The New York Times
OBITUARIES INDEX

The New York Times
OBITUARIES INDEX

1858-1968

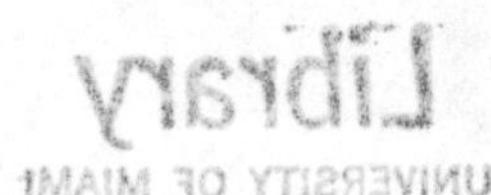

The New York Times

New York 1970

Library of Congress Catalog Card Number 72-113422

Manufactured in the United States of America
by Arno Press, Inc.

The paper in this edition is acid free long life. The cloth is buckram and the book is bound to library standards.

INTRODUCTION

Among the reference works and information services offered by The New York Times, this volume is a "first" in several respects: It is the first to be largely derived from past issues of The Times Index, the first to utilize the computer system developed for the Index, and the first to have been generated by the suggestion of an Index user (a librarian who complained about the tedium of searching a number of issues of the Index for any one name).

This book is designed to facilitate such searches. It brings together, in a single alphabetical listing, all the names entered under the heading "Deaths" in the issues of The New York Times Index from September 1858 through December 1968, augmented by entries for the years 1907 through 1912 (for which the Indexes are still in preparation) and by names from the period 1913 through 1925, not listed in the published Indexes — a total of over 353,000 names.

Entries consist of the name of the deceased, title if given in the original Index entries, pseudonym or nickname if any (in parentheses), and the reference, by year, date, section (if any), page and column, to the original news story. Thus 1939, Mr 19, III, 6:7 indicates the issue of March 19, 1939, section III, page 6, column 7.

Entries are made for news stories only, not for paid notices. Entries for stories other than the obituaries themselves, such as stories about the funeral, memorial services, estate accounting and the like, are included in many cases, and appear in parentheses between the name and the date reference for the obituary. In some of the 19th-century Indexes, when there were several stories about the death of a given individual, complete date, page and column references were not given. In this volume, at least one complete reference for these has been supplied, coupled with earlier but incomplete references. Entries about deceased persons having identical names and no distinguishing titles or pseudonyms are run together, that is, the name appears only once, followed by the several date, page, and column references in chronological order, separated by semicolons.

In the course of the more than 110 years of Indexes synthesized in this volume, the editorial policy on the handling of obituaries underwent numerous changes, and this has resulted in several inconsistencies of inclusion and exclusion, and of style. For example, in some years, accidental deaths and suicides were included under "Deaths," in other years they were not; in some years titles were given and in others omitted; in some years last name and initials only were given; in some years entries were limited to the news story of the death itself, in others they included stories on the preceding illness and on the aftermath. Our aim in producing this volume was to provide a convenient recompilation; to re-edit the material in order to eliminate such inconsistencies would have required an enormous effort that would have increased the cost of this volume to an extent we could not justify.

We hope that we have accomplished what we planned, to provide an efficient new service for our users at low cost. We hope, also, that in the future we will be able to provide many other new services, by similarly exploiting computer technology to open up the vast stores of information in the past issues of The New York Times.

John Rothman, Director of Information Services
Byron A. Falk, Jr., Project Manager

KEY TO ABBREVIATIONS

First Names

Abr	Abraham
Alb	Albert
Alf	Alfred
Arth	Arthur
Benj	Benjamin
Cath	Catherine
Chas	Charles
Danl	Daniel
Edw	Edward
Eug	Eugene
Fredk	Frederick
Geo	George
Hy	Henry
Jas	James
Jno	John
Jos	Joseph
Kath	Katherine
Margt	Margaret
Michl	Michael
Patk	Patrick
Richd	Richard
Robt	Robert
Saml	Samuel
Steph	Stephen
Theo	Theodore
Thos	Thomas
Wm	William

Other

acctg	accounting
cor, corr	correction
ed	editorial
est	estate
funl	funeral
lr	letter
mem	memorial
por	portrait
ser	service
trb	tribute

Titles

Abp	Archbishop
Adm	Admiral
Bp	Bishop
Capt	Captain
Col	Colonel
Com	Commander
Dr	Doctor
Gen	General
Gov	Governor
Lt	Lieutenant
Maj	Major
Mgr, Msgr	Monsignor
Mme	Madame
Pres	President
Prof	Professor
Repr	Representative
Rev	Reverend
Sec	Secretary
Sen	Senator
Sgt	Sergeant

Months

Ja	January
F	February
Mr	March
Ap	April
My	May
Je	June
Jl	July
Ag	August
S	September
O	October
N	November
D	December

The New York Times OBITUARIES INDEX

1858-1968

A

AA, Jan S van der, 1944, Ap 13,19:5
Aadland, Florence Mrs, 1965, My 11,39:3
Aagaard, Harold W, 1945, Ja 1,21:5
Aagaard, Walter S, 1947, Mr 26,25:5
Aage, Prince, 1940, Mr 1,21:3
Aage, Princess of Denmark, 1949, O 17,23:4
Aagesen, Katherine G, 1954, F 1,23:5
Aakesson, Aug, 1938, Je 18,15:6
Aakjer, Jens J Sr, 1946, O 1,23:3
Aal, Alfred D, 1955, N 20,89:2
Aandhal, Fred G, 1966, Ap 8,31:1
Aanrud, Hans, 1953, Ja 11,90:5
Aaroe, Christian C, 1951, Ja 20,15:2
Aaroe, Jensine Mrs, 1948, Ja 28,23:5
Aaroe, Petra M, 1937, F 7,II,9:2
Aaron, Abraham, 1950, My 11,29:1
Aaron, Albert, 1947, Jl 15,23:5
Aaron, Arthur, 1955, F 9,27:1
Aaron, Barney, 1907, Je 4,7:5
Aaron, Bernard J, 1963, N 5,31:3
Aaron, E George, 1960, My 14,23:4
Aaron, Edward I, 1937, Jl 10,15:2
Aaron, Edwin W, 1954, F 22,19:3
Aaron, Gloster B, 1967, My 25,47:4
Aaron, Gloster B Mrs, 1967, Ja 6,35:3
Aaron, Herman, 1939, Ap 21,23:4
Aaron, Hyman, 1950, Je 6,29:3
Aaron, Isaac, 1949, F 20,60:5
Aaron, Israel Rev Dr, 1912, My 16,11:4
Aaron, Jack, 1967, Ag 19,25:3
Aaron, Joseph I, 1951, Mr 21,33:4
Aaron, Michael, 1963, Ap 30,35:3
Aarons, A E, 1936, N 17,27:1
Aarons, Alex A, 1943, Mr 16,19:5
Aarons, Henry M, 1961, S 25,33:5
Aarons, Jacob, 1945, Mr 28,23:4
Aaronsohn, Ephraim, 1939, F 2,19:1
AAronson, Ira N, 1962, S 26,39:1
Aaronson, Irving, 1945, S 22,17:6
Aaronstamm, A Stephen, 1940, D 23,19:2
Aas, Oliver S, 1950, Mr 23,29:4
Aasen, Abraham, 1956, Je 22,23:2
Aasen, John, 1938, Ag 3,19:6
Aasen, Neils W, 1925, D 31,15:6
Aasgaard, Johan A, 1966, Ja 15,27:4
Aba-Novak, William, 1941, N 9,IX,9:8
Abada, Esteban, 1954, D 18,15:4
Abadia Mendez, Miguel, 1947, My 17,16:3
Abadie, Jules, 1953, Ag 11,27:4
Abajian, Mesrob M, 1965, Ap 17,19:6
Aballi, Angel A, 1952, Jl 24,27:5
Abamelek-Lazarew, Maria Princess, 1955, Jl 22,23:4
Abano, Lillian, 1903, D 22,9:5
Abaranell, Lina, 1963, Ja 8,8:7
Abarbanell, Jacob R, 1922, N 11,13:5
Abare, Toney L, 1961, Je 11,54:6
Abashidze, David P, 1952, Jl 12,13:6
Abaunza, Alejandro de Mrs, 1949, O 2,81:1
Abaunza, Carlos, 1944, Mr 19,42:1
Abaunza, Gustavo, 1949, N 27,105:1
Abbadess, Nicholas J, 1961, Ag 18,21:5
Abbane, Ramdane, 1958, My 28,6:5
Abbas, Abdul Baha, 1921, D 1,17:5
Abbas Hilmi II, 1945, O 26,19:4
Abbate, Dominick, 1939, D 31,19:2
Abbate, Grazia Mrs, 1942, Ja 6,23:4
Abbate, Jacob, 1957, F 22,21:1
Abbate, Stephen S, 1965, F 2,33:1
Abbatiello, Joseph Mrs, 1950, Ap 19,29:4
Abbazia, Joseph, 1953, Ap 18,19:5
Abbe, Alanson J, 1949, Ja 4,19:2
Abbe, C S, 1932, Je 17,19:1
Abbe, Cleveland Prof, 1916, O 29,23:1
Abbe, Constant, 1875, Je 21,2:6
Abbe, Earl C, 1948, Je 22,25:3
Abbe, George C, 1949, O 9,93:1
Abbe, J G, 1868, S 22,5:2
Abbe, Paul O, 1954, Mr 12,22:4
Abbe, R, 1928, Mr 8,25:5
Abbe, Robert Mrs, 1920, S 28,13:2
Abbe, William Colgate, 1920, D 4,13:4
Abbelen, P M Msgr, 1917, Ag 25,7:6
Abbell, Maxwell, 1957, Jl 10,27:3
Abbell Hamid, Badis, 1940, Ap 18,23:2
Abbene, Marius L, 1941, D 11,27:6
Abberley, Lester S, 1964, Ag 8,19:3
Abbett, Edward B, 1955, Ap 8,21:4
Abbett, Leon, 1894, D 5,5:4
Abbett, Leon (por), 1949, Ag 16,23:5
Abbett, Lillian A H Mrs, 1938, Jl 2,13:2
Abbett, Sheldon, 1963, S 21,21:5
Abbett, Sheldon Mrs, 1966, My 24,47:2
Abbey, C F, 1884, Ja 12,5:3
Abbey, Charles G, 1952, Mr 6,31:4
Abbey, Edward N, 1940, Ja 21,34:8
Abbey, Edward W Rev Dr, 1937, O 1,21:5
Abbey, Edwin A, 1911, Ag 2,7:5
Abbey, Edwin A Lt, 1917, My 6,19:3
Abbey, H E, 1896, O 18,9:1
Abbey, H E Mrs, 1883, My 10,5:5
Abbey, Henry, 1911, Je 9,13:4
Abbey, L H, 1881, Mr 17,8:2
Abbey, Lorenzo H, 1942, Jl 19,30:8
Abbey, S Legrand, 1908, Mr 10,7:5
Abbey, Westminster, 1922, Je 11,30:3
Abbey, William B, 1954, Ag 22,93:2
Abbiati, F A, 1952, Ag 14,23:2
Abbihl, Jacob H Mrs, 1946, My 31,23:4
Abbink, John, 1958, Ag 4,21:3
Abbit, Benjamin B, 1940, Je 7,23:1
Abbot, Alfred E, 1962, Ja 29,27:2
Abbot, Allan, 1956, Mr 23,27:3
Abbot, Charles G Mrs, 1944, Je 3,13:5
Abbot, Charles W Gen, 1923, D 1,13:4
Abbot, Charles W Rear-Adm, 1907, D 27,7:5
Abbot, Edward A, 1913, O 5,IV,17:5
Abbot, George E, 1952, N 24,23:4
Abbot, Henry W Mrs, 1953, O 10,17:4
Abbot, Jack, 1950, N 10,27:4
Abbot, Leon T Mrs, 1959, Ja 5,29:4
Abbot, W J, 1934, My 20,31:3
Abbot, Walter Lt-Com, 1873, Mr 4,1:4
Abbott, A Theodore, 1955, Ap 3,86:3
Abbott, Albert, 1950, S 23,17:6
Abbott, Albert C, 1957, F 12,27:5
Abbott, Alfred H, 1960, F 17,35:2
Abbott, Allan Mrs, 1945, Je 2,15:4
Abbott, Alson M, 1945, Ag 16,19:3
Abbott, Arthur L, 1952, Jl 27,57:1
Abbott, Arthur P, 1957, D 9,35:5
Abbott, Arthur P Mrs, 1943, S 6,17:4; 1952, F 25,21:3
Abbott, Benjamin Mrs, 1939, D 28,21:2
Abbott, Boyd R Sr, 1947, Je 30,19:3
Abbott, C F, 1933, O 27,19:1
Abbott, C Fred, 1948, D 28,21:3
Abbott, Cary, 1948, O 6,29:5
Abbott, Charles C, 1943, Ap 27,23:1
Abbott, Charles D, 1961, F 5,80:8
Abbott,,Charles F Mrs, 1948, D 31,16:2
Abbott, Charles H, 1954, Ag 22,93:2
Abbott, Charles R, 1939, Jl 9,31:3
Abbott, Charles S, 1956, Mr 16,23:4
Abbott, Charles W, 1941, Je 28,15:5
Abbott, Charlotte E Mrs, 1950, Mr 22,27:4
Abbott, Christopher J, 1954, Ja 11,5:4
Abbott, Clara B Mrs, 1956, Ag 30,25:2
Abbott, Cleve L, 1955, Ap 15,23:1
Abbott, Clifton S, 1945, D 12,27:4
Abbott, Clinton G, 1946, Mr 7,25:2
Abbott, Com, 1869, N 11,5:1
Abbott, Cornelius S Rev, 1910, N 14,9:4
Abbott, Donald B, 1948, O 13,25:1
Abbott, E H, 1931, Ag 9,22:1
Abbott, E Prof, 1884, Mr 23,3:4
Abbott, Eben S, 1956, Ag 25,15:6
Abbott, Edith, 1957, Jl 30,23:1
Abbott, Edith R, 1964, Je 19,31:3
Abbott, Edward P, 1967, My 9,47:3
Abbott, Edward P Mrs, 1965, N 28,88:4
Abbott, Edward T, 1946, S 24,30:2
Abbott, Edwin M, 1940, N 9,17:3
Abbott, Elizabeth Bradford Mrs, 1858, D 17,4:6
Abbott, Elizabeth Mrs, 1941, D 2,23:5
Abbott, Ellis P, 1960, Ap 9,23:3
Abbott, Emma (Mrs E Wetherell), 1891, Ja 6,2:7
Abbott, Ernest H Mrs, 1943, Ap 14,23:4
Abbott, Essex S, 1944, O 18,21:3
Abbott, F V, 1928, S 27,29:5
Abbott, Floyd N Mrs, 1953, S 6,50:1
Abbott, Frances M, 1939, S 22,23:4
Abbott, Francis A Sr, 1949, S 22,31:2
Abbott, Frank D, 1944, D 2,13:6
Abbott, Frank Frost Prof, 1924, Jl 28,11:5
Abbott, Frank H, 1938, O 3,15:5
Abbott, Frank H Mrs, 1957, N 11,29:4
Abbott, Frank S, 1965, Mr 2,35:4
Abbott, Fred, 1903, Jl 9,7:6
Abbott, Frederic K, 1957, Mr 16,19:3
Abbott, G J, 1879, F 2,9:2
Abbott, Gardner, 1904, Ap 10,1:5; 1948, F 7,15:3
Abbott, George B, 1942, F 6,19:5
Abbott, George B Justice (funl, F 13,9:5), 1908, F 11,7:6
Abbott, George B Mrs, 1940, Je 27,23:5
Abbott, George E, 1954, Ap 4,88:1
Abbott, George F, 1952, Je 4,27:2
Abbott, George Henry Jr, 1920, Ag 30,9:6
Abbott, George K, 1959, Jl 3,17:4
Abbott, George N, 1958, F 5,28:1
Abbott, George S, 1938, O 11,25:4
Abbott, Gordon, 1937, Ja 26,21:3
Abbott, Gordon Mrs, 1948, S 7,25:4
Abbott, Gordon W, 1954, Ag 20,19:4
Abbott, Gorham D Rev, 1874, Ag 6,4:6
Abbott, Grace, 1939, Je 20,21:3
Abbott, Guilford C, 1962, Jl 25,33:6
Abbott, H P Almon, 1945, Ap 5,23:4
Abbott, Harlan P, 1947, F 3,19:2
Abbott, Harry, 1942, Mr 11,19:1
Abbott, Harry Jr, 1944, S 20,23:3
Abbott, Helen P, 1947, D 28,40:4
Abbott, Henry, 1943, D 20,23:3
Abbott, Henry A Mrs, 1949, Ja 9,72:4
Abbott, Henry W, 1942, Mr 28,17:2
Abbott, Herbert V Mrs, 1954, F 17,31:2
Abbott, Herman R, 1947, Jl 31,21:5
Abbott, Howard M, 1967, Ap 12,47:1
Abbott, Ira A Ex-Justice, 1921, O 20,17:6
Abbott, J C, 1881, O 9,7:1
Abbott, J S C, 1881, Je 14,5:4
Abbott, J S C Rev, 1877, Je 18,5:5
Abbott, J W P, 1872, Ag 18,1:1
Abbott, Jacob, 1879, N 1,2:3
Abbott, Jacob B, 1950, Jl 16,68:2
Abbott, Jane Mrs, 1962, D 15,14:6
Abbott, Jennie L, 1952, Mr 31,19:4
Abbott, John, 1939, Jl 27,19:5; 1949, O 29,3:3
Abbott, John B, 1963, My 24,31:2
Abbott, John J, 1942, O 19,19:6
Abbott, John J C Sir, 1893, O 31,2:6
Abbott, John Mrs, 1949, O 29,3:3
Abbott, John T, 1914, Mr 9,9:2
Abbott, Joseph D, 1946, Ja 19,13:2
Abbott, Joseph F, 1961, N 10,35:3
Abbott, Julian H, 1946, Ja 21,23:1

Abbott, Karl P, 1950, D 20,31:4
Abbott, Keene, 1941, Jl 6,26:3
Abbott, L F, 1933, F 8,19:1
Abbott, L M, 1932, O 11,21:3
Abbott, Lawrence F Mrs, 1951, N 25,86:3
Abbott, Leonard D, 1953, Mr 20,23:5
Abbott, Llewellyn, 1949, D 19,27:3
Abbott, Marion, 1937, Ja 17,II,8:7
Abbott, Mary Mrs, 1904, F 10,9:6
Abbott, Mary R Mrs, 1939, My 25,25:5
Abbott, Maude E S, 1940, S 3,17:5
Abbott, Nancy A, 1964, Ag 12,35:3
Abbott, Nathan, 1941, Ja 31,19:5
Abbott, Nathan F Mrs, 1948, Ag 5,21:2
Abbott, Norman Mrs (G Hartman), 1955, Ag 9,25:1
Abbott, Norris G Sr, 1953, O 5,27:5
Abbott, Oscar C, 1959, Je 2,35:2
Abbott, Oscar M (will), 1939, D 31,18:2
Abbott, Percy, 1960, Ag 28,83:1
Abbott, Ralph, 1952, O 3,32:3
Abbott, Ralph L, 1938, Mr 14,15:5
Abbott, Ransford J (funl, Jl 23,23:3), 1956, Jl 20,18:1
Abbott, Richard H S, 1948, Ja 12,19:3
Abbott, Robert, 1915, My 19,13:5; 1960, O 11,45:1
Abbott, Robert N, 1964, Ag 26,44:6
Abbott, Robert S, 1940, Mr 1,21:6
Abbott, Robert S Mrs, 1944, Mr 28,19:5
Abbott, Simon Mrs, 1951, Jl 12,25:4
Abbott, Spencer, 1951, D 19,31:4
Abbott, Stephen A, 1938, Je 9,23:5
Abbott, Stuart T, 1956, Jl 25,29:4
Abbott, Thomas Kingsmill Dr, 1913, D 19,11:4
Abbott, Thomas P, 1948, Mr 14,72:6
Abbott, Ulysses V, 1941, D 25,25:2
Abbott, W P Rev (see also D 25,5:3), 1878, D 23,5:5
Abbott, Waldo, 1864, Ag 13,4:6; 1964, N 15,86:3
Abbott, Walter W, 1954, Mr 27,17:1
Abbott, Wenonah S, 1950, Mr 17,23:2
Abbott, Wheeler W, 1937, F 13,13:3
Abbott, Wilbur C, 1939, S 26,23:1
Abbott, William A, 1953, Ja 6,29:6
Abbott, William E, 1949, F 22,23:3
Abbott, William H, 1938, Je 9,23:5
Abbott, William H Mrs, 1952, Jl 5,15:3
Abbott, William Henry, 1919, F 1,13:4
Abbott, William M, 1941, N 15,17:6
Abbott, William O, 1943, S 16,21:5
Abbott, William P, 1937, Ja 30,17:5
Abbott, William R, 1950, Mr 3,26:2
Abbott, William S, 1955, Jl 7,27:3
Abbott, William T, 1922, My 30,13:6
Abbott, William T Rev, 1925, My 29,17:6
Abbott, Wilson R, 1938, D 6,23:2
Abbott, Yarnall, 1938, Je 25,15:6
Abboud, Ahmed M, 1963, D 30,21:3
Abbruzzese, Michael, 1963, O 30,39:4
Abbruzzi, Anthony, 1957, My 24,25:3
Abd-el-Kader, 1873, N 12,1:5; 1883, My 27,7:1
Abd-El-Kader of Algeria, 1879, N 12,5:1
Abd-el Krim, 1908, D 15,9:5
Abd el Krim el Khattabi (funeral, F 8,18:2), 1963, F 7,1:1
Abdella, H I, 1949, Ag 25,23:1
Abdo, Azma (will), 1940, Mr 20,24:3
Abdul-latif, Ismail A, 1949, Ap 25,32:2
Abdul Majeed Didi, Sultan Amir, 1952, F 23,11:5
Abdul-Medjid I, Sultan of Turkey, 1861, Jl 7,4:6
Abdul Razek, Mustafa, 1947, F 16,57:2
Abdullah, Achmed, 1945, My 13,20:3
Abdullah, Mustafa, 1966, Ap 14,1:1
Abdullah al-Salim al-Sabah, Sheik (cor, D 4,31:2), 1965, N 25,35:2
Abdullah bin Khalifa, Sultan of Zanzibar (funeral, Jl 3,6:4), 1963, Jl 2,29:4
Abdur Rahman Khan, Ameer of Afghanistan, 1899, F 25,7:2
Abe, Isoo, 1949, F 11,23:3
Abe, Katsuji, 1939, O 24,4:4
Abe, Nobuyuki, 1953, S 8,31:4
Abe, Paul, 1965, Mr 15,31:2
Abe, Shozo, 1940, Mr 25,15:3
Abeel, Alan C, 1959, O 8,39:2
Abeel, Ansel R Sr, 1952, D 30,19:2
Abeel, Edward Marshall Capt, 1918, Ag 25,19:1
Abeel, Fred S, 1942, Je 26,21:2
Abeel, G N, 1884, Ja 5,2:6
Abeel, Henry F, 1923, Mr 18,6:3
Abeel, John H, 1946, Mr 15,22:3
Abeel, Neilson, 1949, O 17,23:6
Abegg, Henry A, 1904, Ja 29,5:6
Abegg, John Henry, 1920, D 8,17:3
Abel, Adam Mrs, 1948, Jl 13,27:2
Abel, Alice G, 1953, Ag 3,17:5
Abel, Barbara, 1966, My 25,47:4
Abel, Bernard J, 1942, Ag 24,15:4
Abel, Clarence R Mrs, 1949, Ag 26,20:2
Abel, E G, 1907, Je 15,9:7
Abel, Ezra, 1950, Ap 21,23:5
Abel, F A Sir, 1902, S 9,9:5
Abel, Frederic W, 1961, D 5,43:2
Abel, Gerard T, 1943, Mr 16,19:4
Abel, Harold A, 1965, S 1,37:2
Abel, Harry C, 1938, N 25,23:4
Abel, Hazel Mrs, 1966, Ag 1,27:5
Abel, Henry C L, 1950, O 4,31:3
Abel, Howard, 1925, S 15,25:3
Abel, J L, 1903, Ag 21,9:6
Abel, Jack Mrs, 1943, Mr 10,19:5
Abel, James F, 1950, Ja 8,78:3
Abel, Jean Baptiste, 1921, O 1,13:1
Abel, John, 1944, Mr 21,19:3
Abel, John J (por), 1938, My 27,17:3
Abel, John J Mrs, 1938, Ja 21,20:4
Abel, John Mrs, 1948, Jl 22,23:5
Abel, L Hosford, 1943, Ap 10,17:4
Abel, Oscar, 1948, N 29,23:4
Abel, Oscar J, 1951, O 9,29:2
Abel, Samuel E, 1959, Ap 24,27:3
Abel, Stuart, 1937, Ag 12,19:6
Abel, Taffy (Clarence), 1964, Ag 2,77:1
Abel, Theodore, 1949, O 28,23:3
Abel, Victor D, 1949, Ja 15,17:4
Abele, Albert V, 1962, O 21,89:1
Abele, Clarence, 1944, S 14,23:6
Abele, Earl M, 1947, Jl 16,23:5
Abele, Frank M, 1941, D 3,25:3
Abele, Lester J, 1950, S 26,31:3
Abeles, Herbert R, 1960, N 2,39:4
Abeles, Jacob I Mrs, 1964, Jl 28,29:4
Abeles, James A, 1961, Je 18,88:4
Abeles, James A Mrs (cor, My 9,33:1), 1956, My 8, 33:1
Abeles, Jules, 1945, N 4,44:1
Abeles, Leo, 1966, My 9,39:1
Abeles, Peter A, 1952, S 13,17:1
Abeles, Sheldon A, 1938, S 25,38:8
Abell, Arthur H, 1957, N 28,31:5
Abell, Arthur M, 1958, F 9,89:1
Abell, C S, 1875, D 5,2:7
Abell, Charles S (will, Ja 31,17:8), 1953, Ja 15,27:1
Abell, Charles T, 1944, O 14,13:6
Abell, D H Col, 1872, Mr 15,1:6
Abell, Edmund, 1884, Ag 10,5:3
Abell, Edward F, 1904, F 29,7:6
Abell, Elizabeth (Sister Mary Lucy), 1964, O 2,37:4
Abell, Elvira D, 1948, D 9,33:1
Abell, Frank D, 1964, N 23,37:4
Abell, Gurdon R, 1951, Ap 30,21:3
Abell, Harry C, 1948, D 16,29:5
Abell, Harry C Mrs, 1945, Jl 29,39:2
Abell, Irvin, 1949, Ag 29,17:4
Abell, James M, 1925, Je 24,17:4
Abell, John T, 1946, S 13,7:2
Abell, John T Mrs, 1962, Jl 7,17:2
Abell, John W, 1942, Mr 23,15:2
Abell, Louis G, 1962, O 27,25:1
Abell, Mary Joseph Sister, 1922, N 25,13:4
Abell, Oliver J, 1948, Je 1,23:4
Abell, Walter R, 1939, N 17,21:1
Abell, Walter W, 1941, Ja 21,21:4
Abell, William, 1924, Ap 28,15:4
Abell, William T, 1958, Jl 26,15:3
Abell, Winfield V, 1955, Je 1,33:2
Abells, Harry D, 1958, Mr 4,29:1
Abelman, Abram Mrs, 1950, F 24,23:2
Abelman, Max, 1960, O 18,39:3
Abelman, Max Mrs, 1955, S 15,33:4
Abelov, Saul S, 1955, Ap 28,29:2
Abelove, Barney, 1953, O 14,29:3
Abelow, Jacques, 1958, S 16,27:1
Abelow, Jules, 1955, F 11,23:1
Abelow, Samuel P, 1948, N 15,25:5
Abelow, Samuel P Mrs, 1960, O 8,23:4
Abelow, Solomon, 1955, F 26,15:2
Abels, Edward S, 1919, Jl 11,11:3
Abels, Gerald, 1964, S 24,41:1
Abels, Jules C, 1947, Je 15,60:1
Abels, Morris, 1943, My 9,40:4
Abels, Simon, 1950, My 22,21:4
Abels, Simon Mrs, 1956, N 21,27:3
Abelson, Alter, 1964, D 22,27:4
Abelson, Eula M, 1963, Jl 17,31:1
Abelson, Henry, 1943, Je 1,23:1
Abelson, Milton I, 1957, Ja 28,23:3
Abelson, Mortimer S, 1945, Mr 10,17:3
Abelson, Mortimer S Mrs, 1943, F 25,21:3
Abelson, Paul, 1953, N 5,31:5
Abemethy, Ann S, 1954, My 20,31:4
Abemethy, Samuel C, 1954, Ap 22,29:3
Abend, Hallett, 1955, N 28,31:1
Abendroth, Hermann, 1956, My 30,21:6
Abendroth, William P, 1964, D 2,47:1
Abendschein, Ludwig, 1945, Jl 12,11:5
Aber, Emmett A, 1948, Ap 12,21:4
Aberconway, Lord, 1934, Ja 24,17:1
Aberconway, Lord (H D McLaren), 1953, My 24, 89:3
Abercorn, Duke of (Jas Hamilton), 1913, Ja 4,9:3
Abercorn, Duke of (J A E Hamilton), 1953, S 14,27:3
Abercrombe, William D, 1939, F 26,38:7
Abercrombie, Charles S, 1907, Mr 24,9:6
Abercrombie, Charles W, 1953, Jl 25,11:2
Abercrombie, D T, 1931, Ag 30,II,6:1
Abercrombie, Daniel P, 1950, Jl 14,21:6
Abercrombie, David, 1937, Mr 12,25:5
Abercrombie, Francis P, 1939, N 13,19:4
Abercrombie, Fred C, 1945, D 27,19:2
Abercrombie, J J Gen, 1877, Ja 7,7:2
Abercrombie, John W, 1940, Jl 3,17:2
Abercrombie, Lascelles, 1938, O 28,23:3
Abercrombie, Patrick, 1957, Mr 25,87:1
Abercrombie, Peter H, 1950, O 1,104:1
Abercrombie, R M Rev Dr, 1884, D 8,5:2
Abercrombie, Ralph, 1954, Jl 8,23:6
Abercrombie, Ralph H, 1946, Mr 4,23:4
Abercrombie, Robert M, 1940, My 22,23:4
Abercrombie-Miller, Alice (Countess de Castellane), 1965, My 27,37:4
Abercrombie-Miller, Frederick A Com, 1909, N 9,9:6
Aberdare, Clarence N B Lord, 1957, O 6,4:2
Aberdeen, Dowager Marchioness of, 1939, Ap 19,23:3
Aberdeen, Earl of, 1864, Ap 10,3:4
Aberdeen, Lady (Mrs G Gordon), 1949, Mr 14,19:4
Aberdeen and Temair, Marchioness, 1937, Ja 6,23:5
Aberdeen and Temair, Marquess of, 1934, Mr 8,19:1
Aberdein, Robert Dr, 1903, O 19,7:6
Aberenz, Norman R, 1961, Ap 1,17:2
Abergavenny, Lord (G T M Larnach-Nevill), 1954, Mr 31,27:1
Aberhart, William C, 1943, My 24,15:5
Aberhart, William Mrs, 1966, Ja 15,27:2
Aberini, Filoteo, 1937, Ap 14,25:5
Aberle, William F, 1949, S 18,92:4
Aberlin, Edward H Mrs, 1955, Mr 21,25:5
Abernathy, Abel B, 1940, Je 23,31:3
Abernathy, Charles L, 1955, F 24,27:4
Abernathy, Ernest H, 1964, Ag 17,25:5
Abernathy, Leo, 1954, Ja 20,27:6
Abernathy, M A, 1955, N 4,29:4
Abernathy, Sara McLean Mrs (will), 1906, Ja 12,2:6
Aberneth, J J, 1879, O 29,5:5
Abernethy, Albert, 1956, F 16,29:2
Abernethy, Alfred C, 1937, F 13,13:2
Abernethy, Charles T, 1950, Jl 14,21:5
Abernethy, H B, 1944, F 17,19:2
Abernethy, James A, 1938, Ag 23,17:3
Abernethy, Julian Willis Dr, 1923, Jl 4,13:3
Abernethy, William S, 1959, Ag 20,25:2
Abertay, Lord, 1940, D 7,17:4
Abesser, Anna L Mrs, 1940, O 3,25:5
Abetz, Otto, 1958, My 6,9:1
Abetz, Otto Mrs, 1958, My 6,9:1
Abi-Rezk, Paul, 1952, Ja 7,19:5
Abieniste, Gabriel J, 1958, O 15,39:3
Abingdon, William L, 1918, My 19,23:2; 1918, My 20, 11:4
Abinger, Helen Lady, 1915, F 16,9:5
Abkarian, Sarkis H, 1948, Je 25,24:3
Able, Arthur G, 1949, S 15,27:4
Able, Augustus H Mrs, 1947, S 2,21:6
Ables, Harry T, 1951, F 9,25:2
Ablett, Frank S, 1950, O 14,19:2
Ablett, John R, 1943, Ja 30,15:5
Abney, Philip C, 1953, Mr 8,90:2
Abney, William de Wiveleslie Sir, 1920, D 4,13:4
Aboff, Gdalia, 1954, O 26,27:3
Aboff, Gdalia Mrs, 1947, N 4,25:2
Abood, Assad, 1966, Jl 7,37:2
Aborelli, Joseph Mrs, 1968, My 8,47:1
Aborn, Albert C, 1964, Je 8,29:3
Aborn, Carlton N, 1946, Mr 4,23:4
Aborn, M, 1933, N 13,17:1
Aborn, Sargent, 1956, F 7,31:4
Abott, Bessie, 1919, F 10,13:3
Abott, Walter, 1939, F 14,19:1
Abouchar, Raymond P, 1963, Je 9,86:8
Abounader, Toufik F, 1948, S 9,27:4
Aboussleman, Michael, 1938, Mr 2,19:5
About, E F V (funl), 1885, Ja 16,5:5
Abraham, Abraham (funl, Je 30,9:4), 1911, Je 29, 11:3
Abraham, Arthur, 1951, My 29,25:2
Abraham, Benjamin, 1963, N 26,38:5
Abraham, Benjamin L, 1948, Mr 28,48:2
Abraham, Charles, 1955, D 19,27:2
Abraham, Ernest G, 1959, Ag 19,30:1
Abraham, Ernest G Mrs (M Jonas), 1959, Jl 5,56:4
Abraham, Herbert, 1967, Ap 5,47:2
Abraham, James H Mrs, 1962, Ag 17,23:4
Abraham, Joseph H, 1942, O 10,15:5; 1954, Je 4,23:4
Abraham, Lawrence E, 1945, Jl 26,19:4
Abraham, Leonard, 1967, Ja 21,31:2
Abraham, Marcel, 1955, F 18,22:2
Abraham, Otto, 1948, My 9,68:4
Abraham, Paul, 1960, My 9,29:2
Abraham, Phil S, 1955, D 24,13:5
Abraham, Rose Mrs (will, Jl 1,4:6), 1938, My 27,17:4
Abraham, William, 1922, My 15,17:7
Abrahamer, Isidor, 1960, Ap 11,31:2
Abrahams, Abraham, 1955, Jl 20,27:1
Abrahams, Alex I, 1960, Ag 5,23:2
Abrahams, Bernard, 1960, Mr 29,37:3
Abrahams, David J, 1958, N 19,37:4
Abrahams, Elsie R, 1938, Je 9,23:6
Abrahams, Isidor, 1943, Ja 12,23:2
Abrahams, Israel Dr, 1925, O 7,27:4
Abrahams, Jacob, 1950, D 20,31:2
Abrahams, Joseph L, 1948, Mr 24,25:3
Abrahams, M B, 1928, Jl 8,21:1

Abrahams, Mark L, 1940, N 26,23:3
Abrahams, Morton, 1963, Ap 2,47:1
Abrahams, Morton S, 1965, O 19,43:2
Abrahams, Nathan, 1953, Ag 10,23:4
Abrahams, Raymond Mrs, 1960, F 3,33:4
Abrahams, Sidney, 1957, My 15,35:4
Abrahams, Sol H, 1959, Ap 13,31:4
Abrahams, William Mrs, 1950, S 13,28:2
Abrahamsen, Harry, 1964, Ap 15,39:4
Abrahamson, Alex, 1964, F 23,84:8
Abrahamson, Alexander Mrs, 1967, S 16,33:1
Abrahamson, Emanuel M, 1956, Mr 20,50:4
Abrahamson, I, 1933, Jl 19,17:1
Abrahamson, L G, 1946, N 5,25:4
Abraitys, George, 1959, Ja 4,87:2
Abraitys, George Mrs, 1958, F 7,21:1
Abramo, Charles, 1952, Je 16,17:5
Abramovich, Raphael R, 1963, Ap 12,27:4
Abramovitz, Albert, 1963, Jl 14,61:1
Abramovitz, Bing (trb lr), 1953, Je 28,II,1:6
Abramowitsch, Sholem Jacob, 1917, D 16,23:2
Abramowitz, Abram, 1941, Jl 5,11:3
Abramowitz, Alex Mrs, 1942, Mr 3,24:3
Abramowitz, E William (por), 1949, Je 14,31:1
Abramowitz, Herman, 1947, S 26,23:2
Abramowitz, Isaac Mrs, 1953, Ap 15,31:2
Abramowitz, Nathan, 1964, Ja 8,37:4
Abramowitz, Reuben Mrs, 1949, Ag 29,17:3
Abramowitz, Samuel Mrs, 1952, Jl 1,23:5
Abrams, Abe, 1951, S 28,31:4
Abrams, Abraham, 1947, N 29,13:1
Abrams, Albert B, 1955, Ag 18,23:3
Abrams, Albert Dr, 1924, Ja 15,19:3
Abrams, Albert J Mrs, 1959, F 11,39:3
Abrams, Alfred, 1938, Ap 3,II,7:4
Abrams, Ben C, 1949, Mr 9,25:5
Abrams, Benjamin, 1948, S 11,15:4; 1950, N 4,17:3; 1967, Je 24,29:2
Abrams, Benjamin F Mrs, 1947, N 18,30:2
Abrams, Blanche V, 1965, N 16,43:4
Abrams, C E, 1903, Ap 28,9:6
Abrams, Edwin H Mrs, 1953, Ap 21,27:3
Abrams, Ernest R, 1958, N 3,37:1
Abrams, Frank D Rev, 1909, Ap 10,9:5
Abrams, H, 1926, N 16,27:2
Abrams, Harry F, 1944, Je 12,19:3
Abrams, Harry L, 1960, N 21,29:2
Abrams, Henry W, 1955, D 3,17:5
Abrams, Herbert T, 1940, N 11,19:3
Abrams, Isaac, 1938, Ja 31,19:5
Abrams, Jack, 1959, N 2,31:4
Abrams, James E, 1949, Mr 26,17:2
Abrams, Jess M, 1953, My 4,23:3
Abrams, John, 1938, Je 29,19:2
Abrams, John Nelson, 1906, D 23,7:6
Abrams, Joseph D, 1962, Ag 12,80:2
Abrams, Joseph S, 1956, F 23,27:4
Abrams, Joshua, 1953, F 22,61:1
Abrams, Lawrence B (corr, Jl 2,19:3), 1944, Jl 1,15:3
Abrams, Leo, 1965, Ja 25,37:4
Abrams, Lewis A, 1963, Ap 30,35:5
Abrams, Louis, 1939, Ja 16,15:2; 1959, F 25,31:3; 1963, Ag 16,28:1
Abrams, Lucien, 1941, Ap 15,23:2
Abrams, Melville E, 1966, O 11,43:5
Abrams, Mollie Mrs, 1953, My 18,21:3
Abrams, Morris, 1963, S 17,35:2
Abrams, Nathan, 1941, My 1,23:2; 1956, Ag 9,25:2
Abrams, Norman B, 1968, Ag 29,35:5
Abrams, Norman Mrs, 1967, Mr 9,39:1
Abrams, Percy R, 1953, D 18,29:5
Abrams, Peter, 1963, S 10,39:4
Abrams, Philip, 1947, O 10,25:4
Abrams, Quincy I, 1962, O 27,25:4
Abrams, Samuel, 1943, O 5,25:4
Abrams, Samuel J, 1951, Ag 1,23:2
Abrams, Samuel M, 1966, N 26,35:3
Abrams, Sarah, 1939, N 3,21:4
Abrams, Seymour H, 1965, N 18,47:3
Abrams, Sidney, 1965, Ag 17,33:1
Abrams, Stanley B, 1950, O 20,28:2
Abrams, Stanley L, 1954, My 9,88:4
Abrams, Victor H, 1961, N 15,43:2
Abrams, Walter L, 1952, D 8,41:4
Abrams, Weston Mrs, 1903, My 24,3:4
Abrams, William, 1954, Ag 1,84:3
Abrams, William I, 1951, O 29,23:4
Abrams, Zachariah Mrs, 1949, My 9,25:4
Abramsohn, Isadore, 1964, S 9,43:3
Abramson, Etta Mrs, 1937, Je 24,25:3
Abramson, Freda, 1955, D 20,31:2
Abramson, H L, 1934, Ap 18,19:1
Abramson, Henry, 1967, S 4,21:2
Abramson, Ivan Mrs, 1945, Ja 16,19:5
Abramson, Martin J, 1962, My 11,31:1
Abramson, Max, 1956, Ap 12,31:3; 1962, Je 3,88:1
Abramson, Max Mrs, 1955, Mr 17,45:2
Abramson, Meyer, 1949, Je 3,25:4
Abramson, Morris, 1964, Mr 11,39:3
Abramson, Nathan M, 1959, My 14,33:4
Abramson, Philip, 1961, N 30,37:4
Abramson, Richard A, 1955, Je 30,25:3; 1957, D 30, 23:5
Abramson, Sherman C, 1942, My 18,15:2
Abranches, Adelina, 1945, N 23,23:2
Abranches, Joaquin A, 1939, Ap 22,17:5
Abrantes, Helena d', 1947, F 13,23:2
Abrash, Samuel, 1952, F 5,29:2
Abrashkin, Raymond, 1960, Ag 26,26:1
Abrecht, Otto, 1948, Ja 25,57:1
Abreo, Mme, 1881, Jl 4,3:5
Abrera, Sofronio V, 1962, F 27,33:4
Abresch, James, 1959, Ap 17,25:3
Abreu, Diego W Mrs, 1957, Mr 5,31:1
Abrew, Forrest G, 1942, Ja 26,15:3
Abrial, Jacques, 1962, D 21,8:6
Abrian Francis, Bro (J Wagner), 1949, F 17,23:2
Abricosov, A I, 1955, Ap 12,29:1
Abrolat, Gustav Sr Mrs, 1948, N 12,23:2
Abromeit, Carl M, 1965, My 16,88:3
Abromowitz, David, 1953, Jl 16,21:1
Abromowitz, Morris (por), 1938, Ja 23,II,8:7
Abronski, John V, 1938, Ap 18,15:3
Abrosimov, Pavel, 1961, Mr 24,31:3
Abruzzese, Ronald Mrs (I Kramarich), 1967, Ag 13, 80:8
Abruzzi, Duke of the, 1933, Mr 19,33:1
Abry, Charles L, 1944, Je 20,19:3
Abry, Charles L Jr Mrs, 1958, Ag 16,17:5
Abson, Eric, 1948, O 16,15:1
Abstein, Bill, 1940, Ap 10,25:6
Abt, August, 1950, S 10,92:4
Abt, Carl, 1951, F 26,23:2
Abt, Franz, 1885, Ap 2,1:2
Abt, Henry E, 1962, N 30,33:1
Abt, Issac A, 1955, N 24,29:3
Abu Bakar, Tunku Prince, 1956, My 2,31:5
Abu-Khair, Dahir E and James, 1955, Mr 26,35:4
Abuza, Philip, 1945, My 12,13:5
Abzac, Paul d' Vicomte, 1904, D 9,6:4
Abzac, Vicomte Paul d', 1904, D 9,6:4
Abzug, Lionel, 1964, O 21,47:1
Acampora, Julian, 1958, Ap 25,27:2
Acaster, David, 1942, Jl 11,13:6
Acaster, Helen R, 1952, My 31,17:4
Accas, George A (por), 1949, O 28,24:2
Accellaro, Joseph, 1944, My 25,21:5
Acchione, John B, 1947, Je 21,17:3
Accioly, Hildebrando, 1962, Ap 7,25:6
Ace, Harry Mrs, 1958, My 30,21:1
Acebedo y Flores, Manuel, 1958, Jl 26,12:4
Acel, Ervin S, 1958, F 25,27:1
Acer, Ella Mrs, 1941, Ja 9,21:5
Acer, Frank Adams, 1924, D 11,23:5
Acer, John H A, 1939, F 26,38:5
Acerra, Anthony, 1949, Ja 11,27:4
Acevedo, Francisco, 1946, Ap 24,25:5
Acevedo Diaz, Eduardo, 1959, S 3,27:4
Acevedo Torres, Luis, 1951, Ag 1,23:3
Aceves, Julius G, 1953, Ag 19,29:2
Achard, Louis Amedee Eugene, 1875, Mr 28,6:6
Achelis, Friedrich, 1917, My 22,13:4
Achelis, Fritz, 1924, D 24,15:2
Achelis, Johnfritz, 1965, O 11,39:4
Achelis, Thomas, 1911, Ap 7,13:4
Achenbach, Anne, 1962, Ja 7,88:7
Achenbach, George A W, 1953, Ap 28,27:2
Achenbach, Moore S, 1963, Ap 11,33:3
Achenbach, Thomas, 1952, N 26,23:3
Achenbach, William J, 1953, My 10,88:2
Acher, Albert H Col, 1924, Ag 28,17:6
Acher, Herman Mrs, 1958, Je 25,29:1
Acheson, A Glen, 1961, Je 7,41:3
Acheson, Albert R, 1941, F 26,21:6
Acheson, Archibald Brabazon Sparrow (Earl of Gosford), 1922, Ap 12,21:5
Acheson, Arthur M, 1952, My 12,25:4
Acheson, Barclay, 1957, D 6,30:3
Acheson, Barclay Mrs, 1968, My 19,86:2
Acheson, E C, 1934, Ja 29,15:1
Acheson, E G, 1931, Jl 7,23:3
Acheson, Edward C, 1966, S 30,47:3
Acheson, Edward C Mrs, 1958, Jl 26,15:6
Acheson, Edward G, 1962, Ja 7,89:1
Acheson, Edward G Mrs (will, S 20,35:6), 1950, F 3, 23:1
Acheson, Ernest F, 1917, My 17,13:4
Acheson, George, 1957, Mr 15,25:1
Acheson, H Stuart, 1945, Mr 14,19:2
Acheson, John C Dr, 1937, N 26,21:3
Acheson, John H, 1938, S 22,23:4
Acheson, John M, 1967, N 19,84:2
Acheson, Marcus W Judge, 1906, Je 22,7:6
Acheson, Robert F Mrs, 1949, D 4,108:4
Acheson, William R, 1942, Je 20,13:6
Achey, Webster Schimmel, 1953, F 2,21:3
Achi, William C Jr, 1947, Je 19,21:3
Achilles, Gertrude S Mrs, 1955, Ap 2,17:5
Achilles, Harold E Mrs, 1949, N 13,92:4
Achilles, Lillian, 1941, Ap 18,21:1
Achilles, Louis H, 1938, D 12,19:3
Achilles I, King of Pategonia, 1902, Mr 20,9:2
Achim, Levi J, 1944, Ap 7,19:5
Achinstein, Hyman, 1955, Je 3,23:6
Achron, Bertha M Mrs, 1942, My 14,19:5
Achron, Isidor, 1948, My 13,25:3
Achron, Joseph, 1943, My 1,15:5
Achs, Ruth Silbowitz Dr, 1968, S 29,80:5
Achstetter, Robert J, 1945, N 24,20:2
Achten, Ralph B, 1955, My 7,17:6
Achurch, William H, 1951, N 13,29:5
Ackeley, Carl E Mrs, 1966, Jl 22,31:3
Acken, Charles C, 1949, My 9,25:2
Acken, David Mrs, 1964, S 14,33:3
Acken, Henry S, 1939, Mr 11,17:5
Acken, Herbert A, 1952, Ja 13,89:1
Acken, John B, 1944, My 18,19:4
Acken, Luella Mrs, 1952, D 12,29:3
Acken, Ronald G, 1958, O 22,35:4
Acker, A Lincoln, 1950, Jl 23,56:4
Acker, Ambrose B Mrs, 1959, Ag 3,25:5
Acker, Augustus, 1906, N 22,9:5
Acker, Benjamin C, 1925, Ag 31,15:6
Acker, Charles E, 1952, D 2,31:2
Acker, Charles Ernest, 1920, O 19,11:4
Acker, Edwin F, 1951, Jl 6,23:2
Acker, Ernest Mrs, 1952, F 18,19:4
Acker, Finley, 1913, F 13,15:5
Acker, Henry W, 1938, F 16,21:5
Acker, Herman A, 1962, Mr 9,19:5
Acker, J P, 1877, Jl 24,8:6
Acker, James, 1937, Je 14,23:4
Acker, Joseph, 1956, Jl 26,25:4
Acker, Karl, 1958, My 27,31:5
Acker, Lewis H, 1952, Je 26,29:2
Acker, Marion A, 1948, Mr 21,60:6
Acker, Marshall W, 1966, Ja 12,21:2
Acker, Mary, 1947, Mr 27,3:2
Acker, Mary W C Mrs, 1937, Jl 20,23:1
Acker, Milton, 1956, Ag 17,19:4
Acker, Roger D, 1955, Je 1,33:3
Acker, Sarah I, 1944, N 5,54:3
Acker, Willis C, 1951, Mr 19,27:1
Ackerley, Anna L Mrs, 1946, Mr 28,25:5
Ackerley, Edward, 1952, Je 16,17:5
Ackerley, William, 1945, Ja 30,20:3
Ackerley, William C, 1945, Mr 15,23:4
Ackerlind, Carl U, 1961, Ag 5,17:4
Ackerly, Clarence E, 1955, My 31,27:1
Ackerly, Clifford B Mrs, 1943, N 21,56:5
Ackerly, Dana T, 1952, S 21,88:5
Ackerly, H Davis Jr, 1964, O 25,89:1
Ackerly, H Russell, 1963, O 14,29:2
Ackerly, Jerome W, 1950, O 13,29:2
Ackerly, S Leroy, 1949, Mr 26,17:2
Ackerly, William J, 1916, Je 5,11:6
Ackerly, William J Jr, 1944, Ja 6,23:4
Ackerman, A Henry, 1947, S 7,63:3
Ackerman, Adolph, 1947, Ag 2,13:1
Ackerman, Albert, 1955, S 19,25:4
Ackerman, Albert A, 1949, Mr 4,21:3
Ackerman, Albert C Mrs, 1953, O 12,27:5
Ackerman, Andrew J, 1960, Je 22,35:1
Ackerman, Annie M, 1944, D 31,25:2
Ackerman, Arthur C, 1955, F 6,89:2; 1965, Jl 11,68:5
Ackerman, Arthur W, 1958, Ja 15,29:1
Ackerman, Bernard B, 1941, S 16,23:3
Ackerman, Berthold C E Capt, 1937, Jl 28,19:5
Ackerman, Carl W Mrs (funl, Ag 26,27:5), 1954, Ag 23,17:2
Ackerman, Charles F, 1914, Ap 13,11:4; 1953, Mr 19, 29:5
Ackerman, Charles W, 1938, My 11,19:2
Ackerman, Clarence B, 1949, N 25,31:1
Ackerman, David, 1948, D 4,13:5
Ackerman, David Greenlie, 1968, Ap 21,80:6
Ackerman, Edgar M, 1961, Je 3,23:6
Ackerman, Edward D, 1943, N 27,13:5
Ackerman, Edward S, 1941, Ap 9,25:6
Ackerman, Edwin C, 1949, S 29,29:3
Ackerman, Elizabeth Mrs, 1925, O 3,15:4
Ackerman, Emil Mrs, 1958, Je 17,29:4
Ackerman, Ernest A, 1953, S 24,33:4
Ackerman, Frederick L, 1950, Mr 18,13:5
Ackerman, Frederick Mrs, 1962, F 1,31:4
Ackerman, Garret N, 1943, O 23,13:3
Ackerman, Garrett J, 1960, O 4,43:4
Ackerman, Gilbert F, 1909, My 10,9:3
Ackerman, Gorline D Mrs, 1907, N 20,9:6
Ackerman, Grace S Mrs, 1940, Jl 30,19:5
Ackerman, Gunther K, 1924, Jl 29,15:5
Ackerman, Harold, 1956, F 15,31:5
Ackerman, Harold Mrs, 1956, F 15,31:5
Ackerman, Harry, 1959, D 6,86:1
Ackerman, Irving, 1959, Jl 29,29:4
Ackerman, J Fred Maj, 1908, My 23,9:3
Ackerman, Jack, 1963, D 23,25:1
Ackerman, Jacob, 1942, D 30,23:4; 1945, O 2,23:4
Ackerman, Jacob Capt, 1915, Mr 18,11:5
Ackerman, Jacob Mrs, 1945, O 2,23:4
Ackerman, James F Mrs, 1951, O 20,15:4
Ackerman, John A, 1907, Ap 9,9:6
Ackerman, John E Jr, 1967, O 4,51:2
Ackerman, John J, 1943, Ja 4,15:5
Ackerman, John J Sr, 1947, Jl 3,21:4
Ackerman, John L, 1943, Ja 14,21:3
Ackerman, Kenneth, 1963, O 12,13:4
Ackerman, Louis A, 1940, Jl 4,15:3
Ackerman, Marion S, 1943, D 17,28:2

Ackerman, Mary E Mrs, 1915, O 14,11:5
Ackerman, Michael J, 1960, Ag 7,85:1
Ackerman, Morris, 1950, Ja 17,27:4
Ackerman, Phil Mrs, 1942, O 9,21:4
Ackerman, Philip, 1943, D 6,23:3
Ackerman, Ralph H, 1957, Ja 14,23:6
Ackerman, Ramsey D, 1965, Ja 8,29:4
Ackerman, Robert B, 1958, Ap 30,33:4
Ackerman, Robert M, 1961, Je 4,86:3
Ackerman, Robert M Mrs, 1967, O 7,29:1
Ackerman, Robert V, 1958, N 18,37:2
Ackerman, Samuel Mrs, 1950, My 11,30:3
Ackerman, Sarah Mrs, 1949, Ja 6,23:1
Ackerman, Sherman Mrs, 1950, Ja 9,25:2
Ackerman, Silas, 1922, My 23,17:4
Ackerman, Simon, 1959, F 15,86:2
Ackerman, Stephen H, 1943, Jl 4,21:3
Ackerman, Stewart, 1954, S 10,23:1
Ackerman, Theodore, 1949, Ap 5,30:6
Ackerman, Theodore E, 1951, Je 24,72:6
Ackerman, Theron, 1940, Ag 13,19:6
Ackerman, Tunis, 1951, D 18,31:2
Ackerman, Walter, 1946, Je 2,44:3
Ackerman, Warren, 1968, Ag 7,43:4
Ackerman, William A, 1955, Ap 19,31:3
Ackerman, William A Mrs, 1946, S 27,23:4
Ackerman, William Mrs, 1904, S 16,7:7
Ackerman, William R, 1950, O 27,29:1
Ackermann, Frederick T, 1941, S 2,17:5
Ackermann, Leonard E, 1968, Ja 4,37:3
Ackermann, Louis J Mrs, 1948, O 14,29:2
Ackermann, Susan K, 1949, F 15,23:3
Ackerson, Alexander, 1966, F 25,31:3
Ackerson, Charles, 1937, N 12,21:4
Ackerson, Eugene J, 1960, Ap 1,33:2
Ackerson, Fred M, 1956, D 29,15:2
Ackerson, Garret G, 1955, F 10,31:2
Ackerson, Gilbert E Mrs, 1942, D 30,23:5
Ackerson, John, 1944, Je 19,19:4
Ackerson, John H, 1940, Ap 21,39:4
Ackerson, John M Jr, 1965, Ag 13,29:3
Ackert, Burt G, 1946, D 4,31:4
Ackert, Charles Mrs, 1916, My 12,11:6
Ackert, Gilbert B, 1938, O 6,23:4
Ackert, Harry, 1942, N 26,27:1
Ackert, James M, 1948, Mr 1,23:1
Ackert, William E, 1951, Ag 8,25:5
Ackert, Winfred R, 1945, Ja 12,15:5
Ackert, Winfred R Mrs, 1938, N 12,15:1
Ackhart, Chester H, 1948, Je 16,29:2
Ackland, Constance Mrs, 1940, O 15,23:1
Ackland, James E, 1967, Ja 15,84:5
Ackland, James E Mrs, 1944, Jl 25,19:5
Ackley, Alfred H, 1960, Jl 7,31:4
Ackley, Bentley D, 1958, S 5,27:2
Ackley, C Edward, 1938, My 6,21:3
Ackley, Charles B, 1964, Jl 27,31:4
Ackley, Charles S, 1951, D 17,32:3
Ackley, Charles S Mrs, 1958, My 26,29:2
Ackley, Edwin C, 1949, Ap 29,23:4
Ackley, Gabriella J D, 1941, N 7,24:4
Ackley, Howard, 1947, F 13,24:3
Ackley, Howard C, 1957, O 24,33:3
Ackley, John L, 1938, Ag 22,13:4
Ackley, John W, 1964, My 9,27:3
Ackley, Lewis A, 1957, Ag 15,21:1
Ackley, Oliver S, 1908, O 25,13:3
Ackley, Seth M Rear-Adm, 1908, F 9,11:5
Ackley, Willard D, 1952, Ap 17,29:1
Ackman, Herman Mrs, 1953, Ja 20,25:3
Ackroyd, Joseph, 1915, Mr 16,11:4
Ackroyd, William Rev Dr, 1914, My 25,11:6
Acland, Francis D, 1939, Je 10,17:4
Acomb, Clifford N Mrs, 1948, N 5,25:2
Acorn, Herbert H, 1939, D 7,27:4
Acosta, Baldomero, 1943, D 4,13:4
Acosta, Bertrand B, 1954, S 2,21:3
Acosta, Carmen Mrs, 1947, Ap 13,1:2
Acosta, Julian A, 1942, My 20,19:4
Acosta, Julian A Jr, 1947, Mr 21,21:4
Acosta, Margaret C Mrs, 1942, Jl 15,19:5
Acosta, Maximo, 1944, Ap 16,42:4
Acosta, Virgilio, 1962, O 6,20:3
Acosta Garcia, Julio, 1954, Jl 7,31:3
Acosta Mejia, Hernan, 1955, My 14,3:4
Acquario, William J, 1964, Mr 29,60:6
Acquavella, A Lawrence, 1968, D 21,37:2
Acquaviva, Frank P, 1957, My 5,89:1
Acquino, Benigno S, 1947, D 22,3:1
Acre, Robert H, 1947, D 13,15:2
Acree, Farley, 1957, O 30,29:4
Acremant, Albert, 1942, Jl 29,17:3
Acres, Henry G, 1945, S 5,23:5
Acritelli, Peter P, 1912, Mr 4,11:6
Acton, Howard, 1953, O 16,27:5
Acton, John Adams, 1910, N 1,9:5
Acton, John E, 1961, D 23,23:3
Acton, John R Jr, 1960, N 11,31:2
Acton, John S, 1941, My 6,21:4
Acton, Joseph H, 1949, O 25,27:2
Acton, Lord, 1902, Je 20,9:3
Acton, Martg R, 1949, N 10,32:2
Acton, Susan Z, 1951, My 13,90:1
Acton, T C, 1898, My 2,5:6
Acton, Thomas C, 1909, D 16,9:5
Acuff, Herbert, 1951, N 3,17:3
Acuff, Joel A, 1945, Ap 5,23:3
Acuff, John K, 1964, D 18,33:4
Acuff, William S, 1949, Je 18,13:5
Acworth, William Sir, 1925, Ap 3,19:7
Adachi, M, 1934, D 29,15:3
Adair, Cornelia Mrs, 1921, S 24,11:4
Adair, F Robin, 1955, F 9,27:3
Adair, Frank E Mrs (Marion), 1965, Ap 30,35:2
Adair, Harry D, 1960, Ja 8,25:2
Adair, Howard A, 1956, D 16,86:4
Adair, J Dunlop Lt-Col, 1903, N 8,7:6
Adair, Jackson L, 1956, Ja 21,21:4
Adair, Jean, 1953, My 12,27:5
Adair, John P, 1958, Mr 20,29:5
Adair, Julian, 1945, N 3,15:4
Adair, Neal G, 1952, F 24,85:1
Adair, Neal G Mrs, 1951, My 5,17:5
Adair, Oliver P, 1953, Je 1,23:4
Adair, Robert, 1937, Mr 25,25:3
Adair, Robert Ewing, 1968, Ag 31,23:3
Adair, Sadie B, 1944, Ja 18,19:1
Adair, Ward W, 1941, Mr 18,23:4
Adalbert, Prince of Prussia, 1873, Je 7,5:4
Adalbert Ferdinand, Prince of Hohenzollern, 1948, S 24,25:5
Adam, Archibald, 1955, My 21,17:4
Adam, Arthur R, 1950, Ag 19,13:5
Adam, Charles F F, 1913, Ja 29,11:4
Adam, Daniel P, 1938, Ap 1,23:2
Adam, Edmond, 1877, Jl 1,5:7
Adam, Elizabeth Mrs, 1950, My 10,31:1
Adam, George A, 1952, D 29,19:3
Adam, George T, 1920, Jl 28,13:5
Adam, James Noble, 1912, F 10,11:6
Adam, Jesse C, 1939, My 26,23:3
Adam, John D, 1949, Ap 16,15:2
Adam, Lajos, 1946, N 22,23:4
Adam, Lena S Mrs, 1940, Ag 2,15:3
Adam, Medora C Mrs, 1939, O 19,24:2
Adam, Paul, 1920, Ja 3,11:2
Adam, Robert B, 1940, Ap 12,23:3
Adam, Robert W, 1911, Je 19,9:5
Adam, W P, 1881, My 25,4:7
Adami, Fred H Mrs, 1954, F 7,88:2
Adami, J G Dr, 1926, Ag 30,15:5
Adamiak, John J, 1940, D 8,71:3
Adamic, Louis Mrs, 1961, F 16,31:3
Adamik, Frank, 1952, Ja 10,29:3
Adamkiewicz, George, 1958, Ap 5,15:4
Adamo, F S Hunter, 1965, Je 1,39:3
Adamo, Frank, 1952, O 1,33:5
Adamo, John, 1922, O 6,23:4
Adamo, Martin E, 1954, Jl 6,23:5
Adamo, Pedro, 1922, O 6,23:4
Adamowska, Antoinette S, 1938, Ag 19,19:2
Adamowski, Timothee, 1943, Ap 19,19:5
Adamowski, Timothee Mrs, 1951, Jl 9,25:1
Adams, A (funl, S 6,5:6), 1877, S 2,7:6
Adams, A Elizabeth, 1962, F 16,29:3
Adams, A Emmett, 1938, O 31,15:6
Adams, Aaron, 1918, Ap 3,13:4
Adams, Abigail, 1955, F 17,22:8
Adams, Adam A, 1952, S 16,29:2
Adams, Adam C, 1952, Jl 1,23:2
Adams, Albert G, 1938, My 29,II,6:7
Adams, Albert S, 1952, Mr 7,23:2
Adams, Albert V, 1948, Ap 7,27:7
Adams, Albertus M, 1952, F 8,23:3
Adams, Alex M Mrs, 1943, Mr 31,19:5
Adams, Alexander, 1947, Je 24,23:1
Adams, Alfred E Sr, 1952, N 8,17:4
Adams, Alice P, 1937, My 10,19:4
Adams, Allison Leland, 1920, Ap 28,11:4
Adams, Alma E, 1951, Mr 2,25:1
Adams, Alma H Mrs, 1941, N 22,19:4
Adams, Alonzo, 1913, Ja 16,17:4; 1940, Je 19,23:5
Adams, Alva, 1922, N 2,19:4
Adams, Alva B, 1941, D 2,23:1
Adams, Amanda H Mrs, 1947, Ja 28,24:3
Adams, Ambrose R, 1918, Je 10,11:8
Adams, Annette A, 1956, O 27,21:6
Adams, Anton C, 1945, Jl 18,27:2
Adams, Arch, 1937, O 22,24:3
Adams, Arthur, 1943, My 20,21:4; 1960, Je 22,35:4
Adams, Arthur F, 1958, Mr 30,88:6
Adams, Arthur H, 1938, S 26,17:2
Adams, Arthur H Sr Mrs, 1945, Jl 30,19:4
Adams, Arthur S Mrs, 1954, Ag 13,15:4
Adams, Augustus J, 1957, Ap 17,31:6
Adams, Avery C, 1963, D 12,39:3
Adams, Avon F, 1924, Ja 7,19:4
Adams, B M Rev, 1902, D 24,9:6
Adams, Benjamin, 1950, Mr 5,93:1
Adams, Benjamin W Mrs, 1950, Ap 26,29:5
Adams, Bert, 1955, Mr 3,27:1
Adams, Bob, 1948, Mr 1,23:4
Adams, Bowdwine W, 1953, Mr 9,29:2
Adams, Braman B, 1944, Je 28,23:5
Adams, Braman B Mrs, 1940, D 25,27:3
Adams, Bristow, 1957, N 20,32:2
Adams, Burdette S Dr, 1937, Ap 3,19:1
Adams, Burton A, 1951, D 17,32:2
Adams, Burton A Mrs, 1952, O 11,19:5
Adams, C E, 1924, F 24,21:3
Adams, C F, 1886, N 22,4:4; 1950, Ja 22,76:6
Adams, C H, 1902, D 16,9:5
Adams, C K Dr, 1902, Jl 27,7:6
Adams, C Robert, 1948, Mr 4,25:5
Adams, Calvin F, 1943, Ag 12,19:4
Adams, Carl, 1937, O 13,23:5
Adams, Carl F, 1946, O 15,25:2
Adams, Carleton E, 1957, Ap 2,31:3
Adams, Caswell, 1957, D 10,35:3
Adams, Cedric M, 1961, F 19,86:5
Adams, Chaim, 1950, Ja 11,10:6
Adams, Chaim Mrs, 1950, Ja 11,10:6
Adams, Charles, 1904, F 4,9:6
Adams, Charles A, 1961, O 5,37:5
Adams, Charles B, 1944, O 19,23:5
Adams, Charles C, 1938, Mr 31,23:2; 1948, Mr 10, 27:1; 1955, My 23,23:3
Adams, Charles Collard, 1925, My 5,21:4
Adams, Charles D, 1938, My 30,11:3
Adams, Charles E, 1957, Ja 28,23:5
Adams, Charles Edson, 1968, N 29,45:4
Adams, Charles F, 1944, N 17,20:3; 1947, S 15,17:2; 1947, O 3,25:5
Adams, Charles F (funl, Je 13,88:4; will, Je 19,16:7), 1954, Je 12,15:1
Adams, Charles F Mrs, 1950, D 20,31:4; 1956, Ap 10, 31:4
Adams, Charles Follen, 1918, Mr 9,13:8
Adams, Charles Francis, 1915, Mr 21,3:3
Adams, Charles H, 1941, F 5,20:3
Adams, Charles Hemmenway, 1915, Ag 29,15:6
Adams, Charles J, 1955, S 5,11:3
Adams, Charles Joshua Rev Dr, 1924, Jl 7,15:5
Adams, Charles L, 1965, Je 22,35:2
Adams, Charles Laden Prof, 1914, S 18,9:6
Adams, Charles P, 1942, O 17,15:3; 1950, F 18,15:1
Adams, Charles R, 1938, D 23,19:5
Adams, Charles S, 1947, D 6,15:2
Adams, Charles T, 1942, D 16,25:6
Adams, Charles Thornton, 1925, F 17,23:3
Adams, Charles W, 1949, Mr 14,19:6
Adams, Chester M, 1953, N 14,17:4
Adams, Clarence H, 1944, Ag 26,11:5
Adams, Claris, 1960, My 4,45:1
Adams, Claude M, 1958, Mr 27,33:4
Adams, Clayton, 1965, Ap 5,31:5
Adams, Cleve F, 1949, D 30,19:2
Adams, Clinton, 1903, F 19,9:6
Adams, Clyde S, 1939, D 21,23:4
Adams, Comfort A, 1958, F 23,93:1
Adams, Crittenden H, 1943, O 7,23:3
Adams, Crosby, 1951, F 28,27:4
Adams, Crosby Mrs, 1951, N 10,17:5
Adams, Dan, 1947, D 1,21:4
Adams, Daniel C Jr, 1962, O 11,39:5
Adams, Daniel G, 1952, Mr 20,29:4
Adams, Daniel W Gen, 1872, Je 15,3:6
Adams, Darwin J, 1967, F 20,37:1
Adams, David, 1942, My 20,19:1
Adams, David E, 1952, S 8,21:4
Adams, David G, 1952, Je 21,8:7
Adams, David M, 1945, Mr 23,19:3
Adams, David S, 1939, F 6,13:4
Adams, Dean Mrs (Margt), 1964, O 31,29:6
Adams, Demarest, 1950, My 22,21:5
Adams, Donald G, 1962, Mr 5,23:2
Adams, Donald Q, 1940, F 14,21:5
Adams, Dunbar Mrs, 1919, Ja 2,9:3
Adams, E (see also O 29), 1877, N 2,5:3
Adams, E D, 1931, My 21,27:1
Adams, E J Mrs, 1941, Ja 14,21:3
Adams, Earl F, 1956, N 2,27:3
Adams, Earl H, 1962, Je 16,19:4
Adams, Edgar F, 1937, D 22,25:5
Adams, Edgar L, 1940, O 8,25:6
Adams, Edgar W, 1947, Mr 11,27:3
Adams, Edith, 1957, Ap 22,25:2
Adams, Edson F, 1946, Jl 28,40:4
Adams, Edward, 1943, F 8,19:2
Adams, Edward A, 1947, Mr 8,13:2
Adams, Edward E, 1949, Ag 21,68:5
Adams, Edward E B, 1941, Ag 24,34:6
Adams, Edward L, 1944, N 21,25:5
Adams, Edwin Dean Mrs, 1921, D 6,19:5
Adams, Edwin G, 1958, Je 24,31:5; 1959, Mr 5,31:6
Adams, Edwin P, 1957, Ja 3,33:5
Adams, Eliot S Mrs, 1955, S 16,23:2
Adams, Elizabeth, 1938, Ag 14,33:5; 1948, D 15,33:4
Adams, Elizabeth C, 1903, Je 14,1:6
Adams, Elizabeth M Mrs, 1941, Jl 22,19:6
Adams, Elizabeth S Mrs, 1944, Ap 12,21:5
Adams, Ella K Mrs, 1939, N 28,26:2
Adams, Ellis, 1956, Ja 16,21:3
Adams, Elmer E, 1944, Ag 22,17:2
Adams, Emily B, 1937, Ag 19,19:4
Adams, Emma G Mrs, 1946, Jl 30,23:3
Adams, Emmor K Jr Mrs, 1954, Mr 2,25:4
Adams, Ernest G, 1954, N 16,29:1
Adams, Ernest J, 1953, N 25,23:4

Adams, Ernest L, 1939, Je 17,15:5
Adams, Estelle K Mrs, 1941, Je 9,19:2
Adams, Evelyn (will, F 21,29:5), 1961, F 20,31:7
Adams, Everett E, 1954, Ja 20,27:4
Adams, Ewing, 1947, Mr 20,28:3
Adams, F Marion Mrs, 1948, My 25,27:1
Adams, Florence L, 1952, Ja 17,27:2
Adams, Floyd H Mrs, 1946, Jl 14,36:3
Adams, Francis Granger, 1903, Jl 14,7:6
Adams, Francis M, 1949, Jl 27,23:4; 1956, Mr 14,33:4
Adams, Francis M Sr, 1945, S 25,25:1
Adams, Francis T, 1962, Je 20,35:4
Adams, Francis W, 1938, S 26,17:4
Adams, Frank D, 1942, D 28,19:4; 1962, Ja 28,77:1
Adams, Frank D Mrs, 1937, My 17,19:3
Adams, Frank H, 1958, Ap 8,29:1
Adams, Frank J Mrs, 1941, My 17,15:2
Adams, Frank M, 1952, Ag 29,23:2
Adams, Frank R, 1957, Ja 6,89:2; 1963, O 9,43:3
Adams, Frank S, 1964, F 11,39:3
Adams, Frank Stewart, 1964, F 23,84:8
Adams, Frank W, 1937, O 5,25:2; 1952, Ja 21,16:5
Adams, Franklin P, 1940, O 11,21:6
Adams, Franklin P (funl, Mr 26,21:4; cor, Mr 27,86:8), 1960, Mr 24,1:2
Adams, Franklyn A, 1955, Ap 12,29:1
Adams, Franklyn S Mrs, 1961, Ja 26,29:1
Adams, Fred, 1946, D 24,17:3
Adams, Fred R, 1952, Jl 18,19:6
Adams, Fred W, 1945, My 22,19:6
Adams, Frederick, 1923, Jl 26,15:4; 1949, Ap 13,29:3
Adams, Frederick B, 1938, F 14,17:2; 1942, Ja 22,17:3; 1961, O 24,37:1
Adams, Frederick C, 1955, Ap 29,23:4
Adams, Frederick J, 1945, My 4,19:4
Adams, Frederick M, 1964, Jl 16,31:1
Adams, Frederick Morse, 1917, F 8,13:7
Adams, Frederick S Dr, 1907, S 22,9:6
Adams, Frederick T, 1910, D 4,13:4
Adams, Frederick Upham, 1921, Ag 30,15:4
Adams, Frederick W, 1949, Ja 19,28:2
Adams, Freeman W, 1954, Ag 25,27:3
Adams, George B, 1943, Mr 30,26:5
Adams, George B Judge, 1911, O 11,11:6
Adams, George C J, 1938, N 27,48:4
Adams, George E, 1956, Jl 20,17:1; 1960, S 5,15:5; 1966, Mr 14,31:4
Adams, George Edward Rev Dr, 1921, O 27,19:6
Adams, George Elder, 1924, O 30,19:5
Adams, George H Mrs, 1919, O 23,13:4
Adams, George M, 1939, D 14,27:3; 1962, O 29,29:4
Adams, George Mrs, 1948, S 1,48:7
Adams, George P, 1961, Ap 21,33:2
Adams, George P Mrs (por), 1937, Jl 18,II,7:1
Adams, George Quincy, 1911, Ja 15,13:4
Adams, George S, 1938, Jl 6,23:2
Adams, George T, 1946, D 3,31:2
Adams, George W, 1945, Mr 17,13:5; 1953, O 24,15:4; 1955, O 14,36:7
Adams, Gerald L, 1954, Je 19,15:3
Adams, Glenn, 1953, Je 23,29:2
Adams, Glenn D, 1948, Jl 15,23:2
Adams, Grace C Mrs, 1937, Jl 5,17:4
Adams, Graham, 1950, N 22,25:4
Adams, Gridley, 1958, Je 24,31:2
Adams, Gridley Mrs, 1958, Ja 17,25:3
Adams, H D Prof, 1901, Jl 31,2:3
Adams, Hamilton, 1964, Ag 15,21:3
Adams, Hampton, 1965, Je 16,44:1
Adams, Harold B, 1945, Jl 9,11:6
Adams, Harold J, 1951, S 20,31:6
Adams, Harold S, 1943, D 6,23:5
Adams, Harold T, 1945, S 28,21:2
Adams, Harry A, 1946, O 26,17:5
Adams, Harry C, 1952, Je 4,27:5
Adams, Harry L, 1960, F 18,33:4
Adams, Harvey S, 1955, Je 25,15:4
Adams, Hazel M, 1937, D 5,II,9:1
Adams, Helen C (funl plans, Ap 2,93:1), 1967, Ap 1, 32:5
Adams, Henri-Georges, 1967, Ag 29,37:1
Adams, Henry, 1918, Mr 28,11:5
Adams, Henry A, 1962, Ja 2,30:7
Adams, Henry E, 1946, Je 1,13:6
Adams, Henry Frederick Dr, 1925, My 19,21:4
Adams, Henry H, 1946, Ja 16,24:2
Adams, Henry H Col, 1906, My 8,9:6
Adams, Henry H Gen, 1907, Ja 27,7:6
Adams, Henry L, 1947, D 15,25:4
Adams, Henry M Brig-Gen, 1909, D 3,11:4
Adams, Henry N, 1941, My 5,17:5
Adams, Henry P, 1945, My 26,15:5
Adams, Henry P Mrs, 1946, S 5,27:2
Adams, Henry S, 1940, Ap 27,15:2; 1948, S 8,29:5
Adams, Herbert, 1945, My 22,19:3; 1960, D 11,88:8
Adams, Herbert M Mrs, 1946, Ag 15,25:5
Adams, Herbert Mrs, 1948, Jl 3,15:3
Adams, Herbert W, 1960, My 9,29:3
Adams, Horace G, 1949, Ja 19,27:2
Adams, Horatio H, 1945, F 15,19:5
Adams, Horatio M, 1956, Ja 28,17:6
Adams, Hugh L (will, Ag 10,15:5), 1956, Ag 8,25:4
Adams, Hugh L Mrs, 1956, Jl 21,15:3
Adams, Hugh R, 1949, Ag 27,13:7
Adams, Hugh W, 1938, D 6,23:4
Adams, Huntington, 1938, My 18,21:6
Adams, Ida C Mrs, 1938, D 2,23:5
Adams, Ida M, 1960, N 5,23:2
Adams, Ira J, 1958, D 6,23:1
Adams, Isaac, 1883, Jl 23,2:7
Adams, Isabela H Mrs, 1938, Ap 2,15:5
Adams, Ivers S, 1955, Je 12,87:2
Adams, J C, 1935, Ja 30,20:1
Adams, J D (will), 1940, Ap 17,8:5
Adams, J Donald, 1968, Ag 24,27:4
Adams, J Fred, 1955, Je 11,15:4
Adams, J G Dr, 1884, Je 24,5:2
Adams, J Horace, 1956, N 28,35:1
Adams, J Kirk, 1942, Je 8,15:3
Adams, J Lee Dr, 1905, Ap 17,9:4
Adams, J McGregor, 1904, S 18,7:7
Adams, J Ottis, 1907, D 15,13:5
Adams, J Q, 1894, Ag 15,8:1
Adams, J Sidney, 1947, S 22,23:5
Adams, J T, 1881, D 13,5:1
Adams, Jack, 1940, Je 26,23:5
Adams, Jack (Jno Jas Adams), 1968, My 2,47:3
Adams, Jacob Mrs, 1948, Jl 22,23:2
Adams, James B, 1941, Ja 11,17:2; 1946, S 30,25:5
Adams, James E, 1953, Ja 25,86:5
Adams, James R, 1956, N 7,31:4; 1959, O 9,29:3
Adams, James R Mrs, 1953, Ag 27,25:1
Adams, James T, 1949, My 19,29:1
Adams, James W, 1953, D 17,37:1
Adams, Jameson B, 1962, My 2,37:3
Adams, Jeannie H Mrs, 1937, Mr 27,15:5
Adams, Jesse E, 1945, Mr 10,17:6
Adams, Jessie, 1941, Ja 7,23:1
Adams, Jessie B Mrs, 1941, Mr 11,24:3
Adams, Jessie S Mrs, 1940, My 28,23:4
Adams, Jewett W Ex-Gov, 1920, Je 19,13:4
Adams, Joe H, 1959, Je 3,35:4
Adams, John, 1941, D 21,40:7; 1964, S 1,35:3
Adams, John B, 1939, Je 9,21:4; 1968, Mr 22,44:3
Adams, John C, 1918, Jl 24,11:4; 1949, F 19,15:1; 1952, O 11,19:1
Adams, John C Mrs, 1948, Ag 23,17:4
Adams, John D, 1942, Ap 5,41:2; 1943, N 16,23:5; 1954, My 29,15:7
Adams, John D Mrs, 1947, O 17,21:1
Adams, John E, 1945, My 25,19:5
Adams, John G, 1952, F 19,29:2
Adams, John H Sr, 1952, S 7,86:4
Adams, John M, 1960, Jl 22,23:4
Adams, John Mrs, 1943, Ap 10,17:2
Adams, John N Mrs, 1950, N 16,31:3
Adams, John P, 1962, Jl 3,23:1
Adams, John Q, 1940, Ja 3,21:4
Adams, John Quincey, 1908, Mr 28,9:6
Adams, John Quincy, 1916, Ag 17,11:4
Adams, John Quincy Col, 1919, Ag 6,9:2
Adams, John Quincy Dr, 1919, F 13,15:5
Adams, John Quincy Mrs (est), 1911, Je 8,11:5
Adams, John S, 1903, S 14,3:2; 1954, Ap 5,25:3; 1966, Ag 23,39:5
Adams, John T, 1939, O 29,41:1; 1962, N 21,33:2
Adams, John T Mrs, 1943, Ap 21,25:1
Adams, John W, 1949, Mr 12,17:5; 1949, O 1,13:4; 1964, Ag 28,29:1
Adams, John Wolcott, 1925, Je 4,19:5
Adams, Joseph, 1957, Ap 19,21:2
Adams, Joseph H, 1924, Ag 21,11:4; 1941, F 10,17:3
Adams, Joseph H Mrs, 1943, My 28,22:3
Adams, Joseph Mrs, 1958, Mr 22,17:6
Adams, Joseph O, 1953, O 10,17:4
Adams, Joseph Q, 1946, N 11,27:3
Adams, Julia Anne Baker, 1915, D 22,11:4
Adams, Julius, 1949, O 15,15:4
Adams, Justin, 1937, F 2,23:2
Adams, Justus C, 1904, Ja 27,9:7
Adams, K C, 1956, Jl 1,56:4
Adams, Karl, 1943, S 23,21:5
Adams, Kate, 1938, Jl 28,19:4
Adams, Kathryn (Mrs J Magnin), 1959, F 19,31:1
Adams, Kenneth, 1943, Je 14,17:4; 1954, S 21,19:2
Adams, Kenneth C, 1967, Jl 9,60:8
Adams, Kenneth S, 1953, Ap 21,27:2
Adams, L, 1936, Mr 27,21:5
Adams, L Sherman, 1959, Mr 13,29:4
Adams, L W Mrs, 1952, My 9,23:3
Adams, Laurena G, 1947, Ja 29,25:3
Adams, Lawrence B, 1952, Ja 29,25:5
Adams, Lee F, 1948, O 16,15:6
Adams, Lee W, 1940, Ja 8,15:1
Adams, Leon, 1945, Jl 26,20:2
Adams, Leonard Mrs, 1947, My 6,28:2
Adams, Lewis B H, 1937, S 28,23:3
Adams, Lewis R, 1940, D 8,71:3
Adams, Lida S, 1940, My 17,19:2
Adams, Lillian B, 1949, Ap 1,25:1
Adams, Louis W, 1953, Je 10,29:3
Adams, Louise, 1940, My 9,23:6
Adams, Lucretia Mrs, 1937, F 26,22:1
Adams, Lucy P, 1954, D 30,17:5
Adams, Lyman D, 1953, Ja 4,76:4
Adams, Lyndon E, 1938, Ap 10,II,6:6
Adams, Lynn G, 1965, D 4,31:3
Adams, Marada F, 1938, Ja 25,22:4
Adams, Marcus, 1959, Ap 11,21:4
Adams, Marion, 1877, Je 29,5:1
Adams, Mark, 1940, O 4,23:5
Adams, Mark H, 1956, O 19,27:3
Adams, Martha R Mrs, 1959, Je 29,29:5
Adams, Mary M Mrs, 1908, D 30,9:6
Adams, Maude, 1953, Jl 18,1:3
Adams, Melvin J, 1953, F 4,27:3
Adams, Melvin O, 1920, Ag 10,13:5
Adams, Michael J, 1967, N 16,14:1
Adams, Michael T, 1940, Mr 15,23:5
Adams, Miles R, 1951, Je 4,27:4
Adams, Millie J Mrs, 1939, Ap 20,23:2
Adams, Milward, 1923, Je 19,19:2
Adams, Morley P, 1954, F 2,27:1
Adams, Morris, 1952, Jl 16,25:4
Adams, N Rev, 1878, O 9,4:6
Adams, Nicholas B Mrs, 1950, Mr 18,13:5
Adams, Nick, 1968, F 8,49:5
Adams, Norman I, 1951, My 13,89:1
Adams, Oliver S, 1924, My 2,19:6
Adams, Orson Jr Mrs (C Wood), 1961, My 24,41:4
Adams, Oscar Fay, 1919, My 1,17:5
Adams, Oscar Mrs, 1937, N 2,25:2
Adams, Patrick H, 1960, Ja 1,19:2
Adams, Patrick Mrs, 1945, My 3,23:3
Adams, Paul B (por), 1937, Ap 3,19:5
Adams, Paul C Mrs, 1950, Mr 5,93:1
Adams, Paul D, 1966, Mr 17,39:2
Adams, Paul P, 1957, My 29,27:2
Adams, Pearl N Mrs, 1949, O 29,15:4
Adams, Percy D, 1937, D 31,16:2
Adams, Phineas H Mrs, 1957, My 16,31:1
Adams, Platt, 1961, Mr 3,27:1
Adams, Porter H, 1945, D 6,28:2
Adams, Queenie, 1937, Ja 18,19:6
Adams, Quincy, 1964, O 10,29:5
Adams, R Hall, 1960, My 17,37:1
Adams, R High, 1948, Ja 16,21:3
Adams, R Ranney, 1953, Ja 17,15:1
Adams, Randolph G, 1951, Ja 5,21:2
Adams, Raphel, 1946, N 8,23:4
Adams, Ray H, 1953, Ap 13,27:3
Adams, Raymond A, 1950, Ja 23,23:4
Adams, Raymond F, 1955, My 19,29:6
Adams, Rebecca, 1957, D 27,20:1
Adams, Richard C Mrs, 1955, Jl 19,27:3
Adams, Richard H, 1925, Jl 16,19:6
Adams, Richard L, 1957, N 7,35:4
Adams, Robert, 1942, Mr 1,45:1; 1955, My 29,45:2
Adams, Robert A, 1950, Mr 13,21:3; 1954, Ja 8,21:5
Adams, Robert B, 1956, Je 29,21:6
Adams, Robert C (por), 1938, O 6,23:5
Adams, Robert C Mrs, 1954, N 27,13:3
Adams, Robert E, 1947, Je 29,48:3
Adams, Robert Franklin, 1923, My 24,19:4
Adams, Robert J, 1951, Ag 28,23:5; 1967, Ap 5,47:1
Adams, Robert K, 1961, Mr 19,89:1
Adams, Robert M, 1955, F 11,23:1
Adams, Robert S, 1938, Mr 2,19:6
Adams, Robert W, 1951, Jl 14,13:4; 1966, My 11,47:2
Adams, Roe R Jr, 1946, O 12,19:4
Adams, Rogers Mrs, 1964, F 2,89:1
Adams, Roscoe C, 1946, Ap 25,21:5
Adams, Rowland K, 1944, Ag 1,15:6
Adams, Ruby, 1954, My 9,88:6
Adams, Russell V, 1965, Ap 7,43:4
Adams, S, 1928, Je 12,27:5
Adams, S Clarence, 1945, My 16,19:4
Adams, S Clarence H Mrs, 1937, F 11,23:3
Adams, S Sterling Jr, 1950, Jl 13,25:5
Adams, Samuel B, 1938, Mr 21,15:4
Adams, Samuel F Jr Mrs, 1967, O 11,47:1
Adams, Samuel H, 1958, N 17,31:2
Adams, Samuel H Mrs, 1946, S 9,9:2
Adams, Samuel S Mrs, 1958, S 27,21:5
Adams, Samuel T, 1942, D 16,25:6
Adams, Sanford W Mrs, 1955, Ag 9,25:1
Adams, Sara E, 1940, F 29,19:5
Adams, Sara J, 1937, F 13,13:4
Adams, Sarah C, 1879, Ja 2,8:2
Adams, Selden C, 1948, S 28,27:4
Adams, Sessions L, 1956, O 27,21:5
Adams, Sidney I, 1943, N 21,56:5
Adams, Soren S, 1963, O 21,31:4
Adams, Spencer S, 1960, Mr 16,37:3
Adams, Stanley H, 1949, Jl 2,15:4
Adams, Stephen (Michl Maybrick), 1913, Ag 27,7:6
Adams, Susan B Mrs, 1937, F 4,21:2
Adams, T, 1878, Jl 6,5:3
Adams, T Albeus, 1940, S 15,49:1
Adams, T Albeus Mrs, 1948, N 15,25:5
Adams, T Rawlins, 1950, Ap 4,29:4
Adams, T S, 1933, F 9,17:5
Adams, Taylor Mrs, 1956, S 15,17:4
Adams, Theodore F, 1939, Mr 28,24:2
Adams, Theodore P, 1949, F 21,23:3
Adams, Thomas, 1905, F 8,9:5; 1940, Mr 25,15:5; 1942, F 7,17:3; 1949, N 19,17:4
Adams, Thomas D, 1923, O 28,23:2; 1939, F 3,15:5
Adams, Thomas F, 1956, Ap 7,19:4

Adams, Thomas Father, 1908, N 23,9:4
Adams, Thomas S, 1963, O 31,34:2
Adams, Thurston, 1961, Jl 29,21:7
Adams, Uriah M, 1939, Jl 22,15:4
Adams, Viola R, 1955, O 28,25:2
Adams, W A, 1941, N 24,17:4
Adams, W Herbert, 1957, S 29,86:5
Adams, W I Lincoln, 1946, Ja 21,23:5
Adams, W R, 1957, Jl 27,17:4
Adams, W S, 1877, Ap 25,4:6
Adams, W T (Oliver Optic), 1897, Mr 28,8:7
Adams, Waldemar Mrs, 1949, Mr 6,73:1
Adams, Waldo, 1955, My 30,13:5
Adams, Walter C Mrs, 1956, Ja 6,23:3
Adams, Walter S, 1949, Ag 30,27:1; 1956, My 12,19:3
Adams, Walton H, 1949, My 22,88:8
Adams, Warren A, 1944, Ag 29,17:5
Adams, Warren S, 1958, O 21,33:4
Adams, Warren S Mrs, 1938, S 24,17:1
Adams, Wayman, 1959, Ap 9,31:2
Adams, Wendell F, 1964, Jl 22,33:2
Adams, Wesley, 1943, Ja 28,19:4
Adams, Wilbur H, 1958, N 7,28:2
Adams, Wilbur L, 1937, D 5,II,9:3
Adams, Wilfred M, 1941, N 18,25:1
Adams, William, 1951, Ag 1,23:3; 1956, Mr 11,88:5
Adams, William A Mrs, 1949, Jl 12,27:4
Adams, William C, 1948, Je 14,23:3
Adams, William Curtis Dr (funl, Jl 26,5:3), 1925, Jl 23,19:5
Adams, William D, 1951, Ag 19,86:3
Adams, William E, 1941, Ag 6,17:3; 1950, Ap 18,31:3
Adams, William E Dr, 1937, N 8,23:2
Adams, William F Mrs, 1956, Mr 13,27:4
Adams, William Forbes Bp, 1920, Mr 6,11:6
Adams, William G, 1965, Ag 31,33:5
Adams, William H, 1954, F 5,19:3; 1966, Je 21,43:2
Adams, William H Judge, 1903, O 13,9:6
Adams, William J Mrs, 1960, Ja 2,13:3
Adams, William Jr, 1954, N 5,15:1
Adams, William L, 1945, N 18,43:2
Adams, William M, 1957, Ap 11,31:3
Adams, William Mrs, 1951, D 4,33:4
Adams, William R, 1937, Ag 11,23:5; 1943, Je 12, 13:2; 1959, O 8,39:5
Adams, William Rev Dr, 1880, Ag 29,1:6
Adams, William S, 1939, Ja 29,33:2
Adams, William T, 1949, Ja 10,25:3; 1961, S 7,35:4
Adams, William W, 1943, Jl 23,17:5; 1961, F 4,19:3
Adams, Willis, 1947, D 31,15:2
Adams, Winnie Mrs, 1960, O 9,86:4
Adams, Winthrop C, 1951, F 26,23:4
Adams-Connor, Harry G, 1939, Je 8,25:3
Adamsen, William, 1951, Ap 24,29:3
Adamski, Andrew J, 1948, Ja 18,60:6
Adamski, George, 1965, My 1,31:4
Adamsky, Max, 1938, S 9,21:2; 1960, O 12,43:2
Adamson, Austin A, 1943, D 25,13:5
Adamson, C, 1931, My 28,27:3
Adamson, Edward E, 1951, S 15,15:4
Adamson, Frederick G, 1946, D 31,18:3
Adamson, H G, 1955, Jl 7,27:3
Adamson, Han Christian, 1968, S 12,47:3
Adamson, James, 1940, My 12,49:1
Adamson, R, 1935, S 20,21:4
Adamson, Rodney, 1954, Ap 9,1:1
Adamson, Roy L, 1956, Ag 11,13:4
Adamson, W C, 1929, Ja 4,25:5
Adamson, W S Rev, 1913, O 9,13:5
Adamson, William M, 1945, O 26,19:1
Adamus, Louis W, 1959, Mr 9,29:3
Adan, John M, 1953, D 9,11:6
Adaskin, Edward, 1951, D 10,29:3
Adb-el-Aziz, Muley, 1943, Je 11,19:4
Adby, Richard, 1951, Ja 26,23:4
Adcock, Clarence L, 1967, Ja 11,25:1
Adcock, Lee C, 1948, D 5,92:2
Adcock, Sarah Mrs, 1942, F 13,21:2
Addams, Clifford I, 1942, N 8,50:1
Addams, G S, 1933, Ap 15,13:3
Addams, Homer, 1953, Jl 4,11:7
Addams, J, 1935, My 22,1:7
Addelson, Harry, 1958, Ja 9,33:3
Addelston, William M, 1941, D 7,77:2
Addems, William J, 1951, O 24,31:2
Addenbrooke, Henry E, 1940, Je 22,15:3
Adderley, Alfred F, 1953, Je 17,38:3
Adderly, Fred C, 1940, Ja 24,21:2
Addi Ou Bihi, 1961, Ja 31,29:3
Addicks, Frank F, 1954, D 8,35:3
Addicks, Fred P, 1911, N 2,11:4
Addicks, J Edward, 1919, Ag 8,9:3
Addicks, W R, 1931, Ap 15,27:3
Addicks, Weda C Mrs, 1937, Ag 29,II,7:4
Addie, C Barton, 1960, N 4,33:4
Addie, Jack, 1939, Ag 4,13:4
Addie, John Mrs, 1962, F 15,29:4
Addieg, Michael, 1908, F 3,9:5
Addington, George Judge, 1921, O 8,13:6
Addington, Keene H, 1922, O 19,21:5
Addinsell, Harry M Mrs, 1961, Mr 24,27:5
Addis, Albert E, 1952, N 10,25:2
Addis, Dorothy C Mrs, 1938, Ja 15,15:1
Addis, Emerson W, 1922, Ag 24,15:6; 1937, Mr 8,19:4
Addis, Ethel, 1949, Je 17,23:3
Addis, J Stanley Mrs, 1946, Ag 21,27:5
Addis, John F Mrs, 1948, F 19,23:3
Addis, John S, 1937, S 30,23:5
Addis, Leonard M, 1951, My 8,31:2
Addis, Thomas, 1949, Je 6,19:3
Addis, Thomas Emmet Col, 1909, Ag 11,7:4
Addison, Albert P, 1952, N 16,89:2
Addison, Carlotta, 1914, Je 16,9:6
Addison, Charles M, 1947, Ja 14,25:4
Addison, Florence E, 1949, Ag 9,25:1
Addison, James, 1941, D 29,15:6
Addison, James Thayer Rev Dr, 1953, F 14,17:6
Addison, John Edmund Wentworth Judge, 1907, Ap 24,9:5
Addison, Michael, 1955, Je 11,15:5
Addison, Viscount, 1951, D 12,37:1
Addison, William H F Mrs, 1948, D 20,25:5
Addiss, Edward F, 1954, Je 14,21:2
Addleman, Samuel W, 1939, Ja 31,21:2
Addoms, Arnold H, 1945, Je 23,13:4
Addoms, Charles, 1881, D 7,5:5; 1944, D 27,20:3
Addoms, Jessie, 1958, Ag 19,27:1
Addoms, Lewis P Mrs, 1960, F 15,27:2
Addoms, Mortimer C Jr, 1955, Ja 1,13:6
Addoms, Samuel Kissam, 1903, N 22,7:6
Addonizio, Anthony, 1949, S 17,17:4
Addonizio, Frank, 1952, Je 24,29:5
Addy, Arthur R, 1940, D 13,26:7
Addy, Richard, 1903, Jl 21,9:6
Addy, Richard C, 1940, Mr 17,49:2
Ade, George, 1944, My 17,19:1
Ade, John, 1914, Ap 29,11:6
Ade, John Mrs, 1907, Ja 27,7:6
Adeane, Charles R W Mrs, 1941, Ag 2,15:6
Adee, Alvey A (por), 1924, Jl 6,21:1
Adee, Ernest R, 1903, D 14,7:4
Adee, Ernest R Mrs, 1956, My 6,86:5
Adee, G T, 1884, N 21,5:1
Adee, George A, 1908, Ag 13,7:4
Adee, George E, 1946, O 8,23:3
Adee, George T, 1948, Ag 1,56:4
Adee, Graham M, 1952, S 12,21:1
Adee, Philip Henry, 1912, My 30,11:6
Adee, Theodore L, 1913, Je 26,9:5
Adel, Frank F, 1967, F 15,41:3
Adel, Milton P, 1965, My 16,88:3
Adelaide, Sister, 1937, My 8,19:5
Adelbert, Justus Dr, 1869, Je 7,5:5
Adelbert, Prince of Bavaria, 1875, S 22,4:7
Adele, Sister (Cath Daughters of Charity of St Vincent de Paul), 1952, Ja 10,29:1
Adelgunda, Sister, 1939, S 26,23:2
Adelhelm, John S, 1951, D 19,31:3
Adeline, Sister, 1942, My 25,15:6
Adelman, Allan J, 1955, Ap 9,13:2
Adelman, Arthur A, 1956, Ag 30,25:5
Adelman, Edward A, 1950, D 26,23:2
Adelman, Henry Mrs, 1938, N 18,22:2
Adelman, Hyman, 1951, N 26,25:1
Adelman, Mary Mrs, 1939, F 10,23:4
Adelman, Max, 1967, S 25,45:2
Adelman, Meyer, 1951, O 31,29:1
Adelman, Meyer A, 1948, Ap 17,15:2
Adelman, S Martin, 1961, S 6,31:6
Adelmann, Hans, 1944, Ap 5,19:3
Adelmar George, Bro (J A Korphage), 1953, Je 22, 21:1
Adelphus Joseph, Bro (J Veno), 1955, Ja 20,31:5
Adelphus Patrick, Bro (J McKenzie), 1953, Mr 28, 17:5
Adels, Joseph, 1951, Ag 9,21:4
Adelsberger, Bransford, 1939, My 10,5:2
Adelsberger, Ignaz, 1945, Ag 27,19:4
Adelsberger, Ignaz Mrs, 1955, Mr 10,27:1
Adelson, Abe N, 1949, My 2,25:1
Adelson, Fred W, 1944, Ag 21,15:3
Adelson, Harry L, 1954, O 31,89:1
Adelson, Irving Mrs, 1957, D 23,23:4
Adelson, Max, 1957, Je 24,23:5
Adelstein, Samuel, 1962, Jl 3,23:3
Adelstein, Thomas, 1960, Ag 15,23:5
Adelung, George W, 1950, N 30,33:2
Adelung, John H, 1952, F 3,85:1
Aden, Chester V, 1939, Ag 22,19:2
Adenauer, August, 1952, O 11,19:1
Adenauer, Konrad (funl, Ap 26,1:2), 1967, Ap 20,1:4
Ader, Clement, 1925, My 4,19:6
Ader, Morris, 1940, Mr 19,25:1
Aderente, Vincent, 1941, Je 15,36:7
Aderer, Hugo, 1964, D 29,27:2
Aderholt, Morris, 1955, Mr 19,15:6
Adgate, Ray J, 1948, O 21,27:2
Adian, Bro, 1948, F 21,13:6
Adiches, Franz Dr, 1915, F 5,11:6
Adickes, Hermann E, 1966, My 9,39:3
Adie, David C, 1943, F 24,21:3
Adie, Ernest R, 1956, Ag 22,29:4
Adikes, Catherine E, 1947, F 6,23:5
Adikes, John, 1921, Ag 30,15:3
Adikes, John Mrs, 1945, Ag 1,19:3; 1956, Ja 7,17:2
Adikes, Laurence, 1967, Jl 31,27:5
Adikes, Thomas, 1937, O 31,II,11:1
Adil, Salahhatin, 1961, Mr 1,33:1
Adion, Henry West, 1916, N 26,21:1
Adir, Ephraim Mrs (Mme Y Majeska), 1959, O 30, 27:1
Adivar, Abdulhak A, 1955, Jl 31,69:3
Adivar, Adnon Mrs (Halide Edib), 1964, Ja 11,23:3
Adjemoff, Moise S, 1953, Ap 1,29:3
Adjutor, Bro (Patrick Goscelin), 1912, N 19,15:4
Adkins, Charles, 1941, Ap 1,23:6
Adkins, Creed T, 1948, S 14,25:6
Adkins, H M, 1926, N 26,19:5
Adkins, Harry C, 1951, Ja 16,29:4
Adkins, Homer, 1949, Ag 13,12:2
Adkins, Homer M, 1964, F 27,31:5
Adkins, Jack, 1954, O 6,25:3
Adkins, Jess, 1940, Je 26,23:2
Adkins, Leonard D, 1967, N 3,45:1
Adkins, Lucien M, 1921, Ag 19,13:5
Adlam, Thomas N, 1952, O 23,31:2
Adlan, William C, 1964, D 9,47:3
Adle, Richard T, 1949, F 19,15:3
Adleblum, Morris, 1945, O 13,15:1
Adler, Abraham, 1946, S 4,24:2
Adler, Abram, 1922, Ja 10,19:3
Adler, Adeline (Mrs A A Victorson), 1958, Je 5,31:6
Adler, Adolph J, 1961, D 24,37:2
Adler, Adolphe, 1957, Je 15,17:5
Adler, Albert A, 1955, N 27,88:8
Adler, Alex E Mrs, 1957, Ag 21,27:1
Adler, Alfred, 1907, S 19,7:6
Adler, Alfred Dr (por), 1937, My 29,17:1
Adler, Alfred Mrs, 1962, Ap 22,80:7
Adler, Allen A, 1964, F 1,23:6
Adler, Alphonse, 1939, Ja 14,17:4
Adler, Arthur, 1948, N 3,27:6
Adler, Arthur H Mrs, 1950, N 16,31:5
Adler, Bert, 1939, Mr 19,III,7:4
Adler, Buddy (E Maurice, funeral, Jl 15,23:4), 1960, Jl 13,35:1
Adler, Carlos, 1957, O 4,23:4
Adler, Caroline Mrs, 1918, D 6,15:4
Adler, Charles S (funl, Ap 8,13:3; trb, Ap 10,13:4), 1911, Ap 6,11:4
Adler, Clarissa W Mrs, 1953, Mr 9,29:1
Adler, Cyrus, 1940, Ap 8,1:3; 1945, Mr 14,19:4
Adler, Cyrus M Mrs, 1939, Ag 7,15:6
Adler, Cyrus Mrs, 1952, Mr 21,23:4
Adler, David A, 1949, S 28,27:2
Adler, Edna, 1924, Ja 30,19:3
Adler, Edward A, 1956, S 9,84:1
Adler, Eleanor H, 1954, Jl 17,13:5
Adler, Elkan N, 1946, S 16,5:3
Adler, Elmer, 1962, Ja 12,35:1
Adler, Emanuel P (por), 1949, Mr 3,25:4
Adler, Emma T, 1938, F 15,25:4
Adler, Ernest, 1965, F 12,29:1
Adler, Ernest F, 1955, My 27,23:2
Adler, Estelle C Mrs, 1954, Ja 24,84:6
Adler, Ethel B C Dr, 1937, Ja 13,23:4
Adler, Eugene C, 1955, My 14,19:4
Adler, F, 1933, Ap 26,15:1
Adler, F Charles, 1959, F 18,33:2
Adler, Felix, 1960, F 2,35:4
Adler, Felix Mrs, 1948, Mr 21,60:2
Adler, Francis, 1964, D 14,36:1
Adler, Francis E, 1906, D 31,7:5
Adler, Francis H Mrs, 1968, Ag 2,33:2
Adler, Frank, 1943, D 15,28:2
Adler, Frederick M, 1946, Ja 30,25:2
Adler, Frederick M Mrs, 1953, O 21,30:6
Adler, Frederick S, 1950, Ja 8,76:3
Adler, Friedrich, 1960, Ja 3,88:4
Adler, George J Prof, 1868, Ag 25,4:6
Adler, Guido, 1941, Ap 3,23:2
Adler, Harry, 1952, Ag 11,15:4
Adler, Harry C, 1940, Mr 28,23:1
Adler, Harry C Mrs, 1956, F 8,33:5
Adler, Harry Dr, 1937, N 2,25:4
Adler, Henrietta F Mrs, 1940, Jl 12,15:3
Adler, Henry L, 1958, Ap 3,31:3
Adler, Herbert M, 1961, Je 12,29:2
Adler, Herman, 1914, Jl 15,9:7
Adler, Herman Mrs, 1908, D 31,9:6
Adler, Hermann Rev Dr, 1911, Jl 19,9:6
Adler, Howard S, 1961, Mr 14,35:1
Adler, Hugo C, 1955, D 27,23:3
Adler, Irving H Mrs, 1966, Ja 13,25:3
Adler, Irving Mrs, 1952, N 7,23:1
Adler, Irving Mrs (Ruth), 1968, Mr 31,81:1
Adler, Isaac, 1941, Je 25,21:4
Adler, Isaac Dr, 1918, My 6,13:8
Adler, Isaac Mrs, 1960, N 2,39:2
Adler, Isaac S, 1941, F 3,20:1
Adler, J, 1926, Ap 1,25:3
Adler, Jack Mrs, 1962, Jl 23,21:3
Adler, Jacob H, 1939, Jl 17,19:5
Adler, Jesse, 1946, F 9,13:4
Adler, Joel S, 1948, Ag 13,15:3
Adler, John Mercer Dr, 1904, F 13,9:5
Adlcr, Joseph, 1953, Ja 25,85:1
Adler, Jules, 1952, Je 13,23:4
Adler, Julius O (funl, O 7,18:1; will, O 21,28:1), 1955, O 4,1:2

Adler, Laurence, 1960, S 3,17:4
Adler, Lena Mrs, 1923, Ag 13,13:4
Adler, Leo, 1954, S 5,50:8; 1958, N 30,86:7
Adler, Leon N, 1960, O 24,29:3
Adler, Leopold, 1948, Ja 14,25:5
Adler, Leopold Mrs, 1942, Ja 10,18:2
Adler, Lewis H Dr, 1915, Jl 16,9:6
Adler, Lothar, 1966, Ja 31,39:2
Adler, Louis, 1938, Ap 14,23:5; 1947, S 10,27:4; 1952, F 28,27:4; 1957, Ag 15,21:1; 1959, Mr 10,35:3
Adler, Louis K, 1958, Ja 25,20:1
Adler, Ludwig, 1958, Ag 9,13:6
Adler, Martin M, 1937, S 20,23:4
Adler, Mary A, 1952, Ag 4,15:5
Adler, Max, 1916, Ja 17,11:4; 1937, Jl 1,27:4; 1952, N 6,29:4
Adler, Max Mrs, 1955, My 8,88:3
Adler, Max P, 1952, N 3,27:2
Adler, Milton, 1962, Jl 4,21:2
Adler, Milton J, 1961, Mr 13,29:4
Adler, Milton S, 1946, O 10,27:4
Adler, Morris B, 1964, Ja 6,47:4
Adler, Morris H, 1967, Jl 8,25:2
Adler, Mortimer, 1950, O 5,31:3
Adler, Morton L (will, F 29,42:1), 1940, F 21,19:3
Adler, Murray L, 1960, O 28,31:5
Adler, Noah, 1939, D 12,27:6
Adler, Oscar, 1956, Mr 2,23:2
Adler, Paul (por), 1938, My 24,19:3
Adler, Phyllis, 1958, Ag 25,21:1
Adler, Polly, 1962, Je 10,65:2
Adler, Reuben S, 1950, S 27,31:5
Adler, Richard M, 1938, Je 23,21:5
Adler, Rudolph S, 1945, Ja 21,40:2
Adler, S L, 1934, My 24,23:1
Adler, Sam, 1959, D 22,31:4
Adler, Samuel, 1943, My 11,21:5
Adler, Samuel M Mrs, 1964, D 7,35:5
Adler, Sarah L Mrs, 1953, Ap 29,29:1
Adler, Sarah Mrs, 1925, Ja 8,25:5
Adler, Sarah P Mrs, 1940, Ag 6,19:5
Adler, Saul, 1966, Ja 26,37:3
Adler, Seymour, 1957, D 26,19:4
Adler, Sidney J, 1952, Ag 12,19:2
Adler, Sidney L, 1956, Mr 10,17:3
Adler, Siegfried, 1958, Je 15,77:2
Adler, Siegmund, 1959, My 23,25:3
Adler, Siegmund Mrs (Estelle), 1968, Je 27,43:3
Adler, Solomon Alfred Rev, 1910, D 1,11:5
Adler, Theresa, 1941, S 6,15:4
Adler, W H, 1942, D 25,18:2
Adler, W Scott, 1944, O 7,13:5
Adler, Yankel, 1949, Ap 27,27:5
Adlerberg, W Count, 1884, Mr 21,5:4
Adlerblum, David, 1937, D 24,17:5
Adlerblum, Morris Mrs, 1951, O 23,29:1
Adlerman, Israel J P, 1941, S 4,21:4
Adlersberg, David, 1960, Ja 11,45:5
Adlersheim, Henry, 1966, My 18,47:2
Adlerstein, Nathan, 1959, Ja 19,27:2
Adlman, Joseph M, 1952, F 12,27:5
Adlon, Gregory G, 1943, Mr 19,19:1
Adlon, Lorenz, 1921, Ap 8,13:5
Adlon, Louis, 1947, Ap 1,27:3
Adly, Hagir Hanum el, 1949, Je 18,13:1
Admas, John Q, 1938, Ap 25,15:5
Admas, John T, 1938, D 20,25:2
Adney, Edgar T, 1950, O 12,31:5
Adolf, Grand Duke of Luxembourg, 1905, N 18,9:6
Adolph, Alfred W, 1914, Ap 25,15:7
Adolph, Frances T, 1949, Ap 14,25:4
Adolph, Frank L, 1950, F 3,23:3
Adolph, Henry F, 1947, Mr 20,28:2
Adolph, J Harry, 1948, N 17,27:3
Adolph, William A, 1958, S 25,33:4
Adolph Leo, Brother, 1937, Ja 20,22:1
Adolphe, Albert J, 1940, N 13,23:2
Adolphe, Edward, 1958, S 30,31:3
Adolphine, Sister, 1948, Ap 17,15:6
Adolphson, Harry B, 1951, Ja 18,27:4
Adolphy, Fritz, 1903, Ag 23,1:2
Adona, John J, 1949, S 25,92:8
Adonas, Thomas (Bro T Lee), 1963, S 17,35:2
Adoree, R, 1933, O 6,17:4
Adoue, Jean B Jr, 1956, N 19,31:4
Adrain, G B, 1878, Ag 18,7:6
Adreani, Leopold, 1948, D 4,13:3
Adrian, Charles L, 1914, Mr 19,9:6
Adrian, Cyril J, 1963, N 5,31:1
Adrian, Francis L, 1952, Je 14,15:2
Adrian, George M, 1952, O 1,33:2
Adrian, George M Mrs, 1963, Je 12,43:3
Adrian, Gilbert (will, O 28,42:3), 1959, S 14,29:3
Adrian, John, 1945, O 9,21:5
Adrian, Joseph M, 1921, Mr 5,13:5; 1944, N 25,13:6
Adrian, Lewis (Bro LaFontaine), 1966, F 1,35:2
Adrian, Louis J, 1950, N 1,35:4
Adrian, Michael Joseph, 1907, F 16,9:6
Adrian, Robert, 1911, Ja 31,9:5
Adrian Luke, Bro, 1952, F 7,27:5
Adriance, Edwin H, 1946, O 31,25:4
Adriance, Everett Mrs, 1948, Ja 5,19:3
Adriance, Francis H Mrs, 1957, F 15,23:4
Adriance, Harris E, 1940, Jl 12,15:1
Adriance, Harris E Jr, 1959, Jl 14,29:5
Adriance, Harris E Mrs, 1953, My 31,72:1
Adriance, I Reynolds, 1923, Ap 18,21:5
Adriance, J E, 1926, My 24,19:6
Adriance, John, 1874, N 5,8:4
Adriance, John P Mrs, 1964, N 18,47:2
Adriance, Mary H Mrs, 1941, Ag 28,19:2
Adriance, Robert I Mrs, 1951, Je 8,27:1
Adriance, Samuel W, 1943, D 20,23:3
Adriance, T M, 1878, Ja 3,3:2
Adriance, Vanderpoel, 1949, Ag 23,24:3
Adriance, Walter M, 1957, Mr 28,31:2
Adriance, Walter Mrs, 1944, Je 13,19:3
Adriance, William A, 1953, Ap 2,27:4
Adsit, Charles C, 1944, Ap 22,15:5
Adsit, Edgar H Mrs, 1946, S 26,25:4
Adsit, Elon B, 1950, O 12,31:5
Adsit, George A, 1951, F 1,25:5
Adsit, Harry B, 1963, D 24,17:2
Adsit, Martin, 1903, D 22,9:5
Adsit, Newman W, 1949, Ap 16,15:5
Adsit, S Rev, 1883, My 20,7:1
Adson, Alfred W, 1951, N 13,29:5
Adt, Leo F Dr, 1937, D 4,17:5
Aduchefsky, Sidney, 1949, My 25,29:5
Adzima, Andrew, 1943, F 14,48:6
Adzima, Andrew L, 1947, Mr 25,25:3
Adzit, Louis, 1949, N 21,25:6
Aebischer, Joseph M, 1952, My 29,27:3
Aeby, Paul, 1955, Ag 5,19:5
Aegeltinger, William F L Mrs, 1948, Jl 24,15:6
Aegerter, Ernest Mrs, 1961, F 21,21:5
Aelred, Rev Bro, 1909, N 2,9:3
Aende, Pascual Dr, 1925, S 29,27:5
Aery, Charles, 1944, Mr 16,19:5
Aery, William A, 1963, O 17,35:4
Aeschbach, Frederick W Sr Mrs, 1949, Ja 4,19:1
Afanassief, Alexis P, 1946, My 5,46:5
Affachiner, Fanny Y Mrs, 1940, Ja 17,21:3
Affeld, Francis O, 1939, Jl 18,19:4
Affeld, Francis Otto, 1953, F 12,28:5
Affeld, Oscar C, 1939, Ag 25,15:5
Affelder, Louis J Mrs, 1960, D 13,31:5
Affelder, William M, 1937, My 13,25:6; 1957, S 22, 86:7
Afferica, Stephen, 1954, N 28,87:3
Affleck, Benjamin F, 1944, F 14,17:4
Affleck, Charles M, 1954, Ja 16,15:2
Affleck, Charles M Mrs, 1948, Mr 14,72:3
Affleck, James G, 1951, O 22,23:5
Affleck, James G Mrs, 1943, F 20,13:3
Affleck, John B, 1955, Ap 26,29:6
Affleck, Joseph F, 1951, Je 15,23:4
Affronti, Joseph, 1952, Ap 28,19:3
Afghanistan, Queen Mother of, 1941, D 15,19:3
Afinogenov, Alex Mrs, 1948, S 26,76:5
Afong, Wing, 1906, S 28,9:5
Afonsky, Nicholas, 1943, Je 17,21:2
Afritsch, Josef, 1964, Ag 27,33:2
Aftenie, Basil, 1950, Jl 18,5:6
Aga, Nazare Gen, 1912, My 14,11:4
Aga Khan III (Rt Hon Aga Sulton Sir Mohamed Shah), 1957, Jl 12,1:4
Aga-Oglu, Mehmet, 1949, Jl 6,30:1
Agabian, Samuel, 1962, Jl 5,25:4
Agagarian, Berdj, 1944, S 7,23:2
Agamennone, Giovanni, 1949, O 7,31:2
Agan, William B, 1946, F 7,23:5
Agar, Calvin A Sr, 1956, O 31,33:6
Agar, Edgerton W, 1939, O 2,17:3
Agar, George P, 1913, Ap 1,11:5
Agar, J G, 1935, S 21,15:1
Agar, John G Mrs, 1943, Ap 2,21:2
Agar, John T, 1948, Ag 28,16:2
Agar, Philip S Mrs, 1958, Jl 23,27:4
Agard, Charles G, 1938, S 14,23:4
Agard, Clarence M, 1947, Ap 6,60:1
Agard, Henry L, 1964, F 25,31:1
Agassiz, Alexander Mrs, 1873, D 24,1:7
Agassiz, Alexander Prof, 1910, Mr 30,12:1
Agassiz, Elizabeth Cabot, 1907, Je 28,7:6
Agassiz, Georges Col, 1910, Jl 19,7:5
Agassiz, Goe R (will, Mr 23,41:7), 1951, F 6,27:3
Agassiz, Louis J A Prof (funl, D 19,1:5;trb, D 16,8:2), 1873, D 15,1:3
Agassiz, Maria D Mrs, 1942, Ja 4,49:2
Agassiz, Maximilian, 1943, S 22,24:2
Agastino, Father, 1921, Ap 7,15:6
Agate, Cecil C, 1956, Jl 8,65:1
Agate, Frederic J, 1951, N 22,31:3
Agate, John H, 1948, D 7,32:2
Agate, Ludwig, 1941, Jl 10,19:2
Agatha, Sister Sacred Heart, 1955, F 24,27:2
Agatha Maria, Sister, 1966, Ja 1,17:1
Agathon, Norman H, 1958, Mr 21,21:2
Agati, Dominick Mrs, 1961, Ja 11,47:2
Agati, Pasquale (Packy O'Gatty), 1966, O 11,47:1
Agatston, Sigmund A, 1945, Mr 7,21:5
Agayants, Ivan Ivanovich Maj Gen, 1968, My 15,47:3
Agayants, Mikhail I, 1959, Ag 26,10:6
Agee, Alva, 1943, D 11,15:3
Agee, Cyril C, 1950, Ag 15,29:4
Agee, James, 1955, My 18,31:4
Agee, William H, 1954, D 4,17:2
Ager, John C Rev Dr, 1913, Je 14,11:5
Ager, Louis C, 1944, My 20,15:4
Ager, Simon H, 1948, F 10,23:3
Ager, Waldemar T, 1941, Ag 2,15:2
Ageton, Richard V, 1937, Mr 4,23:4
Agganis, Harry (funl plans, Je 29,34:7; funl, Jl 1,21:1), 1955, Je 28,27:2
Aggas, Reed A, 1953, S 29,29:1
Aggeler, William T, 1937, Jl 16,19:5
Aggiman, Jacques N, 1942, Jl 24,19:4
Aghetto, Vittorio Rev, 1937, Ap 4,II,10:6
Agid, Samuel, 1914, D 17,13:6
Agins, Aaron, 1961, Mr 12,86:4
Agius, Francis J, 1958, Ja 26,88:3
Agius, Msgr, 1911, D 14,13:4
Aglassinger, Andreas, 1940, F 22,23:5
Aglipay, Gregorio, 1940, S 2,15:4
Agman, Abraham F Mrs, 1961, Jl 6,29:4
Agne, Charles L, 1952, F 12,27:1
Agne, Charles L Mrs, 1947, D 5,25:4
Agnelli, Giovanni, 1945, D 17,21:3
Agnes, Countess of Winchilsea and Nottingham, 1964, Je 24,37:4
Agnes, Philomena Sister (McCruden), 1950, Ap 1, 15:7
Agnes, Stanislaus Sister (Cullum), 1950, Jl 23,56:2
Agnes, Veronica Sister, 1939, F 8,23:4
Agnes Aloysius Scott, Sister, 1937, Je 10,23:5
Agnes Cecilia, Sister, 1937, Mr 24,25:4
Agnes Claire, Sister (Order of St Dominic), 1958, Je 3,31:1
Agnes de Jesus, Mother, 1951, Jl 29,69:3
Agnes de Sales, Sister(Sisters of Charity),1956, D 1, 21:2
Agnes Dolores, Sister (M Maher), 1962, S 15,25:2
Agnes Eusebius, Sister (Sisters of Charity), 1954, Ap 14,29:5
Agnes Frances, Sister (Dominicans), 1960, Je 4,23:6
Agnes Jerome, Sister, 1923, Ja 8,17:6
Agnes Leo, Sister, 1944, N 18,13:4
Agnes Mary, Sister, 1948, D 11,15:4
Agnes Teresa, Sister(Sisters of Charity of Nazareth), 1955, Ja 17,23:2
Agneta, John, 1961, Mr 8,33:3
Agnew, Andrew, 1955, Mr 5,17:4
Agnew, Andrew D, 1951, D 21,27:2
Agnew, Anna M, 1957, Ja 8,31:5
Agnew, Austin A, 1967, Ja 4,41:1
Agnew, C R Dr, 1888, Ap 19,8:3
Agnew, C Rutledge, 1940, F 14,21:3
Agnew, Charles A, 1941, Je 4,23:5
Agnew, Charles H, 1944, N 3,21:2
Agnew, Charles J, 1938, Ja 27,21:1
Agnew, Clark M, 1959, My 3,86:4
Agnew, Cornelius R, 1954, N 24,23:3
Agnew, Cyrus F, 1940, Ag 28,19:2
Agnew, Daniel Judge, 1902, Mr 10,9:7
Agnew, David Q, 1941, F 9,48:2
Agnew, Edward J, 1944, Jl 2,22:1
Agnew, Em C, 1956, Jl 19,27:3
Agnew, Fletcher Mrs, 1947, D 11,33:6
Agnew, George B (will, Jl 15,16:7), 1941, Je 22,32:3
Agnew, George W, 1941, D 20,19:5
Agnew, Harold A, 1947, F 21,19:1
Agnew, Hobart M'V, 1965, Ap 16,29:4
Agnew, Hugh E, 1955, Jl 31,69:3
Agnew, Hugh E Mrs, 1957, O 6,84:3
Agnew, J L, 1931, Jl 10,19:1
Agnew, J Stuart, 1937, N 19,23:3
Agnew, James Mrs, 1952, D 1,23:6
Agnew, John A, 1939, Ag 4,13:1
Agnew, John C, 1953, S 16,33:3
Agnew, John H, 1953, Je 20,17:6
Agnew, Minnie Mrs, 1941, S 16,23:2
Agnew, Neil, 1958, Je 12,31:4
Agnew, Paul G, 1954, Ja 10,86:2
Agnew, Peter H, 1953, Ja 21,31:4
Agnew, Sam, 1951, Jl 21,13:4
Agnew, Seth M, 1967, Ag 12,25:4
Agnew, Seth Mrs (M E Edes), 1962, O 27,25:4
Agnew, Susan Mrs, 1903, D 8,9:5
Agnew, Walter N, 1942, Ag 1,11:6
Agnew, Willard F Jr, 1961, Mr 15,39:3
Agnew, William G, 1960, Jl 13,35:2
Agnew, William J C, 1955, Ja 27,23:3
Agnew, William L, 1946, D 27,19:4
Agnew, William Sir, 1910, N 1,9:5
Agnini, Armando, 1960, Mr 28,29:2
Agnini, Gregorio, 1945, O 7,44:2
Agnus, Felix Gen, 1925, O 31,17:5
Agoglia, John F, 1939, Ap 12,23:1
Agolia, Michael W, 1963, Ap 6,19:5
Agoncillo, Felipe, 1941, O 1,21:2
Agoos, Samuel L, 1945, Mr 19,19:5
Agoos, Solomon (will, F 7,16:7), 1953, Ja 31,15:2
Agor, Joseph, 1952, O 15,31:4
Agostini, Carlo, 1952, D 28,51:3; 1953, Ja 1,23:2
Agostini, Giovanni de, 1941, N 24,17:4
Agostini, Giuseppe, 1951, Jl 28,11:5
Agostini, Joseph, 1912, Mr 31,15:3

Agostini, Pierre, 1959, Ja 28,31:4
Agoston, Emanuel, 1946, D 20,23:2
Agote, Carlos M, 1950, O 24,29:2
Agramonte, A, 1931, Ag 18,21:1
Agramonte, Ignacio Gen, 1873, My 24,2:7
Agraphiotis, Rudolph, 1952, D 27,9:5
Agrella, Giuseppe, 1950, N 2,31:2
Agrella, Joseph R, 1940, Mr 18,17:5
Agress, Leo, 1958, O 27,27:2
Agrinaldo, Emelio Mrs, 1921, Mr 11,15:5
Agron, Gershon, 1959, N 2,31:1
Agry, Warren C, 1958, Ja 18,15:4
Aguais, H Raymond, 1946, F 18,21:4
Aguero, Joaquin W de, 1920, Mr 18,11:5
Aguero, Miguel E de, 1920, S 19,22:2
Aguero y Betancourt, A de, 1933, Je 22,19:3
Auglia, Francesco Sen, 1921, Ap 16,11:5
Aguiar, Americo de, 1956, Jl 17,21:1
Aguiar, Braz D de, 1947, D 18,30:3
Aguilar, Francisco, 1947, Ja 18,15:4
Aguilar, John, 1953, S 18,24:3
Aguilar, Raymond G, 1954, Mr 2,25:5
Aguilar, Roberto, 1959, Ja 1,31:5
Aguilera, F V (funl, F 27,8:4), 1877, F 24,5:3
Aguinaldo, Emilio (trb, F 7,32:6), 1964, F 6,1:6
Aguinaldo, Leopoldo R, 1958, My 1,31:4
Aguinaldo, Pio I, 1964, Ja 4,23:4
Aguirre, Jorge de, 1947, Je 24,23:5
Aguirre, Jose A de, 1960, Mr 23,37:4
Aguirre, Salvador, 1947, Jl 24,21:6
Aguirre Cerda, Pedro, 1941, N 26,10:1
Aguirre y Gonzalo, Antonio M de, 1963, Mr 13,7:1
Aguirrezadal, Valentine, 1963, Je 26,7:3
Agutter, George, 1968, N 20,57:8
Ahaesey, Thomas F, 1945, S 11,23:4
Ahders, Rebecca E F Mrs, 1945, Ap 16,23:2
Ahearn, Andrew J, 1956, Mr 19,31:1
Ahearn, Bertram J, 1949, N 11,25:1
Ahearn, Charles, 1940, Ap 27,15:4
Ahearn, Daniel F, 1949, Ja 11,27:1
Ahearn, E J, 1934, Ag 24,15:4
Ahearn, Edward G, 1959, D 13,86:6
Ahearn, Elizabeth A Mrs (will, N 23,21:6), 1937, N 12,21:4
A'Hearn, Frank B, 1962, N 16,32:1
Ahearn, Frank H, 1952, D 28,48:7
Ahearn, George P, 1942, My 14,19:2
Ahearn, James A, 1960, Jl 12,35:3
Ahearn, James F, 1938, Ja 4,23:5
Ahearn, John F, 1920, D 20,13:5
Ahearn, John J, 1938, O 12,27:2
Ahearn, Joseph Francis, 1924, Jl 29,15:5
Ahearn, Lawrence J, 1947, Ap 19,15:2
Ahearn, Michael F, 1948, F 6,26:6
Ahearn, Michael T, 1950, Ja 1,43:1
Ahearn, Paschal, 1952, S 19,24:3
Ahearn, Patrick J, 1949, O 29,15:4
Ahearn, Richard L, 1949, Je 22,31:3
Ahearn, T J, 1933, F 17,20:1
Ahearn, Thilliam Rev, 1907, Jl 29,9:5
Ahearn, Thomas (por), 1938, Je 29,19:4
Ahearn, Thomas A, 1946, Ap 22,21:1
Ahearn, Thomas J Jr, 1968, Je 25,41:5
Ahearn, Timothy T, 1941, S 17,23:5
Ahearn, William J, 1957, Mr 8,25:1
Aheken, Dr, 1872, Ag 26,5:5
Ahern, Cornelius J, 1945, S 14,23:1
Ahern, Daniel B, 1941, S 5,21:1
Ahern, Eugene L, 1960, Mr 7,29:2
Ahern, Francis J, 1958, S 2,25:2
Ahern, Francis X, 1943, Ap 17,17:2
Ahern, Frank G, 1952, Mr 19,29:4
Ahern, Fred J Mrs, 1948, D 14,29:5
Ahern, Fred M, 1950, S 19,29:6
Ahern, Frederic J, 1953, D 2,2:7
Ahern, Frederick, 1958, N 16,89:1
Ahern, Hilary R, 1954, D 15,31:4
Ahern, James F Rev (funl, Ag 13,19:6), 1925, Ag 10, 13:6
Ahern, James L, 1960, F 27,19:6
Ahern, John F, 1939, Ap 2,III,7:2
Ahern, John J, 1950, O 29,92:7
Ahern, John W, 1945, Je 10,32:5
Ahern, Leonard L A, 1951, N 3,17:5
Ahern, Mary E, 1938, My 25,23:4
Ahern, Maurice J Mrs, 1947, My 3,17:2
Ahern, Michael J, 1951, Je 6,31:5
Ahern, Neal, 1960, O 23,88:5
Ahern, Patrick, 1925, F 26,21:4; 1940, Ap 23,23:5
Ahern, Patrick J, 1940, S 5,23:5
Ahern, Phil E Father, 1903, D 25,7:6
Ahern, Thomas J, 1951, Ag 16,27:6
Ahern, William D, 1948, Ap 13,27:2
Aherne, Daniel, 1945, My 20,32:5
Ahi, Majid, 1946, S 15,9:7
Ahlberg, Eda M Sister, 1959, Jl 29,29:2
Ahlborn, Emil, 1964, Ja 30,29:4
Ahlbum, Sumner P, 1964, N 14,29:2
Ahle, William B, 1948, S 19,78:4
Ahlers, Carl, 1947, Je 9,21:4
Ahlers, L Paul, 1957, My 30,19:5
Ahlert, Fred E, 1953, O 21,30:3
Ahles, John William, 1915, Ag 20,11:6
Ahles, Robert Lawrence, 1921, O 18,17:2
Ahlfeldt, Alfred, 1941, Ap 12,15:2
Ahlgren, Harry, 1941, O 8,25:5
Ahlgren, Oscar A, 1955, F 15,27:2
Ahlgrim, William H, 1960, Je 10,31:2
Ahlin, Karl A, 1953, N 18,31:3
Ahlman, Einar, 1937, Mr 9,23:4
Ahlquist, Harald, 1938, S 8,23:3
Ahlschlager, Walter W, 1965, Mr 30,47:2
Ahlstrom, Carl F, 1945, D 28,15:2
Ahlstrom, John, 1937, Ap 24,19:3
Ahmad, Zia-Uddin, 1947, D 26,15:4
Ahmad Seif al-Islam, Imam of Yemen (funl, S 21,8:5), 1962, S 20,1:4
Ahmanson, Howard Fieldstead, 1968, Je 18,47:1
Ahmed, 1875, Mr 30,6:6
Ahmed Mukhtar Pasha, 1879, N 29,5:4
Ahmed Seif el Din, Prince, 1937, N 20,17:1
Ahn Changho, 1938, Mr 23,7:3
Ahnelt, William P (por), 1949, O 6,31:1
Ahner, George P, 1959, Ja 16,27:2
Ahner, John M, 1940, My 2,23:5
Ahner, Walter F, 1954, O 21,27:5
Ahner, Walter Mrs, 1937, Ja 30,17:5
Ahnert, Otto C, 1949, N 30,27:1
Ahnert, Paul, 1947, Mr 11,27:4
Aho, Andrew, 1950, S 7,31:3
Ahr, George, 1959, Ap 12,87:2
Ahr, George A Mrs, 1961, N 18,23:5
Ahrberg, Fred, 1951, N 25,86:4
Ahrend, David H, 1950, F 28,29:5
Ahrendt, Carl, 1909, Ja 12,9:4
Ahrens, Adolf, 1957, Ja 23,29:3
Ahrens, Adolph G, 1955, Ja 12,27:2
Ahrens, August C, 1949, Je 24,23:5
Ahrens, Charles E, 1949, O 24,23:6
Ahrens, Edward H, 1947, F 3,20:2
Ahrens, Frank E, 1956, S 12,37:4
Ahrens, Gerard W, 1959, Ag 28,23:3
Ahrens, Gustav E Mrs, 1944, N 8,17:3
Ahrens, Harry A, 1949, Ja 4,40:2
Ahrens, Harry B (Mr and Mrs), 1960, O 9,73:3
Ahrens, Henry A, 1951, My 9,33:1
Ahrens, Herman F, 1958, S 30,31:3
Ahrens, Irving B, 1948, Mr 18,27:2
Ahrens, John, 1953, My 21,31:5
Ahrens, John P Jr, 1940, My 25,17:6
Ahrens, Minnie H, 1943, Je 26,13:3
Ahrens, Robert H Sr, 1954, Je 24,27:3
Ahrens, Rudolph P, 1958, My 24,21:6
Ahrens, Theodore, 1938, Je 13,19:4
Ahrens, Thomas J, 1948, F 22,48:2
Ahrens, William A Jr, 1952, Ag 14,23:3
Ahrens, William E, 1949, Jl 21,25:5
Ahrens, William F, 1954, Ja 30,17:3
Ahrens, William F Mrs, 1943, Ap 13,25:5
Ahrling, Walter F, 1948, O 11,23:5
Ahronovitz, Josef, 1937, Mr 29,19:5
Ahuja, Manchar Mrs, 1962, Ag 8,34:5
Ahumada, Miguel, 1916, Ag 28,9:5
Aibinder, Arthur M, 1964, Ag 29,21:6
Aicard, Jean, 1921, My 14,9:4
Aichberger, Carl, 1962, O 21,88:8
Aichele, George J, 1960, Ag 16,19:5
Aichele, Henry P, 1956, F 15,31:4
Aichinger, Benno, 1951, S 24,27:2
Aickelin, Hans W, 1944, Jl 17,15:4
Aidala, Francesco Mrs, 1952, Mr 22,13:4
Aide, Gerald F X, 1950, O 31,27:4
Aiello, Adamo R, 1947, Je 26,23:2
Aiello, Anthony, 1947, My 28,25:2
Aiello, Joseph, 1964, Ja 16,25:3
Aiello, Nick, 1945, Mr 18,42:3
Aierstok, Leonard G, 1964, Mr 24,33:2
Aievoli, John, 1961, D 8,37:1
Aigeltinger, Albert E, 1957, N 21,30:1
Aigeltinger, Arthur, 1942, Ja 1,25:6
Aigler, Ralph W, 1964, My 25,33:3
Aigler, Ralph W Mrs, 1943, Ja 23,13:5
Aigner, Martin Mrs, 1945, N 10,15:4
Aiguier, Gabriel, 1903, D 7,7:3
Aiken, Alfred L, 1946, D 14,15:3
Aiken, Alfred L Mrs, 1942, Mr 21,17:2
Aiken, Alfred Mrs, 1960, Ap 15,24:1
Aiken, Ann Cleveland, 1903, N 24,9:5
Aiken, Arthur M, 1941, D 6,17:6
Aiken, Chae A, 1965, F 12,29:5
Aiken, Charles Francis Rev, 1925, Jl 9,19:4
Aiken, Charlotte A, 1949, O 22,17:7
Aiken, Cloris, 1952, Mr 25,27:3
Aiken, Donald H, 1960, Ag 27,19:3
Aiken, E C, 1933, Jl 7,17:4
Aiken, Edward L, 1941, F 7,19:2
Aiken, Edward W, 1943, Ag 1,38:7
Aiken, Edwin E, 1951, Ja 7,78:3
Aiken, Frank A, 1963, S 26,36:1
Aiken, Frank Eugene, 1910, O 18,9:4
Aiken, Frank L Mrs, 1957, O 29,31:3
Aiken, G Randolph, 1941, S 26,23:4
Aiken, George D Mrs, 1966, My 11,47:2
Aiken, Howard, 1959, D 8,90:5
Aiken, James W, 1961, N 2,37:5
Aiken, Janet, 1944, F 6,42:2
Aiken, John B, 1964, Ag 16,92:7
Aiken, John H, 1956, Jl 8,64:2
Aiken, John W, 1968, D 25,31:2
Aiken, Louis E, 1949, Je 30,23:2
Aiken, Mary T, 1951, S 3,13:3
Aiken, Matthew M, 1953, Ag 28,17:1
Aiken, Max, 1946, S 20,31:3
Aiken, Pauline, 1956, Ja 16,21:5
Aiken, R Eugene, 1951, Ag 3,21:4
Aiken, Rachel Mrs, 1915, Ag 1,15:5
Aiken, Samuel, 1919, Mr 30,22:5
Aiken, Thomas G, 1956, D 23,30:8
Aiken, William A, 1957, S 27,19:2
Aiken, William M, 1908, D 8,9:4
Aiken, William S Sr, 1952, Mr 20,29:3
Aikenhead, Henry A, 1943, Je 4,21:5
Aikenhead, J Ray, 1952, Ag 21,19:6
Aikens, Andrew J, 1909, Ja 23,9:4
Aikens, H Hayes, 1942, F 8,50:2
Aikens, Walter W, 1948, Je 22,25:1
Aikin, Raymond A Mrs, 1945, F 18,34:6
Aikin, William A, 1939, Jl 28,17:3
Aikins, Frederick H, 1955, D 1,35:2
Aikman, Charles R, 1937, Ap 6,23:5
Aikman, Duncan, 1955, D 15,75:3
Aikman, Hugh, 1942, Je 22,15:6
Aikman, John, 1948, Jl 15,23:1
Aikman, Myra H Mrs, 1942, S 12,13:4
Aikman, Robert, 1960, O 18,39:4
Aikman, Walter M, 1939, Ja 4,21:4
Aikman, Walter Monteith, 1923, Jl 7,11:7
Aileran Edward, Bro (E P Gilvey), 1957, F 13,35:2
Ailes, Milton E, 1925, O 31,17:6; 1943, O 27,23:4
Ailes, Sally C Mrs, 1961, D 18,35:4
Ailesbury, Marquess of (Geo W J C Brudenell-Bruce), 1961, Ag 6,85:1
Ailesbury, Marquis of (Hy Augustus Brudenell-Bruce), 1911, Mr 11,13:5
Ailleret, Charles Gen, 1968, Mr 10,1:7
Ailsa, Marchioness of (F Kennedy), 1949, N 1,27:2
Ailsa, Marquess of, 1938, Ap 10,II,6:5; 1943, Mr 2, 19:5
Ailsa, Marquess of (C Kennedy), 1956, Je 3,86:6
Ailsa, Marquess of (C Kennedy), 1957, Je 3,27:6
Ailshie, Margaret C Mrs, 1959, Ag 27,27:5
Aim, Frank, 1950, F 24,23:2
Aim, Frank Mrs, 1949, Jl 14,27:2
Aiman, Arnold, 1955, N 12,19:1
Aimard, G, 1883, My 2,5:5; 1883, Jl 9,3:6
Aime, Frank L Mrs, 1967, O 21,31:4
Aimee, Joseph A, 1966, Ap 30,31:2
Aimee, Marie, 1887, O 4,5:3
Aimes, Hubert H S, 1949, Jl 22,19:1
Aims, Joseph F, 1957, F 17,92:3
Ain, Wolf, 1946, Ap 10,27:1
Ainey, W D B, 1932, S 5,11:5
Ainey, William H, 1907, N 13,9:6
Ainge, Edith, 1948, O 26,31:2
Ainger, D B Gen, 1913, Ap 3,9:6
Ainley, Allan B, 1955, F 18,21:3
Ainley, Henry, 1945, N 1,23:2
Ainley, William H, 1941, F 7,19:4
Ainslie, Douglas, 1948, Mr 30,23:1
Ainslie, George F Jr, 1954, F 22,19:1
Ainslie, H, 1878, Mr 15,5:5
Ainslie, James Mrs, 1963, Ag 9,23:4
Ainsworth, Albert A, 1943, Ag 11,19:5
Ainsworth, Bertram W, 1957, D 8,87:4
Ainsworth, Clinton W Col, 1908, F 19,7:7
Ainsworth, Cyril (cor, D 15,43:3), 1964, D 14,35:4
Ainsworth, Ed (Edw Maddin Ainsworth), 1968, Je 18,44:4
Ainsworth, F C, 1934, Je 6,21:1
Ainsworth, Forester F, 1955, S 23,25:3
Ainsworth, George C, 1948, S 26,76:6
Ainsworth, H, 1882, Ja 17,6:2
Ainsworth, Harry, 1965, Ag 6,27:1
Ainsworth, Helen, 1961, Ag 20,86:6
Ainsworth, Thomas H, 1958, N 25,33:2
Ainsworth, W H (Novelist), 1882, Ja 4,5:2
Ainsworth, William A Mrs, 1951, Je 19,29:4
Ainsworth, William N, 1942, Jl 8,23:2
Ainsworth, William T, 1947, Jl 18,17:3
Aird, Alex N, 1958, S 9,35:4
Aird, Allan E, 1955, N 12,19:2
Aird, Ian, 1962, S 18,39:4
Aird, John (por), 1938, D 1,23:1
Aird, John Sir, 1911, Ja 7,9:5
Aird, Thomas, 1876, Ap 29,5:2
Airedale, Lord, 1944, Mr 13,15:3
Airedale, Lord (R D Kitson), 1958, Mr 21,21:1
Airey, Edwin, 1955, Mr 15,29:3
Airey, Guy, 1953, D 14,31:5
Airey, James, 1937, S 10,24:1
Airey, Lord, 1881, S 15,5:2
Airey, Richard, 1948, F 3,25:2
Airlie, Earl, 1881, O 17,2:3
Airlie, Earl of (David Lyulph Gore Wolseley Ogilvy), 1968, D 29,52:3
Airlie, Mabell Dowager Countess of, 1956, Ap 9,27:4
Aisen, Maurice, 1942, F 28,17:6
Aisenbrey, Edward J, 1946, Mr 1,21:2
Aisenman, Wolf, 1917, Ag 2,9:6

Aisenstadt, Isaia, 1937, Jl 23,19:5
Aisenstein, Louis, 1943, Mr 11,21:5
Aisenstein, Morris Mrs, 1957, Ap 16,33:4
Aisenstein, Simon M, 1962, S 4,33:4
Aishton, Richard H, 1946, O 4,24:2
Aita, Vincent, 1948, O 9,19:5
Aitchison, Clyde B, 1962, Ja 17,33:3
Aitchison, Clyde B Mrs, 1944, Ja 6,23:5
Aitchison, Edgar A, 1963, Ap 24,35:3
Aitchison, George Prof, 1910, My 17,9:6
Aitchison, Lord, 1941, My 3,15:4
Aitchison, Robert G, 1949, My 6,25:2
Aitchison, Robert J, 1961, F 7,33:4
Aitchison, Stephen, 1942, Ag 27,19:6
Aitchison, William W, 1965, Ag 24,31:4
Aitken, Allan A, 1959, Ja 25,92:6
Aitken, Ambrose S, 1959, Ap 26,87:1
Aitken, Andrew W, 1959, D 29,25:2
Aitken, Annie, 1942, Ap 26,39:2
Aitken, Beekman, 1962, My 17,37:5
Aitken, Charles S, 1955, Mr 3,27:5
Aitken, Douglas V, 1958, F 16,86:1
Aitken, H Frederick, 1939, Je 25,37:1
Aitken, Harry E, 1956, Ag 2,25:6
Aitken, Herbert M, 1939, F 10,23:6
Aitken, J B, 1881, Ap 20,8:2
Aitken, J Manus, 1950, F 22,30:8
Aitken, J Mauns Mrs, 1954, Mr 3,27:2
Aitken, James, 1903, O 2,7:6
Aitken, John W, 1915, S 4,7:6
Aitken, John W Mrs, 1909, D 30,9:5
Aitken, Margaret, 1958, Ap 5,15:4
Aitken, Peter, 1939, Ap 1,19:6; 1947, Ag 5,23:6
Aitken, R T D, 1939, F 23,23:2
Aitken, Robert C, 1965, Mr 12,33:2
Aitken, Robert G, 1951, O 30,29:3
Aitken, Robert I, 1949, Ja 4,19:1
Aitken, Samuel (por), 1938, Ag 13,13:4
Aitken, Samuel R Mrs, 1953, O 26,21:3
Aitken, Tommy, 1941, Jl 10,19:4
Aitken, William M (Lord Beaverbrook),(will, Ag 14,14:1), 1964, Je 10,1:4
Aitken, William T, 1964, Ja 20,43:3
Aitken, William W, 1950, N 7,27:2
Aitkenhead, Arthur, 1949, N 3,29:4
Aitkin, Charles S, 1944, Ja 1,13:3
Aitkon, Arthur S, 1955, D 31,13:2
Aitoro, Nicholas, 1946, Ap 30,22:3
Ajalbert, Jean, 1947, Ja 16,25:1
Ajas, Paul, 1911, S 14,9:5
Ajello, Antonino (por), 1938, Ag 9,19:4
Ajello, Antonino, 1964, O 25,88:8
Ajello, Joseph, 1918, Ag 24,7:4
Ajello, Rose Mrs, 1943, Ja 21,21:1
Ajello, Vincent J, 1949, Ap 30,13:3
Ajootian, Khosrov, 1958, N 29,21:2
Ajuti, Andrea Cardinal, 1905, Ap 29,11:6
Ajzenberg, Mojzesz A, 1962, My 16,41:4
Akamatsu, Norik, 1945, Ag 5,38:7
Akashi, Lt-Col, 1919, O 31,13:6
Akbar, Hydari Sir, 1942, Ja 9,21:4
Akberg, Charles W N, 1937, Ja 26,21:3
Aked, Charles F, 1941, Ag 13,17:6
Akehurst, Herbert F Mrs (M W Smith), 1961, My 4, 37:5
Akelaitis, Andre J, 1955, N 26,19:3
Akeley, C, 1926, D 1,1:2
Akeley, H C, 1912, Ag 1,11:5
Akerberg, Herbert V, 1964, N 7,27:4
Akerhielm, George H, 1958, S 21,86:8
Akerlof, Gosta C, 1966, My 11,34:7
Akerly, Lucy D (will), 1938, F 10,21:1
Akerman, A T, 1880, D 23,4:7
Akerman, Alex, 1948, Ag 22,63:3
Akerman, J C, 1950, O 31,27:4
Akerman, Joseph, 1943, D 11,15:2
Akeroyd, Andrew G S, 1948, Ja 6,23:5
Akeroyd, James, 1953, Ap 22,29:2
Akers, Arthur K Mrs, 1955, Mr 29,29:1
Akers, Dwight, 1968, Mr 14,43:2
Akers, E W Mrs, 1953, Ja 28,27:1
Akers, Edward L, 1942, O 5,19:1
Akers, Forest H, 1966, D 10,37:5
Akers, J Keith, 1964, N 15,86:4
Akers, John S, 1946, S 7,15:4
Akers, John S Mrs, 1946, Jl 24,27:2
Akers, Wallace A, 1954, N 2,27:3
Akerson, George E (por), 1937, D 22,25:3
Akerson, George E Mrs, 1965, My 18,39:2
Akhmatova, Anna (cor, Mr 9,41:4), 1966, Mr 6,92:5
Akhremenko, Ivan, 1950, Je 1,7:4
Akhunbabayev, Juldash, 1943, Mr 1,19:2
Akimov, Georgi V, 1953, Ja 29,27:1
Akimov, Nikolai Pavlovich, 1968, S 7,29:4
Akin, A J, 1903, Ja 13,9:7
Akin, A John, 1962, N 25,86:7
Akin, Albert J, 1942, My 28,17:2
Akin, Charles G, 1953, S 27,87:2
Akin, Charles G Mrs, 1950, Mr 11,15:2
Akin, Edward A, 1940, Ag 10,13:6
Akin, Elwood S, 1937, My 20,21:2
Akin, Frank, 1951, Ja 16,29:4
Akin, John W Judge, 1907, O 19,9:6
Akin, Moses, 1949, Jl 12,27:5
Akin, Robert M, 1948, N 12,23:5
Akin, Thomas B, 1951, N 12,25:1
Akins, Anna B, 1949, Mr 12,18:3
Akins, Bryant L, 1943, O 4,17:4
Akins, Ellis R, 1962, Ag 10,19:3
Akins, Thomas J, 1924, S 18,21:6
Akins, Thomas J Mrs, 1941, S 18,25:2
Akins, Zoe, 1958, O 30,31:1
Akira Ariyoshi, 1937, Je 27,II,6:8
Akita, Kiyoshi, 1944, D 5,23:2
Akizuki, Satsuo, 1945, Je 30,17:6
Aklonis, Boleslavas, 1949, Ap 13,29:6
Akopov, Stepan, 1958, Ag 10,92:6
Akoun, Gaston, 1943, Je 24,22:2
Akramoff, Igor Mrs, 1950, F 10,23:2
Aksamovic, Anton (funl), 1959, O 11,86:3
Akselrod, Joseph, 1947, My 13,25:3
Akst, Harry L, 1963, Ap 3,47:1
Akst, Joseph, 1941, My 18,44:1
Akst, Maurice, 1940, D 28,15:5
Akulin, Mikhail, 1951, Ap 9,25:5
Ala, Hussein, 1964, Jl 14,33:4
Aladdi, Peter, 1924, S 4,19:4
Alam Pasha, Sabry Abu, 1947, Ap 14,27:3
Alam-Tadema, Laurence, 1912, Je 26,13:3
Alamayu, Abyssinian Prince, 1879, N 28,6:6
Alamo, Antonio, 1953, Mr 7,15:3
Alanbrooke, Alan F B, 1963, Je 18,37:1
Alanbrooke, Benita Blanche Lady, 1968, My 5,87:2
Aland, William A Mrs, 1916, S 15,11:4
Alanova, Kyra (Mrs R Hubbell), 1965, S 3,27:3
Alanson, Bertram E, 1958, My 27,29:5
Alanson, Lionel M, 1958, Ap 20,84:2
Alasheieff, Sergei, 1951, O 12,27:1
Alashin, Eugence, 1952, Je 19,27:4
Alaxander, Louis, 1950, Jl 30,61:2
Alb Gustave, Bro (Marists), 1953, F 22,60:8
Alba, Duchess of, 1860, O 9,2:1
Alba, Duke of, 1901, O 16,1:4
Alba, Duke of (J F Stuart y Falco), 1953, S 25,21:1
Alba, Pedro de, 1960, N 11,29:1
Alba, Ralph T, 1952, Ag 12,19:3
Alba, Santiago, 1949, Ap 9,17:4
Alba de Tormes, Duchess of, 1934, Ja 12,23:1
Albach, George H, 1961, O 29,89:1
Al Bachir, Mohammed, 1942, Ap 28,21:4
Albala, David, 1942, Ap 5,42:2
Alban, Bro (J Meenagh), 1961, Je 20,33:5
Alban, Edelwald, 1942, F 14,15:5
Alban, Walter Bro, 1961, Ja 28,19:1
Alban Aloysius, Bro (Thos McKenny), 1966, Mr 19, 29:4
Alban Faber, Bro (J F Shallew), 1956, O 17,35:2
Alban Raymund, Bro (Terro), 1964, Je 28,57:1
Albani, E, 1930, Ap 4,25:3
Albani, Olga Countess, 1940, Je 4,23:2
Albano, Joseph, 1959, Jl 17,21:6
Albano, Vincent F, 1966, Ap 16,33:2
Albarda, Horatius, 1965, My 18,7:2
Albarda, J, 1947, My 24,15:7
Albareda, Anselmo M, 1966, Jl 21,33:2
Albarran, Pierre, 1960, F 25,29:6
Albaugh, Hamilton C, 1963, Ag 9,23:1
Albaugh, John W, 1909, F 12,13:5
Albaugh, Olive M Mrs, 1938, Jl 27,17:2
Albaugh, R Inde, 1944, Mr 7,17:5
Albeck, Charles F, 1923, N 16,17:3
Albeck, George F, 1951, Je 20,27:5
Albeck, Harry F, 1945, Ag 25,11:4
Albeck, Jacob Mrs, 1956, Ap 5,29:1
Albeck, Stephen E, 1939, My 31,23:1
Albeck, Walter C, 1957, My 24,26:1
Albee, E F, 1930, Mr 12,32:2
Albee, Edward F Mrs, 1947, Je 14,15:4
Albee, Frank C, 1947, Ap 18,21:3
Albee, Fred H, 1945, F 16,23:1
Albee, George C Mrs, 1952, My 9,23:5
Albee, George S, 1964, Ja 30,30:2
Albee, Harley C, 1937, Je 1,23:5
Albee, Percy F, 1959, N 28,21:5
Albee, Reed A, 1961, Ag 3,23:3
Albee, William N, 1942, S 1,19:3
Albemarie, Earl of, 1942, Ap 13,15:2
Alber, Fred C, 1944, Ap 3,21:6
Alber, George W, 1944, Ja 20,19:3
Alber, Harry C, 1945, F 9,15:4
Alberg, Manus, 1942, O 15,24:3
Alberga, Adriaan J, 1952, D 5,27:3
Alberghetti, Daniele, 1957, F 1,25:2
Alberghini, Giuseppe, 1954, D 8,35:3
Alberini, Alessandro, 1956, D 15,25:4
Alberque, Ernest G, 1943, Ag 11,19:5
Albers, Anna A Mrs, 1937, Ja 29,19:5
Albers, August F, 1960, Jl 5,28:1
Albers, Bernard M, 1944, Jl 3,11:6
Albers, Capt, 1902, Ap 30,9:1
Albers, Charles E, 1964, My 5,43:4
Albers, Clarence, 1952, S 28,77:1
Albers, Frederick M Dr, 1937, Jl 13,20:2
Albers, Frederick M Mrs, 1955, My 16,23:5
Albers, Hans, 1960, Jl 25,23:4
Albers, Henry, 1940, Ja 19,19:5
Albers, Henry H Mrs, 1954, Ap 15,29:1
Albers, Homer, 1947, Ja 10,21:3
Albers, Joseph H, 1965, D 2,41:4
Albers, Martha, 1942, F 23,21:3
Albers, William H, 1954, Je 7,23:4
Albers, William H Mrs, 1951, D 2,91:1
Albert, Abraham, 1944, F 29,17:5
Albert, Anthony, 1947, Ja 15,25:3
Albert, Archduke of Hapsburg-Lorraine, 1955, Ag 12, 19:4
Albert, C Frederick, 1950, N 23,35:5
Albert, Calvin D, 1959, S 25,29:1
Albert, Charles, 1949, F 3,24:3
Albert, Charles J Mrs, 1946, Ag 24,11:5
Albert, Charles Stanley Rev Dr, 1912, Ja 29,11:5
Albert, Charles Sumner, 1923, Mr 28,19:3
Albert, Clifford E, 1960, S 30,27:2
Albert, Don, 1959, My 9,21:3
Albert, E d', 1932, Mr 4,19:3
Albert, Edward, 1952, Je 30,19:2
Albert, Ernest, 1946, Mr 26,29:1; 1955, Je 18,17:5
Albert, F, 1933, N 24,21:3
Albert, Fanning P, 1921, N 15,19:4
Albert, Francis X E, 1947, N 29,13:6
Albert, George, 1938, Ag 7,32:8
Albert, Harry, 1951, S 10,21:3
Albert, Harry S, 1944, Ja 6,23:5
Albert, Helen H Mrs, 1945, Mr 25,38:3
Albert, Henry J, 1952, O 9,31:5
Albert, Herman M, 1947, F 5,23:4
Albert, Howard J, 1963, Je 16,84:3
Albert, Isaac, 1960, Je 12,86:8; 1966, O 25,48:1
Albert, J S, 1880, Jl 6,5:6
Albert, Jacob, 1961, Jl 5,33:4
Albert, Joseph C, 1954, O 5,27:4
Albert, Joseph f, 1960, O 6,41:4
Albert, Lillian S (Mrs Alphaeus H), 1964, N 18,47:4
Albert, Linda C, 1953, Je 27,15:5
Albert, Lionel L, 1942, S 7,19:5
Albert, Louis, 1944, Ja 26,19:5
Albert, Louis H, 1948, O 9,19:2
Albert, Martin Rev, 1913, S 19,9:4
Albert, Michael G, 1952, Je 22,68:4
Albert, Morris, 1937, Ag 28,15:2
Albert, Nathan, 1962, Je 10,86:5
Albert, Paul R, 1916, Mr 8,11:7
Albert, Prince (Alb Chas Augustus Emmanuel), 1861, D 24,1:2
Albert, Robert L, 1961, Ja 2,25:3
Albert, Sigmund S, 1957, My 8,37:2
Albert, Sigmund S Mrs, 1961, Ap 13,35:2
Albert, Simon, 1953, My 4,23:4
Albert, Thomas B Mrs, 1944, Ap 21,19:1
Albert, Thomas V, 1968, Jl 6,19:1
Albert, William F, 1948, N 27,18:2; 1962, F 10,23:5
Albert I, King of the Belgians, 1934, F 18,1:8
Albert of Monaco, Prince, 1922, Je 27,15:4
Alberta Marie, Sister (A Hanley), 1952, F 5,29:2
Albertanti, Francis P, 1958, F 21,23:3
Albertario, Luigi M, 1949, Je 30,23:2
Alberti, Antonio, 1956, Ag 3,19:3
Alberti, Charles R, 1959, Ap 13,31:5
Alberti, Fleeda (Mrs A Speth), 1955, D 23,17:3
Alberti, John, 1940, Ja 18,23:6; 1954, Jl 31,13:6
Alberti, Mario, 1939, Ja 20,19:4
Alberti, William, 1964, F 8,23:4
Alberti, William A, 1964, Mr 18,41:5
Albertine, Mother, 1947, D 28,40:3
Albertini, Alberto, 1954, Ja 26,27:4
Albertini, Augene, 1941, F 27,19:4
Albertini, Luigi, 1941, D 31,17:1
Albertini, Oscar D, 1955, D 15,37:4
Albertini, Stockwell R, 1942, Je 9,23:2
Albertinus, Bro (Bros of the Sacred Heart), 1959, D 12,23:2
Alberto, Paul J, 1958, My 4,89:1
Alberts, Conrad J, 1954, Mr 8,27:1
Alberts, Gerard H, 1967, N 1,47:3
Alberts, Max W, 1945, Je 12,19:2
Alberts, Robert H, 1915, Ja 29,9:6
Alberts, Sarah S Mrs, 1942, F 4,19:4
Albertson, Benjamin S Jr, 1951, Ap 29,88:7
Albertson, Charles C, 1959, My 16,23:3
Albertson, Charles C Mrs, 1949, Ja 31,19:4
Albertson, Chauncey I, 1944, Ja 3,21:4
Albertson, E Joe, 1965, My 1,31:5
Albertson, Edmund F, 1945, My 19,19:3
Albertson, Edwin R, 1965, Ap 5,31:4
Albertson, Frank, 1964, Mr 4,37:1
Albertson, Harry M, 1957, S 21,19:3
Albertson, Harry V, 1950, F 23,27:3
Albertson, Herbert M, 1947, Ja 31,23:2
Albertson, James H, 1967, Mr 25,3:3
Albertson, John A Mrs, 1916, Mr 12,19:5
Albertson, Kerr T, 1939, D 17,49:1
Albertson, Lewis A, 1942, N 23,23:3
Albertson, Noel C, 1940, My 25,17:3
Albertson, Otto Mrs, 1943, Mr 18,19:3
Albertson, Ralph, 1951, Ja 25,25:5
Albertson, Thomas Willis, 1925, F 20,17:4
Albertson, Townsend W, 1949, Je 7,31:3
Albertson, Walter E, 1956, Je 2,19:6
Albertus, Hegula W Mrs (will), 1938, Ap 10,27:4

Albiez, John, 1956, S 2,57:2
Albig, W Espey, 1952, F 23,11:4
Albin, Abe, 1968, Je 18,47:3
Albin, Abner O, 1948, N 18,27:3
Albin, Chauncey D, 1938, Ja 27,21:3
Albin, James E, 1942, Je 7,42:1
Albin, Leland D, 1957, F 14,27:2
Albin, Leland D Mrs, 1946, N 7,31:5
Albinger, Albert, 1940, D 14,10:8
Albinola, G Count, 1883, Je 6,4:7
Albinson, J Warren, 1948, N 27,17:2
Albion, James F, 1948, Ap 7,25:4
Albizu Campos, Pedro, 1965, Ap 22,33:4
Albizzati, Carlo, 1950, O 16,27:5
Albornoz y Liminiana, Alvaro de, 1954, O 22,27:3
Alboum, Emanuel, 1965, Jl 22,31:5
Albracht, Conrad, 1950, O 27,30:3
Albray, Raymond A Mrs, 1956, S 18,35:1
Albray, Raymonde A Dr, 1968, Je 7,36:6
Albrecht, Archduke of Austria, 1872, S 13,4:4
Albrecht, Arthur E Mrs, 1966, Mr 31,40:1
Albrecht, Bruno J, 1964, Ag 7,29:4
Albrecht, Edward H Mrs, 1947, Je 12,25:4
Albrecht, Elmer W, 1959, Mr 3,33:2
Albrecht, Emil P Mrs, 1956, Ag 6,23:4
Albrecht, Ernest, 1903, Ap 13,14:2
Albrecht, Fred, 1949, Ag 29,17:5
Albrecht, George W, 1939, O 6,25:1
Albrecht, Gustav, 1951, F 23,27:5
Albrecht, H Carl, 1958, Ap 29,29:3
Albrecht, Henry W, 1950, Jl 4,17:2
Albrecht, John Sr, 1951, N 28,31:5
Albrecht, Karl Archduke, 1951, Mr 20,29:2
Albrecht, Lewis, 1950, Ja 4,35:1
Albrecht, Max J, 1943, O 23,13:4
Albrecht, Paul L, 1948, O 1,26:2
Albrecht, Prince of Prussia, 1906, S 14,7:5
Albrecht, Prince of Schleswig-Holstein, 1948, Ap 24, 15:6
Albrecht, Walter M, 1966, D 21,39:3
Albrecht, William J Mrs, 1942, N 9,23:4
Albrecht, William P, 1942, O 31,15:4
Albrecht Eugen, Duke of Wuertemberg, 1954, Je 26, 13:2
Albrechtsen, Oluf, 1955, N 21,29:5
Albrect, Johann Duke, 1920, F 18,11:3
Albright, Adam E, 1957, S 14,19:2
Albright, Andrew, 1905, Mr 19,9:4
Albright, Augustus D, 1939, Ap 18,23:3
Albright, Charles, 1880, S 29,5:2
Albright, Charles E, 1946, Je 15,21:6
Albright, Charles L, 1949, Mr 11,25:1
Albright, Chester E, 1949, Mr 31,25:1
Albright, Edgar Mrs, 1960, O 23,88:5
Albright, Edward (por), 1937, My 26,25:3
Albright, Edward, 1946, S 12,7:2
Albright, Edward A, 1941, O 24,23:3
Albright, Evelyn M, 1942, Ap 18,15:6
Albright, George J, 1952, My 30,15:4
Albright, George J Mrs, 1952, Ja 14,19:5
Albright, George P Mrs, 1960, Ja 17,86:3
Albright, H F, 1926, My 13,25:1
Albright, Henry J, 1951, Ja 23,27:2
Albright, J J, 1931, Ag 21,17:5
Albright, John C, 1953, Jl 5,49:1
Albright, John F, 1955, N 12,19:2
Albright, Leonard, 1948, Mr 2,23:3
Albright, Paul W, 1960, Je 16,33:4
Albright, Ralph W, 1960, S 1,27:5
Albright, Raymond W, 1957, F 20,33:4
Albright, Robert, 1950, N 26,89:4
Albright, Robert C, 1962, S 8,19:4
Albright, Rolland G, 1953, Ag 3,17:4
Albright, Samuel C, 1943, F 17,21:1
Albright, William Brownlee, 1925, D 30,17:4
Albright, William E, 1947, N 30,76:3
Albright, William H A, 1942, Mr 17,21:2
Albright, William Hervey Rev, 1907, D 8,11:5
Albright, William Mrs, 1950, Mr 25,13:2
Albritton, Elmer S, 1952, Ja 11,21:5
Albro, Addis, 1911, O 17,11:5
Albro, Arthur F Mrs, 1941, Ja 16,21:4
Albro, Frank T, 1947, Ag 26,23:1
Albro, James Mrs, 1955, Jl 9,15:5
Albro, Louis Colt, 1924, Mr 3,17:5
Albro, Merlin Z, 1947, Ap 25,21:4
Albro, William H Mrs, 1912, Jl 9,9:5
Albu, George, 1963, F 19,8:8
Album, Leon, 1960, Mr 27,86:8
Albun, S H Rabbi, 1921, Je 13,13:4
Albuquerque, Cerveira de, 1940, Mr 24,31:1
Alburn, John A, 1954, Ag 23,17:4
Alburn, Wilfred H, 1952, S 11,31:2
Alburqurque, Mousinho de, 1942, Ja 26,15:2
Albury, Charles E, 1946, D 6,23:3
Alcala Zamora, Niceto, 1949, F 19,15:1
Alcantara, Pres of Venezuela, 1878, D 9,5:5
Alcarzar, Jacob, 1947, Ja 1,33:3
Alchesay, Baha, 1952, O 14,31:4
Alciatore, Gaston A, 1940, D 24,15:1
Alcock, Bechtel, 1961, Je 29,33:1
Alcock, George W, 1968, F 28,47:4
Alcock, Harold L, 1941, Ja 22,21:2
Alcock, J Curtis, 1942, Jl 7,20:4
Alcock, John H, 1941, D 14,69:3
Alcock, John J, 1944, Ja 8,13:5
Alcock, John L, 1957, O 20,86:4
Alcock, Nathaniel G, 1953, D 11,34:4
Alcock, William A, 1944, D 14,23:3
Alcofarado, Alfredo, 1918, Ag 10,7:5
Alcombrack, Reginald W Mrs, 1950, Jl 11,31:2
Alcorn, Ernest A, 1937, F 4,21:6
Alcorn, Hugh M Mrs, 1961, O 2,31:1
Alcorn, Hugh M Sr, 1955, My 27,23:5
Alcorn, Isabel L, 1951, Ag 21,27:2
Alcorn, J W, 1949, Ap 23,13:2
Alcorn, James E, 1949, Jl 16,13:3
Alcorn, James S, 1940, N 7,25:1
Alcorn, John H Mrs, 1951, N 20,31:3
Alcorn, Meade Mrs, 1947, Jl 30,21:4
Alcorn, Roscoe H, 1952, N 30,87:4
Alcorn, S Stewart Jr, 1965, Ap 1,35:3
Alcorn, Thomas Grant, 1925, N 28,15:4
Alcorn, William c, 1946, Ag 30,17:3
Alcorn, William F, 1939, N 5,49:2
Alcott, A B, 1888, Mr 5,5:3
Alcott, Carroll, 1965, My 16,88:6
Alcott, Charles W, 1910, My 14,9:4
Alcott, Clarence F, 1957, O 24,33:2
Alcott, Clarence F Mrs, 1961, Jl 27,31:4
Alcott, Frank H, 1953, Mr 17,35:6
Alcott, Louisa M, 1888, Mr 7,5:3
Alcott, William, 1950, Ja 20,25:3
Alcott, William A Dr, 1859, Mr 31,4:5
Alda, Frances (Mrs R Vir Den), 1952, S 19,23:1
Aldan, Andrei, 1957, Ja 12,19:4
Aldanov, Mark, 1957, F 26,29:1
Alday, John H Rev, 1911, O 23,11:5
Aldea, Mercedes, 1954, O 30,17:1
Alden, A Mrs, 1936, Ap 12,II,11:1
Alden, C W Mrs, 1931, Ja 9,26:2
Alden, Carlos, 1955, Ag 5,19:2
Alden, Charles Henry Brig-Gen, 1906, Je 10,9:6
Alden, Charles Mrs, 1938, Ag 31,15:4
Alden, Charles R, 1941, S 28,48:2
Alden, Chester W, 1940, Ap 22,17:5
Alden, David J, 1955, Je 25,15:3
Alden, E M Mrs, 1873, My 8,1:6
Alden, E S, 1927, Jl 14,23:5
Alden, Eben Dr, 1937, Jl 22,19:6
Alden, Edward S, 1946, Je 9,40:5
Alden, Elizabeth A, 1943, Je 30,21:4
Alden, Emma L, 1939, S 5,23:5
Alden, Ezra H, 1945, Je 14,19:6
Alden, Frederic A Mrs, 1952, Je 10,27:5
Alden, Frederick A, 1964, S 30,43:1
Alden, George A, 1937, S 24,21:1; 1952, Mr 19,29:4
Alden, George D, 1941, S 10,24:4
Alden, George N, 1943, D 30,17:1
Alden, H O, 1882, Ap 16,2:7
Alden, Harold B, 1950, Ag 1,23:2
Alden, Harriet C, 1921, F 24,13:6
Alden, Harry W, 1945, N 4,44:1
Alden, Henry B, 1939, Ag 21,13:5
Alden, Henry Leroy Judge, 1913, N 22,15:4
Alden, Henry Mills (funl, O 9,15:2), 1919, O 8,19:3
Alden, Herbert W, 1950, N 12,92:5
Alden, I M, 1930, Ag 6,21:5
Alden, J, 1934, Mr 5,15:1
Alden, J M, 1901, Jl 8,7:6
Alden, James (funl, F 25,6:7), 1877, F 7,4:6
Alden, John A, 1944, Ap 13,19:3
Alden, John B, 1924, D 6,15:5
Alden, John E, 1910, S 17,9:6
Alden, John Ferris, 1917, Mr 2,11:6
Alden, John G, 1962, Mr 4,86:5
Alden, John H H, 1947, Mr 10,22:2
Alden, John P C (will), 1949, Ja 20,40:7
Alden, John W, 1925, F 7,15:5
Alden, Joseph R, 1951, S 19,31:3
Alden, Lyman P, 1904, Ja 4,9:6
Alden, Oliver Sr, 1942, F 7,17:6
Alden, Percy S, 1955, Je 8,29:1
Alden, Raymond Dr, 1924, S 29,15:3
Alden, Robert Percy, 1909, Ap 5,7:4
Alden, Schuyler G, 1950, Ap 20,29:4
Alden, William H, 1957, O 17,33:3
Alden, William L, 1946, F 27,25:6
Alden, William Livingston, 1908, Ja 16,9:5
Aldenham, Lord (Hy Hucks Gibbs), 1907, S 15,9:6
Alder, Kurt, 1958, Je 22,77:1
Alder, Thomas P, 1942, Je 15,19:2
Alderdice, F C, 1936, F 27,19:5
Alderdice, G F, 1934, Ap 6,23:6
Alderdice, James Rev, 1903, N 11,3:2
Alderdice, Lawrence, 1937, My 8,19:2
Alderdice, William H Com, 1911, O 7,13:6
Alderdice, Winslow Com, 1907, S 5,9:5
Alderfer, Alvin C, 1941, S 23,23:7
Alderfer, Clement J, 1946, D 2,25:5
Alderman, Abraham, 1940, F 27,21:6
Alderman, Bernard L, 1955, My 16,23:5
Alderman, Charles E, 1953, Ap 7,29:5
Alderman, E A Dr, 1931, Ap 30,26:4
Alderman, Henry O, 1948, Mr 6,13:5
Alderman, Solomon, 1943, Je 16,21:1
Alderson, E Sir, 1927, D 15,29:3
Alderson, George P, 1947, F 11,27:1
Alderson, James Sir, 1882, S 16,5:3
Alderson, Robert, 1961, Ap 30,86:8
Alderson, Victor C, 1946, F 28,23:4
Alderson, William H, 1937, F 15,17:4; 1938, F 7,15:1
Alderson, Wroe, 1965, Je 2,45:2
Aldert, Joseph B (J Bennett), 1967, S 2,25:5
Alderton, Charles H, 1956, Ja 23,25:3
Alderton, George H, 1937, Mr 4,23:4
Alderton, John H Jr, 1949, My 5,27:2
Aldet, Antoine de, 1942, S 4,23:2
Aldham, T Edward, 1954, Ag 10,19:2
Aldhelm, Joseph Bro (A Desrosiers), 1950, Jl 27,25:6
Aldinger, Albert H Sr, 1942, F 11,21:4
Aldington, Richard, 1962, Jl 29,60:7
Aldis, Graham, 1966, Ap 22,41:2
Aldis, O W, 1903, My 1,9:5
Aldis, Owen F, 1925, Ag 6,19:7
Aldobrandini, Giuseppe (Prince), 1939, Je 27,23:2
Aldom, Ira W, 1965, Je 15,41:3
Aldous, Montague, 1946, My 26,32:5
Aldred, Frederick W, 1954, N 17,31:1
Aldred, John E, 1945, N 22,35:2
Aldred, John E Mrs, 1948, N 1,23:5
Aldrich, Amey O, 1963, N 29,37:3
Aldrich, Bertrand F (will), 1955, O 18,45:4
Aldrich, Bess S, 1954, Ag 4,21:1
Aldrich, Charles A, 1949, O 7,27:5
Aldrich, Charles E (will), 1953, Ja 11,88:6
Aldrich, Charles H, 1945, Jl 21,11:2
Aldrich, Charles T, 1953, N 22,88:5
Aldrich, Charlotte Mrs, 1938, My 28,15:6
Aldrich, Chester, 1941, Ja 23,24:6; 1952, Je 27,23:5
Aldrich, Chester H, 1940, D 27,19:1
Aldrich, Chester W Mrs, 1958, Ag 12,29:5
Aldrich, Clarence A, 1916, F 2,11:4
Aldrich, Cora B Mrs, 1948, F 18,27:4
Aldrich, Donald B (mem ser set, Ja 28,19:1), 1961, Ja 19,29:1
Aldrich, Edgar H, 1947, Mr 24,25:3
Aldrich, Edward B, 1957, O 26,21:3
Aldrich, Edward I Mrs, 1950, N 9,33:1
Aldrich, Edward K, 1947, O 22,29:3
Aldrich, Elizabeth, 1948, Ap 30,23:1
Aldrich, Fred A, 1957, Jl 14,73:1
Aldrich, Frederick C, 1948, Je 1,23:4
Aldrich, Frederick J, 1942, Ap 9,19:3
Aldrich, George A, 1941, Mr 8,19:2
Aldrich, George H, 1948, Ap 16,23:4
Aldrich, H D, 1880, Ap 6,5:4
Aldrich, H E, 1942, D 17,37:2
Aldrich, Harold B, 1951, Jl 19,23:6
Aldrich, Harriette H D Mrs, 1937, Ap 3,19:2
Aldrich, Henry E, 1961, N 26,88:8
Aldrich, Herbert L, 1948, Mr 28,48:2
Aldrich, Herman D Mrs, 1904, Ja 20,9:5
Aldrich, James Herman, 1917, Ja 3,11:2
Aldrich, Jay Mrs, 1951, Jl 11,23:6
Aldrich, John G, 1952, Ja 21,15:5
Aldrich, John J, 1903, O 19,7:6
Aldrich, Leland M, 1941, F 12,21:3
Aldrich, Lucy T (will, F 9,11:1), 1955, Ja 13,27:3
Aldrich, M A Col, 1921, Mr 27,22:3
Aldrich, Mary L (trb lr, S 22,30:6), 1948, S 16,29:4
Aldrich, Mary S, 1965, Je 9,47:5
Aldrich, Nelson W Ex-Sen (funl, Ap 19,9:4), 1915, Ap 17,11:1
Aldrich, Nelson W Sen, 1917, F 18,17:2
Aldrich, Newton G, 1909, Jl 24,7:2
Aldrich, P D, 1933, N 23,21:5
Aldrich, Paul I, 1943, My 16,43:1
Aldrich, Raymond E, 1947, Ja 23,23:1
Aldrich, Richard (por), 1937, Je 3,25:1
Aldrich, Richard C, 1961, N 6,37:2
Aldrich, Richard Mrs (Mar 19), 1963, Ap 1,35:1
Aldrich, Richard S, 1941, D 26,13:5
Aldrich, Robert H, 1967, Jl 24,27:3
Aldrich, Roger C, 1956, F 12,89:1
Aldrich, Roger C Mrs, 1958, My 3,19:3
Aldrich, Roy W, 1955, Ja 31,19:4
Aldrich, Stanley A Mrs, 1956, Ja 22,89:1
Aldrich, Stuart M, 1960, Ag 13,15:5
Aldrich, Stuart M Mrs, 1952, Ja 15,27:2
Aldrich, Thomas Bailey (funl, Mr 23,9:6), 1907, Mr 21,9:6
Aldrich, W F, 1878, N 15,4:7
Aldrich, William H, 1958, My 20,34:4
Aldrich, William H Mrs, 1951, Ap 13,23:4
Aldrich, William L, 1946, Je 9,40:4
Aldrich, William P, 1916, Je 22,11:6; 1939, Ja 5,
Aldrich, William S, 1949, Mr 2,25:5
Aldrich, William T, 1966, Je 5,86:4
Aldrich, Winthrop William Jr, 1921, F 27,22:4
Aldrich-Blake, Louisa Dame, 1925, D 30,17:5
Aldridge, A B, 1937, Ag 30,21:4
Aldridge, Alfred H, 1948, S 30,27:4
Aldridge, Amanda I, 1956, Mr 11,88:4
Aldridge, Arthur Frederick (funl, O 25,19:6), 1
O 24,19:5
Aldridge, C Fred, 1941, O 12,53:2
Aldridge, Clayson W, 1944, Ap 2,39:3
Aldridge, Darwin R, 1945, F 18,34:2

Aldridge, George P, 1960, O 19,45:1
Aldridge, George W (trb, Je 16,17:7; funl, Je 13,13:6), 1922, Je 15,19:4
Aldridge, Hardy C, 1953, Jl 7,27:6
Aldridge, Ira, 1867, Ag 12,5:1
Aldridge, Walter H, 1959, Ag 17,23:1
Aldunate, Santiago, 1918, Ap 18,13:5
Aldworth, Richard, 1943, S 19,48:2
Aleardi, A, 1878, Ag 5,3:7
Alegre, J B, 1931, Je 15,19:5
Alegria, Ciro, 1967, F 18,29:5
Aleinikoff, Alex, 1956, Ag 13,19:6
Aleinikoff, Nicholas, 1921, Je 24,15:6
Aleinikoff, Sophia, 1945, S 5,23:3
Aleinkoff, Alex S Mrs, 1945, Je 1,15:5
Aleinkoff, Vera Mrs, 1938, Jl 12,19:4
Alejandrino, Jose M, 1951, Je 2,19:3
Alekhine, Alexander A, 1946, Mr 25,25:1
Aleksandrov, Nikolai M, 1964, Ap 22,47:3
Aleksandrowicz, Ignacy, 1964, Je 11,33:5
Aleman Casharo, Jose, 1950, Mr 26,92:6
Alemany, Jose B, 1951, Jl 17,27:5
Alemparte, Arturo, 1944, Ja 5,17:4
Alencar, Augusto C de Mrs, 1958, Mr 17,29:1
Alencon, Ferdinand Phillippe d' Duke (funl, Jl 8,7:6), 1910, Je 30,7:6
Alenick, Daniel, 1951, D 16,91:1
Alenikoff, Philip, 1961, My 9,39:4
Alenson, Augustine W P, 1961, D 12,57:8
Alenson, William R, 1952, O 10,25:2
Aleon, Armen P, 1952, Jl 17,23:5
Alerding, Herman J Bp, 1924, D 7,7:2
Alero, Marquis of (I Herrero de Collantes), 1961, D 10,89:1
Alers, Augustus L, 1945, My 25,19:3
Alers-Hankey, Lionel Mrs, 1908, D 22,9:6
Aleshire, Arthur W, 1940, Mr 12,23:6
Aleshire, Edward, 1965, Ja 30,27:1
Aleshire, Oscar R, 1942, My 17,46:2
Alesker, Monroe C, 1937, Ag 18,19:4
Alessandri, Marcel Gen, 1968, D 31,27:2
Alessandri, Sen, 1923, N 16,17:2
Alessandri y Palma, Arturo, 1950, Ag 25,21:3
Alessandro, Traditi, 1942, My 7,19:2
Alessandroni, Walter E, 1966, My 10,25:1
Alessandroni, Walter E Mrs, 1966, My 10,25:1
Alessi, Cataldo, 1939, D 13,27:4
Alexander, Albert A, 1954, Je 4,23:3
Alexander, Albert E, 1942, Mr 27,23:2
Alexander, Alex, 1940, Ja 11,23:6; 1948, N 17,27:2
Alexander, Alex L, 1955, N 21,29:5
Alexander, Alex R, 1954, Mr 6,15:3
Alexander, Alexis Mrs, 1941, Ja 5,45:1
Alexander, Alfred H, 1938, Jl 21,21:3
Alexander, Andrew, 1904, Ag 1,7:6
Alexander, Andrew J Mrs, 1922, Ag 2,17:7
Alexander, Anthony, 1948, F 21,13:4
Alexander, Archibald S Col, 1912, Ag 31,7:4
Alexander, Archibald Stevens Col, 1912, S 2,9:6
Alexander, Archie A, 1958, Ja 5,86:3
Alexander, Arthur Douglas, 1919, Ap 24,11:4
Alexander, Arthur S, 1949, Je 11,17:2
Alexander, B Howard, 1950, Ja 29,69:2
Alexander, Basil, 1948, Jl 10,15:5
Alexander, Ben, 1944, Jl 7,15:6
Alexander, Bernard, 1966, Mr 2,41:5
Alexander, C B, 1927, F 8,23:5
Alexander, C B Mrs, 1935, Jl 17,19:4
Alexander, Charles, 1866, O 1,2:4
Alexander, Charles B, 1945, F 7,21:2
Alexander, Charles C, 1945, O 8,15:4
Alexander, Charles C Jr, 1938, Mr 5,17:6; 1956, Je 29, 21:5
Alexander, Charles E, 1943, Ap 5,19:4; 1953, S 22,31:2
Alexander, Charles J, 1939, F 23,23:5; 1965, Ja 31,89:2
Alexander, Charles J Mrs, 1956, Ap 20,25:2
Alexander, Charles McCallon, 1920, O 14,13:3
Alexander, Charles W Mrs, 1960, O 5,41:1
Alexander, Clarence, 1954, Je 21,23:4
Alexander, Clarence H, 1953, F 14,17:4
Alexander, Clarence Mrs, 1953, N 28,15:4
Alexander, Clifford L Mrs (Edith M), 1965, Je 29, 32:7
Alexander, Colin C, 1947, O 30,25:2
Alexander, Colin C Mrs, 1943, O 18,15:4
Alexander, Cornelius Jr Mrs, 1954, N 1,27:5
Alexander, Cruikshank M, 1961, F 4,19:3
Alexander, David, 1950, Ja 15,84:5
Alexander, David E, 1960, D 26,23:2
Alexander, David M, 1940, Mr 14,23:2
Alexander, Deborah Mrs (Mrs Widrevitz), 1901, D 30,7:6
Alexander, Donald, 1959, Jl 22,27:4
Alexander, Donald Mrs, 1943, Jl 1,19:3
Alexander, Dorothy (Mrs C Gilbert), 1960, Je 23, 29:5
Alexander, Douglas (will, Je 14,35:1), 1949, My 23, 22:2
Alexander, Douglas Lady, 1923, Mr 20,21:4
Alexander, E B Gen, 1881, Mr 15,5:3
Alexander, E P Gen, 1910, Ap 29,9:6
Alexander, Earle, 1958, Jl 1,31:4
Alexander, Earle Mrs, 1954, Ag 23,17:2
Alexander, Eben Dr, 1910, Mr 13,II,11:3
Alexander, Edgar M, 1956, My 26,17:5
Alexander, Edward A, 1948, D 18,19:1
Alexander, Edward A Mrs, 1956, N 23,27:2
Alexander, Edward J, 1948, Mr 27,13:5
Alexander, Edward R Sr, 1964, S 23,47:1
Alexander, Edwin H, 1949, My 27,22:2
Alexander, Edwin I, 1941, S 25,25:6
Alexander, Ernest, 1937, Ja 13,23:1
Alexander, Ernest F Dr, 1903, S 5,2:4
Alexander, Ernest R, 1960, S 28,39:3
Alexander, Ernest R Mrs, 1957, S 15,84:4
Alexander, Ernest W, 1949, F 1,26:2
Alexander, Eugene D, 1956, Mr 1,34:5
Alexander, F B Mrs, 1928, Mr 8,2:5
Alexander, Francis Rev, 1916, My 22,11:6
Alexander, Frank, 1937, S 9,23:5; 1959, Jl 20,25:4
Alexander, Frank A, 1939, N 22,21:4
Alexander, Frank L, 1948, Je 11,23:4
Alexander, Franklin D, 1954, Ag 25,27:4
Alexander, Franz G, 1964, Mr 9,29:2
Alexander, Fred W, 1954, Ap 7,31:3
Alexander, Frederic L, 1954, Jl 27,21:2
Alexander, G, 1930, D 12,25:3
Alexander, G W Col, 1903, My 6,9:6
Alexander, George, 1937, Ap 14,25:3; 1950, D 8,29:3
Alexander, George B, 1937, Jl 14,21:3
Alexander, George H, 1924, Ap 12,15:3; 1955, Ap 30, 17:6
Alexander, George J, 1940, F 25,38:2
Alexander, George M, 1943, N 23,25:5
Alexander, George Sir, 1918, Mr 16,13:3
Alexander, Gilbert, 1941, D 6,17:4
Alexander, Gross Dr, 1915, S 8,13:6
Alexander, Grover C, 1950, N 5,92:3
Alexander, H Jr, 1878, Jl 25,1:5
Alexander, H P, 1867, F 24,1:7
Alexander, Harold D, 1949, Mr 9,25:4
Alexander, Harry E, 1946, Ja 30,25:3
Alexander, Harry H, 1941, Ja 6,15:2
Alexander, Hartley B, 1939, Jl 28,17:5
Alexander, Hartley K, 1950, My 16,31:5
Alexander, Hattie E Dr, 1968, Je 25,41:2
Alexander, Henry, 1940, Ap 8,20:4
Alexander, Henry A Mrs, 1938, Ag 23,17:5
Alexander, Henry M, 1910, D 20,13:3; 1952, Ap 17, 29:5
Alexander, Henry M Mrs, 1945, N 23,23:1
Alexander, Henry S, 1948, My 9,68:3
Alexander, Herbert M, 1948, N 24,23:1
Alexander, Hollis W, 1951, D 6,33:4
Alexander, Howard T, 1938, Ja 30,II,9:2
Alexander, Hubbard F, 1952, F 20,29:3
Alexander, I Henry, 1951, N 25,86:6
Alexander, J S, 1932, Jl 17,21:1
Alexander, J W, 1936, F 28,21:4
Alexander, Jack, 1958, Jl 3,25:2
Alexander, Jacques, 1940, Mr 11,15:4
Alexander, James, 1945, Ja 12,15:4
Alexander, James A, 1913, D 4,9:6
Alexander, James H, 1919, F 20,13:4
Alexander, James P, 1948, Ja 2,23:1
Alexander, James W (funl, S 25,11:4), 1915, S 22, 11:5
Alexander, Jasper, 1941, Ap 5,17:3
Alexander, Jesse, 1954, Mr 6,15:6
Alexander, Joel, 1937, My 5,25:6
Alexander, John, 1944, N 11,13:7; 1954, Jl 17,13:6; 1964, Mr 22,77:1
Alexander, John C, 1960, O 9,86:3
Alexander, John D, 1940, N 22,23:1
Alexander, John F, 1939, Jl 30,29:1
Alexander, John P, 1938, Ap 25,15:1
Alexander, John R, 1963, N 10,87:1
Alexander, John W Mrs, 1947, Ja 16,25:1
Alexander, John White (funl, Je 4,11:6), 1915, Je 2, 13:5
Alexander, Joseph, 1943, My 22,13:4; 1951, Jl 17,30:6
Alexander, Joseph Addison Rev Dr, 1860, Ja 30,5:1
Alexander, Joseph L, 1964, Jl 20,25:3
Alexander, Joseph Mrs, 1958, Jl 31,23:2
Alexander, Julia S, 1942, F 21,20:3
Alexander, Julian P, 1953, Ja 2,15:3
Alexander, Kenneth W Lt Col, 1968, Ja 16,39:2
Alexander, King of Greece (por), 1920, O 26,17:3
Alexander, Kurt, 1962, F 20,36:1
Alexander, Kurt C, 1941, Ap 24,21:4
Alexander, Lady, 1946, O 21,31:4
Alexander, Lane B, 1956, F 12,88:4
Alexander, Leigh, 1948, O 26,31:5
Alexander, Leon, 1947, Ag 16,13:1
Alexander, Leroy, 1948, Jl 21,23:4
Alexander, Lester J, 1960, N 27,86:3
Alexander, Lillias, 1959, Mr 20,32:1
Alexander, Lowell, 1955, Mr 24,31:1
Alexander, M Burpee, 1952, Mr 27,29:5
Alexander, M Moss, 1959, Mr 1,86:6
Alexander, M W, 1932, S 12,15:3
Alexander, Magnus D, 1916, Jl 6,13:5
Alexander, Maitland, 1940, Ja 4,24:2
Alexander, Marion H S Mrs, 1940, Jl 10,19:5
Alexander, Mary W A Mrs, 1941, N 5,23:1
Alexander, Maurice, 1945, Jl 17,13:6
Alexander, Max, 1968, N 13,47:3
Alexander, Metropolitan, 1953, O 20,29:5
Alexander, Michael Mrs, 1958, Ag 27,29:3
Alexander, Milton M, 1947, Mr 28,23:3
Alexander, Morris, 1954, My 5,31:4
Alexander, Murray Mrs, 1943, My 14,19:3
Alexander, Nathan, 1947, Je 4,27:5
Alexander, Nellie Mrs, 1945, D 18,27:2
Alexander, Nelson Mrs, 1950, My 27,17:5
Alexander, Norman, 1950, Jl 1,15:2
Alexander, Norman S, 1952, Ja 3,46:3
Alexander, Oakley L, 1950, Ja 22,76:8
Alexander, Oscar H, 1963, Je 26,39:4
Alexander, Paul, 1959, S 21,31:4
Alexander, Paul Mrs, 1958, Ag 12,29:2
Alexander, Paul W, 1946, Ag 30,17:3; 1967, Je 30,34:5
Alexander, Paul W Mrs, 1959, Ja 18,89:1
Alexander, Peter, 1940, N 24,51:7
Alexander, Prince of Battenberg, 1893, N 18,1:4
Alexander, Prince of Thurn and Taxis, 1937, Mr 12, 24:3; 1939, Jl 24,13:4
Alexander, R O, 1949, Jl 28,24:2
Alexander, Ralph H Sr, 1952, Ag 23,13:6
Alexander, Ralph V, 1945, Ap 22,35:1
Alexander, Robert, 1941, Ag 27,19:1
Alexander, Robert F Sr, 1954, Ap 14,29:3
Alexander, Robert J, 1967, N 11,33:4
Alexander, Robert Mrs, 1953, Ap 2,27:1
Alexander, Roe A Mrs, 1940, Mr 20,27:1
Alexander, Roger G, 1961, Ap 4,37:2
Alexander, Rue J, 1949, Ja 3,23:4
Alexander, Samuel, 1938, S 14,23:4; 1952, S 4,27:6
Alexander, Samuel Dr, 1910, N 30,11:4
Alexander, Samuel N, 1957, D 4,39:4
Alexander, Sarah J Mrs, 1940, S 2,15:5
Alexander, Sidney A, 1948, F 5,23:3
Alexander, Stanford, 1953, Je 16,27:1
Alexander, Stephen, 1883, Je 27,4:6
Alexander, Stephen R, 1963, Jl 31,29:4
Alexander, Theodore, 1960, N 3,39:4
Alexander, Thomas (mem, Jl 27,7:6), 1912, Jl 25,9:5
Alexander, Vance J, 1967, F 17,37:3
Alexander, Vaughan A, 1951, Ag 10,15:3
Alexander, Verne N, 1948, F 5,23:2
Alexander, Virginia Mrs, 1949, Jl 25,15:5
Alexander, W A Rev Dr, 1915, My 14,13:6
Alexander, W L Rev, 1884, D 23,5:3
Alexander, W Wallace, 1939, Jl 16,30:8
Alexander, Wallace M, 1939, N 23,27:1
Alexander, Walter, 1964, My 23,23:3
Alexander, Walter D, 1942, Ap 4,13:5
Alexander, Walter F, 1938, My 10,21:5
Alexander, Walter G, 1953, F 6,19:5
Alexander, Walter L, 1955, Ja 22,11:6
Alexander, Walter N, 1960, Mr 15,39:1
Alexander, Walter R, 1954, D 15,31:4
Alexander, Welcome T Mrs, 1946, Ap 5,25:4
Alexander, Wilbur, 1955, Ag 9,25:4
Alexander, Wilford S, 1959, Ap 26,86:4
Alexander, Will W, 1956, Ja 14,19:5
Alexander, William (Duke of Luxemburg), 1912, F 27,9:2
Alexander, William, 1937, Mr 26,21:3; 1948, Ap 6, 24:2; 1951, O 2,27:3; 1955, Ja 1,13:2
Alexander, William A, 1943, Jl 10,13:2; 1950, Ap 24, 25:3; 1956, F 21,33:3
Alexander, William C, 1874, Ag 25,4:6; 1943, Je 25, 17:5
Alexander, William C Jr, 1942, D 14,23:4
Alexander, William D, 1954, My 27,27:4
Alexander, William F, 1941, N 2,52:5; 1947, O 6,21:5
Alexander, William Fontaine Jr, 1968, My 5,82:7
Alexander, William H, 1937, F 3,23:3; 1956, S 17,27:4
Alexander, William H (Mr and Mrs), 1960, Ap 4, 21:2
Alexander, William J, 1953, S 9,29:1
Alexander, William M, 1940, O 5,15:4
Alexander, William Mrs, 1951, N 30,23:1
Alexander, William P, 1956, O 1,27:2
Alexander, William Rev Dr, 1906, Je 30,7:6
Alexander, William S, 1940, O 31,23:5
Alexander, William V, 1938, F 31,15:3
Alexander, William 2d, 1938, F 7,15:4
Alexander, Winthrop, 1941, F 8,15:1
Alexander I, King of Yugoslavia, 1934, O 10,1:8
Alexander III, Russian Czar, 1894, N 2,1:7
Alexander Karagcorgewitz (Prince of Servia), 1885, My 5,5:3
Alexander Michailovitch, Grand Duke, 1933, F 27, 15:3
Alexander of Hillsborough, Earl (Alb V Alexander), 1965, Ja 12,37:1
Alexanderoff, Alex H, 1940, D 13,28:2
Alexanderson, George, 1954, Mr 27,17:4
Alexanderson, George H Mrs, 1953, Jl 13,25:5
Alexanderson, John A, 1946, My 6,21:2
Alexandra, Queen, 1925, N 23,21:4
Alexandra of Schleswig-Holstein-Sonderburg-Glucksburg, Princess, 1957, Ap 15,29:5
Alexandre, Frederick F, 1968, My 16,47:1
Alexandre, Frederick F Mrs, 1957, Ap 13,19:3
Alexandre, J Henry, 1912, Jl 2,11:5
Alexandre, J Henry Jr, 1956, Jl 24,25:5

Alexandre, J Henry Mrs, 1948, Ap 17,15:2
Alexandre, J Henry 3d, 1963, O 29,36:1
Alexandre, Jerome, 1925, D 25,17:4
Alexandre, John E, 1910, Ag 23,9:6
Alexandrine, Queen Mother of Denmark, 1952, D 28, 13:2
Alexandrine, Sister, 1913, Jl 27,II,9:3
Alexandrof, Vladimir V, 1945, My 21,19:6
Alexandroff, Norman, 1960, My 29,56:4
Alexandros Tahhan, Patriarch of Antioch, 1958, Je 18,33:1
Alexandrov, Alexander V, 1946, Jl 9,21:3
Alexandrova, Vera (Mrs S M Schwarz), 1966, O 3, 47:5
Alexandrovitch, Vladimir Duke, 1909, F 18,7:1
Alexanian, Diran, 1954, Jl 4,30:6
Alexay, Alex Mrs, 1959, F 28,19:6
Alexeev, Vasili, 1950, O 18,33:4
Alexeyevich, Vladimir, 1958, N 12,37:4
Alexiade, Alex, 1961, My 25,37:5
Alexich, George M von, 1949, Jl 16,13:5
Alexion, Alex, 1944, Ag 1,15:6
Alexion, Constantine Mrs, 1950, N 9,33:6
Alexis, Algert D, 1967, Je 13,64:1
Alexis, Nord, 1910, My 2,9:4
Alexis, Nord Mrs, 1908, O 13,9:5
Alexis, Paul, 1901, Jl 20,7:6
Alexis, Sister, 1942, Mr 13,20:3
Alexis, Sister Agnes, 1904, Ja 5,9:5
Aley, Albert Mrs, 1945, Je 24,21:1
Aley, Maxwell, 1953, Jl 17,17:5
Alfange, John Mrs, 1948, D 3,25:4
Alfani, Guido, 1940, N 21,29:3
Alfano, Franco, 1954, O 28,35:4
Alfano, Nicholas F, 1968, Ja 5,24:1
Alfano, Ralph V, 1966, Ap 19,41:3
Alfaro, Colon E, 1957, Ap 13,19:2
Alfaro, Horacio F, 1951, F 10,13:4
Alfaro, Leopold, 1947, My 17,15:3
Alfaro, Prudencio Dr, 1915, D 24,9:4
Alfau, Felipe Gen, 1937, O 1,21:3
Alfer, Alfred, 1965, F 17,43:4
Alferes, John D, 1950, S 9,17:3
Alfers, Bruno Rev, 1916, F 25,11:6
Alfieri, Emilio, 1949, My 11,29:4
Alfieri, Odoardo D, 1966, Ja 6,27:2
Alfieri, Paul A, 1960, N 11,31:4
Alfke, John H, 1940, Ap 29,15:6
Alfone, Sully Sr Mrs, 1967, D 20,45:1
Alfonso, Duke of Oporto, 1920, F 22,20:4
Alfonso, King, 1921, Mr 26,13:5
Alfonso, King of Spain, 1885, N 25,1:1
Alfonso, Prince of Bourbon, 1964, F 4,33:2
Alfonso XIII, former King of Spain, 1941, Mr 1,1:6
Alford, Benjamin A, 1960, My 23,29:3
Alford, Charles C, 1871, My 16,1:4
Alford, Ellen F Mrs, 1946, N 8,23:5
Alford, Eugene L, 1946, Ap 17,25:5
Alford, Fred F Sr, 1964, O 16,39:2
Alford, Frederick R, 1937, Ap 27,23:4
Alford, J Warren, 1937, Ag 6,17:6
Alford, John J, 1959, Mr 12,31:5
Alford, Leon P, 1942, Ja 3,32:1
Alford, Ronald C, 1950, My 23,29:4
Alford, Smith Mrs, 1958, Ja 7,47:3
Alford, Theodore C, 1947, Mr 17,23:1
Alford, Very Rev, 1871, Ja 14,1:3
Alford, William J, 1943, S 29,21:3
Alford, William M, 1925, Ag 25,17:5
Alfred, Bro (Cody), 1962, S 9,84:2
Alfred, Brother (J A Cragin), 1951, Ja 7,76:4
Alfred, Clarence J Mrs, 1960, F 20,23:1
Alfred, Frank H, 1947, O 7,27:5
Alfred, Jeanne, 1964, D 24,19:4
Alfred Eugene, Bro, 1939, S 4,19:5
Alfred Patrick, Bro (J J McAuliffe), 1953, Ap 3,23:2
Alfredina, Sister, 1938, Ag 17,19:1
Alfthan, Johannes, 1957, N 15,28:3
Alfven, Hugo, 1960, My 9,29:1
Algara, Angel, 1963, N 27,27:3
Algase, Gertrude, 1962, Ag 4,19:6
Alge, Henry O, 1947, N 27,32:3
Algeo, Bradley C, 1950, Mr 14,25:4
Algeo, Sarah M Mrs, 1953, N 19,31:2
Alger, David, 1964, Jl 27,15:4
Alger, Drew, 1903, Ag 21,9:4
Alger, Edmund C Mrs, 1948, Ag 14,13:2
Alger, Ellice M, 1945, F 19,17:3
Alger, Frederick M Jr, 1967, Ja 7,27:2
Alger, Frederick W, 1952, Ag 5,19:5
Alger, George R, 1947, S 22,23:5
Alger, George W, 1967, Ap 20,43:1
Alger, Howard H, 1946, S 3,19:4
Alger, Jarvins H, 1953, Ja 16,23:3
Alger, John L, 1943, Ja 12,23:4
Alger, Orin M, 1953, Ag 27,25:5
Alger, Philip L Mrs, 1945, S 5,23:3
Alger, Philip R Capt, 1912, F 24,11:5
Alger, R A Sen, 1907, Ja 28,7:5
Alger, Russell A Mrs, 1919, Ag 25,11:4
Alger, W Leslie, 1948, Ag 9,19:3
Alger, William E, 1917, Mr 22,11:3
Algero, George T Mrs, 1946, N 24,79:5
Algor, Jonathon E, 1958, Mr 22,17:5
Algozer, Alfonso L Dr, 1968, N 10,88:4
Algus, Harris J, 1922, My 22,15:6
Algus, Max, 1950, Mr 2,27:4
Alhan, Chefki, 1947, Je 27,21:4
Alheim, Adam, 1943, F 1,15:5
Alhucemas, Marques de, 1938, S 16,21:5
Ali, Fayyaz, 1959, Ap 9,31:1
Ali, George D, 1942, Mr 24,19:1
Ali, Mohammad, 1963, Je 24,7:2
Ali, Mohammed, 1951, O 14,88:4
Ali, Saiyid Fazl, 1959, Ag 23,92:6
Ali Asaf (Asaf Ali Min), 1953, Ap 3,23:1
Ali ben Hadj, 1954, S 8,31:3
Ali Bey Abed, 1939, O 22,40:7
Ali Khan, Amir (Fakir of Ipi), 1960, Ap 20,39:4
Ali Khan, Lady, 1938, F 6,II,8:7
Alicata, Mario, 1966, D 7,47:3
Alice, Princess of England, 1878, D 15,1:1
Alice, Sister (M R Kelly), 1958, Je 24,31:5
Alice Marie, Sister (O'Meara), 1949, S 1,21:2
Alice Marie, Sister Sisters of Charity, 1955, Ap 3,86:5
Alice Ursula, Mother, 1943, My 27,25:2
Alicoate, John W, 1960, Je 22,35:4
Aliev, Mahmoud Ismail Ogly, 1958, S 28,88:3
Aline de l'Immaculee, Sister (J Lennon), 1954, Jl 15, 27:3
Alington, Cyril A, 1955, My 17,29:1
Alington, Giles, 1956, F 26,89:2
Aliotti, Carlo Baron, 1923, F 9,15:4
Alison, Alex A Jr, 1948, Ja 26,19:1
Alison, Archibald Sir, 1867, My 25,1:6
Alison, Christina H Mrs, 1937, Je 30,23:4
Alison, Gertrude Mrs, 1941, Mr 30,48:6
Alison, Valentine S Mrs, 1946, S 25,27:2
Aliyah, Queen Mother of Iraq, 1950, D 22,23:2
Aljoe, David W, 1952, D 3,33:5
Alkas, Isaac A, 1953, Jl 29,23:5
Alke, Stephen Mrs, 1938, Ap 9,17:3
Alker, Carroll B, 1946, Ag 2,19:5
Alker, Edward P, 1938, N 19,17:2
Alker, Henry A, 1951, N 15,29:4
Alkins, George C, 1954, D 24,13:1
All, William L, 1949, Jl 7,25:4
Allai Ben Abdel Malek, 1954, F 22,19:4
Allaimble, Pierre, 1917, My 30,9:4
Allaire, A J Capt, 1903, Ag 10,9:5
Allaire, Hal, 1901, O 19,3:3
Allaire, J W Capt, 1879, Ap 12,8:2
Allaire, John (por), 1937, F 8,17:5
Allan, Adrian R, 1953, S 7,19:4
Allan, Alex J, 1952, Jl 13,60:5
Allan, Alex Mrs, 1961, D 7,43:4
Allan, Andrew, 1915, Jl 7,11:6
Allan, Andrew A, 1919, F 12,13:6
Allan, Annie, 1950, F 17,23:4
Allan, Bert J, 1950, F 2,27:5
Allan, Boyce, 1874, My 25,1:5
Allan, Bryce J, 1924, Ag 31,14:2
Allan, C J Stuart, 1960, Mr 3,29:4
Allan, Carlisle V, 1965, D 9,47:4
Allan, Douglas G, 1947, O 30,25:2
Allan, Edward L, 1940, Ag 5,13:6
Allan, Evelyn W, 1957, F 1,25:5
Allan, G S Dr, 1911, Ja 16,11:3
Allan, George H, 1955, Mr 30,29:5
Allan, George W, 1940, D 7,17:4
Allan, Glenn H, 1955, Jl 25,41:3
Allan, Harold, 1953, F 19,23:3
Allan, Harry C, 1954, Je 24,27:4
Allan, Herbert J, 1958, S 8,29:5
Allan, Hugh A, 1938, Ja 29,15:5
Allan, Hugh M, 1951, S 27,31:5
Allan, Hugh Sir, 1882, D 10,7:5
Allan, J Capt, 1881, Ap 12,5:3
Allan, James, 1948, My 25,27:4
Allan, John A, 1946, D 17,38:5
Allan, John B Mrs, 1947, Ap 5,19:5
Allan, John J, 1960, N 2,39:1
Allan, John L, 1956, Je 20,33:1
Allan, John S, 1942, S 4,24:2
Allan, Joseph W, 1949, F 23,27:1
Allan, L G Mrs, 1881, Ap 26,1:6
Allan, Maude Mrs, 1956, N 9,29:2
Allan, Percy, 1945, N 15,19:3
Allan, Robert W, 1956, Mr 29,27:3
Allan, Vina M J, 1953, Jl 15,25:3
Allan, William Sir, 1903, D 29,9:4
Alland, Raymond A, 1951, O 6,19:1
Allard, Frank E Mrs, 1949, Ja 9,72:4
Allard, John S, 1967, O 4,51:4
Allard, Joseph, 1948, Ag 7,15:4
Allard, Joseph C Rev, 1925, Jl 1,23:4
Allard, Leola, 1951, O 2,28:2
Allard, Louis, 1955, Je 4,15:4
Allard, Sydney, 1966, Ap 13,40:2
Allardice, James, 1937, Jl 8,23:4
Allardice, James J, 1945, Je 5,19:4
Allardice, James K, 1962, Ag 19,88:2
Allardice, Robert B, 1946, Ja 6,40:2
Allardt, Frederick E A, 1964, O 24,29:3
Allaun, Jacob, 1939, Ja 21,15:2
Allbutt, Clifford C Sir, 1925, F 23,17:6
Allchin, Stanley D, 1958, F 16,86:8
Allcock, John W, 1949, F 15,23:5
Allcorn, Ernest H, 1948, Jl 27,25:4
Allcorn, Frank W, 1942, D 11,23:3
Allcorn, Samuel, 1946, F 8,19:2
Allcroft, Arthur N Sr, 1945, Ap 29,37:1
Allderdice, Ellen H Mrs, 1937, My 12,23:6
Alldredge, E P Dr, 1953, F 24,25:1
Alldredge, J Haden, 1962, D 7,39:4
Allds, Jotham P, 1923, S 12,19:4
Allebach, Henry D, 1953, O 10,27:4
Allebach, Leroy, 1943, Ja 19,19:4
Allee, Douglas C, 1937, Jl 23,19:5
Allee, Frank, 1938, O 14,23:4
Allee, James F Mrs, 1943, My 16,43:1
Allee, Warder C, 1955, Mr 19,15:5
Allee, Warder C Mrs, 1945, My 1,23:2
Allegretti, Ignaz, 1903, Mr 12,9:6
Alleman, Gellert, 1946, S 7,15:6
Alleman, Herbert C, 1953, F 10,27:4
Allemang, Herbert J, 1962, Je 16,19:4
Allen, A Brom, 1943, Ag 13,17:5
Allen, A G, 1873, Ag 11,1:6
Allen, A Herbert, 1955, My 27,23:4
Allen, A J, 1956, N 22,33:3
Allen, A Vail, 1944, N 25,13:5
Allen, A Vail Sr Mrs, 1950, F 17,23:1
Allen, Aaron, 1957, D 9,35:4
Allen, Abbott W, 1953, Ag 3,17:6
Allen, Ada, 1951, Jl 10,27:2
Allen, Addison Mrs, 1949, O 14,27:1
Allen, Alarik, 1959, Mr 10,35:5
Allen, Albert G, 1956, Ag 14,25:3
Allen, Albert J, 1945, Ap 17,23:5
Allen, Albert W, 1947, Jl 14,21:4
Allen, Alele L Mrs, 1939, Jl 14,19:2
Allen, Alex, 1941, D 3,25:4; 1953, Je 11,29:2
Allen, Alfred G Mrs, 1958, Ja 1,25:5
Allen, Alfred J, 1957, Mr 7,29:5
Allen, Alma H, 1957, Ja 8,31:2
Allen, Alonzo G, 1949, D 28,25:1
Allen, Alvoni R Mrs, 1939, My 12,21:3
Allen, Amos L, 1911, F 21,11:4
Allen, Andrew J, 1937, Ag 19,19:3
Allen, Andrew W, 1960, Ja 20,31:2
Allen, Ann L Mrs, 1938, O 22,17:7
Allen, Annie T, 1922, F 6,13:4
Allen, Arlene, 1949, Ja 17,19:3
Allen, Artemus W, 1939, O 17,25:3
Allen, Arthur, 1940, S 24,23:3; 1958, O 18,21:6
Allen, Arthur A, 1964, Ja 18,23:2
Allen, Arthur B, 1947, Ag 26,23:3
Allen, Arthur C, 1947, Mr 4,25:2
Allen, Arthur C Mrs (S Spitz), 1956, Ag 11,13:4
Allen, Arthur D, 1949, Ap 9,17:2; 1963, S 5,31:2
Allen, Arthur F, 1946, Ap 2,27:2; 1949, Ag 23,23:5
Allen, Arthur H, 1942, Ja 6,23:4
Allen, Arthur H Rev Dr, 1923, Ap 21,11:5
Allen, Arthur Mrs, 1956, D 29,15:4
Allen, Arthur Mrs (S Steel), 1959, N 14,21:6
Allen, Arthur S, 1944, Ap 11,19:5; 1959, Ja 26,29:3
Allen, Arthur W, 1951, Mr 10,13:2; 1958, Mr 20,29:3
Allen, Arvol D, 1951, F 3,15:4
Allen, Augustus F, 1875, Ja 22,6:6
Allen, Augustus N, 1958, Mr 26,34:5
Allen, B M, 1951, S 8,17:5
Allen, B S, 1935, Mr 30,15:6
Allen, Barbara (see also Ap 11), 1878, Ap 12,8:2
Allen, Barney, 1925, My 12,23:5; 1939, F 13,15:5
Allen, Ben S, 1963, F 28,4:3
Allen, Benjamin, 1958, O 15,39:5
Allen, Benjamin F, 1942, D 6,76:1
Allen, Benjamin L, 1939, N 6,23:4
Allen, Benjamin Mrs, 1952, F 13,29:3
Allen, Benjamin W P, 1965, D 25,13:6
Allen, Bennie, 1953, D 6,2:8
Allen, Bernard M, 1949, S 16,27:2
Allen, Bertha, 1965, D 8,47:2
Allen, Berton A, 1948, N 25,31:4
Allen, Bertram s, 1961, Ag 27,84:8
Allen, Bessie B Mrs, 1952, D 9,33:5
Allen, Billy Mrs (B Montrose), 1964, O 27,39:2
Allen, Boyd S, 1953, Ap 10,21:5
Allen, C B, 1949, F 7,19:3
Allen, C B Mrs, 1950, Ag 5,15:6
Allen, C Edmonds Mrs, 1963, D 16,33:4
Allen, C Frank, 1948, Je 8,26:2
Allen, C Loomis, 1941, S 8,15:6
Allen, C Loomis Mrs, 1940, Jl 6,15:4
Allen, Calvin H, 1918, Jl 15,11:8
Allen, Carey L Sr, 1950, Ap 18,31:2
Allen, Carey L Sr Mrs, 1950, Je 10,17:5
Allen, Carl, 1951, Je 29,6:7
Allen, Carleton K, 1966, D 12,47:2
Allen, Carlton B Mrs, 1939, My 17,23:6
Allen, Caroline W O Mrs, 1940, N 23,17:4
Allen, Catherine, 1952, D 17,33:2
Allen, Catherine A Mrs, 1939, My 13,15:6
Allen, Catherine L H Mrs, 1941, Ag 15,17:4
Allen, Cecil J (por), 1937, D 17,25:3
Allen, Charles, 1869, Ag 7,1:6
Allen, Charles A, 1925, Je 4,19:5; 1946, Ja 28,19:3
Allen, Charles D, 1958, S 8,29:4

Allen, Charles E, 1954, Ag 27,21:3
Allen, Charles E Mrs, 1955, Je 29,29:3
Allen, Charles F, 1942, Ap 2,21:5
Allen, Charles G Mrs, 1938, Ja 5,21:3
Allen, Charles H, 1950, My 21,106:4; 1955, Ja 30,84:3
Allen, Charles H Capt, 1907, O 23,11:6
Allen, Charles I, 1940, Ap 18,23:2
Allen, Charles J, 1916, Je 18,18:4; 1944, Ag 26,11:5
Allen, Charles Julius Gen, 1915, Je 16,11:6
Allen, Charles Kissam, 1925, S 7,11:5
Allen, Charles L, 1940, N 5,34:1; 1948, Ap 17,15:4
Allen, Charles Leslie, 1917, F 24,9:6
Allen, Charles M, 1942, Ap 6,15:4; 1950, Ag 16,29:3
Allen, Charles Mrs, 1948, S 2,23:5
Allen, Charles R, 1938, Jl 7,19:4
Allen, Charles Stirling Mrs, 1912, D 3,15:4
Allen, Charles T, 1954, N 13,15:4
Allen, Charles W, 1941, N 11,23:2; 1948, D 4,13:5
Allen, Charles W Dr, 1906, Je 1,9:5
Allen, Chauncey B Mrs, 1947, N 22,15:2
Allen, Chauncey N Mrs, 1954, D 6,27:4
Allen, Chester A, 1961, Jl 30,68:1
Allen, Chester S, 1952, Ja 8,27:2
Allen, Chris A, 1959, Ag 12,29:5
Allen, Clair J, 1942, N 25,23:1
Allen, Clara B, 1941, N 29,8:4
Allen, Clarence F, 1950, Ja 21,17:5
Allen, Clarence W, 1939, O 4,25:2
Allen, Claxton E, 1960, Ja 16,21:4
Allen, Clayton T, 1967, F 10,35:3
Allen, Cleveland G, 1953, O 14,29:4
Allen, Clinton L, 1960, S 30,27:1
Allen, Clyde I, 1939, Ag 3,19:4
Allen, Crombie, 1946, Mr 3,44:5
Allen, Curtis Mrs, 1961, O 15,88:6
Allen, Daisy C, 1949, D 21,30:5
Allen, Daniel, 1937, D 8,25:2
Allen, Daniel Mrs, 1940, Ja 6,13:5
Allen, Dave, 1955, Ja 5,23:2
Allen, David, 1955, F 5,15:2
Allen, David E, 1942, S 22,21:5
Allen, David E Mrs, 1943, D 12,71:2
Allen, David Wilson, 1919, Je 19,13:4
Allen, Devere, 1955, Ag 28,84:3
Allen, Don, 1959, Je 17,35:2
Allen, Don B (A L Dimmittz), 1966, Je 11,31:5
Allen, Douglass M, 1949, Ag 13,11:6
Allen, Douglass M Jr, 1966, D 10,37:2
Allen, Dudley Peter Dr, 1915, Ja 8,11:5
Allen, E H, 1883, Ja 2,5:2
Allen, E R, 1944, Je 3,13:5
Allen, Earle W, 1967, Jl 1,23:4
Allen, Edgar, 1943, F 4,23:1; 1945, O 11,23:5
Allen, Edgar F (por), 1937, S 21,25:4
Allen, Edgar H, 1942, N 18,26:3
Allen, Edgar P, 1943, Ap 10,17:6
Allen, Edgar S, 1945, O 2,23:3
Allen, Edgar V, 1949, N 12,15:4; 1961, Je 16,33:5
Allen, Edgar W, 1947, Mr 5,26:2
Allen, Edith, 1949, Ag 20,11:5
Allen, Edith D Mrs, 1939, N 16,23:2
Allen, Edith H Mrs, 1938, Ag 26,17:5
Allen, Edward, 1949, Mr 19,15:4; 1956, Je 14,33:2
Allen, Edward B, 1947, D 27,14:2
Allen, Edward C, 1953, Jl 16,21:5
Allen, Edward Dr, 1882, N 16,5:5
Allen, Edward E, 1950, Ap 15,15:3
Allen, Edward E Mrs, 1952, Ja 15,27:4
Allen, Edward H, 1950, My 1,25:2
Allen, Edward H B, 1937, F 5,2:6
Allen, Edward J, 1939, Ag 25,15:1
Allen, Edward N Mrs, 1961, S 29,35:5
Allen, Edward P, 1943, Mr 1,19:6
Allen, Edward P Capt, 1909, N 26,9:6
Allen, Edward P H Mrs, 1957, Ap 1,37:2
Allen, Edward W, 1955, Ap 10,88:1
Allen, Edwin A, 1947, N 3,23:5
Allen, Edwin W, 1940, Ja 2,20:1
Allen, Elbert R, 1947, S 9,32:2
Allen, Elisha H, 1906, My 7,9:6
Allen, Elizabeth Akers Mrs, 1911, Ag 9,9:5
Allen, Elizabeth T, 1948, Je 12,15:2
Allen, Ellery L, 1938, Jl 1,19:1
Allen, Ellis D Sr, 1953, Jl 2,23:6
Allen, Elmer A, 1912, Je 18,11:6
Allen, Elwood C Sr, 1961, Jl 14,23:5
Allen, Emma F P Dr, 1913, Ag 11,7:6
Allen, Emmett H, 1952, Jl 28,15:3
Allen, Ephraim, 1940, Mr 20,27:2
Allen, Eric W, 1944, Mr 6,19:3
Allen, Ernest L, 1947, Je 28,13:2
Allen, Ernest T, 1952, Ja 26,13:3
Allen, Ethan, 1884, Ja 23,5:4
Allen, Ethan Col, 1911, D 9,13:4
Allen, Ethel B, 1941, Ja 3,19:1
Allen, Ethel M, 1953, D 20,77:1
Allen, Eugene, 1950, S 16,19:4
Allen, Eugene T, 1964, Jl 20,25:1
Allen, Eugene Y, 1953, My 6,31:2
Allen, Eunice Mrs, 1948, F 28,15:4
Allen, Everest J, 1939, Ap 6,25:5
Allen, Everett E, 1951, O 20,15:6
Allen, Ezra G, 1952, Ja 5,11:1

Allen, F D, 1902, D 17,3:2
Allen, F H Rev, 1926, D 25,13:3
Allen, F Leroy, 1948, D 7,31:3
Allen, F W, 1933, N 25,15:1
Allen, Florence C, 1952, O 15,31:4
Allen, Florence E, 1966, S 14,47:1
Allen, Francis B, 1952, N 4,30:3
Allen, Francis G, 1946, F 9,13:1
Allen, Francis H, 1953, O 25,88:5
Allen, Francis J, 1951, Mr 27,29:1; 1960, S 19,31:1
Allen, Francis O, 1953, Ap 14,27:5
Allen, Francis P, 1941, Je 29,32:4; 1956, Jl 7,13:5
Allen, Francis W, 1938, O 11,25:4
Allen, Frank, 1925, Jl 26,5:3; 1947, Je 24,23:2
Allen, Frank A, 1951, Mr 26,23:4
Allen, Frank B, 1945, Ap 9,19:5; 1957, S 28,17:5
Allen, Frank C, 1963, D 11,47:4
Allen, Frank D, 1940, Je 10,17:6; 1955, O 12,29:1
Allen, Frank G, 1940, S 1,20:6; 1950, O 10,31:1
Allen, Frank L, 1942, Je 20,13:3; 1962, O 17,39:1
Allen, Frank R, 1952, My 31,14:7
Allen, Franklin, 1939, F 4,15:5
Allen, Fred (funl plans, Mr 19,31:1; funl, Mr 21,37:4), 1956, Mr 18,1:1
Allen, Fred (estate tax appraisal filed), 1960, O 1, 10:7
Allen, Fred C, 1942, Ap 29,21:3
Allen, Fred W Jr, 1954, Ag 12,25:5
Allen, Frederick C, 1953, S 11,21:5
Allen, Frederick E, 1952, Mr 1,15:3; 1960, O 30,86:4
Allen, Frederick H, 1937, N 14,II,10:2; 1964, Ja 17, 43:1; 1965, D 2,41:4
Allen, Frederick H Col, 1937, D 4,17:2
Allen, Frederick I, 1938, My 19,21:6
Allen, Frederick L, 1938, Jl 31,32:8
Allen, Frederick L (funl plans, F 15,23:2; funl, F 17,31:1), 1954, F 14,1:5
Allen, Frederick M, 1964, Ja 13,35:3
Allen, Frederick S, 1954, Ag 21,17:6
Allen, Frederick Sturgis, 1920, Ag 9,9:6
Allen, Frederick W, 1942, N 16,19:2; 1945, Jl 26,19:4; 1961, Ja 7,19:3
Allen, Freeman C Mrs, 1951, Ja 1,17:1
Allen, Freeman H, 1942, Je 13,15:5
Allen, G A, 1878, D 27,5:2
Allen, G Herbert, 1940, Jl 26,17:2; 1943, My 7,19:4
Allen, Gary L, 1963, Jl 5,26:5
Allen, George, 1876, Je 1,6:7; 1953, F 10,27:1
Allen, George A Mrs, 1946, Ag 1,23:1
Allen, George C, 1950, Ap 27,33:1; 1950, Jl 29,13:3
Allen, George D, 1944, Jl 26,19:3; 1950, Jl 22,15:6
Allen, George E B, 1955, Ja 14,19:5
Allen, George G, 1960, O 11,45:2
Allen, George H, 1938, Mr 10,21:2; 1950, N 21,32:3; 1968, Mr 27,47:4
Allen, George H Mrs, 1944, My 10,19:1
Allen, George Henry, 1919, Ap 3,11:3
Allen, George M, 1941, N 21,17:5
Allen, George Mrs, 1949, Ja 7,21:3
Allen, George R, 1951, O 27,19:3
Allen, George T, 1952, S 28,77:2
Allen, George W, 1947, My 6,27:4; 1961, Ja 14,23:4
Allen, George Y, 1925, N 16,19:6; 1938, F 2,19:5
Allen, Gracie (Mrs Geo Burns),(funl, S 1,36:1; will, S 5,10:1), 1964, Ag 29,1:8
Allen, Grant Mrs, 1946, Mr 24,44:5
Allen, Grosvenor Mrs, 1952, Jl 23,23:6
Allen, Grosvenor N, 1954, S 6,15:2
Allen, Guy C, 1954, D 24,13:5
Allen, H A, 1884, F 2,5:4
Allen, H B, 1948, Ag 25,25:3
Allen, H Marshall, 1939, F 11,15:3
Allen, H T, 1930, Ag 31,1:4
Allen, Hamilton, 1947, Je 17,28:4; 1959, O 20,39:4
Allen, Harley, 1960, Ap 30,23:5
Allen, Harley E, 1958, My 27,31:2
Allen, Harmon G, 1958, S 21,86:7
Allen, Harold B, 1945, S 4,23:4
Allen, Harold L, 1948, Ag 31,23:3
Allen, Harold S Mrs, 1947, S 18,25:1
Allen, Harold W, 1951, Mr 12,25:4
Allen, Harold W Mrs, 1951, Jl 13,21:4
Allen, Harrison Gen, 1904, S 24,9:6
Allen, Harrison H, 1964, Ja 1,25:5
Allen, Harry, 1943, Je 1,17:8
Allen, Harry H, 1965, My 20,43:3
Allen, Harry I, 1942, My 12,19:3
Allen, Harry L, 1945, Jl 7,13:7
Allen, Harry N, 1965, Je 27,64:4
Allen, Harry R, 1947, N 13,28:3
Allen, Harvey A, 1882, S 21,4:7
Allen, Harvey S, 1955, My 31,27:2
Allen, Hector J B, 1942, F 4,19:5
Allen, Helen, 1950, N 1,35:5
Allen, Henry, 1917, Ag 10,9:5
Allen, Henry A, 1944, Mr 12,38:3; 1950, Ag 20,77:1
Allen, Henry A Jr, 1944, Mr 1,19:5
Allen, Henry B, 1962, Mr 22,35:1
Allen, Henry C, 1942, Mr 8,42:2
Allen, Henry C Col, 1905, Ja 5,7:4
Allen, Henry F Rev Dr, 1914, Je 14,15:5
Allen, Henry H, 1955, Ag 14,80:4
Allen, Henry J, 1937, Ap 27,23:4; 1950, Ja 18,31:1

Allen, Henry J Mrs, 1951, D 30,25:2
Allen, Henry L, 1948, Mr 31,25:3
Allen, Henry S, 1904, F 2,9:5; 1953, Ap 5,76:3
Allen, Henry W, 1964, Ja 11,23:5
Allen, Henry W Mrs, 1950, Ja 25,27:3
Allen, Herbert, 1957, My 19,88:3
Allen, Herbert E, 1947, O 25,19:2
Allen, Herbert F L, 1950, O 6,27:3
Allen, Herbert G, 1944, Je 24,13:3
Allen, Herbert I, 1937, Ja 12,23:4
Allen, Herbert M Rev, 1911, Ja 26,11:5
Allen, Herbert R, 1945, Mr 16,15:4
Allen, Hervey, 1949, D 29,25:1
Allen, Hilton R Mrs (R Kelly), 1965, S 2,31:1
Allen, Hope E, 1960, Jl 2,17:6
Allen, Horace D, 1951, N 29,33:5
Allen, Horace L, 1940, Ja 7,48:5; 1954, Mr 31,27:4
Allen, Horatio C, 1955, Je 30,25:2
Allen, Howard A, 1952, D 7,89:2
Allen, Howard C, 1967, Ag 13,80:8
Allen, Howard N, 1953, Ja 8,27:3
Allen, Howard S, 1947, Jl 7,17:4
Allen, Howard W, 1957, D 7,21:4
Allen, Hubert A, 1942, My 4,19:2
Allen, Hugh, 1946, F 21,21:5
Allen, Hugh A, 1946, F 13,23:5
Allen, Hugh E, 1945, Ap 18,23:3
Allen, I Lathrop, 1957, Ap 12,25:2
Allen, Ira R, 1903, D 10,9:5
Allen, Irvin L Brig-Gen, 1968, N 28,37:5
Allen, Isaac A Jr, 1953, Ap 4,13:2
Allen, Isaac W, 1948, N 4,29:5
Allen, J, 1879, S 18,8:3
Allen, J B ex-Sen, 1903, Ja 30,9:5
Allen, J Burns, 1937, O 28,23:3
Allen, J Edward, 1907, S 14,9:5
Allen, J F, 1930, S 20,19:7
Allen, J R, 1928, D 22,17:2
Allen, J Ross, 1950, Ap 21,24:2
Allen, J S, 1935, Je 4,23:3
Allen, J W, 1876, Je 16,4:7
Allen, J Warner, 1939, My 11,25:3
Allen, J Weston, 1942, Ja 2,23:3
Allen, J Wilford, 1948, Jl 19,19:3
Allen, J William, 1938, Ag 31,15:4
Allen, James C, 1912, Ja 31,11:5
Allen, James F, 1925, Jl 22,19:5
Allen, James J, 1962, Jl 9,31:5
Allen, James Lane (por), 1925, F 19,19:4
Allen, James M, 1955, Ap 5,29:4
Allen, James N, 1939, Ag 5,15:5
Allen, James P, 1946, O 23,27:5; 1951, Ja 5,22:2
Allen, James P Mrs, 1951, Ja 5,22:2
Allen, James R, 1967, N 24,46:4
Allen, James S, 1947, Jl 15,23:3
Allen, James T, 1948, S 30,27:5
Allen, James T Mrs, 1945, F 16,24:3
Allen, James W, 1940, Mr 6,23:2
Allen, Jay J, 1942, O 19,19:2
Allen, Jean G, 1955, S 22,31:1
Allen, Jean M, 1958, Ap 14,25:4
Allen, Jesse, 1875, N 20,8:5
Allen, Jesse B, 1944, Jl 26,19:6
Allen, Jesse H, 1946, Ap 16,25:2
Allen, Jewett M, 1957, S 15,83:1
Allen, Joel Asaph Dr, 1921, Ag 30,15:1
Allen, Joel N, 1940, Mr 12,23:2
Allen, John, 1917, O 31,13:5; 1939, D 26,19:5; 1943, O 30,15:4; 1951, N 14,31:5
Allen, John A, 1946, F 1,23:1
Allen, John B, 1910, Ag 11,7:6
Allen, John C, 1937, N 18,23:2; 1946, Ap 13,17:5; 1949, Jl 28,23:1; 1950, D 26,23:3
Allen, John C Mrs, 1954, My 11,14:6
Allen, John Clarence Rev Dr, 1917, Ag 22,7:4
Allen, John D, 1964, Mr 10,37:3; 1966, S 1,35:5
Allen, John Dr, 1883, Ag 12,7:3
Allen, John E, 1903, Ag 30,7:6; 1945, Jl 25,23:5; 1947, Ja 3,21:1; 1947, Ja 4,15:2; 1947, Jl 13,44:5; 1949, N 6,94:3
Allen, John H, 1922, D 12,19:4; 1947, F 20,25:2; 1953, Ja 15,27:2; 1958, Ja 21,29:5
Allen, John H Mrs, 1946, Mr 18,21:3; 1949, Mr 28,21:3
Allen, John J, 1937, F 4,21:3; 1940, S 21,19:3
Allen, John J Jr Mrs, 1957, My 16,31:1
Allen, John J Sr, 1945, D 28,15:2
Allen, John K, 1943, N 16,23:2
Allen, John Kimball, 1912, Ja 9,13:6
Allen, John M, 1937, O 30,19:4; 1954, Je 18,23:2
Allen, John M L, 1914, O 30,9:6
Allen, John Mrs, 1942, D 2,25:5
Allen, John P, 1941, Ap 6,48:7
Allen, John S, 1938, Ja 15,15:2; 1954, Ja 15,20:3
Allen, John T, 1923, Je 9,11:7
Allen, John W, 1921, Ag 29,11:1; 1937, O 12,25:3
Allen, Johnny, 1959, Mr 30,31:2
Allen, Joseph, 1884, Mr 15,4:7; 1946, Mr 5,25:4; 1952, S 10,29:6
Allen, Joseph C, 1943, F 23,21:5
Allen, Joseph D, 1965, Mr 4,31:2
Allen, Joseph D Mrs, 1940, O 1,23:5
Allen, Joseph H, 1948, Je 15,27:4; 1951, F 9,26:2
Allen, Joseph H D, 1940, Mr 2,13:4

Allen, Joseph V, 1964, Mr 17,35:2
Allen, Joshua, 1942, N 10,27:5
Allen, Judson W, 1957, F 7,27:2
Allen, Julian, 1967, O 23,45:4
Allen, Kelcey, 1951, Jl 24,25:5
Allen, L, 1883, My 31,5:5
Allen, Laura (will), 1937, D 10,28:4
Allen, Laverne A, 1944, Mr 11,13:3
Allen, Leo, 1950, F 24,23:2
Allen, Leon, 1945, S 19,25:2
Allen, Leon M, 1946, Mr 20,23:3
Allen, Leon Mrs, 1958, Ap 27,86:4
Allen, Leonard L, 1949, D 6,31:2
Allen, Leonard S, 1903, N 22,7:5
Allen, Lester E, 1943, Je 5,15:4
Allen, Lester R, 1941, Je 10,23:3
Allen, Lewis G, 1948, My 30,34:3
Allen, Lewis M, 1949, My 3,25:1
Allen, Lewis W, 1939, Je 14,23:4; 1944, Jl 12,19:5
Allen, Lloyd E, 1950, D 14,35:5
Allen, Louis, 1905, Ap 24,6:2; 1909, Ja 5,9:5
Allen, Louis D, 1939, Mr 16,23:4
Allen, Louis E, 1948, N 29,23:5
Allen, Louis J Rear-Adm Ret, 1905, Je 30,9:3
Allen, Louis L, 1948, My 8,15:5
Allen, Louisa W Mrs, 1941, O 5,49:1
Allen, Lt-Com, 1875, F 8,5:4
Allen, Lucy C, 1937, Ja 9,17:4
Allen, Lucy E, 1943, N 13,13:5
Allen, Luther M, 1956, O 25,33:5
Allen, Lyman, 1961, F 3,23:1
Allen, Lyman H, 1953, My 7,32:3
Allen, Lyman R, 1950, My 5,21:4
Allen, M Adele, 1944, My 20,15:4
Allen, M M Mrs, 1926, Je 20,26:6
Allen, M May, 1944, Ja 11,20:2
Allen, Malvern H, 1955, F 14,19:3
Allen, Mansfield, 1903, F 26,2:3
Allen, Mariet S Mrs, 1939, Ja 29,33:2
Allen, Marion B Mrs, 1941, D 29,15:5
Allen, Marion H, 1952, S 10,29:5
Allen, Mark A Mrs, 1945, Je 7,19:5
Allen, Mark C, 1952, Mr 27,29:1
Allen, Mark W Sr, 1958, O 13,29:2
Allen, Marshall J Mrs, 1914, Jl 21,9:5
Allen, Marston, 1947, Je 14,15:3
Allen, Martin A, 1940, N 6,23:5
Allen, Mary G Mrs, 1938, Mr 23,23:3
Allen, Mary H, 1947, N 19,27:4
Allen, Mary J Mrs, 1960, Ag 28,83:4
Allen, Mary M Mrs, 1938, Je 30,23:5
Allen, Mathew, 1949, S 5,17:6
Allen, Maurice, 1914, O 20,13:5
Allen, Michael J, 1939, Ag 2,19:6
Allen, Millard F, 1955, S 7,31:1
Allen, Morse S, 1967, D 5,47:2
Allen, Murray C, 1954, O 2,17:6
Allen, Nathan Hale, 1925, My 11,17:4
Allen, Norman M, 1909, N 15,9:3
Allen, O K, 1936, Ja 29,5:2
Allen, Orrin T, 1946, Ap 17,25:5
Allen, Oscar K Mrs, 1938, Mr 31,23:3
Allen, Oswald C, 1959, My 5,33:1
Allen, Paul, 1948, N 21,88:6
Allen, Paul H, 1952, O 1,33:2
Allen, Pearl B, 1956, Ap 5,29:4
Allen, Pearl J Mrs, 1942, Ja 16,21:1
Allen, Perry S Mrs, 1947, Mr 6,25:3
Allen, Pheobe S, 1940, N 12,23:5
Allen, Phil Mrs, 1952, D 12,29:2
Allen, Phil S Prof, 1937, Ap 28,23:1
Allen, Philetus, 1957, N 14,33:2
Allen, Philip D, 1965, Jl 29,27:5
Allen, Philip Ex-Gov, 1865, D 17,1:7
Allen, Philip R, 1962, My 3,33:1
Allen, Philip S B, 1967, Jl 11,37:2
Allen, Pliny A, 1943, Ja 23,13:4
Allen, R David Mrs, 1940, Ap 2,26:3
Allen, Ralph, 1966, D 3,39:4
Allen, Ralph H Mrs, 1962, D 6,43:2
Allen, Ray, 1938, Mr 6,II,8:8
Allen, Raymond, 1965, Ja 6,39:2
Allen, Raymond C, 1941, Je 21,17:4
Allen, Raymond D, 1953, Ja 20,25:5
Allen, Raymond D Mrs, 1959, D 21,27:4
Allen, Red (Henry Allen), 1967, Ap 19,45:3
Allen, Reginald B, 1938, Mr 6,II,8:2
Allen, Richard B, 1954, N 3,29:1
Allen, Richard D, 1945, Ag 24,20:2
Allen, Richard F, 1957, Ag 27,29:1
Allen, Richard S Jr, 1948, Mr 13,15:5
Allen, Richard W, 1949, Ag 18,21:2
Allen, Riley H, 1966, O 3,47:4
Allen, Riley H Mrs, 1950, Jl 7,19:5
Allen, Rita (Mrs Milton E Cassel), 1968, Jl 4,19:1
Allen, Robert, 1955, Ag 20,17:5
Allen, Robert E, 1955, Ag 9,25:2
Allen, Robert E L, 1951, F 1,25:5
Allen, Robert G, 1943, My 16,43:2; 1963, Ag 11,85:1
Allen, Robert H, 1949, O 12,29:5
Allen, Robert J, 1950, Mr 7,27:4
Allen, Robert J F, 1952, S 21,88:4
Allen, Robert L, 1949, My 17,25:1; 1959, Ag 2,80:3
Allen, Robert M, 1948, Ap 3,15:6
Allen, Robert P, 1963, Je 29,23:4
Allen, Robert W, 1949, Jl 21,26:2
Allen, Robert W Mrs, 1944, Je 16,19:1
Allen, Rolland C, 1948, Jl 19,19:2
Allen, Ronald H, 1949, Jl 26,27:2
Allen, Russell H, 1945, My 31,5:5
Allen, Russell M, 1967, S 18,47:3
Allen, Russell W, 1945, Ag 7,23:3
Allen, S, 1929, Ap 22,1:2
Allen, S J M Mrs, 1948, D 5,92:5
Allen, Sam G, 1956, O 17,35:3
Allen, Samuel, 1905, Ap 21,9:5
Allen, Samuel A, 1950, D 13,35:5; 1959, Jl 23,27:5
Allen, Samuel E, 1963, Ag 11,84:7
Allen, Samuel E Mrs, 1942, Mr 9,19:5
Allen, Samuel G Mrs, 1944, O 22,45:2
Allen, Sarah E, 1949, S 14,31:5
Allen, Sarah Mrs, 1951, D 11,33:3
Allen, Selden R, 1952, Mr 22,13:5
Allen, Sherman P, 1938, D 31,15:6
Allen, Sidney P, 1966, Ap 3,84:5
Allen, Simeon C, 1962, F 21,45:3
Allen, Spencer, 1955, Ap 18,23:3
Allen, Stuart, 1943, Jl 7,19:2
Allen, T F Dr, 1902, D 6,9:5
Allen, Theodore A, 1903, N 10,9:5
Allen, Theodore C, 1958, Mr 30,88:8
Allen, Theophilus P, 1943, Ja 28,19:1
Allen, Thomas, 1882, Ap 9,2:3; 1924, Ag 27,17:6; 1948, Ap 12,21:5
Allen, Thomas B, 1903, Ap 29,9:6
Allen, Thomas D, 1956, F 15,31:1
Allen, Thomas D Jr, 1953, S 8,31:4
Allen, Thomas E, 1948, My 29,15:5
Allen, Thomas E Sr, 1959, N 10,47:2
Allen, Thomas F Mrs, 1945, Je 1,15:5
Allen, Thomas J, 1951, Ja 14,86:2
Allen, Thomas P, 1945, Ja 14,39:2
Allen, Thomas 3d, 1947, Mr 28,23:2
Allen, Thornton W, 1944, Jl 31,13:5
Allen, Timothy F, 1959, F 7,19:2
Allen, Travers, 1923, F 2,15:4
Allen, Truman E Rev, 1903, S 29,9:2
Allen, Truman J Dr, 1937, D 30,19:5
Allen, Van Etten, 1948, N 9,27:4
Allen, Victor, 1939, S 10,49:3
Allen, Victor M, 1916, S 27,11:6
Allen, Viola, 1948, My 10,21:1
Allen, Vivian B Mrs, 1962, O 12,31:2
Allen, W Burton, 1947, Je 30,19:4
Allen, W F, 1878, Je 4,5:6
Allen, W G, 1939, Ja 10,19:4
Allen, W H, 1882, Ag 30,4:7
Allen, Walter, 1907, F 8,9:6; 1938, Ap 21,19:5
Allen, Walter B, 1946, My 22,21:4; 1957, N 29,29:3
Allen, Walter C, 1945, N 14,19:3
Allen, Walter F, 1958, Ag 17,86:5
Allen, Walter H Mrs, 1952, Mr 28,24:3
Allen, Walter S, 1966, F 10,37:1
Allen, Watson, 1948, Ja 14,25:3
Allen, Weatherford P, 1937, Ap 13,25:1
Allen, Webster D, 1950, D 15,31:5
Allen, Whiting, 1911, Jl 28,9:6
Allen, Willard H, 1957, F 27,27:2
Allen, William, 1879, Jl 12,1:1
Allen, William (funl, Mr 17,11:6), 1917, Mr 4,21:2
Allen, William, 1947, D 21,54:1; 1967, S 18,47:3
Allen, William A, 1946, Je 28,21:2; 1953, O 5,27:5; 1954, Je 23,25:3
Allen, William C, 1925, Ap 14,23:5; 1950, N 21,31:4
Allen, William C Mrs, 1955, Je 3,23:3; 1958, F 9,88:7
Allen, William E, 1964, Jl 11,25:5
Allen, William E Mrs, 1947, O 14,27:4
Allen, William F, 1940, N 12,23:2; 1946, Je 15,21:5; 1949, Mr 22,25:1; 1952, My 24,19:5
Allen, William F Col, 1906, F 7,9:5
Allen, William Frederick, 1915, N 10,13:3
Allen, William G Maj, 1924, N 29,13:4
Allen, William H, 1903, N 26,7:6; 1941, My 21,23:5; 1951, N 13,29:1; 1955, Ja 13,27:1
Allen, William H (Feb 23), 1963, Ap 1,35:1
Allen, William H Capt, 1907, F 24,7:6
Allen, William H Jr, 1943, Je 7,13:3
Allen, William H Rear Adm, 1951, F 11,88:3
Allen, William J Judge, 1868, Je 27,5:2
Allen, William J Sr, 1947, S 11,27:5; 1965, D 22,31:3
Allen, William L, 1938, Ja 7,19:2; 1950, S 29,27:2
Allen, William M, 1947, D 12,27:1
Allen, William P, 1941, My 18,43:3; 1962, Jl 4,21:6; 1965, O 20,47:3
Allen, William R, 1955, Ap 8,21:5
Allen, William R Justice, 1921, S 9,15:4
Allen, William S, 1918, Mr 1,11:4; 1941, F 17,15:3; 1944, Ap 4,21:4; 1948, Ag 14,13:4; 1955, F 15,27:1; 1961, O 15,88:8
Allen, William T, 1948, Ag 29,56:3
Allen, William V Judge, 1924, Ja 13,23:1
Allen, William W, 1939, N 21,16:5
Allen, William W Jr, 1954, S 25,15:6
Allen, Willis B, 1938, S 12,17:5
Allen, Wilmar M, 1956, Ja 16,21:2
Allen, Wilmot B, 1956, O 13,19:2
Allen, Wilmot B Mrs, 1952, O 14,31:5
Allen, Wing B, 1951, D 8,11:2
Allen, Yorke, 1940, Je 8,15:5
Allen of Hurtwood, Lord, 1939, Mr 4,15:6
Allenberg, Bertram, 1958, N 28,30:7
Allenby, A R, 1936, Mr 20,23:3
Allenby, Francis S, 1954, D 1,31:4
Allenby, Peggy (Mrs J McGovern), 1966, Mr 25,41:2
Allenby, Viscountess, 1942, Mr 24,19:4
Allenby of Megiddo, Viscount, 1936, My 15,25:1
Allendale, Lady, 1945, Ag 1,19:3
Allendale, Viscount (Wentworth Canning Blackett-Beaumont), 1923, D 13,21:5
Allender, Edwin M, 1942, Je 3,23:1
Allender, Nina E Mrs, 1957, Ap 3,31:5
Allendesalazar, Manuel, 1923, Mr 14,19:4
Allendorf, Elbert J, 1922, F 1,19:5
Allendorf, Emma, 1945, Ja 16,19:4
Allendorf, Hans, 1948, Jl 27,25:3
Allenton, Joseph, 1939, Ja 6,21:4
Aller, Howard L, 1954, Ap 22,29:5
Aller, Johnson, 1948, Ja 27,25:2
Allerdice, David W, 1963, Je 28,30:6
Allerdice, Norman, 1961, Jl 29,19:7
Allerhand, Max, 1943, S 20,21:5
Allers, George Mrs, 1939, O 4,25:3
Allerton, Lord (Wm Lawles Jackson), 1917, Ap 5, 13:6
Allerton, Robert, 1964, D 23,27:4
Allerton, Rufus K, 1958, Jl 14,21:3
Alles, George, 1944, Ag 8,17:4
Alles, Gordon A, 1963, Ja 23,7:6
Allesandoni, Anthony P, 1948, O 23,15:4
Alleva, Frank Mrs, 1943, Ja 3,42:5
Alleva, Pina Mrs, 1957, O 12,19:5
Allex, Jake (J A Mandushich), 1959, Ag 29,17:4
Alley, A Bryan Mrs, 1937, S 11,17:3
Alley, Albert R Mrs, 1960, Jl 23,19:1
Alley, E Newt, 1947, O 29,27:4
Alley, Edward E Jr, 1949, F 18,24:2
Alley, Ernest V, 1944, O 17,23:2
Alley, G B, 1883, O 17,4:6
Alley, George P, 1951, Jl 15,60:6
Alley, Howard C, 1948, Ja 24,15:4
Alley, Howard C Mrs, 1948, Ja 30,24:2
Alley, James C, 1942, Jl 27,15:4
Alley, John S, 1942, Ap 22,24:2
Alley, Rayford W, 1965, Ap 2,35:2
Alley, Thomas W, 1953, Mr 29,92:1
Alley, Uriah T, 1947, O 28,25:1
Alley, William P Mrs, 1948, D 25,18:2
Alleyne, A P, 1967, Ag 5,23:3
Alleyne, C C Mrs, 1944, My 17,19:3
Alleyne, Cameron C, 1955, Mr 26,15:6
Allez, Jacques A Mrs, 1950, Jl 30,60:1
Allfeier, Frederick, 1957, Jl 11,25:3
Allgair, George Sr, 1945, Ag 22,23:4
Allgair, William A, 1951, O 23,29:3
Allgarer, Fred W, 1937, My 10,19:2
Allgood, Andrew P D, 1956, Ja 25,16:6
Allgood, B F, 1951, Je 15,23:1
Allgood, Dwight M, 1967, O 30,45:4
Allgood, Sara (trb, S 24,II, 3:4), 1950, S 14,31:1
Allgor, Roderick A, 1946, Ag 9,19:6
Allgor, Wendell P, 1940, D 24,15:3
Allgyer, S E, 1953, N 17,31:4
Allhands, George R, 1938, N 23,21:3
Alliaume, Curtis F, 1952, S 2,23:1
Allibone, S A, 1889, S 4,5:2
Allie, Reuben, 1960, Ja 24,88:3
Alliger, Frank I, 1948, O 16,15:3
Alliger, Lewis A, 1952, Mr 1,30:8
Alliger, Lewis A Mrs, 1946, O 4,24:2
Allileuv, Sergei, 1945, Jl 30,19:4
Alliluyeva, Anna S, 1964, Ag 8,19:2
Alliluyeva, Olga E, 1951, Mr 13,31:4
Allin, Alfred T, 1967, O 21,31:2
Allin, C Clark, 1949, D 25,26:6
Allin, George Albert, 1911, F 3,9:5
Allin, George L, 1960, Je 25,21:4
Allin, George L Mrs, 1954, Je 5,17:4
Allin, Horatio N, 1939, D 14,27:5
Allin, R Fred, 1954, O 29,21:2
Allin, Rosabel, 1958, Ap 23,33:2
Alling, Arthur B, 1940, My 3,21:2
Alling, Arthur N, 1949, Mr 16,27:2
Alling, Benjamin W, 1950, Ja 25,27:4
Alling, Charles B, 1903, N 6,9:6; 1965, D 5,89:1
Alling, E Roy, 1948, F 3,25:1
Alling, F Kenneth, 1954, F 10,29:4
Alling, Frank P, 1945, D 16,40:1
Alling, Frederic A, 1949, O 21,26:2
Alling, Frederic A Mrs, 1961, Ap 23,86:5
Alling, Harold L, 1960, Jl 29,25:1
Alling, Harry H, 1949, Jl 2,15:1
Alling, J Sackett, 1905, Je 29,9:2
Alling, Joseph T, 1937, S 21,25:3
Alling, Marian M Mrs, 1939, Ag 16,23:3
Alling, Nels, 1955, Mr 10,27:2
Alling, Newton D, 1948, Ag 16,19:5
Alling, Paul H, 1949, Ja 19,27:1
Alling, Stephen, 1948, O 7,29:2
Alling, Wilbur M, 1953, My 27,31:4

Alling, Wilbur M Mrs, 1952, D 16,31:3
Alling, Willard, 1940, N 19,23:3
Allingham, Margery, 1966, Jl 1,35:1
Allingham, Ralph R, 1957, D 25,31:5
Allington, Earl W, 1945, Je 23,13:5
Allington, H Clifford, 1960, Je 29,33:2
Allinson, James, 1964, Je 22,27:1
Allinson, Josiah T, 1937, Je 16,23:3
Allinson, May, 1918, D 28,11:3
Allis, Amber Mrs, 1941, Mr 5,21:3
Allis, Barney L, 1962, Ap 19,31:4
Allis, Charles, 1918, Jl 24,11:4
Allis, Edward P 2d Mrs, 1947, F 18,25:3
Allis, Frederick S, 1941, Jl 24,17:2
Allis, J P, 1904, Ja 1,7:5
Allis, John, 1939, Je 12,17:5
Allis, John W, 1951, F 21,27:3
Allis, Marguerite, 1958, Ag 8,19:2
Allis, Marjorie, 1944, Ap 13,19:4
Allis, W F Packer, 1945, Ag 20,19:5
Allison, Alex B, 1943, S 17,21:4
Allison, Arnold, 1946, O 29,25:1
Allison, Calvin T, 1949, My 19,29:2
Allison, Charles R, 1945, Je 8,19:4
Allison, Denis J, 1942, Ja 2,34:3
Allison, E F Col, 1937, Jl 18,II,7:2
Allison, Edward, 1943, Ag 16,15:3
Allison, Eli, 1941, N 13,28:2
Allison, Ethel T Mrs, 1951, Ja 17,27:3
Allison, Florence M, 1958, S 10,33:2
Allison, Frank Mrs, 1944, Ap 1,13:7
Allison, George, 1943, Ap 2,21:3; 1951, S 12,31:2
Allison, George D, 1949, My 14,13:2
Allison, George W, 1939, D 18,23:5; 1958, S 19,27:3
Allison, Giles B, 1914, D 25,11:4
Allison, Harry E Dr, 1904, N 13,7:6
Allison, Harvey, 1939, Ja 21,15:2
Allison, Henry Maj, 1909, Ja 20,9:2
Allison, Howard Jr, 1956, Ap 4,29:1
Allison, J (see also Mr 24), 1878, Mr 25,1:3
Allison, J M Ali, 1954, N 12,21:4
Allison, Jack, 1953, O 10,17:5
Allison, James B, 1964, S 27,85:3
Allison, James E, 1955, Jl 5,29:1
Allison, James H, 1962, Mr 14,39:4
Allison, James M, 1940, D 25,27:5
Allison, James N Mrs, 1957, N 28,31:5
Allison, John D R, 1949, Ap 10,76:7
Allison, John M S, 1944, Ap 7,20:2
Allison, John P, 1967, Mr 9,39:1
Allison, John W, 1941, Ap 26,15:2; 1951, Jl 21,13:4
Allison, Joseph, 1924, F 28,19:5
Allison, Joseph Nichols Brig-Gen, 1918, My 27,13:5
Allison, Keith Mrs, 1941, Ap 1,23:3
Allison, Latham L Mrs, 1944, Ag 30,17:2
Allison, Le Roy W, 1955, My 2,21:5
Allison, Leonard B, 1961, D 20,33:4
Allison, Leroy W Mrs, 1954, F 13,13:6
Allison, M S, 1881, My 24,5:2
Allison, Mary D Mrs, 1941, My 11,45:1
Allison, N Dwight Mrs, 1962, My 16,41:3
Allison, R G, 1946, Mr 22,21:5
Allison, Ralph D, 1961, Mr 25,25:3
Allison, Richard J, 1958, O 1,37:5
Allison, Robert H, 1960, Ja 2,13:1
Allison, Robert P, 1957, D 22,40:4
Allison, Robert Price, 1953, F 25,27:4
Allison, Sverre, 1968, Ag 3,25:4
Allison, Thomas Ex-Judge, 1917, My 16,13:6
Allison, Walter L, 1944, Ap 12,21:2
Allison, William, 1945, Jl 30,19:1
Allison, William B Sen, 1908, Ag 9,9:4
Allison, William H, 1939, S 26,23:5; 1941, S 21,45:2
Allison, William M, 1946, Ag 22,27:4
Allison, William M Mrs, 1957, F 3,77:2
Allison, William Mrs, 1959, Je 20,21:5
Allison, William Outis, 1924, D 19,21:3
Allison, William S Sr, 1949, D 17,17:3
Allison, William T, 1941, F 5,19:3
Allison, Wilmer L Sr, 1949, O 22,17:5
Allitson, Frances, 1912, O 4,13:5
Allman, Alfred F, 1938, N 19,17:5
Allman, Charles A, 1959, Je 19,25:3
Allman, David B Mrs, 1964, Mr 26,35:4
Allman, James P, 1956, F 25,19:6
Allman, Justin P, 1945, Mr 13,23:4
Allman, Ray B Mrs, 1941, My 13,23:5
Allman, Sydney K, 1940, My 3,21:5
Allmang, Harold E, 1951, My 12,21:4
Allner, Frederick A, 1942, Jl 19,31:3
Allocca, John H, 1956, D 12,39:6
Allom, Charles, 1947, Je 4,27:1
Allot, Betsy, 1953, F 4,18:3
Allott, Alfred J, 1950, Jl 4,17:5
Allott, Henry E, 1912, S 18,11:2
Allott, Leonard R, 1961, Jl 29,20:8
Alloway, Arthur R, 1957, My 23,33:5
Alloway, Henry, 1939, My 21,III,7:1
Alloway, J Lionel, 1954, F 9,27:5
Alloway, Joseph E, 1962, Je 27,32:7
Allport, Fayette W, 1957, D 6,29:1
Allport, Gordon W, 1967, O 10,47:1
Allport, Lewis, 1946, F 7,23:4
Allred, James V, 1959, S 25,29:2
Allshouse, Harry R, 1951, Ja 8,17:2
Allsop, Thomas, 1937, S 25,17:3
Allsopp, Clinton B, 1962, O 14,85:3
Allsopp, Fred W, 1946, Ap 11,25:2
Allsopp, George A, 1941, O 24,23:2; 1959, Ag 5,27:1
Allton, Wilbur F, 1954, S 8,32:4
Allward, Walter S, 1955, Ap 26,29:2
Allwell, Louis, 1956, Mr 30,19:1
Allwork, Ronald Mrs (Eleanor), 1968, Je 30,53:1
Allyn, Arthur C (will, O 15,23:3), 1960, O 8,23:5
Allyn, Arthur V, 1946, D 27,2:6
Allyn, Charles G, 1952, Ap 22,29:4
Allyn, David F, 1948, N 9,27:2
Allyn, Gurdon S, 1951, D 30,24:5
Allyn, Harriet M, 1957, Jl 9,27:1
Allyn, Herman B, 1939, N 7,25:4
Allyn, Hugh H, 1952, Mr 13,30:4
Allyn, John C, 1946, F 6,23:4
Allyn, Louis M, 1946, Je 1,13:2
Allyn, Robert S, 1956, Ja 2,21:5
Allyn, T M, 1882, Ag 26,5:5
Allyn, W Ellery, 1956, Ap 23,27:5
Alm, Ingvald W, 1951, S 27,31:4
Alma Concilio, Sister (Moran), 1950, Ap 15,15:4
Alma de Paul, Sister (Sisters of Charity), 1954, Ja 7, 31:4
Alma-Tadema, Lawrence Lady, 1909, Ag 17,9:6
Alman, Samuel, 1947, Jl 21,17:3
Almandos Almonacid, Vincente, 1953, N 18,31:3
Almani, Dante, 1949, Ja 7,21:3
Almarez y Santos, Cardinal, 1922, Ja 24,15:4
Almazan, Juan A, 1965, O 11,39:4
Almberg, Harry E, 1943, Ja 12,24:2
Almeader, George L, 1945, My 30,19:4
Almeida, Miguel O de, 1953, D 9,11:2
Almerico, Tony, 1961, D 6,47:1
Almesan, Aurelius, 1945, D 30,14:8
Almfelt, Gustav A, 1946, Ap 16,25:5
Almgren, August E, 1951, N 24,11:1
Almi, Eli A (E A Sheps), 1963, S 25,43:1
Almirall, Joseph J Mrs, 1911, Ag 3,7:5
Almirall, Juan A (cor, O 29,19:1), 1955, O 28,25:5
Almirall, Raymond F, 1939, My 19,21:2
Almodovar, Duke of, 1906, Je 24,9:6
Almon, Andrew B, 1904, My 22,7:5
Almond, David, 1956, My 25,23:3
Almond, David J, 1949, F 4,23:3
Almond, George B Jr, 1949, Ja 28,21:4
Almond, James E, 1960, Mr 14,29:4
Almond, John M, 1939, S 18,19:2
Almond, Nina, 1964, O 2,37:6
Almond, Thomas R Mrs (trb lr, Je 20,16:6), 1953, Je 19,22:3
Almont, Albert, 1945, My 7,17:3
Almonte, Juan, 1869, Mr 24,7:1
Almonti (Ted),(see also Ap 11), 1878, Ap 15,8:2
Almour, Henry I, 1950, Ja 18,32:4
Almour, Ralph, 1953, Mr 28,17:3
Almquist, Aug J, 1942, F 21,19:3
Almquist, Nils T, 1960, S 14,43:1
Almstead, Morris, 1948, Mr 4,25:2
Almy, Charles, 1954, Ja 24,85:1
Almy, Commodore Mrs, 1871, D 11,1:5
Almy, Edward T Mrs, 1941, F 4,21:1
Almy, Frederick, 1965, Ap 22,33:2
Almy, George O, 1953, D 10,47:1
Almy, Gertrude M, 1958, N 13,33:5
Almy, Helen C Mrs, 1938, Ap 11,15:1
Almy, J H, 1878, D 18,2:4
Almy, J J Adm, 1895, My 17,7:1
Almy, John H, 1967, Jl 23,60:7
Almy, John H Mrs, 1947, Ag 25,17:4
Almy, Roland R, 1954, F 11,29:3
Almy, Samuel C, 1959, D 7,31:4
Almy, Thomas, 1882, My 18,5:6; 1946, S 7,15:5
Almy, W E, 1901, Ag 2,7:6
Almy, William, 1940, Je 30,33:3
Almy, William C, 1939, Jl 18,19:2
Aloe, Louis P Mrs (will), 1957, Ja 6,19:3
Alofs, John, 1949, Mr 7,21:1
Alofsin, Isaac F, 1955, F 5,15:2
Alofsin, Louis M (will, Je 6,19:2), 1939, Je 2,23:4
Alois, Prince of Liechtenstein, 1955, Mr 18,27:3
Aloisi, Pompeo, 1949, Ja 16,68:8
Aloisi-Masella, Cardinal, 1902, N 23,4:4
Alondo, Gilberto P, 1941, Mr 9,41:3
Alonge, Paolo, 1954, F 24,25:2
Alonso, Amado, 1952, My 27,27:5
Alonso Lopez, Francisco, 1948, My 19,27:4
Alonzo, Felix Ferrer, 1875, F 14,7:3
Alonzo, James, 1938, Mr 5,17:3
Alonzo, Severo Fernandez, 1925, Ag 15,11:5
Alotrico, Eugene, 1952, Ja 15,27:4
Aloysia, Mother (C A Kelly), 1953, D 30,23:2
Aloysia Concepta, Sister (H Morrisey), 1954, F 7, 88:2
Aloysius, Bro, 1946, Ag 2,19:3
Aloysius, Mary Mother (Rose Keefe), 1913, O 11, 15:4
Aloysius Marie, Sister (E Metz), 1961, S 4,15:4
Alpaugh, J Jorman, 1943, O 3,48:5
Alpaugh, Norman, 1954, N 17,31:4
Alpaugh, Wesley F Mrs, 1961, Je 24,21:2
Alper, Maurice, 1957, Ap 10,33:6
Alper, Michael, 1955, Ja 31,19:3
Alperin, David H, 1963, D 31,19:4
Alperin, Henry, 1903, Ap 26,12:3
Alperin, Joseph, 1962, N 11,88:4
Alperin, Louis I, 1956, S 25,33:2
Alpern, Hymen, 1967, Jl 7,33:3
Alpern, Isaac, 1961, Jl 14,23:1
Alpern, Melvin, 1962, O 14,86:7
Alpers, August C, 1952, F 21,27:5
Alpers, Ernest, 1960, Jl 3,32:5
Alpers, Matilda C, 1952, N 4,29:1
Alpers, William A, 1950, My 14,106:8
Alpers, William C, 1917, F 22,11:4
Alpers, William J, 1914, Mr 3,9:4
Alperson, William, 1907, My 7,9:5
Alperstein, Abraham L Rabbi, 1917, Ja 29,11:5
Alperstein, Bernard B, 1967, Mr 24,31:2
Alpert, Abraham, 1939, S 3,19:2
Alpert, Augusta Dr, 1968, Ja 23,39:3
Alpert, Barnet, 1954, Ja 24,85:1
Alpert, Barnet Mrs, 1959, Ap 14,35:2
Alpert, David, 1963, Ap 7,85:6
Alpert, Edward, 1952, F 28,27:4
Alpert, Frances Mrs, 1937, Mr 14,II,8:5
Alpert, George Mrs, 1967, Ja 22,77:1
Alpert, Isidor, 1955, N 5,19:3
Alpert, Joseph, 1954, N 16,29:5
Alpert, Milton I (Mickey),(Sept 22), 1965, O 11,61:1
Alpert, Myer M, 1955, Ja 21,23:3
Alpert, Phil, 1950, Ap 21,23:1
Alpert, Phillip Mrs, 1960, S 7,43:4
Alpert, Samuel, 1940, Je 21,22:3
Alpert, Simon, 1951, My 19,15:4
Alpert, Zusman, 1941, Ap 14,17:1
Alphand, Charles H, 1942, S 18,22:3
Alphenaar, Gerard, 1965, F 13,21:4
Alpheus James, Bro (J J Gorman), 1961, Mr 10,27:3
Alphonse, Louis, 1942, My 22,21:2
Alphonse Marie, Sister, 1937, Jl 5,17:4
Alphonsus, Bro (F J Wachlski), 1966, D 31,19:1
Alphonsus Cyril Brother (Gingras), 1950, Ap 17,23:4
Alphonsus Edwin Bro (Christian School Bros), 1967, F 1,39:3
Alphonsus Fidelis (Bro A P Linn), 1960, F 4,31:4
Alpin, Edward J, 1965, F 8,25:4
Alpine, John R, 1947, Ap 22,27:4
Alpiner, Benjamin W, 1946, Jl 16,23:5
Alpoim, Amancio, 1948, Jl 21,23:5
Alprin, Joseph, 1943, Jl 22,19:4
Alrich, Herbert W, 1938, Mr 26,15:3
Alsberg, Carl H, 1950, F 10,23:1
Alsberg, Carl L, 1940, N 2,15:3
Alsberg, William J, 1962, F 9,29:5
Alschuler, Alfred S, 1940, N 7,25:4
Alschuler, Samuel, 1939, N 10,23:1
Alsdorf, Claude I, 1948, S 11,15:5
Alsdorf, Edgar Mrs, 1943, N 19,19:1
Alsdorf, Frank J, 1945, N 21,21:2
Alsdorf, Henry J, 1951, Je 3,92:6
Alsdorf, Simon P, 1946, Ja 16,23:3
Alsdorf, Ulysses J, 1952, Je 5,31:1
Alsip, Charles H, 1962, Ap 7,25:5
Alsip, Robert, 1947, S 14,60:6
Alski, John P, 1950, N 19,92:6
Alski, Victor L, 1957, N 7,35:5
Alson, Jacob, 1957, Ag 23,19:5
Alsop, Edward Brown, 1922, N 14,19:4
Alsop, Edward H, 1966, O 10,41:3
Alsop, J W (see also F 28), 1878, Mr 2,8:3
Alsop, James N, 1948, My 29,15:5
Alsop, Jessie M, 1951, Ja 9,30:4
Alsop, John T, 1958, My 12,29:5
Alsop, Joseph W, 1953, Mr 18,31:5
Alsop, Reese D, 1954, Ag 2,17:4
Alsop, Reese F Rev Dr, 1922, O 18,19:4
Alsop, Samuel, 1949, Jl 8,19:1
Alspaugh, John W, 1955, Ap 17,86:6
Alssid, L B, 1937, S 12,29:5
Alster, Emanuel, 1954, N 23,35:2
Alston, David S, 1942, Ag 16,V,4:2
Alston, G W, 1885, Ja 24,8:2
Alston, George L, 1964, Jl 23,27:3
Alston, Granville F Mrs, 1945, N 20,21:5
Alston, Hal B, 1947, My 18,60:4
Alston, Lenora Mrs, 1968, Ag 17,27:2
Alston, Robert C, 1938, F 5,15:3
Alston, Robert S, 1945, Ap 25,23:4
Alston, Roland, 1955, F 19,15:6
Alston, William H, 1947, D 30,23:2
Alstone, Alex Mrs, 1958, S 27,21:1
Altai, Henry S, 1915, F 3,11:7
Altamirano, Luis, 1938, Jl 26,19:3
Altberg, Brita S, 1958, D 29,15:3
Altberg, Harry Z, 1956, N 11,86:3
Alte, Viscount d', 1933, O 4,23:1
Altemus, James D, 1966, My 25,47:2
Altemus, Jamison Torr (funl), 1906, N 12,7:3
Altemus, Lemuel C, 1940, D 9,19:2
Altemus, Rosalie S P Mrs, 1959, My 24,89:1
Altenberg, Leo, 1945, S 16,44:4
Altenburg, Alex, 1940, Mr 13,23:6

Altenburg, Edgar, 1967, Ag 29,37:3
Altenburg, Otto G, 1944, Mr 13,15:1
Altenburger, Ulrich Mrs, 1951, D 21,27:2
Altenkirch, Charles, 1952, Jl 11,17:2
Alter, Arthur G, 1954, D 7,33:1
Alter, Bernard, 1958, Ag 25,21:4
Alter, Blanche, 1947, O 16,27:3
Alter, David, 1947, D 14,80:6; 1948, O 6,29:5
Alter, Dinsmore Dr, 1968, S 24,47:1
Alter, Franklin Jr, 1949, Ja 9,72:5
Alter, George E, 1940, Ag 19,17:6
Alter, Herman, 1955, N 22,35:4
Alter, Joseph C Mrs, 1960, N 24,29:1
Alter, Louis H, 1957, Ap 6,19:4
Alter, Louis P, 1954, Mr 19,24:4
Alter, William, 1937, Ag 26,21:5
Alter, William R, 1950, O 6,27:4
Alteria, Ramsey Sr, 1952, Ja 26,13:3
Alterman, Lewis B, 1966, N 15,41:5
Alterman, Louis L, 1937, N 8,23:3
Alterman, Louis L Mrs, 1955, S 7,31:3
Alterman, Montague T, 1963, Jl 10,35:3
Alterman, Murray L, 1956, Jl 11,29:4
Alterman, S James, 1955, Ag 12,19:4
Alters, Samuel, 1949, Ja 27,23:2
Altfeld, Isaac Mrs, 1937, O 29,21:3
Altfoulish, Emma Mrs, 1914, Ag 11,9:4
Altgeld, J P Gov, 1902, Mr 13,9:4
Altglass, Max, 1952, F 15,25:3
Altham, Harry S, 1965, Mr 13,25:4
Althaus, G A, 1949, S 9,25:4
Althause, Samuel B, 1938, S 13,23:3
Althauser, Norman R, 1962, Ap 10,43:2
Altheimer, Abram S, 1946, Mr 10,46:3
Altheimer, Ben (por), 1938, My 1,II,6:3
Altheimer, Ben J, 1946, My 30,21:4
Althenn, Henry J, 1953, Mr 31,31:5
Altheus Matthew, Bro (V Hardart), 1961, N 10,35:4
Althoff, Henry J, 1947, Jl 4,13:6
Altholz, Nathaniel, 1959, S 16,39:4
Altholz, Nathaniel Mrs, 1939, My 27,15:3
Altholz, Samuel Mrs, 1962, My 4,33:3
Althouse, Calvin O, 1950, N 23,38:3
Althouse, Clarence E, 1955, Ap 22,25:2
Althouse, Daniel M, 1949, S 4,41:2
Althouse, Harry J, 1937, Ja 8,19:1
Althouse, John G, 1956, Ag 4,15:4
Althouse, Margaret L Mrs, 1938, D 31,15:4
Althouse, Mary Mrs, 1942, N 19,25:4
Althouse, Paul, 1954, F 7,88:1
Althouse, William L P, 1955, Ja 19,27:4
Altic, Hattie L, 1950, Je 24,13:3
Altick, Sherman B, 1943, Ja 19,20:2
Altieri, Andrew, 1947, Mr 13,27:3
Altieri, Anthony J Mrs, 1963, My 2,35:4
Altimari, Frank, 1949, Je 17,23:1
Altio, Karlo F, 1956, F 19,92:5
Altmaier, Carl L, 1948, O 10,76:2
Altman, Adolph Mrs, 1961, D 24,36:1
Altman, Alexander, 1946, O 25,24:2
Altman, Arthur, 1963, D 22,35:1
Altman, Benjamin, 1913, O 10,11:5; 1954, O 24,88:8; 1958, My 2,27:2
Altman, Charles D, 1951, Ja 24,27:5
Altman, David, 1948, Ag 7,15:2
Altman, Emil, 1942, S 12,13:3
Altman, Fannie Mrs, 1948, My 29,23:3
Altman, George J, 1937, S 28,23:5
Altman, Harold, 1961, Mr 17,31:1
Altman, Harry E, 1950, Jl 19,31:2
Altman, Henry H, 1943, D 10,27:1
Altman, I I, 1965, S 4,21:6
Altman, Irving, 1954, O 7,23:2
Altman, Jack, 1959, Ja 30,27:1
Altman, Jerome, 1952, F 26,27:1
Altman, Joseph P, 1951, D 8,11:6
Altman, Julius, 1964, Ag 12,35:2
Altman, Louis, 1938, Mr 23,23:1
Altman, Ludwig, 1945, Ja 21,39:2
Altman, Minnie B Mrs, 1951, Ap 26,29:4
Altman, Morris, 1876, Jl 14,4:7
Altman, Murray, 1948, F 18,27:4
Altman, Orven R, 1939, My 17,23:5
Altman, Oscar L, 1968, D 24,20:4
Altman, Samuel C, 1944, Je 4,42:3
Altmann, Bernhard, 1960, D 3,23:4
Altmann, Edward, 1957, My 23,33:3
Altmann, Franz Dr, 1968, S 5,47:4
Altmann, George O, 1955, Ap 15,23:3
Altmann, Manfred, 1954, S 3,18:3
Altmann, Manfred Mrs, 1954, S 3,18:3
Altmann, Moses, 1946, N 21,31:4
Altmann, Siegfried, 1963, S 18,39:2
Altmayer, Leon S, 1940, N 1,25:1
Altmayer, Sanders B, 1937, Jl 15,19:5
Altmeyer, David E, 1966, F 9,36:1
Altmeyer, George, 1939, Mr 8,21:1
Alto, Antonio D, 1937, D 14,25:3
Altomari, Genarro, 1946, Je 22,19:5
Altomari, Michael, 1968, Ja 27,29:2
Alton, Abraham H, 1941, My 31,11:4
Alton, Alfred E, 1940, Je 27,23:5
Alton, Anna H Mrs, 1941, N 25,25:5
Alton, Charles D Dr, 1937, Ja 11,19:3
Alton, Ernest H, 1952, F 19,29:1
Alton, Robert, 1957, Je 13,32:1
Alton, W E, 1948, Jl 11,53:1
Altounian, Asadour, 1957, N 17,86:8
Altreuter, Louis B, 1956, Mr 15,31:4
Altrincham, Lord (E Grigg), 1955, D 2,27:5
Altritt, Arthur, 1938, Mr 10,21:4
Altrocchi, Rudolph, 1953, My 15,23:2
Altrock, Nick, 1965, Ja 21,31:1
Altscheler, Joseph Alexander, 1920, D 9,13:3
Altschiller, Samuel, 1962, F 23,29:2
Altschul, Arthur G Mrs (funl plans, Jl 20,55:2; funl, Jl 21,23:4), 1961, Jl 19,1:3
Altschul, Charles Mrs, 1952, Je 7,19:3
Altschul, David S, 1944, Mr 25,15:5
Altschul, Harold, 1940, S 17,23:6
Altschul, Julius, 1953, Mr 1,93:2
Altschul, Julius Mrs, 1953, Ap 15,31:5
Altschul, Louis, 1943, Mr 23,19:1
Altschul, Louis Mrs, 1958, O 5,86:3
Altschule, Herman, 1962, Mr 5,23:5
Altschuler, Alex A, 1954, Ja 8,21:3
Altschuler, Benjamin M, 1965, F 4,31:4
Altschuler, Benjamin M Mrs, 1968, N 2,37:3
Altschuler, Jacob, 1947, Ag 28,23:5
Altschuler, Milton, 1963, Jl 12,25:1
Altsheler, Joseph Alexander, 1919, Je 7,13:6
Altsheler, Leonard, 1964, D 26,17:5
Altshuler, Bernard, 1948, Jl 26,17:3
Altshuler, Ira M, 1968, Mr 18,45:2
Altshuler, Murray, 1960, O 20,35:5
Altwater, John P, 1950, D 1,25:1
Altz, Harold, 1951, Ag 1,23:4
Aluigi, Mother Superior, 1946, D 20,23:1
Alustiza, Frank, 1953, Jl 28,19:5
Alvarado, Felipe J, 1937, Ja 2,14:3
Alvarado, Guillermo, 1965, Ag 9,25:2
Alvarado, J B, 1882, Jl 15,5:2
Alvarado, Manuel R, 1953, My 12,27:4
Alvares, Raoul, 1942, My 28,17:3
Alvarez, Alejandro, 1960, Jl 19,29:2
Alvarez, Andrew, 1952, O 15,31:3
Alvarez, Augustine R Sr, 1952, N 12,27:6
Alvarez, Enrique H, 1938, N 3,23:2
Alvarez, George G, 1955, F 13,86:1
Alvarez, Jesus R, 1944, O 30,19:2
Alvarez, John M Mrs, 1944, F 29,17:6
Alvarez, Jose, 1921, Mr 23,13:5
Alvarez, Luis F Dr, 1937, My 26,25:6
Alvarez, Manuel C, 1966, Ja 23,88:7
Alvarez, Rafael, 1946, D 27,19:4
Alvarez, Victor, 1945, My 24,19:1
Alvarez Calderon, Jorge, 1940, Mr 19,25:3
Alvarez de la Vega, Aurelio, 1949, Ja 2,60:7
Alvarez del Castillo, Juan M Mrs, 1953, My 9,19:5
Alvarez de Real, Evelio, 1953, D 27,60:8
Alvarez de Sotomayor, Fernando, 1960, Mr 19,21:2
Alvarez Lleras, Jorge, 1952, Ap 22,29:3
Alvaro, Corrado, 1956, Je 12,35:5
Alvaro, Moacyr E, 1959, Jl 24,25:2
Alvaro da Silva, Augusto Cardinal, 1968, Ag 15,37:3
Alvary, M, 1898, N 9,7:5
Alvear, Marcelo de Mrs, 1965, S 20,7:2
Alverez, Gregory J, 1953, O 13,29:1
Alvergue, Humberto R, 1953, Je 12,27:4
Alverson, Claude B Justice, 1922, D 24,20:3
Alverson, Frank J, 1944, Mr 19,42:1
Alverson, James C, 1942, Je 4,19:5
Alverson, Jesse M Sr, 1952, D 28,50:6
Alverson, Joseph C, 1953, Je 24,25:4
Alverson, Walter S, 1942, F 4,19:3
Alverstone, Lord (Dick Webster), 1915, D 16,15:5
Alverz, Henry, 1921, Je 22,15:3
Alves, Francisco, 1952, S 30,4:8
Alves, Francisco de Dr, 1919, Ja 17,13:5
Alvey, Richard H Judge, 1906, S 15,4:4
Alvich, Joseph P, 1965, Ja 9,25:3
Alviene, Claude M, 1946, Ap 25,21:4
Alvin, Forrest J, 1943, O 27,23:2
Alvord, Arthur M, 1955, N 2,35:4
Alvord, B, 1927, Ap 14,27:4
Alvord, Benjamin, 1884, O 18,5:1
Alvord, Charles H, 1955, F 21,21:3
Alvord, Charles P, 1946, Jl 28,40:4
Alvord, Clark (will), 1938, Ja 14,20:3
Alvord, Cornelius Lansing, 1912, S 11,11:5
Alvord, D W, 1871, Ag 4,1:4
Alvord, Dean, 1941, Ap 19,15:5
Alvord, E S Mrs, 1955, Mr 28,27:3
Alvord, Elias C Mrs, 1957, O 12,19:2
Alvord, Ellsworth C, 1964, Ja 17,43:2
Alvord, Emory D, 1959, My 9,21:3
Alvord, George N, 1961, Ap 1,17:6
Alvord, George S, 1946, N 24,79:4
Alvord, Germania Goodrich, 1907, Je 9,9:5
Alvord, Harold C, 1948, N 12,23:1
Alvord, Henry B, 1939, Ap 21,23:3
Alvord, John F, 1924, Mr 14,17:3
Alvord, John W, 1943, Ag 1,39:1
Alvord, Raymond M, 1949, O 25,27:5
Alvord, William Mrs, 1903, My 25,9:6
Alwar, Maharajah of, 1937, My 21,21:3
Alward, Mary E, 1954, Ap 8,27:3
Alward, Vaughn L, 1938, Jl 6,23:4
Alward, Vaughn L Mrs, 1947, Jl 19,13:6
Alweis, Benjamin, 1942, Mr 22,48:7
Alwin, Carl O, 1945, O 17,19:3
Alwood, William B, 1946, Ap 14,46:1
Aly Khan, Prince (funl plans, My 15,31:2; My 17,5:6), 1960, My 13,1:2
Alyea, Jane B, 1946, Ag 26,23:1
Alymer, Frank C, 1945, N 11,42:4
Alymov, Nikolai, 1955, My 6,23:1
Alzate Avendano, Gilberto, 1960, N 27,86:2
Alznauer, Alfred G, 1952, Ag 24,89:1
Amabile, R Dr, 1877, S 19,4:6
Amada, David, 1952, My 29,27:4
Amade, Albert G L D, 1941, N 14,23:4
Amadei, Maria A Mrs, 1950, Ag 27,89:3
Amadeo, Temas, 1950, D 19,29:3
Amadeus, Duke of Aosta, 1890, Ja 19,5:3
Amado, Maurice Mrs, 1958, S 29,27:5
Amado, Raphael, 1937, N 19,23:1
Amadon, Charles S, 1951, Ag 27,19:1
Amadon, Frank E, 1945, Ja 13,11:1
Amador, Juan Neftali, 1916, Ag 11,9:5
Amador, Manuel Dr, 1909, My 3,9:6
Amador, Manuel E, 1952, N 13,31:5
Amador-Guerrero, Manuel Mrs, 1948, Jl 6,23:1
Amand, Gabriel, 1937, Ap 8,23:3
Amandus Henry, Bro (G F Kargl), 1952, F 15,25:3
Amann, Douglas M, 1960, Ag 11,27:2
Amann, Edward J Sr, 1963, Ap 5,47:3
Amann, Eugene, 1948, Ap 3,15:1
Amann, Max, 1957, Ap 2,31:2
Amann, Paul, 1958, F 26,27:2
Amanullah, Ex-King of Afhanistan, 1960, Ap 26,37:2
Amar, James S, 1948, Ap 16,23:2
Amarjit Singh, Sonia Princess, 1947, Jl 4,13:5
Amaro, Joaquin, 1952, Mr 17,21:5
Amaro, Mauricio S, 1942, Je 11,23:1
Amaros, Dominique, 1939, Ag 1,19:5
Amat, Cardinal, 1872, N 9,3:7
Amateis, Louis Prof, 1913, Mr 19,13:5
Amatel, Charles Sr, 1948, Ag 12,21:5
Amato, Dominic, 1950, F 7,27:4
Amato, Frank, 1947, Ap 2,27:2; 1965, Je 12,31:5
Amato, Giuseppe, 1964, F 5,35:5
Amato, Irene Mrs, 1945, S 20,23:5
Amato, Joseph A, 1960, Je 7,35:2
Amato, Matthew, 1940, Ja 14,42:7
Amato, Pasquale, 1942, Ag 13,19:6
Amatruda, Catherine S, 1949, S 3,13:3
Amaya, Carmen (funeral, N 21,39:4), 1963, N 20, 43:3
Amaya, Enrique, 1943, D 11,15:3
Amazon, Maurice, 1963, S 26,35:4
Ambach, David, 1908, N 9,7:5
Ambacher, Henry F, 1950, My 24,29:1
Ambedkar, Bhimrao R (funl, D 8,19:6), 1956, D 7, 27:1
Amber, Harrison L, 1957, N 15,27:3
Amber, Mabel, 1945, O 9,21:4
Amberg, Charles R, 1955, Mr 25,33:6
Amberg, Emil J, 1952, F 24,86:3
Amberg, Gustave, 1921, My 24,15:4
Amberg, Herman A, 1948, Ag 10,21:2
Amberg, Joseph O, 1948, Jl 5,15:2
Amberg, Joseph Sr, 1955, Mr 27,87:1
Amberg, Joshua L, 1949, S 25,92:6
Amberg, Julius H, 1951, Ja 25,25:3
Amberg, Max W, 1937, F 21,II,10:5
Amberg, Paul G, 1939, F 17,19:2
Amberg, Richard H, 1967, S 4,21:2
Amberger, Fritz L, 1950, Mr 27,23:4
Amberley, Viscount (see also Ja 11), 1876, Ja 30,1:2
Amberman, George, 1938, Ag 10,21:7
Amberson, J Burns, 1943, Je 15,21:1
Ambert, Rufma Mrs, 1957, Ja 26,21:7
Ambient, Mark, 1937, Ag 12,19:2
Ambis, John Sr, 1945, Ag 31,17:4
Ambler, Andrew B Gen, 1918, Jl 29,11:6
Ambler, Charles A, 1940, Ag 30,19:3
Ambler, Harry S Jr, 1939, Ap 13,23:4
Ambler, Henry S, 1905, S 18,2:1
Ambler, John J, 1962, N 8,39:2
Ambler, Joseph A, 1948, O 7,29:2
Ambler, Mason G, 1947, Ap 17,27:2
Ambler, William S, 1941, O 17,23:4
Amborn, Fred E, 1943, S 17,21:2
Ambos, Carl L, 1939, Jl 25,19:4
Ambrette, Paul, 1961, Je 28,35:1
Ambro, Peter A, 1965, Je 25,33:2
Ambroise, Louis J, 1938, O 20,23:4
Ambrose, Arthur P, 1959, S 3,27:1
Ambrose, Arthur W, 1952, D 30,6:6
Ambrose, Bro (E F Hanily), 1952, O 14,31:5
Ambrose, C Arthur, 1940, N 24,51:8
Ambrose, George E, 1967, S 29,47:3
Ambrose, Helene (Mrs W N Greaza), 1966, N 12, 29:2
Ambrose, I, 1933, F 14,15:5
Ambrose, Jake, 1951, My 23,35:3
Ambrose, James P, 1954, My 14,23:4
Ambrose, Oliver S, 1955, F 19,15:4

Ambrose, Paul, 1941, Je 2,17:4
Ambrose, Thomas E, 1962, Ag 19,88:2
Ambrose, William, 1944, Ag 14,15:5
Ambrose of Jesus, Bro (F J Delaney), 1956, Ag 16, 25:4
Ambrosini, Valentine, 1952, N 29,17:2
Ambrosini, Valentino Mrs, 1948, D 12,92:7
Ambrosio, Joseph, 1953, S 5,17:8
Ambrosio, Vittorio, 1958, N 22,21:2
Ambrosius, Robert S, 1949, N 7,27:4
Ambrus, George, 1941, N 16,56:2
Ambruster, Charles, 1937, S 28,23:1
Ambruster, Cornelius, 1958, Je 15,77:1
Amchanitzky, Samuel, 1956, Mr 21,38:3
Amchanitzky, Samuel Mrs, 1959, N 11,35:2
Amchin, Maurice, 1959, O 18,86:8
Amdur, Meyer K, 1943, Jl 18,34:3
Amedy, Basilian, 1939, Je 2,23:5
Amee, Jennie T Mrs, 1942, F 25,19:4
Ameer, Leon 4X, 1965, Mr 14,57:4
Ameli, Howard W, 1959, Jl 30,27:5
Amelia, ex-Queen of Greece, 1875, My 21,1:7
Amelia, Ex-Queen of Portugal, 1951, O 26,23:1
Amelia, Queen of Saxony, 1877, N 9,5:1
Amelia, Sister (Buscher), 1950, Ag 2,25:2
Amelkin, Solomon S, 1959, Ag 9,88:8
Amella, Giovanni G, 1949, O 20,29:2
Amelung, Fred, 1947, N 4,25:3
Amelung, J A, 1883, S 19,4:7
Amen, Elizabeth W, 1968, Ja 21,77:1
Amen, Harlan Page, 1913, N 10,9:3
Amen, John H (funeral, Mr 13,86:6), 1960, Mr 11, 25:2
Amend, Alfred J Mrs, 1956, My 23,31:5
Amend, Bernard G, 1911, Ap 7,13:3
Amend, Carl G, 1949, N 29,29:2
Amend, Daniel G, 1959, Mr 17,33:4
Amend, Edward B Justice (funl, O 24,13:6), 1914, O 21,11:5
Amend, Elenore R Mrs, 1942, D 23,19:6
Amend, Karle O, 1944, Ja 3,21:2
Amend, Robert F, 1914, Ja 8,11:4
Amend, Thelma, 1961, S 4,31:2
Amend, William H, 1968, N 11,47:3
Amend, William J, 1947, O 20,23:1
Amende, Charles G Sir, 1916, Ja 15,9:6
Amendt, Anna L, 1938, F 3,23:4
Ament, Fred M, 1945, Ja 3,17:2
Ament, Paul, 1943, Je 1,23:2
Ament, Robert S, 1937, Ap 23,21:4
Ament, Walton Campbell, 1968, Ja 25,40:1
Ament, William S Rev Dr, 1909, Ja 9,9:6
Amer, Alfred S, 1959, O 28,37:3
Ameri, Louis, 1961, My 9,39:1
America, Frank M, 1942, Mr 27,23:4
American, Sadie, 1944, My 4,19:3
Ameringer, Oscar (cor, N 12,21:1), 1943, N 7,56:5
Amerling, Charles H, 1946, O 9,27:4
Amerling, Charles H Jr, 1964, Ja 13,35:3
Amerman, Frederick H, 1944, Mr 19,41:3
Amerman, Harry L, 1948, N 10,29:2
Amerman, Helen, 1951, Jl 21,15:3
Amerman, Henry, 1939, O 15,49:3
Amerman, J W, 1876, Ja 9,6:5
Amerman, John, 1904, F 7,7:6
Amerman, Peter, 1882, Je 28,5:4
Amerman, Ralph A, 1941, Je 6,21:5
Amerman, Willard, 1945, Ja 18,19:3
Amerman, William Mrs, 1945, Mr 24,17:5
Amery, Leopold S, 1955, S 17,15:3
Ames, A, 1933, Ap 14,19:1
Ames, Adelbert Jr, 1955, Je 4,11:3
Ames, Adelbert Mrs, 1939, D 28,22:3
Ames, Adrienne, 1947, Je 1,60:1
Ames, Albert Alonzo, 1911, N 18,13:6
Ames, Alfred K, 1950, My 20,15:4
Ames, Alfrederick S, 1944, Ag 16,19:6
Ames, Allan W, 1966, Ja 18,37:2
Ames, Allen, 1942, Ap 2,21:6
Ames, Azel Dr, 1908, N 13,9:6
Ames, Azell, 1942, N 24,25:4
Ames, Bliss C, 1948, Ag 19,21:5
Ames, Butler, 1954, N 7,88:3
Ames, Carol H Mrs, 1956, O 6,21:4
Ames, Charles Gordon Rev, 1912, Ap 16,13:5
Ames, Charles W, 1921, Ap 14,13:5
Ames, Charles Wilberforce, 1921, Ap 5,19:5
Ames, Chester C, 1941, N 3,19:5
Ames, Clark T Jr, 1957, Jl 21,60:8
Ames, Clifford W, 1942, Jl 31,15:2
Ames, Cortlandt F Jr, 1945, Ja 20,11:6
Ames, E R Bishop (see also Ap 26), 1879, Ap 29,5:4
Ames, Earl O, 1960, Ja 15,31:3
Ames, Edward S, 1958, Jl 1,31:3
Ames, Edward W Mrs, 1949, F 12,17:5
Ames, Eleanor, 1914, Je 28,15:4
Ames, Elisha, 1946, F 20,25:3
Ames, Ella E (will), 1946, O 31,17:4
Ames, Ervin, 1948, Ja 16,21:4
Ames, Ervin Mrs, 1941, O 29,23:2
Ames, Frank, 1947, F 12,25:5
Ames, Frank D, 1938, Mr 7,17:5
Ames, Frederick Lothrop, 1921, Je 20,13:2
Ames, George T, 1949, Je 15,29:2
Ames, Grace E, 1943, F 13,11:6
Ames, H V, 1935, F 8,21:1
Ames, Harry L Mrs, 1950, N 13,27:4
Ames, Helena M Mrs (Helena Kirk), 1908, Je 25,9:5
Ames, Henry C Mrs, 1949, S 22,31:3
Ames, Henry Semple, 1916, Ja 18,11:3
Ames, Herbert B, 1954, Ap 1,31:3
Ames, Hobart, 1945, Ap 23,19:2
Ames, Ira J, 1949, Ja 26,25:4
Ames, Isaac, 1877, Mr 10,2:6
Ames, J B, 1881, Ja 22,8:4
Ames, James Barr Prof, 1910, Ja 9,9:4
Ames, James C, 1943, Mr 28,25:1
Ames, James W, 1944, F 2,21:5; 1955, S 12,25:5
Ames, James W Mrs, 1957, Mr 29,21:2
Ames, John H Mrs, 1949, My 20,27:4
Ames, John L, 1953, Mr 21,17:5
Ames, John S, 1959, Je 25,29:5
Ames, John T Mrs, 1952, Mr 12,27:3
Ames, John W, 1954, D 18,15:4
Ames, John W Jr, 1963, N 12,41:2
Ames, Joseph, 1872, N 2,10:2
Ames, Joseph Blanchard, 1915, Ja 26,9:5
Ames, Joseph S, 1943, Je 25,17:3
Ames, Kirk D Mrs, 1939, F 27,15:3
Ames, Knowlton L Jr, 1965, O 16,27:4
Ames, Leon, 1948, N 28,94:4
Ames, Leslie R, 1947, N 3,23:2
Ames, Louis A, 1952, N 29,13:5
Ames, Louis A Mrs, 1939, Mr 11,17:4
Ames, Lydia M Mrs, 1946, O 3,27:2
Ames, Marion A, 1943, Je 5,15:5
Ames, Nelson, 1907, Mr 9,9:6
Ames, Oakes, 1873, My 9,5:1; 1950, Ap 29,15:3
Ames, Oliver, 1877, Mr 10,2:6; 1895, O 23,9:1
Ames, Paul K, 1938, Jl 9,13:2
Ames, R, 1931, N 28,15:3
Ames, Ralph H, 1949, S 16,27:1
Ames, Reginald M, 1945, My 4,20:2
Ames, Richard B Mrs, 1950, Je 24,13:1
Ames, S P, 1879, Mr 23,10:6
Ames, Samuel, 1865, D 21,1:5; 1875, Jl 6,4:5
Ames, Seth, 1881, Ag 17,5:5; 1949, Ja 22,14:2
Ames, Seth K (will), 1937, Jl 31,17:7
Ames, Stephen, 1954, Ap 23,27:4
Ames, Sullivan D, 1880, N 23,2:4
Ames, Theodore Mrs, 1940, O 28,17:5
Ames, Walter H, 1953, S 15,20:2
Ames, Wilbur F Mrs, 1949, N 15,25:2
Ames, William G, 1938, D 10,17:5
Ames, William Gen, 1914, Mr 10,9:4
Ames, William W, 1949, D 21,30:5
Ames, Winthrop (por), 1937, N 4,25:1
Amesbury, Benjamin C, 1938, Ja 4,23:2
Amespil, Gratien, 1966, N 12,29:4
Amesti, Felix de, 1954, Ja 22,27:1
Amestoy, Michael F, 1950, F 10,23:2
Amet, Edward H, 1948, Ag 18,25:3
Amette, Adolphe Cardinal, 1920, Ag 30,9:5
Amezaga, Juan J, 1956, Ag 21,29:1
Amezua, Agustin G, 1956, Je 11,31:5
Amherst, Baron (Wm Amhurst Tyson-Amherst), 1909, Ja 18,9:4
Amherst, F K, 1883, Ag 23,5:7
Amherst, William Archer Earl, 1910, Ag 15,7:6
Amian Elrick, Bro (T J Bansfield), 1959, D 2,43:4
Amicis, Edmondo De, 1908, Mr 12,7:7
Amick, George, 1959, Ap 5,V,1:7
Amick, Myron J, 1906, Ja 31,11:5
Amick George, Bro, 1959, F 26,31:5
Amidon, Beulah Mrs (Mrs P Ratliff), 1958, S 25,33:2
Amidon, Charles F (ed, D 29,20:4), 1937, D 28,21:3
Amidon, Charles F Mrs, 1950, Ja 21,17:5
Amidon, David E, 1951, Ap 21,17:5
Amidon, Ralph C, 1944, Ap 7,19:1
Amidon, Royal W, 1938, Jl 10,29:4
Amidon, Thomson S, 1940, Je 29,15:5
Amiel, Daniel, 1959, Mr 17,30:4
Amiel, Jack Mrs, 1956, My 19,19:5
Amiel, Moshe A, 1945, Mr 28,23:1
Amiel Gentile Mrs, 1956, O 28,88:8
Amigo, Henry J, 1946, Ag 14,25:5
Amigo, Peter, 1949, O 1,13:3
Amijo, 1871, Jl 19,1:6
Amir, Michel, 1954, Je 17,29:6
Amis, Thomas Mrs, 1954, D 28,23:2
Amitin, Alex, 1947, Je 25,25:3
Amitrano, Louis, 1948, F 29,60:3
Amkenbrand, Robert, 1939, Je 29,26:4
Amlicke, Manfield G Mrs, 1944, O 1,46:2
Amlie, Hans Mrs (M Bennett), 1960, N 7,35:3
Amling, H, 1928, Mr 19,21:3
Amm, Charles J, 1959, My 3,86:4
Amm, John L, 1942, N 22,53:1
Amma, Sivakamu Mme (Mrs S Radhakrishnan), 1956, N 27,37:2
Ammann, George S, 1956, Mr 26,29:5
Ammann, Hannah Mrs, 1939, Ap 8,15:6
Ammann, Ludwig, 1939, O 12,14:6
Ammann, Othmar H, 1965, S 24,6:4
Ammel, Roy W, 1963, D 7,28:4
Ammen, D Adm, 1898, Jl 12,7:5
Ammerman, Benjamin Mrs, 1953, Ag 30,88:5
Ammerman, Edgar, 1954, N 6,17:2
Ammerman, William H, 1944, Jl 4,19:3
Ammidown, H Philip, 1959, Ag 1,17:5
Ammon, Charles G (Lord), 1960, Ap 3,86:8
Ammon, Jay, 1953, Jl 17,17:4
Ammon, John D Rev, 1937, Mr 10,23:3
Ammon, John H, 1948, Ap 2,23:1
Ammon, John H Col, 1904, N 29,9:1
Ammon, Peter, 1941, Mr 18,23:5
Ammon, Robert A Col, 1915, My 16,16:4
Ammon, Roscoe A, 1961, D 17,82:2
Ammon, William B, 1959, Ag 17,23:3
Ammon, William H Mrs, 1939, My 21,III,7:4
Ammons, Albert C, 1949, D 4,108:7
Ammons, Elias Morton Ex-Gov, 1925, My 21,23:5
Amodio, Alessandro, 1861, Jl 6,3:5
Amols, Sadie, 1957, Jl 23,27:4
Amols, Samuel Mrs, 1938, F 11,23:5
Amon, Alexander, 1947, F 1,15:3
Amon, Joseph, 1955, S 2,17:4
Amon, Will R, 1939, D 12,27:4
Amoreaux, Jesse S L' Ex-Judge, 1918, Je 5,11:3
Amoroso, Peter F, 1952, D 28,48:8
Amoruso, Carmelo, 1952, Ap 26,23:3
Amory, Arthur, 1911, Ag 10,7:4
Amory, Copley, 1960, Ap 18,29:6
Amory, Edward L Com, 1911, N 20,11:5
Amory, Eugene H, 1944, My 16,21:5
Amory, Harcourt, 1925, N 28,15:6
Amory, Harcourt Mrs, 1947, My 17,15:4
Amory, James F Mrs, 1957, O 26,21:5
Amory, John M, 1925, N 18,23:4
Amory, Robert Dr, 1910, Ag 28,II,9:6
Amory, Walter, 1937, O 4,21:3
Amory, William, 1907, Je 18,7:6; 1954, Ja 17,92:5
Amos, Barrett V, 1950, Ja 19,27:2
Amos, Benjamin F Mrs, 1957, Ap 13,19:1
Amos, Charles I, 1955, Jl 4,11:5
Amos, Ernest C, 1962, Ja 7,88:7
Amos, Frank B, 1965, Jl 20,33:4
Amos, Harold C, 1948, S 24,26:3
Amos, Howard A, 1944, Jl 22,15:4
Amos, James E, 1953, D 29,23:5
Amos, James E (will), 1954, Ja 15,6:4
Amos, John W, 1950, Ap 15,15:2
Amos, Laysander B Mrs, 1946, Ja 7,19:5
Amos, Lindsay C, 1965, F 2,33:3
Amos, Lindsay C Mrs, 1948, Ag 20,17:5
Amos, Mathilde Mrs, 1967, Ja 15,17:4
Amos, Thomas H Jr, 1942, Ag 10,19:4
Amos, Thyrsa W, 1941, My 6,21:2
Amos, Waldo A, 1947, N 27,32:2
Amos, William D, 1951, O 19,27:2
Amos, William Mrs, 1938, Jl 15,17:2
Amos, WM, 1951, Mr 10,13:5
Amoss, Harold L, 1956, N 4,86:2
Amoss, Ulius L, 1961, N 10,35:1
Amott, Harry R, 1965, F 25,31:4
Amouroux, Charles, 1885, My 26,5:4
Amper, Richard L (funeral, F 14,84:6), 1960, F 13, 19:4
Ampere, Jacques Antoine (author), 1864, My 8,5:3
Ampthill, Lord, 1935, Jl 8,15:4
Amram, David W, 1939, Je 28,21:3
Amron, Jacob Mrs, 1966, Ag 11,33:3
Amrouche, Jean, 1962, Ap 17,35:4
Ams, Emil A Mrs, 1950, Jl 1,15:1
Amsbary, Frank C Jr, 1960, F 3,33:2
Amsbary, Wallace B, 1954, Je 5,17:6
Amsbary, Wallace Mrs, 1950, Ja 25,27:1
Amsdell, Theodore H, 1903, N 10,9:5
Amsden, Charles, 1941, Mr 6,21:6
Amsden, Charles J, 1944, S 13,19:2
Amsden, George S, 1966, N 29,43:4
Amsden, Louis A, 1940, Ag 10,13:2
Amsden, Sherman C, 1958, N 11,30:1
Amsden, Walter A, 1942, D 15,27:3
Amshein, Joseph Msgr, 1914, Ap 27,11:6
Amsinck, Arnold, 1939, N 2,23:1
Amson, Max J, 1939, N 9,23:4
Amster, Henry, 1953, F 13,21:2; 1956, Je 16,19:1
Amster, J Lewis, 1960, My 5,35:2
Amster, J Lewis Mrs, 1948, Je 19,15:3
Amster, Joseph, 1960, Mr 17,33:5
Amster, Nathan L (died intestate, O 8,41:8), 1939, S 23,17:1
Amster, Nathan L Mrs, 1956, S 7,23:5
Amster, Samuel S, 1955, Jl 15,21:2
Amster, Sol, 1961, O 2,31:5
Amsterdam, Alton L, 1946, O 3,27:4
Amsterdam, Charles J, 1957, Ja 1,23:5
Amsterdam, Edward, 1966, F 19,27:5
Amsterdam, Essie S Mrs, 1953, Ag 25,21:4
Amsterdam, Herman J, 1966, My 2,37:1
Amstutz, Clarence E, 1937, S 10,23:4
Amstutz, Frank W, 1959, S 5,15:7
Amstuz, John O, 1964, Ap 30,35:5
Amter, Israel (funl, N 27,13:2), 1954, N 25,29:3
Amulree, Lord, 1942, My 7,19:3
Amundsen, Aaron L, 1947, Ag 5,23:1
Amundsen, Agnes I, 1958, N 2,88:6
Amundsen, Omar, 1951, Ja 25,25:3

Amundson, August, 1949, O 10,23:4
Amundson, Phil G, 1952, D 20,17:3
Amussen, Theodore Mrs, 1961, O 1,86:2
Amussen, Theodore S Mrs, 1958, N 19,37:4
Amweaver, Chester, 1939, O 5,23:1
Amy, Albert, 1958, N 22,21:2
Amy, Alfred V, 1947, D 16,33:4
Amy, Henry Mrs, 1947, D 18,29:2
Amy, LeRoy V, 1961, S 18,29:2
Amyot, J A, 1940, F 14,21:2
Anable, Anna M S, 1947, Mr 30,56:8
Anable, Courtland V, 1924, Ap 4,19:6
Anable, Eliphalet Mrs, 1945, Mr 17,13:4
Anagnos, Michael, 1906, Jl 6,7:5
Ananda, Gajapatatiraj V, 1965, D 4,31:6
Ananikian, Madiros H Prof, 1924, Ag 6,13:4
Anapoell, Joshua Mrs, 1946, Je 18,25:4
Anapoell, William S, 1963, Ag 4,80:6
Anast, James L, 1964, Ag 8,19:7
Anastasi, Leonidas, 1940, Ja 18,23:3
Anastasi, Salvator Rev Father, 1915, My 21,13:5
Anastasia, Albert, 1959, Jl 26,42:6
Anastasia, Anthony, 1963, Mr 2,7:2
Anastasie, 1941, O 10,23:2
Anastasio, Gerardo (Jerry), 1958, D 6,46:3
Anastasio, Joseph, 1956, My 16,70:1
Anastasius Maria, Father, 1947, Ja 10,21:3
Anastassy, Metropolitan (A Gribanovsky),(funl, My 26,47:4), 1965, Mr 24,31:4
Anathan, Lawrence G, 1964, Ja 21,29:2
Anba Youssab II, Patriarch, 1956, N 14,35:3
Ancaster, Countess of, 1953, D 15,39:4
Ancaster, Earl of (Baron W de Eresby), 1951, S 20, 31:4
Ancelin, Pierre, 1948, Ja 30,23:2
Ancier, Morris, 1948, Ja 1,23:4
Ancizar, Roberto Dr, 1920, S 5,19:4
Ancker, Louis, 1937, Ag 8,II,6:6
Ancliffe, Charles, 1952, D 21,53:2
Ancona, Ezio L D, 1941, Mr 29,15:5
Ancona, Sydenham S, 1913, Je 21,9:6
Andate, Julia R Mrs, 1961, D 8,37:3
Andel, Edward M, 1958, Mr 27,33:3
Andelfinger, George C, 1950, Mr 18,13:3
Andelfinger, George V Mrs, 1946, D 24,17:5
Andelhof, Auguste, 1947, O 7,27:4
Anderber, Edward, 1947, Ja 20,25:1
Anderegg, Gustavus A, 1943, Ag 15,39:2
Anderegg, Martin T, 1942, Jl 23,19:4
Anderegg, Rupert A, 1947, Jl 20,44:7
Anderiman, Surreya, 1959, S 30,3:1
Anderman, Albert, 1953, F 10,27:2
Anderman, Henry B, 1940, Ap 9,24:3
Anderman, William E, 1966, Mr 20,86:8
Anderman, Zwi, 1958, Je 18,33:4
Anderosn, Guy, 1938, Je 1,6:2
Anderosn, John J, 1949, Jl 24,52:6
Anderosn, Otto M, 1949, O 23,84:1
Anderosn, Robert V, 1949, Je 7,31:4
Anders, D Webster, 1955, D 30,19:5
Anders, Frank L, 1966, Ja 25,41:1
Anders, Howard S, 1954, Mr 8,27:3
Anders, J Wesley, 1955, Je 19,92:5
Anders, Peter, 1954, S 11,17:5
Anders, William H, 1958, N 9,89:2
Andersen, A C, 1943, D 24,13:5
Andersen, Adolph, 1966, Jl 7,37:1
Andersen, Alfred, 1945, Mr 6,21:4
Andersen, Alsing, 1962, D 6,43:4
Andersen, Arthur, 1941, Je 14,17:4; 1947, Ja 11,19:3
Andersen, Arthur O, 1958, Ja 14,33:4
Andersen, Carl N, 1961, D 23,23:4
Andersen, Edward C, 1951, Jl 25,23:2
Andersen, Ellef, 1951, Ja 10,27:2
Andersen, Fred, 1949, Ap 10,77:1
Andersen, H Viggo, 1964, D 18,33:2
Andersen, Hans C, 1951, F 7,29:4
Andersen, Hans Christian (funl, Ag 12,1:3), 1875, Ag 5,4:6
Andersen, Harald, 1955, D 2,27:4
Andersen, Hendrik C, 1940, D 20,25:5
Andersen, Inga H, 1959, O 3,19:3
Andersen, Janet L, 1959, O 4,86:6
Andersen, Joachim, 1909, My 9,11:4
Andersen, Johannes, 1944, Mr 28,19:5
Andersen, Jonas C, 1956, Ap 6,25:3
Andersen, Lauritz W, 1948, O 4,23:2
Andersen, Olaf, 1941, Jl 20,31:3
Andersen, Paul C, 1947, N 18,29:2; 1948, D 15,33:5
Andersen, Peder, 1948, Mr 23,25:3
Andersen, Sophronia, 1937, S 24,21:3
Andersen, Tage, 1965, Jl 24,21:4
Anderson, A C M Mrs, 1940, Jl 23,19:5
Anderson, A E, 1959, Ap 28,36:1
Anderson, A E Capt, 1914, Jl 14,9:6
Anderson, A Frank, 1945, N 20,21:2
Anderson, A H Mrs, 1884, Ja 7,4:6
Anderson, A L, 1928, D 6,31:5
Anderson, Abraham A, 1940, Ap 28,37:1
Anderson, Abraham A Mrs, 1921, F 22,13:3
Anderson, Adelbert L, 1943, Je 11,19:3
Anderson, Agnes C Mrs, 1949, Mr 2,26:3
Anderson, Alan G, 1952, My 6,29:5
Anderson, Albert, 1948, O 19,28:2
Anderson, Albert A, 1948, My 22,15:3
Anderson, Albert B, 1938, Ap 28,23:1
Anderson, Albert D, 1953, S 6,50:6
Anderson, Albert S Mrs, 1955, Ja 24,23:5
Anderson, Alden, 1944, S 24,46:5
Anderson, Alex, 1954, F 12,25:4
Anderson, Alex C, 1957, Je 4,35:4
Anderson, Alex E, 1942, D 25,17:1
Anderson, Alex L, 1944, D 12,23:2
Anderson, Alex P, 1943, My 9,40:4
Anderson, Alex T, 1944, S 16,13:5
Anderson, Alex W, 1944, N 14,23:3
Anderson, Alfred, 1941, My 12,17:2; 1942, Ag 17,15:5
Anderson, Alfred G, 1960, F 20,23:5
Anderson, Alfred H, 1914, Ap 22,15:7
Anderson, Alfred O, 1953, Ap 17,26:4
Anderson, Alfred S, 1968, N 26,47:2
Anderson, Algernon A, 1949, O 4,27:5
Anderson, Alton Sr, 1951, F 28,27:2
Anderson, Amos R, 1959, Je 8,27:1
Anderson, Andrew, 1942, Je 20,13:7; 1954, Ag 6,17:2; 1954, N 2,27:5
Anderson, Andrew B, 1947, Ag 29,17:4
Anderson, Andrew E, 1943, My 26,23:5
Anderson, Andrew J, 1957, Mr 12,33:2; 1967, Ag 3, 33:3
Anderson, Andrew M, 1940, N 22,23:4
Anderson, Andrew P, 1945, Jl 30,19:3
Anderson, Andrew W, 1949, Je 23,27:5
Anderson, Anna, 1939, O 30,12:5
Anderson, Anna D Mrs, 1964, Ja 11,23:3
Anderson, Annie Mrs, 1948, F 20,27:5
Anderson, Anthony, 1939, Mr 13,17:5
Anderson, Anthony C, 1947, F 24,19:5
Anderson, Arch W, 1946, S 16,5:3
Anderson, Archie A, 1963, N 21,39:4
Anderson, Arthur C, 1953, My 31,74:1
Anderson, Arthur D, 1945, Je 19,19:4
Anderson, Arthur E, 1947, O 11,17:4; 1955, N 25,27:3
Anderson, Arthur J, 1964, Ag 1,21:2
Anderson, Arthur M, 1966, Ag 11,33:4
Anderson, Arthur M Mrs, 1961, Ag 29,31:1
Anderson, Arthur N, 1950, Ag 5,30:3
Anderson, Arthur V, 1956, Ja 5,33:4
Anderson, Arthur V Mrs, 1948, Mr 10,27:4
Anderson, Aug A, 1938, Ja 1,19:2
Anderson, August Mrs, 1948, Ag 6,17:5
Anderson, Augustus T, 1942, Ag 1,11:6
Anderson, Austin B, 1946, S 6,21:1
Anderson, Axel, 1948, My 7,23:4
Anderson, B B Mrs, 1952, Jl 17,23:3
Anderson, B L, 1946, D 21,19:6
Anderson, B P, 1878, D 28,2:3
Anderson, Barbara D Mrs, 1958, Ja 23,27:4
Anderson, Belle B, 1937, My 13,25:2
Anderson, Benjamin, 1938, F 24,19:3
Anderson, Benjamin M, 1949, Ja 20,27:1
Anderson, Bernard M, 1945, O 4,23:5
Anderson, Bernhard, 1949, D 6,31:2
Anderson, Bert G, 1961, Je 17,21:6
Anderson, Bertha F, 1944, My 9,19:6
Anderson, Bjarne B, 1954, My 8,17:6
Anderson, Brice, 1958, S 29,27:2
Anderson, Bruce J, 1943, Ja 23,13:4
Anderson, Burt T, 1950, N 11,15:3
Anderson, Byron W, 1938, D 31,15:6
Anderson, Byrtene C Mrs, 1950, Ap 4,29:4
Anderson, C Edgar, 1939, O 3,23:5
Anderson, C M Dr, 1937, Ag 11,24:4
Anderson, C M Mrs, 1944, Ap 16,42:3
Anderson, C P, 1930, Ja 31,21:3; 1936, Ag 3,15:3
Anderson, C Vivian, 1959, F 2,25:2
Anderson, Carl A, 1940, Ag 27,21:2; 1953, O 3,17:6
Anderson, Carl A Rev, 1937, Ja 25,19:1
Anderson, Carl E, 1954, N 12,15:1; 1965, D 3,39:2
Anderson, Carl G, 1948, O 7,29:2
Anderson, Carl J H, 1938, S 18,45:2
Anderson, Carl L, 1945, D 19,25:3; 1954, Ag 27,21:2
Anderson, Carl S, 1940, Jl 25,17:4
Anderson, Carl T, 1948, N 5,11:7
Anderson, Carl W, 1950, N 9,33:5; 1950, D 22,20:6
Anderson, Carlotta B Mrs, 1956, Mr 8,29:5
Anderson, Carolina M Mrs, 1939, O 8,49:1
Anderson, Caroline G, 1949, F 10,27:2
Anderson, Carroll N, 1946, S 27,23:5
Anderson, Cecil, 1968, N 21,47:4
Anderson, Charles, 1949, Ag 6,17:5; 1954, D 24,13:1
Anderson, Charles A, 1941, Ap 6,48:6; 1948, D 28, 21:2; 1951, D 24,13:3; 1960, Ap 12,33:6; 1962, Ja 24, 33:2
Anderson, Charles A Mrs, 1944, S 29,21:2
Anderson, Charles D, 1951, Mr 9,25:2
Anderson, Charles F, 1944, Jl 23,36:1
Anderson, Charles H, 1939, D 31,19:2
Anderson, Charles K, 1948, O 20,29:4
Anderson, Charles L, 1922, My 17,19:5; 1948, Ap 14, 27:1
Anderson, Charles M, 1908, D 29,9:5; 1938, Jl 16,13:5; 1939, S 23,17:3
Anderson, Charles R, 1957, Je 20,29:3
Anderson, Charles S, 1942, Je 21,37:2
Anderson, Charles W, 1938, Ja 29,15:6; 1940, Ja 25, 21:4; 1946, Ag 28,27:3; 1947, Ag 20,21:3
Anderson, Claire M, 1964, Mr 27,27:1
Anderson, Clarence W, 1938, Mr 19,15:4
Anderson, Claude E, 1941, Ap 11,21:4
Anderson, Claude E Mrs, 1959, N 18,41:5
Anderson, Clifford A, 1946, Mr 17,43:1
Anderson, Clifford C, 1951, Ag 9,21:2
Anderson, Clifford L, 1943, S 9,25:2
Anderson, Clifford O Mrs, 1950, Ap 28,21:3
Anderson, Clifford S, 1954, N 12,21:3
Anderson, Conrad E, 1958, Jl 23,27:4
Anderson, Conrad V Jr, 1960, N 15,39:2
Anderson, Cornelia, 1939, Ag 30,17:5
Anderson, D C, 1884, O 17,5:2
Anderson, D G Rev, 1882, My 16,5:3
Anderson, D M, 1936, O 30,24:1
Anderson, D R, 1938, D 17,15:5
Anderson, Dan C, 1960, My 3,39:4
Anderson, David, 1947, S 12,21:2; 1947, D 22,22:3
Anderson, David J, 1952, O 1,33:2
Anderson, David M, 1968, N 6,23:7
Anderson, Denton C, 1939, Ag 28,19:2
Anderson, Dice R, 1942, O 24,15:3
Anderson, Donald B Mrs, 1961, O 25,37:1
Anderson, Donald W, 1949, My 13,23:1; 1964, O 14, 45:3
Anderson, Douglas C, 1952, D 31,15:5
Anderson, Douglas G, 1956, S 21,25:1
Anderson, Douglas S, 1954, Mr 3,27:5
Anderson, Dwight, 1953, D 15,44:6; 1962, D 27,7:2
Anderson, E B C Mrs, 1905, F 28,9:3
Anderson, E Chauncey, 1941, F 19,21:3
Anderson, E Ellery, 1903, F 25,2:3
Anderson, E J Mrs, 1946, Je 25,21:2
Anderson, Ed M, 1958, Je 25,29:4
Anderson, Eddie Mrs, 1954, Ag 7,13:6
Anderson, Edmund G, 1966, Ap 24,86:8
Anderson, Edmund G Mrs, 1965, O 14,47:3
Anderson, Edward, 1955, Ja 6,27:4
Anderson, Edward Brig Gen, 1937, N 3,23:1
Anderson, Edward D, 1940, My 23,24:2
Anderson, Edward E Mrs, 1965, Ja 21,31:2
Anderson, Edward L, 1904, F 16,9:6
Anderson, Edward M, 1937, O 8,23:3; 1938, My 1,II, 6:8
Anderson, Edward Rev, 1916, My 22,11:6
Anderson, Edward S, 1949, Jl 22,19:2
Anderson, Edward U, 1951, N 4,87:2
Anderson, Edwin, 1951, Mr 10,13:5
Anderson, Edwin B, 1949, Ag 10,21:2
Anderson, Edwin H, 1947, My 1,25:1
Anderson, Elam J, 1944, Ag 18,13:4
Anderson, Eleanor C Mrs, 1942, O 31,15:6
Anderson, Elise Mrs, 1955, My 28,17:3
Anderson, Elizabeth, 1957, D 1,88:2
Anderson, Elizabeth Garrett Dr, 1917, D 19,11:7
Anderson, Ella M Mrs, 1948, Jl 20,23:4
Anderson, Ellery O, 1942, S 17,25:4
Anderson, Elliott M, 1957, F 18,27:5
Anderson, Elmer T, 1943, Je 11,19:3
Anderson, Elmo M, 1951, O 21,92:8
Anderson, Emil, 1939, F 14,19:4; 1948, F 4,23:4
Anderson, Emma H D, 1937, Jl 27,21:2
Anderson, Eric G, 1941, N 22,19:3
Anderson, Ernest B, 1954, Ap 5,25:2
Anderson, Ernest H B, 1963, My 4,25:5
Anderson, Eroy H, 1946, D 18,29:2
Anderson, Ethel M, 1949, S 29,29:1
Anderson, Eugene S, 1951, F 9,25:2
Anderson, Evald, 1941, Jl 21,15:5
Anderson, F Richard Mrs, 1964, D 2,47:2
Anderson, F W Dr, 1903, Ap 22,9:5
Anderson, Florence W, 1945, D 7,21:2
Anderson, Ford S, 1954, Ag 4,21:5
Anderson, Ford S Mrs, 1953, F 4,27:3
Anderson, Frances, 1941, My 12,17:1
Anderson, Frances D, 1958, Ap 23,33:2
Anderson, Francis A Mrs, 1958, Ag 25,21:4
Anderson, Francis N, 1949, D 11,92:5
Anderson, Frank, 1941, Ag 24,35:3; 1954, Je 12,15:5
Anderson, Frank B Mrs, 1952, S 3,29:2
Anderson, Frank Capt, 1921, Ap 5,19:5
Anderson, Frank E, 1955, Je 23,29:4
Anderson, Frank H, 1944, N 17,19:3; 1947, Ap 24,25:3
Anderson, Frank O, 1944, My 2,19:6
Anderson, Frank P, 1937, D 18,21:1
Anderson, Frank R Mrs, 1945, Mr 20,19:4
Anderson, Frank T, 1948, S 27,23:6
Anderson, Franklin C, 1951, S 27,31:5
Anderson, Fred, 1946, S 4,23:4
Anderson, Fred E, 1939, O 21,15:6
Anderson, Frederick, 1957, S 24,35:2
Anderson, Frederick C, 1954, O 5,27:4
Anderson, Frederick G, 1952, Jl 17,23:3
Anderson, Frederick I, 1947, D 25,21:1
Anderson, Frederick J, 1955, Mr 19,15:5
Anderson, Frederick L, 1943, Ap 13,25:1
Anderson, Frederick T, 1951, Jl 29,69:3
Anderson, Frederick W, 1937, Ja 10,II,10:4
Anderson, Garland, 1939, Je 1,25:2
Anderson, Garrett L, 1949, S 30,23:1
Anderson, Gen (funl), 1872, Ap 4,1:6
Anderson, George A Mrs, 1947, Ap 20,63:1; 1965, Jl 13,33:5

Anderson, George B, 1910, Mr 3,9:4
Anderson, George B Jr, 1966, Jl 6,42:2
Anderson, George B Sr, 1961, Ja 12,29:2
Anderson, George C, 1944, Ja 3,22:2; 1962, Ja 9,47:4
Anderson, George D, 1941, My 22,21:5; 1949, S 5,17:5
Anderson, George E, 1940, Mr 18,17:4
Anderson, George F, 1941, Ag 10,37:1; 1947, F 2,57:2
Anderson, George H Mrs, 1949, Je 29,27:1
Anderson, George L, 1938, O 22,17:7
Anderson, George M, 1945, Je 22,15:5; 1947, Je 18, 25:4; 1952, S 3,29:3
Anderson, George S Brig-Gen, 1915, Mr 8,9:3
Anderson, George Sr, 1963, Jl 26,25:1
Anderson, George W, 1938, F 15,26:3; 1965, My 19, 47:4
Anderson, George W Mrs, 1942, My 23,13:3
Anderson, Gertrude, 1942, Ap 16,21:4
Anderson, Gertrude S Mrs, 1943, O 17,4:4
Anderson, Gotthard E, 1967, Ja 24,37:3
Anderson, Grace L, 1946, Ag 21,27:6
Anderson, Graham H, 1950, My 21,104:8
Anderson, Grenville T, 1957, D 21,19:4
Anderson, Gunnard A, 1944, Mr 16,19:2
Anderson, Gus Mrs (Florence), 1962, N 27,37:2
Anderson, Gustave F, 1963, O 15,39:2
Anderson, Gustave W, 1953, O 14,29:4
Anderson, Guy A, 1956, Ag 31,17:4
Anderson, H Alban, 1942, Ap 19,44:3
Anderson, H J, 1881, Je 1,5:6
Anderson, H J Dr, 1876, Ja 18,8:4
Anderson, H N, 1937, D 31,15:4
Anderson, H Randolph, 1942, Ap 20,21:6
Anderson, H Wyndham, 1940, Ap 2,26:3
Anderson, Hans Capt, 1909, Ap 23,9:4
Anderson, Hans Peter, 1914, My 6,11:6
Anderson, Harold, 1967, Je 15,47:4
Anderson, Harold C S, 1963, Ap 26,35:4
Anderson, Harold D, 1950, Je 24,13:6
Anderson, Harold E, 1945, N 26,21:2
Anderson, Harold H Mrs (Gladys L), 1965, Je 19, 29:5
Anderson, Harold M, 1940, D 27,19:3
Anderson, Harold M Mrs, 1940, Ag 18,37:2
Anderson, Harry, 1951, N 25,86:6; 1958, O 15,39:4
Anderson, Harry B, 1954, N 9,27:1
Anderson, Harry C, 1960, N 14,31:2
Anderson, Harry C Mrs, 1958, Ag 31,56:6
Anderson, Harry E, 1949, Ja 1,13:6
Anderson, Harry G, 1957, Ap 5,27:3
Anderson, Harry M, 1947, My 8,25:4
Anderson, Harry N, 1954, D 26,61:2
Anderson, Harry P, 1949, Mr 9,25:2
Anderson, Harry W (funl, N 21,14:7), 1959, N 19,1:2
Anderson, Hattie B, 1946, Je 25,21:2
Anderson, Hayward M, 1950, Ag 3,23:3
Anderson, Helen N Mrs, 1949, My 17,25:1
Anderson, Henry, 1954, F 4,25:4; 1956, O 13,19:5
Anderson, Henry A C Dr, 1909, Ja 6,11:5
Anderson, Henry B, 1938, Mr 18,19:4
Anderson, Henry C, 1939, O 15,49:1
Anderson, Henry H, 1945, Ag 17,17:5
Anderson, Henry James, 1875, D 14,5:2
Anderson, Henry S, 1941, My 7,25:5
Anderson, Henry W, 1954, Ja 8,21:1
Anderson, Herbert C, 1944, Ap 1,13:1
Anderson, Herbert E, 1949, D 13,38:2
Anderson, Herbert V, 1954, O 16,17:3
Anderson, Herman S, 1948, Mr 26,21:2
Anderson, Hettie, 1956, Ag 5,77:2
Anderson, Hilding, 1961, S 4,15:2
Anderson, Hilding C Mrs, 1941, N 13,27:4
Anderson, Hjalmar, 1940, D 9,19:6
Anderson, Howard S Jr, 1960, Jl 22,23:4
Anderson, Hu C, 1953, My 9,19:4
Anderson, Hugh A, 1965, N 11,47:3
Anderson, Hugh C, 1941, Ja 24,17:1
Anderson, Hugh M, 1943, D 24,13:3
Anderson, HY M, 1937, O 3,II,9:2
Anderson, I M, 1952, Ja 11,22:2
Anderson, Ida E Mrs, 1957, S 22,86:5
Anderson, Ida J, 1957, N 19,33:4
Anderson, Ira L, 1962, Ap 9,29:4
Anderson, Isaac, 1920, Je 12,13:4; 1961, N 13,31:2
Anderson, Ivan H, 1959, Ag 20,25:3
Anderson, Ivy, 1949, D 30,19:1
Anderson, J Alfred Mrs, 1964, Mr 31,35:5
Anderson, J Aubrey, 1946, N 25,27:4
Anderson, J Courtney Mrs, 1958, Je 8,88:5
Anderson, J E, 1947, F 5,23:5
Anderson, J F, 1927, Ja 25,21:4
Anderson, J F Jr, 1905, Ja 20,9:2
Anderson, J G, 1933, Je 16,17:3
Anderson, J H A Rev, 1937, D 13,27:4
Anderson, J Hubert, 1966, Jl 23,25:5
Anderson, J Starr, 1959, F 3,31:2
Anderson, J T M, 1946, D 30,22:2
Anderson, J W, 1925, O 26,19:5
Anderson, James A, 1953, Jl 17,17:5; 1954, Ap 13,31:2
Anderson, James B, 1938, N 21,19:2; 1943, D 26,32:8
Anderson, James B Jr, 1959, Ag 8,17:5
Anderson, James B Mrs, 1961, Mr 13,29:5
Anderson, James C Sr, 1968, N 22,47:1
Anderson, James E, 1958, Jl 11,23:2
Anderson, James H, 1966, Je 1,47:1
Anderson, James H Mrs, 1959, Ap 3,27:2
Anderson, James J, 1959, F 16,29:3
Anderson, James McCulloch, 1924, S 25,23:4
Anderson, James N, 1945, Je 18,19:1
Anderson, James P, 1937, Ja 16,17:4; 1947, D 26,15:2
Anderson, James R, 1949, Mr 25,23:2
Anderson, James S, 1959, Ja 21,31:2
Anderson, James W, 1937, N 16,23:5; 1947, O 29,28:3; 1959, Je 20,21:5
Anderson, Jerome A Dr, 1903, D 27,7:7
Anderson, Jessie M Mrs, 1950, N 27,25:4
Anderson, Joel M Mrs, 1945, D 15,17:3
Anderson, Johan G, 1960, O 31,31:5
Anderson, John, 1881, N 25,5:2
Anderson, John (funl), 1882, Ja 4,8:3
Anderson, John, 1911, F 20,7:5; 1914, Mr 10,9:4; 1939, Ap 10,17:2; 1940, O 6,48:2; 1941, S 28,48:1; 1943, Jl 17,13:3; 1948, Jl 13,27:5; 1948, Ag 4,21:4; 1949, Ja 1,13:6
Anderson, John (Viscount Waverly), 1958, Ja 5,86:1
Anderson, John A, 1940, S 6,21:3; 1959, D 4,31:3; 1948, Ap 3,15:2
Anderson, John A Sr, 1965, D 10,47:1
Anderson, John B, 1947, Ap 3,25:5; 1947, My 6,27:1; 1951, Mr 24,13:4
Anderson, John B Mrs, 1942, O 5,19:2
Anderson, John C, 1938, Mr 31,23:4; 1940, Ap 28,36:3; 1965, D 25,13:5
Anderson, John E, 1941, Jl 13,29:1
Anderson, John F, 1939, My 9,23:4; 1954, Ja 11,25:5; 1958, O 1,37:1
Anderson, John F Sr, 1951, Ap 24,29:2
Anderson, John G, 1967, Ja 3,37:1
Anderson, John H Mrs, 1904, Ja 26,9:6
Anderson, John Henry Prof, 1874, F 5,2:6
Anderson, John J, 1939, Je 1,25:5
Anderson, John L, 1953, F 22,63:3
Anderson, John Lewis, 1952, D 15,25:4
Anderson, John M (funl, F 3,23:3; trb lr, F 7,II,3:8), 1954, Ja 31,88:2
Anderson, John Mrs, 1949, F 13,77:2
Anderson, John O, 1955, S 24,19:4
Anderson, John R, 1939, Je 27,23:6; 1941, Mr 8,19:5
Anderson, John R (por), 1949, My 5,27:4
Anderson, John S Sr, 1958, Mr 2,89:2
Anderson, John W, 1939, Mr 25,15:6; 1945, N 24,19:6; 1948, Jl 15,23:4; 1967, S 30,33:4
Anderson, Joseph, 1965, O 23,31:5
Anderson, Joseph B, 1944, Jl 18,19:5
Anderson, Joseph C, 1948, Jl 6,23:2
Anderson, Joseph Rev Dr, 1916, Ag 19,9:5
Anderson, Joseph W, 1957, N 23,19:6
Anderson, Jules E, 1959, Je 21,92:6
Anderson, Julia, 1950, Jl 5,31:4
Anderson, Julia G Mrs, 1938, Ag 25,4:8
Anderson, Karl, 1956, My 19,19:3
Anderson, Karl M, 1946, D 13,24:2
Anderson, Karl Mrs, 1950, Ag 31,26:2
Anderson, Karl P, 1959, N 17,35:6
Anderson, Katherine F, 1953, D 27,60:6
Anderson, Kenneth, 1959, Ap 30,31:2
Anderson, Kenneth W, 1957, My 23,33:2
Anderson, L Jansen, 1951, D 28,21:1
Anderson, Larz, 1878, F 28,4:7; 1902, Je 27,1:2
Anderson, Larz (will, My 9,15:2), 1937, Ap 14,25:1
Anderson, Larz Mrs (will, N 11,36:1), 1948, N 4,29:3
Anderson, Lee, 1955, Jl 13,25:2
Anderson, Lewis B, 1954, O 5,27:6
Anderson, Lewis N, 1939, N 12,48:7
Anderson, Lindsay, 1945, Mr 15,23:1
Anderson, Louis, 1954, Ap 30,23:4
Anderson, Louis B, 1946, My 29,24:3
Anderson, Louis C, 1954, Je 7,23:3
Anderson, Louis M, 1955, Ag 3,23:3
Anderson, Louis Mrs, 1954, Ap 30,23:4
Anderson, Louisa G, 1943, N 17,25:3
Anderson, Luard C, 1951, Je 14,27:6
Anderson, Luis, 1948, Je 16,29:4
Anderson, Lulu Mrs, 1942, F 6,19:5
Anderson, Luther, 1940, Jl 28,27:4
Anderson, Lydia E, 1939, Ap 12,23:4
Anderson, Malcolm E, 1950, O 28,17:6
Anderson, Marjorie D (trb lr, D 14,32:6), 1954, D 1, 31:3
Anderson, Martin, 1943, Ap 4,41:1
Anderson, Mary, 1940, My 30,17:1; 1953, Je 30,23:5; 1964, Ja 30,29:3
Anderson, Mary A Mrs, 1941, S 11,23:4
Anderson, Mary C, 1880, Je 4,3:4
Anderson, Mary Mrs, 1942, My 11,17:2
Anderson, Matilda H Mrs, 1957, Ap 8,23:4
Anderson, Matthew, 1952, F 10,92:3
Anderson, Matthew A, 1967, O 11,47:2
Anderson, Maurice A, 1938, My 4,23:1
Anderson, Max C, 1915, Mr 9,9:4
Anderson, Maxwell (funl plans, Mr 2,27:4; cor, Mr 5,31:1), 1959, Mr 1,1:6
Anderson, Milerd J, 1953, N 27,27:1
Anderson, Miller, 1965, O 30,35:4
Anderson, Milton H, 1952, Ag 15,16:6
Anderson, Monroe D, 1939, Ag 7,15:4
Anderson, Morton H, 1955, Mr 5,17:5
Anderson, Murray, 1955, My 16,47:4
Anderson, N (Uncle Tom), 1926, N 16,27:3
Anderson, N R, 1948, Ag 2,21:4
Anderson, Nathan, 1950, Ja 28,13:1
Anderson, Nelson, 1967, O 27,45:3
Anderson, Nelson P, 1957, D 3,35:5
Anderson, Nils, 1965, Mr 24,46:4
Anderson, Nils Mrs, 1956, Jl 2,21:2
Anderson, O E, 1953, Mr 24,31:2
Anderson, Ollie, 1945, Jl 8,11:5
Anderson, Omer, 1968, N 23,47:1
Anderson, Orvil (more details, Ag 25,39:4), 1965, Ag 24,31:4
Anderson, Orville L, 1943, Ag 6,15:3
Anderson, Orville L Capt, 1918, S 2,9:2
Anderson, Oscar, 1940, Ja 3,15:7; 1949, Mr 31,25:4; 1951, Ag 14,23:4; 1954, Ap 18,88:8
Anderson, Oscar A, 1949, Ap 4,23:5
Anderson, Oscar C, 1962, Ja 27,21:5
Anderson, Oscar W, 1954, My 27,27:4
Anderson, Otto H, 1953, Je 30,23:1
Anderson, Paul G, 1951, O 12,27:3
Anderson, Paul L, 1956, S 17,27:3
Anderson, Paul M, 1966, F 27,84:4
Anderson, Paul Y, 1938, D 8,27:2
Anderson, Percy L, 1944, F 22,24:3
Anderson, Peter, 1943, O 16,13:2
Anderson, Peter A, 1940, O 6,48:3
Anderson, Peyton F, 1945, O 12,23:4
Anderson, Peyton T Sr, 1944, F 10,15:2
Anderson, R B, 1936, Mr 3,21:3
Anderson, R C, 1878, Ja 12,5:4
Anderson, R Earle, 1967, Mr 18,29:1
Anderson, R H, 1879, Je 28,2:5
Anderson, R L, 1959, N 4,35:1
Anderson, R M, 1959, Je 15,27:2
Anderson, Ralph H, 1956, Ja 25,31:5
Anderson, Ralph O, 1950, Ag 25,21:2
Anderson, Ralph W, 1964, Ag 23,87:2
Anderson, Rand, 1948, My 20,29:4
Anderson, Rand Mrs, 1943, Ag 7,11:6
Anderson, Raymond C, 1947, O 31,23:4; 1959, Ag 24, 21:4
Anderson, Reuben M, 1948, My 6,25:5
Anderson, Richard D, 1961, D 1,30:3
Anderson, Richard R, 1943, Ap 3,15:1
Anderson, Richard W, 1954, My 31,14:5
Anderson, Robert, 1944, Jl 6,15:7; 1946, My 16,21:5; 1959, Jl 19,69:3
Anderson, Robert A, 1942, Ja 30,19:2; 1952, Jl 12,13:3
Anderson, Robert C, 1955, F 22,21:3
Anderson, Robert F, 1956, S 2,56:3
Anderson, Robert G, 1939, My 22,17:1; 1950, S 26,31:4
Anderson, Robert G Mrs, 1943, Ag 22,36:5
Anderson, Robert H Jr, 1942, Ag 24,15:1
Anderson, Robert J, 1953, O 20,29:5
Anderson, Robert L, 1951, Je 9,19:4; 1958, F 27,27:1
Anderson, Robert M, 1941, O 2,25:5
Anderson, Robert Maj-Gen, 1871, O 28,7:3
Anderson, Robert Mrs, 1919, Ag 23,7:7; 1956, N 29, 35:2
Anderson, Robert W, 1949, N 30,27:4
Anderson, Robert W Mrs, 1959, Jl 9,27:1
Anderson, Robert Young, 1923, S 13,19:3
Anderson, Robin Robinson Mrs, 1921, My 16,15:4
Anderson, Ronald T, 1953, Ag 15,15:6
Anderson, Roscoe, 1951, Ja 20,15:4
Anderson, Rosemary O Mrs, 1938, N 11,25:4
Anderson, Roulhac, 1961, My 17,37:1
Anderson, Roy, 1949, F 20,V,6:6
Anderson, Roy A Sr, 1947, Mr 6,25:3
Anderson, Roy Scott, 1925, Mr 13,19:1
Anderson, Rudolph E, 1943, F 2,19:3
Anderson, Rudolph J, 1961, Ap 7,31:2
Anderson, Rufus, 1880, Je 2,4:7
Anderson, Rupert M, 1940, Je 1,15:1
Anderson, Rupert W K, 1950, N 10,27:5
Anderson, Rupert Wentworth, 1925, Ag 27,19:6
Anderson, S Lane, 1943, N 12,21:2
Anderson, S Theodore Mrs, 1956, Ap 26,33:2
Anderson, Samuel, 1941, My 27,24:3; 1943, S 29,21:5
Anderson, Samuel H, 1956, D 21,23:5
Anderson, Samuel J Gen, 1905, N 20,2:6
Anderson, Sarah N Mrs, 1940, Mr 26,21:4
Anderson, Seth M Mrs, 1948, Ap 11,72:2
Anderson, Sherwood, 1941, Mr 9,41:1
Anderson, Sidney, 1948, O 9,19:1
Anderson, Soren, 1947, F 4,25:5
Anderson, Spencer, 1947, My 23,24:2
Anderson, St George Mason Mrs, 1925, O 16,21:5
Anderson, Stanley E, 1965, Ja 21,31:2
Anderson, Stanley S, 1951, Jl 23,17:4
Anderson, Stephen H, 1940, Je 10,17:3
Anderson, Stewart, 1939, O 7,17:5
Anderson, Stuart M, 1954, My 24,27:4
Anderson, Subbeal S, 1961, F 22,25:1
Anderson, Susan D, 1883, O 5,8:2
Anderson, Sven A, 1955, Ag 19,19:1
Anderson, Sven E, 1950, Je 21,27:4
Anderson, Swen E Mrs, 1951, S 25,29:4
Anderson, T D Rev, 1883, D 20,4:7
Anderson, T Hart, 1939, Ag 16,23:2
Anderson, T Hart Jr, 1962, Ap 29,29:1
Anderson, Thomas H, 1950, Ap 1,15:1
Anderson, Thomas Henry Justice, 1916, O 2,11:5

Anderson, Thomas J Jr, 1967, Jl 2,35:2
Anderson, Thomas James, 1925, Ja 17,15:4
Anderson, Thomas M, 1939, Mr 25,15:2
Anderson, Thomas McArthur Brig-Gen, 1917, My 10, 13:4
Anderson, Thomas Mrs, 1944, D 27,19:5; 1946, Ap 3, 25:4
Anderson, Thomas N, 1956, D 15,25:2
Anderson, Thompson J, 1948, S 22,31:1
Anderson, Tom, 1913, D 23,9:6
Anderson, Troyer S, 1948, Ap 4,61:1
Anderson, Vernon, 1938, Mr 10,21:5
Anderson, Victor C, 1937, Jl 11,II,5:1
Anderson, Victor E, 1948, S 13,21:3; 1962, Ag 16,27:1
Anderson, Victor H, 1951, Jl 7,13:5
Anderson, Victor O Rev, 1937, O 8,23:4
Anderson, Victor V, 1960, Jl 27,29:1
Anderson, W A, 1903, My 24,7:4
Anderson, W C, 1945, D 20,23:2
Anderson, W C Dr, 1882, O 4,5:5
Anderson, W D Jr, 1937, Ja 29,19:3
Anderson, W H, 1950, My 20,15:3
Anderson, W H P, 1942, D 31,15:4
Anderson, W P, 1940, F 10,15:6
Anderson, W T, 1945, N 24,20:2
Anderson, W W, 1939, O 27,23:3
Anderson, Walter, 1945, D 16,39:1
Anderson, Walter A, 1964, O 26,31:2
Anderson, Walter B, 1952, My 25,93:1
Anderson, Walter C, 1939, N 25,17:1
Anderson, Walter F, 1948, My 13,25:2
Anderson, Walter L, 1963, D 15,86:3
Anderson, Walter M, 1938, D 21,23:4
Anderson, Walter S, 1937, My 2,II,9:2
Anderson, Ward P, 1952, Ag 14,23:5
Anderson, Warren R, 1955, N 24,29:3
Anderson, Wayne C, 1955, Je 28,27:5
Anderson, Wells F, 1958, S 22,31:5
Anderson, Wendell W, 1959, O 21,43:3
Anderson, Wesley H, 1953, Ag 25,21:4
Anderson, Willard P, 1952, S 6,17:6
Anderson, William, 1907, Ag 14,7:5; 1911, Ag 21,9:6
Anderson, William A, 1944, S 11,17:4; 1954, D 14, 33:4; 1962, Ag 15,31:4
Anderson, William B, 1940, Ja 8,15:2
Anderson, William C, 1947, S 5,19:3; 1949, Mr 15,27:4
Anderson, William D, 1946, F 28,23:4; 1947, Ap 4, 23:1; 1951, Ag 2,21:3; 1952, D 27,17:6; 1957, Ja 22, 29:4
Anderson, William E, 1903, S 16,9:6; 1954, O 17,86:7; 1960, D 4,88:4
Anderson, William F, 1944, Jl 23,35:1
Anderson, William F Mrs, 1950, D 6,33:3
Anderson, William Finley, 1905, S 5,7:4
Anderson, William G, 1947, Jl 10,21:3; 1948, F 7,15:4
Anderson, William G Mrs, 1941, Ag 12,19:4
Anderson, William H, 1940, Ja 4,23:4; 1940, O 2,23:2; 1950, Je 27,29:2; 1953, N 6,27:2; 1955, Ap 14,36:3
Anderson, William H Mrs, 1947, Ag 30,15:4; 1951, D 14,31:2
Anderson, William J, 1951, D 7,28:2
Anderson, William K, 1947, F 8,17:2
Anderson, William Kyle, 1909, Ag 29,9:5
Anderson, William L, 1958, O 22,35:2
Anderson, William M, 1951, Mr 23,21:4
Anderson, William O, 1964, Ja 3,23:3
Anderson, William O Jr, 1938, Ja 1,19:2
Anderson, William P, 1951, F 27,27:4
Anderson, William R, 1945, S 12,25:2
Anderson, William R Mrs, 1940, O 8,25:3
Anderson, William Sr, 1947, O 21,23:1
Anderson, William T, 1943, Ap 20,24:3; 1950, My 19, 33:6; 1954, Ap 15,29:5
Anderson, Willisford C, 1950, Mr 21,29:2
Anderson, Wingate M, 1952, Mr 23,94:3
Anderson, Wingate M Mrs, 1961, Jl 3,15:2
Anderson, Winslow, 1948, N 15,26:2
Anderson, Winston D, 1952, N 13,31:1
Anderson, Woodford D, 1951, D 9,91:1
Anderson, Woodford D Mrs, 1968, Ap 4,47:2
Andersson, Alfred O, 1950, My 12,27:4
Andersson, E Einar, 1961, Je 3,23:1
Andersson, Gunnar, 1946, O 20,60:4
Andersson, Gustaf, 1961, N 13,31:4
Andersson, Oscar B, 1955, Jl 28,23:2
Anderstrom, Robert, 1954, My 8,11:3
Anderton, Caroline, 1939, F 28,19:5
Anderton, Harry, 1962, Mr 4,86:5
Anderton, Stephen P, 1947, Mr 10,22:3
Anderton, Walter P, 1967, My 18,47:4
Anderton, William Bancroft Dr, 1917, F 24,9:6
Anderton, William Leigh Jr, 1915, My 6,13:6
Andes, George S, 1920, O 16,13:4
Andes, Henry P, 1952, My 18,93:2
Andes, Hugh W, 1967, Jl 4,19:2
Ando, Kisaburo, 1954, My 11,29:1
Andolsek, William, 1955, N 15,33:4
Andon, Andon E, 1943, F 26,20:2
Andra, Anita, 1960, Ap 8,31:1
Andra, Erich, 1952, My 24,19:4
Andrada, Antonio C de, 1946, Ja 3,19:5
Andrada, David D, 1941, Ja 4,13:2
Andrada, Marco A, 1958, Je 19,31:5
Andrada e Silva, Jose B De, 1954, F 27,13:3
Andrade, Cipriano Rear-Adm, 1911, Je 20,9:5
Andrade, Eduardo, 1958, O 31,26:5
Andrade, Jose, 1902, Mr 21,9:4
Andrade, Manuel J, 1941, Ja 28,19:4
Andrade, Roberto, 1938, N 2,24:2
Andrae, Gabriel, 1876, F 14,1:5
Andrae, William, 1955, Ap 4,29:4
Andralouis, Joseph P, 1962, O 23,37:5
Andrao, Tor, 1947, F 25,26:2
Andrassy, Geza Count, 1938, Ap 30,17:3
Andrassy, Gyula Count, 1890, F 19,2:5
Andrassy, J Count, 1929, Je 12,29:1
Andre, Alphonse B, 1961, F 15,35:5
Andre, Brother, 1937, Ja 6,23:3
Andre, Engel, 1942, My 5,21:1
Andre, Francois, 1962, My 4,33:1
Andre, Frank K, 1944, Je 1,19:5
Andre, Gwili A (Mrs W D Cross Jr), 1959, F 7,12:1
~~Andre, Henri, 1967, O 14,27:4~~
Andre, Hoyt, 1957, Ap 18,29:4
Andre, J F G, 1878, N 28,5:3
Andre, John Mrs, 1943, Ag 2,15:3
Andre, John R, 1949, N 17,29:3
Andre, Jorge R, 1940, Mr 13,23:5
Andre, Jorge R Jr, 1955, S 11,85:1
Andre, Joseph S, 1954, My 17,23:3
Andre, Louis Joseph Nicolas, 1913, Mr 19,13:5
Andre, Marc, 1954, Ag 3,19:4
Andre, Paul, 1947, Ag 22,15:5
Andrea, Frank A D, 1965, D 23,28:3
Andreae, Frank W, 1957, Ja 4,23:3
Andreae, Gottlieb Rev, 1925, Jl 9,19:5
Andreae, Hope L Mrs, 1945, Jl 10,11:6
Andreae, Volkmar, 1962, Je 20,32:5
Andreas, Jeremiah John, 1920, S 24,15:2
Andreasian, Mihran K, 1963, O 7,31:4
Andreeff, Leonid Mrs, 1948, Mr 13,15:3
Andreen, Allan E, 1968, O 7,47:4
Andreen, Gustav A, 1940, O 2,23:4
Andreen, Gustave B, 1952, D 25,29:5
Andreev, Fedor, 1950, Je 2,24:2
Andren, Gustav T, 1967, S 22,47:4
Andreozzi, Louis G, 1962, Je 14,33:3
Andrepont, Paul E, 1966, My 19,47:4
Andres, Alex, 1942, Je 1,13:5
Andres, Benjamin F Mrs, 1950, Jl 25,27:4
Andres, Charles A, 1957, Ag 26,23:3
Andres, Harold, 1963, D 22,34:8
Andres, Henry G, 1921, Ag 29,11:5
Andres, John B Mrs, 1947, D 7,76:3
Andres, Lasar N, 1945, O 17,19:2
Andres, Louis Mrs, 1945, F 26,19:3
Andresen, Albert F R, 1961, Ja 26,29:2
Andresen, Arthur E, 1949, O 10,23:5
Andresen, August H, 1958, Ja 15,29:1
Andresen, August H Mrs, 1957, My 25,21:2
Andresen, Chris Mrs, 1968, F 16,37:1
Andresen, Louis, 1955, Ja 25,25:5
Andress, Clarence S, 1941, Ap 30,19:6
Andress, J Mace, 1942, F 8,49:3
Andress, Joseph C, 1938, Ag 5,18:1
Andress, Mary V, 1964, My 17,87:1
Andress, William N, 1955, Ja 7,22:2
Andretta, Salvador A, 1965, O 20,47:2
Andreve, Grullermo, 1940, O 4,23:5
Andrew, A P Jr, 1936, Je 3,21:3
Andrew, Bishop, 1871, Mr 5,5:5
Andrew, Edward, 1946, My 22,21:1
Andrew, Father, 1946, Ag 29,27:2
Andrew, Felix Bro, 1964, S 10,35:1
Andrew, Flynn L Mrs, 1968, Ap 23,44:2
Andrew, Fred D, 1944, D 12,23:4
Andrew, Gerald W L, 1968, Jl 21,57:1
Andrew, Harold E, 1953, Mr 3,27:2
Andrew, Harriet F Mrs, 1939, N 17,21:2
Andrew, Herman B, 1942, Ja 16,21:2
Andrew, James D, 1937, Mr 25,25:2
Andrew, James H Dr, 1937, N 29,23:5
Andrew, Jess C, 1955, Ap 24,86:5
Andrew, John A Ex-Gov, 1867, O 31,4:7
Andrew, John C S, 1955, Jl 10,74:6
Andrew, John E, 1940, Jl 1,19:3
Andrew, Kenneth, 1952, Ja 23,27:2
Andrew, Kenneth E Sr, 1954, D 4,17:6
Andrew, Kenneth E Sr Mrs, 1954, F 19,27:2
Andrew, Leroy S, 1954, D 12,88:3
Andrew, Lewis C Rev, 1937, Je 16,23:4
Andrew, Norman C, 1958, N 3,37:5
Andrew, Prince, 1944, D 4,23:6
Andrew, Richard M, 1958, Ap 16,33:4
Andrew, Russel G Dr, 1909, Jl 8,7:6
Andrew, Seymour L, 1965, O 24,86:5
Andrew, Thomas W, 1948, Ag 12,21:5
Andrew, Walter S Mrs, 1943, Je 11,19:4
Andrew, William E, 1937, Mr 26,22:2
Andrew (Bro J J Lynch), 1960, My 7,23:5
Andrew Philip, Bro, 1945, O 25,21:3
Andrewa, Charles William Dr, 1924, My 27,21:4
Andrews, A W, 1945, D 29,14:6
Andrews, Adolphus, 1948, Je 20,60:2
Andrews, Adora, 1956, S 19,37:2
Andrews, Albert G, 1950, N 28,32:2
Andrews, Albert G Mrs, 1950, O 18,33:6
Andrews, Albert H, 1945, O 3,19:2
Andrews, Albert L, 1961, N 5,88:8
Andrews, Albert W, 1953, Ja 15,27:3
Andrews, Alex S, 1960, Ap 26,37:2
Andrews, Alexander, 1873, N 25,3:1
Andrews, Alice M Mrs, 1938, Mr 17,21:1
Andrews, Alida Mrs, 1942, Jl 2,21:4
Andrews, Amma M, 1946, Je 25,21:2
Andrews, Annie G Mrs (will, Ap 18,4:5), 1939, Ap 15,19:2
Andrews, Archie M, 1938, Je 18,15:5
Andrews, Arthur E, 1952, Jl 29,21:1
Andrews, Arthur L, 1938, S 17,17:5
Andrews, Austin W, 1958, N 5,35:4
Andrews, Avery D, 1959, Ap 20,31:2
Andrews, Avery D Mrs, 1945, Ja 18,19:3
Andrews, Benjamin P, 1938, F 8,21:5
Andrews, Benjamin R, 1963, Ap 29,31:2
Andrews, Benjamin V, 1955, My 5,33:2
Andrews, Bert, 1953, Ag 22,15:3
Andrews, Buel C, 1940, N 26,23:5
Andrews, C A, 1884, Mr 12,5:5
Andrews, C B Judge, 1902, S 13,9:4
Andrews, C E, 1885, Ja 26,2:3
Andrews, Caroline J Mrs, 1937, Ja 15,22:2
Andrews, Charles, 1950, Ja 29,68:4
Andrews, Charles A, 1940, N 12,24:3
Andrews, Charles A Mrs, 1951, S 2,48:7
Andrews, Charles B, 1950, Ap 20,29:2; 1961, F 6,23:3
Andrews, Charles E, 1939, Ag 29,21:2; 1949, Ja 15, 17:2; 1964, Ja 10,43:1
Andrews, Charles E Jr, 1958, O 16,37:4
Andrews, Charles Ex-Judge, 1918, O 23,13:1
Andrews, Charles F, 1939, S 19,25:2; 1940, Ap 5,21:3
Andrews, Charles L, 1948, S 1,48:7
Andrews, Charles L Mrs, 1938, Ja 5,21:2
Andrews, Charles M, 1943, S 11,13:1
Andrews, Charles M Mrs, 1962, F 26,27:1
Andrews, Charles O, 1942, Ap 23,23:5; 1946, S 19,31:3
Andrews, Charles S, 1957, F 14,27:2
Andrews, Charles T Mrs, 1943, Je 26,13:2
Andrews, Charles W, 1946, Ag 10,13:4
Andrews, Charlotte L, 1942, My 8,21:2
Andrews, Charlton, 1939, Ag 15,19:2
Andrews, Chase, 1925, D 29,23:5
Andrews, Chauncey H Mrs, 1917, Mr 23,9:4
Andrews, Creighton S, 1950, Ag 26,13:3
Andrews, Daisy H, 1921, Mr 5,13:6
Andrews, David, 1964, F 16,65:4
Andrews, David B Jr, 1959, Ja 17,19:4
Andrews, David Curran, 1913, F 22,11:5
Andrews, David Z, 1951, F 22,31:1
Andrews, Delano, 1958, F 1,19:5
Andrews, Donald C, 1952, Jl 14,17:6
Andrews, Donald L Mrs, 1941, D 13,21:4
Andrews, E T, 1866, Ap 9,8:5
Andrews, Edna D Mrs, 1938, S 21,25:5
Andrews, Edward D, 1964, Je 13,23:2
Andrews, Edward Gayer, 1908, Ja 2,9:7
Andrews, Edward Gayer Bp (por), 1908, Ja 1,9:4
Andrews, Edward Gayer Mrs, 1915, O 9,9:3
Andrews, Edward L, 1919, D 18,13:3
Andrews, Edward M Sr, 1947, Ag 22,15:4
Andrews, Edwin C, 1967, Je 26,33:2
Andrews, Edwin C Mrs, 1964, Ap 30,35:4
Andrews, Elisha Benjamin, 1917, O 31,13:5
Andrews, Elizabeth B, 1953, Mr 10,29:2
Andrews, Elmer F, 1964, Ja 18,23:1
Andrews, Emily S Mrs, 1937, O 9,19:6
Andrews, Emmett F, 1963, Ag 16,27:4
Andrews, Eugene P, 1957, S 22,86:4
Andrews, Ferdinand, 1947, S 13,11:3
Andrews, Francis D, 1945, F 17,13:5
Andrews, Francis X, 1952, F 25,21:3
Andrews, Frank C, 1918, D 13,15:2
Andrews, Frank D, 1937, Ja 29,19:3
Andrews, Frank H, 1948, Mr 11,27:2
Andrews, Frank L, 1939, Ja 17,22:2; 1946, S 19,31:5; 1966, My 10,45:2
Andrews, Frank M, 1940, N 27,23:5; 1948, S 3,19:1
Andrews, Frank T, 1940, N 9,17:3
Andrews, Fred, 1948, S 14,29:5
Andrews, Fred A, 1949, Je 20,19:5
Andrews, Fred L, 1941, S 23,23:4
Andrews, Frederick J, 1953, My 29,25:5
Andrews, Frederick W, 1964, O 11,85:6
Andrews, Frederick W Mrs, 1950, Ag 2,25:3
Andrews, G H Mrs, 1880, N 7,7:4
Andrews, G Osgood, 1944, Mr 2,17:3
Andrews, G P Judge, 1902, My 24,1:5
Andrews, Garnett Sr, 1946, N 13,27:6
Andrews, Garrett V, 1946, Ag 4,45:1
Andrews, George, 1938, Mr 30,21:4; 1944, Ag 15,17:4; 1956, F 15,31:4
Andrews, George C, 1940, Jl 11,19:4
Andrews, George C Jr, 1959, O 6,39:2
Andrews, George F, 1949, D 1,31:1
Andrews, George H, 1957, Je 14,25:2
Andrews, George H Mrs, 1958, N 25,33:5

Andrews, George J, 1952, Ja 2,25:5
Andrews, George L, 1938, S 17,17:1
Andrews, George Lippitt Brig-Gen, 1920, Jl 27,13:5
Andrews, George Mrs, 1922, Mr 19,28:3
Andrews, George R, 1941, F 22,15:2
Andrews, George S, 1961, N 12,86:6
Andrews, George S Mrs, 1946, O 7,31:3
Andrews, George W, 1955, Je 15,31:4
Andrews, George Wakeman Rev Dr, 1918, S 15,23:1
Andrews, H Percy Mrs, 1948, Je 17,25:2
Andrews, Hardage L, 1955, Ag 6,15:2
Andrews, Hardage L Sr Mrs, 1952, O 8,31:3
Andrews, Harry, 1924, Je 30,15:3
Andrews, Harry G, 1958, F 15,17:3
Andrews, Harry G Mrs, 1960, F 24,32:2
Andrews, Harry V (funl, S 17,23:3), 1924, S 16,23:4
Andrews, Henry E, 1939, F 11,15:4
Andrews, Horace Ellsworth, 1918, D 2,13:8
Andrews, Horace J, 1951, Mr 25,27:4
Andrews, Horace M Mrs, 1950, Mr 6,22:2
Andrews, Howard E, 1948, F 11,28:2
Andrews, Hugh A, 1949, S 18,94:4
Andrews, Hugh B, 1952, Ja 8,27:1
Andrews, Ilett E, 1960, O 13,37:4
Andrews, Isaac, 1950, Je 18,76:7
Andrews, J De W, 1928, Ap 12,27:3
Andrews, J Munn, 1943, Jl 8,19:2
Andrews, J Munn Mrs, 1944, F 18,17:5
Andrews, J R, 1915, Mr 26,13:3
Andrews, J U, 1883, D 8,2:2
Andrews, J Willis, 1951, Je 21,27:4
Andrews, J Winthrop Mrs, 1948, N 14,77:1
Andrews, James, 1951, F 19,23:2
Andrews, James Bruyn, 1909, Ag 31,7:5
Andrews, James C Mrs, 1967, Ja 17,39:4
Andrews, James F, 1915, F 12,9:6; 1942, My 2,13:7
Andrews, James H M, 1948, F 11,27:3
Andrews, James H Mrs, 1954, Je 1,27:1
Andrews, James S, 1938, Jl 12,19:2
Andrews, Jane A, 1912, Je 1,11:4
Andrews, Jennie Mrs Rev, 1906, Ja 31,11:5
Andrews, Jerome, 1958, My 16,23:6
Andrews, Jesse, 1961, D 30,19:1
Andrews, John, 1950, My 24,29:3
Andrews, John B, 1943, Ja 5,20:2
Andrews, John E, 1958, D 2,37:5
Andrews, John H, 1942, Ag 11,19:3
Andrews, John K, 1966, Ja 1,17:2
Andrews, John M, 1956, Ag 6,23:5
Andrews, John Newman Gen, 1903, D 28,1:6
Andrews, Joseph (por), 1937, S 30,23:3
Andrews, Joseph, 1943, O 4,17:5; 1943, O 20,21:4
Andrews, Joseph E, 1949, F 14,19:2
Andrews, Joseph I, 1944, Jl 15,13:3
Andrews, Joseph L, 1965, Je 12,31:6
Andrews, Joseph Mrs, 1949, Mr 19,15:4
Andrews, Julia du Pont Mrs (est acctg), 1956, Ja 27, 11:6
Andrews, Julian B, 1948, N 12,23:3
Andrews, Justin M, 1967, Jl 2,35:3
Andrews, Kenneth L, 1954, My 2,88:5
Andrews, Kornelia T, 1913, D 5,11:6
Andrews, L Gaylord, 1945, O 16,23:2
Andrews, Launcelot W, 1938, Ap 15,19:5
Andrews, Laverne (Mrs L A Rogers),(funl plans, My 10,47:2), 1967, My 9,47:3
Andrews, Lawrence G Mrs, 1950, Ag 31,25:2
Andrews, Lee, 1962, Jl 11,35:4
Andrews, Leon H, 1949, My 31,24:2
Andrews, Lincoln C, 1950, N 26,90:5
Andrews, Lois (Mrs Leonard Kleckner), 1968, Ap 6, 40:2
Andrews, Loring, 1875, Ja 24,6:7
Andrews, Louis M, 1955, S 12,25:2
Andrews, Lyle D, 1950, Ja 19,28:2
Andrews, M Neil, 1967, S 2,25:5
Andrews, M S, 1936, Ag 3,15:1
Andrews, Marie Mrs, 1949, Ap 4,23:3
Andrews, Mark, 1939, D 11,23:4
Andrews, Mark E Mrs, 1946, Je 9,40:4
Andrews, Matthew P, 1947, Je 22,52:2
Andrews, Maude A, 1943, Ja 9,13:5
Andrews, Minor H, 1950, Ag 8,29:2
Andrews, Nathaniel R, 1950, O 7,19:1
Andrews, Neal R, 1953, Ap 6,19:3
Andrews, Oliver B, 1937, Ja 23,17:2
Andrews, Orvin G Mrs, 1941, Ap 8,25:1
Andrews, Paul S, 1967, Ap 7,34:4
Andrews, Paul S Mrs, 1961, Mr 18,23:3
Andrews, Percival J, 1952, Jl 16,25:5
Andrews, Peter, 1949, O 12,29:3
Andrews, Peter B, 1964, Ap 20,29:2
Andrews, Polly, 1968, Ag 14,39:1
Andrews, Preston L, 1959, N 28,21:4
Andrews, R S Gen, 1903, Ja 7,9:6
Andrews, Ralph J, 1925, D 28,15:2; 1947, Mr 8,13:3
Andrews, Robert C, 1947, D 23,23:1
Andrews, Robert E, 1958, Jl 30,29:4
Andrews, Robert M, 1955, F 20,89:1
Andrews, Robert Mrs, 1949, N 15,25:4
Andrews, Robert S, 1955, N 19,19:5
Andrews, Robert W, 1952, My 30,15:2
Andrews, Rodney D, 1961, Ag 20,87:1
Andrews, Roger M, 1943, Ag 10,19:3
Andrews, Roscoe, 1944, N 8,17:5
Andrews, Roy C (funeral plans, Mr 13,85:1), 1960, Mr 12,1:3
Andrews, Samuel, 1904, Ap 16,1:5
Andrews, Samuel Howe, 1923, F 8,19:5
Andrews, Speer, 1956, Je 5,35:4
Andrews, St George S, 1956, S 1,21:5
Andrews, Steffan, 1953, Jl 3,19:4
Andrews, Susan B Mrs, 1903, S 16,9:6
Andrews, T P Col, 1868, Mr 13,4:7
Andrews, T Wingate Dr, 1937, F 12,23:1
Andrews, Thomas G, 1967, N 6,47:3
Andrews, Thomas H S, 1954, My 24,27:1
Andrews, Thomas S, 1941, D 3,25:5
Andrews, Thomas W, 1952, O 13,21:5
Andrews, W, 1936, S 6,20:1
Andrews, W E B Capt, 1864, Je 20,4:6
Andrews, W E Mrs, 1947, My 7,31:1
Andrews, W Earle (Oct 7), 1965, O 11,61:1
Andrews, W Earle Mrs, 1963, N 2,25:5
Andrews, W S, 1929, Jl 2,27:1
Andrews, Walter E, 1966, S 10,29:4
Andrews, Walter G, 1949, Mr 6,73:1; 1958, Je 1,86:4
Andrews, Walter S, 1946, D 6,23:4
Andrews, Walter S Jr, 1960, Ap 7,35:5
Andrews, Walter S Mrs, 1956, S 5,27:4
Andrews, Walter T, 1957, D 5,35:4
Andrews, Wesley R Col, 1910, F 6,II,11:5
Andrews, Willett B, 1912, F 29,11:5
Andrews, William, 1940, Jl 22,17:6
Andrews, William A Mrs, 1962, F 24,27:2
Andrews, William E, 1922, Jl 10,13:5
Andrews, William H, 1923, Je 21,19:5; 1942, Mr 15, 42:6
Andrews, William H Mrs, 1905, My 5,9:4
Andrews, William L T, 1959, Jl 20,25:2
Andrews, William Loring, 1920, Mr 21,22:3
Andrews, William N, 1923, My 18,19:3; 1937, D 28, 21:1
Andrews, William S, 1912, D 30,7:4; 1941, Jl 5,11:5
Andrews, William V, 1954, S 2,21:2
Andrews, William W, 1942, Mr 15,42:8
Andrews, Winthrop J, 1964, Je 21,84:5
Andrews, Yvette Mrs, 1959, Ap 14,2:4
Andreyeff, Leonid, 1919, S 15,11:6
Andreyev, Leonid, 1919, N 1,11:6
Andreyev, Vassili P, 1950, N 29,33:1
Andriesse, A Albert, 1965, D 22,31:3
Andriesse, Albert Mrs, 1955, S 27,35:1
Andriessen, Willem, 1964, Ap 1,39:2
Andriessen, Wim, 1944, Jl 20,19:6
Andrieu, P P, 1935, F 15,19:4
Andring, Gerhard Mrs, 1944, F 7,15:3
Andring, Gerhard P, 1950, Ap 30,102:5
Andring, John, 1946, Ap 30,21:3
Andromedas, Nicholas J, 1967, Je 15,47:4
Andron, Israel, 1944, My 11,19:6
Andron, Jacob L, 1956, Ja 17,33:5
Andron, Jacob L Mrs, 1948, S 15,31:3
Andron, Martin J, 1946, S 8,46:3
Andron, Philip, 1944, My 23,23:6
Andronov, Alex, 1952, N 2,88:3
Andross, Elmer E, 1950, Ag 23,29:5
Androvette, Charles M, 1943, D 24,13:3
Androvette, William, 1953, Je 4,29:3
Andrus, Alfred D, 1938, F 2,19:5
Andrus, Clift Maj-Gen, 1968, O 2,39:2
Andrus, Elon O, 1949, Ap 30,13:6
Andrus, Ethel Percy, 1967, Jl 15,25:2
Andrus, Frank B, 1942, F 15,45:1
Andrus, Frank Burton Maj, 1924, S 24,19:3
Andrus, Hamlin F, 1957, Jl 11,25:3
Andrus, Harold C, 1965, Ja 19,33:2
Andrus, Harold H Mrs, 1942, S 14,15:3
Andrus, J C Mrs, 1943, Ag 10,19:6
Andrus, J E, 1934, D 27,21:1
Andrus, J Holmes, 1948, Jl 16,19:5
Andrus, John H, 1942, My 2,13:6
Andrus, Vincent D, 1962, Mr 11,87:1
Andrus, Waddel P, 1937, Mr 27,15:6
Andrus, William D, 1951, Ja 21,76:7
Andrus, Winfield, 1962, Mr 25,88:2
Andruss, Alfred A Mrs, 1940, Ja 26,17:5
Andruss, Elias Van Arsdale Brig-Gen, 1910, Ap 5,11:4
Andruss, Frank E, 1943, Mr 3,23:2
Andruss, William H, 1937, Mr 26,22:3
Andrykovich, Michael, 1939, Jl 26,19:5
Andrysiak, Stanley F, 1949, Ja 13,23:1
Andryszak, Jan, 1952, Ap 14,19:6
Ane, Peter F, 1968, N 26,47:2
Anello, Vincent, 1959, Ap 21,35:3
Aneser, Kenneth, 1960, O 25,35:4
Anesius Maurice, Bro (P J Gorman), 1958, Jl 22,27:3
Anethan, Albert d' Baron, 1910, Jl 24,7:6
Anfanger, Ludwig, 1956, Jl 28,17:4
Anfenger, Milton L, 1952, D 11,33:4
Anfuso, Filippo, 1963, D 14,27:6
Anfuso, Ross, 1967, N 23,33:2
Anfuso, Victor L, 1966, D 30,25:1
Angarica, J G, 1878, N 18,8:2
Angarica, J G de (see also Mr 6), 1878, Mr 7,8:1
Angas, W Mack Mrs, 1952, D 13,21:4
Angas, William M, 1960, D 13,31:4
Angel, Charles Fitzhugh, 1917, F 28,11:4
Angel, Jimmy, 1956, D 9,87:4
Angel, John, 1960, O 17,29:2
Angel, John J, 1948, Ap 26,23:4
Angel, John Mrs, 1942, Ja 6,24:2
Angel, Laurance Mrs, 1947, Ap 8,28:2
Angel, William H, 1951, O 31,29:1
Angela, Rev Mother, 1866, S 8,2:2
Angelacci, Frank G, 1965, D 28,25:2
Angelbeck, Chris O Jr, 1942, Jl 12,36:2
Angeles, Bert, 1950, Je 1,27:6
Angelescu, Constantin, 1948, S 15,31:1
Angelescu, Paul, 1949, F 9,27:2
Angeli, Heinrich von, 1925, O 22,25:5
Angelilli, Frank, 1956, F 4,19:2
Angelilli, Frank Mrs, 1958, Mr 26,37:3
Angelin, T W Mrs, 1923, O 26,17:3
Angelina, Praskovya N Mme (Pasha), 1959, Ja 23, 25:1
Angelini, Armando Sen, 1968, Ap 19,47:3
Angelini-Rota, Luigi, 1956, S 3,13:6
Angelis, Edmund M de, 1943, O 27,23:3
Angelis, P de Cardinal, 1877, Jl 9,1:3
Angelis, Salvatore de, 1941, My 17,15:1
Angell, Charles A (will), 1938, Mr 29,21:1
Angell, Charles R, 1953, S 26,17:1
Angell, Edward B, 1947, Ap 24,25:2
Angell, Edwin G, 1903, D 16,9:5
Angell, Frank, 1939, N 3,21:5
Angell, Frank Stanleigh, 1924, Ag 19,15:4
Angell, Frederic Allen, 1903, D 17,9:4
Angell, George Thorndike, 1909, Mr 17,9:3
Angell, Gladys E Mrs, 1962, Jl 22,64:3
Angell, H Kenyon, 1944, My 30,21:3
Angell, Henry P, 1956, S 24,27:1
Angell, J R Mrs, 1931, Je 24,23:1
Angell, James R, 1949, Mr 5,17:1
Angell, Jas B Mrs, 1903, D 18,9:5
Angell, Keith, 1938, D 8,27:5
Angell, Montgomery B, 1959, N 27,29:4
Angell, Norman, 1967, O 9,47:1
Angell, Oscar F Capt, 1864, Je 23,2:3
Angell, Paul, 1938, Je 13,19:3
Angell, Ralph C, 1948, F 26,23:6
Angell, Robert C, 1959, N 28,21:5
Angell, Sallie S Mrs, 1941, Mr 5,21:3
Angell, Sarah L, 1939, Ja 20,19:2
Angell, Sidney L, 1950, Je 2,23:2
Angell, Stephen H, 1950, F 16,23:1
Angell, Stephen L Mrs, 1959, Ag 9,88:4
Angelo, Bro (P Conroy), 1949, My 10,25:3
Angelo, Charles P, 1951, S 13,31:1
Angelo, Robert Prati, 1907, O 12,9:6
Angels, Felipe Mrs, 1919, D 8,15:1
Angelucci, F S Rev, 1937, N 27,17:3
Angelus, Bro, 1922, My 28,22:3
Angelus, Bro (F Curry), 1952, Ag 31,45:1
Angelus, Louis, 1945, Jl 29,39:2
Angelus Gabriel, Bro (J A Cashin), 1958, S 12,25:1
Angelus Thomas, Brother, 1951, My 13,88:6
Angemeier, George, 1902, Je 22,10:1
Angeny, Ferdinand C, 1940, Je 23,30:6
Angeny, Granville L, 1950, Mr 31,32:5
Anger, Edward E, 1962, My 3,33:5
Anger, Harry M, 1963, Jl 24,31:5
Anger, Lou, 1946, My 22,21:4
Angeren, Johannes R M, 1959, Mr 21,21:5
Angers, Auguste Real Sir, 1919, Ap 16,13:2
Angers, Real, 1956, Ja 28,17:7
Angert, Joseph T, 1947, Ag 31,36:6
Angert, Louis V, 1957, Jl 18,25:5
Angevine, Edward, 1912, Ja 14,II,16:2
Angevine, Harry W Sr, 1959, Jl 17,21:5
Angevine, Henry, 1881, S 1,3:3
Angevine, J J, 1903, My 9,9:6
Angevine, Mary, 1949, My 12,31:3
Angevine, Onderdonk, 1904, My 10,9:6
Anghinelli, Edward D, 1943, Ap 30,21:2
Angier, Donald H, 1949, S 5,17:5
Angier, Roswell P, 1946, Je 26,25:5
Angin, Joseph A, 1940, F 14,21:3
Anglada, J Alfred, 1959, D 17,37:5
Angle, Charles M, 1948, My 14,23:2
Angle, Edward J, 1940, Ap 26,21:2
Angle, F Purcell, 1941, F 3,17:3
Angle, Fred E, 1945, O 31,23:4
Angle, George B, 1952, My 28,29:1
Angle, Johnson B, 1946, Mr 8,21:3
Angle, Wesley M, 1960, S 5,15:3
Angleman, Ida, 1937, Ja 26,21:4
Angleman, Winfield S, 1941, Jl 22,19:5
Anglemyer, Howard G, 1953, My 27,31:4
Angler, John C, 1911, O 28,13:5
Anglesey, Lady, 1946, N 5,25:1
Anglesey, Lord, 1905, Mr 15,9:4
Anglim, Daniel F, 1948, O 5,25:3
Anglim, Francis X, 1950, My 4,27:2
Anglin, Basil H Mrs, 1954, N 29,25:4
Anglin, Margaret (Mrs H Hull), 1958, Ja 8,47:1
Angliss, William C, 1957, Je 16,85:1
Anglum, Daniel F Col, 1912, Ja 2,11:5
Anglun, Edward F, 1951, S 22,17:2

Angly, Edward, 1951, D 8,11:1
Angly, Edward Mrs (Eliz), 1968, Jl 31,27:1
Angos, R L, 1949, F 20,60:2
Angott, George, 1945, Je 10,32:3
Angowski, John M, 1951, N 20,31:1
Angrist, Harry Mrs, 1960, O 16,88:8
Angrist, Morris, 1953, Ap 25,15:5
Angstadt, Earl K Mrs, 1952, O 13,21:5
Angsten, Peter J, 1949, O 18,27:1
Angstreich, Mayer, 1951, O 25,29:3
Anguish, Charles A, 1948, N 26,23:4
Angulo, Armand W, 1956, F 23,27:2
Angus, Charles Capt, 1905, Ja 12,7:2
Angus, Charles D Mrs, 1951, N 2,23:4
Angus, Charles Mrs, 1951, Ap 1,92:4
Angus, D Forbes, 1943, Ja 27,21:1
Angus, Frank H, 1939, My 15,17:5
Angus, Howard Mrs, 1948, Ag 31,26:2
Angus, Howard W, 1956, F 13,27:3
Angus, James, 1939, Mr 22,23:3
Angus, John W, 1953, Mr 18,31:4
Angus, R B, 1922, S 18,13:5
Angus, Robert, 1960, Jl 3,32:4
Angus, Robert C, 1954, Ja 7,31:5
Angus, Samuel, 1943, N 18,23:1
Angus, Samuel F, 1908, F 7,7:6
Angus, Walter P, 1945, Ja 14,39:1
Angus, William F, 1951, O 15,25:5
Angus, William T, 1945, Ja 18,19:4
Angus, Willis W, 1958, Ag 29,23:3
Angwin, Francis, 1950, O 20,28:2
Angwin, Stanley, 1959, Ap 23,31:5
Angyal, Joseph Jr, 1954, Je 27,60:3
Anhalt, Duke of, 1904, Ja 25,7:6
Anhalt, Julian, 1955, Ap 16,19:1
Anhalt, Lawrence J, 1946, Ap 23,21:4
Anhalt, Sydney Mrs, 1966, Ap 5,39:1
Anheier, Arthur F, 1951, N 24,28:6
Anheier, Harry D, 1958, Ag 20,27:1
Anheuser, Eberhard, 1963, Jl 30,29:3
Anibal, Samuel G, 1943, D 22,24:3
Anicetus, M, 1948, Ag 22,60:7
Anichkov, Nikolai N, 1964, D 11,39:1
Anido, Severiano M, 1938, D 25,14:5
Anigstein, Ludwik Mrs, 1957, Ap 15,29:3
Anik, Harry, 1959, Ag 31,21:3
Anilionis, Dominick, 1950, N 22,25:4
Anilonis, Donald D, 1950, Ap 1,15:6
Anish, Anth F, 1948, Je 23,27:1
Anisman, James S, 1959, Ag 8,17:4
Anita Maria, Sister (Sisters of St Joseph's), 1955, Mr 15,29:2
Anjou, Gustave, 1942, Mr 3,24:2
Ankenbrand, Frank Sr, 1942, Ap 19,44:2
Ankenbrand, William W, 1945, N 9,19:5
Ankeny, Levi Ex-Sen, 1921, Mr 30,13:6
Anker, Edward R, 1950, D 8,29:2
Anker, Frank P, 1945, Ja 8,17:4
Anker, Fred, 1944, O 31,19:1
Anker, John, 1940, O 12,17:6
Anker, Morris L, 1943, D 23,19:1
Anker, Samuel L, 1941, Jl 9,21:2
Ankerson, Gustav H, 1959, D 22,31:4
Ankrum, Morris, 1964, S 4,29:4
Ann, Sister, 1937, Je 16,23:2
Ann Joseph, Sister, 1937, My 1,19:5
Ann Marita, Mother, 1937, S 27,21:2
Ann of Jesus, Sister (Sarah Flaherty), 1913, Ja 26, 17:2
Anna, Sister (A R McHugh), 1959, O 11,86:8
Anna, Walter, 1952, Je 6,23:4
Anna De Paul, Sister, 1948, Jl 10,15:3
Anna Gabriel, Sister (Hurley), 1965, Mr 18,33:4
Anna Gertrude Forsyth, Sister, 1937, Ag 11,23:2
Anna Mary, Sister (Margt M Doran), 1942, Ja 30, 19:3
Anna Regina, Sister, 1947, Mr 4,26:2
Anna Roselie, Sister, 1937, Je 4,23:2
Anna Vincent, Sister (Mulrooney), 1950, F 18,15:3
Annabel, Floyd W, 1944, Ja 14,19:4
Annabi, Mohammed Ali, 1962, Ap 5,33:4
Annable, Burt A, 1958, F 19,27:4
Annable, Weldon G, 1940, Jl 23,19:5
Annabring, Joseph J, 1959, Ag 29,17:7
Annan, Charles, 1956, Jl 24,25:5
Annan, Elizabeth L Mrs, 1943, Ja 13,23:1
Annan, George H, 1949, D 9,32:4
Annan, John, 1908, O 29,9:5
Annand, Percy N, 1950, Mr 31,32:4
Annear, James, 1946, D 4,38:8
Annenberg, John M, 1941, F 4,21:2
Annenberg, Max, 1941, F 8,15:3
Annenberg, Max J, 1957, Je 28,23:5
Annenberg, Max Mrs, 1963, S 10,39:1
Annenberg, Moses L, 1942, Jl 21,19:1
Annenberg, Moses L Mrs (Sadie F), 1965, Jl 7,37:4
Annenberg, Roger, 1962, Ag 15,31:3
Annenkoff, M Gen, 1899, Ja 23,7:1
Annese, William V, 1951, N 14,31:4
Anneser, Adolphe, 1951, Ja 3,25:1
Annesley, Beresford C B, 1957, Jl 8,23:2
Annesley, Richard Law Mrs, 1905, Mr 18,11:5
Anness, Edward C, 1953, Mr 30,21:4

Annett, Cecil B, 1947, D 9,29:4
Annett, Edward B Mrs, 1937, Mr 31,24:1
Annett, Fred A, 1959, O 17,23:3
Annett, James W, 1951, F 3,15:2
Annette, Sister (S A Rogers), 1953, Ja 30,22:5
Annette, Walter M, 1955, Ag 24,27:2
Annexy, Jaime, 1956, D 17,31:5
Annin, Emma Paddock Mrs, 1925, N 28,15:4
Annin, Joseph P, 1956, D 25,25:1
Annin, William E Jr, 1966, Mr 25,41:3
Annin, William S, 1957, Ap 28,86:6
Annino, Joseph, 1956, F 18,36:3
Annis, Arthur, 1937, Je 10,5:3
Annis, Edith, 1947, Ja 2,28:2
Annis, Ibrahim, 1961, O 19,35:2
Annis, John H, 1962, My 11,31:1
Annis, Newton, 1940, My 31,19:3
Annis, Ralph B, 1953, Ap 14,35:1
Annothe, Maurice, 1937, My 18,23:1
Annunciata, Sister, 1946, Jl 8,29:2
Annunciata, Sister (Donnelly), 1953, S 9,29:1
Annunziata, Augustine J, 1953, N 21,13:4
Annunziato, Nemesio, 1958, My 24,21:5
Annunzio, Gabriele d', 1938, Mr 2,1:2
Ansaldo, Juan A, 1958, Ap 29,29:2
Ansalvi, Michael M Y, 1953, O 13,29:5
Ansart, H Rowena L Mrs, 1942, Jl 23,19:4
Ansbacher, Adolph B (est, F 27,11:3), 1917, F 21, 11:4
Ansbacher, Benno, 1952, O 31,25:4
Ansbacher, Henry C, 1939, My 1,23:4
Ansbacher, Jessie, 1964, Jl 14,33:4
Ansberg, John H, 1954, Je 9,31:3
Ansberry, Timothy T, 1943, Jl 6,21:4
Ansboury, Pat, 1952, S 29,23:2
Anschelewitz, Jacob, 1946, F 22,25:1
Anschuetz, Carl, 1870, D 31,2:3
Anschutz, Lewis R, 1945, S 9,47:3
Anschutz, Thomas P, 1912, Je 17,9:6
Anscombe, E Muriel, 1959, D 16,41:3
Anseele, Edouard, 1938, F 19,15:4
Ansel, Martin F, 1945, Ag 25,11:6
Ansel, Philip, 1963, D 19,33:2
Ansell, A D, 1914, O 22,11:4
Ansell, Henry A, 1949, F 13,77:2
Ansell, Jack, 1955, My 29,44:5
Ansell, John, 1948, D 15,33:3
Ansell, Samuel T, 1954, My 28,23:5
Anselm, August, 1953, O 23,23:5
Anselm, Bro, 1903, Je 24,9:6; 1945, Ag 4,11:3
Anselm, Edwin Bro, 1968, N 23,47:3
Anselma Ruth, Mother (Sisters of St Dominic), 1957, Ja 14,23:2
Ansen, William, 1948, Mr 20,13:5
Ansen, William Mrs, 1947, O 18,15:2
Ansermier, Louis, 1954, F 8,23:3
Anshutz, J Phillip, 1966, Je 29,47:4
Ansin, David, 1950, Jl 2,24:6
Ansley, Clark F, 1939, F 15,23:1
Anslinger, Harry J Mrs, 1961, O 11,47:3
Anslow, William P Jr, 1966, Mr 20,86:6
Anson, Adrian C (funl, Ap 17,17:6), 1922, Ap 15,15:5
Anson, Alfred, 1944, Mr 25,15:2
Anson, Alfred Mrs, 1953, Jl 16,21:4
Anson, Bernard O, 1946, Ag 9,17:6
Anson, Edward H, 1959, N 5,35:3
Anson, Frank Harris, 1923, N 2,17:3
Anson, Grant W, 1942, O 27,25:4
Anson, I Arthur, 1955, Je 12,86:7
Anson, John William H Sir, 1873, Ag 3,1:7
Anson, Lyman Mrs, 1967, Ja 1,52:5
Anson, Raymond S, 1947, Ag 22,15:5
Anson, Ruth E, 1963, My 28,37:2
Anson, Thomas Francis (Earl of Lichfield), 1918, Jl 31,9:5
Anson, William Mrs, 1952, F 12,27:2
Anson, William Reynell Sir, 1914, Je 5,11:5
Ansorge, Herbert C, 1947, D 31,15:2
Ansorge, Martin C, 1967, F 6,29:3
Anspach, Bernard, 1941, Ap 5,17:3
Anspach, Brooke M, 1951, Jl 10,27:2
Anspach, Helene Mlle, 1875, Mr 29,7:4
Anspach, J William, 1958, F 2,86:2
Anspach, Roxanna W Mrs, 1964, Jl 15,35:1
Anspach, Samuel, 1960, F 27,19:3
Anspacher, Louis K, 1947, My 11,60:2
Anspake, George W, 1938, Ag 19,19:1
Anstadt, Peter Rev, 1903, My 13,9:5
Anstay, Arthur H, 1955, N 23,23:3
Anstead, Taylor W, 1937, N 22,19:3
Anstei, D T, 1880, My 22,2:6
Anstendig, Jack, 1957, O 30,29:3
Anstett, Charles E, 1941, Ag 8,15:6
Anstett, Michael A, 1948, S 24,25:3
Anstett, Robert Sr, 1953, D 12,19:6
Anstey, Alfred J, 1945, D 1,23:3
Anstey, Louise L Mrs, 1938, Jl 1,19:4
Anstey, Thomas C, 1873, Ag 14,6:7
Anstice, Henry Rev Dr, 1922, D 19,19:5
Anstice, Josiah, 1920, My 27,11:3
Anstice, Mary R Mrs, 1940, Je 9,44:3
Anstine, Harry B, 1942, O 31,15:2
Anstruther, Robert H, 1938, S 27,21:3

Ant, Morris, 1960, Je 26,72:6
Antal, Eugene, 1952, F 14,27:4
Antas, William, 1953, F 9,27:2
Antek, Samuel, 1958, Ja 28,27:3
Antel, Dorothea, 1938, F 3,24:4
Antell, Anna J Mrs, 1941, D 28,28:6
Antell, Henry, 1960, Ap 25,29:6
Antell, Leon, 1958, Mr 4,29:1
Antell, Samuel H, 1963, D 17,39:3
Antheil, George, 1959, F 13,17:1
Antheil, Henry W, 1945, Je 16,13:3
Anthes, Augustus, 1944, F 10,15:1
Anthes, Christian F, 1947, My 22,27:2
Anthes, Henry G, 1940, N 24,48:3
Anthes, John E, 1958, Mr 16,86:5
Anthes, Lawrence L, 1954, N 24,23:4
Anthes, William F, 1946, Jl 16,23:4
Anthoine, Edward S Mrs, 1965, Je 25,33:1
Anthon, Archibald, 1951, D 15,13:3
Anthon, C E, 1883, Je 9,2:3
Anthon, Emilia, 1877, F 5,8:3
Anthon, Emily, 1903, O 4,7:5
Anthon, John, 1863, Ap 12,6:3
Anthon, John H, 1874, O 30,4:6
Anthon, Judith, 1875, D 7,5:6
Anthon, Prof, 1867, Ag 11,3:5
Anthon, W H, 1875, N 9,4:7
Anthon, William Henry Mrs, 1911, Ap 16,II,11:4
Anthoney, George W, 1937, Mr 18,25:5
Anthony, A F X Mrs, 1958, My 31,15:5
Anthony, Albert W Sr, 1952, Ag 8,17:3
Anthony, Alfred, 1952, Jl 15,21:3
Anthony, Alfred W, 1939, Ja 21,15:1
Anthony, Allen C, 1962, My 11,31:4
Anthony, Aloysius F X, 1943, Mr 25,21:3
Anthony, Ann, 1962, O 10,51:1
Anthony, Arthur H, 1940, Mr 1,21:1
Anthony, Benjamin, 1906, N 7,9:5
Anthony, Bessie (Mrs Bernard C Horne), 1912, N 23,15:6
Anthony, Bro (Herr), 1964, Mr 26,35:1
Anthony, Brother, 1939, Je 14,23:2
Anthony, Charles H, 1921, N 2,17:5
Anthony, Charles L (trb), 1874, My 28,4:6
Anthony, Charles Prof, 1867, Jl 30,4:7
Anthony, Claude, 1951, O 17,32:6
Anthony, Clifford M, 1949, Jl 7,25:1
Anthony, D R Col, 1875, My 23,10:5
Anthony, D R Jr, 1931, Ag 5,19:5
Anthony, Dan Reed, 1904, N 13,7:7
Anthony, Daniel, 1940, F 21,19:2
Anthony, Daniel R 4th, 1959, Je 27,12:4
Anthony, E Peter Mrs, 1966, Mr 4,33:4
Anthony, Earle C, 1961, Ag 8,29:4
Anthony, Earle C Mrs, 1954, Mr 29,19:4
Anthony, Elisabeth M, 1964, Jl 1,35:5
Anthony, Elizabeth, 1954, My 12,31:5
Anthony, Elizabeth S Mrs, 1937, Mr 28,II,8:8
Anthony, Ella T Mrs, 1938, S 10,17:6
Anthony, Emile P, 1961, S 11,27:3
Anthony, Francis, 1903, Ag 30,1:1
Anthony, Francis W, 1951, Mr 29,27:2
Anthony, Frank, 1942, N 20,23:2
Anthony, Frank L, 1938, D 17,15:6
Anthony, Gardner C Dr, 1937, N 29,23:6
Anthony, George J, 1950, Je 15,31:4
Anthony, Geraldine W, 1912, O 21,11:6
Anthony, Graham H, 1967, D 29,27:1
Anthony, H B, 1884, S 3,2:2
Anthony, H T, 1884, O 12,2:5
Anthony, Henry A, 1948, Je 25,23:3
Anthony, Henry Mark, 1915, My 8,15:5
Anthony, Henry S, 1952, My 7,27:3
Anthony, Hubert L, 1957, Jl 14,72:6
Anthony, J G Prof, 1877, O 28,3:7
Anthony, Jack, 1954, Jl 11,73:1
Anthony, Jack M, 1967, Je 15,47:3
Anthony, James, 1876, Ja 13,4:7
Anthony, Joseph J, 1941, Jl 8,19:5
Anthony, Julia B, 1944, Je 28,23:2
Anthony, Katharine, 1965, N 22,37:1
Anthony, Leonard H, 1937, Jl 23,19:4
Anthony, Lucy, 1944, Jl 6,15:7
Anthony, Luke, 1950, O 31,27:3
Anthony, Luther B, 1955, Ap 21,29:2
Anthony, Mary B, 1947, My 23,23:5
Anthony, Mary Mrs, 1906, N 3,9:4
Anthony, Mary S, 1907, F 6,9:7
Anthony, Nicholas Walter, 1919, D 3,15:1
Anthony, Norman, 1968, Ja 22,44:2
Anthony, Orville, 1950, Mr 5,92:3
Anthony, Owen, 1941, S 13,17:4
Anthony, Rev Bro (Wm W Brynes), 1915, Mr 16,11:4
Anthony, Robert L, 1950, N 17,27:4
Anthony, Robert W, 1960, Jl 9,19:4
Anthony, S Reed, 1914, Mr 11,11:5
Anthony, Stuart, 1942, Ap 30,19:5
Anthony, Susan Brownell (funl, Mr 16,9:4; will, Mr 18,11:1), 1906, Mr 13,1:3
Anthony, Theodore V W, 1954, Jl 20,19:3
Anthony, Thomas G, 1937, Ja 30,17:2
Anthony, Watson S, 1955, Jl 24,64:2
Anthony, Wilfrid E, 1948, Jl 25,49:2

Anthony, William A Prof, 1908, Ap 30,7:6
Anthony, William G W Rev Dr, 1953, F 19,23:2
Anthony, Willis B, 1949, Ap 5,29:1
Anthony Marie, Sister (Sisters of St Francis of Allegany), 1955, Mr 23,31:3
Antiga, Juan, 1939, F 10,23:1
Antikainen, Eero, 1960, Ja 13,2:7
Antin, Benjamin, 1956, O 23,33:3
Antin, Harry, 1968, Ag 5,39:3
Antin, Mary, 1949, My 18,27:3
Antinello, Anthony F, 1968, Ja 13,31:3
Antinori, H Marquis, 1882, N 5,8:7
Antisdale, Louis M, 1923, Je 29,17:2
Antisdel, Clarence B, 1943, O 29,19:2
Antkies, Murray, 1960, My 16,31:5
Antl, F William, 1950, O 12,31:3
Antliff, Joseph A, 1941, D 12,25:4
Antmann, Isaak, 1957, N 8,29:3
Antoine, Andre, 1943, O 22,17:5
Antoine, Charles, 1939, Je 20,21:2
Antoine, La Vern, 1949, N 21,25:5
Antoine, Lucien, 1916, Ag 20,15:5
Antoine, Marguerite, 1953, O 21,29:3
Antoine, Maurice P, 1955, My 13,25:3
Antokal, Jack I, 1968, Ap 11,45:4
Antolini, Dante, 1968, D 20,47:2
Antolini, Dante Mrs, 1952, My 13,23:2
Anton, Benjamin D, 1955, Ap 24,87:1
Anton, Carl M, 1950, Ja 16,26:3
Anton, Francis L, 1951, Jl 31,21:2
Anton, George, 1941, Mr 2,43:1
Anton, Percival J, 1948, Jl 29,21:2
Antonelli, Amerigo, 1948, N 12,23:5
Antonelli, Camillo Count, 1916, N 21,11:3
Antoni, Adolph, 1959, My 4,29:4
Antonia, Princess of Bavaria, 1954, Ag 2,17:4
Antonini, Luigi, 1968, D 30,31:2
Antonini, Luigi Mrs, 1966, N 21,45:2
Antoninus Leo, Bro (Bros of the Christian Schools), 1966, My 4,47:5
Antonius, Bro (Saml Jaquay), 1925, Ja 27,13:2
Antonov, Aleksei I, 1962, Je 20,35:1
Antonov, N V, 1948, O 27,27:2
Antonucci, Cardinal, 1879, Ja 29,5:4
Antony, Charles L Mrs, 1949, F 22,24:2
Antony, Emile, 1940, F 6,21:3
Antony of Mary, Bro, 1959, O 2,29:3
Antor, Albert, 1964, Ja 27,23:3
Antos, Istvan, 1960, Ja 6,35:3
Antouelli, Giacomo Cardinal, 1876, N 7,4:6
Antoville, Louis, 1942, D 2,25:3
Antrim, B Frank, 1942, F 18,19:2
Antrim, Clarence D, 1937, My 1,19:5
Antrim, Countess of, 1949, Ap 5,29:4
Antrim, Doron K, 1960, D 6,37:1
Antrim, Doron K Mrs, 1964, S 3,29:2
Antrim, Elbert M, 1961, D 10,88:4
Antrim, Eugene M, 1953, Je 5,27:5
Antrim, Harold T, 1947, Ap 29,27:3
Antrim, Hugh S Sr, 1942, Jl 6,15:6
Antrim, Lillian Mrs, 1941, F 15,15:6
Antrim, William L, 1941, Ag 6,17:2
Antsey, Thomas W, 1937, D 28,21:2
Anurov, Peter V, 1950, Mr 6,21:4
Anuskewicz, Benjamin T, 1967, Je 4,86:5
Anuskewicz, Frank J, 1940, Ap 25,23:4
Anway, Harry B, 1938, Jl 31,33:3
Anwyl, Edward Sir, 1914, Ag 10,7:5
Anyan, Walter R, 1957, Jl 28,61:3
Anzalone, Carmine P, 1968, Je 1,27:4
Anzani, Alessandro, 1956, Jl 25,29:1
Anzelowitz, Louis, 1955, D 18,92:5
Anzer, John Sr, 1946, Je 4,23:1
Anziano, Marco, 1951, Jl 11,23:4
Anziano, Samuel, 1964, Mr 15,86:5
Anzilotti, Dionisio, 1950, Ag 26,13:2
Anzueto, Manuel Mrs, 1946, F 7,23:2
Aosta, Duke of, 1931, Jl 5,13:1; 1942, Mr 4,19:1; 1948, Ja 30,23:1
Aparicio, Julio, 1960, Ag 5,23:3
Apel, Adolph E, 1941, Ag 10,37:3
Apel, Gustave E, 1941, Ap 5,17:5
Apelbaum, Murray, 1960, O 6,41:5
Apelgreen, Carl E, 1950, D 28,26:4
Apelles, Jasper Bro (J L Scanlon), 1944, F 21,15:1
Apenszlak, Jacob, 1950, Mr 30,29:2
Apery, Telemaque E d' Col, 1913, N 18,11:6
Apetz, William R, 1954, Ja 29,19:3
Apezteguia, Marquis, 1902, Ap 16,9:5
Apfel, Arthur H Mrs, 1944, Jl 31,13:5
Apfel, Benjamin, 1951, Je 11,25:4
Apfel, Charles L, 1947, Ap 18,21:3
Apfel, Isadore, 1950, Ap 23,96:2
Apfel, M Marion, 1956, Mr 6,31:4
Apfel, Oscar C, 1938, Mr 23,23:4
Apfel, Sidney K, 1950, Ap 23,96:2
Apfel, William H, 1943, D 20,23:1
Apfelbach, Carl W, 1943, Je 27,32:1
Apfelbaum, Leon J, 1954, O 20,30:1
Apfelbaum, Murray, 1952, Mr 3,21:5
Apfelbaum, Violette C, 1940, S 13,23:3
Apfelroth, Mortimer D, 1955, N 25,27:3
Apgar, Andrew M Mrs, 1951, O 30,29:1
Apgar, Charles E, 1950, Ag 19,13:4
Apgar, Chester P Sr, 1955, Je 24,21:4
Apgar, F K, 1885, Ag 19,5:4
Apgar, Francis A, 1941, Ja 1,23:3
Apgar, Frank L, 1945, D 3,21:2; 1956, Je 1,23:3
Apgar, Fred R, 1950, S 23,17:3
Apgar, Frederick W, 1953, Jl 16,21:5
Apgar, George L Mrs, 1951, S 3,13:4
Apgar, George W, 1963, Je 25,33:2
Apgar, Harry C, 1947, My 27,25:3
Apgar, Harry S Mrs, 1965, Ag 2,29:2
Apgar, Howard G Mrs, 1952, Ja 21,15:3
Apgar, Howard W, 1964, My 27,39:4
Apgar, James K, 1940, S 22,48:3
Apgar, John V, 1954, Ja 31,89:1
Apgar, Leon A, 1950, My 24,29:2
Apgar, LeRoy Howard, 1968, Jl 10,39:3
Apgar, Lester E Mrs, 1949, Ap 27,27:5
Apgar, Mahlon, 1940, My 8,23:3
Apgar, Neaf, 1949, My 1,88:8
Apgar, Peter E, 1947, O 12,76:3
Apgar, Willard N, 1946, Jl 21,40:3
Apgar, Willard R, 1949, Ja 25,23:5
Apice, Parito, 1961, Jl 26,31:1
Apicella, James, 1952, Mr 15,7:7
Apisdorf, Louis, 1967, N 8,47:3
Aplanalp, Elbert E, 1944, S 25,17:2
Apley, Levi H, 1943, Mr 11,21:6
Aplustille, Frank H, 1940, F 15,19:3
Apollinaire, Guillaume Mrs, 1967, Ag 23,51:7
Apollinary, Archbishop, 1933, Je 20,19:4
Aposporos, George T, 1957, Mr 29,21:3
Apostle, Nicholas C, 1968, O 5,35:5
Apostol, Macedonian leader, 1905, Mr 17,3:3
Apostolos, Gus, 1953, O 11,88:6
Apostolu, Demetrios, 1943, Jl 10,13:5
App, Daniel W, 1945, Mr 20,19:5
App, Frank, 1967, Ja 2,19:3
App, John W, 1955, Jl 14,23:5
Appel, A Hirst, 1945, Mr 15,23:5
Appel, Alex, 1948, Ap 11,72:3
Appel, Anna, 1963, N 21,39:3
Appel, Augusta Mrs, 1940, N 25,17:2
Appel, Charles P, 1939, Mr 24,21:1
Appel, Daniel Mitchell Col, 1914, Ap 25,15:6
Appel, David H Mrs, 1958, F 18,27:4
Appel, Edward, 1940, D 28,15:2
Appel, Gerold J, 1965, Jl 4,37:1
Appel, Harry J, 1950, Ap 21,23:5
Appel, Irving I, 1958, S 9,35:3
Appel, Isaac H, 1937, My 25,27:3
Appel, John J E (funl, Ja 13,27:4), 1955, Ja 11,25:4
Appel, John W Jr, 1942, Ag 26,19:3
Appel, Joseph H, 1949, Jl 27,23:1
Appel, Joseph Mrs, 1953, D 25,17:2
Appel, Louis, 1966, My 7,31:4
Appel, Michael G, 1944, Mr 3,15:2
Appel, Nancy E, 1962, Ag 3,23:5
Appel, Reuben B, 1940, D 1,62:2
Appel, Ronald B, 1945, F 12,20:2
Appel, Sidney J, 1964, S 7,19:3
Appel, Theodore P Dr, 1937, Ag 1,II,7:1
Appel, William N, 1937, O 11,21:5
Appelbaum, Joseph H, 1955, Mr 3,27:2
Appelbaum, Myer Rev, 1937, Ag 22,II,7:1
Appelbaum, Nat Mrs, 1956, N 23,27:1
Appelbaum, Sam A, 1953, F 25,27:3
Appelbaum, Sol J, 1945, Ap 11,23:6
Appelbee, Frank J, 1962, Mr 28,39:4
Appelby, T Frank Mrs, 1950, Je 30,23:4
Appelius, Mario, 1946, D 29,35:8
Appell, Agnes S Mrs, 1937, O 6,25:1
Appell, Albert J, 1950, O 2,23:4
Appell, Charles, 1958, O 2,37:5
Appell, Charles J, 1944, Ja 2,38:4
Appell, G, 1929, Ja 20,29:4
Appell, Harry S, 1965, N 20,35:6
Appell, James S, 1964, S 15,37:3
Appell, Louis J, 1951, Je 25,19:4
Appell, Paul D, 1938, Je 29,19:4
Appell, Samuel I Dr, 1968, N 16,37:1
Appelman, Herman, 1960, N 28,31:2
Appelo, Samuel N, 1950, Ap 4,29:2
Appelt, Ewald P, 1954, Ag 11,25:4
Appelt, Frank R, 1939, F 19,39:2
Appelt, Frank R Mrs, 1937, My 4,25:3
Appelt, Rudolf, 1955, Jl 3,32:1
Appelton, D, 1929, Mr 16,19:3
Appenheim, Samson D, 1921, D 11,22:3
Appenzellar, Donald C, 1941, Jl 1,23:5
Appenzellar, Paul, 1953, Ag 18,23:1
Appenzeller, Alice, 1950, F 22,29:5
Appenzeller, Charles D, 1950, Ja 26,27:4
Appenzeller, Kenneth, 1947, Ja 18,15:6
Apperman, Isaac, 1952, Mr 18,27:1
Apperson, Edgar L, 1959, My 14,33:1
Apperson, Elbert C Mrs, 1948, O 5,25:5
Apperson, Harvey B, 1948, F 3,25:1
Apperson, John Mrs, 1952, Je 16,17:2
Apperson, R W Mrs, 1904, Ja 23,9:5
Appert, Edward P, 1943, F 6,13:4
Appey, Carl P Sr, 1952, Ja 28,24:2
Appino, Felix, 1956, D 13,37:2
Apple, B F Rev, 1914, N 23,11:5
Apple, Henry H, 1943, My 20,21:2
Apple, Herman, 1938, O 14,23:4
Apple, Theodore Rev Dr, 1907, S 29,9:6
Applebaum, Emanuel, 1948, D 10,25:3
Applebaum, Henry, 1944, Ja 29,13:5
Applebaum, Jack, 1962, Jl 19,27:2
Applebaum, Jacob, 1966, N 14,41:5
Applebaum, Julius, 1960, My 8,88:7
Applebaum, Max, 1939, Mr 7,21:4
Applebaum, Ralph, 1963, O 8,43:1
Applebaum, William Mrs, 1948, S 17,26:2
Applebee, Ellen O Mrs, 1908, Ja 12,9:5
Applebee, J Kay Rev, 1903, Ap 25,9:4
Applebome, Louis A, 1961, Ja 9,39:5
Appleby, Alfred N, 1965, Mr 25,37:2
Appleby, Bertram G, 1954, D 5,89:1
Appleby, Charles E, 1913, D 17,11:5
Appleby, Charles H, 1956, S 6,25:5
Appleby, Edgar O Mrs, 1959, Ap 5,86:6
Appleby, Edgar T, 1958, O 25,21:1
Appleby, Forrest L, 1941, Je 20,21:5
Appleby, John D, 1938, D 7,23:2
Appleby, John S, 1950, My 30,17:5
Appleby, John S Mrs, 1945, Ja 19,20:2
Appleby, John T, 1945, Ap 2,19:4
Appleby, Lucien O, 1910, O 5,11:6
Appleby, Paul A, 1967, My 7,87:1
Appleby, Paul H, 1963, O 22,37:3
Appleby, Phil T Mrs, 1954, S 16,21:5
Appleby, Ralph Q, 1937, Mr 19,23:4
Appleby, Robert R, 1966, Jl 4,15:5
Appleby, Scott B, 1965, Mr 22,33:2
Appleby, T Frank, 1924, D 16,25:4
Appleby, Theodore F, 1964, Ap 18,29:3
Appleby, Troy W, 1947, Ap 22,27:6
Appleby, William R, 1941, Ap 9,25:6
Applegarth, Robert, 1924, Jl 14,15:4
Applegate, Charles L, 1950, F 9,29:3
Applegate, Chester A, 1944, F 11,19:2
Applegate, Daniel B, 1909, Je 4,7:5
Applegate, Daniel H, 1947, Ap 12,17:4
Applegate, Elias H, 1939, O 17,25:3
Applegate, George E, 1949, Ag 28,72:5
Applegate, George Jr, 1948, Ag 25,25:3
Applegate, George S, 1947, Jl 29,21:4; 1955, S 27,35:1
Applegate, Grover T, 1946, N 5,25:5
Applegate, Hamilton C, 1960, S 10,21:2
Applegate, Harold R, 1944, Ag 24,13:1
Applegate, Harry E, 1949, Mr 8,25:1
Applegate, Howard T, 1961, My 27,38:1
Applegate, John D, 1941, My 8,23:3
Applegate, John J Sr, 1950, Je 18,76:3
Applegate, John S Sr, 1950, Mr 24,25:3
Applegate, Mary C, 1944, Ja 9,42:1
Applegate, Melbourne S, 1953, Je 23,29:3
Applegate, Paul C, 1948, O 23,15:2
Applegate, Paul R, 1962, D 6,43:4
Applegate, Theodore E, 1955, My 27,23:6
Applegate, William, 1905, Je 27,9:5
Applegate, William B, 1943, My 16,43:2
Applegate, William S, 1940, F 7,21:3
Applegate, Wilton T, 1941, D 19,25:2
Applegath, A, 1871, F 28,2:4
Appleget, Helen G Mrs, 1942, D 11,23:4
Appleget, Lee R, 1948, N 18,28:3
Appleman, Earl (por), 1938, Jl 14,21:5
Appleman, Glen, 1958, N 30,87:2
Applequist, Eric J, 1957, Je 29,17:6
Appler, Walter F, 1956, S 14,23:3
Applestein, Harry J, 1962, Mr 4,86:3
Applestone, Leon, 1949, O 14,27:3
Appleton, Adeline C Mrs, 1958, N 7,28:4
Appleton, Arthur, 1960, O 27,37:5
Appleton, Arthur B, 1950, Ap 23,95:2
Appleton, Bertram A, 1957, Mr 9,19:5
Appleton, Carolyn T, 1948, N 22,21:4
Appleton, Charles A, 1943, My 12,25:5
Appleton, Charles Lanier Maj (funl, D 9,17:5), 1921, D 8,19:5
Appleton, Charles W, 1945, Ja 11,23:1
Appleton, Charles W Mrs, 1958, O 22,35:4
Appleton, Chester F, 1958, S 10,33:4
Appleton, Clifford de P, 1939, Mr 18,17:6
Appleton, Daniel F, 1904, F 6,2:3
Appleton, Daniel Sidney, 1908, Mr 19,7:5
Appleton, David McL Mrs, 1960, Ag 30,29:4
Appleton, Edward D, 1942, Ja 30,20:3
Appleton, Edward V, 1965, Ap 23,35:3
Appleton, Floyd F, 1952, Mr 19,29:5
Appleton, Floyd Mrs, 1954, Ag 10,19:4
Appleton, Francis H, 1939, Ap 6,25:2
Appleton, Frank H, 1946, Ag 20,28:3
Appleton, Franklin F, 1951, S 20,31:3
Appleton, Frederick P, 1963, S 24,39:2
Appleton, G L F Mrs, 1878, Jl 31,2:7
Appleton, G S (funl), 1878, Jl 7,7:3
Appleton, George A, 1952, Ag 17,77:2
Appleton, George M, 1951, Jl 8,60:1
Appleton, George N, 1949, Ag 19,17:2
Appleton, George Webb, 1909, Je 15,7:4
Appleton, H Sargent, 1956, D 2,86:2
Appleton, Henry Cozzen, 1925, Mr 18,21:4

Appleton, J A, 1881, Jl 14,2:4
Appleton, James W, 1942, Ag 27,19:4
Appleton, Jean W, 1939, Je 16,23:2
Appleton, John, 1939, O 11,30:2
Appleton, John A, 1966, D 6,47:1
Appleton, John B, 1953, Je 25,27:5
Appleton, John C, 1960, Je 23,29:2
Appleton, John T, 1943, N 22,19:4
Appleton, John W M Gen, 1913, O 28,11:6
Appleton, Joseph W, 1958, Ja 16,29:2
Appleton, Libbie E, 1939, Je 15,23:2
Appleton, Louis R, 1953, Ja 20,25:1
Appleton, Margaret S, 1962, Jl 28,19:5
Appleton, Montauk, 1915, My 22,11:4
Appleton, Paul, 1948, D 26,52:6
Appleton, R R, 1928, F 14,23:5
Appleton, Ralph, 1961, Mr 16,37:4
Appleton, Randolph, 1940, Jl 27,13:6
Appleton, Rev, 1873, D 2,8:4
Appleton, Robert (will, Mr 28,17:3), 1945, Ja 20,11:1
Appleton, Robert Mrs, 1948, O 14,30:3
Appleton, S F, 1883, O 26,4:7
Appleton, Samuel, 1925, My 23,15:6
Appleton, T G, 1884, Ap 18,5:4
Appleton, W H, 1899, O 20,7:1
Appleton, William C, 1940, N 4,19:4
Appleton, William Gardiner, 1920, Ap 8,11:4
Appleton, William H, 1951, Ag 5,72:4
Appleton, William Worthen, 1924, Ja 28,15:3
Appleton, Wolf, 1962, F 26,27:1
Appley, Clarence W Lt, 1918, S 16,11:6
Appley, Joseph E, 1945, O 24,21:2
Appleyard, Margaret, 1944, N 11,13:5
Appleyard, Rollo, 1943, Mr 3,24:2
Applin, George F, 1950, F 3,23:1
Applington, Horace F, 1952, My 24,19:5
Appo, Alice M M, 1953, O 16,27:3
Appo, Garnette B Mrs, 1954, Jl 25,69:2
Appo, Locksley A, 1943, N 6,13:2
Appollonio, Theron A, 1939, D 23,15:3
Apponyi, A (Count), 1933, F 8,19:3
Apps, Edward, 1946, Ap 18,27:1
Apps, Josiah O, 1941, Ag 14,17:6
Appuzzo, Cardinal, 1880, Jl 31,5:2
Appy, Henry, 1903, N 17,9:6
April, Abraham, 1964, Mr 15,86:1
April, Elsie, 1950, Mr 19,92:3
April, Phil, 1957, N 5,31:4
Apropo, Jack J, 1957, Mr 9,19:1
Apsley, Viola, 1966, Ja 21,47:3
Apt, Milburn G, 1956, S 28,1:3
Apted, Charles R, 1941, Je 6,21:1
Apter, Ellie M, 1947, F 21,19:3
Aptheker, Alex, 1955, My 30,13:4
Aptheker, Beckie Mrs, 1942, Jl 18,13:6
Apthorp, Charles H, 1953, Jl 14,27:3
Apthorp, John V, 1939, S 26,23:5
Apthorp, William F, 1913, F 22,11:5
Apy, Chester, 1958, Je 8,88:5
Aquamarian, Louis, 1947, Jl 30,15:7
Aquaro, John, 1940, O 18,21:4
Aquaro-Deodati, Beniamino, 1960, N 24,29:1
Aquillar, Henry Mrs, 1914, My 2,9:5
Aquinata, Sister (Dominican), 1964, O 17,29:5
Aquino, Michael Mrs, 1945, D 25,23:5
Ara, U, 1936, D 27,II,6:3
Arabi Pasha, Ahmed, 1911, S 22,11:5
Arabian, Krikor, 1951, Ja 31,25:2
Arace, Albert, 1965, F 10,41:1
Arace, Dominick, 1954, D 28,23:1
Arace, Pasquale, 1958, O 6,31:3
Arago, Francois, 1937, Mr 9,23:2
Aragon, Angel, 1952, Ja 26,13:5
Aragona, Stanley M, 1965, Je 3,35:4
Arai, Kampoo, 1945, Ap 25,23:2
Arai, Kentaro, 1938, Ja 30,II,9:2
Arai, Riochiro Mrs, 1949, Je 12,76:1
Arai, Rioichiro, 1939, Ap 11,23:2
Arak, Samuel, 1957, Mr 25,25:2
Arakelian, Krikor, 1951, F 27,28:4
Arakelian, Krikor Mrs, 1947, F 28,24:2
Araki, Eikichi, 1959, F 1,84:8
Araki, Sadao, 1966, N 3,39:1
Aramanda, Joseph Mrs, 1946, O 7,31:5
Arambarri, Jesus, 1960, Jl 12,35:1
Arana, Felipe N, 1962, Je 4,29:3
Arana, Guillermo B, 1939, Jl 5,17:3
Arana, Julio, 1952, S 13,17:2
Araneta, Jorge L, 1940, Je 1,15:3
Aranez, Maria A S, 1939, N 2,23:5
Arango, Carmelo, 1942, F 10,19:5
Arango, Francisco, 1943, Mr 8,15:3
Aranguren, Antonio, 1954, S 2,21:2
Aranha, Da Graca, 1956, Ja 4,27:4
Aranha, Luiza D V Mrs, 1948, Je 2,30:3
Aranha, Oswaldo (funeral, Ja 29,25:4), 1960, Ja 28, 31:1
Aranow, Harry, 1952, Ag 2,15:3
Arant, Herschel W, 1941, Ja 15,23:2
Arant, Walter S, 1949, My 6,25:1
Arantes, Ronaldo D, 1959, S 8,27:1
Arantzadi, Angracio de, 1937, F 14,34:6
Aranyi, Francis, 1966, My 7,31:1
Araquistain, Luis, 1959, Ag 7,23:2
Arar, Raymond, 1962, Ap 27,35:3
Arata, Antonio, 1948, Ag 26,22:2
Arata, George F Mrs, 1949, Ja 18,24:2
Arata, Joseph, 1937, F 2,23:5
Arata, Joseph S Jr, 1946, Ag 27,27:1
Arata, Joseph S Mrs, 1954, Ja 27,27:4
Arata, Ubaldo, 1947, D 13,15:1
Arator, Bro, 1947, Je 9,21:2
Aratow, Michael, 1956, Mr 20,23:1
Araujo, Abraham, 1951, Je 23,15:2
Araujo, Alfonso, 1961, F 5,81:2
Araujo, Arturo, 1967, D 3,84:2
Araujo, Miguel A, 1942, Ag 3,15:6
Araulio, Manuel Justice, 1924, Jl 27,23:4
Aravjo, Armando, 1958, N 22,21:1
Arbaiza, John M, 1955, D 7,39:1
Arberg, Carl P, 1961, N 24,28:5
Arbes, Spero, 1946, D 15,77:1
Arbib-Costa, Alfonso, 1950, N 17,27:4
Arbiter, Emanuel, 1951, Je 14,27:5
Arbiter, Joseph Mrs, 1961, Jl 23,69:3
Arbiter, Leo, 1953, Ja 13,27:3
Arbogast, Albert J Sr, 1955, Ag 11,21:5
Arbogast, George A, 1950, Je 6,29:3
Arbogast, Glen E, 1961, Ag 26,17:6
Arboit, Ennio, 1954, S 13,23:3
Arborio-Mella di St Elia, Alberto, 1953, Mr 21,17:3
Arbos, E Fernandez, 1939, Jl 11,45:1
Arbour, Joseph, 1944, My 15,19:4
Arbuckle, Alex W, 1937, Jl 25,II,7:5
Arbuckle, James, 1921, Je 2,13:4
Arbuckle, James W, 1947, Ja 27,23:4
Arbuckle, John, 1912, Mr 28,11:3; 1912, Mr 30,13:5
Arbuckle, M, 1883, My 24,5:1
Arbuckle, Marion A, 1940, My 6,17:4
Arbuckle, Mary Alice, 1907, Je 25,7:6
Arbuckle, R C, 1933, Je 30,17:4
Arbuckle, W Chantler, 1948, F 19,23:3
Arbuckle, W Dewitt, 1937, S 3,17:6
Arbuckle, Woodruff J, 1955, Jl 21,23:6
Arbuckley, Howard B, 1945, Jl 21,11:5
Arbuse, David Mrs, 1957, Je 18,33:4
Arbuthnot, Charles Jr, 1940, Jl 27,13:4
Arbuthnot, Charles 3d, 1951, Ja 3,27:5
Arbuthnot, Duane, 1952, My 9,23:3
Arbuthnot, Harold N, 1955, O 15,15:5
Arbuthnot, Thomas S, 1956, D 3,39:2
Arbuthnot, Wilson S, 1938, N 2,24:2
Arbuzov, Aleksandr Y Prof, 1968, Ja 24,42:4
Arcadius, Arthur Bro, 1907, D 23,9:5
Arcand, Didace, 1952, F 14,27:5
Arcaris, Gaetano, 1941, O 15,21:6
Arcaro, Flavia, 1937, Ap 9,21:2
Arce, Jose Dr, 1968, Jl 29,20:1
Arce Arnao, Juan, 1948, Ag 6,17:6
Arce de Gomez, Encarnacion Mrs, 1942, My 9,13:4
Arce y Ochotorena, Manuel, 1948, S 17,25:2
Arcedeckne, Andrew, 1871, Je 7,1:7
Arcenius, Bro (Finnegan), 1964, Je 25,33:1
Arcentales, Louis A, 1946, S 14,7:4
Arcese, Alfonso, 1949, D 29,26:3; 1950, Ja 1,42:5
Arcese, Gaetano, 1953, D 24,15:4
Arcese, Peter A, 1941, My 29,19:3
Arcese, Vincent J, 1946, Jl 8,29:2
Archaimbaud, Joseph, 1941, My 31,11:5
Archainbaud, George, 1959, F 21,21:6
Archambault, A Margaretta, 1956, Jl 1,56:6
Archambault, Alberic A, 1950, N 27,25:3
Archambault, Albert E Sr, 1957, F 17,92:5
Archambault, Catherine V Mrs, 1951, O 30,29:1
Archambault, Charles F, 1937, N 3,23:2
Archambault, E J, 1940, Ag 12,15:5
Archambault, Frank A, 1912, N 13,15:4
Archambault, Gaston H, 1951, My 22,31:3
Archambault, Horace Sir, 1918, Ag 27,9:7
Archambault, J B, 1937, N 3,23:6
Archambault, James E, 1962, F 28,33:4
Archambault, John Rev, 1910, D 24,9:6
Archambault, Serephin, 1949, N 23,29:2
Archambault, Thomas J H, 1941, Ap 15,23:3
Archambeault, L J Dr, 1902, Ja 24,3:4
Archambo, David P, 1952, F 29,23:2
Archambualt, La Salle, 1940, S 29,44:2
Archard, Howell O Mrs, 1960, Jl 10,72:1
Archard, Percy, 1962, Je 3,60:1
Archbald, Charles E, 1940, N 9,17:4
Archbald, Geoffrey, 1938, D 6,17:2
Archbald, Harry R, 1951, Ap 20,29:2
Archbishop of Canterbury, 1868, O 29,4:7
Archbold, Anne Mrs, 1968, Mr 28,47:3
Archbold, Armar E, 1957, Jl 22,19:4
Archbold, George, 1907, S 18,9:6
Archbold, J F, 1930, Ja 7,31:1
Archbold, John D, 1916, D 6,9:3
Archbold, John D Mrs, 1939, Je 24,17:5
Archbold, May B Mrs, 1939, D 12,27:5
Archbold, Michael J, 1961, Jl 21,23:2
Archbold, Paul L, 1960, Ag 1,23:5
Archbold, William K, 1948, O 27,27:5
Archdale, Edward, 1943, N 4,23:3
Archdeacon, Ernest, 1950, Ja 4,35:5
Archdeacon, John P, 1941, My 21,23:4
Archdeacon, Maurice J, 1954, S 6,15:2
Archdeacon, Peter M, 1937, Ag 20,17:4
Archduchess Sophia of Austria, 1872, My 29,1:6
Archduke Albrecht of Austria, 1872, S 13,4:4
Archduke Charles Ferdinand of Austria, 1874, N 21, 1:2
Archer, Benjamin H, 1956, Ag 30,25:1
Archer, Charles, 1923, Ag 18,9:6
Archer, Clement C, 1942, Mr 1,45:1
Archer, F Morse, 1950, F 3,24:2
Archer, Finch R, 1938, D 4,60:5
Archer, Francis L, 1949, O 21,25:2
Archer, Frank, 1947, N 29,13:3
Archer, Frank M, 1937, Ap 9,21:3
Archer, George, 1960, S 22,27:5
Archer, George D Judge, 1907, My 1,9:6
Archer, George E, 1903, D 5,9:4
Archer, George F, 1943, O 5,25:5
Archer, Georgia A Mrs, 1952, F 28,27:3
Archer, Harold P Mrs, 1942, Ja 14,21:5
Archer, Harry (will), 1940, N 17,28:5
Archer, Harry, 1960, Ap 24,88:1
Archer, Harry M, 1954, My 18,29:1
Archer, Henry B, 1905, Ap 1,11:5
Archer, Herman N, 1947, Ag 17,54:2
Archer, Isaac J, 1945, F 22,27:3
Archer, James, 1904, S 6,7:4
Archer, James J, 1921, My 25,17:4; 1958, Mr 2,88:7
Archer, Jimmy, 1958, Mr 31,27:4
Archer, John, 1956, F 17,21:1
Archer, John A, 1963, Ag 22,27:1
Archer, John B, 1954, F 7,88:5
Archer, John C, 1957, Jl 8,23:5
Archer, John G, 1939, D 7,27:5
Archer, Joseph W, 1937, My 15,19:1
Archer, Julian M, 1965, N 22,37:2
Archer, Kenneth L, 1948, Ja 27,25:3
Archer, Mary, 1963, Mr 30,7:7
Archer, May B Mrs, 1942, Jl 3,17:4
Archer, Minnie W Mrs, 1939, Jl 20,19:5
Archer, Nellie L, 1944, Ja 3,21:4
Archer, O H P Mrs, 1910, S 17,9:6
Archer, Olin W, 1961, F 5,80:3
Archer, Ralph C, 1957, Ag 13,27:1
Archer, Robert H, 1942, F 7,17:4; 1948, Ag 1,56:5
Archer, Robert W, 1948, Ap 9,23:3
Archer, Samuel H, 1941, Ja 17,17:3
Archer, Shreve M, 1947, N 11,27:3
Archer, Storm W, 1946, Ap 12,27:4
Archer, Susan B Mrs, 1947, F 8,17:2
Archer, T V, 1947, N 1,15:4
Archer, Theodore F, 1950, My 20,15:1
Archer, Thomas P, 1949, Ag 11,24:4
Archer, walter P, 1950, S 28,31:5
Archer, William (por), 1924, D 29,15:3
Archer, William C, 1950, Ag 21,19:6
Archer, William H, 1945, Je 9,13:5
Archer-Gilligan, Amy E Mrs, 1962, Ap 24,28:6
Archer-Shee, Francis Lady, 1959, D 14,31:5
Archey, Jimmy, 1967, N 20,47:4
Archibald, A E Capt, 1921, O 25,17:5
Archibald, Alexander Mayor, 1922, F 11,13:2
Archibald, E B, 1881, F 19,8:3
Archibald, E M Sir, 1884, F 9,2:1
Archibald, Eldred J, 1958, F 18,28:3
Archibald, Frank B, 1944, D 20,23:5
Archibald, Fred A, 1956, D 13,37:5
Archibald, George H, 1938, F 6,II,9:1
Archibald, George W, 1940, Ag 16,15:1
Archibald, Grant, 1941, Je 7,17:3
Archibald, Gray Dr, 1916, Ap 13,13:5
Archibald, Harry A, 1949, Ag 9,25:2
Archibald, Harry A Mrs, 1950, Je 9,23:3
Archibald, James P, 1913, S 8,7:4; 1953, Ja 10,17:5
Archibald, Jay, 1955, N 12,19:1
Archibald, Lauren S, 1946, Je 7,20:2
Archibald, Ray C, 1955, Jl 27,23:5
Archibald, Robert, 1939, My 28,III,7:1
Archibald, Robert G, 1953, My 6,31:2
Archibald, Robert J Mrs, 1953, Ja 19,23:4
Archibald, Robert W Jr, 1950, Mr 8,27:2
Archibald, T D Sir (trb), 1876, N 17,2:2
Archibald, Trainor, 1944, Ja 12,23:1
Archibald, W W Mrs, 1952, Ag 22,21:1
Archibald, William, 1953, O 7,29:1
Archibald, William Jr, 1950, Ag 13,77:2
Archibald, William Sr, 1946, Ja 16,23:4
Archibold, Arthur B, 1937, Je 3,25:4
Archibold, Frances, 1940, N 13,28:3
Archibold, Robert L Sr, 1941, Jl 30,18:4
Archila Duran, Gabriel, 1952, S 15,25:3
Archinard, Paul, 1966, Ag 21,93:1
Archinger, James, 1943, F 26,19:5
Archipenko, Alex, 1964, F 26,32:5
Archipenko, Alex Mrs, 1957, D 6,29:1
Archo, Morris, 1961, Ap 9,86:6
Arcieri, Emil, 1949, Mr 19,15:2
Arciszewski, Tomasz, 1955, N 21,29:3
Arco, Georg von Count (por), 1940, My 8,23:5
Arco-Valley, Count von, 1909, Jl 15,7:4
Arco-Valley, von Count Ludwig, 1891, O 16,2:6
Arcolato, Nicholas, 1907, N 11,7:2
Arconada, Cesar M, 1964, Mr 14,23:4

Arcos Cuadra, Carlos (Count of Bailen), 1964, Ap 23,39:5
Arcoverde de Albuquerque Cavalcanti, J, 1930, Ap 19,17:6
Arctander, Arthur J, 1956, Ja 18,31:5
Arctowski, Henryk, 1958, F 23,92:4
Arcularius, Edward R, 1946, F 3,40:2
Ard, Frank C, 1938, Ag 24,21:6
Ard, John L, 1937, My 5,25:1
Ard, William T, 1960, Mr 14,29:3
Ardagh, John Charles Maj-Gen, 1907, O 2,11:6
Ardant, George, 1946, O 8,23:2
Ardell, Herbert S, 1951, Ap 12,33:5
Arden, Edwin, 1918, O 3,13:2
Arden, Elaine, 1954, Ap 13,35:5
Arden, Elizabeth (Eliz N Graham),(funl, O 22,31:1; will, O 28,31:4), 1966, O 19,1:2
Arden, G DeP, 1885, My 27,5:5
Arden, George Baillie-Hamilton (Earl of Haddington), 1917, Je 12,13:2
Arden, Helen, 1957, My 22,33:2
Arden, Henry, 1912, Jl 7,II,11:5
Arden, Thomas R, 1965, O 21,47:1
Arden, Victor (L J Fulks), 1962, Ag 1,31:1
Arden, Wallace Mrs, 1946, Jl 7,36:2
Arden-Close, Charles, 1952, D 22,25:5
Ardent, Charles H, 1946, Mr 4,23:2
Ardia, Joseph M Rev, 1907, Mr 1,9:5
Ardiel, Arthur H, 1949, O 15,15:6
Ardilaun, Lord (Arth Edw Guiness), 1915, Ja 21,9:5
Ardis, Leon T, 1943, O 23,13:3
Ardis, W Frederic, 1954, Mr 27,17:3
Arditi, Luigi, 1903, My 2,9:4
Ardizzoni, Carlo, 1945, N 17,17:5
Ardolino, Edward, 1945, Ap 13,17:4
Ardolino, Ralph J Sr, 1937, Ja 17,II,8:1
Ardrey, J Howard, 1939, F 24,19:1
Ardrey, William J Sr, 1942, S 30,23:3
Ardron, Samuel, 1938, F 17,21:2
Areamunco, Alejandro, 1951, N 25,86:3
Arehart, William M, 1949, F 13,76:4
Arell, Ruth, 1954, Ag 4,21:5
Arellano, Cayetano, 1921, Mr 5,13:4
Arellano, Rafael Remirez, 1921, D 23,13:6
Arena, Angello, 1947, O 8,25:1
Arenas, German, 1948, Ap 22,27:2
Arenberg, Emil, 1942, S 29,23:4
Arenberg, Prince, 1907, Mr 26,9:6
Arend, Ernest A, 1950, Ag 29,27:3
Arend, Francis J, 1942, Ag 25,23:3
Arends, Katherine W, 1951, N 26,25:2
Arendse, Sophie, 1952, Ag 9,13:7
Arendt, Morton, 1958, Ag 24,86:6
Arendt, William Sr, 1946, Jl 24,27:4
Arenoff, Max, 1961, D 23,23:6
Arens, Egmont, 1966, O 2,87:1
Arens, Lidolph A, 1947, N 29,13:3
Arens, Otto, 1910, Ag 27,7:5
Arens, Robert A, 1962, Je 2,19:3
Arens, Winfried B, 1956, N 12,29:5
Arensberg, Walter C, 1954, Ja 30,17:1
Arenson, Albert, 1959, F 12,27:5
Arenstein, Max, 1958, N 22,21:1
Arenstein, Yetta, 1965, F 1,23:2
Arents, Charles R, 1953, Ap 27,23:2
Arents, George (will, D 17,30:6), 1960, D 14,36:1
Arents, George Mrs, 1948, Jl 28,23:4
Arese, F, 1881, Je 29,4:7
Areson, William H, 1959, Mr 10,35:1
Aresoni, Enrico, 1943, Ag 9,13:6
Aretin, Erwin von, 1952, F 26,27:2
Aretz, Carl W, 1942, D 24,15:3
Arevalo, Mariano, 1948, O 19,27:1
Arevalo, Tomas D (Count of Rodezno), 1952, Ag 11,15:1
Arey, Albert L, 1938, S 15,25:2
Arey, Gordon C, 1948, N 4,29:4
Arey, Wayne, 1937, Jl 3,15:2
Argall, T M, 1884, S 3,2:3
Argenio, Louis, 1954, N 5,21:2
Argenlieu, Georges T d', 1964, S 8,29:3
Argent, Claudia G, 1966, Ap 28,43:4
Argenta, Ataulfo, 1958, Ja 22,27:4
Argenteau, Mercy D (Princess Montglyon), 1925, Jl 28,13:6
Argenti, John P, 1950, Jl 1,15:3
Argentina (La), 1936, Jl 20,15:4
Argento, Frances N Mrs, 1942, Je 25,23:3
Argento, Valentino, 1941, S 12,22:3
Argetsinger, George F, 1951, F 12,23:2
Argetsinger, J Cameron, 1955, Je 18,17:5
Arghezi, Tudor, 1967, Jl 24,27:3
Argondizza, Anthony J, 1958, Je 22,76:6
Argov, Moir, 1963, N 25,20:4
Argow, W Waldemar W, 1961, Jl 10,21:4
Argue, John F, 1956, Jl 16,21:3
Argue, Robert D, 1938, Jl 28,19:2
Argue, Robert D Mrs, 1958, My 10,21:5
Argue, William L, 1939, My 26,23:3
Arguedas, Alcides, 1946, My 7,21:5
Arguelles, Frederick S, 1953, Ja 20,25:1
Arguelli Gil, Ivan, 1952, O 28,31:3
Arguello, Alberto, 1945, Mr 9,19:5
Arguello, Benjamin, 1954, Mr 7,91:1
Arguello, Gertrudes Mrs, 1942, Ag 13,21:4
Arguello, Joaquin P, 1947, Ja 22,23:1
Arguello, Leonardo, 1947, D 16,33:6
Arguello, Leonardo Jr, 1947, Mr 10,21:3
Arguello, Narciso, 1943, Ap 20,23:2
Arguello, Santiago, 1940, Jl 5,13:6
Arguello Gil, Hugo, 1961, Mr 13,29:1
Arguimbau, Frank M, 1943, Je 19,13:4
Arguimbau, Frank M Mrs, 1942, Ja 16,22:4
Arguimbau, Vincent C, 1941, Jl 7,15:1
Argyle, William R, 1964, Je 8,29:1
Argyll, Dowager Duchess of, 1939, D 4,23:1
Argyll, Dowager Duchess of (Princess Louise Caroline Alberta), 1940, F 10,2:4
Argyll, Duke of, 1900, Ap 24,9:1
Argyll, Duke of (N D Campbell), 1949, Ag 21,69:1
Ariaga, Camilo, 1945, Je 28,19:3
Arian, Walter, 1953, Ja 17,15:1
Arias, Adbiel J, 1950, S 6,29:1
Arias, Francisco S, 1916, N 13,13:5
Arias, Harmodio, 1962, D 24,8:5
Arias, Henry R, 1965, Ja 5,33:4
Arias, Jorge B, 1950, Jl 6,28:2
Arias Bernal, Antonio, 1961, Ja 1,49:1
Arias Blanco, Rafael, 1959, O 2,2:1
Arias Salgado, Gabriel, 1962, Jl 27,25:2
Ariav, Haim, 1957, Je 18,29:1
Arico, Ralph, 1943, O 2,13:4
Aricson, Ira, 1941, Je 15,36:8
Arida, Antoine, 1955, My 20,25:6
Ariel, Israel, 1937, Jl 21,21:1
Ariel, Wallace A, 1945, S 20,23:3
Arif, Abdel S Pres (funl set, Ap 15,14:4; plans, Ap 16,8:4,5), 1966, Ap 14,1:1
Arifin, Hadji Z (Mar 2), 1963, Ap 1,35:1
Arikan, Saffet, 1947, N 28,27:3
Arima, Yoriyasu, 1944, My 2,19:4
Arimondi, Aurelia, 1941, Jl 29,15:2
Aring, Milton W, 1952, Ag 20,25:6
Arink, Barner, 1903, Ag 11,7:7
Arinkin, Mikhail, 1948, S 10,23:1
Arino, Luis, 1938, My 12,23:1
Aris, Bernardus J, 1947, O 11,17:3
Arisaka, Nariaki Lt-Gen, 1915, Ja 12,9:5
Arita, Hachiro, 1965, Mr 5,33:1
Arjona, Jaime H, 1967, Ja 27,45:4
Arkell, Bartlett, 1946, O 14,29:3
Arkell, James, 1902, Ag 15,9:5
Arkell, Reginald, 1959, My 2,23:4
Arkell, W Clark, 1962, O 9,41:3
Arkema, Edward Mrs, 1951, Mr 7,33:4
Arkett, A Edgar Mrs, 1941, D 15,19:1
Arkin, Abel J, 1942, O 5,19:5
Arkin, Bernard, 1946, Ag 11,46:2
Arkin, Harry, 1951, Jl 10,27:3
Arkin, Jack W, 1959, O 29,33:4
Arkin, Joseph, 1939, My 16,23:4
Arkin, Leon, 1953, O 1,29:3
Arkin, Morris Mrs, 1949, Ja 18,23:4
Arkin, William L, 1958, Ja 21,29:1
Arkins, Francis J, 1945, Ag 24,20:3
Arkins, Vincent P, 1955, Mr 17,45:3
Arkinson, Benjamin R, 1938, S 28,25:3
Arkinstall, John H Mrs, 1950, F 28,29:3
Arkison, Thomas W, 1961, Mr 1,33:3
Arkush, Ralph M, 1965, Ag 17,33:3
Arkush, Reuben, 1951, Ja 9,29:5
Arkwright, Preston S, 1946, D 3,31:4
Arkwright, Preston S Jr, 1947, N 7,23:2
Arky, Adolph, 1939, Ap 12,23:1
Arlen, Michael, 1956, Je 24,76:6
Arlen, Michael Mrs, 1964, S 11,33:5
Arless, George C, 1952, N 16,88:8
Arlinghaus, Frank H, 1964, Ag 26,39:3
Arlington, Argentine H, 1945, Mr 29,23:5
Arlington, Billy, 1913, My 25,IV,7:7
Arlington, Edward, 1947, O 29,27:2
Arlington, Edward Mrs, 1943, N 30,27:4
Arlington, George, 1923, D 3,17:3
Arliss, George, 1946, F 6,23:1
Arliss, Jay E, 1952, Jl 31,23:2
Arlitz, William J, 1944, Ag 25,13:6
Arluck, Cantor S, 1953, Mr 2,23:5
Arm, Harry, 1943, D 14,27:4
Arm, Harry Mrs, 1943, D 14,27:4
Arm, Nathan, 1961, Je 5,31:1
Armagh, Archbishop of, 1869, S 17,1:1
Armaghdale, Lord (Jno Brownlee Lonsdale), 1924, Je 9,17:6
Armagnac, Arthur S, 1945, D 22,19:2
Armaly, Amelia S, 1944, Mr 10,15:3
Armand, Brother, 1949, Ja 15,17:3
Armand-Delille, Paul, 1963, S 7,19:4
Armanet, Crescent, 1955, D 27,23:3
Armao, Joseph, 1957, Mr 26,33:1
Armao, Michael C, 1965, Je 30,37:1
Armas Perez, Ramon, 1960, Je 25,1:6
Armat, Thomas, 1948, O 1,25:4
Armato, Michael, 1947, Mr 1,15:1
Armau, Gerard, 1961, O 26,35:2
Armbrister, Victor S, 1962, O 8,23:3
Armbrust, Arnold T, 1946, Je 7,19:1
Armbruster, Dorothy M, 1967, Ap 23,92:2
Armbruster, Ernest O, 1954, S 26,86:8
Armbruster, Eugene L, 1943, S 23,21:5
Armbruster, Frederick, 1925, N 13,19:5
Armbruster, Howard M, 1961, Ja 12,29:4
Armbruster, Peter, 1937, Ap 10,19:6
Armel, Lyle O, 1948, D 6,25:4
Armel, William N, 1945, O 18,23:4
Armelli, Giuseppe, 1958, Jl 17,18:2
Armenise, Giovanni Count, 1953, F 21,13:6
Armentrout, Lt-Com, 1875, Ag 15,6:7
Armes, Irene H, 1955, S 14,35:4
Armes, Oscar St J, 1952, Ja 24,27:2
Armes, Roland Kingman, 1953, F 4,27:2
Armes, Willard O, 1950, Ap 27,29:4
Armetta, Henry, 1945, O 23,17:3
Armfield, Lucian C, 1949, O 31,25:4
Armhold, R, 1877, Mr 4,12:5
Armhold, William Rabbi, 1924, Mr 6,17:4
Armiger, Benjamin F, 1955, Ap 27,31:4
Armiger, Benjamin F Mrs, 1939, Ag 21,13:1
Armijo, Vego de Marquis, 1908, Je 15,7:4
Armington, Anna K, 1924, Ap 3,21:6
Armington, Frank M, 1941, S 23,23:5
Armington, Frank M Mrs, 1939, O 28,15:6
Armington, Herbert A, 1959, Ag 13,27:2
Armington, Sarah, 1968, Mr 21,47:3
Arminio, Joseph J, 1962, Ja 19,31:2
Armistead, Daniel W Mrs, 1954, S 9,31:3
Armistead, George H Sr, 1950, D 22,24:3
Armistead, George Jr, 1960, F 29,27:1
Armistead, W H, 1904, O 18,9:3
Armistead, William M, 1955, N 7,29:5
Armistead, William M (est acctg), 1956, F 15,32:7
Armitage, Albert B, 1943, N 3,25:3
Armitage, Albert L, 1961, My 15,31:5
Armitage, Alice W Mrs, 1964, D 5,31:5
Armitage, Charles H, 1947, N 30,76:7
Armitage, Charles M, 1923, Ja 31,19:6
Armitage, Elwood S, 1954, F 27,13:4
Armitage, Elwood S Mrs, 1960, D 6,37:6
Armitage, Frederick Wilson, 1907, Ag 21,7:7
Armitage, George L Jr, 1964, Jl 28,29:5
Armitage, John W, 1960, S 22,27:3
Armitage, Joshua D, 1949, F 14,19:4
Armitage, Paul, 1949, Je 29,27:2
Armitage, Walter W, 1953, F 24,25:3
Armitage, William C, 1949, N 5,13:5
Armitage, William Edmond Bp, 1873, D 8,1:6
Armitt, Samuel, 1941, My 1,23:5
Armknecht, Philip G, 1944, Mr 26,42:1
Armm, David, 1925, Jl 7,19:5
Armor, George G, 1941, Ja 23,21:4
Armor, George M, 1955, S 17,15:6
Armot, Louise, 1919, Ag 16,7:6
Armour, A A Mrs, 1904, D 14,9:3
Armour, A W, 1881, Mr 29,4:7
Armour, A Watson (will, N 17,27:3), 1953, N 7,17:6
Armour, A Watson 3d Mrs, 1963, Ja 3,15:7
Armour, Albert P, 1960, Ja 27,33:3
Armour, Alex W, 1956, F 18,19:2
Armour, Allison, 1955, D 10,21:5
Armour, Allison V, 1941, Mr 7,21:4
Armour, Bernard R, 1949, D 2,29:1
Armour, C W, 1927, Mr 23,25:1
Armour, Ethel B Mrs (will), 1949, F 12,19:1
Armour, G, 1881, Je 14,5:4
Armour, G A, 1936, Je 9,24:1
Armour, George D, 1949, F 19,15:5
Armour, H O (see also S 9), 1901, S 12,7:6
Armour, J O, 1927, Ag 17,23:3
Armour, J Ogden Mrs, 1953, F 7,15:5
Armour, J Ogden Mrs (est acctg), 1954, Mr 27,15:4
Armour, James B M, 1947, O 27,21:6
Armour, James M, 1952, S 7,86:3
Armour, John Sir Justice, 1903, Jl 12,7:5
Armour, K B, 1901, S 28,9:6
Armour, Laurance H, 1952, D 30,19:5
Armour, P D, 1901, Ja 7,1:7
Armour, Phil D Mrs, 1950, S 2,15:5
Armour, Philip D (will, F 7,22:8), 1958, Ja 20,23:5
Armour, Philip D Jr, 1965, Mr 14,86:8
Armour, Simeon B Mrs, 1915, N 12,11:5
Armour, Tommy (Thos Dickson Armour), 1968, S 14,31:2
Armour, William, 1958, O 24,20:1
Arms, Dorothy N, 1955, Ja 13,27:2
Arms, E W, 1877, Ja 24,4:7
Arms, Frank T, 1948, Ap 19,23:5
Arms, George, 1912, Mr 17,15:3
Arms, H P Rev, 1882, Ap 7,5:2
Arms, John T, 1953, O 15,33:1
Arms, Samuel D, 1961, Ap 9,86:5
Armsby, George N, 1942, O 26,15:1
Armsley, J H Dr, 1875, D 4,4:7
Armstead, George B, 1950, Mr 8,27:2
Armstead, Henry H, 1940, O 4,23:2
Armstead, Kate H Mrs, 1947, My 12,21:3
Armstring, Arthur D, 1937, N 30,23:3
Armstrong, A Joseph, 1952, Ag 15,27:2; 1954, Ap 1, 31:4
Armstrong, A Weiant, 1946, O 8,23:2
Armstrong, Addison C, 1944, D 7,25:2

Armstrong, Albert H, 1944, Je 1,19:5
Armstrong, Albert J Mrs, 1954, D 20,29:4
Armstrong, Albert L, 1942, O 29,23:4
Armstrong, Alex, 1939, N 21,26:5
Armstrong, Alex F, 1959, Ag 2,80:6
Armstrong, Alex G, 1938, Mr 31,23:6
Armstrong, Alexander C, 1925, My 24,7:2
Armstrong, Allan G, 1939, Ap 8,15:2
Armstrong, Allen, 1950, O 10,31:4
Armstrong, Andrew R, 1968, D 12,47:1
Armstrong, Annie W Mrs, 1958, Mr 18,29:3
Armstrong, Arch F Mrs, 1950, Je 30,23:3
Armstrong, Arthur P, 1956, S 8,17:1
Armstrong, Arthur S, 1938, Ja 14,23:2
Armstrong, Augustus T, 1919, Mr 14,13:3
Armstrong, Austin E, 1953, S 18,29:1
Armstrong, B Dixon, 1908, N 4,11:7
Armstrong, Benjamin H, 1962, F 12,23:5
Armstrong, Bolton S, 1951, Je 16,15:5
Armstrong, C, 1926, F 11,21:2
Armstrong, C Dudley, 1954, Je 10,31:4
Armstrong, C M, 1934, S 10,17:2
Armstrong, C Wesley Sr, 1947, O 2,27:4
Armstrong, Charles, 1967, Je 23,31:1
Armstrong, Charles A, 1953, Ja 3,15:5
Armstrong, Charles A G, 1950, S 2,15:3
Armstrong, Charles C Mrs, 1942, Ap 9,19:2
Armstrong, Charles F, 1965, Mr 9,35:3
Armstrong, Charles G, 1922, S 12,21:5
Armstrong, Charles M, 1925, Ap 2,21:4
Armstrong, Charles N F, 1948, N 3,27:1
Armstrong, Charles Philip, 1910, Je 29,7:5
Armstrong, Charles R, 1942, N 11,25:5
Armstrong, Charles S, 1939, D 6,25:1
Armstrong, Clyde, 1937, O 1,22:2
Armstrong, Cole A, 1968, Je 5,47:1
Armstrong, D A, 1944, Mr 30,21:4
Armstrong, Daniel W, 1947, Jl 17,19:2
Armstrong, David Mrs, 1966, D 21,39:1
Armstrong, David W (Fla), 1963, F 8,18:2
Armstrong, David W (NJ), 1963, O 10,41:2
Armstrong, Dessie, 1914, S 28,9:3; 1914, O 5,11:4
Armstrong, Donald, 1939, S 25,20:2
Armstrong, Donald B Dr, 1968, Ag 27,41:4
Armstrong, Douglas S, 1958, O 29,35:1
Armstrong, Dwight L, 1944, S 11,17:4
Armstrong, E A, 1932, My 3,21:3; 1950, F 16,23:3
Armstrong, Edgar R, 1949, Jl 5,24:5
Armstrong, Edmund G, 1939, O 14,19:6
Armstrong, Edward A Lt (funl, Jl 28,9:4), 1915, Jl 27,9:6
Armstrong, Edward C, 1944, Mr 6,19:3
Armstrong, Edward C Mrs, 1958, Ap 23,33:4
Armstrong, Edward F, 1945, D 16,40:7
Armstrong, Edward H (por), 1938, Ja 3,21:3
Armstrong, Edward Kent Maj, 1919, Je 11,15:4
Armstrong, Edward M, 1961, Je 13,35:1
Armstrong, Edward Maitland, 1915, Jl 17,7:6
Armstrong, Edward McP, 1957, S 11,33:3
Armstrong, Edward Mrs, 1945, Mr 15,15:1
Armstrong, Edward R, 1955, Jl 7,27:4
Armstrong, Edward S, 1941, O 27,17:3
Armstrong, Edward V Dr, 1903, Jl 17,7:6
Armstrong, Edwin, 1961, Jl 14,23:5
Armstrong, Edwin F, 1958, Ja 1,25:4
Armstrong, Edwin S, 1942, Je 2,23:5
Armstrong, Elizabeth H, 1957, D 25,31:5
Armstrong, Ella M, 1940, Ag 2,15:6
Armstrong, F Douglas, 1943, Ja 18,15:4
Armstrong, F Wallis (por), 1949, F 9,28:3
Armstrong, F Wallis Jr, 1956, Ag 16,25:1
Armstrong, Francis P, 1944, Ja 8,13:3
Armstrong, Frank C Gen, 1909, S 9,9:4
Armstrong, Frank C Sr, 1958, S 19,27:1
Armstrong, Frank Mrs, 1945, My 14,17:4
Armstrong, Frank S, 1924, N 12,23:2
Armstrong, Frederick W, 1940, My 9,23:3
Armstrong, G B, 1871, My 6,5:2
Armstrong, Gayle G, 1950, O 16,27:5
Armstrong, George, 1950, Jl 8,13:5
Armstrong, George A, 1957, F 7,27:5
Armstrong, George E, 1914, F 17,11:4; 1947, F 27,21:3
Armstrong, George F, 1937, Jl 2,21:5
Armstrong, George H, 1951, F 16,25:4
Armstrong, George J, 1952, O 17,27:1
Armstrong, George P, 1946, Jl 16,23:3
Armstrong, George S, 1962, S 13,37:3
Armstrong, George W Sr, 1954, O 2,17:5
Armstrong, Geralda Mrs, 1942, Ag 12,19:3
Armstrong, Glendon H, 1958, Ap 25,27:2
Armstrong, Glenn V, 1955, Ag 4,25:3
Armstrong, Gordon, 1959, Ap 29,33:3
Armstrong, H Logie, 1945, D 23,18:7
Armstrong, H Palmer, 1965, F 11,39:4
Armstrong, Hal B, 1957, Je 24,23:4
Armstrong, Harold H, 1950, Jl 19,31:4
Armstrong, Harold M, 1955, F 12,15:1
Armstrong, Harrison, 1916, F 4,9:6
Armstrong, Harry G (por; will, My 14,1:7), 1938, F 7,15:1
Armstrong, Harry G Mrs Lady, 1953, My 29,25:3
Armstrong, Harry H, 1961, Je 6,37:5
Armstrong, Harry M Mrs, 1944, N 17,19:2
Armstrong, Hatley K Mrs, 1947, S 17,25:2
Armstrong, Hector Mrs, 1915, Ap 16,13:4
Armstrong, Helen M, 1948, N 27,17:3
Armstrong, Henry Beekman, 1912, S 3,11:6
Armstrong, Henry E, 1937, Jl 14,21:4; 1939, Ag 24, 19:6
Armstrong, Henry E Mrs, 1946, F 27,25:5
Armstrong, Henry H, 1951, Jl 30,17:6
Armstrong, Henry W (Harry), 1951, Mr 1,27:1
Armstrong, Henry W, 1963, D 24,17:4
Armstrong, Herbert N, 1948, Ag 11,21:3
Armstrong, Homer V, 1940, N 16,17:5
Armstrong, Horace W, 1947, My 10,13:3
Armstrong, Hugh, 1911, D 2,13:4
Armstrong, J, 1883, My 19,5:3
Armstrong, J C, 1931, F 10,21:1
Armstrong, J Gillespie, 1964, Ap 24,33:1
Armstrong, J Gillespie Mrs, 1949, O 30,84:8
Armstrong, J H, 1922, F 20,11:4
Armstrong, J P, 1953, F 22,61:1
Armstrong, Jacob W, 1948, Mr 29,21:5
Armstrong, James, 1867, Ag 24,8:4; 1952, Ja 12,13:2; 1953, Ja 6,29:2
Armstrong, James A, 1938, Ja 10,17:4; 1952, O 8,31:5
Armstrong, James J, 1918, F 5,13:8
Armstrong, James L, 1952, Mr 17,21:2
Armstrong, James M, 1941, My 9,21:6
Armstrong, James Mrs, 1942, Je 24,19:4
Armstrong, James N, 1948, Ap 15,25:4
Armstrong, James S Sr, 1953, My 25,25:5
Armstrong, James Simmons, 1920, Ap 18,22:3
Armstrong, James W, 1955, S 13,31:4
Armstrong, James W Mrs, 1948, Ap 13,28:2
Armstrong, Jesse, 1942, My 17,47:1
Armstrong, John, 1873, D 12,5:5; 1962, Ja 27,21:4
Armstrong, John Allen, 1925, S 24,25:4
Armstrong, John C, 1952, Je 27,23:4
Armstrong, John D Mrs, 1941, O 4,15:3
Armstrong, John G, 1950, My 29,17:3
Armstrong, John Hill, 1914, D 9,13:5
Armstrong, John L, 1943, O 21,27:2
Armstrong, John P T, 1962, N 12,29:4
Armstrong, John S Jr, 1960, F 20,14:7
Armstrong, John T, 1937, Ja 14,22:1
Armstrong, Joseph B, 1943, D 26,32:7
Armstrong, Julian, 1946, My 21,23:1
Armstrong, Julian G, 1950, Jl 18,29:4
Armstrong, Lancelot, 1946, Jl 16,23:2
Armstrong, Lawrence S, 1952, Je 23,19:3
Armstrong, Leon J, 1952, Ap 26,23:5
Armstrong, Lilias, 1937, D 11,19:6
Armstrong, Lord, 1900, D 28,7:2; 1941, O 17,23:2
Armstrong, Lorenzo D, 1947, N 17,21:5
Armstrong, Louis, 1941, N 28,24:2
Armstrong, M, 1903, O 3,9:6
Armstrong, Maitland, 1918, My 27,13:6
Armstrong, Malcolm W, 1956, Mr 4,88:8
Armstrong, Marcus P Mrs, 1953, Jl 28,19:6
Armstrong, Margaret H Mrs, 1942, Je 13,15:5
Armstrong, Margaret N, 1944, Jl 19,19:3
Armstrong, Mary E Mrs, 1945, Mr 15,23:2
Armstrong, Matthew C, 1944, Ja 14,19:2
Armstrong, Noel, 1938, S 8,23:3; 1952, Mr 15,13:6
Armstrong, Obadiah P, 1966, Ag 19,33:2
Armstrong, Oscar S, 1942, Ag 14,17:5
Armstrong, P C, 1952, Mr 26,29:4
Armstrong, Paul (funl, S 2,9:3), 1915, Ag 31,9:5
Armstrong, Paul G, 1958, Ja 13,29:2
Armstrong, Paul S Mrs, 1950, Ap 15,15:2
Armstrong, Percy A, 1949, Ag 8,15:2
Armstrong, Percy A E Mrs, 1948, Ja 3,13:5
Armstrong, Phil E, 1937, Mr 19,23:4
Armstrong, Philip E Mrs, 1960, My 8,88:2
Armstrong, Ralph, 1940, N 5,34:1
Armstrong, Richard, 1938, Ag 5,17:2
Armstrong, Robert, 1946, My 31,23:4
Armstrong, Robert A, 1953, Je 26,19:4
Armstrong, Robert B, 1946, Ag 6,25:1
Armstrong, Robert B Jr, 1955, Ap 4,29:5
Armstrong, Robert D, 1957, D 8,88:6
Armstrong, Robert G, 1956, Jl 27,21:1
Armstrong, Robert H, 1961, Ja 31,29:5
Armstrong, Robert H Mrs, 1956, D 29,15:4
Armstrong, Robert R, 1942, Ap 7,22:4
Armstrong, Robert V, 1943, Ag 17,17:4
Armstrong, Roger W, 1952, Ag 25,17:1
Armstrong, Rolf, 1960, F 24,37:4
Armstrong, Roselle W, 1942, D 15,27:6
Armstrong, Rosetta Mrs, 1947, Mr 29,15:4
Armstrong, S Howard, 1961, Mr 12,86:4
Armstrong, Samuel C Mrs, 1958, O 20,29:4
Armstrong, Samuel Mrs, 1951, Ap 13,23:3
Armstrong, Samuel R, 1942, D 12,17:5
Armstrong, Samuel T, 1944, S 1,13:3
Armstrong, Stanley C, 1950, Jl 13,25:2
Armstrong, Stanley E, 1943, D 10,27:2
Armstrong, Thaddeus G, 1963, Jl 6,15:3
Armstrong, Thaddeus G Mrs, 1959, Ja 3,17:1
Armstrong, Thomas, 1942, Ja 31,17:4; 1949, My 17, 25:3
Armstrong, Thomas F, 1953, S 9,29:2
Armstrong, Thomas N Jr, 1963, Je 7,31:3
Armstrong, Thomas R, 1954, Mr 28,88:3
Armstrong, Traverse A, 1945, Ap 7,15:4
Armstrong, Victor C, 1958, Je 10,33:5
Armstrong, W Park Jr Mrs, 1962, O 13,25:5
Armstrong, Walter E, 1967, N 18,37:2
Armstrong, Walter H, 1938, My 7,15:3; 1949, O 28, 23:4
Armstrong, Walter J, 1946, Jl 11,23:1
Armstrong, Walter P Sr, 1949, Jl 28,23:1
Armstrong, Warwick, 1947, Jl 14,21:3
Armstrong, William, 1922, Mr 23,13:4; 1942, My 23, 13:6; 1943, Jl 4,21:2
Armstrong, William (por;will, Ag 6,17:1), 1949, Ag 5,19:4
Armstrong, William, 1952, Ap 3,35:1
Armstrong, William B, 1937, O 9,19:5
Armstrong, William C, 1949, Ag 7,60:5
Armstrong, William E, 1948, S 19,76:6
Armstrong, William F H, 1949, My 21,13:5
Armstrong, William Farley, 1920, My 3,13:4
Armstrong, William H, 1939, D 1,23:1; 1946, F 14,25:4
Armstrong, William H H, 1916, F 24,13:4
Armstrong, William H Mrs, 1964, S 19,27:6
Armstrong, William J Mrs, 1950, O 25,35:5
Armstrong, William L, 1943, S 23,21:4
Armstrong, William P Mrs, 1964, N 22,86:8
Armstrong, William R, 1953, Ap 24,23:1
Armstrong, William S, 1949, My 30,13:3
Armstrong, William S Sr, 1947, F 18,25:2
Armstrong, William W, 1944, Jl 22,15:3
Armstrong, William W Maj, 1905, Ap 22,5:6
Armstrong, Wynn, 1947, Ja 4,15:2
Armstrong-Jones, Robert, 1943, Ja 31,45:1
Armstrong-Jones, Ronald O L, 1966, Ja 28,47:2
Armsworthy, Hannah Mrs, 1907, Ap 18,11:6
Armsy, Henry Prentiss Dr, 1921, O 20,17:6
Armus, Alex, 1965, My 31,17:5
Arn, Elmer R, 1951, D 28,21:2
Arnade, Ameline B Mrs, 1951, Mr 24,13:3
Arnall, Curtis C, 1964, S 24,41:3
Arnaud, Charles E, 1947, N 30,76:3
Arnaud, F, 1878, Je 2,7:5
Arnaud, Yvonne, 1958, S 21,87:2
Arnaud Cazenave-Conte, Leon B, 1948, My 31,19:3
Arndt, Abraham, 1956, N 25,89:1
Arndt, Charles H, 1940, Ja 19,19:1
Arndt, Christian, 1937, O 30,19:5
Arndt, Christian O, 1966, F 4,31:1
Arndt, Gustave, 1950, N 29,33:1
Arndt, Howard A, 1947, Jl 30,21:6
Arndt, J G, 1879, Ap 13,2:6
Arndt, Karl M, 1956, F 23,27:2
Arndt, Robert V, 1950, Ap 25,31:2
Arndt, Siegfried, 1958, Je 24,31:3
Arndt, W T, 1932, Ja 2,18:3
Arndt, William F, 1957, F 26,29:5
Arneberg, Arnstein, 1961, Je 11,86:4
Arneke, Arthur H, 1947, Jl 7,17:5
Arnel, Mortimer Mrs, 1956, N 29,35:4
Arnell, Artie, 1968, D 20,42:3
Arnerich, Matthew E, 1948, O 10,76:3
Arnesen, Arne C, 1961, Mr 30,29:2
Arnesen, Erling H, 1945, F 3,11:2
Arnesen, Peter, 1942, Je 2,23:2
Arnesen, Sigurd J, 1966, N 1,41:1
Arnesen, Victor H, 1960, F 21,92:7
Arneson, Ben A, 1958, F 14,24:1
Arneson, Sorren R, 1943, Ap 12,24:2
Arnessen, Aksel A, 1946, N 16,19:5
Arnett, Benjamin W, 1948, Ap 23,23:2
Arnett, Benjamin William Bishop, 1906, O 9,7:6
Arnett, Charles D, 1940, D 4,27:5
Arnett, Eugene, 1938, Ja 25,22:3
Arnett, S D, 1946, Mr 28,25:4
Arnett, Trevor, 1955, Ap 1,27:5
Arnett, Trevor Mrs, 1950, Jl 19,31:3
Arnett, William W Mrs, 1961, Mr 19,88:5
Arney, C E Jr (Bee), 1956, N 5,31:4
Arnfeld, Maurice, 1946, Ap 9,27:1
Arnheim, Ernest E, 1962, O 13,25:6
Arnheim, Gus, 1955, Ja 20,31:6
Arnheim, Marks (funl), 1912, Mr 25,11:5
Arnheim, Minnie Mrs, 1941, S 23,23:1
Arnheim, N Gosta, 1964, F 29,21:2
Arnheim, Samuel Walter Lt (funl, Mr 26,13:4), 1918, Mr 23,13:4
Arnheimer, H Irving, 1956, Jl 14,15:6
Arnheiter, Theodore, 1951, Ja 3,27:2
Arnhold, Hans, 1966, S 9,45:3
Arnhold, Harry E, 1950, Ja 3,25:2
Arni, Samuel N, 1953, F 12,27:2
Arniches, Carlos, 1943, Ap 17,17:6
Arnihac, Gaston Mrs, 1954, D 1,31:5
Arnim, Josephine von, 1953, Ja 10,17:2
Arnim, Malvine von, 1908, Ap 1,7:6
Arnn, Charles E, 1955, Ag 14,80:3
Arno, Peter, 1968, F 23,1:2
Arnold, A Judson Mrs, 1955, My 1,88:6
Arnold, A Judson Rev, 1937, D 10,26:4
Arnold, Aaron, 1876, Mr 19,7:1
Arnold, Abraham S, 1951, Ap 18,31:1
Arnold, Ainsworth, 1953, D 19,15:6
Arnold, Albert, 1940, Jl 22,17:1
Arnold, Albert A, 1940, My 3,21:4

Arnold, Alfred C, 1956, Ap 10,31:2
Arnold, Alfred C N, 1941, S 16,25:1
Arnold, Alfred C Rev, 1906, Ja 31,11:6
Arnold, Almon P, 1944, D 25,19:5
Arnold, Arthur H, 1947, Jl 19,13:5
Arnold, Arthur Z, 1965, D 30,21:4
Arnold, Asa H, 1946, N 6,23:4
Arnold, August W, 1956, F 27,23:4
Arnold, Belin, 1962, Ap 5,33:1
Arnold, Benjamin W Mrs, 1945, N 6,19:3
Arnold, Bion J, 1942, Ja 31,17:1
Arnold, C Russell, 1955, S 30,25:3
Arnold, Carl R, 1964, N 26,33:4
Arnold, Charles, 1905, My 7,1:6
Arnold, Charles E, 1949, Ja 25,23:1
Arnold, Charles H, 1951, Ja 17,27:3
Arnold, Charles L, 1943, My 1,15:6
Arnold, Charles W, 1967, Ap 13,43:3
Arnold, Charlotte, 1924, N 28,15:4
Arnold, Charlotte E, 1946, O 22,25:6
Arnold, Chester J, 1941, Mr 18,23:2
Arnold, Clifford, 1952, Ja 30,25:4
Arnold, Clyde N, 1949, Je 21,25:2
Arnold, Conway Hillyer Rear-Adm, 1917, Jl 17,9:3
Arnold, Craig, 1948, S 15,32:3
Arnold, D H, 1885, Mr 19,5:4
Arnold, D S, 1879, My 15,2:6
Arnold, Dan H, 1937, Ag 16,19:2
Arnold, Dan H Mrs, 1955, Ap 19,31:4
Arnold, Daniel J Sr, 1955, F 5,15:5
Arnold, David P, 1942, My 2,13:3
Arnold, De Witt R, 1946, D 22,42:4
Arnold, Donald D, 1946, Ja 5,13:4
Arnold, Dorothy, 1944, Ap 21,19:3
Arnold, Edgar H Mrs, 1962, My 17,37:4
Arnold, Edgar Sr, 1963, Ag 11,85:2
Arnold, Edward, 1940, Je 11,25:2; 1956, Ap 27,27:1
Arnold, Edward A, 1952, Mr 3,21:1
Arnold, Edward Everett, 1925, D 16,25:4
Arnold, Edwin, 1956, Jl 13,19:5
Arnold, Edwin G, 1960, O 18,39:1
Arnold, Edwin Sir, 1904, Mr 25,9:4
Arnold, Ernest L, 1946, S 26,25:5
Arnold, Ernest M, 1919, Mr 1,13:4
Arnold, Eugene H, 1937, D 16,27:4
Arnold, Everett D, 1924, Je 7,13:4
Arnold, Felix (por), 1938, O 2,49:1
Arnold, Florine, 1925, Jl 4,11:6
Arnold, Francis A Jr, 1967, D 4,47:3
Arnold, Francis Benjamin, 1906, F 6,9:6
Arnold, Francis R, 1922, Ap 2,29:3
Arnold, Frank, 1941, My 11,45:2
Arnold, Frank A, 1958, Jl 17,27:3
Arnold, Frank B, 1937, S 24,21:2
Arnold, Frank J, 1953, N 5,31:3
Arnold, Frank J Mrs, 1956, S 22,17:3
Arnold, Frederick, 1951, Ag 1,23:5
Arnold, Frederick H, 1945, N 11,35:2
Arnold, Frederick J, 1959, F 26,31:5
Arnold, Frederick W, 1945, Mr 22,23:3; 1956, Je 8,25:6
Arnold, Gene, 1954, Ap 13,31:3
Arnold, George, 1865, N 11,8:2; 1912, Jl 12,9:4
Arnold, George A, 1954, Je 13,88:2
Arnold, George C, 1938, S 21,25:3
Arnold, George H, 1956, Ja 30,8:8
Arnold, George J, 1943, O 26,23:4
Arnold, George S, 1942, Ja 20,20:2
Arnold, George S Mrs, 1952, My 15,31:1
Arnold, Giles, 1938, Jl 21,21:2
Arnold, Glenn, 1945, Jl 22,38:2
Arnold, Gohen C, 1939, Je 11,44:8
Arnold, Grace, 1937, Ap 20,25:3
Arnold, H Bruno, 1960, Ja 9,21:1
Arnold, H Denham, 1949, N 13,92:8
Arnold, H F, 1933, Jl 11,17:4
Arnold, Harold, 1937, N 10,25:4
Arnold, Harold C, 1960, Mr 14,29:2
Arnold, Harold E, 1952, D 3,33:6
Arnold, Harold S, 1950, Ag 8,20:5; 1951, D 22,15:5
Arnold, Harriet C Mrs, 1942, Ap 30,19:3
Arnold, Harry, 1960, Mr 5,19:5
Arnold, Harry C Mrs, 1944, My 11,19:2
Arnold, Harry J, 1961, Ja 24,29:2
Arnold, Harry L, 1968, Jl 27,27:5
Arnold, Harry S, 1939, Jl 26,19:2
Arnold, Harry W, 1943, D 2,27:5; 1963, N 21,39:3
Arnold, Hazen S, 1953, S 15,31:2
Arnold, Henry, 1942, Je 29,15:6
Arnold, Henry C, 1957, D 24,15:1
Arnold, Henry H Gen, 1950, Ja 16,1:2
Arnold, Henry J, 1959, Ap 7,33:5
Arnold, Henry N, 1939, Je 8,25:3
Arnold, Henry P, 1954, Jl 12,19:4
Arnold, Herbert E, 1957, Mr 4,27:4
Arnold, Hicks, 1903, Ja 29,9:6
Arnold, Hugo F, 1946, Ja 3,19:2
Arnold, I Clinton, 1954, S 9,31:4
Arnold, I N, 1884, Ap 25,5:5
Arnold, J Frederick, 1946, Jl 25,21:5
Arnold, Jack (A J Gluck), 1962, Je 16,19:2
Arnold, James, 1949, My 24,27:4
Arnold, James A, 1948, Jl 31,15:4
Arnold, James C, 1947, Je 7,13:6
Arnold, Jennie O, 1949, F 22,23:1
Arnold, John, 1873, N 18,4:7
Arnold, John C, 1958, N 10,29:2
Arnold, John E, 1963, O 1,39:1
Arnold, John H, 1903, D 8,9:4
Arnold, John Mrs, 1951, Je 28,25:4
Arnold, John P, 1942, Ap 17,17:1; 1956, D 9,89:2
Arnold, John W, 1953, Je 5,12:6
Arnold, Joseph, 1950, Mr 26,94:3
Arnold, Joseph Dr, 1913, N 7,9:3
Arnold, Joseph M, 1958, F 16,86:4
Arnold, Karl, 1958, Je 30,19:3
Arnold, Katherine D Mrs, 1949, Ag 1,17:4
Arnold, Katherine I, 1943, N 23,25:5
Arnold, L C, 1956, S 26,33:2
Arnold, L H, 1907, D 29,9:5
Arnold, L J, 1943, Mr 1,19:5
Arnold, Laura, 1962, Ag 19,88:8
Arnold, Lauren Mrs, 1961, N 26,87:2
Arnold, Lawrence S, 1954, Ap 27,29:4
Arnold, Leslie P, 1961, Mr 22,41:1
Arnold, Linton B, 1940, Je 6,25:2
Arnold, Lois Mrs, 1947, Ja 28,23:3
Arnold, Lord, 1945, Ag 4,11:5
Arnold, Louis P, 1943, Ja 26,19:5
Arnold, Louise F, 1947, N 7,23:4
Arnold, Lynn John, 1968, Ag 24,29:5
Arnold, Lynn U Judge, 1920, My 28,13:4
Arnold, Martha C Mrs, 1950, O 12,31:1
Arnold, Mary, 1966, Jl 12,43:1
Arnold, Mary S (will), 1939, Ag 29,12:6
Arnold, Matthew, 1888, Ap 17,5:2
Arnold, Matthew Mrs, 1901, Jl 1,7:5
Arnold, Michael Judge, 1903, Ap 25,9:4
Arnold, Moody W, 1944, Ag 23,19:6
Arnold, Mortimer P, 1959, My 10,86:6
Arnold, Nason H, 1949, O 18,27:3
Arnold, Olney, 1916, Mr 7,11:4; 1916, Ap 5,13:5
Arnold, Olney Mrs, 1948, Je 24,25:3
Arnold, Oscar M, 1961, N 22,33:4
Arnold, Oswald J, 1949, Je 16,29:4
Arnold, Percy W Col, 1919, F 20,13:4
Arnold, Perry, 1946, D 13,23:2
Arnold, Phil N, 1956, S 15,17:1
Arnold, R Gen, 1882, N 9,5:5
Arnold, Rich H Sr Mrs, 1954, Mr 12,31:3
Arnold, Richard, 1918, Je 22,11:6
Arnold, Richard J, 1941, Ja 20,17:4
Arnold, Robert, 1956, Ja 30,8:8
Arnold, Robert B, 1957, Mr 20,37:6
Arnold, Robert W, 1943, Ja 21,21:4
Arnold, Samuel B, 1961, Ja 30,23:2
Arnold, Samuel Bland, 1906, S 22,1:6
Arnold, Samuel T, 1956, D 13,37:5
Arnold, Sarah L, 1943, F 27,14:8
Arnold, Seth, 1955, Ja 4,21:2
Arnold, Tom M, 1967, Ja 12,39:5
Arnold, Victor E, 1943, Mr 20,15:1
Arnold, W Richmond, 1957, Jl 3,23:3
Arnold, Walter C (will), 1937, S 10,24:2
Arnold, Walter R, 1946, My 1,26:2
Arnold, Wayne R, 1955, N 16,35:4
Arnold, William B Mrs, 1958, S 30,31:3
Arnold, William C, 1955, Ag 2,17:4
Arnold, William C 2d, 1952, N 28,25:1
Arnold, William Campbell, 1925, Jl 21,21:5
Arnold, William E, 1940, My 12,49:1; 1951, Ap 4,29:3
Arnold, William F, 1959, Ag 22,17:6
Arnold, William G, 1959, Jl 1,25:6
Arnold, William Mrs (will), 1945, S 6,26:3
Arnold, William R, 1940, Jl 22,17:3; 1965, Ja 8,29:3
Arnold, William W, 1957, N 25,31:4
Arnold Edward, Bro (J S Saunders), 1952, D 29,19:1
Arnold-Forster, Hugh Oakley, 1909, Mr 13,7:6
Arnolds, Edward W C, 1954, F 8,23:2
Arnolds, Laura, 1938, Je 17,21:5
Arnoldson, C, 1943, S 30,21:2
Arnoldson, K F, 1916, F 21,11:6
Arnolt, Frederick M, 1960, S 22,27:5
Arnolt, Mary E Mrs, 1938, Ja 3,21:5
Arnolth, Samuel, 1903, Jl 21,9:6
Arnon, David, 1968, My 4,39:1
Arnone, Alphonse, 1951, N 24,11:2
Arnone, Eugenia L Mrs, 1950, Je 13,27:2
Arnot, Clinton D, 1967, Ap 28,41:2
Arnot, George B, 1949, D 15,35:2
Arnot, John P, 1951, D 3,31:1
Arnot, Matthias H, 1910, F 16,9:4
Arnot, S T, 1884, N 19,2:4
Arnott, Charles E, 1967, Ap 16,82:6
Arnott, David, 1959, Ja 31,19:3
Arnott, David Mrs, 1962, Je 22,25:4
Arnott, Fred S, 1954, Ja 11,25:4
Arnott, J M, 1885, Je 9,5:4
Arnott, John, 1940, Jl 27,13:4
Arnott, Lauriston J, 1958, Jl 4,19:5
Arnott, Neil Dr, 1874, Mr 16,5:6
Arnott, Robert, 1951, Mr 31,15:5
Arnott, Robert F, 1955, F 4,19:8
Arnoux, Gabriel, 1912, Ja 17,13:4
Arnoux, William H, 1907, Ap 24,9:5
Arnovich, Morrie, 1959, Jl 21,29:1
Arnow, Arthur, 1937, Ap 15,23:2
Arnowitz, Max Mrs, 1948, F 18,27:3
Arns, Charles W, 1938, Jl 13,21:5
Arnsdorf, Henry G, 1941, O 18,19:3
Arnson, Ludwig, 1958, Ap 13,83:6
Arnson, Richard B, 1948, Ag 13,15:4
Arnsparger, James D, 1949, F 28,19:4
Arnst, F Hugo, 1965, Jl 13,4:5
Arnstein, Alex H, 1959, Ap 30,31:3
Arnstein, Alexander E, 1968, S 29,80:6
Arnstein, Daniel G, 1960, Ag 20,19:1
Arnstein, Elizabeth (will, Mr 5,25:2), 1940, F 24,13:2
Arnstein, Hugo, 1957, Je 10,27:4
Arnstein, Leo, 1944, Ag 15,17:3
Arnstein, Leo Mrs (trb lr, My 7,30:6), 1953, Ap 2, 28:3
Arnstein, Max B, 1961, Je 21,37:3
Arnstein, Max L, 1965, Mr 13,25:2
Arnstein, Moritz, 1955, O 30,89:2
Arnstein, Rudolph, 1937, My 6,25:2
Arnstein, Samuel, 1942, N 14,15:2
Arnswalde, Paul A, 1947, S 6,17:4
Arntz, Friedrich M L, 1956, Jl 14,15:5
Arntzen, Viggo S, 1952, Mr 21,23:3
Arnulf Paul, Bro (C A MacDonald), 1959, Je 26,25:3
Arnup, Jesse H, 1965, Ap 6,39:2
Arny, Charles, 1956, D 25,25:4
Arny, Charles F, 1954, Ja 25,19:2
Arny, Frank J, 1946, Ja 3,19:4
Arny, Henry V, 1943, N 4,23:3
Arnzen, Frank E, 1947, Ap 15,25:5
Aro, Toivo, 1951, Mr 19,30:7
Aroh, Calvin H, 1942, Ap 11,13:4
Aron, Albert W, 1945, N 2,19:2
Aron, Benedict, 1950, D 9,15:3
Aron, Elias, 1956, Jl 21,15:2
Aron, Frederick S, 1962, Ja 23,33:4
Aron, Herman M, 1939, Ja 31,21:1
Aron, Jacob, 1964, Ag 31,25:1
Aron, Max, 1950, F 5,84:5
Aron, Milt, 1942, Mr 7,17:2
Aron, Paul, 1955, F 10,31:1
Aron, Sol Mrs, 1956, Ap 2,23:4
Arone, Robert A, 1954, Jl 14,38:1
Aronoff, Isaac, 1965, Jl 23,29:3
Aronoff, Jacob B, 1952, N 18,31:1
Aronoff, Marcus, 1950, F 27,19:1
Aronovici, Carol, 1957, Ag 1,25:3
Aronovitch, A H, 1952, S 9,31:3
Aronovitz, Berl, 1967, F 18,29:4
Aronow, Boris A S, 1950, S 6,29:1
Aronow, Edward I, 1958, O 22,35:5
Aronow, Gustave I, 1947, N 11,27:2
Aronowitz, Alex, 1958, Mr 15,17:6
Aronowitz, Alex Mrs, 1965, D 11,33:3
Aronowitz, Max, 1941, D 15,19:2
Aronowitz, Morris, 1954, F 1,23:3
Aronowitz, Samuel, 1964, N 13,32:7
Arons, Adolph, 1945, D 21,21:3
Arons, Ben L, 1966, F 9,39:1
Arons, Isidore, 1958, N 12,37:5
Arons, Louis, 1943, N 7,56:5
Aronsberg, Michael Mrs, 1952, Mr 6,31:1
Aronsohn, Isaac, 1953, Ag 12,31:3
Aronsohn, Samuel J, 1957, Ap 28,87:1
Aronson, Albert S, 1952, Ap 4,33:5
Aronson, Albert Y, 1957, Ap 12,23:1
Aronson, Alex H, 1960, Ag 10,31:4
Aronson, Alexander S, 1947, Je 11,27:2
Aronson, Carrie G Mrs, 1938, Jl 10,30:7
Aronson, David, 1962, Jl 10,33:4
Aronson, Edward A Dr, 1922, Je 26,13:7
Aronson, Frederick H, 1920, D 2,11:3
Aronson, George C, 1949, N 22,29:1
Aronson, Henry, 1965, Ap 16,29:4
Aronson, Irving J, 1961, D 11,31:4
Aronson, Israel H, 1948, Ja 11,56:4
Aronson, Jacob, 1951, Ja 14,85:1; 1966, Ap 17,87:1
Aronson, Jacob J, 1941, Ag 5,19:6
Aronson, Joseph D, 1958, O 19,87:2
Aronson, Jules E, 1947, O 12,76:5
Aronson, L S, 1934, F 2,17:1
Aronson, Louis Mrs, 1959, S 25,24:3
Aronson, Louis V, 1940, N 3,57:1
Aronson, Maurice, 1946, O 9,27:4
Aronson, Max, 1951, Jl 1,51:2; 1959, Ja 9,25:2
Aronson, Max Mrs, 1965, Mr 2,38:6
Aronson, Mayer, 1917, Mr 13,11:4
Aronson, Morris, 1954, My 12,31:3
Aronson, Moses, 1939, Mr 18,17:3
Aronson, Naoum, 1943, O 1,19:3
Aronson, Nathan, 1949, My 17,25:2
Aronson, Phil, 1952, Ag 1,17:3
Aronson, Rudolph, 1919, F 6,11:3
Aronson, Samuel, 1950, Jl 18,29:5
Aronson, Samuel M, 1955, S 24,19:4
Aronson, Seth, 1966, N 15,41:6
Aronstam, Charles S, 1950, Ag 27,88:3
Aronstein, William, 1954, Mr 14,88:1
Arosema, Louisa L, 1907, Mr 28,9:6
Arosemena, Albino H, 1937, Ap 19,21:5
Arosemena, Alcibiades, 1958, Ap 9,36:1
Arosemena, Carlos C, 1946, Jl 12,17:1
Arosemena, Carlos J, 1952, F 21,27:5

Arosemena, Carlos Mrs, 1948, My 8,15:4
Arosemena, Florencio H, 1945, Ag 31,17:1
Arosemena, Juan D, 1939, D 16,17:6
Arosemena, Pablo, 1947, O 7,27:3
Arostegui, Gonzalo E, 1962, Ag 20,23:4
Arostegui y del Castillo, Gonzalo, 1940, N 19,23:5
Arostegul, Martin Mrs, 1944, Ja 27,19:1
Arouet, Jacques S, 1951, Ap 2,25:6
Arouet, Jacques S Mrs, 1960, Jl 14,27:3
Arp, Benjamin, 1958, Je 27,25:5
Arp, Bill (C H Smith), 1903, Ag 25,7:6
Arp, Jean, 1966, Je 8,43:1
Arpels, Julien, 1964, Ap 10,35:4
Arpert, Eric, 1965, Jl 16,27:2
Arpin, Leo Mrs, 1967, D 23,23:1
Arps, George F, 1939, S 18,19:4
Arquette, Frank, 1945, O 21,46:2
Arra, Gabriel, 1957, Ag 18,83:1
Arraiz, Antonio, 1962, S 17,31:4
Arrants, William, 1955, My 14,19:5
Arras, Edmund F, 1951, O 20,15:4
Arrau, Lucretia L de (Donna), 1959, O 27,37:2
Arredondo, Eliseo, 1923, O 20,15:4
Arrel, George F Judge, 1923, Ap 8,6:2
Arrell, John Rev, 1885, Ja 31,5:3
Arrhenius, S, 1927, O 3,23:2
Arriaga, Manuel de, 1917, Mr 6,11:6
Arrick, Clifford, 1922, Jl 14,13:5
Arries, Leslie G, 1966, N 26,35:2
Arrieta, Alfredo J L, 1950, Je 13,27:3
Arrieta Rossi, Reyes, 1957, My 31,19:1
Arrighi, Antonio Andrea Rev, 1923, F 26,13:4
Arrighi, Charles T, 1949, Jl 24,52:2
Arrighi, Charles T Mrs, 1944, Ap 20,19:4
Arrighi, Roswell S, 1955, N 3,31:4
Arrigo, Leon, 1949, Je 8,29:3
Arrigona, Luis, 1948, Jl 7,46:1
Arrigoni, Dionigi, 1957, Jl 30,23:5
Arrigoni, Frank, 1942, Je 13,15:5
Arrington, John W, 1938, N 15,23:5
Arrington, Peter, 1916, Ag 13,15:6
Arrison, Howard W, 1952, N 25,29:2
Arrivabene, Giovanni, 1881, Je 13,5:6
Arrol, William Sir, 1913, F 21,13:5
Arronet, Lina E Mrs, 1938, My 28,15:4
Arronson, Jacob, 1953, Je 20,17:4
Arrott, Charles F, 1942, My 24,43:2
Arrott, William Mrs, 1951, Ap 9,25:5
Arrowood, Stacy D, 1938, F 14,17:2
Arrowsmith, Eusebius, 1907, O 3,9:4
Arrowsmith, George A, 1952, Mr 11,27:6
Arrowsmith, Harold Mrs, 1950, N 30,33:2
Arrowsmith, Harold Rev, 1918, S 16,11:8
Arrowsmith, John E, 1958, F 10,23:3
Arrowsmith, Leighton M, 1961, My 14,86:6
Arrowsmith, Mary A Mrs, 1940, Ja 20,15:2
Arrowsmith, Mary N, 1965, O 11,39:3
Arrowsmith, R, 1928, Je 3,25:5
Arrowsmith, Stephen V, 1910, Ja 18,11:4
Arrowsmith, Thomas V, 1946, N 3,62:4
Arrowsmith, William B, 1953, S 20,86:6
Arroyo, Julian A, 1959, Ap 4,19:2
Arruza, Carlos (funl, My 23,26:4), 1966, My 21,31:1
Arscott, Allan E, 1952, O 15,31:5
Arsene Karageorgevitch, Prince, 1938, O 24,17:5
Arsenius Cassian, Bro (J Harvey), 1949, F 23,28:3
Arslan, Adel, 1954, Ja 24,84:4
Arslan, Mazhar, 1948, My 28,23:3
Art, Adolphus E, 1937, Je 19,15:4
Artale, Paul J, 1966, Ag 22,33:3
Artaserse, Ambrose, 1946, Jl 5,19:5
Artaserse, Peter P Mrs, 1940, My 28,23:5
Artayeta, Eduardo A, 1944, Ag 26,11:2
Arteaga, Miguel, 1952, S 5,27:3
Arteaga y Betancourt, Manuel (Cardinal), 1963, Mr 22,9:2
Artelt, Theodore W, 1954, Ag 31,21:5
Artemiuk, Platon, 1951, Ag 7,25:2
Arter, J Charles, 1923, D 30,20:1
Arter, Roy C, 1946, S 24,29:4
Arters, John M, 1943, F 20,13:4
Artesani, Arthur L, 1946, N 24,79:3
Arthur, Anne Elizabeth, 1915, Ap 11,11:5
Arthur, C A, 1886, N 19,4:2
Arthur, C A Mrs, 1880, Ja 14,5:2
Arthur, C S, 1884, Jl 7,5:2
Arthur, Cecil B, 1947, Je 22,52:6
Arthur, Charles G, 1953, Ja 25,84:5
Arthur, Chester A, 1937, Jl 19,16:2
Arthur, Chester A Mrs, 1965, N 13,29:1
Arthur, Daniel V, 1939, D 7,27:6
Arthur, Donald, 1956, Ag 3,19:5
Arthur, Edward C, 1963, Jl 30,29:4
Arthur, George, 1946, Ja 15,23:4
Arthur, George D, 1937, Ja 2,14:1
Arthur, George D Mrs, 1955, N 2,35:4
Arthur, George M, 1949, Mr 9,25:2
Arthur, George Maj, 1901, Je 7,9:5
Arthur, George N, 1907, Ag 29,7:4
Arthur, George R, 1941, My 28,25:5
Arthur, Grant A, 1954, D 7,33:4
Arthur, Hayward B, 1955, Ag 14,81:2
Arthur, Helen, 1939, D 10,68:5
Arthur, Henry W, 1939, Je 8,25:4
Arthur, Herbert S, 1952, Je 14,15:1
Arthur, James B McK, 1963, Jl 19,25:3
Arthur, James H, 1943, O 27,23:5
Arthur, James Jr, 1951, Jl 19,23:5
Arthur, John P, 1951, My 9,33:2
Arthur, John W, 1937, Mr 19,23:2
Arthur, Joseph C, 1942, My 1,19:3
Arthur, Julia, 1950, Mr 30,29:5
Arthur, Lee, 1917, D 11,15:6
Arthur, M Wilson, 1952, Ja 5,11:1
Arthur, Mary Mrs, 1925, Ap 21,21:6
Arthur, P M Chief, 1903, Jl 17,1:6
Arthur, Paul H, 1962, Ap 10,43:2
Arthur, Prince of Connaught, 1938, S 12,17:3
Arthur, R Amos A, 1948, F 6,23:3
Arthur, Robert, 1914, O 22,11:6
Arthur, Stanley C Mrs, 1959, D 3,37:3
Arthur, T S, 1885, Mr 7,1:5
Arthur, W Albert, 1960, Ja 22,27:3
Arthur, William C Mrs, 1942, Ag 5,19:5; 1953, Ag 28, 17:5
Arthur, William G, 1943, Jl 20,19:1
Arthur, William Rev Dr, 1875, O 30,6:7
Arthur of Connaught, Princess, 1959, F 27,52:6
Arthurs, Glenn W, 1948, F 11,27:3
Arthurs, James Lt Col, 1937, O 8,24:3
Arthurs, Stanley M, 1950, Mr 20,21:3
Arthurs, Walter F, 1949, Mr 17,25:4
Arthurs, William E, 1951, Ag 10,15:4
Articola, Frank J, 1955, S 29,33:2
Artieda, Helen S Mrs, 1938, My 2,17:3
Artieres, Louis, 1957, S 2,13:2
Artin, Emil, 1963, Ja 4,4:1
Artingstall, Margaret, 1951, F 20,25:3
Artman, Lawrence P, 1954, Ja 3,89:1
Arts, Anthony H, 1958, Ag 24,87:2
Artsay, Nicholas C, 1956, Je 21,31:2
Artz, Webb C, 1941, Jl 3,19:1
Artzybasheff, Boris, 1965, Jl 18,69:1
Artzybasheff, Boris Mrs, 1955, N 13,89:2
Arum, George, 1963, O 7,31:3
Arundale, George S, 1945, Ag 13,19:5
Arundel, George W, 1903, S 1,7:6
Arundel, Martin D Mrs, 1963, My 11,25:5
Arundell, Daniell, 1946, F 22,25:3
Arundell, Everard Aloysius Rev, 1907, Jl 12,7:6
Arutyunov, Bagrat N, 1953, Ja 27,25:3
Arvey, Mary P Mrs, 1955, Ja 1,13:2
Arvidson, Carl E, 1954, O 22,28:1
Arvin, Neil C, 1953, Mr 18,31:3
Arvin, Newton (Mar 22), 1963, Ap 1,35:1
Arvine, Earliss Porter, 1914, Je 24,11:6
Arvintz, Fannie W Mrs (F Wolff), 1961, N 29,41:1
Arvold, Alfred G, 1957, Ap 18,29:5
Arwine, John S Com, 1924, Ag 30,9:6
Ary, Ray, 1947, Jl 9,23:5
Arze, Jose A, 1955, Ag 24,27:3
Arzee, Paul T, 1968, Je 8,31:2
Arzouyan, A, 1933, Je 2,19:5
Arzt, Leopold, 1955, My 22,88:7
Asada, Haime, 1952, Jl 18,19:6
Asada, Keiichi, 1944, D 20,23:3
Asaf Ali (Min), 1953, Ap 3,23:1
Asaf Jah Nizam-ul-Mulk,Nizam of Hyderabad, 1911, Ag 30,7:5
Asafieff, Boris V, 1949, Ja 29,14:2
Asakawa, Kan-Ichi, 1948, Ag 12,21:1
Asam, Charles L, 1951, S 4,27:4
Asano, Chokun Marquis, 1937, F 2,23:5
Asart, William F, 1954, Jl 11,73:1
Asay, A Roy, 1947, Ag 29,17:2
Asay, Mary Mrs, 1937, Je 3,28:2
Asbjornsen, Sigvald H, 1954, S 10,23:3
Asboth, Alex Gen, 1868, Mr 6,4:7
Asbury, Clement DeM, 1963, N 26,38:2
Asbury, Frank H, 1946, F 16,13:3
Asbury, Harry E, 1937, Ap 17,17:1
Asbury, Herbert, 1963, F 25,16:6
Asbury, John C, 1941, S 3,24:4
Ascalesi, Alessio, 1952, My 11,92:5
Ascari, Alberto, 1955, My 27,21:2
Ascari, Maria, 1940, Jl 28,27:4
Ascenzi, Sante, 1941, Ja 15,23:5
Asch, Abraham, 1966, Ja 3,27:4
Asch, Arthur S, 1962, Ag 18,19:3
Asch, Ben M, 1958, N 25,33:4
Asch, David, 1945, Ja 18,19:4
Asch, Jeanne (Mrs A J Ezickson), 1963, S 15,87:1
Asch, Joseph, 1956, Ap 5,29:4; 1962, My 4,33:4
Asch, Max, 1956, S 7,24:3
Asch, Nathan, 1964, D 25,29:2
Asch, Noel Mrs, 1950, F 21,25:2
Asch, Oswald S, 1905, Ja 21,9:6
Asch, Samuel, 1958, S 2,25:1
Asch, Sholem (will, D 18,44:6), 1957, Jl 11,25:1
Asch, Sholem Mrs, 1962, My 26,25:5
Asch, Solomon Mrs, 1952, Mr 11,27:6
Asch, William W, 1951, Ap 11,29:3
Asche, Herman T (por), 1949, Mr 13,76:6
Asche, O, 1936, Mr 24,23:3
Ascheim, Jules, 1938, O 1,17:4
Aschenbach, Charles H, 1938, S 10,17:5
Aschenbach, Cyril G, 1960, O 16,88:7
Aschenbach, Walter J Mrs, 1956, F 23,27:3
Aschenbrenner, Walter C, 1947, F 5,23:5
Ascher, Anita L, 1957, Ag 17,15:5
Ascher, Charles S Mrs, 1960, Mr 6,86:8
Ascher, Leo, 1942, Mr 3,23:2
Ascher, Leopold, 1941, N 14,23:3
Ascher, Samuel W, 1960, Je 3,31:1
Ascher, Sidney, 1949, Mr 17,25:4
Ascherfeld, Louis H, 1950, Je 13,27:1
Aschner, Bernard, 1960, Mr 11,25:1
Asciutto, Otto, 1966, Ap 12,39:2
Ascoli, Alberto, 1957, S 29,86:6
Ascoli, Enrico, 1951, My 4,27:3
Ascroft, Eileen (death held accidental, My 4,6:3), 1962, Ap 30,5:5
Asdang, Chao Fa Prince, 1925, F 11,21:3
Aseltine, Alverton H, 1942, S 26,15:5
Asen, Abraham, 1965, Ag 7,21:4
Asensio, Jose, 1961, F 25,21:1
Aseyev, Nikolai, 1963, Jl 18,27:3
Asfalg, Joseph G, 1968, Ja 4,34:5
Ash, Charles B, 1943, Ja 11,15:3
Ash, Charles E, 1939, Mr 9,21:2
Ash, Charles F, 1938, Ja 27,21:2
Ash, Edward, 1967, Jl 8,25:1
Ash, Edward B, 1941, Mr 28,23:6
Ash, Francis W, 1967, Ja 30,26:4
Ash, Frank C Mrs, 1950, Ja 1,42:5
Ash, Harrison B, 1944, My 16,21:6
Ash, Jerome H, 1953, Ja 6,29:2
Ash, Max, 1964, Ap 28,37:3
Ash, Maxwell, 1961, Mr 28,35:2
Ash, Patrick A, 1939, Ja 19,19:2
Ash, Paul R, 1958, Jl 14,21:4
Ash, Paul T, 1961, N 19,88:1
Ash, Robert E Sr, 1946, Ag 31,15:4
Ash, Roland C, 1942, S 22,21:4
Ash, Theodore E, 1945, D 16,40:1
Ash, Thomas E, 1953, Ag 30,90:1
Ash, William, 1915, Ja 15,11:4
Ash, William C, 1958, O 27,27:5
Ashauer, Louis C, 1944, N 26,57:1
Ashbaugh, Homer T, 1938, Ap 21,19:2
Ashbaugh, John L, 1959, F 10,33:1
Ashbee, Charles F, 1962, My 28,29:4
Ashbee, Charles R, 1942, My 29,17:5
Ashbourne, Lord (Edw Gibson), 1913, My 23,13:5
Ashbourne, Lord, 1942, Ja 25,40:1
Ashbourne, Marianne Lady, 1953, Ag 22,15:6
Ashbridge, Eliza H, 1938, D 15,27:5
Ashbridge, Emily R, 1940, Jl 19,19:4
Ashbridge, Fred A Jr, 1953, Ap 7,29:1
Ashbridge, Samuel H, 1906, Mr 25,9:6
Ashbridge, Thomas L, 1952, Jl 17,23:5
Ashbrook, H Raymond, 1948, Jl 13,28:3
Ashbrook, M Forest Rev Dr, 1968, My 7,47:1
Ashbrook, Paul, 1949, Ag 26,19:2
Ashbrook, Stanley B, 1958, Ja 25,20:1
Ashbrook, William A, 1940, Ja 2,19:3
Ashbrooke, Harriet, 1946, Je 6,21:4
Ashburn, Frank D Mrs, 1964, My 1,35:4
Ashburn, Percy M, 1940, Ag 21,19:4
Ashburn, Sam, 1937, Ag 21,15:5
Ashburn, Thomas Q, 1941, My 3,15:5
Ashburnham, Countess of, 1938, O 10,19:3
Ashburnham, Fleetwood, 1953, Mr 7,15:4
Ashburnham, Thomas Lord, 1924, My 13,21:3
Ashburton, Lord, 1864, Ap 10,3:4; 1938, Mr 28,15:5
Ashby, Albert H, 1953, N 2,25:4
Ashby, Alfred T Mrs, 1943, Jl 13,21:4
Ashby, Arthur W, 1953, S 11,21:5
Ashby, George F, 1950, My 17,29:1
Ashby, Ida N Mrs, 1955, D 5,31:5
Ashby, John L, 1945, Je 20,23:4
Ashby, Thomas E, 1953, Ja 31,15:3
Ashby, William E, 1946, Je 9,40:3
Ashcraft, Alan E, 1961, My 7,86:5
Ashcraft, Edward R, 1938, Ap 27,23:4
Ashcraft, Garland, 1967, Ag 20,88:4
Ashcraft, Lee Mrs, 1945, O 9,21:3
Ashcraft, Leon T, 1945, Ja 20,11:3
Ashcraft, Raymond M, 1946, Je 20,23:1
Ashcroft, Carrie, 1952, Je 30,19:3
Ashcroft, Earl F, 1957, My 21,35:2
Ashcroft, Joseph, 1961, D 1,33:2
Ashcroft, R W, 1947, Ja 9,24:2
Ashcroft, Theodore V, 1951, Je 8,27:1
Ashcroft, William T, 1955, Ja 26,25:2
Ashdown, Cecil S, 1948, Jl 26,17:4
Ashe, Bowman F, 1952, D 17,33:2
Ashe, Charles E, 1940, F 23,15:2
Ashe, Edward J, 1968, Ap 4,47:1
Ashe, Elizabeth H, 1954, Ja 27,27:4
Ashe, Frederic W, 1947, My 23,23:4
Ashe, Gladys C Mrs, 1947, Je 29,48:6
Ashe, James, 1950, Ap 18,31:5
Ashe, John E, 1924, Je 17,19:4
Ashe, Samuel A, 1938, S 2,17:5
Ashe, Sidney W, 1947, Mr 4,25:2
Ashe, Stanley P, 1954, O 1,23:5
Ashe, William F, 1950, Ag 12,13:6
Ashen, David J, 1953, Jl 15,25:5

Ashendorf, Herman P, 1942, Je 30,21:5
Ashenfelter, Robert, 1952, Je 15,84:3
Ashenhurst, Frederick W, 1941, Je 5,23:4
Asher, Abraham, 1948, O 3,64:5
Asher, Ephraim M, 1937, O 30,19:2
Asher, Herman, 1940, Jl 3,17:6
Asher, James, 1958, Ja 13,29:5
Asher, Joseph Mayer Rev Dr, 1909, N 10,9:4
Asher, Leo, 1953, Mr 26,31:5
Asher, Maurice, 1949, Jl 11,17:4
Asher, Max, 1967, N 16,47:2
Asher, William Mrs, 1937, F 3,23:4
Asherman, Edward H, 1940, Mr 3,45:1
Ashfield, Albert W, 1947, Je 19,21:1
Ashfield, Albert W Mrs, 1950, My 28,44:3
Ashfield, John R Sr, 1948, O 9,19:5
Ashfield, Lord, 1948, N 5,25:1
Ashford, B K, 1934, N 2,23:4
Ashford, Mahlon, 1954, Je 6,86:6
Ashford, Taylor J, 1950, O 29,93:1
Ashford, Theodore H, 1940, S 30,17:3
Ashford, William K Mrs, 1938, Ja 24,23:2
Ashforth, A B, 1929, S 5,29:5
Ashforth, Albert B Jr, 1958, Ja 4,15:4
Ashforth, Edward Capt, 1903, S 13,7:5
Ashforth, Frida de Gebele, 1924, Jl 22,15:5
Ashhurst, Harriet, 1938, S 11,II,11:1
Ashhurst, Sarah W, 1937, O 28,25:3
Ashhurst, William W, 1952, F 19,29:1
Ashida, Hitoshi, 1959, Je 21,92:4
Ashinsky, Aaron M, 1954, Ap 3,16:5
Ashkenazi, Meier, 1954, Ag 27,21:6
Ashley, Allen C, 1953, Ag 7,19:3
Ashley, Charles E, 1939, Ja 21,15:6
Ashley, Charles L, 1957, D 30,23:5
Ashley, Charles S, 1941, F 7,19:1
Ashley, Charles S Jr, 1952, Je 4,27:3
Ashley, Clarence De Grand Dr, 1916, Ja 28,9:6
Ashley, Clifford W, 1947, S 20,15:4
Ashley, Daniel W Mrs, 1962, Ja 31,31:4
Ashley, Delos R, 1873, Jl 19,1:6
Ashley, Dexter D, 1949, O 16,88:5
Ashley, Dominic C, 1946, F 5,23:3
Ashley, E, 1931, Mr 31,27:3
Ashley, Edmund A, 1949, F 13,76:2
Ashley, Edward E Jr, 1958, F 4,29:3
Ashley, Edward G, 1939, Jl 15,15:5
Ashley, Edward S, 1947, Jl 29,21:5
Ashley, Edward W, 1938, Je 19,29:2
Ashley, Elizabeth Mrs, 1939, S 7,25:1
Ashley, Ellaphine, 1947, D 16,33:1
Ashley, Florence I, 1940, Ja 9,24:2
Ashley, Frank M, 1942, O 7,25:4
Ashley, Fred B, 1951, Jl 16,21:4
Ashley, Frederick W, 1942, Je 15,19:4
Ashley, George, 1908, O 2,9:6
Ashley, James L, 1945, Mr 7,21:4
Ashley, Jessie, 1919, Ja 22,11:3
Ashley, John S, 1941, Jl 30,17:3
Ashley, Joshua B 3d, 1950, Mr 30,29:3
Ashley, Lucien Seymour, 1912, O 27,II,17:4
Ashley, Lydia R, 1944, My 9,19:2
Ashley, Marjorie, 1951, Ag 24,15:2
Ashley, May, 1951, Ag 23,23:4
Ashley, Ossian D, 1904, D 17,9:5
Ashley, Percy, 1945, S 15,15:3
Ashley, Robert L, 1948, Ap 6,23:2
Ashley, Thomas, 1939, Ag 26,15:4
Ashley, W, 1927, Jl 25,19:4
Ashley, Wilfred Mrs, 1911, F 7,9:6
Ashley, William H Mrs, 1909, My 18,9:5
Ashley, William John, 1921, O 11,19:5
Ashley-Cooper, A (Earl of Shaftesbury), 1885, O 2, 5:5
Ashley-Cooper, Anthony (Earl of Shaftesbury), 1961, Mr 27,31:2
Ashmall W E, 1927, Mr 3,23:3
Ashman, A L (see also O 22,25), 1902, O 28,9:2
Ashman, Alfred, 1952, Je 12,34:6
Ashman, Edward T, 1960, Mr 17,33:1
Ashman, John E, 1946, Jl 22,21:2
Ashman, Walter, 1947, S 28,40:2
Ashmead, Arthur L, 1943, S 11,13:4
Ashmead, Duffield Jr, 1952, My 28,29:4
Ashmead, Graham, 1945, S 10,19:2
Ashmead, Joseph L, 1945, Mr 14,19:1
Ashmead, Percy H, 1919, N 12,13:2
Ashmead, Warren B, 1947, N 25,29:3
Ashmead-Bartlett, E, 1931, My 5,27:1
Ashmore, Edith B Mrs (will), 1939, Mr 26,III,5:2
Ashmore, Edward B, 1953, O 7,29:3
Ashmore, Elmer W J, 1948, Mr 10,28:2
Ashmore, H Warren Sr, 1944, Jl 22,15:6
Ashmore, Lena Ashmore, 1923, F 23,13:4
Ashmore, M E Mrs, 1904, F 21,7:6
Ashmore, Sidney B, 1960, Jl 20,29:1
Ashmore, Sidney G Prof, 1911, My 23,11:5
Ashmun, Bernard I, 1955, Ap 26,29:4
Ashmun, Gilbert A, 1940, My 4,17:5
Ashmun, Margaret E, 1940, Mr 18,17:4
Ashner, Joseph, 1954, D 15,31:4
Ashner, Rudolph M, 1963, N 23,29:5
Ashplant, John S, 1940, Je 7,23:2
Ashraf, Mohammad Agha, 1962, F 11,86:5
Ashten, Charles M, 1949, Mr 22,25:3
Ashton, Amos Turner Rev Dr, 1911, Ja 11,13:4
Ashton, Augustus T (will, O 17,24:8), 1951, O 11, 37:1
Ashton, Charles H, 1966, Ap 4,31:2
Ashton, David G, 1968, My 11,25:6
Ashton, Donald, 1954, Jl 25,69:2
Ashton, Dorothy L, 1958, Mr 21,21:3
Ashton, Elmer, 1947, F 4,25:3
Ashton, Frederick T, 1959, O 9,29:1
Ashton, George, 1953, Ag 3,17:6
Ashton, Herbert Mrs (Jean), 1965, F 27,25:4
Ashton, J Hubley, 1907, Mr 16,9:5
Ashton, James J, 1948, Ap 3,15:2
Ashton, John D, 1942, D 15,28:2
Ashton, John D Mrs, 1918, O 10,11:2
Ashton, Joseph N, 1946, Ag 3,15:2
Ashton, Josie, 1912, Ap 30,11:5
Ashton, Leonard C, 1956, Ap 13,25:1
Ashton, Marvin O, 1946, O 8,23:2
Ashton, Randolph, 1964, F 20,29:2
Ashton, S Algernon B L, 1937, Ap 12,18:1
Ashton, Seth H, 1954, Ap 21,29:1
Ashton, Sylvia, 1940, N 19,24:2
Ashton, William, 1945, F 26,19:1; 1963, S 2,15:2
Ashton, William E, 1957, Jl 24,25:5
Ashurst, Henry F, 1962, Je 1,27:1
Ashurst, Henry F Mrs, 1939, N 2,23:3
Ashurst, Lewis R, 1874, My 6,4:7
Ashvord, Stephen J, 1968, F 27,43:1
Ashwell, Edward Smith, 1914, My 18,9:6
Ashwell Jos A Mrs, 1938, Mr 16,23:5
Ashworth, Abram S, 1952, D 16,31:5
Ashworth, Frederic W, 1941, N 26,23:3
Ashworth, George, 1952, Ja 27,77:2
Ashworth, Harold S, 1959, S 16,39:3
Ashworth, James J, 1953, N 19,31:2
Ashworth, Joseph A, 1948, N 4,29:5
Ashworth, Marie Mrs, 1963, My 9,28:3
Ashworth, Osbourne O, 1945, Jl 7,13:5
Ashworth, Ray, 1960, D 23,19:3
Ashworth, Robert A, 1959, My 9,21:6
Ashworth, Robert A Mrs, 1963, Je 21,29:1
Ashworth, Robert J, 1951, O 7,86:4
Ashworth, Thomas H, 1948, F 23,25:3
Asiala, John J, 1956, Ja 30,27:2
Asiel, Elias, 1920, N 11,13:2
Asiel, Nelson I, 1965, N 4,47:5
Asiel, Robert R, 1961, F 17,24:6
Asimus, William, 1951, Je 24,72:5
Asin y Palacio, Miguel, 1944, Ag 15,17:5
Asinari, Enrico, 1938, Jl 29,17:6
Asinof, Max, 1947, O 27,21:6
Asinof, Morris, 1950, Mr 11,15:5
Asinoff, Jesse Mrs, 1965, D 16,48:1
Asinoff, Morris Mrs, 1941, Ag 18,13:4
Asip, James W, 1965, F 17,43:4
Asip, William, 1938, My 27,17:5
Askew, Curral A, 1950, Mr 23,36:4
Askew, Sarah B, 1942, O 21,21:4
Askey, Edwin G Mrs, 1946, S 6,21:1
Askey, William J, 1940, My 22,23:5
Askin, H, 1934, O 1,17:4
Askin, John M, 1944, O 14,13:3
Askin, Joseph S, 1953, D 20,76:3
Askin, Morris W, 1954, Ja 26,27:2
Askin, William F, 1952, F 28,27:4
Askland, Jon Alfred, 1968, Jl 10,39:3
Askonas, Charles, 1946, Ag 21,27:2
Askowith, Dora, 1958, O 25,21:2
Askwith, Charles, 1953, O 27,27:2
Askwith, Lord, 1942, Je 4,19:3
Asmus, Fred J, 1959, My 23,25:3
Asmus, Henry, 1939, Mr 2,21:2
Asmuth, William A, 1947, Mr 28,23:2
Asnas, Max, 1968, D 12,47:2
Asofsky, Abraham, 1943, Ag 6,15:2
Asofsky, Morris, 1962, My 5,27:5
Aspbury, George, 1946, N 29,25:3
Aspbury, George Mrs, 1951, D 22,15:5
Aspegren, John, 1924, N 9,7:2
Aspel, Elizabeth J, 1952, N 21,25:3
Aspell, Lillian, 1944, My 18,19:5
Aspell Thos A, 1938, Ag 3,19:6
Aspenburg, Charles A, 1957, F 11,29:5
Asper, George H, 1943, F 26,20:2
Asper, Mark W, 1945, D 7,21:2
Aspettati, Antonio M, 1949, Ja 19,28:2
Aspillaga, Antero, 1922, Ja 12,17:6
Aspinall, John A, 1953, Ap 9,27:1
Aspinall, John Sir, 1937, Ja 20,21:5
Aspinall, Joseph (will, Jl 23,15:1), 1939, My 9,24:4
Aspinall, William, 1903, D 17,9:4
Aspinall, William Mrs, 1903, N 28,9:5
Aspinwall, Clarence A, 1964, Mr 1,83:2
Aspinwall, Ernest E, 1948, O 3,64:3
Aspinwall, John, 1949, Ap 29,23:3
Aspinwall, John Abel Rev, 1913, F 15,15:4
Aspinwall, John L (funl), 1873, My 17,12:4
Aspinwall, L Gen, 1886, S 5,7:4
Aspinwall, Lane, 1942, My 4,19:3
Aspinwall, Ny P, 1953, O 24,15:4
Aspinwall, W H (funl, Ja 22,12:2), 1875, Ja 19,8:3
Aspinwall, William, 1955, Ja 7,21:4
Aspinwall, William H, 1910, N 16,11:4
Asplund, Karl, 1949, Ag 11,23:3
Asplund, Rupert F, 1952, D 8,41:2
Asplundh, Carl Sr, 1967, Jl 4,19:1
Asprinio, Maria I Mrs, 1952, Ja 6,93:1
Asquini, Fabro Cardinal, 1879, Ja 12,8:2
Asquith, Anthony, 1968, F 22,32:3
Asquith, Arthur M, 1939, Ag 26,15:4
Asquith, Cyril Lord, 1954, Ag 25,27:4
Asquith, Frank, 1943, Mr 21,26:6
Asquith, Herbert, 1947, Ag 8,17:5
Asquith, Mary, 1942, D 24,15:4
Assaf, Simcha, 1953, O 19,21:6
Assalta, Raffaele Dr, 1909, Jl 7,4:2
Assante, Pasquale, 1947, N 25,29:3
Assaykeen, Ivan V, 1947, Ja 10,21:4
Asscher, Abraham, 1950, My 3,29:1
Asscher, Ellis, 1958, Ap 16,33:1
Asscher, Joseph, 1937, Ag 20,17:3
Asselin, Hector, 1953, O 12,27:6
Asselin, Joseph O, 1961, Jl 28,21:6
Asselin, Olivar, 1937, Ap 19,21:4
Asselineau, Charles (funl), 1874, Ag 16,1:1
Assell, Jeanette, 1946, D 16,47:5
Assell, Peter H, 1949, O 26,27:5
Assemani, Paul, 1958, N 7,14:3
Asser, John, 1949, F 5,15:6
Asser, Tobias Michael Carel, 1913, Jl 30,7:4
Asserson, Alice M B Mrs, 1940, My 18,15:3
Asserson, Christian, 1939, Jl 10,19:2
Asserson, M Alice, 1943, Ja 11,15:2
Asserson, Peter C Rear-Adm, 1906, D 7,11:6
Asserson, Raymond Sr, 1955, F 5,15:4
Asset, Henri L, 1962, Mr 28,39:2
Assier, Emilio, 1946, N 10,62:4
Assing, James, 1952, N 24,23:3
Assissium, Sister Mary, 1875, S 4,5:2
Assmann, F A, 1936, F 20,19:3
Assmann, Frank A, 1966, Jl 25,27:4
Assmann, Frank A Mrs, 1948, Jl 13,27:2
Assmann, Frederick P, 1947, S 2,21:5
Assmann, Heinz, 1954, O 19,27:2
Assmus, Albert L, 1937, O 29,21:4
Assmuth, Joseph A, 1954, Jl 9,17:2
Assur, Samuel, 1950, S 11,23:4
Ast, Abraham W, 1959, S 21,31:2
Ast, Abraham W Mrs, 1942, N 5,25:4
Ast, Philip, 1903, My 9,9:6
Astahov, Paval, 1964, O 10,29:4
Astaire, Fred Mrs, 1954, S 14,27:4
Astakhov, Fyodor A, 1966, O 14,43:4
Astangov, Mikhail F, 1965, Ap 22,33:2
Astarita, Frank W, 1958, Mr 9,86:4
Astarita, Joseph, 1966, O 24,39:4
Astbury, John Sir, 1939, Ag 23,21:6
Aste, Anthony L, 1954, D 9,33:5
Astel, I, 1937, Ag 12,43:1
Astifan, Louis, 1956, My 5,19:4
Astill, William E, 1948, F 11,27:1
Astin, Waldemar, 1940, My 5,52:1
Astler, Katherine A, 1949, F 24,23:4
Astlett, Harry, 1954, My 12,31:4
Astley, Albert E D (Lord Hastings), 1956, Ja 19,33:5
Astley, Fred C Mrs, 1946, S 17,7:5
Astley, G Mason, 1954, Ja 16,15:1
Astley, George M Mrs, 1911, My 6,13:6
Astley, Philip, 1958, D 29,15:4
Aston, Edward R, 1964, D 2,50:5
Aston, Felia, 1883, N 11,9:5
Aston, Francis W, 1945, N 22,36:2
Aston, Fred A Sr, 1958, Mr 9,86:5
Aston, George, 1938, D 3,19:2
Aston, J L Mrs, 1957, S 9,25:2
Aston, John H Mrs, 1953, Je 10,29:2
Aston, Ralph Adm, 1904, D 13,9:6
Aston, Walter R, 1944, S 6,19:4
Astor, Frank, 1944, My 27,15:7
Astor, Henry, 1918, Je 8,11:5
Astor, J J, 1890, F 23,1:5
Astor, J J Mrs, 1887, D 12,1:2
Astor, Jacob, 1910, Ag 20,7:5
Astor, Louis, 1966, Je 20,33:1
Astor, Nancy (Dowager Viscountess),(est appr, Ag 25,29:4), 1964, My 3,1:3
Astor, Vincent (will, F 6,27:8; funl, F 7,19:3), 1959, F 4,1:2
Astor, Vincent (estate tax appraisal), 1960, Jl 1,16:5
Astor, Viscount (por), 1919, O 20,15:2
Astor, Viscount (Wm W Astor),(will, Ap 26,3:1), 1966, Mr 8,39:1
Astor, W B (funl, Nov 27), 1875, N 25,1:1
Astor, W B Mrs (funl), 1872, F 20,1:5
Astor, W W Mrs, 1894, D 23,1:5
Astor, Waldorf, 1952, O 1,33:1
Astor, William, 1892, Ap 27,1:5
Astor, William Mrs (funl), 1908, N 1,9:6
Astor of Hever, Lady (Violet),(est acctg, Mr 18,11:5), 1965, Ja 4,29:1
Astori, Alda, 1949, S 11,95:3
Astrab, Peter, 1941, N 1,15:4
Astrachan, Girsch D, 1946, My 2,21:3

Astrana Marin, Luis, 1959, D 6,86:8
Astray, Jose M, 1954, Ja 2,11:3
Astray, Pilar M, 1949, My 23,23:5
Astrid, Queen of the Belgians, 1935, Ag 30,1:8
Astrom, Carl P, 1944, Ja 31,17:4
Astronsky, Louis, 1942, D 28,20:2
Astry, Perry D, 1953, Ja 7,31:5
Astwood, Charles H, 1941, S 9,23:1
Astwood, Edgar, 1937, Je 3,28:2
Astwood, Edwin P, 1948, Ap 17,15:3
Asunsolo, Jesus L, 1940, Jl 20,9:1
Aswell, Edward C, 1958, N 6,37:3
Aswell, Ella F Mrs, 1937, S 14,23:6
Aswell, James, 1955, F 24,27:3
Aszman, Frank G, 1943, F 23,21:1
Aszman, Harry, 1950, Jl 8,13:5
Aszman, Mary J Mrs, 1948, S 1,23:3
Aszman, Paul H, 1944, Ja 6,23:2
Atadan, Makbule Mme (funl, Ja 20,23:1), 1956, Ja 19,33:2
Atanasio, Charles, 1940, Ap 12,12:3
Atassi, Hashem al, 1960, D 7,43:1
Ataturk, M K, 1938, N 11,1:4
Atcherley, Llewellyn W, 1954, F 18,31:5
Atcherly, Rowland C, 1940, Ap 18,23:4
Atcheson, George Jr, 1948, Ja 10,15:2
Atcheson, Harold G, 1951, Mr 11,95:1
Atcheson, James, 1956, N 16,27:3
Atchinson, Thomas R (T O'Grady), 1942, S 2,23:2
Atchison, Herman S, 1949, Jl 31,61:1
Atchison, Orin, 1957, Ap 21,88:4
Atchison, William S, 1939, Mr 5,48:8
Aten, Norman E, 1938, Ag 20,15:6
Ates, Roscoe, 1962, Mr 2,29:1
Ates, Roscoe Mrs, 1955, My 20,25:3
Atha, Albert H, 1956, F 6,23:3
Atha, Benjamin, 1925, O 26,19:6
Atha, George R, 1942, Ag 4,19:3
Atha, Henry G, 1943, Ap 7,26:2
Atha, Howard D, 1943, F 24,21:4
Athanas, Verne, 1962, Je 23,23:4
Athanase-Emile, Bro (L A Ritiman), 1952, S 11,31:2
Athanassakis, John, 1953, D 31,19:2
Athearn, Fred, 1949, O 4,27:2
Atheling, Edith Mrs, 1944, N 24,23:4
Athenagoras, Archbishop, 1962, O 16,39:1
Atheras, Allen M, 1961, D 31,48:5
Atherhold, Arthur F, 1915, Ap 16,13:4
Atherton, A B Dr, 1921, Mr 9,13:5
Atherton, Agnes, 1950, Ap 3,23:4
Atherton, C C, 1947, F 21,20:3
Atherton, Daisy, 1961, D 20,33:1
Atherton, David F, 1944, F 7,15:3
Atherton, Dudley R, 1959, Ja 14,27:4
Atherton, Edwin N, 1944, S 2,11:4
Atherton, Frank C, 1945, My 30,19:4
Atherton, Fred B, 1967, Ja 28,27:4
Atherton, George W Dr, 1906, Jl 25,7:6
Atherton, Gertrude, 1948, Je 15,27:1
Atherton, Henry F, 1949, F 11,23:1
Atherton, J B, 1903, Ap 9,9:4
Atherton, J Ballard, 1962, F 6,35:4
Atherton, J M, 1932, Je 6,15:2
Atherton, J William, 1967, S 5,43:1
Atherton, James B, 1959, S 16,39:4
Atherton, John, 1952, S 18,29:2
Atherton, John J, 1950, Ag 22,27:3
Atherton, John R, 1953, F 4,27:4
Atherton, John W, 1947, Je 3,25:1
Atherton, June (Mrs T Cornelia Soper),(Sereno), 1912, My 29,11:4
Atherton, Louis M, 1950, F 25,17:4
Atherton, Marian B, 1956, N 13,37:1
Atherton, Percy A, 1940, Mr 23,13:2
Atherton, Percy L, 1944, Mr 9,17:3
Atherton, Ray, 1960, Mr 17,33:1
Atherton, Robert, 1903, Ag 6,7:5
Atherton, Thomas H, 1939, Ag 5,15:6
Atherton, Walter, 1945, N 25,50:2
Athey, Edgar W, 1947, N 19,28:3
Athey, Katherine D, 1952, Ap 28,19:2
Athey, W H Mrs, 1961, N 13,31:4
Athison, John M Rev, 1914, Mr 26,11:5
Athlone, Earl of (A A F W A G Cambridge),(funl, Ja 20,92:8), 1957, Ja 17,29:1
Athoie, Duke of, 1864, F 6,8:2
Athole, G C Rev, 1884, O 4,5:5
Atholl, Duchess of (Katherine Marjory), 1960, O 22, 23:3
Atholl, Duke of (Jno Jas Stewart-Murray), 1917, Ja 21,17:2
Atholl, Duke of, 1942, Mr 17,21:1
Atholl, Duke of (J Stewart-Murray), 1957, My 9,31:1
Atholstan, Lady, 1941, D 27,19:3
Atholstan, Lord, 1938, Ja 29,15:1
Atholz, Samuel, 1965, O 17,86:3
Atienza, Carlos, 1954, Jl 12,19:2
Atiles, Pedro D Dr, 1937, N 2,25:5
Atkey, Albert, 1947, N 10,29:3
Atkin, Charles G, 1952, D 6,21:6
Atkin, Donald R, 1967, F 16,44:4
Atkin, I C Raymond, 1957, Ja 26,19:3
Atkin, I C Raymond Mrs, 1961, Ap 11,37:4
Atkin, Ida Mrs, 1942, Je 8,17:2
Atkin, Irving M, 1968, Ja 21,77:2
Atkin, Isador, 1955, Jl 6,27:4
Atkin, Jack P, 1938, My 15,II,6:7
Atkin, Lord, 1944, Je 26,15:6
Atkin, Louis, 1956, O 24,37:2
Atkin, Meyer, 1953, Jl 20,17:3
Atkin, Robert, 1967, Ap 20,44:1
Atkin, William, 1943, S 29,21:2; 1962, Ag 22,33:1
Atkins, Albert H, 1951, Mr 13,31:2
Atkins, Ben E Sr, 1960, My 2,29:2
Atkins, Benjamin Mrs, 1946, O 8,23:3
Atkins, Bernard M, 1957, N 18,31:4
Atkins, Charles D, 1964, My 8,34:1
Atkins, Charles H, 1947, Ap 16,25:3
Atkins, Daniel H, 1958, N 19,37:5
Atkins, Daniel Mrs, 1946, Jl 15,25:5
Atkins, Edward (will), 1939, Ap 2,3:6
Atkins, Ethel, 1942, N 1,53:2
Atkins, Frederick, 1946, N 18,23:1
Atkins, Frederick M, 1962, O 6,25:5
Atkins, G W E, 1936, N 10,21:1
Atkins, Gaius G, 1956, Ap 6,25:4
Atkins, George B, 1950, D 13,35:4
Atkins, George S, 1951, S 8,17:5
Atkins, Henry A, 1950, Ag 11,19:5
Atkins, Henry M, 1941, Ja 7,23:4
Atkins, Henry M Mrs, 1956, Ja 16,21:2
Atkins, Herbert E, 1949, S 8,29:5
Atkins, Herbert E Mrs, 1943, O 8,19:3
Atkins, Herman V, 1954, My 5,31:3
Atkins, Ira S, 1947, My 9,21:2
Atkins, Ivor A, 1953, N 28,15:3
Atkins, Jacob, 1938, O 10,19:4
Atkins, James Bp, 1923, D 6,19:4
Atkins, James E Jr, 1951, F 23,27:4
Atkins, James S, 1944, N 12,49:2
Atkins, Jeannette B, 1942, O 8,27:4
Atkins, John B Sr, 1954, Ja 11,5:6
Atkins, John R, 1945, F 25,37:1
Atkins, Joseph, 1948, D 18,19:3
Atkins, Kenneth N, 1954, My 21,27:3
Atkins, Matilda H Mrs, 1937, My 29,17:5
Atkins, Max, 1952, Ap 29,27:4
Atkins, Morris F, 1943, D 23,19:1
Atkins, Pauline McDowell Mrs, 1968, N 21,47:4
Atkins, R T, 1933, Je 28,21:1
Atkins, R W Mrs, 1950, O 3,31:1
Atkins, Robert W, 1947, D 22,22:2
Atkins, Samuel W, 1945, Ap 20,19:2
Atkins, T Augusta, 1958, N 21,29:4
Atkins, Thomas Astley, 1916, F 12,11:7
Atkins, William H, 1942, O 9,21:3; 1965, Je 16,43:3
Atkins, William T, 1940, Ag 14,19:4
Atkins, Wilson H, 1951, Ja 7,76:3
Atkinson, Alex H, 1962, Mr 2,29:1
Atkinson, Alton T, 1947, S 19,23:4
Atkinson, Amy Mrs, 1950, S 29,27:4
Atkinson, Antoinette W W Mrs, 1941, O 3,23:3
Atkinson, Arthur K, 1964, S 14,33:4
Atkinson, Asher, 1946, Ja 5,13:2
Atkinson, Charles H, 1909, F 3,9:4
Atkinson, Charles T, 1943, F 1,15:3
Atkinson, Chester J, 1947, D 29,17:2
Atkinson, Clifford Mrs, 1956, S 29,19:4
Atkinson, Condit S, 1953, F 12,28:3
Atkinson, Cora, 1917, Ag 27,9:6
Atkinson, E A Rev, 1902, Ag 2,1:4
Atkinson, E M, 1907, Jl 30,7:7
Atkinson, E M Mrs, 1907, Jl 30,7:7
Atkinson, Edward, 1905, D 12,9:3; 1941, Ja 7,23:2
Atkinson, Edward A, 1962, Mr 28,39:2
Atkinson, Edward H T, 1957, D 27,20:2
Atkinson, Edward J, 1920, F 5,9:4
Atkinson, Edward Spear, 1916, Mr 22,13:6
Atkinson, Edward W, 1940, D 7,17:4
Atkinson, Eleanor Mrs, 1942, N 11,25:3
Atkinson, Florence, 1939, Je 19,15:3
Atkinson, Francis R, 1951, Ja 9,30:2
Atkinson, Fred, 1959, O 13,39:4
Atkinson, Fred H, 1955, Je 20,11:1
Atkinson, Fred W, 1941, O 22,23:2
Atkinson, Frederick C Jr, 1944, D 27,19:4
Atkinson, Frederick G, 1940, Jl 23,19:4
Atkinson, G H Dr, 1884, D 28,2:3
Atkinson, Geoffroy, 1960, N 28,31:3
Atkinson, George, 1941, Mr 25,23:6; 1944, Jl 5,11:2
Atkinson, George C, 1954, Ja 8,21:5
Atkinson, George H, 1955, O 11,39:5
Atkinson, George Mrs, 1937, D 23,22:2
Atkinson, George T, 1942, Ag 25,23:2
Atkinson, Guy F, 1968, S 13,47:1
Atkinson, H Col, 1901, N 29,7:7
Atkinson, Harold B, 1963, Ap 10,39:5
Atkinson, Harry, 1946, Ap 13,17:4
Atkinson, Helen U Mrs, 1941, F 19,21:2
Atkinson, Henry A, 1960, Ja 26,33:1
Atkinson, Henry A Mrs, 1954, Mr 9,27:3
Atkinson, Henry M, 1939, Ja 22,34:6
Atkinson, Herbert S, 1952, Ja 12,13:4
Atkinson, Herschel Sr, 1966, Mr 7,27:2
Atkinson, Homer, 1945, Ap 1,36:3
Atkinson, J B Mrs, 1942, F 6,19:1
Atkinson, J Clarence, 1952, S 1,17:6
Atkinson, J Harry, 1950, Mr 15,29:1
Atkinson, J Robert, 1964, F 3,27:4
Atkinson, James, 1905, My 5,5:4
Atkinson, James Ford, 1924, F 18,13:2
Atkinson, James J, 1940, Ap 25,23:2; 1957, My 30,19:5
Atkinson, James P, 1959, N 2,31:4
Atkinson, John, 1941, N 15,17:2
Atkinson, John A, 1943, Jl 8,19:6
Atkinson, John L Rev, 1908, F 18,7:6
Atkinson, John R, 1941, Mr 20,21:4
Atkinson, Jonathan H, 1944, Ag 27,33:2
Atkinson, Jonathan H Mrs, 1963, Ag 9,23:3
Atkinson, Joseph E, 1948, My 10,21:5
Atkinson, Joseph S, 1968, N 4,47:4
Atkinson, Joseph S Mrs, 1960, Ap 15,23:4
Atkinson, Lilleis C Mrs, 1940, Ja 7,48:1
Atkinson, Llewelyn B, 1939, Ag 10,19:5
Atkinson, Louis E, 1910, F 6,II,11:5
Atkinson, Luther, 1952, Ja 4,40:4
Atkinson, Mahlon H Dr, 1968, Ag 11,72:5
Atkinson, O'Brien, 1947, Ag 27,23:2
Atkinson, Percy, 1950, My 9,29:3
Atkinson, Percy C, 1941, D 21,40:7
Atkinson, Pierre, 1962, S 30,86:4
Atkinson, Ralph W, 1961, My 19,32:2
Atkinson, Robert T, 1947, F 12,25:2
Atkinson, Roy, 1938, D 28,26:2
Atkinson, Roy R, 1959, Jl 20,25:3
Atkinson, Ruth V, 1944, N 27,23:5
Atkinson, Samuel C, 1942, O 6,24:2
Atkinson, Samuel P, 1937, Ap 4,II,10:8
Atkinson, Stephen B, 1948, N 30,27:5
Atkinson, T Rev, 1881, Ja 5,5:3
Atkinson, Thomas E, 1960, Jl 1,25:2
Atkinson, Ulrich S, 1937, D 30,19:4
Atkinson, Wade H, 1942, N 15,56:3
Atkinson, Wade Mrs, 1952, Ja 14,19:4
Atkinson, Walter E, 1959, Ap 23,31:2
Atkinson, Walter E Mrs, 1952, My 29,27:4
Atkinson, Walter F, 1940, Je 21,21:3
Atkinson, William E, 1940, My 20,17:3
Atkinson, William F, 1958, Mr 20,29:2
Atkinson, William H, 1941, N 19,23:4
Atkinson, William M, 1938, O 29,19:2; 1961, D 10,88:
Atkinson, William P, 1943, Ja 23,13:2
Atkinson, William Y, 1953, S 30,31:2
Atkinson, Wilmer, 1920, My 11,9:4
Atkiss, A Lincoln, 1949, Ap 2,15:6
Atkisson, Earl J, 1941, S 20,17:4
Atlas, Benjamin J, 1955, Je 4,15:4
Atlas, Edward, 1968, Je 9,84:6
Atlas, Leopold, 1954, O 2,17:6
Atlas, Meyer, 1965, O 16,27:5
Atlas, Mortimer D, 1955, Jl 10,75:3
Atlass, Albert C, 1939, O 29,40:7
Atlass, Frank, 1938, S 3,13:5
Atlass, H Leslie (will, N 29,26:8), 1960, N 19,21:6
Atlay, James Rev Bp of Hereford, 1894, D 25,5:3
Atlee, Edwin I Jr, 1963, Ap 12,27:3
Atlee, John L, 1950, Ap 5,31:3
Atlee, Louis W Dr, 1937, Jl 9,21:4
Atlee, Potter F, 1940, Mr 25,15:4
Atmore, George W, 1942, O 24,15:4
Atonna, Carmelo, 1951, Ag 31,15:4
Atonna, Carmelo Mrs, 1964, Jl 12,68:4
Ator, Harry W Mrs, 1947, D 8,26:2
Atran, Frank Z, 1952, Je 12,33:1
Atran, Frank Z Mrs, 1962, My 26,25:5
Attalla, Tofic A, 1962, N 3,25:5
Attarian, Edward G, 1945, O 17,19:3
Attaway, Douglass, 1957, Jl 2,27:4
Attaway, Emelie C Mrs, 1948, Ap 17,15:5
Atterbury, Albert H, 1955, N 22,35:2
Atterbury, Albert H Mrs, 1950, O 18,33:4
Atterbury, Allen A, 1916, Je 9,13:6
Atterbury, Anna R Mrs, 1939, N 27,17:4
Atterbury, Charles Larned, 1914, N 11,13:4
Atterbury, George Mrs, 1947, Ja 11,19:3
Atterbury, Grosvenor, 1956, O 19,27:1
Atterbury, Howard E, 1950, My 31,29:2
Atterbury, Isabel N, 1959, Ja 19,27:4
Atterbury, John Turner, 1912, D 11,13:4
Atterbury, John Turner (est), 1913, Jl 11,9:5
Atterbury, Justina, 1907, S 23,9:6
Atterbury, Lawrence, 1940, S 29,44:2
Atterbury, Robert Bakewell, 1917, D 30,19:1
Atterbury, Robert R, 1941, S 2,17:2
Atterbury, Robert R Mrs, 1951, O 6,19:3
Atterbury, W W, 1935, S 21,1:2
Atterbury, Walter B, 1953, My 20,29:2
Atterbury, William W Mrs (will, My 4,12:5), 1937, Ap 25,II,9:2
Atteridge, Harold R, 1938, Ja 17,19:3
Attfield, William A Dr, 1937, Jl 18,II,7:1
Attia, Mrs, 1873, Je 15,8:4
Attig, Chester J, 1947, Ap 3,25:1
Attig, Harry D, 1964, Jl 29,33:3
Attix, James C, 1944, Ap 21,19:2
Attlee, Bartram W, 1950, D 19,30:2
Attlee, Bernard H B, 1943, Mr 30,26:3
Attlee, Clement, 1967, O 8,1:2
Attlee, Mary, 1956, S 7,24:3

Attlee, Robert B, 1953, My 16,19:6
Attlee, Violet H (Countess),(est appr, Ag 20,46:1), 1964, Je 8,29:4
Attoh, K D, 1966, D 27,32:6
Attolico, Bernardo, 1942, F 10,19:4
Attrabasca, Bp of (Rev Geo Holmes), 1912, F 4,13:4
Attride, Roy R B Mrs, 1942, D 16,25:1
Attridge, Richard, 1964, S 25,41:1
Attridge, Thomas W, 1959, N 18,41:6
Attwater, Allan, 1949, Ja 15,17:2
Attwater, Charles E, 1946, F 26,25:4
Attwell, Ernest T (por), 1949, Ag 7,60:3
Attwell, J S Rev, 1881, O 10,5:6
Attwood, E A, 1938, N 9,23:5
Attwood, Frank, 1952, Ap 14,19:5
Attwood, Stanley R, 1953, Je 23,29:3
Attwood, Stephen S, 1965, Je 9,47:3
Attwood, William E, 1950, My 4,27:5
Attwool, Stanley C, 1957, Mr 24,86:4
Aturan, Adrien, 1956, My 11,27:4
Aturia, Angel, 1947, S 10,27:4
Atwater, Benjamin L, 1943, Je 16,21:6
Atwater, Bert L, 1954, S 8,32:7
Atwater, Bert L Mrs, 1959, Ja 18,88:3
Atwater, Charles W, 1946, Mr 25,25:3
Atwater, Charles W Mrs, 1950, My 11,29:2
Atwater, Christopher G, 1947, Jl 15,23:4
Atwater, Christopher G Mrs, 1949, F 12,17:4
Atwater, David Fisher, 1916, My 3,13:7
Atwater, David H, 1944, S 26,23:4; 1949, F 8,25:4
Atwater, De Nyse W, 1948, Ap 14,27:5
Atwater, Dorance, 1910, N 30,11:5
Atwater, Edward S Jr, 1949, Ag 12,17:4
Atwater, Eliot, 1945, Mr 7,21:5
Atwater, Elsie W, 1948, Ap 1,25:4
Atwater, F, 1933, F 24,17:1
Atwater, Frances E, 1968, Ap 8,47:1
Atwater, Frederick Mrs, 1957, My 25,21:5
Atwater, G P, 1932, O 22,15:1
Atwater, George W, 1943, D 11,15:4
Atwater, Helen W, 1947, Je 27,21:3
Atwater, Henry G, 1904, Jl 17,7:6; 1950, Jl 21,19:2
Atwater, Hubert F, 1965, Ja 25,37:4
Atwater, Huntington C Mrs, 1960, D 2,29:2
Atwater, James, 1903, D 20,7:6
Atwater, James B, 1959, Ag 27,27:4
Atwater, John G, 1937, N 23,23:2
Atwater, John J, 1961, D 25,23:6
Atwater, L H Rev, 1883, F 18,7:4
Atwater, Leroy W, 1940, Je 16,38:6
Atwater, Lucy J, 1942, My 18,15:3
Atwater, Mary B, 1941, Je 3,21:4
Atwater, Mary M Mrs, 1956, S 8,17:3
Atwater, Pierce, 1944, Mr 27,19:4
Atwater, Reginald M, 1957, O 20,86:6
Atwater, Walter H, 1944, N 6,19:3
Atwater, Wilbur Olin Prof, 1907, S 23,9:6
Atwater, William, 1882, Jl 17,8:5
Atwater, William B, 1937, Ja 16,17:3
Atwater, William C, 1940, F 23,15:5
Atwater, William C Jr, 1948, O 6,29:3
Atwater, William C Jr Mrs, 1956, Jl 14,15:6
Atwell, Albert G, 1944, D 6,23:3
Atwell, Ambrose A Mrs, 1946, D 6,23:4
Atwell, Aubrey Mrs, 1949, F 7,19:1
Atwell, Ben H, 1951, F 22,31:3
Atwell, Ben H Mrs, 1937, Ja 14,21:2
Atwell, C L, 1880, Mr 20,8:2
Atwell, Charles B Prof, 1937, S 14,23:2
Atwell, David R, 1953, Mr 6,23:3
Atwell, Edward, 1914, D 18,13:5
Atwell, Floyd J, 1940, Ag 26,15:1
Atwell, George G, 1945, D 9,44:4
Atwell, George G Mrs, 1946, Ja 1,27:3
Atwell, George J, 1944, Ag 30,17:3; 1944, S 2,11:2
Atwell, George J Mrs, 1954, Ap 29,31:4
Atwell, Harry A, 1957, N 6,35:4
Atwell, John L, 1962, Jl 11,35:2
Atwell, Lyman, 1961, Ag 25,25:1
Atwell, Robert B, 1963, Ag 6,31:4
Atwell, Roy, 1962, F 7,34:3
Atwell, Wayne J, 1941, Mr 28,23:4
Atwell, William H, 1961, D 23,23:1
Atwell, William P, 1911, Jl 30,9:5
Atwell Marion G, 1938, Ap 13,25:5
Atwill, Edward R Bp, 1911, Ja 25,9:5
Atwill, Lionel, 1946, Ap 23,21:1
Atwill, William, 1942, N 28,13:5
Atwood, A Harlow, 1952, Mr 3,21:4
Atwood, A Harlow Mrs, 1962, S 1,19:3
Atwood, Bertram H de Mrs, 1941, My 21,23:2
Atwood, Charles B, 1941, Jl 23,19:4
Atwood, Donald, 1950, My 12,36:2
Atwood, Ellis D, 1950, D 1,25:5
Atwood, Eugene Mrs, 1942, Ag 27,19:1
Atwood, Frank E, 1943, Mr 6,13:1
Atwood, George D, 1962, My 7,31:3
Atwood, George H, 1938, Mr 17,21:5; 1952, Ja 5,11:3
Atwood, George M, 1943, Ja 7,19:5
Atwood, George S Prof, 1917, F 20,9:4
Atwood, H G, 1941, Je 29,32:6
Atwood, Harley F, 1937, Je 24,25:5
Atwood, Harrison, 1956, N 24,19:3
Atwood, Harrison H, 1954, O 23,15:4
Atwood, Harrison Mrs, 1967, Ap 3,33:1
Atwood, Harry H, 1948, Jl 24,15:4
Atwood, Harry N, 1967, Jl 15,25:4
Atwood, Henry A, 1946, Ag 6,25:5
Atwood, Henry B, 1908, Mr 25,9:5
Atwood, Henry E, 1950, Ag 30,32:3
Atwood, Horace, 1950, Ag 28,17:4
Atwood, Horace F, 1938, Ag 7,33:3
Atwood, Isaac Morgan Rev Dr, 1917, O 28,21:2
Atwood, Ivan J, 1949, F 2,27:4
Atwood, J Arthur, 1949, S 27,28:2
Atwood, James M Col, 1925, O 13,23:4
Atwood, John M, 1951, N 5,31:2
Atwood, John Rev, 1873, My 2,5:5
Atwood, Julius W, 1945, Ap 11,23:1
Atwood, Leon R, 1940, N 18,19:3
Atwood, M V Mrs, 1954, Ja 31,89:1
Atwood, Martha (Mrs G R Baker), 1950, Ap 8,13:4
Atwood, Millard V, 1941, N 4,23:5
Atwood, Nora, 1948, Ja 13,25:2
Atwood, Norman N, 1948, F 16,21:3
Atwood, Raymond, 1951, Ag 22,23:3
Atwood, Roy F, 1963, Jl 27,21:4
Atwood, Roy L, 1954, Jl 13,23:4
Atwood, Roy S, 1953, D 17,37:2
Atwood, Wallace W, 1949, Jl 26,27:1
Atwood, Will G Sr, 1955, N 30,33:4
Atwood, William G, 1948, Ja 25,56:6
Atwood, William P, 1954, D 29,23:4
Atwood, William W, 1938, Ap 23,15:5
Atwood, Winfield A, 1950, Ja 26,27:1
Atz, Jacob, 1945, My 23,19:4
Atz, Joseph, 1941, Je 21,17:3
Aub, Theodore, 1918, S 11,13:1
Aub, Therese, 1952, Ap 16,27:2
Aubel, Fred F Mrs, 1951, My 31,27:3
Aubepin, Henry, 1938, Je 28,19:5
Auber, D F E, 1871, My 15,4:7
Aubert, Eugene Prof, 1917, D 8,15:6
Aubert, Jacques Charles, 1915, Je 9,13:5
Aubert, Louis, 1944, Je 3,13:3
Aubert, Lucien J, 1946, Jl 19,19:5
Aubert Bro (F C Zehetner), 1960, Ja 22,25:1
Aubertin, Albert A, 1955, Ag 23,34:1
Aubin, Thomas S, 1938, Ja 13,21:2
Auble, Robert N, 1952, F 24,84:6
Auboyneau, Philippe, 1961, F 23,27:1
Aubrey, Edwin E, 1956, S 12,37:5
Aubrey, Joseph, 1950, N 20,25:3
Aubrey, Melbourne E, 1957, O 20,86:4
Aubrey, Will, 1958, Ja 4,15:1
Aubrey, William Hickman Smith, 1916, F 12,11:5
Aubril, E Rev, 1881, Je 1,2:5
Aubry, Augusto Vice-Adm, 1912, Mr 5,11:5
Aubry, Octave, 1946, Mr 29,12:7
Aubry, Regina F Mrs, 1955, Mr 2,27:3
Auburn, Charles J Mrs, 1957, S 15,83:1
Aucaigne, Felix, 1914, Mr 28,13:4
Auch, David M, 1952, F 2,13:6
Auch, Wayne, 1951, D 16,91:1
Auchincloss, C Russell, 1958, Ag 5,27:5
Auchincloss, Charles C, 1961, My 15,31:2
Auchincloss, Charles C Mrs, 1953, F 5,23:6
Auchincloss, Elizabeth Ellen, 1925, Je 30,19:5
Auchincloss, Emma B Mrs (will, S 20,20:3), 1942, S 12,13:4
Auchincloss, F L, 1878, D 25,8:5
Auchincloss, Gordon, 1943, Ap 17,17:1
Auchincloss, Hugh, 1947, S 22,23:1
Auchincloss, Hugh D, 1913, Ap 22,11:6
Auchincloss, J Howland, 1968, S 1,53:1
Auchincloss, James C Mrs, 1959, Ag 1,17:2
Auchincloss, James S Mrs, 1960, S 4,69:1
Auchincloss, John, 1876, Je 29,4:7; 1876, Jl 1,5:1; 1948, Ag 29,56:6
Auchincloss, John W, 1938, Ja 25,21:4
Auchincloss, Mary C Mrs, 1903, N 14,9:6
Auchincloss, Samuel S Mrs, 1953, Mr 7,15:6
Auchincloss, William K, 1960, Ja 25,27:5
Auchinleck, Alexander, 1875, Jl 12,4:5
Auchmoody, Francis E, 1941, O 25,17:2
Auchmoody, J W, 1881, Mr 9,5:2
Auchmoody, Llewellyn, 1954, F 28,92:3
Auchmuty, E S Mrs, 1927, O 4,29:3
Auchmuty, R T Col, 1893, Jl 19,4:5
Auchter, Paul P, 1953, N 25,23:4
Auchterlonie, Laurie, 1948, Ja 21,25:4
Auchterlonie, William P, 1937, S 18,19:3
Auchu, Alvah G, 1947, F 11,27:4
Auckland, Dowager Lady, 1955, Ap 24,86:5
Auckland, Lady, 1946, D 26,25:5
Auckland, Lord (G M Eden), 1955, Je 23,29:4
Aucock, Arthur M, 1958, My 25,86:3
Aucock, John, 1962, My 16,41:5
Aucock, Mary, 1942, My 17,47:4
Aucoin, Gertrude M (A De Foe), 1960, Ag 8,21:2
Aud, Joseph Z, 1955, Ja 18,27:2
Aude, Herman T R, 1955, Je 3,23:3
Aude, Robert M, 1961, Ag 22,29:4
Audelewicz, Michael E, 1953, Ja 16,23:2
Audenreid, J C, 1880, Je 4,4:7
Audenreid, William G Mrs, 1944, Ap 14,19:4
Audette, Louis G, 1962, O 16,39:1
Audi, Adele, 1947, N 7,23:3
Audi, Elias J (funl, Ap 21,80:3), 1968, Ap 20,33:3
Audibert, Frank, 1950, S 16,19:6
Audibert, Xavier M, 1956, Ap 4,29:2
Audiberti, Jacques, 1965, Jl 12,27:2
Audley, Baron (T P H Tuchet-Jesson), 1963, Jl 4,17:3
Audley, Frank H, 1916, My 11,11:6
Audley, Henry L, 1947, Ag 20,21:3
Audoux, Marguerite, 1937, F 3,24:1
Audrain, Lawrence A, 1957, S 11,33:4
Audran, Dora, 1956, Jl 11,29:6
Audran, Edmond, 1901, Ag 19,7:7
Audsley, Berthold, 1962, Ja 24,33:4
Audsley, Charles S Mrs, 1950, Je 29,29:4
Audsley, George Ashdown, 1925, Je 24,17:4
Audubon, Leonard, 1951, Ag 28,24:2
Audubon, Maria, 1925, D 23,19:5
Audubon, Mrs (trb, Je 29,8:2), 1874, Je 20,4:6
Audubon, Raymond A, 1956, D 14,29:2
Aue, Charles F, 1962, S 10,29:5
Aue, Charles F Mrs, 1958, Je 2,27:3
Auel, Carl B, 1937, Ap 6,23:2
Auel, Charles, 1908, Je 2,7:6
Auer, Anthony A, 1950, O 14,19:1
Auer, Charles, 1940, O 1,23:2
Auer, Ellis F, 1951, Ja 5,21:4
Auer, Florence, 1962, My 15,39:3
Auer, George J, 1966, Ap 5,39:1
Auer, Ignaz, 1907, Ap 11,11:5
Auer, John, 1948, My 2,76:3
Auer, John F, 1961, D 29,24:4
Auer, Joseph L, 1963, My 26,92:2
Auer, L, 1930, Jl 16,23:1
Auer, Leopold Mrs, 1961, O 7,23:3
Auer, Martha V Mrs, 1940, Je 29,15:6
Auer, Milo A, 1955, Ja 1,13:5
Auer, Milo Mrs, 1950, D 6,33:2
Auer, Mischa, 1967, Mr 6,29:2
Auer, Philip W, 1922, N 1,19:6
Auer, Stephen, 1954, F 16,25:4
Auer, William H, 1967, Je 25,68:5
Auerbach, Arthur, 1957, O 4,23:2
Auerbach, Beatrice Fox Mrs, 1968, D 1,86:2
Auerbach, Berthold, 1882, F 10,5:5
Auerbach, Charles, 1937, Ja 17,II,8:6
Auerbach, Charles G, 1904, Ja 4,9:6
Auerbach, Erich, 1957, O 15,33:1
Auerbach, Frank L, 1964, S 22,39:1
Auerbach, Fred S, 1938, My 29,II,7:2
Auerbach, Harry A, 1953, Ag 28,17:4
Auerbach, Irwin E, 1960, Je 22,35:3
Auerbach, J Dr, 1878, Ag 28,8:5
Auerbach, John H, 1962, O 15,29:2
Auerbach, Joseph, 1942, S 20,40:8
Auerbach, Joseph S, 1944, S 18,19:4; 1949, D 21,29:4
Auerbach, Katherine Hone Mrs, 1923, D 1,13:3
Auerbach, Leo I, 1964, F 13,31:2
Auerbach, Maurice Mrs, 1960, S 21,32:4
Auerbach, Meyer Mrs, 1960, Mr 21,29:5
Auerbach, Morris, 1939, Je 23,19:5
Auerbach, Romeo Winton Dr, 1968, Je 11,44:2
Auerbach, Sam, 1952, Ja 21,15:4
Auerbach, Samuel, 1965, Jl 25,69:2
Auerbach, Sidney, 1965, Je 23,41:1
Auerbach-Levy, William, 1964, Je 30,33:4
Auerbacher, L H, 1903, Ja 8,7:6
Auerbacher, Louis J, 1946, F 22,25:4
Auernheimer, Raoul O, 1948, Ja 8,25:3
Auernheimer, Raoul O Mrs (mem ser), 1967, N 3, 45:2
Auersperg, Franz Prince, 1953, My 12,14:4
Auersperg, Prince, 1885, Ja 7,5:5
Auezov, Mukhtar O, 1961, Je 28,35:4
Auf der Heide, Henry G, 1954, My 18,30:5
Auf der Heide, Oscar, 1945, Mr 30,15:4
Aufderhar, Charles F, 1960, My 22,87:1
Auffmordt, Clement A, 1903, N 26,7:6
Aufhauser, David, 1949, Jl 13,27:5
Aufhauser, Siegfried, 1949, Ja 29,13:5
Aufiero, Emanuel R, 1945, F 6,19:4
Aufiero, Paul A, 1950, Je 27,29:1
Aufmuth, Eugene F, 1951, N 19,23:5
Aufseher, Aaron, 1947, S 2,21:5
Aufsesser, Bertrand M, 1961, N 11,23:3
Aufsesser, Moses F, 1940, Ag 31,13:6
Aug, Edna, 1938, D 2,23:5
Augarde, Adrienne, 1913, Mr 19,13:3
Auge, Albert H, 1951, O 13,17:1
Auge, George O, 1952, Ag 22,21:2
Auge, Leon George, 1904, Ja 22,2:1
Augenblick, Gilbert L Mrs, 1954, N 6,17:2
Augenblick, Harry A, 1948, Ag 31,23:2
Auger, Charles L, 1939, Ja 6,22:2
Auger, Charles L Jr, 1961, Mr 2,27:4
Auger, Joseph J Rev, 1904, Ja 12,7:5
Auger, Walter L, 1952, Ag 20,25:4
Augerias, Pierre, 1925, My 30,9:6
Aughiltree, J S, 1880, Ja 23,8:7
Aughinbaugh, B A, 1959, D 16,41:4
Aughinbaugh, William E, 1940, D 19,25:3
Augier, E, 1889, O 26,4:6
Augostini, Peter, 1946, Mr 18,21:3

Augsburger, Anita, 1943, D 22,24:2
Augsbury, Frank A, 1954, D 30,17:2
Augsbury, Willard S, 1939, Ag 17,21:5
Augspurg, Anita, 1944, Ja 1,13:3
Augur, Ammon A Lt-Col, 1908, Je 27,9:4
Augur, J A Col, 1909, Ap 19,9:6
Augur, J P J, 1884, Ja 10,8:2
Augur, Robert C, 1953, Jl 18,14:8
August, Abraham J, 1943, Je 10,21:3
August, Bro, 1923, Jl 2,15:6
August, Jacob, 1938, N 4,23:4
August, Joseph, 1947, S 26,23:3
August, Leo, 1943, F 22,17:3
August, Max W, 1961, F 18,19:4
August Wilhelm, Prince of Prussia, 1949, Mr 26,17:3
Augusta, Dowager Empress of Germany, 1890, Ja 8, 1:3
Auguste, Harmon S, 1949, O 30,87:3
Augustin, Caroline Mrs, 1924, F 21,17:6
Augustin, Joseph A, 1955, Jl 8,23:4
Augustin, William C, 1943, Je 1,23:3
Augustine, Addison E, 1938, O 4,25:1
Augustine, Edward, 1939, Ag 6,29:8
Augustine, Father, 1941, Ag 12,19:4
Augustine, Henri, 1955, Ag 31,25:3
Augustine, Marcel M, 1944, N 1,23:5
Augustine, Mary Sister (Eliz Higgins), 1914, Ap 14, 11:6
Augustine, Michael F, 1949, Mr 5,18:3
Augustine, Peter, 1956, S 29,19:5
Augustine, William F, 1947, F 11,27:5
Augustine George, Bro Christian Bros, 1956, Je 24,77:1
Augustine Maxwell, Bro, 1944, Ap 13,19:2
Augustowski, Anthony, 1948, Ja 7,25:4
Augustus, Duke, 1881, Jl 27,2:6
Augustus, Ellsworth H, 1964, My 17,87:2
Augustus, Louis A, 1955, Mr 23,31:4
Augustyn, Godfrey W, 1944, S 12,19:5
Auifiero, John M, 1955, S 10,17:4
Aul, Harold E, 1955, O 2,86:1
Auld, George P, 1962, S 9,84:6
Auld, Joseph, 1921, Je 25,11:6
Auld, Robert C M, 1937, Ap 23,21:5
Auld, T Capt, 1880, F 11,2:3
Auld, William M, 1941, Je 6,21:5
Aulenbacher, Frank, 1956, Jl 8,64:2
Auler, Henry, 1951, Ja 7,76:5
Auleta, Francis A, 1938, Mr 11,19:4
Auleta, Michael J (will), 1914, Mr 29,5:6
Auleta, Vincent H, 1961, S 30,25:1
Aulick, John H Commodore, 1873, Ap 28,4:7
Aulick, Will W Mrs, 1964, Ja 23,31:4
Aulick, William W, 1913, D 27,9:5
Aull, Arthur, 1948, My 9,70:1
Ault, Charles, 1948, Je 18,23:3
Ault, Charles S, 1950, O 14,19:4
Ault, George C Mrs, 1953, O 19,21:4
Ault, Gilbert E, 1965, Ap 16,29:3
Ault, Gilbert E Mrs, 1943, N 1,17:2
Ault, Ivan R, 1948, O 14,29:1
Ault, James F, 1965, Ag 28,21:3
Ault, Marie, 1951, My 10,31:1
Ault, Norman, 1950, F 9,29:3
Ault, William, 1951, Mr 27,29:1
Aultman, Merwyn L, 1953, Ag 23,89:3
Aumack, Harold, 1950, Ap 19,29:2
Aumack, Harry P, 1937, D 10,25:3
Auman, Orrin W, 1951, Mr 30,24:3
Auman, Russell F Mrs, 1948, Ap 25,69:1
Aumann, Henry, 1961, O 10,43:3
Aumann, Herbert P, 1950, Jl 2,24:8
Aumann, Luis, 1949, Jl 23,11:5
Aumonier, S, 1928, D 24,13:4
Aunt Judy (A Negress 110 Years Old), 1867, My 17,2:7
Auphelle, Robert, 1962, D 1,25:3
Aupperle, Jacob Mrs, 1943, O 21,27:2
Aurea, Baierl Sister, 1946, N 26,29:1
Aurelio, William G, 1951, D 30,24:3
Aurelius, Herbert Mrs, 1950, N 7,27:3
Aurelius, Marcus A, 1957, Mr 24,86:4
Aurell, Alvin K, 1961, Jl 20,27:1
Aurie, Larry, 1952, D 13,21:2
Auriema, Adolph, 1965, N 30,41:5
Auringer, Obadiah C Rev, 1937, O 3,II,8:4
Auriol, Vincent, 1966, Ja 2,72:5
Auriol (Clown), 1881, O 9,6:7
Aurner, Clarence R, 1948, Ja 24,15:2
Aurobindo, Sri, 1950, D 6,33:3
Auroroff, Constantine, 1960, Je 24,27:3
Aus, Gunvald, 1950, Je 7,29:6
Auser, Wallace V C, 1947, Ap 29,27:2
Auslander, Abe A, 1942, Je 26,21:4
Auslander, George Mrs, 1967, Jl 4,19:5
Auslander, Jack H Mrs, 1964, My 13,47:5
Auslander, Jacob, 1958, Je 4,33:2
Auslander, Joseph, 1965, Je 23,41:1
Auslander, Joseph Mrs (A Wurdemann), 1960, My 20,31:3
Auslander, Morris, 1959, Ja 7,33:2
Ausnit, Edgar M, 1968, F 25,76:7
Ausnit, Max, 1957, Ja 19,15:1
Auspitz, John, 1953, Ag 26,27:2
Auspitz, Julius, 1915, Jl 10,7:5
Auspitz-Kolar, Mme, 1879, F 7,2:7
Auspitzer, Richard G, 1957, S 10,33:3
Austen, Alice, 1952, Je 10,27:5
Austen, David E Gen (funl, Jl 19,11:2), 1917, Jl 17, 9:5
Austen, Ernest E, 1938, Ja 18,23:2
Austen, George, 1938, Ap 25,15:5
Austen, George Mrs, 1949, Ja 22,13:3
Austen, James Jr, 1938, Mr 26,15:3
Austen, Peter T Mrs, 1948, Ag 13,15:5
Austen, Peter Townsend, 1907, D 31,7:6
Austen, Willard E, 1963, D 27,25:2
Austenrieth, Frederick, 1945, D 12,27:5
Auster, Max, 1953, Ag 3,17:5
Auster, Max Mrs, 1957, D 12,29:2
Austerlitz, Louis L, 1937, Ap 6,23:3
Austermuhl, Albert, 1947, Ja 5,53:4
Austin, A E Gloucester, 1937, F 15,17:1
Austin, A Everett Jr, 1957, Mr 31,89:2
Austin, Abram Mrs, 1945, N 6,19:4
Austin, Albert, 1953, Ag 19,29:2
Austin, Albert E, 1942, Ja 27,22:3
Austin, Albert L, 1950, F 1,29:1
Austin, Albert M, 1963, Jl 3,25:1
Austin, Alfred, 1913, Je 3,9:1
Austin, Allen C, 1937, Je 12,15:5
Austin, Alonzo E, 1948, Je 22,25:6
Austin, Anne M Mrs, 1941, Je 13,19:4
Austin, Anthony H, 1943, Ag 6,15:5
Austin, Augustine A, 1959, D 31,21:2
Austin, Berkeley C, 1952, Ap 4,33:7
Austin, Bernard, 1959, Ja 7,33:1
Austin, Bessie G, 1961, Jl 11,31:1
Austin, Britten, 1941, Mr 13,21:1
Austin, Byron W, 1937, Ap 5,3:3
Austin, C, 1936, D 3,25:4
Austin, C A, 1929, D 14,19:3
Austin, Carl B Mrs, 1943, My 30,26:1
Austin, Carl C, 1948, Ja 22,27:3
Austin, Carl E, 1954, Jl 23,17:4
Austin, Carlos, 1953, Ag 6,21:6
Austin, Caroline E, 1938, S 21,25:1
Austin, Carrie E F Mrs, 1937, Ap 14,26:2
Austin, Charles, 1944, Ja 15,13:3
Austin, Charles A Rev, 1937, Mr 9,23:3
Austin, Charles C, 1964, Ag 12,35:4
Austin, Charles E Jr, 1951, Mr 25,73:1
Austin, Charles J, 1940, Ap 5,21:5
Austin, Charles L, 1963, My 16,35:3
Austin, Charles M, 1938, My 17,23:1
Austin, Chauncey G, 1948, O 9,3:1
Austin, Clifford, 1946, My 25,15:2
Austin, D Rev, 1877, D 6,4:7
Austin, David A, 1961, N 10,35:4
Austin, David C, 1949, Ja 3,23:4
Austin, David F Mrs, 1957, Jl 20,15:5
Austin, David P, 1951, Ja 3,27:4
Austin, David Penfield Dr, 1918, Mr 20,13:4
Austin, Donald F, 1949, Ag 16,23:1
Austin, Dwight B, 1955, Mr 9,27:4
Austin, Dwight E, 1941, Je 9,19:2
Austin, Edmund O, 1964, Ja 21,29:5
Austin, Edward C, 1946, Mr 3,44:5
Austin, Edward H, 1960, Ap 18,29:5
Austin, Edward O, 1948, Mr 25,27:4
Austin, Edwin S, 1966, O 23,88:3
Austin, Elmer J, 1940, My 5,52:8
Austin, Elmore F, 1942, N 28,13:3
Austin, Erastus L, 1948, Ja 23,23:4
Austin, Eugene K, 1948, Ja 6,23:4
Austin, Eugene M, 1962, Je 17,81:2
Austin, Everett L, 1951, Ja 6,15:6
Austin, Francis M Mrs, 1948, S 29,29:2
Austin, Frank, 1952, Ja 5,11:6
Austin, Frank R, 1946, Ja 24,21:5
Austin, Fred T (por), 1938, F 27,II,8:8
Austin, Frederic, 1952, Ap 11,23:3
Austin, Frederick A, 1961, My 2,37:5
Austin, Frederick A Mrs, 1947, Je 28,13:3
Austin, George M Sr, 1952, Ja 18,27:3
Austin, George W, 1955, O 5,35:5
Austin, Gerald W, 1963, Ag 30,21:4
Austin, Gilbert V, 1962, Jl 7,17:3
Austin, Hannah G Mrs, 1941, Mr 11,23:2
Austin, Harold R Mrs, 1957, My 3,27:1
Austin, Harold W, 1960, Mr 1,33:4
Austin, Harriett B Mrs, 1937, Ag 23,19:3
Austin, Henry H, 1954, S 27,21:5
Austin, Henry W Jr, 1947, Je 26,23:5
Austin, Herbert, 1947, Jl 21,17:6; 1949, Ag 18,21:2
Austin, Herbert H Brig Gen, 1937, Ap 28,23:4
Austin, Herbert J, 1940, My 13,17:5
Austin, Herbert S (por), 1949, Jl 6,27:1
Austin, Horace P, 1941, O 8,23:1
Austin, Ira B, 1938, Jl 15,17:4
Austin, Isabelle C, 1967, Ja 21,31:5
Austin, J Clayton Mrs, 1942, Mr 19,21:4
Austin, J McM, 1881, D 4,9:3
Austin, James C, 1955, Ag 23,24:1
Austin, James H, 1952, Mr 31,19:1
Austin, James M, 1957, Ag 21,27:2
Austin, James M Mrs, 1951, Je 3,93:1
Austin, Jean K Mrs, 1946, D 12,29:1
Austin, John, 1921, Mr 26,13:6
Austin, John A, 1938, D 22,21:2
Austin, John Brander Jr, 1923, Je 30,11:4
Austin, John F, 1948, D 9,33:2
Austin, John H Mrs, 1952, D 25,29:5
Austin, John M, 1947, Mr 7,25:3
Austin, John M Mrs, 1946, O 31,25:3
Austin, John T, 1943, Jl 3,13:2
Austin, John T Mrs, 1949, Ja 22,14:2
Austin, Joseph E, 1937, S 21,25:4
Austin, Joseph M, 1942, Jl 26,31:3
Austin, Joseph S, 1938, Mr 17,21:3
Austin, Josiah, 1947, Mr 3,21:5
Austin, K O Dr, 1903, S 8,1:2
Austin, Kate H Mrs, 1942, My 25,15:5
Austin, L Carlton, 1939, Ag 17,21:3
Austin, Lawrence C, 1955, D 12,31:4
Austin, Leon H, 1953, Je 3,31:3
Austin, Lewis S, 1943, N 16,23:3
Austin, Lloyd D, 1948, Jl 11,52:7
Austin, Lord, 1941, My 24,15:3
Austin, Lyman T, 1938, Ap 6,23:3
Austin, M, 1934, Ag 14,17:1
Austin, Mabel, 1941, Ap 12,15:6
Austin, Martin F, 1946, N 14,29:4
Austin, Mary Sister, 1914, Mr 9,9:3
Austin, Maurice S, 1964, F 19,39:1
Austin, Oliver L, 1957, N 27,31:2
Austin, Oliver L Mrs, 1948, Ap 6,23:2
Austin, Phil N, 1939, My 24,23:2
Austin, Philip J Mrs, 1946, S 21,15:4
Austin, R F, 1885, Ap 1,5:6
Austin, Ray W, 1950, O 28,17:3
Austin, Raymond M, 1949, Ag 24,25:3
Austin, Reginald M, 1950, Jl 5,31:1
Austin, Richard L, 1948, S 11,15:6
Austin, Richard S, 1948, My 2,15:2
Austin, Richard W, 1937, My 10,19:5
Austin, Richard Wilson, 1919, Ap 21,15:3
Austin, Robert J, 1948, Je 23,27:4
Austin, Roswell M Mrs, 1949, Ap 10,76:4
Austin, Samuel, 1876, Mr 13,1:6
Austin, Samuel C, 1947, D 23,24:2
Austin, Samuel Y, 1958, Jl 12,15:2
Austin, T Merrill, 1939, F 6,13:5
Austin, Theodore, 1947, Ap 23,25:4
Austin, Thomas B, 1937, Mr 23,23:2
Austin, Thomas D, 1967, Ag 2,37:3
Austin, Valorous Mrs, 1948, O 2,15:5
Austin, Walter G, 1937, Ja 15,21:2
Austin, Walter S, 1965, My 11,39:2
Austin, Warren R (trb, D 27,7:2), 1962, D 26,1:4
Austin, William D, 1943, My 28,21:3
Austin, William E Mrs, 1943, Je 9,21:5
Austin, William H, 1947, S 23,25:2; 1952, D 7,88:3; 1960, N 29,37:3
Austin, William H A, 1940, Jl 19,19:5
Austin, William H Mrs, 1955, Ja 1,13:4
Austin, William L, 1949, O 11,34:5
Austin, William L Mrs, 1939, N 2,23:6
Austin, William M, 1947, Ap 29,27:5
Austin, William W, 1919, F 10,13:2
Austin, Willis R, 1955, Ag 30,27:4
Austin, Zed H, 1940, Mr 24,31:1
Austin-Ball, Thomas, 1944, O 4,19:1
Austin Julian, Bro, 1939, D 29,15:4
Austin-Small, Peter O C, 1968, Ap 20,34:3
Austine, William Col, 1904, S 5,5:6
Austral, Florence Mary (Florence Mary Wilson), 1968, My 17,44:1
Austria, Archduchess of (Princess Maria Thresa), 1912, O 25,13:2
Austrian, Ben, 1921, D 14,17:6
Austrian Archduke Charles Louis, 1896, My 20,5:2
Autch, John A, 1951, Je 6,31:2
Auten, Edward Sr, 1941, O 1,21:4
Auten, George M (por), 1949, Je 1,31:4
Auten, George M Mrs, 1937, N 19,23:3
Auten, Harold, 1964, O 7,47:1
Auten, James E, 1947, O 3,25:3
Autenrieth, George C, 1967, Jl 24,27:2
Autenrieth, Joseph F, 1963, My 30,17:2
Auth, Frank J, 1938, F 18,19:2
Auth, Harry J, 1953, D 21,31:6
Auth, Henry J Mrs, 1944, F 16,17:4
Auton, Jesse D, 1952, Ap 1,59:1
Autori, Franco Mrs, 1946, Jl 7,36:2
Autran, J (see also Mr 7 and 24), 1877, Mr 27,2:1
Autremont, Hubert H d', 1947, Ap 17,27:3
Autrey, John L Mrs, 1939, F 18,15:5
Autry, Martin G, 1950, Ja 27,23:2
Auwaerter, Albert F, 1946, Ag 23,19:3
Auwaerter, Paul, 1953, F 23,25:2
Avakian, Agob G, 1940, Mr 3,44:1
Avakian, Hovhannes, 1959, Je 12,27:1
Avalle, Pierino, 1952, My 5,27:6
Avallone, Albert A, 1955, My 29,44:4
Avallone, Peter F, 1938, My 6,21:5
Avalos, Alfredo A, 1953, S 21,25:3
Avanozian, Ghazar, 1953, N 25,23:3
Avard, Clement C Mrs, 1955, Ja 28,20:1
Avayou, David, 1965, F 12,30:1

Avebury, Lord (Jno Lubbock), 1913, My 29,11:5
Avedikian, Zacharia H, 1941, My 18,43:2
Avedikian, Zacharia H Mrs, 1965, S 1,37:4
Avegno, J Bernard, 1957, Jl 12,21:3
Aveling, Christian W Mrs, 1954, Ja 30,17:6
Avelino, Georgino, 1959, Ap 4,19:4
Avella, Angelo, 1948, Ap 7,25:4
Avelline, Mother (Sisters of St Dominic), 1952, Ap 12,11:2
Avendano, Victor, 1960, Mr 23,11:1
Avenol, Joseph, 1952, S 3,29:3
Avent, George J, 1942, Ja 26,15:5
Avent, John M, 1955, Ag 21,93:1; 1958, D 10,39:4
Avent, Joseph E, 1958, F 13,29:1
Averbuck, Samuel H, 1963, O 25,31:4
Averell, Eva, 1959, Ap 11,21:5
Averell, George W, 1951, S 23,87:1
Averell, James George, 1904, N 21,7:2
Averell, James P Mrs, 1963, Ag 28,33:5
Averell, William H, 1946, D 30,22:3
Averescu, Alexandru (por), 1938, O 3,15:5
Averett, Elliott, 1942, N 27,23:1
Averett, Jane, 1953, Mr 19,29:4
Averett, Mary J, 1961, Ja 12,29:3
Averill, Alex M Rev, 1904, F 14,7:6
Averill, Alfred W, 1957, Jl 8,23:5
Averill, Charles E Mrs, 1944, My 26,19:5
Averill, David M, 1938, Jl 18,13:5
Averill, Earl E, 1951, Ap 4,29:4
Averill, Edward W, 1948, F 3,25:2
Averill, Ernest L, 1942, S 14,15:3
Averill, Frank, 1948, Jl 24,15:3
Averill, George C, 1954, S 20,23:4
Averill, Harry, 1945, O 17,19:2
Averill, Harry B, 1960, D 31,17:2
Averill, Mary, 1954, Ja 13,31:4
Averill, Mary H, 1955, O 14,36:7
Averill, Nathan K, 1947, O 28,26:2
Averill, Porter W, 1951, My 27,69:1
Averill, Roger, 1883, D 11,4:7
Averill, Samuel M, 1943, Jl 28,15:5
Aversa, John F, 1940, Ap 16,23:5
Avery, Albert E, 1939, N 22,21:2
Avery, Alfred H, 1957, My 30,19:4
Avery, Angelina L Mrs, 1937, My 24,19:2
Avery, B P, 1875, D 2,4:5; 1876, Ja 27,5:5
Avery, Benjamin B, 1941, F 17,15:2
Avery, Brainard, 1947, F 7,23:4
Avery, Burt M, 1942, D 10,25:6
Avery, Burt Mrs, 1949, Ag 24,25:2
Avery, Charles F, 1922, D 8,17:4; 1962, S 5,40:1
Avery, Charles M, 1940, My 10,24:4
Avery, Charles W Mrs, 1949, My 22,88:1
Avery, Christopher L, 1956, My 7,27:2
Avery, Clarence R, 1953, S 29,29:2
Avery, Clarence W (por), 1949, My 14,13:4
Avery, Cyrus H, 1954, Je 12,15:5
Avery, Edward Woodbridge Dr, 1917, F 14,9:5
Avery, Emma Wait Mrs, 1924, D 28,5:2
Avery, F Charles, 1952, Ag 17,76:6
Avery, Frank E, 1944, Mr 15,19:5
Avery, Frank H, 1943, Ja 18,15:2
Avery, Frank L, 1950, Ja 21,17:2
Avery, Frederick B, 1942, Jl 26,30:6
Avery, Frederick D, 1946, N 17,68:2
Avery, Frederick W, 1939, Mr 16,23:3
Avery, G S, 1936, Mr 4,21:4
Avery, Georges, 1955, N 25,27:3
Avery, Henry C, 1959, N 26,37:4
Avery, Henry W, 1944, S 12,19:3
Avery, Herbert F, 1940, D 14,17:7
Avery, Ira S, 1940, F 5,17:2
Avery, Irving M Col, 1909, Ag 12,7:6
Avery, John, 1940, S 10,23:3
Avery, John M Jr, 1942, Ag 10,19:6
Avery, Kent, 1962, S 8,19:1
Avery, M N, 1942, S 11,21:4
Avery, M P (Living Skeleton), 1882, Jl 17,5:3
Avery, Melanie, 1955, F 3,23:5
Avery, Milton C, 1965, Ja 4,29:1
Avery, Myron C, 1952, D 2,31:2
Avery, Myron H, 1952, Ag 1,17:4
Avery, Myrtilla, 1959, Ap 5,86:7
Avery, Nathan P, 1947, Ap 13,60:4
Avery, Oswald T, 1955, F 21,21:4
Avery, Phil S, 1940, Ap 14,45:3
Avery, Philander M, 1945, Ja 20,11:6
Avery, Richard T, 1951, Ja 27,13:3
Avery, Robert Gen, 1912, O 2,13:6
Avery, Russ, 1953, Ja 26,19:4
Avery, Russell Mrs, 1952, Ap 6,88:4
Avery, Samuel P, 1920, S 26,22:4
Avery, Samuel P Mrs, 1911, Ap 30,II,13:4
Avery, Samuel Putman, 1904, Ag 13,7:6
Avery, Sewell L (will, N 8,24:5), 1960, N 1,1:6
Avery, Sewell L (est acctg), 1961, Ap 19,25:3
Avery, Sewell L (est acctg), 1962, Mr 1,29:3
Avery, Sewell L Mrs (will, Ap 29,61:3), 1956, Ap 9, 27:3
Avery, Sewell Mrs (est appr), 1957, Jl 9,31:2
Avery, Stephen M, 1948, F 12,23:2
Avery, Susan, 1915, F 3,11:6
Avery, Susan J Mrs, 1941, N 4,23:2
Avery, W T, 1880, My 23,1:6
Avery, Waldo A (est acctg), 1959, F 4,25:6
Avery, Walter T, 1904, Je 11,9:6
Avery, Warren J, 1955, My 18,31:6
Avery, William A, 1942, Mr 5,23:5
Avery, William F, 1951, My 14,25:5
Avery, William G, 1964, S 1,35:2
Averyt, Gordon M, 1952, D 9,30:4
Aves, Dreda, 1942, Ap 18,15:4
Avey, Guy R, 1955, Jl 14,23:5
Avezzana, Camillo R, 1949, Je 18,13:4
Avezzana, Giuseppe Gen, 1879, D 26,1:4
Avezzano, Anthony Mrs, 1949, D 5,23:1
Avezzano, Romano, 1923, O 11,21:3
Aviad, Yeshayahu, 1957, Ag 3,15:6
Avidan, Maurice S, 1941, O 18,19:5
Avidon, Frederick, 1967, Ag 17,37:4
Avila Camacho, Manuel (funl, O 15,15:2), 1955, O 14,27:1
Avila Camacho, Maximino, 1945, F 18,34:5
Avildsen, Clarence J, 1964, Jl 6,29:2
Aviles Tiscar, Luis, 1948, N 16,29:1
Avinoff, Andrey, 1949, Jl 17,58:2
Avirett, William G, 1961, Ag 10,27:1
Avis, H Wheaton, 1966, O 14,43:1
Avis, John B, 1944, Ja 22,13:2
Avis, S Walter, 1941, D 19,25:2
Avis, William H, 1944, Ja 18,19:5
Avison, Douglas B, 1952, Ag 7,21:2
Avison, J, 1882, Je 11,7:3
Avitabile, Salvatore, 1957, My 18,19:6
Avitus, Sister, 1924, D 30,17:5
Avlas, Eustis, 1950, D 31,42:8
Avnet, Charles Mrs, 1962, Ja 24,33:4
Avnet, Robert, 1964, Jl 29,21:2
Avni, Joshua, 1964, Ag 25,33:3
Avnsoe, Thorkild, 1958, S 11,33:1
Avolio, Frank Mrs, 1951, F 3,15:4
Avonmore, Lord (W C Yelverton), 1883, Ap 7,1:1
Avory, Edward J, 1944, Je 1,19:3
Avram, David A, 1966, S 8,47:2
Avram, Elias H, 1949, Jl 16,13:1
Avray, Robert, 1949, Ap 21,25:2
Avrick, Harry, 1953, Jl 28,19:6
Avril, Jane, 1943, F 5,21:2
Avshalomov, Aaron, 1965, Ap 28,45:1
Avxentieff, Nicholas D, 1943, Mr 5,17:2
Aw Boon-haw, 1954, S 6,15:3
Awalt, Francis G, 1966, D 31,19:1
Awe, Edward F H, 1950, Mr 9,29:3
Awkerman, Charles H, 1950, My 8,23:4
Awtrey, Robert King Mrs, 1923, Ag 8,15:3
Axe, Emerson W, 1964, Mr 28,19:4
Axe, Emerson W Mrs, 1967, Ap 17,37:1
Axel, Julius, 1961, D 8,37:2
Axel, Prince of Denmark (details, Jl 16,31:1), 1964, Jl 15,32:7
Axelrad, Jacob, 1944, Ag 11,15:5
Axelrad, John, 1957, Mr 2,21:5
Axelrod, Bernard J Mrs, 1959, Je 25,29:4
Axelrod, Charles, 1966, Mr 11,33:2
Axelrod, Herman, 1967, S 19,47:2
Axelrod, Jacob, 1957, Je 9,70:5
Axelrod, Louis, 1949, Jl 5,42:3
Axelroth, Harry R, 1954, Je 5,17:7
Axelsson, George, 1966, Ag 20,25:4
Axenzoff, Max, 1949, F 14,19:2
Axford, W Homer, 1942, S 18,21:5
Axford, William B, 1948, Jl 29,21:2
Axilbund, Samuel, 1950, My 24,29:3
Axley, Robert C, 1954, Mr 30,27:4
Axline, Dean W, 1966, Je 22,47:2
Axline, Edward S, 1947, O 13,23:3
Axline, H E, 1952, Je 18,27:5
Axman, Charles D, 1937, D 7,25:4
Axman, Charles D Mrs, 1945, Mr 3,13:5
Axman, Frederick J, 1954, Ag 2,17:5
Axselrod, Edward, 1950, D 7,33:3
Axson, Edward W, 1905, Ap 30,2:3
Axson, Edward W Mrs, 1905, Ap 30,2:3
Axson, S, 1935, F 27,19:1
Axt, Aug Sr, 1939, Mr 8,21:5
Axt, Harry J, 1944, D 12,23:4
Axt, Robert L M, 1956, S 17,27:1
Axt, William L, 1959, F 15,86:6
Axtell, Albert P, 1938, Je 15,23:6
Axtell, Decatur Mrs, 1925, S 12,15:4
Axtell, E Earle, 1937, N 15,23:4
Axtell, Frederick S, 1937, Ja 27,21:1
Axtell, Leo-Rae, 1959, O 24,21:6
Axtell, Lucien V, 1947, Mr 28,24:2
Axtell, Silas B, 1962, My 1,37:3
Axten, John, 1954, Mr 21,88:6
Axthelm, Ralph, 1959, My 17,84:2
Axtman, John Charles, 1953, Ja 15,27:2
Axtmann, Adolph, 1941, S 21,42:5
Axtmann, C August, 1944, Je 20,19:1
Axton, J T, 1934, Jl 22,22:1
Axworthy, H Harold, 1941, Ag 5,19:3
Ayala, Eusebio, 1942, Je 5,17:3
Ayala, Ramon Gen, 1920, Ag 31,9:1
Ayars, C G, 1902, N 8,1:6
Ayars, Charles H, 1951, Ja 4,29:2
Ayars, Eugenia G Mrs, 1951, D 21,27:4
Aycock, Charles B Ex-Gov, 1912, Ap 5,13:6
Aycock, Nathaniel M, 1952, Ja 12,13:2
Aycock, Roy, 1956, Mr 12,27:3
Aycock, Thomas B, 1948, Ja 9,21:3
Aycock, William L, 1951, O 25,29:2
Aycrigg, Benjamin Arthur, 1925, Je 25,21:6
Aycrigg, George B (Jan 19), 1963, Ap 1,35:1
Ayd, Joseph J, 1957, D 4,39:4
Aydelott, James H, 1966, Je 6,41:1
Aydelotte, Frank (services set, D 19,31:4), 1956, D 18,31:1
Aydelotte, Frank Mrs, 1952, Je 15,84:6
Aye, Maryon, 1951, Jl 22,61:2
Ayed, Farhat B, 1948, Jl 30,17:3
Ayer, Albert C, 1949, O 25,27:5
Ayer, Charles F, 1956, Ja 16,21:5; 1961, S 24,87:2
Ayer, Charles M, 1942, Jl 24,19:3
Ayer, Coburn H, 1957, Ap 4,33:2
Ayer, Francis Wayland, 1923, Mr 6,21:3
Ayer, Frederick, 1918, Mr 15,13:5
Ayer, Frederick Fanning, 1924, Je 10,11:4
Ayer, Harriet Hubbard, 1903, N 26,7:5
Ayer, Harry B, 1942, F 10,19:1
Ayer, Henry P, 1940, My 30,18:4
Ayer, I Winslow Col, 1909, My 1,9:4
Ayer, Ira, 1939, Jl 10,19:2
Ayer, Ira Col, 1903, F 4,9:5
Ayer, J C Dr, 1878, Jl 4,5:4
Ayer, James C, 1939, Mr 21,24:2
Ayer, John V, 1877, My 3,4:7
Ayer, Joseph C, 1944, Ap 17,23:1
Ayer, Lester C, 1940, N 11,19:3
Ayer, Lloyd P, 1952, Ap 1,29:4
Ayer, Luther S, 1951, Ja 27,13:5
Ayer, Nathaniel D (Nat), 1952, S 21,89:3
Ayer, Nathaniel F, 1948, Jl 26,17:4
Ayer, Oliver G, 1952, N 25,29:2
Ayer, Ray S, 1948, D 10,25:1
Ayer, Waldo Emerson Lt-Col, 1916, Mr 12,19:5
Ayer, Walter Mrs, 1951, O 19,27:2
Ayer, Will E, 1952, F 24,85:1
Ayer, Will F, 1947, S 10,27:6
Ayers, A Benedict Bro (Richd A Ayers), 1967, Ja 30,29:4
Ayers, Abram, 1937, D 31,15:5
Ayers, Albert, 1947, D 19,25:3
Ayers, Arthur W, 1948, N 20,13:5
Ayers, Charles F, 1938, F 12,15:2
Ayers, Edward A Mrs, 1951, Ja 13,30:3
Ayers, Emma F M, 1949, S 6,27:3
Ayers, Ernest M, 1952, S 9,31:2
Ayers, Frank W, 1943, N 30,27:4
Ayers, Fred W Mrs, 1953, Ag 16,77:1
Ayers, Frederic M, 1940, My 16,23:4
Ayers, Frederick B, 1941, Jl 31,17:1
Ayers, Frederick Mrs, 1950, Ag 10,25:5
Ayers, George A Sr, 1947, Mr 19,25:3
Ayers, Harry M, 1964, O 8,43:4
Ayers, Henry G, 1947, Ja 20,25:2
Ayers, Herbert D, 1959, D 7,31:2
Ayers, Horace E, 1967, Ja 1,53:2
Ayers, Ira C Mrs, 1959, Ag 9,89:2
Ayers, James A, 1943, O 10,48:6
Ayers, John H, 1943, Mr 30,26:3
Ayers, John H Mrs, 1937, S 2,21:4
Ayers, Jule Mrs, 1945, Ap 4,21:2
Ayers, Lemuel (trb lr, S 11,3:5), 1955, Ag 15,15:2
Ayers, Lemuel Mrs, 1967, Je 24,29:5
Ayers, Milton I, 1961, My 22,41:3
Ayers, Minnie M H Mrs, 1942, D 24,15:2
Ayers, Richard H, 1966, Je 24,37:2
Ayers, Samuel J, 1957, Mr 26,33:2
Ayers, Stuart Mrs, 1955, O 4,35:1
Ayers, Theodore A, 1965, S 11,27:1
Ayers, Wallace Mrs, 1938, F 14,17:4
Ayers, Watson R, 1937, Ap 30,21:3
Ayers, William, 1941, Jl 9,21:6
Ayers, William B, 1953, Jl 6,17:3
Ayers, William L, 1950, O 26,31:6
Ayers, William S, 1954, N 6,17:2
Ayers, Winfield Dr, 1937, Ap 13,25:3
Ayguade, Jaime, 1943, My 31,17:5
Aylen, Henry, 1940, Je 15,15:5
Aylen, James P, 1942, Ap 30,19:2
Aylesbury, Marquis, 1878, Ja 7,1:4
Aylesford, Earl of, 1885, Ja 15,5:3
Aylesworth, Allen B, 1952, F 14,27:6
Aylesworth, Merlin H, 1952, O 1,33:3
Aylesworth, Ray W, 1950, Ag 25,21:2
Ayliffe, J E, 1878, O 29,8:6
Ayling, William J Dr, 1924, Je 15,23:1
Aylmer, Gerald Sir, 1939, Ap 5,25:5
Aylmer, Udo Sir, 1901, D 1,7:6
Aylward, Joseph J, 1966, N 8,39:1
Aylward, Joseph M, 1954, D 18,15:5
Aylward, William J, 1956, F 28,31:5
Aymar, Jose Mrs, 1923, D 21,17:4
Aymar, Reynold A, 1968, Mr 29,41:1
Aymar, W T, 1883, Mr 20,8:2
Ayme, Edward L, 1953, F 5,23:5
Ayme, Louis H, 1912, My 17,13:6
Ayme, Marcel, 1967, O 15,85:1

Ayon, Alfonso, 1944, S 12,19:4
Ayotte, Joseph L, 1956, My 29,27:3
Ayoub Khan, 1887, O 12,1:2
Ayrault, Ernest Fitzhugh, 1920, Mr 18,11:5
Ayrault, Guy, 1957, N 18,31:4
Ayrault, J Allen, 1940, N 6,23:5
Ayre, Amos L, 1952, Ja 15,27:1
Ayre, Charles P, 1937, D 16,27:4
Ayre, James W Mrs, 1949, Jl 26,27:5
Ayre, Samuel, 1956, Ag 26,84:7
Ayre, Thomas D, 1958, Mr 31,27:2
Ayres, A R, 1939, O 17,25:5
Ayres, Agnes, 1940, D 26,19:5
Ayres, Alfred (T E Osmun), 1902, O 27,9:4
Ayres, Anne G Mrs, 1952, Je 28,19:3
Ayres, Arthur B, 1948, S 27,23:3
Ayres, Arthur J Jr, 1955, My 19,29:5
Ayres, Brown Dr, 1919, Ja 29,13:5
Ayres, Charles Greenlief Lt-Col (funl, S 29,11:5), 1909, S 27,9:5
Ayres, Charles Hamilton, 1917, My 10,13:4
Ayres, Charles J, 1953, Mr 23,23:2
Ayres, Charles L, 1963, O 25,32:1
Ayres, Chauncey Dr, 1903, Ap 15,9:6
Ayres, Chauncey P, 1948, Mr 28,48:4
Ayres, Chester T, 1939, Ap 8,15:3
Ayres, Clarence L, 1941, S 6,15:3
Ayres, Clifford H, 1940, Ap 17,23:5
Ayres, Crittenden Mrs, 1949, N 27,105:1
Ayres, David C Rev, 1925, Ap 15,19:3
Ayres, Florence, 1944, Jl 27,17:2
Ayres, Francis O, 1941, Je 20,21:4
Ayres, Harry A, 1960, D 31,17:3
Ayres, Harry M, 1948, N 22,21:1
Ayres, Henry, 1880, O 7,2:7
Ayres, Henry M, 1946, N 21,31:4
Ayres, Herbert B, 1951, Ag 8,25:6
Ayres, Hiram J, 1907, Jl 3,7:5
Ayres, Howard, 1940, D 13,23:5
Ayres, James B, 1940, Je 20,23:5
Ayres, John, 1909, Ag 3,7:4
Ayres, Leonard P, 1946, O 30,27:1
Ayres, Leslie F, 1952, S 8,21:3
Ayres, Louis, 1947, D 1,21:2
Ayres, Milan C Mrs, 1938, N 21,19:3
Ayres, Morgan W, 1948, Mr 28,48:7
Ayres, Morgan W Mrs, 1940, My 21,23:1
Ayres, Nelson M, 1940, Jl 13,13:3
Ayres, Philip W, 1945, N 5,19:3
Ayres, Quincy C, 1963, My 4,25:5
Ayres, Robert M, 1957, D 27,19:3
Ayres, Ruby M, 1955, N 15,29:1
Ayres, Russell R, 1959, O 5,31:5
Ayres, S B, 1929, Je 3,23:3
Ayres, Samuel, 1904, F 4,9:6; 1941, Ap 5,17:3
Ayres, Samuel L P Rear-Adm, 1917, Ap 30,13:5
Ayres, Stanley W, 1952, My 17,19:4
Ayres, Stephen Cooper, 1921, S 3,9:6
Ayres, Theodore V, 1948, N 10,29:3
Ayres, W E, 1951, S 7,29:3
Ayres, Warren W, 1968, Ja 5,24:1
Ayres, William, 1941, D 3,26:2
Ayres, William A, 1923, D 9,23:2; 1952, F 19,29:1
Ayres, William Warren Rev, 1915, Jl 20,11:6
Ayrton, Hertha, 1923, Ag 28,17:4
Ayrton, Robert, 1924, My 20,21:6
Ayscough, J (Mgr Count F B D Bickerstaffe-Drew), 1928, Jl 5,19:5
Aytoun, Prof, 1865, Ag 23,1:4
Ayulo, Manuel, 1955, My 18,41:7
Ayulo, Manuel L, 1941, Ja 2,23:6
Ayvad, Hachig A, 1940, Ag 20,19:6
Ayvad, Parnac M, 1940, Mr 31,44:1
Ayvasian, Haig, 1955, N 28,31:1
Ayyangar, N Gopalaswami Min, 1953, F 10,27:4
Ayyoubi, Atta, 1950, Ja 30,17:3
Azad, Abul Kalam Maulana (funl, F 23,92:5), 1958, F 22,17:2
Azades, Raphael Bro, 1961, Mr 29,33:1
Azades Gabriel, Bro (J A Mahar), 1966, Ja 4,31:4
Azana, Manuel, 1940, N 5,25:1
Azarate y Rosell, Carlos, 1946, Ag 26,23:5
Azariah, Vedanayakam S, 1945, Ja 12,15:3
Azarias, Bro (J C King), 1965, S 3,27:4
Azaroff, Vladimir, 1949, Ap 27,27:2
Azcarate, Gumersindo de, 1917, D 16,23:1
Azcarate, Pablo de Mrs, 1944, Jl 15,13:1
Azeltine, Frederick W, 1942, Ja 20,19:3
Azevedo, Diogenes L, 1944, Mr 6,19:4
Azevedo Gomes, Mario de (funl, D 15,7:1), 1965, D 13,39:5
Azevedo Neves, Alberto, 1955, Ap 16,19:4
Azhayev, Vasily N, 1968, Ap 29,43:4
Azimow, Isadore I, 1955, My 7,17:4
Azin, Simon, 1963, D 25,33:5
Aziz, Abdul, 1948, Mr 30,23:5
Aziz Bou Atour, Mohammed el, 1907, F 15,11:4
Aziz Fahmy, Abdel, 1951, Mr 5,21:3
Azizul Huque, Mohamed, 1947, Mr 23,60:3
Azlauzu, Justo, 1943, F 12,19:3
Azm, Khaled el-, 1965, F 19,35:4
Azmi, Mahmoud, 1954, N 4,1:1
Aznar Embid, Severino, 1959, N 20,31:3
Azodi, Yadullah, 1961, Ag 15,29:4
Azogue, Ramon, 1945, Jl 14,11:6
Azouni, Omar, 1968, N 5,47:1
Azoy, Anastasio C M Jr, 1965, F 6,25:1
Azoy, Mary L Mrs, 1938, N 2,24:3
Azpiroz, Senor Don Manuel de, Mexican Ambassador, 1905, Mr 25,9:3
Azuela, Mariano, 1952, Mr 2,92:3
Azy, Benoist d' Comtesse, 1919, N 13,13:2
Azzara, Casper J, 1967, Ja 24,37:2
Azzariti, Gaetano, 1961, Ja 6,27:4
Azzolino, Anthony, 1944, My 30,21:3

B

Ba, Dr, 1963, N 10,87:1
Baab, John A Mrs, 1952, Je 23,19:4
Baab, Otto J, 1958, S 30,31:5
Baach, Emil, 1944, Ag 8,17:3
Baach, Harry, 1958, Ag 6,25:2
Baad, Charles, 1956, D 22,19:4
Baade, Paul W, 1959, O 12,19:5
Baade, Walter, 1960, Je 28,31:1
Baake, Otto C, 1954, Ja 17,93:2
Baals, Harry W, 1954, My 10,23:6
Baar, Arnold R, 1954, O 16,17:5
Baar, Herman Mrs, 1904, F 22,5:6
Baar, Hermann Dr, 1904, S 5,5:6
Baar, Jacob, 1949, Ap 23,13:2
Baar, Lincoln F, 1960, N 30,37:4
Baar, Rudolph F, 1968, F 14,51:1
Baar, Salomon, 1941, Ap 12,15:2
Baart, P A Rev, 1908, F 13,9:6
Baas, Rudolf, 1952, O 14,31:4
Baatnes, Conrad M, 1946, Ag 25,45:1
Bab, Julius, 1955, F 13,86:7
Baba, Daniel, 1950, Ag 6,72:8
Baba, Eiichi, 1937, D 21,23:2
Baba, Tsunego, 1956, Ap 7,19:5
Babaras, Michael, 1948, F 4,23:3
Babayan, Levon, 1951, Je 7,33:1
Babb, Charles E, 1954, Mr 21,88:4
Babb, Charles H, 1952, N 16,89:1
Babb, Charles W Sr, 1956, Jl 11,29:4
Babb, Cyrus C, 1937, O 4,21:6
Babb, Frank H, 1941, Jl 14,13:3
Babb, George W, 1920, F 16,11:5
Babb, J Vance Mrs, 1966, Ag 13,25:5
Babb, James T, 1968, Jl 22,35:5
Babb, John A, 1948, D 31,15:3
Babb, Maurice J, 1945, O 30,19:4
Babb, Max W, 1943, Mr 14,26:1
Babb, Thomas E, 1940, Jl 19,19:4
Babb, Tony O, 1938, N 17,25:3
Babb, W E, 1948, Mr 24,25:1
Babbage, Andress P Mrs, 1940, Ag 2,15:3
Babbage, Edgar W, 1957, Ag 9,19:4
Babbage, John D, 1949, Mr 12,17:2
Babbage, Mildred, 1949, D 16,31:1
Babbage, Mr, 1871, N 13,2:4
Babbage, Richard G, 1944, Je 3,13:5
Babbin, Hosea J, 1907, O 27,9:6
Babbington, A R, 1940, Ag 13,19:2
Babbitt, Dean Jr Mrs, 1939, Je 17,15:1
Babbitt, Dean R, 1905, Jl 22,7:5
Babbitt, E B, 1881, D 11,2:5
Babbitt, Edwin B, 1939, D 10,68:7
Babbitt, Edwin V Sr, 1967, D 15,94:3
Babbitt, Emma L, 1941, My 25,36:5
Babbitt, Franklin Rev, 1918, Ja 25,11:8
Babbitt, George D, 1919, D 6,11:5
Babbitt, I, 1933, Jl 16,20:1
Babbitt, James A, 1944, O 17,23:3
Babbitt, Josephine H Mrs, 1940, Jl 14,31:1
Babbitt, Kurnal B, 1920, Ja 26,7:2
Babbitt, Lelia P, 1951, F 7,29:3
Babbitt, Robert O, 1904, Ja 2,9:4
Babbitt, Searles, 1940, Ja 31,19:2
Babbott, F L, 1933, D 8,23:1
Babcock, A Emerson Mrs, 1944, Jl 8,11:3
Babcock, Adelbert H, 1949, Jl 7,25:1
Babcock, Agnes D, 1942, Je 5,17:4
Babcock, Alfred Jerome, 1920, N 15,15:5
Babcock, Alfred R, 1949, Ag 29,17:3
Babcock, Andrew B, 1953, O 4,89:2
Babcock, Archer D, 1939, My 26,23:6
Babcock, Arthur E, 1949, Ag 11,23:3
Babcock, Austin L, 1938, N 8,23:2
Babcock, Barry J, 1961, My 19,33:3
Babcock, Beulah E, 1938, O 27,23:3
Babcock, Birton E (will, Ap 28,9:4), 1941, Ap 8,25:6
Babcock, C A, 1876, Jl 4,4:6
Babcock, C H Prof, 1903, Mr 25,9:6
Babcock, Charles A, 1940, Ja 21,34:7
Babcock, Charles E, 1948, Ap 12,21:5
Babcock, Charles H, 1920, D 17,17:4; 1967, D 15,47:1
Babcock, Charles H Jr Mrs (will, Ag 19,24:2), 1953, Jl 18,13:1
Babcock, Charles Henry Rev Dr, 1916, Ja 8,9:7
Babcock, Charles J, 1942, Mr 8,42:7; 1959, Ja 26,29:3
Babcock, Charles L Mrs, 1948, D 7,31:5
Babcock, Charlotte S Mrs, 1937, My 11,25:4
Babcock, Clarence J, 1958, F 26,27:1
Babcock, Clay, 1943, My 4,23:2
Babcock, Clinton L, 1957, F 12,27:2
Babcock, Clinton LeR Mrs, 1963, N 10,86:5
Babcock, Conrad S Mrs, 1962, Ag 22,34:6
Babcock, D, 1884, N 14,2:3
Babcock, David, 1950, F 28,29:4
Babcock, Donald S, 1962, Ap 8,86:8
Babcock, Donald S Mrs, 1948, Je 8,25:3
Babcock, Dr (funl), 1901, Je 8,9:5
Babcock, Dwight H, 1944, D 9,15:5
Babcock, E B, 1935, Mr 2,15:1
Babcock, Edmund C, 1940, Ja 4,24:2
Babcock, Edward S, 1943, My 23,42:5
Babcock, Edward V, 1948, S 3,19:1
Babcock, Edwin C, 1942, Ap 21,23:2
Babcock, Edwin G, 1941, Jl 9,21:3; 1951, F 3,15:5
Babcock, Edwin G Mrs, 1937, Ja 23,17:1
Babcock, Elisha J, 1924, Ap 24,19:4
Babcock, Elizabeth, 1925, Jl 30,19:5; 1952, F 5,29:1
Babcock, Elizabeth D, 1946, D 4,31:2
Babcock, Ernest B, 1954, D 9,33:2
Babcock, F G, 1901, Je 29,2:5
Babcock, F Huntington Mrs, 1964, N 13,35:1
Babcock, F Lawrence, 1960, My 1,86:7
Babcock, Frank D, 1957, Ag 29,27:2
Babcock, Franklin L, 1950, Jl 30,60:4
Babcock, Fred H Mrs, 1937, N 17,23:5
Babcock, Frederic L, 1940, Mr 22,19:3
Babcock, G I, 1934, My 12,15:5
Babcock, George D, 1942, Ja 13,22:6
Babcock, George Sgt, 1871, Ag 24,8:4
Babcock, George T, 1955, S 6,25:3
Babcock, George W, 1938, Jl 17,26:5; 1944, Jl 19,19:4
Babcock, George W Sr, 1950, N 22,25:2
Babcock, Guilford C, 1945, Ag 25,11:3
Babcock, Guilford C Mrs, 1957, Ap 15,29:5
Babcock, Harmon S, 1937, Ja 5,23:2
Babcock, Harold, 1953, Ja 22,23:3
Babcock, Harold Delos, 1968, Ap 11,45:3
Babcock, Harry A, 1960, My 2,29:2
Babcock, Harry S, 1965, Je 17,33:4
Babcock, Henry Denison, 1918, Je 2,21:2
Babcock, Henry H, 1903, D 1,9:6
Babcock, Herbert D, 1966, My 3,44:6
Babcock, Howard E, 1950, Jl 13,25:4
Babcock, Howard L, 1939, O 16,19:5
Babcock, Howell E, 1957, Ap 8,23:4
Babcock, Irving B, 1964, F 8,23:1
Babcock, J C, 1884, D 21,2:5
Babcock, James W Dr, 1922, Mr 4,15:4
Babcock, John A, 1940, My 6,17:3
Babcock, John Breckinridge Gen, 1909, Ap 28,9:4
Babcock, John C Col, 1908, N 21,9:2
Babcock, John R (por), 1938, Jl 2,13:4
Babcock, John W, 1948, Ja 20,23:1
Babcock, Joseph N, 1942, Je 9,23:6
Babcock, Joseph N Mrs, 1937, F 14,II,8:6
Babcock, Joseph W, 1909, Ap 28,9:4
Babcock, Josiah, 1954, Ap 26,25:3
Babcock, Katherine Roosevelt Mrs, 1925, S 11,23:5
Babcock, L Kent, 1959, Ap 29,33:2
Babcock, Lemuel Hollingsworth, 1915, Ja 11,9:5
Babcock, Lester F, 1955, Ag 29,19:6
Babcock, Lewis Hamilton Mrs, 1911, D 5,13:4
Babcock, Louis A, 1938, Jl 14,21:4
Babcock, Louis L, 1956, N 6,35:4
Babcock, Maltbie Mrs, 1943, S 22,23:4
Babcock, Marcus Dr, 1937, S 3,17:5
Babcock, Marie C, 1955, Mr 19,15:4
Babcock, Mary F, 1956, Mr 4,88:2
Babcock, Newton B, 1957, Ag 14,25:5
Babcock, O E Gen, 1884, Je 4,5:1
Babcock, Paul, 1903, O 7,9:5
Babcock, Perley S, 1951, Ag 14,23:3
Babcock, R E, 1872, Mr 7,1:6
Babcock, Reuben L Jr, 1955, Je 3,23:6
Babcock, Richard F, 1954, F 23,27:1; 1967, Ja 10,40:3
Babcock, S B Rev, 1873, O 27,5:4
Babcock, S M, 1931, Jl 3,19:1
Babcock, Samuel D, 1918, Ap 17,13:4
Babcock, Samuel G, 1942, Je 22,15:2
Babcock, Samuel G Mrs, 1947, Ag 29,17:3
Babcock, Susan P, 1905, Ap 10,1:6
Babcock, Theodore S, 1946, Je 23,40:6
Babcock, W Irving Mrs, 1924, My 8,19:4
Babcock, W Wayne (Feb 23), 1963, Ap 1,35:1
Babcock, Walter C Col, 1937, Ag 10,19:4
Babcock, William E Mrs, 1951, O 6,19:2
Babcock, William F Mrs (Bernie), 1962, Je 15,27:4
Babcock, William Gustavus Rev, 1911, Jl 31,7:6
Babcock, William T, 1950, Ja 24,31:1
Babcock, William W, 1945, O 20,11:4
Babcock, Woodward, 1938, Mr 22,21:4
Babe, John J, 1960, Mr 20,86:3
Babela, Douglas J, 1951, S 14,25:4
Babenroth, Donald, 1940, O 8,25:5
Baber, Asa J, 1960, Jl 28,27:1
Baber, John F, 1951, N 5,31:2
Baber, Leonard K, 1955, Je 19,92:7
Baber, Ray E, 1960, Je 23,29:5
Baber, Willard H, 1940, F 17,13:6
Babes, Horia I G, 1959, Jl 7,33:4
Babich, I Y, 1948, D 11,15:6
Babics, Joseph, 1948, D 22,23:4
Babig, Wolodymyr J, 1952, Ja 20,84:7
Babin, Hosea Mrs, 1914, My 10,IV,7:6
Babinet, M, 1872, N 8,1:5
Babington, J M, 1936, Je 16,25:2
Babini, Valentino, 1952, D 29,3:3
Babinski, Waclaw, 1957, Jl 24,26:3
Babits, Seth, 1965, My 8,31:5
Babitsky, John, 1948, Ap 8,25:4
Babitsky, Samuel Mrs, 1948, N 5,25:2
Babize, Auguste C Mrs, 1955, Jl 19,27:4
Babka, John J, 1937, Mr 23,24:2
Babkin, A N, 1950, N 11,15:2
Babkin, Boris P, 1950, My 4,27:1
Babkowski, John Sr, 1948, N 2,25:5
Babler, Jacob L, 1945, Je 1,15:6
Babock, Elmer F, 1952, Ag 4,15:5
Babock, Frederick H, 1941, S 1,15:6
Babock, Harriet, 1952, D 18,29:3
Babock, John R, 1952, Ja 27,76:6
Babonet, Charles, 1950, Ag 19,30:6
Babor, Anthony A, 1959, S 13,84:4
Babor, William F, 1952, O 30,31:6
Babson, Arthur Clifford, 1906, N 10,9:4
Babson, Joseph E, 1875, Ap 26,2:3
Babson, Rea E, 1959, N 14,21:6
Babson, Roger W (will, Ap 6,29:8), 1967, Mr 6,33:4
Babson, Roger W Mrs, 1956, My 1,33:1
Babson, Susan, 1947, S 15,17:2
Babst, Earl D, 1967, Ap 25,43:2
Babst, Earl D Mrs, 1945, Jl 6,11:5
Babst, William J, 1948, F 26,23:6
Babtle, William Gen, 1920, S 15,9:1
Babula, Sigmund P, 1968, S 28,33:2
Babulski, Stanley, 1952, O 23,31:1
Baburizza, Pascual, 1941, Ag 14,17:5
Babus, William J, 1957, Jl 21,60:5
Baby, Double-Headed, 1871, Jl 24,6:3
Baby, Emily G Mrs, 1940, Jl 5,13:5
Bac, Ferdinand, 1952, N 19,29:4
Baca, Elfego, 1945, Ag 29,23:5
Baca-Flor, Carlos, 1941, My 20,23:5
Bacal, Jacques W, 1951, Ja 22,17:5
Bacarat, Georges, 1943, O 6,23:4
Bacardi, Emile, 1922, Ag 30,15:6
Bacardi, F, 1926, N 24,23:3
Baccante, Enzo, 1938, Ap 7,23:2
Baccaro, Michael, 1948, D 10,26:2
Baccelli, Alfredo, 1955, S 14,35:3
Baccelli, Germano P, 1939, Mr 6,15:2
Bacchelli, Mario, 1951, O 20,34:4
Bacchi, Frank, 1965, Ag 4,35:6
Bacchiani, Louis Mrs, 1961, O 31,31:3
Bacchus, John G Rev Dr, 1919, Ag 3,22:5
Bacchus, Thomas W, 1944, D 31,25:1
Baccouche, Salaheddine, 1959, D 27,61:2
Bacevicz, Anthony M Dr, 1937, Ag 12,19:4
Bach, Albert F, 1954, My 11,29:3
Bach, Alfred Dr, 1937, Jl 7,23:1
Bach, Charles T, 1955, My 5,33:4
Bach, David P, 1961, O 1,86:2
Bach, Edward J Mrs, 1961, Ag 18,21:4
Bach, Elbert A, 1944, Ja 3,22:2
Bach, Elias, 1907, Ag 14,7:6
Bach, Francis E, 1952, Je 16,17:3
Bach, Frederick C, 1952, Ag 3,61:3
Bach, Frederick F, 1962, Je 22,25:2
Bach, Gustav, 1925, Ag 15,11:6; 1943, Ja 19,19:5
Bach, Hugo, 1939, Jl 6,23:4
Bach, J C, 1885, Ja 16,2:7
Bach, Jacob C, 1959, Ja 18,88:1
Bach, James A Mrs, 1942, Ap 2,22:3
Bach, Joe, 1966, O 25,48:2
Bach, John F Mrs, 1947, Ja 23,23:4
Bach, John S (Lord Stopford), 1961, Mr 7,35:2
Bach, Joseph S, 1920, Ap 16,13:4
Bach, Julian Mrs, 1962, F 16,27:2
Bach, Julian S, 1958, Ag 28,27:1
Bach, Julius M, 1946, N 30,15:3
Bach, Lawrence B, 1943, Ap 10,17:6
Bach, Matthew, 1949, N 19,17:4
Bach, Nicholas, 1947, Je 24,23:5
Bach, Oscar B, 1957, My 5,88:1
Bach, Otto, 1946, F 16,13:2
Bach, Reginald, 1941, Ja 7,23:3
Bach, Reynold H Mrs, 1957, S 20,25:2
Bach, Richard F, 1968, F 18,80:7
Bach, Siegmund J, 1909, N 14,13:5
Bach, Thoe F, 1962, Ja 20,21:5
Bach, William, 1880, Ag 1,12:5
Bachanche, Clement M, 1958, Jl 6,56:5
Bacharach, Abraham, 1947, O 7,27:6
Bacharach, Fanny Mrs (will), 1938, Jl 6,19:6
Bacharach, George, 1943, S 22,23:3
Bacharach, Harry, 1947, My 14,25:1
Bacharach, Harry Mrs, 1955, Je 22,30:1
Bacharach, Isaac, 1956, S 6,25:5
Bacharach, Lester S, 1957, Ap 10,33:4
Bacharach, Sidney Mrs, 1954, D 25,11:4
Bacharov, Toayan, 1949, Ja 9,72:1
Bache, A D Prof, 1867, F 20,2:2
Bache, B F, 1881, N 3,5:3
Bache, Charles, 1942, D 19,19:6
Bache, Edith M, 1966, Ag 2,33:4
Bache, Frank S, 1953, S 20,87:1

Bache, Franklin, 1946, S 18,31:5
Bache, Harold L (funl), 1968, Mr 18,45:4
Bache, John W, 1948, Mr 13,15:1
Bache, Kay, 1966, Ja 24,35:5
Bache, L S, 1927, O 11,1:7
Bache, Leopold S Mrs, 1950, Mr 11,15:3
Bache, Louise F, 1948, Ag 1,56:6
Bache, Max, 1956, Jl 30,21:5
Bache, Richard L, 1949, D 14,31:5
Bache, Violet, 1947, Ag 17,54:5
Bachelard, Gaston, 1962, O 17,39:2
Bachelder, Walter F Mrs, 1960, Ag 9,27:4
Bachelet, Emile, 1946, My 5,44:2
Bacheller, Irving Mrs, 1924, Mr 29,15:4; 1949, D 8, 33:5
Bacheller, J Henry, 1939, D 13,27:5
Bacheller, J Henry Mrs, 1938, S 10,17:5
Bacheller, Wheelock T Col, 1910, F 9,7:5
Bachellor, Fremont J, 1938, Jl 24,28:5
Bachem, Albert, 1957, Ap 12,25:1
Bachenheimer, Albert, 1961, Ap 29,23:2
Bachenheimer, Emil, 1943, Ja 23,13:4
Bachenheimer, Leon J, 1939, Ap 25,23:1
Bachenheimer, Marshall F, 1966, My 2,37:2
Bacher, Edward J, 1947, O 1,26:7
Bacher, John R Mrs, 1954, S 2,21:2
Bacher, Otto D, 1943, Mr 7,38:3
Bacher, Otto H, 1909, Ag 18,9:6
Bacher, William A, 1941, S 22,15:4
Bacherman, Samuel, 1953, N 16,25:4
Bachiocchi, Count, 1866, O 10,1:1
Bachman, Absalom P, 1942, Je 6,13:5
Bachman, Andrew J, 1955, Ja 28,19:1
Bachman, Arthur Mrs (will), 1959, Jl 31,8:3
Bachman, Bert P, 1958, O 25,21:4
Bachman, Chauncey C, 1946, F 24,44:6
Bachman, Earle, 1938, Ja 7,19:2
Bachman, Ennis W, 1948, Ap 17,15:3
Bachman, Eugene, 1947, D 28,30:7
Bachman, Florence E, 1950, Mr 7,27:2
Bachman, Francis J, 1947, Ja 27,23:1
Bachman, Frank H, 1956, N 15,35:4
Bachman, Frederick, 1966, My 15,88:7
Bachman, Ida C Mrs, 1937, Jl 5,17:5
Bachman, Ivan C, 1959, Ja 27,33:4
Bachman, John H, 1958, Ag 19,28:5
Bachman, John T, 1961, My 28,64:3
Bachman, Jonathan Dr, 1924, S 27,16:4
Bachman, Joseph, 1908, F 26,7:6
Bachman, Joshua, 1949, O 17,23:4
Bachman, Nathan L Sen, 1937, Ap 24,19:1
Bachman, Paul R, 1959, Ap 15,33:3
Bachman, Paul S, 1957, Ja 11,23:1
Bachman, Pearl D Mrs, 1938, F 20,II,8:4
Bachman, Ray A, 1955, Jl 19,27:6
Bachman, Valentine Mrs, 1944, Mr 7,17:4
Bachman, William A, 1942, Ap 15,21:5
Bachman, William W, 1938, N 29,23:4
Bachmann, Fdk S I, 1905, Ja 6,5:2
Bachmann, George, 1952, F 6,29:4
Bachmann, George Jr, 1953, Jl 11,11:6
Bachmann, Isaac D (por), 1949, Ja 1,13:5
Bachmann, Jack G, 1952, Je 12,34:4
Bachmann, Joseph A, 1948, Mr 16,27:1
Bachmann, Louis, 1947, Ag 2,13:5
Bachmann, Max, 1921, Ja 15,13:4
Bachmann, Norbert H, 1951, Ja 3,27:4
Bachmann, Norbet H Mrs, 1937, Ja 9,17:6
Bachmann, Walter J, 1937, Ja 23,17:3
Bachmann, Werner E, 1951, Mr 23,21:1
Bachmeyer, Arthur C, 1953, My 23,15:6
Bachner, Louis, 1945, D 28,15:3
Bachof, William B, 1947, Ap 20,60:5
Bachofer, John G, 1952, Ap 8,29:3
Bachrach, Arthur N, 1959, Ap 3,27:3
Bachrach, Benjamin C, 1951, Ja 1,17:2
Bachrach, Clarence G Mrs, 1962, Je 19,35:1
Bachrach, David, 1948, O 16,15:1
Bachrach, Donald, 1958, Ja 29,27:2
Bachrach, Emil M, 1937, S 29,23:4
Bachrach, Herman S (por), 1949, Mr 30,25:1
Bachrach, Lester Mrs, 1940, Mr 10,49:2
Bachrach, Louis F, 1963, Jl 26,25:3
Bachrach, Louis Mrs, 1953, Mr 12,27:2
Bachrach, Marion Mrs, 1957, O 17,33:4
Bachrach, Max, 1960, My 2,29:3
Bachrach, Walter K, 1963, O 4,35:2
Bachrach, William, 1959, Jl 17,21:4
Bachruch, Carl, 1925, D 5,19:4
Bachtler, Frederick, 1950, My 24,29:3
Bachur, Robert A, 1941, N 3,19:5
Bachursky, Jacob J, 1960, Ap 8,31:3
Bacigalupi, Eugene M, 1954, Ag 27,21:6
Bacigalupi, James A, 1950, Jl 28,21:4
Bacilieri, Bartholomew Cardinal, 1923, F 15,19:4
Back, Edward, 1953, My 20,29:4
Back, Ernest A, 1959, My 23,25:4
Back, George Adm Sir, 1878, Ja 26,5:4
Back, Harry E Sr, 1956, D 19,31:3
Back, Howard, 1946, N 15,23:3
Back, John J, 1951, My 11,27:2
Back, Joseph J, 1941, N 27,23:4
Back, Philip S, 1965, Je 18,35:2
Backas, William F, 1946, O 9,27:5
Backenbury, Henry B, 1942, Mr 11,19:4
Backer, Cora K, 1955, My 13,25:2
Backer, Franklyn E, 1949, Ag 4,23:2
Backer, Henry, 1915, Ja 18,9:5
Backer, Jack, 1937, Jl 28,14:4
Backer, Jacob, 1955, D 26,19:4
Backer, Leslie H, 1956, O 29,29:1
Backer, Samuel, 1957, Ap 21,88:5
Backes, Peter, 1941, D 18,27:4
Backes, Thoe, 1950, D 24,36:1
Backes, William J, 1942, Ja 21,18:3
Backhouse, E T, 1884, S 29,4:7
Backhouse, Frederick N, 1952, Ag 8,17:5
Backhouse, Hugo, 1961, Mr 3,27:1
Backhouse, Oliver, 1943, Mr 26,19:3
Backhouse, Roger Sir, 1939, Jl 16,31:1
Backhouse, Thomas M, 1955, S 17,15:4
Backhus, John B Sr, 1966, O 9,86:3
Backlund, Knute M, 1944, N 13,19:6
Backman, Hyman, 1955, My 26,31:4
Backster, Frank O, 1954, O 18,25:4
Backstrand, Clifford J, 1968, O 4,47:1
Backus, Allen D, 1945, D 21,22:2
Backus, Anna H, 1965, Ag 8,64:7
Backus, Arthur O Mrs, 1950, Mr 19,92:5
Backus, August C Sr, 1952, Mr 8,13:4
Backus, Charles, 1883, Je 22,8:1
Backus, Charles De Witt, 1917, F 17,11:6
Backus, E W, 1934, O 30,19:1
Backus, E Y, 1914, N 13,11:6
Backus, E Y Mrs, 1960, Ag 19,23:1
Backus, Electus T, 1938, Mr 12,17:4
Backus, Foster L, 1907, Mr 11,7:6
Backus, Frederick D, 1937, F 15,17:5
Backus, Frederick P, 1947, F 22,13:4
Backus, George, 1939, My 22,17:4
Backus, George Mrs, 1938, S 4,17:3
Backus, Grosvenor H Mrs, 1915, Ap 30,13:3
Backus, Harold, 1968, Jl 26,33:4
Backus, Henry Clinton (funl, My 6,7:5), 1908, My 4, 7:4
Backus, I Wyckoff Mrs, 1951, Ag 16,27:3
Backus, J C Rev, 1884, Ap 10,2:3
Backus, James H, 1938, Je 7,23:3
Backus, John E, 1911, Mr 24,11:3
Backus, Leslie H, 1963, Ap 9,32:1
Backus, N D, 1954, Je 9,31:5
Backus, Peter J, 1942, Je 26,21:3
Backus, Richard, 1945, Ag 21,21:3
Backus, Richard M, 1937, Ja 6,23:4
Backus, Russell G, 1954, My 5,31:4
Backus, Standish, 1943, Jl 14,19:5
Backus, T F, 1880, F 15,5:3
Backus-Behr, Ella, 1947, F 4,26:2
Bacmeister, Theodore, 1941, My 18,45:1
Bacoats, J A (Sept 25), 1965, O 11,61:1
Bacon, A Dewey, 1943, D 20,23:4
Bacon, Addie, 1939, Mr 6,15:3
Bacon, Alexander S, 1920, My 31,11:4
Bacon, Anna F, 1938, Je 29,19:5
Bacon, Asa, 1945, S 12,25:2
Bacon, Augustus Jr, 1957, Ap 11,31:3
Bacon, Augustus Octavius Gen, 1914, F 15,5:4
Bacon, C A Prof, 1901, N 7,9:6
Bacon, C E T, 1882, Jl 31,5:4
Bacon, Charles B, 1953, Je 15,29:4
Bacon, Charles C, 1950, Jl 25,27:4
Bacon, Charles E, 1958, Mr 16,86:8
Bacon, Charles J, 1968, N 19,40:6
Bacon, Charles K, 1944, Ag 26,11:3
Bacon, Charles M, 1945, Jl 13,11:6; 1952, Jl 22,25:5
Bacon, Charles P, 1916, Je 20,11:6
Bacon, Charles R, 1937, Jl 13,19:3; 1943, Ap 21,25:6
Bacon, Charles W, 1938, N 11,25:6
Bacon, Clara L, 1948, Ap 16,23:3
Bacon, Clarence E, 1941, F 16,40:2
Bacon, Clarence F, 1946, F 3,40:2
Bacon, Cleveland F, 1956, S 15,17:1
Bacon, Curtis S, 1943, D 24,13:4
Bacon, D W Bp, 1874, N 6,5:3
Bacon, Daniel, 1912, D 1,II,17:2
Bacon, Douglas, 1952, Ja 24,27:1
Bacon, Edgar B Mrs, 1966, O 26,47:1
Bacon, Edward, 1938, Je 6,17:4
Bacon, Edward A, 1968, O 6,84:3
Bacon, Edward Everett Rev, 1917, My 24,13:3
Bacon, Edward I, 1946, Jl 30,23:3
Bacon, Edward L, 1961, Ag 25,25:4
Bacon, Edward P Mrs, 1951, Ap 2,25:5
Bacon, Edward Rathbone, 1915, D 3,11:5
Bacon, Edwin Monroe, 1916, F 25,11:6
Bacon, Elliot C (funl, S 20,23:3), 1924, S 29,15:3
Bacon, Elmore C, 1956, S 22,17:4
Bacon, Enos, 1951, Je 23,15:2
Bacon, Ethel K, 1949, D 13,31:3
Bacon, Eugene E, 1949, Je 12,76:2
Bacon, Francis Dr, 1912, Ap 27,13:4
Bacon, Francis H, 1940, F 8,23:4
Bacon, Francis L, 1958, Ja 21,29:2
Bacon, Francis M Mrs, 1951, Jl 9,25:3
Bacon, Francis McNeil, 1912, S 22,II,17:4
Bacon, Francis S, 1941, Mr 16,40:8
Bacon, Frank, 1905, Mr 21,11:4
Bacon, Frank (funl, N 23,21:6), 1922, N 21,19:4
Bacon, Frank Mrs, 1956, S 29,19:1
Bacon, Frank R, 1949, O 7,27:3
Bacon, Frederic S, 1961, Mr 18,23:3
Bacon, Frederick T H, 1952, S 3,30:6
Bacon, Frederick W, 1951, Jl 18,29:6
Bacon, Gaspar G, 1947, D 26,15:5
Bacon, Geoffrey, 1962, Ag 3,3:1
Bacon, George A Mrs, 1937, S 18,19:1
Bacon, George P, 1941, S 20,17:5
Bacon, George T, 1948, Ag 8,57:2
Bacon, George T Mrs, 1953, Ag 23,89:3
Bacon, George W, 1953, Jl 23,24:3
Bacon, Gertrude, 1949, D 24,15:5
Bacon, Gilbert C, 1942, D 2,25:3
Bacon, Gorham, 1940, Mr 6,23:5
Bacon, H Churchill, 1951, Mr 10,13:2
Bacon, Harry S C, 1942, O 19,19:3
Bacon, Henry, 1912, Mr 14,11:4; 1915, Mr 26,13:3
Bacon, Henry (funl, F 20,19:5), 1924, F 17,23:1
Bacon, Henry H, 1937, Ap 7,3:3
Bacon, Henry Mrs, 1945, My 13,20:8
Bacon, Henry S, 1954, F 22,19:5
Bacon, Hickman B, 1945, Ap 14,15:4
Bacon, Horatio W, 1947, My 23,23:1
Bacon, Howard A, 1953, Ap 20,25:1
Bacon, Howard N, 1948, N 13,15:6
Bacon, I R, 1932, D 14,21:3
Bacon, Irving R, 1962, N 24,23:4
Bacon, J Clarence, 1937, My 19,23:5
Bacon, J Prof, 1881, D 1,4:7
Bacon, James F Mrs, 1952, Mr 3,21:3
Bacon, James Mrs, 1958, My 15,29:5
Bacon, Jeremiah I, 1938, Jl 13,21:6
Bacon, John, 1954, Mr 9,27:5
Bacon, John K, 1952, Je 14,15:7
Bacon, John L, 1940, My 25,17:5
Bacon, John M Brig-Gen, 1913, Mr 21,13:2
Bacon, John P, 1942, N 30,23:4
Bacon, John Philip Maj, 1911, S 3,II,9:4
Bacon, John Watson, 1907, F 28,9:6
Bacon, Katherine, 1922, O 15,30:3
Bacon, Katherine D Mrs, 1942, Jl 11,13:6
Bacon, L R, 1902, Ja 20,2:4
Bacon, L R Mrs, 1902, Ja 17,7:5
Bacon, Lavinia C, 1937, Jl 13,20:1
Bacon, Leon B, 1952, S 26,21:3
Bacon, Leonard, 1881, D 25,9:1; 1954, Ja 2,12:3
Bacon, Leonard B, 1944, F 17,19:4
Bacon, Leonard W, 1939, Ja 10,19:4
Bacon, Lloyd, 1955, N 16,35:4
Bacon, Louis P, 1954, Mr 20,15:1
Bacon, Mark R, 1941, Ag 22,15:5
Bacon, Marshal C, 1939, Ag 12,13:6
Bacon, Martha W Mrs, 1940, N 23,23:3
Bacon, Nathaniel T, 1925, O 27,23:3
Bacon, Nicholas H, 1947, Ja 3,21:2
Bacon, Paul V, 1949, N 10,31:3
Bacon, Paul V (will), 1950, Ja 11,25:6
Bacon, Radcliffe, 1946, Ag 23,19:3
Bacon, Ralph F, 1942, Ag 31,17:4
Bacon, Ralph W, 1963, Je 26,39:4
Bacon, Raymond C, 1953, Jl 10,19:6
Bacon, Raymond F, 1954, O 15,24:3
Bacon, Reginald, 1947, Je 10,27:3
Bacon, Reginald K, 1952, D 30,19:3
Bacon, Robert Col (por),(funl, My 31,13:2), 1919, My 30,9:4
Bacon, Robert E, 1959, Jl 19,68:6
Bacon, Robert L, 1938, S 13,1:3
Bacon, Robert O, 1939, My 9,23:5
Bacon, Robert O Sr Mrs, 1958, Je 15,56:2
Bacon, Rogers H, 1962, My 22,38:1
Bacon, Rogers H Mrs, 1940, S 19,23:5
Bacon, Ross F, 1937, Mr 14,II,8:7
Bacon, Selden, 1946, Je 26,25:1
Bacon, Selden Mrs (Josephine), 1961, Jl 31,19:2
Bacon, Susan A, 1946, O 29,25:4
Bacon, Theodore L, 1940, Jl 30,19:4
Bacon, Tyree Capt, 1937, N 3,23:4
Bacon, W B, 1950, Jl 4,17:5
Bacon, W T Rev, 1881, My 19,3:2
Bacon, Walter Rathbone, 1917, N 15,13:4
Bacon, Walter Rathbone Mrs, 1919, Ap 8,11:4
Bacon, Walter W, 1962, Mr 20,37:1
Bacon, William B Mrs, 1920, D 25,7:6
Bacon, William F, 1937, S 13,21:5; 1942, Je 21,37:
Bacon, William M, 1951, Ag 17,17:5
Bacon, William P Col, 1918, Ag 7,9:8
Bacon, William R, 1953, N 27,27:1
Bacon, William S, 1955, Mr 19,15:2
Bacon, Winifred W L Mrs, 1955, Je 3,46:8
Bacone, Arthur E, 1945, Ag 16,19:2
Bacot, John V, 1921, O 31,15:6
Bada, Angelo, 1941, Mr 27,23:2
Badalick, Bertalan, 1965, O 13,47:2
Badaloni, Rosa A, 1949, Ja 9,72:5
Badame, George, 1955, D 21,29:5
Badanes, Bernard H, 1947, Ap 23,25:1
Badanes, Ida, 1946, Ja 29,25:1
Badanes, Saul, 1940, Ap 25,23:6
Badawi, Abdel H, 1965, Ag 6,27:1

Badawi, Helmy B, 1957, Mr 5,31:4
Badayev, Alexei G, 1951, N 5,31:1
Baddeley, J J Sir, 1926, Je 29,23:4
Baddeley, Walter, 1960, F 12,27:3
Baddour, Slyman, 1941, D 3,25:1
Bade, Anthony N, 1963, Ja 21,7:8
Bade, Harry A, 1968, D 9,55:3
Bade, Henry F, 1942, Ag 11,19:2
Bade, Louis W, 1952, Ja 5,11:1
Bade, W F, 1936, Mr 6,21:1
Bade, Wilbur E, 1954, Mr 31,27:3
Bade, William A, 1951, Ap 10,28:2
Bade, William H, 1938, N 19,17:4
Badeau, Adam Gen (see also Mr 21), 1895, Mr 23, 9:7
Badeau, Adam Mrs, 1915, My 18,13:5
Badeau, B, 1883, D 11,4:7
Badeau, Carroll, 1948, S 14,29:3
Badeau, Charles H, 1922, Jl 9,26:4
Badeau, Edward C, 1953, My 25,25:2
Badeau, Harry U, 1947, Ja 30,25:4
Badeau, Isaac F, 1949, Ja 18,23:4
Badeau, John E, 1924, My 13,21:5
Badecker, Ernest A, 1947, N 17,21:2
Badeley, Henry J F Lord, 1951, S 28,31:1
Baden, Berthold von (Margrave),(funl, N 2,8:1), 1963, O 29,36:5
Baden, Hyman, 1966, My 16,37:2
Baden-Powell, Agnes, 1945, Je 4,19:6
Baden-Powell, Baden F S Maj, 1937, O 5,25:1
Baden-Powell, G S Sir, 1898, N 21,7:1
Baden-Powell, Lord, 1941, Ja 9,10:3
Badenberger, Henry D, 1961, Ap 15,21:2
Badenhausen, Adolph H, 1950, D 11,25:4
Badenhausen, Adolph Mrs, 1957, S 14,19:3
Badenhausen, Capt, 1902, O 7,9:5
Badenhausen, Otto A, 1966, S 14,47:2
Badenhop, Conrad F, 1949, Ja 8,15:5
Badenhop, Robert, 1959, S 21,31:2
Badeni, Casimir Count, 1909, Jl 10,7:4
Badenoch, Helen, 1942, D 21,19:4
Bader, Abraham, 1959, Ag 11,27:3
Bader, Albert J Father, 1917, Ag 5,17:3
Bader, Anton G, 1952, O 1,33:4
Bader, Charles, 1918, Ag 12,9:3
Bader, Charles A, 1955, N 11,25:3
Bader, Charles L, 1954, F 6,19:5
Bader, Daniel Mrs, 1940, My 31,19:4
Bader, Daniel S, 1946, N 24,79:4
Bader, David A, 1967, O 16,45:3
Bader, E L, 1927, Ja 29,15:3
Bader, Frank E, 1950, O 14,19:6
Bader, Frank L Mrs, 1940, Mr 31,46:3
Bader, Frank X, 1946, Ja 5,14:2
Bader, Gallus J, 1938, D 10,17:5
Bader, George B, 1952, Ap 20,92:5
Bader, Gershom, 1953, N 13,27:4
Bader, Gustave P, 1959, Ap 23,31:5
Bader, Jesse M, 1963, Ag 20,33:3
Bader, John J, 1946, S 4,24:2
Bader, Lawrence (J F Johnson), 1966, S 17,29:3
Bader, Louis, 1948, Ag 24,24:2
Bader, Louis F S, 1942, S 14,15:2
Bader, Murray H, 1945, N 30,23:3
Bader, Paul O, 1953, S 27,86:1
Bader, Samuel Mrs, 1953, Ag 6,21:6
Bader, William, 1953, Jl 13,25:5
Badge, Wilbur J, 1946, Ag 9,17:5
Badge, William H, 1948, Ap 17,15:2
Badger, Albert E, 1942, My 26,21:6
Badger, Blanche B Mrs, 1939, S 9,17:5
Badger, C J, 1932, S 9,19:1
Badger, Clarence, 1964, Je 20,25:2
Badger, D D, 1884, N 19,2:3
Badger, Daniel, 1944, Ag 13,35:1
Badger, Daniel W, 1952, Mr 27,30:3
Badger, F Preston, 1953, F 5,23:4
Badger, Frank S, 1949, Mr 20,76:4
Badger, George E Hon, 1866, My 21,5:1
Badger, Grace M Mrs, 1941, Jl 19,13:2
Badger, Herbert L, 1952, O 19,88:8
Badger, Merritt O Dr, 1923, S 27,7:3
Badger, Milton Dr, 1873, Mr 4,1:4
Badger, Oscar C, 1958, D 1,29:3
Badger, Paul B, 1943, D 15,28:2
Badger, Philip O Mrs, 1965, D 17,39:2
Badger, Randell W, 1951, Mr 26,23:3
Badger, Robert A, 1942, D 21,23:1
Badger, Sarah F C Mrs, 1942, Jl 3,17:3
Badger, Shreve C, 1956, D 4,39:1
Badger, Shreve C Mrs, 1954, F 11,29:3
Badger, Walter H, 1951, O 23,29:4
Badger, Walter I Jr Mrs, 1956, Je 5,35:5
Badger, Walter L, 1958, N 20,35:5
Badger, Walter S Mrs, 1952, F 4,17:4
Badger, William A Mrs, 1951, Ja 15,17:4
Badger, William Dr, 1908, F 14,7:7
Badger, William O 2d, 1954, Jl 7,31:4
Badger, William W Mrs, 1914, Mr 21,13:4
Badgerow, George W Sir, 1937, My 10,19:5
Badgett, William E, 1960, F 2,35:1
Badgley, Charles W, 1941, Jl 24,17:6
Badgley, Frank, 1955, S 11,84:8
Badgley, Franklin I, 1937, Jl 21,21:5
Badgley, Henry C, 1959, Ja 14,27:2
Badgley, Henry F, 1956, Ap 9,27:4
Badgley, Oliver K, 1945, Mr 21,23:2
Badgley, Ollie V, 1954, O 21,27:5
Badgley, Ralph A, 1958, Ag 25,21:4
Badgley, Richard E, 1961, My 11,37:4
Badgley, Richard E Mrs, 1964, D 9,61:2
Badgley, Robert H, 1966, Ja 27,33:4
Badgley, Theodore J, 1956, Ja 12,27:3
Badham, William, 1957, Ag 1,25:6
Badinelli, William B, 1958, Ja 13,29:2
Bading, Gerhard A, 1946, Ap 12,27:3
Badiullah, Baha'i, 1950, N 3,27:1
Badland, Jane, 1958, Ja 11,17:3
Badley, Brenton T Mrs, 1946, My 7,21:2
Badlishah (Sultan of Kedah), 1958, Jl 14,21:1
Badman, Theodore, 1941, F 27,20:3
Bado, John A, 1964, F 9,88:6
Badoglio, Mario, 1953, F 11,29:4
Badoglio, Pietro, 1956, N 1,39:1
Badry, John G, 1937, Ja 7,21:3
Bady, Louis, 1959, Ag 11,27:1
Baeazler, Alfred T, 1954, F 6,19:3
Baechle, Cecelia I, 1953, O 4,87:1
Baeck, Eugene C, 1945, My 19,19:3
Baeck, Leo, 1956, N 3,23:3
Baeck, Leo Mrs, 1937, Mr 9,23:3
Baeck, William F, 1963, N 16,27:6
Baecker, C Frederick, 1939, Ag 31,19:4
Baecker, Frederick H, 1945, D 12,27:1
Baedeker, Fritz, 1925, Ap 11,13:5
Baedelow, Herman, 1952, D 11,33:2
Baeder, Albert W, 1948, O 9,17:4
Baeder, William, 1957, Ap 20,17:4
Baehler, Charles A (cor, S 30,23:5), 1937, S 28,23:3
Baehm, Peter, 1954, S 19,89:2
Baehr, Albert, 1958, My 22,29:2
Baehr, Alex G, 1958, Mr 2,89:2
Baehr, Eugene R, 1958, D 2,37:3
Baehr, Fred E, 1940, Ag 14,19:3
Baehr, Harry W, 1941, D 21,40:6
Baehr, Herman C, 1942, F 5,21:4
Baehr, John W, 1953, Mr 2,23:5
Baehr, William H, 1943, F 19,19:2
Baekeland, George, 1919, Ja 16,13:2; 1966, F 1,35:4
Baekeland, Leo H, 1944, F 24,15:1
Baekeland, Leo H Mrs, 1957, Mr 1,23:2
Baekey, Arthur A, 1966, N 9,39:2
Bael, Henrie Mrs, 1950, Jl 11,31:2
Baels, Henri, 1951, Je 15,23:3
Baensch, Emil, 1939, Ag 18,19:4
Baenziger, Albert F, 1955, S 22,31:1
Baepler, Walter A, 1958, O 11,23:6
Baer, A R, 1952, My 10,21:1
Baer, Albert M Mrs, 1964, Ja 28,31:1
Baer, Arthur Mrs, 1950, N 15,31:5
Baer, August C, 1950, S 22,31:4
Baer, B L C, 1956, Ap 2,23:4
Baer, Ben, 1921, Jl 28,13:5
Baer, Benjamin F Jr, 1938, D 20,25:3
Baer, Berthold Mrs, 1955, D 26,19:2
Baer, Carl, 1944, Ap 28,20:2
Baer, Charles, 1950, N 11,15:2
Baer, Charles J, 1946, Ap 4,25:2
Baer, David, 1940, My 20,17:4
Baer, Dora Mrs, 1938, Ag 8,13:4
Baer, Emil L, 1942, D 14,28:2
Baer, Felix, 1959, N 7,23:2
Baer, Fred, 1946, My 17,22:3
Baer, Fred E, 1960, N 6,88:8
Baer, Frederick A, 1940, D 17,25:1
Baer, George F (por),(funl, Ap 30,11:6), 1914, Ap 27,11:3
Baer, George F Mrs, 1915, O 22,11:5
Baer, Gustave E, 1951, Ag 29,25:5
Baer, Harry, 1967, Jl 24,27:2
Baer, Harry Mrs, 1949, My 30,13:5
Bae'r, Harry W Mrs, 1963, N 27,27:3
Baer, Herman H, 1951, Ap 5,29:3
Baer, Herschel I, 1957, F 25,25:6
Baer, Herschel Mrs, 1960, Je 1,39:4
Baer, Isaac, 1958, My 30,21:3
Baer, Jacob, 1938, My 3,23:2
Baer, Jacob S, 1940, S 14,17:4
Baer, John A Mrs, 1961, My 1,29:5
Baer, John L, 1924, My 31,15:4
Baer, Joseph A, 1958, Ag 31,57:3
Baer, Julius B, 1966, Ja 2,76:1
Baer, Julius I, 1924, O 23,21:4
Baer, Lazarus, 1924, Ag 3,24:4
Baer, Louis Mrs, 1951, D 9,91:2
Baer, M J (will), 1946, My 26,23:7
Baer, Mabel Mrs, 1937, Je 8,25:4
Baer, Marian E, 1965, S 13,35:2
Baer, Max (funl plans, N 23,31:1), 1959, N 22,1:3
Baer, Michael Mrs, 1937, O 11,21:3
Baer, Morris B, 1921, Mr 24,17:6
Baer, Richard, 1963, Je 19,22:2; 1965, Ap 12,35:1
Baer, Sam Mrs, 1954, S 9,31:3
Baer, Sidney R, 1956, Ag 26,84:8
Baer, Theodore C, 1956, My 27,89:2
Baer, W S, 1931, Ap 8,23:3
Baer, Werner, 1957, Ap 9,33:5
Baer, William B, 1958, Ja 22,28:1
Baer, William C, 1962, Ag 12,80:2
Baer, William J, 1941, S 23,23:1
Baer, William J Mrs, 1949, Je 2,28:2
Baere, Emmanuel, 1954, Je 25,21:4
Baerenklau, Albert G, 1960, O 4,43:5
Baerer, Henry, 1908, D 9,13:4
Baerer, Laura Z Mrs, 1940, Jl 5,13:4
Baerthelote, Victor, 1920, Je 4,13:4
Baerthlein, George, 1950, Ja 11,23:5
Baertschiger, Elizabeth B Mrs, 1943, Mr 18,20:2
Baerwald, Emil, 1948, Ja 22,27:2
Baerwald, Ernest A, 1952, Jl 27,57:1
Baerwald, Hellmut, 1953, Ap 21,27:6
Baerwald, Paul, 1961, Jl 3,15:3
Baerwald, Paul Mrs, 1965, Ag 10,29:4
Baerwald, Rudy, 1955, Jl 29,17:4
Baeseman, R W, 1956, F 3,23:4
Baeslach, Rolland J, 1949, F 16,25:4
Baeszler, Fred J, 1955, D 15,37:5
Baeszler, Joseph D, 1953, Ap 22,29:2
Baetjer, Charles H, 1950, Jl 29,13:1
Baetjer, Edwin G, 1945, Jl 22,38:1
Baetjer, F H H, 1933, Jl 18,17:6
Baetz, Gerard, 1959, Mr 5,31:2
Baetzel, Herman, 1938, Je 2,23:3
Baetzhold, August, 1937, Ja 31,II,8:6
Baeyer, Adolf von Prof, 1917, Ag 25,7:6
Baez, Cedilio, 1941, Je 19,21:3
Baeza, Marco A, 1965, N 7,88:7
Baeza, Walter J, 1960, Ag 17,31:5
Baff, Abraham, 1945, D 16,40:6
Baffa, Alfred J, 1937, Ag 26,21:5
Baffler, Jean, 1920, Ap 20,9:5
Bagaini, Giovanni, 1940, My 7,25:2
Bagan, Gus, 1951, Jl 2,23:4
Baganz, Crawford N, 1955, D 22,23:2
Bagar, Guy M, 1961, Ag 12,17:2
Bagar, Robert, 1957, My 7,35:2
Bagarotti, Giovanni Mrs, 1959, N 7,23:4
Bagarozy, Armand, 1943, O 13,23:2
Bagby, Albert M, 1941, F 27,19:1
Bagby, Alfred Jr, 1948, Jl 8,23:4
Bagby, Arthur P Sen, 1858, S 22,4:4
Bagby, English, 1955, Ja 16,93:1
Bagby, English Mrs, 1937, N 16,23:1
Bagby, George L, 1962, N 14,39:1
Bagby, J Walter, 1952, O 9,31:5
Bagby, James C J Sr, 1954, Jl 29,23:3
Bagby, Jim Mrs, 1956, Je 14,33:1
Bagby, Robert C, 1938, My 7,15:3
Bagby, Robert T Sr, 1956, D 21,23:1
Bagdanavicius, Bladas Mrs, 1954, F 16,25:4
Bagdanavicius, Vladas, 1960, Ap 30,23:6
Bagdasar, Dimitrie, 1946, Jl 18,25:2
Bagdasarov, Andrey, 1961, Ag 28,25:3
Bagdonas, Mikas Dr, 1937, Mr 30,23:5
Bageant, Daniel C, 1960, Ag 25,29:5
Bagehot, W, 1877, Mr 27,5:6
Bagenstose, Harvey L, 1941, Ag 28,19:6
Bagg, Allen H (will, Ag 24,30:7), 1942, Ag 17,15:4
Bagg, Clinton L Dr, 1924, S 21,29:1
Bagg, Halsey J, 1947, Ap 15,25:6
Bagg, James E, 1943, Ag 29,38:3
Bagg, James G Mrs, 1950, My 10,31:2
Bagg, Laurence G, 1943, F 15,15:6
Bagg, Lyman Hotchkiss, 1911, O 24,13:4
Bagg, Robert M, 1917, S 4,11:3
Bagg, Sadie P E Mrs, 1942, Ag 18,21:3
Baggaley, William, 1959, Je 12,27:4
Baggaley, William B, 1947, Ag 30,15:5
Bagge, Goesta A, 1951, Ja 6,15:2
Bagger, Frank E, 1958, Ja 19,86:5
Bagger, Henry H, 1967, Mr 16,47:4
Bagger, Palline, 1946, O 16,27:4
Baggerley, Hiland L, 1944, Ag 7,15:4
Baggerly, Arthur C, 1950, D 10,104:6
Baggett, Lynne, 1960, Mr 24,67:2
Baggett, Sam, 1964, D 30,23:1
Baggot, King, 1948, Jl 13,27:4
Baggs, Frederick C, 1966, Ja 6,27:1
Baggs, Harold E, 1959, Mr 5,31:4
Baggs, Harriet, 1952, Ap 8,29:4
Baggs, Thomas Alexander Mrs, 1922, S 12,21:6
Baggs, William H, 1940, N 13,23:4
Bagioli, Antonio, 1871, F 12,5:2
Bagley, Alfred H, 1947, Ap 12,17:4
Bagley, Alfred M MRs, 1952, N 13,31:2
Bagley, Alfred N, 1942, Je 5,17:4
Bagley, Arthur E, 1952, Mr 12,27:4
Bagley, Belle W, 1939, My 26,23:3
Bagley, Charles C F Mrs, 1955, Je 7,33:2
Bagley, Charles E, 1943, N 25,25:5
Bagley, Charles G, 1952, Ag 21,19:4
Bagley, Charles Jr, 1957, N 4,29:5
Bagley, David W, 1960, My 26,33:1
Bagley, Edward C, 1937, Ag 9,20:2
Bagley, Francis H, 1941, Ag 31,22:8
Bagley, Frank, 1942, Je 23,19:2
Bagley, J, 1876, D 25,8:5
Bagley, J H, 1902, O 24,9:6
Bagley, J J, 1881, Jl 29,5:1

Bagley, Jacob, 1948, N 30,27:1
Bagley, James E, 1910, Je 18,9:5
Bagley, James F, 1940, O 27,44:2
Bagley, John P, 1947, My 7,27:4
Bagley, Melvin E, 1938, Ap 13,25:5
Bagley, Richard, 1961, F 28,33:1
Bagley, S V, 1885, Ap 23,2:3
Bagley, William, 1874, S 26,8:2
Bagley, William C, 1946, Jl 2,25:3
Bagley, William R, 1938, Ag 30,17:5
Bagley, Willis G C, 1943, O 21,27:6
Baglioli, Charles, 1882, Jl 24,5:3
Baglioni, Ennio, 1954, Ap 5,32:1
Bagnall, Francis A, 1950, Jl 30,60:3
Bagnall, Ruth L, 1953, Mr 2,23:4
Bagnall, Vernon B, 1956, Ap 12,31:2
Bagnall, W Ellsworth, 1937, Jl 21,21:5
Bagnall, William E, 1949, Je 20,19:4
Bagnasco, Josephine M, 1939, Mr 26,III,6:7
Bagnell, James, 1924, Je 2,17:6
Bagnell, James F, 1942, D 30,23:3
Bagnell, James J, 1937, N 25,31:5
Bagnell, Robert, 1946, Ap 26,21:4
Bagnoli, Bruno, 1955, O 19,33:4
Bagnulo, Edmund, 1951, O 25,29:3
Bagoe, George, 1954, Ja 17,74:7
Bagoe, George T, 1948, Ag 10,22:3
Bagoin, Thomas Campbell, 1915, Ag 16,9:6
Bagoon, Samuel, 1949, Ag 13,11:2
Bagot, Caryl E, 1961, Ag 6,85:2
Bagot, John (correction, D 31,17:2), 1960, D 30,20:1
Bagot, Richard, 1921, D 13,19:4
Bagratuni, James, 1944, Ja 3,21:2
Bagshaw, John, 1951, D 2,90:4
Bagshaw, Kirk, 1948, Je 3,25:6
Bagshaw, Kirk Mrs, 1941, D 28,28:2
Bagster-Collins, Elijah W, 1954, S 4,11:4
Bagwell, Harry, 1946, N 14,29:5
Bagwell, Samuel R, 1960, Mr 16,37:2
Bahadur, Bhopal Sinhji Maharaja Sir, 1955, Jl 5,29:2
Bahadur, Kanthirara N W (Yuvaraja of Mysore), 1940, Mr 11,15:3
Bahadur, Krishnarajah Wadiyar (Maharajah of Mysore), 1940, Ag 4,33:4
Bahan, William H, 1949, Jl 1,19:1
Bahe, William F, 1946, O 22,25:5
Bahen, J W, 1955, N 13,89:3
Bahler, John M, 1945, O 31,23:2
Bahlke, Alfred F, 1961, Mr 2,27:4
Bahlman, William T, 1951, N 3,17:5
Bahm, John F, 1957, Jl 2,27:4
Bahn, Chester B, 1962, Ja 9,48:1
Bahner, Leo A, 1963, N 26,37:1
Bahney, Luther W, 1961, S 15,33:2
Bahooshian, Joseph, 1952, Jl 16,25:1
Bahr, Abel W, 1959, Mr 3,33:5
Bahr, Augustus J, 1904, F 23,7:6
Bahr, Conrad C, 1959, O 16,31:3
Bahr, Frederick Charles, 1949, Jl 26,27:5
Bahr, Fritz, 1947, Jl 9,23:4
Bahr, George A, 1938, N 7,19:4
Bahr, Gerhard V Mrs, 1954, My 28,23:3
Bahr, Milon F, 1940, D 12,27:4
Bahr, Walther, 1943, Mr 2,19:3
Bahrawi Bey, Awad el, 1948, Ag 30,17:3
Bahrein, Sheikh of, 1942, F 21,19:4
Bahrenburg, Henry W, 1924, My 27,21:4
Bahrenburg, John H, 1951, F 6,27:2
Bahrenburg, John H (will), 1955, S 29,65:1
Bahrenburg, Louis P H, 1940, O 16,23:2
Bahrenburg, William H, 1954, Ap 30,23:1
Bahret, Charles H Mrs, 1949, Je 20,19:5; 1952, Ja 24, 47:3
Bahret, John G, 1948, Je 20,60:6
Bahret, Percy C Mrs, 1948, My 10,21:3
Bahret, Ruth A, 1954, F 20,17:6
Bahret, William F, 1953, Jl 10,19:4
Bahriany, Ivan, 1963, Ag 27,31:4
Bahrs, Henry E, 1940, My 23,23:1
Baiden, A Clifford, 1964, Ap 1,39:5
Baiden, Arthur G Mrs, 1940, Jl 17,21:2
Baier, Adelbert, 1953, F 17,27:3
Baier, David, 1967, Ag 30,43:5
Baier, Donald E, 1963, N 18,33:2
Baier, J Leonard, 1939, O 27,23:5
Baier, Joseph G, 1954, Ap 14,29:2
Baier, Louise (will), 1939, Mr 10,25:6
Baier, Max, 1952, F 3,85:1
Baier, Victor, 1921, Ag 12,13:5
Baier, William J, 1946, N 20,31:4
Baierl, Joseph J, 1955, Jl 9,15:2
Baikie, Alfred, 1947, O 23,25:3
Baikov, Alexander A, 1946, Ap 8,27:4
Baikov, Alexei P, 1955, Mr 12,19:6
Bail, Bernard H, 1912, Ap 11,11:5
Bailby, Leon, 1954, Ja 20,27:3
Bailden, Geoffrey, 1939, Ja 22,35:1
Baildon, Charles M, 1950, O 4,31:1
Bailen, Count of (C Arcos Cuadra), 1964, Ap 23,39:5
Bailen, Samuel L, 1948, Jl 2,21:4
Bailer, Anton, 1958, N 12,37:1
Bailey, A M, 1879, Ap 30,1:5
Bailey, Abe, 1940, Ag 11,31:1
Bailey, Abraham L, 1939, S 28,25:4
Bailey, Albert C, 1946, Je 4,23:4
Bailey, Albert E, 1951, N 1,29:4
Bailey, Albert T, 1956, S 21,25:2
Bailey, Alex D, 1965, Je 19,29:3
Bailey, Alfred J, 1964, S 12,25:2
Bailey, Alfred M, 1943, S 26,48:2
Bailey, Algernon, 1913, Mr 31,13:4
Bailey, Almon L, 1940, O 17,26:3
Bailey, Arthur L, 1940, F 18,41:3; 1943, Ja 22,19:5
Bailey, Arthur S, 1949, O 18,27:3
Bailey, Aubrey C, 1956, F 7,31:5
Bailey, Belle R Mrs, 1940, N 25,17:4
Bailey, Benjamin, 1879, Jl 6,2:3
Bailey, Benjamin F, 1914, D 2,13:5; 1954, Ja 10,86:4
Bailey, Buster (Wm C Bailey), 1967, Ap 14,39:4
Bailey, Calvin W, 1947, Ja 7,27:4
Bailey, Carl E, 1948, O 24,76:3
Bailey, Carolyn S (Mrs E C Hill), 1961, D 25,23:3
Bailey, Charles A, 1939, Jl 12,19:4
Bailey, Charles E, 1950, Ap 27,29:3
Bailey, Charles F, 1953, O 24,15:4
Bailey, Charles Fifield, 1968, Ja 15,47:4
Bailey, Charles H Dr, 1907, D 19,9:5
Bailey, Charles J, 1946, S 22,63:5
Bailey, Charles L, 1938, My 9,17:2
Bailey, Charles O, 1937, Mr 7,II,8:3; 1943, D 17,27:3
Bailey, Charles S Mrs, 1949, O 22,17:5
Bailey, Charles W, 1951, Ja 30,25:5; 1963, My 1,39:3
Bailey, Charles Weaver Maj, 1922, D 11,17:5
Bailey, Clarence D, 1958, Jl 13,68:5
Bailey, Clayton E, 1918, Ag 10,7:5
Bailey, Cleveland M, 1965, Jl 14,37:4
Bailey, Corrine, 1942, F 25,19:1
Bailey, Daniel, 1947, N 25,32:2; 1961, N 22,33:4
Bailey, Daniel D, 1940, N 23,17:3
Bailey, Daniel K, 1947, O 3,25:2
Bailey, David W Mrs, 1960, Mr 31,33:2
Bailey, De Witt, 1948, Jl 8,23:2
Bailey, Eben H, 1943, Ja 22,20:2
Bailey, Edmund Smith, 1908, N 6,7:3
Bailey, Edward G, 1940, O 23,23:2
Bailey, Edward G Mrs, 1944, Je 2,15:4
Bailey, Edward H, 1953, Ja 25,86:5
Bailey, Edward M, 1948, Ap 14,27:4
Bailey, Edward W, 1920, Ja 3,11:3
Bailey, Edwin B Mrs, 1956, F 13,27:3
Bailey, Edwin Ex-Sen (funl), 1914, Jl 11,7:6
Bailey, Edwin T, 1954, Ja 7,31:5
Bailey, Eliza S Mrs, 1939, S 11,19:1
Bailey, Ernest A, 1947, My 3,17:1
Bailey, Ezra B Mrs, 1924, Ag 2,9:6
Bailey, Foster Mrs, 1949, D 17,17:4
Bailey, Frances S, 1946, Ap 26,21:1
Bailey, Frank (will, S 5,12:8), 1953, Ag 27,25:1
Bailey, Frank F, 1944, Mr 17,17:3
Bailey, Frank H Rear-Adm, 1921, Ap 10,22:3
Bailey, Frank M Mrs, 1955, S 25,93:1
Bailey, Frank Mrs, 1964, F 20,29:4
Bailey, Frank P Mrs, 1951, O 9,29:5
Bailey, Frank R, 1949, F 26,15:2
Bailey, Frank T, 1956, O 17,35:4; 1959, Ja 22,32:1
Bailey, Frank T Mrs, 1955, S 29,33:1
Bailey, Frankie, 1953, Jl 9,25:4
Bailey, Frazer A, 1960, My 3,39:3
Bailey, Fred, 1953, Ja 18,93:2
Bailey, Frederick H, 1912, Ap 13,13:5
Bailey, Frederick M, 1967, Ap 20,44:1
Bailey, Frederick R Dr, 1968, S 23,35:5
Bailey, Frederick R Mrs, 1950, N 15,32:2
Bailey, Frederick Randolph, 1923, S 17,15:3
Bailey, G A, 1877, D 28,1:3
Bailey, G F, 1903, F 22,7:4
Bailey, Gamaliel Dr, 1859, Je 22,4:4
Bailey, George D, 1966, D 4,89:2
Bailey, George Dr, 1911, Je 23,11:4
Bailey, George F, 1946, Je 29,19:4
Bailey, George H, 1916, N 26,21:1; 1954, My 6,33:5
Bailey, George M, 1965, D 30,23:4
Bailey, George O, 1964, My 6,47:2
Bailey, George R, 1964, F 2,88:6
Bailey, George T, 1964, Mr 29,60:8
Bailey, George W, 1945, My 2,23:4; 1947, D 17,30:2
Bailey, George W Dr, 1916, D 20,13:4
Bailey, George W Sr, 1946, Mr 10,46:3
Bailey, Gilbert L Dr, 1937, Mr 8,19:3
Bailey, Guy W, 1940, O 23,23:3
Bailey, H Pierson, 1961, Ap 1,17:2
Bailey, Hackliah, 1910, Mr 7,9:4
Bailey, Harland L Mrs, 1963, Je 7,31:4
Bailey, Harold J, 1961, F 11,23:4
Bailey, Harold W, 1939, N 12,49:2
Bailey, Harriet, 1953, My 24,88:2
Bailey, Harry, 1941, O 16,21:5
Bailey, Harry G, 1952, Jl 31,23:1
Bailey, Harry L, 1962, My 28,29:5
Bailey, Harry R, 1941, My 3,15:2
Bailey, Harry U, 1943, S 21,23:5
Bailey, Henry J, 1949, Je 25,13:3
Bailey, Henry L, 1943, Ja 27,21:2; 1961, My 20,23:6
Bailey, Henry L Mrs, 1958, O 21,33:3
Bailey, Herbert, 1939, Mr 19,III,7:2
Bailey, Herbert B Mrs, 1948, N 1,23:5
Bailey, Herbert S, 1962, Ap 22,80:3
Bailey, Hiram P, 1949, Ja 16,69:1
Bailey, Irving, 1947, D 29,17:3
Bailey, Irving W, 1967, My 18,47:3
Bailey, Isabella M Mrs, 1938, Mr 1,21:1
Bailey, Ivon A, 1963, F 12,4:7
Bailey, J A, 1883, Je 18,5:6
Bailey, J F Mrs, 1874, Ap 11,4:4
Bailey, J G, 1929, Ja 5,19:3
Bailey, J H, 1883, Ap 3,5:1
Bailey, J M Judge, 1903, S 28,7:5
Bailey, J W, 1902, Mr 2,7:7; 1929, Ap 14,29:1
Bailey, J W Mrs, 1906, N 19,9:3; 1950, N 25,13:5
Bailey, James A (funl, Ap 15,9:5), 1906, Ap 12,1:3
Bailey, James A, 1954, F 8,23:3
Bailey, James B, 1948, O 3,64:8
Bailey, James D, 1952, Ja 20,84:6
Bailey, James E Mrs, 1947, Je 27,21:3
Bailey, James H, 1958, Je 4,33:1; 1965, Je 22,35:1
Bailey, James M, 1940, Jl 26,17:5
Bailey, James R, 1941, Mr 27,23:4
Bailey, Jason S, 1918, Ag 2,11:6
Bailey, Jennings, 1963, Ja 11,4:1
Bailey, John H, 1952, S 11,31:2
Bailey, John J, 1951, My 21,27:3
Bailey, John M, 1946, F 14,25:5
Bailey, John M Maj, 1916, F 22,11:5
Bailey, John R, 1942, D 22,25:2
Bailey, John T, 1907, Ja 7,7:4; 1942, S 4,23:4
Bailey, Joseph, 1952, Mr 4,27:2
Bailey, Joseph A, 1951, N 15,29:3
Bailey, Joseph Brig-Gen, 1867, Ap 5,5:3
Bailey, Joseph Capt, 1952, Jl 8,27:4
Bailey, Joseph L, 1939, My 16,23:5; 1952, D 4,35:5
Bailey, Joshua L, 1916, D 7,13:5
Bailey, Julius A, 1940, Jl 7,25:4
Bailey, L R Mrs, 1869, F 26,2:2
Bailey, Lansing C, 1913, Mr 30,IV,7:5
Bailey, Leon E, 1941, Mr 8,19:3
Bailey, Leon O Mrs, 1946, Ap 28,44:4
Bailey, Leonard W, 1959, Ja 7,33:1
Bailey, Lester, 1942, N 2,23:6
Bailey, Lew, 1937, Je 25,21:4
Bailey, Lewis M, 1943, S 29,21:4
Bailey, Liberty H, 1954, D 27,17:3
Bailey, Louis J, 1962, O 18,39:3
Bailey, Louise A Mrs, 1947, Je 4,27:3
Bailey, Lydia H Mrs, 1966, N 8,39:3
Bailey, M Claire, 1954, N 19,23:5
Bailey, Margaret E (por), 1949, O 30,84:3
Bailey, Margery, 1963, Je 20,33:2
Bailey, Mary, 1949, D 25,12:2
Bailey, Mary D, 1951, Ja 30,25:3
Bailey, Mary Lady, 1960, Ag 30,29:2
Bailey, Melville C, 1956, O 5,25:5
Bailey, Melville K, 1948, D 14,29:2
Bailey, Middlesex A Prof, 1923, N 26,17:4
Bailey, Mildred (M Rinker), 1951, D 13,33:4
Bailey, Morton S, 1957, S 4,33:5
Bailey, Oliver G, 1952, S 21,88:3
Bailey, P J, 1902, S 7,9:6
Bailey, Paul, 1962, S 16,86:5
Bailey, Pearce Dr, 1922, F 12,22:1
Bailey, Percy L Jr Mrs, 1941, My 28,25:3; 1964, F 20, 29:1
Bailey, Philip S, 1958, Mr 6,27:5
Bailey, Prentiss (will, Jl 7,3:4), 1939, Je 25,36:5
Bailey, Prentiss (will), 1941, Ja 3,11:6
Bailey, R B, 1942, Mr 18,23:5
Bailey, Ralph B, 1947, N 30,76:3
Bailey, Ralph E, 1954, D 4,17:6
Bailey, Ralph Sargent, 1968, D 10,77:6
Bailey, Ralph W, 1953, Je 13,15:6
Bailey, Ray W, 1951, F 23,27:2
Bailey, Raymond E, 1940, Ja 8,15:4
Bailey, Raymond N Jr, 1948, Ja 13,25:1
Bailey, Reginald, 1953, F 11,29:3
Bailey, Richard J, 1956, O 30,37:4
Bailey, Robert L, 1938, Mr 1,21:2
Bailey, Robert M Jr, 1951, D 4,33:5
Bailey, Robert Mrs, 1950, Mr 17,23:4
Bailey, Robert O, 1945, D 27,20:3
Bailey, Robert R, 1949, Je 25,13:1
Bailey, Robert Taylor, 1945, Jl 6,13:8
Bailey, Roswell I, 1945, D 7,21:2
Bailey, Rufus W, 1960, My 15,86:5
Bailey, Russell T (Sept 30), 1965, O 11,61:1
Bailey, S I, 1931, Je 6,17:5
Bailey, S Leonard, 1942, S 8,24:2
Bailey, Samuel A, 1882, Ap 28,2:5
Bailey, Samuel F, 1940, Ja 17,21:3
Bailey, Samuel H, 1945, Mr 23,19:1
Bailey, Sara H Mrs, 1943, D 31,15:2
Bailey, Sarah D, 1940, S 26,23:2
Bailey, Stephen A Mrs, 1952, D 22,25:2
Bailey, Sumner P Jr, 1941, F 14,18:3
Bailey, Sydney, 1942, Mr 31,21:6
Bailey, T, 1877, F 11,6:7
Bailey, Temple, 1953, Jl 8,27:3
Bailey, Theodore L Mrs, 1961, O 19,35:1
Bailey, Theodore W, 1962, N 22,29:3
Bailey, Theodorus, 1947, S 26,23:4
Bailey, Theodorus Mrs, 1964, Ap 19,85:1

Bailey, Thomas, 1912, S 26,11:4
Bailey, Thomas L, 1946, N 3,63:3
Bailey, Thomas P, 1949, F 9,27:5
Bailey, Townsend F, 1944, Ag 20,33:2
Bailey, Townsend F Mrs, 1955, Ag 6,15:5
Bailey, Truman E, 1959, D 25,21:4
Bailey, Vernon, 1942, Ap 22,23:4
Bailey, Vernon H, 1953, O 28,29:1
Bailey, Vernon N, 1944, D 11,23:4
Bailey, W H, 1876, Je 4,5:2
Bailey, Walter C, 1938, Ag 1,13:5
Bailey, Walter P, 1952, Ag 1,17:3
Bailey, Warren W Mrs, 1952, D 3,33:4
Bailey, Whitman, 1954, N 4,31:3
Bailey, William, 1949, Je 16,29:2; 1957, Je 26,31:2
Bailey, William A, 1924, F 4,19:4
Bailey, William B, 1952, Ja 11,21:1
Bailey, William C, 1953, Mr 28,17:2
Bailey, William D, 1925, N 22,9:1
Bailey, William E, 1941, F 22,15:5
Bailey, William H, 1948, N 13,15:1; 1949, N 17,29:2
Bailey, William Henry Sir, 1913, N 23,IV,7:5
Bailey, William Holloway, 1908, O 6,9:7
Bailey, William J A, 1949, My 18,27:4
Bailey, William L, 1941, D 8,23:2
Bailey, William M, 1942, My 6,19:3
Bailey, William T, 1943, Ja 17,44:2
Bailey, William Whitman Prof, 1914, F 21,11:4
Bailhe, Mellysa Mrs, 1959, Jl 16,27:5
Bailie, Albert E, 1957, N 1,27:2
Bailie, Earle, 1940, N 16,17:1
Bailie, George S, 1940, O 5,15:3
Bailie, Joseph T, 1950, My 12,27:3
Bailie, William, 1957, Jl 3,23:4
Bailin, Harry, 1950, F 21,26:2
Bailin, Israel B, 1961, My 1,29:4
Baillard, Victor H Mrs, 1967, F 19,88:5
Baillargeon, Harman, 1941, My 12,17:3
Baille, Frank Sir, 1921, Ja 3,15:6
Baille-Wright, Cronhope Lt Col, 1937, Ja 20,15:4
Bailleres, Raul, 1967, Ja 4,43:4
Baillet, Philip F, 1961, Ag 27,85:2
Baillet-Latour, Henry de Count, 1942, Ja 8,21:1
Bailleul, L C, 1941, S 26,23:5
Bailley-Blanchard, Jeanne Eliza, 1909, Ag 4,7:6
Baillie, Albert, 1955, N 4,29:5
Baillie, Albert Rev, 1923, Mr 21,17:5
Baillie, Charles R, 1946, Jl 25,21:2
Baillie, David G, 1937, Ag 15,II,6:8
Baillie, Donald M, 1954, N 1,27:4
Baillie, Hugh (funl Mr 3,33:4; mem ser set Mr 5,27:2), 1966, Mr 2,41:2
Baillie, Hugh Mrs, 1962, Mr 8,31:2
Baillie, John, 1960, S 30,27:3
Baillie, Robert A, 1961, N 7,33:5
Baillie, W A, 1883, Jl 19,1:4
Baillie, William N, 1948, N 8,21:3
Baillie-Saunders, Margaret, 1949, Ap 25,23:2
Baillie-Stewart, Norman, 1966, Je 8,47:2
Baillieu, Maurice H L, 1961, Jl 28,21:5
Baillieu of Sefton, Lord (Clive Latham Baillieu), 1967, Je 20,39:3
Bailloud, Maurice Camille Gen, 1921, Jl 2,9:7
Bailly, Edward C, 1961, Ja 9,39:3
Bailly, Edward C Jr, 1953, S 29,29:3
Bailly, Emma A, 1955, S 1,23:3
Bailly, Raymond A, 1962, My 1,37:4
Bailly-Blanchard, Arthur, 1925, Ag 25,17:5; 1958, Ap 18,23:4
Bailor, Ford L, 1960, D 28,27:3
Bailwitz, Alex, 1959, My 30,17:5
Baily, Harold J, 1964, N 17,41:4
Baily, Henry P, 1945, F 23,17:4
Baily, J Ralph, 1945, D 1,23:1
Baily, T Carey, 1942, My 21,19:6
Baily, Tom W, 1946, Ag 15,25:5
Baily, W H, 1882, My 21,9:1
Baily, William L, 1947, Ap 8,27:3
Baily, William L Mrs, 1954, Ag 3,19:5
Bailyn, Benjamin, 1967, Jl 23,60:5
Baime, Israel, 1956, Ag 23,27:3
Bain, Alexander, 1877, Ja 12,5:6; 1879, Jl 29,2:4
Bain, Alexander Prof, 1903, S 19,7:6
Bain, Christopher, 1950, My 14,108:2
Bain, Donald, 1954, My 25,21:5
Bain, Elizabeth I Mrs, 1938, Ap 15,19:2
Bain, Ferdinand R, 1945, Ag 16,19:4
Bain, Frederick, 1950, N 24,36:2
Bain, George A, 1939, Ap 18,23:2
Bain, George G, 1944, Ap 21,19:1
Bain, H Foster, 1948, Mr 10,27:1
Bain, H Rupert, 1952, Mr 26,29:3
Bain, J Milo, 1961, S 4,15:4
Bain, James Adger, 1874, D 3,5:6
Bain, James W, 1961, Ja 3,29:4
Bain, Leslie B, 1962, F 8,32:1
Bain, Matty, 1945, S 19,25:3
Bain, Roy S, 1945, D 19,25:4
Bain, Thomas, 1950, F 14,25:4
Bain-Marais, Colin, 1942, Ag 15,11:4
Bainbridge, Barbara C, 1965, My 15,26:2
Bainbridge, Benjamin H, 1940, My 31,19:2
Bainbridge, E C Col, 1903, Ap 2,9:6

Bainbridge, Edmond F, 1945, Jl 20,19:6
Bainbridge, Gale Mrs, 1963, My 29,11:8
Bainbridge, Henry, 1904, Ja 22,9:6
Bainbridge, Henry C, 1916, Mr 11,11:5; 1956, Ag 29, 29:1
Bainbridge, John G, 1963, D 30,21:1
Bainbridge, John K, 1948, Ap 21,27:4
Bainbridge, John K Jr, 1951, S 10,21:6
Bainbridge, Lawrence M, 1950, Je 25,68:4
Bainbridge, Marshall Jr, 1966, Je 27,35:2
Bainbridge, Richard Warin, 1918, Ag 8,11:6
Bainbridge, William, 1958, Jl 27,61:4
Bainbridge, William C, 1950, Jl 9,68:7
Bainbridge, William H Mrs, 1967, F 17,37:3
Bainbridge, William S, 1947, S 23,25:3
Bainbridge, William S Mrs, 1967, Jl 15,25:1
Bainbridge, William W, 1965, My 15,26:2
Bainbridge, William W Mrs, 1965, My 15,26:2
Bainbridge-Bell, Eleanor L M Mrs, 1938, N 4,23:4
Bainbridge-Hoff, William, 1903, My 23,9:3
Baine, Harry M, 1945, Mr 30,15:1
Bainer, Harry M, 1949, Ap 24,76:6
Baines, C Robert, 1962, Mr 7,35:2
Baines, Charles S, 1961, Mr 10,27:4
Baines, Edmund, 1914, Ap 5,15:3
Baines, Huffman (funl, Je 30,15:6), 1967, Je 27,39:2
Bains, Edward, 1949, Jl 11,17:3
Bains, James Jr, 1960, N 2,39:4
Bains-Griffiths, David Rev, 1919, F 6,11:2
Bainter, Fay (funl plans, Ap 18,47:4), 1968, Ap 17, 47:3
Bainton, William L, 1957, Ag 23,19:3
Bainville, J, 1936, F 10,17:3
Bair, Charles E, 1939, D 17,48:6
Bair, Charles S, 1942, O 26,15:5
Bair, Harold, 1960, Jl 10,72:2
Bair, Olga Mrs, 1947, Jl 27,45:2
Baird, Absalom Gen, 1905, Je 15,9:6
Baird, Adam C, 1951, Je 27,29:2
Baird, Alexander, 1945, F 6,19:2; 1967, N 25,39:2
Baird, Andrew B, 1940, S 23,17:3
Baird, Andrew D Col, 1923, S 5,15:1
Baird, Andrew J 2d, 1957, N 30,21:1
Baird, Andrew M, 1967, My 10,44:5
Baird, Andrew Mrs, 1966, Ag 23,39:3
Baird, Bruce, 1960, O 3,31:3
Baird, Cameron, 1960, My 7,23:3
Baird, Campbell A, 1949, Jl 25,15:3
Baird, Charles, 1940, Ja 4,23:2
Baird, Charles E, 1937, Je 26,2:2
Baird, Charles E Mrs, 1937, Je 26,2:2
Baird, Charles L, 1937, Ap 17,17:3
Baird, Charles R, 1940, Ap 11,25:4
Baird, Charles W, 1947, My 26,21:1
Baird, Clay M, 1944, Je 29,23:5
Baird, Coe M, 1942, F 26,19:6
Baird, Cora Mrs, 1967, D 7,52:4
Baird, D, 1927, F 26,15:3
Baird, David Graham, 1913, O 9,13:5
Baird, David Jr, 1955, Mr 1,25:1
Baird, Edgar W Jr, 1957, Ja 17,29:3
Baird, Edward A, 1950, Mr 7,28:2
Baird, Edward K, 1951, Ja 31,25:3
Baird, Frank B, 1939, N 16,23:5; 1950, O 25,35:5
Baird, George, 1962, Je 9,25:2
Baird, George D, 1944, Ag 22,17:2
Baird, George H, 1951, N 15,29:2
Baird, George Mrs, 1958, O 23,31:1
Baird, George William Gen (funl, D 2,7:3), 1906, N 30,9:6
Baird, Harry W Mrs, 1956, N 8,39:4
Baird, Henry L, 1939, Ag 23,14:5
Baird, Henry M Jr Mrs, 1954, Ag 24,21:5
Baird, Henry Martyn Rev Dr, 1906, N 12,8:5
Baird, Henry W, 1943, N 4,23:3; 1963, O 10,41:3
Baird, Henry W Mrs, 1948, Mr 21,60:4
Baird, Irvin, 1964, Ja 31,27:1
Baird, Isabella S Mrs, 1942, Ap 12,44:1
Baird, J A, 1879, Je 19,8:3
Baird, J Francis Mrs, 1960, O 30,86:4
Baird, James (see also Je 21), 1876, Je 25,2:2
Baird, James, 1876, Jl 6,2:1; 1953, My 17,89:1
Baird, James A, 1945, Je 20,23:2
Baird, James Mrs, 1962, O 21,88:8
Baird, James S, 1950, Mr 5,92:4
Baird, Jean Mrs, 1960, S 3,36:8
Baird, Jesse H Mrs, 1951, Mr 17,15:6
Baird, John C, 1964, Je 10,45:3
Baird, John L, 1946, Je 15,21:1
Baird, John Mrs, 1949, D 5,23:4
Baird, John Stuart, 1918, My 25,13:4
Baird, Josephine B Mrs, 1939, N 18,17:4
Baird, Julian W Prof, 1911, Je 27,9:5
Baird, Katherine H, 1949, O 30,84:4
Baird, Llewellyn G T, 1949, Ap 2,15:4
Baird, Lucius O, 1948, D 21,25:2
Baird, Marcus H Capt, 1915, N 11,13:6
Baird, Mary R, 1939, Ap 16,III,7:1
Baird, Matthew, 1914, S 17,9:6
Baird, Mowbrey D, 1939, N 8,23:5
Baird, Rebecca, 1907, Ja 28,7:4
Baird, Richard Loper, 1921, F 4,11:3
Baird, Richard Loper Mrs, 1921, F 4,11:3

Baird, Robert, 1905, Je 28,4:2
Baird, Robert L, 1942, N 17,25:4
Baird, Robert P, 1947, My 18,60:1
Baird, Robert Rev, 1863, Mr 17,8:4
Baird, S F, 1887, Ag 20,5:2
Baird, Stewart, 1947, O 30,25:3
Baird, Stewart Mrs, 1949, N 27,104:6
Baird, Thomas, 1946, D 25,29:6; 1963, Jl 19,25:5
Baird, Tom, 1962, Jl 4,21:4
Baird, W H Lt-Col, 1864, Je 26,5:4
Baird, Walter H, 1948, Ag 2,21:4
Baird, William, 1946, D 30,19:4; 1948, S 16,29:1
Baird, William A, 1940, My 31,19:2
Baird, William J, 1951, F 21,27:3
Baird, William Mrs, 1948, O 31,88:4
Baird, William R, 1917, Mr 16,11:4
Baird, William S, 1954, D 25,11:4
Baird, William T, 1941, Jl 30,18:2
Baird, Willis A, 1954, Ag 12,25:5
Baired, William J Mrs, 1951, Mr 21,33:2
Bairnsfather, Bruce, 1959, S 30,37:3
Bairstow, Edward C, 1946, My 3,22:2
Bairstow, Ernest, 1962, S 15,25:5
Baisden, John S, 1944, S 18,19:3
Baise, Joseph E, 1955, Jl 22,23:1
Baisley, Charles E, 1941, Ag 26,19:1
Baisley, Robert, 1951, Ap 18,31:5
Baisley, Sylvester, 1944, S 21,19:4
Baisslere, Eugene F Mrs, 1958, N.15,23:5
Baist, Henry G, 1948, S 23,29:6
Baiter, George R, 1956, S 7,23:1
Baiter, Jacob P, 1955, Jl 25,19:4
Baiter, Jacob P Mrs, 1954, D 30,17:4
Baiter, Jacob Philip (funl, O 6,27:5), 1925, O 4,5:2
Baity, R F, 1951, O 1,23:5
Baivier, Paul V, 1937, O 2,21:3
Baizan, Celestino, 1941, Je 14,17:6
Baizerman, Saul, 1957, S 1,56:1
Baizerman, Saul Mrs, 1949, D 31,15:5; 1950, Ja 1,43:1
Bajart, Charles N, 1942, Je 4,19:1
Bajpai, Girja S, 1954, D 5,88:1
Bajpai, Ramlal B, 1962, N 17,25:3
Bajpai, Seetle P, 1947, F 2,57:3
Bajus, Lewis, 1954, Ag 27,21:2
Bakal, Harry, 1968, Mr 31,81:2
Bakaleinikoff, Vladimir, 1953, N 6,28:3
Bakenhus, R E Mrs, 1946, D 5,31:5
Bakenhus, Reuben E, 1967, O 7,29:2
Baker, A B, 1928, Jl 31,21:3
Baker, A C, 1884, Mr 12,8:2
Baker, A C Capt, 1926, My 6,28:5
Baker, A E, 1945, Ja 3,17:2
Baker, A Sidney, 1953, S 8,31:2
Baker, A Sidney Mrs, 1946, Je 11,23:3
Baker, A Thornton, 1949, Ag 4,23:2
Baker, A Walter, 1942, Ap 23,24:3
Baker, Adelaide, 1942, Ap 29,21:5
Baker, Adelbert S, 1960, F 3,33:3
Baker, Adeline P, 1948, My 22,15:6
Baker, Al, 1951, O 25,29:6
Baker, Albert, 1942, O 31,15:6; 1945, My 11,19:3
Baker, Albert A, 1959, Mr 25,35:2
Baker, Albert B, 1956, N 21,27:3
Baker, Albert C Justice, 1921, S 1,15:4
Baker, Albert L, 1953, My 6,31:1
Baker, Alfred, 1943, Ap 3,15:1
Baker, Alfred E, 1941, Ap 30,19:2
Baker, Alfred J, 1920, N 28,22:4
Baker, Alice S, 1955, Ja 29,15:1
Baker, Alpheus W, 1905, Ap 12,9:4
Baker, Alton F, 1961, O 28,21:5
Baker, Amy, 1947, Ja 14,25:1
Baker, Andrew, 1924, Mr 1,13:6
Baker, Anice Mrs, 1952, O 4,17:5
Baker, Anne, 1949, F 17,23:5
Baker, Anson C, 1941, Mr 1,15:2
Baker, Archer, 1910, Ja 17,7:4
Baker, Archie M, 1950, S 25,23:2
Baker, Art, 1966, Ag 27,29:3
Baker, Arthur, 1939, My 25,25:5
Baker, Arthur J M, 1953, S 14,27:2
Baker, Arthur M, 1941, S 24,23:3
Baker, Arthur N Sr, 1953, O 2,21:3
Baker, Asa G, 1940, S 11,26:2
Baker, Augustus Sr, 1952, D 10,35:4
Baker, Auval, 1948, Jl 9,19:3
Baker, B, 1933, Jl 5,19:1
Baker, B F, 1939, Ap 11,24:4
Baker, Bartholomew H, 1950, F 25,17:3
Baker, Belle, 1957, Ap 30,29:1
Baker, Ben, 1955, F 17,27:1
Baker, Ben L, 1944, Ap 3,21:3
Baker, Benedict J, 1948, N 20,13:6
Baker, Benjamin, 1951, S 10,21:2
Baker, Benjamin F, 1958, D 22,2:4
Baker, Benjamin Henry, 1943, Je 18,22:3
Baker, Benjamin S, 1945, Ag 17,17:4
Baker, Benjamin Sir, 1907, My 20,9:6
Baker, Bert T, 1955, Ja 23,85:3
Baker, Bertha K, 1943, O 13,23:4
Baker, Berthold N, 1951, F 8,23:5
Baker, Bessie, 1942, Je 25,23:3
Baker, Bruce K, 1965, Je 17,33:4

Baker, Byron W, 1941, Ag 8,15:2
Baker, C B, 1936, O 20,25:3
Baker, C Dwight, 1957, Ag 20,27:2
Baker, C Dwight Mrs, 1951, Je 5,31:3
Baker, C E, 1880, D 21,2:6
Baker, C Ex-Gov, 1885, Ap 29,5:6
Baker, C Graham, 1950, My 17,29:5
Baker, C T, 1881, Mr 2,5:5
Baker, Carroll R, 1940, Ap 25,23:6
Baker, Carson DeW (funl, Ag 16,27:2), 1962, Ag 12, 81:2
Baker, Catherine C, 1947, O 11,17:2
Baker, Catherine E Mrs, 1938, Ag 12,17:3
Baker, Charles, 1904, Ja 13,2:5; 1906, Ag 20,6:6; 1942, Je 11,23:3; 1954, Jl 5,11:6; 1957, O 23,33:4; 1960, Jl 16,19:1
Baker, Charles A, 1937, D 31,16:2; 1945, D 8,17:6; 1949, Je 11,18:8
Baker, Charles C, 1953, N 13,27:2
Baker, Charles D, 1917, Ja 9,13:3
Baker, Charles F, 1944, Mr 8,19:6
Baker, Charles H, 1939, Ag 23,21:3; 1943, Jl 27,17:6
Baker, Charles H C, 1959, Jl 6,27:3
Baker, Charles H Sr, 1965, Je 2,45:5
Baker, Charles J, 1946, D 24,17:4; 1959, Je 25,29:1
Baker, Charles L, 1954, Ag 7,13:6
Baker, Charles M, 1941, My 22,21:5
Baker, Charles P, 1965, Ja 24,81:2
Baker, Charles R, 1952, Mr 29,15:4; 1955, My 25,33:5
Baker, Charles T, 1938, Ap 11,15:1
Baker, Charles W, 1937, Jl 28,19:3; 1938, Ag 9,19:2; 1941, Je 7,17:4
Baker, Charles W Jr, 1950, O 21,17:5; 1954, Ag 28, 15:3
Baker, Charles W Mrs, 1943, Jl 23,17:4
Baker, Chester A, 1948, O 17,76:2; 1952, Mr 5,29:3
Baker, Chris C, 1941, Ap 20,43:1
Baker, Christain E, 1937, Jl 24,15:4
Baker, Clarence C, 1938, Je 2,23:4
Baker, Clarence G, 1948, Ja 2,24:1
Baker, Claude M, 1962, Jl 11,35:4
Baker, Clifton H, 1948, Je 13,68:8
Baker, Clifton L, 1962, Ap 5,33:4
Baker, Clinton H, 1958, Ja 16,29:1
Baker, Clinton M, 1947, Ap 15,25:4
Baker, Colgate, 1940, Je 27,23:4
Baker, Colley S Sr, 1958, F 1,19:4
Baker, Conrad S, 1948, N 14,77:1
Baker, Cornelius, 1944, Ap 12,21:5
Baker, Courts A, 1949, Ja 17,19:2
Baker, Crosby F, 1954, D 11,13:1
Baker, Cyrus Osborne, 1918, Je 16,21:3
Baker, D K, 1903, O 10,9:6
Baker, Daniel E, 1939, D 7,27:2
Baker, Daniel F, 1874, O 13,1:6
Baker, Daniel Mrs, 1954, D 27,17:1
Baker, David Charles, 1919, Mr 28,13:1
Baker, David D, 1950, Je 28,27:3
Baker, David M, 1963, Ag 6,31:3
Baker, David S, 1906, Ja 28,7:6
Baker, Day, 1943, Mr 5,17:4
Baker, Dell A, 1912, Jl 20,7:7
Baker, Dermot O, 1958, Ap 17,31:4
Baker, Donald T, 1939, S 22,23:2
Baker, Dorothy (Mrs Howard Baker), 1968, Je 19, 47:1
Baker, Duron F, 1940, Ap 7,44:7
Baker, Dwight M, 1961, O 27,33:4
Baker, E Brown, 1942, Jl 13,15:3
Baker, E D Maj, 1883, Ja 27,2:2
Baker, E G Mrs, 1950, F 27,19:4
Baker, E H, 1933, S 27,21:1
Baker, E J L, 1883, Ja 1,5:3
Baker, E M, 1884, D 21,2:5
Baker, E Mills Dr, 1909, S 27,9:6
Baker, E N, 1939, O 8,49:2
Baker, Earl C Mrs, 1948, O 14,29:1
Baker, Earle A, 1958, N 7,27:1
Baker, Eddie, 1937, My 16,II,3:1
Baker, Edward, 1937, O 7,27:3; 1944, Ja 12,23:2
Baker, Edward B, 1959, D 24,20:1
Baker, Edward C, 1952, Mr 15,13:5
Baker, Edward E, 1959, O 28,37:5; 1966, Mr 22,42:1
Baker, Edward H, 1943, O 23,13:3
Baker, Edward J (will, F 12,14:6; est appr, Jl 25,19:8), 1959, Ja 18,88:2
Baker, Edward J Mrs, 1940, Jl 2,21:5
Baker, Edward M, 1957, F 18,27:4
Baker, Edward P, 1939, D 31,18:6; 1945, Je 5,19:2
Baker, Edward P Mrs, 1945, S 25,25:2
Baker, Edwin G, 1961, Ja 26,29:5
Baker, Edwin H, 1941, Je 26,23:2
Baker, Edwin M, 1943, My 29,13:2
Baker, Elias B, 1947, Je 13,23:2
Baker, Elizabeth T Mrs, 1953, Ap 30,31:4
Baker, Ellery A, 1943, N 21,56:5
Baker, Ellis B, 1943, N 29,19:4
Baker, Elsie, 1958, Ap 29,29:4
Baker, Elsie A, 1942, Ja 23,19:1
Baker, Elwood T, 1938, N 22,23:4
Baker, Elwood W, 1962, F 19,31:4
Baker, Emma S, 1943, O 28,23:3
Baker, Erwin G, 1960, My 11,39:5
Baker, Eugene, 1940, O 15,23:1
Baker, Everett M, 1950, S 1,1:7
Baker, F Cecil, 1961, N 6,37:3
Baker, F L, 1936, Ja 14,21:3
Baker, Fay (Mrs J Kirk), 1954, N 15,27:4
Baker, Fisher Ames Col, 1919, My 31,13:4
Baker, Florence M Mrs, 1959, O 21,43:3
Baker, Forrest W, 1937, F 26,21:3
Baker, Frances, 1947, My 26,21:2
Baker, Frances A, 1938, Je 5,45:3
Baker, Francis B, 1964, Ja 12,92:8
Baker, Francis E Judge, 1924, Mr 16,23:2
Baker, Frank F, 1948, Je 27,52:6; 1960, F 1,27:4
Baker, Frank H, 1951, My 8,31:4
Baker, Frank J, 1944, Mr 2,17:4
Baker, Frank K, 1951, Ap 18,31:4
Baker, Frank M, 1916, Ja 24,11:2; 1950, Ap 6,29:2
Baker, Frank N, 1952, Je 8,86:7
Baker, Franklin H, 1941, Ap 4,21:3
Baker, Franklin Sr, 1923, F 6,19:4
Baker, Franklin T (por), 1949, F 4,23:1
Baker, Franklin T Mrs, 1951, Mr 4,92:4
Baker, Fred, 1938, My 18,21:6
Baker, Frederick B Mrs, 1960, Ja 31,92:3
Baker, Frederick C, 1938, F 4,21:3
Baker, Frederick H, 1939, O 2,17:6
Baker, Frederick J, 1949, Je 27,27:3
Baker, Frederick Mrs, 1945, Je 6,21:4
Baker, Frederick S A, 1963, D 10,50:7
Baker, Frederick Van V, 1964, D 20,68:6
Baker, Frederick W, 1949, Jl 5,23:4
Baker, G A, 1880, Ap 3,3:3
Baker, G F Sr, 1931, My 3,1:8
Baker, G J, 1928, S 27,1:6
Baker, G P, 1935, Ja 7,17:1
Baker, Genevra W, 1943, Ap 19,19:2
Baker, George, 1924, O 3,21:3; 1944, Ag 13,35:1; 1948, My 4,25:3
Baker, George A, 1955, N 22,35:4
Baker, George B, 1937, My 3,19:6; 1948, Jl 31,16:2; 1948, O 8,25:3
Baker, George B Mrs, 1943, S 17,21:6
Baker, George C, 1943, F 10,25:1; 1946, Ag 21,27:4; 1952, D 4,35:2; 1957, Jl 20,15:4
Baker, George C Mrs, 1958, N 6,37:2
Baker, George D, 1949, Ja 29,13:2
Baker, George D Mrs, 1946, Ag 22,27:2
Baker, George D Rev, 1903, D 18,9:5
Baker, George F, 1937, My 31,1:3; 1947, Ap 17,27:4
Baker, George F Mrs, 1913, Jl 29,7:5
Baker, George H, 1939, F 10,23:5; 1950, Ja 6,21:4; 1954, F 13,13:2
Baker, George Hall, 1911, Mr 28,13:5
Baker, George J, 1944, D 28,20:2; 1967, F 25,28:1
Baker, George M Mrs (est), 1914, Jl 4,7:5
Baker, George Mrs, 1944, F 4,15:5
Baker, George N, 1944, N 25,13:4
Baker, George P Mrs, 1959, D 1,39:3
Baker, George R, 1941, My 3,15:4; 1944, O 25,21:4
Baker, George R Mrs, 1955, Ap 4,29:1
Baker, George S, 1949, Ag 18,21:6
Baker, George Stuart Rev Dr, 1918, F 19,13:6
Baker, George T, 1940, D 15,61:4; 1963, N 5,31:1
Baker, George W, 1940, O 19,17:2; 1941, Mr 9,40:5; 1967, Mr 17,41:1
Baker, Gilbert H, 1939, N 30,21:5
Baker, Gladys (Mrs R L Patrick), 1957, D 18,35:1
Baker, Gordon E, 1955, Ja 11,25:3
Baker, Gordon H, 1963, Ap 9,31:5
Baker, Gordon L, 1953, My 3,89:2
Baker, Gussie Mrs, 1961, Ag 16,31:3
Baker, H H, 1928, Mr 9,25:3
Baker, H Warren, 1951, D 18,31:3
Baker, Halsey H Rev, 1907, Ja 30,9:6
Baker, Hamilton W, 1946, Je 16,40:7
Baker, Harlan F Mrs, 1956, O 29,29:3
Baker, Harold A, 1964, Mr 29,60:7
Baker, Harold C, 1956, D 5,39:4
Baker, Harold C Mrs, 1956, Je 20,31:1
Baker, Harold M, 1954, Je 28,19:5
Baker, Harold M Mrs, 1945, Je 17,26:4
Baker, Harold R, 1967, Ag 10,37:4
Baker, Harold V, 1947, Mr 4,25:3; 1955, Ja 6,27:3
Baker, Harold V Mrs, 1945, N 29,23:2
Baker, Harold W, 1947, N 10,29:5; 1948, F 15,60:6
Baker, Harold W Mrs, 1953, Mr 27,23:1
Baker, Harriet E G Mrs, 1941, Mr 14,21:4
Baker, Harrison V, 1957, N 17,87:2
Baker, Harry B, 1956, D 11,39:2
Baker, Harry C, 1939, Ag 24,19:6
Baker, Harry F, 1944, My 1,15:5
Baker, Harry J, 1953, Ap 6,19:4
Baker, Harry Mrs, 1909, Ja 16,11:6
Baker, Harry T, 1939, Mr 19,III,6:7
Baker, Harvey A, 1951, Mr 29,27:3
Baker, Helen, 1955, Ja 11,25:1
Baker, Henry, 1961, F 14,34:3
Baker, Henry Capt, 1873, Ag 31,8:3
Baker, Henry D, 1939, S 15,23:2
Baker, Henry F, 1941, N 7,23:2
Baker, Henry G, 1939, Mr 8,21:6
Baker, Henry H, 1940, Ja 14,43:2
Baker, Henry H Mrs, 1967, Jl 4,19:2
Baker, Henry I Jr, 1949, S 11,94:3
Baker, Henry M, 1941, Mr 11,23:2
Baker, Henry M Gen, 1912, My 31,15:6
Baker, Henry Rockwell, 1914, Ap 29,11:5
Baker, Herbert (will, Jl 15,13:5), 1939, Jl 5,17:5
Baker, Herbert A, 1940, N 26,23:1
Baker, Herbert G, 1949, Ja 29,13:1
Baker, Herbert J, 1939, Ja 7,15:6
Baker, Herbert L Mrs, 1949, My 19,29:5
Baker, Herbert S Mrs, 1950, D 25,19:4
Baker, Herman C, 1942, S 18,22:3
Baker, Hettie G, 1957, N 15,28:3
Baker, Hezekiah C, 1948, S 13,21:4
Baker, Hiram Wilson, 1918, D 22,17:4
Baker, Hollis S, 1966, Je 14,47:2
Baker, Homer L, 1953, S 10,25:1
Baker, Horace, 1918, Mr 8,11:5
Baker, Horace R, 1952, Jl 9,27:2
Baker, Horace S, 1940, Mr 29,22:2
Baker, Howard F, 1954, Jl 28,23:3
Baker, Howard H (funl, Ja 10,43:3), 1964, Ja 8,37:3
Baker, Howard S, 1950, Je 23,25:2
Baker, Howard W, 1952, N 5,27:4
Baker, Howard W Mrs, 1961, D 28,27:2
Baker, Hubert J, 1950, D 9,15:5
Baker, Hugh B, 1964, D 16,44:1
Baker, Hugh B Mrs, 1954, Je 27,68:2
Baker, Hugh P, 1950, My 25,29:3
Baker, Hugh W, 1956, My 2,31:5
Baker, I Webster, 1949, D 1,31:3
Baker, Ida S Mrs, 1941, Mr 4,23:4
Baker, Irving E, 1951, Jl 30,17:4
Baker, Isaac V Jr, 1912, D 15,17:4
Baker, Iva B, 1937, Je 28,19:6
Baker, J A, 1903, Ap 30,9:6
Baker, J Arthur, 1951, Jl 18,29:4
Baker, J Edwards, 1950, Jl 17,21:4
Baker, J F, 1876, O 3,4:7
Baker, J Frederick, 1956, Je 3,86:7
Baker, J H Mrs, 1873, Mr 21,1:6
Baker, J Milton, 1948, O 15,23:3
Baker, J Stewart, 1966, S 7,47:1
Baker, J Thompson, 1919, D 8,15:4
Baker, J Whitney, 1949, N 2,12:3
Baker, Jack S, 1951, Ja 31,25:4
Baker, Jacob, 1967, S 20,47:1
Baker, James, 1885, Mr 10,2:3; 1943, S 13,19:5
Baker, James A, 1941, Ag 3,35:2
Baker, James Barnes (funl, Je 6,13:6), 1918, Je 4,13:7
Baker, James H, 1960, D 22,23:4
Baker, James H Gen, 1913, My 27,11:6
Baker, James Hutchins Dr, 1925, S 12,15:6
Baker, James M, 1940, N 22,23:2
Baker, James Mrs, 1948, Mr 15,23:4
Baker, James Shaw, 1904, N 22,5:3
Baker, James T, 1939, O 28,15:4
Baker, James T Mrs, 1914, Ag 10,7:4
Baker, Jane Mrs, 1953, S 14,27:4
Baker, Janie A Mrs, 1959, O 25,75:3
Baker, Jehu, 1903, Mr 2,9:5
Baker, Jewett C, 1942, F 11,21:4
Baker, John A Jr Mrs, 1962, S 15,25:4
Baker, John C, 1953, N 26,31:2
Baker, John C Jr, 1952, Mr 5,29:1
Baker, John C Mrs, 1948, N 23,29:2
Baker, John Earl, 1957, Jl 28,61:2
Baker, John Eugene, 1957, My 15,35:4
Baker, John F (Home Run), 1963, Je 29,23:2
Baker, John H, 1946, Ja 9,23:4; 1954, Ag 28,15:4
Baker, John H Mrs, 1952, My 29,27:2
Baker, John J, 1942, D 6,77:3; 1948, Je 23,27:2
Baker, John L, 1939, Ja 6,22:3; 1949, Jl 20,25:2; 1961, Ap 24,29:2
Baker, John L Mrs, 1959, Ag 13,27:5
Baker, John Lewis, 1873, Mr 23,5:5
Baker, John M, 1942, Mr 25,21:2
Baker, John Mrs, 1964, Jl 18,19:5
Baker, John P Mrs, 1911, S 11,9:3
Baker, John T, 1962, N 10,25:4
Baker, John W, 1939, Ja 30,14:2; 1945, Mr 14,19:2; 1966, D 30,25:1
Baker, John W Dr, 1925, Jl 26,5:3
Baker, John W Mrs, 1950, Mr 16,31:4
Baker, Johnny Mrs, 1956, Jl 17,23:2
Baker, Jonathan, 1948, Je 2,29:1
Baker, Joseph, 1947, Je 8,60:2
Baker, Joseph A, 1956, F 27,23:1
Baker, Joseph B, 1944, My 20,15:6; 1947, D 26,15:2
Baker, Joseph C, 1938, Mr 3,21:1
Baker, Joseph D, 1938, O 7,23:4
Baker, Joseph J, 1938, Mr 5,17:6
Baker, Joseph M, 1942, Ap 24,17:5
Baker, Joseph Mrs, 1960, S 22,27:5
Baker, Joseph R, 1946, Ja 10,23:1
Baker, Joseph S, 1947, S 2,21:4
Baker, Joseph W, 1937, Ag 29,II,7:1
Baker, Joshua, 1885, Ap 17,5:4
Baker, Joshua H, 1949, Jl 16,13:1
Baker, Joshua S, 1949, Je 4,13:5
Baker, Josiah Henry, 1903, Jl 18,7:6
Baker, Julian E, 1910, O 20,13:4
Baker, K Lanneau, 1962, Ja 28,76:5
Baker, Katherine, 1919, S 24,17:6

Baker, L H (L H Levy), 1960, My 28,21:2
Baker, Lafayette C, 1868, Jl 4,5:4
Baker, Lee, 1948, F 26,23:5
Baker, Leonard T, 1938, Je 18,15:4; 1955, Ja 7,21:3
Baker, Lester V, 1961, Ag 7,23:5
Baker, Leyland V, 1960, D 31,17:4
Baker, Lincoln T, 1961, Mr 15,39:5
Baker, Lorenzo D, 1950, Ja 17,27:2
Baker, Lorenzo Dow Capt, 1908, Je 22,7:4
Baker, Louis B Dr, 1907, F 27,9:6
Baker, Lucien Ex-Sen, 1907, Je 23,7:6
Baker, Lynn, 1968, Jl 30,39:1
Baker, Mae H, 1965, Jl 24,21:3
Baker, Marcus A, 1903, D 13,18:3
Baker, Margaret R, 1948, D 26,52:5
Baker, Marjorie M W Mrs (will), 1960, N 1,47:2
Baker, Martha A, 1952, Mr 18,27:2
Baker, Mary A, 1951, N 18,91:2
Baker, Mary C D Mrs, 1938, O 7,23:4
Baker, Mary E, 1949, O 18,27:2
Baker, Mary E Mrs, 1938, Je 10,21:5
Baker, Mary H Mrs, 1965, My 7,41:4
Baker, Mary J Mrs, 1938, Jl 19,21:5
Baker, Mary L, 1961, Jl 14,23:2
Baker, Matthew A, 1941, D 30,19:3
Baker, May A, 1925, O 2,23:5
Baker, Melville P, 1958, Ap 12,19:3
Baker, Mercy E, 1957, My 31,19:3
Baker, Mitchell, 1943, Mr 17,21:4
Baker, Moses N, 1955, F 7,21:1
Baker, Moses N Mrs, 1955, Mr 15,26:7
Baker, N B, 1876, S 15,2:6
Baker, N H, 1936, Jl 30,19:3
Baker, Newcombe C, 1952, Ag 3,60:1
Baker, Newcombe C Mrs, 1965, My 8,31:3
Baker, Newton D, 1937, D 26,1:3
Baker, Newton D Mrs, 1951, Ag 24,15:3
Baker, Nina B Mrs (Mrs S J Brown), 1957, S 3,27:2
Baker, Norman B, 1968, Ja 19,47:2
Baker, Norman B Mrs, 1967, D 4,47:2
Baker, Norman H Dr, 1937, Je 6,II,9:2
Baker, Norman R, 1938, O 21,23:4
Baker, O C Bishop, 1871, D 21,2:6
Baker, Oliver, 1939, Ap 12,23:4
Baker, Orrin H, 1949, Jl 14,27:5
Baker, Osborne E, 1949, Ja 16,68:4
Baker, Page M, 1910, My 29,II,7:4
Baker, Paul C, 1943, Ja 21,21:1
Baker, Paul G, 1960, N 29,37:2
Baker, Paul P, 1951, Je 6,31:1
Baker, Percy A, 1943, Je 5,15:5
Baker, Percy W, 1951, O 16,31:2
Baker, Peter S, 1953, Ja 30,22:5
Baker, Peter T, 1956, My 18,25:2
Baker, Phil, 1940, Je 5,25:4
Baker, Phil D, 1963, D 2,37:1
Baker, Purley Albert Dr, 1924, Mr 31,17:3
Baker, R Ray, 1949, My 3,25:5
Baker, R T, 1935, Ap 29,15:1
Baker, Ralph, 1939, Ag 24,19:6
Baker, Ralph J, 1952, F 26,27:2; 1966, N 6,89:1
Baker, Ray B, 1954, N 5,15:1
Baker, Ray S, 1946, Jl 13,14:2
Baker, Ray S Mrs, 1962, My 16,41:5
Baker, Raymond C, 1964, N 20,37:3
Baker, Raymond J, 1941, Ja 3,19:2
Baker, Reginald, 1953, D 9,11:1
Baker, Richard A, 1940, O 14,19:3
Baker, Richard C, 1910, D 19,9:4
Baker, Richard L, 1951, Ja 5,21:2
Baker, Richard W, 1937, F 9,23:3
Baker, Robert, 1943, Je 17,21:4
Baker, Robert D, 1951, D 5,35:2
Baker, Robert E Mrs, 1943, Ja 12,23:2
Baker, Robert P, 1940, S 6,21:5
Baker, Robert R Mrs, 1959, Jl 8,29:4
Baker, Robert W, 1958, D 4,39:4
Baker, Rowland T Mrs, 1942, O 14,25:3
Baker, Roy M, 1956, My 6,86:5
Baker, Roy W, 1945, N 6,19:5
Baker, Russell I, 1951, D 12,37:5
Baker, Russell J, 1961, S 16,19:6
Baker, S Josephine, 1945, F 23,17:1
Baker, Samuel, 1951, N 15,29:2
Baker, Samuel (Oct 2), 1965, O 11,61:1
Baker, Samuel H, 1947, My 28,26:2
Baker, Samuel S, 1938, S 6,21:4
Baker, Samuel White Sir (false report of), 1873, Ap 18,8:4
Baker, Seward, 1910, F 25,9:5
Baker, Shirley, 1948, F 12,23:4
Baker, Sidney T, 1950, Ag 26,13:2
Baker, Sidney T Mrs, 1956, D 23,30:7
Baker, Simon Mrs, 1943, Je 5,15:6
Baker, Somerville N, 1950, Ag 10,25:2
Baker, Stanley, 1940, D 9,19:1
Baker, Stephen (will, Ja 8,25:2), 1947, Ja 1,33:1
Baker, Stephen D, 1944, Mr 30,21:5
Baker, Stephen Mrs, 1948, Ja 19,23:2
Baker, Stetson, 1956, Jl 21,15:6
Baker, T Nelson Mrs, 1937, Je 28,19:3
Baker, Tarkington, 1924, Ja 2,17:3
Baker, Theodore C, 1944, O 8,44:2
Baker, Theodore Mrs, 1940, Ap 12,24:2
Baker, Thomas A, 1950, Ag 8,29:1
Baker, Thomas B, 1941, F 6,22:2
Baker, Thomas F, 1943, My 19,25:5
Baker, Thomas N, 1941, F 25,23:4
Baker, Thomas S, 1939, Ap 8,15:1
Baker, Thorne, 1942, Mr 14,15:5
Baker, Ulysses S G, 1954, F 5,19:5
Baker, Valentine, 1948, O 27,27:1
Baker, Valentine Gen, 1887, N 18,2:1
Baker, W F, 1930, D 5,25:3
Baker, W R G, 1960, O 31,31:3
Baker, W Ray, 1966, Je 9,47:2
Baker, W Reginald, 1953, Mr 8,91:2
Baker, Walter C, 1955, Ap 27,31:3
Baker, Walter C Mrs, 1946, Ap 22,21:5
Baker, Walter E, 1952, S 8,21:5
Baker, Walter H, 1947, Je 27,21:2
Baker, Walter Samuel Dr, 1914, O 27,11:3
Baker, Warren, 1949, Je 4,13:4
Baker, Webb, 1901, N 15,7:2
Baker, Wendell, 1943, Jl 27,17:4
Baker, William, 1872, My 25,1:5
Baker, William A, 1938, Ag 2,19:5; 1942, My 30,15:2
Baker, William B, 1911, My 18,11:6
Baker, William B Col, 1922, Mr 9,17:3
Baker, William C, 1942, My 24,43:3
Baker, William C Jr, 1966, O 8,31:1
Baker, William C Prof, 1937, D 6,27:5
Baker, William Cass, 1922, Ja 7,13:6
Baker, William E, 1942, N 26,27:5; 1954, Je 5,17:5
Baker, William Edgar, 1921, N 8,19:5
Baker, William G, 1948, D 29,21:5
Baker, William H, 1875, Je 2,6:6; 1915, F 26,9:6; 1915, S 22,11:6; 1938, My 13,20:2; 1943, Je 15,21:4; 1957, D 22,40:8
Baker, William H Dr, 1914, N 27,11:6
Baker, William H Jr, 1951, Mr 5,21:3
Baker, William H Maj, 1917, Ja 24,9:4
Baker, William H Mrs, 1960, S 11,82:5
Baker, William J, 1940, Ap 11,25:6; 1945, Mr 31,19:6; 1951, Ag 12,79:5
Baker, William L, 1967, D 21,37:4
Baker, William N T, 1941, My 30,15:3
Baker, William O, 1941, Jl 12,13:2
Baker, William P, 1951, Jl 13,21:1
Baker, William Wilson Prof, 1917, O 14,23:2
Baker, Willis Mrs, 1944, Ap 4,21:2
Baker, Wm J, 1903, O 8,9:5
Baker, Word Mrs, 1966, Je 14,47:1
Baketal, H Sheridan, 1955, Jl 8,23:1
Baketel, Annie M Mrs, 1942, O 6,23:1
Baketel, Oliver S Rev Dr, 1937, F 5,21:3
Baketel, Roy V, 1952, Mr 27,27:3
Bakewell, Allan Campbell Col, 1919, Mr 16,20:5
Bakewell, Charles M, 1957, S 20,25:1
Bakewell, Charles M Mrs, 1947, My 16,23:3
Bakewell, Claude Jr, 1962, Ap 1,75:1
Bakewell, Donald C, 1949, S 12,21:5
Bakewell, Paul Mrs, 1949, Ja 7,21:1
Bakewell, Thomas W, 1909, Jl 8,7:6
Bakh, Alexai N, 1946, My 16,21:3
Bakhmeteff, Boris A, 1951, Jl 22,60:3
Bakhmeteff, G, 1928, Ag 31,19:5
Bakhmeteff, George Mrs, 1925, Je 28,5:3
Bakic, Mitar, 1960, N 27,86:2
Bakius, Frank, 1941, N 24,8:2
Bakkar, Mohammed El, 1959, S 9,41:5
Bakke, C L, 1950, My 7,108:2
Bakken, Elmaar H, 1967, Mr 16,47:1
Bakken, S A, 1950, Ag 22,27:1
Bakker, Cornelis J, 1960, Ap 24,52:4
Bakker, Frederick J Rev, 1937, Ag 26,21:5
Baklanoff, George (por), 1938, D 7,23:4
Bakrow, Julian A Mrs, 1943, Ap 15,25:3
Bakst, Aaron, 1962, O 19,31:3
Bakst, Abraham, 1960, Ap 4,29:2
Bakst, Isaac Mrs, 1961, S 22,33:4
Bakst, Joseph, 1941, Ap 14,17:4
Bakst, Leon, 1924, D 28,5:1
Bakst, Max, 1943, N 13,13:6
Bal, William, 1944, N 23,31:5
Balaban, A J, 1962, N 3,25:3
Balaban, Burton, 1965, O 15,45:5
Balaban, David, 1949, Je 2,27:5
Balaban, David Mrs, 1950, Jl 10,21:2
Balaban, Gloria, 1953, Je 11,34:3
Balaban, John (will, Ap 16,24:1), 1957, Ap 5,27:4
Balaban, John Mrs, 1957, D 22,40:4
Balaban, Sophrony, 1949, O 11,34:5
Balabanoff, Angelica, 1965, N 26,37:3
Balabon, Carolina Mrs, 1945, D 21,21:1
Balaguer, Enrique M, 1947, Ap 21,27:2
Balagur, Martin, 1954, Mr 30,27:4
Balagur, Martin Mrs, 1946, Je 14,21:4
Balakian, Diran Mrs, 1954, Ja 16,15:5
Balakian, Krikor G, 1956, S 28,27:4
Balakin, Yakov, 1950, Je 10,17:3
Balance, Joseph, 1939, Ap 5,25:2
Balandin, Aleksei A, 1967, My 25,47:3
Balaniz, Carl R, 1958, S 9,35:3
Balanos, Nicholas, 1942, S 24,27:5
Balas, Bela C, 1958, F 17,23:2
Balaski, Les, 1964, S 2,43:6
Balassone, Peter, 1943, S 1,19:4
Balaszi, Albert, 1949, F 15,23:3
Balazs, Jeno, 1962, N 27,37:3
Balbach, Edward Jr, 1911, Ja 1,11:2
Balbirnie, Cadwalader D B, 1939, Ja 1,25:2
Balboa, Caesar, 1914, Jl 18,7:6
Balcells, Marian Rev (S J), 1911, O 3,13:5
Balcerak, Daniel, 1955, Jl 26,25:2
Balcerak, Joseph A, 1959, N 3,35:7
Balcerak, Victor, 1960, O 6,41:4
Balch, Allan C, 1943, My 1,15:3
Balch, Allan C Mrs, 1943, Ag 5,15:2
Balch, David R, 1966, F 15,36:4
Balch, Edward C Mrs, 1945, My 2,23:5
Balch, Edwin S Mrs, 1953, Jl 4,11:6
Balch, Emily G, 1961, Ja 11,47:1
Balch, Ernest B, 1938, Ap 30,15:5
Balch, Evertt P, 1959, D 17,37:1
Balch, Frank, 1937, O 31,II,10:7
Balch, Frank A, 1939, D 13,27:2
Balch, Frederic S, 1959, Je 6,21:4
Balch, George O, 1945, Mr 7,21:1
Balch, Glen E, 1944, N 24,23:2
Balch, Glen E Mrs, 1957, Ag 6,27:4
Balch, Harry N, 1964, Ap 16,37:1
Balch, John, 1944, My 26,19:3
Balch, Lewis Maj, 1909, Ag 11,7:5
Balch, Samuel W, 1940, Jl 23,19:1
Balch, Wallace W Mrs, 1944, F 12,13:1
Balch, William Ralston, 1923, Mr 9,15:4
Balckwood, Norman J (por), 1938, Ap 3,II,7:1
Balcoff, Theodore Mrs, 1945, Mr 7,21:4
Balcom, Alfred B, 1943, S 22,23:5
Balcom, Arthur G, 1942, Mr 1,44:3
Balcom, Arthur Mrs, 1956, Jl 22,61:3
Balcom, Homer G (por), 1938, Jl 5,17:3
Balcom, Homer G Mrs, 1947, Je 10,27:3
Balcom, Lowell L, 1938, Mr 13,II,8:8
Balcom, Max F, 1966, Ja 19,41:4
Balcom, Sarah M Mrs, 1923, Ag 25,7:5
Balcombe, Bertram G, 1952, Je 15,84:4
Bald, Edward C Sr, 1946, Jl 2,25:2
Bald, Robert C, 1965, Ag 24,31:4
Baldauf, Herman, 1954, Jl 14,27:3
Balder, Sylvan C, 1957, Mr 1,23:4
Balderson, Robert, 1940, Ap 13,17:4
Balderston, Ella M Mrs, 1939, N 5,49:2
Balderston, Henry L, 1953, F 12,27:4
Balderston, Henry L Mrs, 1953, F 12,27:4
Balderston, John C, 1905, Mr 22,9:6
Balderston, John L, 1954, Mr 10,25:1
Balderston, Joseph W, 1939, S 8,23:2
Balderston, Joseph W Mrs, 1956, Ap 11,33:5
Balderston, Lydia R, 1951, F 27,27:2
Balderston, Mark, 1960, D 21,31:2
Balderston, William Mrs, 1950, N 6,27:4
Baldi, Joseph A, 1948, N 7,89:1
Baldin, Siluan F, 1961, Ap 29,23:5
Balding, Alice H, 1960, Mr 6,84:4
Balding, Gerald M, 1957, S 17,35:1
Balding, John B, 1963, S 10,39:2
Baldini, Gino A, 1960, Ag 19,23:5
Baldomir, Alfredo, 1948, F 26,23:3
Baldowski, George H Jr, 1948, Ja 21,25:3
Baldrick, Charles, 1940, F 7,21:4
Baldridge, Anthony O R (funl plans, D 26,19:4), 1957, D 25,31:6
Baldridge, Carl, 1949, Jl 2,15:7
Baldridge, Claude C, 1961, S 20,29:4
Baldridge, Fanny M (Mrs B V Butterfield), 1961, S 6,37:2
Baldridge, Felix E Mrs, 1961, Jl 25,27:4
Baldridge, H Clarence, 1947, Je 9,21:6
Baldridge, Harry A, 1952, Ja 10,29:1
Baldridge, J Lakin, 1967, Ag 8,39:3
Baldridge, J Lakin Mrs, 1940, Ap 23,24:3; 1952, My 15,31:4
Baldridge, Ralph B, 1946, Jl 16,24:2
Baldus, Francis G, 1947, N 24,23:1
Baldus, Simon A, 1957, Ja 21,25:6
Baldwin, A Clyde, 1952, N 27,31:2
Baldwin, A M, 1866, S 12,2:4
Baldwin, A Stuart, 1922, Je 28,15:5
Baldwin, A W, 1869, N 16,5:1
Baldwin, Aaron G, 1952, N 26,23:1
Baldwin, Abraham R, 1950, O 23,23:5
Baldwin, Albert D Mrs, 1945, Ag 14,21:2
Baldwin, Albert F, 1967, Ja 14,31:5
Baldwin, Albert Jr, 1915, Mr 12,11:6
Baldwin, Albertus H, 1944, Mr 22,19:5
Baldwin, Alfred C, 1957, D 22,40:6
Baldwin, Alice M, 1960, O 13,37:5
Baldwin, Allen T Mrs, 1958, O 10,31:4
Baldwin, Anita M Mrs, 1939, O 26,23:3
Baldwin, Anna L, 1945, O 17,19:2
Baldwin, Arthur C, 1960, F 25,29:6
Baldwin, Arthur D, 1955, Mr 11,25:3
Baldwin, Arthur J, 1939, Jl 22,15:3
Baldwin, Arthur L, 1951, Ja 1,17:2
Baldwin, Arthur M, 1954, F 9,27:6
Baldwin, Arthur Mrs, 1944, N 9,27:4
Baldwin, Austin R Mrs, 1943, Mr 16,19:3

Baldwin, Baldwin M Mrs, 1940, D 4,27:3
Baldwin, Beecher H, 1967, Je 19,35:2
Baldwin, Bruce, 1941, My 29,19:3
Baldwin, C C, 1897, My 13,7:6
Baldwin, C Colmbus, 1924, My 10,13:5
Baldwin, Caleb Cook Rev Dr, 1911, Jl 21,9:6
Baldwin, Caleb E, 1955, Jl 27,23:5
Baldwin, Carroll, 1918, My 15,13:4
Baldwin, Charles, 1937, Mr 8,19:5
Baldwin, Charles A, 1949, Mr 12,18:3
Baldwin, Charles B, 1913, Mr 25,13:4
Baldwin, Charles C, 1955, Ja 22,11:2; 1963, O 26,27:1
Baldwin, Charles E, 1956, My 13,86:7
Baldwin, Charles E Mrs, 1957, Ja 13,84:1
Baldwin, Charles F Maj, 1912, N 6,15:4
Baldwin, Charles G, 1939, Ag 31,19:4
Baldwin, Charles H, 1937, Ja 11,19:2; 1942, Mr 14, 15:6; 1948, Ja 27,26:3; 1949, S 12,21:5; 1958, My 3, 19:3
Baldwin, Charles H Mrs, 1940, Ja 22,15:3
Baldwin, Charles M, 1952, S 30,31:1
Baldwin, Charles T, 1944, D 14,23:1
Baldwin, Charles W, 1938, Jl 16,13:4; 1939, Jl 16,30:7; 1960, O 21,33:2
Baldwin, Chauncey Clark, 1923, Je 8,19:5
Baldwin, Clarence F, 1949, Ap 15,23:3
Baldwin, Clarence M, 1947, Ap 19,15:2
Baldwin, Clarke T, 1939, Ja 3,17:2
Baldwin, Clifford A, 1946, N 21,32:2
Baldwin, Clifford A Sr, 1953, Ap 14,27:4
Baldwin, Clinton A, 1948, My 4,25:1
Baldwin, Conrad A Mrs, 1961, Ap 7,31:3
Baldwin, Dale S, 1952, Jl 18,19:3
Baldwin, Dalton G, 1959, My 29,7:2
Baldwin, Dalton G Mrs, 1959, My 29,7:2
Baldwin, David Asa, 1919, N 12,13:3
Baldwin, David H, 1941, Mr 19,21:5
Baldwin, Dayton, 1942, Mr 19,21:5
Baldwin, Dayton A, 1953, Je 11,29:2
Baldwin, Duncan M, 1952, Jl 14,17:2
Baldwin, E Arthur (por), 1947, S 30,25:3
Baldwin, E F, 1914, N 20,9:7
Baldwin, Eben, 1903, O 10,9:6
Baldwin, Edna K Mrs, 1948, F 15,60:3
Baldwin, Edward C, 1940, Jl 10,19:1
Baldwin, Edward H, 1938, Ja 31,19:4
Baldwin, Edward J, 1906, Ja 11,9:5
Baldwin, Edward R (por), 1947, My 7,27:1
Baldwin, Edward R Mrs, 1957, Ap 7,88:1
Baldwin, Edwin, 1918, My 9,13:8
Baldwin, Edwin Candee Dr, 1913, O 4,13:4
Baldwin, Elbert, 1947, D 7,78:4
Baldwin, Elbert F Mrs, 1944, N 22,19:7
Baldwin, Elbert H, 1906, Je 27,7:6
Baldwin, Eleanor D, 1951, Ja 17,27:3
Baldwin, Eli N, 1946, D 31,17:4
Baldwin, Elias B Capt, 1913, Ja 12,II,17:1
Baldwin, Elias B Col, 1921, Mr 27,22:3
Baldwin, Elias Johnson (Lucky Baldwin), 1909, Mr 2,9:5
Baldwin, Elizabeth, 1939, N 30,21:4
Baldwin, Elizabeth G, 1964, Ag 21,29:3
Baldwin, Elizabeth J, 1948, N 6,13:5
Baldwin, Ellis K, 1951, D 28,21:4
Baldwin, Ernest C, 1947, N 3,23:4
Baldwin, Ernest E, 1949, Jl 11,17:3
Baldwin, Ernest H, 1939, Jl 30,29:1
Baldwin, F Elmore, 1957, Je 24,23:5
Baldwin, F W, 1928, Mr 28,27:4
Baldwin, Florence, 1965, Mr 7,82:8
Baldwin, Florence Mrs, 1918, Jl 22,11:6
Baldwin, Francis M, 1951, F 3,15:6
Baldwin, Francis W, 1961, Je 5,31:3
Baldwin, Francis X, 1948, S 24,25:2
Baldwin, Frank, 1959, O 22,37:6
Baldwin, Frank C, 1945, N 26,21:5
Baldwin, Frank C Mrs, 1954, My 4,29:2
Baldwin, Frank D Gen, 1923, Ap 24,21:4
Baldwin, Frank E, 1943, Ag 10,19:2
Baldwin, Frank G, 1905, My 8,9:6; 1943, Ap 20,23:5
Baldwin, Frank L, 1946, Ap 16,25:1
Baldwin, Frank O, 1937, Ja 25,19:2
Baldwin, Frank P, 1956, My 29,27:5
Baldwin, Frank S, 1925, Ap 9,23:5
Baldwin, Frank T Sr, 1945, Mr 16,15:3
Baldwin, Frank V, 1956, Ja 10,31:1
Baldwin, Fred C, 1939, My 2,23:5; 1952, Jl 23,23:3
Baldwin, Fred D, 1948, Ap 15,25:6
Baldwin, Fred H, 1938, N 12,15:1
Baldwin, Fred J, 1941, O 2,25:4
Baldwin, Fred S, 1958, N 21,29:3
Baldwin, Frederick S, 1948, F 7,15:2
Baldwin, Frederick W, 1948, Ag 8,56:5; 1958, Ja 16, 30:1
Baldwin, G J, 1927, Mr 6,26:1
Baldwin, Ganson J, 1954, Ap 7,31:4
Baldwin, Geoffrey P, 1951, Ag 26,9:4
Baldwin, George, 1914, Jl 24,9:6
Baldwin, George A, 1944, S 6,19:5
Baldwin, George C, 1948, O 4,23:3
Baldwin, George D, 1946, N 12,29:1
Baldwin, George E, 1907, Ap 17,9:6; 1967, N 10,47:3
Baldwin, George E Jr, 1959, Ag 14,21:2
Baldwin, George F, 1958, Jl 1,31:1
Baldwin, George H, 1949, F 2,27:3
Baldwin, George L, 1954, Ja 27,27:2
Baldwin, George S, 1948, S 17,25:5
Baldwin, George Van N, 1943, Ag 25,19:1
Baldwin, George Van Ness, 1908, F 25,7:4
Baldwin, George W, 1905, Je 25,7:2; 1939, N 10,23:4
Baldwin, Gilman E, 1942, O 21,21:5
Baldwin, Grove, 1951, O 17,31:1
Baldwin, Grover C, 1953, O 5,27:5
Baldwin, H M Lt, 1864, N 22,2:2
Baldwin, H R Dr, 1902, F 4,9:5
Baldwin, H Reed, 1952, F 23,26:6
Baldwin, Hannah J Mrs, 1941, Je 22,32:6
Baldwin, Harold A Mrs, 1961, Ja 6,27:3
Baldwin, Harold W, 1954, Mr 17,31:1
Baldwin, Harris H, 1950, N 14,31:3
Baldwin, Harry B, 1942, Je 25,23:5
Baldwin, Harry C, 1939, O 18,25:5
Baldwin, Harry R, 1950, Ag 12,13:2
Baldwin, Harry S, 1948, Ap 10,13:4
Baldwin, Harry W, 1945, D 4,29:5
Baldwin, Harry Wilbur, 1921, Jl 27,15:5
Baldwin, Harvey, 1942, My 9,13:6
Baldwin, Helen, 1946, Ap 20,13:3
Baldwin, Helen M, 1943, Ja 20,19:2
Baldwin, Helen R Mrs, 1938, Jl 30,13:4
Baldwin, Henry D (por), 1947, My 19,21:4
Baldwin, Herbert B, 1939, My 15,17:6
Baldwin, Herbert L, 1950, O 14,19:4
Baldwin, Herbert Mrs, 1950, My 4,27:5
Baldwin, Howard, 1961, Ag 2,29:4
Baldwin, Howard C, 1963, Je 28,29:2
Baldwin, Howard Mrs, 1948, Je 25,23:2
Baldwin, Hugh C, 1942, Je 30,21:4
Baldwin, Ivy, 1953, O 10,17:4
Baldwin, J, 1884, D 30,5:5
Baldwin, J A Col, 1903, Mr 16,9:4
Baldwin, J D, 1883, Jl 9,4:7
Baldwin, J Dixon Roman, 1912, Jl 6,7:6
Baldwin, J Frank, 1968, Mr 10,92:6
Baldwin, J Frank Mrs, 1955, D 27,23:1
Baldwin, J M, 1934, N 9,21:3
Baldwin, James, 1925, S 3,25:6
Baldwin, James C, 1910, O 2,II,13:4; 1956, S 26,33:3
Baldwin, James F, 1950, O 7,17:1
Baldwin, James H, 1941, Ap 22,21:1; 1953, Ja 24,15:6
Baldwin, James L, 1938, My 29,II,6:6
Baldwin, James M Mrs, 1963, Jl 6,15:4
Baldwin, James R Mrs, 1948, Mr 7,68:3
Baldwin, Janet S (Mrs H C Maier), 1958, S 19,28:1
Baldwin, Jesse H, 1914, F 9,7:4
Baldwin, John C, 1939, Jl 4,13:5
Baldwin, John D Mrs, 1943, My 27,25:4
Baldwin, John F, 1966, Mr 10,33:1
Baldwin, John H Gen, 1912, Ag 3,7:4
Baldwin, John J, 1951, Ag 16,27:3
Baldwin, John L, 1938, S 20,23:6
Baldwin, John L Mrs, 1960, My 5,35:2
Baldwin, John M, 1958, Ja 7,47:2
Baldwin, Joseph, 1954, Ja 30,17:5
Baldwin, Joseph A, 1949, Ja 6,23:1
Baldwin, Joseph C, 1937, D 30,19:5; 1957, O 28,27:1
Baldwin, Joseph C Mrs, 1948, Ja 9,22:3
Baldwin, Joseph M Dr, 1937, Ja 6,23:5
Baldwin, Joseph S, 1950, Ja 9,26:4
Baldwin, Julius, 1941, Ja 8,19:3
Baldwin, Lathrop E, 1945, N 6,19:3
Baldwin, Lauris B, 1940, O 9,25:2
Baldwin, LaVerne, 1968, Jl 16,39:4
Baldwin, Lemuel Grant Dr, 1923, Ja 1,15:5
Baldwin, Leonard, 1962, Ap 27,35:1
Baldwin, Leroy W, 1939, Mr 7,22:3
Baldwin, Lewis A, 1949, Jl 29,21:3
Baldwin, Lewis L, 1959, Jl 10,25:4
Baldwin, Lewis W, 1946, My 15,21:3
Baldwin, Llewellyn, 1941, N 27,23:4
Baldwin, Lucien E, 1937, My 1,19:4
Baldwin, Lucille F Mrs, 1942, O 8,27:5
Baldwin, Marc L, 1958, O 10,31:4
Baldwin, Margaret B, 1957, O 11,27:2
Baldwin, Margaret Mrs, 1939, Ap 14,23:4
Baldwin, Mary C Mrs, 1950, Jl 6,27:4
Baldwin, Mary E, 1942, Jl 30,21:3
Baldwin, Mary G, 1945, D 16,40:2
Baldwin, Mary G Mrs, 1938, D 11,60:5
Baldwin, Mary M L Mrs, 1957, Jl 22,19:3
Baldwin, Merritt W Mrs, 1962, N 27,37:2
Baldwin, Morris G, 1954, Ja 5,27:3
Baldwin, Neil S, 1948, Ja 20,23:3
Baldwin, Norman L, 1945, O 19,23:6
Baldwin, O P, 1878, Jl 18,5:5
Baldwin, Octavius D, 1904, Mr 29,9:5
Baldwin, Oliver P Jr Mrs, 1950, D 13,35:3
Baldwin, Percival B, 1958, Je 20,23:5
Baldwin, Perry Oakley Rev, 1914, Ap 11,11:5
Baldwin, R D (Pete), 1951, My 30,21:3
Baldwin, R L Sr, 1950, S 25,23:1
Baldwin, Ralph L, 1943, O 1,19:3; 1960, O 30,86:3
Baldwin, Richard G, 1945, Ja 15,19:2
Baldwin, Richard J, 1944, Je 16,19:6
Baldwin, Rignal W, 1937, Ja 3,II,8:6
Baldwin, Robert H, 1955, N 18,25:5
Baldwin, Robert M, 1953, Ja 29,28:3
Baldwin, Robert T, 1960, Jl 14,27:4
Baldwin, Roger S (por), 1949, Mr 24,27:3
Baldwin, Roger S Mrs, 1960, Ap 22,31:3
Baldwin, Rogers N Mrs, 1962, Je 13,41:4
Baldwin, Roy A, 1941, N 1,15:4
Baldwin, Runyon S, 1963, O 3,35:2
Baldwin, S E, 1927, Ja 31,17:3
Baldwin, S W, 1927, Jl 19,23:3
Baldwin, Samuel A (por), 1949, S 16,27:3
Baldwin, Samuel H, 1950, Ja 25,27:2
Baldwin, Samuel P, 1939, Ja 1,24:7
Baldwin, Samuel P Mrs, 1948, D 28,21:5
Baldwin, Samuel Y, 1924, My 27,21:5
Baldwin, Simeon, 1918, F 12,11:2
Baldwin, Spencer D, 1951, Je 11,25:5
Baldwin, Stanley E, 1950, Mr 21,29:1
Baldwin, Stanley Everett Dr, 1968, Jl 26,33:2
Baldwin, Stanley Mrs, 1945, Je 19,19:3
Baldwin, Stephen C, 1923, Jl 29,6:3
Baldwin, Stephen C Mrs, 1956, Ja 9,25:1
Baldwin, Summerfield 3d, 1955, Ja 17,23:5
Baldwin, Sylvester D, 1923, N 8,19:5
Baldwin, Theodore A Gen, 1925, S 3,25:4
Baldwin, Thomas F, 1923, Ap 28,13:3
Baldwin, Thomas Scott, 1923, My 18,19:3
Baldwin, Thomas W, 1944, F 7,15:4; 1948, Ja 19,23:1
Baldwin, Tillie (Mrs A M W Slate), 1958, O 24,33:3
Baldwin, Townsend Burnet, 1919, S 29,13:1
Baldwin, W B, 1902, F 2,7:2
Baldwin, W B Adm, 1866, Ja 15,2:7
Baldwin, W Baron Mrs, 1961, Ap 19,39:3
Baldwin, W Barton, 1945, F 4,38:7
Baldwin, Walter, 1951, Ja 26,23:1
Baldwin, Wilbur M, 1938, N 7,19:3
Baldwin, Willard A Mrs, 1918, O 18,13:2
Baldwin, William A, 1945, D 16,40:1
Baldwin, William B Mrs, 1948, Jl 17,15:5
Baldwin, William E, 1952, My 25,92:8
Baldwin, William F, 1950, N 11,15:6
Baldwin, William H, 1946, Jl 27,17:4; 1958, Ja 21,26:7
Baldwin, William H Jr, 1960, Ap 20,39:3
Baldwin, William Henry, 1905, Ja 4,9:3; 1909, Je 9, 7:3; 1917, Mr 7,11:6
Baldwin, William J, 1944, Ap 4,21:6
Baldwin, William J Jr, 1945, My 29,15:3
Baldwin, William James, 1924, My 8,19:4
Baldwin, William L, 1945, Jl 30,19:5
Baldwin, William M, 1942, Ja 5,17:5
Baldwin, William M Mrs, 1938, Ap 2,15:4
Baldwin, William O Mrs, 1955, Mr 11,25:3
Baldwin, William S, 1947, S 5,19:4
Baldwin, William W, 1954, O 18,25:5
Baldwin, Winfield H, 1950, Je 18,76:7
Baldwin of Bewdley, Oliver Earl, 1958, Ag 11,21:3
Baldy, Frederic C, 1959, N 15,87:1
Bale, Albert B, 1943, My 8,15:1
Bale, Frederick S, 1968, Ap 3,51:1
Bale, Frederick S Mrs, 1964, S 21,31:1
Bale, Henry B, 1939, Jl 20,19:6
Bale, Henry D, 1951, My 10,31:2
Bale, John, 1882, Ap 3,5:3
Balek, Frank, 1947, My 26,21:2
Balen, Harry, 1962, Ap 17,35:3
Balendonck, Armand, 1956, Je 28,29:4
Balentine, Edward D, 1951, Ja 31,25:5
Balentine, James R, 1942, O 21,21:5
Balentine, Percy L, 1951, D 12,37:2
Balentine, William H, 1948, N 19,27:4
Bales, James A, 1961, F 18,19:5
Balester, Henry Wolcott Mrs, 1919, Mr 24,13:3
Balestier, B S, 1936, Jl 30,19:6
Balestier, Elliot, 1939, O 19,23:4
Balestier, W, 1891, D 9,8:2
Balestrieri, Michael, 1953, Ag 14,19:3
Balfe, Harry, 1944, Ap 24,19:3
Balfe, Harry Mrs, 1951, Ja 24,27:3
Balfe, Harry R, 1965, Ap 4,87:3
Balfe, Joseph, 1881, S 6,2:1
Balfe, Kieran, 1953, Jl 31,19:2
Balfe, M W, 1870, O 22,1:2
Balfe, Thomas W, 1962, Ja 16,33:2
Balfe, Thomas W Mrs, 1956, Ap 12,31:3
Balfour, Arthur (Lord Riverdale), 1957, Jl 8,23:4
Balfour, David A, 1956, D 4,39:4
Balfour, Donald C, 1963, Jl 27,17:5
Balfour, Earl of, 1930, Mr 20,1:2
Balfour, Earl of (Robt Arth Lytton Balfour), 1968, D 4,43:2
Balfour, Eustace James Col, 1911, F 15,9:4
Balfour, F M Prof, 1882, Ag 7,5:1
Balfour, George, 1941, S 28,48:3
Balfour, H L, 1946, D 29,37:2
Balfour, Henry, 1939, F 10,23:3
Balfour, Henry H, 1960, Mr 24,17:2
Balfour, Jabez Spencer, 1916, F 24,13:5
Balfour, Lord, 1945, Ja 16,20:2
Balfour, Murray, 1965, Je 1,39:3
Balfour, Robert, 1952, O 14,31:2
Balfour, Robert A, 1915, F 12,9:6
Balfour-Meville, Leslie, 1937, Jl 17,15:7
Balfour of Burleigh, Lord (G J G B Balfour), 1967, Je 7,51:3

Balgarnie, William H, 1951, Jl 18,29:1
Balgleish, James R, 1954, N 17,31:1
Balicer, Simon, 1953, Mr 13,27:4
Balieff, N, 1936, S 4,19:4
Balin, Mireille, 1968, N 10,88:8
Balina, Pedro, 1949, My 4,29:6
Balinas, Bolivar, 1950, N 15,31:4
Baline, Benjamin M, 1953, My 13,29:5
Balinsky, Charles V, 1947, Ag 22,15:4
Balint, Alex, 1948, Jl 5,15:5
Baliozian, Mardick L, 1943, N 11,23:4
Balke, Clarence W, 1948, Jl 9,19:5
Balke, Richard, 1949, O 27,27:2
Balke, Rudolph F, 1942, Je 5,17:6
Balken, Edward D, 1960, Ap 12,33:4
Balkovic, Samuel Mrs, 1941, Je 26,23:1
Balkwill, Percy S, 1937, F 18,21:3
Ball, A M Rev, 1903, Je 9,9:6
Ball, Abraham, 1945, Ja 25,19:5
Ball, Albert H Rev Dr, 1937, D 4,17:3
Ball, Alfred A, 1939, D 30,15:2
Ball, Alfred J, 1966, O 2,86:5
Ball, Alice E, 1948, Ap 25,71:3
Ball, Alice L, 1942, Ja 18,42:4
Ball, Alpheus M, 1968, F 15,43:1
Ball, Alwyn Jr, 1937, Mr 15,23:5
Ball, Alwyn 3d, 1944, N 11,13:2
Ball, Amos, 1954, D 26,61:2
Ball, Ancell H, 1943, Ja 9,13:3
Ball, Archey D, 1955, Ap 13,29:4
Ball, Arthur A Sr, 1956, Ag 21,29:4
Ball, Arthur E, 1957, N 2,21:1
Ball, Austin, 1948, Jl 25,48:6
Ball, Beatrice V, 1963, O 24,33:2
Ball, Bobby, 1954, F 28,92:6
Ball, Caroline P Mrs, 1938, O 3,15:2
Ball, Cecil, 1951, Jl 2,23:2
Ball, Charles, 1953, My 22,27:1
Ball, Charles F, 1941, O 29,23:4; 1961, Ja 12,29:1
Ball, Clarence E, 1944, Mr 9,17:5
Ball, Clarence F, 1949, My 16,21:4
Ball, Claude C, 1952, Ja 20,85:2
Ball, David C, 1951, Mr 25,72:3
Ball, David H, 1940, F 4,40:8
Ball, David W, 1940, O 31,23:5
Ball, E Arthur, 1947, Ap 18,22:2
Ball, Edmund B Mrs, 1957, O 9,35:3
Ball, Edward E Mrs, 1950, O 26,31:4
Ball, Edward H, 1941, S 10,23:5
Ball, Eliza Mrs, 1942, Ag 8,8:4
Ball, Ella C, 1942, N 20,23:2
Ball, Elmer D, 1943, O 6,23:4
Ball, Emma W Mrs, 1942, N 16,19:5
Ball, Ernest E, 1948, Mr 17,25:2
Ball, Eva L, 1939, My 7,III,7:3
Ball, Francis K, 1942, Je 10,21:2
Ball, Frank A, 1943, Mr 8,15:4
Ball, Frank C, 1943, Mr 20,15:1
Ball, Frank C Mrs, 1944, Jl 1,15:4
Ball, Frank M, 1938, Ap 12,24:2
Ball, Frank P, 1944, Je 18,36:3
Ball, Frederick H, 1940, Jl 23,19:3
Ball, Frederick S, 1958, Ap 23,33:3
Ball, Frederick W Jr, 1944, Ja 26,19:5
Ball, George, 1940, F 18,43:6
Ball, George A, 1955, O 23,87:1
Ball, George E A, 1966, N 27,86:8
Ball, George H Dr, 1907, F 22,9:6
Ball, George L, 1945, O 9,21:1
Ball, George M Jr, 1956, Jl 26,25:3
Ball, George M Mrs, 1960, D 23,19:1
Ball, Gordon R, 1959, Mr 1,86:6
Ball, Grant A Mrs, 1946, Ap 29,22:2
Ball, Halsey J, 1941, Je 2,19:7
Ball, Hampton E Mrs, 1904, F 24,9:6
Ball, Harold A, 1953, O 1,29:3
Ball, Harold H, 1942, N 21,13:5
Ball, Helen, 1943, O 18,15:6
Ball, Henry A, 1914, Ap 28,13:5
Ball, Henry P, 1941, My 3,15:6
Ball, Herman F, 1955, N 27,88:5
Ball, Hibbard O, 1959, Mr 15,89:1
Ball, Hugh G, 1951, F 1,25:3
Ball, Jay O (por), 1947, Mr 27,27:5
Ball, John, 1940, D 3,25:1
Ball, John C, 1950, Ap 21,23:3
Ball, John D, 1945, F 11,38:3
Ball, John N, 1938, F 4,21:1
Ball, John R, 1941, Ja 7,23:3; 1953, Mr 3,27:4
Ball, John W, 1952, O 25,17:4
Ball, Joseph, 1945, Ap 24,19:3
Ball, Joseph A, 1951, Ag 31,15:3
Ball, Joseph Mrs, 1947, S 12,22:3
Ball, Katherine, 1938, N 25,23:4
Ball, L H, 1933, O 19,19:3
Ball, Laurence A, 1938, O 17,15:4
Ball, Louise C, 1946, Je 2,44:6
Ball, Lucy O Mrs, 1941, Ja 24,17:1
Ball, Margaret, 1952, Ja 5,11:3
Ball, Margaret C, 1949, Ja 14,23:2
Ball, Martin A, 1941, Ap 9,25:4
Ball, Max W, 1954, Ag 30,17:5
Ball, Mendel, 1960, Jl 21,27:2
Ball, Nattie L, 1947, O 11,17:4
Ball, Neal, 1957, O 16,32:6
Ball, Nelson A Sr, 1949, Ap 30,13:4
Ball, Norman, 1951, O 13,17:2
Ball, Otho F Mrs, 1945, D 8,17:2
Ball, P de C, 1933, O 23,15:4
Ball, Phil H, 1938, F 4,21:1
Ball, Philip M, 1947, Ja 8,23:2
Ball, Ralph H Mrs, 1954, D 1,31:2
Ball, Richard G, 1948, N 29,23:3
Ball, Robert, 1953, Ja 23,19:1
Ball, Robert S, 1961, Jl 10,21:4
Ball, Robert Stawell Sir, 1913, N 26,11:6
Ball, Roome Van B, 1960, S 21,29:6
Ball, Russell C Sr, 1966, F 12,27:5
Ball, Sarah B, 1962, O 26,31:3
Ball, Stanley C, 1956, Ag 11,13:6
Ball, Stephen C, 1942, Ap 1,21:5
Ball, Stephen J, 1925, N 15,13:1
Ball, Suzan (funl, Ag 10,25:3), 1955, Ag 6,15:3
Ball, Sydney H (por), 1949, Ap 10,77:1
Ball, Sydney H Mrs, 1945, D 7,21:3
Ball, T A, 1914, Je 26,13:6
Ball, T W, 1934, Ja 26,17:3
Ball, Thomas, 1911, D 12,11:5
Ball, Thomas A, 1946, N 16,19:4
Ball, Thomas H, 1938, Je 20,15:3; 1943, O 19,19:6; 1944, My 8,19:6
Ball, Thomas L, 1968, Mr 23,31:4
Ball, Thomas R, 1943, Je 18,22:2
Ball, Thomas Richard, 1911, D 22,13:5
Ball, Thomas V Sr, 1951, Ap 29,88:6
Ball, Walter, 1944, Ag 6,38:1
Ball, Walter S, 1938, N 4,23:3
Ball, Warren P, 1950, Ja 28,13:5
Ball, Webb C, 1922, Mr 9,17:2
Ball, Wilbur L, 1941, N 16,56:4
Ball, William, 1943, Jl 18,34:8
Ball, William A Capt, 1911, Ap 23,11:5
Ball, William B, 1964, My 4,29:2
Ball, William G, 1945, Jl 19,23:4
Ball, William H, 1937, S 15,23:5
Ball, William H Mrs, 1951, Jl 22,61:3
Ball, William W, 1952, O 15,31:4
Ball, Willis M (por), 1947, S 13,11:3
Ball-Hughes, Georgina, 1911, O 11,11:6
Balla, Franz, 1937, F 22,17:2
Balla, Paul de, 1961, D 18,35:4
Ballagh, James C, 1944, S 29,21:1
Ballaine, Francis K, 1964, N 3,31:2
Ballaine, John E, 1941, Ja 17,17:1
Ballance, William A Mrs, 1949, Je 3,25:2
Ballantine, Arthur A, 1960, O 12,39:2
Ballantine, Arthur A Mrs, 1966, Ja 25,41:4
Ballantine, E J (Edw Jas Ballantine), 1968, O 22, 47:4
Ballantine, Henry W, 1951, D 5,36:2
Ballantine, Henry W Rev Dr, 1919, Jl 29,9:2
Ballantine, Isabel A, 1946, Je 23,40:3
Ballantine, J, 1877, D 19,4:7
Ballantine, John H, 1946, Je 8,21:5
Ballantine, John Holme Mrs, 1919, N 16,22:4
Ballantine, Josephine P Mrs, 1940, N 18,19:2
Ballantine, Norman A, 1968, Ja 21,77:1
Ballantine, P H, 1882, S 17,7:5
Ballantine, Percy, 1954, My 29,15:4
Ballantine, Peter, 1883, Ja 24,5:4
Ballantine, Peter S, 1957, D 18,41:8
Ballantine, Robert F, 1905, D 11,7:2
Ballantine, William G Rev Dr, 1937, Ja 11,20:2
Ballantyne, Charles C, 1950, O 20,28:3
Ballantyne, John, 1937, D 28,22:4; 1938, Mr 31,23:1
Ballantyne, John (por), 1949, Je 11,18:6
Ballantyne, Lewis B (por), 1947, S 30,25:4
Ballantyne, Robert A, 1953, F 6,20:4
Ballard, Aaron Edward Dr, 1919, N 28,13:1
Ballard, Addison Rev, 1914, D 3,13:3
Ballard, Alfred H, 1923, My 1,21:4
Ballard, Arba C, 1952, Je 23,19:4
Ballard, Arthur M, 1951, Je 7,33:4
Ballard, Arthur M Mrs, 1961, S 19,35:4
Ballard, Benjamin H, 1957, Mr 7,29:4
Ballard, Bland Judge, 1879, Jl 30,1:6
Ballard, Charles C, 1949, Ag 1,17:4
Ballard, Charles D, 1942, O 16,19:5
Ballard, Charles S, 1949, Ja 15,17:2
Ballard, Charles W, 1963, Je 29,23:3
Ballard, Colin R, 1941, Je 19,21:5
Ballard, Cora P Mrs, 1938, Jl 9,13:4
Ballard, Edward F, 1948, Mr 20,13:6
Ballard, Edward H Mrs, 1959, Ag 2,81:2
Ballard, Edward L, 1938, Ja 1,19:4
Ballard, Edward L Mrs, 1964, Je 16,39:2
Ballard, Edward T, 1944, Mr 21,19:6
Ballard, Edwin M, 1951, F 15,31:1
Ballard, Ellis, 1875, N 3,4:5
Ballard, Ellis A (por), 1938, Je 14,21:3
Ballard, Ellis A Mrs, 1937, O 24,II,8:4
Ballard, Ernest E, 1955, O 1,19:4
Ballard, Ernest S, 1952, Mr 19,29:2
Ballard, Eugene S, 1949, Ag 8,15:3
Ballard, Everett G, 1955, S 24,19:6
Ballard, Frank W, 1945, Ap 20,19:2
Ballard, Fred, 1957, S 26,25:1
Ballard, Frederic L, 1952, D 27,9:2
Ballard, Frederick L, 1925, D 31,15:5
Ballard, Frederick P Mrs, 1949, Mr 10,27:3
Ballard, George G Jr Rev, 1913, Ja 31,11:5
Ballard, George S, 1942, Mr 10,20:2
Ballard, George W, 1950, Ap 7,25:6
Ballard, Grover Jr, 1953, Ag 2,72:6
Ballard, Harlan H Mrs, 1949, F 6,76:2
Ballard, Harlan Jr Mrs, 1948, Mr 13,15:4
Ballard, Harold F, 1954, Ja 16,15:2
Ballard, Harry D, 1947, Ag 8,17:5
Ballard, Helen A, 1949, O 23,86:4
Ballard, J F, 1931, Ap 24,23:3
Ballard, Jason H Mrs, 1949, My 2,25:3
Ballard, Jessie L Mrs, 1941, Mr 9,40:5
Ballard, John H Mrs, 1938, N 18,21:1
Ballard, Marshall (trb lr, Ap 3,22:7), 1953, Mr 25, 31:3
Ballard, Melvin J, 1939, Jl 31,13:2
Ballard, Pat (Francis D), 1960, O 28,31:1
Ballard, Paul H, 1951, Mr 13,31:4
Ballard, Samuel M (Jan 25), 1963, Ap 1,35:1
Ballard, Seymour, 1937, O 28,25:5
Ballard, Sumner, 1941, O 25,17:3
Ballard, Wallace A, 1921, Jl 2,9:7
Ballard, Warren E, 1942, Ap 28,21:3
Ballard, William C, 1939, S 6,23:2; 1952, Je 13,23:3
Ballard, William F R Mrs (Bettina), 1961, Ag 5,17:6
Ballard, William R, 1959, My 17,83:1
Ballard, Willis D, 1950, Jl 1,15:4
Ballardini, Gaetano, 1953, My 27,31:2
Ballay, Joseph, 1947, Je 17,25:4
Ballen, William J, 1940, N 14,48:1
Ballenger, William L Mrs, 1952, Ja 11,21:4
Ballentine, Albert W, 1962, Mr 22,35:5
Ballentine, Emma C Mrs, 1955, Mr 30,29:4
Ballester y Nieto, Carmelo, 1949, Ja 28,22:2
Ballesteros, Antonio, 1949, Jl 18,17:4
Ballestrem, Franz Karl Wolfgang von Count, 1910, D 25,9:2
Ballet, Gilbert, 1916, Mr 18,11:6
Balley, Joseph, 1920, F 1,22:2
Balley, William, 1925, Ap 20,17:5
Ballfeller, Miriam M Mrs, 1944, D 28,19:4
Ballhorn, George E, 1943, My 6,19:2
Balliet, Edgar J, 1950, S 9,17:2
Balliet, Thomas M, 1942, F 19,19:4
Balliet, Thomas M Mrs, 1953, Ap 23,29:3
Balliett, Carlton J Mrs, 1957, S 26,25:4
Ballin, Albert, 1918, N 11,15:1
Ballin, David B, 1956, Ap 16,27:4
Ballin, E S, 1885, Je 24,5:3
Ballin, Gustav Mrs, 1910, Je 26,II,9:4
Ballin, Henry, 1916, F 6,15:5
Ballin, Hugo, 1956, N 28,35:6
Ballin, Hugo Mrs, 1958, Jl 28,23:5
Ballin, Julius, 1923, D 3,17:3
Ballin, Milton (por), 1947, S 13,11:6
Ballin, Oscar E, 1917, Ap 4,15:6
Ballin, William, 1919, N 7,13:1
Balling, Francis X, 1952, Ag 7,21:4
Balling, Frank M, 1955, Ja 2,77:1
Ballinger, Charles, 1950, N 19,92:7
Ballinger, Charles C Mrs, 1951, Mr 13,31:2
Ballinger, Charles P, 1952, N 6,29:5
Ballinger, Charles P Mrs, 1945, S 4,23:4
Ballinger, Edwin G, 1943, D 7,27:2
Ballinger, J G Capt, 1924, Ap 4,19:6
Ballinger, John R, 1943, D 31,15:3
Ballinger, Josiah R, 1945, Jl 26,19:5
Ballinger, Reeve L, 1946, Jl 20,13:5
Ballinger, Rich A, 1922, Je 7,19:5
Ballinger, Sydney J Mrs, 1939, Mr 4,15:2
Ballinger, W Evens, 1949, O 11,34:1
Ballinger, William H, 1941, O 14,23:3
Ballinger, William W Mrs, 1939, Mr 4,15:6
Ballinger, Willis J, 1962, Mr 3,21:3
Ballintine, Harriet I, 1951, F 10,13:3
Ballog, Bella, 1953, F 24,25:2
Ballon, Herman, 1952, F 3,84:3
Ballon, Samuel, 1948, F 3,25:4
Ballord, Herbert C, 1937, O 24,II,9:1
Ballot, Paul L, 1965, Ag 27,29:4
Ballou, Adin, 1960, My 25,39:4
Ballou, Albert D, 1949, N 30,27:3
Ballou, Charles E Rev, 1909, Ap 24,7:3
Ballou, Clarence M, 1948, Je 9,29:3
Ballou, Edward C, 1953, Mr 20,23:3
Ballou, Ellis Rev, 1903, F 4,9:4
Ballou, Frank E Mrs, 1949, Ag 8,15:2
Ballou, Frank H, 1962, Mr 24,25:6
Ballou, Frank P, 1951, Jl 17,27:5
Ballou, George L, 1947, O 28,25:4
Ballou, George M Mrs, 1942, N 30,23:5
Ballou, H A, 1937, N 4,25:6
Ballou, Henry L, 1945, Mr 5,19:6
Ballou, Hosea S, 1943, D 7,27:6
Ballou, John B, 1957, O 6,85:1
Ballou, Latimer W, 1954, N 30,29:1
Ballou, Marion Mrs, 1939, Mr 28,23:5
Ballou, Mary, 1953, O 18,86:4
Ballou, Merician, 1947, D 3,29:1

Ballou, Norris P, 1951, N 15,29:6
Ballou, Richard B, 1955, Ap 20,33:3
Ballou, Walter S, 1938, Ja 27,21:5
Ballou, Willard A, 1950, N 21,31:5
Ballou, William B, 1945, D 3,21:5
Ballou, William H Dr, 1937, D 1,23:5
Ballow, H, 1883, My 30,5:3
Ballreich, Charles A, 1940, F 19,17:1
Balls, Daniel, 1950, Mr 21,29:3
Balls, William H, 1938, Jl 29,17:6
Ballu, Theodore, 1885, My 24,2:3
Balluff, William V, 1948, Ap 13,27:1
Balm, J Horace, 1950, D 9,15:1
Balmanno, Charles G, 1916, Mr 8,11:6
Balme, Gaston F, 1957, Ap 9,33:5
Balmer, Edwin, 1959, Mr 22,86:5
Balmer, Edwin B Mrs, 1959, N 30,31:4
Balmer, Harold F, 1964, Jl 27,31:4
Balmer, Katherine Machaig Mrs, 1925, N 28,15:5
Balmer, Thomas, 1917, Je 14,11:6; 1959, Ag 2,81:1
Balmer, William J, 1961, S 22,33:4
Balmos, John, 1920, N 8,15:5
Balnau, James (Jas Murphy), 1908, My 25,7:2
Balog, Mary Mrs, 1943, Ja 10,48:2
Balog, Max Mrs, 1959, Ag 16,82:7
Balogh, Harry W (funl, Ag 19,17:1), 1961, Ag 17, 27:1
Balokovic, Zlatko, 1965, Mr 31,39:2
Balph, Eleanore H, 1945, My 23,19:5
Bals, Frank C, 1954, Ja 16,15:4
Bals, Joseph, 1968, Ap 11,45:4
Balsam, Aldo R Mrs, 1954, F 28,92:1
Balsam, Berisch, 1963, Je 17,25:1
Balsamo, Pasquale, 1963, Jl 9,31:4
Balsan, Jacques (funl, N 9,29:4), 1956, N 6,35:6
Balsan, Jacques Mrs (Consuelo Vanderbilt, ex-Duchess), 1964, D 7,1:8
Balsan, Jacques Mrs ex-Duchess Marlborough (Consuelo Vanderbilt), 1965, Ja 2,17:3
Balsiger, Eugene J, 1949, O 2,80:6
Balsley, Clyde, 1942, Jl 24,20:3
Balston, J Harris, 1915, N 17,11:6
Baltazzi, S A Warner, 1959, N 16,31:1
Baltes, W Frank, 1948, My 27,25:2
Balthazar, August, 1952, Jl 24,27:5
Baltic, Jack, 1950, F 15,27:5
Baltimore, Margaret Mrs, 1941, D 23,21:5
Baltimore, Richard L Sr, 1961, N 29,41:3
Baltimore, Sam R, 1942, S 29,23:6
Baltimore, Walter A, 1951, Je 24,72:2
Baltodano, Francisco, 1948, Je 21,21:6
Baltodano, Jose F, 1944, Je 28,23:5
Baltrusaitis, Johanna T, 1950, D 25,19:4
Baltushi-Zhemaitis, Felix R, 1957, Je 5,35:5
Baltz, Charles E, 1959, D 24,19:1
Baltz, George, 1883, F 7,5:5
Baltz, Harry R, 1951, Mr 29,27:4
Baltz, Harry R Mrs, 1967, Jl 19,39:2
Baltzell, Alice Mrs, 1938, N 4,34:6
Baltzell, George F Col, 1937, Ag 7,15:1
Baltzell, Robert C, 1950, O 19,31:2
Baltzell, William H, 1942, S 4,24:4
Baltzell, William H 3d Mrs, 1955, Ag 2,23:1
Baltzer, Adolf C G, 1941, F 13,19:5
Baltzer, Armin S, 1963, S 13,30:1
Baltzer, Charles F, 1954, Ag 9,17:5
Balut, Stephen Sr, 1949, N 27,104:4
Baluta, Joseph F, 1952, S 18,29:3
Baluvelt, Benjamin L, 1965, Je 23,41:3
Balvere, John H, 1941, Ag 15,17:2
Balz, Albert G A, 1957, O 3,29:3
Balz, George A, 1939, F 25,15:2
Balzac, Richard, 1949, Ja 11,27:1
Balzar, F B, 1934, Mr 22,22:3
Balzaro, Amadeo, 1955, Ap 8,21:2
Balze, Enrique de la, 1912, O 26,11:6
Balzer, Albert T, 1952, Mr 20,29:2
Balzer, Emil G, 1948, Mr 12,23:2
Balzer, Stephen M, 1940, O 1,23:3
Bam, Frederick K, 1956, D 6,37:4
Bambach, George F, 1954, Ag 2,17:2
Bamber, Beatrice M, 1942, S 6,30:8
Bamber, William C, 1949, D 16,31:2
Bamberger, Abram, 1912, Mr 18,11:3
Bamberger, Alfred D, 1956, Mr 23,27:1
Bamberger, Alfred H, 1948, Ap 28,27:4
Bamberger, Alvin S, 1949, D 3,15:2
Bamberger, Alvin S Mrs, 1953, F 25,27:3
Bamberger, Anton, 1950, D 29,19:2
Bamberger, Edgar S, 1952, Je 30,19:4
Bamberger, Edward S, 1909, Ag 1,9:6
Bamberger, Gus, 1943, Mr 7,38:6
Bamberger, Herman, 1920, Je 2,11:4
Bamberger, Hugo, 1950, Ja 1,42:4
Bamberger, Ira Leo, 1919, D 29,9:3
Bamberger, Leo, 1961, F 25,21:3
Bamberger, Leon J, 1967, Ap 27,45:2
Bamberger, Levi, 1912, Jl 8,9:5
Bamberger, Louis (will, Mr 24,15:5), 1944, Mr 12, 38:1
Bamberger, Max, 1962, Ag 7,29:4
Bamberger, Michael Mrs, 1953, Jl 2,23:3
Bamberger, Milton M, 1954, Ja 8,21:2
Bamberger, Raymond S, 1957, Je 18,33:2
Bamberger, Reba C M Mrs, 1937, My 22,15:2
Bamberger, Robert B, 1942, My 27,23:4
Bamberger, Theron, 1953, S 15,31:3
Bamberger, William Mrs, 1952, Ap 30,27:2
Bambrick, James E, 1937, Mr 12,23:4
Bambrick, James J, 1951, Ag 1,23:2
Bambrick, Richard J, 1953, My 28,14:3
Bambridge, George, 1943, D 19,49:1
Bambridge, Juliette Mrs, 1938, Ap 8,19:2
Bame, Joseph, 1968, N 27,47:3
Bamford, Beatrice Mrs, 1945, F 14,19:4
Bamford, F E, 1932, Je 28,21:1
Bamford, Frank S, 1962, Ag 28,31:2
Bamford, Richard L, 1938, Jl 24,28:5
Bamford, William B, 1945, Ap 12,23:4
Bamford, William H, 1938, Ja 19,23:3
Bamforth, Arthur H, 1958, N 28,27:2
Bamonte, Grace (Mrs W H Damour), 1961, F 11, 23:3
Bampton, Henrietta H Mrs, 1951, Je 20,27:1
Bampton, Samuel W, 1944, N 4,15:4
Ban, Antal, 1951, Ag 27,19:4
Banac, Bozo N, 1945, Ap 16,23:4
Banach, Leon, 1951, Mr 16,31:3
Banach, Stefan, 1945, O 13,15:3
Banachiewicz, Tadeusz, 1954, D 3,27:5
Banagan, Edward J, 1943, S 8,23:2
Banash, Sydney H, 1944, F 27,38:1
Banass, Ladislaus, 1949, Ap 21,12:3
Banaytis, Stanislav, 1954, F 7,88:1
Banbach, Henry C, 1944, My 23,23:1
Banbury, Fernley H, 1963, My 29,33:2
Banbury, George E, 1965, D 21,37:1
Bance, Harrison, 1958, Mr 16,86:7
Bancel, Henry A, 1961, Ap 20,33:2
Bancel, Henry A Mrs, 1957, Je 3,27:6
Bancker, A Capt, 1878, N 13,2:5
Bancker, Adrian, 1868, Mr 15,1:7
Bancker, James W Sr, 1954, S 26,87:2
Bancker, John W, 1952, Ja 17,27:2
Bancker, William F, 1953, O 13,29:3
Bancks, James C, 1952, Jl 2,25:4
Bancroft, Aaron, 1918, O 9,11:2
Bancroft, Albert F, 1943, N 19,19:3
Bancroft, Amos R, 1950, Ja 19,28:2
Bancroft, Burdette M, 1940, Jl 30,19:5
Bancroft, Charles G, 1955, Ja 3,27:6
Bancroft, Charles G Mrs, 1955, Ja 12,27:1
Bancroft, Edgar Addison (por), 1925, Jl 29,21:4
Bancroft, Edward S, 1958, O 25,21:2
Bancroft, Elizabeth H Mrs, 1941, O 29,23:3
Bancroft, Elizabeth M Mrs, 1958, D 29,15:3
Bancroft, Francis S, 1957, O 22,33:5
Bancroft, Frederic (will), 1945, Mr 3,11:6
Bancroft, Frederic W, 1963, Ap 26,35:1
Bancroft, George, 1891, Ja 18,5:1; 1917, D 18,15:5
Bancroft, George (funl plans, O 5,25:4), 1956, O 4, 33:4
Bancroft, Griffing, 1955, My 5,33:5
Bancroft, Guy, 1953, O 27,27:3
Bancroft, Howland, 1964, S 14,33:5
Bancroft, Hubert Howe, 1918, Mr 3,23:1
Bancroft, Hugh Jr, 1953, O 21,29:2
Bancroft, Hugh Mrs, 1949, D 22,23:2
Bancroft, Jessie H, 1952, N 14,23:1
Bancroft, John C, 1964, N 5,45:2
Bancroft, Malcolm, 1942, Ap 9,19:2
Bancroft, Marie Lady, 1921, My 23,13:6
Bancroft, Milton H, 1947, D 12,27:1
Bancroft, Nellie K, 1949, S 9,26:7
Bancroft, S Sir, 1926, Ap 20,27:1
Bancroft, W P, 1942, S 1,19:1
Bancroft, Wilder D Dr, 1953, F 8,89:1
Bancroft, Wilder D Mrs, 1942, F 23,21:5
Bancroft, Wilfred, 1955, D 20,31:1
Bancroft, Wilfred Mrs, 1948, Mr 26,21:3
Bancroft, William, 1947, Mr 19,25:5
Bancroft, William A Gen, 1922, Mr 12,30:3
Bancroft, William Channing Rev Dr, 1923, D 16,23:3
Bancroft, William S Mrs, 1919, F 24,13:2
Band, Samuel, 1941, N 6,23:4
Bandalier, Adolph Francis Alphonse, 1914, Mr 21,13:4
Bandeira, Manuel, 1968, O 15,47:4
Bandekow, Kurt R, 1958, D 2,37:5
Bandel, Ernest, 1876, S 29,5:2
Bandel, Fred W, 1944, D 23,13:7
Bander, Isidore H, 1951, S 10,10:4
Bander, Louis, 1948, F 28,15:2
Bander, Louis Mrs, 1948, Mr 9,23:3
Bander, Morris, 1940, O 23,23:5
Bandera, Stefan, 1959, O 17,5:5
Banderas, Juan, 1918, F 12,11:3
Bandfield, Harold G, 1950, My 11,29:3
Bandholtz, Harry A Maj-Gen, 1925, My 8,19:3
Bandini, Carlo Prince, 1941, Je 17,21:5
Bandini, Lorenzo, 1967, My 11,62:4
Bandler, Clarence G, 1957, N 17,87:1
Bandler, David, 1947, Ja 10,21:3
Bandler, Edna M Mrs, 1939, Jl 7,17:3
Bandler, Harry S, 1962, Ag 20,23:5
Bandler, Meyer, 1951, N 23,29:2
Bandmann, Daniel Edward, 1905, N 25,9:5
Bandmann, Eugene, 1948, O 21,27:2
Bando, Tasumasaburo, 1953, Jl 8,27:5
Bandre, George Sr, 1956, Ap 29,86:5
Bandrow, Louis Mrs, 1911, S 30,13:5
Bane, Baldwin B, 1962, My 25,33:3
Bane, Frank Mrs, 1953, Mr 13,27:3
Bane, J Donald Mrs, 1968, Ap 16,44:1
Bane, John B, 1948, N 2,25:4
Bane, Suda L, 1952, N 20,31:4
Banek, William A, 1954, My 30,45:1
Baner, William Llewellyn Dr, 1921, D 10,13:5
Banerjea, Surendranath, 1925, Ag 8,11:6
Baney, James V Sr, 1961, Jl 2,33:2
Banffy, Desiderius Baron, 1911, F 27,9:3
Banfi, Alfredo, 1956, Mr 16,14:6
Banfield, F J, 1883, Mr 5,5:2
Banfield, T H, 1950, S 1,21:6
Banfill, Bradford, 1944, S 15,19:5
Bang, Anton Christian Rev, 1913, D 31,9:5
Bang, Arthur C, 1947, Mr 1,15:1
Bang, Axel F, 1963, Jl 13,17:4
Bang, Frederick, 1906, Mr 21,9:5
Bang, Hermann, 1912, Ja 30,9:5
Bang, Maia, 1940, Ja 4,24:2
Bange, John A, 1951, Ja 29,19:3
Bangert, Edward Mrs, 1951, D 7,28:2
Bangert, Lawrence C, 1958, Je 17,29:1
Bangert, Louis P Mrs, 1950, Je 4,92:3
Bangha, Bela, 1940, Ap 30,21:4
Banghart, Emma M Mrs, 1937, Ag 23,19:4
Banghart, Harry S, 1940, Je 4,23:4
Banghart, Percy, 1941, Ap 7,17:5
Bango, William McKendree, 1914, Jl 6,7:5
Bangor, Viscount (M R C Ward), 1950, N 18,15:3
Bangs, Andrew G, 1952, Je 6,23:4
Bangs, Archie R, 1951, My 1,29:2
Bangs, Bleeker Capt, 1921, My 29,22:3
Bangs, Charles T, 1939, My 9,23:5
Bangs, Edith, 1959, Ag 31,21:1
Bangs, Eugene F, 1957, Je 23,84:4
Bangs, F N, 1885, D 2,5:3
Bangs, Fletcher H, 1919, Mr 11,11:2
Bangs, Francis H, 1964, My 31,76:6
Bangs, Francis N, 1968, Mr 11,41:2
Bangs, Francis N Mrs, 1966, Jl 25,27:4
Bangs, Francis S, 1920, Mr 3,11:4
Bangs, Frank C, 1908, Je 14,11:5
Bangs, Frederick A, 1938, Je 7,23:1
Bangs, Frederick C, 1964, My 11,31:3
Bangs, G H, 1883, S 15,8:3
Bangs, G S, 1877, N 18,6:7
Bangs, George A, 1955, Je 17,23:4
Bangs, George D, 1923, Ap 17,21:4
Bangs, H Rev, 1869, N 4,1:7
Bangs, Henry M, 1942, F 8,49:2
Bangs, Howard R, 1941, F 12,21:5
Bangs, I S Gen, 1903, My 31,7:6
Bangs, Jessie B Mrs, 1907, Ap 21,9:3
Bangs, John K Jr, 1942, Ag 21,19:6
Bangs, John Kendrick, 1922, Ja 22,22:3
Bangs, Lemuel Bolton Dr, 1914, O 5,11:5
Bangs, Lois A, 1940, F 28,21:4
Bangs, N H Rev, 1884, Ap 3,4:7
Bangs, N J (see also Jl 22), 1878, Jl 23,8:2
Bangsberg, Harry F, 1967, Mr 25,3:3
Banigan, Leon F, 1957, My 25,21:5
Banigan, Louis Mrs, 1950, D 28,25:4
Banilower, Morris Mrs, 1963, S 8,86:7
Banister, Alan B, 1963, N 2,25:4
Banister, Blair Mrs, 1951, O 1,23:4
Banister, Earl A, 1944, Ag 23,19:6
Banister, James B, 1943, D 2,27:2
Banister, James B Mrs, 1942, F 11,21:2
Banister, Seth W Mrs, 1954, Mr 13,15:5
Banister, William B, 1958, My 3,19:4
Bank, Clarence C, 1942, D 6,77:3
Bank, Samuel B, 1939, Ja 15,38:2
Bank, William R, 1955, Mr 23,31:1
Bankard, Edgar H Jr, 1947, N 14,23:1
Bankart, Henry R, 1939, F 1,21:4
Banke, Fred, 1959, Ja 21,31:4
Banker, Arthur W, 1959, Jl 23,27:5
Banker, Charles F, 1947, F 19,25:5
Banker, Clark W, 1939, Ja 25,21:3
Banker, Edmund Jr, 1944, Ag 27,33:4
Banker, Franklin A, 1937, F 16,23:5
Banker, Garrett N Mrs, 1956, D 15,25:5
Banker, George J, 1948, Je 9,29:3
Banker, George Mrs, 1945, S 16,43:1
Banker, George T, 1949, Mr 8,25:2
Banker, Gordon D, 1938, Ag 3,19:4
Banker, Harry Mrs, 1951, Mr 20,29:4
Banker, Henry J, 1952, S 22,23:2
Banker, J H, 1885, F 11,5:5
Banker, Louis G, 1954, O 21,27:1
Banker, Nels O, 1950, S 17,104:5
Banker, P Walter, 1953, Ag 28,17:4
Banker, Silas J, 1954, Jl 30,17:6
Bankes, John E, 1947, Ja 2,27:2
Bankhardt, Elmont V, 1951, Jl 13,21:3
Bankhardt, Frederick Mrs, 1943, F 27,13:3
Bankhead, Henry M, 1957, O 28,27:5
Bankhead, Henry M Mrs, 1938, S 5,15:4

Bankhead, John H, 1946, Je 13,27:1
Bankhead, John L Sen, 1920, Mr 2,11:4
Bankhead, Tallulah (funl, D 15,86:1), 1968, D 13,1:3
Bankhead, William B, 1940, S 15,1:2
Bankhead, William B Mrs, 1952, Jl 3,25:6
Bankroft, Charles P, 1946, F 25,25:1
Banks, Agnes H Mrs, 1940, Jl 15,15:3
Banks, Alex F, 1948, N 8,21:4
Banks, Alex S, 1949, O 14,28:2; 1949, O 17,23:6
Banks, Alfred E, 1951, Ja 17,27:4
Banks, Andrew D, 1966, D 10,37:4
Banks, Andrew Jr, 1955, O 29,19:2
Banks, Anthony Bleecker, 1910, Ag 8,7:5
Banks, Bradley W, 1938, S 23,27:2
Banks, C G, 1934, Ap 28,15:6
Banks, C Whitney, 1961, O 14,23:4
Banks, Caroline, 1925, S 29,27:4
Banks, Charles, 1909, N 17,9:3; 1962, My 22,37:1
Banks, Charles A, 1961, S 29,35:4
Banks, Charles L, 1938, Ag 20,15:5
Banks, Charles Mrs, 1956, O 24,37:6
Banks, Charles O, 1944, Jl 22,15:7
Banks, Charles S, 1939, N 9,23:4
Banks, Charles S Mrs, 1948, Ja 7,25:4
Banks, Charles T, 1958, Mr 9,86:3
Banks, Charles W, 1944, Jl 23,35:4
Banks, Clarence C, 1948, F 24,25:2
Banks, Clayton F, 1947, Ag 15,18:2
Banks, Dave, 1952, Ag 25,25:2
Banks, David, 1945, D 14,27:1
Banks, Edgar J, 1945, My 9,23:2
Banks, Elizabeth, 1938, Jl 19,22:5
Banks, Elizabeth A, 1951, F 8,34:2
Banks, Elizabeth L, 1947, Ap 18,21:2
Banks, Emanuel S, 1956, O 20,21:2
Banks, Eugene B, 1941, Mr 5,21:2
Banks, Fannie M Mrs, 1940, My 9,23:4
Banks, Frank A, 1957, D 16,29:1
Banks, Frederick, 1964, D 19,29:4
Banks, Gardner Col, 1871, Jl 13,8:4
Banks, George M, 1946, Jl 2,25:3
Banks, George W, 1924, Je 10,11:4
Banks, Guy F, 1966, D 8,47:3
Banks, Harold P, 1968, O 12,37:3
Banks, Harvey M Dr, 1910, My 6,9:5
Banks, Henry W Mrs, 1958, S 12,25:3
Banks, Hugh, 1947, Je 30,19:1
Banks, J L, 1883, Je 4,5:1
Banks, James H, 1941, N 19,23:1
Banks, James L, 1950, O 2,23:4
Banks, James L Jr, 1946, Ag 1,23:2
Banks, John H, 1941, Ja 24,17:2
Banks, John W, 1958, Mr 9,87:2
Banks, Kieran P, 1943, My 4,23:1
Banks, Lenox, 1951, O 5,27:1
Banks, Leslie J, 1952, Ap 23,29:3
Banks, Lucian (Sonny), 1965, My 14,27:6
Banks, Monty (will, F 25,10:3), 1950, Ja 9,25:3
Banks, Mrs, 1873, My 2,5:5
Banks, N P Gen, 1894, S 1,1:6
Banks, Nathan, 1953, Ja 25,84:4
Banks, Oliver C Mrs, 1951, My 17,31:3
Banks, Reginald M, 1965, F 18,33:5
Banks, Reginald M Mrs, 1918, Ja 29,15:6
Banks, T C, 1881, D 15,5:3
Banks, T H, 1933, Je 9,17:1
Banks, Talcott M, 1951, N 1,29:5
Banks, Talcott M Mrs, 1966, My 9,39:3
Banks, Thoe H Mrs, 1949, D 14,31:4
Banks, Thomas A, 1952, Je 10,27:3
Banks, Varian, 1941, Ag 29,19:7
Banks, Virgil, 1962, Ja 5,29:5
Banks, Warren S, 1942, Mr 12,19:2
Banks, William, 1882, Ap 20,5:2; 1946, Ja 7,19:4
Banks, William F, 1947, S 28,60:7
Banks, William L, 1924, O 23,21:4
Banks, William P, 1948, Ja 31,19:5
Banks, William S, 1939, F 10,23:4; 1945, Ag 17,17:2
Banks, William Sir, 1904, Ag 10,7:6
Banks, Winifred D, 1954, Ja 2,11:6
Banks, Wright, 1884, My 1,2:4
Banks, Zoe E, 1914, F 25,9:5
Bankson, John P Mrs, 1956, D 22,19:5
Bankson, Lloyd, 1940, Mr 6,23:1
Bankson, Paul A, 1942, N 17,25:5
Bankson, Paul A Mrs, 1939, Ap 18,23:5
Bankson, Philetus C, 1950, O 9,25:3
Banlian, Aram, 1944, My 15,19:4
Bannan, Francis F, 1943, My 30,26:2
Bannard, Charles H, 1938, My 10,21:3
Bannard, Homes, 1966, Je 18,31:5
Bannard, O T (por), 1929, Ja 17,25:1
Bannard, William Heath, 1913, Mr 23,IV,7:5
Bannell, Samuel, 1938, Ja 9,42:3
Banner, Chauncey W, 1950, S 12,27:4
Banner, Harry Mrs, 1961, Ja 27,23:4
Banner, Henry, 1938, Ag 24,21:4
Banner, James M, 1963, N 3,88:7
Banner, John, 1938, Ag 24,21:4
Banner, John H, 1968, Ag 20,41:2
Banner, Michael J, 1941, O 31,23:2
Bannerman, David B, 1957, Jl 8,23:3
Bannerman, Francis, 1918, N 28,17:1
Bannerman, Frank, 1946, S 1,36:1
Bannerman, George, 1964, Ap 18,29:2
Bannerman, Parry E, 1951, My 22,31:5
Bannerman, Robert C, 1940, F 28,21:5
Bannerman, William B Mrs, 1946, O 31,25:5
Bannerot, Frederick G, 1949, D 4,108:4
Bannier, Richard W, 1951, O 26,23:3
Bannigan, Eugene F (funl, Jl 9,27:5), 1958, Jl 5,17:1
Bannigan, Frank, 1953, Ag 23,88:4
Bannigan, John J, 1909, Ja 1,11:5
Bannigan, John P, 1941, Jl 21,15:5
Bannigan, Thomas J, 1941, Je 29,32:8
Bannin, Michael E, 1912, Ag 8,9:6
Banning, Archibald Mrs, 1945, Ja 30,19:2
Banning, Archibald T Dr, 1924, N 10,17:2
Banning, Forrest D, 1957, Jl 27,17:2
Banning, George W, 1951, Ap 15,92:2
Banning, H B, 1881, D 11,2:6
Banning, Kendall, 1944, D 28,19:3
Banning, M, 1879, Je 29,9:4
Banning, William, 1946, Ja 28,19:4
Banning, William L Jr, 1950, S 25,23:2
Banning, William P, 1962, Je 19,35:4
Banninga, John J, 1963, Ag 31,17:6
Bannister, Eleanor C, 1939, Ja 21,15:5
Bannister, H Rev, 1883, Ap 16,1:3
Bannister, Harry, 1961, F 27,27:4
Bannister, Harry (funl plans, Ap 29,35:4), 1967, Ap 28,41:1
Bannister, James A, 1906, F 6,9:6
Bannister, Kimball, 1940, Ja 31,19:2
Bannister, L Ward, 1958, Ja 18,15:5
Bannister, Lemuel, 1906, Ap 14,11:4
Bannister, Murdock, 1949, S 23,23:1
Bannister, William F, 1942, S 10,27:5
Bannister, William P, 1939, Ja 10,19:5
Bannon, Charles, 1907, Ja 3,9:5
Bannon, David J Mrs, 1940, O 29,25:4
Bannon, George H, 1949, N 13,92:4
Bannon, Henry T, 1950, S 8,32:3
Bannon, James H, 1948, Mr 25,38:4
Bannon, James J Mrs, 1961, S 19,35:4
Bannon, John F, 1921, D 25,20:3
Bannon, Joseph D, 1967, Ap 5,47:3
Bannon, Joseph Mrs, 1950, My 18,29:5
Bannon, Kate R, 1904, Ja 2,3:3
Bannon, Leo M, 1948, Ap 13,27:4
Bannon, Margaret S Mrs, 1921, D 25,20:3
Bannon, Selina L (will), 1938, Ja 25,22:4
Bannon, Thomas F, 1958, Ag 30,15:6
Bannon, Thomas J, 1942, Mr 29,44:1
Bannon, Timothy J, 1939, Ja 9,15:2
Bannow, Rudolph F, 1962, Je 24,68:4
Bannvart, Eugene J K, 1952, My 20,25:3
Bannwart, Carl, 1959, Ag 18,29:1
Banome, Salvatore, 1953, Ja 7,31:5
Banon, Edward M, 1944, Ap 15,11:3
Banovsky, Julius, 1950, O 17,31:1
Banse, George J, 1955, Ag 3,23:4
Banse, Oscar F, 1958, N 2,88:5
Banse, Oscar F Mrs, 1956, D 15,25:5
Banser, John C, 1953, Ap 27,23:4
Bansfield, Thomas J (Bro A Elrick), 1959, D 2,43:4
Banta, A Ackerman, 1947, N 16,76:6
Banta, A Ackerman Mrs, 1947, N 25,32:2
Banta, Alfred, 1912, Ag 13,9:5
Banta, Anna M Mrs, 1942, S 12,13:5
Banta, Arthur M, 1946, Ja 3,19:1
Banta, Arthur P, 1949, Ja 25,24:3
Banta, Clare W, 1954, F 28,93:1
Banta, Frank E, 1968, D 31,27:3
Banta, H Raymond, 1959, Ja 31,19:1
Banta, John R, 1940, S 7,15:6
Banta, Lorenz J, 1954, F 22,19:4
Banta, Russell V, 1945, F 19,17:3
Banta, Theodore M, 1910, S 18,II,13:5; 1953, My 19, 29:2
Banta, Warren C, 1937, My 8,19:3
Banta, William C, 1946, Ag 19,25:4
Bantel, Charles F, 1960, S 24,23:5
Bantel, Mattaus, 1952, My 28,29:4
Bantel, William, 1940, N 1,25:5
Bantelman, Henry L, 1948, Ja 19,3:3
Bantelman, Henry L Mrs, 1943, N 10,23:4
Bantick, Horace J, 1942, Jl 23,19:4
Banting, John W, 1941, S 6,15:3
Banting, Margaret G Mrs, 1940, D 4,27:4
Bantleon, Frederick A, 1948, Ap 21,27:2
Bantock, Granville, 1946, O 17,23:3
Banton, Joab H, 1949, Jl 21,25:3
Banton, Joab H Mrs, 1956, Ja 21,21:5
Banton, Travis, 1958, F 3,23:4
Bantz, William, 1949, N 1,27:2
Banyard, John C, 1959, My 14,33:2
Banyard, Leslie F, 1958, Ap 29,29:3
Banz, Otto (Otto Botto), 1968, Ja 8,39:3
Banzer, John, 1949, O 16,90:5
Banzett, Henry, 1941, My 4,53:2
Banzhaf, Henry I, 1951, Mr 7,33:4
Bapst, Frank L, 1941, Ag 9,15:6
Bapst, Robert T, 1959, O 19,29:4
Baptie, Norval, 1966, N 30,47:1
Baptist, William C, 1948, My 9,68:3
Baptiste, Emanuel, 1948, F 18,27:4
Baptiste, George, 1937, Jl 14,21:5
Baque, John W, 1950, Jl 11,31:4
Bar-Yehuda, Israel, 1965, My 5,47:2
Bara, Pauline L Mrs, 1957, Jl 8,23:1
Bara, Theda (funl plans, Ap 9,13:4; funl, Ap 10,88:1), 1955, Ap 8,21:1
Barab, Max B, 1941, Ag 2,15:1
Barabas, Andrew J, 1940, My 3,21:3
Barac, Abraham, 1940, Mr 5,12:6
Baracco, James, 1960, S 30,27:1
Barach, Joseph H, 1954, Mr 10,25:5
Barad, Martin, 1962, Ap 26,33:1
Baradel, Joseph R, 1966, S 15,43:1
Baradoro, Henry D, 1946, Ap 30,22:2
Baraga, Bishop (Canada), 1868, Ja 27,5:5
Baraguey-d'Hilliers, Comte A, 1878, Je 7,1:6
Baragwanath, John G, 1965, Je 28,29:2
Barakat, Layyah A Mrs, 1940, D 6,27:3
Baraldi, George A, 1965, Ap 20,39:1
Baran, Andrew T, 1967, Mr 15,47:3
Baran, Charles, 1945, F 1,23:2
Baran, Joseph T, 1953, My 16,19:1
Baran, Julius Mrs (will, S 12,27:4), 1951, Ap 19,31:5
Baran, Milan L Sr, 1955, Jl 20,27:5
Baran, Paul A, 1964, Mr 28,19:4
Baranco, Meyer J, 1961, D 29,23:1
Barandon, Robert, 1949, Ap 5,29:1
Baraniak, Anton, 1955, Mr 11,3:6
Baranoff, Michael Dr, 1924, N 24,17:3
Barany, R, 1936, Ap 9,23:3
Baranyai, Zoltan, 1948, O 26,31:5
Barasch, Harry, 1937, Mr 15,23:4
Barasch, Louis, 1962, Jl 22,64:4
Barasch, Michael, 1944, S 24,46:3
Barasch, Morris, 1937, D 27,15:4
Barasch, Morris Mrs, 1949, Mr 23,27:5
Barash, David H, 1959, Mr 20,31:2
Barash, Louis, 1959, Jl 9,27:1
Barash, Pincus J, 1966, Ag 25,37:4
Barashick, Aaron, 1941, Jl 7,15:1
Baratelli, Charles C, 1925, N 13,19:4
Baratier, Paul J A, 1939, F 3,15:2
Baratieri, Ores Gen, 1901, Ag 9,7:5
Baratov, Leonid, 1964, Jl 24,27:4
Baratta, Achille F, 1949, My 14,13:5
Baratta, Umberto, 1945, Jl 18,27:4
Baravalle, Victor, 1939, Mr 13,17:4
Barb, Brian, 1968, O 15,47:4
Barb, Charles S, 1948, My 25,27:4
Barb, Jacob S Mrs, 1964, My 8,33:1
Barb, Kirk B, 1954, Jl 24,13:1
Barba, Horace M, 1956, Ja 16,21:6
Barba, Milton B, 1961, O 6,35:2
Barba, William P, 1951, Mr 23,21:4
Barbanel, Joseph, 1949, S 19,23:4
Barbanell, Solon, 1941, N 30,69:2
Barbano, Louis John, 1968, Jl 7,53:2
Barbara, Joseph M Sr (est tax appr), 1962, Ag 23, 11:4
Barbara, Joseph Sr (funl plans, Je 19,11:1; funl, Je 23,67:2), 1959, Je 18,1:1
Barbash, Jacob, 1945, N 22,35:2
Barbash, Leo, 1952, Jl 4,13:4
Barbash, Samuel, 1946, N 15,24:2
Barbato, Theodore, 1953, Ap 7,29:2
Barbe, Waitman Dr, 1925, O 31,17:6
Barbe, William F, 1957, Ap 12,25:1
Barbeau, Antonio, 1947, Je 15,62:3
Barbee, Algernon K, 1967, S 5,43:1
Barbee, Dave R, 1958, Mr 8,17:3
Barbee, Hiram G, 1955, Je 17,23:2
Barbee, James E, 1948, Jl 22,23:3
Barbee, Margaret, 1966, F 3,31:1
Barbee, Robert E, 1938, Ag 6,13:4
Barbehenn, Edwin W, 1958, S 24,27:1
Barbelet, Edward C, 1951, Ag 1,23:5
Barbella, Nicholas, 1954, My 6,33:4
Barbelle, Albert W, 1957, F 6,25:4
Barber, A E Brig-Gen, 1875, N 25,2:7
Barber, A J, 1942, Ag 15,11:6
Barber, A T, 1938, Ap 27,23:5
Barber, Albert L, 1951, D 17,31:3
Barber, Alex W, 1949, Ap 6,29:4
Barber, Amos W Dr, 1915, My 20,11:5
Barber, Archer H, 1949, S 26,25:2
Barber, Archer H Mrs, 1949, S 20,29:4
Barber, Benjamin R, 1954, Jl 11,73:2
Barber, Benjamin R Mrs, 1955, Mr 30,29:4
Barber, Benn, 1965, D 9,47:1
Barber, Bruce G, 1963, Jl 9,31:2
Barber, Charles A, 1957, Ag 18,83:2
Barber, Charles E, 1909, My 21,9:3
Barber, Charles N, 1958, Ap 23,33:2
Barber, Charles W, 1943, Ja 8,20:2
Barber, Cicero Rev, 1911, Mr 11,13:5
Barber, Clarence L, 1918, D 9,13:4
Barber, Clarence S, 1949, O 29,15:4
Barber, Claude C, 1954, Ja 30,17:4
Barber, Courtenay, 1951, My 6,92:5
Barber, David, 1961, S 20,29:4
Barber, David M, 1948, O 7,30:2
Barber, Donn (funl, My 31,5:1), 1925, My 30,9:5

Barber, Dudley M, 1958, D 3,37:4
Barber, Edgar M, 1945, Ap 16,23:3
Barber, Edith M, 1963, Ag 20,33:2
Barber, Edward, 1951, Mr 12,25:2
Barber, Edward J, 1953, Je 14,85:1
Barber, Elliot B, 1951, My 3,29:2
Barber, Elsie Y Mrs, 1939, Mr 18,17:4
Barber, Emanuel, 1951, My 27,69:2
Barber, Emery G, 1937, Mr 2,21:5
Barber, Ernest, 1945, Ja 8,17:3
Barber, Florence H Mrs, 1940, Jl 11,19:3
Barber, Frank I, 1949, N 22,29:3
Barber, Franklin, 1957, Ja 13,85:1
Barber, Frederick C, 1937, Ja 2,11:4
Barber, Frederick C Mrs, 1962, N 22,29:3
Barber, George E, 1940, N 22,23:2
Barber, George G, 1943, Jl 11,34:8
Barber, George H, 1938, Ag 27,13:5
Barber, George J, 1946, S 23,23:1
Barber, George W, 1948, D 8,31:2
Barber, Grace E, 1942, My 1,19:5
Barber, Guthrie Y, 1941, My 8,23:6
Barber, H R, 1903, My 21,9:4
Barber, Henry A Jr, 1956, My 1,33:4
Barber, Henry G, 1961, Mr 17,31:1
Barber, Henry O, 1938, Ag 21,32:8
Barber, Herbert, 1915, N 17,11:6
Barber, Herbert G, 1947, O 6,21:4
Barber, Hiram, 1924, Ag 7,15:5
Barber, Hiram Dr, 1905, Ap 25,11:6
Barber, Howard M, 1954, N 8,21:6
Barber, Hugh L, 1948, N 10,29:5
Barber, J Frank, 1949, Jl 20,25:3
Barber, J W, 1928, F 19,II,7:1
Barber, James W Mrs, 1945, N 16,19:5
Barber, Jess, 1951, Mr 4,64:4
Barber, Jess Mrs, 1951, Mr 4,64:4
Barber, Jesse E, 1957, My 24,25:2
Barber, Joel D, 1952, Ja 6,94:1
Barber, John, 1942, Ja 21,17:3; 1946, F 28,23:4; 1951, Ap 19,31:5
Barber, John K, 1959, Ja 26,29:3
Barber, John M, 1942, My 12,19:3
Barber, John O, 1949, Ap 20,27:3
Barber, John W, 1939, N 14,23:4
Barber, Joseph A, 1951, Je 21,27:3
Barber, Josephine A Mrs, 1945, F 21,19:2
Barber, Leon J, 1946, D 24,17:5
Barber, Lincoln E, 1951, N 1,29:2
Barber, Louis D, 1941, Ja 12,44:2
Barber, Louis E, 1942, N 18,26:2
Barber, Martha Mrs, 1921, D 2,17:6
Barber, Mary E Mrs, 1941, D 25,25:3
Barber, Mayo H, 1939, Ja 17,21:5
Barber, Moses J, 1947, Ja 19,53:4
Barber, Nellie L Mrs, 1948, Ag 20,17:5
Barber, Ohio Columbus, 1920, F 5,9:4
Barber, Oscar E, 1950, Mr 21,32:4
Barber, P J, 1954, F 16,25:1
Barber, Raymond J, 1955, O 30,88:8
Barber, Robert F, 1958, O 7,35:2
Barber, Roderick C, 1955, Ap 1,27:3
Barber, Roy S Col, 1968, My 28,47:1
Barber, S Leroy, 1947, Ag 14,23:4
Barber, S LeRoy Mrs, 1967, F 28,34:2
Barber, Sara M, 1958, Ap 24,31:4
Barber, Stanley, 1954, Ag 3,19:4
Barber, T H Gen, 1905, Mr 17,3:1
Barber, Theodore S, 1939, O 26,23:6
Barber, Thomas A, 1961, D 4,37:3
Barber, Thomas E Mrs, 1937, Je 5,17:4
Barber, Thomas H, 1962, N 13,37:3
Barber, Walter, 1947, Ja 20,25:2
Barber, Walter H, 1951, Je 29,21:4
Barber, Wayne B, 1944, F 29,17:1
Barber, William, 1874, My 5,2:3
Barber, William A, 1947, Jl 21,17:5; 1950, F 9,29:5
Barber, William E, 1941, Mr 18,23:3
Barber, William L, 1945, Je 29,15:4
Barber, William R Mrs, 1953, N 20,23:2
Barber, William W, 1937, D 8,25:2
Barberena, Nicolasa, 1947, Ja 9,23:3
Barberi, Albert P, 1965, Jl 24,21:4
Barberini, Enrico U Prince, 1958, Ap 24,31:4
Barberini, Maria Princess, 1955, Je 19,92:8
Barberis, Alberto, 1957, Jl 29,3:8
Barberis, Eligio G, 1960, D 4,88:6
Barbetta, Anthony L, 1957, O 11,27:1
Barbey, Henry G (por), 1938, Jl 26,19:1
Barbey, Henry I, 1906, Jl 10,7:5
Barbey, John, 1939, D 25,23:2
Barbey, John E, 1956, O 23,33:5
Barbey, Pierre L, 1956, Ap 4,29:3
Barbier, Charles A, 1957, F 7,27:1
Barbier, George Mrs, 1939, Je 10,17:2
Barbier, George W (will, Ag 2,22:1), 1945, Jl 21,11:3
Barbier, H A, 1882, F 15,5:1
Barbieri, Cesare, 1956, My 26,17:2
Barbieri, Frank A G, 1950, My 23,29:1
Barbieri, Joseph P, 1948, Ap 13,28:3
Barbieri, Nick, 1961, D 26,25:2
Barbieri, Peter, 1945, Jl 31,19:2
Barbieri, Thomas, 1942, Je 16,23:3
Barbirolli, Louise Mrs, 1962, O 6,25:2
Barbone, Emilio M, 1957, S 7,19:5
Barbosa, Joao T, 1948, D 16,29:2
Barbosa, Jose C Dr, 1921, S 23,15:6
Barbosa, Ruy Sen, 1923, Mr 2,15:4
Barbosa de Magalhaes, Jose M, 1959, Ap 6,27:5
Barbot, Wingate P, 1950, My 30,17:6
Barbot, Wingate P Mrs, 1950, D 24,34:1
Barbour, A M Maj, 1866, Ap 15,5:5
Barbour, Alexander L, 1945, Mr 24,17:3
Barbour, Anna, 1941, My 16,23:5
Barbour, Anna Edwards Mrs, 1941, S 12,21:5
Barbour, Bertelle A Mrs (will), 1950, S 10,57:4
Barbour, Clarence A Dr (will, F 14,11,8:2), 1937, Ja 17,II,9:1
Barbour, Clarence A Mrs, 1946, Jl 25,21:2
Barbour, Dave, 1965, D 13,39:4
Barbour, Edmund D, 1925, Mr 6,19:4
Barbour, Ensley, 1942, F 26,19:5
Barbour, Fannie Cooley Williams, 1908, Je 14,11:5
Barbour, Francis E, 1948, F 6,26:8
Barbour, Francis E Mrs, 1950, Jl 31,17:4
Barbour, Frederick M Mrs, 1956, O 5,25:2
Barbour, Frederick S, 1952, Ag 6,21:4
Barbour, George C A, 1961, O 14,23:4
Barbour, George H, 1949, Jl 31,60:3
Barbour, Gordon, 1958, Ag 10,94:1
Barbour, Henry E, 1945, Mr 22,23:4
Barbour, Henry G, 1943, S 24,23:5
Barbour, Henry G Mrs, 1943, S 18,17:2
Barbour, Herbert V, 1944, Mr 25,15:5
Barbour, Herman H, 1875, Je 30,4:6
Barbour, Isabell D Dr, 1925, Ja 29,19:4
Barbour, J Foster Mrs, 1943, F 17,21:4
Barbour, J M, 1881, D 9,5:3
Barbour, J Milne, 1951, O 4,33:5
Barbour, James J, 1946, Mr 30,15:5
Barbour, John C, 1962, My 27,92:6
Barbour, John D, 1942, O 29,23:3
Barbour, John E (will, Ag 11,21:7), 1943, Jl 25,31:1
Barbour, John H, 1946, S 27,23:4
Barbour, Joseph L, 1915, F 4,9:5
Barbour, Laurence, 1912, Je 24,9:4
Barbour, Lyell, 1967, My 25,47:2
Barbour, Marshall, 1942, D 7,27:2
Barbour, Najib G, 1949, My 28,15:2
Barbour, Oliver, 1968, Ap 13,25:4
Barbour, Percy E, 1943, My 7,19:1
Barbour, Philips T Mrs, 1962, Jl 4,21:5
Barbour, Phillips T, 1952, Ja 10,29:4
Barbour, Ralph H, 1944, F 20,36:3
Barbour, Robert E, 1961, Mr 16,37:1
Barbour, Robert P, 1956, D 8,19:3
Barbour, Robert S, 1938, F 8,22:2
Barbour, Russell, 1944, Ag 12,11:6
Barbour, Samuel, 1959, D 8,45:3
Barbour, T, 1885, Ja 21,5:5
Barbour, Thomas, 1946, Ja 9,23:1
Barbour, Thomas S Rev Dr, 1915, S 27,9:4
Barbour, Violet Prof, 1968, S 5,57:3
Barbour, W Miller, 1957, Mr 21,31:2
Barbour, W Warren, 1943, N 23,1:6
Barbour, William Col (funl, Mr 5,11:5), 1917, Mr 2, 11:5
Barbour, William Col, 1923, My 10,19:5
Barbour, William D, 1915, Je 2,13:6
Barbour, William R, 1943, Je 27,32:7; 1955, O 1,19:5; 1962, Je 27,32:6
Barboux, Henri, 1910, Ap 26,11:5
Barbusse, H, 1935, Ag 31,13:3
Barc, John J, 1948, O 19,27:4
Barcalow, Theresa, 1908, Je 14,11:5
Barcelo, Alberto, 1946, N 14,29:4
Barcelo, Antonio R, 1938, O 16,45:1
Barcelo, Jose R, 1942, O 27,25:4
Barcham, Irving S, 1944, My 29,15:4
Barchard, John L, 1937, Ja 31,II,8:7
Barchfeld, George, 1949, Ag 19,17:4
Barchfeld, Louis D Mrs, 1943, Ap 3,15:5
Barck, Oscar T, 1953, O 26,21:3
Barcklow, J Harry, 1951, D 7,28:2
Barclay, Albert H Sr, 1951, Mr 17,15:2
Barclay, Alex J, 1950, My 27,17:6
Barclay, Alex M, 1941, Ja 30,21:2
Barclay, Arthur (cor, Jl 24,8:3), 1938, Jl 12,19:5
Barclay, Charles James, 1909, S 28,9:7
Barclay, Edwin J (funl, N 9,33:2), 1955, N 8,29:2
Barclay, Ezekiel S, 1955, Ja 2,76:5
Barclay, Ezekiel S Mrs, 1953, Ag 19,29:5
Barclay, Florence L, 1921, Mr 11,15:4
Barclay, Frank Mrs, 1945, Jl 20,19:4
Barclay, George A, 1964, My 19,37:3
Barclay, George O Dr, 1909, Ap 4,13:4
Barclay, George Sir, 1921, Ja 27,13:4
Barclay, Gordon L Mrs, 1949, O 11,34:3
Barclay, Harold Dr, 1922, Jl 27,17:6
Barclay, Hedworth T, 1944, Jl 27,17:3
Barclay, Henry A, 1905, Mr 9,14:5
Barclay, Hjalmar V, 1941, Je 24,19:1
Barclay, Hugh Brig-Gen, 1968, Jl 24,50:1
Barclay, J Searle, 1945, Ja 31,21:5
Barclay, James C Mrs, 1943, Je 19,13:5
Barclay, James L, 1924, My 18,7:1; 1925, Jl 4,11:5
Barclay, John A, 1940, D 2,23:5
Barclay, John C Mrs, 1962, My 16,41:2
Barclay, Joseph Crews Maj, 1924, My 20,21:5
Barclay, Julian H, 1923, O 7,6:2
Barclay, Lady, 1946, Ja 1,27:3
Barclay, Louise F Mrs, 1903, Jl 28,7:5
Barclay, Mary F, 1950, Mr 25,13:3
Barclay, McKee, 1947, Ap 28,23:2
Barclay, Nathaniel B, 1963, Ap 9,32:1
Barclay, Reginald, 1925, Je 3,23:3
Barclay, Reginald Mrs, 1964, F 9,89:1
Barclay, Robert H, 1960, Mr 28,29:2
Barclay, Samuel, 1950, Mr 27,23:2
Barclay, Shepard G, 1955, Ja 9,86:3
Barclay, Thomas, 1941, F 6,21:3
Barclay, Wade C, 1965, Ja 16,27:1
Barclay, Wade C Mrs, 1952, Ap 26,23:6
Barclay, William D, 1945, S 1,11:6
Barclay, William K Jr, 1954, Mr 20,15:4
Barclay, William K Sr, 1954, Jl 30,17:6
Barclay, William L, 1938, F 14,17:4
Barclay, William Mrs, 1950, Jl 21,19:2
Barclay, Williams R, 1938, S 17,17:5
Barclay, Wright, 1945, F 23,18:2
Barclay, Wright Mrs, 1946, Je 5,23:3
Barclay-Smith, Edward, 1945, Jl 6,11:5
Barcon, Irving, 1958, Je 8,88:8
Barcroft, Joseph, 1947, Mr 22,13:3
Barcume, George R, 1949, Mr 13,76:1
Barcus, James M, 1946, Ag 20,27:5
Barcus, James S, 1920, My 5,11:4
Barcus, Nathan H, 1959, Ap 9,31:2
Bard, Albert S (Mr 26), 1963, Ap 1,35:2
Bard, Alex E, 1941, Ag 21,17:6
Bard, Charles, 1921, Ja 15,13:4
Bard, Charles H, 1954, Je 16,31:2
Bard, Charles H Mrs, 1945, Je 22,15:3
Bard, Charles R Mrs (will), 1959, S 19,16:7
Bard, Charles W Mrs, 1948, O 19,28:3
Bard, Dracie Mrs, 1957, Ag 18,82:2
Bard, E H, 1903, My 15,9:6
Bard, Edward L, 1957, S 4,34:6
Bard, Eva M Mrs, 1939, Ap 1,19:5
Bard, Francis Mrs, 1940, Ap 29,15:4
Bard, Francois, 1944, Ap 2,39:3
Bard, Frederic B, 1950, Je 6,29:5
Bard, George M Mrs, 1947, Mr 10,21:5
Bard, George W, 1925, S 24,25:4
Bard, Guy K, 1953, N 24,30:3
Bard, Harry D, 1948, My 19,27:2
Bard, Harry E, 1955, Jl 13,25:4
Bard, Harry E Mrs, 1956, Ap 24,32:1
Bard, Harry H, 1963, D 12,39:2
Bard, Helen (Mrs A Nixon), 1967, Ap 25,43:1
Bard, Joan, 1964, Ag 11,33:1
Bard, Maria, 1944, Ap 7,19:2
Bard, Phil, 1966, Mr 17,43:7
Bard, Phil L Mrs, 1952, My 28,29:4
Bard, Ralph A Mrs, 1949, Mr 30,25:3
Bard, Sam, 1878, S 20,4:7
Bard, Silas K, 1944, D 22,17:5
Bard, Thomas R Ex-Sen, 1915, Mr 6,11:4
Bard, Wilkie, 1944, My 6,15:4
Bard, William H, 1937, Mr 15,23:1
Bardac, Jacques, 1957, Jl 29,19:3
Bardach, Paul, 1955, D 29,23:1
Bardeen, Charles W, 1924, Ag 20,13:4
Bardell, Rowland P, 1942, N 29,64:7
Barden, E R, 1870, My 18,2:3
Barden, Graham A, 1967, Ja 30,29:1
Barden, John J, 1938, D 4,61:2
Barden, John P, 1954, F 24,25:1
Barden, Joseph A, 1942, D 25,17:4
Barden, Leonard O, 1949, N 22,30:3
Barden, Levi W Col, 1915, S 2,9:5
Barden, Susan T, 1966, Ja 15,27:1
Barden, William J, 1956, O 4,33:2
Bardenhagen, Charles, 1950, F 28,29:1
Bardenheuer, H Ernest, 1939, O 22,40:8
Bardes, Henry, 1943, My 25,23:2
Bardez, Harry M, 1949, F 7,19:2
Bardgett, Edward R, 1962, O 13,25:6
Bardgett, Walter A, 1953, F 9,27:4
Bardin, George, 1910, Je 15,9:4
Bardin, Ivan P, 1960, Ja 8,25:3
Bardin, Kalman Rabbi, 1924, Mr 19,21:5
Bardin-Bouchart, Etienne, 1950, My 4,27:1
Bardo, Clinton L (will, Ag 14,11:5), 1937, Ag 3,23:3
Bardoloi, Gopinath, 1950, Ag 6,72:5
Bardoly, Emery A, 1949, N 12,15:6
Bardomian Edw, Bro, 1958, O 16,37:3
Bardon, Fred B, 1916, Mr 19,19:6
Bardon, Joseph T, 1958, Mr 1,17:3
Bardon, Patrick F, 1940, Je 9,44:1
Bardon, Thomas, 1964, Jl 28,35:4
Bardon, Thomas Mrs, 1957, D 26,19:3
Bardos, Bela, 1948, D 7,31:3
Bardoux, Jacques, 1959, Ag 18,29:4
Bardsley, Charles H Mrs, 1953, Ja 22,23:2
Bardsley, Chester T, 1964, F 13,31:3
Bardsley, Edward, 1954, Ja 15,20:3
Bardsley, George H, 1961, Mr 2,27:4
Bardsley, Robert V, 1952, Jl 29,21:1

Bardsley, William W, 1958, Je 19,31:5
Bardua, Frank W Mrs, 1937, Je 12,15:3
Bardusch, Jacob, 1940, Ja 12,17:5
Bardwell, Charles M, 1953, O 21,24:4
Bardwell, Conrad M, 1949, Ap 29,23:3
Bardwell, Darwin L, 1915, S 7,13:5
Bardwell, George E, 1939, S 16,17:3
Bardwell, Harry B, 1956, N 7,31:1
Bardwell, Josiah, 1875, O 23,4:6
Bardwell, Ralph B, 1938, Ja 28,21:5
Bardwell, Robert D, 1943, N 26,23:1
Bardwell, Willie A, 1908, Mr 28,9:6
Bardy, Edward, 1961, Ag 4,21:2
Bardy, Jack, 1967, F 18,29:1
Bardy, Louis C, 1956, S 7,23:4
Bare, Howard F, 1950, Ja 20,25:2
Bare, Walter, 1937, F 6,17:4
Bare, William F, 1955, N 17,35:3
Barea, Arturo, 1957, D 28,17:4
Barefoot, William, 1954, Jl 17,13:5
Bareford, Frank I, 1968, Ag 17,27:2
Bareford, Frank I Sr, 1951, Je 19,30:3
Bareford, Roxanna Mrs, 1946, Ag 9,19:6
Bareham, Harry U Mrs, 1944, Ap 29,15:4
Bareis, Joseph E, 1959, Mr 6,25:3
Bareish, Philip, 1968, S 27,47:4
Barell, Emil C, 1953, Mr 19,29:4
Barella, Giulio, 1942, D 27,35:1
Baremore, Arnold W, 1951, S 9,89:1
Baremore, Henry R Jr, 1948, Mr 5,22:3
Barenbach, Philip G, 1960, Ja 2,13:5
Barenberg, Louis H, 1957, D 19,31:2
Barenz, Harold W, 1965, My 4,44:1
Barer, C Gregory, 1957, F 10,85:6
Barere, Simon, 1951, Ap 3,1:2
Barere, Simon Mrs, 1958, F 21,23:4
Baretz, Louis H, 1955, Mr 4,23:5
Bareuther, Joseph, 1950, Je 11,92:4
Barfield, Charles V, 1966, F 28,27:2
Barford, Burns F Sr, 1958, N 3,37:2
Barg, Moshe L, 1963, Je 5,41:2
Bargar, Allen E, 1959, Jl 20,25:4
Bargelt, Louis J Mrs, 1951, Ag 29,25:5
Barger, Allen Jr, 1939, F 5,41:3
Barger, Edgar, 1948, Ja 8,25:1
Barger, Fred C Maj, 1923, O 6,15:4
Barger, George, 1939, Ja 7,15:2
Barger, James B, 1947, D 3,29:1
Barger, James H, 1947, Jl 7,17:3
Barger, Milton S, 1925, Mr 19,21:3
Barger, Milton S Mrs, 1911, My 18,11:4
Barger, Milton Sanford, 1925, Mr 6,19:4
Barger, Samuel F, 1914, Ap 8,13:4
Barger, William H, 1952, Mr 22,13:3
Bargeron, Carlisle, 1965, Mr 24,46:4
Barget, Carl W Sr, 1967, Mr 8,45:5
Bargh, Samuel J, 1955, D 28,23:3
Barghash Bin Said, Sultan of Zanzibar, 1888, Mr 28, 2:3
Bargman, Ewald F, 1945, N 23,23:4
Barguet, Eugene B, 1943, Mr 4,20:1
Barham, Albert D, 1945, N 20,21:4
Barham, Frank F, 1953, Ag 7,19:4
Barham, Guy, 1922, Je 10,11:6
Barham, Harry W Sr, 1956, My 11,28:2
Barham, Henry C, 1949, S 29,29:5
Barham, Lewis A, 1958, Mr 14,25:2
Barham, Lillard B, 1945, O 4,23:5
Barham, Marie B Mrs, 1941, D 15,19:2
Barham, Murray H, 1956, D 27,25:1
Barham, Tracy, 1949, D 28,32:2
Barhash, Abraham Z, 1953, D 25,17:3
Barhato, Joseph, 1921, Jl 13,9:2
Barhite, Jared, 1921, Ja 23,22:3
Barhite, John E, 1924, Ap 4,19:5
Barhydt, Charles, 1949, Ap 15,23:2
Barhydt, David Parish, 1908, F 15,7:4
Barhydt, James A, 1939, Jl 17,19:2
Barhydt, James A Mrs, 1939, Jl 17,19:2
Bari, Tony, 1960, S 17,23:4
Barich, Harold J, 1964, F 27,31:5
Baright, Elijah Mrs, 1945, Ja 29,13:1
Baright, Frederick, 1952, Jl 26,13:6
Baright, George F, 1950, F 18,15:2
Baright, George F Mrs, 1961, Ja 9,39:2
Baright, Mary L, 1948, Jl 19,19:6
Baril, Georges, 1953, O 9,27:3
Baril, Samuel J, 1960, Ap 22,29:1
Baril, Wilbur A, 1946, N 4,25:5
Barile, Frank P, 1956, My 21,25:5
Barili, Cardinal, 1875, Mr 9,7:3
Barinbaum, Moses, 1960, My 27,31:1
Baring, Alex Mrs, 1953, Ja 6,29:6
Baring, Cecil Mrs, 1922, Ap 4,17:5
Baring, Charles Bp, 1879, S 17,5:4
Baring, Esmond C, 1963, N 26,37:4
Baring, Evelyn (Lord Cromer), 1917, Ja 30,9:3
Baring, Godfrey, 1957, N 26,33:4
Baring, Harold H J Mrs, 1940, Ap 5,21:5
Baring, Maurice, 1945, D 16,40:1
Baring, Rowland T (Lord Cromer), 1953, My 14,29:5
Baring, Thomas, 1873, N 20,1:7; 1923, Je 6,21:4
Baring, Windham, 1922, D 29,13:5
Baring-Gould, S Rev, 1924, Ja 3,17:3
Baring-Gould, William D, 1921, Ag 20,7:6
Baring-Gould, William S, 1967, Ag 12,25:5
Baringer, Edward M, 1945, Jl 23,19:4
Baringer, Irwin Y, 1952, Ag 4,15:4
Barish, Max Mrs, 1966, Ag 20,25:2
Baritz, Sidney, 1963, My 14,39:3
Barjansky, Alexandre Mrs (Cath), 1965, F 7,92:2
Barjot, Pierre, 1960, F 2,35:3
Bark, Henry Mrs, 1948, S 2,24:2
Bark, Peter Sir, 1937, Ja 18,17:3
Barkalow, Clifton T, 1964, S 29,43:4
Barkalow, Eawin R, 1946, Ja 16,24:3
Barkalow, John S, 1910, Mr 30,12:1
Barkan, Georg, 1945, Mr 8,23:2
Barkan, Otto, 1958, Ap 28,23:5
Barkdull, Charles J, 1953, Ap 23,29:3
Barke, Robert, 1956, Mr 11,88:3
Barkelew, J Ervene, 1945, D 1,23:5
Barkeloo, Miss, 1870, S 27,2:3
Barkentin, George S, 1953, Jl 11,11:6
Barkentin, William S, 1962, F 12,23:4
Barker, Abraham, 1906, Ap 9,1:2
Barker, Albert S, 1942, Ag 23,43:1
Barker, Albert Smith Rear-Adm, 1916, Ja 31,11:4
Barker, Albert W, 1947, D 6,15:5
Barker, Alex C, 1956, Je 20,31:2
Barker, Alex E W, 1948, Ja 5,19:2
Barker, Anthony, 1921, Ja 6,11:3
Barker, Arthur E, 1924, Ja 4,13:4
Barker, Bradley, 1951, S 30,72:3
Barker, C W (see also Ap 6), 1877, Ap 9,8:2
Barker, C W, 1880, Je 1,2:3
Barker, Catherine D Mrs, 1940, N 20,21:4
Barker, Charles E, 1948, Mr 31,25:6
Barker, Charles Francis, 1909, Jl 7,9:5
Barker, Charles H, 1947, Ap 2,27:3
Barker, Charles W T, 1938, Ap 30,15:3
Barker, Clarence A, 1954, S 10,23:1
Barker, Creighton, 1960, Ap 11,31:2
Barker, Curtis H, 1945, N 16,19:4
Barker, Daniel A, 1922, My 29,11:4
Barker, Daniel D, 1954, Ap 2,27:4
Barker, David, 1874, S 16,4:7
Barker, Edgar E, 1948, F 14,13:3
Barker, Edward F, 1949, N 12,15:2
Barker, Ellen B Mrs, 1938, D 22,21:5
Barker, Ellen F, 1944, Je 8,21:6
Barker, Ellen M Mrs, 1937, Jl 3,24:3
Barker, Elsa Mrs, 1954, Ag 26,27:5
Barker, Ernest, 1960, F 20,23:6
Barker, Estelle M, 1956, N 1,39:4
Barker, Ezra D, 1903, N 17,9:6
Barker, F Dr, 1891, Je 1,5:3
Barker, F Marion, 1950, F 22,29:3
Barker, Ford O, 1957, Jl 4,19:2
Barker, Fordyce Dwight Mrs, 1925, Ap 25,15:5
Barker, Francis M, 1944, Jl 22,15:4
Barker, Frank C, 1943, Ap 6,21:3
Barker, Frank M, 1954, Jl 17,13:2
Barker, Frederick A, 1938, Ag 23,17:5
Barker, G W (see also S 27), 1878, S 29,5:6
Barker, George H, 1941, N 19,23:2; 1945, F 7,21:4
Barker, George H Mrs, 1955, My 11,31:1
Barker, George Jr, 1967, D 31,44:8
Barker, George O, 1903, Jl 22,7:6
Barker, George W Mrs, 1952, Ja 29,25:1
Barker, Gerard, 1957, F 19,31:5
Barker, Grace S T, 1954, Mr 8,27:2
Barker, Guy A, 1941, Je 19,21:4
Barker, H, 1914, D 24,9:4
Barker, H Lawrence, 1953, F 26,25:1
Barker, Harold R, 1965, My 31,17:3
Barker, Harriet R Mrs, 1941, F 26,21:4
Barker, Harry, 1963, Je 23,85:2
Barker, Harry L, 1939, My 30,17:4
Barker, Henrietta F, 1941, S 24,23:2
Barker, Henry W, 1943, O 3,48:6
Barker, Herbert A, 1950, Jl 22,15:2
Barker, Herbert L, 1954, Mr 25,29:2
Barker, Herbert T Mrs, 1952, F 18,19:3
Barker, Hilda J Mrs, 1941, My 13,23:4
Barker, Howard W, 1947, F 21,19:4
Barker, J Wesley, 1948, Jl 20,23:4
Barker, Jacob, 1871, D 27,1:4
Barker, James, 1922, F 25,13:4; 1955, Jl 20,27:2
Barker, James Madison, 1905, O 4,9:6
Barker, James McD, 1965, Je 21,29:3
Barker, James P, 1946, Ag 10,13:1
Barker, James W, 1869, Je 27,4:6
Barker, John Col, 1924, My 21,19:1
Barker, John W Brig-Gen, 1924, My 15,19:4
Barker, Joseph, 1949, My 1,88:4
Barker, Joseph D, 1965, S 11,27:4
Barker, Joseph E, 1946, D 6,23:3
Barker, Joseph L, 1956, Ja 2,21:5
Barker, Joseph W Mrs, 1937, O 1,21:5
Barker, Katharine, 1947, O 3,25:2
Barker, Lewellys F, 1943, Jl 14,19:1
Barker, Lilian Dame, 1955, My 23,23:1
Barker, Lottie S Mrs, 1944, Mr 10,15:5
Barker, Louis H, 1939, F 21,19:4
Barker, Marion H, 1947, Ag 15,18:2
Barker, Mary A Mrs (will), 1940, F 10,18:4
Barker, Mary B Mrs, 1942, Ja 8,21:5
Barker, Oliver D, 1946, N 6,23:4
Barker, Otis W, 1951, My 25,27:4
Barker, Otis Y, 1904, O 19,16:2
Barker, P C, 1903, Ag 22,9:6
Barker, Percival M Mrs, 1921, D 21,19:4
Barker, Phil, 1952, Ap 19,15:2
Barker, R Delmar, 1948, Ag 5,21:2
Barker, Rayner C, 1945, My 17,19:1
Barker, Reginald, 1945, F 24,11:3
Barker, Reginald C, 1937, O 22,19:5
Barker, Richard G, 1962, N 27,37:3
Barker, Richard H Dr, 1968, Mr 9,29:3
Barker, Rosa D Mrs, 1937, D 9,26:3
Barker, Roy T, 1959, Jl 15,29:4
Barker, Samuel G, 1942, Ja 2,23:2
Barker, Samuel H, 1939, S 14,23:4
Barker, Stephen, 1946, Ag 18,44:6
Barker, Stephen F, 1948, O 7,29:4
Barker, T J, 1882, Ap 12,4:7
Barker, Thomas, 1941, Jl 1,23:2
Barker, Thomas H, 1954, My 16,76:2
Barker, W Halsey, 1949, Mr 27,78:6
Barker, W MacFarlane, 1948, Ag 11,22:2
Barker, Walter C, 1941, D 29,15:4
Barker, Walter D, 1938, Ap 14,23:2
Barker, Walter G, 1958, O 28,35:4
Barker, Wendell P, 1941, Ap 8,25:5
Barker, Wharton, 1921, Ap 9,11:4
Barker, Willard C, 1954, Ap 17,13:5
Barker, Willard M, 1948, Mr 29,21:4
Barker, William B, 1940, Je 25,23:6
Barker, William E, 1947, D 22,21:5; 1954, My 22,15:2
Barker, William H, 1955, F 13,87:1
Barker, William Henry Maj, 1924, S 11,23:6
Barker, William L, 1937, Ja 16,15:1
Barker, William P, 1947, N 20,29:2
Barker, William P Mrs, 1938, D 11,60:7
Barker, William S, 1950, Jl 28,21:5
Barker, William T, 1951, O 20,15:6
Barker, William W, 1954, N 10,33:2
Barkes, Lewis C, 1966, D 18,85:1
Barkey, Jacob A, 1961, F 8,31:4
Barkhaus, Louis H, 1947, S 28,61:1
Barkhausen, Dr, 1903, S 1,7:6
Barkhausen, Louis H, 1962, Mr 17,25:5
Barkhorn, Charles J, 1961, Jl 1,17:5
Barkhorn, Henry C, 1949, Jl 28,23:3
Barkhorn, Henry C Jr Mrs, 1967, Ap 16,83:1
Barkhouse, Julius, 1921, O 4,15:7
Barkhouse, Louis, 1916, My 6,11:5
Barkhouse, R, 1953, N 6,27:1
Barkin, Samuel, 1958, Mr 16,86:4
Barkin, Samuel Mrs, 1962, Ja 26,31:2
Barkla, Charles G, 1944, O 25,21:3
Barkley, Alben W (funl, My 3,1:4), 1956, My 1,1:1
Barkley, Alben W Mrs, 1947, Mr 11,27:5; 1964, S 7, 19:2
Barkley, Albert H, 1941, Ap 1,23:4
Barkley, Alonzo H, 1949, Ja 3,23:5
Barkley, Augustus P, 1942, Jl 2,21:2
Barkley, Edmond L, 1937, D 8,25:1
Barkley, Florence, 1954, F 3,23:4
Barkley, Frederick R, 1963, N 17,87:2
Barkley, Harry W, 1948, N 12,23:1
Barkley, J E, 1928, Mr 29,27:5
Barkley, James R, 1948, Jl 27,25:4
Barkley, John W Mrs, 1945, D 24,15:1
Barkley, Littleton Mrs, 1946, Ag 21,27:3
Barkley, Paul H, 1963, O 21,31:4
Barkley, Ralph, 1953, N 17,31:5
Barkley, William H, 1953, D 15,39:4
Barkley, William J, 1958, F 10,23:1
Barkley, William Mrs, 1940, Jl 25,17:1
Barklie, Arch, 1937, F 6,17:2
Barklie, Arch Mrs, 1937, Ja 17,II,8:3
Barklie, Mabel D Mrs, 1940, D 4,27:5
Barkman, Edward A Mrs, 1950, Ap 13,29:4
Barkoff, Henry H, 1949, D 28,32:1
Barksdale, Hamilton, 1918, O 19,15:1
Barksdale, John S, 1947, F 4,26:2
Barkstedt, Henry C, 1962, N 17,25:2
Barlas, Harry, 1950, My 30,18:2
Barlas, Mordecai, 1962, Ja 23,33:4
Barlassina, Louis, 1947, S 28,61:1
Barleben, Karl A, 1964, My 10,83:2
Barler, William R, 1959, F 12,27:3
Barletta, Heraclio, 1961, Ja 2,14:5
Barley, Alfred L, 1944, Je 2,15:2
Barley, Henry, 1939, Ja 16,15:1
Barlin, G Msgr, 1909, S 7,9:5
Barling, Edward E, 1943, Je 2,25:3
Barling, Joseph A Mrs, 1946, Jl 15,25:5
Barling, Walter H, 1965, Ap 4,87:1
Barlor, John P (will), 1938, Mr 26,17:8
Barlotti, James A, 1948, Je 9,29:2
Barlow, Aaron, 1946, F 10,42:8
Barlow, Abel J, 1939, Mr 7,21:6
Barlow, Arthur E, 1963, Jl 29,19:4
Barlow, Charles, 1880, Jl 26,4:7
Barlow, Charles H, 1964, N 10,47:1
Barlow, De Witt D, 1945, S 25,25:5

Barlow, E Dudley, 1941, Ag 30,13:2
Barlow, Edgar C, 1951, Jl 22,61:1
Barlow, Edward S, 1952, Jl 13,60:5
Barlow, Elbert S, 1948, D 6,25:3
Barlow, Elmer E, 1948, Je 28,19:4
Barlow, Elmer H, 1966, Ap 20,47:1
Barlow, Faith C, 1949, N 8,31:4
Barlow, George H, 1954, My 7,23:2
Barlow, George W, 1918, S 21,9:8
Barlow, Harry E, 1952, Mr 20,29:1
Barlow, Helen A Mrs, 1946, S 28,17:6
Barlow, Henry M, 1959, D 31,21:5
Barlow, Henry N Mrs, 1961, My 26,33:4
Barlow, Herbert H, 1946, Ja 4,21:2
Barlow, Hildegarde, 1958, N 2,89:2
Barlow, Howard L, 1938, F 21,19:3
Barlow, James F, 1958, O 5,86:6
Barlow, Jane, 1917, Ap 20,13:6
Barlow, Jenny, 1949, N 21,25:2
Barlow, John, 1944, N 27,23:4; 1959, F 1,84:7
Barlow, John C, 1938, My 2,17:5
Barlow, John E Rev, 1937, F 27,17:6
Barlow, John H, 1959, S 2,29:3
Barlow, John P, 1955, N 15,33:4
Barlow, John W Gen, 1914, Mr 3,9:4
Barlow, Joseph H, 1956, Ag 4,15:5
Barlow, Joseph W, 1956, Ap 19,31:2
Barlow, Lester P, 1967, S 6,47:1
Barlow, Mark, 1954, Ag 14,15:3
Barlow, Mason, 1957, F 17,92:7
Barlow, Milt G, 1904, S 29,9:6
Barlow, Moses, 1912, Ja 15,13:5
Barlow, Myron, 1937, Ag 17,19:2
Barlow, Perry Mrs (D H Smith), 1955, D 18,92:6
Barlow, Peter T (funl, My 11,17:5), 1921, My 10,17:3
Barlow, Peter T Mrs, 1905, Ap 26,11:5
Barlow, Reginald, 1943, Jl 7,19:3
Barlow, Robert L, 1966, D 25,49:1
Barlow, Robert S, 1943, S 4,13:1
Barlow, Ronald H Mrs, 1958, Ag 28,27:3
Barlow, S B, 1876, F 29,5:4
Barlow, S L M, 1889, Jl 11,5:2
Barlow, Stephen H, 1962, Jl 9,31:3
Barlow, Thomas, 1945, Ja 15,19:4
Barlow, Waldo D, 1965, Ja 1,17:1
Barlow, Walter, 1941, My 15,23:3
Barlow, Walter J Dr, 1937, S 5,II,6:7
Barlow, Walter L, 1937, D 3,24:2
Barlow, Willard A, 1950, O 11,33:2
Barlow, Willard A Mrs, 1950, O 11,33:2
Barlow, William, 1937, Jl 25,II,7:4
Barlow, William E, 1945, My 11,19:1
Barlow, William H, 1962, S 23,86:7
Barlow, William L, 1951, Je 3,93:1
Barlow, William Mrs, 1914, O 10,11:5
Barlow, William N Mrs, 1947, N 19,27:4
Barma, Gustav (funl, S 23,13:5), 1910, S 22,9:4
Barmack, Joseph E Mrs, 1965, Je 1,39:2
Barmat, Jules, 1938, Ja 7,12:3
Barmettler, Otto H, 1951, Je 19,29:5
Barmore, Alfred, 1875, My 15,10:3
Barmore, Alida, 1953, F 15,93:2
Barmore, Austin Mrs, 1960, Ap 1,33:4
Barmore, G Newell, 1942, S 11,21:4
Barnabas, Bro, 1929, Ap 24,29:3
Barnaby, Frank A, 1941, F 18,23:1
Barnaby, Nathaniel Sir, 1915, Je 16,11:5
Barnar, Bradford, 1914, Ja 28,9:5
Barnard, Albert E, 1950, O 30,27:5
Barnard, Alton, 1959, Jl 6,27:4
Barnard, Amelia J Mrs, 1941, Ap 26,15:4
Barnard, Arthur E, 1948, F 24,25:3
Barnard, Arthur M, 1966, D 12,47:3
Barnard, Arthur Mrs, 1946, D 29,35:8
Barnard, Charles D, 1944, N 6,19:5
Barnard, Charles I, 1942, My 15,20:2
Barnard, Charles J, 1944, Ap 26,19:3
Barnard, Chester I, 1961, Je 8,35:4
Barnard, Clinton L, 1948, F 2,19:5
Barnard, E S, 1931, Mr 28,24:6
Barnard, Edward E Prof, 1923, F 7,15:5
Barnard, Emily V, 1938, O 12,27:1
Barnard, Evan G, 1938, Ja 5,21:2
Barnard, Everett L, 1958, Je 22,76:6
Barnard, Everett L Mrs, 1964, F 7,32:1
Barnard, Everett P, 1957, N 3,89:1
Barnard, F A P, 1889, Ap 28,5:3
Barnard, Frank E, 1903, D 19,9:5
Barnard, Frederic, 1939, Mr 5,48:5
Barnard, Fuller Jr, 1937, Mr 25,25:4
Barnard, G G, 1879, Ap 28,5:1
Barnard, George (mem ser), 1876, O 20,8:4
Barnard, George, 1944, Je 24,13:4
Barnard, George D, 1915, Je 1,15:6
Barnard, George G, 1938, Ap 25,1:4
Barnard, George G Mrs, 1947, N 18,29:2
Barnard, George Gorham, 1919, Ag 23,7:7
Barnard, George M, 1949, Ja 4,19:5
Barnard, George P Mrs, 1925, Jl 7,19:5
Barnard, George T, 1937, D 22,25:4
Barnard, Glenn H, 1941, My 7,25:4
Barnard, Harold H, 1964, Ap 2,33:4
Barnard, Harry E, 1947, Ja 2,27:3
Barnard, Harry W, 1957, O 29,31:5
Barnard, Hayden S Mrs, 1953, Ja 31,15:5
Barnard, Henry, 1907, Ja 28,7:4
Barnard, Herbert W, 1946, O 7,31:5
Barnard, Horace, 1954, Mr 27,17:3
Barnard, J Augustus, 1958, D 5,31:2
Barnard, J Lyon Mrs, 1946, N 17,68:2
Barnard, James L, 1941, Ag 11,13:4
Barnard, John, 1947, D 3,29:1
Barnard, John G Maj Gen, 1882, My 15,5:5
Barnard, Joseph, 1947, Ap 22,27:3
Barnard, Joseph F Judge, 1904, Ja 7,9:5
Barnard, Julia G Mrs, 1960, O 12,39:3
Barnard, Leroy L, 1944, My 6,15:3
Barnard, Leslie F, 1944, Mr 23,19:4
Barnard, Leslie G, 1961, O 31,31:5
Barnard, Margaret B, 1950, Ag 26,13:2
Barnard, Montrose Maj, 1914, Jl 30,9:4
Barnard, Oscar G, 1952, D 29,19:4
Barnard, Phil E, 1938, S 29,25:2
Barnard, Seymour, 1959, Je 15,27:3
Barnard, Seymour Mrs, 1944, N 26,57:1
Barnard, Thomas M, 1944, O 28,15:5
Barnard, Thurman L, 1953, My 6,31:3
Barnard, W F, 1903, Mr 21,9:3
Barnard, William F, 1949, S 2,17:3
Barnard, William H, 1946, F 26,25:2
Barnard, William L, 1942, Mr 26,23:5
Barnard, William N (por), 1947, Ap 4,23:3
Barnardiston, Nathaniel Walter Gen, 1919, Ag 20,15:2
Barnardo, Thomas John, 1905, S 21,9:3
Barnason, Charles F, 1949, D 24,15:4
Barnato, Peter W, 1959, F 23,23:4
Barnato, Woolf, 1948, Jl 28,23:5
Barnatone, Charles Mrs, 1943, F 11,19:2
Barnby (Lord Francis Willey), 1929, F 17,II,8:1
Barndt, Harold J, 1944, Ja 22,13:3
Barnead, Aviassaf, 1957, N 7,35:2
Barnecott, Charles F, 1943, Jl 27,17:6
Barnekow, Charles W, 1950, F 2,27:3
Barner, Earl E, 1956, Mr 6,31:3
Barnert, Fannie, 1947, F 13,24:2
Barnert, N, 1927, D 24,15:3
Barnes, A G, 1931, Jl 26,II,4:1
Barnes, A H Rev, 1878, My 10,4:7
Barnes, Albert C, 1951, Jl 25,1:2
Barnes, Albert C Mrs, 1966, My 6,47:1
Barnes, Albert J, 1943, Jl 29,19:4
Barnes, Albert M, 1952, Ap 4,33:7
Barnes, Albert M Mrs, 1963, My 17,33:5
Barnes, Albert Rev, 1870, D 27,5:4
Barnes, Alfred C Gen, 1904, N 29,5:6
Barnes, Alfred V, 1944, N 8,17:4
Barnes, Amos, 1906, My 31,7:6
Barnes, Amos F, 1938, My 23,17:4
Barnes, Amos W, 1953, F 6,20:7
Barnes, Amy, 1949, Ja 23,68:4
Barnes, Andrew N, 1952, Ag 28,23:4
Barnes, Arthur D, 1965, Je 23,41:4
Barnes, Arthur E, 1937, O 11,21:6
Barnes, Arthur F, 1942, D 15,27:5
Barnes, Arthur H, 1957, S 10,33:5
Barnes, Arthur K, 1950, Ja 14,15:6
Barnes, Arthur L, 1939, S 27,25:5
Barnes, Arthur S, 1956, D 26,27:1
Barnes, Arthur S Mrs, 1950, O 3,31:2
Barnes, Aubrey T, 1950, Ap 18,31:3
Barnes, Benjamin F, 1909, O 21,9:4
Barnes, C C Capt, 1903, My 8,9:7
Barnes, C Montgomery, 1961, Ag 31,27:1
Barnes, Cecil, 1949, Je 27,27:4
Barnes, Charles A, 1913, D 30,9:5
Barnes, Charles E 3d, 1966, Jl 18,27:4
Barnes, Charles F, 1952, Jl 22,25:1
Barnes, Charles H, 1952, Ja 25,21:4
Barnes, Charles J, 1921, Jl 12,13:3
Barnes, Charles P, 1951, D 15,13:4
Barnes, Charles P Mrs, 1951, O 17,31:2
Barnes, Charles S, 1940, D 30,17:4
Barnes, Charles Y, 1943, Ap 5,19:2
Barnes, Claire L (por), 1947, Ja 18,15:3
Barnes, Clarence A, 1944, N 11,13:5
Barnes, Clifford W, 1944, S 19,21:3
Barnes, Clifford W Mrs, 1938, My 14,15:6
Barnes, Cora F (est), 1914, Ag 8,9:5
Barnes, Cornelius E, 1941, Mr 13,21:4
Barnes, Courtlandt D, 1952, F 25,21:4
Barnes, Courtlandt T Mrs, 1958, F 23,92:4
Barnes, Cyrus, 1956, Ag 2,25:5
Barnes, Cyrus L, 1943, Ap 24,13:1
Barnes, Daniel, 1922, Ap 21,13:4
Barnes, David Mrs, 1952, O 27,27:2
Barnes, David R, 1940, O 29,25:2
Barnes, Diantha M Mrs, 1939, Jl 14,19:6
Barnes, Dollie A Mrs, 1937, My 22,15:2
Barnes, Donald L, 1962, Jl 21,19:2
Barnes, Dorothy P Mrs, 1957, Je 18,33:4
Barnes, E Mortimer, 1955, F 16,29:1
Barnes, Earl D, 1951, Ag 13,17:2
Barnes, Edgar S, 1948, Mr 17,25:2
Barnes, Edward A Mrs, 1949, Jl 19,29:3
Barnes, Edwin C, 1954, S 24,24:2
Barnes, Edwin S, 1948, Mr 1,23:2
Barnes, Edwin S Mrs, 1946, N 28,27:3; 1950, Mr 11, 15:2
Barnes, Elmer, 1951, N 23,29:3
Barnes, Emile D, 1959, Jl 5,57:1
Barnes, Emily, 1937, Mr 10,23:5
Barnes, Esther W, 1903, My 26,9:6
Barnes, Eugene F, 1921, F 1,11:2
Barnes, Frank G P, 1942, S 7,19:3
Barnes, Frank H, 1953, S 15,31:4
Barnes, Frank K, 1947, Ja 14,26:3
Barnes, Frank X, 1957, D 14,21:3
Barnes, Franklin B, 1945, Ja 16,20:2
Barnes, Fred A, 1950, Ap 7,25:6
Barnes, Frederic M, 1961, F 4,19:5
Barnes, Frederick Edmund, 1923, Ap 26,19:5
Barnes, Frederick G Sir, 1939, Mr 18,17:5
Barnes, Frederick J, 1948, N 22,21:2
Barnes, Fuller F, 1955, Je 23,29:2
Barnes, G Kingsbury, 1916, My 6,11:4
Barnes, George A, 1965, Ja 11,45:5
Barnes, George E, 1948, D 30,19:1
Barnes, George F, 1951, Jl 22,61:3
Barnes, George H, 1925, Ag 29,11:5; 1938, D 8,27:5
Barnes, George N, 1940, Ap 23,23:4
Barnes, George O, 1944, S 20,23:5
Barnes, George R, 1961, Ap 11,37:4
Barnes, George S, 1953, Je 1,23:5
Barnes, George Z, 1951, Jl 17,27:2
Barnes, Gladeon M, 1961, N 16,39:2
Barnes, Grace R, 1954, Jl 9,17:5
Barnes, H Edgar, 1940, O 7,17:4
Barnes, Haldor, 1943, S 15,27:6
Barnes, Harold A, 1953, Ag 12,31:6
Barnes, Harold F, 1945, My 10,23:3
Barnes, Harold O, 1956, Ap 20,25:4
Barnes, Harriet E, 1881, O 28,8:1
Barnes, Harris C, 1945, Mr 14,20:2
Barnes, Harry C, 1953, Jl 24,13:5
Barnes, Harry Elmer Dr, 1968, Ag 28,44:4
Barnes, Harry G, 1955, Je 23,29:2
Barnes, Harry J, 1953, S 11,21:3
Barnes, Hattie D Mrs, 1941, Ap 19,15:2
Barnes, Henry, 1907, N 29,9:6
Barnes, Henry A Comr (funl plans, S 18,47:1; funl, S 20,47:5), 1968, S 17,1:4
Barnes, Henry Burr, 1911, Ja 13,9:3
Barnes, Henry J, 1950, My 17,29:4
Barnes, Henry Mrs, 1956, My 14,25:5
Barnes, Herbert O, 1947, Ap 14,27:3
Barnes, Horace M, 1952, Ap 26,23:4
Barnes, Howard, 1945, O 21,46:1; 1968, Mr 13,53:1
Barnes, Howard Mrs (K Vincent), 1962, My 28,29:5
Barnes, Howel H Jr, 1963, D 9,35:4
Barnes, hugh E, 1965, Mr 8,29:5
Barnes, Hugh E Mrs, 1961, O 27,30:8
Barnes, Hugh S, 1940, F 16,19:5
Barnes, I C, 1903, My 3,9:6
Barnes, Ira W, 1953, N 18,31:2
Barnes, J, 1936, My 1,21:3
Barnes, J Carroll, 1947, Ag 12,23:2
Barnes, J K Gen, 1883, Ap 6,4:7
Barnes, James, 1950, Ag 26,13:5; 1962, D 27,7:1; 1966, My 26,47:1
Barnes, James A Mrs, 1957, Ag 17,15:6
Barnes, James G Mrs, 1967, S 11,45:4
Barnes, James H, 1912, Jl 12,9:4; 1951, Je 23,15:2
Barnes, James M, 1958, Je 9,23:2
Barnes, James R, 1942, My 17,46:3
Barnes, James W, 1949, Mr 15,27:3
Barnes, Jay P, 1943, My 9,40:8
Barnes, Jesse L, 1961, S 11,27:3
Barnes, John E, 1938, O 16,45:3; 1964, Ap 23,39:4
Barnes, John H, 1952, My 15,31:2
Barnes, John H Mrs, 1947, Je 5,25:1
Barnes, John K, 1961, O 31,31:4
Barnes, John P, 1954, S 3,17:2; 1959, Ap 11,21:3
Barnes, John Pierce Sr, 1954, My 27,27:5
Barnes, John S, 1942, My 1,19:5
Barnes, John Sanford, 1911, N 22,13:5
Barnes, John W, 1940, Ap 23,23:5; 1964, D 18,33:1
Barnes, Joseph F Col, 1937, O 9,19:6
Barnes, Joseph M, 1960, S 28,39:5
Barnes, Julian F, 1961, D 25,23:5
Barnes, Julian L, 1952, F 16,13:5
Barnes, Julius H, 1959, Ap 18,23:3
Barnes, Julius H Mrs, 1957, My 25,21:3
Barnes, Justin L Dr, 1907, Ap 14,9:6
Barnes, Justus D, 1946, F 8,19:2
Barnes, Kenneth, 1957, O 18,23:3
Barnes, Le Van R, 1948, Ap 15,25:2
Barnes, Lemuel C (por), 1938, Jl 19,22:3
Barnes, Leon E, 1953, D 25,17:5
Barnes, Lillian L Mrs, 1951, O 30,29:3
Barnes, Louisa Mrs, 1941, S 14,50:6
Barnes, Luman W, 1938, S 21,25:5
Barnes, Luther E, 1942, D 14,23:2
Barnes, Lyman E, 1904, Ja 17,7:5
Barnes, M H Mrs (funl, D 27,3:2), 1875, D 24,4:6
Barnes, Maj Gen, 1869, F 13,1:2
Barnes, Malcolm H, 1965, D 11,33:5
Barnes, Margaret Ayer, 1967, O 26,47:2
Barnes, Margaret C Mrs, 1962, Ap 3,39:5
Barnes, Mark H, 1967, S 13,47:4

Barnes, Mary Adelaide, 1909, Mr 13,9:4
Barnes, Mary E, 1944, Ja 12,23:4
Barnes, Matthew, 1951, Ap 25,31:1
Barnes, Morton A, 1949, N 5,13:6
Barnes, Myra S, 1962, Ap 20,27:4
Barnes, Nathaniel W, 1953, N 22,89:1
Barnes, Nelson L, 1939, O 22,41:2
Barnes, Noah T, 1962, F 2,29:2
Barnes, Oliver Weldon, 1908, N 15,9:5
Barnes, Orlando M, 1924, My 4,23:2
Barnes, Otis Tiffany Rev, 1919, F 21,13:4
Barnes, Paul F, 1961, O 3,39:4
Barnes, Percival S, 1952, Je 28,19:1
Barnes, Philip W, 1958, S 10,33:3
Barnes, Phineas, 1871, Ag 22,8:3
Barnes, R W, 1954, F 10,29:2
Barnes, R W P, 1952, Mr 28,23:1
Barnes, Rachel (est acctg), 1959, My 7,18:7
Barnes, Ralph W, 1947, O 24,23:2
Barnes, Raymond F (por), 1949, Ag 11,23:3
Barnes, Raymond L, 1956, F 16,29:1
Barnes, Robert A, 1947, Mr 4,26:3
Barnes, Robert E, 1968, D 7,47:2
Barnes, Robert L, 1947, N 28,27:3
Barnes, Robert M J, 1961, Ja 8,86:6
Barnes, Roderic B, 1954, My 14,23:1
Barnes, Roy T, 1937, S 29,23:2
Barnes, Stanley, 1955, Ag 13,13:1
Barnes, Stuart K, 1968, F 22,31:3
Barnes, Susan Bainbridge Mrs, 1915, My 17,9:4
Barnes, T George, 1956, Jl 21,15:2
Barnes, T Roy, 1937, Mr 31,24:2
Barnes, Theodore, 1939, N 26,42:5
Barnes, Thurlow Weed, 1918, Je 28,11:6
Barnes, Virgil J (Zeke), 1958, Jl 27,61:2
Barnes, W, 1930, Je 26,1:4
Barnes, Walter F, 1945, N 22,35:2
Barnes, Walter F Mrs, 1943, Ap 6,21:3
Barnes, Walter K, 1948, Ag 11,21:4
Barnes, Walter S Jr, 1940, F 14,21:5
Barnes, Ward, 1947, Mr 17,23:4
Barnes, Wesley, 1940, Mr 29,21:3
Barnes, Will R, 1939, N 28,25:5
Barnes, Willard J, 1948, Jl 22,23:4
Barnes, William C, 1952, Je 23,19:2
Barnes, William E, 1939, Ag 19,15:2
Barnes, William F Mrs, 1941, Ap 9,25:6
Barnes, William H, 1918, My 7,13:6; 1938, Mr 10, 21:5; 1944, Ap 7,19:2; 1952, Ap 10,29:5
Barnes, William H Jr, 1940, Ja 4,23:4; 1965, Ja 6,39:4
Barnes, William J, 1954, Je 18,23:4; 1955, Je 7,33:5
Barnes, William Jr, 1950, Mr 28,31:2
Barnes, William O, 1960, Ja 7,29:4
Barnes, William R, 1945, F 10,11:1
Barnes, William Sr, 1913, F 24,11:5
Barnes, William T, 1949, My 15,90:3
Barnes, William V, 1941, Ag 20,19:1
Barnes, William W, 1951, Jl 27,19:4
Barnes, Wilson F, 1951, S 5,31:4
Barnes, Zack (Canal Giant), 1879, Jl 3,2:4
Barnesdale, Harold, 1941, D 27,19:4
Barneson, John, 1941, F 26,21:5
Barnet, Fred J, 1941, O 3,23:3
Barnet, Henry B, 1951, Jl 25,23:4
Barnet, Herbert L Mrs, 1958, Je 8,89:1
Barnet, I Milton, 1950, Ja 21,17:1
Barnet, Isadore, 1952, Ag 31,44:8
Barnet, Louis, 1944, Ja 2,38:3
Barnet, Morris S, 1921, D 25,20:3
Barnet, Robert A Mrs, 1957, Je 27,25:4
Barnet, Sarah J S Mrs, 1942, S 18,21:4
Barnet y Vinageras, Jose A, 1945, S 20,23:6
Barnett, Abraham, 1940, N 17,49:3
Barnett, Abraham Mrs, 1958, Ja 11,17:3
Barnett, Albert, 1938, Je 3,21:5
Barnett, Alfred N, 1968, Ap 26,43:3
Barnett, Alfred W, 1940, My 4,17:6
Barnett, Anna L L Mrs, 1952, Ag 10,60:5
Barnett, Bernard Mrs, 1964, Ja 20,43:3
Barnett, Beverly T, 1960, F 15,27:3
Barnett, Brodie D, 1961, My 4,37:4
Barnett, Caryl A, 1962, Je 8,31:5
Barnett, Charles, 1949, S 1,21:3
Barnett, Charles H J, 1954, Mr 4,25:1
Barnett, Charles M, 1940, Ap 27,15:6
Barnett, Charles M Jr, 1947, D 13,15:2
Barnett, Charles T, 1950, D 19,29:3
Barnett, Chester A, 1947, S 24,23:3
Barnett, Claude A, 1967, Ag 3,33:1
Barnett, Edith, 1919, Ag 29,11:6
Barnett, Edward L, 1942, Je 9,23:3
Barnett, Francis F B, 1949, O 16,89:1
Barnett, G, 1930, Ap 28,21:3
Barnett, G Stanley, 1956, My 14,25:2
Barnett, Griff (M Griffith), 1958, Ja 17,25:3
Barnett, Gustave G, 1952, O 31,25:4
Barnett, H Mrs, 1936, Je 11,25:3
Barnett, Harold L, 1964, Ap 2,33:4
Barnett, Harris, 1944, Je 8,21:4
Barnett, Harry, 1953, Mr 13,27:1
Barnett, Harvey, 1950, Je 23,26:3
Barnett, Helen, 1943, Ap 26,19:4
Barnett, Hyman Mrs, 1948, Je 15,27:4
Barnett, Isaac L, 1943, Ap 26,19:2
Barnett, J, 1934, My 30,17:3
Barnett, Jack A, 1956, Ag 7,27:3
Barnett, James H, 1946, Ap 24,26:2
Barnett, James M, 1940, Jl 25,17:3
Barnett, James R, 1967, D 16,41:3
Barnett, John, 1942, Mr 18,23:1
Barnett, John H, 1952, Ag 25,17:1
Barnett, John Mrs, 1957, O 23,33:1
Barnett, John T, 1942, F 2,15:4
Barnett, Joseph, 1915, F 20,11:5; 1939, Ag 5,15:4
Barnett, Joseph Mrs, 1959, Ap 9,31:3
Barnett, Lawrence, 1967, Jl 20,37:4
Barnett, Lee J Mrs, 1964, D 5,31:4
Barnett, Leo, 1949, Ap 16,15:1
Barnett, Leon H, 1946, D 22,41:2
Barnett, Lissa M Dr, 1924, Ag 13,15:3
Barnett, Louis, 1946, O 29,25:2
Barnett, Marcus D, 1952, Jl 2,25:5
Barnett, Martin M, 1968, Jl 27,27:4
Barnett, Mary A (Mother Mary Claire), 1956, Ag 28,27:3
Barnett, Michael J, 1941, O 10,23:2
Barnett, Moses, 1909, My 5,11:6
Barnett, Nathaniel, 1958, N 2,89:2
Barnett, Nathaniel Mrs, 1942, O 5,19:6
Barnett, Otto R, 1945, Mr 29,23:4
Barnett, Paul, 1949, Ja 16,68:4
Barnett, Paul W, 1958, My 14,33:3
Barnett, Robert H, 1942, Je 6,13:1
Barnett, Robert H Mrs, 1955, Ag 16,49:3
Barnett, Robert M, 1953, Ja 3,15:1
Barnett, Roy J, 1954, My 16,86:1
Barnett, Roy W, 1968, Ap 13,25:5
Barnett, Samuel Augustus, 1913, Je 18,9:4
Barnett, Sarah Mrs, 1941, F 20,19:3
Barnett, Sidney N, 1963, S 30,29:3
Barnett, Solomon S, 1940, O 31,23:1
Barnett, Theodore Dr, 1968, D 13,47:1
Barnett, Wells H Jr, 1967, S 8,40:2
Barnett, William, 1953, Ja 9,22:3
Barnett, William E, 1913, O 11,15:3
Barnett, William F, 1957, F 14,27:1
Barnett, William J Sr, 1953, Je 11,29:5
Barnett, William L, 1956, F 12,89:2
Barnett, William R, 1962, Mr 21,39:5
Barnewall, George A, 1952, Ap 16,27:3
Barney, Arie, 1901, O 17,9:7
Barney, Arthur L, 1955, N 9,33:5
Barney, Ashbel H, 1945, S 29,15:4
Barney, C H Gen, 1904, Ja 12,7:6
Barney, C Neal (por), 1949, Ap 25,23:3
Barney, Charles D, 1945, O 25,21:1
Barney, Charles E, 1952, My 18,93:2
Barney, Charles T Mrs, 1946, Ja 13,44:5
Barney, Danford N Jr, 1952, My 22,27:5
Barney, Delbert, 1948, Mr 22,23:4
Barney, E J Mrs, 1954, Ap 21,31:2
Barney, Edgar S (por), 1938, D 26,23:3
Barney, Edgar S (will), 1939, Ja 10,15:3
Barney, Eugene S, 1947, D 20,17:4
Barney, Everett H, 1916, Ap 1,13:4
Barney, Frank A, 1954, D 15,31:5
Barney, Fred M Dr, 1937, Ag 18,19:1
Barney, George C, 1945, My 13,20:2
Barney, George F Mrs, 1947, My 23,23:2
Barney, Harold, 1960, D 31,17:3
Barney, Hiram, 1925, Jl 6,11:6
Barney, Hiram Mrs (Maginel), 1966, Ap 19,41:2
Barney, Isabelle Mrs, 1950, Ja 18,31:4
Barney, J Clyde, 1950, Mr 28,32:2
Barney, J Stewart, 1964, O 11,85:7
Barney, James W, 1948, Ja 25,56:8
Barney, John Stewart, 1925, N 23,21:5
Barney, Joseph, 1937, Ap 14,27:5
Barney, Laura D Mrs, 1940, F 11,49:2
Barney, Loren A, 1950, N 28,31:3
Barney, Mary Chase Mrs, 1872, Jl 3,8:3
Barney, Morgan, 1943, Je 24,21:4
Barney, Raymond L, 1938, Jl 10,31:4
Barney, Samuel E, 1940, F 24,13:1
Barney, Samuel S Ex-Justice, 1920, Ja 1,15:2
Barney, Stanley, 1950, Ja 5,26:5
Barney, William G, 1942, Ag 5,19:4
Barney, William J, 1954, D 14,33:3
Barnham, Henry T, 1937, My 20,21:1
Barnhard, Thomas, 1954, Ap 14,17:2
Barnhardt, George H, 1948, D 25,17:4
Barnhart, Allen K, 1953, Jl 19,56:3
Barnhart, Alvin J, 1938, Mr 15,23:2
Barnhart, Byron P, 1942, O 11,56:4
Barnhart, Clara H Mrs, 1937, Je 16,23:4
Barnhart, Dickson L, 1940, Je 4,23:6
Barnhart, Emmett P, 1951, My 10,31:4
Barnhart, George E, 1962, Ap 27,35:4
Barnhart, Harry, 1948, S 5,41:1
Barnhart, Harvey D, 1946, Ja 21,23:3
Barnhart, Harvey D Mrs, 1946, Ja 21,23:3
Barnhart, I Charles Dr, 1916, Jl 15,9:6
Barnhart, John H, 1949, N 12,15:5
Barnhart, Joseph C, 1957, D 10,35:4
Barnhart, Noah C, 1939, N 9,23:6
Barnhart, Thomas F, 1955, Ja 8,13:3
Barnhart, William N, 1957, Ja 31,27:4
Barnhill, John F, 1943, Mr 12,17:3
Barnhill, O P, 1934, Mr 19,1:7
Barnhill, William R, 1956, F 6,23:1
Barnhouse, Donald G, 1960, N 6,89:1
Barnickel, Peter, 1946, Je 1,13:3
Barnickel, William S, 1923, My 21,15:5
Barnicle, Charles, 1943, D 11,8:8
Barnicle, Valentine B, 1947, S 28,60:5
Barnicle, William J, 1947, S 18,25:4
Barning, Henry F, 1946, F 22,25:3
Barning, John H, 1939, Mr 27,15:3
Barnitt, J Vincent, 1952, Ja 18,27:3
Barnitt, Robert A, 1952, Ja 22,29:4
Barnitz, G B, 1927, Je 9,27:5
Barnouw, Adriaan J, 1968, S 28,33:5
Barnouw, Adriaan J Mrs, 1960, O 3,31:4
Barnowsky, Victor, 1952, My 9,23:5
Barns, Everett, 1947, Je 5,25:3
Barns, Frank V, 1966, Je 4,29:3
Barns, Norman W, 1954, S 13,23:4
Barnsback, H Edward, 1952, Mr 17,21:4
Barnsdall, Aline, 1946, D 19,29:5
Barnsdall, Noel B, 1941, Ap 26,15:4
Barnsdall, Theodore N, 1917, F 28,11:6
Barnsley, Joseph C, 1959, Ag 12,29:3
Barnstein, Eduard, 1948, Ja 28,23:6
Barnston, Henry, 1949, D 13,31:2
Barnstyn, Lowet C, 1953, D 26,13:5
Barnum, A S, 1878, Mr 25,2:6
Barnum, Agnes L, 1938, Je 21,19:5
Barnum, Carl F, 1948, S 21,28:2
Barnum, Charles K, 1950, Mr 27,23:2
Barnum, E N, 1881, S 30,5:2
Barnum, E S, 1878, F 21,2:3
Barnum, Edmund Bragdon, 1921, Ja 22,11:4
Barnum, Enoch Mrs, 1908, F 20,7:6
Barnum, Frederick Stone, 1925, S 10,25:6
Barnum, George S, 1943, N 30,27:1; 1952, O 31,25:1
Barnum, George W, 1937, Ap 1,23:3
Barnum, Gertrude, 1948, Je 19,15:4
Barnum, H A Gen, 1892, Je 30,8:4
Barnum, Harry H, 1939, Je 29,23:4
Barnum, Isaac H, 1904, Jl 29,7:6
Barnum, Jay H, 1962, S 14,31:5
Barnum, Jerome D, 1965, Ja 17,89:1
Barnum, Joseph I, 1912, Je 16,II,17:5
Barnum, Louis E, 1945, Ap 14,15:3
Barnum, Madalene D, 1961, Ag 30,33:1
Barnum, Malvern H, 1942, F 19,19:3
Barnum, P T, 1891, Ap 8,1:7; 1901, D 6,6:3
Barnum, Peter Deacon, 1873, Ag 23,1:6
Barnum, R Allan, 1961, Ap 3,33:2
Barnum, R F, 1928, Je 27,25:3
Barnum, Richard L, 1950, D 30,13:6
Barnum, T, 1878, Mr 25,2:6
Barnum, Thomas R, 1938, Ja 22,15:2
Barnum, W H (see also My 1), 1889, My 4,5:5
Barnum, W R, 1876, Jl 16,7:2
Barnum, Walter M, 1943, F 20,13:4
Barnum, William H, 1963, Ap 30,35:5
Barnum, William H Mrs, 1954, D 7,33:1
Barnum, William L, 1940, O 24,25:6
Barnum, William N, 1939, Ja 18,20:3
Barnum, Zenas, 1865, Ap 8,3:3
Barnwell, Arthur, 1955, Ap 21,29:4
Barnwell, John B, 1966, My 5,48:1
Barnwell, John C, 1959, Ja 12,39:3
Barnwell, Middleton S, 1957, My 7,35:2
Barnwell, Walter, 1943, Jl 31,13:4
Baroche, Pierre Jules, 1870, N 3,1:7
Baroda, Ex-Guikwar's Death, 1882, Jl 28,2:3
Baroda, Gaekwar of (Sir Pratap Singh), 1968, Jl 20, 27:1
Baroff, Benjamin, 1947, Jl 10,21:5
Baroja y Nessi, Pio (funl, N 1,39:4), 1956, O 31,33:3
Baron, Aaron, 1953, Mr 18,31:2
Baron, Abner, 1953, Je 29,21:6
Baron, Abraham, 1949, D 8,33:3
Baron, Adolph Dr, 1937, Ja 4,29:2
Baron, Albert G, 1941, F 10,20:3
Baron, Anna S, 1955, Ja 3,27:5
Baron, Auguste, 1938, Je 4,15:5
Baron, Ben F, 1951, S 10,21:5
Baron, Benjamin Mrs, 1937, N 3,24:2
Baron, Charles R, 1943, F 19,20:2
Baron, Colin F, 1958, Ag 17,85:4
Baron, David, 1940, Ap 2,26:3; 1957, S 5,29:2
Baron, Frank J, 1953, S 3,22:8
Baron, Harry, 1941, D 19,25:3
Baron, Harry Mrs, 1948, Ap 7,25:2
Baron, Harry W, 1964, Mr 6,28:5
Baron, Henry A Mrs, 1963, Ap 17,41:2
Baron, Herman, 1961, Ja 28,19:1
Baron, Hugo S, 1944, Mr 21,19:3
Baron, Hyman, 1944, Mr 12,38:4; 1952, Ag 26,25:1
Baron, Isidor, 1955, Jl 6,27:2
Baron, J Victor, 1945, N 17,17:2
Baron, Jan Capt, 1924, F 6,19:5
Baron, Louis G, 1948, S 20,25:2
Baron, Louis J, 1947, Ag 11,23:2
Baron, Maurice, 1964, S 9,43:1
Baron, Michael A, 1941, Ja 18,15:1

Baron, Paul, 1942, Je 23,19:3
Baron, Pierre, 1939, F 11,15:5
Baron, S Muriel (Mrs D M Raskind), 1961, Ag 14, 25:3
Baron, Samuel, 1946, Jl 14,36:6
Baron, Saul J, 1951, Jl 14,13:3
Baron, Thomas R, 1967, Ap 30,44:4
Baron Fermoy, 1874, S 18,5:5
Baron Von Matzean, 1874, Mr 16,5:6
Baroncelli, Jacques, 1951, Ja 15,17:2
Barondess, Benjamin, 1960, N 29,37:4
Barondess, J, 1928, Je 20,25:5
Barone, Alfred, 1950, Jl 31,17:2
Barone, Franco, 1949, N 3,29:4
Barone, Pep (Jos Barone), 1968, F 20,44:1
Barone, Rose Mrs, 1952, My 20,33:7
Baroni, William J Sr, 1942, S 10,27:2
Baronian, Harry, 1965, Ag 4,35:2
Baronsky, Nikolai N, 1963, D 1,84:5
Barosa, Manuel, 1937, Ag 30,25:4
Barotte, Felix, 1881, My 5,1:3
Barou, Noah (funl, S 8,31:4), 1955, S 6,25:4
Baroux, Lucien, 1968, My 23,47:3
Baroway, Solomon, 1918, Mr 8,11:5
Barowsky, Seymour I, 1956, D 30,32:7
Barquin, Ramon C, 1942, S 11,21:4
Barr, Albert E, 1951, S 6,31:5
Barr, Albert J, 1912, F 25,II,11:3
Barr, Amelia E, 1919, Mr 12,11:3
Barr, Arthur A, 1950, O 30,27:2
Barr, Brevoort B, 1964, D 27,64:3
Barr, Caroline, 1940, F 5,19:3
Barr, Charles Capt (funl, Ja 29,11:2), 1911, Ja 25,9:3
Barr, Charles H, 1947, Ja 11,19:5
Barr, David, 1963, O 17,35:2
Barr, David G, 1964, N 17,41:2
Barr, David Mrs, 1948, S 29,30:2
Barr, David P Mrs, 1954, O 19,27:2
Barr, Donald, 1949, S 3,13:7
Barr, Duncan M, 1958, S 20,19:4
Barr, Fannie, 1919, My 5,13:2
Barr, Frank T, 1953, Ja 5,21:4
Barr, Franklin E, 1949, S 1,21:6
Barr, George, 1967, Jl 13,37:3
Barr, George A, 1945, Ja 27,11:3
Barr, Harry K Sr, 1953, D 9,11:1
Barr, Henry J, 1942, O 7,25:6
Barr, Hugh C, 1960, Je 10,31:2
Barr, Isaac M, 1937, Ja 23,17:4
Barr, James, 1923, Mr 22,19:5; 1938, N 18,21:4
Barr, James A, 1944, O 18,21:1
Barr, James Capt, 1937, Mr 31,23:2
Barr, Jehu Dr, 1904, Mr 21,6:2
Barr, Jere H, 1955, My 28,15:1
Barr, John (funl), 1911, F 27,9:3
Barr, John, 1957, Ag 11,80:6
Barr, John A Mrs, 1949, Je 23,27:4
Barr, John Capt, 1909, Ja 12,9:5
Barr, John H, 1937, Mr 29,19:1; 1953, Je 15,29:4
Barr, John H Mrs, 1950, Je 13,27:2
Barr, John W Jr, 1941, Mr 5,21:3
Barr, John Watson Judge, 1908, Ja 1,9:5
Barr, Joseph, 1951, S 1,11:6; 1959, Je 13,21:6
Barr, Joseph F, 1965, Je 26,29:6
Barr, Joseph Mrs, 1949, My 3,25:5
Barr, Joseph R, 1950, My 8,23:5
Barr, Joseph R Mrs, 1959, Ag 17,23:2
Barr, Joseph W Sr, 1955, Ja 8,13:4
Barr, Lockwood C, 1951, Je 26,29:1
Barr, Louis, 1937, S 1,19:2
Barr, Mark, 1950, D 16,17:3
Barr, Martin W, 1938, D 26,23:2
Barr, Mary G Mrs, 1938, Mr 24,23:3
Barr, Max, 1946, Mr 31,46:3
Barr, Morris L Mrs, 1944, My 13,19:2
Barr, Norman B, 1943, Ap 2,21:3
Barr, Percy M, 1960, Ag 28,82:8
Barr, Phil, 1942, Je 16,23:4
Barr, Richard J, 1951, Je 12,29:3
Barr, Robert, 1912, O 23,13:5; 1958, Ja 24,23:2
Barr, Robert A, 1959, Ag 16,82:2
Barr, Robert C, 1958, O 2,37:4
Barr, Robert I Mrs, 1951, S 5,31:4
Barr, Robert M Mrs, 1944, Ap 3,21:5
Barr, Robert Ross, 1962, Mr 26,31:1
Barr, Robert Rutherford, 1962, My 30,19:4
Barr, S Seymour, 1963, Ja 12,14:5
Barr, Samuel, 1910, My 30,11:5; 1954, Ap 23,27:4
Barr, Samuel Mrs, 1910, My 30,11:5
Barr, Sidney U, 1941, Mr 2,42:2
Barr, T J, 1881, Mr 28,5:5
Barr, Thomas Carson, 1908, F 27,7:7
Barr, Thomas M, 1915, N 1,11:6
Barr, Thomas M Mrs, 1957, D 10,35:2
Barr, Thomas T, 1949, Ap 15,23:2
Barr, Thomas Turner, 1912, Ap 23,13:4
Barr, W Manning, 1966, N 17,47:4
Barr, Walter S, 1957, Jl 5,17:1
Barr, William, 1908, Je 17,9:5
Barr, William C Jr, 1950, Ag 22,27:3
Barr, William G, 1964, Je 3,43:2
Barr, William H, 1944, N 19,50:4
Barr, William John, 1913, D 2,11:6
Barr, William M, 1945, N 5,19:3
Barr, William Mrs, 1944, Ag 21,15:4
Barr, William R, 1909, My 30,9:6
Barra, Anthony, 1948, Je 30,25:3
Barra, Caesar B F (por), 1949, O 1,13:3
Barra, Luigi, 1959, Ap 9,31:4
Barra, Peter (funeral plans, Jl 5,31:4), 1960, Jl 3,V, 11:2
Barracca, S Peter, 1950, Mr 23,36:3
Barrack, Isidore, 1961, Ap 1,17:4
Barrack, William C, 1949, Ja 25,23:2
Barradale, E Morgan, 1964, F 26,35:2
Barradale, E Morgan Mrs, 1954, N 25,29:1
Barradale, William D, 1952, Ja 17,27:1
Barragry, Thomas H, 1938, D 25,14:2
Barraja-Frauenfelder, Joseph, 1966, F 27,85:1
Barral, J A, 1884, S 13,5:2
Barrally, Thomas W, 1944, Ja 18,20:3
Barran, John, 1952, Jl 9,27:2
Barran, Lady, 1939, Jl 2,15:2
Barran, Rowland H, 1949, Ag 7,61:1
Barranco, Cesar A, 1950, Ap 26,29:1
Barranque, Jesus M, 1944, F 9,19:3
Barraquer, Vidal y, 1943, S 15,27:2
Barras, Charles M, 1873, Ap 1,5:5
Barras, Louis R, 1939, Ag 16,23:2
Barras, Madeline D Mrs, 1941, O 6,17:1
Barrasford, Thomas, 1910, F 21,9:5
Barratt, John A, 1944, Mr 3,15:4
Barratt, Thomas J, 1914, Ap 27,11:3
Barratt, Thomas L, 1955, Ja 1,13:4
Barratt, Tom, 1957, Mr 22,23:4
Barratt, Walter A, 1947, Ap 15,25:3
Barratt, Watson, 1962, Jl 8,65:2
Barratt, Watson Mrs, 1949, S 4,41:2
Barratt, William C, 1947, D 28,40:6
Barre, A H, 1944, D 31,26:2
Barre, M Benedict, 1948, Ja 11,56:1
Barreda, Enrique D, 1944, D 11,23:6
Barreda, Juan P, 1943, Ja 10,50:2
Barreiro, Juan Bautista Dr, 1913, D 13,13:6
Barrell, J S, 1904, F 6,9:6
Barrell, Wilbur Fiske, 1909, Ag 9,7:6
Barrera, Frank Mrs, 1948, D 28,21:4
Barrera, Jose, 1949, N 17,29:4
Barrera, S Eugene, 1952, My 26,23:5
Barrera, Stephen F, 1961, O 5,37:5
Barreras, Alberto, 1949, N 2,27:1
Barrere, Camille, 1940, O 10,25:2
Barrere, Claude, 1966, D 4,88:7
Barrere, Georges, 1944, Je 16,19:1
Barrere, Joseph M, 1949, Ja 30,60:8
Barres, Maurice (funl, D 7,21:5), 1923, D 6,19:4
Barrese, Anthony, 1955, My 14,19:4
Barret, Cecil, 1956, N 16,27:3
Barret, J Richard, 1903, N 3,7:7
Barret, LeRoy C, 1960, Jl 17,60:8
Barret, Mayor of St Louis, 1875, Ap 28,4:6
Barret, R C L Mrs, 1939, S 17,48:8
Barret, Robert L C, 1941, My 24,15:2
Barreto, Pedro, 1943, D 6,23:4
Barrett, A H Mrs, 1903, Jl 19,7:6
Barrett, Agnes M, 1959, Ja 22,31:4
Barrett, Alfred J, 1955, N 10,35:2
Barrett, Alfred M Mrs, 1961, Ja 5,31:1
Barrett, Alfred T B, 1939, N 16,23:4
Barrett, Alva P, 1953, Mr 25,31:4
Barrett, Andrew L, 1951, O 3,36:2
Barrett, Andrew L Mrs, 1947, O 4,17:4
Barrett, Anna, 1956, Mr 6,20:4
Barrett, Anna M, 1914, O 3,11:4
Barrett, Anthony J, 1922, My 2,19:5
Barrett, Anton J, 1944, Je 5,19:1
Barrett, Arthur A, 1946, Ag 23,19:5
Barrett, Arthur F, 1940, O 14,19:2
Barrett, Arthur H, 1948, My 14,23:1
Barrett, Arthur J, 1939, N 1,23:6
Barrett, Beatrice F, 1950, N 21,31:4
Barrett, Benjamin W, 1959, Mr 10,35:4
Barrett, Brian N, 1955, Je 14,29:1
Barrett, Catherine Mrs, 1910, My 22,II,11:5
Barrett, Channing Mrs, 1950, D 8,29:3
Barrett, Channing W, 1958, Ja 30,23:5
Barrett, Charles, 1939, Jl 6,24:2
Barrett, Charles A, 1943, Mr 3,23:5; 1953, Je 29,21:5; 1956, Je 14,33:4
Barrett, Charles C, 1918, O 7,13:4
Barrett, Charles E, 1954, Jl 7,31:5; 1956, D 25,25:3
Barrett, Charles E Mrs, 1950, O 29,92:4
Barrett, Charles F, 1941, Ap 2,23:3; 1949, S 16,27:1
Barrett, Charles J, 1907, My 15,9:6; 1963, Jl 2,26:6
Barrett, Charles R, 1962, Ap 10,43:3
Barrett, Daniel J, 1945, Mr 7,21:3
Barrett, Darwin Jr, 1943, F 9,23:2
Barrett, David L, 1966, Jl 9,27:6
Barrett, David R, 1942, Mr 13,19:4
Barrett, Don C, 1943, Ja 21,21:5
Barrett, Douglas L, 1963, My 24,31:1
Barrett, E Commodore, 1880, Ap 2,2:4
Barrett, E W, 1922, Jl 11,15:3
Barrett, Edmund E, 1961, F 26,92:4
Barrett, Edward C, 1940, Jl 31,17:2
Barrett, Edward E, 1943, Ap 23,17:5
Barrett, Edward F, 1958, Jl 1,31:3
Barrett, Edward G, 1962, Ag 9,25:5
Barrett, Edward J, 1953, D 9,11:1
Barrett, Edward J Mrs, 1948, Ja 26,19:4
Barrett, Edward M, 1956, F 19,92:1
Barrett, Edward P, 1965, Ja 1,17:2
Barrett, Edward S, 1944, Ag 24,19:2
Barrett, Elisha T (funl, My 13,41:3), 1966, My 9,39:3
Barrett, Elisha T Mrs, 1956, Jl 8,64:1; 1967, Mr 25, 23:2
Barrett, Elizabeth N, 1958, N 19,37:5
Barrett, Ella M W Mrs, 1937, Ja 3,II,9:1
Barrett, Eva, 1950, Ag 25,21:5
Barrett, Eva M Mrs, 1942, O 15,23:1
Barrett, F Howard, 1962, Ja 23,33:2
Barrett, Father of Lawrence, 1882, N 1,4:7
Barrett, Francis A Mrs, 1937, Ap 26,19:3
Barrett, Frank A, 1962, My 31,27:1
Barrett, Frank A Mrs, 1956, F 18,19:3
Barrett, Fred, 1967, N 28,51:4; 1968, Mr 19,44:1
Barrett, Fred W, 1952, Jl 22,25:4
Barrett, Frederick D, 1961, Jl 24,23:6
Barrett, Frederick W, 1949, N 9,27:1
Barrett, George C (will, Je 13,8:6), 1906, Je 8,9:1
Barrett, George F, 1937, Mr 2,21:2
Barrett, George L, 1938, N 9,23:3
Barrett, George T, 1939, Mr 21,23:5; 1954, O 12,27:6
Barrett, George W, 1949, Je 1,31:4
Barrett, Harold J, 1964, S 6,56:8
Barrett, Harry A, 1959, Mr 8,86:6
Barrett, Harry M, 1949, D 29,25:4
Barrett, Henry A, 1953, F 5,23:4
Barrett, Henry R (will, F 21,40:1), 1940, F 5,17:5
Barrett, Henry R Jr, 1964, Ap 19,84:1
Barrett, Herbert, 1943, Jl 28,15:4
Barrett, Horace F, 1941, D 11,27:2
Barrett, Hugh C, 1950, My 22,21:4
Barrett, Irving, 1942, S 24,27:4
Barrett, Isaac Judge, 1916, N 5,23:4
Barrett, J Harry, 1957, Jl 20,15:4
Barrett, J Harry Mrs, 1948, Ag 18,25:5
Barrett, J P, 1934, My 30,17:2
Barrett, J Russell, 1957, N 2,21:5
Barrett, J W Rev, 1903, My 14,9:6
Barrett, James, 1941, F 12,21:4
Barrett, James A, 1940, Je 28,19:2
Barrett, James E, 1967, Ag 2,37:3
Barrett, James E Mrs, 1941, Mr 24,17:4
Barrett, James E V, 1948, D 6,25:4
Barrett, James H, 1946, O 29,25:3
Barrett, James J, 1956, Je 19,29:4; 1964, Jl 11,25:2
Barrett, James J Mrs, 1949, D 12,34:2
Barrett, James M, 1938, S 30,21:2; 1940, Jl 10,19:2
Barrett, James M (mem ser, O 17,35:4; funl, O 18,-33:1), 1956, O 15,25:4
Barrett, James R, 1948, D 9,33:4
Barrett, John (por), 1938, O 18,25:3
Barrett, John, 1940, Ja 21,34:6
Barrett, John D, 1920, O 22,15:5; 1948, Jl 7,46:4
Barrett, John D Mrs, 1948, N 23,29:4
Barrett, John E, 1947, D 9,29:5; 1949, O 5,29:3
Barrett, John F, 1947, Ja 2,27:4
Barrett, John H, 1940, My 2,24:2
Barrett, John Ignatius Msgr (funl, S 2,7:7), 1913, Ag 29,9:6
Barrett, John J, 1940, D 13,23:4; 1941, Jl 25,15:2; 1947, Ap 7,24:2; 1954, Jl 7,31:2
Barrett, John J Jr, 1941, Ap 9,25:5
Barrett, John J Mrs, 1947, F 14,22:2
Barrett, John L, 1949, Ap 16,15:2
Barrett, John M, 1950, Jl 4,17:5; 1964, F 13,31:4
Barrett, John M Mrs, 1951, Ja 3,27:1; 1960, Jl 29,25:2
Barrett, John Mrs, 1937, Je 10,23:1; 1949, S 30,23:2
Barrett, John P, 1946, N 3,64:2
Barrett, Joseph, 1882, Ja 27,5:4
Barrett, Joseph A, 1966, Ag 28,93:3
Barrett, Joseph L, 1953, My 31,72:4
Barrett, Joseph W, 1942, O 5,19:3
Barrett, Julia, 1945, Je 9,13:5
Barrett, Lawrence, 1891, Mr 21,1:7
Barrett, Lawrence C Jr, 1950, N 27,25:2
Barrett, Leland, 1945, Mr 8,23:2
Barrett, Leo F, 1945, My 25,19:2; 1949, Je 13,19:6
Barrett, Leonard A, 1945, Mr 1,21:2
Barrett, Lucia L Mrs, 1940, D 18,25:2
Barrett, Lucius A, 1939, S 6,23:3
Barrett, Marty, 1950, Jl 5,26:5
Barrett, Mary D Mrs, 1947, My 5,23:1
Barrett, Maurice, 1963, Je 10,31:3
Barrett, Michael E Mrs, 1963, S 29,86:5
Barrett, Michael T, 1940, Ag 24,13:6
Barrett, Mignon A, 1941, N 25,26:2
Barrett, Minnette, 1964, Je 22,27:2
Barrett, Monmouth, 1943, Mr 14,26:1
Barrett, Monte, 1949, O 9,93:2
Barrett, Myron, 1876, My 11,7:4
Barrett, Myron K, 1954, N 18,33:5
Barrett, Nathan Franklin, 1919, O 18,13:4
Barrett, Nicholas J, 1957, Je 18,33:3
Barrett, O Slack, 1953, Ap 5,77:1
Barrett, Ois W, 1950, O 11,33:3
Barrett, Oliver C, 1955, Jl 20,27:5
Barrett, Oliver R, 1950, Mr 6,22:2

Barrett, Pat, 1959, Mr 27,23:3
Barrett, Patrick H Rev, 1914, F 9,7:5
Barrett, Patrick W, 1952, N 19,29:2
Barrett, Paul A, 1947, My 8,25:1
Barrett, Percy S Mrs, 1959, Je 23,33:3
Barrett, R Earl, 1959, Jl 4,15:6
Barrett, Ralph E, 1945, Mr 24,17:5
Barrett, Ralph L, 1962, N 14,39:2
Barrett, Ralph L Mrs, 1951, Jl 19,23:6
Barrett, Raymond F, 1959, O 28,37:2
Barrett, Raymond L, 1954, D 12,88:6
Barrett, Reginald, 1940, F 8,23:4; 1966, Ag 27,30:3
Barrett, Richard, 1946, S 16,5:4
Barrett, Richard C, 1941, N 4,26:2
Barrett, Richard N, 1945, Ag 31,17:3
Barrett, Richard W, 1937, N 2,25:5
Barrett, Robert, 1951, Ja 14,84:6
Barrett, Robert B, 1957, F 9,19:5
Barrett, Robert E, 1954, Je 15,29:2
Barrett, Robert S, 1959, F 25,31:1
Barrett, Robertson T, 1962, O 13,25:5
Barrett, Robertson T Mrs, 1943, Ap 7,26:2
Barrett, Roger, 1968, N 19,40:1
Barrett, Roscoe J, 1938, S 15,25:4
Barrett, Rose M, 1961, Ja 19,29:5
Barrett, Russell S, 1955, My 15,87:2
Barrett, S Ruth, 1961, Mr 10,27:3
Barrett, Sallie Currie Mrs, 1905, Mr 29,9:3
Barrett, Sampson K, 1948, D 24,18:4
Barrett, Samuel A, 1965, Mr 12,33:5
Barrett, Sidney F, 1958, Je 20,23:3
Barrett, Sidney H, 1944, Ap 11,19:4
Barrett, Storrs B Dr, 1937, N 26,26:3
Barrett, T Jr, 1934, Je 12,23:5
Barrett, Thomas A, 1960, Mr 18,26:3
Barrett, Thomas F, 1925, Je 11,19:4; 1955, Ja 22,11:2
Barrett, Thomas H Capt, 1908, Mr 30,7:5
Barrett, Thomas M, 1948, Mr 28,48:2
Barrett, Thomas T, 1958, F 18,27:1
Barrett, Thomas W, 1944, Ja 22,13:1
Barrett, Walter E, 1956, Mr 19,31:1
Barrett, Walter F, 1942, D 27,34:6
Barrett, Walter W, 1951, O 31,29:3
Barrett, William A Jr, 1968, O 31,47:1
Barrett, William E, 1938, Ja 26,23:4; 1942, D 8,25:5
Barrett, William Emerson, 1906, F 13,7:6
Barrett, William F, 1955, My 25,33:5
Barrett, William Fletcher Sir, 1925, My 28,21:4
Barrett, William H, 1949, F 5,15:2; 1950, Je 17,15:6; 1951, S 18,31:3; 1955, Ag 5,19:1; 1967, Jl 29,25:3
Barrett, William J, 1951, Ja 27,13:2; 1967, Ja 23,43:3
Barrett, William M, 1937, Mr 26,21:4
Barrett, William M (will), 1938, D 31,2:8
Barrett, William Z, 1947, Ag 27,23:3
Barrett, Wilson, 1904, Jl 23,7:4
Barrett, Wilton A, 1940, F 19,17:4
Barrett, Wright L, 1946, Jl 10,23:5
Barrette, Antonio, 1968, D 16,50:1
Barretto, Francis, 1942, Ja 15,19:2
Barrias, Louis E, 1905, F 5,7:6
Barricini, Jack, 1952, Je 15,84:1
Barricini, Mac, 1956, Jl 19,27:3
Barrick, Shirley G, 1942, Ja 11,45:1
Barrick, William C, 1904, Ja 6,9:4
Barrie, Archibald, 1948, Ag 27,18:3
Barrie, Caswell Mrs, 1958, Jl 13,69:3
Barrie, Charles J, 1961, Jl 21,23:4
Barrie, Clyde, 1945, D 7,21:5
Barrie, Cyril, 1942, Ap 10,17:4
Barrie, James M Sir, 1937, Je 20,II,1:6
Barrie, John C, 1957, Ap 27,19:5
Barrie, John H Sr, 1956, My 21,25:2
Barrie, Robert Sr, 1952, Jl 26,13:2
Barriere, Joseph, 1910, S 18,II,13:5
Barriero, Manuel, 1940, Jl 15,15:3
Barriger, John Walker Gen, 1907, Ja 1,9:6
Barringer, Barry, 1938, My 23,17:3
Barringer, Benjamin S, 1953, Mr 16,19:3
Barringer, Benjamin S Mrs, 1961, Ap 9,86:3
Barringer, Daniel M, 1873, S 2,1:7; 1962, D 27,7:6
Barringer, Daniel M Mrs, 1957, O 7,27:4
Barringer, Henry G, 1962, O 25,39:4
Barringer, John H, 1940, Mr 14,23:5
Barringer, Leonidas, 1951, Jl 30,17:5
Barringer, Lewis, 1947, D 24,21:3
Barringer, Paul B, 1941, Ja 10,20:2
Barrington, Charles S, 1962, S 10,29:2
Barrington, Finley D, 1951, Jl 23,17:5
Barrington, George W, 1955, Jl 21,23:2
Barrington, John H, 1953, Mr 6,23:2
Barrington, Joseph L, 1966, D 5,45:2
Barrington, Robert W, 1948, Jl 18,52:4
Barrington, Rutland, 1922, Je 2,17:6
Barrington, Thomas H, 1960, O 15,23:5
Barrington, Walter (Rink), 1937, Jl 16,19:3
Barrington, William F, 1941, O 26,43:3
Barrington-Ward, John G, 1946, Je 7,20:2
Barrington-Ward, Lancelot, 1953, N 18,31:4
Barrington-Ward, Robert M, 1948, Mr 1,23:3
Barrington-White, Ivan, 1947, S 11,27:5
Barrios, Antonio Gen, 1915, Jl 27,9:5
Barris, Harry, 1962, D 15,14:6
Barrish, Edith, 1948, N 4,29:3
Barriskill, James M, 1960, Ap 16,17:5
Barrison, Lyseus, 1905, Ap 7,9:5
Barrison, Philip S, 1946, Ap 9,27:4
Barrist, David, 1951, S 16,85:2
Barrister, William H, 1904, Ja 4,16:4
Barritt, Leon, 1938, F 2,19:6
Barritt, William J Sr, 1944, Mr 11,13:5
Barrodale, Barry J, 1957, Jl 27,17:6
Barrois, George A Mrs, 1950, Je 23,25:2
Barroll, F Lewis, 1959, Ag 6,27:5
Barroll, F Lewis Mrs, 1952, Mr 11,27:6
Barroll, Hope H Jr, 1948, O 1,25:2
Barroll, Lee, 1948, Ja 14,25:2
Barroll, Morris K, 1947, Ag 19,23:4
Barron, Albert M, 1962, Ap 3,39:3
Barron, Basil A, 1938, Mr 31,23:3
Barron, Bernard S, 1959, My 17,84:4
Barron, Bessie B Mrs, 1963, D 18,41:4
Barron, C W, 1928, O 3,1:4
Barron, Carter T, 1950, N 17,27:5
Barron, Charles A, 1952, Jl 26,13:5
Barron, Daniel A, 1950, My 17,29:4
Barron, E S Guzman, 1957, Je 27,25:2
Barron, Fred H, 1941, Ap 28,15:6
Barron, Frederick C, 1955, O 11,39:3
Barron, George D, 1947, Ap 2,27:4
Barron, George D Mrs, 1917, My 27,19:4; 1951, Je 12, 29:2
Barron, George D Mrs (est tax appr), 1954, S 1,29:2
Barron, George H, 1942, Je 26,21:2
Barron, George Mrs, 1943, O 13,23:5
Barron, Harry R, 1955, My 20,25:3
Barron, Henri Mrs (Marion Weeks), 1968, Ap 22, 47:4
Barron, Henry F, 1913, S 12,11:2
Barron, Hollis, 1952, Jl 15,21:2
Barron, J D Maj, 1910, Je 12,II,13:4
Barron, J V, 1878, Mr 7,4:7
Barron, J W, 1875, S 27,6:6
Barron, Jacob T, 1950, Mr 13,21:5
Barron, Jacob T Jr, 1952, S 28,77:3
Barron, James, 1942, Jl 28,17:4
Barron, James F, 1940, D 15,61:2
Barron, James L, 1947, S 23,25:4
Barron, John Connor Dr, 1908, F 8,7:6
Barron, John F, 1940, Ja 24,21:5
Barron, John H, 1943, Ag 13,17:4
Barron, John J, 1940, Jl 28,27:2; 1941, Mr 6,21:3
Barron, John J Mrs, 1946, S 12,7:2
Barron, John P, 1942, F 25,19:2
Barron, Julia A, 1952, Ap 30,27:3
Barron, Leonard, 1938, Ap 10,II,7:2
Barron, Mark (funeral plans, Ag 17,31:1), 1960, Ag 16,29:1
Barron, Maurice E, 1938, Ag 23,17:4
Barron, Oscar G Col, 1913, Ja 5,17:2
Barron, Osmond M, 1951, O 11,37:4
Barron, Oswald, 1939, S 26,23:2
Barron, Patrick J, 1951, Je 22,25:4
Barron, Paul L, 1938, Mr 28,15:5
Barron, Samuel Mrs, 1921, N 5,13:5
Barron, William A Jr, 1964, O 1,35:3
Barron, William Jr Mrs, 1945, Ag 25,11:3
Barron, William L, 1944, Mr 4,13:5
Barron, William N, 1963, S 7,19:6
Barron, William W, 1958, Ja 16,29:3
Barron y Ortiz, Fernando, 1953, Je 17,27:2
Barros, Rose Mrs, 1946, S 29,62:2
Barros Azevedo, Philadelpho de (trb, My 19,6:7), 1951, My 10,31:4
Barros y de Braganza, Rodolfo M de, 1962, N 11,88:4
Barroso, Ary, 1964, F 11,39:2
Barroso, Gustavo, 1959, D 4,32:1
Barroso, Sabino, 1919, Je 16,13:5
Barrot, C H O, 1873, Ag 7,5:4
Barrot, V F, 1883, N 14,2:2
Barrow, Alfred C, 1948, Ag 25,25:2
Barrow, Archibald C, 1955, Ap 7,27:4
Barrow, Edward G, 1953, D 16,1:4
Barrow, Edward G Mrs, 1957, O 30,29:4
Barrow, George, 1949, F 25,23:1; 1959, D 29,25:1
Barrow, George Mrs, 1946, Ap 2,28:3
Barrow, Harry, 1954, S 6,26:3
Barrow, Harry Y, 1962, F 6,35:3
Barrow, John Shelby, 1908, D 21,9:5
Barrow, Lonnie, 1960, Je 15,35:3
Barrow, Mary, 1956, N 4,87:2
Barrow, Pope Judge, 1903, D 24,1:4
Barrow, Rosamund Lady, 1906, Ja 11,9:3
Barrow, Washington, 1948, D 20,25:4
Barrow, Wilfred Sir, 1922, F 22,15:6
Barrow, William E, 1957, O 29,31:5
Barrow, William M, 1938, F 14,17:3
Barrow, William Mrs, 1948, Ja 31,19:4
Barrow, William O, 1952, Mr 23,92:1
Barrowcliff, Bayard, 1955, My 7,17:5
Barrowman, John T, 1948, Ap 25,68:4
Barrows, Albert L, 1942, N 9,23:5
Barrows, Alice P, 1954, O 3,86:5
Barrows, Allen Campbell, 1908, Ja 20,9:4
Barrows, Anna, 1948, F 12,23:3
Barrows, Arthur S, 1963, S 21,21:3
Barrows, Charles Clifford Dr, 1916, Ja 3,13:2
Barrows, Daniel A, 1941, S 26,23:2
Barrows, David N, 1965, Ja 31,88:7
Barrows, David P, 1954, S 6,15:5
Barrows, Dudley H, 1947, D 27,13:2
Barrows, Edward M, 1940, D 16,23:3
Barrows, Edwin A, 1948, Ap 20,27:3
Barrows, Eliot T Mrs, 1942, Ja 16,21:2
Barrows, Ella C Mrs, 1944, Mr 13,15:4
Barrows, Elliott T, 1945, Je 17,25:1
Barrows, Frank E, 1962, My 30,19:5
Barrows, Frank L, 1938, Ap 17,II,7:1
Barrows, Franklin Mrs, 1952, Ag 5,19:1
Barrows, Franklin W, 1949, My 27,21:4
Barrows, George M Mrs, 1953, Ja 18,92:5
Barrows, Harold K, 1954, Mr 16,29:5
Barrows, Harry E, 1946, N 27,26:2
Barrows, Ira, 1944, Ja 13,21:2
Barrows, Isabelle C Mrs, 1951, Ap 18,31:4
Barrows, J H, 1902, Je 4,9:4
Barrows, John S, 1943, N 15,19:5
Barrows, Lee E, 1948, Jl 23,19:5
Barrows, Lewis O, 1967, D 31,31:4
Barrows, Louise, 1944, Mr 4,13:5
Barrows, Nat S, 1965, Ap 13,37:1
Barrows, Nathaniel H Sr, 1952, S 10,29:5
Barrows, Oswald C, 1953, My 3,88:4
Barrows, R C, 1881, D 23,2:2
Barrows, Raymond H, 1958, O 23,31:2
Barrows, Richard Mrs (D Roland), 1959, Mr 28,17:1
Barrows, Robert L, 1967, Ja 24,28:8
Barrows, Samuel June Dr, 1909, Ap 22,9:6
Barrows, Samuel June Mrs, 1913, O 26,15:5
Barrows, Theodora L Mrs, 1946, Jl 29,21:5
Barrows, Thomas N, 1962, Ag 14,31:3
Barrows, William P, 1951, F 12,23:1
Barrows, William S, 1940, Ja 28,33:2
Barrus, C, 1931, Ap 5,26:1
Barrus, Dudley C, 1954, Jl 28,23:4
Barrus, Ernest P, 1944, Ja 9,43:1
Barry, Alma, 1950, Ag 21,19:3
Barry, Arthur G, 1942, Ag 23,43:3
Barry, Arthur Hugh Smith (Lord Barrymore), 1925, F 23,17:6
Barry, Bartholomew J, 1951, Je 6,31:2
Barry, Benjamin E, 1956, My 16,35:4
Barry, Bobby, 1964, Mr 27,27:2
Barry, Charles A, 1946, Je 6,21:5
Barry, Charles D, 1943, Ag 1,35:4
Barry, Charles E, 1950, Mr 17,23:4
Barry, Charles H, 1949, Ap 13,29:5
Barry, Charles P, 1964, Ja 2,27:3
Barry, Claud B Sir, 1951, D 29,11:5
Barry, Cornelius B, 1948, S 24,25:5
Barry, Daniel, 1942, O 18,53:2
Barry, Daniel J, 1967, Ap 26,44:5
Barry, Daniel J Mrs, 1953, Jl 17,17:4
Barry, Daniel J Sr, 1937, Jl 13,19:1
Barry, David J, 1953, Jl 8,27:6
Barry, David S, 1951, Jl 2,23:4
Barry, Donald B, 1950, S 24,105:1
Barry, Douglas C, 1948, N 7,88:5
Barry, E M, 1880, Ja 30,5:4
Barry, Edmond P Mrs, 1944, Ap 13,19:6
Barry, Edmund D, 1946, My 8,25:5
Barry, Edward, 1938, Jl 7,19:5
Barry, Edward B, 1938, N 28,15:6
Barry, Edward C Mrs, 1960, N 3,39:2
Barry, Edward J, 1951, Ap 28,15:6
Barry, Edward L, 1943, Ag 13,17:5
Barry, Edward W, 1964, D 28,29:4
Barry, Edward W Jr, 1958, Mr 11,29:5
Barry, Elizabeth M, 1943, Ap 23,17:2
Barry, Ellen (Mother Mary Elenita), 1955, Ja 13,27:5
Barry, Eugene P, 1956, Ja 22,88:3
Barry, Francis J R, 1914, F 27,11:5
Barry, Fred, 1964, Ag 19,37:3
Barry, Frederick, 1943, Ap 6,21:4
Barry, Frederick C, 1943, Ja 18,15:3; 1952, Je 3,29:1
Barry, Frederick L, 1960, O 6,41:2
Barry, G E, 1876, F 28,5:2
Barry, G J, 1877, N 11,6:7
Barry, G Lynn, 1949, D 8,33:3
Barry, Gerald Reid Sir, 1968, N 22,47:3
Barry, H C, 1957, F 10,86:8
Barry, Harold F, 1940, S 14,17:5
Barry, Harry S, 1937, F 10,23:3
Barry, Harry W, 1940, Ja 19,19:5
Barry, Henry A, 1955, Mr 6,88:1
Barry, Henry A Mrs, 1944, Ja 27,19:3
Barry, Henry A Rev, 1907, Ja 11,9:5
Barry, Herbert, 1947, Je 20,19:3
Barry, Herbert H, 1962, My 2,37:4
Barry, Herbert Mrs, 1956, Ap 27,27:3
Barry, Horace Mansfield, 1910, Je 3,7:4
Barry, J H (Jack), 1955, N 5,19:3
Barry, J T, 1928, Mr 6,27:2
Barry, J Weldon, 1945, F 11,38:4
Barry, Jack, 1961, Ap 24,29:3
Barry, James, 1947, Mr 24,25:3
Barry, James A, 1943, O 30,15:4
Barry, James F, 1956, F 23,27:3
Barry, James R, 1950, N 19,93:2
Barry, Jeremiah H, 1946, Mr 24,44:5

Barry, John A Col, 1937, Ja 12,24:1
Barry, John D, 1942, N 4,23:2
Barry, John F, 1940, D 11,28:3; 1954, D 24,13:2; 1968, F 7,47:3
Barry, John G, 1943, Mr 5,17:3
Barry, John H, 1944, Mr 11,13:3
Barry, John H Sr, 1959, Je 1,27:5
Barry, John J, 1910, Ag 26,7:6; 1939, N 17,21:1; 1944, S 28,19:3; 1952, Je 25,29:1; 1953, Ag 10,23:5
Barry, John L, 1947, Mr 2,60:3; 1947, Ag 20,21:4
Barry, John P, 1937, Ag 7,15:4
Barry, John R, 1965, N 14,89:1
Barry, John S, 1953, My 17,89:2
Barry, John Wolfe Sir, 1918, Ja 24,9:2
Barry, Joseph, 1941, F 15,15:4
Barry, Joseph T, 1950, F 3,23:3
Barry, Josephine A, 1964, My 22,35:2
Barry, Justin, 1951, Jl 16,21:4
Barry, Kathleen E Mrs, 1938, Je 26,27:4
Barry, L Frank, 1922, N 10,17:3
Barry, Lawrence, 1903, My 19,7:1
Barry, Lizzie B Mrs, 1940, O 9,25:6
Barry, Llewellyn, 1937, My 29,17:3
Barry, Maurice D, 1942, Ap 17,17:4
Barry, Michael, 1952, Ag 28,23:4
Barry, Michael J, 1942, Ja 10,18:2; 1950, N 19,93:1
Barry, Michael J Mrs, 1948, Ap 27,25:2
Barry, Napolean Bonaparte, 1912, O 22,11:5
Barry, Nicholas, 1948, Ja 14,25:1
Barry, Patrick, 1940, Ag 14,19:2
Barry, Patrick J, 1956, N 25,88:4
Barry, Patrick Mrs, 1925, Mr 4,19:5
Barry, Patrick Thomas, 1925, Mr 4,19:5
Barry, Paul J, 1937, S 29,23:5
Barry, Paul V, 1951, F 17,15:3
Barry, Pete, 1968, Ag 30,33:2
Barry, Phil, 1949, D 4,108:3
Barry, Philip J, 1915, N 7,21:6
Barry, Ralph A, 1939, D 11,23:1
Barry, Redmond, 1913, Jl 12,7:6
Barry, Richard A, 1945, S 11,23:5
Barry, Richard F Sr, 1951, F 27,27:4
Barry, Richard J, 1955, S 21,33:5
Barry, Richard J Mrs, 1964, Mr 28,19:2
Barry, Richard Mrs, 1946, My 24,19:3
Barry, Richard T, 1945, O 31,23:3
Barry, Robert, 1882, Ja 7,5:6; 1952, F 16,13:3
Barry, Robert M, 1938, Ap 23,15:5
Barry, Robert P, 1948, S 20,25:2
Barry, Robert Peabody Maj, 1912, O 10,11:4
Barry, Sam, 1950, S 24,104:8
Barry, Susan S Mrs, 1941, Je 22,32:5
Barry, Thomas, 1937, S 9,23:2; 1951, Ap 2,25:4
Barry, Thomas A, 1947, D 29,18:3; 1966, Je 20,33:4
Barry, Thomas D, 1959, S 21,31:5
Barry, Thomas F, 1925, Jl 1,23:3; 1955, F 14,19:5
Barry, Thomas H, 1921, O 6,17:6
Barry, Thomas Henry Maj-Gen, 1919, D 31,7:5
Barry, Thomas J, 1944, D 23,13:5; 1947, Ja 1,33:4; 1951, Ag 17,17:4; 1966, Jl 31,72:4
Barry, Thomas W Chaplain, 1904, F 25,9:5
Barry, Timothy E, 1946, O 29,25:3
Barry, Timothy P Jr, 1954, S 10,23:3
Barry, W F Gen, 1879, Jl 19,5:2
Barry, Walter D, 1952, N 28,25:3
Barry, Walter F Jr, 1951, Ag 26,38:1
Barry, Walter F Sr, 1942, Jl 7,19:6
Barry, Walter R, 1949, O 6,31:4; 1953, S 29,29:6
Barry, William, 1967, N 18,37:2
Barry, William B, 1946, O 21,31:3
Barry, William D Mrs, 1954, Jl 23,17:6; 1955, F 2,27:4
Barry, William F, 1941, Ja 24,17:3
Barry, William G, 1938, N 24,27:5
Barry, William J, 1948, Je 16,29:5; 1949, My 13,23:2; 1967, Ja 11,25:3
Barry, William Mrs, 1943, O 18,15:2
Barry, William R, 1954, D 8,35:1; 1960, N 4,33:3
Barry, William S, 1944, F 23,19:4
Barry, William T, 1943, My 20,21:3
Barrymore, Diana (funl, Ja 30,21:2; med examiner rept, F 5,19:7), 1960, Ja 26,27:2
Barrymore, Ethel (funl plans, Je 20,21:3; rites, Je 22,25:4), 1959, Je 19,1:5
Barrymore, John, 1942, My 30,1:3
Barrymore, Lionel (funl, N 19,32:2; will, D 3,31:1), 1954, N 16,1:3
Barrymore, Lord (Arth Hugh Smith Barry), 1925, F 23,17:6
Barrymore, Maurice, 1905, Mr 26,9:5
Barsa, Abdala, 1965, Ag 5,29:4
Barsamian, Barsam M, 1945, S 16,43:2
Barsby, William H, 1955, Mr 7,27:6
Barse, Dane, 1960, Mr 1,33:5
Barseghian, Armen, 1949, Ap 12,29:3
Barsel, Solomon, 1952, F 16,13:6
Barsescu, Agata, 1939, N 22,21:2
Barshak, Max, 1956, Ag 12,85:2
Barshak, Simon, 1944, Mr 21,20:2
Barskov, Aleksei, 1951, N 24,11:4
Barsky, Bud, 1967, D 21,37:4
Barsky, David, 1948, D 4,13:5
Barsky, Joseph C, 1954, Mr 28,88:4
Barsky, Joseph M, 1948, Ag 1,58:2
Barsky, Mayer, 1952, Mr 7,23:3
Barsky, Phillip, 1952, Ag 20,25:6
Barson, Elie, 1952, D 9,33:3
Barsotti, C, 1927, Mr 31,23:3
Barsova, Valeria, 1967, D 15,94:3
Barss, Edward M, 1952, My 21,27:4
Barss, John E, 1944, N 23,31:2
Barster, Thomas G, 1904, Ap 10,7:2
Barstow, Beverly C, 1965, Jl 18,68:2
Barstow, Caleb, 1880, My 21,5:4
Barstow, Col Ex-Gov, 1865, D 15,5:1
Barstow, Francis V, 1941, Mr 4,23:5
Barstow, Frank Quarles, 1909, Ag 21,7:1
Barstow, Henry H, 1944, N 22,19:3
Barstow, Henry W, 1940, My 30,17:3
Barstow, J Whitney Dr, 1922, D 18,17:5
Barstow, James S, 1941, My 12,17:2
Barstow, James S Mrs, 1962, Mr 28,39:3
Barstow, James Stuart Jr, 1968, Je 25,41:3
Barstow, John Lester Ex-Gov, 1913, Je 29,5:5
Barstow, John P, 1937, Ja 29,19:1
Barstow, Louis B Mrs, 1938, Ap 5,21:4
Barstow, Nelson A (will), 1954, D 15,33:5
Barstow, Richard I Mrs, 1941, Je 18,21:2
Barstow, Robbins W, 1962, S 19,39:2
Barstow, S F Gen, 1882, Ag 2,5:6
Barstow, William A, 1922, F 11,13:2
Barstow, William S, 1942, D 28,19:1
Barstow, William S Mrs, 1958, Ag 23,15:3
Barstow, Wilson Gen, 1869, Mr 17,7:4
Barszcak, Francis, 1951, F 12,23:1
Bart, Benjamin F, 1948, F 15,60:5
Bart, Blasius, 1957, O 5,17:6
Bart, Jean Mrs, 1955, Mr 8,27:2
Bart, Michael, 1949, Mr 12,17:6
Bart, St Ludwig of Bremen, 1903, Ja 29,2:4
Barta, George L, 1953, Je 12,27:3
Bartak, Joseph P Mrs, 1953, Ag 20,27:5
Bartecchi, Ferdinand A, 1953, O 24,15:5
Bartee, Eldred H, 1941, N 27,23:2
Barteld, Hermann H, 1941, My 8,23:5
Bartell, Floyd E, 1961, Mr 7,35:4
Bartell, Gustave H, 1954, S 10,23:4
Bartelme, Mary M, 1954, Jl 26,17:3
Bartelme, Phil, 1954, My 4,29:4
Bartels, Edward, 1948, N 5,25:3
Bartels, Emil C, 1951, S 29,17:2
Bartels, George M, 1959, My 23,25:3
Bartels, Harold C, 1950, S 12,27:3
Bartels, Herman, 1910, Ag 27,7:6
Bartels, Jerome, 1961, Ja 3,29:1
Bartels, John M, 1944, O 6,23:2
Bartels, John R Mrs, 1967, S 21,47:2
Bartels, Julius, 1964, Mr 12,35:3
Bartelson, Henry C Dr, 1937, O 4,21:3
Bartelstone, Herman, 1950, N 12,94:4
Bartelstone, Jacob, 1948, F 18,27:5
Bartelstone, Louis, 1958, Mr 5,31:2
Bartelt, Arthur H, 1952, Ja 21,15:3
Bartelt, William, 1938, O 14,23:3
Barter, Alfred, 1949, D 1,31:5
Barter, Richard J, 1954, F 19,27:4
Bartet, Julia, 1941, N 21,17:4
Bartfeld, Adolph, 1952, Mr 3,21:1
Bartfield, Samuel, 1947, Jl 16,23:2
Barth, Andrew, 1951, Jl 12,25:3
Barth, Aron, 1957, Je 3,27:4
Barth, Arthur, 1944, Ja 21,17:2; 1956, Ja 28,17:4
Barth, Bernard, 1962, Ag 5,81:2
Barth, C H Brig Gen, 1926, D 6,23:5
Barth, Carl G, 1939, O 30,17:6
Barth, Charles R, 1956, Ap 20,25:4
Barth, Chester A, 1960, Mr 12,21:2
Barth, Dr, 1865, D 14,1:7
Barth, Edward F, 1952, N 25,29:3
Barth, Edwin J, 1964, O 19,33:3
Barth, Eleazer, 1941, Jl 14,13:4
Barth, Fred W, 1952, Mr 5,29:4
Barth, Frederick C, 1941, O 7,23:5
Barth, Gustav, 1951, My 11,27:4
Barth, Hans, 1956, D 9,88:4
Barth, Harry, 1937, Ag 27,19:3
Barth, Henry, 1958, Jl 6,57:2
Barth, Henry L, 1960, Jl 23,19:4
Barth, Jay F, 1959, Je 29,29:6
Barth, John J, 1953, Ja 25,85:1
Barth, John L, 1954, F 22,19:4
Barth, Karl (funl plans, D 12,47:4; mem ser plans, D 14,45:3), 1968, D 11,1:3
Barth, Louis, 1957, My 16,31:3
Barth, Roll, 1951, Ag 26,80:5
Barth, Theodore Dr, 1909, Je 4,7:4
Barth, Theodore H, 1967, Je 21,47:1
Barth, Theodore N, 1961, Ag 23,33:1
Barth, Vincnet D, 1951, Ap 12,33:5
Barth, William, 1958, Je 8,89:1
Bartha, Albert, 1960, D 3,23:4
Bartha, Frank Sr, 1950, S 14,31:3
Bartha, Gyula, 1955, Je 20,21:6
Bartha, Joseph, 1968, D 17,47:1
Barthel, George A Rev, 1915, Ja 16,9:4
Barthel, Otto F, 1941, S 13,17:2
Barthel, Peter J, 1937, Je 23,25:1
Barthel, William J, 1958, Ap 14,25:3
Barthelemy, Joseph, 1945, My 16,10:4
Barthelemy, Pierre de Marquis, 1940, O 31,23:4
Barthelemy, Rene, 1954, F 17,31:1
Barthelmess, Caroline H Mrs, 1937, Ap 24,9:4
Barthelmess, Richard (funeral Ag 21,33:3), 1963, Ag 18,80:2
Barthelmess, Richard Mrs, 1965, Ap 22,33:4
Barthen, Charles, 1942, Jl 23,19:3
Barthman, Henry C, 1941, Mr 26,23:6
Barthman, William, 1914, Ja 18,5:4
Barthman, William C, 1968, Jl 2,41:2
Barthold, Charles, 1943, My 18,23:4
Barthold, John, 1946, N 6,23:4
Barthold, Lee G, 1953, Ag 27,25:3
Barthold, William H, 1949, Ap 12,30:2
Bartholdi, Albert, 1954, O 14,29:3
Bartholdi, F Auguste, 1904, O 5,9:5
Bartholemew, Kathryn Mrs, 1921, Jl 6,15:6
Bartholet, Max, 1967, Ja 20,43:1
Bartholet, Paul, 1962, Mr 17,25:2
Bartholf, Herbert B, 1954, Jl 2,19:3
Bartholmew, Herbert, 1955, Je 28,27:1
Bartholomae, Frederick, 1938, My 31,19:3
Bartholomae, Philip H, 1947, Ja 6,23:5
Bartholomew, A R, 1933, N 28,21:5
Bartholomew, Alanson D Sr, 1949, Ja 18,23:3
Bartholomew, Albert J Mrs, 1966, Mr 24,39:4
Bartholomew, Arthur P, 1943, O 11,19:3
Bartholomew, Charle E Mrs, 1945, Ja 2,19:4
Bartholomew, G W, 1903, Je 9,9:6
Bartholomew, George H, 1968, S 12,47:3
Bartholomew, Harry G, 1962, My 5,27:3
Bartholomew, Henry S, 1960, N 25,27:1
Bartholomew, Herbert A Sr, 1958, O 27,27:5
Bartholomew, J H, 1884, Je 2,5:4
Bartholomew, James K, 1957, D 30,23:3
Bartholomew, John, 1952, D 13,21:3
Bartholomew, John O, 1905, S 18,7:7
Bartholomew, Julia H Mrs, 1940, O 22,23:5
Bartholomew, Lin, 1880, Ag 25,3:4
Bartholomew, Morey C, 1948, O 26,31:5
Bartholomew, Perry Capt, 1903, O 9,7:4
Bartholomew, Ralph I, 1948, D 21,31:1
Bartholomew, Robert, 1966, N 26,36:3
Bartholomew, Robert J, 1950, D 29,19:1
Bartholomew, William H, 1919, S 3,13:4; 1963, Ja 2, 4:1
Bartholomew, William J, 1962, Ja 23,33:1
Bartholomew, Zelina R Mrs, 1937, O 13,23:4
Bartholone, Catherine Mrs, 1956, Jl 3,25:3
Bartholow, J M, 1903, Ap 21,9:5
Bartholow, Otho, 1951, S 27,31:3
Bartholow, Otho F Mrs, 1938, Ap 18,15:4
Barthou, L, 1934, O 10,1:8
Barthouski, John J, 1957, Ag 1,25:4
Bartilucci, Joseph P, 1940, Ja 21,34:4
Bartine, D W, 1881, Ag 14,7:6
Bartine, John D Ex-Judge, 1908, Jl 4,5:4
Bartine, Oliver H, 1955, Jl 8,23:1
Bartinique, Leo J F, 1964, Ap 11,25:1
Bartko, George F Sr, 1951, Ja 3,25:1
Bartky, Walter, 1958, Mr 20,29:4
Bartl, Frank E, 1953, Mr 3,27:1
Bartle, George H, 1938, N 28,15:4
Bartle, Jesse, 1946, Mr 31,46:6
Bartleman, George F, 1951, O 2,28:3
Bartleson, Edward E, 1959, D 29,25:3
Bartless, Charles, 1883, Je 14,4:7
Bartlet, James V, 1940, Ag 7,19:3
Bartlett, Adeline C, 1955, N 30,33:2
Bartlett, Adolphus Clay, 1922, My 31,15:1
Bartlett, Albert A, 1945, Jl 14,11:4
Bartlett, Albert F, 1939, Mr 29,23:2
Bartlett, Alice H Mrs, 1949, S 15,27:1
Bartlett, Arthur C, 1964, Jl 14,33:4
Bartlett, Boyd W, 1965, Je 25,33:2
Bartlett, Brenniman P, 1948, My 1,15:2
Bartlett, C G Gen (funl), 1901, Je 22,9:6
Bartlett, C Julian Mrs, 1959, N 15,86:4
Bartlett, Charles, 1955, Ag 11,21:2
Bartlett, Charles G, 1948, O 20,29:5; 1951, My 5,17:1
Bartlett, Charles Griswold, 1912, N 13,15:4
Bartlett, Charles H, 1937, Mr 2,21:1; 1937, S 3,17:1; 1941, Ja 22,21:3; 1947, Jl 29,21:4; 1952, F 19,29:4
Bartlett, Charles J, 1956, Mr 8,29:3
Bartlett, Charles L, 1909, Mr 8,7:4; 1938, Ap 22,19:4; 1939, Mr 21,23:1; 1950, Jl 16,68:5
Bartlett, Charles M, 1948, Ap 19,23:2
Bartlett, Charles W, 1940, Ap 18,23:1
Bartlett, Clay, 1955, D 14,39:5
Bartlett, Clifton W, 1950, Ja 3,25:4
Bartlett, Craig S, 1963, S 18,40:1
Bartlett, D K, 1881, Ja 12,5:4
Bartlett, David L, 1904, F 23,7:6
Bartlett, David S, 1940, O 28,17:5
Bartlett, David W, 1912, Je 26,13:4
Bartlett, E A Sir, 1902, Ja 19,9:6
Bartlett, E L Sen (Edw Lewis Bartlett),(Bob), 1968, D 12,43:2
Bartlett, E O, 1942, Ag 28,19:2
Bartlett, Edmund C, 1954, Ja 29,19:3
Bartlett, Edward E, 1942, S 25,21:5

Bartlett, Edward E Jr, 1961, Jl 7,25:5
Bartlett, Edward E Jr Mrs, 1944, Mr 22,19:1
Bartlett, Edward R, 1952, Ap 17,29:1
Bartlett, Edward T Judge (trb My 5,11:5), 1910, My 4,11:3
Bartlett, Edwin I, 1954, F 23,27:4
Bartlett, Edwin R, 1957, D 11,31:4
Bartlett, Elizabeth Mrs, 1941, D 10,25:2
Bartlett, Ella F Mrs, 1940, Ap 13,17:1
Bartlett, Ellen C, 1944, Mr 18,13:4
Bartlett, Elvina C Mrs, 1938, O 14,24:3
Bartlett, Enoch J, 1956, Mr 28,31:4
Bartlett, Ernest J, 1956, Jl 5,25:4
Bartlett, Ewell T, 1960, N 24,29:6
Bartlett, Ezra K, 1912, Ag 30,9:6
Bartlett, Florence, 1951, Mr 27,29:3
Bartlett, Floyd J, 1952, D 4,35:3
Bartlett, Francis, 1913, S 25,13:6
Bartlett, Francis A, 1963, N 22,31:6
Bartlett, Francis Wayland, 1903, N 26,7:6
Bartlett, Franklin Col (funl, Ap 27,11:4), 1909, Ap 24,7:2
Bartlett, Franklin Mrs, 1920, S 5,19:5
Bartlett, Frederic, 1948, O 20,29:3
Bartlett, Frederic C, 1953, Je 26,19:3
Bartlett, Frederic H Mrs, 1952, Ap 20,92:3
Bartlett, Frederick B Mrs, 1940, Mr 26,21:2
Bartlett, Frederick Clay Mrs, 1925, O 26,19:6
Bartlett, Frederick E, 1911, Je 10,13:4
Bartlett, Frederick O, 1945, N 5,19:2
Bartlett, Frederick W, 1942, Ap 9,19:3; 1953, F 28,17:6
Bartlett, G Donald, 1945, My 20,32:2
Bartlett, Geoffrey Mrs, 1944, Jl 25,19:6
Bartlett, George, 1955, Ap 13,29:4
Bartlett, George A, 1951, Je 4,27:4
Bartlett, George Alonzo Prof, 1908, N 28,9:5
Bartlett, George F, 1965, N 15,37:3
Bartlett, George G, 1946, Ap 6,17:5; 1952, O 9,31:2
Bartlett, George R, 1945, D 6,27:3; 1953, D 10,47:2
Bartlett, George S, 1945, O 22,17:4
Bartlett, George T, 1949, Mr 12,18:3
Bartlett, George W, 1954, N 20,17:5
Bartlett, Gray, 1951, Jl 26,21:2
Bartlett, Harold J, 1954, S 19,89:1
Bartlett, Harold T, 1955, S 16,23:2
Bartlett, Harriet L, 1948, My 14,23:1
Bartlett, Harry G, 1952, Jl 5,15:6
Bartlett, Harry Mrs, 1937, Mr 12,23:3
Bartlett, Harry S, 1965, Je 27,65:2
Bartlett, Henry, 1943, Ap 1,23:3
Bartlett, Henry Mrs, 1954, N 10,33:4
Bartlett, Herbert A, 1954, Jl 6,23:3
Bartlett, Homer L, 1940, Mr 12,23:3
Bartlett, Homer L Dr, 1905, F 4,9:1
Bartlett, Homer N, 1920, Ap 4,22:2; 1967, Je 18,76:6
Bartlett, Ike F Mrs, 1953, O 4,87:1
Bartlett, Ike Mrs, 1950, Ag 24,27:5
Bartlett, Irving T, 1968, My 16,47:2
Bartlett, J, 1927, Ap 5,27:3
Bartlett, J C, 1903, Je 3,9:6
Bartlett, J F (funl) (see also F 4), 1877, F 6,8:4
Bartlett, J H Mrs, 1925, D 21,21:4
Bartlett, J Henry, 1946, Jl 6,15:5
Bartlett, J Henry Mrs, 1942, D 9,27:6
Bartlett, J Hobart Mrs, 1957, N 16,19:4
Bartlett, J R Adm, 1904, N 23,9:4
Bartlett, J W (mem ser), 1883, O 1,5:2
Bartlett, James E, 1945, F 24,11:4
Bartlett, James H, 1945, O 6,13:5
Bartlett, James L, 1943, O 27,23:2
Bartlett, John, 1905, D 4,1:4
Bartlett, John F, 1950, Ja 30,17:2; 1951, O 19,27:1
Bartlett, John H, 1952, Mr 20,29:3
Bartlett, John P, 1948, Mr 4,25:2
Bartlett, John P Mrs, 1955, Jl 24,65:2
Bartlett, John R, 1918, Je 8,11:5
Bartlett, John R Mrs, 1943, Ag 15,39:2
Bartlett, John T Mrs, 1949, N 29,29:3
Bartlett, John W, 1940, My 19,43:2; 1948, Je 29,23:4; 1961, O 31,31:2; 1965, F 1,23:4
Bartlett, John W Dr, 1937, Jl 14,32:2
Bartlett, Joseph R, 1940, Ap 7,45:2
Bartlett, Josephine (Mrs Harold Perry), 1910, O 16, II,13:4
Bartlett, Lawrence Dr, 1924, Ag 31,14:3
Bartlett, Levi S, 1940, Jl 7,25:3
Bartlett, M N Mrs, 1903, Je 11,9:7
Bartlett, Maitland, 1944, Ja 18,19:1
Bartlett, Matthew, 1945, N 27,23:1
Bartlett, Maud W, 1954, Ap 12,29:4
Bartlett, Max C, 1952, D 10,35:1
Bartlett, Murray (por), 1949, N 14,27:1
Bartlett, Murray, 1949, N 17,29:2
Bartlett, Murray Mrs, 1961, N 28,37:2
Bartlett, Nath Edward, 1924, Ap 24,19:3
Bartlett, North E, 1952, Je 10,27:5
Bartlett, Owen, 1950, Mr 27,23:2
Bartlett, P, 1881, Ap 12,8:2
Bartlett, Paul, 1965, Ap 4,87:2
Bartlett, Paul B Prof, 1953, F 1,89:1
Bartlett, Percy, 1951, Jl 8,61:3
Bartlett, Percy H, 1942, Jl 25,13:6
Bartlett, Philip G Mrs, 1944, F 9,19:3
Bartlett, Ralph A, 1950, F 21,26:2
Bartlett, Randolph I, 1943, O 2,13:5
Bartlett, Raymond S, 1961, My 4,37:4
Bartlett, Robert, 1941, S 7,50:1
Bartlett, Robert A (Bob), 1946, Ap 29,21:1
Bartlett, Rodman, 1881, F 8,5:5
Bartlett, Rolla W, 1946, Mr 8,21:2
Bartlett, Royal, 1948, Ag 14,13:4
Bartlett, Russell S, 1945, S 11,23:6
Bartlett, S, 1889, Mr 8,5:2
Bartlett, Samuel C Rev, 1937, F 3,23:6
Bartlett, Samuel L, 1952, N 27,31:1
Bartlett, Stanley F, 1937, Jl 15,19:5
Bartlett, Theodora, 1962, Jl 15,61:1
Bartlett, Valentine C, 1953, F 12,14:4
Bartlett, W D, 1948, F 7,15:4
Bartlett, W F, 1876, O 17,8:4
Bartlett, W O, 1881, S 24,5:2
Bartlett, Walter A, 1946, Ag 11,46:1
Bartlett, Warren T, 1947, D 23,23:4
Bartlett, Washington A, 1865, F 10,8:5
Bartlett, Willard (funl, Ja 20,21:5), 1925, Ja 18,7:1
Bartlett, Willard, 1950, Ap 5,31:3
Bartlett, William Allen Dr, 1921, Ja 6,11:3
Bartlett, William Alvin Rev Dr, 1917, Ja 16,9:2
Bartlett, William D, 1946, Je 10,21:4
Bartlett, William H, 1937, Mr 23,23:5
Bartlett, William J Mrs, 1943, Ja 17,44:3
Bartlett, William L, 1942, Ap 26,39:2
Bartlett, William O, 1960, Jl 9,19:3
Bartlett, William R, 1943, N 16,23:4
Bartlett, Winifred, 1947, F 14,22:3
Bartley, Alex F, 1938, D 6,23:1
Bartley, Charles E, 1940, Mr 27,21:2
Bartley, David W, 1955, Ap 9,13:3
Bartley, E H Mrs, 1925, Jl 7,19:4
Bartley, Edward L, 1945, O 27,15:6
Bartley, Elias H Dr (por), 1937, Ja 13,23:1
Bartley, J Sims Mrs, 1948, Je 7,19:3
Bartley, John, 1954, Jl 12,19:4
Bartley, Jonathan, 1938, N 23,21:4
Bartley, Joseph C, 1962, S 8,19:4
Bartley, Joseph S, 1953, N 24,29:3
Bartley, Ollie B, 1957, Ja 15,3:3
Bartley, Patrick, 1956, Je 26,35:6
Bartley, Robert J, 1957, Ap 23,31:3
Bartley, S Potter, 1952, Je 11,29:6
Bartley, S Potter Mrs, 1953, Ag 12,31:4
Bartley, William J, 1949, O 29,15:4
Bartley, William R, 1954, Ja 27,27:3
Bartling, Earl F, 1954, S 4,11:3
Bartnett, Edmond J, 1963, Je 24,27:3
Bartnett, John, 1946, O 5,17:3
Bartnett, Kathleen M, 1961, O 12,29:1
Bartnett, Michael F Sr, 1951, Jl 29,69:3
Bartnett, Robert J, 1949, Jl 9,13:6
Barto, Henry D Gen, 1873, D 17,1:6
Barto, James O, 1952, Ap 29,27:2
Bartoccini, Renato, 1963, O 11,37:3
Bartochevitch, Leonty, 1956, Ag 21,29:3
Bartok, Bela, 1945, S 27,21:1
Bartol, George E Mrs, 1953, Jl 30,16:3
Bartol, Grier, 1960, Mr 22,37:3
Bartol, Henry G, 1950, F 25,17:2
Bartol, William C, 1940, N 1,25:6
Bartold, Hugo H, 1948, My 10,21:3
Bartoldi, Auguste Mrs, 1914, O 16,11:5
Bartoli, Eugene, 1948, S 18,17:5
Bartoli, Eugene Mrs, 1950, Mr 1,27:2
Bartoli, Joseph F, 1956, D 11,39:1
Bartolini, Luigi, 1963, My 18,27:6
Bartolo, Augustus Sir, 1937, F 21,II,10:6
Barton, Albert, 1951, Je 7,33:1
Barton, Albert O, 1947, O 23,25:5
Barton, Alfred T Lt, 1917, My 7,9:4
Barton, Artemas D, 1944, Mr 30,21:4
Barton, Arthur J, 1942, Jl 21,19:4
Barton, Arthur W, 1962, S 23,86:8
Barton, Benton G, 1948, N 17,27:3
Barton, Bernard G, 1945, Ag 30,21:5
Barton, Bernard G Mrs, 1951, F 26,23:2
Barton, Betsey, 1962, D 13,5:5
Barton, Bruce (est appr, Jl 25,16:8), 1967, Jl 6,1:3
Barton, Bruce Jr (funl plans, O 1,39:2), 1963, S 30, 29:1
Barton, Bruce Mrs, 1951, N 21,25:1
Barton, C Fred, 1953, O 6,29:6
Barton, Charles, 1917, F 23,11:5; 1951, S 6,31:5
Barton, Charles B, 1939, O 20,23:1
Barton, Charles Day, 1905, Mr 15,9:6
Barton, Charles K, 1958, Ja 25,19:3
Barton, Charles Mrs, 1952, Jl 3,25:3
Barton, Charles Sumner, 1914, Jl 13,9:7
Barton, Charles W, 1956, O 23,33:4
Barton, Charles W Mrs, 1944, Ag 25,13:6
Barton, Clara (por),(funl, Ap 16,13:5), 1912, Ap 13, 13:1
Barton, Clarence, 1925, D 7,21:4; 1948, Ja 6,24:3
Barton, Clarence W, 1956, D 21,23:4
Barton, Cornelius Vanderbilt Mrs, 1968, F 13,43:2
Barton, Craig, 1967, Jl 1,23:4
Barton, Dilmore C, 1938, F 4,21:5
Barton, Donald C, 1939, Jl 10,19:5
Barton, Edmund Sir, 1920, Ja 8,17:3
Barton, Emma W Mrs, 1941, N 10,17:5
Barton, Enos M, 1916, My 5,11:6
Barton, Fannie L A Mrs, 1941, Ja 31,19:5
Barton, Francis A, 1939, Ap 22,17:2
Barton, Francis C Jr Mrs, 1940, My 8,23:6
Barton, Frank A, 1946, Ag 22,27:6
Barton, Frank E, 1961, O 23,29:4
Barton, Frank L, 1941, O 8,23:5
Barton, Fred, 1938, N 11,25:4
Barton, Fred H, 1964, N 19,39:5
Barton, Fred Otis, 1904, F 15,7:6
Barton, Frederick C, 1939, O 28,15:2
Barton, G H, 1933, N 26,33:3
Barton, George, 1940, Mr 17,51:3; 1955, S 23,26:5
Barton, George A, 1942, Je 29,15:3
Barton, George E, 1955, Ja 18,27:2
Barton, George F, 1949, Ja 26,25:4
Barton, George T, 1961, Mr 14,35:1
Barton, H Allen, 1947, F 6,23:2
Barton, Harry L Mrs, 1956, Ag 2,25:3
Barton, Henry, 1946, Jl 28,40:6; 1948, Ja 21,26:3
Barton, Henry J, 1943, Ag 8,37:1
Barton, Henry S, 1941, D 11,27:5
Barton, Herbert C, 1948, Je 18,23:5
Barton, Howard S, 1960, S 22,27:5
Barton, Isaac Duell, 1914, Ag 22,7:4
Barton, J G Prof, 1877, My 23,2:4
Barton, J L, 1936, Jl 22,19:3
Barton, James E (mem ser planned, My 1,37:1), 1962, F 20,35:1
Barton, James H, 1940, O 3,25:3
Barton, James M, 1950, Ap 16,106:5; 1951, My 16,35:5
Barton, James Mrs, 1949, Je 21,25:1
Barton, James P, 1943, D 29,18:2
Barton, John, 1946, D 24,17:1
Barton, John A Dr, 1948, F 28,15:3
Barton, John E, 1945, Jl 30,19:4
Barton, John F, 1941, Je 3,21:3
Barton, John H, 1943, My 11,21:1; 1968, Ja 17,47:1
Barton, John Kennedy Rear-Adm, 1921, D 24,11:6
Barton, John L Mrs, 1949, O 24,23:6
Barton, John Mrs, 1947, N 16,77:1; 1954, D 29,23:4
Barton, John R, 1942, N 15,58:2
Barton, Joseph A L, 1925, N 23,21:4
Barton, Joseph F, 1938, Je 7,23:4
Barton, K and T, 1942, Mr 30,19:3
Barton, LeRoy, 1959, N 29,86:5
Barton, Loren C, 1946, D 21,19:6
Barton, Louis N, 1952, N 18,31:3
Barton, Lyman G, 1944, N 22,19:6
Barton, M A Dr, 1937, N 6,17:4
Barton, Michael R, 1964, N 22,86:6
Barton, Natt L, 1946, N 5,25:5
Barton, Nelson E, 1937, F 9,23:5
Barton, Olive R Mrs, 1957, Ag 16,19:5
Barton, Oliver Grant, 1908, D 7,9:5
Barton, Oliver M, 1949, O 2,82:7
Barton, Phineas, 1866, F 19,4:7
Barton, Plunket Sir, 1937, S 13,21:6
Barton, R M, 1928, Ap 6,23:3
Barton, Ralph A, 1949, N 29,29:1
Barton, Ralph M, 1941, N 16,56:7
Barton, Raymond C, 1954, Jl 6,23:2
Barton, Raynold O, 1963, F 28,4:6
Barton, Richard J, 1939, D 18,23:3
Barton, Robert S, 1954, Ja 17,92:8
Barton, Roy E, 1955, Mr 10,27:3
Barton, Roy F, 1947, Ap 28,23:2
Barton, Sam, 1941, O 9,25:1
Barton, Samuel E, 1947, N 20,29:3
Barton, Samuel G, 1958, Je 4,33:3
Barton, Sidney, 1945, Ap 22,35:1; 1946, Ja 22,27:2
Barton, T H, 1960, D 25,42:2
Barton, Theophilus F, 1963, N 2,25:4
Barton, Thomas F, 1938, O 16,45:2
Barton, Thomas R Mrs, 1946, Je 22,19:3
Barton, Vincent Bro, 1958, Jl 17,27:4
Barton, W E, 1930, D 8,21:1
Barton, W Fred, 1954, O 13,31:2
Barton, W H Dr, 1902, Je 21,3:2
Barton, Walter E, 1948, S 14,29:2
Barton, Ward J, 1963, Ap 14,92:6
Barton, Warren H, 1957, Ag 28,27:3
Barton, William, 1884, S 3,2:2
Barton, William E, 1946, Je 4,23:4
Barton, William E Dr, 1925, N 10,25:4
Barton, William H Jr, 1944, Jl 8,11:1
Barton, William O, 1959, F 10,33:1
Barton, William P, 1954, Mr 16,29:5
Barton, William S, 1957, Mr 14,29:3
Bartow, Aquilla P, 1940, N 26,23:3
Bartow, Carl W, 1952, Mr 10,21:5
Bartow, Charles W, 1957, Ap 21,88:2
Bartow, Edward, 1958, Ap 14,25:4
Bartow, Francis D, 1945, S 25,25:3
Bartow, Francis D Jr, 1962, Mr 17,25:6
Bartow, Henry S Mrs, 1963, D 21,23:6
Bartow, Josiah B, 1941, Ja 15,23:2
Bartow, Moncure Mrs, 1937, Mr 30,24:2
Bartow, Nelson A, 1954, N 26,29:4
Bartow, Nevett S Mrs, 1954, My 31,13:3
Bartow, Philip K, 1962, Ja 15,27:3
Bartow, William N, 1958, O 16,37:4

Bartram, Edward, 1961, Ag 3,23:1
Bartram, Edward W, 1957, S 7,19:3
Bartram, Edwin B, 1964, D 5,31:2
Bartram, Elwood W, 1944, Ap 3,21:6
Bartram, Floyd B, 1946, Mr 6,27:4
Bartram, Gus M, 1951, O 9,29:2
Bartram, Isaac N, 1913, N 20,11:4
Bartram, Joseph P, 1948, Mr 10,28:3
Bartram, Rensselaer W (will, N 30,27:2), 1954, N 21,87:2
Bartrop, Frederic F L, 1939, N 11,15:2
Bartsch, Edward, 1966, N 4,39:4
Bartsch, Hans, 1952, Jl 12,13:2
Bartsch, Rudolf H, 1952, F 9,13:5
Bartsch, Valentine, 1949, S 25,92:4
Bartscherer, Jacob, 1947, Ja 24,21:3
Barttelot, Brian H F, 1942, F 6,19:2
Bartunek, John, 1940, Jl 4,15:6
Bartuski (Geo Nayulas), 1903, Je 21,1:3
Baruc, Edgar S, 1952, Je 14,15:4
Baruch, Alfred, 1964, O 21,47:2
Baruch, Alfred B, 1941, My 9,21:5
Baruch, Belle W (will, My 28,33:7), 1964, Ap 26,88:5
Baruch, Bernard, 1966, Ap 8,31:3
Baruch, Bernard M (funl, Je 24,39:5; will, Jl 9,1:2), 1965, Je 21,1:6
Baruch, Bernard M Mrs (por);(will, Ja 20,13:4), 1938, Ja 17,19:2
Baruch, E de Marnay, 1935, Jl 2,21:3
Baruch, Earle E, 1962, Jl 14,21:1
Baruch, Edward, 1938, Ap 27,23:5
Baruch, Edward Mrs, 1967, S 11,45:3
Baruch, George J, 1939, Mr 30,23:6
Baruch, Hartwig N, 1953, Mr 2,23:6
Baruch, Herman B (will, Mr 25,33:7), 1953, Mr 16, 19:4
Baruch, Joseph M Mrs, 1967, My 7,87:1
Baruch, Kurt M, 1957, Ap 25,31:4
Baruch, Mannes, 1946, F 18,21:2
Baruch, Max, 1938, D 14,25:3
Baruch, Paul L, 1953, F 10,27:2
Baruch, Robert P, 1965, F 5,31:5
Baruch, Sailing P Jr, 1956, F 11,17:3
Baruch, Sailing W, 1962, Je 15,27:3
Baruch, Simon Dr, 1921, Je 4,13:5
Baruch, Simon Mrs, 1921, N 25,15:5
Baruch, Solomon Dr, 1916, S 6,9:5
Baruch, Sydney N, 1959, S 24,37:2
Barudin, Nathan J, 1954, O 19,27:3
Barus, C, 1935, S 21,15:3
Barusch, Walter, 1945, Ja 2,19:5
Baruth, Ralph H, 1947, N 25,32:4
Barve, S G, 1967, Mr 9,4:4
Barvian, Eugene J, 1940, Ap 9,23:2
Barvoets, Ernest A, 1938, O 27,23:2
Barwell, John W, 1938, O 5,23:5
Barwid, Charles H, 1951, D 15,13:6
Barwis, Elizabeth, 1958, O 8,35:1
Barwood, Lydia M, 1949, Mr 5,17:3
Bary, Jean B de, 1959, Mr 15,88:4
Barye, Antoine Louis, 1875, Je 29,4:7
Barysh, Max, 1964, O 26,31:2
Baryshev, S F, 1949, D 17,17:5
Barzelata, Lorenzo, 1943, Jl 15,21:4
Barzilai, Salvatore, 1939, My 5,23:2
Barzilauskas, Anth, 1948, S 22,31:2
Barzini, Luigi Mrs, 1941, Jl 10,19:3
Basalyga, Basil (Abp Benjamin), 1963, N 16,27:4
Basanta, Raymond I, 1964, Ap 25,29:1
Basch, Felix, 1944, My 18,19:2
Basch, Fred, 1943, Ja 5,19:5
Basch, Harriet E, 1952, F 27,29:7
Basch, Joseph, 1945, Ap 13,17:4
Basch, Martin G, 1952, Jl 16,25:5
Basch, Samuel H Dr, 1937, Ag 8,II,6:8
Basch, William E R Mrs, 1966, Mr 3,33:4
Baschein, Jacob, 1939, O 10,23:4
Bascher, Jay, 1944, N 25,13:2
Bascom, Florence, 1945, Je 20,23:1
Bascom, Francis S, 1948, D 24,17:3
Bascom, Frederick L, 1962, Mr 14,39:3
Bascom, George J, 1916, N 2,13:4
Bascom, George J Mrs, 1940, O 24,25:4
Bascom, Henry M, 1950, Mr 15,29:5
Bascom, John Prof, 1911, O 4,13:5
Bascom, O, 1869, N 9,5:3
Bascom, Perry C, 1943, N 2,25:2
Bascom, Wyman S, 1966, Je 26,73:3
Bascome, Henry L, 1909, Jl 19,7:5
Bascome, W Radford, 1940, Je 15,15:4
Bascum, William, 1920, Jl 31,7:6
Basdevant, Jules, 1968, Ja 7,85:1
Basehart, Richard Mrs, 1950, Jl 29,13:1
Basel, Alex, 1941, Je 12,23:5
Basel, Bridget Mrs, 1946, D 4,31:2
Basel, Morris, 1955, Ag 2,23:1
Baseler, Dorothy J Mrs, 1964, D 5,31:3
Basenfelder, Don, 1945, Ja 6,11:4
Basford, George M, 1925, O 28,25:3
Basford, Harold R, 1954, S 2,21:3
Bash, C Clementine, 1942, Ja 23,19:5
Bash, Louis H, 1952, My 25,92:5
Basham, Rhys A, 1954, Ap 19,23:2
Bashaw, Alex, 1953, F 5,23:4
Bashevkin, David, 1964, Jl 17,27:3
Bashford, Coles, 1878, My 3,5:4
Bashford, Edward E, 1949, Je 17,23:5
Bashford, George S, 1952, Mr 9,92:3
Bashford, James D, 1937, Ja 27,21:5
Bashford, Moore, 1949, My 14,13:3
Bashford, Nellie W Mrs, 1941, S 20,17:5
Bashir, Antony (funl, F 24,37:1), 1966, F 17,33:1
Bashlow, Julius, 1961, N 9,35:1
Bashore, Mae, 1960, My 8,37:4
Basie, Harvey L, 1960, Ap 12,33:1
Basil, Bro (P Reid), 1953, O 14,29:2
Basil, Constantine J, 1962, Mr 1,31:1
Basil, Father, 1878, Ap 12,2:5
Basil, Wassily de, 1951, Jl 28,11:3
Basil Jerome, Bro (R Dewhurst), 1957, N 22,25:4
Basile, Arturo, 1968, My 23,47:5
Basile, Joseph A, 1961, Je 24,21:4
Basile, Pierino, 1946, D 23,23:3
Basilevski, Count, 1878, My 22,8:2
Baskcomb, Daniel A W, 1939, D 11,23:4
Basker, Mitchell R, 1966, N 8,39:2
Baskervill, William M, 1953, My 19,29:2
Baskerville, Charles Dr, 1922, Ja 30,11:2
Baskerville, Charles Mrs, 1957, My 29,27:5
Baskerville, Earl S, 1951, Ja 3,27:3
Baskerville, Harry, 1962, Ap 2,31:4
Baskerville, Thomas H, 1946, Ap 14,46:5
Baskerville, Thomas H Mrs, 1951, Ja 17,28:3
Baskett, James, 1942, Jl 31,15:5; 1948, Jl 10,15:6
Baskette, Billy, 1949, N 11,25:2
Baskie, George E, 1954, Ja 14,29:5
Baskin, Herbert K, 1966, O 28,31:3
Baskin, Joseph, 1952, Je 27,23:2
Baskin, Salem N, 1947, Jl 5,11:5
Baskind, Herman D, 1965, D 15,47:3
Baskowitz, H, 1882, D 27,5:2
Basloe, Frank J Mrs, 1956, Jl 4,19:5
Baslow, Isador, 1954, Ap 5,25:2
Bason, Harry, 1951, Ag 10,15:2
Bason, Jack, 1950, F 6,25:5
Bason, William Mrs, 1951, Jl 24,25:5
Basov-Verkhoyantsev, Sergei, 1952, S 3,29:1
Basquin, Olin H, 1946, Ap 3,25:3
Bass, Abraham, 1950, F 4,15:6
Bass, Abraham M, 1958, N 16,89:1
Bass, Basil N, 1956, N 19,31:5
Bass, Charles H, 1904, Ap 27,9:6
Bass, Edgar W Col, 1918, N 7,15:4
Bass, Edward D, 1960, Mr 13,86:3
Bass, Elizabeth, 1956, Ja 28,17:5
Bass, Ella Mrs, 1953, F 18,31:2
Bass, Ernest C, 1939, N 18,17:3
Bass, Ernest L, 1938, F 18,19:3
Bass, George, 1943, Ja 15,17:3
Bass, George G Mrs, 1965, Ap 20,39:3
Bass, George Mrs, 1950, Ag 26,13:5
Bass, Herman (Feb 4), 1963, Ap 1,35:2
Bass, Hyman Mrs, 1951, Jl 10,27:5
Bass, Irving M, 1961, S 17,86:8
Bass, Isidore, 1946, S 18,31:3
Bass, Ivan E, 1967, N 3,48:8
Bass, Jacob, 1954, Ja 3,89:1
Bass, John, 1939, D 23,15:5
Bass, John H, 1922, D 18,17:5
Bass, John R, 1963, Ag 25,82:8
Bass, John W, 1947, Ag 23,13:3
Bass, Joseph Parker, 1919, Mr 28,13:2
Bass, Leo, 1951, F 21,27:5
Bass, Leonard, 1957, Je 20,29:2
Bass, Leopold, 1951, Jl 17,27:4
Bass, Lyman M, 1955, Jl 10,75:1
Bass, Michael Arthur (Baron Burton), 1909, F 2,9:6
Bass, Murray H, 1962, Mr 10,21:3
Bass, Nathaniel I, 1949, Je 2,27:2
Bass, Noreen, 1949, My 27,21:3
Bass, Olin E, 1947, O 29,28:3
Bass, Robert P, 1960, Jl 31,68:4
Bass, Robert P Mrs, 1950, Mr 24,25:1
Bass, Rose, 1953, Ap 17,25:2
Bass, S Lena, 1953, F 3,25:2
Bass, Samuel, 1944, Ap 7,19:5
Bass, Samuel M, 1953, Ap 13,27:2
Bass, Stanley H, 1959, Je 27,23:5
Bass, T W, 1939, Ag 23,21:5
Bass, Walter A, 1942, S 24,27:3
Bass, Walter H, 1958, Je 7,19:4
Bass, Willard S, 1956, F 11,17:1
Bass, William, 1952, Mr 1,15:4
Bass, William F, 1949, My 29,36:6
Bass, William R, 1951, O 27,19:2
Bassano, Bucco, 1950, O 10,31:3
Bassano, Patrick, 1941, Mr 31,15:4
Bassarear, John A, 1940, N 17,49:2
Basseches, Jacob T, 1962, Je 4,29:5
Bassen, Frank Mrs, 1965, Je 17,33:5
Basserman, Albert, 1952, My 16,23:5
Bassermann, Ernst Maj, 1917, Jl 26,11:6
Basset, Leon, 1942, Mr 30,17:3
Basset, William R, 1953, Ja 10,17:2
Basset, Wyatt M, 1914, D 15,13:5
Bassett, Annie Mrs, 1947, N 24,23:2
Bassett, Arthur E, 1951, Ja 27,13:2
Bassett, Augusta A, 1940, D 25,27:3
Bassett, B Stockton, 1939, Mr 16,23:4
Bassett, Benjamin F R, 1950, Mr 13,21:1
Bassett, Carroll P, 1952, Ja 10,29:5
Bassett, Carroll P Mrs, 1954, Mr 2,25:2
Bassett, Charles A 2d (mem ser, Mr 3,33:3; funl, Mr 5,9:2), 1966, Mr 1,1:4
Bassett, Charles E, 1942, My 29,17:4
Bassett, Charles F Mrs, 1959, Ap 21,38:1
Bassett, Charles Franklin, 1916, D 22,9:3
Bassett, Charles R, 1940, N 15,21:3
Bassett, David I, 1960, S 25,88:3
Bassett, E Gordon, 1951, Je 11,25:5
Bassett, Edward M, 1941, Ag 4,13:5; 1948, O 28,29:3
Bassett, Edward S, 1953, Mr 11,29:1
Bassett, Elmer C, 1947, N 23,72:3
Bassett, Fannie D Mrs, 1940, My 22,23:6
Bassett, Frank H, 1950, Ag 6,72:5
Bassett, Frederic B Mrs, 1952, Ja 14,19:3
Bassett, Frederic H, 1956, Ap 30,23:4
Bassett, George J, 1954, F 25,31:3
Bassett, George J Mrs, 1953, Ag 14,19:1
Bassett, Geraldine C, 1938, Je 21,19:4
Bassett, H Ellsworth, 1943, My 23,42:6
Bassett, H H, 1926, O 18,21:3
Bassett, Harry L, 1958, S 14,84:5
Bassett, Howard M, 1965, N 6,29:6
Bassett, I Capt, 1895, D 19,9:1
Bassett, J, 1884, F 6,1:6
Bassett, J Edward Jr, 1957, Ap 4,33:4
Bassett, James G Mrs, 1954, D 6,27:4
Bassett, James V, 1964, S 19,27:3
Bassett, John, 1958, F 13,29:5
Bassett, John A, 1956, O 20,21:3; 1959, Ap 28,35:3
Bassett, John D Jr, 1966, My 26,47:4
Bassett, John D Sr, 1965, F 28,89:1
Bassett, John S Mrs, 1950, Ap 5,32:2
Bassett, John Seymour Dr, 1912, Ag 1,11:5
Bassett, Katherine S V, 1967, Ap 17,37:2
Bassett, Lavern, 1954, S 23,33:3
Bassett, Leonard C, 1959, N 28,21:5
Bassett, Marcus G, 1951, Ag 11,28:8
Bassett, Mary Imogene Dr, 1922, O 23,15:4
Bassett, Melvin E, 1942, Jl 27,15:5
Bassett, Neal, 1947, My 5,23:2
Bassett, Nelson B, 1949, S 7,29:4
Bassett, Noll, 1913, O 23,11:4
Bassett, Prentice Mrs, 1967, Ap 24,33:3
Bassett, Raymond E, 1956, D 5,39:3; 1957, S 3,27:1
Bassett, Richard O, 1945, Jl 16,11:7
Bassett, Robert J, 1967, Ap 8,31:4
Bassett, Russell, 1918, My 9,13:5
Bassett, Russell Mrs, 1925, Ag 12,21:5
Bassett, Samuel H, 1943, My 6,19:3
Bassett, Samuel Mrs, 1945, Ja 30,19:4
Bassett, Theodore S, 1908, O 10,9:5
Bassett, Thomas B Mrs, 1943, Mr 11,21:4
Bassett, Thomas O, 1953, D 29,23:3
Bassett, Ulysses G, 1942, D 17,37:2
Bassett, W H, 1934, Jl 22,23:1
Bassett, Wallace S Mrs, 1941, Mr 26,23:2
Bassett, Wallace T, 1954, Ag 11,25:4
Bassett, Walter G R, 1968, F 10,34:1
Bassett, Warren L, 1950, S 26,31:5
Bassett, William G Judge, 1923, My 26,15:6
Bassett, William H Mrs, 1956, Je 23,17:5
Bassett, William M, 1960, Jl 18,44:6
Bassett, William M Mrs, 1942, Ja 23,19:4
Bassett, William R, 1940, N 30,17:6
Bassett, William W, 1956, Je 28,29:2
Bassett, Winford L, 1952, O 18,19:7
Bassevitch, Julius, 1951, Je 18,23:6
Bassewitz, Philip, 1959, F 27,25:3
Bassford, Edward D, 1873, Je 16,8:6
Bassford, George W, 1905, Ap 20,9:7
Bassford, Homer, 1938, Ja 11,23:2
Bassford, Horace R, 1952, Mr 13,30:3
Bassford, Stephen A, 1922, Je 19,15:5
Bassford, Stephen A Col, 1904, D 21,9:5
Bassford, Thomas S, 1921, Ja 25,11:4
Basshe, Emjo, 1939, O 29,40:7
Basshor, C Hazeltine, 1914, Ag 23,13:6
Bassi, Amadeo, 1949, Ja 15,17:5
Bassi, Antonio Mrs, 1940, F 4,40:8
Bassi, Charles E, 1952, Jl 18,19:3
Bassi, Victor L, 1956, Ja 25,31:4
Bassichis, Jacob, 1953, S 17,29:4
Bassick, Edgar W, 1948, Ap 15,25:5
Bassier, Marie Louis Gaston, 1908, Je 11,7:4
Bassil, Paul F, 1948, Mr 4,25:3
Bassill, John E, 1959, Ap 18,23:1
Bassin, Max, 1963, Jl 11,29:1
Bassingthwaighte, George, 1950, Mr 22,27:4
Bassler, Anthony, 1959, Ag 22,17:1
Bassler, Anthony Jr, 1965, Mr 9,35:3
Bassler, Anthony Mrs, 1951, D 16,91:3
Bassler, John, 1939, My 6,17:5
Basso, Charles E, 1952, Jl 20,52:4
Basso, Frederick Mrs, 1947, Mr 20,27:4
Basso, Hamilton, 1964, My 14,35:3
Bassoe, Peter, 1945, N 7,23:4

Bassols, Narciso, 1959, Jl 26,68:3
Basson, Howard M, 1941, My 24,15:6
Basson, Joseph D, 1955, S 9,23:4
Bassuk, Jacob, 1964, D 10,47:3
Bast, A Robert, 1960, Ja 1,19:2
Bast, Edwin B, 1952, Je 26,29:3
Bast, Lucille, 1923, Mr 24,13:5
Bastable, Edward H, 1961, D 25,23:6
Bastedenbeck, Katherine, 1962, D 5,47:4
Bastedo, A Beekman, 1953, My 25,25:3
Bastedo, Albert E, 1957, Jl 13,17:6
Bastedo, Joseph Albert, 1907, D 24,7:5
Bastedo, Paul H, 1951, Ap 19,31:2
Bastedo, Walter A, 1952, Jl 21,19:6
Basten, Louis B, 1951, Ja 9,30:4
Baster, James, 1957, Ag 26,23:5
Bastiaanse, Wilhelm A F, 1947, Je 15,60:1
Bastian, Charles B Dr, 1937, Ja 14,21:5
Bastian, Frederick E, 1944, F 28,17:4
Bastian, Henry Charlton Dr, 1915, N 19,11:5
Bastian, Robert, 1959, O 13,39:2
Bastianelli, Giuseppe Mrs (cor, Je 20,21:2), 1941, Ja 5,44:7
Bastianelli, Raffaele, 1961, S 3,60:2
Bastiani, Donato, 1953, Ja 16,23:3
Bastianini, Ettore, 1967, Ja 27,45:4
Bastible, Francis X, 1937, Jl 2,21:5
Bastide, Jules, 1879, Mr 4,5:4
Bastie, Maryse, 1952, Jl 7,3:4
Bastien, Cleophas, 1943, F 12,19:3
Bastien, John E, 1957, D 9,35:5
Bastien, Joseph G, 1939, F 8,23:5
Bastien, Joseph J, 1952, O 25,17:5
Bastien-Lepage, J, 1884, D 12,3:3
Bastine, Andrew J, 1940, Ag 31,13:5
Basting, Anton, 1915, F 12,9:6
Baston, George H, 1953, Ap 28,27:1
Bastow, Frank, 1952, D 23,23:4
Bastress, Arthur M, 1961, O 1,86:2
Basy, Alex (por), 1937, Ja 15,21:3
Basye, Arthur H, 1958, Je 16,23:6
Bat-Ochir, Oydovyn, 1962, Ja 11,5:4
Bata, Jan A, 1965, Ag 25,39:1
Bata, Josef, 1949, Ag 14,68:6
Bata, Thomas Mrs, 1954, Mr 1,25:4
Bataille, Achille F, 1919, My 30,9:6
Bataille, H J, 1882, Ja 9,5:5
Bataille, Henry, 1922, Mr 3,13:5
Batastini, Emilio, 1948, S 6,13:5
Batavin, Michael, 1950, N 19,92:7
Batch, Paul O, 1950, N 15,31:4
Batchelar, Edward J, 1960, D 2,29:1
Batchelder, Ann, 1955, Je 19,93:2
Batchelder, Charles C, 1946, My 6,21:1
Batchelder, Charles F, 1947, S 5,20:3; 1954, N 9,27:5
Batchelder, David H, 1966, F 20,88:5
Batchelder, Edward T, 1950, Ap 18,31:4
Batchelder, F Winthrop, 1944, N 2,19:5
Batchelder, Francis J, 1937, D 15,25:6
Batchelder, Frank R, 1947, F 6,23:4
Batchelder, Fred M, 1948, My 16,70:1
Batchelder, Frederick P, 1942, F 15,45:1
Batchelder, George A Col, 1875, My 19,5:1
Batchelder, Harold H, 1961, Ag 26,17:6
Batchelder, Henri, 1938, My 3,23:3
Batchelder, J Franklin, 1949, N 27,104:5
Batchelder, James Locke Rev, 1909, Ap 5,7:4
Batchelder, John L Mrs, 1962, Ag 25,22:2
Batchelder, May Mrs, 1955, Ja 10,23:4
Batchelder, Nathaniel H, 1956, Ja 23,25:4
Batchelder, R F Mrs, 1954, Ap 22,29:4
Batchelder, Roger, 1947, D 15,25:3
Batchelder, Walter J, 1950, Je 9,23:4
Batcheller, Adams Jr, 1951, F 21,27:3
Batcheller, Adams Mrs, 1940, Mr 20,27:4
Batcheller, Birney C, 1950, N 28,31:3
Batcheller, Franklin A, 1942, D 9,27:4
Batcheller, Franklin A Mrs, 1960, D 23,19:4
Batcheller, G S Mrs, 1903, My 15,9:6
Batcheller, George Clinton, 1915, Ja 26,9:5
Batcheller, George H, 1913, N 20,11:4
Batcheller, George R, 1938, S 29,25:5
Batcheller, George Sherman Gen, 1908, Jl 3,7:3
Batcheller, Katherine, 1943, Ja 6,27:1
Batcheller, Tryphosa B, 1952, S 10,29:3
Batcheller, Walter R Mrs, 1952, My 3,21:4
Batchellor, Fred G, 1944, Ap 20,19:3
Batchelor, Alex, 1955, Ja 11,25:2
Batchelor, Bronson, 1948, Jl 7,46:3
Batchelor, C D Mrs, 1959, My 17,84:4
Batchelor, Edwin A, 1961, O 4,45:2
Batchelor, George H, 1939, S 26,23:1
Batchelor, Harry D, 1952, Ja 24,27:4
Batchelor, Henry A, 1912, Ag 22,9:5
Batchelor, James M, 1948, My 18,23:2
Batchelor, John C (cor, D 30,23:3), 1967, D 29,27:1
Batchelor, Louis E, 1944, N 11,13:6
Batchelor, Rosanna Mrs, 1942, Mr 20,19:1
Batcher, John J, 1949, F 20,60:2
Batdorf, Grant D, 1954, S 23,33:1
Bate, Arthur D, 1954, F 24,25:4
Bate, Henry C, 1943, F 5,21:5
Bate, Herbert, 1951, Je 7,33:5
Bate, Herbert N, 1941, My 20,23:3
Bate, J Victor, 1953, Ag 8,11:5
Bate, Oscar M, 1944, Ag 29,17:3
Bate, Richard H, 1950, Mr 30,29:3
Bate, Rutledge, 1964, O 11,88:3
Bate, Stuart C, 1959, Mr 27,23:3
Bate, T Percival Rev, 1920, Ja 13,13:2
Bate, William B US Sen, 1905, Mr 10,6:1
Bateholts, Clinton L, 1943, D 6,23:3
Batelle, Louis, 1946, Jl 3,25:5
Batelli, Enrico, 1944, Ag 1,15:3
Bateman, Benjamin, 1965, My 26,47:1
Bateman, C R Prof, 1883, F 7,5:5
Bateman, Charles J, 1940, My 4,17:2
Bateman, Floyd L, 1949, My 5,27:3
Bateman, Frederic Sir, 1904, Ag 11,7:6
Bateman, Frederick Mrs, 1946, Ja 6,40:4
Bateman, Frederick W, 1948, S 3,19:4
Bateman, George C, 1963, F 6,4:7
Bateman, George F, 1948, Ja 30,23:1
Bateman, H L, 1875, Mr 23,7:3; 1875, Ap 5,5:4
Bateman, Harry, 1946, Ja 24,21:5
Bateman, Herbert R, 1941, My 11,45:2
Bateman, James, 1959, Ag 3,25:4
Bateman, John H, 1953, Ag 25,21:1
Bateman, John T, 1940, S 20,23:2
Bateman, Kate Josephine, 1917, Ap 12,11:6
Bateman, Leo C, 1960, Ja 10,87:1
Bateman, Leslie V, 1946, S 14,7:7
Bateman, Mrs, 1881, Ja 14,5:4
Bateman, Niles C, 1948, Mr 8,23:2
Bateman, Robert J, 1943, Ap 19,19:5
Bateman, Samuel I, 1959, D 15,39:1
Bateman, Thomas R, 1958, Je 11,36:1
Bateman, Virginia (Mrs E Compton), 1940, My 5, 52:3
Bateman, William, 1949, D 20,31:5
Bateman, William Q, 1955, Mr 6,88:1
Bateman, William R, 1959, Ap 15,33:4
Bateman, William S, 1948, D 7,31:1; 1953, Ja 15,27:5
Bater, Herbert W Mrs, 1947, Je 9,21:4
Bates, A Elliott, 1965, My 12,47:5
Bates, Aaron Tiffany, 1909, Ja 6,11:6
Bates, Ada C Mrs, 1939, Mr 21,23:4
Bates, Albert E, 1938, Ag 5,17:2; 1965, Je 9,47:1
Bates, Albert J, 1955, F 12,15:5
Bates, Alexander B Rear-Adm, 1917, F 20,9:5
Bates, Alfred Elliott Maj-Gen, 1909, O 14,9:5
Bates, Amada Mrs, 1942, Jl 29,17:5
Bates, Anna, 1939, N 9,23:4
Bates, Anne G Mrs, 1939, N 3,21:1
Bates, Arlo, 1918, Ag 26,11:4
Bates, Arthur L, 1938, Jl 24,28:8
Bates, Arthur W, 1947, Je 20,19:4
Bates, Bennett, 1957, D 28,17:3
Bates, Blanche, 1941, D 26,13:1
Bates, Carleton J, 1941, Ja 5,44:5
Bates, Charles F, 1944, Jl 9,35:4
Bates, Charles L, 1952, O 2,29:4
Bates, Charles S, 1904, D 9,6:4
Bates, Claude E Mrs, 1953, O 14,29:5
Bates, Clyde, 1950, My 23,29:1
Bates, Clyde J Mrs, 1937, S 5,II,6:6
Bates, Daniel J M, 1941, My 10,15:3
Bates, Daniel M, 1953, F 27,21:4
Bates, Denis H, 1959, S 14,29:5
Bates, Earl R W, 1943, N 2,25:3
Bates, Edward, 1869, Mr 27,6:6
Bates, Edward A, 1923, D 14,21:5
Bates, Edward W Mrs, 1946, N 10,63:1
Bates, Eli, 1912, N 10,17:5
Bates, Ellis A, 1947, My 31,13:4
Bates, Eloise M Mrs, 1941, Je 10,23:5
Bates, Ernest, 1939, D 5,27:1
Bates, Eunice Mrs, 1938, N 20,39:3
Bates, Florence, 1954, F 1,23:5
Bates, Frances E, 1939, O 1,53:2
Bates, Frances Wren, 1908, Je 2,7:3
Bates, Francis E, 1937, S 6,17:6
Bates, Frank G, 1955, N 8,29:2
Bates, Fred D Mrs, 1946, Je 13,27:4
Bates, Fred E, 1953, Jl 3,19:3
Bates, Frederic A, 1957, Je 25,29:2
Bates, Frederick H, 1938, Je 6,17:5
Bates, Frederick H Sr, 1953, Je 8,29:2
Bates, G L, 1940, F 2,17:5
Bates, George, 1916, My 22,11:6; 1952, Jl 31,23:3
Bates, George E, 1944, F 2,21:5; 1946, Je 22,19:5; 1955, Mr 3,27:5
Bates, George E Mrs, 1942, Mr 17,21:5; 1943, F 10, 25:5
Bates, George F, 1938, Jl 19,21:5; 1944, Mr 7,17:3
Bates, George G, 1942, My 8,21:5; 1950, S 9,17:6
Bates, George H, 1965, F 3,35:3
Bates, George Handy, 1916, N 1,11:4
Bates, George Handy Mrs, 1925, Jl 1,23:5
Bates, George J, 1949, N 2,1:8
Bates, George V, 1943, F 20,13:2
Bates, Granville, 1940, Jl 10,19:2
Bates, Hamilton C Sr, 1955, S 3,15:5
Bates, Harry, 1952, D 17,33:1
Bates, Harry C, 1948, F 15,60:2
Bates, Harry O Mrs, 1945, D 5,25:3
Bates, Henry D, 1953, Mr 23,23:4
Bates, Henry L A, 1953, F 21,13:5
Bates, Henry M (por), 1949, Ap 16,15:3
Bates, Henry O, 1956, F 5,86:2
Bates, Henry P, 1942, Mr 4,19:2
Bates, Henry S Jr, 1953, Je 18,29:1
Bates, Isaac Mrs, 1948, Ja 29,23:4
Bates, J L Gen (funl), 1875, N 15,1:5
Bates, J M, 1878, N 12,8:3
Bates, J Stuart, 1945, My 4,19:2
Bates, James L Sr, 1962, O 19,20:5
Bates, James T, 1914, D 25,11:4
Bates, Jeannette A Mrs, 1942, O 19,19:5
Bates, Jeff B, 1966, Ag 19,33:5
Bates, John, 1944, Ja 15,13:3
Bates, John A, 1948, Je 25,24:2
Bates, John G, 1944, F 3,19:3
Bates, John H, 1946, Mr 18,21:3; 1950, Ja 29,68:4
Bates, John L, 1946, Je 9,40:6
Bates, John R, 1940, Mr 14,23:2; 1965, Mr 14,86:8
Bates, Joseph D, 1951, N 28,31:1
Bates, Josephine R, 1941, F 16,40:2
Bates, Joshua, 1864, O 16,8:2
Bates, Julius A, 1940, Jl 9,21:5
Bates, Kahl C, 1941, F 26,21:2
Bates, Kinzie Capt, 1884, F 26,5:3
Bates, Kirk, 1953, Mr 27,23:2
Bates, Lewis B Rev, 1909, Ag 29,9:6
Bates, Lillian, 1945, My 1,23:4
Bates, Lindell T Maj, 1937, Ap 15,24:1
Bates, Lindon, 1924, Ap 23,21:5
Bates, Lindon W (mem), 1915, Je 9,13:5
Bates, Lot B Jr, 1950, N 8,29:3
Bates, Louisa B Mrs, 1940, D 8,69:2
Bates, Madison C, 1961, F 19,86:6
Bates, Margaret D Mrs, 1937, O 10,II,9:2
Bates, Marie, 1923, Mr 14,19:4
Bates, Mark, 1879, Ja 17,3:4
Bates, Martin, 1883, Ja 3,5:4
Bates, Maxwell Mrs, 1952, Je 4,27:3
Bates, Minnie, 1941, S 29,17:4
Bates, Morgan, 1874, Mr 5,5:3
Bates, Moses, 1873, Je 17,1:4
Bates, Nicholas E, 1947, Ja 25,17:2
Bates, Nicholas E Jr, 1940, Ja 23,21:2
Bates, Oscar F, 1949, Je 1,31:3
Bates, Percy (corr, O 18,23:2), 1946, O 17,23:1
Bates, Putman A Sr, 1938, Ja 29,15:6
Bates, Ray T, 1953, F 26,25:2
Bates, Rebecca, 1881, D 15,2:6
Bates, Richard D, 1949, Je 11,17:4
Bates, Robert, 1952, O 19,V,9:1
Bates, Robert C, 1942, D 2,25:2; 1950, My 3,29:1
Bates, Robert J, 1951, Ag 19,86:2
Bates, Robert P, 1944, Jl 2,20:5
Bates, Royal M, 1943, My 24,15:2
Bates, Samuel, 1955, O 22,19:1
Bates, Samuel L Mrs, 1964, Ap 2,33:3
Bates, Sarah L Mrs, 1948, D 4,19:3
Bates, Sidney J, 1943, Ap 17,17:5
Bates, Silas E, 1903, Ap 21,9:5
Bates, Spencer E, 1956, Ap 25,35:5
Bates, Stewart, 1964, My 25,33:1
Bates, T Towar, 1938, Ag 30,17:1
Bates, Thomas B, 1940, Ap 9,23:3
Bates, Thomas S Mrs, 1949, My 25,30:2
Bates, Thornton C, 1937, My 25,28:2
Bates, Walter S, 1943, Jl 12,15:5
Bates, Wilfred G, 1946, Mr 14,25:2
Bates, William A, 1922, Jl 29,7:6; 1949, F 25,23:1
Bates, William C, 1952, S 11,31:5
Bates, William C Mrs, 1957, O 12,19:4
Bates, William E Mrs, 1950, D 15,31:3
Bates, William G, 1944, Je 11,45:1
Bates, William G Mrs, 1953, S 28,25:2
Bates, William J, 1949, F 1,26:2
Bates, William Miller, 1914, S 27,15:5
Bates, William N, 1949, Je 12,79:3
Bates, William W, 1945, Jl 8,11:5
Bateson, Charles E Mrs, 1950, Mr 24,25:4
Bateson, J W, 1966, Jl 7,37:3
Bateson, W Dr, 1926, F 9,25:3
Bateson, William O, 1954, S 7,25:3
Bath, Anna A Mrs, 1944, D 13,23:5
Bath, Edward M, 1951, O 30,29:2
Bath, Frank J, 1952, F 18,19:2
Bath, James M, 1957, Ap 5,27:3
Bath, John T, 1947, Je 24,23:5
Bath, Marquess of, 1946, Je 10,21:3
Bath, Richard G, 1947, Ag 4,17:4
Bath, Stanley, 1941, S 22,15:5
Bath, William A, 1943, S 21,23:4
Bath, William F, 1957, S 22,86:2
Bathe, Hugo G de Sir, 1940, Ag 7,19:2
Bathelt, J Paul Mrs, 1939, Mr 9,4:3
Bathey, Joe, 1953, O 15,33:1
Batho, Charles (por), 1938, Ja 30,II,8:4
Batholf, George Waldron, 1916, Ap 14,9:1
Bathrick, E R, 1917, D 25,15:4
Bathrick, Helen C Mrs, 1941, Ja 31,19:2
Bathrick, Willis A, 1947, My 27,25:2
Bathurst, Charles (Viscount Bledisloe), 1958, Jl 4, 19:4

Bathurst, Clyde, 1938, O 18,26:3
Batie, Franklyn A, 1950, Ja 2,23:2
Batista, Robert A, 1944, N 22,19:5
Batista y Zaldivar, Francisco Jr, 1943, O 29,19:1
Batjer, Henry, 1916, Jl 9,19:5
Batjer, Louis, 1951, N 16,25:5
Batjer, Mariana, 1946, Mr 12,25:6
Batkin, Hyman, 1966, Ja 22,29:5
Batkin, Jacques, 1967, F 7,26:2
Batley, Clinton D Mrs, 1948, Jl 21,23:2
Batley, James A, 1938, D 29,19:3
Batlle Berres, Luis, 1964, Jl 16,31:2
Batlle Pacheco, Lorenzo, 1954, D 4,17:6
Batman, Robert G, 1950, D 13,35:2
Batocki, Adolf von, 1944, Je 9,15:3
Batolov, Constantin, 1938, Ag 3,19:4
Baton, Henry E, 1949, Ap 7,30:3
Baton, Rene, 1940, O 10,26:2
Batonyi, Leopold, 1909, O 26,9:5
Bator, Antoni, 1950, Mr 3,25:4
Bator, Victor, 1967, D 13,47:4
Batroff, Warren C, 1938, Je 21,19:3
Batsch, Albert, 1950, N 5,93:1
Batson, George, 1912, My 15,11:6
Batson, George D, 1941, O 29,23:1
Batson, H E, 1958, N 7,28:1
Batson, Roland R, 1953, F 1,89:2
Batstone, Stephen H, 1952, D 15,25:4
Batt, Jack, 1940, Je 13,23:3
Batt, Ludwig J, 1922, Jl 25,11:6
Batt, Paul J Mrs, 1950, Je 18,76:1
Batt, Paul Mrs, 1962, Ja 14,84:3
Batt, William L Sr, 1965, F 12,29:1
Battaglia, Joseph, 1960, O 8,23:2
Battaglia, Joseph C, 1965, Ap 12,35:3
Battaglia, Louis, 1964, Ja 24,24:3
Battaglia, Salvatore, 1951, N 23,29:2
Battalino, Carmen, 1939, N 19,38:7
Batte, Pryor H, 1950, Ja 30,17:5
Batteau, Wayne (Dr), 1967, O 30,45:3
Batteiger, Rufus L, 1958, Je 30,19:5
Batteiman, Henry, 1912, Ja 11,13:5
Battelle, Charles N, 1939, Ag 1,19:5
Battelle, John Gorden Mrs, 1925, Mr 24,23:2
Battelle, Seavey, 1953, Je 16,27:5
Battelle, Seavey Mrs, 1966, D 29,31:4
Battelstein, Phil, 1955, Jl 7,27:4
Batten, Arthur, 1946, Ja 26,13:4
Batten, Clarence A, 1957, Ja 6,89:1
Batten, George Mrs, 1949, Jl 21,25:4
Batten, George W, 1922, S 15,19:6
Batten, Harry A, 1966, Jl 28,33:1
Batten, Howard W, 1949, Ap 8,26:2
Batten, John M, 1940, Je 7,23:2
Batten, John W, 1945, Jl 3,13:6
Batten, Loring W, 1946, Ja 7,19:3
Battenfeld, Fred W, 1945, Mr 16,15:2
Battenfeld, Theresa, 1961, Jl 5,33:4
Battenfield, C Edwin, 1952, My 8,31:4
Battenhausen, Frank Mrs, 1947, O 5,71:2
Batterberry, John, 1882, N 8,3:2
Batterman, Henry L, 1939, Je 30,19:6; 1961, Jl 5,33:1
Batterman, Henry L Mrs, 1951, My 25,27:2
Batters, Charles J, 1953, Ja 8,27:5
Batters, Henry, 1962, Ag 4,19:4
Battersby, Alzamorah H, 1912, Ja 29,11:5
Battersby, George E, 1943, Mr 30,21:3
Battersby, John D Sr, 1958, S 14,84:3
Battersby, John J, 1959, Ap 2,31:5
Battersby, Mary, 1963, My 15,40:2
Battersby, Michael J, 1962, Ja 25,31:2
Battersby, Michael J Mrs, 1945, Je 8,19:2
Battersby, Richard T, 1947, Ap 14,27:2
Battersea, Baron (Cyril Flower), 1907, N 28,7:4
Battersea, Lady, 1931, N 23,19:3
Battershall, Frederic S, 1952, N 24,23:4
Battershall, Jesse, 1945, My 5,15:2
Battershall, Walton W Rev, 1920, Mr 20,11:6
Battershill, William, 1913, Ap 13,IV,7:5
Batterson, Bert, 1940, O 19,17:6
Batterson, H G Rev, 1903, Mr 12,9:5
Batterson, James Goodwin, 1909, Ag 5,7:6; 1923, Ja 18,15:4
Batterson, James S, 1952, S 26,21:2
Batterson, John P, 1943, Ja 22,20:2
Batterson, Lincoln S Mrs, 1944, My 4,19:4
Batterson, Walter E, 1957, Ja 10,29:2
Batterson, William E, 1938, Ag 12,17:4
Battes, Jacob H, 1947, Je 21,17:5
Battet, Robert M J Adm, 1950, Jl 15,13:6
Battey, Donald E Mrs, 1963, Jl 24,31:4
Battey, Herman M, 1941, F 23,41:3
Batthyany, Prince, 1883, My 16,4:4
Battier, George H, 1942, Jl 14,20:2
Battilana, Charles, 1958, F 13,29:1
Battin, A William, 1968, O 19,37:2
Battin, Charles R, 1950, Jl 30,61:3
Battin, Hamilton S, 1959, F 13,17:2
Battin, Howard H Mrs, 1949, F 11,23:1
Battin, Isaac L Mrs, 1959, Mr 28,17:4
Battin, John R, 1942, Jl 17,15:7
Battin, Joseph V, 1937, D 12,II,8:8
Battin, William C, 1953, My 27,31:3
Battin, William F, 1964, Mr 5,33:3
Battis, Walter T, 1967, My 8,41:2
Battista, Joseph, 1968, Jl 14,65:2
Battisti, Achille Mrs, 1947, Ap 16,25:1
Battle, Charlton E Mrs, 1963, D 3,43:2
Battle, Cullen A Maj Gen, 1905, Ap 9,9:6
Battle, Elizabeth, 1957, S 15,83:1
Battle, George G, 1949, Ap 30,13:1
Battle, George G Mrs, 1954, F 11,29:1
Battle, Henry W Mrs, 1953, Ag 20,27:5
Battle, John, 1948, My 17,19:3
Battle, John T, 1962, N 3,25:2
Battle, Kemp Plummer Dr, 1919, F 6,11:2
Battle, Raymond A, 1962, Jl 12,29:4
Battle, Robert C, 1965, N 5,37:2
Battle, Robert T, 1944, Ap 16,41:3
Battle, Samuel J (funl, Ag 10,41:2), 1966, Ag 7,81:1
Battle, Stephen, 1937, Ja 20,21:4
Battle, W H, 1879, Mr 18,5:2
Battle, William J, 1955, O 10,27:3
Battle, William S Jr, 1947, O 27,21:2
Battles, Donald R, 1941, Ja 21,21:4
Battles, Frank Mrs, 1955, Ja 25,25:5
Battles, H H, 1939, Ap 19,23:3
Battles, S S Mrs (Sally O'Neill), 1968, Je 20,45:4
Battles, William W, 1956, N 7,31:1
Batto, Michael, 1937, F 28,II,9:2
Batts, Arthur A, 1953, Ja 9,21:2
Batts, H Thompson, 1956, Je 3,85:1
Batts, William H, 1954, Ag 16,17:4
Battson, Edwin F, 1966, O 11,47:2
Batty, Basil S, 1952, Mr 20,29:4
Batty, James H Dr, 1906, My 29,20:3
Batty, S Walter, 1947, O 30,26:2
Battye, Edwin H, 1956, Mr 8,29:4
Batwell, Charles D, 1954, S 17,27:2
Baty, Gaston, 1952, O 14,31:2
Baty, John, 1939, Jl 1,17:6
Baty, Thomas, 1954, F 10,29:1
Batyrov, Shadzha B, 1965, O 16,27:4
Batzes, Harry, 1951, D 16,89:1
Batzle, Carolyn D Mrs, 1942, Mr 2,19:2
Batzle, Fred A, 1960, Ap 12,33:1
Batzle, George F, 1947, Je 2,25:4
Batzle, Louis J, 1944, S 5,19:6
Bauch, Emil C, 1940, S 27,23:3
Bauchens, Anne, 1967, My 9,41:8
Bauchle, George Y, 1939, Jl 11,20:3
Bauchle, Thomas H Jr, 1951, D 7,27:5
Bauchmann, John F, 1962, Ap 4,43:3
Bauchner, Harry Mrs, 1950, Ja 20,26:2
Baucus, J Irving, 1937, S 23,27:1
Baudendistel, Clarence F, 1937, O 13,23:1
Bauder, Arthur R, 1952, My 28,29:1
Bauder, Charles F, 1952, O 16,29:4
Bauder, George T, 1937, S 23,27:1
Bauder, John F, 1950, Ap 10,19:5
Bauder, Perry Mrs, 1942, Mr 26,23:5
Baudermann, Michael T, 1956, O 23,33:5
Baudier, A, 1879, Je 19,2:3
Baudier, Joseph R Sr, 1960, N 13,89:1
Baudin, Pierre, 1917, Ag 1,9:3
Baudinelli, John Rev, 1908, S 18,7:4
Baudinot, Truman E, 1945, D 24,16:3
Baudistel, Adolph, 1946, Je 14,21:3
Baudoin, Raymond, 1953, Ag 13,25:5
Baudoine, John F, 1925, D 18,23:3
Baudouin, Heir to Belgian Throne, 1891, Ja 24,1:3
Baudouin, Manuel, 1917, Ja 25,9:3
Baudouine, Charles, 1919, My 11,22:4
Baudrillart, Alfred, 1942, My 20,19:4
Baudry, F, 1885, Ja 4,2:1
Bauer, Albert F, 1954, D 4,17:4
Bauer, Aleck, 1944, Je 12,19:5
Bauer, Alfred D, 1921, Ag 23,15:6
Bauer, Anna R Mrs, 1953, N 3,32:6
Bauer, Anton Archbishop, 1937, D 8,25:5
Bauer, Arthur, 1952, D 28,48:8
Bauer, Arthur J, 1947, F 22,13:1
Bauer, August, 1964, O 21,47:3
Bauer, Bobby (Robt T), 1964, S 17,43:2
Bauer, Bogdan, 1967, My 2,47:1
Bauer, Bruno, 1882, Ap 19,5:5
Bauer, Carl, 1959, Jl 25,17:4
Bauer, Charles C, 1947, Mr 16,60:1
Bauer, Charles E, 1953, D 12,19:5
Bauer, Charles G, 1955, S 20,31:1
Bauer, Charles H, 1939, Ag 30,17:5
Bauer, Charles L Jr, 1960, D 18,84:3
Bauer, Clarence E, 1954, D 27,17:2
Bauer, Conrad, 1958, Ja 3,23:3
Bauer, David, 1938, F 7,15:2
Bauer, Edmond S, 1957, D 12,30:1
Bauer, Edward, 1947, Mr 2,60:3
Bauer, Edward E Mrs (F Myers), 1964, My 30,17:5
Bauer, Elizabeth F, 1938, Je 4,15:4
Bauer, Ernest R, 1967, F 21,47:2
Bauer, Francis S Cardinal, 1915, N 27,15:4
Bauer, Frank M, 1938, Jl 21,21:5
Bauer, Frank M Mrs, 1961, F 15,35:5
Bauer, Frank X, 1958, Je 16,23:3
Bauer, Frederic G, 1964, Ap 16,37:4
Bauer, Frederic G Mrs, 1967, Ja 8,88:6
Bauer, Frederick, 1951, Ag 18,11:3
Bauer, Frederick E, 1945, N 1,23:1
Bauer, Frederick M, 1939, Jl 6,23:5
Bauer, Frederick R, 1963, N 9,25:4
Bauer, Fritz Dr, 1968, Jl 2,26:1
Bauer, G G, 1905, Ap 11,1:2
Bauer, George, 1953, Ag 13,25:3
Bauer, George F, 1949, Mr 5,18:2; 1949, N 16,29:5
Bauer, George J, 1961, My 27,23:6
Bauer, George Mrs, 1948, Ag 19,21:3
Bauer, George N, 1952, O 14,31:1
Bauer, George Sr Mrs, 1944, Mr 7,17:5
Bauer, Gerard, 1967, S 5,43:2
Bauer, Gustav, 1944, S 28,19:4
Bauer, Harold, 1951, Mr 13,31:1
Bauer, Harold Mrs, 1940, My 11,19:4
Bauer, Henry, 1961, Jl 21,23:1
Bauer, Henry C, 1941, My 2,21:1
Bauer, Henry J, 1961, D 13,43:5
Bauer, Henry L, 1950, Mr 15,29:3
Bauer, Herman G, 1938, Jl 28,19:4
Bauer, Hermann, 1958, F 13,29:3
Bauer, Jacob L, 1940, My 15,25:6
Bauer, Johannes, 1949, S 15,27:3
Bauer, Johannes H, 1961, Mr 5,87:1
Bauer, John G Mrs, 1947, O 23,25:6
Bauer, John Granger, 1912, Ja 21,II,13:2
Bauer, John J, 1941, Ap 12,15:1
Bauer, Joseph, 1938, O 13,23:5
Bauer, Joseph H, 1961, Ag 28,25:6
Bauer, Julius, 1944, Jl 22,15:5
Bauer, L Demme, 1940, Mr 30,15:2
Bauer, Lawson H, 1954, Ja 28,27:1
Bauer, Louis H (trb lr, F 12,32:4), 1964, F 3,27:1
Bauer, Louis Mrs, 1946, N 7,31:5
Bauer, M, 1929, My 7,31:3
Bauer, Marie L Dr, 1937, Mr 19,24:1
Bauer, Marion E, 1955, Ag 11,21:3
Bauer, Morris D Mrs, 1948, My 12,27:2
Bauer, Nelson W, 1954, D 4,17:3
Bauer, Oswald A, 1925, D 25,17:5
Bauer, Otto, 1938, Jl 5,17:2
Bauer, Paul, 1903, Jl 26,1:4
Bauer, Philip Mrs, 1960, Ja 8,23:1
Bauer, Philipp, 1946, My 15,21:3
Bauer, Ralph A, 1963, Ag 11,85:2
Bauer, Ralph S, 1941, Jl 14,13:3
Bauer, Reuben B, 1952, Mr 12,27:4
Bauer, Robert, 1960, F 7,84:7
Bauer, Robert C Mrs, 1948, Je 24,26:3
Bauer, Rudolph, 1953, N 30,2:8
Bauer, Russell J, 1962, My 20,87:1
Bauer, S, 1927, F 1,27:4
Bauer, Samuel, 1948, Jl 10,15:4
Bauer, Samuel L, 1951, F 20,25:4
Bauer, Samuel Mrs, 1950, F 12,84:1
Bauer, Shackelford, 1938, D 26,23:4
Bauer, Siegfried, 1948, Je 19,15:3
Bauer, Simon H, 1950, F 17,23:1
Bauer, Theodore H, 1950, F 26,79:3
Bauer, W G, 1960, S 4,69:2
Bauer, Walter, 1963, D 3,43:1
Bauer, Walter C Mrs, 1963, S 22,86:8
Bauer, Willard T, 1949, Ja 6,23:1
Bauer, William C, 1943, Ag 22,36:3
Bauer, William D, 1945, My 3,23:5; 1949, F 15,23:5
Bauer, William D Mrs, 1946, S 14,7:6
Bauer, William F, 1966, N 18,43:1
Bauer, William J, 1954, Ap 21,29:2
Bauer, William W, 1967, D 27,34:3
Bauerband, Louis P, 1945, My 22,19:5
Bauerberg, Paul J, 1950, Mr 13,21:5
Bauerdorf, Charles Frederick, 1915, Ja 20,9:4
Bauerdorf, Walter J, 1925, Je 12,19:6
Bauerkeller, Rudolf, 1922, F 5,22:3
Bauerle, Albert T, 1944, My 2,19:3
Bauerle, Harry T, 1942, Ap 11,13:4
Bauerlein, Edward J, 1948, Ag 21,16:2
Bauermann, Robert, 1947, F 5,23:2
Bauermeister, Otto, 1956, Ja 6,24:7
Bauers, Joseph J, 1956, Ag 31,17:2
Bauersfeld, Walther, 1959, O 29,33:2
Baufeld, William, 1949, Jl 14,27:4
Baugh, Daniel, 1921, Mr 1,13:4
Baugh, Edwin Pugh, 1921, O 13,15:4
Baugh, Paul R, 1947, Jl 21,17:5
Baughan, Edward A, 1938, N 27,49:2
Baughan, Jay T, 1950, F 19,76:2
Baugher, A Charles, 1962, N 3,25:2
Baugher, Jacob I, 1949, Ag 26,20:4
Baugher, Norman J Rev Dr, 1968, Ap 21,80:6
Baugher, William F, 1962, O 20,25:6
Baughman, E Austin, 1946, Ag 2,19:3
Baughman, Greer, 1941, D 3,25:2
Baughman, L Victor Gen, 1906, D 1,9:4
Baughman, Lon H, 1944, Jl 12,19:6
Baughman, Roland O, 1967, O 26,47:4
Baughmann, J W Mrs, 1904, Mr 3,9:6
Bauguess, Vaughn, 1953, Jl 14,27:2
Bauhan, Alice M, 1962, Jl 21,19:6
Bauhan, Charles W, 1938, Jl 6,23:5
Bauhan, Louis, 1941, Ja 30,21:5
Bauhan, Rolf W, 1966, D 6,47:2

Baukhage, Frederick R, 1943, O 4,17:2
Baukney, George H, 1925, Ag 25,17:5
Bauldry, Carleton E, 1951, O 11,37:3
Baum, Agatha B, 1948, Je 2,29:4
Baum, Aug H, 1954, Jl 15,27:3
Baum, Bernard H, 1966, N 10,47:1
Baum, C, 1939, Ag 12,13:4
Baum, Charles, 1938, O 27,23:3
Baum, Dwight J, 1939, D 14,27:1
Baum, Ellis C, 1961, Ap 8,19:5
Baum, Ellis C Mrs, 1960, Ja 21,31:5
Baum, Emmett M, 1942, S 5,13:5
Baum, Felix, 1958, Ja 9,33:2
Baum, Francis G, 1943, D 25,13:5
Baum, George, 1956, My 5,19:6
Baum, Gustave, 1941, Jl 25,15:5
Baum, Harry, 1959, Je 7,86:5
Baum, Harvey A, 1968, My 26,84:6
Baum, Harvey A Mrs, 1945, Ag 5,38:3
Baum, Isidor, 1966, Ap 12,35:3
Baum, Jacob, 1954, D 3,28:1
Baum, James E, 1959, O 20,39:1
Baum, John F, 1958, Je 15,77:2
Baum, John H, 1964, Ja 19,76:5
Baum, Joseph, 1948, Ap 10,13:6
Baum, Joseph M, 1946, Ja 8,23:4
Baum, Joseph Mrs, 1941, My 15,23:2
Baum, Julia M Mrs, 1952, F 22,21:1
Baum, L Frank, 1919, My 8,17:2
Baum, Lester Mrs, 1954, D 14,34:5
Baum, Maud Mrs, 1953, Mr 8,90:4
Baum, Max Mrs (Else), 1966, F 22,23:4
Baum, Millicent, 1943, Mr 25,21:1
Baum, Milton G, 1948, O 27,27:5
Baum, Morton, 1968, F 8,43:3
Baum, Morton J, 1963, Ag 2,27:3
Baum, Moses, 1961, Mr 25,25:3
Baum, Paull F, 1964, Jl 16,31:2
Baum, Samuel, 1944, Ap 29,15:5; 1944, N 14,23:3; 1946, Ja 30,25:2; 1948, Mr 30,23:4
Baum, Samuel M, 1961, D 14,43:3
Baum, Seymour J, 1960, Ja 19,35:4
Baum, Seymour J Mrs, 1962, N 10,25:4
Baum, Solomon Mrs, 1956, N 26,27:3
Baum, Vicki (Mrs R Lert), 1960, Ag 30,29:1
Baum, Walter E, 1956, Jl 13,19:5
Baum, Wilhelm L Mrs, 1940, Ja 6,13:1
Baum, William, 1939, Mr 31,21:5
Baum, William A, 1964, O 27,39:4
Bauman, Alfred, 1952, Je 22,68:3
Bauman, Allen, 1950, Ap 28,21:3
Bauman, Annie Mrs, 1941, My 10,15:3
Bauman, E Guilford, 1950, S 23,17:3
Bauman, Elwood T, 1948, D 10,25:3
Bauman, Frederick J, 1941, Ap 27,38:2
Bauman, George M, 1951, Mr 27,29:4
Bauman, Harry F, 1952, Jl 31,23:4
Bauman, John S, 1956, Ag 31,17:2
Bauman, Jules, 1947, D 27,13:4
Bauman, Julius Mrs, 1959, Mr 22,86:8
Bauman, Louis, 1922, S 12,21:5; 1954, N 2,27:2; 1965, My 24,31:5
Bauman, Milton P, 1943, Ja 30,15:5
Bauman, Paul, 1968, Je 14,47:1
Bauman, Ralph Mrs, 1950, Ag 25,21:4
Bauman, Robert R, 1959, Ap 5,86:4
Bauman, William J, 1939, N 4,15:6; 1961, N 20,31:3
Baumann, Adolph H, 1947, N 29,13:4
Baumann, Albert E, 1948, Ap 14,27:2
Baumann, Albert V, 1956, Ja 28,17:4
Baumann, Berenice L Mrs, 1937, Ag 27,19:3
Baumann, C Ludwig, 1956, Ja 8,87:1
Baumann, C Ludwig Jr, 1960, Ag 2,29:5
Baumann, Frederick W, 1947, Ap 8,27:2
Baumann, Frederick W Mrs, 1948, S 8,29:6
Baumann, George J, 1942, Mr 17,21:2
Baumann, Harold J, 1956, Jl 17,23:1
Baumann, John A, 1949, Ap 25,23:5
Baumann, John R, 1940, Ap 25,23:1
Baumann, Joseph Mrs, 1946, D 5,31:3
Baumann, Joseph W, 1946, N 24,79:4
Baumann, Karl Mrs, 1951, Ap 5,29:3
Baumann, Lucien K, 1943, O 27,23:3
Baumann, Ludwig, 1904, F 21,7:6; 1909, Je 15,7:4
Baumann, Maximillian, 1951, My 20,89:1
Baumann, Michael Jr, 1947, Jl 27,44:7
Baumann, Morris, 1937, D 30,19:4
Baumann, Rudolph W, 1948, Jl 7,46:3
Baumann, Samuel, 1925, My 4,19:5
Baumann, Sidney J Mrs, 1956, Ja 30,27:5
Baumann, Simon, 1944, My 24,19:4
Baumann, Wilbur N Sr, 1948, Ap 23,23:4
Baumann, William C, 1941, Ja 16,21:3
Baumann, William H, 1962, S 24,29:3
Baumbach, Frederick W, 1960, Ag 21,84:7
Baumbach, Werner, 1953, O 21,4:4
Baumbach, William C, 1962, My 5,27:5
Baumbach, William T, 1951, S 13,31:3
Baume, P H J, 1875, N 22,3:1
Baumeister, George Mrs, 1946, Jl 24,27:3
Baumeister, John (por), 1938, Mr 4,23:3
Baumeister, Theodore, 1941, S 9,23:5
Baumeister, Willi, 1955, S 2,17:6

Baumer, Frederick W, 1951, Ap 26,29:3
Baumer, J Peter, 1951, F 16,25:1
Baumer, Minnie, 1941, S 25,25:1
Baumert, Joseph A, 1950, Je 20,27:5
Baumes, Caleb H, 1937, S 26,II,8:1
Baumfeld, Maurice Dr (mem, Mr 8,15:4), 1913, Mr 5,17:4
Baumgardner, Earl G Mrs, 1947, My 19,21:1
Baumgardt, David, 1963, Jl 22,23:4
Baumgardt, Mars F, 1950, N 26,89:5
Baumgart, Adrian, 1965, Je 23,41:3
Baumgart, Charles F, 1948, Ja 24,16:3
Baumgart, Charles K, 1954, My 24,27:1
Baumgart, Samuel Mrs, 1947, N 1,15:5
Baumgartel, Otto R, 1940, Mr 4,15:3
Baumgarten, David Louis, 1923, Jl 14,11:6
Baumgarten, Edward, 1964, Je 1,29:4
Baumgarten, Elmer H, 1961, Mr 27,31:4
Baumgarten, Emile, 1922, F 5,22:3
Baumgarten, Joseph, 1960, My 28,46:5
Baumgarten, Moses Mrs, 1958, Ja 10,26:3
Baumgarten, Otto, 1949, N 6,92:5
Baumgarten, Paul J, 1950, F 25,17:5
Baumgarten, William, 1906, Ap 29,11:6
Baumgartner, Austin L, 1949, Ap 19,26:5
Baumgartner, Edwin A, 1942, Mr 16,15:5
Baumgartner, Elmer J, 1956, My 21,25:4
Baumgartner, Gottlieb, 1937, F 11,23:2
Baumgartner, Henry W Mrs, 1955, Jl 30,17:2
Baumgartner, J Harry, 1947, N 5,28:3
Baumgartner, John, 1946, Je 21,23:2
Baumgartner, Robert E, 1961, Mr 27,31:1
Baumgartner, Stanwood F (Stan), 1955, O 5,35:2
Baumgartner, Warren W, 1963, S 13,29:1
Baumgartner, William J, 1959, Ap 13,31:2
Baumgold, Jack Mrs, 1961, Ap 17,29:5
Baumgold, Jacob, 1964, Ap 13,29:4
Baumgold, Samuel, 1946, D 19,29:2
Baumis, Frank J, 1961, Ja 10,47:5
Baumle, Charles E, 1958, Mr 6,27:5
Baumle, Hulda L, 1966, O 7,43:4
Baumol, Osias, 1948, S 9,27:3
Baumring, Samuel J, 1949, O 18,28:2
Baumritter, Herman K, 1963, Jl 30,29:4
Baumuller, Lewis W Mrs, 1956, Ag 18,17:5
Baun, William G Sr, 1962, F 22,25:2
Baur, Albert C, 1938, My 27,17:3
Baur, Bertha, 1940, S 19,23:6
Baur, Christian, 1960, Mr 18,25:1
Baur, Franklyn, 1950, F 25,17:4
Baur, Harry, 1943, Ap 9,21:1
Baur, Jacob Mrs, 1967, Jl 12,43:2
Baur, Paul V, 1951, Je 6,31:2
Baur, Phil S Sr, 1951, S 16,84:6
Baureis, John T, 1951, D 22,15:6
Baurhenn, Louis P, 1937, Ja 5,23:3
Baury, Louis, 1924, Ag 20,13:3
Bausano, Augusto, 1940, F 6,21:5
Bausch, Edward, 1944, Jl 31,13:3
Bausch, Edward Mrs, 1940, Jl 15,15:5
Bausch, Ernst, 1938, My 25,23:2
Bausch, Henry J, 1944, Mr 17,17:5
Bausch, J J, 1926, F 15,19:3
Bausch, Jacob J, 1943, O 31,48:4
Bausch, John J Mrs, 1945, Ag 3,17:6
Bausch, Kenneth R, 1953, Mr 17,21:1
Bausch, William, 1944, O 20,19:4
Bausch, William Mrs, 1942, N 11,25:5
Bauscher, Abner H, 1950, F 25,17:2
Bauscher, William F, 1947, Jl 13,44:8
Bause, Herman M, 1946, Ja 22,27:3
Bause, Herman Mrs, 1962, Je 27,32:6
Bausewein, Carl, 1946, F 28,23:2
Bausewine, George, 1947, Jl 30,21:2
Baush, J A, 1883, Ja 3,5:4
Bausher, Charles L Jr, 1949, My 14,13:6
Bausher, Earl F, 1950, S 4,17:3
Bausher, Solon D, 1946, Ja 10,23:1
Bauskett, Frank N, 1921, Ja 4,13:3
Bausman, Benjamin Rev Dr, 1909, My 9,11:7
Bausman, George A, 1947, O 12,76:3
Bausman, Joseph E, 1942, Ja 18,42:5
Bausman, Paul R, 1952, Jl 16,25:5
Bausman, R Fenby, 1956, D 11,39:4
Bausman, Richard F Mrs, 1949, D 6,31:4; 1953, Ja 20, 25:2
Bautista, Antonio Maria, 1920, Je 7,15:4
Baux, Arthur T, 1941, Ap 8,25:5
Bavaria, King of, 1864, Ap 3,2:4; 1868, Mr 1,5:1
Bavely, Ernest, 1950, Ap 15,15:5
Bavendam, Frederick A, 1950, F 15,27:4
Bavier, Emma C Mrs, 1941, Ag 5,19:4
Bavier, Robert N, 1967, D 17,92:8
Bavier, Robert N Mrs, 1954, O 14,29:5
Bavier, Stuart, 1949, N 12,15:2
Baviera y Bourbon, Fernando M (Duke of Durcal),(corr, Ap 7,21:2), 1958, Ap 6,88:2
Bavli, Hillel, 1961, Jl 7,25:3
Bavly, Yehudah M, 1943, Jl 8,19:2
Bavona, Alexander Msgr, 1912, Ja 20,13:6
Bawden, Ernest, 1945, N 28,27:5
Bawden, George A, 1949, My 6,25:3
Bawden, Grace M, 1940, Jl 24,21:2

Bawden-Allen, Leslie, 1946, F 12,28:1
Bawhtair, Boris V de, 1943, O 31,49:1
Bawlf, Edward J, 1952, My 14,27:1
Bawlf, Nicholas, 1947, Je 7,13:3
Bawn, Edmund J, 1954, N 20,17:3
Bax, Arnold, 1953, O 4,88:3
Bax, Clifford, 1962, N 19,31:4
Bax, Emily, 1944, Ja 4,17:4
Baxendale, Alfred E, 1963, Jl 5,19:2
Baxeras de Alzugaray, Jose Dr, 1937, Je 14,23:3
Baxeres de Alzugaray, Lola Mrs, 1941, Ja 22,21:3
Baxley, Ira L, 1953, My 13,29:4
Baxley, Isaac R Mrs, 1949, N 25,31:2
Baxt, Samuel H, 1944, Jl 12,19:4
Baxt, Theodore, 1956, S 11,35:4
Baxter, Aaron P, 1951, Ja 1,17:4
Baxter, Abram C B Mrs, 1917, Je 7,11:5
Baxter, Ada R Dr, 1937, Ja 18,17:2
Baxter, Allen K, 1945, F 11,40:4
Baxter, Andrew, 1942, F 6,19:2; 1959, Ja 8,29:1
Baxter, Andrew G, 1945, F 16,23:1
Baxter, Ann C, 1954, D 19,85:1
Baxter, Archibald Easton Col, 1925, O 7,27:5
Baxter, Arthur R, 1957, D 15,86:4
Baxter, Barry, 1922, My 31,15:2
Baxter, Batsell, 1956, Mr 6,31:1
Baxter, Beverly, 1964, Ap 27,31:2
Baxter, Billy, 1914, Jl 14,9:6
Baxter, Bruce R, 1947, Je 22,52:3
Baxter, Charles H, 1943, F 16,19:5
Baxter, Charles J, 1915, D 31,9:5; 1946, N 27,25:1
Baxter, Charles M, 1941, F 27,19:3
Baxter, Charles M Jr Mrs, 1954, Ap 24,17:3
Baxter, Charles M Mrs, 1951, Ap 7,15:5
Baxter, Charles S, 1955, Mr 15,29:2
Baxter, Charles W Capt, 1906, Mr 22,9:5
Baxter, D Freeman, 1949, D 20,31:3
Baxter, David M, 1964, Ap 6,31:1
Baxter, De W C, 1881, My 11,5:5
Baxter, Dow V, 1966, Ja 4,27:1
Baxter, Dudley, 1875, My 21,1:7
Baxter, Edmund F, 1967, My 28,61:1
Baxter, Edna D Mrs, 1959, Jl 28,27:4
Baxter, Edward J, 1945, My 27,26:1
Baxter, Edward O Mrs, 1956, D 6,37:3
Baxter, Elijah, 1939, Ag 23,21:4
Baxter, Eric, 1944, My 11,19:1
Baxter, Florus R, 1944, D 4,23:2
Baxter, Frank H, 1958, S 4,29:2
Baxter, Frankie, 1950, Ja 5,26:5
Baxter, G S, 1928, Jl 3,21:3
Baxter, G W, 1929, D 19,27:5
Baxter, George, 1944, F 10,15:6
Baxter, George G, 1960, S 14,43:3
Baxter, George L, 1956, Mr 1,34:5
Baxter, George W, 1941, Mr 2,42:3; 1948, Ja 27,25:2
Baxter, Gregory P, 1953, F 11,29:3
Baxter, H H Gen, 1884, F 18,5:1
Baxter, Harry T, 1940, Ap 9,23:2
Baxter, Henry F, 1944, Jl 29,13:3
Baxter, Henry Gen, 1874, Ja 2,5:6
Baxter, Hugh, 1946, O 19,21:3
Baxter, Hugh H, 1945, D 29,13:6
Baxter, Irving K, 1957, Je 14,25:1
Baxter, Irving S, 1966, Ap 16,33:4
Baxter, J B M, 1946, D 28,15:2
Baxter, James C, 1956, S 21,25:4
Baxter, James H, 1948, Je 19,15:5
Baxter, James M, 1909, D 29,9:4
Baxter, James P Jr, 1939, S 26,23:4
Baxter, James P Jr Mrs, 1955, My 6,23:2
Baxter, James P Mrs, 1962, My 5,27:1
Baxter, James Phinney, 1921, My 9,11:4
Baxter, John B, 1940, Je 24,15:6
Baxter, John E, 1958, O 6,31:3
Baxter, John E Mrs, 1953, My 16,19:5
Baxter, John L Mrs, 1945, Mr 23,19:4
Baxter, John R, 1962, S 7,59:4
Baxter, John R Mrs, 1962, S 7,59:4
Baxter, John W, 1950, O 11,33:3
Baxter, John W D, 1956, Ja 15,47:5
Baxter, Joseph A Jr, 1964, Ap 26,88:6
Baxter, Lance Mrs, 1959, F 8,86:5
Baxter, Leslie F, 1952, Jl 20,52:4
Baxter, Lora, 1955, Je 18,17:5
Baxter, Louise I Mrs, 1946, F 27,25:4
Baxter, Lydia, 1874, Je 24,5:6
Baxter, Mabel, 1958, Jl 24,25:4
Baxter, Margaret W Mrs, 1942, Ap 1,21:6
Baxter, Michael A, 1954, S 20,23:5
Baxter, Milton S, 1938, O 16,44:5
Baxter, Norman W, 1952, S 14,86:3
Baxter, Peter J, 1938, Ap 28,23:4
Baxter, Richard M, 1951, Je 10,92:7
Baxter, Robert G, 1951, My 8,31:4
Baxter, Robert W, 1957, O 29,31:4
Baxter, Rowena Mrs, 1937, Jl 11,II,4:2
Baxter, Rupert H, 1960, Jl 5,31:3
Baxter, Samuel N, 1945, S 26,23:4
Baxter, Thomas F, 1941, Je 28,15:4
Baxter, Thomas G, 1948, Ag 26,21:3
Baxter, Thomas J, 1938, F 18,19:2
Baxter, Thomas J Rev, 1915, S 22,11:5

Baxter, Thomas O Mrs, 1959, O 28,37:1
Baxter, Victor, 1949, S 8,29:4
Baxter, W R E, 1965, D 22,31:3
Baxter, Walter Capt, 1916, Je 18,18:5
Baxter, Warner, 1951, My 8,31:1
Baxter, William, 1951, Je 28,25:3; 1954, S 24,23:1
Baxter, William C, 1962, Ja 26,31:1
Baxter, William D Mrs, 1940, S 4,23:4
Baxter, William H, 1950, Ja 21,18:2
Baxter, William J, 1944, F 13,41:1; 1948, S 8,38:2; 1952, S 23,33:4
Bay, Burt R, 1951, F 1,25:1
Bay, Charles A, 1940, Ap 24,23:2
Bay, Charles U (funl, Ja 6,23:5), 1956, Ja 1,51:1
Bay, Charles U (est acctg), 1962, Je 30,20:2
Bay, Harry E, 1952, Mr 22,13:6
Bay, Jens C, 1962, Ap 13,35:2
Bay, Marie H Mrs, 1941, S 15,17:5
Bay, Myron E, 1964, S 12,25:2
Bay, Robert P, 1940, Ja 2,20:2
Bay, William Dr, 1865, S 12,4:6
Bayard, Albert W, 1950, Ap 12,27:4
Bayard, Burton L, 1949, Ja 16,68:1
Bayard, Emile, 1937, D 24,20:4
Bayard, Fairfax, 1951, N 13,30:7
Bayard, G P, 1903, Ag 24,7:7
Bayard, George R, 1954, Je 15,29:2
Bayard, J A, 1880, Je 14,5:1
Bayard, Louis P, 1922, Jl 4,13:6
Bayard, Louis Pintard, 1920, Ag 22,20:5
Bayard, Maurice F, 1921, Ap 4,13:5
Bayard, Richard H Hon, 1868, Mr 8,5:3
Bayard, T Alexis Mrs, 1960, Jl 12,35:3
Bayard, T F, 1898, S 29,1:3
Bayard, T F Mrs, 1886, F 1,1:1
Bayard, Thomas F, 1942, Jl 13,15:1
Bayart, Charles R, 1952, Ap 10,29:2
Baybutt, Richard, 1948, My 23,70:1
Bayden, Seth, 1870, Ap 1,5:1
Baydur, Huseyin R, 1955, F 28,19:4
Bayen, Malaku E, 1940, My 9,23:5
Bayer, Alfred J, 1945, Je 27,19:4
Bayer, Arthur G Mrs, 1954, Jl 1,25:3
Bayer, Charles L, 1938, Jl 18,13:6
Bayer, Charles M, 1966, My 21,31:3
Bayer, Clemons H, 1954, Ja 23,13:3
Bayer, E S, 1929, Ja 1,29:5
Bayer, Frederick, 1939, My 22,17:1
Bayer, Frederick J, 1949, D 25,26:6
Bayer, George, 1964, D 11,39:2
Bayer, Gustave, 1943, My 19,25:2
Bayer, Harold F, 1950, Mr 21,32:2
Bayer, Harry A, 1944, My 3,19:3
Bayer, Harry W, 1948, S 30,27:2
Bayer, Henry, 1955, Mr 2,27:3
Bayer, Henry L I, 1947, Jl 26,13:4
Bayer, Herman J, 1950, Je 10,17:4
Bayer, Hinde Mrs, 1941, Ag 25,15:5
Bayer, Howard G, 1966, Mr 11,33:3
Bayer, Julius, 1953, D 9,11:5
Bayer, Lloyd F, 1958, S 30,31:5
Bayer, Maria Mrs, 1941, S 11,23:5
Bayer, Phil Mrs, 1956, Ap 22,86:5
Bayer, Robert J, 1956, Je 7,31:5
Bayer, Robert K, 1967, Mr 28,39:3
Bayer, Robert S, 1953, Ap 17,26:4
Bayer, Stephen D Mrs (will), 1949, Ap 9,17:1
Bayer, Theodore, 1959, Mr 8,86:2
Bayes, N, 1928, Mr 20,27:3
Bayes, Norman, 1950, My 27,17:2
Bayes, Robert R, 1965, F 26,29:2
Bayes, William R, 1964, N 29,87:1
Bayes, William R Mrs, 1957, N 2,21:2
Bayevsky, Herbert I, 1964, Ag 2,77:2
Bayevsky, Herbert I Mrs, 1950, S 10,9:2
Bayfield, St Clair, 1967, My 21,87:1
Bayford, Lord, 1940, F 26,15:2
Bayha, Charles, 1957, Mr 2,21:6
Bayle, George F, 1939, Mr 11,17:3
Bayle, George F Jr, 1949, My 16,21:2
Bayle, James W, 1915, S 18,9:6
Bayle, Luis De, 1938, Mr 25,19:4
Bayles, Aaron, 1964, O 6,39:1
Bayles, Alfred C, 1941, Ag 12,19:4
Bayles, Burton B, 1954, Ap 28,31:2
Bayles, Edward P, 1955, My 28,15:5
Bayles, Edwin A, 1950, Ap 27,29:2
Bayles, Hattie M, 1942, Ap 30,19:5
Bayles, James C Mrs, 1905, Ja 10,9:2
Bayles, James Cooper, 1913, My 9,11:6
Bayles, Lewis C, 1946, D 24,17:5
Bayles, Oscar O, 1909, Jl 16,7:6
Bayles, Samuel Y, 1948, My 29,15:6
Bayles, Theodore, 1952, Ja 21,15:5
Bayles, William H Mrs, 1937, Mr 25,25:6
Bayless, Aaron Mrs, 1960, O 9,86:2
Bayless, George C, 1923, Mr 6,21:4
Baylet, Albert, 1961, Je 27,33:3
Baylet, Jean, 1959, My 30,6:8
Bayley, Archbishop (see also O 4 and 6), 1877, O 10,2:3
Bayley, Charles Clive, 1923, Ja 24,13:5
Bayley, Guy Carleton Mrs, 1921, My 26,13:2
Bayley, Guy L, 1940, Ap 22,17:2
Bayley, Harold R, 1951, Ag 7,25:4
Bayley, John, 1952, Ap 29,27:3
Bayley, Neville, 1948, N 1,23:3
Bayley, Robert W, 1958, Jl 17,27:1
Bayley, Warren, 1964, D 28,29:3
Bayley, Willard J, 1947, Ja 7,28:3
Bayley, William H, 1940, D 18,25:3
Bayley, William S, 1943, F 16,19:1
Baylies, Charlotte U Mrs, 1939, Ap 25,23:3
Baylies, E L, 1932, Ap 30,15:1
Baylies, Edmund L Mrs, 1945, D 2,46:5
Baylies, Edward Lincoln, 1912, D 10,15:4
Baylies, Edward W, 1951, Ja 11,25:5
Baylies, Lincoln, 1958, Ag 6,25:1
Baylies, Theodore B, 1948, N 18,27:3
Baylies, Willard Le Baron Dr, 1917, F 10,9:2
Baylinson, A S, 1950, My 7,106:5
Baylis, A B, 1882, Jl 16,7:2
Baylis, Adelaide B, 1965, Je 23,41:4
Baylis, Alvah M, 1945, F 2,19:3
Baylis, Arthur E Mrs, 1952, Ap 23,29:4
Baylis, C S (funl, Ap 29,9:7), 1903, Mr 21,9:5
Baylis, Carl B, 1942, O 15,23:5
Baylis, Chester, 1961, Ja 1,49:2
Baylis, Edward, 1944, D 10,54:3
Baylis, Frederic J, 1941, Je 12,23:5
Baylis, Henry W, 1949, Je 11,18:4
Baylis, Herbert S Mrs, 1941, S 19,24:2
Baylis, Hiram A, 1950, Ap 24,25:2
Baylis, Lilian, 1937, N 26,21:3
Baylis, W B, 1881, F 19,2:7
Baylis, Walter F, 1947, Mr 26,25:2
Baylis, William, 1944, S 29,21:3
Baylis, William H, 1954, Ja 13,31:2
Bayliss, George, 1958, O 6,31:5
Bayliss, James W, 1949, Ap 21,25:3
Bayliss, Jefferson, 1937, Ap 4,II,10:8
Bayliss, Lucien S Justice, 1916, Ag 29,9:5
Bayliss, William M Sir, 1924, Ag 28,17:6
Bayliss, Wyke Sir, 1906, Ap 7,9:5
Baylitts, Austin W, 1955, Ag 11,21:5
Baylor, Courtenay Mrs, 1945, Jl 28,11:4
Baylor, Harry B, 1954, Ja 1,23:1
Baylor, Percival C, 1951, Ap 13,23:2
Bayly, Charles, 1954, Mr 23,27:2
Bayly, Charles B, 1957, Jl 28,61:1
Bayly, Lewis (por), 1938, My 17,23:4
Bayne, Arthur P Mrs, 1960, S 25,88:6
Bayne, Bushrod R, 1916, Ap 26,13:7
Bayne, Carroll S, 1964, S 23,47:1
Bayne, Donald, 1948, Je 21,21:3
Bayne, Elwood M, 1943, Ja 24,42:3
Bayne, Fred D, 1961, D 28,27:2
Bayne, George G, 1939, D 7,27:1
Bayne, Howard, 1958, Ag 25,21:3
Bayne, Hugh A, 1954, D 26,60:7
Bayne, Jasper, 1941, Ag 10,36:7
Bayne, Marion S, 1938, Ag 30,17:3
Bayne, Reed T, 1954, Je 9,31:4
Bayne, Samuel Gamble, 1924, Ap 21,17:3
Bayne, Stephen F (funl, Ag 26,85:3), 1956, Ag 23, 27:3
Bayne, Thomas L Mrs, 1950, Ja 14,15:4
Bayne, William, 1922, Je 8,19:4; 1955, O 23,86:3
Baynes, Ernest Harold, 1925, Ja 22,19:4
Baynes, John, 1903, S 30,9:6
Baynes, Norman H, 1961, F 13,27:4
Baynes, Sydney, 1938, Mr 10,21:1
Baynes, William C, 1968, Ag 23,27:8
Baynton, Harold, 1963, O 20,88:8
Baynton, Henry, 1951, Ja 4,30:3
Bayo, Alberto, 1967, Ag 5,23:3
Bayrd, Frank Mrs, 1952, Mr 3,21:4
Bays, Alfred W, 1957, D 24,15:2
Bays, George S, 1949, O 21,25:2
Bayuk, Samuel, 1954, N 13,15:5
Bayumi, Hassah A, 1963, Je 25,33:2
Bazaine, F A, 1880, Ag 16,5:2
Bazame, F A Marshal, 1888, S 24,5:4
Bazan, Carlos, 1966, Ja 15,21:5
Bazata, Charles F, 1952, O 2,29:5
Bazavoff, Serge B, 1958, S 24,27:1
Baze, J D, 1881, Ap 18,5:5
Bazerque, Jean, 1952, Ag 29,23:5
Bazett, Henry C, 1950, Jl 13,25:3
Bazhov, Paval, 1950, D 5,31:3
Baziak, Eugene, 1962, Je 19,35:2
Bazin, George F, 1959, Jl 10,25:4
Bazin, John Henry, 1904, O 7,9:6
Bazinet, Addison, 1947, Ap 29,27:4
Bazinet, John, 1953, My 10,89:2
Baziotes, William, 1963, Je 7,31:1
Bazley, Thomas Sir, 1885, Mr 20,2:4
Bazmi, Abu Said, 1951, S 16,84:5
Bazuro, Anna, 1943, Je 21,17:4
Bazykin, Vladimir I, 1965, Ag 14,23:2
Bazzi, Maria, 1959, Ag 25,31:4
Bea, Augustin Cardinal (rites, N 20,57:7), 1968, N 16,1:5
Beach, A B Rev, 1885, Ja 16,2:7
Beach, A F, 1880, O 5,5:3
Beach, Adelaide T Mrs (will, N 20,25:2), 1940, N 14,23:1
Beach, Albert F Jr, 1954, Ja 13,31:2
Beach, Allen C, 1918, O 19,15:2
Beach, Allen P, 1963, N 27,37:2
Beach, Arthur Mrs, 1945, Ap 11,23:4
Beach, Augustus F Lt, 1918, Ja 23,9:5
Beach, Austin Col, 1917, O 17,13:3
Beach, Bennett S, 1939, S 14,23:5
Beach, Burton T, 1939, Ja 5,23:3
Beach, C Edward, 1940, Ja 13,15:6
Beach, C Rev, 1881, Mr 10,5:5
Beach, Calvin B, 1937, Ap 27,23:5
Beach, Charles A, 1954, Je 24,27:2
Beach, Charles C, 1948, F 12,23:2
Beach, Charles E, 1945, Je 19,19:3; 1954, Ap 6,29:3
Beach, Charles H, 1948, Mr 8,23:1
Beach, Charles L, 1951, D 13,33:2
Beach, Charles S, 1947, Mr 24,25:6
Beach, Charles Yale, 1917, O 18,15:2
Beach, Chester, 1956, Ag 8,25:5
Beach, Chester C, 1958, Ap 21,23:4
Beach, Chester Mrs, 1965, Ja 2,19:4
Beach, Chisholm, 1918, N 6,17:3
Beach, Clarence W, 1940, O 15,15:5
Beach, D N Rev Dr, 1926, O 19,29:3
Beach, Daniel, 1913, F 23,II,7:4
Beach, Daniel M Sr, 1948, Jl 23,19:6
Beach, David P, 1955, S 2,17:3
Beach, David S, 1943, My 12,25:3; 1948, Mr 24,25:3
Beach, Don, 1957, My 18,19:5
Beach, E J, 1877, My 22,2:2
Beach, Edward L, 1943, D 21,27:1
Beach, Edward W, 1943, D 23,20:2
Beach, Edwin, 1941, N 9,53:2
Beach, Edwin E, 1963, D 28,23:4
Beach, Ella, 1938, O 23,41:2
Beach, Emmett L, 1947, S 5,20:2
Beach, Erasmus Darwin, 1924, Jl 18,13:5
Beach, Eugene A, 1939, Ap 8,23:8
Beach, F W, 1952, Ja 18,27:3
Beach, Fred J, 1938, Ap 24,II,7:1
Beach, Frederick B, 1947, Jl 22,23:5
Beach, Frederick C, 1918, Je 9,21:5
Beach, Frederick G, 1938, Ja 3,21:4
Beach, Frederick H, 1956, D 17,31:3
Beach, Frederick Odgen, 1918, D 18,15:3
Beach, George, 1951, Ap 30,21:4
Beach, George A, 1918, Ja 23,9:5
Beach, George C Jr, 1948, N 19,28:3
Beach, George L, 1954, Mr 29,19:5
Beach, Grace B, 1946, My 11,27:4
Beach, H P, 1933, Mr 5,26:1
Beach, H Prescott, 1943, Jl 19,15:4
Beach, H Prescott Mrs, 1955, Ag 7,72:8
Beach, Harold K, 1958, Mr 2,88:6
Beach, Harold K (will), 1959, S 4,9:7
Beach, Henry C Sr, 1941, O 21,23:3
Beach, Henry H Mrs, 1944, D 28,19:1
Beach, Horatio S, 1950, Ag 15,29:3
Beach, Howard W, 1942, D 31,15:2; 1962, Jl 31,30:2
Beach, James C, 1906, Mr 22,9:5
Beach, Jessie, 1954, Ag 19,23:3
Beach, John A, 1953, S 23,31:3
Beach, John K, 1938, Jl 7,19:3
Beach, John P, 1953, N 7,17:3
Beach, John R, 1949, Ag 24,25:2
Beach, John R Mrs, 1950, D 13,35:4
Beach, John S, 1905, Mr 15,9:6; 1943, Jl 13,21:4
Beach, Joseph P, 1911, Ja 10,11:3
Beach, Joseph W, 1957, Ag 20,27:2
Beach, Lila A, 1956, Ag 23,27:4
Beach, Lindsley D, 1943, Ja 26,19:1
Beach, Mary A, 1946, S 3,19:4
Beach, Maynard P, 1953, N 1,87:1
Beach, Miles Judge, 1902, My 20,9:4
Beach, Moses Y, 1868, Jl 21,2:6
Beach, Oren M Jr, 1941, O 22,23:2
Beach, Paul M, 1954, Ja 1,23:1
Beach, Phil E Mrs, 1949, F 12,18:3
Beach, Ralph H, 1957, Ap 25,31:5
Beach, Ralph M, 1942, Ap 2,21:3
Beach, Raymond W Mrs, 1941, Je 16,15:5
Beach, Rex Mrs, 1947, Ap 15,25:5
Beach, Robert James, 1916, F 8,11:3
Beach, Robert K, 1937, Je 22,23:2; 1959, My 21,31:1
Beach, Robin Dr, 1968, My 22,47:4
Beach, S Harry Jr, 1953, Jl 1,29:4
Beach, Samuel C, 1943, Ag 2,15:5
Beach, Samy H, 1940, N 23,17:2
Beach, Stanley, 1957, Ag 16,19:4
Beach, Surveyor Gen, 1873, My 2,5:5
Beach, Sylvester J, 1953, F 13,21:3
Beach, Sylvester W, 1940, N 17,49:3
Beach, Sylvia, 1962, O 10,47:2
Beach, Theodore, 1953, S 19,15:2
Beach, Treat S, 1922, D 4,17:3
Beach, W A, 1884, Je 29,1:5
Beach, W D, 1932, Je 19,27:3
Beach, W Edwards, 1956, My 14,25:5
Beach, W N, 1883, F 14,5:1
Beach, Walter G, 1948, O 7,30:2
Beach, Walter Rogers, 1915, D 28,11:5
Beach, Warren C Capt, 1922, Ja 17,17:3

Beach, Will G, 1942, Mr 5,23:4
Beach, Willard P, 1942, Ap 19,44:6
Beach, William, 1943, D 3,23:3
Beach, William C, 1948, D 31,16:3
Beach, William D, 1959, N 28,21:4
Beach, William D Mrs, 1948, My 5,25:4
Beach, William E, 1937, Ja 1,23:3
Beach, William H Mrs, 1959, N 14,21:4
Beach, William N, 1955, My 6,23:4
Beach, Wooster Dr, 1868, Ja 30,8:5
Beacham, Joseph W, 1958, Jl 29,23:3
Beachem, Charles W, 1937, Ja 28,25:2
Beacher, Jacob, 1937, N 18,23:1
Beackwell, William Bayard, 1915, D 1,13:4
Beacom, Andrew J, 1945, S 10,19:3
Beaconsfield, Countess of (Mrs Disraeli), 1872, D 31,1:2
Beaconsfield, Earl, 1881, Ap 19,1:7
Beaconsfield, Viscountess, 1873, Ja 5,5:3
Beadel, Edward M, 1925, My 11,17:5
Beadenkopf, Charles G, 1941, N 6,23:4
Beadle, E L, 1882, Ap 6,2:5
Beadle, E R Rev Dr, 1879, Ja 7,5:4
Beadle, Edmund P, 1951, Ja 31,25:4
Beadle, Edward R, 1945, F 22,27:2
Beadle, Elias R, 1946, N 19,31:2
Beadle, Fritz, 1914, Ap 20,9:5
Beadle, R Cameron, 1968, Je 26,47:5
Beadle, William A Mrs, 1946, S 14,7:4
Beadle, William Henry Harrison Brig-Gen, 1915, N 14,19:6
Beadleston, Alfred N, 1917, Ag 10,9:5
Beadleston, C Perry, 1940, Jl 28,26:6
Beadleston, Edith, 1957, Je 18,33:4
Beadleston, Henry C Mrs, 1958, O 9,37:1
Beadon, Canon, 1879, Ag 8,3:6
Beagary, H Clinton, 1952, My 21,27:3
Beaghen, Thomas E, 1937, Ag 21,15:3
Beaghen, Thomas Mrs, 1951, Mr 31,15:2
Beaird, Robert L Mrs, 1952, Ag 27,27:2
Beakbane, Lionel S, 1949, D 14,31:2
Beake, James A Dr, 1914, Je 10,11:6
Beakes, Albert S, 1940, Ag 30,19:4
Beakes, Charles H C 3d, 1957, O 21,25:4
Beakes, Crosby J, 1948, My 16,68:4
Beakes, Crosby J Mrs, 1946, D 19,29:3
Beakes, John G, 1947, D 9,29:4
Beakes, William E, 1951, Mr 31,15:6
Beal, Abraham, 1872, F 26,5:3
Beal, Carl H, 1946, S 9,9:6
Beal, Catherine, 1941, Mr 26,23:5
Beal, Charles A, 1950, Jl 19,31:4
Beal, Charles W, 1942, Ag 8,9:7
Beal, Edmond, 1948, F 23,25:4
Beal, Edward, 1949, Mr 13,76:1
Beal, Frank P, 1965, S 12,86:4
Beal, Fred E, 1954, N 16,11:3
Beal, Frederick Earl Dr, 1912, Ag 9,7:5
Beal, Genevieve E Mrs, 1949, Ja 23,68:4
Beal, George, 1945, S 12,25:2; 1948, F 5,23:2
Beal, George B, 1957, Ap 10,33:2
Beal, Harry, 1944, N 23,31:6
Beal, Henry C, 1960, Ja 1,19:1
Beal, Howard J Mrs, 1961, Mr 9,29:2
Beal, J Frank, 1941, Ag 22,15:1
Beal, James H, 1945, S 23,44:6
Beal, John M, 1957, Ja 18,21:2
Beal, John P, 1939, D 21,23:4
Beal, Junius E, 1942, Je 25,23:4
Beal, Lizzie Mrs (por), 1938, My 15,II,7:1
Beal, Louise L, 1952, N 19,29:3
Beal, Lyle E, 1952, Ja 19,15:5
Beal, R, 1881, N 26,3:4
Beal, Ralph R, 1947, Ja 25,17:1
Beal, Reynolds, 1951, D 19,31:4
Beal, Robert C, 1937, O 28,25:4
Beal, Thomas M, 1944, S 13,19:5
Beal, Thomas Prince, 1923, My 26,15:6
Beal, William D, 1952, Jl 12,13:5
Beal, William F, 1939, Ja 24,19:4
Beal, William Reynolds, 1912, Je 6,11:5
Beal, Willis P, 1962, Ja 27,21:5
Beale, Alfred M A, 1939, Jl 30,29:4
Beale, Blaine Mrs, 1958, Ja 29,27:4
Beale, Caroline M Mrs, 1956, D 11,36:1
Beale, Constance R, 1937, Ja 11,20:3
Beale, Frank D, 1950, N 22,25:5
Beale, Frederick, 1953, Ja 6,29:3
Beale, George H, 1958, My 14,33:2
Beale, George Nancreade, 1912, Jl 7,II,11:6
Beale, Harry P, 1948, My 19,27:1
Beale, Isola Earle Mrs, 1921, Ja 7,13:5
Beale, J Edward, 1945, O 26,19:2
Beale, James H, 1922, Ag 19,11:6
Beale, Jesse D Mrs, 1948, Ap 29,24:3
Beale, Joseph H, 1943, Ja 21,21:4
Beale, Katherine C Mrs, 1937, Mr 16,23:3
Beale, Leonard T, 1966, S 28,47:4
Beale, Louis D, 1943, Mr 7,38:7
Beale, Phelan, 1956, Je 13,37:5
Beale, Robert B, 1938, S 13,23:5
Beale, Rupert G, 1954, N 13,15:4
Beale, Thomas, 1940, Ja 30,20:3
Beale, Truxton Mrs (mem ser, O 31,33:6), 1956, Je 12,35:3
Beale, William L Mrs, 1960, Je 9,33:1
Beale, Wilson T M, 1959, O 9,29:1
Beales, E, 1881, Je 23,5:2
Beall, Almon L, 1950, Je 19,21:6
Beall, Carrie, 1949, D 29,25:2
Beall, Charles R Mrs, 1950, Je 21,27:3
Beall, Charles W, 1939, F 15,23:3
Beall, Charles W Mrs, 1957, D 31,17:3
Beall, Jeremiah, 1938, F 19,15:3
Beall, Joseph H Judge, 1917, My 15,13:1
Beall, Kenneth, 1942, S 6,30:6
Beall, Ramona, 1947, Mr 25,26:2
Beall, W M, 1959, S 5,15:5
Beall, William H, 1950, Jl 25,27:1
Beals, Alfred T, 1955, N 11,25:2
Beals, Arthur G, 1938, Ap 15,20:3
Beals, Charles O, 1937, My 8,19:2
Beals, Clyde A Mrs, 1967, N 20,47:4
Beals, Donald M, 1960, Mr 11,25:2
Beals, George C, 1940, S 9,15:5
Beals, H Warren, 1948, Mr 15,23:2
Beals, Hallock W, 1954, F 8,23:2
Beals, J Whitney, 1938, Mr 29,21:3
Beals, Jessie T Mrs, 1942, My 31,39:2
Beals, John E L, 1950, Mr 10,28:2
Beals, Morell B, 1939, D 6,25:2
Beals, Oliver W Mrs, 1947, Ja 29,25:4
Beals, Ralph A, 1954, O 15,23:1
Beals, Rose F, 1955, Mr 30,29:2
Beals, Walter B, 1960, S 21,37:3
Beals, William, 1916, Je 27,11:4
Beals, William Col, 1902, My 18,7:1
Beam, Allen W, 1937, Ja 27,21:2
Beam, Charles F, 1938, F 6,II,8:3
Beam, David R Mrs, 1911, Mr 4,11:5
Beam, Edith D Mrs, 1940, Ap 26,21:4
Beam, Henry L, 1943, Ag 4,17:2
Beam, Howard C, 1957, D 4,39:4
Beam, Jacob N, 1954, F 10,29:5
Beam, James B, 1947, D 28,40:3
Beam, Mary G, 1939, S 26,23:4
Beam, Mary H, 1945, My 10,23:4
Beam, Paul O, 1957, Mr 11,27:7
Beam, Stewart N, 1943, S 21,23:3
Beam, Walter I, 1957, S 17,35:5
Beam, William U, 1948, Ja 6,23:2
Beam, Wilson, 1952, O 24,23:1
Beaman, A Gaylord, 1943, O 23,13:6
Beaman, Bartlett, 1947, N 15,17:4
Beaman, Charles C Mrs, 1917, My 5,13:6
Beaman, Charles O, 1938, Ja 19,23:6
Beaman, David W, 1944, N 1,23:5
Beaman, F C, 1882, S 28,4:7
Beaman, George William Rear-Adm, 1917, My 4,11:5
Beaman, Harry C, 1947, Je 6,23:4
Beaman, Marshall E, 1952, Ag 9,13:5
Beaman, Middleton, 1951, S 18,31:5
Beaman, Roy E Mrs, 1957, S 3,28:6
Beaman, William E, 1945, Jl 6,11:7
Beame, Philip, 1962, Ja 28,76:7
Beamer, Elmer A, 1941, My 15,23:2
Beamer, P C Mrs, 1952, S 28,76:7
Beames, Clare F Lt-Col, 1923, Ap 23,15:6
Beamish, Edgar T, 1951, Je 24,72:6
Beamish, James F, 1958, O 27,27:3
Beamish, Lawrence F, 1943, Jl 8,19:3
Beamish, Richard J, 1945, O 2,23:4
Beamish, Tufton P H, 1951, My 3,29:1
Beams, Elliot C, 1941, My 9,21:2
Beamsley, Foster G, 1960, Mr 12,21:3
Bean, A H, 1883, D 27,5:4
Bean, Barton A, 1947, Jl 20,44:5
Bean, Carlos Capt, 1937, Mr 18,25:3
Bean, Charles D, 1938, F 2,19:3
Bean, Clarence H, 1953, Ag 15,15:6
Bean, Clinton, 1957, Jl 24,25:2
Bean, D B, 1905, Je 6,9:5
Bean, Delcie D, 1964, Ja 28,31:5
Bean, Edgar R, 1942, F 23,21:4
Bean, Edward H, 1945, S 6,25:6
Bean, Francis A, 1955, Ag 21,93:3
Bean, Fred R, 1941, My 18,44:1
Bean, Frederick A, 1943, My 17,15:4
Bean, George E M Mrs, 1967, Mr 31,37:3
Bean, George J Sr, 1948, N 27,17:4
Bean, George T, 1959, N 27,29:2
Bean, George W, 1950, N 21,31:3
Bean, Guy C, 1951, Je 8,27:3
Bean, Harold C, 1950, My 22,21:5
Bean, Harold E, 1955, Mr 26,15:3
Bean, Harry, 1948, D 11,15:6
Bean, Henry J, 1941, My 10,15:3
Bean, L L (Leon L Bean), 1967, F 7,39:1
Bean, Oscar, 1937, Ag 28,6:7
Bean, Oscar O, 1943, F 25,21:4
Bean, Rebecca Mrs, 1924, Je 12,17:5
Bean, Richard S, 1968, Je 21,41:3
Bean, Robert B, 1944, S 3,26:7
Bean, Robert H, 1960, My 5,35:3
Bean, Rodney, 1942, D 24,15:4
Bean, Roy S, 1939, Ag 12,13:4
Bean, Susan A, 1956, My 12,19:5
Bean, T, 1926, Ag 6,15:6
Bean, T H Dr, 1916, D 29,9:4
Bean, Theodore L, 1943, S 21,24:3
Bean, Theodore L Mrs, 1952, D 5,27:5
Bean, Thomas, 1950, D 10,104:4
Bean, W Ward, 1952, Jl 13,61:1
Bean, William, 1953, O 7,29:4
Bean, William B, 1948, Ap 23,23:1
Bean, William S, 1944, N 27,23:5
Bean, Willie E, 1941, Ag 21,17:5
Beane, Alger S, 1941, Ag 27,19:4
Beane, Alpheus C, 1937, S 19,II,7:2
Beane, Alpheus C Mrs, 1961, N 23,31:5
Beane, Clarence E, 1956, D 2,86:2
Beane, Howard H, 1948, D 11,15:4
Beane, Ida R Mrs, 1938, Mr 30,21:2
Beane, W S R, 1940, O 14,19:5
Beans, Hal T, 1960, Jl 9,19:2
Bear, Charles H, 1949, S 28,27:5
Bear, Donald J, 1952, Mr 18,27:5
Bear, Firman Edward Dr, 1968, Ap 7,92:7
Bear, George, 1945, F 27,19:3
Bear, John T Mrs, 1949, F 2,27:3
Bear, Joseph A, 1955, Jl 14,23:3
Bear, Joseph A Mrs, 1947, Ap 18,21:2
Bear, Montague M, 1945, Ag 24,19:3
Bear, Theodore, 1940, N 21,21:2
Bearak, Joseph, 1939, Mr 28,23:1
Bearce, Beatrice, 1956, F 23,27:4
Bearce, George D, 1965, Ja 19,33:1
Bearchell, Charles J, 1947, Ja 4,15:3
Beard, Adelaide Mrs, 1942, N 13,23:3
Beard, Adelia Belle, 1920, F 17,9:4
Beard, Billy, 1954, N 15,27:5
Beard, Billy Mrs, 1945, Jl 5,13:5
Beard, Caroline M Mrs, 1938, Ap 6,23:6
Beard, Charles A, 1948, S 2,23:1
Beard, Charles E Mrs, 1963, S 19,27:5
Beard, Charles N, 1943, F 18,23:2
Beard, Clifford, 1950, Ja 25,14:2
Beard, Daniel C, 1941, Je 12,23:1
Beard, Daniel C Mrs, 1940, D 14,17:5
Beard, Dewey, 1955, N 4,29:2
Beard, Edward C, 1952, Ja 25,21:2
Beard, Edward L Jr, 1952, N 16,88:6
Beard, Eliza M, 1940, Mr 13,23:5
Beard, Francis, 1943, Jl 5,15:5
Beard, Frank, 1905, S 30,9:4
Beard, Frank S, 1922, Ag 7,13:5
Beard, G M Dr, 1883, Ja 24,5:3
Beard, Gerald H Rev Dr, 1921, O 11,19:5
Beard, Henry Summerfield, 1905, Ja 8,9:7
Beard, Hollis Mrs, 1958, Jl 30,29:1
Beard, J N Rev, 1904, Ja 5,9:6
Beard, James H, 1967, Mr 4,27:1
Beard, James H Mrs, 1960, Ja 14,33:1
Beard, James R, 1959, Ap 15,33:4
Beard, James T, 1941, D 27,19:1
Beard, James W Mrs, 1957, Mr 23,19:3
Beard, John G, 1946, Ap 24,25:2
Beard, John J, 1955, F 3,23:1
Beard, L, 1933, Ag 14,13:1
Beard, Louis A (funl plans, Ap 15,29:4), 1954, Ap 14,29:3
Beard, Louise S Mrs, 1950, Ja 30,17:2
Beard, Malcolm C, 1960, F 22,17:4
Beard, Mary, 1946, D 5,31:1
Beard, Mary R (Mrs Chas A), 1958, Ag 15,22:1
Beard, Ollin W, 1951, My 11,28:3
Beard, Oswald, 1955, F 25,21:5
Beard, Ralph W, 1948, Jl 18,52:3
Beard, Richard O Mrs, 1955, O 29,19:5
Beard, Robert F, 1965, Mr 12,33:1
Beard, Sydney H, 1938, O 21,23:4
Beard, Theodora, 1949, N 8,31:4
Beard, V V, 1943, O 19,19:2
Beard, Walter E, 1957, F 17,92:6
Beard, Wiley, 1953, O 17,15:5
Beard, William, 1959, N 8,88:8
Beard, William D Justice, 1910, D 8,13:4
Beard, William E, 1950, D 23,15:3
Beard, William K, 1943, Je 11,19:4
Beard, William K Jr Mrs, 1953, Mr 27,24:3
Beard, William M, 1941, O 29,23:4
Beard, William S Mrs, 1949, D 15,35:3
Beard, Williard L Mrs, 1953, S 9,29:5
Beard, Wolcott L, 1939, F 14,19:4
Beardall, William V, 1966, D 27,32:4
Bearden, Humphrey W, 1950, Ja 14,15:6
Bearden, R Howard Mrs, 1943, S 17,21:5
Beardmore, William W Mrs, 1952, D 21,52:6
Beardshaw, David F, 1960, Je 11,21:5
Beardslee, Alice L F, 1939, F 2,19:4
Beardslee, Clark S Rev, 1914, Ap 15,13:6
Beardslee, Clyde E, 1954, Ap 10,15:5
Beardslee, Harry C, 1948, Ja 4,52:3
Beardslee, John W, 1962, My 11,31:4
Beardslee, L A Adm, 1903, N 12,9:5
Beardslee, Lester E Jr, 1951, F 14,29:4
Beardslee, Lisle R, 1963, Ag 15,29:3
Beardslee, Paul C, 1964, S 25,41:3
Beardslee, W Russell, 1955, N 11,25:5

Beardslee, William E, 1941, Ap 28,15:2
Beardsley, A, 1898, Mr 17,7:2
Beardsley, Alling P, 1950, S 24,104:5
Beardsley, Arthur L, 1944, Ja 4,18:3
Beardsley, Arthur L Mrs, 1942, N 1,52:4
Beardsley, Charles S Mrs, 1948, D 31,15:4
Beardsley, Charles Shepard, 1917, Jl 11,9:5
Beardsley, Clarence L, 1940, N 11,19:6
Beardsley, Clifford R, 1957, F 10,86:3
Beardsley, Clifford R Mrs, 1960, Mr 2,37:3
Beardsley, Douglas, 1949, My 28,15:4
Beardsley, Edmond, 1938, N 12,15:2
Beardsley, Frank G, 1954, Ag 2,17:4
Beardsley, Frank H, 1945, F 7,21:5
Beardsley, George A, 1943, N 7,57:2
Beardsley, George A Mrs, 1967, Mr 14,47:1
Beardsley, Glover, 1961, Jl 30,68:2
Beardsley, Grenville, 1960, Je 4,23:4
Beardsley, Guy W, 1942, Je 14,46:1
Beardsley, Harber C, 1951, Ja 19,25:2
Beardsley, Harry M, 1952, F 1,21:1
Beardsley, J A, 1883, Ap 1,2:4
Beardsley, James W, 1944, My 17,19:7
Beardsley, John Hamilton, 1910, D 4,13:4
Beardsley, May B Mrs, 1937, Mr 3,23:3
Beardsley, Myron F, 1952, O 5,89:2
Beardsley, Nelson A, 1944, O 25,21:4
Beardsley, Orville L, 1946, O 1,23:5
Beardsley, Ralph, 1920, Mr 20,11:6
Beardsley, Ralph J, 1951, Je 3,92:5
Beardsley, Reed D, 1946, Ag 20,27:2
Beardsley, Roswell, 1902, N 8,9:5
Beardsley, Rudolf, 1921, Ag 16,15:4
Beardsley, Samuel E E, 1941, O 5,48:4
Beardsley, Samuel R, 1909, D 6,9:4
Beardsley, Sterling S, 1950, F 14,26:3
Beardsley, Sterling S Mrs, 1953, Ag 18,23:2
Beardsley, Ten Eyck R, 1959, S 7,13:6
Beardsley, Thomas H, 1962, My 23,45:4
Beardsley, Wallace P, 1952, My 19,17:6
Beardsley, William A, 1946, D 29,37:3
Beardsley, William H, 1925, D 14,21:5
Beardsley, William J Mrs, 1951, O 31,29:3
Beardsley, William P, 1939, F 18,15:5
Beardsley, William P Mrs, 1944, N 25,13:3
Beardsley, William S (funl, N 25,29:3), 1954, N 22, 1:4
Beardsley, William W, 1965, Ja 10,93:1
Beare, Gene K Mrs, 1964, Mr 30,29:5
Beare, Mary O Mrs, 1960, O 27,37:4
Bearman, Harry W, 1947, Jl 20,44:3
Bearmore, Alvan L Mrs, 1950, Je 2,23:6
Bearnard, Charles J, 1953, Jl 22,27:4
Bearnot, Benjamin, 1960, Ap 22,31:2
Bearns, James Sterling, 1913, F 20,11:3
Bearns, Melville H, 1954, Jl 9,17:3
Bearns, Melville H Mrs, 1952, Mr 30,92:6
Bearns, William, 1944, Jl 18,19:1
Bearry, Eda R Mrs, 1940, Ja 3,21:4
Bearse, George F, 1945, My 5,15:3
Bearshear, William M, 1957, F 26,29:1
Bearsted, Lord, 1948, N 10,29:5
Bearsted, Viscount, 1927, Ja 18,25:4
Bearup, Albert J Mrs, 1947, Ap 10,26:2
Beary, Alice L, 1952, Jl 2,25:4
Beary, Arthur L, 1943, Ap 25,34:7
Beary, Daniel H Mrs, 1954, Ag 12,25:4
Beary, Donald B, 1966, Mr 10,33:1
Beary, Edward J, 1939, Ja 18,19:5
Beary, Frank D, 1950, Ap 2,94:3
Beary, John J, 1940, Mr 16,15:5
Beary, Joseph A, 1943, Jl 17,13:4
Beary, Mary E, 1942, Je 13,15:1
Beary, Michael, 1956, O 10,39:6
Beaser, William, 1953, F 4,27:4
Beasley, Albert, 1939, F 15,23:2
Beasley, Charles S, 1956, D 13,37:2
Beasley, Chauncey H Mrs, 1960, N 30,37:5
Beasley, Chauncy H, 1913, S 6,7:3
Beasley, Dorald D, 1948, Jl 24,15:3
Beasley, F W, 1878, D 31,5:4
Beasley, Frank, 1940, Jl 10,19:2
Beasley, James H M, 1949, D 15,35:2
Beasley, John A (por), 1949, S 3,13:4
Beasley, John E, 1955, Je 10,25:4
Beasley, Marion M, 1942, My 3,52:6
Beasley, Matilda Mrs, 1903, D 22,1:2
Beasley, Mercer Judge, 1897, F 20,2:7
Beasley, Norman, 1963, Jl 4,17:1
Beasley, Oscar N, 1960, N 20,86:7
Beasley, Peter, 1957, Ag 10,15:5
Beasley, Rex W, 1961, F 27,27:5
Beasley, Tom, 1950, O 14,19:4
Beasley, William, 1942, O 1,23:4
Beasom, William H, 1944, Mr 5,35:1
Beason, Ross, 1964, Ja 30,29:5
Beaston, Harry D, 1939, My 17,23:5
Beat, Stanley Mrs, 1948, O 19,27:4
Beaten, Wallace B, 1948, D 29,21:3
Beath, Ribert B Col, 1914, N 26,13:4
Beatie, Arthur Y, 1945, Ap 23,19:4
Beatman, Augustus S, 1937, Ja 10,II,10:5
Beatman, Joseph W, 1965, N 3,35:4
Beaton, Alexander, 1967, Je 24,18:1
Beaton, John J, 1944, S 26,23:4
Beaton, John S, 1943, Jl 4,20:5
Beaton, John W, 1951, D 7,27:1
Beaton, Kendall, 1968, Ja 26,47:2
Beaton, Leslie, 1967, Ja 16,41:1
Beaton, Ralph H, 1943, Jl 7,19:6
Beaton, Sidney, 1947, My 23,23:2
Beaton, Welford, 1951, D 12,37:6
Beaton, William F, 1941, Mr 15,17:3
Beatrice, Princess, 1944, O 27,23:4
Beatrice, Theodore, 1953, Ja 31,15:3
Beatrix, Mother, 1939, Ja 30,13:4
Beattie, A Donald, 1967, Mr 25,3:4
Beattie, Anne O, 1956, Ap 12,31:1
Beattie, Carl M, 1945, Mr 1,21:4
Beattie, Charles N, 1940, Je 20,23:5
Beattie, Clifford S, 1952, Jl 31,23:3
Beattie, David J Mrs, 1956, S 29,19:5
Beattie, Denny B Sr, 1952, F 20,29:4
Beattie, Douglas, 1951, S 19,31:3
Beattie, Edward W Sr, 1944, Je 26,15:7
Beattie, Frank H, 1954, Jl 19,19:4
Beattie, Franklin, 1955, F 8,31:7
Beattie, George A, 1947, S 17,25:5
Beattie, George G Mrs, 1961, N 20,31:5
Beattie, George H, 1949, Jl 9,13:3
Beattie, Harold M, 1944, N 22,19:5
Beattie, Hugh W, 1953, Je 21,84:8
Beattie, J Col, 1885, Mr 8,2:5
Beattie, James, 1908, O 18,VII,11:5
Beattie, John, 1941, S 13,17:3
Beattie, John A, 1955, Mr 15,29:1
Beattie, John C, 1946, S 12,7:2
Beattie, Joseph H, 1953, Ag 18,23:3
Beattie, Lawrence, 1958, Jl 11,23:5
Beattie, Lee W Rev Dr, 1937, F 2,23:1
Beattie, Paul, 1908, My 11,7:5
Beattie, R Leslie, 1953, Je 11,29:3
Beattie, Robert B, 1946, O 10,27:6
Beattie, Robert B Mrs, 1940, Je 25,23:5
Beattie, Robert H, 1938, Mr 27,II,6:7
Beattie, Wilfred P, 1957, Ja 15,29:4
Beattie, William, 1942, S 10,27:1
Beattie, William E, 1950, O 17,31:5
Beattie, William H, 1949, Ap 20,27:2
Beattie, William J, 1949, D 10,17:2; 1959, Je 10,37:3
Beattie, William R, 1966, F 28,27:2
Beattie, William T, 1909, Jl 18,9:6
Beattle, Hans Stevenson, 1919, F 24,13:2
Beattle, John J Judge, 1924, Jl 25,13:5
Beattle, Roy H, 1948, F 23,25:5
Beatty, Alfred C Mrs, 1952, Ag 7,21:6
Beatty, Alvah M, 1955, D 2,27:4
Beatty, Arthur, 1943, F 28,49:3
Beatty, Asher Sr, 1939, Ag 4,13:2
Beatty, Bessie, 1947, Ap 7,23:1
Beatty, Blake H Sr, 1957, S 7,19:2
Beatty, C Earl, 1949, O 31,25:6
Beatty, Charles, 1924, S 18,21:6
Beatty, Claude H, 1945, My 2,23:6
Beatty, Clyde Mrs, 1950, O 26,31:2
Beatty, Clyde R, 1965, Jl 20,33:3
Beatty, Countess, 1932, Jl 18,13:3
Beatty, D, 1936, Mr 11,1:6
Beatty, Dana C, 1950, Je 9,23:4
Beatty, David C, 1940, My 28,23:5
Beatty, Edward (will, Ap 14,4:4), 1943, Mr 24,23:1
Beatty, Elijah D, 1951, F 25,84:6
Beatty, F E Rear Adm, 1926, Mr 18,23:3
Beatty, George W, 1955, F 22,21:2
Beatty, George W Dr, 1937, F 9,23:3
Beatty, Harold C, 1948, Mr 12,23:2
Beatty, Harold D, 1957, O 18,23:4
Beatty, Harry W, 1942, My 2,13:5
Beatty, Henry T, 1949, D 11,93:1
Beatty, Herman C Mrs, 1968, My 9,47:2
Beatty, Horace A, 1940, Mr 10,48:4
Beatty, Howard H, 1947, Ag 5,23:2
Beatty, J Frank, 1955, My 24,31:3
Beatty, J G, 1967, My 9,40:4
Beatty, James, 1949, Mr 29,25:1
Beatty, James A, 1959, N 29,86:7
Beatty, James F, 1951, S 13,31:2
Beatty, James J, 1954, My 4,29:2
Beatty, James M, 1937, N 25,31:4
Beatty, Jerome Mrs, 1961, D 19,33:3
Beatty, John B Mrs, 1959, Je 6,21:6
Beatty, John Gen, 1914, D 22,13:5
Beatty, John H, 1955, Jl 26,25:5
Beatty, John L, 1942, Ap 20,21:5
Beatty, John W Mrs, 1949, D 10,17:3
Beatty, John Wesley Sr, 1924, S 30,23:1
Beatty, Kenneth A, 1941, Ap 6,49:2
Beatty, Mary M, 1955, S 5,11:2
Beatty, May, 1945, Ap 3,19:3
Beatty, Morgan Mrs, 1957, My 27,23:2
Beatty, Ogden, 1963, O 23,41:5
Beatty, Olive Mrs (will), 1952, N 12,29:4
Beatty, Owen I, 1963, Ag 31,17:1
Beatty, Parker, 1940, N 4,19:5
Beatty, Richmond C, 1961, O 11,47:3
Beatty, Robert A, 1957, N 12,37:2
Beatty, Robert C, 1942, N 18,26:3
Beatty, Roy H, 1947, D 6,15:2
Beatty, Sadie C Mrs, 1937, F 13,13:3
Beatty, Sarah F, 1942, N 29,65:2
Beatty, Suzanne S, 1945, Mr 13,23:2
Beatty, Wallace A, 1938, D 2,23:2
Beatty, Willard W, 1961, S 30,25:7
Beatty, William, 1957, Jl 17,27:1
Beatty, William E, 1957, F 18,27:1
Beatty, William V, 1953, Ja 24,15:4
Beattys, Harry H, 1939, Mr 11,17:3
Beatus, Lawrence, 1959, My 30,17:4
Beaty, Amos L, 1939, Ap 30,45:1
Beaty, Arthur H, 1941, Ja 31,19:6
Beaty, Herman C (corr, O 31,49:1), 1943, O 30,15:2
Beaty, John O, 1961, S 13,45:5
Beaty, Richard A D, 1951, F 5,23:3
Beaty, Richard N, 1965, F 6,25:2
Beaty, Terence A, 1951, D 14,31:3
Beaty-Pownall, Charles, 1938, Ag 18,19:2
Beau, Annie M Mrs, 1943, S 3,19:2
Beaubaire, Stanley S, 1949, Mr 21,25:6
Beaubien, Alexander, 1907, Mr 26,9:5
Beaubien, C P, 1949, Ja 19,27:3
Beaubien, Joseph, 1949, Mr 4,21:2
Beaubien, Louis de G, 1939, N 14,23:3
Beaucage, George, 1951, N 5,31:2
Beauchamp, Earl of, 1938, N 15,23:5
Beauchamp, Edwin F, 1958, O 10,31:3
Beauchamp, Harold, 1938, O 5,23:4
Beauchamp, Henry, 1948, Ap 27,25:2
Beauchamp, James M, 1958, N 15,23:4
Beauchamp, John W, 1957, My 18,19:5
Beauchamp, Joseph G, 1953, Je 1,23:6
Beauchamp, Reginald Proctor Sir, 1912, N 12,13:5
Beauchamp, Wilbur L, 1962, Mr 1,31:3
Beauchamp, William M Rev Dr, 1925, D 14,21:3
Beauchat, Augustus Mrs, 1952, Ag 15,15:3
Beauclair, Josephine F, 1941, Ap 11,21:2
Beauclerk, Henry W, 1937, Ja 22,21:3
Beauclerk, Osborne de V (Duke of St Albans), 1964, Mr 3,35:2
Beaudet, Louise, 1948, Ja 1,23:2
Beaudette, Fred R, 1957, Ja 18,22:4
Beaudette, O J, 1944, Ja 7,17:3
Beaudine, Harold, 1949, My 10,25:5
Beaudine, Milton J, 1961, Mr 22,41:5
Beaudouin, Harry E, 1948, Je 6,73:1
Beaudrias, Isidore J, 1949, Ap 5,29:3
Beaudry, Ernest G, 1943, Ja 7,19:3
Beaudry, George, 1940, D 8,71:1
Beaudry, George H, 1966, Ja 1,17:3
Beaudry, Joseph O, 1943, Je 1,23:4
Beauer, Harry, 1937, F 22,17:5
Beaufort, Altha C Mrs, 1937, My 10,19:3
Beaufort, Duke of (Hy Adelbert Wellington Somerset), 1924, N 28,15:4
Beaufort, Jan D H de, 1946, Ap 4,25:3
Beaufort, Leo J C, 1965, Je 10,35:2
Beaufort, Louis Prof, 1937, Mr 20,19:4
Beaufort, W H de, 1918, Ap 3,13:4
Beaufrere, Gustave A Jr, 1948, N 30,27:2
Beauharnais, Guillaume de Count, 1948, Ap 22,22:3
Beaujon, Austin L, 1960, Mr 18,25:3
Beauley, Harriet Mrs, 1959, Mr 18,38:1
Beaulieu, William C, 1964, S 5,19:4
Beaulisisant, G Capt, 1878, S 28,2:6
Beaumister, Otho S, 1938, N 19,17:5
Beaumont, Andre A, 1944, N 25,13:3
Beaumont, Arthur, 1956, Ap 5,29:1; 1961, F 11,23:5
Beaumont, Charles, 1967, F 23,35:3
Beaumont, Clarence, 1956, Ap 12,31:5
Beaumont, E B Col, 1916, Ag 18,9:4
Beaumont, Etienne de Count, 1956, F 6,23:4
Beaumont, Florence S, 1964, Mr 30,29:2
Beaumont, G Berry, 1946, Ag 29,27:1
Beaumont, Gabriel, 1962, Jl 23,12:3
Beaumont, Hartford, 1962, Ja 23,33:2
Beaumont, Henry, 1947, F 22,13:2; 1949, D 18,89:1
Beaumont, Hubert, 1948, D 3,26:3
Beaumont, Hubert Mrs, 1917, Ag 17,9:7
Beaumont, J C Rear Adm, 1882, Ag 4,5:2
Beaumont, James Brown Rev Dr, 1916, F 11,11:5
Beaumont, Jean G D de, 1955, O 15,15:3
Beaumont, John C, 1942, Ap 13,15:4
Beaumont, John W, 1941, Jl 19,13:2
Beaumont, Joseph Mrs, 1945, D 22,19:2
Beaumont, Lewis Lady, 1907, D 2,9:5
Beaumont, Louis D, 1942, O 2,25:1
Beaumont, Louis D (will), 1943, Ap 23,22:7
Beaumont, Lucy, 1937, Ap 25,II,8:2
Beaumont, Martha C, 1943, Ja 30,15:4
Beaumont, Nellie, 1938, O 27,23:5
Beaumont, Oliver, 1953, D 30,23:1
Beaumont, Ralph H, 1953, S 22,31:1
Beaumont, Thomas W, 1942, F 14,15:2
Beaumont-Vassy, Vicompte de, 1875, Jl 27,4:6
Beaunier, Andre, 1925, D 11,23:4
Beaupre, Arthur M, 1919, S 15,11:6
Beaupre, Arthur M Mrs, 1947, Ag 8,17:4
Beauregard, Augustin T, 1951, Ap 10,27:3
Beauregard, Joseph A (Bro Elie Justin), 1953, M 88:4

Beauregard, Marie-Chas-Albert de, 1909, F 16,9:5
Beauregard, P G T Gen, 1893, F 21,1:3
Beauregard, Paul, 1919, Mr 23,20:4
Beaurepaire, Frank, 1956, My 30,21:4
Beausejour, Felis Mrs, 1937, Je 4,23:3
Beaussart, Roger, 1952, Mr 1,15:3
Beauvais, Emile, 1967, Ag 19,25:2
Beauvalet, Pierre, 1942, N 22,52:3
Beauvelt, John W, 1914, D 18,13:6
Beaux, Cecilia, 1942, S 18,21:1
Beavan, Albert W, 1943, Ja 25,14:2
Beaven, Albert W Mrs, 1938, Ap 16,13:5
Beaven, Robert, 1920, S 20,15:5
Beaven, Thomas D Bp, 1920, O 6,15:5
Beaver, Charles W, 1944, S 26,23:5
Beaver, Donald E, 1950, My 21,104:5
Beaver, George, 1961, Ap 16,87:1
Beaver, George W, 1944, Je 24,13:6
Beaver, Gilbert A, 1952, Ap 19,15:3
Beaver, Harry C, 1947, Ap 4,24:2
Beaver, Howard T, 1962, S 16,86:2
Beaver, Hugh, 1967, Ja 18,43:1
Beaver, John, 1917, Ap 21,13:6
Beaver, John A, 1942, Jl 14,19:5
Beaver, Rex P Mrs (Jennie), 1965, Ag 3,31:2
Beaver, Walter S, 1957, Je 7,24:2
Beaverbrook, Lord (Wm M Aitken),(will, Ag 14,14:1), 1964, Je 10,1:4
Beavers, George, 1941, N 24,17:5
Beavers, James L, 1942, N 10,28:3
Beavers, John M Mrs, 1950, D 28,25:2
Beavers, Julia H Mrs, 1941, Je 17,21:6
Beavers, Louis (Mrs L Moore), 1962, O 27,25:2
Beavers, Vernon E, 1951, Mr 23,21:5
Beaverson, James H Y, 1965, O 20,47:5
Beavin, Ambrose H, 1942, Jl 29,17:4
Beazell, William P, 1946, Mr 13,30:2
Beazley, Charles, 1939, S 10,49:3
Beazley, Richard G, 1950, My 4,27:4
Beazley, Rosalind R Mrs, 1924, Ap 23,21:4
Beazley, Samuel W, 1944, S 18,19:4
Beazley, Wayland L Mrs, 1944, N 10,19:4
Beban, G, 1928, O 6,19:4
Bebb, Charles H, 1942, Je 22,15:2
Bebb, Joseph C, 1957, S 23,27:3
Bebee, Edwin H, 1962, S 28,33:5
Bebek, Tibor K J, 1960, S 29,35:2
Bebel, August F, 1913, Ag 14,9:6
Bebel, F A, 1882, S 16,5:3
Bebelheimer, Bruce G Dr, 1937, O 24,II,8:3
Bebie, Edwin W, 1959, S 17,39:4
Bebie, Jules, 1956, Je 11,31:4
Bebilacqua, Duardo, 1941, Jl 29,15:1
Bebout, Frank, 1940, Ag 24,13:6
Bebout, Gaylord N, 1941, Ap 11,21:2
Bebout, Thomas L, 1949, Je 29,27:4
Bebrits, Lajos, 1963, Ag 11,84:3
Becan, John, 1956, Ag 19,93:1
Becatoros, Spyros, 1938, N 15,23:4
Beccari, Filippo M, 1938, D 1,23:4
Beccaris, Frank C, 1954, Mr 26,21:3
Becerra, Leon Dr, 1921, Mr 5,13:4
Bech, Georg, 1951, F 9,26:2
Bechdel, Samuel I, 1948, S 14,29:2
Bechdolt, Adolph F, 1938, My 7,15:2
Bechdolt, Jack Mrs, 1961, S 9,19:3
Bechdolt, John E, 1955, Ja 1,13:6
Becher, Arthur E, 1960, N 5,23:3
Becher, B, 1877, My 18,4:7
Becher, Charles, 1943, Jl 18,34:7
Becher, Harold, 1967, Je 1,44:1
Becher, Johannes R, 1958, O 12,86:4
Becher, Lady (Miss O'Neill), 1872, N 15,5:6
Becherer, Frank H, 1951, Ja 26,23:3
Bechert, Fred J, 1960, F 24,37:1
Bechert, Paul, 1953, Mr 4,27:4
Bechet, Alfred C Mrs, 1941, Mr 13,21:4
Bechet, Alfred C Sr, 1947, D 27,13:4
Bechet, Paul E, 1962, Ja 4,34:1
Bechet, Sidney (funl, My 20,35:3), 1959, My 15,29:1
Bechhold, Siegfried, 1956, F 8,33:2
Becht, Francis C, 1950, Ag 19,13:5
Becht, J George, 1925, Ap 27,17:5
Bechtel, Charles P, 1941, Ja 3,19:2
Bechtel, Edwin D, 1957, Jl 6,15:4
Bechtel, Frederick H, 1945, D 12,27:3
Bechtel, George M, 1952, Mr 23,92:1
Bechtel, John, 1882, My 28,6:6
Bechtel, John C, 1940, Mr 15,23:1
Bechtel, Joseph B, 1946, F 25,25:2
Bechtel, Laura A, 1963, N 28,39:1
Bechtel, Oliver P Ex-Judge, 1919, S 23,17:3
Bechtel, Ralph, 1912, Ja 14,II,16:2
Bechtel, V Richard, 1967, O 6,39:2
Bechtel, W A, 1933, Ag 29,17:1
Bechtel, William H, 1957, My 25,21:6
Bechthold, A H Rev, 1884, N 17,5:5
Bechtol, Lula C Mrs, 1942, N 1,52:4
Bechtold, Edward S, 1953, Ag 24,23:4
Bechtold, George H, 1954, Jl 7,31:2
Bechtold, Gustavus, 1965, D 9,47:1
Bechtold, John J, 1949, Ja 8,15:5; 1953, Ag 10,23:6
Bechtold, Julian F, 1955, My 26,31:1
Bechtold, Lena K Mrs, 1938, Ja 4,23:2
Bechtold, Lewis, 1953, N 11,31:5
Bechtold, William S, 1941, Je 12,23:5
Bechtold, William V, 1949, N 24,31:5
Bechyne, Rudolf, 1948, Ja 3,13:5
Beck, A J, 1949, S 21,32:3
Beck, Adam L, 1939, Ag 11,15:5
Beck, Adam Lady, 1921, O 18,17:4
Beck, Adam Sir, 1925, Ag 17,15:5
Beck, Albert, 1962, Je 2,19:2
Beck, Albert A, 1947, D 5,25:2
Beck, Albert L, 1948, F 14,13:1
Beck, Alex S, 1955, Ap 13,29:2
Beck, Alga M, 1951, Jl 11,23:5
Beck, Alvin B Mrs, 1966, Je 25,31:4
Beck, Andre, 1957, F 21,27:4
Beck, Andrew, 1944, N 8,17:4
Beck, Anna S, 1945, My 9,23:5
Beck, Anthony, 1948, My 18,24:2
Beck, August B, 1951, Je 15,23:4
Beck, August L, 1958, Jl 8,28:1
Beck, Bodog F, 1942, Ja 2,23:4
Beck, C Weston, 1953, S 1,23:2
Beck, Carl, 1952, Jl 23,23:6; 1965, Je 7,37:2
Beck, Carl Dr, 1911, Je 9,13:5
Beck, Carol H, 1908, O 16,9:5
Beck, Celia, 1949, Ap 18,25:2
Beck, Charles E, 1948, Ap 30,23:2; 1949, F 1,25:1
Beck, Charles J, 1947, N 4,25:2
Beck, Charles W, 1939, Mr 20,17:4
Beck, Charles W Jr, 1960, N 8,29:1
Beck, Charleston T, 1946, Ja 24,22:3
Beck, Christian H Mrs, 1960, Je 19,88:6
Beck, Christian J (por), 1949, Je 18,13:3
Beck, Cornelius, 1925, Mr 23,17:4
Beck, Dave Mrs, 1961, N 25,23:1
Beck, David M, 1956, D 9,88:2
Beck, Edward Anthony, 1916, Ap 13,13:5
Beck, Edward C, 1954, My 4,29:2
Beck, Edward E Mrs, 1949, D 9,31:2
Beck, Edward L, 1962, O 17,39:1
Beck, Edward L Mrs, 1948, My 22,15:3
Beck, Edward S, 1942, D 26,11:3
Beck, Edward S Mrs, 1960, My 13,31:4
Beck, Edwin, 1943, O 10,48:4
Beck, Edwin F, 1941, D 20,19:3
Beck, Elsie R Mrs, 1941, Je 10,23:2
Beck, Emil, 1939, N 25,17:2
Beck, Ernest W, 1951, Mr 13,31:2
Beck, Eugene (Gene), 1953, F 27,14:8
Beck, Eugene M, 1946, Ap 30,21:1
Beck, Evelyn E, 1944, Jl 23,35:3
Beck, Ferdinand L, 1946, Je 26,25:4
Beck, Frank H, 1962, Mr 23,33:2
Beck, Frank J, 1947, Ap 13,61:1
Beck, Fred M, 1962, My 7,31:2
Beck, Frederick, 1907, Ap 23,9:4
Beck, Frederick G, 1957, Ag 25,86:6
Beck, Frederick J, 1951, O 11,37:4
Beck, George, 1939, Ap 7,22:3; 1962, F 18,92:5
Beck, George B, 1961, Ja 7,19:5
Beck, George P Sr, 1961, Mr 25,25:5
Beck, George W T, 1943, D 3,24:2
Beck, Gilbert M, 1953, Ja 10,17:6
Beck, Harold E, 1957, My 27,31:1
Beck, Harry, 1956, Mr 2,23:1
Beck, Harry B, 1951, Jl 9,25:4
Beck, Harry M, 1952, Jl 24,27:2
Beck, Henry A W, 1939, F 19,39:2
Beck, Henry C, 1948, D 7,31:1
Beck, Henry E, 1952, Je 4,27:2
Beck, Henry M, 1943, F 3,19:5
Beck, Herman, 1954, O 15,23:3
Beck, Herman C, 1952, Mr 28,23:3
Beck, Howard S, 1937, S 23,27:6
Beck, Irving, 1962, Ja 29,25:3
Beck, Israel, 1958, Ap 21,23:4
Beck, J Alfred, 1952, D 7,89:2
Beck, J D, 1936, N 10,25:5
Beck, J Frank, 1941, F 13,19:4
Beck, J M, 1936, Ap 13,1:2
Beck, J M Mrs, 1950, Jl 5,31:3
Beck, J T Von Dr, 1879, F 3,2:7
Beck, Jacob Mrs, 1949, D 16,31:5
Beck, James, 1875, Mr 17,1:6
Beck, James M Mrs, 1956, Ag 2,25:4
Beck, Jean B, 1943, Je 24,21:3
Beck, Jerome, 1946, D 25,29:2
Beck, John, 1875, My 9,10:5; 1938, D 2,14:2
Beck, John K, 1952, D 4,35:3
Beck, John R, 1947, Ja 5,53:4
Beck, John W, 1951, Ap 7,15:4
Beck, Joseph, 1944, Je 7,19:1
Beck, Joseph A, 1965, F 9,37:3
Beck, Joseph W, 1965, Je 29,32:7
Beck, Julius E, 1949, Ag 9,25:3
Beck, Lafayette D, 1939, Ap 22,17:2
Beck, Lawrence T Mrs, 1954, Jl 8,23:1
Beck, Lester E, 1955, F 3,23:4
Beck, Louis R, 1948, D 15,33:4
Beck, Ludger Rev, 1909, Ag 11,7:4
Beck, Marcus W, 1943, Ja 22,19:5
Beck, Martin, 1940, N 17,49:1
Beck, Mary Mrs, 1946, Jl 6,15:6
Beck, Mitchel, 1954, F 8,23:4
Beck, Morey M, 1938, D 19,23:4
Beck, Morris B, 1957, My 17,25:3
Beck, Morris Mrs, 1963, O 20,88:8
Beck, Otto, 1938, Ja 9,43:2
Beck, Otto O, 1950, F 1,29:4
Beck, Paul, 1955, F 5,15:2
Beck, Peter L, 1962, Mr 17,25:1
Beck, Phil, 1950, N 11,15:3
Beck, R Donald, 1957, D 9,35:4
Beck, Rachel Mrs, 1938, Je 25,15:4
Beck, Raymond, 1953, S 18,23:4
Beck, Raymond W, 1946, Jl 12,17:5
Beck, Richmond J, 1952, N 13,31:3
Beck, S Scott, 1944, Mr 14,19:4
Beck, Thomas C, 1944, S 3,27:2
Beck, Thomas H, 1951, O 17,31:3
Beck, Thomas H Mrs, 1946, O 9,27:3; 1954, Ag 2,17:3
Beck, Walter, 1954, S 6,15:2
Beck, Walter Mrs, 1959, D 30,21:4
Beck, William, 1925, D 1,25:4; 1952, Ap 30,27:5
Beck, William E, 1949, My 11,29:3
Beck, William F, 1949, Mr 24,27:2
Beck, William H, 1955, S 11,84:6; 1957, Mr 31,89:1
Beck, William H Brig-Gen, 1911, N 28,13:4
Beck, William J A, 1944, Je 28,23:5
Beck, William L, 1955, Mr 1,25:4
Beck, William Mrs, 1940, N 6,23:2; 1953, Ja 26,19:3
Beck, William P, 1952, F 13,29:2
Becka, John W, 1949, Ag 2,19:2
Beckaustin, Rosalind M Mrs, 1938, Mr 20,II,9:1
Beckel, Joseph, 1904, Ap 8,9:6
Beckelman, Moses W, 1955, D 11,88:3
Beckelman, Moses W (mem ser), 1956, Ja 12,27:4
Beckenbaugh, John K, 1940, O 7,17:5
Beckendorf, Max, 1968, Je 2,76:8
Beckenstein, Nathan Dr, 1968, O 18,47:1
Becker, A G, 1925, My 15,19:5
Becker, Abigail, 1905, Mr 24,9:6
Becker, Adolph E Mrs, 1955, N 3,31:2
Becker, Adolph F, 1938, Ap 7,23:3
Becker, Adolph F Mrs, 1950, S 30,17:3
Becker, Albert F, 1938, Jl 18,13:5
Becker, Alfred D, 1950, Jl 3,15:5
Becker, Alfred L, 1948, Jl 14,23:3
Becker, Andrew, 1937, N 19,23:3
Becker, Anna C Mrs (will), 1940, Ag 24,7:2
Becker, Arman E, 1965, Ap 30,35:4
Becker, Arthur D, 1947, Mr 17,23:2
Becker, August, 1871, Ap 5,2:3
Becker, Benjamin O, 1953, N 28,15:6
Becker, Bernard J, 1960, N 1,39:4
Becker, Bernard J Mrs, 1953, Jl 26,69:2
Becker, Bobby (J J Emerling), 1954, N 27,13:4
Becker, Burton A, 1956, Jl 11,29:3
Becker, Carl, 1943, Ja 4,15:5
Becker, Carl E, 1938, My 10,21:5
Becker, Carl E G, 1953, O 31,17:3
Becker, Carl L, 1945, Ap 11,23:5
Becker, Charles, 1952, N 15,17:2; 1961, Ag 31,27:1
Becker, Charles A, 1959, O 7,43:1
Becker, Charles F, 1948, Je 11,23:3; 1951, Jl 24,25:1
Becker, Charlotte L, 1946, F 6,23:3
Becker, Clarence D, 1947, Ag 29,17:4
Becker, Claude M, 1960, Jl 16,19:2
Becker, Conrad L, 1940, Ap 2,25:2
Becker, David, 1954, My 7,23:3
Becker, Edward F, 1954, Je 11,23:5
Becker, Edward J, 1965, Ja 25,37:5
Becker, Edward L, 1963, Jl 22,23:5
Becker, Edwin J, 1925, Ja 9,17:3
Becker, Eleanor E, 1963, Je 17,25:1
Becker, Elizabeth T Mrs, 1955, Mr 31,27:5
Becker, Emil, 1938, Ja 18,23:2
Becker, Emily A Mrs, 1940, N 24,49:3
Becker, Emily F, 1941, F 25,23:3
Becker, Frank A, 1938, Ja 1,19:5
Becker, Frank J, 1941, Ap 7,17:5
Becker, Frederick G, 1953, O 27,27:4
Becker, Frederick J, 1952, Ag 9,13:4
Becker, Frederick W, 1938, Je 25,15:5
Becker, Gabe B, 1962, Ja 21,88:5
Becker, George, 1905, Mr 31,9:6
Becker, George F, 1953, D 20,77:2
Becker, George F Dr, 1919, Ap 22,17:2
Becker, George H, 1954, F 23,27:4
Becker, George J, 1943, N 10,23:4
Becker, George L Gen, 1904, Ja 8,7:5
Becker, George Mrs, 1946, N 27,25:1
Becker, George O, 1964, O 4,88:5
Becker, Gilbert Mrs, 1945, My 15,19:2
Becker, Gustaf L, 1947, Ja 13,21:2
Becker, Gustave L, 1959, F 27,25:3
Becker, H Kirke, 1949, Je 22,31:3
Becker, Harrison, 1941, Ap 4,21:3
Becker, Helene S Mrs, 1940, Ag 15,19:3
Becker, Henry, 1956, My 22,33:5
Becker, Henry A, 1939, Je 20,21:1
Becker, Henry B, 1940, O 11,21:4
Becker, Henry C, 1938, Je 11,15:2; 1962, O 19,31:3
Becker, Henry C Mrs, 1958, Jl 17,27:5
Becker, Henry E, 1941, S 24,23:6

Becker, Henry L, 1948, Je 30,25:4
Becker, Henry M, 1950, Mr 26,92:6
Becker, Herman, 1957, S 10,33:4
Becker, Hiram E, 1940, O 26,15:6
Becker, Hiram Mrs, 1953, F 28,17:7
Becker, Hubert, 1948, O 30,15:2
Becker, I Newton Mrs, 1957, My 27,31:5
Becker, Ida, 1943, D 27,19:1
Becker, Ike, 1950, Jl 6,28:2
Becker, Irving N, 1953, O 14,29:1
Becker, Isidor S, 1963, Je 5,41:3
Becker, Ivan S Mrs, 1951, Je 13,29:4
Becker, Jacob S, 1960, S 20,39:1
Becker, Jacques, 1960, F 22,17:4
Becker, John, 1938, Ag 12,17:3
Becker, John I, 1939, Mr 16,23:3
Becker, John J, 1961, Ja 22,84:6
Becker, John L, 1957, Ap 11,31:4
Becker, Joseph, 1966, F 27,84:5
Becker, Joseph A, 1961, Jl 13,29:6
Becker, Joseph F, 1944, Ag 16,19:3
Becker, Joseph P, 1947, Ag 24,56:4
Becker, Joseph W, 1949, Je 14,31:2
Becker, Jules, 1962, Ja 9,94:6
Becker, Jules Mrs, 1962, Ja 9,94:6
Becker, Julius, 1942, My 9,13:5; 1948, Ag 26,21:2
Becker, Julius A Dr, 1916, D 26,11:5
Becker, Karl, 1940, Ap 9,24:3
Becker, Kurt, 1960, Ag 12,19:3
Becker, Lawrence F, 1947, Mr 14,23:2
Becker, Lawrence M, 1968, Mr 5,41:3
Becker, Le Roy, 1949, Ap 29,23:3
Becker, Leo V, 1956, O 24,37:5
Becker, Lewis W, 1964, F 9,88:6
Becker, Lillian S, 1947, Ag 31,36:7
Becker, Louis, 1937, Jl 26,19:6; 1945, S 2,31:2; 1960, D 19,27:1
Becker, Louis C, 1944, Mr 28,19:5
Becker, Louis J, 1953, Jl 3,19:1
Becker, Louis Mrs, 1939, Ap 19,23:2
Becker, Louis T, 1939, F 22,21:4
Becker, Louise E, 1941, Ap 17,23:2
Becker, Matthew G, 1954, Je 11,23:4
Becker, Max, 1960, Jl 31,69:1
Becker, Max J Mrs, 1948, O 24,76:5
Becker, May L Mrs, 1958, Ap 29,29:4
Becker, Michael J, 1946, Ja 26,13:4
Becker, Morris, 1871, Ap 14,8:4; 1961, O 14,23:6
Becker, Morris S, 1965, Mr 31,39:3
Becker, Murvin B Mrs, 1948, Jl 17,15:1
Becker, N Folke, 1962, Jl 22,64:2
Becker, Neal D, 1955, My 17,29:1
Becker, Niles R Mrs, 1965, Jl 22,31:3
Becker, Norman W, 1945, Mr 25,38:4
Becker, O Godfrey, 1922, Ag 10,11:6
Becker, Ole L, 1949, Mr 30,25:4
Becker, Otto E, 1954, Ag 25,27:2
Becker, Paul, 1966, Je 24,37:3
Becker, Phil Mrs, 1955, N 29,29:2
Becker, Philip L, 1960, D 18,84:3
Becker, Ralph C, 1951, F 11,88:4
Becker, Reinhold S, 1945, D 10,21:4
Becker, Robert, 1942, S 15,24:2
Becker, Robert A, 1961, Ja 22,85:2
Becker, Robert A Mrs, 1947, Je 9,21:3
Becker, Robert B, 1959, Jl 1,31:1
Becker, Robert H, 1940, F 9,19:3
Becker, Rose S Mrs, 1946, Ap 17,25:1
Becker, Rudolph, 1961, Ap 18,37:3
Becker, Rudolph W, 1955, F 15,27:4
Becker, Samuel, 1944, D 27,19:5
Becker, Samuel B, 1942, D 27,34:6
Becker, Sarah Mrs, 1940, N 5,34:1
Becker, Sherburn M, 1949, F 6,77:1
Becker, Sidney D, 1962, Mr 20,37:3
Becker, Theodore H, 1942, S 23,25:5
Becker, Thielo, 1944, D 18,19:1
Becker, Ulrich, 1912, Je 22,13:5
Becker, Willard D, 1945, Ja 26,21:3
Becker, William, 1921, My 7,11:3
Becker, William A, 1951, S 21,24:3
Becker, William J, 1941, Mr 17,17:5; 1949, F 8,25:4; 1949, D 25,26:5
Becker, William J Mrs, 1952, Je 22,68:3
Becker, William J Sr, 1961, Ag 18,21:2
Beckerle, Anne, 1967, Ag 17,37:4
Beckerle, Laurence T Sr, 1966, Je 14,47:1
Beckerle, Peter, 1942, Ja 16,21:2
Beckerman, Abraham I, 1964, Ag 3,23:4
Beckerman, Benjamin, 1939, N 22,21:1
Beckerman, Bernard, 1958, Mr 26,37:4
Beckerman, Henry A, 1949, O 15,15:5
Beckerman, Louis, 1945, Mr 8,23:1
Beckerman, Milton Mrs, 1966, Ag 18,35:3
Beckerman, Simeon J Mrs, 1960, Ag 4,25:4
Beckers, William G, 1948, N 5,26:2
Beckers, William Gerald Mrs, 1924, Jl 14,15:4
Beckert, Ernest G, 1950, S 21,31:1
Beckert, Walter A, 1947, Ap 20,63:1
Becket, Frederick M, 1942, D 2,25:1
Becket, George C, 1947, N 13,27:3
Becket, George C Mrs, 1942, Ag 28,19:4
Becket, J Fred, 1954, D 1,31:2
Becket, Maria a, 1904, S 8,7:6
Beckett, Charles Henry, 1917, N 30,13:6
Beckett, Eric, 1966, Ag 30,41:3
Beckett, Ernest William (Lord Grimthorpe), 1917, My 10,13:6
Beckett, Estelle J N Mrs, 1941, Jl 2,21:4
Beckett, Frederick W, 1953, Mr 24,42:3
Beckett, George Rev, 1907, D 15,13:4
Beckett, Gervase, 1937, Ag 25,21:5
Beckett, Gervase (will), 1938, Ja 20,3:6
Beckett, Harry, 1880, O 25,2:4
Beckett, Herbert P, 1953, Jl 23,23:5
Beckett, James J, 1949, O 13,27:2
Beckett, Katherine B Mrs, 1937, Jl 1,27:5
Beckett, Richard C, 1948, D 17,27:1; 1954, Ja 16,15:5
Beckett, Rupert E, 1955, Ap 26,29:4
Beckett, Samuel W, 1939, Ag 1,19:3
Beckett, Scotty, 1968, My 16,47:2
Beckett, Theodore Mrs, 1953, Ja 8,30:1
Beckford, Vern, 1960, My 7,23:2
Beckham, Henry F, 1954, O 7,23:4
Beckham, John C W, 1940, Ja 10,21:1
Beckham, Joseph C, 1954, N 23,33:1
Beckham, Walter H, 1960, O 25,35:2
Beckhard, Arthur Mrs (E Dale), 1961, Jl 24,23:4
Beckhard, Martin A, 1942, S 28,17:3
Beckhardt, Adolf, 1962, Ja 3,33:3
Beckhardt, Moses, 1940, Ap 15,17:4
Beckingham, Daniel F, 1941, O 29,23:3
Beckingham, Harry B, 1953, My 12,27:5
Beckington, Alice, 1942, Ja 6,23:4
Beckjord, Walter C, 1966, Ja 1,17:3
Beckles, Winslow A, 1965, Jl 23,26:7
Beckley, Albert J Mrs, 1949, My 27,21:3
Beckley, Frank E, 1966, Jl 2,23:5
Beckley, George H Bp, 1924, D 25,17:6
Beckley, Harold R (funl, Ap 2,13:8), 1955, Mr 30, 29:3
Beckley, J Harold, 1947, Je 3,25:1
Beckley, John, 1948, Ag 12,21:4
Beckley, John G, 1942, N 18,25:4
Beckley, John T Rev Dr, 1908, F 15,7:6
Beckley, Leonard W, 1945, My 15,19:3
Beckley, Pendleton, 1955, Mr 26,15:4
Beckley, Stewart D, 1962, F 8,31:4
Beckley, William, 1948, D 30,22:2
Beckley, William B, 1916, Mr 25,13:6
Beckley, William S Jr, 1950, Ja 13,23:5
Beckley, Zoe, 1961, Ja 15,86:6
Beckly, Chester C Dr, 1921, F 6,22:4
Beckman, Albert, 1952, S 7,84:5
Beckman, Charles D, 1948, D 30,19:5
Beckman, Clarence P, 1953, D 19,15:3
Beckman, Ernst, 1924, Ap 18,19:5
Beckman, Francis J L, 1948, O 18,23:2
Beckman, Frederic Mrs, 1947, Ja 23,23:1
Beckman, Frederick W, 1957, Jl 11,25:5
Beckman, H D, 1942, Mr 18,23:3
Beckman, Harold E, 1964, F 22,21:1
Beckman, Harold W, 1942, D 29,21:1
Beckman, Herman C, 1966, D 11,88:8
Beckman, John A Sr, 1950, N 7,27:2
Beckman, Johnny, 1968, Je 24,37:2
Beckman, Leo J, 1953, D 23,26:3
Beckman, Mary (Mrs Clarkson Cranmer), 1968, F 13,43:3
Beckman, Thomas J, 1939, Mr 5,48:6
Beckman, Vincent H Sr, 1951, N 17,17:3
Beckman, William, 1953, F 11,31:2
Beckman, William Mrs, 1948, O 6,29:3
Beckman, William W, 1951, Ap 14,15:5
Beckmann, Charles F, 1940, O 14,19:2
Beckmann, Charles O Dr, 1968, Ap 10,47:2
Beckmann, Francis, 1963, O 31,33:3
Beckmann, Fred, 1941, O 18,19:2
Beckmann, Henry C, 1939, Je 27,23:4
Beckmann, J William, 1950, S 9,17:4
Beckmann, John H, 1949, O 27,27:2
Beckmann, John M (will, O 3,12:5), 1961, Mr 26,55:3
Beckmann, Max, 1950, D 28,25:1
Beckmann, Rudolf R, 1960, Jl 8,21:1
Beckmans, Bruce Mrs, 1961, Je 28,70:4
Beckmeyer, E F, 1948, Ap 22,27:3
Beckmeyer, John H, 1945, Je 18,19:2
Beckner, Algernon S, 1954, Je 12,15:5
Beckner, Walter, 1950, F 28,19:3
Becks, Hermann, 1962, Jl 17,25:3
Beckstein, Gustave F, 1949, N 7,27:4
Beckton, Maxwell W, 1951, Ja 3,25:2
Beckurts, Charles L, 1939, Je 18,37:1
Beckus, J P, 1946, D 20,23:4
Beckwith, Alfred T, 1945, O 28,44:3
Beckwith, Anson J, 1954, Je 28,19:4
Beckwith, Bertha D, 1967, Ag 22,34:8
Beckwith, Carroll, 1917, O 25,15:3
Beckwith, Charles Barnes, 1925, Ja 21,21:5
Beckwith, Charles C, 1956, D 21,23:2
Beckwith, Charles D, 1941, O 11,17:3
Beckwith, Charles D Mrs, 1947, Jl 11,15:1
Beckwith, Charles F, 1945, D 3,21:6; 1957, D 17,35:3
Beckwith, Charles H, 1944, Ap 8,7:1
Beckwith, Charles L, 1952, Jl 7,21:6
Beckwith, Charles S, 1944, My 19,19:2
Beckwith, Daniel Mrs, 1947, N 17,21:1
Beckwith, Edgar W, 1957, S 26,25:2
Beckwith, Edmund R, 1949, D 18,90:2
Beckwith, Edward P, 1966, Jl 7,37:2
Beckwith, Frank, 1954, S 10,23:1
Beckwith, Franklin H, 1949, Jl 14,27:4
Beckwith, Fred A, 1952, Mr 25,27:2
Beckwith, Freeman B, 1937, F 9,23:5
Beckwith, George, 1949, N 21,25:4
Beckwith, George H, 1938, N 26,15:5; 1949, N 11,25:4
Beckwith, George S, 1937, Jl 31,15:4
Beckwith, Henry, 1942, Ap 8,19:3
Beckwith, Henry S, 1943, F 26,19:3
Beckwith, Hiram W, 1903, D 24,9:5
Beckwith, James L, 1948, My 8,13:6
Beckwith, James S, 1951, D 18,31:3
Beckwith, Julius H, 1954, N 11,36:7
Beckwith, Laurence, 1946, Je 1,13:1
Beckwith, Oliver R, 1949, Ja 30,60:6
Beckwith, Richard L Mrs, 1955, F 13,86:8
Beckwith, Robert W, 1940, Jl 6,15:6
Beckwith, S R Dr, 1905, Ja 21,7:2
Beckwith, Sanford Mrs, 1948, Ag 8,57:3
Beckwith, T Arnold, 1951, Ap 11,29:1
Beckwith, Theodore D, 1946, Jl 19,19:3
Beckwith-Ewen, Starr L, 1951, My 15,31:5
Beckwitt, Harry J, 1937, Ag 12,19:5
Beckx, P J Father, 1887, Mr 5,5:3
Becmer, Stephen Mrs, 1950, F 21,26:3
Becquerel, Henri, 1908, Ag 26,7:6
Becquerer, M, 1871, Mr 31,1:3
Becton, Maxwell W Mrs, 1938, N 17,25:3
Becton, Simeon I, 1939, Jl 12,19:6
Bedard, Avila, 1960, My 4,45:1
Bedard, Frederick S Jr, 1947, My 9,21:2
Bedbrook, Ernest A St George Maj (funl, My 5,23:1), 1918, My 2,13:3
Beddall, Anna M Mrs, 1943, N 2,25:2
Beddall, Edward Fitch, 1918, D 9,13:4
Beddingfield, Talmadge J, 1959, D 6,86:2
Beddington-Behrens, Edward Sir, 1968, D 1,86:4
Beddoe, Dan (por), 1937, D 28,21:1
Beddow, Clarence E, 1952, Ag 22,21:4
Beddow, Ira A, 1950, Ap 5,31:3
Beddows, Richard, 1922, F 17,15:5
Bede, J Adam, 1942, Ap 12,44:6
Bedea, Charles A, 1948, Ag 31,26:1
Bedel, John Gen, 1875, F 28,6:7
Bedel, Maurice, 1954, O 16,17:4
Bedell, Alan T, 1918, F 26,13:4
Bedell, Alanson S, 1943, Je 29,19:3
Bedell, Alfred M, 1951, Jl 15,60:6
Bedell, Arthur, 1948, D 14,29:3
Bedell, Arthur G, 1916, Ag 6,17:6
Bedell, Arthur S, 1946, Mr 31,46:3
Bedell, Augustus C, 1937, S 4,15:4
Bedell, Chester S, 1954, O 16,17:5
Bedell, Cornelia F, 1951, Je 3,92:6
Bedell, Daniel J Mrs, 1947, O 3,25:4
Bedell, Edward J, 1948, S 25,17:5
Bedell, Edwin F, 1912, N 22,13:3
Bedell, Francis H Mrs, 1968, Mr 10,92:6
Bedell, Frank L, 1943, S 23,21:3
Bedell, Frank M, 1949, D 13,38:4
Bedell, George A, 1940, O 6,48:3
Bedell, George V, 1948, O 11,23:4
Bedell, Harry E, 1937, S 30,23:2
Bedell, Harvey S, 1914, Ap 26,IV,7:5
Bedell, Henry, 1938, Mr 12,17:4
Bedell, James, 1950, Je 3,15:6
Bedell, James W Jr, 1937, Ag 6,17:5
Bedell, John H Mrs, 1948, Je 14,23:3
Bedell, Louis, 1947, Mr 21,21:3
Bedell, Mabel E Mrs, 1937, Jl 12,18:2
Bedell, Max, 1960, O 4,43:3
Bedell, Myron, 1950, F 2,27:1
Bedell, Nettie Mrs, 1940, D 26,19:3
Bedell, Walter H Mrs, 1951, Je 16,15:4
Bedell, William E, 1951, Je 27,29:2
Bedell, William M, 1954, Jl 27,21:5
Bedenkapp, Glen R, 1966, Je 6,41:1
Beder, Henry M Mrs, 1951, My 9,33:4
Beder, William J, 1923, Ja 13,13:5
Bedford, Albert M, 1940, Ap 5,21:1
Bedford, Alfred, 1912, O 9,13:6
Bedford, Alfred C Mrs, 1944, Mr 2,17:3
Bedford, Alfred Cotton (funl, S 23,25:4), 1925, S 2 25:3
Bedford, Alfred Cotton (por), 1925, S 22,25:4
Bedford, Alfred Cotton, 1925, N 9,19:4
Bedford, Bruce Sr, 1962, Jl 29,61:2
Bedford, C Reynolds, 1944, O 16,19:3
Bedford, Charles E, 1961, O 28,21:5
Bedford, Daniel H, 1943, N 17,25:1; 1949, O 25,27
Bedford, Dowager Duchess of, 1960, O 3,31:4
Bedford, Duke of (Wm Russell), 1872, My 28,1:5
Bedford, Duke of, 1893, Mr 25,2:2
Bedford, Duke of (will, D 17,9:1), 1940, Ag 28,19
Bedford, Duke of (will, N 11,27:5), 1953, O 12,1
Bedford, E T, 1931, My 22,25:1
Bedford, Edgar A, 1938, S 29,25:6
Bedford, Edward B, 1953, O 14,29:3
Bedford, Edward H, 1939, Ap 4,25:1

Bedford, Edward T, 1952, F 14,27:2
Bedford, Frank A Jr, 1944, F 24,15:3
Bedford, Frederick H Jr, 1952, D 4,35:1
Bedford, Frederick H Mrs, 1910, D 26,7:6
Bedford, Frederick J Mrs, 1946, S 30,25:4
Bedford, Frederick T, 1963, My 9,37:2
Bedford, Gunning S Dr, 1870, S 6,2:7
Bedford, H M, 1880, Ag 21,5:6
Bedford, Harry, 1941, F 5,20:2
Bedford, Henry C, 1959, N 28,21:3
Bedford, Henry E, 1961, My 6,31:4
Bedford, Henry E Mrs, 1964, Mr 8,87:1
Bedford, Henry P, 1944, Ap 20,19:3
Bedford, J Claude, 1942, F 22,27:2
Bedford, Joseph H, 1951, Ag 25,11:2
Bedford, Lyman O, 1947, Jl 23,23:6
Bedford, Morris, 1937, N 5,23:5
Bedford, Paul, 1967, Ag 18,30:6
Bedford, Paul Mrs (Gertrude V), 1964, N 22,86:7
Bedford, Richard W, 1941, D 5,24:2
Bedford, Sarah J Mrs, 1920, Je 12,13:3
Bedford, Stephen R, 1942, My 10,42:5
Bedford, William H, 1915, Ap 17,11:4
Bedford-Jones, H, 1949, My 7,13:5
Bedichek, Bachman G, 1964, Ja 25,23:4
Bedient, Sidney A Mrs, 1958, My 18,87:1
Bedier, Joseph, 1938, Ag 31,15:2
Bedikian, Dikran M, 1945, F 20,19:3
Bedilion, August K Mrs, 1952, S 6,17:5
Bedinger, George R, 1945, My 8,19:3
Bedingfield, Alfred W, 1943, N 14,57:3
Bedingfield, Victor G L, 1956, O 14,87:2
Bedingfield, Victor G L Mrs, 1963, S 26,35:2
Bedingfield, Victor L, 1906, N 27,9:5
Bedini, Jean, 1956, N 9,29:4
Bedle, A Mrs, 1882, Jl 9,12:2
Bedle, Bennington Randolph, 1917, Ag 14,9:4
Bedle, J D, 1894, O 22,2:6
Bedle, Joseph D, 1942, D 26,11:4
Bedle, Joseph Dorset Ex-Judge, 1917, S 21,9:6
Bedlington, Ann E, 1944, D 13,23:2
Bedlington, Thomas, 1952, Je 30,19:1
Bedloe, Edward Dr, 1915, Jl 25,15:4
Bedlow, Henry, 1914, My 31,5:6
Bedlow, Henry Alfred, 1949, Jl 26,28:3
Bedman, Frank S, 1955, Jl 15,21:4
Bedman, Leon, 1942, D 22,25:5
Bednarchak, Joseph, 1949, N 25,31:4
Bednarczyk, Antoni Mrs, 1943, Ag 29,38:2
Bednarek, George J, 1953, D 18,29:3
Bednarek, Joseph L, 1948, S 8,29:4
Bednarick, John C, 1952, Ag 17,76:6
Bedno, Jacob, 1964, N 14,29:5
Bednorz, Filip, 1954, Ja 16,15:6
Bedow, Vincent Mrs, 1955, Ap 8,21:3
Bedoya, Alfonso (Indio), 1957, D 17,35:3
Bedrick, Emanuel, 1967, D 1,47:3
Bedrick, John, 1942, D 26,11:3
Bedrosian, John, 1949, My 26,30:2
Bedrossian, Edward H, 1948, Ap 19,23:4
Bedsole, Neftel, 1949, Ja 31,19:2
Bedwell, Bettina, 1947, My 1,25:2
Bedwell, Charles F, 1950, F 19,76:1
Bedwell, H Guy, 1952, Ja 2,25:3
Bee, Albert W Jr, 1949, F 16,25:4
Bee, Edward Mrs, 1946, N 16,19:1
Bee, Peter A, 1966, F 3,31:4
Bee, Raymond, 1952, S 3,29:4
Bee, Robert J, 1948, Jl 11,50:8
Beebe, A, 1880, Jl 8,3:2
Beebe, Albert E, 1950, D 12,33:5
Beebe, Albert Rev, 1937, Je 16,23:4
Beebe, Alonzo M, 1954, N 27,13:6
Beebe, Benton L, 1904, Ja 6,9:5
Beebe, Carl V, 1951, Jl 25,23:1
Beebe, Clarence E Mrs, 1917, My 12,11:6
Beebe, Claude S, 1938, My 25,23:1
Beebe, Clifford D, 1937, F 19,19:6
Beebe, David C, 1950, Mr 30,29:1
Beebe, Dwight S Mrs, 1943, Mr 24,24:3
Beebe, E Starks, 1951, D 7,27:3
Beebe, Edward O, 1951, Jl 30,17:5
Beebe, Eleanor H Mrs, 1939, Je 22,23:5
Beebe, Emerson Pratt, 1920, Ja 16,9:5
Beebe, Frank G, 1940, N 26,23:4
Beebe, Frank N, 1903, S 29,9:5
Beebe, Frederick E W, 1952, Mr 5,29:3
Beebe, Frederick H, 1950, F 18,15:7
Beebe, George J, 1943, O 26,23:2
Beebe, George W, 1961, Ag 22,29:4
Beebe, Gilbert, 1881, My 3,5:3; 1952, Je 8,87:1
Beebe, H F, 1927, My 24,25:3
Beebe, Harold S, 1948, Mr 19,24:2
Beebe, Harry, 1909, My 15,9:5
Beebe, Harry W, 1960, Je 11,21:5
Beebe, Helen L T, 1944, Mr 14,19:2
Beebe, Henry R, 1942, N 27,23:2; 1943, Ap 30,21:4
Beebe, Herbert, 1951, Ja 18,27:2
Beebe, Herbert H, 1908, F 14,7:5
Beebe, J, 1934, Mr 31,12:8
Beebe, J Ross, 1955, My 19,29:4
Beebe, J Warren, 1903, S 25,7:5
Beebe, James W, 1943, Ja 1,23:5
Beebe, John B, 1945, Ja 27,11:6
Beebe, John H, 1939, Ag 14,15:5; 1962, S 24,29:3
Beebe, John L, 1965, O 26,45:2
Beebe, Lewic C, 1951, F 18,77:1
Beebe, Lewis A, 1951, Ja 25,25:4
Beebe, Lucius (will, Ap 12,35:6), 1966, F 5,26:1
Beebe, Lucius Sr, 1947, Mr 30,56:4
Beebe, Lynn C, 1957, Je 15,17:7
Beebe, Marcus, 1968, Ap 16,47:2
Beebe, Marcus Jr, 1954, F 25,31:1
Beebe, Merton L, 1945, Je 13,23:2
Beebe, Minnie M, 1955, Ag 17,27:2
Beebe, Raymond W, 1950, F 28,29:4
Beebe, Richard C, 1947, Ap 7,23:1; 1954, Ap 11,87:1
Beebe, Roderick, 1962, Je 4,29:2
Beebe, Royden E Jr, 1959, My 3,86:3
Beebe, Royden E Mrs, 1951, D 3,31:3
Beebe, S W Mrs, 1944, D 29,15:4
Beebe, Silas E Mrs, 1943, N 9,21:2
Beebe, Stanton, 1883, Mr 2,5:2
Beebe, Theodore Chapin Dr, 1925, N 3,25:6
Beebe, W J, 1877, O 25,8:6
Beebe, W R, 1884, My 23,8:2
Beebe, Walter B, 1925, Jl 27,13:4
Beebe, Walter E, 1941, O 19,47:1
Beebe, Warren S, 1965, Ap 24,29:2
Beebe, William, 1962, Je 6,41:1
Beebe, William H H, 1906, Ja 17,11:6
Beebee, Frederick G, 1943, Mr 7,38:3
Beeby, George S, 1942, Jl 19,31:4
Beeby, Nell V, 1957, My 18,19:3
Beech, Alfred J Mrs, 1959, Je 28,69:1
Beech, Walter, 1950, D 1,25:4
Beecham, Betty Lady, 1958, S 3,33:5
Beecham, Joseph Sir, 1916, O 24,12:3
Beecham, Thomas (funl, Mr 11,21:6), 1961, Mr 9,1:4
Beecham, William, 1876, Mr 11,2:6
Beecher, Amourette M, 1905, N 11,9:6
Beecher, Catherine E (see also My 13), 1878, My 15,5:1
Beecher, Charles Emerson Prof, 1904, F 15,7:6
Beecher, E Rev Dr, 1895, Jl 29,1:1
Beecher, Eugene F, 1917, Ja 30,9:2
Beecher, Frederick E, 1941, Ag 5,20:3
Beecher, Frederick H Lt, 1868, S 27,5:5
Beecher, George A, 1951, Je 15,23:1
Beecher, H W, 1887, Mr 6,1:5
Beecher, H W Mrs, 1897, Mr 9,12:1
Beecher, Howard, 1941, N 23,51:6
Beecher, Lucas J, 1954, Ja 27,27:5
Beecher, Luther F Rev, 1903, N 6,9:6
Beecher, Lydia Mrs, 1869, Mr 14,5:1
Beecher, Lyman (funl, Ja 15, 5:2), 1863, Ja 12,5:2
Beecher, Mabel C, 1937, N 25,31:2
Beecher, Mary Howell Mrs, 1923, My 24,19:6
Beecher, Matthew, 1957, N 29,27:3
Beecher, Norman B, 1965, Ja 30,27:4
Beecher, Patrick A, 1940, Je 4,24:2
Beecher, Thomas S Mrs, 1914, Ap 12,15:4
Beecher, W C, 1928, S 20,29:5
Beecher, Walter D, 1966, Jl 22,31:4
Beecher, William (Willie), 1957, Ap 2,31:2
Beecher, William L, 1925, Ag 28,13:4
Beechey, C M, 1881, Jl 12,2:5
Beeching, Charles W, 1953, Jl 2,23:2
Beechinor, Arthur E, 1956, My 20,87:1
Beechinor, Robert J Capt, 1909, Jl 22,7:5
Beechler, Glenn C, 1954, Ja 16,15:2
Beechwood, Christian T, 1945, Ja 21,39:2
Beeck, Elmer E, 1942, Jl 17,15:6
Beeck, Otto A, 1950, Jl 6,27:5
Beeckman, Gilbert L Mrs, 1904, Ap 20,9:6
Beecroft, Chester, 1959, Ja 8,29:1
Beecroft, David, 1943, N 6,13:3
Beecroft, David Mrs, 1941, N 23,53:1
Beecroft, Edgar C, 1939, Ag 27,35:4
Beecroft, Edgar S Mrs, 1938, S 14,23:4
Beecroft, Edward J, 1952, F 5,29:1
Beecroft, John W R, 1966, S 22,47:4
Beecroft, Katherine H Mrs, 1939, N 5,49:2
Beecroft, Victor R, 1958, Mr 28,25:2
Beede, Carl G, 1952, Je 6,23:3
Beede, Charles A Mrs, 1945, D 8,17:3
Beede, Herbert G, 1943, Mr 7,38:7
Beede, Ivan, 1946, Ag 19,25:5
Beedee, Edgar C, 1940, F 25,39:2
Beedle, Marvin L, 1950, D 5,31:1
Beedy, Carroll L, 1947, Ag 31,36:7
Beedy, Howard E, 1937, S 4,15:4
Beegel, Morris, 1958, Je 22,76:4
Beeghly, Wood D, 1938, My 30,11:5
Beegle, Albert E, 1966, S 22,47:5
Beegle, Caroline D, 1959, Ag 28,23:4
Beegle, G Fred, 1953, Je 15,29:3
Beegle, Isaac N Dr, 1903, Jl 21,9:6
Beegle, May, 1943, D 9,28:3
Beegle, Thomas P, 1946, Jl 27,17:3
Beehan, William E Mrs, 1958, My 9,23:1
Beehan, William H, 1950, Jl 10,21:2
Beehler, John C, 1940, Ap 28,37:1
Beehler, Weyman P, 1943, Ap 11,19:4
Beehler, William H Commodore, 1915, Je 24,11:5
Beek, J Alonzo, 1941, S 8,15:5
Beek, Jory van, 1951, Mr 16,38:4
Beekel, Fred, 1946, N 5,25:4
Beeken, Alfred D, 1937, N 29,23:6
Beeken, Axel V, 1954, Mr 15,25:6
Beeken, Axel V Mrs, 1951, Je 8,27:4
Beeken, Valdemar, 1958, Ja 27,27:3
Beekley, Waldron C Mrs, 1952, F 5,29:3
Beekman, A M Judge, 1926, Mr 22,19:3
Beekman, Abraham, 1908, My 11,7:5
Beekman, Alston, 1951, Jl 21,13:5
Beekman, Barclay (H M Shelley), 1956, D 12,39:2
Beekman, Ben, 1946, O 5,17:3
Beekman, Benjamin F, 1875, F 11,4:7
Beekman, Bernard E, 1959, N 7,23:5
Beekman, Charles K, 1941, F 26,21:5
Beekman, Cornelia Augusta, 1917, My 12,11:6
Beekman, Cornelius Mrs (Mrs D Butler), 1967, F 2, 35:2
Beekman, Cortlandt, 1915, Ja 12,9:4
Beekman, Daniel D, 1916, O 22,23:3
Beekman, Daniel H, 1951, F 3,15:2
Beekman, Douw, 1945, Mr 5,19:1
Beekman, Edgar, 1955, Ag 8,21:5
Beekman, Fenwick, 1962, N 22,29:2
Beekman, Frederick W, 1964, Mr 23,29:2
Beekman, Frederick W Mrs, 1946, Ja 7,20:3
Beekman, Gerard, 1918, N 10,23:1
Beekman, Henry M T, 1939, Je 4,49:2
Beekman, Henry R, 1938, Ag 24,21:3
Beekman, Henry W, 1948, Je 5,15:6
Beekman, J W (see also Je 16), 1877, Je 20,8:4
Beekman, James William, 1908, Ag 9,9:4
Beekman, John B, 1940, Jl 11,19:5
Beekman, John B Mrs, 1944, My 26,19:5
Beekman, John H, 1937, Mr 18,25:3
Beekman, Mary E, 1944, Ag 27,33:3
Beekman, Milton R, 1947, Ja 18,15:3
Beekman, Royce A, 1953, Ap 2,17:1
Beekman, S A, 1882, My 22,5:3
Beekman, W H (W H Griffiths), 1885, Mr 21,1:4
Beekman, Walter N, 1962, Ag 2,25:1
Beekman, William Schuyler Lt-Col, 1917, Ap 11,13:7
Beeks, Mack W, 1944, N 29,23:3
Beeks, Mack W Mrs, 1944, Ag 8,17:4
Beeler, Roy H, 1954, S 25,15:4
Beeler, W E, 1963, F 13,9:2
Beeler, William J, 1961, Ap 7,31:4
Beeman, Charles A, 1940, O 11,21:2
Beeman, Edward E, 1953, My 13,29:5
Beeman, Edwin E Dr, 1906, N 7,9:5
Beeman, Raymond F, 1952, D 17,33:3
Beemer, Brace, 1965, Mr 2,35:1
Beemer, Charles Mrs, 1955, Ja 15,13:6
Beemer, Edwin F, 1965, Jl 13,33:5
Beemer, Frank, 1958, Mr 30,88:6
Beemer, James G, 1921, My 8,22:3
Beemer, Louise E Mrs, 1937, My 25,28:2
Beemer, Miles W, 1942, O 27,25:3
Beemer, William C, 1954, Mr 2,25:5
Beene, Dow B, 1952, Ap 18,25:4
Beene, James C, 1950, Jl 9,68:8
Beer, Andrew E, 1954, D 22,23:4
Beer, Charles H Mrs, 1953, Ja 27,25:2
Beer, Edwin (por), 1938, Ag 15,15:4
Beer, Edwin Mrs, 1950, N 3,27:4
Beer, Frederick M, 1963, Je 24,27:5
Beer, George E, 1938, My 23,17:1
Beer, George L Mrs, 1952, Jl 27,57:1
Beer, George Louis, 1920, Mr 16,9:4
Beer, Israel, 1966, My 2,6:4
Beer, Jacob Mrs, 1958, O 30,31:2
Beer, Jacques S, 1954, N 25,29:4
Beer, John E, 1949, My 20,27:2
Beer, Louis, 1915, Mr 26,13:3
Beer, Max, 1965, O 28,43:1
Beer, Max Mrs, 1965, Jl 24,21:2
Beer, Oscar, 1957, Ap 13,19:1
Beer, Richard C, 1959, My 22,27:3
Beer, Thomas, 1940, Ap 19,21:1
Beer, Walter E, 1944, F 19,13:5
Beer, William C, 1916, O 10,11:5
Beer-Hofmann, Richard, 1945, S 27,21:3
Beerbohm, Arthur M, 1937, Mr 4,23:5
Beerbohm, Lady, 1951, Ja 14,86:2
Beerbohm, Max (to be cremated, My 21,25:6; funl, My 22,33:2), 1956, My 20,86:1
Beerbohm, Max Mrs, 1959, Ja 10,17:2
Beere, Bernard Mrs, 1915, Mr 27,11:4
Beerer, Mary H Mrs, 1951, My 22,31:4
Beeres, Louis, 1951, Ja 10,27:6
Beermaert, Auguste, 1912, O 7,11:5
Beerman, Isidore, 1968, D 23,39:1
Beers, Alfred B Judge, 1920, Mr 31,11:6
Beers, Arthur F, 1956, Jl 3,25:5
Beers, Arthur H, 1949, Ja 27,23:2
Beers, Callie H Mrs, 1940, N 13,23:4
Beers, Catherine V, 1949, Ap 24,76:2
Beers, Charles H, 1952, Jl 24,27:6
Beers, Clarence W, 1961, O 23,29:3
Beers, Clifford W, 1943, Jl 10,13:1
Beers, E La Grand, 1942, Mr 14,15:5
Beers, Edmund O Brig-Gen, 1913, Mr 14,9:2
Beers, Frank, 1948, Je 12,15:4

Beers, Frederick, 1956, Ja 18,31:2
Beers, George A, 1937, N 29,23:5
Beers, George E, 1947, D 26,15:3
Beers, H A Prof, 1926, S 8,25:2
Beers, Helen L, 1955, Je 6,27:4
Beers, Helena D Mrs, 1941, Jl 2,21:3
Beers, Henry M, 1961, D 5,39:3
Beers, Herbert P, 1949, D 22,23:5
Beers, Hugh H A, 1944, Jl 25,19:5
Beers, J Maxwell, 1941, N 30,68:3
Beers, James R Capt, 1904, S 4,9:6
Beers, Jessica E, 1942, D 13,73:2
Beers, John W, 1915, S 9,11:6
Beers, Julie Hart (Mrs P Tertius Kempson), 1913, Ag 15,7:6
Beers, Leo, 1938, D 29,19:4
Beers, Leroy A, 1946, My 25,15:3
Beers, Lucius H, 1948, O 3,65:1
Beers, Lucius H Mrs, 1952, F 4,17:3
Beers, Mary E, 1945, N 4,43:1
Beers, Mary H Mrs, 1938, Ja 7,19:2
Beers, Matthew H, 1910, Ap 11,7:4
Beers, Merritt I, 1953, D 12,19:5
Beers, Nathan Perry, 1915, F 19,9:5
Beers, Nellie Mrs, 1873, Jl 15,5:2
Beers, Norman C Mrs, 1939, Jl 8,32:1
Beers, Norman R, 1950, Je 29,29:3
Beers, Paul D, 1962, Mr 7,35:2
Beers, Richard C S, 1958, My 27,29:1
Beers, Robert A, 1950, D 21,29:4
Beers, Sidney J, 1956, D 2,86:7
Beers, Wayne M (por), 1949, Mr 22,25:5
Beers, William F Capt, 1872, Je 8,1:2
Beers, William H, 1949, Jl 3,26:7
Beers, William L, 1955, Ja 15,13:6
Beers, William W, 1950, Ja 1,43:1
Beersman, Charles G, 1946, Ag 1,23:3
Beery, Edwin M, 1939, Ja 31,21:5
Beery, Edwin M Mrs, 1961, D 17,82:5
Beery, John M, 1960, Jl 22,23:2
Beery, Noah Sr, 1946, Ap 2,28:2
Beery, Noah Sr Mrs, 1955, D 28,23:4
Beery, P B, 1883, S 4,5:2
Beery, Wallace, 1949, Ap 17,77:1
Beery, William, 1956, Ja 30,27:3
Beery, William C, 1949, D 26,29:4
Beese, Robert, 1940, Mr 26,21:6
Beesley, Maurice E, 1953, S 8,31:3
Beesley, Theodore Mrs, 1953, Mr 7,15:5
Beeson, Charles H, 1949, D 28,25:2
Beeson, Ernest G, 1941, Ag 5,19:5
Beetem, Edward C, 1938, Ja 13,21:3
Beetem, Robert N, 1938, My 8,II,6:3
Beetha, John H, 1945, My 12,13:4
Beetle, Ralph D Prof, 1937, Jl 11,II,4:5
Beetle, William H, 1950, D 19,29:3
Beeton, Mayson, 1947, Je 25,26:2
Beeton, William A, 1951, Je 2,19:3
Beetson, Fred W, 1953, Ap 1,29:3
Beetson, Frederick W (cor, My 17,15:4), 1947, My 16,23:1
Beeuwkes, C John, 1942, F 5,21:1
Beeuwkes, Henry, 1956, F 2,25:2
Beezley, Willard, 1953, Ja 2,16:4
Beffel, John Mrs, 1946, Ag 23,19:5
Begam, Arthur B, 1959, O 24,21:5
Begas, Karl, 1916, F 23,13:6
Begas, Oskar, 1883, N 11,9:5
Begelman, David Mrs, 1958, F 16,86:2
Begen, Frank R, 1948, Jl 31,15:2
Begen, James Dr, 1925, O 9,23:4
Beger, John H, 1958, F 17,23:3
Begert, John E, 1960, D 15,43:3
Begg, Alex S, 1940, S 27,23:3
Begg, Colin L, 1941, Ja 17,17:1
Begg, Harold K, 1943, Jl 15,21:2
Begg, Howard B, 1967, Mr 2,35:3
Begg, James A, 1940, D 21,17:3
Begg, John W, 1940, Mr 4,15:5
Begg, Joseph R, 1924, My 13,21:5
Begg, Mrs (funl), 1859, Ja 8,8:3
Begg, Norman D, 1956, My 25,23:5
Begg, Roderick, 1943, S 25,15:2
Begg, William C D, 1947, Ag 12,23:2
Begg, William S, 1954, N 19,25:1
Beggans, J J, 1934, Ag 31,18:1
Beggi, Frank (will, Mr 24,24:3), 1938, Mr 22,23:7
Beggi, Peter L, 1965, My 4,43:5
Beggs, Alan H, 1956, Ag 23,27:4
Beggs, Arthur E, 1966, O 22,31:4
Beggs, Charles A, 1939, N 3,21:4
Beggs, Fordyce W, 1957, Je 11,35:4
Beggs, Frederic, 1941, D 2,23:6
Beggs, George, 1954, S 2,21:5
Beggs, George E, 1939, N 24,23:1
Beggs, J Dilworth, 1949, N 30,27:2
Beggs, James D, 1949, Ag 22,21:6
Beggs, James G Sr Mrs, 1956, Ja 10,31:1
Beggs, John I, 1925, O 19,21:4
Beggs, Lee, 1943, N 19,19:5
Beggs, R A (see also N 23), 1878, N 25,2:1
Beggs, Robert B, 1942, Ag 27,19:3
Beghe, Almo, 1946, N 12,29:6
Begin, Louis Nazaire (por),(funl, Jl 26,5:4), 1925, Jl 20,15:4
Begland, Thomas, 1956, Je 22,23:5
Begle, Nathan G, 1948, Ap 6,23:4
Begle, Ned G Mrs, 1959, Ap 1,37:1
Begley, Edward J, 1966, Ag 5,31:5
Begley, Frank M (funl, Ja 30,27:2), 1965, Ja 27,35:1
Begley, Hugh H Mrs, 1945, Ap 20,19:5
Begley, Joseph, 1948, Je 4,23:3
Begley, Joseph A, 1951, Jl 27,19:2
Beglinger, Fred M Judge, 1937, N 19,23:5
Begoon, Harry, 1945, S 5,23:3
Begovitch, Matty, 1966, N 22,45:2
Begrisch, Frank, 1963, S 24,39:4
Begue, Mme (Eliz Ketenring), 1906, O 21,9:2
Beguerre, Antoine, 1960, O 25,35:5
Beguinot, Augusto, 1940, Ja 5,20:3
Begun, Harry M, 1960, S 13,37:2
Beh, Emile L, 1962, My 14,29:4
Beha, James A, 1945, N 15,19:3
Beha, Joseph L, 1950, O 8,105:1
Beha, Joseph Mrs, 1924, Ap 12,15:3
Behal, Auguste, 1941, F 5,19:3
Beham, Jehuda, 1954, N 23,35:3
Behan, Albert S, 1965, Ja 5,33:4
Behan, Brendan (funl, Mr 24,35:1), 1964, Mr 21,25:3
Behan, Edmund T, 1956, Je 24,76:8
Behan, James F, 1948, O 20,29:5
Behan, James F Mrs, 1959, Mr 24,39:3
Behan, James J Sr, 1950, D 8,29:4
Behan, John A, 1948, Je 18,23:5
Behan, Joseph C, 1949, D 2,29:4
Behan, Lawrence W, 1941, Je 18,21:4
Behan, Margaret E, 1956, F 1,31:4
Behan, Purves Mrs, 1954, O 15,23:3
Behan, Stephen, 1967, Jl 14,31:3
Behan, T F, 1931, F 17,25:5
Behan, Warren P, 1952, D 12,29:2
Behan, William A, 1945, F 25,37:2
Behan, William A Mrs, 1950, My 3,29:3
Behanzin, Ex-King of Dahomey, 1906, D 11,4:3
Behar, Cooch, 1922, D 21,15:3
Behar, Ely M, 1951, Ag 7,25:4
Behar, Manoel F D, 1958, Ag 3,80:6
Beharrell, George, 1959, F 21,21:4
Behee, Grant A C, 1943, D 27,19:3
Behel, Vernon W Jr, 1954, S 17,27:3
Behine, William, 1947, My 28,25:2
Behlen, Robert, 1948, Ap 9,23:1
Behling, William P, 1939, Jl 8,15:2
Behm, Peter, 1949, F 1,25:2
Behman, L C (will, Mr 5,9:5), 1902, F 28,9:5
Behn, Arnold G, 1944, Ja 20,19:5
Behn, Edward J, 1966, My 5,47:2
Behn, H, 1933, O 8,38:1
Behn, Hernand Mrs, 1960, O 16,88:8
Behn, Karl Edward Dr, 1906, Je 23,16:6
Behn, Michele L, 1966, F 25,18:8
Behn, Sosthenes, 1957, Je 7,23:4
Behncke, David L, 1953, Ap 16,29:4
Behncke, Nile J, 1954, O 12,27:1
Behncke, Paul Adm, 1937, Ja 5,23:5
Behnee, Harriet (Mrs K Spiekerman), 1963, S 29,86:5
Behner, Ann C, 1958, Ap 17,31:2
Behnert, August F, 1946, Ja 5,13:3
Behnke, Frederick W, 1940, Jl 6,15:7
Behnken, Herman, 1943, F 19,19:4
Behnken, John W Mrs, 1954, Ja 22,27:2
Behnken, John W Rev Dr, 1968, F 25,76:7
Behoteguy, Henry G Mrs, 1948, O 27,27:1
Behr, Arthur C Sr, 1952, D 21,52:7
Behr, Benjamin L, 1938, Mr 5,17:5
Behr, Frederick, 1956, D 10,31:2
Behr, Frederick H, 1944, F 7,15:5
Behr, Frederick Mrs, 1956, Ag 20,21:5
Behr, George A Mrs, 1948, Ja 15,23:4
Behr, Howell, 1961, S 12,33:4
Behr, Hubert J, 1943, O 11,19:6
Behr, John G, 1939, Ap 13,23:2
Behr, John W, 1956, Je 27,31:6
Behr, Karl H, 1949, O 16,90:3
Behr, Louis, 1946, N 13,27:5
Behr, Robert, 1921, Je 16,15:3
Behr, S C Mrs, 1932, N 6,39:1
Behr, Vladimir, 1952, Mr 29,15:1
Behr, Vladimir A Mrs, 1964, Jl 6,29:4
Behra, Jean (funl, Ag 11,30:6), 1959, Ag 2,V,1:7
Behre, Charles H Mrs, 1952, N 6,29:3
Behre, Gerhard F, 1952, Ag 13,21:5
Behre, Karl H, 1952, Ja 9,29:5
Behrend, Ernest R, 1940, S 23,17:5
Behrend, Max, 1950, O 19,31:4
Behrend, Otto F, 1957, My 22,33:1
Behrendt, Alse A, 1952, F 18,19:5
Behrendt, Frances J, 1952, My 20,25:2
Behrendt, Leo A, 1959, F 12,27:4
Behrendt, Walter C, 1945, Ap 27,19:3
Behrens, Alvin, 1953, Ag 4,21:1
Behrens, August, 1924, Ag 25,13:4
Behrens, Charles A Mrs, 1960, Ag 7,84:7
Behrens, Charles D, 1964, F 7,32:1
Behrens, Earl C Mrs, 1954, Ap 8,27:5
Behrens, Edith, 1960, My 4,45:2
Behrens, Ernest, 1945, N 18,43:1
Behrens, Ernest H, 1953, S 14,27:3
Behrens, Ernest Mrs, 1953, Ag 9,77:1
Behrens, Everett E, 1937, Ag 12,19:6
Behrens, Frederick, 1951, Ja 22,17:3
Behrens, Frederick W, 1940, Ap 5,21:1
Behrens, George H, 1968, Mr 1,43:6
Behrens, Herman Mrs, 1937, O 29,22:3
Behrens, Leo F, 1949, Mr 24,27:2
Behrens, Manfred I, 1961, Mr 25,25:4
Behrens, Max, 1952, N 13,31:6
Behrens, Nathaniel, 1913, My 31,11:6
Behrens, Norman H, 1959, Je 9,37:5
Behrens, Otto A, 1952, O 10,6:6
Behrens, Siegfried, 1912, N 6,15:4
Behrens, William H, 1966, Ja 19,38:1
Behrens, William W, 1965, Ja 29,29:4
Behring, Frank H, 1949, S 29,29:5
Behringer, Alfred K, 1961, N 22,33:1
Behringer, Charles A Rev Dr, 1937, O 28,23:3
Behringer, John S, 1955, Ja 31,19:5
Behringer, Louis Mrs, 1945, Ag 4,11:3
Behrle, Fred F, 1941, My 21,23:5
Behrman, Abraham, 1957, D 3,35:4
Behrman, Bernard F, 1952, O 31,25:3
Behrman, Charles, 1957, Mr 5,31:4
Behrman, Emanuel, 1961, Jl 5,33:4
Behrman, Harry, 1959, Ja 21,31:1
Behrman, Harry Mrs, 1957, S 7,19:2
Behrman, Henry, 1947, S 29,21:2
Behrman, Irving E Mrs, 1951, Ag 5,72:6
Behrman, Isidor P, 1945, Ag 5,38:4
Behrman, Meyer, 1959, Mr 14,23:5
Behrman, William S, 1953, N 9,35:2
Behrmann, Arthur E, 1945, F 28,24:2
Behrmann, Clarence H, 1953, Ja 23,20:3
Behrmann, Harry, 1947, S 2,21:2
Behrmann, Helen Mrs, 1948, Jl 13,27:2
Behrmann, Henry F Jr, 1953, Ja 25,86:4
Behrmann, John H, 1946, Mr 27,27:4
Behson, Joseph M Sr, 1953, Ap 5,76:4
Behymer, Arthur L, 1951, Mr 22,31:2
Behymer, F A, 1956, Jl 17,21:1
Behymer, L E, 1947, D 17,29:3
Behymer, L E Mrs, 1958, O 4,21:4
Beichert, John M, 1954, Jl 16,21:2
Beichler, William K, 1953, Ja 6,29:5
Beidas, Youssef K, 1968, N 29,45:1
Beidleman, E E, 1929, Ap 10,29:1
Beidler, George C, 1945, Jl 24,23:3
Beidler, J A, 1912, S 14,13:6
Beidler, Theodore F, 1948, N 18,27:1
Beidoun, Darwish, 1961, Jl 16,54:5
Beier, Benjamin, 1948, O 20,29:5
Beier, Carl L, 1954, Mr 31,27:3
Beier, Paul O Mrs, 1949, F 10,28:3
Beierle, Henry G, 1966, Ja 15,27:5
Beiermeister, James M, 1956, Ja 16,21:3
Beierschmidt, John M, 1943, O 4,17:6
Beiersdorf, Otto W, 1952, Jl 22,25:2
Beierstedt, Harold, 1948, Jl 11,52:6
Beigbeder y Atienza, Juan, 1957, Je 8,19:4
Beigel, Albert, 1964, F 8,23:5
Beiger, Martin, 1903, S 27,7:6
Beigert, Mathias, 1942, N 28,13:2
Beighle, James L, 1960, Je 12,86:6
Beihoff, George J, 1937, O 19,26:2
Beijma, Julius M van, 1944, Jl 13,17:5
Beil, Arthur R, 1960, My 5,35:1
Beilby, George E, 1959, Mr 17,30:5
Beilenson, Peter, 1962, Ja 21,88:2
Beiley, Murray R, 1956, My 1,33:1
Beilin, Asher, 1948, S 14,29:4
Beimel, Jacob, 1944, N 18,13:2
Beimfohr, Otto H, 1937, F 18,21:5
Bein, Albert, 1963, My 4,25:3
Bein, Austin, 1947, F 8,17:5
Bein, William A, 1943, My 31,17:5
Beinecke, Johanna E Mrs, 1938, Mr 22,21:2
Beinecke, Richard S, 1966, N 5,31:1
Beinecke, Walter, 1958, S 4,29:3
Beinert, George H, 1952, Ja 4,23:2
Beinert, Robert L, 1963, Je 5,41:3
Beinhauer, Karl, 1966, O 6,47:2
Beinner, Max, 1962, O 13,25:2
Beinum, Eduard van, 1959, Ap 14,35:4
Beir, Edwin, 1943, My 21,19:6
Beir, Mildred, 1920, O 5,11:2
Beira, Bernardo, 1959, Jl 16,28:1
Beirach, Robert, 1951, Ja 4,29:3
Beirn, Joseph M Mrs, 1961, My 23,39:4
Beirn, Martin J, 1944, Je 2,15:2
Beirne, Eleanor F, 1945, Mr 23,19:2
Beirne, Hugh J, 1924, Je 10,11:4
Beirne, Hugh P, 1944, D 27,19:4
Beirne, John, 1938, F 4,21:2
Beirne, Joseph T Mrs, 1944, Je 5,19:4
Beirne, Michael, 1904, N 3,9:5
Beirne, Nanna G, 1948, Ja 13,25:4
Beirne, Peter, 1905, Mr 24,9:6
Beirne, Richard F, 1950, F 7,27:1
Beirne, T Frank, 1937, F 21,II,11:2
Beisch, Walter, 1939, My 15,17:3

Beise, Sheldon, 1960, Ap 2,24:3
Beisel, R Alvin, 1937, Ja 11,19:4
Beiser, Arthur J, 1945, D 21,21:3
Beiser, Joseph W Dr, 1937, My 25,28:1
Beiser, Rufus W, 1963, Jl 9,32:1
Beisgen, Martin, 1951, N 4,87:1
Beisheim, George, 1955, Ja 26,25:2
Beisheim, John B, 1937, N 21,II,9:2
Beisheim, William F, 1945, N 19,21:3
Beisler, Henry Sr, 1964, Ag 12,35:1
Beisman, Paul, 1958, O 20,29:5
Beiss, Howard Sweetser Dr, 1920, My 3,13:3
Beissig, Lewis C, 1947, Jl 3,21:5
Beistegul, Don Eduardo de, 1908, Mr 7,7:7
Beistle, Morton J Mrs, 1949, F 28,19:4
Beit, Alfred, 1906, Jl 17,7:1
Beit von Speyer, E Baron, 1933, Mr 9,13:5
Beitenman, Florence B, 1943, N 26,23:4
Beiter, John J, 1947, O 16,27:4
Beith, Alex, 1958, Mr 11,29:1
Beith, Alex Mrs, 1954, D 29,23:2
Beith, John H (I Hay), 1952, S 23,33:3
Beitler, Brooks H, 1949, D 21,29:4
Beitler, Joseph, 1967, Mr 14,47:2
Beitler, Julia L Mrs, 1937, Ja 26,21:4
Beitler, Lewis E Col, 1920, D 14,17:4
Beitter, Eugene, 1938, D 11,61:2
Beitz, William E, 1939, F 4,15:2
Bejach, Albert, 1948, N 3,27:4
Bejarano, Jose M, 1954, O 21,27:4
Bejarano, Jose M Mrs, 1967, Ag 28,31:3
Bek, William G, 1948, Ag 15,60:8
Beke, Charles T, 1874, Ag 2,4:7
Beker, Henry H Maj, 1915, S 1,9:4
Bekeros, Peter D, 1961, S 21,35:1
Bekins, John, 1948, N 12,23:3
Bekir, Nedjib M, 1957, Ap 7,88:6
Bekkai, M'barek, 1961, Ap 14,30:1
Bekker, Paul, 1937, Mr 8,19:5
Bel-Jon, Nikos, 1966, Ag 12,31:1
Bela, Nicholas, 1963, N 24,23:1
Belahouane, Alala, 1958, My 10,21:4
Belair, Felix J Mrs, 1947, Mr 22,13:2
Belair, Felix Sr, 1950, F 17,24:3
Belais, D, 1933, Je 7,21:4
Belais, David Mrs, 1944, F 15,17:3
Belais, Henry, 1940, Je 3,15:4
Beland, Leon L, 1908, Mr 8,7:5
Belanger, Cyprien J, 1940, Ag 28,19:5
Belanger, John W, 1968, S 25,47:2
Belanger, Joseph, 1943, Jl 3,13:2
Belanger, Pierre, 1939, My 16,23:5
Belanoff, Charles, 1955, O 25,33:2
Belanske, William E, 1945, O 28,44:2
Belardi, Ray J, 1955, Jl 22,12:8
Belasco, Abe, 1911, Ap 12,13:4
Belasco, D, 1931, My 15,1:3
Belasco, D Mrs, 1926, F 23,23:3
Belasco, Edward, 1937, O 10,II,8:2
Belasco, Frederick Mrs, 1907, Mr 23,9:5
Belasco, Genevieve, 1956, N 19,31:1
Belasco, Henry Mrs, 1951, Ap 3,27:4
Belaunde, Victor A (trb, D 16,47:4), 1966, D 15,47:4
Belbenoit, Rene, 1959, F 27,52:4
Belber, Harry C, 1949, Mr 25,24:2
Belber, Herman S, 1946, Mr 29,23:1
Belber, Marcus Y, 1939, Ja 5,23:5
Belcastro, James, 1945, Ag 25,13:4
Belch, Joseph, 1924, Je 27,19:5
Belch, Keith R, 1954, Ja 4,19:3
Belcham, William, 1938, My 25,23:1
Belchee, Charles E, 1940, Ag 28,19:1
Belcher, Arnold L, 1962, Ja 6,19:5
Belcher, Benjamin H, 1945, Ag 2,19:3
Belcher, Benjamin H Mrs, 1956, Ap 28,17:4
Belcher, Charles, 1904, F 22,5:6
Belcher, Charles L, 1937, Ag 6,17:3
Belcher, Donald, 1966, My 31,43:4
Belcher, Duncan, 1937, N 3,23:3
Belcher, E, 1877, Mr 20,5:3
Belcher, Earl Mrs, 1953, F 22,60:5
Belcher, Frank H, 1947, F 28,24:3
Belcher, Frank J Jr, 1952, Je 25,29:2
Belcher, Frank J Rev, 1922, Je 28,15:6
Belcher, Frederick E, 1919, S 13,11:5
Belcher, George F A, 1947, O 5,68:3
Belcher, Harold, 1950, Ja 1,42:5
Belcher, Harry B, 1952, Ap 26,23:5
Belcher, Hilda, 1963, Ap 28,88:6
Belcher, Horace G, 1959, Je 30,31:2
Belcher, J S, 1883, F 21,2:4
Belcher, John G, 1952, S 2,25:5
Belcher, John W, 1964, O 27,39:3
Belcher, Merwin R, 1952, Ja 26,8:1
Belcher, Robert Mrs, 1954, O 17,87:2
Belcher, Wallace E, 1959, Ag 25,31:2
Belcher, Walter H, 1943, F 14,48:5
Belcher, Ward C, 1941, Ja 26,35:7
Belcher, William H, 1939, My 6,17:6
Belches, John W, 1937, Je 23,25:2
Belcourt, N A, 1932, Ag 8,15:3
Belden, Alfred Goodwin, 1918, My 22,13:6
Belden, Arthur L, 1958, Jl 8,27:4
Belden, Charles F, 1951, O 18,29:4
Belden, Corinne C Mrs, 1942, S 18,22:3
Belden, Ellsworth B, 1939, Mr 12,III,7:1
Belden, Ernest T, 1944, Ap 2,39:1
Belden, Frank A, 1944, Mr 6,19:5
Belden, Frank M, 1941, Ap 23,21:5
Belden, Frank O, 1946, Ap 16,25:3
Belden, H Rev, 1884, Je 26,5:1
Belden, Harry A, 1925, O 31,17:3
Belden, Henry, 1937, Je 21,19:4
Belden, J H, 1949, N 2,27:4
Belden, James J Mrs, 1910, D 27,9:5
Belden, James Jerome, 1904, Ja 2,9:3
Belden, John H, 1937, F 5,21:1
Belden, Joseph C, 1939, F 18,15:6
Belden, Leo V, 1949, Ag 29,17:5
Belden, Louis I, 1963, Jl 9,31:4
Belden, Mary M, 1963, D 21,23:5
Belden, N A W (funl), 1872, Ap 17,5:2
Belder, Francis, 1924, Mr 5,17:5
Belding, Alvah Norton, 1925, D 19,17:5
Belding, David W, 1907, Mr 6,9:6
Belding, Frederick N, 1945, N 13,22:3
Belding, Lewis A, 1964, My 20,43:5
Belding, Milo M, 1917, My 24,13:6
Belding, Milo M Mrs, 1944, S 6,19:3
Belding, Paul H, 1953, Je 5,27:3
Belding, Samuel B Prof, 1937, Ag 7,15:1
Belding, wm S, 1939, Je 20,21:2
Beldock, George, 1958, Ap 10,29:4
Beldon, Samuel W, 1913, D 1,9:4
Beldon, William M, 1938, N 1,23:2
Bele, Refet (Refet Pasha), 1963, O 7,31:2
Belenkov, V K, 1952, Mr 22,13:6
Beless, James, 1903, S 13,7:5
Belewsky-Joukovsky, Maria Countess, 1954, Mr 28, 89:2
Belfield, T Dun, 1957, F 16,17:3
Belford, Alex, 1953, N 26,32:4
Belford, Alex J, 1952, Ap 12,11:5
Belford, George V, 1937, My 12,23:4
Belford, Gilbert S, 1946, N 21,31:4
Belford, Irving, 1950, D 15,31:3
Belford, J Eugene, 1948, F 15,60:3
Belford, J Frank, 1946, Ap 7,46:1
Belford, James B Mrs, 1921, Ja 28,11:4
Belford, John L, 1951, D 13,33:1
Belford, Joseph H, 1968, Ja 14,84:5
Belford, Joseph M, 1917, My 5,13:6
Belfour, Alvin W, 1948, Je 24,25:2
Belgam, Joseph P, 1943, Je 16,21:5
Belgrano, Frank N Jr, 1959, N 12,35:3
Belgrano, Mario, 1947, O 28,25:4
Belhaven and Stenton, Lord (R E A Udny-Hamilton), 1950, O 29,93:2
Beliakoff, Thoedore J, 1962, Ap 3,39:5
Belic, Aleksandar, 1960, F 27,19:5
Belichenko, Peter, 1954, Ag 22,93:2
Belier, Alfred L, 1949, Ag 4,23:3
Belikoff, Samuel, 1914, Jl 20,7:2
Belin, F Lammont Mrs, 1945, Mr 4,38:4
Belin, Ferdinand L, 1961, Jl 7,25:5
Belin, G D'Andelot, 1941, Mr 3,15:3
Belin, G d'Andelot, 1954, My 6,33:3
Belin, Henry Jr, 1917, D 26,9:3
Belin, Henry 3d Mrs, 1959, Ja 1,31:4
Belin, Paul B Mrs, 1948, Ag 5,21:5
Belinfante, Johan J, 1947, Ja 9,23:1
Beling, Christopher C, 1946, D 2,25:3
Beling, Demetrius, 1949, Je 2,27:5
Beling, G A, 1883, O 10,5:2
Beling, George A, 1954, Ap 15,29:1
Belinkoff, Samuel, 1956, Jl 20,17:3
Belinky, Heyman Mrs, 1937, Ap 27,23:5
Belisle, Albert E, 1962, O 26,31:4
Belisle, Fernand, 1956, Ja 8,87:1
Belisle, Hector L, 1950, Ap 25,31:1
Beliveau, Arthur Mrs, 1957, Ag 3,15:4
Beljean, Eugene, 1939, D 5,28:2
Belk, Harrison L, 1940, Ja 7,51:1
Belk, Harry C, 1954, Jl 10,13:6
Belk, William H, 1952, F 22,22:2
Belkin, Michael A, 1950, Ag 5,15:6
Belkin, Solomon Mrs, 1949, Ja 19,27:2
Belkind, Alexandria, 1943, S 22,23:4
Belkind, Samuel, 1962, F 2,30:8
Belkind, Shimshon, 1937, Mr 29,19:4
Belknap, Arthur T, 1942, My 3,53:2
Belknap, Charles, 1954, D 30,17:1
Belknap, Charles A, 1942, O 24,15:4
Belknap, Charles A Mrs, 1942, O 24,15:4
Belknap, Charles B, 1953, N 10,31:5
Belknap, Charles Commander, 1901, Je 16,7:6
Belknap, Edith B, 1947, Ap 12,17:5
Belknap, Ethelbert, 1942, Ag 22,13:7
Belknap, Eugene W Dr, 1925, N 22,9:1
Belknap, Francis P, 1948, F 16,21:3
Belknap, Francis W Mrs, 1961, Jl 29,19:5
Belknap, G F Adm, 1903, Ap 8,9:1
Belknap, H R Maj, 1901, N 14,9:6
Belknap, James B, 1923, Je 6,21:3
Belknap, John Dexter Rev Dr, 1925, O 29,25:6
Belknap, Leverett, 1942, Ja 30,19:2
Belknap, Maitland, 1958, Ap 11,25:1
Belknap, Morris B Col, 1910, Ap 14,11:4
Belknap, Mrs, 1870, D 30,1:5
Belknap, Raymond H, 1966, Ap 26,45:3
Belknap, Reginald R (funl, Ap 3,27:1), 1959, Mr 31, 29:1
Belknap, Seth H, 1940, O 21,17:5
Belknap, W W Gen, 1890, O 14,9:1
Belknap, Waldron, 1943, O 28,23:1
Belknap, Waldron P, 1949, D 15,35:3
Belknap, Waldron P Mrs, 1960, Ja 1,19:3
Belknap, Warren H, 1949, D 1,31:5
Belknap, William C, 1942, Ja 14,21:1
Belknap, William L, 1944, Je 8,21:5
Belknap, William Mrs, 1940, D 5,25:5
Bell, Aaron, 1959, Ag 27,27:3
Bell, Adam Carr, 1912, O 31,13:5
Bell, Agrippa N Dr, 1911, O 17,11:5
Bell, Albert D, 1941, F 15,5:4
Bell, Albert E, 1941, Ap 8,25:5
Bell, Albert J, 1952, F 26,27:3
Bell, Albert M, 1946, Jl 20,13:6
Bell, Albert R, 1955, F 17,27:4
Bell, Albert T, 1943, S 4,13:5
Bell, Alex, 1941, Jl 6,26:4
Bell, Alex W, 1943, Je 24,22:2
Bell, Alexander Graham (por),(funl, Ag 4,15:6), 1922, Ag 3,13:1
Bell, Alexander Graham Mrs, 1923, Ja 4,19:4
Bell, Alfred D, 1961, Je 25,77:2
Bell, Alonzo C, 1945, Ap 13,17:5
Bell, Alphonzo E, 1947, D 28,40:4
Bell, Annie L Mrs, 1938, Ag 8,13:4
Bell, Archie, 1943, Ja 27,21:2
Bell, Arthur G, 1947, Mr 14,23:3
Bell, Arthur R, 1952, Ag 11,15:6
Bell, Arthur V, 1940, F 9,19:4
Bell, Austin, 1941, Ap 5,17:3
Bell, Barbara L Mrs, 1958, Ap 20,85:1
Bell, Berkeley, 1967, Je 16,43:2
Bell, Bernard I, 1958, S 6,17:6
Bell, Bert (deBonneville),(will, N 1,27:1), 1959, O 12,1:3
Bell, Bertrand Faugeres, 1917, Jl 16,9:4
Bell, Betty, 1957, My 11,6:2
Bell, Beulah A Mrs, 1951, F 14,29:2
Bell, Billy, 1952, Je 5,31:3
Bell, Brian, 1942, Je 9,23:3
Bell, Brian Mrs, 1963, S 17,35:4
Bell, C Edwin, 1962, N 11,88:3
Bell, C Herbert, 1954, F 1,23:6
Bell, C J, 1929, O 2,31:4
Bell, C S, 1879, F 24,3:6
Bell, Charles, 1954, F 16,25:3
Bell, Charles A, 1945, Mr 11,39:2
Bell, Charles E, 1949, O 16,90:5
Bell, Charles Frederic Moberly, 1911, Ap 6,11:5
Bell, Charles H Rear Adm, 1875, F 20,7:3
Bell, Charles H Sr, 1949, Ja 9,72:7
Bell, Charles J Ex-Gov, 1909, S 27,9:4
Bell, Charles J Mrs, 1948, Jl 18,53:2
Bell, Charles S, 1945, Ag 24,19:5
Bell, Charles W, 1938, F 9,19:2; 1944, O 14,13:5
Bell, Charlie (C D Chase), 1964, S 26,23:3
Bell, Charlotte, 1925, Ap 9,23:4
Bell, Chester A Mrs, 1950, Ag 20,76:3
Bell, Christ, 1947, Ag 24,56:5
Bell, Chss A Mrs, 1954, N 15,27:5
Bell, Clarence, 1966, D 27,35:2
Bell, Clarence D, 1957, My 6,29:5
Bell, Clarence W, 1954, O 17,87:2
Bell, Clark, 1918, F 23,13:3
Bell, Cleveland R Mrs, 1946, D 7,21:2
Bell, Clive, 1964, S 20,88:3
Bell, Clyde C, 1946, My 1,25:4
Bell, Colin C, 1937, Ag 7,15:1
Bell, Colley W, 1962, Jl 2,29:4
Bell, Cullen M, 1946, D 12,29:2
Bell, D C, 1902, O 29,9:5
Bell, Daniel H V, 1957, Je 25,29:3
Bell, David A, 1948, Je 13,69:1
Bell, David C, 1941, Ag 15,17:5
Bell, David M, 1961, Ja 14,23:5
Bell, Davis H, 1943, Jl 27,17:2
Bell, Dennistoun M, 1954, D 17,31:2
Bell, Digby, 1917, Je 21,13:4
Bell, Digby Mrs, 1904, My 30,5:6
Bell, E D, 1884, Ag 7,5:2
Bell, E Gordon, 1946, S 24,29:1
Bell, E T, 1880, N 5,3:5
Bell, Earl H, 1963, O 19,25:4
Bell, Edward A, 1953, Jl 6,17:4
Bell, Edward Bryce, 1968, My 17,47:3
Bell, Edward H, 1950, Ja 13,23:3
Bell, Edward J, 1940, D 23,19:5
Bell, Edward M, 1952, S 22,23:1
Bell, Edward P, 1943, S 24,23:3
Bell, Edwin, 1951, My 2,31:4
Bell, Edwin C, 1923, Jl 19,15:4
Bell, Edwin H, 1937, Ap 21,23:3
Bell, Edwin J, 1938, Je 21,19:6
Bell, Eliza D Mrs, 1941, N 23,51:4
Bell, Elizabeth, 1941, F 27,19:4

Bell, Elizabeth Mrs, 1937, Ap 21,23:5
Bell, Enoch, 1945, Je 11,15:4
Bell, Enoch Chamberlain, 1916, My 27,11:4
Bell, Eric T, 1960, D 22,23:3
Bell, Ernest, 1955, Ja 9,87:1
Bell, Ernest A, 1968, Jl 27,27:1
Bell, Ernest E, 1956, N 25,88:3
Bell, Ernest Lorne Dr, 1925, Ap 20,17:4
Bell, Frances M, 1966, Ap 13,40:1
Bell, Francis A, 1952, D 12,29:3
Bell, Frank, 1948, My 6,25:5
Bell, Frank A, 1944, Jl 16,31:3
Bell, Frank B, 1949, My 7,13:6
Bell, Franklin Maj-Gen (funl, Ja 11,13:4), 1919, Ja 9,11:1
Bell, Fred S, 1958, F 18,20:3
Bell, Frederick H Sr, 1949, Mr 22,25:5
Bell, G, 1929, Ja 14,23:3
Bell, G Jr Maj Gen, 1926, O 29,23:5
Bell, G Lindsay, 1939, Mr 3,24:2
Bell, Galt, 1949, Jl 7,25:4
Bell, George, 1881, D 10,5:1; 1903, Ag 3,7:6; 1923, Jl 30,13:5; 1943, O 4,17:4; 1944, Mr 6,19:2; 1944, My 2,19:3; 1947, Mr 5,26:3
Bell, George Brig-Gen, 1907, Ja 3,9:5
Bell, George C, 1940, O 19,17:3
Bell, George E Jr, 1960, Ja 12,47:1
Bell, George F, 1946, S 8,46:4
Bell, George G, 1948, F 20,27:1
Bell, George Gen Sir, 1877, Jl 13,4:5
Bell, George H, 1943, O 7,23:3; 1965, Je 27,65:1
Bell, George I, 1942, Ap 12,45:3
Bell, George K A, 1958, O 4,21:3
Bell, George L, 1958, O 10,31:2
Bell, George N, 1945, Ja 13,11:6
Bell, George W, 1960, D 8,35:3
Bell, George W Mrs, 1944, Jl 21,19:1
Bell, Gertrude G M L, 1926, Jl 13,21:5
Bell, Gilbert E O, 1955, Je 10,25:1
Bell, Gilbert J, 1945, Ap 30,19:5
Bell, gordon K Sr, 1955, Ag 29,19:5
Bell, H H Adm, 1868, F 19,5:1
Bell, H H Rear-Adm, 1868, F 19,5:1
Bell, H Sir, 1931, Je 30,25:1
Bell, Hans, 1949, O 22,17:6
Bell, Hariam Parks Col, 1907, Ag 17,7:6
Bell, Harold K, 1967, Je 25,69:2
Bell, Harold S, 1961, Ag 27,85:1
Bell, Harry, 1941, N 19,23:1; 1947, N 11,27:3; 1949, F 18,23:4; 1959, Je 26,25:4
Bell, Harry B, 1944, Je 22,19:6
Bell, Harry J, 1943, O 2,13:3
Bell, Harry Jr, 1958, Ag 19,27:3
Bell, Harry L, 1965, D 24,17:3
Bell, Harry P, 1957, Ap 1,25:5
Bell, Harvey W, 1958, D 11,13:4
Bell, Harvey W Mrs, 1960, D 15,43:3
Bell, Helen Mrs, 1960, Je 25,44:5
Bell, Herbert C F, 1966, Ap 13,43:2
Bell, Herbert M, 1943, Ja 2,11:5
Bell, Herbert W, 1944, Jl 9,35:3
Bell, Herman, 1949, Je 8,30:3
Bell, Hermon F, 1961, S 21,35:2
Bell, Heywood Jr, 1968, Ja 29,31:1
Bell, Hillary, 1903, Ap 10,9:2
Bell, Horace G, 1959, My 30,2:7
Bell, Howard P, 1908, My 8,7:5
Bell, Hugh P, 1961, Ja 30,23:4
Bell, I Jr, 1889, Ja 21,2:3
Bell, Ida F, 1944, Mr 27,19:2
Bell, Irene P Mrs, 1941, My 30,15:6
Bell, Isaac, 1897, O 1,7:5
Bell, J F Capt, 1917, N 7,13:4
Bell, J Frank, 1944, Ag 25,13:2
Bell, J Spencer, 1967, Mr 20,31:5
Bell, J Walter, 1957, Ja 10,29:4
Bell, Jack Mrs, 1941, Je 16,15:4
Bell, James, 1922, O 1,28:4; 1948, F 19,23:5; 1949, N 2,27:4
Bell, James A, 1954, Jl 16,21:2
Bell, James A Mrs, 1953, Ja 11,90:4
Bell, James B, 1967, Jl 9,61:2
Bell, James C, 1946, Mr 1,21:3
Bell, James Christy, 1924, Ja 1,23:2
Bell, James D, 1949, Ag 10,22:2
Bell, James D Col, 1919, N 2,22:4
Bell, James F, 1961, My 8,35:2
Bell, James F Mrs, 1943, D 23,19:4
Bell, James H, 1939, Ag 9,17:2; 1961, Jl 25,28:1
Bell, James M Gen, 1919, S 18,13:5
Bell, James S, 1915, Ap 8,13:5
Bell, James W, 1966, D 23,25:2
Bell, Jared Weed, 1923, F 16,13:5
Bell, Jesse C, 1946, F 19,25:2
Bell, Jesse T, 1939, N 10,23:4
Bell, John, 1869, S 11,1:6; 1885, Mr 23,8:5; 1941, Mr 30,41:6
Bell, John A, 1938, O 8,17:6
Bell, John B, 1946, Ap 8,27:3
Bell, John C Mrs, 1944, Ja 12,23:5
Bell, John F, 1951, My 9,33:6
Bell, John F Mrs, 1950, D 15,31:2
Bell, John G, 1963, My 23,37:4
Bell, John Gen Sir, 1876, N 23,4:6
Bell, John H Gen, 1875, Ap 22,7:2
Bell, John H Mrs, 1955, F 27,86:1
Bell, John J, 1945, Je 9,13:3
Bell, John M, 1941, Mr 25,23:5; 1941, Je 4,23:2
Bell, John Mrs, 1941, Ja 13,15:5
Bell, John S Col, 1917, Je 20,11:5
Bell, John T R Mrs, 1956, Mr 26,29:4
Bell, John W, 1939, My 3,23:4
Bell, Joseph Asbury Dr, 1968, O 31,47:2
Bell, Joseph B, 1955, F 28,19:5
Bell, Joseph C, 1948, Ag 3,25:5; 1960, Ap 27,37:3
Bell, Joseph Dr, 1911, O 5,11:5
Bell, Joseph H Mrs, 1944, My 16,21:2
Bell, Joseph Sr, 1952, Ap 19,15:4
Bell, Kenneth C, 1956, Jl 4,19:3
Bell, Kenneth N, 1951, O 17,31:5
Bell, Laird, 1965, O 22,43:1
Bell, Landon C, 1960, Ag 11,25:4
Bell, Lawrence D (funl plans, O 22,29:3; funl, O 24,37:2), 1956, O 21,87:1
Bell, Leslie, 1962, Ja 20,21:4
Bell, Lisle, 1952, O 8,31:1
Bell, Lloyd W, 1959, Ja 25,92:8
Bell, Louis, 1959, F 5,31:4
Bell, Louis Dr, 1923, Je 15,19:6
Bell, Louis H, 1944, My 3,19:6; 1958, O 18,21:5
Bell, Louis V, 1925, Ja 27,13:2
Bell, Lowthian Sir, 1904, D 21,6:1
Bell, Luke, 1946, Je 18,25:3
Bell, M J, 1947, My 29,21:3
Bell, Marcus L, 1945, Je 16,13:4
Bell, Margaret D J Mrs, 1947, Ap 9,25:5
Bell, Martin P, 1947, N 18,30:2
Bell, Mary L, 1958, Je 7,19:3
Bell, Monta, 1958, F 5,28:1
Bell, Neil, 1964, Je 9,35:3
Bell, Nelson B, 1961, Ja 27,23:3
Bell, Oliver, 1952, F 9,13:1
Bell, Orrin D, 1943, Ag 7,11:4
Bell, Oscar C, 1943, Ag 18,19:4
Bell, P F, 1876, Mr 23,2:4
Bell, Park E, 1925, Mr 2,17:6
Bell, Patrick, 1952, Ja 28,17:6
Bell, Paul W, 1956, S 12,37:2
Bell, Pearl Doles, 1968, Mr 13,53:5
Bell, Phil T, 1939, Mr 10,23:2
Bell, Ralph P Mrs, 1943, Mr 18,19:3
Bell, Raymond E, 1956, Ja 26,29:1
Bell, Raymond L, 1948, S 21,27:2
Bell, Rex (funl, Jl 10,33:1; will, Jl 12,18:3), 1962, Jl 5,23:5
Bell, Richard Dana Dr, 1925, D 8,25:4
Bell, Robert, 1937, Ag 26,21:6; 1944, Jl 4,19:1
Bell, Robert A, 1953, F 26,25:1
Bell, Robert B, 1948, Mr 23,25:4
Bell, Robert Goodman, 1904, Ja 7,9:5
Bell, Robert P, 1950, N 3,27:5
Bell, Robert W, 1947, Je 25,25:3
Bell, Samuel, 1959, Jl 1,25:5
Bell, Samuel D, 1966, N 23,39:4
Bell, Samuel Dana Hon, 1868, Ag 2,5:5
Bell, Samuel Jr, 1937, O 3,II,8:5
Bell, Samuel W, 1942, F 21,19:6
Bell, Sanford, 1948, N 11,27:1
Bell, Spurgeon, 1968, D 24,20:7
Bell, Stephen M, 1940, O 18,21:5
Bell, Susie E Mrs, 1942, Ag 8,11:2
Bell, Sylvia C, 1952, Je 13,23:4
Bell, Thaddeus R, 1941, S 26,23:6
Bell, Thomas, 1946, Je 26,25:5; 1952, Ja 11,21:1; 1961, Ja 18,33:2
Bell, Thomas B, 1947, S 13,11:4
Bell, Thomas C, 1940, O 21,17:5
Bell, Thomas L, 1956, Ag 13,19:5
Bell, Thomas M, 1941, Mr 19,21:3
Bell, Thomas P, 1948, O 23,15:4
Bell, thos, 1880, Mr 17,5:2
Bell, Ulric, 1960, Ja 18,27:1
Bell, Van Saunders, 1940, D 5,25:3
Bell, Vaughn Y, 1954, O 29,21:2
Bell, Vernon, 1942, Mr 31,21:1
Bell, W H, 1946, Ap 14,46:4
Bell, W Howard (died Ap 7; mem ser set), 1967, Ap 21,39:2
Bell, W J, 1948, Jl 20,23:5
Bell, W M, 1903, Je 6,1:2
Bell, Wallace A, 1944, Je 5,19:3
Bell, Walter B, 1949, S 4,40:6
Bell, Walter H, 1947, S 26,23:2
Bell, Walter L, 1946, Ag 18,47:1
Bell, Walter R, 1949, S 9,25:4
Bell, Watson, 1937, Je 7,19:5
Bell, Watson H, 1937, My 8,19:2
Bell, Webster, 1945, Mr 18,42:5
Bell, Will J, 1943, Jl 16,17:2
Bell, Willard S, 1954, Je 12,15:5
Bell, William B, 1949, Ap 1,25:2; 1950, D 22,23:5
Bell, William B Mrs, 1949, N 5,13:4
Bell, William E Mrs, 1940, F 24,13:6
Bell, William F, 1939, D 3,61:1
Bell, William H, 1941, N 12,23:4; 1944, F 14,17:3; 1961, S 14,31:3
Bell, William H Mrs, 1944, Jl 22,15:7; 1957, Je 15,17:5
Bell, William J, 1944, Jl 4,19:3
Bell, William L Jr, 1956, Mr 20,23:4
Bell, William M, 1946, F 18,21:4
Bell, William Mara, 1907, N 3,9:7
Bell, William P, 1953, Je 23,29:3
Bell, William R Capt, 1915, My 4,15:5
Bell, William Rev, 1871, Ap 22,4:2
Bell, William T, 1939, N 23,27:5; 1943, Ap 5,19:3; 1962, Ja 22,23:3
Bell, William W, 1961, D 28,27:4
Bell, Winslow M, 1946, Ja 19,13:3
Bella, Daniel, 1955, Ja 15,13:5
Bellachioma, Attilio, 1952, Ja 10,30:3
Bellah, J Warner Lt, 1910, S 26,13:5
Bellah, Robert G, 1951, F 9,25:2
Bellaing, Edouard Moreau de, 1952, D 22,25:5
Bellairs, Carolyn W Mrs, 1939, N 20,19:5
Bellairs, Henry Rev, 1872, My 6,1:6
Bellairs, Kenneth G, 1940, D 25,27:6
Bellak, Charles M, 1944, N 1,23:3
Bellak, Frederick, 1950, Ja 29,68:8
Bellaman, Henry, 1945, Je 17,26:1
Bellaman, Katherine J Mrs, 1956, N 10,19:2
Bellamann, Caroline Mrs, 1942, Je 23,19:2
Bellamy, David, 1960, N 24,29:1
Bellamy, E, 1898, My 23,7:5
Bellamy, Edward Mrs, 1956, S 6,25:4
Bellamy, F Wilder, 1955, O 25,33:1
Bellamy, John D, 1942, S 27,48:3
Bellamy, John M, 1958, Mr 15,17:5
Bellamy, John S, 1948, F 16,21:1
Bellamy, Paul, 1956, Ap 13,25:1
Bellamy, Rexford Mrs, 1962, Je 16,19:6
Bellanca, Andrew, 1957, D 2,27:5
Bellanca, August Mrs, 1946, Ag 17,13:3
Bellanca, Frank M, 1962, Je 21,31:4
Bellanca, Giuseppe M, 1960, D 27,29:2
Bellanca, Leo, 1942, O 21,21:6
Bellantoni, Raphael, 1958, O 30,31:4
Bellantoni, Thomas G, 1945, Je 22,15:2
Bellatoni, Anthony, 1925, N 29,13:1
Bellatoni, Anthony Mrs, 1925, N 29,13:1
Belle, Victor, 1943, Ja 25,13:2
Belle-Isle, Armand G, 1954, Je 14,21:2
Belle-Isle, David, 1947, Ja 10,22:2
Bellefeuille, Henry, 1939, Ag 25,15:2
Bellegarde, Louis D, 1966, Je 16,47:4
Belleisle, Albert J, 1950, S 22,31:2
Bellenger, Frederick J, 1968, My 12,85:1
Beller, Abraham, 1952, Ap 14,19:3
Beller, Abraham J, 1960, Ja 16,21:2
Beller, Abraham J Mrs, 1945, Ja 1,21:2
Beller, Hans Mrs, 1950, Ap 11,31:3
Beller, Robert, 1951, N 25,87:2
Bellerjeau, Randall, 1960, My 21,23:4
Bellerose, Jean B, 1949, D 26,29:3
Bellerose, Maurice N, 1949, D 29,26:2
Belles, Ella U Mrs, 1957, F 28,27:2
Bellesheim, Frederick, 1942, Ap 22,23:2
Bellesheim, Henry J, 1947, O 24,23:2
Bellessort, Andre, 1942, Ja 23,19:4
Belleville, Henry O, 1953, D 16,35:5
Belleville, Jeanne de, 1953, Ja 13,27:3
Bellevue, Fernand S, 1916, Mr 19,19:6
Bellew, John C M, 1874, Jl 9,4:7
Bellew, John C M Y, 1874, Je 20,5:3
Bellew, Kyrle (funl, N 5,15:5), 1911, N 3,11:4
Bellew, Patrick J, 1958, Ja 16,29:1
Bellew, Robert J, 1937, Jl 30,19:6
Bellew, Thomas J, 1948, S 3,19:2
Bellezza, Russell G, 1958, Ja 15,39:3
Bellezza, Vincenzo, 1964, F 9,88:5
Bellfenville, Edward, 1937, Ja 22,22:3
Bellfort, David, 1958, O 24,33:2
Belli, Andrew F, 1951, F 24,13:4
Bellia, Bruno S, 1959, F 14,21:5
Bellimer, Edward F, 1956, My 17,31:3
Bellin, Jacob H, 1956, F 5,86:3
Bellin, Maurice, 1963, My 19,86:6
Bellinger, Charles, 1948, F 10,23:5
Bellinger, Clarence H, 1952, Ag 14,23:3
Bellinger, Ezra D, 1947, D 24,21:2
Bellinger, F P, 1876, F 16,4:7
Bellinger, Franz Mrs, 1960, Ja 6,35:4
Bellinger, Frederic C, 1941, S 10,23:2
Bellinger, Herman C, 1941, Jl 29,15:4
Bellinger, J B, 1931, S 24,25:1
Bellinger, John B Mrs, 1951, Mr 12,25:3
Bellinger, Patrick N L (funl, Je 2,19:2), 1962, My 27:4
Bellinger, Vernon C, 1946, Ja 11,22:2
Bellinger, Walter E, 1946, Mr 2,13:3
Bellinger, William H, 1948, Jl 11,50:8
Bellinger, William W, 1943, Ap 7,25:5
Bellingham, James C, 1949, F 14,19:3
Bellinghausen, Herman, 1958, Jl 29,23:3
Bellingrath, Elizabeth C Mrs, 1939, D 21,23:4
Bellingrath, Leon, 1945, Jl 28,11:5
Bellingrath, Walter D, 1955, Ag 10,25:4
Bellings, Otto A, 1938, My 13,19:3
Bellini, Ettore, 1943, Ja 22,20:3
Bellini, Renato, 1957, Je 5,35:3

Bellino, Vincenzo, 1952, D 23,23:5
Belliotti, Joseph L, 1948, O 28,29:3
Bellis, A Malcolm Mrs, 1949, F 11,23:4
Bellis, Alfred P S, 1959, N 12,35:4
Bellis, Bernard, 1954, Mr 31,27:3
Bellis, David D, 1952, My 20,25:4
Bellis, Edgar S Mrs, 1962, S 3,15:4
Bellis, Edwin H, 1938, Je 10,21:6
Bellis, Horace D, 1950, N 6,27:4
Bellis, John R, 1949, Ja 5,25:1
Bellis, John W, 1947, O 31,23:2; 1949, O 15,15:6
Bellis, Parks I, 1950, Ag 13,77:1
Bellis, W Oliver, 1957, Je 26,31:2
Bellison, Simeon, 1953, My 5,29:3
Bellman, Edmund R, 1939, D 11,23:5
Bellman, Harold, 1963, Je 3,29:2
Bellman, Will E Mrs, 1945, Jl 23,19:5
Bellmarre, Jacques, 1946, S 4,23:5
Bellmer, Herman F, 1945, D 16,39:1
Bellner, Peter, 1909, Ja 4,9:4
Bello, Jean Mrs, 1958, Je 12,31:3
Bello, Leonardo M, 1944, N 29,23:3
Bello, Vincent, 1957, Mr 9,19:6
Bello Codecido, Emilio, 1963, Mr 5,16:1
Bello y Ahedo, Mariano, 1938, S 7,36:6
Belloc, Bessie Rayner, 1925, Mr 24,23:2
Belloc, Hilaire (will, S 20,38:6), 1953, Jl 17,17:1
Bellon, August, 1943, O 16,13:5
Belloni, Ambrogio, 1950, Jl 23,12:5
Belloni, Sadie H, 1950, Ag 1,23:3
Belloso y Sanchez, Jose A Archbishop of San Salvador, 1938, Ag 11,17:5
Bellow, Harry, 1965, Mr 1,27:3
Bellow, Jacob I, 1967, Ag 26,28:1
Bellows, A Alonzo, 1947, Mr 30,56:4
Bellows, A F, 1883, N 25,2:5
Bellows, Albert H, 1948, Jl 29,21:3
Bellows, Albert Mrs, 1951, D 10,29:1
Bellows, Anna Langden, 1906, Ja 13,9:5
Bellows, Brian C, 1943, D 22,23:3
Bellows, Charles, 1963, My 27,29:4
Bellows, Charles H, 1943, Jl 1,19:2
Bellows, Charles Mrs, 1957, Ag 6,27:5
Bellows, Chief Justice, 1873, Mr 12,5:1
Bellows, Clarence E S, 1937, Jl 8,23:5
Bellows, Daniel E, 1943, O 17,48:6
Bellows, Donald Mrs, 1959, O 7,43:3
Bellows, Edward, 1903, My 21,9:4
Bellows, Elbert E, 1951, My 18,27:1
Bellows, Frederick E, 1954, My 8,17:6
Bellows, George Mrs, 1959, My 12,35:4
Bellows, George Wesley (funl, Ja 11,5:2), 1925, Ja 9,17:3
Bellows, H W (mem ser, F 13,1:7), 1882, Ja 27,2:3
Bellows, Harold A, 1960, O 6,41:6
Bellows, Harold H, 1960, O 5,41:3
Bellows, Henry A, 1939, D 30,15:4
Bellows, Howard C, 1940, D 29,24:8
Bellows, John, 1945, Ap 20,19:1
Bellows, John Mrs, 1940, Mr 15,23:1
Bellows, Johnson M, 1949, Ap 9,17:5
Bellows, Marjorie T, 1961, Jl 14,23:3
Bellows, Oscar F, 1949, My 22,88:5
Bellows, Robert P, 1957, My 25,21:6
Bellows, Russell H, 1949, N 11,25:2
Bellows, S D, 1879, Ja 6,5:6
Bellows, William Mrs, 1950, N 23,38:4
Bellows, Willis A Mrs, 1954, Jl 17,13:5
Bellucci, Antonio, 1916, My 25,13:4
Bellucci, Frank A, 1968, Ag 25,88:6
Bellus, Jean, 1967, Ja 16,41:3
Bellusci, Nicola, 1952, Ja 16,25:3
Belluscio, Frank Sr, 1957, O 22,33:6
Belluzzo, Giuseppe, 1952, My 23,21:4
Bellwald, August M, 1946, F 9,13:4
Belmar, Maurice, 1953, D 16,35:3
Belmont, August, 1890, N 25,1:7
Belmont, August Jr (funl, Ag 1,11:4), 1919, Mr 30, 22:2
Belmont, August Maj, 1924, D 12,21:4
Belmont, Earle A, 1953, F 26,25:4
Belmont, Earle A Mrs, 1953, Mr 2,23:6
Belmont, Edgar, 1953, Ap 3,24:4
Belmont, Frank J Jr, 1960, S 9,29:1
Belmont, Frederick Mrs, 1945, D 9,44:2
Belmont, Ira J, 1964, O 23,39:1
Belmont, Joan M Mrs, 1952, My 24,19:4
Belmont, Morgan, 1953, S 19,15:3
Belmont, Morgan Mrs, 1945, N 3,15:2
Belmont, O H P Mrs, 1933, Ja 26,17:1
Belmont, Oliver H P (funl, Je 12,7:2), 1908, Je 11,7:3
Belmont, P Mrs, 1935, O 21,19:3
Belmont, Perry, 1947, My 26,1:5
Belmont, Peter F, 1950, N 11,15:2
Belmont, Roy, 1946, O 23,27:4
Belmonte, Gloria, 1955, S 14,35:5
Belmonte, Juan, 1962, Ap 9,1:6
Belmonte, Peter, 1949, S 6,27:3
Belmonte Pool, Waldo, 1954, My 9,88:2
Belmore, Bertha, 1953, D 16,35:5
Belmore, Daisy, 1954, D 13,27:4
Belmore, Earl of, 1948, F 14,13:2
Belmore, Earl of (C Lowry-Corry), 1949, Mr 3,25:4
Belmore, George (funl, N 18,2:4), 1875, N 16,4:7
Belmore, Herbert, 1952, Mr 16,91:2
Belmore, Leonard, 1951, O 17,31:1
Belmore, Lionel, 1953, F 3,25:4
Belnap, H W, 1918, O 13,23:2
Belo, A H Mrs, 1913, F 6,11:5
Belo, Alfred H Mrs, 1954, Ap 4,88:1
Belo, Antonio, 1948, Jl 17,15:4
Beloe, William, 1966, Ap 4,24:8
Belosselsky-Beloserski, Constantin Prince, 1920, My 30,22:3
Belosselsky-Belozersky, Andre, 1961, Ap 12,41:3
Belosselsky-Belozersky, Serge Prince, 1951, Ap 22,88:6
Belote, Theodore G, 1967, F 14,43:1
Belous, Charles, 1966, Jl 15,31:3
Belous, Meyer, 1943, Ja 9,13:3
Beloussoff, Evsei, 1945, D 3,21:5
Beloussoff, Evsei Mrs, 1961, My 13,19:5
Below, Otto von, 1944, Mr 16,19:4
Belowsky, Morris Mrs, 1959, Jl 27,25:3
Belper, Baron (Hy Strutt), 1914, Jl 27,7:7
Belper, Lord (E Strutt), 1880, Jl 2,5:1
Belrose, Louis, 1960, Mr 11,25:1
Belsey, Francis Flint Sir, 1914, My 26,11:5
Belshaw, Charles, 1919, N 25,11:4
Belshaw, Charles Mrs, 1919, N 25,11:4
Belshaw, Harold, 1966, Ja 27,33:4
Belshaw, Horace, 1962, Mr 22,35:3
Belsinger, Harry P, 1941, My 31,11:6
Belsky, Abraham, 1958, Jl 9,27:5
Belsky, Hyman, 1962, Ap 2,31:3
Belsky, Isidore, 1938, Jl 26,19:5
Belsky, Max, 1950, Je 15,31:4
Belson, J Harry, 1947, Mr 15,13:3
Belsterling, Charles S, 1959, D 27,60:3
Belt, Benjamin L, 1937, S 16,25:3
Belt, Benjamin L (will), 1939, F 17,22:8
Belt, Glen, 1940, S 6,21:5
Belt, Henry Dr, 1910, My 7,9:6
Belt, O C, 1961, S 13,45:1
Belt, William L, 1908, D 14,9:3
Beltaire, John B, 1957, Je 9,89:1
Belth, Irving, 1952, Je 26,29:6
Belth, Norton, 1965, Mr 20,27:3
Belting, Herbert J, 1948, F 29,60:8
Belton, Austin J, 1962, N 25,86:6
Belton, Joseph, 1952, Ag 5,19:4
Belton, Patrick J, 1951, Ag 5,73:2
Belton, Samuel G, 1958, F 11,31:1
Beltran, Basil R, 1949, Ja 21,22:2
Belts, Theodore E, 1951, Je 6,31:3
Beltz, Frederick, 1944, Je 17,13:7
Beltz, Harry B, 1949, My 8,76:4
Beltz, W B T, 1942, F 9,15:2
Beltz, William E, 1960, N 23,29:3
Beltzhoover, George G, 1942, O 31,15:7
Belven, John L, 1941, O 7,23:1
Belville, J Edgar, 1939, My 31,23:2
Belviso, Thomas H, 1967, D 29,27:2
Belvoir, Wilbur H, 1909, Jl 8,7:4
Belwin, Alma, 1924, My 4,23:2
Belyayev, Ivan, 1967, Mr 25,23:4
Belyayev, Nikolai I, 1966, O 30,89:1
Belz, Emil O, 1953, D 15,39:1
Belz, John C, 1955, Je 9,29:5
Belz, Joseph A, 1937, O 1,21:4
Belzer, Adolf, 1958, Ja 29,27:1
Belzer, Max W, 1951, Ap 3,27:3
Belzner, Theodore, 1955, N 21,29:4
Belzner, William J, 1940, S 2,15:3
Bemak, Louis, 1948, N 26,23:3
Beman, James G, 1949, My 17,25:5
Beman, John B Sr, 1954, Ja 2,11:5
Beman, N S S Rev Dr, 1871, Ag 16,3:1
Bemardone, Carmino, 1908, Ja 28,9:4
Bembaron, David, 1955, My 3,31:1
Bemberg, Federico O, 1949, Ap 1,25:2
Bembo, P L Count, 1882, F 3,5:3
Bembridge, John F, 1959, S 19,23:5
Bembridge, William A, 1941, O 14,23:4
Bemelmans, Ludwig, 1962, O 2,39:4
Bement, Alon Mrs (K Emmet), 1960, Je 7,35:5
Bement, Clarence S, 1923, Ja 28,6:2
Bement, Douglas, 1943, My 16,42:4
Bement, Frederick, 1917, Jl 9,9:5
Bement, L Dennison Jr, 1960, F 20,23:4
Bement, Louis M, 1944, S 5,19:5
Bement, Martin O, 1944, Je 1,19:2
Bemis, Anthony J, 1942, Mr 22,49:1
Bemis, Earl W, 1939, Ap 29,17:5
Bemis, G E, 1901, O 26,9:4
Bemis, George H, 1962, Jl 20,25:4
Bemis, George M, 1943, Ap 5,19:1
Bemis, Harry P, 1947, My 25,60:5
Bemis, Willard, 1950, Mr 4,17:5
Bemish, Donald M, 1946, Ag 11,46:1
Bemont, Alon, 1954, N 24,23:1
Bena, Victor A, 1947, Mr 15,13:4
Benach, Martin L, 1949, My 31,23:2
Benaderet, Bea, 1968, O 14,47:3
Benaglia, Angelo E, 1956, Mr 5,23:4
Benaglia, Arthur, 1944, Je 9,15:4
Benahm, Vernon A Mrs, 1953, My 24,88:2
Benaim, Joseph F, 1958, Ag 6,25:1
Ben Ali, Hassan, 1914, Jl 22,9:5
Ben-Ami, Jacob Mrs, 1966, O 22,31:4
Benanti, Phil J, 1949, S 22,31:3
Benard, Aime, 1938, Ja 10,17:6
Benard, Edmond D, 1961, F 5,10:1
Benares, Maharajah of, 1939, Ap 6,25:1
Benari, Benjamin, 1967, D 30,23:2
Ben-Ari, Raikin, 1968, Ja 9,32:3
Benas, John M, 1948, Mr 11,27:3
Benas, Maurice E Mrs, 1966, F 12,25:2
Ben-Asher, Samuel L, 1954, O 22,27:1
Ben-Asher, Solom J, 1949, Ap 28,31:4
Benassi, Memo, 1957, F 25,25:5
Benatar, Louis, 1945, D 28,16:2
Benathen, Morris B, 1966, Ag 21,92:7
Benatzky, Ralph, 1957, O 18,23:2
Benavente, Maurice, 1959, S 6,72:5
Benavente y Martinez, Jacinto (cor, Jl 30,17:2), 1954, Jl 15,27:1
Ben Avi, Ittamar, 1943, Ap 19,19:3
Benavides, Oscar H, 1945, Jl 3,13:5
Ben Ayad, Prince, 1946, N 20,31:2
Benbough, Percy J, 1942, N 5,25:5
Benbow, John, 1944, F 22,24:2
Benbow, William, 1939, Ag 16,23:2
Benbrook, Albert, 1943, Ag 16,15:3
Bence, John G, 1947, F 3,19:4
Bence, Logan C, 1943, S 11,13:4
Bence, Miguel A Mrs, 1947, Ja 21,23:4
Bencel, Joseph, 1945, N 18,44:1
Bench, John J, 1947, D 10,31:3
Benchley, Robert C, 1945, N 22,35:1
Benckendorff, Alexandre C Count, 1917, Ja 12,13:4
Bencsik, Michael, 1950, D 23,15:6
Benda, Jean, 1949, Ag 3,23:1
Benda, John Mrs, 1963, S 13,29:1
Benda, Julien, 1956, Je 8,25:3
Benda, Rosel F, 1954, Je 14,21:4
Benda, Wladyslaw T, 1948, D 1,29:2
Bendann, Laurence, 1938, Mr 28,15:5
Bendel, Aug, 1938, Ja 26,23:2
Bendel, Henri W (will), 1939, Ja 7,13:8
Bendel, Leon, 1950, F 5,84:5
Bendelari, Arthur E, 1952, F 13,29:2
Bendelari, Augusto, 1903, My 16,9:6
Bender, Abraham L, 1963, Ap 11,33:1
Bender, Albert F, 1949, Ag 10,21:2
Bender, Albert M, 1941, Mr 5,21:2
Bender, Anton A (Tony), 1955, F 25,21:5
Bender, Arthur, 1908, F 14,7:7
Bender, August F, 1950, Jl 23,57:2
Bender, Augustus J, 1965, S 7,39:3
Bender, Charles A (funl, My 28,23:3; A Daley on Career, My 28,27:2), 1954, My 23,88:4
Bender, Charles A Mrs, 1961, Mr 2,27:1
Bender, Charles M Sr, 1950, Mr 15,29:2
Bender, Clifford A, 1966, D 1,47:5
Bender, Daniel H, 1953, D 28,21:4
Bender, Edward, 1947, F 15,15:2
Bender, Edward A, 1947, Ag 11,23:4
Bender, Edwin A, 1950, Je 21,27:2
Bender, Edwin P, 1952, F 3,85:1
Bender, Ezra Mrs, 1943, My 27,28:6
Bender, Frank B, 1958, Je 12,31:3
Bender, Frederick W, 1963, Je 9,87:1
Bender, George A, 1948, O 6,29:5
Bender, George E, 1954, N 8,21:4
Bender, George F, 1941, Ag 27,19:2
Bender, George H, 1961, Je 19,27:3
Bender, George Mrs, 1949, My 6,25:2
Bender, Harold H, 1951, Ag 17,17:6
Bender, Irwin H, 1951, D 19,31:4
Bender, James P, 1960, D 6,41:3
Bender, John B, 1966, Ap 28,34:6
Bender, Joseph B, 1948, D 1,29:5
Bender, Karl Mrs, 1948, N 4,29:2
Bender, Louis Mrs, 1949, D 31,15:5
Bender, Maurice B Mrs, 1957, My 12,86:8
Bender, Melvin T Mrs, 1940, O 28,17:6
Bender, Milton, 1964, Mr 4,37:2
Bender, Olive Mrs, 1950, Jl 6,28:3
Bender, Oscar G, 1955, F 9,25:3
Bender, Oscar G Mrs, 1964, N 5,45:5
Bender, Paul B, 1941, My 14,21:1
Bender, Peter, 1940, My 19,42:4; 1940, D 9,19:3
Bender, Richard V, 1948, Ag 4,21:5
Bender, Robert W, 1937, D 27,32:2
Bender, Simon Mrs, 1952, N 29,17:3
Bender, Welcome W, 1947, O 30,25:3
Bender, Welcome W Mrs, 1941, O 6,17:5
Bender, William, 1954, Ja 3,88:6
Bender, William F, 1948, S 1,23:2
Bender, William I, 1961, S 11,27:6
Bender, William J, 1944, Mr 12,38:2
Bendere, Edward C, 1951, O 26,23:4
Benderly, Samson, 1944, Jl 10,15:6
Bendern, Arnold Maurice de Count, 1968, O 8,47:2
Bendet, Louis, 1942, Mr 3,24:2
Bendheim, Arthur H, 1950, Je 13,27:3
Bendheim, Fritz, 1955, O 1,19:2
Bendheim, Henry J, 1962, D 10,17:2
Bendheim, Nanette Felsentein Mrs, 1968, N 24,87:2

Bendheim, Siegfried, 1960, Mr 3,29:2
Bendick, Charles Mrs, 1950, Je 8,31:3
Bendick, George A, 1956, Ja 30,27:3
Bendick, Harry L, 1949, Ap 16,15:1
Bendiner, Alfred, 1964, Mr 20,33:3
Bendiner, Irvin, 1946, N 6,23:6
Bendiner, Milford, 1955, Je 13,23:4
Bendiner, Sabato M, 1957, N 18,31:4
Bendinger, Henry J, 1964, F 1,23:3
Bendinger, Jacob Mrs, 1950, D 19,29:2
Benditzsky, Naoum Mrs (M Kerr), 1963, S 20,33:4
Bendix, Carlheinz, 1959, Je 9,37:2
Bendix, Earnest O, 1948, D 1,29:3
Bendix, Emil, 1962, Ap 24,27:6
Bendix, Ernest, 1944, Je 24,13:4
Bendix, J E Gen (see also O 9), 1877, O 11,8:1
Bendix, Max, 1945, D 7,22:3
Bendix, Paul R, 1943, D 28,18:2
Bendix, Vincent, 1945, Mr 28,23:1
Bendix, William (funl, D 18,33:4), 1964, D 15,43:1
Bendixen, Bernhard C, 1959, F 2,25:3
Bendixen, J Henry, 1940, D 5,25:2
Bendixsen, Aage, 1950, F 26,79:3
Bendove, Raphael A, 1951, S 22,17:5
Bendy, William S Mrs, 1949, D 11,92:6
Bene, Joseph, 1937, N 3,17:8
Benecke, Alex, 1952, Mr 25,27:3
Benedek, Beatrice Mrs, 1963, D 28,23:2
Benedek, L von, 1881, Ap 28,5:2
Benedetti, Joseph, 1954, Ag 28,15:5
Benedetti, le Comtesse Mme, 1873, Je 29,1:2
Benedetti, Vincent de Count, 1900, Mr 29,6:7
Benedetti-Pichler, Anton A, 1964, D 12,31:4
Benedetto, N Warren, 1953, F 24,25:4
Benedetto, Vincenzo, 1943, Ag 1,38:7
Benedict, A K, 1878, Mr 1,8:5
Benedict, A L, 1950, Ja 16,25:5
Benedict, Abner R Maj, 1867, My 19,5:4
Benedict, Abraham, 1943, Mr 5,17:3
Benedict, Abraham Z, 1945, Mr 1,21:3
Benedict, Agnes E, 1950, Ja 7,17:4
Benedict, Albert C, 1940, O 30,23:2
Benedict, Albert N, 1941, Je 4,23:3
Benedict, Albert R, 1953, Ap 19,90:1
Benedict, Alfred C, 1943, My 29,13:5
Benedict, Amos C, 1950, Mr 24,26:2
Benedict, Andrew B Sr, 1953, My 19,29:2
Benedict, Basil D, 1961, Ja 29,47:3
Benedict, Benjamin Lincoln, 1920, Jl 14,9:6
Benedict, C A, 1933, N 2,21:1
Benedict, C Ray, 1939, My 5,23:3
Benedict, Carrie B Mrs (C Bridewell), 1955, Ja 8,13:2
Benedict, Charles, 1881, N 3,5:3; 1938, S 20,23:2
Benedict, Charles A, 1944, N 5,54:7
Benedict, Charles C, 1951, F 1,25:5
Benedict, Charles C Mrs, 1956, Je 1,23:3
Benedict, Charles H, 1940, Ja 14,42:6; 1948, O 21,27:4
Benedict, Charles S Dr, 1937, Ap 17,17:5
Benedict, Charles W, 1941, Ag 22,15:6
Benedict, Claire (Mrs J Collamore), 1954, Jl 20,19:4
Benedict, Clara E, 1949, Jl 6,27:4
Benedict, Cleveland K Mrs (will, S 30,15:1), 1959, Jl 18,15:6
Benedict, Cooper Procter, 1968, Je 6,47:4
Benedict, E C, 1880, O 23,2:7; 1936, My 12,23:3
Benedict, E C Com, 1919, F 27,11:2
Benedict, Edwin C Mrs, 1957, Jl 7,61:1
Benedict, Edwin P, 1915, My 12,13:4
Benedict, Eleanore B Mrs, 1954, D 25,11:5
Benedict, Eli, 1941, Jl 17,19:6
Benedict, Elias C Mrs, 1907, S 29,9:4
Benedict, Elias Cornelius Commodore, 1920, N 25,15:5
Benedict, Erastus D, 1915, S 21,11:6
Benedict, Ernest L, 1939, Mr 8,21:4
Benedict, Farrand N, 1956, N 4,87:1
Benedict, Felicia L Mrs, 1939, Jl 11,19:4
Benedict, Florence, 1937, Mr 2,21:5
Benedict, Francis G, 1957, My 16,31:2
Benedict, Frank E, 1911, F 5,II,11:3
Benedict, Frank L, 1967, Ja 11,25:3
Benedict, Frank R Mrs, 1950, My 11,29:2
Benedict, Fred I, 1947, Mr 29,15:3
Benedict, Frederic P, 1967, Jl 3,17:5
Benedict, G H, 1876, My 15,5:6
Benedict, George E, 1942, N 22,52:7
Benedict, George G Mrs, 1963, Ag 30,21:2
Benedict, George Greenville, 1907, Ap 9,9:6
Benedict, George W, 1871, S 25,4:7
Benedict, Grace S Mrs, 1937, Jl 24,15:2
Benedict, H Augusta Mrs, 1939, Ja 28,15:1
Benedict, H Kimball, 1958, My 14,33:5
Benedict, H Morrison, 1953, D 10,47:3
Benedict, Harry, 1963, Ap 5,48:1
Benedict, Harry E Mrs, 1956, My 4,25:1
Benedict, Harry H Mrs, 1948, S 11,15:1
Benedict, Harry H Sr, 1956, O 1,27:1
Benedict, Harry Y Dr, 1937, My 11,25:2
Benedict, Henry H Mrs (will, N 1,41:1; est acctg, N 4,14:2), 1961, O 30,29:2
Benedict, Henry Mrs, 1924, O 11,15:5
Benedict, Herschel A, 1941, Ap 21,19:6
Benedict, Hobart L, 1960, Mr 17,33:5
Benedict, Homer B, 1947, D 1,22:2
Benedict, Homer E, 1951, Ag 8,25:1
Benedict, Howard O, 1953, S 24,33:5
Benedict, Howard W, 1946, Ap 26,21:4
Benedict, James A, 1955, Ag 11,21:4
Benedict, James Augustus, 1924, O 3,21:3
Benedict, James D, 1944, N 3,21:5
Benedict, James D Mrs, 1958, N 21,29:3
Benedict, James H, 1925, Mr 11,21:4
Benedict, Jay L, 1953, S 17,29:4
Benedict, Jerome, 1946, O 9,27:3
Benedict, Jesse L, 1956, O 28,89:1
Benedict, John C, 1939, Jl 13,19:4
Benedict, John Mrs, 1949, Ja 22,13:2
Benedict, John N, 1958, O 1,37:6
Benedict, Julius Sir, 1885, Je 6,5:2
Benedict, Le Grand L, 1923, O 29,15:4
Benedict, Lemuel C, 1943, S 16,21:5
Benedict, Leroy, 1943, Jl 31,13:2
Benedict, Lewis L Col, 1864, Ap 24,5:3
Benedict, M Elizabeth, 1939, Ag 16,23:4
Benedict, Margaret DeW, 1960, My 21,23:5
Benedict, Mary K, 1956, F 13,27:3
Benedict, Mary von B Mrs, 1941, Ap 22,21:5
Benedict, Nathan, 1943, Je 15,21:5
Benedict, Paul M, 1938, Ag 19,19:1
Benedict, Percy L, 1952, O 8,31:1
Benedict, Pierce E, 1937, F 12,23:2
Benedict, Purdy F, 1957, Mr 19,37:2
Benedict, R, 1936, N 30,21:3
Benedict, Ralph C, 1965, Ag 7,21:1
Benedict, Ralph T, 1962, D 8,27:5
Benedict, Raymond G, 1938, Ap 10,II,6:2
Benedict, Read, 1914, S 21,7:4
Benedict, Robert A, 1954, S 29,31:5
Benedict, Robert Dewey, 1911, Jl 30,9:5
Benedict, Ruth F, 1948, S 18,17:1
Benedict, S R, 1936, D 23,21:3
Benedict, S W, 1880, My 5,8:2
Benedict, Sarah Seaman Mrs, 1914, Ja 1,15:4
Benedict, Sumner L, 1957, Je 9,88:4
Benedict, Susan, 1942, Ap 10,18:2
Benedict, Victor E, 1951, D 12,37:4
Benedict, Wallace, 1941, F 9,49:2
Benedict, Walter L, 1953, My 9,19:1
Benedict, Walter L Mrs, 1950, Ap 13,29:4
Benedict, Walter S, 1950, Je 16,25:5
Benedict, Warren D Mrs, 1952, Jl 11,17:2
Benedict, Wayland R Prof, 1915, Jl 23,9:6
Benedict, William H, 1938, Ja 4,23:5
Benedict, William L Mrs, 1951, Ja 24,27:4
Benedict, Williston, 1961, Mr 12,86:8
Benedict Victor Brother (D Cronin), 1966, Ja 20,30:4
Benedictis, Benjamin, 1916, Jl 12,11:7
Benedicto, Jose A, 1924, Jl 27,23:4
Benedictus, Pierre E, 1954, Je 17,29:3
Benedikt, Moriz, 1920, Mr 20,11:6
Benedikt, William G (will), 1953, Jl 14,25:1
Benedite, Leonce, 1925, My 13,21:5
Benedix, Hans Ehrlich, 1916, Ag 1,9:5
Benedix, John Robert, 1873, S 28,4:7
Benedum, Michael L (funl, Ag 2,80:4; will, Ag 5,17:2), 1959, Jl 31,23:1
Benedum, Michael L (est appr), 1961, Jl 3,9:2
Benedum, Michael L Mrs, 1951, Ag 12,78:8
Benedum, Ralph C, 1955, Ja 16,95:6
Benefield, Barry Mrs, 1960, Ap 15,23:4
Beneke, William Sr, 1942, S 4,23:2
Benelli, Sem, 1949, D 19,27:2
Benemelis, Lorenzo M, 1948, F 29,60:3
Benenson, Isador, 1946, F 21,21:4
Benenson, Jacob, 1949, Je 23,27:2
Benenson, Jacob Mrs, 1953, Ap 12,89:1
Benenson, Robert, 1955, S 4,56:1
Benes, Eduard, 1948, S 4,1:2
Benes, Eduard Mrs (death rept denied, Ja 10,87:1), 1954, Ja 9,15:2
Benes, Jara, 1949, Ap 12,30:3
Benes, John A, 1957, F 5,23:5
Benes, Vaclaw, 1943, N 25,26:3
Benes, Vojta, 1951, N 21,25:5
Benesch, Aaron G, 1966, Ag 17,36:4
Benesch, Anna M, 1951, Ja 16,29:5
Benesch, Edward A, 1950, S 4,17:5
Benesch, John T Mrs, 1952, Jl 24,27:1
Benesch, Otto, 1964, N 28,21:5
Benesch, William Mrs, 1958, Je 20,23:3
Benesi, Oscar, 1956, Ja 20,23:3
Beneson, Benjamin (por), 1938, Ja 27,21:5
Benet, Christie, 1951, Mr 31,15:4
Benet, Francis N R Mrs, 1940, Jl 9,21:5
Benet, Laurence V, 1948, My 22,15:3
Benet, Stephen V, 1943, Mr 14,25:1
Benet, Stephen V Mrs, 1962, Ag 19,88:2
Benet, William R, 1950, My 5,21:1
Benet, William R Mrs (Marjorie Flack), 1958, Ag 31,56:8
Beneville, Prosper V Mrs, 1961, Mr 30,29:3
Beneway, Frank Mrs, 1943, D 31,15:2
Benezet, Louis P, 1961, My 4,37:5
Benfield, Thomas, 1922, S 29,19:5
Benford, Edward M, 1937, Ja 6,23:4
Ben-Gavriel, Moshe Y, 1965, S 20,7:2
Benge, Wilson, 1955, Jl 3,33:2
Bengelsdorf, Albert A, 1956, S 16,84:4
Benger, Ernest B, 1954, My 28,23:3
Bengert, L A, 1957, Mr 31,89:1
Bengis, Abraham, 1952, Ja 11,21:4
Bengough, Benny, 1968, D 23,39:2
Bengough, Margaret L Mrs, 1945, My 23,19:3
Bengs, Hilding A, 1958, F 2,87:1
Bengsten, Holger S, 1951, N 19,23:4
Bengston, Anna L, 1938, F 15,25:6
Bengston, Carl JDr, 1937, Jl 10,15:5
Bengtson, John C, 1948, Ja 5,19:2
Bengtsson, Frans G, 1954, D 20,29:4
Benguiat, Benjamin, 1953, O 28,29:2
Benguiat, Vital, 1937, Mr 18,25:1
Ben Gurion, David Mrs, 1968, Ja 30,41:1
Benham, Albert, 1952, F 17,85:2
Benham, Charles M, 1959, Ap 29,33:5
Benham, Clarence H, 1943, Je 22,20:2
Benham, Clyde G, 1960, Je 1,39:4
Benham, De Witt M, 1938, Je 11,15:4
Benham, F Darius, 1960, Ja 26,35:7
Benham, Frederick W Mrs, 1953, N 1,87:1
Benham, George F, 1961, Jl 26,31:4
Benham, George W, 1941, F 18,23:1
Benham, H C, 1901, Jl 15,1:5
Benham, H K, 1905, Ag 12,7:6
Benham, H W Maj Gen, 1884, Je 2,5:3
Benham, Harry K, 1961, Ag 12,17:4
Benham, Henry Hill Maj, 1911, Mr 22,11:5
Benham, James R, 1961, My 5,29:2
Benham, James T Jr, 1947, Ja 10,21:2
Benham, Rhoda W, 1957, Ja 19,15:4
Benham, Sidney S, 1944, N 15,27:3
Benham, Victor B, 1955, Je 17,23:4
Benham, Wales A, 1946, S 14,7:4
Benham, Wallace C Mrs, 1945, Jl 7,13:7
Benham, Wesley H, 1945, Jl 11,11:6
Benham, William, 1939, Je 9,21:5
Ben-Horin, Eliahu, 1966, S 6,47:3
Benignus, Bro (J Gerrity), 1953, Ja 28,27:3
Benignus Joseph, Bro (W Sheffield), 1953, D 30,23:1
Benilde Patrick, Bro, 1943, Jl 19,15:5
Benin, Harry, 1967, Jl 16,64:5
Benington, Arthur, 1924, Mr 21,19:4
Benington, Eugene C, 1941, Ag 5,19:1
Benington, George A, 1964, Ap 22,47:1
Benioff, Hugo Dr, 1968, Mr 2,29:3
Benisch, Charles J, 1959, F 5,31:5
Benish, George A, 1951, Jl 17,27:3
Benish, Victor Sr, 1950, Ag 31,26:2
Benisovich, Michael N, 1963, O 22,37:2
Benitz, Adolph G, 1944, Ag 17,17:6
Benitz, William L, 1942, Je 2,24:3
Benj Jos, Bro, 1961, F 24,21:3
Benjamin, Aaron, 1960, O 3,31:5
Benjamin, Albert D, 1950, F 10,23:3
Benjamin, Alfred H, 1925, O 6,27:5; 1957, D 18,35:3
Benjamin, Arthur, 1943, S 25,15:2; 1960, Ap 10,86:3
Benjamin, Bro (D F Burke), 1955, My 13,25:2
Benjamin, Bruce, 1959, D 24,19:3
Benjamin, Charles E, 1941, Ja 1,23:2
Benjamin, Charles F, 1915, My 6,13:5
Benjamin, Cletus J, 1961, My 16,37:2
Benjamin, D P, 1883, O 30,8:4
Benjamin, D W Dr, 1903, Ap 30,9:6
Benjamin, David, 1942, Ja 21,18:2
Benjamin, David J Mrs, 1952, F 22,21:1
Benjamin, David K, 1950, Ag 9,29:4
Benjamin, David W, 1952, N 18,31:2
Benjamin, Earl L, 1942, F 1,43:3
Benjamin, Edward Wade, 1903, D 22,9:5
Benjamin, Ernest H, 1943, My 10,19:3
Benjamin, Eugene S, 1941, Je 22,32:5
Benjamin, Eugene S Mrs, 1953, O 28,29:4
Benjamin, Eugenia B, 1943, My 16,43:2
Benjamin, Everett E Capt, 1903, D 18,9:5
Benjamin, Everett S, 1948, Jl 29,21:5
Benjamin, Everett S Mrs, 1942, Ap 21,23:5
Benjamin, F Everett, 1939, My 1,23:4
Benjamin, Flora A, 1960, Je 30,29:3
Benjamin, Frank, 1945, F 16,23:5
Benjamin, George, 1948, Je 8,25:4
Benjamin, George H, 1951, Je 8,27:1
Benjamin, George R, 1947, Ap 30,25:3
Benjamin, George W, 1925, N 4,23:4
Benjamin, Gilbert G, 1941, My 29,19:2
Benjamin, Hamilton F, 1938, O 27,23:3
Benjamin, Harry, 1967, Ag 10,37:3
Benjamin, Henry, 1945, O 28,44:2
Benjamin, Henry R, 1967, F 23,35:3
Benjamin, Henry R Mrs, 1960, Mr 5,19:4
Benjamin, Isadore L, 1953, Ag 15,15:3
Benjamin, Isidor, 1964, O 28,45:2
Benjamin, J P, 1884, My 8,1:6
Benjamin, Jacob A, 1948, Jl 11,53:1
Benjamin, James W, 1943, Ag 4,17:3
Benjamin, John, 1906, Ja 16,11:5
Benjamin, John F, 1951, O 25,29:2
Benjamin, John J, 1958, F 2,87:1
Benjamin, Joseph, 1923, F 22,15:4
Benjamin, Joseph A, 1940, Je 30,32:6
Benjamin, Joseph J Mrs, 1950, S 6,29:5
Benjamin, Judson E, 1957, N 15,28:3

Benjamin, Karl, 1951, N 30,23:4
Benjamin, Leo, 1954, Je 25,21:1
Benjamin, Lester N, 1942, O 23,21:2
Benjamin, Louis, 1949, O 17,23:4; 1959, My 15,29:2
Benjamin, Louis (L Lorimer), 1959, D 8,45:2
Benjamin, M Wells, 1951, O 3,33:2
Benjamin, Martin, 1954, Jl 30,17:4
Benjamin, Martin Chase, 1905, F 30,9:7
Benjamin, Mary L, 1904, Ja 28,9:5
Benjamin, Maurice C Mrs, 1951, D 27,21:1
Benjamin, Max E, 1954, S 9,31:4
Benjamin, Maxwell W, 1941, Je 29,32:6
Benjamin, Mlle, 1878, F 20,5:1
Benjamin, Morris W, 1922, Jl 29,7:6
Benjamin, Nathan, 1940, F 24,13:3; 1954, O 30,17:2
Benjamin, Park (funl, Ag 24,15:6), 1922, Ag 22,17:5
Benjamin, Park, 1959, Jl 12,73:1
Benjamin, Park Mrs, 1906, D 31,7:5; 1922, S 13,21:5; 1956, O 4,33:5
Benjamin, Patriarch, 1946, F 19,25:5
Benjamin, Paul R (funl, Je 16,17:5), 1912, Je 1,11:4
Benjamin, Philip B, 1915, Ja 5,15:4
Benjamin, Philip R, 1966, Ap 19,41:1
Benjamin, Raphael Rabbi, 1906, N 16,9:6
Benjamin, Raymond, 1952, Je 19,27:1
Benjamin, Rene, 1948, O 5,25:5
Benjamin, Richard, 1944, Ja 24,17:6
Benjamin, Robert M, 1966, Ja 18,34:1
Benjamin, Robert S Mrs, 1961, Ap 21,33:4
Benjamin, Roland, 1949, Jl 3,26:4
Benjamin, Romeyn P, 1939, D 7,27:3
Benjamin, S G W, 1914, Jl 20,7:4
Benjamin, Samuel C, 1947, Ja 10,21:4
Benjamin, Samuel L, 1961, Je 9,33:3
Benjamin, Scott R, 1944, My 20,15:5
Benjamin, Sidney H, 1948, N 21,88:1
Benjamin, Sidney Mrs, 1965, Ja 26,37:2
Benjamin, Susan E, 1940, O 2,23:4
Benjamin, Thaddeus Mrs, 1950, F 27,19:1
Benjamin, Thomas P, 1950, Mr 11,15:2
Benjamin, W M, 1928, F 18,17:3
Benjamin, W Wallace Mrs, 1952, F 28,52:1
Benjamin, Walter P, 1966, D 1,47:4
Benjamin, Walter R, 1943, S 29,21:1
Benjamin, Walter R Mrs, 1954, Ja 14,29:4
Benjamin, Ward Mrs, 1945, Mr 17,13:4
Benjamin, Wayland E, 1913, S 12,11:6
Benjamin, William B, 1946, Jl 2,25:2
Benjamin, William E, 1940, F 26,15:1
Benjamin, William Evarts Mrs, 1924, S 9,19:3
Benjamin, William H Rev, 1907, F 1,9:4
Benjamin, William R, 1951, Ag 21,27:3
Benjamin (Abp B Basalyga), 1963, N 16,27:4
Benjamin I, Patriarch of Istanbul, 1945, N 21,21:4
Benjamine, W W, 1882, Jl 21,5:1
Benjumea Burin, Joaquin, 1963, D 31,19:1
Benkard, Gerald, 1941, N 8,19:4
Benkard, Harry H Mrs, 1945, Ag 11,13:6
Benke, Ernest, 1957, Ap 10,33:4
Benke, Herman C, 1946, D 13,23:4
Benkert, Ambrose W, 1962, Mr 12,31:4
Benkert, George M, 1952, S 3,29:2
Benkert, William R, 1965, D 28,25:3
Benkiser, Robert F C, 1953, My 22,27:4
Benkiser, Walter A, 1965, Je 13,84:7
Benlian, Ben A, 1952, D 5,27:5
Benlliure y Gil, Mariano, 1947, N 10,29:5
Ben-Meir, Moshe, 1959, Ja 19,27:4
Benmosche, Moses, 1951, S 6,31:1
Benn, Carl, 1939, N 16,23:3
Benn, Ernest, 1954, Ja 18,23:3
Benn, George W Mrs, 1954, My 14,23:2
Benn, Gottfried, 1956, Jl 8,65:1
Benn, Gwendolen, 1967, Ja 3,37:1
Benn, Henry E, 1951, O 13,17:5
Benn, James S, 1958, Ja 5,87:1
Benn, James S Jr, 1955, Ag 16,49:3
Benn, Marcus A, 1947, Ja 25,17:3
Benn, Theodore, 1964, My 25,33:1
Benn, William W (Viscount Stansgate), 1960, N 18, 31:4
Bennan, James B, 1955, F 21,30:4
Bennard, George, 1958, O 11,23:6
Bennehoff, L D, 1947, O 29,27:3
Bennehoff, Olton R, 1950, Jl 20,25:1
Bennekamper, Otto W, 1950, S 14,32:4
Bennell, Raymond J, 1959, Je 30,31:3
Bennenson, Grigori, 1939, Ap 6,25:3
Benner, Albert P, 1948, O 27,27:3
Benner, Allen L, 1950, Mr 13,21:1
Benner, George, 1951, F 25,87:5
Benner, Harold F, 1950, S 30,17:4
Benner, Harvey, 1966, Ja 29,27:3
Benner, Ida S L Mrs, 1938, S 7,36:3
Benner, John, 1940, F 22,23:5
Benner, John W, 1955, Ja 23,85:1
Benner, Louis H, 1944, S 12,19:3
Benner, Nathaniel A, 1905, Ap 12,9:4
Benner, Nathaniel W, 1946, D 2,25:3
Benner, Samuel Armstrong, 1921, Mr 29,15:6
Benner, W O, 1939, Ap 15,6:8
Benner, Walter G, 1946, O 24,27:2
Benner, Willis Mrs, 1959, Je 15,27:4
Benner, Winthrop W, 1950, Je 12,27:4
Benners, Alfred Jr Mrs, 1953, My 12,27:5
Benners, Edwin Henry, 1923, Mr 10,13:4
Benners, John, 1868, F 29,5:2
Benners, Royal W, 1952, Jl 4,13:5
Benners, William J Jr, 1940, Ap 5,21:4
Bennet, Alfred L, 1939, Ap 7,22:3
Bennet, Chester L, 1938, N 20,39:2
Bennet, Emily J Mrs, 1938, My 29,II,7:2
Bennet, George H Dr, 1904, Ja 28,9:6
Bennet, Harold L Mrs, 1956, F 8,33:5
Bennet, Joseph E Mrs, 1944, O 12,27:5
Bennet, Leslie J, 1944, Ap 26,19:3
Bennet, O, 1880, Jl 13,5:4
Bennet, William S, 1962, D 3,32:1
Bennet, William S Mrs, 1959, Mr 18,37:5
Bennet-Thompson, Lilian Mrs, 1942, Ap 11,13:2
Bennett, A, 1931, Mr 28,1:2
Bennett, A Frank, 1944, Ap 3,19:2
Bennett, A James, 1942, Je 28,32:4
Bennett, A Norman, 1959, Jl 1,31:2
Bennett, A P Col, 1883, N 25,2:5
Bennett, A S, 1878, S 13,1:6
Bennett, Adolphus, 1908, F 5,7:5
Bennett, Adolphus Mrs, 1908, F 5,7:5
Bennett, Alberta, 1948, Ap 1,26:3
Bennett, Alden L Rev, 1923, Je 9,11:5
Bennett, Alfred S, 1950, D 7,33:3
Bennett, Alfred T, 1951, N 29,33:4
Bennett, Alice Dr, 1925, Je 1,15:3
Bennett, Andrew W, 1951, Ap 4,29:3
Bennett, Archibald S, 1957, My 25,21:4
Bennett, Arthur A, 1949, Ja 15,30:4
Bennett, Arthur B, 1951, D 2,91:1
Bennett, Arthur B Mrs, 1948, My 26,25:4
Bennett, Arthur E, 1948, Jl 20,23:5
Bennett, Arthur F, 1961, Ag 31,27:5
Bennett, Arthur V, 1952, Ag 1,17:4
Bennett, Arthur W, 1950, Ap 4,29:3
Bennett, B, 1932, N 6,38:1
Bennett, Barbara (Mrs L Surprenant), 1958, Ag 10, 93:1
Bennett, Belle H, 1922, Jl 21,11:5
Bennett, Ben J, 1938, S 1,23:5
Bennett, Bernard (Poco), 1913, D 21,IV,5:5
Bennett, Bessie, 1939, Mr 25,15:3
Bennett, Billy, 1942, Jl 1,25:5
Bennett, Birchard G, 1960, Ag 1,23:5
Bennett, Boyd A, 1958, N 9,89:1
Bennett, Burton E, 1942, Ag 3,15:5
Bennett, C S, 1949, Mr 4,21:3
Bennett, Carlyle, 1962, Ap 14,25:2
Bennett, Carrie E Mrs, 1938, D 5,23:3
Bennett, Charles, 1947, Je 15,60:3; 1948, O 3,64:3
Bennett, Charles A, 1943, D 21,28:3; 1954, Mr 17, 31:2; 1966, My 25,47:4
Bennett, Charles B, 1961, S 8,32:1
Bennett, Charles E, 1941, O 2,25:4; 1956, S 2,57:2
Bennett, Charles E Mrs, 1949, S 12,21:1
Bennett, Charles E Prof, 1921, My 3,17:4
Bennett, Charles G, 1914, My 26,11:6
Bennett, Charles H, 1956, S 18,35:3
Bennett, Charles J, 1941, Mr 25,23:3
Bennett, Charles L, 1941, Je 9,19:3; 1948, S 12,72:4; 1952, Jl 21,19:3
Bennett, Charles M, 1950, S 8,31:1
Bennett, Charles U S A Col, 1905, Ja 19,9:3
Bennett, Clarence E, 1913, Ap 7,9:6
Bennett, Clarence F, 1950, D 26,23:1
Bennett, Claude E, 1952, Ag 28,23:5; 1961, D 3,88:3
Bennett, Claude G, 1955, Ap 21,29:1
Bennett, Claude H, 1953, Je 20,17:5
Bennett, Claude H Jr, 1961, My 17,37:3
Bennett, Clifford, 1964, Mr 26,35:3
Bennett, Colbert A, 1953, F 7,15:2
Bennett, Constance (Mrs J T Coulter),(funl, Jl 28,-35:4), 1965, Jl 26,23:1
Bennett, Cortland Mrs, 1948, Je 10,25:4
Bennett, Courtenay W Sir, 1937, D 17,32:3
Bennett, Cyril, 1957, My 27,31:3
Bennett, Cyrus A Mrs, 1943, D 21,27:3
Bennett, D D, 1939, F 2,19:6
Bennett, D M, 1882, D 7,5:1
Bennett, David C, 1956, Ap 11,33:2
Bennett, David Mrs, 1945, Je 16,13:1
Bennett, David P, 1947, N 3,23:2
Bennett, David T, 1937, Ja 23,18:8
Bennett, Don, 1960, Ap 7,35:4
Bennett, E P Dr, 1882, O 29,9:2
Bennett, Earl A, 1947, Jl 8,23:4
Bennett, Earl J, 1965, F 13,21:5
Bennett, Earl S, 1951, Je 8,27:2
Bennett, Eben H, 1944, S 1,13:2
Bennett, Edgar Mrs, 1951, F 12,23:3
Bennett, Edmund J, 1950, Ap 13,29:3
Bennett, Edmund R, 1949, My 17,5:4
Bennett, Edward, 1942, O 20,21:3; 1954, Je 2,31:3
Bennett, Edward C Mrs, 1951, Ap 1,94:1
Bennett, Edward H, 1949, O 27,27:3; 1954, O 16,17:4
Bennett, Edward J, 1965, F 18,33:2
Bennett, Edward Mrs, 1951, S 6,31:4
Bennett, Edwin A, 1946, Jl 11,23:3
Bennett, Edwin E, 1951, F 24,13:3
Bennett, Edwin H, 1912, F 23,11:4
Bennett, Edwin L, 1952, O 18,19:3
Bennett, Edwin S Lt, 1918, Je 16,21:3
Bennett, Elbert Anderson, 1919, Je 17,15:4
Bennett, Elbert G, 1950, Ap 3,23:5
Bennett, Elizabeth D, 1960, Ag 28,82:6
Bennett, Elliott C, 1950, Mr 28,31:4
Bennett, Ellsworth W, 1949, Jl 16,13:2
Bennett, Elmer L, 1950, D 11,25:2
Bennett, Emily M, 1963, S 7,19:5
Bennett, Ernest A, 1938, D 1,23:2
Bennett, Ernest H, 1953, F 20,20:4
Bennett, Ernest H Sr, 1955, Ap 1,28:3
Bennett, Ernest L, 1942, S 9,23:2
Bennett, Estelline, 1948, Ja 23,24:2
Bennett, Eugene B, 1952, F 24,85:2
Bennett, Everett, 1948, Ag 17,21:2
Bennett, F, 1928, Ap 26,1:8
Bennett, Floyd B, 1952, F 19,29:2
Bennett, Forrest, 1959, D 13,86:5
Bennett, Francis L Mrs, 1944, O 20,20:2
Bennett, Francis Xavier, 1920, D 2,11:3
Bennett, Frank A, 1939, Ap 24,17:4
Bennett, Frank D, 1958, Ap 10,29:3
Bennett, Frank I, 1925, D 21,21:4
Bennett, Frank O, 1960, My 29,57:3
Bennett, Frank P, 1965, Jl 10,25:4
Bennett, Frank W, 1946, N 27,25:2; 1960, Je 26,72:7
Bennett, Fred, 1946, N 16,19:5; 1957, My 14,35:3
Bennett, Fred S Mrs, 1950, Ap 12,27:4
Bennett, Frederick A, 1950, S 19,29:2
Bennett, Frederick J Capt, 1937, Mr 23,23:4
Bennett, G A, 1883, D 19,2:7
Bennett, G C, 1885, Ja 4,2:1
Bennett, George A, 1958, F 28,21:3
Bennett, George C, 1950, Mr 26,92:6; 1952, Ja 19, 15:3; 1959, F 5,31:5
Bennett, George D Mrs, 1949, N 12,15:1
Bennett, George E, 1952, F 17,86:4; 1962, Jl 19,27:4; 1965, Mr 27,27:2
Bennett, George E Mrs, 1952, Ap 5,15:3
Bennett, George H, 1938, Ja 25,21:6; 1954, Je 21,23:2
Bennett, George L, 1941, Je 4,23:4; 1953, Ag 13,25:5; 1962, O 31,37:2
Bennett, George S, 1951, F 28,27:1
Bennett, George Sr, 1940, S 27,23:5
Bennett, George W, 1913, S 19,9:4; 1943, Ja 28,19:3
Bennett, Gertrude E, 1964, Je 14,84:6
Bennett, Grena, 1946, Ap 5,25:4
Bennett, H M, 1902, Ap 12,9:6
Bennett, Harold E, 1943, S 2,19:4
Bennett, Harold F M, 1948, Ap 29,23:4
Bennett, Harry, 1937, D 20,27:2; 1947, D 25,21:3; 1949, Mr 23,27:5; 1955, Ja 22,11:5
Bennett, Harry C, 1939, My 30,17:1
Bennett, Harry F, 1949, F 19,15:2
Bennett, Harry L, 1949, Ja 16,68:5
Bennett, Harry R, 1941, F 17,15:1
Bennett, Harry T, 1949, Ja 9,72:5
Bennett, Helen F, 1959, Ag 17,23:3
Bennett, Hendrick L, 1947, Je 23,23:4
Bennett, Henry, 1940, Mr 14,23:4
Bennett, Henry A, 1947, O 18,15:2
Bennett, Henry G, 1951, D 24,1:1
Bennett, Henry G Mrs, 1951, D 24,1:1; 1967, S 22,47:2
Bennett, Henry J, 1956, My 23,31:3
Bennett, Henry Mrs, 1947, My 16,23:2
Bennett, Henry Sir, 1913, Je 3,9:4
Bennett, Herbert, 1937, Mr 24,25:3
Bennett, Herbert H, 1959, Jl 22,27:2
Bennett, Herbert H Mrs, 1940, S 19,23:5
Bennett, Herbert I, 1955, N 8,31:2
Bennett, Homer L, 1940, Mr 26,21:2
Bennett, Hubert D, 1951, S 9,88:4
Bennett, Hugh H, 1960, Jl 8,21:2
Bennett, Hugh S, 1950, Mr 23,36:2
Bennett, Ira, 1949, Ap 12,29:2
Bennett, Ira E, 1957, Mr 27,31:6
Bennett, Irving T (death ruled suicide, O 19,25:6), 1955, O 4,35:3
Bennett, Irwin G, 1955, Ap 1,27:3
Bennett, J Frank, 1938, Mr 21,16:1
Bennett, J Louis, 1960, My 22,86:8
Bennett, J S, 1955, Jl 14,23:6
Bennett, Jack, 1962, F 18,92:4
Bennett, James, 1950, O 24,29:3
Bennett, James A Dr, 1915, Jl 13,11:6
Bennett, James B Mrs (D Graham), 1959, Je 26,25:5
Bennett, James C (por), 1938, Ja 5,21:5
Bennett, James C, 1942, O 11,56:7; 1968, My 4,39:3
Bennett, James E, 1948, D 22,23:3
Bennett, James G Mrs, 1946, F 5,23:1
Bennett, James Gordon (funl, Je 14,5:3), 1872, Je 2, 4:7
Bennett, James Gordon Mrs, 1873, Ap 1,5:5
Bennett, James H, 1946, Mr 7,25:3; 1956, My 9,33:5
Bennett, James J, 1951, My 6,92:5
Bennett, James M, 1941, Ja 28,19:6
Bennett, James M Jr, 1962, O 22,29:4
Bennett, James M Mrs, 1953, Je 11,29:2
Bennett, James N, 1954, Ap 20,29:2
Bennett, James O, 1940, F 28,21:3
Bennett, James W, 1903, Ap 15,9:6

Bennett, Joe (J B Aldert), 1967, S 2,25:5
Bennett, John, 1956, D 30,32:6
Bennett, John A, 1951, Jl 19,23:3
Bennett, John A Sr, 1959, D 31,21:5
Bennett, John B, 1940, Ja 3,22:3; 1964, Ag 10,31:3
Bennett, John C, 1950, My 18,29:5
Bennett, John D, 1944, N 19,50:4
Bennett, John F, 1941, Ja 28,19:2
Bennett, John F Mrs, 1949, S 15,27:2; 1958, Mr 19,31:5
Bennett, John H, 1938, N 23,21:5
Bennett, John J, 1947, My 22,27:5; 1957, O 24,33:3; 1967, O 5,39:2
Bennett, John J Sr, 1941, F 10,20:3
Bennett, John Jr, 1940, O 8,25:5
Bennett, John L, 1966, Je 7,47:2
Bennett, John R, 1905, Je 22,1:1; 1941, O 24,23:5
Bennett, John S, 1938, Mr 20,II,8:4
Bennett, John S Mrs, 1943, S 21,23:4
Bennett, John S Sr, 1948, My 23,68:6
Bennett, John W, 1953, Je 4,29:4
Bennett, John W F, 1943, S 1,19:3
Bennett, Johnstone, 1906, Ap 15,9:6
Bennett, Joseph, 1957, N 19,30:3
Bennett, Joseph A, 1954, Ja 7,31:3
Bennett, Joseph A Rev, 1925, O 29,25:6
Bennett, Joseph Gordon (funl), 1918, My 24,13:7
Bennett, Joseph R, 1953, F 23,25:5
Bennett, Joseph S, 1955, O 15,15:5
Bennett, Josiah K, 1958, Je 29,69:1
Bennett, Josiah Quincy, 1916, N 30,13:3
Bennett, Julia L Mrs, 1940, Ja 30,3:1
Bennett, Laura, 1939, S 26,23:4
Bennett, Lee, 1954, O 11,27:3
Bennett, Leon D Mrs, 1955, F 8,27:1
Bennett, Leroy T, 1952, O 17,27:4
Bennett, Leslie L, 1960, Mr 19,21:5
Bennett, Lewis J, 1925, Ap 17,21:5
Bennett, Lois M, 1946, Mr 8,21:1
Bennett, Loren E, 1966, Je 23,39:3
Bennett, Louis, 1959, Mr 31,29:2
Bennett, Louis H, 1947, O 20,23:6
Bennett, Lucy Mrs, 1941, Je 26,23:5
Bennett, M, 1930, Ja 17,1:2
Bennett, M H B Mrs, 1871, F 10,2:7
Bennett, M Toscan, 1940, D 17,25:4
Bennett, Martha M Mrs, 1943, Ja 17,44:7
Bennett, Mary E Mrs, 1941, S 7,50:1; 1955, Ja 24,23:5
Bennett, Mary U Mrs, 1947, S 2,21:3
Bennett, May F, 1924, Mr 20,19:5
Bennett, Melvin S, 1940, Je 11,25:3
Bennett, Merton W, 1941, O 11,17:6
Bennett, Michael, 1946, Mr 21,25:4
Bennett, Michael A, 1951, Ag 2,21:1
Bennett, Milly (Mrs H Amlie), 1960, N 7,35:3
Bennett, Minot D, 1941, D 9,31:2
Bennett, Myra Mrs, 1959, My 4,29:4
Bennett, Myron, 1951, F 8,23:5
Bennett, Noel S, 1944, Ag 6,37:4
Bennett, O P, 1924, Ap 23,21:4
Bennett, Ollie J B, 1957, F 8,23:4
Bennett, Otto R Sr, 1949, N 23,29:3
Bennett, P E O, 1938, Mr 24,23:2
Bennett, Paul, 1959, Ja 16,28:1
Bennett, Paul A, 1966, D 19,37:6
Bennett, Perry R, 1942, N 25,23:6
Bennett, Peter E, 1966, Ja 15,27:6
Bennett, Peter F B Lord, 1957, S 29,86:5
Bennett, Phil A, 1942, D 8,26:2
Bennett, Philip E, 1961, Ja 30,23:5
Bennett, R H, 1945, My 13,20:2
Bennett, Ralph E, 1939, My 1,23:6; 1945, F 13,28:1
Bennett, Raymond F, 1949, D 10,18:2
Bennett, Reo, 1938, Mr 25,19:1
Bennett, Reuben R, 1966, D 1,47:3
Bennett, Richard B Viscount, 1947, Je 28,13:1
Bennett, Richard H, 1950, F 27,19:2; 1955, D 23,17:3
Bennett, Richard R, 1955, Ag 22,21:5
Bennett, Robert, 1967, S 19,47:2
Bennett, Robert A Mrs, 1943, O 9,13:5
Bennett, Robert B Mrs, 1958, My 26,29:3
Bennett, Robert J, 1950, Jl 14,21:2
Bennett, Robert Mrs, 1955, Ag 11,21:4
Bennett, Robert W, 1943, F 26,20:2
Bennett, Roger W, 1950, Ap 8,13:6
Bennett, Ross G, 1937, N 10,25:5
Bennett, Ruth H, 1947, F 21,19:1
Bennett, Samuel, 1951, F 14,30:3; 1955, F 13,86:2
Bennett, Samuel E, 1951, Mr 9,25:2
Bennett, Samuel E Mrs, 1955, My 17,29:1
Bennett, Samuel Jerome, 1921, D 27,13:6
Bennett, Samuel M, 1963, Ap 11,33:1
Bennett, Samuel O Mrs, 1967, F 23,35:2
Bennett, Samuel T, 1941, Ap 25,19:5
Bennett, Sarah W Mrs, 1941, Mr 11,23:3
Bennett, Spencer M, 1946, Je 30,38:5
Bennett, Stanley K, 1955, Ja 16,92:7
Bennett, Stephen A, 1955, F 17,27:5
Bennett, T E, 1870, S 7,1:7
Bennett, T Francis, 1958, Ja 31,21:4
Bennett, T L, 1932, My 10,24:4
Bennett, Theodore, 1956, Mr 16,23:4
Bennett, Theodore Mrs, 1954, Mr 8,27:2
Bennett, Theron C, 1937, Ap 7,25:3
Bennett, Thomas, 1885, Mr 27,6:1
Bennett, Thomas H Mrs, 1958, F 1,19:1
Bennett, Vernon, 1960, Je 24,27:3
Bennett, W, 1871, Ap 6,2:3
Bennett, Walter H, 1954, N 26,29:5; 1963, O 9,43:4
Bennett, Walter J, 1911, D 16,13:5
Bennett, Walter M, 1938, Ja 14,23:3
Bennett, Walter W, 1948, Je 18,23:4
Bennett, Warren, 1954, D 29,23:1
Bennett, Wendell C, 1953, S 7,7:4
Bennett, Whitman, 1968, Ap 19,47:4
Bennett, Wilbur K, 1961, My 28,64:3
Bennett, Wilda, 1967, D 23,23:2
Bennett, Will L, 1950, My 8,25:7
Bennett, Willa B, 1940, Ap 16,23:3
Bennett, William, 1938, Ap 3,II,7:3; 1948, My 12,28:3; 1956, Je 25,23:5; 1958, Mr 13,29:3
Bennett, William C Col, 1923, Ap 2,17:5
Bennett, William E, 1939, D 22,19:4
Bennett, William H, 1937, Jl 8,23:5; 1945, N 9,19:3; 1948, Je 13,68:4
Bennett, William H Capt, 1910, N 3,9:5
Bennett, William H Jr, 1962, Je 17,80:7
Bennett, William M, 1955, O 30,88:1
Bennett, William M Jr, 1940, Jl 5,28:1
Bennett, William N, 1937, Ja 26,21:4
Bennett, William R, 1945, D 31,17:2
Bennett, William S, 1937, N 8,23:4
Bennett, William Sternoale Sir, 1875, F 2,5:5
Bennett, William Van Brunt, 1914, Je 19,13:5
Bennett, William W, 1963, My 20,31:5
Bennett, William W Mrs, 1956, Ap 17,31:2
Bennett, William Winslow Col, 1914, Jl 16,9:6
Bennett, Winchester, 1953, Ja 19,23:5
Bennett, Winfield S Mrs, 1950, Jl 22,15:4
Bennetter, Harold J, 1944, N 12,49:2
Bennetto, John, 1946, O 28,27:4
Bennetts, Benjamin H, 1940, F 14,21:3
Bennetts, Mary F, 1941, D 9,31:5
Bennetts, Thomas Mrs, 1946, Jl 28,39:2
Benney, Trevoes W, 1967, Jl 25,32:5
Benneyan, Hachadoor G, 1944, My 20,15:7
Bennhoff, Gustav A Mrs, 1949, Jl 3,27:1
Bennie, James R, 1948, D 15,33:6
Bennigsen, Rose Mrs, 1948, Ja 25,57:1
Benning, May, 1948, My 14,23:5
Benninger, Albert C Marshal, 1937, Mr 19,23:2
Benninger, August H, 1956, S 1,15:4
Benninger, Leo, 1945, D 4,30:2
Benninger, Leo Mrs, 1955, My 6,23:5
Benninghoff, Harry B, 1949, Ap 26,26:2
Benningsen, R, 1902, Ag 9,9:6
Bennington, Elmer E, 1949, Ap 8,25:4
Bennington, John H, 1937, O 23,15:7
Bennion, Adam S, 1958, F 12,29:5
Bennion, Edward G, 1963, O 30,39:2
Bennion, Percy H, 1964, My 3,87:1
Bennion, Percy H Mrs, 1957, Ap 20,17:2
Bennion, Samuel O, 1945, Mr 9,19:2
Bennion, Theron, 1956, D 13,37:4
Bennis, David A, 1954, Jl 1,25:5
Bennis, Joseph H, 1963, D 9,35:2
Bennison, Harold B, 1944, Mr 18,13:3
Bennison, John F, 1956, Mr 16,23:4
Bennison, Richard T, 1958, My 22,29:2
Bennison, William T, 1941, Mr 19,21:2
Bennitt, Chandler, 1958, F 17,14:5
Bennitt, Chandler Mrs, 1962, N 21,30:1
Bennitt, George S Rev, 1915, Mr 17,11:5
Benns, Charles P, 1945, Mr 6,21:2
Benny, Allan, 1942, N 8,50:3
Benny, George A, 1925, Ja 31,13:5
Benny, James, 1937, Ap 7,25:1
Benny, John R Mrs, 1957, My 31,19:1
Benois, Aleksandr, 1960, F 10,37:4
Benoist, Andre, 1953, Je 20,17:5
Benoist, Condie L, 1953, Mr 24,42:2
Benoit, Hector W, 1942, Je 28,33:2
Benoit, Leon, 1957, S 11,33:4
Benoit, Pierre, 1962, Mr 4,86:4
Benoit, Remi A Mrs, 1962, Je 24,68:8
Benoit, Richard C, 1948, Ag 16,19:3
Benoit, Walter E Mrs, 1950, My 21,104:4
Benoit-Levy, Jean, 1959, Ag 4,27:1
Benrimo, J Harry, 1942, Mr 27,23:4
Benrimo, Thomas, 1958, My 21,33:4
Bens, S J Mrs, 1928, Mr 12,21:5
Bensberg, F William, 1940, Ap 15,17:4
Bense, Thomas A, 1950, My 28,44:5
Bensel, Arlington, 1941, Jl 1,23:5
Bensel, John A Maj, 1922, Je 20,19:4
Bensel, Mary A Mrs, 1940, Ap 14,44:8
Bensel, Peter C Capt, 1905, Ap 30,8:2
Bensel, Walter, 1959, S 17,39:2
Bensel, Walter Mrs, 1956, Ja 17,33:4
Benseler, Theodore M, 1952, Ja 3,27:2
Bensen, Wilhelm G Mrs, 1954, F 18,31:1
Bensen, 1942, Jl 27,15:6
Benshoof, Lou, 1950, My 10,31:3
Bensing, Earle, 1951, Mr 14,33:2
Bensing, Roy, 1953, S 30,31:3
Bensinger, C G, 1963, Ap 1,27:5
Bensinger, C Raymond, 1954, N 12,21:2
Bensinger, Daniel E, 1950, Ap 30,102:6
Bensinger, Guy A, 1958, Jl 10,27:3
Bensinger, Norman E, 1967, Ap 13,43:2
Bensky, Arthur, 1946, N 14,29:2
Bensky, Nathan J, 1939, N 20,19:2
Bensley, David L, 1963, Ag 12,21:4
Bensley, Harry, 1956, My 28,27:5
Bensley, Robert, 1956, Je 13,37:5
Benson, A G, 1878, Ap 20,8:1
Benson, Al B, 1955, Ja 1,13:2
Benson, Alexander, 1947, N 10,29:2
Benson, Allan L, 1940, Ag 20,19:3
Benson, Arline T Mrs, 1943, S 7,23:3
Benson, Arthur Christopher, 1925, Je 17,21:5
Benson, Arthur D, 1941, F 12,21:2
Benson, Arthur W, 1946, N 21,31:3
Benson, Audrey, 1948, My 14,23:5
Benson, Ben, 1959, My 1,29:1
Benson, Benjamin G, 1939, O 9,19:5
Benson, Bernard A, 1961, O 30,29:5
Benson, Bernhard, 1953, Ja 3,15:2
Benson, Betsy, 1924, Mr 27,19:5
Benson, Blair V, 1956, N 25,89:1
Benson, C Beverley, 1957, Ap 4,33:2
Benson, C H, 1905, Mr 17,9:4
Benson, Charles Mrs, 1922, Ap 11,19:4
Benson, Clara M, 1940, Jl 29,13:6
Benson, David H W, 1950, Je 6,29:4
Benson, E W Rev Archbishop of Canterbury, 1896, O 12,1:2
Benson, Edgar A, 1946, Je 27,22:2
Benson, Edward A, 1968, F 17,26:1
Benson, Edward F, 1940, Mr 1,21:1
Benson, Edward G, 1948, F 4,23:3
Benson, Edward G Mrs, 1965, O 26,45:4
Benson, Edwin J Mrs, 1951, D 28,21:2
Benson, Edwin N Jr, 1954, S 8,31:3
Benson, Elmer E, 1946, Ja 5,13:5
Benson, Ernest C, 1947, Je 10,27:2
Benson, Francis B Jr, 1941, F 19,21:1
Benson, Francis C 3d, 1962, S 28,25:8
Benson, Frank, 1940, Ja 1,23:3
Benson, Frank Sherman, 1907, Mr 1,9:5
Benson, Frank W, 1951, N 16,25:2
Benson, Frederic C, 1941, Jl 26,16:7
Benson, Frederick Shepherd Col, 1920, F 25,11:4
Benson, G S, 1883, Mr 23,5:2
Benson, Gabriel, 1945, D 8,17:2
Benson, George A Sr, 1959, F 28,19:3
Benson, George T, 1944, N 7,27:4
Benson, George W, 1944, Ag 30,17:2
Benson, Georgianna W Mrs, 1941, Mr 31,15:4
Benson, Goodman A, 1938, Ag 16,6:2
Benson, Grenville R Mrs, 1913, F 8,13:4
Benson, Hadley S, 1948, Ja 27,25:2
Benson, Harry B, 1953, My 1,21:4
Benson, Hevlyn D, 1948, N 1,23:2
Benson, Hilmer O, 1957, Mr 22,23:2
Benson, Horatio S, 1947, My 1,25:2
Benson, J Alfred, 1950, Ja 1,42:8
Benson, James, 1920, Jl 2,11:5
Benson, James A, 1943, D 16,28:2
Benson, James H, 1905, Ap 16,1:6
Benson, John, 1962, Ag 24,22:6
Benson, John C, 1944, D 26,19:4
Benson, John G, 1940, Ap 16,23:2; 1953, Ag 28,17:5
Benson, John H, 1956, F 24,25:1
Benson, John M, 1947, Je 1,60:3
Benson, John O, 1940, Jl 4,15:2
Benson, John P, 1947, N 17,21:5
Benson, John R Mrs, 1939, Ja 1,25:1
Benson, John T (will, S 26,51:7), 1943, S 20,21:5
Benson, Joseph H, 1941, S 28,49:1
Benson, Joseph W, 1949, O 28,23:3
Benson, L S, 1903, Ja 30,9:7
Benson, Lawrence J, 1961, Mr 30,29:2
Benson, Leland W, 1952, S 20,15:5
Benson, Marion T, 1962, Je 8,2:4
Benson, Maxwell F, 1964, D 17,41:1
Benson, Mitchell M, 1966, F 8,39:1
Benson, Nelson Mrs, 1952, Ja 5,11:1
Benson, Ole E, 1952, Mr 3,21:2
Benson, Oscar H, 1951, Ag 17,17:5
Benson, Otis O Jr Mrs, 1961, O 13,35:2
Benson, Ovid P, 1940, Mr 31,45:1
Benson, Peter, 1949, Jl 30,1:1
Benson, Philip A, 1946, O 17,23:5
Benson, R Dale Jr, 1949, Ag 5,19:5
Benson, Raymond D, 1958, Mr 30,88:2
Benson, Raymond E, 1950, N 27,17:6
Benson, Reuel A, 1956, Ag 7,27:4
Benson, Rex Lt-Col Sir, 1968, S 28,33:4
Benson, Richard E Jr, 1957, Jl 3,23:3
Benson, Richard Meux Rev, 1915, Ja 15,11:4
Benson, Richard Mrs, 1964, D 1,41:4
Benson, Robert, 1916, Ja 27,11:5
Benson, Robert D Mrs, 1949, Mr 5,17:4
Benson, Robert Hugh Msgr, 1914, O 20,13:5
Benson, Rudolph, 1954, Ja 1,23:6
Benson, Samuel J, 1949, Je 20,19:4
Benson, Stella, 1933, D 8,23:3
Benson, Swan, 1949, O 23,84:4
Benson, Thomas, 1937, Ap 11,II,8:5

Benson, Tillman C, 1939, F 16,21:3
Benson, Victor, 1949, S 1,21:5
Benson, Walter L, 1940, My 17,19:6
Benson, Wilfrid, 1963, O 17,32:5
Benson, William C Jr, 1953, My 25,25:1
Benson, William Capt, 1874, Jl 19,8:2
Benson, William G, 1968, Ap 2,47:1
Benson, William S, 1942, Je 1,13:4
Benson, William W, 1953, N 23,27:2
Benson, William W Mrs, 1943, N 20,13:5
Bent, Arthur C, 1955, Ja 1,13:2
Bent, Arthur S, 1939, F 18,15:3
Bent, Erling S, 1955, Ap 19,31:1
Bent, Francis P, 1951, D 3,31:4
Bent, Frederick W, 1915, Ap 16,13:4
Bent, George E Sr, 1948, D 4,13:4
Bent, John J, 1949, Mr 4,21:2
Bent, Lester H, 1941, D 22,17:6
Bent, Luther Stedman Maj, 1915, Ap 20,15:4
Bent, Maurice H, 1957, N 28,31:3
Bent, Newell, 1938, Ag 30,17:5
Bent, Quincy, 1955, My 6,23:3
Bent, Ralph H Mrs, 1959, O 22,37:4
Bent, Richard M Mrs, 1943, My 21,19:4
Bent, Rupert G, 1948, D 24,17:2
Bent, Samuel A, 1951, D 11,33:3
Bent, Samuel Arthur, 1912, N 23,15:6
Bent, Samuel S, 1938, Je 7,23:2
Bent, Sarah P, 1938, N 29,23:2
Bent, Silas, 1945, Jl 31,19:5
Bent, Silas Mrs, 1949, N 2,12:7
Bent, Thomas C, 1938, S 17,17:4
Bent, Walter D, 1921, O 2,22:3
Benta, George A Mrs, 1951, D 28,21:3
Benta, J George, 1945, My 23,19:1
Benter, Charles, 1964, D 5,31:2
Benthale, Edward J, 1948, Mr 27,13:3
Benthall, Thomas, 1938, My 24,19:4
Bentham, Chris, 1948, Ap 24,15:3
Bentham, George, 1914, Ap 9,11:5
Bentham, Myron S, 1948, Mr 21,61:1
Benthin, Howard A, 1968, My 20,47:2
Benthysen, John, 1953, F 5,23:2
Bentinck, Baron (R F Carel), 1943, S 4,13:1
Bentinck, Godard Count, 1940, Ja 5,19:5
Bentinck, H C Lord, 1931, O 7,25:1
Bentinck, Norah, 1939, My 25,25:3
Bentkowski, Edmund J, 1952, Jl 12,13:6
Bentley, Alex N, 1953, N 6,27:3
Bentley, Alys E, 1951, Ja 9,30:5
Bentley, Arthur, 1944, S 28,19:3
Bentley, Arthur B, 1954, Ja 5,27:2
Bentley, Arthur F, 1957, My 22,33:2
Bentley, Bede, 1939, My 11,25:4
Bentley, Bert H, 1947, N 20,29:3
Bentley, Bertha M (por), 1949, N 6,92:3
Bentley, Cyril E, 1957, Ja 12,19:3
Bentley, Daniel B Mrs, 1955, My 17,29:2
Bentley, David G, 1947, Ag 3,52:6
Bentley, E C, 1956, Mr 31,15:3
Bentley, Edward M Mrs, 1938, Ja 22,15:4
Bentley, Elizabeth, 1963, D 4,47:1
Bentley, Floyd J, 1939, F 8,23:3
Bentley, Frank R, 1939, F 3,15:4
Bentley, Gerald E Mrs, 1961, D 9,27:4
Bentley, Harold W, 1939, Mr 20,17:6
Bentley, Harry C, 1967, N 9,47:4
Bentley, Harry K, 1949, My 10,26:4
Bentley, Henry, 1938, O 22,17:6
Bentley, Herbert L, 1947, Jl 12,13:5
Bentley, Horace M, 1967, Ap 10,35:2
Bentley, Irene (Mrs I Smith), 1940, Je 4,23:5
Bentley, J V, 1881, O 6,5:3
Bentley, James, 1955, Je 21,31:2
Bentley, James B, 1949, Ag 2,20:5
Bentley, James H, 1949, O 24,23:2
Bentley, Jerome H, 1961, F 23,27:3
Bentley, John Mrs, 1945, N 14,19:2
Bentley, John R Jr, 1951, Ap 19,31:5
Bentley, John W, 1950, N 16,31:3
Bentley, Julian, 1968, Mr 13,53:2
Bentley, Lawrence F Mrs, 1966, N 16,47:3
Bentley, Lawrence W, 1937, F 24,23:3
Bentley, Leverett D G, 1949, Mr 29,25:3
Bentley, Linden E, 1944, Mr 7,17:2
Bentley, M Julia, 1959, N 15,86:7
Bentley, Madison, 1955, My 30,13:6
Bentley, Martha C Mrs, 1942, My 4,19:4
Bentley, Nellie W, 1956, Ag 30,25:1
Bentley, Oswald L, 1940, D 27,20:2
Bentley, Perce J, 1962, My 9,43:2
Bentley, Peter, 1875, S 28,6:7
Bentley, R Sr, 1928, Ja 22,29:1
Bentley, Raymond, 1940, Mr 1,21:4
Bentley, Robert O, 1957, D 30,23:4
Bentley, Robert Prof, 1871, S 14,1:7
Bentley, Robert W, 1947, S 22,23:4
Bentley, Spencer, 1963, N 30,27:1
Bentley, W A, 1931, D 24,17:1
Bentley, W Clemens, 1962, F 16,27:2
Bentley, Walter E, 1962, Je 10,86:6
Bentley, Walter H, 1945, F 1,23:4
Bentley, William H, 1948, D 2,29:2
Bentley, William L, 1941, S 30,23:3
Bentley, Wilmer H, 1958, N 13,33:1
Bentley, Wray A, 1949, Ja 20,27:5
Benton, C R, 1955, My 12,29:1
Benton, Charles, 1947, O 3,25:2
Benton, Charles A, 1939, Mr 16,23:2
Benton, Charles Edward, 1877, F 12,4:7
Benton, Charles M Mrs, 1958, D 10,40:1
Benton, Charles Montgomery, 1922, Ap 11,19:4
Benton, Charles V, 1965, My 18,39:2
Benton, Cleveland F, 1940, S 27,23:5
Benton, Curtis, 1938, S 15,25:5
Benton, Dwight, 1903, My 10,7:5
Benton, Elbert J, 1946, Mr 30,15:5
Benton, Elma H Mrs, 1942, O 7,25:2
Benton, Frank A, 1942, F 3,19:5
Benton, Frederick A, 1955, S 27,35:4
Benton, Frederick D, 1938, My 13,19:2
Benton, Frederick J, 1943, O 21,27:6
Benton, George A, 1949, D 6,31:2
Benton, George A Ex-Justice, 1921, S 11,21:1
Benton, George W, 1952, Je 24,29:5
Benton, Guy P Mrs, 1947, Ag 16,13:3
Benton, Hale P, 1946, Ap 3,25:2
Benton, Harold L, 1943, O 19,19:4
Benton, Helen V Mrs, 1939, Jl 6,23:5
Benton, Isaac, 1905, Ap 6,6:4
Benton, J G, 1881, Ag 24,2:4
Benton, J Webb, 1947, O 24,23:5
Benton, James C, 1951, Je 30,15:4
Benton, James W, 1947, O 26,70:4
Benton, James W Mrs, 1948, Ag 24,23:4
Benton, Jane Mrs, 1950, Ap 3,23:1
Benton, Jay Bayard, 1918, My 26,23:2
Benton, Jay R, 1953, N 4,33:4
Benton, Jay W, 1941, Ag 18,13:5
Benton, Joel, 1911, S 16,7:5
Benton, John B, 1920, N 7,22:5
Benton, John E, 1948, Je 22,25:4
Benton, John K, 1956, Ag 22,29:2
Benton, John W, 1964, S 27,85:4
Benton, Josiah H, 1917, F 7,13:6
Benton, Kenneth H, 1950, Ja 31,23:1
Benton, Lawrence (Larry), 1953, Ap 4,13:5
Benton, Lawrence J Mrs, 1950, D 14,35:6
Benton, Louis M, 1948, Je 28,19:2
Benton, Mary L, 1955, Ag 16,23:2
Benton, Mary V, 1949, Ja 8,15:2
Benton, Morris F, 1948, Jl 1,23:6
Benton, N S, 1869, Jl 1,5:5
Benton, Nelson K, 1961, Ap 20,33:4
Benton, O H, 1938, My 11,19:2
Benton, Oliver L, 1952, F 28,27:3
Benton, Stephen Olin Dr, 1915, O 25,9:4
Benton, Stuart Harry Dr, 1915, Mr 4,9:5
Benton, W P Gen, 1867, Mr 24,3:7
Benton, Waldo T, 1940, N 17,50:2
Benton, Walter G, 1954, Ja 4,19:3
Benton, William E, 1951, Mr 20,29:4
Benton, William S, 1945, O 23,17:4
Benton, Woodie, 1952, Mr 14,23:1
Bentz, Charles A Dr, 1937, Jl 26,19:6
Bentz, Harry, 1941, Ja 25,15:3
Bentz, Herman B, 1940, Ag 5,13:5
Bentz, John F, 1950, Ag 3,23:5
Bentzig, Peter J, 1950, S 8,32:2
Benvenuti, Lodovico, 1966, My 29,8:2
Benvenuto, Michael, 1947, Jl 23,23:5
Benvie, William Y, 1940, Mr 20,27:6
Benvignati, Mario, 1953, Ag 6,21:4
Benware, Rex K, 1952, S 6,17:4
Benway, Joseph A, 1954, S 12,85:1
Benwell, T H, 1955, Ap 30,17:6
Ben-Yahuda, Elieser, 1922, D 18,17:5
Benyon, Edward, 1949, Je 4,13:3
Benz, Emma, 1947, O 4,17:3
Benz, Ferdinand, 1909, Ja 29,9:5
Benz, Francis E, 1954, Ap 16,21:1
Benz, Henry, 1947, N 30,76:6
Benz, Henry Mrs, 1937, S 29,23:5
Benz, Joe, 1957, Ap 23,31:6
Benz, Margaret G (Mrs L L Benz), 1967, My 31,43:3
Benza, Philip L, 1966, N 19,33:3
Benzecry, Benjamin Mrs, 1937, D 8,25:3
Benzell, William Mrs, 1967, S 6,47:2
Benzier, Erwin E, 1962, Jl 5,23:6
Benziger, Adelrick, 1956, My 31,27:4
Benziger, Aloysius M, 1942, Ag 22,13:2
Benziger, August, 1955, Ap 14,36:2
Benziger, Bruno, 1955, N 25,27:3
Benziger, Bruno Mrs, 1965, F 8,25:1
Benziger, Nicholas C, 1925, O 19,21:4
Benzing, Alice P Mrs, 1948, O 24,76:4
Benzing, Andrew, 1944, Ja 18,19:3
Benzing, Ferdinand K, 1954, Ag 11,25:5
Benzing, Joseph H, 1960, Mr 18,25:1
Benzing, Magnus A, 1945, S 29,15:3
Benzing, Otto T, 1954, D 25,11:3
Benzinger, Bernard A, 1958, Ja 26,88:6
Benzinger, Frederick, 1923, D 6,19:3
Benzinger, Peter L, 1965, N 30,41:1
Benzoni, Sculptor, 1871, Ap 6,2:3
Ben Zvi, Itzhak (funl plans, Ap 24,32:1; funl, Ap 25,33:4), 1963, Ap 23,1:4
Beradi, Guiseppi Marguis, 1919, N 21,11:3
Beradi, Terresa Marchioness, 1919, N 13,13:1
Berado, Nicholas, 1949, My 30,13:4
Beradt, Martin, 1949, N 27,104:5
Beran, Rudolf, 1954, Ap 25,86:2
Berard, Alexandre, 1923, Ap 21,11:4
Berard, Christian (por), 1949, F 13,76:1
Berard, Eugene Michel, 1922, Mr 21,19:6
Berard, Leon, 1960, F 26,27:2
Berard, Norbert H, 1946, S 21,15:2
Berard Joseph, Bro (W B De Coste), 1956, F 20,23:3
Berardi, G Cardinal, 1878, Ap 7,1:2
Berardini, Alphonse A, 1945, My 30,19:4
Berardini, Michele, 1924, Ja 15,19:2
Berardis, Anthony, 1943, Jl 7,19:4
Berardis, Anthony Mrs, 1951, D 20,31:5
Berardo, Anthony J, 1954, My 10,23:5
Berau, Philip, 1943, O 20,21:5
Beraud, Henri, 1958, O 25,21:4
Berault, William V, 1948, Ap 7,25:5
Berbauer, Francis S, 1941, D 10,25:4
Berberich, Clement, 1953, Jl 13,25:6
Berberich, Henry G, 1950, Mr 7,28:3
Berberich, Hugo Dr, 1968, Mr 27,47:2
Berbert, Lyn, 1943, Ap 10,17:6
Berce, William, 1958, F 23,92:8
Berch, Samuel H, 1951, O 30,29:3
Berchmans, John Mother (Sisters of St Joseph), 1951, Ag 2,21:4
Berchmans, Mother (Most Pure Heart of Mary), 1951, Jl 24,25:4
Berchtold, Fanny von Countess, 1912, S 28,13:6
Berchtold, Leopold von Count, 1942, N 22,52:3
Berckmans, Louis A, 1939, O 30,17:7
Berckmans, Prosper J A, 1910, N 9,9:2
Bercoe, Peter, 1963, N 20,43:4
Bercovici, Joseph, 1967, F 16,44:3
Bercovici, Konrad, 1961, D 28,27:1
Bercovici, Konrad Mrs, 1957, O 24,33:4
Bercovici, Leonardo Mrs, 1951, My 24,32:3
Bercovitch, Pete, 1942, D 28,19:2
Bercu, Bernard, 1966, S 11,87:2
Berczeller, Adolf, 1966, O 6,47:4
Berczeller, Arpad, 1959, N 29,86:7
Berdan, H Gen, 1893, Ap 1,1:6
Berdan, Harry C, 1940, S 27,23:5
Berdan, Henry L, 1920, Ap 30,13:5
Berdan, Jacob M, 1960, Jl 12,35:2
Berdan, John M, 1949, Ap 4,23:1
Berdanier, Anthony F, 1951, Mr 31,15:3
Berdanier, Paul F, 1961, Ap 25,35:4
Berdell, Theodore V, 1950, Ja 26,27:4
Berdick, John E, 1944, Ag 31,17:2
Berdick, William, 1965, S 5,57:2
Berdine, Harold S, 1966, Mr 16,45:4
Berdyaev, Nicholas, 1948, Mr 25,28:2
Berea, Alejandro Mrs, 1945, Ap 5,23:3
Berea, Pedro, 1961, F 21,35:4
Berean, Harold C, 1963, S 10,39:4
Bereano, Phil L, 1949, My 23,23:5
Bereano, Phil L Mrs, 1954, S 21,27:3
Bereford, Richard, 1955, Ap 2,17:6
Beregekoff, Dimitry, 1961, Jl 8,19:5
Berenato, Anthony M, 1947, S 3,25:2
Berend, Harry Mrs, 1953, F 28,17:4
Berenger, Henri, 1952, My 19,17:5
Berenger, Rene Sen, 1915, Ag 30,7:5
Berenguer, D'Amaso, 1953, My 20,29:1
Berenguer-Cesar, Jacome B, 1957, N 5,31:2
Berenice, Mother (McDonough), 1951, N 30,23:4
Berens, Conrad (Mar 2), 1963, Ap 1,35:2
Berenschot, Berend W, 1964, Ja 24,24:4
Berenson, Arthur, 1944, Ag 13,35:2
Berenson, Bernard (funl, O 9,29:4), 1959, O 8,1:3
Berenson, Irving H, 1968, F 10,34:1
Berenson, Robert L, 1965, F 3,35:2
Berenstein, Max A, 1954, D 8,35:1
Berentsen, Richard B, 1941, Ja 24,17:3
Berentsen, Thomas B, 1948, N 22,21:6
Berenyi, Vera Mrs, 1960, N 28,31:2
Berenzweig, Elias, 1954, My 12,31:2
Beresford, Arch, 1938, Jl 13,21:5
Beresford, Charles Baron, 1919, S 8,13:3
Beresford, Frank E, 1967, My 28,60:7
Beresford, George C, 1938, Mr 1,21:5; 1940, O 13,49:3
Beresford, H G, 1938, Je 14,21:4
Beresford, Harry, 1944, O 5,23:3
Beresford, John D, 1947, F 4,25:4
Beresford, John George, 1916, My 25,13:6; 1925, My 11,17:4
Beresford, Percival, 1943, Mr 8,15:3
Beresford, Robert F, 1966, D 21,39:1
Beresford, S B Dr, 1873, O 15,4:7
Beresford, S R de la P H, 1928, My 30,19:3
Beresford, Walter C, 1942, Ja 31,17:6
Beresford-Peirse, Noel M D P, 1953, Ja 16,23:3
Bereswill, Edward A, 1952, Ag 6,21:4
Berets, Carl H, 1938, Mr 2,19:2
Beretta, Pietro, 1957, My 4,21:2
Beretta, Walter, 1968, F 28,47:3
Beretti, Francesco, 1955, Ap 29,23:3
Beretz, Basil, 1946, Ja 1,28:2

Beretz, O Paul, 1961, O 6,35:1
Berezina, Nicholas Mrs, 1955, N 30,33:3
Berezowsky, Nicolai, 1953, Ag 28,17:1
Berg, A, 1935, D 25,27:1
Berg, Albert, 1919, My 8,17:2
Berg, Albert A, 1950, Jl 2,24:3
Berg, Albert M, 1960, Jl 21,27:5
Berg, Albert W, 1915, Ja 2,9:6
Berg, Andrew, 1939, Mr 4,15:1
Berg, Anthony, 1948, F 18,27:4
Berg, Arthur T, 1958, Jl 5,17:3
Berg, Axel A, 1959, Je 28,68:3
Berg, Bernard, 1942, Ja 15,21:7
Berg, Bernard Mrs, 1957, Ja 8,31:2
Berg, C I, 1926, O 14,25:3
Berg, Carl, 1956, My 12,19:2; 1964, Je 21,84:4
Berg, Carl E, 1938, F 11,23:1
Berg, Carl J van den, 1959, Ag 27,27:5
Berg, Casper R, 1951, Mr 14,33:2
Berg, Charles, 1942, Je 24,19:2
Berg, Charles W, 1944, My 9,19:5; 1951, S 4,27:4
Berg, Christian H, 1950, D 14,35:4
Berg, Emil A, 1952, Mr 7,23:4
Berg, Ernest, 1962, O 5,5:3
Berg, Ernst J, 1941, S 10,23:1
Berg, Evelyn V (Mrs W A Sturgeon), 1960, Ja 26, 33:3
Berg, Frank O, 1953, F 1,88:4
Berg, Frantz F, 1957, D 31,17:5
Berg, Fred T, 1964, N 4,39:4
Berg, Frederick, 1908, F 22,7:5
Berg, Frederick (will, D 6,5:6), 1938, N 18,21:6
Berg, George L, 1941, Jl 4,13:5
Berg, Gertrude (Mrs Lewis Berg),(will filed, O 18,- 26:5), 1966, S 15,43:3
Berg, Gunnar, 1955, Ja 11,25:5
Berg, Gustave H, 1940, D 8,71:2
Berg, H L Mrs, 1939, D 26,19:5
Berg, Hart O, 1941, D 10,25:3
Berg, Henry, 1938, Ap 21,19:6
Berg, Henry H, 1958, N 6,37:5
Berg, Henry W (por), 1938, D 23,19:1
Berg, Henry 3d, 1958, N 29,21:5
Berg, Herbert, 1942, O 10,15:6
Berg, Herman, 1952, Ag 20,25:5
Berg, Herman L, 1962, N 16,31:1
Berg, Hugo van den, 1938, D 6,23:2
Berg, Irving H, 1941, Ag 30,13:3
Berg, J Frederic, 1958, Ap 5,15:5
Berg, Jacob, 1956, My 31,27:4
Berg, Jacob D, 1963, Je 19,37:5
Berg, Jan van den, 1961, N 17,35:2
Berg, Jay, 1945, O 13,15:3
Berg, John D, 1949, Jl 1,19:5
Berg, Joseph, 1964, Jl 8,35:1
Berg, Joseph W, 1941, Jl 12,13:5
Berg, Katherine Mrs, 1949, Ja 30,60:5
Berg, L Rodney, 1941, Ja 11,17:2
Berg, Leo J, 1962, Jl 29,60:7
Berg, Leo Mrs, 1950, Mr 13,21:3
Berg, Leon M, 1944, Ja 28,23:1
Berg, Lev, 1950, D 26,23:1
Berg, Louisa van den Mrs, 1947, Ag 23,13:5
Berg, Max, 1958, Je 18,33:2
Berg, Michael C, 1964, Jl 11,25:4
Berg, Moncure B, 1955, D 3,17:6
Berg, N V, 1884, Ag 16,2:6
Berg, Nettie L Mrs, 1967, Jl 27,35:3
Berg, Oliver J, 1955, Ag 23,23:5
Berg, Oscar E Mrs, 1939, D 12,27:1
Berg, Phil, 1948, Je 4,23:1
Berg, R Howard, 1965, Jl 26,23:5
Berg, Reuben Mrs, 1964, N 19,39:6
Berg, Rockwell H, 1941, Ag 31,23:2
Berg, Samuel, 1950, Jl 16,69:1; 1963, Ap 26,36:1
Berg, Samuel M, 1959, Ap 6,27:4
Berg, W I, 1937, Je 7,19:5
Berg, Walter Gilman, 1908, My 13,7:5
Berg, Walter P, 1952, F 4,17:5
Berg, William A (will), 1950, Ap 23,67:1
Berg, William H, 1940, Je 27,23:5; 1962, N 27,38:1
Berg, William M, 1950, Je 21,27:3
Berg, William Mrs, 1937, Ja 18,17:2; 1953, Ag 19,29:5
Berga, Pablo, 1939, Jl 17,19:5
Bergali, Marcelino, 1943, Ap 19,19:4
Bergamasco, Eugenio, 1940, Je 13,23:2
Bergamin, Francisco, 1937, F 13,13:3
Bergamo, Guido, 1953, Je 27,15:3
Bergan, Francis T, 1966, Ap 17,87:1
Bergan, Joseph E, 1945, Ap 2,19:4
Bergan, William F, 1947, D 24,22:3
Bergbauer, Fred J, 1963, O 29,36:5
Bergdoll, Erwin R, 1965, Mr 23,39:2
Bergdoll, Grover C (est appr, Mr 30,36:2), 1966, Ja 29,27:2
Bergdoll, Louis Mrs, 1944, D 5,38:4
Bergdorf, Eugenie Mrs, 1938, Ja 7,20:1
Berge, Edward W, 1915, Mr 18,11:5
Berge, Peter, 1946, S 29,62:3
Berge, Wendell, 1955, S 26,23:1
Berge, William E, 1958, Mr 14,25:2
Berge, William H, 1940, Jl 15,15:4
Bergeim, Frank H, 1965, Ap 14,42:1
Bergeler, Charles A, 1941, My 2,21:5
Bergen, Adolph A Mrs, 1956, F 16,29:1
Bergen, Benjamin, 1937, Ja 28,25:1
Bergen, Charles A, 1945, Je 2,15:4
Bergen, Cornelius J, 1940, Ap 2,26:3
Bergen, Cornelius R Jr, 1949, O 12,30:6
Bergen, Daniel, 1951, My 6,92:1
Bergen, Daniel Mrs, 1949, Je 10,27:3; 1951, O 6,19:2
Bergen, DeHart, 1944, Ja 29,13:3
Bergen, Edmond S, 1960, Mr 18,25:2
Bergen, Edward J, 1946, Je 26,25:1
Bergen, Elston H, 1957, Je 13,32:1
Bergen, F Willard, 1968, Je 17,39:2
Bergen, Fannie M Mrs, 1941, N 1,15:4
Bergen, Fenwick W Mrs, 1959, N 15,87:1
Bergen, Francis P, 1942, N 24,26:2
Bergen, Frederick I, 1960, F 27,19:5
Bergen, George E Mrs, 1951, N 2,24:3
Bergen, Harold B, 1942, N 5,25:2
Bergen, Jacob I, 1944, Ap 16,41:1
Bergen, James C, 1906, D 23,7:6
Bergen, James J Justice, 1923, O 21,23:2
Bergen, John, 1939, S 28,25:2
Bergen, John A, 1942, D 11,23:4
Bergen, John F, 1943, Mr 13,13:2; 1945, Jl 21,11:6
Bergen, John G, 1867, Jl 19,8:3
Bergen, John Q, 1946, Ja 2,19:3
Bergen, Joseph A, 1942, O 24,15:3
Bergen, Leffert L, 1904, F 24,9:6
Bergen, Leigh B, 1943, F 5,21:3
Bergen, Lydia G Mrs, 1948, F 28,15:2
Bergen, Martin, 1906, O 10,7:2
Bergen, Martin V, 1941, Jl 9,21:3
Bergen, Mary P Mrs, 1940, Mr 28,23:3
Bergen, Meta J Mrs, 1939, Je 2,23:4
Bergen, Nella, 1919, Ap 26,15:4
Bergen, Patrick, 1951, N 15,29:1
Bergen, Peter G, 1865, Ag 4,8:3
Bergen, Pierron, 1941, My 2,44:2
Bergen, Thomas D, 1946, S 19,31:1
Bergen, Ward V, 1965, O 19,43:3
Bergen, William C, 1925, S 26,17:6
Bergener, A E M, 1950, My 16,31:1
Bergener, August G, 1946, Ja 10,23:1
Bergener, Walter T, 1948, D 16,29:2
Bergenrun, Werner, 1964, S 5,19:4
Bergenstal, Delbert M, 1959, S 14,29:5
Bergenthal, Bruno A, 1951, Ja 22,17:4
Bergenthal, Hugo, 1956, Ag 30,25:4
Berger, Aaron, 1960, Ag 12,19:3
Berger, Abraham, 1950, Jl 2,24:6; 1956, Jl 15,60:5
Berger, Adolf, 1962, Ap 9,29:4
Berger, Adolph, 1961, Ap 16,86:6
Berger, Alex, 1940, Ap 12,23:3; 1953, Ja 26,19:4
Berger, Alexandre, 1968, D 7,47:3
Berger, Andrew B, 1942, O 27,25:2
Berger, Andrew B Jr, 1957, D 8,89:1
Berger, Arch E, 1941, Je 18,21:2
Berger, Arthur, 1959, N 1,86:3; 1960, Ja 13,47:1
Berger, Arthur V Mrs, 1960, O 24,29:4
Berger, Benjamin M, 1938, Je 25,15:6
Berger, Boniface, 1940, My 27,19:4
Berger, Carl, 1917, Ap 18,13:5
Berger, Carl P, 1947, Mr 15,13:5
Berger, Charles (Heinie), 1954, F 11,29:3
Berger, Charles A, 1966, S 24,23:6
Berger, Charles E, 1948, My 3,21:3
Berger, Charles P Jr, 1955, N 9,33:3
Berger, Clyde D, 1959, Jl 31,23:2
Berger, David, 1947, N 25,32:3
Berger, David H, 1959, Ja 27,33:1
Berger, Edla G, 1960, Je 12,86:6
Berger, Edward, 1960, F 24,37:1
Berger, Edward C, 1961, Jl 13,29:2
Berger, Edward H, 1952, My 14,27:3
Berger, Edward L, 1951, Ag 9,21:6
Berger, Elmer S, 1955, F 26,15:5
Berger, Fernand A, 1951, S 27,31:6
Berger, Florence Mrs, 1941, Ag 4,13:5
Berger, Fred, 1949, Jl 30,15:6
Berger, G Frederick, 1953, S 24,33:3
Berger, George A Sr, 1953, S 18,24:3
Berger, George H, 1952, Je 18,27:1
Berger, Gisella L Mrs, 1937, Jl 3,15:6
Berger, Gustav, 1958, O 19,87:3
Berger, H William, 1963, Ag 11,85:1
Berger, Hans, 1941, Je 10,23:5
Berger, Herbert L, 1968, Ap 23,44:2
Berger, Herman L Mrs, 1944, My 15,19:5
Berger, Hulda E, 1951, Ag 26,77:2
Berger, Irving, 1961, N 22,33:4
Berger, Isaac, 1953, D 28,21:1
Berger, Isidor, 1954, Ap 19,23:4
Berger, Jacob A, 1952, Jl 19,15:2
Berger, Jean, 1937, Mr 11,23:2
Berger, John B, 1937, S 2,21:4
Berger, John J, 1966, Mr 21,33:5
Berger, Joseph E, 1953, Ja 3,15:4
Berger, Joseph J, 1949, Ag 12,17:2
Berger, Joseph L, 1956, Ja 9,25:2
Berger, Josephine Mrs, 1941, Ja 3,21:4
Berger, Karl A, 1966, N 7,47:2
Berger, Kitty, 1925, Ap 23,21:2
Berger, Kornel C, 1967, Jl 29,25:6
Berger, Leo A, 1953, N 12,43:8
Berger, Louis, 1948, S 2,23:4; 1952, Mr 27,29:5
Berger, Louis D, 1966, Mr 11,33:2
Berger, Mac, 1967, Ap 29,35:3
Berger, Marcy I, 1951, F 25,85:1
Berger, Maurice W, 1968, Jl 27,27:1
Berger, Max, 1951, Je 13,29:6; 1955, D 30,19:4; 1964, Jl 2,31:5
Berger, Max A, 1966, Je 16,47:4
Berger, Max Mrs, 1944, Ag 29,17:5; 1951, Ap 3,27:2
Berger, Meyer (Mike),(funl plans;trb, F 11,39:4,5), 1959, F 9,29:1
Berger, Milton (Dick), 1956, O 22,29:2
Berger, Milton, 1958, Ap 28,23:4
Berger, Milton Mrs, 1964, D 13,86:6
Berger, Morris A, 1952, S 6,17:6; 1958, Ag 1,21:4
Berger, Murray Mrs, 1948, S 29,29:4
Berger, Nathan H, 1968, N 1,47:1
Berger, Nathan I, 1956, Je 4,29:5
Berger, Paul H, 1962, S 20,33:4
Berger, Phyllis, 1950, Ja 8,76:5
Berger, Rudolph (funl, Mr 3,11:5), 1915, Mr 1,9:5
Berger, Samuel, 1923, Ap 19,19:4
Berger, Samuel A, 1962, Je 22,25:3
Berger, Samuel A Mrs, 1941, Mr 29,15:6
Berger, Samuel E, 1949, D 26,29:6
Berger, Samuel L Mrs, 1967, O 16,45:2
Berger, Samuel M, 1941, Ag 7,17:4
Berger, Samuel S, 1956, S 20,33:4
Berger, Solomon, 1959, D 1,39:4
Berger, Stephen C, 1939, Ag 19,15:6
Berger, V, 1929, Ag 8,25:1
Berger, Victor L Mrs, 1944, Je 17,13:2
Berger, William, 1953, My 28,23:5; 1959, N 30,31:4
Berger, William J, 1950, S 29,27:1
Berger, William T, 1956, Je 29,21:5
Berger the Billiard Player, 1875, O 15,1:5
Bergere, Llewellyn K, 1952, O 6,25:3
Bergere, Ramonda Mrs, 1941, Ap 27,38:3
Bergeron, Edgar P, 1948, Je 18,24:2
Bergeron, Lionel M, 1950, O 17,31:4
Bergeron, Robert E, 1962, N 11,88:7
Bergerson, Emile F, 1948, Ja 2,23:2
Berges, Frederick H, 1951, N 29,33:4
Berges, Frederick H Mrs, 1940, My 24,19:2
Berges, Phillip J, 1943, Ag 27,17:4
Bergesen, Berge S, 1965, Jl 11,69:1
Bergesson, Raymond A, 1953, Ja 20,25:3
Bergey, Daniel, 1951, Ja 1,17:1
Bergey, David H Dr, 1937, S 6,17:4
Berggrav, Eivind, 1959, Ja 15,33:5
Berggren, Elof, 1950, Je 7,29:3
Berggren, Ernest J, 1943, S 10,24:2
Berggren, Karl A, 1947, F 14,21:4
Bergh, Albert van der, 1943, O 19,19:1
Bergh, Arthur, 1962, F 14,35:2
Bergh, Coba de, 1946, Ag 17,13:2
Bergh, Edward R, 1953, Ag 8,11:3
Bergh, Edwin, 1876, My 14,5:4
Bergh, Henrik, 1952, Jl 16,25:4
Bergh, Henry, 1888, Mr 13,8:4
Bergh, Joseph F Dr, 1871, Jl 22,4:6
Bergh, Leo V, 1941, N 28,24:3
Bergh, Lillie D, 1941, Jl 13,29:2
Bergh, Louis O, 1955, N 30,33:4
Bergh, Louis O Mrs, 1944, My 14,45:1
Bergh, T, 1881, Ag 6,5:4
Bergh, William R, 1953, Ag 12,31:3
Berghane, Frederick A, 1945, Je 22,15:4
Berghane, Henry Mrs, 1942, Ja 12,15:3
Bergherm, C Russell, 1966, O 30,88:6
Berghes, De Landas, 1920, N 19,15:4
Berghoff, Walter E, 1948, F 24,25:3
Berghold, William M, 1949, Ag 13,12:2
Bergholtz, Herman, 1938, N 17,25:5
Bergida, Adolf, 1939, My 2,23:4
Bergin, Daniel T, 1968, O 10,47:5
Bergin, Frank J, 1958, O 8,35:1
Bergin, Frank T, 1951, Jl 1,51:2
Bergin, James A, 1944, Ap 7,20:2
Bergin, Joseph V, 1947, S 12,21:5
Bergin, Paul D Rev, 1915, Ag 10,11:7
Bergin, Thomas, 1945, Je 1,15:2
Bergin, William J, 1959, Jl 14,29:4
Bergius, Friedrich, 1949, Mr 31,25:2
Bergland, Eric L, 1953, D 31,19:5
Berglass, Solomon, 1942, N 7,15:5
Bergler, Edmund, 1962, F 7,37:2
Berglind, Harry R, 1956, Je 21,31:2
Berglund, Abraham, 1942, My 30,15:3
Berglund, Alex G, 1944, N 14,23:5
Berglund, Arnold W, 1968, Mr 24,93:1
Berglund, Erick B, 1965, Ap 11,92:4
Berglund, Hilding, 1962, My 19,27:4
Berglund, Milford P, 1948, O 13,25:1
Berglund, William C, 1958, F 28,21:1
Bergman, Alfred C, 1960, Ap 15,23:2
Bergman, Bernard A Mrs, 1965, O 27,47:4
Bergman, Bo, 1967, N 18,37:4
Bergman, Carl, 1876, Ag 13,6:7
Bergman, Charles, 1944, S 28,19:2
Bergman, Clarence, 1942, D 20,45:2

Bergman, George B, 1949, Ag 23,23:2
Bergman, Gustav, 1938, Jl 21,21:5
Bergman, H A, 1948, Ja 21,25:3
Bergman, Harold C, 1961, D 17,82:5
Bergman, Harry Mrs, 1957, F 26,29:2
Bergman, Henry, 1917, Ja 11,15:4; 1946, O 24,27:2; 1962, N 9,26:2
Bergman, J A Mrs, 1938, D 21,23:4
Bergman, Jacob, 1966, Jl 27,39:1
Bergman, Justin Mrs, 1948, Ap 22,27:2
Bergman, Justin Sr, 1960, Jl 6,33:1
Bergman, Leonard E, 1942, S 6,30:5
Bergman, Louis Mrs, 1967, Ap 23,94:3
Bergman, Maury, 1961, D 27,27:3
Bergman, Nathaniel B, 1950, My 24,29:3
Bergman, Ray, 1967, F 19,88:7
Bergman, Raymonde M Mrs, 1949, Mr 31,25:3
Bergman, Robert H, 1947, Je 14,15:5
Bergman, Robert S Mrs, 1948, O 18,23:1
Bergman, Samuel, 1947, S 26,23:2
Bergman, Samuel H, 1950, O 17,31:5
Bergman, Sidney M, 1957, Ja 24,29:4
Bergman, Simon, 1939, My 11,25:3
Bergman, Sven R, 1944, N 27,23:4
Bergman, William E Mrs, 1962, Je 21,31:4
Bergmann, Albert D, 1958, My 30,21:1
Bergmann, Augustus H, 1968, S 20,47:4
Bergmann, C, 1935, S 27,21:5
Bergmann, Clifford L Mrs, 1960, Jl 1,25:5
Bergmann, Edgar E, 1942, D 6,76:2
Bergmann, Ernst von, 1907, Mr 26,9:5
Bergmann, Federico C Mrs, 1948, D 8,31:5
Bergmann, Frederick J, 1950, Ap 21,23:2
Bergmann, George W, 1949, S 13,29:3
Bergmann, Henry J, 1951, D 4,33:1
Bergmann, Joseph A, 1958, Mr 4,29:3
Bergmann, Louis, 1962, O 29,29:4
Bergmann, Max, 1944, N 8,17:5
Bergmann, Paul, 1945, Je 9,13:3
Bergmann, Paul J, 1941, Ja 27,15:4
Bergmann, Paul Sr, 1951, S 18,31:2
Bergmann, Rudolph C, 1963, O 10,41:1
Bergmann, S, 1927, Jl 8,19:3
Bergmann, Werner, 1959, N 4,35:3
Bergmark, Anna L L Mrs, 1940, Ag 18,37:2
Bergmark, Olaf, 1939, Je 13,23:5
Bergner, C William, 1903, My 5,9:6
Bergner, Gustavus W, 1937, My 23,II,11:3
Bergner, Otto C, 1950, S 22,31:1
Bergoff, Pearl L, 1947, Ag 13,5:3
Bergold, Frank J, 1962, Ja 4,34:1
Bergold, Joseph Mrs, 1959, Mr 16,31:5
Bergougnan, Mathieu, 1940, F 27,21:1
Bergquist, Charles W, 1956, Mr 1,33:4
Bergquist, Clarence H, 1958, S 7,87:2
Bergquist, G William, 1967, My 30,21:4
Bergquist, John G, 1938, S 1,23:6
Bergquist, Robert F Mrs, 1955, Ag 12,19:4
Bergren, David E, 1947, Ag 23,13:5
Bergren, Ellen H, 1949, S 22,31:4
Bergren, Nellie Mrs, 1943, O 20,21:5
Bergsaker, Anders J, 1951, N 24,11:6
Bergsma, Ennius H, 1946, My 2,21:2
Bergsmann, Max Sr, 1950, Je 17,15:2
Bergsmark, Daniel R, 1945, Je 27,19:4
Bergson, Henri, 1941, Ja 6,15:1
Bergson, Louis J, 1942, Ag 5,19:6
Bergson, Peter H Mrs (B Keane), 1964, Mr 4,34:6
Bergstraser, Samuel L, 1958, Jl 5,17:2
Bergstrasser, Arnold, 1964, F 26,35:4
Bergstresser, Fred L, 1949, Ag 15,17:3
Bergstresser, Ross K, 1951, Ap 15,92:3
Bergstresser, Samuel W Mrs, 1951, Ag 26,80:2
Bergstrom, Albert R, 1941, S 10,23:3
Bergstrom, Carl J, 1956, O 3,33:6
Bergstrom, Charles A Mrs, 1952, Je 18,27:2
Bergstrom, Francis W, 1946, Mr 31,46:5
Bergstrom, George E, 1955, Je 21,31:2
Bergstrom, Jeremiah K, 1949, N 9,27:5
Bergstrom, John N, 1951, Je 21,27:4
Bergstrom, Karl G, 1940, Je 15,15:2
Bergstrom, Richard J, 1965, Je 24,35:3
Bergstrom, Willis C, 1951, N 24,11:5
Bergstrom, Willis C Mrs, 1958, O 29,35:1
Bergton, Bernard J, 1966, N 5,31:3
Berguido, Carlos, 1951, N 25,86:4
Berguido, Carlos Sr Mrs, 1947, Je 29,48:5
Bergus, Fredrich, 1949, Ap 1,26:2
Bergvall, Jakob L, 1945, Ag 31,17:3
Bergvall, John, 1959, Ag 12,29:2
Berhard, L Dr, 1884, Ap 22,5:4
Berhold, John A, 1952, My 13,23:2
Berhold, Susan B, 1949, Je 16,29:1
Berigan, Bernard, 1942, Je 3,23:5
Berilla, John J, 1948, Mr 2,23:4
Bering, Donald A, 1951, Je 28,25:2
Beringer, George M, 1948, F 16,21:5
Beringer, Gerson W, 1948, Je 27,52:4
Beringer, Marx H, 1907, S 12,7:6
Beringer, Viola R H Mrs, 1938, D 9,25:2
Berini, Stanislaw, 1943, Mr 13,13:4
Berinstein, Benjamin, 1950, F 23,27:5
Beris, Samuel, 1959, Je 17,35:1
Berisford, Joseph S Mrs, 1967, Je 4,86:4
Berisford, Reta V Mrs, 1941, F 3,17:4
Berish, Archie, 1963, Ag 30,21:4
Berish, John Mrs, 1951, N 20,31:5
Beristain, Leopoldo, 1948, Ja 7,25:2
Berizzi, Louis, 1951, Mr 21,33:4
Berizzi, Stefano, 1960, O 31,31:6
Berk, Ben A Mrs, 1954, Mr 16,29:2
Berk, Benjamin A, 1956, D 8,19:2
Berk, Henry, 1946, S 14,7:5
Berk, Milton, 1957, Mr 31,88:2
Berk, Paul F, 1942, My 1,19:3
Berk, William, 1965, My 1,31:1
Berkander, George F, 1937, O 5,25:1
Berke, Henry H Mrs, 1946, My 13,21:2
Berke, Joseph H, 1938, Je 17,21:6
Berke, Kalman (corr, My 22,29:4), 1958, My 19,25:1
Berke, Kiva, 1961, N 17,35:1
Berke, Phil H, 1951, Jl 30,19:4
Berkebile, John W, 1968, F 10,34:3
Berkeley, Alfred, 1938, My 17,23:3
Berkeley, Alfred R Mrs, 1939, My 27,15:3
Berkeley, Bernard H, 1949, F 2,27:5
Berkeley, Earl of, 1942, Ja 16,21:4
Berkeley, Frederick G, 1962, F 14,33:1
Berkeley, Norborne, 1964, My 27,39:1
Berkeley, Randolph C, 1960, F 1,27:3
Berkeley, Robert G C, 1949, Ap 12,30:2
Berkeley, Robert Maurice Rev, 1916, Ap 29,11:5
Berkeley, Sidney S, 1968, Je 6,47:4
Berkeley, T M F Earl, 1882, S 11,5:5
Berkeley, William N, 1945, N 26,21:2
Berkeley, Wilson E Mrs, 1946, Je 16,40:5
Berkell, Charles, 1938, N 20,39:2
Berkemeier, Susetta K Mrs, 1937, Jl 7,24:1
Berkenbosch, Willem, 1957, Ja 18,21:3
Berker, Anna, 1941, Mr 19,21:1
Berkery, Martin Mrs, 1949, N 5,13:4
Berkery, Thomas F, 1963, O 28,27:4
Berkery, Thomas F Mrs, 1952, My 23,21:4
Berkes, Harvey A, 1940, N 1,25:4
Berkey, Charles A, 1942, O 1,23:4
Berkey, Charles F, 1957, Ap 28,86:2
Berkey, Charles P, 1955, Ag 24,27:4
Berkey, Charles P Mrs, 1940, Ja 11,23:5
Berkey, Russell S Mrs, 1947, Ag 11,23:6
Berkfield, Edward, 1958, Jl 25,19:4
Berkfield, Edward Mrs, 1965, Je 5,31:6
Berkhemer, William F, 1948, Ap 10,13:2
Berkhofer, William R, 1965, Mr 25,37:1
Berking, Max B Mrs (Dorothy), 1962, Ap 26,33:4
Berkley, Gerald J, 1947, Jl 16,23:4
Berkley, Harold (mem ser set, S 7,39:2), 1965, Jl 21, 37:5
Berkley, Henry J, 1940, Ap 7,44:7
Berkley, Hugh K, 1947, Jl 13,44:7
Berkley, Jerold, 1967, F 25,28:2
Berkman, Harry, 1960, Jl 20,29:1
Berkman, Joseph, 1957, F 12,27:2
Berkman, Moses, 1956, Jl 20,17:4
Berkmark, Gustave Mrs, 1948, My 18,23:4
Berkner, Lloyd V, 1967, Je 5,43:3
Berko, William, 1950, D 16,17:6
Berkovsky, Max, 1949, S 7,29:1
Berkow, Samuel G, 1961, S 2,15:4
Berkowitz, Adolph Mrs, 1946, D 25,29:6
Berkowitz, Benjamin, 1957, O 27,86:7
Berkowitz, Chaim, 1952, O 15,31:1
Berkowitz, George, 1947, Jl 12,13:4
Berkowitz, H Chonon, 1945, Ja 19,19:5
Berkowitz, Harry, 1944, N 18,13:5
Berkowitz, Harry M, 1956, Ja 1,51:1
Berkowitz, Henry J, 1949, Mr 2,25:2
Berkowitz, Henry W Rev, 1924, F 8,19:5
Berkowitz, Isaac D, 1967, Mr 30,45:2
Berkowitz, James, 1962, N 7,39:4
Berkowitz, Joseph, 1953, Mr 3,27:2
Berkowitz, Joseph J, 1952, Ja 2,25:2
Berkowitz, Maurice H Mrs, 1946, Ja 25,23:1
Berkowitz, Max E, 1958, Ap 16,35:1
Berkowitz, Michael, 1941, Ag 3,34:6
Berkowitz, Milton, 1962, Ag 21,33:1
Berkowitz, Morris, 1951, Jl 14,13:4
Berkowitz, Mortimer, 1966, O 27,47:3
Berkowitz, Nathan, 1947, D 16,34:2
Berkowitz, Nathan S, 1957, Ja 15,30:2
Berkowitz, Samuel, 1966, Ap 30,31:3
Berkowitz, Samuel S, 1963, Je 5,41:3
Berkowitz, Sidney, 1957, My 28,33:3
Berkson, Irving, 1953, F 14,17:1
Berkson, J Count, 1938, Jl 24,29:4
Berkson, J Count Mrs, 1945, D 19,25:3
Berkson, Seymour (funl plans, Ja 6,34:1; funl, Ja 8,29:5), 1959, Ja 5,29:2
Berkstresser, Gordon A, 1963, O 7,31:4
Berl, Alexander, 1947, O 22,29:4
Berl, C Waggaman, 1953, O 8,29:4
Berl, E Ennalls, 1954, Ap 2,27:2
Berl, Ernest, 1946, F 17,44:3
Berla, Samuel, 1956, Je 1,23:3
Berlack, Harris, 1968, D 5,47:3
Berlage, H P, 1934, Ag 13,13:1
Berlan, Alan J, 1965, N 30,41:1
Berlan, Seward Coe von Mrs, 1917, Jl 14,7:5
Berland, Joseph, 1938, N 20,39:1
Berle, Adam, 1941, N 4,23:4
Berle, Adolf A Mrs, 1940, F 8,23:5
Berle, K, 1934, My 7,17:3
Berle, Sarah Mrs, 1954, Je 1,27:2
Berlenbach, Katherine Mrs, 1937, D 30,19:3
Berlenbach, Paul Mrs, 1966, Je 3,39:1
Berlenbach, Phil H, 1938, Mr 26,15:2
Berlepsch, H H von Baron, 1926, Je 4,23:6
Berlew, Gilderoy O, 1940, N 30,17:1
Berlewi, Henry K, 1967, Ag 4,29:1
Berley, Max, 1958, Ja 12,86:8
Berley, Thomas F, 1955, D 7,39:1
Berlfein, Jacob Mrs, 1951, Je 3,95:3
Berliet, Leon, 1942, Ag 6,19:6
Berlin, Bernard S, 1947, Mr 31,23:4
Berlin, Carl E, 1940, Jl 10,19:4
Berlin, Charles, 1952, Jl 1,23:4
Berlin, David, 1954, Ag 21,17:4
Berlin, David A (will), 1966, D 10,75:4
Berlin, Henry Clay, 1921, My 10,17:4
Berlin, Jessie K Mrs, 1947, S 15,17:4
Berlin, Joseph I, 1964, O 1,35:4
Berlin, Louis, 1960, F 15,27:4
Berlin, Max J, 1959, Je 16,35:5
Berlin, Meyer, 1949, Ap 18,25:4
Berlin, Michael, 1946, Ja 14,19:3
Berlin, Moe, 1956, F 19,92:4
Berlin, Richard S, 1903, Jl 14,5:2
Berlin, Sarah Mrs, 1943, F 12,19:5
Berlin, Sarah N Mrs, 1938, D 30,15:1
Berlin, Simon, 1963, Ap 16,35:3
Berlin, Theodore, 1962, N 18,86:7
Berlin, William F, 1960, Mr 6,86:1
Berlind, Hyman, 1954, Ja 28,27:3
Berlind, Peter S, 1959, D 22,31:5
Berliner, Abraham, 1966, Jl 2,23:4
Berliner, Alfred, 1944, S 13,19:3
Berliner, E, 1929, Ag 4,24:4
Berliner, Harold, 1963, Ag 5,29:5
Berliner, Irwin M, 1966, O 8,31:4
Berliner, Jac, 1903, F 15,2:6
Berliner, Leo E, 1903, F 9,9:3
Berliner, Leonard H, 1967, Ap 12,47:2
Berliner, Louis M, 1961, D 2,23:4
Berliner, Marcus, 1908, S 12,7:6
Berliner, Morris, 1954, Ag 19,23:2
Berliner, Samuel (funl, S 15,17:2), 1956, S 13,35:3
Berliner, Solomon, 1910, N 15,11:4
Berliner, William M, 1964, Mr 25,41:1
Berlinger, Edward F, 1953, Mr 5,27:2
Berlinger, Joseph (cor, Ja 7,78:4), 1951, Ja 5,21:4
Berlingeri, Dominick, 1965, Je 5,14:6
Berlinghoff, Henry, 1954, Ja 11,25:5
Berlinghoff, William H Mrs, 1968, Ja 22,47:3
Berlingieri, Raffaele G, 1964, My 2,27:1
Berlioz, Hector, 1869, Mr 22,1:3
Berliss, John J, 1941, O 7,24:3
Berlitz, Maximilian D, 1921, Ap 7,15:6
Berlizheimer, David T, 1952, Ag 20,25:6
Berlowe, Matilda, 1952, N 20,24:6
Berls, Rudolph, 1960, Je 26,73:1
Berman, Aaron, 1947, Je 24,23:4
Berman, Abraham B, 1957, N 24,87:3
Berman, Abram, 1962, Jl 28,19:2
Berman, Alex, 1954, O 16,17:1
Berman, Alfred, 1961, Je 24,21:6
Berman, Barnet V, 1951, N 18,90:2
Berman, Barney, 1946, Ja 1,27:2
Berman, Benjamin H, 1960, D 7,43:4
Berman, Cotelle R, 1942, F 25,20:3
Berman, Daniel M, 1967, N 23,33:3
Berman, David (NJ), 1959, Ag 25,31:5
Berman, David (NY), 1959, S 7,15:6
Berman, David P, 1966, Mr 29,41:3
Berman, Edward (cor, Je 7,23:2), 1938, Je 3,21:5
Berman, Edward, 1953, Ap 16,29:1
Berman, Eli, 1938, O 23,41:3
Berman, Elias, 1937, Jl 20,23:5
Berman, Emil, 1960, Ja 11,45:4
Berman, George J, 1961, D 17,82:1
Berman, Harold, 1949, My 31,23:4
Berman, Harold Mrs, 1949, Je 14,31:4
Berman, Harry M, 1955, F 16,29:1
Berman, Harry S, 1944, F 18,17:5
Berman, Howard M, 1967, Mr 23,35:2
Berman, Ira B, 1950, N 30,33:4
Berman, Israel, 1956, Ja 6,24:6; 1960, Je 21,34:1
Berman, J Phil, 1938, Ja 25,21:5
Berman, Jacob, 1922, My 15,17:4
Berman, Jacob H, 1953, O 21,30:6
Berman, Jeremiah J, 1955, Ja 6,27:3
Berman, Lee, 1967, Ja 30,29:1
Berman, Lionel, 1968, Mr 1,43:3
Berman, Louis, 1946, My 17,21:1
Berman, Louis B, 1964, O 26,31:3
Berman, Louis E, 1944, Mr 21,19:5
Berman, Louis G, 1954, Jl 23,17:2
Berman, Louis K, 1960, D 2,29:2
Berman, Louis L, 1963, Ag 23,25:1
Berman, Mark, 1953, N 26,31:4
Berman, Matthew, 1968, Mr 25,41:3

Berman, Maurice L, 1958, Mr 27,33:4
Berman, Max, 1951, Jl 26,21:5; 1954, Ja 24,84:4; 1956, Mr 11,88:5
Berman, Meyer, 1961, O 18,43:3
Berman, Meyer Mrs, 1941, O 30,23:3
Berman, Morris, 1945, N 1,23:1
Berman, Morris Brig Gen, 1945, N 13,21:4
Berman, Morton M Mrs, 1949, Je 11,18:4
Berman, Nathan, 1965, My 7,41:2
Berman, Oscar, 1951, D 3,31:5
Berman, Phil, 1954, Ja 9,16:3
Berman, Robert B, 1954, Je 2,23:5
Berman, Sam, 1950, Ap 27,29:5
Berman, Sidney (cor, S 18,35:1), 1956, S 12,37:3
Berman, Sidney M, 1959, Ap 19,86:1
Berman, Stanley, 1968, F 26,32:7
Berman, Sydney D, 1966, My 23,41:1
Berman, Victor H, 1953, O 1,29:4
Berman, William, 1956, Mr 14,33:4
Bermann, Richard A, 1939, S 6,23:1
Bermann, Robert B, 1953, S 23,31:2
Bermant, Henry, 1965, N 13,29:5
Bermant, Jacob W, 1950, Jl 2,24:8
Bermard, Robert W (por), 1949, Mr 11,26:3
Bermas, George W, 1938, F 20,II,9:1
Bermel, Joseph, 1921, Jl 29,13:5; 1921, S 1,15:2
Bermes, Daniel Mrs, 1903, D 6,7:6
Bermingham, Edward J, 1958, Jl 14,21:4
Bermingham, Edward J Dr, 1922, Jl 18,11:3
Bermingham, Frank L, 1946, S 13,7:3
Bermingham, George A, 1939, N 13,19:5
Bermingham, Jennie, 1937, Je 5,17:1
Bermingham, John F, 1942, Ag 26,19:6
Bermingham, Richard A, 1939, N 15,23:1
Bermingham, Rutledge, 1953, Ap 20,25:4
Bermingham, Simon Sr, 1948, Ja 8,25:2
Bermudez, R M Col, 1894, Ap 3,1:5
Bern, Edward G, 1956, N 24,19:6
Bernacchi, L C, 1942, Ap 25,13:5
Bernadotte, Neomi, 1953, My 26,29:4
Bernadotte, Princess Ebba, 1946, O 17,23:2
Bernadou, John B Com, 1908, O 3,9:2
Bernal Jimenez, Miguel, 1956, Jl 28,17:6
Bernales, Jose C, 1944, Ap 19,23:2
Bernan, Louis Mrs, 1945, O 2,23:2
Bernanos, Georges, 1948, Jl 6,23:3
Bernard, Abner, 1950, Ja 9,25:2
Bernard, Adm, 1903, Jl 17,7:6
Bernard, Adolph F, 1952, D 25,29:2
Bernard, Agnes F, 1919, Jl 20,21:2
Bernard, Al, 1949, Mr 7,21:2
Bernard, Anthyme Prof, 1882, F 8,5:5
Bernard, Barney, 1924, Mr 22,15:6
Bernard, Baruch, 1953, F 28,17:6
Bernard, Benjamin F, 1949, O 11,34:2
Bernard, Benjamin F Mrs, 1961, N 30,34:4
Bernard, Bernard, 1963, Jl 19,25:3
Bernard, C, 1878, F 28,5:1
Bernard, Caroline Richings, 1882, Ja 15,5:5
Bernard, Dorothy, 1955, D 16,29:3
Bernard, E George, 1952, F 26,27:2
Bernard, Elizabeth, 1944, S 30,13:6
Bernard, Emile, 1941, Ap 20,44:1
Bernard, Felix, 1944, O 24,23:4
Bernard, Francis P Mrs, 1948, N 25,32:3
Bernard, Frank L, 1951, O 12,27:5
Bernard, Frederick, 1954, Ap 4,88:3
Bernard, George, 1951, S 18,31:5
Bernard, George J Sr, 1954, Jl 24,13:2
Bernard, George M Mrs, 1960, Ap 15,23:3
Bernard, George Mrs, 1951, O 8,21:4
Bernard, Helen, 1923, N 3,16:5
Bernard, Henry P Sr, 1951, My 1,29:4
Bernard, Herman J, 1967, N 26,85:1
Bernard, Herman R, 1948, Ja 21,26:3
Bernard, Hermann Ernest (Prince of Hohelohe-Langenburg), 1913, Mr 12,11:4
Bernard, Jack, 1966, F 14,29:2
Bernard, James L, 1943, Je 20,34:6; 1961, F 2,29:5
Bernard, John, 1903, Ap 25,6:3
Bernard, John J, 1954, Ja 17,93:2
Bernard, John N, 1873, Mr 23,4:7
Bernard, Jules E, 1955, Jl 3,33:2
Bernard, Lawrence V, 1950, Mr 1,27:4
Bernard, Levi Robins, 1915, D 21,13:5
Bernard, Louis E, 1958, O 24,33:4
Bernard, Luther L, 1951, Ja 25,25:2
Bernard, M, 1883, O 24,2:6
Bernard, Maurice G, 1963, O 24,30:4
Bernard, Maurice G Mrs, 1948, Ag 31,23:2
Bernard, Merrill, 1951, Ap 14,15:4
Bernard, Montague, 1882, S 6,5:2
Bernard, Murray, 1952, F 15,25:1
Bernard, Nat, 1957, O 20,86:8
Bernard, Nicholas, 1967, S 29,47:2
Bernard, O G, 1882, Je 5,2:3
Bernard, Oliver P, 1939, Ap 17,17:2
Bernard, Oswald, 1952, Mr 16,91:1
Bernard, Paul, 1954, Je 17,29:3; 1958, My 5,29:5
Bernard, Pierre A, 1955, S 28,35:2
Bernard, Reuben F Gen, 1903, N 18,9:3
Bernard, Robert, 1951, Ag 28,23:1
Bernard, Robert Mrs, 1937, S 2,21:3
Bernard, Robert Y, 1937, Mr 6,17:2
Bernard, Roger, 1954, S 18,15:6
Bernard, S, 1927, My 19,27:3
Bernard, Sam, 1950, Jl 7,19:6
Bernard, Sam Jr, 1954, D 14,33:2
Bernard, Stanilaus, 1961, F 18,19:1
Bernard, Tristam, 1947, D 8,26:2
Bernard, W Carlton, 1967, Ag 25,35:3
Bernard, W S, 1938, My 8,II,6:5
Bernard, W Stuart, 1956, D 20,29:2
Bernard, Walter C, 1947, Jl 3,21:4
Bernard, Walter J, 1952, Ag 22,21:6
Bernard, William Boyle (see also Ag 9), 1875, Ag 23,4:6
Bernard, William H, 1949, Mr 31,25:3
Bernard, William J, 1946, Ag 10,13:6
Bernard, William M (por), 1949, My 4,27:4
Bernarda, Mother (Josephine Weiler), 1940, Je 26, 23:4
Bernardes, Arthur D, 1955, Mr 24,31:1
Bernardi, Mario de, 1959, Ap 9,31:3
Bernardine, Lewis (Bro B McEneaney), 1963, My 1, 39:5
Bernardine Marie, Sister, 1942, My 20,19:6
Bernardini, Filippo, 1954, Ag 27,21:6
Bernardo, Nicola, 1951, F 20,25:4
Bernath, Louis, 1906, Je 30,1:6
Bernatz, John G, 1948, Jl 2,21:4
Bernau, Frederick W, 1951, My 23,35:4
Bernau, Raymond B, 1950, N 14,32:3
Bernauer, Rudolph, 1953, N 28,15:7
Bernauer (Sister Hildegarde), 1959, N 1,86:3
Bernay, Eric, 1968, N 5,44:5
Bernays, A C Dr, 1907, My 23,9:6
Bernays, Ely, 1923, O 9,21:5
Bernays, Ely Mrs, 1955, Mr 12,19:3
Bernays, Lewis Mrs, 1940, D 17,26:3
Bernazza, Charles L, 1945, D 21,21:3
Bernbaum, Ernest, 1958, Mr 9,86:7
Bernbaum, Henry L, 1951, Ja 1,17:1
Bernd, Arthur E, 1947, Ag 1,17:5
Berndt, Edward C Sr, 1952, D 27,10:3
Berndt, Edward Jr, 1940, F 29,19:3
Berndt, Herman D, 1937, F 9,23:4
Berndt, Karl, 1952, Je 27,23:5
Berndtson, Charles A, 1948, My 10,21:3
Berne, Gustave M Mrs, 1965, Mr 29,33:1
Berne, Robert E, 1954, Jl 12,19:4
Berne, Sammy, 1966, Ja 16,82:8
Bernecker, Edward M, 1955, Je 28,27:1
Bernegau, Carl M, 1948, S 7,25:1
Berneker, Louis F, 1937, Ja 28,25:5
Bernell, Charles S, 1949, Je 24,23:2
Berner, Charles E, 1924, Je 26,23:5
Berner, Frank, 1955, Ag 6,15:6
Berner, Fred L, 1940, Je 15,15:4
Berner, Fred Mrs, 1941, O 9,23:1
Berner, George C, 1950, Ag 22,27:3
Berner, Marie J, 1942, Ja 7,19:2
Berner, Paul, 1954, N 12,21:2
Berner, Pincus, 1961, Ag 8,29:1
Berner, Walter C, 1964, Ag 8,19:2
Berner, William G, 1947, Ap 16,25:5
Bernerd, Jeffrey, 1950, Ag 11,19:2
Berneri, Marie-Louise, 1949, Ap 18,25:6
Bernero, John, 1943, F 28,49:1
Berners, E C, 1939, Jl 2,15:3
Berners, Lord (G H Tyrwhitt-Wilson), 1950, Ap 20, 29:3
Bernes, Henri, 1941, My 22,21:6
Bernet, Albert G, 1952, Je 26,29:5
Bernet, Otto, 1945, O 14,42:5
Bernet, William M, 1951, F 10,13:3
Bernetha, Harry, 1940, Ag 25,35:3
Bernetta, Clara, 1925, S 14,19:5
Berney, William, 1961, N 25,23:2
Bernezzo, G M Asinari di, 1943, Je 7,13:4
Bernfeld, Henry Mrs, 1950, My 4,27:4
Bernfeld, Lupescu, 1943, N 15,19:6
Bernfeld, Mollie Mrs, 1954, Jl 20,19:4
Bernhard, Adolph, 1954, D 2,31:2
Bernhard, Adolph E, 1942, Je 27,13:2
Bernhard, Alva D, 1955, Jl 25,19:2
Bernhard, Charles F, 1949, Je 12,76:1
Bernhard, Charles H, 1964, O 18,89:2
Bernhard, Frederick P, 1955, O 31,25:5
Bernhard, Georg, 1944, F 11,19:3
Bernhard, Henry, 1943, My 9,40:3
Bernhard, Jacob G, 1939, S 2,17:4
Bernhard, James M, 1947, Ag 26,23:2
Bernhard, James M Mrs, 1965, Ag 28,21:4
Bernhard, Jesse, 1937, Ja 20,22:1
Bernhard, John A, 1942, O 27,26:3
Bernhard, John E, 1941, My 5,17:4
Bernhard, Joseph, 1954, Jl 16,21:4
Bernhard, Louis M, 1949, O 1,13:6
Bernhard, Morris, 1938, Ag 6,13:5
Bernhard, Richard, 1947, F 4,25:2
Bernhard, Richard J, 1961, Ja 28,19:3
Bernhard, Sadie L, 1954, Je 10,31:3
Bernhardi, F von, 1930, Jl 11,19:1
Bernhardt, Abraham A, 1963, Ap 19,43:3
Bernhardt, Carol L, 1952, F 27,27:4
Bernhardt, Frank X, 1937, Je 14,23:6
Bernhardt, Frederick I, 1940, Ag 2,15:4
Bernhardt, Lawrence E, 1952, Je 18,27:3
Bernhardt, M, 1928, D 22,17:2
Bernhart, Joseph, 1948, N 1,23:3
Bernheim, Bernard, 1925, Ag 1,11:5
Bernheim, Bertram M, 1958, N 29,21:3
Bernheim, Eli H, 1943, Ap 4,40:7
Bernheim, George B, 1968, Mr 4,37:3
Bernheim, Henry, 1917, Je 13,13:4
Bernheim, Henry J, 1946, N 29,25:5
Bernheim, Hugo S, 1943, Jl 5,15:6
Bernheim, Julius C Mrs, 1959, Mr 22,86:7
Bernheim, Lemuel F, 1953, O 12,27:6
Bernheim, Leonard Henly, 1968, My 18,33:1
Bernheim, Ruth G, 1953, S 12,17:5
Bernheimer, Abraham, 1940, Jl 23,19:2
Bernheimer, Adolph L, 1944, Mr 20,17:2
Bernheimer, Charles L, 1944, Jl 2,19:3
Bernheimer, Charles S, 1960, N 10,47:4
Bernheimer, Clarence G Mrs, 1967, D 13,47:4
Bernheimer, Edwin E, 1942, Jl 31,15:5
Bernheimer, Leopold Mrs, 1945, O 14,43:1
Bernheimer, Louis, 1948, D 9,34:2
Bernheimer, Mayer S, 1909, Ag 21,7:2
Bernheimer, Richard, 1958, Je 7,19:5
Bernheimer, Stephen R, 1925, Jl 20,15:3
Bernheisel, Charles F, 1958, S 10,33:3
Bernholz, Francis T, 1958, Jl 25,19:2
Bernholz, Martin J, 1952, Ap 21,21:5
Bernhouse, William H, 1944, Je 24,13:6
Bernie, Ben, 1943, O 21,27:1
Bernier, Ann E, 1959, D 1,39:2
Bernier, Art, 1953, My 22,27:3
Bernier, Paul, 1964, N 22,68:2
Berniger, William I, 1955, Mr 18,27:5
Berning, Wilhelm, 1955, N 26,19:5
Berninger, Dominique, 1949, D 7,31:6
Berninger, Louis V, 1956, Ag 14,25:5
Berninghaus, Oscar E, 1952, Ap 28,19:2
Bernini, Ferdinando, 1954, Mr 14,89:2
Bernis, William Edward, 1915, N 30,13:5
Bernis, William J, 1942, Mr 5,23:5
Bernius, George Jr, 1951, F 8,23:8
Bernius, Odell M, 1948, S 9,27:4
Berno, Harry, 1951, N 24,11:3
Berno, Noble, 1922, F 17,15:5
Bernoff, Benjamin, 1922, Mr 17,17:3
Bernoff, Benjamin Mrs, 1922, Mr 17,17:3
Bernon, Maurice, 1954, Mr 24,27:1
Berns, Max A, 1947, N 20,29:4
Berns, Morris, 1949, S 6,27:5
Berns, Morris W, 1966, Je 6,41:3
Berns, William (will), 1962, My 3,35:1
Bernsdorff, Frank J, 1950, N 27,25:1
Bernshouse, Salonia L Mrs, 1940, Je 13,23:5
Bernson, Ernest J, 1947, Ap 14,27:5
Bernsteen, A C, 1952, O 16,29:3
Bernstein, Abe, 1968, Mr 9,29:4
Bernstein, Abraham, 1937, Je 23,25:2; 1938, N 23, 21:3; 1958, Ap 5,28:1
Bernstein, Abraham I, 1945, Ag 22,23:4
Bernstein, Abraham N, 1941, Jl 29,15:5
Bernstein, Aline Mrs, 1955, S 8,31:1
Bernstein, Allen M, 1951, Je 19,29:2
Bernstein, Ann S, 1958, Ap 11,25:5
Bernstein, Arthur I, 1966, My 7,31:4
Bernstein, Arthur L, 1947, Ja 22,23:1
Bernstein, Ben, 1938, Je 14,21:4
Bernstein, Benjamin, 1903, My 27,2:3
Bernstein, Benjamin M, 1964, Ja 20,43:2
Bernstein, Benjamin M Mrs, 1963, Jl 7,52:6
Bernstein, Bernard, 1922, Ag 31,15:5; 1922, S 4,13:7; 1941, Ap 6,48:6; 1957, Je 1,17:6; 1958, Ja 23,21:5
Bernstein, Bernard Mrs, 1960, Ap 10,86:4
Bernstein, Chanon Mrs, 1958, My 15,29:4
Bernstein, Charles, 1942, Je 14,46:3; 1964, My 25,33:1
Bernstein, David, 1945, N 11,42:3
Bernstein, David (cor, N 24,29:1), 1953, N 23,27:5
Bernstein, David, 1955, N 17,35:2
Bernstein, David A, 1954, D 18,15:5
Bernstein, David Mrs, 1958, My 9,23:2
Bernstein, E, 1932, D 19,15:1
Bernstein, Elias, 1950, Je 10,17:2; 1956, Jl 18,27:4
Bernstein, Ephraim Mrs, 1941, O 31,23:4
Bernstein, Ephraim R, 1957, D 14,21:1
Bernstein, Eugene B Mrs, 1949, D 31,15:6
Bernstein, George, 1967, Je 14,47:4
Bernstein, George J, 1955, Ag 5,19:5
Bernstein, Gerson J, 1965, N 15,37:4
Bernstein, H, 1935, S 1,18:1
Bernstein, Harold, 1950, Ap 4,29:2
Bernstein, Harry Mrs, 1951, Ag 11,11:5; 1954, O 14, 29:2
Bernstein, Henri, 1953, N 28,15:1
Bernstein, Henry H, 1947, F 9,62:7
Bernstein, Herman, 1947, Jl 30,21:3
Bernstein, Herman (funeral, N 6,41:1), 1963, N 4, 35:2
Bernstein, Herman J Mrs, 1964, Ja 9,31:3
Bernstein, Herman Mrs, 1954, My 27,27:3
Bernstein, Hirsch, 1907, Ag 2,7:6
Bernstein, Isaac Mrs, 1949, O 18,27:3

Bernstein, Isadore, 1944, O 20,20:2
Bernstein, Isidor, 1938, My 10,21:2
Bernstein, Israel, 1967, Je 30,37:4
Bernstein, Israel I Dr, 1937, Mr 11,23:4
Bernstein, J E, 1934, O 13,14:2
Bernstein, J Sidney, 1943, D 10,27:1
Bernstein, J Sidney Mrs, 1963, N 24,23:1
Bernstein, Jacob, 1947, D 6,15:2
Bernstein, James, 1959, Je 30,31:5
Bernstein, Jefferson D, 1911, Ag 4,7:6
Bernstein, John L, 1952, Ag 23,13:4
Bernstein, Joseph, 1938, Ag 14,32:7; 1951, Jl 20,21:6; 1968, S 27,47:4
Bernstein, Joseph B, 1952, Ap 25,23:4
Bernstein, Joseph J, 1950, S 29,27:2; 1951, O 30,29:2
Bernstein, Julian L, 1967, O 7,29:2
Bernstein, Julius, 1937, D 3,23:4
Bernstein, Leo D, 1953, F 19,23:3
Bernstein, Leon I, 1950, Mr 14,25:3
Bernstein, Louis, 1962, F 16,29:2
Bernstein, Louis G, 1958, Jl 29,23:2
Bernstein, Louis Rabbi, 1922, N 1,19:6
Bernstein, Ludwig B, 1944, D 28,19:1
Bernstein, M C, 1962, Mr 30,33:4
Bernstein, Max, 1914, Ag 2,15:6; 1942, Ja 7,19:6; 1944, Mr 31,21:1; 1946, D 14,15:4; 1952, S 15,25:2
Bernstein, Max Dr, 1925, Mr 10,21:3
Bernstein, Mayer, 1955, My 28,15:5
Bernstein, Meier Mrs, 1967, Ja 12,39:6
Bernstein, Mordecai, 1966, Ap 22,41:1
Bernstein, Moriz, 1944, Jl 15,13:6
Bernstein, Morris, 1924, My 30,15:5
Bernstein, Morris H, 1916, Mr 19,19:7
Bernstein, Morris L, 1962, S 8,19:2
Bernstein, Myer, 1968, O 23,47:3
Bernstein, Nahum A Mrs, 1965, D 28,25:2
Bernstein, Nathan C, 1966, O 23,88:1
Bernstein, Oscar, 1958, Jl 16,29:1
Bernstein, Phil, 1939, Mr 10,23:4; 1951, Je 14,27:5
Bernstein, Phil M, 1949, D 5,23:2
Bernstein, Phil M Mrs, 1956, O 28,89:2
Bernstein, Philip, 1964, F 15,23:2
Bernstein, R Alexander Mrs, 1954, F 10,29:3
Bernstein, Rachel A Mrs, 1948, Ja 17,17:4
Bernstein, Ralph, 1948, N 20,13:5
Bernstein, Reuben, 1940, Ap 9,23:4
Bernstein, Ruth, 1953, Ap 1,29:3
Bernstein, Samuel, 1905, Je 9,2:3; 1957, F 20,33:2
Bernstein, Samuel D, 1954, S 5,51:2
Bernstein, Samuel E, 1951, Mr 18,89:1
Bernstein, Samuel E Mrs, 1953, Ag 28,1:7
Bernstein, Samuel L, 1951, Ja 16,29:3
Bernstein, Samuel Mrs, 1945, D 26,19:2; 1952, S 16, 29:1
Bernstein, Saul, 1967, N 2,47:1
Bernstein, Saul Mrs, 1944, My 18,19:4
Bernstein, Sidney (funl plans, Jl 24,60:5), 1966, Jl 23, 25:2
Bernstein, Sigismund, 1910, Ja 30,II,11:1
Bernstein, Solomon, 1948, S 12,72:1
Bernstein, Solon S, 1953, Jl 12,65:3
Bernstein, Theodore, 1957, N 7,35:4
Bernstein, Theodore F, 1949, Mr 12,17:5
Bernstein, William, 1939, Ag 19,15:3; 1953, F 20,20:4
Bernstein, Zion de F, 1937, Ap 10,19:4
Bernstorf, Bernhard, 1956, S 16,85:1
Bernstorff, Count, 1873, Mr 27,5:6
Bernstorff, Frank A, 1966, Ap 8,31:3
Bernstorff, Jeanne von, 1943, Ap 27,23:2
Bernstorff, Johann H von Count, 1939, O 7,17:1
Berntano, Arthur, 1944, Ja 30,38:4
Bernthaler, Carl, 1925, N 3,25:6
Berntsen, Harry, 1952, Ja 12,15:7
Berntson, Charles A, 1940, Jl 24,21:4
Bernus, Pierre, 1951, D 23,22:5
Bernuth, Oscar M, 1958, Ja 15,29:2
Bernys, Georges, 1960, My 9,29:3
Beroldt, Meno, 1943, Je 4,21:3
Berolzheimer, Edwin M (por), 1949, Mr 16,27:3
Berolzheimer, Emil, 1922, My 26,19:6
Berolzheimer, Emil Mrs, 1948, F 4,23:5
Berolzheimer, Howard Mrs, 1937, Ja 9,17:3
Berolzheimer, Phil, 1942, My 23,13:3
Berolzheimer, Ruth, 1965, D 8,47:3
Berquist, Bernard M, 1958, Jl 9,27:3
Berr, Georges, 1942, Jl 22,19:6
Berra, Franco, 1955, F 20,88:6
Berra, Peitro, 1961, N 8,27:4
Berrall, James, 1950, My 28,44:2
Berrent, Herbert I, 1959, Mr 24,39:4
Berres, Abraham, 1966, Ag 30,41:1
Berres, Abraham Mrs, 1958, S 9,35:5
Berres, Albert J Jr, 1947, Ag 14,23:6
Berresford, Arthur B, 1946, Ap 17,25:2
Berresford, Arthur W, 1941, My 31,11:5
Berresford, Richard C, 1954, F 8,23:4
Berreta, Tomas, 1947, Ag 3,53:1
Berreta, Tomas Mrs, 1951, S 8,17:1
Berri, Herbert, 1948, Mr 19,23:4
Berri, William (funl, Ap 22,21:1), 1917, Ap 20,13:5
Berri, William Mrs, 1910, Je 13,7:5
Berrian, Charles A, 1921, D 6,19:5
Berrian, John E, 1954, D 30,17:1
Berrian, Louis C, 1953, Ag 12,31:2
Berrian, William E, 1942, O 22,21:3
Berrick, Alfred A, 1950, O 2,23:6
Berrien, Cornelius R, 1944, O 1,46:2
Berrien, Cornelius R Mrs, 1959, N 12,35:5
Berrien, D, 1878, F 14,5:2
Berrien, Edward M, 1953, S 25,21:4
Berrien, Frank D, 1951, F 2,23:2
Berrien, Frank D Mrs, 1962, Mr 26,31:1
Berrien, J M, 1883, N 22,2:5
Berrien, James G Mrs, 1953, My 26,29:4
Berrien, William E Mrs, 1953, Ap 28,27:3
Berrier, D Roy, 1952, O 3,23:2
Berrigan, John F, 1955, Jl 15,21:3
Berriman, Edward, 1962, Ag 26,82:6
Berriman, John W, 1941, My 17,16:2
Berring, David B, 1950, N 2,31:2
Berrio, Pedro J, 1950, O 16,27:6
Berro, Robert, 1956, S 7,17:6
Berry, A S Judge, 1908, Ja 8,9:7
Berry, Abe S, 1952, Ag 9,13:4
Berry, Albert G, 1938, My 14,15:2
Berry, Alfred F, 1951, My 12,21:2
Berry, Alice, 1942, F 16,17:5
Berry, Arthur D, 1941, F 12,21:3
Berry, Arthur H, 1948, Ja 7,25:6
Berry, Bertram, 1958, My 24,21:3
Berry, Burton J, 1921, Ag 31,13:3
Berry, C Harold, 1965, Mr 18,33:3
Berry, Carroll, 1924, Ja 26,13:2
Berry, Carroll Mrs, 1924, Ja 28,15:4
Berry, Catherine E, 1957, F 25,25:5
Berry, Cecil R, 1968, N 16,37:1
Berry, Charles, 1952, Ja 2,25:3
Berry, Charles A, 1948, Jl 14,23:1
Berry, Charles B, 1947, Ja 14,25:3
Berry, Charles D, 1943, N 4,23:2
Berry, Charles J, 1940, Ja 24,21:2
Berry, Charles W, 1941, My 1,23:1
Berry, Charlotte M, 1940, O 9,25:4
Berry, Clarence E, 1945, F 10,11:3
Berry, Clyde A, 1946, D 27,19:3
Berry, Daniel S Sr, 1966, Ja 6,27:2
Berry, David Mrs, 1947, O 9,25:4; 1950, Jl 9,69:2
Berry, De Loss W, 1964, Mr 3,36:1
Berry, E Milton, 1955, O 19,27:4
Berry, Earl D, 1919, D 23,9:2
Berry, Earl E, 1943, N 11,23:3
Berry, Earl H Mrs, 1957, Ag 6,27:2
Berry, Edward B, 1963, My 24,31:2
Berry, Edward B Mrs, 1950, S 4,17:5
Berry, Edward E, 1941, My 24,15:3
Berry, Edward F, 1944, Ag 29,17:3
Berry, Edward Mrs, 1943, Ap 6,21:4
Berry, Edward S, 1948, D 7,31:2
Berry, Edward W, 1945, S 21,21:3
Berry, Elwood S, 1954, Jl 3,11:7
Berry, Erwin W, 1960, Ap 14,37:6
Berry, Frank, 1954, S 14,27:3
Berry, Frank B, 1937, Je 13,II,7:2
Berry, Frank D, 1965, Mr 28,27:1
Berry, Fred, 1955, Ag 9,25:3
Berry, Fred K, 1966, S 11,86:7
Berry, Fred M, 1952, Ap 28,19:4
Berry, Fred N, 1955, My 26,31:5
Berry, Frederic S Mrs, 1950, S 13,27:5
Berry, Frederick, 1947, S 9,22:1
Berry, Frederick J, 1946, Ja 28,19:2
Berry, G T, 1956, N 18,89:2
Berry, George A, 1940, Je 21,21:6; 1962, N 10,25:4
Berry, George F, 1938, Ap 17,II,6:6
Berry, George R, 1945, My 26,15:6
Berry, Gibson T, 1940, F 24,13:5
Berry, Harold H, 1961, Ag 16,31:4
Berry, Harold L, 1962, Ag 19,89:2
Berry, Harriet M, 1940, Mr 25,15:3
Berry, Hattie M Mrs, 1942, Mr 5,24:2
Berry, Helen Mrs, 1941, F 15,15:1
Berry, Henry A, 1944, Mr 14,19:2
Berry, Henry T, 1952, N 16,88:4
Berry, Herbert H, 1945, Jl 20,19:4
Berry, Hiram B, 1908, D 28,7:6
Berry, Hobert G, 1939, My 11,25:5
Berry, Howard, 1958, Ap 29,29:1
Berry, Irving M, 1960, S 9,29:2
Berry, Isabelle W Mrs, 1937, N 25,31:5
Berry, J F, 1931, F 12,21:1
Berry, J Howard Sr, 1961, Mr 15,39:5
Berry, J Willets, 1938, N 1,23:4
Berry, James, 1957, Ag 25,63:6
Berry, James D, 1941, Ap 2,23:1
Berry, James E, 1966, N 23,39:4
Berry, James Gomer (Viscount Kemsley), 1968, F 7, 47:1
Berry, James H, 1950, S 23,17:1
Berry, James L Mrs, 1961, Je 29,33:1
Berry, John, 1915, D 9,15:5; 1955, S 23,25:4
Berry, John D Mrs, 1944, D 29,15:2
Berry, John F, 1950, Ja 17,27:3
Berry, John F Mrs, 1940, Ap 27,15:2
Berry, John G, 1959, N 3,35:6
Berry, John J, 1939, Ag 6,37:4; 1940, Mr 8,21:4
Berry, John J Capt, 1905, Mr 26,9:4
Berry, John P, 1945, D 19,25:2
Berry, Joseph F, 1953, O 1,29:2
Berry, Joseph I, 1952, O 21,29:3
Berry, Jules, 1951, Ap 24,29:5
Berry, Julian, 1937, Mr 30,24:2
Berry, Kenneth K, 1945, My 25,19:5
Berry, Lawrence F, 1951, Mr 9,25:5
Berry, Lee W, 1945, Ap 1,36:4
Berry, Lenora K Mrs, 1950, Mr 16,32:2
Berry, Leon, 1941, O 31,23:4
Berry, Llewellyn L, 1954, N 26,29:4
Berry, Lucien G, 1938, Ja 1,19:2
Berry, M F, 1915, Mr 5,9:6
Berry, Maja L, 1961, S 1,17:1
Berry, Mark, 1939, My 12,21:3
Berry, Martha M (will, Mr 6,14:1), 1942, F 27,17:1
Berry, Maxwell R, 1944, Ja 27,19:5
Berry, Michael, 1949, F 11,23:4
Berry, Milton H, 1939, D 5,28:2
Berry, Milton Jr, 1954, Ap 13,31:5
Berry, Milton L, 1938, Ja 4,24:3
Berry, Modena L Mrs, 1942, F 1,42:7
Berry, Oswald, 1952, Je 9,23:3
Berry, Perley M, 1939, F 14,19:5
Berry, R L, 1933, My 10,17:1
Berry, R M, 1929, My 20,25:5
Berry, Richard, 1883, O 23,5:3
Berry, Richard J, 1960, Mr 29,37:4
Berry, Robert, 1956, Ap 15,88:7
Berry, Robert H, 1953, D 20,64:5
Berry, Robert W, 1960, Ap 2,23:3
Berry, Romeyn, 1957, Mr 23,19:6
Berry, Samuel, 1948, Ag 25,25:1
Berry, Samuel C, 1954, D 29,23:2
Berry, Samuel J, 1947, Ag 2,13:5
Berry, Schofield, 1942, Ag 25,23:1
Berry, Standish E, 1959, Ap 10,29:2
Berry, Sydney G, 1966, S 22,47:2
Berry, Sydney G Mrs, 1939, Ap 13,23:4
Berry, Theodore M, 1953, F 5,23:5
Berry, Thomas J, 1943, Ap 9,21:2
Berry, Thomas S, 1962, Jl 22,64:5
Berry, Tom, 1951, O 31,29:4
Berry, Vivian E, 1954, Ag 26,27:5
Berry, Volney W, 1951, Jl 1,50:5
Berry, W C Capt, 1869, Ag 17,5:6
Berry, W H, 1951, My 4,27:4
Berry, Walter S, 1944, Jl 15,13:4
Berry, Ward L, 1967, Je 19,35:4
Berry, Watson B, 1963, Ag 19,25:5
Berry, William, 1950, Je 28,27:6
Berry, William E, 1960, S 13,37:3
Berry, William G, 1949, Je 28,27:4
Berry, William H, 1963, O 7,31:4
Berry, William J C Capt, 1912, Ap 20,15:6
Berry, William J Sir, 1937, Ap 6,23:3
Berry, William Mrs, 1944, N 30,23:4
Berry, Z D, 1967, S 2,22:7
Berryhill, John H, 1941, Je 17,21:3
Berryhill, Porter, 1953, Jl 12,65:1
Berryman, Charles H Mrs, 1912, S 24,13:6
Berryman, Clifford K, 1949, D 12,33:1
Berryman, Henry W, 1908, Jl 11,7:5
Berryman, Henry Whitney, 1908, Jl 14,5:4
Berryman, J C Rev, 1906, My 9,9:5
Berryman, John B, 1945, Ag 12,39:3
Berryman, Robert N Mrs, 1965, Ja 7,31:4
Berryman, W A, 1952, Ag 4,15:6
Bers, Harold T, 1961, O 15,88:4
Bers, Julian E, 1968, Ag 18,88:3
Bersch, George W (cor, D 20,19:2), 1941, D 14,68:8
Berse, Samuel, 1938, Ag 18,42:4
Bersell, P Olof, 1967, My 3,45:2
Bersenev, Ivan N, 1951, D 28,21:4
Bersey, James T Sr, 1965, O 21,47:5
Bersin, David D, 1959, D 14,31:5
Berson, Abraham, 1956, Jl 28,17:5
Berson, B Irving, 1959, Jl 20,25:5
Berson, George J, 1957, O 23,33:4
Berson, Hyman L, 1966, Jl 18,27:2
Berson, Joseph S, 1956, Je 14,33:1
Berson, Richard D, 1956, S 14,23:2
Bersot, Pierre, 1880, F 2,5:3
Berstecher, J Frederick, 1950, Ag 11,19:2
Berstler, George J, 1958, O 17,29:1
Berstler, Robert A Mrs, 1950, N 15,31:3
Berston, J James, 1944, F 28,17:2
Berston, James L Mrs, 1952, Mr 10,21:3
Bert, Arthur A, 1953, O 14,29:1
Bert, Berthe, 1967, Jl 10,28:5
Bert, Frederick W (funl, My 5,11:4), 1911, My 4,11:4
Bert, J Weimer, 1939, S 27,25:5
Bert, James B, 1942, F 6,19:3
Berta, Archie, 1948, F 25,23:4
Berta Hummel, Sister, 1946, D 25,29:4
Bertan, Cornelius J, 1957, D 13,27:4
Bertanzel, Carl F, 1949, D 7,31:4
Bertasso, Joseph S A, 1950, N 13,28:4
Bertauld, C A, 1882, Ap 10,5:5
Bertaut, Clarence J, 1948, S 16,29:5
Berte, Stephen J, 1964, O 8,43:4
Berteau, Gerald F, 1952, Mr 21,24:3
Bertel, Joseph Mrs (Helena), 1965, Mr 31,39:1

Bertelli, Riccardo, 1955, O 19,33:2
Bertelli, Riccardo Mrs (Ida Conquest), 1937, Jl 13, 19:1
Bertels, W Raymond, 1946, My 24,19:4
Bertelsen, Aage, 1948, Ja 15,23:2
Bertelsen, Elius M, 1941, Ja 19,40:1
Bertermann, Irwin, 1945, Je 9,13:5
Bertero, Michael, 1957, Je 15,17:5
Bertez, Andre, 1940, Ja 11,23:2
Bertha, John, 1952, Ag 21,19:4
Bertha Marie, Mother, 1946, N 30,15:3
Berthaut, J A, 1881, D 27,5:3
Berthe Lecroix, Mother, 1944, O 11,21:5
Berthelot, H, 1931, Ja 29,23:3
Berthelot, Louis, 1956, Je 10,89:1
Berthelot, P, 1934, N 23,19:3
Berthelot, P E Marcelin, 1907, Mr 19,9:5
Berthelsen, Holger P, 1963, My 26,92:3
Berthiaume, Eugene, 1946, S 2,17:6
Berthiaume, Jean, 1946, O 31,25:1
Berthiaume, Val C, 1941, Ap 25,19:4
Berthold, Frank A, 1939, Ap 7,21:5
Berthold von Baden, Margrave (funeral, N 2,8:1), 1963, O 29,36:5
Bertholf, Ellsworth P Commodore, 1921, N 12,13:5
Bertholf, Henry, 1885, F 21,5:5
Bertholf, Lester V, 1938, Mr 27,II,7:3
Bertholf, Neilson, 1961, O 14,23:2
Bertholf, Ralph J, 1957, Je 15,17:4
Bertholon, Albert C, 1962, Ja 20,21:3
Berti, Ettore, 1940, My 8,23:3
Bertie, Francis Levenson Lord, 1919, S 28,22:3
Bertillon, Alphonse, 1914, F 14,11:3
Bertillon, Jacques Dr, 1922, Jl 8,11:7
Bertin, George, 1943, Ap 15,25:2
Bertin, Harry, 1946, Jl 26,21:5
Bertin, Jean, 1943, D 3,24:2
Bertin, John Bro (C Brady), 1957, Jl 4,19:4
Bertin, John G, 1945, S 27,21:4
Bertin, Laura, 1953, Ja 1,23:1
Bertin, Louis E, 1924, O 25,15:6
Bertin, Michel J, 1957, Je 11,35:3
Bertin Leo, Bro (J Sullivan), 1955, Jl 11,23:3
Bertine, Arthur W, 1938, My 12,23:2
Bertine, Edwin K, 1960, My 8,88:6
Bertine, Eleanor, 1968, Ja 4,37:2
Bertine, Mabel E Mrs, 1942, Ag 2,38:7
Bertine, Samuel W, 1951, Ap 16,25:5
Bertine, Samuel W Mrs, 1950, N 10,27:1
Bertine, Walton D Mrs, 1947, Je 19,21:5
Bertini, A A, 1931, Mr 3,29:1
Bertini, Bartholomew Mrs, 1946, F 3,39:1
Bertino, Giovanni, 1949, D 31,15:4
Bertner, Ernest W, 1950, Jl 29,13:3
Bertol, Rodrigue P, 1967, Ja 14,31:2
Bertola, Enrico, 1949, O 6,47:4
Bertole, Carlo F, 1940, Ja 7,48:2
Bertolet, Charles D, 1956, Jl 14,15:4
Bertolet, Elmer C Sr, 1956, Jl 18,27:5
Bertolet, John A, 1956, Ap 8,84:3
Bertolet, Samuel E, 1948, N 15,25:1
Bertolet, Ulysses S G, 1943, O 21,27:3
Bertolet, Walter M Dr, 1953, F 9,27:3
Bertolette, Ralph, 1944, Ja 3,21:1
Bertolini, Pietro, 1920, N 29,15:6
Bertolino, Angelo, 1943, N 2,25:5
Bertolino, Vincent Father, 1903, N 13,9:6
Bertollo, Arturo, 1952, Ag 21,19:2
Bertolotti, Angelo Mrs, 1954, My 6,33:3
Berton, Edmond D, 1959, S 25,24:6
Berton, Samuel R, 1953, O 11,89:1
Bertona, Attilio, 1955, S 15,33:6
Bertoncini, Paul, 1953, My 4,23:3
Bertoni, Louis P, 1964, O 13,39:8
Bertram, Adolf, 1945, Jl 13,11:6
Bertram, Albert J, 1944, N 6,19:4
Bertram, Anton Sir, 1937, S 18,19:5
Bertram, Bertrand W, 1951, F 1,25:3
Bertram, Carl F, 1946, N 12,29:4
Bertram, Francis G L, 1938, Mr 26,15:4
Bertram, George, 1941, Jl 16,17:2
Bertram, H Henry, 1946, S 25,27:4
Bertram, H Henry Mrs, 1944, F 8,15:5
Bertram, J, 1934, O 24,23:1
Bertram, James Mrs, 1949, Jl 5,23:4
Bertram, John, 1944, S 6,19:5
Bertram, John F, 1958, Mr 10,23:3
Bertram, Liston C, 1948, Mr 13,15:6
Bertram, Louis, 1917, F 20,9:3
Bertram, Wilfred, 1953, F 27,21:1
Bertram, William H, 1949, Ja 1,11:8
Bertrand, Aime Charles, 1903, O 19,1:2
Bertrand, Anna E Mrs, 1947, F 21,19:3
Bertrand, Ernest, 1958, O 13,29:6
Bertrand, F Dr, 1926, Jl 19,15:6
Bertrand, Jules A Brig Gen, 1939, D 7,27:6
Bertrand, Louis, 1941, D 7,77:2
Bertrand, Louis 3d, 1958, Ap 16,33:3
Bertrand, Louise Mrs, 1953, O 22,29:6
Bertrand, M Louis, 1940, F 25,38:3
Bertrand, Marshall, 1942, O 31,15:3
Bertrand, Matthew W, 1945, Jl 19,23:6
Bertrand, Ruth W Mrs, 1954, Ap 13,31:4
Bertrand, William Capt, 1937, O 29,21:1
Bertranda, Sister, 1947, N 11,27:4
Bertrandias, Victor E, 1961, Mr 21,37:4
Bertron, Samuel R (por), 1938, Jl 1,19:3
Bertsch, Emily H, 1903, Ag 16,10:2
Bertsch, Fred S, 1953, Je 29,21:2
Bertsch, Frederick J, 1945, Je 7,19:4
Bertsche, Ambrose, 1951, F 27,27:2
Bertschmann, Jacob, 1918, O 30,11:3
Bertschmann, Jean J Mrs, 1958, Ag 24,86:2
Bertschy, Bertha V Mrs, 1937, S 29,23:3
Bertschy, Melville P, 1965, Jl 16,27:2
Bertuccio, George E, 1955, S 22,31:3
Bertuzzi, Albert, 1955, My 15,86:6
Bertuzzi, Albert Mrs, 1952, D 22,25:6
Beruff y Mendieta, Antonio, 1952, O 2,29:5
Berul, Zalman, 1952, Je 16,17:4
Berutti, Arturo, 1938, Ja 4,23:3
Berwald, Joseph M, 1943, D 18,15:5
Berwald, Joseph M Mrs, 1949, Jl 3,27:1
Berwald, Robert F, 1955, Mr 26,15:2
Berwald, William, 1948, My 11,25:1
Berweiler, Peter F, 1944, N 15,27:3
Berwick, George A, 1949, Jl 25,15:2
Berwick, Lord, 1947, Je 13,24:3
Berwin, Albert J, 1941, Ja 10,19:1
Berwind, E J, 1936, Ag 19,21:1
Berwind, Edward J Mrs, 1922, Ja 7,13:6
Berwind, J E, 1928, My 24,29:3
Berwind, John E (will, Mr 29,25:6), 1945, Ja 1,21:4
Berwind, Julia A, 1961, My 18,35:2
Beryl, Edwin, 1922, N 28,21:5
Berzen, Nathan E, 1959, Mr 12,31:3
Besanceney, Louis E, 1952, My 24,19:4
Besancon, Julien, 1952, Ap 17,29:4
Besant, A, 1933, S 21,19:1
Besant, Walter Sir, 1901, Je 11,9:5
Besas, Jacob, 1940, D 8,69:3
Besas, Max Mrs, 1951, F 6,27:1
Besaw, Josephine C, 1948, Ag 12,21:3
Besch, Carl A, 1962, Jl 3,23:2
Besch, Joseph, 1943, Jl 1,19:2
Beschorman, William C, 1946, Mr 30,15:2
Beseler, Hans von Gen, 1921, D 23,13:6
Besemer, Howard B Dr, 1918, F 9,15:8
Besen, Eli, 1962, S 14,31:1
Beser, Nicholas, 1950, Ap 24,25:4
Beshar, Arteen H, 1951, Ja 31,25:2
Beshgetour, Horace, 1941, Ap 9,25:5
Beshirian, Paul, 1954, Jl 25,68:6
Besiegel, Walter E, 1962, Je 2,19:2
Besier, Rudolf, 1942, Je 15,19:5
Beskin, Israel S, 1964, Ja 25,23:5
Beskronov, P M, 1955, Je 1,33:4
Besler, William G, 1942, My 21,19:4
Besley, Frederic A, 1944, Ag 17,17:3
Besnard, Leo E Rev, 1925, Ag 11,21:4
Besner, Aaron, 1958, F 16,86:5
Besner, Louis Mrs, 1948, S 4,15:3
Besnier, Ernest Dr, 1909, My 17,9:6
Beson, Warren, 1959, O 26,29:5
Besredka, Alexandre, 1940, Mr 1,21:2
Besrodni, Boris, 1966, O 11,43:4
Bess, Demaree C, 1962, Je 3,88:5
Bessborough, Earl of (V B Ponsonby), 1956, Mr 11, 88:1
Besschastnov, T A, 1948, F 11,27:2
Besse, Antonin, 1951, Jl 5,25:6
Besse, Arthur, 1951, N 25,87:1
Besse, Edward L, 1951, D 8,11:2
Besse, Max, 1954, S 22,29:4
Besse, Seth J, 1947, D 27,13:4
Besse, Seth J Jr Mrs, 1947, My 10,13:5
Besseling, Jacobus Mrs, 1943, Je 30,21:5
Bessell, Wesley S, 1967, D 27,37:1
Bessell, William W, 1940, Ap 2,25:1
Bessella, Anthony, 1938, Jl 26,19:2
Bessels, E Dr, 1888, Ap 3,5:2
Bessemer, Henry Sir, 1898, Mr 16,7:2
Bessen, Harry, 1955, D 13,39:4
Bessen, Jack, 1948, F 11,27:3
Bessenyey, Georges B, 1959, F 20,25:4
Besser, Charles, 1941, D 3,52:3
Besser, Herman, 1942, O 6,23:3
Bessey, Arthur A Mrs, 1949, D 26,29:4
Bessey, Ernest A, 1957, Jl 18,25:1
Bessey, Mabel A, 1943, Ja 27,21:5
Bessie, Abraham, 1951, Jl 19,23:4
Besson, Harlan, 1949, Ja 11,27:3
Besson, Joseph, 1938, Ja 27,21:3
Besson, Leonidas H Mrs, 1957, Jl 11,25:3
Besson, Philibert H M, 1941, Mr 19,21:1
Besson, Robert J, 1957, Ja 11,23:2
Besson, Samuel A, 1937, Ja 15,21:5
Besson, Violet, 1938, D 22,22:2
Best, A Starr, 1950, Je 18,76:3
Best, Alfred M, 1958, My 7,35:2
Best, Alfred M Mrs, 1949, Je 6,19:3
Best, Andrew, 1958, Jl 15,25:4
Best, Arthur A, 1960, O 26,39:2
Best, Arthur C, 1940, Jl 24,21:2
Best, Charles B, 1953, Jl 22,27:3
Best, Charles J, 1941, Jl 11,15:4
Best, Clarence L, 1951, S 23,85:1
Best, Cleremont Livingston Mrs, 1923, My 24,19:6
Best, Clermont L Maj, 1903, Ap 15,9:6
Best, Dionysus F Rev (funl, Ap 30,11:2), 1914, Ap 28,13:5
Best, Edgar, 1949, My 31,23:1
Best, Edgar L, 1950, O 3,31:3
Best, Edwin, 1966, Jl 12,43:3
Best, Elizabeth, 1948, O 6,29:2
Best, Ernest M, 1963, N 1,33:3
Best, Floyd C, 1948, Jl 8,23:4
Best, Francis J, 1947, F 16,57:3
Best, Frederick C, 1945, Ag 18,11:5
Best, Frederick W, 1951, My 10,31:5; 1953, Mr 18,31:5
Best, Gary L, 1964, Jl 11,11:3
Best, Harry, 1942, Mr 10,20:2
Best, Harry M, 1947, Ja 7,27:3
Best, Herman Mrs, 1945, D 25,23:6
Best, Howard R, 1958, Ag 10,92:2
Best, Isabelle Mrs, 1938, Ag 5,34:1
Best, J, 1880, Ap 6,5:4
Best, Jacob, 1946, Jl 5,19:4
Best, James B Mrs, 1947, S 27,15:3
Best, James H, 1951, Je 9,19:3
Best, John A Mrs, 1949, Ag 22,21:4
Best, Leigh, 1924, Ap 28,15:4
Best, Leonard E, 1967, D 15,47:3
Best, Lindsey, 1941, Je 16,15:5
Best, Lucius P Mrs, 1962, Ag 8,32:1
Best, Margaret, 1942, Ap 19,43:3
Best, Mary A, 1942, O 15,23:4
Best, Matthew R, 1940, O 15,23:6
Best, Oscar S Mrs, 1950, Jl 18,29:5
Best, Otto, 1937, Mr 6,17:3
Best, Ralph Mrs, 1958, O 2,37:3
Best, Richard, 1939, F 24,19:2
Best, Richard I, 1959, S 27,86:5
Best, Robert A, 1949, N 27,105:1
Best, Robert H, 1952, D 21,8:3
Best, Roy, 1954, My 28,23:4
Best, Samuel M Dr, 1968, D 21,37:4
Best, Thomas A V, 1941, N 25,26:2
Best, Thomas W, 1945, D 9,44:5
Best, Wesley Capt, 1937, N 5,23:2
Best, William, 1955, S 22,31:3
Best, William A, 1943, O 31,50:5
Best, William E, 1961, N 28,37:3
Best, William H, 1942, Je 5,17:1; 1960, O 29,23:6
Best, William Newton, 1922, Ap 13,19:6
Best, William R Sr, 1945, Je 8,19:5
Beste, Henry, 1914, Ag 19,9:6
Bestebreurtje, Anton D, 1956, Ag 20,21:2
Besteiro, J, 1940, S 28,17:5
Bestelmeyer, German, 1942, Jl 4,17:3
Bester, Harold, 1945, My 20,32:2
Beston, Henry, 1968, Ap 17,47:1
Bestor, Arthur E, 1944, F 5,15:1
Bestor, Paul, 1962, Je 27,35:3
Besuden, David R, 1956, Jl 5,25:5
Besunder, Max, 1959, Ja 27,33:1
Beswick, Arthur B, 1945, D 30,14:5
Beswick, William, 1940, Je 28,19:5
Betancourt, Julian Gen, 1914, Ag 3,11:5
Betanzos, Jose M, 1948, D 28,22:2
Betaque, Harry A, 1950, N 22,25:4
Betbeder, Onofre, 1915, Ja 25,9:4
Betche, Frederick Mrs, 1949, F 17,23:3
Betelle, Howard E, 1963, Ag 31,17:5
Betelle, James O Mrs, 1959, Ag 30,82:2
Betensky, Rubin, 1949, N 11,26:3
Beteta, Arturo, 1942, D 25,17:6
Beteta, Ramon (Oct 5), 1965, O 11,61:1
Bethard, Douglas H, 1944, Mr 22,19:4
Bethea, J, 1928, Jl 3,11:3
Bethea, Solomon Hicks Judge, 1909, Ag 4,7:6
Bethel, Arthur W, 1941, Jl 14,13:6
Bethel, Bruce Mrs, 1959, D 18,29:2
Bethel, John P, 1958, My 31,15:6
Bethel, Thomas, 1951, Je 2,19:3
Bethel. Lawrence L, 1965, Mr 1,27:4
Bethell, Adrian, 1941, Jl 17,19:2
Bethell, Florence Mrs, 1956, My 10,31:1
Bethell, Frank H, 1959, Ap 23,31:6
Bethell, Hugh K, 1947, Mr 7,25:1
Bethell, James G, 1962, My 24,35:3
Bethell, Monsaquila, 1946, N 17,68:3
Bethell, Richard (Lord Westbury), 1873, Jl 21,5:4
Bethell, Richard M T (Lord Westbury), 1961, Je [illegible] 27:3
Bethell, Stanislaus, 1941, N 2,53:2
Bethell, U N, 1933, Ja 14,13:3
Bethke, Gunter, 1966, D 3,39:4
Bethke, William, 1966, S 30,47:1
Bethlehem, Louis, 1940, S 23,17:2
Bethon, Kate, 1903, F 24,14:3
Bethune, George W Rev Dr, 1862, My 16,8:2
Bethune, John N, 1955, Ag 17,27:3
Bethune, Mary M (funl plans, My 20,25:2; funl, M[illegible] 24,31:2), 1955, My 19,29:1
Bethune, Norman, 1939, N 26,43:3
Bethune, Norman G, 1955, D 31,13:5
Betjeman, Anna H, 1945, N 6,19:2
Betner, Benjamin C, 1951, F 2,24:2

Betram, Louis J, 1940, D 18,25:5
Betrone, Annibale, 1950, D 12,33:1
Betrone, Piero, 1956, F 26,88:2
Betros, Louis, 1950, My 26,23:2
Betsch, William G, 1959, Je 28,69:1
Betschick, Augustus R, 1954, F 13,13:4
Betsky, Joseph Mrs, 1955, Ap 29,23:3
Bett, Henry, 1953, Ap 8,29:4
Bettag, Joseph G, 1953, Je 3,31:3
Bettan, Edward, 1951, Ja 29,19:5
Bettan, Israel, 1957, Ag 6,27:3
Bettand, Earl of, 1873, My 7,5:4
Bettany, George K, 1949, O 27,27:3
Bettcher, Louis F, 1949, Ap 30,13:5
Bette, Bud (Sidney Bette), 1968, Mr 2,29:1
Bettelheim, Anton Mrs, 1953, N 4,33:1
Bettelheim, Edwin S, 1938, Ja 16,II,8:7
Bettelheim, Ernst, 1945, S 14,23:3
Bettelheim, Spencer D, 1937, N 8,24:1
Bettelin, Rev Bro, 1920, Ap 13,9:3
Bettels, Otto C, 1944, Je 10,15:5
Betten, Francis S, 1942, D 9,27:4
Bettencourt, Edmund, 1943, O 17,49:1
Bettenhausen, Tony (funl, My 17,47:2), 1961, My 13,13:5
Bettens, Edward Detray, 1920, Ja 22,17:2
Betteridge, William Mrs, 1949, Mr 28,21:2
Betters, Harry R, 1961, O 13,35:1
Betters, Paul V, 1956, My 14,25:3
Bettes, Charles R, 1937, O 30,19:4
Bettes, Harrison C, 1942, My 23,13:4
Bettes, T J, 1949, Ap 27,27:2
Betti, Adolfo, 1950, D 3,88:4
Betticher, Charles Eugene Rev, 1922, Mr 17,17:6
Bettina, Vincent Mrs, 1954, Je 22,27:4
Bettinger, H B, 1950, My 19,29:4
Bettinger, Joseph M, 1941, Ag 28,19:6
Bettinghaus, Harry W, 1947, D 1,21:4
Bettis, C K Lt, 1926, S 2,21:1
Bettis, Louis T Mrs, 1943, Jl 23,17:1
Bettle, Robert Mrs, 1951, Jl 21,13:4
Bettler, H C, 1944, My 24,19:3
Bettman, Alfred, 1945, Ja 23,19:2
Bettman, Alfred Mrs, 1948, Jl 20,23:2
Bettman, Gilbert, 1942, Jl 18,13:1
Bettman, Irvin Sr Mrs, 195[illegible], Ag 20,17:4
Bettmann, Hans Mrs, 195[illegible], Je 24,13:5
Bettoja, Maurizio, 1964, Ag 25,33:5
Bettolo, Giovanni Adm, 1916, Ap 8,15:4
Betton, Elizabeth L, 1938, Jl 7,19:5
Betts, Albert A, 1943, D 29,17:2
Betts, Allan R, 1948, D 10,25:2
Betts, Anna D, 1943, S 3,19:6
Betts, Anna L Mrs, 1941, N 21,17:3
Betts, Benjamin F Mrs, 1964, Ja 16,25:2
Betts, C C, 1882, S 20,3:7
Betts, C Fred, 1954, Jl 17,13:6
Betts, Charles A, 1960, O 30,87:1
Betts, Clarence D, 1945, Ap 12,23:2
Betts, Cortland S, 1943, My 14,20:3
Betts, Craven L, 1941, Jl 31,17:6
Betts, Edgar H Sr Mrs, 1941, Ja 4,13:3
Betts, Edgar K, 1908, N 17,7:3
Betts, Edward C, 1946, My 8,25:3
Betts, Edward H, 1951, Mr 28,29:5
Betts, Edward K, 1954, Ap 13,31:1
Betts, Edwin, 1944, Ja 21,17:3
Betts, Edwin M, 1958, S 29,27:2
Betts, Ernest D, 1948, Mr 16,27:5
Betts, Esther M E Mrs, 1959, My 2,23:5
Betts, F J, 1879, O 15,5:2
Betts, Frank, 1950, Je 3,15:3
Betts, Frank C, 1963, S 12,37:4
Betts, Frederic H, 1905, N 13,9:5
Betts, George F, 1942, Je 6,13:5
Betts, George H, 1940, Jl 9,21:2
Betts, George N Mrs, 1948, N 9,27:1
Betts, George W Jr, 1959, Ja 10,17:2
Betts, Harrison, 1952, Jl 15,21:4
Betts, I Watson Sr, 1939, Ja 9,15:5
Betts, J A, 1928, My 8,27:3
Betts, James A, 1951, Ap 3,27:5
Betts, John R Sr, 1940, Ag 15,19:4
Betts, Judge (New York), 1868, N 6,5:1
Betts, Karl S, 1962, Je 12,37:3
Betts, L F H, 1926, Jl 1,23:3
Betts, Leila, 1953, S 19,15:6
Betts, Lillian P Mrs, 1938, Ap 7,23:3
Betts, Louis, 1961, Ag 14,25:2
Betts, Paul C, 1956, F 9,32:1
Betts, Philander (por), 1945, F 6,19:1
Betts, Philander Mrs, 1959, F 25,31:3
Betts, Raymond L Sr, 1967, D 31,44:7
Betts, Ritchie G, 1951, Ag 21,27:1
Betts, Ritchie G Mrs, 1939, O 7,17:4
Betts, Roland W, 1954, S 16,29:4
Betts, Romeo T, 1953, S 14,27:6
Betts, Romeo T Mrs, 1968, Ja 8,35:3
Betts, W, 1884, Jl 6,7:4
Betts, Wyllys R, 1967, Ap 4,44:1
Betty, Lee I, 1945, Ja 25,19:2
Betty, Lee I Mrs, 1951, N 1,29:1
Betulli, Ancaleto, 1953, Ag 8,11:6

Betyeman, Charles F Jr, 1957, O 26,21:5
Betz, Arthur B, 1947, My 31,13:5
Betz, Basilian Joseph Bro, 1966, F 20,88:4
Betz, Charles F Sr, 1952, Jl 20,53:2
Betz, Frank S, 1940, F 29,19:2
Betz, George H, 1941, N 4,26:3
Betz, George N Sr, 1943, Ag 23,15:6
Betz, George W, 1952, S 4,27:4
Betz, J Fred, 1942, F 22,27:1
Betz, James J, 1959, Jl 7,33:2
Betz, John F, 1908, Ja 17,9:6
Betz, Margaret Mrs, 1922, D 21,15:3
Betz, Philip F, 1967, Mr 14,47:2
Betzing, Henry F, 1960, D 18,84:3
Betzler, Stacy B, 1949, Ja 29,14:2
Betzner, E, 1931, Mr 31,27:1
Beuchert, Theresa, 1949, Ap 6,29:5
Beucke, Aug Jr, 1942, S 1,19:4
Beucler, Harry T, 1947, S 25,29:3
Beucus, Robert V, 1947, Mr 13,27:4
Beuermann, Henry R, 1954, Ag 6,17:5
Beuermann, Henry R Mrs, 1944, N 5,53:1
Beuf, Carlo Countess, 1923, My 3,19:3
Beugler, Hugh M, 1939, Jl 17,19:6
Beukema, Henry S (mem ser set, Ja 23,13:2), 1954, Ja 20,7:2
Beukema, Herman, 1960, N 27,86:2
Beule, Charles Ernest, 1874, Ap 6,1:7
Beulhausen, Carl A, 1952, Ja 23,27:4
Beulhausen, Edgar A, 1954, Ag 23,17:5
Beulshausen, Minna, 1953, Mr 9,29:4
Beumer, E J, 1946, O 8,23:2
Beuningen, Daniel-Georges van, 1955, Je 12,28:1
Beunke, J William, 1941, D 1,19:2
Beurerlein, Joseph A, 1950, O 9,25:3
Beurermann, Raymond H, 1944, Ag 19,11:2
Beuret, Jean E C Viscount, 1952, Ag 24,88:5
Beury, Charles E, 1953, Mr 10,29:1
Beury, J L Col, 1903, Je 3,9:6
Beuscher, Philip, 1943, Jl 21,15:4
Beuse, Walter, 1957, Ag 27,29:3
Beusoleil, Leonard D, 1959, My 11,27:4
Beust, F von Baron, 1886, O 25,5:2
Beust, Theodore B Dr, 1937, N 25,31:3
Beute, Christopher A, 1955, F 28,19:3
Beuter, Andrew, 1940, My 26,34:1
Beutler, Hans G, 1942, D 19,20:2
Beutler, Seymour, 1912, O 14,15:5
Beutner, Reinhard H, 1964, Ap 16,37:3
Bevan, Aneurin (funl plans, Jl 8,4:8; funl, Jl 9,4:6), 1960, Jl 7,1:8
Bevan, Arthur D, 1943, Je 11,19:1
Bevan, Billy, 1957, N 29,29:2
Bevan, Charles, 1948, O 24,76:2
Bevan, Charles J, 1955, S 10,17:6
Bevan, Edwin J, 1956, F 10,21:3
Bevan, Edwyn R, 1943, O 20,21:6
Bevan, Frank J, 1941, Ag 12,19:6
Bevan, James M, 1944, S 15,19:3
Bevan, John R, 1945, F 8,19:5
Bevan, Llewelyn D Rev Dr, 1918, S 28,13:4
Bevan, Phoebe Mrs, 1949, F 14,19:3
Bevan, Ralph H, 1952, Mr 19,29:2
Bevan, Roland, 1957, Ag 17,15:3
Bevan, Thomas H, 1938, Jl 25,15:3
Bevan, William, 1951, O 3,33:3
Bevans, Clem, 1963, Ag 13,31:2
Bevans, David, 1968, S 9,1:1
Bevans, Irma S, 1951, S 25,29:5
Bevans, James L, 1944, F 6,42:1
Bevans, James W, 1949, N 12,15:6
Bevans, Lionel, 1965, F 20,25:4
Bevans, Philippa, 1968, My 11,35:5
Bevans, W S, 1941, Ja 16,21:4
Bevans, William H, 1949, D 2,29:5
Beven, John L, 1945, Ja 4,19:3
Beverage, Albion P, 1951, Ja 31,25:2
Beverett, Henry J, 1951, O 11,37:3
Beveridge, A J, 1927, Ap 28,23:1
Beveridge, Alven, 1922, Ag 23,13:6
Beveridge, Edwin, 1948, Ap 16,23:1
Beveridge, Frank S, 1956, D 5,39:4
Beveridge, Hugh P, 1962, Ja 1,23:4
Beveridge, James B, 1915, F 23,13:3
Beveridge, Lady (Mrs J Mair), 1959, Ap 27,27:4
Beveridge, T Byron, 1946, D 29,35:3
Beveridge, Thomas, 1907, O 18,11:6
Beveridge, William H, 1963, Mr 18,15:1
Beverley, Alton R, 1956, F 2,25:5
Beverley, George, 1961, Jl 9,77:1
Beverly, Arthur L, 1961, D 13,43:2
Beverly, Bert I, 1948, S 28,27:3
Beverly, Philetus Rev, 1921, O 17,15:3
Beverly, William, 1950, Jl 26,25:6
Bevers, Adolph W, 1952, N 8,17:3
Bevers, Adolph W Mrs, 1940, Je 30,32:7
Bevers, Carl H, 1950, Jl 19,32:3
Beverstock, Berthan M Mrs, 1947, Je 18,25:4
Beves, Arthur S, 1945, Jl 24,23:3
Beviano, Felice, 1952, F 29,23:3
Bevier, Gilbert H, 1951, F 25,86:5
Bevier, I, 1942, Mr 18,23:3
Bevier, Kenneth M, 1946, S 25,27:4

Bevier, Louis Dr, 1925, My 6,23:4
Bevilacqua, Alfred, 1954, D 5,88:2
Bevilacqua, Anthony, 1953, Ap 24,23:3
Bevilacqua, Carmen C (Tommy McFarland), 1954, O 26,27:5
Bevilacqua, Giulio Cardinal, 1965, My 7,41:1
Bevilacqua, Giuseppe, 1951, Ap 6,25:4
Bevilacqua, Louis, 1967, Mr 18,29:1
Bevilacqua, Pasquale, 1954, Ap 11,86:4
Bevilacqua, Pasquale Mrs, 1949, Je 27,27:3
Bevilaqua, Clovia, 1944, Jl 27,17:4
Beville, Monty, 1955, Ja 26,25:1
Bevin, Chauncey G, 1948, N 8,21:4
Bevin, Ernest, 1951, Ap 15,1:2
Bevin, Leander A, 1919, Mr 26,15:4
Bevin, Sydney, 1960, My 30,17:2
Bevington, Martin Lt-Com, 1903, O 26,7:6
Bevington, Merle M, 1964, Ag 17,25:5
Bevins, Charles Lovatt, 1925, D 22,21:4
Bevins, M Spencer, 1914, Mr 25,11:6
Bevis, Howard L Dr, 1968, Ap 25,47:2
Bew, George A, 1944, N 12,48:6
Bewer, Julius A, 1953, S 1,23:1
Bewley, William, 1953, N 7,17:4
Bewoor, Guranath, 1950, N 30,33:2
Bexel, J A, 1938, F 7,15:3
Bey, A S, 1941, My 7,25:4
Bey, Cattaul, 1925, Je 13,15:4
Bey, Hranoush A Mrs, 1942, Ja 31,17:3
Bey, Ismail Kemal, 1919, Ja 28,9:4
Bey, Izzet, 1920, Ja 12,9:1
Bey, Peter, 1950, N 20,25:2
Bey, Simon C, 1948, Ap 5,21:4
Beydts, Louis, 1953, S 17,29:4
Beye, Henry K, 1964, Ap 10,35:1
Beye, William, 1941, O 28,23:3
Beyea, Benjamin D, 1938, Je 15,23:4
Beyea, George M, 1963, Je 5,41:2
Beyea, Samuel Dr, 1907, Ag 20,7:5
Beyer, Agnes A, 1946, Mr 20,23:2
Beyer, Albert W Sr, 1937, Je 2,23:4
Beyer, Alida, 1941, My 22,21:1
Beyer, Barnet J, 1947, F 25,25:3
Beyer, Charles W, 1953, N 30,2:8
Beyer, Charlotte B Mrs, 1938, Ja 13,21:5
Beyer, David S, 1937, Je 28,19:5
Beyer, Ehrenfried, 1953, Je 6,17:3
Beyer, Ernest, 1954, F 6,19:5
Beyer, Eugene, 1940, Jl 27,5:7
Beyer, Ferdinand A, 1955, F 10,31:4
Beyer, Ferdinand A Mrs, 1949, N 27,105:1
Beyer, Frank J Mrs, 1943, Ap 25,35:2
Beyer, Frank L, 1945, My 23,19:2
Beyer, Frederick, 1954, Ag 7,13:6
Beyer, George J, 1954, Je 13,88:2
Beyer, H Otley, 1967, Ja 2,19:1
Beyer, H William, 1967, Ag 26,27:3
Beyer, Henry A, 1950, My 10,31:4
Beyer, Herman W, 1940, Ap 15,17:4
Beyer, Michael Sr, 1939, Jl 8,15:2
Beyer, Nicholas L, 1952, O 11,19:4
Beyer, Otto S, 1948, D 9,33:1
Beyer, Robert L, 1937, N 18,23:2
Beyer, Russell B Mrs, 1938, Ja 8,15:1
Beyer, Walter, 1946, N 27,25:3
Beyer, Walter E, 1959, O 14,43:3
Beyer, Walter F, 1950, S 20,31:3
Beyer, William P, 1947, O 29,27:5
Beyers, Fredrik W, 1938, S 16,21:4
Beyers, Nicholas K, 1943, Ag 4,17:4
Beyersdorfer, Frank, 1945, Ag 24,19:2
Beyfus, Gilbert H, 1960, O 31,31:4
Beyfus, Gustav, 1903, Jl 27,7:6
Beyfuss, Andrew John, 1968, My 14,47:3
Beygrau, Frederick R, 1941, O 25,17:5
Beyhl, William F, 1948, Ja 9,22:3
Beymer, Merritt C, 1953, Mr 9,29:3
Beynon, George W, 1965, Je 11,31:1
Beynon, H L, 1966, Je 25,31:5
Beynon, Lee J Jr, 1966, D 30,47:7
Beyrer, George S, 1949, Jl 17,56:8
Bezancon, Fernand, 1948, Je 29,23:1
Bezanson, Osborne, 1961, Mr 1,33:4
Bezazian, John B (will, Jl 7,5:3), 1959, Je 28,68:8
Bezdek, Hugo, 1952, S 20,15:3
Bezemer, Tammo J, 1944, Jl 14,13:3
Bezner, Frederick, 1951, O 18,60:3
Bezrukov, Nokolai, 1953, My 28,23:5
Bhabha, Homi J, 1966, Ja 25,16:5
Bharati, Baba, 1914, F 21,11:3
Bhatnagar, Shanti S, 1955, Ja 2,77:1
Bhojrajji, Maharajah of Gondal, 1952, Ag 1,17:3
Bhopal, Nawab of (Sir H Kahn), 1960, F 5,27:4
Bhowal, Rajah of, 1946, Ag 5,23:6
Bhutan, Maharajah of (Wangchuk Jigmey), 1952, Mr 30,93:1
Biadene, Giovanni, 1948, D 13,23:1
Biagetti, Biagio, 1948, Ap 4,60:5
Biagi, Vincenzo, 1954, Jl 12,19:1
Biagini, Luigi, 1942, My 16,13:6
Bialdyga, Ignatius, 1962, My 5,27:5
Bialek, Thaddeus L B Mrs, 1946, Mr 5,11:2
Biales, Samuel, 1947, Je 20,20:2

Bialik, Manoah L, 1962, O 7,82:5
Bialosky, Abraham J, 1951, N 21,25:3
Bialostotzky, Benjamin J, 1962, S 23,86:6
Biamonte, Dominick, 1952, Jl 28,15:4
Biancheri, Giuseppe, 1908, O 27,9:5
Bianchi, Albert W, 1956, Je 13,37:2
Bianchi, Angelo R, 1966, D 6,47:3
Bianchi, Augusto G, 1951, My 13,90:1
Bianchi, Charles A, 1967, Je 24,29:5
Bianchi, Clemente J, 1958, Ap 4,24:1
Bianchi, Emilio, 1941, S 13,17:4
Bianchi, Eugene J, 1950, O 25,35:4
Bianchi, Frank, 1940, Ja 21,34:6
Bianchi, Gerolamo, 1951, Mr 31,15:2
Bianchi, John, 1914, Ag 21,9:6; 1939, F 15,23:6; 1957, O 17,33:2
Bianchi, Juan, 1937, Ja 2,14:4
Bianchi, Martha D, 1943, D 22,23:4
Bianchi, Ovid C, 1957, Ap 16,33:2
Bianchi, William, 1949, F 6,76:4
Bianchi, William Mrs, 1948, Mr 1,23:2
Bianchi-Cagliesi, Vincenzo, 1950, N 10,27:5
Bianchini, Charles, 1944, D 27,19:2
Bianco, Alberto, 1939, D 29,15:3
Bianco, Allesandro, 1954, S 18,15:2
Bianco, Carmine, 1949, Mr 7,21:3
Bianco, Francesco, 1946, Jl 22,21:5
Bianco, Margery W, 1944, S 5,19:6
Bianco, Pieretto, 1937, Mr 8,19:4
Bianco, Pio, 1960, Ag 11,27:2
Biancolli, Charles, 1945, Mr 13,23:3
Biancolo, James, 1946, Jl 30,23:6
Bianculli, Pasquale, 1940, Je 12,25:5
Bianu, Cornel V (cor, Je 20,33:1), 1966, Je 19,84:3
Biard, A, 1882, Jl 9,6:7
Biard, A F, 1882, Je 25,7:1
Biard, Philip W Mrs (Cath), 1968, Jl 17,43:2
Biart, Victor, 1952, Mr 27,29:4
Biauvelt, George A, 1924, O 17,21:3
Bibb, Peyton B, 1906, Jl 5,4:3
Bibb, William G, 1941, Ag 17,39:3
Bibbins, A Leal, 1951, Ap 1,93:1
Bibbins, Royal E, 1950, Mr 9,29:3
Bibbins, Ruthella M Mrs, 1942, My 26,21:6
Bibbo, Henry T, 1957, Je 22,15:6
Bibbs, Arthur D, 1949, Je 7,31:4
Bibby, Albert Father, 1925, F 20,17:3
Bibby, Harold, 1942, F 12,23:5
Bibby, Julia Livingston, 1925, F 10,23:3
Bibby, Thomas F A, 1940, F 3,13:1
Bibby, W H K, 1880, Jl 10,8:2
Biber, Alphonse, 1954, My 15,15:2
Biberstein, Hans, 1965, N 22,37:3
Bibesco, Elizabeth (por), 1945, Ap 9,19:3
Bibesco, George V Prince, 1941, Jl 4,13:4
Bibiana, Sister, 1946, Jl 16,24:2
Bible, Charles F, 1957, S 16,31:4
Bible, Cleo W Mrs, 1954, Ja 27,27:1
Bible, Dana X Mrs, 1942, Ja 23,19:2
Bible, Frank W Rev Dr, 1937, N 16,23:3
Bible, Howard W, 1951, Jl 31,21:4
Bible, J D, 1942, N 22,55:2
Bible, Thomas, 1945, My 11,19:2
Bible, William, 1958, My 25,87:1
Bibo, Irving, 1962, My 3,33:3
Bibolotti, Aladino, 1951, F 25,86:5
Bibring, Edward, 1959, Ja 12,39:5
Bicester, Lord (V H Smith), 1956, F 18,19:3
Biche, John L, 1950, N 10,28:2
Biche, L L, 1941, O 25,17:4
Bichelonne, Jean, 1944, D 28,19:1
Bicher, Leo B, 1940, N 23,17:6
Bichowsky, Francis R, 1951, Ap 6,25:4
Bick, Carl E, 1955, Jl 30,17:2
Bick, Chaim M, 1964, My 26,39:1
Bick, Chaim Mrs, 1960, F 5,27:2
Bick, Herman J, 1954, Ag 13,15:5
Bick, Karl H, 1957, Je 17,29:1
Bick, Louis R, 1950, N 3,27:4
Bickar, Elsie M, 1942, D 9,27:4
Bickar, Jacob C, 1938, Ja 18,23:4
Bickard, Charles, 1953, Ja 29,27:3
Bickel, August C, 1949, My 11,29:5
Bickel, George L, 1941, Je 7,17:6
Bickel, John F, 1941, N 29,17:3
Bickel, Karl Mrs, 1964, S 1,35:2
Bickel, Luke Capt, 1917, Je 13,13:4
Bickel, Mildred, 1924, My 3,15:4
Bickelhaupt, Carroll D, 1954, My 17,23:2
Bickelhaupt, George, 1939, Je 22,23:4
Bickell, Charles H, 1938, Je 6,17:4
Bickendorff, Victor P, 1947, Jl 31,21:6
Bickerdyke, M A (Mother), 1901, N 9,1:3
Bickers, Frank C, 1951, Ja 24,27:2
Bickers, Joseph E Mrs, 1944, S 26,23:4
Bickers, Thomas E, 1951, S 20,31:1
Bickerstaph, George L Mrs, 1945, Jl 15,15:5
Bickersteth, R Rev, 1884, Ap 16,4:2
Bickersteth, Samuel Mrs, 1954, D 3,27:3
Bickersteth, Samuel Rev Dr, 1937, My 19,23:2
Bickert, Gordon W, 1967, Mr 18,29:3
Bickerton, J G Mrs, 1948, Je 16,29:2
Bickerton, J P Jr, 1936, Ag 21,15:3
Bickett, Thomas Walter Ex-Gov, 1921, D 29,15:4
Bickett, William J Mrs, 1945, My 2,23:5
Bickett, William P (will, O 4,15:5), 1938, S 22,23:3
Bickett, William P (will), 1940, Mr 1,41:1
Bickford, Annie E C Mrs, 1941, F 1,17:1
Bickford, Arthur F, 1952, Je 17,27:4
Bickford, Charles N (funl, N 11,33:1), 1967, N 10, 47:1
Bickford, Edward C, 1943, S 24,23:4
Bickford, Francis H, 1958, My 19,25:2
Bickford, Francis S Mrs, 1948, O 13,25:5
Bickford, Hamilton J, 1967, Jl 14,29:1
Bickford, Harold C, 1952, Ag 31,45:1; 1956, F 19,92:4
Bickford, Herbert J, 1937, D 19,II,9:1
Bickford, Lydia A Dr, 1918, Mr 12,13:7
Bickford, Nelson N, 1943, D 6,23:1
Bickford, Samuel L, 1959, Jl 19,68:6
Bickford, Willis C, 1945, N 6,19:5
Bickhart, Monroe L, 1943, N 13,13:3
Bicking, S Austin, 1951, S 16,84:4
Bickle, Edward W, 1961, My 3,37:1
Bickley, Catherine, 1949, S 30,23:3
Bickley, Emil B, 1963, Jl 3,25:1
Bickley, Ervin Felton, 1953, F 21,13:5
Bickley, George H Bp, 1924, D 26,15:5; 1924, D 28,5:2
Bickley, Robert S, 1957, D 28,17:5
Bickley, William P, 1958, Ja 21,26:5
Bickman, Alex J, 1951, Je 8,27:1
Bickmann, Frederick W, 1942, Je 9,23:5
Bickmore, Albert H, 1949, Mr 2,25:2
Bickmore, Albert H Mrs, 1953, Ag 8,11:4
Bickmore, Albert Smith Prof, 1914, Ag 14,11:6
Bickmore, Jesse O Mrs, 1942, Je 7,42:1
Bicknell, Clarence F, 1920, Mr 19,13:4
Bicknell, Clarence W, 1950, Mr 27,23:5
Bicknell, Eugene P, 1925, F 11,21:2
Bicknell, Frank B, 1951, D 6,33:2
Bicknell, G A Rear-Adm, 1925, Ja 29,19:4
Bicknell, George J, 1944, Ag 4,13:2
Bicknell, George W Rev Dr, 1916, Je 4,21:5
Bicknell, Helen, 1955, Je 1,33:2
Bicknell, Helen (est tax appr filed), 1956, Mr 27,29:2
Bicknell, John Mrs, 1958, O 30,31:4
Bicknell, John P, 1951, Ag 23,23:1
Bicknell, John W, 1961, Je 23,29:3
Bicknell, John W Mrs, 1950, N 3,27:5
Bicknell, Roscoe G, 1947, D 9,33:5
Bicknell, Thomas W, 1925, O 7,27:4
Bicknell, Warren M, 1941, Ag 8,15:4
Bicknell, William H, 1947, N 22,15:4
Bicks, Alex, 1963, My 10,34:1
Bickum, Dorothy, 1952, Ap 4,25:4
Bickwit, George S mrs, 1955, D 12,31:5
Biddeman, Margaret S, 1954, S 5,51:1
Bidder, G P, 1878, S 21,5:4
Biddinger, Charles H, 1940, Ap 29,15:6
Biddison, Mark M, 1960, S 20,39:2
Biddison, Ned D, 1950, Ap 16,104:3
Biddison, Norbert R, 1949, Ap 26,25:5
Biddison, Thomas N, 1958, Ag 8,19:3
Biddle, A Mercer, 1946, S 5,27:5
Biddle, Albert N Mrs, 1947, Jl 9,23:2
Biddle, Alfred A, 1967, Ag 27,89:2
Biddle, Alfred A Mrs, 1942, Je 28,32:2
Biddle, Andrew P, 1944, Ag 4,13:3
Biddle, Anthony J D (funl, N 17,35:3), 1961, N 14, 39:2
Biddle, Anthony J D Sr, 1948, My 28,23:1
Biddle, Anthony J Sr Mrs, 1947, Jl 26,13:2
Biddle, Arney Sylvenus Rev Dr, 1914, My 22,13:6
Biddle, Caldwell K Col, 1915, Je 3,11:5
Biddle, Charles, 1923, Jl 12,17:4
Biddle, Charles J Col (trb, O 1,1:6), 1873, S 29,5:2
Biddle, Charles J Mrs, 1950, My 2,29:4
Biddle, Charles M Jr, 1957, Mr 4,27:3
Biddle, Christine, 1944, Ja 26,19:3
Biddle, Clement M, 1959, S 3,27:1
Biddle, Clement M Mrs, 1960, O 29,23:7
Biddle, Clement Mrs, 1956, Ja 6,24:7
Biddle, Clinton P, 1939, Ap 12,24:4
Biddle, Constance E, 1952, O 8,31:2
Biddle, Craig, 1910, Jl 27,9:5; 1947, D 23,23:3
Biddle, Craig Mrs, 1925, O 28,25:5
Biddle, David H, 1949, S 16,27:2
Biddle, E, 1933, F 25,15:4
Biddle, Edith F, 1938, Je 11,15:5
Biddle, Edward M, 1950, Mr 14,25:3
Biddle, Edward Mrs, 1949, F 21,23:3
Biddle, Edward W Mrs, 1950, Jl 22,15:3
Biddle, Frances R Mrs, 1937, Mr 30,23:3
Biddle, Francis, 1968, O 5,35:1
Biddle, Frank C, 1952, D 15,25:6
Biddle, Frederick, 1950, F 27,19:5
Biddle, G H Col, 1884, Je 12,2:4
Biddle, George D, 1952, N 16,88:4
Biddle, Harry W, 1950, Ag 24,15:2
Biddle, Henry C, 1937, Ag 26,21:6
Biddle, J, 1936, Ja 19,38:4
Biddle, James Brig-Gen, 1910, Je 10,9:4
Biddle, James G, 1947, D 22,22:3
Biddle, James Mrs, 1922, Jl 1,13:6
Biddle, John, 1903, Ag 2,7:5
Biddle, Josephine P Mrs, 1948, Ap 24,15:5
Biddle, Katherine C, 1912, Mr 15,9:4
Biddle, Livingston L Sr, 1959, Jl 9,27:5
Biddle, Louis A, 1940, O 8,25:4
Biddle, Lynford, 1941, Ja 25,15:5
Biddle, Margaret T Mrs (funl, Je 13,37:2; mem ser set, Je 25,23:1), 1956, Je 9,17:4
Biddle, Mary D Mrs (funl, Je 16,33:5; will, S 2,5:5), 1960, Je 15,41:4
Biddle, Mary H R Mrs, 1940, Je 16,39:1
Biddle, Maurice W, 1955, S 30,25:3
Biddle, Moncure, 1956, O 3,33:5
Biddle, Moncure Mrs, 1959, Mr 23,31:3
Biddle, Nicholas, 1909, O 30,9:5; 1923, F 19,15:5
Biddle, Nicholas Mrs, 1909, N 3,11:7; 1943, D 29, 17:3; 1962, Jl 18,29:5
Biddle, Sydney G, 1954, O 30,17:1
Biddle, Thomas, 1875, My 17,1:6
Biddle, Ward G, 1946, My 29,24:2
Biddle, William Baxter, 1923, F 20,17:3
Biddle, William C, 1942, Ap 12,45:3
Biddle, William M, 1903, D 10,9:5
Biddle, William P Gen, 1923, F 27,19:4
Biddlecombe, Conrad H, 1946, Mr 29,24:2
Biddulph, George W, 1952, Ap 28,19:4
Biddulph, Howard, 1965, D 16,48:1
Biddulph, John M Lord, 1949, D 8,33:2
Biddulph, Simeon, 1952, N 26,23:5
Bidinger, Julius F, 1954, Ja 14,29:4
Bidlingmeyer, Charles, 1946, Mr 5,25:4
Bidou, Henri, 1943, F 15,15:2
Bidstrup, Frederick M S, 1949, Je 2,27:3
Bidwell, A, 1899, Mr 9,3:6
Bidwell, Addison, 1945, Ja 21,40:6
Bidwell, Alice P Mrs, 1950, O 23,23:3
Bidwell, Daniel D, 1937, Ap 25,II,8:5
Bidwell, Edward J, 1941, Ag 12,19:5
Bidwell, Edwin C, 1905, N 16,11:4
Bidwell, Frederick D, 1947, D 23,23:3
Bidwell, George, 1905, My 7,12:7
Bidwell, George L, 1961, Jl 27,31:2
Bidwell, George R, 1948, Mr 17,25:5
Bidwell, Horace Gilbert Dr, 1925, D 8,25:5
Bidwell, Howard F, 1944, S 25,17:3
Bidwell, Jennie, 1947, O 26,70:3
Bidwell, John Mrs, 1918, Mr 25,11:4
Bidwell, Lawrence K, 1946, Jl 13,15:5
Bidwell, Marshal S, 1872, O 28,5:6
Bidwell, Raymond A, 1954, Ja 7,31:4
Bidwell, Richard M, 1964, Jl 28,29:1
Bidwell, Roger Edward Shelford Rear-Adm, 1968, N 4,47:2
Bidwell, Samuel C, 1951, Jl 28,11:1
Bidwell, Stephen L, 1951, Ja 12,27:3
Bidwell, W H, 1881, N 16,5:3
Bidwill, Charles W, 1947, Ap 20,60:2
Bie, Hans, 1956, Mr 14,33:2
Biear, Wendell C, 1945, Mr 13,23:5
Biebel, Clarence A, 1965, N 28,89:2
Biebel, Franklin M, 1966, S 24,23:3
Bieber, Herbert W, 1953, Ag 25,21:2
Bieber, Hugo, 1950, O 2,23:3
Bieber, Milton J, 1949, Mr 31,25:2
Bieber, Siegfried, 1960, N 26,21:6
Bieberstein, Baron Marshall von (por), 1912, S 25, 13:1
Bieberstein, Baron von, 1920, N 15,15:5
Bieberstein, Szymon Z, 1960, Mr 19,21:3
Bieberstein, Waldemar Alexander von Baron, 1907, N 30,7:4
Biechler, Elmer G, 1948, Jl 6,23:5
Bieckly, Logan E, 1907, Mr 7,9:6
Biedenfeld, Curt von Baroness, 1911, S 7,9:2
Biedenharn, Lawrence C, 1954, Ja 17,92:7
Biedenharn, Ollie L, 1949, F 4,23:2
Biedenkapp, John H, 1958, Je 14,21:5
Biederbick, Henry, 1916, Mr 26,21:4
Biederman, Charles, 1937, S 11,17:5
Biederman, Julius, 1962, Jl 8,65:2
Biederman, Martin, 1945, Ja 8,17:4
Biederman, Solomon J, 1966, D 5,45:3
Biedermann, Arno W, 1959, Je 6,21:2
Biedermann, Aug, 1939, Mr 26,III,6:6
Biedermann, Leo F, 1949, Mr 17,25:2
Biedermann, Louis, 1957, Jl 17,27:5
Biedermann, Walter R, 1952, O 26,89:1
Biederwolf, William E, 1939, S 3,19:1
Biedrzycki, Ceslaus S E, 1952, N 27,31:5
Bieg, Charles E, 1945, S 2,32:2
Bieg, Frederick C Com, 1909, O 15,11:4
Biegen, Eugene A, 1945, D 25,23:2
Biegler, Phil S, 1948, Ja 14,26:2
Biehl, Charles, 1949, Mr 23,27:4
Biehoff, Frederic Dr, 1937, Ag 1,II,6:2
Bieksa, John A, 1948, S 23,29:5
Biel, Clara von Arnim von, 1962, O 16,39:1
Biel, Josephine P, 1944, Ja 22,13:6
Biel, Louis, 1915, Ag 24,11:5
Biel, Louis Mrs, 1947, Je 30,19:3
Bielaski, A Bruce, 1964, F 20,29:1
Bielaski, Frank B, 1961, Ap 6,26:1
Biele, Herbert E, 1968, Ja 4,37:1
Bielecki, Andre, 1959, Jl 1,25:3
Bielefeldt, Herbert F, 1953, Jl 18,13:1

Bielek, Irvan, 1943, N 2,25:2
Bieler, Herman C, 1949, Ap 20,27:2
Bieler, Samuel L Rev Dr, 1917, F 20,9:5
Bieley, Paul Mrs, 1962, Je 8,31:4
Bielinis, Kipras, 1965, D 8,47:4
Bieliukas, Bronius Mrs, 1966, Je 30,39:3
Biello, Joseph A, 1962, My 2,37:3
Bielohlawek, Herman, 1918, Jl 4,13:6
Bielovucic, Juan B, 1949, Ja 15,17:5
Bielschowsky, Alfred, 1940, Ja 7,48:8
Bien, Charles B F, 1954, Jl 29,23:6
Bien, Charles B F Mrs, 1954, Jl 29,23:6
Bien, Frank A, 1945, O 20,11:5
Bien, Franklin, 1924, S 28,27:3
Bien, Joseph R, 1947, F 21,20:3
Bien, Julius, 1909, D 22,11:5
Bien, Robert T (R Warwick), 1964, Je 7,86:4
Bien, Sylvan, 1959, My 13,37:3
Bienemann, Walter J, 1942, Mr 6,21:4
Bienenfeld, Henry L, 1943, Ja 6,27:3
Bienenfeld, Jesse, 1945, Je 18,19:5
Biener, David, 1953, Jl 7,27:2
Bienerth, Count von, 1918, Je 6,13:6
Bienfang, Daisy Mrs, 1947, D 3,29:2
Bieniek, Andrew, 1937, N 11,25:4
Bienroth, Conrad, 1908, O 8,9:2
Bienstock, Herbert W, 1941, Jl 31,17:5
Bienstock, Michael, 1954, S 26,87:1
Bienstock, Samuel, 1937, O 29,21:3
Bienstock, Samuel J, 1945, My 13,20:2
Bienvenu, Emile Mrs, 1939, D 30,15:3
Bienvenu-Martin, Yvonne, 1943, D 12,68:2
Bier, Arthur S, 1951, O 24,31:3
Bier, August, 1949, Mr 17,25:4
Bier, Edward, 1958, S 19,27:2
Bier, Joseph A, 1965, Mr 17,45:4
Bier, Kupper, 1925, Je 11,19:3
Bier, Moses, 1922, Je 5,13:6
Bier, Oscar R, 1944, D 2,13:2
Bierau, Henry J, 1949, Je 16,29:2
Bierbauer, Charles A, 1950, F 17,23:3
Bierce, Fred J, 1949, O 20,29:6
Bierce, George H, 1937, Jl 16,19:5
Bierce, Stella B, 1946, Ap 22,21:4
Bierck, Adolph, 1905, Ap 2,9:6
Bierck, John E, 1962, N 26,29:1
Bierd, William G, 1944, F 22,23:5
Bieri, John C, 1951, Ap 1,93:1
Bierkan, Andrew T, 1947, Ja 20,25:4
Bierman, George, 1940, S 22,48:1
Bierman, Hendrik, 1948, Ja 22,27:4
Bierman, Isaac Mrs, 1913, Je 20,9:4
Biermann, Georg, 1949, Ap 8,25:3
Bierne, George, 1951, D 14,31:3
Bierne, Marie G, 1956, Jl 31,23:1
Bierring, Walter L, 1961, Je 26,31:4
Biers, Carl L, 1960, Je 10,31:2
Biers, Howard, 1967, Mr 18,29:5
Bierstadt, Albert, 1902, F 19,9:5
Bierstadt, Harold, 1948, Jl 13,27:3
Biertuempfel, Albert H, 1953, O 29,31:2
Biertuempfel, Frederick A, 1963, My 1,39:3
Biertuempfel, Hugo C, 1966, S 19,43:2
Biertuempfel, Oscar A, 1958, Ap 29,29:1
Bierut, Boleslaw (funl, Mr 17,3:4), 1956, Mr 14,1:8
Bierweiler, Louis C, 1964, D 13,86:4
Bierwirth, Frederick W, 1964, My 4,29:3
Bierwirth, Heinrich C, 1940, F 5,17:4
Bierwirth, John H, 1952, F 27,27:2
Bierwirth, Leopold, 1874, O 31,12:3
Biery, Hudson R, 1967, Jl 6,29:4
Biery, Joseph F, 1952, Ag 16,15:4
Biery, Walter L, 1937, Ap 18,II,8:5
Biesecker, Edgar W, 1942, Ag 7,17:3
Biesecker, Guy A, 1958, F 12,29:2
Biesel, Augustus, 1915, Je 14,9:4
Biesel, Charles, 1945, Ag 7,24:3
Biesemeyer, Walter, 1953, Ag 30,89:1
Bieser, Augustus E, 1946, O 29,25:5
Bieser, Edward J, 1948, Je 25,23:5
Biester, Harry L, 1947, Ap 12,17:6
Bietry, Pierre Mrs, 1950, F 1,29:4
Biever, Nicolas, 1965, Jl 17,25:1
Bifarini, Ugolino, 1945, Ja 25,19:4
Biffar, Sarah Mrs, 1942, Je 6,13:4
Biffen, Rowland, 1949, Jl 15,19:4
Biffer, Dominick A, 1946, O 18,23:3
Biffle, I, 1934, Ap 8,32:1
Biffle, Leslie L, 1966, Ap 7,39:2
Biffle, Solon, 1938, Ja 28,21:2
Big Mountain, Sebastian, 1954, My 13,29:5
Big Tree, John (Chief), 1967, Jl 7,33:1
Bigalow, William E, 1947, Ja 14,25:4
Bigart, Alice V Mrs, 1959, Mr 26,31:3
Bigart, Anna Mrs, 1949, Jl 27,23:4
Bigart, Homer S, 1956, N 17,21:6
Bigbee, Homer L, 1949, N 3,29:4
Bigden, Myrtle, 1955, N 16,35:3
Bigelow, Agnes E Mrs (est acctg), 1954, Ap 7,36:4
Bigelow, Alice H, 1956, My 11,28:1
Bigelow, Anson A, 1958, D 4,39:4
Bigelow, Anson A Mrs, 1961, Mr 7,35:4
Bigelow, Archie P, 1942, D 26,11:3
Bigelow, Arthur C, 1922, Ag 27,28:3
Bigelow, Arthur L, 1967, Mr 10,36:2
Bigelow, Arthur S Mrs, 1949, Ja 4,40:2
Bigelow, Asa, 1882, Ap 8,5:4
Bigelow, Ashley, 1962, My 20,86:8
Bigelow, Bruce M, 1954, D 29,23:3
Bigelow, Burt M Mrs, 1966, Ap 26,45:3
Bigelow, Carle M, 1955, My 11,31:3
Bigelow, Carlotta H Mrs, 1952, F 14,30:4
Bigelow, Caroline P Mrs, 1942, F 10,19:5
Bigelow, Charles A (funl, Mr 14,11:4), 1912, Mr 13, 11:4
Bigelow, Charles E, 1939, Ag 29,21:5
Bigelow, Charles H, 1939, Je 11,45:1
Bigelow, Clara L, 1942, Ap 6,15:5
Bigelow, Clarence O, 1937, Mr 29,19:2
Bigelow, D Jackson, 1872, S 14,10:5
Bigelow, David, 1950, My 14,72:2
Bigelow, David Mrs, 1966, F 24,37:4
Bigelow, Doris C, 1949, Ag 30,27:5
Bigelow, Edith J Mrs, 1939, My 4,23:1
Bigelow, Edward, 1946, My 7,21:3
Bigelow, Edward F, 1938, Jl 15,17:6
Bigelow, Edward Mrs, 1947, Je 7,13:4
Bigelow, Edward Payson, 1925, Jl 21,21:6
Bigelow, Edward S, 1961, S 7,35:1
Bigelow, Edwin Moses, 1905, Ap 23,3:4
Bigelow, Emerson, 1966, Ja 13,25:4
Bigelow, Emma F G Mrs (will), 1938, Ap 15,20:4
Bigelow, Ernest A (por), 1945, Ja 9,19:4
Bigelow, Ernest A Mrs, 1944, O 6,23:4
Bigelow, Florence I, 1939, Ag 31,19:2
Bigelow, Francis H, 1941, O 13,17:4
Bigelow, Frank, 1954, Ap 28,31:5
Bigelow, Frank B, 1949, My 31,23:3
Bigelow, Frank H Rev, 1937, Mr 20,19:2
Bigelow, Frank Mrs, 1924, Mr 8,11:6
Bigelow, Franklin O, 1949, My 24,28:2
Bigelow, Franklin O (est appr), 1953, D 24,17:8
Bigelow, Frederic R, 1946, S 10,7:3
Bigelow, Frederick A, 1941, Ja 25,15:3
Bigelow, Frederick S, 1954, S 30,31:3
Bigelow, G T, 1878, Ap 13,4:7
Bigelow, Grace, 1952, Ja 24,27:1
Bigelow, Harry A, 1950, Ja 9,25:4
Bigelow, Harry M, 1940, D 5,25:2
Bigelow, Harry W, 1946, Mr 9,13:2
Bigelow, Henry B, 1967, D 12,47:2
Bigelow, Herbert E, 1950, My 8,23:4
Bigelow, Herbert S, 1951, N 13,29:2
Bigelow, Horace E, 1942, N 12,25:2
Bigelow, Isabella L Mrs, 1941, My 19,17:4
Bigelow, J, 1879, Ja 13,3:4
Bigelow, J Dr, 1879, Ja 31,8:2
Bigelow, J W, 1928, Je 25,21:4
Bigelow, John (funl), 1911, D 23,9:3
Bigelow, John D, 1943, Ja 30,15:6
Bigelow, John F Mrs, 1943, Mr 31,19:3
Bigelow, John L, 1938, D 4,60:4
Bigelow, John Mrs, 1948, S 5,40:7
Bigelow, John P, 1872, Jl 6,1:3
Bigelow, John W Mrs, 1906, D 18,9:5
Bigelow, Karl W Mrs, 1960, Je 14,37:1
Bigelow, Lester B, 1938, S 16,21:5
Bigelow, Lewis S Mrs, 1944, Jl 19,19:5
Bigelow, Lucius S Mrs, 1944, F 2,21:3
Bigelow, M T, 1902, D 30,9:6
Bigelow, Mabel C Mrs, 1941, N 28,23:3
Bigelow, Mason H Mrs, 1964, Mr 24,33:1
Bigelow, Maurice A, 1955, Ja 7,21:5
Bigelow, Melville Madison Prof, 1921, My 5,17:4
Bigelow, Moses, 1874, Ja 11,8:6; 1959, S 18,32:1
Bigelow, Otis M, 1939, Jl 1,17:7
Bigelow, Paul, 1961, Mr 18,23:5
Bigelow, Paul Mrs, 1942, D 2,25:2
Bigelow, Poultney (funl plans, My 30,45:1; funl, Je 1,27:4), 1954, My 29,15:2
Bigelow, Prescott, 1937, O 28,25:2
Bigelow, Richard, 1948, D 11,15:3
Bigelow, Richard L, 1948, S 6,13:6
Bigelow, Robert P, 1955, S 7,31:1
Bigelow, Robert R L, 1952, D 17,33:4
Bigelow, Roger L, 1952, Ag 12,19:4
Bigelow, S Lawrence, 1947, D 6,15:3
Bigelow, Samuel, 1913, Mr 21,13:2
Bigelow, Samuel F, 1915, Mr 9,9:4
Bigelow, Talman Mrs, 1968, Mr 30,33:5
Bigelow, Thomas S, 1904, Jl 21,3:2
Bigelow, Uriah S Dr, 1873, F 27,1:6
Bigelow, W S Dr, 1926, O 7,27:3
Bigelow, Willard D, 1939, Mr 7,21:3
Bigelow, William F, 1966, Mr 7,27:5
Bigelow, William F Mrs, 1956, Ag 11,13:3
Bigelow, William P, 1941, Mr 18,23:6
Bigelow, William Richards, 1915, Ap 15,13:5
Bigelow, Willoughby C, 1940, Ja 22,15:5
Bigelow, Willoughby C Mrs, 1950, Ag 9,29:4
Biger, Pierre, 1967, Jl 12,43:4
Bigg, Howard P, 1948, Ap 21,27:2
Bigg, William A, 1955, S 11,84:7
Biggar, J L, 1938, Je 3,21:2
Biggar, J L Maj-Gen, 1922, F 19,22:3
Biggar, James, 1954, O 25,27:3
Biggar, O M, 1948, S 6,13:4
Biggar, W H, 1922, Jl 10,13:5
Biggar, Walter, 1940, N 21,29:2
Biggart, William, 1939, S 28,25:5
Bigger, Edward C, 1942, Je 2,23:5
Bigger, Frederick, 1963, Je 19,37:3
Bigger, Gilbert L, 1949, Jl 24,52:4
Bigger, H F Dr, 1926, N 30,29:3
Bigger, Henry J, 1941, N 4,23:5
Bigger, Henry P, 1938, Jl 27,17:2
Bigger, Isaac A Jr, 1955, Ja 28,19:2
Bigger, T B, 1880, My 6,2:2
Biggerman, Carl P, 1942, Mr 30,17:5
Biggers, E D, 1933, Ap 6,17:1
Biggers, Emma E Mrs, 1950, My 7,106:1
Biggers, George C, 1963, Mr 26,9:5
Biggers, George P, 1951, Ap 5,29:3
Biggers, John D Mrs, 1942, Ag 17,15:4
Biggers, Joseph M, 1940, N 29,21:5
Biggerstaff, Robert A, 1957, Je 22,15:3
Biggert, Cassius F, 1941, O 14,23:3
Biggert, F C Jr, 1952, F 11,25:4
Biggi, John F, 1968, O 4,47:1
Biggie, Marcia, 1947, Jl 29,22:3
Biggin, Florence I, 1951, O 20,15:5
Biggin, Harry M, 1942, Je 16,23:6
Biggins, Edward H, 1940, S 7,15:5
Biggins, John E, 1952, D 15,25:5
Biggio, Giovanna Mrs, 1947, N 5,27:3
Biggs, A Hermione, 1950, O 19,31:3
Biggs, Asa Judge, 1878, Mr 7,4:7
Biggs, Burch E Sr, 1954, S 13,23:3
Biggs, Carl S, 1940, Ap 24,23:5
Biggs, Charles L, 1942, D 22,25:3
Biggs, Francis S, 1939, N 15,23:5
Biggs, George, 1946, N 6,5:5
Biggs, George P, 1955, D 19,27:2
Biggs, George W Jr, 1953, Ja 26,19:4
Biggs, Harold A, 1937, Ja 16,15:2
Biggs, Hermann Dr, 1923, Je 29,17:3
Biggs, J Crawford, 1960, F 1,27:2
Biggs, John D, 1954, D 9,33:4
Biggs, John E, 1953, Ja 8,27:4
Biggs, John G, 1949, Jl 7,26:2
Biggs, John R, 1950, Ja 5,25:3
Biggs, John Sr, 1937, Ap 4,II,10:7
Biggs, Ralph L, 1964, D 5,31:4
Biggs, Richard J Jr, 1938, Mr 6,II,8:1
Biggs, Walter, 1968, F 12,39:2
Biggs, William A, 1939, Je 20,21:6
Biggs, William P, 1947, Je 13,23:2
Biggstaff, B F Rev, 1905, My 23,9:6
Bigham, Charles C (Lord Mersey), 1956, N 22,33:4
Bigham, L Thomas, 1954, O 19,27:1
Bigham, Reginald B, 1964, Jl 31,23:5
Bigham, Thomas J Jr Mrs, 1961, O 25,37:2
Bigham, Trevor, 1954, N 26,29:3
Bigham, Truman C, 1952, D 31,15:2
Bighum, Edward, 1951, Je 18,23:7
Biglan, Albert M, 1964, Mr 15,86:1
Bigler, Alex B, 1939, N 18,17:3
Bigler, Frank S, 1942, Ap 20,21:5
Bigler, George R, 1937, S 25,17:5
Bigler, Harry C, 1950, F 14,26:3
Bigler, John Ex-Gov, 1871, D 2,1:4
Bigler, Paul G Mrs, 1952, S 14,87:1
Bigler, S C Mrs, 1904, F 20,1:1
Bigler, William, 1880, Ag 10,5:5
Bigler, William H Dr, 1904, D 11,1:6
Bigley, Frank G, 1943, D 24,13:4
Bigley, Joseph H, 1952, O 14,31:1
Bigley, Joseph H Mrs, 1949, S 20,29:4
Biglin, Bernard, 1924, My 12,17:6
Biglow, Charles W Mrs, 1943, Ap 10,17:1
Biglow, Ernest C, 1962, O 6,25:5
Biglow, William K, 1948, Mr 14,72:3
Bignami, Ugo, 1949, D 10,17:4
Bignell, Edward, 1947, Ag 27,23:4
Bignell Jos, 1953, Mr 3,27:1
Bigoney, Elmer E Mrs, 1950, F 11,15:1
Bigoney, Newton, 1922, Jl 28,13:5
Bigongiari, Dino, 1965, S 8,47:2
Bigongiari, Dino Mrs, 1966, Jl 31,72:3
Bigongiari, Gino, 1962, F 11,87:1
Bigongiari, Terese P Mrs, 1955, Ja 13,27:5
Bigras, Jean Baptiste Mrs, 1917, S 29,11:7
Bigsby, Charles S Mrs, 1950, Ja 10,29:3
Bigsby, Robert Dr, 1873, O 3,4:7
Bigue, Philippe, 1955, Ja 6,27:4
Bigum, Anton M, 1950, S 2,15:6
Bijay Chand Mahtab, Maharajah of Burdwan, 1941, Ag 30,13:4
Bijl, Hendrik van der, 1948, D 3,26:3
Bijlaard, Paul P, 1967, Mr 11,29:1
Bijur, Abraham, 1922, My 2,19:6
Bijur, Asher, 1880, F 13,4:7
Bijur, N, 1930, Jl 9,23:4
Bijur, Nathan Mrs, 1944, Ja 28,18:3
Bijur, Samuel H, 1942, Ag 15,11:3
Bijur, Samuel H Mrs, 1963, N 20,40:2
Bijur, Sherman M, 1968, F 29,37:1
Bijur, Sherman M Mrs, 1962, F 14,35:4
Bijur, William L, 1960, O 30,86:3

Bikaner, Prince of, 1950, S 26,31:6
Bikelas, M, 1908, Jl 22,5:6
Bikle, Charles E, 1949, Mr 27,78:2
Bikle, Henry W, 1942, Ja 27,22:2
Biladeau, Clarence J, 1939, D 27,21:4
Bilak, Stefan J, 1950, O 22,93:1
Bilbee, William H, 1940, Je 13,23:5
Bilbo, Theodore G, 1947, Ag 22,1:2
Bilden, Howard M, 1960, N 2,39:1
Bilder, Jacob O Mrs, 1956, My 11,27:2
Bilder, Nathaniel Mrs, 1952, Ja 21,15:1
Bilder, Robert M, 1961, Je 11,86:5
Bilder, Walter Mrs, 1939, Mr 4,15:2
Bildersee, Barnett, 1908, F 28,7:5
Bildersee, Isaac, 1952, Ag 24,88:1
Bildner, Morris, 1951, Je 22,25:4
Bildt, Axel R, 1944, Ag 26,11:7
Bildt, Lillian M de Baroness, 1912, Ja 6,13:5
Biles, George H, 1943, S 21,24:2
Biles, J H Sir, 1933, O 28,15:6
Bilgrey, Max, 1948, O 21,27:5
Bilinski, Andrew T, 1952, Ag 26,25:2
Bilkerd, H A, 1929, Ja 22,1:4
Bilkey, Charles L, 1938, Ap 21,19:3
Bilkey, H Edward, 1950, Ja 19,27:3
Bill, Albert C, 1944, D 15,19:4
Bill, Alfred H, 1964, Ag 12,35:4
Bill, Carroll Mrs, 1950, Jl 28,21:3
Bill, Cecil A, 1925, Ap 25,15:6
Bill, Charles A, 1942, S 6,31:1
Bill, Charles G, 1952, Ag 8,17:3
Bill, E, 1880, Ap 2,2:4
Bill, Edward, 1947, Ja 16,25:2
Bill, Edward L, 1956, Ap 24,31:4
Bill, Edward L Mrs, 1948, N 5,26:2
Bill, Edward W, 1937, Jl 29,19:4; 1946, Ja 2,19:3
Bill, Frank R, 1947, Mr 15,13:2
Bill, Freeman M, 1941, F 17,15:1
Bill, Harry L, 1954, Ap 16,21:1
Bill, John G, 1959, D 29,26:2
Bill, Joseph A, 1960, Ap 14,37:6
Bill, Ledyard, 1907, O 7,9:5
Bill, Phil W, 1941, D 30,19:2
Bill, Raymond, 1957, Je 14,25:3
Billard, F C, 1932, My 18,21:1
Billard, Frederick C Mrs, 1940, My 20,17:5
Billard, Frederick H, 1952, Ap 5,15:4
Billaudot, Rene, 1944, N 9,27:6
Billaut, Marc, 1955, Ap 8,25:5
Bille, Frank Ernest, 1918, Je 11,11:5
Bille, T de, 1883, Je 12,4:7
Biller, David W, 1966, Jl 21,33:2
Biller, Ernest C, 1945, D 28,16:2
Biller, George Jr Rev, 1915, O 26,11:5
Biller, George Mrs, 1952, Ag 7,21:4
Biller, Newman M, 1963, O 14,29:4
Biller, Samuel B, 1946, Ja 21,23:2
Billerbeck, Harry M, 1962, Je 6,41:3
Billes, John W, 1956, N 18,89:2
Billhardt, Fred A, 1968, Je 26,47:5
Billhardt, Philip, 1966, F 20,88:5
Billhartz, William M, 1941, Je 1,40:4
Billie, John Mrs, 1939, Ag 16,23:1
Billiet, Ernest, 1939, Mr 22,23:1
Billig, Max C, 1961, Jl 10,21:4
Billigmeyer, Henry, 1946, Ja 16,23:3
Billikopf, Jacob, 1951, Ja 1,17:3
Billing, Archibald, 1881, S 6,2:1
Billing, Berta S Mrs, 1938, O 18,25:6
Billing, F W, 1914, Jl 25,7:5
Billing, W Henry, 1947, O 17,21:3
Billingham, Frank L, 1939, Mr 1,21:5
Billingham, Fred F, 1944, N 13,19:3
Billingham, James R, 1959, D 6,86:8
Billinghurst, Guillermo, 1915, Je 29,13:6
Billings, A M, 1926, Je 21,19:3
Billings, Andrew, 1880, Je 10,5:4
Billings, Andrew Mrs, 1913, Mr 31,13:4
Billings, Benjamin L, 1865, Jl 18,5:2
Billings, Charles Ethan, 1920, Je 6,22:4
Billings, Charles K, 1945, N 14,19:5
Billings, Charles M Mrs, 1956, D 29,15:4
Billings, Charles T, 1942, O 3,15:5
Billings, Chester Sr, 1952, S 24,33:2
Billings, Cornelius K G, 1937, My 7,25:4
Billings, Cornelius K G Mrs (will, My 21,2:3), 1937, My 17,19:4
Billings, Elizabeth, 1944, S 11,17:7
Billings, Ernest E, 1946, O 8,23:5
Billings, Frank (Josh), 1957, Mr 14,29:5
Billings, Franklin S Mrs, 1964, Ja 30,30:1
Billings, Fred, 1890, O 1,2:2; 1903, Ag 23,1:2
Billings, George W Jr, 1953, My 7,31:2
Billings, Hammatt, 1874, N 16,5:1
Billings, Harry F Sr, 1943, Mr 2,19:4
Billings, Haskell C, 1941, Jl 27,31:1
Billings, Henry M, 1915, O 14,11:5
Billings, Howard Mrs, 1949, S 27,27:3
Billings, J S, 1928, Ap 28,19:3
Billings, James L, 1951, Ja 4,29:3
Billings, John A Mrs, 1944, S 13,19:5
Billings, John S Mrs, 1925, Jl 6,11:7
Billings, John Shaw (funl, Mr 13,11:4), 1913, Mr 12, 11:4
Billings, Leonard L, 1939, O 23,19:2
Billings, Myra I, 1953, S 25,21:2
Billings, Oliver C, 1950, Mr 6,21:2
Billings, Oliver C Jr, 1967, Jl 17,29:4
Billings, Oliver C Mrs, 1947, Je 16,21:5
Billings, Percy, 1947, Ap 16,25:2
Billings, R Bloss, 1941, Jl 3,19:3
Billings, Samuel O, 1954, Mr 30,27:2
Billings, William H, 1943, My 12,25:1
Billings, William L, 1942, Ag 18,21:5
Billingsley, Allen L, 1954, O 8,23:1
Billingsley, Floyd M, 1951, My 3,29:2
Billingsley, Horace M, 1948, Ja 9,21:4
Billingsley, Hugh M, 1965, F 11,39:2
Billingsley, Logan, 1963, Ag 5,29:2
Billingsley, Sherman, 1966, O 5,47:1
Billington, Cecil, 1950, Mr 19,95:6
Billington, Cornelius E Dr, 1904, Ja 9,9:6
Billington, Frederick, 1938, F 26,15:2
Billington, George W, 1951, S 14,25:1
Billington, James J, 1944, N 24,23:2
Billington, James J Mrs, 1942, O 13,23:4
Billington, Percy R, 1946, S 29,62:4
Billington, Stephen H, 1946, Ja 4,21:3
Billington, W Stanley, 1939, Ap 14,23:3
Billington, William, 1946, Ap 2,27:3
Billington, William Mrs, 1947, F 12,25:2
Billipp, Ernest, 1940, Ap 4,23:1
Billipp, Ernest H, 1951, Je 10,92:3
Billman, Frederick H, 1964, F 5,35:5
Billman, Howard, 1905, Mr 14,9:6
Billman, William C, 1943, Mr 3,23:6
Billmeir, Jack A, 1963, D 24,17:5
Billmeyer, Charles E, 1959, Ap 13,31:3
Billmyer, Alexander, 1924, My 26,17:6
Billmyre, Joseph F, 1956, Ag 17,19:5
Billner, Karl P, 1965, Je 9,47:1
Billo, Geoffroy Mrs, 1962, Mr 7,35:3
Billo, Otto, 1951, Ag 14,23:1
Billot, Gen, 1907, Je 2,7:5
Billotte, Alfred C, 1961, N 30,37:4
Bills, Arthur, 1958, Mr 10,23:1
Bills, Daniel, 1945, Ag 29,23:1
Bills, Marcella M Mrs, 1948, Je 21,21:4
Bills, Nathan D, 1947, Jl 12,13:6
Bills, William E, 1937, S 27,21:4
Billson, William H, 1941, D 26,13:2
Billstrom, Nels J, 1939, S 12,25:4
Billwiller, Charles J Jr, 1951, Ap 11,29:3
Billwiller, Henrietta H Mrs (Henrietta Hudson), 1942, Ap 4,13:2
Billyeald, Joseph, 1905, Mr 14,9:6
Bilmanis, Alfred, 1948, Jl 27,25:1
Bilodeau, Marie L (Mother P Claver), 1953, S 13, 84:8
Bilofsky, Molly, 1907, S 7,9:6
Biloon, Sol, 1964, N 18,47:3
Bilotti, Anton, 1963, N 12,38:1
Bilotti, Salvatore, 1953, Ja 22,23:4
Bilson, Thaddeus W Mrs, 1944, Jl 16,31:2
Bilstein, Louis C, 1947, O 22,29:1
Bilt, Cornelius L van der, 1947, D 7,76:4
Biltz, Robert O, 1947, Ag 31,36:6
Bily, A F (Dan), 1949, N 27,104:8
Bilyou, George Mrs, 1950, N 12,93:2
Bimanski, Francis X, 1952, Ap 29,27:4
Bimberg, Benjamin, 1950, N 28,31:2
Bimberg, Bernard A Mrs, 1940, N 24,48:2
Bimberg, Charles, 1924, D 4,21:4
Bimberg, Edward, 1937, My 10,19:3
Bimberg, Edward Mrs, 1951, O 10,23:6
Bimberg, Meyer H, 1908, Mr 30,7:5
Bimboni, Alberto, 1960, Je 19,88:2
Bimko, Fischel, 1965, Ap 10,30:1
Bimson, John, 1937, N 4,25:5
Binacum, Thomas Bp, 1911, F 5,II,11:4
Binch, Francis, 1947, Je 25,25:3
Binday, Morris L, 1955, Ap 26,29:1
Bindenberger, J Fred, 1939, D 30,15:5
Binder, Abraham, 1945, O 8,15:4; 1959, Ja 25,92:8
Binder, Abraham W, 1966, O 11,47:1
Binder, Abraham W Mrs, 1953, Ap 6,19:4
Binder, Adolf, 1954, Je 1,27:5
Binder, Carroll, 1956, My 2,31:1
Binder, Charles F, 1965, Ag 13,26:8
Binder, Elmer C, 1955, Jl 10,73:2
Binder, Henry F, 1951, Ag 19,86:3
Binder, Hyman, 1948, N 22,21:2
Binder, Jacob W, 1955, Ja 16,93:2
Binder, John Mrs, 1946, Jl 23,25:1
Binder, Lewis, 1961, My 13,19:6
Binder, Louis, 1952, My 20,25:3
Binder, Louis R, 1944, Ja 10,17:4
Binder, Raymond S, 1941, Ja 1,23:6
Binder, Rudolph M, 1950, O 17,31:2
Binder, Rudolph M Mrs, 1943, Je 8,22:2
Binder, Samuel, 1940, F 1,21:2
Binder, Walter J, 1959, Ap 24,27:2
Binderman, Nahum T, 1943, Ja 23,13:1
Binderman, Saul A, 1952, D 31,15:3
Bindewald, George F, 1950, Je 27,29:5
Bindewald, George F Mrs, 1946, S 20,31:3
Bindewald, Theodore L B, 1954, Ag 1,85:1
Binding, Rudolf, 1938, Ag 6,13:4
Bindler, Sol Mrs, 1956, My 16,35:5
Bindley, John, 1921, D 17,13:3
Bindloss, Harold, 1946, Ja 2,19:4
Bindsell, Nicholas W, 1944, Je 18,36:3
Binen Michael Bro (M P Lenihan), 1962, Mr 26,31:2
Binet, George, 1962, O 27,25:5
Binet, H, 1936, Jl 16,17:1
Binetter, Bruno B, 1952, My 13,23:5
Binford, Jesse H, 1952, Je 11,29:4
Binford, Jessie, 1966, Jl 12,43:4
Binford, Lloyd T, 1956, Ag 28,27:1
Binford, Morton C, 1946, D 27,19:3
Bing, Benjamin M, 1939, Ja 16,15:5
Bing, Ernst, 1961, Mr 17,24:1
Bing, Hans N, 1939, Ja 6,21:5
Bing, Joseph M, 1950, D 10,104:3
Bing, Otto, 1937, N 15,23:5
Bing, William A, 1952, Mr 13,29:3
Bingay, Guy C, 1953, My 11,27:2
Bingay, Malcolm W, 1953, Ag 22,15:5
Bingeman, Charles W Mrs, 1946, Ag 25,46:2
Binger, Arnold, 1945, Ag 28,19:5
Binger, Frances N Mrs, 1942, F 18,19:3
Binger, Frank C Mrs, 1953, Je 2,29:4
Binger, George M, 1951, S 28,31:4
Binger, Henry Mrs, 1946, S 4,23:1
Binger, Robert E, 1959, Je 7,86:3
Binger, William H, 1966, Ja 6,27:1
Bingesser, Carl, 1950, My 16,31:5
Bingham, A, 1927, S 2,17:5
Bingham, A W, 1928, Je 11,21:3
Bingham, Abbie, 1910, D 25,9:2
Bingham, Albert B, 1957, N 9,27:6
Bingham, Albert H Mrs, 1949, My 15,90:2
Bingham, Anson H, 1949, Ap 23,13:1
Bingham, Arthur C, 1956, N 7,31:5
Bingham, Arthur W, 1943, My 20,21:3; 1967, Ja 30, 29:5
Bingham, Arthur W Mrs, 1943, Mr 27,13:2
Bingham, C, 1934, Je 1,23:5
Bingham, Charles, 1947, Je 20,20:2
Bingham, Charles L, 1941, Ja 5,44:5
Bingham, Charles Mrs, 1949, Ja 21,21:1
Bingham, Charles T, 1946, Jl 19,19:4
Bingham, David (funl, Ag 18,9:6), 1923, Ag 17,13:4
Bingham, David, 1956, Je 25,23:5
Bingham, David S, 1965, F 24,42:1
Bingham, Donald C, 1946, Jl 25,21:1
Bingham, Edward, 1939, S 25,19:5
Bingham, Eugene C, 1945, N 7,23:5
Bingham, Frederick C, 1944, N 18,13:5
Bingham, George, 1945, Ap 9,19:4; 1965, D 19,84:3
Bingham, George B, 1938, F 13,II,7:2
Bingham, George C P (Earl of Lucan), 1964, Ja 22, 37:2
Bingham, George H Mrs, 1948, N 9,27:4
Bingham, Gertrude E, 1913, N 19,9:6
Bingham, Goundry W, 1945, F 1,23:2
Bingham, H H, 1950, Ag 21,19:5
Bingham, Hamilton Capt, 1908, Ap 4,9:7
Bingham, Hamilton W, 1943, N 23,25:5
Bingham, Harold C, 1964, Ag 27,33:5
Bingham, Harry P (will), 1955, Mr 31,55:3
Bingham, Henrietta Worth, 1968, Je 18,47:3
Bingham, Henry H, 1912, Mr 27,13:4
Bingham, Henry H Gen, 1912, Mr 24,15:3
Bingham, Hiram (est acctg, Jl 10,34:2), 1956, Je 7, 31:1
Bingham, Hiram Dr, 1908, O 27,9:5
Bingham, Howard H C, 1956, Jl 12,23:6
Bingham, Isaac E Mrs, 1950, F 10,23:1
Bingham, J Clarke, 1962, D 6,43:1
Bingham, J Grace, 1958, N 8,21:4
Bingham, James, 1940, Ag 20,19:2
Bingham, James G, 1949, My 19,30:2
Bingham, Jeremiah, 1938, Mr 30,21:2
Bingham, Joel F Mrs, 1908, Ag 22,7:5
Bingham, Joel Foote Rev, 1914, O 20,13:5
Bingham, John E Sir, 1915, Mr 19,11:6
Bingham, John George Barry (Baron Clanmorris), 1916, N 5,23:4
Bingham, John J, 1953, N 26,31:1
Bingham, Kenneth Fisher, 1912, Ja 2,11:6
Bingham, L A, 1885, F 21,2:2
Bingham, Leroy W, 1964, S 21,31:5
Bingham, Lloyd, 1915, D 23,13:4
Bingham, Lloyd (funl), 1916, Ja 26,11:6
Bingham, Mary G, 1953, Jl 25,11:2
Bingham, Mary Mrs, 1905, O 28,9:6
Bingham, Millicent Todd Mrs, 1968, D 3,47:3
Bingham, Norman W, 1958, N 14,27:1
Bingham, R, 1927, My 9,21:3
Bingham, Robert F, 1947, S 7,60:8
Bingham, Robert H, 1964, Jl 16,31:3
Bingham, Robert W Amb, 1937, D 19,1:4
Bingham, Robert W Mrs, 1953, Mr 19,29:3
Bingham, Robert Worth (Genoa, Nev), 1966, Ja 1 17:4
Bingham, Robert Worth Mrs, 1917, Jl 28,7:5
Bingham, Rose L, 1961, S 24,86:3
Bingham, Rowland V, 1942, D 9,27:2

Bingham, Rudolph, 1904, Je 13,2:2
Bingham, T, 1934, S 7,21:1
Bingham, Theodore A Brig-Gen, 1920, O 29,15:5
Bingham, Walter V, 1952, Jl 9,27:5
Bingham, Will, 1967, Ag 14,31:2
Bingham, William 2d, 1955, F 19,15:3
Bingham, Worth (Robt W), 1966, Jl 13,43:1
Bingham-Spencer, Reginald A Mrs, 1966, Ap 26,46:1
Bingle, Ernest J, 1957, Je 1,17:6
Bingle, Peter J, 1950, Ap 6,29:1
Bingler, Adolph E Mrs, 1953, O 25,89:2
Bingley, Henry C A, 1939, My 17,23:5
Bingley, Lord, 1947, D 12,27:2
Bining, Arthur C, 1957, O 2,33:3
Bininger, Abraham, 1870, O 15,2:7
Bininger, Byron (see also D 27), 1903, D 28,7:4
Bininger, Elizabeth D, 1923, F 28,17:3
Bininger, William Burger, 1908, My 16,7:4
Binion, Samuel Augustus Prof, 1914, Ja 10,9:6
Binkley, Charles C, 1960, Je 29,33:5
Binkley, Christian K, 1938, Ap 30,15:5
Binkley, George E, 1956, Mr 16,23:2
Binkley, Robert C, 1940, Ap 12,23:2
Binkley, Wilfred E, 1965, D 10,47:1
Binkovitz, Louis, 1951, Ap 22,89:2
Binkovitz, Morris, 1942, S 2,23:2
Binkow, Aaron, 1945, D 19,25:3
Binkowski, Edward S, 1954, O 27,29:1
Binks, Harry D, 1954, F 8,23:4
Binks, John W, 1939, F 6,13:3
Binks, William T, 1945, Ap 16,23:5
Binn, Louis, 1967, O 10,47:2
Binn, Mary Mrs (autopsy rept, Ag 20,69:6), 1967, Ag 19,23:6
Binney, Edwin Mrs, 1960, S 10,21:5
Binney, Henry P, 1940, Ja 3,22:3
Binney, Horace, 1875, Ag 13,4:6
Binney, Horace (will, Ja 21,7:3), 1937, Ja 8,19:5
Binney, Horace Mrs, 1955, Jl 24,65:3
Binney, Hugh, 1953, Ja 11,91:1
Binney, John Rev Dr, 1913, Je 14,11:5
Binney, Ralph M, 1965, Jl 11,68:5
Binney, Thomas Rev, 1874, F 25,5:6
Binney, William G, 1909, Ag 4,7:6
Binney, William G Mrs, 1908, Ja 27,7:4
Binney, William Mrs, 1914, Ag 10,7:4
Binnie, James W, 1957, D 27,19:1
Binning, Edward G (funl plans), 1961, My 29,19:5
Binning, George Baillie-Hamilton Col, 1917, Ja 13,11:4
Binns, Dorothy R Mrs, 1958, O 8,35:4
Binns, Frank E Mrs, 1947, F 15,15:3; 1962, O 10,47:1
Binns, H Stanley, 1948, Jl 24,15:6
Binns, John R, 1959, D 9,42:1
Binns, Walter P, 1966, D 5,45:4
Binsse, Henry B Mrs, 1952, O 21,29:3
Binsted, John H, 1950, S 8,31:3
Binsted, Norman S, 1961, F 22,25:5
Binswanger, Hyman P, 1938, Jl 4,13:5
Binswanger, Isadore, 1955, Je 27,21:4
Binswanger, Max Mrs, 1964, Ag 6,29:2
Binyon, Laurence, 1943, Mr 11,21:3
Binyon, Millard P, 1954, N 24,23:4
Binz, Max E, 1955, Mr 26,15:1
Binzen, Frederick W, 1961, S 30,25:1
Biondetti, Clemente, 1955, F 25,21:3
Biondi, Jean, 1950, N 11,4:7
Bioren, John S, 1951, S 20,31:3
Biorkman, Claes G A, 1944, D 29,15:2
Biornberg, Adolph, 1876, Ap 23,2:2
Biossat, Harry A, 1951, Jl 27,19:6
Biosson, Pierre F, 1948, Jl 22,23:4
Biow, Louise B Mrs, 1965, Ap 30,35:5
Biow, Milton H Mrs, 1943, F 27,13:3
Biow, Seymour L, 1960, N 9,35:2
Bippart, C Herbert, 1966, Mr 29,41:2
Bippus, George J, 1904, Ja 8,7:5
Bippus, Rupert F, 1951, S 13,31:5
Biquerel, A C, 1878, Ja 22,8:2
Biram, James H, 1948, O 31,88:4
Birbeck, Lady, 1939, My 31,23:2
Birch, A Otis, 1967, Mr 18,29:4
Birch, Abner H, 1945, Je 15,19:2
Birch, Alan, 1961, D 14,43:2
Birch, Charles A, 1945, N 20,21:4
Birch, Charles E, 1953, My 12,27:2
Birch, Florence A Mrs, 1942, N 15,57:1
Birch, Francis A, 1949, My 12,31:6
Birch, Frank E, 1948, Mr 19,23:1
Birch, Frank H, 1951, My 16,35:6
Birch, Frederick H, 1940, Jl 13,13:5
Birch, G W Rev, 1902, Ap 27,7:7
Birch, George W Mrs, 1944, My 12,19:4
Birch, Helen B Mrs, 1937, N 16,23:3
Birch, Helen L Mrs, 1938, N 8,23:2
Birch, Hugh T, 1943, Ja 9,13:5
Birch, James, 1945, Jl 18,27:3
Birch, James F N, 1939, F 4,15:2
Birch, James Mrs, 1957, My 29,27:6
Birch, James P, 1965, Je 2,45:5
Birch, John, 1937, Je 19,15:5
Birch, John H, 1950, Jl 13,25:5
Birch, John H S, 1949, Jl 24,53:1
Birch, Joseph M, 1952, N 24,23:4
Birch, Louisa Mrs, 1941, Ja 20,12:1
Birch, Marcus Mrs, 1949, Jl 1,19:4
Birch, Reginald B, 1943, Je 18,21:3
Birch, Roy, 1945, Ag 17,18:3
Birch, Stephen, 1940, D 30,17:1
Birch, Stephen M (por), 1945, Ap 11,23:4
Birch, T H, 1929, F 2,17:3
Birch, Thomas J, 1944, O 29,43:2
Birch, William F, 1946, Ja 26,13:6
Birchall, Charles, 1952, Ag 31,45:1
Birchall, Emma S Mrs, 1937, Ja 28,25:6
Birchall, Frederick T (funl plans, Mr 8,27:2; funl, Mr 12,19:3), 1955, Mr 7,27:1
Birchall, Frederick T Mrs, 1955, F 22,21:4
Birchall, John, 1941, Ja 7,23:2
Bircham, Bernard H, 1945, Jl 12,11:4
Birchansky, Leo, 1949, Mr 10,27:4
Birchard, A, 1879, S 15,5:4
Birchard, Arthur R, 1949, D 17,17:3
Birchard, Cecil C, 1951, Jl 31,22:2
Birchard, Clarence C, 1946, F 28,23:2
Birchard, Glen R, 1967, Je 5,16:1
Birchard, Glenn R, 1937, S 25,17:3
Birchard, Mary, 1942, F 10,20:4
Birchard, Matthew Mrs, 1908, N 10,9:4
Birchard, Paul I, 1959, Mr 21,21:4
Birchenough, Allen O, 1951, Mr 4,92:3
Birchenough, Harry, 1951, Mr 21,33:3
Birchenough, Henry Sir, 1937, My 13,25:5
Bircher, Rudolf P, 1966, O 6,47:4
Bircher-Brenner, M O, 1939, Ja 26,21:3
Birckhead, Fred H, 1903, D 30,7:2
Birckhead, H, 1929, Jl 11,23:5
Birckhead, Oliver W, 1962, F 17,19:4
Birckhead, Phil G, 1938, Jl 10,29:1
Bird, Adriel U, 1950, Ap 16,104:3
Bird, Alan L, 1968, N 18,47:3
Bird, Anna C Mrs, 1942, N 21,11:5
Bird, C I, 1951, N 7,29:2
Bird, C S, 1927, O 10,21:6
Bird, Charles A, 1925, N 12,25:5
Bird, Charles A Gen, 1920, Mr 23,9:6
Bird, Charles C, 1958, Je 10,33:3
Bird, Charles O, 1953, Je 26,19:4
Bird, Charles R, 1960, Ja 22,25:3
Bird, Clarence, 1950, Ap 5,31:2
Bird, Constant M, 1920, My 25,11:4
Bird, Cyrus M, 1944, Ja 3,21:1
Bird, Edith A, 1954, N 27,14:3
Bird, Edward D, 1947, O 14,27:5
Bird, Edward D Mrs, 1938, My 13,19:4
Bird, Edward J, 1937, D 16,27:6
Bird, Elias H, 1943, F 17,21:4
Bird, Elisha B, 1943, Ap 10,17:6
Bird, Elmer Mrs, 1950, Ja 25,27:3
Bird, Emerson P, 1941, Je 30,17:4
Bird, Erroll S, 1944, My 6,15:3
Bird, Ethel, 1960, O 8,23:2
Bird, Eugene H, 1960, Jl 20,29:2
Bird, Eugene S, 1953, O 20,29:5
Bird, Eustace G, 1950, Ap 4,29:2
Bird, Floyd J, 1966, My 5,48:1
Bird, Frank, 1956, D 9,89:1
Bird, Frank L, 1954, My 11,29:5
Bird, Frank W, 1950, N 8,29:3
Bird, Fred, 1951, S 20,31:2
Bird, George H, 1939, N 9,23:3
Bird, George L, 1954, S 28,29:4
Bird, George M, 1949, Ap 19,25:5
Bird, Georgianna, 1950, Jl 20,25:3
Bird, Grace E, 1955, D 2,27:5
Bird, Harriet (will), 1938, O 21,3:3
Bird, Harrison K, 1961, My 25,37:3
Bird, Harrison K Mrs, 1946, Ap 9,27:3
Bird, Harry, 1956, Ag 22,29:4
Bird, Henry, 1903, My 1,9:5
Bird, Henry D, 1966, Je 5,87:1
Bird, Herbert J, 1949, Ag 9,25:3
Bird, Hobart S, 1960, Jl 22,23:1
Bird, Hobart S Mrs, 1952, Ja 8,27:1
Bird, Ira H, 1872, F 17,3:5
Bird, J Sterling, 1944, Je 17,13:1
Bird, James Rufus Dr, 1922, Mr 29,17:5
Bird, John H, 1909, My 27,9:4
Bird, John J, 1911, My 7,II,11:4; 1964, S 19,27:4
Bird, John J Mrs, 1958, Ag 30,15:5
Bird, John W, 1951, O 29,23:5
Bird, Joseph, 1917, Mr 9,7:6
Bird, Joseph E Dr, 1937, Je 28,19:4
Bird, Joseph Edward, 1914, N 2,9:5
Bird, Joseph M Mrs, 1944, Ap 26,19:2
Bird, Leonard, 1957, Ja 23,29:4
Bird, Louis E, 1942, F 22,26:3
Bird, Louis F, 1951, Mr 11,94:5
Bird, Louis W, 1948, N 23,29:3
Bird, Lucy Mrs, 1951, Mr 11,94:5
Bird, Matthew, 1881, Ja 16,2:7
Bird, Patrick H, 1940, Ap 19,21:5
Bird, Paul, 1963, S 9,27:1; 1968, Ag 24,29:4
Bird, Phil, 1948, Je 11,23:2
Bird, Ralph P, 1940, F 27,21:6
Bird, Robert M, 1942, My 10,42:7
Bird, Robert T, 1941, Mr 22,15:6
Bird, Roger P, 1945, Jl 2,15:3
Bird, S Curtis, 1963, S 3,33:3
Bird, Samuel, 1951, Mr 7,33:3
Bird, Sarah L A Mrs, 1939, Mr 7,21:3
Bird, Stanley P, 1968, D 30,31:4
Bird, Thomas, 1952, Mr 20,29:5
Bird, Thomas F Sr, 1954, D 8,35:3
Bird, Thomas J, 1943, Ap 24,13:1
Bird, Timothy J, 1938, Jl 16,13:5
Bird, W Gillette, 1941, Jl 3,19:6
Bird, Walter R Mrs, 1957, Ag 29,27:4
Bird, Wellington D Mrs, 1950, N 2,31:3
Bird, Whitworth F, 1968, Ja 16,39:3
Bird, William, 1903, D 21,7:5; 1963, Ag 6,31:2
Bird, William E, 1950, F 20,25:4
Bird, William H Mrs, 1949, O 22,17:5
Bird, William S, 1948, Jl 22,23:1; 1966, O 24,39:3
Birdlebough, Laverne, 1949, Jl 12,27:3
Birdlebough, Laverne Mrs, 1949, Jl 12,27:3
Birdoff, Harry Mrs, 1953, Ja 6,29:5
Birdsall, Albert T Dr, 1913, S 25,13:4
Birdsall, Andrew F, 1947, My 30,21:2
Birdsall, Annie F Mrs, 1938, Jl 26,19:4
Birdsall, Arthur M, 1955, F 27,87:2
Birdsall, Carl A, 1956, N 20,37:5
Birdsall, Catherine B, 1946, Je 25,21:4
Birdsall, Charles H, 1965, Ja 12,37:2
Birdsall, Clarence Jr, 1947, My 21,25:5
Birdsall, Claude H, 1939, Ag 29,21:6
Birdsall, D Kingsley, 1952, N 11,30:3
Birdsall, Daniel, 1920, O 26,17:4
Birdsall, E T, 1933, N 7,23:3
Birdsall, Edward, 1949, Ap 28,31:2
Birdsall, Estella J, 1941, Ap 29,19:5
Birdsall, George W, 1911, Ja 24,9:5; 1967, Je 2,41:3
Birdsall, Godfrey, 1948, N 19,27:2
Birdsall, Herbert, 1955, F 6,88:4
Birdsall, Hudson, 1944, O 27,23:4
Birdsall, J Lewiston, 1938, S 1,23:5
Birdsall, Joel M Mrs, 1941, F 2,45:2
Birdsall, Joseph, 1938, O 2,49:2
Birdsall, Lawrence E, 1945, N 16,19:2
Birdsall, Lester J, 1949, S 8,29:5
Birdsall, Luther, 1908, Jl 29,7:4
Birdsall, M, 1944, Je 14,19:5
Birdsall, Sam, 1882, My 30,5:5
Birdsall, William E, 1954, Ap 10,15:3
Birdsall, William J, 1947, Mr 2,60:3
Birdsall, William W Prof, 1909, Mr 18,9:5
Birdsell, J Frank Mrs, 1957, N 15,28:3
Birdsell, Rudolph W, 1937, Ag 11,24:2
Birdseye, Clarence, 1956, O 9,35:4
Birdseye, Claude H, 1941, Je 1,41:1
Birdseye, Henry M, 1964, Ag 20,29:1
Birdseye, Lewis E Sr, 1942, D 25,18:2
Birdsong, John M Mrs, 1956, O 25,33:5
Birdsong, Silas A, 1953, Ap 2,27:2
Birdwell, Russell Jr, 1946, Ag 16,21:3
Birdwell, Russell Mrs, 1965, Ja 23,25:1
Birdwood, Christopher B, 1962, Ja 8,39:5
Birdwood, George Sir, 1917, Je 30,11:6
Birdwood, William R, 1951, My 18,27:1
Bireley, Frank W, 1960, O 22,23:5
Birely, Charles W, 1951, My 5,17:1
Biren, Henry S, 1954, Jl 31,13:5
Biren, Robert I, 1963, Jl 16,31:4
Birenbach, Samuel, 1950, N 27,25:5
Birge, Charles, 1942, N 23,23:3
Birge, Edward S, 1958, Jl 8,28:1
Birge, J Kingsley, 1952, Ag 17,77:1
Birge, Julius, 1958, Ja 30,49:3
Birge, Morton B, 1941, Mr 24,17:4
Birge, Nathan R, 1950, Ap 9,84:3
Birge, Walt W, 1952, Je 15,84:5
Birge, William R, 1957, Ag 5,21:2
Birgess, Wilfrid L, 1937, Ag 19,19:5
Birgfeld, Adolph, 1874, F 5,2:6
Biringer, Edward, 1955, S 9,23:5
Biringer, Henry F, 1958, Ag 9,13:4
Birinyi, Louis K, 1941, S 5,21:1
Birk, Benedict, 1946, Ag 16,21:2
Birk, Benjamin J, 1947, Je 30,19:1
Birk, Louis C Mrs, 1957, O 10,33:3
Birk, Louis P, 1953, Je 20,17:6
Birke, William D, 1963, My 31,25:1
Birkel, A Henry Mrs, 1953, O 6,29:1
Birkenhauer, John, 1950, S 5,27:4
Birkenhead, Earl of, 1930, O 1,17:1
Birkenmeier, August G, 1951, D 12,37:3
Birkenstock, Gregory J, 1951, Ag 23,25:7
Birkett, Edwin K, 1950, My 15,21:5
Birkett, H S, 1942, Jl 20,13:1
Birkett, James R, 1956, My 16,35:3
Birkett, Lillian, 1943, F 23,21:4
Birkett, Norman, 1962, F 12,23:4
Birkett, Raymond J, 1938, Ap 25,15:3
Birkhead, Leon M, 1954, D 2,31:3
Birkhead, May, 1941, O 29,24:2
Birkhimer, William Edward Brig-Gen, 1914, Je 11,11:6
Birkhoff, George D, 1944, N 13,19:5
Birkholz, Benjamin L, 1938, Je 24,19:3
Birkholz, Chester R, 1964, Jl 8,35:4
Birkholz, Joseph A, 1949, My 18,27:5

Birkholz, Joseph A Mrs, 1954, F 23,27:3
Birkigt, Marc, 1953, Mr 16,19:2
Birkinbine, Carl P, 1942, F 28,17:3
Birkinbine, John, 1915, My 15,13:6
Birkinbine, John L W, 1938, Jl 18,13:5
Birkinbine, Olaf W, 1950, Ag 23,29:4
Birkmire, William H, 1924, F 10,23:3
Birks, Gerald W, 1950, O 14,19:2
Birks, John E, 1948, Mr 20,13:5
Birks, John H M, 1949, Mr 25,23:2
Birks, T R, 1883, Jl 23,5:4
Birks, William M, 1950, Jl 6,27:6
Birla, Jugan K, 1967, Je 25,68:4
Birla, Raja B, 1956, Ap 2,23:4
Birley, Oswald, 1952, My 7,27:3
Birling, Leon B, 1947, Je 4,27:4
Birman, Philip E, 1947, D 14,76:4
Birmingham, Daniel Moschel Rev Dr (funl, Je 28,9:6), 1915, Je 20,15:6
Birmingham, Edward H, 1950, N 19,93:1
Birmingham, Edward J, 1955, Jl 31,68:3
Birmingham, Edward S, 1911, Mr 20,9:5
Birmingham, Frank, 1945, O 31,23:5
Birmingham, George A, 1950, F 3,23:2
Birmingham, Harry C, 1947, D 31,15:2
Birmingham, J Edward, 1954, Jl 19,19:3
Birmingham, James B, 1952, D 19,32:3
Birmingham, James F, 1925, N 14,15:4
Birmingham, John, 1939, O 13,23:2
Birmingham, John F, 1950, N 9,33:1
Birmingham, Louise de Viscountess, 1877, Je 27,8:5
Birmingham, Mark, 1914, D 24,9:4
Birmingham, Martin J, 1959, Mr 25,35:1
Birmingham, Mary, 1945, S 1,11:3
Birmingham, Michael J, 1964, F 4,33:2
Birmingham, Richard, 1952, Je 11,29:5
Birmingham, Rose A, 1939, Ja 23,13:4
Birmingham, Stirling, 1938, O 3,15:6
Birmingham, Thomas, 1912, S 27,13:5
Birmingham, Thomas F, 1949, My 2,25:5
Birmingham, Thomas J, 1951, O 20,15:7
Birmingham, William G, 1958, F 16,86:5
Birn, A Otto, 1953, Ap 18,19:3
Birn, Edward S, 1952, S 3,29:5
Birnbach, Fred, 1942, N 4,23:4
Birnback, Ralph J, 1961, F 7,33:2
Birnbaum, Abe, 1966, Je 20,30:3
Birnbaum, Abraham, 1964, F 5,35:4
Birnbaum, Emanuel, 1960, Ja 5,31:4
Birnbaum, Gipel Mrs, 1937, D 4,17:4
Birnbaum, Joyce E, 1960, F 14,84:5
Birnbaum, Karl K, 1950, Ap 2,94:5
Birnbaum, Louis, 1961, N 30,34:6
Birnbaum, Louis H, 1966, D 30,25:3
Birnbaum, Nathan Dr, 1937, Ap 5,19:6
Birnbaum, Philip S, 1947, D 6,15:6
Birnbaum, Rubin, 1950, My 28,44:8
Birnbaum, Samuel M, 1961, Mr 7,35:4
Birnbaum, Uriel, 1956, D 11,39:1
Birney, Bryan T, 1944, F 17,19:3
Birney, Charles O, 1939, Ja 6,22:2
Birney, D B Maj-Gen, 1864, O 20,4:5
Birney, Frank C Ensign, 1871, Jl 19,8:2
Birney, Hoffman, 1958, Je 4,31:1
Birney, Josephine Mrs, 1915, My 7,13:6
Birney, Lauress J Bishop, 1937, My 11,25:3
Birney, Theodore William Mrs (Alice M Birney), 1907, D 21,9:5
Birney, William W, 1954, My 13,29:3
Birnholz, James, 1956, D 14,29:5
Birnholz, Marco, 1965, S 6,15:6
Birnie, Christine, 1953, F 26,30:4
Birnie, Douglas P Rev Dr, 1937, Mr 22,23:6
Birnie, Harold T, 1960, F 26,27:3
Birnie, James, 1951, D 30,24:3
Birnie, James J, 1951, My 15,31:4
Birnie, Loraine F H Mrs, 1940, Ap 14,45:1
Birnie, Robert A, 1949, My 19,29:4
Birnie, Rogers, 1939, S 27,25:2
Birnie, Samuel G, 1938, S 9,21:1
Birnie, Upton, 1957, O 18,23:1
Birns, Saul, 1963, O 15,40:1
Birns, Stanley, 1914, Jl 17,9:4
Birns, William, 1948, Ja 11,56:4
Biro, Benedict, 1952, Ja 18,27:4
Biro, Ernest P, 1965, D 28,27:4
Biroli, Alessandro P, 1962, My 22,37:3
Biroli, Luigi N P, 1952, Je 8,87:1
Biron, Benjamin, 1954, Ap 20,29:2
Birrell, A, 1933, N 21,19:1
Birrell, Augustine Mrs, 1915, Mr 11,11:4
Birrell, George V, 1945, O 21,46:1
Birs, Alonzo Mrs, 1942, Ag 25,23:4
Birsh, Abraham S, 1952, F 19,29:1
Birstein, Bernard, 1959, Jl 10,25:3
Birsztien, Stanley A, 1954, Jl 14,27:2
Birt, Albert E, 1964, My 16,25:2
Birtchiel, Charles E, 1939, Ag 23,21:6
Birtles, Francis, 1941, Jl 2,21:6
Birtwhistle, Hezekiah, 1911, O 9,11:5
Birtwhistle, Thomas, 1907, F 26,11:6
Biryuzov, Sergei S, 1964, O 20,1:7
Bisbane, L L Mrs, 1904, Ja 23,9:5
Bisbe y Alberni, Manuel (funl plans, Mr 22,3:1), 1961, Mr 21,7:2
Bisbee, Edgar C, 1957, Ag 1,25:3
Bisbee, Eldon, 1952, Ja 8,27:3
Bisbee, Eldon Mrs, 1949, D 14,31:1
Bisbee, Eleanor, 1956, Ap 20,25:2
Bisbee, Frederick A Rev Dr, 1923, N 27,19:1
Bisbee, Frederick C, 1940, O 23,23:6
Bisbee, Genevieve, 1955, Ag 4,25:5
Bisbee, H Rev, 1879, Jl 8,2:7
Bisbee, Harlan N, 1954, Ap 28,31:1
Bisbee, Marvin Davis Rev Dr, 1913, S 2,7:7
Bisbee, Spaulding, 1958, Ag 30,15:6
Bisbee, Warren A, 1941, O 3,23:2
Bisbee, William H, 1942, Je 12,21:1
Bisbing, H S, 1933, N 28,21:3
Biscardi, Alphonso, 1952, O 11,19:2
Biscaretti, Roberto Count, 1940, Ag 14,19:6
Bisceglia, Alphonse F, 1952, Ap 10,29:3
Bisch, Louis E, 1963, S 8,86:4
Bischke, Julius, 1949, Mr 19,15:2
Bischof, Charles M, 1961, O 4,45:3
Bischof, George J, 1953, F 27,21:3
Bischoff, Alfred M, 1950, Je 29,29:4
Bischoff, Carl, 1940, N 29,21:2
Bischoff, Charles J, 1959, F 18,33:2
Bischoff, Edward T, 1940, My 26,35:2
Bischoff, Ernest A, 1958, Jl 8,27:3
Bischoff, Henry, 1902, Mr 8,9:5
Bischoff, Henry Justice, 1913, Mr 31,13:5
Bischoff, Henry S, 1947, Mr 13,27:4
Bischoff, Henry W, 1945, N 6,19:3
Bischoff, John H, 1967, Ja 22,76:4
Bischoff, John M Sr, 1950, O 7,19:4
Bischoff, John W, 1925, My 22,19:6
Bischoff, John W Dr, 1909, My 31,7:7
Bischoff, Morris, 1939, Ja 27,19:1
Bischoff, Norbert, 1960, Jl 2,17:4
Bischoff, Otto J, 1953, My 12,27:1
Bischoff, R, 1934, F 2,17:3
Bischoff, Robert Mrs, 1961, F 6,23:2
Bischoff, Rudolph, 1953, Ja 12,27:3
Bischoffsheim, Banker of Paris, 1873, N 15,1:7
Biscoe, Earl, 1964, N 22,86:4
Biscoe, Earl Mrs, 1959, Ap 23,31:3
Biscoe, Howard M, 1951, Mr 26,23:5
Biscoll, George, 1953, Ag 6,21:5
Biscuccia-VillaFranca, Silvio N Count, 1918, My 16, 13:6
Biseo, Attilio, 1966, Jl 9,27:6
Bisgood, Arthur G, 1963, Ap 5,47:3
Bisgyer, Gustave, 1967, Ja 4,43:2
Bisgyer, Sarah F Mrs, 1941, N 1,15:5
Bish, Frederick F, 1954, Ag 10,19:6
Bisher, Peter Dr, 1953, F 18,31:3
Bishof, Anthony E Mrs, 1941, Je 4,13:5
Bishop, A McC Lt Commander, 1885, Ap 24,5:4
Bishop, A Thornton, 1958, O 3,29:2
Bishop, Alfred L Mrs, 1958, My 27,31:3
Bishop, Alice, 1924, S 21,29:1
Bishop, Ancil H, 1956, Jl 31,23:2
Bishop, Archibald S, 1961, Jl 13,29:5
Bishop, Arete, 1942, D 23,19:4
Bishop, Arthur C, 1953, Ja 3,15:6
Bishop, Arthur G, 1944, Ja 23,38:1
Bishop, Arthur V, 1955, Ja 7,21:5
Bishop, B, 1935, Ja 27,27:5
Bishop, Benjamin L, 1946, F 13,23:3
Bishop, Bernice P, 1884, N 14,5:4
Bishop, Burton T, 1945, Ag 11,13:2
Bishop, C F, 1935, Mr 31,36:1
Bishop, Carl, 1946, Jl 28,39:1
Bishop, Carl W, 1942, Je 17,23:5
Bishop, Carlos E, 1946, Jl 9,21:3
Bishop, Cassius, 1952, Jl 15,21:4
Bishop, Charles, 1959, O 20,40:1
Bishop, Charles King, 1904, Mr 3,9:6
Bishop, Charles M, 1948, F 25,23:2; 1949, D 2,29:5
Bishop, Charles P, 1951, Mr 19,27:5
Bishop, Chester, 1937, My 24,19:2
Bishop, Clarence A, 1945, Ap 5,23:5
Bishop, Clifford E, 1962, Jl 28,19:3
Bishop, Clifford M, 1960, Mr 23,37:2
Bishop, Coleman Mrs, 1916, N 23,13:4
Bishop, Cornelius W, 1962, N 6,33:3
Bishop, Cortland Field, 1911, D 2,13:4
Bishop, Davis Jr Mrs, 1923, S 29,7:2
Bishop, Dwight S, 1967, O 19,47:1
Bishop, E F, 1883, D 8,1:2
Bishop, Edgar R, 1947, Ja 23,26:2
Bishop, Edith, 1943, Ja 30,15:2
Bishop, Edward C, 1944, O 27,23:5
Bishop, Edward E, 1944, Mr 8,19:4
Bishop, Edwin, 1946, Jl 21,40:2
Bishop, Elizabeth C Mrs, 1953, D 16,35:1
Bishop, Elliot, 1954, Jl 26,17:1
Bishop, Elwell Alexander Dr, 1925, D 23,19:4
Bishop, Emily, 1912, Mr 3,15:3
Bishop, Ernest E, 1948, Je 15,27:3
Bishop, Ernest H, 1951, Ja 30,25:4
Bishop, Ernest Simons Dr, 1926, N 17,25:4
Bishop, Eugene L, 1951, F 28,27:3
Bishop, F Warner, 1947, Mr 24,25:1
Bishop, Floyd D, 1947, D 18,29:2
Bishop, Francis C Mrs, 1953, O 15,33:5
Bishop, Francis Nathaniel Holmes, 1968, Ja 27,29:5
Bishop, Frank, 1944, F 1,20:2; 1944, Ag 14,15:3
Bishop, Fred A, 1961, Ag 28,25:5
Bishop, Fred S, 1951, S 29,17:1
Bishop, Frederic L, 1947, O 13,23:4
Bishop, Frederick A, 1941, Ja 26,38:3
Bishop, Geneva Johnstone, 1923, D 22,13:3
Bishop, George, 1947, Mr 16,60:1; 1953, O 4,32:3
Bishop, George D, 1943, N 28,68:3
Bishop, George E, 1959, Ap 12,86:4
Bishop, George F, 1939, D 6,25:5; 1954, Jl 21,27:3
Bishop, George H Jr, 1952, Je 16,17:2
Bishop, George R, 1959, Ja 7,33:4
Bishop, George S Rev Dr, 1914, Mr 13,9:4
Bishop, George T, 1940, Ag 26,15:1
Bishop, Gertrude A Goewey Dr, 1921, S 7,13:4
Bishop, Gilbert C, 1941, S 28,49:3
Bishop, Gilbert L Jr, 1941, D 27,19:4
Bishop, Giles Col, 1925, Ap 11,13:4
Bishop, Harold L, 1940, Ag 8,19:5
Bishop, Harold S, 1943, O 24,44:6
Bishop, Harry F, 1950, Jl 10,21:1
Bishop, Harry Mrs, 1949, F 15,24:3
Bishop, Heber R, 1902, D 11,9:3
Bishop, Henry, 1907, N 4,9:5; 1937, O 5,25:4; 1938, Jl 31,33:4; 1939, Mr 7,21:3; 1944, N 30,23:5
Bishop, Henry A Mrs, 1944, Je 19,19:4
Bishop, Henry F, 1910, Ja 15,9:4
Bishop, Henry G, 1964, S 25,41:4
Bishop, Henry M, 1957, Ap 21,89:1
Bishop, Henry O, 1954, Ag 3,19:4
Bishop, Howard B, 1961, F 8,31:2
Bishop, Howard E, 1943, Jl 26,19:2
Bishop, Howard F, 1946, N 18,23:4
Bishop, Hubert E, 1949, My 21,13:2
Bishop, Hutchens C Rev, 1937, My 19,23:4
Bishop, Isabella Bird, 1904, O 8,9:1
Bishop, J, 1879, Ja 30,8:3
Bishop, J A, 1944, N 13,19:5
Bishop, J B, 1928, D 14,29:3
Bishop, J M, 1910, Jl 11,7:5
Bishop, J R T, 1956, Ja 24,31:4
Bishop, J Warren, 1944, O 29,44:2
Bishop, Jacob, 1952, D 13,21:6
Bishop, James F, 1948, N 11,27:2
Bishop, James H, 1961, My 13,44:1
Bishop, Jane E Dr, 1922, Ap 12,21:6
Bishop, Jennie Mrs, 1957, Ag 6,27:5
Bishop, Jim Mrs, 1957, O 11,27:2
Bishop, John A, 1958, Mr 16,87:1
Bishop, John H, 1940, O 25,21:1
Bishop, John J, 1952, Ag 11,15:6
Bishop, John M Mrs, 1908, N 27,9:4
Bishop, John P, 1944, Ap 6,23:6
Bishop, John T, 1945, N 17,17:4
Bishop, John W, 1923, O 23,21:4
Bishop, John W Mrs, 1956, Mr 26,29:3
Bishop, Joseph E, 1959, Je 25,29:2
Bishop, Joseph L, 1938, F 24,19:5
Bishop, Julian T, 1966, S 9,45:1
Bishop, Justin L, 1939, My 16,23:4
Bishop, L A H, 1943, Mr 14,26:2
Bishop, L O, 1937, S 7,21:5
Bishop, Leo, 1941, Je 19,21:1
Bishop, Louis F, 1941, O 7,23:1
Bishop, Lucie Mrs, 1940, N 6,23:2
Bishop, Mabel L, 1946, D 1,78:3
Bishop, Mariano, 1953, Ja 3,15:2
Bishop, Mary C, 1948, F 4,24:1
Bishop, Mary F, 1939, Mr 18,17:3
Bishop, Mary R Mrs, 1939, D 7,27:5
Bishop, Matthew H, 1945, Ap 25,23:4
Bishop, Maude E Mrs, 1937, Mr 22,23:2
Bishop, Max, 1962, F 26,27:3
Bishop, Merle J, 1962, Jl 8,64:4
Bishop, Morgan E, 1958, Je 23,23:4
Bishop, Mortimer, 1942, S 16,15:5
Bishop, Nathan, 1880, Ag 8,5:6
Bishop, Nathaniel W Mrs, 1947, D 21,52:5
Bishop, Oakes E, 1955, Mr 14,23:2
Bishop, Ogden M, 1955, S 23,26:6
Bishop, Paul R, 1949, Ap 3,76:2
Bishop, Philip E, 1964, My 13,47:5
Bishop, Reed R, 1950, F 3,23:5
Bishop, Richard, 1953, N 16,25:5; 1956, My 29,27:2
Bishop, Robert E, 1950, Ja 29,68:3
Bishop, Robert F, 1942, O 6,23:4
Bishop, Robert H Jr, 1955, S 30,25:2
Bishop, Robert Mrs, 1955, S 26,23:4
Bishop, Roswell P, 1920, Mr 5,13:5
Bishop, Roy N, 1938, D 21,23:6
Bishop, Roy T, 1950, Je 25,70:2
Bishop, Rufus F, 1953, D 11,31:5
Bishop, Samuel Henry (funl), 1914, Je 1,11:6
Bishop, Samuel R, 1963, My 4,25:1
Bishop, Sarah E Mrs, 1937, Ja 21,23:4
Bishop, Seth Scott Dr, 1923, S 7,15:4
Bishop, Shelton H (funl plans, Ag 30,29:2; funl, Ag 31,21:4), 1962, Ag 25,19:5
Bishop, Sherman C, 1951, My 29,25:3
Bishop, Simon K, 1944, Jl 16,31:4

Bishop, Stanley W, 1951, Je 8,27:1
Bishop, Storrs M, 1940, Jl 10,19:3
Bishop, Theodore Sr, 1937, F 7,II,9:2
Bishop, Thomas J, 1958, Jl 31,23:4
Bishop, Victor, 1876, Mr 12,7:5
Bishop, W Howard, 1953, Je 12,27:2
Bishop, W I (funl), 1889, My 14,8:1
Bishop, W M Mrs, 1949, D 23,21:4
Bishop, Walter, 1956, Ja 17,33:5
Bishop, Warren L, 1939, D 18,23:4
Bishop, William, 1959, O 4,87:1
Bishop, William A (funl, S 16,85:1), 1956, S 12,37:1
Bishop, William A, 1957, Jl 10,27:3
Bishop, William A Col, 1919, Mr 19,11:2
Bishop, William A Mrs, 1949, Mr 8,25:2
Bishop, William D, 1904, F 5,3:3; 1912, Ja 24,11:4
Bishop, William Franklin, 1923, O 30,19:3
Bishop, William H, 1909, Mr 8,7:4; 1943, Mr 10,19:1
Bishop, William H Jr, 1923, Ap 14,13:4
Bishop, William H Mrs, 1912, S 16,13:6
Bishop, William I, 1941, O 1,21:3
Bishop, William J, 1948, Ag 17,21:4
Bishop, William M Mrs, 1944, Ap 17,23:4
Bishop, William S, 1944, Mr 16,19:5
Bishop, William W, 1955, F 22,21:2
Bishop, Yale D, 1943, S 27,19:5
Bishop-Schultz, Anna, 1884, Mr 20,5:4
Bishopp, Newton C, 1946, Ag 27,27:3
Biskey, Walter H Mrs, 1961, Je 28,35:1
Bisland, Margaret W, 1953, Je 22,22:7
Bisland, Pressley E, 1947, Jl 25,17:2
Bisland, Pressly E Mrs, 1950, Ja 27,23:3
Bisland, Thomas Sheilds, 1908, Jl 18,7:5
Bisleti, Gaetano Card, 1937, Ag 31,23:1
Bismarck, Herbert Prince, 1904, S 19,7:5
Bismarck, Johanna F C E Princess, 1894, N 28,5:2
Bismarck, Prince Wife of, 1873, S 23,5:5
Bismarck, William Count, 1901, My 31,6:2
Bispham, Charles P, 1939, Ap 27,25:6
Bispham, David, 1921, O 3,13:3
Bispham, David Charles, 1917, N 7,13:2
Bispham, David S Mrs, 1943, O 27,23:5
Bispham, George T, 1949, Mr 30,25:3
Bispham, George Tucker, 1906, Jl 29,9:6
Bispham, H C, 1882, D 23,4:7
Bispham, Harrison A, 1960, Ap 26,37:4
Bisschop, Willem R, 1944, F 24,15:5
Bissel, Frederick, 1946, N 29,25:2
Bissel, George Edwin, 1920, Ag 31,9:1
Bissel, Mary Mrs, 1923, Ap 26,19:5
Bissel, W H Gov, 1860, Mr 22,5:1
Bissell, Addison H, 1952, N 22,23:4
Bissell, Addison H Sr Mrs, 1956, Jl 16,21:1
Bissell, Alliston P, 1944, Jl 6,15:6
Bissell, Arthur H Mrs, 1958, Mr 10,23:1
Bissell, Arthur T, 1942, F 7,17:5
Bissell, Charles M, 1909, Ag 6,7:4
Bissell, Chester W, 1962, Ag 15,31:1
Bissell, Clarence H, 1912, Jl 3,11:6
Bissell, Clinton T, 1956, F 16,29:4
Bissell, Dwight E, 1956, My 9,33:4
Bissell, Elias, 1937, D 7,25:4
Bissell, Elmer J, 1940, Ja 5,20:2
Bissell, Emily P, 1948, Mr 9,24:2
Bissell, Eugene, 1909, Ag 30,7:5
Bissell, Frank, 1943, Ag 17,17:3
Bissell, Frank H, 1957, D 21,19:4
Bissell, Frederick E, 1958, D 29,15:3
Bissell, George Capt, 1909, N 5,9:4
Bissell, George E, 1920, S 2,9:2
Bissell, George P, 1952, Ap 3,36:3
Bissell, H Woodruff, 1955, F 21,21:4
Bissell, Harold W, 1955, D 7,39:2
Bissell, Harry, 1921, N 30,17:4
Bissell, Herbert P, 1919, My 1,17:5
Bissell, Howard, 1937, O 25,19:3
Bissell, Irving J, 1961, My 16,37:2
Bissell, John B Mrs, 1960, Mr 20,87:1
Bissell, John Henry, 1925, O 12,21:5
Bissell, Joseph Bidleman Maj, 1918, D 3,15:4
Bissell, Joseph H, 1962, O 25,39:3
Bissell, Leon, 1947, Je 27,22:3
Bissell, Luther B, 1941, My 10,15:4
Bissell, Nicol Mrs, 1959, My 5,33:4
Bissell, Pelham S, 1943, S 9,25:3
Bissell, Pelham S Mrs, 1948, Ja 29,23:2
Bissell, Pelham St George Rev, 1918, Ap 3,13:4
Bissell, Richard M, 1941, Jl 19,13:3
Bissell, Robert A, 1947, Ap 4,23:3
Bissell, Robert P, 1962, Ap 14,25:1
Bissell, Robinson K, 1948, Je 13,69:1
Bissell, Washington, 1923, Mr 24,13:5
Bissell, Whit Mrs, 1958, Ja 12,87:1
Bissell, William E, 1949, F 10,27:2
Bissell, William G Dr, 1919, N 15,11:3
Bissell, Wilson S, 1903, O 7,9:5
Bisset, George S, 1949, Je 27,27:2
Bisset, Thomas B, 1925, S 22,25:4
Bisset, William J Jr, 1945, Ag 7,23:1
Bissett, Clyde A, 1945, Je 14,19:2
Bissett, Enid Mrs, 1965, Ap 26,31:1
Bissett, Florence G, 1946, Ja 31,21:3
Bissett, J J Dr, 1915, Jl 21,11:4
Bissett, Roderick J, 1952, Mr 1,15:4
Bissier, Julius, 1965, Je 19,29:4
Bissiere, Roger, 1964, D 4,40:3
Bissig, Aug, 1949, Je 2,28:6
Bissig, Charles, 1949, Ja 18,24:2
Bissing, Harry Mrs, 1963, Ap 7,86:3
Bissing, Moritz Ferdinand von Gen, 1917, Ap 19,15:6
Bissinger, Allan H, 1944, F 28,17:3
Bissland, John R, 1922, Jl 27,17:5
Bissolati, Leonida, 1920, My 7,11:2
Bisson, Alexandre Charles, 1912, Ja 29,11:4
Bisson, Louis A, 1953, Je 26,19:1
Bisson, Percival N, 1949, Ap 14,1:1
Bissonnette, Thomas H, 1951, D 2,90:3
Bissonnette, Wesley S, 1943, Ja 20,19:4
Bistany, Khalil A, 1940, Je 22,15:2
Bistor, James E, 1945, Mr 5,19:1
Bistrong, Charles, 1966, Je 4,29:3
Bistrong, Jacob, 1952, My 2,25:3
Bistrong, Jacob Mrs, 1951, S 1,11:2
Bistrong, Joseph, 1957, Je 5,35:5
Bistrong, Nathan H, 1968, My 21,47:3
Bistrup, Frank V, 1949, O 1,13:5
Biswanger, Wilhelmina, 1948, Ja 30,23:2
Bitar, Thomas K, 1950, S 13,27:5
Bitensky, Abraham, 1968, Jl 22,35:4
Bitensky, Abraham Mrs, 1966, O 14,43:2
Bitgood, Ellsworth M, 1952, Ja 20,84:8
Bitker, Jacob L, 1945, D 6,27:4
Bitler, Reuben O Commodore, 1937, Je 24,25:5
Bitner, Edgar F, 1939, Ap 13,23:2
Bitner, Harry M, 1960, Mr 8,24:3
Bitomley, Frank P, 1950, Jl 30,61:2
Bitte, George, 1947, Ap 16,25:1
Bittel, John J, 1938, Ja 20,23:6
Bittenbender, Glace, 1957, Ap 17,31:5
Bittenbender, H A, 1945, Mr 9,19:1
Bittenbinder, Michael Mrs, 1949, Mr 5,18:3
Bittencourt, Paulo, 1963, Ag 3,17:3
Bittenfeld, Herwarth von, 1943, Ja 1,23:4
Bitter, Francis, 1967, Jl 27,35:1
Bitter, Francis Mrs (R Devi), 1958, Jl 15,25:5
Bitter, Marguerite, 1950, Ja 10,29:2
Bitterman, Louis, 1942, O 14,25:1
Bitterman, Peter J Jr, 1942, D 11,23:4
Bitterman, Samuel, 1958, Ag 14,29:5
Bitterman, Sidney, 1951, F 7,29:5
Bitting, Franklin B, 1956, Je 25,23:3
Bitting, Fred E, 1953, My 22,27:2
Bitting, Mary L E, 1940, My 24,13:6
Bitting, Samuel T, 1960, Mr 30,37:1
Bitting, William, 1941, Jl 18,19:4
Bitting, William C, 1940, O 19,17:4
Bittinger, Albert, 1922, Je 29,15:5
Bittinger, Benjamin F Rev, 1913, S 21,II,15:4
Bittinger, J E, 1942, F 17,21:2
Bittinger, Leigh N, 1960, S 25,88:6
Bittle, Oscar T, 1947, Mr 23,60:7
Bittles, Francis L, 1937, N 19,23:2
Bittles, William, 1943, Ag 31,17:6
Bittmann, Charles, 1964, Ja 15,31:1
Bittner, Frederick J, 1943, Ap 24,13:2
Bittner, George, 1943, D 14,27:3
Bittner, Herbert G, 1960, Jl 14,27:6
Bittner, John J, 1961, D 15,37:3
Bittner, Julius, 1939, Ja 11,19:2
Bittner, Van A, 1949, Jl 20,25:1
Bittner, W Emmet, 1949, S 4,41:2
Bittong, R Arthur, 1945, D 22,19:4
Bittorf, Max, 1953, Ap 3,23:3
Bitts, W A, 1884, Jl 28,1:3
Bitz, Herbert G, 1956, D 17,31:4
Bitzer, Charles J, 1968, Je 7,39:1
Bitzer, G W, 1944, My 2,19:1
Bitzer, George L, 1951, Ja 5,22:2
Bitzig, Ferdinand Mrs, 1949, D 2,29:5
Bitzky, Louis F, 1952, Je 29,56:4
Bivens, Burke, 1967, N 9,47:3
Bivens, James R, 1956, S 21,25:2
Bivings, William T, 1943, Je 16,21:4
Bivins, Alice E, 1937, D 21,23:4
Bivins, L, 1929, Ja 18,23:4
Bix, Bert J (will), 1950, Ja 21,30:5
Bixbee, William Johnson, 1921, Jl 15,11:7
Bixby, Allen B, 1941, D 3,25:6
Bixby, Bert J, 1948, S 8,29:5
Bixby, Clayton E, 1956, O 5,25:3
Bixby, David E, 1947, Ap 5,19:1
Bixby, Dianna Mrs, 1955, Ja 4,7:2
Bixby, Edson K, 1940, Mr 18,17:4
Bixby, Frank E, 1958, O 1,37:5
Bixby, Frank L, 1918, F 9,15:8
Bixby, Fred H, 1952, My 18,92:4
Bixby, George H Mrs, 1946, Ja 2,19:4
Bixby, Harold M, 1965, N 20,35:2
Bixby, Herbert D, 1949, Ja 25,23:2
Bixby, James S, 1967, F 23,35:2
Bixby, James Thompson Rev, 1921, D 28,15:5
Bixby, Joel H, 1940, D 2,23:4
Bixby, Joseph, 1948, Je 26,17:3
Bixby, Jotham W, 1945, Ja 28,38:5
Bixby, Laura R Mrs, 1958, Ja 11,17:3
Bixby, Leland C, 1949, Ja 10,25:1
Bixby, Llewellyn, 1942, Ja 27,21:5
Bixby, Raymond O, 1961, My 23,39:4
Bixby, Samuel M, 1912, Mr 12,13:4
Bixby, W H, 1928, S 30,31:5
Bixby, W K, 1931, O 30,23:1
Bixby, William H, 1967, S 12,47:1
Bixio, Gen, 1873, D 21,1:7
Bixio, O, 1877, F 4,2:5
Bixler, Albert G, 1943, My 27,25:4
Bixler, Albert G Mrs, 1952, Jl 1,23:4
Bixler, C E Mrs, 1940, My 24,19:4
Bixler, Cassius E, 1952, D 9,33:6
Bixler, Frank, 1921, S 7,13:4
Bixler, Harry C, 1965, Jl 3,19:5
Bixler, Heister C, 1949, Ag 20,11:6
Bixler, James W, 1943, Ag 24,19:1
Bixler, Rena C, 1942, Ap 8,19:3
Bixy, Alfred L, 1942, D 16,25:7
Bize, L A, 1946, Ja 11,22:2
Bizel, Frederick W, 1949, Mr 29,25:3
Bizel, John S, 1938, O 21,23:4
Bizzarri, Ubaldo L, 1955, Ap 6,29:4
Bizzell, James A, 1944, N 3,21:5
Bizzell, William B, 1944, My 15,19:6
Bjarnasoin, Leifus B, 1954, F 13,13:1
Bjerknes, Vilhelm, 1951, Ap 11,29:3
Bjerre, Paul, 1964, Jl 17,27:2
Bjerregaard, Carl Henry, 1922, Ja 29,22:3
Bjerregaard, James A, 1958, Ag 15,21:2
Bjoerling, Jussi (funl, S 20,39:2), 1960, S 10,21:1
Bjoernson, Bjoern, 1942, Ap 24,17:8
Bjoernsson, Sveinn, 1952, Ja 26,13:1
Bjork, David K, 1962, Mr 7,35:1
Bjork, Oscar, 1945, Ag 19,40:3
Bjork, R William, 1964, Ag 10,31:1
Bjork, Waino, 1950, Jl 11,31:3
Bjorklund, C Arthur, 1956, Jl 29,65:1
Bjorkman, Carl, 1961, Jl 27,31:5
Bjorkman, Carl E, 1947, O 31,23:3
Bjorkman, Carol, 1967, Jl 6,35:1
Bjorkman, Edwin, 1951, N 17,17:7
Bjorkman, Gordon S, 1966, O 25,48:2
Bjorkman, Olaf, 1946, Mr 7,25:4
Bjorkman, Valentine, 1939, Jl 12,19:5
Bjorksten, Walter, 1953, Mr 21,17:6
Bjorling, C O Bishop, 1884, F 2,5:4
Bjorn, John, 1939, Je 1,25:5
Bjornbom, Carl A, 1961, Ap 19,39:1
Bjornson, Bjornstjirne, 1910, Ap 27,9:1
Bjornson, John S, 1944, S 27,21:5
Bjurberg, Emily K Mrs, 1941, S 10,23:3
Blaber, Harry P, 1961, Ja 22,84:3
Blaber, O, 1956, Ag 9,26:6
Blabon, George W 3d, 1962, My 22,37:1
Blache, Hans H, 1952, Mr 18,27:2
Blacher, Charles Mrs, 1945, S 14,23:3
Black, Abraham B, 1941, S 13,17:4
Black, Adalbert, 1944, Ap 19,23:4
Black, Adam, 1874, Ja 26,4:7
Black, Adam H, 1959, O 22,37:3
Black, Albert, 1961, Ap 3,33:3
Black, Albert G, 1966, My 19,47:3
Black, Albert H, 1966, O 25,48:3
Black, Alec, 1942, Je 30,21:3
Black, Alex, 1940, My 9,23:1
Black, Allen J, 1941, Je 26,23:3
Black, Arch, 1952, Ag 20,25:6
Black, Archibald Mrs, 1943, D 2,27:4
Black, Arthur, 1953, My 6,31:5
Black, Arthur D (Dean), 1937, D 8,25:1
Black, Avery J, 1958, My 22,29:5
Black, Ben, 1950, D 27,27:2
Black, Benjamin F, 1967, Ja 2,19:4
Black, Benjamin W, 1945, D 3,21:2
Black, Bertram H, 1951, S 13,31:4
Black, Bill, 1965, O 22,43:2
Black, Blanchard A, 1942, S 6,31:2
Black, Burton A, 1959, Je 18,31:3
Black, Carl E, 1946, Ja 14,19:2
Black, Carlos E, 1940, Ag 1,21:2
Black, Catherine, 1949, O 8,13:2
Black, Charles, 1950, N 25,13:1
Black, Charles C, 1947, S 16,24:2; 1947, D 24,21:1
Black, Charles C Mrs, 1915, Mr 23,9:4; 1950, Mr 30, 29:5
Black, Charles E, 1954, Je 23,26:8; 1967, O 6,39:1
Black, Charles F, 1950, My 1,25:3
Black, Charles G, 1944, S 29,21:3
Black, Charles G Mrs, 1956, F 13,27:3
Black, Charles O Mrs, 1950, Ap 19,30:2
Black, Chauncey F, 1904, D 3,9:3
Black, Clinton R Jr, 1963, O 9,43:2
Black, Clyde E, 1951, Mr 19,27:3
Black, Conrad, 1905, Mr 22,9:6
Black, Daniel, 1945, Ap 6,15:4
Black, Daniel D Mrs, 1951, Ap 29,89:2
Black, David W, 1965, Ap 15,34:1
Black, Don, 1959, Ap 22,33:1
Black, E Charlton Mrs, 1945, Jl 7,13:7
Black, E R, 1934, D 20,23:1
Black, Edward, 1942, Je 21,36:8; 1948, D 1,29:3
Black, Edward B, 1939, My 4,23:2
Black, Edward E, 1944, Je 27,19:1; 1966, Ap 24,86:8

Black, Edward J, 1949, Ja 25,23:3
Black, Elizabeth, 1965, S 8,47:3
Black, Elizabeth M, 1939, Jl 1,17:5
Black, Ellis M, 1961, D 26,25:3
Black, Elmer E, 1909, My 31,7:6
Black, Ernest B, 1949, Jl 5,24:5
Black, Ethel C, 1964, F 4,33:4
Black, Ewd R, 1903, N 25,9:5
Black, Francis, 1960, Je 9,33:3
Black, Francis P, 1950, Mr 30,29:3
Black, Frank B, 1937, D 20,27:4
Black, Frank F, 1944, Je 15,19:6
Black, Frank J, 1948, N 18,28:3
Black, Frank Swett Ex-Gov (por),(funl, Mr 26,11:4), 1913, Mr 22,13:1
Black, Fred C, 1966, My 24,50:1
Black, Garland C, 1951, Ja 26,23:4
Black, George, 1942, Ag 29,15:3; 1945, Mr 6,21:6; 1946, Ap 13,17:6; 1961, D 7,43:2
Black, George Ashton Mrs, 1916, F 21,11:5
Black, George E, 1941, Je 25,21:3
Black, George Evans, 1907, D 22,9:4
Black, George F, 1948, S 8,29:1
Black, George H, 1952, F 26,27:1; 1965, Jl 31,21:4
Black, George H Mrs, 1952, Ap 2,33:5
Black, George L, 1943, Je 2,25:5
Black, George M, 1959, Jl 7,33:6
Black, George Mrs, 1957, N 2,21:6
Black, Harold E, 1954, My 3,25:3
Black, Harry, 1949, S 15,27:4
Black, Harry C, 1956, N 26,27:1
Black, Harry C Mrs, 1952, Ap 19,15:2
Black, Harry K Mrs, 1947, Mr 11,27:1
Black, Harry S Mrs, 1961, Je 11,86:4
Black, Harry T, 1949, Ja 1,13:3
Black, Harvey W, 1912, Jl 31,9:5
Black, Henry, 1940, Mr 14,23:6
Black, Henry E, 1951, Mr 26,23:3
Black, Henry M Mrs, 1938, Je 16,23:4
Black, Henry V, 1941, Je 13,19:6
Black, Henry V D Mrs, 1945, S 21,21:5
Black, Herbert A, 1952, Ag 9,13:4
Black, Herbert G, 1953, My 12,27:4
Black, Herbert L, 1965, D 16,47:2
Black, Herbert L Mrs, 1967, N 13,47:1
Black, Herman, 1942, Jl 16,19:3
Black, Herman Mrs, 1952, O 25,17:3
Black, Howard, 1967, Jl 14,31:3
Black, Howard D, 1949, Ag 27,13:4
Black, Howie, 1951, Ja 21,76:5
Black, Hugh, 1942, My 22,21:2; 1953, Ap 8,29:1
Black, Hugo L Mrs, 1951, D 8,11:5
Black, Ira Woodruff Col, 1968, Mr 24,92:7
Black, Irwin M, 1946, D 3,31:3
Black, Israel P, 1903, My 23,9:3
Black, J Frank, 1952, N 23,88:2
Black, J Hunter, 1945, Je 2,15:5
Black, J S, 1883, Ag 20,5:4
Black, James, 1905, Je 17,6:2
Black, James D, 1938, Ag 6,13:1
Black, James M, 1949, O 19,29:2
Black, James R, 1957, Ja 1,23:5
Black, James T, 1955, S 2,17:5
Black, Jessie B Mrs, 1940, Mr 26,21:2
Black, Jimmy, 1949, D 2,29:1
Black, John, 1911, Ag 14,7:5; 1918, Ja 28,13:5
Black, John A, 1923, D 15,13:3
Black, John C, 1947, Ja 29,25:2
Black, John C Gen, 1915, Ag 18,11:6
Black, John C Mrs, 1945, Ag 26,44:6
Black, John D, 1960, Ap 13,40:1
Black, John D Mrs, 1945, F 18,34:2
Black, John J, 1958, Jl 6,56:5
Black, John Janvier Dr, 1909, S 28,9:5
Black, John M, 1956, Jl 13,19:2
Black, John P, 1957, Je 8,19:6
Black, John T, 1967, Jl 22,25:3
Black, John W, 1956, S 29,19:3
Black, John W Mrs, 1940, O 23,23:6
Black, Joseph I Mrs, 1950, O 22,94:3
Black, L M, 1952, F 19,29:3
Black, Leonard F Jr, 1963, O 14,29:5
Black, Lester C, 1942, D 12,17:3
Black, Lewis M, 1945, Ag 7,23:3
Black, Loring M, 1956, My 22,42:5
Black, Louis W, 1948, Ag 25,25:5
Black, Malcolm S, 1960, Ap 14,37:4
Black, Malcolm W, 1967, N 11,33:1
Black, Matthew W, 1955, Ja 20,31:4
Black, Maurice, 1938, Ja 19,23:2
Black, Milton M, 1942, F 4,19:3
Black, Morris Mrs, 1955, My 30,13:6; 1960, Ja 12,47:4
Black, Nathaniel R, 1949, Ja 8,15:4
Black, Norman B Mrs, 1951, Ag 17,17:2
Black, Norman D, 1944, Ag 5,11:2
Black, O Otis, 1961, D 13,43:1
Black, Olive P, 1948, Jl 2,21:4
Black, Orla E, 1949, Ja 28,21:3
Black, Paul L, 1962, O 30,35:4
Black, R C, 1931, Ja 27,23:1
Black, Ralph, 1909, Ap 12,7:3
Black, Raymond C, 1938, D 2,23:1
Black, Rene, 1963, Ag 7,33:1
Black, Robert, 1951, Jl 13,21:2
Black, Robert C, 1907, Jl 18,7:5
Black, Robert Lee, 1954, Ap 27,29:5
Black, Robert Lounsbury, 1954, Ja 26,27:3
Black, Robert M, 1951, S 11,29:2
Black, Robert W, 1955, Jl 7,27:3
Black, Ruby A, 1957, D 16,15:2
Black, S Bruce, 1968, D 11,47:2
Black, S Duncan, 1951, Ap 16,25:4
Black, Samuel Charles, 1921, Jl 26,15:6
Black, Samuel P, 1967, Ag 5,23:4
Black, Silas D Dr, 1912, Ja 3,13:4
Black, Thomas, 1938, Ap 20,23:1
Black, Van Lear Jr, 1956, Mr 3,19:6
Black, Van Lear Mrs, 1949, Ag 26,19:2
Black, Vete George, 1968, Jl 24,50:2
Black, Victor, 1952, Je 28,19:4
Black, Victor E, 1949, Ag 4,23:4
Black, W J, 1941, D 23,22:2
Black, Walter J, 1958, Ap 17,31:3
Black, Walter J Mrs, 1963, Jl 6,15:5
Black, Warren G, 1950, Jl 7,19:2
Black, Wendell W, 1952, Je 8,86:8
Black, William, 1898, D 11,7:4
Black, William A, 1956, Ag 26,84:3
Black, William C, 1952, S 2,23:1
Black, William C Mrs, 1939, N 6,23:5
Black, William D Mrs, 1910, Ag 14,II,9:5
Black, William G, 1955, Ag 28,84:4
Black, William H, 1916, Ap 16,21:4; 1943, Mr 3,24:3; 1955, Ag 24,27:1
Black, William M, 1957, My 25,21:4
Black, William Perkins Capt, 1916, Ja 5,13:5
Black, William R, 1962, Mr 21,39:5
Black, William T, 1903, D 19,9:5; 1948, Je 11,23:3; 1968, O 9,47:4
Black, William T Sr, 1938, D 11,62:2
Black, William W, 1967, S 2,25:6
Black, Witherbee, 1959, Ag 9,89:3
Black Bela, 1947, S 6,17:4
Blackadder, Thomas, 1953, Mr 29,93:1
Blackall, Brewer Mrs, 1949, Mr 17,25:2
Blackall, Christopher Rubey Rev Dr, 1924, Ja 26,13:2
Blackall, Clarence H, 1942, Mr 6,21:2
Blackall, F S, 1928, O 7,30:3
Blackall, Frederick S Jr, 1963, Jl 8,20:1
Blackall, Frederick S Mrs, 1952, Ja 24,47:3
Blackall, R C, 1903, S 1,2:6
Blackall, Robert M, 1964, Ja 1,25:4
Blackburn, A S, 1960, N 25,27:3
Blackburn, Alex M, 1960, F 21,92:4
Blackburn, Alex Mrs, 1954, Mr 16,29:5
Blackburn, Benn, 1938, Je 28,19:5
Blackburn, Casper K, 1951, Ja 25,25:3
Blackburn, Claud A C, 1941, Ap 26,15:6
Blackburn, D Asa (funl, O 1,9:6), 1909, S 29,11:3
Blackburn, Edward J, 1955, Ja 6,27:2
Blackburn, Floyd Mrs, 1941, Ag 15,17:2
Blackburn, Frank L, 1947, Ap 28,23:3
Blackburn, Grace, 1943, Ag 26,17:5
Blackburn, Henry W Mrs, 1951, O 27,19:5
Blackburn, J C Jr, 1902, F 13,9:5
Blackburn, Jack, 1942, Ap 25,18:8
Blackburn, James W, 1954, Jl 14,27:2
Blackburn, Jason A, 1959, My 2,23:5
Blackburn, John H, 1952, D 23,23:4
Blackburn, John H Mrs, 1946, Mr 20,15:5
Blackburn, Joseph C, 1950, Ag 15,29:4
Blackburn, Joseph C S Gen, 1918, S 13,11:2
Blackburn, L P ex-Gov, 1887, S 15,5:2
Blackburn, Robert, 1942, Ja 3,32:1; 1955, S 11,84:8
Blackburn, Robert Mrs, 1947, My 11,62:4
Blackburn, Susan M, 1946, O 7,31:1
Blackburn, Thomas L, 1941, S 24,23:2
Blackburn, Tom (Leonard T), 1964, Mr 7,23:2
Blackburn, Veran Sr, 1945, Ja 2,19:3
Blackburn, Walter Mrs, 1951, Jl 5,25:6
Blackburne, George, 1961, Je 19,27:5
Blackburne, John H, 1924, S 2,19:3
Blackburne, Lena (Russell Blackburne), 1968, Mr 2, 29:4
Blackburne, Thomas F, 1942, Jl 27,6:2
Blackburne, Walter, 1938, Ag 15,15:6
Blacker, L V Stewart, 1964, Ap 20,29:1
Blackerby, Phil E, 1948, Je 26,17:3
Blackett, B, 1935, Ag 16,3:5
Blackett, Charles S, 1937, Ap 20,26:1
Blackett, William C Mrs, 1953, Ap 1,29:3
Blackett, William Cameron, 1925, Ag 24,13:6
Blackett-Beaumont, Wentworth Canning (Viscount Allendale), 1923, D 13,21:5
Blackfan, Agnes, 1925, Mr 5,19:5
Blackfan, Joseph, 1883, N 25,2:5
Blackfan, Kenneth D, 1941, N 30,69:3
Blackford, Alfred Mrs, 1945, Ap 8,35:1
Blackford, Ambler M, 1942, My 12,19:3
Blackford, Charles E Jr, 1951, Jl 19,23:1
Blackford, Douglas L, 1953, D 15,39:1
Blackford, Eugene G, 1904, D 29,2:4; 1964, S 17,43:3
Blackford, Francis W, 1942, Mr 27,23:5
Blackford, Frank C, 1949, Ap 1,25:2
Blackford, Frank Sr Mrs, 1947, Ag 28,23:4
Blackford, Fred, 1954, F 21,59:4
Blackford, H J Sr, 1955, Jl 29,17:5
Blackford, John, 1903, D 8,9:5
Blackford, John J, 1955, Mr 25,24:4
Blackford, John J Mrs, 1954, F 10,29:2
Blackford, Mary, 1937, S 26,II,9:3
Blackford, Mary E Mrs, 1946, Mr 5,25:4
Blackford, Staige D, 1949, Jl 18,17:4
Blackford, Wilton F Dr, 1942, Ap 4,13:2
Blackhall, Walter L, 1946, O 26,17:2
Blackhurst, James, 1903, My 3,9:6
Blackhurst, Laurence, 1947, F 1,15:1
Blackie, C, 1883, Ap 24,5:1
Blackie, Ernest M, 1943, Mr 6,13:4
Blackie, J S, 1895, Mr 3,5:3
Blackie, John Sr, 1874, Je 30,4:7
Blackie, William R, 1946, F 19,25:2
Blackington, Alton H, 1963, Ap 25,33:4
Blackinton, Amos S, 1949, Je 20,19:3
Blackiston, Henry C, 1951, Ja 24,27:1
Blackledge, Edgar S, 1951, F 25,87:1
Blackledge, Frank A, 1962, Mr 14,39:3
Blackler, Charles E, 1948, Ap 16,23:3
Blackley, Agnes B Mrs, 1941, F 25,23:3
Blackley, Norman M, 1940, F 13,23:5
Blackley, William A, 1961, N 8,35:2
Blacklock, Robert, 1907, Ag 1,7:6
Blackman, Abraham, 1952, Ja 8,27:5
Blackman, Albert E, 1954, Jl 13,23:5
Blackman, Alfred A, 1946, O 19,21:1
Blackman, Arthur W, 1945, F 1,23:1
Blackman, Aylward M, 1956, Mr 10,17:6
Blackman, Benjamin D, 1949, O 27,27:2
Blackman, Blanche A, 1950, F 24,23:2
Blackman, Carl P, 1937, Mr 5,21:3
Blackman, Christopher, 1947, Je 25,25:2
Blackman, Clifford A, 1919, My 22,15:5
Blackman, Edward L, 1960, N 14,31:3
Blackman, Elinor, 1942, Jl 16,19:5
Blackman, George L Dr, 1871, Jl 20,1:4
Blackman, Gertrude I, 1947, Ap 29,27:5
Blackman, Irwin N, 1964, O 28,45:2
Blackman, J B, 1937, F 11,23:1
Blackman, J Newcomb, 1958, Jl 5,17:2
Blackman, J Newcomb Mrs, 1962, O 6,25:4
Blackman, Lee R, 1942, N 19,25:4
Blackman, Maurice R, 1946, Ap 11,25:5
Blackman, Ralph B Mrs, 1951, Ja 25,25:1
Blackman, Stanley J, 1952, My 13,23:4
Blackman, Walter W, 1939, D 31,18:5
Blackman, William A Mrs, 1937, S 25,17:6
Blackman, William W, 1943, O 22,17:3
Blackmar, A E, 1931, F 16,19:3
Blackmar, Adele M Mrs, 1942, D 30,23:2
Blackmar, H E, 1952, Je 20,23:3
Blackmar, Milton W, 1950, S 16,19:4
Blackmar, Milton W Mrs, 1959, Jl 5,57:1
Blackmar, W W, 1905, Jl 17,7:7
Blackmer, Charles F, 1950, Ag 17,27:5
Blackmer, Henry M (will, Je 12,23:1), 1962, My 27, 93:1
Blackmer, John E Mrs, 1953, Ag 10,23:4
Blackmer, Myron K, 1955, Jl 17,60:5
Blackmer, Robert M, 1957, Jl 14,73:1
Blackmer, Samuel H, 1951, D 26,25:2
Blackmer, Walter S Mrs, 1949, D 5,23:2
Blackmere, Friedrich A R von S Count, 1941, Ja 22, 21:4
Blackmon, Fred L, 1921, F 9,9:4
Blackmore, Arthur E, 1921, D 17,13:4
Blackmore, Arthur E Mrs, 1925, Jl 8,17:4
Blackmore, Charles T, 1944, O 10,23:5
Blackmore, E Willard, 1949, N 22,30:2
Blackmore, George A, 1948, O 3,64:4
Blackmore, George C, 1942, My 22,21:3
Blackmore, George H Mrs, 1943, D 29,17:3
Blackmore, Jess H, 1956, S 25,33:1
Blackmore, Joseph J, 1941, F 12,21:2
Blackmore, Richard D, 1900, Ja 22,7:2
Blackmore, W H Mrs (Eliza Newton), 1882, F 8,8:
Blackmur, Richard P (mem ser set, Mr 18,30:4), 1965, F 3,35:1
Blackney, William W Mrs, 1951, D 1,13:4
Blacksnake, Owen, 1881, Ja 3,8:6
Blackstead, Eric N, 1967, D 22,31:1
Blackstock, Thomas G Mrs (cor, S 15,15:2), 1951, S 14,25:4
Blackstone, A E, 1951, Ja 31,26:4
Blackstone, Earl, 1950, Je 6,29:5
Blackstone, Ernest G, 1950, Jl 6,27:3
Blackstone, Harriet, 1939, Mr 17,21:6
Blackstone, Harry (biog, N 18,47:1), 1965, N 17,4
Blackstone, Michael, 1956, My 21,25:4
Blackstone, Paul J Mrs, 1950, Jl 23,57:2
Blackstone, Samuel, 1959, Ap 22,33:1
Blackstone, Wyllis, 1885, F 23,5:2
Blackton, Henry Mrs, 1959, F 15,86:7
Blackton, J Stuart, 1941, Ag 14,17:3
Blackwelder, Gertrude B Mrs, 1938, Jl 5,17:4
Blackwell, Antoinette Brown Rev Dr, 1921, N 6,2
Blackwell, Arthur, 1882, N 11,5:1
Blackwell, Bruce C, 1966, Ag 20,25:3
Blackwell, Carlyle, 1955, Je 18,17:3
Blackwell, Charles A, 1966, My 2,37:4

Blackwell, Edward D, 1955, Ap 8,21:5
Blackwell, Emily Dr, 1910, S 9,9:5
Blackwell, Ernest C, 1960, My 15,86:1
Blackwell, Francis O, 1943, Ap 13,25:4
Blackwell, Frank E, 1911, Ja 12,13:4; 1951, Ap 30,21:3
Blackwell, Frederick S, 1956, S 5,27:5
Blackwell, G E, 1926, D 15,27:5
Blackwell, George, 1942, S 17,25:5
Blackwell, George C, 1954, My 1,15:5
Blackwell, George E Mrs, 1961, Ja 4,33:2
Blackwell, George M Mrs, 1957, D 2,27:4
Blackwell, George R Mrs, 1938, O 12,27:1
Blackwell, Gurdon S, 1965, F 3,35:1
Blackwell, Henry B Dr, 1909, S 8,9:4
Blackwell.Horace F Jr, 1958, Jl 7,27:3
Blackwell, Hubert C, 1955, Ja 19,27:1
Blackwell, Hugh B, 1957, N 4,29:5
Blackwell, J A Lt-Com, 1923, Jl 29,6:4
Blackwell, James Hancock Mrs, 1968, S 27,47:3
Blackwell, James M, 1938, D 14,25:5 ;1961, D 22,23:3
Blackwell. L B Mrs, 1933, Ap 14,19:3
Blackwell Lucy Stone, 1893, O 19,5:5
Blackwell Richd R Mrs, 1953, O 13,29:1
Blackwell, Robert E (por), 1938, Jl 8,17:3
Blackwell, Roy C, 1961, D 28,27:5
Blackwell, Sadie C, 1943, Jl 16,17:4
Blackwell, W J Col, 1903, N 13,1:6
Blackwell, William H, 1963, N 5,31:4
Blackwell Wm T, 1952, S 16,29:4
Blackwell, William T Mrs, 1961, Ja 27,23:1
Blackwell, Wilson H, 1940, D 8,69:2
Blackwell, Wilson H Mrs, 1958, F 13,29:5
Blackwood, Algernon, 1951, D 11,33:5
Blackwood, Arthur E Mrs, 1950, Ja 31,23:2
Blackwood, Arthur T, 1953, Jl 20,17:4
Blackwood, Henry P T, 1948, S 4,15:4
Blackwood, John, 1923, Ag 11,9:6
Blackwood, Oswald H, 1953, Mr 24,42:3
Blackwood, Paul, 1944, O 26,23:5
Blackwood, Peter P, 1938, Jl 13,44:4
Blackwood, S Temple, 1959, N 28,21:6
Blackwood, Samuel T, 1943, Je 12,13:1
Blackwood, William, 1912, N 12,13:5
Blackwood, William E, 1944, O 11,21:6
Blackwood, William R Brig-Gen, 1922, Ap 28,17:6
Blackwool, John, 1879, N 10,2:4
Blacoc, Robert E, 1962, Mr 22,35:4
Blacque, Kate R Mrs (will), 1938, Je 8,2:5
Bladel, George, 1945, O 22,19:4
Bladen, John T, 1948, Je 14,23:1
Blades, Ansley O, 1948, Ag 14,13:1
Blades, Archie L, 1944, Ja 23,38:3
Blades, Lawrence J K, 1961, My 26,33:4
Blades, Rowland (Lord Ebbisham), 1953, My 25,25:2
Bladet, Gaston D, 1938, Ap 14,23:5
Bladt, Olaf, 1943, O 22,17:2
Bladworth, George C, 1956, Mr 29,27:5
Blaedel, Nicolai, 1943, D 4,13:5
Blaesi, J George F, 1956, S 26,33:4
Blaetz, Harry M, 1950, S 2,15:2
Blaffer, Robert L, 1942, O 24,15:5
Blagden, Augustus S, 1960, My 12,35:1
Blagden, Crawford Lt Col, 1937, Ja 13,23:2
Blagden, Dexter, 1948, N 22,21:3
Blagden, Dexter Mrs (Mabel), 1968, Jl 16,39:3
Blagden, Francis Meredith Mrs, 1968, Je 5,47:3
Blagden, G, 1934, Mr 23,23:3
Blagden, G W, 1884, D 19,2:4
Blagden, George Mrs, 1925, D 12,15:5
Blagden, Isa, 1873, F 11,1:5
Blagden, Phillips Mrs, 1958, Je 21,19:3
Blagden, Samuel P, 1949, My 6,25:4
Blagden, Thomas, 1938, O 5,23:2; 1959, O 9,21:3; 1962, Ag 27,23:6
Blagden, Thomas Mrs, 1962, Mr 17,25:4
Blagden, Wendell P, 1938, D 20,25:5
Blagoeva, Stela Mrs, 1954, F 17,31:4
Blagrove, Henry, 1873, Ja 6,5:3
Blague, Giles, 1957, Mr 14,29:4
Blaha, Joseph C, 1944, Ap 3,21:5
Blaha, Mathew, 1949, D 20,31:3
Blaicher, Arthur A, 1957, Jl 12,21:4
Blaicher, Hilmar E, 1945, D 13,29:1
Blaidell, A Leo, 1947, Je 17,25:5
Blaier, O William, 1962, Ja 5,29:2
Blaik, William D, 1947, Ja 5,53:4
Blaikie, George W, 1949, My 6,25:3
Blaikie, Ralph L, 1964, S 21,31:4
Blaikie, William, 1904, D 7,9:3
Blain, Hugh M, 1938, D 31,15:2
Blain, J D, 1876, Jl 19,4:7
Blain, James M, 1937, Ag 24,22:1
Blain, Thomas J Mrs, 1945, Ja 13,11:4
Blaine, Anita M Mrs (est acctg filed), 1955, Je 10, 15:6
Blaine, Anna Mrs, 1938, Ja 6,19:6
Blaine, Arthur M, 1966, Je 29,47:2
Blaine, Charles H, 1937, F 12,23:4
Blaine, Chester G, 1945, F 7,21:2
Blaine, Daniel T, 1958, N 5,35:1
Blaine, Emmons, 1892, Je 19,9:6
Blaine, Emmons Mrs (will, F 20,29:4; est acctg, N 19,7:4), 1954, F 13,13:3
Blaine, Grace S Mrs, 1938, My 19,21:2
Blaine, Graham B Mrs, 1968, My 22,47:3
Blaine, Harriet G, 1945, N 7,23:1
Blaine, J J, 1934, Ap 17,21:1
Blaine, James G, 1893, Ja 28,1:6
Blaine, Jimmy (Jas W Bunn), 1967, Mr 19,92:7
Blaine, Joan, 1949, Ap 20,27:5
Blaine, Mrs, 1871, My 7,1:7
Blaine, W, 1890, Ja 16,1:6
Blaine, W Frank, 1909, Ja 24,11:5
Blair, Allan J, 1968, Ap 23,47:2
Blair, Alonzo, 1879, Jl 17,2:7
Blair, Andrew G, 1907, Ja 26,9:5
Blair, Arthur, 1947, F 5,23:2
Blair, Bruce, 1954, S 7,26:1
Blair, Burton D, 1950, S 1,21:4
Blair, C Ledyard, 1949, F 8,25:1
Blair, C Ledyard Mrs, 1953, F 11,29:3
Blair, Charles Austin Justice, 1912, Ag 31,7:4
Blair, Charles B, 1953, Ag 11,27:3
Blair, Charles H, 1964, Ja 24,27:1
Blair, Chauncey J, 1916, My 11,11:6
Blair, Clarence M, 1944, My 23,23:2
Blair, Clay C Sr, 1967, Ja 1,52:5
Blair, Clyde S, 1956, Ja 13,23:3
Blair, David G, 1948, Ap 5,21:5
Blair, David H, 1944, S 14,23:3; 1960, My 15,86:3
Blair, De Witt Clinton, 1915, Je 4,11:4
Blair, Emma D Mrs, 1941, D 20,19:6
Blair, Esther Dr, 1937, D 12,II,8:7
Blair, Eugene, 1884, Jl 25,3:6
Blair, Eugene K, 1940, F 4,40:3
Blair, Eugenie (funl, My 18,19:7), 1922, My 15,17:7
Blair, Ezra C, 1942, Je 23,19:3
Blair, F P, 1876, O 20,2:1
Blair, Floyd G, 1965, O 30,35:1
Blair, Frank, 1939, Ja 13,19:2
Blair, Frank A, 1937, My 6,25:4
Blair, Frank P Gen (funl, Jl 11,7:4), 1875, Jl 10,4:6
Blair, Frank P Mrs, 1954, Ap 27,29:6
Blair, Frank R, 1954, Ag 8,85:3
Blair, Frank R Mrs, 1954, D 4,17:5
Blair, Frank T, 1953, Ja 13,27:1
Blair, Frank W Mrs, 1938, F 14,17:5
Blair, George, 1920, Ja 8,17:2; 1957, Mr 17,87:1
Blair, Gilbert B, 1949, S 20,29:3
Blair, Gist, 1940, D 17,25:3
Blair, Harold A, 1921, D 11,22:2
Blair, Harriet Brown Mrs (will), 1953, F 18,33:3
Blair, Harry M, 1939, D 29,23:4
Blair, Harry N, 1949, N 29,29:4
Blair, Harry W Mrs, 1951, Ag 4,15:3
Blair, Henry P, 1948, O 5,25:6
Blair, Henry T, 1967, Mr 7,41:1
Blair, Henry W, 1920, Mr 15,15:5
Blair, J A Jr, 1934, Ag 16,17:4
Blair, J Insley Mrs, 1951, N 19,23:6
Blair, J Mrs, 1930, N 6,25:3
Blair, James, 1942, S 11,21:3; 1944, N 19,50:2; 1950, D 12,33:4
Blair, James A (cor, D 2,17:6), 1939, N 29,23:4
Blair, James A Mrs, 1955, Ag 1,19:2
Blair, James Carroll, 1953, F 3,25:3
Blair, James H, 1955, F 25,21:6
Blair, James R, 1961, Jl 16,69:1
Blair, James T, 1962, Jl 13,24:1
Blair, James T Mrs, 1962, Jl 13,24:1
Blair, James W, 1952, F 19,29:2
Blair, Jesse H, 1968, S 14,28:1
Blair, John, 1942, Ja 21,17:2
Blair, John A, 1924, N 12,23:2
Blair, John B, 1946, D 2,25:5; 1963, O 24,33:4
Blair, John I, 1939, Ag 1,19:4
Blair, John Inslee, 1899, D 3,4:5
Blair, John L Mrs, 1967, D 20,45:3
Blair, John V, 1948, My 1,15:2
Blair, Joseph A, 1943, D 25,13:2
Blair, Joseph P, 1942, N 16,19:6
Blair, Lafayette G Mrs, 1945, Ap 12,23:2
Blair, Livingston L, 1966, Ap 27,47:2
Blair, Lovisa I, 1944, D 29,15:4
Blair, Mary, 1947, S 19,23:5
Blair, Mary A I M Mrs, 1940, Ag 6,22:6
Blair, Mary M, 1962, Je 9,25:1
Blair, Matthew J, 1948, Ja 26,19:3
Blair, Milton J, 1952, Ag 13,21:4
Blair, Montgomery, 1883, Jl 28,5:3
Blair, Mrs, 1877, Jl 6,4:6
Blair, Orlan R, 1944, O 23,19:3
Blair, Orrin C, 1947, Ag 5,23:3
Blair, Pierpont, 1939, My 14,III,6:8
Blair, Raymond H, 1963, Je 16,84:5
Blair, Richard H Mrs, 1948, O 28,29:4
Blair, Robert H, 1952, Ag 28,23:6
Blair, Robert S, 1958, O 14,37:4
Blair, Sam, 1938, O 22,17:6
Blair, Thomas D, 1949, Ja 3,23:5
Blair, Thomas H, 1942, S 17,25:3
Blair, Thomas S, 1953, N 1,87:1
Blair, W Dyer, 1952, Ap 4,25:3
Blair, W Reid (por), 1949, Mr 2,25:3
Blair, W Reid Mrs, 1965, Ja 3,84:7
Blair, Walter D, 1953, Ja 12,27:1
Blair, Walter D Mrs (E H Frost), 1958, Ap 11,25:3
Blair, Walter E, 1953, Mr 25,31:2
Blair, Walter W, 1959, My 6,40:1
Blair, Wiley Jr, 1962, S 10,29:1
Blair, William, 1912, S 17,11:6
Blair, William G, 1957, Je 17,23:4
Blair, William H, 1943, My 19,25:3
Blair, William J, 1960, Ap 30,23:6
Blair, William N Mrs, 1942, Ap 11,13:5
Blair, William R, 1962, S 3,15:3
Blair, William S, 1956, Je 10,89:2
Blair, William W, 1948, Ja 21,26:2
Blair, Wolcott, 1966, My 18,47:1
Blair-Smith, Christopher D, 1959, F 14,21:4
Blair-Smith, H, 1933, Ja 12,17:1
Blairon, Paul E, 1964, My 21,35:2
Blais, A A Bp, 1919, Ja 25,11:2
Blais, Joseph M, 1948, My 3,21:4
Blaisdell, Alfred Osgood, 1919, O 23,13:4
Blaisdell, Bertram S, 1949, Ja 30,60:3
Blaisdell, Bruce, 1956, Jl 19,27:4
Blaisdell, C Carroll, 1942, S 17,25:3
Blaisdell, D, 1875, Ag 26,1:2
Blaisdell, E Thurston Mrs, 1947, S 24,23:4
Blaisdell, Edward K Mrs, 1903, N 28,9:5
Blaisdell, Edwin C, 1945, N 21,21:5
Blaisdell, Ferren F, 1958, F 2,86:8
Blaisdell, Frank C, 1943, F 9,23:3
Blaisdell, Harry W, 1944, Mr 7,17:2
Blaisdell, James A, 1957, Ja 30,29:3
Blaisdell, James W, 1942, F 28,17:4
Blaisdell, Russell E, 1965, Mr 7,82:5
Blaisdell, Thomas C, 1948, D 12,93:1
Blaisdell, William B, 1940, Ja 30,20:3
Blaisdell, William L, 1941, F 13,19:5
Blaisdell, William Mrs, 1949, Ja 1,13:2
Blake, A, 1881, S 8,5:4
Blake, Adelaide S, 1942, N 21,13:3
Blake, Alfred, 1950, D 16,17:4
Blake, Amy B Mrs, 1938, Jl 8,17:4
Blake, Anna, 1940, Ap 30,13:2
Blake, Anna M Mrs, 1941, F 18,23:5
Blake, Anne S, 1949, F 1,25:1
Blake, Arthur, 1944, O 24,23:3; 1954, Je 29,27:3
Blake, Basil F, 1950, N 3,27:2
Blake, Bruce, 1957, Ja 9,31:4
Blake, C F, 1881, F 22,8:1; 1883, Jl 11,5:1
Blake, Charles Dupee, 1903, N 25,9:2
Blake, Charles F, 1948, Mr 21,60:5
Blake, Charles R, 1947, N 27,31:3
Blake, Chauncey E, 1943, N 4,23:5
Blake, Clarence J Dr, 1919, Ja 30,13:3
Blake, Clinton H, 1916, My 20,11:4; 1947, Ja 26,53:5
Blake, Clinton H Mrs, 1967, My 11,47:1
Blake, Corinne E, 1941, D 27,19:2
Blake, Daniel B, 1950, F 9,56:2
Blake, David B, 1956, Mr 23,27:2
Blake, E Nelson, 1921, D 17,13:3
Blake, E Wilson, 1947, Jl 5,11:3
Blake, Eben N, 1960, Ag 28,83:3
Blake, Edgar, 1943, My 27,25:1
Blake, Edmund M, 1961, F 18,19:4
Blake, Edward, 1912, Mr 2,13:4; 1949, Ja 25,24:2
Blake, Edward E, 1947, S 10,27:3
Blake, Edward H, 1922, Jl 21,11:5
Blake, Edwin M, 1955, D 21,29:5
Blake, Elmore E, 1948, Ja 23,24:3
Blake, Ernest, 1961, Jl 17,21:5
Blake, Euph Mrs, 1904, O 23,7:6
Blake, Florencine M Mrs, 1937, Mr 7,II,8:5
Blake, Francis, 1913, Ja 20,11:6
Blake, Francis G, 1952, F 2,13:1
Blake, Francis S, 1944, O 23,19:2
Blake, Frank, 1948, Je 29,23:1
Blake, Frederick H, 1951, Ap 2,25:6
Blake, Frederick H Mrs, 1951, Jl 18,29:2
Blake, Freeman D, 1940, Jl 22,17:2
Blake, Geoffrey Vice-Adm Sir, 1968, Jl 25,33:4
Blake, George, 1955, O 8,19:4; 1961, Ag 31,27:3
Blake, George Batty, 1875, Ag 7,8:2
Blake, George E, 1871, F 25,1:3
Blake, George H, 1955, D 28,23:5
Blake, George H Mrs, 1944, O 2,19:6
Blake, George J, 1941, Jl 12,13:1
Blake, Grenfill Mrs (Lillie Devereaux Blake), 1913, D 31,9:5
Blake, H C Commodore, 1880, Ja 22,5:5
Blake, H N, 1933, N 30,40:5
Blake, Harry W, 1955, N 24,29:3
Blake, Helen N, 1953, Ap 23,29:4
Blake, Helen V, 1955, Jl 16,15:5
Blake, Henrietta F Mrs, 1941, D 4,25:2
Blake, Henry C, 1949, D 21,29:2
Blake, Henry C Mrs, 1948, S 22,31:1
Blake, Henry S, 1956, Mr 12,27:4
Blake, Henry T, 1922, Ap 8,15:4
Blake, Henry W Mrs, 1952, Ap 7,25:4
Blake, Herbert C, 1948, S 24,25:1
Blake, Herbert S, 1948, Ja 21,25:4
Blake, Ida M, 1939, D 31,18:6
Blake, Irving E, 1940, N 18,19:4
Blake, Isaac D, 1924, Ag 15,13:6

Blake, Israel O, 1942, Ag 13,19:4
Blake, Israel O Mrs, 1942, Jl 23,19:5
Blake, J E, 1880, S 29,5:2
Blake, J W, 1935, My 25,15:1
Blake, James, 1948, S 9,27:2
Blake, James G, 1947, Jl 6,41:2
Blake, James G Mrs, 1952, N 10,25:4
Blake, James J, 1937, Je 4,23:5
Blake, James Sr Mrs, 1947, Ja 1,34:3
Blake, James Vila Rev, 1925, My 1,19:5
Blake, John A L, 1938, My 11,19:5
Blake, John B, 1943, Ag 20,15:4
Blake, John D, 1942, My 16,13:3
Blake, John G Col (funl, Ja 28,7:6), 1907, Ja 25,9:5
Blake, John J Sr, 1949, Ag 12,17:5
Blake, John M, 1943, Jl 10,13:6
Blake, John S, 1911, O 5,11:6
Blake, John T, 1943, O 8,19:3
Blake, Joseph A Dr, 1937, Ag 13,17:4
Blake, Joseph A Mrs, 1946, Ap 28,42:3
Blake, Joseph M, 1949, O 3,17:4
Blake, Julia, 1959, F 1,85:1
Blake, K D Mrs, 1930, Ap 20,25:1
Blake, Kaisley, 1948, My 19,27:3
Blake, Kenneth M, 1958, O 20,29:2
Blake, Kenneth M Mrs, 1944, Mr 27,19:5
Blake, Lewis W Dr, 1872, S 18,4:6
Blake, Lillie Devereaux Mrs, 1914, Ja 10,9:5
Blake, Louise A J Mrs, 1942, S 9,23:5
Blake, Lucien Ira, 1916, My 6,11:7
Blake, Lucy A, 1947, Ja 18,15:5
Blake, Luther L, 1953, Jl 4,11:6
Blake, Margaret A, 1959, Ap 25,21:2
Blake, Martin J, 1939, Ja 14,17:2
Blake, Mary E Mrs, 1907, F 28,9:6
Blake, Maurice A, 1947, D 15,25:1
Blake, Maurice A Mrs, 1940, Ja 19,19:2
Blake, Michael, 1923, Ap 10,21:5
Blake, Monroe W, 1955, F 10,31:5
Blake, Montgomery S, 1957, O 26,21:5
Blake, Morgan, 1953, Jl 28,19:5
Blake, Norman H, 1948, Mr 5,21:3
Blake, P, 1878, O 20,6:7
Blake, Preston Mrs, 1961, Mr 1,33:3
Blake, Ralph M, 1950, Ap 17,23:3
Blake, Ralph V, 1941, O 7,23:3
Blake, Richard, 1954, S 26,86:6
Blake, Robert E, 1962, My 10,37:5
Blake, Robert F, 1949, D 4,108:7
Blake, Robert H, 1945, Ja 4,19:1; 1950, Mr 11,15:5
Blake, Robert J Mrs, 1949, Ap 19,25:3
Blake, Robert P, 1950, My 10,31:3
Blake, Samuel Parkman Mrs, 1923, Ag 18,9:6
Blake, Stafford A, 1951, Je 25,19:5
Blake, Sue A, 1955, F 4,21:1
Blake, T Whitney, 1919, N 28,13:1
Blake, Theodora, 1949, O 19,29:2
Blake, Theodore E, 1949, Jl 4,13:5
Blake, Thomas F, 1938, Jl 6,23:5; 1944, Ja 15,13:6
Blake, Thomas Mrs, 1964, N 2,39:2
Blake, Thomas Rev, 1937, Ag 2,19:6
Blake, Tiffany, 1943, S 29,21:6
Blake, Virginia J, 1954, Ag 17,21:1
Blake, Wainright D, 1953, O 4,89:2
Blake, Walter S, 1940, Jl 15,15:3
Blake, Warren A, 1954, F 27,13:5
Blake, William, 1968, F 21,47:2
Blake, William B (Comedian), 1863, Ap 24,4:6
Blake, William C, 1951, Ap 20,29:1
Blake, William F, 1964, Ap 3,33:4
Blake, William H, 1951, N 17,17:4; 1965, My 11,39:4
Blake, William J, 1944, D 18,19:1; 1948, Mr 19,23:3
Blake, William J Mrs, 1946, Ap 28,44:3
Blake, William L Rev, 1915, Je 7,11:4
Blake, William M, 1946, F 14,25:3
Blake, William M Jr, 1967, Ja 23,43:2
Blake, William Mrs, 1946, N 6,23:5
Blake, William P, 1910, My 23,7:6
Blake, William Robert, 1968, My 28,47:1
Blake, William S, 1903, D 21,7:4
Blakeley, Archibald Col, 1915, Ag 27,9:6
Blakeley, Bertha E, 1962, Jl 19,27:6
Blakeley, George H, 1942, D 26,9:1
Blakeley, George H Mrs, 1940, Mr 21,25:4
Blakeley, Margaret M Mrs, 1954, Ap 10,15:1
Blakeley, T Arthur, 1938, N 18,21:3
Blakeley, William S, 1914, Jl 21,9:5
Blakelock, Clarence L, 1947, Ja 20,25:5
Blakelock, Ralph, 1919, Ag 11,11:1
Blakelock, Ralph A (funl, Ag 15,11:6), 1919, Ag 13, 11:3
Blakely, Aloysius J, 1938, N 29,23:3
Blakely, Aloysius Rev, 1912, N 1,13:4
Blakely, Charles A, 1950, S 14,31:3
Blakely, Charles R, 1947, Je 17,25:4
Blakely, Charles R Mrs, 1939, Mr 11,17:6
Blakely, Edward W, 1947, S 30,25:5
Blakely, Ellen M, 1937, F 22,17:3
Blakely, Gilbert Sykes, 1925, O 22,25:5
Blakely, Hugh J, 1958, Jl 19,15:4
Blakely, James, 1915, O 21,11:5
Blakely, James R Y, 1942, Ja 31,17:4
Blakely, John, 1941, D 6,17:5
Blakely, Julius W Mrs, 1945, My 17,19:3
Blakely, Lamotte, 1941, Jl 30,17:4
Blakely, Mary B Mrs, 1903, Jl 31,7:6
Blakely, Paul L, 1943, F 27,13:5
Blakely, Quincy, 1945, Je 14,19:3
Blakely, Stuart B, 1952, F 28,27:2
Blakeman, Alexander M Col, 1912, Ap 8,11:5
Blakeman, Alfred E, 1961, S 13,45:1
Blakeman, Andrew W, 1910, F 28,9:5
Blakeman, Andrew W Mrs, 1910, F 28,9:5
Blakeman, Birdseye Mrs, 1912, Ag 22,9:6
Blakeman, Caldwell Robertson, 1924, Ja 24,17:4
Blakeman, Chester B, 1950, My 3,29:4
Blakeman, Earle C Mrs, 1945, S 28,21:3
Blakeman, John P, 1864, Ag 25,3:2
Blakeman, Sterling B, 1942, Jl 20,13:5
Blakemore, Paul, 1967, Ap 24,33:1
Blakeney, Albert A, 1924, O 16,25:4
Blakeney, Alfred, 1957, My 13,31:2
Blakeney, W E Dr, 1903, Je 6,7:6
Blaker, Ernest H, 1947, O 22,29:3
Blaker, Ora M, 1945, Ag 6,15:5
Blakeslee, Albert F, 1954, N 17,31:5
Blakeslee, Albert F Mrs, 1947, Mr 28,23:1
Blakeslee, Alice C Mrs, 1940, Jl 31,17:5
Blakeslee, Bert N, 1942, Mr 28,17:5
Blakeslee, Charles G, 1954, Ja 9,15:1
Blakeslee, Clarence, 1954, Je 27,69:1
Blakeslee, Clarence E, 1941, Ja 10,19:1
Blakeslee, Clifford L, 1949, Ja 24,19:3
Blakeslee, Dwight S Sr, 1945, S 22,17:3
Blakeslee, Eben, 1950, Ja 26,27:3
Blakeslee, Edward G Com, 1919, Mr 1,13:4
Blakeslee, Edwin M, 1962, Mr 24,25:5
Blakeslee, Elmer F, 1939, S 5,23:4
Blakeslee, Elmer F Mrs, 1949, Ag 8,15:3
Blakeslee, Francis D, 1942, S 13,53:1
Blakeslee, G H, 1955, Mr 19,2:3
Blakeslee, George A (daughter contests will, Jl 15,- 34:4), 1954, Je 11,23:1
Blakeslee, George A Mrs, 1953, D 25,17:3
Blakeslee, George E, 1920, Ja 11,22:4
Blakeslee, George H, 1954, My 6,33:1
Blakeslee, Henry J, 1941, Ja 20,17:2
Blakeslee, Howard W, 1952, My 3,21:1
Blakeslee, M Grant, 1956, D 11,39:2
Blakeslee, Victor F, 1947, Ap 7,23:2
Blakeslee, Victor F Mrs (I Skariatina), 1962, N 18, 86:5
Blakeslee, Walter H, 1940, Mr 31,45:2
Blakeslee, Walter H Mrs (will), 1946, Ap 6,15:3
Blakeslee, Wilbur B Mrs, 1942, S 22,21:2
Blakesley, J W Rev, 1885, Ap 19,8:7
Blakesly, Phil I, 1949, My 28,15:6
Blakey, Benjamin W, 1966, S 16,37:4
Blakey, John W, 1941, D 19,25:1
Blakiston, Herbert E D, 1942, Jl 30,21:4
Blakiston, Kenneth M, 1937, Ja 21,23:4
Blakley, Edward B, 1965, Ag 23,31:3
Blakley, G A, 1878, N 12,5:2
Blakley, John J, 1941, Mr 20,21:2
Blakley, John L, 1951, My 7,25:5
Blakley, Samuel G, 1942, Ap 24,17:5
Blakslee, Paul J Mrs, 1954, Ja 23,13:5
Blakstone, Nan, 1951, S 26,31:5
Blalock, A O, 1943, N 6,13:6
Blalock, Alfred, 1964, S 16,31:2
Blalock, Myron G, 1950, D 29,19:5
Blamey, Thomas, 1951, My 27,68:1
Blamy, John F, 1941, Ap 21,19:4
Blan, Samuel A, 1954, F 19,27:4
Blanc, Alberto C, 1960, Jl 5,31:3
Blanc, Auguste, 1882, Ja 18,5:1
Blanc, Edmond, 1920, D 13,15:4
Blanc, Edward H Mrs, 1953, S 24,33:2
Blanc, Eugene, 1945, Ap 7,15:2
Blanc, Gian Alberto, 1967, Ja 3,37:2
Blanc, Henry, 1941, Mr 22,15:3
Blanc, Louis, 1882, D 7,4:7
Blanc, Louis Mme, 1876, My 14,10:5
Blanc, May, 1918, My 6,13:1
Blanc, Mme, 1881, Jl 27,2:6
Blanc, Phil J, 1948, O 19,27:1
Blanc, Philip R, 1963, Jl 13,17:6
Blanc, Samuel O, 1964, D 21,29:1
Blanc, Sidney F, 1950, Je 3,15:6
Blanc, Victor H, 1968, D 17,50:3
Blanc (Gambler), 1877, S 17,2:6
Blancand, Gus, 1954, O 22,27:3
Blancard, Rudolph C, 1953, F 17,27:4
Blancard, William, 1953, Je 8,29:4
Blancett, Truman, 1945, Ja 26,21:4
Blanch, Arnold, 1968, O 24,47:3
Blanch, Norman F, 1925, Je 11,19:5
Blanch, Norman H, 1950, S 24,105:2
Blanch, Pedro, 1946, Ag 29,27:3
Blanchar, Pierre, 1963, N 22,31:6
Blanchard, Agnew C, 1938, F 16,21:4
Blanchard, Arthur, 1943, O 29,19:5
Blanchard, Arthur A, 1956, Mr 26,29:5
Blanchard, Arthur N, 1959, Ap 10,29:3
Blanchard, Charles A, 1925, D 21,21:3
Blanchard, Charles L, 1942, S 7,19:4
Blanchard, Clinton R, 1942, Mr 14,15:4
Blanchard, Curtis B, 1954, Mr 25,31:4
Blanchard, Elmer Mrs, 1954, Mr 25,31:4
Blanchard, Fessenden S, 1963, N 11,31:2
Blanchard, Finla A, 1942, Ag 6,19:5
Blanchard, Fred C, 1966, F 15,39:1
Blanchard, Frederick K, 1952, D 19,31:4
Blanchard, G R Mrs, 1903, My 4,7:6
Blanchard, George D B, 1903, D 19,9:4
Blanchard, George H, 1940, My 24,19:1
Blanchard, George L Mrs, 1947, S 11,27:5
Blanchard, George W, 1939, Ja 19,19:4
Blanchard, Georges, 1954, N 25,29:5
Blanchard, Gilbert W, 1941, Je 4,23:4
Blanchard, Gordon, 1956, S 11,35:4
Blanchard, Harold F, 1958, D 31,19:2
Blanchard, Harold I, 1955, My 11,31:5
Blanchard, Harold M, 1960, Mr 11,25:4
Blanchard, Harold W, 1952, Mr 20,29:1
Blanchard, Harry, 1960, F 1,32:6
Blanchard, Harry W, 1939, O 6,25:1
Blanchard, Henry Mrs, 1948, My 12,27:2
Blanchard, Herbert H, 1949, My 24,28:3
Blanchard, I H, 1931, D 12,19:3
Blanchard, J Cliff, 1951, Jl 21,13:3
Blanchard, James A Mrs, 1923, D 29,13:6
Blanchard, Jamie M, 1941, O 5,48:1
Blanchard, John D, 1954, Ja 11,6:6
Blanchard, John F, 1944, N 19,50:6
Blanchard, John O Mrs, 1956, Je 23,17:6
Blanchard, Joseph Armstrong (funl, Jl 12,11:7), 1916, Jl 10,11:6
Blanchard, Joseph Nathaniel Rev Dr, 1912, N 29,15:5
Blanchard, Julian, 1967, Mr 28,39:2
Blanchard, Kitty (Mrs McKee Rankin),(funl, D 17,- 13:4), 1911, D 15,13:5
Blanchard, Lawrence E, 1943, D 14,27:2
Blanchard, Lee B Mrs, 1956, Mr 6,31:4
Blanchard, Leon N Mrs, 1951, F 24,13:4
Blanchard, Lloyd A, 1952, Jl 28,15:4
Blanchard, Louis L, 1950, Je 29,29:2
Blanchard, Loyal, 1959, Mr 24,39:1
Blanchard, Marie G, 1950, My 13,17:4
Blanchard, Phineas B, 1962, Ap 24,37:1
Blanchard, Ralph F, 1938, Mr 28,15:5
Blanchard, Raymond I, 1951, O 6,19:6
Blanchard, Robert H, 1939, My 18,25:4
Blanchard, Rolla F Sr, 1949, My 24,28:2
Blanchard, Rollo K, 1953, Ap 26,85:4
Blanchard, S Turner Mrs, 1957, D 15,86:6
Blanchard, Schuyler C Mrs, 1958, My 10,21:4
Blanchard, Thomas, 1864, Ap 24,3:5
Blanchard, W Scott, 1953, Mr 18,31:3
Blanchard, Walter A, 1967, Ag 14,31:2
Blanchard, William A, 1948, Ag 12,22:2
Blanchard, William C, 1968, N 12,43:3
Blanchard, William H, 1947, Je 11,27:4; 1951, D 27, 21:3
Blanchard, William H Mrs, 1948, F 2,19:2
Blanchard, William L, 1937, Je 27,II,7:3
Blanchard, William M, 1942, D 22,25:5
Blanche, Jacques E, 1942, O 6,23:5
Blanchet, G, 1881, N 20,2:7
Blanchet, Georges, 1946, Ap 14,46:6
Blanchet, Gladys Mrs, 1954, Je 2,24:2
Blanchet, Louis B, 1923, F 6,19:4
Blanchet, Louis J, 1956, Je 7,31:4
Blanchette, George E, 1943, Ja 18,15:4
Blanchfield, James A, 1957, O 21,25:3
Blanchfield, James A Mrs, 1967, Ja 19,35:1
Blanchfield, John I, 1940, Je 28,19:2
Blanchfield, Patrick J, 1943, S 21,23:3
Blanchfield, Walter W, 1956, Je 2,19:3
Blanchot, Henri F, 1957, Jl 15,19:4
Blanck, Alex P, 1956, N 23,27:1
Blanck, Joseph G, 1955, F 5,15:3
Blancke, Frederick G, 1949, Jl 29,21:6
Blancke, Frederick Mrs, 1951, F 4,77:2
Blancke, Harold Mrs, 1951, Ja 25,25:2
Blancke, Henry L Mrs, 1952, Jl 13,61:1
Blancke, Kate, 1942, Je 25,23:2
Blancke, Leo M, 1966, N 29,43:2
Blancks, E Raymond Sr Mrs, 1944, Jl 28,13:3
Blanco, Andres E, 1955, My 22,27:2
Blanco, Antonio Guzman Gen, 1899, Jl 30,7:2
Blanco, Bugamo Col, 1925, D 6,13:1
Blanco, Eugenio A, 1964, Ag 6,29:1
Blanco, John R, 1945, D 18,27:1
Blanco, Juan C, 1952, My 4,90:6
Blanco, Raymon Gen, 1906, Ap 5,9:4
Blanco-Fombona, Horacio, 1948, Mr 26,21:4
Blanco Herrera, Julio, 1955, O 19,33:4
Blanco-Soler Perez, Carlos, 1962, O 31,37:3
Blanco y Gonzales, Alfredo, 1937, Mr 22,23:1
Blancpain, Claude Mrs, 1967, Ap 24,28:3
Bland, Francis L, 1941, Ag 27,19:2
Bland, H Willis Judge, 1913, N 16,IV,7:6
Bland, Harry M, 1960, Ap 14,37:4
Bland, Hubert Mrs, 1924, My 6,21:5
Bland, John R, 1923, Ja 7,7:3
Bland, Leonard H, 1967, Ja 1,53:2
Bland, Louisa H A Mrs, 1938, Je 1,23:1
Bland, Mose E, 1940, Mr 1,21:5

Bland, Oscar E, 1951, Ag 4,15:4
Bland, Percival M, 1965, Ja 14,35:3
Bland, Reuben C, 1941, Mr 24,17:2
Bland, Richard Parks, 1899, Je 16,8:1
Bland, Schuyler O, 1950, F 17,23:1
Blandin, Amos N, 1949, Ja 2,60:6
Blandin, Charles K, 1958, F 10,23:2
Blandina, Sister, 1941, F 25,23:4
Blandine, Rev Mother, 1937, My 20,21:4
Blanding, Donald B, 1957, Je 10,27:4
Blanding, Fred J, 1950, Jl 18,30:4
Blanding, P Howard, 1938, N 8,23:3
Blanding, Richard W, 1939, My 8,17:5
Blandori, Hugo P, 1965, Jl 15,29:4
Blandy, Charles, 1918, My 1,13:5; 1965, Je 30,37:3
Blandy, Harold F, 1922, My 19,17:6
Blandy, Isaac C, 1937, D 23,22:3
Blandy, William H P (funl, Ja 19,25:4), 1954, Ja 13, 31:1
Blaney, Catherine F X, 1937, N 19,23:1
Blaney, Catherine Mrs, 1937, S 23,27:2
Blaney, Charles E, 1944, O 22,46:2; 1966, F 10,37:2
Blaney, Dwight, 1944, F 3,19:4
Blaney, H Clay Mrs, 1966, Ap 28,43:1
Blaney, J D, 1904, Mr 22,9:7
Blaney, J Van Zandt Dr, 1874, D 14,1:6
Blaney, John E, 1922, N 14,19:4
Blaney, William, 1943, O 7,23:4
Blaney, William B, 1907, O 13,9:6
Blaney, William C, 1922, D 15,19:5
Blanford, Benjamin Mrs, 1947, F 21,19:2
Blanford, Sidney E, 1941, O 31,23:2
Blanford, William, 1920, F 19,11:4
Blanger, Bernard A Mrs (Lady M Greaves), 1955, F 24,15:1
Blank, A H Mrs, 1952, O 16,29:2
Blank, Albert S, 1954, N 5,15:1
Blank, Aristide, 1960, Ja 9,21:3
Blank, Charles H, 1951, D 13,33:4
Blank, Frederic Mrs, 1946, Mr 30,15:4
Blank, Frederick C, 1942, Ag 6,19:4
Blank, Harry J, 1966, F 8,36:5
Blank, Henry, 1949, Mr 18,25:1
Blank, Jack A, 1961, Ja 20,26:2
Blank, Joost de, 1968, Ja 2,37:2
Blank, Joseph J, 1965, Ja 18,70:5
Blank, Joseph S, 1956, Ap 21,17:2
Blank, L, 1934, S 9,34:3
Blank, Louis, 1958, Ag 21,25:2
Blank, Margaret H, 1952, My 30,15:2
Blank, Phil Mrs, 1940, O 31,23:1
Blank, Philip, 1963, My 30,17:4
Blankaert, Louis, 1945, O 23,3:4
Blanke, David M, 1955, Je 25,15:5
Blanke, Donald C, 1959, Mr 30,31:3
Blanke, George Christian, 1911, F 13,11:5
Blanke, George J, 1957, Ap 26,25:3
Blanken, Anna M, 1954, Ap 2,28:6
Blankenagel, John C Mrs, 1963, O 17,32:6
Blankenburg, Clarence L, 1953, Mr 28,17:2
Blankenburg, Lucretia L Mrs, 1937, Mr 29,19:3
Blankenburg, Rudolph, 1918, Ap 13,13:4
Blankenhorn, David E, 1940, O 20,49:3
Blankenhorn, Heber, 1956, Ja 2,21:3
Blankenhorn, Jacob F, 1940, Mr 28,23:6
Blankenhorn, Mary D Mrs, 1958, Je 12,31:2
Blankenship, Ted, 1945, Ja 15,19:5
Blankevoort, N, 1947, N 25,32:2
Blankfeld, Nathan, 1951, N 4,86:7
Blankford, Walter J, 1938, Ja 5,21:4
Blankfort, Bella Mrs, 1919, Ja 25,11:4
Blankfort, Bernard, 1967, Ag 14,31:3
Blankfort, Isaac M, 1947, Jl 7,17:2
Blankfort, Walter A, 1958, Ja 1,25:4
Blankman, Bernard, 1939, F 6,13:3
Blankman, Carlton S, 1948, Ag 15,60:4
Blankmeyer, Harrison C Mrs, 1955, Mr 23,31:1
Blankner, Frederick Mrs, 1956, N 17,21:2
Blankner, William F, 1947, Jl 13,44:2
Blankstein, Alan H, 1955, Ap 20,33:5
Blanpied, Ralph D, 1951, Mr 19,27:3
Blanqui, L A (see also Mr 2), 1876, Mr 3,5:4
Blanqui, L A (see also Ja 1), 1881, Ja 3,5:5
Blanshard, Brand, 1966, D 12,47:4
Blanshard, Paul Mrs (Mary H), 1965, Mr 11,33:4
Blanton, Albert B, 1959, My 23,25:4
Blanton, Charles L Sr, 1948, Ja 10,15:1
Blanton, Darrell E, 1945, S 14,23:4
Blanton, H J (Jack), 1955, Ja 9,86:8
Blanton, Smiley, 1966, O 31,35:3
Blanton, Thomas L, 1957, Ag 13,27:1
Blanton, William B, 1959, Jl 18,15:1
Blanton, Wyndam B, 1960, Ja 7,29:5
Blasberg, Arthur, 1961, N 27,29:5
Blasberg, Harry, 1939, Ja 26,21:4
Blasberg, William, 1962, Ag 8,31:1
Blascheck, Joseph, 1917, Jl 22,15:3
Blaschka, Rudolph, 1939, My 3,23:4
Blasco, Ibanez V, 1928, Ja 29,23:1
Blasdell, H H, 1903, My 11,1:2
Blasdell, H H Mrs, 1903, My 11,1:2
Blasdell J H, 1905, Mr 24,6:7
Blase, John H, 1951, F 22,31:2
Blase, Theodore, 1963, N 10,86:4
Blasenbrey, Frederick, 1950, Jl 29,13:1
Blasenstein, Joseph E, 1947, Ap 4,23:4
Blaser, Charles, 1937, My 12,23:2
Blaser, Fred Rev Dr, 1925, O 12,21:5
Blaser, Frederick E, 1937, F 19,19:4
Blaser, Herman J, 1957, O 10,86:6
Blasewitz, Julius, 1949, F 23,27:2
Blasey, Joseph, 1942, D 14,23:1
Blash, Rudolph F, 1956, Ap 7,19:3
Blashfield, Albert Dodd, 1920, F 10,9:1
Blashfield, E H, 1936, O 13,27:1
Blashfield, Edwin H Mrs (will, Mr 13,36:2), 1947, Ja 29,25:2
Blashow, Samuel, 1961, Jl 15,19:3
Blasi, Peter C, 1940, Ap 5,21:5
Blaslock, Richard E, 1937, Ap 2,23:4
Blass, Ethyl Mrs, 1951, Mr 1,27:1
Blass, Gustaf, 1963, Ag 8,27:4
Blass, J Lewis, 1966, Je 17,45:3
Blass, Julian G, 1939, Ag 12,13:6
Blass, Paul C, 1954, Mr 3,27:3
Blasser, George A, 1948, My 1,15:2
Blatch, Harriot S Mrs, 1940, N 21,29:1
Blatchford, Antoinette B Mrs, 1937, Jl 5,17:3
Blatchford, B M (see also S 5), 1875, S 17,8:2
Blatchford, C F Mrs, 1901, Je 13,9:6
Blatchford, Charles H Mrs, 1952, Ag 30,13:6
Blatchford, Robert, 1943, D 18,15:4
Blatchford, Samuel Justice, 1893, Jl 8,1:3
Blatchford, Samuel M, 1912, S 12,11:5
Blatchford, Thomas W Dr, 1866, Ja 10,4:7
Blatchley, Allison H, 1946, Jl 18,25:4
Blatchley, Jacob E, 1948, Ja 9,21:3
Blatchley, Willis S, 1940, My 29,23:5
Blatherwick, Norman R, 1961, Ja 14,23:5
Blatnik, Margaret Mrs, 1964, Ap 10,23:8
Blatt, Carl C, 1952, D 29,19:5
Blatt, Kurt B, 1960, D 21,31:4
Blatt, Lester J, 1965, Mr 31,39:2
Blatt, Maurice L, 1944, D 11,23:3
Blatt, Max E, 1962, Jl 20,25:1
Blatt, Max E Mrs, 1964, D 23,25:2
Blatt, Meyer H G, 1967, Je 24,29:3
Blatt, Philip, 1946, Ja 12,15:5
Blatt, Sidney Mrs, 1947, F 27,21:5
Blatt, Solomon, 1963, D 16,1:2
Blatt, William M, 1958, Ja 31,21:2
Blattberg, Wolf, 1958, Je 27,25:4
Blatteis, Simon R Dr, 1968, Je 13,47:3
Blatti, Albert L, 1947, O 20,23:3
Blattner, Adolph A Mrs, 1966, Ja 17,47:4
Blattner, Benjamin, 1956, Mr 11,88:7
Blatz, Edward B, 1961, Ap 13,35:5
Blatz, Emil, 1944, My 16,21:6
Blatz, Eva C Mrs, 1941, Ja 5,44:5
Blatz, Francis J Mrs, 1946, Mr 21,25:2
Blatz, Frederick W, 1962, Jl 23,21:4
Blatz, Frederick W Mrs, 1954, F 16,25:2
Blatz, Max L, 1950, Je 9,23:2
Blatz, Warren J D, 1950, Ag 4,21:5
Blatz, William E, 1964, N 2,39:2
Blatzheim, Henry J, 1954, Jl 24,13:5
Blatzheim, William A, 1941, Ja 29,17:4
Blau, Albert S, 1954, Ja 5,27:1
Blau, Arthur I, 1959, Ja 10,17:5
Blau, Bela, 1940, O 22,23:1
Blau, Joseph, 1968, Jl 15,31:4
Blau, Leo, 1952, Jl 2,25:2
Blau, Max F Mrs, 1949, O 24,23:5
Blau, Max Friedrich, 1923, N 26,17:4
Blau, Moses, 1954, S 3,17:3
Blau, Sidney, 1965, My 25,41:1
Blau, Thomas, 1948, N 30,28:2
Blau, William, 1941, O 9,23:3
Blauer, William E, 1957, F 12,27:1
Blaul, William V, 1939, Je 26,15:6
Blauner, Harry, 1949, Je 27,27:4
Blauner, Harry Mrs, 1943, Ap 19,19:5
Blauner, Max, 1962, Je 8,31:2
Blauner, Samuel A, 1942, My 18,15:2
Blaurock, Otto E, 1947, N 10,29:4
Blauspahn, Alfred Mrs, 1950, F 27,19:1
Blaustein, Clara, 1952, Je 18,27:3
Blaustein, David Dr (funl, Ag 29,9:5), 1912, Ag 28, 9:5
Blaustein, Joseph, 1960, Ag 23,29:4
Blaustein, Lazarus, 1962, S 17,31:4
Blaustein, Louis, 1937, Jl 28,19:1
Blaustein, Louis (will), 1938, Ap 8,19:3
Blaustein, Louis Mrs (Henrietta), 1965, D 9,47:2
Blaut, Arthur, 1967, N 8,40:2
Blauvelt, Adele P Mrs, 1938, Ap 23,15:6
Blauvelt, Bula C Mrs, 1942, Je 18,21:2
Blauvelt, C J, 1881, Ap 21,2:7
Blauvelt, Chester L, 1942, O 11,56:5
Blauvelt, Clifford L, 1940, F 29,19:4
Blauvelt, Cornelius, 1914, My 5,11:6
Blauvelt, Cornelius Mrs, 1945, My 5,15:2
Blauvelt, Edgar E, 1941, N 25,25:2
Blauvelt, Elmer, 1938, Ap 19,22:2
Blauvelt, Elmer Mrs, 1961, D 2,23:1
Blauvelt, Gerrit F, 1947, N 13,27:3
Blauvelt, Harold, 1947, F 8,17:1
Blauvelt, Hiram B D, 1957, O 17,33:3
Blauvelt, Isaac, 1925, Mr 30,17:5
Blauvelt, J Hudson, 1958, N 2,89:1
Blauvelt, James G, 1946, My 11,27:3
Blauvelt, James P, 1954, N 8,21:5
Blauvelt, jane Mrs (will), 1910, Ap 23,11:5
Blauvelt, John J Jr, 1952, Ag 27,27:1
Blauvelt, Lester J, 1950, Mr 5,92:4
Blauvelt, Lillian, 1947, S 1,19:5
Blauvelt, Louis L, 1959, Je 4,31:5
Blauvelt, Mary T, 1952, Jl 3,25:4
Blauvelt, Reginald T, 1944, Je 28,23:7
Blauvelt, Roswell P, 1963, S 5,31:1
Blauvelt, Susan C, 1950, Ap 27,33:1
Blauvelt, William L, 1942, Ap 28,21:5
Blavatsky, Mme, 1891, My 9,1:6
Blaver, James A Ex-Gov, 1914, F 1,5:6
Blaw, Morris, 1915, Ja 3,IX,3:6
Blaxter, Henry V, 1948, O 31,88:5
Blay, Carmelo B, 1941, Mr 4,23:6
Blayer, Albert R, 1964, Je 20,25:4
Blayer, Albert Sr Mrs, 1968, Ap 3,47:2
Blaylock, Selwyn G, 1945, N 20,21:4
Blayney, Charles A, 1949, Jl 13,27:3
Blayney, May, 1953, F 11,29:6
Blazas, Henrikas, 1965, N 3,39:1.
Blazejewski, Stanley W, 1943, Ap 14,23:5
Blazer, Albert, 1959, Ag 21,21:2
Blazer, Alfred, 1965, My 25,41:2
Blazer, Harry, 1948, D 26,52:6
Blazer, John, 1903, Ag 26,7:6
Blazer, Paul G Sr, 1966, D 10,37:4
Blazier, John F, 1966, Mr 5,27:3
Blazy, Sterling, 1953, N 28,15:3
Bleach, Maz, 1966, O 9,86:2
Bleakley, A, 1881, Ap 19,5:3
Bleakley, Charles A, 1955, D 31,13:5
Bleakley, Clarence L, 1963, D 29,43:1
Bleakley, H Harriet R Mrs, 1938, My 15,II,7:2
Bleakley, Rollin R, 1962, Mr 14,39:4
Bleakley, Rosalie A, 1952, F 28,27:4
Bleakley, William F Mrs, 1951, O 31,29:2
Bleakney, Frank M, 1947, N 9,74:5
Bleakney, Guy G, 1949, My 7,13:2
Bleasdale, Fred G, 1952, F 21,27:3
Blease, Cole L, 1942, Ja 20,19:1
Blease, Walter R, 1952, Ja 8,27:4
Blease, Warren T, 1955, D 21,29:1
Bleau, J Edward, 1954, D 10,27:1
Blech, Leo, 1958, Ag 26,29:1
Blecher, Max, 1943, Mr 22,19:5
Blechle, Joseph W, 1942, O 9,22:2
Blechman, Nathan, 1952, Ja 10,29:2
Blechman, Simon Mrs, 1940, O 23,23:5
Blechschmidt, Hans, 1951, Ap 15,93:2
Blechschmidt, Jules, 1947, S 7,60:6
Blechschmidt, Paul, 1961, D 27,8:8
Blecke, Edward, 1942, Mr 12,19:3
Bleckert, Harvey, 1951, O 22,29:4
Bleckwenn, Frederick W, 1912, Ja 19,11:5
Bleckwenn, William J, 1965, Ja 9,25:1
Bledisloe, Viscount (C Bathurst), 1958, Jl 4,19:4
Bledsoe, Benjamin B, 1938, O 31,15:2
Bledsoe, Jules, 1943, Jl 16,17:3
Bledsoe, Samuel T, 1939, Mr 9,21:3
Bledsoe, Samuel T Mrs, 1943, My 11,21:1
Bledsoe, Walter A, 1950, Mr 2,27:3
Bleeck, John, 1963, Ap 24,35:1
Bleecker, A J, 1884, Ja 18,8:1
Bleecker, Anthony J, 1941, N 9,52:2
Bleecker, Bache Mrs, 1964, N 14,29:3
Bleecker, Benjamin De Witt, 1916, Ja 10,11:2
Bleecker, Benjamin DeW, 1959, O 18,86:1
Bleecker, Charles M, 1946, F 1,23:1
Bleecker, E Dr, 1878, Mr 20,5:3
Bleecker, Emily R O Mrs, 1937, N 27,17:5
Bleecker, Evelyn De Witt, 1912, D 29,15:2
Bleecker, L Augustus Mrs, 1919, Je 2,15:6
Bleecker, Leonard A, 1950, Mr 3,25:1
Bleecker, Louisa O, 1939, F 15,23:5
Bleecker, Russell Mrs, 1947, N 28,27:2
Bleecker, Rutger, 1944, Ag 25,13:5
Bleecker, T Bache, 1951, D 8,11:3
Bleecker, Victor E, 1944, D 10,53:2
Bleecker, William H, 1939, F 26,38:7
Bleeker, Theodore B, 1966, O 3,47:3
Bleekman, George, 1912, Ap 4,13:3
Bleeth, Philip, 1945, My 5,15:5
Bleezarde, Edward J, 1943, Jl 18,35:1
Bleezarde, Edward J Mrs, 1951, O 21,92:6
Bleezarde, Ruth, 1962, N 26,29:1
Blegen, Julius, 1942, D 21,23:2
Blegvad, Harald, 1951, Ag 23,23:6
Blei, Jacob, 1957, Je 20,29:1
Bleibtreu, Hedwig, 1958, Ja 26,88:5
Bleich, Abraham H, 1952, N 10,25:3
Bleich, Judah, 1961, Je 1,35:2
Bleich, Samuel D, 1937, Ag 19,19:5
Bleicher, Clarence E, 1952, S 25,31:3
Bleichroder, Hans von, 1917, Ja 12,13:4
Bleichroeder, James von, 1937, My 1,19:3
Bleichroeder, Paul, 1943, Ap 11,49:2

Bleick, Theodore E, 1951, F 21,27:4
Bleick, William D, 1954, My 12,31:4
Bleicker, Ernest H, 1949, Je 22,31:2
Bleier, Michael M, 1956, D 5,39:2
Bleier, Phil, 1957, Je 24,23:5
Bleier, Willard B, 1951, S 2,48:6
Bleier, William D, 1955, My 17,29:3
Bleiler, Charles M, 1941, Ja 9,21:4
Bleiman, Max, 1904, O 29,9:4
Bleistein, J Henry (por), 1949, O 29,15:5
Bleloch, Charles E, 1940, S 27,23:2
Blenckstone, Olaf, 1953, Ja 22,23:2
Blender, Irving J, 1942, Ja 2,23:4
Blenderman, Harry J Mrs, 1961, My 17,37:2
Blenis, Charles R, 1944, S 20,23:5
Blenk, James Hubert Rev, 1917, Ap 21,13:4
Blenker, Louis Gen, 1863, N 4,5:1
Blenkner, Fred C, 1946, Je 16,40:5
Blenner, Burghard, 1909, Jl 26,7:7
Blenner, Carle J, 1952, Ap 14,19:6
Blennis, George D, 1946, D 8,77:2
Bleriot, L, 1936, Ag 2,II,7:1
Bleser, Daniel C, 1939, N 27,17:3
Bleser, Walter, 1946, O 9,27:5
Blesse, Frederick A, 1954, Je 5,17:6
Blesse, Paul, 1925, O 28,25:5
Blessing, Charles, 1948, F 6,23:3
Blessing, Earl C, 1955, Mr 29,29:1
Blessing, Edgar F, 1939, Jl 20,19:5
Blessing, Francis, 1903, D 1,9:5
Blessing, Francis Lt, 1920, Mr 16,9:6
Blessing, Frederick W, 1958, D 11,13:4
Blessing, George F Mrs, 1954, Je 15,29:6
Blessing, George Frederick, 1921, Je 26,22:3
Blessing, Henrik G Dr, 1916, My 23,11:5
Blessing, Henry F, 1945, F 23,18:2
Blessing, John G, 1952, Je 20,23:5
Blessing, Leroy C, 1949, My 24,27:3
Blessing, Peter E, 1957, Je 16,84:8
Bleston, Walter S, 1965, N 6,29:4
Bletcher, George J, 1948, F 11,27:2
Blethen, Alden J, 1915, Jl 13,11:5
Blethen, C B, 1941, O 31,23:5
Blethen, C B Mrs, 1957, Ag 31,15:7
Blethen, Joseph, 1937, O 8,24:3
Blethen, William K, 1967, Mr 1,43:4
Bletz, Alex L, 1948, Ap 2,23:2
Bleuel, C T, 1940, S 18,23:2
Bleustone, Nathan B, 1948, Ag 26,22:2
Bleuze, August, 1947, S 23,25:5
Blevins, Leonard C Mrs, 1957, F 18,27:4
Blevney, May H Mrs, 1939, Ja 8,42:6
Blewett, George F, 1963, N 2,37:6
Blewett, William E (Oct 6), 1965, O 11,61:1
Blewis, Bernard Alec, 1968, Ja 8,35:1
Blewitt, William E, 1938, Mr 14,16:2
Bley, David L, 1940, F 20,21:4
Bley, Kenneth, 1953, My 9,19:3
Bley, Walter F, 1951, D 2,90:1
Bleyer, Adrien S, 1964, O 26,31:3
Bleyer, Alfred, 1950, Ap 5,31:4
Bleyer, Arthur, 1962, O 21,89:1
Bleyer, Julius Mount Dr, 1915, Ap 5,11:5
Bleyer, Le Roy M, 1952, Jl 10,31:2
Bleyler, Charles B, 1949, Je 14,31:2
Bleyler, Clarence, 1943, Ap 17,17:4
Blichfeldt, Hans F, 1945, N 17,17:5
Blick, Ida S, 1946, Mr 31,46:3
Blick, Samuel, 1937, My 29,17:4
Blickensderfer, George C, 1917, Ag 16,11:6
Blickensderfer, Jesse S, 1949, Mr 8,25:3
Blickensderfer, Joseph P, 1960, O 7,35:1
Blickman, Harry, 1939, F 12,44:7
Blickman, Harry Mrs, 1960, Je 15,41:1
Blickman, Saul, 1960, D 4,88:4
Blickman, Saul Mrs, 1962, F 20,35:3
Blidden, David Rabbi, 1909, Ja 18,9:3
Bliden, Flora Mrs, 1922, Ap 26,19:5
Blidstein, Abraham B, 1962, Jl 3,23:2
Blieberger, Charles, 1939, Mr 7,8:4
Blied, Frank C, 1951, F 2,23:1
Bliem, Daniel, 1945, O 26,19:2
Bliesmann, Gus, 1959, Jl 16,27:4
Bligh, Esme I Earl of Darnley, 1955, My 30,13:1
Bligh, George R, 1948, Mr 16,28:3
Bligh, Robert W, 1922, D 28,17:5
Bligh, Walter E, 1967, My 9,41:8
Blight, Arthur H, 1964, F 27,31:3
Blight, Atherton, 1909, N 5,9:7
Blight, Robert Rev, 1907, Mr 29,9:6
Blind, Rudolf, 1916, F 4,9:6
Blindauer, Adam P, 1953, S 23,31:2
Blinder, Naoum, 1965, N 22,37:2
Blinn, Albert K, 1939, D 22,19:1
Blinn, Ernest Henry, 1904, My 24,5:6
Blinn, Frederick B, 1910, Ag 9,9:4
Blinn, H, 1928, Je 25,21:3
Blinn, Irving L Mrs, 1956, Jl 22,61:2
Blinn, Oscar S, 1958, D 11,13:5
Blinn, Randolph, 1943, F 5,21:2
Blinn, Robert J, 1962, S 10,29:3
Blinn, Rollie H, 1957, N 28,31:2
Blinn, William A, 1938, Ja 3,21:4
Blinn, William C, 1947, N 3,23:1
Blish, Asa, 1948, Je 25,23:1
Blish, C D, 1883, N 21,4:6
Blish, Sylvester, 1945, My 29,15:4
Blish, Sylvester Mrs, 1956, O 25,33:4
Bliss, A Rev, 1881, Mr 24,2:4
Bliss, A Stanley, 1944, Ag 20,33:2
Bliss, A W, 1903, Ag 26,7:6
Bliss, Aaron Thomas, 1906, S 17,9:5
Bliss, Alfred F, 1951, My 17,31:4
Bliss, Alfred V, 1949, Mr 4,21:2
Bliss, Alice Mrs, 1947, Jl 8,23:1
Bliss, Archibald M, 1923, Mr 20,21:4
Bliss, Arthur H, 1957, F 9,19:5
Bliss, Arthur T, 1938, S 14,23:2
Bliss, Benjamin B, 1940, N 30,17:5
Bliss, Benjamin B Mrs, 1946, Ja 4,21:3
Bliss, Cassandra H, 1879, My 2,4:6
Bliss, Catherine D, 1884, O 2,8:4
Bliss, Charles A, 1949, Mr 7,21:2
Bliss, Charles F, 1947, Ja 8,24:2; 1960, My 21,23:4
Bliss, Charles L, 1939, O 2,17:5
Bliss, Chester, 1945, Jl 12,11:5
Bliss, Chester W, 1925, Mr 3,23:4
Bliss, Clara A, 1948, F 3,25:1
Bliss, Collins P, 1946, D 29,35:2
Bliss, Collins P Mrs, 1954, Jl 3,11:5
Bliss, Cornelius N (funl), 1911, O 11,11:4
Bliss, Cornelius N, 1949, Ap 6,29:1
Bliss, Daniel Rev Dr, 1916, Ag 8,9:5
Bliss, Don C, 1945, My 22,19:4
Bliss, Douglas S, 1949, Ap 3,76:7
Bliss, Edward L, 1960, Ja 23,21:4
Bliss, Edwin Munsell Dr, 1919, Ag 8,9:4
Bliss, Elizabeth M Mrs, 1923, S 29,7:3
Bliss, Elizabeth W, 1903, Jl 22,7:6
Bliss, Elmer J, 1945, Jl 2,15:2
Bliss, Ernest C, 1916, Jl 23,17:7
Bliss, Francis Edward, 1915, N 10,13:3
Bliss, Francis W, 1957, Ja 21,25:5
Bliss, Frank W, 1939, D 3,61:3
Bliss, Franklin B, 1948, Mr 28,48:4
Bliss, Franklin W Mrs, 1944, F 7,15:4
Bliss, Frederick Dr, 1937, Je 5,17:3
Bliss, Frederick G, 1967, My 11,47:2
Bliss, George, 1873, Ap 21,5:2; 1896, F 3,1:7
Bliss, George B, 1939, Jl 24,13:4
Bliss, George Col, 1897, S 3,7:5
Bliss, George D Dr, 1923, Je 8,19:5
Bliss, George S, 1943, S 24,23:5
Bliss, George Y Mrs, 1954, S 23,33:5
Bliss, George Y Rev, 1924, Jl 11,13:6
Bliss, Gilbert A, 1951, My 9,33:2
Bliss, H C ex-Sen, 1903, S 30,9:6
Bliss, Harold H, 1956, S 21,25:1
Bliss, Harry F Mrs, 1948, Ag 23,17:2
Bliss, Helen M Mrs, 1941, Jl 7,15:5
Bliss, Henry E (cor, Ag 16,23:4), 1955, Ag 10,25:1
Bliss, Henry E Mrs, 1943, S 8,23:2
Bliss, Henry W, 1947, N 3,23:4
Bliss, Hiram A, 1944, N 15,27:2
Bliss, Homer C, 1941, F 22,15:5
Bliss, Howard S Mrs, 1941, Je 29,32:4
Bliss, Ida E (will, S 19,12:3), 1942, Ag 1,11:5
Bliss, Jay C, 1940, Jl 5,13:4
Bliss, John, 1903, S 17,7:6
Bliss, John Collins Rev Dr, 1909, Ap 12,7:4
Bliss, John H, 1945, O 3,19:5
Bliss, John S Col, 1907, S 29,9:6
Bliss, Joseph H, 1959, Mr 18,37:3
Bliss, Joshua I, 1966, Mr 6,92:7
Bliss, Julius, 1946, Ja 22,27:4
Bliss, Laura A, 1944, F 7,15:4
Bliss, Mary Newton, 1925, Ag 15,11:6
Bliss, Monte M, 1959, D 9,45:4
Bliss, Olney B, 1944, O 30,19:4
Bliss, P C, 1885, F 2,5:6
Bliss, P P, 1877, Ja 4,4:6
Bliss, Phil E, 1939, Ap 13,23:4
Bliss, Ralph P, 1949, S 9,25:4
Bliss, Reginald T Mrs, 1944, F 20,35:1
Bliss, Robert P, 1946, D 20,23:3
Bliss, Robert W, 1962, Ap 20,27:2
Bliss, Sydney R, 1939, Ag 15,19:5
Bliss, T H, 1930, N 9,18:1
Bliss, Valentine, 1937, My 14,23:2
Bliss, W Dr, 1889, F 22,5:2
Bliss, W E, 1880, D 13,1:4
Bliss, W H Mrs, 1935, F 23,11:3
Bliss, Walter P Mrs, 1961, F 7,33:2
Bliss, Walter Phelps (funl, Ja 13,23:1), 1924, Ja 11, 17:3
Bliss, Walter T, 1941, F 11,23:2
Bliss, William, 1942, Jl 4,17:7; 1951, Je 5,31:3
Bliss, William B Jr, 1958, F 4,29:3
Bliss, William E, 1948, N 3,27:4; 1968, My 18,33:3
Bliss, William Hallowell Rev, 1925, Ja 18,7:1
Bliss, William J, 1908, S 29,9:7
Bliss, William J A, 1940, D 28,15:2
Bliss, William L, 1944, D 6,23:3
Bliss, William L Sr, 1948, Mr 9,23:2
Bliss, William S, 1941, Ag 18,13:2
Bliss, Zenas W, 1957, Ja 11,23:1
Bliss, Zenas W Mrs, 1950, Ja 20,25:1
Blithe, Wesley L, 1946, My 21,23:5
Blitz, Anne D, 1951, F 20,25:2
Blitz, Antonio (see also Ja 2), 1877, Ja 30,3:6
Blitz, Daniel, 1961, Ag 1,31:4
Blitz, Hyman, 1946, Ap 2,27:4
Blitz, John D, 1960, Mr 23,37:2
Blitz, Myer, 1953, My 14,29:5
Blitz, Signor (E Harding), 1880, N 18,2:7
Blitz, William S, 1948, Ja 23,23:4
Blitzer, B, 1928, F 4,15:4
Blitzer, Jacob, 1948, N 28,92:5
Blitzer, Leo, 1959, O 1,35:3
Blitzer, Moses D, 1967, My 17,47:4
Blitzstein, Samuel M, 1945, Ap 28,15:1
Bliven, Alonzo Perry, 1912, Ag 17,9:6
Bliven, C Frank, 1945, D 27,20:3
Bliven, Emma A, 1951, My 21,27:4
Bliven, George H, 1943, S 11,13:2
Bliven, William L, 1941, Ja 26,25:4
Bliven, William W, 1942, S 25,21:1
Bliwise, Harry, 1960, Ja 7,29:1
Blixen-Finecke, Baroness (I Dinesen), 1962, S 8,1:5
Blizard, Everitt P, 1966, F 24,38:1
Blizzard, Alpheus W, 1957, O 23,33:4
Blizzard, George W, 1948, Ag 24,23:4
Blizzard, William, 1958, Ag 1,21:2
Blizzare, John W, 1941, Ja 30,21:4
Bloch, A W, 1903, S 1,7:6
Bloch, Achille, 1938, Ap 26,21:4
Bloch, Adam E, 1940, My 10,23:1
Bloch, Adolph, 1948, S 8,29:5
Bloch, Andre, 1960, Ag 10,31:1
Bloch, Armand Rev, 1923, S 2,22:3
Bloch, Arthur Sr, 1953, Jl 30,23:3
Bloch, Barney, 1943, S 2,19:3
Bloch, Bella Mrs, 1939, F 24,19:4
Bloch, Benjamin M, 1959, Ap 27,27:5
Bloch, Bernard, 1945, Je 22,15:2; 1950, N 22,26:2; 1965, N 29,35:1
Bloch, C E, 1952, F 15,25:4
Bloch, Camille, 1949, F 16,25:5
Bloch, Chaim, 1948, Mr 19,24:2
Bloch, Charles E, 1940, S 3,17:4
Bloch, Claude C, 1967, O 7,29:1
Bloch, Curt, 1952, O 4,17:3
Bloch, Dave E, 1943, Ja 6,25:2
Bloch, David, 1943, Ag 12,19:3
Bloch, Edward H Mrs, 1955, Ag 9,25:4
Bloch, Elijah M, 1955, Ja 24,23:5
Bloch, Emanuel H (funl, F 3,9:3), 1954, Ja 31,51:3
Bloch, Ernest, 1959, Jl 16,27:1
Bloch, Ernest Mrs, 1948, Ja 6,23:2; 1963, Je 8,25:1
Bloch, Henri, 1942, My 4,19:4
Bloch, Henry, 1903, Jl 15,7:6
Bloch, Henry L, 1941, D 9,31:1; 1943, Ap 22,23:1
Bloch, Henry W, 1943, Je 7,13:4
Bloch, Herbert A, 1965, My 26,47:1
Bloch, Herbert A Mrs, 1968, Ap 29,43:2
Bloch, Herbert R Jr Mrs, 1967, S 8,40:1
Bloch, Herbert R Sr, 1957, Mr 21,31:4
Bloch, Herman W Mrs, 1959, Ja 25,94:1
Bloch, Hyman H, 1964, D 23,27:3
Bloch, Irving M, 1952, F 22,22:2
Bloch, Isidor, 1944, Ja 24,17:3
Bloch, Jacob, 1941, S 18,25:5
Bloch, Jacques O, 1958, My 10,21:5
Bloch, Jean R, 1947, Mr 16,60:5
Bloch, Joseph, 1941, O 31,23:1
Bloch, Joseph C, 1946, Ag 16,21:5
Bloch, Joseph Dr, 1923, O 4,23:3
Bloch, Joseph M, 1949, My 16,21:3
Bloch, Joshua, 1957, S 27,19:5
Bloch, Julius T, 1966, Ag 24,51:4
Bloch, Kurt J, 1956, N 10,19:2
Bloch, Leopold, 1908, Je 25,9:5
Bloch, Louis, 1951, Je 13,29:4
Bloch, Louis M, 1963, Jl 1,29:2
Bloch, Louisa Mrs, 1941, F 25,23:2
Bloch, M, 1929, D 6,27:1
Bloch, Martin, 1967, S 20,47:3
Bloch, Maurice I, 1948, N 6,13:4
Bloch, Max, 1952, D 30,19:5
Bloch, Max E, 1956, Ap 7,19:3
Bloch, Monroe P Mrs, 1941, D 27,19:2
Bloch, Nathan, 1952, Mr 24,25:6
Bloch, Robert I, 1967, O 30,45:4
Bloch, Sam, 1945, O 1,19:3
Bloch, Samuel, 1951, Ja 28,76:2
Bloch, Samuel Jr, 1952, D 5,27:1
Bloch, Samuel S, 1937, O 3,II,8:3
Bloch, Sol M, 1941, S 10,23:5
Blochberger, Charles H, 1950, Ja 15,84:4
Block, Abraham Mrs, 1957, Ap 7,89:1
Block, Alex, 1953, Je 3,31:4
Block, Alexander, 1921, Ag 13,9:6
Block, Alfred L, 1949, Ja 15,17:5
Block, Alvin P, 1957, Ap 5,27:1
Block, Anita C Mrs, 1967, D 13,47:1
Block, Arthur, 1939, Ap 24,17:4; 1958, Ja 5,87:2
Block, Benjamin, 1950, Mr 6,22:3
Block, Bernard, 1951, Ja 11,25:4
Block, Bernard B, 1962, N 27,37:1

Block, Carl E D, 1948, O 9,19:5
Block, Charles, 1951, Jl 29,68:6
Block, D Finnie, 1942, Jl 29,17:3
Block, Daniel, 1958, Mr 3,27:4
Block, David J, 1939, Ap 9,III,6:7
Block, Edmond, 1946, Jl 19,19:5
Block, Edward, 1961, Ja 5,31:1
Block, Elmer, 1955, Je 7,33:1
Block, Emamuel J, 1939, Mr 6,15:5
Block, Frederick, 1945, Je 2,15:3
Block, George M, 1940, Je 22,15:5
Block, George W, 1904, Ja 16,3:5; 1940, O 31,23:5
Block, Giles, 1950, N 16,31:1
Block, Harris, 1958, O 3,29:4
Block, Henry, 1921, My 21,13:4; 1938, Ja 24,23:4
Block, Herbert, 1964, N 15,86:7
Block, Herman, 1951, Mr 9,25:4
Block, Irving, 1961, S 24,87:2
Block, Irwin, 1960, Ag 4,25:2
Block, J Horace, 1961, Jl 12,31:1
Block, Jack M, 1951, Je 3,93:1
Block, Jeanette P Mrs, 1942, Ag 2,38:7
Block, Jesse, 1957, Ap 17,31:4
Block, John, 1944, O 18,21:2
Block, John G, 1966, Je 11,31:4
Block, John Mrs, 1941, O 22,23:2
Block, John W, 1952, Mr 6,32:3
Block, Joseph, 1943, F 7,48:1; 1958, F 15,17:3
Block, Karl M (funl plans, S 22,31:4), 1958, S 21,87:1
Block, Karl M Mrs, 1945, F 16,23:2
Block, Lazare, 1943, N 24,21:3
Block, Leopold E, 1952, N 13,31:1
Block, Leslie A, 1945, F 20,19:3
Block, Lester G, 1953, D 19,15:3
Block, Louis, 1922, D 4,17:4
Block, Louis (est acctg), 1955, D 29,24:2
Block, Louis, 1962, O 12,32:6
Block, Louis C, 1940, Mr 11,15:2
Block, Louis H, 1965, N 5,37:2
Block, Maurice, 1961, Jl 7,25:1
Block, Meier S, 1967, Je 22,39:3
Block, Melvin A, 1963, Mr 12,7:5
Block, Monroe, 1954, D 24,13:3
Block, Ottomar, 1953, S 15,31:4
Block, Paul (will, Jl 1,17:5), 1941, Je 23,17:1
Block, Paul Jr Mrs, 1960, O 1,19:6
Block, Phil D (will, N 22,49:1), 1942, Jl 1,25:5
Block, Reuben, 1967, Mr 2,35:3
Block, Roy A, 1967, N 27,47:3
Block, Rudolph, 1954, Jl 24,13:2
Block, S John, 1955, Je 1,33:1
Block, Seymore R, 1960, D 22,26:2
Block, Siegfried, 1955, O 19,33:5
Block, Simon E, 1949, Ap 6,29:3
Block, Simon J, 1944, Je 16,19:5
Block, Solomon, 1943, Ja 24,42:2
Block, Wilhelm F Mrs, 1957, My 2,31:2
Block, William, 1919, My 18,22:5; 1919, My 19,17:5
Block, William J, 1958, Je 23,23:3
Blocker, Harry T, 1955, Ja 10,23:4
Blocker, Walter A, 1963, S 26,36:1
Blocker, William P, 1947, Mr 1,15:4
Blocki, Frederick W Mrs, 1947, Ap 24,25:4
Blocki, Gale, 1937, F 17,21:4
Blocksidge, Garnet (Pete), 1956, Jl 28,17:3
Blockus, Elias, 1946, Jl 4,19:6
Blockx, Jan, 1912, My 24,13:6
Blodget, Ada C Mrs, 1940, F 27,21:5
Blodget, Alden S, 1964, Je 12,32:7
Blodget, Arba, 1949, S 3,13:6
Blodget, Francis M, 1950, N 25,13:5
Blodget, H Townsend, 1937, Jl 9,21:5
Blodget, Robert W, 1953, D 13,87:1
Blodget, Rufus Ex-Sen, 1910, O 4,11:5
Blodgett, Albert M, 1942, My 30,15:6
Blodgett, Charles A, 1952, Ja 3,27:4
Blodgett, Delos A, 1908, N 2,7:5
Blodgett, Delos A Mrs, 1947, Ag 2,13:4
Blodgett, Delos A 2d (cor, Mr 25,23:1), 1967, Mr 24, 31:1
Blodgett, Elbert D, 1953, N 7,17:4
Blodgett, Foster, 1877, N 17,1:5
Blodgett, Frank D, 1954, Jl 11,72:3
Blodgett, Frank J, 1943, N 1,17:3
Blodgett, Frank J Mrs, 1943, Ap 16,22:2
Blodgett, Frederick S Mrs, 1941, S 29,17:5
Blodgett, Gardner S Maj, 1909, Ap 19,9:6
Blodgett, George L, 1938, Ja 17,19:2
Blodgett, Henry W Judge, 1905, F 10,7:4
Blodgett, John Taggart, 1912, Mr 5,11:5
Blodgett, John W, 1951, N 22,32:2
Blodgett, M E Mrs, 1933, My 12,17:3
Blodgett, Mary Louise, 1907, F 11,9:5
Blodgett, P S (see also O 28), 1902, O 30,9:5
Blodgett, Robert F, 1948, F 10,23:4
Blodgett, Russell, 1958, F 28,13:6
Blodgett, Thomas H, 1964, O 5,33:3
Blodgett, Thurston P Mrs, 1961, Mr 24,27:4
Blodgett, W T (funl, N 7,5:4), 1875, N 6,6:7
Blodgett, William E, 1947, Jl 21,17:3
Blodgett, William H, 1950, Jl 13,25:5
Blodgett, William T Mrs, 1904, Jl 9,9:6
Blodgett, William Tilden, 1917, F 1,11:5

Blodgett, Willis E, 1963, O 11,37:2
Blodnieks, Adolfs, 1962, Mr 23,33:4
Bloede, Victor G, 1937, Mr 30,23:3
Bloedow, F A, 1939, Ja 29,33:1
Bloemecke, Charles B, 1943, O 1,19:1
Bloemecke, Henry J, 1923, My 30,15:4
Bloeser, Willy F, 1958, O 26,88:5
Bloesinger, J Edward, 1954, Ja 5,27:1
Bloeth, William J, 1939, Mr 26,III,7:2
Blogg, Henry G, 1954, Je 15,3:1
Blohm, Christian, 1902, N 4,1:4
Blohm, Edward E Capt, 1925, O 10,15:4
Blokland, F Beelaerts van, 1956, Mr 28,31:5
Blom, Eric W, 1959, Ap 13,31:2
Blom, Frans, 1963, Je 24,27:5
Blomberg, Emma von Mrs, 1938, Ja 19,23:5
Blomberg, Eva von Baroness, 1937, Je 26,17:3
Blomberg, Harry, 1950, F 2,27:1
Blomberg, John A, 1944, S 13,19:6
Blomberg, Werner von Field Marshal Gen, 1946, Mr 14,8:2
Blomdahl, Karl-Birger, 1968, Je 18,47:2
Blomfield, Frank, 1942, Ja 22,17:2
Blomfield, Reginald, 1942, D 29,21:1
Blomgren, Gustaf, 1940, Ap 10,25:4
Blomgren, Mary, 1951, D 21,27:3
Blommers, Johannes Bernandus, 1914, D 15,15:5
Blomquist, Hugo L, 1964, N 30,33:5
Blomstergren, Axel W, 1941, F 25,23:2
Blonay, Godefroy de Baron, 1937, F 15,17:2
Blond, Maurice, 1955, F 13,87:1
Blondel, John J, 1939, Je 9,21:5
Blondel, John J Mrs, 1967, Jl 16,65:1
Blondell, Ed, 1943, Mr 29,15:3
Blondell, J C (see also My 9), 1877, My 10,8:5
Blondell, Kathryn Mrs, 1952, O 7,29:2
Blondin, the Ropewalker, 1897, F 23,7:4
Blonger, Lou, 1924, Ap 21,17:5
Blonski, Albert, 1945, F 8,19:2
Blonstein, Albert Mrs, 1956, F 21,33:2
Blood, A Curtis, 1948, Je 23,27:2
Blood, Bindon, 1940, My 17,19:3
Blood, Bryant H, 1946, Ag 19,25:4
Blood, Charles, 1924, Ap 30,19:2
Blood, Charles A, 1946, My 5,44:5
Blood, Charles I, 1963, Je 6,35:3
Blood, Edward Sr, 1938, Ap 27,23:4
Blood, Emily, 1943, Jl 15,21:5
Blood, Ernest A, 1955, F 7,21:5
Blood, George D, 1944, My 8,19:6
Blood, George Mrs, 1966, Jl 16,25:1
Blood, H, 1885, Je 18,5:6
Blood, Henry H, 1942, Je 20,13:3
Blood, Imogene M Mrs, 1939, Ja 28,15:2
Blood, Isaiah, 1870, D 1,2:7
Blood, John R, 1955, O 13,32:1
Blood, Leighton H, 1961, Mr 31,27:2
Blood, Mary G Mrs, 1942, F 5,21:1
Blood, Maurice, 1940, Ap 3,23:5
Blood, Robert M, 1950, Ag 5,15:4
Blood, S William Mrs, 1951, Mr 3,13:2
Blood, Sylvester Lawton, 1915, D 18,11:4
Blood, W J Jr, 1933, F 14,15:1
Blood, Wilfred D, 1938, Mr 2,19:6
Blood, William E, 1967, Jl 24,27:1
Bloodgood, Ada F Mrs, 1948, Mr 11,27:2
Bloodgood, Albert C, 1943, O 24,44:3
Bloodgood, Arthur F, 1938, Mr 31,23:1
Bloodgood, Clara Mrs (will, D 25,7:5), 1907, D 8, 11:4
Bloodgood, Clifford, 1957, O 10,33:3
Bloodgood, Del Dr, 1902, Ap 6,7:6
Bloodgood, Dudley T, 1955, S 14,35:2
Bloodgood, Francis Jr, 1937, S 10,23:3
Bloodgood, Fred L, 1952, N 25,29:4
Bloodgood, Hildreth K Mrs, 1911, Ja 5,9:4
Bloodgood, Hildreth Kennedy, 1918, F 21,11:3
Bloodgood, Howard, 1948, Mr 25,27:2
Bloodgood, Isaac L, 1938, S 30,21:5
Bloodgood, J B, 1877, Ag 2,4:6
Bloodgood, John W, 1959, Mr 4,31:4
Bloodgood, Joseph C Mrs, 1961, F 14,37:2
Bloodgood, Robert H, 1937, O 3,II,8:7
Bloodgood, Wilber A, 1923, Ap 8,6:2
Bloodgood, William D, 1940, Ap 10,25:2
Bloodworth, Ben, 1954, Ja 5,27:5
Bloom, Abraham, 1946, O 13,59:4
Bloom, Arthur Mrs, 1951, O 31,29:5
Bloom, Ben, 1940, N 24,49:2
Bloom, Benjamin, 1952, Ja 2,25:3
Bloom, Benjamin N, 1958, S 10,33:1
Bloom, Bernard D, 1958, Mr 31,27:3
Bloom, Casper, 1937, O 19,25:3
Bloom, Chauncey B, 1942, Je 1,13:2
Bloom, Daniel B, 1954, O 1,23:2
Bloom, David, 1904, Ja 24,2:6
Bloom, Dewey D, 1952, O 18,19:5
Bloom, Edgar S, 1955, Ag 15,15:4
Bloom, Edward L (funl, Jl 22,19:5), 1925, Jl 21,21:4
Bloom, Emanuel, 1950, D 20,31:4
Bloom, Frank, 1950, Ap 15,15:3
Bloom, Frank Mrs, 1945, N 26,21:3
Bloom, Harold E, 1963, Jl 19,25:3

Bloom, Harry, 1945, N 1,23:3
Bloom, Harry J, 1950, Ap 10,19:1
Bloom, Harry Mrs, 1953, Ja 4,76:3
Bloom, Henry T Mrs, 1947, F 2,57:2
Bloom, Herbert I, 1966, Ja 19,38:1
Bloom, I Mortimer, 1956, Ja 11,31:4
Bloom, Ira, 1954, F 6,19:5
Bloom, Isadore, 1959, Ja 25,61:6
Bloom, Isidore F, 1954, D 26,61:2
Bloom, Israel H, 1938, O 6,23:4
Bloom, Jacob, 1937, D 22,25:4; 1962, Ja 16,33:3
Bloom, Jacob H, 1964, F 29,21:5
Bloom, Joseph F, 1958, Ja 25,19:1
Bloom, Joseph H, 1955, Ap 13,29:4
Bloom, Lawernce H, 1946, Je 17,21:3
Bloom, Louis, 1952, S 25,31:5
Bloom, Louis H, 1964, N 2,39:4
Bloom, Lucian R, 1959, S 30,29:5
Bloom, Maurice J, 1965, Jl 14,37:3
Bloom, Max, 1952, My 23,21:1; 1966, Mr 9,41:4
Bloom, Mayer L, 1925, Jl 10,17:6
Bloom, Moses Mrs, 1951, Je 28,25:4
Bloom, Myer S, 1960, My 5,35:2
Bloom, Nathan, 1959, F 21,21:5
Bloom, Peter A, 1944, F 22,23:1
Bloom, Richard D, 1948, Ja 17,17:2
Bloom, Rubin, 1952, Ag 27,27:3
Bloom, Samuel, 1956, Jl 27,21:3
Bloom, Samuel I, 1952, My 26,23:2
Bloom, Sarah J, 1961, My 9,39:2
Bloom, Selig, 1943, My 8,15:4
Bloom, Sol, 1940, N 21,30:2; 1949, Mr 8,1:6
Bloom, Sol Mrs, 1941, Je 25,21:2
Bloom, Solomon F (funl, Ja 9,47:1), 1962, Ja 7,76:4
Bloom, Vera, 1959, Ja 11,88:2
Bloom, Warren J, 1958, My 14,33:4
Bloom, Warren J Mrs, 1946, Jl 22,21:3
Bloom, William, 1938, D 16,26:1; 1943, N 24,21:2
Bloomberg, Augustus Rev, 1906, D 3,9:4
Bloomberg, David, 1941, My 31,11:3
Bloomberg, Harry Mrs, 1955, Je 10,25:4
Bloomberg, Louis M, 1948, O 2,15:6
Bloomberg, Maxwell H Dr, 1968, O 12,37:4
Bloomberg, Theodore G, 1965, Mr 16,39:2
Bloome, Harris S Mrs, 1960, O 24,29:3
Bloomer, Armanda C C Mrs, 1951, Ag 15,27:2
Bloomer, Charles, 1947, Jl 21,17:4
Bloomer, Charles E, 1938, N 30,23:4
Bloomer, Charles F, 1951, Jl 17,27:4
Bloomer, Charles H, 1938, My 28,15:5
Bloomer, Charles H Mrs, 1949, Ja 28,21:2
Bloomer, Edgar N, 1952, O 26,88:1
Bloomer, Edward, 1940, O 9,25:5
Bloomer, George A, 1941, O 29,23:1
Bloomer, Harvey N, 1946, Je 8,21:3
Bloomer, Howard B, 1953, Jl 24,13:6
Bloomer, J J, 1931, N 11,23:1
Bloomer, James R, 1963, N 13,41:4
Bloomer, Joseph F, 1946, D 25,29:2
Bloomer, Melville H, 1940, Jl 2,22:3
Bloomer, Millard J, 1949, S 16,28:2
Bloomer, Robert A S, 1953, Je 22,21:1
Bloomer, Ruth H, 1959, Ap 18,23:6
Bloomer, Steve, 1938, Ap 17,II,7:3
Bloomfield, Arthur J, 1962, Jl 6,25:4
Bloomfield, Daniel, 1963, S 18,39:3
Bloomfield, Harry N, 1953, O 23,23:4
Bloomfield, Harry W, 1950, Jl 14,21:5
Bloomfield, Howard W, 1948, D 12,92:7
Bloomfield, James T, 1961, My 1,29:5
Bloomfield, Joseph, 1911, Jl 31,7:6
Bloomfield, Lady, 1905, My 23,9:6
Bloomfield, Leo J, 1955, N 5,19:1
Bloomfield, Leonard, 1949, Ap 19,25:1
Bloomfield, Louis A, 1953, My 3,88:2
Bloomfield, M, 1928, Je 14,27:5
Bloomfield, Mary E, 1938, My 17,23:2
Bloomfield, Maximilian D, 1949, My 7,13:3
Bloomfield, Meyer (por), 1938, Mr 15,23:3
Bloomfield, Meyer Mrs, 1949, Mr 4,21:5
Bloomfield, Robert W, 1951, Ja 14,84:4
Bloomgarden, Elias, 1965, My 19,47:4
Bloomgarden, Hyman, 1951, Jl 12,25:6
Bloomgarden, Saul, 1952, S 9,31:5
Bloomingdale, Charles, 1942, F 25,19:3
Bloomingdale, Donald, 1954, Mr 5,10:5
Bloomingdale, E W, 1928, F 7,27:5
Bloomingdale, Gertrude, 1955, O 4,35:1
Bloomingdale, Harry, 1962, Ja 6,19:4
Bloomingdale, Hattie C Mrs, 1941, Mr 5,21:5
Bloomingdale, Hiram C, 1953, Mr 17,29:1
Bloomingdale, Joseph B, 1904, N 23,9:2
Bloomingdale, Lewis M, 1939, S 30,17:2
Bloomingdale, Lyman G (funl, O 16,9:6), 1905, O 14,9:6
Bloomingdale, Rosalie B Mrs, 1956, Ja 21,21:2
Bloomingdale, Samuel J Mrs, 1956, Mr 1,33:3
Bloomingdale, Samuel Joseph, 1968, My 11,35:1
Blooms, Louis I, 1962, Ag 17,23:4
Bloor, Alfred Johnson, 1917, N 20,13:4
Bloor, Mother, 1951, Ag 11,11:1
Bloor, Walter R, 1966, F 12,27:1
Bloore, John, 1942, O 25,44:4

Blore, George W, 1950, N 29,33:4
Bloss, Claire H (Mrs D Halsted), 1958, Ap 10,29:3
Bloss, Edward B, 1941, F 19,21:1
Bloss, Frank E, 1951, Ag 14,23:2
Bloss, G D (see also My 29), 1876, My 31,8:4
Bloss, James O, 1918, D 16,15:2
Bloss, James R, 1951, Ap 23,25:1
Blosser, Matt D, 1941, Ap 12,17:7
Blossfield, Charles, 1963, Je 19,37:4
Blossom, Betty (Mrs E T B Johnston), 1957, S 22, 87:2
Blossom, Dudley S (will, O 19,19:3), 1938, O 9,45:3
Blossom, Dudley S Jr, 1961, Ag 5,17:4
Blossom, Francis, 1956, Mr 14,33:3
Blossom, Francis Mrs, 1954, F 3,23:2
Blossom, Frederick F, 1941, F 20,19:3
Blossom, George W, 1960, D 14,39:3
Blossom, George W Sr, 1942, Ja 1,25:3
Blossom, Harry F, 1956, Mr 10,17:5
Blossom, Henry Martyn (funl, Mr 27,13:2), 1919, Mr 24,13:3
Blossom, Herbert, 1958, Jl 10,27:3
Blossom, Herbert Mrs, 1953, O 8,29:4
Blossom, John T, 1946, O 11,23:3
Blossom, Peter A, 1959, Mr 6,25:4
Blossom, Virgil T, 1965, Ja 16,27:2
Blosveren, Baron B, 1955, Jl 2,15:4
Blott, Harold, 1951, Ag 31,15:4
Blott, Jack L, 1964, Je 13,23:1
Blough, Christian E Mrs, 1956, D 22,19:6
Blough, P J Mrs, 1951, My 12,21:4
Blouin, Alfred Mrs, 1943, D 9,27:2
Blouin, Robert E, 1947, Ag 31,36:8
Blouke, Milton Baker Dr, 1922, F 14,17:5
Bloundelle-Burton, John Edward, 1917, D 12,15:6
Blounk, W M, 1919, Jl 28,11:4
Blount, Bessie, 1938, Ag 20,15:6
Blount, Charles H, 1951, Ja 15,17:3
Blount, F Nelson, 1967, S 2,10:5
Blount, J H Rep, 1903, Mr 9,9:6
Blount, John A, 1948, Ag 22,60:5
Blount, John J, 1946, Je 23,40:6
Blount, Lynn H, 1965, Ja 9,25:5
Blount, Nelson, 1943, S 2,19:5
Blount, W Oscar, 1949, Ja 11,27:4
Blount, William A Judge, 1921, Je 16,15:3
Blount, William Mrs, 1911, Ag 19,7:5
Bloustein, Samuel, 1960, Ag 15,23:5
Blow, Allmand W, 1948, Mr 22,23:4
Blow, George, 1947, F 19,25:3
Blow, George W, 1960, O 30,86:7
Blow, George W Mrs (Kath), 1965, Mr 26,35:2
Blow, H T (see also S 12), 1875, S 13,4:7
Blow, J G Mrs, 1935, Ja 27,27:1
Blow, Susan Elizabeth, 1916, Mr 29,11:5
Blower, Tom, 1955, F 18,21:4
Blowers, Clayton, 1941, Jl 22,20:3
Blowers, Oscar D, 1949, D 11,92:5
Blowitz, Joseph, 1949, Jl 18,17:6
Blowitz, Opper de, 1903, Ja 19,9:5
Blowitz, William F, 1964, Mr 15,86:3
Bloxham, William, 1957, D 20,24:3
Bloxom, Angeline Mrs, 1903, N 29,7:5
Bloy, Robert K Sr, 1959, My 28,31:5
Bloy, Robert K Sr Mrs, 1953, My 27,31:5
Blucher, Irene Countess, 1954, Ag 9,19:1
Bluckhorn, Harvey W, 1941, D 28,28:2
Blue, Alex G, 1941, Ap 12,15:2
Blue, Arch, 1940, Je 22,15:5
Blue, Cary D Mrs, 1965, Jl 3,19:4
Blue, Charles E, 1947, O 5,68:5
Blue, Charles W, 1963, D 14,27:2
Blue, Harold G, 1940, O 6,48:2
Blue, Hugh, 1965, Jl 4,37:1
Blue, Leonard A Dr, 1916, Ag 19,9:6
Blue, Luzerne (Lu), 1958, Jl 29,23:1
Blue, Monte (Gerald M), 1963, F 19,8:6
Blue, Monte Mrs, 1956, Mr 24,19:3
Blue, Rupert, 1948, Ap 13,27:6
Blue, V Rear Adm, 1928, Ja 23,21:3
Blue, Walter Mrs, 1951, Mr 26,23:3
Blue Cloud, Chief, 1951, Ja 24,27:4
Bluecher, Alma von, 1961, S 13,45:4
Bluecher, Franz (funl, Ap 2,31:2), 1959, Mr 27,23:1
Bluefeather, Princess, 1947, Mr 15,13:3
Bluege, Adam, 1952, Jl 21,19:4
Bluege, Ossie Mrs, 1937, Ag 29,II,6:8
Blueitt, Virgil F, 1952, Ap 30,27:4
Bluestein, Abram I, 1947, My 11,60:2
Bluestein, Max, 1957, My 30,19:3
Bluestein, Samuel, 1949, Ja 7,21:2
Bluestine, Arthur M, 1963, O 20,88:7
Bluestone, Jesse F, 1954, Ag 3,19:1
Bluestone, Moses A, 1956, D 21,23:3
Bluethner, Julius, 1910, Ap 14,11:4
Bluhm, Conrad L, 1950, Ja 3,25:2
Bluhm, Julius, 1942, Mr 22,49:4
Bluhm, Kilian, 1950, O 7,19:1
Blum, Aaron Mrs, 1966, Ag 20,25:5
Blum, Abe J, 1950, N 3,27:1
Blum, Abraham, 1952, Ap 18,25:3
Blum, Abraham Mrs, 1959, Ap 13,31:4
Blum, Abraham Rabbi, 1921, Ag 7,22:5
Blum, Albert (will, My 8,28:7), 1940, My 3,21:4
Blum, Asher, 1960, Ja 5,31:4
Blum, Caroline, 1903, Ag 14,7:6
Blum, Charles, 1952, N 29,17:5; 1965, Jl 3,19:5
Blum, Charles B, 1957, Jl 1,23:3
Blum, Charles M, 1962, F 15,29:3
Blum, Charles Mrs, 1958, S 7,86:4
Blum, Daniel, 1941, Ja 4,13:2; 1965, F 25,31:3
Blum, David, 1965, Je 14,33:2
Blum, Edward, 1944, Mr 28,19:6
Blum, Edward C, 1946, N 22,23:1
Blum, Edward C Mrs, 1959, F 11,39:1
Blum, Emery, 1951, Mr 6,27:4
Blum, Emile M Col, 1924, S 11,23:6
Blum, Eugene, 1958, Mr 20,29:2
Blum, Ferdinand H, 1953, My 24,88:3
Blum, Francis H, 1962, N 22,29:5
Blum, George E, 1966, D 10,37:5
Blum, Gustav, 1963, Ag 1,27:3
Blum, Harold L, 1945, Jl 22,37:1
Blum, Harriet, 1943, D 4,13:4
Blum, Harry, 1947, My 20,25:6; 1952, D 13,21:6
Blum, Harry H, 1966, D 8,47:1
Blum, Harry Mrs, 1952, D 13,21:6
Blum, Henry L, 1945, Ag 23,23:4
Blum, Henry Mrs, 1939, Ap 27,25:1
Blum, Isador, 1966, N 5,31:3
Blum, Isidor, 1968, D 22,52:7
Blum, Jacob, 1938, F 26,15:2; 1955, Mr 13,86:1
Blum, Jacques L, 1947, My 3,17:5
Blum, James R, 1961, Ja 19,29:5
Blum, Jerome (cor, Ag 7,27:1), 1956, Jl 26,25:3
Blum, Jerome W Mrs, 1949, F 11,23:5
Blum, John M, 1958, My 11,87:2
Blum, Joseph K, 1961, Jl 26,31:3
Blum, Joseph K Mrs, 1956, F 8,33:1
Blum, Julius, 1942, F 28,17:2; 1954, Jl 15,27:3
Blum, Leon, 1950, Mr 31,31:1
Blum, Leon Mme, 1938, Ja 23,II,8:6
Blum, Mabel L, 1965, My 2,88:2
Blum, Max, 1941, S 6,15:3
Blum, Max L Mrs, 1946, My 5,46:4
Blum, Milton C, 1963, D 22,34:4
Blum, Milton W, 1964, N 30,33:4
Blum, Morton G, 1957, Mr 19,37:4
Blum, Myrt T, 1960, Jl 2,17:4
Blum, R F, 1903, Je 9,9:6
Blum, Ralph, 1950, My 3,29:4
Blum, Raymond J, 1945, My 24,19:1
Blum, Richard, 1948, Je 3,25:3
Blum, Richard J Mrs, 1949, F 20,60:4
Blum, Richard L Sr, 1950, My 21,104:5
Blum, Richard W, 1966, My 6,47:4
Blum, Robert, 1965, Jl 10,25:3
Blum, Robert L, 1954, F 6,19:5
Blum, Sammy, 1945, Je 2,15:1
Blum, Seymour, 1955, N 19,19:1
Blum, Sidney J, 1938, N 26,15:1
Blum, Simon, 1945, Ag 4,11:5
Blum, Theodor, 1962, Jl 25,33:4
Blum, Theodor Mrs, 1953, Ap 17,25:4
Blum, Victor G, 1954, Mr 4,25:3
Blum, William, 1942, F 3,19:2
Blumberg, Abram M, 1952, F 13,29:6
Blumberg, Bernard G, 1950, O 1,104:3
Blumberg, George, 1960, Ja 19,35:1
Blumberg, Harry Mrs, 1963, D 24,17:1
Blumberg, Herman, 1956, F 18,19:3
Blumberg, Hyman Mrs, 1965, O 20,47:2
Blumberg, Jack, 1964, D 7,35:4
Blumberg, Jack Mrs, 1959, Je 22,25:5
Blumberg, Joseph, 1944, Ap 26,19:3
Blumberg, Julius, 1955, My 11,31:4
Blumberg, Leo, 1955, Ag 21,93:1
Blumberg, Leon J, 1966, Ja 31,39:4
Blumberg, Leonard A, 1937, Mr 11,23:5
Blumberg, Louis, 1957, Ap 5,27:2; 1965, Mr 18,30:4
Blumberg, Max (por), 1938, N 10,27:3
Blumberg, Max Mrs, 1966, O 10,41:3
Blumberg, Meyer, 1954, Je 22,27:2
Blumberg, Meyer S, 1959, Mr 31,29:4
Blumberg, Milton L, 1965, My 26,47:4
Blumberg, Nate J, 1960, Jl 25,23:3
Blumberg, Samuel, 1966, Jl 15,31:1
Blumberg, Theodore L, 1959, D 5,23:6
Blumberg, Valentin (corr, Ag 4,21:5), 1961, Ag 3,23:1
Blumberg, William I Mrs, 1942, D 16,25:5
Blumberg, William L, 1938, Mr 9,23:4
Blumberg, William L Mrs, 1958, My 24,21:6
Blumberg, Yuli (Mrs B Kopman), 1964, N 14,29:6
Blume, Charles, 1963, S 19,27:5
Blume, Conway M, 1950, Ag 3,23:5
Blume, Edgar J, 1959, Jl 29,29:2
Blume, Frederick J Jr, 1960, Ap 28,35:4
Blume, Jack T Mrs, 1961, Mr 22,41:4
Blume, Joseph S, 1949, Mr 26,17:6
Blume, Julius, 1944, Ag 4,13:5
Blume, Louis F, 1946, Ag 15,25:2
Blume, Louis Mrs, 1950, N 30,33:3
Blume, Milton E, 1959, Ap 29,33:2
Blume, Paul, 1952, Jl 22,25:1
Blume, T Prof, 1883, Ag 21,2:6
Blume, William H, 1948, F 25,24:3
Blumen, Henrietta Mrs, 1952, My 2,25:2
Blumenau, Herman, 1938, Je 10,21:5
Blumenberg, John, 1916, My 10,13:7
Blumenberg, Louis, 1916, F 24,13:6
Blumenberg, Marc A, 1913, Mr 28,15:5
Blumenberg, Milton W, 1913, N 27,13:6
Blumenfeld, Adolph Mrs, 1956, O 3,33:5
Blumenfeld, Diana (Mrs J Turkow), 1961, S 5,35:2
Blumenfeld, Israel I, 1962, Mr 29,33:2
Blumenfeld, Jacob, 1955, Ja 23,85:2
Blumenfeld, Murry H, 1958, O 24,33:2
Blumenfeld, Ralph D, 1948, Jl 18,53:1
Blumenfeld, Siegmund, 1950, Je 24,13:5
Blumenkrantz, Abraham, 1961, Ag 19,17:1
Blumenschein, Ernest L, 1960, Je 8,39:4
Blumenschein, Fred W, 1946, Jl 14,38:5
Blumenson, Louis T, 1956, My 4,25:4
Blumenstein, Isabel Mrs, 1937, Mr 13,19:5
Blumenstiel, Albert, 1954, Ap 19,23:2
Blumenstiel, Alexander, 1905, Je 17,9:5
Blumenstock, David I, 1963, Ag 29,29:1
Blumenstock, Frank G, 1953, D 19,15:3
Blumenstock, James A, 1963, Ag 1,27:5
Blumenstock, Louis, 1958, O 30,31:2
Blumenstock, Mort, 1956, Jl 19,27:5
Blumenthal, A C, 1957, Jl 31,23:3
Blumenthal, A Pam, 1953, Ja 28,27:2
Blumenthal, Aaron, 1937, D 14,25:1
Blumenthal, Abraham, 1949, D 24,15:2
Blumenthal, Abraham Mrs, 1953, D 13,87:1
Blumenthal, Albert, 1912, Ja 12,13:5
Blumenthal, B, 1912, D 7,15:5
Blumenthal, Benjamin (funl, Ag 31,13:5), 1921, Ag 29,11:5
Blumenthal, Burton R, 1962, Jl 19,27:2
Blumenthal, C E, 1883, O 13,4:6
Blumenthal, Carl, 1952, Ap 13,76:4
Blumenthal, Ernest, 1954, Je 9,31:4
Blumenthal, Eugene, 1953, Mr 13,27:4
Blumenthal, F Mrs, 1930, S 22,19:4
Blumenthal, Ferdinand, 1914, O 22,11:4
Blumenthal, George (will, Jl 12,28:6), 1941, Je 27, 17:1
Blumenthal, George, 1943, Jl 28,15:3
Blumenthal, Gustav Mrs, 1957, Je 25,29:1
Blumenthal, Harold, 1951, N 21,25:4
Blumenthal, Harold B, 1961, O 26,35:3
Blumenthal, Hart, 1941, F 4,21:6
Blumenthal, Hugo (will, Ag 14,19:8), 1943, Ag 10, 19:1
Blumenthal, Hugo Mrs, 1947, Ap 23,25:2
Blumenthal, Irving, 1946, Mr 14,25:5
Blumenthal, J Leon, 1949, D 15,35:3
Blumenthal, Jacob, 1938, D 18,48:8
Blumenthal, Joseph, 1949, N 29,29:4; 1957, Ag 14,25
Blumenthal, Julius, 1959, Je 2,35:2
Blumenthal, Louis, 1957, O 10,33:2; 1966, My 12,45:
Blumenthal, Louis E, 1959, Ap 26,86:8
Blumenthal, Louis F, 1940, N 14,23:2
Blumenthal, Mark Dr, 1921, Ja 12,15:5
Blumenthal, Maurice, 1940, F 28,21:3
Blumenthal, Maurice B, 1948, Mr 10,28:2
Blumenthal, Meyer, 1951, My 19,15:2
Blumenthal, Milton M, 1942, D 22,17:2
Blumenthal, Morris, 1949, O 18,28:2
Blumenthal, Morton H, 1954, Ap 11,87:2
Blumenthal, Moses L, 1955, My 29,45:1
Blumenthal, Myron S, 1957, Jl 7,60:8
Blumenthal, R G, 1933, Ja 15,25:4
Blumenthal, Samuel, 1925, F 1,7:2
Blumenthal, Sherman C, 1968, My 4,39:4
Blumenthal, Sidney, 1948, Ja 6,24:2
Blumenthal, Sol, 1946, S 19,31:4
Blumenthal, Walter, 1937, N 3,24:3
Blumenthal, William, 1963, Ap 15,29:2
Blumer, Frank H, 1954, Mr 4,25:4
Blumer, Fred J, 1956, Mr 21,25:4
Blumer, G Adler, 1940, Ap 26,21:3
Blumer, George, 1962, My 17,37:4
Blumer, Thomas S, 1954, Mr 22,27:2
Blumeyer, Arthur A, 1959, Je 27,23:4
Blumfeld, Kurt, 1963, My 23,37:4
Blumgart, Leonard, 1959, Mr 21,21:4
Blumgarten, Allan S, 1958, Mr 15,17:3
Blumin-Kursky, Maximillian, 1950, Ja 18,31:4
Blummer, George Mrs, 1907, Ag 28,7:6
Blumoehr, Clarence, 1960, S 27,37:3
Blumoehr, Victor L Jr, 1955, Ag 26,19:1
Blumrick, Edward H, 1947, Jl 24,21:4
Blumstein, Fannie H Mrs, 1940, O 30,23:4
Blumstein, Louis M, 1920, Ja 27,15:2
Blumstein, William, 1960, Ag 30,29:5
Blumt, Alfred W F, 1957, Je 4,35:1
Blundell, Charles Mrs, 1947, Mr 23,60:2
Blundell, George, 1959, D 23,27:1
Blundell, James S, 1968, D 4,47:3
Blunt, Anne Lady (Baroness Wentworth), 1918, Ja 22,11:5
Blunt, Charles R, 1940, Ap 29,15:5
Blunt, Edward J, 1950, Jl 29,13:2
Blunt, Edwin F, 1946, S 5,27:2
Blunt, Elijah Sir, 1916, Je 20,11:7
Blunt, G W (see also Ap 20), 1878, Ap 23,8:3

Blunt, Grace L, 1954, Je 27,69:2
Blunt, James G, 1943, F 16,19:2
Blunt, John, 1913, Ja 4,9:3
Blunt, Katherine (will, Ag 6,19:1), 1954, Jl 30,17:3
Blunt, Matthew M Gen, 1907, My 15,9:6
Blunt, Orison, 1879, Ap 22,2:3
Blunt, Percy C, 1953, Mr 21,17:4
Blunt, W W, 1933, F 28,19:3
Blunt, Wilfred S, 1922, S 12,21:5
Blunt, Wilfrid M, 1967, My 14,86:5
Blunt-Lytton, Judith A D (Baroness Wentworth), 1957, Ag 10,15:3
Bluntschli, Robert W, 1958, S 15,21:6
Blutau, Theodore C, 1954, D 28,23:2
Bluth, Paul Mrs, 1939, Ag 9,17:5
Blutreich, David, 1915, F 5,11:6
Bly, James F, 1959, Jl 30,27:2
Bly, Nellie, 1922, Ja 28,13:4
Bly, Vincent T, 1951, Jl 30,17:5
Blyden, Edward Wilmot Dr, 1912, F 9,9:5
Blydenburg, Jules, 1960, Mr 6,86:7
Blydenburg, Kate Mrs, 1937, My 12,23:2
Blydenburgh, Charles E Justice, 1921, Ap 21,13:5
Blydenburgh, Earl D, 1944, N 25,13:4
Blydenburgh, Vail, 1943, My 21,20:2
Blye, Henry Clay, 1922, F 24,12:5
Blye, John H Jr, 1957, Mr 7,29:1
Blyley, Katherine G, 1961, N 3,35:1
Blymyer, William H, 1939, Ap 16,III,6:8
Blyn, Henry, 1941, N 20,27:1
Blystone, Ernest L, 1963, D 18,47:1
Blystone, John G, 1938, Ag 7,32:6
Blyth, Bertram, 1949, Je 25,13:2
Blyth, Charles Allen, 1916, Jl 6,13:7
Blyth, Charles R, 1959, Ag 26,29:1
Blyth, James A, 1944, Ja 4,17:5
Blyth, James Lord, 1925, F 9,17:4
Blythe, Betty, 1917, Ag 21,9:2
Blythe, Brent W, 1956, Je 13,37:2
Blythe, George E, 1957, My 26,93:1
Blythe, Gerard S Mrs, 1949, Jl 10,57:1
Blythe, Joe L, 1949, Ja 24,19:2
Blythe, John J Rev, 1937, D 16,27:3
Blythe, Joseph William, 1909, Mr 7,11:6
Blythe, Milton M, 1940, D 14,17:2
Blythe, Rowland P, 1961, Je 20,33:2
Blythe, Samuel E Sr, 1941, D 4,25:1
Blythe, Samuel G, 1947, Jl 19,13:1
Blythe, Walter E, 1966, Mr 25,41:3
Blythin, Edward, 1958, F 15,17:2
Blythswood, Baron (Barrington Bulkeley Campbell-Douglas), 1918, Mr 14,13:6
Blyton, Enid, 1968, N 29,45:2
Bo, Florenzo, 1954, Jl 6,23:5
Boadwee, Russell K, 1960, Mr 10,31:1
Boag, David C, 1945, My 7,17:4
Boag, Gaillard T, 1959, Mr 9,29:3
Boag, William, 1939, Je 2,23:4
Boak, James E, 1956, Ap 3,29:5
Boak, Jud D, 1952, F 25,21:2
Boak, Mabel, 1951, My 11,27:4
Boal, Adam Mrs, 1945, Je 18,19:5
Boal, David J, 1954, S 3,17:3
Boal, Donald G, 1953, Ag 1,11:6
Boal, Pierre de L, 1966, My 25,47:2
Boal, Sam J, 1964, S 29,18:5
Boal, Theodore D, 1938, Ag 23,17:4
Boan, Henry Jr, 1957, F 13,35:2
Boaney, James J, 1937, Ap 6,23:3
Board, Frederick Z, 1959, Ja 15,33:4
Boardingham, George, 1957, Ag 4,80:7
Boardman, Andrew, 1881, My 12,8:3
Boardman, Bradford, 1940, S 17,23:5
Boardman, Brewer G, 1948, Ag 30,17:1
Boardman, Charles S, 1939, Ap 20,23:4
Boardman, Dixon, 1954, O 18,25:3
Boardman, Edward L, 1939, Ag 15,2:4
Boardman, Edwin A, 1943, Ag 28,11:5
Boardman, Francis, 1943, D 14,28:2
Boardman, Frank C, 1938, Mr 8,19:3
Boardman, G Dana Dr, 1903, Ap 29,9:5
Boardman, George G, 1940, Ag 23,15:5
Boardman, George M, 1923, N 27,19:2
Boardman, George Nye Rev Dr, 1915, N 10,13:2
Boardman, Gerald D, 1961, S 26,40:1
Boardman, H A, 1880, Je 16,2:3
Boardman, Henry B, 1940, Jl 18,19:6
Boardman, Henry B Mrs, 1947, Mr 24,25:4
Boardman, Henry F, 1937, D 25,15:6
Boardman, J Griffith, 1960, Ag 14,55:4
Boardman, John L, 1954, N 17,31:5
Boardman, Kenneth, 1964, N 10,47:5
Boardman, Landsdale, 1903, S 10,7:6
Boardman, Lester W, 1953, Mr 14,15:5
Boardman, Lot, 1939, F 28,20:2
Boardman, Mabel T, 1946, Mr 18,21:1
Boardman, Nell, 1968, Mr 1,43:3
Boardman, Phil W, 1948, Ap 30,23:2
Boardman, Richard M, 1942, S 12,13:2
Boardman, Richard M Mrs, 1946, Ja 19,13:3
Boardman, Robert H, 1915, Jl 27,9:6
Boardman, Samuel W, 1956, Jl 9,23:5
Boardman, Samuel W Rev Dr, 1917, Ag 31,7:8
Boardman, Sidney Sewell, 1908, Mr 24,7:5
Boardman, Simon, 1950, Mr 26,94:4
Boardman, Thomas J, 1942, O 9,21:4
Boardman, W, 1930, O 24,23:3
Boardman, Wallace S, 1951, Jl 19,23:6
Boardman, William B, 1961, Jl 12,31:5
Boardman, William H, 1914, F 17,11:3
Boardman, William Jarvis, 1915, Ag 3,9:7
Boardman, William Mrs, 1945, F 24,11:3
Boardman, William P, 1908, My 23,9:3
Boardman, William Whiting, 1871, Ag 29,4:7
Boarman, C Rear Adm, 1879, S 16,5:3
Boarman, Marcus D, 1959, Jl 1,25:4
Boas, Belle, 1953, D 28,21:4
Boas, Edwin C Mrs, 1951, O 22,23:3
Boas, Emanuel, 1879, My 22,5:3
Boas, Emil L (por),(mem, My 5,15:5), 1912, My 4, 13:1
Boas, Ernest P, 1955, Mr 10,27:1
Boas, Francis J, 1954, D 31,13:4
Boas, Franz, 1942, D 22,25:1
Boas, Frederick S, 1957, S 2,13:3
Boas, Herbert Allan, 1917, F 2,11:5
Boas, Ismar, 1938, Mr 28,15:6
Boas, Louis M, 1938, Ja 18,23:5
Boas, Ralph P, 1945, D 8,17:3
Boasberg, Al, 1937, Je 19,17:1
Boasberg, Emanuel, 1937, Je 3,25:6
Boase, William N, 1938, Mr 8,19:3
Boatner, Victor V, 1950, F 13,21:2
Boatwright, Frederic W Mrs, 1946, Ja 30,25:1
Boatwright, Frederick W, 1951, N 1,29:2
Boatwright, Herbert L Mrs, 1955, N 9,33:5
Boatwright, John L Mrs, 1959, F 12,27:2
Boatwright, Leslie G, 1959, My 13,32:4
Boatwright, Priscilla Mrs, 1958, N 19,37:5
Bob, Charles V, 1944, D 1,25:8
Bob, Harry A, 1953, Je 10,29:4
Bob, Herman D, 1941, S 10,23:3
Bob, Maurice H, 1941, F 17,15:4
Bobadilla, William, 1964, Je 9,35:5
Bobal, Thomas J, 1953, Ap 21,27:3
Bobbink, Lambertus C, 1950, D 8,29:1
Bobbitt, Louis M, 1947, Ap 10,25:2
Bobbs, William C, 1926, F 12,19:3
Bobek, Anton, 1947, Ap 26,13:6
Bober, Herbert, 1922, Ap 18,17:4
Bobilin, Gustav, 1943, S 29,21:4
Bobker, Charles, 1960, O 21,33:2
Bobo, Robert L, 1962, Ap 19,31:5
Bobo, Stephen N, 1945, N 25,48:5
Bobola, Stella, 1949, O 11,31:3
Bobrick, Arthur L, 1957, N 15,27:2
Bobrick, Louis, 1954, N 3,29:4
Bobrick, Louis Mrs, 1956, O 31,33:5
Bobrick, Mayo A, 1939, D 14,27:1
Bobrow, Jacob Mrs, 1958, Ja 12,86:4
Bobrowski, Adam Z, 1949, Jl 12,27:2
Bobsin, Harry, 1953, N 6,28:3
Bobst, E Walton, 1964, Ag 1,21:4
Bobst, Elmer H Mrs, 1953, Mr 4,27:6
Bobst, George O, 1947, O 12,76:4
Bobzin, William H, 1947, Mr 15,13:6
Bocande, Eugene De, 1905, Je 9,9:5
Boccasile, Gino, 1952, My 12,25:3
Bocchetti, Ferdinando, 1955, Jl 3,32:3
Bocchini, Arturo, 1940, N 21,29:2
Boccia, Charles, 1951, Ap 28,15:3
Boccini, Manuel F, 1962, Ap 9,29:4
Bochau, Carl T, 1952, O 30,31:5
Bocher, Maxime Prof, 1918, S 13,11:2
Bochetti, Silvio, 1946, O 4,24:2
Bochkor, Stephen, 1954, S 10,23:2
Bochman, John L sr, 1958, Jl 9,27:4
Bochner, Philotheus, 1955, My 23,23:4
Bock, Charles E, 1940, Ja 15,15:6
Bock, Edward L, 1942, Mr 31,21:3
Bock, George F, 1949, Jl 7,25:3
Bock, George R, 1959, O 20,39:3
Bock, Gustav, 1910, F 16,9:3
Bock, H Anton, 1953, Jl 22,27:5
Bock, Harry, 1949, O 14,27:4; 1957, D 10,35:1
Bock, Harry S, 1950, My 2,29:3
Bock, Helene, 1962, Jl 1,56:6
Bock, J Henry, 1940, N 2,15:5
Bock, Lee C, 1951, F 4,76:5
Bock, Ludwig R, 1958, F 10,23:3
Bock, Margarethea A R, 1942, My 1,19:2
Bock, Nicholas, 1962, Mr 1,31:3
Bock, Oscar F, 1948, S 3,19:5
Bock, Otto, 1942, Ag 17,15:5
Bock, Walter A, 1947, N 8,17:5
Bock, William E, 1943, Jl 10,13:4
Bock, William E Mrs, 1954, Mr 2,25:4
Bock, William G, 1950, Mr 1,27:4
Bocke, William, 1946, My 6,21:3
Bockee, Elizabeth P, 1956, My 29,27:3
Bockelmann, John F, 1967, Mr 16,47:3
Bockenek, Aaron, 1949, S 16,27:3
Bocker, Charles L, 1950, F 21,25:4
Bockes, George L, 1940, Ap 29,15:3
Bockhorst, John A, 1954, Mr 19,23:1
Bockius, Morris R, 1939, Ap 14,23:2
Bockoven, Harry E, 1949, D 6,31:3
Bockstahler, Walter, 1965, Ag 22,83:2
Bockstein, Benjamin, 1952, My 24,19:7
Bockus, Charles E, 1940, Je 29,15:6
Bockus, Harry N, 1963, Jl 1,29:2
Bocock, Branch, 1946, My 25,15:3
Bocock, J P, 1903, Je 18,9:6
Bocock, Willis H, 1947, N 1,15:5
Bocqueraz, Leon, 1959, S 24,37:2
Bocqueraz, Roger, 1941, Mr 2,42:5
Bocquet, Albert Guillaume, 1910, Jl 19,7:5
Bodansky, Aaron, 1960, Mr 19,21:2
Bodansky, Meyer, 1941, Je 15,36:8
Bodanzky, Artur, 1939, N 24,1:2
Boddam-Whetham, Edye K, 1944, Mr 31,21:5
Boddie, Mary G Mrs, 1941, Jl 30,17:6
Boddily, William W, 1905, Mr 10,9:7
Boddington, Arthur T, 1948, S 9,27:5
Boddington, Clement, 1962, S 6,31:1
Boddington, Fanny C, 1946, My 29,24:3
Boddy, Edmund C, 1940, Ja 14,42:7
Boddy, John, 1952, Mr 17,21:3
Boddy, Manchester, 1967, My 14,87:1
Bode, Boyd H, 1953, Mr 30,21:5
Bode, George M, 1937, Ap 5,19:2
Bode, Herman, 1937, S 20,25:2
Bode, Milton, 1938, Ja 11,23:4
Bode, W von, 1929, Mr 2,21:6
Bode, William, 1946, O 15,25:3
Bodecker, Charles F, 1965, F 12,29:2
Bodecker, Charles F Mrs, 1957, N 13,35:3
Bodee, Lew (L P Bodenstein), 1961, F 16,31:4
Bodel, John K Mrs, 1956, O 20,21:2
Bodell, Frederick, 1938, Je 22,23:2
Bodell, Joseph J, 1950, Jl 2,24:5
Bodelschwingh, Friedrich von, 1946, Ja 12,15:3
Bodelsen, Otto N, 1940, Jl 6,15:3
Boden, Cecil C, 1959, Ja 6,33:1
Boden, Ernest J, 1948, Jl 11,53:2
Boden, George, 1950, D 27,27:3
Boden, Harry C 4th, 1955, D 2,27:1
Boden, Howard B Jr, 1942, Ag 15,11:4
Boden, James, 1955, Ja 25,25:1
Boden, John, 1913, Ag 25,5:2
Boden, John Jr, 1906, D 23,7:6
Boden, Joseph, 1965, D 23,28:1
Boden, Joseph J Mrs, 1963, Jl 17,31:3
Boden, Joseph L, 1953, Ag 16,77:2
Boden, Oliver, 1940, Mr 7,23:4
Boden, Paul B, 1937, My 18,23:5
Boden, Percy L, 1946, Ja 5,13:3
Bodenhamer, O L, 1933, Je 20,19:1
Bodenhamer, William Dr, 1905, Ap 1,11:5
Bodenheimer, Henri, 1937, D 29,21:4
Bodenheimer, John A, 1943, Ag 25,19:5
Bodenheimer, Lawrence E, 1953, F 1,88:5
Bodenheimer, Leon M, 1946, Ja 7,19:3
Bodenheimer, Milton, 1949, Mr 26,17:4
Bodenhoff, G Bertram, 1953, Jl 26,69:3
Bodenlos, John J, 1954, Je 27,17:4
Bodenos, Robert I, 1949, Je 30,23:2
Bodenstab, Theolinda I Mrs, 1941, O 10,23:4
Bodenwein, Edna S Mrs, 1951, O 2,27:5
Bodenwein, Theodore (will, Ja 28,13:2), 1939, Ja 13, 19:1
Bodenwieser, Elias, 1952, O 2,29:5
Bodfish, Clarence Julius, 1916, N 27,11:2
Bodfish, Harton H, 1945, F 2,19:4
Bodfish, Morton, 1966, My 21,31:2
Bodge, Harriet J Mrs, 1923, N 20,19:4
Bodge, Thomas H, 1942, Jl 12,35:2
Bodger, Elizabeth, 1943, Mr 28,II,16:5
Bodger, John C, 1950, Mr 28,31:1
Bodhananda, Swami, 1950, My 20,15:6
Bodian, Jack, 1949, O 14,23:6
Bodie, Ping (F S Pezzolo), 1961, D 19,29:3
Bodie, Robert J, 1947, Jl 14,21:4
Bodie, W S, 1879, O 29,5:3
Bodin, Francis E, 1943, Jl 31,13:3
Bodin, Fred H, 1962, Ja 13,21:4
Bodine, Alfred V Mrs, 1958, My 21,33:4
Bodine, Clarence H, 1952, N 21,25:2
Bodine, Cornelius, 1939, My 6,17:3
Bodine, Eleanor H Mrs, 1913, O 17,11:4
Bodine, Frederick J, 1955, Mr 31,27:1
Bodine, Frederick J Mrs, 1948, N 5,25:3
Bodine, George, 1952, Ap 24,31:4
Bodine, George I Jr, 1947, Jl 11,15:4
Bodine, Helen S, 1957, Ag 9,19:1
Bodine, John A Dr, 1919, F 25,11:3
Bodine, Joseph H, 1954, Jl 24,13:3
Bodine, Joseph L, 1950, Je 11,92:3
Bodine, S Laurence, 1937, O 2,21:5
Bodine, Samuel L, 1958, S 16,27:1
Bodine, Tom, 1937, Jl 31,15:5
Bodine, William B, 1955, D 1,35:3
Bodine, William B Rev, 1907, S 29,9:4
Bodine, William H, 1960, N 5,23:2
Bodine, William H Mrs, 1968, N 28,37:4
Bodine, William L, 1951, N 27,31:2
Bodine, William W, 1959, S 20,86:6
Bodkin, Gertrude (Rev Mother), 1966, O 19,38:7
Bodkin, Henry, 1938, O 23,40:7

Bodkin, John A, 1968, My 14,47:3
Bodkin, Martin L, 1948, D 2,29:3
Bodkin, S A Mrs, 1943, My 29,13:6
Bodkin, Thomas, 1961, Ap 25,35:3
Bodkin, Thomas C, 1950, Je 2,23:1
Bodley, George Frederick, 1907, O 22,9:4
Bodley, Harley R, 1951, My 12,38:4
Bodley, James Edward Courtenay, 1925, Je 9,21:4
Bodley, Joseph L, 1950, Mr 27,23:3
Bodley, Temple, 1940, N 24,51:1
Bodman, Fenimore L, 1957, Je 4,35:1
Bodman, George M, 1950, My 7,106:7
Bodman, George M Mrs, 1955, F 14,19:4
Bodman, Herbert L, 1958, Mr 5,31:1
Bodmer, Hulburt D, 1940, My 6,17:5
Bodmer, John A, 1960, Je 2,33:4
Bodner, Max, 1957, D 7,21:4
Bodner, Seymour, 1964, D 27,64:2
Bodo, Andre, 1953, D 23,25:2
Bodtke, Harold R Mrs, 1955, Ja 13,27:1
Boduky, Joseph, 1945, Je 28,19:3
Bodvin, Napoleon F Mrs, 1951, Jl 25,23:1
Bodwell, Charles S, 1941, Ap 5,17:4
Bodwell, Frank W, 1945, My 12,13:5
Bodwell, J C, 1876, Jl 25,4:6
Bodwell, William P, 1940, Ja 17,21:1
Body, Charles William Edward Rev, 1912, S 25,13:2
Bodziak, Edmund J Mrs, 1947, Mr 21,22:3
Boe, Gerhard M, 1942, Mr 7,17:4
Boe, Lars W, 1942, D 28,20:2
Boe, Robert R Mrs, 1943, Je 26,13:4
Boebinger, Carl S, 1952, Je 10,27:2
Boeche, Guy A, 1937, D 10,26:1
Boeck, Wilhelm Prof, 1876, Ja 7,5:2
Boeck-Greissau, Josef C, 1953, Ap 22,29:2
Boeckel, Richard M Mrs, 1952, Jl 4,13:3
Boecker, Alex Mrs, 1957, S 17,35:3
Boecker, Alexander, 1947, D 6,15:4
Boeckh, Charles B, 1940, Ap 27,15:3
Boecking, Ewald, 1950, Ag 20,76:2
Boeckler, Hans, 1951, F 17,15:1
Boecklin, Werner, 1953, F 21,13:2
Boeddinghaus, Hugo, 1963, O 3,35:2
Boedecker, H B, 1911, Ap 6,11:5
Boedecker, Karl A, 1959, My 2,23:4
Boedecker, William C, 1941, S 13,17:3
Boeder, Leo, 1958, My 2,27:1
Boeder, Robert C, 1937, Je 7,19:6
Boegborn, Gerrit A, 1953, Jl 7,27:4
Boege, Arthur S, 1963, O 29,36:3
Boege, Fred W, 1954, D 27,17:4
Boeger, Marius, 1954, F 23,27:2
Boegner, Franz, 1943, Je 30,21:5
Boegner, Marc Mrs, 1951, D 6,33:2
Boehler, Hans, 1961, S 19,35:5
Boehling, J Frederick, 1948, Je 8,25:4
Boehling, J Joseph, 1941, D 9,23:5
Boehm, Abraham, 1912, Jl 4,7:6
Boehm, Alfred P, 1942, O 9,21:5
Boehm, Charles A, 1952, O 2,29:4
Boehm, Daniel A, 1951, Ap 3,27:4
Boehm, Edward, 1952, O 12,88:5
Boehm, Frank J, 1957, Jl 9,29:5
Boehm, Fred, 1953, Mr 1,92:3
Boehm, Frederick W, 1944, Mr 2,17:4
Boehm, George A, 1959, D 17,37:5
Boehm, George J Jr, 1949, Jl 17,57:2
Boehm, Henry, 1959, F 17,31:3
Boehm, Henry Father, 1875, D 30,4:7
Boehm, Henry Father (funl), 1876, Ja 1,8:3
Boehm, J Henry, 1955, My 7,17:5
Boehm, Jacob F Mrs, 1949, S 11,96:3
Boehm, John, 1923, Mr 12,15:4
Boehm, Joseph L, 1943, Je 30,21:2
Boehm, Julius B, 1961, Ag 30,33:3
Boehm, Lewis Covington, 1921, Je 14,15:3
Boehm, Louis, 1962, O 5,33:2
Boehm, William H, 1957, Ja 27,84:3
Boehm-Ermolli, Eduard von Baron, 1941, D 10,25:5
Boehmcker, Johann H, 1944, Je 18,35:1
Boehme, Adolph J, 1946, O 22,25:3
Boehme, Anna W Mrs, 1942, D 20,44:6
Boehme, Herman O, 1938, F 2,19:5
Boehmer, Harry F, 1944, D 21,21:4
Boehmer, Louis Mrs, 1943, Mr 2,19:4
Boehmer, Ludwig A, 1954, D 25,11:3
Boehn, Hans von Gen, 1921, F 20,22:1
Boehnel, Joseph, 1956, F 9,32:1
Boehnel, William, 1942, Jl 19,31:3
Boehnel, William Mrs (Molly Ricardel), 1963, Ap 3, 47:3
Boehner, Reginald S, 1945, Ag 10,15:3
Boehrer, John J Mrs, 1953, Je 17,27:2
Boehrer, Otto F, 1950, Mr 18,13:5
Boehringer, Randall S, 1960, Ja 20,31:1
Boeing, William E, 1956, S 29,19:5
Boekemann, Berthold W, 1953, Ja 21,31:3
Boeker, Helma, 1962, Je 14,33:5
Boeker, Leopold, 1947, S 1,19:4
Boelaere, Fernand T van, 1947, My 1,25:2
Boelker, George O, 1948, Jl 22,23:2
Boelter, William G Mrs, 1945, F 17,13:3
Boelzle, Aug H Mrs, 1954, S 18,15:3

Boenau, Charles G, 1957, My 21,35:4
Boening, Louis A, 1957, O 13,86:2
Boenning, Henry D, 1943, Je 8,21:2
Boenning, William M, 1956, D 28,21:3
Boepple, Paul Mrs, 1942, F 5,21:4
Boerger, Franz, 1953, Ag 28,17:3
Boericke, Gideon, 1950, Mr 20,21:2
Boericke, William F (Feb 14), 1963, Ap 1,35:2
Boerke, Frederick G, 1938, Mr 8,19:5
Boerner, Eugene S, 1966, S 7,47:3
Boerner, Fred, 1948, S 18,17:6
Boerner, William, 1951, D 23,22:3
Boero, Filip, 1958, Ag 11,21:3
Boers, William J Sr, 1947, Ap 10,26:3
Boershmann, Ernst, 1949, My 3,25:5
Boerum, Folkert R, 1903, N 15,7:6
Boerum, John Mrs, 1910, S 12,9:6
Boes, Herbert W, 1948, Ja 13,25:5
Boesch, Gustav, 1937, Ja 10,II,10:4
Boesche, Edwin L, 1937, N 10,25:6
Boeschenstein, Charles, 1952, Jl 4,13:6
Boeschenstein, Charles Mrs, 1947, N 15,17:4
Boese, Alonzo, 1881, O 5,5:6
Boese, Clifford, 1922, Mr 21,19:6
Boese, Edwin (will), 1953, Ja 10,19:8
Boese, Quincy W (will), 1947, O 4,9:4
Boese, Thomas, 1904, Mr 26,9:6
Boese, William H, 1959, D 6,86:6
Boesel, Albert G Mrs, 1939, Ap 13,23:4
Boesel, Richard E, 1958, Mr 22,17:6
Boesen, William J J, 1941, Ja 28,19:2
Boeshore, Erwin, 1943, N 24,21:2
Boesiger, Henry L, 1954, My 8,17:5
Boesiger, Leroy E, 1953, Ag 6,21:3
Boesser, G Frederick, 1948, My 18,24:3
Boetcher, Ane Mrs, 1953, My 30,15:4
Boetcher, Walter C, 1951, O 7,87:2
Boetcher, Walter C Mrs, 1938, My 29,II,6:7
Boetel, John G Jr, 1951, F 8,23:6
Boetselaer, J C van Baron, 1943, Mr 14,26:1
Boettcher, Charles, 1948, Jl 3,15:6
Boettcher, Charles 2d, 1963, Ap 16,35:2
Boettcher, Claude K, 1957, Je 10,27:5
Boettcher, Claude K Mrs, 1958, O 8,35:2
Boettger, George F, 1954, My 10,23:3
Boettger, Robert, 1945, O 22,17:3
Boettger, Theodore Martin, 1914, Ja 9,11:5
Boetticher, Emma C, 1960, Ag 25,29:2
Boetticher, Henry O, 1953, Ag 17,15:6
Boetticher, Karl Heinrich von Dr, 1907, Mr 7,9:6
Boetticher, Otto, 1945, My 22,19:5
Boettiger, Adam C, 1940, My 21,23:6
Boettiger, Carol, 1939, F 2,19:6
Boettiger, Elizabeth F, 1941, Mr 20,21:5
Boettiger, George, 1940, Ag 3,15:5
Boettjer, Herman, 1967, Je 20,39:2
Boettke, Charles, 1951, Je 12,29:4
Boettke, Henry Sr, 1949, D 9,31:1
Boettler, William F, 1965, Mr 20,27:1
Boettner, Frank A, 1965, My 21,35:2
Boettner, Henry O, 1952, S 7,86:5
Boettner, John A, 1961, Mr 18,23:6
Boettner, Victor, 1955, Ap 3,86:6
Boetto, Pietro, 1946, F 1,23:1
Boetzelaer, E Baroness, 1942, Jl 14,20:5
Boeuf, Randall J, 1939, S 15,23:2
Boewig, Henry, 1939, Ap 1,19:2
Boex, Clem J, 1955, Ag 16,23:2
Boeyen, Hendrik van, 1947, Mr 31,23:5
Boezi, Ernesto, 1947, Ja 1,33:5
Boezinger, Bruno, 1939, Ap 13,23:5
Boff, David Mrs, 1966, F 3,31:3
Boff, Felix M Msgr, 1912, Mr 21,11:4
Boff, Jacob, 1953, My 3,89:2
Boffa, Marietta Mrs, 1952, S 16,29:4
Boffa, Paul, 1962, Jl 7,17:6
Boffey, Gertrude C, 1960, D 26,23:5
Boffey, Kenneth M, 1939, S 19,26:3
Boffey, William H, 1913, S 18,11:5
Bofinger, David T, 1949, D 20,31:3
Bog, William A, 1944, O 8,42:8
Bogacz, John S Jr, 1954, O 27,29:1
Bogaev, Harry A, 1956, Ap 22,86:6
Bogan, Berg, 1952, D 30,19:3
Bogan, L Bernard, 1958, Ap 6,88:6
Bogan, Ralph A L, 1962, Mr 25,88:3
Bogan, Simon, 1944, D 28,19:5
Bogan, William J, 1958, O 10,31:1
Bogan, William J Mrs, 1948, D 5,92:2
Bogan, William Mrs, 1958, Ja 28,27:1
Boganda, Barthelemy, 1959, Ap 1,10:4
Bogar, Joseph E, 1947, Ja 22,23:3
Bogard, Gertrude, 1940, Ag 5,13:2
Bogardus, A N Capt, 1913, Mr 24,11:5
Bogardus, C A, 1911, Je 15,9:5
Bogardus, Edgar, 1948, Je 24,26:3; 1958, My 13,22:5
Bogardus, Egbert H Jr, 1960, Ja 7,29:2
Bogardus, Frank W, 1953, N 21,13:5
Bogardus, George W, 1955, F 5,15:2
Bogardus, Henry J Dr, 1924, O 22,21:5
Bogardus, J S, 1903, Je 16,7:6
Bogardus, John C, 1953, Ag 11,27:3
Bogardus, John C Mrs, 1924, Ag 3,24:4

Bogardus, John H, 1940, Mr 21,25:4
Bogardus, Obadiah C, 1943, Ja 22,20:2
Bogardus, Obediah Mrs, 1947, S 6,17:5
Bogardus, Peter, 1868, Ap 3,5:3
Bogardus, William E Rev, 1908, Ja 6,7:4
Bogarin, Juan Sinforiano, 1949, F 26,15:6
Bogart, Arthur H, 1954, S 4,11:4
Bogart, Belmont L, 1950, Ja 8,76:5
Bogart, Charles R, 1942, My 11,17:5
Bogart, Charles W, 1919, Ja 14,11:3
Bogart, Cyril D Mrs, 1943, My 31,17:4
Bogart, David F, 1944, N 16,23:6
Bogart, Donald W, 1955, Ja 29,15:2
Bogart, Edith E, 1958, O 28,35:1
Bogart, Edwin B, 1947, Ap 23,25:4
Bogart, Elliot S, 1956, My 25,23:4
Bogart, Elmer E, 1952, S 2,23:4
Bogart, Elmer E Mrs, 1956, Jl 18,27:5
Bogart, Ernest L, 1958, N 5,35:2
Bogart, Florence, 1961, Ja 4,33:2
Bogart, George A, 1951, S 27,31:3
Bogart, George E, 1951, Je 27,29:5
Bogart, Gilbert B, 1957, Ap 28,87:1
Bogart, Gilbert Ditmas, 1913, N 29,13:6
Bogart, Harold E, 1943, D 21,27:3
Bogart, Humphrey (funl plans, Ja 16,31:1; funl, Ja 18,22:5), 1957, Ja 15,1:1
Bogart, J Z, 1881, Mr 30,8:2
Bogart, James P, 1903, D 25,7:6
Bogart, Jessie B Mrs, 1941, Mr 22,15:2
Bogart, John, 1941, My 24,15:4
Bogart, John B, 1921, N 18,17:5; 1939, Ja 19,19:3
Bogart, John Col, 1920, Ap 26,13:3
Bogart, John D, 1959, Jl 11,19:4
Bogart, John L, 1942, Ja 12,15:3
Bogart, Lloyd S, 1952, Ag 21,19:6
Bogart, Louis O, 1943, My 23,42:3
Bogart, Maude H Mrs, 1940, N 24,49:1
Bogart, Morgan L, 1915, Jl 3,7:5
Bogart, Robert C, 1947, O 24,23:1
Bogart, Rudolphus Ritzema, 1907, Ja 25,9:4
Bogart, Sarah H, 1947, N 9,72:5
Bogart, Stanley, 1960, D 26,23:4
Bogart, Walter Thompson Dr, 1968, O 8,47:1
Bogart, Warren H, 1956, D 28,21:1
Bogart, William J B, 1961, Jl 12,32:5
Bogart, William S, 1954, F 12,25:4
Bogatko, Anthony S, 1963, D 5,45:4
Bogatko, Frank X Mrs, 1949, S 11,96:4
Bogats, Benjamin, 1939, Mr 13,17:3
Bogda, Russell W, 1958, F 24,19:3
Bogdan, Francis R, 1947, N 12,27:5
Bogdanoff, Rose (mem plans, Ja 28,23:5), 1957, Ja 20,93:1
Bogdanov, Semyon I, 1960, Mr 16,37:1
Bogdanove, A J, 1946, Ag 25,45:2
Bogdanovich, Martin J, 1944, Je 20,19:4
Bogeaus, Benedict, 1968, Ag 25,88:7
Bogen, Eugene F, 1953, D 18,29:3
Bogen, Isidore, 1966, D 5,45:2
Bogen, Jules I, 1963, My 18,27:1
Bogen, Michael Mrs, 1959, Mr 25,35:2
Bogenshutz, William J, 1939, My 15,17:6
Boger, Edwin L, 1937, D 18,21:4
Boger, H Batterson, 1965, My 2,88:1
Boger, Robert F, 1968, D 13,47:1
Boger, Robert F Mrs, 1956, F 15,31:5
Bogert, A C, 1882, Je 28,8:2
Bogert, Albert Z, 1942, S 16,23:5
Bogert, Anna M, 1940, Mr 5,23:2
Bogert, Beverley, 1959, Ja 31,19:6
Bogert, Blanche, 1948, Je 3,25:2
Bogert, C R Dr (see also N 11), 1877, N 14,8:3
Bogert, Charles A, 1945, My 6,38:1; 1947, D 3,29:
Bogert, Charles H, 1946, My 18,19:4
Bogert, Charles W, 1939, Jl 13,19:2
Bogert, Clarence A, 1949, D 20,31:3
Bogert, Daniel G, 1953, Mr 23,23:2
Bogert, David, 1915, S 28,11:5
Bogert, Edward H, 1945, Ja 6,11:2
Bogert, Edward S Capt, 1924, Ap 6,27:1
Bogert, Edward Strong, 1911, F 17,9:4
Bogert, Eugene Thurston, 1915, O 22,11:5
Bogert, George H, 1944, D 14,23:1
Bogert, H K, 1875, Ag 31,5:5
Bogert, Henry L, 1965, Mr 7,81:6
Bogert, J Calvin Mrs, 1939, Ja 2,16:6
Bogert, John Augustus, 1921, Je 22,15:4
Bogert, John L, 1956, Ag 12,84:2
Bogert, John M Mrs, 1939, O 6,25:4
Bogert, John W Ex-Judge, 1919, F 14,13:6
Bogert, Marie C Mrs, 1942, Ja 19,17:2
Bogert, Marston T, 1954, Mr 22,27:5
Bogert, Peter, 1905, Mr 19,9:4
Bogert, Seba M, 1903, Je 9,9:6
Bogert, Stanley W, 1938, O 29,19:2
Bogert, Walter L, 1959, Ag 14,21:5
Bogert, Willet A, 1938, D 20,25:4
Bogert, William B, 1948, F 21,13:1
Boggess, Arthur C, 1955, S 7,31:1
Boggess, Dusty (Lynton R Boggess), 1968, Jl 9,
Boggia, B Franklyn, 1957, Ap 4,33:5
Boggiana, Adolfio I, 1949, Je 22,31:6

Boggiani, Tommaso P, 1942, F 27,17:6
Boggis, Bertram S Sr, 1958, Ja 27,27:4
Bogglid, Steen S B, 1947, Ja 7,27:5
Boggs, A Maris Dr, 1937, Jl 14,21:4
Boggs, C S Rear Adm, 1888, Ap 23,5:2
Boggs, Charles R, 1940, Ap 2,25:4
Boggs, Dexter S, 1941, N 21,17:3
Boggs, Frank, 1938, F 17,21:5
Boggs, Frank C, 1950, Ap 20,29:2
Boggs, Gilbert H Sr, 1941, My 15,23:5
Boggs, Henry, 1872, Ja 15,1:6
Boggs, Henry A, 1949, D 28,25:4
Boggs, John G, 1939, Ag 23,21:7
Boggs, John L, 1943, F 22,17:2
Boggs, John W, 1914, Ag 9,15:7
Boggs, Robert Dr, 1967, O 26,47:5
Boggs, Robert H, 1945, Ap 3,19:4
Boggs, Samuel W, 1954, S 15,33:1
Boggs, Thomas K, 1952, N 18,32:3
Boggs, Thomas Kelly Maj, 1916, F 17,11:7
Boggs, Thomas R, 1938, S 3,13:6
Boggs, Viola C Mrs, 1938, My 21,15:5
Boggs, W D C, 1878, F 4,4:7
Boggs, William Brenton, 1875, Mr 12,7:6
Boggs, William R Sr, 1962, Jl 21,19:2
Boggs, William Robertson Gen, 1911, S 16,7:5
Boghassian, Sarah Mrs, 1909, Ag 18,9:5
Boghetti, Giuseppi, 1941, Jl 8,19:4
Boghosian, Vagharshag, 1959, Ja 27,33:2
Boghossian, Missag, 1958, S 18,31:1
Boghossian, Paul O, 1962, Jl 26,27:1
Bogia, Reuben A, 1957, D 13,27:1
Bogie, Mord M, 1952, Jl 9,27:4
Bogin, Harris Mrs, 1956, Jl 23,23:4
Bogin, Maurice, 1943, Je 17,21:4
Bogin, Moris, 1957, Jl 12,21:1
Bogin, Morris Mrs, 1963, D 10,50:8
Bogin, Solomon, 1949, Ag 30,27:1
Bogislav, Ruano, 1956, F 8,33:5
Bogle, James, 1873, O 13,4:7
Bogle, R E, 1952, O 1,16:5
Bogle, Robert B, 1941, My 26,19:4
Bogle, Ronald F, 1949, Ap 1,25:3
Bogle, S, 1932, Ja 12,23:1
Bogner, Ferdinand E, 1941, Mr 14,21:2
Bogner, P Joseph, 1966, S 8,47:3
Bogolyubov, Efim, 1952, Je 19,27:4
Bogomoletz, Alexander A, 1946, Jl 20,1:2
Bogorad, George, 1962, Ap 21,19:1
Bogorad, Joseph, 1949, S 2,17:3
Bogoslovsky, Boris B, 1966, D 3,39:4
Bogoten, George, 1945, N 14,19:2
Bogran, Luis Jr, 1937, Ag 4,19:1
Bogslowsky, Joseph Mrs, 1959, Jl 5,57:1
Bogue, Edward Augustus Dr, 1921, N 24,19:6
Bogue, F A, 1946, N 19,31:5
Bogue, Galen, 1951, S 6,31:4
Bogue, H P Rev, 1872, Ja 16,1:6
Bogue, Harold J, 1959, Ap 9,28:6
Bogue, Horace P V, 1939, Ja 28,13:5
Bogue, Jesse P, 1960, F 7,84:8
Bogue, Morton D Mrs, 1945, Mr 21,23:3
Bogue, Perry D, 1941, O 19,47:1
Bogue, Richard, 1943, Ap 20,23:4
Bogue, Sarah L Mrs, 1939, N 26,42:5
Bogue, Virgil Gay, 1916, O 16,11:3
Bogus, Morton G, 1955, Jl 12,25:1
Boguslav, David, 1962, S 6,31:3
Boguslav, Peggy Mrs, 1945, Jl 24,3:7
Boguslawski, Moissaye, 1944, Ag 31,17:4
Bogutz, Albert H, 1962, Ap 11,43:4
Bogy, L V Sen (see also S 20), 1877, S 21,1:6
Bogy, Marie Mrs, 1876, F 22,5:6
Bogy, Ramsay C, 1914, Mr 12,9:4
Bohachevsky, Constantine, 1961, Ja 8,86:4
Bohack, H C, 1931, S 18,23:1
Bohack, Paul Sr Mrs, 1952, S 3,30:4
Bohan, Charles A, 1944, Je 13,19:2
Bohan, Charles J, 1942, O 17,15:7
Bohan, James J, 1960, Jl 1,25:1
Bohan, John C, 1948, Jl 28,23:3
Bohan, Joseph D, 1947, My 25,60:3
Bohan, Katherine, 1943, S 17,21:1
Bohan, Owen W (funl plans, D 7,31:4), 1959, D 6, 86:3
Bohan, Richard M, 1950, Ag 20,32:8
Bohan, William E, 1943, F 25,21:4
Bohan, William L, 1966, Ja 17,47:3
Bohane, Edward, 1940, Ja 14,42:6
Bohannon, Elbert Mrs, 1965, D 30,23:1
Bohannon, Mary E, 1963, S 29,87:1
Bohanon, Paul, 1954, S 1,27:4
Bohart, William H Mrs, 1953, N 1,87:2
Bohdanowicz, Karol, 1947, Je 8,60:3
Bohem, Anthony O, 1939, Je 17,15:5
Bohen, Joseph F, 1941, S 29,17:4
Bohen, Leo J, 1942, Ap 10,17:4
Bohen, Thomas M, 1961, D 21,27:1
Bohenk, John J, 1950, Mr 5,92:6
Bohl, Alfred J, 1944, My 20,15:5
Bohl, Ann D (will), 1959, Ag 9,27:1
Bohl, Louis J Rev Father, 1917, Ja 31,11:6
Bohland, Charles H, 1947, My 14,25:4

Bohle, Ernst W, 1960, N 13,88:6
Bohle, Herman, 1943, Jl 14,19:5
Bohleber, William, 1958, D 10,39:1
Bohlen, Charles J, 1948, Mr 16,27:5
Bohlen, Charles Mrs, 1947, Ag 15,18:2
Bohlen, Frank H, 1942, D 10,25:5
Bohlender, James G, 1956, Jl 31,23:2
Bohlenund Halbach, Sophie Mrs, 1915, Jl 3,7:6
Bohlig, Fred, 1947, O 25,19:2
Bohlig, Georg Gustav, 1918, O 31,13:3
Bohlin, G Samuel, 1952, N 18,31:4
Bohlin, Howard G, 1950, Ja 26,27:3
Bohlin, Torsten, 1950, Ag 29,27:3
Bohlinger, Alfred J Mrs (Kath), 1968, My 29,36:4
Bohlman, William, 1952, Ag 19,14:4
Bohm, Leo W, 1946, Mr 9,13:1
Bohm, Max, 1923, S 21,4:7
Bohm, Max B, 1950, Ag 9,29:2
Bohm, Oscar H, 1948, Ja 30,23:2
Bohm, Oscar Mrs, 1949, O 1,13:4
Bohm, Victor C, 1955, D 22,23:4
Bohman, Edward D, 1945, Ap 30,19:1
Bohmer, John, 1958, Je 2,27:4
Bohmert, William R, 1948, O 17,76:2
Bohmfalk, Charles W Mrs, 1951, Mr 13,31:2
Bohn, Alfred C, 1955, D 28,23:2
Bohn, Arthur, 1948, Ja 15,23:1
Bohn, Charles B, 1953, Ap 3,24:3
Bohn, Charles R, 1948, Je 7,19:4
Bohn, Emil, 1953, O 4,89:2
Bohn, H G, 1884, Ag 25,5:6
Bohn, Harry A, 1957, Jl 6,15:1
Bohn, John V Mrs, 1944, Ap 29,15:4
Bohn, William E, 1967, D 5,50:7
Bohnard, William A, 1945, N 29,23:3
Bohne, Arthur G, 1941, F 25,23:1
Bohne, Arthur J, 1954, Ja 19,25:3
Bohne, Gustave J, 1949, N 29,29:4
Bohnen, Carl A, 1952, Ja 2,25:3
Bohnen, Michael, 1965, Ap 27,37:1
Bohnen, Roman, 1949, F 26,15:6
Bohner, William J, 1940, O 10,25:2
Bohnert, Herbert A, 1967, Ag 20,88:3
Bohning, Henry H, 1947, N 27,31:4
Bohnsack, Christie R, 1964, Ja 21,29:4
Bohnsack, Christie R Mrs, 1958, N 7,27:3
Bohnsack, Frieda, 1959, F 20,25:5
Boho, George, 1915, Ag 14,7:5
Bohr, Harald, 1951, Ja 23,27:4
Bohr, Niels (trb, N 19,35:3; trb lr, N 27,36:6), 1962, N 19,1:2
Bohr, Raymond H, 1968, D 17,50:5
Bohrer, George G, 1938, Je 2,23:4
Bohrer, George Mrs, 1940, Je 26,23:5
Bohrer, John V, 1945, D 7,21:3
Bohrer, John V Mrs, 1964, O 1,35:4
Bohsung, Harold F, 1959, Ja 18,88:1
Boice, Alfred E, 1948, D 11,15:1
Boice, Charles D, 1946, Ap 10,27:4
Boice, Delancey, 1952, My 13,23:4
Boice, Hugh K, 1963, Jl 2,26:6
Boice, James E, 1953, Ja 21,31:3
Boice, Jason S, 1947, Ap 16,25:3
Boice, Jason S Mrs, 1947, Ap 16,25:3
Boice, John, 1938, S 11,II,11:2
Boice, Lee, 1947, My 5,23:5
Boice, Michael, 1950, Je 20,27:1
Boice, Theodore H, 1925, F 5,19:4
Boice, William L Mrs, 1963, My 2,35:3
Boice, William T, 1954, Jl 20,19:2
Boichenko, Alex, 1950, Je 1,7:4
Boichut, Edmund J V, 1941, Je 6,21:4
Boicourt, Marie L, 1961, D 12,57:8
Boieldleu, Adrian, 1883, Jl 13,2:7
Boies, Edward B, 1947, O 7,27:2
Boies, Horace, 1923, Ap 7,13:6
Boies, Horace Ex-Gov, 1908, Ja 4,9:2
Boies, Loren E, 1944, Mr 9,17:2
Boies, Louis, 1903, Ap 18,9:4
Boies, Sherman H Capt, 1919, D 30,13:3
Boies, W B Dr, 1919, Jl 18,11:3
Boies, William A, 1948, Je 6,72:3
Boies, William A Mrs, 1950, O 22,94:3
Boiko, Harold S Mrs, 1962, Jl 28,19:4
Boileau, Charles C, 1949, Mr 8,26:3
Boileau, Edwin C, 1941, F 20,19:4
Boileau, Phil Mrs, 1951, My 16,35:2
Boileau, Philip, 1917, Ja 19,7:2
Boileau, Raymond F Lady, 1942, Ja 17,17:1
Boillin, Joseph A, 1941, N 26,23:2
Boillod, Charles A, 1959, D 6,86:1
Boillot, Felix, 1961, Ag 18,21:6
Boire, Aime P, 1947, D 21,54:1
Boire, Victor B, 1940, S 29,44:1
Bois, Elie J, 1941, Ap 29,19:4
Bois, Henri-Charles, 1962, Jl 19,27:3
Boisdeffre, Le Mouton de Gen, 1919, Ag 25,11:4
Boise, James V, 1940, Jl 18,19:3
Boise, Otis Bardwell Prof, 1912, D 4,13:4
Boise, Philip, 1924, O 4,13:4
Boisen, Anton T (Oct 1), 1965, O 11,61:1
Boisett, Ralph, 1940, Ap 5,22:2
Boisfleury, Robert de, 1940, Ap 5,22:3

Boisgelin, Yolande de Marquise, 1964, D 30,25:3
Boisliniere, Louis C, 1941, Ja 12,44:6
Boisot, Emile K, 1941, F 3,17:2
Boisrouvray, Countess Guy du, 1958, N 8,21:1
Boissard, George A, 1947, Mr 26,25:1
Boisseau, Blair M, 1959, My 31,76:4
Boissevain, A A H, 1921, Ap 20,13:6
Boissevain, Adolphe, 1951, S 12,31:4
Boissevain, Charles H, 1946, O 19,21:1
Boissevain, Daniel G, 1940, N 28,23:2
Boissevain, Ernest W Mrs, 1948, Jl 17,15:5
Boissevain, Eugen J, 1949, Ag 31,23:6
Boissevain, G Louis (funl, Ap 28,15:4), 1924, Ap 26, 15:4
Boissevain, Henri F, 1958, S 28,88:3
Boissevain, Henri Mrs, 1957, Je 9,88:5
Boissevain, Inez, 1916, N 27,11:1
Boissevain, Robert, 1938, Ap 25,15:5
Boissevain, Walrave, 1944, Ap 21,19:2
Boissier, Arthur P, 1953, O 5,27:4
Boissier, Leopold, 1968, O 23,47:1
Boisson, Pierre F, 1948, Jl 22,23:4
Boit, Edward D, 1915, Ap 23,13:4
Boiteux, Diable (Baron de Vaux), 1915, D 30,13:5
Boivin, August A, 1959, D 14,31:5
Boivin, G H, 1926, Ag 8,16:1
Boivin-Champeaux, Jean, 1954, D 19,84:2
Bojar, Stephen, 1953, Mr 29,93:1
Bojer, Johan, 1959, Jl 4,15:3
Bok, Curtis (estate appraisal), 1963, My 28,33:1
Bok, Edward W, 1930, Ja 10,21:1
Bok, Flora L Mrs, 1937, O 24,II,9:1
Bok, W Curtis, 1962, My 23,45:1
Bokanowski, M, 1928, S 3,1:5
Bokelund, Chester S, 1953, O 9,27:3
Boker, Bela, 1964, Ag 24,27:3
Boker, Carl F Jr, 1948, Je 15,27:5
Boker, G H, 1890, Ja 3,5:2
Boker, H, 1884, F 9,5:2
Boker, Hermann D, 1962, Ag 17,23:5
Bokhara, Emir of (Sayid Abdul Ahad), 1911, Ja 6,9:4
Bokhari, Ahmed S (funl, D 7,88:2), 1958, D 6,23:3
Bokor, Margit (por), 1949, N 10,31:3
Bokras, Andrew J, 1951, Ag 10,15:2
Bokros, Mary B, 1948, F 7,15:4
Bokser, Maurice A, 1959, S 16,39:3
Bokum, Norris H, 1937, My 23,II,11:1
Bol, Cornelis, 1965, Ag 1,76:5
Bolam, Robert Sir, 1939, Ap 30,44:6
Bolam, Silvester, 1953, Ap 28,27:5
Bolan, Daniel J, 1941, My 9,21:5
Bolan, James S, 1952, My 27,27:1
Bolan, John E, 1940, My 2,24:3
Bolan, John J, 1942, D 15,27:3; 1951, Je 27,29:2
Boland, Berchmans J, 1952, D 27,9:4
Boland, Bridget G Mrs, 1943, S 16,21:5
Boland, Charlie, 1961, My 6,35:8
Boland, Clay A, 1963, Jl 25,25:3
Boland, Daniel L, 1959, My 6,39:3
Boland, Ellen S M, 1949, S 7,29:2
Boland, Francis J, 1961, Ja 2,25:2
Boland, Francis P, 1948, My 16,68:3
Boland, Frank A K, 1967, Jl 3,17:4
Boland, Frank K, 1953, N 12,31:4
Boland, Frederick A, 1940, D 28,15:4
Boland, Helen, 1948, F 16,21:3
Boland, Helen C, 1955, My 24,31:3
Boland, Henry B, 1947, Ap 2,28:3
Boland, James C, 1947, F 19,25:3
Boland, James J, 1940, D 3,25:2
Boland, James J (funl, Ja 18,27:5), 1955, Ja 14,21:4
Boland, James J (funl, My 19,88:4), 1957, My 15, 35:1
Boland, James P, 1949, Ap 29,23:5
Boland, John, 1940, Ap 20,17:2; 1947, Jl 26,13:6
Boland, John F, 1956, F 21,33:4
Boland, John F Jr, 1962, F 17,19:4
Boland, John J, 1956, O 5,25:4
Boland, John J Sr Mrs, 1952, Ag 14,23:3
Boland, John L, 1905, Mr 22,9:6
Boland, John P, 1952, Ag 16,27:4; 1964, Ag 8,19:3
Boland, John P Msgr, 1968, Jl 1,33:1
Boland, Joseph, 1960, F 27,19:4
Boland, Joseph E, 1952, Ag 23,13:4
Boland, Joseph J, 1964, S 13,86:7
Boland, Joseph M, 1950, Ap 28,21:2
Boland, Joseph M Mrs, 1966, D 24,19:5
Boland, Joseph P, 1948, D 13,23:3
Boland, Lilian C, 1965, D 10,42:6
Boland, Mary, 1965, Je 24,35:1
Boland, Mary A, 1947, Ja 10,22:2
Boland, Matthew J, 1953, Jl 17,17:4
Boland, Michael J, 1961, D 21,27:4
Boland, Patrick, 1950, Jl 27,25:4
Boland, Patrick J, 1957, F 16,17:5
Boland, Patrick M, 1942, My 19,19:1
Boland, Paul A Bro, 1953, Jl 24,13:7
Boland, Rev, 1908, S 27,11:7
Boland, Russell, 1954, N 6,17:2
Boland, Thomas, 1952, F 4,17:3
Boland, Thomas F, 1957, Ap 18,29:1
Boland, William T Mrs, 1956, S 19,37:1
Bolande, Frank W, 1916, O 16,11:5

Bolander, Arthur, 1951, Mr 12,25:4
Bold, George A, 1951, Ja 24,27:4
Bold, Peter, 1937, Je 22,23:2
Bolde, Conrad, 1950, N 12,94:7
Boldenweck, William, 1922, Ag 24,15:5
Boldrewood, Rolf, 1915, Mr 12,11:6
Boldt, George (por),(funl, D 7,13:4), 1916, D 6,9:1
Boldt, George C Jr, 1958, Ja 27,27:1
Boldt, George C Mrs, 1904, Ja 9,9:2
Boldt, Hans, 1938, Je 14,15:3
Boldt, Joseph R, 1966, My 23,41:2
Bolduan, Charles F, 1950, Jl 5,32:2
Bolduc, J E, 1950, Ap 7,25:4
Bolduc, Joseph Sen, 1924, Ag 15,13:7
Bole, Benjamin P, 1941, N 28,23:1
Bole, Benjamin P Mrs, 1950, O 30,27:3
Bole, Hamilton B, 1953, Ja 5,21:3
Bole, James P, 1940, Mr 27,21:2
Bole, Joseph K, 1952, Jl 25,17:3
Bole, Joseph K Jr, 1956, Jl 21,15:4
Boleman Jno R, 1956, My 22,33:1
Bolen, David D, 1950, S 25,23:3
Bolen, Edwin S, 1940, Je 4,24:2
Bolen, Grace R, 1941, Ag 23,13:4
Bolen, John K, 1938, S 6,21:4
Bolen, Newton W, 1939, D 31,19:1
Bolender, Alfred T Mrs, 1950, Ja 25,27:4
Bolenius, A W Maj, 1885, Ap 29,5:6
Bolens, Walter L, 1937, Mr 1,20:1
Boles, Abigail J, 1950, S 30,17:3
Boles, David E, 1939, Ag 3,19:4
Boles, Dexter, 1950, Ag 21,19:3
Boles, Edgar H, 1950, F 6,25:1
Boles, Edgar H Mrs, 1954, Ag 9,17:3
Boles, George, 1944, F 28,17:2
Boles, John M Mrs, 1950, Jl 21,19:3
Boles, Leo A, 1943, Je 20,34:4
Boles, William R, 1950, Mr 4,17:3
Boleschka, Charles F, 1939, Mr 3,23:4
Boleslawski, Richard, 1937, Ja 18,17:1
Bolet, Nicanor, 1920, Ag 6,9:6
Bolet, Nicanor L, 1939, Ag 3,19:5
Boley, Henry B, 1967, O 25,47:1
Boley, Henry M Mrs, 1942, Ag 10,19:4
Boley, Jean, 1957, O 8,36:1
Boley, Joseph A, 1965, Je 1,39:2
Boley, Orville F, 1965, S 1,37:6
Boley, William S, 1955, Je 7,33:4
Boleyn, John, 1946, Ja 6,40:7
Bolger, Edwin A, 1924, Ap 6,27:1
Bolger, Frank, 1955, D 1,35:1
Bolger, Frank J, 1956, Je 30,17:2
Bolger, James C, 1951, D 8,11:2
Bolger, John A, 1942, O 31,15:2
Bolger, Leo, 1948, Je 27,52:6
Bolger, Patrick A, 1966, Ag 18,35:5
Bolger, Paul S L, 1961, Mr 26,93:1
Bolger, Paul S 3d, 1961, D 14,43:4
Bolger, William H, 1957, My 29,27:2
Bolger, William M, 1949, My 20,27:5
Bolhack, Samuel, 1966, Ag 25,37:1
Bolich, Daniel A, 1966, F 24,37:2
Bolig, Harry, 1956, Mr 30,19:5
Bolin, Gaius C, 1946, Ap 17,25:4
Bolitho, Gordon Mrs, 1956, Ag 1,23:5
Bolitho, James H, 1943, F 16,19:5
Bolitho, W (W B Ryall), 1930, Je 4,27:3
Bolitz, Wendel Jr, 1937, Ag 12,19:3
Bolivar, Bert A, 1953, My 1,22:4
Bolivar, Clemencia P, 1942, S 11,21:3
Bolk, Klass, 1953, F 19,23:4
Bolkestein, Hendrik, 1942, S 25,21:4
Boll, Arthur J, 1941, D 16,27:6
Boll, George Mrs, 1956, Ja 18,31:2
Boll, Henry P, 1949, S 3,13:4
Boll, John J, 1951, Ag 9,21:3
Bolland, Mary H Mrs, 1939, Mr 6,15:3
Bollard, Ralph H Mrs, 1942, My 22,21:5; 1961, O 17, 39:4
Bollard, Robert G, 1964, N 3,31:3
Bollati, Ambrogio, 1950, Mr 30,29:4
Bollati, Riccardo, 1939, O 14,19:4
Bolle, Edward C, 1938, O 30,41:3
Bolle, Raymond J, 1952, Ap 8,29:4
Bollee, Amedee, 1917, Ja 22,11:3
Bollee, Leon, 1913, D 18,9:6
Bollenbacher, John C, 1939, Mr 5,48:4
Bollens, Ann M Mrs, 1941, D 24,17:1
Bollens, Lilly A, 1948, S 28,27:2
Boller, Alfred Pancoast, 1912, D 11,13:4
Boller, Edward O, 1954, S 15,33:3
Boller, Frank H Mrs, 1965, Ag 12,27:1
Boller, Vernon Wright, 1919, Je 26,9:3
Bollerman, Howard, 1966, Ag 16,39:3
Bolles, Albert S, 1939, My 9,24:4
Bolles, Enoch Sen, 1865, Jl 7,2:2
Bolles, Frederick N, 1960, Ag 29,25:2
Bolles, George E, 1955, S 24,19:4
Bolles, Harriet M Mrs, 1941, Ja 27,15:5
Bolles, Henry J, 1942, Jl 8,23:3
Bolles, John A, 1951, D 14,31:1
Bolles, Lemuel L, 1957, Jl 2,27:4
Bolles, Lillie H Mrs, 1943, F 10,25:4
Bolles, Randolph, 1939, Jl 22,15:6
Bolles, Reuben C, 1941, My 21,23:6
Bolles, Richard J, 1917, Mr 27,11:5
Bolles, Robert E, 1944, Jl 11,15:2
Bolles, Stephen, 1941, Jl 9,21:1
Bolles, William E M, 1950, O 3,31:2
Bolles, William L, 1951, S 27,31:2
Bolletieri, Angelo R, 1965, O 24,86:6
Bollettieri, James Jr, 1951, O 12,22:6
Bolley, Leo, 1949, O 28,23:1
Bolli, Hugo, 1967, Ap 5,4:6
Bolling, Alex R, 1964, Je 4,37:1
Bolling, Bertha, 1937, S 21,25:1
Bolling, Charles E Mrs, 1947, Ja 19,53:1
Bolling, George E, 1945, My 21,19:3
Bolling, George M, 1963, Je 3,29:3
Bolling, George W, 1940, Je 14,21:4
Bolling, John A, 1939, O 27,23:4
Bolling, Powhatan, 1921, Ag 12,13:6
Bolling, Raynal C Mrs, 1961, D 14,43:1
Bolling, Robert H, 1955, My 9,23:4
Bolling, Rolfe E Mrs, 1944, Ap 13,19:5
Bolling, Stith Gen, 1916, N 9,13:6
Bolling, Thomas A Mrs, 1956, Ja 9,25:1
Bolling, William Mrs, 1925, N 22,9:2
Bollinger, Anne (Mrs J T Nielsen), 1962, Jl 17,25:3
Bollinger, Arthur F, 1950, Ap 15,15:2
Bollinger, Charles, 1957, S 27,19:2
Bollinger, Conrad, 1946, N 4,25:5
Bollinger, Henry W, 1951, D 2,91:1
Bollinger, Jacob, 1948, D 14,29:3
Bollinger, James W, 1951, F 1,25:3
Bollinger, William W, 1947, Mr 16,60:3
Bolljahn, John T, 1960, Je 26,72:8
Bollman, William H, 1954, N 25,29:2
Bollman, William P 3d, 1968, N 8,47:4
Bollschweiler, Albert, 1937, Ag 11,24:3
Bollt, Max, 1967, Ap 14,39:3
Bolm, Adolf, 1951, Ap 17,29:2
Bolmer, Daniel G, 1962, Ja 31,31:4
Bolmer, Gertrude S Mrs, 1943, N 23,26:2
Bolmer, William B 2d, 1955, O 5,35:5
Bolo, Msgr, 1921, Mr 20,22:2
Bolognesi, Aldo, 1949, Jl 11,17:5
Bolognesi, Giulio, 1963, D 20,29:1
Bolognino, John R, 1940, O 23,23:4
Bolognino, Laurence S, 1963, N 10,87:2
Bolon, Gordon K, 1961, Jl 1,17:2
Bolotovsky, Julius J, 1957, Ag 26,23:4
Bolsaubin, Edward L, 1915, Jl 30,9:7
Bolser, Charles E, 1957, Jl 30,23:4
Bolser, Claude M, 1968, Mr 6,47:2
Bolsey, Jacques, 1962, Ja 21,88:3
Bolshaw, Harris, 1947, Jl 9,23:4
Bolsover, Edward C Sr, 1938, N 19,17:5
Bolster, Calvin L, 1948, F 16,22:2
Bolster, Charles E, 1945, Ja 27,11:2
Bolster, Frelon E, 1940, N 24,51:2
Bolster, Jeanie T Mrs, 1937, Mr 13,19:1
Bolster, Wilfred, 1947, My 4,60:4
Bolster, William W, 1944, Ag 12,11:3
Bolt, George W, 1951, Ag 7,4:6
Bolte, Charles, 1938, Jl 25,15:3
Bolte, Frank B, 1955, Ja 18,10:5
Bolte, Guy W, 1947, S 22,23:6
Bolte, Herman, 1908, D 17,9:4
Bolte, John C, 1947, O 15,27:2
Bolte, John C Mrs, 1955, S 4,56:2
Bolte, William H, 1956, Ap 7,19:4
Bolte, William J, 1967, Ap 27,45:2
Bolten, Claus Sr, 1951, Jl 21,13:4
Bolter, Hyman, 1949, Ap 29,23:2
Boltey, Richard D, 1954, N 20,17:5
Boltman, Gustavus Mrs, 1918, Jl 23,13:5
Bolton, Arthur D, 1954, O 31,89:1
Bolton, Barton A, 1951, Ag 6,21:3
Bolton, Bennett M, 1960, Je 29,33:5
Bolton, Burton, 1925, Jl 3,13:3
Bolton, C Hope, 1954, F 16,25:3
Bolton, Charles Edward Mrs (Sarah Knowles Bolton), 1916, F 22,11:5
Bolton, Charles W, 1942, N 18,25:6
Bolton, Chester C, 1939, O 30,17:5
Bolton, Clarence H, 1944, S 7,23:2
Bolton, Cornelius Winter Rev, 1906, Ag 29,7:4
Bolton, Edward J, 1961, O 8,87:2
Bolton, Edward T, 1952, Je 9,12:3
Bolton, Elliott Mrs, 1957, S 24,35:3
Bolton, Elmer K Dr, 1968, Jl 31,27:1
Bolton, Eric I, 1950, Ja 18,31:5
Bolton, Eugene Mrs, 1948, My 2,76:7
Bolton, Frank C, 1961, F 1,35:3
Bolton, Frank L, 1954, S 17,27:5
Bolton, George, 1959, Jl 31,23:3
Bolton, George B, 1961, Jl 26,31:3
Bolton, Guy R Jr, 1961, Ag 8,29:1
Bolton, Henry C, 1903, N 20,9:5
Bolton, Herbert E, 1953, Ja 31,15:5
Bolton, Irving C, 1953, F 12,27:3
Bolton, Irving C Mrs, 1953, F 12,27:3
Bolton, Isabel M, 1956, F 24,25:3
Bolton, James R, 1939, F 26,38:8; 1941, Ap 17,23:2
Bolton, Jennie L Mrs, 1939, D 12,27:5
Bolton, John B, 1939, Mr 26,III,6:6
Bolton, John E, 1914, Je 11,11:6
Bolton, John H, 1956, Jl 31,23:5
Bolton, John W, 1943, O 3,48:5
Bolton, Joseph R, 1950, Ap 3,23:2
Bolton, Julian C, 1944, F 26,13:4
Bolton, Lawrence J, 1958, S 30,31:4
Bolton, Lord, 1944, D 13,24:2
Bolton, Mary Laycock Mrs, 1968, N 25,47:2
Bolton, Mother Margaret, 1943, F 28,49:1
Bolton, Newell C, 1947, D 29,17:3
Bolton, Nina M, 1942, O 2,25:4
Bolton, Norman C, 1945, D 3,21:5
Bolton, Reginald P, 1942, F 19,19:6
Bolton, Reginald P Mrs, 1945, D 30,14:8
Bolton, Richard, 1949, Je 17,23:3
Bolton, Richard J, 1954, My 10,23:4
Bolton, Richard M, 1965, Ag 5,29:3
Bolton, Robert L, 1950, D 12,33:5
Bolton, Samuel, 1946, Ja 13,44:3
Bolton, Thaddeus L, 1948, Ja 4,52:2
Bolton, William, 1945, Ap 5,23:1; 1962, N 23,29:1
Bolton, William A, 1955, D 3,17:6
Bolton, William A Mrs, 1954, Ag 5,23:2
Bolton, William C, 1937, N 29,23:5
Bolton, William J, 1952, Ap 9,31:2
Bolton, William R, 1967, Ap 17,37:2
Bolton, William R Mrs, 1940, S 10,23:2
Boltuch, Salo M Dr, 1968, D 4,47:2
Boltwood, Edward, 1924, S 11,23:6
Boltwood, Harvey, 1938, S 3,13:2
Boltz, Joseph, 1948, My 19,27:5
Bolze, Dorothea, 1950, Je 14,31:3
Bolze, Rudolph A, 1950, Je 19,21:6
Boman, Robert P, 1949, O 24,23:6
Boman, Theodore, 1925, N 13,19:4
Bomann, Donald, 1966, Ap 24,86:7
Bomann, George A Mrs, 1947, Ja 1,34:2
Bomann, George A Sr, 1963, Ap 16,35:3
Bomar, Edward E, 1953, O 28,29:3
Bomash, Louis, 1942, N 28,13:1
Bombardier, Armand, 1964, F 20,29:3
Bombarger, Avo P, 1954, Ja 16,15:6
Bombe, Arnold W, 1949, N 16,29:2
Bomberger, C M, 1950, S 10,92:5
Bomeisler, Carl, 1953, Ag 28,17:2
Bomeisler, Douglass M, 1953, D 29,23:1
Bomeisler, Louis E, 1941, Ag 14,17:6
Bomeisler, Paltiel M, 1947, My 11,60:4
Bomer, Walter L, 1947, Ja 3,21:3
Bomhard, Theodor von, 1945, Mr 21,3:1
Bomm, John C, 1960, Ag 11,27:2
Bommer, Emil Mrs, 1950, S 25,23:3
Bommer, Peter C Mrs, 1913, Ag 14,9:3
Bommer, Peter C Rev Dr, 1913, Ag 14,9:3
Bommer, William J, 1951, F 3,15:4
Bompard, Maurice Mrs, 1951, N 15,29:4
Bomzon, O Samuel M, 1943, O 24,45:1
Bon, Albert, 1964, Jl 22,8:6
Bona, Joseph L, 1951, Mr 30,23:2
Bona, Sister (R Breuning), 1942, My 12,19:4
Bona, Thomas P, 1950, Je 29,29:3
Bonacchini, Frank, 1951, S 5,31:5
Bonaccini, Paolo, 1925, My 7,19:5
Bonachea, Raul A, 1965, D 3,39:2
Bonachini, Romolo, 1943, My 26,23:1
Bonacker, Harry J, 1950, Ag 6,72:8
Bonacossa, Alberto Count, 1953, F 1,88:1
Bonafax, Cayetano Senor, 1875, S 23,1:6
Bonafede, John D, 1963, Jl 20,19:4
Bonafield, Harold H Mrs, 1960, F 4,31:5
Bonaiuti, Ernesto, 1946, Ap 21,46:1
Bonan, Salvator, 1946, My 9,21:5
Bonanno, Menotti, 1955, Ap 9,13:5
Bonanno, Raoul, 1944, Ap 9,34:3
Bonaparte, Antoine Prince, 1877, Mr 29,5:2
Bonaparte, Charles J, 1921, Je 29,15:3
Bonaparte, Charlotte Contesse Prinoli Princess, 190 O 1,9:4
Bonaparte, Claude A, 1948, Ap 30,23:4
Bonaparte, J N Mrs, 1881, S 16,5:2
Bonaparte, Jeanne Princess, 1905, O 29,III,4:1
Bonaparte, Jerome N, 1945, N 11,42:6
Bonaparte, Jerome N Mrs, 1950, Jl 29,13:6
Bonaparte, Jerome Napoleon, 1870, Je 10,5:2
Bonaparte, Jerome Napoleon Mrs, 1911, N 20,11:
Bonaparte, Louis Prince (Napoleon IV), 1879, Je 1:3
Bonaparte, Lucien Cardinal, 1895, N 20,5:2
Bonaparte, Marie (trb, O 13,24:5), 1962, S 22,25
Bonaparte, P N Prince, 1881, Ap 11,5:5
Bonaparte, Prince Napoleon, 1899, F 13,1:4
Bonaparte, Roland Mme, 1882, Ag 21,5:6
Bonaparte, Roland Prince, 1924, Ap 15,21:3
Bonaparte-Patterson, Mme, 1879, Ap 5,1:7
Bonaparte-Wyse, Andrew N, 1940, Je 2,45:3
Bonaparte-Wyse, Mrs, 1871, Ap 12,1:2
Bonaparte-Wyse, Napoleon G, 1946, Ag 26,23:6
Bonar, George, 1938, Ap 8,19:5
Bonar, Ronald E, 1915, My 22,11:4
Bonar, Susan D Mrs, 1937, F 14,II,9:2
Bonard, Louis, 1871, My 17,8:4
Bonardi, Giovacchino, 1941, Ja 18,15:3

Bonaschi, Alberto C, 1948, Ag 5,21:1
Bonaventure, Bro (P J Dunne), 1954, F 16,25:3
Bonaventure, Edmond F, 1918, S 11,13:4
Bonaventure, Edmund F Mrs, 1942, D 9,27:5
Bonaventure, Father (Jno Anthony Frey), 1912, Jl 6, 7:4
Bonaventure, George A, 1962, O 17,39:1
Bonaventure, Mother (M H Fay), 1966, N 8,39:2
Bonavita, Auguste, 1943, Ap 25,34:2
Bonawit, David J, 1953, Ap 24,23:2
Bonawit, Henry, 1951, S 6,31:2
Bonbright, George D B, 1939, S 7,25:4
Bonbright, George D Mrs, 1943, Mr 12,17:3
Bonbright, Howard, 1942, Je 20,13:7
Bonbright, Irving W (will, Ag 20,14:2), 1941, Ag 3, 35:1
Bonbright, Irving W Mrs, 1961, D 28,27:3
Boncan, Marcelo T, 1948, Jl 12,19:4
Bonch-Bruyevich, Vladimir, 1955, Jl 15,21:4
Bonci, Alessandro (por), 1940, Ag 11,31:3
Bond, A Curtis, 1923, O 23,21:4
Bond, Albert Mrs, 1944, N 5,54:3
Bond, Alex R, 1937, Je 5,17:5
Bond, Alfreda A Mrs, 1946, O 9,27:4
Bond, Allan, 1950, Je 15,31:1
Bond, C Carter, 1955, N 12,19:1
Bond, Carrie J Mrs, 1946, D 29,35:4
Bond, Carrol T, 1943, Ja 20,20:3
Bond, Charles, 1954, Ag 25,27:2
Bond, Charles A, 1943, Ja 6,25:5; 1943, Je 10,21:4
Bond, Charles A Jr, 1947, Mr 5,25:3
Bond, Charles E, 1942, S 13,53:4
Bond, Charles H Jr, 1937, F 16,23:3
Bond, Charles J, 1939, N 24,23:4
Bond, Charles M, 1967, S 11,45:3
Bond, Charles P, 1942, Ag 8,11:4
Bond, Christiana, 1944, N 9,27:5
Bond, Clayton E, 1964, Ag 5,33:4
Bond, Daniel J, 1955, My 16,23:5
Bond, Daniel W Judge, 1911, Ja 23,7:4
Bond, David K Lt, 1937, O 9,19:6
Bond, E A Mrs, 1903, Ap 1,9:7
Bond, Edward A Mrs, 1907, O 3,9:4
Bond, Edward F, 1941, Je 17,21:5
Bond, Edward J, 1941, N 13,27:4
Bond, Edward L Sr, 1954, S 22,29:3
Bond, Edward N, 1919, Mr 28,13:2
Bond, Edwin E, 1966, N 3,39:2
Bond, Eleanor, 1963, O 24,33:2
Bond, Elizabeth L, 1943, Ap 14,23:3
Bond, Elmer J, 1954, S 4,11:5
Bond, F Fraser, 1965, D 27,25:1
Bond, Ford, 1962, Ag 16,27:4
Bond, Francis M, 1949, Je 3,26:2
Bond, Frank A, 1960, My 20,31:2
Bond, Frank S, 1912, F 28,11:4
Bond, Frederic D, 1951, Ap 3,27:4
Bond, Frederick, 1914, F 9,7:6
Bond, Frederick E Mrs, 1939, Ap 9,III,7:2
Bond, George, 1938, F 20,II,8:6
Bond, George A, 1966, Ja 26,37:5
Bond, George B, 1946, Ap 15,27:3
Bond, George H, 1954, My 9,89:2
Bond, George M, 1939, Ap 12,23:1
Bond, George W, 1907, Jl 3,7:6
Bond, Giles B, 1944, Je 22,19:6
Bond, Glenn C, 1950, Mr 8,27:3
Bond, Henry, 1925, Ag 10,13:6
Bond, Henry Whitelaw Justice, 1919, S 30,19:2
Bond, Hubert, 1945, Ap 19,27:4
Bond, J R H Mrs, 1943, Je 12,13:1
Bond, James Jr, 1946, Mr 16,13:6
Bond, Jay, 1954, My 17,23:4
Bond, Jessie, 1942, Je 18,21:6
Bond, John, 1940, O 27,45:1
Bond, John A, 1941, D 10,25:5
Bond, John R S, 1872, D 2,1:6
Bond, Joseph A, 1954, Mr 7,91:1
Bond, Joseph H Mrs, 1952, Ag 5,19:5
Bond, Kate, 1924, Mr 27,19:5
Bond, L L, 1903, Ap 16,9:6
Bond, Lewis Rev, 1919, S 8,13:4
Bond, M Nelson, 1942, Ap 15,21:5
Bond, MacGregor, 1958, Mr 12,31:2
Bond, Margaret L, 1948, S 14,29:4
Bond, Marion E, 1953, Ja 21,31:5
Bond, Mary A Mrs, 1937, Ag 31,23:3
Bond, Paul S, 1955, Ja 11,25:4
Bond, Phil E, 1949, Ag 19,17:2
Bond, Prof, 1865, F 21,2:1
Bond, Ridgely B Mrs, 1937, Ag 24,21:5
Bond, Robert A, 1939, Je 29,23:4
Bond, Robert Sir, 1927, Mr 18,21:3
Bond, Robert T, 1951, Jl 20,21:5
Bond, Rollin Mrs (G Farnell), 1961, D 4,37:3
Bond, Samuel B, 1942, Ja 10,15:3
Bond, Samuel J, 1938, Ap 23,15:6
Bond, Seth M, 1940, Je 17,15:6
Bond, St George, 1949, N 6,92:2
Bond, Stanley F, 1959, My 25,29:3
Bond, Stanley S, 1943, F 16,20:2
Bond, Stephen N, 1940, S 22,49:2
Bond, Thomas E, 1949, D 10,17:2
Bond, Thomas H, 1941, Ja 26,36:7
Bond, Thomas P, 1952, D 1,23:5
Bond, Walter, 1967, S 16,33:1
Bond, Walter J, 1948, N 24,24:3
Bond, Ward (funl, N 8,29:3; will, N 24,47:3; D 15,-34:6), 1960, N 6,87:4
Bond, William, 1951, N 22,31:5
Bond, William A, 1943, Je 12,13:2
Bond, William H, 1921, Je 12,22:2; 1942, My 1,17:2
Bond, William S, 1950, D 30,13:4; 1952, S 12,21:2
Bond, William S Mrs, 1949, Ag 18,21:5
Bond, William T (Tiny the Clown), 1963, Ag 15,29:2
Bondance, Antonio, 1940, Jl 9,23:5
Bondarenko, Fyodor P, 1961, Mr 27,31:5
Bondarenko, Igor I, 1964, My 9,27:2
Bonde, Reiner, 1959, Jl 14,29:3
Bonde, William R, 1953, F 3,25:2
Bondell, Murray, 1945, Jl 12,13:6
Bondfield, Margaret, 1953, Je 18,29:3
Bondi, J Rev Dr, 1874, Mr 12,2:3
Bondoll, Michael, 1948, D 25,17:3
Bondurant, Alex L Dr, 1937, Ja 13,23:2
Bondurant, Charles W, 1953, S 25,21:4
Bondy, Charles F, 1945, D 14,28:2
Bondy, Joseph, 1945, D 22,19:4
Bondy, Karl Frederick, 1924, My 14,19:5
Bondy, Leo J, 1944, O 30,19:3
Bondy, Leo J Mrs, 1959, Ap 8,37:2
Bondy, Lewis, 1938, S 9,22:6
Bondy, Louis, 1958, N 12,37:5
Bondy, Manuel H, 1950, My 30,17:4
Bondy, Maurice S, 1925, D 11,23:2
Bondy, Max, 1951, Ap 18,31:3
Bondy, Richard C Jr, 1945, N 15,20:2
Bondy, Robert E Mrs, 1967, D 31,44:5
Bondy, William, 1964, Mr 31,35:3
Bondy, William S, 1938, Jl 12,20:1
Bone, Albert J, 1937, O 14,25:4
Bone, David, 1959, My 18,27:3
Bone, David F, 1944, Je 21,19:4
Bone, F Darcy, 1946, My 6,21:2
Bone, Gavin D, 1942, Ap 10,17:4
Bone, George P, 1951, Ap 20,29:2
Bone, George Sr Mrs, 1947, Jl 31,21:3
Bone, James, 1962, N 24,23:4
Bone, Muirhead, 1953, O 23,23:3
Bone, S C, 1936, Ja 28,19:3
Bone, Scott C Mrs, 1948, Je 29,23:3
Bone, Stephen, 1958, S 16,28:1
Bone, Walter A, 1958, My 26,29:4
Bone, William A, 1938, Je 13,19:2
Bonechi, Paolo, 1949, Ja 9,72:1
Bonegan, John Mrs, 1945, Ag 9,21:2
Bonehill, Bessie, 1902, Ag 22,9:2
Bonelli, Luigi, 1954, F 14,92:2
Bonelli, Pauline Mrs, 1952, My 5,25:7
Boneo, R Etcheverry, 1947, N 11,27:2
Boner, Herbert E, 1946, Ag 26,23:5
Boner, Mary F, 1954, Je 22,27:4
Bones, Helen W, 1951, Je 6,31:5
Bones, Iva H Mrs, 1940, Ap 2,26:4
Bones, Walter I Sr, 1961, Ag 1,31:4
Bonesteel, Charles H, 1964, Je 6,23:1
Bonesteel, Edward W, 1948, O 19,27:2
Bonesteel, James E, 1943, Ja 19,20:2
Bonet, Willaumez Count, 1871, S 11,1:7
Bonetti, Julio, 1952, Je 19,27:5
Boney, Daniel C, 1942, S 8,23:2
Bonfig, Henry C, 1962, My 1,37:1
Bonfiglio, Giuseppe, 1947, Je 3,25:4
Bonfils, Charles A, 1955, Ag 27,15:3
Bonfils, F G, 1933, F 3,17:1
Bonfils, F W, 1958, My 23,23:3
Bonfils, W B Mrs, 1936, My 26,26:2
Bongard, Robert R, 1956, F 5,87:2
Bongarzone, Andrea, 1943, Je 22,19:3
Bonggren, Jakob, 1940, Jl 26,17:4
Bongiovanni, Carmine A, 1967, My 11,54:5
Bongiovanni, Joseph L, 1949, Ag 18,21:1
Bongiovanni, Manlio, 1944, Jl 2,20:2
Bonhag, George V, 1960, N 1,40:1
Bonham, Arthur F, 1953, My 17,89:1
Bonham, Ernest E (Tiny), 1949, S 16,27:1
Bonham, Frederick T, 1958, S 22,31:4
Bonham, Frederick T Mrs, 1952, My 21,27:1
Bonham, Guy L, 1942, Je 1,13:1
Bonham, John L, 1914, Jl 5,5:6
Bonham, Milledge, 1943, Je 24,21:5
Bonham, Milledge L Jr, 1941, Ja 23,22:2
Bonham, Milledge L Jr Mrs, 1958, Mr 17,29:3
Bonham, W B Lt, 1903, D 3,9:5
Bonham-Carter, Charles, 1955, O 22,19:5
Bonheur, Lucien L, 1918, Ag 15,11:5
Bonheur, Rosa, 1899, My 27,3:1
Bonhoeffer, Karl, 1949, Ja 10,25:4
Bonhoeffer, Karl F (cor, My 26,93:1), 1957, My 21, 35:6
Boni, Giacomo Prof, 1925, Jl 11,11:6
Boniarczyk, Charles, 1962, Ja 28,77:1
Boniel, Robert D, 1945, Ja 8,17:3
Boniface, Alfred S, 1949, O 22,17:4
Boniface, Arthur, 1943, Jl 19,15:2
Boniface, Arthur Mrs, 1959, D 8,45:1
Boniface, G C Mrs, 1883, O 15,4:7
Boniface, George C, 1912, Ja 4,13:4; 1917, Mr 28,13:6
Boniface, Harry, 1938, F 27,II,8:5
Boniface, Joseph, 1954, My 4,29:4
Boniface, Marie, 1879, F 2,2:7
Boniface, Mike, 1910, S 19,7:4
Boniface of Mary,Bro (J M McGarr), 1960, F 22, 17:5
Bonifas, Issac, 1947, My 14,25:4
Bonifaz, Neptali, 1952, Ag 25,17:1
Bonilla, P, 1926, S 13,21:5
Bonilla, Roderigo H, 1946, Je 27,21:2
Bonillas, I, 1944, F 1,19:1
Bonillas, Ignacio Mrs, 1941, D 4,25:4
Bonime, Josef, 1959, N 10,47:4
Bonin, David, 1956, My 8,33:2
Bonin, George, 1957, O 15,33:3
Bonin, Judge, 1922, Ap 14,17:6
Bonine, Charles E, 1948, O 27,27:1
Bonine, Fred N, 1941, Ag 24,35:4
Bonisteel, Pearl B, 1950, Ja 29,68:5
Bonisteel, William J, 1949, D 17,17:4
Bonito, Alan H, 1937, D 14,25:3
Bonitto, Vernon O, 1945, O 15,17:4
Bonitus Paulian Bro, 1960, Je 29,33:4
Bonitz, Edgar A, 1958, Ap 18,23:3
Bonitz, Howard E, 1957, My 13,31:1
Bonjer, F H Capt, 1910, F 27,II,11:4
Bonkoski, Vincent J, 1953, Je 23,30:4
Bonn, August L, 1949, Je 28,27:1
Bonn, Frank P, 1952, D 19,32:5
Bonn, Harry K, 1948, F 9,17:5
Bonn, Hugo L, 1949, Ja 25,23:3
Bonn, Max J, 1943, Mr 26,19:1
Bonn, William B, 1910, O 29,11:6
Bonna, Thomas C, 1950, Je 13,28:2
Bonnafay, Archbishop, 1920, Ap 21,9:4
Bonnaffon, Samuel A, 1940, D 29,24:8
Bonnafoux, Lucien H, 1953, Ja 23,19:1
Bonnal, Edmond, 1915, O 20,11:4
Bonnard, Abel, 1968, Je 2,89:1
Bonnard, Andre, 1959, O 21,43:4
Bonnard, Leo, 1945, Ap 24,19:6
Bonnard, Mario, 1965, Mr 24,43:1
Bonnard, Pierre, 1947, Ja 25,17:3
Bonnat, Leon, 1922, S 9,13:5
Bonnaure, Gaston, 1942, F 28,17:5
Bonne, Alfred (cor, D 21,27:4), 1959, D 19,27:2
Bonne, Willem M, 1963, Mr 9,7:3
Bonneau, Joseph A, 1948, Jl 5,19:3
Bonneau, Lincoln, 1953, D 13,87:1
Bonneau, Selina Mrs, 1909, N 27,9:4
Bonneau, Treffle, 1937, D 7,25:3
Bonnechose, Francois Paul Emile, 1875, Mr 15,8:2
Bonnechose (De), H G B Cardinal, 1883, O 29,5:4
Bonnefous, Georges, 1956, My 28,27:3
Bonnel, Benjamin L, 1953, D 31,19:6
Bonnel, Harold R, 1951, My 17,31:5
Bonnell, Adelaide, 1949, F 1,25:2
Bonnell, Duncan J, 1959, Mr 3,33:1
Bonnell, Eleanor V (Sister Mary Angela), 1943, Ag 26,17:6
Bonnell, Elias H, 1914, Jl 21,9:5
Bonnell, Geoffrey H, 1962, S 26,39:2
Bonnell, George C, 1944, O 6,23:1
Bonnell, George P Mrs, 1944, Ag 11,15:2
Bonnell, Horace A, 1954, My 19,31:4
Bonnell, Isaac, 1881, N 23,4:7
Bonnell, J Fearnely, 1952, S 1,17:6
Bonnell, John Harper, 1912, Je 18,11:5
Bonnell, Lawrence C, 1952, N 7,23:4
Bonnell, Lawrence T Sr, 1948, Je 24,25:5
Bonnell, Russell L, 1951, O 23,29:2
Bonnell, William L, 1960, D 25,42:5
Bonnelly, Paul F Mrs, 1949, Ja 11,31:2
Bonnemaison, Manuel E, 1961, F 18,19:6
Bonnencontre, Ernest C, 1955, Ap 21,29:2
Bonner, Adolph, 1951, Ap 21,17:5
Bonner, Agnes, 1914, S 26,11:5
Bonner, Albert S, 1945, F 10,11:2
Bonner, Amy, 1956, Ja 5,33:2
Bonner, Campbell, 1954, Jl 13,23:4
Bonner, Charles E, 1951, Ag 17,17:5
Bonner, Charles G, 1951, F 9,25:2
Bonner, Charles W, 1965, Mr 23,39:3
Bonner, Christine, 1948, F 16,22:2
Bonner, Clark J Sr, 1947, Ja 15,26:2
Bonner, Crenshaw Mrs, 1954, D 29,15:5
Bonner, David, 1917, D 31,7:6; 1958, Ja 16,29:3
Bonner, David T, 1958, O 31,26:6
Bonner, Douglas E, 1943, Ag 22,36:6
Bonner, Douglas G, 1960, D 30,20:1
Bonner, Edward J, 1946, Ja 22,27:3
Bonner, Eugenie, 1924, Mr 16,23:2
Bonner, Francis A, 1954, Mr 8,27:4
Bonner, Francis H, 1943, Jl 11,34:7
Bonner, Frank, 1906, Ja 2,9:6
Bonner, Frederic, 1911, Ja 4,9:3
Bonner, Frederick D Mrs, 1943, S 9,25:2
Bonner, G S, 1902, O 4,9:5
Bonner, George Mrs, 1953, O 22,29:2
Bonner, George T, 1924, Je 2,17:6
Bonner, Herbert C, 1965, N 8,35:1

Bonner, Isabel (Mrs J Kramm),(funl plans, Jl 6,28:1), 1955, Jl 2,12:8
Bonner, Jack, 1938, Ja 16,II,9:2
Bonner, John Houghton Maurice, 1917, Ja 31,11:6
Bonner, John J, 1945, N 28,27:2
Bonner, John M, 1952, Ja 26,13:2
Bonner, John M D Mrs, 1941, Ja 2,23:3
Bonner, Joseph C, 1944, S 29,21:2
Bonner, Joseph F, 1954, Mr 15,25:4
Bonner, Kenneth, 1965, D 22,31:4
Bonner, Mannes, 1943, F 22,17:3
Bonner, Moses J, 1939, S 3,18:5
Bonner, Paul Ed, 1922, Ja 21,13:4
Bonner, Paul H Mrs, 1962, Ja 2,30:6
Bonner, Paul Hyde, 1968, D 15,85:1
Bonner, Paul R, 1959, Ja 26,29:2
Bonner, R Mrs (see also Ap 3), 1878, Ap 6,8:3
Bonner, Reginald E, 1949, My 4,29:5
Bonner, Robert, 1899, Jl 7,1:5
Bonner, Robert E, 1924, O 7,23:4
Bonner, Robert J, 1946, Ja 26,13:2
Bonner, Walter D, 1956, Ja 4,27:5
Bonner, William A, 1953, Je 25,27:3
Bonner, William J, 1949, Ja 12,27:4
Bonnet, Edgar, 1942, F 18,19:2
Bonnet, Henri Mrs, 1962, Ap 6,35:1
Bonnet, Jacob, 1907, Ap 11,11:5
Bonnet, Joseph, 1944, Ag 3,19:5
Bonnet, Joseph L, 1967, Je 3,31:4
Bonnet, Marie T Mrs, 1954, Mr 23,27:4
Bonnet, P Mrs, 1903, Je 12,9:1
Bonnet-Duverdier, M, 1882, N 28,2:2
Bonneto, Felice, 1953, N 22,V,1:2
Bonnett, D Blake, 1938, Ja 28,21:3
Bonnett, Earl C, 1963, N 23,29:3
Bonnett, Louis B, 1951, D 12,37:4
Bonnett, William D, 1940, Ja 31,19:3
Bonnetti, Joseph, 1947, N 29,13:4
Bonneville, B L, 1878, Je 13,1:2
Bonneville, Christophe de, 1947, Jl 15,23:5
Bonneville, Joseph H, 1961, D 23,23:1
Bonneville, Roy C, 1962, Mr 30,33:5
Bonney, Alvero G, 1943, O 16,13:2
Bonney, C C, 1903, Ag 24,7:5
Bonney, Caroline S Mrs, 1966, F 16,43:4
Bonney, Charles W, 1956, Jl 24,25:1
Bonney, Clinton H, 1949, Ja 14,23:1
Bonney, Edmund A, 1944, Ap 1,13:6
Bonney, Francis A, 1954, Ag 25,27:1
Bonney, George B, 1909, N 12,11:5
Bonney, James B, 1946, Je 1,13:4
Bonney, John J, 1952, O 31,25:5
Bonney, Josephine, 1938, Ap 3,II,7:1
Bonney, Kenneth C, 1939, Jl 21,19:1
Bonney, Leonard W Mrs, 1967, Ja 29,76:7
Bonney, Ralph M, 1945, Ja 5,15:5
Bonney, Thomas George Prof, 1923, D 11,21:3
Bonney, Virginia L, 1963, Jl 6,15:6
Bonnier, Karl O, 1941, My 30,15:6
Bonnin, Paul C, 1957, S 23,27:4
Bonnin, Raymond T Mrs, 1938, Ja 27,21:2
Bonniwell, Eugene C, 1964, Je 5,31:1
Bonniwell, Fred H, 1940, Mr 5,23:2
Bonnor, James, 1949, Jl 31,60:7
Bonnot, Paul, 1951, Ag 3,21:4
Bonnot, Paul P, 1962, S 14,31:3
Bonnyman, Alex, 1953, Ap 16,29:4
Bonnyman, Douglas D Mrs, 1955, My 29,45:1
Bonnyman, James, 1937, Ap 10,19:4; 1945, Jl 11,11:5
Bonnyman, John H, 1951, S 15,15:3
Bono, Emilio de, 1941, N 14,24:2
Bonoff, Charles A, 1952, Je 9,23:3
Bonoff, Harold, 1946, F 1,23:4
Bonoff, Harold C, 1948, F 10,23:1
Bonomi, Bessie G Mrs, 1939, Mr 26,III,6:7
Bonomi, Ivanoe, 1951, Ap 20,29:3
Bonomo, Albert A Mrs, 1959, Ja 25,92:8
Bonomo, Michael V, 1945, F 7,21:5
Bonomo, Umberto, 1958, My 13,29:4
Bonsack, Henry W, 1948, Ap 14,28:2
Bonsal, Alonzo F, 1966, D 23,25:1
Bonsal, Frank Adair, 1924, O 29,21:2
Bonsal, J Purviance, 1937, N 12,21:1
Bonsal, Leigh, 1940, Ap 9,23:4
Bonsal, Mary M P Mrs, 1940, Ap 16,23:4
Bonsal, Stephen, 1951, Je 9,19:1
Bonsal, Stephen Jr, 1950, O 29,92:5
Bonsal, Stephen Mrs, 1955, Jl 17,61:3
Bonsall, Amos, 1915, F 2,7:6
Bonsall, Edward H Jr, 1954, My 26,29:2
Bonscher, John J, 1941, Je 24,19:4
Bonsels, Waldemar, 1952, Ag 2,15:5
Bonsib, Henry S, 1939, N 30,21:5
Bonsib, Roy S, 1955, Ap 22,25:5
Bonsteel, Leo A, 1949, Ag 13,11:6
Bonstelle, J, 1932, O 15,15:3
Bonta, Del, 1912, Je 3,9:6
Bonta, Edwin W, 1959, Jl 19,69:2
Bonta, Leon R, 1939, O 10,23:4
Bonta, Wilma B Mrs, 1950, N 28,31:5
Bonte, George W, 1946, Mr 14,25:3
Bontecou, Alvin F Mrs, 1948, N 13,15:1
Bontecou, Francis, 1914, Jl 9,7:3
Bontecou, Frederic H, 1959, S 18,31:1
Bontecou, Nathalie Mrs, 1941, D 31,18:2
Bontempelli, Massimo, 1960, Jl 23,19:6
Bontempo, Elly, 1956, Jl 6,21:5
Bontempo, Michael A Mrs, 1961, Jl 5,33:1
Bontemps, Aldo, 1939, N 26,43:1
Bonter, Claude C, 1957, D 21,19:6
Bonthron, William D, 1950, N 29,33:2
Bonties, Harry P, 1937, Ja 28,25:3
Bonvicino, Louis A, 1957, O 3,29:5
Bonvillian, William D, 1967, My 2,47:1
Bonvin, Ludwig, 1939, F 19,39:1
Bonwell, Charles, 1953, O 18,86:4
Bonwit, Lester R Mrs, 1944, D 6,23:5
Bonwit, Paul J, 1939, D 11,23:1
Bonx, Nathan J, 1950, O 25,35:6
Bonynge, Albert W, 1939, Mr 30,23:5
Bonynge, Henry A, 1956, D 12,39:4
Bonynge, Paul Justice (will, Jl 14,44:2), 1937, Je 30, 23:5
Bonynge, Robert W, 1939, S 23,17:3
Bonynge, Robert W Mrs, 1937, Ag 9,19:3
Bonynge, Russell, 1958, S 12,25:1
Bonynge, William, 1950, Ag 29,27:3
Bonynge, William H, 1921, Ja 13,13:5
Bonython, Lavington, 1960, N 7,35:5
Bonzani, Emil, 1954, N 24,23:3
Bonzano, J Cardinal, 1927, N 27,1:5
Bonzano, Max F, 1920, N 2,17:5
Bonzer, Arthur F, 1951, Je 20,27:2
Bonzo, Valfre di Cardinal, 1922, Je 26,13:7
Bonzogno, Eduard, 1920, Mr 17,11:3
Boochever, George B, 1959, F 15,86:6
Boochever, Louis C, 1952, D 2,36:5
Boochever, Louis C Mrs, 1952, N 10,25:3
Boochever, Samuel, 1940, Ag 7,19:4
Boock, Charles M, 1950, My 23,60:4
Boocock, Murray, 1942, F 18,19:5
Boocock, R Dr, 1903, D 30,7:2
Boodberg, Alexis P, 1945, D 18,27:1
Boodell, John C, 1958, Jl 10,27:4
Boodin, John E, 1950, N 15,31:1
Boody, D A, 1930, Ja 21,25:1
Boody, Edgar, 1962, Je 22,25:1
Boody, Edgar Jr, 1963, S 4,40:3
Boody, Irving R, 1951, Mr 21,33:5
Boogar, Isaac P, 1945, D 25,23:5
Boogher, Albert W G, 1963, Ap 3,47:5
Booher, Charles F, 1921, Ja 22,11:4
Booher, Jay C, 1942, Je 29,15:3
Booht, Wright J, 1947, F 12,25:4
Book, Dorothy L, 1955, Ag 10,25:2
Book, William F, 1940, My 24,19:2
Book, William H, 1946, Jl 11,23:3
Bookbinder, Coleman, 1944, Jl 28,13:1
Bookbinder, Max, 1945, Ag 12,40:3
Booker, Archy S Jr, 1964, N 12,37:4
Booker, Caroline R Mrs, 1954, O 15,23:4
Booker, George W, 1950, Ap 26,29:1
Booker, John A, 1942, O 12,34:4
Booker, John M, 1948, Mr 13,15:4
Booker, Joseph, 1949, D 27,23:4
Booker, Joseph R, 1960, Ag 2,29:5
Booker, Major, 1949, Mr 1,25:2
Booker, Norman L, 1952, Ja 10,29:2
Booker, William D Dr, 1921, Mr 16,9:4
Booker, William M, 1945, Ja 28,37:1
Bookhout, Raymond C, 1959, O 21,44:1
Bookin, Boris W, 1946, Mr 12,25:2
Bookman, Abraham Mrs, 1965, Mr 7,83:1
Bookman, Adolph, 1909, N 19,11:4
Bookman, Harold L, 1968, N 23,47:3
Bookmeyer, Raymond A, 1945, F 15,19:2
Bookmyer, Edwin H, 1956, My 9,33:3
Bookmyer, Roy T, 1948, N 23,29:1
Books, William J, 1954, Ag 17,21:5
Bookstaber, Harry Mrs, 1943, D 28,17:2
Bookstaber, Irving A, 1965, O 13,47:3
Bookstaber, Morris, 1951, Ja 20,15:3
Bookstaber, Philip D, 1964, My 21,35:5
Bookstaver, Barnet S, 1951, Je 27,29:5
Bookstaver, Harry S, 1938, Jl 4,13:6
Bookstaver, Henry W, 1907, S 25,9:5
Bookstaver, Henry Weller, 1907, S 22,9:6
Bookstaver, Joseph D Mrs, 1949, F 18,24:3
Bookstaver, Samuel, 1966, My 17,47:2
Bookstaver, William Brooks, 1925, D 23,19:4
Bookstein, Hyman, 1940, My 27,19:3
Bookstein, Hyman Mrs, 1939, Ap 15,19:4
Bookstein, Jack, 1961, My 10,45:2
Bookwalter, Alfred G, 1939, Ap 3,15:1
Bookwalter, Charles F, 1961, My 27,23:7
Bookwalter, Charles S, 1948, Ap 29,23:5
Bookwalter, Charles S Mrs, 1953, N 21,13:2
Bookwalter, John W, 1915, S 28,11:5
Bookwalter, Lulu G, 1958, S 7,87:1
Bookwalter, O P M, 1903, Ag 7,7:7
Boole, Ella A Mrs, 1952, Mr 14,23:1
Boole, Francis I A, 1869, S 3,5:2
Boole, Samuel E Mrs, 1948, Je 14,24:3
Boom, Aire, 1950, Je 25,68:7
Boom, Olin S, 1948, Mr 24,25:4
Boomer, Joseph F, 1946, D 23,23:3
Boomer, L B, 1881, Mr 7,5:2
Boomer, Lucius, 1947, Je 27,21:1
Boomer, Robert DeF, 1966, O 6,47:1
Boon, Daniel J, 1947, F 14,22:3
Boon, Henry G, 1953, N 12,43:8
Boon, James A, 1945, O 23,17:5
Boon, John H, 1958, O 17,29:2
Boone, Andrew R, 1955, Ja 17,23:5
Boone, Annie J Mrs, 1937, Ja 31,II,8:3
Boone, Blair F, 1940, D 8,69:1
Boone, C Daniel, 1957, Jl 26,19:1
Boone, Charles, 1955, Jl 25,19:4
Boone, Daniel, 1944, N 27,23:4
Boone, Daniel E Col, 1903, O 13,9:7
Boone, Emmett E Mrs, 1941, Ja 17,17:3
Boone, F E Sr, 1954, Jl 3,11:4
Boone, Ike, 1958, Ag 3,81:1
Boone, Ilsley Dr, 1968, D 12,47:1
Boone, James L, 1961, O 18,43:3
Boone, John H, 1955, Je 4,15:3
Boone, John T, 1945, F 10,11:1
Boone, John Talbot Col, 1916, Ja 25,9:4
Boone, Leona K Mrs, 1950, O 28,17:4
Boone, Levi G, 1940, D 16,23:2
Boone, Lewis C, 1945, F 20,19:4
Boone, Louis C, 1950, N 20,25:3
Boone, Perley, 1948, S 7,26:2
Boone, Ransloe, 1955, My 10,29:1
Boone, Robert, 1948, N 23,29:4
Boone, Rodney E, 1943, Jl 28,15:5
Boone, Rowan Mrs, 1949, Ag 2,19:4
Boone, W C Dr, 1926, F 14,28:5
Boone, W J, 1936, Jl 11,15:5
Boone, W J Bishop (Shanghai),(cor, O 16,8:2), 1864, O 7,2:3
Boone, William A, 1943, Jl 21,15:4; 1959, Ag 13,27:3
Boone, William Constantine Pise, 1912, Ja 1,13:3
Boone, William G, 1952, Ap 25,23:3
Boone, William K Mrs, 1941, F 12,21:5
Boone, Wilmot D, 1949, Ja 30,60:8
Boonwatt, S Mrs, 1967, O 16,15:1
Boor, Frank, 1938, Ap 11,15:2
Boor, John, 1967, D 10,86:8
Booraem, Alfred W, 1955, F 8,27:4
Booraem, Francis, 1947, O 10,25:4
Booraem, John Van Vorst, 1923, My 25,21:5
Booraem, Theodore B, 1912, F 27,9:2
Boord, Willa (will), 1939, My 3,25:5
Boorman, James, 1866, Ja 26,2:3
Boorman, Kitchell, 1946, N 8,23:2
Boorse, Howard F, 1951, D 8,11:2
Boorse, Michael, 1952, O 2,21:5
Boorse, Paul C, 1962, My 19,27:3
Boorstein, Samuel W, 1967, Mr 30,45:3
Boos, Charles Mrs, 1949, My 4,29:3
Boos, Herman J Mrs, 1957, F 21,27:5
Boos, J Kenneth Mrs, 1940, Jl 20,15:4
Boos, John W, 1948, Ja 6,24:2
Boos, Ludwig C, 1959, D 9,45:2
Boos, Richard N Mrs, 1967, Mr 28,39:5
Boos, William F, 1949, Ag 13,11:6
Booshard, Everett B, 1959, My 11,53:6
Boostein, Stanley R, 1964, Ja 12,92:3
Boot, John C (Lord Trent), 1956, Mr 10,17:4
Boote, Charles W, 1960, O 8,23:6
Boote, James B, 1945, N 18,43:2
Boote, Mabel L, 1945, Ja 13,11:2
Bootes, Harry V, 1938, Mr 9,23:5
Bootes, James T, 1945, Ag 31,17:2
Booth, Abram E, 1952, N 21,25:3
Booth, Agnes (Mrs Jno B Schoeffel), 1910, Ja 3,9:
Booth, Albert J, 1939, D 30,15:4
Booth, Albert J (Albie),(funl, Mr 5,31:6), 1959, M 27:2
Booth, Albert Rev, 1917, Jl 22,15:3
Booth, Alexina G, 1955, F 1,29:4
Booth, Alfred, 1914, N 3,11:4; 1948, Mr 14,72:2
Booth, Alfred B, 1949, D 29,25:2
Booth, Alfred E Gen, 1914, My 12,11:5
Booth, Alfred J Col, 1937, F 16,23:3
Booth, Alfred J Mrs, 1943, Je 3,21:3
Booth, Alfred Mrs, 1943, D 14,27:3
Booth, Alice Treat, 1908, My 3,11:4
Booth, Almond E, 1957, Ap 24,33:2
Booth, Almond E Mrs, 1951, Mr 16,31:2
Booth, Arthur R Mrs, 1942, S 17,25:5
Booth, Arthur W, 1951, O 23,29:2
Booth, Ballington, 1940, O 6,49:1
Booth, Ballington Mrs, 1948, Ag 27,19:1
Booth, Bradford A, 1968, D 2,47:4
Booth, C Douglas, 1944, F 23,19:5
Booth, Charles, 1916, N 24,13:2
Booth, Charles A, 1953, F 3,25:1
Booth, Charles G, 1949, My 23,23:3
Booth, Charles H Mrs, 1941, Ja 3,19:4
Booth, Charles J, 1947, F 21,19:2
Booth, Charles L, 1946, O 4,23:4
Booth, Chris, 1939, Ap 20,23:2
Booth, Christopher H H Mrs, 1962, Ja 23,33:4
Booth, Clarence H, 1952, O 27,27:2
Booth, Clarence M, 1939, Ja 20,19:2
Booth, E W, 1927, Ja 9,30:1
Booth, Edmund, 1905, Mr 30,5:5

Booth, Edmund H Mrs, 1954, D 12,89:2
Booth, Edmund W Mrs, 1964, F 8,23:5
Booth, Edward H, 1937, S 6,17:4
Booth, Edward J, 1943, N 20,13:6
Booth, Edward T, 1964, Mr 14,23:4
Booth, Edwin, 1893, Je 7,1:5
Booth, Edwin Mrs (wife of actor), 1863, F 22,1:6
Booth, Edwin Mrs, 1881, N 14,5:4
Booth, Emma J Mrs, 1948, O 25,23:6
Booth, Enos S, 1946, S 28,17:6
Booth, Ernest, 1952, S 23,33:2
Booth, Evangeline C, 1950, Jl 18,29:1
Booth, Fenton W, 1947, Jl 28,15:1
Booth, Ferris, 1955, Ag 15,15:3
Booth, Francis A, 1964, D 21,29:4
Booth, Frank, 1939, Ap 23,III,7:1
Booth, Frank H Mrs, 1959, Je 26,25:3
Booth, Franklin, 1948, Ag 26,21:4; 1956, Ja 11,29:1
Booth, Franklin Mrs, 1955, Mr 26,15:1
Booth, Frederick A, 1913, Je 30,7:4
Booth, Frederick H, 1941, Ag 14,17:6
Booth, G Raymond, 1953, N 16,25:3
Booth, George E, 1945, F 25,37:1
Booth, George F, 1955, S 2,17:1
Booth, George F Mrs, 1954, D 31,13:3
Booth, George G (por), 1949, Ap 12,29:4
Booth, George G Mrs, 1948, Ja 25,56:6
Booth, George O, 1948, F 20,27:4
Booth, George W, 1951, O 3,33:3
Booth, George W Capt, 1914, Ja 7,11:5
Booth, H, 1926, S 26,27:1
Booth, Hal E, 1942, Mr 9,20:2
Booth, Hanson, 1944, F 27,38:3
Booth, Harold S, 1950, Je 24,13:5
Booth, Harry G, 1942, O 24,15:2
Booth, Henley C, 1947, Ja 9,24:3
Booth, Henry, 1952, F 5,29:2
Booth, Henry Francis, 1916, N 3,13:5
Booth, Henry K, 1942, O 18,52:7
Booth, Henry Wood, 1925, Mr 18,21:4
Booth, Hilliard Mrs, 1954, Je 17,29:3
Booth, Hubert C, 1955, Ja 15,13:3
Booth, Irving E (est tax appr), 1957, S 14,11:6
Booth, Isaac S, 1949, Mr 24,28:2
Booth, J A, 1879, Ag 3,1:6
Booth, J B, 1883, S 16,6:7
Booth, J F Rev, 1865, N 27,5:1
Booth, J W, 1876, S 15,2:6
Booth, Jack, 1966, Je 25,31:4
Booth, Jack R, 1944, Je 13,19:3
Booth, James, 1903, Ag 17,7:5
Booth, James A, 1938, D 31,15:4
Booth, James H, 1945, Mr 3,13:2
Booth, James R, 1952, Ap 18,25:3
Booth, James S, 1954, S 14,27:2
Booth, James S Mrs, 1942, Ag 2,38:7
Booth, Jesse Mrs, 1943, Je 20,34:5
Booth, John, 1880, D 30,1:4; 1943, F 21,32:8
Booth, John H, 1943, My 4,23:2; 1960, D 4,88:4
Booth, John H Jr, 1958, Je 21,19:3
Booth, John J, 1938, O 12,27:6
Booth, John R, 1925, D 9,27:3; 1941, O 10,23:5; 1942, O 22,21:5; 1954, Ag 11,25:4
Booth, Josie Mrs, 1875, O 12,4:7
Booth, Knox, 1915, O 25,9:4
Booth, Kyle Rev, 1937, S 16,25:3
Booth, Levis M, 1938, N 8,23:4
Booth, Louis, 1953, Je 8,29:3
Booth, Lydia A Mrs, 1923, N 1,21:4
Booth, Lynn, 1937, N 23,23:4
Booth, Marion, 1937, Ja 6,23:1
Booth, Marshall J Mrs, 1952, Ja 5,11:5
Booth, Mary A, 1922, S 16,15:3
Booth, Mary F Mrs, 1955, Jl 7,27:1
Booth, Mary H C, 1865, Ap 12,4:5
Booth, Mary L, 1889, Mr 6,5:2
Booth, Mary Lady, 1924, N 8,15:5
Booth, Mr (Lyceum Theater, London), 1872, Je 16, 1:6
Booth, Neil W, 1943, Jl 4,20:7
Booth, Newell S Rev Dr, 1968, My 19,86:4
Booth, Palmer G, 1948, Mr 15,23:4
Booth, Paul L, 1947, My 22,27:5
Booth, Paul Mrs, 1950, O 11,33:5
Booth, R H, 1931, Je 21,20:1
Booth, R W, 1884, F 15,4:6
Booth, Rachel H Mrs, 1939, Je 29,23:6
Booth, Ralph D, 1960, N 22,35:1
Booth, Ralph H Mrs, 1951, S 5,31:1
Booth, Robert J, 1939, N 21,23:4
Booth, Robert M, 1961, Mr 14,35:1
Booth, Ronald, 1950, D 1,25:3
Booth, Roy N, 1965, F 28,88:6
Booth, Samuel, 1947, Ap 18,21:3
Booth, Samuel P, 1939, Ap 3,15:5
Booth, Sydney B, 1937, F 7,II,9:3
Booth, Thomas E, 1940, Jl 11,19:4; 1953, My 7,31:4
Booth, Victor J, 1964, Ja 6,47:4
Booth, Vincent R, 1950, D 27,27:4
Booth, Vincent R Mrs, 1957, Ja 13,85:1
Booth, W Bramwell, 1929, Je 17,1:4
Booth, W Bramwell Gen, 1924, O 9,23:5
Booth, W C, 1876, Je 26,4:6
Booth, W Vernon Lt, 1918, Jl 16,13:6
Booth, Walker C, 1944, Ap 7,19:2
Booth, Walter, 1955, Jl 6,27:1
Booth, William B, 1938, N 2,24:2
Booth, William Bramwell Mrs, 1957, Je 11,35:4
Booth, William C, 1955, S 25,93:3
Booth, William C Mrs, 1960, Je 1,39:4
Booth, William E, 1945, F 28,23:4; 1948, Ag 22,63:5
Booth, William G, 1946, D 26,25:3
Booth, William R, 1948, S 7,25:2; 1953, Jl 26,69:3
Booth, William R Mrs, 1951, N 1,29:1
Booth, Willis H (est acctg, S 12,52:6), 1958, F 22, 17:4
Booth, Willis H Mrs, 1957, My 12,86:4
Booth, Willis H Mrs (est acctg), 1958, S 12,52:6
Booth, Winfield S, 1954, My 1,15:4
Booth-Clibborn, Arthur, 1939, F 15,23:4
Booth-Clibborn, Arthur S Mrs, 1955, My 10,29:5
Booth-Hellberg, Lucy Mrs, 1953, Jl 19,57:3
Booth-Tucker, F, 1929, Jl 18,21:3
Boothby, Alfred, 1937, F 7,II,8:6
Boothby, Clarence S, 1949, Mr 22,25:5
Boothby, Clark, 1944, Ja 19,19:5
Boothby, Clayton D, 1944, N 26,58:4
Boothby, Ernest L, 1952, O 18,19:2
Boothby, George H, 1945, S 1,11:3
Boothby, Guy Newell, 1905, F 28,9:6
Boothby, John William, 1923, Mr 20,21:4
Boothby, Oren C, 1940, Ag 10,13:4
Boothby, Robert, 1941, F 8,15:5
Boothby, Silas, 1949, My 28,15:2
Boothe, Earle, 1949, S 14,31:1
Boothe, Edwin M, 1941, Je 10,23:2
Boothe, Viva B, 1964, O 10,29:3
Boothman, John N, 1958, Ja 1,25:1
Boothy, Arthur V, 1951, N 20,31:5
Bootman, Harris D, 1951, Jl 13,21:3
Boots, Norman J, 1964, Ag 26,39:1
Boots, Ralph Henderson Dr, 1968, O 22,47:1
Boots, Rose E, 1960, F 26,27:3
Booty, Alfred, 1938, D 22,22:2
Booz, Edward D, 1939, Je 6,23:5
Booz, Edwin G, 1951, O 15,25:4
Booz, Horace C, 1951, Mr 15,29:4
Booz, S Graham, 1943, S 28,25:1
Boozan, William E, 1943, F 6,13:6
Boozan, William E Mrs, 1958, Ja 19,86:7
Booze, Albert, 1908, Mr 27,9:6
Bopes, Robert F, 1946, Mr 2,13:5
Bopf, Arthur P, 1940, My 13,17:4
Bopha, Kantha Princess (funl), 1953, Ja 5,21:4
Bopp, Augustus F, 1953, Je 9,27:4
Bopp, Paul S, 1956, N 17,21:5
Bopp, Robert P, 1940, Jl 23,19:5
Bopp, Werner, 1955, Ap 4,37:1
Boppe, Auguste, 1921, My 17,17:5
Boppel, John F, 1947, S 2,21:2
Bor, Gen (T Komorowski), 1966, Ag 26,33:1
Borah, William E, 1940, Ja 20,1:1
Boraisha, Manachem, 1949, F 13,76:2
Borak, Jonas (por), 1949, Ap 6,29:3
Boras, Samuel Mrs, 1951, N 3,17:1
Borba, Tomas, 1950, F 14,25:4
Borberg, William, 1958, My 18,86:1
Borbey, Pierre, 1954, O 26,27:2
Borch, George, 1950, My 19,27:3
Borchard, Edwin M, 1951, Jl 23,17:3
Borchardt, Albert H, 1962, Je 15,27:3
Borchardt, Frederick W, 1956, Ap 16,27:4
Borchardt, Herman, 1951, Ja 24,27:1
Borchardt, Ludwig, 1938, S 9,21:3
Borchardt, Selma Munter, 1968, F 1,34:7
Borcher, Aug, 1942, N 26,28:3
Borcher, John H, 1940, D 31,15:2
Borcher, William F, 1964, Ja 6,47:4
Borcherdt, Walter O, 1939, Ap 26,23:4
Borchers, Bernard W, 1953, N 27,27:3
Borchers, Harry J Sr Mrs, 1952, D 18,29:5
Borchers, Herbert, 1953, N 28,20:2
Borchers, Richard, 1954, D 26,61:1
Borchert, Ernest G, 1949, Jl 10,56:5
Borchert, Frank W, 1947, Jl 5,11:5
Borchmans, Mary Mother (Julia Gorman), 1912, Jl 2,11:3
Bordages, Ellen F, 1950, O 15,55:1
Bordanaro, Charles X, 1948, Mr 6,13:2
Bordeau, Chester, 1966, Jl 26,32:1
Bordeaux, David J, 1948, F 13,21:4
Borden, Albert G, 1950, Ja 28,13:3
Borden, Albert R, 1947, Ap 16,25:5
Borden, Alfred, 1949, Mr 20,76:6
Borden, Allen L Mrs, 1961, Ag 15,29:2
Borden, Alpheus H Mrs, 1957, Je 30,68:6
Borden, Andrew Mrs, 1915, Mr 30,11:4
Borden, Bertram H, 1956, My 1,33:4
Borden, Carleton G, 1938, S 27,21:3
Borden, Caroline, 1922, Mr 21,19:6
Borden, Carrie L, 1946, Ap 30,21:1
Borden, Charles Henry, 1913, Mr 10,9:4
Borden, Daniel C, 1964, O 17,29:4
Borden, Edwin F, 1944, Je 24,13:2
Borden, Fanny, 1954, F 1,23:6
Borden, Frank C, 1944, My 17,19:4
Borden, Frank P Mrs, 1958, S 27,21:3
Borden, Fred W, 1959, S 26,23:4
Borden, Gail, 1940, My 6,17:5
Borden, Garrick Mallory, 1912, My 25,13:6
Borden, George C Jr, 1955, Jl 9,15:5
Borden, George Pennington Gen, 1925, Ap 27,17:5
Borden, H L, 1902, N 26,2:4
Borden, Harry, 1957, Ag 1,25:3
Borden, Henry, 1914, Jl 30,9:4
Borden, Henry J, 1950, Je 2,24:2
Borden, Herbert L, 1943, Ag 6,15:6
Borden, Horace L, 1964, O 13,43:3
Borden, Howard L, 1948, Ap 3,15:4
Borden, Howard L Mrs, 1947, Ja 7,27:3
Borden, Howard S, 1950, D 10,107:3
Borden, Howard S Mrs, 1940, Ag 6,19:6
Borden, Ivey L, 1949, F 20,60:3
Borden, J, 1877, Mr 10,2:6
Borden, Jacob R, 1939, Mr 21,23:2
Borden, James B, 1939, Ja 24,19:2
Borden, John, 1961, Jl 30,69:1
Borden, John A, 1925, My 3,5:2
Borden, John C, 1960, Ap 10,86:6
Borden, John E, 1938, Jl 19,22:4
Borden, John F, 1938, Ja 17,19:4
Borden, John T, 1946, Je 27,21:4
Borden, John W, 1937, D 7,25:4
Borden, Joseph C, 1944, Mr 13,15:1
Borden, Joseph W, 1961, N 30,34:3
Borden, Julia H, 1940, Je 8,15:4
Borden, Laura Lady, 1940, S 8,49:3
Borden, Lisbeth A, 1927, Je 3,21:3
Borden, Martin L Mrs (D Weston), 1960, Jl 29,25:2
Borden, Mary, 1968, D 3,50:4
Borden, Matthew Chaloner Durfee, 1912, My 28,11:3
Borden, Milo S, 1962, N 10,25:2
Borden, N B, 1865, Ap 11,4:2
Borden, Olive, 1947, O 2,27:4
Borden, Parker G, 1947, Jl 7,17:4
Borden, Rebecca C Mrs, 1937, Ja 14,21:4
Borden, Richard P, 1942, S 24,27:2
Borden, Robert L Sir (will, Ag 13,15:8), 1937, Je 11, 23:1
Borden, Spencer, 1957, F 1,25:3
Borden, Spencer Col, 1921, O 18,17:4
Borden, Stephen W, 1948, My 16,68:6
Borden, T J Col, 1902, N 22,2:5
Borden, W Col, 1882, S 22,2:3
Borden, William B, 1949, My 17,25:5
Borden, William E, 1947, F 25,25:2
Borden, William H, 1951, N 6,29:4
Borden, William W, 1913, Ap 10,11:5
Bordenave, Enrique, 1940, Ja 25,21:6
Bordenet, Jean P, 1963, Ag 18,80:8
Borders, Harry L, 1948, Ja 24,15:4
Borders, J B, 1913, Ag 13,9:5
Borders, J B Mrs, 1913, Ag 13,9:5
Borders, Karl, 1953, Ja 31,15:6
Bordes, Charles, 1909, N 9,9:5; 1909, D 10,11:4
Bordes, Pierre, 1943, Jl 25,30:8
Bordet, Jules, 1961, Ap 7,31:1
Bordewich, Harold L Mrs (L Madigan), 1962, Ag 23,59:1
Bordick, Charles M, 1961, My 14,86:3
Bordley, John, 1941, D 18,27:6
Bordman, Clyde Mrs, 1937, Ag 4,19:6
Bordman, John, 1943, S 19,48:5
Bordner, Delores W, 1966, O 21,41:5
Bordoni, Irene, 1953, Mr 20,23:1
Borduas, Paul E, 1960, F 24,37:1
Bordwell, Hudson J, 1937, N 17,23:2
Bordwell, Lavern, 1953, S 8,31:3
Borea, William, 1968, Ja 3,47:1
Boree, Mathias J, 1872, S 15,1:3
Borein, Edward, 1945, My 21,19:5
Boreing, Vincent, 1903, S 17,7:7
Borel, Antoine, 1915, Mr 29,9:4
Borel, Charles B, 1960, Mr 17,33:5
Borel, Emile, 1956, F 5,87:1
Borel, Guadalupt, 1949, D 24,15:6
Borel, J L Gen, 1884, F 24,7:4
Borella, Victor Mrs, 1956, Jl 7,13:5
Borelli, Joseph, 1918, D 16,15:1
Borelli, Jules, 1941, F 12,21:3
Boreman, Arthur I, 1966, Je 18,31:4
Boreman, Kenner S, 1940, Ja 15,15:3
Boren, Addison, 1949, N 5,13:1
Boren, Saul, 1961, D 6,48:1
Boren, Wallace R, 1963, S 20,33:1
Borenius, Tancred, 1948, S 5,40:8
Borenski, Vincent, 1955, Ja 2,61:4
Borenstein, Julius, 1942, Mr 14,15:3
Borenstein, Louis, 1961, Ap 26,39:1
Boreo, Emil, 1951, Jl 28,11:2
Borer, Robert C, 1953, Mr 28,17:4
Borer, William, 1941, Mr 24,17:2
Bores, Joseph, 1952, Ag 30,13:5
Boresch, Thomas Mrs, 1950, D 30,13:5
Boret, Victor, 1952, Ap 25,23:3
Boretz, Mary E (por), 1949, Ag 30,27:1
Borg, Adolph F, 1959, Ap 19,87:1
Borg, Carl O, 1947, My 10,13:7
Borg, Charles W, 1946, N 27,25:5

Borg, Evelyn E (Mrs A F Landeker), 1961, O 9,35:4
Borg, George W, 1960, F 22,17:2
Borg, John (funl, My 11,27:3; will, Je 1,23:2), 1956, My 8,33:1
Borg, John Mrs, 1955, Ja 23,85:2
Borg, Kenneth D, 1954, Ag 29,16:4
Borg, Marie Mrs, 1947, O 28,7:3
Borg, Myron I Jr, 1962, D 7,34:3
Borg, Myron I Mrs, 1958, Ag 17,86:3
Borg, S C, 1934, Ja 10,21:1
Borg, Sidney C Mrs (funl, Ja 12,27:5), 1956, Ja 10, 31:1
Borg, Simon, 1904, F 12,9:5
Borg, Simon Mrs (funl, Ag 3,7:5), 1905, Jl 31,7:5
Borgading, Alvin A, 1964, N 14,29:5
Borgatta, Marco R, 1956, N 13,37:5
Borgatti, Giuseppe, 1950, O 19,31:3
Borge, Manuel Jr, 1940, N 17,48:4
Borgeaud, Henri, 1964, My 27,39:3
Borgenicht, Louis, 1942, O 13,23:5
Borgenicht, Max Mrs, 1952, Ap 15,27:2
Borgenicht, S William, 1946, Je 19,21:3
Borgenicht, Sadie (Mrs S B Finn), 1962, N 22,29:4
Borger, Edward M, 1953, S 22,31:1
Borger, Frank, 1941, Mr 29,15:3
Borger, John H, 1959, D 30,21:1
Borgerding, Thomas, 1956, D 1,21:5
Borgerhoff, Elbert B O Dr, 1968, Jl 1,33:4
Borgerhoff, Joseph, 1950, Ag 4,21:6
Borges, Esteban G, 1942, Ag 4,19:5
Borges, John A, 1946, Ag 21,27:3
Borges, Waldemar B, 1952, N 1,11:4
Borgese, Giuseppe A, 1952, D 5,27:2
Borgeson, Eric W, 1961, Ag 27,84:4
Borgeson, Melvin B, 1963, N 23,29:3
Borgeson, Sidney E, 1955, Ag 4,25:3
Borgeson, Sydney E Mrs, 1938, Je 19,29:2
Borgetti, Leonard, 1948, Ag 30,25:1
Borgfeldt, George, 1903, N 22,7:5
Borgford, Helgi I S, 1957, Je 3,27:4
Borghard, Anthony W, 1961, F 26,92:6
Borghese, Rodolfo (Prince), 1963, Ag 10,17:1
Borghi, Armando, 1968, Ap 30,47:2
Borghi, Joseph, 1947, Jl 18,17:4
Borgia, Domenico, 1937, F 8,17:2
Borgin, Frank Jr, 1924, Jl 15,9:3
Borgioli, Dino, 1960, S 14,43:1
Borglum, Gutzon, 1941, Mr 7,21:1
Borglum, Gutzon Mrs, 1955, Ag 17,27:2
Borglum, Lincoln Mrs, 1963, N 27,37:3
Borglum, Paul, 1968, S 23,35:5
Borglum, Solon H, 1922, Ja 31,12:5
Borgman, Albert S, 1954, D 10,28:2
Borgmann, Aug, 1949, O 8,13:5
Borgmann, Joseph H Rev, 1937, Ag 27,19:4
Borgmeier, Wilhelmina K Mrs, 1940, Mr 19,25:1
Borgnis, Horace, 1941, My 1,23:2
Borgonini Duca, Francesco, 1954, O 5,27:4
Borgstede, John G, 1945, S 10,19:4
Borgstedt, Henning, 1952, D 2,31:3
Borgwald, Harold, 1966, Mr 3,33:4
Borgward, Carl F, 1963, Jl 30,29:4
Borgzinner, Albert, 1951, Jl 11,23:3
Borgzinner, Siegmund, 1944, My 11,19:5
Bori, Lucretia (est appr), 1966, O 2,86:8
Bori, Lucrezia (funl, My 18,41:3; will, My 24,25:1), 1960, My 15,1:4
Borican, John, 1942, D 23,19:2
Borie, A E, 1880, F 6,2:5
Borie, Adolphe E, 1954, Ap 28,31:4
Borie, C Louis, 1964, Mr 13,34:5
Borie, Charles L Jr, 1943, My 12,25:5
Borie, Charles L Mrs, 1944, S 1,13:3
Borie, Lawrence M, 1952, Ja 15,27:1
Borie, Patty D N Mrs, 1940, O 26,15:1
Boring, Edwin Garrigues, 1968, Jl 2,26:2
Boring, William A, 1937, My 6,25:1
Boring, William A Mrs, 1946, Je 29,19:4
Borinsky, Charles, 1966, Je 17,45:3
Borinsky, Samuel, 1962, My 2,37:4
Boris, Anthony H, 1954, Ag 13,15:3
Boris, Grand Duke of Russia, 1943, N 10,23:5
Boris, M I (B Majdrakoff), 1962, Jl 17,25:5
Boris, William, 1947, Mr 18,27:1
Boris III, King of Bulgaria, 1943, Ag 29,1:6
Borisoglebsky, Viktor V, 1964, F 6,29:5
Borisov, Nikolai A, 1955, S 16,23:4
Borisov, Sergei A, 1964, S 29,43:2
Borissyak, Alexy, 1944, F 27,38:2
Borjes, Fritz H, 1954, Ja 5,27:3
Borjes, Henry, 1959, Ag 11,27:5
Borkel, John, 1921, Ap 3,22:3
Borkland, William, 1942, Jl 2,21:5
Borkow, Phil S, 1956, Ja 9,36:1
Borkowski, Eustazy, 1960, My 21,23:4
Borland, Andrew A, 1958, O 14,37:5
Borland, Bertha, 1952, Ja 20,88:3
Borland, Bessie, 1951, N 23,30:3
Borland, Charles, 1946, Ja 4,21:2
Borland, Hal Mrs, 1944, O 30,19:3
Borland, J Nelson 2d, 1950, Ap 27,29:3
Borland, James B, 1939, My 20,15:5
Borland, John E Dr, 1937, My 17,19:5
Borland, John M, 1946, Ag 13,27:2
Borland, John Mrs, 1959, Jl 20,25:2
Borland, Mary A Mrs, 1938, Je 17,21:4
Borland, Nettie A, 1952, Ja 28,17:5
Borland, Reuben, 1925, D 13,13:1
Borland, Walter S, 1959, D 24,19:6
Borland, William P, 1919, F 22,9:3
Borland, William S Jr, 1967, Mr 27,33:3
Borlenghi, Angel G, 1962, Je 19,32:1
Borlund, Robert D, 1956, Jl 26,25:5
Borman, Adolph H, 1915, Ag 21,7:6
Borman, Helen, 1941, Jl 24,17:4
Borman, Paul de, 1948, Ap 22,27:2
Born, Edward, 1941, Ja 7,23:1
Born, Frank A, 1937, Ap 1,23:4
Born, Herman, 1957, O 7,27:4
Born, John, 1943, Ag 31,17:3
Born, John A, 1942, D 13,75:6
Born, Louis, 1950, My 9,29:4
Born, Wolfgang (por), 1949, Je 16,29:2
Bornand, Adrian V, 1949, O 27,28:2
Borncamp, Edward Rev, 1912, Ag 14,9:4
Borncamp, William F, 1923, Jl 13,15:5
Borne, Charles A, 1953, F 14,17:5
Borne, John E (funl, Jl 13,7:4), 1910, Jl 12,7:5
Borne, Lucien, 1954, D 24,13:3
Borneman, Henry S, 1955, Ja 14,19:6
Borneman, Herman Jr, 1946, F 21,21:2
Borneman, John A, 1955, Ap 10,89:1
Borneman, William J Mrs, 1954, Jl 31,13:5
Bornemann, Charles J, 1947, Mr 31,23:5
Bornemann, Louis W, 1954, N 18,33:2
Bornemann, R Nelson, 1958, O 6,31:5
Bornemann, William H, 1952, Ja 22,29:4
Bornewasser, Franz R, 1951, D 21,27:3
Bornhoeft, Susanna W Mrs, 1942, My 14,19:1
Bornhold, John, 1951, Ag 23,23:5
Bornkesel, August L, 1946, Ap 9,27:2
Bornman, Ralph H Mrs, 1951, O 13,17:4
Bornmann, Carl F, 1954, Je 8,27:2
Bornmann, J George, 1943, Je 29,19:2
Borno, Louis, 1942, Jl 30,21:3
Bornoff, Louis R, 1963, D 11,47:4
Bornschein, Franz C, 1948, Je 10,25:4
Bornscheuer, Henry A, 1937, Jl 15,19:5
Bornstein, Benjamin, 1954, Je 13,88:2
Bornstein, Garner H, 1954, Ag 8,85:3
Bornstein, Harry, 1950, Ap 1,15:4; 1950, Je 3,15:5
Bornstein, Isadore, 1953, F 4,27:1
Bornstein, Jack J, 1956, F 14,29:2
Bornstein, Jack Mrs, 1960, S 11,82:5
Bornstein, Joseph, 1952, Je 26,29:5
Bornstein, Joseph M, 1949, Jl 19,30:4
Bornstein, Morris Maj, 1923, Jl 9,13:3
Bornstein, Newton A, 1959, My 7,33:4
Bornstein, Sol, 1967, Je 2,46:7
Borochowicz, Leo, 1953, F 4,27:2
Borodin, Dmitry N, 1957, Je 21,25:2
Borodin, Michael (M Gruzenberg), 1953, S 3,21:1
Borodin, Nicholas A Prof, 1937, D 23,21:5
Borodkin, Michael, 1966, D 10,38:3
Borodkin, Morris B Mrs, 1965, O 11,39:3
Boroff, Abraham, 1961, Ja 14,23:2
Boroff, David (funl plans, My 17,35:5), 1965, My 16,88:5
Boroff, George, 1968, Je 23,73:1
Boroff, Isaac Mrs, 1947, Jl 3,21:3
Boros, Henry, 1952, Jl 6,49:1
Boros, Julius Mrs, 1951, S 10,21:4
Boross, Eugen, 1942, O 9,21:1
Borough, Randal, 1951, F 6,27:5
Borovsky, Alexander, 1968, Ap 28,83:1
Borow, Henry, 1956, S 10,27:5
Borowetz, Edmund W, 1950, Mr 17,24:3
Borowiak, Stanislaus N, 1944, Jl 13,17:6
Borowitz, David Mrs, 1956, N 19,31:5; 1959, Ja 26, 29:2
Borowski, Anastasia Mrs, 1938, O 6,23:1
Borowski, Felix, 1956, S 7,24:2
Borowsky, F Gordon, 1961, Je 26,31:6
Borowsky, Michael, 1959, Jl 22,27:1
Borowsky, Samuel J, 1966, Ap 25,31:4
Borquist, Edwin A, 1947, Mr 31,23:2
Borr, Mischa, 1957, My 7,35:2
Borras, Peter, 1950, Ag 23,29:2
Borre, Cesar, 1950, Ap 13,29:2
Borrell, Frank N, 1957, S 11,24:3
Borrell, James H, 1939, O 1,53:1
Borrell, Leonard L, 1961, S 10,86:2
Borrelli, Francis, 1954, Ap 28,31:3
Borrelli, Frank, 1951, Je 15,23:3
Borrelli, Josephine P Mrs, 1952, My 18,92:3
Borrelli, Luigi, 1960, Jl 28,27:5
Borrero, Pablo, 1950, Je 16,25:6
Borrett, Oswald C, 1950, Jl 29,13:1
Borrok, Archie, 1957, Mr 5,31:4
Borromeo, Cardinal, 1881, D 2,2:7
Borromeo, Guido Count, 1942, Ja 23,20:2
Borrone, Milton, 1964, Jl 12,69:1
Borrow, George, 1881, Jl 31,6:7
Borrowe, Hallet Alsop Maj, 1921, My 23,13:5
Borrowes, George H, 1953, D 15,39:3
Borrowman, George, 1946, Mr 28,25:3
Bors-Koefoed, Axel, 1949, Jl 26,27:1
Borsa, Mario, 1952, O 7,29:2
Borschinino, Jens Waldemar, 1903, Ag 11,7:7
Borshaw, Hyman, 1962, F 3,21:1
Borsky, Louis R, 1954, Mr 30,27:5
Borst, Doris G B Mrs, 1948, My 16,68:7
Borst, Eugene A, 1949, My 24,28:2
Borst, George, 1944, D 15,19:2
Borst, Guernsey J, 1955, S 22,31:1
Borst, Henry V Ex-Justice, 1925, N 27,17:4
Borst, Homer J, 1956, Jl 2,21:4
Borst, Homer W, 1954, O 21,27:5
Borst, Nelson R, 1940, Mr 30,15:6
Borst, Victor D, 1961, Ap 6,26:1
Borst, W H, 1882, O 31,5:2
Borst, Warren R, 1952, O 19,88:5
Borsum, Louis, 1942, D 4,25:2
Bortel, James G, 1952, My 25,94:4
Borten, Isadore, 1944, Ap 25,23:6
Borth, John C, 1939, F 7,19:4
Borth, John C Mrs, 1953, My 7,31:3
Borthwick, James, 1958, O 5,86:8
Borthwick, Pringle, 1948, D 31,15:3
Borthwick, William S, 1951, S 13,31:2
Bortnowski, Wladislaw, 1966, N 22,45:5
Bortolotti, Tino, 1954, O 16,17:3
Borton, Alwyn E, 1950, F 16,23:4
Borton, C Stanley, 1950, N 12,92:3
Borton, Fred S, 1942, O 27,25:1
Borton, John Mrs, 1959, Jl 21,30:5
Borton, John N Mrs, 1942, F 11,21:3
Borton, May W Mrs, 1956, Jl 1,56:8
Borton, Neville T, 1938, Je 3,21:4
Bortzner, Christian, 1953, Ag 15,6:3
Boruchoff, Ber, 1939, Ap 6,25:1
Boruff, Blanche Mrs, 1951, N 12,25:1
Boruff, Kate C P Mrs, 1942, S 6,30:6
Borum, L P, 1949, Ag 20,11:5
Borup, Andrew, 1947, My 4,60:3
Borup, Doan, 1944, O 4,19:1
Borup, George, 1912, My 2,11:4
Borup, Henry D Col, 1916, My 27,11:4
Borup, P A, 1952, O 25,23:5
Borvig, T H, 1938, Ag 23,17:3
Borwell, Frank J C, 1944, O 16,19:6
Borwick, Leonard, 1925, S 17,23:6
Borwin, Karl (Duke of Mecklenburg), 1908, Ag 26 7:6
Borzage, Frank, 1962, Je 20,32:4
Borzage, Mary Mrs, 1947, Jl 1,25:2
Borzilleri, Charles R, 1942, Je 2,24:2
Bos, Arie, 1962, Ja 18,29:5
Bos, Coenraad V, 1955, Ag 6,15:1
Bos, Gerard J W, 1952, N 12,27:5
Bos, Karel J, 1943, D 3,23:4
Bosan, Alonzo, 1959, Jl 9,27:4
Bosanquet, William S B, 1966, Mr 8,30:2
Bosart, Louis, 1947, Je 22,52:3
Bosbyshell, William F Mrs, 1941, Je 20,21:2
Boscarelli, Raffaele, 1942, Ap 24,17:2
Bosch, Arthur, 1952, S 9,31:5
Bosch, Carl, 1940, Ap 28,36:5
Bosch, Charles A, 1947, O 28,25:5
Bosch, Dorothea I, 1962, Ja 8,39:3
Bosch, Edmund A Mrs, 1949, My 16,21:4
Bosch, Ernesto, 1951, Ag 23,23:2
Bosch, Frederick H, 1944, Ap 2,39:1
Bosch, Frederick H Mrs, 1959, Jl 16,27:4
Bosch, Herbert M, 1962, S 17,31:2
Bosch, Herman J, 1957, Ap 7,88:1
Bosch, I van den, 1942, Jl 12,15:2
Bosch, Johannes A L van den, 1945, Mr 13,23:4
Bosch, Louis, 1939, D 10,59:3
Bosch, Robert, 1942, Mr 13,19:3
Bosche, Aloysius Rev, 1916, O 19,9:4
Boschen, C D Mrs, 1903, Je 23,7:6
Boschen, Frederick, 1949, Ap 18,25:3
Boschen, Frederick W, 1942, Ap 3,21:6
Boschen, Henry L, 1946, Jl 27,17:3
Boschen, Otto, 1959, O 7,43:1
Boschen, Otto Mrs, 1953, Je 30,23:2
Boschert, Frederick H, 1960, Jl 18,27:5
Boschot, Adolphe, 1955, Je 2,29:4
Boschwitz, Carl, 1937, Jl 13,20:3
Boscia, John, 1914, Ag 27,11:5
Boscia, Michael J, 1955, N 9,33:4
Bosco, Giuseppe, 1951, Je 16,15:4
Bosco, James V, 1956, Mr 23,27:3
Bose, Charles H, 1903, Jl 31,7:6
Bose, Edwin, 1945, Ap 17,23:5
Bose, Fritz, 1949, N 27,104:3
Bose, Herman, 1917, N 24,13:5
Bose, Herman H, 1955, N 24,29:2
Bose, Jagadis C Sir, 1937, N 24,23:1
Bose, Ludolph, 1940, D 31,15:4
Bose, Rash B, 1945, Ja 23,10:2
Bose, Sarat C, 1950, F 21,25:1
Bose, Subhas Chandra (death confirmed Ag '45) 1956, S 12,10:5
Bose, William, 1875, D 27,5:4
Boser, Alfred W, 1937, Ag 4,19:1
Boser, Louis A, 1949, D 22,23:3
Boshart, William H, 1966, N 7,47:4

Boshell, James A, 1953, Je 18,29:2
Boshell, Jorge Dr, 1924, My 5,15:3
Bosher, Martha C Mrs, 1941, F 19,21:5
Bosher, Robert S, 1904, Ja 14,9:2
Bosio, A J, 1876, Jl 7,4:6
Bosio, Madame, 1859, Ap 30,5:1
Boskamp, A J, 1950, O 18,33:4
Boskerck, Lucas J von, 1908, Ap 20,7:4
Boskowitz, George W Dr, 1917, Mr 16,11:4
Bosler, Clinton D, 1903, D 23,9:6
Bosler, J W, 1883, D 18,4:7
Bosler, William D, 1944, D 7,25:3
Bosley, Frederick A, 1942, Mr 23,15:4
Bosley, John Jr, 1951, O 13,17:5
Bosley, John W, 1943, Je 16,21:6
Bosley, Lewis W, 1952, Ja 29,25:2
Bosley, William B, 1960, O 21,33:4
Boslow, Harry, 1957, Ja 25,21:2
Bosman, Bertram S, 1949, Mr 15,27:4
Bosman, David, 1919, O 26,22:3
Bosman, David Mrs, 1944, My 31,19:5
Bosman, George W, 1954, D 13,27:1
Bosmans, Henriette, 1952, Jl 4,13:4
Bosmans, Martin, 1948, My 19,28:3
Bosniak, Jacob, 1963, Ag 26,27:4
Bosquett, Thomas J, 1947, D 12,27:3
Boss, Andrew, 1947, Ja 14,25:1
Boss, Benson B, 1938, Ja 11,23:6
Boss, Charles E, 1940, Mr 19,25:5
Boss, Charles R, 1940, S 2,15:4
Boss, Edward J, 1943, Mr 30,26:3
Boss, Ernest A, 1947, D 25,21:2
Boss, Frederick Mrs, 1946, Ag 27,27:6
Boss, Harley, 1964, My 16,25:3
Boss, Herbert A, 1958, Ap 1,31:6
Boss, Innocent, 1962, N 7,39:5
Boss, Lawrence, 1956, Jl 25,29:5
Boss, Lewis Prof, 1912, O 6,II,17:4
Boss, Nelson R, 1951, Ja 22,17:2
Boss, Theodore H, 1966, F 25,31:4
Boss, Thomas B, 1940, N 20,21:4
Boss, William, 1951, Ag 26,79:3
Boss, Winfield L Mrs, 1956, Ap 12,31:1
Bossa, Harold V, 1961, S 6,37:4
Bossa, Simon, 1950, Mr 3,25:2
Bossak, Gen, 1871, Mr 2,8:2
Bossak, Joseph M, 1941, Ap 19,15:4
Bossak, S Mrs (Fania), 1962, Ag 25,19:3
Bossak, Solomon, 1959, D 26,31:3
Bossan, Lola, 1945, Ag 19,39:1
Bossange, Edouard R, 1947, N 18,29:4
Bossard, F Edgar, 1966, Mr 10,33:3
Bossard, Harry B, 1950, Ap 13,29:3
Bossard, James H S, 1960, Ja 30,21:5
Bossard, Lester, 1948, Je 14,24:2
Bossard, Louis R, 1945, O 28,44:3
Bosscher, J P, 1942, My 16,13:3
Bosse, Benjamin Maj, 1922, Ap 5,17:5
Bosse, Charles R, 1963, Ap 21,86:3
Bosse, Harriet, 1961, N 7,33:3
Bosse, Henry, 1943, O 7,23:4
Bosse, Henry P Col, 1903, D 16,9:5
Bosse, Marie L Mrs, 1952, Mr 17,21:5
Bosselman, William, 1947, Ap 22,27:4
Bossert, Charles L, 1941, N 14,23:2
Bossert, Charles V, 1953, Mr 12,25:1
Bossert, John, 1944, S 23,13:3
Bossert, John L, 1942, Jl 11,13:5
Bossert, Louis, 1913, Ja 31,11:5; 1945, D 13,29:5
Bosshart, John H, 1964, My 18,26:6
Bosshart, John H Mrs, 1943, Mr 5,17:5
Bossi, Enea, 1963, Ja 12,14:5
Bossi, Frederick G, 1945, Mr 4,36:6
Bossi, Marco Enrico, 1925, F 22,19:2
Bossidy, Bart, 1948, F 22,48:2
Bossieux, Helen L, 1948, My 16,70:2
Bossom, Alfred C, 1965, S 5,57:1
Bosson, Edward P, 1942, D 14,28:4
Bossong, Werner, 1950, Ja 5,23:1
Bossoutrot, Lucien, 1958, S 2,25:3
Bost, Bernice C Mrs, 1944, F 6,41:1
Bost, Charles, 1943, Mr 21,26:6
Bost, J R, 1950, Mr 18,13:2
Bost, Ralph W, 1951, S 23,85:3
Bost, William D, 1962, N 3,25:1
Bosted, Donald C, 1956, Ap 23,27:5
Bostelman, Ben A, 1958, Ap 6,88:5
Bostelmann, Louis J, 1965, D 29,29:4
Bostelmann, Monroe Mrs (Else), 1961, D 29,24:4
Bostetter, Charles F, 1943, F 3,19:4
Bosthwick, Oliver, 1905, Mr 24,9:3
Bostic, Earl, 1965, O 29,43:2
Bostick, J Wallace, 1941, Ja 2,23:2
Bostin, J W, 1952, O 19,V,9:1
Bostock, Edward H, 1940, S 19,23:6
Bostock, Frank C, 1912, O 9,13:3
Bostock, Frank T, 1945, Je 12,19:5
Bostock, H, 1930, Ap 30,25:5
Bostock, Herbert A, 1947, Mr 6,25:1
Bostock, Lillian F, 1913, Jl 18,9:6
Bostock, Thomas, 1951, My 18,27:1
Bostock, Walter J Mrs, 1950, Ap 26,29:3
Bostock, William T Sr, 1954, Ap 10,15:6

Bostom, Ernest F, 1963, N 8,31:3
Boston, C, 1930, Ja 5,18:1
Boston, C A, 1935, Mr 9,15:1
Boston, Carlton E, 1945, N 28,27:1
Boston, Charles A Mrs, 1967, Ap 25,43:1
Boston, Clarence E, 1941, Ag 27,19:2
Boston, Frank E, 1960, F 9,31:3
Boston, Grace, 1954, S 26,87:1
Boston, Harold Mrs, 1937, F 26,21:4
Boston, Joseph H, 1954, Mr 16,29:3
Boston, Paul M, 1947, F 6,23:3
Bostrom, Erik G B, 1907, F 22,9:5
Bostrom, Otto H, 1952, Je 11,29:4
Bostrom, Wollmar F, 1956, N 15,35:2
Bostwick, Arthur E, 1942, F 14,15:4
Bostwick, Blanche (Mrs T N Page), 1959, Mr 2,27:1
Bostwick, C Livingston, 1940, O 12,17:6
Bostwick, Carl E, 1944, F 29,17:3
Bostwick, Charles A, 1937, Jl 26,19:4
Bostwick, Charles D, 1937, D 17,25:2
Bostwick, Charles E, 1944, O 13,19:3
Bostwick, Charles P, 1923, Je 22,17:5
Bostwick, Elwood F, 1958, Ja 15,29:3
Bostwick, Franchesa Mrs, 1967, Jl 30,64:5
Bostwick, Frank M, 1945, D 22,19:3
Bostwick, Henry Anton Col, 1917, Jl 26,11:6
Bostwick, Henry M, 1940, N 26,23:1
Bostwick, Jabez A Mrs, 1920, Ap 28,11:4
Bostwick, Larry C, 1944, O 27,23:3
Bostwick, Leonard, 1945, S 13,23:1
Bostwick, Louis R, 1943, Jl 25,31:2
Bostwick, Lucius A, 1940, Ja 16,23:1
Bostwick, Richmond F, 1955, My 31,27:4
Bostwick, Robert L Mrs, 1951, F 3,15:5
Bostwick, W H Mrs, 1903, Je 1,7:7
Bostwick, William C, 1959, Ja 31,19:4
Bostwick, William W, 1959, Ja 13,47:3
Boswell, Alfred C, 1944, S 2,11:7
Boswell, Alfred Mrs, 1947, Jl 7,17:5
Boswell, Charles R, 1940, Jl 29,13:2
Boswell, David C, 1961, O 9,35:3
Boswell, H Robertson Jr, 1960, N 28,31:2
Boswell, Helen V, 1942, Ja 6,23:3
Boswell, Lawrence T, 1954, Je 20,62:4
Boswell, Maitland C, 1952, My 4,90:3
Boswell, Martha (Mrs G L Lloyd), 1958, Jl 3,25:2
Boswell, P, 1936, D 19,19:6
Boswell, Peyton Jr (cor, Je 29,27:4), 1950, Je 24,13:5
Boswell, Robert S, 1954, Ag 22,93:1
Boswell, Russell T, 1951, N 22,31:1
Boswell, Walter O Mrs, 1956, D 13,37:1
Boswich, Samuel, 1952, Jl 25,17:4
Bosworth, Anne, 1961, Jl 28,21:3
Bosworth, Boardman M, 1950, O 11,33:1
Bosworth, David N, 1959, Ag 10,27:4
Bosworth, Foster Mrs, 1907, D 21,9:6
Bosworth, Francke H, 1949, Ap 29,23:1
Bosworth, Francke H Mrs, 1949, My 15,90:5
Bosworth, Frank A, 1940, Ap 25,23:4
Bosworth, Frank S Mrs, 1950, N 8,29:4
Bosworth, George M, 1925, Jl 27,13:4
Bosworth, Halliam, 1954, O 12,27:2
Bosworth, Harold B, 1964, S 3,29:5
Bosworth, Hobart V, 1943, D 31,15:1
Bosworth, J S, 1884, My 22,5:2
Bosworth, Lloyd Sr, 1950, D 2,13:7
Bosworth, Sofia B Mrs, 1941, F 19,21:1
Bosworth, Thomas S, 1957, D 18,35:3
Bosworth, William B, 1948, N 3,27:2
Bosworth, William W, 1966, Je 5,86:6
Bosze, Anthony P, 1956, Mr 15,31:5
Botassi, Demetrius N, 1924, S 28,27:3
Botbyl, George W, 1937, S 16,25:2
Botbyl, Justus G, 1938, Mr 9,23:5
Botbyl, William G, 1955, F 25,21:2
Botchford, Clement Mrs, 1957, S 30,31:4
Botein, Herman W Mrs, 1967, S 17,84:8
Boteler, Andrew K Mrs, 1960, S 29,35:2
Boteler, Elijah S Jr, 1938, Ja 26,23:4
Botelho, Abel Col, 1917, Ap 25,11:7
Botello Muniz, Jose V, 1951, S 27,31:2
Botens, George W, 1945, My 2,23:3
Botero, Roberto, 1957, O 7,27:5
Both, John, 1938, Mr 25,19:3
Both, Paul C, 1941, S 23,23:2
Botha, Annie C E Mrs, 1937, My 22,18:1
Botha, Hermanus N, 1950, Ja 23,23:3
Botha, Jaap, 1966, Mr 18,39:2
Botha, Louis, 1952, Ag 7,21:2
Botha, Louis Gen, 1919, Ag 29,11:6
Bothe, Albert E, 1955, N 12,19:2
Bothe, Henry, 1947, N 11,27:4
Bothe, Walther, 1957, F 9,19:5
Bothezat, George De, 1940, F 3,30:5
Bothman, Louis, 1949, Ja 20,27:2
Bothmer, Felix von Gen Count, 1937, Mr 20,19:6
Bothner, Charles A, 1948, Ap 23,23:4
Bothner, George, 1954, N 21,86:5
Bothwell, Charles W, 1957, F 3,76:1
Bothwell, Edward J, 1957, Jl 25,23:1
Bothwell, James W, 1944, Ja 27,19:4
Bothwell, John F, 1967, Mr 9,39:2
Bothwell, W Earl, 1949, O 13,27:2

Bothwell, Walter J, 1947, Ag 29,17:6
Botini, Piero C de, 1944, Ag 22,17:3
Botke, Cornelis, 1954, S 18,15:4
Botker, Christian, 1945, Mr 11,39:1
Botkin, Jeremiah D Rev, 1921, D 30,15:6
Botkin, L C, 1942, O 24,15:3
Botkin, Samuel J Mrs, 1946, Jl 7,36:6
Botrel, Jean, 1925, Jl 28,13:5
Botsford, Alfred M, 1967, My 17,47:5
Botsford, Alfred Pomeroy Rev, 1925, S 5,13:6
Botsford, E Herbert, 1952, Mr 28,23:4
Botsford, E Herbert Mrs, 1962, D 6,43:4
Botsford, Elliott A, 1942, Jl 20,13:4
Botsford, George Willis Prof, 1917, D 14,13:5
Botsford, Samuel B, 1941, Ag 4,13:4
Botsford, Sarah Flagler Mrs, 1915, Ja 19,9:5
Botsford, Stephen B, 1967, D 22,28:7
Botsford, William H, 1942, N 5,25:2
Botsford, William Judge (Nova Scotia), 1864, My 26,2:6
Bott, Ethel M, 1953, Je 26,19:3
Bott, Frederick V, 1956, Ja 20,23:1
Bott, George R, 1937, Ag 16,19:1
Bott, James H, 1957, Mr 25,25:3
Botta, Carlo, 1875, S 27,4:6
Botta, Luca (funl, O 3,13:5), 1917, S 30,23:5
Botta, Maude Mrs, 1952, N 27,31:1
Botta, Robert A, 1954, Jl 8,23:1
Bottai, Giuseppe, 1959, Ja 10,17:3
Bottazzi, Filippo, 1941, S 21,45:1
Bottcher, William G, 1948, O 12,25:5
Bottelli, Romolo Sr, 1957, Je 6,31:4
Botten, Edward W, 1949, Je 7,32:2
Botten, John, 1947, Ag 19,23:1
Bottenfield, L S Mrs, 1952, Mr 21,23:5
Bottenwiesser, Paul, 1942, Mr 14,15:6
Botter, David E, 1963, My 11,25:3
Bottger, Emil, 1906, Je 29,9:7
Bottger, O C, 1941, Jl 13,29:3
Botthof, Frank W Sr, 1942, My 31,39:2
Botti, Andrew P, 1960, N 19,21:1
Botti, Anthony J, 1963, Ag 9,23:4
Botti, Carmelita, 1951, Mr 19,27:1
Botti, Edmond, 1943, Ag 24,19:3
Botti, John D, 1955, Jl 2,15:6
Bottiger, K N, 1879, Ja 26,8:5
Bottiglieri, Antoinette Mrs, 1956, D 28,21:3
Botting, Richard A Mrs, 1948, Je 22,25:2
Bottl, Louise, 1924, N 1,15:3
Botto, Arrigo Sen, 1918, Je 11,11:5
Botto, Otto (Otto Banz), 1968, Ja 8,39:3
Bottolisen, C A, 1964, Jl 19,64:3
Bottom, Raymond B, 1953, O 30,23:3
Bottome, Harry H, 1963, Ap 4,47:5
Bottome, Margaret Mrs (funl, N 18,7:2), 1906, N 15, 9:6
Bottome, Phyllis (Mrs A E F Dennis, Ag 23,25:1), 1963, Ag 24,19:2
Bottome, Willard B, 1955, Mr 15,29:3
Bottomley, Albert E, 1950, Ag 26,13:6
Bottomley, Charles, 1950, Ag 30,31:1
Bottomley, Florence, 1945, D 4,29:5
Bottomley, Gordon, 1948, Ag 27,18:4
Bottomley, H, 1933, My 27,6:3
Bottomley, Harold S, 1951, N 8,29:3
Bottomley, Howland W, 1955, F 25,21:4
Bottomley, James L (Sunny Jim), 1959, D 12,23:3
Bottomley, John (funl, Je 18,13:6), 1918, Je 17,13:8
Bottomley, Roland, 1947, Ja 6,23:4
Bottomley, William A, 1957, Ag 25,87:1
Bottomley, William L, 1951, F 2,23:3
Bottoms, George W, 1952, Ag 27,27:5
Bottoms, Maitland, 1955, Ag 19,19:1
Bottoms, Norman Mrs, 1946, Mr 30,15:5
Bottoms, Sam F F, 1942, My 3,53:2
Bottoni, Robert J Sr, 1958, S 7,87:2
Botts, C T Mrs, 1937, Je 4,23:4
Botts, Edward W, 1943, F 15,15:5
Botts, Hugh F, 1956, O 15,25:5
Botts, Hugh P, 1964, Ap 27,31:5
Botts, John Minor, 1869, Ja 6,5:1
Botwin, Max, 1948, My 7,23:4
Botwin, Max Mrs, 1947, Jl 1,25:2
Botwinick, Harry, 1950, F 14,25:2
Botwinik, Berl, 1945, Ag 30,21:6
Botwinik, Meyer, 1954, My 21,27:5
Botwinik, Samuel, 1954, Ap 18,89:2
Botzow, Stephanie E, 1958, My 5,29:2
Bou, John M, 1953, Ja 28,28:3
Boucas, Valentim F, 1964, D 3,49:1
Boucas, Valentin F Mrs, 1946, Je 18,25:2
Boucaut, James Penn Sir, 1916, F 2,11:4
Boucek, Anthony J, 1942, Mr 10,19:4
Boucek, Charles F, 1948, Ja 18,60:3
Bouchard, Eva, 1949, D 27,24:2
Bouchard, Frederick, 1941, F 24,15:5
Bouchard, Georges, 1956, Ag 4,15:5
Bouchard, Jack, 1954, Jl 16,21:1
Bouchard, Louis C, 1950, Je 16,25:6
Bouchard, Napoleon L, 1941, S 15,11:6
Bouchardon, Pierre, 1950, N 12,94:5
Bouche, Henri L Mrs, 1959, F 20,25:3
Bouche, Henry L, 1908, D 4,11:4

Bouche, Rene R, 1963, Jl 7,52:5
Boucher, Anthony (Wm Anthony Parker White), 1968, My 1,47:1
Boucher, Bertha Mrs, 1945, Mr 1,21:5
Boucher, Billy, 1958, N 12,37:3
Boucher, Charles H, 1951, N 16,36:1
Boucher, Chauncey S, 1955, Ag 14,81:3
Boucher, Frank Mrs, 1950, My 26,23:5
Boucher, Frank R, 1957, Ja 14,23:4
Boucher, Frederick W, 1951, Ap 21,34:1
Boucher, George, 1960, O 18,39:3
Boucher, George V, 1954, N 18,33:3
Boucher, H E, 1935, Ap 28,32:1
Boucher, Henry N, 1963, D 19,33:3
Boucher, Jean, 1939, Je 19,15:4
Boucher, John W, 1939, Mr 1,21:5
Boucher, Osias, 1955, My 14,19:6
Boucher, Pierre Lamhire, 1905, Ap 9,9:6
Boucher, Samuel A, 1945, D 17,21:4
Boucher, Stephen F, 1946, S 28,17:6
Boucher, Victor, 1942, F 23,21:6
Boucher, William J, 1947, Ap 9,25:1
Boucherville, Charles Eugene Boucherde Sen, 1915, S 12,17:4
Bouchery, Albert, 1942, Ja 10,15:6
Bouchery, Desire, 1944, N 8,17:2
Bouchett, Msgr, 1903, Ap 13,9:5
Bouchon, Andre, 1954, My 3,31:1
Boucicault, Aubrey (funl, Jl 13,11:4), 1913, Jl 11,9:5
Boucicault, D G, 1929, Je 26,25:3
Boucicault, Dion, 1890, S 19,5:1
Boucicault, Nina, 1950, Ag 6,73:3
Boucicault, William, 1881, Je 17,1:2
Bouck, C Worcester, 1941, My 24,15:4
Bouck, Francis E, 1941, N 25,25:1
Bouck, Gabriel Col, 1904, F 22,5:6
Bouck, Peter C, 1903, Jl 17,7:6
Bouck, Rodman B, 1903, D 24,9:5
Bouck, Roland O, 1953, N 28,15:5
Bouck, William C ex-Gov, 1859, Ap 21,4:5
Bouck, Zeh, 1946, Ag 29,27:2
Boucot, Louis, 1949, Mr 30,25:1
Bouden, Milton L, 1938, Ag 21,32:5
Bouden, Thomas H, 1907, Mr 23,9:5
Boudet, Paul, 1877, N 19,5:3
Boudin, Louis B, 1952, My 31,17:1
Boudin, Louis B Mrs, 1959, O 26,29:5
Boudinot, Jane J, 1914, Ja 24,9:4
Boudinot, Watson H, 1952, Je 3,29:5
Boudou, Gaston, 1948, Ap 30,23:4
Boudousquie, Charles, 1866, S 2,5:3
Boudreau, Susan M, 1880, Mr 7,9:4
Boudren, Thomas Maj, 1913, O 16,11:4
Boudro (New Orleans Caterer), 1867, O 26,2:2
Boudrow, S Mrs, 1903, F 2,1:3
Bough, Joseph F, 1949, O 17,23:4
Boughan, John P, 1948, D 9,33:3
Bougher, Herbert J, 1948, Mr 19,23:3
Bougher, John T, 1948, F 20,27:2
Boughner, Homer D, 1938, S 10,17:4
Boughner, Joseph L, 1944, O 18,21:4
Boughner, Raymond T, 1968, N 20,47:1
Boughton, Albert S, 1947, S 27,15:5
Boughton, Alfred C, 1948, Ag 8,56:4
Boughton, Alice, 1943, Je 23,21:5
Boughton, Arthur C, 1956, D 29,15:2
Boughton, Edward S Mrs, 1946, My 13,21:5
Boughton, Everett W, 1968, N 18,47:1
Boughton, Frederick S, 1945, O 15,17:5
Boughton, George E, 1940, Ap 5,22:3
Boughton, George H, 1866, My 8,4:4
Boughton, George W, 1948, Ja 26,19:2
Boughton, Ralph H, 1951, Ag 17,17:5
Boughton, Van Tuyl, 1964, S 25,41:1
Boughton, Wilfred E, 1949, Je 20,19:6
Boughton, William C, 1960, N 14,31:4
Boughton, Willis, 1942, Je 17,23:3
Bougle, Celestin, 1940, Ja 26,17:5
Bouglione, Alexandre, 1954, Je 1,27:3
Bougrat, Pierre, 1962, Ja 12,16:6
Bouguereau, A G, 1922, F 1,19:5
Bouguereau, Adolphe William, 1905, Ag 21,7:5
Bouichou, J Ernest, 1939, N 7,25:3
Bouille, Pierre, 1950, Mr 11,15:1
Bouillon, Lincoln, 1966, O 3,47:3
Bouilloux-Lafont, Maurice, 1937, Jl 30,19:6
Bouimistrow, Wladimir V O, 1948, Mr 30,23:4
Bouisson, Fernand, 1959, D 30,22:1
Boujard, Claude, 1952, Ap 9,31:5
Bouker, Andrew A, 1925, Je 18,21:5
Bouker, John A, 1903, D 25,7:6
Boulanger, G E J M Gen, 1891, O 1,1:7
Boulanger, Lucien, 1941, My 9,21:5
Boulanger, Mrs, 1909, O 1,9:4
Boulanger, Pierre, 1950, N 12,40:1
Boulaye, Andre D Mrs, 1950, Ag 25,21:3
Boulden, C J Dr, 1909, D 10,11:5
Boulden, Henry J, 1943, O 19,19:4
Boulden, John N, 1954, Je 25,21:3
Bouldin, Pawhatan, 1907, Mr 9,9:6
Bouldin, William Jr, 1943, Ja 6,27:2
Boule, Marcellin, 1942, Jl 21,19:5
Boulicault, Marcel, 1961, F 4,19:4
Boulinguiez, Marie, 1951, D 28,21:4
Boulle, Maurice, 1961, Ag 14,3:4
Boulrice, Alfred, 1952, Je 11,29:3
Boult, Samuel Rev, 1916, O 12,11:7
Boult, William T, 1943, Mr 20,15:2
Boulter, Howard T, 1953, Ap 26,86:2
Boulter, John W, 1964, N 25,37:4
Boultes, Jake, 1955, D 26,19:4
Boulton, A C Forster, 1949, Mr 15,27:6
Boulton, Alfred J, 1944, Mr 2,17:3
Boulton, Alfred J Mrs, 1954, Ja 28,27:3
Boulton, Eleanor F, 1955, N 23,23:5
Boulton, Eric B, 1962, Mr 27,38:1
Boulton, Frank F, 1921, Ag 19,13:4
Boulton, Harold K, 1950, D 30,13:4
Boulton, Henry L, 1963, S 15,86:2
Boulton, Schroeder Mrs, 1964, S 1,35:2
Boulton, Theodore H, 1940, D 19,25:2
Boulton, William Bowen, 1922, S 18,13:2
Boulton, William Henry, 1874, F 3,1:7
Boulware, Aubin L, 1924, Je 13,19:6
Bouman, Frans C, 1950, Ja 31,23:5
Bouman, K H, 1947, N 12,27:2
Boumphrey, Pauline F H Mrs, 1959, Ja 26,29:3
Boumphrey, Stanley M, 1941, Ja 6,18:1
Bound, Charles Fiske, 1924, Jl 26,9:6
Bound, Wade G, 1956, Je 9,17:6
Boundy, Samuel, 1942, Ja 27,21:5
Bounsall, Alfred E, 1946, N 10,62:4
Bounty, Joseph, 1879, Ja 19,2:4
Bounty, Royal S, 1944, Mr 8,19:5
Bouquet, Sebastian Gen, 1925, F 24,19:2
Bouquio, John, 1952, Ap 2,33:5
Bour, Charles J, 1940, N 19,23:1
Bour, Kendrick M, 1950, N 16,31:4
Bourassa, Henri, 1952, S 1,17:4
Bourbaki, C D S Gen, 1871, F 5,1:7; 1897, S 23,7:2
Bourbaki, Peter, 1948, S 10,23:1
Bourbeau, Ernest C J, 1947, S 2,21:4
Bourbeau, M, 1877, O 29,2:4
Bourbeau, William R, 1954, F 21,68:1
Bourbon, Charles Princess, 1904, O 18,9:5
Bourbon, Henri de Duke of Normandy, 1937, Jl 15,19:4
Bourbon, Philippe de Prince of Deux-Seciles, 1949, Mr 9,25:4
Bourbon-Busset, Francois de Count, 1954, Jl 26,17:5
Bourbon de Braganza, Phillippe Prince, 1922, Jl 13, 13:2
Bourbon-Orleans, Prince Louis Ferdinand, 1945, Je 23,13:6
Bourbon-Parma, Prince Joseph of, 1950, Ja 8,76:3
Bourbon-Parma, Prince Louis of, 1967, D 6,51:4
Bourbon y de la Torre, Francisco Duke of Seville, 1952, D 7,88:7
Bourchier, A, 1927, S 15,29:2
Bourchier, Anna-Marie, 1944, My 12,19:2
Bourcier, Emmanuel, 1955, Mr 31,27:4
Bourdelle, Pierre, 1966, Jl 8,35:1
Bourdet, Edouard, 1945, Ja 19,20:2
Bourdette, George C, 1947, Mr 21,22:2
Bourdillon, Bernard, 1948, F 8,60:3
Bourdillon, Tom, 1956, Ag 1,12:6
Bourdin, Henri, 1949, Je 13,19:3
Bourdon, Blin de Viscount, 1940, Ap 19,21:1
Bourdon, Rosario, 1961, Ap 25,35:4
Bourdon, William A, 1951, My 22,31:3
Boureau, H W, 1912, O 22,11:5
Bourgeois, Alfred, 1938, Jl 30,13:2
Bourgeois, B G, 1943, Ja 29,19:5
Bourgeois, Charles, 1940, My 16,23:2
Bourgeois, George A, 1943, Ja 14,21:4
Bourgeois, Henri S Mrs, 1963, D 23,25:1
Bourgeois, Leon (por),(funl, S 3,15:6), 1925, S 30,23:3
Bourgeois, Pierre, 1925, S 8,21:6
Bourgeois, William, 1955, Ag 13,13:5
Bourgeois, William L, 1951, D 7,27:2
Bourges, Albert R, 1955, N 15,33:4
Bourget, Ignace Archbishop, 1885, Je 9,3:3
Bourget, P, 1935, D 25,27:3
Bourgknecht, Jean, 1964, D 24,19:1
Bourgoine, Joseph J, 1955, Mr 2,21:6
Bourgoing, Baron de (Philippe la Beaume), 1882, Ap 21,5:2
Bourguard, George H, 1948, N 28,92:3
Bourguardez, Joseph P, 1917, D 28,11:5
Bourguignon, Joseph, 1941, O 18,19:6
Bouring, William Benjamin Sir, 1916, O 22,23:3
Bourjerdi, Hassan T, 1961, My 31,27:1
Bourke, Anthony, 1962, F 8,32:1
Bourke, Anthony E, 1950, F 14,26:4
Bourke, Charles Francis, 1914, Ag 5,13:6
Bourke, Charles W, 1958, Jl 6,56:6
Bourke, Edward J, 1945, Ja 24,21:5
Bourke, Fan, 1959, Mr 11,35:1
Bourke, Henry S, 1952, Je 10,27:5
Bourke, John W, 1956, O 31,25:4
Bourke, Leonard W, 1949, My 12,31:5
Bourke, Martin, 1939, Ap 10,17:3
Bourke, Matthew C, 1945, Jl 31,19:4
Bourke, Ted, 1940, N 3,57:1
Bourke, Ulich H Earl of Mayo, 1962, D 21,8:6
Bourke, Valentine V Dr, 1968, S 4,47:3
Bourke, Victor G Mrs, 1956, Ag 8,25:5
Bourmont, Armand de Capt, 1917, Jl 25,11:7
Bourn, Augustus O Ex-Gov, 1925, Ja 30,17:4
Bourn, W B, 1874, Ag 19,5:6
Bourn, William G, 1916, S 13,9:5
Bourne, Alan, 1967, Je 27,39:1
Bourne, Alexander P, 1946, S 6,21:3
Bourne, Alfred S, 1956, Mr 2,23:4
Bourne, Alfred S Mrs, 1955, Mr 20,89:1
Bourne, Alvah Wayland Jr, 1968, Ja 24,42:4
Bourne, Arthur K, 1954, Ap 4,88:4
Bourne, Charles G, 1948, O 22,25:4
Bourne, Charles G Mrs, 1963, S 25,43:2
Bourne, Edmund W, 1939, Je 11,45:3
Bourne, Edward G Mrs, 1943, F 19,19:1
Bourne, Edward Gaylord Prof, 1908, F 25,7:4
Bourne, Edward R, 1962, N 7,39:3
Bourne, Ella, 1947, Jl 5,11:4
Bourne, Elvira S Mrs, 1942, Jl 17,15:5
Bourne, Emily Howland, 1922, Mr 26,27:2
Bourne, Emma S K Mrs, 1916, S 1,9:6
Bourne, Ernest L, 1939, Ap 8,15:6
Bourne, F, 1935, Ja 1,27:1
Bourne, Francis Gilbert (funl, Mr 13,11:3), 1919, Mr 10,11:4
Bourne, George G, 1945, My 3,23:6
Bourne, George L, 1940, My 26,34:5
Bourne, George Q, 1950, My 26,23:1
Bourne, George Q Mrs, 1950, D 6,33:4
Bourne, George W, 1948, F 29,61:1
Bourne, George Watson, 1916, F 4,9:6
Bourne, Henry A, 1942, Jl 18,13:7
Bourne, Hope K Mrs, 1951, Mr 18,88:4
Bourne, Howard, 1918, N 16,13:4
Bourne, Isaac H Capt (funl, D 24,3:3), 1874, D 2 8:1
Bourne, John A Mrs, 1945, N 1,23:2
Bourne, Jonathan Jr, 1940, S 3,17:5
Bourne, Leonard, 1965, Ag 23,31:5
Bourne, Linnie M Mrs, 1937, Mr 12,23:4
Bourne, Phil H, 1949, Ja 4,19:4
Bourne, Randolph, 1918, D 23,11:3
Bourne, Richard C, 1944, My 13,19:5
Bourne, Richard S Jr, 1954, D 31,13:3
Bourne, Robert C, 1938, Ag 9,19:3
Bourne, S H, 1957, O 15,30:1
Bourne, Shearjashub Mrs, 1908, O 25,13:3
Bourne, Sidney H, 1937, My 21,22:2
Bourne, Stephen N, 1925, Mr 26,23:4
Bourne, Theodore F, 1941, F 20,19:3
Bourne, Theodore Mrs, 1954, Ag 17,21:3
Bourne, Theodore Rev, 1910, Mr 23,11:4
Bourne, W O, 1901, Je 7,9:5
Bourne, William, 1915, Mr 22,9:5
Bourne, William C, 1957, F 1,25:1
Bourne, William S, 1946, Ag 30,17:4
Bournier, Charles A, 1952, Mr 5,29:5
Bournique, Alvar L, 1938, Jl 24,29:5
Bourquardez, Alfred P, 1945, F 1,23:1
Bourque, Thomas J, 1952, F 17,84:7
Bourquin, Eugene C, 1945, D 1,23:2
Bourquin, George M, 1958, N 17,31:2
Bourquin, Mary Mrs, 1946, S 18,31:3
Bourquin, Paul A, 1945, Ap 4,21:4
Bourquin, William E, 1940, Ap 16,23:4
Bours, George G, 1952, Ja 17,27:5
Bours, William A, 1968, Ap 6,39:4
Bourskaya, Ina, 1954, Je 29,27:4
Bourtzeff, Vladimir L, 1942, O 30,19:1
Boury, Adrien, 1948, Je 3,25:5
Boury, Louis J, 1937, S 8,23:4
Bouse, Elmer E, 1945, F 26,19:5
Bouse, Frank C, 1945, Ag 1,19:3
Bouse, George, 1925, F 22,19:2
Bouse, John H D, 1952, Jl 31,23:2
Bouse, Joseph, 1949, Ap 29,23:4
Bouse, Robert L, 1946, N 22,23:1
Bousfield, Alfred H, 1937, Mr 21,II,8:4
Bousfield, Cyril E Mrs, 1946, Jl 23,25:5
Bousfield, Midian O, 1948, F 17,25:3
Boushall, Joseph D, 1966, Ag 30,36:8
Bousher, Frank, 1939, Je 13,23:5
Bousman, H Hugh, 1953, N 28,15:4
Bousman, H Hugh Mrs, 1955, Je 14,29:2
Bousquet, Annie, 1956, Jl 1,V,3:3
Bousquet, Jacques, 1939, N 20,19:4
Boutelle, C Arthur, 1940, Ap 21,42:3
Boutelle, Clarence Miles, 1903, S 18,7:3
Boutens, Pieter C, 1943, Mr 15,14:2
Bouterse, Peter V, 1962, Jl 22,64:3
Boutet de Monvel, Louis, 1913, Mr 17,11:4
Boutilier, Napeen, 1955, Je 21,31:1
Boutiller, Elizabeth Le, 1908, O 27,9:6
Boutillier, Emanuel F, 1944, N 22,19:2
Boutin, W J, 1948, F 9,17:3
Bouton, Adrian F Mrs, 1941, Je 15,37:1
Bouton, Arch L, 1941, Ap 19,15:6
Bouton, Arthur G, 1948, N 12,23:3
Bouton, Arthur G Mrs, 1948, Jl 14,23:6
Bouton, Clarence E, 1962, Jl 18,29:3
Bouton, D'or, 1873, S 26,5:6
Bouton, Edward L, 1944, Jl 25,19:6
Bouton, Edward Sr Mrs, 1946, Ja 18,19:3
Bouton, Eugene, 1951, Ap 1,93:1

Bouton, Frank R, 1952, O 19,89:1
Bouton, George R, 1957, Jl 25,23:4
Bouton, Harold, 1940, D 15,61:2
Bouton, Harry R, 1946, Ap 16,25:4
Bouton, J W, 1902, O 7,9:5
Bouton, Jessie E, 1947, D 14,76:6
Bouton, Mabel, 1903, F 5,3:4
Bouton, N, 1878, Je 7,5:6
Bouton, Sanford P Mrs, 1949, Je 2,27:4
Boutot, Arthur E, 1960, Ja 22,27:3
Boutot, Victor O, 1948, O 31,88:6
Boutroux, Emile, 1919, N 2,22:3
Boutwell, Alfred H, 1966, Ja 26,37:3
Boutwell, George Sewall, 1905, F 28,9:5
Boutwell, Louis E, 1949, O 27,27:3
Bouve, Thomas T, 1938, F 1,21:1
Bouverie, Alice Pleydell- Mrs (est acctg), 1958, S 4, 17:5
Bouvet, Marie M, 1915, Je 3,11:5
Bouvier, Arthur L, 1946, S 28,17:3
Bouvier, Charles A, 1943, N 27,13:2
Bouvier, Danielle, 1961, My 30,6:1
Bouvier, John V, 1948, Ja 17,18:2
Bouvier, John V Mrs, 1940, Ap 3,23:6
Bouvier, John V 3d, 1957, Ag 4,81:3
Bouvier, M C, 1935, Jl 30,19:3
Bouvier, Maurice, 1952, Ap 14,19:4
Bouvier, Michael A, 1954, Mr 16,29:5
Bouwman, Philippe M, 1948, O 16,15:2
Bouwmeester, Louis, 1925, Ap 29,21:5
Bouy, Jules, 1937, Je 29,22:2
Bouzek, Josef, 1950, N 24,35:1
Bovaird, Joseph H, 1947, My 4,60:5
Bovard, Everett W, 1956, Mr 24,19:4
Bovard, Grace I, 1953, Jl 23,12:8
Bovard, Mellville Y, 1938, Mr 7,17:2
Bovard, Oliver K, 1945, N 5,19:5
Bovay, Harry E, 1952, Ja 27,77:1
Bove, Angelo, 1950, Je 17,15:4
Bove, J Henry, 1962, S 17,31:3
Bove, James V, 1956, Jl 6,45:1
Bove, Raphael, 1902, D 2,9:4
Bovee, Arthur G, 1961, My 6,31:5
Bovee, C N, 1904, Ja 20,9:5
Bovee, Christina N, 1913, Mr 5,17:4
Bovell, Henry, 1938, Ag 30,17:5
Bovello, Vincent, 1953, Ja 21,22:3
Bovenizer, George W, 1961, My 11,37:4
Boveri, Marcella Mrs, 1950, O 25,35:1
Boveri, Theodore Prof, 1915, O 17,15:5
Bovers, William H Mrs, 1966, Ag 3,37:3
Boves, Lawrence Mrs, 1952, Ap 1,29:1
Bovey, Wilfrid, 1956, O 12,29:2
Bovie, V M, 1926, Mr 12,19:3
Bovie, William T, 1958, Ja 2,27:1
Bovill, William Sir, 1873, N 2,1:7
Boville, Robert G Rev Dr, 1937, N 9,23:1
Bovis, Louis W, 1950, O 17,31:4
Bovy-Lycherg, Charles, 1873, Mr 19,5:6
Bow, Clara (funl, O 2,3:7), 1965, S 28,1:6
Bow, Clara H Mrs, 1937, F 9,23:1
Bow, Homer, 1961, Ap 29,23:6
Bow, Warren E, 1945, My 13,19:1
Bowater, Eric V, 1962, Ag 31,21:2
Bowater, Frank H, 1947, N 11,27:4
Bowater, Vansittart, 1938, Mr 29,21:5
Bowcher, Frank, 1938, D 8,27:2
Bowden, Andrew, 1882, Ag 18,5:5
Bowden, Charles W, 1954, Ja 17,93:2
Bowden, Daniel T, 1937, D 16,27:5
Bowden, Frank Sir, 1921, Ap 26,15:4
Bowden, Fred, 1938, Jl 23,13:7
Bowden, Frederick P Mrd, 1955, Jl 27,23:3
Bowden, Gardiner S Mrs, 1959, Ja 28,31:3
Bowden, Garfield A, 1945, D 11,25:3
Bowden, George K, 1951, Jl 14,13:3
Bowden, Harold, 1960, Ag 25,29:2
Bowden, James T, 1946, F 8,19:2
Bowden, John, 1951, D 1,13:5
Bowden, John L, 1955, Je 8,29:6
Bowden, John N, 1964, N 25,37:5
Bowden, John W, 1959, Mr 4,31:4
Bowden, Louis H, 1959, Je 16,35:5
Bowden, Muriel Dr, 1968, My 19,86:7
Bowden, Smith Nathaniel Sir, 1921, Ap 30,11:4
Bowden, William, 1955, Ap 23,19:5
Bowden, William Dougherty, 1968, S 28,33:5
Bowden, William Jr, 1948, Ja 7,25:5
Bowdish, Jennie C Mrs, 1905, Je 15,9:6
Bowdish, Wellesley Wellington Rev Dr, 1915, O 10, 17:6
Bowditch, Charles P, 1921, Je 2,13:4
Bowditch, Edward, 1965, Ap 7,43:2
Bowditch, Frederick Mrs, 1951, Je 18,23:4
Bowditch, Henry Pickering Dr, 1911, Mr 14,11:4
Bowditch, Ingersoll, 1938, F 13,II,7:2
Bowditch, John P, 1945, D 23,18:3
Bowditch, Manfred, 1960, Je 30,29:2
Bowditch, Nathaniel I, 1945, Ap 4,21:5
Bowditch, Richard L, 1959, Ag 1,17:1
Bowditch, William C, 1952, O 7,29:5
Bowdle, John H, 1937, D 16,27:2
Bowdoin, George E, 1959, Mr 5,31:2
Bowdoin, George E Mrs (Harriet S), 1965, F 22,21:4
Bowdoin, George Sullivan, 1913, D 17,11:6
Bowdoin, George T, 1967, Ja 28,27:3
Bowdoin, Harold M (cor, D 2,29:3), 1949, N 30,27:2
Bowdoin, Harriette, 1947, My 18,60:2
Bowdoin, James S, 1961, Ag 20,86:2
Bowdoin, Temple, 1914, D 3,13:4
Bowdoin, William G, 1904, N 13,1:4; 1947, Mr 25,25:3
Bowdren, Thomas C, 1950, S 22,31:3
Bowe, Frank, 1939, Mr 1,21:4
Bowe, James F, 1942, Jl 21,19:6
Bowe, John, 1914, Ja 6,13:6
Bowe, John E, 1951, O 2,28:3
Bowe, John E Mrs, 1946, Jl 16,24:2
Bowe, John J, 1937, Ap 10,19:4
Bowe, Joseph L, 1967, Je 23,1:7
Bowe, Michael, 1881, Ag 20,8:6
Bowe, Peter, 1903, Mr 3,3:6
Bowe, Thomas A, 1951, D 9,90:5
Bowe, William J, 1943, Ja 22,20:3
Bowell, MacKenzie Sir, 1917, D 11,15:6
Bowen, A E Mrs, 1951, My 1,29:3
Bowen, A L, 1945, Jl 9,11:5
Bowen, Aberdeen O, 1946, F 12,28:1
Bowen, Agnes E, 1925, Ja 29,19:4
Bowen, Albert E, 1953, Jl 16,21:2
Bowen, Amos M, 1951, Ap 17,29:5
Bowen, Andrew J, 1941, Jl 25,15:3
Bowen, Arnold E, 1948, O 16,15:1
Bowen, Arthur J, 1944, Jl 30,35:2; 1962, F 18,92:6
Bowen, Arthur J Mrs, 1938, Ja 18,23:4
Bowen, Arthur V, 1949, Ap 20,27:4
Bowen, C Aubrey, 1948, F 20,27:3
Bowen, C C, 1880, Je 24,2:5
Bowen, C W, 1935, N 3,II,9:1
Bowen, Charles C, 1946, My 2,21:1
Bowen, Charles Clement, 1909, My 2,11:5
Bowen, Charles H, 1941, My 31,11:6
Bowen, Charles P, 1938, Jl 29,17:2
Bowen, Charles R, 1959, Je 16,35:4
Bowen, Cloyd L Mrs, 1948, Jl 7,23:3
Bowen, Cornelius L, 1943, Ja 23,13:3
Bowen, David C, 1952, Je 3,29:2
Bowen, David R, 1939, S 7,25:5
Bowen, Edmund I, 1954, Je 22,27:4
Bowen, Edward J, 1956, S 8,17:2
Bowen, Edwin F, 1953, Je 24,21:2
Bowen, Eli, 1924, My 5,15:3
Bowen, Elizabeth B C Mrs (will, N 18,31:8), 1941, N 4,26:4
Bowen, Ernest C, 1953, N 4,33:4
Bowen, Eugene B, 1952, Ap 21,21:4
Bowen, Ezra, 1945, D 28,16:3
Bowen, F, 1890, Ja 22,2:3
Bowen, Francis M, 1951, Ap 30,21:5
Bowen, Frank H, 1952, Ap 20,92:5
Bowen, Frank W, 1915, Ap 19,9:5
Bowen, Franklin D, 1940, S 6,21:5
Bowen, Frederick S, 1940, Ja 14,43:3
Bowen, Frederick S Mrs, 1955, Mr 4,23:3
Bowen, G W, 1885, F 7,3:6
Bowen, George A, 1945, My 11,19:4
Bowen, Gwen O Mrs, 1940, Ja 5,19:2
Bowen, H C Mrs, 1863, My 3,5:5
Bowen, H W, 1927, My 30,15:5
Bowen, Harold G, 1965, Ag 2,29:4
Bowen, Henry C, 1896, F 25,8:1
Bowen, Henry Elliott, 1919, Je 16,13:6
Bowen, Herbert L, 1940, Jl 1,19:4
Bowen, Herbert R, 1946, N 16,19:2
Bowen, Herbert W Mrs, 1949, Ap 6,29:4
Bowen, Isaac R Mrs, 1946, O 1,23:2
Bowen, J Gen, 1886, S 30,5:5
Bowen, James, 1949, My 31,23:1
Bowen, James Sr, 1954, F 14,93:1
Bowen, James V, 1940, Mr 7,23:3
Bowen, James W, 1940, Je 22,15:6
Bowen, Jesse N, 1938, My 19,21:2
Bowen, Jesse P, 1953, Ag 13,25:3
Bowen, John D, 1950, Ja 19,27:1
Bowen, John J, 1953, Ap 28,27:2
Bowen, John T, 1940, D 7,17:2
Bowen, Joseph H, 1961, D 24,36:8
Bowen, Joseph R, 1946, D 14,15:1
Bowen, Joseph T Mrs, 1953, N 10,31:4
Bowen, Katherine, 1959, Jl 15,29:2
Bowen, Kathryn E Mrs, 1950, Je 16,25:3
Bowen, Laurance, 1947, S 3,25:2
Bowen, Marcellus Dr, 1916, O 6,11:4
Bowen, Marian H Mrs, 1951, O 9,29:4
Bowen, Mary M, 1945, Ag 24,19:3
Bowen, Norman L, 1956, S 12,25:6
Bowen, Norris L, 1952, Ap 10,29:3
Bowen, Orley G, 1959, Ap 14,35:1
Bowen, Paul S, 1947, Mr 8,13:3
Bowen, R T, 1879, S 3,2:5
Bowen, R W, 1948, Je 28,19:1
Bowen, Rees H Mrs, 1950, Jl 28,21:4
Bowen, Reuel C Rev, 1923, S 14,19:5
Bowen, Robert A, 1958, Ag 13,27:3
Bowen, Robert J, 1945, Je 20,23:1
Bowen, Robert W, 1942, D 10,25:5
Bowen, Russell A, 1946, Je 27,21:3
Bowen, Russell H, 1954, Ja 10,87:1
Bowen, Samuel B, 1943, S 22,23:4
Bowen, Samuel R, 1944, Ag 9,17:2
Bowen, Scott H, 1941, D 24,17:4
Bowen, Sherry, 1956, Ag 5,76:8
Bowen, Sherry Mrs, 1961, D 4,37:3
Bowen, Stirling, 1955, F 14,19:3
Bowen, Temple G, 1960, D 10,23:3
Bowen, Thomas M Ex-Sen, 1907, Ja 1,9:5
Bowen, Trevor P, 1960, D 19,27:2
Bowen, Ward C, 1956, My 24,31:5
Bowen, West, 1904, F 18,9:5
Bowen, William A, 1924, F 4,19:4; 1937, S 19,II,7:1; 1955, N 13,88:8
Bowen, William F, 1940, My 28,23:5
Bowen, William J, 1948, Jl 29,21:3
Bowen, William M, 1937, D 23,22:4
Bowen, William M P, 1955, Ap 10,88:8
Bowen, William S, 1951, My 20,89:2; 1959, Ag 12,29:3
Bowen, William S Mrs, 1955, Ag 22,21:5
Bowen, Willis E, 1944, Jl 12,19:5
Bowen, Winnifred C, 1953, My 18,21:3
Bower, Albert G, 1960, Ag 3,29:5
Bower, Alex, 1952, Ag 7,21:4
Bower, Alfred L, 1948, N 17,27:4
Bower, Andrew P, 1949, O 25,27:3
Bower, Arthur B, 1915, F 22,9:4
Bower, Bertha M, 1940, Jl 24,21:5
Bower, Charles T, 1954, N 13,15:1
Bower, Edwin E, 1947, Jl 2,23:2
Bower, Elsie S Mrs, 1940, Mr 22,19:3
Bower, Frank, 1908, S 22,9:6
Bower, Frank A, 1964, Jl 31,24:1
Bower, Frederick O, 1948, Ap 12,21:5
Bower, George, 1942, D 29,21:5
Bower, George M, 1939, Ap 5,25:5
Bower, Hamilton, 1940, Mr 7,23:2
Bower, Harry F, 1949, F 20,60:2
Bower, Jacob, 1950, Je 28,27:2
Bower, John L, 1955, D 7,39:3
Bower, John O, 1960, N 1,40:1
Bower, Joseph M, 1953, S 10,25:3
Bower, Joseph Mrs, 1940, Jl 10,19:5
Bower, Julius J, 1960, D 8,35:4
Bower, Justus H, 1958, Jl 29,23:5
Bower, Kate L (will), 1940, Ja 26,9:2
Bower, Michael A, 1945, Ap 15,14:7
Bower, R F, 1882, My 21,10:2
Bower, Ralph S, 1953, N 20,23:1
Bower, Roy E B, 1950, F 16,24:2
Bower, Stella, 1954, N 28,87:2
Bower, W Frank, 1943, Je 5,15:4
Bower, Wallace A, 1955, Jl 11,23:2
Bower, Walter J, 1949, N 16,29:5
Bower, William C, 1954, F 18,31:5
Bower, William H, 1956, S 22,17:4
Bowerhan, Robert C, 1939, My 19,21:4
Bowering, W Gilbert, 1958, S 15,21:4
Bowerman, Arthur E, 1943, Ja 10,48:2
Bowerman, Arthur L, 1958, F 12,29:3
Bowerman, Benjamin Franklin, 1915, S 11,9:7
Bowerman, Charles W, 1947, Je 12,25:6
Bowerman, Frank, 1948, D 1,29:5
Bowerman, Frank H, 1951, D 23,22:5
Bowerman, George H, 1961, Je 15,43:5
Bowerman, Guy E, 1940, Mr 18,17:5
Bowerman, Harvey C, 1943, My 7,19:3
Bowerman, Judah P, 1944, My 6,15:5
Bowerman, Richard Neville, 1920, Ag 11,9:5
Bowers, Alvin T Mrs, 1943, D 31,16:6
Bowers, Arthur E, 1925, N 11,23:4
Bowers, Arthur F, 1905, N 4,9:5
Bowers, C Edward, 1951, Je 15,23:2
Bowers, Chester H, 1949, Ag 14,68:8
Bowers, Clarence H, 1943, Ap 18,48:5
Bowers, Claude G (funl, Ja 26,88:7), 1958, Ja 22,27:1
Bowers, Claude G Mrs, 1964, D 5,31:2
Bowers, Clayton, 1941, Jl 25,14:3
Bowers, Cornelius, 1946, Ja 14,19:5
Bowers, E Stanley Sr, 1952, My 13,23:3
Bowers, Edward C, 1947, S 8,21:4
Bowers, Elory Mrs, 1948, Je 28,19:3
Bowers, Ethel B, 1942, Ap 17,17:2
Bowers, F K, 1930, O 16,25:1
Bowers, Frank J, 1947, Ag 27,23:3
Bowers, Frank N Mrs, 1947, Mr 31,23:1
Bowers, Frederick A, 1940, Mr 2,13:5
Bowers, Frederick V, 1961, My 2,37:1
Bowers, Freeman, 1939, Ja 20,19:3
Bowers, G V (see also Ag 19), 1878, Ag 21,8:2
Bowers, George H, 1943, F 28,47:5; 1962, Ja 9,20:6
Bowers, George H Mrs, 1962, Ja 9,20:6
Bowers, George Mead, 1925, D 9,27:4
Bowers, George W, 1943, O 30,15:4
Bowers, Harold, 1958, N 7,19:5
Bowers, Harry S, 1946, F 23,13:4
Bowers, Henry, 1940, Jl 16,17:4
Bowers, Henry F, 1963, Mr 29,7:5
Bowers, Henry K, 1956, D 3,29:3
Bowers, Howard E, 1946, Ja 3,19:3
Bowers, Ida, 1943, Ap 20,23:1
Bowers, Jacob, 1915, Ap 26,9:6
Bowers, Jacob E, 1942, Ag 6,19:5
Bowers, James F, 1925, N 12,25:4

Bowers, Joel F, 1959, N 30,31:2
Bowers, Lamont M, 1941, Je 3,21:1
Bowers, Lloyd W (funl, S 13,9:6), 1910, S 10,9:3
Bowers, Lloyd W Mrs, 1943, S 11,13:3
Bowers, Maurice A, 1954, O 25,27:5
Bowers, Michael (Mickey), 1966, Je 28,45:3
Bowers, Newcombe Mrs, 1949, Ap 2,15:1
Bowers, Ogden H, 1959, N 29,86:4
Bowers, Paul E, 1938, F 16,21:2
Bowers, Percy W, 1948, My 19,27:4
Bowers, Philip, 1946, O 31,14:5
Bowers, Raymond H, 1946, Ap 28,44:3
Bowers, Raymond R, 1956, F 28,8:4
Bowers, Robert H, 1941, D 31,18:2
Bowers, Russell W, 1956, Ja 9,25:1
Bowers, Samuel, 1962, Mr 14,39:2
Bowers, Spotswood D, 1939, D 23,15:3
Bowers, Spotswood D Mrs, 1952, D 23,23:5
Bowers, Stewart M, 1962, Ag 21,33:2
Bowers, T S Col, 1866, Mr 7,1:3
Bowers, Thomas W, 1950, Mr 17,23:5
Bowers, Walter D, 1937, Je 20,II,7:1
Bowers, Walter P, 1947, Jl 23,23:5
Bowers, Wesley C, 1963, Je 28,29:1
Bowers, Wesley C Mrs, 1957, Ag 25,86:1
Bowers, Whitman W, 1939, Ja 1,24:7
Bowers, William C Mrs, 1958, Mr 10,23:2
Bowers, William G, 1958, S 18,31:3
Bowers, William G Mrs, 1947, N 23,72:3
Bowers, William H, 1953, D 23,26:3
Bowers, William S, 1942, S 5,13:5
Boweryem, G, 1864, Jl 15,8:4
Bowes, A K Mrs, 1937, Ag 16,19:5
Bowes, Carleton F, 1962, Ja 26,31:1
Bowes, Edward, 1946, Je 14,21:1
Bowes, Frank A, 1957, F 25,25:3
Bowes, Frank B, 1939, F 16,21:4
Bowes, Frank S, 1937, Jl 14,22:1
Bowes, Frederick Mrs, 1958, Ja 19,86:7
Bowes, John A, 1952, Jl 29,21:4
Bowes, Katherine, 1940, D 18,25:2
Bowes, Robert M, 1945, Je 25,17:4
Bowes, Russell W, 1960, Je 25,21:6
Bowes, Thomas D, 1965, Jl 3,19:2
Bowes, Walter H, 1957, Je 25,29:3
Bowes, Walter H Mrs, 1949, Ag 20,11:3
Bowes-Lyon, David, 1961, S 14,31:1
Bowes-Lyon, Ernest Mrs, 1945, Jl 18,27:4
Bowes-Lyon, Francis, 1948, F 19,23:2
Bowes-Lyon, Lillian, 1949, Jl 26,28:5
Bowes-Lyon, Malcolm, 1957, Ag 24,15:4
Bowes-Lyon, Mary F (Lady Elphinstone), 1961, F 9, 31:3
Bowes-Lyon, Maude A Lady, 1941, Mr 2,42:2
Bowes-Lyon, Michael C H, 1953, My 2,15:5
Bowes-Lyon, Michael Mrs, 1959, Ja 21,31:1
Bowes-Lyon, Nancy Lady, 1959, F 13,17:2
Bowes-Lyon, Patrick, 1946, O 8,23:3
Bowhill, Frederick, 1960, Mr 13,85:2
Bowie, Allen S, 1945, O 6,13:4
Bowie, Archibald E, 1960, My 28,21:5
Bowie, Arthur, 1966, O 26,47:3
Bowie, Augustine J, 1966, F 8,36:4
Bowie, Barbara A, 1947, Ap 29,55:3
Bowie, Beverley M, 1958, N 16,88:1
Bowie, Carter L, 1948, Je 23,27:5
Bowie, Edward H, 1943, Ag 1,38:8
Bowie, Fred T, 1951, Ap 5,29:5
Bowie, Friedlander W, 1938, Ja 7,19:3
Bowie, James A, 1949, S 3,13:2
Bowie, John M, 1937, S 12,II,7:3
Bowie, R H Bayard, 1961, Je 7,41:3
Bowie, R J, 1881, Mr 14,5:1
Bowie, Thomas F, 1869, N 5,5:3
Bowie, Walter R Mrs, 1963, Je 23,85:1
Bowie, Walter W, 1938, O 28,23:6
Bowie, William D Col, 1873, Jl 21,1:4
Bowker, Alice M Mrs, 1941, Ja 18,15:3
Bowker, Clarence C, 1950, N 6,27:6
Bowker, Edwin L, 1948, Ap 20,27:2
Bowker, Elmer E, 1939, Ja 23,13:5
Bowker, F Dexter, 1937, Ap 4,II,11:3
Bowker, Harry D, 1953, F 23,25:3
Bowker, Heber D, 1940, Ja 21,34:5
Bowker, Horace, 1954, My 26,29:2
Bowker, Horace Mrs, 1938, Ap 21,19:4
Bowker, John H, 1916, F 27,17:5
Bowker, John L Mrs, 1948, Je 16,29:4
Bowker, R R, 1933, N 13,17:4
Bowker, T Harry, 1941, Ag 23,13:4
Bowker, Theodore, 1950, N 13,27:4
Bowker, Walter S, 1959, Ja 10,17:5
Bowker, William S, 1948, D 3,25:3
Bowkley, Harry T, 1959, Je 26,25:2
Bowkley, Raymond E, 1965, Ap 21,45:1
Bowlby, Dorothy O, 1952, Je 20,23:3
Bowlby, E O, 1937, Mr 13,19:5
Bowlby, George, 1951, Mr 4,93:1
Bowlby, Harry L, 1966, N 18,43:1
Bowlby, Jeol M Mrs, 1951, D 7,27:3
Bowlby, Joel M, 1957, Ag 27,29:4
Bowlby, John W Mrs, 1946, F 7,23:1
Bowlby, Robert Archer Lt, 1918, O 18,13:2
Bowlby, Robert M Mrs, 1943, D 1,21:1
Bowlby, Robert O, 1945, Ag 14,21:2
Bowlby, Robert W, 1949, Ja 16,68:4
Bowlby, Rosewell S, 1957, O 19,21:1
Bowlen, Maurice E, 1952, Ja 31,27:1
Bowler, A K Mrs (see also Ag 22 and 23), 1876, Ag 25,5:4
Bowler, E R, 1937, N 11,25:5
Bowler, G P, 1878, Mr 25,5:3
Bowler, Harold T, 1965, Jl 24,21:4
Bowler, James B, 1957, Jl 19,19:1
Bowler, John W, 1938, D 28,21:6
Bowler, Robert B, 1943, S 17,22:3
Bowler, Robert Pendleton, 1919, My 29,13:3
Bowler, Sarah, 1877, F 7,4:7
Bowler, Walter S Mrs, 1960, O 23,88:6
Bowler, William G, 1956, Je 28,29:4
Bowler, William H, 1951, My 9,33:4
Bowles, Albert E, 1944, My 11,19:2
Bowles, Alfred H, 1954, My 11,29:3
Bowles, Arthur R, 1941, S 5,21:2
Bowles, B F, 1876, My 5,5:4
Bowles, Basil S, 1953, Jl 21,23:5
Bowles, Charles A, 1946, Ag 2,19:5
Bowles, Charles A Mrs, 1943, N 26,23:5
Bowles, Charles E, 1957, Jl 31,23:5
Bowles, Elliot A, 1957, Je 28,23:2
Bowles, F T, 1927, Ag 4,21:3
Bowles, Frank W, 1957, S 2,13:4
Bowles, George A, 1956, Je 4,29:5
Bowles, Harry H, 1948, My 30,34:2
Bowles, Janet P Mrs, 1948, Jl 19,19:2
Bowles, Peter W, 1942, Ag 30,43:3
Bowles, R Pearson, 1953, Ja 8,27:1
Bowles, Robert H, 1948, Ap 13,27:3
Bowles, S (mem ser, Ja 24,1:7), 1878, Ja 17,4:7
Bowles, Samuel, 1915, Mr 17,11:5
Bowles, Sherman H, 1952, Mr 4,27:3
Bowles, Susan h, 1951, N 19,23:4
Bowles, William H, 1953, Jl 15,25:4; 1959, Je 10,37:1
Bowles, William J, 1941, Je 13,19:6
Bowley, Albert J, 1945, My 24,19:5
Bowley, Freeman W, 1944, Mr 2,17:2
Bowley, George, 1938, Ja 29,15:2
Bowling, Abner F Rev, 1937, Mr 26,21:2
Bowling, Charles B Mrs, 1948, Mr 23,25:5
Bowling, Edgar S, 1950, Ap 16,104:3
Bowling, Elmer, 1950, O 13,29:2
Bowling, Harry R, 1955, Mr 4,23:2
Bowling, Thomas C, 1952, D 26,15:3
Bowlus, Edward L, 1942, Ja 3,32:1
Bowly, George H, 1943, F 6,13:6
Bowly, Harry H, 1937, S 10,23:2
Bowly, Jane Vanderhorst Mrs, 1922, My 19,17:6
Bowman, A A, 1936, Je 13,17:5
Bowman, A H Col, 1865, N 12,4:6
Bowman, Abraham M, 1950, F 8,27:1
Bowman, Abram H, 1943, Jl 20,19:6
Bowman, Albert C, 1937, S 18,19:2
Bowman, Albert M, 1953, Ag 14,19:1
Bowman, Alfred C, 1955, My 13,25:4
Bowman, Alfred W, 1962, N 10,25:1
Bowman, Andrew W, 1952, Ap 27,91:1
Bowman, Annie L Mrs, 1937, F 16,23:3; 1946, Mr 28, 25:1
Bowman, Archibald, 1955, My 12,29:4
Bowman, Austin L, 1915, Je 4,11:5
Bowman, Border Mrs, 1942, Ap 26,40:2
Bowman, C Luckey, 1965, D 27,25:4
Bowman, Charles C, 1941, Jl 4,13:4; 1967, S 3,52:7
Bowman, Charles V Rev, 1937, Ag 6,17:3
Bowman, Charles W, 1943, S 29,21:4
Bowman, Chester H, 1948, D 17,27:5
Bowman, Claes W, 1939, Ap 1,19:3
Bowman, Clellan A Dr, 1937, Ja 8,20:2
Bowman, Curtis R, 1954, My 6,33:1
Bowman, D Hudson (Sept 28), 1965, O 11,61:1
Bowman, David, 1964, D 29,21:1
Bowman, De Witt W, 1943, Mr 27,13:2
Bowman, Earl M, 1945, My 30,19:2
Bowman, Edgar J, 1947, N 13,28:3
Bowman, Edward, 1938, F 17,21:1
Bowman, Edward L, 1957, Mr 14,29:3
Bowman, Edward N Mrs, 1961, Ag 20,86:2
Bowman, Edward S, 1940, Ag 21,19:6
Bowman, Edward W, 1949, S 2,17:1
Bowman, Elizabeth, 1922, N 6,15:4
Bowman, Elsa, 1960, Jl 17,61:1
Bowman, Ernest M, 1942, Ja 29,19:2
Bowman, Ethel, 1955, Ap 9,13:3
Bowman, F C, 1884, O 31,5:6
Bowman, Florence M, 1944, N 1,23:1
Bowman, Foster H, 1956, Jl 18,27:2
Bowman, Frank, 1948, Ja 22,27:5
Bowman, Frank K, 1942, My 14,19:4
Bowman, Frank S, 1904, Ja 11,7:6
Bowman, Franklin, 1961, N 4,19:1
Bowman, Fred Mrs, 1925, Ag 18,19:6
Bowman, George, 1903, S 16,9:6
Bowman, George A (por), 1938, My 6,21:4
Bowman, George C, 1950, My 24,30:2; 1961, N 8,35:3
Bowman, George E, 1941, S 7,49:2
Bowman, George T, 1951, F 16,25:5
Bowman, Gertrude L Mrs, 1967, My 13,33:3
Bowman, H H, 1946, Ag 11,46:1
Bowman, Hank, 1966, Ja 9,V,1:7
Bowman, Harold M, 1949, N 22,29:4
Bowman, Harry L, 1965, My 26,47:2
Bowman, Harry L Mrs, 1956, F 15,31:5
Bowman, Hazel (Mrs J J Leonard), 1956, D 3,29:5
Bowman, Henry A Mrs, 1943, N 25,25:1
Bowman, Henry N, 1955, Mr 6,89:2
Bowman, Herschel V, 1939, N 19,39:1
Bowman, Howard A Mrs, 1949, Jl 22,19:1
BowmaN, Isaiah, 1950, Ja 7,17:1
Bowman, Isaiah Mrs, 1952, My 13,30:1
Bowman, J Harkness Mrs, 1956, Ap 21,17:3
Bowman, J Hayes, 1963, Ap 7,86:1
Bowman, J M, 1931, O 28,12:2
Bowman, J Warren, 1962, F 10,23:1
Bowman, James, 1940, My 3,21:6
Bowman, James C, 1961, S 28,41:2
Bowman, James E, 1954, S 19,89:2
Bowman, James H, 1952, O 13,21:4
Bowman, James L, 1951, S 14,25:3
Bowman, Jay K Mrs, 1946, Ap 16,25:5
Bowman, Joanna Mrs, 1942, Ja 15,19:4
Bowman, John, 1946, D 28,16:2
Bowman, John A, 1955, Ja 15,13:6
Bowman, John A Mrs, 1951, Ja 25,25:4
Bowman, John A 3d, 1954, Ag 27,21:3
Bowman, John E (will, Ag 4,8:6), 1938, Jl 22,18:3
Bowman, John G, 1962, D 3,31:4
Bowman, John J, 1966, Mr 15,39:1
Bowman, Katherine F Mrs, 1942, Jl 10,17:1
Bowman, L W, 1947, Jl 10,21:3
Bowman, Laura, 1957, Mr 31,89:1
Bowman, Leon, 1940, F 12,13:2
Bowman, Linn, 1953, Mr 31,31:2
Bowman, Lloyd D, 1962, Ag 20,23:6
Bowman, Lynn, 1942, Jl 13,16:4
Bowman, Milton S, 1966, Ag 8,27:3
Bowman, Orville S, 1940, Mr 16,15:6
Bowman, Otis, 1944, Jl 23,35:2
Bowman, Ralph M, 1949, Je 21,25:2
Bowman, Richard G, 1968, O 24,47:4
Bowman, Robert J, 1958, Ja 24,23:1
Bowman, Robert M, 1957, D 11,31:2
Bowman, Rufus, 1952, Ag 20,25:4
Bowman, S L Mrs, 1925, D 11,23:4
Bowman, Samuel O H, 1915, S 11,9:5
Bowman, Samuel Rev, 1861, Ag 11,3:4
Bowman, Selwyn Rice, 1903, Ag 29,7:5
Bowman, Sidney B, 1949, Ja 4,19:5
Bowman, Stephen C V, 1961, S 21,35:4
Bowman, Theodore Mrs, 1943, O 20,21:5
Bowman, Thomas Bp, 1914, Mr 4,11:5; 1923, Mr 20, 21:4
Bowman, Vernon A, 1963, Ag 11,85:2
Bowman, Walter Mrs, 1952, Ag 11,15:6
Bowman, Wilbur J, 1956, Ap 23,27:1
Bowman, Willard, 1959, F 28,19:4; 1962, Mr 8,31:2
Bowman, William, 1940, Ap 24,23:5
Bowman, William F, 1943, O 11,19:5
Bowman, William J, 1950, S 15,26:3
Bowman, William L, 1947, Ja 8,23:4
Bowman, William M, 1966, D 10,37:4
Bowman, William P, 1937, Ja 23,18:5
Bowman-Manifold, John, 1940, Mr 15,23:3
Bown, Emma Col, 1924, D 17,21:3
Bown, Herbert G, 1951, D 5,35:1
Bown, William E, 1951, F 3,15:6
Bowne, Borden P Prof, 1910, Ap 3,II,11:2
Bowne, Charles B, 1952, F 13,29:1
Bowne, Charles S Mrs, 1947, Ag 11,23:5
Bowne, Clifford B, 1946, Je 14,21:4
Bowne, Edward Randolph, 1920, Ag 14,7:5
Bowne, Eugenia J, 1943, Jl 12,15:4
Bowne, Frederic, 1937, Ap 16,23:2
Bowne, Frederic Mrs, 1954, Je 21,23:3; 1968, Mr 2 45:1
Bowne, Frederick B, 1941, Ja 2,23:2
Bowne, Herbert S, 1951, Ja 2,23:4
Bowne, Jacob Titus Prof, 1925, O 17,15:4
Bowne, R Frank Mrs, 1944, Jl 13,17:4
Bowne, R H, 1881, My 3,8:5
Bowne, Samuel Barry, 1913, D 28,II,15:5
Bowne, Samuel W, 1910, O 30,II,13:5
Bowne, Sidney B, 1959, S 17,39:6
Bowne, Sydney B, 1915, Jl 28,9:4
Bowne, Walter Mrs, 1953, Mr 29,92:1
Bowne, William B, 1940, Ja 5,20:3
Bowness, Robert A, 1960, Jl 18,27:2
Bowns, Edward E Mrs, 1946, Ap 11,25:3
Bowran, Thomas, 1951, Ja 2,23:1
Bowring, Charles C, 1945, Je 16,13:5
Bowring, Charles W, 1940, N 2,15:2
Bowring, Edgar R, 1943, Je 24,21:3
Bowring, F C, 1936, Mr 25,21:1
Bowring, John Sir, 1872, N 24,5:2
Bowring, Thomas Benjimin Sir, 1915, O 19,11:4
Bowron, Charles W, 1952, D 17,33:4
Bowron, Fletcher, 1968, S 12,47:1
Bowron, J C, 1884, O 3,5:3
Bowron, Thomas W, 1944, Ag 21,15:6
Bowron, William Lloyd, 1916, O 19,9:4

Bowser, Alfred W, 1951, N 2,23:3
Bowser, Arreta Mrs, 1954, N 7,86:1
Bowser, Edward A Prof, 1910, F 23,9:4
Bowser, George, 1960, F 1,27:5
Bowser, James L, 1950, Je 16,25:4
Bowser, James M Sr, 1944, Mr 17,17:2
Bowser, John W, 1941, Ja 14,21:3; 1956, Mr 31,15:6
Bowser, Paul F, 1960, Jl 18,27:2
Bowser, W J, 1933, O 26,19:5
Bowser, William J, 1945, D 21,21:3
Bowsfield, Colvin C, 1940, Ja 30,19:5
Bowsher, C Forest, 1950, Je 27,29:3
Bowsky, Charles A, 1964, S 11,33:5
Bowtell, David W, 1941, Je 13,19:4
Bowyer, G Sir, 1883, Je 8,5:2
Bowyer, John M Rear-Adm, 1912, Mr 16,13:5
Bowyer, Leonard L, 1942, D 20,44:4
Bowyer, Samuel H, 1938, My 26,25:4
Bowyer, Ward M, 1949, F 7,19:3
Box, Albert H, 1947, Je 15,62:5
Box, George E, 1943, Ap 26,19:2
Box, Harold K, 1956, My 26,17:5
Boxall, William Sir, 1879, D 7,7:1
Boxell, Vern M Mrs, 1966, O 11,43:4
Boxer, George E Dr, 1968, Mr 15,39:1
Boxer, Henry Dr, 1924, O 23,21:4
Boxer, J I, 1957, Je 2,86:3
Boxer, Max A, 1966, O 19,38:6
Boy-ed, I Mrs, 1928, My 14,21:4
Boyajian, Abcar, 1946, Ja 6,39:1
Boyajian, Osgan M, 1945, F 15,19:4
Boyan, James F, 1947, Jl 14,21:5
Boyan, James J, 1950, O 19,31:2
Boyar, Benjamin A, 1964, F 22,21:3
Boyce, Addisone S (cor, O 27,21:2), 1956, O 19,27:2
Boyce, Adolphe L, 1955, N 7,29:2
Boyce, Alex R, 1937, D 4,17:6
Boyce, Arthur C, 1959, S 1,29:4
Boyce, C Prevost, 1955, Ja 16,95:6
Boyce, Charles W, 1960, Ja 13,47:2
Boyce, Eli, 1944, Mr 7,17:3
Boyce, Ella R, 1943, Jl 18,34:6
Boyce, Ernest C, 1948, Ap 23,23:5
Boyce, Erskine, 1952, O 1,33:3
Boyce, Frank J, 1962, F 11,87:1
Boyce, Fred G Jr, 1960, Ap 26,37:5
Boyce, Frederick G, 1938, O 10,19:3
Boyce, George H, 1966, N 7,47:3
Boyce, George M, 1942, Ap 20,21:5
Boyce, George R, 1942, My 23,13:6
Boyce, Gerald E, 1963, Ap 13,19:5
Boyce, Harold A, 1945, D 14,27:2
Boyce, Hawley M, 1944, Mr 23,19:1
Boyce, Henry C, 1943, Ag 14,11:4
Boyce, Henry J, 1955, S 29,33:4
Boyce, Heyward E, 1950, Jl 24,17:2
Boyce, Ignatius, 1949, Ag 21,68:6
Boyce, Ira W, 1955, F 27,87:2
Boyce, Isaac, 1942, Mr 10,19:1
Boyce, Isaac N, 1939, Ag 14,15:5
Boyce, Isaac N Mrs, 1950, N 16,31:4
Boyce, James (see also Jl 11), 1876, Jl 13,3:4
Boyce, John, 1954, O 9,17:6
Boyce, John F, 1945, Ap 22,35:1
Boyce, John J, 1948, D 25,17:3
Boyce, John N, 1940, Ap 2,25:2
Boyce, John W, 1951, D 8,11:1
Boyce, Leslie, 1955, Je 1,33:3
Boyce, Paul L, 1941, Je 5,23:5
Boyce, Richard, 1958, Ag 6,25:4
Boyce, Robert H, 1943, Je 7,13:6
Boyce, Robert R, 1949, S 14,31:3
Boyce, Rodney S, 1941, N 27,23:4
Boyce, Samuel C, 1940, Jl 20,15:7
Boyce, Sidney Smith, 1924, My 30,15:6
Boyce, Thomas B, 1959, N 15,86:7
Boyce, Thomas E, 1943, Mr 22,19:4
Boyce, W Graham, 1942, Jl 5,30:2
Boyce, Wallace H, 1968, N 11,47:2
Boyce, Walter H, 1951, D 27,21:5
Boyce, Walter H Dean, 1968, N 10,88:7
Boyce, William D Mrs, 1959, Jl 7,33:1
Boyce, William G B Maj Gen Sir, 1937, Jl 20,23:2
Boyce, William H, 1937, N 10,25:4; 1942, F 7,17:6
Boyce, William L 2d, 1943, Ap 18,49:1
Boyce, Willis G, 1951, Je 3,93:1
Boyce, Willis G Mrs, 1960, F 13,19:2
Boycheff, Helen, 1914, Ag 21,9:6
Boycott, St John, 1940, O 28,17:6
Boyd, A C Prof, 1910, S 12,9:6
Boyd, A H H Rev, 1866, Ja 6,1:6
Boyd, A P, 1905, My 5,5:2
Boyd, A Rev, 1883, Jl 12,2:5
Boyd, Alex, 1937, Je 15,23:2
Boyd, Alex R, 1962, Ag 31,21:1
Boyd, Alice M, 1947, S 23,25:4
Boyd, Allan Stuart Capt, 1920, Ag 25,9:3
Boyd, Allen R, 1947, Mr 31,23:4
Boyd, Anna, 1916, Je 6,13:4
Boyd, Archie, 1914, Ap 18,11:5
Boyd, Arnold R, 1955, Mr 27,86:3
Boyd, Augusto S, 1957, Je 18,33:4
Boyd, Benjamin J, 1942, Ag 8,11:1
Boyd, Bert A, 1952, Ap 1,29:4
Boyd, Bevie L, 1949, Je 17,23:3
Boyd, Carl Col, 1919, F 15,11:5
Boyd, Charles A, 1950, N 7,27:4; 1961, Ap 24,29:3
Boyd, Charles E J, 1959, Je 29,29:3
Boyd, Charles P Sr, 1964, Ag 6,29:4
Boyd, Clarence J, 1959, Ap 11,21:1
Boyd, D Knickerbocker, 1944, F 22,24:2
Boyd, D M, 1877, Ap 4,4:7; 1881, Jl 17,12:2
Boyd, Daniel H, 1918, Mr 1,11:3
Boyd, Daniel L, 1959, Ja 4,2:4
Boyd, David F, 1954, Ap 1,31:6
Boyd, David K Mrs, 1959, My 2,23:3
Boyd, Denis W, 1965, Ja 24,80:7
Boyd, Dora S Mrs, 1938, Ap 21,19:5
Boyd, Edward B, 1943, N 4,23:5
Boyd, Edward Jr, 1955, N 23,23:1
Boyd, Edward R Mrs, 1945, Jl 12,11:4
Boyd, Elmer B (funl, F 10,31:2), 1955, F 8,28:1
Boyd, Ernest, 1946, D 31,17:2; 1947, Ja 3,21:2
Boyd, Everett M, 1957, Ja 8,31:4
Boyd, Federico, 1924, My 27,21:3
Boyd, Foster J, 1951, S 6,31:4
Boyd, Francis P, 1950, My 13,17:5
Boyd, Frank L Mrs, 1941, Ag 18,13:5
Boyd, Frank W, 1947, S 18,25:1
Boyd, Frederick C C, 1958, S 9,35:1
Boyd, George H, 1944, Ap 16,42:1
Boyd, George M, 1939, My 22,17:2
Boyd, George McCrea, 1916, Mr 14,11:2
Boyd, George N, 1951, Je 9,19:6
Boyd, George W, 1917, S 23,23:3
Boyd, George William, 1903, N 29,7:6
Boyd, Gilbert D, 1938, Ap 1,23:2
Boyd, Grover W, 1958, Ja 10,26:2
Boyd, Harold J, 1945, O 22,17:6
Boyd, Harry R, 1940, Mr 11,15:4
Boyd, Harry T, 1954, Jl 10,13:6
Boyd, Henry A, 1959, My 30,17:5
Boyd, Henry E, 1939, O 27,23:6
Boyd, Henry W, 1958, F 23,92:8
Boyd, Homer V, 1952, Ag 2,15:7
Boyd, Howard C, 1955, Ag 26,19:1
Boyd, Howard L, 1937, Ja 30,17:2
Boyd, Hugh, 1923, N 20,19:4
Boyd, Ingram F Sr, 1950, O 29,92:5
Boyd, Irwin H, 1944, N 4,15:3
Boyd, J C Maj-Gen, 1910, D 19,9:5
Boyd, J P, 1881, My 11,5:5
Boyd, Jackson Mrs, 1960, My 14,23:4
Boyd, James, 1941, My 14,21:3; 1944, F 26,13:3; 1947, F 14,21:1; 1949, Ap 21,25:3
Boyd, James A, 1949, O 26,27:2
Boyd, James C, 1951, N 17,17:3
Boyd, James E, 1950, My 12,27:4; 1960, N 28,31:5
Boyd, James H, 1946, Ja 4,21:1
Boyd, James J, 1950, S 8,31:3
Boyd, James L, 1950, Ag 27,89:2
Boyd, James N, 1915, S 7,13:5
Boyd, James O, 1947, Ag 15,17:4
Boyd, James O Mrs, 1959, S 2,29:2
Boyd, Jennie M, 1941, Jl 21,15:3
Boyd, John, 1881, D 2,2:7; 1902, D 5,9:7
Boyd, John B, 1962, O 24,39:4
Boyd, John D Mrs, 1949, Je 10,27:4
Boyd, John H, 1957, O 16,32:3
Boyd, John J, 1939, Ja 23,13:4
Boyd, John Mrs, 1954, S 23,33:3
Boyd, John O, 1952, S 12,21:2
Boyd, John P, 1871, Jl 21,1:6
Boyd, John R, 1951, F 14,29:2
Boyd, John Scott, 1904, D 13,9:6
Boyd, John T, 1948, N 13,15:5; 1950, Je 8,31:1; 1967, Ap 10,35:4
Boyd, John Thomas, 1904, My 4,9:6
Boyd, John W, 1940, N 23,17:1
Boyd, Joseph, 1952, Ja 15,27:2
Boyd, Joseph A, 1958, Ja 24,23:2
Boyd, Joseph E, 1947, O 2,27:3
Boyd, Joseph F, 1907, Mr 24,9:6
Boyd, Joseph H, 1937, O 21,24:1
Boyd, Joseph M, 1947, Mr 13,27:5; 1956, Mr 16,23:3
Boyd, Julius Rev, 1937, Ja 19,23:5
Boyd, Lillian K, 1942, Mr 21,17:2
Boyd, Lloyd T, 1914, N 9,9:5
Boyd, Lyford S, 1946, Jl 8,29:4
Boyd, Lynn, 1859, D 27,5:2
Boyd, Marcus, 1949, Jl 7,25:3
Boyd, Margaret M Mrs, 1942, Jl 28,17:3
Boyd, Margaret R, 1955, S 12,25:5
Boyd, Mary B Mrs, 1964, Jl 9,33:3
Boyd, Matthew F, 1937, Ap 11,II,8:4
Boyd, Maurice C, 1949, Mr 24,27:4
Boyd, Melville, 1959, F 5,31:2
Boyd, Oran C Sr, 1952, Ja 7,19:6
Boyd, P Ivor, 1947, F 19,25:1
Boyd, Penleigh, 1923, N 29,21:4
Boyd, Phoebe A, 1952, N 18,32:3
Boyd, Pliny A, 1958, N 22,21:5
Boyd, R Earl Maj, 1937, My 29,17:6
Boyd, Robert A, 1959, O 15,39:5
Boyd, Robert M, 1917, D 21,11:5
Boyd, Robert M Jr, 1943, Jl 24,13:4
Boyd, Robert M Jr Mrs, 1950, My 20,15:5
Boyd, Robert S, 1953, Ja 21,31:2
Boyd, Robert W, 1946, Mr 23,13:5
Boyd, Roy M, 1958, Je 4,31:6
Boyd, Roy Mrs, 1937, Mr 9,2:7
Boyd, Sam B, 1953, Ja 8,27:2
Boyd, Samuel B Sr Mrs, 1958, Ja 27,27:1
Boyd, Samuel G Dr, 1937, Ja 24,35:1
Boyd, Stan Mrs, 1960, My 28,21:6
Boyd, Stuart Capt, 1920, Ag 26,15:4
Boyd, Thomas, 1952, D 2,31:2
Boyd, Thomas P, 1957, Je 16,84:2
Boyd, Vernon D, 1965, Je 2,45:2
Boyd, Walter A, 1968, Mr 15,39:1
Boyd, Walter D, 1949, Mr 29,26:2
Boyd, Willard A Mrs, 1949, Je 20,19:5
Boyd, William (will, O 16,3:7), 1937, S 29,23:4
Boyd, William (will), 1938, Jl 22,4:2
Boyd, William, 1961, F 6,23:3
Boyd, William A, 1918, Ja 25,11:8; 1948, F 22,48:7; 1951, F 3,15:5
Boyd, William B, 1941, Je 25,21:4
Boyd, William E Jr, 1955, O 2,87:2
Boyd, William J Mrs, 1940, Je 23,30:5
Boyd, William K, 1938, Ja 20,23:2
Boyd, William M, 1949, F 17,23:4; 1956, Mr 12,27:4
Boyd, William Mrs, 1937, Ag 19,19:5
Boyd, William N Sr, 1951, F 11,88:1
Boyd, William P, 1944, F 8,15:3
Boyd, William R Jr, 1959, N 8,88:2
Boyd, William W, 1943, S 24,23:5
Boyd-Carpenter, William, 1954, Ap 20,19:2
Boyd-Rochfort, Arthur, 1940, Ag 8,19:2
Boyd-Rochfort, Winifred, 1941, F 10,17:4
Boyden, Albert A, 1925, My 4,19:5
Boyden, Arthur R, 1937, Jl 31,15:3
Boyden, Charles W, 1955, My 24,31:5
Boyden, Obadiah S, 1907, D 10,9:4
Boyden, R W, 1931, O 26,19:1
Boyden, Roland W Mrs, 1924, My 6,21:4
Boyden, Ulysses H, 1945, Ag 19,39:1
Boyden, W C Jr, 1955, D 22,1:7
Boyden, Wallace C, 1937, S 9,23:5
Boye, Burton L, 1942, Jl 10,17:3
Boye, Martin M Dr, 1909, Mr 6,7:4
Boyeman, Harriette Mrs, 1950, My 6,15:5
Boyen, Joseph F, 1965, Ja 24,80:7
Boyer, Alden S, 1953, Je 18,29:1
Boyer, Alvah O Mrs, 1958, My 24,21:4
Boyer, Annie-Marie Mrs, 1956, S 19,37:1
Boyer, Arsenius, 1939, Ja 2,23:2
Boyer, Arthur I, 1961, O 31,31:5
Boyer, Arthur I Mrs, 1945, F 16,23:1
Boyer, Arthur T, 1954, Jl 17,13:2
Boyer, Auguste, 1956, O 22,29:1
Boyer, Budd Mrs, 1953, Mr 15,92:1
Boyer, C Valentine, 1954, Ag 1,84:3
Boyer, Calvin S, 1951, Ag 11,11:5
Boyer, Charles B, 1942, Ag 12,19:6
Boyer, Daniel S, 1949, S 28,27:2
Boyer, David, 1949, O 16,88:2
Boyer, Edward D Mrs, 1960, D 7,43:4
Boyer, Edwin S, 1950, F 22,29:4
Boyer, Fred C, 1939, Ja 11,19:3
Boyer, George B Capt, 1903, N 25,9:5
Boyer, Harry A, 1944, My 23,23:5
Boyer, Harry T, 1939, Ag 27,35:2
Boyer, Harvey M, 1938, Ag 25,19:3
Boyer, Henry A, 1964, Je 18,35:4
Boyer, Henry P, 1949, Ag 26,19:5
Boyer, James M, 1948, Mr 17,25:4; 1959, Jl 26,68:3
Boyer, John R, 1940, O 13,49:3
Boyer, John R C Mrs, 1940, My 1,24:3
Boyer, Kenneth H, 1957, S 19,29:2
Boyer, Lucien, 1942, Je 18,21:1
Boyer, Martha E, 1939, S 28,25:3
Boyer, Maurice P, 1957, O 30,29:4
Boyer, Maurice W, 1944, Mr 7,17:5
Boyer, Merce E, 1948, Ag 24,23:5
Boyer, Napoleon, 1938, Ja 26,23:5
Boyer, Nathalie Mrs, 1940, D 20,25:2
Boyer, Pearce F, 1949, Jl 23,11:2
Boyer, Phil, 1950, D 15,31:4
Boyer, Philip B, 1946, Ag 25,46:1
Boyer, Ralph L, 1952, My 21,27:2
Boyer, Richard J F, 1961, Je 6,37:4
Boyer, Robert A, 1950, Ap 16,106:4
Boyer, Rosario G, 1953, Je 2,29:3
Boyer, Russell L, 1940, O 19,17:5
Boyer, W Charles Sr, 1951, O 7,87:1
Boyer, Walter T, 1950, Ap 11,31:4
Boyer, Wanda M Mrs, 1950, Ag 4,21:3
Boyer, William, 1952, F 16,13:6
Boyer, William C, 1957, O 31,31:1
Boyer, William H, 1950, Ag 25,21:4
Boyers, John C, 1957, S 24,35:2
Boyes, Edward J, 1951, D 1,13:5
Boyes, Henry R, 1959, My 12,35:5
Boyes, John, 1947, Je 15,62:3; 1951, Jl 21,13:7
Boyes, John W, 1948, Mr 23,25:1
Boyes, Kurwin R, 1957, F 1,25:2
Boyes, Truman L, 1956, O 19,27:4
Boyesen, H H Prof, 1895, O 5,5:3

Boyhan, John J (will), 1940, Ag 29,19:1
Boyhan, William J Ex-Justice, 1919, Ap 12,15:4
Boyington, Charles L, 1953, Ag 15,15:3
Boyione, Vivian, 1953, Mr 6,14:4
Boyke, Charles M, 1953, Je 30,23:3
Boykin, Charles S Mrs, 1953, D 11,31:1
Boykin, Clarence E, 1949, Ag 15,17:3
Boykin, H M Col, 1937, Ap 27,23:5
Boykin, Hamilton G, 1943, Je 29,19:1
Boykin, Richard M, 1950, Ja 30,17:5
Boykin, Robert H, 1958, Ja 15,29:1
Boykin, Samuel F, 1953, Jl 27,19:6
Boykin, Samuel V, 1956, Mr 20,23:4
Boyko, Fred S, 1951, Jl 6,23:6
Boyko, Jacob, 1938, F 13,II,6:6
Boykoff, Abraham S, 1968, Ag 4,68:1
Boykoff, Max, 1954, Ag 20,19:1
Boylan, Alice V, 1944, My 4,19:3
Boylan, Anne J, 1960, Mr 14,50:5
Boylan, Arthur A, 1957, My 21,35:3
Boylan, Arthur A Mrs, 1942, F 22,26:5
Boylan, Bridget Mrs, 1945, Jl 5,13:1
Boylan, Charles E, 1963, Jl 14,61:2
Boylan, Charles N, 1956, S 6,25:6
Boylan, Daniel C, 1954, S 23,33:3
Boylan, Francis J, 1954, Ja 1,23:4
Boylan, Frank, 1959, O 5,31:4
Boylan, James J, 1942, Je 10,21:2
Boylan, James P, 1945, S 26,23:5
Boylan, James R, 1914, D 15,13:5
Boylan, James T, 1939, Ap 19,23:3
Boylan, James W, 1963, Ag 7,33:1
Boylan, John, 1951, My 3,29:3
Boylan, John C, 1966, N 24,35:4
Boylan, John C Mrs, 1937, Ja 6,25:5
Boylan, John J, 1938, O 6,23:1
Boylan, John J (will), 1940, Je 1,31:6
Boylan, John P, 1960, Jl 20,29:2
Boylan, John S, 1965, N 20,35:1
Boylan, Matthew A, 1945, S 28,21:4
Boylan, Matthew R, 1945, My 1,23:1
Boylan, Michael J, 1943, D 30,17:2
Boylan, Patrick, 1941, My 13,24:2
Boylan, Patrick W, 1947, S 3,25:3
Boylan, Peter, 1943, D 1,21:3
Boylan, Peter N, 1941, Ag 29,17:2
Boylan, Richard J, 1966, D 27,35:2
Boylan, Robert J Mrs, 1947, D 30,23:2
Boylan, Robert P, 1960, Je 23,29:4
Boylan, Thomas E, 1956, O 1,27:4
Boylan, Thomas V, 1952, Ap 6,1:8
Boylan, William A, 1940, Jl 9,21:1
Boylance, Frank D Mrs, 1943, My 22,13:3
Boyland, George E, 1957, Ag 31,15:6
Boyland, James P, 1950, D 8,29:2
Boyland, John W, 1960, N 11,29:1
Boyland, William L, 1950, F 21,25:5
Boyle, Aileen, 1965, Je 4,35:1
Boyle, Albert J (will, N 27,25:8), 1957, N 3,88:2
Boyle, Alex, 1943, Ap 20,23:3
Boyle, Alex R M, 1959, S 11,27:1
Boyle, Algernon D E H, 1949, O 16,89:1
Boyle, Andrew J, 1944, Mr 9,17:5
Boyle, Angus J, 1957, N 17,87:2
Boyle, Boyle G Mrs, 1949, Ag 16,23:1
Boyle, Bridget Mrs, 1917, Ap 25,11:5
Boyle, Cavendish Sir, 1916, S 18,13:3
Boyle, Charles, 1948, Ja 10,15:3
Boyle, Charles A, 1959, N 5,27:8
Boyle, Charles E Jr, 1949, Jl 4,13:4
Boyle, Charles J, 1947, Ap 23,26:3
Boyle, Condy O, 1938, Je 2,23:5
Boyle, Cornelius, 1957, D 20,27:3
Boyle, Cornelius J, 1949, Mr 8,25:1
Boyle, Cosmas, 1955, O 12,31:4
Boyle, David, 1961, Ap 21,33:2
Boyle, Donald F, 1954, Mr 30,27:3
Boyle, Donald Rev, 1937, N 4,25:3
Boyle, E D, 1926, Ja 4,19:5
Boyle, E K, 1874, Ap 18,3:4
Boyle, Edward, 1945, Ap 3,19:1
Boyle, Edward F, 1943, D 15,27:1
Boyle, Eilwood P, 1947, Ap 22,28:3
Boyle, Elmer E, 1956, Jl 21,15:6
Boyle, Ferdinand Thomas Lee, 1906, D 4,9:5
Boyle, Francis J, 1940, Jl 2,21:5
Boyle, Frank J, 1952, Mr 27,29:5; 1965, Ja 11,45:2
Boyle, George, 1956, O 21,86:8
Boyle, George F, 1948, Je 21,21:5
Boyle, Grace M, 1951, S 12,31:4
Boyle, Hal Mrs, 1968, O 27,82:2
Boyle, Harold L, 1952, D 19,31:2
Boyle, Harry J, 1953, O 17,15:2
Boyle, Havey J, 1947, Mr 19,25:3
Boyle, Helen M, 1959, O 12,19:4
Boyle, Henry E S, 1941, O 16,21:4
Boyle, Hugh C, 1946, O 23,27:2; 1950, D 23,15:4
Boyle, J Edward Jr, 1954, Ag 25,27:1
Boyle, J F, 1930, Jl 3,21:3
Boyle, J Joseph, 1951, Ap 26,29:1
Boyle, J Leo, 1954, F 16,25:1
Boyle, J Leonard, 1960, N 25,27:4
Boyle, J T Gen, 1871, Jl 29,1:4
Boyle, James, 1939, Je 12,17:6; 1954, Je 4,23:3
Boyle, James A, 1937, Ap 3,19:1
Boyle, James D, 1945, D 27,19:1
Boyle, James E, 1938, S 19,19:1; 1954, Je 6,86:5
Boyle, James F, 1954, F 11,29:3; 1966, Ja 5,31:2
Boyle, James J, 1951, D 16,91:2; 1964, Ag 11,33:1
Boyle, James J Mrs, 1968, N 6,47:3
Boyle, James P, 1939, S 25,19:3
Boyle, James P Mrs, 1951, Ja 14,85:1
Boyle, James S, 1961, Mr 26,92:8
Boyle, James T, 1961, Jl 4,19:5
Boyle, John, 1885, Ja 9,8:5; 1943, Ap 12,25:3
Boyle, John A, 1950, Mr 7,27:3
Boyle, John Douglas, 1968, My 30,25:2
Boyle, John E Dr, 1968, Ja 16,39:3
Boyle, John E Jr Mrs, 1949, Je 22,31:2
Boyle, John F, 1947, Ap 26,13:5; 1950, Je 26,27:3; 1953, D 9,11:6
Boyle, John H, 1940, Ja 21,34:7; 1940, S 5,23:5; 1956, Mr 13,27:3
Boyle, John Howard, 1968, Ap 3,51:1
Boyle, John J, 1917, F 11,23:3; 1948, N 24,23:3; 1967, My 15,43:3
Boyle, John J Mrs, 1947, N 8,17:4; 1958, Ja 18,15:3
Boyle, John J Rev, 1916, My 26,11:4
Boyle, John S, 1944, Mr 11,13:5
Boyle, John W, 1924, Mr 28,17:4
Boyle, Joseph A, 1948, My 26,25:6; 1960, O 19,45:4
Boyle, Joseph B, 1946, N 28,27:2
Boyle, Joseph E, 1956, D 4,39:1
Boyle, Joseph F Mrs, 1949, My 18,27:1
Boyle, Joseph P, 1956, S 28,27:2
Boyle, Joseph S, 1963, D 25,33:3
Boyle, Joseph W Col (funl, Ap 18,21:5), 1923, Ap 16,17:5
Boyle, Juan A Lt, 1905, My 5,1:4
Boyle, Louis M, 1953, Ag 3,17:4
Boyle, Luke J, 1942, Je 30,21:4
Boyle, Luke Sr, 1943, Je 6,44:1
Boyle, McKinley, 1918, Mr 25,13:8
Boyle, Michael A, 1942, Mr 14,15:6
Boyle, Michael H, 1964, S 27,86:3
Boyle, Michael J, 1946, Ag 12,21:3; 1952, Ag 10,61:3; 1958, My 19,25:3
Boyle, Mortimer Lt-Col, 1925, My 2,15:5
Boyle, Nina, 1943, Mr 5,17:4
Boyle, Norman T, 1968, Ja 2,41:5
Boyle, Patrick A, 1938, F 23,23:3
Boyle, Patrick J, 1923, Ja 31,19:6
Boyle, Peter A, 1942, Ja 4,48:4
Boyle, Ress H, 1941, S 10,23:2
Boyle, Robert E, 1941, Ja 29,17:1
Boyle, Robert H (Earl of Shannon), 1963, D 30,2:3
Boyle, Robert M, 1945, Ag 24,19:2
Boyle, Roger, 1940, Ja 27,13:3
Boyle, Terence J, 1952, N 30,87:4
Boyle, Theresa, 1906, Mr 6,9:5
Boyle, Thomas, 1871, Ap 30,1:3
Boyle, Thomas E, 1940, Ja 3,21:5; 1951, Ap 27,23:2
Boyle, Thomas F, 1955, Je 16,31:5
Boyle, Thomas J, 1938, Ap 29,21:5
Boyle, Thomas P, 1948, Ja 27,25:4
Boyle, Thomas R Mrs, 1938, D 14,26:1
Boyle, Thomas S, 1941, Jl 6,27:4; 1956, F 14,29:3
Boyle, Walter F, 1956, F 15,31:5
Boyle, Walter G, 1943, D 9,27:5
Boyle, William A, 1948, D 27,22:2; 1950, Ja 13,23:3
Boyle, William A Sr Mrs, 1960, O 27,37:4
Boyle, William E, 1941, F 8,15:2
Boyle, William F, 1960, D 24,15:1
Boyle, William H, 1949, Ag 2,19:3
Boyle, William H Col, 1919, Ap 24,11:4
Boyle, William H D (Earl of Cork and Orrery), 1967, Ap 20,43:2
Boyle, William J, 1951, Je 27,29:3
Boyle, William M Jr, 1961, S 1,17:4
Boyle, William T, 1951, S 23,87:1
Boylen, Alfred W, 1940, F 10,15:6
Boyles, Joshua A Mrs, 1946, F 24,44:2
Boyles, Robert E, 1947, N 11,27:3
Boylhart, Frederick, 1944, D 7,25:4
Boylston, Arthur C, 1949, My 12,31:1
Boylston, Caleb Dudley, 1912, D 18,15:4
Boylston, Edward J Mrs, 1941, Ap 15,23:1
Boylston, John, 1938, N 2,23:2
Boylston, John W, 1940, Je 5,25:5
Boylston, Samuel D, 1939, N 26,42:6
Boyne, Ava L, 1960, Ap 16,17:5
Boyne, Matthew L, 1940, Ja 30,20:3
Boyne, Peter, 1958, Ap 26,19:3
Boyne, Viscount, 1942, Ja 20,19:4
Boyne, William E Mrs, 1943, Ap 24,13:3
Boynge, Charles William Mrs, 1914, Je 30,11:5
Boyno, Edward E, 1956, Ag 28,27:4
Boynton, Albert E, 1945, F 23,17:4
Boynton, Alexander, 1944, S 22,19:4
Boynton, Allan G, 1955, Ap 17,86:2
Boynton, Ben L, 1963, Ja 24,7:3
Boynton, C B Rev, 1883, Ap 28,5:3
Boynton, C Whitman, 1965, Mr 26,35:3
Boynton, Charles A, 1915, S 6,9:6
Boynton, Charles B Mrs, 1945, S 24,19:2
Boynton, Charles E Jr, 1940, S 26,23:4
Boynton, Charles F, 1937, My 3,19:2
Boynton, Charles H Mrs, 1943, F 19,20:2; 1952, My 6, 29:2
Boynton, Charles Rev, 1908, F 19,7:7
Boynton, Charles W Mrs, 1937, Mr 24,25:2
Boynton, Clancy D, 1950, O 8,104:5
Boynton, Donald S, 1966, Ag 27,29:6
Boynton, Edward B, 1948, F 7,15:4
Boynton, Edward E, 1939, D 29,15:3
Boynton, Floyd A, 1948, Mr 27,13:3
Boynton, Frank L, 1945, F 21,19:5
Boynton, George B Capt, 1911, Ja 20,11:3
Boynton, George G, 1954, Je 4,23:3
Boynton, George R, 1945, Ja 7,37:1
Boynton, H V Gen, 1905, Je 4,9:5
Boynton, Henry W, 1947, My 12,21:3
Boynton, L R, 1938, Mr 11,19:2
Boynton, Mark H, 1939, N 24,23:4
Boynton, Melbourne P, 1942, Je 18,21:4
Boynton, Myra L, 1953, O 25,89:1
Boynton, Neil, 1956, F 2,25:5
Boynton, Paul W, 1965, Jl 29,27:3
Boynton, Percy H, 1946, Jl 9,21:1
Boynton, Perry S, 1961, F 19,86:4; 1965, F 10,41:3
Boynton, Perry S Sr Mrs, 1950, S 9,17:5
Boynton, Richard W Mrs, 1938, N 8,23:5
Boynton, Roland E, 1942, F 7,17:2
Boynton, Stephen Emerson, 1907, My 10,7:6
Boynton, Thomas J, 1945, Ap 14,15:3
Boynton, William P, 1955, Mr 12,19:5
Boyrer, William C, 1940, S 29,44:2
Boys, Charles V, 1944, Mr 31,21:3
Boys, William H, 1938, F 21,19:5
Boysen, Charles C, 1957, Jl 6,15:4
Boysen, Otto H, 1937, F 6,17:3
Boysen, Rudolph, 1950, N 26,89:5
Boyt, Alex, 1956, O 3,33:4
Boyteaux, Gilbert L La, 1914, Ap 20,9:4
Boyton, Paul Capt, 1924, Ap 20,22:1
Boza, Ricardo, 1948, O 19,27:3
Bozanta, Charles Count, 1914, Mr 24,9:4
Bozell, Leo B, 1946, Mr 25,25:5
Bozeman, Nathan Gross Dr, 1916, Mr 18,11:6
Bozios, James A, 1916, Ap 3,13:6
Bozorth, Loriot D Jr, 1958, My 2,27:2
Bozsan, Eugene J, 1941, D 5,23:5
Bozyan, Arkel H, 1950, O 27,29:1
Bozyan, Arkel H Mrs, 1968, N 2,37:4
Bozyan, H Frank, 1965, D 29,29:4
Bozza, Fausto, 1961, Ag 9,33:5
Bozza, Joseph D, 1961, Jl 23,69:2
Bozza, Michael, 1944, F 23,23:4
Bozzo, Ralph, 1951, Je 29,21:2
Braaf, Fetih P, 1942, Ja 13,19:3
Braakensiek, John, 1940, F 29,19:5
Braam, John F, 1956, Je 2,20:2
Braasch, William, 1940, Jl 3,17:3
Braatoy, Bjarne, 1957, Mr 16,19:6
Brabant, Edward Yewd Maj-Gen, 1914, D 14,11:5
Brabazon of Tara, Lord (John-Theodore Cuthbert Moore-Brabazon), 1964, My 18,29:3
Brabin, Charles J, 1957, N 6,35:4
Brabourne, Lord, 1939, F 23,23:2
Bracalello, Dominic A, 1957, Ag 29,27:5
Bracato, James (Diamond Jim Moran), 1958, Ap 14, 25:1
Bracci, Francesco (Cardinal), 1967, Mr 25,23:3
Bracco, Roberto, 1943, Ap 24,14:8
Brace, Arthur C, 1950, Mr 23,36:2
Brace, C L Rev, 1890, Ag 14,8:1
Brace, Charles C Mrs, 1957, Ag 8,23:4
Brace, Charles L (por), 1938, My 26,25:1
Brace, Charles L Mrs, 1947, My 31,13:2
Brace, Donald C, 1955, S 22,31:1
Brace, Donald E, 1955, Ja 25,25:3
Brace, Duff S, 1948, D 8,31:2
Brace, Edgar S, 1947, Ja 15,25:2
Brace, Ivor L, 1952, O 25,17:3
Brace, J P (see also O 10), 1881, O 13,8:3
Brace, James H, 1956, Ap 12,31:1
Brace, John P, 1872, O 22,4:7
Brace, Joseph, 1937, Jl 18,II,7:3
Brace, Norman C, 1954, Je 22,27:4
Brace, Richard A, 1938, Ag 18,20:4
Brace, Robert N, 1938, D 26,23:3
Brace, William H Dr, 1909, S 2,9:6
Bracelen, Charles M, 1942, O 9,21:3
Bracewell, John Mrs, 1945, O 1,19:3
Bracewell, Russell, 1954, D 14,33:1
Bracey, Hugh O, 1946, Mr 23,13:5
Brach, Charles L, 1944, F 20,36:3
Brach, Edwin J, 1965, Ja 29,29:3
Brach, Edwin J (est appr), 1966, Je 22,28:6
Brach, Emil J, 1947, N 1,15:3
Brach, Otto W, 1954, D 23,19:2
Brachear, Gaylord C, 1949, Jl 14,27:5
Brachen, Joseph R, 1947, Jl 20,44:3
Brachetti, Giulio C, 1950, Je 20,27:3
Brachocki, Alex, 1948, Ja 7,25:6
Bracht, Frank J, 1961, Mr 13,29:3
Brack, Annabelle, 1958, Mr 29,36:2
Brack, Frederick, 1965, My 26,47:2
Brack, Harry, 1949, O 22,17:6

Bracken, Brendan Viscount, 1958, Ag 9,13:4
Bracken, Clio Hinton Mrs, 1925, F 13,17:4
Bracken, Edward A, 1947, F 13,24:2
Bracken, Francis B, 1937, F 2,23:2
Bracken, John J, 1954, Jl 19,19:4
Bracken, Joseph L Jr, 1955, F 22,21:4
Bracken, Leonidas L, 1942, Je 22,15:4
Bracken, Olin, 1952, My 8,31:6
Bracken, Stanley, 1966, Ap 2,29:3
Bracken, Thomas F (ed, F 24,28:1), 1959, F 23,23:5
Bracken, Thomas Mrs, 1959, Jl 31,24:1
Bracken, William A, 1961, S 18,29:5
Brackenbury, Georgina, 1949, F 1,25:5
Brackenridge, Alex, 1964, My 24,92:4
Brackenridge, Gavin, 1965, Ag 16,27:4
Brackenridge, John C, 1947, F 4,25:2
Bracker, Alfred F (will), 1939, My 14,44:3
Bracker, Charles Mrs, 1951, Je 5,31:4
Bracker, Henry G Mrs, 1965, D 6,37:4
Bracker, Milton (trb, Ja 31,26:5; interment, F 2,89:1), 1964, Ja 29,33:2
Bracker, Murray, 1947, My 15,25:2
Bracket, James Mrs, 1951, S 19,31:2
Brackett, Anna C, 1911, Mr 19,II,11:2
Brackett, Charles Mrs, 1948, Je 9,29:1
Brackett, Cyrus Fogg Prof, 1915, Ja 30,9:6
Brackett, Edgar Truman (funl, F 29,17:6), 1924, F 28,19:5
Brackett, Edward S, 1951, Mr 2,26:2
Brackett, Elliott G, 1942, D 31,15:2
Brackett, F Ernest, 1938, D 18,48:7
Brackett, Frederick Maj, 1914, F 16,7:5
Brackett, G B Col, 1915, Ag 4,11:5
Brackett, George Callender, 1911, My 22,11:4
Brackett, George F, 1942, Ap 6,15:2
Brackett, Jeffrey R, 1949, D 6,32:4
Brackett, John C, 1945, D 18,27:1; 1967, Je 22,39:4
Brackett, Minnie R Mrs, 1938, Ap 15,20:4
Brackett, Quincy A, 1951, Ag 13,17:3
Brackett, Raymond O Lt Comdr, 1937, Jl 30,19:6
Brackett, Richard N Dr, 1937, N 28,II,8:5
Brackett, Sarah Mrs, 1904, Je 27,7:6
Brackett, W Oliver, 1945, Jl 28,11:4
Brackett, W Warren, 1940, Ag 20,19:3
Brackett, Walter M, 1919, Mr 5,11:3
Brackett, William, 1941, Ag 6,17:6
Brackett, William S, 1959, Ja 9,27:3
Brackett, Winslow M, 1956, F 12,88:8
Brackley, Albert J, 1937, D 15,25:2
Brackmann, Albert, 1952, Mr 21,23:4
Bracons, Adolfo Mrs, 1948, N 23,29:4
Bracy, Clara T Mrs, 1941, F 25,23:5
Bradburn, George, 1944, D 11,23:4
Bradbury, Albert W Col, 1909, Mr 28,13:6
Bradbury, Arthur F, 1953, My 24,53:5
Bradbury, Christopher H, 1952, Ag 29,23:2
Bradbury, Frank E Mrs, 1943, D 21,28:2
Bradbury, Harold M, 1942, Ap 22,23:5
Bradbury, Harold Mrs, 1952, Je 14,15:6
Bradbury, Harry B, 1923, My 17,19:4
Bradbury, Howard W, 1964, N 4,39:5
Bradbury, J P Justice, 1915, Jl 18,15:6
Bradbury, James, 1940, O 15,23:3
Bradbury, Joseph, 1914, Je 28,15:5
Bradbury, Kittie H Mrs, 1940, F 23,3:8
Bradbury, Lord (J Swanwick),(will, Ag 2,23:4), 1950, My 4,27:4
Bradbury, Robert H, 1949, Mr 28,21:5
Bradbury, Ruth C, 1964, My 3,86:6
Bradbury, Samuel, 1947, Ag 31,37:1
Bradbury, Samuel L, 1943, Je 24,21:3
Bradbury, Stella L, 1951, My 24,35:3
Bradbury, W B Prof, 1868, Ja 9,1:7
Bradbury, W C, 1925, O 6,27:4
Bradbury, William C Mrs, 1937, S 8,23:3
Bradbury, William Frothingham Prof, 1914, O 23,11:5
Bradbury, William Mrs, 1951, Ja 6,15:5
Bradbury, William P, 1939, Ja 17,21:4
Bradcock, Henry R, 1941, Ja 24,17:4
Braddicks, Robert P, 1965, Ag 25,39:3
Braddock, C W, 1927, Ag 7,26:4
Braddock, Charles S Jr Dr, 1917, Mr 24,11:3
Braddock, Elizabeth Mrs, 1937, D 31,15:4
Braddock, Harold, 1958, Je 28,17:4
Braddock, Joseph, 1945, Mr 28,23:5
Braddock, O L, 1947, D 10,31:2
Braddon, E Kate Mrs, 1941, Jl 25,15:6
Braddon, Edward Nicholas Sir, 1904, F 3,9:5
Braddon, Mary E, 1915, F 5,11:6
Braddon, William H, 1905, F 14,9:3
Braden, Charles W, 1953, S 22,31:3
Braden, Frank, 1962, My 3,33:4
Braden,Frank L, 1949, N 24,31:3
Braden, George C, 1942, Ja 9,21:1
Braden, George L, 1943, Je 4,21:3
Braden, H Robert, 1952, Jl 15,21:3
Braden, J Noble, 1957, F 16,17:1
Braden, James A, 1955, Je 30,25:1
Braden, James S, 1961, Ja 22,85:1
Braden, Luther D, 1947, My 15,25:3
Braden, Norman S, 1944, S 28,19:3
Braden, Paul (Paul Lepaul), 1958, Je 10,33:1
Braden, Robert G, 1949, Ag 2,21:6
Braden, Roy S, 1951, My 2,31:3
Braden, Spruille Mrs, 1962, My 26,25:6
Braden, William, 1942, Jl 19,30:6
Braden, William A, 1947, Jl 1,25:4
Braden, William Mrs, 1950, Je 25,68:8
Braden, William Mrs (will), 1953, F 19,25:1
Brader, Reid B, 1966, My 6,47:3
Bradfield, Clarence H Jr, 1962, S 14,31:5
Bradfield, Harold W, 1960, My 2,29:1
Bradfield, Harriet, 1953, Mr 21,17:1
Bradfield, William Walter, 1925, Mr 19,21:5
Bradford, A L Mrs, 1954, Ap 18,88:4
Bradford, A W, 1867, N 7,8:2; 1881, Mr 2,5:5
Bradford, A W Mrs, 1875, F 28,6:7
Bradford, Alan N, 1943, D 28,18:3
Bradford, Arthur H, 1955, Ag 20,17:5
Bradford, Benjamin Boyland Mrs, 1944, Jl 10,15:6
Bradford, Charles C, 1953, Mr 9,29:2
Bradford, Clarence D, 1947, O 28,26:3
Bradford, Douglas, 1958, Ja 26,88:4
Bradford, E A, 1928, My 5,17:3
Bradford, E G, 1928, Mr 31,19:5
Bradford, E H Dr, 1926, My 8,17:3
Bradford, Earl of (O Bridgeman), 1957, Mr 24,86:1
Bradford, Edward Anthony Mrs, 1920, D 16,17:3
Bradford, Edward G, 1948, Ag 13,15:4
Bradford, Edward H Mrs, 1955, Mr 31,27:5
Bradford, Edward S, 1957, Mr 30,19:4
Bradford, Elliott, 1947, Jl 27,45:2
Bradford, Ernest S, 1965, Mr 16,39:3
Bradford, Ernest S Mrs, 1954, F 23,27:4
Bradford, Eugene, 1957, Je 19,35:4
Bradford, Francis S, 1961, O 3,39:4
Bradford, Frank W Mrs, 1957, N 28,31:4
Bradford, Frederick C, 1950, Je 29,29:3
Bradford, G, 1932, Ap 12,21:1
Bradford, Gamaliel Mrs, 1954, N 25,29:4
Bradford, George G, 1952, Ag 23,13:2
Bradford, George H, 1937, D 5,II,9:2; 1953, O 6,29:4
Bradford, George Mrs, 1950, Ag 30,31:2
Bradford, George W, 1947, N 12,27:5
Bradford, Gerard, 1955, N 6,86:3
Bradford, Glen, 1952, Ag 18,17:2
Bradford, Harmon M Mrs, 1960, O 20,35:5
Bradford, Harriet A, 1948, My 20,29:1
Bradford, Herbert A, 1947, Jl 19,13:5
Bradford, J E, 1882, Ag 15,5:2
Bradford, J O, 1879, Je 28,2:5
Bradford, James C, 1941, My 13,24:2
Bradford, Jennie O Mrs, 1947, Ja 4,15:4
Bradford, John, 1940, D 10,25:3; 1948, O 18,23:4; 1967, N 7,39:3
Bradford, John H Gen, 1908, My 21,7:6
Bradford, Joseph Capt, 1872, Ap 17,1:6
Bradford, Kingsland Mrs, 1955, My 14,19:5
Bradford, Lindsay, 1959, O 7,43:3
Bradford, Lindsay Mrs, 1964, Mr 23,29:4
Bradford, Louis C, 1912, Ap 23,13:3
Bradford, Marcus C, 1950, N 14,31:1
Bradford, Marion N Mrs, 1953, Ag 21,17:1
Bradford, Mary C Mrs, 1938, Ja 16,II,9:1
Bradford, Mary E, 1940, Ap 6,17:4
Bradford, Mary L Mrs, 1938, Jl 24,28:8
Bradford, O M, 1881, F 22,4:7
Bradford, Roark, 1948, N 14,76:5
Bradford, Royal Bird Rear-Adm, 1914, Ag 6,11:6
Bradford, Russell L, 1937, N 10,25:6
Bradford, S D, 1866, Ja 7,1:7
Bradford, Saxton, 1966, Ap 26,45:2
Bradford, Stella S, 1959, Ja 21,31:5
Bradford, T Hewson Dr, 1915, Je 28,9:6
Bradford, T W, 1883, My 11,2:2
Bradford, Taul, 1883, O 29,5:4
Bradford, Thomas C (funl), 1872, Ja 17,1:3
Bradford, V L, 1884, Ag 9,4:7
Bradford, Walter R, 1925, Je 6,15:5
Bradford, Walton, 1952, S 7,86:4
Bradford, William, 1938, Ja 1,19:5; 1946, Jl 3,25:5; 1950, F 24,23:4
Bradford, William B, 1965, Ja 17,88:8
Bradford, William H, 1948, N 17,27:4; 1958, Ag 23, 15:4
Bradfute, Blaine W, 1949, D 30,20:4
Bradfute, Jack, 1963, Ap 27,25:2
Bradfute, Walter S, 1957, Ap 15,29:4
Bradin, Clara A C Mrs, 1938, Ag 9,19:2
Bradin, James W, 1938, S 7,25:3
Bradin, Percival H, 1942, S 19,15:3
Bradin, Robert L, 1952, Ap 20,92:6
Bradish, Donald D, 1949, S 28,27:4
Bradish, Luther Hon, 1863, S 2,2:6
Bradish, Peter H, 1947, Ap 20,60:5
Bradlaugh, Charles, 1891, Ja 31,5:1
Bradlee, Arthur T, 1925, S 1,21:5
Bradlee, Henry G, 1947, S 5,19:5
Bradlee, John R Mrs, 1944, Ja 21,17:3
Bradlee, Reginald, 1943, My 21,19:5
Bradlee, Roger Wainwright, 1907, N 24,9:6
Bradley, A C Judge, 1902, My 16,5:2
Bradley, A D, 1885, Mr 4,2:5
Bradley, Albert W, 1953, N 24,29:5
Bradley, Alex, 1958, S 4,29:5
Bradley, Alfred, 1908, Ap 11,7:5
Bradley, Alfred E Col (funl, D 18,17:5), 1922, D 17, 6:4
Bradley, Allan B A, 1952, F 13,29:1
Bradley, Allen R, 1954, Mr 31,27:1
Bradley, Alpeora, 1882, O 23,5:5
Bradley, Alva, 1953, Mr 30,21:4
Bradley, Alvin F, 1948, Ja 11,56:3
Bradley, Ambrose E Capt, 1905, Ap 4,11:6
Bradley, Ann E Mrs, 1937, Ja 31,II,9:3
Bradley, Anon H, 1916, Ag 24,9:3
Bradley, Archie, 1948, S 28,27:4
Bradley, Arthur G, 1943, Ja 29,19:3
Bradley, Benjamin, 1942, D 29,21:3
Bradley, Benjamin H, 1965, Ja 6,39:4
Bradley, Brenton T (por), 1949, F 3,23:1
Bradley, Bruce E Mrs, 1962, F 11,87:2
Bradley, C Cole Dr, 1910, D 31,9:3
Bradley, C Cole Mrs, 1944, Ag 1,15:5
Bradley, Carolyn G, 1954, D 10,27:4
Bradley, Charles, 1938, S 5,15:3; 1939, Ag 6,37:2
Bradley, Charles B, 1960, My 8,88:4
Bradley, Charles C, 1939, Jl 27,19:2
Bradley, Charles F, 1957, Mr 22,23:3
Bradley, Charles H, 1916, Jl 21,9:6
Bradley, Charles H Jr, 1916, F 23,13:4
Bradley, Charles L, 1943, D 19,48:5
Bradley, Charles O, 1954, F 1,23:4
Bradley, Charles W, 1946, My 6,21:3
Bradley, Chris Mrs, 1902, Ja 12,1:3
Bradley, Clarence H, 1938, D 28,26:2
Bradley, Claude J, 1947, O 13,24:3
Bradley, Claude L, 1950, Je 15,31:4
Bradley, Dan F, 1939, N 12,48:8
Bradley, Daniel Ex-Sen, 1908, F 24,7:5
Bradley, Daniel J, 1950, Ap 25,31:5
Bradley, David C, 1939, S 28,25:2
Bradley, Dean of Westminster, 1903, Mr 13,9:5
Bradley, Dennis M Bp, 1903, D 14,7:5
Bradley, Dwight A, 1939, N 8,25:6
Bradley, Dwight J, 1957, D 29,49:1
Bradley, Dwight J Mrs, 1966, O 30,89:2
Bradley, E Mrs, 1929, Ag 23,21:3
Bradley, Ed H, 1939, Ap 6,25:1
Bradley, Eduardo, 1951, My 5,17:4
Bradley, Edward C, 1959, D 17,37:5
Bradley, Edward E, 1938, S 21,25:1
Bradley, Edward J, 1938, Ap 10,II,7:1; 1941, My 4, 53:3
Bradley, Edward M, 1950, F 16,23:2
Bradley, Edward P, 1942, Jl 20,13:3
Bradley, Edward R, 1946, Ag 16,21:1
Bradley, Edwin J, 1948, Mr 3,23:5
Bradley, Ernst, 1947, N 13,27:2
Bradley, Erving E, 1947, Ag 20,21:6
Bradley, Floyd, 1949, Ap 21,26:3
Bradley, Follett, 1952, Ag 5,19:3
Bradley, Frances S, 1949, F 12,17:2
Bradley, Francis H, 1924, S 20,15:6
Bradley, Frank, 1947, My 31,13:2
Bradley, Frank J, 1950, F 25,17:3
Bradley, Franklin N, 1949, Ja 4,40:2
Bradley, Fred, 1947, My 25,60:7
Bradley, Fred B, 1947, F 2,57:5
Bradley, Fred J, 1939, Mr 2,21:2
Bradley, Frederick T, 1940, F 3,13:1
Bradley, Gamble, 1938, Ja 22,18:2
Bradley, George, 1942, Je 10,21:6
Bradley, George A, 1953, D 20,76:3
Bradley, George B, 1916, Ja 10,11:2
Bradley, George F, 1952, Mr 6,31:1
Bradley, George G Mrs, 1954, S 14,27:2
Bradley, George H, 1938, F 6,II,9:2
Bradley, George P, 1914, Je 15,9:6
Bradley, George Rev, 1871, Ap 17,8:2
Bradley, George V, 1968, Jl 31,27:1
Bradley, Harold C Mrs, 1952, Ja 28,17:1
Bradley, Harold J, 1949, Je 15,29:4
Bradley, Harold S, 1952, D 11,33:3
Bradley, Harry, 1938, Mr 24,23:4
Bradley, Harry B, 1956, Je 19,29:2
Bradley, Harry L, 1965, Jl 24,21:3
Bradley, Henry, 1923, My 24,19:5
Bradley, Henry M Jr, 1939, N 29,23:3
Bradley, Henry N, 1950, Ag 11,19:5
Bradley, Henry T, 1955, Ja 11,25:3
Bradley, Herbert W, 1949, S 20,29:2
Bradley, Horace, 1946, Jl 10,23:3
Bradley, Howard A, 1950, My 25,29:4
Bradley, Howard M, 1953, F 24,25:1
Bradley, Hugh, 1964, Ap 18,29:4
Bradley, Hugh F, 1949, Ja 28,21:2
Bradley, Hugh G W Mrs, 1956, D 7,27:4
Bradley, Irwin C, 1949, Je 23,27:3
Bradley, Isaac V Jr Mrs, 1940, Jl 13,14:7
Bradley, J P Justice, 1892, Ja 23,3:1
Bradley, Jack, 1960, S 2,23:2
Bradley, James, 1925, Ag 21,13:6
Bradley, James A (funl, Je 8,17:5), 1921, Je 7,17:3
Bradley, James A Mrs, 1915, F 15,7:5
Bradley, James B, 1940, Jl 5,13:6
Bradley, James E, 1948, Ja 9,21:4
Bradley, James J, 1943, S 4,13:6
Bradley, James L, 1957, Ag 1,25:1

Bradley, James P, 1958, Jl 23,27:4
Bradley, James P Mrs, 1955, Mr 30,29:3
Bradley, James S, 1955, Je 17,23:2
Bradley, Jane Anne Mrs, 1907, O 23,11:6
Bradley, Jean, 1955, Ag 12,19:4
Bradley, Jerome, 1951, Ja 15,17:3
Bradley, John, 1937, Ja 20,21:3; 1943, Ag 18,19:4; 1952, Jl 11,17:3
Bradley, John A, 1967, Ap 28,41:3
Bradley, John E, 1938, Ap 5,21:2; 1966, Ag 25,37:4
Bradley, John E Dr, 1912, O 9,13:6
Bradley, John H, 1920, Ja 19,9:2; 1962, Ag 24,25:4
Bradley, John J, 1948, My 23,68:5
Bradley, John J Mrs, 1949, S 23,24:2; 1956, Mr 3,19:1
Bradley, John M, 1951, O 28,84:4
Bradley, John R, 1953, Ap 28,27:5
Bradley, John W, 1946, F 3,40:2
Bradley, Joseph, 1948, O 6,29:4
Bradley, Joseph F, 1939, My 15,6:6
Bradley, Joseph H Rev, 1919, Ag 20,15:2
Bradley, Joseph S, 1961, Ja 18,30:4
Bradley, Judson S, 1962, S 12,39:1
Bradley, Justin B, 1941, Mr 29,15:4
Bradley, L L P Brig-Gen, 1910, Mr 15,7:4
Bradley, Lawrence, 1924, N 22,15:5
Bradley, Lillian E Mrs, 1961, My 31,33:4
Bradley, Linn, 1956, N 1,39:2
Bradley, Luke C, 1944, My 13,19:4
Bradley, Lydia K Mrs, 1908, Ja 17,9:6
Bradley, Lynde, 1942, F 10,19:4
Bradley, Manlon O Mrs, 1943, Ap 2,21:1
Bradley, Manson J, 1946, F 9,13:5
Bradley, Mary S Mrs, 1940, S 26,23:5
Bradley, Michael J, 1960, F 28,83:1
Bradley, Moses Mrs, 1949, Ja 18,24:2
Bradley, Newell C, 1957, Mr 6,31:2
Bradley, Oliver, 1950, Ag 31,25:4
Bradley, Omar N Mrs, 1965, D 2,41:2
Bradley, Oscar, 1948, S 1,24:2
Bradley, Otis T, 1950, N 23,35:5
Bradley, Patrick J, 1946, D 29,35:3
Bradley, Paul T, 1950, Ag 2,25:3
Bradley, Phil R, 1949, Ja 1,13:4
Bradley, Preston Mrs, 1950, My 28,44:3
Bradley, Richard M, 1943, F 12,19:3
Bradley, Robert B, 1953, Je 3,31:5
Bradley, Robert M, 1944, F 15,17:5
Bradley, Robert S, 1908, Jl 28,5:4; 1945, S 8,15:4; 1946, D 2,25:4
Bradley, Ruth (Mrs F D Jones), 1963, Ag 8,27:5
Bradley, Samuel S, 1947, Ap 10,25:1; 1966, Jl 16,25:2
Bradley, Samuel S Mrs, 1958, Ag 17,86:3
Bradley, Sarah, 1922, S 26,17:5
Bradley, Sarah Mrs, 1944, My 12,19:2
Bradley, Sheldon B Mrs, 1951, O 19,27:3
Bradley, Stephen R, 1941, F 21,19:3
Bradley, Stuart R, 1951, Mr 28,29:5
Bradley, Thomas A, 1950, F 17,24:2
Bradley, Thomas A Mrs, 1903, S 21,7:6; 1962, F 13, 35:4
Bradley, Thomas C, 1946, D 12,29:3; 1948, N 14,76:8
Bradley, Thomas Dr, 1866, Ag 29,3:1
Bradley, Thomas E D, 1943, S 2,19:6
Bradley, Thomas F, 1950, O 13,29:2
Bradley, Thomas H, 1968, My 11,35:1
Bradley, Thomas W, 1920, My 31,11:4
Bradley, Tom, 1961, Ja 5,31:1
Bradley, Victor J, 1923, S 17,15:3
Bradley, W H, 1903, Ja 8,1:3
Bradley, Walter, 1943, Jl 24,13:4; 1958, S 28,88:8
Bradley, Walter H, 1945, Je 19,19:5
Bradley, Walter H Mrs, 1940, Je 7,23:5
Bradley, Walter P, 1947, S 15,17:5
Bradley, Walter P Mrs, 1957, Ag 31,15:3
Bradley, William, 1921, Jl 21,15:5; 1924, F 22,15:4; 1954, Mr 13,15:6; 1955, My 9,23:3
Bradley, William A, 1939, Ja 11,19:5; 1947, My 25, 60:3
Bradley, William A Mrs, 1943, Ag 26,17:5
Bradley, William B, 1940, Jl 11,19:3
Bradley, William C, 1947, Jl 27,45:1; 1949, My 6,25:2
Bradley, William H, 1922, Ja 19,17:6; 1948, My 24, 19:2; 1949, Ag 5,19:4; 1953, My 11,27:5
Bradley, William H Mrs, 1916, S 30,11:4; 1955, F 24, 27:2
Bradley, William J, 1916, O 14,11:2
Bradley, William N, 1957, Ap 11,31:1; 1962, Ap 19, 31:2
Bradley, William O'Connell, 1914, My 24,IV,7:5
Bradley, William T, 1949, O 14,27:1
Bradley, William V (Bill), 1955, N 25,55:5
Bradley, Willis W, 1954, Ag 29,89:3
Bradly, Thomas S, 1940, N 19,23:3
Bradna, Ella, 1957, N 13,32:2
Bradna, Fred, 1955, F 22,21:2
Bradner, Curtis C, 1940, Ag 8,19:3
Bradner, Frank E, 1937, Je 8,25:2
Bradner, Frank W, 1952, My 6,29:2
Bradner, Fred, 1945, Jl 17,13:8
Bradner, Morris R, 1963, D 8,86:3
Bradner, R Maxwell, 1948, N 16,29:3
Bradner, Robert D, 1954, Mr 25,29:4
Bradner, William H G, 1950, Jl 30,60:2
Bradney, James O, 1948, Jl 15,23:5
Bradney, Joseph J, 1955, Mr 6,88:2
Bradsby, Frank W, 1937, My 12,23:4
Bradshaw, Albert M Capt, 1915, S 4,7:5
Bradshaw, Archibald H Rev, 1923, Je 10,6:2
Bradshaw, Arthur W Mrs, 1940, F 23,15:3
Bradshaw, C Kevin, 1965, Je 19,29:3
Bradshaw, Charles H, 1912, Je 3,9:5
Bradshaw, Chester A, 1953, Je 1,23:5
Bradshaw, Claude Mrs, 1937, O 20,23:4
Bradshaw, De Emmett, 1960, Ap 13,39:2
Bradshaw, Edward D, 1941, D 23,22:2
Bradshaw, Ernest C, 1955, S 18,87:2
Bradshaw, Francis E Mrs, 1946, S 28,17:4
Bradshaw, Frederick H Mrs, 1959, Ja 2,25:1
Bradshaw, George B, 1958, D 9,41:1
Bradshaw, George F Maj, 1925, O 5,21:4
Bradshaw, Hamilton, 1945, S 8,15:5
Bradshaw, Henrietta M, 1938, F 6,II,9:2
Bradshaw, Jack, 1948, Ap 15,25:5
Bradshaw, James A, 1950, F 19,79:3
Bradshaw, Jeanette D Mrs, 1941, My 27,23:4
Bradshaw, John H, 1941, Jl 6,27:2
Bradshaw, John J, 1951, O 16,31:3
Bradshaw, John L Mrs, 1949, Ja 15,17:2
Bradshaw, Joseph L, 1950, Mr 12,93:1
Bradshaw, Joseph P, 1937, D 21,23:1
Bradshaw, Laura Hale, 1924, F 28,19:6
Bradshaw, Leslie H, 1950, D 29,19:2
Bradshaw, Louis C, 1952, Je 27,23:4
Bradshaw, Mary F, 1945, F 10,11:5
Bradshaw, Olive, 1917, Jl 7,9:5
Bradshaw, Percy H, 1946, S 21,15:2
Bradshaw, Richmond Mrs, 1966, O 19,47:4
Bradshaw, Robert C, 1953, O 6,29:4
Bradshaw, Thomas, 1939, N 11,15:6
Bradshaw, Walter, 1957, O 1,33:1
Bradshaw, William H, 1940, Ja 27,13:2
Bradshaw, William K, 1953, N 2,25:5
Bradshaw, William L, 1964, S 21,31:5
Bradshaw, William M, 1948, My 2,77:2
Bradshaw, William R, 1952, Ap 27,90:6
Bradsher, A B, 1951, Ja 30,25:2
Bradsher, Earl V, 1954, N 16,29:6
Bradspies, Joseph, 1955, Ap 25,23:5
Bradstreet, A G, 1883, Je 18,5:6
Bradstreet, Andrew J, 1939, Jl 27,19:3
Bradstreet, E P, 1931, F 15,30:1
Bradstreet, Howard, 1937, Ap 18,II,9:2
Bradstreet, Samuel W, 1946, F 2,13:4
Bradt, Elbert F, 1953, My 6,31:4
Bradt, Frederick W, 1967, Mr 25,23:3
Bradt, Gay, 1916, F 14,13:4
Bradt, George M, 1919, D 2,13:2
Bradt, George M Mrs, 1911, My 6,13:6
Bradt, Harlan H, 1953, Ap 22,29:4
Bradt, Helmut L, 1950, My 26,23:4
Bradt, Kate K Mrs, 1938, My 26,25:3
Bradt, Morris Mrs, 1912, Ap 4,13:4
Bradt, Roy, 1956, Je 26,29:5
Bradt, Walter J, 1917, O 3,13:5
Bradt, Warren L, 1939, Mr 5,49:2
Bradt, William C, 1947, O 17,21:3
Bradt, William D, 1943, S 29,21:2
Bradway, Irving E, 1944, Ag 6,37:3
Bradway, Joseph S, 1913, Jl 8,7:6
Bradwell, James B, 1943, Ap 10,17:2
Bradwell, James B Judge, 1907, N 30,7:4
Bradwell, S D, 1903, My 16,9:6
Bradwin, Edmund W, 1954, F 21,68:3
Brady, A, 1883, Ja 23,5:2
Brady, Abner S Mrs, 1915, D 17,11:4
Brady, Alexander, 1879, Jl 29,2:2
Brady, Alfred F, 1961, Mr 11,21:6
Brady, Alfred S Jr Mrs, 1955, Ja 29,15:2
Brady, Alice, 1939, O 30,17:1; 1949, My 3,25:1
Brady, Ambrose C, 1954, Ja 31,88:8
Brady, Ambrose Mrs, 1953, D 13,86:6
Brady, Andrew J, 1949, Jl 6,27:3
Brady, Andrew J Jr, 1958, Ja 28,27:1
Brady, Anthony N, 1913, Jl 24,7:1
Brady, Anthony N Mrs, 1921, My 1,22:3
Brady, Anthony R, 1947, S 1,19:3
Brady, Arthur A, 1951, Mr 31,15:1
Brady, Arthur C, 1944, Ap 29,15:2
Brady, Arthur O, 1947, F 15,15:1
Brady, Augustine M Rev, 1909, O 10,13:6
Brady, Bernard A Rev, 1906, Ja 31,11:6
Brady, Bernard A Sr, 1959, F 13,17:1
Brady, Bernard F Rev, 1921, Mr 28,11:6
Brady, Bernard J, 1953, Jl 19,56:3
Brady, Bruce B, 1939, Jl 13,19:3
Brady, Catherine A, 1945, Je 17,26:1
Brady, Charles (Bro Bertin John), 1957, Jl 4,19:4
Brady, Charles A Mrs, 1951, Ja 12,27:3
Brady, Charles D, 1946, S 8,44:2
Brady, Charles H, 1968, Ap 25,47:4
Brady, Charles N, 1938, Jl 7,19:2; 1950, Jl 6,27:5
Brady, Charles R, 1950, D 25,19:2
Brady, Charlotte, 1942, O 6,24:2
Brady, Clarence H, 1943, F 28,49:1
Brady, Cyrus Townsend Dr, 1920, Ja 25,22:1
Brady, Daniel J, 1956, My 3,31:1
Brady, Daniel M Mrs, 1945, Je 11,15:2
Brady, E W CApt, 1903, My 4,7:6
Brady, Edmund Mrs, 1955, Mr 1,25:3
Brady, Edward, 1939, Jl 2,14:2; 1940, O 5,15:5
Brady, Edward A, 1951, Ja 14,84:3
Brady, Edward J Sr, 1957, Ja 9,31:2
Brady, Edwin S, 1949, My 13,23:5
Brady, Ellen F Mrs, 1943, Ja 5,20:2
Brady, Eugene J, 1961, D 26,25:3
Brady, F L Dr, 1902, D 26,7:6
Brady, Francis, 1937, Ap 9,21:2; 1940, My 29,23:5; 1944, Mr 31,21:4
Brady, Francis A, 1944, My 23,23:5
Brady, Francis C, 1951, Jl 2,23:4
Brady, Francis I, 1955, Mr 31,27:5
Brady, Francis X Rev, 1911, Mr 14,11:4
Brady, Frank, 1957, S 3,27:1
Brady, Frank A, 1940, Je 9,44:4
Brady, Frank F, 1914, Ag 2,15:6
Brady, Frank J, 1940, F 6,21:4; 1946, S 28,17:6
Brady, George A Mrs, 1955, Ja 14,21:1
Brady, George C, 1941, Je 18,21:2
Brady, George F, 1950, Ja 16,25:5; 1951, Ja 12,27:4
Brady, George W, 1955, Je 26,77:1
Brady, Gerald H, 1968, O 18,53:6
Brady, Gerald H Mrs, 1958, F 12,29:5
Brady, Harold J, 1946, Ap 10,27:2; 1949, Jl 25,15:2
Brady, Harry B, 1940, Mr 7,23:3
Brady, Harry J, 1946, Je 15,21:3
Brady, Henry, 1954, Jl 9,17:4
Brady, Henry S Jr, 1941, N 11,24:2
Brady, Henry 2d, 1960, Ja 19,36:1
Brady, Hugh, 1951, Ja 7,76:3
Brady, Hugh D Mrs, 1954, My 12,31:2
Brady, Irish Bobby (R J Kroemmelbein), 1967, My 2,47:2
Brady, Irving L, 1953, Je 10,29:4
Brady, Irving L Mrs, 1950, Mr 15,29:4
Brady, J C, 1927, N 11,23:3
Brady, J H, 1885, F 16,2:5
Brady, J R Judge, 1891, Mr 17,8:1
Brady, Jack, 1949, N 17,29:4
Brady, James, 1938, Ag 28,33:3; 1941, F 22,15:2; 1941, O 6,17:2; 1950, N 13,45:8
Brady, James A, 1949, N 4,23:4; 1959, Ag 21,21:3
Brady, James A Mrs, 1947, N 24,23:4
Brady, James Boyd Rev, 1912, Jl 23,9:5
Brady, James Buchanan (Diamond Jim), 1917, Ap 14,13:1
Brady, James C, 1941, D 7,77:1
Brady, James Cox Mrs, 1918, D 27,11:6
Brady, James F Sr Mrs, 1959, Ja 25,94:1
Brady, James H Mrs, 1945, N 21,21:4
Brady, James H Sen (funl, Ja 17,13:4), 1918, Ja 14, 11:4
Brady, James I, 1949, O 16,90:2
Brady, James J, 1944, Ja 11,19:4; 1945, Ja 3,17:2; 1959, F 18,33:1
Brady, James L, 1949, Mr 18,25:1; 1951, My 16,35:5
Brady, James M Mrs, 1942, Mr 27,23:6
Brady, James P, 1938, Jl 21,21:4
Brady, James R, 1950, F 18,15:6
Brady, James T (funl, F 12,10:3), 1869, F 10,5:1
Brady, James T, 1939, Je 10,17:6; 1941, Ja 15,23:4
Brady, James W, 1903, Jl 9,3:2; 1947, Ag 23,13:3
Brady, John, 1949, My 24,27:4
Brady, John A, 1949, Je 24,10:3
Brady, John A Mrs, 1961, Ja 23,23:3
Brady, John B, 1959, N 11,35:4
Brady, John C, 1955, N 16,35:2
Brady, John E, 1947, O 28,25:1; 1954, D 30,17:4
Brady, John E Mrs, 1952, F 20,29:2
Brady, John F, 1938, Ap 2,15:2; 1940, D 29,25:1
Brady, John F (will, Ja 29,13:5), 1941, Ja 1,23:6
Brady, John F, 1944, Je 2,15:2; 1958, S 9,35:4
Brady, John F Mrs, 1953, Ap 10,21:2
Brady, John G, 1943, Ap 8,23:6
Brady, John G Mrs, 1951, F 7,29:2
Brady, John J, 1943, My 11,21:4; 1948, My 18,23:3; 1950, Ja 10,29:4; 1950, Ag 17,27:1; 1951, F 21,27:2; 1962, N 21,33:2
Brady, John J Justice (funl, Ja 9,17:5), 1916, Ja 8,9:4
Brady, John R, 1921, D 15,19:4; 1946, Ap 9,27:5; 1967, F 3,31:2
Brady, John R Mrs, 1912, S 10,11:4
Brady, John Rev, 1910, Ja 7,9:4
Brady, John T, 1907, Ag 7,7:6; 1948, Ja 23,23:4
Brady, John T Mrs, 1948, D 30,19:3
Brady, Joseph A, 1939, Ag 27,35:2; 1939, D 21,23:3; 1958, Ap 26,19:2
Brady, Joseph B, 1966, F 17,33:3
Brady, Joseph E, 1955, Jl 18,21:2
Brady, Joseph F, 1943, Ap 13,25:2
Brady, Joseph H, 1961, Jl 4,19:3
Brady, Joseph P, 1945, Mr 6,22:2
Brady, Joseph W, 1961, Jl 31,19:6
Brady, L Rev, 1912, D 30,7:4
Brady, Lawrence P, 1957, N 16,19:2
Brady, Louis S, 1958, Jl 26,15:5
Brady, Lynn E, 1939, N 25,17:5
Brady, Margaret L, 1943, Ag 16,15:6
Brady, Marguerite W Mrs, 1937, Ag 29,II,7:1
Brady, Mary Mrs, 1922, F 27,13:6

Brady, Matthew A, 1941, N 1,15:4
Brady, Matthew F, 1959, S 22,35:3
Brady, Matthew P, 1955, F 27,86:2
Brady, Maurice Mrs, 1951, Ag 29,27:8
Brady, Michael E, 1941, My 13,23:5
Brady, Michael J Mrs, 1951, Jl 2,23:4
Brady, Mifflin B, 1940, D 10,25:4
Brady, N F, 1930, Mr 28,18:2
Brady, Neal J, 1947, Je 19,21:4
Brady, Nicholas R, 1940, S 11,26:3
Brady, Owen P, 1948, Mr 15,23:2
Brady, Patrick, 1941, Jl 25,15:2
Brady, Patrick Mrs, 1957, D 7,21:2
Brady, Patrick Rev, 1911, Mr 19,II,11:2
Brady, Peter, 1947, N 1,15:4
Brady, Peter P, 1938, O 18,25:2
Brady, Ralph R, 1950, D 12,33:4
Brady, Richard F, 1954, Mr 16,29:5
Brady, Richard V, 1968, Mr 29,45:2
Brady, Robert A, 1963, Ap 28,88:1
Brady, Robert A Mrs (Mildred E), 1965, Jl 29,27:1
Brady, Robert C, 1949, My 9,25:4
Brady, Robert T, 1944, S 18,19:5
Brady, Rose, 1940, N 4,19:2
Brady, Sarah Mrs, 1951, N 9,27:2
Brady, Simeon Jr, 1954, Mr 28,88:4
Brady, Simeon Sr Mrs, 1954, Mr 9,27:2
Brady, Stanley, 1949, N 23,29:3
Brady, Stephen J, 1874, Mr 11,8:1
Brady, Susan M, 1939, Jl 4,13:4
Brady, Terence A, 1956, Je 28,29:4
Brady, Terence A Mrs, 1958, My 26,29:3
Brady, Thomas A, 1941, Je 24,19:1
Brady, Thomas C, 1941, Je 13,19:3; 1963, My 5,87:1
Brady, Thomas F, 1952, Je 14,15:6
Brady, Thomas J, 1924, S 7,31:3; 1948, Ag 17,22:2; 1955, N 12,19:3
Brady, Thomas J Gen, 1904, Ap 24,7:6
Brady, Thomas J Mrs, 1964, Ap 28,37:2
Brady, Thomas L, 1940, Mr 22,19:5
Brady, Thomas S, 1957, Jl 7,60:7
Brady, Thomas V, 1963, Jl 1,29:1
Brady, Tom W, 1946, Mr 7,25:4
Brady, W Malcolm, 1950, Jl 8,13:4
Brady, W U, 1870, Ap 1,5:1
Brady, William A, 1945, Jl 16,11:7; 1950, Ja 8,76:1
Brady, William A Mrs (G George), 1961, My 20,23:5
Brady, William E Mrs, 1961, Mr 18,23:3
Brady, William G Jr, 1966, O 10,41:3
Brady, William H, 1961, Ja 21,21:3; 1964, Ag 5,33:2
Brady, William O (rites, O 5,37:5), 1961, O 2,31:4
Brady, William P, 1965, Ag 26,33:5
Brady, William S, 1957, F 2,19:3
Brady, William T Rev, 1937, My 14,23:4
Braegger, Victor, 1966, Ja 2,72:3
Braekeleer, George de Mrs, 1912, My 17,13:5
Braelow, Harry A, 1944, D 20,23:3
Braelow, Joseph C, 1957, Ag 13,27:4
Braen, Abram, 1956, Ag 3,19:5
Braender, Harry, 1957, Ap 20,17:6
Braendle, Edward E, 1954, O 19,27:5
Braff, Bernard, 1941, Ja 9,21:3
Braff, Joseph P, 1951, Ap 30,22:2
Braga, Bernardo, 1960, D 24,15:4
Braga, Theophil Dr, 1924, Ja 29,19:3
Bragan, George W, 1961, Jl 28,21:2
Bragantini, Boniface Rev Father, 1916, F 21,11:6
Braganza, Miguel de Prince, 1923, F 22,15:3
Bragaw, Allen C Mrs, 1944, Ag 9,17:4
Bragaw, Emma H Mrs, 1948, Ag 21,16:3
Bragaw, Henry S, 1940, Ag 29,19:6
Bragaw, Janet Mrs, 1925, D 23,19:4
Bragaw, Marjorie P Mrs, 1942, S 17,25:2
Bragaw, Richard, 1942, O 8,27:5
Bragdon, Anne E, 1949, My 30,13:6
Bragdon, Charles R, 1964, N 19,39:5
Bragdon, Claude F, 1946, S 18,31:5
Bragdon, Clifford S, 1956, Ja 20,23:2
Bragdon, Edmund V, 1939, N 4,15:4
Bragdon, Edward Mrs, 1948, F 25,23:1
Bragdon, George Chandler, 1910, Ag 8,7:5
Bragdon, George H, 1951, My 13,88:3
Bragdon, John S, 1964, Ja 8,37:2
Bragdon, Millicent Mrs, 1924, Ap 17,19:4
Bragdon, Walter L, 1948, My 24,20:2
Brager, Harry E, 1966, Ag 6,23:5
Brager, Louis, 1958, Ag 4,21:3
Bragers, Achille P, 1955, My 30,13:4
Bragg, Braxton Mrs, 1908, S 26,7:6
Bragg, Braxton T, 1876, S 28,7:3
Bragg, Caleb S, 1943, O 26,23:1
Bragg, Charles E, 1953, O 11,89:2
Bragg, Charlotte A, 1957, S 2,13:5
Bragg, Cyrus, 1943, N 11,23:6
Bragg, E S Mrs, 1914, Ap 12,15:4
Bragg, Edward S Gen, 1912, Je 21,13:5
Bragg, Harry G, 1964, My 2,27:2; 1968, D 12,43:6
Bragg, Henry E, 1951, Ja 2,23:1
Bragg, Homer, 1951, D 14,32:6
Bragg, J B Sr, 1947, N 27,31:1
Bragg, James E, 1957, O 18,23:3
Bragg, Ralph O, 1952, N 13,31:5
Bragg, Thomas E Mrs, 1961, S 8,31:2
Bragg, Thomas J, 1946, S 30,25:4
Bragg, William H (por), 1942, Mr 13,19:1
Bragger, Joseph E, 1954, My 15,15:1
Braginskaya-Fishson, Anna Mrs, 1951, My 5,17:6
Bragle, Francis K, 1960, Mr 16,37:4
Braglia, Alberto, 1954, F 6,19:4
Bragno, Francesco, 1952, Ap 26,23:3
Brague, L Harry Jr, 1968, Mr 23,31:1
Braham, Aaron D, 1959, O 16,31:2
Braham, Alex E, 1951, N 12,15:1
Braham, David, 1905, Ap 13,11:5
Braham, David Jr, 1915, Jl 1,11:5
Braham, David Mrs, 1920, O 9,15:4
Braham, George, 1952, Jl 21,19:2
Braham, Harry A, 1938, Ja 16,II,9:1
Braham, Herbert J, 1950, Ap 17,23:5
Braham, Herbert J Jr, 1948, Jl 9,19:1
Braham, Horace, 1955, S 8,31:3
Braham, John Joseph, 1919, O 29,13:5
Braham, Lionel, 1947, O 9,25:1
Braham, Melbourne A H, 1939, D 3,61:2
Braham, William, 1941, My 3,15:5
Brahdy, Alfred, 1950, D 28,26:2; 1951, Ja 1,17:4
Brahdy, Max B, 1964, Jl 17,27:1
Brahe, Karl, 1951, D 17,31:3
Brahe, Lewis, 1873, My 19,5:5
Brahe, May, 1956, Ag 17,19:3
Braheney, Bernard F, 1954, Ja 4,19:2
Brahinsky, Mani L, 1953, O 5,27:4
Brahm, Ferdinand J, 1949, Mr 25,24:2
Brahm, Joseph, 1914, Ag 18,9:4
Brahm, Lawrence, 1959, Jl 18,15:6
Brahmachari, Rishi S, 1966, D 1,15:1
Brahms, Benjamin I, 1943, S 8,23:6
Brahms, J, 1897, Ap 4,16:4
Brahn, Charles R Mrs, 1937, My 15,19:1
Brahney, John C, 1944, Ja 28,17:4
Braid, James, 1950, N 28,31:1
Braidwood, Andrew H, 1943, Ap 3,15:3
Braidwood, William D, 1957, O 29,31:3
Braidy, Fozi, 1958, My 14,33:3
Brailey, James S, 1916, Ag 3,11:6
Brailove, S Alex, 1960, F 26,27:1
Brailow, Anatole P Mrs, 1942, S 24,27:3
Brailsford, H N, 1958, Mr 24,27:2
Brailsford, Walter R, 1949, Mr 10,27:1
Brain, Dennis, 1957, S 2,10:6
Brain, Francis W T Sir, 1921, S 2,13:2
Brain, George L, 1964, Ap 6,31:3
Brain, Walter R (Lord), 1966, D 30,25:3
Brainard, Alfred H, 1913, O 27,9:4
Brainard, Alson L, 1962, Ja 7,88:8
Brainard, C Brewster, 1956, My 9,33:4
Brainard, C Green Sr, 1944, N 15,27:5
Brainard, Daniel Dr, 1866, O 14,5:4
Brainard, David L, 1946, Mr 23,13:3
Brainard, Dudley, 1960, Ja 7,58:6
Brainard, Dudley Mrs, 1960, Ja 7,58:6
Brainard, Edward W, 1943, F 23,21:3
Brainard, Elliot R, 1937, My 24,19:3
Brainard, Estelle M, 1943, D 31,16:5
Brainard, Eugene F, 1950, S 7,31:4
Brainard, Frank S, 1958, Mr 6,27:1
Brainard, Harry P, 1940, Ag 4,33:4
Brainard, J Edwin, 1942, S 9,23:3
Brainard, James E, 1910, N 2,11:4
Brainard, Jean S Mrs, 1941, N 14,23:3
Brainard, John Rev Dr, 1909, N 26,9:5
Brainard, Lyman B, 1916, O 12,11:5
Brainard, Mabel H Mrs, 1955, Mr 9,27:4
Brainard, Millar, 1953, Je 9,27:3
Brainard, Morgan B, 1957, Ag 29,27:3
Brainard, Morgan B (will), 1959, Ap 12,76:5
Brainard, Morgan B Jr, 1960, My 31,31:1
Brainard, Morgan B Mrs, 1958, N 27,29:4
Brainard, Newton C, 1964, Jl 17,27:1
Brainard, Owen, 1919, Ap 3,11:3
Brainard, Seymour, 1937, Jl 7,23:6
Brainard, William H, 1937, Ag 7,15:3; 1949, Jl 24,53:3
Brainard, William S, 1938, Je 24,19:3
Brainari, R C, 1879, Ja 4,5:3
Braine, Bancroft G, 1958, N 22,21:5
Braine, Clinton E, 1951, Ja 13,15:6
Braine, D L Adm, 1898, Jl 31,1:7
Braine, Son of Commander Braine, 1874, Ja 1,2:6
Braine, Theodore, 1916, D 14,15:5
Brainerd, Arthur L, 1958, Je 19,31:6
Brainerd, Charles W, 1940, O 15,23:3
Brainerd, Dwight, 1941, Ap 22,21:1
Brainerd, E Leroy, 1948, O 12,25:6
Brainerd, Edwin A Mrs, 1955, Mr 3,27:1
Brainerd, Eleanor H Mrs, 1942, Mr 19,21:2
Brainerd, Erastus, 1922, D 26,13:4
Brainerd, Eveline W, 1948, Ag 1,56:2
Brainerd, Ezra Dr, 1924, D 10,23:2
Brainerd, George Cotton, 1912, Ja 11,13:4
Brainerd, George W, 1956, F 16,29:4
Brainerd, Harvey B, 1951, S 7,29:1
Brainerd, Helen C, 1943, S 25,15:1
Brainerd, I H, 1935, My 2,21:1
Brainerd, Lawrence, 1925, Mr 13,19:3
Brainerd, Louis J, 1951, O 5,27:2
Brainerd, Lucy M Mrs, 1939, F 20,17:5
Brainerd, Mary B B Mrs, 1939, Jl 30,29:2
Brainerd, W H H, 1880, D 14,2:4
Brainerd, Warren C, 1961, Ag 7,23:4
Brainerd, William H, 1917, Ap 28,13:5; 1941, My 9, 21:3
Braines, Louis, 1941, Ja 31,19:2
Brainin, Clement S, 1959, Jl 21,29:3
Brainin, Reuben, 1939, D 1,23:3
Brainin, Simon M Dr, 1911, Ap 3,9:5
Brainina, Balbina, 1951, Ja 28,76:3
Braislin, Edward Rev Dr, 1915, Jl 26,9:6
Braislin, John G Mrs, 1945, N 13,21:3
Braislin, William C, 1948, D 4,19:2
Braisted, Abraham A Capt, 1915, D 22,11:4
Braisted, Charles H Mrs, 1945, My 24,19:3
Braisted, Cornell B, 1943, My 9,40:8
Braisted, George W, 1947, S 20,15:4
Braisted, John M Sr, 1956, Ag 12,84:6
Braisted, William C, 1941, Ja 18,15:1
Braisted, William C Capt, 1916, F 6,15:4
Braithwaite, Albert N, 1959, O 21,44:1
Braithwaite, Charles H, 1946, Ap 17,25:3
Braithwaite, John S, 1948, Ag 31,23:3
Braithwaite, Lilian, 1948, S 18,17:5
Braithwaite, Walter P, 1945, S 10,19:4
Braithwaite, William A, 1951, F 1,25:5
Braithwaite, William S B, 1962, Je 9,25:4
Braitmayer, Otto E, 1940, Mr 1,21:4
Braitsch, William J, 1951, Jl 20,21:2
Brake, Howard, 1964, Ag 6,29:2
Brakeley, George A, 1961, Je 15,43:1
Brakeley, Joseph E, 1937, My 7,25:2
Braker, Conrad M, 1938, F 19,15:2
Braker, Henry J, 1908, S 2,7:6
Braley, Anna E, 1959, Mr 7,21:6
Braley, Berton, 1966, Ja 27,33:1
Braley, H K, 1929, Ja 18,23:3
Braley, Silas A, 1966, O 12,43:5
Brall, Ira, 1966, Ja 3,27:2
Brall, Joshua Mrs, 1957, Jl 12,21:1
Brallia, Floyd B, 1951, S 6,31:5
Brallier, Paul S, 1961, Mr 30,29:2
Braloff, Henry E, 1945, D 24,16:2
Braloff, Herman M, 1953, Ap 26,86:3
Bralove, Harry M, 1961, Mr 25,25:6
Bralovic, Stojan, 1968, N 19,40:6
Bram, Israel, 1955, S 9,23:3
Bram-Soroko, Louis Mrs, 1954, Ja 13,31:4
Bramah, Ernest (E B Smith), 1942, Je 28,32:5
Braman, Chester A, 1964, Ja 14,31:5
Braman, Chester A Mrs, 1947, Ap 18,21:3
Braman, Grenville D Mrs, 1959, N 7,23:5
Braman, Harold A, 1949, Ag 26,19:5
Braman, Henry T, 1937, Mr 25,25:1
Braman, James L, 1957, My 15,35:4
Braman, Joseph Balch Mrs, 1924, N 12,23:2
Braman, William A, 1905, Ap 14,9:6
Braman, Winifred W Prof, 1937, Mr 25,25:6
Brame, Ervin, 1949, N 24,32:4
Brame, J L J, 1878, F 2,2:4
Bramer, John P, 1964, N 8,88:8
Bramer, Samuel E, 1949, Mr 25,24:2
Bramfeld, William H, 1958, O 29,35:4
Bramhall, Frank J Col, 1907, N 27,7:6
Bramhall, George, 1957, Mr 6,31:3
Bramhall, George W, 1925, Ja 28,17:3
Bramhall, H Keasbey, 1968, N 7,47:3
Bramhall, Jacques, 1943, Jl 1,19:6
Bramhall, Jacques Mrs, 1946, N 28,27:1
Bramhall, Walter M Col, 1913, S 30,13:4
Bramham, William G, 1947, Jl 9,23:1
Bramkamp, Richard A, 1958, S 3,33:2
Bramlee, John B Col, 1872, F 12,1:3
Bramlette, Thomas E ex-Gov, 1875, Ja 13,5:6
Bramley, Frank, 1915, Ag 12,9:6
Bramley, Frederic, 1925, O 11,5:1
Bramley, Herbert W, 1945, Ap 16,23:5
Bramley, Matthew F, 1941, My 31,11:5
Bramley, Sylvanus W, 1953, N 19,31:4
Bramley, William H, 1950, Ag 15,30:3
Bramman, Catherine A, 1952, Ap 22,29:3
Brammer, Frederick H, 1949, Ja 21,21:1
Brammer, George L, 1947, F 17,19:4
Bramnick, David, 1959, Ag 10,27:4
Bramnick, David Mrs, 1962, N 21,33:4
Bramnick, Jacob Mrs, 1959, F 2,25:4
Brampton, Jean, 1955, Je 30,25:4
Brampton, Lord (Hy Hawkins), 1907, O 7,9:5
Brams, Daniel M, 1964, D 28,29:2
Bramson, Leon, 1941, Mr 4,23:6
Bramson, Leon Mrs, 1952, S 4,27:2
Bramson, Sam (funl, Ap 7,25:2), 1962, Ap 5,33:2
Bramstedt, William F Mrs, 1949, My 13,23:2
Bramuglia, Juan A, 1962, S 5,39:1
Bramwell, Cora M Mrs, 1938, Ja 29,15:3
Bramwell, George M, 1943, O 27,23:6
Bramwell, William M, 1962, Ag 6,25:2
Bramwell Jos, 1905, F 7,9:5
Bran, Florian A Mrs, 1949, O 30,84:4
Brana, Trinidad Mrs, 1944, Mr 7,19:4
Branagan, Frank, 1949, Mr 10,27:3
Branca, John, 1956, Mr 13,27:5; 1964, Mr 14,23:5
Brancaccio, Elizabeth Princess, 1909, Ap 12,7:5

Brancati, Vitaliano, 1954, S 26,87:3
Brancato, Dominick R, 1958, Je 17,29:2
Brancato, Madeline Mrs, 1942, S 14,15:3
Branch, Anna H, 1937, S 9,23:5
Branch, Blythe W, 1942, My 23,13:4
Branch, Dennis, 1964, Ja 10,43:1
Branch, Edward R, 1949, O 20,29:1
Branch, G Irving, 1961, Ag 10,27:1
Branch, Gerald E K, 1954, Ap 16,21:2
Branch, Harllee Sr, 1967, Mr 16,47:3
Branch, Harold W, 1950, D 5,32:4
Branch, Harry, 1953, Je 19,21:2
Branch, Henry 2d, 1945, D 2,46:3
Branch, Irving L, 1966, Ja 4,5:2
Branch, John K Mrs, 1952, N 2,88:3
Branch, John Patterson, 1915, F 3,11:7
Branch, Lenora, 1960, My 29,56:3
Branch, Leslie W, 1940, F 20,21:2
Branch, Louise, 1959, D 14,31:4
Branch, Mary E, 1944, Jl 9,36:1
Branch, Matthew D, 1961, Jl 11,31:4
Branch, Randolph W, 1955, Ap 8,21:2
Branch, W, 1865, Ja 23,8:5
Branch, William E, 1964, F 29,21:1
Branchard, Catherine R Mme, 1937, Ja 10,II,10:1
Branchard, Emile (por), 1938, F 16,21:3
Branchaud, Henry H, 1942, Ja 27,21:2
Brancusi, Constantin, 1957, Mr 16,19:4
Brand, Aaron, 1958, My 21,33:1
Brand, Abraham, 1955, Mr 28,27:4
Brand, Albert, 1954, D 7,33:5
Brand, Albert R, 1940, Mr 29,21:1
Brand, Alex, 1956, Ja 25,31:2
Brand, Allan D Sr, 1947, F 15,15:4
Brand, C H, 1933, My 18,19:3
Brand, Caesar, 1941, N 26,23:4
Brand, Carl W, 1942, S 6,30:8
Brand, Charles, 1954, Jl 13,23:5; 1966, My 25,47:1
Brand, Charles Com, 1872, My 31,1:7
Brand, Charles J (por), 1949, Je 30,23:3
Brand, Clarence, 1940, Ja 20,15:1
Brand, E Thomas, 1946, D 24,18:2
Brand, Edwin W, 1959, Je 29,29:2
Brand, Enoch J, 1948, O 5,25:5
Brand, Erwin, 1953, Jl 14,27:3
Brand, Fred Sr, 1943, My 15,15:4
Brand, Frederick, 1949, Ja 2,60:5
Brand, George A, 1940, Mr 7,23:4
Brand, Gustav A, 1944, My 29,15:4
Brand, H Russell, 1950, Ja 6,21:5
Brand, Harry, 1958, Ap 17,31:3
Brand, Henry Robert, 1906, N 23,9:2
Brand, Herbert Mrs, 1967, Jl 27,35:2
Brand, Herman A, 1937, Ja 6,23:1
Brand, Hugo, 1951, F 28,27:2
Brand, Irving, 1948, My 6,26:5
Brand, Isaac F, 1958, N 24,29:1
Brand, James T, 1964, F 29,21:3
Brand, Joel, 1964, Jl 15,35:4
Brand, John W, 1939, F 15,23:4
Brand, Joseph L, 1942, Je 28,33:1
Brand, Louise F Mrs, 1955, F 27,35:2
Brand, Mathilda K Mrs, 1937, My 12,23:5
Brand, Max J, 1942, O 26,15:5
Brand, Morris A Dr, 1968, N 20,47:1
Brand, Norton F, 1947, Ap 11,25:2
Brand, Otto, 1958, Ap 26,19:2
Brand, Philip R, 1947, Jl 4,13:6
Brand, R A Mrs, 1945, D 28,16:2
Brand, Robert H, 1963, Ag 24,19:4
Brand, Robert H Mrs, 1937, Ja 21,23:3
Brand, Sylvester S, 1959, Jl 17,43:3
Brand, Walter W, 1944, O 4,20:3
Brand, William A Sr, 1961, F 4,19:6
Brand, William Francis Rev Dr, 1907, F 19,9:7
Brandaleone, Joseph, 1957, D 10,35:4
Brandao, Artur, 1960, N 30,37:4
Brandao de Melo, Antonio, 1950, F 14,26:4
Brandau, Gustav, 1948, Ag 9,19:2
Brandau, Gustav Mrs, 1943, Ag 24,19:4
Brande, Dorothea, 1948, D 18,19:6
Brandeaux, Palmere, 1965, My 23,85:1
Brandeberry, J Kermit, 1953, Jl 8,27:3
Brandeberry, John B, 1953, S 25,21:4
Brandebury, Carl S, 1942, S 16,23:2
Brandegee, Frank B, 1924, O 18,15:6
Brandeis, Erich, 1954, N 19,23:2
Brandeis, George, 1948, My 17,19:4
Brandeis, Louis D Mrs (will, O 23,19:5), 1945, O 13, 15:3
Brandeis, Madeleine Mrs, 1937, Je 29,21:2
Brandeis, Paul, 1963, Jl 21,64:8
Brandeis, Samuel, 1945, My 22,19:6
Brandeis, Zerlina F Mrs, 1937, D 11,19:4
Brandel Chas F, 1949, Ag 1,17:3
Brandell, Milton, 1951, O 30,29:4
Brandell, William, 1951, Mr 9,25:1
Branden, Paul M, 1942, Ja 5,20:3
Brandenberger, Jacques, 1954, Jl 15,27:3
Brandenburg, Charles H Dr, 1920, Jl 18,22:5
Brandenburg, George A, 1962, F 20,71:2
Brandenburg, Joseph F, 1942, S 15,24:2
Brandenburg, Matthew H, 1968, Jl 8,39:4
Brandenburg, Nora B (Mrs J V Johansen), 1950, Je 2,23:4
Brandenburg, William A, 1940, O 30,23:6
Brandenstein, Lewis F, 1949, F 25,24:3
Brandes, Fred E, 1952, Ap 14,19:3
Brandes, Frederick C, 1962, Ja 3,33:2
Brandes, G, 1927, F 20,II,9:1
Brandes, Herman, 1960, Ja 29,25:1
Brandes, Julius E, 1953, Ap 11,17:3
Brandes, William P, 1953, Ap 10,21:3
Brandin, Nils F, 1946, Ja 26,13:2
Brandin, William H, 1945, Ap 20,19:4
Brandis, Augustus, 1942, O 21,21:4
Brandl, Alois, 1940, F 11,49:2
Brandle, Theodore M, 1949, N 29,29:2; 1949, D 3,15:5
Brandle, Theodore M Mrs, 1948, Ap 2,23:1
Brandler, Charles H, 1941, Je 20,21:3
Brandley, George C, 1939, N 27,17:4
Brandmarker, J Leon, 1957, N 15,27:1
Brandmarker, J Leon Mrs, 1962, F 26,27:3
Brandmarker, Sanford, 1967, Ap 7,37:4
Brandmier, John F, 1941, S 3,23:3
Brandner, Louis F, 1947, D 14,80:6
Brando, Marlon Sr, 1965, Jl 19,27:5
Brando, Marlon Sr Mrs, 1954, Ap 1,31:2
Brandon, Daniel B, 1951, O 21,92:4
Brandon, E M, 1948, Ja 10,15:3
Brandon, Edgar E, 1957, Je 9,88:4
Brandon, Edmund J, 1946, N 2,15:5
Brandon, Harriet E, 1945, Ag 5,38:4
Brandon, J Kell, 1967, My 11,47:4
Brandon, J Kell Mrs, 1959, F 1,85:1
Brandon, James B, 1951, O 11,37:5
Brandon, James G, 1943, My 22,13:2
Brandon, John J, 1941, Ag 28,19:6
Brandon, John R, 1940, D 12,27:6
Brandon, Marie G Mrs, 1942, Ag 22,13:5
Brandon, Melvin C, 1951, S 4,27:3
Brandon, Stuart K, 1960, D 17,23:5
Brandon, W W, 1934, D 8,15:1
Brandon, Washington D, 1953, Jl 2,23:2
Brandon, William R, 1961, Je 13,35:1
Brandow, Aaron G, 1949, S 5,17:4
Brandow, Isabella Mrs, 1944, O 4,20:2
Brandram, Rosina, 1907, Mr 2,9:6
Brandreth, B, 1880, F 20,2:6
Brandreth, Courtenay, 1947, N 4,26:3
Brandreth, John Breckinridge Maj, 1919, D 10,13:1
Brandreth, Paulina, 1946, Ap 21,46:2
Brands, George J, 1965, F 13,21:1
Brandschain, Herman, 1950, Je 8,31:3
Brandsma, Titus, 1942, Ag 26,19:5
Brandstein, Abraham, 1944, Mr 17,17:3
Brandstein, Joseph S, 1955, Ap 8,21:4
Brandsten, Ernst, 1965, My 18,39:4
Brandstrom-Ulich, Robert Mrs, 1948, Mr 5,22:2
Brandt, Arthur J, 1944, My 31,19:4
Brandt, Arthur W, 1943, Je 12,13:1
Brandt, Aug H, 1942, Je 14,46:8
Brandt, C Edwin, 1939, Ja 9,15:4
Brandt, Carl, 1957, O 14,27:1
Brandt, Carl A W, 1942, Ap 26,40:5
Brandt, Carl A W Mrs, 1944, Je 2,15:2
Brandt, Carl P, 1965, Ja 24,80:6
Brandt, Charles J Jr, 1950, O 8,104:4
Brandt, Christopher F, 1950, My 7,106:2
Brandt, D Bailey, 1941, Jl 22,19:4
Brandt, Edward, 1951, N 8,29:2
Brandt, Erdmann N, 1966, Je 14,47:4
Brandt, Ernst, 1940, F 4,40:4
Brandt, Ernst H, 1945, O 26,19:5
Brandt, Francis B, 1939, S 5,23:6
Brandt, Frank E, 1938, Jl 20,19:2
Brandt, Fred H, 1950, F 21,25:1
Brandt, Frederic C, 1957, F 17,92:4
Brandt, Frederic F, 1950, N 18,15:6
Brandt, George N, 1943, Je 7,13:2
Brandt, George W, 1963, N 13,41:1
Brandt, Gunnar, 1949, Mr 15,27:1
Brandt, Gusti Mrs, 1952, F 1,21:2
Brandt, Harry J, 1958, Jl 30,29:6
Brandt, Harry R, 1949, Ap 20,27:3
Brandt, Harvey F Mrs, 1962, Jl 3,23:1
Brandt, Henry T, 1945, N 7,23:6
Brandt, Henry W, 1959, Je 27,23:2
Brandt, Herbert W, 1955, Mr 9,27:2
Brandt, Herman, 1910, D 31,9:3; 1956, Mr 23,27:2
Brandt, Herman Carl George, 1920, D 21,13:4
Brandt, Herman Mrs, 1955, Ap 23,19:1
Brandt, Jennie K Mrs, 1949, Ag 13,11:3
Brandt, Joe, 1939, F 23,23:6
Brandt, John, 1953, Mr 6,20:7
Brandt, John F, 1966, Ap 24,87:1
Brandt, John W, 1949, N 12,15:4
Brandt, Kathe, 1902, Ja 14,9:5
Brandt, Lilian, 1951, Je 6,31:3
Brandt, Louis, 1949, Ja 29,13:4
Brandt, Ludwig, 1942, N 12,25:3
Brandt, Marianne, 1921, S 9,15:4
Brandt, Maurice L, 1960, F 13,19:4
Brandt, Nathan H, 1945, My 14,17:4
Brandt, Olaf E, 1940, F 21,19:6
Brandt, Oskar, 1948, D 14,29:4
Brandt, Paul Mrs, 1944, D 17,38:3
Brandt, Robert G, 1952, S 15,25:4
Brandt, Robert L Mrs, 1962, F 23,29:1
Brandt, Rudolph C, 1941, Ja 27,15:2
Brandt, Ruth E, 1954, Ag 6,17:5
Brandt, Sophie, 1946, F 5,23:2
Brandt, Walther I, 1958, F 7,21:3
Brandt, William C, 1943, My 29,13:4
Brandt, William E, 1963, N 20,43:3
Brandt-Ericksen, Viggo Mrs, 1944, O 26,23:2
Brandwein, Fishel Mrs, 1953, N 14,17:6
Brandwein, Henry G, 1950, Je 6,30:2
Brandwein, Julius, 1944, Mr 8,19:4
Brandwein, Peter (funl, Jl 4,19:1), 1956, Jl 3,25:3
Brandwen, Maxwell Mrs (Adele D), 1964, Ag 14, 27:3
Brandwynne, Azriel D, 1955, D 26,19:1
Brane, DeForest Mrs, 1959, N 19,39:3
Branegan, Joseph M, 1940, Ag 14,19:6
Braney, Joseph P, 1949, D 2,29:2
Branfladt, Ole A, 1941, N 24,17:3
Branfman, Theodore G, 1954, D 27,17:5
Brangan, Charles S, 1964, S 24,41:2
Brangwyn, Frank, 1956, Je 13,37:3
Branham, Ben P, 1942, Je 27,13:6
Branham, Leroy, 1956, O 28,64:5
Branham, Sara E (Mrs P S Matthews), 1962, N 19, 31:2
Branham, Vernon C, 1951, O 25,29:1
Braniff, Paul R, 1954, Je 2,31:5
Braniff, Thomas E, 1954, Ja 11,1:7
Braniff, Thomas E Mrs, 1954, Ag 25,27:5
Branigan, Edward R, 1943, N 11,23:4
Branigan, Edward W Prof, 1911, Mr 24,11:3
Branigan, James E, 1956, My 9,33:4
Branigan, James S Sr, 1948, S 24,25:4
Branigan, Josiah H, 1948, N 12,23:4
Branigan, William F, 1944, N 24,23:3
Branion, Clark, 1940, N 19,24:3
Branion, John M, 1965, Jl 3,19:6
Branique, William J Dr, 1914, Je 16,9:7
Brank, Rockwell S, 1947, F 26,25:2
Branly, Edouard, 1940, Mr 25,15:1
Brann, Emmett R, 1953, Ap 14,27:1
Brann, George, 1954, Je 15,29:1
Brann, Henry, 1962, Ag 11,17:3
Brann, Henry A Msgr, 1921, D 29,15:3
Brann, Louis J, 1948, F 4,23:1
Brann, Oliver C, 1945, Ap 9,19:1
Brann, Ralph M, 1967, My 16,45:2
Brann, William L (will), 1951, My 1,38:5
Brann, William Mrs, 1961, Ag 4,21:2
Brannan, Barrington L, 1941, F 5,19:2
Brannan, Dana Mrs, 1960, My 20,31:3
Brannan, E D Mrs, 1936, N 15,II,9:1
Brannan, Frank C, 1966, O 24,39:3
Brannan, J M Gen, 1882, F 14,5:1
Brannan, J W, 1936, Ag 31,15:3
Brannan, William F, 1956, D 3,29:2
Brannen, Bernard, 1949, D 6,32:2
Brannen, Hugh, 1956, Ja 7,17:4
Branner, Bernard Mrs, 1947, S 11,27:3
Branner, H C, 1966, Ap 25,31:5
Branner, John Casper Dr, 1922, Mr 2,21:5
Branner, Martin M Mrs, 1966, Ja 3,27:4
Branney, William H Jr, 1949, Jl 9,13:5
Brannick, Edward Mrs, 1942, Mr 19,21:4
Brannick, Frank L Mrs, 1956, My 6,87:2
Brannigan, Israel, 1903, Ja 10,9:5
Brannigan, James F, 1959, My 20,35:5
Brannigan, Joseph W, 1943, N 18,23:5
Brannigan, Robert Mrs, 1944, Ap 27,23:6
Brannigan, William G, 1950, S 20,31:1
Branning, Walter Mrs, 1948, Ap 2,23:4
Brannon, Drysdale, 1957, Ag 18,83:2
Brannon, George W, 1943, D 13,23:5
Brannon, James M, 1943, Ja 22,19:2
Brannon, Martin J, 1952, Je 13,23:2
Brannon, Melvin A, 1950, Mr 27,23:4
Brannon, Rebecca C Dr, 1923, O 1,7:3
Brannon, Robert M, 1944, O 4,20:3
Brano, Gonzales, 1871, S 9,1:7
Branower, Edmund I, 1956, Ja 21,21:6
Branower, Jacob, 1954, Mr 17,31:6
Branower, Solomon, 1960, F 11,35:1
Branower, William, 1943, Ja 19,19:4
Branscombe, Arthur, 1924, F 15,15:6
Bransen, Walter, 1941, D 23,21:6
Bransfield, Jerold F, 1958, Ap 7,21:3
Bransfield, William E, 1947, My 2,22:3
Bransky, Oscar E, 1958, O 4,21:5
Bransom, Paul Mrs, 1963, Ap 11,33:1
Branson, Ada, 1954, Ja 5,27:2
Branson, Ernest L, 1960, D 16,33:4
Branson, George R Mrs, 1952, S 13,17:3
Branson, J Scott, 1951, Je 2,19:3
Branson, John H, 1951, My 8,31:4
Branson, Lottie L Mrs, 1940, Ap 25,23:5
Branson, Marriette de Tellier (est appr), 1958, Ap 26,14:2
Branson, Robert N, 1965, N 11,47:2
Branson, Roswell H, 1956, N 12,29:4
Branson, William H, 1961, Ja 22,85:2

Branstater, Henry F, 1956, Mr 7,33:4
Branstetter, Otto F, 1924, Ag 5,17:4
Brant, A Earl, 1967, O 4,47:2
Brant, Alfred, 1965, Ja 27,35:2
Brant, Alvin E, 1964, O 28,45:4
Brant, Cornelia C, 1959, Mr 10,36:1
Brant, David J Mrs, 1955, Ag 15,15:1
Brant, Frank W, 1950, Ag 24,27:5
Brant, Frederick R, 1951, Ap 10,27:1
Brant, Howard N, 1937, Ja 6,23:2
Brant, Moses J, 1951, My 2,31:6
Brant, Thomas H, 1937, Ap 29,21:5
Brant, Walter C, 1951, O 26,23:4
Branthwaite, Isaac W, 1956, My 25,23:3
Branting, Hjalmar (por), 1925, F 25,19:3
Branting, Hjalmar Mrs, 1950, D 14,35:3
Brantingham, Charles H Capt, 1918, Ja 8,15:2
Brantly, Jack B, 1941, My 11,45:1
Brantly, Theodore L, 1961, Ag 17,27:5
Brantly, Theodore L Jr, 1951, Ag 9,15:2
Branton, A F Sr, 1955, Jl 28,23:3
Branton, G Ralph, 1957, D 4,39:5
Branwell, Auckland Mrs, 1941, O 24,23:4
Braque, Georges (funeral, S 4,39:2; tribute, S 8,-11,19:2), 1963, S 1,1:4
Braren, Cornelius S, 1940, Je 7,23:5
Brarens, Caroline, 1950, O 7,17:1
Brasch, Arno A, 1963, My 5,86:6
Braschi, Giovanni, 1959, Ja 6,33:4
Brase, Fritz, 1940, D 2,23:4
Brase, Hagbard, 1953, Mr 19,29:5
Brasefield, Edgar N, 1962, Je 19,35:3
Brasefield, L N, 1946, Ag 14,25:5
Braselton, Chester A, 1951, S 26,31:1
Brash, Douglas W, 1947, Mr 4,25:4
Brash, Samuel, 1944, Ag 16,21:7
Brash, William Dr, 1937, Ap 6,23:3
Brashear, Douglas W, 1954, S 20,23:6
Brashear, John A Mrs, 1910, My 19,9:4
Brashear, John Alfred Dr, 1920, Ap 9,13:3
Brashear, Peter C, 1943, Ap 20,23:2
Brashear, Peter C Mrs, 1963, Ap 24,35:3
Brashear, Roy P, 1951, Ap 23,25:2
Brashears, Andrew D, 1957, S 10,33:1
Brasher, Philip, 1961, D 16,25:5
Brasher, Rex, 1960, Mr 1,33:3
Brasic, Ilija, 1951, Mr 16,31:4
Brasier, George M Mrs, 1950, Je 27,29:1
Brasier, Henri, 1941, N 12,23:4
Brasington, William L, 1947, Mr 14,23:4
Braskamp, Alydia, 1947, N 5,27:6
Braslau, Abel Dr, 1925, O 21,23:4
Braslau, S, 1935, D 23,19:1
Braslow, Charles, 1945, My 7,17:5
Braslow, David, 1963, Jl 21,64:4
Braslow, Hyman, 1954, Mr 20,15:3
Brass, L, 1946, F 24,33:2
Brass, Leonard J Mrs, 1954, Je 21,23:3
Brass, Louis F, 1954, Ja 24,84:5
Brass, Oliver, 1957, Mr 4,27:2
Brassard, Lucien D, 1955, F 20,88:7
Brassard, Melina N Mrs, 1947, O 17,21:2
Brassel, Roger S, 1954, Jl 15,27:5
Brassert, Herman A, 1961, Je 19,27:5
Brassey, Ann Lady, 1887, O 13,5:3
Brassey, Bernard T (Lord), 1967, Jl 1,23:4
Brassey, Countess, 1934, F 22,21:1
Brassey, Earl Lord, 1919, N 14,13:3
Brassil, Daniel S, 1937, Ja 31,II,8:4
Brassil, Janet T, 1965, F 23,33:4
Brassil, John E, 1954, F 16,25:4
Brassington, Frank G, 1949, Jl 19,29:4
Brassler, Hans, 1962, Ja 29,25:2
Brasted, Howard S, 1945, Ag 29,23:4
Brastow, Lewis L, 1947, Ja 10,22:2
Brastow, Lewis Orsmond Prof, 1912, Ag 11,II,11:5
Brastow, Virginia, 1952, Ap 30,27:5
Brastrup, Frederick T, 1951, Ap 12,33:2
Brasure, John W, 1937, S 24,21:3
Bratenahl, Carl F, 1939, Mr 1,21:1
Brathwaite, Frederick G (por), 1939, O 31,23:3
Brathwaite, Woolsey Mrs, 1939, My 26,23:5
Bratianu, J T C, 1927, N 25,1:7
Bratley, Cyril O, 1948, My 11,25:3
Bratney, John F, 1949, Ja 16,69:1
Bratone, Clement, 1966, F 11,33:3
Bratt, H Albert Mrs, 1956, D 29,15:5
Bratt, Ivan, 1956, Ja 26,29:1
Bratt, Lewis, 1945, Mr 24,17:5
Brattain, Keren G, 1957, Ap 12,25:2
Bratten, Clifton E, 1948, F 13,21:3
Bratten, George H, 1949, Mr 3,26:2
Bratten, Walter H, 1952, Ap 24,31:3
Bratter, David Mrs, 1959, Jl 15,29:3
Bratter, Edward M, 1957. N 27,31:1
Bratter, William J, 1960, Jl 23,19:3
Brattig, Adolph, 1948, D 20,1:8
Bratton, Edward W, 1955, D 26,19:4
Bratton, Howard Mrs, 1951, S 19,31:2
Bratton, John S, 1907, S 20,9:6
Bratton, John W, 1947, F 9,61:1
Bratton, Leslie E, 1959, Ag 4,27:4
Bratton, Luther B, 1943, Ap 21,25:4
Bratton, Meredith J, 1967, F 20,37:2
Bratton, Norman Mrs, 1945, Ap 27,19:2
Bratton, Rufus S, 1958, Mr 21,21:4
Bratton, Sam G, 1963, S 23,29:4
Bratton, Theodore D, 1944, Je 28,23:4
Brattstrom, C Alfred, 1957, Je 1,17:4
Brau Zuzuarregui, Mario, 1941, Ag 26,19:4
Brauburger, George P, 1954, D 12,88:6
Brauch, Arthur, 1962, Je 22,25:2
Braucher, Ernest, 1949, F 10,27:2
Braucher, Frank, 1968, O 1,48:1
Braucher, Howard S (por), 1949, My 24,27:5
Braucher, Mavolta Mrs, 1949, Ap 19,25:1
Braucher, William M, 1958, N 15,23:4
Brauchitsch, Walther von, 1948, O 20,7:1
Braude, Emil, 1937, F 22,17:2
Braude, Henry W, 1942, Jl 23,19:4
Braude, Johann, 1968, Ja 15,47:1
Braude, Morris, 1959, Je 19,25:5
Braudling, George, 1922, O 28,13:5
Braudo, Alexander Dr, 1924, N 11,23:3
Braue, Olive L Mrs, 1953, D 25,5:2
Brauer, Aug, 1938, F 26,15:4
Brauer, Samuel S, 1960, F 14,84:7
Brauff, Herbert D, 1955, Je 16,31:6
Braukhage, Alice D Mrs, 1937, Je 5,17:3
Brauman, Julius S, 1954, My 5,31:2
Brauman, Seymour J, 1966, F 9,39:2
Braumuller, Herman, 1940, N 20,21:3
Braun, Abraham, 1940, N 24,49:3
Braun, Adolph L, 1951, S 23,84:8
Braun, Alfred W, 1951, Ja 25,25:1
Braun, Arthur C, 1955, F 23,27:5
Braun, Ascher, 1943, Ap 20,16:2
Braun, Bernard, 1964, S 13,86:4
Braun, Beulah M Mrs (B McFarland), 1964, Ag 11, 33:2
Braun, C J Jr, 1939, D 5,27:2
Braun, Carl F, 1954, F 5,20:3
Braun, Carl J, 1962, Mr 24,25:3
Braun, Carl R B, 1942, F 7,15:1
Braun, Charles F Mrs, 1953, Ja 5,21:5
Braun, Conrad, 1946, My 9,21:5
Braun, Daniel, 1954, Mr 15,25:3
Braun, David, 1947, D 12,27:3
Braun, E A, 1950, Jl 11,31:1
Braun, Edward, 1957, Ap 17,31:4
Braun, Emmy von, 1959, D 29,26:2
Braun, Eugene, 1965, Ap 10,29:3
Braun, Ferdinand Dr, 1918, Ap 22,11:8
Braun, Francis G, 1956, Jl 18,27:2
Braun, Frederick, 1945, F 10,11:3
Braun, Frederick S, 1961, Ag 9,33:4
Braun, Fritz, 1950, Ja 18,31:2
Braun, George C, 1873, Mr 11,5:2
Braun, Gustave F, 1949, Mr 13,76:5
Braun, H Dudley, 1949, D 7,31:2
Braun, Harald, 1960, S 26,33:4
Braun, Jacob Dr, 1937, Ja 30,17:4
Braun, Jacob T, 1949, F 22,23:5
Braun, John F, 1939, N 19,39:3
Braun, John J, 1942, Je 24,19:3; 1942, Jl 15,19:2
Braun, John W, 1967, S 29,40:1
Braun, Jurgen J, 1952, Mr 14,23:2
Braun, Konrad F, 1965, S 10,35:4
Braun, Leo, 1954, N 14,89:3; 1961, Mr 14,35:3
Braun, Leopold L S, 1964, Jl 19,65:1
Braun, Louise E, 1942, F 6,19:6
Braun, Ludwig, 1916, F 22,11:5
Braun, Marcus, 1921, F 28,11:4; 1921, Mr 5,13:5
Braun, Mary Mrs, 1941, Ag 13,17:6
Braun, Matthias Mrs, 1959, F 18,33:1
Braun, Maurice, 1941, N 9,53:2
Braun, Maurice Mrs, 1946, Mr 24,46:4
Braun, Max (por), 1945, Jl 4,13:3
Braun, Max, 1958, Ja 4,15:3
Braun, Michael J, 1950, O 14,19:3
Braun, Moritz, 1963, Ag 30,21:3
Braun, Morris, 1954, Ja 29,19:2
Braun, Otto, 1955, D 29,23:3
Braun, Paul, 1941, Ja 31,19:4
Braun, Peter M, 1941, My 28,25:4
Braun, Robert, 1953, N 14,17:5; 1955, Mr 9,27:4
Braun, Samuel G, 1956, D 3,29:3
Braun, Samuel J, 1938, F 19,15:2
Braun, Valentine, 1948, Jl 30,18:6
Braun, Walter C, 1949, Ap 29,23:2
Braun, Wendelin, 1957, Ag 22,27:4
Braun, Wilhelm A, 1954, O 14,29:4
Braun, Will C, 1948, S 14,29:3
Braun, William, 1942, F 26,19:3; 1943, N 22,19:3
Braun, William J, 1944, Mr 6,19:4
Braun, William Mrs, 1951, Mr 15,29:3
Braun, William P, 1946, Ja 16,24:3
Brauneis, Francis A Dr, 1905, Ap 26,2:4
Brauner, Olaf M, 1947, Ja 5,53:5
Brauner, Olaf M Mrs, 1966, Ja 12,21:3
Brauner, Pincus, 1965, N 13,29:1
Brauner, Victor, 1966, Mr 13,87:1
Brauner, William J Sr, 1952, Ap 24,31:1
Braunfeld, Samuel, 1951, Mr 16,31:2
Braunhut, Jeanette Mrs, 1960, Ja 10,45:2
Braunlich, Arthur R, 1943, Ja 9,13:5
Braunschweig, Edward U, 1945, F 18,34:1
Braunschweig, Julius, 1939, S 14,23:2
Braunschweig, Morris, 1945, Jl 18,27:5
Braunschweig, Phil A, 1941, O 8,23:3
Braunsdorff, R Kenneth, 1959, N 17,35:6
Braunstein, Harry, 1941, My 9,21:2
Braunstein, Joseph E, 1954, O 18,25:5
Braunstein, Julius, 1950, My 15,21:2
Braunstein, William P, 1953, Je 25,27:4
Braunworth, Arthur F, 1956, My 22,33:1
Braus, A Leon, 1955, F 27,21:5
Braus, Paul, 1946, Ja 20,42:6
Brause, Archie, 1966, Ag 14,88:2
Brause, Edward, 1967, S 3,53:1
Brautigam, Charles R, 1952, My 2,25:3
Brautigam, George A, 1958, Ag 19,27:4
Brav, Louis, 1950, My 23,29:4
Braveman, Abraham, 1963, Ap 7,85:6
Braverman, Benjamin, 1964, Mr 20,33:1
Braverman, Gabriel Mrs, 1956, Je 27,31:4
Braverman, Gabriel Mrs (L Putlitz), 1962, S 14,31:4
Braverman, Henry, 1966, N 20,88:8
Braverman, Herb, 1958, Je 3,31:1
Braverman, Lewis Mrs, 1963, Jl 24,31:5
Braverman, Marcus, 1939, Je 9,21:5
Braverman, Samuel, 1946, O 11,23:1
Braverman, Sigmund, 1960, Mr 29,37:3
Braverman, Solomon, 1951, Ap 21,17:2
Bravman, Barney O, 1952, F 22,21:2
Bravo, Ignacio, 1918, Ap 13,13:5
Bravo, Mario, 1944, Mr 19,41:1
Bravo, Samuel, 1953, Je 4,29:1
Brawer, Abram, 1958, O 25,21:5
Brawer, Arthur, 1946, N 27,25:1
Brawer, Arthur Mrs, 1943, F 25,21:2
Brawer, Milton, 1968, O 26,37:2
Brawer, Samuel, 1941, Jl 1,23:2
Brawley, Arthur L Mrs, 1963, D 4,9:5
Brawley, Benjamin, 1939, F 7,19:4
Brawley, Charles F, 1951, Ag 26,77:1
Brawley, Edwin J, 1945, Ag 3,17:4
Brawley, Frank, 1962, Ja 21,88:6
Brawley, Jack, 1953, F 9,27:3
Brawley, William H, 1955, Jl 11,23:5
Brawn, John P, 1943, Je 17,21:4
Brawn, William L, 1951, Ap 12,33:3
Brawn, Worthen E, 1947, Jl 18,35:5
Braxton, Harry, 1952, My 14,27:2
Braxton, James H, 1954, F 3,23:3
Braxton, Wister W (will), 1938, Ap 23,4:4
Bray, Albert C, 1943, Ap 5,19:4
Bray, Anderson Mrs, 1954, Ag 18,29:4
Bray, Andrew Watson, 1916, Ap 20,13:6
Bray, Archie W, 1942, N 19,25:4
Bray, Arthur, 1945, Je 8,19:5
Bray, C E, 1932, F 15,17:5
Bray, Daniel P, 1942, Jl 23,19:3
Bray, Ella W, 1954, Je 5,17:4
Bray, Fannie P, 1940, Ag 3,15:5
Bray, Frank C (por), 1949, Mr 25,23:3
Bray, Frank M Mrs, 1959, My 5,33:4
Bray, Frederick W, 1953, Mr 22,86:1
Bray, George S, 1937, Ap 8,23:5
Bray, George W, 1957, Ja 10,29:1
Bray, George W Mrs, 1960, N 14,31:2
Bray, Harold J, 1942, O 30,19:2
Bray, Harry A, 1956, N 17,21:5
Bray, Harry L, 1949, F 9,27:3
Bray, Henry Dr, 1925, D 9,27:5
Bray, Henry J, 1948, Mr 2,23:5
Bray, James A, 1944, S 2,11:2
Bray, James L, 1961, O 6,35:1
Bray, John G, 1950, D 19,29:4
Bray, John L, 1952, D 8,41:5
Bray, Joseph C, 1910, Ag 16,7:5
Bray, Joseph E, 1939, D 29,15:3
Bray, Joseph F, 1959, O 15,39:4
Bray, M William (corr, Ja 19,29:5), 1961, Ja 18,33:1
Bray, Michael, 1939, My 1,23:4
Bray, Orville, 1924, My 30,15:5
Bray, Patrick A, 1953, Je 18,29:4
Bray, Romeo J Mrs, 1948, Jl 7,46:5
Bray, T J, 1933, D 12,23:5
Bray, Thomas H, 1940, D 14,17:6
Bray, Thomas J, 1943, My 19,25:2
Bray, Walter C, 1942, Jl 9,21:5
Bray, William B, 1943, Mr 8,15:3
Bray, William C, 1946, F 25,25:4
Bray, William G, 1949, Ap 26,25:4
Bray, William L, 1953, My 26,29:4
Bray, William M, 1942, Mr 6,22:2
Bray, Yvonne de, 1954, F 3,23:5
Braybrooke, Lord, 1904, Ja 13,9:6
Braydon, Robert B, 1968, O 28,96:1
Braye, Baron (A Verney-Cave), 1952, F 13,29:3
Brayer, E Harold, 1948, Je 25,23:1
Brayley, Alex, 1925, Mr 3,23:4
Braymer, Lawrence, 1965, D 2,41:3
Braymes, Mark, 1966, Ap 26,45:1
Brayn, Abraham, 1943, Ja 29,19:4
Brayshaw, Elmore A, 1955, My 30,13:4
Brayshaw, G Leslie, 1943, Jl 8,19:4
Brayton, Aaron M, 1949, Ja 21,22:3

Brayton, Ada M Mrs, 1941, Ag 27,19:3
Brayton, Arthur, 1952, D 24,17:4
Brayton, Arthur E, 1938, Je 6,17:4
Brayton, Charles R Gen, 1910, S 24,11:5
Brayton, Harry J, 1939, S 21,23:4
Brayton, John S, 1961, N 13,31:1
Brayton, Lily (will, O 17,11:6), 1953, My 2,15:2
Brayton, Maxwell H, 1953, O 1,29:4
Braz Pereira Gomes, Wenceslay, 1966, My 16,37:5
Brazaitis, Joseph, 1947, O 18,15:2
Brazao, Alfred C, 1953, Ja 29,27:1
Brazeau, Jean Mrs (E Turner), 1966, Ja 15,27:2
Brazeau, Marie T, 1956, Ja 25,31:4
Brazee, Cornelius F Mrs, 1950, Ja 11,23:5
Brazee, Irving Mrs, 1940, S 21,19:7
Brazell, James C, 1943, Ja 11,15:1
Brazer, Clarence W, 1956, My 8,33:3
Brazer, Clarence W Mrs, 1945, N 1,23:3
Brazer, G Herbert, 1937, Ap 21,23:5
Brazier, Elizabeth L, 1944, Ap 20,19:3
Brazier, Frederick O, 1943, My 3,17:3
Brazier, George A, 1950, Ag 27,89:3
Brazier, Henry B, 1946, My 31,24:3
Brazier, James W, 1939, Je 21,23:3
Brazier, William E, 1947, Ag 14,23:1
Brazil, Dowager Empress of, 1873, Ja 27,1:7
Brazo, Mary B Mrs, 1939, D 7,27:3
Brazos, Julia, 1947, D 25,21:4
Brazza, Pierre P F C Savorgnan de, 1905, S 16,9:6
Brazzi, Stella, 1944, D 20,23:5
Brdey, Walter J, 1959, N 12,35:5
Brdlik, Vladislav, 1964, Ja 30,29:3
Breadner, L S, 1952, Mr 16,91:1
Breadon, Grace, 1938, Ap 24,II,7:2
Breadon, Sam, 1949, My 11,29:1
Bready, William R, 1950, S 18,23:5
Breaker, John C, 1941, Je 7,17:2
Breaker, William D, 1953, My 21,31:3
Breakstone, Benjamin, 1956, O 19,27:4
Breakstone, Benjamin H, 1945, Ap 24,19:2
Breakstone, David, 1962, S 19,39:1
Breakstone, Isaac, 1945, N 10,15:3
Breakstone, Morris, 1952, My 21,27:5
Breakstone, Moses, 1947, Jl 26,13:6
Breakwith, J B, 1923, Ja 4,19:4
Brearley, Harry, 1948, Jl 16,19:6
Brearley, Harry C, 1940, F 11,49:2
Brearley, Samuel M Mrs, 1962, N 14,40:1
Brearley, William H, 1909, Mr 27,9:4; 1949, D 3,15:4
Brearly, Mary C, 1925, N 13,19:6
Brearton, James F, 1940, Jl 9,21:1
Brearton, Patrick J, 1947, F 7,23:2
Breasted, F H Mrs, 1934, Jl 16,15:3
Breasted, J H, 1935, D 3,25:1
Breath, James (will, My 19,18:7), 1938, Ap 24,II,7:1
Breath, Melvin B, 1950, Jl 2,25:1
Breault, Oscar E, 1949, Ja 1,13:3
Breaux, Gustave A, 1953, Ag 6,21:2
Breaznell, Eugene H, 1960, Ja 6,35:4
Brebbia, Carlos, 1947, Je 19,21:4
Brebner, John B, 1957, N 11,29:1
Brecard, Charles, 1952, D 24,17:4
Breccia, Evaristo, 1967, Jl 29,25:5
Brechemin, Charles, 1949, F 19,15:2
Brecher, Edward M Mrs, 1966, O 23,89:2
Brecher, Egon, 1946, Ag 14,26:2
Brecher, Jacques, 1938, My 12,23:4
Brecher, Max, 1968, D 2,47:4
Brechlin, Lina Sister, 1938, N 24,27:2
Brecht, Bertolt, 1956, Ag 16,25:5
Brecht, Charles, 1948, Ja 16,21:3
Brecht, Elmer P, 1947, N 30,76:5
Brecht, Samuel K, 1939, Ap 21,23:1
Brecht, Vincent B, 1959, F 6,25:2
Brecht, Walther, 1950, Jl 6,27:2
Brechtel, Andrew J, 1942, N 6,23:4
Brechter, Frederick A, 1951, N 24,11:6
Breck, Charles A Mrs, 1943, O 19,19:4
Breck, Daniel, 1938, Ap 24,II,7:3
Breck, E, 1929, My 15,31:5
Breck, George William, 1920, N 23,13:4
Breck, J, 1933, Ag 3,17:1
Breck, John H Sr, 1965, F 18,33:2
Breck, John H Sr Mrs, 1957, Ja 6,88:2
Breck, Joseph, 1873, Je 17,1:4
Breck, Luther A, 1947, O 22,29:3
Breck, Mary Duer, 1907, Jl 15,7:7
Breck, Mary E, 1953, Ag 25,21:3
Breck, Richard A, 1874, N 18,5:4
Breck, Samuel, 1880, S 13,5:3
Breckenridge, Ben J, 1939, Mr 24,21:5
Breckenridge, Clarence E Mrs, 1951, S 4,27:2
Breckenridge, Edwin L, 1946, My 3,21:3
Breckenridge, Edwin L Mrs, 1939, Ja 14,17:3
Breckenridge, Fred F, 1940, N 15,21:1
Breckenridge, George P, 1950, O 5,31:3
Breckenridge, Gerald, 1964, Ag 9,77:1
Breckenridge, Hugh H, 1937, N 5,23:1
Breckenridge, John C, 1941, Jl 19,13:4
Breckenridge, John E Mrs, 1945, D 5,25:2
Breckenridge, Karl S, 1941, Ja 29,17:3
Breckenridge, Leland D, 1960, My 7,23:2
Breckenridge, Lester P, 1940, Ag 24,13:4
Breckenridge, Lucien S, 1941, O 14,23:3
Breckenridge, Mary E, 1941, D 20,19:5
Breckenridge, R J Rev, 1871, D 28,1:6
Breckenridge, Robert P, 1964, Je 27,25:1
Breckenridge, Scott D, 1941, Ag 2,15:2
Breckenridge, William E, 1961, Ag 20,86:6
Breckenridge, William E Mrs, 1944, D 13,23:5
Breckenridge, William H, 1950, Je 24,13:2
Brecker, S Charles Dr, 1968, D 19,47:2
Breckinridge, Aida de A Mrs, 1962, My 29,31:3
Breckinridge, D, 1935, F 19,21:1
Breckinridge, Desha Mrs, 1920, N 26,13:4; 1949, Je 14,31:3
Breckinridge, Henry, 1960, My 3,39:4
Breckinridge, James C (por), 1942, Mr 4,19:3
Breckinridge, John C Gen (last moments, My 19,5:2), 1875, My 18,1:6
Breckinridge, John C Mrs, 1907, O 10,9:4; 1961, F 9, 31:5
Breckinridge, John S, 1958, S 17,32:6
Breckinridge, Mary Mrs, 1965, My 17,35:2
Breckinridge, Samuel P Rev Dr, 1907, N 12,9:5
Breckinridge, Sophonisba P, 1948, Jl 31,15:1
Breckinridge, W C P, 1904, N 20,3:2
Breckon, W O, 1947, Mr 20,27:5
Breckwoldt, Julius, 1941, Ap 24,21:6
Breckwoldt, Leonard, 1947, S 3,25:1
Bredamus, James, 1942, S 10,27:5
Brede, A, 1934, Ap 30,15:5
Brede, Ella M, 1959, N 11,35:4
Brede, Henry, 1940, N 5,25:3
Brede, William J, 1968, Mr 10,92:6
Brede, William P, 1952, Ja 27,76:4
Bredemeyer, William F, 1941, Je 5,24:3
Bredenfoerder, Charles, 1938, F 4,21:4
Breder, Charles M, 1937, Ap 30,21:4
Breder, Frank O, 1955, Mr 19,15:5
Breder, Frank O Mrs, 1946, Jl 23,25:3
Breder, Henry W, 1937, Mr 2,21:2
Bredestege, Francis, 1939, Mr 15,23:5
Bredig, Georg, 1944, Ap 28,19:3
Bredin, Walter, 1955, N 23,23:3
Bredius, Abraham, 1946, Mr 16,13:5
Bredow, Hans, 1959, Ja 11,88:4
Bredow, John T, 1940, Ap 28,36:3
Bredow, Leopold von Mrs, 1907, Ag 23,7:4
Bredt, Carl V, 1961, Ap 1,17:4
Bredt, Julia F, 1949, Je 5,92:3
Bredt, Paul F, 1940, N 29,21:2
Bredull, August Mrs, 1946, Je 9,42:3
Bree, Chester, 1958, Ja 28,27:4
Bree, Malvine, 1937, F 21,X,8:4
Bree, wm A, 1951, N 17,17:6
Breece, George E, 1942, Ja 24,15:8; 1950, N 3,27:1
Breech, Joseph Mrs, 1951, Jl 28,11:7
Breed, A F, 1876, My 10,8:1
Breed, Alan R, 1954, Ag 21,17:2
Breed, Arthur H Sr, 1953, Ap 29,29:6
Breed, Charles B, 1958, Ag 12,29:3
Breed, Charles B Mrs, 1957, Ag 18,83:2
Breed, Charles H, 1950, Jl 31,17:5
Breed, Charles N, 1937, F 19,19:2
Breed, Charles Orrin, 1910, N 16,11:4
Breed, Florence Mrs, 1943, Ap 2,21:3
Breed, Francis S, 1940, Je 16,38:6
Breed, Frederick S, 1952, My 17,19:5
Breed, George, 1939, Ag 9,17:2
Breed, George C, 1950, Jl 2,24:5
Breed, George H, 1956, Je 26,29:4
Breed, George Mrs, 1952, D 16,31:2
Breed, Henry E, 1954, Ap 7,31:1
Breed, Howard, 1947, Jl 1,25:4
Breed, James M Mrs, 1945, Je 19,19:4
Breed, Julia P Mrs, 1941, Ag 16,15:2
Breed, Lewis B, 1951, N 12,25:2
Breed, Mary B, 1949, S 16,28:3
Breed, Nathaniel P, 1947, My 11,60:3
Breed, R E, 1926, O 15,23:4
Breed, Robert S, 1956, F 11,17:6
Breed, Stephen A, 1948, F 28,15:4
Breed, William C, 1951, D 4,33:1
Breed, William C Jr Mrs, 1957, O 14,27:2
Breede, Walter, 1961, Ag 25,25:3
Breeden, C E, 1903, Ag 26,7:6
Breeden, William C, 1942, F 7,17:5
Breeding, Earl B Mrs, 1960, Ja 23,21:1
Breeding, Earle G, 1958, Ja 18,15:6
Breeding, Edwin C, 1949, F 20,60:6
Breeding, Edwin C Mrs, 1957, My 2,31:2
Breeding, Hollis P, 1950, D 21,29:1
Breeding, Robert H, 1946, Mr 18,21:5
Breeding, William P, 1950, Ag 30,31:3
Breedlove, Joseph P, 1955, My 25,33:5
Breedy, Paul J, 1945, O 5,23:2
Breeghly, Robert E, 1951, Jl 1,29:2
Breeman, George A, 1937, Ap 12,17:2
Breen, A E, 1938, S 12,17:4
Breen, Aloysius, 1960, Ja 14,33:4
Breen, Daniel A, 1948, F 11,27:2
Breen, David J, 1941, S 17,23:2
Breen, Dennis M, 1954, Jl 6,23:4
Breen, Edward B, 1950, Je 9,23:5
Breen, Eugene L, 1956, Je 2,20:3
Breen, Francis W, 1945, D 17,22:3
Breen, Frank J, 1943, F 28,47:7
Breen, George F, 1957, Jl 3,23:3
Breen, Harry D, 1941, N 1,15:7
Breen, Henry C, 1966, My 16,37:3
Breen, Hyman, 1950, Jl 11,31:2; 1954, My 3,25:2
Breen, J Robert, 1964, Mr 24,33:1
Breen, James E, 1959, Jl 9,27:4; 1967, D 10,87:1
Breen, James J, 1949, Jl 19,30:2
Breen, James M, 1947, Je 1,60:3
Breen, Jay W, 1957, Ap 9,33:1
Breen, John, 1957, S 8,84:7
Breen, John J, 1941, Je 25,21:3; 1941, Ag 28,19:4; 1957, F 18,27:4
Breen, John M, 1957, F 16,17:4
Breen, John Mrs, 1948, Ap 11,72:1
Breen, John T, 1916, O 11,11:4
Breen, Joseph I, 1965, D 8,47:3
Breen, Joseph V, 1950, My 10,31:5
Breen, Joseph W, 1944, Ag 19,11:7
Breen, Joseph W Mrs, 1951, O 26,23:4
Breen, Katherine M, 1956, Mr 3,19:2
Breen, Lott R, 1952, N 7,23:1
Breen, Margaret J, 1948, Mr 27,13:5
Breen, Mary E Mrs, 1937, O 21,23:2
Breen, Matthew P, 1921, Ag 23,15:7
Breen, Michael F, 1952, D 24,17:3
Breen, Paul M, 1945, Jl 20,19:5
Breen, Peter J, 1953, Jl 27,19:5
Breen, Rebecca Mrs, 1957, Jl 19,19:5
Breen, Richard L, 1967, F 2,35:2
Breen, Robert A, 1959, S 4,21:4
Breen, Thomas, 1954, F 2,27:2
Breen, Thomas B, 1958, Ap 6,88:7
Breen, Thomas C, 1961, Ag 23,33:5
Breen, Walter L, 1956, Jl 23,23:3
Breen, William D, 1959, Je 21,92:8
Breene, Edmond C, 1961, Ag 25,25:4
Breese, Charles, 1944, My 18,19:5
Breese, E, 1936, Ap 7,25:1
Breese, Georgianna S Mrs, 1939, N 18,17:5
Breese, Harriet Mrs, 1940, Mr 27,21:3
Breese, James L, 1959, Ap 3,27:3
Breese, James Lawrence Mrs, 1917, Mr 13,11:4
Breese, K R Capt, 1881, S 14,5:2
Breese, Murray, 1960, Je 27,25:1
Breese, Robert P, 1958, Jl 18,21:2
Breese, S L Rear-Adm, 1870, D 18,1:7
Breese, Sidney Judge, 1878, Jl 2,2:7
Breese, Vinton P, 1940, Ag 14,19:6
Breese, William E, 1958, O 1,37:3
Breese, Zona G Mrs, 1938, D 28,21:1
Breg, W Roy, 1954, N 4,31:6
Bregel, Frank Sr, 1948, O 29,26:2
Bregler, Charles, 1958, S 28,88:2
Breglio, John B, 1951, S 11,30:2
Bregman, Abner, 1957, Je 11,35:1
Bregman, Adolph, 1951, O 5,28:2
Bregman, David, 1949, D 31,15:3
Bregman, George R, 1940, F 13,23:4
Bregman, Irving L Mrs, 1953, Ja 5,21:4
Bregman, Jack, 1967, S 11,45:3
Bregman, Josef, 1946, My 15,21:4
Bregman, Louis I, 1958, Ja 12,86:8
Bregold, Frank, 1940, Ag 12,15:4
Bregowsky, Ivan M, 1939, S 11,19:4
Breguet, Anne H, 1961, Mr 25,25:4
Breguet, Jacques (por), 1939, Mr 22,23:1
Breguet, Louis, 1883, O 28,8:7; 1955, My 5,33:3
Bregy, Edith M, 1952, Jl 8,27:2
Brehaut, Howard G, 1941, Mr 6,21:4
Brehaut, Lemuel, 1945, Je 15,19:3
Breheny, Raphael, 1950, S 28,31:2
Brehier, Emile, 1952, F 5,29:3
Brehm, A E, 1884, N 16,2:6
Brehm, Alfred, 1884, D 17,2:3
Brehm, Allen K, 1956, N 21,27:2
Brehm, Frederick W, 1950, Ap 6,29:2
Brehm, John S, 1946, N 3,64:2
Brehm, Ludvig T, 1949, Ap 20,27:1
Brehm, Paul A, 1949, My 1,88:4
Brehm, William H, 1954, N 13,15:6
Brehovsky, Nicholas, 1945, Ag 2,19:6
Breidenbach, Frederick C, 1955, My 22,88:3
Breidenbach, John R, 1949, S 29,29:3
Breidenbach, Mary C Mrs, 1941, Ja 10,19:3
Breidenthal, Willard J, 1960, D 27,29:1
Breidt, Joseph P, 1962, S 2,57:1
Breiel, George I, 1951, F 2,23:1
Breier, Benjamin, 1956, O 31,33:2
Breier, Louis S, 1960, S 14,43:1
Breingan, Irene S Mrs, 1937, My 28,21:5
Breining, Chester G, 1952, D 13,21:5
Breining, Mary M Mrs, 1941, Ag 17,38:2
Breintnall, R Heber Gen, 1925, Jl 7,19:5
Breisach, Paul, 1952, D 27,9:3
Breisacher, Edward H Sr, 1963, Je 14,29:2
Breisch, Howard R Mrs, 1958, Mr 30,88:7
Breisch, Phil J Jr, 1952, N 27,31:5
Breish, Phil J, 1942, Ap 4,13:4
Breit, Harvey (cor, Ap 13,25:3), 1968, Ap 10,47:
Breit, Jan J, 1959, O 22,37:2
Breitbard, Abraham, 1949, My 12,31:2

Breitbart, Bernard, 1967, N 6,47:1
Breitbart, Bernard Mrs, 1942, Je 2,24:3
Breitbart, Charles H, 1961, Ap 3,33:1
Breitbart, Charles H Mrs, 1963, Je 10,31:2
Breitbart, Lawrence M, 1943, D 22,23:3
Breitbart, Sigmund, 1925, O 13,23:5
Breitel, Herman Mrs, 1954, Jl 24,13:4
Breitel, Sharon, 1944, Mr 28,19:4
Breitenbach, Fred, 1953, D 30,23:4
Breitenbach, John E, 1963, Mr 26,9:7
Breitenbach, John F, 1968, Je 13,47:2
Breitenbach, John R Maj, 1875, Mr 16,7:5
Breitenbach, Max J Mrs, 1944, O 18,25:4
Breitenbach, William, 1937, My 14,23:3
Breitenberg, Frank P, 1925, Mr 9,17:4
Breitenbrook, Harold C, 1964, S 30,43:4
Breitenfeld, Frederick, 1966, F 9,39:2
Breitenfeld, Siegmund Mrs, 1943, S 29,21:1
Breitenstein, Reginald H, 1960, Je 5,86:3
Breiter, Edward G, 1953, N 17,31:1
Breitfuss, Leonid, 1950, Jl 22,15:5
Breithack, Frederick D, 1953, Mr 30,21:4
Breithack, Frederick D Mrs, 1956, Je 13,37:5
Breithaupt, Harry W, 1947, Mr 11,27:2
Breithaupt, William J, 1944, O 10,21:3
Breithut, Frederick E, 1962, My 13,88:8
Breitinger, J Louis, 1953, Ag 18,23:4
Breitmeyer, Phil, 1941, N 11,23:4
Breitner, Burghard, 1956, Mr 29,27:5
Breitner, Fred, 1942, S 22,21:2
Breitner, Hugo, 1946, Mr 7,26:2
Breitnitz, Lawrence W, 1968, O 9,47:3
Breitt, Albert, 1937, Je 25,22:1
Breitt, Fred, 1937, Je 25,22:1
Breitung, Charles F, 1937, Jl 25,II,7:4
Breitung, Edward N, 1924, O 3,21:3
Breitung, Max, 1937, Ag 20,17:4
Breitwieser, Joseph V, 1950, Mr 9,54:4
Breitwieser, Theodore J, 1959, Ap 23,31:4
Breitwisch, Cora, 1964, O 8,43:3
Brekke, David, 1951, O 14,82:3
Breland, Keller, 1965, Je 19,29:3
Brelland, Maria E Mrs, 1947, F 14,21:1
Brelsford, John H, 1951, Mr 15,29:4
Brelsford, John H Mrs, 1957, S 26,25:3
Brelsford, Mrs, 1874, Ag 16,1:6
Brelvi, Syed A, 1949, Ja 10,25:5
Brem, Walter V Dr, 1937, N 20,17:5
Brema, Marie, 1925, Mr 24,23:4
Bremen, Henry von, 1943, D 24,13:1
Bremer, Adolph, 1939, O 11,27:2
Bremer, Alex M, 1939, F 25,15:6
Bremer, Alexander H W, 1921, Ja 9,23:1
Bremer, Arthur E, 1946, Je 28,21:3
Bremer, Edward G, 1965, My 6,39:3
Bremer, Frank V, 1961, Je 25,76:4
Bremer, George John, 1925, Mr 5,19:5
Bremer, Harry H, 1955, N 11,25:2
Bremer, John L, 1959, D 27,60:8
Bremer, Karl, 1953, Jl 19,56:4
Bremer, Lawrence H, 1956, F 4,19:4
Bremer, Lloyd P Mrs, 1962, Jl 15,60:1
Bremer, N, 1880, Ja 9,2:1
Bremer, Otto, 1951, F 19,23:2
Bremer, Peter H, 1948, Jl 5,15:3
Bremmer, Frank E, 1941, My 2,21:3
Bremner, Andrew Augustus Col, 1907, Je 8,9:4
Bremner, David F, 1965, Mr 17,45:1
Bremner, Donald J, 1945, Mr 22,23:2
Bremner, Frank M, 1945, Mr 31,19:1
Bremner, James, 1960, F 23,31:1
Bremner, John R, 1949, N 2,27:4
Bremner, Will F, 1964, Jl 2,31:4
Bremond, Lulu J S Mrs, 1941, Ja 22,21:4
Bremont, Anna de Countess, 1922, O 19,21:4
Bremont, E L de Count (funl), 1882, My 24,3:5
Brems, Carl P, 1967, S 13,44:4
Brenaman, Edgar M, 1942, S 8,23:4
Brenan, John F, 1953, Ja 15,27:4
Brenan, Ralph S, 1952, Ag 16,15:3
Brenauer, Gabriel Mrs, 1917, Ja 14,19:1
Brenauer, Joseph B, 1946, Ap 18,27:3
Brenchley, Frederick, 1938, Mr 11,19:5
Brendan, Bro (B McGillicuddy), 1960, Mr 9,33:1
Brendel, El, 1964, Ap 10,35:1
Brendel, Henry W, 1940, S 15,48:3
Brendel, Samuel (est inv;left no will), 1953, D 10,54:8
Brendel, Samuel J, 1952, N 7,23:2
Brendle, Frederick H, 1940, F 6,21:3
Brendler, Charles, 1965, Jl 31,21:4
Brendler, Ralph, 1963, S 16,35:2
Brendlinger, E Leidy, 1945, N 14,19:2
Brendlinger, Margaret R, 1952, Ag 12,19:5
Brendlinger, William B, 1951, Je 27,29:3
Breneman, Mark, 1953, Ag 21,18:5
Breneman, Paul B, 1952, N 1,21:5
Breneman, Tom (will, My 20,24:5), 1948, Ap 29,23:1
Brenenstuhl, Charles H, 1948, My 28,23:4
Brenenstuhl, Orvis A, 1948, F 15,60:4
Brener, Abram Rabbi, 1968, Ja 6,29:4
Brener, Daniel A, 1968, N 26,53:3
Brener, Samuel, 1945, O 3,19:6
Brenes Jarquin, Carlos, 1942, Ja 3,19:5
Brenes-Mesen, Roberto, 1947, My 23,23:5
Brengle, Henry G, 1943, N 12,21:2
Brengle, S L, 1936, My 21,23:5
Breniser, Ross D, 1942, Jl 12,35:2
Brenk, Robert J, 1940, Ja 9,23:4
Brenman, Morris, 1967, Mr 27,33:3
Brenn, William G, 1949, Ap 23,13:4
Brennan, Agnes C, 1956, O 31,33:5
Brennan, Alfred L Jr Mrs, 1963, D 24,17:3
Brennan, Alfred T V, 1940, S 3,17:2
Brennan, Ambrose K Dr, 1937, My 25,28:2
Brennan, Amy S, 1948, O 20,29:2
Brennan, Andrew J, 1956, My 24,31:3
Brennan, Andrew P, 1939, My 30,17:5
Brennan, Andrew V, 1941, Ap 11,21:2
Brennan, Anna B Mrs, 1937, Mr 9,24:1
Brennan, Arthur A, 1954, Ja 15,20:3
Brennan, Arthur J, 1955, D 16,29:3
Brennan, Arthur J Mrs, 1959, Ag 1,17:4
Brennan, Baldwin Peter Bro, 1944, Mr 26,42:1
Brennan, Bernard J Jr, 1954, My 1,15:3
Brennan, Beulah B, 1952, F 25,21:2
Brennan, Charles E, 1948, My 26,25:1
Brennan, Charles H, 1942, F 20,17:3
Brennan, Charles J, 1937, Jl 10,15:4; 1950, My 7, 108:1; 1962, F 27,33:1
Brennan, Charles Mrs, 1948, Ag 29,56:6
Brennan, Cornelius P, 1965, O 16,27:2
Brennan, Daniel J, 1958, Ja 22,27:4
Brennan, David J, 1942, F 22,26:4
Brennan, Dennis B, 1939, Jl 6,23:1
Brennan, Dennis J, 1950, N 1,32:7
Brennan, Edmund T, 1964, N 19,39:4
Brennan, Edward F, 1944, Ja 28,17:4
Brennan, Edward F Dr, 1923, N 30,15:2
Brennan, Edward J, 1954, O 3,86:7; 1964, Ag 11,33:2
Brennan, Edward J Rev, 1937, Ja 16,15:1
Brennan, Edward M, 1956, N 11,86:4
Brennan, Edward P, 1942, Ja 11,46:1
Brennan, Edward T, 1960, O 14,33:3
Brennan, Ellen E, 1953, Ja 13,27:2
Brennan, Eugene T Sr, 1965, N 24,39:4
Brennan, Francis, 1950, F 1,29:2
Brennan, Francis Cardinal (funl, Jl 6,21:2), 1968, Jl 3,35:2
Brennan, Francis G, 1948, My 3,21:3
Brennan, Francis J, 1954, Ag 14,15:4
Brennan, Francis P, 1951, Ap 2,25:5
Brennan, Frank, 1950, N 6,27:2; 1968, O 2,39:3
Brennan, Frank A, 1937, S 26,II,9:3
Brennan, Frank A (por), 1945, N 28,27:5
Brennan, G E, 1928, Ag 9,19:1
Brennan, G J, 1934, O 24,21:4
Brennan, George D, 1954, D 29,23:3
Brennan, H Mott, 1968, Jl 20,27:4
Brennan, Hannah, 1943, F 11,19:1
Brennan, Hannah Mrs, 1869, N 18,5:2
Brennan, Harry, 1949, Mr 14,19:6
Brennan, Harry J, 1944, F 4,15:2; 1964, N 14,29:1
Brennan, Henry D, 1939, Mr 30,23:5
Brennan, Henry F, 1955, Jl 22,23:4
Brennan, Henry M, 1948, My 30,34:4
Brennan, Herbert J, 1954, Ja 5,27:4
Brennan, Isaac Bell (funl, O 2,9:7), 1908, S 29,9:7
Brennan, J Donald, 1953, Ap 27,23:5
Brennan, J Keirn, 1948, F 5,24:2
Brennan, James, 1938, O 9,V,8:5
Brennan, James A, 1942, S 12,13:2; 1956, Ag 25,15:6
Brennan, James C, 1937, F 8,17:3
Brennan, James F, 1958, S 28,88:3
Brennan, James H, 1945, N 27,23:2
Brennan, James J, 1958, My 4,89:1; 1965, Mr 8,29:5
Brennan, James J Prof, 1965, S 9,42:2
Brennan, James L, 1952, My 31,17:2
Brennan, James M, 1946, F 28,23:4
Brennan, James P Mrs, 1945, S 2,32:2; 1952, D 21,52:6
Brennan, James S, 1946, Ja 21,23:3
Brennan, James T, 1950, Je 9,23:4
Brennan, James W Mrs, 1957, Ag 21,27:2
Brennan, Jane (Mother Mary Florence), 1940, D 4, 27:1
Brennan, Jay (Jas J), 1961, Ja 17,37:2
Brennan, Joanna A Mrs, 1942, D 5,15:7
Brennan, Joe, 1945, F 20,19:4
Brennan, John, 1903, Ap 26,7:6; 1907, Ag 28,7:5; 1924, Jl 4,13:5; 1949, D 8,33:4; 1950, Ja 14,15:3
Brennan, John A, 1942, Ag 21,19:4
Brennan, John C, 1943, F 3,19:3; 1944, Ag 13,35:2
Brennan, John E, 1942, Ja 10,18:1
Brennan, John E Mrs, 1951, F 14,29:4
Brennan, John F, 1924, Je 24,21:5; 1946, Ap 2,27:2; 1958, F 10,23:3; 1959, Mr 24,39:2
Brennan, John G, 1944, F 26,13:3
Brennan, John J, 1938, F 27,II,9:2; 1945, N 6,19:5; 1947, D 9,33:7; 1952, D 24,17:2; 1954, O 27,29:1; 1958, D 7,88:7; 1964, N 19,39:4; 1967, N 18,37:1
Brennan, John J Mrs, 1944, S 28,19:5
Brennan, John M, 1945, Je 28,19:4
Brennan, John M Jr, 1952, Ja 30,26:2
Brennan, John N, 1954, My 26,29:3
Brennan, John P, 1952, N 19,29:3
Brennan, John T Mrs, 1952, Mr 30,93:2
Brennan, Johnny (R Dotina), 1960, N 3,39:1
Brennan, Joseph B, 1958, Je 14,21:5
Brennan, Joseph F, 1948, Mr 2,23:2
Brennan, Joseph H, 1954, N 3,29:1; 1961, Ap 20,33:3
Brennan, Joseph J, 1949, O 11,34:1
Brennan, Joseph P, 1939, Ja 10,19:5; 1953, Ja 20,25:4
Brennan, Joseph R, 1953, S 22,31:2
Brennan, Kyran, 1939, My 24,23:5
Brennan, Lawrence N, 1948, Ap 18,68:4
Brennan, Leonard A, 1949, O 7,27:3
Brennan, Lucy A, 1957, Ag 1,25:2
Brennan, M T, 1879, Ja 20,5:4
Brennan, Madeleine, 1968, Je 28,41:3
Brennan, Madge T Mrs, 1940, Ag 13,19:3
Brennan, Margaret M Mrs, 1906, My 29,4:3
Brennan, Martin A, 1941, Jl 5,11:6
Brennan, Martin Mrs, 1948, Mr 1,23:4
Brennan, Mary, 1938, O 26,23:4
Brennan, Mary (Sister Mary Clement), 1967, O 27, 45:4
Brennan, Mary B (Countess of Strathmore), 1967, S 9,31:5
Brennan, Mary C, 1949, My 19,30:2
Brennan, Mary H, 1941, Mr 25,23:4
Brennan, Mary W, 1964, O 17,29:6
Brennan, Matthew F, 1941, Ap 7,17:1
Brennan, Matthew T Mrs, 1907, S 26,9:5
Brennan, Michael J, 1938, N 26,15:3
Brennan, Michael J Capt, 1937, Ja 6,23:2
Brennan, O W, 1884, O 30,5:2
Brennan, Owen B, 1961, My 29,19:3
Brennan, Owen E, 1955, N 5,19:6
Brennan, Patrick, 1948, My 29,15:6
Brennan, Patrick F Mrs, 1946, O 20,60:3
Brennan, Patrick J, 1961, Jl 14,47:4
Brennan, Paul J, 1942, My 8,21:2
Brennan, Paul M, 1962, F 16,27:1
Brennan, Philip A, 1944, Jl 3,11:5
Brennan, Philip A Mrs, 1968, Ag 4,69:1
Brennan, Philip F, 1953, Ja 5,21:3
Brennan, Philip J Mrs, 1967, Ag 13,80:7
Brennan, Raymond, 1940, S 18,23:3
Brennan, Raymond D, 1953, N 20,23:1
Brennan, Raymond E, 1954, Mr 26,21:3
Brennan, Redmond S, 1948, Ag 18,25:1
Brennan, Richard A, 1968, Je 14,47:3
Brennan, Robert, 1964, N 13,36:1
Brennan, Robert A, 1940, D 18,25:5
Brennan, Robert G, 1947, Ap 11,25:2
Brennan, Robert J, 1940, O 2,23:4; 1941, O 24,23:2; 1957, D 15,86:4
Brennan, Robert W, 1957, S 10,33:3
Brennan, Russell H, 1942, N 3,24:2
Brennan, Sebastian Rev, 1937, F 1,19:2
Brennan, Thomas, 1912, D 21,13:4
Brennan, Thomas A, 1912, Ag 15,9:3; 1952, Jl 1,23:5
Brennan, Thomas Col, 1914, Mr 2,9:4
Brennan, Thomas E, 1953, Jl 14,27:2
Brennan, Thomas E Mrs, 1947, Ag 19,23:1
Brennan, Thomas F, 1937, F 15,17:2
Brennan, Thomas F Mrs, 1946, Ap 23,21:2
Brennan, Thomas H, 1940, Je 17,15:3; 1946, O 3,27:2
Brennan, Thomas J, 1921, S 2,13:3; 1940, D 25,27:4; 1949, Ja 17,19:4; 1950, N 13,27:3; 1952, S 8,21:5; 1953, Ja 30,22:4
Brennan, Thomas J Sr, 1954, My 18,29:3
Brennan, Thomas M (Bklyn), 1957, Ap 12,23:1
Brennan, Thomas M (Stony Pt, NY), 1957, O 10,33:3
Brennan, Thomas P, 1965, D 20,35:5
Brennan, Thomas W, 1950, Jl 29,13:7
Brennan, Timothy, 1881, D 4,7:3
Brennan, W D (see also Mr 8), 1881, Mr 9,1:3
Brennan, W H, 1935, Ap 26,19:2
Brennan, W J, 1930, My 15,27:5
Brennan, Wallace A, 1967, S 12,47:1
Brennan, Wallace A Mrs, 1949, F 18,23:2
Brennan, Walter H, 1941, S 26,23:4
Brennan, William, 1944, Ja 6,23:5; 1944, N 16,23:3; 1946, F 2,13:3; 1946, F 16,17:2; 1948, Je 10,25:4
Brennan, William A, 1961, Jl 15,19:4
Brennan, William E Jr, 1957, Jl 8,23:6
Brennan, William F, 1938, S 19,19:5; 1945, D 3,21:2; 1953, S 29,29:6
Brennan, William H, 1963, F 5,4:8
Brennan, William H Mrs, 1953, N 7,17:3
Brennan, William J, 1954, N 27,14:2; 1961, Ap 10,31:5
Brennan, William J Mrs, 1964, O 7,47:2
Brennan, William J Sr, 1964, S 16,31:2
Brennan, William Mrs, 1947, O 15,27:2
Brennan, William P, 1941, D 28,29:2; 1955, Ag 19,19:1
Brennar, Reuben G (will), 1937, Ag 12,17:4
Brennard, Everett C Mrs, 1938, Ag 21,32:6
Brennecke, Cornelius G, 1954, Ag 3,19:5
Brennecke, Ernest, 1950, Ap 7,25:4
Brennecke, Henry, 1962, Ap 30,27:1
Brenneis, Alfred G, 1950, Ag 10,25:3
Brenneman, Gustave W, 1906, F 7,9:5
Brenneman, L Leslie, 1949, F 12,17:4
Brenneman, Mary E, 1949, Mr 10,27:2
Brenneman, Nettie Mrs, 1959, O 12,19:4
Brennen, Hugh J, 1948, S 21,27:5
Brennen, John H, 1946, Ag 16,21:4
Brennen, John J, 1951, Mr 29,27:3
Brennen, Joseph D, 1940, D 13,23:2

Brennen, Stefance F Mrs, 1937, F 13,31:1
Brennen, Thomas A, 1959, S 24,19:5
Brennen, Thomas J, 1961, Mr 27,31:5
Brennen, William J, 1924, Ap 16,23:5
Brenner, Adolph L, 1946, Ap 25,21:1
Brenner, Aug, 1948, S 25,17:6
Brenner, Aug Mrs, 1954, N 8,21:3
Brenner, C William, 1953, Jl 12,42:1
Brenner, Camille Mrs, 1914, Ap 8,13:3
Brenner, Charles Mrs, 1947, Je 7,13:2
Brenner, Edward C, 1958, Jl 25,19:3
Brenner, Frederick L M, 1960, Mr 7,29:4
Brenner, George A Mrs, 1966, O 22,31:3
Brenner, George H, 1943, Ag 10,19:3
Brenner, George J, 1947, Mr 1,15:6
Brenner, Harry, 1948, My 8,15:4
Brenner, I Morton, 1961, F 25,21:1
Brenner, Jacob, 1921, O 17,15:3; 1953, O 27,31:5; 1955, Ap 12,29:4
Brenner, James E, 1963, Ap 27,25:2
Brenner, John, 1937, Ap 4,II,10:7
Brenner, John L, 1955, Je 26,76:4
Brenner, Joseph G, 1937, Ja 4,29:5
Brenner, Louis F Mrs, 1952, F 13,29:2
Brenner, Mildred F Mrs, 1942, S 19,15:6
Brenner, Morris, 1956, Ap 2,23:5
Brenner, Nathan I, 1939, F 12,44:6
Brenner, Oscar C, 1947, Jl 19,13:2
Brenner, Philip I, 1967, N 21,48:1
Brenner, Robert L Mrs, 1961, Mr 21,37:2
Brenner, Sam, 1922, Je 7,19:7
Brenner, Samuel, 1937, D 30,19:4
Brenner, Victor David, 1924, Ap 6,27:1
Brenner, Victor Mrs, 1952, Ag 24,89:1
Brenner, W Nissen, 1962, Je 24,69:2
Brenner, William H, 1942, Je 22,15:4
Brenner, William N, 1962, F 21,45:1
Brennesholtz, Gilbert C, 1944, D 6,23:2
Brennig, Charles C, 1966, Ap 22,41:2
Brennock, Gregory, 1950, Je 2,23:5
Brennock, Michael A Mrs, 1946, Je 11,23:1
Brennock, Thomas M, 1947, Ap 4,23:2
Brennon, John C, 1939, D 3,60:6
Brenon, Algernon S Mrs, 1946, O 2,29:4
Brenon, Chandos, 1925, F 7,15:5
Brenowitz, Harris Mrs, 1957, My 1,37:2
Brensilber, Jennie Mrs, 1942, Ap 30,19:2
Brenson, Herbert, 1958, Je 23,23:3
Brenson, Theodore, 1959, S 23,39:1
Brenson, Theodore Mrs, 1967, O 23,45:3
Brent, Brandy, 1953, D 23,26:6
Brent, C H, 1929, Mr 28,29:1
Brent, Henry K, 1946, S 17,7:2
Brent, Henry K Mrs, 1940, D 27,19:4
Brent, Martin, 1952, S 9,31:3
Brent, Romney Mrs (G Malo), 1963, D 3,43:4
Brent, Rudolph, 1966, Je 12,87:1
Brent, Stuart Mrs, 1955, O 11,39:3
Brent, Theodore, 1953, Je 10,29:2
Brentano, Arthur Mrs, 1940, Je 28,19:3
Brentano, Felix, 1961, Je 25,77:1
Brentano, Heinrich von, 1964, N 15,86:4
Brentano, L, 1931, S 10,25:1
Brentano, Lowell, 1950, Jl 9,69:1
Brentano, Peter von, 1956, Je 12,35:4
Brentano, Rowena L, 1967, F 11,29:2
Brentano, Sara Mrs, 1924, D 7,7:2
Brentano, Simon, 1915, F 16,9:5
Brentano, Simon Mrs, 1957, N 29,29:3
Brentano, Theodore, 1940, Jl 3,17:4
Brentford, Lord, 1932, Je 9,21:1
Brentlinger, John M, 1946, D 2,25:2
Brenton, Cranston Rev, 1937, D 23,21:5
Brenton, J J, 1881, Ag 17,8:6
Brenton, Merwyn R, 1946, O 14,29:6
Brenton, Reginald Carry Capt, 1921, My 18,17:5
Brenton, William P, 1955, D 30,19:2
Brenwasser, Charlotte, 1944, O 15,44:3
Brenza, John B, 1955, F 12,15:1
Brenzel, Henry I, 1949, Ag 16,23:2
Brenzinger, Julius F, 1947, S 7,60:5
Breon, Earl H, 1961, O 24,37:4
Brereton, Arthur M, 1938, Je 18,15:3
Brereton, Cloudesley Dr, 1937, Jl 14,22:1
Brereton, Edward E, 1955, F 12,15:5
Brereton, George, 1952, N 11,29:2
Brereton, Henry E H, 1957, My 15,35:5
Brereton, Henry H, 1956, Je 12,35:1
Brereton, Lewis H, 1967, Jl 21,31:2
Bresca, Vittorio A, 1954, O 11,27:5
Breschel, Gustav, 1959, My 9,21:3
Brescher, Joseph, 1950, Ag 24,27:5
Brescher, Joseph Mrs, 1957, D 10,35:5
Bresco, Adolfo, 1944, Ja 6,23:4
Bresee, Fred H, 1964, Jl 19,65:2
Bresee, P F Rev Dr, 1915, N 14,19:5
Breshkovsky, C, 1934, S 13,23:1
Breshnan, Daniel J, 1950, Je 26,27:1
Bresky, Bertil H, 1967, Je 4,86:3
Bresky, Hillard, 1957, Ag 3,15:5
Breslauer, Bernard, 1950, Je 1,27:2
Breslauer, Lewis R, 1958, F 11,31:2
Breslauer, Milton K, 1968, N 12,47:1
Breslaw, Alfred, 1965, Mr 27,27:5
Breslaw, Joseph, 1957, Jl 4,19:2
Breslaw, William J, 1942, S 29,23:4
Breslawsky, John J, 1953, Je 15,29:3
Bresler, Moses H, 1962, Ag 29,29:2
Breslin, Annie E, 1903, Ap 28,9:6
Breslin, Charles D, 1941, Jl 10,19:1
Breslin, Howard, 1964, My 31,76:4
Breslin, James E, 1951, N 20,31:3
Breslin, James H, 1906, Ap 1,11:5
Breslin, John A, 1939, Je 13,23:4
Breslin, John J, 1942, O 23,21:4
Breslin, John J Mrs, 1959, D 21,27:3
Breslin, John J Sr, 1947, S 9,31:3
Breslin, John V, 1960, D 31,17:5
Breslin, John W Mrs, 1942, Jl 11,13:5
Breslin, Joseph A, 1947, Mr 8,14:2
Breslin, Patrick N (por), 1938, Je 29,19:3
Breslin, Samuel S, 1959, Ja 1,31:4
Breslin, Susan, 1925, Ag 7,15:6
Breslin, Thomas, 1911, Ap 14,11:4
Breslin, Thomas J, 1951, Jl 30,17:4
Breslin, Timothy, 1905, Ap 14,9:6
Breslin, William J (J Britton), 1962, Mr 28,39:1
Bresloff, Herman, 1954, Ja 18,25:4
Breslow, David, 1958, Ap 23,33:1
Breslow, Henry, 1968, N 7,47:4
Breslow, Louis G, 1952, Ap 22,29:4
Breslow, Meyer, 1946, My 1,25:1
Breslow, Noah, 1959, F 22,88:5
Breslow, Stanley, 1955, My 20,25:4
Bresnahan, George T, 1964, Ag 7,29:1
Bresnahan, John F, 1956, Jl 3,25:5; 1966, Mr 13,86:3
Bresnahan, Patrick F, 1940, Ja 31,19:4
Bresnahan, Roger, 1944, D 5,23:3
Bresnahan, William H, 1947, My 15,26:2
Bresnan, P H, 1904, Ja 21,9:6
Bresnick, Carl S, 1959, S 25,24:1
Bresnihan, Benjamin J, 1943, My 7,19:2
Bresnihan, John J, 1945, Ja 1,21:5
Bresnik, Benjamin, 1966, Ja 24,35:3
Bressan, Anthony J, 1945, Ag 18,11:6
Bressant, Jeremiah Mrs, 1951, O 12,27:1
Bressart, Felix, 1949, Mr 23,27:2
Bresse, Burtis B, 1939, Ag 1,19:5
Bresselsford, Millard, 1946, Mr 22,22:2
Bressey, Charles H Sir, 1951, Ap 15,92:4
Bressler, Arthur L, 1908, N 7,7:4
Bressler, David M (por), 1942, D 17,29:5
Bressler, Isadore Mrs, 1964, Jl 4,13:2
Bressler, J Walter Rev, 1937, F 21,II,10:4
Bressler, Martin M, 1948, Ap 13,27:5
Bressler, Max, 1966, F 17,34:1
Bressler, Mordecai, 1957, My 7,35:3
Bressler, Raymond G, 1948, My 10,21:3
Bressler, Raymond G Jr Dr, 1968, Ja 12,27:2
Bressler, Samuel, 1959, Je 1,27:4
Bressler-Pettis, Charles W, 1954, My 14,23:2
Bressmer, Mary, 1955, Mr 5,17:6
Bret, Walter E, 1948, F 10,23:3
Bretch, Paul, 1955, My 7,17:3
Breteuil, Charles de, 1960, S 26,33:2
Bretfield, Maurice E, 1944, N 25,13:2
Breth, Ferdinand W, 1957, Ja 9,31:5
Brethauer, Charles J, 1952, Ag 14,23:2
Brethauer, Frederick L, 1945, Jl 22,38:1
Bretherick, Arthur P, 1958, N 12,37:4
Bretherick, Henry, 1943, D 18,15:1
Bretnall, Francis E, 1948, S 3,19:2
Bretnall, G H Mrs, 1952, Jl 31,23:4
Bretnall, George H, 1961, Ja 12,29:3
Bretnall, Reginald J, 1955, O 15,15:3
Bretnall, Walter T, 1952, Mr 16,90:3
Breton, Andre, 1966, S 29,47:5
Breton, Jules Adolphe, 1906, Jl 6,7:5
Breton, Jules L, 1940, Ag 26,15:2
Breton, Leon, 1940, Jl 26,17:3
Breton, Raoul, 1959, Ap 24,27:2
Bretonne, May, 1952, S 30,31:5
Bretsch, Homer L, 1940, Je 8,15:3
Bretsch, Lawrence E, 1960, O 25,35:2
Bretschey, Stanton L, 1955, Ja 22,11:1
Brett, Adelaide D Mrs, 1938, S 11,II,11:1
Brett, Agnes B Mrs, 1955, D 27,23:3
Brett, Amy D, 1945, My 8,19:1
Brett, Charles H, 1906, Mr 6,9:6
Brett, Charles Leferich, 1968, Ja 15,47:1
Brett, David E, 1953, Ag 25,21:4
Brett, Everett A, 1957, My 22,33:6
Brett, Francis J, 1941, Mr 24,17:3
Brett, Francis J Mrs, 1943, F 25,21:2
Brett, Frederick P, 1950, Jl 18,29:3
Brett, G P, 1936, S 20,II,10:8
Brett, George B, 1948, F 27,21:3
Brett, George J, 1940, Ap 19,21:2
Brett, George S, 1944, O 28,15:3
Brett, Harvey, 1951, Je 24,73:1
Brett, Homer, 1965, N 27,31:4
Brett, John A, 1937, Ag 13,17:3
Brett, L M, 1927, S 24,17:4
Brett, Morgan L, 1962, Ag 5,81:1
Brett, Mortin W, 1879, N 24,8:5
Brett, Philip M, 1960, Jl 3,32:2
Brett, Philip M Mrs, 1960, F 2,35:2
Brett, Robert, 1945, O 4,23:6
Brett, Sereno E, 1952, S 10,29:5
Brett, Thomas Mrs, 1963, S 13,13:3
Brett, William G, 1913, N 29,13:5
Brett, William T, 1940, S 10,23:5
Brettauer, Joseph, 1941, D 27,20:2
Brettell, A R, 1903, Je 6,7:7
Bretthauer, Emilie, 1940, F 15,19:5
Brettle, Howard A, 1958, Je 26,27:6
Brettman, William H, 1944, Je 3,13:6
Brettner, Otto L, 1946, D 28,15:5
Brettschneider, Leonard, 1954, My 15,15:4
Bretz, Alice Mrs, 1953, D 24,15:2
Bretz, Edward F, 1939, Jl 20,19:5
Bretz, John L, 1920, D 26,22:2
Bretz, Ross B, 1943, Ag 7,11:5
Bretzfelder, Charles B, 1946, Ja 18,19:3
Bretzfield, Silas Wright, 1916, Ap 23,19:4
Breuchaud, Jules Mrs, 1959, N 22,86:1
Breuer, Henry, 1959, O 27,37:2
Breuer, Regina, 1956, Je 25,23:2
Breuer, S Rabbi, 1926, Jl 21,19:2
Breuer, Walter H, 1961, My 12,58:5
Breugelmans, Jef, 1947, Je 14,15:1
Breuil, Francis W, 1944, O 29,43:2
Breuil, Henri, 1961, Ag 22,29:1
Breuner, Katherine, 1949, F 1,26:2
Breunich, Frank F, 1948, Mr 19,23:3
Breunich, Hieronymus Mrs, 1941, My 17,15:5
Breunig, Herman Jr, 1948, My 11,25:4
Breuning, Gustave, 1946, N 30,15:5
Breuning, Rose (Sister Bona), 1942, My 12,19:4
Breuninger, Harold F Sr, 1965, Je 4,35:1
Breusing, Friedrich A Adm, 1914, O 9,9:4
Brevoort, Benjamin H, 1941, Ap 23,21:4
Brevoort, Carson, 1944, Mr 24,19:5
Brevoort, Henry, 1941, Mr 20,21:4
Brevoort, Henry W Maj, 1910, Ap 5,11:5
Brevoort, James Renwick, 1918, D 16,15:3
Brevoort, William H Jr, 1959, Je 3,35:4
Brevoort, William H Jr Mrs, 1940, Ja 15,17:6
Brew, Arthur H, 1937, Je 20,II,6:6
Brew, Russell O, 1957, Ap 26,25:2
Brew, William P, 1953, My 29,25:4
Brew, William P Mrs, 1943, Ap 8,23:2; 1951, S 19,31:2
Brewer, Addison P, 1905, My 6,9:6
Brewer, Albert D, 1954, My 12,31:4
Brewer, Bert B, 1951, D 3,31:5
Brewer, Charles B, 1944, Ja 20,19:1
Brewer, Charles E, 1908, Je 16,9:6; 1941, My 2,21:4
Brewer, Charles H, 1963, My 5,87:1
Brewer, Charles R, 1946, O 6,58:6
Brewer, Chauncey M, 1938, Mr 3,21:2
Brewer, Chester L, 1953, Ap 17,25:5
Brewer, Clavert, 1949, D 25,26:3
Brewer, Clifford M, 1940, Ag 2,15:6
Brewer, Clifton H, 1947, S 30,25:6
Brewer, Clifton H Mrs, 1948, Ap 4,60:2
Brewer, Clyde Mrs, 1959, Ap 21,38:1
Brewer, E P, 1932, Je 19,21:3
Brewer, Earl L, 1942, Mr 11,20:2
Brewer, Edward A, 1952, Ag 23,13:3
Brewer, Edward N, 1942, F 23,21:5
Brewer, Eliza M, 1949, Je 19,68:2
Brewer, Elliott, 1952, F 20,29:5
Brewer, Erle G, 1950, O 22,92:5
Brewer, Everard C, 1925, My 15,19:5
Brewer, Francis E Mrs, 1950, Mr 18,13:4
Brewer, Frank G, 1948, O 25,23:2
Brewer, George E, 1939, D 25,23:3
Brewer, George Emerson Jr, 1968, F 22,31:3
Brewer, George Emerson Mrs, 1925, Ap 2,21:3
Brewer, George M Mrs, 1960, O 5,41:4
Brewer, Graham H Mrs, 1956, Je 19,29:5
Brewer, Griffiths, 1948, Mr 2,24:3
Brewer, Harry F, 1942, Jl 20,13:2
Brewer, Harry G, 1951, Ja 14,85:1
Brewer, Harry J, 1938, F 22,21:4
Brewer, Hilton C, 1965, Ja 16,27:2
Brewer, Hugh G, 1967, Ag 20,88:5
Brewer, Isaphene, 1951, My 20,88:4
Brewer, J H, 1931, D 1,27:5
Brewer, James A, 1957, Mr 7,29:2
Brewer, John D, 1952, Jl 8,27:4
Brewer, John H, 1961, My 4,37:3
Brewer, John J, 1951, D 28,21:2
Brewer, John K, 1950, S 28,31:2
Brewer, John M, 1950, Ag 26,13:4
Brewer, John M Mrs, 1952, Ap 25,23:3
Brewer, John W, 1962, N 1,31:4
Brewer, Joseph E Mrs, 1953, S 30,31:3
Brewer, Joseph H, 1943, F 11,19:4
Brewer, L A, 1933, My 7,31:2
Brewer, L O Mrs, 1953, O 6,29:6
Brewer, Leigh Richmond Bp, 1916, Ag 29,9:4
Brewer, Malcolm O, 1954, Ag 1,87:6
Brewer, Mary Mrs, 1954, Je 24,27:4
Brewer, Maurice, 1956, O 2,35:5
Brewer, Nathan A, 1940, Je 8,15:2
Brewer, Nicholas R (por), 1949, F 16,25:2
Brewer, Pinckney P, 1955, F 2,27:1
Brewer, R P, 1933, Je 15,17:3

Brewer, Randolph E, 1944, Ja 19,19:5
Brewer, Reuben P Mrs, 1956, Jl 18,27:5
Brewer, Richard Jr, 1947, Ap 6,60:2
Brewer, Robert B, 1951, Je 19,29:2
Brewer, Robert D, 1949, Ja 11,27:4
Brewer, Robert K, 1945, Mr 23,19:3
Brewer, Robert W A, 1957, D 8,88:3
Brewer, Ruben P, 1960, Ap 14,37:4
Brewer, Sam S Mrs, 1952, Ap 30,27:6
Brewer, Sarah L, 1954, Ja 9,15:2
Brewer, Stephen M, 1961, Jl 21,23:3
Brewer, Theodore H, 1940, S 20,23:4
Brewer, Willard, 1942, F 6,19:3
Brewer, William A, 1922, D 17,6:3
Brewer, William B, 1957, O 5,17:5
Brewer, William G, 1949, O 15,15:6
Brewer, William Henry Prof, 1910, N 3,9:5
Brewer, William J, 1953, Ag 13,25:5
Brewer, William R, 1907, N 17,9:5; 1941, Mr 13,21:4
Brewerton, Arthur, 1951, Mr 14,33:2
Brewerton, H Gen, 1879, Ap 18,5:2
Brewerton, Henry Feltus Lt-Col, 1913, N 3,9:6
Brewerton, Ridgley, 1946, S 7,15:5
Brewing, Willard, 1960, Ag 14,93:2
Brewis, Edward, 1916, Ag 18,9:4
Brewster, Abraham, 1874, Jl 28,4:6
Brewster, Adelaide L Mrs, 1952, Ag 12,19:3
Brewster, Albert S, 1941, My 22,21:5
Brewster, Albert V, 1956, Mr 4,88:2
Brewster, Alfred A, 1953, Ja 31,15:5
Brewster, Andre W, 1942, Mr 28,17:3
Brewster, Andre W Mrs, 1948, F 15,60:3
Brewster, Angus, 1871, S 27,1:6
Brewster, B A, 1888, Ap 5,4:7
Brewster, Benjamin, 1941, F 3,17:3
Brewster, Benjamin H Jr, 1941, Ja 29,17:2
Brewster, Benjamin Mrs, 1925, Ap 21,21:5
Brewster, C Barton, 1958, S 1,13:3
Brewster, Carroll H, 1952, Mr 27,29:3
Brewster, Charles H Mrs, 1957, Mr 8,25:1
Brewster, Charles N, 1949, Mr 27,76:7
Brewster, Chauncey B, 1941, Ap 10,24:2
Brewster, D P, 1876, F 22,5:6
Brewster, David L S (por), 1945, Jl 12,11:5
Brewster, David Sir, 1868, F 12,4:6
Brewster, E Franklin, 1947, N 28,27:2
Brewster, E H Mrs, 1945, F 18,34:3
Brewster, Edson S, 1954, Mr 13,15:2
Brewster, Edward. 1960, F 27,19:3
Brewster, Edwin T, 1960, Mr 15,39:3
Brewster, Elisha H, 1946, Ap 30,21:3
Brewster, Eugene V, 1939, Ja 2,23:3
Brewster, F Carroll 3d, 1950, Jl 12,29:3
Brewster, F Raymond, 1956, D 29,15:2
Brewster, Francis, 1952, Ag 20,25:3
Brewster, Francis E, 1939, My 27,15:6
Brewster, Francis Mrs, 1947, Ag 4,17:3
Brewster, Frank, 1961, O 18,43:1
Brewster, Frank H, 1943, D 30,18:2
Brewster, Frank M, 1953, Je 1,23:5
Brewster, Frederick F, 1948, Je 1,23:3
Brewster, Frederick F (will, O 5,131:4), 1958, S 17, 32:3
Brewster, Frederick F Mrs, 1963, D 16,33:5
Brewster, G H, 1903, My 13,9:5
Brewster, George F, 1964, F 13,31:4
Brewster, George W, 1940, F 5,18:2
Brewster, George W W, 1939, S 27,25:3
Brewster, H D, 1928, Ag 8,21:3
Brewster, Harold, 1956, F 5,86:3
Brewster, Harold N, 1965, Jl 7,37:2
Brewster, Harold P, 1925, Je 16,21:6
Brewster, Harold S, 1948, Ap 8,25:1
Brewster, Henry B, 1948, Ap 21,27:5
Brewster, Horace Austin, 1903, D 20,7:6
Brewster, J B, 1902, Mr 11,9:5
Brewster, J Newton, 1949, D 20,31:4
Brewster, J Riggs, 1949, Mr 19,15:5
Brewster, James, 1866, N 25,1:7
Brewster, James H, 1920, Ag 5,7:5
Brewster, James H Jr, 1959, My 5,33:6
Brewster, James N S Jr, 1938, N 14,19:5
Brewster, James R, 1948, Ag 19,21:1
Brewster, John, 1949, D 18,88:4
Brewster, John A, 1947, Jl 29,21:4
Brewster, Joseph, 1923, My 4,17:3
Brewster, Lewis O, 1938, Ag 1,13:3
Brewster, Lyman D Judge, 1904, F 15,7:6
Brewster, Mabel T Mrs, 1941, O 30,23:4
Brewster, Marg P (Mrs J Kieley), 1960, Mr 8,33:2
Brewster, Mary J, 1938, Je 11,15:5
Brewster, O Byron, 1953, O 28,29:5
Brewster, Owen (funl, D 29,23:1), 1961, D 26,25:1
Brewster, Percy D, 1952, O 30,31:2
Brewster, Richard Caldwell Dr, 1907, My 20,9:6
Brewster, Richard L, 1916, Mr 3,11:4
Brewster, Robert S, 1939, D 25,23:5
Brewster, Ruby T Mrs, 1937, D 31,15:2
Brewster, S Edward, 1941, Je 18,21:1
Brewster, S Edward Mrs, 1943, O 10,48:5
Brewster, S M, 1902, O 14,1:4
Brewster, Samuel Dwight, 1920, Ja 10,11:4
Brewster, Seabury, 1884, S 21,2:7
Brewster, Sergeant B Sr, 1957, Ag 15,21:4
Brewster, Sidney W, 1939, Ap 9,III,6:7
Brewster, Stanley, 1950, F 14,25:4
Brewster, Stephen V, 1949, Ag 30,27:2
Brewster, T P, 1945, Ja 9,19:4
Brewster, Ulysses Mrs, 1947, Jl 22,23:4
Brewster, Walter S, 1954, S 17,27:2
Brewster, Walter S Mrs, 1947, S 25,29:5; 1950, Ap 1, 15:5
Brewster, Walter Shaw, 1913, Mr 31,13:4
Brewster, Willard E, 1949, Ja 25,23:5
Brewster, Willard E Mrs, 1950, F 28,30:2
Brewster, William, 1949, N 26,15:1; 1953, N 4,33:5; 1966, Ag 3,37:4
Brewster, William E, 1945, D 8,17:4; 1949, D 20,31:2
Brewster, William J, 1952, Ap 1,29:5
Brewster, William M, 1961, Je 27,33:5
Brewster, William Mrs, 1907, F 25,9:6
Brewster, William N Mrs, 1955, Mr 18,28:3
Brewster, William R Mrs, 1909, Mr 31,11:4
Brewster, William T, 1961, Mr 28,35:5
Brewster, Winfield, 1962, N 3,25:3
Brewton, Alice, 1956, Mr 22,35:5
Brewton, William G Mrs, 1944, O 21,17:6
Brex, Frank E, 1944, S 12,19:4
Brexendorf, Alex M, 1943, Mr 15,13:2
Breydrick, Thomas J Msgr, 1915, O 6,11:7
Breyer, Frank G, 1966, Jl 27,39:4
Breyer, Frederick William, 1907, Jl 28,7:5
Breyer, Henry W Mrs, 1967, Jl 12,43:3
Breyer, Moe Mrs, 1951, My 1,29:2
Breyfogel, S C, 1934, N 25,30:3
Breyfogle, Willis C, 1945, S 23,46:5
Breynat, Gabriel, 1954, Mr 11,31:1
Breywood, Henry, 1947, Ag 14,23:1
Brezee, Dorothy N, 1949, Ja 16,68:5
Brezee, Fred, 1949, Je 10,28:5
Brezing, Herman, 1945, Jl 2,15:6
Breznak, John, 1953, Ap 12,80:3
Brialmont, A H Gen, 1885, Ap 19,9:5
Brian, Alexander J Mrs, 1966, Ja 31,39:4
Brian, Donald, 1948, D 23,19:1
Brian-Schaninoff, Nicholas, 1943, Je 18,21:1
Brianceau, Henry, 1950, Ag 24,27:3
Briand, A, 1932, Mr 8,1:2
Briant, Alfred E, 1951, Ja 28,76:5
Briant, Clarence H Mrs, 1943, D 15,27:3
Briant, Raymond C, 1954, Ap 27,29:6
Briante, Rocco, 1942, D 8,25:5
Briante, Rocco Mrs, 1948, D 19,76:4
Briarly, Frank L, 1937, Ja 26,21:4
Briarly, John W, 1967, Jl 7,31:1
Brice, Andrew T, 1942, Mr 16,15:5
Brice, Arthur H Mrs, 1937, Je 6,II,9:1
Brice, Brooks A, 1960, S 23,29:2
Brice, C S, 1898, D 16,1:7
Brice, Charles F Mrs, 1961, S 10,86:1
Brice, Elizabeth (B Shaler), 1965, Ja 26,37:2
Brice, Fanny, 1951, My 30,21:1
Brice, Helen O, 1950, Ja 21,17:2
Brice, James H, 1955, Ja 24,23:5
Brice, John A, 1946, Ja 10,23:4
Brice, John F, 1937, Mr 8,19:5
Brice, Katherine, 1911, Jl 28,9:6
Brice, Monte, 1962, N 9,35:1
Brice, Rose Mrs, 1941, My 1,23:1
Brice, Stewart M (funl, Je 11,11:5), 1910, Je 10,9:5
Brice, Wilson B, 1947, Ag 2,13:6
Briceno-Iragorry, Mario, 1958, Je 7,19:3
Brichant, Leon, 1941, My 17,15:4
Brichler, George W, 1939, S 14,23:4
Brick, Abraham Lincoln, 1908, Ap 8,7:4
Brick, Alyea M, 1960, Ja 2,13:2
Brick, Arthur H, 1963, Je 14,29:1
Brick, Francis A Jr, 1968, Ap 4,47:4
Brick, Harry, 1949, Jl 23,11:4
Brick, Seymour, 1960, Ag 15,23:2
Brick, Walter F, 1951, Jl 8,61:2
Brick, William T, 1954, D 15,31:1
Bricka, H V, 1958, Mr 17,29:3
Bricka, William, 1943, My 15,15:5
Brickel, A C J, 1950, S 12,27:4
Brickel, Jack, 1968, F 21,47:1
Brickel, Ralph, 1952, Mr 23,92:4
Brickell, Donal J F, 1952, My 18,93:1
Brickell, Elsie A, 1945, D 10,21:4
Brickell, Fred G Sr, 1961, Ap 10,31:5
Brickels, John L, 1964, Mr 18,41:5
Bricken, Abraham, 1947, Jl 8,24:2
Bricker, Charles E, 1939, F 18,15:3
Bricker, Clarence, 1947, Je 29,48:6
Bricker, Frederick M, 1940, Jl 10,19:4
Bricker, Harry C, 1965, Jl 29,27:4
Bricker, Laura Mrs, 1942, Ja 24,15:7
Bricker, Luther O, 1942, Ag 14,17:6
Bricker, Mead L, 1964, Ja 30,30:1
Bricker, Mervin W, 1948, S 14,29:5
Bricker, Sacks, 1961, S 3,60:4
Brickert, Carlton, 1943, D 24,14:6
Brickert, Carlton Mrs, 1949, Je 29,27:3
Brickett, Beatrice H, 1951, D 11,33:5
Brickham, Judal, 1954, N 26,29:3
Brickhouse, Ephraim L, 1958, Ap 23,33:3
Brickley, Bartholomew A, 1959, Ja 19,27:2
Brickley, Charles E, 1949, D 29,46:4
Brickman, Chaffee S Mrs, 1959, Ja 21,31:1
Brickman, Franklin L, 1961, Ag 26,17:6
Brickman, Gerald, 1950, O 30,20:7
Brickman, Harry, 1956, N 18,88:4
Brickman, Signe Theresa, 1924, Ap 10,23:4
Brickner, Barnett R, 1958, My 15,29:5
Brickner, David, 1908, Ja 31,7:5
Brickner, Edwin S, 1946, Ap 17,25:2
Brickner, Edwin S Mrs, 1950, D 3,89:2
Brickner, Isaac M Mrs, 1944, Ap 26,19:5
Brickner, Joseph, 1943, Ap 30,21:4
Brickner, Max, 1920, N 24,17:3
Brickner, Richard M, 1959, Ap 27,27:2
Brickner, Samuel M Dr, 1916, My 6,11:5
Brickner, Samuel M Mrs, 1923, Mr 15,19:5
Bricks, Ambrose G, 1954, N 12,21:3
Bridegum, John C, 1948, Jl 20,23:2
Bridenbaugh, Carl Mrs, 1943, Mr 25,21:2
Bridenbaugh, John H, 1953, Jl 30,23:5
Bridenbaugh, Richard G, 1951, S 2,49:1
Bridenbecker, Judson, 1952, My 9,23:2
Brides, Arthur E Dr, 1937, S 26,II,8:3
Bridewell, Carrie (Mrs C B Benedict), 1955, Ja 8,13:2
Bridge, Arthur H, 1937, Je 3,28:3
Bridge, Benjamin, 1950, O 23,23:3
Bridge, Charles A, 1908, O 30,9:6
Bridge, Cyprian Sir, 1924, Ag 17,24:4
Bridge, David A, 1946, Ap 7,44:2
Bridge, Don U Mrs, 1960, My 16,31:6
Bridge, Edward H, 1939, S 29,23:3
Bridge, Frank, 1941, Ja 12,46:1
Bridge, Frederick Sir, 1924, Mr 19,21:5
Bridge, George S, 1938, Je 9,23:4
Bridge, Hamilton G, 1955, S 30,25:3
Bridge, James H, 1939, My 29,15:3
Bridge, Josiah, 1940, Ap 16,23:2
Bridge, Norman Dr, 1925, Ja 11,5:2
Bridge, Samuel D, 1944, Mr 10,15:2
Bridge, Walter G, 1943, Ag 21,11:5
Bridge, William F, 1911, My 4,11:5
Bridge, William H Rev, 1937, Mr 5,21:3
Bridge, William J, 1946, Ap 5,25:2
Bridgeford, John R, 1942, Ja 5,20:2
Bridgeforth, Harold W, 1965, Ap 11,93:2
Bridgeman, Alfred, 1903, My 22,9:4
Bridgeman, Andrew Mrs, 1942, Ja 3,19:1
Bridgeman, Arthur Milnor, 1925, Jl 19,7:4
Bridgeman, Charles T, 1967, My 7,87:1
Bridgeman, F A, 1928, Ja 17,29:3
Bridgeman, F Sir, 1929, F 19,29:1
Bridgeman, Frederick B Rev, 1925, Ag 24,13:5
Bridgeman, Linden W, 1943, D 29,17:3
Bridgeman, Orlando (Earl of Bradford), 1957, Mr 24,86:1
Bridgeman, Wentzel A Mrs, 1947, Ap 1,27:2
Bridgens, Albert, 1941, Jl 7,15:1
Bridger, Edgar, 1946, Jl 2,25:4
Bridger, Felix J, 1952, N 26,23:1
Bridger, James S, 1956, Ap 20,25:3
Bridges, Amelia C Mrs (will, Jl 20,17:5), 1940, F 18, 41:3
Bridges, Benjamin F Gen, 1922, O 9,15:6
Bridges, Bernice, 1965, N 24,39:5
Bridges, Calvin B, 1938, D 28,26:1
Bridges, Capt, 1909, Ag 16,7:4
Bridges, Charles, 1950, My 31,29:2
Bridges, Charles H, 1948, S 12,74:1
Bridges, Charles S, 1961, N 26,88:1
Bridges, Elisha Hall Dr, 1903, D 10,9:5
Bridges, Ellen Mrs, 1952, Ap 24,31:4
Bridges, F M, 1885, Mr 21,2:7
Bridges, Florence E L Mrs, 1963, Ap 6,19:5
Bridges, Frank E, 1943, My 22,13:2
Bridges, Frederick J, 1950, Ag 7,19:4
Bridges, George T M Sir, 1939, N 27,17:3
Bridges, H F G, 1947, Ag 11,23:5
Bridges, H Styles Mrs (por), 1938, My 26,25:3
Bridges, Henry P, 1957, Ap 24,33:3
Bridges, Henry W, 1943, Ag 6,15:3
Bridges, Horace J, 1955, O 9,86:2
Bridges, John J, 1941, S 21,45:1; 1948, Je 18,23:5
Bridges, John J Rev, 1918, O 23,13:1
Bridges, John S, 1937, Ja 16,17:3
Bridges, Kenneth L, 1962, Je 5,41:1
Bridges, Kenneth L Mrs, 1967, Ap 24,33:4
Bridges, Lucas, 1949, Ap 6,29:5
Bridges, Milton A, 1939, Ag 20,32:4
Bridges, R S, 1930, Ap 22,29:1
Bridges, Ralph L, 1946, Ap 19,29:1
Bridges, Robert, 1941, S 3,24:3
Bridges, Samuel, 1937, Ja 11,20:3
Bridges, Samuel W, 1943, Mr 1,19:2
Bridges, Styles (funl, N 29,41:5; will, D 6,24:1), 1961, N 27,1:4
Bridges, Styles (est inventory), 1962, My 4,25:3
Bridges, Thomas, 1937, Ja 13,4:3
Bridges, Thomas Mrs, 1955, Ja 11,25:1
Bridges, Thomas R, 1943, Je 8,21:3
Bridges, Tommy, 1968, Ap 20,33:3
Bridges, William, 1951, S 28,31:1
Bridges, William Mrs, 1949, Je 21,25:3; 1968, My 3, 54:4

Bridges-Adams, William, 1965, Ag 19,31:5
Bridgett, Charles R, 1946, My 12,45:3
Bridgett, George E, 1960, F 6,19:6
Bridgett, Nora Mrs, 1937, Ap 25,4:4
Bridgetts, Frank E, 1952, F 4,17:3
Bridgetts, Harry W, 1963, D 31,19:3
Bridgetts, John Jr, 1959, My 19,33:4
Bridgewater, John Jr, 1951, S 8,17:4
Bridgham, Joseph, 1865, Ap 2,8:4
Bridgham, William Haliburton, 1916, Ag 1,9:6
Bridgham, William Haliburton Mrs, 1916, Ag 1,9:6
Bridgman, Burt N, 1951, My 24,35:5
Bridgman, Donald W, 1953, My 21,31:4
Bridgman, Edwin B, 1958, My 11,87:1
Bridgman, Elise, 1881, Jl 10,12:2
Bridgman, Fred L, 1941, Jl 9,21:5
Bridgman, Frederick B Rev Dr, 1925, Ag 27,19:6
Bridgman, George B, 1943, D 17,27:1
Bridgman, George Herbert Dr, 1925, Jl 11,11:6
Bridgman, Harry B, 1954, D 2,31:4
Bridgman, Herbert (funl, O 1,19:3), 1924, S 27,16:3
Bridgman, Herbert L, 1924, S 30,23:1
Bridgman, Hugh, 1968, Je 7,39:1
Bridgman, Laura D, 1889, My 25,5:2
Bridgman, Louis W, 1960, My 13,31:5
Bridgman, Mary Layton Mrs, 1915, N 11,13:5
Bridgman, Oliver B Mrs, 1938, Je 30,23:6
Bridgman, Ray C, 1951, N 26,45:3
Bridgman, Robert (funl, Mr 25,11:6), 1914, Mr 22, 15:4
Bridgman, Thomas F, 1955, S 19,25:2
Bridgman, Walter R, 1947, Je 24,23:6
Bridgman Amy S, 1949, O 15,15:5
Bridgmen, O B, 1933, Je 24,13:1
Bridgwater, William, 1966, D 16,47:5
Bridie, Alex L, 1952, Ag 24,88:6
Bridie, James, 1951, Ja 30,25:1
Bridle, Augustus, 1952, D 22,25:6
Bridoux, Eugene, 1955, Je 7,33:4
Bridwell, John C Mrs, 1942, D 17,37:2
Brieant, Charles L, 1966, F 3,31:4
Bried, James L, 1951, Mr 5,21:4
Briederbach, Rudolph, 1914, Ag 17,7:1
Briegel, George F, 1968, My 14,47:3
Briegel, Jesse, 1964, Ja 6,47:2
Brieger, Fritz, 1948, N 6,13:4
Brieger, Fritz Mrs, 1959, Mr 29,81:1
Briegleb, Gustave A, 1943, My 22,13:5
Briel, Rebecca Mrs, 1925, Ag 15,11:5
Brien, Donald G Mrs (Louise Lerch), 1967, Ja 6,35:4
Brien, William M, 1947, N 20,29:3
Brienza, Giosue, 1949, Je 23,27:5
Brienza, James V, 1964, Je 6,23:2
Brier, Charles, 1959, My 25,29:3
Brier, Frank L, 1957, S 6,21:2
Briere, Emilie Mrs, 1941, F 3,20:2
Brierley, James Mrs, 1941, D 23,21:2
Brierley, John R, 1961, O 15,88:1
Brierley, William W, 1950, Jl 13,25:6
Brierly, G Mrs, 1926, Je 6,II,9:1
Brierly, J Ernest, 1967, N 21,47:2
Brierly, Ralph C, 1960, D 3,23:4
Brierton, Robert S, 1957, Je 9,88:5
Brierton, Sylvester L, 1956, F 12,88:4
Brierton, Thomas F, 1945, Ap 7,15:6
Briese, Lester E, 1959, My 31,76:6
Briesemeister, Otto, 1910, Jl 6,7:5
Briesemeister, William A, 1967, My 11,54:5
Briest, Joseph I, 1903, Je 10,9:6
Brietz, Eddie, 1946, My 15,21:2
Brieux, E, 1932, D 7,21:1
Briffault, Robert, 1948, D 14,29:1
Brigance, William N, 1960, F 1,27:5
Brigantic, Margaret, 1922, Ja 26,17:6
Brigden, Frederick H, 1956, Mr 27,35:4
Brigden, George, 1941, My 8,23:3
Brigden, George I, 1966, Jl 25,27:4
Briggie, William E, 1962, S 14,31:6
Briggin, George, 1947, Ja 28,24:3
Briggs, Ada W Mrs, 1942, Jl 26,31:3
Briggs, Alanson T, 1946, F 3,40:1
Briggs, Albert W, 1910, Ag 6,7:6
Briggs, Alison Capt, 1905, Ja 21,9:4
Briggs, Alonzo M Mrs, 1946, S 19,31:2
Briggs, Arthur C, 1939, Ja 26,21:5
Briggs, Asa S, 1949, Mr 11,26:3
Briggs, Benjamin F Mrs, 1964, D 29,27:3
Briggs, Benjamin M Dr, 1924, O 2,23:3
Briggs, Bernard R, 1949, Jl 26,27:3
Briggs, Bertrand S, 1939, O 8,49:2
Briggs, C A, 1930, Ja 4,17:3
Briggs, C F, 1877, Je 22,5:4; 1877, D 23,3:5
Briggs, C Frank, 1962, Ja 1,23:4
Briggs, Cabel T Mrs, 1952, Je 8,86:5
Briggs, Caspar W (por), 1942, Jl 11,13:3
Briggs, Catherine, 1957, O 18,23:1
Briggs, Charles, 1943, N 4,23:5
Briggs, Charles A, 1942, D 15,28:2
Briggs, Charles Augustus Dr (funl), 1913, Je 12,9:6
Briggs, Charles E Dr, 1937, Ja 31,II,8:5
Briggs, Charles G Capt, 1919, Mr 4,11:3
Briggs, Charles J, 1941, N 28,23:2
Briggs, Charles Mrs, 1903, Ap 19,7:4
Briggs, Charles S, 1943, S 14,23:2
Briggs, Christie B, 1946, Je 14,21:5
Briggs, Clifton D, 1939, Mr 24,21:2
Briggs, D C, 1903, My 17,7:6
Briggs, D D (see also Jl 5), 1876, Jl 9,8:6
Briggs, David H, 1949, O 16,88:6
Briggs, Dwight N, 1954, Jl 28,23:3
Briggs, Dwight N Mrs, 1946, F 24,44:1
Briggs, E Fred, 1944, Ap 1,13:2
Briggs, Edmund F, 1945, Jl 11,8:1
Briggs, Edward F, 1959, My 22,27:2
Briggs, Ella de M L Mrs, 1941, N 23,52:1
Briggs, Elmer L, 1948, Ja 13,25:5
Briggs, Emilie G, 1944, Je 16,19:4
Briggs, Emily W Mrs, 1955, My 18,31:4
Briggs, Ernest, 1947, O 16,27:4
Briggs, Frank C Mrs, 1950, F 19,76:2
Briggs, Frank H, 1938, Ja 14,23:3
Briggs, Frank H Mrs, 1943, N 24,21:6
Briggs, Frank O Ex-Sen (funl, My 11,7:6), 1913, My 9,11:5
Briggs, Frank W, 1941, F 6,21:5
Briggs, Frankland, 1944, Mr 18,13:1
Briggs, Frankland B Mrs, 1938, N 18,21:1
Briggs, Franklyn F, 1948, N 1,23:5
Briggs, Fred, 1945, S 6,25:4
Briggs, Frederic F, 1940, D 2,23:5
Briggs, Frederick W, 1942, O 20,21:3; 1959, Ag 2,81:1
Briggs, Garland B, 1959, S 7,15:5
Briggs, George, 1869, Jl 1,5:5; 1947, Je 30,19:4
Briggs, George E, 1944, F 14,17:6
Briggs, George E Mrs, 1949, O 20,29:1; 1953, N 12, 31:4
Briggs, George I, 1944, My 5,19:2
Briggs, George M Mrs, 1941, S 25,25:4
Briggs, George N, 1944, O 6,23:5
Briggs, George W, 1966, Ap 19,41:2
Briggs, Gilmore W, 1872, F 22,5:4
Briggs, Glen W, 1952, Ap 28,19:2
Briggs, Glenn, 1956, Ag 6,23:2
Briggs, Gray C, 1942, Ja 25,41:1
Briggs, Hal, 1925, Ap 30,21:4
Briggs, Harlan, 1952, Ja 27,76:6
Briggs, Harold R, 1952, O 28,31:5
Briggs, Henry B, 1952, D 21,53:2
Briggs, Henry B H Mrs, 1945, Jl 2,15:6
Briggs, Herbert J, 1940, My 16,23:3
Briggs, Herbert Mrs, 1946, S 4,23:4
Briggs, Herbert W, 1957, Ap 3,31:5
Briggs, Isaac, 1882, Ag 15,5:2
Briggs, J Albert, 1956, Ap 14,17:3
Briggs, J Emmons, 1942, Ja 5,20:1
Briggs, Jacob, 1938, My 20,19:5
Briggs, James F, 1952, O 3,23:1
Briggs, James H, 1937, Ap 14,25:4
Briggs, James M, 1938, O 20,23:2
Briggs, Jeremiah, 1876, My 30,5:2
Briggs, John A, 1952, Ap 3,35:5
Briggs, John B, 1952, Je 10,27:3
Briggs, John E, 1937, D 28,22:4
Briggs, John H Mrs, 1943, My 13,21:3
Briggs, John Mrs, 1946, Ja 11,21:1
Briggs, Joseph, 1937, Mr 31,23:5
Briggs, Joseph W, 1872, Mr 10,5:5
Briggs, Josiah A, 1941, My 28,25:1
Briggs, Katherine M Mrs, 1947, F 16,57:2
Briggs, Kenneth M, 1946, Mr 26,29:3
Briggs, L B R, 1934, Ap 25,21:1
Briggs, Leland S, 1964, F 4,30:8
Briggs, Llewellyn R, 1960, N 16,41:4
Briggs, Lloyd A, 1950, Ja 6,21:3
Briggs, Lloyd V, 1941, Mr 1,15:3
Briggs, Lucia R, 1960, Ja 11,45:5
Briggs, Lucius W, 1940, S 11,25:1
Briggs, Lyman J, 1963, Mr 27,4:6
Briggs, Mary, 1954, N 8,21:3
Briggs, Mathias J (Matt), 1962, Je 13,41:2
Briggs, Merton L, 1948, N 3,27:4
Briggs, N S, 1884, D 10,5:4
Briggs, Olive M, 1961, D 14,43:2
Briggs, P Dixon, 1954, Ja 22,27:1
Briggs, P Zamor, 1948, Je 29,23:3
Briggs, Philip H Gen, 1914, Ag 28,9:6
Briggs, Raymond W, 1959, D 25,21:5
Briggs, Reginald J, 1942, F 7,17:5
Briggs, Robert H, 1953, Je 4,29:6
Briggs, Robert W, 1957, Ap 6,19:6
Briggs, S Ellis Maj, 1921, O 2,22:4
Briggs, Samuel A, 1963, S 24,39:3
Briggs, Stephen A, 1965, Ap 14,42:1
Briggs, Stephen D, 1941, Ap 17,23:3
Briggs, Stephen H, 1913, Jl 22,7:6
Briggs, Stuart E, 1945, D 22,19:3
Briggs, Thomas H, 1941, My 21,23:4
Briggs, Thomas H 3d Mrs, 1940, Ja 11,23:6
Briggs, Thomas R, 1952, Ag 12,19:7; 1961, Jl 13,29:6
Briggs, Thomas W, 1964, Mr 3,35:1
Briggs, Victor H Sr, 1945, Jl 24,23:1
Briggs, Walter B, 1943, N 2,25:4
Briggs, Walter O, 1952, Ja 18,27:1
Briggs, Walter O Sr Mrs, 1955, F 14,19:4
Briggs, Walter P, 1962, S 7,30:1
Briggs, Wanton, 1923, Mr 3,13:5
Briggs, Wilbur L, 1947, Ag 28,23:5
Briggs, William H, 1952, Ag 1,17:5
Briggs, Winfield S, 1961, Mr 18,23:4
Brigham, A De L, 1881, N 8,5:2
Brigham, A P, 1932, Ap 1,21:1
Brigham, Albert P Mrs, 1948, N 29,23:3
Brigham, Alex F, 1949, O 13,27:6
Brigham, Arthur W Mrs (Ethel Frank), 1968, S 28, 33:4
Brigham, Carl C, 1943, Ja 25,14:3
Brigham, Cecil E, 1956, S 6,25:4
Brigham, Charles H, 1947, O 19,66:6
Brigham, Clarence S, 1963, Ag 14,33:1
Brigham, Cyril A, 1952, Ag 6,21:1
Brigham, Elbert S, 1962, Jl 6,25:3
Brigham, Ernest L Mrs, 1941, Jl 1,23:2
Brigham, Fred C, 1951, D 25,31:4
Brigham, Frederick L, 1953, Ja 19,23:2
Brigham, George J, 1962, Ag 29,29:4
Brigham, Harry, 1937, Je 9,25:4
Brigham, Harry H, 1941, O 3,23:2
Brigham, Henry D, 1944, F 3,19:5
Brigham, Henry H, 1940, D 25,27:1
Brigham, Henry H Jr, 1959, O 26,29:5
Brigham, Henry M, 1938, S 9,21:4
Brigham, Henry R, 1947, O 30,26:3; 1964, D 26,17:3
Brigham, Henry R Mrs, 1943, Ja 24,43:2
Brigham, James G, 1952, Ag 29,23:1
Brigham, John H, 1912, F 12,11:5
Brigham, Loriman S, 1903, D 20,7:6
Brigham, Lucius W, 1943, Ag 26,17:4
Brigham, Mrs (A A Young), 1882, Jl 5,8:6
Brigham, Oshea S, 1938, O 20,23:3
Brigham, Percy T (funl), 1966, O 9,44:1
Brigham, Robert H, 1957, D 27,19:2
Brigham, Ruben, 1946, D 7,21:3
Brigham, Susan, 1912, Mr 4,11:4
Brigham, Theodore W Jr, 1949, My 20,28:6
Brigham, William E Mrs, 1954, O 21,27:3
Brigham, William H, 1940, Ap 16,23:2
Brighouse, Harold, 1958, Jl 26,15:3
Bright, Alan, 1940, Mr 10,49:1
Bright, Arthur A Jr, 1953, My 15,23:3
Bright, Arthur D, 1940, D 13,23:5
Bright, Charles Sir, 1937, N 22,19:5
Bright, Clarence E (por), 1949, F 22,23:3
Bright, David E, 1965, Ap 13,37:1
Bright, E, 1931, Mr 19,23:3
Bright, Fred E, 1925, O 8,27:4
Bright, George H, 1946, Mr 13,29:5
Bright, George W, 1949, Mr 21,23:4
Bright, Golding Mrs, 1945, Ag 14,21:4
Bright, J B, 1880, Ja 9,5:2
Bright, J Fulmer, 1953, D 31,19:3
Bright, J L, 1947, Ag 13,23:5
Bright, James C, 1947, N 13,28:2
Bright, James H, 1959, Ja 6,33:2
Bright, Jesse D, 1875, My 21,6:7
Bright, John, 1889, Mr 27,1:1; 1943, F 7,48:3
Bright, John I, 1940, Je 26,23:5
Bright, John M Mrs, 1943, Ag 17,17:5
Bright, John Mrs, 1878, My 14,5:3; 1952, Ag 25,17:3
Bright, Kenneth L, 1948, N 30,27:5
Bright, L V, 1933, O 24,21:3
Bright, Marshal H Maj, 1907, Mr 1,9:5
Bright, Mary A Mrs, 1924, Ap 21,17:5
Bright, O Percy, 1938, My 8,II,6:3
Bright, Orville T 3d, 1958, Mr 23,88:3
Bright, R G, 1941, Ap 17,23:5
Bright, Robert, 1943, D 19,48:3; 1957, Ag 22,27:4
Bright, Robert A, 1953, S 5,15:2
Bright, Robert L Mrs, 1924, D 26,15:5
Bright, Robert S Mrs, 1966, F 22,23:2
Bright, Samuel, 1870, F 17,3:6
Bright, Stanley, 1957, S 28,17:1
Bright, William H, 1946, Mr 8,21:2
Bright, William H Mrs, 1960, S 5,15:5
Bright, William J, 1907, Jl 8,7:6
Bright, William T, 1949, Jl 4,13:4
Bright, Willis C, 1966, My 20,47:4
Brightly, Frederick C, 1947, Je 16,21:2
Brightly, Walter H, 1950, Je 28,27:4
Brightman, Edgar S, 1953, F 27,21:1
Brightman, Horace I, 1941, Ap 4,21:5
Brightman, Joseph F, 1942, Je 30,21:1
Brightmeyer, John, 1925, Ag 2,5:4
Brighton, Alfred R Jr, 1942, Je 24,17:5
Brigman, Bennett M, 1938, F 9,20:3
Brignall, H Warren, 1948, Ag 12,21:3
Brignoll, P, 1884, O 31,1:7
Brikoff, Paul, 1952, Ag 13,16:3
Bril, Henry, 1947, Jl 27,46:2
Bril, Jacques L Mrs, 1962, Ag 16,27:4
Brilant, Saul Mrs, 1964, Ag 12,35:4
Brilioth, Yngve T, 1959, Ap 30,31:4
Brill, A A Mrs, 1963, Ag 21,33:1
Brill, A Henry, 1958, Jl 19,15:5
Brill, Abraham, 1943, F 21,32:5; 1950, My 9,29:4
Brill, Abraham A, 1948, Mr 3,23:1
Brill, Charles, 1940, Jl 20,15:5
Brill, Charles S, 1951, O 11,37:4
Brill, Edward G, 1914, Je 9,11:4

Brill, Edward Mrs, 1937, Je 27,II,6:6
Brill, Frederick W, 1937, O 24,II,8:3
Brill, George M, 1959, Jl 6,27:3
Brill, Jacob S Mrs, 1945, Mr 24,17:5
Brill, Jeanette G, 1964, Mr 31,35:3
Brill, Maurice, 1951, Jl 7,13:3
Brill, Max D (por), 1938, Ja 20,23:5
Brill, Morris M, 1947, F 10,29:2
Brill, Morris Mrs, 1941, F 5,19:2
Brill, Nathan E, 1925, D 17,23:5
Brill, Nathan E Mrs, 1950, My 24,30:2
Brill, Nathaniel E, 1925, D 14,21:4
Brill, Regina Mrs, 1906, Ap 28,11:6
Brill, S, 1931, My 14,23:1
Brill, Samuel, 1957, Jl 14,73:2
Brill, Samuel S, 1953, Ap 1,29:4
Brill, Sidney D, 1951, Ja 28,76:3
Brill, Sol Mrs, 1960, Ja 2,13:3
Brill, Thomas, 1951, Ag 11,11:4
Brill, Thomas G, 1948, Jl 29,42:2
Brill, Thomas Mrs, 1951, Ag 26,80:2
Brill, Walter J, 1937, Ap 27,23:2
Brill, Walter P, 1943, N 18,23:2
Brill, William F, 1907, N 18,7:7
Brilleman, Aaron, 1954, N 4,31:1
Briller, Louis G Mrs, 1961, Ag 27,85:2
Brillhart, Robert W Mrs, 1958, Mr 31,6:8
Brilliant, Paul, 1954, Mr 24,27:3
Brillinger, Fred, 1956, Ja 11,29:1
Brilmayer, William L, 1937, Ap 14,25:1
Brim, Charles J, 1963, Je 10,31:4
Brimberg, Henry A, 1959, O 4,86:2
Brimberg, Samuel N, 1963, Je 14,31:3
Brimmer, Lester G, 1942, O 3,15:6
Brin, Arthur Mrs, 1961, S 7,35:1
Brin, Joseph C, 1952, Mr 22,13:2
Brina, Ernest C, 1960, N 4,33:4
Brincard, Baron C, 1953, Jl 2,23:2
Brincherhoff, Frank R, 1950, S 20,31:1
Brinckerhoff, Arthur F, 1959, Jl 1,31:2
Brinckerhoff, Charles Owens, 1916, Ja 6,13:5
Brinckerhoff, Charles R, 1941, S 13,17:2
Brinckerhoff, Clarence V, 1947, Je 12,25:5
Brinckerhoff, Edwin O, 1915, D 9,15:6
Brinckerhoff, Elbert A, 1875, Mr 8,2:4; 1943, N 12,21:2
Brinckerhoff, Elbert Adrian, 1913, Mr 24,11:3
Brinckerhoff, Garret, 1944, Je 4,42:2
Brinckerhoff, H Everett, 1959, S 20,86:4
Brinckerhoff, H Rockwood, 1942, N 7,15:5
Brinckerhoff, Henry M, 1949, O 13,27:1
Brinckerhoff, Henry M Mrs, 1942, Ap 23,23:2
Brinckerhoff, Herbert C Sr, 1960, Mr 9,33:2
Brinckerhoff, Howard F, 1950, S 9,17:4
Brinckerhoff, J Howard, 1957, O 18,23:3
Brinckerhoff, Julia F Mrs, 1940, Ag 22,19:3
Brinckerhoff, La Tourette, 1942, N 1,53:2
Brinckerhoff, Matthew V B, 1938, D 20,25:6
Brinckerhoff, T H Capt, 1901, D 3,9:5
Brinckerhoff, Theodore Mrs, 1961, Mr 21,37:4
Brinckerhoff, Walter Remsen Dr, 1911, Mr 3,11:5
Brinckerhoff, Walter W, 1957, Jl 29,19:5
Brinckerhoof, James E, 1958, S 5,27:3
Brinckman, Theodore Sir, 1937, S 10,24:1
Brind, Harold C, 1941, Je 12,23:2
Brind, Patrick, 1963, O 5,25:4
Brinda, Dowager Princess Maharani of Kapurthala, 1962, Ag 9,25:2
Brindamoor, George W, 1941, Ag 3,35:1
Brindeau, P L E, 1882, Mr 11,5:3
Brindell, R P, 1926, D 31,13:4
Brindis, Joseph, 1951, O 14,88:4
Brindle, Herbie, 1949, N 19,13:5
Brindley, Alma H, 1943, S 9,25:4
Brindley, Audley Jr, 1957, N 21,33:3
Brindley, Augustus R, 1947, Mr 22,13:6
Brindley, Elias B, 1946, Je 18,25:5
Brindley, Henry L, 1958, Je 22,76:8
Brindley, Oscar A Maj, 1918, My 3,15:3
Brindley, Stephen, 1940, D 18,25:3
Brindley, Theodore H, 1950, O 28,17:5
Brindley, Wallace Mrs, 1948, Jl 7,23:2
Brindley, William A Sr, 1961, Ag 18,21:5
Brine, Mary Dow Mrs, 1925, Jl 21,21:5
Brine, Paul B, 1967, N 4,33:3
Brinegar, Edgar P, 1943, Mr 4,19:2
Briner, Emil A, 1944, O 9,23:5
Briner, George C Mrs, 1955, D 14,39:1
Brines, Osborne A, 1960, My 19,37:5
Briney, Mark R, 1948, My 2,76:3
Briney, Robert M, 1967, N 4,33:2
Briney, William N Mrs, 1950, Ap 24,25:4
Bring, Karl, 1949, N 1,27:2
Bring, Louis H, 1961, Jl 17,21:4
Bringer, Randolph, 1943, My 6,19:3
Bringham, Arthur H, 1907, Mr 18,7:2
Bringhurst, Edward, 1939, D 9,15:4
Bringhurst, Robert R, 1949, Ap 17,76:8
Bringhurst, Robert R Mrs, 1952, My 31,14:7
Bringhurst, Robert Ralston, 1912, Ag 4,II,11:6
Bringhurst, William, 1962, Je 11,31:5
Bringhurst, William Mrs, 1945, Ja 1,22:3
Bringloe, Bill, 1937, D 31,15:3
Bringuier, Paul, 1946, My 15,21:2
Brini, Giuseppe, 1941, Ja 19,40:3
Brinin, Roche-Leah Mrs, 1951, Ap 14,15:4
Brininstool, Earl A, 1957, Jl 31,23:4
Brink, A J E, 1947, O 18,15:3
Brink, A M, 1937, Jl 21,21:3
Brink, Aug, 1941, N 18,25:5
Brink, Benjamin Myer, 1915, O 4,9:6
Brink, Charles E, 1939, Ag 2,19:5
Brink, Eben C, 1964, Je 23,33:2
Brink, Francis G, 1952, Je 25,15:1
Brink, Frank M, 1944, Mr 23,19:5
Brink, Fred, 1949, S 15,27:3
Brink, Frederick, 1968, My 28,47:1
Brink, George W, 1950, O 24,29:5
Brink, Henry W, 1950, Jl 26,25:3
Brink, Hobart D, 1948, Ag 22,60:6
Brink, James W, 1942, Jl 26,31:3
Brink, Joel, 1940, Ja 3,22:2
Brink, John E, 1950, O 7,21:8
Brink, Mary A Mrs, 1942, F 27,17:4
Brink, Mary L (Sister Teresa), 1954, Jl 2,19:5
Brink, P H, 1903, Ag 18,7:6
Brink, Persen M Mrs, 1959, My 2,23:4
Brink, William Rea, 1905, Mr 31,9:6
Brinker, Eugene F, 1958, Je 11,35:2
Brinker, J M Capt, 1903, Je 10,9:6
Brinker, Robert C, 1967, Jl 8,25:4
Brinker, Robert H, 1959, Je 2,35:1
Brinker, Una A, 1952, N 13,31:3
Brinker, Vivian H, 1950, Ap 7,25:5
Brinkerhoff, Abraham S Dr, 1919, N 9,22:3
Brinkerhoff, Charles F, 1917, D 22,11:5
Brinkerhoff, David Mrs, 1924, Je 9,17:5
Brinkerhoff, Frederick W, 1966, Ag 14,88:2
Brinkerhoff, Harry A, 1949, My 4,29:1
Brinkerhoff, J H, 1903, Ja 18,7:5
Brinkerhoff, R B Gen, 1911, Je 6,9:5
Brinkerhoff, Richard S, 1947, Ap 26,13:5
Brinkerhoff, Robert M, 1958, F 18,28:2
Brinkerhoff, Robert M Mrs, 1961, D 10,88:5
Brinkerhoff, Walter Mrs, 1909, Ap 3,9:5
Brinkerhoff, William J, 1954, F 27,13:4
Brinkherhoff, Frederic, 1943, Jl 29,17:2
Brinkley, Carlin L, 1952, Ja 23,27:4
Brinkley, Edward S, 1949, Jl 26,27:4
Brinkley, Edwin T, 1949, Ap 28,31:5
Brinkley, Frank Capt, 1912, O 29,13:5
Brinkley, Harry A, 1956, F 21,33:1
Brinkley, Hugh L, 1904, Ja 8,7:5
Brinkley, John R (por), 1942, My 27,24:2
Brinkley, Nell, 1944, O 22,47:3
Brinkley, Nell (will), 1945, Mr 21,16:2
Brinkley, Robert S Mrs, 1948, Mr 16,27:2
Brinkley, Roberta F, 1967, Je 11,87:2
Brinkman, Aug, 1941, S 17,23:4
Brinkman, Ernest, 1938, D 30,15:4
Brinkman, Eugene J, 1967, Je 27,39:3
Brinkman, Frank H, 1962, S 22,25:1
Brinkman, Louis H, 1937, F 12,23:5
Brinkman, William M, 1942, N 4,23:6
Brinkmann, Reginald R, 1954, D 1,31:4
Brinkop, Harry, 1949, O 25,27:3
Brinkworth, John J, 1966, Ja 23,88:8
Brinley, C Coapes, 1960, Jl 14,27:2
Brinley, Charles E, 1963, Jl 9,31:3
Brinley, Daniel P, 1963, Ag 1,27:3
Brinley, Gordon (Mrs Danl P), 1966, Ja 9,56:8
Brinley, Harold L, 1939, Jl 11,19:4
Brinley, Henry, 1949, D 28,32:2
Brinley, Henry D, 1957, My 13,31:4
Brinley, John R, 1946, F 2,13:2
Brinley, John R Jr, 1954, Mr 21,89:2
Brinley, Richard, 1939, Jl 6,23:4
Brinnier, William D, 1924, Ja 31,15:5
Brinser, Harry L, 1945, D 10,21:3
Brinsley, George, 1875, My 25,6:7
Brinsley, Henry John (Duke of Rutland), 1925, My 9,15:5
Brinsley, Rev Dr (funl), 1873, N 2,3:4
Brinsley, Richard E, 1947, F 16,57:6
Brinsmade, Frederick G, 1945, Ap 17,23:4
Brinsmade, H N Rev, 1879, Ja 19,7:4
Brinsmade, J B, 1884, Ja 4,5:2
Brinsmade, J N Mrs, 1905, Mr 22,9:6
Brinsmade, Louis L, 1920, Je 20,18:4
Brinsmade, Mary G Mrs, 1939, D 5,27:6
Brinsmade, Paul S, 1964, Ap 10,39:8
Brinsmade, Thomas C, 1941, F 16,40:2
Brinsmade, William B, 1942, S 24,27:3
Brinson, Samuel Mitchell, 1922, Ap 14,17:6
Brinson, Stanley W, 1951, Mr 22,31:1
Brintenstool, Harry, 1960, Mr 8,33:2
Brintnall, P, 1880, S 20,1:4
Brinton, Caleb S, 1942, Ap 25,13:2
Brinton, Caleb S Mrs, 1941, Ap 5,17:5
Brinton, Charles M Mrs, 1946, Jl 10,23:5
Brinton, Charles W, 1950, Je 2,23:3
Brinton, Christian, 1942, Jl 15,19:2
Brinton, Clement S, 1963, Jl 27,17:2
Brinton, Crane Dr, 1968, S 8,84:2
Brinton, Douglas E, 1946, Ja 18,19:1
Brinton, Edward Mrs, 1939, Ja 24,19:4
Brinton, Ferree Sr, 1941, N 13,27:3
Brinton, Francis D, 1951, O 20,15:5
Brinton, Frederick S, 1938, O 15,17:2
Brinton, Gertrude W Mrs, 1942, F 27,18:2
Brinton, Helen C, 1946, Ag 3,15:3
Brinton, Howard T, 1966, N 30,47:2
Brinton, John H Mrs, 1924, D 23,19:4
Brinton, Robert F, 1946, Ja 20,42:5
Brinton, W B, 1937, D 21,23:5
Brinton, Willard C, 1957, N 30,21:3
Brintzenhoff, Jonathan S, 1949, S 27,28:3
Brintzinghoffer, Theodore C, 1952, Ag 28,23:5
Briody, Henry E, 1945, N 28,27:3
Briody, William F, 1964, Mr 1,83:2
Brion, Adolph E, 1925, Ja 29,19:3
Brion, Oscar P, 1941, F 17,15:5
Brion, Paul F, 1943, S 27,19:2
Briones, Manuel, 1957, O 1,33:3
Brior, Bennie, 1914, Jl 17,9:4
Briordy, William J, 1966, Ag 2,33:3
Brioschi, Pedro A, 1943, N 15,19:2
Bris, Pierre Le, 1940, F 14,21:4
Brisacher, Emil, 1951, Ja 28,76:1
Brisban, George Mrs, 1943, Jl 16,17:5
Brisbane, A, 1936, D 26,1:5
Brisbane, Arthur Mrs, 1967, O 31,49:4
Brisbane, Emily, 1959, My 2,23:3
Brisbane, George, 1942, D 8,25:6
Brisbin, John, 1880, F 4,3:4
Brisbin, Willsie E, 1948, N 18,27:4
Brisch, Edward G, 1960, Ap 10,86:1
Brisco, Norris A, 1944, My 10,19:1
Briscoe, A M Judge, 1901, N 10,7:6
Briscoe, Benjamin (por), 1945, Je 28,19:1
Briscoe, Benjamin B, 1946, N 11,27:1
Briscoe, Chesleigh H, 1944, D 4,23:2
Briscoe, Frank J, 1953, My 28,23:3
Briscoe, Henry V A, 1961, S 26,39:3
Briscoe, Herman T, 1960, O 10,31:3
Briscoe, Hugh V, 1940, D 26,19:3
Briscoe, J C Gen, 1869, My 26,4:7
Briscoe, James, 1950, N 6,27:5
Briscoe, James Mrs, 1937, Je 29,21:2
Briscoe, James T, 1903, Ap 23,1:2
Briscoe, John S, 1943, Jl 7,19:5
Briscoe, Lottie, 1950, Mr 22,27:3
Briscoe, N Butler, 1945, Ja 15,19:6
Briscoe, Peter F, 1955, Mr 29,29:3
Briscoe, Robert Pearce Adm, 1968, O 16,47:1
Briscoe, Samuel M, 1940, Mr 15,23:4
Briscoe, William E, 1938, Ag 20,15:2
Brisebois, Joseph M, 1954, Ag 6,17:2
Brisk, A Lincoln, 1957, D 23,23:4
Brisk, Charles S Mrs, 1951, F 7,29:4
Brisker, Dani, 1959, S 30,37:2
Briskin, Jehuda, 1948, Ag 26,21:4
Briskin, Sam, 1961, My 16,43:1
Briskin, Samuel J, 1968, N 15,47:1
Briskman, Samuel, 1967, F 16,39:1
Briskovich, Joseph, 1952, O 15,31:5
Brislin, Henry C, 1946, Je 17,21:2
Brislin, Hugh J, 1945, O 13,15:1
Brislin, James F, 1948, Mr 10,28:3
Brislin, John, 1907, Mr 28,9:6
Brislin, John A, 1944, Je 27,19:2
Brislin, Thomas J, 1962, Mr 2,29:2
Brisman, Harry, 1962, My 3,33:2
Brison, Peter Van V, 1964, F 26,21:1
Brisotti, Albert A, 1964, Ag 10,31:3
Brissel, Arthur R, 1966, O 8,31:3
Brissel, Arthur R Mrs, 1955, Jl 15,31:8
Brissette , Frederick J, 1941, Ja 5,44:6
Brissie, Eugene F, 1961, Mr 29,33:2
Brisson, Adolphe, 1925, Ag 29,11:6
Brisson, Alphonse V, 1959, Mr 27,23:4
Brisson, Carl (C Pedersen),(funl, S 30,31:5), 1958, S 26,27:3
Brisson, Henri, 1912, Ap 15,9:5
Brisson, Pierre, 1965, Ja 1,19:3
Bristed, Charles Astor, 1874, Ja 16,4:7
Bristel, Richard C, 1943, S 3,19:2
Brister, Charles J, 1955, D 18,92:5
Brister, Charles J Mrs, 1937, D 18,21:6
Brister, Emma S Mrs, 1937, S 28,23:2
Brister, Frederick E, 1946, Mr 18,21:4
Brister, Miller M (por), 1949, Je 12,76:1
Brister, Wilbur L, 1944, D 11,23:3
Bristley, Frank D, 1941, O 2,25:5
Bristol, Arthur E, 1954, My 6,33:3
Bristol, Arthur L (por), 1942, Ap 22,23:3
Bristol, Augusta Cooper Mrs, 1910, O 6,11:4
Bristol, Bennet B, 1942, N 13,23:2
Bristol, Claude M, 1951, D 17,31:2
Bristol, Edgar H, 1944, Jl 25,19:2
Bristol, Edith Mrs, 1946, F 17,42:3
Bristol, Edward N, 1946, Mr 4,23:2
Bristol, Effie R Mrs, 1942, O 7,25:4
Bristol, Ellen G Mrs, 1940, Je 25,23:2
Bristol, Emmett A, 1937, Je 4,23:3
Bristol, Eugene S Mrs, 1943, Mr 14,26:3
Bristol, Frances L, 1953, D 21,31:5
Bristol, George W, 1939, Ag 30,17:6
Bristol, Henry P, 1959, Ap 16,33:1
Bristol, Henry P Mrs, 1968, Mr 3,89:2

Bristol, Homer C, 1914, Ja 23,11:5
Bristol, Howard H, 1951, Je 4,27:2
Bristol, J E, 1928, My 6,7:3
Bristol, John Bunyan, 1909, S 2,9:3
Bristol, Lawrence, 1946, Ja 10,23:5
Bristol, Lee H, 1962, S 24,29:1
Bristol, Lee H Mrs, 1951, D 25,31:5
Bristol, Leverett D, 1957, F 21,27:6
Bristol, Lucius M, 1953, My 11,27:4
Bristol, Marchioness of (D F Emblim de Zulueta), 1953, Mr 29,92:1
Bristol, Mark L, 1939, My 14,III,7:1
Bristol, Mark L Mrs, 1945, D 17,21:2
Bristol, Marquess of (F W F Hervey), 1951, O 25, 29:1
Bristol, Marquess of (Earl Jermyn), 1960, Ap 6,41:3
Bristol, Marquis of, 1864, N 15,2:2
Bristol, Mary A, 1947, My 5,23:4
Bristol, Milton A, 1957, D 2,27:3
Bristol, Roscoe C, 1950, My 10,31:4
Bristol, Samuel R, 1956, F 20,23:2
Bristol, Theodore L Sr, 1955, D 6,38:1
Bristol, Walter W, 1945, O 23,17:2
Bristol, Warren H, 1943, S 28,25:4
Bristol, William, 1944, N 29,23:5
Bristol, William M Mrs, 1947, Jl 16,23:4
Bristor, Robert E, 1942, Ja 25,41:2
Bristow, Algernon Thomas Dr (funl, Mr 28,15:5), 1913, Mr 27,11:1
Bristow, Allen S, 1943, Je 22,19:5
Bristow, Claude S, 1939, Mr 24,21:6
Bristow, Frederick W, 1945, S 1,11:3
Bristow, George W, 1961, N 13,29:4
Bristow, James J R, 1965, Ja 30,27:3
Bristow, Joseph L, 1944, Jl 15,13:4
Bristow, Myon E, 1955, N 12,19:5
Bristow, William B, 1955, D 22,23:4
Bristow, William B Mrs, 1950, Jl 15,13:6
Bristowe, Orme C, 1938, D 30,15:2
Britan, Halbert H, 1945, Ag 6,15:4
Britan, Joseph T Rev, 1953, F 11,29:2
Brite, L C, 1941, S 5,21:5
Britell, Patrick, 1967, S 19,47:2
Brites, Geraldino de, 1941, Ag 25,15:3
Brito, Gene, 1965, Je 9,47:4
Britt, Aaron M, 1948, My 4,25:5
Britt, Albert J, 1940, Jl 27,13:4
Britt, Alice M, 1945, My 15,19:3
Britt, Arthur D, 1955, Jl 28,23:1
Britt, Benjamin T, 1949, O 24,23:4
Britt, Daniel J, 1938, F 23,23:4
Britt, Edmund J, 1937, Ag 29,II,7:2
Britt, George Mrs, 1944, D 6,23:2
Britt, Howard L, 1953, S 25,21:2
Britt, J Gabriel, 1914, N 7,11:6
Britt, James B, 1953, Jl 29,23:5
Britt, James E, 1940, Ja 23,21:4
Britt, James J, 1939, D 27,24:1
Britt, John J, 1942, F 28,17:2
Britt, John M, 1944, Ap 20,19:2
Britt, Laurence V, 1964, Jl 1,35:4
Britt, P J, 1931, Ap 6,21:1
Britt, T Louis A, 1942, Jl 15,19:6
Britt, Thomas J, 1958, O 26,88:6
Britt, Walter D, 1956, S 4,29:2
Britt, Walter D Mrs, 1953, O 26,21:5
Brittain, Alfred, 1943, Jl 2,19:2
Brittain, Arch, 1940, Ja 22,15:4
Brittain, Charles J, 1942, Ja 13,22:2
Brittain, Charles P, 1946, Jl 12,17:2
Brittain, F Edward Mrs, 1945, S 30,46:7
Brittain, Henry L, 1959, Ag 16,82:3
Brittain, Jeremiah R Rev, 1903, D 28,7:4
Brittain, Joseph K, 1942, Ja 14,21:4
Brittain, Richard J, 1957, My 26,92:4
Brittain, William Franklin, 1912, Jl 21,II,11:4
Brittain, William S, 1966, D 31,19:1
Brittan, Marion L, 1953, Jl 2,23:1
Brittan, Roswell S, 1951, F 4,77:2
Britten, Clarence M, 1958, Ap 10,29:4
Britten, E T, 1936, O 29,25:1
Britten, Edwin F Jr, 1966, Ap 2,29:2
Britten, Edwin F Mrs, 1945, Ap 16,23:4
Britten, Edwin F Sr, 1942, Ag 9,42:6
Britten, Edwin F 3d, 1956, D 9,88:1
Britten, Ernest, 1943, D 16,27:4
Britten, Fred A, 1946, My 5,44:3
Britten, Walter A, 1957, S 24,35:1
Brittin, Bennett, 1915, O 26,11:6
Brittin, E A, 1903, N 24,9:5
Brittin, Frank L, 1955, My 6,23:2
Britting, Charles H, 1914, Mr 9,9:3
Brittingham, Arthur H, 1958, S 5,27:2
Brittingham, Bettie S (por), 1949, Ap 30,13:5
Brittingham, Ellen R Mrs, 1937, F 10,23:2
Brittingham, George W, 1944, Ja 4,17:2
Brittingham, Harry L, 1945, N 14,19:2
Brittingham, John L Mrs, 1949, Ap 9,17:7
Brittingham, Juan F, 1940, O 29,25:2
Brittingham, Lorenzo W, 1943, Je 27,32:6
Brittingham, Thomas E Jr, 1960, Ap 18,29:1
Brittingham, Thomas H, 1949, O 14,27:2
Brittingham, Wilson H Mrs (E L Travers), 1958, Ap 15,33:4
Brittlebank, Julius, 1937, Jl 26,19:2
Brittner, William Mrs, 1947, Ja 26,53:1
Britto, Morris S, 1955, S 1,23:2
Britton, Alexander Hamilton Mrs, 1911, Ap 8,13:5
Britton, Alexander Harrison, 1915, F 8,7:4
Britton, Arthur W, 1962, Jl 27,25:5
Britton, B F, 1881, Je 16,5:2
Britton, Byron O, 1951, Mr 9,25:4
Britton, Charles Price, 1917, F 28,11:6
Britton, Charles W, 1955, S 23,26:6
Britton, Edgar C, 1962, Ag 2,25:4
Britton, Edward E, 1925, N 10,25:5
Britton, Edward E Col, 1921, O 24,15:5
Britton, Emily, 1965, Jl 29,27:1
Britton, Everett L, 1910, My 20,9:5
Britton, Frank H, 1916, Jl 27,9:6
Britton, Frederic H Mrs, 1954, Je 17,29:3
Britton, George C, 1954, Mr 4,25:4
Britton, George E, 1949, Mr 13,76:1
Britton, Grace E, 1949, Ja 16,68:3
Britton, Harry, 1958, Jl 25,19:4
Britton, Harry B, 1955, Jl 31,69:3
Britton, Howard, 1944, Mr 24,19:3
Britton, Howard Mrs, 1957, Mr 15,25:1
Britton, J A Mrs, 1948, Jl 2,21:5
Britton, J Raymond, 1951, S 29,17:5
Britton, Jack (W J Breslin), 1962, Mr 28,39:1
Britton, James H, 1937, S 2,21:2
Britton, James L, 1948, Mr 10,27:3
Britton, Joanna Mrs, 1939, F 6,13:4
Britton, John A Jr, 1954, D 17,31:3
Britton, John S Sr, 1950, F 16,23:5
Britton, John T Sr, 1944, My 20,15:6
Britton, John W 2d, 1943, Ap 8,23:2
Britton, Maurice William Rev, 1914, D 10,13:4
Britton, Milt, 1948, Ap 30,24:2
Britton, N L, 1934, Je 26,19:1
Britton, Richard E, 1947, Je 11,27:4
Britton, Richard H, 1956, Je 22,23:4
Britton, Russel H, 1952, F 26,27:4
Britton, William J, 1943, N 8,19:6
Britton, William R, 1947, O 31,23:1
Britton, William W, 1947, Jl 22,23:1
Britton, Wilton E (por), 1939, F 16,21:3
Britton, Winchester (cor, Ag 8,29:1), 1950, Ag 4,21:5
Britvan, Louis, 1957, N 16,19:1
Britz, Everett F, 1958, Ag 29,23:2
Britz, Francis, 1956, S 15,17:5
Brix, Harry J, 1966, Ap 5,39:3
Brix, Lou, 1941, F 5,20:3
Brixey, Austin D, 1937, My 20,21:4
Brixey, Richard D, 1943, Mr 15,13:4
Brixey, William Richard, 1911, Je 10,13:6
Brizendine, M Evans, 1968, My 1,47:3
Brizi, Alessandro, 1955, Ja 17,23:3
Brizi, Ugo, 1949, N 8,31:1
Brizzie, James, 1948, S 17,25:1
Brizzolara, James Col, 1913, S 25,13:6
Broaca, John P, 1938, Ja 28,21:1
Broach, Howard, 1950, Ap 16,104:7
Broach, Howard E, 1943, Mr 7,38:4
Broach, John C, 1945, N 15,19:4
Broad, George B, 1961, D 7,43:4
Broad, Gordon T, 1947, F 19,26:2
Broad, Harry R, 1958, Ja 21,26:6
Broad, Henry, 1903, Jl 29,2:3
Broad, J Payson Mrs, 1910, F 28,9:5
Broad, Maurice C, 1945, Ja 28,38:2
Broad, William, 1947, Je 12,27:1
Broadbent, Ernest W, 1943, Ja 14,21:1
Broadbent, George A, 1946, Jl 12,17:5
Broadbent, Harry I, 1948, O 20,29:1
Broadbent, J Wilson, 1962, Ap 2,31:1
Broadbent, Jack H, 1955, N 30,33:1
Broadbent, James A, 1956, N 1,39:5
Broadbent, James T, 1947, Je 4,27:3
Broadbent, John, 1938, Je 10,21:2
Broadbent, Samuel N, 1952, O 8,31:3
Broadbent, Wallace M, 1965, Ja 5,33:3
Broadbent, Wilfred O, 1952, Ja 30,26:5
Broadbent, William Henry Sir, 1907, Jl 11,7:6
Broadbridge, George T Baron, 1952, Ap 17,29:3
Broaddus, Bower, 1949, D 12,33:2
Broadfield, Charles J, 1939, Je 29,23:7
Broadfoot, Grover L, 1962, My 19,27:1
Broadfoot, Hibbard E, 1957, D 7,21:2
Broadfoot, Martin A, 1942, Ag 30,42:5
Broadfoot, William A, 1957, My 12,87:1
Broadhead, Almet N, 1925, My 6,23:4
Broadhead, George M, 1943, My 31,17:4
Broadhead, Sheldon B, 1925, Ag 31,15:5
Broadhead, W, 1879, Ap 14,5:6
Broadhurst, Arthur E, 1942, Ja 30,19:3
Broadhurst, Edward T, 1955, D 14,39:4
Broadhurst, Edwin B, 1965, Ap 5,31:2
Broadhurst, George, 1952, F 1,21:1
Broadhurst, George Mrs, 1959, Ja 8,29:2
Broadhurst, Henry, 1911, O 12,9:6; 1949, Ap 3,76:3
Broadhurst, Henry Mrs, 1947, N 21,27:1
Broadhurst, Jean, 1954, S 6,15:1
Broadley, Edward, 1947, N 25,32:5
Broadley, Harrison Col, 1914, D 30,11:5
Broadley, John E, 1950, Jl 12,29:5
Broadman, Joseph, 1966, F 26,25:3
Broadmeadow, Maximilian D, 1953, Ag 6,21:2
Broadnax, Mary E, 1950, Jl 11,31:5
Broads, Samuel, 1952, Mr 1,15:2
Broads, Samuel Mrs, 1954, F 11,29:4
Broadsword, Israel A, 1952, Jl 26,13:6
Broadwater, Charles C, 1954, D 28,23:1
Broadwater, Henry S, 1941, Ap 8,25:5
Broadwater, J A B, 1957, Ag 29,27:2
Broadwater, Norman I, 1940, Ja 5,19:4
Broadway, Joseph B, 1955, Mr 11,25:1
Broadway, Robert, 1945, Jl 24,23:5
Broadway, William G, 1937, Jl 16,19:6
Broadwin, David, 1942, D 2,25:3
Broadwin, I Lawrence, 1963, Ap 4,47:3
Broadwin, Isra T, 1953, Ag 8,11:5
Broady, Harry W, 1945, Ja 2,19:2
Broady, Joseph M, 1951, O 22,23:5
Broaker, Frank, 1941, N 13,27:3
Broatch, Frederick W, 1960, O 26,39:3
Broatch, John A, 1950, My 28,44:3
Brobst, David R, 1965, D 19,84:1
Brobst, John E, 1943, O 2,13:4
Brobst, Verda M Mrs, 1946, Jl 27,17:4
Brobston, Mary A, 1947, Jl 23,23:4
Broca, Benjamin Auguste, 1924, O 4,13:4
Broca, Paul, 1880, Jl 11,7:2
Brocard, Antonin, 1950, My 30,18:2
Broccoli, Albert R Mrs, 1958, S 24,27:3
Broch, Edward, 1920, Jl 2,11:5
Broch, Erich, 1956, My 29,27:4
Broch, Hermann, 1951, My 31,27:6
Brochado da Rocha, Francisco, 1962, S 27,37:2
Brochet, Jean (J Bruce), 1963, Mr 27,4:5
Brochu, Edward, 1960, O 19,45:4
Brock, Albert G, 1938, D 16,25:4
Brock, Anson A, 1963, Ag 29,29:5
Brock, Arnold J, 1958, F 6,27:2
Brock, Arthur, 1938, Jl 15,17:2
Brock, Elbert H, 1941, N 9,53:1
Brock, George A, 1938, Mr 18,19:4
Brock, Gustav F (por), 1945, F 6,19:4
Brock, Harry, 1948, N 23,29:4
Brock, Henry, 1902, N 5,9:6
Brock, Henry G, 1940, O 11,21:6
Brock, Henry I (trb lr, Ap 29,22:6), 1961, Ap 27,21:3
Brock, Henry J Mrs, 1957, Ap 28,86:4
Brock, Isaac, 1908, My 16,7:6; 1909, S 5,9:6
Brock, James Capt, 1921, F 22,13:5
Brock, John, 1953, Ja 19,23:4
Brock, John D, 1953, Ap 7,29:4
Brock, Loren E Mrs, 1949, My 15,90:7
Brock, Louis M, 1958, Ja 7,47:2
Brock, Louis M Mrs, 1937, Ap 9,21:4
Brock, Mary L T Mrs, 1940, Mr 21,26:4
Brock, Michael L Mrs, 1956, Ap 28,17:6
Brock, Osmond D, 1947, O 15,28:2
Brock, R Allan, 1965, My 4,43:2
Brock, Ray, 1968, F 19,39:1
Brock, Raymond E, 1962, F 3,21:4
Brock, Roger J, 1957, N 19,33:3
Brock, W S, 1932, N 14,20:1
Brock, Walter L, 1952, S 13,17:1
Brock, William E, 1950, Ag 6,73:1
Brockaway, Charles A, 1945, F 8,19:5
Brockbank, Harrison, 1947, D 1,21:3
Brockbank, J I, 1946, Ja 11,22:3
Brockbank, Mary A P Mrs, 1941, Ag 20,19:2
Brockdorff, Ahlett von, 1943, My 11,21:2
Brockdorff-Rantzau, von Count, 1928, S 10,23:5
Brockelman, Frederick Mrs, 1944, D 19,21:5
Brockelmann, Karl, 1956, My 14,25:4
Brockenbrough, John C, 1903, Ag 30,7:6
Brockenbrough, Robert L Mrs, 1923, Ag 23,15:4
Brockett, Ada Mrs, 1950, Ap 8,13:4
Brockett, Albert L, 1952, Mr 8,13:4
Brockett, Homer, 1946, Mr 28,25:6
Brockett, Lewis A, 1960, S 20,39:3
Brockett, Roy R, 1953, Ap 14,27:4
Brockett, Samuel, 1910, My 29,II,7:5
Brockett, Walter D, 1940, Mr 8,21:3
Brockhagen, Carl N, 1941, D 3,25:5
Brockhaus, Edward, 1948, F 12,23:2
Brockhaus, Fritz, 1952, Jl 13,61:2
Brockhaven, Eugene F, 1967, Ap 12,47:3
Brockhaven, Walter H, 1955, S 16,23:2
Brockhurst, Harry B, 1945, Je 3,32:7
Brockie, Arthur H, 1946, S 24,29:2
Brockie, William, 1909, N 5,9:4
Brocking, Aug, 1948, S 1,24:2
Brockington, Charles E, 1942, D 2,25:5
Brockington, George A, 1955, Ag 27,15:5
Brocklebank, Charles A W, 1948, N 2,25:1
Brocklebank, Claude E Jr, 1958, O 25,21:3
Brocklebank, Thomas, 1953, S 17,29:6
Brocklebank, Thomas Sir, 1911, Ja 13,9:3
Brockman, Ann, 1943, Mr 31,19:3
Brockman, Fletcher S, 1944, N 13,19:4
Brockman, James, 1967, My 24,47:1
Brockman, John B, 1958, Jl 4,19:3
Brockman, John W, 1940, Ag 25,35:2
Brockman, Karl Jr, 1963, S 28,19:5

Brockman, Samuel J, 1938, Mr 24,23:2
Brockman, Whitefield W, 1939, D 15,25:4
Brockmeier, Wesley A, 1944, Ag 31,17:2
Brockmeyer, Aug W, 1937, Ja 25,19:4
Brockson, F, 1942, Mr 18,23:4
Brockway, A, 1933, Je 26,15:3
Brockway, Alonzo W, 1953, Je 12,27:2
Brockway, Asahel Norton Dr, 1910, Jl 5,13:6
Brockway, Ezra S, 1948, N 5,26:3
Brockway, Francis Asbury, 1908, Ja 3,9:5
Brockway, George, 1953, Ag 19,29:2
Brockway, Henry A, 1903, O 14,9:6
Brockway, Horace H, 1910, D 6,13:2
Brockway, Howard, 1951, F 21,27:2
Brockway, Leverett E, 1914, Je 24,11:5
Brockway, Marion T Mrs, 1940, Je 4,23:4
Brockway, Robert B N Sr, 1950, Ap 1,15:1
Brockway, Zebulon Reed, 1920, O 22,15:6
Brockwell, Maurice W, 1958, D 9,41:4
Brod, Alex E, 1955, Jl 23,17:2
Brod, B Harold, 1938, D 9,25:3
Brod, Max, 1968, D 21,37:1
Brod, Robert Mrs, 1945, Ag 5,38:4
Brod, Sam, 1940, Ja 31,19:3
Brod, William, 1943, Ag 25,19:4
Broda, Marjan F, 1963, N 10,86:5
Broda, Norman L, 1949, D 11,93:1
Brodbeck, Andrew R, 1937, F 28,II,8:7
Brodbeck, Emil, 1949, Ag 11,23:4
Brodbeck, George, 1951, F 2,24:2
Brodden, Lillian Mrs, 1922, O 11,19:6
Brode, Charles G, 1962, D 7,39:1
Brode, Leo, 1955, Ja 2,76:4
Brodeen, Hilding, 1944, Jl 24,15:5
Brodel, John Mrs, 1949, D 16,31:3
Broder, Aaron, 1955, Je 3,23:4
Broder, Abraham V Mrs, 1950, Mr 13,21:3
Broder, Charles L, 1951, Ja 16,29:2
Broder, Edward W, 1943, F 6,13:6
Broder, H C, 1945, Ag 11,13:5
Broder, Harry, 1948, F 11,28:2; 1955, S 2,17:5
Broder, Nathan, 1967, D 18,47:3
Broder, Nathan E, 1954, Mr 11,31:4
Broder, Thomas F, 1944, Ap 29,15:4
Broderick, Arthur F, 1948, My 13,25:2
Broderick, Bonaventure F, 1943, N 19,19:1
Broderick, Catherine Mrs, 1942, F 17,22:3
Broderick, Clement H, 1903, Jl 18,7:6
Broderick, David C, 1963, My 26,93:1
Broderick, David C Mrs, 1955, Jl 16,15:6
Broderick, David F, 1940, Ja 3,22:4
Broderick, David Mrs, 1950, Ag 12,13:4
Broderick, Edmund D, 1939, Ja 18,19:4
Broderick, Edward F, 1939, O 11,27:1
Broderick, Edward J, 1942, D 2,25:3; 1963, S 18,39:4
Broderick, Edward V, 1957, My 11,21:4
Broderick, Eugene, 1950, D 10,105:1
Broderick, Francis I, 1945, O 11,23:3
Broderick, Frank B, 1943, Je 19,13:3
Broderick, Helen (Mrs L Crawford),(funl plans, S 28,31:5), 1959, S 27,86:1
Broderick, J Lawrence, 1959, O 29,33:2
Broderick, J Sir, 1933, Je 3,13:3
Broderick, James, 1944, F 26,13:1; 1875, F 3,5:4
Broderick, James G, 1940, Ja 4,23:5
Broderick, Jennette M, 1950, Ag 17,27:3
Broderick, John, 1939, Ag 10,19:5
Broderick, John A Maj, 1937, My 26,25:2
Broderick, John C, 1956, S 5,27:3
Broderick, John H, 1951, Mr 6,27:1; 1955, Jl 3,33:3
Broderick, John J, 1947, My 29,21:2; 1949, Ap 9,17:3; 1966, Ja 18,37:3
Broderick, John J Mrs, 1949, Ap 15,24:3
Broderick, John R, 1945, O 21,46:3
Broderick, John T, 1947, Mr 22,13:2
Broderick, Joseph A, 1951, Je 5,31:1; 1959, Ap 7,33:2
Broderick, Joseph V, 1945, Je 11,15:5
Broderick, Matthew, 1940, F 27,21:2
Broderick, Matthew J, 1950, D 21,29:5
Broderick, Michael J, 1951, S 13,31:4
Broderick, Michael Mrs, 1950, N 9,33:2
Broderick, Michael S, 1955, D 29,23:2
Broderick, Patrick, 1948, Mr 29,21:6
Broderick, Paul J, 1949, Ja 28,22:3
Broderick, Stephen J Mrs, 1961, Jl 20,27:5
Broderick, Thomas E, 1949, O 2,80:6
Broderick, Thomas J, 1946, Mr 28,25:3
Broderick, Vere H, 1958, Ag 6,25:4
Broderick, Vivian, 1943, Ag 11,19:2
Broderick, William E Mrs, 1948, F 18,27:3
Broderick, William J Sr, 1962, Je 16,19:6
Broderick, William L, 1950, F 7,27:4
Brodersen, O Charles, 1956, S 20,33:6
Broderson, Hans C, 1953, Ag 25,21:3
Broderzon, Moishe, 1956, Ag 21,29:1
Brodesser, Frederick A, 1948, Ap 10,13:2
Brodesser, George L, 1952, Ap 8,29:5
Brodetsky, Selig, 1954, My 19,31:2
Brodeur, Edward L, 1957, Je 11,35:3
Brodeur, Francois-Xavier, 1951, F 19,23:2
Brodeur, J A A, 1927, N 18,23:6
Brodeur, Joseph A C A, 1946, Mr 27,27:3
Brodeur, L P Lt-Gov, 1924, Ja 3,17:3
Brodge, Howard, 1955, D 13,39:4
Brodhay, O Chester, 1954, Ap 15,29:2
Brodhead, Barton, 1916, Ja 6,13:4
Brodhead, Calvin E, 1945, Mr 21,23:3
Brodhead, Cecile Mrs, 1944, Ap 23,43:2
Brodhead, Conrad K, 1951, N 4,86:6
Brodhead, Elbert H, 1953, Mr 10,29:1
Brodhead, Frank M, 1951, My 19,15:6
Brodhead, G H, 1903, Mr 3,9:6
Brodhead, George H, 1940, My 26,34:2
Brodhead, George L, 1952, My 14,27:2
Brodhead, Harold N, 1949, D 22,23:3
Brodhead, J A, 1884, Ap 5,5:3
Brodhead, J Davis Judge, 1920, Ap 25,22:4
Brodhead, J M, 1880, F 24,5:6
Brodhead, James, 1943, N 11,23:6
Brodhead, John Romeyn, 1873, My 17,5:5
Brodhead, Nathaniel B, 1956, Mr 3,19:2
Brodhead, Nathaniel B Mrs, 1964, Jl 21,33:2
Brodhead, Richard T Mrs, 1944, N 7,27:3
Brodhead, Thornton, 1947, Jl 3,21:6
Brodie, Alex Oswald Col, 1918, My 12,21:2
Brodie, Andrew M, 1943, F 22,17:1
Brodie, Benjamin R, 1961, O 8,87:1
Brodie, Charles F, 1950, Jl 22,15:4
Brodie, Edward E, 1939, Je 29,23:6
Brodie, Edwin W, 1942, My 23,13:3
Brodie, George W, 1957, Mr 26,33:4
Brodie, Ian, 1943, F 17,21:3
Brodie, Israel B (cor; he was a widower), 1965, Ag 2,29:2
Brodie, Israel B Mrs, 1961, S 2,15:6
Brodie, James F, 1938, Ap 26,21:2
Brodie, James F Rev Dr, 1910, Ag 17,7:5
Brodie, John G, 1946, Ag 10,13:2
Brodie, John W, 1873, Ja 30,5:4
Brodie, Mary C, 1948, S 1,23:1
Brodie, Maurice, 1939, My 12,21:2
Brodie, Orrin L, 1943, O 6,23:1
Brodie, Orrin L Mrs, 1955, My 12,29:4
Brodie, Ralph E, 1944, Ja 11,20:2
Brodie, Ralph E Mrs, 1941, O 10,23:4
Brodie, Robert B, 1959, D 28,23:2
Brodie, Roger, 1953, Ja 21,13:5
Brodil, Franklin V, 1964, Ja 7,33:3
Brodkin, Nathan D, 1967, F 8,31:4
Brodmann, Robert W, 1955, N 11,25:3
Brodmerkel, Adolph, 1947, D 19,25:3
Brodnax, George H Sr, 1949, Jl 15,19:3
Brodnax, James Mrs, 1945, Je 5,19:2
Brodrick, George Charles, 1903, N 9,7:6
Brodrick, William (Viscount Midleton), 1907, Ap 19, 9:5
Brodsky, David, 1967, Mr 16,47:2
Brodsky, Harold, 1965, F 17,43:2
Brodsky, Hyman, 1949, D 14,31:3
Brodsky, Hyman Rabbi, 1937, F 26,22:2
Brodsky, Irving, 1958, My 20,33:1
Brodsky, Israel J, 1942, Ag 6,19:4
Brodsky, Jacob A, 1962, Je 24,68:8
Brodsky, John E, 1910, D 29,9:4
Brodsky, Joseph R, 1947, Jl 29,21:4
Brodsky, Lew, 1923, Jl 27,13:6
Brodsky, Louis B Mrs, 1957, S 14,19:6
Brodsky, Peter Mrs (cor, Mr 30,37:1), 1960, Mr 29, 37:2
Brodsky, Sarah Mrs, 1938, My 21,15:4
Brodsky, Selig, 1945, Jl 21,11:5
Brodsky, William P, 1959, D 18,29:2
Brodstein, Louis, 1952, Jl 8,27:4
Brodt, Herm J, 1963, My 22,41:4
Brodt, John Henry Rev, 1875, S 15,4:6
Brodt, Philip E, 1946, Je 29,19:5
Brody, Albert, 1947, D 29,17:4
Brody, Alexander Dr, 1968, O 22,47:2
Brody, Allen M, 1948, Ag 25,25:1
Brody, Ann, 1944, Jl 17,15:6
Brody, Charles M, 1947, Ja 28,23:2
Brody, Harry, 1964, Ag 9,76:4
Brody, Henry W, 1946, S 22,62:4
Brody, I James, 1966, Jl 30,25:5
Brody, Iles, 1953, N 12,31:2
Brody, Irving T, 1948, Ja 29,23:2
Brody, Joseph, 1937, Ag 17,19:2; 1944, Je 29,23:6
Brody, Joseph M, 1940, S 6,21:5
Brody, Julius K, 1959, F 19,31:4
Brody, Lawrence D, 1961, Ja 3,29:3
Brody, Leonard Mrs, 1966, Mr 14,31:1
Brody, Michael J Mrs, 1952, N 18,31:4
Brody, Nathan S, 1944, F 2,21:5
Brody, Samuel, 1956, Ag 9,25:6
Brody, Samuel S, 1967, Je 30,34:3
Broeck, Renselaer Ten, 1918, My 31,13:6
Broecker, F William, 1944, D 28,19:3
Broecker, T H, 1965, S 16,47:3
Broedel, Max, 1941, O 28,23:6
Broek, Albertus T, 1944, F 6,42:4
Broek, Johannes van den, 1946, O 23,27:5
Broek, John Y, 1963, Ap 18,35:4
Broek, John Y Mrs, 1955, O 30,88:8
Broeker, Emil, 1937, Ap 6,23:3
Broeker, Ewald, 1948, S 8,29:1
Broekman, David H, 1958, Ap 2,31:3
Broekman, Theodore J, 1953, Ag 26,27:5
Broekstra, Martin E, 1940, Mr 19,25:4
Broening, George H Mrs, 1944, O 19,23:3
Broening, William F, 1953, O 13,29:5
Broenniman, Edward G, 1949, Jl 26,28:2
Broeser, Henry V, 1938, Je 30,23:5
Brof, Leon L, 1964, Ap 22,47:2
Broff, Irving, 1954, O 30,17:2
Broff, Stanley R, 1963, Je 16,84:3
Brogan, A Leo, 1949, Je 9,31:5
Brogan, Anne R, 1947, O 31,23:3
Brogan, Arthur, 1939, Je 13,23:4
Brogan, Bridget A, 1962, My 28,29:2
Brogan, Daniel J, 1949, Jl 8,19:1
Brogan, Edward J, 1941, F 24,15:3
Brogan, Francis J, 1944, Mr 15,19:2
Brogan, Helen A, 1956, S 23,84:2
Brogan, James C, 1937, F 2,23:4
Brogan, James J, 1950, Je 7,29:4
Brogan, James M, 1939, O 9,19:5
Brogan, John A, 1951, F 12,23:4
Brogan, John A Mrs, 1945, O 9,21:1
Brogan, John H, 1944, Je 16,19:4
Brogan, John J, 1953, Je 11,29:2
Brogan, John W, 1946, Jl 5,19:6
Brogan, Joseph E, 1957, F 3,76:1
Brogan, Michael, 1953, O 22,1:3
Brogan, Patrick F, 1942, Mr 25,21:3
Brogan, Thomas G, 1945, S 20,23:2
Brogan, Thomas J, 1965, My 30,50:6
Brogan, Thomas J Mrs, 1964, Mr 29,60:6
Brogan, W T, 1878, S 27,10:4
Brogan, William J, 1943, My 10,19:1
Brogan, William P Mrs, 1943, N 17,25:2
Brogden, Edward A, 1951, My 9,33:5
Brogdon, William C, 1957, Je 21,25:4
Broge, Walter E, 1951, Ja 15,17:4
Brogger, Ivar W, 1963, Ap 22,27:1
Brogger, Ruth G, 1942, D 31,15:4
Broggi, Carl J, 1956, Mr 9,23:3
Brogi, Ambrose, 1959, F 1,85:1
Brogi, Myron M, 1954, S 4,11:5
Brogle, Albert P, 1949, D 5,23:5
Broglie, Maurice de (Duc), 1960, Jl 16,19:6
Brogren, Stanley C Mrs, 1958, S 23,33:1
Broh, Julius, 1940, D 31,15:4
Brohawn, Charles E, 1953, S 13,85:2
Brohee, Abel, 1947, My 3,17:5
Brohel, Joseph A, 1942, My 27,23:4
Brohm, George H, 1940, Ja 26,17:4
Brohm, William L, 1967, O 2,47:1
Brohmer, William A, 1967, N 29,40:4
Broich, William, 1940, Mr 23,26:3
Broidy, Edward W, 1950, N 3,27:2
Broidy, Julius, 1964, Mr 11,39:3
Broidy, Julius Mrs, 1948, F 3,25:4
Broidy, William F, 1959, Jl 15,29:1
Brokaw, Abraham, 1907, S 24,11:6
Brokaw, Albert D, 1966, Jl 5,27:1
Brokaw, Charles F Mrs, 1944, D 9,15:4
Brokaw, Clifford V, 1956, Jl 14,15:3; 1959, Ja 4,88:5
Brokaw, Clifford V Mrs, 1951, Jl 31,21:1
Brokaw, DeWitt P, 1954, Ag 30,17:4
Brokaw, Eugene, 1940, D 17,26:2
Brokaw, F Joseph M, 1940, O 26,15:2
Brokaw, George J, 1937, Ag 7,15:5
Brokaw, George Jr Mrs, 1949, F 25,23:3
Brokaw, Howard C, 1960, Mr 19,21:2
Brokaw, Howard C Mrs, 1960, O 26,39:5
Brokaw, Irving (por), 1939, Mr 20,17:3
Brokaw, Irving Mrs, 1937, S 12,II,6:7
Brokaw, Isaac V, 1913, S 30,13:6
Brokaw, James O, 1947, D 8,25:5
Brokaw, John B Mrs, 1948, Jl 27,25:4
Brokaw, Lee W, 1962, O 23,37:5
Brokaw, Lester N, 1908, O 15,9:7
Brokaw, Lester W, 1954, O 30,20:2
Brokaw, Marmaduke I, 1952, Je 13,23:3
Brokaw, N H Mrs, 1948, My 19,23:3
Brokaw, Raymond V, 1965, Mr 16,39:4
Brokaw, Richard H, 1937, My 22,15:5
Brokaw, Robert W Mrs, 1949, Ja 22,13:5
Brokaw, Thomas P, 1912, Ag 14,9:4
Brokaw, Thorton F, 1960, My 14,23:6
Brokaw, William B Mrs, 1944, Ag 19,11:2
Brokaw, William G, 1941, F 18,23:2
Brokaw, William Vail, 1907, My 9,9:5
Broke, Willoughby de Baron, 1923, D 17,17:4
Brokenshire, Charles D, 1954, My 30,44:5
Brokenshire, Norman E, 1965, My 5,47:1
Brokmeyer, Eugene C, 1951, S 22,17:5
Broley, Charles L, 1959, My 5,33:2
Brolli, Edward J Mrs, 1958, D 3,37:1
Brombaugh, M G, 1930, Mr 15,19:5
Bromberg, Aaron, 1953, Ja 10,17:5
Bromberg, Arthur C, 1956, Jl 4,19:4
Bromberg, David, 1957, Ag 20,27:1
Bromberg, J Edgar, 1951, D 7,28:2
Bromberg, Jacob, 1948, Je 9,29:6
Bromberg, Joseph C, 1940, O 15,23:3
Bromberg, Max H, 1959, O 23,29:1
Bromberg, Mayer D, 1952, Ap 8,29:3

Bromberger, A, 1878, O 18,3:3
Bromberger, Edgar, 1956, Mr 18,88:4
Bromberger, Ignatz Mrs, 1948, S 25,17:2
Bromer, Albert W, 1964, Ja 4,23:5
Bromer, Ralph S, 1957, S 26,25:4
Bromfield, Charles, 1944, Ap 24,19:5
Bromfield, Charles Mrs, 1947, Ja 9,23:2
Bromfield, Edward Thomas Rev, 1908, Jl 28,5:4
Bromfield, Louis (funl plans, Mr 20,23:5; funl, Mr 23,27:4), 1956, Mr 19,1:2
Bromfield, Louis Mrs, 1952, S 16,29:2
Bromfield, Percy R, 1953, Ag 11,27:5
Bromfield, Percy R Mrs, 1951, Ap 3,27:3
Bromhead, Alfred, 1963, Mr 7,7:4
Bromiley, Irving Mrs, 1955, Jl 6,27:3
Bromilow, Walter, 1939, Je 27,23:6
Bromley, Byron G, 1940, F 17,13:3
Bromley, Calvin D, 1939, Mr 26,III,6:7
Bromley, Charles S, 1950, Ag 8,29:4
Bromley, Charles S Jr, 1956, Je 6,33:3
Bromley, Henry W, 1957, Je 25,29:1
Bromley, John E, 1942, O 27,25:4
Bromley, John E Mrs, 1943, Je 10,21:3
Bromley, John M Mrs, 1943, N 20,13:4
Bromley, John S Mrs, 1951, Jl 31,22:2
Bromley, Joseph, 1953, Ag 6,21:3; 1953, N 4,33:4
Bromley, Joseph H, 1947, S 6,17:6
Bromley, Robert E, 1956, Je 19,29:5
Bromley, Stanley W, 1954, F 17,31:4
Bromley, Theodore, 1914, F 5,9:5
Bromley, Worthington K, 1951, Ja 27,13:5
Bromm, John H, 1938, My 22,II,7:1
Bromme, Lou, 1953, Je 30,24:6
Brommer, Charles F, 1949, O 25,27:5
Bromund, Jesse F Mrs, 1946, Jl 16,23:3
Bromwell, Charles S Lt-Col, 1915, D 11,13:6
Bromwell, Laura, 1921, Je 8,17:5
Bronander, Wilhelm B Sr, 1956, My 20,86:7
Bronaugh, Anne, 1961, Je 18,88:4
Bronaugh, Fred L, 1946, D 12,29:4
Bronaugh, Welbourne F Mrs, 1939, O 11,30:4
Brond, Harry H, 1948, N 22,22:3
Brondel, John Bp, 1903, N 4,9:6
Brondum, Howard W, 1960, F 29,27:2
Bronfenbrenner, Jacques J, 1953, Ag 14,19:6
Bronfin, I D, 1934, Ag 1,17:3
Bronfman, Abe, 1968, Mr 19,47:2
Bronfman, Abe Mrs, 1967, S 4,21:4
Bronfman, Harry, 1963, N 13,41:3
Brong, Edgar J, 1958, Ap 29,29:4
Brong, Karl S, 1955, Jl 31,59:3
Broniewska, Janina, 1947, Ag 25,17:2
Broniewski, Wladyslaw, 1962, F 11,87:1
Bronk, Isabelle, 1955, F 4,21:2
Bronk, John Parker, 1904, Ja 24,5:6
Bronk, Mitchell, 1950, N 1,35:4
Bronk, Mitchell Mrs, 1940, D 20,25:3
Bronk, William M, 1941, O 16,21:2
Bronkema, Frederick, 1960, N 16,41:4
Bronne, David, 1948, N 4,30:2
Bronner, Finn J, 1954, Ap 14,29:2
Bronner, Harry (will, D 28,13:2), 1940, D 22,31:1
Bronner, Joseph H Mrs, 1950, Ag 13,76:1
Bronner, Leonard, 1941, N 27,23:6
Bronner, Leonard J, 1951, O 3,33:2
Bronner, Wilber M Mrs, 1946, Jl 12,17:5
Bronnes, Hanna Mrs, 1941, O 21,23:5
Bronock, John J, 1951, Ag 21,27:4
Bronowicz, Frank, 1954, Jl 15,27:2
Brons, William S, 1947, Ap 29,27:2
Bronson, Alvin, 1881, Ap 3,7:3
Bronson, Arthur, 1956, Ap 22,86:3
Bronson, Barbara G, 1959, Ap 12,86:4
Bronson, Bennet, 1950, N 25,13:4
Bronson, Bernard S, 1943, Mr 16,19:1
Bronson, Charles Tracey (funl, O 6,27:5), 1925, O 5, 21:5
Bronson, Clara W Mrs, 1942, D 26,6:2
Bronson, Edgar B, 1947, D 10,31:5
Bronson, Edgar Beecher, 1917, F 5,11:6
Bronson, Edgar S, 1924, Je 8,26:1
Bronson, Edwin H, 1949, Mr 5,17:5
Bronson, Ezekiel S, 1957, Ag 21,27:2
Bronson, Francis W, 1966, S 9,45:4
Bronson, Frank A Mrs, 1950, Ap 20,15:5
Bronson, Frank E, 1942, Jl 9,21:3
Bronson, Frank P, 1953, N 8,88:5
Bronson, George A, 1953, O 6,29:6
Bronson, Greene C Hon, 1863, S 5,4:6
Bronson, Helen Mrs, 1950, Ag 23,29:3
Bronson, Howard E, 1937, Mr 22,23:5
Bronson, J Harmar, 1948, N 22,21:6
Bronson, James, 1966, F 6,92:3
Bronson, James H, 1909, N 28,11:5
Bronson, Julia H Mrs, 1940, N 1,25:2
Bronson, Karl H, 1953, Ja 24,15:6
Bronson, Louis E, 1954, My 15,15:5
Bronson, Melvin A Mrs, 1921, Ja 27,13:4
Bronson, Miles Jr, 1946, D 2,25:4
Bronson, Milton M, 1951, D 18,31:4
Bronson, Nathaniel R, 1949, Ap 21,25:1
Bronson, Oliver, 1918, Je 30,19:1
Bronson, Oliver H, 1950, O 22,92:2
Bronson, Owen, 1948, Ap 12,21:6
Bronson, Paul Mrs, 1924, F 12,17:3
Bronson, Robert T, 1942, D 31,15:4
Bronson, Sarah S Mrs, 1940, Ap 10,25:5
Bronson, T B, 1881, D 8,5:3
Bronson, Thomas A, 1914, F 25,9:4
Bronson, Thomas B, 1948, D 5,92:7
Bronson, William M, 1952, Ag 19,23:3
Bronson, William S, 1942, F 12,23:3
Bronson, William T, 1955, Ap 29,23:5
Bronsteen, Edward, 1965, Je 20,72:8
Bronstein, Benjamin, 1961, O 15,88:7
Bronstein, Ida, 1950, Je 24,13:2
Bronstein, Irving Mrs, 1948, F 15,60:5
Bronstein, Jesse B, 1951, N 22,31:3
Bronstein, Martin L, 1955, S 25,92:6
Bronstein, Sammy, 1958, Je 24,31:2
Bronsten, Irvin C, 1957, Mr 6,31:5
Bronx, Isabelle, 1943, Ja 11,15:5
Broodbank, Joseph G, 1944, Jl 16,31:3
Brooder, John F, 1947, N 24,23:3
Brook, Arthur H, 1960, S 8,35:2
Brook, Arthur S, 1947, Mr 9,60:2
Brook, Avylen H, 1946, Ap 16,25:4
Brook, Charles H, 1957, Ap 13,19:1
Brook, George, 1912, Ja 16,13:3
Brook, Herbert Mrs, 1955, D 9,27:4
Brook, John Robert, 1968, Jl 4,19:2
Brook, John T, 1942, O 29,23:3
Brook, Norman C (Lord Normanbrook), 1967, Je 16, 43:2
Brook, Percy, 1947, Ja 26,53:2
Brook, Warner F (por), 1945, My 31,15:3
Brook, William A D, 1953, Ag 18,2:3
Brook-Jones, Elwyn, 1962, S 6,31:4
Brooke, Alan E, 1939, O 31,23:3
Brooke, B Hayes Mrs, 1950, My 14,106:3
Brooke, Basil V, 1945, D 13,29:1
Brooke, Bertram Mrs, 1952, Je 13,23:2
Brooke, C F Tucker, 1946, Je 24,31:5
Brooke, Charles, 1963, My 10,33:1
Brooke, Charles Sir, 1917, My 18,13:5
Brooke, Collin S, 1954, Ap 12,29:4
Brooke, Cynthia, 1949, S 12,21:4
Brooke, Donald W, 1954, Ja 31,89:2
Brooke, Edward Sr, 1940, N 21,29:5
Brooke, Ellen T, 1959, S 21,31:5
Brooke, Estelle B, 1946, My 31,24:2
Brooke, Flavius L Justice, 1921, Ja 22,11:4
Brooke, Francis Key Bp, 1918, O 23,13:1
Brooke, Francis M, 1949, F 3,23:1
Brooke, Frederick H, 1960, D 26,23:3
Brooke, Frederick H Mrs, 1967, Je 10,33:2
Brooke, George A Jr, 1956, O 25,33:5
Brooke, George H, 1938, N 17,25:4
Brooke, H Percy Mrs, 1946, O 1,23:3
Brooke, Henry L, 1939, Ja 25,22:1
Brooke, Howard, 1941, Jl 12,13:3
Brooke, Hugh F, 1948, Ap 14,27:1
Brooke, Jack, 1924, Jl 15,9:3
Brooke, James J, 1957, D 5,35:4
Brooke, John A, 1967, Ja 30,29:3
Brooke, John Mercer Col, 1906, D 15,11:6
Brooke, Milton M, 1953, Mr 21,17:3
Brooke, Raymond W, 1959, Je 14,87:1
Brooke, Robert E, 1942, Jl 22,19:3
Brooke, Robert Fulton, 1904, N 24,7:5
Brooke, Robert H, 1944, F 4,15:2
Brooke, Roger, 1940, D 19,25:5
Brooke, Stopford Augustus Rev, 1916, Mr 20,11:3
Brooke, Stopford W W, 1938, Ap 25,15:2
Brooke, Walter S, 1961, My 19,31:2
Brooke, Zachary N, 1946, O 8,23:6
Brooke-Popham, Robert, 1953, O 21,29:3
Brooker, Albert G, 1957, Ap 23,31:5
Brooker, Bertrand, 1955, Mr 22,31:2
Brooker, C F, 1926, D 21,23:3
Brooker, Utica V Mrs, 1873, Jl 11,5:2
Brookes, Macy Dr, 1924, Je 6,17:5
Brookes, Norman Sir, 1968, S 28,33:2
Brookes, Thomas R, 1947, Ag 17,53:1
Brookfield, Charles H E, 1913, O 21,9:6
Brookfield, Frank, 1940, Ap 27,15:3
Brookfield, Robert M, 1940, D 22,31:2
Brookfield, Thomas W, 1948, O 22,26:3
Brookhart, Della, 1946, F 7,23:2
Brookhart, Leslie S, 1945, Je 26,19:3
Brookhart, Smith W, 1944, N 16,23:1
Brookhart, Smith W Mrs, 1944, Ja 1,13:3
Brookings, R S, 1932, N 16,17:1
Brookings, Robert S Mrs (Isabel V J), 1965, Ap 9, 33:4
Brookings, Walter D, 1950, Jl 25,27:6
Brookins, Charles R, 1960, Ag 17,31:3
Brookins, Charles S, 1951, Ja 16,29:5
Brookins, Homer D, 1938, Ap 4,17:4
Brookins, Homer T, 1957, Jl 25,23:4
Brookins, John C, 1942, Ag 20,19:2
Brookins, Louis C, 1943, Ja 23,13:4
Brookins, Walter, 1953, Ap 30,31:1
Brookman, Frank E Mrs (will), 1952, D 26,20:1
Brookman, Henry D Mrs, 1925, Je 22,15:5
Brookman, Irving Mrs, 1962, Jl 10,33:4
Brookman, John J, 1904, S 24,6:1
Brookman, Louis Jr, 1945, Ag 12,39:2
Brookmire, S Kenard, 1957, D 17,35:2
Brooks, A Clinton, 1939, Ag 28,19:3
Brooks, A Palmer, 1945, Jl 10,11:7
Brooks, A Palmer Mrs, 1937, Ja 17,II,8:7
Brooks, Albert, 1957, N 29,29:3
Brooks, Albert J, 1948, D 18,19:2
Brooks, Aleck G, 1950, S 1,21:6
Brooks, Alex M, 1940, S 23,17:3
Brooks, Alfred C, 1947, Jl 20,44:8
Brooks, Alfred H, 1924, N 23,7:1
Brooks, Alfred M, 1963, D 22,34:5
Brooks, Alice M C, 1957, D 11,22:4
Brooks, Alida W, 1942, S 10,27:2
Brooks, Allan, 1946, Ja 5,13:3
Brooks, Allan L, 1960, Ag 21,84:8
Brooks, Allerton F, 1955, Ap 14,36:4
Brooks, Allerton F Mrs, 1959, N 7,23:4
Brooks, Anna G, 1949, Ap 17,76:4
Brooks, Anson S, 1937, Ag 4,19:4
Brooks, Archibald A, 1953, O 24,89:2
Brooks, Arthur A (will), 1941, Mr 11,26:4
Brooks, Arthur B, 1950, Jl 20,25:4
Brooks, Arthur D, 1951, Ag 10,15:5
Brooks, Arthur G, 1948, F 13,21:1
Brooks, Arthur Rev Dr, 1895, Jl 14,5:6
Brooks, Arthur W, 1948, Jl 8,23:5
Brooks, Aubrey L, 1958, Ja 11,17:6
Brooks, Babert V Sr, 1966, S 5,64:6
Brooks, Belvidere, 1916, F 11,11:5
Brooks, Belvidere Mrs, 1913, Jl 26,7:6
Brooks, Benjamin, 1948, F 2,19:5
Brooks, Benjamin T, 1962, Ag 7,30:1
Brooks, Bert, 1967, My 20,35:4
Brooks, Bryant B, 1944, D 10,53:2
Brooks, Byron Alden, 1911, S 29,9:4
Brooks, Byron E, 1944, Mr 28,19:4
Brooks, C S, 1934, Je 30,15:2
Brooks, C T Rev, 1883, Je 15,5:4
Brooks, C Wayland, 1957, Ja 15,30:1
Brooks, Charles, 1872, Jl 12,2:3
Brooks, Charles A (will, D 27,30:2), 1950, D 18,31:3
Brooks, Charles A, 1953, S 13,72:5
Brooks, Charles Dr, 1924, Ag 19,15:5
Brooks, Charles E, 1949, F 14,19:2
Brooks, Charles F, 1951, N 12,25:4; 1958, Ja 9,36:1
Brooks, Charles G, 1952, Jl 10,31:5
Brooks, Charles H, 1948, F 2,19:3
Brooks, Charles J, 1966, My 1,87:5
Brooks, Charles Mrs, 1944, My 14,46:1
Brooks, Charles Shirley, 1874, F 24,5:4
Brooks, Charles W, 1953, Mr 2,23:6
Brooks, Charley, 1944, Mr 20,18:3
Brooks, Christine Mrs, 1955, S 5,11:5
Brooks, Christopher, 1949, Ag 16,23:4
Brooks, Christopher J, 1949, Mr 18,25:3
Brooks, Clara W V Mrs, 1942, D 21,23:4
Brooks, Conrad F, 1945, O 12,23:1
Brooks, Curtis J, 1948, F 4,24:2
Brooks, Don, 1950, Ap 9,85:1
Brooks, Edith L, 1942, N 14,15:2
Brooks, Edward J, 1946, Jl 6,15:4
Brooks, Edward S, 1873, My 1,7:2; 1875, My 1,7:2; 1957, Jl 14,72:6
Brooks, Edwin E, 1951, O 12,27:3
Brooks, Edwin F, 1959, Ap 30,63:3
Brooks, Elwood M (Feb death noted), 1965, My 18, 58:5
Brooks, Emerson, 1948, Jl 24,15:3
Brooks, Erastus, 1886, N 26,1:7
Brooks, Ernest, 1957, N 14,34:1
Brooks, Eugene C, 1947, O 20,23:2
Brooks, Eugene S, 1968, Mr 8,39:3
Brooks, Forrest E Mrs, 1960, O 26,39:2
Brooks, Francis E, 1924, Ag 27,17:4
Brooks, Frank, 1944, Mr 10,15:3
Brooks, Frank A, 1945, Ap 19,27:2
Brooks, Frank G, 1955, Mr 6,88:1
Brooks, Frank H, 1937, S 6,17:4
Brooks, Frank N, 1939, S 28,15:2
Brooks, Frank W, 1923, Je 29,17:1
Brooks, Frank W Jr, 1943, Ja 6,27:2
Brooks, Franklin E, 1916, F 9,11:6
Brooks, Fred E, 1951, Je 7,33:4
Brooks, Frederick Mrs, 1945, N 18,43:1
Brooks, Frederick Rev, 1874, S 21,1:2
Brooks, Frederick W, 1959, N 5,35:2
Brooks, George, 1907, O 23,11:6
Brooks, George B, 1966, Je 22,47:3
Brooks, George G (will, Je 24,29:6), 1941, My 1[illegible] 43:6
Brooks, George G Mrs, 1940, S 29,43:2
Brooks, George M, 1941, Ja 3,20:2
Brooks, George S, 1948, My 8,15:6
Brooks, George W Dr, 1904, Je 8,9:7
Brooks, George W Mrs, 1952, Je 28,19:2
Brooks, Gregory S, 1963, Ag 9,23:2
Brooks, H, 1929, S 16,27:3; 1936, Ap 14,21:1
Brooks, H F, 1937, Jl 15,10:5
Brooks, H Mortimer Mrs, 1920, Ag 19,9:4
Brooks, H Quintus, 1916, F 20,15:4
Brooks, Harold, 1937, Mr 13,19:6

Brooks, Harry B, 1944, Jl 12,19:4
Brooks, Harry L, 1947, Ag 26,23:6
Brooks, Harry M, 1943, Ag 18,19:4
Brooks, Harry S, 1924, Je 10,11:4
Brooks, Henry G, 1944, My 3,19:5
Brooks, Henry S, 1938, Jl 28,19:6
Brooks, Henry T, 1946, Ja 2,19:3
Brooks, Henry T Mrs, 1959, F 12,27:3
Brooks, Henry W, 1941, My 12,17:6
Brooks, Horace J, 1957, Jl 5,17:1
Brooks, Howard G, 1937, Ag 10,19:4
Brooks, Irving, 1958, Ap 6,88:4
Brooks, Isaac W, 1916, O 18,11:6
Brooks, J, 1877, My 1,1:6
Brooks, J Wilton, 1916, Jl 7,11:5
Brooks, James B, 1954, D 28,23:1
Brooks, James B Mrs, 1947, Mr 22,13:4
Brooks, James E, 1945, Ja 12,15:4; 1954, Ap 25,87:3
Brooks, James H, 1941, O 14,23:2
Brooks, James J, 1937, Jl 23,19:6
Brooks, James W, 1961, Je 18,89:1
Brooks, Jane P Mrs, 1951, F 11,88:1
Brooks, Jere H, 1937, My 18,23:1
Brooks, Jerome, 1954, My 11,29:1
Brooks, John, 1943, D 7,27:5
Brooks, John A J Capt, 1915, F 15,7:5
Brooks, John C, 1944, Ap 27,23:1
Brooks, John Cotton Rev Dr, 1907, Ja 5,9:5
Brooks, John E, 1913, F 22,11:5
Brooks, John G, 1938, F 9,19:4; 1948, Je 3,25:1
Brooks, John Graham Mrs, 1968, F 23,33:2
Brooks, John H, 1945, O 12,24:2; 1945, D 23,18:2
Brooks, John N, 1941, Ap 8,25:6
Brooks, John P, 1957, Je 19,35:4
Brooks, John W, 1960, Ag 28,83:1
Brooks, Jonas H, 1937, My 30,18:7
Brooks, Joseph, 1916, N 28,13:1
Brooks, Joseph D, 1946, Ap 25,21:3
Brooks, Joseph Judson, 1914, Ap 11,11:5
Brooks, Joseph Mrs, 1925, O 21,23:4
Brooks, Joshua L, 1949, F 17,23:2
Brooks, L W, 1953, N 23,27:2
Brooks, Lawrence, 1878, My 13,8:4
Brooks, Lawrence B, 1954, My 20,31:1
Brooks, Lawrence R, 1954, D 4,17:3
Brooks, Leon, 1967, O 29,84:3
Brooks, Leon Q Mrs, 1962, Ja 5,29:3
Brooks, Leverich V V, 1962, S 27,34:6
Brooks, Lewis (see also Ag 10), 1877, Ag 13,2:3
Brooks, Lewis F, 1950, F 8,27:3
Brooks, Lilly B B Mrs, 1953, D 14,31:2
Brooks, Lloyd T, 1956, F 5,87:1
Brooks, Lon A, 1961, O 22,86:7
Brooks, Louis C Mrs, 1965, Je 1,39:2
Brooks, Louise D D Mrs, 1941, D 13,21:4
Brooks, M L Mrs, 1882, Ag 12,5:2
Brooks, Mark S, 1946, Ap 23,21:1
Brooks, Mary, 1941, My 9,21:5
Brooks, Mary C Mrs, 1940, D 19,25:5
Brooks, Mary Mrs, 1953, Mr 27,23:4
Brooks, Mary W, 1949, Ag 18,21:1
Brooks, Max, 1956, Jl 13,19:4
Brooks, Morgan, 1947, Ap 25,21:4
Brooks, Morgan Mrs, 1947, S 3,25:2
Brooks, Morris, 1968, My 23,47:4
Brooks, Myre J Dr, 1937, D 12,II,9:2
Brooks, Neil C, 1949, Mr 14,19:5
Brooks, Nelson, 1945, O 9,21:5
Brooks, Nicholas, 1925, Jl 25,11:5
Brooks, Nicholas J, 1950, Jl 15,13:5
Brooks, Noah, 1903, Ag 18,7:6
Brooks, Norman K, 1961, My 21,87:2
Brooks, Norval C, 1944, Ap 4,21:2
Brooks, Olin L, 1963, Jl 25,25:2
Brooks, Olin L Mrs, 1959, Jl 1,31:2
Brooks, Oliver, 1940, O 30,23:5
Brooks, Overton (funl plans, S 18,29:1), 1961, S 17, 86:1
Brooks, Paul, 1952, F 29,5:2
Brooks, Paul D, 1958, O 25,21:3
Brooks, Pauline Mrs, 1910, F 10,7:4
Brooks, Percival W, 1959, Mr 10,35:2
Brooks, Percy C, 1937, O 16,19:4
Brooks, Peter A, 1948, My 17,19:4
Brooks, Peter C, 1946, N 6,23:5
Brooks, Phillips Bishop, 1893, Ja 24,1:6
Brooks, Phillips R, 1945, Ja 14,40:2
Brooks, Ralph G (funl, S 13,37:4), 1960, S 10,21:3
Brooks, Randy, 1967, Mr 22,47:2
Brooks, Ransome J, 1947, N 8,17:4
Brooks, Raymond, 1960, Ag 20,19:6
Brooks, Raymond E, 1960, Ap 5,37:4
Brooks, Reese G, 1907, Je 13,7:6
Brooks, Reuben R, 1906, F 12,7:4
Brooks, Ricard, 1954, Je 23,26:3
Brooks, Richard A E Mrs, 1966, S 25,84:2
Brooks, Richard S, 1962, F 18,93:1
Brooks, Ritchie Jr Mrs, 1938, Jl 22,17:6
Brooks, Robert B, 1960, My 1,86:4
Brooks, Robert C, 1941, F 4,21:4
Brooks, Robert E L, 1947, My 6,28:2
Brooks, Robert N, 1953, Ag 5,23:2
Brooks, Robert S Jr, 1948, O 20,29:4

Brooks, Roelif H (funl, S 28,39:2), 1960, S 26,33:2
Brooks, Roswell F Jr, 1955, Mr 4,23:1
Brooks, S P, 1931, My 15,23:1
Brooks, Sarah Blake, 1903, Ag 25,7:6
Brooks, Sheldon D, 1946, S 5,27:4
Brooks, Sidney J, 1955, O 19,33:1
Brooks, Silas, 1906, Ap 8,9:6
Brooks, Solomon J, 1945, S 28,21:2
Brooks, Stephen, 1954, O 30,17:5
Brooks, Stephen A, 1950, Ap 1,15:5
Brooks, Stratton D, 1949, Ja 20,27:4
Brooks, Stratton D Mrs, 1941, Ja 19,40:4
Brooks, Sumner C, 1948, Ap 24,15:4
Brooks, T E, 1948, O 6,29:4
Brooks, Thomas A, 1959, S 24,37:4
Brooks, Thomas E, 1945, Ja 9,19:3; 1950, Je 7,29:2
Brooks, Thomas F, 1949, D 17,17:2
Brooks, Thomas L, 1955, Ag 30,27:3
Brooks, Thomas P, 1959, My 25,29:1
Brooks, Thomas R, 1939, Ag 15,19:5
Brooks, Toler P, 1943, D 31,16:8
Brooks, Tom A, 1951, Je 20,27:5
Brooks, Van Wyck, 1963, My 3,31:1
Brooks, Van Wyck Mrs, 1946, Ag 31,15:3
Brooks, Vernon H, 1938, Ag 15,15:4
Brooks, W, 1933, Mr 27,15:4
Brooks, W Baxter, 1939, Ap 13,23:1
Brooks, W H Rev Dr, 1923, My 26,15:6
Brooks, Walter, 1968, N 12,47:3
Brooks, Walter B Jr, 1937, Mr 26,22:3
Brooks, Walter G, 1943, Mr 18,19:3
Brooks, Walter H, 1958, My 2,27:2
Brooks, Walter R, 1951, D 23,22:3; 1958, Ag 19,28:5
Brooks, Walter R Mrs, 1952, O 12,89:2
Brooks, William, 1951, Ja 17,27:2
Brooks, William A Jr, 1959, F 25,31:1
Brooks, William Allen Dr, 1921, My 21,13:3
Brooks, William C, 1957, Mr 18,27:5
Brooks, William E Mrs, 1949, N 12,15:4
Brooks, William F, 1950, Mr 7,27:2
Brooks, William G, 1911, Ag 24,7:5; 1953, My 3,88:2
Brooks, William H, 1943, Jl 27,21:5
Brooks, William L, 1952, Jl 14,17:5
Brooks, William Mrs, 1963, Ap 16,35:2
Brooks, William O, 1954, Ap 10,15:4
Brooks, William P, 1938, Mr 9,23:3
Brooks, William R Dr, 1921, My 4,5:3
Brooks, Wilson A, 1966, N 20,88:7
Brooks, Winfield S, 1963, My 13,29:3
Brooks, Winthrop H, 1963, My 22,41:2
Brooks, Woodford, 1942, Ja 26,15:5
Brooksbank, Hubert A, 1942, D 2,25:5
Brooksbank, William G, 1941, Ag 12,19:3
Brookwell, George, 1941, Ag 9,15:5
Broom, Robert, 1951, Ap 7,15:2
Broom, Samuel, 1923, O 15,15:5
Broomall, Carolus M, 1942, N 2,21:5
Broomall, Carolus M Mrs, 1956, S 20,33:5
Broomall, J J, 1937, N 17,23:4
Broomall, John M 3d, 1941, Mr 2,42:5
Brooman-White, Richard C, 1964, Ja 27,23:2
Broome, Edwin C, 1950, Ap 18,32:2
Broome, Ernest L, 1938, S 11,II,11:2
Broome, Frank H, 1940, Je 8,15:2
Broome, G T, 1881, N 10,3:2
Broome, Harvey, 1968, Mr 10,92:8
Broome, Isaac, 1922, My 5,17:6
Broome, Joseph, 1916, Je 4,21:7
Broome, Montague W, 1951, D 19,31:2
Broome, Robert E, 1966, D 6,47:1
Broome, Robert W, 1959, Je 21,92:6
Broome, Thornhill, 1946, F 23,13:3
Broomell, Chester C, 1937, Ja 10,II,10:5
Broomell, Francis E, 1942, S 17,25:4
Broomell, I N, 1941, Mr 24,17:4
Broomfield, Fred, 1955, Ja 7,21:4
Broomfield, John C, 1950, Ja 9,25:2
Broomhall, George J S, 1938, Je 25,15:4
Broomhall, J Duke, 1966, N 12,30:3
Broonzy, William L C (Big Bill), 1958, Ag 16,17:3
Brophy, Albert T, 1955, Ja 7,21:4
Brophy, Alice E, 1948, Je 12,15:2
Brophy, Arnold, 1962, Ap 11,43:2
Brophy, Charles B, 1963, D 5,45:2
Brophy, Charles H A, 1957, Mr 15,25:4
Brophy, Daniel E, 1950, S 13,27:2
Brophy, Daniel F, 1960, D 19,27:3
Brophy, David T, 1953, Ap 23,29:5
Brophy, Edward, 1960, My 31,31:1
Brophy, Edward A, 1949, O 18,27:1
Brophy, Edward V, 1942, My 23,13:4
Brophy, Eleanor A Mrs, 1939, S 21,23:3
Brophy, Esther S Mrs, 1942, Mr 11,19:3
Brophy, George O, 1949, Ag 16,23:5
Brophy, H W (Dutch), 1951, Je 14,27:1
Brophy, Harold, 1966, My 24,43:5
Brophy, Harry J, 1954, Mr 27,17:3
Brophy, Helen M, 1950, Mr 30,29:1
Brophy, James C, 1950, D 14,35:5
Brophy, James E, 1953, N 22,89:1
Brophy, John, 1943, My 13,21:4; 1943, S 25,17:6; 1963, F 21,9:4; 1965, N 16,47:3
Brophy, John B Jr, 1941, O 8,23:5

Brophy, John F, 1941, Mr 23,45:1
Brophy, John J, 1960, O 1,19:5
Brophy, John P, 1939, Ap 19,23:3
Brophy, John S, 1944, Ja 20,19:4
Brophy, John W, 1946, Ag 29,27:4
Brophy, Joseph A, 1949, F 24,23:1
Brophy, Joseph A Mrs, 1967, My 16,45:3
Brophy, Joseph H, 1962, Ag 11,17:6
Brophy, Joseph P, 1968, Ap 24,47:2
Brophy, Loire Mrs, 1947, Mr 5,26:2
Brophy, Mary A, 1953, My 25,25:4
Brophy, Matthew J, 1949, Jl 21,25:1
Brophy, P J Mrs, 1948, S 29,29:3
Brophy, P J Rev, 1875, Je 28,8:6
Brophy, Patrick, 1924, F 22,15:4
Brophy, Patrick J, 1945, O 23,17:3
Brophy, T W, 1928, F 5,II,7:3
Brophy, Thomas, 1967, Jl 30,65:1
Brophy, Thomas P, 1962, Mr 25,89:1
Brophy, Vincent P, 1954, Ja 1,23:5
Brophy, William A, 1940, O 15,23:2
Brophy, William A Mrs, 1948, Ap 13,27:5
Brophy, William J, 1942, Ja 10,15:4
Broquet, Edward, 1938, Ag 5,18:2
Brorein, William G, 1937, D 13,27:6
Brosemer, Albert E, 1948, Mr 14,72:2
Brosen, Julius J, 1943, Je 12,13:2
Brosius, Albert M, 1944, O 10,21:3
Brosius, Carlton L, 1956, S 30,87:1
Brosius, Thomas H, 1953, Je 28,60:5
Brosius, Warren A, 1954, Je 27,69:1
Broski, John A, 1942, Jl 25,13:3
Brosman, Paul W (mem ser), 1956, F 16,29:1
Brosmith, Allan E, 1947, Ja 30,25:4
Brosmith, William, 1937, Ag 23,19:3
Brosnahan, Thomas, 1940, O 8,25:4
Brosnahan, Thomas F, 1948, Mr 17,25:4
Brosnahan, Timothy J Rev, 1915, Je 5,9:6
Brosnan, Dennis J, 1951, Ap 26,29:3
Brosnan, Edward J, 1948, Ag 6,17:3
Brosnan, John, 1947, Ag 1,17:3
Brosnan, John J, 1957, Ja 8,31:4
Brosnan, Lorenz J, 1943, Ap 14,23:4
Brosnan, Timothy P, 1941, Je 2,17:3
Brosnan, W L, 1933, F 25,15:3
Brosnan, William J, 1951, Ap 23,25:4
Bross, Ernest, 1923, F 1,11:4
Bross, Martin G, 1949, Je 8,30:2
Bross, Minton D, 1946, Je 28,21:4
Bross, Rachel K, 1967, O 21,31:4
Bross, Steward R, 1963, Ap 11,33:1
Bross, William Collier, 1903, D 2,9:5
Bross, William W Mrs, 1940, Ap 26,21:5
Brossard, Charles E, 1948, Je 3,25:5
Brossard, John, 1965, O 16,8:5
Brossard, John Mrs, 1965, O 16,8:5
Brosseau, A J, 1936, S 25,23:4
Brosseau, Alfred J Mrs, 1959, Ap 21,35:3
Brosshard, Henry M, 1949, N 23,29:4
Brossman, Charles F, 1944, My 6,15:2
Brossman, H Franklin, 1955, Ap 30,17:6
Brossman, William C, 1953, F 16,12:6
Brost, Frederick G, 1944, O 26,23:3
Brost, Lawrence F Mrs, 1948, My 12,27:4
Broster, Dorothy K, 1950, F 11,15:4
Brostrom, Dan, 1925, Jl 25,11:5
Brostrom, Ethel, 1959, N 2,31:3
Brother, Doran P, 1965, Ja 22,44:1
Brother Agelbert, 1875, My 7,7:2
Brotherhood, Percy M Jr, 1941, Ja 16,21:1
Brothers, Arthur M, 1958, S 17,32:4
Brothers, Eli, 1942, Ap 20,21:6
Brothers, Elmer D, 1937, Ap 7,25:3
Brothers, Frank J, 1945, Ag 26,43:2
Brothers, G N, 1933, Mr 4,13:1
Brothers, George R, 1957, F 13,35:4
Brothers, James H, 1956, Ja 25,31:2
Brothers, John J, 1941, Mr 29,15:5
Brothers, Katherine A Mrs (will, N 28,28:1), 1940, O 28,17:3
Brothers, Lawrence J, 1961, My 7,86:8
Brothers, Leo V, 1950, D 24,29:3
Brothers, Rubin, 1954, S 24,24:3
Brothers, Samuel Dr, 1918, D 19,15:4
Brothers, William A Rev, 1913, D 23,9:6
Brotherston, Bruce W, 1947, Ap 18,21:3
Brotherton, Albert, 1949, Ja 8,15:3
Brotherton, Charles F R, 1949, Jl 30,15:5
Brotherton, Charles W, 1958, S 8,29:2
Brotherton, George C, 1941, F 16,41:2
Brotherton, George C Sr, 1924, Ag 31,14:2
Brotherton, Horatio Rev, 1903, O 23,7:5
Brotherton, John, 1941, Mr 9,40:5
Brotherton, John R, 1937, F 24,24:1
Brotherton, Nina C, 1949, My 28,15:4
Brothwell, Nelson, 1958, F 16,80:6
Brothwick, John G, 1937, Ja 19,17:4
Brotton, Church E, 1952, F 13,29:2
Brotz, Anton F, 1945, Ap 18,23:2
Brotzman, Irvin C, 1950, Ag 18,21:4
Brouard, Clarence, 1952, My 28,29:3
Brouard, Daisy M, 1950, D 10,104:4
Brouard, Elmer B, 1941, Mr 28,23:3

Brouard, Elmer B Mrs, 1941, Mr 28,23:3
Brouard, Gabrielle, 1944, S 4,19:4
Brouckere, Louis de, 1951, Je 5,31:3
Broudy, Jesse, 1951, Jl 4,17:4
Broudy, Michael, 1951, Ag 17,17:3
Brouet, Auguste, 1941, N 12,23:1
Brough, Alex, 1940, F 28,21:4
Brough, Alex Mrs, 1957, O 21,25:4
Brough, Fanny Whiteside, 1914, D 2,13:5
Brough, Gov, 1865, Ag 30,5:4; 1865, Ag 31,1:4
Brough, John A Sr Mrs, 1966, Ap 20,47:4
Brough, Lionel, 1909, N 9,9:5
Brough, Louise M J, 1947, N 15,17:3
Brough, Robert, 1905, Ja 22,9:3
Brough, Sydney, 1911, Mr 29,13:5
Brougham, Frances E L, 1942, O 27,25:2
Brougham, Frederick I, 1949, Mr 30,25:1
Brougham, Herbert B, 1946, Ap 19,29:3
Brougham, John, 1880, Je 8,5:1
Brougham, Lady, 1865, Ja 29,8:1
Brougham, Lord, 1868, My 10,4:5
Broughel, Andrew J, 1925, N 22,9:1
Brougher, William E, 1965, Mr 7,81:7
Broughshane, Lord (Sir W H Davison), 1953, Ja 20, 25:4
Broughton, Charles D, 1962, O 22,29:2
Broughton, Charles E, 1956, N 1,39:4
Broughton, Charles F Mrs, 1947, Ap 1,27:3
Broughton, E P, 1903, N 9,7:6
Broughton, Geoffrey, 1954, S 11,17:4
Broughton, Harry T, 1948, Ja 22,27:4
Broughton, J Melville, 1949, Mr 7,21:3
Broughton, Lord, 1869, Je 5,5:2
Broughton, Luke D, 1947, D 7,78:5
Broughton, Luke D Mrs, 1937, Ag 23,19:2
Broughton, Luke J, 1948, Je 17,25:1
Broughton, Nathaniel, 1940, Ag 11,31:2
Broughton, P, 1926, Jl 22,19:6
Broughton, Rhoda, 1920, Je 7,15:2
Broughton, Urban H R (Lord Fairhaven), 1966, Ag 21,92:8
Broughton, William C, 1914, O 21,11:5
Broughton, William H C, 1938, Ja 30,II,9:2
Broughton, William S, 1951, Ja 11,25:5
Brougniart, A T, 1876, F 20,7:3
Brouha, Lucien A Dr, 1968, O 19,37:5
Brouillette, L C, 1937, Ap 24,19:4
Broun, Daniel S Mrs (J Wolf), 1958, F 25,55:5
Broun, E Fontaine Mrs, 1949, S 7,29:2
Broun, Heywood, 1939, D 19,23:1
Broun, Heywood C Mrs, 1951, My 16,35:2
Broun, Le Roy Dr, 1925, Ap 23,21:2
Broun, Rae H Mrs, 1939, Jl 7,17:4
Brounet, Arthur, 1941, F 28,19:5
Brounoff, Platon, 1924, Jl 13,22:4
Brous, Bernard Mrs, 1961, Ag 29,21:1
Brouse, H Grace, 1944, D 16,15:3
Broussard, James F, 1942, N 3,23:2
Broussard, Joseph C, 1966, F 8,36:5
Broussard, Robert F Sen, 1918, Ap 13,13:4
Brousse, Abel A, 1944, S 28,19:2
Brousseau, Kate, 1938, Jl 10,29:4
Brouthers, D, 1932, Ag 3,15:3
Brouthers, Edward Mrs, 1951, Mr 29,27:2
Brouwer, Dirk, 1966, F 1,31:7
Brouwer, Dirk W, 1963, N 4,35:5
Brouwer, John H, 1939, F 16,21:3
Brouwer, Stephen J, 1946, Ap 6,17:4
Brouwer, Theophilus A, 1911, Je 16,9:6
Brouwers, Frans M J C, 1947, Mr 5,25:5
Brovenitch, Ellen, 1922, O 30,15:5
Brovitz, Phil, 1949, Ja 16,68:1
Brow, Arthur A, 1952, My 28,29:2
Brow, N W, 1877, F 8,5:3
Broward, Napoleon Bonaparte Ex-Gov, 1910, O 2,II, 13:4
Browd, Ephraim K Dr, 1922, My 17,19:4
Browder, Basil D, 1960, Ap 2,23:2
Browder, Earl Mrs, 1955, Ja 9,86:4
Browder, Ella J Mrs, 1947, Mr 27,27:1
Browder, George R, 1944, N 4,15:4
Browder, Jonathan B, 1958, Ap 9,36:1
Brower, A Vedder, 1942, Mr 2,19:4
Brower, Alice V, 1958, D 2,37:4
Brower, Ancel J, 1943, N 25,25:4
Brower, Bailey Sr, 1964, Ap 6,31:1
Brower, Bloomfield, 1912, Ja 7,II,15:3
Brower, Charles C, 1944, O 22,46:4
Brower, Charles C Mrs, 1952, Jl 15,21:2
Brower, Charles D, 1945, F 13,23:2; 1945, N 4,43:1
Brower, Charles D Jr, 1942, Jl 13,15:3
Brower, Cyril D, 1954, O 18,25:5
Brower, David Capt, 1916, F 16,11:7
Brower, Edna, 1950, Ag 5,15:4
Brower, Edward C, 1961, My 11,37:5
Brower, Ernest C, 1925, Jl 28,13:5
Brower, Frank, 1874, Je 7,7:6
Brower, Frederick, 1947, Ap 20,63:2
Brower, Frederick I Mrs, 1955, F 5,15:5
Brower, Frederick W Jr, 1905, Ja 12,7:2
Brower, Garret, 1922, Ja 3,17:3
Brower, George E, 1961, Ag 26,17:4
Brower, George G Mrs, 1947, Ja 9,23:1
Brower, George Vanderhoof, 1921, O 16,22:4
Brower, Gilbert, 1949, D 29,25:5
Brower, Harold S, 1954, Je 6,86:4
Brower, Harry, 1947, Mr 26,25:2
Brower, Harry V Mrs, 1957, O 19,21:3
Brower, Herbert D Mrs, 1960, D 1,35:4
Brower, Herbert S, 1937, D 2,25:6
Brower, Howard Stanley, 1968, Mr 6,47:2
Brower, J H, 1881, Je 16,5:2
Brower, Jacob L, 1939, O 16,19:5
Brower, John I, 1957, S 5,29:4
Brower, John L, 1872, S 21,2:2
Brower, John Lefoy, 1922, Jl 19,13:6
Brower, John Van Alst, 1910, N 9,9:2
Brower, Kate, 1941, Jl 23,19:5
Brower, Lawrence C, 1955, D 28,24:7
Brower, Lawrence G, 1954, My 7,23:2
Brower, Leonard J, 1950, D 25,15:4
Brower, Lorenzo Sr Mrs, 1952, F 28,27:3
Brower, Max P, 1954, Ap 27,29:4
Brower, Melvin H, 1939, N 18,17:3
Brower, Mott R, 1947, Ja 29,26:2
Brower, Ogden, 1943, Ag 5,15:2
Brower, Oliver A, 1952, My 13,23:4
Brower, Otto, 1946, Ja 26,13:4
Brower, Paul, 1968, Ap 25,47:4
Brower, Percy Mrs, 1960, Ap 17,93:1
Brower, R Frank Mrs, 1962, S 26,39:4
Brower, Rebecca R Mrs, 1943, O 12,27:3
Brower, Richard L, 1958, Ja 19,86:1
Brower, Roy, 1952, Je 12,33:3
Brower, Sarah Louise Mrs, 1921, Mr 12,11:6
Brower, Thomas H, 1940, My 24,19:2
Brower, Walter S, 1962, F 11,86:6
Brower, William L, 1940, My 10,24:3
Brower, William P, 1954, Ap 23,27:1
Brower, Wilson S, 1938, O 9,44:7
Brower, Winfield C, 1951, O 23,29:2
Brower, Winifield S, 1949, S 17,17:5
Browers, Mr, 1872, F 29,4:7
Brown, A Ellicott, 1948, Ag 20,17:4
Brown, A G, 1880, Je 14,5:1
Brown, A Glenn, 1956, Je 29,21:2
Brown, A H, 1941, Mr 19,22:3
Brown, A L, 1885, Ja 29,4:7
Brown, A Mason, 1951, Ag 6,21:4
Brown, A Maurice, 1952, My 8,31:4
Brown, A Roy, 1944, Mr 10,15:3
Brown, A Seymour, 1947, D 24,21:4
Brown, A Ten Eyck, 1940, Je 10,17:2
Brown, Aaron, 1945, Ja 25,19:2
Brown, Aaron J Mrs, 1956, Ja 24,32:5
Brown, Aaron Venable (funl, Mr 11,1:4), 1859, Mr 9,4:1
Brown, Abe M, 1952, My 26,23:5
Brown, Abner B, 1938, D 20,25:4
Brown, Abraham, 1947, Ag 31,37:1; 1962, O 13,25:3; 1967, D 14,47:2
Brown, Abraham A, 1937, My 17,19:3
Brown, Abraham J, 1953, Mr 25,31:3
Brown, Abram L, 1944, S 29,21:2
Brown, Adams E Jr, 1952, F 20,29:4
Brown, Addison, 1913, Ap 10,11:5
Brown, Addison Mrs, 1943, Mr 1,19:4
Brown, Addison R Sr, 1956, S 20,33:1
Brown, Adelaide, 1940, Jl 30,19:4
Brown, Adelaide H Mrs (will, F 5,12:6), 1937, Ja 8, 19:1
Brown, Adeline P Mrs, 1938, D 13,25:6
Brown, Adon P, 1942, Ap 24,17:2
Brown, Alan, 1960, S 9,29:4
Brown, Alanson C Jr Mrs, 1955, S 27,35:5
Brown, Alanson D Mrs, 1915, My 26,13:5
Brown, Albert, 1950, D 4,29:2
Brown, Albert C, 1943, Mr 28,24:2; 1945, S 24,19:1; 1953, Ag 30,88:1
Brown, Albert F, 1939, Je 28,21:6
Brown, Albert I Mrs, 1952, F 22,21:3
Brown, Albert J, 1938, N 17,25:3
Brown, Albert L, 1942, Ja 9,21:2; 1963, Je 11,37:4
Brown, Albert O (will, Ap 20,23:8), 1937, Mr 29,19:4
Brown, Albert O, 1945, Mr 6,21:5
Brown, Albert S, 1950, Ag 27,88:1
Brown, Albert W, 1937, O 7,27:5; 1950, N 29,33:3
Brown, Alec, 1962, S 11,33:4
Brown, Alex, 1941, Ap 30,19:4
Brown, Alex (will), 1949, My 21,28:2
Brown, Alex A, 1960, Ag 16,29:4
Brown, Alex C, 1964, Ap 11,25:3
Brown, Alex C Mrs, 1956, Ja 30,27:3
Brown, Alex S, 1956, Ja 31,29:2
Brown, Alfred, 1955, Ja 7,21:1
Brown, Alfred G, 1953, D 15,39:1
Brown, Alfred J, 1960, Ag 23,29:4
Brown, Alfred R, 1939, F 8,23:4
Brown, Alfred Seely Dr, 1968, Ag 17,27:5
Brown, Alfred W (por), 1938, S 8,23:1
Brown, Alfred W, 1955, My 27,23:2
Brown, Algernon, 1960, O 6,14:7
Brown, Algernon W, 1952, N 3,29:2
Brown, Alice, 1948, Je 22,25:2
Brown, Alice C, 1942, F 23,21:4
Brown, Alice E, 1938, Ag 17,19:5; 1949, Jl 11,17:5
Brown, Alice H, 1950, F 23,27:4
Brown, Alice S Mrs, 1941, F 23,39:6
Brown, Alice V, 1949, O 19,29:3
Brown, Alpheus L, 1949, Jl 15,19:3
Brown, Alphonse, 1951, Ap 13,23:1
Brown, Alvan S Mrs, 1954, Jl 4,31:1
Brown, Alvia K, 1938, My 25,23:5
Brown, Alvin F Mrs, 1947, N 19,27:2
Brown, Ames, 1947, My 26,21:1
Brown, Ames T (funl, My 24,41:5), 1961, My 20,23:2
Brown, Amy H, 1948, O 15,23:5
Brown, Andrew B, 1939, Ja 10,10:5
Brown, Andrew H, 1937, Je 19,17:4
Brown, Andrew H Jr, 1945, Jl 16,11:7
Brown, Andrew J, 1939, Ag 10,19:4
Brown, Andrew L, 1940, My 13,17:3
Brown, Andrew M, 1948, Ag 12,21:4
Brown, Andrew Mrs, 1953, Ap 10,21:5
Brown, Andrew W, 1946, D 20,23:3
Brown, Anna B Mrs, 1949, Mr 22,25:3
Brown, Anna L Mrs, 1939, O 28,15:4
Brown, Anna Mrs, 1961, Jl 12,32:1
Brown, Anne, 1940, F 4,40:6
Brown, Annie M Dr, 1914, My 1,13:6
Brown, Anson, 1949, My 18,27:3
Brown, Anthony, 1960, Jl 4,15:4
Brown, Anthony J, 1937, Je 11,23:3
Brown, Archer, 1904, S 24,9:7
Brown, Archer H Mrs, 1960, D 10,23:6
Brown, Archibald G, 1922, Ap 4,17:5
Brown, Archibald M, 1956, N 30,23:3
Brown, Archibald W, 1959, D 25,21:6
Brown, Arden Mrs, 1957, Ja 26,19:4
Brown, Arlo A, 1961, D 20,33:3
Brown, Armstead, 1951, O 30,29:5
Brown, Arthur, 1951, D 13,33:4; 1954, N 10,33:2
Brown, Arthur C, 1941, Ap 12,15:6; 1950, Mr 7,27:3
Brown, Arthur E, 1940, N 29,21:5
Brown, Arthur F, 1947, S 29,21:1; 1952, My 4,91:2
Brown, Arthur G, 1925, N 20,21:3
Brown, Arthur H, 1944, O 5,23:4; 1961, D 8,37:2
Brown, Arthur J, 1958, Ap 11,25:3
Brown, Arthur J Jr, 1959, F 20,26:1
Brown, Arthur J Mrs, 1945, D 26,19:3
Brown, Arthur Jr, 1957, Jl 9,29:1
Brown, Arthur K Mrs, 1958, Ap 4,21:1
Brown, Arthur L, 1951, Jl 11,23:5; 1954, Mr 21,89:2
Brown, Arthur M, 1945, Jl 17,13:6
Brown, Arthur M Sr, 1950, N 6,27:2
Brown, Arthur R, 1950, Ap 7,25:3
Brown, Arthur T, 1942, Je 16,10:4; 1951, My 18,28:3; 1954, N 17,31:2; 1960, S 26,33:1
Brown, Arthur V, 1949, Ap 16,15:6
Brown, Arthur W, 1958, Ja 7,47:3; 1966, O 25,45:3
Brown, Arthur W Mrs, 1965, My 7,41:4
Brown, Ashmun N, 1948, Ja 13,19:3
Brown, Augustus Cleveland, 1915, Ja 4,11:5
Brown, Austin H Capt, 1903, Ag 13,7:6
Brown, Austin L, 1953, Ja 11,90:2
Brown, B, 1936, S 17,23:6
Brown, B G Prof, 1903, S 30,9:6
Brown, B Ross, 1953, My 6,31:1
Brown, Bache H Sr, 1957, F 5,23:1
Brown, Barnum, 1963, F 6,4:8
Brown, Bartholomew F, 1948, Je 7,19:4
Brown, Baxter L, 1952, N 11,29:4
Brown, Bayard, 1926, Ap 9,19:1
Brown, Beatrice, 1954, Ap 3,15:2
Brown, Belden B Mrs, 1920, Jl 3,15:6
Brown, Benjamin (por), 1939, F 13,15:3
Brown, Benjamin, 1940, F 5,17:4
Brown, Benjamin C, 1942, Ja 21,18:2
Brown, Benjamin F, 1949, F 11,23:3
Brown, Benjamin F S, 1920, Ag 27,11:4
Brown, Benjamin H, 1955, My 19,29:6
Brown, Benjamin W, 1949, Ag 16,23:2; 1955, Ja 8,1
Brown, Beriah, 1939, Mr 5,49:2
Brown, Bernard C, 1951, F 13,31:2
Brown, Bertram O, 1938, Ap 2,15:6
Brown, Bertrand, 1964, Je 4,37:5
Brown, Bessie H, 1945, Ja 10,23:3
Brown, Bettina L, 1960, Ja 1,19:3
Brown, Bill, 1939, Ja 21,15:5
Brown, Bonnar, 1961, My 14,86:8
Brown, Boyce (Bro Matthew), 1959, Ja 31,19:2
Brown, Boyd S, 1951, Je 10,92:8
Brown, Brian, 1958, N 14,27:4
Brown, Buford M, 1966, O 19,47:5
Brown, Burr R, 1948, My 2,77:1
Brown, Burton B Mrs, 1966, F 3,32:1
Brown, Burton S, 1944, Jl 19,19:6
Brown, Byron C, 1947, N 27,31:1
Brown, C, 1932, D 1,21:4
Brown, C Anna, 1952, Ap 2,33:2
Brown, C Emerson, 1949, D 19,27:4
BRO
Brown, C F, 1929, Je 20,25:5
Brown, C Foster Jr, 1965, Ap 14,41:2
Brown, C H Dr, 1901, O 19,9:2
Brown, C Kimball, 1958, N 20,35:4
Brown, C Stuart, 1946, Mr 27,27:3
Brown, C W, 1928, Mr 7,25:1
Brown, Calvin, 1945, S 12,25:3
Brown, Carl J, 1943, F 13,11:3

Brown, Carl L, 1951, N 10,17:4
Brown, Carl S, 1939, Ag 6,37:4
Brown, Carleton, 1941, Je 26,23:3
Brown, Carlyle, 1964, Ja 5,92:8
Brown, Caroline E, 1884, Jl 17,5:4
Brown, Carroll N (por), 1938, D 16,25:1
Brown, Carroll N Mrs, 1967, Ja 10,40:4
Brown, Catherine H Mrs, 1953, Jl 2,23:3
Brown, Caxton, 1952, Jl 26,13:1
Brown, Cecil L, 1964, Ap 29,41:3
Brown, Cecil R Mrs, 1957, Ag 3,15:6
Brown, Charles, 1940, My 3,21:3; 1948, Ag 3,25:3
Brown, Charles A, 1937, My 4,25:4; 1938, N 24,27:1; 1941, O 19,46:2; 1948, N 24,23:4; 1950, Je 21,27:5
Brown, Charles B, 1944, N 4,15:6; 1959, Mr 14,23:5
Brown, Charles C, 1949, My 28,15:4; 1949, D 19,27:5
Brown, Charles D, 1948, N 27,17:5
Brown, Charles D Sr, 1954, F 9,27:2
Brown, Charles E, 1944, S 5,19:6; 1946, F 17,42:6; 1959, O 20,39:5
Brown, Charles E Jr, 1949, N 9,27:3
Brown, Charles E Mrs, 1938, Ja 6,19:4
Brown, Charles F, 1940, Mr 23,13:3; 1944, Mr 8,19:1; 1948, S 4,15:4
Brown, Charles F Mrs, 1939, Jl 15,15:2; 1948, N 14, 77:1; 1949, Mr 22,25:5
Brown, Charles G Mrs, 1948, My 7,23:4
Brown, Charles H, 1937, Ag 21,15:2; 1947, Je 16,21:3; 1960, Ja 21,31:4
Brown, Charles H Jr, 1962, S 12,39:4
Brown, Charles H Jr Mrs, 1944, My 10,19:5
Brown, Charles H Mrs, 1956, Jl 13,19:1; 1959, Mr 31, 30:5
Brown, Charles H Mrs (cor, N 3,45:3), 1967, N 2, 47:5
Brown, Charles H Sr, 1960, Je 23,29:4
Brown, Charles J, 1948, My 7,23:4
Brown, Charles K, 1944, F 7,15:1
Brown, Charles L, 1947, O 9,25:3; 1950, Ja 22,77:2; 1953, Ap 18,19:2; 1959, D 5,23:4
Brown, Charles M, 1967, D 12,48:1
Brown, Charles P, 1939, Mr 23,23:5; 1950, Je 25,70:1
Brown, Charles R, 1950, N 29,33:1
Brown, Charles R Mrs, 1962, Ja 25,31:4
Brown, Charles Rufus Rev, 1914, F 3,11:6
Brown, Charles T, 1950, Mr 9,29:4
Brown, Charles W Mrs, 1952, D 7,88:3
Brown, Charlotte A, 1948, D 8,31:2
Brown, Charlotte C Mrs, 1937, Ja 20,21:1; 1941, Mr 7, 21:6
Brown, Charlotte H, 1961, Ja 12,29:2
Brown, Charlotte S Mrs, 1940, My 7,25:3
Brown, Chester C, 1950, Jl 27,25:6
Brown, Chester J Mrs, 1942, My 9,13:4
Brown, Chester R, 1952, Ja 21,15:4; 1967, S 22,47:2
Brown, Chester T, 1953, N 13,27:1
Brown, Claire H, 1951, Ap 8,92:3
Brown, Clara, 1938, F 16,42:5
Brown, Clara K Mrs, 1950, F 17,23:1
Brown, Clara M Mrs, 1937, D 13,27:2
Brown, Clarence, 1918, Jl 31,9:5
Brown, Clarence E, 1955, Ja 6,27:3
Brown, Clarence Eugene, 1924, S 6,11:7
Brown, Clarence F G, 1950, Je 5,23:3
Brown, Clarence J (funl, Ag 28,21:5), 1965, Ag 24, 31:1
Brown, Clarence M (est tax appr, Je 7,19:1), 1958, F 10,23:2
Brown, Clarence R, 1919, Ja 25,11:2
Brown, Clarence T, 1938, Ag 1,13:4
Brown, Clark W, 1951, O 27,19:3
Brown, Claud Mrs, 1962, O 17,39:4
Brown, Claude J, 1944, Ja 6,23:4
Brown, Claude K, 1940, Mr 21,25:5
Brown, Claude O, 1954, Jl 3,11:6
Brown, Clifford K, 1946, Mr 16,13:6
Brown, Clifford W, 1964, My 29,29:5
Brown, Clifton S, 1952, My 12,25:5
Brown, Clint, 1956, Ja 1,50:5
Brown, Clinton B, 1960, My 27,31:1
Brown, Clinton C, 1941, Je 28,15:3
Brown, Clinton Mrs, 1945, My 22,19:4
Brown, Coleman P, 1964, Je 30,33:2
Brown, Colvin W, 1952, Jl 9,27:2
Brown, Constant, 1942, Ag 9,43:4
Brown, Constantine, 1966, F 25,31:2
Brown, Constantine Mrs, 1939, O 30,17:5
Brown, Cora, 1957, Ap 23,31:1
Brown, Corinne Stubbs, 1914, Mr 16,9:3
Brown, Curtis W, 1945, Ag 7,23:2
Brown, Cyril, 1949, O 8,13:4
Brown, Cyril J, 1960, D 24,15:3
Brown, Cyrus W, 1951, F 12,23:1
Brown, D Henry, 1937, Ja 17,II,8:3
Brown, Dan W, 1925, O 27,23:4
Brown, Dana J, 1940, N 19,24:3
Brown, Daniel F, 1952, Je 22,68:3
Brown, Daniel H, 1945, Ja 24,21:4
Brown, Daniel R, 1919, Mr 1,13:4
Brown, David, 1941, S 30,23:3; 1952, S 17,31:5; 1960, O 16,88:8
Brown, David A, 1958, D 24,2:4
Brown, David B, 1960, N 9,35:2
Brown, David C, 1943, My 13,21:4; 1950, S 29,27:3
Brown, David J, 1951, N 14,31:6
Brown, David L, 1966, Ja 10,25:4
Brown, David L Mrs, 1953, N 13,27:2
Brown, David N, 1908, F 22,7:6; 1943, N 12,22:3
Brown, David P, 1965, My 1,31:2
Brown, David Paul, 1872, Jl 12,5:4
Brown, David S Mrs, 1967, My 23,47:1
Brown, David W, 1952, F 6,29:3
Brown, Davis, 1959, S 27,86:3
Brown, De Witt C, 1912, Ap 8,11:6
Brown, Delaplaine, 1906, Je 24,9:6
Brown, Delbert F, 1955, N 18,25:4
Brown, Demarcus C Mrs, 1941, Ja 12,44:2
Brown, Dennis E, 1945, My 8,34:4
Brown, Dickson, 1954, F 2,27:3
Brown, Dickson Q, 1939, S 12,25:3
Brown, Dillon Dr, 1909, Mr 17,9:2
Brown, Don, 1958, My 3,19:3
Brown, Don C, 1963, F 7,7:3
Brown, Donald C Mrs, 1952, F 5,29:2
Brown, Donald L, 1940, Ja 30,19:1; 1966, D 11,89:2
Brown, Donaldson (Oct 2), 1965, O 11,61:1
Brown, Dorothy H, 1967, O 24,47:4
Brown, Douglas, 1946, Mr 27,27:4
Brown, Douglas C (Viscount Ruffside), 1958, My 6, 35:4
Brown, Douglas Dr, 1937, Je 8,25:5
Brown, Douglas W, 1954, Mr 11,31:5
Brown, Douglass E, 1952, Ja 9,29:3
Brown, Downing P, 1954, Ap 3,15:3
Brown, Dr, 1873, Je 1,1:6
Brown, Dwight H, 1944, My 10,19:3
Brown, E A Dr, 1883, Je 20,5:3
Brown, E E, 1934, N 4,1:3
Brown, E F Col, 1903, Ja 11,7:5
Brown, E J, 1880, N 24,5:2
Brown, E Kelly, 1965, Ap 1,35:4
Brown, E Stanley, 1961, Je 13,35:2
Brown, E Winslow, 1948, Ap 22,27:3
Brown, Earl O, 1944, S 18,19:1
Brown, Earl W, 1963, Ap 24,35:2
Brown, Earle, 1944, N 29,23:5
Brown, Earle G, 1962, N 2,31:2
Brown, Earle G Mrs, 1940, D 23,19:2
Brown, Edgar G, 1954, Ap 11,87:2
Brown, Edgar P Dr, 1937, Jl 9,21:4
Brown, Edith, 1956, D 8,19:4
Brown, Edith H, 1951, Ap 25,29:2
Brown, Edith K, 1967, Je 24,29:5
Brown, Edmund G, 1959, Ja 30,27:1
Brown, Edmund J, 1954, S 22,29:3
Brown, Edmund Jr Mrs, 1957, Je 3,27:4
Brown, Edward, 1956, My 28,27:5
Brown, Edward A, 1914, Ap 17,11:6; 1945, Je 5,19:4
Brown, Edward B, 1940, Mr 22,19:3
Brown, Edward B Mrs, 1960, Ap 10,86:7
Brown, Edward E, 1959, Ag 25,31:1
Brown, Edward E Mrs, 1944, O 7,13:3
Brown, Edward Flint, 1909, S 28,9:5
Brown, Edward H, 1938, N 11,25:4; 1949, F 4,24:3; 1959, D 8,45:4
Brown, Edward J, 1950, F 2,28:2; 1953, Ag 1,11:5
Brown, Edward K, 1922, Ja 17,17:3; 1951, Ap 24,29:4
Brown, Edward L, 1949, Ap 7,29:3
Brown, Edward M, 1947, F 8,17:5
Brown, Edward Marsh, 1903, D 2,2:1
Brown, Edward N, 1956, My 3,31:4
Brown, Edward N Mrs, 1944, Jl 20,19:2
Brown, Edward S, 1938, Je 5,45:2; 1942, D 29,21:3; 1955, Jl 13,25:4
Brown, Edward Sir, 1939, Ag 9,17:3
Brown, Edward T, 1922, My 3,21:5
Brown, Edward T Mrs, 1925, Mr 26,23:4
Brown, Edwin, 1950, Ap 12,27:3
Brown, Edwin A Mrs, 1956, Ja 4,27:1
Brown, Edwin C, 1941, Jl 13,29:3
Brown, Edwin C N, 1955, Ag 19,19:2
Brown, Edwin M, 1952, F 5,29:3
Brown, Edwin Mrs (Ned), 1958, Mr 27,33:4
Brown, Edwin P, 1951, S 4,27:5
Brown, Edwin S, 1942, My 16,13:6
Brown, Edwy R, 1942, Ja 26,15:5
Brown, Edwy R Mrs, 1954, D 29,23:1
Brown, Edythe J, 1941, F 26,21:3
Brown, Egbert Brainard Col, 1922, S 10,28:3
Brown, Egbert E, 1956, F 20,23:3
Brown, Egbert W, 1944, Je 4,42:1
Brown, Elanor G, 1964, Jl 22,33:5
Brown, Elbert M Mrs, 1947, D 6,15:2
Brown, Elgar, 1958, S 9,35:4
Brown, Elijah H, 1946, S 3,19:5
Brown, Elijah H Mrs, 1948, Mr 9,23:4
Brown, Eliza Mrs, 1942, O 10,15:5
Brown, Elizabeth, 1940, Ag 6,20:3
Brown, Elizabeth F, 1946, F 28,23:3
Brown, Elizabeth J, 1949, Ap 8,26:3
Brown, Elizabeth S, 1948, Ap 10,13:5
Brown, Elizabeth V Mrs, 1938, My 9,17:3
Brown, Ella C Mrs, 1947, Ap 26,13:4
Brown, Elliot C, 1946, Ja 11,21:2
Brown, Elliott F, 1959, Mr 22,86:8
Brown, Elliott W, 1941, My 26,19:4
Brown, Elliott W Mrs, 1941, Ja 11,17:4
Brown, Ellis E, 1941, Je 21,17:1
Brown, Ellis V, 1938, Ja 3,21:2
Brown, Ellsworth S, 1948, Mr 22,23:3
Brown, Elmer, 1952, O 5,89:2; 1968, F 28,47:1
Brown, Elon R, 1922, S 25,15:4; 1922, S 26,17:4
Brown, Elwood S, 1924, Mr 19,21:5
Brown, Emil, 1958, Jl 16,29:2
Brown, Enoch, 1962, Ap 22,80:6
Brown, Enoch R, 1950, Ap 5,31:1
Brown, Eric, 1939, Ap 7,21:3
Brown, Ernest, 1958, Je 10,33:3; 1962, F 17,19:1
Brown, Ernest A, 1940, Je 2,44:7
Brown, Ernest B Mrs, 1943, N 22,25:3
Brown, Ernest G, 1951, Ag 28,24:2
Brown, Ernest H, 1961, Je 18,88:6
Brown, Ernest L Mrs, 1945, D 27,20:2
Brown, Ernest M, 1938, S 22,23:3
Brown, Ernest W, 1938, Jl 24,29:3; 1945, Ja 21,40:2; 1947, F 7,23:2; 1960, D 25,42:1
Brown, Esther, 1943, D 26,32:4
Brown, Ethel D, 1948, N 10,29:5
Brown, Ethel E, 1948, My 31,19:4
Brown, Ethel M, 1947, Je 3,25:2
Brown, Eugene Sr, 1953, Ag 15,15:6
Brown, Eugene W, 1940, F 22,23:5; 1949, Ap 3,76:8
Brown, Evelyn L, 1944, O 7,13:6
Brown, Everard C, 1954, F 10,29:1
Brown, Everett C, 1937, Ap 12,17:5
Brown, Everett H, 1937, Ap 3,19:4
Brown, Everett H Jr, 1951, My 4,27:3
Brown, Everett J, 1947, Ja 14,25:1
Brown, Everett L, 1944, Ag 7,15:5
Brown, Everett S, 1964, D 22,29:2
Brown, F Herbert, 1947, My 7,27:6
Brown, F J Mrs, 1947, Mr 30,56:4
Brown, F Quentin, 1946, N 30,15:6
Brown, F Roy, 1960, D 1,35:1
Brown, Fannie P Mrs, 1944, Mr 10,15:2
Brown, Fanny W, 1963, S 5,31:1
Brown, Fayette, 1953, F 1,89:1
Brown, Fergus, 1940, N 9,17:2
Brown, Florence G, 1952, Mr 7,24:3
Brown, Florence M, 1943, N 3,25:5
Brown, Floyd deL, 1955, N 8,31:2
Brown, Floyd L, 1944, My 30,21:5
Brown, Floyd S, 1949, F 8,25:4
Brown, Forrest U, 1941, S 4,21:2
Brown, Foster V, 1937, Mr 27,15:4
Brown, Francina, 1942, D 26,11:1
Brown, Francis C, 1939, F 2,19:5; 1940, N 2,15:3; 1966, O 3,50:2
Brown, Francis Gordon, 1911, My 11,11:6
Brown, Francis H, 1950, Jl 15,13:5
Brown, Francis L, 1949, Mr 29,25:3; 1957, O 16,35:1
Brown, Francis Mrs, 1949, D 24,15:4
Brown, Francis Rev Dr, 1916, O 16,11:5
Brown, Francis S, 1940, My 7,25:1
Brown, Francis X, 1951, N 26,25:2
Brown, Frank, 1945, My 5,15:2; 1950, F 7,27:5; 1961, Ap 29,23:1
Brown, Frank A, 1943, My 27,28:6; 1956, Ja 23,25:4; 1962, Ap 3,39:5
Brown, Frank B, 1951, My 24,35:2
Brown, Frank C, 1943, Je 4,21:4; 1955, Jl 3,33:2
Brown, Frank D, 1909, S 15,9:5
Brown, Frank E, 1925, S 30,23:4; 1937, Ag 12,19:4; 1947, D 16,33:4; 1948, F 20,27:2
Brown, Frank Edwin Maj, 1920, Je 25,11:4
Brown, Frank Ex-Gov, 1920, F 4,11:4
Brown, Frank H, 1941, Ja 19,41:2; 1946, D 5,31:3; 1950, My 26,23:1; 1954, Ap 2,27:2
Brown, Frank L, 1922, Mr 25,11:3; 1940, My 30,17:5; 1948, Ag 13,15:4; 1962, Mr 13,32:2
Brown, Frank M, 1945, Ag 25,11:2
Brown, Frank M Capt, 1903, Jl 14,7:7
Brown, Frank Mrs, 1950, My 13,17:5
Brown, Frank Q Mrs, 1950, S 11,23:5
Brown, Frank V, 1940, Mr 2,13:5
Brown, Frank W, 1942, O 7,25:4
Brown, Franklin E, 1953, Je 10,29:2
Brown, Franklin Q, 1955, N 8,31:1
Brown, Franklyn K, 1942, Ap 3,21:6
Brown, Fred A Mrs, 1946, Je 14,22:2
Brown, Fred C, 1955, Ap 5,29:4
Brown, Fred F, 1960, Ag 10,31:5
Brown, Fred G, 1946, D 21,19:6
Brown, Fred H, 1943, N 4,23:4; 1955, F 4,21:1
Brown, Fred J, 1943, O 1,19:1
Brown, Fred L, 1944, Ap 5,19:5
Brown, Fred O Mrs, 1943, F 27,13:3
Brown, Fred R, 1941, S 1,15:6
Brown, Frederic A, 1957, Je 24,23:4
Brown, Frederic N, 1960, Mr 2,37:5
Brown, Frederick, 1960, D 11,88:4
Brown, Frederick A, 1954, F 17,31:3
Brown, Frederick D, 1949, Ap 28,31:2
Brown, Frederick E, 1945, O 4,23:5
Brown, Frederick F, 1958, Je 12,31:4
Brown, Frederick F Mrs, 1956, Ap 27,27:2
Brown, Frederick J, 1939, S 20,27:6
Brown, Frederick L Mrs, 1938, O 29,19:4
Brown, Frederick Mrs, 1940, D 5,23:3

Brown, Frederick R, 1941, N 17,19:2; 1952, Mr 16,91:2
Brown, Frederick R Mrs, 1951, Je 26,29:3
Brown, Frederick Squire, 1915, Ja 14,11:4
Brown, Frederick W, 1947, Mr 15,13:5; 1947, Je 19, 21:2
Brown, G Gilbert, 1946, Ja 12,15:3
Brown, G H Hon, 1865, Ag 6,6:4
Brown, G Preston Mrs, 1952, Mr 21,23:4
Brown, G Victor, 1959, N 3,35:8
Brown, G W Jr, 1903, My 26,9:5
Brown, G Winthrop, 1938, N 4,23:3
Brown, Gabriel S Mrs, 1955, Ja 6,27:4
Brown, Gardner W, 1940, N 26,23:5
Brown, Garrott William, 1913, O 21,9:7
Brown, Gary, 1908, D 22,9:2
Brown, Gay H, 1960, D 13,31:5
Brown, Gay H Mrs, 1946, Mr 12,25:4
Brown, Geoffrey W, 1955, O 16,86:2
Brown, George, 1875, Jl 9,4:6; 1880, My 10,2:4; 1911, Jl 7,9:4; 1912, My 13,9:6; 1945, O 11,23:4; 1946, N 19,31:5; 1950, My 1,25:2; 1954, N 7,88:1; 1962, Ap 13,35:1
Brown, George A, 1939, Jl 10,19:4; 1942, N 19,25:5; 1954, Jl 3,11:6
Brown, George B, 1907, O 2,11:7; 1938, Je 24,19:4; 1939, Ja 19,19:2
Brown, George C, 1919, My 12,13:3; 1939, D 8,25:4; 1940, F 23,15:5; 1952, N 20,31:1
Brown, George E, 1946, D 12,29:1; 1947, S 10,27:5; 1949, Jl 18,17:4; 1955, Ag 19,19:4
Brown, George E Mrs, 1955, S 1,23:4
Brown, George F, 1939, Ap 17,17:2; 1940, D 28,15:4
Brown, George F Mrs, 1959, Je 27,25:1
Brown, George F Rev (funl, Mr 28,13:4), 1914, Mr 25,11:6
Brown, George Fox, 1914, My 1,13:6
Brown, George Francis, 1910, Ja 11,9:4
Brown, George G, 1938, Ap 20,23:5; 1955, D 20,31:1; 1957, Ag 28,27:2
Brown, George G Mrs, 1948, Ja 22,27:3
Brown, George H, 1942, Mr 12,19:2; 1943, F 10,25:4; 1947, D 12,27:3; 1952, N 14,23:4
Brown, George Hay, 1909, N 25,11:6
Brown, George J, 1953, My 8,25:3; 1955, Ja 20,31:5
Brown, George K, 1947, Mr 7,25:3
Brown, George L, 1939, D 19,26:4; 1941, Je 7,17:4
Brown, George L (por), 1949, S 11,95:3
Brown, George M, 1939, Ap 26,23:4; 1953, Ap 17, 25:1; 1953, Ag 11,27:3; 1959, Ap 2,31:5
Brown, George M Mrs, 1951, Ap 15,93:1
Brown, George M Sir, 1939, Je 29,23:5
Brown, George Mrs, 1946, O 4,23:3
Brown, George R, 1941, Jl 6,27:3; 1943, Jl 31,13:7; 1944, S 8,19:3; 1960, Jl 29,25:4
Brown, George Rear-Adm, 1913, Je 30,7:4
Brown, George S, 1941, N 12,24:2; 1943, Ag 10,19:4
Brown, George Sir, 1865, S 12,8:2
Brown, George T, 1941, Mr 4,23:3; 1967, S 22,47:1
Brown, George V, 1937, O 19,26:1; 1948, Ap 4,60:5; 1955, Ap 19,31:2
Brown, George W, 1919, F 18,11:3; 1941, Ap 13,39:1; 1944, Ag 10,17:3; 1946, Ja 25,23:2; 1947, Mr 29,15:2; 1950, Je 2,23:4; 1951, N 28,31:2; 1960, Ja 10,87:2
Brown, George Washington Capt, 1915, Mr 24,11:4
Brown, George William Mrs, 1919, Jl 3,10:2
Brown, Gerald Rudderow, 1925, Ap 11,13:3
Brown, Gerson J, 1957, F 4,19:2
Brown, Gilbert H, 1949, My 21,13:5
Brown, Gilbert P, 1943, F 12,19:5
Brown, Gilmor, 1960, Ja 12,47:5
Brown, Glen D, 1957, N 9,27:4
Brown, Gloria K Mrs, 1952, S 1,17:5
Brown, Godwin M, 1944, S 23,13:4
Brown, Goodwin, 1912, Jl 19,9:6
Brown, Gordon H, 1941, Jl 27,31:2
Brown, Greeley A, 1945, Jl 2,15:5
Brown, Grover C, 1956, N 11,87:1
Brown, Gustave L, 1950, D 5,31:4
Brown, H A, 1878, Ag 22,5:5
Brown, H Bettie Dr, 1937, Ag 14,13:5
Brown, H Fletcher, 1944, F 29,17:1
Brown, H G, 1903, Ja 2,14:2
Brown, H L, 1880, N 27,5:4
Brown, H Lewis, 1955, Je 16,31:1
Brown, H Runham, 1949, D 21,30:3
Brown, H W, 1916, Jl 10,11:4
Brown, Halloran H, 1953, F 2,21:1
Brown, Halstead H, 1941, Ag 15,17:6
Brown, Harlan E, 1943, N 6,13:3
Brown, Harold, 1951, Je 4,27:4
Brown, Harold D, 1949, F 8,25:2; 1952, D 10,35:2; 1962, Ja 7,88:7
Brown, Harold E, 1963, Ag 11,85:1
Brown, Harold H, 1953, Ja 9,21:3; 1954, D 31,13:3
Brown, Harold L, 1960, D 12,29:2
Brown, Harold Mrs, 1960, Ap 26,37:2
Brown, Harold O, 1950, Ag 1,23:5
Brown, Harold S, 1958, O 4,21:6
Brown, Harris N, 1920, Jl 17,7:5
Brown, Harrison, 1945, O 22,17:6
Brown, Harry, 1937, Je 25,21:6; 1946, Mr 5,25:5; 1946, O 31,25:4; 1950, Ap 17,23:1; 1952, Je 28,19:4
Brown, Harry A, 1946, Mr 16,13:3; 1952, F 29,23:2
Brown, Harry C, 1953, Ja 28,27:2
Brown, Harry D, 1942, Mr 27,23:2
Brown, Harry D Jr, 1954, Ja 5,27:4
Brown, Harry F, 1940, N 28,23:3
Brown, Harry F Mrs, 1951, Ag 5,73:1
Brown, Harry G, 1950, D 4,29:4
Brown, Harry H, 1939, Mr 22,23:2
Brown, Harry J, 1949, Je 3,26:3
Brown, Harry J Mrs, 1948, My 24,20:2
Brown, Harry K, 1945, Ap 18,23:2
Brown, Harry L, 1954, F 24,25:5
Brown, Harry M, 1950, D 4,29:3
Brown, Harry P, 1951, My 25,27:4
Brown, Harry S, 1949, Ja 2,60:7; 1950, F 19,79:3
Brown, Harry S Mrs, 1959, Jl 31,23:3
Brown, Harry Sr, 1938, Ja 24,23:4
Brown, Harry V Sr, 1959, O 28,37:3
Brown, Harry W, 1956, N 21,27:3; 1962, Mr 3,21:2
Brown, Hartman H (funl), 1968, Jl 13,17:1
Brown, Harvey D, 1937, Ag 22,II,7:2
Brown, Harvey E Dr, 1937, Ja 2,14:3
Brown, Harvey H Jr, 1950, Ag 12,13:6
Brown, Harvey J, 1951, Ap 17,29:3
Brown, Harvey T, 1937, N 16,23:6
Brown, Hawkins, 1903, D 2,9:5
Brown, Hazel C, 1964, Je 22,27:2
Brown, Helen (Mrs Philip S), 1964, D 7,35:4
Brown, Helen B, 1950, Ag 16,29:5
Brown, Helen D, 1941, S 7,51:5
Brown, Helen D Mrs, 1941, Ap 6,49:1
Brown, Helen W Mrs, 1940, F 10,15:4
Brown, Henry, 1924, Je 23,19:6; 1949, Mr 6,72:2; 1953, Mr 17,29:3
Brown, Henry B Ex-Justice, 1913, S 5,9:3
Brown, Henry B Mrs, 1948, D 3,25:2
Brown, Henry C, 1961, Jl 14,23:1
Brown, Henry Capt, 1907, S 5,9:5
Brown, Henry E, 1958, S 21,87:1; 1960, My 22,86:8
Brown, Henry H, 1947, Ja 20,25:3
Brown, Henry I, 1955, My 7,17:5
Brown, Henry Jr, 1940, Ja 16,23:5
Brown, Henry M, 1916, Ag 1,9:5
Brown, Henry P Jr, 1955, F 22,21:3
Brown, Henry T, 1938, Ag 18,20:4
Brown, Henry T Jr Mrs, 1938, D 20,25:2
Brown, Henry Wentworth, 1911, Ja 20,11:5
Brown, Herbert, 1940, N 16,32:4
Brown, Herbert A Mrs, 1943, N 12,21:4
Brown, Herbert B, 1946, Ag 17,13:6
Brown, Herbert C, 1954, Ap 8,27:3
Brown, Herbert D, 1937, Jl 12,18:1; 1963, Ag 3,17:6
Brown, Herbert F, 1948, O 5,25:3
Brown, Herbert G, 1943, My 4,23:5
Brown, Herbert H, 1947, My 27,25:4; 1949, F 18,23:4; 1958, F 12,29:2
Brown, Herbert J, 1945, Ap 17,23:1
Brown, Herbert Padelford, 1920, D 12,22:4
Brown, Herbert Q, 1955, N 4,29:3
Brown, Herbert Q Mrs, 1949, Ap 8,25:3
Brown, Herbert R Sr, 1954, Ag 19,23:5
Brown, Herbert S, 1959, My 23,25:6
Brown, Herman, 1962, N 16,32:1
Brown, Herman E, 1942, Mr 21,17:3
Brown, Herschel V Mrs, 1942, Ap 9,19:4
Brown, Hezekiah Capt, 1907, Ap 9,9:6
Brown, Hilton U, 1958, S 21,86:3
Brown, Hiram V, 1945, F 13,23:1
Brown, Hobart B, 1955, Je 4,15:5
Brown, Homer, 1938, Je 28,19:4
Brown, Horace, 1949, Ap 16,15:4
Brown, Horace B Mrs, 1942, Ag 27,19:5
Brown, Horace G Mrs (M Davies),(funl plans, S 24,87:1), 1961, S 23,19:2
Brown, Horace S, 1954, Mr 29,19:6
Brown, Howard B, 1960, Ap 6,41:4
Brown, Howard H, 1953, Mr 28,17:4; 1964, Ag 10,31:1
Brown, Howard L, 1946, Ag 16,21:6
Brown, Howard U, 1954, Ap 4,89:1
Brown, Howard W, 1955, Ja 10,23:3
Brown, Howland S, 1941, Je 1,40:1
Brown, Hubert R, 1963, O 19,25:3
Brown, Hugh E, 1952, Ja 2,21:3
Brown, Hugh R, 1957, Mr 8,25:1; 1960, D 9,31:1
Brown, Hugh R Mrs, 1947, Je 13,24:3
Brown, Hugh S, 1961, D 17,82:5
Brown, Hyman S, 1939, N 5,49:3
Brown, I Frank, 1946, Ja 5,13:1
Brown, Irving, 1903, My 19,9:6
Brown, Irving H, 1940, D 29,24:5; 1965, Jl 1,31:5
Brown, Irving S, 1938, F 7,15:2
Brown, Isaac, 1947, N 24,23:5
Brown, Israel, 1964, Je 6,23:3
Brown, Israel Mrs, 1952, D 9,33:2
Brown, Ivan E, 1963, My 25,25:6
Brown, J (see also N 2), 1877, N 4,8:1
Brown, J, 1883, Mr 29,2:4
Brown, J Ashley Mrs, 1951, My 17,31:4
Brown, J C, 1904, D 14,9:2; 1951, Ja 9,29:1
Brown, J Carter, 1874, Je 11,5:4
Brown, J Crawford, 1954, O 26,27:3
Brown, J Earle Mrs, 1966, Ag 11,33:2
Brown, J Epps, 1925, Mr 28,15:5
Brown, J F (funl), 1871, Ap 3,8:4
Brown, J H, 1880, Ag 23,5:1; 1902, Ap 3,9:5; 1939, Jl 30,9:8
Brown, J Hammond, 1955, Ag 14,81:2
Brown, J Harry, 1961, F 25,21:5
Brown, J Herbert, 1952, Ag 2,15:6
Brown, J Howard, 1956, F 11,17:1
Brown, J Leo, 1951, S 26,31:4
Brown, J M, 1932, Mr 4,19:5
Brown, J Marechal Jr, 1940, Ap 2,26:4
Brown, J O, 1903, Mr 16,1:4
Brown, J P, 1872, Ap 29,1:5
Brown, J Rev, 1884, Ag 16,2:4
Brown, J Romaine, 1924, N 6,19:5
Brown, J S, 1934, Ag 19,24:1
Brown, J Spencer, 1945, D 30,14:4
Brown, J Stacy Jr, 1920, N 9,15:1
Brown, J Stanley, 1939, S 8,23:3; 1959, F 17,31:4
Brown, J Stuart, 1948, Ja 1,23:5
Brown, J T, 1880, N 25,2:2
Brown, J W, 1875, S 7,2:1
Brown, J Walter, 1949, Je 8,30:3
Brown, J Willard, 1910, D 8,13:4
Brown, J Woods, 1925, D 27,7:1
Brown, J Wright, 1951, My 13,88:7
Brown, Jack C, 1944, O 23,19:3
Brown, Jack Mrs, 1962, Ap 22,80:7
Brown, Jacob, 1938, S 24,17:3; 1941, My 25,36:4
Brown, Jacob F, 1938, Jl 20,19:6
Brown, Jacob J, 1954, N 27,13:4
Brown, James, 1939, Mr 22,23:4; 1947, D 29,17:4
Brown, James A, 1938, S 12,17:4
Brown, James A Mrs, 1942, O 6,23:4; 1951, N 2,23:4
Brown, James B, 1909, F 3,9:4; 1940, O 26,15:4
Brown, James C, 1939, Ap 5,25:4; 1964, Ja 16,25:1; 1965, My 19,47:3
Brown, James C Mrs, 1939, S 9,17:2
Brown, James E, 1955, My 27,23:3; 1960, F 25,29:6
Brown, James E Jr, 1964, F 3,27:5
Brown, James F, 1937, Ap 25,II,8:2; 1953, O 25,89:1
Brown, James F Jr, 1951, Ag 17,6:7
Brown, James Hudson, 1916, Ag 25,7:6
Brown, James J, 1938, My 4,23:2; 1946, O 19,21:5; 1952, N 29,13:4
Brown, James J Jr, 1959, O 26,29:4
Brown, James M, 1940, Ja 31,19:5; 1941, D 27,19:3; 1951, D 5,35:2
Brown, James M Sr, 1968, Ag 2,33:2
Brown, James Mrs, 1948, My 4,25:1
Brown, James Noel, 1917, S 30,23:2
Brown, James R, 1945, Je 6,21:4
Brown, James S, 1938, Mr 9,23:2; 1950, Mr 3,25:1; 1950, My 2,29:2
Brown, James S Mrs, 1957, N 7,35:5
Brown, James W, 1943, D 28,17:3; 1952, F 25,21:2
Brown, James W (funl, Je 3,35:5; cor on obituary, Je 4,31:4), 1959, My 31,77:1
Brown, James W Mrs, 1945, Mr 29,23:5
Brown, Jasper C, 1966, D 20,43:1
Brown, Jay G, 1942, My 22,21:2
Brown, Jean D, 1963, Ag 10,17:4
Brown, Jean F, 1950, S 21,31:2
Brown, Jenifer S, 1953, Ja 6,29:1
Brown, Jennie A, 1937, Ag 23,19:4
Brown, Jere E, 1951, D 12,38:2
Brown, Jeremiah E, 1954, Jl 27,21:5
Brown, Joannie N Mrs, 1939, O 22,41:2
Brown, Joe, 1945, N 23,23:4
Brown, Joe B Judge, 1968, F 21,47:1
Brown, Joe W (est appr, N 25,57:5), 1959, F 16,2
Brown, Joel B, 1953, Ap 14,27:3
Brown, Joel E, 1949, D 23,21:2
Brown, John, 1938, Mr 31,23:6; 1957, My 18,19:3; 1967, D 21,37:3
Brown, John A, 1873, Ja 1,1:6; 1918, Je 5,11:2; 19 O 14,23:4; 1946, Ja 5,13:3; 1950, Ap 27,29:5; 19 Ag 10,15:1
Brown, John A Jr Mrs, 1940, Ag 22,19:2
Brown, John A S, 1937, My 1,19:5
Brown, John B, 1954, Jl 15,27:2
Brown, John B Marshall, 1907, Jl 21,7:6
Brown, John B Mrs, 1958, N 12,37:2
Brown, John C, 1948, N 24,23:2; 1950, Jl 27,25:1; 1960, F 21,92:7
Brown, John Carter Mrs, 1909, Mr 1,9:2
Brown, John Crosby, 1909, Je 26,7:3
Brown, John Crosby Mrs, 1918, F 16,11:8
Brown, John D M, 1951, Ja 17,27:4
Brown, John Dr, 1882, My 12,5:2
Brown, John E Sr, 1957, F 14,27:4
Brown, John F, 1940, F 16,19:1
Brown, John F Judge, 1924, S 18,21:5
Brown, John F Mrs, 1946, My 10,19:4
Brown, John George (por),(est, Ag 14,9:3), 191 F 9,17:4
Brown, John Gilbert, 1903, S 3,7:7
Brown, John H, 1947, Ap 21,27:2
Brown, John H Jr, 1963, Je 12,43:1
Brown, John Hamilton, 1916, Jl 26,11:6
Brown, John Howard, 1917, Ap 24,11:5
Brown, John J, 1941, Mr 25,23:2; 1943, My 2,45 1946, F 17,42:5; 1947, O 7,27:2; 1948, N 11,27 1960, D 16,33:3; 1965, Mr 7,83:1
Brown, John Jr, 1961, Ja 11,47:6

Brown, John K, 1941, My 4,53:2
Brown, John K A, 1946, My 13,21:1
Brown, John L, 1955, Ag 7,72:7
Brown, John L Mrs, 1948, D 22,23:2
Brown, John M, 1915, D 11,13:4; 1949, O 7,31:2
Brown, John N Mrs, 1950, Mr 31,31:4
Brown, John P, 1909, Ag 24,9:6; 1961, My 5,29:5
Brown, John P Mrs, 1954, Ag 19,23:2
Brown, John R, 1945, O 27,15:4
Brown, John Rev Dr, 1922, Ja 17,17:3
Brown, John S Sr, 1950, D 18,31:4
Brown, John Sir, 1926, Ap 7,23:3; 1958, Ap 8,29:2
Brown, John T, 1949, S 12,21:4
Brown, John W, 1903, D 13,7:5; 1937, Ja 16,17:2; 1941, N 8,19:2
Brown, John W (will), 1951, Ja 11,21:4
Brown, John W, 1956, Jl 11,29:2
Brown, John Young, 1904, Ja 12,7:5
Brown, Joseph, 1950, My 28,44:7; 1952, Ag 13,21:1
Brown, Joseph B, 1953, F 24,25:4
Brown, Joseph C, 1945, Ja 18,19:5
Brown, Joseph C Mrs, 1952, O 14,34:4
Brown, Joseph D, 1952, Mr 13,29:1
Brown, Joseph E (Bro Patrick), 1953, F 27,6:6
Brown, Joseph E, 1968, Ag 1,31:4
Brown, Joseph E Jr Dr, 1937, My 6,25:2
Brown, Joseph Epes, 1918, Ja 18,9:5
Brown, Joseph F, 1905, Ap 11,11:6; 1958, My 9,23:3
Brown, Joseph G, 1962, Mr 29,33:2
Brown, Joseph Jr, 1954, My 23,90:1
Brown, Joseph M, 1959, Jl 13,27:4
Brown, Joseph Mrs, 1949, D 15,35:5
Brown, Joseph O, 1950, O 14,19:5
Brown, Joseph O Mrs, 1941, D 4,25:5
Brown, Joseph P, 1948, D 11,15:2
Brown, Joseph T, 1937, Jl 3,15:3; 1951, N 10,17:5
Brown, Joseph T Mrs, 1943, Ag 19,19:1
Brown, Joseph Thomas, 1918, Je 27,11:5
Brown, Josephine C, 1960, O 1,19:4
Brown, Judson A, 1911, Jl 13,9:5
Brown, Julius, 1949, Ag 24,26:5
Brown, Julius B, 1943, Mr 28,24:3
Brown, Julius L, 1910, S 6,9:6
Brown, Junius G, 1937, Mr 24,25:1
Brown, Justus Morris Brig-Gen, 1912, D 22,15:5
Brown, Karl T, 1951, F 1,25:2
Brown, Kenneth D, 1955, Ap 17,87:2
Brown, Kenneth R, 1958, Mr 19,31:2
Brown, Kenneth W Mrs, 1938, Ja 18,23:3
Brown, Kenyon, 1961, Ap 20,33:5
Brown, Kilburn R, 1955, Ap 22,25:2
Brown, Kingdon W, 1957, S 23,27:1
Brown, Kirk, 1945, Ja 13,11:3; 1949, F 15,23:4; 1953, Jl 15,25:5
Brown, L Greeley Mrs, 1957, D 15,86:8
Brown, L Renton, 1948, Je 7,19:4
Brown, L S, 1924, Ap 3,21:6
Brown, Lady, 1946, O 5,17:4
Brown, Larry G, 1938, D 24,15:1
Brown, Lathrop, 1959, N 29,87:1
Brown, Lawrason Dr, 1937, D 27,16:2
Brown, Lawrence K, 1940, S 19,23:2
Brown, Leggett, 1953, Mr 23,23:3
Brown, Leigh A, 1959, S 14,29:2
Brown, Lennox P, 1943, Jl 2,19:5
Brown, Leo E, 1968, D 9,47:3
Brown, Leo F, 1956, Ja 24,31:3
Brown, Leon, 1942, O 6,23:2
Brown, Leon A, 1954, Ag 6,17:4
Brown, Leonard, 1952, Mr 30,93:2
Brown, Leonard W, 1937, F 15,17:2
Brown, Leroy T, 1956, Ja 24,31:2
Brown, Leslie, 1962, N 17,25:5
Brown, Leslie W, 1941, Ag 15,17:2
Brown, Lester D, 1957, D 10,35:1
Brown, Lester T, 1962, Mr 31,25:4
Brown, Lew, 1948, Mr 30,23:3; 1958, F 6,27:3
Brown, Lew B, 1944, Ag 17,17:7
Brown, Lewis H, 1951, F 27,27:1
Brown, Lewis J, 1940, Ja 13,15:5
Brown, Lewis R, 1951, F 27,27:4
Brown, Lewis T Col, 1911, Mr 20,9:2
Brown, Lillian C Mrs, 1937, D 14,25:5
Brown, Lillian L Mrs, 1963, My 6,29:4
Brown, Llewellyn, 1949, N 26,15:3
Brown, Llewellyn Mrs, 1965, F 11,39:3
Brown, Lloyd, 1950, F 19,76:3
Brown, Lloyd E, 1954, Ap 30,23:2
Brown, Lorenzo D, 1958, Ap 30,33:4
Brown, Louis A, 1947, Mr 19,25:5
Brown, Louis F Mrs, 1951, S 6,31:4
Brown, Louis G, 1940, S 17,23:6
Brown, Louis L, 1955, O 7,25:2
Brown, Louis M, 1942, N 8,50:5
Brown, Louise B, 1946, Ap 21,46:2
Brown, Louise F, 1955, My 7,23:3
Brown, Lourie G, 1952, Jl 14,17:4
Brown, Lowell H, 1965, F 26,29:1
Brown, Lucien M, 1960, Ap 17,93:1
Brown, Lucy Hall Mrs, 1907, Ag 4,7:6
Brown, Luman B Mrs, 1937, Je 28,19:5
Brown, Lyman C, 1961, Ap 3,30:2
Brown, Lyman S, 1937, Ja 17,II,8:7
Brown, Lyndon O, 1966, Ja 25,41:2
Brown, Lynn D, 1963, Je 24,27:3
Brown, Lytle, 1951, My 4,27:4
Brown, M Brooks Mrs, 1963, S 1,56:6
Brown, M S Mrs, 1901, Je 4,9:7
Brown, M Stanley, 1958, Ja 20,23:3
Brown, Mabel W Mrs, 1963, Ap 14,93:1
Brown, Mabelle, 1940, S 14,17:2
Brown, Malcolm, 1939, O 20,28:4
Brown, Malcolm E T, 1939, Ap 8,23:8
Brown, Marcus, 1941, Ag 21,17:5
Brown, Margaret K Mrs, 1948, O 30,15:5
Brown, Margaret S Mrs, 1937, N 20,17:1
Brown, Margaret W, 1952, N 15,17:3
Brown, Marie O, 1951, My 2,31:3
Brown, Marshall, 1944, D 17,37:1
Brown, Marshall L, 1942, N 6,23:1
Brown, Marshall S, 1948, S 20,25:1
Brown, Marshall S Jr, 1960, Mr 21,29:2
Brown, Martha A Mrs, 1942, Jl 23,19:5
Brown, Martha T, 1943, Mr 14,24:4
Brown, Martin J, 1948, D 20,25:3
Brown, Martin M, 1947, S 19,23:2
Brown, Marvin K, 1958, Ap 3,31:2
Brown, Mary, 1948, F 8,60:5
Brown, Mary A, 1938, Ja 26,23:5
Brown, Mary A Mrs, 1944, Mr 3,9:2
Brown, Mary F, 1943, N 4,23:2
Brown, Mary H, 1937, Ja 24,II,9:1
Brown, Mary J, 1938, F 12,15:3
Brown, Mary M Mrs, 1937, Ap 3,19:5
Brown, Mary P, 1961, Jl 27,31:4
Brown, Mary W Mrs, 1939, Jl 26,19:5
Brown, Matilda D, 1950, F 6,25:2
Brown, Matthews, 1953, Mr 9,29:2
Brown, Maurice F, 1943, My 23,42:6
Brown, Maurice H, 1953, Je 25,27:3
Brown, Max S Mrs, 1963, Je 4,39:4
Brown, Maynard W, 1937, Ap 10,19:3
Brown, McKensie, 1955, Ag 19,19:4
Brown, Melford G Mrs, 1946, S 3,19:1
Brown, Melford L, 1956, S 12,37:2
Brown, Melville W, 1938, F 1,21:1
Brown, Meyer L, 1965, N 3,35:1
Brown, Michael, 1947, Ja 24,22:3; 1956, Jl 10,31:5
Brown, Michael A, 1937, D 31,15:4
Brown, Michael H, 1946, O 31,25:1
Brown, Michael J, 1938, Ag 22,13:6; 1952, Ja 17,27:5
Brown, Michigan C, 1957, S 22,86:8
Brown, Millard D, 1957, S 23,27:6
Brown, Millard D Mrs, 1958, Ja 7,47:4
Brown, Milton, 1965, D 16,42:1
Brown, Milton A, 1947, S 22,23:5
Brown, Milton D, 1953, Jl 13,25:5
Brown, Milton Mrs, 1959, Mr 6,25:2
Brown, Minnie A Mrs, 1948, Ag 25,25:3
Brown, Miriam Holton Mrs, 1865, N 22,5:1
Brown, Mordecai, 1948, F 15,61:1
Brown, Mordecai Mrs, 1958, O 7,35:3
Brown, Morris, 1965, Ag 14,23:4
Brown, Morris E, 1955, O 14,27:3
Brown, Mortimer J, 1945, Ap 9,19:4
Brown, Mortimer S, 1943, Mr 26,19:4
Brown, Moses, 1937, D 24,17:4
Brown, Munson S, 1903, Jl 12,7:6
Brown, Myron J, 1940, Ag 2,15:4
Brown, N B, 1875, Mr 15,5:2
Brown, N C, 1956, F 16,5:1
Brown, N Warren, 1940, My 19,43:3
Brown, Nacio H, 1964, S 30,43:4
Brown, Nannie F Mrs, 1942, N 20,23:4
Brown, Nat S Mrs, 1938, N 18,21:1
Brown, Natalie B D Mrs, 1950, Mr 29,29:3
Brown, Nathan, 1875, N 7,7:1
Brown, Nathan C, 1941, Mr 21,21:5
Brown, Nathaniel M, 1939, N 23,27:2; 1954, My 7,23:2
Brown, Nathaniel S, 1943, S 18,17:3
Brown, Nelson D, 1960, Mr 8,33:4
Brown, Nelson P, 1946, Ap 10,27:3
Brown, Neva A Mrs, 1940, Ja 14,43:2
Brown, Nicholas M, 1948, F 7,15:5
Brown, Niles A, 1953, Ja 15,27:3
Brown, Nina A, 1944, Ag 9,17:5
Brown, Norman J, 1963, Ap 23,37:4
Brown, Norris, 1960, Ja 6,35:3
Brown, Norris W, 1952, N 29,17:2
Brown, Odber L W, 1950, N 4,17:6
Brown, Oliver A Mrs, 1945, F 14,19:4
Brown, Oliver A Rev Dr, 1908, Ag 16,7:4
Brown, Oliver H, 1924, Ap 2,19:5
Brown, Omar J, 1951, Jl 9,25:5
Brown, Ona W Mrs, 1960, Ap 2,23:5
Brown, Orella D, 1947, Ap 18,21:1
Brown, Orlando Col, 1867, Ag 4,3:7
Brown, Orton B Mrs, 1942, O 21,21:4
Brown, Orville G, 1958, Mr 18,29:4
Brown, Orville H, 1943, Jl 26,19:6
Brown, Osborne E, 1946, Ja 19,13:2
Brown, Oscar J, 1958, My 17,19:5
Brown, Oswald E, 1939, O 23,19:6
Brown, Otis deR, 1957, S 10,33:1
Brown, Owen C, 1947, F 1,15:5
Brown, Owen N, 1925, Ja 22,19:4
Brown, Owen N Mrs, 1965, Ag 17,33:2
Brown, Owsley, 1952, N 2,88:5
Brown, P B, 1940, Mr 5,24:3
Brown, P P, 1881, Ap 13,5:3
Brown, Parke, 1943, O 1,19:4
Brown, Patrick W Rev, 1937, Jl 16,19:2
Brown, Paul, 1961, S 25,33:3
Brown, Paul D, 1958, D 29,15:3
Brown, Paul E, 1951, S 11,29:3
Brown, Paul F, 1944, D 9,15:6
Brown, Paul G, 1950, Mr 25,11:8
Brown, Paul J, 1947, S 12,21:4
Brown, Paul Mrs, 1941, S 24,23:5
Brown, Paul W, 1937, Ap 7,25:4
Brown, Perc S, 1963, N 16,27:5
Brown, Percy, 1949, Ap 6,29:2; 1950, O 9,25:5
Brown, Percy A, 1962, Mr 5,23:2
Brown, Percy J, 1962, Jl 7,17:4
Brown, Perry, 1951, Mr 2,25:2
Brown, Peter, 1942, S 30,23:5
Brown, Peter A, 1938, D 31,15:5
Brown, Peter B, 1948, O 13,25:1
Brown, Peter E, 1941, N 2,53:2
Brown, Peter H, 1949, Ja 4,19:1
Brown, Peter L, 1942, My 4,19:6
Brown, Phil F, 1953, Mr 25,31:3
Brown, Phil J, 1951, Ja 27,13:3
Brown, Philip Auld Harrison Rev Dr, 1909, S 16,9:6
Brown, Philip H, 1943, Jl 22,19:5
Brown, Philip M, 1966, My 12,45:1
Brown, Philip S Maj, 1915, My 16,16:4
Brown, Philip T, 1967, Je 28,45:4
Brown, Philip Turner, 1924, Ag 26,11:3
Brown, Plumb, 1947, Ap 29,27:2
Brown, Preston, 1948, Jl 1,23:3
Brown, Price, 1938, Ap 5,21:3
Brown, R Alpheus, 1945, Je 26,19:4
Brown, R Alston, 1942, Ag 26,19:6
Brown, R B, 1952, My 22,27:1
Brown, R B Gen, 1916, Jl 31,9:6
Brown, R C, 1880, F 1,5:6
Brown, R Capt, 1885, Je 19,2:5
Brown, R E L, 1902, O 20,9:4
Brown, R M G Comdr, 1906, D 15,11:6
Brown, Ralph, 1948, D 7,31:3
Brown, Ralph A, 1954, S 14,27:3
Brown, Ralph C, 1947, My 16,24:2
Brown, Ralph D, 1952, S 8,45:4
Brown, Ralph F, 1954, N 8,21:2
Brown, Ralph G, 1960, Ja 1,19:2
Brown, Ralph W, 1949, F 28,19:6
Brown, Randall, 1953, My 26,29:6
Brown, Randolph F, 1952, N 4,30:4
Brown, Randolph F Mrs, 1966, Mr 19,29:6
Brown, Ray, 1944, My 1,15:5
Brown, Ray A, 1959, S 9,41:3
Brown, Ray C B, 1951, My 17,31:5
Brown, Ray D, 1955, Jl 21,23:2
Brown, Ray F, 1964, Mr 24,35:1
Brown, Ray G Mrs, 1952, O 18,19:4
Brown, Ray M, 1949, N 11,25:1
Brown, Raymond C, 1942, O 2,25:2
Brown, Raymond D Mrs, 1948, D 17,27:1
Brown, Raymond L, 1960, D 1,35:1
Brown, Raymond L Jr, 1959, Ag 7,23:4
Brown, Raymond Mrs, 1956, Mr 3,19:1
Brown, Raymond W, 1911, Mr 25,11:4
Brown, Reed Jr, 1962, Jl 27,25:4
Brown, Reginald W Rev, 1937, S 14,23:5
Brown, Remington J S, 1940, Mr 3,3:4
Brown, Reuben F, 1949, My 25,29:2
Brown, Rexwald, 1940, Je 22,15:7
Brown, Richard, 1903, S 2,7:6; 1952, Ag 3,61:2; 1962, S 13,37:2
Brown, Richard D, 1949, My 11,29:5
Brown, Richard D Mrs, 1942, Ja 23,20:2
Brown, Richard F Mrs, 1964, Ja 18,12:3
Brown, Richard J, 1942, F 5,21:6
Brown, Richard L, 1960, O 23,89:1; 1963, Ag 21,33:2
Brown, Richard P, 1943, Ap 20,24:3; 1948, Mr 15,23:2
Brown, Richard P Mrs, 1957, My 5,89:1
Brown, Richard T, 1954, Ag 16,17:4
Brown, Richmond L, 1966, O 8,31:4
Brown, Richmond L Mrs, 1952, Mr 11,27:6
Brown, Robert, 1946, Je 14,21:3; 1949, Ag 22,21:6
Brown, Robert A, 1907, S 23,9:6; 1948, F 13,21:5; 1959, S 26,23:6; 1966, Ja 27,33:1
Brown, Robert A Brig Gen, 1937, O 2,21:3
Brown, Robert A Mrs, 1946, My 24,19:5
Brown, Robert B, 1940, D 24,15:1
Brown, Robert C, 1937, N 2,28:2; 1942, F 7,17:3; 1944, D 30,11:4; 1945, Mr 27,19:2; 1959, Ag 8,17:6
Brown, Robert C Mrs, 1961, O 27,33:2
Brown, Robert Campbell, 1916, Jl 19,9:5
Brown, Robert D, 1952, Jl 22,25:2
Brown, Robert E, 1938, N 26,15:2
Brown, Robert F, 1937, Je 14,23:4
Brown, Robert G, 1947, O 3,25:1
Brown, Robert G Ingersoll, 1968, My 2,47:4
Brown, Robert J, 1939, O 27,23:5; 1953, O 3,17:3
Brown, Robert M Dr, 1921, My 2,15:5
Brown, Robert O, 1949, F 2,27:2
Brown, Robert R, 1937, Je 18,21:2; 1950, N 3,28:3; 1959, Je 1,27:5

Brown, Robert R Mrs, 1957, Ja 16,31:4
Brown, Robert S (por), 1938, Ja 19,23:5
Brown, Robert S, 1955, F 22,21:5
Brown, Robert V Jr, 1960, F 12,28:1
Brown, Robert W, 1951, Ja 19,25:3; 1955, Ja 11,25:2
Brown, Robert Wood, 1924, D 29,15:4
Brown, Robie M, 1950, Ap 16,104:3
Brown, Rodney W, 1959, My 4,29:5
Brown, Roland C, 1963, My 9,37:1
Brown, Roland P, 1949, Ja 7,21:4
Brown, Roscoe C E, 1946, D 15,77:1
Brown, Roscoe C E Mrs, 1955, F 28,19:4
Brown, Ross E, 1954, Ap 29,31:5
Brown, Roy, 1956, My 18,25:5; 1957, Je 9,88:4
Brown, Roy H, 1959, Ja 1,31:3
Brown, Royal (cor, N 12,31:3), 1953, N 3,31:1
Brown, Royal C, 1946, Mr 30,15:3
Brown, Royce G Mrs, 1950, O 11,33:3
Brown, Rufus E, 1954, Ag 28,15:5
Brown, Russ, 1964, O 21,43:5
Brown, Russell M, 1950, N 26,90:3; 1956, D 26,27:4
Brown, S E Prof, 1877, Ag 8,3:3
Brown, S Howell Jr, 1963, N 18,33:4
Brown, S K, 1934, Ap 3,21:5
Brown, S Pope, 1948, Ag 4,21:5
Brown, S Seeley, 1946, O 16,27:2
Brown, Sally J (Mrs M S Brunjes), 1960, Jl 5,31:2
Brown, Sam, 1941, Je 5,24:3
Brown, Samuel, 1882, N 16,5:5; 1943, Je 27,32:3; 1961, My 18,35:3
Brown, Samuel A, 1952, Mr 18,27:1
Brown, Samuel B, 1945, N 30,23:4
Brown, Samuel Chester, 1905, Ap 8,1:6
Brown, Samuel D Mrs, 1948, Ag 24,23:3
Brown, Samuel H, 1940, Je 13,23:5; 1958, Je 26,27:5
Brown, Samuel K, 1940, Mr 14,23:4
Brown, Samuel Mrs, 1948, Mr 22,23:4
Brown, Samuel Newell, 1912, Jl 6,7:5
Brown, Samuel Queen Mrs, 1916, Je 29,11:5
Brown, Samuel R Rev, 1937, Ap 13,25:3
Brown, Samuel S (will, D 16,1:4), 1905, D 12,9:4
Brown, Samuel S, 1947, O 23,25:4
Brown, Samuel T, 1953, F 25,27:3
Brown, Samuel W, 1940, Ja 12,17:4
Brown, Sanger 2d Dr, 1968, Mr 21,47:2
Brown, Sarah E Mrs, 1940, Mr 23,13:5
Brown, Sarah Faulkner, 1921, Jl 23,7:7
Brown, Sarah Jane Goodell Mrs, 1920, Je 22,11:4
Brown, Selden S, 1940, Ap 2,26:3
Brown, Sevellon, 1956, D 29,15:1
Brown, Sherman L Mrs, 1960, N 15,39:3
Brown, Shirley E, 1937, Ja 10,II,9:2
Brown, Sidney G, 1948, Ag 9,19:5
Brown, Sidney J Mrs (Mrs N B Baker), 1957, S 3, 27:2
Brown, Sidney L, 1947, Ja 19,53:1
Brown, Sidney S, 1955, Ag 5,19:1
Brown, Simon, 1873, F 28,5:3
Brown, Simon H, 1940, Je 11,25:4
Brown, Sophia M Mrs, 1943, Je 11,19:2
Brown, Spencer G, 1944, Mr 20,18:2
Brown, Spring, 1938, S 28,25:6
Brown, Stanley D, 1967, O 24,47:3
Brown, Stanley L, 1964, S 29,43:3
Brown, Stanley M, 1958, F 14,24:1; 1968, N 18,47:4
Brown, Stanley R, 1951, My 27,68:4
Brown, Stanton, 1959, O 20,39:1
Brown, Stephen D, 1938, Ja 22,15:3
Brown, Stephen D Rev Dr, 1875, F 20,7:3
Brown, Stephen E, 1915, O 21,11:5
Brown, Stephen Howland, 1917, Jl 21,11:7
Brown, Stephen Howland Mrs, 1909, F 4,9:4
Brown, Stephen J, 1944, Mr 9,17:1
Brown, Stephen P, 1919, D 13,13:4
Brown, Stewart, 1880, F 1,5:6
Brown, Stewart Gen, 1917, Ag 21,9:2
Brown, Stimson Joseph Commodore, 1923, D 21,17:4
Brown, Stockton, 1876, Je 24,2:4
Brown, Stuart H, 1943, Ja 21,21:2
Brown, Sumner E, 1940, My 20,17:3
Brown, Susan, 1951, O 29,23:3
Brown, Sydney M, 1952, Ap 8,29:2
Brown, T Allston, 1918, Ap 4,13:8
Brown, T Joseph, 1952, Je 11,29:6
Brown, Th Pearce Capt, 1903, D 3,9:5
Brown, Thaddeus H, 1941, F 26,21:3
Brown, Thalia N, 1945, F 8,19:6
Brown, Thatcher M, 1954, My 3,25:1
Brown, Thatcher M Jr Mrs, 1949, Ag 6,17:2
Brown, Thatcher M Mrs, 1947, Mr 12,25:5
Brown, Theodore (Steve), 1965, S 20,7:2
Brown, Theodore J, 1948, Ja 20,23:2
Brown, Theodore P, 1940, Je 16,38:7
Brown, Thomas, 1907, Ja 4,7:5; 1943, My 10,19:1; 1957, Ja 4,23:3
Brown, Thomas B, 1941, Mr 18,23:4
Brown, Thomas C (por), 1938, Je 3,21:3
Brown, Thomas C, 1948, S 17,25:2; 1952, My 25,94:5; 1967, Ja 2,19:3
Brown, Thomas D Mrs, 1963, O 29,36:8
Brown, Thomas E, 1950, Je 26,27:4
Brown, Thomas E Mrs, 1946, My 2,21:2
Brown, Thomas Ellis, 1923, Ag 16,15:6
Brown, Thomas F, 1946, F 16,13:4; 1962, S 12,39:1
Brown, Thomas H, 1964, Ag 15,21:4
Brown, Thomas H Mrs, 1937, Ag 6,17:2
Brown, Thomas I, 1959, Ap 24,27:4
Brown, Thomas I Mrs, 1946, Mr 6,27:4
Brown, Thomas J, 1940, Ap 29,15:3; 1942, Ja 25,41:1; 1957, Je 27,25:2
Brown, Thomas Jefferson Justice, 1915, My 28,13:6
Brown, Thomas K, 1944, Je 6,17:2
Brown, Thomas K Jr Mrs, 1961, Ag 19,17:6
Brown, Thomas L, 1949, Ja 20,27:2
Brown, Thomas P, 1962, Je 4,29:5; 1965, D 15,47:2
Brown, Thomas R, 1950, S 27,32:3
Brown, Thomas Sr, 1948, F 3,26:2
Brown, Thomas W, 1950, D 1,25:5
Brown, Thompson D, 1951, Je 12,29:3
Brown, Thurmond, 1943, Ag 3,19:3
Brown, Tom, 1958, Mr 26,34:6
Brown, Tom S, 1960, O 3,31:5
Brown, Vachel J, 1952, Ag 1,17:4
Brown, Verna, 1960, Ap 19,37:2
Brown, Vernal Mrs, 1955, My 17,29:4
Brown, Vernon C, 1938, S 2,17:2; 1945, Ja 1,21:4
Brown, Vernon H (funl, Ag 7,7:4), 1913, Ag 6,7:6
Brown, Victor, 1967, Mr 27,33:3
Brown, Victor W, 1949, Jl 23,11:3
Brown, Vincent B, 1958, Je 12,27:1
Brown, W A, 1939, O 17,25:5
Brown, W A Mrs, 1944, Ag 9,17:4
Brown, W C Bishop, 1927, Jl 26,19:3
Brown, W Clark, 1952, Ja 21,15:3
Brown, W Douglas, 1943, Jl 1,19:3
Brown, W G, 1883, My 15,2:6; 1941, Jl 5,11:6
Brown, W H, 1903, Ap 24,9:6
Brown, W Harman, 1902, O 16,9:5
Brown, W Harry Mrs (will, O 26,25:4), 1938, S 4, 17:4
Brown, W Hogan, 1959, Ag 31,21:4
Brown, W K, 1879, Jl 7,8:4
Brown, W N, 1883, Mr 13,5:4
Brown, W R, 1878, N 19,5:5
Brown, W Staples, 1915, S 25,11:4
Brown, W W, 1941, Ja 12,19:2
Brown, W Wallace, 1958, My 5,29:5
Brown, Wade H, 1939, Je 8,25:3; 1942, Ag 6,19:1
Brown, Waldron Post, 1915, My 16,16:6
Brown, Wallace D, 1944, Je 3,13:6
Brown, Wallace E, 1939, N 19,39:3
Brown, Wallace K, 1947, My 13,25:2
Brown, Wallace K Mrs, 1949, Ap 9,17:6
Brown, Wally, 1961, N 15,43:2
Brown, Walter, 1871, Mr 5,5:2; 1879, My 3,8:3; 1949, Je 29,54:3; 1952, N 5,27:2
Brown, Walter A (will, O 23,47:4), 1964, S 8,29:4
Brown, Walter B, 1949, Mr 23,27:3
Brown, Walter E, 1947, Ap 2,27:1; 1954, Mr 26,21:3; 1963, My 30,17:5
Brown, Walter F, 1949, My 24,28:3; 1951, N 19,23:5; 1961, Ja 27,23:1
Brown, Walter H, 1945, N 5,19:4
Brown, Walter Jr, 1961, S 18,29:5
Brown, Walter M, 1961, D 18,35:2
Brown, Walter S, 1942, My 4,19:5
Brown, Walter T, 1954, Ag 6,17:6; 1963, O 9,43:3
Brown, Walter V, 1952, N 8,17:3
Brown, Walter W, 1958, Mr 16,86:8
Brown, Warren D, 1947, Ap 22,27:5
Brown, Warren S, 1954, F 26,19:3
Brown, Warren W, 1966, My 31,43:3
Brown, Washington R, 1942, S 29,23:3
Brown, Wayne A, 1959, My 28,31:3
Brown, Wendell P, 1966, Mr 1,37:3
Brown, Wentworth Mrs, 1966, F 7,29:2
Brown, Whitefield N, 1903, S 18,7:3
Brown, Wilbur F, 1946, Mr 1,21:5
Brown, Wilburt Scott Maj-Gen, 1968, D 15,86:2
Brown, Wilfred A, 1955, S 20,31:1
Brown, Will H, 1953, Ap 3,23:1
Brown, Willard, 1910, D 30,11:4
Brown, Willard E, 1953, F 27,21:1
Brown, Willard Mrs, 1947, My 12,21:5
Brown, Willard P, 1950, F 21,25:4
Brown, Willard S, 1940, N 30,17:5
Brown, William, 1944, D 2,13:4; 1947, F 14,21:5; 1947, N 25,29:4; 1957, Mr 26,33:1; 1960, My 23,29:3
Brown, William A, 1913, D 2,11:6; 1943, D 16,27:1; 1945, F 19,17:4; 1953, My 1,21:4; 1958, Je 8,88:7
Brown, William A A, 1923, F 3,13:4
Brown, William A Jr, 1957, Ap 20,17:1
Brown, William A Mrs, 1942, D 13,75:3
Brown, William B Jr Mrs, 1955, N 6,86:7
Brown, William B Mrs, 1955, Ja 26,25:4
Brown, William C, 1924, D 7,7:1; 1939, My 10,23:2; 1952, Mr 18,27:2; 1954, Mr 20,15:3
Brown, William E, 1940, Je 16,38:8; 1940, S 30,17:2; 1945, My 17,19:1; 1946, Je 25,21:6; 1950, Mr 19, 95:5; 1950, My 10,31:4; 1952, My 6,29:3; 1952, Je 23,19:5; 1955, My 21,2:3; 1960, My 12,35:4
Brown, William Eustis Dr, 1968, Ja 6,29:4
Brown, William F, 1941, F 12,21:4; 1950, S 22,31:3; 1951, D 16,90:1
Brown, William F Mrs (A A Sutherland), 1961, Mr 30,29:2
Brown, William G, 1944, O 22,46:3; 1947, Ap 8,27:2
Brown, William G Mrs, 1956, O 27,21:4
Brown, William H (funl), 1875, Jl 19,4:6
Brown, William H, 1937, S 3,17:4; 1937, O 27,31:5; 1938, Ap 9,17:5; 1939, N 10,23:3; 1945, My 27,26:2; 1946, My 15,21:4; 1946, Ag 23,19:5; 1954, Je 26,13:6
Brown, William H Jr, 1949, D 31,15:6; 1966, Ja 18, 34:1
Brown, William H Mrs, 1945, N 25,50:2; 1947, Ag 24, 58:1; 1952, My 22,27:2
Brown, William Harrison, 1917, Jl 27,9:5
Brown, William Harvey, 1913, My 15,11:6
Brown, William Henry, 1910, Je 26,II,9:4
Brown, William Heren Mrs, 1968, Ja 18,39:3
Brown, William I, 1942, Je 19,23:4
Brown, William I Mrs, 1951, Ap 29,89:3
Brown, William J, 1912, F 29,11:5; 1938, Ja 23,II,8:1; 1942, Ja 10,15:3
Brown, William J (Bill), 1943, S 4,13:4
Brown, William J, 1949, F 3,23:1; 1949, F 18,23:4; 1949, Mr 4,21:1; 1960, O 5,41:3
Brown, William J Mrs, 1938, My 20,19:4
Brown, William K, 1958, Ja 25,19:4
Brown, William L Col, 1906, D 14,11:5
Brown, William L Rev, 1908, D 16,11:5
Brown, William M, 1915, F 1,9:4
Brown, William M (Oct 7), 1965, O 11,61:1
Brown, William M, 1966, Ja 12,21:3
Brown, William M Rev, 1937, N 1,21:1
Brown, William Mrs, 1953, Jl 27,19:4
Brown, William P, 1949, Ap 26,26:2
Brown, William Perry Col, 1914, O 6,11:6
Brown, William R, 1913, O 13,9:4; 1955, Ag 5,19:2; 1958, Ja 4,15:2
Brown, William S, 1937, Mr 24,25:2; 1948, O 4,23:2
Brown, William T, 1944, N 13,19:6; 1953, Ag 24,23:5
Brown, William T Mrs, 1940, Jl 16,17:3
Brown, William Thayer, 1916, My 9,11:5
Brown, William V, 1953, Jl 26,69:2
Brown, William W, 1950, Ag 4,21:4
Brown, Wilson, 1913, N 8,13:6; 1957, Ja 3,33:1
Brown, Winifred A, 1958, Jl 29,23:4
Brown, Wolaston Richmond, 1923, Mr 10,13:4
Brown, Wolf Mrs, 1966, D 1,47:4
Brown, Wolstan C, 1960, My 20,29:1
Brown, Wylie, 1960, My 16,31:3
Brown, Zaidee, 1950, N 29,33:4
Brown, Zoe L Mrs, 1958, S 21,86:7
Brown-Potter, C U Mrs, 1936, F 13,19:1
Brown-Sequard, C E Dr, 1894, Ap 3,5:5
Brownback, J Harold, 1952, Jl 16,25:3
Brownbill, Fannie Mrs, 1948, O 11,23:5
Browne, Albert L, 1940, Mr 5,23:4
Browne, Aldis Birdsey, 1914, Je 3,13:6
Browne, Aldis J Sr, 1961, Jl 18,29:5
Browne, Alex S, 1957, N 18,31:2
Browne, Alexander F, 1920, Jl 8,11:3
Browne, Alfred, 1925, N 7,15:5
Browne, Alfred D, 1952, Mr 8,13:2
Browne, Arch, 1948, N 9,28:3
Browne, Arch Mrs, 1949, My 27,21:1
Browne, Arthur H, 1951, Je 11,25:2
Browne, Bard, 1967, F 16,39:3
Browne, Belmore, 1954, My 3,25:2
Browne, Bennet B Dr, 1922, Mr 11,13:6
Browne, Beverly, 1948, Mr 19,23:3
Browne, Charles, 1947, Ag 18,17:4
Browne, Charles A, 1907, Je 14,7:6; 1947, F 4,25:3
Browne, Charles A Mrs, 1942, Ja 27,22:2
Browne, Charles F (Artemus Ward), 1867, Mr 9,
Browne, Charles F M, 1955, D 22,23:4
Browne, Charles L Dr, 1937, Ag 30,21:4
Browne, Charles Mrs, 1966, My 30,19:3
Browne, Curtis N, 1946, Mr 19,27:3
Browne, Daniel Mrs, 1954, S 17,6:3
Browne, David H, 1917, Mr 31,11:5
Browne, de Courcy Bettingfield Mrs, 1915, Jl 15,9
Browne, Duncan H, 1954, D 10,27:1
Browne, Duncan H Mrs, 1942, N 28,13:3
Browne, Edward A, 1941, Jl 26,15:6
Browne, Edward E, 1945, N 24,19:5
Browne, Edward Ex-Judge, 1911, N 8,13:5
Browne, Edward J, 1955, Ja 5,23:1
Browne, Edward K, 1940, Ag 20,19:4
Browne, Evelyn G Mrs, 1939, Mr 5,48:6
Browne, F Webster, 1968, S 14,31:2
Browne, Francis J, 1968, Mr 13,53:6
Browne, Freeland, 1947, Ag 29,17:3
Browne, G Arthur, 1949, Ja 29,14:2
Browne, G F, 1885, Je 1,2:2
Browne, G H, 1877, N 18,7:2
Browne, G Morgan, 1959, Ja 15,33:1
Browne, George, 1958, Mr 15,10:3
Browne, George B (Byron), 1961, D 26,25:2
Browne, George E, 1946, Jl 14,36:3
Browne, George E Mrs, 1954, D 18,15:5
Browne, George V, 1964, N 26,33:2
Browne, Gilbert G, 1960, Je 25,21:5
Browne, Grant Hugh, 1925, Mr 11,21:4
Browne, H K (Phiz), 1882, Jl 10,5:6
Browne, Harold A, 1940, Je 28,19:6
Browne, Harold F, 1945, F 17,13:3

Browne, Harriet R Mrs, 1939, Mr 24,21:6
Browne, Harris W C, 1965, Ap 11,93:1
Browne, Harry C, 1950, Ag 6,73:3
Browne, Henry E, 1925, S 26,17:5
Browne, Henry F, 1953, Ap 22,29:5
Browne, Horace B Mrs, 1945, Ja 9,19:5
Browne, Howard, 1948, D 10,25:4
Browne, Irene, 1965, Jl 26,23:3
Browne, Israel P H, 1960, Ap 11,32:1
Browne, J Carlind, 1944, Ja 9,42:2
Browne, J L Mrs, 1938, Je 7,23:3
Browne, J Ross, 1875, D 9,4:6
Browne, J W S Gen, 1873, Mr 13,1:6
Browne, James J, 1948, F 18,28:2
Browne, James L, 1952, My 15,31:2
Browne, James Mrs, 1946, N 4,25:5
Browne, Jean A, 1937, N 12,21:3
Browne, John, 1945, N 18,43:1
Browne, John Dean, 1913, Mr 24,11:5
Browne, John J Mrs, 1957, O 12,19:2
Browne, John K, 1939, Mr 24,21:5
Browne, Joseph G M, 1954, Je 4,23:4
Browne, Josiah Mrs, 1944, Ag 14,15:3
Browne, Lewis A, 1937, My 25,27:3
Browne, Lewis R Mrs, 1947, Je 13,23:3
Browne, Louis E, 1951, F 11,89:1
Browne, Mary S Mrs, 1942, F 3,19:5
Browne, Maud Mrs, 1948, O 1,26:2
Browne, Maurice, 1955, Ja 22,11:4
Browne, Michael E, 1945, F 3,11:4
Browne, Miles E, 1941, My 8,23:2
Browne, Newberne A, 1949, Ap 20,27:1
Browne, Oliver G, 1950, O 28,17:4
Browne, Oliver G Mrs, 1947, D 19,25:3
Browne, P E, 1934, S 21,23:3
Browne, Patrick, 1940, S 17,23:6
Browne, Patrick J, 1961, N 23,31:2
Browne, Ralph C, 1960, Ja 7,29:2
Browne, Ralph C Mrs, 1952, Ap 13,77:2
Browne, Richard H, 1956, Je 20,31:3
Browne, Robert A, 1950, Ap 4,29:2
Browne, Robert B, 1959, Je 8,27:1
Browne, Robert Capt, 1923, Ag 20,11:4
Browne, Robert L Sr, 1947, N 17,21:4
Browne, Ross, 1963, S 24,39:4
Browne, Samuel B, 1953, F 7,15:4
Browne, Samuel W, 1941, Mr 6,21:4
Browne, Sara E Mrs, 1939, N 4,15:4
Browne, Sidney J, 1941, Ag 14,17:5
Browne, St Aubyn W, 1955, Jl 14,23:4
Browne, Stewart (por), 1938, Ag 5,17:3
Browne, Stewart (will), 1938, O 2,26:1
Browne, Tara, 1966, D 19,11:1
Browne, Thomas A Mrs, 1952, D 18,29:4
Browne, Thomas Mrs, 1954, O 25,27:2
Browne, Thomas Q Jr, 1914, Ag 28,9:5
Browne, Thorne A, 1945, D 12,27:2
Browne, Tom, 1910, Mr 17,9:4
Browne, Valentine Dr, 1915, N 20,13:6
Browne, Vincent F Mrs, 1956, Je 13,37:2
Browne, W Graham, 1937, Mr 12,23:3
Browne, W Preston, 1952, Je 21,15:4
Browne, Waldo R, 1954, Ja 27,27:1
Browne, Walter (funl, F 11,11:3), 1911, F 10,9:4
Browne, Walter H, 1955, Ja 25,25:2
Browne, Will C, 1940, My 23,24:2
Browne, William A Jr, 1949, Mr 11,25:3
Browne, William B, 1953, Ap 29,29:4
Browne, William G Mrs, 1941, Jl 21,15:6
Browne, William H, 1945, F 22,27:4; 1945, My 15,19:1
Browne, William Hardcastle, 1906, F 25,9:6
Browne, William T, 1949, Mr 9,25:4
Browne, William W, 1959, Mr 28,17:5
Browne, Wynard B, 1964, F 20,29:2
Browne (Mother Mary Agatha), 1964, F 8,23:5
Brownell, Arthur, 1945, Ja 11,23:2
Brownell, Baker, 1965, Ap 8,39:3
Brownell, C L, 1927, F 3,21:5
Brownell, C M Mrs, 1921, Jl 2,9:6
Brownell, Charles Clarence Dr, 1862, Ag 28,3:1
Brownell, Charles M, 1950, Ag 8,29:4
Brownell, Chauncey W, 1938, F 6,II,8:3
Brownell, Clifford W, 1957, Je 18,33:1
Brownell, Eleanor O, 1968, Ag 17,27:3
Brownell, Forrest L, 1957, N 27,31:4
Brownell, Francis H, 1954, Mr 9,27:2
Brownell, Frank A, 1939, F 4,15:3
Brownell, Frank V, 1945, Mr 6,21:3
Brownell, Frederick H, 1953, S 24,33:1
Brownell, Frederick R, 1953, O 6,29:1
Brownell, G F, 1934, Ap 16,17:3
Brownell, G George, 1948, D 1,29:4
Brownell, George F Mrs, 1945, Je 3,31:1
Brownell, George H, 1950, Je 2,23:2
Brownell, George L, 1944, D 19,21:5
Brownell, Gilbert S, 1954, D 28,23:5
Brownell, Harvey A, 1962, O 23,37:4
Brownell, Helen M Mrs, 1951, S 14,25:1
Brownell, Herbert Mrs, 1959, My 30,17:4
Brownell, Hollis L, 1961, S 8,31:3
Brownell, Isaac A Mrs, 1958, My 5,29:3
Brownell, James D, 1951, My 10,31:1
Brownell, John Leonard, 1910, Ag 15,7:6
Brownell, Joseph A, 1951, N 26,25:5
Brownell, Kenneth C, 1958, Ag 5,27:2
Brownell, L F, 1941, Mr 8,19:3
Brownell, Leonard D, 1945, Je 13,23:4
Brownell, Louis M, 1949, S 16,27:1
Brownell, Morris R Jr Mrs, 1952, Jl 29,21:5
Brownell, Myers, 1952, D 12,29:4
Brownell, Randolph H Mrs, 1965, Mr 4,31:4
Brownell, Silas B, 1918, Je 13,13:4
Brownell, T C Bishop, 1865, Ja 14,4:4
Brownell, W C, 1928, Jl 23,17:4
Brownell, Walter D, 1957, Ap 11,31:3
Brownell, William C Mrs (G Hall), 1961, Mr 1,33:4
Brownell, William R Mrs, 1947, Mr 13,27:2
Browner, Adair T, 1939, Ag 8,17:5
Browner, Bertram, 1938, Ag 11,3:2
Brownett, Harry A Sr, 1945, N 21,21:2
Brownewell, Ruth, 1955, D 9,27:3
Brownfield, H O N, 1958, Jl 10,27:4
Brownfield, John, 1939, My 31,23:1
Brownholtz, George W, 1949, N 3,29:3
Browning, Alan, 1960, Mr 6,84:7
Browning, Albert J, 1948, Jl 3,16:2
Browning, Arthur, 1957, N 24,87:1
Browning, Charles P, 1954, Ja 21,31:4
Browning, Charles R, 1945, Ja 27,11:5
Browning, Charles R Mrs, 1958, F 6,27:1
Browning, E W, 1934, O 13,13:1
Browning, Edward Franklin, 1912, My 19,II,15:5
Browning, Edward Jr, 1955, F 14,8:6
Browning, Elizabeth Barrett, 1861, Jl 19,3:2
Browning, Elmer E Jr, 1947, Ja 9,24:2
Browning, Everett E, 1950, Ja 8,78:2
Browning, Frances E, 1937, My 28,21:4
Browning, Frederick A M, 1965, Mr 15,31:2
Browning, George L, 1952, My 6,31:3
Browning, George W, 1952, Ja 30,25:3
Browning, Giles J, 1945, Mr 5,19:3
Browning, Grace, 1951, F 9,25:2
Browning, Guy K, 1954, S 12,84:4
Browning, Henry K Mrs, 1951, Mr 24,13:6
Browning, Henry L, 1948, N 30,28:2
Browning, Henry Mrs, 1947, Je 7,13:3
Browning, J H, 1877, Mr 27,8:6
Browning, J Hull, 1914, O 27,11:5
Browning, J M, 1926, N 27,17:5
Browning, J W, 1942, D 21,23:4
Browning, John S Jr, 1948, Je 13,68:6
Browning, John Scott, 1919, S 1,7:4
Browning, Jonathan E, 1939, My 18,25:6
Browning, Joseph G, 1941, Mr 22,15:3
Browning, Lillie F, 1952, Jl 22,25:2
Browning, Miles R, 1954, S 30,31:6
Browning, Montague E, 1947, N 6,28:2
Browning, Mortimer, 1953, Je 26,19:5
Browning, O H, 1881, Ag 12,5:2
Browning, Oren F, 1963, O 31,33:3
Browning, Peaches (Mrs F H Willson),(will, S 22,7:1), 1956, Ag 24,19:2
Browning, Phil E Dr (will, Ja 11,29:3), 1937, Ja 4, 29:3
Browning, Ralph R Mrs, 1943, Ja 31,46:1
Browning, Robert, 1889, D 13,1:5
Browning, Robert Wiedemann Barrett, 1912, Jl 9,9:3
Browning, Ross E, 1949, N 14,27:2
Browning, S Pearce Jr, 1961, F 26,92:2
Browning, Thomas B Dr, 1968, Ag 24,27:1
Browning, Tod, 1962, O 10,47:4
Browning, Tod Mrs, 1944, My 14,46:1
Browning, Victor R, 1951, F 17,15:4
Browning, W A Col, 1866, Mr 5,4:1
Browning, Walter W, 1938, Ja 17,19:2
Browning, Webster E, 1942, Ap 17,17:4
Browning, William, 1941, Ja 6,15:5
Browning, William Charles, 1904, Ag 5,7:6
Browning, William H, 1947, Mr 16,60:7
Browning, William H Mrs, 1948, D 17,27:1
Browning, William J, 1920, Mr 25,11:6
Browning, William S, 1944, Ap 17,23:5
Browning, Woodson, 1945, Ja 9,19:5
Brownlee, Arthur, 1939, F 13,15:6
Brownlee, Arthur C, 1961, Ap 1,17:3
Brownlee, Frederick L, 1962, N 12,29:5
Brownlee, Harris F Dr, 1937, F 25,23:2
Brownlee, Hugh R, 1946, D 7,21:5
Brownlee, J E, 1961, Jl 16,69:2
Brownlee, J J, 1879, N 12,2:4
Brownlee, James F, 1960, O 13,37:4
Brownlee, James L Jr, 1954, Jl 13,23:4
Brownlee, John H, 1945, O 26,19:1
Brownlee, Millard, 1947, Ag 20,21:2
Brownlee, O L, 1945, Ap 1,36:3
Brownlee, Raymond B Mrs, 1953, F 1,89:1
Brownlee, Royal E, 1940, F 15,19:4
Brownlee, William A, 1950, N 9,33:1
Brownlee, William K, 1938, Mr 25,19:4
Brownlee, William M, 1962, Ap 12,35:4
Brownlie, J E, 1946, D 24,17:4
Brownlie, James T, 1938, O 15,17:3
Brownlie, Walter B M, 1957, Ag 1,25:5
Brownlow, Charles Henry Sir Field Marshall, 1916, Ap 6,13:5
Brownlow, J P Gen, 1879, Ap 29,4:7
Brownlow, John F, 1958, N 13,33:5
Brownlow, Lady, 1952, N 28,25:3
Brownlow, Louis, 1963, S 28,19:6
Brownlow, W G, 1877, Ap 30,4:7
Brownlow, Walter P, 1910, Jl 9,7:6; 1910, Jl 12,7:4
Brownlow, William Gannaway Mrs, 1914, F 12,9:4
Brownmiller, George A Sr, 1943, F 12,19:4
Brownrigg, Abel L Mrs, 1948, My 18,24:3
Brownrigg, Douglas E R, 1939, F 15,23:2
Brownrigg, W Douglas S, 1946, F 9,13:5
Brownscombe, William T, 1955, Ag 10,25:2
Brownson, C M, 1955, Je 25,15:5
Brownson, Carleton L, 1948, S 27,23:4
Brownson, Henry Francis Maj, 1913, D 21,IV,5:5
Brownson, Isabelle K Mrs, 1942, N 2,21:4
Brownson, J M Maj, 1871, Jl 29,1:4
Brownson, James I, 1939, Ja 2,23:2
Brownson, Jane T, 1940, My 17,19:3
Brownson, Josephine, 1942, N 11,25:4
Brownson, Marcus A, 1938, D 19,23:5
Brownson, O A, 1876, Ap 18,7:5
Brownson, W H, 1935, Mr 17,37:1
Brownstein, Aaron Mrs, 1948, Ag 26,21:4
Brownstein, Hannah, 1949, Ap 23,13:5
Brownstein, Simon W, 1945, My 8,19:1
Brownworth, Eugene F, 1948, Ja 21,25:5
Brownworth, Henry Mrs, 1953, Je 20,17:3
Brownyard, George W, 1943, Ap 22,23:1
Browse, Robert T, 1948, D 16,29:5
Broy, Charles C, 1943, S 22,23:6
Broyles, Joseph W, 1945, S 30,46:4
Brozowski, Richard, 1955, D 26,19:4
Bru, Lorenzo L, 1940, Mr 3,45:2
Bruant, Aristide, 1925, F 13,17:4
Brubacher, A R Mrs, 1947, Jl 22,23:2
Brubacher, Abram R, 1939, Ag 24,19:3
Brubacker, Claude Mrs, 1940, Jl 24,21:6
Brubaker, Albert, 1943, Ap 30,21:2
Brubaker, Arthur, 1939, Mr 25,15:5
Brubaker, Henry C, 1957, Ap 28,87:1
Brubaker, Howard, 1957, F 4,19:4
Brubeck, John J Mrs, 1942, Jl 14,20:5
Bruccoli, John, 1948, F 14,13:3
Bruce, A P, 1903, S 14,7:5
Bruce, Albert C, 1964, Ap 1,39:5
Bruce, Alexander, 1944, N 26,57:1
Bruce, Alexander Hugh (Lord Balfour of Burleigh), 1921, Jl 7,11:5
Bruce, Alfred W, 1955, Ja 20,31:2
Bruce, Archie E, 1957, My 18,19:2
Bruce, Arthur, 1938, Ap 20,23:5
Bruce, Arthur C, 1954, O 7,23:3
Bruce, B K, 1898, My 18,7:6
Bruce, C Arthur, 1966, D 23,25:4
Bruce, Charles E Dr, 1924, Ap 20,22:2
Bruce, Charles G, 1939, Jl 13,19:3
Bruce, Charles M, 1938, Je 9,23:4
Bruce, Claire (Mrs J Hendrickson), 1959, Ap 6,27:4
Bruce, Cyrus W, 1943, Jl 29,19:2
Bruce, D, 1931, N 28,17:3
Bruce, Douglas W, 1953, My 29,25:2
Bruce, Earl Mrs, 1940, Ap 2,25:3
Bruce, Edna M, 1954, My 15,11:1
Bruce, Edward, 1943, Ja 27,21:5
Bruce, Edward James (Earl of Elgin), 1968, N 29, 45:3
Bruce, Edwin L, 1944, Ag 19,11:7
Bruce, Elizabeth, 1942, Ap 13,15:5
Bruce, Elizabeth Mrs, 1941, D 26,13:4
Bruce, Ethel S Mrs, 1957, Je 21,25:1
Bruce, Frank, 1940, Jl 7,25:3
Bruce, Frank M Sr, 1953, F 24,25:5
Bruce, Fred A (will), 1938, D 11,34:5
Bruce, Frederick J, 1940, Je 11,25:5; 1955, O 16,87:1
Bruce, Frederick Sir, 1867, S 20,1:5
Bruce, George, 1866, Jl 8,8:4
Bruce, George B, 1940, Mr 21,25:2
Bruce, George H, 1940, Ag 31,13:3
Bruce, Gordon D Mrs, 1945, D 28,15:2
Bruce, H, 1877, S 26,4:7
Bruce, Harold A, 1958, F 11,31:5
Bruce, Harold A Mrs, 1953, Jl 30,23:3
Bruce, Harry, 1949, S 3,13:2; 1961, Mr 21,37:3
Bruce, Harry E, 1951, Ap 12,33:4
Bruce, Henry M W, 1948, N 30,27:5
Bruce, Henry W, 1945, Mr 12,19:5
Bruce, Herbert A, 1963, Je 24,27:5
Bruce, Horace V, 1948, O 15,23:3
Bruce, Howard, 1961, Je 18,88:1
Bruce, J M, 1884, D 19,2:4
Bruce, James D, 1946, S 6,21:2
Bruce, James D Dr, 1923, F 20,17:3
Bruce, James Manning Rev, 1922, My 16,19:5
Bruce, James Mrs, 1907, Ap 20,9:6
Bruce, James P, 1942, S 4,23:2
Bruce, James Rev, 1913, D 3,15:5
Bruce, Jean (J Brochet), 1963, Mr 27,4:5
Bruce, Jesse C Rev Dr, 1922, S 20,21:4
Bruce, John, 1871, Ag 20,5:4; 1952, Ja 28,17:5
Bruce, John Duncan, 1920, Jl 7,11:2
Bruce, John E Eldridge, 1924, Ag 18,13:4
Bruce, John Edward, 1924, Ag 11,13:5
Bruce, John M, 1942, Je 13,15:2

Bruce, Joseph, 1872, Ja 29,1:7
Bruce, Kathleen, 1950, Ap 30,102:5
Bruce, L Frederick, 1948, Ja 15,23:2
Bruce, Lena, 1938, Ap 4,17:3
Bruce, Lenny (L A Schneider), 1966, Ag 4,33:2
Bruce, Leonard E, 1960, Ja 8,23:1
Bruce, Leslie Combes, 1911, Ag 3,7:6
Bruce, Llola, 1952, O 25,17:4
Bruce, Logan Lithgow Rev, 1968, D 6,47:1
Bruce, M Linn, 1940, Ag 6,20:4
Bruce, Malcolm C, 1954, S 10,23:3
Bruce, Malcolm G, 1948, Ap 1,25:3
Bruce, Malcolm G Mrs, 1943, Jl 17,13:3
Bruce, Matilda Wolfe, 1908, Jl 30,5:4
Bruce, Michael, 1957, My 27,31:5
Bruce, Michael Mrs, 1943, F 27,13:1
Bruce, Miriam H, 1949, Je 11,17:3
Bruce, Nigel, 1953, O 9,27:1
Bruce, Oliver Mrs, 1955, Je 21,23:1
Bruce, Robert, 1882, S 24,2:3; 1951, N 22,31:5; 1955, Mr 28,27:2; 1957, My 28,33:4
Bruce, Robert Ambler, 1907, Je 1,9:6
Bruce, Robert M, 1909, F 26,7:3
Bruce, Robert R, 1942, F 22,26:1; 1961, My 18,35:5
Bruce, S D Col, 1902, F 1,9:6
Bruce, Victor Alexander (Earl of Elgin), 1917, Ja 19, 7:2
Bruce, W H, 1944, Ja 1,13:4
Bruce, W W, 1954, Ag 26,27:4
Bruce, Wallace, 1914, Ja 3,11:5
Bruce, Wallace W, 1947, S 17,25:5
Bruce, William, 1944, O 10,23:3
Bruce, William A, 1942, Ja 31,17:5
Bruce, William C, 1946, My 10,19:3; 1949, D 22,23:2
Bruce, William G, 1949, Ag 14,70:3
Bruce, William L, 1952, N 6,29:1
Bruce, William L Mrs, 1949, N 9,27:2
Bruce, William M, 1938, Ja 22,18:2
Bruce, William Speirs Dr, 1921, N 1,19:6
Bruce-Gardner, Charles, 1960, O 2,84:6
Bruce-Jones, David B S, 1938, N 2,23:4
Bruce-Joy, Albert, 1924, Jl 23,15:3
Bruce of Melbourne, Viscount (Stanley M Bruce), 1967, Ag 26,27:4
Bruch, Edward B Lt-Col, 1918, My 14,13:6
Bruch, Max, 1920, O 3,22:1
Bruchesi, Paul, 1939, S 21,23:3
Bruchhausen, Joseph, 1960, S 19,31:4
Bruchhauser, Frederick W, 1950, Mr 30,30:2
Bruchlos, Barron, 1960, D 7,43:2
Bruchlos, Werner C, 1968, O 20,86:3
Bruck, Eberhard F, 1960, O 14,33:2
Bruck, Franklyn Mrs, 1957, Ag 26,23:2
Bruck, Isaac I, 1948, D 9,34:2
Bruck, Samuel, 1958, Ja 12,86:4
Bruck, Sidney, 1960, O 8,23:5
Bruckart, William L, 1940, Ag 5,13:4
Bruckel, Fred H, 1937, Je 19,15:5
Brucker, A William, 1952, Mr 13,29:2
Brucker, Charles Sr, 1955, Ja 14,21:2
Brucker, Henry, 1949, Ja 12,28:2
Brucker, Herbert Mrs, 1950, Ap 10,19:4
Brucker, Raymond, 1875, Mr 15,5:2
Brucker, Wilber M, 1968, O 29,47:1
Bruckheimer, David, 1957, Mr 16,19:5
Bruckheimer, Marcus, 1942, Ap 21,23:4
Bruckheimer, Samuel, 1944, Mr 5,35:1
Bruckheiser, William A, 1945, Jl 17,13:6
Brucklacher, Anna, 1955, S 3,15:6
Brucklacher, Charles, 1950, Mr 17,24:5
Brucklacher, Elise, 1950, Je 7,2:6
Bruckler, John, 1950, Je 29,29:1
Bruckman, Henry E, 1947, F 3,19:1
Bruckman, Henry E Mrs, 1942, Je 6,13:4
Bruckman, J Frank, 1944, Mr 22,19:4
Bruckman, Sarah L G Mrs, 1938, N 15,23:2
Bruckmann, George W, 1959, Je 18,31:6
Bruckner, Aloys L (other details, Je 4,35:3), 1965, Je 3,35:3
Bruckner, Arthur Dr, 1937, Ag 31,23:2
Bruckner, Eugene E, 1944, Ja 29,13:1
Bruckner, Ferdinand, 1958, D 6,23:2
Bruckner, Frank, 1949, Ap 21,25:2
Bruckner, Henry, 1874, Jl 18,8:5; 1942, Ap 15,21:1
Bruckner, Herman A, 1945, Ap 27,19:4
Bruckner, Joseph G, 1958, Ag 30,15:7
Brucks, Lester M, 1952, Ag 2,15:3
Brude, Ole M, 1949, N 5,14:3
Brudenell-Bruce, George W J C (Marquess of Ailesbury), 1961, Ag 6,85:1
Brudenell-Bruce, Henry Augustus (Marquis of Ailesburg), 1911, Mr 11,13:5
Bruder, Adolph, 1944, F 26,13:4
Bruder, Andrew J, 1953, Mr 19,29:2
Bruder, Charles F Jr, 1947, D 15,25:2
Bruder, Gallus, 1943, Ap 14,23:5
Bruder, John G, 1938, Je 23,21:1
Bruder, Louis, 1940, Ja 7,48:4
Bruder, Stephen J, 1943, Ap 17,17:3
Bruder, William H, 1946, Ap 2,27:5
Brudner, Arnold, 1944, Ag 9,17:4
Brudney, Florence G, 1945, S 21,21:1
Brue, Anthony P, 1951, Mr 21,33:4
Brue, John L, 1948, O 18,23:4
Brue, Luigi, 1942, Ag 26,19:4
Brue, William, 1952, My 1,29:4
Bruechig, Emil, 1947, Mr 24,25:2
Brueckmann, Valentine C, 1937, Ag 25,21:3
Brueckner, Alfred, 1957, O 28,28:1
Brueckner, Leo J, 1967, Jl 25,32:5
Brueckner, Oscar J, 1949, S 11,92:2
Brueckner, Wilhelm, 1954, Ag 22,92:2
Brueger, Edward M, 1940, Ap 5,21:5
Brueggemann, Henry L, 1943, S 16,21:4
Bruehl, William A R Sr, 1947, Ap 13,60:1
Bruel, Andree, 1966, Mr 15,39:1
Bruen, Alex J, 1937, F 26,21:5
Bruen, D B, 1880, Mr 4,5:6
Bruen, E B Rev, 1911, O 9,11:5
Bruen, Edward E, 1938, My 12,23:6
Bruen, Edward F, 1952, N 24,23:5
Bruen, Frank J, 1939, My 9,23:4
Bruen, James H, 1961, N 29,41:4
Bruen, John E Mrs, 1958, My 11,86:7
Bruen, Mathew M, 1949, Jl 5,23:3
Bruen, Oscar H, 1949, N 15,25:2
Bruen, William Livingston, 1923, O 26,17:4
Bruening, von Prof, 1883, D 8,1:6
Bruenn, Julius B Mrs, 1949, Ag 26,20:3
Bruenn, Louis S, 1949, My 20,27:2
Bruenner, Louis A, 1945, F 1,23:5
Bruer, Calistus A, 1949, O 4,27:4
Bruere, Alice H, 1946, O 5,17:5
Bruere, Henry, 1958, F 19,27:1
Bruere, Mina M, 1937, Mr 11,23:1
Bruere, Robert W Mrs, 1953, Ag 11,27:4
Brues, Charles, 1955, Jl 24,65:2
Bruestle, David P, 1951, N 11,90:7
Bruestle, George M, 1939, Ag 16,23:2
Bruette, William A, 1952, Ja 27,76:4
Bruff, Austin J, 1958, Jl 20,65:1
Bruff, Judd H, 1947, Ag 17,53:2
Bruff, Lawrence Laurenson Lt-Col, 1911, Ag 5,7:6
Bruffee, Alfred, 1951, O 26,24:2
Brug, George, 1940, Ap 21,43:2
Bruger, Maurice, 1957, N 27,31:4
Brugere, Henri Joseph Gen, 1918, S 2,9:2
Bruggeman, Arthur, 1937, D 1,23:3
Bruggeman, Louis Mrs, 1956, Ag 20,21:5
Bruggemann, Frederick C, 1943, N 25,25:2
Bruggemeier, Albert E, 1952, Jl 8,27:2
Bruggman, George W, 1950, N 11,15:5
Bruggmann, Charles, 1967, S 17,84:5
Bruggy, Frank L, 1959, Ap 7,34:1
Brugh, E S Mrs, 1942, F 16,17:3
Brugh, Jacob A, 1937, Mr 2,21:1
Brugh, Samuel S, 1939, Ap 15,19:1
Brugler, C Edward, 1959, S 2,29:3
Brugler, Van Cleve, 1948, D 30,19:3
Bruguier, Michael, 1967, Mr 17,2:6
Bruguiere, Francis, 1945, My 17,19:2
Bruguiere, Louis S, 1954, Ja 22,28:4
Bruhl, Henrietta Mrs (will), 1939, Ap 26,16:6
Bruhl, J Burleigh, 1942, Ja 31,17:7
Bruhn, John D, 1943, My 23,43:2
Bruhn, Wilhelmina S, 1949, My 4,29:2
Bruhy, Harvey A, 1918, S 9,11:4
Bruin, Frances N, 1938, Je 26,27:3
Bruin, James J, 1949, Ja 27,23:3
Bruina, J Robert, 1964, Ap 20,29:2
Bruine, J R S de, 1941, My 2,21:1
Bruins, Gijsbert W J, 1948, Mr 23,25:1
Bruins, John H, 1954, D 27,17:5
Brukenfeld, Carl M, 1962, Ja 21,88:8
Brukenfeld, Morris, 1958, Mr 14,25:1
Brukenfeld, Morris Mrs, 1968, Ag 25,88:4
Brulat, Paul, 1925, N 26,23:5; 1940, Ag 19,17:5
Brulatour, C Jules, 1961, Mr 12,79:1
Brulatour, C Jules Mrs, 1961, Mr 12,79:1
Brulatour, Dorothy Mrs, 1946, F 21,21:2
Brulatour, Jules E (will, N 27,46:2), 1946, O 27,62:3
Brulatour, Jules E Mrs, 1924, Ag 16,11:6
Brule, Andre, 1953, F 15,92:8
Brumaghim, George S, 1940, Ag 2,15:5
Brumagim, Robert S Mrs, 1954, D 16,37:6
Brumbach, Harry F, 1956, D 20,29:4
Brumback, George S, 1957, D 17,35:1
Brumbaugh, Andrew K, 1958, Ja 13,29:2
Brumbaugh, I Harvey Dr, 1937, Ag 11,23:4
Brumbaugh, Justin J, 1951, Jl 6,23:4
Brumbaugh, Norman Dr, 1953, F 17,27:2
Brumbaum, Theodore F Mrs, 1946, Ja 25,23:3
Brumberger, Martin, 1951, Ap 6,25:4
Brumby, Frank H, 1950, Jl 17,21:3
Brumby, Leonard, 1947, Jl 16,23:5
Brumby, Otis A, 1953, Jl 28,19:3
Brumder, George, 1910, My 10,9:5
Brumerhop, Henry, 1940, Jl 19,19:6
Brumfiel, Daniel M, 1958, Ag 22,21:4
Brumfield, David A, 1966, S 14,43:5
Brumfield, Frank E, 1953, O 29,31:3
Brumfield, Thomas M Sr, 1967, Ag 6,77:2
Brumidi, Fresco Painter, 1880, F 20,5:2
Bruml, Milton, 1958, F 1,19:1
Brumley, Albert L, 1937, Jl 31,15:6
Brumley, Ben B, 1953, Jl 4,11:7
Brumley, Daniel J, 1959, D 8,45:3
Brumley, Edward R, 1955, Ag 19,19:5
Brumley, Horace T, 1910, Ap 24,II,13:4
Brumley, James Lincoln, 1919, Jl 22,9:1
Brumley, Oscar V, 1945, Ja 15,19:5
Brumley, S S, 1881, D 1,3:4
Brumm, G F, 1934, My 30,18:1
Brumm, Herman F, 1952, O 2,29:3
Brumm, John L, 1958, Ag 17,85:4
Brumm, Lester, 1947, F 26,25:2
Brummell, Adonijah Harrison, 1907, O 16,9:5
Brummer, Christopher, 1909, N 26,9:7
Brummer, Edward J, 1952, Je 29,56:2
Brummer, Ernest, 1964, F 23,85:1
Brummer, Imre Mrs, 1952, Ag 17,76:4
Brummer, Joseph, 1947, Ap 15,25:4
Brummer, William F, 1949, O 13,27:4
Brummitt, Dan B, 1939, Ap 6,25:5
Brun, B Lucien, 1954, F 21,68:2
Brun, Charles, 1908, F 22,7:2
Brun, Constanin, 1945, D 25,23:3
Brun, Jean Jules Gen, 1911, F 24,9:4
Brun, John Rev, 1873, F 19,8:4
Brunauer, Stephen Mrs (Esther C), 1959, Je 27,23:2
Brunault, J S H Bishop, 1937, O 22,23:1
Brunck, Fred, 1944, O 3,23:4
Brundage, A H, 1936, Mr 13,23:3
Brundage, Albert P, 1952, Mr 7,24:3
Brundage, Alfred B, 1946, D 21,19:5
Brundage, Annie P, 1946, O 1,23:5
Brundage, Armand C, 1947, Ag 4,17:6
Brundage, Bertha Mrs, 1939, My 7,III,6:7
Brundage, Charlotte H Mrs, 1938, O 24,17:6
Brundage, Frank E, 1949, O 26,27:4
Brundage, Frank T, 1955, Ja 16,93:2
Brundage, George, 1946, F 11,29:2
Brundage, Harriet B Mrs, 1941, N 29,17:2
Brundage, Harry M, 1954, N 30,29:4
Brundage, Henry M, 1937, Jl 18,II,6:4
Brundage, Hiram, 1942, O 11,56:3
Brundage, Howard A, 1961, F 11,23:5
Brundage, Howard D, 1939, D 2,17:2
Brundage, J Arthur, 1948, Ag 2,21:4
Brundage, J Roberts, 1952, D 10,35:5
Brundage, James H, 1964, S 4,29:3
Brundage, John J Mrs, 1941, S 25,25:6
Brundage, John Mrs, 1912, N 5,13:4
Brundage, John N, 1956, Ap 11,33:1
Brundage, Lenore (Mrs David Katz), 1968, Mr 25, 41:4
Brundage, Lillie A, 1954, S 5,50:2
Brundage, Norman L, 1955, Mr 22,31:3
Brundage, Percy H, 1912, My 30,11:6
Brundage, Percy H Mrs, 1954, Jl 10,13:6
Brundage, Stanley E Mrs, 1952, S 2,23:3
Brundage, Teemon M, 1910, O 17,9:5
Brundage, Ulysses G, 1938, D 30,16:4
Brundage, Warren R, 1967, Jl 18,38:1
Brundidge, Harry T, 1961, Ap 20,33:3
Brundige, Albert S, 1951, N 10,17:5
Brune, Herbert M Sr, 1948, Ap 14,27:5
Brune, John A, 1952, N 17,25:4
Brune, William, 1956, O 10,39:5
Bruneau, A E, 1940, D 2,23:2
Bruneau, Armand L, 1945, Ag 22,25:3
Bruneau, Theodule, 1938, F 10,21:3
Brunel, Isambard Kingdom, 1859, S 28,4:6
Brunel, Richard D, 1942, F 11,22:2
Brunelle, Irma L, 1952, Ja 23,27:5
Bruner, Daniel M, 1943, Je 27,32:6
Bruner, Frank, 1949, Jl 19,29:2
Bruner, George E, 1952, Je 23,19:4
Bruner, John H, 1959, Ja 29,27:2
Bruner, Lawrence Prof, 1937, Ja 31,II,8:5
Bruner, Maude D Mrs, 1941, Mr 19,21:2
Bruner, Rudy, 1967, S 30,33:2
Bruner, Wilbur K, 1946, Ap 20,13:5
Brunet, M Emile, 1945, My 13,20:7
Brunet, Walter M, 1947, S 25,29:2
Brunet, William, 1875, Ag 23,4:6
Brunetiere, Ferdinand, 1906, D 10,7:4
Brunett, Fred, 1921, Ag 16,15:2
Brunett, Rock A, 1939, Je 5,17:3
Brunette, Fritzi, 1943, S 30,21:2
Brunetti, Fred R, 1959, N 27,26:7
Brunetti, Joseph J, 1968, D 11,41:2
Brungers, Amelia Mrs (will), 1941, F 4,18:3
Brunhild, Milton, 1949, F 1,25:4
Brunhoff, Jean de, 1937, N 6,17:6
Brunicardi, William F, 1942, N 19,25:3
Brunie, Charles H Sr, 1963, My 8,39:3
Brunie, Henry, 1940, D 6,23:5
Bruning, Baroness von, 1943, Ja 20,19:3
Bruning, George H, 1953, D 28,21:1
Bruning, Henry F, 1959, My 14,33:3
Bruning, Henry L Gen, 1875, Jl 11,7:6
Bruning, William C, 1953, O 2,21:2
Brunini, John B, 1954, N 9,27:1
Brunini, John B Mrs, 1947, S 3,25:1
Brunius, Pauline L, 1954, Ap 1,31:5
Brunjes, Martha S Mrs (S J Brown), 1960, Jl 5,
Brunjes, William H, 1941, F 1,17:1
Brunk, Frank F, 1940, N 20,21:1

Brunk, John H, 1952, My 10,21:4
Brunker, Albert R, 1959, D 31,21:1
Brunker, Anthony, 1949, O 20,29:3
Brunkhorst, Fred W, 1940, F 4,40:8
Brunler, Oscar, 1952, Ag 3,60:5
Brunn, Arthur J (por), 1949, Ag 28,74:3
Brunn, Herman A, 1941, S 23,23:5
Brunn, Joseph, 1951, Ap 10,27:2
Brunn, Joseph F Mrs, 1962, F 1,31:1
Brunn, Julius W, 1908, Ja 1,9:5
Brunn, Paul A, 1957, Jl 23,25:1
Brunn, Robert B J, 1953, Ag 1,11:6
Brunnell, Harry, 1922, Mr 18,13:4
Brunnenmiester, Frank O, 1964, Jl 2,31:2
Brunner, Albert L Jr, 1952, Je 10,27:4
Brunner, Alfred, 1953, Ag 10,23:4
Brunner, Arthur C, 1964, S 27,86:8
Brunner, Bruce Mrs, 1940, Ag 25,35:2
Brunner, Carl B, 1967, Ja 25,43:4
Brunner, Constantin, 1937, S 1,19:3
Brunner, Edward G, 1953, D 29,23:2
Brunner, Emil, 1911, S 16,7:7
Brunner, Emil H, 1966, Ap 7,39:1
Brunner, Emil R, 1963, D 27,23:2
Brunner, Emile C, 1942, Ja 15,19:2
Brunner, Ernest A, 1950, F 2,27:2
Brunner, Eugene A, 1947, Ja 29,25:3
Brunner, Eugene B Mrs, 1952, Je 19,27:4
Brunner, F Edward, 1951, Je 7,33:2
Brunner, Felix, 1950, Jl 7,19:3
Brunner, Frederick C, 1948, Mr 26,22:2
Brunner, George L, 1949, O 29,15:2
Brunner, Harry K, 1939, Jl 20,19:3
Brunner, Heinrich Prof, 1915, Ag 12,9:6
Brunner, Henry, 1921, Ja 9,23:1
Brunner, Horace C, 1944, Mr 21,19:2
Brunner, Howard W, 1964, F 9,89:2
Brunner, James D, 1945, Ap 7,15:3
Brunner, James J, 1947, Ag 21,23:3
Brunner, Jean A, 1951, My 23,35:1
Brunner, John A, 1949, O 21,25:4
Brunner, John E, 1950, Ag 20,76:4
Brunner, John Sir, 1929, Ja 17,25:5
Brunner, Leo J, 1941, F 23,40:2
Brunner, Matthew, 1951, Ja 17,27:3
Brunner, Rudolf, 1944, Mr 9,17:5
Brunner, William, 1937, Ja 26,25:2
Brunner, William F, 1943, Je 27,32:3; 1965, Ap 24,29:1
Brunner, William N, 1944, F 9,19:5
Brunnick, Walter A, 1944, Ap 14,19:5
Brunning, Charles Mrs, 1957, Mr 16,19:3
Brunning, Francis J, 1947, My 8,25:4
Brunnow, Baron, 1875, Ap 15,7:5
Brunnow, Countess, 1874, Mr 15,5:5
Bruno, Andrew L, 1967, F 1,39:4
Bruno, Antonio, 1944, Ja 6,23:3
Bruno, Basil B, 1955, Mr 24,31:2
Bruno, Edwin W, 1944, D 13,23:1
Bruno, Francis, 1956, Jl 17,23:2
Bruno, Frank, 1946, Ag 15,25:6
Bruno, Frank J, 1955, Ag 9,25:2
Bruno, Frank J Mrs (J C Colcord), 1960, Ap 9,23:3
Bruno, Frank T, 1938, Ap 20,23:2
Bruno, Frank V Mrs, 1963, Je 12,43:4
Bruno, Giuseppe (funl, N 14,89:2), 1954, N 11,31:1
Bruno, Gus, 1914, Ag 9,15:5
Bruno, James, 1952, O 1,34:4
Bruno, John C, 1965, Ap 11,93:1
Bruno, Joseph, 1952, D 16,31:3; 1956, O 19,27:1
Bruno, Joseph J (Big Joe), 1951, Jl 11,23:2
Bruno, Joseph M L, 1946, Jl 15,25:5
Bruno, S Frank Mrs, 1963, N 20,43:3
Bruno, Samuel J, 1953, Ap 2,27:1
Bruno, Sylvian, 1948, D 5,92:4
Bruno, William A, 1943, O 19,19:4
Brunot, Felix R, 1942, Ja 6,23:5
Brunot, Ferdinand, 1938, Ja 31,19:4
Brunott, Frederick C, 1946, O 29,26:2
Bruns, Alfred E, 1954, Mr 2,25:3
Bruns, Benjamin, 1959, Je 20,21:2
Bruns, Charles A Mrs, 1952, S 17,31:4
Bruns, Christian, 1950, Ap 23,95:2
Bruns, Cyrus B, 1952, My 17,19:4
Bruns, Edwin G, 1950, Jl 9,68:8
Bruns, Edwin G Jr (will, My 22,43:2;cor, D 2,20:3), 1941, Ja 14,21:5
Bruns, Frank J, 1949, Jl 20,25:2
Bruns, J Bowling, 1950, D 9,15:3
Bruns, J D Dr, 1883, My 21,7:2
Bruns, Viktor, 1943, S 23,21:3
Bruns, William C, 1937, Ja 16,15:1
Bruns, William H, 1965, F 16,35:4
Bruns, William H Mrs, 1960, Ag 29,25:4
Brunschvicg, Leon, 1944, F 2,21:2
Brunsman, Robert, 1949, D 13,38:4
Brunson, Clyde W, 1951, D 21,28:2
Brunson, Mason C Sr, 1950, Ag 23,29:2
Brunson, W A Dr, 1937, D 1,23:5
Brunst, G Rudolph, 1956, Ag 24,19:4
Brunstein, Louis, 1959, Je 14,87:1
Brunstetter, Byron C, 1953, S 17,43:1
Brunston, Gustav F, 1959, Mr 5,31:5
Brunstrom, David L, 1941, Ja 13,15:3
Brunswick, Duke of, 1873, Ag 20,4:7; 1884, O 19,9:4
Brunswick, Ruth M, 1946, Ja 26,13:3
Brunswick-Luneberg, Duke of (Ernst August Wilhelm), 1923, N 15,19:4
Brunswig, Lucien, 1943, Jl 19,15:6
Brunswig, Sarah Mrs, 1939, D 15,25:4
Brunt, Albert Mrs, 1952, Mr 30,92:5
Brunt, Charles C, 1945, D 13,29:1
Brunt, Clarence, 1952, Ag 30,13:6
Brunt, Joseph H, 1947, D 2,29:3
Brunt, Lewis A, 1946, Mr 31,46:4
Brunt, Robert S, 1950, N 30,34:3
Brunt, Shermer D, 1949, Mr 8,25:2
Brunton, John C, 1951, F 17,15:5
Brunton, Thomas Louder Sir, 1916, S 18,13:4
Brunyate, William L, 1939, D 29,15:4
Brusati, Renzo Count, 1918, D 30,9:2
Brusche, Walter H, 1939, Mr 28,24:2
Bruschi, Frank J Mrs, 1950, Je 10,17:5
Bruschi, Marie, 1914, Jl 23,9:1
Bruscoe, Rollin H, 1960, Ap 11,31:4
Brusewitz, Axel, 1950, O 4,31:1
Brush, Alanson P, 1952, Mr 7,24:3
Brush, Alvin G, 1965, Ap 25,87:5
Brush, Arthur T, 1953, Je 23,29:4
Brush, Carrie F Mrs, 1938, Mr 1,21:3
Brush, Charles F, 1929, Je 16,24:3
Brush, Charles H, 1944, My 31,19:5
Brush, Charles N, 1938, O 10,19:2
Brush, Daniel H Brig-Gen, 1920, Mr 9,11:1
Brush, Daniel S, 1938, D 4,60:5
Brush, E A, 1877, Jl 11,1:5
Brush, E F, 1927, O 4,29:4
Brush, Edward, 1920, Ja 7,19:3
Brush, Edward F Mrs, 1945, S 21,21:4
Brush, Edward L, 1953, S 25,21:3
Brush, Edward V, 1948, Jl 16,19:2
Brush, Fletcher, 1949, Jl 19,29:1
Brush, Florence L, 1964, F 12,34:1
Brush, Frederic, 1961, F 21,35:5
Brush, Frederic Mrs, 1961, O 27,33:5
Brush, Frederick M, 1953, Ap 28,27:3
Brush, G W, 1927, N 19,17:5
Brush, George, 1965, O 19,43:2
Brush, George D Mrs, 1949, Jl 30,15:4
Brush, George de F, 1941, Ap 25,19:1
Brush, George E, 1938, Je 11,15:6
Brush, George Jarvis, 1912, F 7,11:3
Brush, George S, 1942, N 8,51:2; 1946, Ap 30,21:2
Brush, George S Jr, 1942, Jl 26,30:8
Brush, Gerome, 1954, S 15,33:5
Brush, Gilbert P, 1967, O 1,84:2
Brush, Graham, 1954, Jl 12,19:5
Brush, Graham M, 1968, N 6,47:2
Brush, H Mortimer, 1917, Mr 29,13:5
Brush, Hamilton M, 1947, Ag 27,23:6
Brush, Harlan W, 1942, D 25,17:2
Brush, Henry L, 1938, Ja 23,II,8:5
Brush, Henry R, 1941, F 1,17:3
Brush, James Edwards, 1908, Jl 15,5:5
Brush, Jane W, 1960, S 23,29:4
Brush, Jerome W Mrs, 1966, Je 15,47:2
Brush, Joel L, 1942, Ap 4,13:5
Brush, John I, 1952, Ap 17,29:4
Brush, John T Mrs, 1957, D 30,23:4
Brush, Joseph, 1940, O 13,49:2
Brush, Joseph W, 1952, Mr 15,13:4
Brush, Joshua C, 1942, Ap 19,43:2
Brush, Katherine, 1952, Je 11,29:4
Brush, Katherine M Mrs, 1940, Je 21,21:5
Brush, Louis H, 1948, Je 25,23:1
Brush, Louis H Mrs, 1966, Ag 20,25:3
Brush, Matthew C, 1940, O 16,23:1
Brush, Nathaniel H, 1940, O 23,23:2
Brush, Ralph E, 1952, N 25,29:4
Brush, S (see also S 18), 1877, S 19,8:3
Brush, Shadrach M, 1903, Jl 13,7:5
Brush, Thomas S, 1938, O 31,15:1
Brush, Walter F, 1919, D 26,11:5
Brush, William D, 1941, Ja 23,22:2
Brush, William Peck Rev, 1919, N 23,22:3
Brush, William W, 1962, O 23,37:1
Brusie, Charles F, 1941, Je 15,36:8
Brusie, Charles I, 1942, N 4,23:5
Brusie, Frank G, 1956, Ap 8,84:4
Brusie, Harry, 1941, Je 17,21:2
Brusie, Maud S Mrs, 1939, D 13,27:2
Brusiloff, Alexei A Gen, 1926, Mr 18,23:4
Brusiloff, Nat, 1951, N 4,87:1
Bruso, O A, 1924, Mr 6,17:4
Brusoff, Valery, 1924, O 10,19:5
Brussel, A Stanley, 1942, Mr 12,19:3
Brussel, George Jr, 1961, S 4,15:6
Brussel, Herbert S, 1953, Je 3,31:2
Brussel, Lillian, 1924, Ag 24,24:4
Brust, George, 1940, D 15,61:4
Brust, Herbert O, 1953, My 1,22:3
Brust, Peter, 1946, Je 24,31:1
Bruton, Frances K Mrs, 1941, Ag 29,17:5
Bruton, Frank, 1954, F 10,29:1
Bruton, Gaston S Jr, 1961, S 4,30:8
Bruton, John F, 1946, Mr 28,25:2
Bruton, Joseph F Mrs, 1947, Jl 31,21:5
Bruton, Thomas B, 1942, F 24,21:3
Brutone, J W B, 1876, N 25,2:5
Brutton, Harry S, 1950, Je 1,27:1
Bruun, Rikard V, 1944, Ja 3,21:4
Bruyn, Casimir de, 1938, Ap 11,15:1
Bruyn, Charles, 1950, Jl 24,17:6
Bruyn, Charles DeW, 1959, My 8,27:4
Bruyn, Francis S, 1959, Jl 10,25:4
Bruyn, William E, 1940, N 2,15:5
Bruzaitis, Anthony J, 1962, Mr 26,31:2
Bry, M Edwin, 1955, S 12,25:2
Bry, Paul, 1953, Je 30,23:6
Bryan, Alfred, 1958, Ap 2,31:5
Bryan, Alfred C, 1964, Ap 1,39:4
Bryan, Alfred S, 1948, Je 2,29:4
Bryan, Alice M, 1948, Ag 3,26:3
Bryan, Ashbel W, 1951, Je 16,15:3
Bryan, Ashbel W Mrs, 1959, Ja 30,28:1
Bryan, Barnabas Jr, 1952, F 6,29:4
Bryan, Benjamin B, 1937, Je 15,23:3
Bryan, Brantz M, 1962, Mr 15,35:2
Bryan, Charles F, 1945, S 11,23:1; 1955, Jl 9,15:2; 1968, D 13,47:1
Bryan, Charles J, 1947, D 6,15:6
Bryan, Charles M, 1941, Ja 15,23:4
Bryan, Charles Page, 1918, Mr 14,13:6
Bryan, Charles S, 1954, F 21,68:4; 1956, Mr 30,19:2
Bryan, Charles T, 1967, My 18,47:5
Bryan, Charles W Jr, 1966, Mr 17,39:4
Bryan, Charles W Mrs, 1949, Jl 22,19:1
Bryan, Claude S, 1951, Jl 31,21:2
Bryan, Edward P, 1910, Ja 25,9:4
Bryan, Einar C, 1948, D 31,15:4
Bryan, Ellen E Mrs, 1937, S 28,23:1
Bryan, Enoch A, 1941, N 7,23:2
Bryan, Ernest R, 1954, D 19,84:5
Bryan, Eugene C Mrs (O Morgan), 1961, Mr 5,86:5
Bryan, Frank, 1939, My 30,17:2
Bryan, Frank C, 1951, Ja 13,15:4
Bryan, Frank H, 1957, Ja 1,23:6
Bryan, Frank H Mrs, 1964, S 22,39:2
Bryan, Frank J, 1943, Mr 11,21:5
Bryan, Frederick C, 1941, Ap 8,26:2
Bryan, Frederick J Mrs, 1961, D 23,23:4
Bryan, George, 1958, Mr 8,17:5
Bryan, George R, 1943, O 4,17:5
Bryan, George S, 1943, D 23,19:1; 1964, Jl 15,35:3
Bryan, Gray, 1958, S 20,40:1
Bryan, H Lewis, 1959, Jl 10,25:4
Bryan, Hal, 1948, Ag 15,60:4
Bryan, Hamilton V, 1944, O 19,23:3
Bryan, Harry C, 1953, Je 5,27:2
Bryan, Henry C, 1922, Ag 29,15:4
Bryan, Henry W, 1939, N 29,23:2
Bryan, Herbert, 1950, O 1,104:6; 1953, Ap 17,25:1
Bryan, Hiram E, 1947, Ag 13,23:1
Bryan, Isaac J, 1940, Ap 15,17:4
Bryan, Isabel, 1957, O 12,19:2
Bryan, J B, 1953, Ja 15,27:1
Bryan, J St George, 1945, Je 15,19:5
Bryan, James E, 1951, D 19,31:2
Bryan, James H, 1961, D 12,43:3
Bryan, James W, 1954, Mr 14,89:2; 1956, Ag 28,27:2
Bryan, Jimmy, 1960, Je 20,40:7
Bryan, John, 1943, Ja 3,46:1
Bryan, John B, 1938, S 20,23:2
Bryan, John H, 1962, Ag 1,31:3
Bryan, John I, 1944, Je 4,42:3
Bryan, John S, 1944, O 17,23:1; 1964, Ja 22,75:1
Bryan, John S Mrs, 1952, S 9,31:5
Bryan, Joseph, 1908, N 21,9:2
Bryan, Joseph H, 1948, O 22,25:5
Bryan, Joseph Mrs, 1910, S 12,9:6
Bryan, Joseph W Mrs, 1946, Ap 4,25:5
Bryan, Kathryn M, 1954, Mr 17,31:1
Bryan, Kirk, 1950, Ag 23,29:6
Bryan, Louis A, 1966, F 28,27:2
Bryan, Lyman Curtis Dr, 1918, F 10,17:1
Bryan, M J Don, 1961, D 28,27:3
Bryan, M K Col (Albany), 1863, Jl 2,5:2
Bryan, Mal B, 1964, F 22,21:1
Bryan, Mary C, 1945, Jl 2,15:5
Bryan, Mary M, 1959, Jl 10,25:4
Bryan, O, 1903, S 30,9:6
Bryan, Paul M, 1944, Ag 5,11:4
Bryan, Reginald E, 1950, Jl 9,68:7
Bryan, Richard, 1907, Ag 1,7:6
Bryan, Richard Williamson D Bryan, 1913, F 12,15:4
Bryan, Robert C, 1941, D 25,25:1
Bryan, Robert E, 1952, S 1,17:5
Bryan, Robert R, 1963, Jl 26,25:3
Bryan, Samuel, 1924, N 16,7:3
Bryan, Samuel Mrs, 1945, O 20,11:3
Bryan, Samuel S, 1947, F 21,20:2; 1955, F 10,31:2
Bryan, Sheldon Martin, 1968, N 8,47:4
Bryan, Stephen J, 1958, Jl 19,15:6
Bryan, Stewart, 1965, My 3,33:4
Bryan, Thomas B, 1906, Ja 27,9:5
Bryan, Thomas J, 1939, Ja 25,21:2
Bryan, Thomas L Jr, 1958, Jl 24,25:4
Bryan, Vincent, 1937, Ap 28,23:5
Bryan, W A, 1940, My 2,23:2
Bryan, W J Mrs, 1930, Ja 22,23:3

Bryan, W S Plummer Rev, 1925, My 29,17:5
Bryan, Walter Dr, 1905, Je 27,4:1
Bryan, Walter G, 1941, Mr 2,43:1
Bryan, Wilhelmus B, 1938, Jl 11,17:5
Bryan, William A, 1942, Je 19,23:2; 1944, N 8,17:4
Bryan, William H, 1940, My 29,23:2
Bryan, William Henry, 1908, F 27,7:7
Bryan, William J, 1968, Mr 19,47:3
Bryan, William James Sen, 1908, Mr 23,7:5
Bryan, William L, 1955, N 22,35:3
Bryan, William L Mrs, 1948, Ag 28,15:4
Bryan, William S, 1940, Jl 14,31:3
Bryan, William Shepard Jr, 1914, Ap 4,15:4
Bryan, William Sr, 1944, Mr 11,13:2
Bryan, Winfield O, 1940, My 2,23:4
Bryan-Ashwell, Henry J, 1947, Ja 4,15:4
Bryan-Ashwell, Henry J Mrs, 1958, My 27,31:4
Bryann, John, 1918, N 29,13:5
Bryans, Andrew E, 1958, Jl 28,23:4
Bryans, James H Mrs, 1950, D 27,27:2
Bryans, William T, 1937, Je 30,23:4
Bryant, Albert, 1956, Ja 17,33:4
Bryant, Albert G, 1915, F 25,9:4
Bryant, Albert H, 1957, O 20,86:4
Bryant, Alex G, 1953, Ag 27,25:1
Bryant, Alice G, 1942, Jl 27,15:6
Bryant, Aloysius J, 1965, Jl 9,26:1
Bryant, Anna G Mrs, 1941, Ja 28,19:4
Bryant, Bernard W, 1943, O 21,27:6
Bryant, C Ralph Mrs, 1957, Ag 13,27:2
Bryant, Carleton E, 1941, Mr 28,23:4
Bryant, Carrie P Mrs, 1952, Ap 2,33:4
Bryant, Charles, 1948, Ag 8,57:1
Bryant, Charles B, 1949, Ag 11,24:2
Bryant, Charles D J, 1937, Ja 23,17:4
Bryant, Charles L, 1945, Ja 31,21:5
Bryant, Charles M, 1945, Ja 15,19:5
Bryant, Charles S, 1943, O 31,48:5
Bryant, Charles W Mrs, 1952, O 8,31:2
Bryant, Cheston M, 1947, Jl 27,44:5
Bryant, D C, 1940, Jl 3,17:4
Bryant, Dan, 1875, Ap 11,7:3
Bryant, Dorothy W Mrs, 1962, N 24,23:5
Bryant, E E Gen, 1903, Ag 12,9:6
Bryant, Earlham, 1968, O 25,47:4
Bryant, Edward A, 1957, S 11,33:1
Bryant, Eleazar, 1942, Ap 11,13:2
Bryant, Eliot H, 1955, O 18,37:3
Bryant, Elwyn R, 1942, O 3,15:5
Bryant, Emmons, 1942, Mr 8,43:2
Bryant, Emmons Mrs, 1948, O 30,15:1
Bryant, Ernest C, 1942, S 8,23:3
Bryant, Esther L Mrs, 1942, S 24,27:4
Bryant, F Edward, 1945, D 8,17:4
Bryant, Fitch C, 1959, N 5,35:4
Bryant, Floyd S, 1965, Ap 11,92:8
Bryant, Francis A, 1960, Je 21,33:4
Bryant, Frank, 1949, D 3,15:5
Bryant, Frank L, 1947, F 26,25:3; 1948, Jl 22,23:1
Bryant, Frank Mrs, 1959, Mr 16,31:3
Bryant, Frederick C, 1967, Je 23,31:7
Bryant, Frederick H, 1945, S 5,23:1
Bryant, Frederick W, 1947, Ag 13,23:2
Bryant, G Frank Col, 1924, N 17,19:4
Bryant, G W Rev, 1901, Je 17,7:4
Bryant, G Willard, 1949, N 9,27:3
Bryant, George A, 1963, Ap 22,27:5
Bryant, George B, 1949, F 15,23:5
Bryant, George C, 1947, Ag 29,17:3
Bryant, George C Mrs, 1949, Ja 10,25:5
Bryant, George R, 1968, Je 15,35:1
Bryant, George W, 1947, My 7,27:4
Bryant, H Arthur Mrs, 1952, O 20,23:5
Bryant, H H, 1938, My 21,15:6
Bryant, Harold Child Dr, 1968, Jl 26,33:2
Bryant, Harry A, 1943, S 16,21:5
Bryant, Henry, 1904, Ja 8,7:5
Bryant, Irving S, 1946, N 10,63:5
Bryant, J H, 1902, Ja 15,9:5
Bryant, James G Mrs, 1954, Ja 5,27:4
Bryant, John A, 1953, My 27,31:6
Bryant, John Dr, 1908, Mr 21,9:6
Bryant, John H Gen, 1906, N 21,9:6
Bryant, John T, 1941, Ja 8,19:5
Bryant, Joseph D Dr (funl, Ap 10,13:3), 1914, Ap 8, 13:5
Bryant, Joseph D Mrs, 1919, S 30,19:3
Bryant, Joseph H Sr, 1944, S 28,19:2
Bryant, Julia S, 1907, Jl 25,7:5
Bryant, L M Mrs, 1933, D 14,23:3
Bryant, Lane Mrs (Mrs L B Malsin), 1951, S 27,31:1
Bryant, Leland A, 1954, Jl 21,27:5
Bryant, Lester Mrs (Edna Hibbard), 1942, D 27,34:3
Bryant, Lewis A, 1948, Mr 3,23:5
Bryant, Lewis T Brig-Gen, 1923, Je 28,15:5
Bryant, Louis M, 1946, Je 9,40:5
Bryant, Louise S, 1956, Ag 31,17:1
Bryant, M D, 1933, Ja 20,17:1
Bryant, Maria O R Mrs, 1940, Je 1,15:2
Bryant, Maude D Mrs, 1946, O 24,27:4
Bryant, Monroe B, 1907, Ag 27,7:6
Bryant, Montgomery Col, 1901, Je 18,7:6
Bryant, Nana, 1955, D 26,19:2
Bryant, Nathan D, 1949, Ja 25,23:4
Bryant, Neil, 1902, Mr 7,9:7
Bryant, Ole H, 1943, Ja 14,21:1
Bryant, Paul K, 1947, Je 6,23:1
Bryant, Ralph C, 1939, F 3,15:1
Bryant, Ralph L, 1942, Ap 12,45:2
Bryant, Randolph, 1951, Ap 25,29:4
Bryant, Raymond F, 1951, D 29,11:2
Bryant, Russell W, 1951, My 31,27:4
Bryant, Ruth W, 1957, O 28,27:2
Bryant, Samuel (por), 1938, S 22,23:1
Bryant, Samuel W, 1938, N 5,19:4
Bryant, Samuel W Mrs, 1945, Jl 22,38:1
Bryant, Scipio G, 1947, Ag 28,23:2
Bryant, Stewart F, 1945, F 7,21:6
Bryant, Theodore K Mrs, 1948, Mr 22,23:2
Bryant, W B, 1932, Je 5,33:3
Bryant, W C, 1878, Je 13,4:7; 1905, F 16,9:4
Bryant, William A Maj, 1918, Ag 12,9:7
Bryant, William B, 1955, D 4,89:1
Bryant, William B Mrs, 1968, N 19,40:1
Bryant, William C, 1956, Mr 21,37:1
Bryant, William Cullen Dr, 1911, Jl 24,7:6
Bryant, William G, 1950, Je 19,21:5
Bryant, William L, 1947, Je 10,27:5
Bryant, William Mrs, 1922, Ag 30,15:5
Bryant, William R, 1941, Ja 10,19:4
Bryant, William S, 1956, Je 27,31:2
Bryant, Willie, 1964, F 15,23:2
Bryant, Windom, 1942, O 16,19:5
Bryce, Carroll, 1911, D 8,13:4
Bryce, Chalmers K, 1964, D 8,45:1
Bryce, Chalmers K Mrs, 1967, Je 15,47:2
Bryce, Clarence H, 1957, Jl 23,25:4
Bryce, David A, 1965, N 4,47:2
Bryce, Edith, 1917, Ja 25,9:3
Bryce, Ellsworth, 1957, Ja 24,29:3
Bryce, James, 1876, Je 25,5:6
Bryce, James Mrs, 1950, Ap 25,31:1
Bryce, James W, 1949, Mr 28,21:4
Bryce, Lloyd S Gen, 1917, Ap 3,13:6
Bryce, Lloyd S Mrs, 1916, Ap 30,19:5
Bryce, Myric W Mrs, 1959, D 16,41:1
Bryce, Ray, 1944, Ja 10,17:3
Bryce, Richard, 1966, N 13,89:1
Bryce, Thomas F, 1939, Mr 13,17:3
Bryce, Viscount, 1922, Ja 25,15:6
Bryce, Viscountess, 1939, D 29,15:5
Bryce, Wallace, 1950, My 16,31:4
Bryde, Edward D, 1951, Jl 24,25:4
Bryde, Frederick J, 1942, My 8,21:2
Bryden, Eugene S, 1951, F 1,25:5
Bryden, James, 1956, S 14,23:2
Bryden, Newton B, 1955, My 8,88:2
Bryden, William T, 1910, Mr 9,9:2
Brydges, Charles Edward, 1911, Mr 22,11:5
Brydle, Fenton R, 1949, N 6,92:2
Brydon, John C, 1939, Mr 10,23:3
Brydon, William Dr, 1873, Ap 11,1:5
Bryer, Charles Mrs, 1953, My 22,27:3
Bryer, Russell K, 1949, My 28,15:4
Brykcznski, Emil S, 1943, Ag 12,19:2
Brylaweki, Edward, 1951, Ap 30,21:3
Brymn, J Tim, 1946, O 4,23:4
Bryn, Aage, 1950, D 29,20:2
Bryn, Elmer H Mrs, 1957, My 18,19:5
Bryne, Laura L Mrs, 1938, Ja 14,23:4
Bryne, Patrick J, 1952, O 30,5:3
Bryner, Ezra H, 1909, Mr 12,7:7
Bryner, Vera, 1967, D 15,94:1
Brynildsen, John O, 1948, N 12,23:2
Bryning, Percy L, 1941, Mr 23,45:1
Bryson, David E Mrs, 1955, Jl 31,68:4
Bryson, Ernest J, 1951, Ja 16,29:3
Bryson, George, 1937, My 9,II,11:1
Bryson, George Eugene, 1912, F 28,11:5
Bryson, Gladys E, 1952, D 19,31:5
Bryson, Hugh E Mrs, 1952, N 29,17:3
Bryson, J H, 1941, N 25,25:2
Bryson, John A, 1967, D 6,51:6
Bryson, John P Dr, 1903, My 6,9:6
Bryson, Joseph R, 1953, Mr 11,33:6
Bryson, Lyman (mem ser set, D 4,31:2), 1959, N 26, 37:1
Bryson, Lyman Mrs, 1944, Mr 24,20:3
Bryson, Margaret E Mrs, 1946, N 5,25:3
Bryson, Mizell, 1953, Ap 1,29:3
Bryson, Robert H, 1938, S 11,II,11:1
Bryson, Thomas B, 1922, S 7,17:5
Bryson, Thomas H, 1943, Mr 24,23:4
Bryson, William C (trb, D 2,14:6), 1943, N 30,27:5
Bryton, Georgia, 1942, Ja 27,22:2
Brzoziewski, Joseph, 1965, Ja 20,39:1
Bsharah, Mary C, 1941, S 23,23:6
Bshop, Henry W, 1945, N 21,21:4
Buat, E A L Gen, 1923, D 31,13:5
Bub, Frank D Sr, 1950, Jl 7,19:3
Bub, Hermann J, 1950, Ap 8,13:3
Bubacz, Richard H, 1962, Je 16,19:3
Bubb, Adam Mrs, 1951, Ag 4,15:5
Bubb, Charles B, 1947, Ag 8,17:5
Bubb, F Alfred, 1948, O 20,29:2
Bubb, Frank W Sr, 1961, My 4,37:4
Bubb, George L, 1955, F 19,15:4
Bubb, John C, 1954, Mr 12,21:5
Bubb, John P, 1940, O 8,25:2
Bubb, N Burrows, 1925, Ja 20,21:5
Bubbard, Dana M, 1954, Ja 28,27:4
Bubeck, Jeanne Mrs, 1942, F 5,22:2
Buber, Martin (trb, Je 14,29:4; ed, Je 14,1:2; funl, Je 15,38:1), 1965, Je 14,1:2
Bubet, Theodore, 1949, S 29,29:4
Bublick, David, 1955, D 31,13:5
Bublick, Gedalia, 1948, Mr 19,23:2
Bublick, Gedalia Mrs, 1949, Ap 25,23:4
Bubnov, Aleksandr P, 1964, Jl 3,21:2
Bubos, Anthony P, 1939, D 1,23:2
Buc, Hyym E, 1950, Ja 24,32:2
Buc, Saul R, 1960, Je 7,35:3
Bucci, Anselmo, 1955, N 20,88:8
Bucci, Leonard A, 1961, F 9,31:4
Bucci, Leopold, 1949, F 14,19:2
Bucci, Nicholas, 1956, N 21,27:1
Bucci, Umberto, 1950, Ja 4,46:4
Bucciante, Alfredo, 1950, D 27,27:1
Buccino, Raul A, 1964, Mr 31,35:1
Buccleuch, Dowager Duchess of, 1954, Ag 8,85:3
Buccleuch, Duke of (Wm Hy Montagu-Douglas-Scott), 1914, N 6,11:5
Bucerzan, John, 1959, S 16,39:1
Buch, Carl F, 1954, Jl 4,22:4
Buch, Elsa A, 1961, Ja 9,39:5
Buch, Joseph G, 1945, Je 22,15:1
Buch, Louis J, 1964, Mr 26,35:3
Buch, Samuel M, 1959, Ja 25,92:3
Buch, William, 1938, F 27,II,8:5
Buchan, Alex, 1954, Jl 8,23:2
Buchan, Anna, 1948, N 25,31:1
Buchan, Edward, 1958, Ja 21,29:3
Buchan, Edward J Mrs (Peerless Annabelle), 1961, D 2,23:5
Buchan, Helen Mrs, 1937, D 19,II,9:1
Buchan, Lawrence Gen, 1909, O 8,9:3
Buchanan, A Sir, 1882, N 15,5:4
Buchanan, A W Patrick, 1939, N 3,21:1
Buchanan, Adelaide Tilden Mrs, 1904, N 15,7:6
Buchanan, Albert W, 1966, N 12,29:2
Buchanan, Allen, 1940, Ja 14,42:7
Buchanan, Andrew, 1912, N 21,13:4
Buchanan, Andrew B, 1952, Je 25,29:3
Buchanan, Arch, 1941, N 18,25:5
Buchanan, Barry Mrs (B Lawford), 1960, N 12,29:5
Buchanan, Beaufort C Mrs, 1955, Ag 19,19:6
Buchanan, Charles J Maj, 1916, Ja 8,9:7
Buchanan, Charles L, 1962, Mr 12,31:1
Buchanan, Charles P, 1941, F 14,17:1
Buchanan, Chester L, 1951, Ap 4,29:4
Buchanan, Douglass, 1945, Ja 16,20:2
Buchanan, Duncan G, 1949, Ag 26,19:2
Buchanan, E Anna, 1922, Ap 5,17:5
Buchanan, E S, 1932, S 7,19:3
Buchanan, Edward R, 1910, D 5,13:4
Buchanan, Edwin C, 1940, O 5,15:4
Buchanan, Edwin L, 1945, Ag 9,21:5
Buchanan, Edwin P, 1955, Jl 13,25:2
Buchanan, Ella, 1951, Jl 17,27:5
Buchanan, Forrest E, 1948, Mr 11,27:3
Buchanan, Frank, 1951, Ap 28,15:1
Buchanan, Franklin, 1874, My 14,5:3
Buchanan, G E, 1938, Ap 10,II,6:2
Buchanan, George, 1955, Je 29,29:5
Buchanan, George A, 1940, My 23,23:4
Buchanan, George A Mrs, 1940, Ag 29,19:3
Buchanan, George B, 1939, Ap 14,23:1
Buchanan, George E, 1939, Mr 25,15:5
Buchanan, George H, 1944, Ja 18,19:2
Buchanan, George Nelson, 1917, D 1,13:7
Buchanan, George V, 1957, F 27,27:1
Buchanan, George W, 1948, Je 13,68:4
Buchanan, Gordon Sr, 1946, O 29,25:4
Buchanan, H L, 1940, Jl 31,17:3
Buchanan, Hugh, 1959, S 19,23:5
Buchanan, Isaac, 1883, O 2,5:5
Buchanan, J Hervey Dr, 1918, Je 8,11:5
Buchanan, Jack, 1957, O 21,25:1
Buchanan, James A, 1945, O 12,23:3
Buchanan, James Ex-Pres, 1868, Je 2,4:7
Buchanan, James J, 1947, D 9,29:3
Buchanan, James L, 1955, D 29,23:4
Buchanan, James W, 1952, Je 29,56:3
Buchanan, John, 1941, Ja 27,15:4
Buchanan, John F, 1941, F 6,21:4
Buchanan, John J Dr, 1937, Ag 25,21:4
Buchanan, John L, 1939, F 25,15:4
Buchanan, John P, 1908, My 22,7:4
Buchanan, John R, 1951, O 14,89:3
Buchanan, John R Sr, 1947, Je 23,23:2
Buchanan, John T, 1949, My 9,25:3
Buchanan, Joseph Ray, 1924, S 15,21:2
Buchanan, Joseph T, 1952, Ja 23,27:2
Buchanan, Kenneth B, 1956, Ap 10,31:4
Buchanan, Laura W Mrs, 1941, D 24,17:3
Buchanan, Livingston, 1952, My 14,27:4
Buchanan, Lynn D, 1939, D 27,21:3
Buchanan, Madeline S Mrs, 1940, S 6,21:6
Buchanan, Malcolm G, 1942, Ja 13,19:1

Buchanan, Mary, 1946, Ag 10,13:4
Buchanan, Myron W, 1957, S 7,19:1
Buchanan, Norman S, 1958, Ap 27,86:3
Buchanan, Oswald C, 1966, Je 29,47:5
Buchanan, Pat, 1950, Mr 24,26:2
Buchanan, Perley J, 1944, F 24,15:5
Buchanan, Phil J, 1948, Jl 12,19:5
Buchanan, R C Col, 1878, N 30,2:4
Buchanan, Richard W, 1951, Mr 24,13:2
Buchanan, Robert, 1901, Je 11,9:6
Buchanan, Robert H, 1942, Ja 4,49:1
Buchanan, Scott Dr, 1968, Mr 29,41:1
Buchanan, Stephen L, 1948, Ag 2,21:5
Buchanan, T Drysale Mrs, 1947, Mr 4,25:1
Buchanan, T McKean Lt, 1863, Ap 26,3:1
Buchanan, Taylor T, 1953, S 30,31:5
Buchanan, Thomas C, 1958, Ap 11,26:1
Buchanan, Thomas D, 1940, Mr 22,19:1
Buchanan, Thomas Jefferson, 1920, Jl 16,11:4
Buchanan, Thomas S (por), 1949, Je 14,31:3
Buchanan, Thompson, 1937, O 16,19:5
Buchanan, Tillie E, 1952, D 20,17:3
Buchanan, Vera D, 1955, N 27,88:3
Buchanan, W D, 1934, F 20,24:2
Buchanan, W Edgar, 1941, Je 3,21:5
Buchanan, William A, 1949, Ja 6,23:4; 1954, Jl 12,19:6
Buchanan, William H Mrs, 1946, Ap 20,13:3
Buchanan, William I, 1909, O 30,9:6
Buchanan, William R, 1943, S 5,28:8
Buchanan, William R Mrs, 1956, D 16,87:1
Buchanan, William W, 1949, F 1,25:4
Buchanan, Willis E, 1950, F 18,15:4
Buchannan, Lester M, 1950, Ja 26,27:4
Buchannan, McKean, 1872, Ap 18,2:5
Buchard, Oscar, 1949, O 29,15:4
Buchard, Stewart, 1950, Je 1,27:5
Bucharoff, Simon, 1955, N 26,19:1
Buchbinder, Jacob R, 1947, S 19,23:1
Buchbinder, Leon, 1965, Mr 5,33:4
Buchbinder, Meyer, 1940, My 31,19:5
Buchbinder, Milton Dr, 1968, F 26,37:2
Buchbinder, Morris, 1914, Je 8,7:4
Buchdahl, Milton G, 1962, Jl 15,61:1
Buchdahl, Milton G Mrs, 1968, Ag 14,43:4
Buchen, Walter, 1961, Je 14,19:2
Bucher, Aug J Dr, 1937, Ja 26,21:2
Bucher, Carl J, 1951, O 12,27:4
Bucher, Elise, 1945, S 10,19:5
Bucher, Elmer E, 1964, Je 15,29:3
Bucher, Emil H, 1954, S 14,27:2
Bucher, Frank C, 1946, D 10,31:1
Bucher, J C, 1937, Jl 6,19:3
Bucher, John C, 1945, Mr 28,23:3
Bucher, Joseph A, 1962, N 8,39:2
Bucher, Paul, 1925, Jl 16,9:3
Bucher, Robert L, 1952, S 16,29:3
Bucher, Walter H, 1965, F 19,36:1
Bucher, William K Mrs, 1950, O 21,17:6
Bucher, William W, 1950, O 5,32:2
Buchhaltz, Henry A, 1945, F 11,40:2
Buchholtz, Arthur F, 1940, Ap 4,23:6
Buchholtz, Jacob, 1966, Ag 20,25:5
Buchholtz, Louis, 1941, Jl 1,23:1
Buchholz, Charles W, 1912, O 21,11:5
Buchignani, Emile C, 1944, S 22,19:5
Buchignani, Emile C Mrs, 1959, D 16,41:4
Buchland, Thomas, 1947, Je 13,23:4
Buchler, Adolph, 1939, F 20,17:4
Buchman, Alexander M, 1947, Jl 24,21:6
Buchman, Edward H, 1945, Jl 29,40:3
Buchman, Frank N D (mem ser, Ag 12,17:1; funl, Ag 19,17:5), 1961, Ag 9,1:1
Buchman, George A Mrs, 1957, O 12,19:3
Buchman, Harry, 1952, Mr 18,27:3
Buchman, Harry G, 1951, S 5,31:5
Buchman, Irving, 1956, Mr 1,33:2
Buchman, Joseph H, 1939, Ja 9,15:2
Buchman, Judah L, 1957, D 9,35:4
Buchman, Moses R, 1957, Ap 17,31:2
Buchman, Robert K, 1951, F 23,27:2
Buchmann, John O, 1965, S 8,47:1
Buchmayr, Sig, 1964, Ja 15,38:1
Buchner, Charles J Mrs, 1957, Ja 10,29:5
Buchner, Edward E, 1951, D 17,31:4
Buchner, Louis, 1937, Ap 3,19:3
Buchner, Louis B, 1945, Mr 2,19:3
Buchner, Ralph, 1952, Je 29,56:6
Bucholz, Gustav, 1925, Je 8,15:4
Bucholz, Otto, 1958, S 15,21:4
Buchsbaum, Aaron, 1918, Je 26,13:5
Buchsbaum, Abraham, 1958, Ap 25,27:1
Buchsbaum, Lawrence M, 1943, Ja 17,44:3
Buchsbaum, Max, 1941, Ap 14,17:1
Buchsbaum, Morris A, 1954, N 25,29:4
Buchsbaum, Rose Mrs, 1941, F 21,19:1
Buchtenkirch, Herman, 1940, S 15,48:3
Buchter, Morris, 1954, Mr 12,21:3
Buchwald, Bruno, 1954, Ja 27,27:4
Buchwald, Ephraim, 1965, D 31,21:4
Buchwald, Maurice G, 1951, Ja 24,27:3
Buchwald, Nathaniel, 1956, Jl 9,23:4
Buchwalter, Ira, 1950, Ja 5,25:4
Buchwalter, Mary K Mrs, 1937, O 1,21:5
Buck, A E, 1902, D 5,9:1
Buck, A Morris, 1958, Je 10,33:4
Buck, Adele, 1912, Ag 28,9:5
Buck, Adrian A Jr, 1960, Jl 4,15:3
Buck, Al (Axford C Buck), 1967, Je 24,29:2
Buck, Alan M, 1966, Ap 10,79:5
Buck, Albert, 1951, Jl 17,27:4
Buck, Albert Henry Dr, 1922, N 17,17:5
Buck, Albert W, 1944, S 13,19:4
Buck, Benjamin A, 1954, O 28,35:5
Buck, Benjamin F, 1922, F 21,17:3; 1941, Ag 6,17:6
Buck, Bradford, 1904, S 2,7:4
Buck, C Austin, 1945, Jl 14,11:7
Buck, C Douglass, 1965, Ja 29,34:1
Buck, Carl D (cor, F 12,15:4), 1955, F 10,31:3
Buck, Carl D Mrs, 1942, Ag 24,15:4
Buck, Carl E, 1953, N 23,27:3
Buck, Caroline, 1950, Ja 16,26:3
Buck, Charles B, 1948, Mr 21,60:4
Buck, Charles H Rev Dr, 1910, Ja 14,9:3
Buck, Charles T, 1958, Ap 10,29:5
Buck, Clarence E, 1944, S 3,26:5
Buck, Daniel Judge, 1905, My 22,7:5
Buck, Dudley (funl, O 10,13:4), 1909, O 7,9:4
Buck, Dudley, 1941, Ja 14,21:5
Buck, Dudley A, 1959, My 22,27:4
Buck, Edith S, 1954, Jl 18,57:2
Buck, Edward, 1948, Ap 28,28:2
Buck, Edward G, 1944, D 28,19:3
Buck, Florence Rev, 1925, O 13,23:4
Buck, Francis D Mrs, 1948, My 13,25:2
Buck, Frank, 1950, Mr 26,92:3
Buck, Frank H, 1942, S 18,21:4
Buck, Fred, 1951, Mr 22,31:1
Buck, Gene (funl, Mr 1,23:3), 1957, F 25,25:4
Buck, Gene Mrs, 1968, Je 1,27:5
Buck, George B, 1961, Ap 14,29:2
Buck, George L, 1942, F 7,17:4
Buck, George W, 1874, D 25,4:7; 1950, N 6,27:2; 1959, F 16,29:4
Buck, Gertrude, 1922, Ja 10,19:3
Buck, Glen, 1938, F 4,21:4
Buck, Grover C, 1955, Ap 7,27:6
Buck, Gurlon (see also Mr 7), 1877, Mr 9,2:4
Buck, Guy, 1949, Mr 6,72:2
Buck, H D Mrs, 1941, O 20,17:4
Buck, Harold M, 1959, D 25,21:1
Buck, Harold M Mrs, 1953, Mr 31,31:4
Buck, Harold W, 1958, Ag 7,25:6
Buck, Harry A, 1944, Ja 22,13:4
Buck, Harry C, 1943, Jl 28,15:5
Buck, Helen Mrs, 1938, Jl 20,19:4
Buck, Henry I, 1942, F 7,17:1
Buck, Howard, 1871, Mr 18,8:4; 1944, Mr 27,36:4
Buck, Howard J, 1962, Jl 4,21:4
Buck, Isaac Jr Mrs, 1963, Ag 2,27:1
Buck, J Clifton, 1952, Je 15,84:6
Buck, J James, 1960, F 25,29:4
Buck, J Mahlon, 1964, N 1,89:1
Buck, Jefferies, 1939, Ag 16,23:2
Buck, Jerome H, 1943, O 30,15:4
Buck, Johannes S, 1956, Ag 11,32:8
Buck, John Henry, 1914, F 1,5:6
Buck, John M, 1938, My 3,23:6
Buck, John R, 1917, F 7,13:6; 1967, S 9,31:4
Buck, Joseph F, 1942, S 16,23:2
Buck, Joseph W, 1955, Jl 11,23:6
Buck, Julia O T Mrs, 1940, Ja 29,15:5
Buck, Junior C Mrs, 1938, F 26,15:1
Buck, Katherine Mrs, 1940, Ja 12,17:5
Buck, Ken, 1954, S 24,24:2
Buck, Leffert Lefferts, 1909, Jl 18,9:5
Buck, Leffert Mrs, 1946, Ja 8,23:2
Buck, Louis I, 1942, Ag 6,19:4
Buck, Louis P, 1955, D 25,48:8
Buck, Norman S, 1964, Ap 12,87:1
Buck, Oscar M, 1941, F 11,23:1
Buck, Otto, 1959, Mr 27,23:3
Buck, Percy C, 1947, O 8,25:3
Buck, Peter H, 1951, D 3,31:1
Buck, Phillip E, 1947, Ja 17,23:5
Buck, Philo Dr, 1924, S 9,19:3
Buck, Philo M Jr, 1950, D 10,104:4
Buck, Philo M Jr Mrs, 1952, N 19,29:5
Buck, Raymond L, 1939, F 15,23:4
Buck, Richard H, 1956, D 12,39:4
Buck, Richard S, 1951, Ag 5,73:1
Buck, Robert J, 1941, N 17,19:5
Buck, Robert O, 1950, Ap 2,94:5
Buck, S Trainer, 1942, Ag 22,13:6
Buck, Salon J, 1962, My 28,29:2
Buck, Samuel L, 1937, My 13,25:2
Buck, Samuel M, 1949, Ag 27,13:4
Buck, Samuel P Mrs, 1951, Ja 5,21:1
Buck, Seaver B, 1950, My 16,31:3
Buck, Thomas Corner, 1904, My 29,7:4
Buck, Vincent M, 1947, Ag 10,52:6
Buck, Vincent M Mrs, 1953, My 24,89:2
Buck, W F, 1912, F 1,13:4
Buck, Walter A, 1955, Je 13,23:4
Buck, Walter F, 1918, S 9,11:4
Buck, Walter S, 1941, Ap 24,21:3
Buck, William A, 1945, O 5,23:2
Buck, Winthrop, 1947, N 7,23:3
Buckalew, Farmer W, 1948, N 19,27:4
Buckalew, John B, 1953, Ap 9,27:5
Buckard, Charles A, 1962, My 8,39:2
Buckbee, John C, 1952, Ap 30,27:5
Buckbee, Lott E, 1953, Ag 21,17:1
Buckbee, Louis R, 1961, Ap 9,86:3
Buckbee, William A, 1951, O 4,33:3
Buckbinder, Morris Rabbi, 1923, D 30,20:1
Bucke, R M Dr, 1902, F 21,9:5
Bucke, Thomas V H, 1962, Ag 13,25:5
Bucke, William H Maj, 1915, Jl 2,11:4
Buckelew, Charles W, 1966, Ja 12,21:3
Buckelew, Eva G Mrs, 1944, My 4,19:5
Buckelew, James, 1948, S 20,25:5
Buckell, Henry W, 1954, N 7,86:1
Buckell, Robert Sir, 1925, Je 24,17:4
Buckelow, Sarah F, 1907, Ap 26,9:6
Buckenham, John E Burnett (will, Ag 24,49:5), 1952, Ag 14,23:5
Buckenmyer, Frederick, 1942, Ja 11,45:2
Buckenmyer, Herbert T, 1958, N 5,39:2
Buckerridge, Guy L, 1944, Jl 17,15:4
Buckey, Mervin C, 1940, Mr 22,19:2
Buckham, Charles W, 1951, Mr 12,25:1
Buckham, Matthew H, 1910, N 30,11:4
Buckham, Robert B, 1947, Mr 25,25:3
Buckhardt, John F, 1946, Ja 5,13:1
Buckholt, Russell, 1962, F 14,33:1
Buckholy, George A, 1914, O 29,11:4
Buckholz, Frederick W, 1944, N 23,31:5
Buckholz, William F, 1955, Jl 17,60:6
Buckhout, Carrie H Mrs, 1943, Ja 16,13:3
Buckhout, Craig E, 1952, F 23,11:6
Buckhout, Edward W, 1943, My 9,40:7
Buckhout, Frank C Mrs, 1943, Ap 13,26:3
Buckhout, George N (will, S 19,17:3), 1953, S 14,27:5
Buckhout, Henry C, 1925, Ap 16,21:4
Buckhout, Lewis W, 1944, D 1,24:2
Buckhout, William H, 1950, Ap 12,28:2
Buckin, Leon, 1941, D 7,76:1
Buckingham, Arthur C, 1944, D 27,19:4
Buckingham, Charles H, 1954, S 30,31:4
Buckingham, Clarence, 1913, Ag 30,7:6
Buckingham, E H, 1877, N 29,4:7
Buckingham, G A, 1882, Ja 11,5:4
Buckingham, G Frederick, 1949, Ja 18,23:5
Buckingham, Garland A, 1951, Mr 2,26:3
Buckingham, John E, 1909, Mr 27,9:4
Buckingham, John Mrs, 1948, O 26,31:5
Buckingham, John R Capt, 1919, Ja 18,11:3
Buckingham, Joseph T, 1861, Ap 12,4:6
Buckingham, Kate S (will, D 24,15:6), 1937, D 15, 25:3
Buckingham, L E W, 1938, My 27,17:4
Buckingham, Laura A, 1937, D 10,25:2
Buckingham, Lee S, 1946, Ja 3,19:1
Buckingham, Leonard, 1953, S 5,16:4
Buckingham, Mary F Mrs, 1942, Ag 27,19:2
Buckingham, Max M, 1951, O 13,17:2
Buckingham, Merritt S, 1949, D 8,34:3
Buckingham, Norman S, 1940, D 1,62:6
Buckingham, O W, 1903, N 1,7:6
Buckingham, Roy, 1944, My 19,19:3
Buckingham, Roy Mrs, 1967, Ag 15,39:2
Buckingham, S McLean, 1965, My 17,35:1
Buckingham, Sam Mrs, 1951, Ap 19,31:3
Buckingham, Samuel L, 1958, F 4,26:5
Buckingham, Thomas L, 1939, D 17,49:1
Buckingham, W A Sen, 1875, F 5,8:3
Buckingham, Walter F, 1967, My 25,47:2
Buckingham, William c, 1940, Mr 9,32:8
Buckingham, William D, 1965, Ja 20,39:2
Buckinghamshire, Earl of (Jno H Mercer-Henderson), 1963, Ja 4,2:3
Buckinham, Richard G, 1939, Mr 12,III,7:2
Buckland, A W J, 1960, Ja 10,86:5
Buckland, Carl P, 1940, N 27,23:3
Buckland, Charles C, 1968, My 28,47:1
Buckland, Charles P, 1937, My 17,19:5
Buckland, Edward G, 1953, Mr 31,31:1
Buckland, Edward G Mrs, 1942, Ap 26,40:4
Buckland, F T, 1880, D 20,5:4
Buckland, Lord, 1928, My 24,1:2
Buckland, William H, 1939, Ap 4,25:4
Buckland, William L, 1964, N 26,33:4
Buckland, William S, 1940, My 31,19:2
Buckland, William W, 1946, Ja 17,23:5
Buckle, G E, 1935, Mr 13,20:3
Buckle, George E Mrs, 1938, F 14,17:2
Buckle, Henry Thomas, 1862, Je 20,4:5
Buckleman, George W, 1950, Mr 23,29:4
Bucklen, Harley R, 1955, Mr 13,86:7
Buckler, Albert, 1939, D 2,17:4
Buckler, Richard T, 1950, Ja 25,28:3
Buckler, Thomas H, 1940, D 29,24:8
Buckles, Doyle L, 1947, D 19,25:2
Buckles, Harold H, 1953, Je 9,27:1
Buckles, Ward M, 1947, Je 15,62:5
Buckley, Albert C, 1939, Ag 18,19:1
Buckley, Albert F, 1954, Je 27,68:4
Buckley, Albion C Mrs, 1951, Jl 10,27:3
Buckley, Aloise (Mrs B W Heath), 1967, Ja 18,43:2

Buckley, Alva A, 1944, My 16,21:2
Buckley, Anne L, 1959, Ap 19,86:2
Buckley, Arthur D, 1961, Jl 9,77:1
Buckley, B L, 1932, D 27,13:1
Buckley, Berthold E Rev, 1968, Mr 21,47:2
Buckley, C W, 1866, Ja 7,4:1
Buckley, Catherine M, 1950, My 17,29:3
Buckley, Charles A, 1944, S 15,19:2; 1955, Mr 8,27:2
Buckley, Charles A (funl plans, Ja 24,25:3; ed, Ja 24,36:2), 1967, Ja 23,1:7
Buckley, Charles B Mrs, 1948, My 26,25:5
Buckley, Charles H, 1939, D 1,23:2
Buckley, Charles H Mrs, 1945, Jl 12,11:7
Buckley, Charles Ramsay, 1918, My 5,23:1
Buckley, Charles W, 1945, Ap 7,15:5
Buckley, Chester L, 1953, O 24,15:2
Buckley, Christopher, 1944, D 22,17:5
Buckley, Christopher A, 1922, Ag 22,9:5
Buckley, Clifford H, 1963, D 25,33:4
Buckley, Cornelius A, 1947, Ja 22,23:5
Buckley, Daniel, 1916, Ap 4,13:4; 1939, My 15,17:5
Buckley, David A, 1948, Ag 27,18:4; 1952, Mr 25,27:1
Buckley, David E, 1946, F 28,23:1
Buckley, E J, 1885, Mr 28,3:4
Buckley, Edgar, 1954, N 4,31:3
Buckley, Edmond J, 1950, O 15,104:3
Buckley, Edward J, 1925, Ja 28,17:3; 1940, Ag 14,19:6
Buckley, Edward L, 1948, My 7,23:1
Buckley, Edward S Jr, 1943, N 16,23:5
Buckley, Eli J, 1961, F 7,33:5
Buckley, Ester C, 1960, Jl 17,60:8
Buckley, Eugene, 1937, Jl 1,27:5
Buckley, Floyd, 1956, N 15,35:2
Buckley, Frederick, 1907, D 18,9:5
Buckley, Frederick M, 1942, F 26,19:3
Buckley, G Swayne, 1879, Je 26,5:2
Buckley, George, 1953, Mr 25,31:6
Buckley, George A Lt Col, 1937, N 13,19:4
Buckley, George L, 1958, Jl 11,23:3
Buckley, Harold R, 1958, Je 17,29:5
Buckley, Harold S, 1941, Mr 9,40:6
Buckley, Harry D, 1955, Je 3,23:4
Buckley, Harry P, 1944, Je 28,23:4
Buckley, Henry, 1903, My 31,7:6
Buckley, Henry W, 1952, O 23,31:2
Buckley, Herbert, 1952, D 31,15:2
Buckley, James, 1921, Ja 29,11:4; 1949, Ja 25,23:5
Buckley, James J, 1939, F 28,19:4
Buckley, James Justice, 1872, O 11,8:5
Buckley, James M Mrs, 1910, Ap 25,9:4
Buckley, James M Rev Dr, 1920, F 9,9:4
Buckley, James V, 1954, Jl 31,13:3
Buckley, Jere D, 1962, Ja 24,33:2
Buckley, Jeremiah D, 1968, N 13,47:3
Buckley, Jeremiah D Mrs, 1951, Ap 25,29:2
Buckley, Jeremiah S, 1960, Ag 26,25:6
Buckley, John A, 1942, N 1,52:6; 1950, S 11,23:4
Buckley, John F Dr, 1937, Jl 22,19:6
Buckley, John G, 1952, S 16,29:2
Buckley, John J, 1944, Mr 1,19:2; 1946, Ja 29,25:3; 1947, S 14,60:3; 1966, Je 3,39:4; 1967, O 3,47:2
Buckley, John L, 1908, My 21,7:6
Buckley, John M, 1907, Ja 28,7:4
Buckley, John Matthew Dr, 1916, Je 11,21:5
Buckley, John P, 1942, My 15,19:2
Buckley, John T, 1950, Ap 26,29:6
Buckley, John Welles Dr, 1910, Ag 25,7:5
Buckley, Johnny, 1963, Ag 7,33:3
Buckley, Joseph, 1950, O 28,17:4
Buckley, Joseph C, 1963, N 9,25:3
Buckley, Joseph F, 1944, S 17,41:2
Buckley, Joseph V, 1946, Ja 4,21:2
Buckley, Joseph W Sr, 1962, Ap 18,39:3
Buckley, Julian G Mrs, 1944, D 24,26:3
Buckley, Leo, 1956, Je 11,31:4
Buckley, Lucius C, 1949, Ja 22,13:2
Buckley, M J, 1960, My 11,39:4
Buckley, Margaret, 1922, Jl 10,13:4
Buckley, Mary M G Mrs, 1940, Ja 15,15:3
Buckley, Michael, 1941, O 11,17:1
Buckley, Michael F Mrs, 1944, Ap 2,39:1
Buckley, Michael H, 1948, D 3,25:3
Buckley, Michael J, 1951, D 26,25:4
Buckley, Minnie A, 1951, Jl 20,21:5
Buckley, Nora C, 1946, Ag 19,25:3
Buckley, Oliver E, 1959, D 15,39:1
Buckley, Patrick E, 1947, Ag 25,17:4
Buckley, Paul O, 1967, N 25,39:4
Buckley, Peter E, 1946, D 29,35:7
Buckley, Peter J Sr Mrs, 1945, Je 27,19:4
Buckley, Phil F, 1955, F 27,87:1
Buckley, Ralph L, 1953, My 17,89:2
Buckley, Reuben N, 1943, S 28,25:5
Buckley, Richard C, 1964, Mr 20,33:5
Buckley, Richard F Dr, 1968, Ag 15,37:2
Buckley, Richard M Lord, 1960, N 13,86:1
Buckley, Richard W, 1910, Ap 22,9:5
Buckley, Robert (Jamaica Kid), 1938, Je 17,28:5
Buckley, Robert E, 1942, Jl 26,31:1
Buckley, Samuel S, 1953, Ag 23,89:1
Buckley, Sarah C, 1942, N 25,23:5
Buckley, T C T, 1874, Jl 14,4:7
Buckley, Thomas, 1941, Jl 25,15:5
Buckley, Thomas C T, 1962, N 4,88:5
Buckley, Thomas J, 1949, Jl 4,13:4; 1964, S 10,35:1
Buckley, Thomas J Mrs, 1943, D 26,32:2
Buckley, Ulick O, 1951, N 18,91:3
Buckley, Wickliffe S, 1938, O 5,23:2
Buckley, William, 1947, D 29,2:4
Buckley, William A, 1942, My 4,19:4; 1953, Mr 24, 42:3
Buckley, William D, 1942, Je 23,19:4
Buckley, William F, 1958, O 6,31:1
Buckley, William H, 1952, My 2,25:3
Buckley, William H Mrs (Kathleen McShane), 1952, Mr 21,24:3
Buckley, William J, 1956, Ag 27,19:6; 1968, Mr 4,37:3
Buckley, William N Mrs, 1950, Ag 28,17:6
Buckley, William R, 1947, D 5,25:4
Bucklin, Charles Aubrey Dr, 1919, F 15,11:5
Bucklin, E C, 1934, Ap 4,21:3
Bucklin, Frank H, 1945, Je 24,21:1
Bucklin, Harris H, 1954, Ap 5,25:4
Bucklin, Harry M, 1964, Je 18,35:3
Bucklin, Walter S, 1965, Ap 24,29:4
Bucklyn, J M K Dr, 1925, S 17,23:4
Buckman, Allan R, 1944, Je 13,19:5
Buckman, Charles L Jr, 1952, Je 24,29:3
Buckman, Clarence J, 1943, F 19,19:5
Buckman, David Lear, 1916, O 27,9:5
Buckman, Frank R Mrs, 1953, Mr 17,29:3
Buckman, Frederick W, 1961, My 30,17:4
Buckman, J, 1884, N 27,5:4
Buckman, J Hibbs, 1950, D 14,35:5
Buckman, Margaret P Dr, 1904, Ja 8,7:5
Buckman, Rosina, 1949, Ja 1,11:8
Buckman, Rudolph, 1949, Ja 11,27:2
Buckman, Thomas E, 1945, Mr 27,19:3
Buckman, William G, 1946, Mr 30,15:2
Buckman, Zina B, 1939, My 20,15:5
Buckmaster, Leland S, 1967, Ja 4,43:3
Buckmaster, Viscount, 1934, D 5,23:6
Buckmiller, Frank C, 1951, Jl 8,60:3
Buckminster, Harold C, 1941, S 28,49:4
Buckminster, Rollin, 1947, My 5,23:5
Buckminster, William R, 1939, O 15,49:2
Bucknall, G Stafford, 1943, F 18,23:1; 1967, Jl 6,35:2
Bucknall, Henry W J, 1942, Je 25,23:5
Bucknam, Clifford, 1950, Ja 8,77:1
Bucknam, Clifford Mrs, 1952, F 13,29:2
Bucknam, Marjorie M, 1952, Je 25,29:4
Bucknell, Howard Mrs, 1949, D 5,23:1
Bucknell, Philip H, 1962, D 4,41:3
Buckner, Albert G, 1941, F 19,21:4
Buckner, Edmund G Col, 1920, Ag 5,7:5
Buckner, Edmund G Mrs, 1947, Jl 29,22:3
Buckner, Emory R (will, Mr 23,40:2), 1941, Mr 12, 21:1
Buckner, Marion H, 1950, F 10,23:2
Buckner, Matthew G, 1945, Ap 11,23:5
Buckner, Mortimer N (will, Mr 13,27:6), 1942, F 26, 19:1
Buckner, Robert L (cor, Ja 27,23:3), 1961, Ja 26,29:2
Buckner, Samuel O, 1945, N 11,42:4
Buckner, Thomas A (will, Ag 28,16:2), 1942, Ag 9, 43:1
Buckner, Thomas A Mrs, 1962, Ap 22,80:7
Buckner, Thomas E, 1956, My 6,86:6
Buckner, Walker (por), 1939, N 13,19:3
Buckner, Walter Mrs, 1953, Ja 5,21:1
Buckner, William A, 1956, Ag 21,29:2
Buckner, William D, 1938, Ag 28,32:8
Buckner, William P (trb, Ag 28,24:5), 1961, Ag 18, 22:1
Bucko, Michael Mrs, 1951, O 10,23:5
Buckout, George E, 1948, Je 18,24:2
Buckout, I C, 1874, S 29,5:2
Buckpitt, Frederick W, 1943, Je 21,17:3
Buckridge, Alfred O, 1939, Ag 26,15:5
Buckridge, Charles D, 1946, N 29,25:2
Buckridge, Thomas A, 1955, Ag 4,25:6
Buckser, Fredel, 1942, O 12,17:5
Buckson, Joseph A, 1947, F 11,27:1
Buckstein, Jacob, 1962, S 20,33:3
Buckstone, J B, 1879, N 1,2:3
Buckstone, Rowland, 1922, S 15,19:5
Buckvar, Oscar, 1954, My 11,29:5
Buckwalter, Brinton, 1949, Ap 12,29:3
Buckwalter, Clarence C, 1951, Jl 6,23:3
Buckwalter, Tracy V, 1948, Mr 16,27:1
Buckx, J M H, 1946, S 24,30:2
Bucky, Jacob D, 1923, Jl 27,13:6
Bucky, Milton G, 1951, D 12,37:2
Bucky, Phil B, 1957, Ag 10,15:6
Bucove, Maurice, 1959, Ag 18,29:3
Bucquet, Harold S, 1946, F 15,26:2
Buda, Alfred M, 1951, Je 5,33:4
Buda, Alfred M Mrs, 1951, Je 5,33:4
Buda, Joseph, 1962, N 20,35:4
Buda, Joseph W, 1951, D 20,31:2
Buda, Marcus, 1950, N 4,17:2
Budahn, Louis A, 1955, My 3,31:5
Budd, Alfred M Mrs, 1952, D 4,35:5
Budd, Beekman, 1962, Ap 24,37:3
Budd, Bern Mrs, 1952, S 3,30:3
Budd, Clarence A, 1953, Je 10,29:3
Budd, Denison M, 1944, N 30,23:3
Budd, Eckard P, 1912, Je 3,9:5
Budd, Edward G, 1946, D 2,25:1
Budd, Edward G Mrs, 1956, My 3,31:5
Budd, Edward G 3d, 1940, N 14,23:5
Budd, Enos Goble Maj, 1907, F 14,9:6
Budd, Frank, 1916, Mr 1,11:5
Budd, Fred D, 1949, Ap 14,25:5
Budd, Frederick W (will, N 16,37:2), 1941, N 7,23:2
Budd, George A, 1942, My 2,13:4
Budd, Harriet, 1943, Ap 1,23:5
Budd, Harry W, 1947, N 2,73:1
Budd, Henry G, 1942, Ag 11,19:4
Budd, Horace, 1940, Ag 14,19:2
Budd, Joseph, 1962, O 23,37:4
Budd, Kenneth P, 1949, Je 27,16:2
Budd, Leon A, 1953, Ag 29,17:4
Budd, Leslie J, 1944, My 29,15:5
Budd, Louis W, 1948, F 19,23:5
Budd, Margaret Hardenbergh, 1905, My 2,11:6
Budd, Mary M Mrs, 1952, N 27,31:4
Budd, Meritt L, 1952, D 31,15:3
Budd, Ogden D, 1938, My 5,23:4
Budd, Ogden D Mrs, 1944, F 2,21:4
Budd, Ralph, 1962, F 3,21:3
Budd, Ralph W, 1959, Jl 15,29:2
Budd, Reynolds, 1908, F 9,11:5
Budd, Samuel, 1912, Jl 18,9:5
Budd, T Earl Mrs, 1943, Mr 19,19:3
Budd, T Earle Dr, 1912, S 14,13:6
Budd, W A, 1871, Mr 1,5:4
Budd, William, 1880, Ja 10,5:4; 1941, Mr 26,23:2; 1944, S 11,17:6; 1953, Jl 7,27:5
Budd, William Hardenburgh, 1912, Je 2,II,13:5
Budd, William J Sr, 1937, Ap 5,19:3
Budde, Albert Orlando, 1924, My 28,23:4
Budde, Arnold Mrs, 1951, Ag 7,25:4
Budde, Frances M Mrs, 1946, Ap 9,27:3
Budde, H F, 1951, Ag 28,23:6
Budde, John N, 1954, Ag 6,17:3
Buddeberg, Charles A Mrs, 1950, N 25,13:3
Buddeberg, Katherine S, 1944, Jl 26,19:4
Buddenbrock, Theodor, 1959, Ja 19,27:5
Buddensiek, Charles, 1901, D 25,5:1
Buddish, Barnett, 1961, Jl 20,27:1
Buddle, Charles D Mrs, 1953, Ja 24,15:5
Budds, Harold H, 1954, F 20,17:5
Buddy, Edward C, 1953, Jl 30,23:4
Buddy, Lewis 3d, 1941, Mr 15,17:5
Buddy, Robert S, 1957, S 30,31:3
Budell, Alfred E, 1967, Mr 16,47:1
Budell, Beatrix, 1967, Ap 27,45:2
Budelman, Abner G, 1955, Je 1,33:2
Budelman, Edward, 1940, S 14,17:6
Budelman, Frederick T, 1954, Mr 14,88:5
Budennaya, Nadezhda, 1925, D 10,25:5
Buder, Frederick L, 1956, Ap 18,31:2
Buder, Gustavus A, 1954, Ap 15,29:3
Buderman, Joseph V, 1945, S 29,15:1
Budge, John, 1945, F 1,23:3
Budge, Norman D, 1958, My 15,29:4
Budge, Ross A, 1950, O 5,31:4
Budil, Frederick, 1948, Jl 27,25:5
Budinger, John, 1951, S 21,23:3
Budinger, John M, 1966, Ag 26,33:4
Budington, Ernest G, 1948, F 18,28:3
Budington, Robert A, 1954, O 26,27:4
Budington, W I Rev Dr, 1879, N 30,7:3
Budington, William G Dr, 1917, Ap 17,11:6
Budisavljevic, Srdjan, 1968, F 21,47:2
Budish, Jacob M, 1966, Je 7,47:1
Budlong, C Montgomery, 1948, D 20,25:5
Budlong, Clarence R, 1946, Ja 26,13:2
Budlong, Edwin C, 1946, Je 20,23:3
Budlong, Frederick G, 1953, S 26,17:3
Budlong, Frederick Mrs, 1946, Je 13,27:3
Budlong, George M, 1945, Mr 22,23:4
Budlong, Lester G, 1946, Ja 8,23:3
Budlong, Milton J (est inventory, D 9,37:5), 194 Jl 7,15:2
Budlong, Theodore W, 1963, Je 2,84:7
Budlong, Ware T, 1967, N 15,47:4
Budnar, George, 1946, Je 15,21:2
Budner, Erwin M, 1958, My 25,86:5
Budner, Philip, 1960, Je 29,33:5
Budney, Clifford, 1952, Ja 10,29:4
Budnitz, Emil, 1944, Ja 14,19:5
Budreau, Alfred Jr, 1948, My 2,77:1
Budrecki, Anthony Mrs, 1953, Ap 11,17:5
Budrecki, Michael C, 1955, My 27,23:3
Budritzki, Gen, 1876, F 17,5:2
Budrock, John, 1951, F 6,27:2
Budrow, Joseph, 1947, D 16,33:1
Budrys, Jonas, 1964, S 3,29:2
Budtz, Bertel K W, 1948, D 18,19:5
Budwig, Ira, 1951, Jl 6,23:5
Budworth, William S, 1938, F 9,19:4; 1952, D 5,
Budziak, John F, 1956, Jl 17,23:4
Budzinski, Stanislaw, 1948, Ap 15,25:4
Bueb, Ivor, 1959, Ag 2,V,14:7
Bueb, John J, 1937, Jl 1,27:4
Buebendorf, Francis X, 1961, Ja 15,86:2
Buebning, Henry, 1946, Ap 12,27:1

Bueche, Harry S, 1957, Ja 29,31:2
Buechel, J F Marvin, 1958, F 25,27:3
Buechler, Aug F, 1948, O 2,15:6
Buechler, Richard K, 1968, O 16,47:2
Buechner, Charles C, 1952, My 23,21:4
Buechner, Frederick L, 1951, Ja 16,29:1
Buechner, George C, 1938, O 26,23:2
Buechner, W H, 1949, Ap 20,27:2
Bueck, Henry Axel, 1916, Jl 7,11:5
Bueffel, Bernard H Mrs, 1950, My 31,29:5
Buegeleisen, Samuel, 1957, F 16,17:5
Buehl, Luigi H, 1950, Je 23,25:4
Buehler, Alice L Mrs, 1940, N 30,17:2
Buehler, Arthur G Mrs, 1961, F 23,27:3
Buehler, Frank S, 1957, My 19,88:4
Buehler, Herman O, 1950, N 28,31:4
Buehler, Huber G Dr, 1924, Je 21,13:5
Buehler, Joseph Jr, 1938, Je 8,23:1
Buehler, Louis C, 1959, D 13,86:4
Buehler, Richard H, 1962, Mr 14,28:2
Buehler, William E, 1938, S 20,23:4
Buehler, William George Rear-Adm, 1919, Ag 11,11:4
Buehrle, Emil G, 1956, N 29,35:3
Buek, Hannah L V Mrs, 1941, F 14,17:4
Buel, Arthur, 1952, N 12,27:4
Buel, C C, 1933, My 23,19:3
Buel, Conrad M, 1939, Ap 30,45:2
Buel, David H Rev, 1923, My 24,19:6
Buel, Emott D, 1948, Ja 31,19:3
Buel, Hillhouse M, 1939, O 18,25:1
Buel, Horace E, 1938, F 25,17:4
Buel, John L Dr, 1937, S 2,21:3
Buel, John L Mrs, 1943, N 3,25:6
Buel, Keenan, 1948, N 6,13:3
Buel, Martin V T Mrs, 1940, Ja 20,15:1
Buel, Walker S, 1957, My 24,26:1
Buell, Aug C Col, 1904, My 24,9:6
Buell, Bradley Mrs, 1960, Mr 19,21:6
Buell, Byron W, 1875, My 16,6:7
Buell, C E, 1903, Je 28,7:5
Buell, Charles C, 1964, Je 15,29:4
Buell, Charles Mrs, 1942, O 10,15:1
Buell, Dai, 1939, Jl 10,19:2
Buell, Don C, 1945, Ap 6,16:2; 1957, My 5,89:1
Buell, Edith M, 1951, Ag 3,21:2
Buell, Ely, 1944, O 12,27:2
Buell, Fisher A, 1956, Ag 2,25:3
Buell, Francis W, 1942, Ag 13,19:3
Buell, G P, 1883, Je 1,5:2
Buell, George J E, 1956, Mr 2,23:3
Buell, Ira W, 1906, Ja 16,11:5
Buell, Irwin A, 1950, My 2,30:3
Buell, James, 1881, Ap 5,5:2
Buell, John J, 1940, O 29,25:4
Buell, Joseph Mrs, 1950, Ja 10,29:2
Buell, Lucy B, 1939, S 28,25:6
Buell, M D, 1933, N 25,15:5
Buell, Martin, 1882, Jl 14,5:3
Buell, Mary R Mrs, 1960, F 24,37:2
Buell, Nina G Mrs, 1947, D 31,15:3
Buell, Oliver P Gen, 1925, O 15,23:5
Buell, R M, 1883, Jl 2,5:1
Buell, Ralph P, 1946, My 19,42:2
Buell, Ralph P Mrs, 1949, Mr 8,25:3
Buell, Raymond L, 1946, F 21,21:1
Buell, Richard A Jr Mrs, 1968, D 16,47:6
Buell, Richard S, 1967, Ap 24,33:2
Buell, Robert C, 1953, F 1,88:1
Buell, Robert L, 1966, Jl 6,42:4
Buell, Theodore E, 1959, Ja 25,92:7
Buell, Walter H, 1944, D 1,23:3
Buell, William H, 1950, D 25,19:4
Buelow, Alfred E, 1944, Jl 15,13:3
Buelow, Alfred von, 1916, Je 27,11:7
Buelow, B von Prince, 1929, O 29,31:1
Buelow, B W von, 1936, Je 22,19:1
Buelow, Blandine von Mrs, 1941, D 19,25:2
Buelow, Charles J, 1951, My 7,25:4
Buelow, Karl W P von Marshal, 1921, S 1,15:2
Buemming, Herman W, 1947, Ap 18,21:3
Buen, Demofilo de, 1946, Je 25,21:4
Buenahora, Victor M, 1948, Jl 7,23:2
Buenger, Wilhelm Justice, 1937, Mr 22,23:5
Buening, Frank H, 1950, Ap 25,31:3
Bueno, Jose R de la T, 1948, My 4,25:2
Bueno, Lucillo A C, 1938, Mr 12,17:4
Buensod, Alfred C, 1957, N 26,30:3
Buensod, Henry S, 1949, Ja 5,25:4
Buensod, Henry S Mrs, 1943, Je 5,15:2
Buenz, Karl, 1918, S 16,11:6
Buenzle, Fred J, 1946, Je 28,22:3
Buerckel, Joseph, 1944, S 30,13:4
Buergel, Bruno, 1948, Jl 10,15:2
Buerger, Charles R, 1939, Ja 4,21:5
Buerger, Kurt, 1951, Jl 30,8:4
Buerger, Leo, 1943, O 7,23:2
Buerk, Charles A, 1952, N 14,23:3
Buerk, Charles A (est tax appr), 1954, S 25,11:4
Buerket, George S, 1960, S 5,15:2
Buermann, August Jr, 1961, S 14,31:1
Buermann, Robert, 1962, Ap 30,27:4
Buermeyer, Henry, 1922, O 11,19:5
Buermeyer, Herbert Arthur Lt, 1918, Jl 14,21:1
Buero, Juan A, 1950, Je 6,30:2
Bues, Artie, 1954, N 8,21:2
Bueschel, William H Mrs, 1967, Je 15,47:2
Buescher, Ferdinand A, 1937, N 30,23:5
Buesing, Hans C P, 1941, Jl 21,15:4
Bueso, Facundo, 1960, Ja 25,7:4
Buesser, Frank Sr Lt, 1937, Ja 13,24:3
Buesser, Frederick G, 1950, Jl 3,15:2
Buesser, Harry, 1959, O 3,19:7
Buesser, Harry Mrs, 1943, Mr 8,15:5
Buetlmann, William F, 1958, Ap 18,23:1
Buettner, J H Mrs, 1938, O 18,25:3
Buettner, Julius, 1941, F 2,45:2
Buettner, William O, 1953, S 7,19:5
Bufano, Remo Mrs, 1954, F 27,13:2
Buff, Johnny, 1955, Ja 18,27:2
Buff, Louis F, 1941, Ag 30,13:4
Buff, William J Jr, 1966, N 12,29:1
Buffa, Paul L, 1951, Mr 3,13:5
Buffalo, Julius S, 1938, Mr 19,15:3
Buffett, Howard, 1964, Ap 30,35:2
Buffey, Ralph H, 1961, Ap 29,23:5
Buffin, Menneth M Mrs, 1953, Je 12,15:4
Buffington, Abraham P, 1942, S 3,19:2
Buffington, Adelbert R, 1922, Jl 11,15:3
Buffington, Angie A G Mrs, 1954, Je 6,86:6
Buffington, Arthur H, 1945, Je 7,19:6
Buffington, Eugene J, 1937, D 10,25:1
Buffington, Everett F, 1947, D 29,18:3
Buffington, Frank H, 1948, My 22,15:4
Buffington, George, 1961, Je 18,88:5
Buffington, Harold S R, 1964, Ag 27,33:5
Buffington, James Sr, 1954, Ja 3,89:1
Buffington, John, 1875, Mr 8,4:7
Buffington, Joseph, 1947, O 22,30:2
Buffington, Richard L, 1939, N 13,19:6
Buffington, Walter J Mrs, 1946, My 6,21:5
Buffington, William E, 1938, My 28,15:6
Buffler, Louis, 1963, Jl 21,64:8
Buffoni, Francesco, 1951, F 2,23:1
Buffum, Charles A, 1941, Jl 20,31:3
Buffum, Charles A Mrs, 1956, Je 18,25:5
Buffum, Charles T Dr, 1914, Jl 30,9:6
Buffum, Douglas L, 1961, Mr 23,33:4
Buffum, E G, 1867, D 27,1:2
Buffum, Harry, 1968, Ap 11,45:4
Buffum, Herbert, 1939, O 11,30:2
Buffum, Vryling, 1944, Ja 29,13:1
Buffum, William H, 1909, Ap 30,9:5
Buffum, William W, 1940, Je 23,30:6
Buford, Charles H, 1960, Ag 19,23:3
Buford, Louis M, 1907, Je 30,7:7
Buford, Marius Bainbridge Capt, 1914, D 10,13:4
Buford, N B, 1883, Mr 30,5:4
Buford, T Col, 1885, F 14,5:2
Buford, Wallace A, 1954, My 8,2:6
Bugas, Andrew P, 1948, Ap 8,25:5
Bugatti, Ettore, 1947, Ag 22,15:2
Bugbee, Arthur G, 1953, Ag 21,17:2
Bugbee, Byron D, 1952, N 29,17:4
Bugbee, E Frank Mrs, 1949, D 25,26:4
Bugbee, Emma A J Mrs, 1939, Jl 31,13:5
Bugbee, Frank E, 1937, D 30,19:4
Bugbee, Henry G, 1945, Ja 19,19:1
Bugbee, James A, 1941, Ja 2,23:4
Bugbee, Julius W, 1955, Jl 22,23:6
Bugbee, Martha R Mrs, 1941, S 25,25:2
Bugbee, Newton A K Mrs, 1937, N 6,17:4
Bugbee, Ripley W, 1938, S 15,25:5
Bugden, Frank E, 1945, D 27,20:3
Bugden, John P, 1948, N 16,29:2
Bugei, John, 1946, Ag 13,27:4
Bugeln, George W, 1951, D 11,33:2
Bugg, Irving, 1955, Ja 29,15:3
Bugge, Jens Col, 1919, Jl 18,11:4
Bugge, Sophus Dr, 1907, Jl 9,7:6
Buggelin, Robert H, 1959, F 6,25:1
Buggeln, Herman M, 1962, Jl 20,25:5
Buggeln, Robert F, 1965, My 25,41:2
Buggeln, Robert F Mrs, 1961, O 18,43:4
Buggey, Townsend Jr, 1952, Ag 23,13:1
Bugher, Frederick H, 1924, N 26,19:3
Bugher, Frederick Mrs, 1960, N 30,37:4
Bugler, Edwin, 1948, S 13,21:2
Bugler, Patrick J, 1945, O 29,19:2
Bugli, Charles A, 1947, My 26,21:2
Buglione, Andrew T, 1966, Ap 27,47:1
Bugnano, Marquis of, 1940, Jl 6,15:2
Bugniazet, Gustave E Mrs, 1953, F 12,28:5
Buhalo, John H, 1950, F 26,79:3
Buhay, Beckie, 1953, D 18,29:1
Buhay, Michael, 1947, Ag 11,23:5
Buhl, Albert K, 1941, D 6,17:5
Buhl, Louise Z Mrs, 1940, Je 11,25:2
Buhl, Theodore D, 1907, Ap 8,9:6
Buhl, Theodore De L Mrs (A Reilly), 1961, D 29, 23:2
Buhler, Augustus, 1920, Ap 22,11:4
Buhler, E Aug, 1940, Ja 2,19:1
Buhler, Edward E Mrs, 1951, Je 17,86:4
Buhler, Eugene, 1958, Je 8,88:8
Buhler, John, 1917, Jl 18,9:5
Buhler, Joseph S, 1961, My 19,32:4
Buhler, Louis L, 1965, Ag 6,27:3
Buhler, Ulysse, 1949, Jl 21,26:2
Buhlig, Richard, 1952, F 1,22:2
Buhr, Arthur H, 1959, Mr 16,31:5
Buhr, Joseph C Sr, 1952, Ja 6,92:2
Buhr, Victor W, 1966, O 9,87:1
Buhre, Alma (funl, O 14,13:3), 1920, O 11,16:4
Buhrendorf, John C, 1961, F 23,27:2
Buhrer, Carl R, 1941, N 29,17:5
Buhrer, John S Mrs, 1938, F 7,15:1
Buhrman, Andrew J Jr Mrs, 1957, N 18,31:4
Buhrman, Arthur, 1965, O 23,31:4
Buhrman, Parker W, 1955, Je 2,29:5
Buhrmaster, Ernest G, 1956, N 22,33:2
Buhrmaster, John H, 1952, Je 24,29:3
Buhrmeister, Aug, 1950, Ja 2,23:4
Buhrmeister, Aug Mrs, 1939, S 25,20:1
Buick, James M, 1941, Jl 27,30:3
Buick, Thomas L, 1938, F 22,21:3
Buigas de Dalmau, Diego, 1960, F 26,27:4
Buines, Francisco, 1924, S 23,23:2
Buissert, Auguste, 1965, Ap 16,29:3
Buisson, Joseph C, 1954, Jl 3,11:4
Buist, George L, 1951, D 30,24:2
Buiton, Wallace Mrs, 1943, Jl 21,15:3
Buitoni, Francesco Mrs, 1949, S 23,23:4
Buivid, Michel, 1962, Je 23,23:3
Buividas, Stephen I, 1962, S 3,15:4
Bujac, Roberts M, 1963, O 31,33:3
Bukantz, Barnett, 1957, S 5,29:2
Bukaski, Burchardt, 1942, Je 9,23:4
Bukata, Walter, 1963, Ag 22,27:4
Bukeley, Rudolph, 1949, F 4,23:4
Buker, Fred M, 1950, Ja 12,27:3
Buker, Henry, 1941, O 1,21:6
Buker, Richard, 1939, Ag 16,23:2
Bukofzer, Manfred, 1955, D 8,37:5
Bukowski, Edward B, 1959, F 22,89:2
Bukowski, John J Mrs, 1940, Ag 3,15:6
Bukowski, Peter I, 1956, Jl 8,64:5
Bukshtynovich, Mikhail, 1950, Jl 1,15:2
Bulach, Zorn von Baron, 1921, Ap 21,13:4
Buland, Harvey A, 1966, Ja 22,29:2
Bulcock, Thomas, 1948, Mr 13,15:5
Buley, R Carlyle Dr, 1968, Ap 26,43:1
Buley, Victor E Mrs, 1950, Mr 9,30:2
Bulfin, Edward S Sir, 1939, Ag 22,19:2
Bulfin, Thomas W, 1941, Ag 4,13:2
Bulfinch, George G, 1944, Mr 17,17:3
Bulfinch, Thomas, 1867, My 31,2:2
Bulford, Marguerite Mrs, 1941, Mr 13,21:2
Bulford, Murray N, 1939, O 23,19:3
Bulgakoff, Sergius, 1944, S 13,19:5
Bulgakov, Leo, 1948, Jl 21,23:3
Bulgakov, Mikhail A, 1940, Mr 11,15:4
Bulgaris, D, 1878, Ja 12,4:6
Bulger, B, 1932, My 23,15:1
Bulger, Craig D Mrs, 1955, S 19,25:2
Bulger, Edward H, 1968, D 23,39:2
Bulger, Hugh, 1945, Je 10,32:3
Bulger, James E, 1963, Ap 23,37:3
Bulger, James J, 1967, Ja 5,37:3
Bulger, Joseph I, 1966, D 4,79:5
Bulger, Niel J, 1961, S 10,86:2
Bulger, Thomas H, 1944, F 17,19:1
Bulk, Jac, 1960, Jl 14,27:4
Bulkeley, Charles C, 1938, My 7,15:2
Bulkeley, Fannie B H Mrs (will, D 2,15:6), 1938, Je 23,21:3
Bulkeley, Harry C, 1948, N 4,30:3
Bulkeley, Howard S, 1943, Ja 20,19:3
Bulkeley, John C Mrs, 1949, Mr 11,25:4
Bulkeley, M G Jr, 1926, Mr 23,27:3
Bulkeley, Morgan Gardner (funl, N 8,15:4), 1922, N 7,17:4
Bulkeley, Robert T, 1950, Ap 24,25:3
Bulkeley, W H, 1902, N 8,9:5
Bulkeley, William E, 1950, Ap 2,95:3
Bulkeley, William T, 1943, F 26,19:4
Bulkley, C W Mrs, 1938, O 3,15:4
Bulkley, C Walter, 1946, Je 15,21:2
Bulkley, Charles G, 1954, Je 28,19:5
Bulkley, Charles S, 1960, O 24,29:6
Bulkley, Duncan, 1942, Ja 18,44:2
Bulkley, Edward, 1881, Jl 10,7:2
Bulkley, Edwin A Rev Dr, 1907, Mr 26,9:5
Bulkley, Edwin M (por), 1949, Je 21,25:1
Bulkley, Edwin M Mrs, 1954, D 29,29:1
Bulkley, Erasmus Walbridge, 1923, D 14,21:5
Bulkley, Everett S Sr, 1961, D 23,23:2
Bulkley, Frank, 1924, Mr 12,19:5
Bulkley, George G, 1940, Je 30,33:2
Bulkley, Harry C, 1943, F 19,19:4
Bulkley, Henry D, 1872, Ja 8,2:4
Bulkley, Henry Deming Maj, 1909, N 26,9:5
Bulkley, Henry W, 1940, Jl 1,19:5
Bulkley, J E, 1879, N 5,5:6
Bulkley, J Nelson, 1958, F 19,27:4
Bulkley, Jonathan, 1939, O 17,25:5
Bulkley, Jonathan O, 1967, Mr 28,45:1
Bulkley, L D, 1928, Jl 21,13:5
Bulkley, Robert J, 1965, Jl 23,26:7
Bulkley, Robert J Jr, 1962, N 24,23:5

Bulkley, Sarah T, 1943, Je 22,19:2
Bulkley, Sereno B, 1943, Ap 13,25:5
Bulkley, Stanley, 1954, Jl 31,13:4
Bulkley, William H Mrs, 1947, Ja 15,25:4
Bull, Archibald H, 1920, F 14,11:3
Bull, Brennan B, 1950, O 18,33:2
Bull, C G, 1931, Je 2,29:5
Bull, C L, 1932, Mr 23,21:1
Bull, Charles C, 1939, N 1,23:2; 1940, Mr 8,21:3
Bull, Charles H, 1942, N 27,23:3
Bull, Charles M, 1953, Ja 26,19:3
Bull, Charles Stedman Dr, 1911, Ap 18,11:5
Bull, Clarence A, 1944, F 25,17:6
Bull, Clifton Banham, 1921, Mr 25,15:5
Bull, Cornelius H, 1944, Je 21,19:1
Bull, David C, 1959, Ap 20,31:2
Bull, Davis Mrs, 1944, Ap 29,15:6
Bull, Duncan O, 1950, O 3,31:3
Bull, E Llewellyn, 1939, N 9,23:4
Bull, E Llewellyn Mrs (will, Ag 17, 18:7), 1939, Jl 27,19:2
Bull, E Myron, 1953, Je 5,27:1
Bull, Ebenezer, 1952, Ag 18,17:5
Bull, Ebenezer Lt, 1918, Je 4,13:4
Bull, Edward, 1921, Jl 2,9:6
Bull, Edward S Mrs, 1949, Jl 27,23:3
Bull, Elsie O, 1951, N 4,87:1
Bull, Ernest M, 1943, O 7,23:1
Bull, Ernest M Mrs, 1946, Je 18,25:5
Bull, Frank A, 1964, Ja 5,92:6
Bull, Frank I, 1956, Ag 10,17:1
Bull, Frederic, 1948, O 2,15:5
Bull, G W, 1879, D 27,4:7
Bull, George D (por), 1939, My 28,III,6:8
Bull, George H, 1943, O 10,48:5
Bull, George S, 1955, S 28,35:3
Bull, George W Dr, 1911, Ja 2,9:5
Bull, H, 1941, O 2,25:4
Bull, Harold A, 1955, Ap 11,23:6
Bull, Harrison, 1903, Je 16,7:6
Bull, Harry S, 1946, Ja 5,13:3
Bull, Henry, 1912, Ap 18,13:2
Bull, Henry A, 1951, N 18,90:2
Bull, Henry A Jr, 1954, D 12,76:3
Bull, Henry A Mrs, 1953, Ja 31,15:1
Bull, Henry W, 1958, Ag 8,17:4
Bull, Horace P, 1945, S 29,15:2
Bull, I M, 1884, S 10,5:6
Bull, Irving, 1952, O 24,23:1
Bull, J Edgar, 1923, O 3,15:3
Bull, Jerome C, 1952, N 18,31:3
Bull, Johan, 1945, S 14,23:1
Bull, John, 1875, Ap 27,1:6; 1947, D 19,25:3
Bull, John S, 1938, O 26,23:4
Bull, La Verne Mrs, 1939, Je 27,23:7
Bull, Lorenzo, 1905, N 3,9:5
Bull, Ludlow, 1954, Jl 2,19:3
Bull, Mary A, 1908, D 3,9:4
Bull, Melville (will, Jl 12,7:5), 1909, Jl 6,7:7
Bull, O B, 1880, Ag 19,5:5
Bull, Ole Mrs, 1911, Ja 19,9:4
Bull, Rene, 1942, Mr 21,17:5
Bull, Rich S, 1939, My 20,15:4
Bull, Robert F Mrs, 1955, N 19,19:2
Bull, Robert G, 1939, D 8,25:3
Bull, Robert H 2d, 1956, D 2,87:2
Bull, Robert Maclay, 1914, N 7,11:5
Bull, Samuel S, 1951, O 28,85:1
Bull, Stephen D Mrs, 1949, O 13,27:5
Bull, Storm Prof, 1907, N 19,9:5
Bull, Theodore, 1958, Ap 21,23:5
Bull, Theodore H Mrs, 1960, N 1,40:1
Bull, Thomas, 1962, Ap 17,35:1
Bull, W Sir, 1931, Ja 24,17:5
Bull, Wellington E, 1947, Ja 31,23:4
Bull, Wellington E Mrs, 1945, My 26,15:5
Bull, Willard E Mrs, 1957, Ap 11,31:1
Bull, William, 1903, My 21,1:1
Bull, William J, 1963, Je 15,23:4
Bull, William L (funl), 1914, Ja 5,9:6
Bull, William P, 1948, Jl 1,23:4
Bull, William R, 1937, Ap 14,25:1; 1943, N 6,13:6
Bull, William S Gen, 1910, D 19,9:4
Bull, William T Mrs (funl, F 12,12:2), 1911, F 8,9:5
Bull, William Tillinghast Dr (trb, F 25,7:4), 1909, F 23,9:1
Bullard, A, 1929, S 11,27:5
Bullard, Addison E, 1938, D 10,17:5
Bullard, Albert M, 1908, S 24,9:4
Bullard, Albert M Mrs, 1950, D 19,42:2
Bullard, Albert W, 1952, Mr 17,21:2
Bullard, Donald A Mrs, 1958, Je 29,69:2
Bullard, Dudley B, 1941, Je 11,21:4
Bullard, E J, 1950, Mr 5,92:3
Bullard, Edward A, 1967, N 19,85:1
Bullard, Edward F, 1944, Ja 24,17:5
Bullard, Edward P, 1953, Je 27,15:6
Bullard, Eugene J, 1961, O 14,23:2
Bullard, Frederick L, 1952, Ag 4,15:2
Bullard, George C, 1966, Ap 16,33:4
Bullard, Harold C, 1949, Je 29,27:3
Bullard, Harold F, 1951, Ap 18,31:5
Bullard, Harry N, 1947, Ja 4,15:5
Bullard, Harry Sir, 1903, D 27,4:1
Bullard, Herbert S, 1945, Je 29,15:4
Bullard, Howard B Mrs, 1956, F 28,31:1
Bullard, Howard O, 1942, Jl 28,17:5
Bullard, John E, 1956, Ap 6,26:2
Bullard, John T Mrs, 1949, Mr 17,25:2
Bullard, Joseph W C Sr, 1956, S 18,35:4
Bullard, Lewis E, 1950, N 22,25:3
Bullard, Percy, 1941, O 29,24:2
Bullard, Ralph H, 1961, N 4,19:3
Bullard, Ralph Mrs, 1950, Jl 25,27:5
Bullard, Richard D, 1943, Ap 24,13:7
Bullard, Robert L, 1947, S 12,21:1
Bullard, Robert Lee Mrs, 1921, D 13,19:3
Bullard, Tenny Fisher Mrs, 1912, Jl 23,9:5
Bullard, Thomas E, 1942, S 21,15:5
Bullard, W H G, 1927, N 25,1:2
Bullard, W Irving, 1948, Je 29,24:2
Bullard, Waldo E, 1905, Mr 31,9:6
Bullard, William Duff Dr, 1906, Je 21,7:6
Bullen, Arthur Henry, 1920, Mr 3,11:4
Bullen, Avery L, 1959, Je 26,25:6
Bullen, Dana Ripley, 1943, My 11,21:2
Bullen, Daniel, 1951, F 27,27:1
Bullen, Frank T, 1915, Mr 2,9:4
Bullen, George R, 1937, D 4,17:5
Bullen, Henry L (por), 1938, Ap 28,23:2
Bullen, Percy S, 1958, Ja 16,29:4
Bullene, Egbert F, 1958, F 23,92:3
Buller, Arthur H, 1944, Jl 5,17:6
Buller, Redvers Sir, 1908, Je 3,7:6
Buller, Walter, 1938, My 22,II,7:2
Buller-Murphy, Basel Mrs (Deborah), 1965, Ap 18, 81:1
Bullett, Alex C, 1868, Je 14,1:2
Bullett, Emma, 1914, F 1,5:5
Bullett, Gerald, 1958, Ja 5,86:6
Bullett, Jim, 1942, Jl 24,19:4
Bulley, George W Mrs, 1946, S 3,19:2
Bulley, Harriet M Mrs, 1938, Ja 15,15:4
Bulliet, C J Mrs, 1946, My 22,21:4
Bulliet, Clarence J, 1952, O 21,29:2
Bullinger, Charles E, 1952, F 9,13:2
Bullington, Orville, 1956, N 25,89:2
Bullington, Richard E, 1943, Ja 22,19:3
Bullion, A O, 1905, Ag 30,9:7
Bullion, George J, 1946, Mr 3,44:5
Bullis, Harry A, 1963, S 29,86:2
Bullis, John L Brig-Gen, 1911, My 27,13:6
Bullis, William J, 1948, O 16,15:4
Bullit, James F, 1941, Mr 28,23:3
Bullitt, A S, 1932, Ap 11,15:3
Bullitt, Cuthbert Col, 1906, Ag 5,9:6
Bullitt, James B Jr, 1957, My 9,31:4
Bullitt, Logan M, 1916, N 22,13:6; 1921, Ja 15,13:4; 1941, O 16,21:5
Bullitt, Logan M Mrs, 1955, My 10,29:1
Bullitt, Thomas W Col, 1910, Mr 4,9:4
Bullitt, William C (funl, F 21,44:5; will, Ag 9,36:8), 1967, F 16,1:5
Bullitt, William M (will, O 30,24:3), 1957, O 4,23:3
Bullitt, William O, 1914, Mr 23,11:4
Bullivant, Carey R Mrs, 1937, F 25,6:3
Bullivant, Fred, 1942, Je 1,13:5
Bullivant, H Clifford, 1953, Ja 16,23:2
Bullivant, Herman C Mrs, 1943, Jl 2,19:4
Bullivant, William A, 1941, S 29,17:4
Bullman, Franklin P, 1941, D 6,17:4
Bulloch, William, 1941, F 12,21:1; 1950, Ap 23,92:8
Bullock, Addie B Mrs, 1943, D 10,28:2
Bullock, Albert T, 1959, D 23,27:2
Bullock, Alexander, 1882, Ja 18,5:1
Bullock, Annie E Mrs, 1939, O 22,40:3
Bullock, Arthur R, 1946, O 6,58:8
Bullock, Arthur R Mrs, 1937, D 29,21:2
Bullock, Berry, 1959, D 14,31:4
Bullock, C W, 1867, Ap 13,4:6
Bullock, Calvin, 1944, Je 22,19:4
Bullock, Calvin Mrs, 1956, Ap 21,17:5
Bullock, Charles C, 1954, Ap 10,15:6
Bullock, Charles J, 1941, Mr 19,22:2
Bullock, Charles S, 1947, My 27,26:3
Bullock, David J Mrs, 1960, Je 30,29:2
Bullock, David M, 1953, O 23,23:3
Bullock, David N, 1955, N 13,89:2
Bullock, Earl S, 1941, My 3,15:4
Bullock, Edgar Q, 1939, F 9,21:4
Bullock, Eugene H, 1956, My 22,33:1
Bullock, F, 1940, N 10,56:4
Bullock, Frederick D Dr, 1937, Ag 17,19:6
Bullock, Frederick F Jr, 1961, Jl 3,15:1
Bullock, George W, 1929, O 11,31:5
Bullock, Georgia P, 1957, Ag 30,19:5
Bullock, Harry A Capt, 1919, Ja 20,15:4
Bullock, Horace D Mrs, 1953, D 13,86:7
Bullock, Hugh, 1958, Ag 20,27:4
Bullock, Joseph J, 1948, Mr 26,22:2
Bullock, Mary E, 1947, Ap 15,25:4
Bullock, Miss, 1874, S 28,8:2
Bullock, Morris C Mrs, 1960, My 7,23:3
Bullock, Nathaniel, 1867, N 15,1:3
Bullock, Ralph W, 1947, D 20,17:2
Bullock, Rufus Brown, 1907, Ap 28,9:5
Bullock, Seth, 1919, S 24,17:4
Bullock, Sheldon Capt, 1908, Ag 3,5:2
Bullock, Turner, 1959, Ap 28,35:2
Bullock, Walter F, 1942, My 3,52:1
Bullock, Walter R, 1949, Mr 8,26:3; 1951, S 13,31:2
Bullock, Warren B Mrs, 1952, My 7,27:6
Bullock, William Ashcom, 1917, My 10,13:5
Bullock, William O, 1946, Je 17,21:3
Bullock, Willoughby, 1950, Ap 23,92:7
Bullock, Winifred D Mrs, 1961, Ja 6,27:3
Bullock-Webster, Aubrey, 1962, Ja 11,33:3
Bullough, George Sir, 1939, Jl 27,19:2
Bullowa, Alma M, 1946, Ap 6,17:2
Bullowa, Emilie M, 1942, O 26,15:3
Bullowa, Ferdinand E M, 1919, F 22,9:4
Bullowa, Jesse G M, 1943, N 10,23:2
Bullowa, Jesse G M Mrs, 1942, Mr 24,19:4
Bullus, Albert Mrs, 1949, F 12,17:6
Bullus, Oscar Commodore, 1871, O 8,5:4
Bullwinkel, Edward J, 1948, Ag 15,60:5
Bullwinkle, George B, 1946, Je 9,40:6
Bullwinkle, Henry Dr, 1920, S 16,9:1
Bulman, William Sr, 1946, D 31,17:3
Bulmer, Alfred A, 1954, Mr 2,25:4
Bulmer, James W, 1942, Ap 21,23:3
Bulmer, Melville S, 1960, D 9,31:2
Bulmer, Roscoe C Capt, 1919, Ag 7,7:4
Bulmer, Stephen A, 1949, O 16,88:3
Bulmer, William A, 1950, N 8,29:5
Bulmer, William B, 1941, Ap 24,21:2
Bulock, Alfred C, 1947, Mr 5,25:3
Bulosan, Carlos, 1956, S 14,23:3
Bulova, Arde (funl, Mr 24,27:6), 1958, Mr 20,29:1
Bulova, Victor, 1954, Ap 27,29:3
Bulow, H Von Dr, 1894, F 14,8:1
Bulow, Harry N, 1965, Mr 18,33:3
Bulow, William J, 1960, F 27,19:4
Bulowa, Hugo, 1938, Mr 10,21:2
Bulowa, Otto, 1952, Mr 12,27:5
Buloz, F, 1877, Ja 13,5:2
Bulson, C Percival Dr, 1916, My 19,11:7
Bulson, Devillo N, 1945, Mr 23,19:2
Bulson, Edward F, 1951, S 1,11:5
Bulsonz, Charles H, 1945, Jl 20,19:6
Bulteel, John C, 1956, F 19,92:2
Bultman, Herbert F B, 1940, My 15,25:3
Bulwer, Henry Sir, 1872, My 28,1:5
Bulwinkle, Alfred L, 1950, S 1,21:3
Bulwinkle, John M, 1915, D 10,13:6
Bulziewicz, Stanislaus, 1938, S 18,44:7
Bumann, Gilbert A, 1946, Ja 29,25:5
Bumatsende, Gonchigin, 1953, S 24,33:1
Bumbaugh, George L, 1952, N 9,90:2
Bumbe, Hans, 1914, Ag 13,9:4
Bumer, Charles T, 1960, Mr 15,39:1
Bumgard, George H, 1941, Ja 15,23:5
Bumgarner, Plato, 1952, Ja 27,77:2
Bumm, Ernst Dr, 1925, Ja 4,7:1
Bump, Arthur S, 1948, D 15,34:3
Bump, Horace P, 1941, Je 12,23:3
Bump, Milan R, 1925, My 6,23:4
Bumpas, George W, 1941, O 19,47:3
Bumphrey, Hiram, 1872, F 26,5:3
Bumpus, Everett C Judge, 1920, Ap 22,11:3
Bumpus, Hermon C, 1943, Je 22,19:1
Bumstead, Albert H, 1940, Ja 10,21:6
Bumstead, Albert Mrs, 1950, Ag 31,26:2
Bumstead, Arthur I, 1958, My 22,29:6
Bumstead, Arthur I Mrs, 1942, Ap 16,21:3
Bumstead, Charles W, 1953, My 4,23:5
Bumstead, Eva R Mrs, 1937, My 12,23:2
Bumstead, F J, 1879, N 29,5:4
Bumstead, Henry A Mrs, 1952, Ag 29,23:4
Bumstead, Ralph W, 1964, Ja 9,31:1
Bumstead, William H, 1874, S 9,8:1
Bumsted, J Howard, 1946, D 1,76:5
Bumsted, Roy, 1949, N 9,28:3
Bun, D J, 1876, Ag 4,4:7
Bunau-Varilla, Jean, 1922, F 3,15:3
Bunau-Varilla, Maurice, 1944, Ag 3,19:4
Bunau-Varilla, Philippe, 1940, My 18,15:1
Bunce, Ada W Mrs, 1937, Mr 23,24:1
Bunce, Alan, 1965, Ap 28,45:3
Bunce, Arthur C, 1953, My 29,25:4
Bunce, Carleton B, 1945, N 9,20:2
Bunce, Chester B, 1957, O 29,31:2
Bunce, F M, 1901, O 20,4:1
Bunce, George W, 1967, Ja 17,39:1
Bunce, Henry C Mrs, 1943, Jl 3,13:4
Bunce, James H, 1943, Mr 29,15:2
Bunce, John Lee, 1907, O 2,11:6
Bunce, Jonathan B, 1912, Mr 7,11:4
Bunce, Richard H, 1949, My 5,27:4
Bunce, Russell, 1874, Ja 22,8:5
Bunce, S A, 1876, Mr 13,1:6; 1882, F 5,12:1
Bunce, William E, 1958, Je 20,23:5
Bunce, William J, 1950, Ag 19,13:3
Bunch, C C, 1942, Je 16,23:5
Bunch, Charles H, 1953, D 13,86:4
Bunch, Richard H Mrs, 1942, F 18,19:6
Bunchuk, Yascha, 1944, S 1,13:4
Buncke, Henry C, 1949, O 12,29:4
Bund, Henry, 1966, My 17,47:2

Bundel, Charles M, 1941, S 17,23:6
Bundesen, Herman N, 1960, Ag 26,25:1
Bundesen, Herman N (est tax acctg), 1961, D 28,9:1
Bundick, John M, 1939, Ag 21,13:5
Bundschuh, Oscar, 1967, My 24,47:4
Bundschuh, Peter C, 1952, Ag 14,23:5
Bundschuh, William I, 1962, F 18,92:3
Bundy, Bruce, 1939, Je 26,15:5
Bundy, C L, 1933, Ag 22,17:4
Bundy, George M, 1951, Ap 7,15:6
Bundy, Harvey H, 1963, O 8,43:1
Bundy, Leroy N, 1943, My 31,17:2
Bundy, Omar, 1940, Ja 21,34:4
Bundy, Omar Mrs (will), 1953, O 30,18:4
Bundy, Robert E, 1960, N 28,31:4
Bundy, Thomas C, 1945, O 14,42:4
Bundy, William, 1940, N 30,17:1
Bundy, William E, 1903, Ag 17,7:5
Bungard, Barnet, 1953, S 19,15:6
Bungard, Barnet Mrs, 1955, F 25,21:5
Bungart, Peter A, 1948, Jl 31,15:1
Bungat, Frederick, 1949, Ap 21,33:2
Bunge, Albert J, 1937, N 15,23:3
Bunge, Alejandro E, 1943, My 25,23:4
Bunge, Augusto, 1943, Ag 3,19:6
Bunge, Francisco, 1949, N 11,25:4
Bunge, William F, 1953, Mr 20,23:2
Bunger, Ferdinand N, 1958, Ag 16,17:6
Bungers, Karl Sr, 1953, F 2,21:3
Bungey, Frederick N, 1941, Ap 2,23:4
Bunim, Joseph J, 1964, Jl 9,33:2
Bunim, Milton, 1954, N 21,86:4
Bunin, Ivan, 1953, N 9,35:3
Bunis, Michael, 1948, Ag 7,15:4
Bunker, Albert Mrs, 1954, Ap 29,31:2
Bunker, Arthur E, 1955, Mr 23,31:1
Bunker, Arthur H, 1964, My 20,43:2
Bunker, Charles W O, 1958, S 18,31:1
Bunker, Dumont, 1962, N 20,35:1
Bunker, Edward A Mrs, 1923, My 25,21:5
Bunker, Ellsworth Mrs, 1964, Ap 20,29:3
Bunker, Fred R, 1946, S 7,15:5
Bunker, Fred R Mrs, 1950, O 3,31:1
Bunker, G R, 1927, Ja 6,27:5
Bunker, George H, 1951, Jl 15,60:3
Bunker, George R Mrs, 1942, Ap 14,21:3
Bunker, Harold, 1957, O 5,17:2
Bunker, Henry A, 1953, Mr 21,17:4
Bunker, Herbert H, 1951, N 19,23:2
Bunker, Homer L, 1938, Ag 23,17:4
Bunker, Horace M, 1938, Ja 10,17:3
Bunker, Mary Hinman Mrs, 1925, D 6,13:1
Bunker, Paul D, 1943, S 15,27:5
Bunker, Paul R, 1960, Ja 31,92:4
Bunker, Ralph, 1966, Ap 29,47:1
Bunker, Raymond U, 1937, Jl 8,23:2
Bunker, Robert E, 1951, Ja 27,13:2
Bunker, Sydney K Dr, 1968, S 24,47:1
Bunker, William L, 1949, F 21,23:2
Bunkley, Jeol W Mrs, 1948, My 20,29:2
Bunkley, Joel W, 1967, D 13,47:3
Bunn, Albert C, 1952, S 4,27:2
Bunn, Albert C Rev, 1912, D 26,9:5
Bunn, Alice, 1953, Ap 10,22:3
Bunn, Benton S, 1942, N 20,23:1
Bunn, Charles E, 1960, N 23,29:4
Bunn, Charles H, 1950, Je 9,23:5
Bunn, Charles W, 1941, Ja 3,20:2
Bunn, David A, 1907, Ap 23,9:4
Bunn, Frank C Dr, 1937, Ja 11,19:3
Bunn, Frank C Mrs, 1952, Je 12,34:7
Bunn, Fred L, 1944, Je 19,19:4
Bunn, George W Sr, 1938, S 16,21:2
Bunn, Howard S, 1964, Ja 13,35:2
Bunn, Isaac O, 1944, D 13,23:4
Bunn, James W (Jimmy Blaine), 1967, Mr 19,92:7
Bunn, John S, 1942, S 20,41:6
Bunn, John W, 1920, Je 8,11:2
Bunn, Mary E Mrs, 1937, D 9,25:4
Bunn, Paul V, 1938, D 9,25:5
Bunn, Walter Hodge, 1918, F 5,13:5
Bunnell, A O, 1923, D 2,23:2
Bunnell, Alfred R Sr, 1954, N 28,87:3
Bunnell, C Holmes, 1945, D 9,45:1
Bunnell, Charles E, 1956, N 3,23:5
Bunnell, Charles H Mrs, 1948, Je 20,60:8
Bunnell, Frank S, 1959, Ja 9,27:2
Bunnell, George B, 1911, My 4,11:5
Bunnell, George C, 1904, F 22,5:6
Bunnell, John A, 1940, D 10,25:5
Bunnell, John B, 1965, Mr 25,37:2
Bunnell, John B Mrs, 1949, F 22,23:1
Bunnell, Milton, 1962, Ja 26,31:3
Bunnell, Sterling, 1957, Ag 22,27:4
Bunnell, Walls W, 1965, Ap 10,29:3
Bunnell, Walter L Mrs, 1948, Ja 18,60:2
Bunnelle, Robert E Mrs, 1959, F 8,86:2
Bunner, H C, 1896, My 12,9:6
Bunny, John, 1915, Ap 27,13:5
Bunny, Rupert, 1947, My 27,25:1
Bunocore, Giuseppe, 1949, O 10,23:3
Bunoz, Emil M, 1945, Je 4,19:6
Bunsen, Christian Karl Josias von Baron, 1860, D 15, 2:3
Bunsen, Robert William Eberhard, 1899, Ag 17,7:2
Bunte, Ludwig C, 1939, Mr 5,48:6
Bunten, Clarence E, 1946, Ag 25,45:1
Bunten, George T, 1938, N 4,23:1
Bunten, William R, 1945, S 27,21:3
Buntin, Bill, 1968, My 12,84:4
Buntin, Thomas C (T D Palmer), 1966, O 5,47:3
Buntin, William C Dr, 1937, D 20,27:5
Buntin-Becker, Ann L, 1950, Ap 15,15:4
Bunting, Alice, 1964, O 11,88:6
Bunting, C A, 1901, Je 9,5:6
Bunting, Carroll M, 1920, Mr 5,13:5
Bunting, Charles H, 1961, My 30,17:4
Bunting, Clarence E, 1949, F 15,23:3
Bunting, Clifton D, 1953, Mr 20,23:3
Bunting, Florence, 1948, S 2,23:4
Bunting, Frank L Sr Mrs, 1953, Ap 21,27:1
Bunting, George A, 1960, Ja 2,13:3
Bunting, George M, 1939, Jl 8,15:1
Bunting, Guy J, 1937, D 25,15:5
Bunting, Henry, 1954, Ap 16,21:3
Bunting, Henry S, 1948, D 3,26:2
Bunting, James, 1940, Jl 16,17:2
Bunting, Josiah T Dr, 1938, Je 1,23:4
Bunting, Lloyd H Mrs, 1960, F 8,29:4
Bunting, Maxwell H, 1957, D 23,23:2
Bunting, Percy William Sir, 1911, Jl 23,9:6
Bunting, Phil D, 1940, Je 30,33:3
Bunting, Robert F, 1938, Jl 18,13:6
Bunting, Russell W, 1962, N 23,30:3
Bunting, Wesley, 1949, Ja 1,13:1
Bunting, William M Col, 1912, F 12,11:5
Buntinx, Benedict Mrs, 1953, F 11,29:2
Bunton, Isaac N Capt, 1907, Je 9,9:5
Bunyan, Edward H, 1952, D 6,21:5
Bunzi, Gustav, 1912, My 26,15:5
Bunzikofer, Fritz, 1907, O 11,9:5
Bunzl, Walter G Mrs, 1968, Ap 10,47:1
Buol, Lawrence R, 1956, My 30,21:4
Buonamici, Carlo, 1920, O 3,22:1
Buoncompagni, B, 1880, D 16,2:7
Buono, Antonio, 1953, Ja 23,20:3
Buono, Mario, 1958, Je 28,17:5
Buonora, Charles P, 1961, Ag 13,88:3
Burack, Aaron D, 1960, O 8,23:3
Burack, Harry, 1952, Ja 5,11:1
Burack, Irving, 1953, F 2,21:4
Burak, Anne, 1947, F 17,19:4
Buranelli, Prosper, 1960, Je 20,31:2
Burani, Michelette, 1957, O 28,27:1
Burant, Felix, 1964, Ag 27,33:3
Burba, George F, 1920, Ag 7,5:7
Burba, James F, 1948, Jl 7,46:1
Burbach, George M, 1959, F 22,89:1
Burbach, Louis R, 1954, Jl 20,19:5
Burbage, Paul H, 1950, Ap 1,15:5
Burbage, Paul H Mrs, 1954, Je 9,31:4
Burbank, Abram L, 1962, Jl 17,25:2
Burbank, Alonzo N, 1921, Jl 24,22:4
Burbank, Ambrose B, 1904, Ja 19,9:6
Burbank, Bertrand L, 1956, F 21,33:5
Burbank, C Everett Mrs, 1953, Jl 1,29:5
Burbank, Daniel W, 1945, N 21,21:5
Burbank, Edward, 1937, Je 2,23:5
Burbank, Elbridge A, 1949, Mr 22,25:3
Burbank, George B Mrs, 1949, My 9,25:3
Burbank, Guy H, 1947, Jl 20,45:2
Burbank, Harold H, 1951, F 7,29:2
Burbank, Jerome B, 1942, Je 14,45:2
Burbank, L, 1926, Ap 11,2:1
Burbank, Mortimer L, 1956, D 14,29:6
Burbank, Reginald Jr, 1949, Je 12,35:5
Burbank, Robert A, 1959, Je 4,31:2
Burbank, Robert A Mrs, 1954, My 11,29:2
Burbank, Sidney Gen, 1882, D 9,2:5
Burbank, Walter C, 1953, S 14,27:5
Burbank, William A, 1945, Mr 21,23:4
Burbank, William H, 1903, O 24,9:6
Burbery, George W, 1951, Mr 27,29:2
Burbidge, Norman E, 1942, Ap 18,15:4
Burbidge, Richard G W, 1966, F 3,31:2
Burbidge, Richard Sir, 1917, Je 2,9:4
Burbridge, William Thomas, 1912, S 17,11:6
Burbridge, Woodman, 1945, Je 4,19:4
Burby, Edward D, 1939, O 12,25:3
Burby, Edward Mrs, 1954, Ja 5,27:2
Burby, Gordon C, 1951, O 19,27:5
Burcel, Juan, 1910, N 19,11:6
Burch, Albert C, 1948, Mr 15,23:2
Burch, Angelus T, 1967, N 20,47:3
Burch, Arthur W, 1943, My 28,21:1
Burch, Benjamin H Rev, 1921, Jl 28,13:4
Burch, Billy, 1950, D 1,25:1
Burch, Bradley, 1967, Ap 16,82:8
Burch, Donald A, 1946, Ja 1,27:4
Burch, Edward C, 1949, D 12,33:2
Burch, Edward C Mrs, 1958, Ja 26,88:5
Burch, Elbert A, 1946, F 7,23:1
Burch, Frank, 1946, Ap 5,25:3
Burch, Frank E, 1957, Jl 3,23:4
Burch, Guy I, 1951, Ja 14,86:2
Burch, H C, 1906, N 26,2:3
Burch, Harold W, 1948, Ag 15,61:1
Burch, J C, 1881, Jl 29,5:2
Burch, James M Mrs, 1940, Ag 28,17:5
Burch, Llyod M, 1957, F 12,27:4
Burch, Louis, 1946, Ag 14,25:6
Burch, Louis H, 1950, Ja 16,26:2
Burch, Lowell R, 1962, Mr 9,29:1
Burch, Lowell R Mrs, 1962, My 23,45:2
Burch, Mark H, 1914, Je 18,11:5
Burch, R A Mrs, 1903, My 5,9:6
Burch, Rousseau A, 1944, Ja 31,17:3
Burch, Selby L, 1941, Jl 29,15:5
Burch, Thomas G (will, Ap 2,27:7), 1951, Mr 21,33:3
Burch, Tracy D Mrs, 1950, D 26,23:1
Burch, William D Jr Mrs, 1954, Ja 20,27:1
Burch, William W, 1960, O 6,41:4
Burchard, A W, 1927, Ja 23,24:1
Burchard, Clarence M, 1966, D 31,19:2
Burchard, Edward L, 1944, D 1,23:2
Burchard, James A, 1960, My 30,17:3
Burchard, Jessie Mrs, 1951, Mr 11,92:4
Burchard, Johann Heinrich Dr, 1912, S 7,11:6
Burchard, Lewis S, 1946, My 17,21:5
Burchard, Malcolm W, 1955, Mr 17,45:4
Burchardi, Bernhard Theodore, 1919, O 23,13:4
Burchell, Edgar B, 1960, My 20,31:1
Burchell, Edgar B Mrs, 1956, F 24,25:1
Burchell, Fford, 1953, F 11,29:2
Burchell, Frank H, 1965, My 29,27:2
Burchell, Frederick, 1951, N 21,25:1
Burchell, Harry D, 1964, Ja 28,31:3
Burchell, Henry J, 1959, Mr 6,25:1
Burchell, Sarah Frances Mrs, 1911, D 4,13:5
Burchell, Thomas H, 1942, My 15,20:2
Burchell, Thomas H Mrs, 1941, O 26,43:2
Burchenal, Charles D, 1962, Mr 18,87:1
Burchenal, Elizabeth, 1959, N 22,86:1
Burchenal, Ruth, 1950, O 4,31:5
Burcher, Reginald H Mrs, 1938, S 5,15:4
Burchett, George, 1953, Ap 4,13:1
Burchfield, Albert H, 1942, F 18,19:2
Burchfield, Charles E (trb, Ja 15,11,29:2), 1967, Ja 11,25:4
Burchfield, Charles W, 1955, D 9,27:5
Burchfield, W G, 1951, O 23,29:3
Burchiel, Sam W, 1953, F 20,19:2
Burchill, John R, 1948, F 13,21:3
Burchill, Joseph M, 1941, F 16,41:3
Burchill, Kenneth A, 1952, Ag 28,23:4
Burchill, Thomas E Mrs, 1968, Mr 2,29:4
Burchill, Thomas F, 1955, Mr 27,87:1
Burchill, William G, 1940, Mr 17,51:3
Burchinal, Thomas L, 1940, Je 28,19:2
Burchman, Philip, 1961, My 17,37:2
Burchmore, John S, 1965, Mr 12,33:4
Burchum, George H, 1958, O 23,31:4
Burck, Arthur R, 1955, F 20,88:6
Burck, Carroll M Mrs, 1942, Ja 23,19:5
Burck, Henry, 1938, My 18,21:1
Burck, William A, 1957, Mr 14,29:4
Burckard, Morris W, 1958, S 11,34:1
Burckhalter, C W Mrs, 1958, My 17,19:2
Burckhardt, Herman V, 1958, D 31,19:1
Burcky, Christian, 1908, Je 23,7:4
Burco, Ferruccio, 1965, Ap 28,45:3
Burd, Abraham M, 1957, Jl 26,19:4
Burd, Abraham M Mrs, 1949, N 11,26:2
Burd, Charles E, 1958, Ap 11,26:1
Burd, Charles G, 1958, F 25,27:2
Burd, Frank J, 1962, Ja 7,89:1
Burd, George Eli Rear-Adm, 1924, F 20,19:5
Burd, Harry, 1945, Ag 1,19:4
Burd, Norman J, 1956, My 12,19:5
Burd, Walter, 1939, Ag 3,19:4
Burd, William M, 1937, D 16,31:3
Burde, Richard J, 1954, D 19,85:2
Burdeau, A L, 1894, D 13,8:2
Burdell, William F, 1945, N 11,42:5
Burden, Arthur Scott, 1921, Je 16,15:3
Burden, Charles, 1949, Jl 30,15:1
Burden, Charles E, 1940, D 28,10:1
Burden, George A, 1955, F 27,86:3
Burden, Henry, 1871, Ja 21,8:5; 1937, F 6,17:5
Burden, Henry J, 1960, Mr 29,37:5
Burden, I Townsend, 1953, Jl 20,17:3
Burden, I Townsend Mrs, 1916, Ap 30,19:5; 1949, Ag 11,24:3
Burden, Isiah Townsend, 1913, Ap 24,11:3
Burden, Jack, 1943, Ja 10,50:4
Burden, James Abercrombie (will, O 19,9:4), 1906, S 24,1:2
Burden, James Abercrombie Mrs, 1920, D 27,13:6
Burden, Joseph Mrs, 1938, Ap 4,17:4
Burden, Joseph W, 1903, My 29,9:6
Burden, Nelson J, 1941, F 2,45:2
Burden, Oliver D, 1947, N 12,27:3
Burden, Peter, 1921, S 7,13:4
Burden, Samuel J, 1942, N 25,23:5
Burden, Verne G, 1951, Je 25,19:5
Burden, Walter P, 1954, Ap 8,27:4
Burden, William Armistead Moale, 1909, F 3,9:5
Burden, Williams P, 1943, Jl 27,17:6
Burdenko, Nikolai N, 1946, N 12,29:1

Burdett, Bernard M, 1948, F 7,15:5
Burdett, Bernard Mrs, 1944, Ap 14,19:2
Burdett, Coleman B, 1945, Jl 17,13:7
Burdett, Cyril H, 1939, Jl 1,17:6
Burdett, Daniel H, 1944, O 24,23:4
Burdett, Donald A, 1958, Mr 13,29:5
Burdett, Edward A, 1909, N 30,9:4
Burdett, Francis, 1951, Ap 18,31:1
Burdett, Frederick A, 1953, Ag 13,25:2
Burdett, George A, 1943, Mr 28,24:7
Burdett, Gilbert U, 1950, Jl 30,61:3
Burdett, J B Dr, 1903, My 23,9:3
Burdett, John L, 1938, O 20,23:1
Burdett, Joseph O, 1943, Jl 31,13:6
Burdett, Manuel, 1961, Ap 3,33:1
Burdett, Norman S, 1948, D 30,19:2
Burdett, Samuel S Capt, 1914, S 26,11:7
Burdett, William C, 1944, Ja 14,19:3
Burdett, William E, 1942, My 20,19:4
Burdett, Winella W Mrs, 1940, Mr 29,21:1
Burdett-Coutts, Lady (Baroness Angela Georgina Burdett-Coutts), 1906, D 31,7:1
Burdett-Coutts, William L Ashmead, 1921, Jl 29,13:3
Burdette, Clara B (est estimate, Ja 12,17:1), 1954, Ja 7,31:4
Burdette, Henry W, 1947, My 19,21:5
Burdette, Mary G, 1907, S 29,9:7
Burdette, Robert J, 1914, N 20,9:5
Burdge, Dwight, 1905, Ap 19,11:6
Burdick, Abram L, 1944, O 29,43:2
Burdick, Carl G, 1946, S 2,17:5
Burdick, Charles B, 1955, F 18,22:2
Burdick, Charles K, 1940, Je 23,31:1
Burdick, Clarence M, 1937, Jl 2,21:4
Burdick, Clark, 1948, Ag 28,16:3
Burdick, David H, 1951, O 27,19:5
Burdick, Donald L, 1967, N 13,47:1
Burdick, Edward D, 1961, Ja 19,29:2
Burdick, Edward Hamilton, 1905, Ap 30,7:6
Burdick, Edward W, 1962, S 7,30:1
Burdick, Ernest W, 1947, F 20,25:3
Burdick, Esther E, 1915, My 26,13:5
Burdick, Eugene L, 1965, Jl 27,33:4
Burdick, Eugene L (est acctg), 1966, Ja 7,9:2
Burdick, Francis Marion, 1920, Je 4,13:4
Burdick, George, 1958, Jl 17,27:5
Burdick, George H, 1953, My 14,29:2
Burdick, Harriet F Mrs, 1962, O 11,39:3
Burdick, Harry, 1957, Mr 28,31:3
Burdick, Henry H, 1953, Ja 19,23:2
Burdick, Horace R, 1942, S 19,15:5
Burdick, Irving E, 1944, Mr 1,19:6
Burdick, Isaac J, 1951, O 11,37:4
Burdick, J Byron, 1951, Mr 28,29:2
Burdick, James T Dr, 1912, My 21,13:5
Burdick, Jervis W, 1962, N 13,38:1
Burdick, John J, 1940, S 29,44:4
Burdick, John T, 1955, N 13,89:2
Burdick, Morton H, 1955, My 1,87:5
Burdick, Reginald H, 1953, D 24,15:4
Burdick, Thomas B, 1938, Mr 26,15:5
Burdick, Usher L (funl plans, Ag 21,84:6; funl, Ag 23,29:1), 1960, Ag 20,19:4
Burdick, Usher L Mrs, 1955, Ag 30,15:8
Burdick, William B, 1949, Jl 2,15:2
Burdin, Albert J Mrs, 1947, F 5,23:2
Burding, W N Mrs, 1963, Ag 1,27:4
Burditt, William F Jr, 1950, Ja 26,27:4
Burditt, William F Mrs, 1952, Je 29,58:5
Burdock, Thomas F, 1940, Mr 10,49:1
Burdon, Williams Proudfoot Mrs (funl, F 25,7:6), 1908, F 24,7:4
Burdsall, E Morris, 1939, Ap 22,17:3
Burdsall, Elwood, 1939, Mr 11,17:4
Burdsall, Richard H, 1915, S 1,9:5
Burdsall, Richard L (will, Mr 14,17:4), 1953, F 27,6:6
Burdwan, Maharajah of (Bijay Chand Mahtab), 1941, Ag 30,13:4
Bure, Emile, 1952, Je 3,29:4
Bureau, Edouard S, 1938, Je 8,23:2
Bures, Adolph, 1950, Ag 1,23:3
Buresch, K, 1936, S 17,23:3
Buret, Hadj A, 1960, Ja 6,35:5
Burfeind, Ethel, 1948, My 4,25:3
Burfeind, Henry W, 1918, O 23,13:1
Burfeind, Louis H, 1966, S 25,85:1
Burford, Archie D, 1945, O 3,19:4
Burford, Lawrence B, 1953, Ag 12,31:4
Burford, M W, 1877, Ap 15,7:5
Burg, Alfred W, 1956, O 12,29:3
Burg, Charles A, 1948, Je 20,60:7
Burg, Copeland C, 1961, O 22,86:6
Burg, De, 1884, Ag 26,4:6
Burg, Frederick, 1953, Mr 8,89:6
Burg, Morris, 1963, D 25,33:1
Burg, Stoddard S Maj, 1925, Ap 10,19:4
Burga, Benjamin F, 1939, O 5,23:1
Burgard, Alfred S, 1946, O 4,23:2
Burgard, Edgar M, 1939, Ag 29,21:4
Burgard, John C, 1962, Je 2,19:4
Burgard, John C Jr, 1947, My 27,25:2
Burgdorf, Alfred L, 1962, O 16,47:6
Burge, Charles, 1943, O 23,13:4
Burge, Hubert Murray Rev Dr, 1925, Je 12,19:4
Burge, Jerome B Mrs, 1966, Mr 9,41:4
Burge, Lofton V, 1948, F 16,21:5
Burge, Robert, 1945, O 12,24:3
Burgee, Joshua A, 1938, Ap 5,21:4
Burger, Aaron L, 1963, Ap 7,86:2
Burger, Abbott Mrs, 1951, Jl 31,21:1
Burger, Alex Mrs, 1941, N 12,23:1
Burger, Alfred G, 1962, D 29,4:7
Burger, Arthur, 1965, My 14,37:4
Burger, Bernard A, 1948, Je 22,25:5
Burger, Carl A, 1937, Mr 21,II,8:7
Burger, Carl V, 1967, D 31,44:2
Burger, Charles A Mrs, 1957, D 26,19:3
Burger, David D, 1938, Mr 13,II,8:7
Burger, David Mrs, 1959, D 7,31:4
Burger, Edward, 1940, Je 10,17:4
Burger, Gen (funl), 1871, My 29,5:2
Burger, Gustav A, 1952, Ja 9,29:1
Burger, Henry Sanford Mrs, 1914, F 21,11:3
Burger, Herbert H, 1967, Ap 30,86:8
Burger, I Victor, 1957, My 1,37:3
Burger, Irving, 1956, Mr 20,23:1
Burger, J, 1933, My 4,17:4
Burger, James C, 1937, Mr 2,21:3
Burger, John D, 1943, N 2,25:6
Burger, John D Mrs, 1958, F 7,21:2
Burger, John F, 1937, F 21,II,10:6
Burger, John F Sr, 1955, N 18,25:3
Burger, Joseph H Mrs, 1946, Jl 23,25:3
Burger, Joseph Mrs, 1944, N 1,23:3
Burger, Joseph P, 1949, Ag 7,61:1
Burger, Laidlaw B, 1958, O 21,33:2
Burger, Laura Mrs, 1941, Mr 1,15:6
Burger, Louis G Brig-Gen, 1914, My 12,11:5
Burger, Martin M, 1960, O 4,43:2
Burger, Max F, 1950, My 31,29:2
Burger, Paul F, 1937, Je 17,23:3
Burger, Pincus, 1949, D 17,17:6
Burger, Rudolph E Mrs, 1962, Jl 7,17:5
Burger, Samuel N, 1964, Ap 21,33:5
Burger, Thomas O, 1952, D 20,17:5
Burger, William, 1964, Ag 25,33:4
Burger, William C, 1959, D 12,23:1
Burger, William H, 1952, Mr 22,13:2; 1964, Ap 28,37:4
Burger, William J, 1949, My 1,88:4
Burgert, Joseph D Mrs, 1944, O 5,23:1
Burgess, Albert F, 1953, F 25,27:5
Burgess, Albert P, 1951, F 6,27:5
Burgess, Alexander Bishop, 1901, O 9,9:6
Burgess, Alfred L, 1941, Ap 30,19:4
Burgess, Alfred S, 1957, O 22,33:5
Burgess, Arthur H, 1948, My 8,15:5
Burgess, Arthur S, 1964, My 23,23:2
Burgess, B L, 1939, S 19,25:2
Burgess, Bliss M, 1956, Ja 21,21:2
Burgess, Caleb A, 1923, Ap 11,21:5
Burgess, Capt, 1874, Ag 12,4:7
Burgess, Charles Capt, 1911, Jl 17,9:5
Burgess, Charles E, 1968, Ap 11,45:4
Burgess, Charles F, 1945, F 14,20:2
Burgess, Charles M, 1950, F 7,28:2
Burgess, Charles O, 1954, Ja 15,19:3
Burgess, Clarence H Mrs, 1955, Ag 23,23:4
Burgess, Daniel Maynard Dr, 1911, Mr 1,11:3
Burgess, Edward, 1891, Jl 13,2:4
Burgess, Edward G, 1919, Je 2,15:6
Burgess, Eleanor H Mrs, 1955, O 7,25:4
Burgess, Elizabeth A Mrs, 1958, Mr 20,29:1
Burgess, Elizabeth C, 1949, Jl 23,11:4
Burgess, Ellis B, 1947, D 22,21:5
Burgess, Ernest W, 1966, D 28,37:3
Burgess, Frank, 1950, S 2,15:3
Burgess, Frank H, 1939, Jl 8,15:6
Burgess, Frederick Bp (funl, O 19,21:5), 1925, O 17, 15:4
Burgess, Frederick H, 1938, D 7,23:3
Burgess, Frederick H Mrs, 1938, D 7,23:3
Burgess, G K, 1932, Jl 3,14:3
Burgess, Gelett, 1951, S 19,31:1
Burgess, Gelett Mrs, 1947, O 13,23:2
Burgess, George F, 1920, Ja 2,11:2
Burgess, George H, 1957, Mr 2,21:4
Burgess, George S, 1942, Jl 8,23:3
Burgess, Grover, 1948, Jl 31,15:4
Burgess, Guy (funeral, S 5,2:6), 1963, S 1,1:6
Burgess, H, 1933, Mr 19,32:1
Burgess, Harold D R, 1939, Je 20,21:5
Burgess, Harriet, 1947, D 5,25:3
Burgess, Harry C, 1940, Ja 2,19:4
Burgess, Harvey J, 1946, O 26,17:1
Burgess, Helen, 1937, Ap 8,23:5
Burgess, Horace T, 1939, Ag 18,19:6
Burgess, J Lester, 1941, S 10,24:4
Burgess, J W, 1931, Ja 14,23:1
Burgess, James K, 1944, Mr 28,19:2
Burgess, James S, 1945, S 22,17:2
Burgess, John E, 1948, Ap 12,21:4
Burgess, John L, 1940, F 11,49:2; 1942, O 30,19:4
Burgess, John S, 1949, Ag 19,17:5
Burgess, Joseph E, 1961, Ja 18,33:1
Burgess, Kenneth E, 1946, F 12,28:1
Burgess, Louis R, 1938, D 18,49:1
Burgess, Louis R Mrs, 1947, Jl 20,44:2
Burgess, Magnus M, 1953, Ag 17,15:6
Burgess, Neil, 1910, F 20,II,9:1
Burgess, Neil Mrs, 1905, S 18,7:6
Burgess, Nellie J, 1950, Jl 23,56:2
Burgess, Newton A, 1953, Ap 2,27:3
Burgess, Nicholas G, 1942, Ag 30,43:2
Burgess, Paul, 1959, Ja 1,31:1
Burgess, Perry, 1962, S 17,31:4
Burgess, Perry Mrs, 1962, Je 12,37:2
Burgess, Roy H Jr, 1954, D 15,31:1
Burgess, Seth M, 1913, Mr 19,13:5
Burgess, Sullivan 3d, 1941, S 22,15:5
Burgess, Thayer, 1949, O 11,34:2
Burgess, Theodore H, 1961, Ap 17,29:3
Burgess, Thomas, 1955, Jl 3,33:2
Burgess, Thornton W (funl plans, Je 7,37:4), 1965, Je 6,84:4
Burgess, Thornton W Mrs, 1950, Ag 17,27:1
Burgess, W C, 1955, Ag 5,19:4
Burgess, W J, 1883, Je 5,2:6
Burgess, W Randolph Mrs (trb lr, Jl 31,18:7), 1953, Jl 16,21:5
Burgess, Waldo S, 1952, F 19,29:5
Burgess, Walter, 1942, Ap 27,15:2
Burgess, Walter E, 1943, Ap 11,48:3
Burgess, William, 1941, Mr 11,24:3
Burgess, William H, 1940, Je 27,23:4
Burgess, William Rev, 1922, Ag 1,19:5
Burgess, William S, 1947, Mr 20,27:1
Burgesser, Eugene T, 1955, Je 23,29:4
Burget, George A Mrs, 1946, O 13,59:4
Burget, Warren L, 1947, Ag 22,15:5
Burgett, Ambrose L (Perry), 1959, O 4,86:3
Burgett, Harold R, 1955, Jl 28,23:4
Burgevin, David, 1944, Ap 23,42:7
Burggraaff, John J, 1938, S 30,21:2
Burggraf, Ephram A, 1948, D 19,76:3
Burgh, Thomas Dr, 1906, Mr 15,5:5
Burghard, Edward M Mrs, 1945, Mr 7,21:4
Burghard, Frederick J Mrs, 1958, O 16,37:3
Burghard, George E, 1963, D 10,50:8
Burghardt, Arthur W, 1941, Ap 21,19:4
Burghardt, Fritz, 1947, Mr 28,23:4
Burghardt, George J, 1903, D 15,9:5
Burghardt, Henry D, 1949, Jl 17,56:6
Burghart, Leon C, 1940, Ja 7,48:4
Burghclere, Baron (Herbert Coulstoun Gardner), 1921, My 8,22:3
Burgheim, Clarence, 1948, O 27,27:2
Burgheim, Clarence Mrs, 1956, Ja 29,93:2
Burgher, Clarence L, 1954, Mr 16,29:1
Burgher, Clarence L Mrs, 1954, Mr 30,27:6
Burgher, Theodore G, 1943, My 14,19:1
Burgi, C Arnold, 1957, Ag 15,21:5
Burgi, Oscar, 1960, F 21,92:8
Burgidge, George A, 1943, S 30,21:3
Burgin, Bryan O, 1947, F 7,23:4
Burgin, Leslie, 1945, Ag 17,17:1
Burgin, Miron, 1957, Mr 14,29:3
Burgin, William O, 1946, Ap 12,27:3
Burgio, Salvator M, 1959, Ag 29,17:3
Burgmeier, John M, 1949, Ag 16,23:4
Burgos, Antonio, 1937, Ag 3,23:5
Burgos, Ernesto B, 1937, D 5,II,9:3
Burgos, Rafael, 1953, My 21,31:6
Burgos Melo, Romilio, 1948, Ag 20,17:4
Burgoyne, Andrew C, 1959, F 16,29:3
Burgoyne, Arthur G, 1955, N 19,19:5
Burgoyne, Charlotte Lady, 1871, D 16,1:6
Burgoyne, Daniel Sr, 1945, Jl 27,15:5
Burgoyne, Henry B, 1950, Ag 4,21:6
Burgoyne, John Fore Sir, 1871, O 10,1:1
Burgoyne, R Gordon, 1950, Je 19,21:3
Burgoyne, Robert A, 1960, Ap 23,23:5
Burgoyne, Sidney J, 1946, Ap 5,25:3
Burgoyne, Thomas F, 1941, Ap 24,21:3
Burgoyne, William L, 1956, N 9,29:3
Burgstaller, Ludwig, 1953, Ja 2,15:2
Burgstresser, Abraham K, 1951, N 27,31:4
Burguente, Ricardo Gen, 1937, Mr 31,4:4
Burgunder, B Bernei, 1948, Ap 21,27:5
Burgwin, George C Jr, 1949, O 9,93:2
Burhaneddin, Mehemed Prince, 1949, My 30,13:5
Burhaneddin, Princess, 1952, My 12,25:6
Burhans, Earl H, 1945, S 18,23:3
Burhans, Edward W, 1948, F 14,13:2
Burhans, Fordyce W, 1951, O 26,23:5
Burhans, Mary A Mrs, 1941, N 5,23:6
Burhard, Edward A, 1939, Je 4,49:1
Burhenne, Andrew, 1912, Ag 2,9:5
Burhoe, Lemuel W, 1949, D 10,17:5
Burhorn, C Alfred, 1947, D 8,25:3
Buriam, Jane Mrs, 1921, S 22,17:6
Burian, Stephen Baron, 1922, O 21,13:5
Burich, Stephen J Sr, 1946, F 5,23:3
Burin, Rafael B (Count Guadalhorce), 1952, S 17:4
Burina, Arveda, 1908, N 16,9:6
Burinskas, William, 1951, Mr 22,31:4
Burisch, Julius A, 1958, My 16,23:6
Burisch, Julius G, 1948, D 15,33:6
Burk, Addison B, 1912, F 28,11:4

Burk, Calamity Jane, 1903, Ag 2,2:5
Burk, Cong Henry, 1903, D 6,7:6
Burk, Frank L, 1959, Ja 31,19:1
Burk, Frederick S, 1950, D 6,33:2
Burk, Gary L, 1946, Ag 27,29:6
Burk, Joseph C, 1945, D 24,15:2
Burk, Joseph E, 1946, O 8,23:2
Burk, Joseph R, 1951, D 14,31:1
Burk, Samuel G, 1946, Mr 28,25:2
Burk, William C, 1956, Je 13,37:2
Burk, William L Mrs, 1940, Ap 14,44:7
Burkam, Elzey G, 1940, Mr 14,23:4
Burkan, N, 1936, Je 7,II,9:1
Burkard, Charles I, 1941, Ja 17,17:1
Burkard, Charlotte A, 1964, Mr 29,60:6
Burkard, John A, 1949, F 23,27:1
Burkard, Oscar R, 1950, F 19,79:3
Burke, Abram F, 1938, Mr 20,II,9:2
Burke, Albert, 1958, N 23,89:1
Burke, Albert V Sr, 1961, My 21,86:3
Burke, Alexander E, 1944, My 20,15:5
Burke, Andrew F, 1939, Jl 26,19:4
Burke, Anna G, 1947, Mr 30,56:4; 1948, D 2,29:2
Burke, Anthony F, 1948, O 21,27:3
Burke, Anthony P, 1948, O 30,15:4
Burke, Armand, 1956, D 16,86:2
Burke, Arthur, 1948, F 26,23:5
Burke, Arthur E, 1950, Ja 17,27:4; 1964, N 16,31:5
Burke, Arthur Mrs, 1954, F 21,68:4
Burke, Bertha A, 1963, N 20,43:3
Burke, Burke I, 1967, N 29,40:6
Burke, Burt S, 1967, Mr 2,35:3
Burke, Carleton F, 1962, Jl 30,23:4
Burke, Charles, 1949, Ja 13,23:2
Burke, Charles C, 1942, Ag 28,19:3
Burke, Charles Clinton, 1924, My 7,21:3
Burke, Charles F (will, F 14,II,2:2), 1937, Ja 23,17:3
Burke, Charles H, 1944, Ap 8,13:5
Burke, Charles Henschel, 1924, F 2,13:6
Burke, Charles W, 1951, S 11,29:5
Burke, Clarence E Col, 1919, My 11,22:4
Burke, Clarence L, 1952, Ag 14,23:2
Burke, Clarence O Mrs, 1951, S 29,17:5
Burke, Cornelius J, 1958, S 14,84:3
Burke, D N Rev, 1913, Ag 7,7:4
Burke, Daniel L, 1938, F 13,II,7:3
Burke, Daniel Mrs, 1945, O 2,23:4
Burke, Daniel W Brig-Gen, 1911, Je 1,11:5
Burke, David A, 1939, Je 1,25:4; 1966, Mr 16,46:1
Burke, David F (Bro Benjamin), 1955, My 13,25:2
Burke, David J, 1949, S 10,17:2
Burke, Dennis J Sr, 1948, S 6,13:4
Burke, E A, 1928, S 25,31:5
Burke, Edmund, 1882, Ja 26,3:3; 1943, Ap 12,23:3; 1947, D 27,13:3; 1949, Ap 19,25:1; 1950, Je 15,31:2
Burke, Edmund G, 1966, My 10,45:3
Burke, Edmund J, 1941, Ja 2,23:4
Burke, Edmund Mrs, 1962, O 21,88:7
Burke, Edmund S, 1966, Ja 23,89:2
Burke, Edmund S Jr, 1962, Ap 8,87:1
Burke, Edward, 1947, Ja 2,27:4
Burke, Edward F, 1937, Ja 20,21:3; 1951, D 22,9:3
Burke, Edward G, 1957, F 15,23:3
Burke, Edward J, 1960, My 16,31:4; 1964, My 14,35:4
Burke, Edward J Sr, 1968, Mr 5,41:1
Burke, Edward L, 1943, F 20,13:1
Burke, Edward R, 1968, N 5,44:3
Burke, Edwin (will, O 20,12:3), 1944, S 27,21:3
Burke, Edwin H, 1924, Mr 1,13:5
Burke, Ellen, 1949, Mr 28,21:5
Burke, Ellen F, 1950, S 12,27:4
Burke, Eugene A, 1953, Ag 12,31:5
Burke, Eugene P, 1961, Ap 13,35:5
Burke, Eugene S, 1938, My 1,II,6:5; 1951, S 5,31:2
Burke, Francis P, 1903, Jl 14,7:6
Burke, Francis X, 1966, O 7,43:2
Burke, Frank, 1943, F 3,19:3; 1945, Jl 18,27:6; 1956, O 16,33:1
Burke, Frank E, 1945, O 27,15:6
Burke, Frank G Jr, 1963, D 31,19:4
Burke, Frank H, 1948, Jl 19,19:4
Burke, Frank J, 1961, Jl 7,25:5
Burke, Frank P, 1946, Mr 31,46:3
Burke, Frank X T, 1954, F 10,29:2
Burke, Fred, 1940, Jl 11,13:2
Burke, Fred H, 1945, Ap 4,21:6
Burke, Frederick A, 1942, Jl 16,19:6
Burke, Frederick J, 1950, Ag 3,23:3
Burke, George H, 1951, Mr 30,23:2
Burke, George J Sr, 1950, O 4,31:2
Burke, Gerald J, 1947, N 26,23:2
Burke, Gordon L, 1963, N 17,86:4
Burke, Grafton, 1938, S 27,21:4
Burke, Grafton Mrs, 1962, N 2,31:2
Burke, H F L, 1950, Ag 13,76:2
Burke, Harold J, 1961, Ag 22,29:2
Burke, Harry, 1945, Mr 28,23:1
Burke, Harry A, 1964, Jl 3,44:6; 1965, F 18,33:2
Burke, Haslett P, 1957, O 6,84:5
Burke, Helen, 1946, My 25,15:4
Burke, Henry J, 1938, S 30,21:3
Burke, Henry J Mrs, 1947, S 1,19:3
Burke, Henry P, 1945, Mr 19,19:4
Burke, Hubert J, 1960, N 13,89:1
Burke, J J, 1936, O 31,19:4
Burke, J T, 1928, Ap 25,27:5
Burke, James, 1939, O 20,23:2; 1940, Ja 23,21:1; 1964, O 3,2:6
Burke, James A, 1945, Jl 22,37:1; 1956, Ja 27,23:5
Burke, James A (requim mass, S 16,47:4), 1965, S 14,39:3
Burke, James A Mrs, 1964, Je 2,37:2
Burke, James D, 1943, O 1,19:5
Burke, James E, 1904, F 24,9:6; 1943, Ap 25,34:3
Burke, James F, 1948, Ja 19,23:4; 1948, O 4,23:4; 1950, Jl 19,31:4
Burke, James H Mrs, 1942, Je 21,36:6
Burke, James J, 1938, N 6,49:3; 1950, Jl 26,25:3; 1962, My 29,31:5
Burke, James M, 1947, F 18,25:2
Burke, James S, 1938, Ap 8,19:6
Burke, James Stranahan, 1913, O 30,9:3
Burke, James T, 1942, Mr 27,23:5; 1961, Ag 6,85:1
Burke, Jefferson D, 1939, D 29,15:1
Burke, Jeremiah, 1938, F 20,II,8:6
Burke, Jeremiah J, 1944, Ag 16,19:3
Burke, Jim (J Valentino), 1951, Ja 23,27:1
Burke, Joanna A Mrs, 1941, N 4,26:4
Burke, John, 1921, Jl 15,11:5; 1937, My 15,19:1; 1942, F 15,44:4; 1951, O 31,29:4
Burke, John A, 1946, N 10,62:4; 1946, D 1,76:5; 1954, F 16,25:3; 1967, O 2,47:2
Burke, John B, 1952, Ja 19,15:3
Burke, John E, 1953, F 13,21:3; 1958, Ag 1,21:2
Burke, John Edward Msgr (funl, My 12,23:5), 1925, My 8,19:3
Burke, John F, 1950, Ap 5,31:4; 1959, My 7,33:3; 1966, Ag 6,23:2
Burke, John J, 1941, Ja 31,19:4; 1943, F 3,19:5; 1945, O 26,19:4; 1951, S 16,84:5; 1951, D 22,16:2; 1957, F 17,92:5; 1958, N 19,37:4; 1963, N 29,34:5; 1964, O 28,45:1
Burke, John M Maj, 1917, Ap 13,13:5
Burke, John P, 1941, Mr 2,43:3
Burke, John R Mrs, 1955, Je 20,21:1
Burke, John S (funl plans, My 2,37:4), 1962, Ap 29, 86:2
Burke, John T, 1943, My 19,25:1; 1950, Ag 5,15:5
Burke, John V, 1947, Je 25,25:4; 1962, Ag 28,31:5
Burke, John W, 1937, S 3,17:5
Burke, John W (Providence, RI), 1959, Ja 28,31:2
Burke, John W (Washington, DC), 1959, O 9,21:3
Burke, John W Mrs, 1948, Je 4,23:2; 1957, Ja 24,29:4
Burke, Johnny, 1964, F 26,35:1
Burke, Joseph, 1939, Jl 20,19:3
Burke, Joseph A, 1950, Je 11,92:5; 1952, O 9,31:1; 1952, D 23,23:3; 1958, Je 8,89:1
Burke, Joseph A (funl plans, O 19,8:4), 1962, O 17, 39:1
Burke, Joseph F, 1948, Ja 22,27:4
Burke, Joseph H, 1941, Ja 1,23:3
Burke, Katherine, 1925, O 20,25:5
Burke, Katherine A, 1946, Ja 19,14:2
Burke, Kenneth K Mrs, 1968, Ag 3,25:1
Burke, Leo G, 1953, My 9,19:6
Burke, Leon, 1953, F 28,17:6
Burke, Liam, 1950, Je 15,31:5
Burke, Luke D, 1951, O 21,92:3
Burke, Luke Mrs, 1962, S 2,57:2
Burke, M, 1933, Jl 11,15:1
Burke, M J Col, 1905, Mr 16,9:6
Burke, Margaret Mrs, 1940, Mr 2,13:1
Burke, Maria H Mrs, 1957, Je 20,29:1
Burke, Martha Jefferson Randolph Mrs, 1915, Ag 10, 11:7
Burke, Martin A, 1948, Je 21,21:4
Burke, Martin E, 1945, Jl 2,15:3
Burke, Mary (Sister Mary Gonsolva), 1953, My 13, 29:3
Burke, Mary L, 1947, F 27,21:1
Burke, Matthew Burke, 1924, Jl 3,15:5
Burke, Matthew F, 1944, F 26,13:6
Burke, Maurice F Rev, 1923, Mr 18,6:3
Burke, Merritt, 1943, N 24,21:4
Burke, Michael, 1925, Ag 24,13:5; 1937, Mr 13,19:2
Burke, Michael E Sr, 1941, Ag 12,19:1
Burke, Michael Mrs, 1945, Je 2,15:5
Burke, Morgan J Jr, 1967, D 23,23:1
Burke, Morris E, 1944, N 12,42:2
Burke, Norbert T, 1967, Mr 30,45:4
Burke, Oliver, 1937, S 16,25:4
Burke, Ormonde J, 1950, Ap 17,23:3
Burke, Oscar M, 1959, D 2,43:2
Burke, Patrick, 1950, Ja 29,68:4
Burke, Patrick J, 1949, Ja 4,40:2
Burke, Patrick J Jr, 1966, F 16,40:6
Burke, Peter, 1940, S 24,23:4; 1958, Ja 25,19:1
Burke, Peter F, 1950, N 9,33:4
Burke, Phil D, 1948, O 30,15:5
Burke, Philip T, 1944, Ap 17,23:4
Burke, Ralph B M, 1945, Mr 11,40:2
Burke, Ralphe H, 1956, Ag 24,19:5
Burke, Randolph F (funl), 1961, Ag 21,23:3
Burke, Raymond A, 1968, D 16,47:1
Burke, Raymond H, 1954, Ag 19,23:5
Burke, Rebecca Mrs, 1939, D 25,20:5
Burke, Regina C M, 1967, Ap 14,39:1
Burke, Richard H, 1958, Ag 31,57:3
Burke, Richard T, 1941, My 30,15:5; 1941, N 24,17:2; 1945, N 23,23:4
Burke, Robert B, 1944, Jl 2,19:1
Burke, Robert E, 1940, F 26,15:4; 1949, N 24,32:4
Burke, Robert Emmett, 1921, Jl 30,9:6; 1925, Ag 10, 13:6
Burke, Robert F, 1952, Je 27,23:4
Burke, Robert M, 1954, D 21,27:4
Burke, Robert P, 1905, Mr 3,9:4
Burke, Russell E, 1948, Ja 27,25:3
Burke, Russell E Mrs, 1953, S 22,31:3
Burke, Ruth B Mrs, 1941, Mr 25,23:2
Burke, Sherman K, 1943, Jl 2,19:3
Burke, Stephen F, 1952, D 30,19:4
Burke, Stephen P, 1945, Mr 11,40:3; 1947, O 30,26:2
Burke, Stevenson Judge, 1904, Ap 25,9:6
Burke, T M A Bp, 1915, Ja 21,9:4
Burke, T N Rev, 1883, Jl 3,4:7
Burke, T P, 1937, D 21,48:4
Burke, Theodore, 1940, O 26,15:4
Burke, Thomas, 1937, S 30,23:4; 1944, Jl 19,19:2; 1945, S 24,19:5; 1954, S 30,11:5
Burke, Thomas A Mrs, 1964, O 26,31:5
Burke, Thomas A Sr, 1949, Jl 19,29:4
Burke, Thomas C, 1950, Ja 19,27:1
Burke, Thomas D, 1954, Ag 21,17:6
Burke, Thomas E, 1941, O 25,17:6
Burke, Thomas F, 1923, Ag 15,17:6; 1941, F 28,19:3; 1941, Mr 28,23:5; 1944, Ja 23,38:2; 1947, S 2,21:1; 1958, Jl 3,25:4
Burke, Thomas H, 1959, S 13,84:1
Burke, Thomas J, 1946, Ja 11,22:2; 1966, Mr 12,27:3
Burke, Thomas Mrs, 1954, Ja 9,15:2
Burke, Thomas P, 1938, Jl 17,26:6; 1954, Ag 4,21:4; 1959, Ag 30,82:2
Burke, Thomas S, 1963, Ap 16,35:2
Burke, Thomas S Mrs, 1945, O 2,23:1
Burke, Vincent P, 1953, D 20,77:2
Burke, W B, 1947, D 21,52:5
Burke, Walter D Jr, 1948, Ag 18,25:2
Burke, Walter F, 1946, D 15,77:4; 1961, O 5,37:2
Burke, Walter J, 1942, S 11,21:5
Burke, Webster H, 1958, Jl 24,25:5
Burke, William, 1942, D 25,18:2; 1944, S 25,17:4; 1946, Je 1,13:1; 1946, O 2,29:3
Burke, William A, 1938, Ag 27,13:3; 1944, O 31,18:3
Burke, William E, 1950, Ja 16,26:2; 1962, Ja 6,19:6
Burke, William F, 1953, My 2,15:5; 1960, Ap 18,29:5
Burke, William F Mrs, 1922, F 8,17:5
Burke, William H, 1948, Ap 25,68:3
Burke, William J, 1923, Mr 27,19:4; 1925, N 8,5:2; 1939, Ag 14,15:4; 1950, S 27,31:4
Burke, William J Sr, 1964, Ag 22,21:4
Burke, William L, 1942, Ap 28,21:1
Burke, William M, 1904, O 10,2:5
Burke, William T, 1953, My 15,23:3
Burke-Gaffney, Noel, 1958, S 21,86:2
Burke-Sheridan, Margaret, 1958, Ap 18,23:4
Burkess, Theodore, 1909, Jl 6,7:5
Burket, H K, 1951, Ap 4,29:4
Burket, Harlan F, 1943, O 21,27:3
Burkett, Charles H, 1903, Je 26,9:6
Burkett, Harry L, 1941, S 27,17:5
Burkett, Jesse C, 1953, My 28,23:3
Burkey, William D, 1957, My 11,21:6
Burkhalter, C, 1884, F 1,5:6
Burkhalter, Peyton B, 1947, Ag 20,21:1
Burkhalter, Ralph M, 1944, D 15,19:6
Burkham, Caroline T, 1937, Mr 5,21:3
Burkhander, Arthur W, 1956, Ag 13,19:7
Burkhard, Henri, 1956, Ja 12,27:4
Burkhard, Herman J, 1950, F 20,25:4
Burkhard, Joseph J, 1953, Ja 19,24:3
Burkhard, Thomas, 1916, F 7,11:2
Burkhard, Willy, 1955, Je 23,29:3
Burkhardt, Charles A, 1960, F 18,33:2
Burkhardt, Charles Mrs, 1951, S 3,27:3
Burkhardt, Christian, 1948, Je 10,25:2
Burkhardt, Edward A, 1940, My 10,23:4
Burkhardt, Ernest R, 1953, S 8,31:1
Burkhardt, Erwin J, 1952, F 26,27:2
Burkhardt, Erwin W, 1957, O 23,33:1
Burkhardt, Frank T, 1943, Ja 14,21:2
Burkhardt, Frederic, 1937, Mr 21,II,8:2
Burkhardt, Frederick K, 1958, D 7,88:5
Burkhardt, George E, 1963, My 31,25:4
Burkhardt, Gustav A, 1956, Ap 6,26:3
Burkhardt, Harry F, 1952, O 19,88:4
Burkhardt, Hilbert A, 1957, Ja 1,23:6
Burkhardt, Howard C, 1953, Jl 12,65:3
Burkhardt, Jaques, 1867, F 23,3:1
Burkhardt, John A, 1937, Je 8,25:4
Burkhardt, John E, 1954, N 3,29:4
Burkhardt, Richard C, 1937, D 9,25:4
Burkhardt, Robert F, 1947, D 21,54:1
Burkhardt, Roger F, 1968, N 14,47:4
Burkhardt, Solon, 1952, F 9,13:6
Burkhardt, Theodore L, 1951, Ap 18,31:1
Burkhart, Addison, 1937, Ja 26,21:2
Burkhart, Catherine F Mrs, 1945, Ja 15,19:1
Burkhart, Edward S, 1942, Ag 18,21:6

Burkhart, Emil W, 1952, Ag 10,61:1
Burkhart, Harvey J, 1946, S 23,23:5
Burkhart, John R, 1941, S 16,23:2
Burkhart, Mary P, 1953, Mr 5,27:4
Burkhart, William R, 1954, Mr 18,31:3
Burkhart, William S, 1941, N 15,17:5
Burkheimer, Harry C, 1955, My 24,31:2
Burkholder, Albert N, 1954, O 4,27:5
Burkholder, Arthur L, 1952, Jl 28,15:2
Burkholder, Charles I, 1948, Mr 15,23:3
Burkholder, E Paul, 1950, S 19,31:2
Burkholder, Jacob F, 1944, Je 9,15:4
Burkholder, John D, 1954, Mr 9,27:1
Burkholder, S K (funl). (see also Ap 1), 1877, Ap 3, 8:2
Burkinshaw, Charles D, 1955, Ja 20,31:3
Burkinshaw, Neil, 1955, S 21,33:3
Burkitt, Garrett Sr, 1959, Ap 2,31:4
Burkitt, John D Mrs, 1950, D 12,34:4
Burkman, Anna B Mrs, 1941, O 18,19:5
Burkman, Eric (por), 1949, F 27,68:5
Burkman, Eric, 1949, Mr 3,25:6
Burkow, Louis, 1925, O 14,25:3
Burks, Edward D, 1961, Jl 29,19:6
Burks, Jesse D, 1942, N 20,24:2
Burks, Sidney L, 1961, Jl 4,6:8
Burlage, R C, 1883, Je 29,5:3
Burland, Joseph A, 1957, Jl 23,27:1
Burland, William H, 1941, Jl 3,19:5
Burlee, William J, 1916, N 10,13:4
Burleigh, Andrew L, 1967, F 20,37:2
Burleigh, Balfour of Lord (Alexander Hugh Bruce), 1921, Jl 7,11:5
Burleigh, Bennet, 1914, Je 18,11:6
Burleigh, C C (See also Je 15), 1878, Je 17,1:2
Burleigh, Celia Mrs Rev, 1875, Jl 28,4:6
Burleigh, Charles A, 1939, Ap 10,17:2
Burleigh, Edwin C Sen, 1916, Je 17,11:4
Burleigh, Francis W, 1947, Mr 21,21:3
Burleigh, George Shepard, 1903, Jl 23,7:6
Burleigh, George W, 1940, Mr 16,15:3
Burleigh, George W Mrs, 1943, Mr 2,19:5
Burleigh, Harry T (por), 1949, S 13,29:1
Burleigh, J H, 1877, D 7,5:3
Burleigh, John J, 1917, F 19,11:5
Burleigh, John L Col, 1909, My 11,9:6
Burleigh, Lemoyne, 1907, D 6,11:4
Burleigh, Perry G, 1954, D 13,27:4
Burleigh, Sydney Mrs, 1952, Jl 19,15:3
Burleigh, W H (funl), 1871, Mr 22,2:7
Burleigh, William P, 1947, Ag 15,17:1
Burleigh, William W 2d, 1940, Jl 20,15:5
Burles, Samuel, 1903, Ag 4,7:6
Burleson, Albert Mrs, 1948, Ja 9,22:3
Burleson, Albert S, 1937, N 25,31:1
Burleson, Charles Mrs, 1950, N 29,33:2
Burleson, D S, 1953, Jl 23,23:4
Burleson, H L, 1933, Ag 2,15:4
Burlew, Charles R, 1955, D 8,37:3
Burlew, Charles R Mrs, 1948, F 3,26:1
Burlew, Ebert E, 1945, O 23,17:5
Burley, Albert W, 1964, Ja 20,43:2
Burley, Andrew B, 1942, Ja 5,17:6
Burley, Augustus H, 1903, N 28,9:5
Burley, Frank, 1951, O 21,92:4
Burley, Harry B, 1954, Ag 24,21:4
Burley, James L, 1942, Ap 21,23:3
Burley, James L Mrs, 1947, O 6,21:3
Burley, John S, 1946, Jl 26,21:3
Burley, John W Mrs, 1949, N 28,27:5
Burley, John W Sr, 1948, Je 21,21:2
Burley, Thomas F Jr, 1944, Mr 8,19:4
Burlie, John D, 1966, F 22,23:3
Burlin, Charles W, 1942, O 4,53:1
Burlin, Natalie Curtis, 1921, O 29,13:6
Burlin, Phil, 1952, Ja 16,25:1
Burling, Albert E, 1960, O 31,31:4
Burling, Charles E, 1941, Mr 29,15:4
Burling, Charles E Mrs, 1950, Je 24,13:5
Burling, Charles H Mrs, 1945, D 1,23:6
Burling, George B Mrs, 1958, Jl 22,27:1
Burling, Gilbert, 1875, F 8,5:4
Burling, John, 1961, Ja 15,86:8
Burling, John Dr, 1937, D 20,27:5
Burling, John L, 1959, D 10,39:5
Burlingame, Alvah W, 1952, My 20,25:1
Burlingame, Anson (funl, Ap 24,5:4), 1870, F 24,5:2
Burlingame, Bertrand C, 1941, S 24,23:6
Burlingame, Bruce O, 1953, My 20,29:3
Burlingame, C Charles, 1950, Jl 23,57:3
Burlingame, Cris M, 1940, N 24,49:3
Burlingame, Dennis M, 1964, Ja 25,23:5
Burlingame, Edward Livermore, 1922, N 17,17:5
Burlingame, Elmer E Mrs, 1951, D 31,13:5
Burlingame, Everett E, 1950, Je 7,29:2
Burlingame, Everett E Mrs, 1942, N 6,23:4
Burlingame, Frederic A, 1939, D 29,15:3
Burlingame, Gayle, 1945, Ap 1,12:4
Burlingame, H C, 1903, Je 8,7:6
Burlingame, Millard P, 1956, My 25,23:2
Burlingame, Rex J, 1952, My 25,92:7
Burlingame, Roger, 1967, Mr 20,31:3
Burlingame, Thomas Mrs, 1944, Ap 3,21:4
Burlingame, Walter D, 1944, O 19,23:2
Burlingame-Cheney, Emeline Mrs, 1923, F 26,13:4
Burlinger, Harry C, 1953, Jl 27,19:1
Burlingham, A H Rev, 1905, Mr 2,9:6
Burlingham, Charles C, 1959, Je 8,1:4
Burlingham, Charles Mrs, 1937, D 8,25:3
Burlingham, Frederick, 1924, Je 11,21:4
Burlingham, Gertrude S, 1952, Ja 14,19:6
Burlingham, James P, 1939, S 24,44:1
Burlingham, Myra, 1937, Mr 30,23:3
Burlingham, William, 1940, Je 14,21:5
Burlington, Arthur J, 1962, Ap 24,37:1
Burlington, Daniel Sr, 1945, Jl 28,11:4
Burlington, Harry J, 1945, Jl 12,11:6
Burliuk, David, 1967, Ja 16,41:4
Burlock, H Victor, 1950, Ja 18,32:2
Burlock, T H, 1883, D 22,8:3
Burlon, Louis J, 1955, Ag 14,81:1
Burman, Borah Z, 1964, O 13,39:1
Burman, Clarence N, 1951, O 15,25:4
Burman, Howard A, 1953, F 1,88:2
Burman, John, 1941, Mr 5,21:4
Burmeister, Edward Capt, 1910, Ja 12,9:5
Burmeister, Henry A, 1952, Je 3,29:1
Burmeister, Louis Jr, 1944, Ap 1,13:5
Burmese King, 1878, D 1,9:1
Burmester, Frank E, 1938, Ja 19,23:4
Burmester, Henry J, 1957, Je 1,17:6
Burmester, J Louis Mrs, 1947, Mr 18,27:5
Burmester, W, 1933, Ja 17,19:1
Burmingham, Bridget Mrs, 1922, Ja 19,17:5
Burn, G F, 1878, O 31,2:5
Burn, Irving, 1955, My 26,31:1
Burn, John H Mrs, 1953, N 1,87:1
Burn, Joseph, 1950, O 13,29:4
Burn, Raymond T, 1921, S 2,13:3
Burn, Walter S, 1937, Mr 23,24:2
Burn, William H, 1938, Ap 1,23:4
Burnaby, Algernon E, 1938, N 14,19:5
Burnaby, Davy (por), 1949, Ap 19,25:5
Burnaby, F Col, 1885, Ja 22,1:2
Burnam, Curtis F, 1947, N 30,76:6
Burnam, Hubert K, 1942, O 15,23:2
Burnaman, G E, 1948, N 20,13:3
Burnand, Francis Cowley Sir, 1917, Ap 22,21:3
Burnap, Alvares M, 1948, F 16,21:3
Burnap, Arthur E, 1965, Ag 7,21:2
Burnap, Clement F, 1938, Ap 9,17:4
Burnap, Robert L, 1949, N 2,27:2
Burne, Alex J, 1950, O 3,31:1
Burne, John C, 1951, My 7,25:3
Burne, Nancy, 1954, Mr 26,21:4
Burnee, Frederick D, 1938, F 26,15:2
Burneer, Frank, 1944, Jl 13,17:4
Burnell, Edward J Jr, 1964, Mr 23,29:2
Burnell, George A, 1942, Ja 29,19:4
Burnell, George C Capt, 1909, Ap 23,9:4
Burnell, George E, 1948, O 25,23:6
Burnell, Levi, 1881, D 13,2:6
Burnell, Max R, 1959, S 20,87:1
Burnell, Vincent R, 1958, D 31,38:5
Burnell-Nugent, Frank, 1942, Mr 14,15:4
Burnelli, Vincent J, 1964, Je 23,33:2
Burner, Daniel Greene, 1903, S 25,1:5
Burner, William A, 1948, S 16,29:4
Burnes, Daniel Sr, 1937, F 26,21:4
Burnes, Edward P, 1944, My 24,19:2
Burnes, Francis X, 1948, S 30,27:4
Burnes, Leo J, 1963, Jl 26,25:2
Burnes, Thomas J, 1943, N 3,25:6
Burnet, Dana, 1962, O 24,39:2
Burnet, David S Elder, 1867, Jl 11,8:3
Burnet, Eleline, 1949, O 19,29:4
Burnet, George H, 1963, S 21,21:3
Burnet, J, 1928, My 28,25:3
Burnet, James Robinson, 1908, Jl 12,9:6
Burnet, John, 1938, Jl 3,12:8
Burnet, Marguerite Du M Mrs, 1965, Mr 28,92:8
Burnet, Samuel, 1963, D 4,47:3
Burnet, Timothy, 1904, D 20,9:5
Burnet, Warren H, 1958, Je 25,29:1
Burnet, William E, 1954, My 21,27:2
Burnet, William H, 1910, My 2,9:4
Burnett, A, 1884, Ap 5,5:3
Burnett, Arthur C, 1953, S 21,25:5
Burnett, Arthur H, 1952, Ag 9,13:5
Burnett, Arthur W, 1947, O 30,26:2; 1948, Ja 5,20:2
Burnett, Bertrand G Mrs, 1952, Ag 25,17:2
Burnett, C H Dr, 1902, Ja 31,9:6
Burnett, Charles, 1939, N 29,23:1
Burnett, Charles A, 1953, Jl 8,27:5
Burnett, Charles G, 1952, D 14,90:5
Burnett, Charles R, 1949, Ja 12,27:3
Burnett, Charles S, 1945, Ap 11,23:4
Burnett, Charles T, 1946, F 1,23:1
Burnett, Curtis R, 1942, D 23,19:1
Burnett, D Frederick, 1940, Ap 23,23:1
Burnett, D Frederick Mrs, 1950, Ja 8,77:1
Burnett, Daniel, 1948, F 19,23:4
Burnett, David Ex-Judge, 1873, Ag 29,4:7
Burnett, Douglass, 1957, My 17,25:1
Burnett, E Rodney, 1956, D 10,31:4
Burnett, Edgar A, 1941, Je 30,17:5
Burnett, Edmund C (por), 1949, Ja 12,27:4
Burnett, Edward, 1925, N 6,23:5
Burnett, Edward F Mrs, 1947, D 15,25:2
Burnett, Edward R, 1953, Ag 5,23:4
Burnett, Emma, 1946, Ag 11,45:1
Burnett, Ernie, 1959, S 12,21:6
Burnett, Frances Hodgson (funl, N 2,7:1), 1924, O 30,19:1
Burnett, Frank C, 1940, Jl 17,21:6
Burnett, Frank T, 1951, Mr 30,23:4
Burnett, Fred H, 1949, F 27,68:4
Burnett, Frederick W, 1953, Ja 5,21:3
Burnett, George, 1950, N 18,15:3
Burnett, George A, 1951, S 23,85:2
Burnett, George H, 1951, F 15,31:5
Burnett, Harold, 1966, Jl 6,45:1
Burnett, Harry A, 1941, My 7,25:5
Burnett, Henry Lawrence, 1918, My 15,13:4
Burnett, Henry Lawrence Gen (funl, Ja 7,13:4), 1916, Ja 5,13:4
Burnett, J Lester, 1952, My 11,92:7
Burnett, J M, 1947, N 1,15:3
Burnett, James E, 1949, F 23,27:4
Burnett, James R, 1939, Mr 29,23:3; 1952, Je 14,1
Burnett, Jean L (funl, F 28,9:6), 1907, F 27,9:6
Burnett, Jerome C, 1946, D 5,32:2
Burnett, John C, 1959, O 30,27:2
Burnett, John C Mrs, 1956, Ja 9,25:3
Burnett, John H, 1959, Ag 14,21:4
Burnett, John L, 1919, My 14,17:7
Burnett, John S, 1942, F 11,22:2; 1946, Mr 22,21:4
Burnett, Joseph H, 1956, N 5,31:2
Burnett, Josephine M, 1945, D 18,27:3
Burnett, Leland J, 1958, O 7,35:2
Burnett, Levi H, 1948, O 28,30:2
Burnett, Levi H Mrs, 1954, Je 12,15:4
Burnett, Lucien D Sr, 1962, O 30,35:1
Burnett, Lyman C, 1950, N 13,28:2
Burnett, N Lowe, 1942, Jl 21,20:3
Burnett, Nathan L Mrs, 1963, Jl 13,17:4
Burnett, Paul M, 1944, N 1,23:4
Burnett, Percy L, 1943, O 31,48:4
Burnett, Phil, 1955, Mr 18,28:3
Burnett, R W, 1955, Je 2,29:5
Burnett, Richard F, 1962, Ag 8,31:4
Burnett, Robert L, 1959, Jl 3,17:2
Burnett, Robert P, 1953, S 15,31:3
Burnett, Ruth (Mother), 1944, Mr 18,13:3
Burnett, S Burk Capt, 1922, Je 28,15:6
Burnett, Sally K, 1965, D 10,42:5
Burnett, Samuel M, 1909, Mr 1,9:2
Burnett, Swan Moses Dr, 1906, Ja 19,11:5
Burnett, Thomas J, 1940, D 20,25:3
Burnett, Thomas O, 1937, Ag 24,21:4
Burnett, Thomas W, 1945, O 20,11:4
Burnett, Tom L, 1938, D 27,17:5
Burnett, Virginia S, 1947, Ag 24,56:1
Burnett, Vivian, 1937, Jl 26,1:4
Burnett, W B Gen, 1884, Je 25,5:3
Burnett, Walter A, 1944, Mr 17,17:2
Burnett, William E, 1946, O 29,25:3; 1952, N 20,3
Burnett, William N, 1956, Jl 9,23:2
Burnett, William W, 1952, Mr 24,25:3
Burnette, A Rex, 1952, My 4,90:7
Burnette, Smiley (Lester A Burnette), 1967, F 18
Burney, Charles Denniston Sir (funl service), 196
N 13,47:2
Burney, Charles Fox Dr, 1925, Ap 16,21:4
Burney, Robert, 1942, S 15,23:2
Burnham, A A, 1879, Ap 13,2:3
Burnham, Addison C, 1939, S 12,25:4; 1951, Ap 1
33:2
Burnham, Alex O, 1959, Ag 13,27:1
Burnham, Ammi 2d, 1903, My 19,9:6
Burnham, Baron, 1943, Je 16,21:4
Burnham, Beverley, 1942, Je 1,13:2
Burnham, C L, 1927, Je 22,27:5
Burnham, Charles, 1938, Ja 20,23:2
Burnham, Charles L, 1924, N 6,19:5
Burnham, Charles Luther, 1917, Mr 2,11:6
Burnham, D H Mrs, 1945, D 25,23:2
Burnham, Daniel H, 1912, Je 2,II,13:5; 1961, N 5,
Burnham, Daniel H Mrs, 1961, N 5,66:1
Burnham, Edmund A, 1950, Ag 23,29:3
Burnham, Elmer S, 1941, Ja 6,15:2
Burnham, Eugene E, 1949, Ap 24,78:1
Burnham, Flora C Mrs, 1939, F 9,21:1
Burnham, Fred C, 1962, My 21,33:4
Burnham, Fred W, 1940, Ap 16,23:3
Burnham, Frederic, 1942, Jl 9,21:2
Burnham, Frederick R, 1947, S 2,21:6
Burnham, Frederick R Mrs, 1939, D 23,15:3
Burnham, G W, 1885, Mr 19,5:4
Burnham, George, 1912, D 12,13:3
Burnham, George R, 1962, Je 13,41:4
Burnham, George W, 1958, Ag 30,15:4
Burnham, Gordon W, 1950, N 23,38:2
Burnham, Gordon W Mrs, 1883, O 10,8:2
Burnham, Guy L, 1957, Je 12,35:5
Burnham, Henry Eben Ex-Sen, 1917, F 9,11:6
Burnham, Homer V, 1945, Jl 22,37:1
Burnham, J Forrest, 1940, Ja 28,33:3
Burnham, J Hampden, 1940, Ap 26,21:4

Burnham, James Kellogg, 1907, Mr 15,9:6
Burnham, James L, 1941, Ap 10,24:2
Burnham, John A, 1944, Je 24,13:3
Burnham, John B (por), 1939, S 26,23:1
Burnham, John B Mrs, 1945, Ap 7,15:5
Burnham, John E, 1941, Ag 21,17:4
Burnham, John L Dr, 1925, S 16,25:4
Burnham, John M, 1957, N 16,19:5
Burnham, Lord, 1916, Ja 10,11:1
Burnham, Lord (E F Lawson), 1963, Jl 5,16:8
Burnham, Louis E, 1960, F 14,84:7
Burnham, Marianne W Mrs, 1945, My 22,19:5
Burnham, Martha C, 1954, O 26,27:4
Burnham, Mary M Mrs, 1937, N 6,17:6
Burnham, Nicholas, 1925, F 3,13:4
Burnham, Percy H, 1954, Jl 15,27:2
Burnham, R Wesley, 1953, Jl 23,23:4
Burnham, Roger N, 1962, Mr 16,31:1
Burnham, Ruth H Mrs, 1966, F 16,43:5
Burnham, Sherburne W Dr, 1921, Mr 12,11:6
Burnham, Smith, 1947, D 15,25:4
Burnham, Stewart H, 1943, S 27,19:4
Burnham, Thomas B, 1925, Ja 30,17:4
Burnham, Viscount, 1933, Jl 21,17:1
Burnham, Walter, 1937, O 3,II,8:8; 1948, Je 18,23:3
Burnham, Walter H, 1968, Je 3,45:2
Burnham, William, 1951, Ap 5,29:4
Burnham, William A, 1922, O 19,21:6
Burnham, William Addison, 1923, Ap 20,17:4
Burnham, William Dixon Capt, 1919, Mr 29,13:4
Burnham, William H, 1941, Je 26,23:6
Burnhan, Brig-Gen, 1864, O 2,5:2
Burnick, William F, 1949, D 8,33:4
Burnie, William Mrs, 1925, Je 10,23:5
Burnofsky, Mayer, 1953, Je 26,19:4
Burnquist, J A Alfred, 1961, Ja 13,27:2
Burns, A Lincíln, 1941, Ja 15,23:8
Burns, Albert, 1959, Mr 7,21:1
Burns, Alex J, 1953, Ag 13,25:3
Burns, Alex S Jr, 1938, S 6,21:3
Burns, Alfred A Mrs (Frances S), 1961, F 28,33:4
Burns, Alfred E, 1948, Ag 5,21:4
Burns, Allan T, 1953, Mr 10,29:3
Burns, Andrew J, 1958, N 14,27:3
Burns, Anna E, 1954, Mr 17,31:5
Burns, Anne Katharine, 1968, S 21,33:3
Burns, Archibald P, 1958, My 26,29:2
Burns, Arthur J, 1948, S 21,27:4
Burns, Arthur L, 1944, Ag 31,17:6
Burns, Arthur L Mrs, 1942, F 17,21:4
Burns, Arthur R, 1959, S 8,35:3
Burns, Barbara, 1962, Ja 2,21:1
Burns, Bob (will, F 28,27:4), 1956, F 3,21:5
Burns, Brendan, 1961, Ja 29,85:2
Burns, C J Walter, 1944, F 4,15:4
Burns, Charles A, 1947, Jl 20,45:2; 1958, F 24,19:1
Burns, Charles B, 1939, O 26,23:6
Burns, Charles F, 1947, My 4,60:8
Burns, Charles S Maj, 1916, F 1,11:7
Burns, Charles V, 1947, Ja 1,34:3
Burns, Charles W (por), 1938, Ja 20,24:2
Burns, Charley (Charles Goes), 1944, F 15,17:6
Burns, Clinton, 1939, F 4,15:1
Burns, Cloyd E, 1951, My 26,17:5
Burns, Cornelius F, 1938, My 24,19:4
Burns, D Joseph, 1942, Ag 21,19:5
Burns, D Joseph Mrs, 1960, O 27,37:5
Burns, Daniel J, 1942, Ag 21,19:2
Burns, Dawson Dr, 1909, Ag 23,7:4
Burns, Dawson J, 1954, N 8,21:4
Burns, Dennis F, 1957, S 11,33:2
Burns, Dexter D, 1954, D 1,31:3
Burns, Dominick F, 1940, F 29,19:4
Burns, Dorothy L, 1947, Ag 20,23:6
Burns, E Stanley, 1945, Je 3,32:3
Burns, Edmund J, 1958, Ja 28,28:1
Burns, Edward, 1914, My 19,9:5
Burns, Edward F, 1944, Jl 27,17:4; 1945, Mr 27,19:3
Burns, Edward H, 1955, Ja 28,19:3
Burns, Edward J, 1944, N 16,23:5; 1946, Ap 23,21:5
Burns, Edward J Mrs, 1951, D 10,29:4
Burns, Edward M, 1952, S 29,23:6
Burns, Edward T, 1948, Ag 12,21:4
Burns, Edwin F, 1947, Ap 16,25:5
Burns, Elbert S, 1951, My 21,27:3
Burns, Eleanor I (trb, F 9,12:7), 1952, F 2,13:5
Burns, Elizabeth, 1941, Ag 26,19:5
Burns, Elizabeth M, 1944, Jl 25,19:5
Burns, Ernest L, 1947, S 2,21:5
Burns, F Hugh, 1961, Jl 15,19:7
Burns, Francis, 1945, Je 10,32:4
Burns, Francis D, 1967, Ag 11,31:4
Burns, Francis J, 1955, Ap 28,29:3
Burns, Francis L, 1952, My 7,27:4
Burns, Francis P, 1955, N 18,25:4; 1960, N 12,21:6
Burns, Francis P Sr, 1955, Ja 3,27:2
Burns, Frank A, 1903, N 3,1:6
Burns, Frank F, 1944, F 25,17:5
Burns, Frank L, 1937, Mr 11,23:2
Burns, Frank T, 1950, My 28,44:7
Burns, Frankie, 1961, Ap 12,41:4
Burns, Franklin L, 1946, F 10,42:4
Burns, Frederick W, 1937, Ap 23,21:5
Burns, George J, 1939, My 22,17:3; 1966, Ag 16,39:3
Burns, George K, 1962, Je 12,37:3
Burns, George M, 1960, D 9,31:2
Burns, George Mrs (G Allen) (funl, S 1,36:1; will, S 5,10:1), 1964, Ag 29,1:8
Burns, George R, 1941, N 6,23:6; 1964, Mr 3,35:3
Burns, George V, 1954, S 28,29:2; 1956, Ja 17,33:2
Burns, Gerald G, 1952, F 17,86:4
Burns, H Boris, 1965, Ag 4,35:1
Burns, Harold, 1949, My 11,29:3
Burns, Harry, 1939, Ja 11,19:2; 1948, Jl 10,15:5
Burns, Harry B, 1950, N 23,35:5
Burns, Harry F, 1951, Ap 8,93:2
Burns, Harvey L, 1958, N 18,37:4
Burns, Henrietta H, 1944, Ja 5,17:4
Burns, Henry F, 1947, Ja 21,23:5
Burns, Henry G, 1943, N 20,13:6
Burns, Herbert D, 1960, Mr 29,37:2
Burns, Irving R, 1950, F 16,23:3
Burns, J Thomas, 1945, D 29,13:5
Burns, Jabez Mrs, 1957, D 15,86:7
Burns, Jabez Rev Dr, 1876, F 2,4:6
Burns, Jack, 1954, O 9,17:5
Burns, James, 1943, Ja 11,31:5; 1944, Jl 14,13:4; 1947, S 24,23:5; 1951, My 22,31:5
Burns, James A, 1940, S 10,23:6
Burns, James A Mrs, 1937, O 19,26:1
Burns, James E, 1940, My 22,23:4; 1962, My 11,31:1
Burns, James Ex-Sen, 1925, D 18,23:2
Burns, James F, 1948, S 19,76:4; 1958, Ja 11,17:4; 1968, My 16,48:1
Burns, James F Mrs, 1951, F 13,31:4
Burns, James H, 1937, My 6,25:5
Burns, James J, 1942, S 20,41:3; 1942, O 10,15:4
Burns, James J Dr, 1914, F 20,9:4
Burns, James L, 1964, O 8,43:2
Burns, James L Mrs, 1962, Ag 1,31:1
Burns, James Mrs, 1954, O 19,27:5
Burns, James T, 1937, N 16,23:3
Burns, John, 1872, F 11,5:5; 1903, My 24,7:4; 1942, Mr 23,15:3; 1943, Ja 25,13:5
Burns, John A, 1937, Ag 10,19:5; 1943, Ap 16,21:2
Burns, John A (Lord Inverclyde), 1957, Je 19,35:3
Burns, John B Sr, 1948, O 23,15:3
Burns, John C, 1910, My 7,9:6
Burns, John F, 1947, My 31,13:4
Burns, John H, 1940, Je 27,23:3; 1953, Ja 15,27:3
Burns, John H Jr, 1947, My 23,23:4
Burns, John H Novelist, 1953, Ag 14,19:1
Burns, John J, 1939, Ja 24,19:6; 1940, F 12,17:3; 1949, Ap 9,17:3; 1950, F 14,26:4; 1951, D 16,91:2; 1957, My 12,86:1
Burns, John N, 1941, N 2,55:8
Burns, John P, 1966, D 23,25:1
Burns, John T, 1950, F 23,27:1; 1953, O 19,21:5
Burns, Joseph, 1946, N 4,25:3; 1958, Ag 11,21:5
Burns, Joseph E, 1942, Ap 17,17:5; 1946, O 21,31:3
Burns, Joseph T, 1958, Je 26,27:4
Burns, Joseph V, 1962, O 9,41:4
Burns, Judson C, 1943, Ja 27,21:4
Burns, Kenneth G, 1949, O 22,17:4
Burns, Kenneth H, 1955, Jl 3,33:2
Burns, L H, 1928, Je 10,23:1
Burns, Lawrence, 1939, Jl 4,13:3
Burns, Lee E Mrs, 1953, Mr 25,25:1
Burns, Leopoldina, 1942, Je 4,19:5
Burns, Lloyd S, 1953, Ag 7,19:6
Burns, Louis J, 1945, My 23,19:5
Burns, M W Col, 1883, D 11,8:1
Burns, Martin, 1937, Ja 9,17:5
Burns, Martin C, 1948, Ag 22,60:6
Burns, Martin H, 1939, O 2,17:3
Burns, Mary, 1923, Jl 29,6:3
Burns, Matthew D, 1965, F 15,27:5
Burns, Michael, 1924, Ap 29,17:1; 1942, Jl 15,19:5
Burns, Michael A, 1938, Mr 9,23:4
Burns, Michael F, 1937, Je 23,25:1
Burns, Michael J, 1949, My 3,25:2
Burns, Michael Mrs, 1949, D 2,29:1; 1951, Ja 9,30:2
Burns, Michael R, 1947, Jl 31,21:5
Burns, Mitchell Mrs, 1945, Je 1,15:4
Burns, Nat (N B Haines),(funl, N 14,40:1), 1962, N 10,25:1
Burns, Ned J, 1953, O 13,29:4
Burns, Owen M, 1952, O 27,27:2
Burns, Patrick, 1937, F 25,23:5
Burns, Patrick C, 1959, Jl 19,69:2
Burns, Patrick C Mrs, 1947, N 29,13:1
Burns, Patrick J, 1946, O 28,27:5
Burns, Paul, 1957, Ap 15,21:2
Burns, Paul H, 1942, Ja 10,15:3
Burns, Paul J, 1959, O 24,86:8
Burns, Peter, 1908, Ag 20,7:6
Burns, R, 1879, Ag 4,5:5
Burns, Randall G Mrs, 1954, D 11,13:2
Burns, Rev Dr, 1869, Ag 20,1:5
Burns, Richard F, 1952, Mr 25,27:3
Burns, Richard J, 1952, Ap 24,31:3
Burns, Robert, 1954, Ap 9,23:2; 1954, O 22,27:2; 1961, Je 17,21:2; 1964, Ag 21,30:5
Burns, Robert A, 1950, O 14,19:2; 1968, S 9,47:2
Burns, Robert E, 1938, Ap 25,15:4; 1938, D 4,60:8
Burns, Robert E (will, Jl 3,36:4), 1955, Je 7,33:1
Burns, Robert F, 1950, Je 6,29:3
Burns, Robert J, 1961, N 16,39:3
Burns, Robert Mrs, 1943, Jl 21,15:4; 1951, O 27,19:4
Burns, Robert P, 1947, Ag 20,21:5; 1955, Je 11,15:1
Burns, Robert P Mrs, 1946, O 14,29:4
Burns, Robert W, 1957, Ap 29,25:5; 1964, S 7,19:5
Burns, Robert W 3d, 1956, O 10,39:2
Burns, Rosalie A, 1958, My 3,19:2
Burns, Sherman M, 1946, D 16,23:1
Burns, Silas, 1940, Ag 11,31:3
Burns, Simon, 1910, F 7,9:5
Burns, St Clair M, 1953, My 12,27:4
Burns, Stilwell C, 1944, N 3,21:3
Burns, Thomas, 1938, Ja 17,19:1; 1944, My 25,21:3
Burns, Thomas E, 1943, Je 4,21:1
Burns, Thomas F, 1937, Ap 12,17:3; 1940, S 3,17:5
Burns, Thomas J, 1951, Ag 27,19:2; 1966, Jl 18,27:3
Burns, Thomas J Mrs, 1950, F 17,23:2
Burns, Thomas Mrs, 1945, D 11,25:2
Burns, Thomas S, 1952, Jl 10,31:1
Burns, Timothy, 1937, D 13,27:5
Burns, Timothy J, 1964, My 9,27:2
Burns, Tommy, 1955, My 11,31:2
Burns, Vincent L, 1960, Ag 27,19:6
Burns, W Chalmers, 1963, Ap 5,47:2
Burns, W G, 1949, N 25,31:1
Burns, W J, 1932, Ap 15,19:1
Burns, Walter, 1940, S 20,23:5
Burns, Walter H Mrs, 1919, Jl 21,11:2
Burns, Walter X, 1946, O 6,59:5
Burns, William, 1951, O 1,23:5; 1962, Mr 8,31:3
Burns, William A, 1951, Je 19,29:1
Burns, William A Mrs, 1947, D 29,17:2; 1954, Ap 28, 31:4
Burns, William A Sr, 1942, Je 30,21:5
Burns, William C, 1955, Ag 6,15:1
Burns, William E, 1943, Jl 23,17:1
Burns, William F, 1913, F 6,11:5
Burns, William G, 1946, Mr 15,21:5; 1953, My 27,31:4
Burns, William H, 1941, My 21,23:3; 1945, Mr 14, 20:2; 1957, Ap 8,23:5; 1968, O 25,47:4
Burns, William J, 1952, O 13,21:3
Burns, William M, 1952, Ap 3,35:4
Burns, William McG, 1966, Jl 29,31:2
Burns, William Mrs, 1967, O 14,27:5
Burns, William Nicol Col, 1872, Mr 13,2:7
Burns, William T, 1951, Jl 25,23:4
Burns, Willis T, 1945, Je 25,17:4
Burns, Willis T Mrs, 1941, Mr 6,21:3
Burnshaw, Edward W Jr, 1941, Je 7,17:2
Burnside, A E, 1881, S 14,5:1
Burnside, Cameron, 1952, Mr 29,15:3
Burnside, Charles H, 1941, Mr 20,21:2
Burnside, Charles V, 1944, Je 15,19:5
Burnside, David, 1942, Ja 6,23:2
Burnside, De Witt L, 1937, Je 28,19:4
Burnside, George D, 1944, S 11,17:6
Burnside, Howard L, 1948, Ag 3,25:3
Burnside, Irving H, 1961, O 20,33:1
Burnside, James H (will, N 27,34:6), 1938, N 22,24:2
Burnside, Malcolm, 1946, Ap 7,46:3
Burnside, Mrs, 1871, Ag 5,6:2
Burnside, R H, 1952, S 15,25:1
Burnside, Robert C (por), 1938, Ag 4,17:1
Burnside, Robert C Mrs, 1943, D 29,17:4
Burnside, Robert H Mrs, 1940, N 25,17:4
Burnstine, David, 1965, Ag 28,21:4
Burnstine, Ruth A, 1941, S 24,23:4
Burnz, Elizabeth B Mrs, 1903, Je 23,7:6
Buro, Louis D, 1946, F 28,23:1
Buron, Edmond, 1942, Ag 3,15:4
Burpeau, Oscar, 1944, N 2,19:3
Burpeau, William P, 1964, Jl 13,29:3
Burpee, Charles B, 1945, My 14,17:5
Burpee, Charles M, 1943, Ag 17,17:3
Burpee, Frank E, 1958, D 1,29:4
Burpee, Frank H, 1954, F 27,13:5
Burpee, Frank W, 1939, O 9,19:4
Burpee, George W, 1967, N 8,47:1
Burpee, George W Mrs, 1968, Jl 13,27:5
Burpee, Hortense R Mrs, 1952, Ja 29,25:2
Burpee, Isaac, 1885, Mr 3,2:3
Burpee, John S, 1939, D 26,19:3
Burpee, Lawrence J, 1946, O 15,25:3
Burpee, Lucien F Justice, 1924, My 10,13:4
Burpee, Moses Mrs, 1943, Mr 19,19:4
Burpee, W Atlee, 1915, N 27,15:5; 1966, Ja 11,27:1
Burpee, W Atlee Mrs, 1948, N 12,24:3
Burpoe, Frank E, 1946, Ag 22,27:3
Burquier, Msgr, 1943, Mr 31,19:3
Burr, Aaron C, 1882, Jl 28,5:4
Burr, Abram D, 1952, Jl 5,15:4
Burr, Alex G, 1951, F 9,25:2
Burr, Allston, 1949, Ja 19,27:5
Burr, Angie S L Mrs, 1939, Ag 11,15:1
Burr, Anna C (will), 1942, Jl 15,21:4
Burr, Anna M, 1938, My 13,19:5
Burr, Borden, 1952, Ag 6,21:6
Burr, C C, 1883, My 3,5:2
Burr, Caril S, 1916, F 27,17:5
Burr, Charles E, 1924, Ag 26,11:3
Burr, Charles H Dr, 1908, Ag 15,7:4
Burr, Charles H Mrs, 1941, S 11,23:2

Burr, Charles W, 1944, F 20,36:5
Burr, Courtney, 1961, O 18,43:1
Burr, Daniel Mrs, 1949, D 21,29:2
Burr, Douglas H, 1951, O 26,20:2
Burr, Edward, 1952, Ap 17,29:3
Burr, Edward H (will), 1943, Ja 27,25:1
Burr, Edward T, 1958, Je 17,29:5
Burr, Edwin, 1866, Mr 14,2:4
Burr, Elizabeth Mrs, 1924, Ag 12,11:2
Burr, Emanuel, 1957, Jl 10,27:4
Burr, Emily T, 1966, F 4,31:2
Burr, Enoch Fitch Rev Dr, 1907, My 10,7:6
Burr, Eugene W, 1961, F 6,23:2
Burr, Frances Ellen, 1923, F 10,13:5
Burr, Frances P Mrs, 1939, Ja 16,15:3
Burr, Francis H, 1910, D 5,13:5
Burr, Frank W Sr Mrs, 1968, Jl 13,44:3
Burr, Frederick S, 1939, Ja 8,43:3
Burr, Freeman F, 1956, Je 11,31:5
Burr, George E, 1939, N 18,17:3
Burr, George H, 1939, D 19,26:3
Burr, George H Mrs, 1964, Ja 31,27:5
Burr, George L, 1938, Je 28,19:6; 1956, Ag 5,77:2
Burr, George L Sr, 1949, D 19,27:4
Burr, George W B, 1959, My 22,27:3
Burr, George W Brig-Gen, 1923, Mr 5,15:4
Burr, Gerard H, 1944, F 22,23:4
Burr, Gertrude S Mrs, 1941, Ja 6,18:6
Burr, H A, 1884, D 26,5:4
Burr, Hanford M, 1941, O 7,23:2
Burr, Harold C, 1955, Jl 7,27:4
Burr, Henry, 1901, N 17,3:3; 1941, Ap 7,17:6
Burr, Henry E Mrs, 1938, Ap 3,II,7:4
Burr, Henry Mrs, 1954, S 18,15:3
Burr, Henry P, 1940, D 6,23:3
Burr, Hudson C, 1949, Ap 21,25:1
Burr, I Tucker, 1952, F 4,17:1
Burr, James M Mrs, 1943, Ag 15,38:7
Burr, Jane B, 1956, Ja 15,93:1
Burr, John Reed, 1968, Ap 9,47:1
Burr, Joseph Arthur Justice, 1915, Ap 20,15:5
Burr, Joseph B, 1947, N 14,23:5
Burr, Karl E, 1945, Jl 10,11:7
Burr, Kate, 1943, Mr 3,23:5
Burr, Leland M, 1951, O 14,88:5
Burr, Lionel C, 1925, N 26,23:5
Burr, Louis Heman, 1909, Ap 17,9:5
Burr, Marcus Rev, 1914, O 17,11:4
Burr, Mary E, 1944, Jl 8,11:5
Burr, Mary L Y D Mrs, 1941, My 30,15:2
Burr, Melancethon, 1915, Ag 22,13:5
Burr, Milton W, 1954, Ja 16,15:6
Burr, Myron S, 1938, N 6,49:2
Burr, N B, 1928, F 12,30:3
Burr, P N, 1947, Mr 19,25:5
Burr, Phil C, 1950, N 6,27:4
Burr, Theodore, 1943, N 5,19:2
Burr, Van Rensselaer, 1946, Mr 1,22:2
Burr, W, 1929, My 7,31:1
Burr, W P, 1930, N 14,23:1
Burr, Walter C, 1940, Ap 4,23:2
Burr, William Fairfield, 1908, Jl 19,7:7
Burr, William Henry, 1908, F 29,7:6
Burr, William J, 1948, Mr 7,70:5
Burr, William P Mrs, 1918, F 19,13:5
Burr, Winthrop Jr, 1923, O 2,7:3
Burrage, A C, 1931, Je 30,25:5
Burrage, Champlin, 1951, Ja 10,27:3
Burrage, Guy H, 1954, Je 18,23:6
Burrage, Harry L, 1952, Mr 27,29:1
Burrage, Helen M, 1919, F 26,11:4
Burrage, John D Mrs, 1966, Jl 28,33:5
Burrage, William S, 1939, Ja 25,21:5
Burrage, William S Mrs, 1955, Ap 18,23:3
Burrard, Sidney G, 1943, Mr 18,19:5
Burras, Charles H, 1955, Je 1,33:1
Burras, Howard K (funl, D 22,21:4), 1925, D 19,17:6
Burrell, C B, 1881, O 18,5:1
Burrell, Charles A, 1950, Je 6,30:2
Burrell, D, 1878, Ap 21,5:1
Burrell, D J Rev, 1926, D 6,23:4
Burrell, David D, 1950, F 23,27:1
Burrell, David J Mrs, 1918, S 23,9:6
Burrell, Edward C, 1924, N 5,19:4
Burrell, Ellen L, 1938, D 5,23:3
Burrell, Frank A, 1962, My 10,37:2
Burrell, George A, 1905, N 8,9:6; 1957, Ag 18,83:3
Burrell, Gustave J, 1965, Ag 28,21:5
Burrell, H B, 1953, N 12,31:2
Burrell, Harold P, 1957, S 3,27:4
Burrell, Harold W, 1950, Je 23,25:3
Burrell, Horace H, 1945, Je 28,19:2
Burrelle, John A, 1957, Je 2,87:2
Burrell, Leo P, 1939, Ag 7,15:6
Burrell, Martin, 1938, Mr 21,15:1
Burrell, Peter Robert (Baron Gwydyr), 1909, Ap 4, 13:4
Burrell, Randal C, 1962, F 12,23:3
Burrell, W D, 1937, Jl 27,10:2
Burrell, William, 1958, Ap 1,31:5
Burrelle, Frank A, 1910, Ja 28,9:4
Burrett, Claude A, 1941, Mr 5,21:1
Burri, Paul, 1943, Mr 25,21:3
Burrian, Carl, 1924, S 27,16:4
Burridge, Lee S, 1915, My 5,13:4
Burridge, Walter W, 1913, Je 26,9:4
Burrier, Walter P, 1954, Ja 31,88:7
Burright, Arthur L, 1958, F 13,29:2
Burright, Arthur L Mrs (Grandma), 1958, F 12,29:4
Burrill, C D, 1902, O 27,9:5
Burrill, Edgar W, 1958, D 7,88:5
Burrill, Edward L, 1937, Ap 20,25:6
Burrill, Ellen M, 1937, D 11,19:3
Burrill, Emmons P Mrs, 1965, F 15,27:4
Burrill, Harvey D (will, D 30,17:8), 1938, D 25,15:3
Burrill, James A, 1953, O 12,27:5
Burrill, Louis D, 1955, Jl 24,65:1
Burrill, Percy Morris, 1925, Mr 19,21:3
Burrill, Thomas J, 1916, Ap 16,21:4
Burrill, William Henry, 1915, Je 4,11:6
Burrill, William P, 1874, Mr 4,3:6
Burris, Alva B, 1938, Mr 26,15:5
Burris, Charles A, 1949, D 27,23:2
Burris, Harry, 1955, O 15,15:4
Burris, Michael M, 1966, Jl 2,23:3
Burris, William P, 1946, N 9,17:2
Burrison, Newton, 1951, D 5,35:1
Burriss, Eli E, 1950, Mr 19,94:6
Burritt, Alan B, 1955, Jl 25,19:5
Burritt, Bailey B, 1954, Je 19,15:3
Burritt, Bailey B Mrs, 1960, Mr 27,87:1
Burritt, Burton T, 1945, Ag 26,44:6
Burritt, Daniel E, 1951, D 6,33:3
Burritt, Elihu, 1879, Mr 8,5:2
Burritt, George H, 1944, Ag 27,33:3
Burritt, Leslie A, 1940, D 8,69:2
Burritt, Leslie D, 1965, Ag 9,25:1
Burritt, Louis L, 1944, N 9,27:5
Burritt, Marion T, 1944, My 6,15:5
Burritt, Maurice C, 1959, O 7,43:2
Burritt, Norman W, 1952, N 29,17:3
Burritt, Olin H, 1949, Jl 8,19:2
Burritt, Stephen D, 1938, Jl 14,21:5
Burros, Hyman, 1944, Je 24,13:5
Burrough, Bertha C Mrs, 1947, Ja 29,25:3
Burrough, Edmund W, 1962, My 10,37:2
Burrough, Ervel B Mrs, 1941, O 5,49:1
Burrough, Henry W, 1938, Ag 8,13:5
Burrough, Lewis F, 1937, Ap 7,25:2
Burrough, William F, 1938, O 27,23:3
Burroughs, Agnes Z Mrs, 1941, Mr 26,23:5
Burroughs, Alan, 1965, My 4,43:1
Burroughs, Aretus P, 1952, Ap 20,92:4
Burroughs, B, 1934, N 17,15:3
Burroughs, Charles F, 1944, Ap 22,15:3
Burroughs, Charles Mrs, 1945, D 29,14:3
Burroughs, Charles W, 1943, F 17,21:4
Burroughs, Claude, 1876, D 7,2:3
Burroughs, Dexter, 1946, Jl 11,23:4
Burroughs, Earl A, 1941, D 22,17:1
Burroughs, Edgar R, 1950, Mr 20,21:3
Burroughs, Frederick S, 1940, Je 21,22:2
Burroughs, G Hartley, 1955, F 10,31:3
Burroughs, G S Rev, 1901, O 23,9:3
Burroughs, Harry E, 1946, D 19,29:3
Burroughs, Harry S, 1965, Mr 7,82:7
Burroughs, Henry C, 1950, My 13,17:5
Burroughs, Henry S, 1940, Ja 22,15:4
Burroughs, Jane J, 1952, D 8,41:3
Burroughs, John, 1917, Mr 7,11:6
Burroughs, Joseph A, 1953, Ag 12,31:2
Burroughs, Joseph H, 1940, Ag 3,15:6
Burroughs, Josephine, 1940, Je 29,15:4
Burroughs, Julian, 1954, D 17,31:4
Burroughs, Malvern C, 1954, Ag 4,21:1
Burroughs, Nannie H, 1961, My 22,31:5
Burroughs, Neal, 1963, O 8,43:3
Burroughs, Preston A, 1955, O 24,27:3
Burroughs, Robert N Mrs, 1949, Jl 23,11:6
Burroughs, Shepard H, 1946, My 18,19:2
Burroughs, Stephen H, 1942, D 5,15:1
Burroughs, William H C, 1948, Ag 13,15:4
Burroughs, William W, 1937, Ap 28,23:4
Burrow, Francis R, 1945, D 18,27:4
Burrow, Henry J, 1954, Jl 18,56:3
Burrow, John D, 1948, Ag 26,21:2
Burrow, Trigant, 1950, My 26,23:5
Burrow, Trigant Mrs, 1951, O 17,31:1
Burrow, William H, 1941, F 18,23:4
Burrowes, Arthur L Rev, 1923, N 1,21:4
Burrowes, Charles Rev, 1914, My 30,11:5
Burrowes, Edward J, 1946, Ja 1,27:3
Burrowes, Edward J Mrs, 1939, F 23,23:4
Burrowes, Harry C, 1947, Ja 25,17:3
Burrowes, Horace S, 1949, Ap 20,27:4
Burrowes, John F, 1944, O 24,23:2
Burrowes, Lon M, 1953, Ag 8,11:6
Burrowes, Paul O, 1948, F 12,23:2
Burrowes, Rosemary, 1951, Ap 27,23:2
Burrowes, Thomas Mrs, 1959, O 23,29:4
Burrows, A Fenton Mrs, 1945, Ag 17,17:4
Burrows, Acton, 1948, N 16,29:4
Burrows, Alfred A, 1947, D 18,29:2
Burrows, Alvin T, 1941, My 22,21:5
Burrows, Andrew A, 1949, N 29,39:5
Burrows, Angie Mrs, 1944, Mr 8.19:2
Burrows, Arthur R, 1947, N 27,31:4
Burrows, Charles E, 1952, S 4,7:5
Burrows, Earle N, 1951, My 8,31:2
Burrows, Edwin G, 1958, Jl 14,21:5
Burrows, Ellen V Mrs, 1940, Ap 20,17:5
Burrows, Frank G, 1949, O 11,34:6
Burrows, Frank G Mrs, 1968, My 14,47:2
Burrows, Frederick T, 1957, N 4,29:3
Burrows, George E, 1966, Mr 13,86:8
Burrows, George F, 1943, S 26,48:2
Burrows, George H, 1943, N 24,21:2
Burrows, George R, 1951, My 14,25:4
Burrows, Grover C, 1963, Jl 7,53:1
Burrows, Harold L, 1965, Jl 27,33:2
Burrows, Harry O, 1956, S 13,35:4
Burrows, Irving L, 1949, Mr 31,25:4
Burrows, J Stanley, 1943, My 13,21:4
Burrows, James D, 1962, F 9,29:3
Burrows, James W, 1939, S 2,17:6
Burrows, John, 1908, F 1,9:5
Burrows, John S Sr, 1960, Ja 21,31:4
Burrows, John T, 1943, Ap 28,23:4
Burrows, Julius Caesar Ex-Sen, 1915, N 17,11:4
Burrows, Lansing Dr, 1919, O 18,13:4
Burrows, Leo C Sr, 1948, O 10,76:5
Burrows, Lorenzo, 1885, Mr 7,5:2
Burrows, Lynn M, 1944, F 11,19:2
Burrows, Raymond M, 1952, Je 1,84:4
Burrows, Robert E, 1957, Ja 29,31:5
Burrows, Robert N, 1950, Ag 10,25:1
Burrows, Samuel, 1947, Jl 9,23:5
Burrows, W A, 1903, Je 5,9:6
Burrows, Walter L Sr, 1966, Ja 13,25:4
Burrows, Warren B, 1952, D 10,35:6
Burrows, Willard S, 1952, Ja 2,25:2
Burrows, William F, 1925, Jl 31,15:6
Burrows, William G, 1947, F 3,19:1
Burrows, William R, 1955, Mr 4,23:3
Burrucker, Harry H, 1941, Je 21,17:4
Burrud, Leland J, 1959, D 14,31:5
Burrus, Florence A, 1950, Ja 4,2:3
Burruss, Julian A, 1947, Ja 5,53:3
Burry, George W (est acctg filed), 1967, Je 2,9:1
Burry, John, 1908, Mr 13,7:4
Burry, Leo A, 1953, Ja 7,31:4
Burry, Solen, 1953, Je 9,27:1
Bursch, Daniel F W, 1948, F 18,27:4
Bursch, Robert H, 1943, O 26,23:2
Burslem, Alex Y, 1946, O 22,25:5
Bursley, Herbert S, 1961, Mr 2,27:3
Burstall, Henry, 1945, F 11,40:3
Burstein, Abraham, 1966, O 4,47:3
Burstein, Harry, 1950, D 2,13:3
Burstein, Samuel H, 1954, Mr 24,27:1
Burstein, Simon P Mrs, 1951, Ag 5,72:3
Burstell, Carl B, 1952, My 21,27:4
Burstell, Edwin C, 1958, Mr 6,27:6
Burstiner, Joseph, 1937, Je 23,25:4
Burstiner, Joseph Mrs, 1966, Ja 14,39:3
Burston, B Elliot, 1954, My 28,23:1
Burston, Harold, 1939, Mr 16,23:5
Burstow, Walter, 1943, O 6,23:2
Burstyn, Joseph (trb, D 13,II,5:7), 1953, N 30,2:8
Burt, A, 1883, O 31,4:6
Burt, A M, 1925, Ap 21,21:5
Burt, Addison Millington, 1909, Ja 16,11:6
Burt, Andrew S Gen, 1915, Ja 13,9:5
Burt, Arthur H, 1963, O 19,25:5
Burt, Arthur W, 1945, Ap 26,23:3
Burt, Bates G, 1948, Ap 6,23:4
Burt, Benjamin H, 1950, S 19,31:3
Burt, C A, 1865, Mr 25,4:2
Burt, Charles A, 1967, N 2,47:4
Burt, Charles C, 1959, Ap 9,31:3
Burt, Charles M, 1944, My 26,19:5
Burt, Charles M Mrs, 1947, D 1,21:4
Burt, Clayton R, 1957, O 22,33:3
Burt, E A, 1939, Ap 29,17:7
Burt, E C, 1884, My 24,4:7
Burt, Edith B, 1952, Mr 16,90:4
Burt, Edward W, 1940, F 15,19:5
Burt, Edwin S, 1953, Ag 3,1:1
Burt, Ella Ney Mrs, 1925, Ap 14,23:4
Burt, Frank A, 1964, Ap 5,86:7
Burt, Frank H, 1942, Ap 25,13:4; 1946, Mr 4,23:6
Burt, Frederic, 1943, O 6,23:1
Burt, Frederick A, 1941, O 24,23:5
Burt, George Albert, 1909, Mr 12,7:5
Burt, George F, 1943, Je 22,19:3
Burt, George H, 1958, O 12,86:2
Burt, George H Mrs, 1943, D 23,19:3
Burt, George W, 1944, My 24,19:3
Burt, Harry P, 1941, Mr 20,21:5
Burt, Henry R, 1937, Ja 2,14:2
Burt, Horace Greeley, 1913, My 20,11:6
Burt, James B, 1937, F 5,21:2
Burt, James D Mrs, 1941, S 14,50:2
Burt, Jane, 1903, Ag 14,7:6
Burt, Laura, 1952, O 17,27:4
Burt, Louis M, 1958, Ja 31,21:3
Burt, Milo C, 1943, O 2,13:2
Burt, Paul G, 1962, Jl 3,23:3
Burt, S P, 1884, My 11,7:2

Burt, Samuel, 1961, Ag 20,86:5
Burt, Samuel S, 1947, Ag 14,23:5
Burt, Struthers, 1954, Ag 30,17:3
Burt, Stuart D, 1965, Ja 11,45:3
Burt, Thomas, 1922, Ap 14,17:6
Burt, Thomas G, 1941, Je 5,24:3
Burt, W, 1936, Ap 10,24:1
Burt, W L, 1882, Ap 22,5:3
Burt, Walter, 1940, O 17,25:4
Burt, Walter D, 1949, D 24,15:3
Burt, Wilbur F, 1965, D 30,23:1
Burt, William B, 1953, Ag 7,19:2
Burt, William F (will), 1947, My 13,27:2
Burt, William G Mrs, 1956, N 20,37:3
Burt, William H, 1940, N 23,17:6
Burt, William Mrs, 1946, Mr 24,46:3
Burt, William P, 1955, F 25,21:3
Burtch, Verdi, 1945, D 29,13:5
Burte, Edgar, 1950, D 8,29:3
Burten, Emanuel, 1961, D 21,27:2
Burtis, Alan M, 1965, My 1,31:1
Burtis, Caroline E Mrs, 1943, S 30,21:4
Burtis, Charles M, 1939, O 5,23:6
Burtis, Clare E, 1939, N 13,19:4
Burtis, Edith M, 1946, Ja 5,13:4
Burtis, F Filmore, 1915, S 28,11:3
Burtis, Frank G, 1964, N 24,39:2
Burtis, George H, 1959, Je 26,25:3
Burtis, Gillette H, 1948, S 20,25:2
Burtis, H Spencer Dr, 1937, Ap 25,II,8:5
Burtis, Harry M, 1949, Ap 1,25:5
Burtis, J H, 1903, Ja 30,9:5
Burtis, John H, 1952, My 7,27:2
Burtis, John H Mrs, 1912, Jl 10,9:4
Burtis, Murray, 1948, N 11,27:2
Burtis, W A, 1884, D 14,2:6
Burtman, Abraham, 1946, Mr 28,25:5
Burtnett, Bertrand G, 1955, N 22,35:6
Burtnieks, John A, 1959, O 6,39:5
Burton, Albert W, 1957, Jl 6,15:2
Burton, Alfred C, 1907, Ap 16,11:6
Burton, Andrew M, 1966, Ag 3,37:4
Burton, Annie C Mrs, 1946, Ag 7,27:2
Burton, Anthony R, 1947, F 27,21:2
Burton, Arthur D, 1948, F 12,23:1
Burton, Baron (Michl Arth Bass), 1909, F 2,9:6
Burton, Benjamin B Mrs, 1964, Jl 11,25:3
Burton, Benjamin T, 1968, N 24,87:1
Burton, Beverly, 1904, Ja 6,9:5
Burton, Birdella, 1943, Jl 21,15:3
Burton, Charles E, 1940, Ag 28,19:6
Burton, Charles L, 1961, Mr 22,41:3
Burton, Charles P, 1947, Ap 1,28:2
Burton, Charles Sr, 1951, N 28,31:3
Burton, Charlotte, 1942, Mr 31,21:2
Burton, Cornelia G Mrs, 1940, F 2,17:3
Burton, Dagsworthy D, 1941, Jl 15,20:2
Burton, Darius E, 1953, Jl 17,17:3
Burton, David, 1963, D 31,19:3
Burton, Doris G, 1965, Ag 29,84:8
Burton, E Earl, 1968, S 30,47:2
Burton, Edgar, 1968, N 10,88:4
Burton, Edgar Gordon, 1968, My 10,44:4
Burton, Edgar O, 1940, Ja 2,19:2
Burton, Edward C, 1946, N 22,23:2
Burton, Edward F, 1962, Ap 28,25:4
Burton, Eli F, 1948, Jl 7,46:1
Burton, Eli K, 1958, F 27,27:1
Burton, Elliot C, 1954, Mr 31,27:1
Burton, Ernest D Dr, 1925, My 27,23:3
Burton, Ernest Dewitt Dr, 1925, My 29,17:5
Burton, Felix A, 1949, N 30,27:4
Burton, Fletcher P, 1949, S 17,17:3
Burton, Florence R Mrs, 1948, Je 24,26:2
Burton, Frances T Mrs, 1940, Ap 21,42:3
Burton, Frank V, 1922, Mr 12,30:3; 1923, S 2,22:3
Burton, Fred, 1945, D 12,27:4; 1959, Je 3,35:1
Burton, Frederick H Mrs, 1941, Ag 20,19:6
Burton, Frederick Russell, 1909, O 2,9:4
Burton, Frederick W, 1956, F 11,17:2
Burton, G W, 1901, Ag 23,7:6
Burton, George A, 1947, My 31,13:3
Burton, George C, 1949, D 1,31:3
Burton, George Hall Gen, 1917, O 21,23:3
Burton, George L, 1916, Jl 20,11:5
Burton, George L Sr, 1960, Jl 23,19:3
Burton, George W, 1939, Ag 22,19:6
Burton, Harold F, 1950, D 25,19:5
Burton, Harold H, 1964, O 29,35:1
Burton, Harold W, 1964, Ag 20,29:5
Burton, Harry, 1954, Jl 16,21:5
Burton, Harry D, 1937, O 4,21:6
Burton, Harry E, 1945, Mr 21,23:4
Burton, Howes, 1960, Je 28,31:1
Burton, Isabel Lady, 1896, Mr 24,5:4
Burton, J H Rev, 1881, Ag 11,1:5
Burton, James C, 1966, F 6,92:3
Burton, Jean, 1952, Ja 20,84:3
Burton, Jennie C D Mrs, 1939, Mr 22,23:2
Burton, Jerry F Mrs, 1960, Ap 14,37:5
Burton, Jessie B S Mrs, 1939, O 17,25:6
Burton, John H, 1946, Ag 2,19:4
Burton, John J, 1944, N 1,23:5
Burton, John N Mrs, 1949, Ja 26,25:5
Burton, John R, 1944, Ja 28,18:2
Burton, Joseph, 1949, O 8,13:2; 1960, Ag 2,29:6
Burton, Joseph R Ex-Sen, 1923, F 28,17:4
Burton, Kenneth M, 1950, Ag 22,27:5
Burton, Laurence V Mrs, 1965, Ag 14,23:1
Burton, Lewis W, 1940, O 18,21:4
Burton, Margaret A, 1938, Ag 24,21:4
Burton, Marion Leroy, 1925, F 21,11:5
Burton, Martin C, 1958, Mr 4,29:4
Burton, Matthew H Mrs, 1950, O 1,104:7
Burton, Montague, 1952, S 22,23:1
Burton, Nat, 1945, Mr 23,19:2
Burton, Nelson, 1947, S 30,25:5
Burton, P C, 1953, My 22,27:2
Burton, Phil (L Samuels), 1959, Ap 29,33:4
Burton, Pomeroy, 1947, O 16,27:3
Burton, R F Sir, 1890, O 21,5:3
Burton, Richard, 1940, Ap 9,23:2
Burton, Robert, 1955, Je 18,17:2
Burton, Robert C, 1961, Mr 19,88:6
Burton, Robert J, 1965, My 30,47:3
Burton, Robert M, 1925, Ag 11,21:4
Burton, Samuel C, 1950, Je 2,23:3
Burton, T E, 1929, O 29,1:4
Burton, Theodore, 1942, Jl 23,19:3
Burton, Thomas, 1943, D 17,27:1
Burton, Thomas J, 1943, Mr 23,23:2
Burton, Thomas L, 1945, D 10,21:2
Burton, Virginia Lee (Mrs Geo Demetrios), 1968, O 16,47:2
Burton, Walter B, 1968, D 20,42:7
Burton, Walter C (funl, Ag 6,15:4), 1923, S 4,17:1
Burton, Walter L Jr, 1960, Ap 17,93:1
Burton, Warren D, 1956, Mr 23,27:3
Burton, Warren J, 1958, Ap 28,23:5
Burton, Wilfred J, 1947, Je 18,25:4
Burton, William, 1966, Mr 11,34:1
Burton, William A, 1949, Ag 7,61:2
Burton, William C, 1946, Ap 19,29:5
Burton, William Evans (funl, F 14,5:1; will, F 27,8:3), 1860, F 11,4:5
Burton, William H, 1955, F 22,21:5
Burton, William L 2d, 1958, Jl 28,23:2
Burton, William M, 1954, D 30,17:1
Burton, William O, 1940, O 22,23:2
Burton, William Shakespeare, 1916, F 5,11:6
Burton-Chadwick, Robert, 1951, My 24,35:4
Burton-Opitz, Russel, 1954, N 19,23:5
Burtsell, P V, 1883, Jl 30,5:5
Burtsell, Richard Labor Msgr (funl, F 9,9:5), 1912, F 5,9:4
Burtsfield, R Read, 1965, N 16,47:2
Burtt, Aaron F, 1954, O 13,31:5
Burtt, Arthur M, 1941, Ap 20,43:2
Burtt, Horatio H, 1968, Mr 6,47:4
Burtt, Howard, 1956, Ap 28,17:6
Burtt, Robert H, 1960, D 4,88:4
Burwash, Lachlin T, 1940, D 22,30:5
Burwasser, Herman, 1948, N 13,15:3
Burwell, Anson C, 1950, Jl 12,29:6
Burwell, C Sidney, 1967, S 4,21:5
Burwell, E Leslie, 1956, Mr 28,31:4
Burwell, E P, 1932, My 23,15:5
Burwell, Edward B, 1945, F 28,24:2
Burwell, G Loring, 1956, S 3,13:4
Burwell, John F, 1947, Jl 22,23:2
Burwell, Joseph S, 1903, S 22,7:5
Burwell, Robert O B, 1950, O 6,27:1
Burwell, William Turnbull Rear-Adm, 1910, Ja 5,11:4
Bury, C W F (Earl of Charleville), 1874, N 3,2:6
Bury, Charles K H, 1963, S 21,21:4
Bury, Clarence E, 1952, Ja 8,27:5
Bury, Edmund, 1956, Je 27,31:5
Bury, George, 1958, Jl 22,28:1
Bury, Harold G, 1963, Ap 22,27:4
Buryan, William, 1961, Ap 21,33:1
Busam, Joseph Rev, 1915, My 15,13:5
Busanovich, Geddie M, 1941, Ag 22,15:5
Busath, Carl H, 1948, Ja 1,23:1
Busbee, Jacques Mrs, 1962, Mr 3,21:4
Busbey, Emily J, 1879, N 18,8:4
Busbey, Fred E, 1966, F 13,84:6
Busbey, L White Mrs, 1959, Ag 5,27:2
Busbey, Leroy W Jr, 1952, F 29,23:4
Busby, Alfred W, 1964, Ag 30,93:1
Busby, Alfred W Mrs, 1964, Je 9,35:4
Busby, Amy, 1957, Jl 15,19:3
Busby, Edith L Mrs, 1964, N 17,41:3
Busby, George, 1949, Mr 22,25:2
Busby, George W, 1942, Ap 3,22:2
Busby, Terrell A, 1952, Ja 10,30:2
Buscaglia, Carlo, 1967, Mr 29,45:1
Buscaglia, Christy J, 1953, O 4,89:2
Buscall, Lewis F, 1950, D 7,33:5
Buscarlet, Jean, 1949, O 26,27:3
Busch, A A Sr, 1934, F 14,9:1
Busch, Adolf, 1952, Je 11,29:1
Busch, Adolphus (funl, O 12,15:2), 1913, O 11,15:1
Busch, Adolphus 3d, 1946, Ag 30,17:5
Busch, Arthur A, 1941, Ag 17,38:1
Busch, Arthur J (B Downes), 1966, Ja 28,47:4
Busch, August A Sr Mrs (will, Je 4,14:6), 1958, My 28,31:2
Busch, Briton N, 1950, Ap 3,24:2
Busch, Carl, 1915, Ap 9,11:5; 1943, D 20,23:2
Busch, Charles R, 1968, N 10,88:8
Busch, David F, 1951, Jl 4,17:6
Busch, Elizabeth O Mrs, 1958, My 6,35:2
Busch, Elsa V, 1956, My 1,33:3
Busch, F William, 1958, Ja 22,28:1
Busch, Fritz, 1951, S 15,15:1
Busch, Fritz Mrs, 1966, N 28,39:2
Busch, George, 1949, F 2,27:3
Busch, George J, 1944, Je 21,19:1
Busch, Gerald A, 1956, Je 13,37:4
Busch, Hans, 1952, O 8,31:5
Busch, Harold V, 1945, D 13,29:5
Busch, Henry, 1943, N 2,25:5
Busch, Henry P, 1942, Ap 26,39:2
Busch, Herman A, 1966, Ja 20,30:6
Busch, Hyman, 1959, Ja 17,19:4
Busch, Irving, 1960, Jl 10,72:4
Busch, John H, 1941, O 6,17:5
Busch, Joseph W, 1938, Ag 27,13:3
Busch, L Mrs, 1928, F 26,27:4
Busch, Mae, 1946, Ap 22,21:4
Busch, Miers, 1943, My 31,17:5
Busch, Milton E, 1941, Ag 28,10:3
Busch, Moritz, 1899, N 17,6:6
Busch, Otto S, 1939, Jl 29,15:6
Busch, Philip, 1905, My 22,9:1
Busch, Theodore L Mrs, 1949, Ap 12,29:4
Busch, Vladimir A, 1964, Jl 28,29:4
Busch, W, 1941, My 13,24:2
Busch, Wilhelm, 1946, D 29,37:4
Busch, William C A, 1948, My 22,15:3
Busch-Greenough, Edmee Mrs, 1955, D 19,27:2
Buschbaum, Joseph C, 1946, Ja 15,23:4
Buschbeck, A Gen, 1883, My 30,5:2
Buschbeck, Ernst H, 1963, My 21,37:3
Buschek, Hermann A, 1953, S 10,25:3
Buscher, George C, 1966, Ja 27,33:3
Buschgen, O W, 1948, F 22,48:3
Buschgen, Otto W Mrs, 1961, Je 3,23:4
Buschigen, Robert W Mrs, 1946, Mr 9,13:2
Buschke, William, 1950, D 22,24:2
Buschman, Sol L, 1945, S 25,25:3
Buschow, Gustav, 1946, Ap 20,13:3
Buse, Henry H, 1955, Ap 19,31:1
Buse, Oscar A, 1953, Jl 5,49:2
Buse, Raymond L, 1955, Ja 20,31:5
Buser, John Jr, 1959, Mr 5,31:4
Buser, Nathaniel E, 1954, D 1,31:2
Buser, Raymond G, 1957, Ap 3,31:2
Buset, Max, 1959, Je 29,29:3
Busey, George W, 1944, Ap 4,21:5
Busey, Henry C, 1942, N 17,26:2
Busey, Norval H Mrs, 1947, Jl 1,25:4
Busey, Paul G, 1950, S 25,23:3
Bush, A McC, 1877, D 21,3:3
Bush, Adrian D, 1947, S 7,63:2
Bush, Almon A, 1941, Ap 2,23:3
Bush, Alvin R, 1959, N 6,30:2
Bush, Amos J, 1941, Mr 20,21:2
Bush, Annie L, 1937, F 23,27:3
Bush, Archer C, 1956, F 11,17:2
Bush, Archibald G, 1966, Ja 17,47:2
Bush, Arthur W, 1873, D 6,12:4; 1950, N 15,31:1
Bush, Asahel N, 1953, F 26,25:1
Bush, B F, 1927, Jl 30,15:5
Bush, Baron De, 1903, Jl 25,7:1
Bush, Barton L, 1951, Ap 1,92:1
Bush, C Abbott, 1943, D 1,21:2
Bush, Carl W, 1962, Je 21,31:4
Bush, Catherine I Mrs, 1954, O 13,31:3
Bush, Charles A Mrs, 1949, O 25,28:3
Bush, Charles G, 1956, Ap 8,84:6
Bush, Charles Green, 1909, My 23,11:6
Bush, Charles S, 1957, F 8,23:5
Bush, Clifford N, 1957, Jl 2,27:3
Bush, D Fairfax Mrs, 1959, Ag 15,17:5
Bush, David H, 1941, S 12,21:5
Bush, Douglas J, 1955, Ag 7,73:2
Bush, Edgar D, 1949, Jl 23,11:6
Bush, Edward, 1919, Je 5,13:4
Bush, Eleanor J Mrs, 1952, Ja 15,27:3
Bush, F Harvey, 1941, My 10,15:5
Bush, Frances C Mrs, 1967, N 23,33:4
Bush, Frank, 1958, S 15,21:3
Bush, Fred S, 1962, F 10,23:3
Bush, Frederika D, 1953, Ap 23,29:6
Bush, George E, 1957, O 20,86:5
Bush, George Mrs, 1952, Jl 8,27:4
Bush, George Prof, 1859, S 22,4:4
Bush, George R, 1944, Ap 30,45:2
Bush, George W, 1944, N 2,19:2
Bush, Guy L, 1958, S 17,32:5
Bush, Harry F, 1950, N 25,13:6
Bush, Henry J, 1953, My 16,19:5
Bush, Henry T, 1945, My 8,34:6
Bush, Humphrey L, 1945, N 22,37:6
Bush, I J, 1939, Mr 11,17:6
Bush, Irving T, 1948, O 22,25:1
Bush, Irving T Mrs, 1946, F 25,25:2
Bush, J Rusell, 1948, Ja 16,21:4

Bush, James C Maj, 1905, Je 13,9:6
Bush, James I, 1961, S 10,86:4
Bush, James M Sr, 1962, Ap 11,43:1
Bush, John, 1945, D 21,21:1
Bush, John F, 1951, N 30,23:5
Bush, John F Mrs, 1941, Ja 3,19:4
Bush, John M, 1942, Je 7,41:1
Bush, Joseph, 1941, My 27,23:3
Bush, Joseph H, 1947, Ag 29,17:5
Bush, Judson R, 1938, Mr 19,15:5
Bush, Julia H, 1962, F 13,35:3
Bush, Leonard T, 1953, Jl 14,27:4
Bush, Lincoln, 1940, D 12,27:3
Bush, Lucius M, 1966, Je 15,47:2
Bush, Margaret Mrs, 1906, N 4,9:6
Bush, Mary S T Mrs (will), 1955, Mr 12,36:1
Bush, Myron, 1903, Je 8,7:6
Bush, Nancy Mrs, 1905, Mr 28,9:4
Bush, Oscar A Mrs, 1951, Jl 26,21:3
Bush, Phil L, 1954, Je 26,13:7
Bush, R Perry Mrs, 1947, N 22,15:4
Bush, Raymond M, 1954, S 2,21:5
Bush, Robert M, 1942, F 4,19:3
Bush, Robert P Dr, 1923, Ja 9,23:4
Bush, Rowland G, 1945, S 16,42:8
Bush, Rowland I, 1946, Ag 31,15:4
Bush, Royal R, 1952, Mr 12,27:5
Bush, Rufus T, 1950, D 5,31:5
Bush, Russell H, 1964, Mr 28,19:3
Bush, S Adeline, 1948, D 31,15:2
Bush, Samuel D 2d, 1946, D 22,42:2
Bush, Samuel G, 1940, Je 16,38:8
Bush, Samuel P, 1948, F 9,17:3
Bush, Sanford Mrs, 1947, Jl 19,13:5
Bush, Seth J T Mrs, 1943, Jl 22,19:4
Bush, Thomas M, 1873, My 16,5:2
Bush, Viola B, 1966, Ag 3,37:3
Bush, Wallace A, 1962, Jl 19,27:5
Bush, Walter E Sr, 1951, D 27,21:1
Bush, Walter G, 1943, F 21,32:7
Bush, Wendell T, 1941, F 11,23:1
Bush, Wendell T Mrs, 1954, Je 8,27:4
Bush, Wesley C, 1942, Ap 1,21:2
Bush, William G, 1953, Ja 17,15:4
Bush, William J, 1952, N 12,27:4
Bush, William L, 1941, O 14,23:4
Bush, William N Mrs, 1939, F 9,21:3
Bush, William S Mrs, 1954, Je 4,23:3
Bush, William T, 1950, Je 19,21:4
Bush-Brown, H K, 1935, Mr 2,15:4
Bush-Brown, Henry K, 1944, N 18,13:2
Busha, John, 1907, D 12,11:5
Busha, Socrates, 1948, Je 24,25:3
Bushart, Louis E, 1941, Mr 30,49:2
Bushby, Alan, 1967, Mr 2,35:2
Bushe, H Grattan, 1961, Ag 25,25:5
Bushee, Alice H, 1956, Ap 30,23:4
Bushel, James, 1955, Je 24,21:2
Bushel, Morris, 1957, Ap 8,23:3
Bushel, Peter, 1949, Ja 5,25:4
Bushell, William G, 1961, Jl 28,21:5
Busher, Charles E, 1939, My 4,23:2
Busher, Eugene J, 1952, My 14,27:5
Busher, Ronald W, 1954, Je 18,23:5
Bushey, Alfred, 1955, Ja 7,21:4
Bushey, Francis S, 1960, D 19,27:4
Bushey, Francis S Mrs, 1961, F 27,27:6
Bushey, Henry Mrs, 1939, F 21,19:2
Bushey, Ira S, 1925, S 24,25:4; 1949, Jl 30,15:6
Bushey, Raymond J, 1956, My 21,25:2
Bushfield, Harlan J, 1948, S 28,27:1
Bushfield, John A, 1940, Ag 9,15:4
Bushick, Frank B Sr, 1952, D 6,21:6
Bushing, Theodore Mrs, 1938, N 16,23:5
Bushman, Charles A, 1941, Ja 2,23:4
Bushman, Edward L, 1948, My 26,25:4
Bushman, Francis X, 1966, Ag 24,1:2
Bushman, Francis X Mrs, 1956, F 6,23:3
Bushman, John H Mrs, 1943, O 17,49:2
Bushman, Josephine F Mrs, 1964, My 29,29:2
Bushman, Louella M, 1943, Jl 4,20:3
Bushman, William M, 1937, Ap 25,II,9:2
Bushnell, A S Ex-Gov, 1904, Ja 16,9:3
Bushnell, Albert, 1880, Ja 18,5:4; 1940, Je 26,23:2
Bushnell, Alvah, 1920, S 29,9:3
Bushnell, Burrus E, 1939, Je 16,23:6
Bushnell, C D, 1945, D 21,21:2
Bushnell, C S, 1896, My 7,1:3
Bushnell, Carl D, 1946, Ag 25,46:3
Bushnell, Charles E, 1938, My 10,21:2
Bushnell, Charles J, 1950, Ap 18,31:1
Bushnell, Douglas S, 1961, Ap 22,25:3
Bushnell, Edward R, 1951, Ja 6,15:6
Bushnell, Eleanor G, 1943, Mr 25,21:2
Bushnell, Elmer A, 1939, Ja 28,13:5
Bushnell, George E (Sept 30), 1965, O 11,61:1
Bushnell, George E Col, 1924, Jl 25,13:5
Bushnell, George H, 1953, My 28,23:1
Bushnell, Guy F, 1954, Ja 9,15:4
Bushnell, Handley Nelson Dr, 1908, N 29,11:5
Bushnell, Henry P, 1960, F 2,35:1
Bushnell, Horace, 1876, F 18,4:7
Bushnell, James H, 1950, D 20,32:2
Bushnell, John L, 1944, O 12,27:2
Bushnell, John L Mrs, 1954, Ag 20,19:4
Bushnell, Paul P, 1951, Ja 23,27:1
Bushnell, Pope, 1881, Ja 28,5:4
Bushnell, Robert H, 1960, Jl 14,27:5
Bushnell, Robert S Mrs, 1950, S 6,29:2
Bushnell, Robert T (por), 1949, O 24,23:4
Bushnell, Vance L, 1948, My 28,23:3
Bushnell, Winthrop G, 1921, O 24,15:5
Bushong, Albert J, 1908, Ag 21,7:5
Bushong, Charles A Mrs, 1946, Ag 6,25:1
Bushong, John R, 1954, Ja 27,27:2
Bushong, Robert G, 1951, Ap 7,15:3
Bushwell, Eben F, 1948, F 2,19:2
Bushy, Archibald H, 1945, Ap 26,23:5
Busi, Aristide, 1939, O 31,23:6
Busicco, Phil S, 1953, Ag 20,27:5
Busichio, John, 1950, Jl 30,61:1
Busichio, Joseph B, 1947, D 27,13:5
Busiel, C A ex-Gov, 1901, Ag 30,7:6
Busing, Ferdinand A, 1962, Ja 3,33:3
Busing, John, 1951, Mr 4,6:5
Busk, Anthony S, 1940, F 29,19:2
Busk, Frederick T, 1949, Je 18,13:5
Busk, Joseph R Mrs, 1916, D 12,11:4
Busk, William H, 1947, Ag 6,23:2
Busk-Jensen, Leif, 1956, My 13,21:1
Buskuhl, Ernst, 1945, S 16,30:7
Busler, Howard S Dr, 1937, N 18,23:4
Busley, Jessie, 1950, Ap 21,23:2
Busloff, Herman S, 1945, My 8,19:4
Busold, Howard B, 1953, Mr 31,32:3
Busoni, Ferruccio, 1924, Jl 28,11:4
Busoni, Rafaello, 1962, Mr 19,29:3
Buss, Charles M, 1946, My 7,21:6
Buss, Fred G Sr, 1954, Mr 9,27:5
Buss, Ralph H, 1940, My 28,23:4
Buss, William, 1944, Mr 9,17:2
Bussabarger, John B, 1957, Ag 7,27:4
Bussard, Lawerence H, 1951, Jl 24,32:8
Bussche-Haddenhausen, Hilmar von dem Baron (por), 1939, N 21,26:3
Busse, Fred A, 1914, Jl 10,9:5
Busse, Frederick H, 1946, Je 3,21:2
Busse, Hans Gen, 1937, Ag 31,23:5
Busse, Henry, 1955, Ap 24,87:1
Busse, Henry H (corr, F 12,25:3), 1946, F 10,42:5
Busse, Joseph H, 1948, Ap 7,25:2
Busse, Julius, 1954, Jl 15,27:4
Busse, William, 1955, Jl 18,21:3
Bussell J H, 1878, My 9,4:7
Busselle, S Marshall Mrs, 1945, Ag 17,17:3
Bussemey, Emil A, 1946, Ja 24,22:3
Bussenius, W O Mrs (Luellen), 1968, D 26,37:5
Busser, Ralph C, 1955, Mr 7,27:5
Busser, Sterling H, 1954, S 26,87:2
Busseti, Pier, 1953, F 21,13:6
Bussewitz, Maxillian A, 1942, S 22,21:6
Bussey, Albert F, 1942, My 27,23:5
Bussey, Bert J, 1949, F 22,23:6
Bussey, Charles J, 1956, D 19,23:6
Bussey, Cyrus Gen, 1915, Mr 5,9:6
Bussey, Gertrude C, 1961, Mr 14,35:2
Bussey, Talmadge, 1949, O 12,44:1
Bussey, Thomas E, 1947, S 8,21:5
Bussey, Thomas E Mrs, 1945, Mr 16,15:1
Bussing, George A Sr, 1941, D 27,19:1
Bussing, John Stuyvesant, 1916, Ja 25,9:5
Bussing, Robert S, 1925, S 25,21:6
Bussmann, A G, 1947, O 9,25:1
Bussom, Thomas W, 1951, N 13,29:4
Bussow, Carl, 1961, Ja 19,29:4
Bustamante, Carlos L, 1950, N 14,32:3
Bustamante y Sirven, A S de, 1951, Ag 26,77:1
Bustamente, Manuel, 1950, Ag 7,19:5
Bustani, Emile (funeral, Mr 18,2:7), 1963, Mr 16,7:2
Bustani, Sulliman el (funl, Je 4,19:5), 1925, Je 3,23:3
Bustanoby, Andre, 1916, F 11,11:7
Bustanoby, Jacques, 1942, Mr 24,19:3
Bustanoby, Louis, 1917, Ag 5,17:3
Bustard, Joseph L, 1953, Je 14,86:1
Bustard, Joseph L Mrs, 1966, Mr 6,93:1
Bustard, Robert E, 1915, Jl 20,11:5
Busteed, Richard, 1950, Ag 11,19:4
Busteed, Walton H, 1958, Jl 9,27:5
Busteed, William H, 1924, S 11,23:7
Bustelo, Gregorio, 1965, F 6,25:5
Buster, Harriet E, 1938, Jl 9,13:4
Buster, William T, 1954, F 26,19:5
Bustillo, Sanchez, 1908, S 21,7:6
Bustin, Henry W, 1956, Je 9,17:2
Busto, Mario J, 1943, O 2,13:2
Buston, Arthur J, 1937, Ja 2,14:5
Bustos, Enrique Mrs, 1965, S 2,31:5
Bustug, Irfan, 1960, S 13,15:2
Buswell, Frederic C Mrs, 1944, Ap 26,19:4
Buswell, Frederick C, 1925, N 29,13:2
Buswell, Henry C (will), 1940, Mr 19,29:1
Buswell, James Oliver Rev Dr, 1922, Ap 7,17:5
Buswell, Leslie, 1964, O 14,45:4
Buswell, Walter M, 1951, O 1,23:5
Butansky, Abraham, 1956, Ja 28,17:3
Butchart, Cuthbert S, 1955, Jl 12,25:2
Butcher, Ben H, 1937, F 13,13:5
Butcher, Charles E Mrs, 1944, F 1,20:2
Butcher, Charles Mrs, 1943, Ja 10,50:1
Butcher, Clifford F, 1957, F 1,25:5
Butcher, Edward W, 1960, D 13,31:2
Butcher, Edwin, 1950, Ag 1,23:2
Butcher, Elvin O Jr, 1957, Je 8,19:5
Butcher, Frank C, 1957, My 25,21:3
Butcher, H Earl, 1955, D 8,37:2
Butcher, Harry H, 1942, Je 20,13:4
Butcher, Henry C, 1938, Mr 8,19:3
Butcher, Howard Jr Mrs, 1957, N 11,29:4
Butcher, John C Mrs, 1923, Je 23,11:6
Butcher, John C Rev, 1923, Je 23,11:6
Butcher, John M A, 1964, Mr 19,33:2
Butcher, John W, 1944, F 22,24:3
Butcher, Max, 1957, S 17,35:2
Butcher, Robert H, 1959, Mr 23,31:2
Butcher, Samuel (see also Jl 31), 1876, Ag 1,5:4
Butcher, Samuel Henry, 1910, D 30,11:4
Butcher, Thomas, 1948, Mr 2,23:3
Butcher, Thomas C, 1960, O 1,9:5; 1961, D 27,25:5
Butcher, Thomas Mrs, 1955, Ap 22,25:2
Butcher, Walter (will), 1954, Ja 14,5:3
Butcher, Walter, 1956, My 5,19:5
Butcher, Willard F Mrs, 1953, My 25,25:5
Butcher, Willard Mrs, 1955, Ja 13,27:2
Butcher, William L, 1931, Ja 16,21:3
Butcher, William L Mrs, 1967, Ja 18,43:1
Bute, Lord (will, D 20,2:4), 1947, Ap 26,13:3
Bute, Marchioness of, 1947, My 17,15:6
Bute, Marquess of (J Crichton-Stuart), 1956, Ag 16, 25:5
Bute, Marquis of, 1900, O 10,7:1
Butenschoen, Ferdinand, 1951, S 6,31:1
Butensky, Jules M, 1947, Mr 1,15:2
Butensky, Louis, 1959, My 3,86:1
Buter, Xander J, 1967, Ag 12,25:5
Buterbaugh, Jesse R, 1958, My 23,23:1
Buteux, Harry C, 1943, My 25,23:4
Buteux, Raymond D, 1967, Jl 8,25:5
Buti, Carlo, 1963, N 19,41:3
Butland, George D, 1941, Ja 10,19:1
Butler, A Leon, 1967, D 16,41:2
Butler, Adelaide, 1878, Je 15,8:6
Butler, Adele B, 1938, Ap 1,23:1
Butler, Albert N, 1947, Je 4,27:5
Butler, Albert N Jr, 1954, N 23,33:1
Butler, Alice D Mrs, 1950, D 29,19:2
Butler, Amos W Dr, 1937, Ag 7,15:6
Butler, Ann Lady, 1953, Jl 24,13:3
Butler, Anna B, 1948, S 14,30:2
Butler, Arthur G, 1947, S 9,31:5
Butler, Arthur J, 1943, D 14,27:4
Butler, Arthur W, 1949, N 22,29:2
Butler, Arthur W Mrs, 1954, O 9,17:2
Butler, B C, 1882, N 27,5:3
Butler, B F, 1884, D 13,5:2
Butler, B F Gen, 1893, Ja 11,1:6
Butler, B F Mrs (see also Ap 9), 1876, Ap 16,9:4
Butler, B Frank, 1904, Ag 3,7:6
Butler, B I, 1881, S 2,2:1
Butler, Basil G, 1945, Je 3,32:4
Butler, Benjamin (trb, D 2,5:3), 1858, N 24,1:5
Butler, Benjamin F, 1925, N 3,25:5
Butler, Bertram T, 1958, O 8,35:3
Butler, Bradford, 1959, O 19,29:5
Butler, Burridge D, 1948, Mr 31,26:2
Butler, Burton D, 1954, Ja 26,16:2
Butler, Byron T, 1957, Mr 26,33:1
Butler, Charles, 1897, D 14,7:5; 1920, S 18,9:2; 19 Je 5,27:4
Butler, Charles E, 1924, F 16,13:5
Butler, Charles E Mrs, 1925, Mr 5,19:5
Butler, Charles H, 1940, F 10,15:5
Butler, Charles M, 1959, D 25,21:2
Butler, Charles N Sr Mrs, 1938, Ag 5,17:2
Butler, Charles P, 1948, My 1,15:3
Butler, Charles R, 1945, Mr 19,19:5
Butler, Charles S, 1944, O 8,44:1; 1954, O 27,29:
Butler, Chauncy, 1937, O 3,II,9:2
Butler, Clarence K, 1941, Ja 7,23:2
Butler, Clarence W Dr, 1904, D 21,9:5
Butler, Claude W, 1951, F 28,27:2
Butler, Dale D, 1943, Ap 9,21:6
Butler, Dan B, 1953, Mr 15,93:2
Butler, Daniel, 1918, My 27,13:6
Butler, David, 1964, Je 7,87:1
Butler, Dudley Mrs (Mrs C Beekman), 1967, F
Butler, E Santley, 1958, Ja 22,27:2
Butler, E T, 1884, Ap 19,5:2
Butler, Earle S, 1946, Je 19,21:4
Butler, Edith A, 1953, Ap 17,25:3
Butler, Edith L, 1939, Mr 23,23:4
Butler, Edmond B, 1956, Mr 22,35:1
Butler, Edmond J, 1937, My 31,16:2
Butler, Edmund L, 1948, Mr 26,21:1
Butler, Edmund W, 1956, N 27,38:1
Butler, Edward, 1905, Mr 19,9:4; 1943, D 4,13:
Butler, Edward B Mrs, 1946, S 8,44:4
Butler, Edward H (funl, Mr 12,9:5), 1914, Mr
Butler, Edward H (funl, F 22,27:3), 1956, F 2
Butler, Edward H (est tax appr), 1960, F 25,2

Butler, Edward J, 1952, Mr 18,27:5
Butler, Edward J Mrs, 1947, Je 1,62:4
Butler, Edward T, 1959, My 5,33:5
Butler, Eli B, 1943, My 27,28:7
Butler, Eliza M, 1959, N 15,86:5
Butler, Ellis P, 1937, S 14,23:1
Butler, Elmer T, 1940, Jl 3,17:5
Butler, Ernest J, 1939, D 10,68:2
Butler, Ernest M, 1948, O 26,31:3
Butler, Ethan F, 1964, Ja 28,31:2
Butler, Etta, 1903, Ja 8,9:7
Butler, Eugene J, 1956, My 20,86:5
Butler, Evelyn M, 1957, Je 11,35:2
Butler, Everett D, 1951, Ag 4,15:5
Butler, F H, 1928, N 28,27:3
Butler, F Warren, 1952, Mr 21,23:2
Butler, Francis, 1874, Je 18,2:5
Butler, Francis E Mrs, 1907, Ap 5,9:7
Butler, Francis Parke Mrs, 1875, Jl 8,4:7
Butler, Frank, 1953, Jl 11,11:5; 1967, Je 13,47:1
Butler, Frank A, 1949, Ja 2,60:5; 1955, Je 20,21:5; 1961, F 21,35:3
Butler, Frank E, 1948, Ja 8,25:1; 1948, S 12,72:1
Butler, Frank F, 1941, Ap 12,15:5
Butler, Frank S, 1967, Ag 27,89:2
Butler, Franklin Crosby, 1914, Ag 22,7:6
Butler, Frederick H, 1949, My 14,13:2
Butler, G M, 1943, F 19,30:3
Butler, G R Dr, 1926, D 7,27:1
Butler, George B, 1907, My 6,9:2
Butler, George E, 1940, Mr 9,15:5
Butler, George Frank Dr, 1921, Je 23,17:2
Butler, George H Houghton Rev, 1921, S 13,17:4
Butler, George M, 1944, Jl 21,19:1
Butler, George P Mrs, 1944, S 15,19:5
Butler, George Prentiss, 1911, Ap 9,13:5
Butler, George R, 1961, Mr 13,29:1
Butler, George S, 1960, Mr 31,33:4
Butler, Gilbert, 1957, O 15,33:1
Butler, Gilbert F, 1938, S 12,17:6
Butler, Goold T, 1942, Ag 4,19:3
Butler, H R, 1934, My 23,19:1
Butler, Hamilton, 1953, Je 1,23:5
Butler, Harcourt, 1938, Mr 3,21:5
Butler, Harold, 1957, Ag 24,15:5
Butler, Harold B, 1951, Mr 28,29:3
Butler, Harold M, 1941, Ag 12,19:5
Butler, Harriet, 1914, Ja 5,9:6
Butler, Harry H, 1948, F 3,25:1
Butler, Harry J, 1965, Mr 9,35:2
Butler, Harry M, 1943, N 26,23:3
Butler, Harry T Mrs, 1957, O 15,30:1
Butler, Henry C, 1942, O 7,25:6
Butler, Henry Clay Capt, 1920, Ap 25,22:4
Butler, Henry E, 1947, Mr 6,25:6
Butler, Henry F, 1964, F 7,31:1
Butler, Henry L, 1940, Mr 15,23:2
Butler, Henry L Mrs, 1912, F 4,13:4
Butler, Henry M, 1940, Ag 23,15:6
Butler, Henry V, 1872, Ag 8,1:7; 1908, Mr 1,9:5; 1957, Ag 7,27:3
Butler, Henry W, 1957, D 26,19:1
Butler, Herbert, 1946, O 8,23:5
Butler, Herman B Mrs, 1954, Je 15,29:6
Butler, Homer F, 1962, Ap 29,86:6
Butler, Howard A, 1959, Je 24,31:4
Butler, Howard C Prof (funl), 1922, S 7,17:5
Butler, Howard Crosby Prof, 1922, Ag 16,9:4
Butler, Howard R Mrs, 1945, D 28,15:3
Butler, Hugh (funl, Jl 4,31:2; will, Jl 21,29:2), 1954, Jl 2,19:1
Butler, Hugh Mrs, 1941, F 16,41:2
Butler, Ida F, 1949, Mr 12,18:8
Butler, Irving D, 1938, Je 1,23:1
Butler, Isabella G, 1948, Ag 24,23:2
Butler, J, 1934, F 21,19:1
Butler, J Ambrose, 1909, O 3,13:5
Butler, J E Mrs, 1903, D 20,7:6
Butler, J G Jr, 1927, D 21,25:2
Butler, J Vernon, 1950, Jl 5,32:6
Butler, James, 1940, N 18,19:2; 1951, O 2,27:1
Butler, James A, 1945, Ap 10,19:4
Butler, James Edward William Theobald Marquess, 1919, O 28,13:2
Butler, James F, 1939, Ag 29,21:6
Butler, James G, 1949, Ja 20,27:4
Butler, James Gay Col, 1916, Ag 23,9:4
Butler, James Glentworth, 1916, D 30,9:4
Butler, James H Maj, 1905, My 22,7:5
Butler, James H Mrs, 1939, Ap 11,24:3
Butler, James J, 1951, Jl 21,13:5; 1959, O 24,21:6
Butler, James K, 1964, O 8,43:3
Butler, James L, 1923, Ja 24,13:6; 1948, O 6,30:2
Butler, James Mrs, 1906, N 7,9:5; 1949, Je 20,19:4; 1961, F 14,37:3
Butler, James P, 1941, F 16,41:1
Butler, James W, 1955, N 8,29:3
Butler, Jeremiah, 1925, D 7,21:5; 1942, Jl 22,19:3
Butler, Jerome A, 1949, Je 1,31:2
Butler, Jessie S Mrs, 1943, My 7,19:4
Butler, John A, 1940, Jl 7,25:5; 1948, O 23,15:4
Butler, John C, 1953, Ag 14,19:4
Butler, John Capt, 1925, O 31,17:4
Butler, John E, 1957, Mr 3,84:7
Butler, John G Rev Dr, 1909, Ag 3,7:4
Butler, John J, 1942, O 8,27:4; 1947, D 2,29:4; 1966, Jl 6,42:3
Butler, John K (Mar 14), 1963, Ap 1,35:2
Butler, John L, 1945, S 19,25:4; 1951, O 11,37:2
Butler, John M, 1913, Ap 11,9:6
Butler, John P, 1945, D 4,29:4
Butler, John R, 1940, N 30,17:3
Butler, John W, 1952, S 26,21:3; 1958, O 12,86:6
Butler, John W Rev Dr, 1918, Mr 18,13:5
Butler, Jonathan F Mrs, 1960, S 30,27:3
Butler, Joseph, 1924, O 13,17:6
Butler, Joseph A, 1958, N 3,37:4
Butler, Joseph H, 1947, Ja 29,25:4
Butler, Kate C, 1945, N 7,23:3
Butler, Kathleen T B, 1950, My 4,27:3
Butler, Kevin, 1938, F 15,26:6
Butler, Lawrence S, 1954, Mr 27,17:6
Butler, Leonard F, 1968, Je 5,47:1
Butler, Lewis J, 1964, Je 8,29:1
Butler, Lily J Mrs, 1941, Mr 2,43:1
Butler, Louis P, 1945, N 10,15:4
Butler, Louise M Mrs, 1942, My 28,17:1
Butler, Lyman C, 1917, Je 21,13:5
Butler, Mannie de S Mrs, 1942, Mr 14,15:5
Butler, Marion, 1938, Je 4,15:3
Butler, Mary, 1946, Mr 17,43:1; 1946, Mr 21,25:4
Butler, Mary J Mother, 1940, Ap 24,23:1
Butler, Mary M, 1948, F 19,23:4
Butler, Mary Mrs, 1921, Ap 14,13:4
Butler, McCoskry Mrs, 1948, Mr 5,21:4
Butler, Michael, 1937, Ap 22,23:6
Butler, Michael H, 1962, Ag 3,23:2
Butler, Michael J, 1942, Ja 21,18:2; 1954, Je 1,27:1
Butler, Mildred, 1941, O 3,23:4
Butler, Montagu, 1952, N 8,17:5
Butler, Montagu Dr, 1918, Ja 15,13:2
Butler, Morgan, 1949, Jl 14,28:2
Butler, Morgan Mrs, 1946, F 4,25:4
Butler, Morris, 1945, Ag 7,24:2
Butler, Myron, 1962, F 24,27:3
Butler, Nat, 1943, My 26,23:5
Butler, Newt C, 1949, Ap 16,15:2
Butler, Nicholas M Mrs, 1948, My 5,25:3
Butler, Nita L, 1944, F 25,17:6
Butler, Ormond, 1915, S 15,9:3
Butler, Ormond R, 1940, O 26,15:2
Butler, Ovid, 1960, F 21,92:3
Butler, P Mrs (Fanny Kemble), 1893, Ja 17,4:7
Butler, Paul D, 1955, F 3,23:3
Butler, Paul L, 1959, Ja 6,34:1
Butler, Paul M, 1961, D 31,1:4
Butler, Paul M (funl plans), 1962, Ja 1,23:5
Butler, Philo W, 1957, Ag 25,86:8
Butler, Pierce, 1939, N 16,1:4; 1953, Mr 29,95:3
Butler, Pierce Jr, 1957, Mr 27,31:5
Butler, Rachel Barton, 1920, N 28,22:4
Butler, Ralph, 1954, Mr 4,25:2
Butler, Ralph A, 1938, N 4,23:5
Butler, Richard, 1902, N 13,9:5
Butler, Richard A, 1955, F 27,86:3
Butler, Richard A Mrs, 1954, D 10,27:1
Butler, Richard J, 1925, Mr 24,23:4; 1947, Jl 1,27:2
Butler, Richard Mrs, 1953, Ag 14,19:2
Butler, Robert, 1955, S 16,23:1
Butler, Robert A, 1951, Ja 23,27:1
Butler, Robert G, 1949, D 13,31:4
Butler, Robert G Mrs, 1951, O 3,36:4
Butler, Robert Gordon, 1906, S 26,9:4
Butler, Robert W, 1946, Mr 7,25:3
Butler, Robert W Mrs, 1948, Je 8,25:6
Butler, Roger, 1954, S 8,42:3
Butler, Roland, 1961, O 21,21:2
Butler, Rush C, 1953, Ja 13,27:2
Butler, Rush C Jr, 1964, Jl 17,27:2
Butler, Samuel, 1902, Je 20,9:2
Butler, Samuel B, 1941, Ag 24,34:5
Butler, Samuel F Sr, 1956, F 2,25:5
Butler, Sanford P, 1955, Ja 26,25:4
Butler, Sheldon L, 1948, Ag 7,15:2
Butler, Sheppard, 1962, N 27,37:3
Butler, Smedley D, 1940, Je 22,34:1
Butler, Smedley D Mrs, 1962, Je 16,19:7
Butler, Spencer W, 1953, My 28,23:3
Butler, Sydney E Mrs (will), 1955, Ja 1,4:2
Butler, T Francis, 1955, Jl 24,65:1
Butler, T L, 1880, O 22,5:3
Butler, T R, 1884, Ja 21,5:6
Butler, T S, 1928, My 27,3:3
Butler, Tait, 1939, Ja 14,17:5
Butler, Theron Mrs, 1910, My 24,9:5
Butler, Thomas, 1914, My 5,11:6; 1945, Ag 21,21:2
Butler, Thomas A, 1941, Ap 22,21:4; 1954, Ag 14,15:6
Butler, Thomas B Chief Justice, 1873, Je 9,1:6
Butler, Thomas Baldwin, 1968, My 22,47:1
Butler, Thomas Coddington, 1912, Mr 7,11:5
Butler, Thomas D Sir, 1937, D 31,16:2
Butler, Thomas E, 1949, My 6,25:1
Butler, Thomas J, 1939, Mr 9,21:5; 1961, My 4,37:3
Butler, Vincent P, 1967, Mr 6,28:8
Butler, W A, 1881, F 2,5:1
Butler, W O (see also Ag 7), 1880, Ag 10,4:7
Butler, Walter C, 1948, S 14,29:5
Butler, Walter E, 1964, Jl 3,21:1
Butler, Walter P, 1942, Ja 9,21:2
Butler, Walter P Mrs, 1938, D 30,15:3
Butler, Warren F, 1949, F 23,27:6
Butler, Watson H Mrs, 1924, F 22,15:5
Butler, Wiley, 1967, Mr 25,23:2
Butler, William, 1948, Ja 23,24:2
Butler, William A, 1904, Ja 8,7:5
Butler, William A Mrs, 1950, Mr 5,92:4
Butler, William Allen (funl, Jl 4,13:4), 1923, Jl 2,15:6
Butler, William Allen Mrs, 1919, F 16,20:4
Butler, William B, 1957, Mr 22,23:3
Butler, William C, 1944, Ja 7,17:4; 1956, My 26,17:5
Butler, William Francis Sir, 1910, Je 8,6:4
Butler, William G, 1925, Ag 29,11:5
Butler, William H, 1946, O 26,17:4
Butler, William J, 1942, Ja 9,21:1; 1944, N 13,19:3; 1951, Ap 6,25:2; 1952, D 1,23:3; 1953, My 9,19:4
Butler, William M, 1940, Je 23,30:7; 1940, Jl 6,15:6; 1946, My 15,21:4
Butler, William M Mrs, 1937, Je 17,23:2
Butler, William R, 1946, My 13,21:3
Butler, William S, 1944, F 20,35:1
Butler, William T, 1943, Je 20,34:8
Butler, William W Sir, 1939, Ap 7,21:5
Butler, Willis A, 1948, Mr 29,21:5
Butler, Wilson W, 1937, Je 19,15:6
Butler-Bowdon, John L W (Lord Grey De Ruthyn), 1963, O 26,27:2
Butleroff, Boris J, 1952, Ja 4,23:4
Butlin, William Sir, 1923, My 15,19:4
Butman, Elizabeth Mother, 1955, N 27,88:6
Butman, George A, 1940, Ap 18,23:5
Butman, Harold A Mrs, 1960, Je 4,23:3
Butman, J W, 1903, O 13,7:4
Butner, Henry W Gen, 1937, Mr 14,II,9:1
Butsch, John Louis Dr, 1925, S 9,25:5
Butsch, Russell L C, 1946, F 10,42:3
Butt, C, 1936, Ja 24,19:3
Butt, Charles S, 1946, D 28,16:2
Butt, Claus D, 1947, Mr 9,60:7
Butt, Ernest, 1956, D 4,39:5
Butt, Fred B, 1946, Mr 30,15:4
Butt, Frederic W, 1946, O 22,25:4
Butt, Isaac, 1879, My 6,5:3
Butt, John D, 1967, S 13,44:4
Butt, Lawrence Havemeyer, 1920, D 25,7:5
Butt, Louis, 1924, Ag 1,11:4
Butt, Richard F Maj, 1907, N 13,9:6
Butt, William E, 1953, O 18,87:1
Butt, William M, 1943, S 18,17:5
Butt, William S, 1962, My 5,27:1
Buttafochi, Emelio, 1941, D 7,76:2
Butte, George C, 1940, Ja 19,19:2
Buttenheim, Edgar J, 1964, N 24,39:4
Buttenheim, Edgar J Mrs, 1961, Ap 11,37:2
Buttenheim, Harold S, 1961, Ja 13,27:1
Buttenheim, Harold S Mrs, 1924, My 27,21:5
Buttenheim, Lester H, 1959, Jl 29,29:1
Buttenwieser, Clarence, 1960, Ag 17,31:1
Buttenwieser, Joseph L (por),(will, Ag 24,19:2), 1938, Ag 18,19:1
Buttenwieser, Joseph L Mrs, 1938, My 14,15:6
Buttenwieser, L Prof, 1901, S 24,7:6
Buttenwieser, Moses, 1939, Mr 13,17:5
Butter, Emanuel, 1961, F 8,31:1
Butterfield, Alfred C, 1965, Ap 2,35:1
Butterfield, Alfred H, 1944, Ap 22,15:6
Butterfield, Beth V, 1956, Jl 21,15:7
Butterfield, Beth V Mrs (F M Baldridge), 1961, S 6, 37:2
Butterfield, Charles B, 1953, Ap 3,23:1
Butterfield, Charles E, 1958, Mr 4,29:3
Butterfield, Daniel Gen, 1901, Jl 1,1:4; 1913, Ag 7,7:4
Butterfield, Elmore E, 1959, My 17,84:3
Butterfield, Everett, 1925, Mr 7,13:7
Butterfield, Frederick, 1883, Je 26,2:4; 1943, Jl 23,17:3
Butterfield, Frederick T R Mrs, 1957, Je 1,17:2
Butterfield, Geraldine B Mrs, 1953, Ag 25,21:3
Butterfield, Harold E, 1950, Ap 23,92:4
Butterfield, Henry I, 1910, F 12,9:4
Butterfield, Herbert, 1957, My 5,89:1
Butterfield, Herbert B, 1945, N 15,19:2
Butterfield, James, 1941, S 24,23:3
Butterfield, John, 1869, N 16,5:1
Butterfield, John H Mrs, 1948, O 27,27:4
Butterfield, Lyman E, 1944, N 11,13:2
Butterfield, Mary L Mrs, 1941, F 5,19:3
Butterfield, Ora Elmer, 1916, D 23,9:6
Butterfield, Robert E, 1946, Ap 28,42:7
Butterfield, Roy L Mrs, 1940, F 29,19:1
Butterfield, Roy Lyman, 1968, F 14,47:3
Butterfield, W, 1884, F 2,5:4
Butterfield, Walter H, 1949, Jl 20,25:6
Butterfield, Walton, 1966, Ag 25,37:2
Butterick, Ebenezer, 1903, Ap 1,9:6
Butterick, Harold E, 1925, Ja 19,17:4
Butterick, Mary E (will), 1941, Mr 28,17:6
Butterly, George P Mrs, 1952, Ja 8,27:4
Butterly, James, 1944, F 26,13:3
Butterly, James N, 1939, O 31,23:4; 1952, F 18,19:4
Butterly, Katherine A, 1946, D 24,17:4

Buttermore, William J, 1947, O 2,27:2
Butters, Alex J, 1952, F 21,27:4
Butters, Frank, 1958, Ja 2,29:4
Butters, George S, 1925, Je 30,19:5
Butterweck, Howard Mrs, 1949, Ja 30,60:4
Butterworth, B, 1898, Ja 17,1:4
Butterworth, Benjamin T, 1953, Mr 17,29:2
Butterworth, Benjamin T Mrs, 1947, Ja 7,28:2
Butterworth, Cyril, 1952, Ja 29,25:4
Butterworth, Emerson M, 1961, D 4,37:3
Butterworth, Frank S, 1950, Ag 22,27:3
Butterworth, G F, 1928, Mr 14,25:1
Butterworth, G Forrest, 1956, Ap 19,31:1
Butterworth, George, 1950, D 4,29:3
Butterworth, George F Mrs, 1943, N 19,19:4
Butterworth, George Forrest Jr, 1919, Mr 31,13:4
Butterworth, George W, 1956, Ja 13,23:3
Butterworth, H H, 1883, Mr 18,9:1
Butterworth, Harry W, 1938, Ag 4,17:5
Butterworth, Harry W Jr, 1952, D 18,29:5
Butterworth, Henry, 1940, My 7,25:2
Butterworth, Hezekiah, 1905, S 6,7:7
Butterworth, Horace, 1939, D 10,68:2
Butterworth, James F, 1937, My 3,19:5
Butterworth, James J, 1937, F 21,10:7
Butterworth, John F, 1873, Mr 7,5:6
Butterworth, John Frederick Rev, 1921, My 18,17:4
Butterworth, John S Mrs, 1955, N 16,35:1
Butterworth, Julian E, 1961, Ap 4,37:4
Butterworth, Marion, 1921, My 8,22:3
Butterworth, Mary L, 1945, F 8,19:1
Butterworth, Ralph N, 1950, Ap 21,23:3
Butterworth, Robert E, 1954, S 28,29:4
Butterworth, Robert H Jr, 1944, Ja 15,13:4
Butterworth, Roger H, 1938, O 22,17:6
Butterworth, Samuel F, 1875, My 8,4:7
Butterworth, Samuel Mrs, 1955, Je 14,29:4; 1956, Mr 4,88:2
Butterworth, Spencer K, 1958, Ap 28,23:1
Butterworth, W, 1936, Je 1,19:4
Butterworth, William Henry, 1921, N 25,15:4
Butterworth, William Mrs (will), 1953, D 23,23:4
Butterworth, William W, 1963, O 25,31:3
Buttery, Fred W, 1956, S 19,37:2
Buttery, George, 1948, Ja 25,56:4
Buttfield, William J, 1948, D 31,16:4
Butti, Charles A, 1964, Ja 18,23:6
Buttikoffer, Thomas J, 1945, O 4,23:5
Buttinghausen, Remi J, 1961, My 11,37:3
Buttini, Aldo, 1957, D 2,27:4
Buttle, Norman A, 1939, Ap 19,23:3
Buttles, John S, 1949, My 19,29:4
Buttles, John S Mrs, 1951, Ja 18,27:1
Buttles, Marvin D, 1939, My 18,25:2
Buttles, Marvin D Mrs, 1954, Mr 18,31:1
Buttles, Marvin Stephen Dr, 1907, My 10,7:5
Buttles, William S, 1940, S 4,23:1
Buttling, Albert J, 1937, F 20,17:1
Buttling, William J (funl, Mr 16,9:5), 1911, Mr 13,9:5
Buttner, Annie Mrs, 1916, F 9,11:4
Buttner, Carl Dr, 1916, N 17,9:3
Buttner, George F, 1958, Ag 19,27:4
Buttner, Louis J, 1949, Jl 20,25:4
Buttny, Joseph Mrs, 1946, Mr 14,25:1
Buttolph, William, 1944, Ag 16,19:1
Button, Charles I, 1939, Ja 3,17:2
Button, Edwin H, 1951, Ag 7,25:1
Button, Forrest C, 1947, My 28,26:2
Button, Frederick R, 1961, F 14,37:4
Button, George, 1966, Ja 3,27:4
Button, H Freeman, 1942, Ja 30,19:4
Button, John C, 1964, Ag 15,21:5
Button, John C Mrs, 1966, F 15,39:2
Button, Joseph, 1943, N 11,23:2
Button, Mary E, 1955, My 3,31:4
Button, William H, 1938, Ag 27,13:3; 1944, My 7,46:2
Buttorff, Simon A, 1939, Ja 3,18:2
Buttram, Frank, 1966, D 19,37:2
Buttress, John B, 1940, S 24,23:2
Buttrick, Allen G, 1954, N 30,29:1
Buttrick, Charles Asa, 1921, Ja 14,11:3
Buttrick, Harold Edgar, 1924, D 11,23:4
Buttrick, R C, 1950, Mr 6,21:4
Buttrick, W Rev Dr, 1926, My 28,21:5
Butts, Alfred M, 1957, Ja 8,31:2
Butts, Anna L Mrs, 1948, My 19,27:3
Butts, Arthur C, 1913, O 13,9:4
Butts, Arthur Jr, 1957, F 24,85:2
Butts, Charles R, 1938, O 7,23:4
Butts, Edmund L, 1950, Je 8,31:6
Butts, Eliza S, 1941, Mr 5,21:1
Butts, Freeman W Mrs, 1952, Mr 29,15:2
Butts, Harold G Sr, 1949, My 13,23:4
Butts, Harry T, 1952, F 16,13:2
Butts, Harvey M, 1938, Ap 15,19:1
Butts, Henry F J, 1950, My 11,29:3
Butts, Isaac, 1874, N 21,1:4; 1907, D 14,9:4
Butts, James De Witt, 1916, Ag 23,9:4
Butts, James E, 1940, S 11,25:5
Butts, James E P, 1937, My 27,23:5
Butts, Joseph S, 1961, Ap 11,37:5
Butts, Katherine C Mrs, 1941, My 27,23:4
Butts, Laverne P, 1949, Mr 10,27:4
Butts, Orpha S Mrs, 1939, N 14,23:6
Butts, Orrin F, 1937, D 2,25:6
Butts, R F, 1933, My 2,17:3
Butts, Susan H, 1957, D 27,20:2
Butts, William D Jr, 1953, O 29,31:3
Butts, William G, 1955, Ag 31,25:3
Buttz, Henry Anson Rev, 1920, O 7,15:3
Butu, Hadji, 1938, F 22,21:5
Butwell, James H, 1956, F 15,31:4
Butwin, Charles, 1967, S 12,47:1
Butz, Allan H, 1954, F 20,17:4
Butz, Arthur N, 1959, S 6,72:3
Butz, Arthur N Jr, 1946, D 8,79:5
Butz, George A, 1937, D 22,25:4
Butz, Henry Mrs, 1952, N 9,90:1
Butz, J S C, 1963, Ap 26,35:3
Butz, Theodore C, 1953, S 25,21:2
Butzel, Fred M, 1948, My 22,15:4
Butzel, Henry M, 1963, Je 8,25:1
Butzel, Lawrence M, 1955, Mr 21,25:4
Butzel, Leo M, 1961, Mr 1,33:4
Butzow, Frank E, 1960, Ag 22,25:3
Buuren, David-Michl van, 1955, S 4,56:4
Buvinger, Henry Edward, 1906, Je 17,9:6
Buvinger, Ralph R, 1946, D 10,31:3
Buwalda, John P, 1954, Ag 21,17:2
Buxbaum, Edward J, 1956, Mr 31,15:4
Buxbaum, Friedrich, 1948, O 8,25:2
Buxbaum, Harry H, 1945, Ap 22,36:1
Buxbaum, Paul, 1965, N 22,37:5
Buxby, John S, 1952, O 30,31:5
Buxhoeveden, Olga O, 1961, Mr 30,29:1
Buxhoewden, Countess, 1905, Ja 24,9:6
Buxman, William, 1954, Ag 28,15:7
Buxton, Bertram H, 1947, F 11,27:3
Buxton, C F, 1903, Ap 24,9:6
Buxton, Charles R, 1942, D 18,28:2
Buxton, Clarence B, 1954, Jl 28,23:3
Buxton, Dana Mrs, 1952, Ja 3,27:3
Buxton, Earl of, 1934, O 16,23:1
Buxton, Edward T Mrs, 1952, Jl 29,21:3
Buxton, Frank E, 1939, Ja 12,19:2
Buxton, Frederic J Mrs, 1939, Ag 11,15:1
Buxton, G Edward (por), 1949, Mr 16,27:1
Buxton, George E, 1942, Je 16,23:6
Buxton, Harrison H, 1955, D 25,48:6
Buxton, Henry J, 1939, S 2,17:4
Buxton, Hugh B, 1967, Je 17,31:4
Buxton, James P, 1947, Ap 15,25:1
Buxton, Leonard H D, 1939, Mr 7,21:4
Buxton, Merritt C, 1951, My 10,31:2
Buxton, Merritt C Mrs, 1950, Je 23,25:3
Buxton, Robert V, 1953, O 3,17:4
Buxton, Thomas Fowell, 1915, O 29,13:6
Buxton, Walter W, 1937, Ag 5,23:4
Buxton, Warner R, 1941, Mr 15,17:4
Buxton, William H, 1937, O 17,II,9:1
Buy, Walter E Mrs, 1966, O 21,41:2
Buyanskii, Nikolai, 1953, My 6,31:1
Buyer, Edith M, 1960, Je 6,29:4
Buyer, Samuel, 1937, O 6,25:5
Buyer-Mimeure de Gen, 1919, D 16,13:4
Buys, Arthur F, 1924, F 5,23:3
Buys, Chris, 1955, F 24,27:4
Buys, Jarrett H, 1961, D 1,30:3
Buys, John L, 1955, My 25,33:3
Buys, Ovid, 1871, Je 15,1:3
Buys, Thomas A Mrs, 1947, Ap 5,19:4
Buys, Thomas Alexander Dr, 1921, Ap 21,13:5
Buys, Vernon N, 1948, N 6,13:3
Buysee, Joseph A, 1958, Ap 20,85:1
Buysse, Leo A, 1954, Ap 24,17:5
Buz, Frederick H, 1939, D 23,15:3
Buz, Katherine Mrs, 1940, Ag 1,21:2
Buza, Frank, 1950, D 28,25:2
Buzalka, Michal, 1962, Ja 10,14:2
Buzby, Benjamin F, 1944, O 24,23:3
Buzby, Clara, 1959, Ag 15,17:5
Buzby, Clarence J, 1956, Jl 21,15:4
Buzby, Duncan L, 1924, Je 26,23:4
Buzby, George R Mrs, 1948, Mr 1,23:5
Buzby, Harold A, 1955, N 27,88:4
Buzby, J Howard Mrs, 1954, Mr 9,27:4
Buzby, Walter J, 1950, D 23,15:4
Buzby, Walter J Mrs, 1950, Mr 21,32:2
Buzby, William D Jr, 1950, My 2,29:5
Buzin, Morris, 1959, Jl 24,25:4
Buzzard, E Farquhar, 1945, D 19,26:2
Buzzee, Raymond, 1948, Mr 23,25:5
Buzzell, Hodgdon C, 1948, S 13,21:2
Buzzell, J W, 1953, O 31,17:3
Buzzell, Josiah W, 1941, Ja 12,45:3
Buzzell, Loring B, 1959, O 21,43:1
Buzzell, Reginald W, 1959, Ja 26,29:4
Buzzell, William O, 1959, Ja 27,33:2
Buzzerd, Simeon S, 1959, Je 2,35:4
Buzzi, Alfred A, 1964, N 13,36:1
Buzzi, William, 1937, N 12,4:8
Buzzi-Peccia, Arturo, 1943, Ag 31,17:3
Buzzini, Leopold, 1960, My 21,23:2
Buzzini, Walter J, 1949, N 11,25:2
Byam, Ernest E, 1938, Ja 22,15:2
Byam, Wally, 1962, Jl 25,33:6
Byam, William M, 1954, O 27,20:3
Byard, Dever S, 1965, Mr 14,87:2
Byard, John K, 1959, S 4,19:3
Byas, Hugh, 1945, Mr 7,21:1
Byas, Hugh Mrs, 1962, N 9,26:3
Bybee, Hal P, 1957, Mr 31,88:1
Byble, Duane, 1946, My 14,21:4
Bye, Carl R, 1960, My 17,37:1
Bye, Charles C, 1942, Mr 23,15:3
Bye, Christine F Mrs, 1941, Ja 15,23:4
Bye, George T (funl, N 28,31:5), 1957, N 25,31:5
Bye, Robert, 1949, N 14,27:4
Byer, Lesser Mrs, 1944, Jl 1,15:5
Byer, Robert J, 1940, F 7,21:3
Byer, Willard E, 1943, Jl 25,30:8
Byergo, John M, 1949, D 23,13:1
Byerly, Raymond N Mrs, 1949, S 9,26:7
Byerly, Robert W, 1957, O 8,35:3
Byerly, W E, 1935, D 21,17:3
Byers, Calvin A, 1949, Jl 19,29:5
Byers, Carl R, 1956, O 28,88:8
Byers, Clarence W, 1945, O 26,19:1
Byers, Dallas C, 1909, Ag 27,7:6
Byers, Eben M, 1932, Ap 1,1:2
Byers, Fred C, 1958, S 15,21:5
Byers, George W, 1938, N 14,19:5
Byers, Grover C, 1943, N 7,56:8
Byers, Horace G, 1956, D 6,37:5
Byers, J Frederic (will, Je 17,19:2), 1949, Je 12,76:4
Byers, J Harvey, 1954, Ap 14,29:3
Byers, Joseph R, 1948, N 8,21:3
Byers, Laud, 1951, Ap 14,15:2
Byers, Lawrence Marshall, 1909, Jl 9,7:6
Byers, Margaret Dr, 1912, F 22,9:4
Byers, Mortimer W, 1962, Mr 6,35:2
Byers, Ralph N, 1954, Ag 12,25:4
Byers, Ralph S, 1949, Ag 21,69:1
Byers, Russell T, 1955, Jl 13,25:4
Byers, S H M, 1933, My 26,19:1
Byers, Thomas J, 1947, F 20,26:2
Byers, Vincent G, 1960, S 14,43:4
Byers, Vincent G Mrs, 1956, Mr 19,31:3
Byers, W L Mrs, 1949, N 21,25:6
Byers, William G M, 1957, Ag 3,15:3
Byfield, Albert H, 1946, Ag 25,46:4
Byfield, Ernest L, 1950, F 11,15:5
Byfield, Robert S, 1955, D 2,28:2
Byford, Henry T, 1938, Je 6,17:3
Byford, Roy, 1939, F 1,21:5
Bygate, Thomas W, 1961, Je 12,29:1
Bygott, Gladys, 1918, O 13,23:1
Byington, A Homer, 1910, D 30,11:4
Byington, Edwin H, 1944, Ja 27,19:1
Byington, Floyd R, 1952, Mr 27,30:4
Byington, Frederic P, 1948, Jl 2,21:5
Byington, George V Mrs, 1937, Je 16,23:2
Byington, Homer M, 1966, Jl 8,35:3
Byington, Lewis F, 1943, My 8,15:6
Byington, Margaret, 1952, Ag 19,23:5
Byington, Moses B Jr, 1937, My 19,23:4
Byington, Roderick, 1904, F 2,9:6
Byington, Roderick Dr, 1937, Je 3,28:2
Byington, William H Jr, 1943, Mr 2,19:2
Byk, Ephraim, 1947, S 30,25:4
Byk, Paul, 1946, Mr 24,46:3
Byler, Frank D, 1954, N 7,88:1
Byler, John G Mrs, 1967, D 10,87:1
Byler, Robert C, 1951, Mr 29,27:6
Byles, Axtell J, 1941, S 29,17:3
Byles, Axtell J Mrs, 1961, O 5,37:4
Byles, Edmund T Mrs, 1946, S 18,31:1
Byles, William E, 1947, D 2,29:1
Byles, William E Mrs, 1952, N 10,25:4
Byles, William Pollaid Sir, 1917, O 19,13:6
Byllesby, Henry Malison, 1924, My 2,19:5
Byllesby, Margaret S B Mrs, 1938, My 17,23:4
Bylund, Walter R, 1960, Mr 29,38:1
Byne, Mildred S Mrs, 1941, D 25,25:6
Byng, Edward C Mrs, 1958, My 6,35:3
Byng, Edward J, 1962, F 16,29:3
Byng, Field Marshal Viscount, 1935, Je 7,21:1
Byng, Viscountess, 1949, Je 22,31:5
Bynner, Edwin T, 1959, Ag 29,17:5
Bynner, George C, 1952, Ja 6,92:4
Bynner, Witter, 1968, Je 3,41:5
Byoir, Carl, 1957, F 4,19:1
Byram, Addison V, 1945, Ja 5,15:4
Byram, Brothers E, 1940, S 24,23:2
Byram, Horace L, 1947, F 13,23:3
Byram, Newton, 1951, Jl 26,21:5
Byram Harry E, 1941, N 12,23:1
Byrd, Catherine, 1940, N 30,17:5
Byrd, David W, 1945, Jl 7,13:6
Byrd, Douglas L Mrs, 1946, My 30,21:1
Byrd, Francis O, 1956, Je 6,33:2
Byrd, George Harrison Mrs, 1923, Ap 19,19:3
Byrd, George R, 1945, My 11,19:2; 1954, Mr
Byrd, H L Dr, 1884, N 30,9:2
Byrd, Harry F Mrs (funl, Ag 28,29:2), 1964, 39:5
Byrd, Harry F Sr (funl, O 24,39:2; funl plans, 22,31:4), 1966, O 21,1:2
Byrd, James C, 1954, D 29,23:4

Byrd, Joseph, 1955, D 25,48:4
Byrd, Linda, 1963, Jl 20,6:2
Byrd, Millard F, 1910, Mr 30,12:4
Byrd, Minnie, 1937, My 15,19:5
Byrd, Orris S, 1950, Mr 4,17:3
Byrd, Phil, 1939, Jl 24,13:3
Byrd, Ralph, 1952, Ag 19,23:4
Byrd, Rhone H, 1944, Je 19,19:5
Byrd, Richard E (funl plans, Mr 13,31:1; funl, Mr 15,25:1), 1957, Mr 12,1:2
Byrd, Richard E Sr Mrs, 1957, S 19,29:4
Byrd, Sam, 1955, N 15,33:2
Byrd, Thomas B Mrs, 1962, Ap 14,25:5
Byrd, Thomas Bolling, 1968, F 25,76:8
Byrd, Westwood B Mrs, 1952, Mr 21,46:1
Byrd, William, 1952, Ag 7,21:5
Byrd, William M, 1874, S 28,4:7
Byrd, William Mrs, 1956, Ja 12,27:4
Byrd, William Sr, 1950, My 11,29:1
Byrdsong, Follie, 1952, Jl 6,1:4
Byrider, John, 1942, Ag 20,19:3
Byrider, William A, 1944, Ap 19,23:5
Byrne, Agnes I, 1950, N 22,25:3
Byrne, Alfred, 1956, Mr 14,33:2
Byrne, Alfred E Mrs, 1961, O 5,37:3
Byrne, Arthur C, 1957, Jl 23,27:3
Byrne, Austin T Mrs, 1947, N 9,74:5
Byrne, Catherine, 1957, Ja 13,84:1
Byrne, Charles Alfred, 1909, Ag 25,9:4
Byrne, Charles E, 1958, Ap 2,31:1
Byrne, Charles G, 1949, N 12,15:4
Byrne, Charles H, 1943, Mr 21,26:7
Byrne, Charles M, 1938, O 13,23:4
Byrne, Charles T, 1943, Ja 23,13:3
Byrne, Chris E, 1950, Ap 2,92:5
Byrne, Colman, 1948, My 14,23:5
Byrne, D, 1928, Je 20,1:2
Byrne, Daniel E, 1945, F 16,23:2
Byrne, Daniel J, 1942, N 24,25:4; 1955, S 25,92:6
Byrne, Dayton C, 1955, Mr 2,27:4
Byrne, Edward, 1925, Jl 1,23:5; 1940, N 12,10:4
Byrne, Edward A, 1938, D 8,28:1
Byrne, Edward F, 1958, Ap 18,23:5
Byrne, Edward J (por), 1939, F 8,23:1
Byrne, Edward J, 1940, F 10,15:6; 1943, Ap 7,25:4; 1952, Ja 7,19:3; 1960, Ap 26,37:2
Byrne, Edward P, 1954, Je 19,15:6
Byrne, Edward V, 1963, Jl 27,17:2
Byrne, Eugene Alexis, 1909, N 3,11:5
Byrne, Eugene H, 1952, S 24,33:3
Byrne, Eugene J Mrs, 1953, Jl 2,23:1
Byrne, Francis A, 1960, O 8,23:5
Byrne, Francis H B, 1948, O 18,25:6
Byrne, Francis J, 1945, N 19,21:2
Byrne, Francis Michael, 1923, F 8,19:6
Byrne, Frank, 1903, O 29,9:5; 1941, Mr 15,17:1
Byrne, Frank T, 1954, O 18,25:1
Byrne, Frederick J, 1942, N 16,19:2
Byrne, George D (Bro Geo Francis), 1953, O 26,21:1
Byrne, George P, 1965, O 31,86:2
Byrne, George R, 1943, Ag 8,37:3
Byrne, Gerald P, 1967, D 17,92:5
Byrne, Harvey J, 1872, Mr 2,1:5
Byrne, Henry H, 1872, Mr 16,2:5
Byrne, J Capt, 1909, Ap 29,9:4
Byrne, J J, 1930, Mr 15,19:1
Byrne, Jack, 1939, Ja 13,19:2
Byrne, James, 1942, N 5,25:3; 1943, F 10,29:3
Byrne, James A, 1949, S 29,29:1; 1959, O 4,86:5; 1961, Je 7,41:2
Byrne, James C, 1942, Je 14,46:1
Byrne, James F, 1940, Mr 23,13:6; 1953, Jl 10,19:3
Byrne, James H, 1950, D 22,23:3
Byrne, James Mrs, 1945, O 19,23:4
Byrne, James P, 1939, Ag 17,21:4; 1943, D 24,13:4
Byrne, James P Mrs, 1952, Mr 18,27:2
Byrne, James W, 1944, Je 16,19:3
Byrne, John, 1905, N 1,9:6; 1940, My 12,48:7
Byrne, John Col, 1909, D 31,9:4
Byrne, John F, 1937, S 20,23:2; 1938, Ag 11,17:4; 1949, Je 5,92:6; 1965, Ag 7,21:6
Byrne, John J, 1940, F 15,19:5; 1940, Ap 15,17:1; 1946, Ap 17,25:2
Byrne, John M, 1952, Je 4,27:3
Byrne, John T, 1947, Ag 14,23:4; 1966, Ag 29,29:4
Byrne, John W, 1946, D 30,19:3; 1948, F 17,25:3
Byrne, Joseph, 1953, Jl 9,25:2; 1961, O 28,21:5
Byrne, Joseph G, 1945, My 14,17:3
Byrne, Joseph J, 1956, Jl 4,19:6
Byrne, Joseph M, 1924, N 25,23:3; 1938, S 15,25:4
Byrne, Joseph M Dr, 1914, Ag 28,9:3
Byrne, Joseph M Mrs, 1951, Ja 13,15:2
Byrne, Julia, 1940, D 16,23:6
Byrne, Katherine, 1942, Ag 28,19:1
Byrne, Kay S, 1948, Ag 25,25:1
Byrne, Kevin J, 1941, Ja 6,7:4
Byrne, Laurence A, 1965, N 2,33:2
Byrne, M J, 1947, S 26,23:1
Byrne, Marie J Sister, 1951, N 12,25:5
Byrne, Martha, 1943, S 27,19:3
Byrne, Mary C Mrs, 1940, My 29,23:4
Byrne, Matthew A, 1951, Mr 3,13:4
Byrne, May A Mrs, 1938, Je 28,19:4
Byrne, Michael J Rev, 1922, Ja 10,19:3
Byrne, Michael S, 1951, Mr 12,25:4
Byrne, Patrick C, 1952, Mr 1,15:4
Byrne, Patrick J, 1948, F 18,28:2; 1953, Ap 18,2:5
Byrne, Patrick Rev, 1907, Je 16,7:6
Byrne, Patrick Sheedy Dr, 1914, Mr 24,9:4
Byrne, Peter D, 1906, Ja 21,7:6
Byrne, Philip J, 1960, N 6,89:1
Byrne, R Leonard, 1959, Ja 19,27:3
Byrne, Richard P, 1958, Jl 19,15:6
Byrne, Robert C, 1951, F 23,27:6
Byrne, Robert J, 1955, F 8,27:1
Byrne, Ruth V, 1937, F 18,21:3
Byrne, Stephen A, 1950, Jl 24,17:5
Byrne, Sylvester J Dr, 1923, D 7,21:6
Byrne, Thomas, 1944, Mr 16,19:5; 1951, O 17,25:1
Byrne, Thomas F, 1908, N 20,9:2; 1943, Ap 5,9:3
Byrne, Thomas J, 1954, Je 11,23:6; 1965, Mr 3,41:4
Byrne, Thomas J Mrs, 1946, Mr 22,21:3
Byrne, Thomas Sebastian Rev, 1923, S 5,15:4
Byrne, Walter S, 1956, O 7,87:2
Byrne, William, 1950, My 5,21:4
Byrne, William E, 1950, O 17,31:4
Byrne, William F, 1949, N 14,27:4
Byrne, William J, 1947, S 9,31:3; 1948, Je 12,15:5
Byrne, William L, 1964, Ja 22,37:1
Byrne, William T, 1952, Ja 28,17:5
Byrne, William T Mrs, 1948, S 14,29:3
Byrnes, Charles F, 1939, Ap 25,23:5
Byrnes, Daniel P Mrs, 1957, S 7,19:3
Byrnes, Edward J, 1941, Je 22,32:7; 1943, D 31,15:2
Byrnes, Edward J Jr, 1957, O 11,27:4
Byrnes, Edward W, 1967, N 11,33:2
Byrnes, Esther F, 1946, S 5,27:5
Byrnes, Francis, 1960, Ag 10,31:4
Byrnes, Francis J, 1959, D 24,19:2
Byrnes, Frank Dr, 1922, Mr 2,21:5
Byrnes, Garrett, 1953, S 24,33:1
Byrnes, George F, 1938, Mr 15,23:5
Byrnes, Helen L, 1939, Je 14,23:3
Byrnes, Horace M, 1965, S 4,21:5
Byrnes, Hugh P, 1948, F 25,24:3
Byrnes, J Leonard, 1952, Jl 12,13:7
Byrnes, J M, 1936, D 20,II,9:2
Byrnes, J P, 1943, F 25,11:2
Byrnes, James A, 1943, Mr 29,15:3
Byrnes, James C Mrs, 1948, O 27,27:3
Byrnes, James J, 1948, Je 24,26:3
Byrnes, James Mrs, 1944, N 20,21:5; 1948, My 18,23:3
Byrnes, James W, 1944, Ag 25,13:4; 1953, S 10,25:5
Byrnes, James W Mrs, 1944, Je 11,45:1
Byrnes, Jimmy, 1941, Ag 2,15:2
Byrnes, John A, 1963, Jl 25,25:1
Byrnes, John F, 1948, Je 20,62:4
Byrnes, John F Sr, 1945, Ja 5,15:4
Byrnes, John J, 1940, Ap 22,17:4; 1943, Ag 29,38:3
Byrnes, John J Mrs, 1957, Ja 27,84:1
Byrnes, John Mrs, 1943, S 5,29:2
Byrnes, John P, 1941, D 31,17:4
Byrnes, Joseph B, 1945, S 29,15:6
Byrnes, Joseph Mrs, 1962, Je 17,80:8
Byrnes, Leo I Jr, 1956, F 12,89:1
Byrnes, Leo J, 1945, Ja 28,38:3
Byrnes, Leonard, 1940, Je 27,23:6
Byrnes, Patricio Rev, 1875, Mr 27,4:7
Byrnes, Patrick J Mrs, 1948, N 30,27:4
Byrnes, Paul T, 1964, S 12,25:6
Byrnes, Ralph L, 1943, F 19,19:3
Byrnes, Ralph R, 1966, F 23,39:4
Byrnes, Robert H, 1948, Ap 19,23:6; 1957, Mr 21,31:3
Byrnes, Sara Mrs, 1904, Ap 28,9:3
Byrnes, Thomas (funl, My 11,9:4), 1910, My 9,7:6
Byrnes, Thomas F, 1916, D 17,19:2
Byrnes, Thomas W, 1963, O 20,88:6
Byrnes, Timothy E, 1944, Mr 20,17:2
Byrnes, Walter E, 1952, Jl 28,15:3
Byrnes, William C, 1953, O 13,29:2
Byrnes, William F, 1954, Ag 25,27:1
Byrnes, William J, 1950, Mr 12,94:3
Byrnes, William M, 1963, S 20,33:2
Byrnes, William W (Rev Bro Anthony), 1915, Mr 16,11:4
Byrns, Chester J, 1924, N 2,7:1
Byrns, J W, 1936, Je 4,1:3
Byrns, Richard S, 1941, O 20,17:3
Byrns, Robert A, 1940, My 9,23:2
Byron, Anne Isabella Milbanke (Baroness Wentworth), 1860, My 31,4:1
Byron, Arthur W, 1943, Jl 18,34:6
Byron, Charles, 1957, D 27,19:2
Byron, Charles E, 1940, My 7,25:5; 1946, Ja 7,19:2
Byron, Charles L, 1964, Je 30,33:3
Byron, Daniel E, 1964, N 26,33:2
Byron, Edward A, 1964, N 22,86:7
Byron, Edward W, 1937, Jl 17,15:4; 1940, My 19,43:2
Byron, Frank H, 1964, Ap 8,43:4
Byron, Frederick E C, 1949, Je 7,32:6
Byron, G de L, 1882, Jl 12,5:3
Byron, George, 1949, Ja 10,25:5
Byron, George Mrs (mem ser set, N 22,86:7), 1959, N 10,18:1
Byron, Gordon M, 1916, Ap 23,19:4
Byron, H J, 1884, Ap 14,5:2
Byron, Helen, 1947, F 19,25:2
Byron, James F, 1950, My 15,21:4
Byron, John J, 1945, Mr 11,40:1; 1949, O 29,15:2
Byron, John W, 1941, Ja 10,19:5
Byron, Joseph W, 1951, Ap 14,15:5
Byron, Leon J, 1967, Ja 19,31:8
Byron, Malcolm R, 1955, S 25,93:2
Byron, Mark B Jr, 1946, D 25,29:6
Byron, Norman, 1956, Je 21,31:4
Byron, Oliver Doud, 1920, O 23,13:6
Byron, Paul, 1959, My 16,23:6
Byron, Percy A, 1957, S 12,31:5
Byron, Percy A Jr, 1959, Ja 9,25:1
Byron, Percy A Mrs, 1941, Je 22,32:2
Byron, Percy C, 1959, Je 11,33:3
Byron, Robert, 1959, My 31,76:6
Byron, Royal J, 1943, Mr 5,17:5
Byron, Stephanie G, 1954, O 8,34:6
Byron, Thomas E, 1940, My 3,21:5
Byron, Victor S, 1944, Mr 26,42:2
Byrt, Arthur W Rev Dr, 1912, Ag 1,11:5
Bystroem, Jakob, 1947, Ag 29,17:6
Bystrom, Elizabeth N Bradley, 1906, Mr 11,9:6
Byszewski, Jan L, 1968, O 29,47:1
Bywater, Hector C, 1940, Ag 18,37:1
Bywater, Selwyn, 1961, Ap 7,31:1
Byxbee, Frank D, 1949, My 21,13:6
Byxbee, Joseph S Capt, 1914, S 11,9:6

C

Caan, Francis, 1942, S 12,13:1
Caballero, F P, 1924, O 18,15:6
Caballero, Joseph E, 1948, F 26,23:5
Caballero, Lucas, 1942, O 14,25:5
Cabana, Oliver Jr, 1938, Ja 22,18:1
Cabanel, A, 1889, Ja 24,2:6
Cabanellas, M, 1938, My 15,33:3
Cabanellas, Miguel, 1953, S 26,17:5
Cabaniss, Edward M, 1960, S 28,39:5
Cabanne, William C, 1950, O 17,31:1
Cabaud, Henry E, 1942, N 6,23:2
Cabaud, Philip G Dr, 1968, Mr 22,47:1
Cabble, Elijah, 1903, Jl 28,7:6
Cabble, Joseph C, 1940, O 8,25:6
Cabe, Thomas, 1955, Ap 4,19:7
Cabecadas, Jose M, 1965, Je 13,84:6
Cabeen, Charles William Dr (funl, Je 18,21:6), 1925, Je 16,21:2
Cabeen, David C, 1965, Mr 31,39:3
Cabel, Jacob, 1925, Ap 10,19:4
Cabell, Edward Carrington Mrs, 1923, O 28,23:2
Cabell, Hartwell, 1955, D 13,39:4
Cabell, Henry L Jr, 1946, Ap 19,29:3
Cabell, James B (funl plans, My 7,35:3), 1958, My 6,1:1
Cabell, James B Mrs, 1949, Mr 30,25:2
Cabell, Robert H, 1947, D 14,80:1
Cabell, Robert H Jr, 1942, Ja 8,22:2
Cabell, Royal E, 1950, S 9,17:4
Cabell, Sears W, 1943, Mr 28,24:8
Cabell, William Lewis Gen, 1911, F 23,9:4
Cabell, Wymond, 1956, F 17,21:1
Cabezas, Frank, 1948, Ja 20,24:2
Cabieses, Oscar R, 1942, Ap 4,13:1
Cabijos, Marcel, 1964, N 24,39:3
Cabinillas, Louis V, 1950, Ap 13,29:3
Cable, Andrew J, 1943, Ja 27,21:4
Cable, Boyd, 1943, Ag 14,11:6
Cable, D Jarvis, 1952, O 26,88:4
Cable, Elmer E Mrs, 1954, Ja 21,31:2
Cable, Frank T, 1945, My 23,19:1
Cable, Frederick W, 1941, Mr 20,21:2
Cable, George W (por), 1925, F 1,7:1
Cable, George W Mrs, 1904, F 28,7:5; 1923, Je 8,19:5
Cable, John R, 1951, D 3,31:5
Cable, Ransom R, 1909, N 13,11:5
Cable, Robert, 1951, F 11,89:1
Cable, Robert P, 1960, Ja 20,31:1
Cable, Sanford G, 1938, My 13,20:4
Cable, Stephen Mrs, 1915, N 20,13:5
Cable, T E, 1903, Jl 26,7:6
Cable, William, 1952, S 22,23:2
Cable, William A, 1960, Ag 12,19:6
Cable, William E Jr, 1965, Je 9,47:2
Cable, William H, 1947, D 24,22:2; 1967, Jl 8,25:4
Cables, Charles T, 1945, Mr 16,15:4
Cables, Ernest D, 1950, Ja 13,23:4
Cables, Preston K, 1949, S 26,25:2
Cables, Ronald W, 1948, N 27,17:5
Cables, William Mrs, 1947, Jl 7,17:4
Cabot, Arthur Tracy Dr, 1912, N 5,13:5
Cabot, Caroline W Mrs, 1951, Ap 28,15:4
Cabot, F Higginson, 1956, F 5,86:3
Cabot, F Higginson Mrs, 1965, Jl 7,37:1
Cabot, Francis, 1905, Ap 13,11:5
Cabot, Francis E, 1938, Ja 9,42:3
Cabot, Francis H, 1939, D 21,26:3
Cabot, Francis H Mrs, 1955, Mr 21,25:1
Cabot, George D, 1961, F 24,21:4
Cabot, George E, 1946, Ap 19,29:5
Cabot, Godfrey L, 1962, N 3,25:4
Cabot, Harry D, 1951, Ag 25,11:6
Cabot, Hugh, 1945, Ag 16,19:3
Cabot, Irving L, 1962, Mr 11,86:5
Cabot, John, 1948, My 14,23:2
Cabot, John B, 1959, D 12,17:6
Cabot, Lucy S, 1944, Jl 18,19:4
Cabot, Mary, 1924, My 24,15:3
Cabot, Phil, 1941, D 26,13:3
Cabot, Powell M, 1956, D 17,31:4
Cabot, Quincy S, 1957, Ap 3,31:5
Cabot, Richard C, 1939, My 9,23:1
Cabot, Sebastian, 1950, Je 23,25:3
Cabot, Stephen P, 1951, D 12,37:5
Cabot, T H, 1938, F 4,21:3
Cabot, T Handasyd Mrs, 1958, F 11,31:2
Cabot, T P, 1902, N 27,2:1
Cabot, Walter K, 1951, Ja 30,25:1
Cabot, William B, 1949, F 1,25:4
Cabral, Anthony P, 1959, Ja 28,31:3
Cabral, Manuel Dr, 1914, Ja 16,9:4
Cabrera, Blas, 1945, Ag 3,17:2
Cabrera, Charles S Mrs, 1947, Mr 8,13:5
Cabrera, Estrada, 1924, S 27,16:2
Cabrera, Francisco, 1959, Ja 28,14:1
Cabrera, Jose R, 1943, My 21,20:3
Cabrera, Luis, 1954, Ap 14,29:2
Cabrera, Luis F, 1952, D 31,15:4
Cabrera, Ramon J, 1966, Ja 10,25:4
Cabrey, John J, 1952, D 24,17:5
Cabrieres, Francis Mary Cardinal, 1921, D 22,15:4
Caburg, Philip Prince of, 1921, Jl 6,15:6
Cacchione, Peter V, 1947, N 7,24:2
Cacciarelli, Robert A, 1950, Jl 13,25:3
Cacciatore, Frank, 1966, Ap 29,47:2
Cacciatti, Simone, 1948, Ja 19,25:5
Caccini, Attilio M, 1953, Ag 29,17:5
Caccini, Virgilio, 1940, F 7,21:5
Caceres, Andres Avelino Gen, 1923, O 11,21:3
Caceres, Julian R, 1950, Jl 19,31:2
Caceros, Harry P, 1947, F 27,21:4
Cachard, Edward Mrs, 1917, Ap 5,13:5
Cachin, Marcel, 1958, F 13,29:1
Cackowi, Francis A, 1948, Ap 13,27:3
Caclamanos, Demetrius, 1949, Je 8,30:4
Cadbury, Barrow, 1958, Mr 10,23:4
Cadbury, Benjamin, 1955, Je 25,15:5
Cadbury, Edward, 1948, N 22,22:2
Cadbury, George, 1922, O 25,19:5; 1954, S 28,29:5
Cadbury, George Mrs, 1951, D 5,35:4
Cadbury, Henry T, 1952, S 26,21:1
Cadbury, John W Jr, 1948, S 12,72:2
Cadbury, William A, 1957, Jl 10,27:5
Cadbury, William E, 1967, O 28,31:5
Cadbury, William W, 1959, O 17,23:4
Cadby, H W, 1942, Mr 18,23:3
Cadby, Robert A, 1949, O 2,80:6
Caddagan, John P (funl, N 3,9:5), 1908, O 30,9:5
Caddell, John B, 1955, Ap 28,29:2
Caddick, George E Mrs, 1948, F 3,25:5
Caddigan, D T, 1884, My 2,8:4
Caddigan, John J, 1952, Ja 3,27:2
Caddle, Bertram B, 1953, D 28,21:3
Caddle, William Sr, 1948, My 21,23:4
Caddock, Earl, 1950, Ag 26,13:4
Caddoo, King H, 1944, Ag 7,15:4
Caddy, Sam, 1959, Ja 25,92:4
Cade, George L, 1950, O 5,31:2
Cade, Seeley D Jr, 1954, Ap 19,23:3
Cade, Seely, 1949, My 19,29:3
Cade, Svend, 1952, Je 26,29:3
Cadell, Francis C B, 1937, D 7,25:4
Cadell, Robert, 1950, F 20,19:3
Cadell, Robert Mrs, 1950, F 20,19:3
Cadenas, George E, 1960, O 25,35:4
Cadenas y Aguilera, Jose M, 1939, N 15,23:5
Cadett, George H Mrs, 1952, Mr 22,13:3
Cadgene, Ernest Mrs, 1967, F 12,92:1
Cadien, Lee (por), 1938, Mr 20,II,9:1
Cadigan, John J Dr, 1937, Je 6,II,9:1
Cadigan, John M, 1944, F 20,35:1
Cadin, Martin L, 1940, O 5,15:3
Cadisch, Gordon F, 1937, O 5,25:3
Cadison, Leo M, 1958, Je 19,31:4
Cadiz, Alvin G, 1961, Jl 5,33:1
Cadle, Charles L, 1937, Jl 5,17:6
Cadle, E Howard, 1942, D 21,19:5
Cadley, Edward F, 1938, Jl 21,21:6
Cadman, Charles W, 1946, D 31,17:1
Cadman, Frederick L, 1958, Je 2,27:4
Cadman, Frederick L Mrs, 1960, D 7,43:3
Cadman, Lord, 1941, Je 2,17:3
Cadman, Maurice D, 1955, My 4,29:5
Cadman, Paul F, 1946, N 12,29:3
Cadman, S P, 1936, Jl 13,1:3
Cadman, S Parkes Mrs, 1952, Ag 12,19:5
Cadman, Samuel Rev Dr, 1906, My 29,11:3
Cadman, William L, 1943, D 5,65:2
Cadmus, Bradford, 1964, D 30,23:2
Cadmus, D J, 1879, Ja 19,2:5
Cadmus, Edgar, 1953, O 25,89:1
Cadmus, Edmund, 1907, Mr 3,7:7
Cadmus, Egbert, 1939, Ag 15,19:4
Cadmus, Eugene L, 1958, Mr 28,25:4
Cadmus, Frank D, 1918, F 21,11:7
Cadmus, George Miller, 1914, F 9,7:4
Cadmus, George W, 1949, Ja 25,23:1
Cadmus, Harold Sr, 1964, Jl 19,64:6
Cadmus, Henry L, 1951, Ja 15,17:3
Cadmus, Nancy E, 1950, F 1,29:4
Cadmus, Nicholas V, 1957, Ap 20,17:1
Cadogan, Alexander Sir, 1968, Jl 10,39:1
Cadogan, Earl of, 1933, O 5,21:6
Cadogan, Henry Arthur (Viscount Chelsea), 1908, Jl 3,7:4
Cadogan, Lady, 1907, F 10,7:6
Cadore, Leon, 1958, Mr 17,29:5
Cadoret, William M, 1941, D 21,40:8
Cadorin, Ettore, 1952, Je 19,27:5
Cadorna, Giovanna B Marchioness, 1941, F 12,21:3
Cadorna, L, 1928, D 22,17:2
Cadot, Jacqueline, 1951, F 1,26:5
Cadoux, Cecil J, 1947, Ag 18,17:3
Cadoy, Paul C, 1943, My 7,19:4
Cadwalader, Charles Evert Dr, 1907, Je 14,7:6
Cadwalader, Gouverneur Mrs, 1948, S 2,23:6
Cadwalader, John, 1925, Mr 13,19:3
Cadwalader, John Lambert, 1914, Mr 12,9:5
Cadwalader, Mary H, 1944, O 24,23:4
Cadwalader, Mary H F Mrs, 1937, D 31,15:5
Cadwalader, Richard M Jr, 1960, S 25,88:8
Cadwalader, Richard M Mrs, 1941, My 16,23:1
Cadwalader, William B, 1957, Je 2,87:1
Cadwallader, Charles G, 1950, Jl 12,29:2
Cadwallader, Frank Irish, 1921, Ap 15,15:4
Cadwallader, George, 1879, Ja 27,1:6
Cadwallader, George B Gen, 1914, O 22,11:5
Cadwallader, Linda M Mrs, 1942, Mr 30,17:2
Cadwallader, T Sidney, 1950, Ja 24,31:3
Cadwallader, William H Mrs, 1942, F 10,19:4
Cadwell, Allen W, 1955, N 12,19:6
Cadwell, Charles A, 1947, Mr 29,15:3
Cadwell, Chester T, 1950, Ja 26,27:3
Cadwell, Clarence J, 1949, Jl 12,27:3
Cadwell, Edward E, 1948, Je 14,23:3
Cadwell, George H, 1963, Ap 19,43:2
Cadwell, Harry B, 1954, Mr 23,27:2
Cadwell, Jean, 1967, O 3,47:3
Cadwell, Lewis E, 1948, My 11,26:2
Cadwell, Lewis E Mrs, 1949, Jl 7,25:1
Cadwell, Mark A, 1938, Ja 21,20:5
Cadwell, Stephen Utley, 1907, Ja 22,9:6
Cady, Bertha Chapman, 1956, Ja 28,17:6
Cady, C H, 1879, D 23,8:1
Cady, Cecil J, 1953, F 1,88:8
Cady, Charles G, 1950, My 18,29:3
Cady, Chauncey Marvin, 1925, N 6,23:5
Cady, Christopher A, 1915, My 6,13:5
Cady, Clarence W, 1940, N 14,23:3
Cady, Claude, 1951, Jl 4,17:4
Cady, Edward E, 1940, Ap 24,23:4
Cady, Edwin W, 1939, Ap 19,23:5
Cady, Ernest, 1908, F 17,7:4
Cady, Everett W, 1964, F 18,35:3
Cady, Frank W, 1963, Ap 22,27:2
Cady, Fred A, 1960, Ag 22,25:4
Cady, George L, 1939, N 25,17:4
Cady, George M, 1955, Ap 18,23:4
Cady, George W, 1912, O 15,15:6
Cady, H Emilie, 1941, Ja 4,13:4
Cady, Hamilton P, 1943, My 27,25:4
Cady, Harriette, 1944, S 24,46:2
Cady, Harrison Mrs, 1956, Ap 17,31:1
Cady, J Cleveland, 1919, Ap 18,13:3
Cady, Joseph H, 1947, S 29,21:3
Cady, Lyndon B Dr, 1920, My 15,15:4
Cady, Mary L, 1952, Mr 11,27:6
Cady, Mayant Mrs, 1871, S 18,1:6
Cady, Paul C, 1944, Ag 7,15:2
Cady, Pierre A, 1945, N 3,15:2
Cady, Ralph H, 1939, D 2,17:5
Cady, Reed W, 1951, Jl 13,21:3
Cady, Samuel H, 1942, O 4,52:1
Cady, Walter P, 1941, O 2,25:2
Cady, Willoughby M, 1953, Jl 1,29:2
Caesar, Arthur, 1953, Je 22,21:3
Caesar, Charles U, 1948, Ap 15,25:3
Caesar, Ellen Mrs, 1921, O 19,19:4
Caesar, George P Mrs, 1952, O 17,27:1
Caesar, Henry A, 1939, D 11,23:3
Caesar, Joseph, 1945, Jl 31,19:5
Caesar, Max Mrs, 1951, Ja 22,17:1
Caesar, Orville S, 1965, My 21,35:2
Caetani, G, 1934, O 24,21:1
Caetani, L, 1935, D 26,17:3
Caetani, Marguerite C (Duchess of Sermoneta), 1963, D 19,33:3
Caetani, Michelangelo Prince, 1941, My 28,25:5
Caetani, Onorato (Duke of Sermoneta), 1917, S 4, 11:5
Caffal, Charles, 1953, Ap 30,31:2
Caffee, Robert H, 1957, Ap 14,64:4
Cafferata, Felicia, 1940, Ap 1,19:3
Cafferty, Harry M, 1948, Ag 31,24:3
Cafferty, James H, 1869, S 9,4:7
Caffery, Charles D, 1943, D 6,23:4
Caffery, Donelson, 1962, Mr 24,25:2
Caffery, Doneson, 1906, D 31,4:2
Caffey, Eugene M, 1961, My 31,33:1
Caffey, Francis G, 1951, S 21,24:2
Caffey, H C, 1880, D 29,5:1
Caffey, Lochlin W, 1942, O 31,15:2
Caffre, Alvara Mrs, 1939, Jl 13,19:4
Caffrey, Edwin C, 1945, Jl 26,19:4
Caffrey, George H, 1953, Ja 1,23:5
Caffrey, James G Sr, 1949, Jl 22,19:3
Caffrey, James J, 1961, Mr 6,25:1
Caffrey, James V Mrs, 1938, S 27,21:3
Caffrey, Leo J, 1951, Ap 9,25:4
Caffrey, Patrick F, 1944, O 11,21:5
Caffrey, Thomas Mrs, 1952, O 19,88:5
Caffrey, Thomas W, 1967, Jl 29,10:4
Caffrey, William, 1937, N 23,23:4
Caffrey, William J, 1939, Ja 14,17:2
Caffrey, William J A Justice (will, S 18,9:6), 19[illegible] S 2,21:2
Cafritz, Morris, 1964, Je 13,23:1

Cage, Fred W, 1945, D 5,25:5
Cage, John M, 1964, Ja 5,92:1
Caggiano, Giovanni, 1941, Ja 25,15:5
Cagle, Clifford E, 1951, Ja 22,17:4
Cagle, Walt, 1938, Je 30,23:4
Cagnetta, Luigi, 1939, S 26,23:3
Cagney, Alfred, 1941, D 19,25:5
Cagney, Caroline Mrs, 1945, O 10,21:2
Cagney, Charles L, 1945, Ja 17,21:2
Cagney, Edward S Dr, 1968, Ja 8,39:1
Cagney, T George, 1946, F 18,21:3
Cagney, Winifred E Mrs, 1942, D 27,34:5
Cahalan, John I, 1940, S 2,18:8
Cahalane, Cornelius F, 1957, Ja 3,33:4
Cahalane, John J, 1925, S 21,19:4
Cahall, Joseph L, 1937, Je 29,21:4
Cahall, Ralph S, 1954, O 28,35:3
Cahan, Abraham, 1951, S 1,11:3
Cahan, Abraham Mrs, 1947, My 2,21:2
Cahan, Charles H, 1944, Ag 16,19:6
Cahan, Jacob M, 1960, Ja 29,25:2
Cahan, Samuel, 1964, O 31,29:5
Cahan, Solomon, 1953, Ja 7,31:2
Cahan, Solomon Mrs, 1952, Je 26,29:2
Cahane, Harry, 1960, Ja 23,21:4
Cahen, Alfred, 1963, S 5,31:2
Cahen, Ceasar G, 1943, Ap 30,21:4
Cahen, Julius Philip, 1918, S 5,11:5
Cahen, Oscar, 1956, N 28,12:5
Cahen, Waldemar M, 1956, D 11,39:1
Cahier, Sarah, 1951, Ap 16,25:3
Cahill, Albert E, 1950, S 14,31:2
Cahill, Alex A, 1938, O 12,27:3
Cahill, Alexander P, 1944, Ja 3,21:3
Cahill, Arthur B, 1960, D 14,39:3
Cahill, Arthur H, 1951, Jl 20,21:3
Cahill, Arthur T, 1962, Ja 26,31:2
Cahill, Carlisle C, 1959, N 11,35:2
Cahill, Charles H, 1945, Ap 5,23:2
Cahill, Charles T, 1946, Je 1,13:5
Cahill, Daniel E, 1945, Ja 27,11:4
Cahill, Daniel J, 1938, Ap 1,23:4
Cahill, Daniel W, 1942, My 19,40:1
Cahill, David V, 1948, N 16,29:3
Cahill, Edward, 1948, Mr 8,23:5
Cahill, Edward A, 1949, My 13,23:1
Cahill, Edward C, 1961, Je 1,35:1
Cahill, Edward G, 1961, Ag 6,84:3
Cahill, Edward W, 1938, D 19,23:3
Cahill, Eugene M, 1940, O 25,21:3
Cahill, Francis J, 1942, Ja 8,21:6; 1961, S 14,31:1
Cahill, Frank R, 1940, My 12,48:1
Cahill, Frank V, 1956, Je 12,35:1
Cahill, George A Mrs, 1950, Ja 11,23:2
Cahill, George F (cor, Jl 28,27:1), 1959, Jl 25,17:1
Cahill, George H, 1949, N 9,27:1
Cahill, Gerald Mrs, 1939, Ag 13,29:1
Cahill, Hannah A Mrs, 1953, N 3,31:3
Cahill, Harry P, 1939, Ja 16,15:4
Cahill, Holger, 1960, Jl 9,19:1
Cahill, Irving J, 1950, Mr 16,31:2
Cahill, James A, 1941, O 26,43:1
Cahill, James A Jr, 1942, O 21,21:2
Cahill, James E, 1942, Ap 24,17:4
Cahill, James E Sr, 1968, N 21,47:1
Cahill, James J, 1942, Ap 8,19:4
Cahill, James P, 1955, Ja 25,25:4
Cahill, John A, 1944, S 1,13:4; 1950, Mr 2,27:5; 1964, S 6,56:3
Cahill, John D, 1957, S 14,19:5
Cahill, John E, 1953, O 18,86:4
Cahill, John H, 1917, Jl 7,9:7; 1949, My 19,29:3; 1965, N 16,47:4
Cahill, John J, 1959, O 23,29:3
Cahill, John R Mrs, 1939, D 6,25:2
Cahill, John T, 1948, My 14,23:3; 1966, N 4,42:1
Cahill, John T Mrs, 1938, D 8,28:1
Cahill, Joseph A, 1948, D 28,22:2
Cahill, Joseph Ambrose, 1947, Ag 3,52:8
Cahill, Joseph F, 1944, S 2,11:3
Cahill, Lily, 1955, Jl 21,23:5
Cahill, M, 1933, Ag 24,15:1
Cahill, Margaret J, 1944, F 24,15:2
Cahill, Maris, 1945, N 13,21:4
Cahill, Martin J (funl, Jl 18,11:4), 1922, Jl 15,9:6
Cahill, Mary E, 1937, Je 10,23:5
Cahill, Michael H, 1939, Ap 30,44:8; 1940, Mr 27,21:3
Cahill, Michael J, 1941, Mr 20,21:4
Cahill, Michael J Mrs, 1946, Mr 26,29:1
Cahill, Patrick, 1907, S 8,7:6
Cahill, Patrick J, 1943, My 27,28:8; 1948, D 14,29:2
Cahill, Ray, 1952, N 6,29:5
Cahill, Raymond, 1957, Mr 6,31:5
Cahill, Santiago P, 1924, Jl 27,23:4
Cahill, Santiago P Mrs, 1944, Ja 9,43:1
Cahill, T Merton Mrs, 1964, S 5,19:3
Cahill, Thomas, 1924, N 13,21:5
Cahill, Thomas F, 1957, O 25,27:2
Cahill, Thomas W, 1951, O 2,28:3
Cahill, William, 1946, O 27,60:6; 1954, N 27,14:2
Cahill, William J, 1947, S 30,25:3; 1954, My 21,27:4; 1963, Ap 22,27:2
Cahill, William Sr, 1947, Jl 30,21:4
Cahill, William T, 1956, Ap 13,25:3
Cahillane, Jude T, 1962, Je 7,35:1
Cahir, Francis J, 1949, N 1,28:2
Cahir, John F, 1967, F 28,34:1
Cahir, Walter F, 1945, F 3,11:6
Cahn, Albert, 1938, Mr 24,23:1
Cahn, Arthur M, 1966, Je 8,47:3
Cahn, Bernard, 1906, Ja 25,9:6
Cahn, Bernard R, 1951, Ap 14,15:1
Cahn, Bertram H, 1950, F 9,29:4
Cahn, Bertram J, 1959, Ag 12,29:1
Cahn, David B, 1959, S 28,31:5
Cahn, Edmond, 1964, Ag 10,31:2
Cahn, Edward Mrs, 1955, Mr 25,23:2
Cahn, Edwin I, 1951, Ap 11,29:4
Cahn, Emanuel S, 1948, D 31,15:4
Cahn, Ernst I, 1962, Mr 6,35:1
Cahn, Ferdinand Mrs, 1950, N 3,27:3
Cahn, Frank B, 1958, Ap 5,15:6
Cahn, Harry, 1957, O 5,17:3
Cahn, Harry Mrs, 1947, F 28,23:5
Cahn, Irving, 1965, N 11,50:8
Cahn, Joel G, 1950, S 9,19:3
Cahn, Julien, 1944, S 28,19:2
Cahn, Julius, 1921, My 16,15:4
Cahn, Julius Mrs, 1913, N 12,9:6
Cahn, Lazard (will), 1940, Je 14,19:2
Cahn, Leopold, 1904, S 11,7:6
Cahn, Louis, 1939, Ag 18,19:5
Cahn, Louis M, 1953, Ag 24,23:5
Cahn, Maurice Mrs, 1957, Ag 14,25:4
Cahn, Moise S Mrs, 1964, Ap 14,34:8
Cahn, Reuben D, 1956, F 1,31:2
Cahn, Samuel, 1955, Ap 14,36:3
Cahn, Samuel J, 1962, O 11,39:1
Cahn, Samuel Mrs, 1945, My 2,23:5
Cahn, Sigmund, 1947, Jl 20,44:2
Cahn, William L Mrs, 1956, D 15,25:4
Cahners, Fulton I, 1966, Mr 17,39:2
Cahoon, Edward D, 1920, N 20,15:4
Cahoon, Ernest L, 1963, O 11,37:3
Cahoon, Helen F Mrs, 1960, Ap 26,37:4
Cahoon, James Blake, 1968, My 30,25:2
Cahoon, Samuel T, 1952, S 1,17:6
Cahoon, William B, 1951, Ja 29,19:4
Cahoone, Andrew Mott, 1919, F 25,11:3
Cahoone, Richards M, 1944, Jl 1,15:5
Cahoone, S, 1884, Mr 7,5:2
Cahuet, Alberic, 1942, F 2,15:4
Caie, John S, 1956, S 16,86:8
Caillaux, Joseph, 1944, N 23,31:1
Caillaux, Joseph Mrs, 1943, Ja 31,46:2
Caillavet, Gaston Armand de, 1915, Ja 14,11:4
Caille, Adolph A, 1937, F 10,23:4
Cailler, Arthur G, 1950, Ap 12,27:2
Cailletet, Louis Paul, 1913, Ja 6,9:5
Caillouet, Adrian J, 1946, D 20,23:4
Caimmi, Riccardo, 1940, D 28,15:3
Cain, Arthur F, 1955, Ap 16,19:2
Cain, B B, 1932, S 20,21:1
Cain, Byron B Jr Mrs, 1958, Mr 7,23:2
Cain, David E, 1965, Je 12,31:4
Cain, Edward A, 1958, Ap 10,29:2
Cain, Edward A Mrs, 1968, Je 22,33:6
Cain, Everett E, 1939, Ap 21,23:5
Cain, George F, 1953, N 2,25:5
Cain, Henri, 1937, N 22,19:3
Cain, Henry E, 1943, S 30,21:6
Cain, J Watson, 1950, Mr 24,25:2
Cain, J Wilbert, 1939, My 1,4:7
Cain, James J, 1937, Ap 2,23:3
Cain, James R, 1950, S 5,27:4
Cain, James W, 1938, O 14,23:3
Cain, John E, 1950, Jl 1,15:3
Cain, John J, 1937, Ja 18,17:4; 1967, My 29,25:4
Cain, John V, 1964, N 2,39:3
Cain, Joseph Stillwell, 1904, My 5,5:4
Cain, Judson V, 1947, My 3,17:3
Cain, Leo J, 1945, Ap 11,23:4
Cain, Nicholas F, 1955, Jl 23,17:4
Cain, Patrick J, 1949, My 14,13:6
Cain, Patrick J Mrs, 1938, Mr 28,15:4
Cain, Robert, 1954, Ap 30,23:4; 1961, N 19,88:2
Cain, William E, 1960, Mr 21,29:4
Cain, William J, 1942, F 21,20:3
Cain, William M, 1938, F 2,19:2
Caine, Charles W, 1948, Jl 18,54:3
Caine, George R, 1924, Ag 23,9:4
Caine, H Sir, 1931, S 1,23:1
Caine, John T 3d, 1955, Jl 7,27:1
Caine, Milton A, 1955, D 27,23:2
Caine, Ralph H, 1939, Ja 17,21:4
Caird, Alex, 1951, O 7,87:1
Caird, Andrew, 1956, D 16,86:7
Caird, Farnam P, 1938, Je 1,23:5
Caird, James Key Sir, 1916, Mr 11,11:4
Caird, James Sir, 1954, S 29,31:5
Caird, John H, 1952, N 30,86:4
Caird, William G, 1955, D 26,19:4
Caire, Adam R, 1943, N 5,19:4
Caire, Caroline M Mrs, 1950, O 11,33:1
Caire, Richard S, 1949, F 20,60:2
Cairnes, J E Prof, 1875, Jl 9,1:2
Cairney, William H, 1939, Ag 18,19:2
Cairns, Adrian G, 1948, Ag 2,21:2
Cairns, Alex D, 1958, Jl 12,15:1
Cairns, Anne S, 1941, Mr 2,43:2
Cairns, Bogardus S, 1958, D 10,20:1
Cairns, Charles H, 1951, Je 4,27:3
Cairns, Clifford I, 1955, D 16,30:2
Cairns, Earl, 1885, Ap 3,5:4
Cairns, Edward, 1943, S 18,17:4
Cairns, Edward Mrs, 1955, Jl 28,25:5
Cairns, Edward T, 1941, Ap 6,49:2
Cairns, Emma E Mrs, 1941, N 16,56:8
Cairns, Emma E N, 1955, O 30,88:7
Cairns, F A, 1879, Je 20,5:2
Cairns, George W, 1947, My 9,22:3
Cairns, Hugh, 1942, D 10,30:2
Cairns, Hugh W B Mrs, 1952, Jl 19,15:4
Cairns, Irvin C, 1950, O 11,33:4
Cairns, Irving, 1939, F 18,15:2
Cairns, John, 1954, F 14,93:2
Cairns, John D, 1958, Mr 10,23:1
Cairns, Joseph Jr, 1962, Ag 14,32:1
Cairns, Laurence B, 1960, Je 10,31:5
Cairns, Mary, 1946, Mr 12,25:1
Cairns, Robert A, 1937, N 25,31:3
Cairns, Thomas F, 1949, Mr 23,27:2
Cairns, William K Jr, 1960, Ja 16,21:6
Cais, Dos Tejos Mario, 1944, Ja 6,23:2
Caithness, Earl of, 1881, Mr 30,8:3; 1947, Mr 28,23:3
Caithness, Earl of (Jas R Sinclair), 1965, My 9,87:2
Caits, Joseph, 1957, Mr 11,25:3
Caivein, Madison Julius, 1914, D 9,13:6
Caizzo, Camillo, 1921, Ag 10,13:6
Cajander, Aimo K, 1943, Ja 22,19:1
Cajetan Theisen, Bro, 1940, S 24,23:3
Cake, Lawrence E, 1944, Jl 8,11:7
Cakmak, Fevzi, 1950, Ap 11,31:1
Calabrese, Frank, 1947, F 12,25:5; 1950, O 18,33:5
Calabrese, Frank A, 1945, D 4,29:4
Calabrese, Giuseppe O, 1966, N 16,47:4
Calace-Mottola, Frank, 1942, O 2,25:5
Calafato, Guy T, 1959, Je 20,21:2
Calahan, Edward A, 1912, S 13,9:6
Calahan, Harold A, 1965, N 27,31:2
Calahan, Harry C, 1953, Ap 27,23:3
Calahan, William W, 1940, My 30,17:5
Calak, Lester Williams Ex-Justice, 1922, S 24,27:4
Calamai, Marco, 1957, Ag 21,7:5
Calame, Charles A, 1961, Ap 12,41:1
Calanan, Eleanor A, 1937, F 16,23:4
Calandriello, Anthony Mrs, 1962, O 23,37:3
Calascione, Anthony Mrs, 1966, My 10,39:3
Calbeton y Planchon, Fermin, 1919, F 6,11:2
Calbridge, Charles H, 1940, My 28,23:3
Calcagni, Ralph, 1948, Ag 30,18:2
Calcagnini, Arthur B, 1965, Je 9,47:3
Calcagnini, George P, 1956, Je 29,21:3
Calcagno, Ross F, 1948, Mr 1,23:3
Calcina, Thomas Sr, 1937, S 10,23:3
Calcott, William S, 1952, F 16,13:6
Calcraft, W, 1880, Ja 1,3:3
Calcraft (Hangman), 1879, D 16,1:4
Caldara, Emilio, 1942, N 4,23:6
Caldarone, Angelo Mrs, 1947, Ag 28,23:4
Caldbeck, Samuel J, 1955, Mr 2,27:5
Caldbeck, Weldon S, 1955, Jl 25,19:3
Caldecote, Lord, 1947, O 12,76:4
Caldecott, Andrew Sir, 1951, Jl 15,61:1
Caldecott, Catherine Philips Mrs, 1968, Jl 9,35:6
Caldecott, Ridgley V Mrs, 1958, N 13,33:4
Calder, A Stirling, 1945, Ja 8,17:1
Calder, Alex Sr, 1962, O 23,37:2
Calder, Alexander G Jr, 1920, F 21,13:4
Calder, Alexander M, 1923, Je 15,19:5
Calder, Curtis E, 1955, Ap 3,87:1
Calder, Elizabeth, 1961, Ja 3,27:7
Calder, Elizabeth H Mrs, 1942, Jl 15,19:3
Calder, Ernest S, 1947, N 29,13:6
Calder, Frank, 1943, F 5,21:1
Calder, Frederick M Justice, 1921, Ja 18,11:4
Calder, Helen I, 1942, Mr 27,23:5
Calder, Isabel M, 1960, D 18,84:8
Calder, J H Mrs, 1903, F 17,3:2
Calder, James A, 1956, Jl 21,15:3
Calder, John K, 1946, N 17,70:1
Calder, John Mrs, 1962, Mr 5,23:4
Calder, John W, 1957, Ap 22,25:2
Calder, King, 1964, Je 29,27:5
Calder, Louis, 1963, Je 20,33:3
Calder, Louis H, 1938, My 21,15:3
Calder, Louis R, 1965, Ag 29,84:7
Calder, William M, 1945, Mr 4,38:1
Calder, William M Mrs, 1953, N 11,31:4
Calderazzo, James J, 1954, S 24,24:2
Calderon, Arcadio Yarnell, 1909, N 8,7:6
Calderon, Ezequiel R, 1942, Ap 2,22:2
Calderon, Francisco Garcia, 1905, S 23,9:4
Calderon, Luis F, 1943, Ag 20,15:4
Calderon, Manuel, 1955, Jl 8,23:2
Calderon, Salvador, 1940, N 11,19:5
Calderon, Victor M Mrs, 1951, Ag 8,25:4
Calderone, Francesco Mrs, 1944, Mr 22,19:4
Calderone, Leonard, 1950, S 29,27:3

Calderone, Salvatore Mrs, 1958, O 16,37:5
Calderwood, Chic, 1966, N 13,V,3:1
Calderwood, John N, 1962, S 24,29:4
Caldroney, Thomas L, 1939, Ag 3,19:5
Caldwell, A, 1936, O 24,17:5
Caldwell, A C, 1952, My 28,29:5
Caldwell, A M, 1948, Ag 9,19:5
Caldwell, Agnes, 1948, D 3,25:3
Caldwell, Albert B, 1958, Je 1,86:5
Caldwell, Albert E (cor, F 17,19:1), 1947, F 16,57:7
Caldwell, Albert J, 1940, Mr 3,44:1
Caldwell, Alexander Dr, 1907, N 4,9:2
Caldwell, Alexander Ex-Sen, 1917, My 21,11:4
Caldwell, Andrew J, 1906, N 23,9:5; 1943, O 16,13:4
Caldwell, Archibald Mrs, 1956, Ja 24,31:4
Caldwell, Benjamin P, 1950, S 22,31:2
Caldwell, Bert, 1951, Jl 28,11:3
Caldwell, Bruce, 1959, F 16,29:1
Caldwell, Burns D, 1922, S 26,17:4
Caldwell, Burns D Mrs, 1948, My 14,23:5
Caldwell, C H B Commodore, 1877, D 2,7:3
Caldwell, Carlyle G Mrs, 1968, D 5,47:1
Caldwell, Charles, 1956, Jl 25,29:1
Caldwell, Charles P, 1940, Ag 2,15:3
Caldwell, Charles W Jr (funl, N 3,89:2; mem ser, N 5,31:1), 1957, N 2,21:3
Caldwell, Chester W, 1945, Je 6,21:4
Caldwell, Clifford D, 1940, Ap 17,23:5
Caldwell, David C, 1953, Mr 6,23:4
Caldwell, David S, 1953, Ja 7,31:5
Caldwell, Dimont M Mrs, 1947, D 8,25:2
Caldwell, Donald L, 1957, N 15,28:3
Caldwell, Edward (por), 1949, Ag 14,69:1
Caldwell, Edward Mrs, 1941, Ag 20,19:2
Caldwell, Edward Richardson, 1924, N 19,21:3
Caldwell, Edward T, 1937, N 13,19:3
Caldwell, Ernest B, 1946, Je 1,13:3
Caldwell, Eugene Wilson Dr (funl, Je 24,11:5), 1918, Je 21,13:3
Caldwell, Everett, 1921, D 27,13:5
Caldwell, Frank C, 1924, My 16,19:2
Caldwell, Frank M Brig Gen, 1937, Mr 9,24:2
Caldwell, Fred T, 1951, D 22,15:6
Caldwell, George W, 1946, Mr 15,22:2; 1949, Ag 5, 19:4; 1954, My 23,89:1
Caldwell, Gerald E, 1948, Jl 17,16:8
Caldwell, Godfrey C B, 1966, Ap 2,29:2
Caldwell, H Wallace, 1940, D 28,15:3
Caldwell, Harold P, 1959, Je 1,27:5
Caldwell, Harry E, 1952, Ja 6,93:2
Caldwell, Harry H, 1939, Ap 28,25:5
Caldwell, Harry R, 1957, D 22,40:6
Caldwell, Helen Mrs, 1940, Ja 6,13:2
Caldwell, Henry Clay, 1915, F 17,11:6
Caldwell, Hugh H, 1943, Jl 30,15:2
Caldwell, Hugh M, 1955, Ja 31,19:2
Caldwell, Ira S, 1944, Ag 19,11:5
Caldwell, J F, 1902, My 23,9:4
Caldwell, James, 1954, N 18,33:2
Caldwell, James E, 1944, S 27,21:4
Caldwell, James H, 1941, Mr 20,21:5
Caldwell, James M, 1943, Jl 20,19:3
Caldwell, James R, 1965, Ap 5,31:3
Caldwell, Jeanne E, 1947, Ag 8,17:1
Caldwell, Jesse C, 1941, F 23,39:6
Caldwell, John, 1909, N 24,9:4
Caldwell, John Lawrence, 1922, D 7,19:6
Caldwell, John R, 1918, Mr 7,11:4
Caldwell, John T Mrs, 1961, F 22,25:5
Caldwell, John W, 1945, F 25,37:2
Caldwell, Joseph D, 1950, My 3,29:4
Caldwell, Joseph G, 1964, N 30,39:3
Caldwell, Joseph P, 1946, Ag 31,15:6
Caldwell, Joseph Pearson, 1911, N 23,11:5
Caldwell, Julius A, 1955, N 24,29:4
Caldwell, Leslie S, 1949, D 29,26:3
Caldwell, Louis G, 1951, D 13,33:5
Caldwell, Louis W, 1937, Ag 7,15:6
Caldwell, Louis W Mrs (M Clemens),(will, Jl 16,-27:7), 1952, Mr 5,29:2
Caldwell, Mary M Mrs, 1946, S 25,27:4
Caldwell, Maurice H, 1957, Ap 16,33:1
Caldwell, Norman W, 1958, Je 1,87:1
Caldwell, Oliver P, 1966, Ja 12,21:4
Caldwell, Orestes H, 1967, Ag 30,43:3
Caldwell, Otis W, 1947, Jl 6,40:6
Caldwell, Otis W Mrs, 1959, My 9,21:5
Caldwell, Ray, 1967, Ag 19,25:2
Caldwell, Rebecca A, 1952, Ja 4,40:3
Caldwell, Rebekah, 1944, N 11,13:6
Caldwell, Robert F Mrs, 1958, F 19,27:3
Caldwell, Robert F Sr, 1959, Ag 30,82:6
Caldwell, Robert J, 1951, D 22,15:1
Caldwell, Robert W, 1954, Je 23,25:1
Caldwell, Rosemary, 1952, My 24,19:5
Caldwell, Sam, 1953, Ag 16,76:6
Caldwell, Samuel A, 1963, S 3,33:2
Caldwell, Samuel Cushman, 1923, Ja 24,13:4
Caldwell, Samuel H, 1960, O 13,37:1
Caldwell, Sarah E, 1954, Ap 28,31:3
Caldwell, Tod R Gov, 1874, Jl 12,4:6
Caldwell, Wilbur F, 1953, Ja 5,21:2
Caldwell, William, 1876, Jl 4,4:6; 1885, Mr 9,5:3; 1942, D 15,27:2
Caldwell, William E, 1943, Ap 2,21:1; 1957, Ag 25, 86:4
Caldwell, William H, 1913, Ja 5,17:2; 1937, Je 28, 19:4; 1941, My 22,21:4; 1947, S 10,27:4
Caldwell, William M, 1939, O 7,17:4
Caldwell, William R, 1966, F 21,39:1
Caldwell, William T, 1941, Ag 15,17:5
Caldwell, William W, 1956, Mr 29,27:5
Caldwell, William W Mrs, 1941, D 9,31:2
Caldwer, Frederick V, 1946, Ag 6,25:1
Caleb, Gideon Norville, 1916, Mr 2,11:7
Calenberg, Ethel P, 1940, My 30,17:3
Calenberg, Harry H, 1962, Ja 15,27:4
Calenda, Raphael, 1943, D 29,17:1
Calenda, Vincent D, 1957, Ag 13,27:3
Calenda, Vincent D Jr, 1946, S 28,17:5
Calenda, Vincent D Mrs, 1943, F 10,25:1
Calender, Albert C, 1954, S 22,29:5
Calender, Samuel A, 1880, D 28,5:4
Caley, Arthur E, 1940, O 12,17:6
Caley, J Clarence, 1947, Mr 6,25:3
Caley, Joseph M Dr, 1937, Jl 6,19:4
Caley, N Herbert, 1956, Ap 11,33:3
Caley, Neville A, 1961, Mr 14,35:4
Calfayan, Mampre (funl plans, Jl 21,23:3), 1961, Jl 18,29:4
Calfee, John E, 1940, N 30,17:6
Calhern, Louis (to be cremated, My 14,25:3; will, My 24,27:4), 1956, My 13,86:3
Calhoun, Alfred R Maj, 1912, S 2,9:6
Calhoun, Alice (Mrs M C Chotiner), 1966, Je 6,41:2
Calhoun, Byron E, 1957, S 5,29:2
Calhoun, Charles, 1916, Ag 25,7:6
Calhoun, Charles L, 1954, My 28,23:1
Calhoun, Clarence C Mrs, 1949, Mr 22,25:4
Calhoun, David R, 1925, F 12,19:3
Calhoun, E Noble, 1941, Ja 26,36:1
Calhoun, Ervin, 1950, Ap 17,23:4
Calhoun, Fillmore, 1967, My 6,31:4
Calhoun, Frank W, 1945, Ap 24,19:5
Calhoun, Fred H H, 1959, My 3,86:3
Calhoun, Frederic S Mrs, 1949, D 12,33:2
Calhoun, Galloway Mrs, 1954, My 24,27:2
Calhoun, George W, 1963, D 8,86:1
Calhoun, Harold G, 1953, My 14,29:3
Calhoun, Harold Mrs (Dorothy D), 1963, D 3,43:2
Calhoun, Hazen, 1957, Je 9,89:1
Calhoun, J Ellwood, 1938, F 9,19:2
Calhoun, John, 1859, O 18,2:5
Calhoun, John C, 1947, F 28,23:4
Calhoun, John Caldwell, 1918, D 19,15:4
Calhoun, John D, 1963, Ag 13,31:1
Calhoun, John E, 1940, F 16,19:5
Calhoun, John F, 1951, Mr 15,29:5
Calhoun, John H, 1946, Mr 2,13:6
Calhoun, John J, 1946, Ag 9,17:4
Calhoun, John Rev, 1937, O 17,II,8:7
Calhoun, Joseph P Rev, 1937, Mr 1,20:1
Calhoun, Mary E, 1963, N 12,41:2
Calhoun, Minnie Mrs, 1952, Ag 20,25:3
Calhoun, P C, 1882, Mr 15,5:3
Calhoun, Patrick, 1943, Je 18,21:5
Calhoun, Philo C, 1964, D 20,69:1
Calhoun, Robert H, 1957, Mr 2,21:6
Calhoun, Roland F, 1944, My 12,19:3
Calhoun, Rose M, 1937, Ag 4,19:3
Calhoun, W B, 1865, N 10,4:6
Calhoun, William A, 1939, My 10,23:5
Calhoun, William J, 1967, D 2,39:5
Calhoun, William L, 1938, Ja 4,23:4; 1963, O 21,31:2
Calif, Amos H, 1914, S 17,9:6
Califano, Augustus E, 1966, O 23,88:7
Califano, Frank, 1939, D 4,23:5
Califf, Joseph M Brig-Gen, 1912, Ja 5,13:5
Calingaert, George, 1960, Ap 19,37:5
Calippe, Abbe C, 1947, Je 17,28:3
Calisch, Edward N, 1946, Ja 8,23:1
Calise, Dominick Sr, 1951, O 12,27:4
Calisher, Joseph H, 1943, Ja 8,20:3
Calissi, John W, 1959, Je 3,35:3
Calitri, Antonio, 1949, Je 5,92:5; 1954, Jl 13,23:3
Caliver, Ambrose, 1962, Ja 30,29:1
Calixtus, Bro (J E Curran), 1952, S 7,87:1
Calixtus, Philip Bro, 1957, N 12,34:1
Calixtus Leo, Bro, 1956, Ja 11,29:1
Calka, John J, 1953, Mr 10,31:8
Calkin, Alonzo A, 1946, Jl 14,37:2
Calkin, Clara H Mrs, 1938, S 3,13:6
Calkin, John B, 1959, Ap 20,31:4
Calkin, John W, 1964, Ag 6,29:4
Calkins, Carlos G Capt, 1916, D 22,9:3
Calkins, Charles E, 1948, Ap 4,60:2
Calkins, Clinch (Mrs Mark Merrell), 1968, D 28,27:3
Calkins, Dick, 1962, My 14,29:4
Calkins, Donald Mrs, 1943, F 8,19:2
Calkins, Earnest E, 1964, O 6,39:1
Calkins, Earnest E Mrs, 1950, Je 9,23:4
Calkins, Edward, 1940, D 17,26:2
Calkins, Elisha, 1942, Ap 8,19:4
Calkins, Elton, 1958, Ja 16,29:1
Calkins, Gary N, 1943, Ja 5,19:5
Calkins, Gary N Mrs, 1965, D 10,42:2
Calkins, George A, 1949, Ap 23,13:4
Calkins, Harlan F, 1962, O 4,39:4
Calkins, Harriet A, 1944, O 21,17:4
Calkins, Harry R, 1956, N 3,23:5
Calkins, Harvey R, 1941, F 17,15:3
Calkins, Hiram, 1905, Ja 10,9:2
Calkins, Irving R, 1958, Ag 28,27:3
Calkins, J Burt, 1949, Ja 6,23:3
Calkins, James J, 1944, Jl 15,13:2
Calkins, James S, 1960, Ja 4,29:5
Calkins, John T, 1941, Ja 23,21:4
Calkins, John U Sr, 1954, Ap 24,17:3
Calkins, Leighton, 1955, D 29,23:4
Calkins, Rollin Mrs, 1956, Jl 25,29:5
Calkins, Truesdel P, 1942, Je 9,2[illegible]:1
Calkins, Wolcott Rev Dr, 1925, Ja 2,15:4
Call, Annie P, 1940, F 6,22:2
Call, Clara E Mrs, 1942, Mr 7,17:4
Call, Clay D, 1945, Jl 24,23:5
Call, Edward P Mrs, 1962, Ag 7,29:4
Call, Edward Payson, 1919, My 20,17:5; 1919, Je 7, 13:6
Call, Loren H Lt, 1913, Jl 9,7:4
Call, Martha C Mrs, 1937, Ja 3,II,8:5
Call, Norman, 1959, My 26,35:4
Call, S Leigh, 1952, N 20,31:4
Call, Wilkinson Sen, 1910, Ag 25,7:5
Call, William, 1950, F 26,77:1
Call, William B, 1960, Ap 19,37:3
Call, William E, 1943, D 13,23:4
Call, William Mrs, 1955, Ja 18,27:3
Call, William Timothy, 1917, N 15,13:5
Callaghan, Bryan, 1912, Jl 9,9:5
Callaghan, Charles W, 1949, Ap 5,29:2
Callaghan, Cornelius H, 1954, My 13,29:4
Callaghan, George Astley Sir, 1920, N 24,17:4
Callaghan, Glenn S, 1952, Ap 1,29:5
Callaghan, Harry J, 1944, Ja 4,17:5
Callaghan, James A, 1941, Je 7,17:4
Callaghan, James G, 1939, Mr 23,23:1
Callaghan, James M, 1950, F 22,30:2
Callaghan, Jeremiah N, 1939, O 25,23:5
Callaghan, Jerome, 1948, Mr 18,27:2
Callaghan, John, 1941, O 29,23:2; 1949, Ag 24,25:2
Callaghan, John E, 1954, Jl 16,21:2
Callaghan, John F, 1937, My 25,28:3
Callaghan, John P, 1943, Ap 22,23:6
Callaghan, John P Rev, 1914, F 26,9:5
Callaghan, John W, 1943, Je 5,15:3
Callaghan, M Mrs, 1878, N 1,2:6
Callaghan, Michael J, 1949, Ap 17,76:5
Callaghan, Phil C, 1941, F 17,15:4
Callaghan, Richard W, 1915, O 28,11:5
Callaghan, Stephen, 1952, O 13,21:6
Callaghan, T F, 1881, Jl 11,8:4
Callaghan, Thomas J, 1958, O 16,37:1
Callaghan, William D, 1960, My 21,23:5
Callagy, Agnes, 1950, Ja 27,23:4
Callagy, Frank M, 1951, Jl 11,23:6
Callagy, Martin F, 1942, Ja 11,46:1
Callagy, Martin V, 1954, Ag 5,23:3
Callahan, Agnes, 1947, N 16,77:1
Callahan, Andrew, 1950, F 21,25:5
Callahan, Andrew C, 1941, O 13,17:5
Callahan, Billy (Mrs V Valenzio), 1964, F 23,85:1
Callahan, Carl C, 1947, N 14,23:2
Callahan, Charles E, 1917, Ja 24,9:3
Callahan, Charles S, 1964, N 14,29:5
Callahan, Daniel J, 1942, F 17,21:2; 1957, O 24,33:
Callahan, Daniel T, 1949, D 26,29:3
Callahan, David, 1903, My 22,9:4
Callahan, Dennis E, 1946, Jl 13,15:5
Callahan, Dominick F, 1944, F 29,17:1
Callahan, Edith T, 1949, Ag 3,23:3
Callahan, Edward C, 1951, F 15,31:2
Callahan, Edward F, 1952, F 20,29:3; 1954, Ja 15,1
Callahan, Edward J, 1943, N 10,23:4
Callahan, Edward M, 1942, N 17,25:3
Callahan, Emmett, 1965, D 31,21:4
Callahan, Eugene, 1940, D 15,60:1
Callahan, Eugene J, 1954, F 23,27:4
Callahan, F Howard, 1962, Ja 21,88:4
Callahan, Francis J, 1948, Je 22,25:4
Callahan, Frank, 1933, F 6,15:1; 1959, F 19,31:4
Callahan, Frank J, 1948, N 27,17:5
Callahan, Frank K, 1942, D 2,25:4
Callahan, Frank P, 1952, D 22,25:2
Callahan, Frank S (will, Jl 20,12:5), 1947, Jl 9,23
Callahan, George E, 1949, Ag 11,24:3
Callahan, George F, 1950, D 11,25:3
Callahan, George J, 1942, D 31,15:3
Callahan, George M, 1939, My 21,III,7:2
Callahan, George W, 1945, Mr 17,13:4
Callahan, Harry C, 1954, F 17,31:2
Callahan, Henry A, 1968, Jl 3,35:2
Callahan, Henry M, 1956, Ap 14,17:6
Callahan, Herbert F, 1955, Ja 14,21:4
Callahan, Jack, 1954, Ag 26,27:2
Callahan, James A, 1948, F 12,23:5; 1956, My 26,
Callahan, James C, 1960, F 24,37:3
Callahan, James E Sr, 1950, Jl 12,29:5
Callahan, James J, 1949, Ja 11,31:6; 1951, Ap 24,

Callahan, James T, 1959, Ap 25,21:4
Callahan, John, 1939, O 23,19:3; 1944, Je 5,19:3; 1946, O 18,23:2; 1948, N 25,31:4; 1956, My 13,86:5
Callahan, John A, 1942, Mr 5,23:6
Callahan, John F, 1948, Ja 21,25:2; 1954, Ag 16,17:2; 1958, S 21,86:2
Callahan, John H, 1941, Ap 26,15:6
Callahan, John J, 1950, O 11,33:4; 1957, Je 16,84:8
Callahan, John L, 1951, D 25,31:2
Callahan, John M, 1941, My 10,15:1; 1949, S 9,25:4
Callahan, John Mrs, 1942, D 24,15:5; 1952, Mr 10, 21:5; 1960, N 7,35:4
Callahan, John P, 1946, Je 18,25:1; 1967, N 9,47:3
Callahan, John P Jr, 1955, D 17,23:5
Callahan, Joseph J, 1949, Ag 18,21:5
Callahan, Joseph T, 1944, Mr 8,19:4
Callahan, Julia F, 1952, Ap 30,27:4
Callahan, Kate, 1867, N 3,2:7
Callahan, M J, 1902, D 11,10:1
Callahan, Martin J, 1958, Jl 3,25:2
Callahan, Mary E, 1959, Je 2,35:3
Callahan, Matthew, 1939, D 31,18:5
Callahan, Maurice Sr, 1956, Ja 23,25:2
Callahan, Michael, 1903, My 26,9:6
Callahan, Michael H, 1948, My 15,15:2
Callahan, Michael J, 1947, Je 26,23:3; 1961, O 31,31:3
Callahan, Michael Mrs, 1962, Mr 13,35:2
Callahan, Neil Mrs, 1951, Ap 26,29:5
Callahan, Neil U Mrs, 1951, Ag 11,11:6
Callahan, Nellie, 1954, Jl 25,69:4
Callahan, Patrick, 1940, Ag 29,19:4
Callahan, Patrick H, 1940, F 5,17:4
Callahan, Robert H, 1954, Je 30,27:5
Callahan, Robert Jr, 1952, Je 10,27:5
Callahan, T Lewis, 1950, Mr 17,23:3
Callahan, Thomas J, 1968, S 22,88:5
Callahan, Thomas M, 1948, Je 6,72:5
Callahan, Thomas M Mrs, 1948, Ap 11,72:2
Callahan, Timothy, 1943, Ap 3,15:6
Callahan, Wilfred D, 1946, F 1,24:2
Callahan, William A, 1958, Jl 5,17:4
Callahan, William B, 1956, Jl 9,23:2
Callahan, William E, 1957, Ja 3,33:1
Callahan, William F (funl), 1964, Ap 24,33:5
Callahan, William H, 1951, Jl 27,19:4
Callahan, William J, 1937, My 5,25:5; 1938, Jl 29, 17:3; 1944, Ap 19,23:4; 1944, Ag 4,15:7; 1947, Ja 16, 25:3; 1952, N 11,29:3
Callahan, William Mrs, 1945, Ag 10,15:2
Callan, Andrew T, 1960, Jl 31,69:2
Callan, Byron K, 1965, Jl 5,17:5
Callan, Charles C, 1941, My 14,21:5
Callan, Charles J, 1962, F 27,34:1
Callan, Claude, 1956, Ap 19,31:1
Callan, Edward J, 1957, My 18,19:2
Callan, Frank D Mrs, 1967, Ja 24,28:7
Callan, James A, 1960, My 26,33:4
Callan, Jessie M, 1951, Jl 25,23:4
Callan, John B, 1949, F 17,23:5
Callan, John G, 1941, Ja 1,23:5
Callan, John H, 1949, Je 27,27:3
Callan, John H Jr, 1949, D 18,90:4
Callan, John L, 1958, O 9,37:2
Callan, John P Col, 1968, S 29,80:4
Callan, Joseph H, 1965, Mr 21,86:2
Callan, Lewis White Dr, 1920, Ja 22,17:2
Callan, Luke H, 1942, S 10,27:3
Callan, Matthew, 1940, F 14,21:4
Callan, Patrick J, 1949, Je 1,31:5
Callan, Peter, 1939, Mr 14,21:2
Callan, Peter J, 1937, Ja 19,23:5
Callan, Robert L Jr (Bob), 1967, Ja 21,31:6
Callan, Thomas J, 1908, Mr 7,7:5; 1952, My 31,17:3; 1960, Ag 17,31:3
Callan, William, 1963, Je 30,57:1
Callan, William Mrs, 1956, Jl 9,23:5
Callanan, Andrew W, 1944, My 10,19:3
Callanan, Edward A, 1956, Ap 15,88:8
Callanan, Francis J, 1940, Ap 22,17:2
Callanan, Lawrence J, 1913, O 18,13:4
Callanan, Neil D, 1958, Mr 7,23:1
Callanan, Richard P, 1963, D 3,43:5
Callanan, Victor J, 1958, N 1,19:6
Callander, George M, 1959, Ap 1,37:4
Callander, Jack O, 1956, S 22,17:5
Callander, James, 1952, My 27,29:6
Callanen, Gardner A, 1948, F 6,26:6
Callans, Lee D, 1958, N 25,33:1
Callary, Thomas R, 1944, Mr 18,13:5
Callaway, Abner K, 1938, F 24,19:6
Callaway, Adah A Mrs, 1951, Je 30,15:5
Callaway, Cason J, 1961, Ap 13,35:3
Callaway, Charles S, 1962, Ja 26,31:3
Callaway, Christopher E, 1945, Ap 23,19:4
Callaway, David H, 1960, Ja 29,25:1
Callaway, Edward L, 1945, N 23,23:2
Callaway, Eli R, 1956, N 7,31:1
Callaway, F E Sr, 1928, F 13,19:5
Callaway, Gertrude L, 1952, Mr 16,91:1
Callaway, Hendley R, 1948, Jl 29,21:3
Callaway, Holt F, 1966, Ag 23,39:3
Callaway, Lew L Mrs, 1966, S 2,31:3
Callaway, Llewellyn L, 1951, Ag 7,25:6
Callaway, Merrel P, 1957, Je 17,23:3
Callaway, Merrel P Mrs, 1942, N 1,52:6; 1953, D 25, 17:3
Callaway, S R, 1904, Je 2,9:6
Callaway, Samuel T, 1943, D 19,48:6
Callaway, Trowbridge, 1963, Je 21,29:1
Callaway, W Elmer, 1956, My 13,86:5
Callaway, William R, 1937, F 11,23:1
Callaway, William T, 1948, N 16,29:2
Callbreath, James F, 1940, Ag 5,13:6
Callear, William M Mrs, 1948, My 9,68:6
Calleia, Pasquale, 1945, Jl 4,13:5
Callejas, Francisco, 1945, Jl 27,15:3
Callejo, Eduardo, 1950, Ja 22,78:2
Callen, Alfred C, 1951, Jl 31,21:3
Callen, Arthur S, 1961, My 10,45:4
Callen, Harold W, 1965, My 10,33:4
Callen, John H, 1958, O 17,29:3
Callen, Peter, 1942, D 15,27:5
Callender, Clark Mrs, 1947, N 2,73:2
Callender, Donald B, 1965, Je 13,84:7
Callender, Geoffrey A, 1946, N 7,31:3
Callender, George B, 1942, O 11,56:2
Callender, Guy Stevens, 1915, Ag 9,7:5
Callender, Harold (trb, O 15,38:6; will, O 15,77:7), 1959, O 9,29:2
Callender, Harold Mrs, 1951, Je 27,29:4
Callender, John A, 1956, Ja 15,92:1
Callender, Joseph E, 1947, S 21,60:7
Callender, Orma C, 1949, Je 27,28:4
Callender, Robert F, 1957, D 15,86:8
Callender, Thomas O, 1938, D 4,60:5
Callender, W R, 1876, Ja 23,6:5
Callender, Wesley P Jr, 1968, Ap 10,43:2
Callender, William E, 1944, Ja 27,19:2
Callender, William H, 1961, Je 25,77:1
Callender, William N, 1939, O 22,40:7
Callery, James F, 1959, Je 12,27:2
Callery, Joseph B, 1949, Ag 9,25:4
Callery, Marguerite M Mrs, 1940, D 7,17:6
Callery, Phil A, 1938, N 10,27:3
Callery, Thomas J, 1943, Mr 28,24:5; 1943, Ap 1,23:4
Callery, William T, 1941, Ag 12,19:6
Calles, N Senora, 1927, Je 3,21:5
Calles, P E Mrs, 1932, N 26,15:1
Calles, Plutarco E, 1945, O 20,11:1
Calley, Russell B, 1952, Mr 25,27:2
Calligan, Bernard, 1962, Ja 1,23:2
Calligan, Ed Mrs (A Jamison), 1961, Ap 18,37:3
Calligan, William J, 1959, O 28,37:3
Callighan, J Rev, 1869, Ja 29,4:7
Callin, A E, 1949, D 30,19:3
Callinan, George H, 1942, My 12,19:1
Callis, Charles A, 1947, Ja 22,23:2
Callis, Harold B, 1965, D 1,47:4
Callis, Harold B Mrs, 1947, Ja 29,25:1
Callis, Theodore E Mrs, 1955, Ja 26,25:3
Callisen, Adolph W, 1940, S 2,15:5
Callistos, Bishop, 1940, N 29,21:6
Callistrat, Patriach, 1952, F 6,29:3
Callman, M Monroe, 1943, Ja 13,23:3
Callner, Irwin H, 1950, N 29,33:3
Callo, Joseph F Mrs, 1947, Je 29,48:1
Callorda, Pedro E, 1949, D 7,31:2
Callow, George W, 1959, D 16,41:4
Callow, John M, 1940, Jl 28,27:1
Callow, Russell S (Rusty), 1961, F 24,29:1
Callow, Walter H, 1950, Ja 8,76:4
Callow, William, 1882, Ap 16,2:7
Calloway, Artemus A, 1948, Ap 9,23:1
Calloway, Roger M, 1943, D 7,27:5
Calloway, Walter B, 1955, My 15,87:2
Callus, Francis Sr, 1938, Ag 22,30:3
Callvert, Ronald G, 1955, F 15,27:1
Callwell, W E (see also Mr 23), 1877, Mr 26,8:3
Calm, James B, 1909, Mr 9,9:6
Calman, Jacob S, 1952, Mr 4,27:4
Calman, Maurice S Mrs, 1963, Je 19,37:2
Calmann-Levy, George, 1937, F 10,23:5
Calmer, Edgar Mrs, 1955, N 25,27:3
Calmer, John S, 1945, O 17,19:2
Calmer, May Mrs, 1953, Mr 12,25:2
Calmette, A, 1933, O 30,12:1
Calnan, Evelyn, 1922, S 22,15:4
Calnan, John L, 1946, F 2,13:4
Calnan, Martha, 1965, Mr 11,33:1
Calnan, William J, 1949, D 18,88:3
Calnen, Henry J, 1941, Mr 6,21:3
Calnon, William J, 1945, S 21,21:4
Calocay, Arpad Sr, 1958, My 4,89:2
Calonkey, Leon, 1953, D 26,13:4
Calrk, Harry R, 1943, Jl 1,19:5
Calrk, William R Mrs, 1939, D 7,27:2
Calrke, Graham W, 1943, My 5,27:5
Calrow, Mary, 1941, Jl 28,13:5
Calthorpe, Baron (Augustus Gough-Calthorpe), 1910, Jl 23,7:6
Calthorpe, Lady, 1940, Jl 5,13:5
Calthrop, Dion C, 1937, Mr 9,23:4
Calthrop, Donald, 1940, Jl 16,17:6
Calthrop, Guy Spencer Sir, 1919, F 24,13:2
Calton, William D, 1948, Mr 25,27:2
Calvano, Mary (Sister Mary Ferdinand), 1952, Ap 23,29:4
Calvano, Michael, 1950, S 16,19:4
Calve, Emma, 1942, Ja 7,19:1
Calvelli, Eugene Sr, 1962, Ap 24,37:3
Calvelli, Vito, 1947, Ag 8,17:5
Calvemine, Frank, 1949, Ag 16,23:3
Calverley, Amice M, 1959, Ap 12,87:1
Calverly, Charles, 1914, F 27,11:5
Calvert, Alex H, 1952, F 11,27:7
Calvert, Allen P, 1965, N 15,37:3
Calvert, Bruce, 1940, Je 1,15:2
Calvert, C, 1879, Je 16,5:4
Calvert, Cecil K, 1948, Ap 20,27:2
Calvert, Charles Mrs, 1921, S 23,15:6
Calvert, Frank, 1884, Jl 22,1:2
Calvert, Frank J, 1947, Ag 30,15:3
Calvert, Frank M, 1949, F 18,23:2
Calvert, George, 1946, My 10,19:2
Calvert, Henry M Maj, 1925, Ja 23,19:4
Calvert, J B, 1928, Ja 14,17:5
Calvert, Jacob G, 1959, S 30,29:6
Calvert, James C, 1915, D 30,13:4
Calvert, Jay H, 1964, Ja 4,23:5
Calvert, John S, 1949, F 22,23:4
Calvert, Leonard H, 1958, F 23,93:1
Calvert, Louis (funl, Jl 20,13:4), 1923, Jl 19,15:5
Calvert, Louis L, 1941, F 10,17:5
Calvert, Lowell V, 1955, Ag 18,23:3
Calvert, Madison R, 1945, N 26,21:5
Calvert, Naidene P Mrs, 1944, My 21,43:2
Calvert, Ralph L, 1952, Ap 2,33:5
Calvert, Robert C, 1952, Je 15,84:1
Calvert, Samuel H, 1954, Je 7,23:5
Calvert, Thomas E P, 1938, Jl 2,13:4
Calvert, William C, 1956, O 1,27:5
Calvert, William J, 1945, Mr 22,23:5
Calvert, William R, 1949, O 6,31:1
Calvert, William W, 1940, F 29,19:4
Calverton, Victor F, 1940, N 21,29:4
Calvet, Marcel, 1952, O 22,27:6
Calvey, Michael W, 1952, Ag 10,60:6
Calvin, Anson B, 1950, F 17,23:3
Calvin, Chester W Mrs, 1960, N 13,88:7
Calvin, D C Mrs, 1877, Ap 23,8:4
Calvin, Edgar E, 1938, Mr 18,19:2
Calvin, Floyd, 1939, S 2,17:6
Calvin, William A, 1962, Ja 28,76:3
Calvo, Carlos, 1942, Je 1,13:2
Calvo, Joaquin B, 1952, N 21,25:3
Calvo, Luis A, 1945, Ap 24,19:3
Calvocoressi, Leonidas J, 1952, Ap 19,15:2
Calvosa, Rocco M, 1960, S 1,27:3
Calvosa, Ulrich, 1952, Ag 25,17:2
Calyer, C Gilbert, 1940, F 22,23:4
Calyer, W Newcomb, 1960, Je 23,29:5
Calyo, Nicolino, 1884, D 11,2:5
Calza, Guido, 1946, Ap 24,25:4
Cam, Helen Maud Dr, 1968, F 13,43:3
Camac, Charles N B, 1940, S 29,43:1
Camac, Julia A M Mrs, 1941, O 11,17:5
Camacho, Angarita A, 1952, S 7,86:3
Camacho, Anna de C Mrs, 1938, My 25,23:4
Camacho, Maurice V, 1941, O 11,17:3
Camacho, Sebastian, 1915, N 10,13:2
Camacho, Simon, 1883, O 4,2:4
Camacho de Avila, Eufrosina Mrs, 1939, N 9,23:5
Camarco, Michael, 1949, Jl 11,17:3
Camargo, Teodora, 1945, Ja 26,21:1
Camarota, Vincent J, 1957, D 28,17:1
Camas, E Filhol de, 1945, Ap 4,21:3
Camassel, Philip Cardinal, 1921, Ja 20,9:4
Cambata, Shiavax C, 1951, F 7,29:4
Cambell, Alexander Douglas, 1915, O 13,15:6
Cambell, Chester W, 1960, S 21,37:1
Cambern, Harriet J Mrs, 1951, F 4,76:4
Cambia, John T, 1951, Ap 17,29:5
Camblos, Alice M Mrs, 1938, Ag 28,33:3
Camblos, Henry S, 1911, Jl 9,11:4
Cambo, Chiquito de (J Apesteguy), 1950, D 28,25:5
Cambon, Camille Vice Adm, 1937, Ja 5,23:4
Cambon, J, 1935, S 20,21:1
Cambon, Paul, 1924, My 30,15:6
Cambria, Frank, 1966, S 18,84:4
Cambria, John, 1952, D 11,33:4
Cambria, John Mrs (Marie), 1952, O 15,31:4
Cambridge, Alex A F W A G (Earl of Athlone),(funl, Ja 20,92:8), 1957, Ja 17,29:1
Cambridge, Duke of, 1904, Mr 18,9:1
Cambridge, Marquess of, 1927, O 25,29:3
Cambridge, Walter H, 1938, Ja 21,19:4
Camburn, Daniel, 1949, O 23,84:1
Camche, Leon J, 1966, O 7,43:3
Camden, Alex T, 1954, Mr 12,21:1
Camden, Harry P, 1943, Ag 12,19:1
Camden, Horace P, 1939, Ap 4,25:2
Camden, Johnson N, 1942, Ag 17,15:1
Camden, Johnson N Ex-Sen, 1908, Ap 26,9:4
Camden, Marquis of, 1872, My 7,4:7
Camden, Sprigg D, 1943, D 21,27:1
Camelon, David, 1956, My 4,25:3
Camera, A U N, 1938, Ag 29,13:6
Camerana, Giancarlo Count, 1955, N 30,33:2
Camerden, Elizabeth H, 1907, Ja 18,7:5

Camerden, William H, 1939, My 13,15:4
Camerer, Prof, 1879, Mr 22,2:7
Camerlengo, Marietta, 1955, Mr 5,17:6
Cameron, A Guyot, 1947, Jl 30,21:5
Cameron, A Guyot Sr Mrs, 1946, Ag 23,19:2
Cameron, Agnes D, 1912, My 14,11:4
Cameron, Alex, 1951, S 15,15:5
Cameron, Alex Jr, 1960, O 13,37:2
Cameron, Alex Mrs, 1958, Ja 22,27:4
Cameron, Alexander, 1915, F 4,9:5
Cameron, Alexander G, 1944, My 31,19:1
Cameron, Allan, 1937, Je 1,23:2
Cameron, Alpin W (will), 1956, Jl 25,23:2
Cameron, Andrew, 1948, Jl 13,28:2
Cameron, Arch, 1948, F 20,28:3
Cameron, Archie G, 1956, Ag 10,17:5
Cameron, Arthur, 1967, Mr 3,35:5
Cameron, Arthur E Mrs, 1938, Mr 14,16:2; 1949, Ja 6, 23:2
Cameron, Augustus G, 1960, S 9,29:2
Cameron, B A, 1925, Ja 3,13:5
Cameron, Ben F, 1964, Ap 4,27:2
Cameron, Charles, 1941, N 18,25:1
Cameron, Charles Alexander Sir, 1921, F 28,11:4
Cameron, Charles E, 1940, F 13,23:3; 1942, N 16,19:2; 1946, F 25,25:3
Cameron, Charles L, 1940, N 3,57:3
Cameron, Charles R Mrs, 1943, Jl 28,15:4
Cameron, D Gen, 1879, Ap 5,5:3
Cameron, Daniel A, 1937, S 6,17:4
Cameron, David, 1945, S 17,19:5
Cameron, Don, 1918, Ag 31,7:5
Cameron, Donald, 1940, F 17,13:2; 1955, Jl 13,25:1; 1961, Ap 12,41:2
Cameron, Donald C, 1948, Ja 10,15:3; 1954, N 18,33:4
Cameron, Donald F, 1941, D 16,27:1
Cameron, Donald J, 1964, Ja 29,33:1
Cameron, Donald L, 1939, My 15,17:4
Cameron, Donald Mrs, 1944, Ag 19,11:3; 1946, D 12, 29:5
Cameron, Donald W, 1951, O 12,27:5
Cameron, Duncan, 1916, Mr 1,11:4; 1960, Ap 20,39:1
Cameron, Duncan E Mrs, 1954, Ja 23,13:4
Cameron, Duncan S, 1947, Ja 17,24:3
Cameron, Edgar S, 1944, N 6,19:4
Cameron, Edward H, 1938, D 21,23:4
Cameron, Edward M, 1942, O 23,21:5
Cameron, Edwin A, 1948, N 18,27:5
Cameron, Edwin J, 1955, Mr 23,31:2
Cameron, Emmett F, 1961, Ja 17,37:1
Cameron, Ewan C D, 1957, D 5,35:2
Cameron, Ewen, 1967, S 9,31:5
Cameron, F G Capt, 1880, D 3,2:5
Cameron, Frederick C, 1939, S 30,17:5
Cameron, Frederick K, 1939, Jl 29,15:7
Cameron, George H, 1944, Ja 29,13:6
Cameron, George T, 1955, O 4,35:1
Cameron, George V, 1944, Ja 25,19:6
Cameron, Gertrude G Mrs, 1961, Ja 21,21:4
Cameron, Glenn M, 1955, My 10,29:5
Cameron, Gordon W, 1955, Ap 30,17:2
Cameron, Gregory D, 1952, Jl 12,13:6
Cameron, H Eugene, 1955, Jl 12,25:4
Cameron, H S, 1875, My 29,1:3
Cameron, Harry A D, 1940, Jl 26,17:6
Cameron, Harry de Haven Dr, 1903, S 6,7:6
Cameron, Henry G, 1940, Ag 8,19:2
Cameron, Hugh, 1918, Jl 16,13:6; 1941, N 10,17:3
Cameron, Hugh Mrs, 1952, Ap 17,29:3
Cameron, Irving G, 1942, F 3,19:5
Cameron, Isabell, 1906, Jl 17,7:6
Cameron, Isabelle J, 1945, My 31,15:4
Cameron, J A, 1885, Ja 29,1:3
Cameron, James, 1953, Jl 2,23:4
Cameron, James B, 1958, Ap 17,31:4
Cameron, James H, 1951, Mr 15,29:5
Cameron, James K, 1958, Ja 6,39:2
Cameron, James M, 1949, O 27,27:4
Cameron, James R, 1946, Ag 23,19:1
Cameron, James Y, 1939, N 14,23:5
Cameron, Jessie V Mrs, 1953, Jl 18,13:6
Cameron, John C Capt, 1909, Mr 15,9:5
Cameron, John Capt, 1873, Ja 2,5:2
Cameron, John F, 1952, Mr 23,92:4
Cameron, John H, 1947, D 6,15:3; 1948, Jl 14,23:5
Cameron, John M, 1939, Ja 3,17:3; 1946, Jl 9,21:5
Cameron, John M Mrs, 1944, S 10,45:2
Cameron, John P, 1957, Je 25,29:1
Cameron, John T, 1944, D 2,13:5
Cameron, Joseph S, 1952, Mr 6,29:4
Cameron, Kenneth, 1941, Mr 13,21:3
Cameron, Kittie H Mrs, 1941, My 7,25:5
Cameron, Lambert V B, 1943, Ja 9,13:4
Cameron, Leon B, 1924, O 3,21:3
Cameron, Leslie G, 1958, N 18,37:3
Cameron, Lewis Rev, 1909, O 31,13:4
Cameron, Lizzie V Mrs (will), 1937, Jl 11,21:3
Cameron, M, 1877, S 12,5:3
Cameron, Malcolm J, 1953, S 15,31:6
Cameron, Malcolm J Mrs, 1951, O 4,33:5
Cameron, Margaret Selina Erne, 1919, Ag 7,7:4
Cameron, Marie, 1916, Ap 5,13:6
Cameron, Martha R, 1938, Ap 13,25:4
Cameron, Mrs, 1879, Jl 3,5:3
Cameron, Norman, 1953, Ap 23,29:1
Cameron, Norman W, 1947, N 27,31:3
Cameron, Peter, 1937, S 1,19:3
Cameron, Philip G, 1962, N 24,23:4
Cameron, Ralph H Jr, 1952, Ap 9,31:2
Cameron, Ralph Henry, 1953, F 13,21:3
Cameron, Ralph M, 1944, Mr 4,13:1
Cameron, Raymond J, 1946, Je 16,40:6
Cameron, Reuben, 1950, Ja 20,25:1
Cameron, Richard, 1949, Ja 31,19:5
Cameron, Robert D, 1949, N 22,30:2
Cameron, Sen Mrs, 1874, Je 21,6:7
Cameron, Simon Sen, 1889, Je 27,1:7
Cameron, Thomas, 1947, Jl 18,17:2
Cameron, Thomas L, 1948, Ag 27,18:4
Cameron, V L, 1894, Mr 28,4:7
Cameron, Violet, 1919, O 26,22:3
Cameron, W Gray L, 1948, F 8,60:6
Cameron, W Roberts, 1950, N 28,31:1
Cameron, William A, 1938, Ja 26,23:5
Cameron, William B, 1955, Je 26,77:1
Cameron, William C (will), 1952, Ja 20,84:1
Cameron, William D, 1951, Ag 2,21:4
Cameron, William H, 1941, N 24,17:1
Cameron, William J, 1955, Ag 3,23:2; 1963, My 12, 87:1
Cameron, William M, 1950, O 3,31:1
Cameron, William P, 1957, F 13,35:1
Cameron-Ramsay-Fairfax-Lucy, Henry W, 1944, Ag 23,19:4
Cameron. Wm H, 1963, S 14,25:1
Camester, Albert, 1908, Je 14,11:4
Camfield, Daniel A, 1914, N 10,11:5
Camfield, William H, 1944, N 11,13:7
Camilieri, Lorenzo (trb lr, Ap 29,II,10:8), 1956, Ap 22,85:4
Camilla, Sister (Mary Campbell), 1941, Mr 19,21:4
Camilla Borden, Sister, 1937, Mr 20,19:4
Camille, Roussan, 1961, D 12,43:1
Camiller, Louis, 1909, D 27,7:2
Camillo, Pasquale, 1963, Ap 21,86:5
Camillone, Michael, 1961, My 12,26:5
Camillus Lellis, Bro (Walsh), 1959, Jl 4,15:6
Caminetti, Anthony, 1923, N 18,23:2
Camira, Adm, 1920, Ja 6,15:1
Camisa, John J, 1939, Ap 19,23:5
Camm, Sydney, 1966, Mr 13,86:6
Cammack, Addison, 1901, F 6,9:3
Cammack, Huette, 1920, F 22,20:3
Cammack, Ira, 1939, S 13,25:3
Cammack, James W Sr, 1939, F 6,13:3
Cammack, John Addison, 1909, S 16,9:4
Cammack, R Edward, 1945, Mr 18,42:2
Cammaerts, Emile, 1953, N 3,31:1
Camman, Eric A, 1956, Ap 5,29:4
Camman, G P Dr, 1863, F 21,2:4
Cammann, Claude D, 1937, Mr 18,25:2
Cammann, Frederic A, 1946, Ag 31,15:2
Cammann, George P, 1920, D 26,22:2
Cammann, H Schuyler, 1965, Mr 4,31:4
Cammann, Henry J, 1920, Ag 25,9:2
Cammann, Henry L Mrs, 1955, D 5,31:2
Cammann, Oswald N, 1944, Ap 21,19:5
Cammarota, Michael, 1951, Mr 30,23:4
Cammerer, Arno B, 1941, My 1,23:3
Cammeyer, Alfred J, 1909, Ag 15,7:4
Cammeyer, Henrietta A, 1956, S 7,24:2
Cammeyer, J E, 1881, Ja 19,5:3
Cammisa, Michael, 1939, Jl 3,13:7
Camnitz, Harry R, 1951, Ja 7,76:3
Camnitz, Samuel H (Howie), 1960, Mr 3,30:1
Camoys, Lord (Ralph Francis Julian Stonor), 1968, Ag 4,69:1
Camoys, Mildred (Mrs R F J Stoner), 1961, N 22, 33:1
Camp, Albert S (funl, Jl 26,17:5), 1954, Jl 24,13:2
Camp, Anna Katherine Mrs, 1925, Jl 23,19:5
Camp, C W, 1936, N 1,II,11:2
Camp, Caleb J, 1909, Je 20,9:4
Camp, Caroline D, 1938, O 8,17:4
Camp, Curtis B, 1949, Ja 9,72:7
Camp, David Nelson Prof, 1916, O 20,9:4
Camp, E Marvin, 1966, Jl 11,29:1
Camp, Edward G, 1944, F 29,17:3
Camp, Edwin, 1955, D 5,31:4
Camp, Ernest W, 1938, My 14,15:5
Camp, Etta J Mrs, 1943, D 27,20:2
Camp, Frank, 1949, Mr 23,27:5
Camp, Frank A, 1944, Je 6,17:5
Camp, Fred Edgar, 1903, D 10,9:5
Camp, Frederic E, 1963, D 17,39:2
Camp, George R, 1947, Je 29,48:4
Camp, George W Mrs, 1951, N 10,17:6
Camp, Glen D, 1966, Mr 3,33:2
Camp, Guy W A, 1939, Je 6,23:5
Camp, Harold, 1962, Ag 12,81:2
Camp, Harold M, 1959, O 18,86:8
Camp, Harold Mrs, 1964, O 1,35:6
Camp, Henry N, 1950, Ap 20,29:3
Camp, Herbert L, 1950, Ja 29,69:1
Camp, Hiram W, 1956, N 1,39:3
Camp, Hugh N, 1921, Ja 18,11:4
Camp, Irving L, 1946, F 15,26:2
Camp, James J, 1963, D 31,19:2
Camp, Jane E Mrs, 1938, Ag 27,13:6
Camp, John D, 1952, S 20,15:2
Camp, John M Mrs, 1954, S 22,29:2
Camp, John S, 1946, F 2,13:5
Camp, John T Col, 1921, S 1,15:2
Camp, Joseph M, 1948, Ag 12,21:4
Camp, Lawrence S, 1947, My 7,31:3
Camp, Morton, 1952, Ap 26,23:2
Camp, Nathan H, 1903, N 9,7:5
Camp, Norman H, 1952, Jl 10,31:5
Camp, Oliver S, 1949, S 23,23:3
Camp, Quintus E, 1951, Ag 14,23:4
Camp, Raymond R, 1962, My 20,86:3
Camp, Roland H, 1948, Ag 16,19:3
Camp, Samuel G, 1952, Ap 28,19:3
Camp, Saul, 1957, My 30,19:6
Camp, Theodore C, 1924, Jl 17,15:5
Camp, Walter, 1925, Mr 17,21:4
Camp, Walter Jr, 1941, Ja 1,23:4
Camp, Walter Jr Mrs, 1949, F 2,27:4
Camp, Wendell, 1963, F 5,4:6
Camp, Wilber E, 1943, O 3,49:1
Camp, Wilbur H T, 1954, Jl 3,11:6
Camp, William D, 1937, Jl 14,21:1
Campa, Miguel A, 1965, Ag 23,31:2
Campagna, Anthony Mrs, 1967, Ag 23,51:4
Campagna, Armono A Mrs, 1959, Jl 17,21:4
Campagna, Joseph J, 1949, Ja 18,23:2
Campagna, Louis, 1955, My 31,52:1
Campaigne, Curtis, 1939, Mr 5,48:7
Campana, Ettore, 1941, Je 30,17:6
Campana, Francis, 1945, Jl 8,11:6
Campana, Vincent R, 1955, Jl 17,60:8
Campanari, Leandro, 1939, Ap 24,17:1
Campanaro, Joseph J, 1958, Ap 2,31:4
Campanella, Charles P, 1941, Mr 18,23:3
Campanella, Domenico, 1946, S 25,27:5
Campanella, Joe, 1967, F 17,37:2
Campanella, Roy Mrs, 1963, Ja 26,7:3
Campanelli, Gaetano T, 1962, S 22,25:1
Campanelli, Guiseppa Mrs, 1945, Jl 3,13:3
Campanini, Cleofonte, 1919, D 20,11:1
Campanini, Italo, 1896, N 24,1:2
Campanole, Nicholas W, 1955, Mr 27,86:5
Campari, David, 1940, Mr 12,23:5
Campau, Alexander, 1908, Ap 2,7:6
Campbell, A, 1883, S 17,5:5
Campbell, A D, 1942, Mr 3,24:2
Campbell, A E Rev Dr, 1875, Ja 2,2:6
Campbell, A G, 1884, Ja 11,5:5
Campbell, Abbey Henrietta, 1920, O 5,11:1
Campbell, Alan, 1963, Je 15,24:2
Campbell, Alan Dirchfield Dr, 1913, Ap 2,11:5
Campbell, Albert C, 1947, Ja 26,53:1
Campbell, Alex, 1940, My 18,15:4; 1942, D 17,29:6; 1951, Jl 29,68:6
Campbell, Alex A, 1951, N 13,30:6
Campbell, Alex G, 1954, Ja 30,17:5
Campbell, Alex Mrs, 1949, D 20,31:4
Campbell, Alexander, 1903, S 28,7:5; 1916, Ap 21,1
Campbell, Alexander Bishop, 1866, Mr 6,5:2
Campbell, Alexander Col, 1882, Ap 17,2:2
Campbell, Alexander Morton, 1968, Ja 6,39:3
Campbell, Alexander Rev, 1866, Mr 11,5:4
Campbell, Alexander S Mrs, 1945, Ja 3,17:3
Campbell, Alfred B, 1947, Ag 11,23:4
Campbell, Alfred S, 1912, Ag 8,9:4
Campbell, Alice B, 1952, Ap 5,15:4
Campbell, Alice Boole Dr, 1909, Ja 1,11:5
Campbell, Allan, 1939, My 16,23:5
Campbell, Allan R, 1957, F 18,27:1
Campbell, Alwyn S, 1952, Ag 27,5:5
Campbell, Andres H Mrs, 1961, S 23,19:1
Campbell, Andrew, 1945, Je 14,19:4
Campbell, Andrew G, 1943, Ja 27,21:3; 1957, Mr 89:1
Campbell, Andrew T Mrs, 1957, Ja 8,31:4
Campbell, Anthony F, 1914, D 30,11:6
Campbell, Anthony Mrs, 1945, S 18,24:2
Campbell, Arch H, 1948, My 12,27:4
Campbell, Arch Mrs, 1950, D 2,13:4
Campbell, Archibald B, 1965, N 3,35:4
Campbell, Archibald S, 1960, Jl 23,19:3
Campbell, Archiblad F Rev Dr, 1925, Ja 13,19:6
Campbell, Archie L, 1951, My 28,21:2
Campbell, Archie W, 1943, Ag 13,17:4
Campbell, Argyle, 1940, Ap 6,17:4; 1944, Ag 15,
Campbell, Argyll, 1943, N 26,23:3
Campbell, Arthur B (will, D 29,16:3), 1954, Jl 2
Campbell, Arthur D, 1956, Ja 16,21:5
Campbell, Arthur J, 1940, O 6,48:2; 1966, Jl 1,35
Campbell, Arthur P, 1955, D 8,37:4
Campbell, Arthur S, 1941, D 24,15:4
Campbell, Augustus Mrs, 1939, N 28,17:5
Campbell, Austin D, 1953, N 22,88:1
Campbell, B J, 1934, Ap 5,21:3
Campbell, Bales M, 1937, Ja 8,20:1
Campbell, Benjamin, 1939, Ag 21,13:2
Campbell, Benjamin Howell, 1925, Ap 4,17:6
Campbell, Bernard, 1943, Ag 26,17:4
Campbell, Bessie, 1943, Mr 18,19:4
Campbell, Braxton W Mrs, 1955, Jl 12,25:1

Campbell, Brayton, 1967, Ja 25,43:3
Campbell, Bruce, 1955, Mr 31,27:2
Campbell, Bruce A, 1954, Ag 29,89:1; 1955, S 30,25:6
Campbell, Bruce D, 1939, Mr 21,23:1
Campbell, C Macfie, 1943, Ag 8,37:3
Campbell, C W, 1937, S 4,15:6
Campbell, Caroline G Brooke Mrs, 1905, F 26,7:6
Campbell, Cassius M, 1952, D 23,23:2
Campbell, Catherine Mrs, 1941, N 19,25:4; 1953, Ag 26,27:3
Campbell, Cecil, 1952, My 12,25:3
Campbell, Chandler, 1956, O 29,29:3
Campbell, Charles, 1950, N 14,31:4; 1964, Jl 27,31:4; 1966, D 2,39:4; 1952, Ag 1,5:4
Campbell, Charles A, 1939, Ja 8,42:3; 1940, S 5,23:3
Campbell, Charles E, 1955, D 30,19:3
Campbell, Charles E Dr, 1913, S 16,11:6
Campbell, Charles E Mrs, 1948, Mr 1,23:2
Campbell, Charles F Mrs, 1957, Ag 9,19:5
Campbell, Charles H, 1912, S 13,9:6; 1956, D 19,31:1
Campbell, Charles J, 1944, Ag 21,15:3
Campbell, Charles L, 1954, My 16,86:4; 1956, Jl 10, 31:2
Campbell, Charles M, 1940, Ag 12,15:6
Campbell, Charles M Mrs, 1946, F 17,42:4
Campbell, Charles Mrs, 1950, My 23,29:1; 1964, O 11,85:6
Campbell, Charles R, 1964, My 4,29:3
Campbell, Charles S, 1954, S 22,29:5
Campbell, Charlotte Mrs, 1913, N 17,9:4
Campbell, Chesser M (funl plans; trb, Jl 12,35:5), 1960, Jl 11,29:4
Campbell, Chester C, 1955, D 25,48:1
Campbell, Chris, 1941, Ap 3,23:4
Campbell, Clarence G, 1956, Ag 12,85:1
Campbell, Clarence G Dr, 1956, Je 17,92:8
Campbell, Clarence L, 1963, Je 16,84:3
Campbell, Claude M, 1950, Ap 22,19:4
Campbell, Clinton D (por), 1938, Jl 12,19:4
Campbell, Clyde B, 1945, My 11,19:4
Campbell, Clyde C, 1947, Ag 13,23:6
Campbell, Clyde H, 1946, D 15,77:4
Campbell, Colin, 1881, Je 27,5:4; 1954, Ap 9,24:6
Campbell, Colin C, 1946, N 12,29:4
Campbell, Colin E Mrs (Lois), 1967, Ag 29,37:4
Campbell, Colin H, 1914, O 27,11:6
Campbell, Colin Lady, 1911, N 3,11:4
Campbell, Colin Sir (Lord Clyde), 1863, Ag 30,6:4
Campbell, Courtney, 1960, Ap 19,37:4
Campbell, Craig (Robt C), 1965, Ja 14,35:3
Campbell, D, 1927, My 10,27:1
Campbell, D Grant, 1956, Jl 21,15:6
Campbell, Dan M, 1967, O 24,47:2
Campbell, Daniel, 1919, N 16,22:4
Campbell, Daniel C, 1944, N 30,23:4
Campbell, Daniel E, 1958, Ap 18,23:4
Campbell, Daniel Mrs, 1955, Ja 28,19:2
Campbell, Daniel T, 1907, D 18,9:5
Campbell, David, 1949, My 28,15:5; 1951, D 4,33:6
Campbell, David C, 1949, Jl 1,19:2
Campbell, David W, 1961, Mr 3,27:3
Campbell, De Witt C, 1937, N 27,17:6
Campbell, Delwin M, 1952, Mr 29,15:6
Campbell, Don E, 1949, N 8,31:2
Campbell, Don J, 1956, O 11,39:4
Campbell, Donald, 1942, D 11,23:3; 1948, F 25,23:2; 1958, S 24,27:4; 1967, Ja 5,1:3
Campbell, Donald A, 1963, Jl 23,29:3;1953, Ap 19,90:1
Campbell, Donald J, 1959, Je 3,35:4
Campbell, Donald K, 1950, Ja 27,24:3
Campbell, Donald M, 1942, Ag 26,19:5
Campbell, Donald W, 1950, Mr 1,27:2
Campbell, Donald W Mrs, 1950, Ag 13,77:1
Campbell, Dorcas E, 1959, S 23,35:3
Campbell, Dorine Mrs, 1962, D 3,31:2
Campbell, Dorothea A, 1958, O 17,29:1
Campbell, Dortch, 1953, N 3,31:2
Campbell, Douglas, 1937, S 27,3:8; 1950, F 7,28:2
Campbell, Douglas A, 1945, S 25,25:1; 1950, Ag 22, 27:4
Campbell, Douglas H, 1953, F 25,27:5
Campbell, Douglas S, 1949, Mr 11,25:5
Campbell, Duncan Lt-Gov, 1871, N 8,5:4
Campbell, Duncan T, 1942, D 21,23:2
Campbell, Ed L, 1965, Jl 31,21:3
Campbell, Edmund Rev, 1925, Ap 16,21:5
Campbell, Edmund S (trb, Je 5,23:5), 1950, My 10, 31:1
Campbell, Edward, 1939, D 17,49:1; 1945, Jl 18,27:5
Campbell, Edward A Brig-Gen, 1917, F 16,11:6
Campbell, Edward A Rev, 1921, Jl 12,13:5
Campbell, Edward B, 1946, Ja 26,13:5
Campbell, Edward F, 1939, Je 20,21:1
Campbell, Edward J, 1951, Ag 13,17:3; 1960, S 22,27:6
Campbell, Edward K, 1938, D 9,25:2
Campbell, Edward Mrs, 1946, S 28,17:6
Campbell, Edward W, 1941, Ja 6,15:2
Campbell, Eldridge H, 1956, F 16,29:3
Campbell, Eleanor R, 1959, D 31,21:2
Campbell, Elizabeth A C Mrs, 1942, F 20,17:4
Campbell, Elizabeth M, 1955, Je 16,31:5
Campbell, Ella J Mrs, 1942, N 24,25:3
Campbell, Ella S Mrs, 1939, D 12,27:4
Campbell, Elmer I, 1942, F 22,27:2
Campbell, Emma, 1950, D 29,20:3
Campbell, Emma Frances Riggs, 1919, F 27,11:2
Campbell, Emmett J, 1953, O 8,29:3
Campbell, Emmett T, 1948, Je 14,23:3
Campbell, Ernest A, 1944, Ap 21,19:1
Campbell, Esther Mrs, 1953, Mr 21,17:3
Campbell, Ethan A, 1940, D 5,25:3
Campbell, Eugene K, 1953, F 11,29:2
Campbell, Everette L, 1966, S 30,47:2
Campbell, F E, 1934, Ja 20,15:4
Campbell, Felix, 1902, N 9,7:5
Campbell, Flora Mrs, 1947, Ap 29,27:2
Campbell, Floyd D, 1962, Ja 21,88:5
Campbell, Francis Alexander Sir, 1911, D 30,11:4
Campbell, Francis C, 1942, Jl 24,19:2; 1943, O 4,17:5
Campbell, Francis J, 1954, Ja 1,23:4; 1958, Je 11,36:1; 1964, My 1,35:1
Campbell, Francis M, 1953, Je 1,23:5
Campbell, Frank, 1924, F 17,23:2; 1924, My 23,19:4; 1964, O 6,77:6
Campbell, Frank C, 1954, Ja 4,19:3
Campbell, Frank C Mrs, 1947, Ap 1,27:4
Campbell, Frank E Mrs, 1954, O 22,27:5
Campbell, Frank J, 1939, O 2,17:4; 1951, S 11,20:2; 1953, Ag 8,11:6
Campbell, Frank S, 1951, My 29,25:2
Campbell, Frank V, 1942, F 21,19:6
Campbell, Fred, 1937, My 13,26:2; 1966, Je 11,31:4
Campbell, Frederick, 1872, D 29,8:1
Campbell, Frederick Archibald Vaughan (Earl Cawdor), 1911, F 9,7:6
Campbell, Frederick B, 1937, D 27,15:4
Campbell, Frederick G, 1940, My 1,24:2
Campbell, Frederick Mrs, 1960, Jl 2,17:3
Campbell, Frederick Rev Dr, 1917, F 24,9:4
Campbell, Frederick V, 1946, My 19,42:8
Campbell, George, 1938, D 12,19:1
Campbell, George A, 1943, Ag 19,19:3; 1954, N 11, 31:5
Campbell, George C Col, 1937, Mr 4,23:2
Campbell, George F, 1939, Je 19,15:4
Campbell, George F (por), 1949, Je 19,68:2
Campbell, George H, 1955, Ag 2,23:4
Campbell, George J, 1922, Ag 4,15:4; 1941, S 11,23:4; 1941, N 25,26:4
Campbell, George M, 1938, Mr 13,II,8:7
Campbell, George R, 1947, O 29,28:2; 1950, F 28,29:2
Campbell, George S Mrs, 1941, My 17,15:4
Campbell, George T, 1957, Ap 27,19:2
Campbell, George W, 1948, N 1,23:2
Campbell, Gerald, 1964, Jl 6,29:4
Campbell, Gilbert W, 1938, Jl 9,13:2
Campbell, Glenn H, 1947, O 21,24:2
Campbell, Gordon, 1953, O 6,29:1
Campbell, Gordon G, 1945, O 14,44:4
Campbell, Gordon Mrs, 1940, Ja 17,21:3
Campbell, Grace M (Mrs H Campbell), 1963, Je 2, 84:7
Campbell, Guy G, 1957, D 5,35:2
Campbell, H, 1877, Ag 21,8:6
Campbell, H Lyle, 1948, D 7,31:2
Campbell, Harold A, 1963, Jl 14,61:1
Campbell, Harold A M, 1959, Ag 1,17:3
Campbell, Harold D, 1955, D 30,20:1
Campbell, Harold G, 1942, Je 17,23:1
Campbell, Harriette R Lady, 1950, Jl 29,13:5
Campbell, Harris W, 1965, Ag 31,33:1
Campbell, Harry, 1914, Jl 27,7:7; 1955, Ap 17,87:2; 1961, My 17,45:7
Campbell, Harry A, 1965, Jl 4,37:3
Campbell, Harry H, 1950, N 21,32:2
Campbell, Harvey, 1938, Ja 28,21:1
Campbell, Harvey J, 1955, Mr 24,31:2
Campbell, Hector R, 1952, O 3,23:1
Campbell, Henry A, 1938, Ap 5,21:1
Campbell, Henry C, 1916, Ja 30,17:4
Campbell, Henry J, 1945, F 19,17:5
Campbell, Herbert R, 1946, D 26,25:2
Campbell, Hoik D, 1903, Jl 31,7:6
Campbell, Horace S, 1941, Ap 21,19:5
Campbell, Howard H Mrs, 1967, Ja 17,39:4
Campbell, Hugh, 1951, O 16,39:6
Campbell, Hugh Gorden, 1920, Je 23,11:4
Campbell, Hugh J, 1961, D 19,29:7
Campbell, Ida S, 1939, Ag 26,15:3
Campbell, Ira A (Mar 7), 1963, Ap 1,35:3
Campbell, Ira A Mrs, 1954, F 5,19:4
Campbell, Isabelle A Mrs, 1941, Jl 25,15:5
Campbell, J, 1876, Ag 8,3:4
Campbell, J A, 1927, Je 26,20:1; 1933, S 21,19:3
Campbell, J B, 1883, N 10,5:2
Campbell, J Bart, 1943, Ja 13,23:3
Campbell, J Burlow, 1940, Je 29,15:6
Campbell, J Hugh, 1954, O 18,25:4
Campbell, J P, 1903, S 30,9:6
Campbell, J R, 1934, Ag 17,15:6
Campbell, J W Rev Dr, 1914, F 21,11:4
Campbell, J Walter, 1953, Mr 29,95:3
Campbell, Jacob G, 1939, My 14,III,7:2
Campbell, James, 1914, Je 13,9:5; 1949, Ja 20,27:3; 1961, O 6,35:3
Campbell, James A, 1949, D 22,23:3
Campbell, James A G, 1941, Ja 3,19:4
Campbell, James A Mrs, 1947, O 27,21:4; 1953, Ja 3, 15:5
Campbell, James Alexander, 1908, My 10,9:4
Campbell, James B, 1946, O 12,19:2
Campbell, James Capt, 1922, Ap 5,17:4
Campbell, James D, 1954, Ap 25,87:2
Campbell, James E, 1940, O 22,23:4
Campbell, James E Ex-Gov, 1924, D 21,5:2
Campbell, James F, 1937, F 23,27:4
Campbell, James G, 1940, Je 3,15:3
Campbell, James G Mrs, 1947, Ap 20,63:4
Campbell, James H, 1954, N 4,31:5
Campbell, James J Mrs, 1949, Ap 19,25:3
Campbell, James Kenneth, 1968, O 21,47:1
Campbell, James L, 1948, Je 12,15:3; 1954, D 6,27:4
Campbell, James L Mrs (Dr Annie S Campbell), 1922, Jl 13,13:2
Campbell, James M, 1948, Mr 20,13:4; 1952, Ag 22, 21:1
Campbell, James R, 1965, Ja 12,37:3
Campbell, James R Gen, 1924, Ag 13,15:3
Campbell, James S, 1939, D 31,18:6
Campbell, James T, 1945, O 27,15:6
Campbell, Jane Elliot Mrs, 1903, D 12,9:6
Campbell, Jessie Mrs, 1939, Ja 17,21:5
Campbell, Jimmy, 1967, Ag 20,88:3
Campbell, Joe F, 1955, Je 18,17:5
Campbell, John, 1861, Jl 7,4:6; 1876, Jl 21,4:6; 1905, Mr 19,7:3; 1905, Ap 12,9:4; 1944, D 6,23:5
Campbell, John A, 1938, Je 3,21:4; 1954, My 2,89:2; 1962, Mr 22,35:4
Campbell, John A Mrs, 1951, S 4,27:3
Campbell, John B, 1938, O 25,23:4
Campbell, John B (will), 1940, Je 7,III,6:1
Campbell, John B, 1941, Ag 10,37:2
Campbell, John B (A Daley on career, Jl 8,29:2; funl, Jl 11,73:1), 1954, Jl 8,23:1
Campbell, John B, 1956, S 5,27:4
Campbell, John B Mrs, 1956, Jl 26,24:5
Campbell, John B T, 1956, Jl 28,17:5
Campbell, John C, 1938, Mr 20,II,8:7
Campbell, John E, 1954, Mr 7,91:2
Campbell, John H, 1922, Ap 6,17:4; 1937, Ag 17,19:5
Campbell, John Henderson, 1915, Ja 5,15:4
Campbell, John J, 1937, Mr 15,23:4; 1939, F 22,21:3; 1940, Je 26,23:4; 1951, N 22,31:1
Campbell, John J Jr, 1960, My 26,33:4
Campbell, John L, 1950, Ag 29,27:5
Campbell, John M, 1920, D 26,22:1; 1945, Ja 17,21:2
Campbell, John Mrs, 1945, Ja 28,38:4; 1948, Ag 2,21:4
Campbell, John Rev Dr, 1937, Mr 19,23:5
Campbell, John T, 1938, O 7,23:6; 1940, Ag 4,33:2
Campbell, John V, 1944, My 23,23:6
Campbell, John W, 1957, Mr 16,19:2; 1967, Jl 30,64:8
Campbell, Johnston, 1947, D 6,15:6
Campbell, Johnston B, 1953, N 7,17:5
Campbell, Joseph, 1942, Ja 6,23:2; 1949, Ja 29,13:5
Campbell, Joseph A, 1941, My 7,25:3; 1951, My 17, 31:6
Campbell, Joseph J, 1957, F 13,35:1
Campbell, Kemper, 1957, Ja 10,29:1
Campbell, Kenneth, 1967, Je 7,51:7
Campbell, Killis Dr, 1937, Ag 9,19:6
Campbell, Kingsley R, 1942, Ja 2,23:2
Campbell, L D, 1882, N 28,2:2
Campbell, L Prince, 1925, Ag 15,11:6
Campbell, Lawrence, 1915, Ag 21,7:5
Campbell, Lawrence B, 1960, Ap 4,29:6
Campbell, Lawrence D, 1940, Je 14,21:3
Campbell, Lawrence G Mrs, 1951, Jl 18,29:3
Campbell, Lawrence N, 1960, F 7,84:7
Campbell, Leon, 1951, My 11,27:2
Campbell, Lester, 1954, My 21,27:1
Campbell, Levin H, 1955, Ap 16,19:4
Campbell, Lily B, 1967, F 19,88:6
Campbell, Louis G, 1952, O 22,27:5
Campbell, Louis J, 1968, D 13,42:2
Campbell, Luther, 1947, D 29,18:2
Campbell, Luther A, 1948, Ja 1,23:5
Campbell, M B Mrs (funl, O 27,2:2), 1875, O 25,8:2
Campbell, M S, 1941, N 8,19:3
Campbell, Malcolm, 1947, Je 2,25:4; 1949, Ja 2,60:3
Campbell, Malcolm G, 1947, Jl 24,21:6
Campbell, Marcus B, 1944, Ag 4,13:3
Campbell, Marie C, 1960, Je 1,39:5
Campbell, Marius, 1940, D 8,71:4
Campbell, Mark V, 1950, F 26,78:1
Campbell, Mary, 1907, Je 3,7:6
Campbell, Mary (Sister Camilla), 1941, Mr 19,21:4
Campbell, Mary, 1942, Mr 19,21:5
Campbell, Mary E, 1948, F 23,25:5
Campbell, Mary P Mrs, 1938, Je 24,19:5
Campbell, Mary Mrs, 1941, D 13,21:3
Campbell, Mason H, 1960, D 1,35:4
Campbell, Maud W G Mrs, 1941, Jl 29,15:6
Campbell, Maurice, 1942, O 17,15:4
Campbell, Maurine, 1943, N 24,21:5

Campbell, Merritt W, 1938, S 25,38:7
Campbell, Michael, 1950, F 17,23:1
Campbell, Milton D, 1950, Ag 12,13:2
Campbell, Minnie S E Mrs (Lachlan), 1940, Je 13, 23:3
Campbell, Morris O, 1948, Ja 19,23:3
Campbell, Morton C, 1952, S 17,31:4
Campbell, Morton R Mrs, 1962, Mr 31,25:3
Campbell, Murdock S, 1943, Je 5,15:4
Campbell, N Demarest, 1958, Mr 29,17:5
Campbell, Nathaniel A, 1944, N 26,58:3
Campbell, Neal P, 1960, Je 21,21:2
Campbell, Neil L, 1950, Je 4,92:2
Campbell, Neil N, 1956, S 8,17:4
Campbell, Nellie, 1943, Ja 24,43:1
Campbell, Nelson, 1943, Jl 12,15:2
Campbell, Nelson S, 1953, Ap 16,29:5
Campbell, O L, 1942, Ag 9,42:7
Campbell, Oliver S, 1953, Jl 12,65:2
Campbell, Oren C, 1953, D 25,17:4
Campbell, Oscar J Mrs, 1964, Ja 28,31:4
Campbell, Palmer, 1925, D 16,25:3
Campbell, Patrick, 1908, My 19,7:4
Campbell, Patrick B, 1907, Je 13,7:5
Campbell, Patrick Mrs, 1940, Ap 11,25:3
Campbell, Patrick T Dr, 1937, F 13,13:1
Campbell, Patrick W, 1955, Jl 11,23:5
Campbell, Paul, 1941, S 10,23:4
Campbell, Peter, 1958, Ag 22,21:2
Campbell, Peter G, 1948, N 8,21:5
Campbell, Peter J, 1954, O 30,17:6
Campbell, Phil P, 1941, My 27,23:1
Campbell, Preston W, 1954, Jl 4,30:8
Campbell, R Erskine Mrs, 1949, Ag 24,25:4
Campbell, R J Mrs, 1964, Mr 30,29:2
Campbell, R Potter, 1953, Ag 30,88:2
Campbell, R Robert, 1950, Ap 4,29:4
Campbell, Ray W Mrs, 1946, My 21,23:3
Campbell, Rebecca Cooper, 1925, F 13,17:3
Campbell, Reginald J, 1956, Mr 3,19:5
Campbell, Rev Dr, 1864, Ap 2,4:6
Campbell, Richard T, 1940, Ag 8,19:4
Campbell, Robert, 1940, Mr 14,23:5; 1949, D 9,32:3; 1954, S 30,31:4; 1957, S 1,57:1; 1961, My 8,35:6; 1952, N 23,88:3
Campbell, Robert A, 1947, N 7,23:2
Campbell, Robert C, 1954, Mr 27,17:2; 1966, O 10,41:1
Campbell, Robert D, 1959, Jl 6,27:4
Campbell, Robert F Mrs, 1952, My 28,29:5
Campbell, Robert F, 1947, Ap 4,23:5
Campbell, Robert G, 1954, O 1,23:2
Campbell, Robert H, 1958, S 16,28:1
Campbell, Robert J, 1950, Ja 31,23:1; 1953, Jl 21,23:3
Campbell, Robert K, 1954, N 13,15:3
Campbell, Robert M, 1953, Je 14,86:1
Campbell, Robert Mrs, 1955, Mr 3,27:2
Campbell, Robert W, 1947, F 16,57:5
Campbell, Ronald H, 1953, N 17,31:5
Campbell, Ronald H Mrs, 1949, F 16,25:3
Campbell, Ronald N, 1965, D 31,21:1
Campbell, Rowland, 1943, O 21,27:4
Campbell, Roy, 1957, Ap 25,15:7
Campbell, S Reed, 1919, Ag 16,7:4
Campbell, Samuel, 1870, D 1,2:7
Campbell, Samuel A, 1946, D 22,41:1
Campbell, Samuel I, 1947, Ag 3,53:2
Campbell, Samuel J, 1944, N 2,19:5
Campbell, Samuel S, 1948, F 23,25:3
Campbell, Samuel S Mrs, 1948, F 20,27:3
Campbell, Sanford Mrs, 1960, Mr 18,25:3
Campbell, Selena M, 1962, Ap 21,20:4
Campbell, Sheppard, 1938, Mr 27,II,6:2
Campbell, Sherwood C, 1874, N 28,4:6
Campbell, Shiras, 1958, F 8,19:1
Campbell, Sinclair Sr, 1948, Ja 22,27:6
Campbell, Stephen James Mrs, 1968, Ap 14,77:2
Campbell, T B, 1885, Mr 6,5:5
Campbell, T William, 1953, My 6,31:3
Campbell, Thaddeus C, 1957, My 23,33:3
Campbell, Thomas, 1941, O 7,23:4; 1949, Mr 13,76:2
Campbell, Thomas A Mrs, 1947, S 15,17:4
Campbell, Thomas C, 1939, Je 29,23:5; 1967, O 12, 45:1
Campbell, Thomas C Col, 1904, Ja 5,16:3
Campbell, Thomas D, 1966, Mr 19,29:2
Campbell, Thomas E, 1944, Mr 2,17:4
Campbell, Thomas F, 1948, Ap 16,23:3; 1957, Mr 8, 25:4
Campbell, Thomas J Rev, 1925, D 15,25:4
Campbell, Thomas Mrs, 1947, My 31,13:4
Campbell, Thomas W, 1950, N 28,31:1
Campbell, Thomas W Rev, 1918, Mr 27,13:2
Campbell, Thurlow J, 1951, Mr 5,21:4
Campbell, Truman W, 1947, D 19,25:1
Campbell, V Floyd, 1906, Ap 23,11:2
Campbell, Virginia E, 1941, Jl 31,17:1; 1957, Ag 29, 27:4
Campbell, Virginia Mrs, 1922, D 19,19:4
Campbell, W B, 1867, Ag 20,4:7
Campbell, W F Dr, 1926, S 8,25:1
Campbell, W J, 1931, S 6,20:3
Campbell, W T Dr, 1906, Mr 5,9:2
Campbell, W W, 1881, S 8,5:4
Campbell, Wallace, 1945, S 6,25:6; 1950, Ap 6,29:6
Campbell, Wallace E, 1968, My 1,47:4
Campbell, Wallace G, 1955, O 12,31:4
Campbell, Wallace H, 1965, Ja 23,25:1
Campbell, Wallace R, 1947, Ag 11,23:3
Campbell, Walter, 1946, Ja 2,19:3; 1962, Ag 15,31:3
Campbell, Walter G, 1958, My 10,21:3
Campbell, Walter J, 1939, Je 13,23:4
Campbell, Walter S, 1945, Ag 24,19:3; 1957, D 26,19:1
Campbell, Wendell B, 1948, Ap 9,23:3
Campbell, Wilbert H, 1950, D 9,15:3
Campbell, Wilbur M, 1940, Je 13,23:6
Campbell, Wilfred Dr, 1918, Ja 2,11:6
Campbell, William, 1941, Mr 11,24:3; 1948, D 17,27:4; 1952, O 11,19:1; 1952, N 1,21:3
Campbell, William A, 1938, D 16,25:5; 1957, O 21, 25:2; 1960, Ap 26,37:5; 1963, D 29,42:8
Campbell, William A Mrs, 1952, N 24,23:4
Campbell, William Alvin, 1917, N 24,13:5
Campbell, William B, 1942, Ja 31,17:5; 1948, Ag 15, 61:2
Campbell, William E, 1947, F 19,25:2
Campbell, William F, 1944, Ja 23,38:1; 1949, N 20, 92:6
Campbell, William H, 1906, N 6,9:5; 1941, Jl 13,28:5; 1944, D 26,19:3; 1952, Ap 16,28:3
Campbell, William J, 1945, Ap 11,23:5; 1946, Mr 4, 23:3; 1951, My 25,27:5; 1963, D 8,86:4
Campbell, William K, 1944, S 22,19:2
Campbell, William L, 1966, F 16,43:4
Campbell, William M, 1951, Jl 12,25:2
Campbell, William N, 1947, S 9,31:4
Campbell, William P Mrs, 1946, Mr 3,45:2
Campbell, William R Mrs, 1948, Mr 31,25:2
Campbell, William S, 1939, Ap 18,23:2; 1946, Ap 19,29:2
Campbell, William S Mrs, 1950, D 3,88:3
Campbell, William T, 1952, S 28,77:2; 1958, Ag 7,25:5
Campbell, William V, 1959, My 9,21:4
Campbell, William V Mrs, 1950, N 27,25:4
Campbell, Willis C, 1941, My 5,17:5
Campbell, Willson R, 1958, N 8,21:3
Campbell, Worthington, 1964, S 1,35:2
Campbell-Bannerman, Henry Mrs, 1906, Ag 31,9:4
Campbell-Bannerman, Henry Sir, 1908, Ap 23,9:3
Campbell-Douglas, Barrington Bulkeley (Baron Blythswood), 1918, Mr 14,13:6
Campe, E Lee, 1950, My 16,31:2
Campeau, Charles, 1952, S 20,15:3
Campeau, Frank, 1943, N 9,21:5
Campeau, Joseph E, 1961, S 4,15:5
Campell, John J, 1952, Je 27,23:4
Campello, Paolo Count, 1903, Jl 4,7:6
Campello, Ranieri de, 1959, My 30,17:4
Campen, Sam M, 1938, Ja 6,19:3
Camperdown, Earl of (Robt Adams Haldane-Duncan), 1918, Je 7,13:6
Camperdown, Earl of, 1933, D 6,23:3
Camperio, Filippo, 1945, Je 12,19:3
Camperlengo, John, 1942, D 16,25:4
Campero, Arturo M, 1942, O 27,25:4
Campesi, Joseph, 1966, Ag 11,33:1
Campfield, William H, 1952, My 17,19:4
Camphausen, Guillaume, 1885, Je 20,2:4
Camphin, R, 1954, Mr 8,4:4
Camphor, Alex T Mrs, 1952, N 1,21:5
Camphor, Alexander Priestly, 1919, D 12,17:2
Campi, Louis Mrs, 1961, D 7,43:2
Campiglia, Louis R, 1954, F 9,27:1
Campillo, G di, 1901, Ag 11,3:5
Campinchi, Cesar, 1941, F 24,15:1
Campion, Alfred H, 1951, F 19,23:3
Campion, Daniel J, 1958, N 5,35:3
Campion, David Mrs, 1942, Ja 31,17:4
Campion, David T, 1942, N 8,52:8
Campion, Edward W, 1961, Mr 2,27:3
Campion, George W, 1949, My 26,29:3
Campion, Gilbert F M, 1958, Ap 7,21:4
Campion, H Clifford Jr, 1945, N 13,21:1
Campion, Horace G, 1962, O 1,31:4
Campion, James G, 1939, Ag 21,13:4
Campion, James Sr, 1937, O 10,II,8:2
Campion, James W Jr, 1968, D 21,37:1
Campion, Jeremiah J, 1916, Mr 25,13:6
Campion, John L, 1939, Je 11,44:7
Campion, Martin J, 1947, My 1,25:4
Campion, Patrick Mrs, 1949, Je 17,23:1
Campion, Raymond J, 1958, My 11,86:8
Campion, Richard R, 1962, Jl 11,36:1
Campion, William H, 1951, N 12,25:3
Campion, William M, 1951, Ap 6,25:2
Campion De Crespigny, Claude Capt, 1910, My 19,9:4
Campisteguy, Juan Dr, 1937, S 5,II,6:8
Campitiello, James L, 1962, Jl 30,23:4
Campman, William H, 1953, N 25,23:4
Campo, Pietro, 1955, My 24,31:3
Campofranco, Vito J, 1962, Ag 15,31:4
Campomenosi, Louis J, 1943, Ap 29,21:4
Campos, Jose, 1940, S 21,19:3
Campos, Marshal Martinez, 1900, S 24,1:6
Campos, Mary, 1951, D 8,11:3
Campos Marquetti, Generoso, 1966, My 21,31:3
Campos-Salles, Manuel Ferraz de Dr, 1913, Je 29,5:7
Camprubi, Augustus A, 1953, Mr 26,31:2
Camprubi, Jose A, 1942, Mr 13,19:5
Camprubi, Jose Mrs, 1955, S 29,33:2
Camps, M Lowell, 1961, Je 5,31:2
Campsall, Frank, 1946, Mr 17,43:2
Campuzano, Felipe Count of Mansilla, 1955, Jl 11,23:5
Camrose, Viscount (W E Berry),(mem ser, Je 24,5:2), 1954, Je 16,31:1
Camus, Albert (funl, Ja 7,30:1), 1960, Ja 5,1:3
Camus, F Edward Mrs, 1944, My 27,15:4
Camwell Chas J, 1953, Je 23,29:2
Canada, Henry G, 1948, Ap 30,23:6
Canada, Paul M, 1955, Je 4,15:4
Canada, William W, 1921, My 18,17:5
Canaday, Miles M Mrs, 1947, Je 2,25:3
Canaday, Paul O, 1962, My 11,31:3
Canaday, Roscoe H, 1948, F 24,25:3
Canaday, Stephen D Ex-Sen, 1923, Ag 27,11:3
Canade, Donald J, 1966, S 17,29:1
Canade, Vincent, 1961, S 4,15:5
Canade, Vincent G, 1954, Je 11,23:2
Canady, Oscar M, 1944, N 7,27:1
Canaipi, Victor V, 1957, Ap 14,86:8
Canale, Cesare, 1962, N 29,37:1
Canale, Ulisse A, 1958, F 6,25:1
Canales, C Gen, 1881, Je 30,5:4
Canali, Nicola Cardinal (funl, Ag 8,29:2), 1961, Ag 4,21:2
Canalizo, Eugene A, 1953, S 17,29:6
Canalizo, Jorge A, 1963, N 11,31:5
Canalizo, Paul E, 1964, D 29,27:3
Canan, Sarah C Mrs, 1922, O 4,23:4
Cananaugh, Joseph F, 1955, Je 25,15:3
Canaris, Constantine, 1877, S 16,4:7
Canarutto, Angelo, 1944, Ag 30,17:2
Canary, William J, 1946, F 7,23:1; 1950, Ap 13,29:2
Canavan, David Mrs, 1951, D 27,21:4
Canavan, David P, 1914, S 22,11:6
Canavan, Edward, 1957, O 14,27:5
Canavan, Edward V, 1940, Ag 20,19:5
Canavan, Frederick L, 1951, Ag 16,27:6
Canavan, James E, 1949, My 28,15:5
Canavan, Joseph, 1950, F 3,24:3
Canavan, Joseph J, 1940, O 11,21:1
Canavan, Martin J, 1942, S 2,23:1
Canavan, Patrick J, 1950, Je 2,23:2
Canavan, Thomas J, 1948, Mr 17,25:1
Canavelli, Jean, 1941, Je 5,24:4
Canazey, Joseph Mrs, 1946, My 2,12:5
Canby, Al H, 1940, O 16,23:3
Canby, C G C, 1873, Je 18,5:4
Canby, E R S Maj-Gen, 1873, Ap 13,1:2
Canby, Ella A S Mrs, 1938, My 20,19:4
Canby, Henry S, 1961, Ap 6,33:1
Canby, William M, 1937, Ja 2,11:4
Cancellieri, Philip, 1965, Ja 31,88:1
Cancro, Louis Mrs, 1949, N 22,29:3
Canda, Adele Mrs (funl), 1871, Je 24,8:3
Canda, Charles J, 1914, D 1,13:6
Canda, Ferdinand E, 1920, O 15,13:4
Candau, Saveur, 1955, S 30,25:5
Candee, Charles E, 1938, Ap 10,II,6:2
Candee, Harold Churchill, 1925, Jl 11,11:6
Candee, Lyman, 1943, Mr 3,23:5
Candee, Nehemiah, 1941, Jl 11,15:6
Candee, Nehemiah Mrs, 1956, O 13,19:4
Candee, Willard L, 1921, Ap 25,11:4
Candela, Michael J, 1959, Ja 2,25:3
Candela, P B, 1956, Ja 10,31:2
Candela, Rosario, 1953, O 7,29:1
Candia, Jose M, 1947, My 25,60:3
Candido, Patrick, 1963, My 28,28:4
Candidus, Louis Mrs, 1945, Ag 5,38:3
Candidus, Otto B, 1958, S 19,27:2
Candidus, Pantaleon, 1907, S 27,9:6
Candie, Francis Dr, 1875, Ap 3,6:7
Candilla, Guiseppi, 1907, S 12,7:7
Candler, A G, 1929, Mr 13,31:3
Candler, Albert E, 1938, Ap 5,21:4
Candler, Allen Daniel Ex-Gov, 1910, O 27,11:4
Candler, Asa G Jr, 1953, Ja 12,27:2
Candler, Beatrice P Mrs, 1954, Ap 21,29:2
Candler, Catherine P, 1947, O 13,23:3
Candler, Charles H, 1957, O 2,33:1
Candler, Charles Howard Sr Mrs, 1968, Ag 26,39:2
Candler, Duncan, 1949, N 14,27:2
Candler, Ezekiel S Jr, 1944, D 20,23:3
Candler, Flamen B, 1914, Ja 3,11:5
Candler, George, 1947, Ap 9,25:1
Candler, J W, 1903, Mr 17,9:5
Candler, John H, 1947, F 16,57:7
Candler, John S, 1941, D 10,25:2
Candler, Marsden B, 1956, S 3,13:5
Candler, Robert W Mrs, 1953, Ag 4,21:5
Candler, Wallace, 1941, O 4,15:2
Candler, Walter B, 1949, Mr 31,25:4
Candler, Walter T, 1967, Ap 26,47:1
Candler, Walter T Jr, 1951, F 12,16:5
Candler, Warren A, 1941, S 26,23:3
Candler, Warren A Mrs, 1943, Jl 25,31:3
Candler, William Jr, 1965, F 7,80:3
Candlin, James E Jr, 1961, F 4,19:6
Candlish, Robert Smith Rev, 1873, O 21,4:7
Candlyn, T Frederick H, 1964, D 18,33:2
Candon, James P, 1953, N 17,31:5

Candor, Thomas H, 1939, N 2,23:3
Candor, Toby (W E S Whitman), 1901, O 8,7:7
Candy, Charles Brig-Gen, 1910, O 30,II,13:5
Candy, Edmund, 1946, Ag 24,11:3
Candy, Harry, 1946, Ja 3,19:2
Candy, Henry T A Capt, 1943, My 30,III,5:4
Candy, John B, 1903, D 30,7:2
Candy, W Warren, 1951, Ap 24,29:4
Cane, Cyril H, 1960, Ja 4,29:5
Cane, Edward T M Mrs, 1937, S 11,17:6
Cane, Guy M, 1948, S 15,31:1
Cane, Melville Mrs, 1952, My 2,25:1
Cane, Oliver S, 1950, Mr 10,27:2
Cane, William F E Mrs, 1957, N 11,29:5
Cane, William H (will, Ap 19,28:4), 1956, Mr 28,31:1
Cane, William H (will), 1957, D 7,19:8
Cane, William H Mrs, 1945, S 21,21:2
Canedy, Helena F Mrs, 1937, F 16,23:5
Canegata, James C, 1951, My 27,69:1
Canegata, James Mrs, 1945, Jl 13,11:6
Canelli, John J, 1965, S 7,39:1
Caner, Delia Mrs, 1953, Mr 9,29:3
Caner, Gerald W, 1955, Ja 19,27:2
Canessa, Roberto E, 1961, Ja 28,3:8
Canestrelli, Rido, 1938, Je 29,19:3
Caneva, Carlo Gen, 1922, S 26,17:6
Caneva, Joseph M, 1942, Ag 8,11:7
Canevari, Alphonse, 1955, Ag 2,23:2
Canevaro, Cesar, 1883, N 27,5:4
Canfield, A Cass, 1904, Mr 25,9:5
Canfield, Albert H, 1939, Ag 4,13:6
Canfield, Amos, 1942, N 15,59:3
Canfield, Andrew A, 1951, Ja 28,76:2
Canfield, Andrew Jackson, 1908, Ag 26,7:6
Canfield, Angelica G Mrs, 1955, Ja 11,25:4
Canfield, Arthur A, 1947, D 6,15:4
Canfield, Carl A, 1944, Ag 29,17:4
Canfield, Charles E, 1941, Jl 14,13:4
Canfield, Charles H, 1941, Ap 13,39:2
Canfield, Edward, 1916, Ag 19,9:5; 1946, Ja 4,22:3
Canfield, Ellen B, 1939, Jl 13,19:5
Canfield, Francis D Mrs, 1955, Ja 26,25:1
Canfield, Francis D 3d, 1944, Mr 6,19:3
Canfield, Frederick P, 1942, F 22,26:4
Canfield, G Allen, 1941, O 8,23:1
Canfield, G F, 1933, N 16,23:3
Canfield, George W, 1950, S 18,23:5
Canfield, Harry L, 1942, Mr 9,19:4
Canfield, Harry S, 1954, Ja 26,27:5
Canfield, Hobart, 1906, N 16,9:6
Canfield, James, 1949, D 7,31:5
Canfield, James A, 1924, Jl 22,15:5; 1959, My 30,17:2
Canfield, James A Mrs, 1946, O 10,27:4
Canfield, James F, 1918, F 27,11:5
Canfield, James Hulme Dr, 1909, Mr 30,9:5
Canfield, John, 1903, N 8,7:7; 1957, S 2,13:1
Canfield, John E, 1941, My 12,17:6
Canfield, John J, 1957, S 18,33:4
Canfield, John L, 1958, Je 19,31:5
Canfield, John 2d, 1949, Mr 6,73:1
Canfield, Mary C, 1966, Ja 30,84:2
Canfield, O L, 1955, S 25,92:6
Canfield, Omer T, 1942, F 3,19:2
Canfield, P A, 1934, Ap 3,21:1
Canfield, Richard A, 1914, D 14,11:4
Canfield, Robert H, 1941, D 21,41:2
Canfield, Sarah L, 1939, Je 28,21:2
Canfield, Sherman D, 1939, Mr 31,21:2
Canfield, Walter L, 1958, Jl 30,29:5
Canfield, William Augustus, 1909, Jl 31,7:5
Canfield, William H V, 1943, D 19,48:3
Canfield, William W, 1937, Ag 29,II,6:7
Canfil, Fred A, 1953, Mr 25,31:4
Cangemi, John F, 1947, O 19,66:5
Cangemi, Salvatore J, 1963, S 1,57:2
Cangin, Frank D, 1961, Ja 21,21:4
Cangro, Anthony P, 1958, My 20,33:1
Canham, Charles D W, 1963, Ag 23,25:1
Canham, Erwin D Mrs, 1967, Ag 19,25:4
Canham, Robert, 1938, My 15,II,6:8
Canham, Vincent W, 1942, O 9,21:4
Canham, Vincent W Mrs, 1952, Mr 12,27:4
Canice Brendan, Bro, 1958, F 18,27:2
Canick, Michael (por), 1948, F 16,21:2
Caniff, John W, 1959, O 28,37:2
Canino, Anthony J, 1953, Ag 1,11:4
Canino, James Sr, 1952, O 16,29:4
Canino, Salvatore F, 1961, S 23,19:1
Canis, Euphemia H Mrs, 1947, My 13,25:1
Canis, Otto F A, 1942, Jl 11,13:1
Canis, Otto P M, 1942, N 8,52:6
Canivan, Charles J, 1944, Mr 15,19:5
Canman, Leo, 1924, Ja 29,19:3
Cann, Alice G Mrs, 1938, Je 23,21:5
Cann, Alice M, 1945, D 20,23:4
Cann, George T Judge, 1937, N 11,25:1
Cann, Isaac H, 1943, D 3,24:2
Cann, James E, 1907, My 3,7:4
Cann, Jessie Y, 1964, F 21,27:4
Cann, John H, 1940, Jl 22,17:4
Cann, John J Mrs, 1954, Ag 7,13:4
Cann, Norman D, 1956, Mr 18,88:2
Cann, Richard T, 1944, F 11,19:1
Cannaday, Frederick C, 1957, Ja 28,23:5
Cannaday, Issac Rev Dr, 1968, Mr 23,31:2
Cannalonga, Maurice J, 1941, Je 13,14:4
Cannan, Charles E, 1952, Mr 19,29:1
Cannan, Fred S, 1950, O 25,35:3
Cannan, George A, 1941, Ap 2,23:4
Cannan, William A, 1967, Jl 20,37:3
Canne, Hugo, 1957, O 24,33:4
Cannefax, R L, 1928, F 28,23:6
Cannel, Louis, 1951, Mr 5,21:4
Cannell, Marshall, 1949, My 31,23:2
Cannell, Paul J (Mar 21), 1963, Ap 1,35:3
Canner, Isadore, 1945, Ag 9,21:3
Canney, Anthony J, 1948, O 19,27:5
Canney, Fred A, 1942, Ja 28,19:5
Canniff, Brownell, 1942, Jl 19,31:2
Canniff, Roy L, 1951, D 2,90:2
Canniff, Timothy, 1940, S 9,15:6
Canniff, Timothy M, 1951, Jl 18,29:3
Canniff, William E, 1945, Jl 1,17:3
Canniff, William H, 1925, S 19,15:5
Cannilla, Luigi, 1949, Mr 3,25:6
Canning, Arthur, 1939, O 10,23:6
Canning, Austin J, 1967, My 8,41:2
Canning, Chester C, 1967, Ja 24,28:6
Canning, Edward S, 1939, My 24,23:6
Canning, Ernest H, 1942, O 1,23:2
Canning, Franklin V Mrs, 1937, Ag 4,19:3
Canning, George A Mrs, 1952, S 1,17:4
Canning, Hubert George de Burgh (Lord Clanricarde), 1916, Ap 14,9:4
Canning, Hugh Mrs, 1941, F 25,23:3
Canning, John, 1940, Ap 10,25:2
Canning, John B, 1962, Jl 6,25:4
Canning, John J, 1942, F 20,17:5; 1954, My 26,29:3
Canning, Joseph A, 1951, Mr 24,13:4
Canning, Kate, 1953, Ap 23,29:4
Canning, Michael, 1941, Mr 30,49:2
Canning, Stratford Sir, 1880, Ag 16,1:1
Canning, William C, 1939, Ap 14,23:2
Canning, William E, 1923, Ag 1,17:5
Canning, William H, 1937, F 7,II,8:5
Cannold, Sidney, 1968, N 16,37:2
Cannon, A Arthur, 1951, N 30,23:4
Cannon, A Arthur Mrs, 1940, F 18,41:2
Cannon, A Benson, 1950, N 28,46:7
Cannon, Alonzo G, 1940, Ja 27,13:2
Cannon, Annie J, 1941, Ap 14,17:3
Cannon, Bernard J, 1962, F 14,33:1
Cannon, C W Alex, 1948, S 15,32:2
Cannon, Cavendish W, 1962, O 8,23:5
Cannon, Charles A Mrs, 1965, D 24,17:3
Cannon, Charles S, 1956, Mr 17,19:4
Cannon, Clarence (funl, My 15,35:1), 1964, My 13, 1:4
Cannon, Daniel B, 1951, N 24,11:1
Cannon, David P, 1945, My 13,20:7
Cannon, David W Jr, 1938, D 16,25:4
Cannon, E B, 1940, Mr 4,17:5
Cannon, E Gaines, 1966, Ag 10,41:2
Cannon, Edward A, 1942, D 9,27:4; 1965, Ag 13,26:8
Cannon, Emma, 1954, Ja 24,84:3
Cannon, Eugene T, 1946, Jl 6,15:6
Cannon, F J, 1933, Jl 27,17:3
Cannon, Frank A, 1958, Je 26,27:5
Cannon, Franklin D, 1953, Ap 5,76:6
Cannon, George C, 1956, O 2,35:3
Cannon, George E Dr (funl, Ap 9,23:4), 1925, Ap 7, 19:5
Cannon, George J, 1960, Ap 3,87:1
Cannon, Gilbert, 1939, Je 26,15:4
Cannon, Gilbert Mrs, 1950, Jl 12,29:2
Cannon, H W, 1934, Ap 28,15:3
Cannon, Harold B, 1959, Ja 9,55:5
Cannon, Harry L, 1944, N 11,13:5
Cannon, Harvey P, 1958, F 12,29:4
Cannon, Helen G, 1947, Ag 27,23:3
Cannon, Henry B, 1940, Ag 2,15:3
Cannon, Henry H, 1940, Ag 3,15:4
Cannon, Herbert C Sr, 1964, F 23,84:8
Cannon, Herbert G Sr, 1953, Mr 26,31:3
Cannon, Herbert L, 1958, Jl 16,29:2
Cannon, Ida M, 1960, Jl 9,19:3
Cannon, J G, 1926, N 13,1:3
Cannon, J W Capt, 1882, Ap 19,5:5
Cannon, J W Sr Mrs (will, Je 3,7:3), 1938, My 5,23:5
Cannon, James E, 1946, My 21,23:2
Cannon, James G, 1963, N 4,35:5
Cannon, James Graham, 1916, Jl 6,13:5
Cannon, James Jr, 1944, S 7,23:1
Cannon, James M, 1950, F 22,29:5
Cannon, James P, 1955, Mr 8,27:3
Cannon, James P Mrs (Rose), 1968, Mr 9,29:5
Cannon, James W, 1938, Ag 24,21:5
Cannon, James 3d, 1960, Mr 10,31:2
Cannon, John, 1941, S 15,17:2
Cannon, John B, 1941, Mr 22,15:5
Cannon, John C, 1923, Mr 29,19:4
Cannon, John G, 1953, S 22,31:3
Cannon, John K (funl, Ja 15,13:4), 1955, Ja 13,27:1
Cannon, Joseph A, 1940, Ja 7,48:7
Cannon, Joseph D, 1952, Ja 5,11:4
Cannon, Joseph E, 1948, O 10,76:6
Cannon, Joseph F (will, Je 29,25:1), 1939, Je 22,23:4
Cannon, Joseph G, 1915, Ap 17,11:2
Cannon, Joseph J, 1945, N 6,19:1
Cannon, LaGrand B Mrs, 1952, F 29,24:6
Cannon, Lawrence A, 1939, D 26,19:2
Cannon, Le Grand B, 1906, N 4,9:6
Cannon, LeGrand B, 1952, F 29,24:6
Cannon, LeGrand Jr Mrs, 1948, My 3,21:4
Cannon, Lucien, 1950, F 15,27:5
Cannon, Marin L Jr, 1957, My 2,31:1
Cannon, Martin A, 1949, F 15,23:3
Cannon, Martin L, 1952, O 31,25:1
Cannon, Mary A, 1962, Mr 18,86:3
Cannon, Michael J, 1938, F 18,19:3
Cannon, Michael R, 1962, N 3,25:2
Cannon, Michael T, 1943, D 31,15:3
Cannon, Pat, 1966, Ja 24,35:2
Cannon, Patrick J Msgr, 1922, Je 1,19:5
Cannon, Peter L, 1962, Ag 13,25:3
Cannon, Raymond J, 1951, N 26,25:2
Cannon, Richard Mrs, 1945, Ag 5,38:3
Cannon, Robert B, 1954, D 29,23:2
Cannon, Sylvester Q, 1943, My 30,26:1
Cannon, T Franklin, 1951, N 11,90:8
Cannon, Thomas B, 1965, D 1,47:3
Cannon, Thomas H, 1946, Ja 11,22:3; 1950, Ap 5,31:1
Cannon, Thomas J Sr, 1954, Ja 22,27:2
Cannon, Timothy J, 1954, Ag 29,89:1
Cannon, Townsend L, 1966, F 1,35:4
Cannon, Victor H, 1950, S 2,15:4
Cannon, Walter B (cor, O 6,13:3), 1945, O 2,23:1
Cannon, William C Lt Col, 1937, Ap 18,II,9:1
Cannon, William G, 1941, O 21,23:2
Cannon, William J, 1946, Jl 4,19:4; 1966, Je 24,37:1
Cannon, Wingate, 1937, Ag 21,15:4
Cannone, Dominick Mrs, 1954, N 12,21:4
Cannone, Nicholas, 1958, Jl 13,68:8
Cannone, Thomas, 1956, O 10,39:5
Canny, Mary E, 1958, Mr 26,37:3
Cano, Harold W, 1956, Ja 14,19:2
Canode, Charles H, 1939, F 26,38:6
Canon, Charles R, 1950, Ja 24,31:4
Canon, Helen, 1954, Jl 10,13:5
Canongo, Don Augustin Valdesy Arostegin Count, 1875, Ap 10,1:5
Canonica, Pietro, 1959, Je 9,37:5
Canonico, Frank A, 1956, My 15,31:3
Canoutas, Seraphim G, 1944, Ap 5,19:4
Canpbell Calvin C Mrs, 1953, My 24,88:5
Canrobert, F C, 1895, Ja 29,7:4
Cansino, Eduardo Mrs, 1945, Ja 27,11:5
Cansten, James H, 1874, O 30,4:7
Cantacuzene, George, 1913, Ap 6,IV,7:4
Cantacuzene, Michael Prince, 1955, Mr 26,15:3
Cantacuzene, Serge Prince, 1953, O 31,17:2
Cantacuzene, Serge Princess (Countess Speransky), 1968, S 12,47:3
Cantacuzenu, Charles A Gen, 1937, O 10,II,8:3
Cantala, Julio, 1950, Ja 31,4:6
Cantalupo, Joseph J, 1958, Ap 19,21:6
Cantarero, Augusto, 1959, F 11,39:2
Cantave, Leon Gen, 1968, F 23,33:1
Cantel, L, 1878, Jl 28,7:2
Cantelli, Guido (mem rites), 1956, D 2,86:8
Cantelmo, Alphonse L, 1961, Ja 2,25:5
Cantelmo, Ercole, 1925, My 11,17:5
Cantelmo, Frank, 1968, My 31,29:1
Canter, Edward A, 1955, Je 10,25:5
Canter, Hall, 1939, S 3,19:1
Canter, Herman H, 1943, Ag 31,17:3
Canter, Orley M, 1938, O 15,17:2
Canter, Sydney J, 1960, Mr 3,29:3
Canter, William I, 1941, Mr 18,23:5
Canterbury, Archbishop of, 1862, S 20,8:5
Canterbury, Archbishop of (A C Tait), 1882, D 4,5:2
Canterbury, Lord, 1941, F 28,19:3
Cantillon, Joe Mrs, 1948, Ap 3,15:1
Cantillon, Matthew, 1961, S 16,19:3
Cantillon, William D, 1914, D 14,11:4
Cantilo, Jose L, 1944, O 12,27:5
Cantilo, Jose M, 1953, Jl 31,19:4
Cantin, Eugene J, 1949, D 30,19:5
Cantine, Charles Freeman, 1912, Jl 15,9:6
Cantine, Edward B, 1924, Je 9,17:5
Cantine, James, 1940, Jl 2,21:5
Cantine, Peter Mrs, 1904, Ja 6,9:5
Cantini, Ernest C, 1960, Ap 16,17:5
Cantley, Walter J, 1960, Je 30,29:3
Cantlin, Thomas A, 1924, Ag 21,11:5
Cantline, Peter Mrs, 1954, O 1,23:4
Canto, Bernardo, 1949, O 17,23:1
Canto, Henry, 1946, Ap 19,29:4
Canto, William U S Consul, 1937, Jl 1,27:6
Canton, Alejandro, 1941, O 6,17:2
Canton, Allen A, 1940, Mr 22,19:4
Canton, Charles, 1913, D 10,13:5
Canton, Herman J, 1964, Ja 24,27:3
Canton, Patrick L, 1950, Ag 17,27:4
Canton, Thomas M Col, 1913, Mr 15,13:4
Cantonaides, Costa, 1938, Je 19,28:8
Cantoni, Aldo, 1948, S 20,25:3
Cantoni, Federico, 1956, Jl 24,25:4
Cantor, Aaron S, 1955, Ap 20,33:2

Cantor, Abraham, 1949, My 4,29:4
Cantor, Allen J, 1943, D 11,15:3
Cantor, Arthur, 1943, My 12,25:1; 1962, My 9,43:3
Cantor, Benjamin, 1948, My 1,15:1
Cantor, Bernard H, 1964, Ja 2,27:1
Cantor, Charles, 1950, F 22,30:3; 1966, S 17,29:4
Cantor, Eddie (funl plans, O 12,29:2; will, O 16,32:2), 1964, O 11,1:2
Cantor, Eddie Mrs (funl, Ag 11,17:4), 1962, Ag 10, 19:3
Cantor, H A, 1902, Ap 3,9:6
Cantor, Harry, 1963, My 9,37:3
Cantor, Herman, 1953, O 13,29:1
Cantor, Hyman, 1959, F 26,31:2
Cantor, Isador, 1949, D 13,38:2
Cantor, Jacob A, 1921, Jl 3,18:3; 1921, Jl 5,15:2; 1955, Ap 24,87:2
Cantor, Julius, 1947, Ap 8,27:4
Cantor, Marjorie, 1959, My 18,30:8
Cantor, Maurice, 1967, F 3,31:3
Cantor, Max, 1942, My 12,19:5
Cantor, Maxwell A, 1954, Je 6,87:1
Cantor, Nat, 1956, Mr 17,19:4
Cantor, Nathaniel, 1957, D 6,30:2
Cantor, Rachel Mrs, 1942, My 4,19:3
Cantor, Reuben, 1956, Ag 14,25:4
Cantor, Sol M, 1965, Mr 6,25:4
Cantor, William, 1945, O 18,23:5; 1958, F 7,21:1
Cantore, Angela Mrs, 1950, Mr 23,29:4
Cantore, Emma, 1965, D 28,27:2
Cantore, Patsy, 1967, Ap 8,31:5
Cantrell, Francis S Jr, 1946, Je 24,31:1
Cantrell, George E, 1950, O 26,31:1
Cantrell, Howard M, 1937, Ja 10,II,9:3
Cantrell, Paul, 1962, Jl 11,35:3
Cantrell, Warren D, 1967, S 20,47:3
Cantrell, William R, 1938, O 29,19:4
Cantril, Simeon T, 1959, S 11,28:1
Cantrill, J Campbell, 1923, S 3,13:4
Cantu, Cesare, 1881, F 8,2:4
Cantu, Giuseppe, 1940, O 26,15:1
Cantwell, Alfred W, 1965, D 30,23:4
Cantwell, Ben, 1962, D 5,47:4
Cantwell, Edward, 1947, Je 3,25:3
Cantwell, Frank G, 1954, D 10,28:3
Cantwell, Fred E, 1945, D 3,21:5
Cantwell, Harry C, 1946, Ja 11,21:2
Cantwell, James P, 1956, N 27,38:1
Cantwell, John A, 1953, Je 13,15:5
Cantwell, John J, 1947, O 31,23:1
Cantwell, John M, 1937, Ag 14,13:3
Cantwell, Leo J, 1956, S 3,13:1
Cantwell, Michael (Bro Ephrem Faber), 1957, N 30, 21:3
Cantwell, Michael J, 1956, Jl 2,21:5
Cantwell, Michael J Mrs, 1949, N 21,25:4
Cantwell, Miles, 1962, Mr 29,33:2
Cantwell, Robert E, 1947, O 29,28:3
Cantwell, Thomas V, 1953, Je 27,15:3
Cantwell, William W, 1950, Ap 24,25:6
Canty, Arthur E, 1946, Ag 10,13:5
Canty, George R (cor, F 7,47:3), 1968, F 6,43:3
Canty, Jeremiah J, 1952, Je 20,23:3
Canty, Samuel, 1875, Ja 22,2:6
Canty, William A, 1924, N 4,21:3
Cantzen, Conrad (will, S 14,20:4), 1945, Je 29,15:2
Cantzlaar, George LaF, 1967, N 13,47:4
Canudo, Raymond Mrs, 1949, O 27,27:3
Canudo, Ricotto, 1923, N 13,21:4
Canuel, John, 1945, Je 29,15:3
Canuso, Francis A Sr, 1953, N 10,31:4
Canute, William F Mrs, 1945, F 17,13:3
Canuti, Robert, 1951, S 18,31:4
Canuto, Young, 1952, Ap 8,38:5
Canzona, Sam, 1957, Je 25,29:5
Canzoneri, Anthony (Tony),(funl plans, D 12,23:5), 1959, D 11,33:3
Capa, Julia F Mrs (Mrs D Friedmann), 1962, Ja 4, 33:1
Capa, Robert (gets Croix de Guerre posthumously, My 29,11:1), 1954, My 26,3:4
Capablanca, Jose R, 1942, Mr 9,19:1
Capablanca, Ramiro, 1944, D 7,25:5
Capaldo, Louis A Mrs, 1958, N 4,27:3
Capalti, Cardinal, 1875, Ap 16,1:6
Capano, Frank X, 1956, F 12,88:6
Caparell, Basil A, 1949, S 22,31:5
Caparn, H A (por), 1945, S 25,25:1
Caparo, Jose A, 1954, Jl 13,23:3
Capart, Jean, 1947, Je 17,25:3
Capasse, Edward, 1956, N 5,31:4
Capdevielle, Aug E, 1940, Jl 14,30:7
Capdevila Alexander, Antonio, 1953, N 6,27:3
Capdeville, Armand, 1912, Ja 29,11:4
Cape, Emily P Mrs, 1953, D 30,23:3
Cape, Herbert J, 1960, F 11,35:2
Capece, Rocco, 1951, My 1,29:4
Capehart, Alvin Mrs, 1959, Ja 20,35:4
Capehart, Charles, 1938, F 15,26:7
Capehart, Edward E Capt, 1917, F 21,11:5
Capehart, Everett D, 1948, Jl 8,23:4
Capehart, Everett D Mrs, 1967, F 25,28:1
Capehart, Ivan, 1950, Mr 26,93:1
Capehart, Sadie P W Mrs, 1938, My 15,II,6:8
Capehart, Thomas C, 1960, Ja 22,1:5
Capehart, Thomas C Mrs, 1960, Ja 22,1:5
Capek, Karel (por), 1938, D 26,23:1
Capek, Karel Mrs (Olga Scheinpflugova), 1968, Ap 17,47:2
Capek, Thomas, 1950, Mr 29,29:2
Capek, Thomas Mrs, 1956, Ag 11,13:4
Capel, Thomas J Msgr, 1911, O 24,13:4
Capelini, John, 1948, O 17,76:3
Capell, Adela Beach Grant (Earl of Essex), 1916, S 26,11:2
Capell, Richard, 1954, Je 22,27:2
Capelle, George S Jr, 1939, Jl 17,19:5
Capelli, Walter L, 1952, Ja 11,21:4
Capello, Anthony, 1956, Ap 23,27:4
Capen, Bessie Tilson, 1920, F 12,11:4
Capen, C Alfred, 1955, My 20,25:1
Capen, Elmer H Rev Dr, 1905, Mr 23,9:6
Capen, James F, 1943, D 19,49:1
Capen, James W Mrs, 1921, Mr 24,17:4
Capen, Julia F, 1967, Ag 3,33:5
Capen, Morris P, 1948, Mr 17,25:5
Capen, Oliver B, 1953, My 3,88:3
Capen, Randall T, 1948, S 4,15:5
Capen, Samuel, 1947, Ag 22,15:6
Capen, Samuel Billings, 1914, Ja 31,11:5
Capen, Samuel D Jr, 1950, F 6,25:6
Capen, Samuel H, 1943, My 25,23:5
Capen, Samuel P, 1956, Je 23,17:1
Capen, Samuel P Mrs, 1951, My 6,93:1
Capen, Welcome I, 1919, Ap 18,13:3
Capen, William H, 1941, Ja 16,23:3
Caperoon, F S, 1942, Mr 17,21:1
Capers, William T, 1943, Mr 30,26:3
Capers, William T Jr, 1954, Jl 18,57:2
Caperton, A T, 1876, Jl 27,4:7
Caperton, William B, 1941, D 22,17:3
Caperton, William B Mrs, 1940, D 1,62:4
Capes, Clarence W, 1968, Ap 6,39:4
Capes, Frances D, 1952, Ja 26,13:4
Capes, Joseph, 1944, S 15,19:3
Capes, William P, 1946, Ag 23,19:1
Capezio, Anthony (Tough Tony), 1955, Jl 9,31:1
Capezio, Salvatore, 1940, Ja 10,21:5
Capiet, Andre, 1925, Ap 25,15:5
Capinpin, Mateo M, 1958, D 29,15:5
Capitain, Adelaide M, 1947, D 8,25:5
Capitain, Harry G, 1941, Ag 30,13:1
Capitani, Lorenzo, 1963, S 6,29:4
Capito, Giuseppe, 1940, My 9,23:3
Caplan, Ephraim, 1943, O 8,19:3
Caplan, George A, 1942, O 19,19:5
Caplan, Henry, 1944, D 1,23:3
Caplan, Isadore J, 1966, D 6,47:2
Caplan, Israel A, 1917, Je 10,23:3
Caplan, Joseph, 1961, N 9,35:5
Caplan, Mordecai, 1947, Jl 28,15:2
Caplan, Oscar, 1961, Ja 21,21:4
Caple, Edward Mrs, 1947, N 15,17:3
Caples, Ralph C (por), 1949, F 8,25:2
Caples, Russel B, 1968, F 6,44:1
Caples, William G, 1940, My 16,23:4
Caplin, Hymie, 1949, D 16,31:4
Caplin, Otto P, 1964, S 9,43:4
Caplin, Otto P Mrs, 1948, S 15,31:5
Caplin, William, 1951, O 13,17:5
Caplow, Aaron J Mrs, 1948, Ag 26,22:2
Capner, Thomas E, 1937, Je 11,23:5
Capobianco, Carmine F, 1948, O 9,19:5
Capocaccia, Domenico, 1956, Jl 30,21:2
Capodici, Albert, 1949, Mr 29,25:6
Capolino, J Joseph Mrs, 1946, Ja 7,19:2
Capon, Charles R, 1954, N 3,29:2
Capon, Robert Mrs, 1949, Jl 28,23:2
Capon, William A, 1947, Ja 12,59:2
Capone, Antonio, 1941, Je 19,21:3
Capone, Arthur J, 1949, Ja 1,13:5
Capone, Gaetano, 1947, N 20,30:2
Capone, James (R J Hart), 1952, O 2,29:4
Capone, Theresa Mrs, 1952, N 30,55:2
Caponegro, Ernest V Jr, 1965, Ap 18,80:6
Caponigri, Joseph F, 1946, Ja 31,21:3
Caporale, Peter, 1965, Je 7,37:2
Caporale, Raphael, 1962, D 2,88:8
Capotosti, Luigi (por), 1938, F 17,21:5
Capowski, William V, 1954, Ag 8,85:2
Capozzi, Francis C, 1957, Ag 22,27:2
Capozzi, Joseph, 1940, D 7,17:2
Capozzi, Louis, 1924, Ag 1,11:5
Capp, John A, 1938, Ja 7,20:1
Capp, Samuel H, 1962, Ag 11,17:6
Cappalo, Fannie, 1908, O 22,9:5
Capparell, James, 1956, Mr 13,27:1
Cappel, Clarence C, 1948, Ap 17,15:6
Cappel, Peter P, 1942, N 30,23:5
Cappel, William, 1949, N 23,29:2
Cappell, Jack (Lucky), 1954, Ja 3,89:1
Cappellaro, Marie E W Mrs, 1952, Jl 28,1:4
Cappelle, J Ernestine, 1937, D 22,25:4
Cappelletto, Giovanni, 1942, Ja 22,17:3
Cappelli, Louis W, 1966, Jl 31,72:2
Cappelli, Rafaele Marquis, 1921, Je 5,22:2
Cappello, Joseph, 1952, Mr 19,29:1
Cappello, Joseph J, 1966, Ag 16,39:2
Capper, Arthur, 1951, D 20,31:1
Capper, Arthur Sen, 1923, Jl 5,15:4
Capper, George H, 1948, Ag 18,25:5
Capper, John, 1955, My 26,31:3
Capper, Mary M, 1939, Ap 2,III,7:2
Capper, Stewart Henbest, 1925, Ja 10,13:4
Cappi, Giuseppe, 1963, Jl 13,17:4
Cappilino, Frank J, 1948, D 5,92:6
Cappinger, John J Gen, 1909, N 5,9:6
Cappio, Peter, 1962, Jl 16,24:7
Cappo, Jeo, 1951, Ja 24,27:5
Cappock, William, 1923, Ag 15,17:6
Cappon, Franklin C, 1961, N 30,34:4
Cappon, James, 1939, S 20,27:3
Capponi, Marquis (see also F 5), 1876, F 26,2:3
Capps, Edward, 1950, Ag 22,27:1
Capps, Edward Mrs, 1937, D 25,15:2
Capps, Edwin M, 1938, Ja 17,19:1
Capps, Frank L, 1943, Je 4,21:1
Capps, Ryland T Jr, 1954, Ja 16,15:6
Capps, Stephen R, 1949, Ja 21,22:3
Capra, Frank, 1939, D 24,14:6
Capra, Peter, 1963, O 24,30:4
Capra, Sarah Mrs, 1941, My 24,15:5
Caprasse, Georges, 1959, Mr 2,27:2
Capraun, Anna M, 1966, N 17,47:3
Caprile, Alberto, 1951, Ap 6,25:1
Caprio, Amerigo F Mrs, 1955, D 12,31:6
Caprivi, von Gen, 1899, F 7,7:3
Capron, Benjamin A, 1945, Ja 25,19:4
Capron, C Alexander Mrs, 1946, Je 19,21:5
Capron, C Gray, 1948, Jl 11,52:7
Capron, Charles A, 1955, F 4,21:2
Capron, Charles B, 1942, D 27,34:4
Capron, Charles P, 1948, Mr 30,23:3
Capron, Florence E, 1951, Je 17,86:3
Capron, H Gen, 1885, F 24,2:3
Capron, Hazen S, 1945, My 5,15:2
Capron, Paul, 1944, O 2,19:6
Capron, T Saxton Mrs, 1957, N 17,86:3
Capron, Winfield B, 1949, My 5,27:2
Caproni, Gianni, 1957, O 30,29:3
Capstaff, Albert L, 1963, S 21,21:2
Capstaff, John G, 1960, F 3,33:5
Capstick, John H, 1918, Mr 18,13:5
Capstick, Thomas, 1964, Mr 22,77:1
Capt, James C, 1949, S 1,21:5
Capthorn, Annie Mrs, 1918, Ag 13,9:4
Capus, Alfred, 1922, N 2,19:5
Capus, Ellison Bp, 1908, Ap 23,9:6
Caputa, Joseph J, 1965, S 9,41:1
Caputi, Sebastian P, 1963, Je 5,41:5
Caputo, Angelo, 1946, Je 25,21:4
Caputo, Emilio, 1951, Mr 1,29:3
Caputo, Jacques, 1962, D 8,27:5
Caputo, John A, 1954, D 18,15:2
Caputo, Joseph O, 1949, N 10,31:1
Caputo, Lorenzo, 1958, My 3,19:4
Caputo, Thomas, 1946, F 26,26:2
Capwell, A B, 1880, Ag 25,5:6
Capwell, Clarence J, 1948, Mr 25,27:4
Car, Stanislaw, 1938, Je 19,29:1
Cara, Benjamin Cozzens Gen, 1916, F 15,11:5
Carabellese, Pantaleo, 1948, S 24,25:1
Caracciolo di Castagneto, Margaret Princess, 1955, Jl 2,15:5
Carafa D'Andria, Duchess, 1951, O 19,27:2
Caragianes, Felix, 1951, Mr 21,33:3
Caragol, Antonio B, 1962, Jl 4,21:2
Caraman Chimay, Alexandre de Princess, 1948, Jl 52:8
Caramazza, Charles, 1920, O 7,15:2
Carano, Ugo, 1959, F 22,89:1
Caravella, Joseph A, 1964, My 16,25:5
Caraway, Henry R, 1944, Ja 31,17:2
Caraway, Henry R Mrs, 1962, O 24,39:2
Caraway, T H, 1931, N 7,1:2
Caraway, Thaddeus Mrs, 1950, D 22,23:1
Carb, Alfred B, 1963, S 2,15:2
Carbajal Pena, Fidencio, 1953, Mr 27,23:3
Carbaugh, Harvey C, 1941, Je 24,20:2
Carbeau, Charles W, 1953, Ap 23,29:4
Carber, Frank H, 1948, F 29,60:5
Carberry, Clifton B, 1940, Je 9,44:7
Carberry, J A, 1903, Je 5,9:7
Carberry, James J, 1960, My 20,29:2
Carberry, John D, 1945, Ja 16,19:3
Carberry, John D Mrs, 1954, Ja 14,29:1
Carberry, John W, 1914, My 24,IV,7:5
Carberry, Morris V, 1944, Mr 28,19:3
Carberry, Rowland P, 1950, Ja 11,23:1
Carberry, Thomas, 1949, S 29,29:3
Carbia, Enrique, 1938, N 27,48:6
Carbin, Hannah M Mrs, 1908, S 21,7:7
Carbine, James T, 1947, Je 15,60:2
Carbo, Luis Felipe, 1913, F 27,13:4
Carbonara, E Vernon Prof, 1968, Je 14,47:1
Carbonara, Teresa, 1951, F 23,27:3
Carbonaro, John, 1951, Ja 8,17:2
Carbone, Agostine, 1915, Mr 29,9:4
Carbone, Francis N, 1961, O 13,35:4

Carbone, Mario G, 1950, Ap 18,31:1
Carbone, William E Sr, 1957, F 20,33:4
Carbonell, Carlos F, 1916, Ag 9,11:4
Carbonell, Cornelius M, 1940, Ja 29,16:2
Carbonnel, Eric D M de (funl, Ag 6,27:2), 1965, Ag 3,31:4
Carbonnier, Claes, 1961, Jl 21,23:2
Carboro, Anthony, 1937, Je 26,3:8
Carbrey, Eugene G, 1938, My 21,15:6
Carbrey, Harry F, 1939, Jl 30,29:4
Carbrey, Thomas J, 1946, Mr 24,44:6
Carcano, Ramon J, 1946, Je 3,21:4
Carcion, Frank, 1937, F 24,23:4
Carco, Francis, 1958, My 27,29:1
Card, Albert N, 1948, D 31,16:3
Card, Carl J, 1955, S 15,33:6
Card, Charles W, 1942, My 1,19:2
Card, Cora P Mrs, 1942, Ja 31,17:4
Card, Daniel P, 1957, Jl 27,17:7
Card, Harry N Mrs, 1954, F 11,29:1
Card, Maria L Mrs, 1938, Mr 27,II,6:2
Card, Mary, 1940, O 15,23:4
Card, Miller Mrs, 1946, Ja 14,19:4
Card, W W, 1948, S 4,15:1
Card, Walton G, 1948, N 12,23:1
Card, Willard S, 1964, O 3,29:4
Card, William C, 1947, Mr 31,23:1
Cardamone, Frank A Sr, 1949, Ap 14,25:2
Cardamone, John M, 1949, O 5,29:5
Cardani, Louis P Mrs, 1951, D 16,90:4
Cardara, Caesar Mrs, 1944, Jl 16,31:3
Cardarelli, Vincenzo, 1959, Je 16,35:5
Cardashian, V, 1934, Je 13,23:1
Carden, George A, 1946, Je 5,23:3
Carden, George A Mrs, 1942, Ap 29,21:5; 1952, N 27, 31:6
Carden, Godfrey L, 1965, Mr 26,35:5
Carden, Herbert, 1941, F 15,15:5
Carden, Lady, 1939, S 21,23:5
Carden, Lionel Sir, 1915, O 17,15:5
Carden, Nellie, 1940, Ja 30,3:1
Carden, Thomas, 1949, S 9,25:4
Carden, William M, 1947, O 25,19:6
Cardenas, Adam Dr, 1916, Jl 14,11:7
Cardenas, Adolfo, 1958, Ap 12,19:5
Cardenas, Ambrose A de, 1943, S 22,24:3
Cardenas, Claire Husted de Mrs, 1922, Ja 16,13:4
Cardenas, Jeremias, 1952, Ag 31,44:7
Cardenas y Rodriguez de Rivas, Juan F de, 1966, Ja 22,29:6
Cardenia, Gennaro (G Scognamiglio), 1965, N 24, 39:2
Carder, Earle W, 1967, S 26,47:3
Carder, Frank M, 1947, Mr 20,27:2
Carder, Frederick, 1963, D 12,39:2
Carder, R A, 1951, Ap 29,89:1
Cardew, Frederic A, 1942, Jl 14,20:4
Cardeza, Charlotte D M Mrs, 1939, Ag 2,19:6
Cardeza, Jnp Martinez Dr, 1921, Ap 1,13:3
Cardeza, Thomas D M, 1952, Je 7,19:2
Cardeza, Thomas D M (will), 1954, Ag 4,14:4
Cardeza, Thomas Mrs, 1943, N 12,21:1
Cardiello, P, 1929, Ja 15,29:2
Cardigan, Lady, 1915, My 27,11:6
Cardijn, Joseph (Cardinal), 1967, Jl 26,36:1
Cardile, Peter E, 1967, D 16,41:3
Cardinal, Adolphe, 1954, Ja 20,27:3
Cardinal, Alexis Billiet, 1873, My 2,1:5
Cardinal, Edward J, 1949, S 30,24:2
Cardinal, Joseph Sr, 1960, Je 16,33:2
Cardinal, Ralph J, 1941, Jl 4,13:2
Cardinal Amat Di San Fillippo E Sosso, 1871, D 28, 1:7
Cardinal Varmicelli-Casoni, 1874, My 30,1:7
Cardinale, Frank J, 1960, Ap 5,37:5
Cardinale, Pasquale F, 1958, Ag 13,27:5
Cardinell, John D, 1940, Ag 27,21:6
Cardoff, Thomas H, 1964, O 10,29:5
Cardon, Martin J, 1955, Mr 9,27:2
Cardon, Orson P, 1961, Ap 21,33:3
Cardon, Philip V, 1965, O 14,47:4
Cardona, Raymond, 1941, Ag 17,38:2
Cardone, Catherine, 1912, Jl 11,9:5
Cardone, John B, 1963, N 19,42:1
Cardonsky, Samuel, 1948, My 26,25:2
Cardozo, Albert, 1909, Ja 25,9:6
Cardozo, Benjamin N, 1938, Jl 10,1:1
Cardozo, Ernest A, 1947, D 26,15:3
Cardozo, Ernest A Mrs, 1945, S 27,21:2
Cardozo, J Lopes Dr, 1914, N 4,7:6
Cardozo, Michael H, 1906, Jl 20,7:6
Cardozo, Michael H Jr, 1951, Mr 24,13:3
Cardozo, Sidney B, 1952, Ag 16,15:6
Cardozo, William, 1940, Je 4,23:3
Cardozza, Frank D, 1954, F 17,31:4
Carducci, Bice, 1951, Ja 13,15:5
Carducci, Giosue (funl, F 17,9:5), 1907, F 16,9:5
Cardwell, Allen D, 1951, O 22,23:5
Cardwell, George A, 1949, O 14,27:4
Cardwell, James R, 1957, D 9,35:1
Cardwell, John, 1940, Ag 5,13:6
Cardwell, Robert, 1961, D 12,43:3
Cardwell, William, 1944, N 26,58:6
Cardwell, William J, 1952, My 8,31:2
Care, James R, 1949, O 14,27:4
Carega, Louis, 1920, F 12,11:4
Carell, William F, 1948, N 6,13:2
Carella, Nicholas A, 1963, O 31,33:3
Carena, Felice, 1966, Je 19,84:1
Carens, George C, 1962, Ja 6,19:6
Carens, James F, 1946, N 2,15:4
Carens, Thomas H, 1960, Jl 1,25:4
Carera, Martin, 1871, Ap 18,1:5
Caresche, Ferdinand A, 1939, Mr 1,21:5
Carette, Julien, 1966, Jl 22,31:2
Carew, C J Lady, 1901, N 13,3:4
Carew, Charles Hallowell, 1872, O 13,5:3
Carew, Gerald A, 1959, My 22,27:3
Carew, James (por), 1938, Ap 5,21:3
Carew, John F, 1951, Ap 14,15:1
Carew, Joseph J, 1947, Mr 20,27:5
Carew, Maurice N, 1960, My 5,35:1
Carew, Nelson M, 1952, Ap 2,33:5
Carew, Paul T, 1953, My 8,25:4
Carew, Paul V, 1947, Mr 17,23:3
Carew, Raymond R, 1938, D 8,27:4
Carew, Robert G, 1947, D 30,23:2
Carew, William N, 1951, Je 23,15:4
Carewe, Edwin, 1940, Ja 23,21:6
Carey, Anna R, 1950, F 7,27:3
Carey, Arthur A, 1952, D 14,90:3
Carey, Arthur M, 1955, O 31,25:5
Carey, Asa Bacon Brig-Gen, 1912, Ap 5,13:4
Carey, Bernard P, 1947, Jl 9,23:4
Carey, Bert, 1948, My 2,76:6
Carey, Charles D, 1942, Ap 16,21:6
Carey, Charles E, 1945, S 3,23:4
Carey, Charles H, 1941, Ag 28,19:3
Carey, Charles W, 1945, Ap 5,23:4
Carey, Clifford B, 1948, Je 11,23:3
Carey, D P, 1949, Ja 16,68:3
Carey, Daniel J, 1950, Ap 26,29:3
Carey, Daniel J Mrs, 1949, Ja 3,23:4
Carey, Donald E, 1961, Je 3,23:3
Carey, E J, 1878, F 4,8:4
Carey, Eben, 1947, Je 6,23:1
Carey, Edward F, 1949, Mr 19,15:2; 1952, Ja 10,30:2
Carey, Edward G, 1953, Jl 3,19:3
Carey, Edward J, 1949, S 12,21:3
Carey, Edwin J, 1968, O 18,53:2
Carey, Eleanor, 1915, My 4,15:5; 1916, Ap 1,13:7
Carey, Elizabeth B, 1966, My 15,88:2
Carey, Elizabeth Mrs, 1937, Jl 29,19:5
Carey, Emmanuel, 1949, F 27,68:5
Carey, Francis (Middletown, NY), 1951, Ag 8,25:5
Carey, Francis (Phila), 1951, D 3,31:3
Carey, Francis J, 1950, My 5,21:4
Carey, Francis K, 1944, O 5,23:5
Carey, Francis K Mrs, 1943, Ja 22,19:2
Carey, Francis L, 1951, Jl 6,23:4
Carey, Frank H, 1938, D 8,27:2
Carey, Frederick R, 1955, O 11,39:3
Carey, G Claude, 1949, D 9,32:2
Carey, George E, 1945, D 1,23:6
Carey, George G S, 1948, Mr 9,23:5
Carey, George H, 1967, Mr 25,23:5
Carey, George J, 1958, Ja 30,23:1
Carey, George R, 1954, My 20,31:4
Carey, Gerald J, 1967, Ap 29,35:3
Carey, H Bissell Sr Mrs, 1962, Ap 4,43:5
Carey, H C, 1879, O 14,5:4
Carey, H Frank Mrs, 1961, O 24,37:2
Carey, Hampson, 1951, Jl 14,13:4
Carey, Harry, 1947, S 22,23:3
Carey, Harry G, 1966, F 7,29:2
Carey, Harry J, 1955, Ja 1,13:2
Carey, Harry K, 1949, N 2,27:3
Carey, Harry W, 1939, My 29,15:1
Carey, Henry De Witt, 1908, O 15,9:6
Carey, Henry M, 1953, O 14,29:1
Carey, Henry T, 1918, Mr 28,11:8
Carey, Henry W, 1911, Ap 29,13:6
Carey, Homer F, 1950, Ag 1,23:1
Carey, Isabella W Mrs, 1938, D 28,26:6
Carey, J A, 1928, O 11,27:5
Carey, J E, 1881, N 15,8:5
Carey, J Frank, 1938, D 16,25:3
Carey, J Newman, 1954, My 18,29:2
Carey, James, 1944, Je 3,13:6
Carey, James A, 1949, My 29,36:6
Carey, James A Rev, 1968, Ap 7,92:5
Carey, James B, 1962, Jl 22,64:3
Carey, James F, 1941, F 14,17:2
Carey, James F Mrs, 1939, O 12,25:5
Carey, James Jr, 1939, O 29,40:7
Carey, James L, 1955, Ja 1,13:3
Carey, James P, 1909, N 30,9:4; 1942, Je 13,15:2
Carey, James P Mrs, 1954, O 10,87:1
Carey, James T, 1940, Je 7,23:3
Carey, Jeremiah J, 1953, O 5,27:1
Carey, John C, 1947, O 2,27:1
Carey, John G, 1939, N 8,23:3
Carey, John H, 1962, Ap 13,35:1
Carey, John J, 1946, O 12,19:4
Carey, John J M, 1940, O 2,23:6
Carey, John J Mrs, 1945, Mr 31,19:2
Carey, John P, 1962, Jl 7,17:5
Carey, John Q, 1958, Ja 7,47:5
Carey, Joseph, 1941, F 6,21:4
Carey, Joseph A Jr, 1966, S 17,29:2
Carey, Joseph M (Newark, Del), 1965, Je 11,31:2
Carey, Joseph M (Toledo, Ohio), 1965, Jl 15,29:4
Carey, Justin, 1947, Ja 18,15:6
Carey, Justin F, 1961, N 11,23:2
Carey, Katherine, 1952, Ap 10,29:5
Carey, Kenan, 1958, Ja 6,39:4
Carey, Lawrence B Mrs, 1946, N 26,29:3
Carey, Lennard Arthur Lt, 1916, Jl 26,11:7
Carey, Martin, 1922, Ap 9,28:3
Carey, Mary E Mrs, 1951, N 2,23:2
Carey, Mary W, 1964, Ap 14,37:2
Carey, Matthew, 1956, Mr 4,89:1
Carey, Michael, 1946, N 8,23:5; 1952, My 23,21:1
Carey, Michael B Mrs, 1949, N 10,31:3
Carey, Mildred A, 1957, D 28,17:3
Carey, Norman W, 1952, F 9,13:5
Carey, Patrick Rev, 1918, Ap 11,13:3
Carey, Peter A, 1940, My 14,24:2
Carey, Peter A Mrs, 1940, Mr 22,19:1
Carey, Peter B, 1943, N 1,18:2
Carey, Peter J, 1949, Jl 22,19:2
Carey, Peter J Mrs, 1939, F 28,19:4
Carey, Phil S Mrs, 1951, Je 28,25:6
Carey, R E, 1935, F 3,30:1
Carey, Ralph W, 1951, Jl 25,23:1
Carey, Richard, 1945, Ja 14,39:1
Carey, Robert, 1963, O 7,31:4
Carey, Robert D, 1937, Ja 18,17:2
Carey, Robert E, 1966, Je 23,39:3
Carey, Robert L, 1962, Ja 1,23:3
Carey, Robert Mrs, 1961, O 29,88:6
Carey, Rosa Nouchette, 1909, Jl 20,7:6
Carey, Roy E, 1964, Ja 3,23:2
Carey, Stephen W, 1920, S 7,15:3
Carey, Stephen W Jr, 1938, Ag 7,33:4
Carey, Thomas, 1925, S 3,25:6
Carey, Thomas A, 1955, D 12,31:4
Carey, Thomas F, 1941, D 16,27:4; 1961, Ja 19,29:3
Carey, Thomas J, 1945, Mr 5,19:4; 1952, N 5,27:3; 1958, Mr 31,27:5; 1958, Je 9,23:5
Carey, Thomas L, 1938, N 19,17:1
Carey, Thomas M, 1947, Mr 12,25:5
Carey, Thomas R, 1940, My 3,21:2
Carey, W H Mrs, 1944, My 28,34:1
Carey, Walter J, 1955, F 19,15:5
Carey, Walter L, 1957, F 26,29:5
Carey, Wilbert F, 1940, Je 18,23:5
Carey, William A, 1945, Ja 2,19:3
Carey, William A Rev, 1947, Je 1,60:8
Carey, William B, 1945, F 20,19:2
Carey, William E (por), 1938, Jl 22,17:6
Carey, William F, 1951, F 24,13:1
Carey, William F Mrs, 1958, Mr 27,33:2
Carey, William Francis, 1907, O 2,11:6
Carey, William H, 1952, D 19,31:5; 1959, Mr 12,31:5
Carey, William H Mrs, 1955, Jl 4,11:4
Carey, William J, 1939, D 26,19:2; 1947, Jl 3,21:4; 1951, My 12,21:5; 1952, My 23,21:2
Carey, William T, 1941, N 18,25:3
Carfagna, Guido, 1948, My 4,25:2
Carfalite, Edwin L, 1939, D 1,23:2
Cargill, George W, 1953, Jl 7,27:5
Cargill, J Lester, 1947, D 20,17:4
Cargill, S D, 1903, Mr 17,9:5
Cargon, Rutherford W, 1938, F 24,19:3
Carhart, Amory S, 1912, Mr 19,11:4
Carhart, Anna G, 1956, Ap 21,17:6
Carhart, Arthur I, 1948, My 26,25:2
Carhart, Charles L, 1951, O 22,23:4
Carhart, Crawford P, 1947, S 16,23:4
Carhart, E R Mrs, 1949, Ap 8,26:5
Carhart, Edmund H, 1944, N 28,23:1
Carhart, George, 1952, Ja 3,46:3
Carhart, George B, 1905, Mr 18,11:5
Carhart, George V, 1955, Je 15,31:2
Carhart, Georgiana P Mrs, 1959, Mr 3,33:2
Carhart, Haroid C, 1945, Jl 7,13:5
Carhart, Harold W, 1960, Je 13,27:5
Carhart, Henry Brigham, 1920, F 12,11:5
Carhart, Henry O, 1940, My 23,23:3
Carhart, James L, 1937, My 6,25:3
Carhart, John B, 1949, Mr 25,23:1
Carhart, William B, 1912, Je 22,13:6
Carhart, William C, 1962, Jl 29,60:8
Carhart, William M Dr, 1937, N 14,II,10:2
Carichoff, Eugene R, 1938, F 1,21:4
Carideo, Angelo M, 1949, D 1,31:4
Caridillo, Joseph, 1948, S 19,76:6
Caril, John, 1901, S 5,7:6
Carillo, Edith H Mrs, 1953, Jl 25,11:3
Carinci, Alfonso, 1963, D 7,27:3
Caring (Sister Mary Athanasius), 1968, Je 9,84:7
Carington, William Henry Peregrine Lt-Col, 1914, O 8,11:5
Carini, Luigi, 1961, Ja 10,47:5
Carisbrooke, Marchioness of (Lady Irene Mountbatten), 1956, Jl 17,23:5
Carisbrooke, Marquess of (A A Mountbatten), 1960, F 24,37:2

Carisi, John, 1960, F 22,17:5
Carkhuff, George B, 1947, Jl 17,19:4
Carkhuff, Joseph D, 1960, Mr 16,37:3
Carkhuff, Lorenzo W Mrs, 1937, O 3,II,9:2
Carkhuff, Lorenzo W Sr, 1944, O 14,13:4
Carkin, Seth B, 1938, Ap 29,21:4
Carkner, James W, 1961, Ja 26,29:1
Carkner, James W Mrs, 1955, Ag 16,49:2
Carl, Frank L, 1945, Mr 21,23:3
Carl, George J P, 1946, N 22,23:4
Carl, Harry, 1950, Ap 20,29:2
Carl, Jack R, 1964, O 24,15:7
Carl, John F Mrs, 1947, Ap 28,23:4
Carl, Max J, 1950, D 11,25:1
Carl, Prince of Sweden, 1951, O 24,31:1
Carl, William P, 1945, D 19,25:4
Carl Eduard, Duke of Saxe-Coburg-Gotha), 1954, Mr 7,90:7
Carland, John Emmett Judge, 1922, N 12,6:4
Carlata, Giovanni, 1917, Je 24,19:4
Carlaw, Mary C Mrs, 1937, N 28,II,9:2
Carlaw, Raymond F, 1953, Je 12,27:5
Carlberg, G, 1881, Ap 28,5:2
Carlborg, Otto, 1954, Ja 22,27:2
Carle, Edward H, 1958, D 24,2:5
Carle, Jean B E, 1951, Je 8,27:2
Carle, John J, 1939, Ja 8,42:5
Carle, Lloyd, 1916, Mr 9,13:5
Carle, Richard, 1941, Je 29,33:1
Carle, Richard Mrs, 1925, Ja 19,17:4
Carle, Robert W (funl, Ag 29,1:1), 1964, Ag 27,33:5
Carle, Robert W Mrs, 1963, My 16,35:4
Carlebach, Azriel, 1956, F 13,27:4
Carlebach, Herbert L (funl, O 12,43:4), 1966, O 9, 86:4
Carlebach, Julius, 1964, O 14,45:4
Carlebach, Naphtali H, 1967, D 25,21:3
Carlen, John C, 1948, F 22,48:5
Carles, Arthur B, 1952, Je 20,23:6
Carleson, Anna, 1915, Ag 17,9:5
Carless, Henry, 1941, Je 28,15:4
Carleton, A Clifford, 1958, N 13,33:1
Carleton, Bernard S (est acctg), 1964, D 17,43:1
Carleton, Burk G Dr, 1914, O 21,11:5
Carleton, C T, 1877, My 28,8:1
Carleton, Charles S, 1957, F 23,17:6
Carleton, Dudley, 1939, Je 9,21:2
Carleton, Edmund Dr, 1912, Je 17,9:6
Carleton, Elmer H, 1952, Je 2,21:1
Carleton, Frederick S, 1953, O 24,15:3
Carleton, G W, 1901, O 12,9:6
Carleton, George M, 1956, Ag 22,29:2
Carleton, Guy E, 1943, Jl 17,13:5
Carleton, Guy O, 1948, Je 13,68:5
Carleton, Harry, 1944, Ja 14,19:1
Carleton, Henry Guy, 1910, D 11,17:3
Carleton, Horace M, 1914, D 26,7:4
Carleton, John M, 1950, Ag 6,73:2
Carleton, Marjorie (Mrs Earle J), 1964, Je 5,31:6
Carleton, Osgood Mrs, 1953, O 6,29:3
Carleton, Ralph Mrs, 1959, D 2,43:3
Carleton, Rich H, 1939, Ag 12,13:6
Carleton, Robert L, 1956, Jl 14,15:2
Carleton, Sara K (Mrs Guy Carleton), 1967, Mr 13, 37:2
Carleton, Spencer, 1939, Jl 12,19:6
Carleton, Sprague, 1967, Jl 8,25:3
Carleton, W T, 1883, Jl 24,5:6
Carleton, Will, 1912, D 19,15:5; 1951, N 27,31:3
Carleton, Will Mrs, 1904, N 11,9:2
Carleton, William, 1944, Ag 5,11:7
Carleton, William S, 1940, Ja 17,21:4
Carleton, William T, 1922, S 27,19:4
Carletti, Ottirino, 1941, Ap 16,23:3
Carley, Earle E, 1945, Mr 25,38:2
Carley, Edmond G, 1951, Ja 28,76:3
Carley, Edward B Mrs, 1968, D 14,45:3
Carley, George H, 1953, Ap 10,22:3
Carley, John Capt, 1912, Ja 5,13:4
Carley, John O, 1962, F 22,25:3
Carley, Neale S, 1952, Ja 20,84:2
Carley, Robert W, 1946, My 28,21:1
Carley, Walter A, 1954, O 8,23:1
Carley, Willard M, 1954, S 16,29:4
Carley, William E, 1965, Ja 5,33:4
Carlfelt, Carl G, 1954, Je 8,27:1
Carli, Hermenegildo, 1959, O 2,2:1
Carlile, Allan Douglas Rev Dr, 1914, Jl 17,9:6
Carlile, Hildred, 1942, S 27,49:1
Carlile, J S, 1878, O 25,3:2
Carlile, James G, 1941, O 25,17:5
Carlile, John C, 1941, Ag 17,38:2
Carlile, John S, 1952, Ja 6,93:2
Carlile, Marie, 1951, D 11,33:5
Carlile, William B, 1945, Je 11,15:3
Carlile, Wilson, 1942, S 27,49:1
Carlin, Andrew F, 1945, Ja 12,15:5
Carlin, Anthony, 1938, Ag 21,33:3
Carlin, Benedict, 1940, My 10,23:5
Carlin, C C Jr, 1966, Mr 24,34:2
Carlin, Christopher L Mrs, 1937, F 22,17:3
Carlin, Edith R, 1961, O 13,35:1
Carlin, Edward J, 1967, Jl 19,39:4
Carlin, Francis (por), 1945, Mr 12,19:4
Carlin, Frank A (funl, D 15,31:1), 1954, D 11,13:6
Carlin, Frank A Mrs, 1963, Ap 7,85:6
Carlin, Frederick W, 1940, Ja 29,15:6
Carlin, Frederick W Jr, 1937, N 14,II,11:2
Carlin, George A (por), 1945, N 29,23:3
Carlin, George A Mrs, 1967, Je 11,87:1
Carlin, George E, 1951, N 30,23:4
Carlin, George P, 1947, Jl 24,21:4
Carlin, Harold, 1962, Ap 1,86:8
Carlin, Harry J, 1963, Ap 7,85:6
Carlin, James R, 1945, N 23,23:2
Carlin, James W, 1946, F 5,23:1
Carlin, Jess J, 1955, F 5,15:5
Carlin, John J, 1968, N 9,33:5
Carlin, Joseph D, 1943, D 31,15:1
Carlin, Joseph P, 1948, Jl 8,23:2
Carlin, Katherine, 1937, O 15,23:5
Carlin, Lewis, 1961, Mr 1,33:5
Carlin, Mack R, 1941, N 21,17:1
Carlin, Malcolm, 1952, N 25,29:4
Carlin, Melvin, 1958, Ap 3,18:2
Carlin, Nellie, 1948, S 6,13:5
Carlin, Patrick J, 1925, My 13,21:3
Carlin, Robert Capt, 1903, D 29,9:6
Carlin, Robert G, 1943, O 4,17:1
Carlin, Samuel Mrs, 1964, Jl 23,27:4
Carlin, Thomas A, 1953, N 20,24:4
Carlin, Thomas G, 1914, Ag 22,7:4; 1959, Mr 2,27:6
Carlin, W E, 1928, Mr 20,27:5
Carlin, Walter J, 1947, Ag 3,52:3; 1958, Ap 25,27:1
Carlin, Walter J Mrs (funl plans, Ag 1,23:1), 1956, Jl 27,1:4
Carlin, Walter L, 1937, My 14,23:4
Carlin, William C M, 1948, O 16,15:2
Carlin, William J, 1946, F 21,21:5
Carlin, William L, 1963, O 22,37:3
Carlin, William P Gen, 1903, O 5,7:7
Carliner, Paul E, 1956, O 15,25:2
Carlinfanti, Giovanni Mrs, 1948, Ap 25,68:6
Carling, Alfred Mrs, 1945, Mr 24,17:2
Carling, Elmer C, 1958, Ja 22,27:5
Carling, Ernest R, 1960, Jl 17,62:1
Carling, John A, 1941, F 7,19:4
Carling, John Sir, 1911, N 7,13:6
Carling, Leo J Sr, 1948, S 20,25:2
Carling, Paul C, 1948, S 28,27:3
Carling, William K, 1964, F 25,31:1
Carling, Willis C, 1960, F 5,27:4
Carlinger, Jacob, 1946, Je 4,23:2
Carlino, Lorenzo C, 1943, Jl 30,15:4
Carlino, Lorenzo Mrs, 1965, F 17,43:3
Carlis, Harry, 1954, O 16,17:5
Carlisle, A, 1926, Mr 6,15:5; 1936, Ap 23,23:1
Carlisle, Arthur, 1943, Ja 6,27:1
Carlisle, Audrey V, 1941, S 25,25:4
Carlisle, Bishop of, 1869, O 3,5:5
Carlisle, Bob, 1951, Mr 3,13:1
Carlisle, Burlington M, 1954, F 22,19:4
Carlisle, Carr Mrs, 1922, S 13,21:4
Carlisle, Charles A, 1938, S 3,13:2
Carlisle, Clifton H, 1951, Jl 28,11:2
Carlisle, Donald T, 1956, Ap 6,26:3
Carlisle, Dowager Countess of (Rhoda), 1957, D 11, 31:1
Carlisle, Earl of (G J L'E Howard), 1963, F 19,8:6
Carlisle, Floyd (por), 1942, N 10,27:4
Carlisle, Floyd L Mrs, 1953, F 12,28:5
Carlisle, Frank J, 1950, My 6,15:2
Carlisle, George L, 1954, D 23,19:5
Carlisle, George L Mrs, 1961, My 15,31:6
Carlisle, Gertrude, 1951, O 19,27:5
Carlisle, Harry E, 1953, Ja 5,21:3
Carlisle, Helen Grace (Mrs Helen Grace Reid), 1968, Ap 4,47:2
Carlisle, Henry C, 1964, Ap 11,25:3
Carlisle, Henry W (por), 1945, D 15,17:2
Carlisle, J M, 1877, My 20,6:7
Carlisle, James Henry Dr, 1909, O 22,7:5
Carlisle, Jay F Mrs, 1937, Mr 27,15:4
Carlisle, Jayn F, 1937, N 18,23:2
Carlisle, Jessie, 1950, Mr 10,27:4
Carlisle, John, 1903, S 1,7:6
Carlisle, John G (por),(funl, Ag 2,7:5), 1910, Ag 1,7:1
Carlisle, John G Mrs (funl, Ag 7,7:5), 1905, Ag 5,7:6
Carlisle, John H, 1964, My 2,27:3
Carlisle, Joseph M, 1937, O 16,19:2
Carlisle, Joseph M N Mrs, 1966, N 7,47:2
Carlisle, Lenore N, 1944, Mr 22,19:3
Carlisle, M Mrs, 1926, N 19,25:4
Carlisle, Mary Helen, 1925, Mr 18,21:4
Carlisle, O H, 1950, N 18,15:3
Carlisle, Ralph S, 1948, F 27,21:1
Carlisle, S R Mrs, 1941, Mr 9,40:5
Carlisle, S Richards, 1942, Mr 15,42:5
Carlisle, William L (Wild Bill), 1964, Je 20,25:3
Carll, Benjamin W, 1940, D 2,23:3
Carll, David, 1948, N 22,21:5
Carll, Edward E, 1937, Ja 27,21:3
Carll, James H Jr, 1956, F 11,17:4
Carll, Lewis Buffett Prof, 1918, Mr 24,13:1
Carll, S Edwards, 1967, Jl 22,26:1
Carll, Zerbino Mrs, 1946, D 5,29:1
Carlo, Alexandre, 1952, F 3,84:3
Carlo, Louis A, 1959, My 7,33:1
Carlo, Monte Mrs, 1956, D 16,86:3
Carlock, Arthur M, 1941, N 4,23:4
Carlock, John E, 1941, O 23,23:2
Carlock, L J Judge, 1903, Ap 21,9:5
Carlon, John D, 1957, Ag 16,19:2
Carlon, John J, 1953, Ja 21,31:1
Carlos, Dr (Baron De Mainey, C Haase), 1880, Mr 15,5:4
Carlos, H (Baron de Maincy), 1880, Mr 15,5:4
Carlos of Bourbon, Prince of Spain, 1949, N 12,15:5
Carlos Pius, Archduke, 1953, D 25,17:2
Carlotta (L Aymar), 1949, F 23,27:4
Carlotti, Marquis, 1920, Ja 24,11:4
Carlough, Elbert, 1941, O 10,23:3
Carlough, Frank V Sr, 1960, My 1,86:8
Carlough, Jass, 1940, D 28,15:2
Carlough, William H, 1950, Mr 10,27:3
Carlow, James P, 1957, Mr 10,88:5
Carlquist, Axel T, 1942, Ag 29,15:5
Carlsen, Bent E, 1951, N 7,29:4
Carlsen, C J, 1884, N 12,2:6
Carlsen, Daniel L, 1956, Ag 21,29:6
Carlsen, Dines, 1966, O 3,47:4
Carlsen, E, 1932, Ja 4,21:3
Carlsen, Haakon, 1968, D 20,42:8
Carlsen, Niels C, 1950, F 8,27:2
Carlson, Albert B, 1950, D 17,84:5
Carlson, Alfred W, 1951, D 1,13:2
Carlson, Alida M Mrs, 1942, Ag 12,19:4
Carlson, Alvin W Mrs, 1960, O 22,23:4
Carlson, Anna Mrs, 1948, F 20,27:1
Carlson, Anton J, 1956, S 3,13:3
Carlson, Arthur C, 1950, O 14,19:6
Carlson, Astie, 1944, S 19,21:3
Carlson, Augusta L Mrs, 1942, O 23,21:4
Carlson, Axel (will), 1952, S 23,23:2
Carlson, Axel B, 1960, My 4,45:4
Carlson, Axel H, 1948, Mr 15,23:4
Carlson, Axel Mrs, 1921, Ag 19,13:4
Carlson, Benjamin, 1950, Je 17,15:7
Carlson, Bernhard, 1952, Mr 2,93:2
Carlson, Carl H, 1954, N 10,33:4
Carlson, Carl O, 1948, Mr 15,23:1
Carlson, Charles B, 1952, F 11,25:5
Carlson, Charles G, 1960, Mr 8,33:3
Carlson, Charles G Mrs, 1960, Mr 8,33:3
Carlson, Chester F, 1968, S 20,47:1
Carlson, Eda, 1947, Je 27,21:5
Carlson, Eric H, 1950, Mr 7,27:5
Carlson, Ernest, 1940, F 8,23:2
Carlson, Ernest A, 1962, Je 14,33:6
Carlson, Ernst A, 1942, S 6,30:7
Carlson, Evans F, 1947, My 28,25:1
Carlson, Francis O P, 1948, Ja 17,17:4
Carlson, Frank H, 1959, Jl 3,17:4
Carlson, Franz J, 1950, S 7,31:1
Carlson, George L, 1962, S 27,37:1
Carlson, Glenn E, 1948, My 26,25:4
Carlson, Hada M, 1949, S 12,21:4
Carlson, Harold, 1964, S 12,25:4
Carlson, Harold C, 1964, N 2,39:3
Carlson, Harry E, 1960, O 14,33:3
Carlson, Harry J, 1957, Je 17,23:4
Carlson, Harry O, 1951, D 13,33:1
Carlson, Helen H, 1942, Ag 29,15:5
Carlson, Helen M, 1965, Ap 20,39:4
Carlson, Herman A, 1951, O 29,23:5
Carlson, Joel Mrs, 1960, Je 24,27:4
Carlson, John, 1939, Ag 17,21:2; 1952, N 27,31:4
Carlson, John A, 1938, D 15,27:5
Carlson, John E, 1941, F 19,21:3
Carlson, John F, 1945, Mr 21,23:1
Carlson, John H, 1960, Ag 28,83:1
Carlson, Lester W, 1950, Ap 12,27:3
Carlson, Ludwig, 1937, My 9,II,11:1
Carlson, Myron L, 1944, F 2,21:5
Carlson, Oscar E, 1955, O 4,28:8
Carlson, Paul H, 1951, Mr 5,21:4
Carlson, Peter Mrs, 1937, Mr 14,II,9:1
Carlson, Robert C, 1957, S 27,19:3; 1958, Jl 26,1
Carlson, Roland P, 1968, Ja 7,84:4
Carlson, Ruth M, 1963, N 6,41:3
Carlson, Samuel A, 1961, My 15,31:5
Carlson, Samuel Mrs, 1956, Jl 15,61:1
Carlson, Seth R, 1947, F 27,21:2
Carlson, Swan, 1946, N 25,7:2
Carlson, Theodore D, 1968, Ag 6,37:2
Carlson, Theodore P, 1959, Mr 12,31:4
Carlson, Walter E, 1967, My 8,41:3
Carlson, Wesley G, 1954, Ap 7,31:2
Carlson, William A, 1951, Je 18,23:5
Carlsrud, Anton Mrs, 1953, Ja 13,27:5
Carlsson, Gunnar F, 1967, Jl 1,23:3
Carlsson, John R, 1953, Mr 31,32:3
Carlsson, Oscar H, 1945, Mr 3,13:1
Carlstedt, Alex B Mrs, 1943, Ap 25,35:1
Carlstedt, Claudia (Mrs F Kistler), 1953, My 3
Carlstrom, Dorothea A, 1952, Je 22,70:5
Carlstrom, Oscar E (por), 1948, Mr 7,70:2
Carlstrom, Victor, 1917, My 10,13:3
Carlstrom, Walter W, 1948, Mr 11,27:2

Carlton, Albert B Mrs, 1951, O 5,28:4
Carlton, C R, 1920, My 19,11:4
Carlton, Caleb Henry Brig-Gen, 1923, Mr 22,19:5
Carlton, Collie E, 1942, Jl 15,19:1
Carlton, Della H Mrs, 1941, Je 24,19:5
Carlton, Edgar P, 1952, Ag 12,19:5
Carlton, Edward, 1953, D 31,19:5
Carlton, Edwin H, 1964, S 6,56:4
Carlton, Effie I C Mrs, 1940, Ja 7,48:6
Carlton, Frank Mrs, 1947, S 22,23:4
Carlton, Guy E, 1950, N 15,31:1
Carlton, Harry, 1949, Ja 15,17:1
Carlton, James C Maj, 1905, F 25,9:3
Carlton, James H Gen, 1873, Ja 9,1:3
Carlton, Leslie G, 1938, S 5,15:5
Carlton, Mary Catherine Rev Mother, 1941, My 13, 23:5
Carlton, Newcomb, 1953, Mr 14,15:1
Carlton, Schuyler C, 1941, O 28,23:5
Carlton, Thomas B, 1940, N 3,57:2
Carlton, Thomas Rev, 1874, Ap 17,4:6
Carlton, William N C, 1943, F 4,23:3
Carlucci, Gaston A, 1965, Ap 17,19:6
Carlucci, Joseph L, 1962, Mr 9,29:2
Carlucci, Sophy P, 1950, F 25,17:5
Carlyle, Alexander J, 1943, My 29,13:4
Carlyle, Alonzo F, 1954, F 13,13:5
Carlyle, Francis, 1916, S 16,11:6
Carlyle, Frank E, 1960, O 3,31:6
Carlyle, Frederick W, 1916, Mr 18,11:6
Carlyle, Hal Newton, 1908, F 24,7:2
Carlyle, Jessie, 1946, Ja 22,27:5
Carlyle, Richard, 1942, Je 14,45:2
Carlyle, Richard F, 1949, D 5,23:5
Carlyle, Thomas (funl, F 11,1:5), 1881, F 6,1:7
Carlyle, Thomas Mrs, 1866, My 7,1:1
Carlyle, William L, 1955, Ag 7,73:3
Carmack, Edward W Mrs, 1947, My 25,60:4
Carmack, Frank S, 1941, Ja 19,40:3
Carmack, George, 1922, Je 7,19:6
Carmalt, A M Mrs, 1931, S 5,13:5
Carmalt, James W, 1937, D 3,23:2
Carmalt, Katherine W, 1946, Jl 16,23:2
Carmalt, Laurence J, 1940, Je 25,23:6
Carman, Ada, 1952, Ja 14,19:4
Carman, Albert R, 1939, O 18,26:2
Carman, Albert R Mrs, 1946, My 21,23:2
Carman, Armin, 1961, My 16,37:4
Carman, Clarence H, 1942, Mr 11,19:4
Carman, Clarence M, 1952, N 27,31:5
Carman, Cornelius, 1947, My 27,25:3
Carman, Edward R, 1963, O 27,88:7
Carman, Edwin C, 1939, Ja 9,15:6
Carman, Edwin S, 1951, Mr 23,21:2
Carman, Eugene A, 1941, Jl 13,28:6
Carman, Ezra Ayres Gen, 1909, D 26,11:6
Carman, Fletcher F, 1964, D 27,64:2
Carman, Francis J, 1943, Ag 5,15:3
Carman, G Herbert, 1937, F 9,23:5
Carman, George N, 1941, Je 25,21:4
Carman, Harry J (ed, D 28,28:2), 1964, D 27,64:5
Carman, Harry J (trb lr, Ja 16,26:4; mem ser, Ja 23,25:1), 1965, Ja 16,26:4
Carman, John H, 1941, Jl 5,11:3
Carman, Lewis C, 1946, O 7,31:1
Carman, Louis E, 1939, O 29,40:4
Carman, Mortimer Capt, 1937, D 21,23:1
Carman, Richard, 1904, Ja 8,7:5
Carman, Richard Sr, 1937, Mr 31,24:3
Carman, Ringgold W, 1944, Je 17,13:3
Carman, Samuel, 1949, Je 30,23:6
Carman, William C, 1941, Ja 12,44:1
Carman, William F, 1952, Ja 30,10:5
Carman, William F Mrs, 1952, Ja 30,10:5
Carman, William W, 1952, Jl 21,19:3
Carman, William W Mrs, 1967, S 30,33:1
Carmardella, Louis, 1947, D 25,21:4
Carmeichael, Otto, 1942, Ap 11,13:3
Carmel, George, 1955, Je 11,15:3
Carmela, Rev Mother, 1923, Ap 7,13:6
Carmelia, Francis, 1947, D 18,30:2
Carmelite Nun, Mother Theresa, 1878, F 17,9:2
Carmell, Daniel D, 1957, Je 4,71:4
Carmen, B, 1929, Je 9,27:2
Carmen, Charles W, 1955, Ja 12,27:2
Carmen, Ellis, 1949, Jl 15,19:2
Carmen, George P, 1949, O 27,27:4
Carmer, Agnes S, 1940, S 4,23:3
Carmer, Bertram H, 1957, My 3,27:2; 1959, Ap 23,31:4
Carmer, Frank T, 1944, Ap 17,23:3
Carmer, Hermon A, 1941, D 11,27:6
Carmer, Mary E Mrs, 1941, Jl 17,19:2
Carmer, Myron E, 1944, N 8,17:3
Carmer, Willis G, 1940, Ja 8,15:2
Carmical, Andrew L, 1955, Ag 29,19:4
Carmichael, Albert Edward, 1919, F 17,13:2
Carmichael, Amy, 1951, F 9,25:2
Carmichael, Archibald H, 1947, Jl 16,23:2
Carmichael, David G, 1950, S 3,38:5
Carmichael, Dougall, 1945, S 18,23:3
Carmichael, George E, 1964, Mr 25,41:2
Carmichael, George T, 1962, Ap 16,29:2
Carmichael, Harry S T, 1949, S 30,23:3
Carmichael, Howard C, 1943, O 13,23:1
Carmichael, Howard Mrs, 1959, Mr 19,33:3
Carmichael, J A Dr, 1911, N 13,9:4
Carmichael, James Bp, 1908, S 22,9:6
Carmichael, James T, 1939, My 1,23:3
Carmichael, John, 1903, Ag 25,7:6
Carmichael, John H Mrs, 1943, F 1,15:4
Carmichael, John P Mrs, 1953, Je 11,29:4
Carmichael, Lewis, 1905, O 6,9:6
Carmichael, Oliver C, 1966, S 27,47:1
Carmichael, Omer, 1960, Ja 10,86:2
Carmichael, Robert, 1945, N 6,19:2
Carmichael, Robert H, 1968, My 21,47:3
Carmichael, Roy, 1954, Mr 2,25:4
Carmichael, W M, 1881, Je 9,5:6
Carmichael, William D, 1959, Jl 26,68:3
Carmichael, William D Jr, 1961, Ja 28,19:2
Carmin, Joseph, 1955, F 24,27:2
Carmine, A Clyde, 1944, Ap 25,23:4
Carmine, George C, 1947, Ap 9,25:3
Carmine, Joseph E, 1944, Je 5,19:1
Carmo, Maria do Carmo Fragoso Senhora, 1956, Mr 14,33:5
Carmody, Barrett, 1965, Ja 15,43:1
Carmody, Charles C, 1938, F 27,II,9:3
Carmody, Charles J, 1954, Ap 20,29:4
Carmody, Cornelius, 1962, S 19,40:1
Carmody, Cyril A, 1952, Ag 19,23:2
Carmody, F, 1928, Ap 29,25:6
Carmody, Francis T, 1965, F 16,35:3
Carmody, Francis X Mrs, 1915, Ag 25,11:6
Carmody, Hudson B, 1943, D 1,21:4
Carmody, John F, 1949, Ag 9,25:2
Carmody, John J, 1944, N 30,23:1
Carmody, John M, 1963, N 12,41:1
Carmody, John P, 1937, Ag 10,19:3; 1953, Jl 7,27:2
Carmody, John R, 1917, Mr 17,13:5
Carmody, Joseph F, 1954, D 3,27:4
Carmody, Martin H, 1950, D 10,105:1
Carmody, Mary J, 1939, Mr 21,23:4
Carmody, Michael H, 1948, Ag 28,15:1
Carmody, Terence F, 1943, Jl 4,20:8
Carmody, Terrence F Mrs, 1947, F 24,19:3
Carmody, Thomas, 1922, Ja 23,11:5; 1954, Ja 28,27:3
Carmody, Thomas J, 1948, N 1,23:5
Carmody, Thomas W Mrs, 1954, Je 15,29:2
Carmody, Timothy A, 1940, Ja 25,21:3
Carmona, Antonio O de F, 1951, Ap 19,31:1
Carnahan, Charles C, 1947, S 9,32:2
Carnahan, Clara G, 1956, Mr 10,17:7
Carnahan, Ella M, 1950, Ja 31,23:3
Carnahan, George A, 1954, Ja 5,27:2
Carnahan, George H, 1941, Mr 21,21:4
Carnahan, James A, 1953, N 16,25:6
Carnahan, John M, 1938, O 25,23:2
Carnahan, Paul H, 1965, D 27,23:6
Carnahan, R B, 1918, Je 24,11:5
Carnahan, William E, 1963, Ag 8,27:5
Carnahan, William L, 1966, Ag 8,27:3
Carnal, Harry A, 1946, F 17,42:5
Carnarvon, Earl of, 1890, Je 29,3:2
Carnarvou, Countess of, 1875, Ja 26,4:6
Carnay, Elliot L, 1961, My 27,23:6
Carncross, John L, 1911, N 14,13:6
Carne, Louis Marcien de Count, 1876, F 14,1:5
Carne, William, 1952, O 16,29:4
Carneal, Mary, 1948, O 7,29:4
Carnegie, Andrew (por),(funl, Ag 13,11:3), 1919, Ag 12,9:1
Carnegie, Andrew Mrs (will, Je 29,21:4), 1946, Je 25,22:1
Carnegie, Andrew 2d, 1947, Je 10,27:2
Carnegie, Andrew 2d Mrs, 1943, Mr 4,19:4
Carnegie, Colman, 1911, Ag 8,9:6
Carnegie, Dale (funl plans, N 3,31:2), 1955, N 2,35:1
Carnegie, Daniel, 1954, D 3,27:3
Carnegie, David L G H (Earl of Northesk), 1963, N 8,32:1
Carnegie, George Lauder, 1921, N 16,19:3
Carnegie, Hattie (Mrs J Zanft),(will, Mr 9,8:4), 1956, F 23,27:1
Carnegie, Jerry Y Mrs, 1949, Ap 4,23:6
Carnegie, Robert K (Andy), 1951, Ja 27,13:5
Carnegie, Thomas M, 1944, S 23,13:4
Carnegie, Thomas M Jr, 1954, Jl 21,27:2
Carnegie, W H, 1936, O 20,25:1
Carnegie, W H Mrs, 1957, My 20,25:1
Carnegie, William C, 1944, Jl 30,35:2
Carnegie, William Coleman Mrs, 1906, Mr 28,9:5
Carnegie, William R, 1945, O 23,17:4
Carnell, Althea J, 1939, Jl 19,19:7
Carnell, E Bradley, 1954, D 23,19:1
Carnell, John F, 1951, Ja 24,27:2
Carnell, Prentiss Sr, 1958, Ap 21,23:3
Carnera, Primo (funl plans, Jl 1,23:4), 1967, Je 30, 37:1
Carnera, Sante, 1941, F 22,15:4
Carnes, George D, 1940, My 15,25:4
Carnes, John W, 1943, N 21,56:4
Carnes, John W Mrs, 1964, O 14,45:5
Carnes, S T Mrs, 1944, Mr 15,19:5
Carnes, Sidney Cecil, 1953, F 14,29:4
Carnes, W E Mrs, 1952, Ja 6,93:1
Carnes, Welcome D, 1938, S 12,17:5
Carnett, J Berton Jr, 1963, O 15,39:4
Carneval, James, 1948, Je 14,24:2
Carneval, James Mrs, 1938, Ag 22,13:6
Carnevalli, Alberto, 1953, My 24,24:4
Carnevari, George, 1950, S 8,31:1
Carney, Andrew A, 1950, D 26,23:4
Carney, Andrew F, 1956, O 25,33:3
Carney, Arthur, 1938, Ap 12,24:1
Carney, Arthur G, 1962, Mr 26,31:5
Carney, Clarence C, 1945, Jl 13,11:4
Carney, Clarence R, 1937, Ja 16,17:2
Carney, Claude S, 1940, F 27,21:5
Carney, Don (Uncle Don), 1954, Ja 16,15:3
Carney, Don Mrs, 1949, D 31,3:6
Carney, Edward B, 1966, Je 9,47:3
Carney, Edward F, 1964, N 26,33:2
Carney, Edward J, 1943, Ja 31,44:2
Carney, Edward L, 1939, N 24,23:4
Carney, Edward M, 1962, F 28,25:3
Carney, Edward M Mrs, 1963, Jl 1,29:1
Carney, Edward O, 1966, Je 12,86:7
Carney, Elizabeth, 1951, Ja 26,23:2
Carney, Elvin P, 1968, S 1,53:3
Carney, Francis J, 1939, Jl 29,15:3
Carney, Frank D Mrs, 1948, Mr 6,13:6
Carney, Frank J, 1951, Je 15,23:3
Carney, George A, 1960, Mr 18,26:5
Carney, George D, 1944, Mr 20,18:2
Carney, Harold, 1943, Je 22,20:3
Carney, Helen Mrs, 1912, Ag 4,II,11:6
Carney, James, 1938, Jl 1,13:5
Carney, James A, 1938, Mr 28,15:3
Carney, James H, 1946, S 24,29:3
Carney, James H Rev-Brother, 1910, Mr 20,II,11:4
Carney, James S, 1924, O 18,15:6
Carney, Jane A, 1966, Ap 29,47:3
Carney, Jim, 1941, S 11,23:4
Carney, John F, 1942, F 22,26:1; 1944, Je 9,15:5
Carney, John J, 1956, My 20,87:1
Carney, John J Sr, 1948, Je 16,29:4
Carney, John L, 1940, F 5,17:3
Carney, John M, 1956, N 29,35:5
Carney, Joseph, 1949, Ja 5,26:2
Carney, Joseph F, 1953, O 1,29:1
Carney, Joseph P, 1941, D 9,31:3
Carney, Joseph V, 1946, O 7,31:4
Carney, Joseph W, 1947, Ja 1,33:2
Carney, Kate, 1950, Ja 2,23:4
Carney, Kenneth, 1957, N 25,31:3
Carney, Luke, 1943, Ap 15,25:3
Carney, Mae, 1938, F 18,19:3
Carney, Margaret Mrs, 1939, Ja 27,21:3
Carney, Matthew Dr, 1937, Mr 25,25:3
Carney, Matthew J, 1942, Ap 2,22:3
Carney, Owen J, 1958, N 25,33:1
Carney, Patrick J, 1943, F 17,21:4; 1953, Ja 11,91:3
Carney, Peter J Mrs, 1948, Je 12,15:3
Carney, Philip L, 1965, Ap 1,35:3
Carney, Richard, 1941, Je 22,32:4; 1950, O 21,17:3
Carney, Robert E Mrs, 1957, D 30,23:4
Carney, Stephen J, 1953, Ag 20,27:3
Carney, Sydney Jr, 1945, Ja 16,20:2
Carney, Thomas F, 1949, Je 5,92:4
Carney, Thomas J, 1942, Je 30,21:1
Carney, Thomas J Mrs, 1941, D 22,17:2
Carney, W H Bruce, 1948, Je 12,15:7
Carney, William J, 1940, N 12,23:2; 1951, Ag 1,23:6
Carney, William M, 1953, F 17,34:2
Carnochan, Frederic G, 1952, Ap 4,15:4
Carnochan, G M Mrs, 1905, Ja 6,10:5
Carnochan, Gouveneur Morris, 1915, Jl 1,11:6
Carnochan, J D, 1928, D 13,29:4
Carnochan, Morris Mrs, 1922, S 7,17:5
Carnock, Lord (F A Nicolson), 1952, Je 3,29:5
Carnot, Adolphe, 1920, Je 22,11:4
Carnot, Joseph Mrs, 1967, Mr 17,41:1
Carnow, Abraham, 1963, S 2,15:5
Carnrick, Millard, 1957, Je 29,17:5
Carnright, George F, 1946, Jl 1,31:3
Carnright, John F, 1942, Jl 1,25:3
Carns, Margaret J Mrs, 1952, F 26,27:2
Carns, Walter T, 1946, Ag 12,21:4
Carns, William L, 1941, S 28,48:1
Carny, Carny C (H LeVan), 1958, N 12,37:2
Caro, Buevantura, 1949, S 28,27:4
Caro, Daniel, 1949, My 10,25:5
Caro, Marcus R, 1962, My 18,31:3
Caro, Miguel Antonio, 1909, Ag 7,9:5
Caro, Nathan L, 1948, Mr 6,13:2
Caro, Raffaele de, 1961, Je 5,31:5
Caro, S Dr, 1881, My 1,5:2
Caro, Samuel Rabbi, 1912, Je 24,9:4
Caro, Theodore, 1964, Ag 19,37:5
Caro Rodriguez, Jose M (funl, D 8,31:5), 1958, D 5, 31:1
Carocia, Michael, 1953, Ap 28,30:8
Caroe, William D, 1938, Mr 1,21:1
Caroff, Julius, 1962, S 29,23:4
Carol, Martine (Mrs E Eland), 1967, F 7,39:3
Carol, Pearl, 1955, N 23,23:4
Carol II, Ex-King of Rumania, 1953, Ap 4,1:4
Carolan, James S, 1943, N 17,25:3

Carolan, Maria (Sister Mary Claudia), 1965, N 16, 47:1
Carolan, Matthew L, 1938, Je 7,23:3
Caroli, Rene D, 1945, Ap 23,19:3
Caroline, Queen of Denmark, 1881, My 10,5:5
Caroline, Sister, 1908, Mr 14,7:6
Caroll, David, 1881, Ag 1,5:2
Caron, Adolphe L, 1959, D 19,27:2
Caron, Paul, 1941, F 16,41:1
Caronia, Joseph B, 1962, F 24,27:5
Carothers, Alice, 1951, Jl 23,17:6
Carothers, Eleanor K, 1951, Ag 12,79:4
Carothers, George C (cor, Ag 23,21:6), 1939, Ag 5, 15:7
Carothers, George C Mrs, 1952, O 26,89:1
Carothers, James M, 1951, D 20,31:2
Carothers, Neil, 1965, Jl 9,26:3
Carothers, Robert, 1954, S 25,15:6
Carow, Emily T, 1939, Mr 21,23:4
Carow, Phil W, 1952, O 15,31:2
Carozza, Frank Sr, 1951, My 29,25:2
Carp, Pierre P, 1919, Je 30,11:3
Carp, Samuel, 1963, F 23,7:3
Carpeaux, Jean Baptiste, 1875, O 14,4:6
Carpendale, Belle M, 1953, Ag 26,27:6
Carpender, John Nellson, 1911, N 22,13:4
Carpender, Sydney B Mrs, 1964, Jl 21,33:3
Carpender, William, 1946, N 28,27:4
Carpender, William Mrs, 1959, F 25,31:2
Carpenter, Aaron E Mrs (will), 1966, F 20,55:6
Carpenter, Agnes, 1958, F 6,27:5
Carpenter, Albert D, 1950, S 23,8:1
Carpenter, Alex H, 1941, Jl 20,31:2
Carpenter, Alfred F, 1955, D 28,23:4
Carpenter, Alice B, 1954, Mr 11,31:4
Carpenter, Allan Mrs, 1950, Ag 15,29:2
Carpenter, Allan W, 1948, Ap 11,72:2
Carpenter, Ann E, 1950, O 6,27:2
Carpenter, Arch B Sir, 1937, My 28,21:6
Carpenter, Arthur, 1924, F 24,21:3
Carpenter, Arthur A, 1958, N 27,29:5
Carpenter, Arthur F, 1943, D 20,23:5
Carpenter, Arthur F Mrs, 1966, Mr 12,27:3
Carpenter, Arthur S, 1960, Ja 11,45:3
Carpenter, B G Mrs, 1879, D 29,5:4
Carpenter, Benjamin Jr, 1947, S 26,23:5
Carpenter, C, 1883, Mr 9,3:2
Carpenter, C Whitney, 1954, Ap 8,27:4
Carpenter, Caroline A, 1907, Je 13,7:6
Carpenter, Charles A, 1951, O 21,93:2
Carpenter, Charles A Mrs, 1954, O 27,29:1
Carpenter, Charles C, 1938, S 9,21:2; 1942, Ja 31,17:2
Carpenter, Charles E, 1942, N 10,27:6
Carpenter, Charles J, 1948, F 17,25:4
Carpenter, Charles K, 1951, S 7,29:3
Carpenter, Charles P, 1945, S 25,25:3
Carpenter, Charles R, 1956, F 24,25:3
Carpenter, Charles S, 1949, Ap 16,15:6
Carpenter, Charles T, 1941, My 1,23:3
Carpenter, Clarence, 1954, Je 19,15:5
Carpenter, Clarence E, 1962, Mr 23,33:2
Carpenter, Clarence W, 1946, F 24,44:3
Carpenter, Cliff D, 1965, Ag 7,21:2
Carpenter, Clifton B, 1952, S 2,23:1
Carpenter, D Frederick, 1944, My 3,19:3
Carpenter, D M, 1883, S 30,1:5
Carpenter, Dan E, 1938, S 8,23:3
Carpenter, Dan Hoagland, 1903, Jl 29,7:6
Carpenter, Dana S, 1940, Ap 12,23:4
Carpenter, Daniel (funl, N 20,8:2), 1866, N 16,5:4
Carpenter, Dayton W, 1941, My 28,25:5
Carpenter, Douglas Boyd, 1916, S 9,11:6
Carpenter, Dunbar F, 1955, O 11,39:2
Carpenter, Dwight C, 1953, Ja 15,27:5
Carpenter, Ebenezer Mrs, 1914, D 21,9:4
Carpenter, Edith L, 1946, Jl 18,25:4
Carpenter, Edmund J, 1924, F 22,15:4
Carpenter, Edward A, 1953, Ap 23,29:4
Carpenter, Edward C, 1950, O 8,104:6
Carpenter, Edward C Mrs, 1959, F 17,31:4
Carpenter, Edward Mrs, 1959, Je 11,33:4
Carpenter, Edward O, 1916, D 19,11:3
Carpenter, Edwin F, 1963, F 13,9:2
Carpenter, Elbert C, 1964, My 14,35:1
Carpenter, Elbert L, 1945, Ja 31,21:2
Carpenter, Elizabeth Mrs (will), 1914, Ag 21,9:6
Carpenter, Elmer E, 1952, Jl 24,27:3
Carpenter, Elnathan Mrs, 1937, Jl 20,23:2
Carpenter, Ernest C, 1942, Ap 23,23:2
Carpenter, Ernest E, 1953, S 5,15:5
Carpenter, Ernest E Mrs, 1949, O 5,29:5
Carpenter, Ernest W, 1937, Jl 20,23:5
Carpenter, Esek C, 1940, Je 6,25:4
Carpenter, Essex P, 1945, S 14,23:4
Carpenter, Evelyn, 1940, Ja 21,34:4
Carpenter, Ezra S, 1952, Mr 17,21:5
Carpenter, Fayette, 1944, Ag 5,11:6
Carpenter, Florence E, 1951, D 9,91:2
Carpenter, Ford A, 1947, N 12,28:2
Carpenter, Francis M, 1919, My 13,17:4
Carpenter, Francis W, 1925, D 27,7:1
Carpenter, Frank, 1943, Je 5,15:2; 1948, F 23,25:3
Carpenter, Frank E, 1956, My 30,21:3
Carpenter, Frank E Mrs, 1956, N 7,31:4
Carpenter, Frank G, 1924, Je 18,19:5; 1952, Ap 12,11:2
Carpenter, Frank M, 1947, O 28,25:2
Carpenter, Frank P, 1938, Ap 14,23:1
Carpenter, Frank S Mrs, 1957, Mr 2,21:5
Carpenter, Frank W, 1945, Mr 2,20:2
Carpenter, Franklin T, 1908, O 31,9:5
Carpenter, Fred E, 1938, Mr 17,21:3
Carpenter, Fred V, 1948, N 9,27:4
Carpenter, Fred W, 1957, Ag 29,27:4
Carpenter, Frederick B Brig-Gen, 1907, N 5,9:5
Carpenter, Frederick W, 1939, Ap 13,23:2
Carpenter, Frederick Walton Dr, 1925, Mr 3,23:5
Carpenter, G S Gen, 1904, Ag 13,7:4
Carpenter, Gardner C, 1952, Mr 9,92:3
Carpenter, George A, 1944, S 14,23:2
Carpenter, George B Mrs, 1958, Ja 19,87:1
Carpenter, George E, 1946, Ap 10,27:3
Carpenter, George Mrs, 1947, Ag 20,21:5
Carpenter, George Rice Prof, 1909, Ap 9,9:4
Carpenter, George S, 1942, Je 5,17:1
Carpenter, George T, 1951, N 27,31:4
Carpenter, George W, 1947, Ag 2,13:2; 1952, Ap 8, 29:5; 1955, D 31,13:2
Carpenter, Gilbert C Mrs, 1958, Jl 10,27:3
Carpenter, Gilbert S Mrs, 1914, Mr 23,11:4
Carpenter, H Beach, 1955, S 28,35:3
Carpenter, H C Harold, 1940, S 16,19:6
Carpenter, H S, 1926, O 27,27:5
Carpenter, H W, 1903, Jl 12,11:3
Carpenter, Harold, 1944, D 27,20:2
Carpenter, Harriet E, 1909, S 29,11:6
Carpenter, Harriet Mrs, 1909, S 27,9:6
Carpenter, Harry, 1946, O 18,24:2; 1952, F 1,22:2
Carpenter, Harry A, 1942, Ap 6,15:2
Carpenter, Harry B Mrs, 1968, Jl 21,56:5
Carpenter, Harry C, 1958, Je 13,23:2
Carpenter, Harry G, 1960, Ag 27,19:5
Carpenter, Harry M, 1941, O 4,15:3
Carpenter, Henry Cannon, 1968, N 7,47:3
Carpenter, Henry Mrs, 1947, N 2,72:6
Carpenter, Herbert L, 1943, O 4,17:1; 1963, Ag 24,19:5
Carpenter, Herbert S Mrs, 1960, O 5,41:3
Carpenter, Horace F, 1937, Mr 1,19:3
Carpenter, Horace T, 1947, My 21,25:2
Carpenter, Howard B, 1946, O 30,17:4
Carpenter, Howard C, 1955, Ap 8,21:4
Carpenter, Howard F, 1942, Jl 28,17:4
Carpenter, Howard L, 1958, My 24,21:4
Carpenter, Howard Mrs, 1948, Ja 29,23:2
Carpenter, Hubert V, 1941, N 16,56:2
Carpenter, Hugh S, 1947, S 30,25:4
Carpenter, Hunter, 1953, F 25,27:3
Carpenter, I George, 1947, Je 18,25:4
Carpenter, J B Mrs, 1948, Ag 30,25:2
Carpenter, J Henry (funl, Je 20,85:2), 1954, Je 18, 23:3
Carpenter, James B, 1950, Mr 15,29:3
Carpenter, James D Mrs, 1960, Ja 4,29:3
Carpenter, James E R Mrs, 1956, O 25,33:2
Carpenter, James F, 1967, Je 5,43:1
Carpenter, James O, 1905, Mr 8,9:5
Carpenter, James W, 1948, N 20,13:2
Carpenter, James W Mrs, 1948, F 14,13:5
Carpenter, Jerusha Mrs, 1940, N 26,23:4
Carpenter, Jesse O Mrs, 1959, Mr 19,33:2
Carpenter, John A, 1951, Ap 27,23:4
Carpenter, John E, 1939, N 25,17:4
Carpenter, John G, 1946, Ja 22,27:5
Carpenter, John H, 1938, Ja 30,II,9:3; 1943, Ap 7,25:1
Carpenter, John H Jr, 1945, My 1,23:1
Carpenter, John M, 1950, My 31,29:4
Carpenter, John S, 1956, Je 21,31:4
Carpenter, John T, 1946, S 18,31:4
Carpenter, John T Jr, 1962, Ag 22,33:2
Carpenter, John T Mrs, 1941, N 13,27:3
Carpenter, Joseph, 1937, Ap 14,25:4
Carpenter, Joseph L, 1942, Mr 31,21:1
Carpenter, Joseph R Jr, 1952, Jl 22,25:4
Carpenter, Joseph R Mrs, 1954, My 25,21:7
Carpenter, Kate D B Mrs, 1942, S 4,23:4
Carpenter, Lansing T, 1959, Jl 25,5:2
Carpenter, Laurence E, 1958, D 5,31:3
Carpenter, Leland S, 1956, D 8,19:5
Carpenter, Leon A Jr, 1963, Je 25,33:4
Carpenter, Les G, 1948, F 26,23:4
Carpenter, Lewis Cass Col, 1908, Mr 8,7:5
Carpenter, Lillian M, 1942, Je 6,13:3
Carpenter, Linn E, 1918, Ag 19,9:8
Carpenter, Linton E, 1954, S 1,27:5
Carpenter, Louis H, 1916, Ja 22,9:5
Carpenter, Louis S, 1942, N 2,21:4
Carpenter, Lucien B, 1946, Ja 25,23:1
Carpenter, Marion S Mrs, 1962, N 3,25:6
Carpenter, Martin R, 1945, Ja 14,40:3
Carpenter, Mary, 1877, Je 16,2:6
Carpenter, Mary J Mrs, 1954, My 6,33:5
Carpenter, Matthew, 1881, F 25,1:7
Carpenter, Maxwell E, 1953, Ag 15,15:1
Carpenter, Newel U, 1957, F 16,17:2
Carpenter, Newton H Mrs, 1943, Je 6,44:2
Carpenter, Oliver, 1880, N 5,8:1
Carpenter, Oliver C, 1959, S 15,39:2
Carpenter, Oliver P, 1937, Mr 7,II,8:3
Carpenter, Orlando Mrs, 1951, Je 1,23:4
Carpenter, Orvis F, 1945, O 19,23:1
Carpenter, Otto, 1958, N 9,89:1
Carpenter, Otto F, 1947, F 26,25:3
Carpenter, P H, 1891, O 23,5:5
Carpenter, Paul, 1952, My 27,27:4; 1964, Je 13,23:4
Carpenter, Perry J, 1951, Ja 2,23:4
Carpenter, Peter J Jr, 1941, S 16,23:2
Carpenter, Philip, 1919, Jl 24,9:1
Carpenter, R D, 1903, S 12,9:6
Carpenter, Ralph E, 1967, Je 10,33:5
Carpenter, Ralph G, 1961, Mr 19,89:1
Carpenter, Raymond V, 1947, Mr 13,27:5
Carpenter, Reese, 1953, My 5,29:3
Carpenter, Richard, 1939, S 5,23:4
Carpenter, Richard F, 1913, Jl 20,II,11:4
Carpenter, Robert F, 1959, F 9,29:4
Carpenter, Robert F Mrs, 1959, F 10,33:2
Carpenter, Robert J, 1955, My 10,29:2
Carpenter, Robert M 3d, 1937, Ja 14,21:2
Carpenter, Robert Purser, 1920, S 16,9:2
Carpenter, Robert R M, 1949, Je 12,76:3
Carpenter, Roger G, 1962, Jl 21,19:3
Carpenter, Rolla C, 1919, Ja 20,15:5
Carpenter, Samuel, 1908, Ja 9,9:5; 1953, Mr 20,23:2
Carpenter, Sarah L, 1947, Ag 2,13:5
Carpenter, Sidney H, 1955, N 1,31:2
Carpenter, Solomon G, 1945, My 20,32:2
Carpenter, Spencer C, 1959, Ag 20,26:2
Carpenter, T Leslie, 1947, Mr 1,15:1
Carpenter, Tailer Mrs, 1953, Ja 2,15:1
Carpenter, Thomas D, 1943, D 21,27:2
Carpenter, Thomas D Mrs, 1943, D 21,27:2
Carpenter, Thomas E Mrs, 1950, D 22,20:6
Carpenter, Thomas H 3d, 1957, Ja 7,25:3
Carpenter, Thomas K, 1951, F 7,29:3
Carpenter, Virgil K, 1946, F 21,21:3
Carpenter, W Irving Mrs, 1962, N 9,26:4
Carpenter, W T Coleman, 1967, Jl 24,27:2
Carpenter, Walter C, 1949, N 28,27:4
Carpenter, Walter H, 1946, Mr 14,25:3
Carpenter, Walter S Jr Mrs, 1949, O 6,31:6
Carpenter, Ward N, 1953, S 15,31:2
Carpenter, Warwick S Mrs, 1949, O 13,27:3
Carpenter, Willard A, 1925, N 18,23:4
Carpenter, Willard Prof, 1924, Mr 1,13:5
Carpenter, William, 1952, Ag 20,25:5
Carpenter, William A, 1941, Ja 5,44:3
Carpenter, William C, 1948, Ag 18,25:4
Carpenter, William E, 1937, Ag 22,II,6:8
Carpenter, William F, 1951, Ap 20,29:2
Carpenter, William G, 1942, F 20,17:2
Carpenter, William H, 1939, Je 9,21:2; 1944, N 4,15 1965, S 7,39:4
Carpenter, William H Mrs, 1941, F 21,19:1
Carpenter, William M, 1961, Je 12,29:3
Carpenter, William R, 1949, Mr 13,76:6
Carpenter, William W, 1945, Ap 29,37:2
Carpenter, Williston C Mrs, 1950, S 12,27:2
Carpenter, Ziba, 1909, S 20,7:6
Carpentier, Charles F, 1964, Ap 4,27:1
Carpentier, Horace W Gen, 1918, F 1,9:5
Carpentieri, Giacomo, 1941, Jl 17,19:4
Carper, Gerald I, 1937, Mr 12,23:3
Carpi, Fernando, 1916, N 10,13:5
Carpi, Fred, 1967, O 30,45:5
Carpinello, Joseph, 1947, Ap 17,27:2
Carr, Albert, 1924, Je 19,21:4
Carr, Alexander, 1946, S 20,31:1
Carr, Ambrose A, 1962, Ap 23,29:3
Carr, Arthur H, 1941, My 28,25:5
Carr, Arthur T, 1954, F 19,34:1
Carr, Arthur W, 1945, N 18,44:1; 1963, F 9,8:2
Carr, Austin H, 1942, F 5,21:5
Carr, Beatrice E, 1957, Ag 7,27:5
Carr, Bill, 1966, Ja 15,27:3
Carr, C Fred, 1946, O 4,23:5
Carr, Camillo Cassatti Cadmus Brig-Gen, 1914, Jl 5:6
Carr, Charles C, 1952, Jl 31,23:3
Carr, Charles E, 1955, My 1,88:6
Carr, Charles L, 1951, O 11,37:2
Carr, Charles Mrs, 1947, Je 19,21:4
Carr, Charlotte E (mem ser, Jl 31,10:3), 1956, J 19:3
Carr, Claiborn M, 1956, Ap 18,31:4
Carr, Clarence Mrs, 1949, D 9,32:3
Carr, Clarence S, 1947, F 10,29:4
Carr, Clark E Col, 1919, Mr 2,21:4
Carr, Clifford C, 1960, D 11,88:6
Carr, Cornelius J, 1938, F 13,II,7:3
Carr, Daniel, 1948, Je 21,21:5
Carr, Donald, 1961, Ag 5,17:7
Carr, E, 1878, My 21,8:4
Carr, Edith Mrs, 1940, D 8,69:4
Carr, Edward J Msgr, 1937, O 23,15:8
Carr, Edward T M, 1959, S 29,36:2
Carr, Edwin H, 1945, Je 9,13:3
Carr, Edwin H Mrs, 1947, N 12,27:1
Carr, Elizabeth F, 1961, F 28,33:2
Carr, Elmer S, 1958, Mr 12,31:1
Carr, Emily, 1945, Mr 3,13:4

Carr, Emma J, 1939, My 11,25:4
Carr, Emsley, 1941, Ag 1,15:2
Carr, Ernest W, 1964, D 17,41:5
Carr, Eugene, 1937, Ja 15,21:4
Carr, Floyd L, 1948, My 24,19:5
Carr, Francis A, 1953, Ap 21,27:4
Carr, Francis C, 1951, Je 24,72:6
Carr, Francis J, 1942, D 12,17:4
Carr, Francis L Rev, 1937, Jl 22,19:5
Carr, Frank A, 1947, Mr 24,25:5
Carr, Frank C, 1956, D 14,29:4
Carr, Frank D, 1937, Ja 11,19:3
Carr, Frank S, 1957, F 5,23:1
Carr, Fred P, 1947, Ja 5,53:1
Carr, Frederick D, 1939, F 14,19:5
Carr, Gene, 1959, D 10,39:2
Carr, George J, 1966, N 25,37:2
Carr, George L, 1941, D 19,25:5
Carr, George S, 1954, F 23,27:3
Carr, George W, 1925, Ag 16,5:2; 1942, Je 19,23:4
Carr, George W Mrs, 1963, S 11,43:2
Carr, Geraldine (Mrs G Carneol), 1954, S 3,12:1
Carr, Gilbert H, 1954, Ap 27,29:1
Carr, Gladys L, 1951, S 15,15:2
Carr, Grace I, 1948, Je 30,25:6
Carr, Grace T Mrs, 1922, O 3,21:5
Carr, Gregory, 1940, O 24,25:5
Carr, Harris B, 1957, F 12,27:2
Carr, Harry C, 1943, D 30,17:3
Carr, Harry J Mrs, 1945, S 20,23:1
Carr, Henry J, 1952, S 6,17:5
Carr, Henry Lovell, 1906, Je 25,7:6
Carr, Homer W, 1942, S 5,13:6
Carr, Horace, 1941, Ap 14,17:3
Carr, Horace Merwin Rev, 1922, N 8,15:4
Carr, Howard, 1945, F 6,19:3
Carr, J Arthur, 1953, F 2,21:4
Carr, J W Comyns, 1916, D 14,15:5
Carr, Jack, 1951, Ap 17,29:5
Carr, James, 1904, F 3,9:5
Carr, James G, 1954, O 19,27:1
Carr, James W Mrs, 1950, My 1,25:6
Carr, Jeptha C, 1950, Jl 24,17:5
Carr, Jesse D, 1903, D 12,9:6
Carr, Jesse F, 1948, Ag 15,60:3
Carr, Jessie R, 1943, Mr 23,19:2
Carr, John, 1937, My 22,15:4
Carr, John C Sr, 1967, Je 29,43:4
Carr, John F, 1940, Ja 1,24:2
Carr, John J, 1949, Jl 30,15:7
Carr, John O, 1948, Ag 25,25:3
Carr, John S, 1904, F 23,7:6
Carr, John W, 1960, F 19,27:2
Carr, Joseph F, 1939, My 21,III,6:6
Carr, Joseph F Mrs, 1950, S 1,21:4; 1951, Ja 22,17:4
Carr, Joseph K, 1940, D 13,23:3
Carr, Joseph W Prof, 1909, Mr 5,9:5
Carr, Josiah, 1903, S 30,9:6
Carr, Julian S Gen, 1924, Ap 30,19:2
Carr, Julian S Jr, 1922, Mr 18,13:5
Carr, Kate Mrs, 1923, O 22,19:3
Carr, Kenneth S, 1966, D 13,47:4
Carr, Lady, 1942, My 25,15:4
Carr, Laurence, 1954, Ap 18,88:7
Carr, Leander K, 1937, S 22,27:5
Carr, Leo T, 1943, D 19,20:5
Carr, Lester H, 1967, Ja 4,43:1
Carr, Lewis J, 1946, S 5,27:2
Carr, Lewis S, 1954, Je 16,31:5
Carr, Lovell H, 1938, Ag 25,19:3
Carr, Lucien, 1915, Ja 29,9:6
Carr, Lyle, 1912, F 18,II,13:4
Carr, Mai Belle Mrs, 1944, Ap 8,13:4
Carr, Maurice J, 1940, N 8,21:4
Carr, Michael J, 1949, F 4,24:3
Carr, Nat, 1944, Jl 8,11:2
Carr, Patrick Francis Rev, 1919, Ap 28,15:4
Carr, Percy W, 1957, Ag 9,19:4
Carr, Phil, 1957, Ag 8,23:4
Carr, Rachel H, 1946, Ag 16,21:5
Carr, Ralph L, 1950, S 23,17:6
Carr, Ralph W, 1946, Je 10,21:5
Carr, Reid L, 1948, O 8,26:3
Carr, Reid L Mrs, 1950, F 25,17:5
Carr, Richard, 1949, Ag 20,11:2
Carr, Richard F Rev, 1937, Ja 29,19:5
Carr, Robert F, 1945, Ja 23,19:5
Carr, Robert J, 1942, Je 1,13:4
Carr, Robert P, 1945, F 28,23:5
Carr, S, 1882, Ap 16,7:1
Carr, Sade, 1940, N 18,19:3
Carr, Samuel, 1922, My 30,13:5
Carr, Steve, 1954, My 29,15:4
Carr, Stuart, 1955, Mr 4,23:4
Carr, Sydney Z, 1955, N 23,50:2
Carr, Thomas Archbishop, 1917, My 7,9:5
Carr, Thomas L, 1948, Mr 13,15:2
Carr, Trem, 1946, Ag 19,25:5
Carr, W S Col, 1880, S 22,8:2
Carr, Walter D, 1950, Ag 16,29:1
Carr, Walter L, 1944, F 4,15:6
Carr, Wentworth C, 1942, My 1,19:4
Carr, Wilbur J, 1942, Je 27,13:1
Carr, Wilbur J Mrs, 1965, Je 1,39:4
Carr, William A, 1940, My 4,17:5
Carr, William B, 1942, O 15,23:4
Carr, William C, 1948, My 30,34:5; 1954, N 16,29:4
Carr, William C D, 1937, F 14,II,8:7
Carr, William C Mrs, 1958, Jl 15,25:3
Carr, William D, 1953, S 7,19:4
Carr, William Dr, 1925, O 16,21:4
Carr, William H, 1946, O 14,29:1
Carr, William I, 1943, Mr 6,13:2
Carr, William J, 1950, Je 2,23:3
Carr, William J G, 1959, O 6,39:2
Carr, William J Justice, 1917, Ag 6,9:4
Carr, William J Mrs, 1917, F 25,19:2
Carr, William J Sr, 1939, Je 30,19:5
Carr, William L, 1959, O 20,39:5
Carr, Wooda N, 1953, Je 30,23:3
Carr-Gomm, Hubert, 1939, Ja 25,21:2
Carra, Carlo, 1966, Ap 14,35:6
Carra, James, 1951, Ag 29,25:2
Carrabine, Martin I, 1965, Ag 18,35:3
Carrabine, Oscar, 1947, Jl 18,17:3
Carrabine, Oscar Mrs, 1966, Je 15,47:4
Carracino, Gennaro, 1951, Mr 29,27:4
Carragan, George, 1925, Ja 20,21:4
Carragan, James F Mrs, 1959, S 18,31:1
Carragan, Sydney B, 1959, Je 7,86:5
Carragan, William H, 1954, D 17,31:4
Carragher, Frank J, 1939, Mr 30,23:5
Carragher, John J, 1948, N 13,15:4
Carragher, Joseph A Sr, 1954, Jl 16,21:4
Carraher, Joseph M, 1949, F 24,24:3
Carraher, Owen, 1946, Ag 28,27:5
Carran, Thomas J, 1937, Mr 3,23:2
Carranza, Enelio, 1938, Jl 13,21:4
Carranza, Estefania de Mrs, 1938, Ag 30,17:4
Carranza, Virginia Sannas, 1919, N 10,13:2
Carras, Theodore L, 1967, D 31,44:7
Carrasco, Don Antonio, 1874, Ja 5,3:1
Carrati, Lorenzo J, 1949, Jl 4,13:5
Carre, Albert (por), 1938, D 13,25:4
Carre, Walter W, 1968, S 23,35:4
Carreau, Cyrille, 1914, Mr 27,11:6; 1956, Ag 31,17:2
Carredine, George H, 1951, D 27,21:2
Carrel, Alexis, 1944, N 6,19:1
Carrel, Frank, 1940, Jl 31,17:4
Carrel, Henry Clay, 1915, O 21,11:5
Carrel, Leonardo, 1940, D 28,15:2
Carrel, Lynn J Jr, 1952, My 9,23:1
Carrel, M Louis, 1962, O 13,25:1
Carrel, Morton D, 1955, Ap 6,29:2
Carrell, Eugene A, 1942, Jl 8,23:5
Carrell, J Wallace, 1940, D 17,26:3
Carreno, Alberto M, 1962, S 7,29:2
Carreno, Teresa (funl, Je 15,9:7), 1917, Je 13,13:6
Carrer Justiz, Francisco, 1947, Jl 6,40:7
Carreras, Maria (Mrs G Carreras), 1966, Ap 18,29:5
Carrere, Emilio, 1947, My 1,25:5
Carrere, Henri Valente, 1919, Jl 18,11:4
Carrere, J Maxwell Mrs, 1941, O 4,15:5
Carrere, J P H, 1948, O 8,25:3
Carrere, John M Mrs, 1920, F 9,9:4
Carrere, John Merven (funl, Mr 3,11:4), 1911, Mr 2, 9:3
Carrere, Robert M, 1959, My 24,89:2
Carres, Peter J, 1952, S 3,29:4
Carret, Jaime E, 1941, S 2,17:2
Carretier, Pierre, 1945, Je 29,15:3
Carretta, Frank A, 1940, D 31,15:2
Carrick, Alice Van L (Mrs P O Skinner), 1961, N 26,88:4
Carrick, Charles L, 1941, Jl 8,19:1
Carrick, Countess of (Mrs T W S H Butler), 1954, Jl 31,13:6
Carrick, Earl of, 1901, D 25,2:2
Carrick, Gerald S, 1963, S 19,27:6
Carrick, Krickel K, 1952, D 21,52:7
Carrick, Lynn, 1965, S 13,35:1
Carrick, Robert E, 1968, Ja 25,40:1
Carrick, William S, 1953, Ja 24,15:4
Carrick, Willington M, 1939, Jl 3,13:6
Carrico, J Leonard, 1944, N 23,31:5
Carrier, Arthur E, 1939, D 19,26:4
Carrier, Charles L, 1944, O 19,23:5
Carrier, Edward B Mrs, 1965, F 1,23:3
Carrier, James F (Bro Fidelis), 1903, N 15,9:5
Carrier, John F, 1952, Mr 8,13:5
Carrier, Louis, 1961, D 16,25:2
Carrier, Marshall H Sr, 1944, Mr 16,19:2
Carrier, Noyes B A, 1947, D 28,40:1
Carrier, Paul, 1948, S 17,25:1
Carrier, Robert M, 1957, S 14,19:4
Carrier, Willis H, 1950, O 8,104:3
Carrier, Willis H Mrs, 1939, Je 4,48:7; 1964, S 27,86:4
Carrier-Belleuse, P, 1933, Ja 2,23:1
Carrier-Belleuse, Robert Louis, 1913, Je 16,9:2
Carriere, Theodore Mrs, 1946, Ja 15,23:2
Carrig, Martin, 1962, Ja 6,19:4
Carrigan, Andrew, 1872, S 6,5:4
Carrigan, Charles E, 1943, S 14,23:3
Carrigan, Edward, 1944, My 10,19:5
Carrigan, Eugene, 1945, Ja 24,21:1
Carrigan, George E, 1942, Mr 10,19:1
Carrigan, James A, 1963, S 15,86:4
Carrigan, James F, 1906, Ag 25,7:6
Carrigan, John E, 1944, My 9,19:4
Carrigan, John J, 1940, Mr 9,15:4
Carrigan, Patrick M, 1943, D 4,13:2
Carrigan, Thomas C Dr, 1921, Ag 6,9:6
Carrigan, Thomas J, 1941, O 3,23:5
Carrigan, William L, 1939, O 28,15:6
Carrigg, John J, 1940, Ja 8,15:5; 1963, Ag 11,84:6
Carrigues, Charles Franklin, 1909, Ag 12,7:6
Carrillo, Julian Mrs, 1949, Ja 29,13:2
Carrillo, Leo (funl plans, S 12,33:1; funl, S 15,30:6), 1961, S 11,27:2
Carrillo, Mario, 1940, Mr 22,19:5
Carrillo, Ramon, 1956, D 22,19:3
Carrillo Flores, Nabor, 1967, F 20,37:2
Carrillo Pedraza, Ramona Mrs, 1955, Ag 20,17:6
Carringer, J Raymond, 1966, Ja 6,27:3
Carrington, Asygell W Rev, 1937, Mr 26,22:1
Carrington, B W, 1946, Ja 30,25:2
Carrington, C R Marquess of Lincolnshire, 1928, Je 14,27:3
Carrington, Campbell Mrs, 1941, O 24,23:3
Carrington, Charles L, 1965, Mr 8,29:4
Carrington, Edward C (por), 1938, D 31,15:1
Carrington, Edward Lt, 1865, Mr 27,4:5
Carrington, Elaine S (Mrs G D Carrington), 1958, My 5,29:4
Carrington, Eva J Mrs, 1942, Ag 7,17:4
Carrington, Fitzroy, 1955, Ja 1,13:4
Carrington, Frank de L, 1940, D 4,27:5
Carrington, Frederick Gen, 1913, Mr 24,11:5
Carrington, George D, 1945, Ap 21,13:5
Carrington, Gordon D, 1944, Ag 22,17:4
Carrington, H B Gen, 1912, O 27,II,17:4
Carrington, Helen, 1963, O 24,33:3
Carrington, Henry O, 1940, My 30,18:3
Carrington, Henry S, 1961, F 18,19:1
Carrington, J B, 1929, Ja 22,29:2
Carrington, John B Mrs, 1968, F 15,43:5
Carrington, John R, 1949, Ag 6,17:6
Carrington, Katherine W, 1953, My 3,88:1
Carrington, Malcolm, 1943, Ja 16,13:1
Carrington, Mary C, 1950, Ag 28,17:5
Carrington, Otis M, 1964, D 4,40:3
Carrington, Richard A Jr, 1960, Mr 22,37:2
Carrington, Susan B Mrs, 1937, Jl 22,19:4
Carrington, W T, 1931, My 5,27:5
Carrington, William J, 1947, Jl 25,17:4
Carriols, Jose S Mrs, 1946, My 9,21:6
Carrion, Ramon, 1966, Ag 13,25:4
Carris, Lewis H, 1950, Mr 21,32:3
Carrizales, Enrique, 1949, O 13,34:7
Carroll, A Rook, 1946, N 3,63:1
Carroll, Agnes F Mrs, 1940, Ap 14,45:3
Carroll, Albert, 1956, D 5,39:5
Carroll, Albert A, 1941, Ja 26,38:1
Carroll, Alex, 1952, D 27,9:6
Carroll, Alfred F, 1947, Ja 11,19:3
Carroll, Alice B Mrs, 1940, F 2,17:2
Carroll, Amelia J Mrs, 1937, Ap 9,21:3
Carroll, Anna Mrs, 1947, D 30,23:4
Carroll, Arthur, 1938, Mr 19,15:6
Carroll, Arthur A, 1937, Jl 1,27:4
Carroll, Arthur T, 1948, Je 12,15:3
Carroll, Augustus J, 1968, Ap 13,25:1
Carroll, B Harvey, 1922, Ap 1,15:4
Carroll, Ben, 1945, Je 7,19:3
Carroll, Benjamin H, 1958, O 23,31:1
Carroll, Benjamin L, 1944, Ag 13,36:1
Carroll, Beryl F, 1939, D 17,48:8
Carroll, Billy, 1909, F 23,9:2
Carroll, Bradish J Jr, 1943, Ja 5,19:2
Carroll, Brockholst L, 1905, Ja 31,9:5
Carroll, Caroline S Mrs, 1938, Mr 9,23:2
Carroll, Catherine, 1944, F 27,38:2
Carroll, Catherine Mrs, 1941, D 12,26:2
Carroll, Charles, 1921, O 7,17:5
Carroll, Charles A, 1947, Ag 1,17:1; 1954, Ap 23,27:3
Carroll, Charles A Mrs, 1944, N 21,25:4
Carroll, Charles E, 1940, My 31,19:3; 1958, Ap 17,31:4
Carroll, Charles F, 1946, My 18,19:6
Carroll, Charles J, 1941, Jl 10,19:1; 1942, Ag 18,21:5; 1955, D 1,35:1
Carroll, Charles L, 1939, My 6,17:2
Carroll, Charles M, 1945, S 4,23:6
Carroll, Charles Mrs, 1947, S 11,27:1
Carroll, Charles P, 1941, Ja 12,44:1
Carroll, Charles Tucker Mrs, 1914, My 24,IV,7:5
Carroll, Curtis C, 1945, S 19,25:5
Carroll, D J, 1927, Mr 7,19:3
Carroll, Dan, 1939, Ag 1,19:4
Carroll, Daniel J, 1948, Ag 29,60:2; 1951, Je 3,92:4
Carroll, Daniel M, 1965, Jl 15,29:2
Carroll, David H Dr, 1912, N 16,15:6
Carroll, David W T, 1959, O 3,19:4
Carroll, Denis, 1956, N 26,27:4
Carroll, Denis R, 1945, F 28,23:3
Carroll, Douglas G, 1945, Ja 13,11:2
Carroll, Eber M, 1959, D 30,21:4
Carroll, Edward A, 1940, Mr 2,13:2; 1959, N 6,29:2
Carroll, Edward C, 1954, Mr 14,89:1
Carroll, Edward F, 1943, F 17,21:1

Carroll, Edward J, 1942, F 28,17:1; 1945, D 23,18:3; 1947, Ap 7,23:5; 1948, Ja 6,23:3
Carroll, Edward R, 1943, F 21,33:1
Carroll, Edward W, 1943, F 14,49:1
Carroll, Eugene H Sr, 1960, N 4,33:2
Carroll, Eugene P, 1938, O 17,15:7
Carroll, Evangeline, 1961, Je 29,33:2
Carroll, Francis A, 1965, D 8,43:3
Carroll, Francis B, 1967, F 27,29:1
Carroll, Francis M, 1941, Mr 30,49:3
Carroll, Francis X, 1962, Je 27,35:3
Carroll, Frank, 1938, Je 29,19:5
Carroll, Frank A, 1947, Ap 24,25:5
Carroll, Frank D Mrs, 1952, Je 20,23:4
Carroll, Frank E, 1941, D 20,19:3
Carroll, Fred L, 1943, Ag 31,17:4
Carroll, Fred M, 1961, N 2,37:1
Carroll, Frederick A, 1945, O 18,23:2
Carroll, George, 1939, Ag 7,15:5
Carroll, George A, 1966, Ap 4,31:3
Carroll, George M, 1956, Je 13,37:4
Carroll, George T, 1943, F 20,13:2
Carroll, George V, 1949, N 26,15:4
Carroll, Gerald J, 1953, N 5,31:2
Carroll, Grace, 1952, Jl 9,27:4
Carroll, H G, 1939, Ag 21,13:4
Carroll, Harry, 1962, D 28,8:6
Carroll, Harry M, 1953, Ap 22,29:2
Carroll, Harry P, 1954, Ap 7,31:1
Carroll, Henry Brig-Gen, 1908, F 14,7:6
Carroll, Henry G, 1948, Ag 12,21:2
Carroll, Henry J, 1950, Ja 13,23:3
Carroll, Hillary G, 1966, F 19,11:6
Carroll, Hiram C, 1947, Ap 16,25:4
Carroll, Howard B (Mar 18), 1963, Ap 1,35:3
Carroll, Howard J, 1960, Mr 22,37:3
Carroll, J B, 1932, Ja 9,17:3
Carroll, J Elmer, 1964, S 24,41:5
Carroll, J H, 1931, N 30,19:5
Carroll, J W, 1881, O 17,5:5
Carroll, James E, 1964, Je 15,29:4
Carroll, James E Sr, 1955, Mr 23,31:5
Carroll, James F, 1924, D 16,25:4; 1941, Ja 17,17:2; 1957, Ap 9,33:5; 1959, Mr 16,31:4; 1968, Ap 7,92:8
Carroll, James H (will, N 13,29:1), 1941, O 22,23:2
Carroll, James J, 1905, Ap 22,13:2; 1907, My 2,11:6; 1959, N 7,23:4; 1962, Ag 1,31:1
Carroll, James J Sr, 1967, O 6,39:4
Carroll, James Maj, 1907, S 18,9:6
Carroll, James T, 1940, O 22,23:2
Carroll, James W, 1920, Je 27,18:2; 1957, Ap 14,86:6
Carroll, James W Col, 1937, Ap 1,23:3
Carroll, John, 1907, Jl 7,7:5; 1938, Je 22,23:3; 1949, My 9,25:5; 1957, D 19,31:3; 1959, N 8,88:3; 1968, Ja 22,47:1
Carroll, John A, 1942, Mr 22,48:8; 1944, O 7,13:5; 1946, My 7,21:6; 1949, Ja 14,23:4
Carroll, John B, 1937, D 15,25:4
Carroll, John C, 1939, Ja 6,21:3
Carroll, John F Mrs, 1960, Ap 26,37:4
Carroll, John Francis, 1911, N 18,13:1
Carroll, John H Dr, 1968, My 25,35:2
Carroll, John J, 1937, O 19,25:2; 1939, Ag 1,19:7; 1941, Je 2,17:5; 1946, N 30,15:5; 1948, Je 10,25:2; 1948, D 24,17:4; 1961, Ja 1,49:1
Carroll, John J Jr, 1947, Je 15,60:3; 1958, Je 17,30:2
Carroll, John Lee, 1873, Mr 27,2:2; 1911, F 28,11:4
Carroll, John M, 1959, My 12,35:5
Carroll, John P, 1942, Ja 2,34:2
Carroll, John P Bp, 1925, N 5,23:5; 1925, N 29,13:1
Carroll, John S Mrs, 1955, Ap 9,13:2
Carroll, John T, 1939, Ag 13,29:4
Carroll, John V, 1955, My 25,33:4
Carroll, John W, 1925, Jl 6,11:6; 1946, Mr 5,26:3
Carroll, Johnnie, 1925, Jl 3,13:7
Carroll, Joseph, 1941, S 5,22:2; 1943, D 27,19:3; 1948, Ja 2,24:1; 1953, Ap 12,89:1
Carroll, Joseph C, 1937, Jl 10,15:3
Carroll, Joseph D, 1912, N 24,II,17:4
Carroll, Joseph F, 1955, D 14,39:2
Carroll, Joseph G, 1939, My 17,5:2
Carroll, Joseph H, 1937, S 28,23:1
Carroll, Joseph M Sr, 1954, S 1,27:3
Carroll, Joseph T, 1948, N 15,25:1
Carroll, Julia A, 1948, Ap 17,15:5
Carroll, Julia W C, 1959, O 21,43:3
Carroll, Katherine B, 1939, Ja 18,19:4
Carroll, Lauren (por), 1945, Mr 30,15:1
Carroll, Lawrence F, 1919, F 6,11:2
Carroll, Lawrence J, 1939, Mr 15,23:4; 1953, O 29,31:2
Carroll, Leonard, 1964, Ap 7,35:2
Carroll, Leslie H, 1950, Ap 11,31:1
Carroll, Lewis (C L Dodgson Rev), 1898, Ja 16,7:4
Carroll, Louis J, 1940, Jl 13,13:6
Carroll, M Rose, 1948, Ag 29,56:4
Carroll, Malcolm B, 1955, D 29,23:3
Carroll, Martin, 1952, N 4,29:4
Carroll, Martin A, 1959, Ap 15,33:4
Carroll, Martin Father (see also Ag 15), 1902, Ag 19,9:5
Carroll, Martin J, 1937, O 9,19:3; 1950, Jl 1,15:5
Carroll, Martin Mrs, 1951, Mr 24,13:5
Carroll, Mary G Mrs, 1942, O 23,21:2
Carroll, Mary Mrs, 1924, Ap 6,27:2; 1939, Je 10,17:1
Carroll, Matthew J, 1957, Ja 9,31:4
Carroll, Matthew J Mrs, 1954, Ap 28,31:2
Carroll, Matthew L, 1955, N 16,12:6
Carroll, Matthew V, 1940, Ap 6,17:4
Carroll, Michael, 1872, Ja 1,1:6
Carroll, Michael B, 1960, O 28,31:2
Carroll, Michael J, 1941, Ag 11,13:4; 1942, Je 6,13:5
Carroll, Michael M, 1946, My 28,23:2
Carroll, Mitchell, 1948, O 14,30:2
Carroll, Morris H, 1951, N 3,17:2
Carroll, Nancy, 1965, Ag 7,13:1
Carroll, Norman, 1967, F 5,89:1
Carroll, Parke, 1961, F 5,81:1
Carroll, Patrick H, 1951, O 2,27:4
Carroll, Patrick J, 1959, S 19,23:3
Carroll, Patrick J Rev, 1959, N 19,39:3
Carroll, Paul T (Pete), (funl, S 21,27.3), 1954, S 18, 15:6
Carroll, Paul V Mrs, 1957, O 17,33:2
Carroll, Paul Vincent, 1968, O 21,47:2
Carroll, Peter E Mrs, 1953, Mr 23,23:4
Carroll, Peter J, 1966, Ag 27,30:2
Carroll, Phil A, 1957, Jl 10,27:5
Carroll, Phil H, 1941, D 7,79:1
Carroll, Philip Dr, 1906, D 17,11:5
Carroll, R Emmett, 1947, S 4,25:6
Carroll, Raymond G, 1943, D 14,27:5
Carroll, Raymond V, 1959, Mr 17,33:1
Carroll, Richard A, 1959, Mr 13,29:2
Carroll, Richard F, 1951, Ap 3,27:3
Carroll, Richard L, 1952, Ja 22,29:3
Carroll, Richard T, 1945, N 25,50:4
Carroll, Robert, 1942, N 29,64:8
Carroll, Robert E Mrs, 1967, D 23,23:1
Carroll, Robert F, 1964, D 30,23:1
Carroll, Robert M, 1937, S 11,17:7
Carroll, Robert P, 1954, Mr 31,27:2
Carroll, Robert S, 1949, Je 27,27:6
Carroll, Robert W, 1940, S 3,17:4; 1963, My 7,43:2
Carroll, Royal P Mrs, 1949, D 1,31:4
Carroll, Royal Phelps, 1922, F 8,17:4
Carroll, Stephen J, 1949, Ag 26,19:4
Carroll, Susan Eliz Mrs, 1905, Je 9,9:5
Carroll, Sydney, 1958, Ag 25,21:2
Carroll, T G, 1934, S 17,17:1
Carroll, T W, 1940, O 6,48:2
Carroll, Thomas, 1945, Ja 29,13:6
Carroll, Thomas C, 1960, O 1,19:4
Carroll, Thomas E Rev, 1916, O 5,11:6
Carroll, Thomas F, 1941, F 9,48:1; 1942, Ja 7,20:2; 1948, D 26,52:6
Carroll, Thomas H, 1964, Jl 28,29:3
Carroll, Thomas J, 1916, O 29,23:1; 1947, Je 6,23:3; 1949, D 13,38:2; 1951, Ap 24,29:4
Carroll, Thomas P, 1965, My 4,43:4
Carroll, Thomas Police Chief, 1937, Jl 24,15:7
Carroll, Timothy E, 1948, My 24,19:2
Carroll, Timothy F, 1943, Mr 27,13:5
Carroll, Vena T Mrs, 1950, Mr 4,17:3
Carroll, Vincent M, 1944, Mr 18,13:6
Carroll, Virginia, 1955, Ja 16,93:2
Carroll, W, 1879, Je 26,2:7
Carroll, W J, 1934, Ja 13,13:3
Carroll, Walter, 1941, N 24,8:2
Carroll, Walter p, 1951, O 22,23:6
Carroll, Walter R, 1955, F 26,15:5
Carroll, Walter S, 1950, F 25,17:3; 1950, Mr 2,28:5; 1953, O 15,33:2
Carroll, William, 1957, S 26,25:5
Carroll, William A, 1937, Je 10,23:2; 1961, Ja 15,86:3
Carroll, William B, 1952, My 1,29:6
Carroll, William C Mrs, 1962, My 17,37:1
Carroll, William D, 1946, D 21,19:4
Carroll, William E, 1950, Mr 1,27:1
Carroll, William E Dr, 1968, F 29,37:3
Carroll, William F, 1951, S 18,31:3
Carroll, William G, 1941, Ag 23,13:6
Carroll, William H, 1950, Mr 28,31:1
Carroll, William H Dr, 1919, Je 21,15:6
Carroll, William J, 1920, N 2,17:5; 1941, Mr 8,19:6; 1946, Ap 26,21:3; 1958, Ag 11,21:3
Carroll, William J Mrs, 1952, F 2,13:4
Carroll, William K, 1942, Ag 18,21:4
Carroll, William L, 1960, D 6,41:2
Carroll, William P, 1941, S 28,49:3
Carroll, William R, 1905, Je 18,9:6
Carroll, Winifred, 1961, Mr 3,27:2
Carroll (Bro Gervase), 1964, Je 25,33:1
Carroll-Coleman, William, 1968, My 9,47:2
Carrolton, Charles A, 1943, O 12,27:3
Carron, Arthur, 1967, My 11,54:1
Carron, Charles, 1946, Ja 21,23:2
Carron, Francois, 1939, Je 9,21:3
Carrora, Joseph (J Dundee), 1965, Ap 23,35:1
Carrott, Orville B, 1951, Ag 16,27:2
Carrow, Howard Judge, 1922, Ap 17,17:6
Carrozzo, Michael, 1940, Ag 5,27:3
Carrubba, Thomas A, 1968, Ap 6,39:3
Carruth, Arthur B, 1946, N 1,23:4
Carruth, C R, 1926, D 29,21:3
Carruth, Clarence U, 1945, Mr 12,19:2
Carruth, David V, 1941, Ap 21,19:2
Carruth, Ed, 1937, Ap 29,21:4
Carruth, Gorton V, 1960, Ap 17,92:7
Carruth, Henry, 1962, Ag 15,31:1
Carruth, Joseph A, 1960, Ag 21,84:6
Carruth, Oliver E, 1943, Mr 11,7:2
Carruth, Paul H, 1961, D 5,39:3
Carruth, Paul H Mrs, 1958, Ap 25,27:2
Carruth, William M, 1943, Ja 24,43:1
Carruthers, Adam Prof, 1937, N 14,II,11:3
Carruthers, Arthur C, 1956, O 5,25:3
Carruthers, Arthur R Mrs, 1948, Mr 19,23:3
Carruthers, Charles B, 1945, O 4,23:4
Carruthers, Frederick W, 1913, Jl 17,7:5
Carruthers, George, 1947, Ap 2,27:2
Carruthers, Harry, 1945, O 20,11:4
Carruthers, James, 1924, S 20,15:6; 1938, Ap 14,23:2; 1949, Mr 27,76:8
Carruthers, James A, 1945, Ap 2,19:3
Carruthers, James Mrs (V Markham), 1959, F 4,26:1
Carruthers, John F B, 1960, Ja 17,86:2
Carruthers, John G, 1955, My 3,31:4
Carruthers, Louis J, 1960, N 30,37:2
Carruthers, Louis Mrs, 1956, Ja 2,21:4
Carruthers, Lyman B, 1957, N 21,30:1
Carruthers, Roy, 1942, N 16,19:4
Carruthers, Samuel J, 1961, Ap 21,33:1
Carruthers, Thomas N, 1960, Je 14,37:2
Carruthers, Walter W, 1951, O 16,31:3
Carruthers, William J G, 1941, Je 6,21:5
Carryl, Guy Wetmore, 1904, Ap 2,9:5
Carscallen, Charles S, 1939, Je 30,19:5
Carse, David B, 1938, O 31,15:6
Carse, Henry R, 1942, Ap 14,21:5
Carse, Henry R Mrs, 1948, D 8,31:1
Carse, J B Gen, 1883, N 30,3:2
Carse, John B, 1945, Je 25,17:3
Carse, Marguerite B S Mrs, 1941, F 9,48:3
Carse, Orlando M, 1951, O 3,36:3
Carse, Robert A, 1950, Ja 17,28:2
Carsky, Joseph, 1962, Mr 28,39:4
Carslake, Bernard, 1941, Jl 30,17:5
Carslake, Walter M (will), 1951, My 12,4:3
Carson, Adam C, 1941, My 25,36:6
Carson, Alex P, 1956, My 1,33:2
Carson, Alfred, 1880, Ap 12,8:3
Carson, Arch I, 1951, D 22,15:4
Carson, Arch I Mrs, 1951, O 21,92:8
Carson, Benjamin, 1967, Je 19,35:2
Carson, Brooks, 1947, F 18,25:1
Carson, Charles H, 1940, Ap 12,23:5
Carson, Christopher A, 1952, Mr 31,19:3
Carson, Clara L, 1940, My 2,24:2
Carson, David R, 1945, S 7,23:4
Carson, Edward J, 1953, Ja 8,27:4
Carson, Edward N, 1954, Ag 11,25:5
Carson, Elmer L, 1950, Mr 8,27:1
Carson, Emily E Mrs, 1939, N 14,23:3
Carson, Frank, 1957, Ap 23,31:5
Carson, Frank W, 1941, Mr 20,21:1
Carson, George, 1941, Jl 27,31:3
Carson, George B, 1949, My 8,76:5
Carson, George W, 1943, Ja 29,19:4
Carson, H L, 1929, Jl 20,15:3
Carson, Hubert F, 1954, Ag 25,27:4
Carson, Hugh A, 1962, O 7,82:3
Carson, J (Jock), 1948, Ag 1,57:2
Carson, J Alex, 1953, Ap 10,21:3
Carson, J E, 1879, Jl 8,5:4
Carson, J T, 1940, O 16,23:4
Carson, Jack, 1963, Ja 3,15:7
Carson, James, 1875, Jl 28,5:3; 1957, S 12,31:5
Carson, James B, 1958, N 21,29:4
Carson, James B Mrs, 1945, Je 10,32:2
Carson, James G Jr, 1941, Ja 15,23:2
Carson, James J, 1950, N 9,33:5
Carson, James M, 1950, Ap 11,31:3
Carson, James S, 1960, Ag 10,31:1
Carson, Jerome S Sr, 1952, Ap 8,29:4
Carson, Jessie M, 1959, S 7,15:2
Carson, John G Mrs, 1952, F 26,27:1
Carson, John Gen Sir, 1922, O 14,13:7
Carson, John J, 1953, My 12,27:2
Carson, John L, 1945, My 19,21:1; 1964, Jl 27,31:
Carson, John M, 1956, Ja 19,33:5
Carson, John M Maj (funl, O 1,13:5), 1912, S 30
Carson, John M Mrs, 1964, S 25,41:2
Carson, John R, 1940, N 1,25:5
Carson, Joseph, 1953, Ag 25,21:6
Carson, Joseph J Jr, 1956, D 21,23:4
Carson, Joseph M, 1943, D 20,23:5
Carson, Kit, 1868, My 30,5:4; 1876, Ap 22,1:4
Carson, Lady, 1966, Ag 8,27:3
Carson, Lewis C, 1947, Ap 10,25:4
Carson, Lord, 1935, O 23,21:1
Carson, Luther F, 1962, Jl 28,19:6
Carson, Matthew B Maj, 1937, Ag 26,21:3
Carson, Oswald B Mrs, 1961, O 10,43:3
Carson, Perry H, 1909, N 1,11:4
Carson, Rachel L (trb lr, Ap 19,IV,8:5; will, My 19,41:3), 1964, Ap 15,1:4
Carson, Robert, 1938, D 1,23:5; 1940, D 27,20:3; Mr 4,25:1
Carson, Robert B, 1960, Mr 11,26:4

Carson, Robert J, 1943, Ja 10,50:3
Carson, Robert L, 1938, O 11,25:1
Carson, Robert N Mrs, 1912, Jl 6,7:4
Carson, Robert W, 1951, Mr 3,13:5
Carson, Robert 3d, 1959, O 16,31:4
Carson, Russell L, 1950, My 17,29:5
Carson, Russell M L, 1961, Ja 8,86:4
Carson, Simeon L, 1954, S 9,32:3
Carson, Stanley T, 1957, Je 6,31:5
Carson, Thomas B, 1941, Ag 3,35:1
Carson, Thomas G, 1913, Mr 12,11:4
Carson, Timothy I, 1946, Ap 26,21:4
Carson, Waid E, 1946, Ap 12,27:5
Carson, William A, 1949, Ap 30,13:2
Carson, William E, 1940, N 5,25:2; 1942, Mr 26,23:5
Carson, William K, 1957, O 27,86:4
Carson, William Mrs, 1952, D 24,17:4
Carstairs, C, 1928, Jl 11,23:3
Carstairs, Carroll, 1948, O 3,65:1
Carstairs, Charles Haseltine, 1919, O 30,13:2
Carstairs, James, 1958, Ap 8,29:2
Carstang, John, 1956, S 14,23:4
Carsten, Adolph S, 1939, F 2,19:6
Carstens, Albert M, 1956, F 4,19:4
Carstens, C C, 1939, Jl 5,17:4
Carstens, Carl C Mrs, 1951, O 20,15:4
Carstens, Henry A, 1941, N 4,23:4
Carstensen, Andrew P, 1953, F 27,21:1
Carstensen, Gustav A, 1941, Je 27,17:4
Carstensen, Henry Sr, 1948, Jl 16,19:3
Carstensen, John, 1922, Ap 15,15:6
Carswell, Alexander Mrs, 1943, Ja 29,19:4
Carswell, David B, 1951, Mr 2,26:3
Carswell, James G, 1945, Ap 14,15:3
Carswell, John S, 1967, Mr 3,35:5
Carswell, Ronald, 1947, Ap 21,27:5
Carswell, William B, 1953, S 8,31:1
Carswell, William B Mrs, 1962, S 21,30:6
Carswell, William H, 1942, Ja 22,17:1
Carswell, William O, 1944, Mr 24,19:1
Cart, Francis G, 1938, D 4,60:5
Cart, Francis G Mrs, 1953, Mr 19,29:6
Cartalis, George, 1957, S 29,86:8
Carten, John L Jr, 1953, F 9,27:4
Carter, A E, 1882, Jl 10,5:6
Carter, A H Mrs, 1934, Ja 27,13:3
Carter, A P, 1903, N 21,9:6
Carter, Adeltha E Mrs, 1942, O 29,23:3
Carter, Alfred E, 1959, Ja 20,35:2
Carter, Alice, 1939, N 4,15:6
Carter, Allan J, 1949, Jl 3,27:2
Carter, Allan L Sr, 1944, N 26,57:1
Carter, Allen Mrs, 1944, Ap 2,15:4
Carter, Alva J, 1943, Ja 25,13:4
Carter, Amon G (funl plans, Je 25,15:6; funl, Je 26,-76:3), 1955, Je 24,21:3
Carter, Amon G (est appr), 1956, My 11,19:4
Carter, Andrew F, 1966, Ag 3,37:2
Carter, Anita, 1945, My 24,19:1
Carter, Anne, 1945, Je 26,19:5
Carter, Arthur (Nick), 1954, N 7,86:1
Carter, Arthur H, 1965, Ja 5,33:3
Carter, Ashby B, 1953, O 29,31:3
Carter, Augustus D (Ad), 1957, Je 26,31:2
Carter, B Frank Mrs, 1947, Je 9,21:5
Carter, Barbara B, 1951, S 7,29:2
Carter, Benjamin, 1906, N 11,9:6
Carter, Benjamin F, 1949, D 11,93:1
Carter, Bernard, 1912, Je 14,11:6
Carter, Bernard S, 1961, N 9,31:4
Carter, Blaine D, 1949, Ja 4,19:3
Carter, Boake, 1944, N 17,20:2
Carter, Charles, 1909, Mr 7,11:6; 1966, Ag 11,33:3
Carter, Charles C, 1937, D 31,16:1
Carter, Charles G Mrs, 1957, Jl 15,19:4
Carter, Charles H, 1950, F 5,84:4
Carter, Charles M, 1955, Ap 2,17:5
Carter, Charles S, 1958, N 10,29:1
Carter, Charles W, 1941, F 7,10:5; 1945, Ag 3,17:5; 1957, O 9,35:2
Carter, Charles W Mrs, 1941, F 7,10:5
Carter, Christopher R, 1925, D 8,25:5
Carter, Clarence E, 1961, S 12,33:4
Carter, Clarissa R Mrs, 1951, Ag 27,19:3
Carter, Clifford C, 1958, Ja 14,33:3
Carter, Clifton C, 1950, S 22,31:1; 1967, Ja 12,39:4
Carter, Clyde Mrs (D Harkins), 1963, S 2,15:5
Carter, D M, 1881, Jl 8,8:2
Carter, David P, 1942, D 25,17:5
Carter, David W, 1956, O 24,37:3
Carter, Desmond, 1939, F 4,15:4
Carter, Dewey J, 1950, S 14,31:4
Carter, Donald P Mrs, 1943, My 3,17:2
Carter, Donald W, 1948, N 21,88:3
Carter, Douglas S, 1957, O 21,25:2
Carter, E M, 1928, Ag 4,13:5
Carter, E Robert, 1955, Mr 11,25:1
Carter, Edmund C, 1949, Je 1,31:4
Carter, Edna, 1963, My 16,35:4
Carter, Edward C, 1919, Je 29,22:4
Carter, Edward C (cor, N 16,27:1), 1954, N 10,33:1
Carter, Edward C Mrs, 1943, Ap 19,19:1
Carter, Edward D, 1958, My 24,21:3
Carter, Edward G, 1946, N 1,23:4
Carter, Edward L, 1960, D 15,43:1
Carter, Edward P, 1955, Ag 3,23:5
Carter, Edward R, 1944, Je 10,15:4
Carter, Edward W, 1939, O 25,23:7
Carter, Edwin F, 1952, Ja 26,13:4
Carter, Elbert A, 1946, Ag 30,17:5
Carter, Elliott C, 1955, D 30,20:1
Carter, Ellis W, 1964, O 25,88:2
Carter, Emma B Mrs, 1953, N 23,27:1
Carter, Emma Downs, 1907, Je 29,7:6
Carter, Ernest F, 1958, Je 4,33:2
Carter, Ernest T (will, Jl 7,25:3), 1953, Je 22,21:3
Carter, Ernest T Mrs, 1952, Ja 1,25:5
Carter, Esther F (Mrs C W Carter Jr), 1966, Ap 30, 31:5
Carter, Eugene Mrs, 1957, O 13,86:6
Carter, Ex-Sen, 1911, S 18,11:5
Carter, Ferdinand S, 1940, Mr 19,25:3
Carter, Francis G, 1960, Je 17,31:4
Carter, Frank, 1920, My 11,9:4; 1937, N 24,23:4
Carter, Frank A, 1956, Ap 6,25:3
Carter, Frank L, 1955, Ap 20,33:3
Carter, Frank W, 1942, Jl 12,36:4
Carter, Franklin, 1919, N 23,22:3
Carter, Fred M, 1951, S 9,88:3
Carter, Frederic D, 1959, Ag 26,29:2
Carter, Frederick B Rev, 1924, N 15,13:5
Carter, Frederick G, 1956, F 21,33:2
Carter, Frederick H, 1945, Ap 5,23:5
Carter, Frederick M, 1943, N 16,23:3
Carter, G Frank, 1961, D 9,27:6
Carter, G Herbert, 1956, Mr 2,23:3
Carter, Gale H, 1951, D 6,33:6
Carter, George, 1942, D 30,23:3; 1945, My 5,16:2
Carter, George C, 1944, Ag 10,17:5; 1944, S 22,19:2; 1950, O 21,17:6
Carter, George H (por), 1948, O 24,76:1
Carter, George R Mrs, 1945, My 29,15:6
Carter, George Sir, 1922, F 10,15:4
Carter, Glenn D, 1951, Jl 18,29:3
Carter, Glenn O, 1964, Mr 22,76:6
Carter, Gordon, 1941, N 17,19:3
Carter, Grace D, 1948, Je 9,29:2
Carter, Hanson, 1948, Je 9,29:4
Carter, Harrison (Nick), 1943, O 25,15:6
Carter, Harry, 1956, Ja 25,31:1
Carter, Harry B, 1955, Jl 4,11:3
Carter, Harry L, 1960, Je 15,41:4
Carter, Harry W, 1937, D 4,3:2
Carter, Helen, 1940, D 23,38:1
Carter, Helene (Mrs H C Silvey), 1961, Ja 2,25:5
Carter, Henry, 1951, Je 21,27:4; 1961, O 26,35:2
Carter, Henry Dr, 1916, Jl 6,13:6
Carter, Henry E, 1943, D 6,23:5
Carter, Henry H, 1952, D 5,27:2
Carter, Henry K, 1952, Je 30,19:2
Carter, Henry R Dr, 1925, S 15,25:4
Carter, Herbert, 1914, Ja 19,9:6
Carter, Herbert S, 1945, Ag 9,21:1
Carter, Herbert S Jr, 1938, S 28,25:4
Carter, Homer W Jr, 1961, N 18,23:5
Carter, Horace A, 1959, My 3,87:1
Carter, Howard, 1939, Mr 3,23:1; 1946, Ja 18,19:4
Carter, Howard F, 1954, Ag 31,21:2
Carter, Hugh, 1950, D 27,27:3
Carter, Huntington T, 1946, Ap 26,22:3
Carter, J Frank, 1948, Jl 4,26:8
Carter, J Franklin, 1948, Ap 1,25:6
Carter, J G, 1954, Jl 22,23:3
Carter, J Madison, 1949, D 16,31:2
Carter, J Nelson, 1959, Je 1,27:2
Carter, J O, 1909, F 28,11:4
Carter, J Stanley, 1954, D 17,31:3
Carter, James, 1944, Ap 11,20:2
Carter, James A, 1940, D 31,15:4
Carter, James Coolidge, 1905, F 15,1:3
Carter, James H, 1944, Ja 7,17:3
Carter, James L Gen, 1919, F 17,13:2
Carter, James M, 1943, N 27,13:5
Carter, James N, 1925, Mr 7,13:6
Carter, James T Mrs, 1938, S 23,27:4
Carter, Jane W Mrs, 1962, Mr 11,87:1
Carter, Jennie Mrs, 1941, Ap 10,23:4
Carter, Jesse Benediet Dr, 1917, Jl 23,9:6
Carter, Jesse S, 1947, O 29,27:2
Carter, Jesse W, 1959, Mr 16,31:3
Carter, John, 1950, S 14,31:5
Carter, John Capt, 1910, O 27,11:4
Carter, John E Mrs, 1938, O 26,23:3
Carter, John F, 1967, N 29,47:1
Carter, John H, 1959, Jl 28,27:2
Carter, John J, 1939, D 10,68:4
Carter, John J Col, 1917, Ja 4,11:5
Carter, John M Mrs, 1957, Ap 21,88:5
Carter, John O Mrs, 1958, D 6,23:2
Carter, John P, 1955, O 23,86:7
Carter, John R, 1944, Je 4,41:1
Carter, John S, 1965, O 23,31:5
Carter, John S Mrs, 1950, Ag 11,19:3
Carter, John W, 1941, O 2,25:1; 1941, D 7,79:1
Carter, Joseph, 1948, Ap 11,72:4
Carter, Joseph A, 1959, Ap 4,19:5
Carter, Joseph H, 1954, My 25,27:4
Carter, Jule P, 1941, Ja 22,21:1
Carter, Larue D, 1946, Ja 23,27:5
Carter, Lawson Averell, 1925, Ja 24,13:5
Carter, LeRoy E, 1967, Mr 11,29:1
Carter, Leslie, 1908, S 26,7:6
Carter, Leslie Mrs, 1937, N 14,II,11:1
Carter, Lester W, 1960, Ja 19,36:1
Carter, Levi, 1903, N 8,7:7
Carter, Lewis S, 1944, F 4,15:3
Carter, Leyton E, 1953, N 18,31:4
Carter, Louis A, 1941, Je 16,15:4
Carter, Lt, 1875, Ja 1,2:5
Carter, Luke B, 1940, Jl 8,17:2
Carter, Lynwood Mrs, 1966, D 10,37:2
Carter, Lyon, 1950, S 21,31:3
Carter, Mabel O Mrs, 1963, S 18,39:1
Carter, Mabel W P Mrs, 1942, O 8,27:5
Carter, Madge P Mrs, 1959, N 9,31:4
Carter, Marguerite Mrs, 1907, S 27,9:5
Carter, Martha L Mrs, 1941, F 26,22:2
Carter, Mary A Mrs, 1944, D 19,21:5
Carter, Mary J Mrs, 1948, F 2,19:4
Carter, Mary W, 1945, Ja 3,17:5
Carter, Merville H, 1939, S 6,23:1
Carter, Milton, 1938, S 20,23:3
Carter, Mrs, 1881, Ja 21,2:2
Carter, Nelson P A Mrs, 1952, D 29,19:1
Carter, O S, 1901, Je 30,7:6
Carter, Oberlin M, 1944, Jl 20,19:2
Carter, Oliver G, 1937, Je 23,25:5
Carter, Oliver G Mrs, 1964, F 18,35:4
Carter, Paul S, 1944, Ja 30,38:3
Carter, Pheobe E Mrs, 1938, Ap 25,15:2
Carter, Phil W, 1951, Je 30,15:6
Carter, R Franklin, 1952, Ap 20,92:3
Carter, Ralph B Sr, 1961, Ag 23,33:4
Carter, Raymond L, 1950, O 18,33:3
Carter, Reginald L, 1950, D 19,29:2
Carter, Richard B, 1949, Je 9,31:2; 1950, Jl 6,27:2
Carter, Robert, 1918, Mr 1,11:5
Carter, Robert A (funl, F 7,17:5), 1924, F 5,23:4
Carter, Robert A Jr, 1943, Ap 4,44:1
Carter, Robert D Mrs, 1957, Mr 22,23:1
Carter, Robert E, 1959, Mr 20,31:3
Carter, Robert E Mrs, 1947, Ja 7,27:4
Carter, Robert L Sr, 1944, N 2,19:1
Carter, Roland Mrs, 1948, Ap 11,72:2
Carter, Roy Mrs, 1956, Ap 27,27:4
Carter, Russell, 1939, Ap 30,44:7; 1966, S 3,23:1
Carter, Russell J Mrs, 1963, My 25,25:5
Carter, Russell S, 1944, Mr 8,19:4
Carter, Russell S Mrs, 1964, Ja 13,35:4
Carter, Sally R, 1939, Je 25,37:3
Carter, Samuel T Jr, 1943, Mr 23,19:1
Carter, Samuel T Jr Mrs, 1966, D 24,19:6
Carter, Shirley, 1937, Ag 10,19:5; 1940, Je 21,21:4
Carter, Solon A, 1918, Ja 30,9:8
Carter, Steven V, 1959, N 5,35:5
Carter, Thomas Coke Bp, 1916, F 28,9:3
Carter, Thomas Francis Prof, 1925, Ag 7,15:7
Carter, Thomas I, 1951, D 19,31:4
Carter, Thomas Mrs, 1943, O 4,17:4
Carter, Vaulx Mrs, 1949, S 17,17:3
Carter, Walter C, 1963, Ag 30,21:3
Carter, Walter Steuben, 1904, Je 4,9:7
Carter, Weld S Mrs, 1963, Jl 22,23:5
Carter, Wesley E, 1950, Je 19,21:4
Carter, William, 1905, Ja 26,8:4; 1912, D 29,15:3; 1947, Ja 27,25:2; 1949, Jl 27,24:2; 1949, Ag 2,19:3
Carter, William D, 1937, S 3,17:4
Carter, William E, 1940, Mr 21,25:5; 1953, Ag 4,21:4
Carter, William E Rev, 1922, S 14,21:6
Carter, William G, 1956, N 6,35:1
Carter, William H, 1955, Ap 24,86:4
Carter, William H Ex-Sen, 1916, Ja 17,11:5
Carter, William H Gen, 1925, My 26,21:4
Carter, William H Mrs, 1955, Ja 20,31:6
Carter, William Hodding Sr, 1955, Ag 5,19:4
Carter, William J, 1941, O 25,17:3; 1943, F 8,20:3; 1946, Ag 7,27:4; 1947, Mr 26,25:3
Carter, William L, 1960, N 8,29:2
Carter, William L Mrs (will), 1937, D 8,28:4
Carter, William Mrs, 1956, Ap 9,27:4
Carter, William S, 1944, My 14,46:1
Carter, William Samuel, 1923, Mr 16,17:5
Carter, William T, 1951, N 13,29:5; 1955, D 22,23:5; 1963, Ag 1,27:5
Carter, William W, 1950, O 14,19:3
Carter, Woodward L, 1962, F 13,35:5
Carter, Zeta Mrs, 1964, Ag 3,25:4
Carter, Zina R, 1922, Ap 20,17:4
Carter-Rosenhauch, Edmund, 1959, O 30,27:3
Carteret, George, 1915, F 23,13:3
Cartey, John J Mrs, 1939, F 9,21:4
Carthy, Albert J Mrs, 1951, D 10,29:4
Carthy, William H, 1942, Ag 27,19:3
Cartier, Alfred, 1925, O 16,21:5
Cartier, Arthur J B, 1953, O 30,23:1
Cartier, G Thomas, 1938, Ja 20,23:5
Cartier, George E Sir (see also My 21), 1873, Je 14, 6:7
Cartier, George R, 1944, O 23,19:5

Cartier, Hortense, 1942, Ja 3,19:4
Cartier, J N, 1955, Jl 22,23:1
Cartier, Jacques, 1941, S 17,23:6
Cartier, Joseph A, 1952, O 15,31:3
Cartier, Julie Mrs (funl), 1906, N 19,6:2
Cartier, Louis J, 1942, Jl 24,19:5
Cartier, Louis J Mrs, 1952, Mr 30,92:4
Cartier, Michel N, 1937, Ag 16,19:5
Cartier, Pierre, 1941, D 18,27:4
Cartier, Pierre C, 1964, O 29,36:1
Cartier, Pierre Mrs, 1959, N 13,29:1
Cartier, Una F Mrs, 1961, Ag 3,23:4
Cartier de Marchienne, Baron de, 1946, My 11,27:5
Cartin, Joseph A, 1949, Ag 18,22:2
Cartinhour, Gaines T, 1949, S 29,34:3
Cartland, Donald L, 1964, Je 10,45:2
Cartledge, Charles F Mrs, 1918, N 5,13:6
Cartledge, J L, 1952, Ja 27,32:4
Cartledge, John, 1910, N 23,9:5
Cartlidge, Harold T, 1955, My 10,29:5
Cartmel, William B, 1940, D 8,68:4
Cartmell, James R, 1950, Ag 14,17:5
Cartmell, John R Sr, 1955, O 28,26:1
Cartmell, Levi, 1945, Ja 12,15:3
Cartmell, N Madison, 1961, Jl 20,27:2
Cartmell, Nate (Nathaniel J), 1967, Ag 24,37:4
Cartmell, Van H, 1922, Ag 24,15:5; 1966, O 31,35:1
Cartmell, William M, 1954, D 7,33:2
Cartnell, Charles, 1938, N 11,25:2
Carton, J R, 1881, S 10,2:5
Carton, James Sr, 1943, F 27,13:4
Carton, Joseph R Rev, 1916, Jl 17,11:5
Carton, Lawrence A, 1952, Je 15,84:1
Carton, Matthew A, 1941, Ja 26,36:6
Cartoon, Ethel G Mrs, 1940, Ja 4,23:2
Cartoon, Michael, 1944, Mr 25,15:4
Cartoon, Nathan, 1939, Ap 27,25:4
Cartotto, Ercole, 1946, O 4,23:2
Cartright, Hervey, 1953, Je 6,17:6
Cartter, Allan M, 1946, D 3,31:4
Cartwright, B Benton, 1947, F 9,63:4
Cartwright, Beatrice B Mrs, 1956, Ag 27,19:4
Cartwright, Ben, 1904, Jl 31,1:4
Cartwright, Charles M, 1951, N 30,23:4
Cartwright, Clermont C, 1967, O 9,47:1
Cartwright, Frank T Mrs, 1958, F 23,92:2
Cartwright, George S, 1959, Ja 18,88:3
Cartwright, Harry E, 1947, Je 8,60:4
Cartwright, Henry R Jr, 1941, N 21,17:3
Cartwright, Henry R Jr Mrs, 1955, Je 23,29:1
Cartwright, Hubert, 1963, Mr 26,9:5
Cartwright, Hubert J, 1958, Mr 7,23:3
Cartwright, James H, 1953, Ag 18,23:3
Cartwright, James H Justice, 1924, My 19,17:3
Cartwright, John A, 1953, O 29,31:3
Cartwright, John S, 1954, Mr 29,19:5
Cartwright, L Russell, 1959, My 7,33:5
Cartwright, L Russell Mrs, 1965, My 30,51:1
Cartwright, Oswald, 1957, Jl 12,21:3
Cartwright, Otho G, 1943, D 1,21:4
Cartwright, Peter Rev, 1872, S 27,5:2
Cartwright, Richard Lady, 1920, D 25,7:6
Cartwright, Richard S (funl, Jl 30,28:6), 1956, Jl 26, 25:4
Cartwright, Richard Sir, 1912, S 25,13:6
Cartwright, Robert H, 1915, Je 19,9:7
Carty, Arthur C Rev, 1937, N 30,23:4
Carty, Donald J, 1954, Ag 23,17:5
Carty, Felix, 1904, Ja 19,9:6
Carty, J J, 1932, D 28,17:1
Carty, James W, 1941, S 6,15:4
Carty, Jerome, 1908, D 31,9:6
Carty, John D, 1958, S 28,89:1
Carty, John R, 1949, Jl 13,27:3
Carty, Joseph C, 1958, Jl 19,15:7
Carty, Joseph G, 1968, Ag 14,43:3
Carty, May M, 1958, Ja 26,88:6
Carty, Patrick J, 1907, Je 16,7:6
Carty, Raymond, 1954, N 24,23:3
Carty, Thomas, 1960, Je 28,31:4
Carty, Thomas F, 1940, D 11,27:5
Carty, Thomas Mrs, 1958, Jl 22,27:2
Caruana, George J, 1951, Mr 27,29:3
Caruana, Maurus, 1943, D 18,15:4
Carus, Edward, 1947, Ag 17,52:6
Carus, Paul, 1919, F 15,11:4
Caruso, Ada G, 1946, O 18,23:3
Caruso, Benjamin O, 1950, D 22,24:3
Caruso, Charles G, 1965, O 11,39:3
Caruso, Clarence, 1945, Je 5,21:7
Caruso, Enrico Mrs (Dorothy), 1955, D 17,23:4
Caruso, Ernest Mrs, 1947, S 9,31:5
Caruso, Giovanni, 1940, Ag 13,19:4
Caruso, Joan, 1956, S 13,70:8
Caruso, Lucille, 1951, Ag 3,8:6
Caruso, Pasquale Mrs, 1961, N 10,35:1
Caruso, Phil, 1950, Jl 12,29:3
Caruso, Saverio S, 1952, D 2,36:6
Caruth, James L, 1948, D 24,18:4
Caruthers, Allen, 1941, Ja 25,15:4
Caruthers, Allen Jr, 1952, Ag 7,21:3
Caruthers, Allen Mrs, 1944, F 6,42:1
Caruthers, F Porter, 1952, My 26,23:2
Caruthers, Frank D, 1942, O 18,19:4
Caruthers, Frank D Jr, 1961, N 4,19:4
Carvajal, Arturo P, 1955, Ag 30,27:2
Carvajal, Federico H, 1952, F 6,29:5
Carvajal-Forero, Jose De, 1949, Ag 5,19:6
Carvalho, Bertram N Mrs, 1938, D 31,15:1
Carvalho, David Nunes, 1925, Je 30,19:5
Carvalho, Flora S de Mrs, 1963, N 28,39:3
Carvalho, Jacob S, 1937, Mr 14,II,8:4
Carvalho, John Bertram, 1968, My 16,48:1
Carvalho, Leon, 1897, D 30,7:2
Carvalho, S S Mrs, 1945, O 29,19:4
Carvalho, Sol S, 1942, Ap 13,15:3
Carvel, Arnold W, 1953, O 22,29:2
Carvel, Arnold W Mrs, 1947, Ja 19,53:3
Carvell, Frank B, 1924, Ag 11,13:6
Carven, Christopher C, 1960, Mr 12,21:6
Carver, Alex B, 1960, N 22,35:3
Carver, Allan B, 1949, D 23,22:4
Carver, Amos D, 1948, S 27,23:5
Carver, Amos D Mrs, 1947, Mr 23,60:8
Carver, Benjamin Mrs, 1948, Ag 24,23:5
Carver, Callie H, 1957, N 2,21:4
Carver, Charles C W, 1942, N 16,19:5
Carver, Clarence J, 1940, Ag 18,37:3
Carver, Clifford N, 1965, Mr 8,29:2
Carver, E Ross, 1956, My 31,27:5
Carver, George, 1949, O 31,25:6
Carver, George W (trb, Ja 10,12:3), 1943, Ja 6,25:1
Carver, Harry E Mrs, 1961, Je 19,27:2
Carver, Harry P, 1952, Mr 12,27:1
Carver, Hartwell Dr, 1875, Ap 19,4:7
Carver, Henrietta P Mrs, 1949, Jl 27,24:3
Carver, Hubert, 1951, Jl 21,18:2
Carver, Humphrey Mrs, 1948, Ja 19,23:4
Carver, J Ward, 1942, Jl 25,13:5
Carver, James, 1948, N 2,25:4
Carver, James Sr, 1950, Ja 24,32:6
Carver, John P, 1948, F 17,26:2
Carver, Leslie J, 1959, N 19,14:4
Carver, Louise, 1956, Ja 21,21:4
Carver, Lynne (Mrs W J Mullaney), 1955, Ag 13, 13:2
Carver, Philip, 1968, Je 3,45:2
Carver, Robert S, 1942, Ja 27,22:2
Carver, Thomas N, 1961, Mr 8,33:5
Carver, Walter B, 1961, Jl 6,29:2
Carver, Walter L, 1958, Ap 14,25:2
Carver, Walter L Mrs, 1966, D 5,45:4
Carver, William O, 1954, My 25,27:2
Carver, William Y, 1941, Jl 18,19:5
Carveth, Hector R Mrs, 1964, Ja 4,23:3
Carvey, Walter S, 1955, Je 15,31:4
Carvil, Joseph, 1960, Je 13,27:5
Carville, Arthur J, 1964, F 9,89:1
Carville, Edward P, 1956, Je 28,29:2
Carvin, Edward T Mrs, 1957, Jl 1,23:5
Carwell, Joseph, 1965, Ja 3,85:1
Carwin, Joseph L, 1964, Jl 1,35:6
Carwithen, Van Court Mrs, 1961, Je 17,21:5
Cary, A Claxton, 1909, Ja 12,9:6
Cary, Albert E Dr, 1937, Ag 5,23:4
Cary, Albert F, 1937, Mr 17,25:2
Cary, Alice, 1871, F 14,5:5; 1871, Ag 4,5:3
Cary, Annie Louise, 1921, Ap 4,13:1
Cary, Arthur J L, 1957, Mr 30,19:1
Cary, Benjamin H, 1917, F 22,11:4
Cary, Byron Plantagenet (Viscount Falkland), 1922, Ja 11,21:6
Cary, Byron Plantagenet Mrs (Viscountess Falkland), 1920, N 19,15:4
Cary, C P, 1943, Je 16,21:5
Cary, Chester H, 1953, D 25,17:5
Cary, Clarence Mrs, 1945, O 17,19:3
Cary, Cornelius J, 1954, Mr 23,27:5
Cary, E G, 1927, O 13,25:3
Cary, E L, 1936, Jl 14,19:1
Cary, Edward (por),(funl, My 25,11:1), 1917, My 24,13:1
Cary, Edward H, 1953, D 12,19:5
Cary, Edward K, 1954, Ag 5,23:4
Cary, Edward V Mrs, 1955, D 31,13:5
Cary, Eliza R, 1918, Ja 6,18:5
Cary, Eugene Judge, 1904, Mr 23,1:6
Cary, Frank Mrs, 1953, My 6,31:2
Cary, George, 1945, My 6,38:1
Cary, George F, 1943, Ag 27,17:6
Cary, George Walton Maj, 1909, Mr 17,9:3
Cary, Guy F, 1950, Ag 28,17:3
Cary, Guy F Mrs (will, D 31,24:4), 1966, D 19,37:6
Cary, Hamilton Wilkes, 1917, F 16,11:5
Cary, Harry F, 1938, My 10,21:4
Cary, Harry M, 1942, D 17,37:7
Cary, Henry A, 1947, O 9,25:1
Cary, Henry N, 1922, N 24,17:4
Cary, Henry N Mrs, 1958, Ja 23,27:4
Cary, Irving B, 1963, Jl 13,17:5
Cary, J C, 1884, Ag 8,5:2
Cary, Justus E, 1943, Jl 23,17:1
Cary, Kate (will, F 17,13:1), 1945, F 11,39:1
Cary, Leland C, 1941, Ag 15,17:1
Cary, Leland C Mrs, 1938, F 16,21:1
Cary, Lewis R, 1956, Jl 12,23:2
Cary, Lillian C Mrs, 1945, D 16,40:3
Cary, Melbert B, 1946, Mr 18,21:3
Cary, Melbert B Jr, 1941, My 29,19:3
Cary, Melbert B Jr Mrs (will), 1968, Ja 14,1:6
Cary, Melbert B Mrs, 1967, D 29,27:1
Cary, Nellie Bostwick, 1906, Ja 14,9:6
Cary, Otis Mrs, 1946, D 27,19:4
Cary, Phebe E Mrs, 1937, F 13,13:2
Cary, Phoebe, 1871, Ag 2,5:7
Cary, Robert, 1866, F 20,4:2
Cary, Robert W, 1967, Jl 17,29:4
Cary, Seward, 1948, S 7,25:1
Cary, Thomas F (funl, D 27,7:1), 1925, D 25,17:6
Cary, Trumbull, 1869, Je 26,5:2
Cary, Van Brunt, 1948, Jl 27,25:5
Cary, Wales L Mrs, 1944, Mr 22,19:3
Cary, Walter, 1937, Jl 4,II,6:6
Cary, William, 1901, O 19,1:4; 1946, N 1,23:3
Cary, William F Mrs, 1904, N 29,9:1
Cary, William H, 1951, O 6,19:5
Cary, William H Mrs, 1953, Ap 15,45:2
Cary, William N, 1924, O 23,21:4
Cary, William P, 1943, S 24,23:5
Cary-Barnard, Dudley P, 1961, Je 1,35:4
Caryl, Eliza J P Mrs, 1915, Ap 29,13:5
Caryl, William L, 1939, F 25,15:1
Caryll, Ivan, 1921, N 30,17:3
Caryll, Leonard H, 1955, Ag 7,73:2
Casabona, Anna, 1959, Ag 8,17:6
Casaccio, Ricardo, 1958, Ag 4,21:6
Casacona, Victor L, 1959, F 12,11:8
Casad, Campbell, 1952, Ap 24,32:3
Casad, Roland C, 1951, Ja 19,25:4
Casaday, Leroy B, 1950, F 7,27:2
Casadesus, Francis, 1954, Je 28,19:3
Casadesus, Henri, 1947, Je 1,60:2
Casadesus, Mathilde (Mrs G Richer), 1965, Ag 31, 33:3
Casado, Segismundo Col, 1968, D 19,47:4
Casady, Thomas Mrs, 1951, Ap 29,88:6
Casagrande, Stephen, 1961, O 9,35:2
Casalaspro, Michael J, 1958, S 16,27:3
Casale, Frank, 1967, F 14,43:2
Casale, James E, 1958, Jl 2,29:2
Casale, John B, 1948, Jl 10,15:3
Casale, Joseph, 1963, Je 13,33:4
Casals, Pablo Mrs, 1955, Ja 23,28:4
Casamassa, Angelo R, 1964, Ap 12,87:1
Casamassa, Vincent Mrs, 1962, Je 5,41:3
Casanas, Benjamin C, 1955, Ja 4,21:4
Casanas y Pages, Salvador Msgr, 1908, O 28,7:5
Casanave, Charles L, 1958, My 9,16:2
Casanave, Garganne, 1884, N 22,3:2
Casanova, Jose M, 1949, D 23,21:2
Casanova, Joseph A, 1966, Ap 4,24:8
Casanova, Mariano Rev, 1908, My 17,9:5
Casanova y Marzol, V, 1930, O 24,23:4
Casarella, Angela Mrs, 1955, Je 3,23:3
Casares Quiroga, Santiago, 1950, F 19,76:1
Casartelli, Louis Charles Bp, 1925, Ja 19,17:5
Casas, Jose J, 1951, O 9,29:3
Casassa, Frank D, 1921, S 22,17:6
Casasus, Joaquin D, 1916, F 27,17:5
Casati, Alessandro, 1955, Je 6,27:2
Casati, Capt, 1902, Mr 8,9:5
Casati, Ettore, 1945, Ag 16,19:3
Casavant, Gustave A, 1949, Jl 4,13:2
Casavis, Jack, 1967, My 5,39:3
Casazza, Albert, 1960, S 25,88:3
Casazza, Charles, 1951, D 20,31:3
Casazza, John W, 1947, Ag 26,23:2
Casazza, Lawrence, 1954, S 21,27:3
Cascales, Joe L, 1946, Je 23,40:3
Cascales, John (Johnny Richards), 1968, O 9,47:
Casci, Paul, 1956, Ap 24,31:4
Casciano, Peter Mrs, 1951, N 11,90:6
Cascioli, Edward M J, 1946, Ap 2,27:4
Case, Adelaide McA, 1967, Ja 12,39:3
Case, Adelaide T, 1948, Je 20,62:1
Case, Albert Clark, 1918, Ja 12,11:4
Case, Albert Willard, 1925, D 23,19:3
Case, Anna, 1938, Jl 20,19:4
Case, Archibald, 1916, Ag 27,17:5
Case, Arthur E, 1946, Ja 21,23:4
Case, Brayton C, 1944, Ag 1,15:2
Case, Charles E, 1947, N 22,15:2
Case, Charles J Mrs, 1937, O 11,21:4
Case, Charles L, 1955, F 11,23:2
Case, Charles Z, 1965, S 10,35:3
Case, Chester H, 1968, My 30,25:1
Case, Clarence E, 1961, S 4,15:1
Case, Clarence E Mrs, 1959, Jl 7,33:5
Case, Clifford P Sr Mrs, 1968, O 28,47:3
Case, Clifford Phillip Dr, 1920, Mr 9,11:1
Case, Clinton P, 1937, Je 14,23:5
Case, David B, 1941, Ag 6,17:3
Case, David K Maj, 1908, Ap 22,9:5
Case, Dean J, 1951, Ap 4,29:4
Case, Eckstein, 1944, D 21,21:2
Case, Edward R, 1949, Jl 14,27:2
Case, Egbert D, 1968, D 7,47:1
Case, Elisha W, 1912, Ap 7,15:3
Case, Elizabeth E, 1951, Ja 24,27:4

Case, Elliot P, 1950, Ja 10,29:1
Case, Elmer E, 1951, S 2,49:1
Case, Ermine C Mrs, 1923, My 24,19:6
Case, Eugene A, 1952, Ap 22,29:2
Case, Everett (will, My 8, V,4:8), 1966, My 1,87:4
Case, Francis (mem ser, Je 25,29:4; trb, Jl 26,27:3), 1962, Je 23,23:2
Case, Frank, 1946, Je 8,21:1
Case, Frank D, 1937, D 1,48:1
Case, Frank M, 1948, Je 28,19:3
Case, Frank Mrs, 1946, F 22,25:1
Case, Gabe, 1904, Je 2,9:5
Case, George B, 1945, Ag 27,19:3; 1955, Jl 20,27:1
Case, George J, 1961, D 2,23:3
Case, George M, 1941, D 14,68:4
Case, George S, 1950, O 12,31:2
Case, Harold C M, 1966, Ja 10,25:5
Case, Harry N, 1956, My 26,17:4
Case, Helen S Mrs, 1939, O 20,23:4
Case, Henry G, 1950, O 8,104:7
Case, Henry J, 1924, S 1,13:4; 1940, F 19,17:4
Case, Henry J Mrs, 1966, S 24,23:4
Case, Henry P, 1938, D 1,23:4
Case, Herbert L Mrs, 1959, Ag 15,17:6
Case, Herbert M, 1941, Ap 2,23:3
Case, Howard G, 1943, Ag 7,11:6
Case, Howard M, 1952, Ja 23,27:5
Case, J Edsal, 1959, S 24,37:2
Case, J Herbert Mrs, 1957, O 8,36:1
Case, J Russell, 1953, S 17,29:5
Case, James D, 1961, Mr 12,77:6
Case, James H Jr, 1965, Jl 13,33:1
Case, James T, 1960, My 25,39:5
Case, Jess A, 1955, Ja 28,20:1
Case, John A Mrs, 1947, Jl 20,44:3
Case, John C Mrs, 1962, O 24,39:1
Case, John F, 1946, D 21,19:5
Case, John P, 1961, Je 15,43:4
Case, John W, 1937, S 12,II,7:4
Case, Joseph D, 1944, Ja 1,13:1
Case, Joseph H T, 1941, Ag 12,19:5
Case, Joseph S, 1911, Ja 7,9:5
Case, L U, 1948, S 12,74:2
Case, Lawrence W, 1944, F 18,17:1
Case, Leon D, 1939, Jl 7,17:5
Case, Leonard, 1880, Ja 7,4:7
Case, Leslie V Dr, 1937, Jl 19,15:2
Case, Lloyd B, 1967, F 17,37:2
Case, Louis M, 1955, Ap 14,29:4
Case, Mary S, 1953, F 2,21:5
Case, Mason N, 1948, Jl 15,23:2
Case, Maurice Dr, 1968, My 4,39:4
Case, Mills E, 1948, My 15,15:2
Case, Montgomery B, 1953, My 9,19:2
Case, Montgomery B Mrs, 1945, O 5,23:5
Case, Peter V Mrs, 1949, Mr 10,27:4
Case, Peter V N, 1925, Ag 6,19:6
Case, Porter J, 1952, S 12,21:2
Case, R L, 1880, F 26,5:2
Case, Ralph E, 1942, Jl 26,30:7
Case, Robert D, 1944, My 31,19:5; 1946, My 20,24:2
Case, Rogers, 1954, Ap 29,31:5
Case, Rolland A, 1947, My 26,21:4
Case, Rolland W, 1957, D 19,31:4
Case, Russell, 1964, O 11,88:6
Case, Sackett L Mrs, 1953, Je 24,25:5
Case, Samuel B, 1949, D 28,32:3
Case, Samuel P, 1948, Ag 12,21:1
Case, Shindel G, 1940, Jl 18,19:4
Case, Shirley J, 1947, D 7,76:1
Case, Stephen, 1945, O 23,17:5; 1955, Je 18,17:5
Case, Theodore W, 1944, My 14,46:5
Case, W Clifford, 1950, D 23,16:2
Case, W E, 1903, Mr 15,7:5
Case, Walter S Mrs, 1966, F 20,88:4
Case, Wesley R Jr, 1950, N 10,27:5
Case, Willard E, 1918, O 28,11:2
Case, Willard E Mrs, 1952, Ja 28,17:5
Case, Willard L, 1958, S 23,33:2
Case, William, 1939, Je 23,15:7
Case, William C, 1946, Ap 22,21:1
Case, William H Mrs, 1952, Je 19,27:2
Case, William L, 1941, Jl 4,15:1
Case, William Scoville, 1921, Mr 1,13:4
Case, William W Rev Dr, 1915, Je 1,15:7
Casebolt, George H Mrs, 1955, Mr 6,88:3
Caseley, Lester S, 1947, F 20,25:4
Casella, Georges, 1922, My 22,15:6
Casella, John, 1945, Ja 9,19:1
Caselton, Gartner W, 1958, Je 21,19:1
Casement, Dan D, 1953, Mr 8,91:1
Casement, James S Gen, 1909, D 14,11:4
Casenove, Henri, 1941, Ja 29,17:2
Caser, Ettore, 1944, Mr 1,19:5
Caserio, Domenick, 1952, Ap 12,11:6
Caserta, Count of, 1934, My 27,28:3
Casertano, Antonio, 1939, D 14,27:4
Casety, Mary Z Mrs, 1946, Ap 30,21:4
Casey, Alphonsus B Mrs, 1960, Ap 11,32:1
Casey, Alphonsus L, 1956, S 8,17:3
Casey, Amedee J, 1950, O 13,29:4
Casey, Austen E, 1964, Ja 3,24:1
Casey, Charles Mrs, 1957, O 20,86:7
Casey, Charles R, 1942, Jl 7,19:4
Casey, Chris C, 1942, Jl 27,15:6
Casey, Clare M, 1959, Ap 19,86:6
Casey, Cyril A, 1943, My 23,43:2
Casey, Daniel, 1951, Jl 4,17:4
Casey, Daniel M, 1943, F 10,25:3
Casey, Daniel M Mrs, 1960, F 4,31:3
Casey, Daniel Mrs, 1943, N 12,21:3
Casey, Daniel V, 1943, S 14,23:5
Casey, Dora (Sister Rita Agnes), 1960, Mr 23,37:1
Casey, Edward B, 1960, Ag 3,29:4
Casey, Edward C, 1940, Mr 12,23:4
Casey, Edward L, 1966, Jl 28,33:3
Casey, Edward P (will, Ja 11,21:2), 1940, Ja 3,21:3
Casey, Edward P Mrs, 1955, My 14,19:2
Casey, Eugene C, 1937, My 11,25:4
Casey, Eugene D, 1965, F 27,25:5
Casey, Eugene R, 1964, Ja 10,43:2
Casey, Francis H, 1953, D 10,47:2
Casey, Frank D, 1944, D 19,21:3
Casey, Frank J, 1964, D 28,29:4
Casey, Frank P, 1950, S 15,26:4
Casey, G Rhoads Sr, 1964, Je 11,33:4
Casey, Gavin S, 1964, Je 27,25:5
Casey, George A, 1951, Ag 29,25:2; 1960, Jl 9,19:5
Casey, George A Mrs, 1959, Ja 1,31:2
Casey, George J, 1963, Jl 6,15:2
Casey, George W, 1949, O 1,13:5; 1955, F 12,15:1
Casey, Gerald P, 1945, Ap 20,19:4
Casey, Grant, 1940, D 25,27:2
Casey, Harry V, 1951, F 24,13:3
Casey, Hugh J, 1961, Ap 18,37:4
Casey, J Schuyler Mrs, 1938, Jl 27,17:2
Casey, James A, 1950, Je 14,31:4
Casey, James B, 1946, D 29,35:5
Casey, James B Mrs, 1957, Je 3,27:6
Casey, James F, 1940, N 20,21:1; 1950, F 12,84:1
Casey, James F (Nixey), 1954, Mr 17,31:3
Casey, James F, 1964, Mr 23,29:4
Casey, James G, 1948, Mr 7,69:1
Casey, James G Mrs, 1954, N 2,27:6
Casey, James H, 1937, D 25,15:3
Casey, James P, 1946, D 10,31:2; 1959, My 6,39:1
Casey, James P Mrs, 1955, Jl 20,27:4
Casey, Jeremiah, 1941, F 22,15:1
Casey, John, 1942, D 30,23:3; 1944, My 7,45:2; 1948, Mr 19,25:5
Casey, John F, 1948, N 8,21:5
Casey, John F Dr, 1952, Mr 7,23:3
Casey, John F Jr, 1962, D 8,27:4
Casey, John F Jr Mrs, 1952, Ap 5,15:2
Casey, John F Sr, 1941, O 8,23:3
Casey, John F Sr Mrs, 1954, O 7,23:2
Casey, John J, 1945, O 19,23:2; 1953, N 16,25:6
Casey, John M, 1959, O 24,21:4
Casey, John P, 1945, O 23,17:3
Casey, John S, 1948, D 3,25:1
Casey, John T, 1947, Jl 26,13:7; 1968, My 17,44:1
Casey, Joseph C Mrs, 1920, Jl 24,9:6
Casey, Joseph D, 1952, Ag 15,16:4
Casey, Joseph F, 1915, N 30,13:5
Casey, Joseph G, 1956, Ap 2,23:3
Casey, Joseph P, 1943, O 14,22:2
Casey, Josephine, 1922, F 27,13:6
Casey, Kellogg K V (por), 1938, O 20,23:2
Casey, Kenneth, 1965, Ag 11,35:3
Casey, Lawrence J Sr, 1952, Je 25,29:2
Casey, Lee T, 1951, Ja 30,25:5
Casey, Leo, 1960, My 24,37:2
Casey, Leo D, 1954, Ag 14,7:2
Casey, Leo Mrs, 1948, My 5,25:3
Casey, Leslie J, 1942, F 19,19:6
Casey, Mary C Mrs, 1943, O 25,15:4
Casey, Michael, 1937, My 3,19:3
Casey, Michael J, 1940, Ag 7,19:2
Casey, Michael T, 1938, Ag 29,13:5
Casey, O R, 1936, N 29,II,9:1
Casey, P J, 1927, O 2,II,9:1
Casey, P J Mrs, 1952, Ja 12,13:5
Casey, Pat, 1962, F 8,31:2
Casey, Patrick, 1941, Ap 26,15:4; 1952, Jl 11,17:2
Casey, Patrick F, 1943, S 18,17:6
Casey, Patrick H, 1941, N 7,23:4
Casey, Patrick J, 1939, S 20,27:5
Casey, Patrick M, 1951, Mr 31,15:1
Casey, Phil, 1904, Jl 13,7:6
Casey, Philip J, 1964, O 3,29:4
Casey, Raymond, 1937, S 23,27:3
Casey, Rita Mrs, 1950, Ja 17,27:3
Casey, Robert J, 1962, D 5,47:2
Casey, Robert J Mrs, 1945, Ja 11,23:5
Casey, Samuel K, 1939, S 13,25:5
Casey, Silas, 1882, Ja 23,5:4
Casey, Silas Rear-Adm, 1913, Ag 15,7:6
Casey, Stephen J, 1948, S 18,17:2
Casey, T, 1931, O 6,27:1
Casey, T L Gen, 1896, Mr 26,1:3
Casey, Terrence F, 1939, Je 4,48:6
Casey, Thomas, 1954, D 31,13:4
Casey, Thomas B, 1937, Ja 21,24:1
Casey, Thomas F, 1944, Mr 28,19:2
Casey, Thomas L Col, 1925, F 4,21:4
Casey, Thomas Mrs, 1949, Mr 24,28:3
Casey, Thomas P, 1949, D 11,92:4
Casey, Thomas S, 1944, My 20,15:1
Casey, Thomas W, 1954, N 11,31:2
Casey, Timothy E, 1943, Mr 12,17:2
Casey, Victor J, 1947, My 28,25:3
Casey, Vincent H, 1959, N 2,31:2
Casey, Walter J, 1952, N 19,29:3
Casey, William C, 1938, D 16,25:2
Casey, William D, 1939, Ja 12,19:5
Casey, William F, 1957, Ap 22,25:3
Casey, William J, 1937, Ja 12,23:2; 1954, F 27,13:2
Casey, William L, 1955, F 11,23:1
Casey, William P, 1938, Ag 15,15:5
Casey, Winifred A Mrs, 1942, D 4,25:4
Casgrain, A Chase, 1941, O 28,23:4
Casgrain, Joseph P B, 1939, Ja 7,15:3
Casgrain, Pierre, 1950, Ag 27,89:2
Casgrain, Thomas, 1916, D 30,9:4
Cash, Albert D, 1952, Ag 4,16:3
Cash, Frank I, 1947, O 9,25:2
Cash, Harold S, 1946, Ap 25,21:4
Cash, Herbert B, 1944, Mr 18,13:2
Cash, James J Sr, 1949, S 9,26:4
Cash, James W, 1950, Ja 21,17:1
Cash, Joe, 1967, Jl 15,25:1
Cash, John A, 1950, F 26,77:1
Cash, John E, 1965, My 20,43:4
Cash, Milton H, 1958, O 29,35:4
Cash, O C, 1953, Ag 17,15:2
Cash, Preston J, 1965, Ag 21,21:6
Cash, Reginald J, 1959, Mr 14,23:3
Cash, Sherman A, 1940, D 20,25:4
Cash, Tim, 1967, Jl 31,34:8
Cash, William T Mrs, 1947, N 19,27:4
Cash, William W, 1955, Jl 19,27:5
Cashal, Francis J, 1948, Mr 5,21:5
Cashal, Michael J, 1951, Ag 21,27:1
Cashal, Michael J Jr, 1942, Jl 21,19:3
Cashan, Nicholas Sr, 1948, S 10,23:4
Cashdan, Isadore, 1948, S 22,31:2
Cashel, William S, 1966, O 29,29:5
Cashen, Eleanor R, 1947, F 28,24:2
Cashen, James A 3d, 1959, O 21,43:2
Cashen, John C Capt, 1875, Mr 13,10:5
Cashen, John F, 1943, O 7,23:2
Cashen, Michael J, 1954, N 10,33:2
Casher, Izadore, 1948, Ap 16,23:3
Cashin, Daniel J, 1948, Mr 19,23:1
Cashin, Daniel J Mrs, 1943, Ag 16,15:3
Cashin, Denis B, 1950, D 18,31:3
Cashin, Harrell T, 1949, Ja 12,27:2
Cashin, Harry F, 1962, Ap 28,25:2
Cashin, J Vincent, 1942, O 20,21:3
Cashin, James F, 1959, F 23,23:4
Cashin, John Mrs, 1945, Ap 3,19:1
Cashin, Joseph A (Bro Angelus Gabriel), 1958, S 12, 25:1
Cashin, Josie, 1943, Jl 16,17:1
Cashin, Martin J, 1946, D 14,15:5
Cashin, Mary, 1943, Jl 16,17:1
Cashin, Mary A, 1937, Je 21,19:2
Cashin, Michael A Mrs, 1954, D 31,13:3
Cashin, Michael P Sir, 1926, Ag 31,17:2
Cashin, Thomas F Sr, 1940, My 24,19:5
Cashin, Thomas P, 1951, S 7,29:4
Cashin, Vincent A, 1960, O 24,29:4
Cashin, William D, 1944, Jl 12,19:5
Cashin, William E, 1945, Ja 18,19:1
Cashion, Edward H, 1949, My 2,25:5
Cashman, Bender Z, 1948, O 9,19:1
Cashman, Benjamin, 1938, Ja 8,15:5
Cashman, Daniel F, 1941, Ja 31,19:3
Cashman, Earl W, 1959, Ag 5,27:5
Cashman, Francis J, 1953, O 2,21:4
Cashman, John, 1946, Je 7,19:1
Cashman, John F, 1940, Ag 4,32:8
Cashman, John J, 1948, O 13,25:5; 1953, D 14,31:6
Cashman, Joseph, 1962, F 16,29:3
Cashman, Joseph F, 1961, F 21,35:4
Cashman, Louis, 1953, Ap 3,24:6
Cashman, Louis P Sr, 1961, N 6,37:2
Cashman, Michael, 1945, Je 6,21:3
Cashman, Michael J, 1947, Ja 28,23:3
Cashman, Nellie, 1925, Ja 8,25:4
Cashman, Sol H, 1951, My 13,89:1
Cashman, Thomas J, 1941, Je 29,32:6
Cashman, Timothy D, 1951, Ap 10,27:3
Cashman, William S, 1951, Ja 27,13:3
Cashmore, Arthur D, 1951, O 11,37:5
Cashmore, C Ernest Sr, 1946, N 16,19:5
Cashmore, Harry, 1952, O 26,89:1
Cashmore, Howard A, 1948, My 5,25:2
Cashmore, John (funl plans, My 9,27:4; funl, My 12,29:2), 1961, My 8,1:2
Casiglia, Arturo, 1954, D 23,19:4
Casimir, Perier M (see also Jl 7), 1876, Jl 20,4:6
Casimir-Perier, Auguste Mrs, 1907, Mr 30,9:7
Casimir-Perier, Jean Paul Pierre, 1907, Mr 13,9:6
Casimir-Perier, Jean Paul Pierre Mrs, 1912, Mr 4,11:6
Casino, Patrick, 1939, F 28,19:2
Casiraghi, Gilbert A, 1949, O 1,13:5
Caskey, Alvin D, 1958, O 24,33:1
Caskey, James S, 1958, My 18,86:2

Caskey, John F, 1961, My 29,19:2
Caskey, Lacey D, 1944, My 23,23:3
Caskey, Wayne F, 1964, S 1,35:3
Caskie, John J K, 1949, Ap 22,24:8
Caskie, Malcolm D, 1948, S 21,28:3
Caskie, Marion M, 1966, N 5,31:3
Caskin, Lida Pickett Mrs, 1907, D 16,9:4
Casko, Stephen F, 1961, O 14,23:3
Casler, C Avery, 1952, D 20,17:3
Casler, Herman, 1939, Jl 22,15:5
Casler, Melvin D, 1937, Ja 29,19:1
Casley, William Mrs, 1953, Jl 17,17:3
Casner, Barry S, 1962, Ap 6,35:1
Casner, Frederick, 1947, D 17,29:4
Casner, Lloyd, 1965, Ap 11,V,1:6
Casnin, J Harold, 1948, N 23,29:3
Caso, Antonio, 1946, Mr 8,21:2
Caso, Dominick, 1954, N 15,27:2
Caso, Joaquin Dr, 1923, Jl 17,19:5
Cason, Charles C (Sept 30), 1965, O 11,61:1
Cason, Julsey, 1951, My 1,29:4
Caspar, Charles J, 1951, D 10,29:5
Caspar, Frank Mrs, 1962, Ja 4,34:1
Caspar, Frederick C Mrs, 1947, O 28,25:2
Casparian, Harry, 1965, Ag 1,77:1
Casparis, Horton R, 1942, N 13,23:3
Caspary, Alfred H (will, Ja 18,24:5), 1955, Ja 9,86:6
Caspe, Maurice (por), 1948, S 2,23:4
Casper, Arthur, 1946, O 15,26:3
Casper, Casper V, 1956, Ag 2,25:1
Casper, Cy (Chas Casper), 1968, Mr 9,29:2
Casper, Edward A, 1962, S 5,39:2
Casper, Edward J, 1949, Mr 18,25:1
Casper, Franklin J (will), 1945, My 30,21:7
Casper, Leopold, 1959, Mr 19,33:2
Casper, Louis, 1959, Jl 2,25:2
Casper, Louis Mrs, 1946, N 6,23:4
Casper, M W, 1903, Je 3,9:6
Casper, Sidney J, 1964, O 22,35:3
Casper, William F, 1947, O 19,66:4
Casper, William R Mrs, 1907, Ja 29,9:6
Casperfield, James D, 1925, My 19,21:3
Casperl, Charles Jr Dr, 1917, O 15,13:4
Casriel, Gertrude, 1948, Ja 26,19:2
Cass, A C, 1903, Jl 6,2:3
Cass, Abraham, 1905, Je 5,9:7
Cass, Allan L Mrs, 1953, D 26,13:1
Cass, Alvin C, 1950, Mr 10,27:2
Cass, Charles A, 1958, Ap 25,27:2
Cass, Charles A Mrs, 1958, N 25,33:4
Cass, Charles W, 1947, F 15,15:5
Cass, Chauncey S, 1942, F 13,5:2
Cass, Claude B, 1944, Jl 24,15:6
Cass, Clinton D, 1944, Jl 28,13:1
Cass, George W Mrs, 1903, D 6,7:6
Cass, Harry, 1962, S 2,57:1
Cass, James M, 1945, Mr 10,17:3
Cass, Joseph K, 1938, N 2,23:4
Cass, Josiah E, 1947, D 3,30:2
Cass, Kate L Mrs, 1950, F 3,23:4
Cass, Lewis Gen, 1866, Je 18,4:5
Cass, Martin J, 1956, S 15,17:2
Cass, Mary A, 1940, S 19,23:5
Cass, Maurice S, 1940, Mr 6,23:5
Cass, Newton R Mrs, 1953, My 10,88:2
Cass, Paul, 1904, Ja 23,9:5
Cass, Phil, 1956, D 5,39:2
Cass, Raymond J, 1955, F 10,31:3
Cass, Richard L, 1948, O 23,15:2
Cass, Saint George W, 1873, Ag 9,5:3
Cassa, Chidane-Maryam, 1951, S 5,31:5
Cassa, M George, 1942, Je 5,17:5
Cassado, Gaspar, 1966, D 27,35:3
Cassady, Frank A Mrs, 1953, Ap 30,31:4
Cassady, John H Mrs, 1958, D 10,39:1
Cassady, Maynard L, 1948, O 25,24:2
Cassagnac, Paul de, 1904, N 5,5:5
Cassano, William J, 1966, S 3,23:2
Cassara, Sylvester, 1952, S 27,17:2
Cassard, Herbert, 1904, O 5,9:6
Cassard, Morris Jr, 1968, F 2,35:3
Cassard, William G, 1919, Je 30,11:3
Cassard, William J Jr, 1942, S 1,19:4
Cassasa, Charles S B, 1943, F 23,21:2
Cassatt, Alexander J, 1907, Ja 1,9:4
Cassatt, Alexander Johnson Mrs, 1920, Ja 10,11:4
Cassatt, Alexander Johnston, 1906, D 29,1:3
Cassatt, Edward Buchanan Col, 1922, F 1,19:4
Cassatt, Gardner, 1911, Ap 7,13:4; 1955, S 10,17:2
Cassatt, M, 1926, Je 16,25:3
Cassatt, Robert K, 1944, S 19,21:2
Cassavant, Charles H Mrs, 1938, Ja 18,23:2
Casscles, Elizabeth V, 1950, N 11,15:4
Casscles, Joshua Mrs, 1947, My 21,25:6
Casse, Alfred J Col, 1910, N 22,11:4
Cassebeer, Frederick, 1915, Ag 21,7:6
Cassebeer, Henry A, 1921, Jl 28,13:4; 1941, D 30,20:2
Cassebeer, Theodore, 1941, O 13,17:6
Casseboom, Frank O, 1956, D 27,25:1
Cassedy, J Townsend, 1946, My 22,21:3
Cassedy, Pierce A, 1949, Ag 9,25:5
Cassel, Ernest Sir, 1921, S 23,15:5
Cassel, George, 1945, Mr 20,19:5
Cassel, Gustav, 1945, Ja 16,19:1
Cassel, Helen, 1947, O 8,25:2
Cassel, Milton E Mrs (Rita Allen), 1968, Jl 4,19:1
Cassel, Morris Mrs, 1937, O 13,23:5
Cassel, Samuel, 1940, Je 12,25:6
Cassel, Samuel S, 1943, Jl 20,19:4
Casselberry, Raymond C, 1954, Ap 21,29:1
Cassell, Clement C, 1939, N 4,15:6
Cassell, George C, 1958, Ag 30,15:5
Cassell, James W, 1939, N 5,49:3
Cassell, Matthew E, 1951, Ag 17,17:5
Cassell, Norman W, 1941, D 23,21:3
Casselli, Patrick J, 1949, My 12,31:2
Casselman, Elbridge J, 1965, N 1,41:1
Casselman, F C, 1941, Mr 22,15:3
Casselman, Theodore E, 1953, N 12,31:3
Casselman, William Jr, 1950, S 22,31:3
Casselmann, Frederick, 1947, Mr 28,23:2
Cassels, Edwin H, 1947, Jl 9,23:2
Cassels, Robert, 1942, Jl 5,30:2; 1959, D 25,21:3
Cassels, Robert C H, 1957, N 23,19:6
Cassen, John J, 1944, D 13,23:2
Casserly, Eugene, 1883, Je 15,5:4
Casserly, Henry L, 1958, O 21,33:4
Casserly, John B Mrs, 1954, My 12,31:5
Casserly, Michael, 1966, D 13,47:4
Casserly, Thomas F Mrs, 1946, Ja 18,19:3
Cassese, John J Mrs, 1966, Mr 19,29:4
Cassese, Philip Mrs, 1945, Mr 20,11:6
Cassett, Louis N, 1950, Mr 25,11:7
Cassetta, Cardinal, 1919, Mr 24,13:3
Cassibry, Reginald E Jr, 1955, Ap 7,27:4
Cassidy, Alice, 1953, N 10,31:5
Cassidy, Bernard F Mrs, 1953, S 11,21:3
Cassidy, Bert A, 1950, Ja 22,78:1
Cassidy, Dennis A, 1946, Jl 6,15:5
Cassidy, Donald J, 1953, N 26,31:1
Cassidy, Edward F, 1937, N 20,17:3
Cassidy, Edward J, 1942, N 15,56:3
Cassidy, Edward V, 1944, D 19,21:5
Cassidy, Edwin E, 1945, N 20,21:4
Cassidy, Eugene Rev, 1876, D 2,8:4
Cassidy, Francis, 1873, Je 17,1:4
Cassidy, Francis J, 1941, N 15,17:2; 1960, Je 20,31:4; 1967, My 4,39:2
Cassidy, Frank L, 1963, Jl 25,25:1
Cassidy, G, 1934, F 13,19:5
Cassidy, George G, 1946, Ap 7,46:2
Cassidy, George J, 1962, My 7,31:4
Cassidy, George L, 1962, O 15,29:4
Cassidy, George Sr, 1961, Mr 11,21:5
Cassidy, George W, 1941, Mr 17,17:3; 1955, Je 20,21:4
Cassidy, Harold H, 1956, N 20,37:5; 1962, O 9,41:4
Cassidy, Harry, 1958, Ja 14,30:4
Cassidy, Harry E, 1962, N 16,31:4
Cassidy, Holland M, 1943, N 16,23:2
Cassidy, James A, 1953, Jl 11,11:6
Cassidy, James B, 1952, Ag 4,15:4
Cassidy, James E, 1951, My 18,27:2
Cassidy, James J, 1949, Ag 4,23:5
Cassidy, James T, 1948, Jl 31,15:5
Cassidy, James W, 1919, Jl 17,13:4
Cassidy, John, 1909, My 19,9:5; 1911, Je 22,11:3; 1940, N 21,29:4
Cassidy, John F, 1955, Ag 27,15:6
Cassidy, John F Mrs, 1942, Ja 11,44:1
Cassidy, John J, 1946, Ap 1,27:5; 1953, Jl 22,27:2
Cassidy, John M, 1941, Ag 24,35:3
Cassidy, John Sr, 1959, Mr 18,38:1
Cassidy, Joseph, 1912, O 15,15:4
Cassidy, Joseph (funl, N 25,15:5), 1920, N 22,15:3
Cassidy, Joseph, 1951, Je 27,29:5
Cassidy, Joseph F, 1956, O 11,39:4
Cassidy, Joseph H, 1961, Je 11,87:1
Cassidy, Joseph Mrs, 1948, Ap 2,24:2
Cassidy, Joseph T, 1942, My 11,15:6
Cassidy, Laurence L, 1960, My 5,35:1
Cassidy, Leslie M, 1967, F 9,39:3
Cassidy, Lewis C, 1949, F 7,19:5
Cassidy, Marshall, 1968, O 24,47:1
Cassidy, Matthew P, 1940, F 6,22:2
Cassidy, Maurice, 1949, O 23,84:3
Cassidy, Morley F, 1968, S 17,47:2
Cassidy, Owen, 1911, Ja 16,11:4
Cassidy, Patrick, 1945, Mr 10,17:6
Cassidy, Robert S Mrs, 1945, N 23,23:1
Cassidy, Thomas A, 1962, Je 28,31:4
Cassidy, Thomas F, 1941, S 4,21:2
Cassidy, Thomas J, 1940, S 29,43:2; 1942, Ja 16,21:3
Cassidy, Thomas P, 1960, F 24,37:1
Cassidy, W J, 1938, N 12,30:2
Cassidy, Wendell P, 1959, Ag 12,29:3
Cassidy, William, 1873, Ja 24,1:4
Cassidy, William P, 1938, Ap 22,19:1
Cassidy, William Rochefort, 1916, F 10,11:4
Cassill, Harold E, 1957, Ag 3,15:6
Cassils, Angus S, 1939, Je 2,23:5
Cassin, Edward, 1954, Jl 19,19:6
Cassin, John, 1869, Ja 14,5:5
Cassin, Morris, 1954, Jl 18,57:1
Cassini, Igor Mrs (mass, Ap 11,15:1; ruling, Ap 16,38:2), 1963, Ap 10,18:1
Cassini, Marguerite, 1961, S 26,39:2
Cassini, Michael Count, 1913, My 10,11:5
Cassinis, Gino, 1964, Ja 14,31:2
Cassino, Anthony, 1943, Jl 13,21:3
Cassino, Jay, 1957, Jl 5,18:7
Cassino, Samuel E, 1937, N 19,23:5
Cassion, John Mrs, 1957, S 9,25:3
Cassirer, Bruno, 1941, O 28,23:5
Cassirer, Ernst (por), 1945, Ap 15,14:5
Cassirer, Ernst Mrs, 1961, Ja 6,27:2
Cassody, John B Justice, 1907, D 31,7:6
Cassola, Filippo, 1942, F 28,17:6
Casson, Henry Col, 1912, S 26,11:4
Casson, Ira, 1950, Ja 13,23:4
Casson, Samuel E, 1957, Ja 16,31:1
Cassone, Frank A, 1962, S 30,86:8
Cassou, Henri P, 1940, O 30,23:6
Cassulo, Andrew, 1952, Ja 11,21:3
Castagnola, Alice F di, 1963, S 26,35:1
Castagnola, Salvatore, 1949, D 9,32:4
Castaldi, Edward, 1948, Mr 10,27:1
Castaldi, Maria, 1940, Ag 12,15:4
Castaldo, Alfonso Cardinal, 1966, Mr 4,33:1
Castaldo, Philip, 1922, D 11,17:5
Castaneda, Carlos E, 1958, Ap 6,88:1
Castanheira de Moura, Antonio, 1952, N 23,89:1
Castator, Fred W, 1940, N 24,51:1
Castegnier, Armand, 1909, Jl 15,7:4
Castegnier, Georges Prof, 1913, Ja 8,11:4
Castel, Jean, 1939, O 10,23:5
Castelao, Alfonso R, 1950, Ja 9,25:3
Castelar, Emilio, 1899, My 28,1:2
Castelbajac, Marquis of, 1949, N 9,28:2
Castell, George O, 1952, F 14,27:2
Castell, Taylor, 1953, Ja 28,27:5
Castell-Castell, Alexandrine L, 1962, Ap 27,35:3
Castellane, Alice de Countess (A Abercrombie-Miller), 1965, My 27,37:4
Castellane, B de, 1932, O 20,21:5
Castellane, Florenz de Marquise, 1922, F 8,17:5
Castellane, Marquis de, 1917, D 10,15:6; 1946, F 8, 19:3; 1956, Ag 28,27:2
Castellani, Giovanni, 1953, S 1,23:3
Castellano, Eugenia Mrs, 1949, Je 2,27:3
Castellano, Graz, 1964, Ag 30,93:1
Castellano, John U, 1962, O 24,39:1
Castellano, Louis J, 1964, Ja 5,92:1
Castellanos, Felix, 1952, Mr 6,31:4
Castellanos, Miguel, 1940, Jl 26,17:4
Castellanos Mena, Manuel, 1945, Ja 6,11:4
Castelle, James, 1964, Mr 22,77:1
Castelli, Alfonso, 1941, Ag 25,15:1
Castelli, Francis J, 1963, D 5,45:1
Castelli, Francis S Mrs, 1949, S 12,21:3
Castelli, John A, 1953, My 25,25:4
Castellini, Joseph J, 1949, My 9,25:5
Castellini, Robert H, 1952, F 7,27:5
Castello, Salvador, 1950, F 19,78:4
Castellon, Camilo, 1942, D 9,28:2
Castellon, Hildebrando, 1943, Ja 14,21:2
Castellon, Simeon Pereira y Bp, 1921, F 2,11:5
Castellott, Eugenio, 1957, Mr 15,29:5
Castells, Julian M, 1951, Ap 18,31:4
Castellucci, Andrew, 1944, D 1,23:4
Castellucci, Oreste C, 1949, D 28,32:2
Castelmary, A, 1897, F 11,1:3
Castelmenardo, Vessicho Gurgo di Countess, 191 My 5,11:6
Castelnau, Edouard de (por), 1944, Mr 20,18:2
Castelnuovo, Guido, 1952, Ap 28,19:2
Castelnuovo-Tedesco, Mario, 1968, Mr 19,44:2
Castelo Branco, Humberto (ed trb, Jl 19,38:2; fun 21,31:1), 1967, Jl 19,16:1
Castelvuchio Frabasilis, J de, 1932, D 20,19:3
Castens, Herman, 1904, Ja 29,9:6
Castenskjold, J G de Grevenkop, 1915, My 22,11
Caster, Louis E, 1960, My 16,31:4
Casterlin, Charles H, 1944, F 22,23:1
Casterlin, Dennis C, 1941, O 3,23:4
Casterlin, George Sr, 1946, D 4,31:1
Casterot, Alexis, 1952, Je 30,19:3
Casterton, J Ward, 1959, Jl 23,27:3
Casterton, Robert J, 1958, My 16,25:1
Castiaux, Joseph F, 1954, My 25,27:1
Castiaux, Joseph W, 1945, Ag 17,17:2
Castiglione, Duchess, 1879, Ag 10,5:7
Castiglioni, Arturo, 1953, Ja 23,19:3
Castiglioni, Camillo, 1957, D 25,31:3
Castiglioni, H V de Count, 1879, S 27,2:5
Castilleo, Jaime, 1938, Ja 1,19:3
Castillo, Antonio J, 1946, Ja 19,14:2
Castillo, Arthur, 1953, O 24,15:2
Castillo, Domingo del, 1943, My 8,4:1
Castillo, Gaspar Betaucourt, 1920, Ag 13,9:5
Castillo, Jose A, 1940, Je 23,30:8
Castillo, Mina A del, 1949, D 6,31:4
Castillo, Ramon S, 1944, O 13,19:1
Castillo, Suri, 1951, S 4,12:4
Castillo, Thomas J, 1948, My 9,68:5
Castillo Najera, Francisco, 1954, D 22,23:1
Castimore, Clarence, 1955, Ja 30,84:8
Castle, Agnes, 1922, My 1,17:2
Castle, Arthur, 1941, My 3,15:2
Castle, Bernard J, 1952, Ag 14,23:3

Castle, Charles C, 1943, Ap 2,21:1
Castle, Davis McFarland Dr, 1924, Ag 7,15:6
Castle, Egerton, 1920, S 18,9:2
Castle, Eli N, 1956, Ag 22,29:4
Castle, Eugene W, 1960, F 10,37:2
Castle, F A Dr, 1902, Ap 29,9:5
Castle, George H, 1954, Je 9,31:4
Castle, Henry N Mrs, 1950, Ap 24,25:4
Castle, James H, 1957, Jl 8,23:1
Castle, Jesse G, 1944, Ap 21,19:4
Castle, John G Mrs, 1955, D 22,23:5
Castle, John H Jr, 1968, O 6,84:6
Castle, Joseph L, 1952, Ag 26,25:3
Castle, Katherine Q Mrs, 1948, Ja 12,19:3
Castle, Lewis G (mem ser, Je 6,29:2), 1960, Je 5,86:2
Castle, M S, 1871, Jl 30,6:5
Castle, Margaret Mrs, 1945, F 3,11:6
Castle, Montague, 1939, Ag 12,13:5
Castle, Nick, 1968, Ag 29,35:5
Castle, Oliver H, 1944, My 24,19:3
Castle, Robert S, 1948, My 8,15:6
Castle, Vernon (funl, F 20,9:5), 1918, F 16,11:1
Castle, Walter L, 1952, Ap 13,76:4
Castle, William E, 1962, Je 5,41:4
Castle, William R, 1963, O 14,29:2
Castle, Wilmot, 1941, O 21,23:1
Castle, Winifred Mrs, 1958, Je 10,33:4
Castle, Worden L, 1949, N 21,25:5
Castleman, Ada R Mrs, 1941, F 4,21:5
Castleman, Francis L, 1954, Jl 19,19:5; 1955, Ja 1,13:4
Castleman, Frank R, 1946, O 10,27:5
Castleman, Harry (Chas Austin Fosdick), 1915, Ag 23,9:5
Castleman, J Warrant Judge, 1920, Ja 3,11:3
Castleman, John B Gen, 1918, My 24,13:7
Castleman, Kenneth G, 1954, Je 17,29:5
Castleman, Mayo, 1943, O 27,23:2
Castlerosse, Doris, 1942, D 13,74:2
Castlerosse, Valentine E C B, 1943, S 21,23:1
Castles, Andrew Mrs, 1907, S 11,9:6
Castles, George C Mrs, 1964, N 5,19:3
Castles, Henry J, 1955, F 17,27:1
Castles, Hiram R, 1938, O 23,40:8
Castles, John W, 1965, Ap 22,33:3
Castles, John W Mrs, 1954, My 18,30:4
Castles, Joseph T, 1938, Jl 11,17:4
Castles, Joseph T Jr, 1945, Ja 7,38:1
Castles, Mary E, 1939, N 13,19:4
Castles, Rita M, 1940, Ap 4,23:2
Castles, Robert W, 1937, Jl 21,21:5
Castlestewart, Earl of (Sir Hy Jas Stuart-Richardson), 1914, Je 7,5:6
Castletown, Lord, 1937, Je 2,23:2
Castner, Cornelius Capt, 1904, D 13,9:7
Castner, Joseph C, 1946, Jl 9,21:5
Castner, Lawrence V, 1949, D 8,34:2
Castner, Philip A, 1943, My 24,15:5
Castner, Richard, 1946, Jl 28,40:7
Casto, C Everett, 1958, Ap 9,33:3
Casto, Door C, 1958, Je 3,20:4
Casto, Theodore D, 1949, My 20,27:4
Castonguay, J Emile, 1956, Je 24,77:1
Castonguay, Jules, 1958, F 21,23:2
Castor, Anna C, 1951, S 5,31:3
Castor, William B, 1938, D 30,15:5
Castor y Jiminez, Otton, 1939, D 15,25:6
Castoris, Bro (Michl F Walsh), 1924, My 30,15:6
Castra, Eugenio de, 1944, Ag 19,11:6
Castree, Robert B Dr, 1937, D 29,21:3
Castrillo, Salvador, 1950, O 1,104:2
Castro, Albert E, 1942, My 18,15:4
Castro, Angel Mrs, 1963, Ag 8,27:4
Castro, Angelo Mrs, 1955, My 26,31:3
Castro, Charles B de, 1960, S 25,88:8
Castro, Cipriano Gen, 1924, D 6,15:5
Castro, Diego de, 1903, Je 24,9:6
Castro, Don M Sr, 1963, S 18,39:1
Castro, Gino J, 1957, Je 23,84:3
Castro, Juan Jose, 1968, S 5,47:1
Castro, Leite de, 1950, D 14,35:3
Castro, Ricardo, 1907, N 30,7:5
Castro Barcelos, Christovao de, 1946, F 17,42:6
Castro Beeche, Ricardo, 1967, O 11,34:2
Castro Leon, Jesus M, 1965, Jl 13,33:2
Castro Ramirez, Manuel, 1954, Ja 27,27:5
Castronovo, Vincent, 1950, Ja 10,29:2
Caswell, Alanson Mrs, 1938, F 22,21:3
Caswell, Annabella, 1951, Ja 18,27:2
Caswell, Burton J, 1951, F 6,27:3
Caswell, Caroline M, 1938, D 19,23:3
Caswell, Daniel Orvis, 1925, Je 23,19:5
Caswell, Edward R, 1956, Ja 14,19:6
Caswell, John (funl), 1871, Ap 2,4:7
Caswell, John, 1954, D 25,11:5
Caswell, John P, 1938, O 6,23:3
Caswell, Lincoln H, 1939, O 14,19:2
Caswell, Myron J, 1949, Ag 11,23:4
Caswell, Pauline S Mrs, 1942, Jl 21,19:4
Caswell, Phil, 1956, Ap 26,33:4
Caswell, Philip, 1881, F 24,4:7; 1947, Ag 24,56:3
Caswell, Thomas Thompson Rear-Adm, 1913, Jl 10,7:3
Caswell, William W, 1940, Ja 1,23:3
Catalan, Miguel A, 1957, N 12,37:2
Catalano, Charles P Dr, 1968, S 17,47:3
Catalano, Donato V, 1949, O 18,28:4
Catalano, Joseph J, 1952, N 11,30:3
Catalanotti, Joseph, 1946, Jl 16,23:3
Cataldo, Angelo, 1944, Ja 30,37:2
Catallo, William J, 1968, Jl 16,39:3
Catania, Nicholas, 1944, F 5,15:6
Catchings, Waddill, 1968, Ja 1,15:1
Catchpole, Margaret Mrs (M Roberts), 1962, O 24, 39:3
Catchpole, Robert A, 1942, Mr 9,20:2
Catchpool, Thomas C, 1952, S 18,29:4
Cate, George W Judge, 1905, Mr 8,9:5
Cate, Leroy V, 1955, Je 5,85:1
Cate, Lucy Mrs, 1937, N 20,17:4
Cate, Rex M, 1963, O 30,39:4
Cate, Russell D, 1937, My 5,25:2
Cate, Sheridan R, 1950, My 9,29:2
Cate, Walter C, 1938, F 12,15:5
Cate, William E, 1937, Ap 25,II,8:2
Catela, Jose, 1950, N 4,17:3
Catelli, Charles H, 1937, O 14,25:2
Caten, Walter E, 1945, Je 10,32:2
Cater, Aymar Mrs, 1952, Ap 4,25:2
Cater, Douglas A, 1943, Jl 15,21:2
Cater, Robert Dupont, 1904, Ja 30,1:3
Cater, William B, 1952, Je 25,29:4
Cater, William H, 1958, My 25,86:4
Caterini, Cardinal, 1881, O 30,2:6
Catero, Elizabeth M, 1960, Ap 23,23:3
Caters, Pierre de, 1944, Ap 8,13:3
Caterson, Eliza A, 1948, N 8,21:4
Caterson, Herbert R, 1968, F 22,32:8
Cates, Dudley, 1954, Ap 25,86:5
Cates, Dudley Mrs, 1956, Ag 20,21:3
Cates, John M, 1955, N 10,35:2
Cates, Junius S, 1949, O 19,29:4
Cates, Louis S, 1959, O 30,27:1
Cates, Morris P, 1953, My 29,25:4
Cathala, Pierre, 1947, Jl 28,15:3
Catharine, Irwin T, 1944, Mr 7,17:4
Catharine, Joseph W (por), 1944, O 10,23:1
Cathart, George C, 1951, Ja 6,15:4
Cathcart, Andrew, 1882, F 13,5:1
Cathcart, Annabel, 1951, N 29,33:3
Cathcart, Arthur M, 1949, N 3,29:4
Cathcart, Charles S, 1945, D 11,25:4
Cathcart, Daniel B, 1959, Ja 24,19:2
Cathcart, Edward, 1949, Ja 26,25:4
Cathcart, Ernest R, 1952, Jl 1,23:5
Cathcart, John B, 1941, My 11,44:4
Cathcart, R H, 1941, Mr 21,21:5
Cathcart, Ray L, 1947, N 21,27:3
Cathcart, Robert Jr, 1943, My 22,13:2
Cathcart, Sue Mrs, 1964, My 29,29:4
Cathcart, W C Mrs, 1952, Ag 27,27:3
Cather, David C, 1944, Je 30,21:6
Cather, Willa S, 1947, Ap 25,21:1
Catherine, Mother, 1948, D 31,15:2
Catherine, Sister (Cath G Whittaker), 1941, Jl 10, 19:3
Catherine Regina, Sister (Sullivan), 1959, N 15,87:1
Catherine Veronica, Sister (White), 1950, N 21,31:3
Cathers, George, 1941, S 12,21:2
Catherwood, B F, 1957, Ja 2,27:5
Catherwood, M H Mrs, 1902, D 27,9:5
Catherwood, Robert, 1947, Ja 20,25:5
Catherwood, Robert B, 1903, N 15,7:5
Catherwood, William S Jr, 1948, Ja 30,23:1
Cathey, John T, 1954, O 17,84:4
Cathles, Lawrence M, 1958, My 12,29:4
Catinella, Frank P, 1946, Je 5,23:2
Catlaw, J Kenneth, 1966, O 15,29:5
Catlaw, Thomas J, 1946, Je 19,21:1
Catlaw, Thomas J Mrs, 1949, Ja 8,15:2
Catledge, Lee J Mrs, 1948, Je 26,17:4
Catlett, Landon C Jr, 1925, Jl 18,13:2
Catlett, Mary Mrs, 1939, N 30,21:4
Catlett, Sidney (Big Sid), 1951, Mr 27,29:3
Catlett, Walter, 1960, N 15,39:1
Catley, William C, 1950, D 1,25:4
Catlin, Abraham E, 1950, N 10,27:4
Catlin, Catherine L R (will), 1906, Je 5,18:4
Catlin, Charles A, 1916, Ap 13,13:6
Catlin, Charles F, 1939, Mr 19,III,6:7
Catlin, Charles Taylor, 1912, Ja 5,13:5
Catlin, Elizabeth D, 1959, N 27,29:2
Catlin, Ephron, 1967, D 13,47:2
Catlin, Frederick T, 1944, Ag 11,15:1
Catlin, George, 1872, D 24,1:6; 1908, Je 8,7:4
Catlin, Harry, 1961, Je 14,19:4
Catlin, Isaac S Gen, 1916, Ja 20,9:5
Catlin, John, 1874, Ag 6,4:6; 1944, Je 13,19:4
Catlin, John B, 1952, O 23,31:5
Catlin, Justa J, 1940, S 9,15:6
Catlin, Leslie A, 1949, S 29,29:3
Catlin, Lynde A, 1915, O 25,9:4
Catlin, Lynde Maj, 1901, O 11,9:6
Catlin, Malcolm B, 1960, Jl 23,19:3
Catlin, Mark Sr, 1956, My 17,31:5
Catlin, Randolph, 1961, N 30,34:4
Catlin, Roy G Rev Dr, 1937, S 18,19:1
Catlin, Rufus O Mrs, 1951, S 11,29:3
Catlin, Sheldon, 1948, Mr 27,13:3
Catlin, Theron E, 1960, Mr 20,86:5
Catlin, Warren B Dr, 1968, Jl 12,31:3
Cato, Lamar Q, 1948, Jl 14,24:2
Catoggio, Anthony, 1959, Ag 26,29:1
Caton, Harry, 1965, O 24,87:1
Caton, Harry B, 1949, Ap 28,31:2
Caton, James H, 1948, Ja 10,15:1
Caton, John E, 1944, Jl 11,15:3
Caton, John J, 1956, My 17,31:5
Caton, W D, 1947, Jl 29,22:2
Caton, Will, 1943, Jl 3,13:2
Catoni, Giulio, 1950, O 21,17:3
Cator, James H, 1903, Jl 28,7:6
Cator, Ralph B P, 1945, Jl 30,19:5
Cator, Sylvio, 1952, Jl 23,23:4
Catozella, Joseph, 1945, Je 24,22:2
Catozella, Joseph Mrs, 1958, Mr 6,27:5
Catricala, V James, 1958, Ja 10,26:3
Catron, Judge, 1865, Je 1,1:3
Catron, Thomas Benton Ex-Sen, 1921, My 17,17:6
Catrow, Herbert G, 1944, O 31,19:2
Cats, Alex, 1954, O 31,89:1
Catt, Carrie C Mrs, 1947, Mr 10,21:1
Cattani, Bey, 1883, Je 1,3:4
Cattani-Amadori, Federico, 1943, Ap 13,25:3
Cattarinich, Joseph, 1938, D 8,27:2
Cattell, Edward J, 1938, Ja 7,19:1
Cattell, Jacques, 1960, D 20,33:2
Cattell, James M (por), 1944, Ja 21,16:3
Cattell, James M Mrs, 1948, O 13,25:5
Cattell, Owen, 1940, Mr 28,23:3
Cattell, Richard B, 1964, S 18,35:3
Cattell, William, 1937, My 12,23:4
Cattell, William C, 1948, D 25,18:2
Cattell, William M, 1953, S 6,50:2
Cattera, Ettore, 1916, D 3,23:2
Catterall, Arthur, 1943, N 29,19:5
Catterall, Joseph J, 1958, Ja 20,23:1
Catterall, Ralph Charles Henry Prof, 1914, Ag 4,11:6
Cattie, Joseph P, 1950, Jl 5,31:4
Cattier, Felicien, 1946, F 5,24:3
Cattier, Jean Mrs, 1961, Je 10,23:5
Cattin, William H, 1911, O 6,13:6
Catto, Thomas S, 1959, Ag 24,21:3
Catts, Robert M, 1942, Ap 23,24:2
Cattus, John V, 1945, Mr 2,20:2
Caturani, Michele G, 1940, F 25,38:5
Cauchois, Frederic Augustus, 1918, Ap 12,13:8
Cauchois, Oscar R, 1941, D 30,19:3
Cauchois, Reginald W, 1960, D 15,43:3
Cauchois, Reginald W Sr Mrs, 1958, Ja 13,29:1
Cauchon, Mme, 1877, D 10,3:4; 1878, Mr 4,4:7
Caudill, Raleigh B, 1955, Jl 15,21:2
Caudle, T Lamar Mrs, 1961, D 5,43:2
Cauer, Ernst L, 1951, Je 22,31:3
Cauer, Minna Mrs, 1922, Ag 4,15:7
Cauffman, Clyde H, 1946, O 30,27:2
Cauffman, David M, 1939, Ja 3,18:2
Cauffman, Stanley H, 1947, F 13,24:3
Caufiel, J, 1932, Jl 11,13:3
Caufield, Edward J, 1959, O 22,37:2
Caufield, James E Jr, 1942, D 1,25:4
Caufield, John P, 1949, S 23,23:2
Caughey, John L, 1955, Ag 30,27:5
Caughey, Milton H, 1958, Jl 16,29:4
Caughey, Samuel Mrs, 1948, N 13,15:3
Caughlan, Thomas B, 1938, D 20,25:5
Caughlan, Walter B, 1952, N 13,31:2
Caughlan, Walter B Jr, 1956, Je 17,92:6
Caulcutt, John, 1943, Ap 30,21:5
Caulcy, Frank W, 1947, D 12,27:2
Cauldwell, Andrew J, 1949, O 10,23:2
Cauldwell, Ebenezer, 1875, Je 20,7:3
Cauldwell, Frederic, 1942, Jl 27,15:6
Cauldwell, Gilbert J, 1939, N 18,17:5
Cauldwell, J A, 1922, D 16,15:5
Cauldwell, John J Mrs, 1958, Je 21,19:2
Cauldwell, Leslie G, 1941, Je 4,23:2
Cauldwell, Mary (Sister Miriam), 1882, O 26,2:2
Cauldwell, Oscar R, 1959, S 9,41:1
Cauldwell, Samuel Millbank, 1916, Mr 9,13:4
Cauldwell, Thomas W, 1909, Ap 12,7:5
Cauldwell, William, 1907, D 3,9:5
Cauley, Mary F, 1940, Je 19,23:6
Cauley, Peter M, 1938, N 21,19:2
Caulfield, Alfred H, 1940, My 4,17:6
Caulfield, Benedict J, 1949, F 7,19:4
Caulfield, Charles E, 1947, Jl 31,21:1
Caulfield, Frank, 1950, D 12,33:5
Caulfield, Frank J, 1956, S 21,25:1
Caulfield, George, 1939, Je 29,23:6
Caulfield, George B, 1944, Ap 5,19:1
Caulfield, Henry S, 1966, My 13,41:3
Caulfield, Joseph A, 1941, Jl 2,21:2
Caulfield, L Frederick, 1958, S 26,27:1
Caulfield, Merville H, 1949, F 13,76:2
Caulfield, Raymond V, 1967, O 9,47:3
Caulfield, Sidney W, 1945, S 14,23:4
Caulk, John R, 1938, O 14,23:2
Caulker, Arthur E, 1953, Je 24,9:6
Caulkins, Eugene D, 1940, Ap 26,21:4
Caulkins, Frederick P Mrs, 1949, Mr 28,21:3

Caulkins, Henry M, 1943, Ap 21,25:5
Caulkins, T Vassar, 1951, Ja 23,27:2
Caulkins, Thomas V Jr, 1953, N 18,31:2
Caulway, John J, 1967, D 9,47:1
Caum, Samuel L, 1941, Ap 8,25:4
Caunitz, Oscar F, 1940, Ag 20,19:4
Causer, Robert L, 1955, My 16,23:3
Causey, Edward H, 1942, Ja 7,19:2
Causey, James H, 1943, Ap 9,21:4
Causey, John W, 1908, O 2,9:7
Causey, Joseph G, 1947, N 8,17:2
Causey, W B, 1936, Ag 11,21:3
Cauthers, James B, 1941, F 20,19:4
Cauthers, William James, 1914, Ja 14,11:5
Cauthorne, Edward E, 1966, My 14,31:1
Cautley, John R, 1951, Ap 26,29:2
Cauty, Arthur B, 1954, Ag 4,21:5
Cauty, Francis H, 1950, N 24,35:3
Cauwelaert, Frans van, 1961, My 18,35:2
Cauwelaert, Louis A van Mrs, 1946, N 7,31:5
Cauwenberg, Jean-Marie van, 1950, Ap 18,32:2
Cauwer, Paul de, 1949, Ag 26,19:4
Cavadore, Joseph, 1957, Ag 16,19:3
Cavagnaro, Angelo, 1903, Ag 14,7:6
Cavagnaro, James F Mrs, 1942, O 16,19:4
Cavagnaro, John, 1903, Ap 22,9:6
Cavagnaro, Mario, 1947, Jl 4,13:4
Cavaguari, Maj, 1879, S 20,3:2
Cavalier, Emil Mrs, 1943, Mr 10,19:4
Cavalier, Jacques, 1937, Mr 23,23:4
Cavalier, William, 1945, O 27,15:4
Cavallari, Aristides Cardinal, 1914, N 25,11:6
Cavallaro, Joseph B (funl, Ag 27,29:4), 1957, Ag 23, 19:1
Cavalli-Molinelli, Achille, 1958, Ag 12,29:4
Cavallo, Michael, 1966, O 27,47:3
Cavallo, Peter A Sr, 1952, Ap 15,27:3
Cavallo, Rafello, 1957, N 17,87:2
Cavan, Earl of, 1946, Ag 30,17:3
Cavan, Earl of (H E S S Lambart), 1950, D 11,25:2
Cavanagh, Austin H, 1941, Ap 23,21:5
Cavanagh, Charles, 1937, O 10,II,8:7
Cavanagh, Edward F, 1957, Ap 30,29:1
Cavanagh, Edward Sr Mrs (funl, O 29,47:7), 1965, O 26,45:3
Cavanagh, Frank Mrs, 1947, O 10,25:3
Cavanagh, Frederick C, 1951, Ja 5,21:2
Cavanagh, Harry G, 1949, Ap 13,29:2
Cavanagh, Harry Jr, 1947, My 20,25:3
Cavanagh, Hiram, 1938, D 13,25:3
Cavanagh, J Albert, 1947, Jl 25,18:2
Cavanagh, James, 1939, Ap 13,23:4; 1951, Je 26,29:5
Cavanagh, James F Mrs, 1965, N 26,34:4
Cavanagh, James Mrs, 1947, S 23,25:3
Cavanagh, Jerome J, 1962, F 15,29:2
Cavanagh, John, 1957, Ja 25,21:3
Cavanagh, John F, 1957, Jl 14,73:2
Cavanagh, John G, 1937, N 24,23:4
Cavanagh, John Mrs, 1957, My 22,33:2
Cavanagh, Martin F, 1942, Ja 10,15:5
Cavanagh, Max J, 1954, Mr 19,24:5
Cavanagh, Paul F, 1957, N 4,29:3
Cavanagh, Paul Mrs, 1960, O 20,10:6
Cavanagh, Richard F, 1940, Je 13,23:1
Cavanagh, Sylvester J, 1968, Mr 18,37:8
Cavanagh, Thomas H, 1963, Ag 11,85:1
Cavanagh, Thomas J, 1941, Jl 1,23:5
Cavanagh, William F, 1955, Ja 8,13:2
Cavanagh, William J, 1942, Ag 26,19:6; 1959, Ag 9, 88:4
Cavanagh, William J Bro, 1962, O 2,39:4
Cavanaugh, Albert J, 1950, Ap 15,15:3
Cavanaugh, Andrew J, 1938, Ap 19,21:2
Cavanaugh, Arthur G, 1948, Je 23,27:2
Cavanaugh, Charles, 1948, O 4,23:5
Cavanaugh, Clair A, 1953, O 15,33:6
Cavanaugh, Clarence F, 1959, N 7,23:3
Cavanaugh, Clay, 1943, O 5,25:3
Cavanaugh, Clifford Edward Maj, 1920, Ja 31,11:3
Cavanaugh, Cortes W, 1953, Jl 7,27:5
Cavanaugh, David F, 1955, O 1,19:3
Cavanaugh, Donald J, 1948, Jl 30,18:2
Cavanaugh, E L, 1937, Ap 27,23:2
Cavanaugh, Edward F, 1957, Je 22,15:2
Cavanaugh, Elanor S, 1959, Mr 20,31:1
Cavanaugh, F W, 1933, Ag 30,19:1
Cavanaugh, Frederick J Mrs, 1920, Ja 31,11:3
Cavanaugh, George W, 1938, Jl 3,12:6
Cavanaugh, Hobart, 1950, Ap 27,33:1
Cavanaugh, Hobart Mrs (F Heston), 1963, Jl 2,26:5
Cavanaugh, James, 1967, Ag 19,25:4
Cavanaugh, James F, 1955, O 23,86:8; 1967, S 29,47:3
Cavanaugh, James J, 1948, My 17,19:2
Cavanaugh, John Mrs, 1959, S 3,27:4
Cavanaugh, Joseph H, 1954, N 12,21:4
Cavanaugh, Joseph J, 1912, S 12,11:5
Cavanaugh, Lawrence J, 1945, Mr 31,19:5
Cavanaugh, Leo D, 1965, Jl 21,37:3
Cavanaugh, Mortimer, 1945, O 8,15:3
Cavanaugh, Pat, 1908, Mr 19,7:4
Cavanaugh, Patrick, 1948, Je 18,23:2
Cavanaugh, Paul V, 1954, My 14,23:2
Cavanaugh, Robert E, 1960, Mr 7,29:4
Cavanaugh, Thomas F, 1959, Ag 10,27:4
Cavanaugh, Thomas F Mrs, 1950, O 15,104:5
Cavanaugh, Wallace Mrs (apparently encased self in plastic bag), 1959, Je 8,23:4
Cavanaugh, William J, 1949, O 25,27:3
Cavanaugh, William P, 1965, F 14,88:2
Cavanillas, Jose M, 1957, Ja 8,31:1
Cavargna, Arthur Mrs, 1947, Ja 8,23:2
Cavarly, Haywood P, 1941, O 30,23:2
Cave, Charles, 1939, My 20,15:3
Cave, Edith S, 1944, D 17,38:2
Cave, Edward, 1951, F 3,15:3
Cave, Eugene M, 1945, Ja 1,21:2
Cave, George A, 1952, Ap 1,29:2
Cave, Harry W, 1953, Je 25,27:4
Cave, Henry W, 1964, My 21,35:3
Cave, James H, 1964, D 22,29:4
Cave, Lord, 1928, Mr 30,25:3
Cave, Stephen, 1880, Je 8,2:7
Cave-Brown-Cave, Rowland H, 1943, D 24,14:7
Cavedon, Antonio Mrs, 1949, S 10,17:4
Caven, Alex, 1948, Jl 6,23:3
Caven, Frank H, 1949, Ag 19,17:2
Caven, George, 1937, F 7,II,9:2
Caven, Joseph E Col, 1912, Je 3,9:5
Caven, Joseph L, 1907, Mr 18,7:5
Cavenaugh, Daniel J, 1940, Ja 11,23:4
Cavenaugh, Ralph W, 1909, D 7,9:4
Cavenaugh, Robert J, 1963, D 10,43:2
Cavender, Glenn W, 1962, F 11,87:1
Cavender, John H, 1940, My 30,17:5
Cavender, Kay Mrs, 1948, D 4,13:3
Cavender, Richard L, 1944, S 10,47:6
Cavendis, Moyra Mrs, 1942, F 8,48:2
Cavendish, Charles Lord (por), 1944, Mr 24,19:4
Cavendish, Emma Lady, 1920, S 27,15:2
Cavendish, Richard Lord, 1946, Ja 8,24:2
Cavendish (H Jones), 1899, F 17,7:1
Cavendish-Bentinck, George Mrs, 1943, N 7,56:6
Cavendish-Bentinck, William George, 1909, Ag 23,7:5
Caveney, John W, 1938, N 6,49:1
Cavens, Frederic, 1962, My 2,37:3
Caver, Robert M, 1953, S 22,31:2
Caverly, Charles E, 1946, My 23,21:6
Caverly, Charles S Dr, 1918, O 17,15:2
Caverly, Edward, 1915, Je 22,15:6
Caverly, John J, 1939, Jl 13,19:6
Caverly, John R, 1939, Ag 5,15:3
Caverly, Orrin G, 1957, D 5,35:3
Caverno, Julia H, 1949, F 5,15:3
Cavero, Salvador, 1940, F 20,21:5
Cavert, David W, 1958, N 11,29:1
Cavert, David W Mrs, 1953, Ja 31,15:1
Cavert, Inez M, 1958, N 29,21:1
Cavey, Arthur T, 1940, S 16,19:2
Cavey, Francis A, 1944, My 22,19:6
Cavia, Mariano de, 1920, Jl 15,7:3
Cavicchia, John, 1961, Ap 5,37:3
Cavies, Valentine, 1961, Jl 25,27:2
Caviglia, Enrico (por), 1945, Mr 24,17:4
Cavignac, Godefroy, 1905, S 26,9:7
Cavin, Evelyn T, 1962, Ag 29,29:2
Cavins, Benjamin F Rev, 1924, Ag 26,11:3
Cavis, Frederick L, 1940, Je 21,21:4
Cavo, John A, 1947, Ag 18,17:5
Cavo, Lawrence A, 1940, S 15,48:3
Cavour, Camillo Benso di Count, 1861, Je 17,8:4
Caw, D J Col, 1882, My 19,2:3
Cawdor, Earl (Fredk Archibald Vaughan Campbell), 1911, F 9,7:6
Cawl, Charles E Mrs, 1966, My 30,19:4
Cawley, Charles M, 1957, S 26,25:4
Cawley, F S, 1941, F 16,40:3
Cawley, Frederick J, 1941, Mr 30,49:2
Cawley, James T, 1961, F 21,35:4
Cawley, John, 1953, Ja 18,93:1
Cawley, John M, 1957, D 6,29:2
Cawley, John P, 1959, Mr 20,31:3
Cawley, Joseph C, 1949, D 26,29:5
Cawley, Peter A, 1949, Ja 17,19:5
Cawley, Sherman, 1946, S 30,25:4
Cawley, Thomas J P, 1950, O 12,31:3
Cawley, William J, 1939, Je 26,15:4
Cawse, Alfred J Sr, 1951, N 19,23:5
Cawse, Alfred J Sr Mrs, 1954, O 23,15:5
Cawthon, Fannie Mrs, 1947, Ag 10,53:2
Cawthorn, Joseph (por), 1949, Ja 23,68:5
Cawthorn, Joseph Mrs (Queenie Vassar), 1960, S 13,37:2
Cawthorne, Harry L, 1949, S 19,23:2
Cawthorne, William B, 1937, Mr 29,19:4
Cayce, Edgar, 1945, Ja 4,19:4
Caye, Webster J Sr, 1959, N 30,31:5
Caye, Weyant D, 1962, Ap 6,35:1
Cayea, Edward, 1957, D 9,35:3
Cayford, Arthur F, 1949, Mr 1,26:2
Caygill, J Ranson, 1952, F 15,25:4
Cayley, Camille Dr, 1968, N 12,43:5
Cayley, Harry G, 1964, Je 7,86:7
Caylus, E, 1878, Ap 2,4:6
Cayou, Frank M, 1948, My 8,15:5
Caypless, Edgar, 1917, Je 9,11:6
Cayser, August B T, 1943, Mr 2,19:4
Cayton, Herbert C, 1947, S 28,60:4
Cayton, Horace R Mrs, 1943, Ag 2,15:4
Cayvan, Alice W, 1903, F 6,7:1
Cayvan, Georgia (will, D 6,3:5), 1906, N 20,1:2
Caywood, David Roosevelt, 1909, Jl 14,7:4
Caywood, Roland B, 1952, Ja 9,29:3
Caywood, Thomas, 1949, Je 24,23:5
Caywood, William A, 1943, Ja 3,42:6
Cayzer, Charles, 1940, F 19,17:5
Cayzer, Charles Sir, 1916, S 29,13:5
Caza, Oliver J, 1945, O 26,19:1
Cazakoff, Jacob, 1954, Mr 22,27:5
Cazalet, Leonora Mrs, 1944, My 18,19:3
Cazalnayou, Raymond, 1952, S 1,1:2
Cazauran, A R, 1889, Ja 28,5:2
Cazazza, Joseph Mrs, 1949, Je 1,31:6
Cazeneuve, Cook, 1880, F 4,3:5
Cazes, Marcellin, 1965, O 11,39:3
Cazneau, Thomas N Gen, 1873, Jl 12,1:6
Cazzolia, John, 1942, My 4,19:4
Cazzolla, Vito, 1950, Ag 22,27:2
Ccoltharp, William H, 1956, Ap 17,31:3
Ceballind, Gen, 1871, Jl 12,5:4
Ceballos, Juan M, 1954, Mr 13,15:6
Cebotari, Maria, 1949, Je 10,27:4
Cebreco, Agustin Gen, 1924, D 20,15:5
Cecchi, Emilio, 1966, S 6,48:1
Cecelia Maria, Sister Sisters of St Joseph, 1953, S 19, 15:4
Cecere, Dominic W, 1948, O 14,29:5
Cech, Joseph, 1938, O 18,II,23:5
Cecil, Edward, 1940, D 15,61:3
Cecil, Eustace Lord, 1921, Jl 4,9:7
Cecil, George, 1923, Jl 7,11:5
Cecil, Hugh R H (Lord Quickswood), 1956, D 11, 39:2
Cecil, J R, 1880, Mr 18,8:2
Cecil, James M, 1954, S 19,89:1
Cecil, John F A, 1954, O 23,15:2
Cecil, John H, 1939, Je 4,49:1
Cecil, Mary, 1940, D 22,31:2
Cecil, Russell LaF, 1965, Je 2,45:3
Cecil, Thomas Lord, 1873, D 29,2:2
Cecil, William, 1943, Ap 17,17:4
Cecil, William T B Marquess of Exeter, 1956, Ag 7, 27:5
Cecil of Chelwood, Eleanor Lady, 1959, Ap 26,86:4
Cecil of Chelwood, Viscount (Edgar Algernon Robt Gascoyne Cecil), 1958, N 25,33:4
Cecilia Clare, Sister (Annie Walls), 1942, Ap 5,41:
Cecilia Rose, Sister (M M Langan), 1950, D 1,25:
Cecilia Rose, Sister (Sisters of Charity), 1958, Ag 23,15:2
Cecilia Treesa, Sister, 1937, Je 15,23:5
Cecilian, Bro (F E Flynn), 1961, My 27,23:3
Cecilie Auguste Marie, Ex-Crown Princess of Pruss 1954, My 7,23:1
Cecire, Bernard F, 1943, Ag 15,38:6
Ceclia Monica, Sister (M Driscoll), 1954, Mr 30,
Cedar, Carl W, 1954, Jl 31,13:4
Cedar, Ephraim, 1959, Ap 23,31:5
Cedar, Philip Mrs, 1925, O 4,5:3
Cederbaum, Morris, 1954, Mr 25,29:1
Cederstrom, Ellen H, 1945, Ja 6,11:1
Cefalo, Joseph, 1938, Mr 20,II,8:2
Cefalu, Sam, 1959, My 1,29:1
Cehanovska, Sophie Mrs, 1955, N 30,33:1
Cehelsky, Longin, 1950, D 15,31:3
Ceia, Benvindo, 1941, D 6,17:4
Cejudo, Alfredo, 1961, S 24,3:6
Celarek, Joseph, 1952, N 8,17:4
Celarier, Robert P, 1959, D 25,21:6
Celauro, John, 1961, O 11,47:2
Celchamber, William H, 1940, Jl 23,19:2
Celebre, John W, 1967, Mr 4,27:1
Celentano, Francis Mrs, 1949, F 15,23:5
Celeste, Mme, 1882, F 20,5:4
Celestia Maria, Mother, 1961, Je 9,33:1
Celestin, Oscar (Papa), 1954, D 16,37:2
Celestine, Sister, 1938, Ag 28,33:4; 1957, D 8,88
Celine, Louis-Ferdinand, 1961, Jl 5,33:2
Celine Gossin, Mother, 1939, O 16,19:6
Celis, Jose de, 1961, N 9,35:2
Celis, Luis de, 1937, O 26,23:3
Cell, George C Dr, 1937, Ap 19,21:2
Cella, Christopher, 1947, N 11,27:2
Cella, Joseph J, 1964, O 8,43:5
Cella, Lorenzo, 1960, Ap 12,33:5
Cella, Peter, 1939, Je 24,17:4
Cella, Richard, 1944, Ap 1,13:4
Cella, Romeo, 1957, S 30,31:4
Cella, Teresa (Apple Mary), 1911, Mr 4,11:6
Cella, Theodore, 1960, S 8,35:2
Cella, Theodore Mrs (M Boll), 1949, Ap 12,3
Celler, Albert A, 1966, N 9,39:1
Celler, Emanuel Mrs (funl, Mr 24,1:2), 1966, 41:3
Celles, Alfred de, 1925, O 7,27:5
Celli, Faith (Mrs Arth Murray), 1942, D 18,2
Celli, Frank, 1949, Ag 2,19:1
Cellier, Frank (por), 1948, S 28,28:2
Cellini, Giuseppe, 1940, My 1,23:5
Cellini, Renato, 1967, Mr 27,33:3

Celona, Frank H, 1960, S 10,21:5
Cembalest, Michael, 1958, F 28,13:4
Cence, Walter, 1950, Ag 6,54:2
Cenci, de Vicovan Princess, 1915, My 13,15:5
Cenci, de Vicovere Prince, 1909, N 7,13:5
Cendrars, Blaise, 1961, Ja 22,84:7
Ceniceros, Francisco, 1940, S 29,44:2
Cennerazzo, Armando, 1962, Ja 11,33:5
Censer, Milton Mrs, 1946, Mr 31,46:4
Centanni, Eugenio, 1942, Ag 21,19:1
Centenarian, Robert Sixbury, 1873, O 26,4:7
Centeno, Antonio, 1947, D 26,15:2
Centeno, Juan A, 1949, Je 21,25:4
Center, Edward C, 1938, F 12,15:5
Center, Edward L, 1957, Ja 30,29:1
Center, Edward W, 1953, N 2,25:4
Center, H Livingston, 1918, Mr 3,23:1
Center, Harry B, 1941, Ja 22,21:4
Center, Samuel L, 1949, Mr 13,76:4
Centkiewicz, Stanislaw L, 1951, Ap 23,25:2
Centlivres, Albert van der S, 1966, S 20,47:3
Centra, Pio, 1904, D 18,7:7
Ceough, Richard, 1947, Ja 10,21:5
Cephas, Mother, 1938, Ag 31,15:4
Cepollaro, John, 1953, N 20,24:4
Cerabone, Victor, 1954, Je 26,13:4
Cerabone, Victor Mrs, 1939, F 15,23:6
Cerar, Peter V, 1966, Jl 17,68:4
Cerdan, Marcel, 1949, O 29,1:8
Cere, Joseph, 1919, Ap 30,11:3
Cerero, Ralph L, 1946, O 26,17:6
Ceres, Anthony V Mrs, 1950, Mr 15,29:3; 1950, Mr 16,32:2
Ceres, Harvey H, 1941, Je 30,17:5
Ceretta, Ralph, 1967, Ja 12,39:2
Cerezo, Saturnino M, 1945, D 4,29:2
Cerf, Barry, 1948, Ap 24,15:1
Cerf, Elizabeth M, 1940, Jl 7,25:4
Cerf, Eugene E, 1938, D 24,15:5
Cerf, Gustave, 1941, O 3,23:2
Cerf, Louis A, 1959, Ja 23,25:3
Cerholm, Frederick, 1951, O 18,29:4
Ceria, Edmond, 1955, Jl 26,25:4
Ceriani, James, 1953, S 1,23:3
Cerilli, Louis, 1939, Je 2,23:4
Cerio, George, 1943, O 29,19:3
Cerio, George Mrs, 1949, N 12,15:4
Cerletti, Ugo, 1963, Jl 27,17:1
Cermak, A J, 1933, Mr 7,1:2
Cermak, Charles Mrs, 1947, Je 18,25:4
Cermak, Emil, 1949, Ag 12,17:5
Cermak, Joseph W, 1964, F 14,29:3
Cerney, William J, 1962, F 18,92:7
Cerniglia, Frank J, 1956, S 5,27:5
Cernikoff, Vladimir, 1940, Jl 25,17:2
Cernivivo, Michael, 1950, D 19,59:7
Cerny, Lawrence J, 1946, Jl 9,21:2
Cerone, May, 1966, Mr 30,45:2
Cerone, Rose, 1952, Ja 31,27:1
Cerone, Salvatore Mrs, 1943, Ja 17,44:5
Ceroni, Otello, 1961, O 7,23:5
Ceroni-Gonzaga, Vittorio F, 1956, O 13,19:6
Cerqua, Aug Edward, 1905, Ja 23,7:5
Cerracchio, Enrico, 1956, Mr 22,35:2
Cerrato, John, 1961, S 24,86:5
Cerre, Albert A, 1942, Mr 28,17:6
Cerretti, B, 1933, My 9,17:3
Cerrute, Edmund P, 1943, Ag 16,15:2
Cerruti, John J, 1948, Ag 16,19:4
Ceruti, Mary L, 1953, Ja 19,24:3
Cerutti, Ernest, 1937, Ja 24,II,8:3
Cerutti, Louis, 1961, N 20,31:5
Cervenka, John A, 1951, Ag 23,23:5
Cervera, Juan, 1952, N 19,29:5
Cervera, Pascual Vice-Adm, 1909, Ap 4,13:5
Cervini, Andrew F, 1963, D 5,41:6
Cervini, Anthony A, 1963, S 3,33:4
Cervini, Anthony Mrs, 1941, Ap 2,23:2
Cervini, Aug, 1940, My 8,23:3
Cervini, Aug Mrs, 1939, Mr 3,23:3
Cervini, John I, 1965, F 18,33:1
Cervini, Joseph G, 1956, O 12,29:2
Cervone, Frank, 1948, N 23,29:2
Cesare, Luigi De, 1959, D 18,29:1
Cesare, Oscar E, 1948, Jl 25,48:5
Cesare, Victor, 1954, My 14,31:6
Cesarin, Alexandre Col, 1907, My 28,9:5
Cesario, Antonio, 1939, F 28,19:2
Cesarone, Nicholas, 1956, F 27,45:1
Cesnola, L P di Mrs, 1902, Je 2,9:2
Cesnola, L P Gen, 1904, N 22,5:1
Cespedes, Carlos M de, 1939, Mr 28,23:3
Cespedes, Cuban Ex-President, 1874, Mr 8,4:1
Cespedes, Miguel de, 1955, Je 9,29:4
Cessna, Clarence M, 1949, N 26,15:2
Cessna, Clyde V, 1954, N 22,23:2
Cestero, Tulio, 1955, O 30,88:5
Cesteros, Jose N, 1958, F 9,88:2
Cetrulo, Gerald I, 1957, Mr 11,25:5
Cetto, Stephen, 1945, N 15,20:2
Cetywayo, 1883, Jl 26,5:3
Cevallos, Bernardo, 1948, N 21,88:6
Cevallos, Larios M, 1941, Je 26,23:5
Cevasco, James J, 1952, D 29,19:4
Cevasco, James J Jr, 1950, Je 4,92:5
Cevasco, Victor J, 1966, Ap 21,39:3
Cevolotto, Mario, 1953, Ap 7,29:5
Ceytlin, Benjamin H, 1955, S 20,31:4
Chabas, Paul, 1937, My 11,25:1
Chabau, Michael, 1952, Ja 31,27:5
Chabaud-Latour, F E H de Baron Gen, 1885, Je 12,5:2
Chabernaud, Leonce, 1953, Mr 21,18:4
Chabon, Jean A, 1948, S 10,23:1
Chabot, August J, 1944, Mr 16,19:4
Chabot, Charles H, 1943, Ag 4,17:3
Chabot, Charles Mrs, 1943, Ja 3,42:5
Chabot, Ernest D, 1955, Jl 4,11:6
Chabot, John T Mrs, 1949, Mr 26,17:5
Chabot, Lorne, 1946, O 11,23:3
Chabot, Theodore J, 1918, N 29,13:5
Chace, A B, 1932, F 29,17:3
Chace, Amos M Mrs, 1938, Mr 16,23:5
Chace, Arnold B Jr, 1950, Jl 2,24:8
Chace, Arthur F, 1966, Ja 7,27:1
Chace, Benjamin B, 1947, Jl 28,15:4
Chace, Benjamin C, 1950, F 10,23:1
Chace, Caril S, 1955, Ja 22,11:3
Chace, Carleton, 1965, Ap 27,37:3
Chace, Charles A (funl, S 19,29:5), 1957, S 17,30:1
Chace, Daniel C, 1946, O 27,60:6
Chace, Fenner A, 1953, Je 5,27:6
Chace, Frederic I, 1958, O 22,35:5
Chace, George H, 1957, Je 12,35:5
Chace, Horace C, 1948, D 3,26:2
Chace, Jonathan Ex-Sen, 1917, Jl 1,19:4
Chace, Lucy F Mrs, 1946, Ja 31,21:2
Chace, Malcolm G, 1955, Jl 17,61:1
Chace, Malcolm G Mrs, 1947, Jl 6,41:2
Chace, Mason S, 1944, Ag 11,15:2
Chace, Morton B, 1939, Ap 24,17:5
Chace, Robert R, 1954, N 25,29:2
Chace, Stanley A, 1939, D 31,18:6
Chace, William G, 1937, Jl 13,19:2
Chach, Michael, 1951, My 7,25:4
Chackes, Jacob Mrs, 1953, My 24,88:2
Chacon, L, 1931, Ap 11,19:3
Chadbourne, Arthur C, 1951, Ag 7,25:2
Chadbourne, Gilbert R, 1942, My 11,15:5
Chadbourne, Humphrey, 1950, O 27,29:4
Chadbourne, Julia M Mrs, 1955, Ap 7,27:4
Chadbourne, Marc, 1941, Ja 5,45:3
Chadbourne, P A, 1883, F 24,5:3; 1884, Je 24,5:3
Chadbourne, Thomas L (por), 1938, Je 16,23:1
Chadbourne, William M (funl plans, My 5,43:5), 1964, My 3,86:6
Chadburn, Mary H Mrs, 1938, O 30,41:1
Chadburn, Thomas, 1949, Ag 25,23:4
Chaddock, Robert E, 1940, O 29,25:7
Chadeayne, David L, 1940, My 10,23:3
Chadeayne, Frank Mrs, 1950, D 18,31:2
Chadeayne, Frank R, 1943, D 9,27:1
Chadeayne, Henry W, 1945, Ap 23,19:3
Chadeayne, Sarah F Mrs, 1939, D 27,21:5
Chadgnon, John I, 1960, Ag 13,15:4
Chadsey, A G, 1881, Jl 17,12:5
Chadwick, Alan S, 1950, Je 23,25:4
Chadwick, Albert A, 1941, Mr 19,21:1
Chadwick, Alfred T, 1951, Jl 23,17:2
Chadwick, Benjamin H Capt, 1916, Mr 2,11:6
Chadwick, Cassie, 1907, O 11,9:6
Chadwick, Charles, 1950, F 25,17:5; 1953, S 29,29:5
Chadwick, Charles L, 1941, O 16,21:4
Chadwick, Charles S, 1959, Mr 26,31:2
Chadwick, Clarence B, 1947, N 29,13:5
Chadwick, Elbridge G, 1945, Mr 24,17:6
Chadwick, Everett D, 1949, F 22,23:3
Chadwick, Frank L, 1937, Mr 17,26:2
Chadwick, Frank Mrs, 1945, D 30,14:5
Chadwick, Frederick P, 1952, Ja 31,27:4
Chadwick, French Ensor Rear-Adm, 1919, Ja 28,9:3
Chadwick, George B, 1961, O 19,35:3
Chadwick, George H, 1953, Ag 17,15:4
Chadwick, Harry P, 1944, Jl 9,36:1
Chadwick, Hector M, 1947, Ja 3,21:3
Chadwick, Helen, 1940, S 6,21:4
Chadwick, Henry, 1908, Ap 21,9:6
Chadwick, Henry W Mrs, 1955, S 26,23:4
Chadwick, Isaac E, 1952, N 20,31:2
Chadwick, J R, 1905, S 25,1:6
Chadwick, James, 1882, My 15,5:6
Chadwick, James A Mrs, 1960, Ap 23,23:4
Chadwick, James W, 1963, My 1,39:1
Chadwick, John, 1961, N 10,35:2
Chadwick, John H, 1938, O 31,15:1
Chadwick, John P, 1940, F 5,17:3
Chadwick, John R Mrs, 1944, Mr 26,42:1
Chadwick, John White Rev, 1904, D 12,9:5
Chadwick, Joseph D, 1943, D 2,27:5
Chadwick, Joseph H, 1948, My 4,25:5
Chadwick, Joseph Mrs, 1945, O 10,36:3
Chadwick, Joseph P Capt, 1914, Ap 23,13:6
Chadwick, Louis G, 1942, S 17,25:3
Chadwick, Louise J Mrs, 1937, Ap 2,23:2
Chadwick, Margaret E Mrs, 1906, Mr 30,9:4
Chadwick, Nat, 1964, F 24,25:3
Chadwick, Richard Sr, 1951, N 5,31:5
Chadwick, Stanley H, 1943, Jl 20,19:2
Chadwick, Stillman P R, 1943, S 21,23:2
Chadwick, Suzanne, 1957, Je 28,23:3
Chadwick, Thomas B, 1955, Je 28,27:5
Chadwick, Tom, 1946, Mr 4,23:2
Chadwick, William L, 1909, Jl 15,7:4; 1948, F 17,25:4
Chadwick-Collins, James Mrs, 1948, My 21,23:1
Chafe, R M, 1949, O 16,89:1
Chafee, Tribbie (funl, O 18,28:8), 1968, O 16,45:3
Chafee, Zechariah, 1943, Jl 9,17:6
Chafee, Zechariah Jr, 1957, F 9,19:3
Chafey, Clarence, 1945, S 4,23:4
Chaffar, Selim A, 1949, Ja 11,27:1
Chaffe, John, 1949, D 28,25:2
Chaffe, John C Mrs, 1946, Ag 14,25:1
Chaffee, A R Lt-Gen, 1914, N 4,7:7
Chaffee, Adna R, 1941, Ag 23,13:1
Chaffee, Adna R Mrs, 1921, Ap 16,11:4; 1945, Ag 26, 44:6
Chaffee, Arthur R, 1948, Mr 21,60:6
Chaffee, Edward James, 1913, S 27,13:5
Chaffee, George Dr, 1922, O 27,17:4
Chaffee, H Almon, 1957, Ja 1,23:5
Chaffee, H Elliott, 1961, Mr 12,86:7
Chaffee, Henry S, 1964, Ja 11,23:3
Chaffee, J H, 1903, Ag 2,7:3
Chaffee, James F Mrs, 1950, O 24,29:3
Chaffee, Jerome S, 1947, N 27,32:2
Chaffee, John W, 1907, Mr 27,9:6
Chaffee, Jonathan I Mrs, 1959, Ap 12,86:8
Chaffee, Julia A Mrs, 1916, Mr 17,11:5
Chaffee, Lawrence, 1956, D 23,30:5
Chaffee, Lawrence D, 1941, Ag 4,13:2
Chaffee, Maurice A, 1967, My 26,39:4
Chaffee, Melzar M, 1947, Je 7,13:4
Chaffee, Newman K, 1944, Ag 5,11:1
Chaffee, Oliver N, 1944, Ap 27,23:3
Chaffee, Roger B (funl and burial plans, Ja 29,49:2; Ja 30,2:7), 1967, Ja 28,1:8
Chaffer, Elmer R Sr, 1944, Jl 8,11:2
Chaffers, William H, 1947, N 30,76:4
Chaffey, Andrew M, 1941, Jl 17,19:6
Chaffey, Richard, 1942, Jl 26,30:6
Chaffin, Andrew D, 1945, Ja 17,21:4
Chaffin, Clarence E, 1943, N 23,25:3
Chaffin, Rafe C, 1958, Mr 26,37:3
Chaffin, Robert F, 1953, Mr 11,29:5
Chafin, Carrie A Mrs, 1942, N 5,26:4
Chafin, Don, 1954, Ag 10,19:2
Chafin, Eugene W, 1920, D 1,15:4
Chafin, Fanny, 1911, Mr 4,11:2
Chagall, Bella, 1944, S 4,19:5
Chagaris, Efthemios F, 1962, Ja 4,33:1
Chagas, Joao, 1925, My 29,17:6
Chagnon, Leon W, 1953, Jl 31,19:2
Chagy, Beryl, 1954, Ap 26,25:4
Chahoon, George Jr, 1951, Ap 16,25:3
Chaiet, Louis, 1950, F 1,29:2
Chaig, Herbert S Mrs, 1944, O 17,23:3
Chaigie, Wallace M, 1944, O 13,19:3
Chaigneau, Auguste, 1941, My 26,19:5
Chaiken, Edward R, 1956, Je 11,31:5
Chaikin, Abraham, 1966, S 20,47:2
Chaikin, Abraham H, 1966, O 10,41:2
Chaikin, Joseph, 1946, Je 3,21:4
Chaikoff, Israel L, 1966, Ja 27,33:4
Chaillaux, Homer L, 1946, F 20,25:1
Chaille, Emerson W, 1939, Ag 29,21:3
Chaille-Long, Charles Col, 1917, Mr 26,11:6
Chaillet, Octave F Mrs, 1953, Mr 3,27:2
Chaim, Adolph Maj, 1924, F 20,19:4
Chain, Kwang-Shi, 1922, Mr 4,15:4
Chaires, Anna E, 1924, Ja 30,19:4
Chairs, Sheriff, 1873, Ja 14,5:4
Chait, Samuel, 1956, Mr 28,31:4
Chaitin, Isaac, 1941, O 25,17:4
Chaitkin, Jacob, 1955, Ag 28,84:4
Chaitovitz, James, 1942, Ja 9,21:5
Chakko, Sarah, 1954, Ja 27,27:3
Chakrin, Harry, 1967, Jl 6,35:2
Chalaire, Alcide Mrs, 1950, Ag 22,27:5
Chalette, Leon, 1958, Mr 4,29:1
Chaleyer, Philip, 1961, S 8,31:1
Chalfant, Edward C, 1942, N 6,23:2
Chalfant, Edward P, 1942, F 22,26:4
Chalfant, Edward T, 1951, Ag 31,15:3
Chalfant, Floyd, 1954, My 28,4:8
Chalfant, Herman S, 1957, Jl 21,60:3
Chalfant, Leroy M, 1939, Ja 19,19:2
Chalfant, Napoleon B, 1939, O 2,17:6
Chalfant, Sidney A, 1943, S 1,19:2
Chalfant, W A, 1943, N 6,13:4
Chalfin, Harry, 1964, My 6,47:1
Chalfin, Jacob L, 1955, N 29,29:4
Chalfin, Paul, 1959, F 16,29:3
Chalfin, Paul M Mrs, 1962, O 23,37:5
Chalfont, Scott, 1952, F 12,16:8
Chalfont, William P, 1950, N 29,33:1
Chaliapin, Julia Mrs, 1965, Ja 7,31:5
Chalif, Louis H, 1948, N 25,31:6
Chalifour, Onesime, 1956, Jl 14,15:6
Chalifoux, Samuel G, 1952, D 18,29:1
Chalk, Peter, 1946, Ap 15,27:4

Chalker, Harold L, 1952, O 13,21:2
Chalkley, Floyd E, 1966, Ja 10,25:6
Chalkley, Otway H, 1956, Mr 23,27:5
Chalkley, Thomas H Mrs (Genevieve), 1965, Jl 30, 25:2
Challan, John P, 1964, Je 1,29:4
Challemel-Lacour, P A, 1896, O 27,16:6
Challen, Paul J, 1949, Je 4,13:5
Challender, Mearl R, 1947, Je 3,25:2
Challenger, Howard S, 1952, Ja 5,11:4
Challenger, Sidney W, 1944, Mr 2,17:4
Challenger, V Winfield, 1957, N 2,21:2
Challenor, George, 1947, Jl 31,21:4
Challinor, David, 1962, Je 25,29:5
Challinor, David Mrs, 1966, Ja 11,29:4
Challinor, George O, 1956, Jl 15,60:7
Challis, James Rev, 1882, D 5,7:4
Challis, William G, 1904, F 29,7:6
Chalmers, Alan R, 1962, O 3,41:4
Chalmers, Allan K Mrs, 1957, Jl 23,27:3
Chalmers, Arthur A Mrs, 1956, Ag 7,27:2
Chalmers, Audrey Mrs, 1957, N 30,21:3
Chalmers, David W, 1950, Ja 18,32:2
Chalmers, Donald, 1937, My 18,23:5
Chalmers, Eliza J, 1951, Mr 29,27:5
Chalmers, George, 1908, Ja 16,9:6
Chalmers, Grace, 1942, O 8,27:3
Chalmers, H, 1932, Je 3,19:5
Chalmers, Henry, 1958, Je 6,23:4
Chalmers, J V, 1927, F 2,25:5
Chalmers, James, 1910, Ap 16,11:6; 1941, Ap 20,42:1
Chalmers, James A, 1937, O 9,19:2
Chalmers, James Dr, 1937, Ja 8,19:5
Chalmers, Jessie J, 1951, Ja 23,27:4
Chalmers, Joan P Mrs, 1940, Ja 26,17:4
Chalmers, John B, 1944, My 25,21:6
Chalmers, John S, 1967, D 6,51:4
Chalmers, Katherine, 1947, N 29,13:5
Chalmers, Lord, 1938, N 18,21:3
Chalmers, Matthew Dr, 1909, Ja 8,9:5
Chalmers, Philip O, 1946, F 16,13:1
Chalmers, S, 1935, D 15,II,10:8
Chalmers, T G Dr, 1884, Je 5,4:7
Chalmers, Thomas, 1903, Jl 14,1:2; 1940, Jl 6,15:2
Chalmers, Thomas H (mem ser, S 14,47:1), 1966, Je 12,87:1
Chalmers, Thomas M Rev Dr, 1937, F 3,23:5
Chalmers, William J, 1938, D 11,60:5
Chalmers, William W, 1944, O 3,23:5
Chaloner, J A, 1935, Je 2,31:1
Chaloner, Tom Mrs, 1944, Mr 6,19:3
Chaloner, William C, 1944, S 24,46:1
Chaloux, Frank, 1953, Ap 3,23:3
Chaloux, Frank Mrs, 1955, Mr 2,27:2
Chaloux, Louis Y, 1962, S 14,31:5
Chalufour, Alex P E, 1948, Jl 10,15:6
Chalupcznski, Mieczyslaw, 1946, Ja 5,13:2
Chalupez, Eleonora Mme, 1954, Ag 25,27:1
Chalzel, Leo, 1953, Jl 18,13:5
Cham (Count Amedee de Noe), 1879, S 20,2:6
Chamales, Thomas T, 1960, Mr 21,10:3
Chamalian, Hacob, 1947, Ap 20,60:6
Chamansky, Adolph B, 1937, Mr 5,21:4
Chamard, Guillaume, 1907, O 29,11:6
Chambellan, Pierre L, 1959, O 8,42:5
Chambellan, Rene P, 1955, N 30,33:3
Chamberlain, A S, 1885, F 19,2:4
Chamberlain, Abiram Ex-Gov, 1911, My 16,13:5
Chamberlain, Ada L, 1942, F 25,19:2
Chamberlain, Aims R, 1951, D 29,11:6
Chamberlain, Albert, 1939, Jl 23,29:3
Chamberlain, Albert H, 1944, Je 29,23:1
Chamberlain, Albert R, 1954, D 1,31:2
Chamberlain, Alexander, 1946, Ja 25,24:2
Chamberlain, Alexander F Dr, 1914, Ap 10,13:6
Chamberlain, Alice F, 1939, Ap 16,III,7:2
Chamberlain, Allen, 1945, Je 25,17:4
Chamberlain, Amos, 1960, Mr 16,37:4
Chamberlain, Arthur, 1913, O 21,9:6; 1941, Ag 9,15:4
Chamberlain, Arthur N, 1958, Mr 4,29:2
Chamberlain, Austen Sir (Jos), 1937, Mr 17,14:1
Chamberlain, B F Maj (funl), 1871, D 29,5:4
Chamberlain, C M, 1879, My 12,5:2
Chamberlain, C W, 1884, Ag 22,5:3
Chamberlain, Callie Mrs, 1954, D 20,29:1
Chamberlain, Carroll W, 1958, Ja 2,29:4
Chamberlain, Charles J, 1943, Ja 6,27:2
Chamberlain, Clark W, 1948, O 14,29:2
Chamberlain, Cyrus, 1903, F 8,1:4
Chamberlain, Cyrus N Mrs, 1917, Jl 8,15:5
Chamberlain, D S Dr, 1903, My 12,9:6
Chamberlain, Daniel H, 1907, Ap 14,9:6
Chamberlain, Dexter H, 1952, O 14,31:5
Chamberlain, Donald E, 1964, D 26,17:3
Chamberlain, Dudley Mrs, 1951, N 1,29:4
Chamberlain, Dwight L, 1955, D 1,35:4
Chamberlain, E J, 1924, Ag 28,17:5
Chamberlain, E M, 1939, Ag 14,15:4
Chamberlain, Edward B, 1948, N 7,89:1
Chamberlain, Edwin C, 1949, My 24,28:5
Chamberlain, Emily Davis Mrs, 1968, N 6,47:1
Chamberlain, Esther R Mrs, 1942, F 10,19:6
Chamberlain, Everett, 1875, F 28,5:2
Chamberlain, Francis N, 1965, O 7,3:8
Chamberlain, Frank C, 1940, Mr 28,24:4
Chamberlain, Frank L, 1951, My 15,31:1
Chamberlain, Fred V, 1958, Mr 9,86:2
Chamberlain, Fred V S Mrs, 1956, Ja 4,27:4
Chamberlain, Frederick H, 1940, Jl 4,15:3
Chamberlain, G E, 1928, Jl 10,23:1
Chamberlain, G Howard, 1961, Je 22,84:3
Chamberlain, George A, 1941, N 17,19:4; 1966, Mr 5, 27:4
Chamberlain, George B, 1943, Jl 14,19:4
Chamberlain, George C Mrs, 1948, Ap 10,13:3
Chamberlain, George D, 1944, F 21,15:1
Chamberlain, George D Mrs, 1952, O 6,25:5
Chamberlain, George F, 1914, F 9,7:6
Chamberlain, George H, 1952, Ag 8,17:5
Chamberlain, Guy C, 1945, S 24,19:5
Chamberlain, H S, 1927, Ja 10,23:2
Chamberlain, Harry B, 1937, Ap 27,23:6
Chamberlain, Harry M, 1939, Ja 1,24:4
Chamberlain, Harry M Mrs, 1947, Je 10,27:4
Chamberlain, Harvey W, 1943, Ap 10,17:1
Chamberlain, Henry, 1954, O 12,27:1
Chamberlain, Henry Richardson (funl, F 18,11:6), 1911, F 16,11:4
Chamberlain, Henry T, 1961, My 11,37:2
Chamberlain, Hiram S Capt, 1916, Mr 16,13:6
Chamberlain, Horlad, 1912, Jl 22,7:6
Chamberlain, Ida, 1943, Ap 3,15:5
Chamberlain, Ivory, 1881, Mr 10,5:5
Chamberlain, Ivy M Lady, 1941, F 14,17:3
Chamberlain, J C Mrs, 1884, Ja 5,1:3
Chamberlain, J Maxwell Dr, 1968, My 27,47:2
Chamberlain, J P, 1878, O 6,2:2
Chamberlain, James L, 1959, D 5,23:3
Chamberlain, Jessie Reeve Mrs, 1968, O 7,47:1
Chamberlain, John A, 1949, O 4,27:2
Chamberlain, John A (cor, My 29,45:1), 1955, My 28,15:1
Chamberlain, John C, 1943, Jl 4,20:3
Chamberlain, John F Mrs (Emily Jordan), 1912, F 20,11:4
Chamberlain, John H Rev Dr, 1921, Ja 11,11:4
Chamberlain, John L, 1948, N 15,25:1
Chamberlain, John L Mrs, 1947, F 11,27:1
Chamberlain, John M, 1959, Mr 6,25:4
Chamberlain, John Mrs, 1955, S 9,23:3
Chamberlain, Joseph (funl, Jl 7,9:5), 1914, Jl 4,7:1
Chamberlain, Joseph, 1947, Ag 23,13:6
Chamberlain, Joseph P, 1951, My 22,31:4
Chamberlain, Joshua L, 1914, F 25,9:5
Chamberlain, Kenneth H, 1942, Ja 11,44:1
Chamberlain, Kenyon F, 1947, D 5,26:2
Chamberlain, Lawrence, 1961, D 19,33:1
Chamberlain, Leander Trowbridge Rev (will, Jl 24,7:5), 1913, My 11,IV,7:6
Chamberlain, Lewis B, 1942, F 26,19:2
Chamberlain, Lewis B Mrs, 1948, Mr 3,24:2
Chamberlain, Lloyd E Judge, 1937, F 17,22:1
Chamberlain, Luther H, 1944, F 9,19:2
Chamberlain, Marcia K Mrs (will), 1955, Ag 3,15:4
Chamberlain, N B, 1878, Je 17,2:3
Chamberlain, N B Sir, 1902, F 19,9:3
Chamberlain, Neville, 1940, N 11,1:4
Chamberlain, Neville Mrs, 1967, F 13,33:4
Chamberlain, Noel B, 1921, Ja 9,23:2
Chamberlain, Orlando E, 1907, Jl 31,7:5
Chamberlain, Park, 1948, Ag 31,26:2
Chamberlain, Paul M, 1940, My 29,23:3
Chamberlain, Philetus, 1937, Ag 6,17:3
Chamberlain, Robert F, 1967, Jl 17,29:5
Chamberlain, Robert L, 1941, Je 24,19:1
Chamberlain, Robert N Justice, 1917, S 21,9:6
Chamberlain, Robert R, 1963, S 20,33:2
Chamberlain, Rodman W, 1966, O 1,32:6
Chamberlain, Roy B, 1967, Ja 14,31:3
Chamberlain, Roy W, 1958, Je 16,23:5
Chamberlain, Rudolph W, 1945, S 17,19:1
Chamberlain, Sam M Mrs, 1905, Ja 19,9:1
Chamberlain, Samuel Selwyn, 1916, Ja 26,11:7
Chamberlain, W J, 1901, Ag 15,7:6
Chamberlain, W Taylor, 1945, My 23,19:5
Chamberlain, W W, 1945, N 26,21:5
Chamberlain, Walker Rev, 1909, Mr 30,9:4
Chamberlain, Walter B, 1961, Ap 5,37:4
Chamberlain, Walter E, 1959, O 31,4:6
Chamberlain, Warner A, 1957, My 1,37:5
Chamberlain, William, 1967, Jl 31,27:4
Chamberlain, William E, 1911, Ag 7,7:6; 1940, O 24, 25:2
Chamberlain, William H, 1943, Ja 24,42:3; 1951, D 15,13:4
Chamberlain, William H H, 1942, F 16,17:2
Chamberlain, William I Rev, 1937, S 29,23:2
Chamberlain, William R, 1949, S 24,13:4
Chamberlain-Wagner, Eva, 1942, My 27,23:5
Chamberlaine, Henry Rev, 1924, O 6,19:5
Chamberlayne, Churchill G, 1939, Ap 4,25:3
Chamberlayne, Edward P, 1963, Je 8,25:4
Chamberlayne, Edward S, 1950, Mr 3,25:2
Chamberlayne, J H, 1882, F 19,9:3
Chamberlin, B C, 1933, N 11,15:6
Chamberlin, Benjamin D, 1962, My 22,37:3
Chamberlin, Benjamin D Mrs, 1962, F 14,33:1
Chamberlin, C A, 1878, S 2,5:1
Chamberlin, Carrie D Mrs, 1944, S 10,46:1
Chamberlin, Clarence V C Mrs, 1950, F 14,25:3
Chamberlin, Clayton P, 1949, Je 4,13:4
Chamberlin, Cornelius C, 1952, Je 14,15:2
Chamberlin, E C, 1938, Jl 5,17:5
Chamberlin, Edward H, 1967, Jl 17,29:2
Chamberlin, Emily Hall, 1916, Mr 1,11:6
Chamberlin, Eugene, 1919, O 2,17:7
Chamberlin, Frederic E, 1939, Mr 14,21:2
Chamberlin, G Howard, 1948, Ja 29,23:2
Chamberlin, Gardner J, 1939, Ja 25,21:2
Chamberlin, Georgia L, 1943, S 8,23:4
Chamberlin, Harry D, 1944, O 1,46:1
Chamberlin, Henry B, 1941, Jl 8,19:4
Chamberlin, J Douglas, 1961, D 3,88:2
Chamberlin, John R, 1950, My 6,15:5
Chamberlin, L Alfred, 1959, My 12,35:2
Chamberlin, Lafayette, 1945, My 26,15:1
Chamberlin, Mary W, 1964, Ap 28,37:4
Chamberlin, Melville P, 1941, S 6,15:5
Chamberlin, Noel, 1943, Ag 17,17:3
Chamberlin, Robert B, 1951, Ap 24,29:3
Chamberlin, Rollin T, 1948, Mr 7,70:4
Chamberlin, Sanford, 1950, My 24,29:2
Chamberlin, Ward B, 1903, N 13,7:5; 1956, Mr 22,35:
Chamberlin, William F, 1943, Jl 30,15:4
Chamberlin, William G, 1953, Je 5,27:3
Chamberlyn, A H, 1903, Ja 11,7:5
Chambers, Adam Rev, 1923, Ja 26,17:3
Chambers, Albert M, 1968, D 17,50:5
Chambers, Alex B, 1950, Jl 6,27:3
Chambers, Ambrose E (funeral plans, My1,39:3), 1963, Ap 26,36:2
Chambers, Arthur, 1876, Je 1,6:7
Chambers, Arthur C, 1925, D 22,21:4
Chambers, Arthur E, 1955, Ap 8,21:5
Chambers, Arthur L, 1940, Ag 16,15:2
Chambers, B Arnold, 1966, My 6,47:4
Chambers, B Stuart Rev Dr, 1918, F 16,11:5
Chambers, C Bosseron Mrs, 1941, Ja 13,15:5
Chambers, Charles, 1958, Ja 30,23:2
Chambers, Charles E, 1939, Mr 21,23:5; 1941, N 6, 23:2
Chambers, Charles Haddon, 1921, Mr 29,15:6
Chambers, Cornelius, 1941, Ag 8,15:5
Chambers, Dennis F, 1951, O 21,93:2
Chambers, Dorothea K L Mrs, 1960, Ja 9,21:3
Chambers, Edward C G, 1940, N 2,23:2
Chambers, Edward J C, 1948, Mr 10,27:4
Chambers, Elizabeth B, 1952, Ja 13,89:2
Chambers, Elsie Mrs, 1939, N 4,15:4
Chambers, Emaline Mrs, 1923, O 17,19:3
Chambers, Ernest J Col, 1925, My 13,21:3
Chambers, Francis T, 1939, N 10,23:4
Chambers, Frank A, 1951, Mr 22,31:5
Chambers, Frank E, 1947, N 26,23:3
Chambers, Frank M, 1939, Je 14,23:4
Chambers, Frank R, 1940, My 1,23:4
Chambers, Frank R Mrs, 1947, O 6,21:3
Chambers, Frank V, 1940, F 7,21:3
Chambers, Frank W, 1950, Mr 16,31:1; 1962, Ap 1 43:3
Chambers, Franklin S, 1947, Mr 2,60:7
Chambers, Fred, 1941, S 15,17:3
Chambers, Frederick, 1908, Mr 29,9:6
Chambers, Frederick C, 1938, F 13,41:4
Chambers, Frederick D, 1953, N 16,25:5
Chambers, George F, 1965, Jl 4,37:2
Chambers, George J, 1954, O 10,87:1
Chambers, George L P Mrs, 1948, Jl 22,23:4
Chambers, Gerald H, 1957, Ag 8,23:1
Chambers, Gordon, 1950, F 28,29:5
Chambers, Hamilton P, 1961, Ap 29,23:6
Chambers, Harry B, 1954, N 15,27:5
Chambers, Harry B Mrs, 1956, Jl 10,31:4
Chambers, Henry K Mrs, 1965, Ag 10,29:2
Chambers, Henry L, 1963, My 13,29:2
Chambers, Henry W, 1965, Ap 12,35:2
Chambers, Herbert J Mrs, 1945, Ap 22,36:3
Chambers, J Wheaton, 1958, F 5,28:1
Chambers, James, 1917, Je 12,13:5
Chambers, James A, 1954, Mr 2,25:2
Chambers, James S, 1923, F 3,13:4
Chambers, Jared J, 1942, O 18,52:4
Chambers, Joanna I, 1958, Ja 29,27:1
Chambers, John B, 1955, Ag 18,23:2
Chambers, John C, 1948, My 28,23:5
Chambers, John J, 1944, S 9,15:2
Chambers, John Rev, 1875, S 24,4:5
Chambers, John W Dr, 1917, Ja 22,11:3
Chambers, Jordan, 1962, Ag 12,80:2
Chambers, Joseph, 1903, O 1,9:5
Chambers, Joseph A, 1953, My 21,31:1
Chambers, Joseph E Sr, 1948, F 20,28:3
Chambers, Julia L Mrs, 1966, O 15,29:2
Chambers, Julius, 1920, F 13,11:3
Chambers, Kenneth, 1950, N 15,31:5
Chambers, L Morgan, 1938, Mr 3,21:2
Chambers, Leverett, 1958, Mr 9,86:8
Chambers, Lyster, 1947, Ja 28,23:4
Chambers, Martin Luther Dr, 1905, Je 13,9:6

Chambers, Maude E, 1937, F 16,23:4
Chambers, Merritt G Mrs, 1940, F 14,21:5
Chambers, Mordaunt, 1945, Ap 28,15:1
Chambers, Myron G, 1961, Ja 1,48:1
Chambers, Norma, 1953, Ja 1,23:5
Chambers, Pauline E Mrs, 1940, D 6,23:2
Chambers, R W, 1933, D 17,36:1
Chambers, Ralph H, 1951, D 24,13:2
Chambers, Raymond R, 1943, Ap 8,23:5
Chambers, Raymond W, 1942, Ap 25,13:3
Chambers, Robert, 1871, Mr 18,1:4; 1957, Jl 24,25:1
Chambers, Robert A, 1951, S 20,31:1
Chambers, Robert C Mrs, 1952, Mr 9,92:5
Chambers, Robert F, 1947, N 19,28:3
Chambers, Robert Mrs, 1961, Ag 2,29:4
Chambers, Robert N, 1954, Je 15,29:5
Chambers, Robert N Mrs, 1942, S 1,19:3
Chambers, Robert Rev, 1917, Ap 4,15:5
Chambers, Robert S, 1943, My 15,15:1
Chambers, Samuel D Sr, 1951, Ap 16,25:4
Chambers, Samuel Mrs, 1947, F 5,26:1
Chambers, Samuel W, 1951, D 7,27:5
Chambers, Sara D, 1953, Jl 28,19:3
Chambers, Stuart M, 1960, Ag 27,19:3
Chambers, Talbot W, 1954, Ap 8,27:2
Chambers, Tileston F, 1947, F 19,25:5
Chambers, Vactor T, 1957, S 21,19:3
Chambers, W, 1883, My 21,7:2
Chambers, Walter, 1903, Je 20,2:2
Chambers, Walter A, 1951, Jl 14,13:3; 1953, Ap 30, 31:3
Chambers, Walter B, 1945, Ap 21,13:6
Chambers, Walter S, 1951, Mr 14,33:4
Chambers, Washington I Mrs, 1945, Jl 27,15:5
Chambers, Whittaker, 1961, Jl 12,1:6
Chambers, Wilber W, 1943, Je 6,44:2
Chambers, Will G, 1949, Ap 17,76:7
Chambers, Willard L, 1943, O 10,48:4
Chambers, William C, 1951, Mr 30,23:1
Chambers, William E, 1952, F 13,31:1
Chambers, William G, 1956, Jl 7,13:4
Chambers, William H, 1950, My 7,108:1
Chambers, William P, 1911, Jl 19,9:6
Chamblin, Gabriel H, 1952, Mr 14,20:6
Chamblin, Walter Jr, 1955, S 24,22:2
Chambliss, Alexander, 1947, O 1,29:2
Chambliss, Anna Mrs, 1954, My 3,25:5
Chambliss, Hardee, 1947, Je 3,25:1
Chambord, Comte de, 1883, Ag 25,5:3
Chambord, Countess de, 1886, Mr 26,1:2
Chambre, A St John Rev Dr, 1911, D 8,13:4
Chambre, Louis, 1955, Ap 23,19:2
Chambrun, Aldebert de, 1962, Ap 24,37:1
Chambrun, Charles de, 1952, N 7,23:5
Chambrun, Comtesse De (C Longworth), 1954, Je 2, 31:3
Chambrun, Marie de Countess, 1951, O 11,37:5
Chambrun, Marquise de, 1902, N 20,9:6
Chambrun, Pierre de Marquis, 1954, Ag 25,27:1
Chambrun, Suzanne Eleanore de, 1921, D 19,15:3
Chambure, Comte de, 1953, S 27,87:2
Chameides, Maximilian, 1963, N 3,88:8
Chameroy, Frank V, 1962, Je 13,41:5
Chamie, Tatiana (trb, D 20,II,10:7), 1953, N 19,31:3
Chamier-Glisezenski, W von, 1943, Ag 21,3:4
Chaminadas, Gabriel Mrs, 1966, Jl 21,33:1
Chaminade, Cecile (por), 1944, Ap 19,23:1
Chamlee, Mario, 1966, N 15,41:5
Chamlin, William, 1958, My 13,29:3
Chamorel, J, 1928, Mr 13,20:3
Chamorro, Agustin, 1946, Mr 26,29:5
Chamorro, Diego M Mrs, 1951, N 17,17:6
Chamorro, Diego Manuel, 1923, O 14,6:2
Chamorro, Emiliano, 1966, F 27,84:7
Chamorro, Emiliano Mrs, 1952, Ap 8,29:3
Chamorro, Pedro J, 1952, D 10,35:4
Chamorro, Rosendo, 1947, Ja 8,24:3
Chamot, Auguste F, 1909, S 30,9:7
Champ, E Oliver, 1954, N 28,87:1
Champ, Walter B, 1940, Je 24,15:5
Champ, William S, 1924, Je 3,17:6
Champagne, Charlotte, 1953, Je 9,27:3
Champagne, Earl O, 1949, Ja 23,68:6
Champagny, Count, 1882, My 1,5:1
Champetier de Ribes, Auguste, 1947, Mr 7,26:2
Champion, Arthur, 1876, F 6,6:7
Champion, Charles W, 1958, F 21,23:3
Champion, D'Arcy Lyndon, 1968, Mr 23,31:5
Champion, Earl M, 1952, Je 11,29:6
Champion, Edouard, 1938, Mr 1,21:4
Champion, Edward L, 1965, My 4,43:3
Champion, F G Bevill, 1961, D 26,25:2
Champion, Frank B, 1960, Je 5,87:1
Champion, George, 1946, S 10,5:3
Champion, Harry, 1942, Ja 15,19:6
Champion, Henry C, 1910, Ja 12,9:4
Champion, James A Mrs, 1942, N 25,23:4
Champion, John B, 1948, Ja 19,24:3
Champion, John W, 1954, Mr 3,27:3
Champion, Joseph G, 1948, N 15,25:4
Champion, Lee Mrs, 1953, Mr 17,29:4
Champion, LeRoy L Mrs, 1964, Ag 8,19:5
Champion, Louis A, 1947, Ag 11,23:4
Champion, Michael, 1904, Ja 10,10:2
Champion, Necols, 1965, N 28,88:8
Champion, Pierre, 1942, Jl 1,25:3
Champion, Raymond, 1940, Ja 23,21:2
Champion, Raymond W, 1949, Ag 5,19:5
Champion, Robert W, 1937, N 3,24:3
Champion, S B, 1903, S 10,7:6
Champion, Stevens, 1956, Mr 11,67:7
Champion de Crespigny, Claude, 1941, My 17,15:1
Champlain, Harold P, 1957, Je 28,23:5
Champlain, M B, 1879, Mr 10,5:6
Champlin, Archie E, 1951, F 6,27:3
Champlin, Charles A Mrs, 1943, S 18,17:3
Champlin, Charles D, 1950, Ag 24,27:6
Champlin, Charles H, 1952, Mr 2,92:1
Champlin, Charles K, 1946, F 14,25:5
Champlin, Charles S Mrs, 1947, S 22,23:4
Champlin, E Frank, 1946, Ap 7,46:4
Champlin, Ellis H, 1961, N 8,35:4
Champlin, Frank E C Mrs, 1925, O 15,23:4
Champlin, George A, 1950, F 22,30:2
Champlin, George A Mrs, 1949, O 30,84:5
Champlin, George B, 1946, O 16,27:2
Champlin, George M, 1948, N 6,13:4
Champlin, H L, 1901, D 22,7:5
Champlin, Henry D, 1946, N 14,29:2
Champlin, James M, 1945, F 21,19:2
Champlin, John, 1954, N 5,7:4
Champlin, John D, 1949, Ag 12,18:2
Champlin, John Denison, 1915, Ja 9,11:4
Champlin, Lawrence W, 1956, Mr 7,33:2
Champlin, Lewis T, 1951, Ap 2,25:5
Champlin, Loren J, 1938, My 27,17:4
Champlin, Louis F, 1948, Ag 30,18:2
Champlin, Paul M, 1950, O 25,35:5
Champlin, Tint, 1938, N 19,17:6
Champney, Benjamin, 1907, D 12,11:5
Champney, Elizabeth Mrs, 1922, O 14,13:5
Champney, Henry T, 1913, N 19,9:6
Chan, Lazard, 1940, My 24,19:1
Chan, Tom Y, 1944, S 5,19:4
Chan Chak, Andrew, 1949, S 1,21:6
Chan Pi-chun, 1959, Je 27,2:7
Chanal, F V A, 1882, Mr 23,5:3
Chanalis, Michael N, 1962, Ja 9,47:1
Chance, Albion S, 1955, N 25,28:1
Chance, Charles Mrs, 1940, O 19,17:3
Chance, Edwin M, 1954, N 28,86:3
Chance, Edwin M Mrs, 1940, N 22,23:3
Chance, Frank L, 1940, O 23,23:4
Chance, Frank Mrs, 1954, F 24,25:1
Chance, George G, 1958, O 3,29:2
Chance, Henry M Dr, 1937, F 21,II,10:5
Chance, James F, 1938, O 19,23:5
Chance, Leslie G, 1959, My 11,27:4
Chance, Pierce M, 1944, Mr 31,21:6
Chance, R Robinson, 1958, Mr 2,89:1
Chance, Samuel J, 1962, Mr 1,31:1
Chancellor, John R, 1952, Ag 2,15:7
Chancellor, Phillip S, 1946, Jl 13,15:3
Chandlee, Benjamin, 1952, Ja 8,27:3
Chandlee, Edward E, 1962, Je 6,41:1
Chandlee, Edward E Mrs, 1958, S 20,19:5
Chandlee, Harry, 1956, Ag 4,15:6
Chandlee, William H, 1951, S 11,29:1
Chandler, Albert B Mrs, 1907, S 16,9:6
Chandler, Albert E, 1954, Ja 30,17:2
Chandler, Albert R, 1957, Mr 25,25:5
Chandler, Alex, 1942, S 10,27:1
Chandler, Alfred A Col, 1937, Ja 13,23:3
Chandler, Alfred N, 1954, Mr 13,15:5
Chandler, Arthur H, 1945, Je 30,17:4
Chandler, Arthur W, 1955, F 6,88:8
Chandler, Asa C, 1958, Ag 24,86:2
Chandler, Asa M, 1954, S 24,23:2
Chandler, Augustus, 1922, Je 20,19:6
Chandler, Bert D, 1947, D 14,76:4
Chandler, Buckingham, 1950, S 6,29:2
Chandler, C H, 1881, Ap 3,5:4
Chandler, C Q, 1943, D 21,27:2
Chandler, Charles, 1960, O 28,31:3
Chandler, Charles de F, 1939, My 19,21:3
Chandler, Charles E, 1948, Ag 3,26:2
Chandler, Charles F Mrs (will, My 13,25:2), 1953, Ap 17,25:1
Chandler, Charles F Prof, 1925, N 17,25:3
Chandler, Charles Frederick (funl, Ag 27,19:5), 1925, Ag 26,19:4
Chandler, Charles H, 1941, D 31,18:2
Chandler, Charles L, 1962, Je 30,19:5
Chandler, Charles W, 1937, Je 29,21:3
Chandler, Christopher D, 1947, Je 3,26:3
Chandler, Dan Mrs (Peggy), 1953, Je 13,15:5
Chandler, David H Mrs, 1955, S 27,35:3
Chandler, Digby W, 1967, O 8,87:1
Chandler, Douglas M H Mrs, 1956, F 3,11:2
Chandler, E Lawrence, 1966, Ja 31,39:2
Chandler, Edward M, 1944, Ap 9,33:1
Chandler, Elmer A, 1947, Ag 19,23:4
Chandler, Etta, 1956, My 9,33:4
Chandler, Frances Mrs, 1952, N 28,28:6
Chandler, Frank M, 1950, Mr 26,92:6
Chandler, Frank W, 1947, Je 14,15:1
Chandler, Frederick B, 1966, D 24,19:4
Chandler, Frederick C, 1945, F 19,17:2
Chandler, Frederick D, 1946, O 31,25:5
Chandler, Fremont A, 1954, D 25,11:3
Chandler, G H, 1883, Ag 14,2:4
Chandler, George A, 1941, D 8,23:5
Chandler, George B, 1905, Je 30,9:4; 1943, N 25,25:3
Chandler, George F, 1947, O 15,27:3; 1964, N 7,27:1
Chandler, George F Mrs, 1945, Mr 15,23:2
Chandler, George W, 1953, My 28,23:4
Chandler, H E Mrs, 1949, Je 15,29:4
Chandler, Harry (por), 1944, S 24,45:1
Chandler, Harry Mrs, 1952, Ag 10,60:7
Chandler, Helen, 1956, Ja 22,88:5
Chandler, Henry A E, 1949, D 29,26:4
Chandler, Henry G Jr, 1967, Je 1,43:3
Chandler, Henry Sweeting, 1906, D 27,7:4
Chandler, Henry T, 1960, Jl 21,27:3
Chandler, Henry W, 1953, D 5,2:7
Chandler, Izora Mrs, 1906, Ag 26,9:6
Chandler, J A C, 1934, Je 1,23:4
Chandler, J J, 1903, Ap 24,9:6
Chandler, J R, 1880, Jl 12,5:4
Chandler, J S, 1934, Je 21,23:5
Chandler, James K, 1963, N 21,39:4
Chandler, Jeff (Ira Grossel),(funl, Je 20,33:1; will, Jl 6,19:1), 1961, Je 18,88:3
Chandler, John F, 1941, Ap 17,23:5
Chandler, John F Mrs, 1957, Je 14,25:4
Chandler, John G, 1939, Mr 24,21:5
Chandler, John Gorham, 1915, Je 23,11:4
Chandler, Joseph D, 1958, Je 2,27:1
Chandler, Joseph E, 1945, Ag 20,19:5
Chandler, Joseph S, 1959, My 25,29:3
Chandler, Joseph S Jr, 1948, Ap 4,60:5
Chandler, Lewis S, 1963, Ag 3,17:3
Chandler, Lilburn, 1948, D 3,25:2
Chandler, Louis B, 1945, My 31,15:4
Chandler, Louis H, 1939, F 1,21:2
Chandler, M L, 1951, Jl 5,28:3
Chandler, Mary A, 1883, Jl 18,2:5
Chandler, Mrs, 1871, Mr 21,1:4
Chandler, N, 1884, Ag 14,5:3
Chandler, Norman, 1944, Ja 28,17:5
Chandler, Norman W, 1945, Jl 17,13:5
Chandler, Percy M, 1944, O 15,44:2
Chandler, Philip, 1968, My 24,47:2
Chandler, Porter R Mrs, 1958, O 26,88:8
Chandler, Ralph J, 1966, Ag 7,81:3
Chandler, Randolph E, 1942, F 7,17:1
Chandler, Randolph E Mrs, 1956, Ag 17,19:2
Chandler, Raymond, 1959, Mr 27,23:4
Chandler, Robert A, 1938, Ag 2,19:4
Chandler, Robert C Mrs, 1903, Jl 1,9:1
Chandler, Robert K, 1967, Ag 23,51:6
Chandler, Samuel Gen, 1867, Jl 26,2:6
Chandler, Sara A Mrs, 1948, F 1,60:6
Chandler, Seth Carlo Prof, 1914, Ja 1,15:4
Chandler, Spencer H, 1947, Ag 26,23:5
Chandler, Susan E, 1952, F 10,93:2
Chandler, Swithin, 1940, D 11,27:2
Chandler, T P, 1928, Ag 18,13:4
Chandler, Thomas W, 1938, Ag 13,13:5
Chandler, Virginia M, 1942, My 6,19:2
Chandler, W D, 1941, Mr 9,41:3
Chandler, W J D Mrs, 1950, F 10,24:2
Chandler, W M, 1935, Mr 17,37:5
Chandler, Walter, 1924, N 18,25:4; 1967, O 2,47:2
Chandler, Walter G, 1960, Jl 7,31:4
Chandler, Willard P, 1941, My 25,37:1
Chandler, William, 1953, My 25,25:2
Chandler, William D, 1948, Ja 21,25:6
Chandler, William E, 1947, Je 1,60:4; 1959, O 26,29:2
Chandler, William Eaton Ex-Sen, 1917, D 1,13:6
Chandler, William G, 1965, Je 17,33:3
Chandler, William H, 1939, D 3,60:7
Chandler, William H Dr, 1906, N 24,11:6
Chandler, William H Mrs, 1938, My 21,15:2
Chandler, William K, 1940, My 25,17:5
Chandler, William R Mrs, 1954, My 15,15:2
Chandler, Z, 1879, N 2,1:1
Chandler, Zach A, 1950, Mr 9,29:4
Chandor, Douglas (trb lr, Ja 20,24:6;will, Ap 19,52:6), 1953, Ja 14,31:4
Chandor, Mary H M Mrs, 1941, My 10,15:6
Chaney, Arthur U, 1941, D 4,25:4
Chaney, Clarence W, 1955, Ja 28,20:2
Chaney, James E, 1967, Ag 22,39:1
Chaney, L, 1930, Ag 27,25:1
Chaney, L Beverley Dr, 1968, Mr 14,43:1
Chaney, Newcomb K, 1966, Jl 14,35:4
Chanfrau, F S, 1884, O 2,5:5
Chanfrau, Frank Mrs, 1909, S 22,9:3
Chang, Chien, 1926, Ag 26,19:3
Chang, Henry K Mrs, 1957, Ap 20,17:2
Chang, John M, 1966, Je 5,87:1
Chang, John Wen-ti, 1961, Je 29,33:2
Chang, Peng Chun, 1957, Jl 21,61:1
Chang Chia, 1957, Mr 5,31:3
Chang-Chih-Tung, 1909, O 6,9:2
Chang Lan, 1955, F 10,31:3
Chang Lin-chih, 1967, F 25,4:6
Chang Nai-Teh, 1947, Jl 28,15:4

Chang Ning Chou, 1957, O 17,26:5
Chang Po-ling, 1951, F 28,27:3
Chang Shan-tze, 1940, O 21,17:6
Chang Shu-chi, 1957, Ag 20,27:4
Chang Tao-fan, 1968, Je 14,47:4
Chang Yung-ni, 1945, Ag 6,15:4
Changarnier, N A T (see also F 16), 1877, Mr 4,10:2
Chanin, Abraham L, 1968, My 3,47:1
Chanin, Nathan, 1965, Ag 9,25:2
Chanin, Simon, 1946, S 7,15:5
Chanis, Daniel (funl, Ja 24,17:4), 1961, Ja 23,23:5
Chankalian, Edward J, 1947, My 8,25:3
Chankalian, James M, 1947, My 13,26:3
Chanler, Ashley Mrs (H Coggeshall), 1966, S 27,47:1
Chanler, J D, 1877, O 25,8:2
Chanler, J W, 1877, O 21,6:7
Chanler, J W Mrs (funl, D 17,8:4), 1875, D 14,5:2
Chanler, L Stuyvesant Jr Mrs, 1952, Je 21,15:6
Chanler, Lewis S, 1942, Mr 2,19:1
Chanler, Lewis S Mrs, 1961, Mr 12,86:2
Chanler, R W, 1930, O 25,17:1
Chanler, Theodore W, 1961, Jl 28,21:2
Chanler, W A, 1934, Mr 5,15:5
Chanler, William A Mrs, 1946, Je 20,23:1
Chanler, Winthrop A Mrs, 1952, D 20,17:6
Channel, William Fry Sir, 1873, F 27,1:7
Channell, Edward C, 1942, Jl 14,38:5
Channell, Wayne, 1950, O 4,31:3
Channer, Earle A, 1948, Je 17,25:1
Channing, Elizabeth Lady, 1925, Ag 29,11:5
Channing, Frank, 1938, Jl 26,19:5
Channing, George, 1957, My 30,19:2
Channing, J Parke, 1942, O 14,25:5
Channing, Lord, 1926, F 23,23:5
Channing, Mark, 1943, D 23,19:1
Channing, Roscoe H, 1961, Ap 4,37:4
Channing, Roscoe Henry, 1916, F 14,13:6
Channing, W H Rev, 1884, D 24,1:1
Channing, Walter, 1954, Ag 16,17:3
Channing-Stetson, Grace E Mrs, 1937, Ap 5,19:5
Channon, Henry, 1958, O 9,37:3
Channon, Irving M, 1942, N 9,23:4
Channon, Veta W Mrs, 1943, Je 18,21:5
Chanslor, Joseph A, 1946, My 22,21:5
Chanslor, Roy, 1964, Ap 17,35:1
Chant, Clarence A, 1956, N 20,37:2
Chant, Frederick H, 1950, Ja 20,26:2
Chant, Laura Ormiston Mrs, 1923, F 17,13:4
Chantanacorun, Waravan, 1952, My 15,31:5
Chantry, Allan J, 1959, Ap 10,29:4
Chanukoff, Leon, 1958, S 26,27:3
Chanute, Charles D, 1911, S 18,11:4
Chanzy, A E A, 1883, Ja 6,1:5
Chao Erh-lu, 1967, F 7,7:1
Chao Tai-Wen, 1943, D 30,17:3
Chapais, Joseph A T, 1946, Jl 16,23:6
Chapaprieta Torregrosa, Joaquin, 1951, O 17,31:1
Chapchal, Jacques, 1947, Mr 20,28:3
Chapel, Eugenia (Mrs H Dardier), 1964, Ap 25,29:4
Chapell, Marcus Henry, 1907, Ap 12,9:6
Chapelle, Charles C, 1958, Je 17,29:5
Chapelle, Henry M, 1952, Je 22,68:4
Chapelle, Placide-Louis (funl), 1905, Ag 11,7:6
Chapelle de Jumilhac, Armand de Duke de Richelieu, 1952, My 31,17:5
Chapelsky, Leo, 1953, Mr 21,17:5
Chapi, Maria Teresa, 1924, Ja 5,13:5
Chapin, A C, 1936, O 3,17:1
Chapin, Albert F, 1957, Ag 6,27:5
Chapin, Alex F, 1937, O 13,23:1
Chapin, Alfred Clark Mrs, 1908, D 11,11:4
Chapin, Alfred H Jr, 1961, Ja 6,27:4
Chapin, Anna Alice, 1920, F 27,13:4
Chapin, Anne M, 1967, Ap 9,92:7
Chapin, Archer L, 1956, S 25,33:4
Chapin, Archibald B, 1962, O 20,25:3
Chapin, Arlo, 1942, O 22,21:3
Chapin, Arthur B, 1943, Mr 20,15:3
Chapin, Arthur F, 1941, N 2,55:4
Chapin, Asahel, 1947, Je 2,25:3
Chapin, Benjamin Chester, 1918, Je 4,13:4
Chapin, C E, 1930, D 14,24:1
Chapin, C W, 1883, Je 11,5:1
Chapin, Carl M, 1938, F 23,23:2
Chapin, Carroll S, 1953, Ag 10,23:6
Chapin, Charles B, 1941, Ag 6,17:1
Chapin, Charles E, 1921, Ja 31,9:4
Chapin, Charles H B, 1943, Ag 15,38:7
Chapin, Charles L, 1937, Je 6,II,9:2
Chapin, Charles M Mrs, 1959, Je 22,25:5
Chapin, Charles V, 1941, F 1,18:2
Chapin, Charles V Mrs, 1947, Jl 1,25:3
Chapin, Charlotte S Mrs, 1942, S 2,23:5
Chapin, Chester W, 1922, N 12,6:4
Chapin, Cornelius K, 1941, My 7,25:2
Chapin, Deliah L, 1942, O 8,27:5
Chapin, E H, 1880, D 28,1:7
Chapin, E H (mem ser), 1881, Ja 10,1:4
Chapin, E H Mrs, 1881, Jl 23,2:6
Chapin, Edmund L, 1944, Mr 23,19:4
Chapin, Edward C, 1948, F 18,28:2
Chapin, Edward H, 1938, N 20,38:8
Chapin, Edward W Sr, 1954, Je 27,69:2
Chapin, Edward Y, 1954, Mr 8,27:1
Chapin, Elizabeth L Mrs, 1937, O 10,II,8:2
Chapin, Emily B Mrs, 1940, My 6,17:2
Chapin, Frank W Mrs, 1948, Ja 6,23:3
Chapin, Franklin G Sr, 1957, Je 13,31:4
Chapin, Frederic H, 1958, Ag 6,25:2
Chapin, Frederic L Mrs, 1941, S 7,51:4
Chapin, Frederick E, 1923, Mr 23,19:5
Chapin, Frederick Lincoln (funl, D 21,IV,5:6), 1913, D 20,13:5
Chapin, George A, 1953, Jl 23,23:2
Chapin, George H, 1939, Ja 6,22:3
Chapin, Gilbert E, 1948, O 27,27:3
Chapin, Gilbert E Mrs, 1964, O 28,45:1
Chapin, H Winfield, 1954, N 19,23:5
Chapin, Harold W, 1943, Ag 25,19:3
Chapin, Harry G, 1954, F 8,23:2
Chapin, Helen B, 1950, Mr 3,25:3
Chapin, Heman Gerald, 1919, S 29,13:1
Chapin, Henry Barton Rev, 1914, Jl 8,9:4
Chapin, Henry D, 1942, Je 28,33:1
Chapin, Henry D Mrs, 1964, F 21,27:3
Chapin, Henry E Mrs, 1954, O 16,17:4
Chapin, Henry J, 1941, F 28,19:4
Chapin, Henry J Mrs, 1957, Jl 27,17:2
Chapin, Herman, 1940, N 10,56:4
Chapin, Howard M, 1940, S 19,23:1; 1953, Ag 15,15:6
Chapin, Huntley Mrs, 1938, Jl 27,17:1
Chapin, James P, 1964, Ap 7,35:1
Chapin, John A, 1953, Ja 2,15:3
Chapin, John Jewett, 1923, Je 10,6:2
Chapin, Jonathan W, 1938, F 11,23:3
Chapin, Joseph E, 1937, Ap 27,23:2
Chapin, Joseph H, 1939, S 23,17:2
Chapin, Joseph H Mrs, 1946, Ja 27,42:7
Chapin, Joseph M, 1938, Mr 20,II,8:2
Chapin, Josiah L Mrs, 1914, F 1,5:5
Chapin, L H Paul, 1938, S 20,23:2
Chapin, L H Paul Mrs, 1967, N 29,40:1
Chapin, Leon A, 1953, O 29,31:3
Chapin, Leonard S, 1954, Jl 8,23:4
Chapin, Lindley Garrison, 1925, Mr 11,21:4
Chapin, Louis W, 1944, Ap 30,46:3; 1954, S 8,31:3
Chapin, Lucius A, 1948, S 3,19:3
Chapin, Lucy E, 1940, N 14,23:5
Chapin, M B, 1934, Mr 9,19:3
Chapin, M E T Mrs, 1932, D 2,21:1
Chapin, Nathaniel, 1937, N 30,23:3
Chapin, Newton, 1948, Ja 17,18:2
Chapin, Philip E Mrs, 1909, Mr 3,9:5
Chapin, R D, 1936, F 17,17:1
Chapin, R S, 1879, Ag 3,6:6
Chapin, Robert C, 1945, O 9,21:2
Chapin, Robert Coit, 1913, S 14,15:7
Chapin, Robert D, 1945, Ja 26,21:1
Chapin, Robert S, 1948, D 23,20:3
Chapin, Robert W, 1938, My 24,19:2
Chapin, Robert W Mrs, 1938, My 19,21:4
Chapin, Rufus F, 1945, Je 13,23:2
Chapin, Russell N Mrs, 1967, Ja 26,33:3
Chapin, Samuel A, 1959, My 14,33:2
Chapin, Selden, 1963, Mr 28,16:8
Chapin, Simeon B, 1949, My 22,88:5
Chapin, Simeon B Mrs, 1946, Mr 26,29:4
Chapin, Simon B, 1945, Ja 5,15:1
Chapin, Stuart Mrs, 1950, Ja 2,23:3
Chapin, W B, 1947, S 27,15:6
Chapin, W Rev, 1865, My 5,4:1
Chapin, Walter S Mrs, 1914, S 19,11:2
Chapin, Warren W, 1957, Je 7,23:1
Chapin, Wilfred H, 1939, N 22,24:7
Chapin, Will E, 1937, O 16,19:6
Chapin, William E, 1953, Mr 9,29:5
Chapin, William W, 1957, N 9,27:6
Chapin, Willis M, 1960, O 16,88:6
Chapiro, Jose, 1962, Ja 18,29:3
Chapius, Arthur, 1949, Ja 14,23:5
Chapla, Charles A, 1951, D 15,13:5
Chapleau, Samuel E Stonge Maj, 1921, Ja 27,13:4
Chapler, Jacob M, 1948, Ag 24,23:3
Chaplin, Charles Spencer Jr (will, My 24,38:1), 1968, Mr 21,54:2
Chaplin, Edith H (Dowager Marchioness of Londonderry), 1959, Ag 24,27:2
Chaplin, Henry Viscount, 1923, My 30,15:3
Chaplin, Herbert H, 1955, Ap 28,29:4
Chaplin, Hugh Mrs, 1956, S 18,35:3
Chaplin, James C, 1948, S 12,72:6
Chaplin, James D, 1937, Ag 24,21:4
Chaplin, Ralph H, 1961, Mr 28,35:1
Chaplin, Richard, 1967, O 23,45:2
Chaplin, Robert T Mrs, 1938, Mr 24,23:4
Chaplin, Stewart, 1940, S 8,49:2
Chaplin, Thomas H A, 1944, O 20,19:4
Chaplin, Walter, 1950, S 6,29:4
Chaplin, William Wilson, 1907, Je 30,7:7
Chaplin, Winfield Scott, 1918, Mr 13,11:8
Chapline, Jesse G, 1937, Jl 6,19:3
Chaplinsky, Joseph, 1941, My 24,15:4
Chaplygin, Sergei, 1942, O 12,17:6
Chapman, A, 1935, D 5,25:3
Chapman, Addelia A Mrs, 1948, Ap 30,24:3
Chapman, Alfred M, 1962, S 5,39:1
Chapman, Almira Mrs, 1922, Ag 31,15:6
Chapman, Alvah H Sr, 1961, Mr 13,29:4
Chapman, Amabel (Lady Eardley-Wilmot), 1961, F 23,27:3
Chapman, Arms S, 1940, My 1,24:2
Chapman, Arms S Mrs, 1957, D 31,18:2
Chapman, Arnold G, 1937, Je 4,23:4
Chapman, Arthur, 1959, Ja 6,33:3
Chapman, Arthur B Mrs, 1948, F 3,25:4
Chapman, Arthur G, 1949, Mr 6,72:3
Chapman, Arthur Mrs, 1960, D 29,25:1
Chapman, Arthur W, 1951, Ap 12,33:4
Chapman, Benjamin E, 1954, F 13,13:3
Chapman, Bert O, 1953, Ag 9,77:2
Chapman, Bertha, 1938, Ag 13,13:4
Chapman, Bertha J Mrs, 1938, D 27,17:5
Chapman, Blanche (Mrs B C Ford), 1941, Je 8,48:6
Chapman, C C, 1956, My 31,27:4
Chapman, C L, 1945, F 8,19:5
Chapman, C Palmer, 1961, Mr 13,29:5
Chapman, C Palmer Mrs, 1955, F 3,23:2
Chapman, C Russell, 1940, F 28,22:2
Chapman, Carlton Mrs, 1949, S 20,29:5
Chapman, Carlton Theodore, 1925, F 13,17:4
Chapman, Cecil, 1938, Je 24,19:5
Chapman, Ch B Mrs, 1903, S 8,7:6
Chapman, Charles C, 1944, Ap 7,19:1
Chapman, Charles E, 1913, Mr 7,11:5; 1941, N 19,23:
Chapman, Charles F, 1937, Ag 4,19:2; 1938, Mr 7, 17:1; 1939, Ja 27,19:4
Chapman, Charles F Mrs, 1954, Ja 6,31:2
Chapman, Charles H, 1940, D 17,25:5; 1956, Ap 6,25:
Chapman, Charles J, 1938, Mr 25,20:4; 1948, Jl 25, 49:2
Chapman, Charles L, 1941, F 26,22:2
Chapman, Charles S, 1962, D 17,15:8
Chapman, Charles T, 1949, D 9,31:2
Chapman, Charles W Mrs, 1950, Jl 13,25:2
Chapman, Chauncey W L, 1946, My 7,21:3
Chapman, Chester W, 1949, D 11,92:6
Chapman, Chief Justice, 1873, Jl 27,1:7
Chapman, Clarence E, 1947, Ap 14,27:2
Chapman, Clarence G, 1958, Ag 19,28:5
Chapman, Clowry, 1950, Mr 30,29:4
Chapman, Cloyd M, 1944, Jl 4,19:5
Chapman, Cora Mrs (will), 1950, D 23,18:6
Chapman, David C, 1944, Jl 28,13:1
Chapman, Earl R, 1958, O 25,21:6
Chapman, Ed Mrs, 1950, Ag 30,31:2
Chapman, Edgar T Mrs, 1962, N 25,86:6
Chapman, Edith P Mrs (will), 1939, N 12,24:4
Chapman, Edmond B, 1954, O 13,31:2
Chapman, Edward M, 1952, My 26,23:4
Chapman, Edwin Nesbitt Mrs, 1916, N 29,11:4
Chapman, Elias S, 1948, Ja 4,52:6
Chapman, Elizabeth C Mrs, 1937, Je 6,II,8:7
Chapman, Elizabeth I Mrs, 1941, O 26,43:3
Chapman, Ella J W Mrs, 1940, O 3,25:4
Chapman, Ellwood B, 1955, Jl 28,23:6
Chapman, Emmanuel (por), 1948, Ap 19,23:3
Chapman, Ernest A, 1938, Ap 2,15:1
Chapman, Ernest H, 1941, Jl 20,30:4
Chapman, Ethelyn B, 1943, Ag 31,17:5
Chapman, Eugene, 1954, Ja 23,13:6
Chapman, Fletcher Mrs, 1938, Ag 18,19:1
Chapman, Francis, 1939, My 3,23:2
Chapman, Francis A, 1937, My 15,19:6
Chapman, Frank, 1966, Jl 28,33:4
Chapman, Frank C, 1951, O 23,29:3
Chapman, Frank H, 1955, Je 9,29:2
Chapman, Frank L, 1942, Je 4,19:5
Chapman, Frank M (por), 1945, N 17,17:1
Chapman, Frank M, 1960, N 18,31:1
Chapman, Frank M Mrs, 1944, S 23,13:6
Chapman, Frank P, 1938, Ap 29,21:3
Chapman, Fred P, 1937, F 13,13:1
Chapman, Frederick B, 1957, F 23,17:3
Chapman, Frederick S, 1941, F 4,21:5
Chapman, George, 1953, Ja 4,76:6
Chapman, George A, 1914, Ja 25,IV,5:5; 1946, D 29:5; 1947, Ap 25,21:4; 1950, D 31,43:1
Chapman, George D, 1948, F 17,25:4
Chapman, George F, 1938, Ag 15,15:3
Chapman, George F Mrs, 1949, Jl 7,25:4
Chapman, George H Mrs, 1945, Ja 24,21:2
Chapman, George J, 1948, O 20,29:4
Chapman, George L, 1962, Ag 16,27:2
Chapman, George L Mrs, 1949, F 12,17:2
Chapman, George Mrs, 1939, Je 26,15:6
Chapman, George S, 1910, Je 8,6:4
Chapman, George T Rev, 1872, O 19,10:2
Chapman, Gertrude W, 1937, F 21,II,10:6
Chapman, Gilbert W Mrs, 1949, Mr 16,27:3
Chapman, Gladys E, 1944, O 18,27:5
Chapman, H G, 1883, Mr 17,5:3
Chapman, H S, 1882, Mr 31,4:7; 1926, Je 7,19:5
Chapman, Hamilton J, 1937, O 26,23:1
Chapman, Harold W, 1955, Ap 24,86:4
Chapman, Harriet L, 1940, S 2,15:5
Chapman, Harry A, 1940, Ap 23,23:6
Chapman, Harry E, 1944, Je 5,19:2
Chapman, Harry J, 1967, O 28,31:2
Chapman, Harry P, 1952, Je 2,21:4
Chapman, Helen S Mrs, 1937, Jl 14,22:1

Chapman, Henry C Dr, 1909, S 9,9:6
Chapman, Henry Grafton Mrs, 1921, Je 11,13:5
Chapman, Henry O, 1967, Mr 6,28:7
Chapman, Henry P Jr, 1938, My 22,II,6:7
Chapman, Henry T Col, 1912, S 9,9:6
Chapman, Henry W, 1941, Mr 13,21:2
Chapman, Herbert R, 1937, N 19,23:3
Chapman, Herbert S, 1946, D 30,22:2
Chapman, Herman H, 1963, Jl 16,31:3
Chapman, Hervey W, 1955, Mr 6,88:6
Chapman, Howard, 1957, Ap 9,33:4
Chapman, Howard R, 1942, D 9,28:2
Chapman, Hugh B Mrs, 1938, Ag 20,15:1
Chapman, Hugh Mrs, 1956, Ja 8,87:1
Chapman, Hyams Jr, 1948, Jl 17,15:5
Chapman, Ira T, 1957, Ag 16,19:4
Chapman, Ira T Mrs, 1947, Ja 25,17:4
Chapman, Isabel M, 1940, Mr 31,45:2
Chapman, J J, 1903, Ag 17,7:5; 1933, N 5,32:1
Chapman, J L Mrs, 1953, Ap 2,27:3
Chapman, J Lewis, 1958, F 11,23:5
Chapman, J Wilbur Jr, 1924, Jl 15,9:4
Chapman, J Wilbur Rev Dr (funl, D 30,9:4), 1918, D 26,11:6
Chapman, Jacob Rev, 1903, Je 6,7:6
Chapman, James, 1947, Jl 31,21:4
Chapman, James A (died Sept 22; will), 1966, O 15, 1:1
Chapman, James F, 1944, Ag 26,11:6
Chapman, James J, 1948, Ja 15,23:4
Chapman, James Lt Comdr, 1937, Ag 8,II,6:5
Chapman, John, 1924, Ap 29,17:3
Chapman, John D Mrs, 1945, Ag 19,39:2
Chapman, John H, 1948, S 25,17:3; 1962, Ja 20,21:6
Chapman, John J, 1953, N 4,33:4; 1958, Ap 29,29:4
Chapman, John L, 1960, O 10,31:2
Chapman, John M, 1947, Mr 21,21:4
Chapman, John Mrs, 1946, Ja 29,25:4
Chapman, John S, 1943, Mr 18,19:4
Chapman, John S Jr Mrs, 1949, D 24,15:2
Chapman, John W, 1939, N 28,25:3; 1945, S 9,46:5
Chapman, John W Mrs, 1952, Jl 27,57:1
Chapman, Joseph, 1945, O 6,19:6; 1952, Ja 24,27:2
Chapman, Joseph L, 1943, D 22,24:3
Chapman, Joseph T Mrs, 1950, Je 5,23:5
Chapman, Judson W, 1951, Ag 8,25:5
Chapman, Kenneth W, 1959, S 19,23:4
Chapman, Lansing Mrs, 1959, Mr 16,31:4
Chapman, Lawrence B, 1965, My 14,37:1
Chapman, Lebbeus Jr, 1876, My 2,6:7
Chapman, Levi S, 1954, F 12,25:5
Chapman, Liza (Mrs A M Heath Jr), 1967, Ja 22, 62:3
Chapman, Louis B, 1943, Ja 10,50:4
Chapman, Louis H, 1944, My 3,19:5
Chapman, Maro S, 1907, Mr 22,11:6
Chapman, Marvin, 1960, Ap 13,40:1
Chapman, Marvin A, 1955, Ag 20,17:4
Chapman, Mary E, 1958, Jl 17,27:3
Chapman, Mary L, 1940, Ja 11,23:3
Chapman, Melville D, 1925, Ag 13,19:6
Chapman, Melvin D Mrs, 1965, My 3,33:5
Chapman, Newton D, 1962, Ap 24,37:1
Chapman, Newton D Mrs, 1944, Mr 4,13:5
Chapman, Niles, 1940, Ap 27,15:2
Chapman, Noah H Mrs, 1907, N 12,9:6
Chapman, Otis P, 1950, My 15,21:4
Chapman, Page, 1947, O 6,21:2
Chapman, Page Sr Mrs, 1937, Je 4,23:4
Chapman, Paul W, 1953, Ap 29,29:3; 1954, Jl 18,56:7
Chapman, Percy A Prof, 1937, S 21,25:1
Chapman, Phil F, 1949, My 22,88:8
Chapman, Preston B Mrs, 1949, Je 12,76:1
Chapman, R Curtis, 1941, Je 18,21:4
Chapman, Ralph E Mrs, 1954, Ag 31,21:6
Chapman, Ralph R, 1945, Ja 22,17:4
Chapman, Reuben, 1882, My 18,5:6
Chapman, Richard D, 1942, Ap 8,19:5
Chapman, Richard D Mrs, 1966, Je 2,43:1
Chapman, Richard M Mrs, 1947, F 7,24:2
Chapman, Richard W, 1947, S 10,27:1
Chapman, Robert A, 1939, My 9,23:1
Chapman, Robert Ferguson Dr, 1912, N 13,15:4
Chapman, Robert Hollister, 1920, Ja 13,13:2
Chapman, Roscoe S, 1939, Jl 21,19:5
Chapman, Rose Mrs, 1923, O 28,23:3
Chapman, Ross M, 1948, S 26,76:6
Chapman, Royal N, 1939, D 3,60:3
Chapman, S H, 1931, S 24,25:3
Chapman, S Spencer, 1923, D 30,20:1
Chapman, silas, 1925, S 11,23:6
Chapman, T P (see also S 15), 1875, S 23,6:7
Chapman, Theodore E Jr, 1950, Mr 2,27:5
Chapman, Theron T, 1964, S 17,43:4
Chapman, Thomas A, 1949, Je 2,27:5
Chapman, Victor, 1916, Je 27,11:7
Chapman, Virgil M, 1951, Mr 9,26:2
Chapman, W H, 1884, Ja 12,5:3
Chapman, W Orr, 1940, Ja 28,32:6
Chapman, Walter H, 1943, O 21,27:2
Chapman, Walter I, 1953, S 28,25:4
Chapman, Walter J, 1961, N 21,39:1
Chapman, Walter W, 1944, D 6,23:4
Chapman, Ward, 1942, Mr 28,17:3
Chapman, Warren S, 1937, Mr 3,23:3
Chapman, William, 1952, Ag 26,25:4
Chapman, William A, 1954, Mr 3,27:2
Chapman, William B, 1946, O 16,28:2
Chapman, William C Mrs, 1950, F 14,26:2
Chapman, William D, 1944, Jl 17,15:4
Chapman, William G, 1945, Je 13,23:2
Chapman, William G Mrs, 1944, D 24,26:4
Chapman, William H, 1940, Jl 28,27:1; 1944, Ag 29, 17:2; 1945, My 16,19:3; 1951, N 18,91:2
Chapman, William H Mrs, 1943, O 11,19:2
Chapman, William Henry, 1907, O 19,9:6
Chapman, William L Mrs, 1959, Ja 6,33:5
Chapman, William P, 1945, S 5,23:5
Chapman, William P Jr, 1947, Mr 22,13:4
Chapman, William P Jr Mrs, 1937, Ag 7,15:4
Chapman, William Porter, 1916, O 10,11:7
Chapman, William R, 1941, My 19,17:3
Chapman, William R Jr, 1949, Ap 26,26:2
Chapman, William Y Rev Dr, 1926, O 28,25:5
Chapman, Wolcott P, 1958, Ja 20,23:4
Chappedelaine, Jean de, 1950, F 24,23:1
Chappedelaine, Louis de, 1939, D 10,69:1
Chappel, Walter J, 1944, N 21,25:2
Chappelear, Claude S, 1943, Je 8,21:4
Chappelear, Edgar S Mrs, 1959, Ag 15,17:2
Chappell, Agnes E, 1942, O 28,23:6
Chappell, Arch B, 1938, Ag 29,13:4
Chappell, Augustus F, 1942, Ja 26,15:1
Chappell, Benjamin B, 1951, F 2,24:3
Chappell, Benjamin Rev-Dr, 1925, My 6,23:3
Chappell, C Raymond, 1953, S 24,33:2
Chappell, Charles, 1925, O 21,23:4
Chappell, Charles E, 1937, My 2,II,9:2
Chappell, D Arch D Mrs, 1954, Ag 28,89:2
Chappell, Delos A, 1916, F 10,11:2
Chappell, Edward A, 1955, D 2,27:3
Chappell, Edwin R, 1961, Jl 22,21:5
Chappell, Elwin, 1940, Ja 18,23:5
Chappell, George S, 1946, N 26,29:2
Chappell, Harry A, 1955, F 5,15:6
Chappell, Howard F, 1924, Jl 18,13:5
Chappell, Howard F Mrs, 1943, Mr 16,19:4
Chappell, Hubert B, 1968, Je 20,45:5
Chappell, J J, 1871, My 25,1:5
Chappell, James E, 1960, Ja 30,21:4
Chappell, Jane M, 1943, D 15,28:3
Chappell, John O, 1958, Ja 24,23:1
Chapput, Louis, 1948, Ja 15,23:3
Chappell, Marie Mrs, 1924, O 5,31:2
Chappell, Matthew N Dr, 1968, F 12,53:4
Chappell, Orlanna W Mrs, 1942, Mr 19,21:3
Chappell, Paul, 1962, Ap 14,25:5
Chappell, Phil W, 1941, N 2,52:2
Chappell, Ralph H Mrs, 1937, Je 8,25:3
Chappell, Ralph L, 1966, Ag 30,36:6
Chappell, William R, 1937, N 23,23:4
Chappelle, Charles C, 1937, F 10,23:2
Chappelle, Marion K Mrs, 1952, My 20,25:1
Chapperon, Harry, 1958, O 19,87:1
Chappetta, Daniel M, 1963, Je 10,31:6
Chapple, Bennett, 1962, My 19,27:2
Chapple, Isaac Mrs, 1952, N 30,89:1
Chapple, Joe M, 1950, Ap 19,30:2
Chapple, John C, 1946, My 2,21:4
Chappoulie, Henri A, 1959, Ja 15,2:6
Chappuis, Friedrich W von, 1942, S 11,2:2
Chapsal, Fernand, 1939, F 11,15:6
Chaptal, Monsignor, 1943, My 29,13:2
Chaput, Henri F, 1940, My 7,25:5
Chaput, Omer, 1951, Je 19,30:3
Chaqueneau, Julien St C, 1958, Ja 27,27:4
Charach, Benjamin, 1937, Ap 2,23:1
Charache, Herman, 1960, Mr 21,29:4
Charash, Jack, 1949, Mr 12,17:5
Charat, Benjamin, 1953, Jl 23,23:3
Charbin, Paul, 1956, O 24,37:2
Charbonneau, Edward, 1958, S 1,13:4
Charbonneau, Eugene G, 1943, Ap 11,48:3
Charbonneau, Henry A, 1946, Jl 12,17:1
Charbonneau, Jean, 1960, O 28,31:2
Charbonneau, Joseph, 1959, N 21,23:5
Charbonneau, Theodore Mrs, 1955, Ja 28,20:1
Charbonnier, Leon A, 1947, S 27,15:5
Charch, William H, 1958, Jl 26,15:5
Charcowsky, Charles, 1966, S 26,41:2
Chard, Eugene W, 1940, My 4,17:5
Chard, James A, 1942, My 11,15:6
Chard, James A Mrs, 1956, S 3,13:4
Chard, Marie L, 1938, Ja 22,15:6
Chardavoyne, Henry, 1943, F 4,23:3
Charde, John J, 1957, Ag 1,25:5
Chardenet, Auguste, 1964, O 24,29:6
Chardonnet, Hilaire Bernigaud Count, 1924, Mr 13, 17:3
Charell, Ludwig, 1956, N 7,31:4
Charest, Clarence M, 1951, Ap 22,88:5
Charet, Charles, 1950, S 15,25:5
Charett, George Mrs, 1943, Ap 1,23:4
Charette, George, 1938, F 7,15:2
Charette, 1871, Ag 1,5:6
Charging, Thunder, 1923, Ja 3,13:4
Chari, R T, 1955, S 4,56:1
Charicius Norbert, Bro, 1940, S 10,23:5
Charig, Philip, 1960, Jl 23,19:2
Charin, Morris, 1963, Ap 7,85:6
Chariott, Frederick J, 1956, My 2,31:4
Charke, Rebecca S (Sophie May), 1906, Ag 18,5:4
Charkoukian, Zkon, 1940, Mr 10,51:3
Charla, Leonardo, 1939, Ja 6,21:3
Charland, Hector, 1962, D 29,4:7
Charlat, Louis W, 1958, N 22,21:1
Charlat, Newman, 1948, My 13,26:2
Charlat, Newman Mrs, 1949, My 22,90:6
Charle, William W, 1959, Mr 24,39:2
Charlebois, O, 1933, N 21,19:3
Charlemont, Viscount (J E Caulfeild), 1949, Ag 31, 23:4
Charles, A Chalmers, 1951, Ja 17,27:5
Charles, A Chalmers Mrs, 1951, N 15,29:1
Charles, Arthur L, 1953, D 21,31:4
Charles, Christine, 1942, F 23,21:1
Charles, Dorothy, 1956, S 3,13:6
Charles, Edward C Col, 1863, Ap 27,5:2
Charles, Edwin H, 1956, Ja 21,21:6
Charles, Emily C, 1944, Jl 11,15:5
Charles, Emperor of Austria-Hungary, 1922, Ap 6,17:4
Charles, Fred, 1947, N 24,23:4
Charles, Frederick H, 1942, Ap 17,17:4
Charles, Harold, 1945, N 29,23:5
Charles, Harry H, 1937, Mr 3,23:3
Charles, Herbert, 1952, Ja 4,40:2
Charles, J Mother, 1885, My 22,1:4
Charles, J Sir, 1928, Jl 16,1:2
Charles, John E, 1949, Ja 4,19:4
Charles, Joseph D, 1966, N 17,47:5
Charles, Martin G, 1966, Ja 13,25:3
Charles, Nona, 1948, Jl 27,25:6
Charles, Perry, 1952, My 8,31:2
Charles, Philip Mrs, 1947, Je 13,24:2
Charles, Prince of Auersperg, 1890, Ja 5,2:5
Charles, Reginald E, 1953, Mr 14,15:5
Charles, Rollin L, 1941, D 14,68:5
Charles, Ronald, 1955, D 26,19:3
Charles, Sister (V G Duclos), 1953, N 16,25:3
Charles, Thomas J, 1961, F 25,21:3
Charles, Walter H, 1955, S 27,35:2
Charles, William A (por), 1945, Ja 23,19:4
Charles, William B, 1950, N 28,31:3
Charles, William R, 1944, O 25,21:5
Charles (Sister Marie Theresa), 1967, S 2,22:8
Charles Ambrose, Bro (F Egan), 1952, Jl 17,23:5
Charles Bruno, Brother, 1965, O 21,47:4
Charles III, Prince of Monaco, 1889, S 12,5:2
Charles-Roux, Francois, 1961, Je 28,35:3
Charleston, John J, 1943, Mr 3,24:3
Charlesworth, Charles A, 1938, O 1,17:5
Charlesworth, H P Mrs, 1937, D 18,21:3
Charlesworth, Hector W, 1945, D 31,17:3
Charlesworth, John D, 1962, O 1,31:4
Charlesworth, M L, 1880, O 20,5:1
Charlety, Sebastien (por), 1945, F 10,11:4
Charleville, Earl of (C W F Bury), 1874, N 3,2:6
Charleville, Joseph, 1955, Mr 17,45:4
Charlick Oliver, 1875, My 1,7:2
Charlier, Alphonse Rev, 1916, O 22,23:3
Charlier, Roger Mrs, 1956, F 23,27:4
Charlock, Marjorie M, 1938, Ap 2,15:3
Charlock, Norman F, 1961, Jl 31,19:2
Charlock, Palmer H, 1920, F 5,9:4
Charlock, William J, 1954, D 5,89:2
Charlot, Andre, 1956, My 21,25:1
Charlot, Andre Mrs, 1956, Ag 22,29:5
Charlotte, Empress of Mexico, 1927, Ja 19,3:1
Charlotte, J C, 1883, O 15,4:7
Charls, George H, 1944, S 12,19:5
Charls, Louis Duke de la Troumaille, 1911, Jl 5,11:6
Charlton, E P, 1930, N 21,25:1
Charlton, Earle P Mrs, 1957, Ag 31,15:4
Charlton, Edward Adm Sir, 1937, O 25,19:6
Charlton, Francis, 1923, Ag 7,17:2
Charlton, Frank R, 1945, Ja 23,19:5
Charlton, H Richard, 1953, My 15,23:3
Charlton, Harry, 1957, My 21,35:5
Charlton, Henry, 1943, Je 9,21:2
Charlton, James, 1913, N 20,11:5
Charlton, John, 1910, F 13,II,11:4
Charlton, John E, 1947, Mr 29,15:6
Charlton, John F, 1942, N 16,19:1
Charlton, John W, 1922, Jl 22,7:5
Charlton, Lionel, 1958, Ap 20,84:7
Charlton, Paul Ex-Judge, 1917, Je 5,11:7
Charlton, Richard Mrs, 1965, My 16,39:1
Charlton, Robert C, 1952, Mr 27,29:1
Charlton, Robert H, 1945, Ja 25,19:3
Charlton, Sidney F, 1965, S 15,47:2
Charlton, Walter G Judge, 1917, F 15,11:5
Charlton, William C, 1940, Ja 10,21:5
Charlwood, Edward, 1952, My 27,27:4
Charman, Walter M, 1951, Je 16,15:3
Charna, Theodore, 1965, D 17,39:1
Charnas, Harry L Mrs, 1955, D 28,23:5
Charnay, Isidore J, 1960, O 13,37:2
Charney, C King, 1958, Je 7,19:2

Charney, Daniel, 1959, Jl 3,17:3
Charney, Herman Mrs, 1967, Jl 14,31:3
Charney, John, 1950, Jl 16,68:8
Charney, Samuel, 1955, D 26,19:5
Charney, William, 1968, Mr 18,45:1
Charnley, Vernon, 1943, Je 29,19:3
Charnwood, Lord, 1945, F 6,19:5
Charon, Jean E, 1950, Je 14,31:6
Charost, A A, 1930, N 8,17:3
Charpentier, Alexandre, 1909, Mr 5,9:7
Charpentier, Arthur M, 1960, Ja 8,25:4
Charpentier, Edouard, 1917, Je 21,13:4
Charpentier, Gustave, 1956, F 20,23:4
Charpentier, Henri, 1961, D 25,23:4
Charpentier, 1871, Ag 8,1:5
Charpo, Charles, 1941, Mr 31,15:3
Charras, Col, 1865, F 12,3:3
Charret, Eugene C, 1953, D 30,24:3
Charrier, Henry, 1950, S 24,105:1
Charruard, John I, 1879, Jl 21,8:1
Charsa, Gordon F, 1941, S 24,23:3
Charsha, Edwin F, 1942, Ap 27,15:5
Charske, Fannin W, 1953, My 5,29:5
Charsky, Boris, 1956, Je 4,29:5
Charte, Vincent J, 1943, N 26,23:1
Charteris, Edmund B, 1939, Jl 4,13:4
Charteris, Evan E, 1940, N 17,50:1
Charters, Clement F, 1966, O 4,47:3
Charters, James A, 1946, Ja 4,21:2
Charters, Werrett W, 1952, Mr 10,21:3
Chartier, Emile-Auguste (Alain), 1951, Je 4,27:4
Chartier, Glen J, 1956, Ja 13,23:2
Chartier, Roy, 1946, Ag 6,25:4
Chartock, Mayer Mrs, 1962, Ap 2,31:2
Chartoff, Hyman, 1966, Jl 25,27:1
Chartoff, William, 1961, Ag 24,29:4
Charton, Paul W Mrs, 1946, Ap 20,13:4
Chartowich, Alex T, 1955, My 27,23:3
Chartrand, Enos F, 1964, Ap 2,33:5
Chartrand, George R Mrs, 1951, Jl 12,25:4
Chartrand, Joseph, 1909, Ag 26,9:6
Chartrand, Maurice, 1938, S 10,12:3
Chartres, William M, 1883, Ja 7,2:1
Charvet, Maurice, 1939, Ja 12,19:4
Chasan, Aaron, 1946, O 16,27:1
Chasan, Harry V, 1948, Je 9,29:1
Chasan, Louis, 1957, N 14,33:4
Chasan, Nathan, 1944, Ja 16,43:2
Chase, A N Mrs, 1951, O 19,27:3
Chase, A S, 1878, Je 14,4:7
Chase, Addison J, 1950, N 21,31:5
Chase, Agnes Mrs, 1963, S 26,35:1
Chase, Al, 1956, Ja 22,88:7
Chase, Albert N, 1950, O 12,31:2
Chase, Almira R Mrs, 1946, S 29,62:2
Chase, Alvin E, 1961, My 12,26:5
Chase, Arthur, 1952, F 23,11:5
Chase, Arthur E, 1955, Ja 25,25:2
Chase, Arthur G Mrs, 1952, Ap 4,33:5
Chase, Arthur L, 1945, Jl 17,13:7
Chase, Arthur M, 1947, S 8,21:2
Chase, Arthur M Mrs, 1944, Ag 16,19:4
Chase, Aurin M, 1953, Jl 10,19:2
Chase, Austin C Col, 1922, N 17,17:5
Chase, Beatrice (O K Parr), 1955, Jl 5,29:3
Chase, Burdell Mrs, 1944, Ja 18,19:2
Chase, C A, 1927, N 17,25:3
Chase, C Thurston, 1944, Ja 20,19:3
Chase, Carl C, 1957, S 18,33:4
Chase, Carrie M Mrs, 1952, N 4,23:1
Chase, Carroll, 1960, My 13,31:1
Chase, Charles, 1923, F 12,13:4
Chase, Charles D (Charlie Bell), 1964, S 26,23:3
Chase, Charles E, 1939, Je 12,17:3
Chase, Charles E B, 1953, F 13,21:1
Chase, Charles F, 1945, D 29,13:5
Chase, Charles F Mrs, 1955, Jl 24,65:1
Chase, Charles S, 1938, O 1,17:6
Chase, Charles W, 1942, My 11,15:5
Chase, Charley, 1940, Je 21,21:4
Chase, Chester W, 1937, D 14,25:1
Chase, Clara R, 1954, Je 4,23:2
Chase, Clement Mrs, 1950, F 11,15:3
Chase, Cleveland K, 1951, N 28,31:5
Chase, Clyde R, 1960, Jl 24,65:2
Chase, Colin, 1937, Ap 26,19:5
Chase, Cornelius T Mrs, 1946, D 28,15:3
Chase, Cornelius W, 1947, Ja 19,53:1
Chase, Daniel, 1872, Jl 28,1:3; 1964, F 6,29:1
Chase, Edith M Mrs, 1945, S 17,19:4
Chase, Edna W Mrs (funl plans, Mr 22,23:3; funl, Mr 24,86:3), 1957, Mr 21,31:2
Chase, Edward E, 1953, Ag 3,1:1
Chase, Edward L, 1965, F 21,76:8
Chase, Edward M, 1939, N 18,17:2; 1962, Jl 4,21:6
Chase, Edward M Mrs, 1949, Ap 8,26:5
Chase, Edward T, 1941, Jl 22,20:2
Chase, Edwin O, 1943, D 11,15:2
Chase, Edwin P, 1949, Jl 12,27:4
Chase, Eleanor Frances Mrs, 1910, O 30,II,13:5
Chase, Emory A Judge, 1921, Je 26,22:4
Chase, Ernest D, 1966, Ag 28,92:2
Chase, Ethel W B, 1949, Ag 29,18:2
Chase, Francis Rev, 1904, O 22,9:5
Chase, Francis S Jr, 1957, F 16,17:1
Chase, Frank D, 1937, Jl 24,15:6; 1949, N 10,31:1
Chase, Frank L (will), 1963, N 10,43:5
Chase, Frank S, 1958, Jl 28,23:3
Chase, Frank W, 1948, Ap 3,15:1
Chase, Franklin H, 1940, My 25,17:3
Chase, Frederick L, 1954, S 15,33:4
Chase, Frederick M, 1921, Ap 9,11:2
Chase, Frederick P S, 1953, O 19,21:6
Chase, Frederick S, 1947, D 7,76:1
Chase, Frederick S Mrs, 1937, Ap 5,19:2
Chase, George, 1924, Ja 9,21:3
Chase, George Colby, 1919, My 28,15:2
Chase, George D, 1948, My 8,15:4
Chase, George E, 1942, N 19,25:4
Chase, George H, 1909, N 3,11:4; 1939, Ja 3,18:1; 1952, F 4,17:1
Chase, George L, 1908, Ja 8,9:6
Chase, George L Mrs, 1904, F 3,9:6
Chase, George M, 1938, N 15,23:1
Chase, George T Mrs, 1951, F 12,23:3
Chase, Giles A, 1947, Jl 16,23:5
Chase, Guy M, 1944, Jl 9,35:2
Chase, H V, 1942, Mr 10,19:5
Chase, Hal, 1947, My 19,21:1
Chase, Halsey, 1951, Jl 6,23:5
Chase, Harold M, 1960, Jl 7,22:2
Chase, Harry A, 1944, Jl 7,15:3
Chase, Harry W (funl plans, Ap 23,19:4), 1955, Ap 21,29:3
Chase, Harvey S, 1946, Ap 10,27:3
Chase, Harvey S Mrs, 1944, Je 11,45:2
Chase, Helen G, 1951, Ja 13,15:4
Chase, Henry M, 1940, Ap 7,44:8
Chase, Herbert, 1947, Jl 29,22:3
Chase, Herbert A, 1944, Ja 30,38:3
Chase, Herbert F, 1942, Ap 17,17:1
Chase, Horace Gair, 1913, F 6,11:5
Chase, Howard A, 1925, Ag 19,19:7
Chase, Howard G, 1952, Ag 1,17:2
Chase, Howard L, 1948, Mr 22,23:3
Chase, Howard W, 1941, Ap 27,39:1
Chase, Ima, 1951, D 23,22:3
Chase, Irving H, 1951, Mr 15,30:2
Chase, Irving H Mrs, 1944, S 19,21:6
Chase, J F, 1882, Jl 26,8:4
Chase, J F Rev, 1926, N 4,27:4
Chase, J Ira, 1953, Je 18,29:3
Chase, James E, 1950, N 22,25:3
Chase, James R, 1952, Jl 17,23:4
Chase, Jehu V Mrs, 1950, S 8,31:1
Chase, Jehu V Rear Adm, 1937, My 26,25:1
Chase, John, 1950, F 2,28:3
Chase, John B Mrs, 1948, My 8,15:6
Chase, John M Mrs, 1951, Ja 21,78:2
Chase, John Mrs, 1903, S 17,7:6
Chase, John W, 1961, Ap 20,33:4
Chase, Joseph C, 1965, Ja 16,27:3
Chase, Joseph C Mrs, 1944, F 3,19:4
Chase, Joshua C, 1948, Ja 8,25:3
Chase, Julia L Mrs, 1959, O 23,29:2
Chase, Julia Mrs, 1946, My 16,21:1
Chase, Lagrand E, 1953, D 25,17:2
Chase, Lawrence S, 1959, N 10,47:4
Chase, Leroy G, 1948, O 25,23:5
Chase, Levi R, 1948, Ap 5,21:5
Chase, Lewis N Dr, 1937, S 24,21:3
Chase, Lewis S, 1950, D 3,88:4
Chase, Lynn B, 1946, N 5,25:4
Chase, Mabel A, 1939, Ap 2,III,6:7
Chase, Mable H, 1953, My 26,29:5
Chase, Marjorie, 1941, N 18,25:1
Chase, Mary E, 1962, Ag 25,19:2
Chase, Maurice L, 1937, Je 12,15:2
Chase, Melville W, 1940, F 20,21:5
Chase, Melvin B, 1948, D 8,31:3
Chase, Merrill Mrs, 1961, Ja 9,39:3
Chase, Morris R, 1960, S 9,29:1
Chase, Nancy G, 1950, F 25,17:4
Chase, Nathan E, 1948, Ag 25,25:4
Chase, Newell, 1955, Ja 27,23:2
Chase, Oliver W, 1946, S 21,15:5
Chase, Orville G Mrs, 1950, Ag 28,17:5
Chase, Oscar J Jr Mrs, 1951, Mr 31,15:5
Chase, Oscar M, 1939, Ap 11,23:5
Chase, Paul A, 1946, Ap 19,29:4; 1963, Ag 1,27:4
Chase, Pauline C, 1962, Mr 5,23:3
Chase, Porter B, 1943, Ag 14,11:4
Chase, Randall, 1940, Jl 21,29:1
Chase, Richard D, 1952, O 21,29:1
Chase, Richard V Jr, 1962, Ag 28,31:2
Chase, Richard W, 1952, Ag 5,19:2
Chase, Rodney, 1957, Jl 16,25:4
Chase, Roy J, 1943, Mr 2,19:2
Chase, Russell D Mrs, 1952, Ja 13,88:7
Chase, S B Mrs, 1902, D 7,7:5
Chase, S O Sr, 1941, Ap 1,23:4
Chase, Salmon P Chief Justice, 1873, My 8,4:7
Chase, Samuel, 1938, N 5,19:6
Chase, Solan, 1909, N 24,9:6
Chase, Stanley P, 1951, Ja 23,27:2
Chase, Stephen A, 1912, Je 7,13:4
Chase, Talbot C Mrs, 1940, Ap 15,17:2
Chase, Theodore L, 1950, F 13,21:5
Chase, Volney O Capt, 1917, Je 26,13:5
Chase, W H, 1881, Je 24,8:4
Chase, Walter B Dr, 1920, N 16,15:4
Chase, Walter I, 1942, O 16,19:4
Chase, Walter M, 1955, Ag 26,19:3
Chase, Walter W, 1949, Mr 27,76:6
Chase, Ward B Mrs, 1954, S 28,29:4
Chase, Warren H Mrs, 1946, S 11,7:2
Chase, Wesley, 1948, F 10,23:3
Chase, Wilbur, 1938, O 16,44:7
Chase, Wilfred L, 1941, O 9,23:2
Chase, William, 1940, O 1,23:2
Chase, William B, 1948, Ag 26,21:1
Chase, William B Mrs, 1954, F 23,27:2
Chase, William Dwight, 1913, Ja 8,11:4
Chase, William E, 1947, Ja 14,25:2
Chase, William G, 1968, Mr 25,41:5
Chase, William H, 1920, Ja 30,15:4; 1938, O 21,23:3; 1955, Mr 19,15:1
Chase, William M, 1916, O 26,11:5; 1916, O 28,13:3
Chase, William R, 1951, Ag 31,15:1
Chase, William S, 1940, Jl 17,21:1
Chase, Willis H, 1945, Jl 3,13:3
Chaseman, Moses H, 1952, Je 24,29:4
Chasen, Samuel Mrs, 1942, Ap 28,21:2
Chasen, Simon, 1963, S 4,40:3
Chasey, Arthur F Sr, 1962, Je 4,29:4
Chasey, James Dr, 1937, Mr 30,24:2
Chasick, Joseph M, 1966, F 26,25:1
Chasis, Nathan H, 1944, O 19,23:3
Chasles, Michel, 1880, D 20,5:4
Chasman, Chellis I, 1950, Je 18,76:3
Chasman, David, 1961, My 18,35:4
Chasmar, James H, 1915, O 10,17:5
Chason, Aaron Mrs, 1955, Je 13,23:2
Chason, Daniel H, 1947, Jl 1,25:4
Chasse, Edmond, 1951, Mr 25,72:6
Chasse, Nicholas A, 1944, Ap 13,19:4
Chasseloup-Laubat, Comte De, 1903, N 21,9:6
Chassen, Jacob, 1948, Ja 21,25:2
Chassin, Asher Rabbi, 1937, My 6,25:4
Chassy, Lon, 1952, My 24,19:6
Chastain, James G, 1954, F 21,68:4
Chastel, Jacques, 1958, Jl 13,68:5
Chastine, Robert, 1911, Ag 21,9:6
Chaszczynski, Aniela Z Mrs, 1948, Jl 26,17:5
Chatard, Francis Silas Marean Bp, 1918, S 8,23:1
Chataug, Louis J, 1950, My 13,17:5
Chatburn, Thomas W, 1941, Ap 22,21:3
Chateaubriand, Assis (Francisco de Assis Chateaubriand Bandeira, 1968, Ap 6,39:1
Chatel, Louis P, 1951, My 12,21:3
Chatel, Yves, 1944, O 14,13:4
Chatelet, Albert, 1960, Jl 1,25:1
Chatellier, Joseph Francis, 1916, Jl 5,11:6
Chater, N W, 1882, Je 6,5:2
Chater, William, 1915, Mr 15,11:5
Chatfield, A G, 1875, O 5,6:6
Chatfield, Albert H Mrs, 1950, D 26,23:2
Chatfield, Albert S, 1941, Jl 26,15:4
Chatfield, Alfred E M Lord, 1967, N 16,47:3
Chatfield, Cyrus H, 1922, My 25,19:4
Chatfield, George H, 1946, S 20,31:3
Chatfield, Hazen, 1959, Ap 28,35:4
Chatfield, John L Col, 1863, Ag 13,5:2
Chatfield, Josiah C Mrs, 1956, S 15,17:1
Chatfield, L S, 1884, Ag 5,5:5
Chatfield, Lyman G, 1945, Ag 25,11:3
Chatfield, Minotte E, 1952, Ag 20,25:5
Chatfield, Morton, 1939, Ja 26,21:3
Chatfield, Paul O, 1958, N 20,35:3
Chatfield, Victor M, 1940, F 23,15:2
Chatfield, Walter H, 1922, Jl 2,16:3
Chatfield, William A, 1943, D 17,27:2
Chatfield-Taylor, Hobart C, 1945, Ja 17,21:5; 1960, O 26,39:2
Chatfield-Taylor, Hobart C Mrs, 1918, Ap 6,15:4
Chatham, Gerald W, 1956, O 11,39:2
Chatham, Herbert G, 1942, Jl 27,15:5
Chatham, Thurmond, 1957, F 6,25:4
Chatham, Thurmond Mrs, 1949, Jl 14,27:5
Chatillon, Albert, 1949, Mr 30,25:3
Chatillon, George E, 1949, Mr 11,25:2
Chatin, Alfred Dr, 1923, Mr 15,19:5
Chatkin, David J, 1947, F 15,15:6
Chatlos, Louis A, 1951, Mr 29,27:3
Chatman, Boris, 1965, Ag 6,27:4
Chatman, John, 1952, Jl 19,13:4
Chatres, John J, 1952, Je 23,19:3
Chatrian, Pierre-Alexandre, 1890, S 5,5:6
Chatry, Raymond J Mrs, 1950, O 16,27:4
Chattaway, Edward, 1956, My 4,25:6
Chattaway, J Thurland, 1947, N 13,27:5
Chatterdon, Arthur E, 1947, O 10,25:3
Chatterjee, Atul, 1955, S 9,23:4
Chatters, Carl H, 1960, D 14,39:4
Chatterson, Edward, 1951, Jl 13,21:5
Chatterton, Edward H, 1964, F 3,27:5
Chatterton, Ernest, 1950, Je 14,31:2
Chatterton, Eyre, 1950, D 12,33:4
Chatterton, Fenimore, 1958, My 10,21:6

Chatterton, John (Signor Perugini), 1914, D 5,13:6
Chatterton, Justus W, 1950, Ja 17,28:3
Chatterton, Robert, 1940, D 6,27:2
Chatterton, Ruth, 1961, N 25,23:1
Chatterton, William T, 1942, N 11,25:3
Chattin, Henry I, 1947, S 11,27:1
Chattin, M Powers, 1945, O 13,15:5
Chattin, Walter R, 1950, Mr 3,25:4
Chattisham, Lord, 1945, Ag 28,19:4
Chatz, John H, 1955, Je 27,21:4
Chauauneuf, Alphonse L de, 1943, Ja 30,15:1
Chauchard, H A, 1909, Je 5,9:5
Chaude, Marius A, 1941, Ap 20,44:2
Chaulnes, Duc de, 1908, Mr 26,7:4
Chaumeix, Andre, 1955, F 24,27:2
Chauncey, Commodore, 1871, Ap 14,2:4
Chauncey, D M, 1881, Jl 7,5:1; 1883, Ja 30,8:2
Chauncey, Daniel, 1921, Ap 27,17:4
Chauncey, Egisto F, 1963, Ap 4,47:2
Chauncey, Elihu, 1916, My 17,11:6
Chauncey, George S, 1945, Je 13,23:1
Chauncey, Louise, 1907, Mr 2,9:5
Chauncey, Lucy, 1945, D 27,19:3
Chaura, Margarita de, 1947, Jl 16,23:5
Chausky, Manuel, 1961, My 12,29:4
Chautemps, Camille, 1963, Jl 2,29:1
Chautemps, Emile, 1918, D 11,15:4
Chauveau, Charles A, 1940, D 18,25:4
Chauveau, Charles F X Alexnader, 1916, Mr 8,11:5
Chauveau, Jean F Dr, 1903, O 18,7:6
Chauvel, Charles E, 1959, N 12,35:2
Chauvel, Henry (por), 1945, Mr 5,19:4
Chauvenet, Regis, 1920, D 7,13:3
Chauvenet, Virginia (por), 1949, Mr 8,25:3
Chauvet, Ernest G, 1958, Ap 7,21:2
Chauviere, Lucien, 1966, Ap 9,25:4
Chauvin, Charles F, 1946, Ag 6,25:2
Chauvin, Hector Judge, 1922, Je 18,28:3
Chavannes, Charles de, 1940, F 9,19:2
Chavannes, P P de, 1898, O 26,7:2
Chavard, Victor S, 1964, S 19,27:5
Chavasse, Christopher M, 1962, Mr 11,86:4
Chavchavadze, Elizabeth Princess, 1962, F 15,6:6
Chavchavadze, George Prince, 1962, F 15,6:6
Chave, Ernest J, 1961, My 17,37:1
Chave, George P, 1938, Ja 30,II,8:2
Chavelle, Edward H, 1951, D 25,31:4
Chaves, Federico Mrs, 1953, Je 7,84:5
Chaves, Felipe, 1905, Ap 12,7:2
Chavez, Carlos A, 1947, D 18,30:3
Chavez, Dennis (funl, N 22,29:4), 1962, N 19,1:3
Chavez, Dennis Jr, 1968, Ag 12,40:4
Chavez, Ezequiel, 1946, D 4,31:5
Chaya, John S, 1953, Je 30,23:5
Chayet, Bernard L, 1963, Mr 9,7:6
Chazick, Aaron, 1939, Ap 23,III,7:3
Chazin, Hirsch L Mrs, 1946, D 31,17:2
Cheadle, Clarence C, 1942, O 7,25:2
Cheatham, Catherine S, 1946, Ja 6,40:4
Cheatham, Jon H, 1950, F 19,76:1
Cheatham, Joseph J, 1942, S 10,27:4
Cheatham, Thaddeus A, 1956, N 5,31:6
Cheatham, Walter B Mrs, 1962, Ag 29,29:3
Cheatle, George L, 1951, Ja 4,29:3
Cheatman, B Frank, 1944, D 4,23:2
Cheavens, John S Mrs, 1952, Ag 5,19:5
Cheben, Milan J, 1947, N 15,17:4
Cheche, Mathew P, 1949, S 24,13:5
Check, David D Mrs, 1964, My 31,76:6
Checkver, Leo Mrs, 1957, N 29,29:2
Chedester, Lawrence D, 1943, O 13,23:3
Chedeville, Charles J, 1940, Mr 6,23:3
Cheek, James S, 1938, Ag 22,13:3
Cheek, Joanne Lloyd-Jones Dr, 1968, S 15,85:1
Cheek, T A Rev, 1884, Ap 6,9:5
Cheeks, Emma V Mrs, 1941, N 5,23:1
Cheeks, William, 1947, Mr 4,26:3
Cheel, Harold W, 1958, O 22,35:1
Cheel, R Duncan, 1943, N 30,27:4
Cheeney, Alfred M, 1950, F 22,29:2
Cheesebrough, L B, 1903, Ag 18,2:4
Cheeseman, Frank E, 1958, My 11,87:1
Cheeseman, Roland G, 1947, D 3,29:5
Cheesman, Al, 1958, Ap 4,21:4
Cheesman, Frank P, 1938, My 5,23:6
Cheesman, Georgiana P Mrs, 1941, Ja 5,44:3
Cheesman, Hobart Dr, 1903, Ap 13,9:6
Cheesman, Hubert, 1955, My 12,29:2
Cheesman, James E Mrs, 1960, Ap 4,29:5
Cheesman, John K Mrs, 1952, S 28,77:1
Cheesman, Joseph R, 1945, Mr 30,15:3
Cheesman, Richard D, 1950, Ja 10,29:2
Cheesman, Robert P Mrs, 1946, My 31,23:1
Cheesman, William S Dr, 1912, My 8,11:4
Cheeswright, Frederick H, 1960, F 15,27:2
Cheetham, Albert C Rev, 1937, F 10,23:1
Cheetham, James F, 1949, D 24,15:2; 1957, Jl 31,23:2
Cheetham, Jose E, 1951, Ap 3,27:3
Cheetham, Milne, 1938, Ja 7,19:5
Cheetham, Walter W Jr, 1959, Ag 6,27:4
Cheever, David, 1955, Ag 15,15:3
Cheever, David Mrs, 1940, Mr 30,15:3
Cheever, David W Dr, 1915, D 28,11:4
Cheever, Helen, 1960, My 6,31:4
Cheever, Louisa S, 1957, D 9,35:5
Cheever, Markham, 1956, D 7,27:4
Cheever, Markham Mrs, 1950, F 1,29:2
Cheever, Ruth Barnard Mrs, 1903, Ag 7,7:7
Cheever, Samuel Judge, 1874, O 1,4:6
Cheevers, Thomas P, 1945, Jl 23,19:4
Cheffetz, Asa, 1965, Ag 25,39:5
Cheh-Yuan, Sung, 1940, Ap 7,45:1
Cheifitz, Abraham Mrs, 1961, Jl 9,77:2
Cheire, Adelaide (Ruth Adelaide Greenfield), 1914, Ap 4,15:4
Cheke, Marcus J, 1960, Je 23,29:2
Chekhov, Maria P, 1957, Ja 18,21:1
Chekhov, Michael, 1955, O 2,86:3
Chekhov, Nicholas, 1949, N 6,92:3
Chekhova, Olga L Knipper- (funl, Mr 26,31:1), 1959, Mr 23,31:4
Chekmenev, Yevgeny M, 1963, Ap 24,35:2
Chekrezi, Constantine A, 1959, Ja 11,88:2
Chelf, Loy N, 1952, S 13,17:2
Chelioti, George, 1951, S 28,31:3
Chelius, Herman P, 1941, Ja 8,19:2
Chelius, M J, 1876, Ag 30,5:6
Chellborg, Julia, 1945, S 26,23:4
Chellborg, Oscar Horton, 1921, S 15,15:4
Chellew, Walter J, 1942, My 30,15:4
Chellis, Eugene Mrs, 1943, Ap 11,49:1
Chellis, Robert E, 1965, Jl 30,22:5
Chellus, Oscar von, 1923, Je 16,11:4
Chelminski, Jan V de, 1925, N 3,25:5
Chelmsford, Lord (F Thesiger), 1878, O 7,5:2
Chelmsford, Lord, 1905, Ap 10,9:6
Chelmsford, Viscount, 1933, Ap 2,31:1
Chelsea, Viscount (Hy Arth Cadogan), 1908, Jl 3,7:4
Chelton, Edgar A, 1940, Ag 20,19:2
Chelton, William H Capt, 1912, S 5,9:5
Chemama, Emile, 1956, Ap 1,V,3:8
Chemberji, Nikolai, 1948, Ap 25,68:3
Chemidlin, Harry L, 1964, S 23,47:4
Chemnitz, Harry D, 1961, D 31,48:2
Chemnitz, Matthew J, 1940, My 12,48:4
Chen, Clarence, 1908, My 12,7:6
Chen, Eugene, 1944, My 21,44:1
Chen Cheng Vice President, 1965, Mr 6,25:1
Chen Chi-Yuan, 1968, Je 2,76:8
Chen Chia-keng, 1961, Ag 12,17:4
Chen Chieh, 1951, Ag 17,17:5
Chen Chih-mai, Mrs, 1953, Ag 31,17:1
Chen Han Kuang, 1957, Mr 18,27:4
Chen Keng, 1961, Mr 17,31:3
Chen Kuo-Fu, 1951, Ag 26,79:3
Chen Pu-lei, 1948, N 14,32:3
Chen Tu-Hsiu, 1942, My 28,17:4
Chenal, Marthe, 1947, Ja 30,25:5
Chenard, Emile J, 1948, O 17,76:3
Chenault, Raymond C, 1953, O 10,17:4
Chenault, Richard S, 1952, D 31,15:4
Chenel, Ernest, 1947, S 14,60:2
Chenery, Charles M, 1948, Mr 2,23:4
Chenery, T, 1884, F 12,5:3
Chenery, William E, 1949, Ja 4,40:2
Cheney, A, 1878, O 16,1:6
Cheney, A N, 1901, Ag 18,7:6
Cheney, Anne W, 1944, My 26,19:6
Cheney, Austin, 1948, O 6,29:5
Cheney, Benjamin A, 1938, O 5,23:4; 1945, O 12,23:5
Cheney, Benjamin P Mrs, 1922, D 12,19:4
Cheney, Charles, 1874, Ag 15,5:4; 1942, Ap 12,44:4
Cheney, Charles B, 1955, Je 15,31:1
Cheney, Charles Edward Bp, 1916, N 16,11:3
Cheney, Charles Mrs, 1953, Ja 20,25:2
Cheney, Charles P W, 1953, Je 16,27:4
Cheney, Charles R, 1949, Je 28,28:2
Cheney, Clarence O, 1947, N 5,28:2
Cheney, Clarence O Mrs, 1968, O 17,47:4
Cheney, Clifford D, 1948, S 8,29:5
Cheney, Coleman B, 1956, Mr 18,89:2
Cheney, E Dow Mrs, 1904, N 20,7:5
Cheney, Edward J Mrs, 1939, Mr 3,23:2
Cheney, Elias H, 1924, Ag 28,17:5
Cheney, Emily G, 1953, Jl 15,25:2
Cheney, Everett W Mrs, 1956, Ap 10,31:1
Cheney, Frank D, 1955, N 21,29:5
Cheney, Frank D Mrs, 1959, D 28,23:5
Cheney, Frank Jr, 1957, Ap 1,25:4
Cheney, Frank Sr, 1904, F 6,9:6
Cheney, Frank W Col, 1909, My 27,9:6
Cheney, George L Mrs, 1944, Ja 30,38:3
Cheney, George N, 1951, O 7,85:6
Cheney, Guy, 1939, Ap 19,23:5
Cheney, Guy W Mrs, 1953, S 2,25:3
Cheney, H R, 1876, D 16,4:6
Cheney, Harry M, 1937, Ja 3,II,9:2
Cheney, Horace B Mrs, 1949, Je 24,23:3
Cheney, Howard A Mrs, 1948, Jl 15,23:4
Cheney, Howell, 1957, Ag 22,27:2
Cheney, J Davenport Capt, 1919, O 14,17:3
Cheney, J L, 1932, N 30,19:5
Cheney, James Judge, 1903, D 14,7:4
Cheney, John Vance, 1922, My 2,19:5
Cheney, Knight Jr Mrs, 1949, Jl 13,27:4
Cheney, Lotta P, 1947, D 11,33:1
Cheney, Louis R, 1944, D 18,19:2
Cheney, Louis R Mrs, 1940, D 23,19:5
Cheney, Louise, 1939, Je 29,23:4
Cheney, Marjory, 1967, N 17,47:2
Cheney, Maurice L, 1954, D 4,17:5
Cheney, Monroe G, 1952, S 29,23:5
Cheney, Nelson W, 1944, N 25,13:5
Cheney, Oren Burbank Rev, 1903, D 23,9:6
Cheney, Orion H, 1939, Ja 18,19:1
Cheney, Phil, 1948, Ja 22,27:3
Cheney, Ray E, 1944, D 26,19:4
Cheney, Richard Otis Sr Mrs, 1916, D 28,9:5
Cheney, Richard P, 1904, F 25,9:5
Cheney, Robert M, 1961, N 4,19:3
Cheney, Rush, 1882, Je 8,5:4
Cheney, Russell, 1945, Jl 13,11:7
Cheney, S L, 1940, Ap 13,17:4
Cheney, Sherwood A, 1949, Mr 14,19:3
Cheney, Stanley, 1956, Je 9,17:6
Cheney, Stephen C, 1950, Ja 6,21:1
Cheney, Thomas P, 1942, Je 12,21:2
Cheney, Walter B Mrs, 1956, Ja 16,21:4
Cheney, Ward, 1876, Mr 23,2:4
Cheney, Ward (Jan22), 1963, Ap 1,35:3
Cheney, Wells W, 1938, My 18,21:5
Cheney, William C, 1941, Mr 3,15:5
Cheney, William F, 1941, Ap 11,22:3
Cheney, William H Lt, 1918, Ja 23,9:5
Cheney, Winslow, 1968, Ag 15,37:4
Cheng, C Y, 1939, N 16,23:2
Cheng, Seymour C Y, 1954, Jl 9,17:2
Cheng Chien, Gen, 1968, Ap 14,76:6
Cheng Chung-chiang, 1950, Jl 21,19:2
Cheng-Fu Wang, 1951, Jl 4,17:6
Cheng Tien-fong, 1967, D 1,47:4
Cheng-Yang Hsu, 1951, F 18,78:5
Chenitz, Jacob, 1949, D 9,32:2
Chenitz, Nathan, 1955, Jl 8,23:4
Chenkin, George B, 1962, S 13,37:5
Chennault, Claire L (funl plans, Jl 29,23:4; funl, Jl 31,23:1), 1958, Jl 28,1:1
Chennault, John S, 1942, Ag 11,19:2
Chenot, James E, 1947, D 2,29:2
Chenoweth, Alexander Crawford, 1922, Ap 15,15:6
Chenoweth, Arthur E, 1955, Ag 20,17:2
Chenoweth, Curtis W, 1944, Jl 13,17:3
Chenoweth, Emory S, 1946, D 9,25:5
Chenoweth, Lawrence B, 1958, O 19,86:4
Chenoweth, William H, 1954, Jl 19,19:3
Cheny, Richard Otis, 1912, N 16,15:6
Cheo, Thomas Mrs, 1955, D 19,27:1
Cheoim Spaho Effendi, 1942, F 16,8:3
Cheon, Henri, 1944, Je 18,36:1
Cheplin, Harry A, 1959, Mr 4,31:4
Chequer, John D, 1965, Ja 13,25:3
Cherashore, A Albert, 1955, F 13,86:4
Cheray, Louis M, 1949, Ap 1,25:4
Cherbonnier, A Victor Mrs, 1968, Ap 23,47:2
Cherbuliez, Charles Victor, 1899, Jl 3,7:2
Cherburg, Rudolph Mrs, 1961, Mr 1,33:4
Cherchesky, L Scott, 1949, N 3,29:4
Cheremukhin, Alexei M, 1958, Ag 22,21:3
Cherey, Henry I, 1953, My 9,19:5
Cheri, Teresa, 1873, Je 24,2:7
Chericone, Domenick C, 1964, S 1,35:3
Cherin, Herbert, 1968, S 26,47:1
Cherington, Charles R, 1967, Je 9,45:1
Cherington, Paul T, 1943, Ap 25,35:1
Cherkasky, Karl S, 1967, F 26,84:2
Cherkasov, Nikolai K, 1966, S 15,49:3
Cherkes, Charles, 1951, O 29,23:4
Cherksey, Leon, 1966, Ja 29,27:4
Chernay, M Henry, 1967, Ag 6,76:5
Cherner, Joseph, 1956, Ap 18,31:4
Chernetsky, Semyen, 1950, Ap 15,15:3
Cherney, Edward Mrs, 1945, Ja 13,11:5
Cherney, Marvin, 1967, Mr 18,29:3
Cherniavsky, Abraham, 1938, Ag 6,13:3
Cherniavsky, Josef, 1959, N 4,35:2
Chernin, Benjamin, 1958, Mr 27,33:3
Chernoff, Vadim, 1954, Ap 20,29:3
Chernov, F, 1950, Je 1,7:4
Chernov, Viktor M, 1952, Ap 16,27:1
Chernow, Ben B, 1953, Ja 19,23:4
Chernow, David L, 1962, S 15,25:5
Chernow, Joseph I, 1966, S 3,23:5
Cherny, Joseph A, 1948, D 15,33:3
Chernyeshev, Ivan, 1951, Ag 23,23:4
Chernyshev, Ilya S, 1962, O 22,3:4
Chernyshov, Vassily V, 1952, S 14,86:2
Cheron, H, 1936, Ap 15,21:5
Cheronis, Nicholas D, 1962, Jl 4,41:2
Cheronnet-Champollion, Rene, 1959, My 8,27:5
Cherpillod, Andre, 1945, D 3,21:2
Cherrie, James P, 1949, O 19,29:3
Cherrill, Fred, 1964, D 24,19:2
Cherrington, Ernest H Mrs, 1949, Ap 25,23:4
Cherrington, Ernest H Sr, 1950, Mr 14,25:1
Cherrington, John D, 1955, Ap 13,29:1
Cherry, Addie R A, 1942, O 27,25:1
Cherry, Blair, 1966, S 11,87:3
Cherry, C Waldo, 1944, O 12,27:2
Cherry, Clem A, 1957, Ag 3,15:6

Cherry, E, 1936, My 13,24:1
Cherry, Effie, 1944, Ag 6,37:1
Cherry, Frances A, 1965, Jl 16,27:1
Cherry, George A, 1940, Ja 18,23:1
Cherry, George R, 1946, Jl 22,21:4
Cherry, Henry H Dr, 1937, Ag 2,19:4
Cherry, Henry I, 1950, My 3,29:4
Cherry, Henry T Jr, 1953, Ag 21,17:3
Cherry, James R, 1937, O 7,27:5
Cherry, John F, 1948, Ag 31,23:3
Cherry, John L, 1968, Ja 13,31:2
Cherry, John Mrs, 1951, Ja 28,65:4
Cherry, Joseph B, 1943, Ag 19,19:5
Cherry, Joseph H, 1953, Jl 2,23:6
Cherry, Moses J, 1965, Ap 13,37:4
Cherry, Patrick J, 1946, D 30,22:8
Cherry, Robert G, 1957, Je 26,31:1
Cherry, Talmadge C, 1941, Mr 30,48:5
Cherry, Thomas F, 1903, D 29,9:6
Cherry, Thomas H, 1944, Ag 31,17:2
Cherry, William J, 1942, Je 19,23:2
Cherry, William S Jr, 1961, Ap 14,29:4
Cherry, William Shaw, 1968, Ja 3,47:2
Cherry, William T, 1941, O 13,17:5
Cherry-Garrard, Apsley, 1959, My 19,34:1
Cherryman, M, 1928, Ag 11,11:3
Chertoff, Paul, 1966, Ja 11,29:4
Chertok, Moses A, 1962, Je 25,29:5
Chertov, Alex, 1961, O 23,29:3
Chertov, Ivan A, 1951, Ag 5,73:2
Cherubini, Guiseppe, 1946, N 22,23:1
Chervenka, Gustave, 1947, Je 5,26:3
Cherwell, Frederick A L, 1957, Jl 4,19:1
Cherwin, Benjamin L, 1949, Mr 14,19:6
Cherwin, Benjamin L Mrs, 1956, Ap 10,31:1
Cherwin, Jack B, 1968, S 8,84:6
Chesbro, George, 1925, O 16,21:4
Chesbro, Ray L, 1954, Mr 26,21:2
Chesbrough, L R, 1878, Ap 4,5:2
Chesbrough, William H, 1939, F 18,15:2
Chesebro', Caroline, 1873, F 18,5:3
Chesebro, Denison P Mrs, 1950, Je 11,92:2
Chesebrough, Helen P, 1949, Ag 29,17:4
Chesebrough, R A, 1933, S 9,13:4
Chesebrough, Robert C Capt, 1871, D 11,5:4
Chesebrough, Robert Maxwell, 1910, Je 5,II,11:4
Chesebrough, William Col, 1905, Je 9,9:5
Cheseldine, Raymond M, 1954, D 25,11:2
Cheserton-Mangle, Elizabeth Mrs, 1951, My 12,21:3
Chesham, Lord of (J C Cavendish), 1952, Ap 26,23:6
Chesher, Earl C 1954, Ap 12,29:5
Cheshire, Fleming Duncan, 1922, Je 14,19:5
Cheshire, Frederic J, 1939, Mr 26,III,7:2
Cheshire, Frederick W, 1939, Ja 26,21:4
Cheshire, J B, 1961, Je 4,86:5
Cheshire, John, 1910, S 27,13:6
Cheshire, Laura B, 1943, Jl 15,21:3
Cheshire, Leslie G, 1966, N 13,89:2
Cheshire, Zoe, 1946, S 16,5:5
Chesire, George, 1941, D 4,25:6
Chesler, Hylan Mrs, 1967, O 25,47:1
Chesler, Isador, 1955, Jl 22,23:3
Chesler, Isadore J, 1953, Ag 29,17:4
Chesley, Albert J, 1955, O 18,37:1
Chesley, Faris F, 1950, S 13,28:2
Chesley, Franklin R, 1951, F 14,29:4
Chesley, Henry H, 1963, Je 11,37:2
Chesley, Mabel L, 1966, O 1,32:5
Chesman, Nelson, 1906, O 27,9:6
Chesmedjeff, Grigor, 1945, S 19,2:4
Chesney, Alan J, 1945, Ja 5,15:3
Chesney, Alan M, 1964, S 23,47:3
Chesney, Arthur, 1949, Ag 30,27:4
Chesney, Cummings C, 1947, N 28,27:1
Chesney, John A, 1947, Ag 17,52:4
Chesney, Robert Mrs, 1952, N 8,17:5
Chesney, William J, 1954, Ap 17,13:6
Chesney, William L, 1947, My 16,23:3
Chesnov, Z S, 1948, F 27,21:3
Chesnut, Emily H, 1966, Ag 3,37:4
Chesnut, Roy, 1950, Je 5,23:1
Chesnut, W Calvin, 1962, O 17,39:5
Chesnut, William, 1940, S 6,21:1
Chesnutt, Scott E, 1948, My 12,27:1
Chess, Benjamin Mrs, 1966, My 14,31:1
Chessar, Charles W, 1946, Ja 25,24:2
Chessar, Elizabeth S, 1940, F 17,13:6
Chessin, Alex, 1955, Jl 12,25:1
Chessin, Meyer, 1950, N 9,33:5
Chessman, Adam P, 1939, O 15,49:2
Chessman, Merle R, 1947, S 2,21:5
Chessman, Violet M, 1947, My 22,27:1
Chester, A, 1934, F 13,19:1
Chester, A H Prof, 1903, Ap 14,9:6
Chester, Alma, 1953, Ja 24,15:4
Chester, C M, 1932, My 5,19:3
Chester, C T, 1880, Ap 14,4:7
Chester, Clarence L, 1958, D 30,35:1
Chester, Colby M Mrs, 1923, Ap 10,21:4; 1956, F 22, 27:3
Chester, Frank D, 1938, Je 15,23:5
Chester, Frederick D, 1943, Ja 3,42:6
Chester, George, 1949, Ap 22,24:7
Chester, George M, 1903, D 20,7:6
Chester, George Randolph, 1924, F 27,17:4
Chester, Hawley T, 1954, O 25,27:2
Chester, Henry, 1953, Ja 14,31:1
Chester, James R, 1942, My 14,19:5
Chester, Jerome, 1954, S 14,27:1
Chester, John, 1951, Jl 11,23:3
Chester, John A Rev, 1906, D 21,9:4
Chester, John N, 1871, O 12,5:6
Chester, Joseph E, 1938, Ja 28,21:3
Chester, Lewis S, 1945, Je 15,19:4
Chester, Manley E, 1937, N 18,23:1
Chester, Margaret B Mrs, 1944, F 16,17:3
Chester, Nellie Mrs, 1944, My 21,44:3
Chester, Raymond V N, 1943, Mr 23,19:4
Chester, Rosalind Kramer Mrs (Mrs Alexander Chester), 1968, D 4,47:1
Chester, S H, 1940, Ap 28,37:3
Chester, Sam K Mrs, 1918, Ap 3,13:4
Chester, Samuel K, 1921, Mr 22,17:4
Chester, Saul W, 1964, S 13,87:1
Chester, Stanley J, 1955, Ag 5,19:2
Chester, Thomas Mrs, 1966, S 20,47:3
Chester, W H Capt, 1863, Jl 14,3:3
Chester, Wayland M, 1945, F 8,19:1
Chesterfield, Earl of, 1871, D 2,1:7; 1933, Ja 25,12:1
Chesterfield, Earl of (E H S Stanhope), 1952, Ag 4, 15:6
Chesterfield, Henry, 1939, Ja 12,20:4
Chesterman, E B, 1903, Ag 11,1:7
Chesterman, Frederick M, 1966, Jl 7,37:1
Chesterman, George B, 1908, My 7,7:6
Chesterton, Frances Mrs, 1938, D 13,26:2
Chesterton, G K, 1936, Je 15,1:2
Chestnut, James C, 1942, Ja 29,19:6
Chestnut, Samuel H, 1949, D 7,31:3
Cheston, Albert D, 1939, Mr 28,24:3
Cheston, Charles S Sr, 1960, F 14,84:6
Cheston, E M, 1922, Mr 18,13:5
Cheston, Frank C, 1955, D 21,29:2
Cheston, G, 1881, Mr 10,5:5
Cheston, Henry C, 1946, D 25,29:2
Cheston, Henry C Mrs, 1948, N 21,88:2
Cheston, J Hamilton, 1966, D 31,19:5
Cheston, James Jr, 1940, S 2,15:5
Cheston, James Mrs, 1967, D 23,23:2
Cheston, James 3d, 1945, Ja 28,37:2
Cheston, Radcliffe Jr, 1968, Mr 23,31:1
Cheston, Radcliffe Jr Mrs, 1961, D 8,37:4
Chetham, Harry R, 1938, S 15,25:2
Chetham, William, 1944, Ag 14,15:4
Chetlain, Arthur H, 1940, Ap 11,26:2
Chetlain, Augustus Louis Mrs, 1923, My 4,17:3
Chettiar, Annamalai, 1948, Je 17,25:1
Chettur, Krishna K, 1956, Ap 30,23:5
Chetty, R K S, 1953, My 6,31:3
Chetwin, William E, 1940, S 14,17:5
Chetwode, George K, 1957, Mr 13,31:2
Chetwode, Lady, 1946, Je 30,38:3
Chetwode, Phil W (Field Marshal Lord), 1950, Jl 7, 19:1
Chetwood, C H, 1952, O 16,29:5
Chetwood, George L Mrs, 1945, Ja 4,19:2
Chetwood, Thomas B, 1952, S 24,33:5
Chetwynd, G Sir, 1935, Ag 29,4:1
Chetwynd, George Mrs (Lady Hastings), 1907, F 4, 9:5
Chetwynd, Rosalind Lady, 1922, O 10,21:4
Chetwynd, Ross, 1952, Ja 15,27:4
Cheude, Leon, 1947, Ja 10,22:2
Chevalier, Albert, 1923, Jl 12,17:3
Chevalier, Charles C Mrs, 1947, Mr 12,25:2
Chevalier, Eugenio Mrs, 1949, O 13,27:2
Chevalier, Gus, 1947, N 21,27:1
Chevalier, Jacques, 1962, Ap 20,27:2
Chevalier, John B, 1955, S 15,33:1
Chevalier, Mercedes G, 1956, Ja 17,33:3
Chevalier, Michel, 1879, N 30,5:3
Chevalier, Stuart, 1956, Jl 4,19:5
Chevalier, Willard, 1961, Je 30,27:3
Chevalier, Willard Mrs, 1962, Mr 1,31:5
Chevalier, William J, 1952, Ag 31,44:3
Chevallier, Francis T, 1951, My 13,88:6
Chevers, L M Rev, 1875, S 15,4:6
Chevers, Marshall Trowbridge Mrs, 1925, D 16,25:4
Cheves, Langdon, 1940, Ja 2,19:4
Chevigny, Hector, 1965, Ap 22,33:1
Chevillard, Camille, 1923, My 31,15:4
Chevillard, Maurice, 1943, Je 24,21:2
Cheviot, John C, 1946, F 17,42:5
Cheviot, Thomas C Mrs, 1941, N 17,19:4
Chevreul, M E, 1889, Ap 10,5:3
Chevrier, Edgar R E, 1956, Ag 27,19:1
Chevrier, Maxine, 1946, Ag 3,15:5
Chevrillon, Andre, 1957, Jl 18,25:3
Chevrolet, Arthur, 1946, Ap 18,27:3
Chevrolet, Louis, 1941, Je 7,17:1
Chew, Alexander Lafayette, 1911, N 19,II,15:5
Chew, Ames Parker, 1924, N 30,7:2
Chew, Benjamin Mrs, 1950, Mr 21,29:1
Chew, Benjamin Sr, 1938, Ap 1,23:6
Chew, Beverly, 1924, My 22,17:5
Chew, Elisha C, 1940, Ag 6,20:4
Chew, Elizabeth B Mrs, 1941, Jl 7,15:2
Chew, J S, 1885, Mr 14,5:2
Chew, John A, 1959, N 23,31:2
Chew, John Hamilton Dr, 1924, Ag 15,13:5
Chew, John M, 1946, Ap 13,17:2
Chew, John M Mrs, 1941, Mr 28,23:1
Chew, Joseph J, 1946, F 11,29:2
Chew, Margaret L, 1941, O 28,23:2
Chew, Oswald, 1949, D 7,31:3
Chew, Oswald Mrs, 1948, N 4,29:4
Chew, Philip F, 1966, Ap 22,29:6
Chew, Philip F Mrs, 1959, Ap 8,37:1
Chew, Phineas P Mrs, 1947, Ag 19,23:2
Chew, Richard S Lt Commander, 1875, Ap 11,7:3
Chew, Robert S, 1873, Ag 4,1:5
Chew, Samuel, 1919, Jl 9,13:3
Chew, Samuel C, 1960, Ja 17,86:3
Chew, Samuel L, 1943, Ap 8,23:5
Chew, Samuel Mrs, 1963, S 3,36:1
Chew, Thomas, 1944, Ag 12,11:4
Chew, William M, 1943, S 6,17:5
Chewey, George S, 1956, Ag 21,29:3
Chewing, William J Mrs, 1955, S 19,25:5
Chewning, Walter L, 1951, N 13,29:2
Chewning, William J Dr, 1937, O 30,19:6
Cheyfitz, Edward T, 1959, My 25,29:1
Cheylesmore, Lady, 1945, S 16,43:2
Cheylesmore, Lord (Herbert Eaton), 1925, Jl 30,19:4
Cheyne, Tho Kelly Rev, 1915, F 18,11:6
Cheyne, Thomas, 1956, Jl 6,21:4
Cheyney, Edward P, 1947, F 2,57:5
Cheyney, John K, 1939, Mr 20,17:5
Cheyney, Peter, 1951, Je 27,29:1
Cheyney, Ralph, 1941, O 16,21:3
Chi Chao-ting, 1963, Ag 10,17:3
Chi Pai-Shih, 1957, S 17,35:2
Chia Ching-te, 1960, O 21,33:1
Chia-tseng Chen, 1959, N 21,23:1
Chiaffarelli, Manfredo, 1944, Ja 3,21:2
Chiampou, Charles P, 1946, F 26,25:4
Chianelli, Russell J, 1967, O 8,86:2
Chiang Monlin, 1964, Je 19,31:3
Chiang Wei-kuo Mme, 1953, Mr 22,86:1
Chiapella, Edward E, 1951, Ja 16,29:3
Chiappe, Andrew J, 1967, My 6,31:5
Chiappero, Piergiorgio, 1963, Jl 16,31:3
Chiappetta, Pasquale, 1960, Je 24,27:5
Chiappinelli, Salvatore, 1948, O 6,29:4
Chiarello, Augustus V, 1961, Ja 27,23:2
Chiarello, Dick, 1963, Ap 5,47:4
Chiarello, Gus G, 1961, F 22,25:3
Chiarello, Gus P, 1963, S 23,29:4
Chiarello, Marion Mrs, 1950, S 25,12:3
Chiari, Joseph P, 1963, S 5,31:3
Chiari, Rodolfo, 1937, Ag 18,19:3
Chiariglione, Hector, 1940, Ap 23,24:2
Chiarini, Angelo, 1943, Mr 24,23:3
Chiarlo, Carlo Cardinal, 1964, Ja 22,37:4
Chiaroni, Federico, 1945, N 19,10:3
Chiasserini, Ada, 1958, F 14,23:1
Chiasson, P A, 1942, F 2,15:1
Chiavacci, Egisto, 1881, F 6,5:1
Chiaventone, Mike, 1922, My 20,15:6
Chiba, Taneaki, 1953, Je 26,19:5
Chibas, Eduardo J, 1941, Ag 22,15:6
Chicharro, Eduardo (lr, Je 2,26:7), 1949, My 25,2
Chichester, Arthur C S (Lord Templemore), 1953 O 5,27:4
Chichester, Aston, 1962, O 25,39:4
Chichester, Bp of (Ernest Roland Wilberforce), 1 S 10,7:4
Chichester, Caroline C, 1948, O 8,25:2
Chichester, Cassius M, 1950, Je 2,23:2
Chichester, Charles D, 1941, Ja 27,15:3
Chichester, Charles F, 1908, F 21,7:7
Chichester, Earl of, 1905, Ap 22,11:7
Chichester, Edward G, 1940, O 1,23:5
Chichester, Edward Rear Adm Sir, 1906, S 18,9:4
Chichester, George H Sgt, 1916, Ag 28,9:6
Chichester, Gerald Sir, 1939, O 11,30:2
Chichester, Harriet A, 1952, F 13,29:4
Chichester, Howard, 1940, N 18,19:4
Chichester, Howard Mrs, 1939, My 21,III,7:2
Chichester, William O Capt, 1937, Je 29,21:5
Chichibu, Prince of Japan, 1953, Ja 4,77:1
Chick, John D, 1961, Ap 14,2:1
Chick, Louis S, 1949, D 22,23:4
Chickering, C C, 1903, Ja 29,9:6
Chickering, Charles F Mrs, 1912, Ja 11,13:4
Chickering, Clifford C, 1942, Ag 5,19:4
Chickering, Clifford G Mrs, 1940, Ja 16,23:3
Chickering, Edward C, 1952, D 27,7:8
Chickering, Frederick W, 1920, O 16,13:4
Chickering, Henry T, 1954, Mr 15,25:3
Chickering, James H, 1950, My 7,106:2
Chickering, John A, 1953, Mr 11,29:3
Chickering, Thomas E, 1871, F 15,1:2
Chickering, William E, 1959, Mr 3,33:3
Chico, Juan, 1941, Ja 11,17:3
Chicoine, Joseph E, 1948, O 28,30:2
Chicoine, Martin J, 1961, Ag 10,27:2
Chicolani, Louis, 1950, Ag 22,27:5
Chideckel, Maurice, 1958, Je 22,76:4

Chidester, Charles E, 1946, Ag 3,15:5
Chidester, Drew, 1948, Ja 19,23:5
Chidester, Floyd E, 1947, Je 21,17:6
Chidester, Harmon O, 1957, F 7,27:1
Chidester, John H, 1959, Mr 22,87:2
Chidester, John Y, 1948, S 4,15:3
Chidester, Samuel W, 1939, My 16,23:4
Chidester, William Mrs, 1947, Mr 23,60:8
Chidlaw, William M Mrs, 1949, Ag 28,72:7
Chidsey, Andrew D, 1944, Je 23,19:5
Chidsey, Andrew D 3d, 1963, Ap 13,19:6
Chidsey, John T, 1946, My 22,21:2
Chidsey, T McKeen, 1958, Ap 20,84:4
Chidwick, J P, 1935, Ja 14,15:1
Chidwick, Richard Mrs, 1912, Je 27,13:5
Chief, Joseph, 1904, S 24,9:6
Chiesa, Ettore D Mrs, 1963, Je 16,84:2
Chiesa, Jules Della Marquis, 1915, Ap 11,11:5
Chievitz, Ole, 1946, D 27,20:2
Chifley, Joseph B, 1951, Je 14,27:1
Chigi, Alfio G, 1950, F 4,15:3
Chigi, Alfred, 1946, F 16,13:2
Chigi-Albani, Mario Prince, 1914, N 5,11:6
Chigi della Rovere-Albani, Ludovico Prince, 1951, N 15,29:4
Chigi Saracini, Guido, 1965, N 20,35:5
Chikako Kuni, Princess, 1956, S 10,27:4
Chilcote, Don, 1948, O 20,29:2
Chilcott, C A Rev, 1866, My 1,3:1
Chilcott, Warden S Sir, 1942, Mr 13,19:4
Child, Albert M, 1940, Mr 24,30:7
Child, Alpha, 1918, My 25,13:5
Child, Anne W Mrs, 1948, Ap 17,15:2
Child, C G, 1880, S 29,5:2
Child, Calvin G, 1943, Je 5,15:4
Child, Charles M, 1954, D 21,27:2
Child, Clarence G, 1948, S 21,27:4
Child, David Lee, 1874, S 28,9:1
Child, Earnest T, 1946, O 27,63:3
Child, Edmund B, 1946, F 13,23:2
Child, Edwin B, 1937, Mr 11,23:5
Child, Ernest, 1954, Je 13,89:1
Child, Francis, 1938, O 20,23:1
Child, Francis Ex-Judge, 1914, S 29,11:1
Child, Francis Mrs, 1913, My 19,9:4
Child, Frank H, 1904, Ja 9,9:2
Child, Frank S Jr, 1959, Mr 24,39:2
Child, Fred S, 1964, Ap 16,37:3
Child, H Eugene, 1952, Ag 3,61:2
Child, Herbert E Mrs, 1942, Ap 24,17:3
Child, John H Mrs, 1951, Ag 29,25:1
Child, Josiah H Mrs, 1948, Ap 6,23:5
Child, Lilian R Mrs, 1941, D 5,23:2
Child, Lydia Maria, 1880, O 21,5:4
Child, R W, 1935, F 1,21:1
Child, Sidney P, 1946, Jl 5,19:4
Child, Stanley G sr, 1953, Jl 24,13:6
Child, Sydney P Mrs, 1953, D 16,35:2
Child, W Stanley, 1946, Ap 1,27:5
Child, Warren G, 1938, Je 10,21:3
Child, William B, 1944, F 6,41:1; 1960, Je 15,41:1
Childe, Carrie G Mrs, 1942, Je 6,13:1
Childe, Cromwell, 1941, Mr 4,23:6
Childe, Henry Langdon, 1874, N 7,8:7
Childe, Vere G, 1957, O 20,28:1
Childers, James S, 1965, Jl 18,68:8
Childers, Louis E, 1961, Mr 3,27:2
Childers, Robert E Mrs, 1964, Ja 3,24:2
Childre, Cecil H, 1966, My 29,56:6
Childress, Avent, 1967, F 24,35:3
Childress, Wade T Mrs, 1948, Ja 21,26:3
Childs, A E, 1933, N 11,15:3
Childs, Albert J, 1944, Mr 17,17:2
Childs, Augusta D, 1942, S 26,15:4
Childs, Beatrice C Mrs, 1942, My 27,23:2
Childs, Benjamin F, 1942, N 5,25:4
Childs, C Frederick, 1955, Mr 16,33:5
Childs, C Frederick Mrs, 1952, Ag 17,77:1
Childs, Caroline G Mrs, 1937, Jl 12,18:1
Childs, Charles A, 1912, D 25,11:5
Childs, Charles F, 1946, Ja 22,27:4
Childs, Chester, 1883, S 29,5:4
Childs, Daniel Brewer, 1925, N 12,25:6
Childs, Dennis H, 1949, My 27,21:3
Childs, E, 1929, Ap 18,29:3
Childs, Edmund S, 1947, Jl 12,13:4
Childs, Edward H, 1944, O 23,19:2
Childs, Edwards H Mrs, 1951, Mr 2,25:2
Childs, Edwin O, 1950, My 18,29:2
Childs, Ella B Mrs, 1941, D 12,26:2
Childs, Esther Mrs, 1945, Mr 23,19:4
Childs, Eversley, 1953, D 21,31:3
Childs, Eversley Jr, 1952, O 30,31:4
Childs, Eversley Mrs, 1944, N 19,50:6
Childs, F Carter, 1918, N 26,15:3
Childs, Frank A, 1965, Ja 27,35:3
Childs, Frank H, 1954, Jl 8,23:2
Childs, Frederick A, 1953, Ag 13,25:4
Childs, Frederick B, 1939, Jl 20,19:4
Childs, Frederick Mrs, 1946, Ap 26,21:3
Childs, Frederick Robbins, 1907, O 24,11:5
Childs, G W (por), 1894, F 3,1:5
Childs, Geoffrey S, 1956, D 8,19:5
Childs, George H, 1963, D 10,43:4
Childs, Harold M, 1941, Ja 11,17:4
Childs, Harold P, 1938, D 28,26:4
Childs, Harris Robbins, 1922, Mr 25,11:3
Childs, Harry E, 1941, Ag 11,13:3
Childs, Harry R, 1949, F 5,15:1
Childs, Henry O, 1940, Ap 4,23:3
Childs, Irving H, 1943, Jl 15,21:2; 1952, D 9,33:5
Childs, J Roll, 1958, N 6,37:5
Childs, James A, 1945, Ag 26,44:7
Childs, Joel H, 1954, Jl 25,68:6
Childs, John Lewis, 1921, Mr 6,21:3
Childs, Joseph W, 1960, Ap 25,29:5
Childs, Lyman W, 1948, Ap 27,25:2
Childs, Marquis W Mrs, 1968, Je 23,73:2
Childs, Mary Mrs, 1941, S 21,45:3
Childs, Maude E, 1946, S 5,27:4
Childs, Nancy J, 1941, Jl 19,13:2
Childs, Nancy Mrs, 1952, O 5,51:4
Childs, Ozro 2d Mrs, 1945, Ap 22,36:2
Childs, Ralph, 1941, D 5,23:4
Childs, Richard A, 1952, O 2,29:2
Childs, Richard S Mrs, 1961, S 26,39:1
Childs, Richard T, 1960, My 30,17:4
Childs, S C, 1932, Ag 5,13:3
Childs, S Winston Jr, 1961, N 27,29:1
Childs, Samuel S, 1925, Mr 18,21:3
Childs, Starling W, 1946, D 21,19:3
Childs, Thomas F, 1945, Ap 24,19:3
Childs, Vernon G, 1939, Ja 17,22:2
Childs, W H, 1928, N 3,19:3
Childs, William (por),(will, Jl 29,17:1), 1938, My 23, 17:1
Childs, William H, 1962, My 26,25:4
Childs, William M, 1939, Je 23,19:5
Childs, William Mrs, 1921, Je 8,17:6; 1952, S 18,29:1
Childs, William S, 1952, F 20,30:4
Childs, William St C Jr, 1965, F 12,29:4
Childs, William St C Jr Mrs, 1965, F 12,29:4
Childs, William T, 1945, O 31,23:4
Childs, Wyndham, 1946, N 30,15:5
Childton, Joshua M, 1947, D 8,25:4
Chiles, Harry L, 1945, Jl 18,27:1
Chiles, Samuel L (por), 1944, Ag 30,17:6
Chilko, Alex J, 1963, D 9,35:2
Chillian, Stephen A Sr, 1967, F 6,29:3
Chillingworth, Felix P, 1938, Jl 2,13:4
Chillis, ex-Lt Gov, 1883, O 7,4:7
Chilowsky, Constantin, 1958, Jl 1,31:4
Chilson, Arthur A, 1938, Ag 13,13:4
Chilson, Edward N, 1960, S 14,43:1
Chilson, Elmer E, 1950, S 20,31:1
Chilson, Eugene, 1950, D 27,27:3
Chilson, Haynes H, 1937, Mr 21,II,8:8
Chilston, Viscount, 1947, Jl 26,13:5
Chilstrom, Nels J, 1947, Ja 2,27:1
Chilton, Alice M Mrs, 1950, Ja 1,42:4
Chilton, Edwin Bailey, 1925, S 3,25:6
Chilton, Eleanor C Mrs, 1949, F 9,28:2
Chilton, Euphemia Deklyn, 1916, Ja 19,11:5
Chilton, Forrest S, 1946, Ag 8,21:4
Chilton, Henry G, 1954, N 22,23:4
Chilton, Joseph E Maj, 1937, F 22,17:4
Chilton, Katherine Lady, 1959, My 29,23:1
Chilton, R H, 1879, F 19,2:6
Chilton, Samuel, 1867, Ja 18,8:5
Chilton, William E Jr, 1950, S 22,31:5
Chilton, William E Sr, 1939, N 8,23:4
Chilton, William H, 1954, Ap 7,31:5
Chilver, Mabel A, 1948, Je 16,29:3
Chilver, William W, 1951, O 21,93:1
Chilver, William W Mrs, 1951, Je 1,26:1
Chilvers, Charles H Capt, 1919, Ap 2,11:2
Chilvers, William Mrs, 1958, Jl 7,27:5
Chimento, Juan, 1946, D 21,19:3
Chimento, Pasquale, 1964, O 22,35:2
Chin, Sam, 1909, Jl 17,7:6
Chin, Stanley Q W, 1955, Ap 30,17:2
Chin Bing, 1962, S 5,39:4
Chin Kung Fong, 1952, F 5,29:1
Chinaglia, Achille G, 1950, Je 13,27:5
Chinaria, Hira S, 1955, My 8,3:4
Chinca, Ugo, 1952, N 9,91:1
Chinda, S Count, 1929, Ja 17,25:3
Chindblom, Carl R, 1956, S 13,35:2
Chindblom, Carl R Mrs, 1956, S 13,35:2
Chinery, A Randolph, 1942, O 27,25:4
Chinese Empress, 1881, Ap 20,1:4
Ching, Cyrus S, 1967, D 28,32:1
Ching, Cyrus S Mrs, 1939, Jl 14,19:3
Ching, Prince, 1917, F 2,11:4
Ching, Thomas, 1954, O 28,35:4
Ching Jun Lin, 1947, Ja 7,28:3
Chinich, Milton J, 1968, Mr 23,31:5
Chiniquy, C P Rev, 1899, Ja 17,1:4
Chinitz, Aaron, 1945, Ap 6,15:3
Chinitz, Samuel, 1968, My 16,47:1
Chinlund, Edwin F, 1960, Ja 12,47:3
Chinn, John M, 1939, D 18,23:1
Chinn, Philip, 1962, F 24,27:1
Chinnery, Albert T, 1947, S 24,23:4
Chinnery, Anna C, 1954, Ap 24,17:6
Chinnery, John B, 1944, Ag 9,17:5
Chinnery, Joseph A, 1959, My 23,25:3
Chinnery, Robert M, 1948, D 22,24:3
Chinnock, Charles E, 1915, Je 12,11:5
Chinnock, Harry E, 1948, Ap 15,25:6
Chinnock, John R, 1964, My 1,35:1
Chiocchetti, Emilio, 1951, Jl 30,17:4
Chiodo, Carmen V, 1945, O 24,23:7
Chiodo, Frank, 1945, O 4,23:6
Chiodo, Mary E, 1947, Mr 16,53:5
Chip, George, 1960, N 7,71:4
Chiperfield, Burnett M, 1940, Je 25,23:5
Chiperfield, Robert B Mrs, 1955, Ap 23,19:5
Chipinick, Morris, 1957, N 25,31:3
Chipkin, Israel S (mem ser, D 20,31:1), 1955, O 27, 33:3
Chipley, Charles A Gen, 1904, Ja 8,7:3
Chipley, Hunt, 1937, O 31,II,10:7
Chipley, William Galt Mrs (Bonnie Hodges), 1968, D 20,47:1
Chipman, Elisha S, 1942, Ja 28,19:1
Chipman, F Sherman, 1950, Ap 9,85:1
Chipman, F Sherman Mrs, 1940, N 8,21:2
Chipman, Frank E, 1942, Je 4,19:4
Chipman, George B, 1947, S 24,23:4
Chipman, Gordon P, 1965, F 9,37:1
Chipman, Henry, 1867, Ap 7,5:4
Chipman, Herbert L, 1938, Mr 1,21:4
Chipman, Holmes S, 1941, S 11,23:2
Chipman, John H, 1957, Je 18,29:1
Chipman, Norris B, 1957, Ag 15,21:3
Chipman, Norton Parker Judge, 1924, F 2,13:6
Chipman, Ralph N, 1956, Ag 21,29:4
Chipman, Reuben T, 1950, S 22,23:5
Chipman, Richmond L, 1960, N 28,31:4
Chipman, W Evan, 1922, S 4,13:6
Chipman, Walter W, 1950, Ap 5,31:1; 1952, Mr 3,21:2
Chipman, Warwick F Mrs, 1949, Ag 8,15:4
Chipman, Wilfred H, 1905, Ap 26,11:5
Chipman, William J, 1950, Je 18,76:7
Chipman, William P Rev Dr, 1937, Mr 1,19:6
Chipman, Wilmon B, 1943, D 27,20:2
Chipp, Elvin D, 1949, Ap 24,76:2
Chipp, J Deyo Mrs, 1938, Ap 6,23:6
Chipp, Rodney A, 1944, Ap 1,13:6
Chipp, Rodney D, 1948, Ag 21,16:3; 1966, D 29,28:5
Chippendale, Cornelius, 1945, Mr 5,19:3
Chippendale, Harry A, 1953, N 3,31:2
Chippiga, Stephen J, 1948, Mr 13,15:2
Chiquette, George F, 1939, D 13,27:5
Chiquoine, Victor L, 1949, N 11,26:2
Chiray, Maurice, 1954, D 15,31:1
Chirdon, Michael D, 1947, O 28,27:8
Chiribiri, Antonio, 1943, Ap 23,17:5
Chisam, Joseph, 1947, My 30,21:1
Chisholm, Alex, 1950, N 5,V,4:1
Chisholm, Alex A, 1939, N 25,17:3
Chisholm, Andre T, 1954, F 10,29:5
Chisholm, Angus V, 1940, F 17,13:6
Chisholm, Donald E, 1951, O 29,23:2
Chisholm, Donald V, 1960, Jl 18,27:4
Chisholm, Duncan, 1939, Jl 26,19:4
Chisholm, Edward D Mrs, 1951, My 10,31:4
Chisholm, Edward de C, 1941, Ap 6,49:1
Chisholm, George E, 1938, Ja 18,23:3
Chisholm, George H, 1943, My 11,21:4; 1952, Je 28, 19:2
Chisholm, Henry L, 1949, N 24,31:4
Chisholm, Herbert E M, 1945, Ag 21,21:2
Chisholm, Horatio P, 1941, Mr 12,21:4
Chisholm, Hugh, 1924, S 30,23:1
Chisholm, Hugh A, 1940, S 27,23:5
Chisholm, Hugh J, 1912, Jl 9,9:3; 1959, D 24,19:2
Chisholm, J A, 1903, Ap 17,9:6
Chisholm, James, 1943, Jl 28,15:4
Chisholm, Julian J Dr, 1903, N 3,7:6
Chisholm, Kenneth J, 1957, Jl 5,17:3
Chisholm, Laura B Mrs, 1949, Ag 16,23:5
Chisholm, Louise B Mrs, 1956, Mr 31,15:6
Chisholm, Raymond D, 1955, Mr 27,86:8
Chisholm, Robert K, 1962, Mr 24,25:6
Chisholm, Robert K Mrs, 1965, Ja 26,34:1
Chisholm, Scotty, 1957, D 26,19:4
Chisholm, Thomas O, 1960, Mr 2,37:2
Chisholm, W, 1880, F 12,2:5
Chisholm, William A, 1949, N 10,32:3
Chisholm, William J, 1942, My 2,13:2; 1950, Ja 23,23:3
Chisholm, William R Mrs, 1945, N 5,19:4
Chism, William F, 1953, Ag 14,19:6
Chisolm, Alexander Col, 1910, Mr 11,9:4
Chisolm, B Ogden (por), 1944, Mr 21,19:1
Chisolm, Benjamin O Mrs, 1940, Je 8,15:4
Chisolm, Dorothy Rogers, 1914, Ap 29,11:6
Chistoserdov, Vadim, 1951, O 21,92:4
Chisum, John G, 1951, Je 13,29:2
Chiswell, Richard R, 1940, F 16,19:1
Chiswell, Robert C Sr, 1951, O 15,25:4
Chitambar, J R, 1940, S 6,21:3
Chitrik, Jacob, 1963, Ap 19,43:2
Chittenden, Albert E Mrs, 1951, O 29,23:1
Chittenden, Alice H, 1945, O 3,19:1
Chittenden, Arthur S, 1948, Ja 4,52:3
Chittenden, Baldwin Jr, 1939, My 11,25:5
Chittenden, Edward A, 1938, F 6,II,8:2; 1948, F 8,60:6

Chittenden, George P, 1952, Ja 14,19:4
Chittenden, Harlow W, 1872, Jl 26,5:6
Chittenden, Horace, 1909, D 27,7:7
Chittenden, Horace W, 1965, My 5,47:1
Chittenden, J Daniel, 1943, N 30,27:3
Chittenden, Jared, 1904, Ja 17,7:6
Chittenden, Joseph H, 1874, D 5,2:2
Chittenden, Lucius E, 1900, Jl 23,2:3
Chittenden, Rhea E, 1952, Ja 9,29:2
Chittenden, Russell H, 1943, D 27,19:1
Chittenden, S B, 1889, Ap 15,5:3
Chittenden, S B Mrs, 1884, Ap 14,5:2
Chittenden, Simeon H Mrs, 1925, N 9,19:5
Chittendon, Hiram M Brig-Gen, 1917, O 10,11:5
Chittendon, Samuel, 1903, Je 27,3:2
Chitterling, Georgia F T Mrs, 1940, My 14,23:5
Chitterling, Nelson M Dr, 1937, O 30,19:6
Chittick, Richard O, 1949, My 17,25:4
Chittison, Herman, 1967, Mr 16,47:3
Chitty, Herbert C, 1956, My 4,25:2
Chitty, Joseph, 1942, F 7,17:5
Chitty, Marion A, 1948, N 3,27:4
Chitty, Reginall Mrs, 1967, F 26,84:8
Chitwood, Leonard N, 1953, S 29,29:1
Chiuchiolo, A Ralph, 1944, D 15,19:3
Chiulli, Alphonse G, 1953, O 17,15:5
Chiurco, Anthony, 1938, Ag 2,19:3
Chiusano, Giuseppe, 1945, Je 4,19:2
Chivacheff, Louis H, 1940, My 17,19:1
Chivers, Arthur B, 1939, D 13,27:3
Chivers, John K D, 1966, Ag 3,37:2
Chivers, Rev Dr, 1907, D 3,9:6
Chivian, Herman, 1938, Jl 2,13:4
Chivian, Howard, 1957, Mr 7,29:1
Chizik, Chana, 1951, D 22,15:2
Chizner, Meyer, 1945, My 12,13:4
Chlapowski, Alfred Count, 1940, Mr 12,10:4
Chloupek, Erwin L, 1948, Ag 31,26:1
Chmela, Stephan, 1947, F 21,19:3
Chmely, Michael A, 1961, Ja 1,49:2
Chmely, Michael J, 1950, Mr 22,28:2
Chmielinska, Josef Mrs, 1939, F 28,20:2
Chmielinski, John M Rev, 1937, F 24,23:4
Chmielnitzki, Melech, 1946, Mr 29,24:2
Chmielski, Peter, 1946, S 8,44:4
Chmura, Paul J, 1950, N 22,25:2
Choate, Alice M Mrs, 1959, S 10,35:3
Choate, Arthur O, 1962, Je 20,35:4
Choate, Arthur O Mrs, 1967, My 18,47:2
Choate, Benjamin C, 1954, O 3,87:3
Choate, C F Jr, 1927, D 1,27:5
Choate, C S Mrs, 1929, N 13,27:4
Choate, Caroline (will, Jl 30,15:8), 1955, Jl 8,23:1
Choate, Charles H, 1941, Ag 26,19:6
Choate, Edward A, 1944, Ap 8,14:7
Choate, George C S Mrs, 1925, Je 25,21:7
Choate, George D, 1909, Ap 20,9:5
Choate, Harold R, 1958, F 24,19:1
Choate, Herbert E, 1942, O 14,25:2
Choate, Homer M, 1937, Ag 24,21:4
Choate, J K, 1928, Je 21,25:5
Choate, James Mrs, 1953, O 19,21:6
Choate, Joseph H (funl, My 18,13:3), 1917, My 16, 13:1
Choate, Joseph H Jr, 1968, Ja 20,29:1
Choate, Joseph H Jr Mrs, 1955, N 12,19:5
Choate, Mabel, 1958, D 29,15:3
Choate, Margaret J, 1954, S 3,17:5
Choate, Margaret M, 1944, My 16,21:6
Choate, Mary K, 1938, Jl 13,21:4
Choate, Nathaniel, 1965, Ag 24,31:1
Choate, Raymond S, 1960, O 6,41:6
Choate, Robert B, 1963, D 22,34:6
Choate, Rufus (funl, Jl 25,2:1), 1859, Jl 15,4:6
Choate, Sarah E, 1937, My 18,23:2
Choate, Ward N, 1939, N 24,23:4
Choate, William A, 1937, Mr 18,25:5
Choate, William Gardner, 1920, N 15,15:5
Choate, Winfield Scott, 1903, Je 30,3:3
Chobot, Robert, 1958, S 28,88:4
Choboy, Elizabeth H, 1943, O 19,11:3
Choboy, Mary T, 1943, O 19,11:3
Chodoff, Louis, 1956, Ja 27,23:2
Chodorcoff, William, 1966, Ap 19,41:2
Chodorov, Frank, 1966, D 29,28:8
Chodzko, Lernard, 1871, Ap 6,2:3
Choffin, Jean A, 1944, My 20,15:1
Choffy, Joseph D, 1961, S 6,37:1
Choi Bol-san Premier, 1952, Ja 28,17:6
Choinard, Arthur J, 1949, Mr 26,17:1
Choiseul, Duchess de (Mrs Chas Coudert), 1919, Mr 14,13:3
Choiseul, Eliza de, 1904, Ja 30,9:5
Choix de Saint Ange, M, 1877, Ja 8,5:5
Choka, E Mrs, 1940, D 25,44:1
Chokla, Louis M, 1953, Je 2,29:6
Chola, Sebastian, 1950, F 8,27:3
Chollar, Harvey W, 1955, Mr 29,29:3
Chollar, Walter E, 1948, Je 13,63:5
Chollet, Burt G, 1964, My 12,37:2
Chollet, Jean, 1952, D 3,33:4
Cholmeley, Montague Sir, 1874, Ja 20,1:7
Cholmeley-Jones, Edward S, 1964, Jl 8,35:2
Cholmeley-Jones, Richard Gilder Lt-Col, 1922, F 22, 15:5
Cholmeley-Jones, Roynon, 1947, Je 17,28:6
Cholmondeley, George Henry Hugh Lord, 1923, Mr 17,13:2
Cholmondeley, Marquess of (former Lord Great Chamberlain), 1968, S 18,47:1
Cholmondeley, Mary, 1925, Jl 16,9:3
Cholodny, Peter D, 1945, Mr 6,21:2
Cholst, William, 1954, S 12,85:1
Choltitz, Dietrich von (funl, N 10,47:3), 1966, N 6, 88:5
Chomel, Marie, 1957, Ja 9,31:1
Chomette, Henri, 1941, Ag 20,19:1
Chomsky, Nathan, 1951, N 18,91:1
Chon, Benjamin W, 1952, D 2,31:5
Choneh (E Mozdof), 1966, Ag 8,27:5
Chong, George T, 1962, N 17,25:3
Chong Oo Kim, Bishop, 1939, S 20,27:5
Choos, George, 1961, Ap 4,37:2
Chopak, Herman, 1951, Mr 1,27:5
Chopin, Alex A Mrs, 1961, N 29,41:2
Chopp, Charles E, 1965, Mr 11,33:3
Choppin, S, 1880, Mr 3,1:4
Choquette, Charles A, 1967, Mr 16,47:1
Choquette, Ernest, 1941, Mr 31,15:5
Choquette, Philippe A, 1948, D 21,31:1
Choquette, Robert H, 1939, Ag 21,13:3
Chorin, Francis (funl, N 10,47:1), 1964, N 6,37:4
Chorley, E Clowes Mrs, 1938, D 14,25:2
Chorley, Edward C (por), 1949, N 4,28:2
Chorley, H F, 1872, Mr 2,5:3
Chorley, John W, 1954, Ap 15,29:2
Chorlton, Harry L, 1955, Ag 24,27:2
Chorlton, William H, 1953, Je 23,30:3
Chormann, Otto I Mrs, 1944, Ap 24,19:4
Choromanski, Zygmunt Most Rev, 1968, D 28,25:8
Chorosh, William H, 1943, F 22,17:1
Chors, Henry A Dr, 1904, Ja 10,7:6
Chosak, Joshua Rabbi, 1937, N 13,19:3
Chosin, Prince, 1871, Jl 17,5:2
Chotiner, Max C Mrs (A Calhoun), 1966, Je 6,41:2
Chott, Hugo J, 1949, Ag 30,27:4
Chotzinoff, Samuel, 1964, F 11,39:3
Chou, Joseph Chi-shih, 1954, Mr 17,14:4
Chou Yin, 1954, D 8,35:3
Chough, Pyung Ok (funl plans, F 21,7:2), 1960, F 16, 7:3
Choumenkovitch, Ilija, 1962, O 9,41:2
Chounaval, Constance, 1923, Ag 25,7:5
Choutea, Pierre Jr, 1865, S 13,2:6
Chouteau, Henri, 1952, Mr 16,90:8
Chow, Albert K, 1957, O 18,23:2
Chow, Hung-ching, 1957, My 8,37:4
Chowla, M L, 1953, F 20,20:3
Chown, A Blake, 1948, O 11,23:3
Choykee, Andrew T, 1963, O 6,88:7
Choynski, Joe, 1943, Ja 26,23:6
Chramer, Fredrik A, 1960, Jl 7,31:6
Chrelkov, Nikola, 1950, Ag 30,31:3
Chresomales, Andrew, 1954, N 19,23:2
Chresomales, James A, 1961, Je 24,21:3
Chretien, Henri, 1956, F 8,33:2
Chretien, John D, 1946, O 12,19:4
Chrilley, Mary, 1937, My 1,19:5
Chris, Bork, 1945, Ja 4,19:2
Chrisdie, Charles, 1915, D 21,13:4
Chrisdie, Charles H Jr Mrs, 1965, Je 14,33:3
Chrisfield, W, 1880, Je 18,2:3
Chrisler, Annie L T Mrs, 1940, My 30,17:3
Chrisler, Dwight J, 1950, N 4,17:3
Chrisman, J J, 1881, Jl 31,2:2
Chrisman, Neil, 1949, O 23,84:3
Chrisman, Wilmer Olin Lt, 1914, Ja 13,9:6
Christ, Charles G Mrs, 1949, Jl 20,25:2
Christ, Frank E, 1944, Jl 26,19:1
Christ, Fred V Rev, 1937, Jl 10,15:3
Christ, George M, 1947, Je 28,13:2
Christ, George R, 1952, F 18,19:2
Christ, Harold J, 1956, Ag 3,19:1
Christ, J Rudolf Mrs, 1948, O 16,15:1
Christ, John, 1953, Ag 30,89:2
Christ, John E Mrs, 1952, My 20,25:2
Christ, Philip J Mrs, 1964, Ja 4,23:1
Christ, Robert A, 1943, Ja 17,44:5
Christal, John, 1951, Ag 16,27:4
Christaller, Hetene, 1953, My 26,29:4
Christatos, Morris, 1949, O 15,15:3
Christatos, Morris Mrs, 1943, Ap 28,23:2
Christatos, Nicholas, 1941, S 4,21:6
Christe, Harriet B W Mrs, 1938, Ap 11,15:2
Christedes, Christ F, 1951, D 13,33:4
Christel, John A, 1955, O 16,87:1
Christel, Ronald R, 1948, My 5,20:3
Christenberry, Charles W, 1963, D 27,23:7
Christenberry, William C Mrs, 1964, D 8,45:1
Christensen, Alfred T, 1950, Ag 16,29:5
Christensen, Andrew F, 1967, My 4,39:2
Christensen, Ann M Mrs, 1947, Jl 25,18:2
Christensen, Arthur C, 1940, Jl 12,15:5
Christensen, C T Gen, 1905, Ja 28,7:5
Christensen, Charles A, 1955, N 6,86:7
Christensen, Charles W, 1954, Ap 16,21:3
Christensen, Chris, 1940, S 24,23:1; 1954, Ja 24,84:3
Christensen, Christ, 1939, Je 25,36:6
Christensen, Christian, 1959, Ap 6,27:4
Christensen, Christian A, 1951, S 7,29:3
Christensen, Einar C, 1956, Jl 7,13:6
Christensen, Ernest H, 1952, Mr 13,29:3
Christensen, Ferdinand W Mrs, 1951, My 6,92:8
Christensen, Fred R, 1942, My 7,19:5
Christensen, Frederick W, 1946, Je 12,27:2
Christensen, H G, 1950, Je 12,27:3
Christensen, Halfdan, 1950, S 18,23:5
Christensen, Hans A, 1950, Ja 4,46:2
Christensen, Helen M, 1945, D 30,14:3
Christensen, Henry F, 1964, D 17,41:3
Christensen, Henry Sr, 1945, N 10,15:4
Christensen, James A (Sept 16), 1965, O 11,61:1
Christensen, Jens P, 1938, Je 8,23:2
Christensen, John, 1937, My 12,23:6
Christensen, Knud, 1956, Ag 16,25:4
Christensen, Leo M, 1955, F 11,23:4
Christensen, Margit H, 1960, Ja 29,25:1
Christensen, Martin, 1949, Ja 31,19:4
Christensen, Niels A, 1952, O 7,29:6
Christensen, Parley P, 1954, F 11,29:3
Christensen, Peter, 1952, Ap 5,15:3
Christensen, Peter Mrs, 1956, Jl 23,23:4
Christensen, Thomas P, 1953, N 28,15:6
Christensen, Viggo, 1960, N 29,37:2
Christensen, William A, 1940, Jl 21,29:2
Christenson, Bernard H, 1938, Jl 22,17:5
Christenson, Charles A, 1956, My 16,35:4
Christenson, Elmo C, 1955, My 25,33:2
Christenson, George Sr, 1955, F 10,31:4
Christenson, John A, 1948, S 14,30:2
Christenson, Joseph, 1944, Ap 5,19:5
Christenson, Louis P, 1962, Ap 27,35:3
Christenson, Sven Maj, 1937, S 4,15:3
Christenson, Walter F, 1963, O 21,31:2
Christenson, William L, 1961, D 8,42:8
Christer, Anthony, 1962, Ag 23,29:2
Christerson, Melbourne, 1957, O 10,33:4
Christiaansen, Annie L Mrs, 1951, Je 13,29:3
Christiaansen, Norman M, 1948, Mr 13,15:3
Christian, A, 1871, O 22,6:1
Christian, Albion C, 1947, Jl 30,21:2
Christian, Andrew D, 1947, Ja 4,15:5
Christian, Andrew W, 1950, Ja 20,26:2
Christian, Bro (Brodie), 1949, N 9,27:4
Christian, Charles J Sr, 1965, D 28,25:1
Christian, Claude (funeral), 1963, Je 2,27:1
Christian, Edgar, 1940, S 18,18:2
Christian, Emily P, 1940, Ag 27,21:2
Christian, Floyd G, 1954, My 17,24:4
Christian, Frank L, 1955, O 20,35:5
Christian, George B Jr, 1951, F 10,13:3
Christian, George L, 1920, Ap 26,13:4
Christian, George Martin Rev, 1913, O 7,13:6
Christian, Harrison, 1954, Ja 17,75:1
Christian, Henry A, 1951, Ag 26,76:5
Christian, James M, 1950, F 7,27:3
Christian, John L, 1968, O 7,47:1
Christian, Lewis E, 1949, O 14,27:3
Christian, Lewis E Mrs, 1957, Mr 10,88:5
Christian, Lewis H, 1949, Mr 13,76:5
Christian, M Osborne Dr, 1918, Je 17,13:8
Christian, Mary Mrs, 1949, S 13,30:3
Christian, Oscar W, 1953, Je 27,15:2
Christian, Palmer, 1947, F 21,20:2
Christian, Princess of Hesse (E Reid-Rogers), 1 F 3,46:1
Christian, Robert M, 1948, Ag 12,21:2
Christian, Robert O, 1944, Mr 11,13:6
Christian, Roy, 1942, Ja 18,42:2
Christian, Stephen B, 1946, S 1,35:1
Christian, T J Jackson, 1952, S 16,29:1
Christian, William J, 1952, S 21,88:2
Christian, William T, 1951, S 20,31:4
Christian IX, King of Denmark and Norway (fun 19,5:1), 1906, Ja 30,5:1
Christian of Mary, Bro (Malloy), 1961, D 7,43
Christian of Schleswig-Holstein, Prince, 1917, O 13:2
Christian Walter, Bro (Gardine), 1961, My 7,8
Christian X, King of Denmark, 1947, Ap 21,1:3
Christiana, Jacob, 1949, N 5,30:4
Christiana, Sister (F Friggs), 1949, Ap 28,31:4
Christiancy, George A C, 1943, O 2,13:4
Christiancy, Lillie, 1883, D 14,2:2
Christiani, Henning O, 1950, Je 2,25:7
Christiani, Rudolf, 1960, D 21,31:1
Christiano, Frank, 1963, Je 10,31:5
Christiano, James, 1958, F 26,27:4
Christians, George F, 1965, Ag 4,35:5
Christians, Marguerita M (Mady), 1951, O 2
Christians, Rudolf, 1921, F 10,7:2
Christians, William F, 1956, Mr 15,31:3
Christiansen, Arthur, 1963, S 28,19:2
Christiansen, Cai L, 1943, D 26,32:4
Christiansen, Donald L, 1948, F 2,19:1
Christiansen, F Melius, 1955, Je 2,29:2
Christiansen, Fred L, 1954, Ja 21,31:5
Christiansen, Hakon, 1960, S 22,27:5
Christiansen, John F, 1947, F 20,25:1

Christiansen, Karl, 1951, Mr 26,23:2
Christiansen, Leif J, 1962, Jl 1,56:3
Christiansen, Otto, 1951, Je 18,23:6
Christiansen, William F, 1951, Je 2,19:5
Christianson, Andrew, 1942, Mr 1,17:2
Christianson, Harry C, 1920, N 18,15:4
Christianson, J O, 1961, Ag 7,23:4
Christianson, John A, 1944, My 12,19:3
Christianson, Joseph P, 1958, D 5,32:1
Christianson, Oscar Mrs, 1947, F 13,23:4
Christianson, Theodore, 1948, D 11,15:5
Christianson, Thomas C, 1948, N 21,88:6
Christie, A L, 1880, Jl 9,1:3
Christie, Al, 1951, Ap 15,93:2
Christie, Alex G, 1964, O 26,31:3
Christie, Alexander Archbishop, 1925, Ap 7,19:5
Christie, Cal, 1947, Jl 8,23:5
Christie, Campbell M, 1963, Je 22,23:2
Christie, Chandler, 1943, My 19,25:4
Christie, Charles H, 1955, O 2,86:1
Christie, Charles R, 1937, Ja 14,21:3
Christie, Chester D, 1939, Ja 29,32:8
Christie, Cornelius, 1924, S 11,23:6
Christie, David, 1910, Ja 4,13:4
Christie, David R Sr, 1948, N 9,27:3
Christie, Edward M, 1962, S 14,31:1
Christie, Francis A, 1938, Ag 5,18:3
Christie, Frederick W, 1966, Ag 7,81:1
Christie, George, 1903, O 10,9:6; 1939, Je 15,23:3; 1949, My 21,13:6
Christie, George I, 1953, Ag 4,21:6
Christie, Haldane H, 1941, Mr 17,17:2
Christie, Harry C, 1939, Mr 7,21:4
Christie, Herbert B, 1958, O 29,35:2
Christie, Howard E, 1954, Ja 5,27:3
Christie, Isabella M Mrs, 1915, Ag 27,9:7
Christie, James Mrs, 1946, My 24,19:4
Christie, John, 1944, Ja 12,23:1; 1953, Ap 11,17:3; 1962, Jl 5,25:4
Christie, John A, 1957, O 15,33:3
Christie, John D, 1924, My 13,21:4
Christie, John E, 1940, N 19,5:5
Christie, John Mrs, 1953, Je 1,23:3
Christie, John R, 1947, Ja 5,53:2
Christie, Joseph F, 1941, Ap 15,23:2
Christie, Lansdell K, 1965, N 17,47:4
Christie, Leonard D Jr, 1961, S 15,33:1
Christie, Loring C, 1941, Ap 9,25:1
Christie, Loring C Mrs, 1939, N 22,21:1
Christie, Luther R, 1939, D 2,17:4
Christie, Margaret, 1967, Je 24,29:6
Christie, Margaret Mrs, 1943, Ag 6,15:5
Christie, Mary B Mrs, 1961, My 1,29:6
Christie, Michael L, 1958, Jl 27,61:2
Christie, Philip, 1947, S 7,60:7
Christie, R E Jr, 1934, Je 26,1:6
Christie, Ralph C, 1957, Ag 4,81:2
Christie, Raymond E, 1956, Je 28,29:4
Christie, Robert, 1923, S 15,15:6
Christie, Robert E, 1947, My 13,25:1
Christie, Robert H, 1962, F 13,35:4
Christie, Robert L, 1947, Mr 31,23:5
Christie, Robert S, 1963, N 5,28:3
Christie, Robert S Mrs, 1953, Je 30,23:5
Christie, Samuel M, 1952, Ja 27,77:1
Christie, Thea A S Mrs, 1940, Mr 19,25:4
Christie, Thomas Davidson Rev, 1921, My 27,17:4
Christie, Walter, 1941, Je 3,21:3; 1958, O 18,21:4
Christie, Walter Mrs, 1951, Ag 13,17:6
Christie, Walter R, 1947, S 15,17:3
Christie, William A, 1956, Jl 11,29:3
Christie, William G, 1951, F 8,33:2
Christiernin, Charles L, 1944, O 19,23:1
Christina, Louis E, 1939, O 5,29:3
Christina, Princess, 1879, Ap 30,1:1
Christina Marie, Mother (McDonald), 1964, Jl 9,33:2
Christine, Henri, 1941, N 28,23:2
Christison, R Sir, 1882, Ja 28,5:3
Christl, Harry O, 1942, Ag 30,42:6
Christl, Joseph, 1925, O 24,15:6
Christman, Albert F, 1959, Mr 11,35:5
Christman, Charles, 1938, F 28,15:4
Christman, Charles N, 1943, F 25,21:4
Christman, Frank H, 1954, Ap 5,25:3
Christman, George J, 1950, F 13,21:4
Christman, Henry, 1943, My 14,20:2; 1945, Je 14,19:5; 1952, N 4,29:4
Christman, Henry Mrs, 1953, Je 16,27:3
Christman, Henry Mrs (Zoe), 1968, S 24,44:2
Christman, Howard S, 1949, F 19,15:2
Christman, Jacob, 1952, N 13,31:4
Christman, Joseph A, 1944, D 14,23:4
Christman, Louise, 1947, Jl 31,21:5
Christman, Richard G, 1952, O 8,31:2
Christman, Warren U, 1944, My 28,34:2
Christman, William, 1946, Ag 4,46:1
Christman, William W, 1937, F 27,17:3
Christmann, Adam Sr Mrs, 1941, O 15,21:6
Christmann, Carl A, 1955, N 27,88:6
Christmas, Albert G, 1953, Jl 30,16:6
Christmas, Albert G Mrs, 1958, My 31,15:4
Christmas, Charles, 1868, S 8,8:4
Christmas, James M, 1939, N 30,21:6
Christmas, John K, 1962, Mr 12,31:2
Christmas, Lee, 1924, Ja 22,17:2
Christmas, William W, 1960, Ap 15,23:1
Christner, Ernest C, 1965, Ja 20,39:4
Christner, Ernest P, 1943, S 9,25:5
Christodoulou, Christ Mrs, 1963, Je 11,37:4
Christofalo, Charles J, 1953, F 1,89:1
Christoff, Frederick J, 1949, Ap 25,23:4
Christoff, Henry G, 1949, My 10,11:2
Christoff, Theodore, 1940, Je 21,21:7
Christoffers, Claus H, 1954, N 9,27:3
Christofferson, Edna E Mrs, 1945, Mr 10,17:2
Christofferson, Harold, 1950, My 9,30:5
Christol, Philip A, 1942, My 26,21:5
Christoph, Charles E, 1962, D 3,31:3
Christoph, Otto J, 1940, N 26,23:1
Christopher, Albert, 1960, N 25,27:2
Christopher, Arthur Jr, 1967, D 11,47:5
Christopher, Donald, 1960, My 26,33:5
Christopher, Franklin, 1964, Ag 29,21:4
Christopher, Frederick W, 1950, F 3,24:3
Christopher, George H (trb, Ja 27,33:1), 1959, Ja 24, 19:6
Christopher, George T, 1954, Je 8,27:3
Christopher, H Ward, 1962, Ag 7,18:4
Christopher, Harry J, 1944, Mr 21,20:3
Christopher, Harry W, 1962, Jl 31,27:4
Christopher, John, 1951, Je 30,15:5
Christopher, John J, 1945, Ja 21,39:2
Christopher, Joseph P, 1964, S 20,89:1
Christopher, Lawrence J, 1947, Jl 28,15:2
Christopher, Margaret, 1937, My 12,2:7
Christopher, Michael J, 1952, Jl 17,23:4
Christopher, Prince of Greece, 1940, Ja 22,15:3
Christopher, Russ, 1954, D 7,33:1
Christopher, Walter S Dr, 1905, Mr 4,9:4
Christopher, William R, 1954, O 19,27:3
Christopher Jos, Bro, 1940, Mr 23,13:4
Christopher Xavier, Bro (J J Nicholson), 1957, N 21, 30:1
Christopherides, Dimitrios, 1949, Mr 24,27:2
Christophersen, Carl, 1947, O 21,24:3
Christophersen, Edward C, 1964, Ag 26,39:6
Christophersen, Herbert, 1945, Ja 4,19:3
Christopherson, C A Sr, 1951, N 3,17:5
Christopherson, Olen W, 1964, My 20,43:2
Christopherson, Stanley, 1949, Ap 7,29:4
Christophides, Miltiades, 1959, F 14,22:1
Christophoros II, Patriarch, 1967, Jl 25,32:3
Christy, Albert W, 1938, Jl 19,22:1
Christy, Arthur E, 1946, Jl 9,21:3
Christy, Bayard H, 1943, Je 22,19:4
Christy, Earl, 1961, S 6,31:5
Christy, Frank T, 1942, O 2,25:2
Christy, George, 1868, My 15,2:4
Christy, Gordon V Mrs, 1959, My 20,35:4
Christy, Harley H, 1950, Je 8,31:3
Christy, Harry, 1948, S 8,29:1
Christy, Howard C (will, Ap 25,25:3), 1952, Mr 4, 27:1
Christy, Howard Chandler, 1919, Ag 15,11:5
Christy, Ivan, 1949, My 10,26:4
Christy, John L, 1955, D 20,31:3
Christy, Louis, 1949, Ap 28,31:1
Christy, Robert C, 1919, S 30,19:3
Christy, Robert J, 1952, Je 8,85:1
Christy, Russ J, 1947, F 4,26:3
Christy, William C, 1957, F 2,19:4
Christy, William G, 1965, D 30,23:3
Chrone, Alex, 1962, My 20,86:7
Chronim James, Bro (T F Flynn), 1954, S 1,27:5
Chrust, Jay F, 1958, Jl 22,27:4
Chrysler, Jack F, 1958, N 8,21:3
Chrysler, Mintin A, 1963, Ag 20,33:1
Chrysler, Phil H, 1948, Ag 15,60:2
Chrysler, Walter P, 1940, Ag 19,1:2
Chrysler, Walter P Mrs (por), 1938, Ag 9,19:1
Chrysostom, Austin Bro (J J Leahy), 1964, Ag 23, 87:2
Chrysostom, John, 1907, Ap 11,11:5
Chrysostom, John Bro, 1917, Ja 24,9:3
Chrysostom Cavouridis, Archbishop, 1955, O 14,27:2
Chrysostomos, Archbishop (por), 1938, O 23,40:7
Chryssanthos, Archbishop, 1949, S 30,24:3
Chryssikos, George Mrs, 1949, N 1,27:2
Chryst, Robert D, 1956, O 11,39:4
Chryst, William, 1958, Je 6,24:1
Chrystal, Charles B, 1964, Ag 16,92:5
Chrystal, David Mrs, 1949, My 27,21:2
Chrystal, Eugene, 1946, Mr 17,45:2
Chrystal, Joseph O, 1949, S 2,17:4
Chrystie, Edward P, 1960, O 25,35:3
Chrystie, Einar, 1949, O 6,31:5
Chrystie, Frank Few, 1925, F 15,7:3
Chrystie, T Ludlow, 1954, Ag 16,17:1
Chrystie, Thomas Mackaness Ludlow Dr, 1914, My 20,13:7
Chrystie, Thomas W, 1956, F 22,27:1
Chrystie, Thomas W Mrs, 1963, O 28,27:5
Chrystie, Walter, 1944, D 10,53:2
Chrystie, Walter Jr, 1948, D 8,31:1
Chrystie, Williams F, 1947, S 8,21:6
Chu, Farn B, 1941, Ap 20,43:3
Chu, King, 1951, Mr 11,92:5
Chu Chao-hsin, 1932, D 12,5:1
Chu Chaw Shong, 1956, Je 10,89:2
Chu Cheng, 1951, N 25,86:4
Chu Chia-hua, 1963, Ja 5,8:4
Chu Foke, 1957, Ap 25,31:3
Chu Pei-teh Gen, 1937, F 18,15:6
Chu Shao-liang, 1963, D 29,43:1
Chu Shen, 1943, Jl 5,15:5
Chu Shih-ming, 1965, O 28,43:5
Chuan, S James, 1962, Ap 15,80:5
Chubb, Charles St John, 1913, Ap 28,11:4
Chubb, Edwin W, 1959, Jl 26,68:3
Chubb, George H, 1954, Jl 31,13:6
Chubb, Henden Mrs, 1955, Ap 21,29:5
Chubb, Hendon, 1960, S 5,15:4; 1965, Je 2,22:2
Chubb, Lewis W, 1952, Ap 3,35:1
Chubb, Lyle R, 1950, F 7,27:5
Chubb, P, 1930, Je 16,21:5
Chubb, Percival, 1960, F 17,35:4
Chubb, Percival Mrs, 1924, Ap 10,23:4
Chubb, R Walston Mrs, 1953, Mr 27,23:4
Chubb, S Harmsted, 1949, My 8,76:3
Chuckrow, David J, 1963, D 16,33:5
Chudleigh, Baron of (Lewis Hy Hugh Clifford), 1916, Jl 20,11:6
Chudnoff, Harry, 1955, O 28,26:2
Chudoba, Frank A, 1944, S 19,21:1
Chudson, Walter A Mrs, 1966, N 4,39:1
Chugerman, Samuel, 1956, N 16,27:3
Chukhnov, Ivan F, 1965, Ap 2,35:3
Chukovsky, Nikolai K, 1965, N 7,88:6
Chula Chakrabongse, Prince, 1963, D 31,19:1
Chumar, Clarence A, 1940, S 7,15:5
Chumar, George P Mrs, 1940, Ag 23,15:5
Chumley, Lee Mrs, 1960, O 6,41:5
Chun Jien-pao Mrs, 1951, O 2,28:3
Chun Lock, 1868, S 20,3:7
Chundrigar, Ismail I, 1960, S 27,37:1
Chung Chang, Hawthorne, 1945, F 24,11:2
Chung Chun-so, 1952, N 14,23:2
Chung-wan, Bing, 1938, Ja 21,19:3
Chung Wing-kwong, 1942, Ja 27,10:8
Churbuck, Leander M, 1940, Ag 15,19:6
Church, A B Rev Dr, 1912, N 18,11:5
Church, A E Prof, 1878, Ap 2,5:1
Church, A L, 1931, Je 27,17:3
Church, A S Dr, 1884, O 26,2:5
Church, Aaron, 1957, My 4,21:2
Church, Albert C, 1965, F 9,37:4
Church, Alfred C Rev, 1937, Ja 8,19:3
Church, Alfred W, 1953, Ag 23,89:2
Church, Allan H Mrs, 1954, O 5,27:1
Church, Alonzo, 1937, F 22,17:3
Church, Alonzo W, 1909, Ag 13,7:6
Church, Archibald, 1952, My 9,23:3
Church, Arthur E, 1955, Jl 7,27:4
Church, Austin, 1960, Mr 31,33:3
Church, Benjamin L, 1952, Je 3,29:2
Church, Benjamin Silliman, 1910, D 10,11:3
Church, Billy, 1942, D 27,34:3
Church, C Edward, 1959, Ap 8,37:1
Church, Charles A, 1945, Mr 19,19:3
Church, Charles A Dr, 1915, N 14,19:6
Church, Charles H, 1946, Je 4,23:2; 1963, S 5,31:4
Church, Charles Mrs, 1956, S 17,27:4
Church, Charles T, 1953, F 17,27:5
Church, Clyde M, 1949, Ap 3,76:2
Church, Denver, 1952, F 23,11:2
Church, E J, 1880, S 30,5:3
Church, Edgar M, 1938, D 28,26:3
Church, Edmund T, 1945, My 19,19:5
Church, Elihu C, 1963, Ag 18,81:1
Church, Elihu D, 1953, Jl 19,57:2
Church, Elmer L, 1951, Jl 9,25:3
Church, Everett L, 1947, N 11,27:3
Church, Francis Pharcellus, 1906, Ap 12,9:5
Church, Frank C, 1952, Ja 30,25:3
Church, Frank E Mrs, 1950, F 26,64:3
Church, Frederic C, 1937, O 18,17:6
Church, Frederick S, 1924, F 20,19:5
Church, G P, 1884, S 2,4:6
Church, Gaylord 3d, 1965, Ja 15,43:1
Church, George Col, 1903, Je 28,7:6
Church, George Earl Col, 1910, Ja 6,9:4
Church, George H Mrs (will, D 14,30:5), 1943, N 10, 23:5
Church, George M, 1946, Ja 18,20:2
Church, George W, 1947, Ja 29,25:3
Church, Gilbert L, 1949, F 28,19:4
Church, Harold B, 1948, N 6,13:3
Church, Henry A, 1941, Ja 20,17:2
Church, Henry C Sr, 1951, Ag 2,21:2
Church, Herman H, 1948, My 22,15:4
Church, Heyliger, 1948, N 16,29:5
Church, Howard W, 1946, O 1,23:1
Church, James B Capt, 1907, F 16,9:6
Church, James C, 1910, My 30,11:7
Church, Jerry Mrs, 1957, F 28,27:5
Church, John A, 1952, N 12,27:5
Church, John Admas, 1917, F 13,11:5
Church, John H, 1953, N 5,31:3
Church, John H C, 1946, S 4,24:2

Church, Joseph F, 1961, My 11,37:5
Church, Joseph K, 1943, Mr 26,19:1
Church, Lewis H, 1955, Ja 6,27:4
Church, Lewis H Mrs, 1956, My 10,31:4
Church, Lincoln S, 1948, D 17,27:4
Church, Lloyd, 1948, Ag 3,25:1
Church, Merton, 1944, S 26,23:3
Church, Milford E, 1950, Ja 11,23:4
Church, Norman W, 1953, Ja 8,27:3
Church, Norval L Mrs, 1942, Ja 1,25:5
Church, Orson S, 1944, F 25,17:5
Church, P Schuyler, 1956, Ja 24,31:3
Church, Ralph E, 1950, Mr 22,27:1
Church, Ranson Mrs, 1949, D 16,31:5
Church, Reginald H, 1942, N 8,53:1
Church, Reuben, 1951, My 27,68:4
Church, Richard Maj, 1911, My 9,11:5
Church, Richard N L, 1943, F 20,13:3
Church, Robert R, 1952, Ap 19,15:2
Church, S E, 1880, My 15,1:7
Church, Samuel H, 1943, O 12,27:1
Church, Samuel S Mrs, 1949, Jl 30,15:5
Church, Walter N, 1940, Je 20,23:6
Church, Walter R, 1946, D 6,24:2
Church, Willard, 1944, My 24,19:5
Church, William B, 1964, Ap 2,33:3
Church, William B Mrs, 1948, N 26,23:2
Church, William Cosant (funl, My 27,19:3), 1917, My 24,13:5
Church, William E, 1945, O 21,45:1
Church, William E Mrs, 1963, Je 12,43:4
Church, William L Mrs, 1908, F 2,9:4
Church, William W, 1941, Ja 20,12:1
Churchill, Alex L, 1948, O 29,25:2
Churchill, Alfred V, 1949, D 31,15:3
Churchill, Allen L, 1940, N 17,49:2
Churchill, Arthur B, 1966, My 5,47:1
Churchill, Arthur H, 1955, Jl 25,19:2
Churchill, B, 1940, O 11,21:3
Churchill, Billy, 1949, Je 9,31:4
Churchill, C W, 1951, F 12,23:1
Churchill, Charles C Maj, 1908, Mr 7,7:5
Churchill, Charles H, 1956, D 9,89:2
Churchill, Chester L, 1958, S 20,19:6
Churchill, Diana (will), 1964, Mr 3,26:6
Churchill, Douglas W, 1942, F 8,49:2
Churchill, Durand Jr, 1963, Ag 4,80:8
Churchill, Dwight W, 1961, Ag 16,31:1
Churchill, E George Spencer-, 1964, Je 25,7:7
Churchill, Everett A, 1959, D 31,21:4
Churchill, Francis M, 1944, Ag 3,19:6
Churchill, Frank N, 1954, My 30,44:7
Churchill, Frank S, 1946, Mr 1,21:1
Churchill, Frederick A, 1949, Mr 16,27:5
Churchill, George B, 1925, Jl 2,19:5; 1925, Jl 3,13:5
Churchill, George B Mrs, 1946, Ap 22,21:6
Churchill, H B, 1937, F 11,23:3
Churchill, H Lloyd, 1960, Jl 19,29:5
Churchill, Harold B, 1962, S 12,39:2
Churchill, Harold S, 1950, Ap 11,31:3
Churchill, Harry R, 1940, Mr 29,21:5
Churchill, Heber B, 1958, Mr 23,88:8
Churchill, Henry W, 1961, F 19,87:1
Churchill, Howard L, 1943, O 19,19:3
Churchill, Hugh C, 1939, Ag 21,13:2
Churchill, Ida L Mrs (will, S 7,21:7), 1938, Ag 18, 19:3
Churchill, Ivor, 1956, S 18,35:2
Churchill, J, 1930, Ja 20,14:5
Churchill, John A E W Spencer Mrs (Duchess of Marlborough), 1961, My 24,41:3
Churchill, John C, 1905, Je 5,9:7
Churchill, John D, 1954, Ag 15,84:4
Churchill, John D I Spencer- Earl of Sunderland, 1955, My 16,9:3
Churchill, John S, 1947, F 24,20:3
Churchill, John S Mrs, 1957, Je 27,25:4
Churchill, Lemuel B, 1938, Mr 26,15:5
Churchill, Marigold, 1921, Ag 24,11:5
Churchill, Marlborough, 1947, Jl 10,22:2
Churchill, Marlborough Mrs, 1947, S 3,25:4
Churchill, Percy, 1962, Ag 5,81:1
Churchill, Preston B, 1956, S 23,84:7
Churchill, R J Mrs, 1902, S 9,9:2
Churchill, Randolph H S Lord, 1895, Ja 25,16:1
Churchill, Randolph Lady (por), 1921, Je 30,17:3
Churchill, Randolph Spencer, 1968, Je 7,36:1
Churchill, Richard, 1911, S 21,13:6
Churchill, S Welles, 1940, Ja 17,21:3
Churchill, Spencer Mrs, 1949, S 28,27:2
Churchill, T W, 1934, My 8,23:2
Churchill, Thomas W Lt, 1918, Jl 10,13:8
Churchill, Viscount, 1934, Ja 4,19:1
Churchill, Wainwright Jr, 1957, D 10,35:4
Churchill, Walter T, 1948, N 27,17:4
Churchill, Warner L Mrs, 1956, D 20,29:4
Churchill, William, 1920, Je 10,11:5; 1949, Ag 29,17:3
Churchill, William H, 1954, Jl 28,23:1
Churchill, William L, 1937, Mr 10,23:2
Churchill, Winston, 1947, Mr 13,27:1
Churchill, Winston L S Sir (funl, Ja 31,1:2; will, F 13,2:2), 1965, Ja 24,1:6
Churchill, Winston Mrs, 1945, My 28,19:5
Churchill-Smith, Harrison, 1956, Mr 11,89:1
Churchman, Day, 1961, Ja 29,47:3
Churchman, George, 1941, S 4,21:3
Churchman, John W Dr, 1937, Jl 14,21:3
Churchman, Phil H, 1954, Ap 15,29:4
Churchman, W Morgan, 1938, My 30,11:4
Churchman, William B Jr, 1952, Je 13,23:2
Churchman, William E, 1944, Jl 7,15:5
Churchwell, William, 1955, Ap 19,31:3
Churgin, Leopold, 1965, Ap 1,35:4
Churgin, Pinkhos M, 1957, N 29,29:3
Churgin, Pinkhos Mrs, 1954, O 26,27:1
Chusmir, Morris, 1950, S 20,31:4
Chussler, Joseph W, 1948, Je 27,52:3
Chute, Charles L, 1953, S 27,85:3
Chute, Edward E, 1954, Ja 3,38:2
Chute, Edward L, 1939, Jl 14,19:3
Chute, H O, 1944, S 21,19:6
Chute, Mortimer H, 1937, D 29,22:3
Chute, Stathern B, 1950, F 19,78:1
Chuter-Ede, James, 1965, N 12,47:1
Chutkowski, Angeline A Countess, 1915, My 26,13:5
Chutkowski, Thaddeus K de, 1914, N 14,11:6
Chutter, Reginald F, 1963, Jl 28,65:1
Chwington, John L, 1922, Ag 31,15:4
Chworowsky, Karl M, 1964, Ap 9,31:2
Chworowsky, Karl M Mrs, 1948, Ap 13,27:4
Chynoweth, Phillips, 1948, D 8,31:1
Chynoweth, Richard M, 1954, Je 2,31:2
Chyriacos, Jonel, 1968, Ap 10,43:3
Ciabatoni, Nick, 1947, Je 22,5:8
Ciaburri, Alfred, 1964, Ag 27,33:5
Ciancia, Mario, 1940, Ja 19,19:5
Cianciabelli, Joseph A, 1962, F 13,35:5
Cianciarulo, Joseph A, 1951, Ag 27,19:4
Cianciulli, Anthony, 1951, Ap 22,88:4
Cianculli, Joseph, 1956, Ag 24,19:5
Cianetti, Ettore, 1949, Mr 27,76:7
Cianfarani, Aristide B, 1960, F 12,27:2
Cianfarra, Camille Mrs, 1944, N 10,19:6
Cianfarra, Camillie M, 1956, Jl 7,1:4
Cianfarra, Joan, 1956, Jl 27,1:4
Ciangiarulo, John A, 1965, D 19,84:2
Ciano, Carolina Countess, 1959, My 14,33:2
Ciano, Costanzo Count, 1939, Je 27,23:4
Ciarlantini, Franco, 1940, F 6,21:4
Ciarlo, Nicholas M, 1949, Ap 13,29:6
Ciavarelli, George, 1949, My 10,25:3
Ciavarelli, Sal J, 1960, Ag 14,55:4
Cibell, George H, 1952, Ap 14,19:3
Cibelli, Alfred J, 1955, Ap 24,86:4
Cibelli, Eugene E, 1961, Ja 3,29:4
Cibelli, Salvatore, 1957, F 20,33:5
Cibulskis, Michael J, 1948, D 18,19:6
Cicala, Nicholas J, 1952, N 18,32:3
Cicarell, Joseph Mrs, 1944, N 11,13:4
Cicasoli-Indolfi, Viuliana, 1959, D 29,25:4
Ciccarelli, Eugene C, 1943, S 25,15:3
Ciccarini, Giovanni Mrs, 1903, S 3,7:6
Ciccolini, Guido, 1963, My 12,86:2
Ciccolini, Guido Mrs, 1953, O 29,31:4
Ciccotti, Eddore (cor, Je 6,22:6), 1939, My 23,23:1
Ciccotti, Francisco, 1937, S 15,23:6
Cicero, John, 1955, Ag 27,15:5
Cicero, Lawrence J, 1954, F 14,93:2
Cichowlas, Basil, 1956, Ap 1,89:2
Cicila, George, 1950, Mr 7,28:2
Cicognani, Gaetano Cardinal, 1962, F 6,35:3
Ciechanow, Julius, 1950, N 29,33:3
Ciechanowicz, Fichel W, 1955, F 17,27:2
Cieciuch, Thomas J, 1951, Ag 2,21:5
Cieciuch, Walter P, 1959, O 20,39:3
Cieplak, John Archbishop, 1926, F 18,23:1
Cierva, Juan de la, 1938, Ja 13,22:1
Ciesielski, George L, 1944, Mr 23,19:5
Ciesla, Theodore R, 1958, S 13,19:2
Cieslicki, Marion E, 1965, Jl 20,20:8
Cifre, Anton, 1944, Mr 21,19:5
Cigelman, Abraham, 1967, Mr 19,92:2
Cigliano, Vincent, 1957, F 9,19:5
Cigliano, William U, 1955, Ag 27,15:7
Cilano, Cosmo A, 1937, S 30,23:4
Cilcennin, Viscount (J P L Thomas), 1960, Jl 14,27:2
Cilea, Francesco, 1950, N 21,31:2
Cilella, Alfred J, 1964, Ag 6,29:1
Cilento, Carlo Mrs, 1947, D 25,21:4
Cilento, Sol, 1959, Mr 12,62:1
Cilette, Alfonso A, 1946, Ap 7,46:1
Cilley, Gordon H, 1938, Ja 18,23:6
Cilley, John Kelley Maj, 1916, D 7,13:4
Cilley, Jonathan P Brig-Gen, 1920, Ap 8,11:4
Cilley, Osborn H, 1958, Ap 17,31:3
Cills, William R, 1956, Ag 5,77:2
Ciminera, Joseph A, 1942, Ja 29,19:5
Cimini, Pietro Mrs, 1956, D 26,27:1
Cimmet, Harry, 1952, S 16,29:1
Cimperman, John A, 1968, F 18,80:4
Cincar-Markovitch, Alex, 1948, Jl 12,19:3
Cinelli, Delfino, 1942, My 5,21:2
Ciner, Emanuel, 1958, F 9,88:2
Cingue, Francisco (cor, Ja 15,16:4), 1954, Ja 14,24:8
Cinnamon, Frank, 1959, O 12,19:6
Cinquegrana, Vincent E, 1956, N 27,37:3
Cinquevalli, Paul, 1918, Ag 5,9:8
Cintas, Oscar B (will, My 29,29:7), 1957, My 12,87:2
Cintas, Oscar B Mrs, 1941, D 28,28:4
Cioffi, Lawrence, 1946, Je 24,31:4
Cioffi, Vincent, 1951, Ag 15,27:2
Ciolli, Augusta (Mrs J de Laurentis), 1967, F 3,31:2
Ciora, Martin, 1939, Mr 7,21:5
Cipiani, Amilcare, 1918, My 28,13:8
Cipolla, Anthony, 1956, Ag 11,13:6
Cipolletti, Emilio D, 1948, D 14,29:6
Cipoth, Jacques S A, 1951, D 25,31:6
Cipperly, Clark, 1956, Je 24,76:4
Cipperly, John C, 1963, S 28,19:5
Cipperly, John H, 1940, Jl 20,15:7
Cipperly, Margaret V H Mrs, 1941, O 18,19:4
Cippico, Giuseppe Count, 1941, Mr 28,23:5
Cipriani, A J, 1956, F 24,25:2
Cipriani, Arthur A, 1945, Ap 19,27:3
Cipriani, Frank J, 1955, My 30,13:5
Cipriani, Leon Nette, 1905, S 26,9:6
Cipriano, Maria Mrs, 1943, Ap 21,20:6
Ciraolo, Frank, 1957, My 14,35:2
Ciraolo, Giovanni, 1954, O 8,23:3
Cirelli, Anthony, 1940, S 25,27:4
Ciriaci, Pietro Cardinal, 1966, D 31,19:3
Ciriani, Anthony Mrs, 1950, S 29,27:2
Ciric, Irinej, 1955, Ap 7,27:1
Cirigliano, Caesar A, 1958, Ag 8,19:1
Cirigliano, Dominic Rev, 1947, Ap 6,61:1
Cirino, Anthony, 1959, Je 26,25:5
Cirker, Mitchell, 1953, F 6,19:4
Cirtautas, Kazyz C, 1963, Ag 29,29:4
Cisar, Alex, 1954, Ja 10,10:5
Cisco, J J, 1884, Mr 24,1:5
Cisco, John J Mrs, 1942, Mr 14,15:5
Cisero, Michael Sr, 1958, O 2,37:4
Cisin, Morris Dr, 1924, Ap 10,23:4
Cisin, Stephen, 1948, Ja 27,25:2
Cisneros, E de, 1934, F 4,31:3
Cisney, Thomas E, 1957, Je 14,25:2
Cisney, Thomas E Mrs, 1960, Ja 9,21:2
Cissel, Helenry M, 1955, Je 5,84:8
Cissel, John A Sr, 1958, My 22,29:5
Cissel, Ross, 1954, My 1,15:5
Cissell, Benjamin M, 1949, Je 1,32:2
Cissell, Chalmers (Bill), 1949, Mr 16,27:4
Cist, Frank, 1967, O 11,47:4
Cist, H M Gen, 1902, D 18,2:3
Cist, Robert W, 1938, F 16,21:4
Citarella, Anthony J, 1966, F 3,31:3
Citlo, Joseph, 1925, Ag 17,15:5
Citro, Anthony V, 1957, Je 16,85:1
Citroen, A G, 1935, Jl 4,15:1
Citron, Bernard, 1962, N 13,38:1
Citron, Edwin, 1961, O 12,29:2
Citron, Israel, 1958, S 21,87:1
Citron, Joseph L, 1948, S 11,15:1
Citron, Louis, 1955, F 7,21:2
Cittadini, Count Pier Adolfo, 1946, O 24,27:5
Cittarelli, Pasquale, 1947, N 24,23:2
Ciuba, Jacob, 1952, F 26,27:1
Ciuci, Joseph, 1958, Jl 18,21:5
Ciudad Rodrigo, Bishop of, 1941, D 28,28:1
Ciufia, Cono, 1944, F 13,41:3
Civello, Charles, 1948, S 2,24:2
Civini, Signor, 1872, Ja 23,1:6
Civkin, Victor, 1968, Ap 15,43:2
Cizek, Frank, 1947, Jl 2,23:1
Claar, Charles F, 1953, O 26,21:5
Claar, Elmer A, 1962, Ap 6,35:4
Claassen, Peter W Prof, 1937, Ag 17,19:3
Clabaugh, Hinton G, 1946, Je 2,44:7
Clabault, Alexander, 1947, Ja 18,15:5
Clabby, John H, 1947, Ja 10,22:3
Clacken, Margaret M, 1951, D 16,91:1
Clackett, Charles W, 1952, O 22,27:2
Clad, Clinton, 1962, My 5,56:1
Clad, Harry J, 1944, Ag 5,11:5
Clad, Noel, 1962, My 5,56:1
Cladek, Walter E Mrs, 1954, F 14,92:2
Claessens, August (funl, D 13,27:5), 1954, D 1(
Claeys, C Donald, 1945, D 30,14:4
Claeys, Charles M, 1939, Jl 11,19:4
Claeys, Harry C, 1954, Ap 8,27:2
Claeys, Leon, 1947, Mr 20,27:3
Clafen, Royal V, 1950, Je 1,27:2
Claffey, Michael E, 1942, D 24,15:3
Claffey, Michael E Mrs, 1951, Ap 20,29:2
Claffy, George, 1940, Jl 11,19:2
Clafin, Nellie G Mrs (will), 1940, F 25,19:6
Claflin, Albert W, 1956, Je 21,31:2
Claflin, Arthur B, 1939, F 2,19:4
Claflin, Edith F, 1953, Mr 8,90:5
Claflin, Fred H, 1946, Ag 11,45:1
Claflin, George E, 1919, Ap 19,17:4
Claflin, Horace B, 1885, N 15,1:7
Claflin, James R, 1949, D 21,29:2
Claflin, John (por), 1938, Je 12,39:1
Claflin, John Mrs, 1949, F 17,23:1
Claflin, Leon R, 1948, Ag 27,18:3
Claflin, Raymond E, 1958, Ja 17,30:1
Claflin, Ward W, 1938, F 9,19:5
Clagett, Arthur N, 1953, S 22,31:5

Clagett, Brice, 1951, O 29,23:5
Clagett, Brice Mrs, 1953, S 19,15:3
Clagett, Henry B, 1952, N 15,17:2
Clagett, Henry N, 1942, D 4,25:2
Claggett, Katherine Mrs, 1940, F 25,39:2
Claggett, Strabo V, 1966, Jl 13,43:3
Claghorn, Charles, 1923, Jl 17,19:6
Claghorn, J L, 1884, Ag 27,5:2
Claghorn, Kate H, 1938, Mr 24,23:4
Claghorn, Martha Holladay Mrs, 1905, Mr 17,9:4
Claghorn, William C, 1942, Ag 19,19:4
Clague, Frank, 1952, Mr 26,29:2
Clague, Phil Mrs, 1950, Ja 31,23:2
Clague, S, 1927, Ja 21,15:3
Clague, Stanley Mrs, 1955, N 4,30:2
Clahane, Francis J, 1961, S 20,29:4
Claherty, Coleman, 1956, Ja 5,34:1
Claiborne, J Herbert Dr, 1922, My 28,22:3
Claiborne, J Herbert Mrs, 1965, Jl 10,25:2
Claiborne, J Tyler Sr, 1948, My 20,29:4
Claimant, Tichborne (Arthur Orton), 1898, Ap 2,9:1
Clair, Edward L, 1951, Je 14,27:2
Clair, Francis W, 1953, Ap 28,27:5
Clair, John D Sr, 1955, Ap 25,23:4
Clair, John J, 1958, Ja 24,23:1
Clair, John M, 1946, F 20,25:2
Clair, Joseph A, 1956, Jl 7,13:4
Clair, Matthew W, 1943, Je 29,19:1
Clair, Pierson E, 1948, Ja 7,25:5
Clair, Samuel H, 1940, N 19,23:3
Clair, Verne, 1952, Ap 11,23:3
Clair, Verne Mrs, 1954, N 17,31:4
Clair, William U, 1960, Mr 31,33:4
Clairborne, Elmer M, 1961, O 29,88:8
Claire, Cora B L Mrs, 1942, N 18,31:3
Claire, Sister, 1940, D 5,25:6
Claire, Ted, 1960, D 10,23:4
Clairmont, Wilfred, 1949, Ap 26,25:2
Clairon, Laura, 1945, F 7,22:2
Clairville, L N, 1879, F 10,2:2
Clairville, M, 1879, Mr 10,2:5
Clairville, William H, 1910, Ja 21,11:7
Clakre, Patrick J, 1948, Ap 25,69:1
Clamage, Edward, 1959, D 8,45:2
Claman, Henry, 1924, Jl 16,11:5
Clamens, Pierre A, 1960, Mr 22,38:1
Clamer, Guiliam H, 1963, Ap 14,92:6
Clancey, Bert, 1951, O 18,29:5
Clancey, John, 1864, Jl 2,8:3
Clancey, John A, 1942, Je 5,17:5
Clancy, Arthur, 1952, O 8,31:3
Clancy, Charles B, 1965, My 6,39:4
Clancy, Charles M, 1952, Je 20,23:6
Clancy, Charles Mrs, 1951, Ja 27,13:3
Clancy, Daniel D, 1938, F 2,19:2
Clancy, Edward A (por), 1949, Ap 20,27:5
Clancy, Elizabeth R Mrs, 1941, D 16,27:4
Clancy, Eugene A, 1952, Mr 30,92:6
Clancy, Eugene A Sr, 1944, S 26,13:8
Clancy, Frank A, 1945, F 22,27:4
Clancy, Frank B, 1945, Je 22,15:1
Clancy, Frank J, 1958, D 29,15:3
Clancy, Frederick M, 1957, Ap 30,29:4
Clancy, George C, 1961, Mr 8,33:4
Clancy, George M, 1960, Ag 3,29:4
Clancy, George M Mrs, 1937, Ap 29,21:5
Clancy, J E, 1927, F 6,26:5
Clancy, James, 1908, D 20,11:5
Clancy, James F, 1962, O 12,31:1
Clancy, James L, 1956, N 2,27:2
Clancy, John E, 1960, My 31,31:4
Clancy, John F, 1925, Ag 31,15:6; 1951, Mr 6,27:4
Clancy, John G, 1948, F 14,13:2
Clancy, John J, 1921, N 30,17:4; 1959, D 7,31:4
Clancy, John M, 1903, Jl 27,7:7
Clancy, John R Mrs, 1944, My 22,19:6
Clancy, Joseph I, 1963, Je 14,29:1
Clancy, Lillian, 1953, Ap 11,17:3
Clancy, Mary, 1958, Mr 19,31:4
Clancy, Patrick J Mrs, 1949, Mr 15,27:3
Clancy, Patrick J Rev, 1905, Mr 23,9:6
Clancy, Paul G, 1956, D 30,33:1
Clancy, Robert J, 1939, F 22,21:6
Clancy, Rose S Mrs, 1946, D 11,31:4
Clancy, Stephen S, 1968, N 30,80:1
Clancy, Terrence A, 1946, Je 4,23:5
Clancy, Thomas F, 1937, F 15,17:2; 1938, S 29,25:1
Clancy, Thomas P V, 1938, Ap 1,23:4
Clancy, William B, 1966, Je 21,43:5
Clancy, William E, 1948, F 11,27:2
Clancy, William L, 1948, Ap 6,24:2
Clancy, William S, 1945, N 3,15:4
Clancy, William T Sr, 1944, Mr 28,19:5
Clanmorris, Baron (Jno Geo Barry Bingham), 1916, N 5,23:4
Clannfhearghuis, Seumas, 1961, Mr 27,31:2
Clanricarde, Lord (Hubert Geo de Burgh Canning), 1916, Ap 14,9:4
Clanricarde, Marchioness of, 1876, F 3,5:2
Clanricarde, Marquis of, 1874, Ap 11,1:7
Clans, J Rev, 1882, Ap 8,5:4
Clanwilliam, Earl of (A V Meade), 1953, Ja 24,15:5
Clanwilliam, Lord, 1907, Ag 5,7:6
Clap, Henry, 1875, Ap 11,7:3
Clapham, Alfred, 1950, O 28,17:5
Clapham, C Griffith, 1942, Ag 31,17:5
Clapham, James, 1940, Ag 17,15:6
Clapham, John, 1946, Mr 30,15:3
Clapham, John F, 1941, Ag 30,13:6
Clapp, A W, 1941, Mr 5,21:6
Clapp, Alfred Sr Mrs, 1950, Ag 30,32:3
Clapp, Arch M, 1951, S 13,31:2
Clapp, Arthur P, 1925, Ag 10,13:7
Clapp, Arthur W, 1942, F 13,21:4
Clapp, C Rev, 1878, F 2,8:5
Clapp, Carlos D, 1950, D 23,15:2
Clapp, Carrie P F (will), 1939, D 15,30:2
Clapp, Cecil F, 1942, F 13,21:3
Clapp, Charles E Jr, 1957, Ja 4,23:4
Clapp, Charles W, 1940, O 6,49:2
Clapp, Clift R, 1945, Mr 20,19:4
Clapp, E Donaldson, 1957, O 24,33:2
Clapp, E L, 1878, Jl 6,8:2
Clapp, Eben P, 1947, My 9,21:4
Clapp, Ebenezer, 1860, Mr 13,3:2; 1881, Je 14,5:4
Clapp, Ella, 1922, Ag 8,11:5
Clapp, Elsie, 1965, Jl 31,21:1
Clapp, Ernest, 1951, Ja 30,25:2
Clapp, Frank L Prof, 1937, Mr 24,25:4
Clapp, Frazier J, 1945, Ag 3,17:3
Clapp, Frederick M Mrs, 1960, F 4,31:2
Clapp, George F, 1945, O 23,17:5
Clapp, George H, 1948, Je 23,27:4; 1949, Ap 1,25:5
Clapp, George Sheppard, 1914, Mr 23,11:2
Clapp, George W, 1958, Ag 11,21:2
Clapp, George W Mrs, 1949, Ja 25,23:4
Clapp, Gordon R, 1963, Ap 29,31:1
Clapp, H D, 1880, Ja 6,5:2
Clapp, Harold H, 1939, Je 14,23:6
Clapp, Harold L, 1961, S 4,15:5
Clapp, Harold T, 1945, My 29,15:3
Clapp, Henry Austin, 1904, F 20,9:2
Clapp, Henry B Mrs, 1949, N 14,27:3
Clapp, Henry L, 1907, My 11,7:2
Clapp, Howard F, 1945, S 1,11:4
Clapp, Howard F Mrs, 1937, Ap 8,23:2
Clapp, Howard H, 1939, F 26,38:7
Clapp, Ira Munsen, 1906, My 21,9:2
Clapp, J Cornell, 1953, F 24,25:5
Clapp, Janet M Mrs (J Mabie), 1961, D 8,37:2
Clapp, John M, 1953, D 30,23:2
Clapp, Joseph E, 1953, Ja 17,15:1
Clapp, Kenneth H, 1951, F 24,13:3
Clapp, Lewis S, 1941, Mr 30,49:2
Clapp, Lloyd A, 1956, N 12,29:2
Clapp, M E, 1929, Mr 7,25:2
Clapp, Martin F, 1903, D 25,7:6
Clapp, Martin H, 1960, N 7,35:5
Clapp, Nicholas D Mrs, 1912, My 21,13:5
Clapp, Paul S, 1953, D 9,11:1
Clapp, Percy E, 1958, Ag 27,29:2
Clapp, Percy O, 1960, Jl 4,15:6
Clapp, Phil G, 1954, Ap 10,15:2
Clapp, Richard H, 1967, Ja 25,43:3
Clapp, Robert G, 1951, Ag 18,11:3
Clapp, Roger H, 1959, My 3,86:2
Clapp, S C, 1933, S 17,37:3
Clapp, Sidney K, 1949, Ag 17,23:3
Clapp, Susan C N Mrs, 1942, Ja 5,20:3
Clapp, T Eaton Rev, 1903, Ag 13,9:7
Clapp, Theodore Rev, 1866, My 21,5:2
Clapp, W R Dr, 1883, Je 7,5:2
Clapp, W W, 1866, My 6,3:5
Clapp, Warren A, 1952, Ap 22,29:3
Clapp, Washington, 1868, Ag 6,1:4
Clapp, Willard M Mrs, 1943, Ag 29,39:4
Clapp, William F, 1951, D 30,24:4
Clapper, Clinton R, 1948, D 23,19:2
Clapper, Frank S, 1944, Jl 22,15:4
Clapper, Fred, 1942, Ag 15,11:6
Clapper, Raymond L Mrs, 1968, N 12,47:2
Clapper, Samuel M D, 1940, Ja 20,15:5
Clapper, William B, 1938, Jl 24,24:3
Clapper, William J, 1950, Ja 23,23:4
Clapperton, George, 1924, Ja 12,13:3
Claps, John, 1944, N 22,19:5
Clara Agnes, Sister, 1941, D 6,17:1
Clara Agnes Lockington, Sister, 1944, Ap 18,21:3
Clarabut, George G, 1955, F 15,27:1
Clardy, Kit, 1961, S 6,37:3
Clardy, Martin L, 1914, Jl 6,7:5
Clare, Arthur E Mrs, 1940, Ap 2,26:4
Clare, Arthur E Sir, 1939, O 26,23:2
Clare, Arthur James, 1915, O 23,11:5
Clare, Daniel Hunt Jr, 1968, Je 23,73:2
Clare, Edwin A, 1967, F 24,35:3
Clare, Henry A Mrs, 1953, Ap 30,31:5
Clare, James, 1939, F 4,15:5
Clare, James L, 1960, Ap 17,93:1
Clare, John, 1912, S 9,9:5
Clare, Philip, 1903, N 26,7:6
Clare, Thomas J, 1940, Ja 17,21:4
Clarek, Richard H, 1911, My 25,11:6
Claren, Thomas, 1954, Ja 18,23:4
Clarence, Duke of (Prince Albert Victor of Wales), 1892, Ja 15,9:6
Clarendon, Alfred W, 1937, O 6,25:5
Clarendon, Charles H Sr, 1942, Ap 25,13:5
Clarendon, Earl of, 1870, Je 28,4:7
Clarendon, Earl of (Edw Hyde Villiers), 1914, O 4, 14:4
Clarendon, Earl of (G H H Villiers), 1955, D 14,39:1
Clarendon, George T Mrs, 1948, S 12,72:5
Clarendon, James P, 1942, S 19,15:5
Clarendon, Louis F, 1952, Ja 4,40:2
Claret, Frank H, 1946, Ap 1,28:3
Claretie, Jules, 1913, D 24,11:7
Clarey, James H, 1914, F 2,7:1
Clarey, John Edward, 1914, F 18,9:5
Clarey, John J, 1941, Je 14,17:3
Clarey, Louis H, 1941, My 17,15:5
Clarey, Northrop, 1966, Ap 2,29:4
Clarges, Verner, 1911, Ag 12,9:6
Clarholm, Magnus, 1946, O 5,17:4
Claridge, John D, 1958, Mr 21,21:3
Clarin, David X, 1967, Ja 17,39:3
Clarina, Sister, 1943, Ja 27,21:1
Clariond, Aime, 1960, Ja 2,13:2
Clark, A, 1877, F 21,5:6
Clark, A B, 1942, D 23,19:4
Clark, A Bowman, 1948, My 25,27:4
Clark, A Clayton, 1951, Je 19,29:3
Clark, A Harry, 1947, Ja 22,23:3
Clark, A J, 1882, O 16,5:3
Clark, A L, 1930, Je 12,25:5
Clark, A M, 1903, O 28,9:5
Clark, A Mortimer, 1962, F 26,27:2
Clark, A N, 1867, Mr 26,5:5
Clark, A Schuyler Mrs, 1944, F 29,17:5
Clark, A W, 1924, D 10,23:2
Clark, Abel S, 1918, Mr 15,13:5
Clark, Abraham L, 1951, F 14,29:2
Clark, Abraham L Mrs, 1944, Ja 5,17:2
Clark, Ada R, 1958, N 27,29:4
Clark, Addison H, 1959, D 25,21:2
Clark, Addison L, 1957, Je 3,27:5
Clark, Ainsworth W, 1955, Ja 14,21:2
Clark, Albert, 1875, Je 14,5:4
Clark, Albert B, 1937, Jl 27,21:5
Clark, Albert M, 1950, Je 11,92:4
Clark, Albert Mrs, 1957, O 29,31:4
Clark, Albion M, 1944, Mr 12,38:5
Clark, Alden H, 1960, My 29,56:4
Clark, Alex, 1950, Ag 29,27:4
Clark, Alex H, 1961, Je 17,21:6
Clark, Alexander, 1903, S 28,7:5; 1968, N 2,37:4
Clark, Alfred, 1950, Je 18,77:1
Clark, Alfred C (will, N 25,47:2), 1961, S 30,25:4
Clark, Alfred G, 1953, Ja 3,15:4
Clark, Alfred S, 1956, Mr 14,33:4
Clark, Alice B, 1956, My 3,31:1
Clark, Allan J, 1965, F 6,25:3
Clark, Almira, 1938, Jl 3,13:1
Clark, Aloysius, 1950, Ja 27,24:4
Clark, Alson S, 1949, Mr 24,28:6
Clark, Alva B, 1955, N 15,33:3
Clark, Alvan H, 1939, D 15,25:2
Clark, Alvin, 1887, Ag 20,5:1
Clark, Alzamore H, 1914, Je 28,15:4
Clark, Ambrose R, 1944, N 19,50:1
Clark, Amelia S, 1949, D 16,31:5
Clark, Amy A Mrs, 1954, Ja 11,25:4
Clark, Ann Mrs, 1924, Ja 19,13:4; 1946, Jl 28,40:6
Clark, Anna B, 1952, Ja 8,27:4
Clark, Anna Mrs, 1948, O 23,15:6
Clark, Anne T, 1942, F 15,44:1
Clark, Anneta I, 1961, O 11,47:2
Clark, Appleton L Mrs, 1945, N 30,23:2
Clark, Arabel W, 1957, D 24,15:4
Clark, Arthur, 1967, My 30,21:3
Clark, Arthur B, 1948, My 15,15:6
Clark, Arthur E, 1946, Ap 23,21:1; 1950, N 7,27:4
Clark, Arthur E Mrs, 1953, My 4,23:5
Clark, Arthur J, 1954, Je 4,23:3
Clark, Arthur L, 1940, F 24,13:5; 1956, S 21,25:5; 1962, O 3,41:2
Clark, Arthur N, 1940, N 26,23:2
Clark, Arthur R, 1945, Mr 31,19:3
Clark, Arthur T, 1942, O 16,19:4
Clark, Asa B, 1947, Ag 8,17:3
Clark, Atherton, 1949, Jl 4,13:6
Clark, Austin H, 1954, O 29,23:5
Clark, Austin W, 1948, N 23,29:2
Clark, Avery B, 1957, Jl 17,27:4
Clark, B P, 1903, My 30,7:5
Clark, Barrett H, 1953, Ag 7,19:1
Clark, Barzilla W, 1943, S 23,21:5
Clark, Ben R, 1967, Ja 31,31:1
Clark, Benjamin P, 1939, Ja 13,19:5
Clark, Bennett C, 1954, Jl 14,27:3
Clark, Bennett C Mrs, 1943, D 28,17:2
Clark, Benton H, 1964, My 23,23:2
Clark, Bernard C, 1947, Jl 27,44:4
Clark, Bernard C Mrs, 1967, Ja 16,41:4
Clark, Bernard H, 1957, Ja 18,21:4
Clark, Bernard S, 1922, F 14,17:4
Clark, Beverly L, 1860, Ap 19,1:5
Clark, Bobby (Robt E),(funl, F 16,37:4; will, F 19,- 20:2), 1960, F 13,19:1

Clark, Bonnell W, 1955, Mr 4,23:3
Clark, Boyd, 1957, Ag 12,19:4
Clark, Bradford J, 1954, F 18,31:2
Clark, Bruce, 1945, O 11,23:1
Clark, Buddy, 1949, O 2,47:3
Clark, Byron, 1967, Jl 28,31:2
Clark, Byron R, 1949, My 26,30:2
Clark, C Albert, 1955, Ja 23,85:1
Clark, C B, 1952, O 25,17:4
Clark, C B Mrs, 1903, Mr 15,9:5
Clark, C C, 1873, F 13,1:6
Clark, C Dismas, 1963, Ag 16,27:3
Clark, C H, 1926, S 6,15:1
Clark, C Howard, 1916, Ja 11,11:6; 1942, My 11,15:4
Clark, C Ralph Mrs, 1945, S 13,23:5
Clark, C S, 1926, Ag 16,15:3
Clark, C W, 1933, Ap 9,30:1
Clark, C W (Merc), 1953, Jl 2,23:1
Clark, Calvin M, 1947, Mr 2,60:3
Clark, Calvin M Mrs, 1942, N 5,25:6
Clark, Cameron, 1957, Mr 24,86:1
Clark, Carlos B, 1947, D 20,17:5
Clark, Carlos M Mrs, 1939, My 2,24:2
Clark, Carlos N, 1960, Je 6,29:4
Clark, Caroline G Mrs, 1937, N 21,II,9:2
Clark, Caroline R, 1944, F 26,13:3
Clark, Carrie R Mrs, 1946, Ap 6,17:3
Clark, Cecil F, 1955, D 1,35:3
Clark, Champ (funl, Mr 4,13:3), 1921, Mr 3,13:1
Clark, Champ Mrs, 1937, Je 16,23:2
Clark, Charles, 1939, Je 1,25:5; 1952, Ap 2,33:4; 1958, F 11,31:2
Clark, Charles A, 1939, Mr 13,17:5
Clark, Charles A Jr, 1960, Je 2,33:2
Clark, Charles B, 1949, Ap 8,26:3
Clark, Charles C, 1944, N 30,23:4; 1949, Ja 27,23:3
Clark, Charles D, 1959, Mr 28,17:3; 1963, S 9,27:2
Clark, Charles D Mrs, 1950, Mr 14,25:2
Clark, Charles E, 1939, Ja 25,21:4; 1942, My 3,53:2
Clark, Charles E (tribute lr, D 24,16:5), 1963, D 14, 27:4
Clark, Charles E Rear-Adm, 1922, O 2,17:6
Clark, Charles F, 1937, Ap 22,23:4; 1942, Je 10,21:5
Clark, Charles Finney, 1904, S 4,9:6
Clark, Charles H, 1873, N 23,4:7; 1919, My 22,15:6; 1942, Je 2,24:2; 1950, D 12,33:3; 1951, Ap 4,29:5; 1951, Ap 10,27:4; 1952, Ja 15,27:1; 1958, Ja 29,27:3
Clark, Charles H Mrs, 1949, Ja 15,17:2
Clark, Charles Heber, 1915, Ag 11,9:6
Clark, Charles Hull, 1925, Ja 19,17:3
Clark, Charles L, 1915, Je 22,15:6
Clark, Charles M, 1942, D 24,15:4; 1945, Ap 7,15:3; 1955, O 16,87:2
Clark, Charles M Mrs, 1950, Jl 1,15:5
Clark, Charles Mrs, 1944, D 3,57:3
Clark, Charles N, 1919, Jl 19,9:7
Clark, Charles P, 1951, Ag 29,25:6; 1953, Ap 4,13:6; 1967, N 30,47:2
Clark, Charles P Mrs, 1945, Ja 26,21:4
Clark, Charles R, 1960, Jl 24,64:3
Clark, Charles S, 1941, Ja 7,23:3; 1947, Je 17,28:1
Clark, Charles U, 1960, S 30,27:2
Clark, Charles W, 1937, D 27,15:1
Clark, Charles W (will), 1938, My 1,38:1
Clark, Charles W, 1942, Ja 16,21:4
Clark, Charles W Mrs, 1904, Ja 28,1:6
Clark, Chase A, 1966, D 31,19:4
Clark, Chauncey I, 1952, Ap 11,23:4
Clark, Chauncey J Mrs, 1960, F 13,19:2
Clark, Chester W, 1960, Mr 15,39:3
Clark, Christopher Timothy Msgr, 1968, Ja 20,29:1
Clark, Clarence E, 1954, Mr 23,27:3
Clark, Clarence H, 1943, Ap 14,23:1
Clark, Clarence M (will, Ag 19,4:6), 1937, Je 30,23:4
Clark, Clarence V, 1954, Ja 25,19:3
Clark, Claude H, 1937, O 4,21:4
Clark, Cleon R, 1945, N 10,15:5
Clark, Clifford P, 1953, Je 6,17:5
Clark, Clinton, 1950, Mr 12,93:1
Clark, Coryell, 1957, S 12,31:4
Clark, Cuyler L, 1943, Mr 30,26:5
Clark, D Crawford Mrs, 1944, Ja 25,19:5
Clark, D W, 1874, Ag 17,1:6
Clark, D Worth, 1955, Je 21,31:3
Clark, Dana E, 1942, Ag 12,19:5
Clark, Daniel D Jr, 1941, Je 27,17:3
Clark, Danny, 1937, My 24,19:4
Clark, David Crawford, 1919, Ap 20,22:2
Clark, David H, 1950, My 29,17:6
Clark, David H Sr, 1968, Jl 4,19:4
Clark, David L, 1939, F 5,40:7
Clark, David Mrs, 1964, S 28,29:5
Clark, David R, 1942, O 11,56:2
Clark, David S, 1939, F 28,19:2
Clark, Delbert, 1953, O 13,29:3
Clark, Donald C G, 1968, S 5,47:1
Clark, Donald G, 1950, Ap 10,19:2
Clark, Donald L, 1966, Je 29,47:4
Clark, Donald L Mrs, 1966, Ja 10,25:4
Clark, Dorothy W, 1957, D 13,18:3
Clark, Dudley S, 1949, Mr 18,26:2
Clark, Duncan C, 1966, Ja 14,39:3
Clark, Duwayne G, 1957, Ag 16,19:4
Clark, Dwight E, 1959, Jl 25,17:6
Clark, Dwight F, 1951, Ja 6,15:6
Clark, Dwight Mrs, 1958, Jl 14,21:3
Clark, E Dr, 1883, Je 9,2:3
Clark, E Horton, 1952, Ag 8,17:4
Clark, E P, 1903, F 17,2:3
Clark, E T, 1935, D 17,23:5
Clark, Earl, 1943, Ja 6,25:2
Clark, Earl J Mrs, 1947, D 5,25:3
Clark, Ed S, 1949, S 3,6:4
Clark, Edgar M, 1955, Ag 1,19:6
Clark, Edith M (will), 1944, Ap 8,20:5
Clark, Edith R, 1954, Ap 10,15:3
Clark, Edmund Sanford, 1907, My 30,7:6
Clark, Edward, 1882, O 17,4:7; 1902, Ja 7,7:5; 1941, Mr 1,15:6; 1962, My 1,37:3
Clark, Edward A, 1940, D 9,19:5
Clark, Edward B, 1941, S 23,23:3; 1947, Jl 22,24:3
Clark, Edward B Mrs, 1940, N 17,50:1
Clark, Edward C, 1937, Ag 2,19:4
Clark, Edward D, 1949, Ap 22,24:6
Clark, Edward Dodge, 1915, Mr 22,9:3
Clark, Edward F, 1958, F 20,25:5; 1960, My 15,85:4; 1963, D 29,42:8
Clark, Edward F Mrs, 1957, O 3,29:2
Clark, Edward H, 1945, D 18,27:5; 1954, N 22,23:3
Clark, Edward H Mrs, 1947, Ap 3,25:2
Clark, Edward J, 1943, Mr 7,38:4; 1944, Ja 3,21:5; 1948, My 11,25:4; 1959, F 11,39:4
Clark, Edward Jr, 1921, Ag 17,11:6
Clark, Edward L, 1941, Ap 8,25:5
Clark, Edward L Rev Dr, 1910, F 6,II,11:5
Clark, Edward M, 1938, S 13,23:4
Clark, Edward N, 1944, Jl 4,19:4; 1950, My 28,44:7
Clark, Edward O, 1937, My 17,19:1
Clark, Edward R, 1951, N 27,31:5
Clark, Edward T, 1951, Ag 19,85:1; 1960, O 21,33:2
Clark, Edward W, 1939, N 17,22:2; 1946, Ap 5,25:3; 1946, Ap 17,25:4
Clark, Edwin H, 1945, S 18,24:2
Clark, Edwin L (death Mar 23 noted), 1967, Ap 26, 32:8
Clark, Edwin W, 1955, O 14,27:1
Clark, Egbert N, 1942, N 17,25:1
Clark, Egbert N Mrs, 1945, S 25,25:5
Clark, Elbert V, 1955, F 26,15:2
Clark, Eleanor G, 1952, Ap 26,23:3
Clark, Eliot R, 1963, N 3,88:4
Clark, Elizabeth F, 1949, Je 30,23:4
Clark, Ella M, 1955, F 19,15:3
Clark, Ellery H, 1949, Jl 28,23:6
Clark, Ellwood, 1956, O 17,35:2
Clark, Ellwood Mrs, 1948, D 28,21:1
Clark, Elmer T, 1966, Ag 31,40:4
Clark, Elmer W, 1958, Ag 30,15:5
Clark, Elsie B, 1960, Je 3,31:1
Clark, Elton, 1943, F 4,23:6
Clark, Elton W, 1958, S 20,40:1
Clark, Emanuel M, 1941, F 15,15:3
Clark, Emerson, 1940, N 25,17:3
Clark, Emma, 1943, My 14,20:2
Clark, Emma K, 1940, F 19,17:2
Clark, Emmons (funl, Ag 13,7:6), 1905, Ag 10,7:5
Clark, Emmons Col, 1906, F 2,18:2
Clark, Ernest, 1951, Ag 27,19:2; 1963, My 19,86:6
Clark, Ernest L, 1965, S 11,27:2
Clark, Ernest R, 1953, Ja 27,25:4
Clark, Estelle M Mrs (will), 1952, Ja 29,16:4
Clark, Estelle P S Mrs, 1937, S 24,21:1
Clark, Eugene B, 1942, Jl 31,15:2; 1942, N 8,III,3:5
Clark, Eugene C Mrs, 1944, Mr 18,13:5
Clark, Eugene Clinton, 1916, O 7,11:3
Clark, Eugene M, 1942, Ap 17,17:2
Clark, Eugene R, 1952, My 13,30:1
Clark, Everett F, 1952, Ap 6,66:5
Clark, Everett M Mrs, 1945, S 6,25:5
Clark, Ezra B, 1950, Ag 22,27:5
Clark, Ezra W, 1949, Ag 13,11:5
Clark, F Ambrose Mrs (will, O 24,36:2), 1950, O 3, 31:3
Clark, F E, 1927, My 27,23:3
Clark, F Hubbard, 1903, O 15,9:7
Clark, F W, 1927, Mr 20,26:1
Clark, F Y, 1903, Ag 22,9:6
Clark, Fannie M Mrs, 1942, F 22,26:3
Clark, Florence, 1957, D 11,22:4
Clark, Florence J, 1951, Ja 19,25:6
Clark, Floyd H, 1958, O 1,37:2
Clark, Fontaine R, 1966, Jl 25,27:2
Clark, Francis E Mrs, 1945, S 25,25:2
Clark, Francis J, 1952, Jl 20,52:4
Clark, Francis Ludlow, 1907, My 28,9:5
Clark, Francis P (O Lamont), 1952, Ja 18,28:8
Clark, Francis R, 1945, Ap 16,23:3
Clark, Francis X, 1965, F 2,33:1
Clark, Frank B, 1937, My 10,19:2
Clark, Frank C, 1939, F 5,40:4; 1941, O 30,23:4
Clark, Frank D Mrs, 1946, Mr 16,13:5
Clark, Frank E, 1950, D 13,35:2
Clark, Frank H, 1950, N 4,17:6
Clark, Frank H Dr, 1937, Mr 5,21:2
Clark, Frank Hodges, 1904, Ja 6,9:5
Clark, Frank K, 1950, S 21,31:3
Clark, Frank M, 1923, Jl 16,11:5
Clark, Frank Mrs, 1949, Jl 13,27:2
Clark, Frank S, 1947, Ap 13,60:2
Clark, Frank T, 1944, My 17,19:4
Clark, Frank W, 1945, Ag 5,38:5; 1948, My 12,28:3
Clark, Franklin J, 1962, Je 21,31:5
Clark, Fred, 1968, D 7,47:3
Clark, Fred E, 1948, N 30,28:3
Clark, Fred W, 1942, Je 26,21:6
Clark, Frederic B, 1959, Ja 22,31:1
Clark, Frederick A, 1947, D 7,77:1
Clark, Frederick C, 1937, Ap 26,19:5
Clark, Frederick D, 1966, Jl 14,35:4
Clark, Frederick E Dr, 1920, O 6,15:5
Clark, Frederick F Mrs, 1955, O 23,86:1
Clark, Frederick H, 1956, Ap 21,17:4
Clark, Frederick H Mrs, 1949, Ja 13,23:4
Clark, Frederick L, 1961, S 16,19:2
Clark, Frederick M, 1947, Jl 17,19:4
Clark, Frederick P, 1953, Mr 19,29:5; 1954, D 17,31:1; 1963, Ap 13,19:4
Clark, Frederick P J, 1948, Mr 19,23:1
Clark, Frederick Pareis, 1968, My 17,47:1
Clark, Frederick W, 1940, Ap 20,17:2
Clark, G B, 1903, Ag 15,7:6
Clark, G H, 1881, Ag 21,7:3
Clark, G S, 1882, Jl 29,2:7
Clark, G William, 1953, Mr 21,17:5
Clark, Gaylord P Dr, 1907, S 2,7:7
Clark, George, 1940, D 20,25:2; 1946, D 22,41:3; 1954, S 17,27:5; 1954, D 26,61:2; 1959, D 27,61:2
Clark, George A, 1873, F 15,8:6; 1943, Ap 6,21:5; 1945, Ag 7,23:3; 1949, F 19,15:1; 1955, My 27,23:2; 1957, O 19,21:5
Clark, George B, 1942, Jl 8,23:4
Clark, George B Mrs, 1940, Mr 23,13:5
Clark, George C, 1944, Mr 6,19:2
Clark, George C Mrs, 1947, Mr 26,25:1
Clark, George Crawford, 1919, F 26,11:5
Clark, George D, 1949, Je 19,68:4
Clark, George D Sr Mrs, 1949, Ja 21,21:4
Clark, George E, 1918, N 29,13:5; 1950, Je 9,23:6
Clark, George F, 1938, F 11,23:2
Clark, George F Mrs, 1946, Je 29,25:1; 1954, Ja 17, 93:1
Clark, George H, 1941, D 1,19:3; 1949, Ja 2,60:4; 1953, S 27,86:5; 1956, Je 4,29:3
Clark, George H Mrs, 1944, S 2,11:3
Clark, George M, 1939, Ap 8,15:1; 1940, N 15,21:4; 1945, Ag 21,21:3
Clark, George Malcolm, 1913, Ja 25,15:5
Clark, George O, 1939, O 29,40:7
Clark, George P, 1938, S 19,19:3
Clark, George Putman, 1914, Mr 18,11:6
Clark, George W, 1965, My 19,47:2
Clark, George W M, 1956, Ja 20,23:1
Clark, George W M Mrs, 1952, Ja 2,25:4
Clark, George W Mrs, 1939, F 12,44:7
Clark, Gilbert G, 1963, Jl 13,17:6
Clark, Glenn, 1956, Ag 28,27:4
Clark, Gordon E, 1949, Jl 16,13:6
Clark, Gordon M, 1952, D 21,53:2
Clark, Gordon R, 1952, F 26,27:4
Clark, Grace D, 1948, D 7,31:1
Clark, Grenville (ed, Ja 14,30:2), 1967, Ja 13,23:4
Clark, Grover, 1938, Jl 18,13:2
Clark, Grover C, 1952, Ja 5,11:2
Clark, Grover Mrs, 1957, Ag 14,25:1
Clark, Guy C, 1957, Jl 3,23:3
Clark, Guy G, 1945, Ap 18,23:5
Clark, Guy G Jr, 1941, Jl 26,15:2
Clark, H Archer, 1949, Ja 11,31:2
Clark, H Burdette, 1950, F 11,15:2
Clark, H F, 1876, Ap 14,7:2
Clark, H Norton, 1965, Jl 3,19:5
Clark, H Ross, 1952, S 16,29:3
Clark, H Schieffelin, 1918, Ja 5,9:2
Clark, Hamilton B Mrs, 1948, My 19,27:3
Clark, Harold, 1942, Ag 26,19:5
Clark, Harold A, 1948, N 10,29:4
Clark, Harold A Sr (autopsy ordered, D 26,62:3), 1954, D 25,17:1
Clark, Harold B, 1956, O 29,29:4
Clark, Harold C, 1958, O 24,33:3
Clark, Harold E, 1944, Ja 1,13:2
Clark, Harold F, 1938, Jl 18,13:6
Clark, Harold G, 1966, Je 2,43:1
Clark, Harold H, 1925, Jl 9,19:3; 1959, Je 6,21:4
Clark, Harold H Mrs, 1955, Jl 2,15:7
Clark, Harold N, 1954, My 21,27:2
Clark, Harold T, 1965, Je 3,35:2
Clark, Harold W, 1947, Ap 16,25:4; 1947, My 28,5
Clark, Harriet, 1954, Mr 23,27:5
Clark, Harriet B Mrs, 1942, Ag 10,19:6
Clark, Harry, 1956, F 27,31:4; 1958, F 21,24:2
Clark, Harry C, 1947, O 17,21:3; 1952, F 22,12:2
Clark, Harry E, 1940, Ap 18,23:5
Clark, Harry H, 1952, F 7,27:2
Clark, Harry K, 1961, Ap 15,21:4
Clark, Harry M, 1946, Ja 31,21:5
Clark, Harry S, 1955, Je 4,15:3
Clark, Harry W, 1950, Mr 18,14:2
Clark, Hazel M D Mrs (will, N 22,24:2), 1940, N

56:7
Clark, Heman, 1902, S 8,7:6
Clark, Henry A, 1944, F 17,19:4; 1951, O 30,29:4
Clark, Henry A Mrs, 1942, Je 24,19:2
Clark, Henry C, 1951, Jl 20,21:5; 1953, Jl 26,69:2
Clark, Henry E, 1949, Ap 28,31:2
Clark, Henry F, 1945, N 20,21:3; 1951, N 20,31:3
Clark, Henry F Jr, 1964, S 6,56:8
Clark, Henry G, 1940, F 7,21:5
Clark, Henry I, 1940, Ja 23,21:5
Clark, Henry L, 1949, Je 9,31:4
Clark, Henry R, 1947, F 26,26:3
Clark, Henry W, 1942, Jl 19,30:8
Clark, Herbert A, 1944, Ap 21,19:5
Clark, Herbert B, 1966, F 12,27:4
Clark, Herbert C, 1937, N 19,23:1
Clark, Herbert H, 1948, S 10,23:5
Clark, Herbert L, 1940, F 27,21:6
Clark, Herbert L Mrs, 1943, Jl 31,13:6
Clark, Herbert M, 1964, S 2,37:2
Clark, Herbert S, 1943, F 14,49:1
Clark, Herbert T, 1948, My 10,21:5
Clark, Herbert W Mrs, 1938, O 6,23:3; 1948, N 24,23:3
Clark, Herman A, 1943, Ap 9,21:4
Clark, Horace, 1876, F 16,4:7
Clark, Horace F, 1873, Je 20,5:3
Clark, Horace P Capt, 1914, F 26,9:5
Clark, Horatio D, 1957, Ap 18,29:3
Clark, Hovey C, 1955, Ja 1,13:6
Clark, Howard A, 1953, Ap 1,29:2
Clark, Howard B, 1944, O 17,23:3
Clark, Howard F Mrs, 1967, Ap 27,45:4
Clark, Howard 2d, 1945, S 19,25:4
Clark, Hubert G, 1946, Ja 23,27:3
Clark, Hubert L, 1947, Ag 1,17:6
Clark, Hugh, 1942, Je 27,13:5
Clark, Hugh H, 1954, D 20,29:5
Clark, Hugh M, 1956, Ja 24,31:2
Clark, Hugh M Mrs, 1953, D 23,25:3
Clark, Ida L, 1954, N 13,15:2
Clark, Ira J, 1950, Ja 11,23:3
Clark, Irving S, 1947, Ag 2,13:6
Clark, Isaac C, 1959, N 26,37:4
Clark, Isaac Rev Dr, 1918, S 3,11:3
Clark, Isabella G Mrs, 1939, D 30,15:6
Clark, Ivor B Sr, 1960, Ja 23,21:3
Clark, J Ambrose, 1964, F 27,31:1
Clark, J Averell, 1960, Mr 12,21:5
Clark, J Bayard, 1947, My 21,25:2; 1959, Ag 27,27:4
Clark, J Dudley Mrs, 1965, Ja 22,44:1
Clark, J F, 1884, Ja 23,5:4
Clark, J F A Mrs, 1949, Ag 24,25:5
Clark, J F Rev, 1888, Je 6,4:6
Clark, J G, 1927, My 5,27:5
Clark, J H, 1881, Je 18,5:2
Clark, J H Col, 1907, Je 28,7:6
Clark, J Harold, 1946, O 24,27:2
Clark, J Henry, 1945, Ja 3,17:6
Clark, J K, 1903, Ja 26,1:6
Clark, J N, 1903, Ja 16,9:7
Clark, J Reuben Jr, 1961, O 7,23:4
Clark, J Reuben Jr Mrs, 1944, Ag 3,19:2
Clark, J Scott Prof, 1911, D 28,9:5
Clark, Jack J Mrs, 1962, Ja 31,31:1
Clark, Jack W, 1952, Ag 22,21:5
Clark, Jacob E, 1952, Ja 29,25:4
Clark, James, 1881, Ag 4,5:5; 1904, Ja 23,9:5; 1941, S 25,25:3; 1946, F 9,13:2; 1947, Ja 10,21:4
Clark, James A, 1950, S 2,15:3; 1950, O 30,27:4
Clark, James A Mrs, 1945, D 2,46:2; 1949, Ja 15,17:1
Clark, James A Sr, 1950, My 5,21:2
Clark, James C, 1952, Ja 20,84:6; 1954, N 2,27:5
Clark, James D, 1937, My 19,23:5
Clark, James D Mrs, 1961, Je 11,87:2
Clark, James E, 1945, Ap 24,19:4; 1960, Mr 31,33:5; 1962, N 8,39:4
Clark, James F, 1944, Ap 18,21:6
Clark, James G, 1940, Mr 22,19:4
Clark, James G Dr, 1915, Ap 10,11:5
Clark, James G Mrs, 1943, Mr 12,17:3
Clark, James H, 1940, D 4,27:1; 1954, D 25,11:4
Clark, James H Rev, 1925, Ap 8,21:4
Clark, James K Mrs, 1949, My 3,25:1
Clark, James O Mrs, 1956, Jl 4,19:2
Clark, James P, 1909, Ja 11,9:7; 1962, Ap 18,39:1
Clark, James P Mrs, 1954, Mr 9,27:2
Clark, James S, 1912, O 24,11:6
Clark, James Smalley, 1905, Je 7,9:5
Clark, James T, 1922, S 9,13:5; 1961, Mr 13,29:1
Clark, James W, 1947, S 21,60:1
Clark, James Wilson, 1913, S 14,15:7
Clark, Jane Mrs, 1953, N 18,31:3
Clark, Jane S, 1952, Ag 9,13:6
Clark, Jay Jr, 1948, F 8,60:2
Clark, Jean P Mrs, 1938, Mr 27,17:2
Clark, Jeannette A, 1955, Jl 28,23:2
Clark, Jefferson, 1918, D 15,22:3
Clark, Jennie D Mrs, 1941, Je 21,17:3
Clark, Jennie Mrs, 1953, Ja 6,29:5
Clark, Jeptha B, 1914, My 18,9:5
Clark, Jerome, 1941, Jl 13,28:4
Clark, Jesse R, 1921, S 26,15:7
Clark, Jesse W Mrs, 1943, Ap 8,23:1
Clark, Jessie M, 1943, F 2,19:1
Clark, Jim (funl plans, Ap 10,61:5; funl, Ap 11,60:5), 1968, Ap 8,1:1
Clark, John, 1866, O 18,1:7
Clark, John A, 1943, Jl 15,21:3; 1951, N 25,86:1
Clark, John B, 1938, Mr 22,21:3; 1944, N 2,19:3; 1952, O 22,27:4; 1953, Mr 8,91:1
Clark, John Blake, 1922, Ag 11,11:5
Clark, John Bullock, 1903, S 8,7:6
Clark, John C, 1946, Je 28,22:2; 1960, Ja 28,31:2
Clark, John C Jr, 1966, Ag 21,93:1
Clark, John C Mrs, 1946, Mr 8,21:1
Clark, John Campbell, 1921, Ja 6,11:3
Clark, John D, 1938, Je 2,23:5
Clark, John E Mrs, 1958, O 24,33:2
Clark, John Emory Prof, 1921, Ja 5,13:6
Clark, John F, 1941, F 9,49:2; 1941, Ag 25,15:5; 1941, Ag 29,17:5; 1955, O 28,25:5
Clark, John G, 1941, Ja 8,19:4; 1946, F 2,13:5; 1949, N 26,15:4
Clark, John H, 1938, D 13,25:5; 1950, Jl 2,25:1
Clark, John H Jr, 1967, F 6,29:2
Clark, John H Jr Mrs, 1957, Ag 8,23:3
Clark, John Howe Dr, 1913, D 2,11:6
Clark, John J, 1903, O 4,7:6; 1941, Ja 16,21:2; 1947, Ap 13,60:4
Clark, John K, 1963, Ja 21,7:8
Clark, John L, 1951, D 13,33:5; 1960, S 6,35:2
Clark, John L Rev, 1951, Mr 12,25:5
Clark, John M, 1906, D 29,6:2; 1963, Je 28,29:1
Clark, John Mitchell, 1913, Mr 11,11:3
Clark, John Mrs, 1958, Je 14,21:6
Clark, John Norwood, 1904, F 18,9:6
Clark, John R, 1952, N 27,31:5; 1956, My 16,35:5; 1967, F 28,34:3
Clark, John S, 1960, Ja 20,31:5
Clark, John S Gen, 1912, Ap 9,11:4
Clark, John T, 1949, D 7,31:2; 1954, Mr 18,31:4
Clark, John W, 1941, Ap 15,23:5; 1948, O 24,76:1
Clark, Joseph, 1937, O 19,26:2
Clark, Joseph A, 1951, Mr 12,25:3; 1960, O 11,45:4
Clark, Joseph B, 1938, Mr 14,15:4
Clark, Joseph Bourne Rev Dr, 1923, Jl 12,17:4
Clark, Joseph D Mrs, 1955, Je 22,29:4
Clark, Joseph Firth, 1918, Ja 23,9:5
Clark, Joseph H Mrs, 1944, F 10,15:2
Clark, Joseph M, 1953, Ja 8,27:3
Clark, Joseph P, 1956, D 5,39:5
Clark, Joseph S, 1911, Jl 17,9:4
Clark, Joseph S Mrs, 1951, Ja 21,77:1
Clark, Joseph S Sr, 1956, Ap 16,28:1
Clark, Joseph Sill Sr (est acctg), 1957, Jl 13,10:6
Clark, Joseph T, 1937, Jl 24,15:4
Clark, Juanita M Mrs, 1955, F 18,22:2
Clark, K U Mrs, 1935, F 18,15:3
Clark, Kate S Mrs, 1940, O 9,25:5
Clark, Kathryn R Mrs, 1942, My 28,17:2
Clark, Keith, 1939, Mr 13,17:2; 1951, O 7,85:6
Clark, Keith Mrs, 1951, Ag 23,23:5
Clark, Kenneth S, 1945, Ja 24,21:3; 1954, Ja 22,27:3
Clark, L C, 1880, F 12,2:5
Clark, L L Mrs, 1932, Ag 2,17:3
Clark, L P Dr, 1933, D 4,19:6
Clark, L Stowell, 1950, Ag 20,77:2
Clark, Lancaster P, 1950, Mr 11,15:4
Clark, LeGrand L, 1959, O 9,21:3
Clark, Leon, 1941, Je 26,23:3
Clark, Leonard B, 1950, Ag 7,21:7
Clark, Leonard P, 1949, F 12,18:2
Clark, Leroy Mrs, 1962, Ag 29,29:3
Clark, Leslie S Mrs, 1944, My 5,19:2
Clark, Lester, 1904, Ap 20,6:2
Clark, Lester W, 1955, Je 28,27:4
Clark, Lester W Jr, 1909, S 14,9:5
Clark, Lester W Mrs, 1945, N 29,23:2
Clark, Lewis Gaylord, 1873, N 5,7:2
Clark, Lewis S, 1941, My 29,19:5
Clark, Lillian W Mrs, 1941, O 15,21:2
Clark, Lois F, 1937, O 2,21:3
Clark, Lois R Mrs, 1959, Je 23,33:2
Clark, Louis, 1940, Ag 11,31:2
Clark, Louis A, 1938, F 1,21:5
Clark, Louis C, 1924, Ag 18,13:4
Clark, Louis H, 1960, Jl 7,31:5
Clark, Louis J Mrs, 1966, Jl 20,41:4
Clark, Louis Jr, 1907, Ag 21,7:6
Clark, Louise Amelia, 1919, Ag 9,9:7
Clark, Lucius C, 1949, Mr 28,21:5
Clark, Lucy S Mrs, 1942, Je 11,23:2
Clark, Luther S Mrs, 1961, Ap 25,35:4
Clark, M Elizabeth, 1967, Ja 22,76:6
Clark, M Eugene, 1940, O 10,25:5
Clark, M H Capt, 1912, F 6,11:5
Clark, M L, 1881, O 29,5:4
Clark, M P, 1881, Ja 4,8:1
Clark, Margaret E, 1949, Mr 8,25:4
Clark, Margaretta C Mrs, 1941, Mr 19,21:3
Clark, Marguerite, 1940, S 26,23:4
Clark, Mark G, 1946, My 13,21:2
Clark, Mark W Mrs, 1966, O 6,47:6
Clark, Marmaduke, 1964, Jl 18,19:4
Clark, Martin S, 1951, Ap 18,31:1
Clark, Mary-Chase, 1945, Mr 15,23:1
Clark, Mary E, 1944, Je 2,15:3; 1958, S 18,31:4
Clark, Mary E Mrs, 1942, Je 15,19:5
Clark, Mary G Mrs, 1940, S 2,15:3
Clark, Mary M, 1945, Ap 27,19:2
Clark, Mary M Mrs, 1940, S 30,17:3
Clark, Mary S Mrs, 1939, Ag 31,19:5
Clark, Mayme S Mrs, 1937, Ag 15,II,6:8
Clark, Melville, 1953, D 12,19:6
Clark, Melvin Reamer, 1952, S 26,21:3
Clark, Merrell E, 1941, My 12,17:3
Clark, Michael A, 1957, Jl 13,17:2
Clark, Michael J, 1946, O 6,59:4
Clark, Miles Heber, 1923, Mr 7,15:4
Clark, Montgomery (por), 1938, Jl 17,27:4
Clark, Morris K, 1955, Je 10,25:2
Clark, Morton G Mrs, 1960, Ja 22,27:2
Clark, Myra S Mrs, 1940, S 3,17:3
Clark, Myron, 1869, Mr 13,5:3
Clark, Myron H, 1953, S 1,23:1
Clark, N Walling Rev Dr, 1918, Mr 13,11:5
Clark, Nalbro B, 1952, S 10,29:5
Clark, Nelson, 1925, Ap 30,21:4
Clark, Nelson E, 1949, Ja 11,31:1
Clark, Noyes D (will, Ap 1,14:4), 1937, Mr 18,25:4
Clark, O P Mrs, 1943, Ap 30,21:2
Clark, Orlo R, 1954, Je 22,8:4
Clark, Orlo R Mrs, 1954, Je 22,8:4
Clark, Oscar N Mrs, 1951, D 30,24:3
Clark, Osman D, 1941, S 12,21:3
Clark, Osroe A, 1947, Je 24,24:3
Clark, Owen C, 1963, My 12,87:1
Clark, P, 1934, Ag 21,17:4
Clark, P L, 1950, F 6,25:5
Clark, P Webster, 1954, D 22,23:1
Clark, Patrick J, 1940, My 16,23:4
Clark, Paul A, 1938, N 24,29:2
Clark, Paul R, 1961, S 19,35:2
Clark, Percy H, 1965, Ag 13,29:4
Clark, Percy H Mrs (funl, Je 27,23:5), 1959, Je 25, 29:3
Clark, Perkins Mrs, 1912, Ja 2,11:5
Clark, Perley M, 1953, S 6,50:4
Clark, Peter, 1937, S 10,24:1
Clark, Peter Mrs, 1944, O 17,23:2
Clark, Peter S, 1942, Ag 1,11:3
Clark, Phebe Mrs, 1940, Ja 28,33:2
Clark, Phil C, 1949, O 1,13:6
Clark, Philip E, 1946, Jl 26,21:4
Clark, Phillips A Mrs, 1938, S 25,38:6
Clark, Primus C, 1944, Jl 9,36:1
Clark, R E Dr, 1903, D 8,9:4
Clark, R Inslee, 1966, O 27,47:3
Clark, R P, 1932, Ap 9,15:6
Clark, Ralp B Mrs, 1957, Ap 20,17:6
Clark, Ralph J, 1949, Je 18,13:4
Clark, Ralph R, 1950, Ag 3,23:3
Clark, Ralph S, 1958, N 30,86:4
Clark, Ray (Toughie), 1951, Ag 18,11:6
Clark, Ray H, 1955, O 28,25:3
Clark, Raymond, 1955, Ja 24,23:4
Clark, Raymond F, 1964, O 5,33:1
Clark, Raymond K, 1947, Jl 4,13:6
Clark, Raymond P, 1948, Je 29,23:4
Clark, Raymond S Mrs, 1966, Ja 3,27:4
Clark, Rensselaer W, 1965, Ap 21,45:4
Clark, Richard Mrs, 1912, S 8,II,13:4; 1956, Jl 12,23:5
Clark, Richard T, 1960, Je 4,23:6
Clark, Robert, 1943, Ap 9,21:3
Clark, Robert B, 1949, F 19,15:6
Clark, Robert B Mrs, 1943, Je 30,21:4
Clark, Robert C, 1939, D 5,27:6
Clark, Robert G, 1955, D 10,21:3; 1956, Ja 27,23:2
Clark, Robert H, 1913, Je 19,11:5; 1941, N 12,23:2; 1947, Mr 25,25:2
Clark, Robert K, 1937, O 10,II,8:8
Clark, Robert K Mrs, 1945, Ap 17,23:3
Clark, Robert Maj, 1905, F 27,7:5
Clark, Robert R, 1951, F 6,27:3
Clark, Robert S (will), 1957, Ja 18,23:8
Clark, Robert S (est tax appr), 1961, Ag 24,59:2
Clark, Robert S Mrs, 1945, D 25,23:2; 1960, Ap 9,23:5
Clark, Robert V, 1952, Ag 28,23:4
Clark, Robert V Jr (will), 1964, O 29,37:8
Clark, Robert W, 1952, Ja 16,25:2; 1962, O 29,29:5
Clark, Robert W Mrs, 1948, My 12,28:3
Clark, Robert Y, 1961, Je 6,37:2
Clark, Robert Y Mrs, 1945, Jl 24,23:5
Clark, Roderick P Mrs, 1949, S 7,29:4
Clark, Roe S, 1955, D 24,13:3
Clark, Roger P, 1940, Je 9,44:3; 1954, Ap 2,28:6
Clark, Roland, 1957, Ap 15,29:5
Clark, Roland W, 1941, Ja 25,15:2
Clark, Roscoe N, 1937, Je 8,25:4
Clark, Roy E, 1941, F 16,40:6
Clark, Roy W, 1948, O 4,23:5
Clark, Rush, 1879, Ap 29,4:7
Clark, Russell C, 1967, Mr 3,35:4
Clark, S A, 1931, N 9,19:5
Clark, S Hoxie, 1944, Je 12,19:3
Clark, S Milton, 1959, Mr 11,35:1
Clark, Samuel A Mrs, 1949, Ja 13,23:3
Clark, Samuel C, 1949, N 10,31:2
Clark, Samuel H, 1941, N 15,17:3

Clark, Samuel H Mrs, 1962, S 12,39:2
Clark, Samuel L, 1957, Ap 22,25:2
Clark, Samuel N, 1954, My 5,31:5
Clark, Samuel S, 1939, Mr 15,23:2
Clark, Samuel T Mrs, 1957, O 24,33:1
Clark, Sarah A P Mrs, 1942, D 11,23:2
Clark, Sarah G, 1941, F 19,21:2
Clark, Satterlee, 1881, S 25,8:4
Clark, Sayles B Mrs, 1967, Je 14,47:4
Clark, Sedgwick A, 1961, Mr 15,39:5
Clark, Seth, 1941, Je 21,17:3
Clark, Seth F, 1951, Mr 16,31:3
Clark, Sheldon, 1952, Ag 16,15:1
Clark, Sigourney F Mrs, 1946, Jl 5,19:2
Clark, Slade F Mrs, 1953, Ap 7,29:3
Clark, Solomon F, 1961, N 16,17:1
Clark, Stanley I Mrs, 1962, My 12,23:1
Clark, Stanley L, 1943, Ag 7,11:4
Clark, Stephen C, 1950, D 1,25:2
Clark, Stephen C (trb lr, S 23,28:5; will, S 30,1:1), 1960, S 18,86:3
Clark, Susan Mrs, 1937, Jl 21,21:6
Clark, Sydney Williams, 1915, Jl 23,9:6
Clark, Sylvester W, 1938, D 6,23:1
Clark, T A, 1932, Jl 19,20:1
Clark, T M Bp, 1903, S 3,8:4
Clark, Taliaferro, 1948, Jl 5,15:2
Clark, Teresa B Mrs, 1947, N 24,23:5
Clark, Thatcher, 1962, Jl 20,25:1
Clark, Theodore F, 1910, S 24,11:5
Clark, Theodore F Rev, 1916, F 26,9:5
Clark, Theodore S, 1937, D 19,II,8:5; 1966, Mr 19,29:5
Clark, Thomas, 1864, N 11,2:2; 1943, S 30,21:1
Clark, Thomas A, 1963, Ag 15,29:5
Clark, Thomas B, 1941, N 12,23:2; 1944, Ag 5,11:5
Clark, Thomas C, 1953, D 9,11:4
Clark, Thomas E, 1962, N 21,33:4
Clark, Thomas Edwards, 1916, Je 1,11:7
Clark, Thomas F, 1944, Mr 14,19:4
Clark, Thomas F Dr, 1937, Ja 14,21:3
Clark, Thomas F Mrs, 1949, Jl 16,13:3
Clark, Thomas F Sr, 1951, Ja 17,27:2
Clark, Thomas J, 1957, Jl 9,27:1
Clark, Thomas M Mrs, 1944, My 3,19:6
Clark, Thomas Mrs, 1945, Mr 14,19:2; 1949, Jl 22,20:2
Clark, Thomas R, 1952, N 21,25:3
Clark, Thomas S, 1945, My 22,19:4; 1964, O 2,37:2
Clark, Thomas S H, 1955, Ja 1,13:2
Clark, Thomas W, 1944, Ap 10,19:3
Clark, Tyler E, 1956, D 12,39:1
Clark, U Grant, 1947, Jl 18,17:1
Clark, Ulysses S, 1941, F 12,21:5
Clark, Vail F, 1950, D 20,31:2
Clark, Victor S, 1946, Ap 3,25:5
Clark, Vincent, 1951, My 4,27:4
Clark, Vincent M, 1962, Ja 18,29:1
Clark, Virginius E, 1948, Ja 31,19:2
Clark, W, 1929, Jl 11,23:3; 1934, Jl 31,17:3
Clark, W A, 1934, Je 15,21:6
Clark, W A Jr Mrs, 1903, Ja 2,9:6
Clark, W C, 1872, Ap 26,1:3
Clark, W C Rev, 1875, S 24,4:5
Clark, W Douglas, 1949, Ag 31,23:2
Clark, W E, 1940, Ja 21,35:2
Clark, W G, 1948, Ja 19,24:3
Clark, W Irving, 1925, Je 6,15:5; 1958, Ap 7,21:1
Clark, W L, 1935, D 19,25:1; 1960, O 10,31:3
Clark, W M, 1915, Ag 31,9:5
Clark, W W, 1873, Ag 11,1:6
Clark, W Wiltshire Capt, 1868, Ag 1,5:3
Clark, Wallace (por), 1948, Jl 5,15:5
Clark, Wallace Mrs, 1962, F 21,45:1
Clark, Wallace V, 1960, Ag 25,29:5
Clark, Wallis H, 1961, F 15,35:3
Clark, Wallis O Maj, 1914, S 17,9:6
Clark, Walter, 1917, Mr 13,11:5; 1951, Ap 27,23:4
Clark, Walter A, 1947, Jl 15,23:6
Clark, Walter Appleton, 1906, D 27,1:4
Clark, Walter E, 1950, F 5,84:7; 1955, My 2,21:3; 1960, O 2,84:2
Clark, Walter G, 1950, D 19,30:2
Clark, Walter H, 1939, O 21,15:5
Clark, Walter J, 1950, Je 21,27:6
Clark, Walter Justice, 1924, My 20,21:6
Clark, Walter L, 1941, Jl 5,11:5
Clark, Walter L Jr, 1951, Ap 17,29:2
Clark, Walter L Lt Col, 1937, Ja 14,21:4
Clark, Walter L Mrs, 1940, N 26,23:2
Clark, Walter R Mrs, 1945, S 20,23:5
Clark, Walter T, 1951, O 1,23:5; 1960, F 11,35:4
Clark, Walter V, 1944, F 27,38:1
Clark, Waltson G Mrs, 1955, S 12,25:4
Clark, Warren, 1964, S 28,29:5
Clark, Watson G, 1937, D 8,25:3
Clark, Webster K, 1954, Jl 27,21:5
Clark, Wilbur, 1965, Ag 28,21:2
Clark, Wilkie C, 1950, O 25,35:2
Clark, Willard B, 1942, N 9,23:2
Clark, Willard F, 1955, My 23,23:2
Clark, Willett H, 1938, My 27,17:4
Clark, William, 1902, Jl 8,9:4; 1907, D 18,9:5; 1939, Ap 8,23:8; 1946, F 7,23:1; 1948, My 18,23:4; 1957, O 11,27:1; 1958, Ap 23,33:4
Clark, William A, 1912, Ap 18,13:5; 1913, N 14,11:6; 1942, Ag 11,19:5; 1943, Ja 11,15:4; 1944, Ap 4,21:3; 1946, My 10,19:2; 1948, Ja 7,26:2; 1948, Ap 12,21:4; 1949, My 11,29:5; 1951, Mr 3,13:1; 1953, Je 7,84:5; 1957, O 18,23:4
Clark, William A Dr, 1951, My 19,15:3
Clark, William A Mrs, 1963, O 12,23:5
Clark, William B, 1942, O 11,57:2
Clark, William B Sr, 1961, O 8,87:1
Clark, William Bell Sr, 1968, N 4,47:3
Clark, William Brewster Dr, 1912, O 12,11:1
Clark, William Bullock Dr, 1917, Jl 28,7:7
Clark, William C, 1912, N 15,13:6; 1940, Ja 7,49:3; 1940, Ja 18,23:3; 1945, My 8,19:5; 1948, F 20,27:4; 1952, D 28,50:1
Clark, William C Mrs, 1938, Mr 31,23:3
Clark, William D, 1941, O 15,21:5
Clark, William E, 1942, Je 27,13:6; 1946, D 7,21:4; 1966, Ag 12,31:4
Clark, William Everitt, 1912, Ja 30,9:5
Clark, William F, 1903, O 6,9:4; 1940, S 10,23:6; 1943, Jl 13,21:2; 1947, F 26,25:5
Clark, William H, 1925, N 10,25:4; 1943, F 22,17:1; 1948, Ja 25,56:6; 1950, S 16,19:5; 1951, O 14,88:5; 1952, N 25,29:3
Clark, William H Jr, 1942, D 19,20:3
Clark, William H Mrs, 1949, Je 5,94:3
Clark, William H Sr, 1946, N 23,15:2
Clark, William Hancock Maj, 1922, Ja 26,17:4
Clark, William J, 1909, O 30,9:6; 1922, Mr 2,21:5; 1942, Ap 21,23:4; 1946, D 23,23:4; 1950, Ja 19,27:3; 1956, Je 18,25:3; 1957, N 29,29:1; 1961, Ap 29,23:1
Clark, William Jared, 1922, D 14,21:4
Clark, William Judson Mrs, 1922, Mr 10,15:5
Clark, William L, 1938, Ag 23,17:5; 1952, My 17,19:3; 1956, My 6,86:6
Clark, William M, 1941, F 8,15:1; 1950, Ag 22,27:4; 1964, Ja 21,29:2
Clark, William Meade Rev, 1914, Ap 30,11:6
Clark, William Mortimer Sir, 1917, Ag 12,17:2
Clark, William Newton, 1920, Ag 6,9:6
Clark, William Newton Dr, 1912, Ja 16,13:4
Clark, William O, 1946, F 14,25:4
Clark, William O Mrs, 1948, Je 12,15:4
Clark, William R Mrs, 1955, Jl 12,25:4
Clark, William Reid Rev, 1925, Ap 20,17:6
Clark, William Sr Mrs, 1945, Ag 15,19:3
Clark, William T, 1925, S 17,23:4; 1939, Mr 11,17:4
Clark, William Thomas, 1905, O 23,9:5
Clark, William W, 1939, My 18,25:4
Clark, Willis G, 1938, N 6,49:1
Clark, Willis W, 1938, N 7,19:4
Clark, Winfield, 1959, Ap 17,25:4
Clark, Woodward D, 1958, S 5,27:2
Clark-Duff, William G, 1945, Je 26,19:6
Clark-Duff, William G Mrs, 1943, N 16,23:6
Clark-Kennedy, W H, 1961, O 28,21:4
Clarke, A Vernon, 1963, N 7,34:2
Clarke, Ada S, 1955, Ag 2,23:2
Clarke, Albert, 1968, Mr 29,41:4
Clarke, Albert Col, 1911, Jl 17,9:5
Clarke, Alexander S, 1909, My 28,9:7
Clarke, Alfred, 1922, Ap 29,15:4
Clarke, Alfred C, 1958, N 8,21:1
Clarke, Alfred G, 1958, Ap 25,27:3
Clarke, Allan G, 1953, Jl 8,27:5
Clarke, Allen H, 1947, N 3,23:5
Clarke, Andrew D, 1948, My 20,29:1
Clarke, Andrew Sir Gen, 1902, Ap 1,9:6
Clarke, Andrew T J, 1955, Ja 30,84:4
Clarke, Anna C, 1958, Ag 20,27:2
Clarke, Ara F Mrs, 1957, Ap 4,33:4
Clarke, Arban Mrs, 1938, Ap 21,19:4
Clarke, Arthur, 1942, D 17,37:1
Clarke, Arthur C, 1949, S 27,27:4
Clarke, Arthur C Mrs, 1944, D 26,19:5
Clarke, Arthur E Col, 1921, O 2,22:3
Clarke, Arthur F Sr, 1963, N 26,37:3
Clarke, Arthur L Mrs, 1966, D 28,43:3
Clarke, Augustus W, 1923, Ag 9,13:6; 1923, Ag 23,15:4
Clarke, B W Mrs, 1909, N 22,9:5
Clarke, Basil, 1947, D 13,15:1
Clarke, Branford, 1947, Jl 8,23:4
Clarke, Bruce A, 1950, Ja 11,23:5
Clarke, C C, 1877, Mr 18,7:4
Clarke, C Herford, 1937, Mr 14,II,8:5
Clarke, C Read, 1956, N 24,19:4
Clarke, C W Actor, 1867, S 23,5:5
Clarke, Calvin, 1960, Ja 4,29:5
Clarke, Carolyn (Mrs H F Strange), 1951, S 11,29:4
Clarke, Casper Lady, 1917, Ag 13,9:5
Clarke, Casper Purdon (funl, Ap 2,13:4), 1911, Mr 30,11:5
Clarke, Charles A, 1944, Ap 29,15:4
Clarke, Charles B, 1944, Ja 29,13:3; 1951, F 17,15:2
Clarke, Charles C, 1910, My 27,9:5
Clarke, Charles J C, 1945, D 7,21:3
Clarke, Charles Kirk Dr, 1924, Ja 21,17:4
Clarke, Charles L, 1941, O 10,23:1
Clarke, Charles Manchester, 1908, Jl 10,7:5
Clarke, Charles N, 1964, My 21,35:4
Clarke, Charles P, 1938, Ap 13,25:2; 1963, D 15,87:1
Clarke, Charles W, 1964, N 10,47:2
Clarke, Cherrie, 1945, Mr 20,19:4
Clarke, Clinton C Mrs, 1953, Jl 17,17:3
Clarke, Creston, 1910, Mr 22,11:4
Clarke, Daniel, 1872, F 29,5:4; 1885, Mr 18,3:3
Clarke, Darius W Bishop (will, Je 3,2:1), 1871, My 24,5:4
Clarke, Deborah Baker Mrs, 1875, Ja 7,5:6
Clarke, Donald B, 1952, Jl 6,48:6
Clarke, Donald H, 1958, Mr 30,88:2
Clarke, Dumont, 1908, Mr 16,7:4
Clarke, Dumont (will), 1910, Ja 8,9:4
Clarke, Dumont, 1960, Je 23,29:1
Clarke, Dumont Mrs, 1946, D 9,25:2
Clarke, E A S, 1931, My 16,17:3
Clarke, E Arthur S Mrs, 1959, Jl 22,27:2
Clarke, E D, 1885, Mr 24,5:1
Clarke, E Thurston, 1962, My 28,29:5
Clarke, Edward (A Moss), 1960, Ag 9,27:2
Clarke, Edward E, 1950, Ag 8,29:4; 1955, Jl 5,29:4
Clarke, Edward S, 1956, O 2,35:2
Clarke, Edward W, 1946, N 20,31:4
Clarke, Edwin, 1953, F 20,20:3
Clarke, Edwin L, 1948, S 16,29:2
Clarke, Eldad L, 1940, Jl 23,19:2
Clarke, Elisabeth I K Mrs, 1940, Je 12,25:5
Clarke, Eric K, 1958, N 21,29:4
Clarke, Eric T, 1968, O 24,47:3
Clarke, Ernest, 1947, S 17,25:4
Clarke, Eugene, 1909, Jl 26,7:7
Clarke, Florence E, 1958, Ap 3,31:3
Clarke, Francis W, 1938, F 21,19:4
Clarke, Francis W Col, 1866, Ag 29,3:1
Clarke, Francis X, 1967, F 28,34:2
Clarke, Frank E, 1937, O 17,II,9:3
Clarke, Frank R, 1961, O 12,29:2
Clarke, Frank T Mrs, 1908, O 16,9:5
Clarke, Frank W, 1967, My 6,31:3
Clarke, Fred, 1949, Ag 6,17:2; 1960, Ag 15,23:1
Clarke, Frederick, 1941, Ag 20,19:5; 1944, Jl 29,13:5
Clarke, Frederick B, 1943, S 22,23:5
Clarke, Frederick E, 1953, F 28,17:4
Clarke, Frederick H, 1947, Ag 24,58:2
Clarke, Frederick L, 1949, Je 1,31:3
Clarke, Gage, 1964, O 25,88:7
Clarke, Galen, 1910, Mr 26,9:5
Clarke, Geoffrey, 1950, O 12,31:5
Clarke, George, 1871, Je 4,1:6; 1906, O 5,9:3; 1962, Jl 6,25:4
Clarke, George B, 1938, Mr 7,17:4
Clarke, George C, 1955, S 7,31:3
Clarke, George C Mrs, 1953, S 11,21:4
Clarke, George Chever, 1911, Ja 12,13:4
Clarke, George E, 1938, Jl 9,13:6
Clarke, George H, 1948, D 30,19:5; 1953, Mr 28,17:3
Clarke, George Hyde, 1914, Ag 2,15:5
Clarke, George J, 1946, Jl 2,25:6
Clarke, George L, 1956, Je 1,23:4
Clarke, George Mrs, 1914, Ap 11,11:6
Clarke, George P B, 1943, D 17,27:3
Clarke, George P F, 1951, Jl 24,25:4
Clarke, George Rev, 1921, Ja 20,9:4
Clarke, George W Dr, 1908, S 16,9:5
Clarke, Gilmore, 1938, N 5,19:2
Clarke, Gilmore D Mrs, 1962, S 5,39:2
Clarke, Grace O, 1958, Je 25,29:4
Clarke, H A, 1929, Ja 19,17:4
Clarke, H Audley Mrs, 1904, O 11,9:5
Clarke, Harley L, 1955, Je 7,33:3
Clarke, Harry C, 1942, F 26,19:5
Clarke, Harry J, 1959, D 18,29:4
Clarke, Harry M, 1947, Jl 27,45:1
Clarke, Harry R, 1951, Ag 14,23:2
Clarke, Hedley L, 1945, Mr 6,22:2
Clarke, Helen M, 1949, D 21,30:3
Clarke, Henry Audley, 1910, D 17,13:4
Clarke, Henry Conquest, 1914, N 16,9:5
Clarke, Henry S, 1919, Ap 10,11:2
Clarke, Henry S Mrs, 1951, D 13,33:5
Clarke, Herbert L, 1945, F 1,23:4
Clarke, Hermann F, 1947, O 31,23:2
Clarke, Howard S, 1904, Ja 23,9:5
Clarke, Hudson, 1946, Mr 21,25:3
Clarke, Hugh M, 1938, Jl 28,19:5
Clarke, Ida, 1938, F 27,II,8:2
Clarke, J Alexander Jr, 1943, F 2,19:1
Clarke, J G, 1880, S 16,2:4
Clarke, J Hervey, 1940, My 21,23:6
Clarke, J Lyell, 1953, My 6,31:2
Clarke, J P, 1932, Ja 13,23:1
Clarke, Jacob O, 1937, S 16,25:2
Clarke, James, 1907, My 18,7:4; 1945, S 6,25:3
Clarke, James A Mrs, 1943, Ag 26,17:4
Clarke, James C, 1938, Ap 17,II,7:2
Clarke, James D, 1953, N 24,29:3
Clarke, James F, 1943, S 5,29:2
Clarke, James Franklin, 1916, Jl 8,9:4
Clarke, James G, 1939, My 12,21:5
Clarke, James H, 1954, N 4,31:4
Clarke, James H Mrs, 1950, Jl 17,21:4
Clarke, James I, 1961, Mr 18,23:6
Clarke, James Mrs, 1923, S 18,21:6
Clarke, James O, 1959, Ag 15,17:1
Clarke, James R, 1948, O 27,27:4

Clarke, James R Mrs, 1963, Je 22,23:5
Clarke, James S, 1942, Jl 9,22:5
Clarke, James W E, 1938, O 14,23:3
Clarke, Jay, 1949, Je 17,23:5
Clarke, Jeremiah, 1964, Je 2,37:4
Clarke, Jesse W, 1950, Ap 28,21:2
Clarke, John, 1879, F 22,2:2; 1943, My 1,15:3; 1943, S 24,23:2
Clarke, John A, 1944, N 24,23:2
Clarke, John D Mrs, 1953, Ap 10,22:3
Clarke, John E, 1955, N 22,35:2
Clarke, John Eastman Prof, 1913, N 23,IV,7:5
Clarke, John F, 1919, Jl 24,9:2; 1943, Jl 7,19:4
Clarke, John H, 1937, N 8,23:3
Clarke, John H (will, Mr 30,16:2), 1945, Mr 23,19:1
Clarke, John J, 1942, Ja 28,19:3
Clarke, John M, 1953, Mr 7,15:4
Clarke, John Mason Dr (funl, Je 2,23:3), 1925, My 30,9:4
Clarke, John Mrs, 1956, My 30,21:3
Clarke, John P, 1944, O 28,15:6; 1949, Jl 5,24:3
Clarke, John Proctor Mrs, 1924, My 6,21:4
Clarke, John S, 1959, F 1,85:1; 1962, My 22,38:1
Clarke, John Sleeper, 1899, S 26,7:3
Clarke, John V, 1911, Je 1,11:5
Clarke, John W, 1937, Ja 11,20:2
Clarke, Joseph F, 1944, F 10,15:3
Clarke, Joseph I C (por), 1925, F 28,13:3
Clarke, Joseph Mrs, 1948, Ag 11,22:2
Clarke, Josephine Miller Mrs, 1909, My 2,11:5
Clarke, Joshua W, 1947, Mr 29,15:2
Clarke, Julius L, 1907, N 24,9:7
Clarke, Kenneth B, 1960, O 29,23:5
Clarke, L Commander, 1885, Je 9,5:4
Clarke, Laurence W Mrs, 1947, F 7,24:2
Clarke, Lewis L, 1964, Jl 8,35:4
Clarke, Lloyd, 1909, My 8,7:5
Clarke, Louis D, 1908, F 12,7:6
Clarke, Louis S, 1957, Ja 7,25:3
Clarke, Louis W, 1921, S 27,19:4
Clarke, Lucian B Mrs, 1954, Ja 17,20:5
Clarke, Marshall, 1943, F 27,13:1
Clarke, Mary B, 1956, Je 18,25:2
Clarke, Mary C, 1898, Ja 15,41:4
Clarke, Mathias (funl), 1872, Mr 17,4:6
Clarke, Maurice, 1946, D 6,23:1
Clarke, Merrill F, 1958, S 5,27:2
Clarke, Michael, 1916, Mr 14,11:5
Clarke, Norman F, 1943, Je 15,21:4
Clarke, Norman R, 1964, N 7,27:5
Clarke, Ormonde S, 1963, Ag 2,27:1
Clarke, Oscar D, 1947, F 23,53:8
Clarke, P J, 1881, D 5,5:1
Clarke, Patrick J, 1939, Ja 4,21:4
Clarke, Phil J, 1952, Ag 2,15:6
Clarke, Philip R, 1966, O 30,88:8
Clarke, Prescott Mrs, 1948, Mr 25,27:3
Clarke, R Morton, 1956, O 15,25:4
Clarke, R W, 1872, My 24,1:2
Clarke, R W (Deadwood Dick), 1930, My 6,29:3
Clarke, R W Mrs, 1877, My 25,2:7
Clarke, Ralph, 1914, Mr 29,5:5
Clarke, Ralph D, 1950, Mr 16,31:4
Clarke, Ralph H, 1947, My 16,23:2
Clarke, Ray S, 1948, Ap 2,23:1
Clarke, Reuben C, 1943, My 12,25:4
Clarke, Richard Floyd, 1921, S 17,13:6
Clarke, Richard H, 1942, Ag 19,19:2
Clarke, Richard W Mrs, 1951, F 25,84:7
Clarke, Robert B, 1950, O 30,27:3
Clarke, Robert D, 1938, Ap 14,23:5
Clarke, Robert J, 1962, Ja 7,88:7
Clarke, Robert S, 1941, Ja 29,17:2
Clarke, Rollin M, 1950, S 17,105:2
Clarke, S M, 1931, Jl 27,15:5
Clarke, Samuel F Mrs, 1951, My 12,21:3
Clarke, St John Mrs, 1944, Ap 29,15:4
Clarke, Stanley, 1953, Je 2,29:3
Clarke, Stanley Mrs, 1953, Je 21,84:5
Clarke, Stephen Greely, 1915, Jl 15,9:4
Clarke, Sydney R, 1944, Jl 30,35:4
Clarke, Sylvester Rev, 1904, S 5,5:6
Clarke, T B, 1931, Ja 19,17:3
Clarke, T C, 1901, Je 17,7:4
Clarke, T James, 1952, Jl 22,25:5
Clarke, T Wood, 1959, D 18,29:3
Clarke, Talcott Hunt Maj, 1918, D 6,15:4
Clarke, Theodore Fullinghuysen Rev Dr, 1916, F 15, 11:4
Clarke, Thomas, 1937, Ag 23,19:3
Clarke, Thomas A, 1907, D 9,7:4; 1940, Ja 26,17:1; 1945, Ag 15,19:2
Clarke, Thomas B Jr, 1958, Ja 26,88:4
Clarke, Thomas B Mrs, 1920, N 20,15:4
Clarke, Thomas Cottrell, 1874, D 24,5:2
Clarke, Thomas Curtis Col, 1921, My 26,13:4
Clarke, Thomas F, 1920, Ap 2,15:1
Clarke, Thomas H, 1941, My 8,23:4
Clarke, Thomas H Mrs, 1956, Ag 29,29:4
Clarke, Thomas L Mrs, 1957, Ja 28,23:2
Clarke, Thomas P, 1944, Ag 1,15:5
Clarke, Thomas S, 1943, N 22,19:1
Clarke, Thomas Shields, 1920, N 16,15:4
Clarke, Tom, 1957, Je 19,35:3
Clarke, Tracy L, 1944, S 9,15:5
Clarke, V A, 1932, Ag 12,15:3
Clarke, Victor H, 1953, Mr 20,23:2
Clarke, W H, 1878, Ag 7,1:5
Clarke, W H Crichton, 1942, Ja 3,19:4
Clarke, W M, 1878, N 23,5:3
Clarke, W T, 1883, D 12,4:7
Clarke, Waldo E, 1953, My 18,21:6
Clarke, Walter A D, 1955, Je 2,29:4
Clarke, Walter J, 1946, S 30,25:2
Clarke, Walter J Dr, 1937, Mr 9,23:4
Clarke, Washington B, 1941, Ja 11,17:3
Clarke, Wendell M, 1940, S 26,23:2
Clarke, Wilfred, 1945, Ap 29,37:1
Clarke, William, 1962, My 25,33:4
Clarke, William B, 1946, Jl 7,35:1
Clarke, William B Dr, 1924, Je 9,17:6
Clarke, William C, 1943, F 16,19:2
Clarke, William E, 1938, My 13,19:2
Clarke, William E Sr, 1958, My 27,31:1
Clarke, William F, 1937, Ag 24,21:1
Clarke, William F Mrs, 1942, Ja 27,21:1
Clarke, William H, 1955, Ag 2,23:5
Clarke, William H Mrs, 1946, Ap 5,25:1
Clarke, William J, 1954, D 2,31:5
Clarke, William J (Bill), 1959, Jl 30,27:4
Clarke, William L, 1952, Mr 30,92:5
Clarke, William McQuade, 1923, D 14,21:5
Clarke, William P, 1937, S 2,21:2; 1955, Ag 5,19:3
Clarke, William R, 1948, Jl 23,19:5
Clarke-Smith, James Mrs, 1922, Mr 4,15:4
Clarken, James V, 1938, Ap 19,21:4
Clarken, Joseph A, 1960, D 29,25:4
Clarkin, Franklin, 1960, Je 13,27:1
Clarkin, James J Mrs, 1950, S 6,29:3
Clarkson, A Vallette Rev, 1907, D 12,11:6
Clarkson, Albert J, 1945, Je 5,19:2
Clarkson, Arthur, 1911, F 6,9:5
Clarkson, Banyer Mrs (will, S 26,21:2), 1937, Ag 22, II,7:3
Clarkson, Blandy B, 1954, D 3,27:3
Clarkson, Charles, 1955, F 4,19:5
Clarkson, Charles F, 1959, N 28,21:4
Clarkson, Clermont Livingston, 1914, Ap 12,15:4
Clarkson, David, 1904, Jl 22,7:2
Clarkson, David A, 1952, F 21,27:1
Clarkson, David A Mrs, 1960, Ja 4,29:2
Clarkson, David B, 1923, Je 30,11:4
Clarkson, David H, 1946, Ja 24,21:4
Clarkson, David H Mrs, 1943, Ja 2,11:2
Clarkson, Grosvenor B, 1937, Ja 24,II,8:1
Clarkson, Herbert W, 1962, O 1,31:4
Clarkson, James O, 1951, Jl 19,23:6
Clarkson, James S Gen (funl, Je 2,21:1), 1918, Je 1, 11:4
Clarkson, James S Mrs, 1922, S 15,19:6
Clarkson, Joel O, 1949, Ap 27,27:3
Clarkson, John G, 1909, F 5,7:5
Clarkson, John H, 1943, My 22,13:3
Clarkson, Lloyd, 1960, My 28,21:1
Clarkson, Matthew, 1913, Mr 13,11:5
Clarkson, Percy W, 1962, S 15,25:3
Clarkson, Peter S, 1950, Ag 23,58:8
Clarkson, R A, 1884, Mr 11,2:2
Clarkson, R Hunter Mrs, 1946, My 11,27:3
Clarkson, Ralph, 1942, Ap 7,21:4
Clarkson, Ralph P Mrs, 1950, F 17,23:3
Clarkson, Richard B, 1949, O 2,80:7
Clarkson, Robert G, 1942, D 15,27:2
Clarkson, Robert L Jr, 1966, My 2,37:4
Clarkson, Robert Mrs, 1952, Je 12,33:3
Clarkson, S F, 1883, Ja 9,5:4
Clarkson, Samuel, 1913, S 25,13:4
Clarkson, Sidney A, 1949, D 6,31:3
Clarkson, Stanley, 1961, Ja 23,23:2
Clarkson, Stewart N, 1955, D 20,31:4
Clarkson, Stuart L, 1957, O 27,85:4
Clarkson, Thomas A, 1956, O 31,33:3
Clarkson, Thomas B, 1942, Je 23,19:4
Clarkson, Walter L, 1938, My 13,19:4
Clarkson, William F, 1942, O 24,15:6
Clarkson, William H, 1943, Ap 21,25:2
Clarkson, William M, 1959, My 13,37:4
Clarkson, Wright, 1943, O 18,15:5
Clarry, Edward J, 1937, Ap 22,23:6
Clarry, Reginald, 1945, Ja 18,19:2
Clary, Edward M, 1960, Ag 17,31:1
Clary, Ernest T, 1943, Ap 11,49:2
Clary, Justin R, 1959, My 26,35:2
Clas, Alfred C, 1942, Jl 9,21:5
Clas, Henry W, 1955, S 11,84:6
Clasby, Josephine L, 1952, Mr 5,29:4
Clasen, Howard W, 1949, Ag 14,70:8
Clash, C Henry, 1946, D 10,32:3
Clash, Charles W, 1959, Mr 27,23:2
Clason, Ernest F, 1948, D 23,20:3
Clason, John, 1917, O 11,13:3
Class, George B, 1954, Ag 4,21:1
Class, John L, 1968, My 22,47:1
Class, Paul T, 1942, Mr 9,19:4
Class, T Sherman, 1945, D 19,25:4
Class, William H, 1910, Ja 6,9:4; 1955, F 16,29:4
Classe, Leon, 1945, F 10,11:3
Classen, Stefan M, 1945, D 8,17:1
Classon, Leon C, 1952, Jl 11,17:6
Claster, Harris, 1941, D 9,31:5
Claster, Lester, 1939, N 10,23:5
Clasz, Edward, 1963, Je 9,86:5
Clattenburg, Albert E, 1951, S 4,27:3
Clatworthy, William, 1917, Mr 7,11:4
Claude, Abram, 1959, Jl 8,29:5
Claude, Abram Mrs, 1958, Ag 23,15:6
Claude, Edward P, 1953, Ap 9,27:2
Claude, Georges, 1960, My 24,37:4
Claude, Gordon H, 1940, O 7,17:4
Claude Ramez, Bro, 1956, F 14,29:2
Claude Stephens, Mother, 1946, My 23,21:4
Claudel, Paul (funl plans, F 24,27:5; funl, Mr 1,25:1), 1955, F 23,27:1
Claudet, Mineau Mrs, 1939, Mr 20,17:5
Claudis, Dane H, 1946, My 1,26:2
Claudius, Josephine A, 1940, F 15,20:1
Claudy, Robert B, 1937, S 26,II,8:7
Clauer, Henry S, 1955, Je 13,23:5
Clauge, Fred, 1951, F 28,27:1
Claughton, Edward N, 1955, My 11,31:3
Claughton, P C Rev, 1884, Ag 13,5:6
Claus, Carl, 1944, O 7,13:5
Claus, Erwin P, 1956, S 24,27:5
Claus, Fritz W, 1967, O 17,47:2
Claus, Henry T, 1966, N 19,33:2
Clause, Robert L, 1964, Ap 5,87:1
Clausen, Bergilot, 1953, O 29,31:1
Clausen, Bernard Dr, 1914, S 25,11:3
Clausen, Carl, 1954, D 3,27:1
Clausen, Christian, 1963, D 11,47:2
Clausen, Christian F W, 1964, O 7,47:4
Clausen, Christian M, 1941, F 6,21:4
Clausen, Claus K, 1958, D 25,2:5
Clausen, Fred H, 1944, O 22,45:2
Clausen, Fred N, 1955, Mr 8,27:2
Clausen, Frederick B, 1942, Ag 7,17:4
Clausen, Frederick R, 1967, Ja 31,31:4
Clausen, Fritz, 1947, D 6,2:2
Clausen, George, 1944, N 24,24:3
Clausen, George C, 1917, My 25,11:5
Clausen, George U, 1957, Ap 27,19:5
Clausen, Henry P, 1949, D 21,30:3
Clausen, Holger S, 1947, N 17,21:1
Clausen, Julia, 1941, My 3,15:3
Clausen, Karl E, 1963, S 29,87:2
Clausen, Leon R, 1965, Ag 15,83:2
Clausen, Mads, 1966, Ag 28,93:2
Clausen, Nan G Mrs, 1937, Mr 14,II,8:6
Clausen, Nicolas C, 1940, S 21,19:4
Clausen, Roy E, 1956, Ag 23,27:4
Clausen, Samuel W, 1952, D 30,19:5
Clausen, Walter B, 1955, O 20,36:1
Clauson, Clinton A, 1959, D 31,21:4
Clauson, J Earl, 1937, Je 25,21:3
Clauss, Eugene A, 1949, N 9,27:4
Clauss, George, 1957, D 15,86:3
Clauss, Henry O, 1939, D 3,60:4
Clauss, Theodore, 1949, F 1,25:3
Claussen, Alma V, 1951, My 11,27:5
Claussen, George, 1948, D 21,31:2
Claussen, Matthew B, 1949, S 17,17:1
Claussen, Matthew B Mrs, 1955, N 5,19:4
Clausz, Charles Mrs, 1946, O 29,25:3
Clauzel, C Count, 1951, Ag 14,23:3
Claverie, Jean B, 1944, Ag 22,17:2
Clavering, Thomas, 1953, Ja 25,85:2
Clavey, Elmer I, 1946, D 22,41:2
Clavin, Hugh F, 1944, Mr 1,19:2
Clawan, Harry, 1951, My 26,17:3
Clawson, Aden R Prof, 1925, Ag 18,19:3
Clawson, C Dudley, 1958, Ja 6,39:4
Clawson, Charlotte V Mrs, 1940, Ja 20,15:4
Clawson, Cortez R, 1950, O 31,27:3
Clawson, Don, 1951, D 18,31:1
Clawson, F T Mrs, 1903, Je 28,7:5
Clawson, Frank A, 1949, S 30,23:2
Clawson, Frank L, 1964, Jl 7,35:1
Clawson, Frank T, 1949, Ag 1,17:4
Clawson, John L, 1945, Ja 3,17:4
Clawson, John W, 1964, O 28,45:1
Clawson, Lawrence D, 1937, Jl 20,23:5
Clawson, Marcus L, 1953, Ja 26,19:3
Clawson, Raymond R, 1963, Jl 9,31:4
Clawson, Rudger, 1943, Je 22,19:3
Clawson, Samuel G, 1942, D 18,27:1
Claxton, Allen E, 1966, S 28,50:6
Claxton, Brooke, 1960, Je 14,34:3
Claxton, David, 1952, Je 18,7:2
Claxton, Herbert H, 1954, F 23,27:3
Claxton, James M, 1949, D 11,92:4
Claxton, Kate, 1924, My 6,21:1
Claxton, Kate's mother, 1904, Je 6,9:6
Claxton, Oliver, 1959, O 10,21:2
Claxton, Philander P, 1957, Ja 13,84:8
Claxton, Philander P Mrs, 1955, Jl 18,21:1
Clay, Albert G Mrs, 1955, S 6,25:2
Clay, Albert Tobias, 1925, S 15,25:3
Clay, Alexander Stephens Sen, 1910, N 14,9:3
Clay, Alfred G, 1938, Ag 25,19:4

Clay, Annie L Mrs, 1942, Mr 7,17:5
Clay, Arthur R, 1964, Je 5,31:3
Clay, Arvah E, 1950, D 29,19:4
Clay, Brutus H, 1946, F 19,25:2
Clay, Cassius M Gen, 1903, Jl 23,7:5
Clay, Cassuis Marcellus Gen, 1914, F 14,11:6
Clay, Cecil Gen, 1907, S 24,11:6
Clay, Clifford F, 1959, Jl 28,27:3
Clay, Curtis L, 1945, S 9,18:6; 1952, Mr 7,23:1
Clay, Edward B, 1960, F 9,31:2
Clay, Ezekiel F Col, 1920, Jl 29,9:4
Clay, George C, 1941, Ag 5,19:1
Clay, Grady E, 1946, Jl 12,17:4
Clay, Harriet Mrs, 1947, Ag 7,21:5
Clay, Henry Mrs, 1864, Ap 8,1:2
Clay, J A, 1881, Mr 19,2:7
Clay, James, 1873, S 27,4:7; 1946, My 13,21:2
Clay, James B, 1864, Ja 28,1:5
Clay, John E, 1951, Ja 25,25:2
Clay, Joseph V F, 1958, Ja 24,23:1
Clay, King of Whist, 1873, O 14,1:1
Clay, Laura, 1941, Je 30,17:2
Clay, Mabel, 1937, Je 7,19:4
Clay, Mary F R Mrs, 1939, My 21,III,7:3
Clay, Phil T, 1948, Ja 11,58:4
Clay, Richard, 1959, F 14,21:5
Clay, Theodore, 1870, My 19,2:2
Clay, Thomas A, 1943, Mr 15,13:3
Clay, Thomas Hart, 1871, Mr 23,2:3
Clay, Thomas J, 1939, Ja 17,22:3
Clay, Wallace L, 1961, N 14,36:1
Clay, Wharton, 1952, Ja 4,40:5
Clay, William H, 1941, S 16,23:5
Clay, William Mrs, 1944, Mr 22,19:2
Clay, William R, 1938, Ag 16,19:4; 1967, Ap 24,33:3
Clayberger, Ray P, 1965, N 11,47:3
Clayborn, John H, 1954, Je 18,23:5
Claybourne, John, 1871, Jl 7,1:6
Claybrook, John N, 1949, D 10,17:4
Clayburg, Henry C, 1952, F 25,21:2
Clayburgh, Albert, 1946, My 15,21:4
Clayburgh, Alma (Mrs Alb), 1958, Ag 6,25:3
Clayburgh, Herbert E Mrs, 1941, Jl 28,13:3
Claycomb, Roy S, 1964, Ja 27,23:3
Claydon, Frank J, 1960, F 1,27:5
Claydon, George T, 1952, D 22,25:5
Clayfield, LeRoy, 1968, Ap 6,39:4
Clayland, John M, 1941, N 24,17:2
Claypool, E M (Bert), 1949, Ag 15,17:6
Claypool, Harold K, 1958, Ag 4,21:3
Claypool, James V, 1965, Ap 27,38:1
Claypool, John M, 1945, Je 13,23:5
Claypoole, Edward B, 1952, Ja 17,27:3
Claypoole, J Arthur Sr, 1957, Mr 5,31:1
Claypoole, Walter, 1962, Je 6,41:2
Clayton, Adelaide H, 1961, My 3,37:2
Clayton, Albert R, 1964, Ja 14,31:4
Clayton, Arthur E, 1950, Ap 17,23:2
Clayton, Bertram T Col, 1918, Je 5,11:3
Clayton, Clara C Mrs, 1951, S 24,27:3
Clayton, Clark W, 1952, Ap 22,29:4
Clayton, Delia A, 1953, Je 12,27:1
Clayton, Edward H, 1946, N 19,31:3
Clayton, Edward U, 1963, S 28,19:3
Clayton, Ernest, 1955, D 28,23:3
Clayton, Estelle, 1917, F 13,11:5
Clayton, Ethel, 1966, Je 12,86:5
Clayton, Frank B, 1951, D 2,91:2
Clayton, Frank E, 1941, My 27,23:3
Clayton, Frederick G, 1946, My 26,32:3
Clayton, Frederick W, 1951, Jl 14,13:3
Clayton, G, 1929, S 12,31:5
Clayton, George C, 1945, Ag 1,19:5
Clayton, George M Rev, 1937, S 8,23:1
Clayton, George R, 1948, Ap 1,25:2
Clayton, Graham, 1903, O 6,9:4
Clayton, Harry B, 1959, S 11,27:2
Clayton, Harry H, 1938, N 28,15:4
Clayton, Harry R, 1951, N 17,17:3
Clayton, Hay Battaile Mrs, 1937, F 22,17:5
Clayton, Henry H, 1946, O 28,27:2
Clayton, Herbert M, 1968, N 27,47:3
Clayton, Howard, 1947, Ag 4,17:5
Clayton, Hugh, 1947, S 29,21:4
Clayton, James, 1907, Ja 4,7:6
Clayton, John B, 1955, F 11,23:5
Clayton, John B Mrs, 1958, Ag 8,19:3
Clayton, John E, 1937, Ap 20,26:1
Clayton, Joseph, 1881, S 18,7:1
Clayton, Joseph J, 1958, Ag 22,21:4
Clayton, Joshua, 1940, F 5,18:2
Clayton, Lawrence, 1949, D 5,23:5
Clayton, Lou, 1950, S 13,27:3
Clayton, Martin G Rev, 1937, Ja 31,II,8:6
Clayton, Max, 1945, Jl 4,13:4; 1957, Jl 2,27:4
Clayton, Nathan W, 1949, My 5,27:4
Clayton, Owen D, 1962, Ap 18,39:2
Clayton, P (see also Ap 7), 1877, Ap 13,5:5
Clayton, Powell Gen, 1914, Ag 26,9:5
Clayton, Powell Maj, 1916, D 28,9:5
Clayton, Powell Mrs, 1917, Ja 18,11:3
Clayton, Richard, 1956, My 29,27:2
Clayton, Robert, 1958, Mr 20,29:5
Clayton, Walter F, 1942, My 9,13:5
Clayton, Walter H, 1956, F 16,29:3
Clayton, Walter I, 1959, My 6,39:1
Clayton, Wilbur H, 1957, F 18,27:5
Clayton, William A, 1963, My 10,33:2
Clayton, William B, 1949, S 7,29:3; 1957, Ag 2,19:2
Clayton, William F, 1959, Mr 5,31:1
Clayton, William H, 1961, Ap 29,23:6
Clayton, William L, 1966, F 9,39:1
Clayton, William L Mrs (will, Ja 15,7:4), 1960, Ja 8, 25:1
Claytor, Thomas A, 1941, Je 6,21:4
Cleage, Thomas A, 1922, Jl 6,19:5
Clear, Albert F, 1960, S 26,33:5
Clear, Edward F Jr, 1959, S 10,35:4
Clear, James T, 1953, Je 9,27:3
Clear, William H, 1950, F 11,15:6
Clearfield, J Schneyer, 1947, Jl 8,23:4
Clearwater, Anna H Mrs, 1937, Jl 26,19:5
Clearwater, Byron, 1938, S 15,25:1
Clearwater, Charles, 1947, Ja 26,53:2
Clearwater, Charles K, 1941, Ja 21,21:5
Clearwater, Esther, 1943, O 9,13:4
Clearwater, Helena, 1956, My 17,31:4
Clearwater, J D, 1947, D 23,19:3
Clearwater, R, 1881, D 7,1:3
Clearwater, Thomas H, 1950, My 4,27:3
Clearwater, Walter M, 1947, N 1,15:3
Clearwater, William H, 1948, S 25,17:1
Cleary, Alfred J, 1950, Ap 25,31:4
Cleary, Anna E Mrs, 1941, Ap 4,21:4
Cleary, Charles, 1945, O 1,19:5
Cleary, Cornelius C Mrs, 1950, Je 15,31:3
Cleary, Cornelius J, 1939, My 29,15:4
Cleary, Daniel F, 1953, D 7,2:3
Cleary, David M, 1951, O 4,33:4
Cleary, Edward, 1939, My 25,25:2
Cleary, Edward L, 1940, N 21,30:2
Cleary, Edwin, 1922, Ag 4,15:6
Cleary, F Stafford, 1959, N 6,29:2
Cleary, Francis A, 1964, Jl 19,64:8
Cleary, Francis A Mrs, 1952, Ja 3,46:3
Cleary, Francis X, 1940, D 27,20:2
Cleary, Frank, 1939, Ap 2,1:1
Cleary, Frank J, 1959, Je 25,29:5
Cleary, Frank L, 1959, My 28,31:4; 1960, S 4,68:4
Cleary, George C, 1945, D 7,22:2
Cleary, Harold J, 1956, Jl 15,60:6
Cleary, Harry J, 1949, D 7,31:4
Cleary, Irene F, 1960, O 22,23:5
Cleary, James, 1948, N 16,29:4
Cleary, James C, 1949, F 7,19:5
Cleary, John, 1954, F 11,29:5
Cleary, John A, 1949, S 8,29:4
Cleary, John F, 1954, S 10,23:2
Cleary, John H, 1940, My 9,23:2
Cleary, John J Capt, 1937, S 30,23:2
Cleary, John M, 1953, D 13,86:8
Cleary, John Mitchell, 1920, Ap 23,13:4
Cleary, Martin J, 1958, Ap 5,15:6
Cleary, Mary R Mrs, 1937, Ap 9,21:2
Cleary, Michael H, 1954, Je 16,31:4
Cleary, Michael J, 1947, F 23,54:3; 1951, Ja 13,15:5; 1967, Jl 30,64:2
Cleary, Michael J Mrs, 1947, N 7,23:1
Cleary, Morris, 1951, Ag 9,21:5
Cleary, Owen J (Pat), 1960, S 11,81:1
Cleary, Patrick F, 1954, F 12,25:2
Cleary, Patrick J, 1919, D 27,9:4
Cleary, Patrick R, 1948, N 24,23:3
Cleary, Peter B, 1941, Jl 13,29:2
Cleary, Peter J, 1937, Je 15,23:4
Cleary, Robert, 1924, My 13,21:4
Cleary, Robert Emmet, 1920, Ap 23,13:4
Cleary, Steve, 1938, Je 22,23:3
Cleary, Thomas, 1903, N 4,16:3; 1948, N 4,29:4
Cleary, Thomas E, 1949, Ag 11,24:3
Cleary, Thomas J, 1947, F 26,25:2
Cleary, W E, 1932, D 21,19:1
Cleary, William A, 1965, D 6,37:4
Cleary, William B, 1956, F 19,92:5
Cleary, William D (por), 1949, Ag 7,61:1
Cleary, William J Sr Mrs, 1944, N 8,21:8
Cleary, William S J, 1951, Ja 23,27:1
Cleater, John F, 1961, Jl 1,17:2
Cleaton, Allen, 1958, Je 12,31:5
Cleave, Leopold, 1943, D 12,45:3
Cleaveland, Arthur B, 1951, Ap 18,31:4
Cleaveland, Charles F, 1908, Mr 1,9:6
Cleaveland, E L Rev, 1866, F 19,4:7
Cleaveland, Frank N Mrs, 1951, N 7,29:1
Cleaveland, John L, 1904, F 19,9:6
Cleaveland, John M, 1939, Je 14,23:4
Cleaveland, Livingston W Mrs, 1943, S 24,23:2
Cleaveland, Stuart W, 1967, Ag 16,41:2
Cleaveland, Trumbull William Dr, 1923, Ag 26,26:4
Cleaveland, Winfield M, 1945, Je 26,19:2
Cleaver, A S Mrs, 1939, Ag 17,21:4
Cleaver, Alonzo L, 1953, My 19,29:3
Cleaver, Arthur D, 1951, Je 27,29:6
Cleaver, Arthur H, 1948, My 12,27:1
Cleaver, C Grant Mrs, 1949, O 16,88:2
Cleaver, Clarence G, 1944, D 12,23:4
Cleaver, Cyril K, 1951, My 20,89:1
Cleaver, Elizabeth B Mrs, 1937, Ap 23,21:4
Cleaver, Helen E, 1948, N 17,27:2
Cleaver, Holstein D, 1948, Ap 3,15:2
Cleaver, James D Jr, 1903, D 11,9:5
Cleaver, Louis A, 1944, Jl 12,19:3
Cleaver, Mary Mrs, 1953, Ag 27,25:3
Cleaver, Pauline Mrs, 1952, Jl 7,21:4
Cleaver, Thoburn G Mrs, 1940, Ag 1,21:5
Cleaver, Thoburn G Sr, 1963, D 23,25:2
Cleaver, Thomas L, 1950, S 11,23:6
Cleaver, Thomas P, 1910, Ag 11,7:6
Cleaver, Thomas R, 1965, My 23,85:2
Cleaves, Charles H, 1937, Jl 29,19:5
Cleaves, Daniel Lunt, 1924, Jl 29,15:5
Cleaves, Edwin L, 1955, F 14,16:5
Cleaves, Eugene L, 1958, Je 28,17:4
Cleaves, Eugene L Mrs, 1950, Jl 10,21:5
Cleaves, Henry B Ex-Gov, 1912, Je 12,II,17:5
Cleaves, Howard H Mrs, 1947, Je 10,27:4
Cleaves, Lincoln L, 1940, Ja 22,15:3
Cleaves, Royal S, 1958, Ja 15,29:2
Cleaves, Willis E, 1964, My 14,35:2
Cleavinger, John S, 1954, D 30,17:2
Cleborne, Christopher J, 1909, O 3,13:5
Clee, Charles Jr, 1944, Ap 13,19:6
Clee, F Raymond, 1951, Ap 12,33:4
Clee, Gilbert H, 1968, Jl 29,31:2
Clee, Henry R M, 1950, Ja 2,23:2
Clee, Lester H, 1962, Mr 16,31:1
Cleeland, John S Dr, 1907, D 9,7:5
Cleeland, Roy, 1955, Ap 17,87:2
Cleeland, Samuel J, 1941, D 29,15:6
Cleene, Eugene de, 1943, Mr 15,13:3
Cleeves, Lulu B, 1945, My 2,23:6
Clegg, Atkin, 1950, My 29,17:3
Clegg, Byard L, 1957, N 11,29:4
Clegg, Charles Sir, 1937, Je 27,II,6:7
Clegg, George B Sr, 1946, N 4,25:5
Clegg, Harry J, 1950, Mr 30,29:4
Clegg, James R, 1948, D 28,5:2
Clegg, John B, 1947, Jl 26,13:4; 1962, Ja 23,33:4
Clegg, John W Jr, 1954, Jl 20,19:4
Clegg, Moses Tran, 1918, S 5,11:3
Clegg, Thomas H, 1939, Jl 18,19:3
Cleghorn, Albert E, 1958, Ja 10,23:3
Cleghorn, Guy F, 1938, F 7,15:4
Cleghorn, Sarah N, 1959, Ap 5,86:3
Cleghorn, Sprague, 1956, Jl 13,19:6
Cleghorn, William J, 1937, Ja 20,22:1
Clehane, Catherine Mrs, 1938, Ap 19,17:6
Clein, Elias, 1961, O 14,23:5
Clejan, Deodat, 1966, Je 17,22:7
Cleland, Alex, 1954, Jl 8,23:3
Cleland, Alex J, 1955, Ap 3,86:4
Cleland, Charles, 1941, Ja 20,17:1
Cleland, Charles S, 1944, S 21,19:6
Cleland, Douglas J, 1951, Ja 3,27:4
Cleland, George A, 1945, Jl 12,11:4
Cleland, Lillian, 1952, F 29,23:4
Cleland, Mabel (Mrs K De W Widdemer), 1964, Ag 6,29:4
Cleland, Robert G, 1957, S 5,29:4
Cleland, Thomas M, 1964, N 10,47:1
Cleland, William B. 1946, Jl 20,13:3
Clelland, Norman, 1954, N 7,43:1
Clelland, Robert B, 1945, N 16,19:3
Clem, Dallas W, 1953, F 7,15:5
Clem, Frank, 1952, Ja 3,27:4
Clem, John L Maj Gen, 1937, My 15,19:4
Clemans, Ezra, 1939, S 26,23:4
Clemans, Harold H, 1953, Ap 14,27:2
Clemen, Paul, 1947, Jl 17,19:4
Clemence, Laura E Mrs, 1939, N 27,17:2
Clemence, William B, 1947, Jl 30,21:4
Clemenceau, Georges Mrs, 1923, Mr 17,13:3
Clemenceau, Michel, 1964, Mr 5,33:2
Clemency, Anne E, 1938, Ag 12,17:6
Clemenko, Michael P, 1948, O 24,76:4
Clemens, Alonzo J, 1950, S 24,104:4
Clemens, Arthur, 1907, Ag 25,7:5
Clemens, Cameron, 1909, F 1,9:5
Clemens, Charles I, 1940, Ap 6,17:5
Clemens, Edward, 1956, Je 21,31:4
Clemens, Edward L, 1941, Mr 3,15:5
Clemens, Emanuel, 1955, Je 23,29:4
Clemens, Hans, 1959, Ag 27,27:2
Clemens, Harold S, 1954, Je 18,23:2
Clemens, Hays H, 1942, Ja 29,19:4
Clemens, James B Mrs, 1943, D 3,23:2
Clemens, Jeremiah Ex-Sen, 1865, My 23,5:1
Clemens, Leonard, 1943, My 12,25:3
Clemens, Lilian A, 1944, Je 9,15:3
Clemens, Mazie (Mrs L W Caldwell), 1952, M[illegible] 29:2
Clemens, Orion Mrs, 1904, Ja 16,9:5
Clemens, Richard A, 1961, O 8,87:1
Clemens, S, 1880, Je 3,5:2
Clemens, Samuel L (Mark Twain),(funl), 1910, Ap 25,9:5
Clemens, Samuel M Mrs, 1904, Je 7,7:6
Clemens, Thomas J, 1951, S 19,31:4
Clemens, Walter C, 1964, Jl 4,13:5

Clemenshaw, Charles Lt, 1918, Mr 28,11:5
Clemenson, Edward G, 1943, Ap 19,19:5
Clement, A E, 1943, Ap 3,15:3
Clement, Ada, 1952, Jl 24,27:4
Clement, Agostino, 1938, N 20,39:1
Clement, Arthur W, 1952, N 1,21:2
Clement, Bertha B, 1950, Mr 18,13:4
Clement, C Francis, 1963, D 25,33:2
Clement, C M, 1934, S 10,17:3
Clement, Clay, 1910, F 22,9:4
Clement, E, 1928, F 24,21:3
Clement, Edward Henry, 1920, F 9,9:4
Clement, Emory F Mrs, 1940, F 7,21:1
Clement, Ernest P Dr, 1937, F 3,23:1
Clement, Ernest W, 1941, Mr 12,22:3
Clement, Felix, 1885, F 1,7:3
Clement, Frederic P Mrs, 1950, S 20,31:3
Clement, Frederick, 1951, S 17,21:5
Clement, G Kimball, 1951, Mr 21,33:1
Clement, George A, 1957, My 31,19:3
Clement, George Ansel, 1919, S 14,22:3
Clement, George C Mrs, 1952, D 28,50:5
Clement, George E Mrs, 1958, F 17,23:4
Clement, George H, 1962, Ja 9,47:2
Clement, Henry, 1939, Ja 16,15:1
Clement, Henry Steiner Col, 1921, O 14,17:4
Clement, Henry Steiner Mrs, 1911, Ja 29,11:2
Clement, J B, 1903, Mr 8,25:4
Clement, James E, 1944, Je 27,19:6
Clement, James J, 1960, Ja 10,86:5
Clement, James W Lt, 1904, Jl 29,7:6
Clement, John S, 1956, Ap 24,32:1
Clement, John S Mrs, 1949, D 30,19:3
Clement, Lavinia B, 1950, N 29,33:4
Clement, Lewis H, 1946, Mr 29,23:3
Clement, Lucius R, 1945, Jl 21,11:2
Clement, Lyman E, 1948, Mr 4,25:3
Clement, Martha J, 1959, O 11,86:3
Clement, Martin W (funl plans, S 1,35:4), 1966, Ag 31,43:1
Clement, Martin W (est acctg filed), 1967, Mr 24,7:1
Clement, Martin W Mrs, 1966, My 5,48:1
Clement, Mary L A (will), 1953, D 20,50:5
Clement, Mary Mother (Sister of St Joseph), 1910, S 13,9:6
Clement, Nathaniel E, 1950, Ap 9,84:5
Clement, Norman P, 1951, Ap 27,23:6
Clement, P W, 1927, Ja 10,23:3
Clement, Robert E, 1938, S 2,23:4
Clement, Roger C, 1960, Jl 1,25:3
Clement, Rufus E, 1967, N 8,40:3
Clement, Stephen, 1943, Mr 2,19:4
Clement, Stephen M Mrs, 1943, D 30,17:3
Clement, William T, 1955, O 18,37:1
Clement Eustace, Bro (J P Kelleher), 1964, N 8,89:1
Clement Peter, Bro (A R Lamoureux), 1962, O 29, 29:4
Clemente, Eugene, 1950, O 19,31:3
Clemente, L Gary, 1968, My 14,47:1
Clemente, Pasquale Dr, 1925, My 19,21:3
Clemente, Victor, 1959, Jl 25,36:6
Clementel, E, 1936, D 27,II,6:4
Clementi, Alberto de, 1960, O 28,31:1
Clementi, Anthony J, 1953, O 24,20:7
Clementi, Cecil, 1947, Ap 7,23:3
Clementian, Bro (Peter Muth), 1912, D 3,15:5
Clementian, Bro (E Donahoe), 1959, Mr 6,25:4
Clementian, Bro, 1961, Ag 27,85:1
Clementine of Saxe-Coburg-Gotha Princess, 1907, F 17,9:6
Clementius, Bro, 1944, Ag 25,13:2
Clements, Alice E, 1954, D 13,27:4
Clements, Andrew V, 1964, Ap 15,39:4
Clements, Berthold A, 1949, N 24,31:2
Clements, Buena Mrs, 1946, Ja 28,19:2
Clements, C Runcie, 1960, Je 1,39:3
Clements, Charles A, 1941, D 21,40:8
Clements, Charles F, 1958, F 10,23:4
Clements, Colin, 1948, Ja 30,23:4
Clements, Dudley, 1947, N 5,27:6
Clements, Dudley M, 1950, Jl 26,25:2
Clements, Earll W, 1957, N 28,31:3
Clements, Edward F, 1939, Mr 20,17:5
Clements, Florence D, 1949, Ag 29,17:5
Clements, Frank P, 1959, N 21,23:4
Clements, Frederic E, 1945, Jl 28,11:6
Clements, Gabrielle D, 1948, Mr 28,48:2
Clements, George H, 1947, Ap 30,25:3
Clements, George W, 1951, S 10,21:5
Clements, H Loren Mrs, 1944, Je 24,13:5
Clements, Hall K (Mrs Geo Clements), 1967, Je 10, 33:4
Clements, Howard P, 1938, O 21,23:3
Clements, Isaac W, 1950, Mr 30,29:1
Clements, Jack, 1941, My 25,36:6
Clements, James R, 1942, Je 12,21:1
Clements, John Harry, 1908, Ja 17,9:6
Clements, Judson C, 1917, Je 19,13:5
Clements, Lyman J, 1940, Ap 14,45:3
Clements, Macmillan, 1961, Ag 24,29:6
Clements, Maude H, 1944, N 23,31:3
Clements, Samuel C, 1947, N 18,29:3
Clements, Thomas, 1943, Je 5,15:5
Clements, Victor, 1903, Ap 27,7:5
Clements, William, 1945, Mr 23,19:4
Clements, William Boles, 1909, My 27,9:4
Clementson, George B, 1962, Mr 16,31:1
Clemes, William W, 1957, N 1,23:7
Cleminson, Haldane Mrs, 1909, My 31,7:2
Clemmens, Stanley M, 1961, My 27,23:3
Clemmensen, Erik C, 1941, My 22,21:5
Clemmer, J Frank Mrs, 1940, Ja 14,42:7
Clemmey, Mary, 1884, Ag 19,2:5
Clemmons, Joe R (por), 1949, Ap 4,23:5
Clemons, Joseph, 1949, F 23,27:3
Clemons, Julia, 1948, Mr 4,25:6
Clemow, Frank G, 1939, F 27,15:3
Clemson, George N Mrs, 1943, N 8,19:5
Clench, H C, 1881, Je 21,7:5
Clendenin, Elinor G Mrs, 1966, My 28,27:4
Clendenin, F M, 1930, Ag 20,19:4
Clendenin, Gabrielle G Mrs, 1937, Mr 6,17:4
Clendenin, James B, 1939, Mr 5,49:1
Clendenin, Joseph (por), 1938, D 3,19:3
Clendenin, William W, 1941, N 21,17:2
Clendenin, William W Mrs, 1944, D 20,23:5
Clendenny, Merseles G, 1945, Ap 3,19:3
Clendinning, Katherine (Mrs C H Durkee), 1956, Ag 18,17:6
Clendon, Clara K, 1950, Ja 10,30:2
Cleophas, Gustave E, 1950, My 9,29:3
Clephane, Arthur H Sr, 1961, F 9,31:4
Clephane, James Ogilvie, 1910, D 1,11:5
Clephane, Malcolm Mrs, 1945, Ja 17,21:1
Clephane, Walter C, 1951, Ag 18,11:5
Clerc, Jean, 1952, N 5,27:1
Clerc, Laurent, 1869, Jl 19,1:7
Clergue, Francis H, 1939, Ja 20,19:1
Clerides, John, 1961, Ja 18,33:2
Clerk, George, 1951, Je 20,27:3
Clerk, Ira, 1946, S 30,25:5
Clerk-Jeannotte, Albert, 1945, Jl 23,19:4
Clerkin, Edward A, 1964, Ap 29,41:4
Clerkin, Patrick, 1948, Ag 18,25:4
Clermont, Harriet K Mrs, 1940, Ag 11,30:8
Clesinger, J B A, 1883, Ja 8,5:5
Cless, George R, 1944, D 10,53:1
Cletus, Glackin (Bro), 1960, Ap 13,40:1
Cleveland, A C, 1903, Ag 25,7:6
Cleveland, Anna (Mrs H B James), 1954, Ja 9,15:4
Cleveland, Arthur H, 1940, Mr 28,23:3; 1949, N 6,92:2
Cleveland, Arthur M, 1954, Ja 11,25:1
Cleveland, Benjamin D Capt, 1925, Je 23,19:5
Cleveland, Blair, 1958, Ja 14,30:4
Cleveland, Burr P, 1958, Je 27,25:2
Cleveland, C D, 1869, Ag 20,1:5
Cleveland, Carleton A, 1954, Jl 24,13:6
Cleveland, Charles D, 1944, D 18,19:3
Cleveland, Charles G, 1964, My 17,86:7
Cleveland, Charles L, 1948, Mr 28,48:7
Cleveland, Chester E, 1949, F 3,23:5
Cleveland, Chester W, 1961, O 25,37:3
Cleveland, Clement, 1950, Ap 15,15:5
Cleveland, Donald E H, 1955, O 25,33:1
Cleveland, Dorothy, 1954, S 26,87:2
Cleveland, Douglas S, 1955, Ap 2,17:5
Cleveland, Douglas S Mrs, 1949, F 7,19:2
Cleveland, Duke of, 1864, F 6,8:2
Cleveland, Edward Spicer, 1903, N 30,7:5
Cleveland, Ellen D G Mrs, 1954, F 18,31:2
Cleveland, Eva L, 1955, Ag 18,23:4
Cleveland, Flaude, 1948, N 13,15:4
Cleveland, Frank, 1953, N 6,27:2
Cleveland, Frank A, 1903, D 10,9:5
Cleveland, Frank E, 1950, Ag 1,23:3
Cleveland, Frank W, 1953, Ap 6,19:5
Cleveland, Frederick A, 1946, Ja 28,19:5
Cleveland, Frederick A Mrs, 1925, My 4,19:6; 1956, Ap 9,27:2
Cleveland, Frederick A Prof, 1914, O 16,11:5
Cleveland, George, 1913, Mr 1,15:5; 1957, Jl 16,25:5
Cleveland, Harold F, 1955, Ja 20,31:2
Cleveland, Harry H, 1946, My 25,15:5
Cleveland, Henry D, 1963, S 27,29:2
Cleveland, Horace G, 1957, Mr 30,19:5
Cleveland, Howard, 1948, O 3,64:4
Cleveland, J Albert, 1949, Jl 10,57:2
Cleveland, J F (see also O 10), 1876, O 13,8:4
Cleveland, J G Rev Dr, 1903, Ag 14,7:7
Cleveland, J Wray, 1937, My 16,II,8:4
Cleveland, Jack E, 1953, Ag 30,88:7
Cleveland, James H, 1950, Mr 22,27:2
Cleveland, James Y, 1958, Je 6,23:4
Cleveland, Jeremiah B, 1905, F 11,9:2
Cleveland, John, 1877, D 1,8:2
Cleveland, Joseph W, 1913, D 4,9:6
Cleveland, Lee N, 1953, D 17,37:3
Cleveland, Leslie L, 1953, Ag 22,15:6
Cleveland, Louis F, 1872, N 20,5:4
Cleveland, Louis K Mrs, 1950, Mr 26,96:2
Cleveland, M A, 1912, My 20,9:5
Cleveland, Mabel, 1914, Jl 23,9:2
Cleveland, Malcolm C, 1941, N 2,52:1
Cleveland, Manzies C, 1938, O 11,25:3
Cleveland, Margaret M Mrs, 1942, F 7,17:3
Cleveland, Mather Mrs, 1967, Jl 10,28:4
Cleveland, Newcomb (will, Ag 15,29:6), 1951, Jl 30, 17:5
Cleveland, Newcomb Mrs, 1948, S 28,27:5
Cleveland, Oren, 1883, Jl 11,4:7
Cleveland, Parker Prof, 1858, O 16,5:1
Cleveland, Paul, 1950, My 21,104:3
Cleveland, Paul W, 1952, Jl 19,15:5
Cleveland, Robert B, 1946, S 10,7:4
Cleveland, Rose Elizabeth, 1918, N 27,13:3
Cleveland, Ruth, 1904, Ja 8,7:4
Cleveland, Ruth S, 1948, S 13,21:4
Cleveland, Sanford E, 1948, Ap 30,24:2
Cleveland, W F, 1883, N 17,2:2
Cleveland, W M Rev, 1906, Ja 17,11:6
Cleveland, William C Prof, 1873, Ja 17,5:6
Cleveland, William L, 1943, My 14,19:4
Cleveland, William S, 1923, Ja 1,15:5
Clevenberg, Christian L, 1947, O 23,25:4
Clevenger, Cliff, 1960, D 14,39:2
Clevenger, Cloyd P (cor, Mr 13,34:8), 1964, F 13,31:3
Clevenger, Esta M (Mrs Jas L Clevenger Jr), 1967, Jl 15,25:3
Clevenger, Frank M, 1949, F 20,61:1
Clevenger, Joseph C, 1955, Ja 21,23:2
Clevenger, Russell R, 1960, My 4,45:3
Clevenger, Salen H, 1953, Ag 4,21:5
Cleverdon, Walter S L, 1945, Mr 27,19:4
Cleverley, Abraham B, 1925, F 26,21:4
Cleverley, Ernest L Mrs, 1962, Mr 1,31:5
Cleverley, Frank T, 1952, Ag 19,23:4
Cleverley, William K, 1952, My 4,90:8
Cleverly, H F Capt, 1882, My 22,5:3
Cleverly, Harry, 1968, D 7,47:2
Cleverly, Martha Jane Mrs, 1912, Ap 2,12:5
Cleverly, Merton, 1948, S 20,25:4
Cleverly, Norman W, 1950, Ag 23,29:4
Cleves, C P, 1874, Je 15,4:7
Clew, Louis J, 1954, Ag 6,17:3
Clewell, John H, 1958, F 12,29:3
Clewell, John H Rev Dr, 1922, F 22,15:5
Cleworth, Cecil H, 1953, Mr 24,31:3
Cleworth, Wilfred Mrs, 1950, Ap 19,29:4
Clews, George D, 1940, D 6,23:2
Clews, Henry (funl), 1923, F 2,15:6
Clews, Henry Jr, 1937, Jl 29,19:5
Clews, Henry Jr Mrs, 1959, Ap 16,33:3
Clews, Henry Mrs, 1945, My 20,31:1
Clews, James, 1903, Je 9,9:6
Clews, James Blanchard Mrs, 1919, Ag 16,7:6
Clews, John Henry, 1907, Ap 11,11:5
Clexton, Edward W, 1966, Ag 25,37:1
Clezie, Leonard J, 1950, Mr 25,13:5
Clibborn, John, 1938, N 1,24:4
Cliburn, J M Mrs, 1965, Je 16,44:4
Click, David G Mrs, 1942, Ag 1,11:3
Clickenger, Joseph K, 1941, Ag 28,19:6
Clickner, Stanley E, 1952, Ja 14,19:5
Cliett, Irene P S Mrs, 1962, D 4,41:2
Cliff, H Cooper, 1939, My 3,23:5
Cliff, Laddie, 1937, D 9,25:5
Cliff, Thomas A, 1916, My 18,11:6
Cliffe, A C, 1928, Je 13,27:5
Cliffe, Albert W, 1958, Ja 1,25:3
Cliffe, Alice B Mrs, 1943, Ag 2,15:5
Cliffe, Edward H, 1956, Mr 8,29:5
Cliffe, George W, 1948, Jl 9,19:1
Cliffe, John W, 1944, D 1,24:2
Cliffe, Sydney H, 1955, F 5,15:3
Cliffe, William, 1938, Ja 16,II,9:2
Cliffer, Mauri, 1948, Je 5,15:7
Clifford, Agnes, 1941, O 9,23:3
Clifford, Albert E, 1947, Ag 25,17:5
Clifford, Alex, 1952, Mr 14,23:4
Clifford, Alex K, 1950, Je 10,17:1
Clifford, C R, 1935, Mr 24,34:3
Clifford, Charles C, 1940, Je 9,44:2
Clifford, Charles E J, 1960, Mr 30,37:2
Clifford, Charles L, 1953, Je 11,29:3
Clifford, Charles P, 1946, Je 11,23:4
Clifford, Cornelius C (por), 1938, D 5,23:4
Clifford, E P, 1928, D 18,31:1
Clifford, Edmund L, 1945, N 29,23:3
Clifford, Edward, 1963, Je 15,23:5
Clifford, Edward Mrs, 1956, S 2,56:5
Clifford, Elmer L, 1920, O 20,13:5
Clifford, Eric, 1964, S 10,35:4
Clifford, Eugene, 1941, Ag 3,34:3
Clifford, Frank A Mrs, 1961, S 3,60:3
Clifford, Frank L, 1941, N 6,23:4
Clifford, Fred W, 1941, Ja 1,23:6
Clifford, George, 1941, Ag 31,22:7
Clifford, George B, 1943, Je 19,13:5
Clifford, George H, 1959, F 4,26:1
Clifford, Gordon, 1968, Je 13,47:4
Clifford, Harold L, 1953, Ap 17,25:2
Clifford, Harry E, 1952, Jl 9,27:1
Clifford, Hugh, 1941, D 20,20:4
Clifford, J H, 1876, Ja 3,1:6
Clifford, Jack, 1951, Ag 16,21:2; 1956, N 11,86:8
Clifford, James, 1957, N 14,33:2
Clifford, James J, 1940, O 4,23:1
Clifford, James V, 1947, N 11,27:2
Clifford, John D Jr, 1956, N 19,31:4

Clifford, John D Sr, 1941, Ag 24,35:4
Clifford, John E, 1947, Mr 4,25:3
Clifford, John H, 1950, My 26,23:3
Clifford, John J, 1944, Ag 5,11:6; 1968, My 5,87:1
Clifford, John Jr Mrs, 1956, S 8,17:4
Clifford, John Rev Dr, 1923, N 21,19:3
Clifford, Joseph A, 1965, S 8,47:4
Clifford, Joseph E, 1941, F 10,17:3
Clifford, Leonard C, 1949, Ja 22,13:6
Clifford, Lewis Henry Hugh (Baron of Chudleigh), 1916, Jl 20,11:6
Clifford, Lord, 1943, Jl 9,17:3
Clifford, Michael A, 1949, Ja 25,23:4
Clifford, Michael F, 1943, S 20,21:3
Clifford, Nathan (see also Jl 26), 1881, Jl 28,5:4
Clifford, Nathan Mrs, 1950, Ap 30,102:8
Clifford, Patrick J M, 1952, Ag 13,21:1
Clifford, Phil H, 1942, N 5,25:4
Clifford, Robert A, 1962, Ja 16,33:4
Clifford, Robert C, 1944, Jl 20,19:3
Clifford, Robert H, 1913, N 3,9:6; 1959, My 17,84:7
Clifford, Rosamond, 1944, Ap 21,19:3
Clifford, Thomas E, 1939, Jl 28,17:2
Clifford, W Capt, 1883, F 25,9:3
Clifford, Walter Mrs, 1952, F 24,86:2
Clifford, William, 1942, Mr 18,23:4
Clifford, William H, 1940, Ja 22,15:6
Clift, Denison H, 1961, D 21,27:4
Clift, Edward H, 1916, N 7,11:5
Clift, Fred W Mrs, 1940, Mr 29,21:4
Clift, John W, 1942, Ja 30,20:2
Clift, John W Mrs, 1940, Mr 31,45:2
Clift, Montgomery (funl plans, Jl 25,27:1; funl, Jl 27,39:4), 1966, Jl 24,61:1
Clift, Robert E, 1944, Je 7,19:4
Clift, Robert E Mrs, 1943, S 23,21:2
Clift, William B, 1964, F 26,32:7
Clifton, Ann, 1943, F 19,19:5
Clifton, C, 1928, Je 22,23:3
Clifton, Chalmers D, 1966, Je 21,43:3
Clifton, Chalmers Mrs, 1967, F 12,92:3
Clifton, Charles E, 1958, N 10,29:1
Clifton, Edward C, 1916, Jl 26,11:6
Clifton, Elmer, 1949, O 17,23:5
Clifton, Eva, 1880, D 28,3:3; 1881, Ja 9,5:6
Clifton, Fanny Mrs, 1908, Ag 29,9:4
Clifton, George B, 1955, S 20,31:5
Clifton, Grace G Mrs, 1940, Ja 30,19:2
Clifton, Harry, 1881, Je 18,5:5
Clifton, Harry P, 1940, Mr 27,21:3
Clifton, J T, 1928, Mr 25,II,2:2
Clifton, John T Mrs, 1961, N 22,33:3
Clifton, Joseph C, 1967, D 26,33:1
Clifton, Joseph H, 1951, Ja 21,77:2
Clifton, Marion P, 1917, N 9,13:6
Clifton, Minnie Mrs, 1939, Mr 1,21:5
Clifton, Ray D, 1940, Ap 28,37:2
Clifton, Robert G, 1952, F 14,27:3
Clifton, Robert R, 1943, Ap 4,41:2
Clifton, Sarah L Mrs, 1908, Je 30,7:6
Clifton, Saul T, 1941, S 29,17:4
Clifton, William A, 1941, O 17,23:4
Clifton-Brown, Edward C, 1944, N 4,15:6
Clifton-Smith, Walter E Mrs, 1909, Mr 25,9:4
Cliggett, Patrick H, 1940, My 5,53:1
Clime, Winfield S, 1958, Mr 15,17:5
Climenko, Hyman Dr, 1920, D 17,17:4
Climenko, Leon, 1966, My 30,19:3
Climes, John A, 1945, Mr 2,20:2
Clinch, Alfred D, 1925, Ag 28,13:5
Clinch, Anna Catherine, 1908, Ap 16,9:4
Clinch, C P, 1880, D 17,8:1
Clinch, Douglas W, 1953, F 11,29:5
Clinch, Edward S, 1960, My 31,31:4
Clinch, Edward Sears Justice, 1924, N 25,23:3
Clinch, Edward Sears Mrs, 1924, Ap 10,23:4
Clinch, Edward Whitney, 1924, O 22,21:5
Clinch, Frank A, 1956, D 21,23:3
Clinch, Frank A Mrs, 1955, O 17,27:5
Clinchy, James H Mrs, 1939, F 4,15:2
Clinchy, John A, 1937, Mr 22,23:2
Cline, Albert G, 1954, S 1,27:4
Cline, Alfred, 1948, Ag 6,36:8
Cline, Allen M, 1963, Ag 15,29:5
Cline, Benjamin F Dr, 1937, D 11,19:4
Cline, Charles F, 1944, Je 16,19:6
Cline, Charles S, 1954, Ap 23,27:2
Cline, Edward F, 1961, My 24,41:5
Cline, Elmer C, 1965, Je 6,85:1
Cline, Hugh C, 1939, O 3,23:3
Cline, Isaac M, 1955, Ag 5,19:2
Cline, James R, 1945, F 10,11:5
Cline, John C, 1954, D 13,27:1
Cline, Joseph L, 1955, Ag 13,13:5
Cline, Lucinda Mrs, 1941, D 24,15:5
Cline, M, 1934, Je 12,23:1
Cline, McMillan B, 1950, O 4,10:6
Cline, Phil, 1951, D 11,4:5
Cline, Pierce, 1943, O 26,23:2
Cline, Robert A, 1958, N 21,29:1
Cline, Thomas L, 1954, N 23,35:4
Cline, Wade L, 1949, S 12,21:4
Cline, Walter D, 1960, Je 25,21:6
Cline, Walter G, 1943, My 29,13:5
Cline, Warren W, 1939, Ap 26,23:4
Cline, William H Jr, 1966, F 1,31:1
Cline, Winfield E, 1947, Ap 20,63:2
Clinedinst, Barnett M, 1953, Mr 18,31:4
Clinedinst, Barnett M Mrs, 1957, Ap 13,19:5
Clineman, Harry W, 1946, Mr 15,21:2
Clineman, William F, 1938, Ap 25,15:5
Clines, J Harry, 1965, S 4,21:4
Clines, Thomas G Sr, 1941, Je 21,17:5
Clingaman, Daniel, 1951, F 19,23:2
Clingen, John, 1960, Ap 17,92:6
Clingen, John J, 1942, Jl 7,20:3
Clink, Joseph J, 1953, Ja 5,21:4
Clinkscales, John G, 1942, Ja 2,23:2
Clinkunbroomer, Henry A, 1964, D 12,31:4
Clinkunbroomer, Henry A Mrs, 1961, F 3,25:1
Clinnin, John V, 1955, S 18,86:5
Clinton, Alex F, 1964, Mr 29,60:8
Clinton, Alexander, 1878, F 20,2:4
Clinton, Alexander James, 1910, D 27,9:5
Clinton, Baron (C J R H Forbes-Trefusis), 1957, Jl 7, 60:7
Clinton, Catherine, 1941, Jl 26,15:6
Clinton, Charles A, 1938, Mr 5,17:5
Clinton, Charles D, 1949, Mr 12,17:3; 1952, Ap 22,29:3
Clinton, Charles W Mrs, 1942, N 4,23:3
Clinton, Charles William, 1910, D 2,9:5
Clinton, De Witt, 1937, N 20,17:4
Clinton, De Witt Col, 1873, Ag 18,4:6
Clinton, De Witt Jr, 1953, F 16,21:6
Clinton, E Raymond, 1952, Ap 12,11:4
Clinton, Frank N, 1942, F 21,20:2
Clinton, George E, 1947, Ag 18,17:3
Clinton, George P Dr, 1937, Ag 14,13:2
Clinton, George W Rev Dr, 1921, My 13,15:6
Clinton, Harry E, 1962, Jl 18,29:2
Clinton, Jacob M Mrs, 1962, Je 6,41:3
Clinton, Jacob S, 1938, Ap 27,23:2
Clinton, James J, 1952, O 11,19:2
Clinton, John, 1922, D 29,13:4; 1946, Ap 7,46:5
Clinton, John T, 1952, Je 23,19:4
Clinton, Joseph A, 1952, Ap 1,29:2
Clinton, Lewis, 1939, Ag 13,29:4
Clinton, Marshall, 1943, S 5,28:7
Clinton, Sadie, 1941, D 12,26:2
Clinton, Thomas M Mrs, 1965, Je 19,29:1
Clinton, William J, 1953, O 27,27:4
Clinton, William R, 1939, My 30,17:4
Clinton, 20th Lord, 1904, Mr 31,9:6
Clinton-Baker, Lewis, 1939, D 13,27:5
Clipperton, Ella E, 1947, Mr 8,13:5
Clippinger, Arthur R, 1958, Jl 19,15:6
Clippinger, Charles H, 1937, F 7,II,8:8
Clippinger, David A, 1938, F 23,23:5
Clippinger, H Foster, 1954, My 23,88:7
Clippinger, Walter G, 1948, O 1,26:2
Cliquennoi, Grover A, 1949, Ja 10,25:5
Clisbee, George Mrs, 1957, Ap 17,31:5
Clisby, Charles K, 1946, Je 17,21:4
Clisby, Daisy I Mrs, 1940, Jl 21,29:1
Clisham, John J, 1956, My 12,19:6
Clissold, Edward T, 1943, F 22,17:1
Clithero, Ray O Mrs, 1939, N 18,17:2
Clitherow, Richard, 1947, Je 4,27:3
Clive, Colin, 1937, Je 26,17:3
Clive, Edward E, 1940, Je 7,23:1
Clive, Henry (H C O'Hara), 1960, D 16,33:1
Clive, Mrs, 1873, Jl 30,3:2
Clive, Robert, 1948, My 14,23:1
Cliver, Alvin B, 1965, My 3,33:3
Clivette, Merton Mrs, 1951, Je 23,15:4
Clo, J Harry, 1947, F 24,20:3
Cloak, Frank V C, 1953, O 5,27:6
Cloak, Leston W, 1959, Mr 18,37:4
Cloak, Samuel Dougherty, 1914, Ap 21,11:5
Cloak, Walter R, 1952, S 10,29:4
Cloak, William A, 1946, Ag 13,27:4
Cloake, Thomas R B, 1946, D 31,18:4
Cloarec, Jerome M Msgr, 1920, F 11,11:4
Clock, George A Mrs, 1943, D 29,18:2
Clock, Harry B, 1944, F 15,17:5
Clock, Hermeo, 1938, Ag 23,17:3
Clock, Josephine S Mrs, 1942, Je 10,21:6
Clocke, T Emory, 1950, Ag 16,29:3
Clode, Edward J, 1941, Ap 12,15:3
Clode, Edward J Jr, 1941, Jl 11,15:4
Clode, Edward J Mrs, 1939, My 30,17:4
Clody, Harry W, 1949, S 30,23:4
Cloetingh, Arthur C, 1954, N 28,86:5
Clofine, Morton, 1943, F 21,32:6
Clogg, Hallye, 1965, Jl 6,33:1
Clogher, Alex C, 1964, N 15,87:1
Clohessy, John, 1956, Jl 31,23:1
Clohosey, Addison B, 1958, N 6,37:1
Clohosey, Thomas A, 1951, Ap 17,29:3
Cloke, Allen D Mrs, 1947, S 26,23:3
Cloke, Paul, 1963, S 27,29:2
Cloke, Peter V Jr, 1958, Je 4,33:1
Cloke, Teddy Mrs, 1960, Ja 21,31:1
Cloke, Thomas J Rev, 1921, Ja 1,9:4
Cloke, William, 1909, F 6,9:4
Clokey, Allison A Mrs, 1948, My 21,23:3
Clokey, Joseph W, 1960, S 15,37:4
Clokey, T Gerald, 1949, My 12,31:3
Cloman, Sydney A Lt-Col, 1923, My 14,15:5
Cloman, Sydney Mrs, 1943, O 14,21:5
Clonin, James E, 1925, Ap 7,19:6
Cloonan, Frank A, 1950, S 19,29:4
Cloonan, John J, 1940, Ja 29,15:6; 1959, Ap 17,25:1
Cloonan, John J Mrs, 1939, Je 17,15:6; 1946, Ja 16, 24:2
Clooney, James T Mrs, 1964, Mr 18,41:5
Clooney, Mary E, 1937, D 26,II,7:2
Clooney, William A, 1955, S 26,23:6
Cloos, Wilmot D, 1956, F 7,31:3
Cloots, W H, 1948, O 13,25:4
Clopton, Malvern B, 1947, Ap 22,28:2
Clopton, William H, 1947, Ag 5,23:3
Cloquet, J Baron, 1883, Mr 23,2:4
Cloran, Edward F, 1952, N 11,29:1
Cloran, Frank J, 1954, Ap 20,29:2
Cloran, Gerard B, 1946, Ap 30,21:3
Clos, Jean H, 1959, Ap 29,33:2
Clos, Phil Mrs, 1948, My 28,23:4
Clos, Philip A, 1945, Jl 17,13:6
Close, Alan M, 1958, Ap 24,31:5
Close, Albert, 1951, Je 29,21:3
Close, Bessie L, 1949, S 16,27:4
Close, Charles M, 1945, S 19,25:2
Close, E H, 1924, Ag 8,13:6
Close, Edward B, 1955, F 6,88:1
Close, Elbert L, 1950, S 19,32:3
Close, F, 1882, D 19,5:1
Close, F N B, 1932, Ap 9,15:1
Close, Francis M, 1951, Jl 14,13:4
Close, Frederick P, 1962, Mr 12,31:2
Close, George I Mrs, 1937, Ag 31,23:5
Close, George R, 1958, F 25,27:4
Close, Gilbert F, 1952, O 27,27:5
Close, Harold W, 1959, Ja 3,17:2
Close, Harry B, 1951, N 17,17:5
Close, J Frederick, 1963, Ag 13,31:1
Close, Lewis R, 1957, S 9,25:5
Close, Mary L Mrs, 1942, Ag 9,42:8
Close, O Bell, 1956, Ap 6,25:2
Close, Peter M, 1937, Ap 17,17:4
Close, Ralph W, 1945, Mr 22,23:3
Close, Robert, 1948, Ja 13,25:1
Close, Robert J, 1942, Ja 8,21:6
Close, Samuel W, 1947, Je 4,27:1
Close, Stuart M, 1942, Jl 24,19:4
Close, Upton, 1960, N 15,22:4
Close, Walter H, 1937, Ja 24,II,9:2
Close, Walter H (will), 1938, S 22,20:6
Close, William Brooks, 1923, S 27,7:3
Close, William R, 1941, D 17,27:4
Closs, Elton H, 1961, O 25,37:2
Closs, Henry W, 1954, Ap 30,23:4
Closs, Michael J, 1961, D 2,23:3
Closs, Warren, 1949, Ap 29,23:2
Closset, George, 1955, Mr 14,23:2
Clossey, William F, 1946, N 23,15:2
Clossick Patk M J, 1949, O 27,28:2
Closson, Grace G Mrs, 1942, D 28,20:3
Closson, Hanford H, 1964, Ag 14,27:3
Closson, Henry B, 1958, S 5,27:3
Closson, Henry B Mrs, 1954, Ja 22,27:1
Closson, Henry Whitney Brig-Gen, 1917, Jl 17,9:5
Closson, Robert E, 1944, Jl 6,15:2
Closterhouse, John Mrs, 1945, Ja 5,15:3
Cloth, Milton, 1949, F 17,23:1
Cloth, Morris Mrs, 1945, Ap 8,36:1
Cloth, William, 1946, D 11,31:5
Clother, Beecher S, 1953, My 11,11:6
Clother, Caleb, 1944, D 24,26:3
Clothier, Albert L, 1953, Ap 15,31:4
Clothier, Caroline, 1950, Mr 11,15:3
Clothier, Florence M Mrs, 1938, D 28,21:3
Clothier, Frank, 1944, Mr 15,19:4
Clothier, Isaac H, 1921, Ja 16,22:4
Clothier, Isaac H Jr, 1961, Ap 28,31:1
Clothier, Isaac H 3d, 1961, Ap 30,86:4
Clothier, James J, 1956, Jl 10,31:3
Clothier, Morris L, 1947, S 9,31:1
Clothier, Robert C Mrs, 1966, Je 23,39:3
Clothier, Walter, 1940, Mr 15,23:3
Clothier, William J, 1962, S 6,31:4
Clothier, William J Mrs, 1955, Ag 7,73:1
Clothier, William R, 1946, F 14,25:4
Clothilde, Maria Therese Louise (Princess Cloth[illegible] 1911, Je 26,9:5
Clothilde, Princess (Maria Therese Louise Cloth[illegible] 1911, Je 26,9:5
Clotilde, Mother (Sisters of Divine Providence), 1954, D 4,17:5
Clotworthy, Russel G, 1944, Je 13,19:5
Cloud, Archibald J, 1957, Je 24,23:6
Cloud, Charles H, 1944, O 7,13:5
Cloud, Charles R L, 1949, Ag 26,20:5
Cloud, Daniel T, 1962, Ap 3,39:4
Cloud, Drummond A, 1959, Mr 31,29:2
Cloud, Frank L, 1952, Jl 23,23:4
Cloud, Henry R, 1950, F 12,84:2
Cloud, Kenneth G, 1950, D 1,25:3
Cloudman, Arthur M, 1949, Ag 9,25:2

Cloudman, Harry H, 1950, D 12,33:4
Cloue, Father, 1943, My 25,23:3
Clough, Albert L, 1940, S 22,48:2
Clough, Bradford W, 1958, Je 18,33:1
Clough, Carlton W, 1947, D 29,17:3
Clough, Charles A, 1961, S 11,27:6
Clough, Charles C, 1954, Mr 18,31:4
Clough, Clarence A, 1947, F 25,26:2
Clough, Clayton C Mrs, 1952, O 5,89:2
Clough, David M Ex-Gov, 1924, Ag 29,11:6
Clough, George H, 1948, O 16,15:6
Clough, George R Mrs, 1956, Ja 15,92:1
Clough, George W, 1958, My 17,19:4
Clough, George W Jr Mrs, 1955, Ag 2,23:3
Clough, Harry D, 1942, O 2,25:4
Clough, Homer W, 1957, O 31,31:3
Clough, Irvin M, 1941, Ag 22,15:5
Clough, John E Rev Dr, 1910, N 25,11:6
Clough, John Mrs, 1947, D 5,26:2
Clough, Joshua, 1948, N 15,25:5
Clough, Lewis W, 1951, D 23,22:5
Clough, O Flint, 1950, Je 3,15:4
Clough, Paul W Mrs, 1938, Mr 13,II,9:2
Clough, Raymond S, 1953, Ja 27,25:3
Clough, Robert H, 1945, Ja 20,11:1
Clough, S DeWitt, 1960, F 1,27:5
Clough, Simeon D (est tax appr), 1961, Je 1,27:4
Clough, William P Col, 1916, Ag 18,9:5
Cloughen, John, 1911, D 28,9:5
Clougher, Edward B, 1949, D 11,92:7
Clous, John Walter Brig-Gen, 1908, S 2,7:6
Clouse, Charles W, 1948, O 21,27:1
Clouse, Morris W Dr, 1937, Ag 29,II,7:3
Clouston, Edward Sir, 1912, N 24,II,17:5
Clouston, Thomas R, 1950, N 2,31:1
Clouston, Thomas Smith Sir, 1915, Ap 20,15:5
Clouter, Gilbert C, 1950, Je 25,68:7
Cloutier, Adrian A, 1946, Jl 3,25:3
Cloutier, Joseph F X, 1939, Ap 22,17:4
Clouting, E Sherman, 1947, My 2,21:1
Clouting, Henry, 1954, F 23,27:2
Clouzot, Vera Mme, 1960, D 16,38:4
Clovelly, Cecil, 1965, Ap 27,37:4
Clover, George F, 1919, O 16,17:2
Clover, George F Rev, 1937, Jl 19,16:1
Clover, Harry F, 1949, F 27,68:7
Clover, Lewis P, 1912, F 12,11:5
Clover, Richardson Mrs, 1920, My 18,11:5
Clovis, Glenn M, 1959, My 27,35:3
Clow, Allan B, 1968, Jl 19,35:2
Clow, Andrew G, 1958, Ja 2,29:3
Clow, Anne H Mrs, 1967, My 27,31:5
Clow, Fred E, 1941, Ja 5,44:3
Clow, H Harden, 1940, Ap 30,21:5
Clow, J Beach, 1953, My 6,31:5
Clow, Kent S, 1952, D 15,25:3
Clow, Percival, 1952, Ap 18,25:3
Clow, R F, 1878, Mr 2,5:1
Clow, Stephen, 1941, Je 7,19:4
Clow, William E, 1942, S 15,23:4; 1953, Ag 7,15:8
Clow, William E Jr Mrs, 1939, Je 7,23:1
Cloward, Donald B, 1956, S 19,37:1
Clowes, B Valentine, 1916, Ag 25,7:5
Clowes, Ernest S, 1957, Ja 9,31:5
Clowes, George H A, 1958, Ag 26,29:3
Clowes, George H Mrs, 1967, My 25,42:4
Clowes, John H, 1945, My 20,31:1
Clowes, William Laird, 1905, Ag 15,7:6
Clowry, Patrick A, 1948, Je 29,23:1
Clowry, W H Rev, 1884, Je 13,5:3
Cloyd, Harold R, 1949, Ap 3,77:1
Clubert, Frederick P, 1956, Ja 26,29:4
Clucas, Edward W, 1948, F 16,21:1
Clucas, George F Lady, 1937, N 12,21:3
Clucas, George F Sir, 1937, N 12,21:3
Clucas, Lowell M, 1951, D 23,22:5
Clucas, Ronald D, 1955, My 2,14:4
Clucas, W Frank, 1952, O 4,17:6
Cluck, James C, 1956, Je 15,25:1
Cluck, Thomas C, 1955, Ap 13,29:1
Cluck, William, 1953, Jl 3,19:4
Cluesmann, Leo, 1966, D 30,25:5
Cluett, Albert E, 1949, Ja 5,25:1
Cluett, Albert E Mrs, 1963, Ag 4,80:2
Cluett, E Harold, 1954, F 5,19:1
Cluett, E Harold Mrs, 1943, O 2,13:4
Cluett, Edmund Mrs, 1937, Je 24,25:4
Cluett, George A, 1955, Jl 8,23:3
Cluett, George A Mrs, 1950, S 2,15:3
Cluett, George B, 1912, Je 29,11:3
Cluett, George B Jr, 1939, Ag 10,19:3
Cluett, George B 2d, 1957, My 5,76:8
Cluett, John P, 1965, D 31,21:5
Cluett, Nellie A, 1959, S 5,15:4
Cluett, Robert Jr, 1951, My 16,35:5
Cluett, Robert 3d (Jan 18), 1963, Ap 1,35:3
Cluett, Sanford L, 1968, My 19,86:5
Clufelli, Augusto, 1921, Ja 7,13:5
Cluff, Charles C, 1937, N 15,23:1
Cluff, Edward R, 1954, Ap 26,25:5
Cluff, Walter, 1943, Ap 27,23:3
Cluff, Walter E Mrs, 1957, Ja 8,31:2
Clulow, Frederick S, 1962, Mr 30,33:4
Clum, Charles, 1942, Jl 6,15:4
Clum, Harold D, 1959, Je 4,31:4
Clum, Woodworth, 1946, Ap 11,25:5
Clunan, John J, 1966, Ja 22,29:5
Clune, Brendan, 1952, N 26,23:4
Clune, Charles L, 1941, S 3,23:5
Clune, George H, 1946, D 4,31:2
Clune, John, 1948, F 19,23:2
Clune, Joseph T, 1964, My 29,29:3
Clune, Mary C, 1956, Ag 5,77:2
Clune, Patrick H, 1950, S 21,31:1
Clune, Patrick J, 1947, N 16,76:7
Clune, Timothy, 1938, Jl 3,12:7
Clunet, Edouard, 1922, O 13,17:6
Cluney, John Mrs, 1947, Jl 13,44:1
Clunies-Ross, Ian, 1959, Je 21,93:1
Clurman, Morris J, 1961, O 12,29:5
Clurman, Will N, 1957, My 17,25:3
Cluseret, Gen, 1871, My 31,5:6
Cluseret, Gustave Paul, 1900, Ag 24,2:6
Clustin, Ivan, 1941, N 28,23:4
Clutch, Robert M, 1945, My 6,38:2
Clute, Frank M, 1940, My 1,23:6
Clute, Harry W, 1955, F 11,23:1
Clute, Horace E Mrs, 1937, Ja 5,23:2
Clute, J D, 1879, N 13,3:4
Clute, James M, 1947, F 22,13:3
Clute, James M Mrs, 1948, My 25,27:3; 1949, N 17, 29:3
Clute, James S, 1942, My 7,19:5
Clute, John D, 1879, N 13,3:4
Clute, John G (cor, Jl 3,17:6), 1940, Je 28,19:4
Clute, Katherine, 1948, O 9,19:3
Clute, Richard C Jr, 1953, Ja 22,23:3
Clute, Warren W, 1938, Ap 8,19:6
Clute, William K, 1942, Ap 11,13:2
Clutia, Harry H, 1938, N 25,23:2
Clutter, Raymond Mrs, 1946, D 21,19:4
Clutton, Francis Mrs, 1944, My 9,19:4
Clutton, Fred H, 1946, Je 4,23:3
Clutton, Ralph M, 1941, D 23,21:1
Clutz, Jacob Rev, 1925, S 9,25:5
Clutz, John J, 1966, Jl 22,31:2
Cluverius, Wat T, 1952, O 29,29:3
Cluverius, Wat T Mrs, 1938, Ja 21,19:3
Cluysenaar, Alfred, 1902, N 25,9:5
Cluytens, Andre, 1967, Je 5,43:4
Clyce, Thomas S, 1946, Mr 7,25:5
Clyde, Andy, 1967, My 19,39:1
Clyde, David, 1945, My 18,19:5
Clyde, Francis J Mrs, 1950, D 17,85:1
Clyde, George M Mrs, 1948, O 3,67:2
Clyde, George Sr, 1948, F 11,27:4
Clyde, James T, 1941, O 24,23:4
Clyde, Lord (Sir Colin Campbell), 1863, Ag 30,6:4
Clyde, Lord, 1944, Je 18,36:3
Clyde, Marshall H, 1946, N 19,31:4
Clyde, Melton A, 1875, Ja 25,1:7
Clyde, Samuel D, 1955, N 8,31:2
Clyde, Thomas (will, Mr 17,9:2), 1937, Mr 8,19:4
Clyde, William P, 1923, N 19,15:3
Clydesmuir, Lord (J Colville), 1954, N 2,27:5
Clyma, Walter, 1950, F 22,30:2
Clyman, Joseph H, 1942, F 19,19:5
Clymer, Hiester, 1884, Je 13,1:6
Clymer, John, 1937, My 25,28:2
Clymer, Meredith Dr, 1902, Ap 21,9:4
Clymer, R W, 1879, F 10,3:4
Clymer, Robert L, 1949, Ag 1,17:3
Clymer, Virgil H, 1952, S 6,17:5
Clymin, Irving H, 1964, N 5,45:4
Clyne, Frances, 1944, F 13,42:1
Clynes, John R (por), 1949, O 25,28:2
Clyve, Gunnar S, 1953, D 29,23:2
Cmar, John, 1944, S 30,13:3
Coad, Clifford J, 1945, Jl 19,23:3
Coad, J Francis, 1938, Jl 24,28:7
Coad, Peter A Dr, 1968, Je 12,47:1
Coad, William J, 1943, D 30,18:3
Coady, Charles B, 1953, Ja 28,27:5
Coady, James D, 1940, O 3,25:1
Coady, Michael M, 1959, Jl 29,29:5
Coady, Robert J, 1921, Ja 7,13:5
Coaffee, Cyril, 1945, Jl 4,13:5
Coaker, William, 1938, O 30,40:8
Coakley, Andy (Andrew J), 1963, S 28,19:4
Coakley, Daniel, 1945, Ap 30,19:4
Coakley, Daniel H, 1952, S 20,15:5; 1964, Mr 28,19:6
Coakley, Edward L, 1957, My 26,93:2
Coakley, James C, 1949, Jl 2,15:5
Coakley, James J, 1949, Mr 4,21:4; 1958, S 16,27:3
Coakley, James J Sr Mrs, 1949, Ag 23,24:3
Coakley, John, 1947, Ag 18,17:3
Coakley, John A, 1950, My 20,15:3
Coakley, John J, 1937, F 8,17:3; 1946, N 17,68:3; 1960, Mr 9,33:1
Coakley, John P, 1950, S 19,32:2
Coakley, John T, 1950, D 13,35:1
Coakley, Joseph A, 1951, N 8,29:5
Coakley, Joseph T, 1962, Ap 19,31:1
Coakley, Thomas F, 1949, Jl 2,15:5; 1951, Mr 6,27:4
Coakley, Walter A, 1951, N 18,90:5
Coakley, William R, 1950, Mr 26,96:2
Coale, Griffith B, 1950, Ag 21,19:3
Coale, James J, 1947, S 25,29:2
Coale, S Chase, 1962, My 28,29:6
Coale, W Archer, 1937, Ap 18,II,9:2
Coale, William E, 1955, S 10,17:2
Coalter, Roger G, 1938, Ap 30,15:3
Coan, Francis P, 1938, Ja 12,21:5
Coan, Francis X, 1957, D 20,24:8
Coan, Frederick G, 1943, Mr 24,23:2
Coan, Frederick G Mrs, 1939, Jl 4,13:7
Coan, J J, 1926, Jl 21,19:2
Coan, Luke, 1949, F 26,15:3
Coan, Matthew J, 1966, Je 13,39:3
Coan, Michael J, 1946, Jl 6,15:5
Coan, Philip M, 1968, Ap 23,47:2
Coan, Robert A, 1945, Ap 13,17:4
Coan, Titus, 1883, Ja 4,5:3
Coan, Titus Munson Dr, 1921, My 9,11:4
Coan, William, 1939, Ap 2,III,7:2
Coan, William J, 1943, S 5,28:5
Coane, William J, 1946, Ag 1,23:3
Coaney, Charles F, 1955, Ag 31,25:3
Coaney, George D, 1945, O 18,23:1
Coapman, Wall G, 1956, Mr 7,33:3
Coapman, Walter L, 1950, S 13,27:1
Coar, John F, 1939, Je 28,21:4
Coastas, Charles, 1950, Ap 20,29:4
Coate, Armitt H Mrs, 1938, D 20,25:5
Coates, Albert, 1953, D 12,19:1
Coates, Azael, 1942, Ag 20,19:4
Coates, Charles F, 1957, S 13,44:5
Coates, Charles H, 1953, O 10,17:3
Coates, Crawford, 1944, O 11,21:5
Coates, Edward Fletcher Sir, 1921, Ag 15,13:2
Coates, Edward Hornor, 1921, D 24,11:5
Coates, Edwin Morton Brig-Gen, 1913, S 14,15:7
Coates, Eric, 1957, D 22,41:1
Coates, F E, 1927, Ap 8,23:3
Coates, Foster (funl, N 22,3:4), 1914, N 18,11:6
Coates, Francis Jr, 1948, F 7,15:3
Coates, Frank R (por), 1938, Je 28,19:3
Coates, George C, 1943, Mr 28,24:4
Coates, George M Mrs, 1954, O 30,17:6
Coates, Harry, 1961, My 7,86:5
Coates, Henry T, 1910, Ja 23,II,11:3; 1960, D 8,35:4
Coates, Howard W, 1904, F 12,9:6
Coates, J Lloyd Mrs, 1952, D 7,89:2
Coates, James A, 1952, Ag 23,13:2
Coates, John, 1937, D 16,27:5; 1941, Ag 17,39:2
Coates, John R, 1952, O 20,23:2
Coates, Joseph G, 1943, My 28,22:3
Coates, Joseph S, 1951, S 21,24:3
Coates, Ora B, 1949, My 27,36:6
Coates, Paul, 1968, N 18,47:2
Coates, Robert, 1941, Ja 29,17:4
Coates, Sherman G, 1952, Ag 29,23:3
Coates, Wells W, 1958, Je 19,31:3
Coates, William A, 1955, Ja 7,22:3
Coates, William J Dr, 1916, D 20,13:4
Coates, William M, 1937, My 26,25:1
Coates, William M Mrs, 1952, Mr 25,27:1
Coats, Alfred M, 1942, Jl 22,19:5
Coats, Charles E, 1947, F 6,23:4
Coats, Fred M, 1949, F 5,15:5
Coats, James Sir, 1913, Ja 21,13:6
Coats, Randolph, 1957, Je 23,84:7
Coats, Robert H, 1960, F 9,31:5
Coats, Robert H Mrs, 1938, D 20,25:2
Coats, W H, 1928, Ag 22,21:4
Coats, Willard, 1956, Je 16,19:4
Coats, Wilson P Mrs (Carolyn D), 1965, Jl 11,68:8
Coatsworth, Caleb J Jr, 1939, S 27,25:4
Coatsworth, Emerson, 1943, My 12,25:5
Cobb, Albert A Sr, 1958, Ag 24,86:2
Cobb, Albert W, 1941, My 27,23:3
Cobb, Allen R, 1961, N 28,32:4
Cobb, Andrew G Mrs, 1947, My 17,15:2
Cobb, Andrew L, 1922, Jl 29,7:6
Cobb, Andrew L Jr, 1967, F 11,29:5
Cobb, Andrew L 3d Mrs, 1967, Ap 24,33:4
Cobb, Arthur Jr, 1954, N 15,27:3
Cobb, Arthur Sr, 1951, Mr 4,92:3
Cobb, Beatrice, 1959, S 12,21:2
Cobb, Bernard C, 1957, O 1,33:2
Cobb, C (see also S 18), 1877, S 19,8:3
Cobb, C, 1934, N 29,31:4
Cobb, C L, 1879, My 1,1:2
Cobb, C M, 1944, Jl 19,19:2
Cobb, Candler (funl, My 28,15:6), 1955, My 25,33:1
Cobb, Charles A, 1945, Ap 2,19:3
Cobb, Charles L, 1953, Mr 16,22:5
Cobb, Charles N, 1939, My 9,23:4
Cobb, Clement B P, 1955, Mr 12,19:3
Cobb, Cleveland, 1945, Mr 18,42:4
Cobb, Cyril, 1938, Mr 9,16:4
Cobb, Cyril R, 1950, Je 29,29:2
Cobb, Cyrus, 1903, Ja 30,1:6
Cobb, Darius, 1919, Ap 24,11:4
Cobb, Duane P Mrs, 1957, Ap 19,21:1
Cobb, E M Lt, 1883, O 30,5:3
Cobb, Eben B, 1940, O 16,23:4
Cobb, Eben B Mrs, 1956, Jl 13,19:5
Cobb, Edward B (will, D 1,24:2), 1938, N 25,23:4

Cobb, Edward W, 1954, Je 2,31:3
Cobb, Edwyn H W, 1955, Mr 28,27:4
Cobb, Elisabeth (Mrs E C Rogers), 1959, My 27,35:2
Cobb, F Gordon, 1952, Jl 30,24:7
Cobb, Farrar, 1944, My 30,21:2
Cobb, Francis H, 1949, Ja 10,25:2
Cobb, Frank C, 1953, Mr 9,29:1
Cobb, Frank I Mrs, 1965, F 4,31:4
Cobb, Frank Irving, 1923, D 23,20:4
Cobb, Fred, 1954, Mr 18,31:5
Cobb, Gardner, 1908, Ap 7,9:4
Cobb, George, 1943, Je 18,21:5
Cobb, George A, 1955, Je 18,17:2
Cobb, George H, 1940, N 8,21:3; 1943, Ja 12,24:3
Cobb, George H Mrs, 1938, Mr 13,II,9:2
Cobb, George W, 1916, S 17,19:1; 1945, F 28,23:4
Cobb, George W Jr, 1948, Mr 16,27:3
Cobb, Guy W, 1940, Jl 24,21:3
Cobb, H I, 1931, Mr 28,19:1
Cobb, Harold A, 1947, Mr 31,23:1
Cobb, Harold E, 1951, O 13,17:3
Cobb, Helen A, 1954, My 12,31:4
Cobb, Henry E, 1943, Ag 18,19:2
Cobb, Henry I Mrs, 1944, Ag 2,15:5
Cobb, Henry N Rev, 1910, Ap 18,9:2
Cobb, Herbert C M, 1953, Je 8,29:3
Cobb, Herschel R, 1951, Ap 14,15:1
Cobb, Howard, 1948, N 20,13:4
Cobb, Howell, 1868, O 10,4:7
Cobb, Humphrey, 1944, Ap 26,19:4
Cobb, Humphrey M Mrs, 1960, Ap 3,86:2
Cobb, Irvin S, 1923, Ap 4,17:4
Cobb, Irvin S Mrs, 1967, N 2,47:2
Cobb, J H, 1882, Mr 13,5:2
Cobb, J Storer, 1904, F 19,9:5
Cobb, Jacob Blackwell, 1923, Ap 10,21:3
Cobb, James A, 1958, O 16,37:2
Cobb, James Judge, 1903, Je 5,9:6
Cobb, James S, 1954, My 2,89:2
Cobb, John R, 1952, S 30,1:2; 1967, Mr 25,23:1
Cobb, Joseph S, 1958, O 9,37:4
Cobb, Kate A V Mrs, 1939, Je 30,19:2
Cobb, Kenneth R, 1961, N 29,41:3
Cobb, L H Rev Dr, 1906, F 6,9:6
Cobb, L Henry, 1946, D 27,19:4
Cobb, Lawrence C, 1959, Ag 8,17:5
Cobb, Leigh E Mrs, 1950, Jl 19,31:4
Cobb, Martha W Mrs, 1953, Je 29,21:6
Cobb, Matilda M Mrs, 1937, N 28,II,9:1
Cobb, Murray A Maj, 1937, Jl 27,21:1
Cobb, Murray A Mrs, 1948, D 9,33:4
Cobb, Phil H, 1953, Jl 19,56:6
Cobb, Ralph G, 1947, Ja 15,25:3
Cobb, Ross B, 1940, My 20,17:2
Cobb, Rufus E Jr, 1956, My 27,89:1
Cobb, Samuel, 1880, S 18,3:7
Cobb, Sanford, 1876, My 24,5:6
Cobb, Sanford Ellsworth, 1915, Jl 14,9:6
Cobb, Scribner, 1951, Ag 1,23:5
Cobb, Stanley Dr, 1968, F 26,37:1
Cobb, Stephen A Dr, 1968, D 6,47:1
Cobb, Theodore, 1919, D 31,7:4
Cobb, Tyrus R (trb, Jl 18,21:1; funl, Jl 20,20:3), 1961, Jl 18,1:3
Cobb, Tyrus R Jr, 1952, S 10,29:4
Cobb, Virginia S Mrs, 1939, F 26,39:3
Cobb, W Bruce, 1959, N 13,29:3
Cobb, Willard H, 1959, My 6,40:1; 1967, S 6,44:7
Cobb, William O, 1949, O 19,29:4
Cobb, William T, 1954, Ja 10,87:2
Cobb, William T Ex-Gov, 1937, Jl 25,II,7:1
Cobb, Willis S, 1940, O 6,49:2
Cobb, Zack L, 1951, D 21,27:3
Cobban, George Jr Mrs (D H Hughes), 1960, Jl 2, 17:2
Cobbe, Frances P, 1904, Ap 6,5:2
Cobbett, Alfred R, 1940, D 18,25:3
Cobbett, Frederick B, 1957, F 7,27:6
Cobbett, Louis, 1947, Mr 11,27:3
Cobbett, W, 1878, Ja 13,6:7
Cobbett, Walter W, 1937, Ja 23,18:7
Cobbold, R, 1877, Ja 7,7:2
Cobbs, James Henry, 1906, Ag 13,7:6
Cobbs, James M, 1957, Ja 31,27:2
Cobbs, John L Jr Mrs, 1957, Ja 16,31:4
Cobbs, Novel C, 1938, D 5,23:5
Cobbs, Rudolph Dr, 1968, My 27,47:1
Cobby, Arthur, 1955, N 12,19:1
Cobden, Isabel M Mrs, 1941, S 12,22:2
Cobden, R, 1865, My 14,8:3
Cobden, Richard, 1865, Ap 17,5:1; 1940, S 6,21:6
Cobden-Sanderson, Thomas Doves, 1922, S 20,21:4
Cobe, Andrew J, 1924, D 12,21:3
Cobean, Sam, 1951, Jl 3,15:5
Coberly, Edward D, 1949, Jl 19,29:2
Coberly, William B Jr Mrs, 1948, N 27,17:4
Cobey, Harry, 1953, Mr 5,27:4
Cobey, Louis Mrs, 1950, Mr 23,36:1
Cobham, Gladys M, 1961, O 21,21:6
Cobham, James L, 1939, O 10,23:2
Cobham, Lady, 1937, S 29,23:3
Cobham, Lady (will), 1938, D 1,21:2
Cobham, Viscount (J C Lyttleton), 1949, Ag 1,17:4
Cobin, Peter K Mrs, 1950, Mr 10,51:1
Coble, Charles L, 1959, Ag 2,81:2
Coble, Joe, 1951, S 17,21:3
Coble, Morris S, 1966, Jl 3,34:7
Cobleigh, Annie W Mrs, 1938, O 30,41:2
Cobleigh, N S, 1927, Mr 4,21:4
Coblens, Pauline E Mrs, 1937, Mr 18,25:5
Coblentz, Edmond D, 1959, Ap 17,25:1
Coblentz, Gaston, 1942, Je 19,23:6
Coblentz, Lambert B, 1949, Ja 30,60:7
Coblentz, Lloyd E, 1938, Ag 10,19:2
Coblentz, William E, 1962, S 19,39:1
Coblenz, Adolph, 1949, O 29,15:5
Coblenz, Edward, 1940, Ag 2,15:2
Coblenz, Sigmund Rabbi, 1923, O 14,6:2
Cobley, Harold D, 1962, Ja 5,29:1
Cobo, Albert E, 1957, S 13,23:1
Cobo, Alfredo V, 1941, F 2,44:8
Coborn, Charles, 1945, N 24,19:3
Cobos Batres, Manuel, 1953, Ap 5,76:4
Cobrin, Isadore Mrs, 1951, Jl 11,23:6
Coburn, Aaron C, 1942, D 3,25:6
Coburn, Alonzo, 1902, S 7,7:4
Coburn, Andrew, 1940, S 23,17:3
Coburn, Charles, 1950, Ap 30,77:5
Coburn, Charles (funl plans, S 1,17:2; funl;will, S 3,60:4), 1961, Ag 31,27:1
Coburn, Charles A, 1960, F 18,33:2
Coburn, Charles D Mrs, 1937, Ap 28,23:1
Coburn, Charles H Sr, 1954, Ja 24,85:1
Coburn, Clyde G, 1941, D 4,25:2
Coburn, Elmer R, 1957, Mr 19,37:2
Coburn, Fred R, 1945, D 6,27:4
Coburn, Frederick W, 1953, D 16,35:2
Coburn, George A, 1955, Ja 1,13:5
Coburn, Harry H, 1958, S 26,27:1
Coburn, Howard L, 1918, Je 20,11:5
Coburn, John, 1954, My 22,15:2
Coburn, John A, 1943, Mr 6,13:4
Coburn, John P, 1938, Ag 11,17:4
Coburn, Leroy C, 1951, O 11,37:5
Coburn, Lewis Larned, 1910, O 24,9:6
Coburn, Louise H, 1949, F 8,25:4
Coburn, Nelson F, 1944, S 16,13:4
Coburn, Oscar E, 1953, N 24,29:2
Coburn, Paul N, 1948, My 20,29:3
Coburn, Richard, 1952, O 31,25:1
Coburn, Walter S Mrs, 1953, Ag 23,88:2
Coby, Oliver J Rev, 1937, Je 23,25:2
Coca, Arthur F, 1959, D 13,87:1
Coca, Arthur F Mrs, 1966, My 29,56:3
Cocalis, Soteros D, 1939, Ap 23,III,7:2
Cocanougher, Greenwood O Mrs, 1951, D 23,22:4
Coccia, Aurelia, 1938, O 2,49:2
Cochefert, Armand, 1911, S 7,9:5
Cochel, Wilbur A, 1955, My 3,31:1
Cochems, Edward B, 1953, Ap 10,21:6
Cochenour, Thomas S, 1939, O 8,48:8
Cocheo, Stephen, 1960, S 1,27:1
Cocheo, Thomas, 1959, Je 12,27:3
Cocheu, Henry B, 1958, O 28,35:2
Cocheu, Henry B Mrs, 1938, Ja 13,21:4
Cocheu, Josephine Mrs, 1952, S 7,83:3
Cocheu, Lindsley F, 1965, F 9,37:1
Cochin, Denys Baron, 1922, Ap 12,21:5
Cochise, Indian Chief, 1871, S 19,4:1; 1874, Je 15,1:6
Cochran, A S, 1929, Je 21,25:1
Cochran, Albert E, 1910, O 13,11:4
Cochran, Alex Sr, 1949, N 14,27:5
Cochran, Alexander, 1908, My 1,8:5
Cochran, Arch A, 1941, Mr 26,23:2
Cochran, Arthur W, 1957, S 3,28:5
Cochran, Bernard, 1944, D 4,23:1
Cochran, Bernard J Mrs, 1959, Ag 4,27:2
Cochran, Charles B, 1951, F 1,25:1
Cochran, Charles Tremont, 1906, D 20,9:4
Cochran, Crandel A, 1966, Ag 25,37:3
Cochran, David H Dr, 1909, O 5,9:5
Cochran, Emery Ellsworth Dr, 1968, Jl 9,35:7
Cochran, Emeth T Mrs, 1940, D 22,31:2
Cochran, Frank J, 1960, My 21,23:3
Cochran, Fred, 1951, S 21,24:3
Cochran, G A, 1930, D 6,19:1
Cochran, George, 1912, Ja 26,11:4
Cochran, George C, 1905, Mr 14,9:6
Cochran, George D (will), 1938, Ag 6,14:7
Cochran, George I, 1949, Je 28,27:2
Cochran, Grace H, 1944, Mr 25,15:2
Cochran, Harrington W, 1942, Ap 28,21:3
Cochran, Harry A, 1940, Jl 23,19:5
Cochran, Harry B, 1946, F 9,13:4
Cochran, Helen D Mrs, 1939, S 8,23:3
Cochran, Henry J (will, S 24,68:3), 1952, S 11,31:3
Cochran, Henry J Mrs, 1961, My 21,86:6
Cochran, Howard A, 1949, N 4,27:3
Cochran, James, 1942, N 17,25:3
Cochran, James B Mrs, 1912, S 24,13:5
Cochran, James B Rev, 1921, S 1,15:2
Cochran, James D, 1938, D 22,21:5
Cochran, James Y, 1947, Ag 16,32:2
Cochran, John J, 1947, Mr 7,25:3
Cochran, John J Mrs, 1938, My 31,19:5
Cochran, John Jr, 1947, S 28,60:5
Cochran, John W, 1938, D 18,48:8
Cochran, Joseph W, 1961, Ag 18,21:3
Cochran, Mabel, 1966, My 15,88:8
Cochran, Myron E Mrs, 1956, D 15,25:2
Cochran, N Guy, 1950, S 26,31:1
Cochran, Negley D, 1941, Ap 14,17:5
Cochran, R, 1880, D 16,2:7
Cochran, Richard E, 1937, Ap 16,23:3
Cochran, Richard Ellis, 1919, F 22,9:4
Cochran, Robert Le R (Feb23), 1963, Ap 1,35:3
Cochran, Sadie L Mrs, 1956, Mr 24,19:4
Cochran, Samuel, 1952, D 28,49:1
Cochran, Sen, 1903, Ag 13,3:7
Cochran, Stella S Mrs, 1938, O 21,23:5
Cochran, Steve (Robt A),(more details, Je 28,3:5), 1965, Je 27,64:2
Cochran, T, 1936, O 30,23:1
Cochran, Thomas (will), 1940, Jl 12,13:5
Cochran, Thomas Mrs, 1924, My 23,19:5
Cochran, Thomas P, 1942, D 6,76:3
Cochran, W E, 1927, Ap 28,23:4
Cochran, Welker, 1960, Jl 30,17:4
Cochran, William, 1917, Ja 4,11:4
Cochran, William A, 1944, F 6,42:3
Cochran, William Edgar, 1924, F 8,19:5
Cochran, William F, 1950, Jl 4,17:1
Cochran, William F Jr, 1946, O 19,21:4
Cochran, William H, 1949, F 20,60:6
Cochran, William J, 1925, Ag 2,5:4
Cochran, William S, 1938, Ja 13,21:5
Cochran, Williams, 1944, Ap 26,19:4; 1960, Mr 30,
Cochrane, A, 1878, Mr 11,2:4
Cochrane, A B, 1877, Jl 3,4:6
Cochrane, A De Witt, 1918, O 26,11:2
Cochrane, Aaron V, 1943, S 8,24:2
Cochrane, Alexander, 1919, Ap 11,11:3
Cochrane, Allister, 1954, O 22,27:2
Cochrane, Archibald D, 1958, Ap 18,23:3
Cochrane, Arthur, 1954, Ja 13,31:2
Cochrane, Bert G, 1954, Ap 2,28:5
Cochrane, Charles A (will), 1940, S 7,17:4
Cochrane, Charles E, 1941, Mr 21,21:1
Cochrane, Charles H, 1940, S 17,23:2
Cochrane, Charles P (will), 1940, N 21,31:6
Cochrane, Charles S, 1959, S 6,72:7
Cochrane, David, 1951, Je 26,29:3
Cochrane, David K, 1947, Mr 16,60:6
Cochrane, Douglas, 1941, Ap 15,23:4
Cochrane, Edward L (funl, N 19,39:2), 1959, N 31:1
Cochrane, Edward W, 1954, Ag 9,17:1
Cochrane, Frank, 1916, F 17,11:7
Cochrane, George, 1967, O 9,47:3
Cochrane, George Dr, 1872, N 20,2:2
Cochrane, Gordon S (Mickey), 1962, Je 29,27:2
Cochrane, Harry H, 1946, S 21,15:5
Cochrane, Henry A Sr, 1949, Je 5,94:3
Cochrane, Henry C Mrs, 1952, Ag 6,21:1
Cochrane, Henry Clay Brig-Gen, 1913, Ap 28,11:
Cochrane, Henry D, 1943, Ag 18,19:1
Cochrane, Herbert A, 1960, S 19,31:3
Cochrane, James A, 1947, Ag 10,53:1
Cochrane, James H, 1944, Ag 3,19:2
Cochrane, James K, 1949, Ja 4,19:2
Cochrane, James P, 1961, O 29,88:6
Cochrane, John, 1950, Ja 9,25:5
Cochrane, John C Sr, 1952, My 28,29:5
Cochrane, John F, 1949, Je 9,31:1
Cochrane, John M, 1963, S 11,43:4
Cochrane, John Mrs, 1942, N 13,23:3
Cochrane, John T, 1938, Ja 13,22:2
Cochrane, John W, 1910, Mr 10,9:4
Cochrane, Josephine, 1953, Mr 29,94:4
Cochrane, Lewis, 1937, My 7,25:5
Cochrane, Moses, 1937, S 22,27:3
Cochrane, Phil D, 1958, Ag 10,92:3
Cochrane, Raymond E, 1949, Je 2,28:6
Cochrane, Robert C, 1950, S 3,39:1
Cochrane, Robert J, 1948, O 19,27:3
Cochrane, T T Adm Sir, 1872, O 22,4:7
Cochrane, Thomas J (funl plans, S 19,37:3), 19 S 7,23:2
Cochrane, Thomas L, 1941, N 27,23:5
Cochrane, Thomas Lord, 1860, N 13,5:1
Cochrane, Tom D, 1937, N 10,25:1
Cochrane, William, 1941, Mr 29,15:3
Cochrane, Witt K, 1943, Mr 14,24:7
Cochrun, James L Sr, 1964, D 21,29:1
Cock, Thomas Dr, 1869, Je 18,4:7
Cock, Townsend Daniel, 1913, Je 20,9:4
Cockayne, Charles A, 1949, Mr 1,25:3
Cockayne, William J, 1951, My 17,31:4
Cockburn, Albert E, 1941, Mr 22,15:3
Cockburn, Alexander Sir, 1880, N 22,5:6
Cockburn, Andrew, 1955, Ag 16,49:2
Cockburn, Dugald B S, 1903, D 7,7:3
Cockburn, James, 1883, Ag 15,5:2
Cockburn, James H, 1939, Je 3,15:6
Cockburn, Robert, 1940, N 29,21:1
Cockburn, Samuel C, 1946, Ag 7,27:2
Cockburn, William H, 1938, D 5,23:1
Cockcroft, James, 1911, N 13,9:5
Cocke, Henry T, 1944, S 27,21:3

Cocke, Matty L (por), 1938, Ag 17,19:1
Cocke, Nathaniel C, 1944, Ag 2,15:4
Cocke, Nathaniel C Mrs, 1953, My 16,19:3
Cocke, William H, 1938, Je 11,15:2
Cockefair, Alfred G, 1939, Mr 21,23:3
Cocken, William Y, 1958, N 12,37:5
Cocker, Frederick W, 1952, Mr 1,15:4
Cocker, George B, 1938, N 9,23:3
Cocker, Marjorie B Mrs, 1941, My 3,15:6
Cockeram, Alan, 1957, S 12,31:2
Cockeram, Arthur H, 1950, D 30,13:5
Cockerell, Sydney, 1962, My 2,37:2
Cockerill, George, 1957, Ap 20,17:5
Cockerill, John F, 1942, Je 17,23:6
Cockerill, John F Mrs, 1950, My 2,29:5
Cockerline, Walter H, 1941, F 14,17:4
Cockey, Charles T Jr, 1938, Mr 13,II,9:2
Cockey, Melchior G, 1943, Ag 3,19:3
Cockey, O S, 1915, My 11,15:4
Cockfield, Alan S, 1956, Jl 21,15:5
Cockfield, Henry R, 1942, Ja 8,21:3
Cockill, George Sr, 1937, N 3,23:5
Cocking, Walter, 1950, My 7,80:4
Cocking, Walter D, 1964, Ja 15,31:1
Cockings, Burton A, 1942, S 4,23:5
Cocklin, James T, 1940, Ja 5,4:1
Cockram, W E, 1946, F 23,13:3
Cockran, W Bourke, 1923, Mr 2,15:2
Cockran, W Bourke Mrs, 1945, Ja 8,17:5
Cockrell, Ewing, 1962, Ja 29,25:2
Cockrell, Francis Marion, 1915, D 14,13:5
Cockrell, Fred, 1950, Mr 16,31:3
Cockrell, Irvin, 1951, D 29,11:4
Cockrill, Edgar H Mrs, 1953, My 30,15:5
Cockroft, Grace A, 1961, D 9,27:3
Cockrum, James W, 1937, N 7,II,9:3
Cocks, Arthur W, 1952, Je 8,86:4
Cocks, Charles J, 1958, S 6,17:5
Cocks, Edmund L, 1958, S 20,19:5
Cocks, Frederick S, 1953, My 30,15:4
Cocks, Gilbert T, 1944, S 13,19:2
Cocks, Henry P, 1949, My 28,15:2
Cocks, Howard O, 1949, D 25,26:2
Cocks, Isaac H, 1910, Je 13,7:5
Cocks, Jessie W Mrs, 1938, N 14,19:4
Cocks, John H, 1938, Ja 29,15:3
Cocks, Orrin G, 1962, O 23,37:5
Cocks, Rowland E, 1952, Ag 4,15:4
Cocks, Rowland E Mrs, 1941, Ap 23,21:6
Cocks, W Burling, 1913, My 22,11:4
Cocks, W W, 1932, My 25,19:1
Cocks, William H, 1948, D 14,29:3
Cockshutt, Henry, 1944, N 27,23:6
Cockshutt, William F, 1939, N 23,27:3
Cocoris, John M, 1944, Ap 10,19:4
Cocozza, Alfred A (M Lanza),(funl plans, O 9,29:3), 1959, O 8,39:1
Cocozza, Joseph H, 1950, N 27,25:3
Cocozza, Michael A, 1941, D 27,19:1
Cocroft, Reginald B, 1958, Ja 11,17:6
Cocroft, Samuel, 1925, Ap 15,19:4
Cocroft, Thoda, 1943, Ag 10,19:2
Cocteau, Jean (funeral, O 17,32:5), 1963, O 12,1:3
Cocu, Adolphe, 1949, Ja 30,60:8
Codding, Edwin H Mrs, 1949, D 29,25:3
Codding, George M, 1964, S 24,41:2
Codding, James H, 1919, S 14,22:3
odding, Katherine D Mrs, 1941, Je 26,23:4
odding, Laurence W, 1957, My 2,31:3
odding, William A, 1965, N 24,39:3
oddington, Alpheus Mrs, 1943, Jl 19,15:5
oddington, C C, 1928, D 4,31:5
oddington, Charles E, 1907, Ag 25,7:5
oddington, D S, 1865, S 4,5:1
oddington, Dave H, 1956, Je 27,31:1
oddington, David H Mrs, 1922, O 14,13:5
oddington, Dewey, 1949, Ap 27,27:3
oddington, Edward G, 1951, F 3,15:4
oddington, Edwin D, 1943, D 27,19:4
oddington, Edwin D Mrs, 1959, Ja 3,17:4
oddington, Henry K Mrs, 1949, F 27,69:1
oddington, James I, 1960, Ap 30,23:7
oddington, Jefferson, 1876, Ag 4,4:7
oddington, Jesse C, 1951, Ag 14,23:3
oddington, Lyman B, 1953, D 12,19:4
oddington, Martin D Mrs, 1946, Je 18,25:4
oddington, Mary I Mrs, 1945, Mr 29,23:3
oddington, Paul, 1951, F 10,30:2
oddington, Seeley C, 1948, D 7,31:4
oddington, William A, 1945, D 31,17:4
ode, Harold M, 1941, My 15,23:2
ode, John M, 1959, D 10,39:4
ode, William E, 1945, O 31,23:5; 1957, F 28,27:2
odee, Ann (Mrs F Orth), 1961, My 22,31:4
odella, Pasquale, 1941, F 18,23:1
odella, Vincent, 1948, S 18,17:3
oder, Fred C, 1947, Ap 5,19:5
odere, Napoleon, 1955, D 10,21:2
odet, Alex C, 1940, S 24,23:5
odey, Frank J, 1953, S 25,21:2
odling, Ursula W Mrs, 1950, Mr 7,27:5
odling, William, 1947, Mr 29,15:6
odling, Wilson C, 1955, Jl 19,27:2

Codman, Alfred, 1944, F 7,15:5
Codman, Charles A, 1911, F 4,13:4
Codman, Charles A E, 1952, S 2,23:6
Codman, Charles R, 1956, Ag 26,84:7
Codman, Charles R Jr, 1946, Ag 30,17:4
Codman, Ernest A, 1940, N 25,17:2
Codman, James M, 1925, O 10,15:6
Codman, John T Dr, 1907, D 17,9:5
Codman, Robert Bp, 1915, O 8,11:6
Codman, Russell S, 1941, My 17,15:2
Codman, Russell S Mrs, 1962, Mr 22,35:2
Codman, Stephen Mrs, 1945, D 29,13:2
Codner, Maurice, 1958, Mr 11,29:3
Codner, W Valentine Mrs, 1947, F 16,57:1
Codori, John M, 1947, My 15,26:3
Codos, Paul, 1960, Ja 31,93:1
Codreanu, Ion Z, 1941, N 22,19:1
Codrington, Alfred E, 1945, S 14,23:1
Codrington, George W, 1961, Ap 27,21:4
Codrington, Herbert R, 1952, Mr 25,27:3
Codrington, W J Gen Sir, 1884, Ag 9,4:7
Codwise, George W, 1952, Ag 19,23:3
Codwise, Henry R, 1946, Mr 9,13:1
Cody, Alton J, 1947, Jl 27,44:5
Cody, Arta, 1904, F 2,9:6
Cody, Bessie, 1960, Ja 6,35:4
Cody, Edward J, 1953, My 17,88:2
Cody, Ellen (Sister Mary Malachy), 1951, D 26,25:5
Cody, Ernest J, 1946, N 1,23:3
Cody, Ethel Mrs, 1957, N 23,19:6
Cody, Francis M, 1959, Jl 28,27:3
Cody, Frank, 1946, Ap 9,27:5
Cody, Frank D, 1948, O 24,76:3
Cody, Frank M, 1937, Ap 9,21:2
Cody, Guy B, 1954, F 20,17:4
Cody, H A, 1948, F 11,27:1
Cody, Helen, 1921, Jl 24,22:3
Cody, Henry J, 1951, Ap 28,15:3
Cody, Jack, 1963, Ap 13,19:5
Cody, James J, 1922, F 23,15:5; 1952, Ja 8,27:3
Cody, John C, 1963, D 6,36:1
Cody, John J, 1965, My 20,43:3
Cody, John K I, 1944, O 10,23:5
Cody, John P, 1959, F 22,89:1
Cody, Josh, 1961, Je 19,27:2
Cody, L, 1934, Je 1,23:1
Cody, Leila M Mrs, 1939, F 7,20:2
Cody, Leon C, 1943, O 6,23:5
Cody, Margaret A, 1949, D 6,31:4
Cody, Mary A, 1946, My 5,46:4
Cody, Maurice E, 1951, D 22,15:3
Cody, Maxwell B, 1957, F 25,25:5
Cody, Michael J, 1950, Ja 9,25:4
Cody, Morrill S Mrs, 1957, N 7,35:2
Cody, Morris J, 1916, Je 15,11:6
Cody, Nellie, 1958, Je 21,19:5
Cody, Patrick, 1920, Jl 12,9:4
Cody, Sherwin, 1959, Ap 6,27:3
Cody, Sidney E, 1954, N 21,87:2
Cody, Vivian, 1961, O 4,45:1
Cody, William F Col (funl, Je 15,9:4), 1917, Ja 11, 15:3
Cody, William Frederick Mrs, 1921, O 22,13:6
Cody, William J, 1959, Jl 26,68:4
Cody (Bro Alf), 1962, S 9,84:2
Codyer, Henry, 1951, Je 27,29:5
Coe, Aaron Mrs, 1904, S 27,9:5
Coe, Andrew, 1952, My 17,19:4
Coe, Augustus V R, 1941, N 21,17:4
Coe, C A, 1883, O 13,4:6
Coe, Charles F (funl plans, D 31,13:4), 1956, D 29, 15:3
Coe, Charles H, 1938, My 9,17:5
Coe, Charles W, 1945, Ag 20,19:4
Coe, Colles J, 1961, Ag 5,17:2
Coe, E Holloway, 1939, My 24,23:4
Coe, Edward Benton Rev Dr, 1914, Mr 20,11:4
Coe, Edward Prince, 1917, F 10,9:4
Coe, Edwin M, 1942, D 22,25:3
Coe, Edwin M Mrs, 1940, Ag 28,19:2
Coe, Ella S, 1944, S 24,46:2
Coe, Ernest F, 1951, Ja 2,23:1
Coe, Eugene W, 1941, S 19,23:2
Coe, Eva J Mrs, 1941, Mr 22,15:6
Coe, Frank E, 1924, My 29,19:5
Coe, Frank G, 1937, F 22,17:3
Coe, Frank S, 1942, Je 30,21:5
Coe, Frank S Mrs, 1941, S 8,15:3
Coe, Franklin, 1940, F 21,19:5
Coe, Franklin E Mrs, 1950, S 23,17:2
Coe, Fred J, 1951, D 8,11:5
Coe, G S, 1896, My 4,8:1
Coe, George A, 1951, N 10,17:3
Coe, George W, 1941, N 14,23:3
Coe, H C Mrs, 1936, O 16,25:3
Coe, Harold E, 1938, Je 18,15:6
Coe, Henry C, 1940, Ap 22,17:3
Coe, Henry E, 1954, Ja 13,31:2
Coe, Herbert W, 1957, Ja 26,19:3
Coe, Jack, 1956, D 17,31:3
Coe, James D, 1947, F 15,15:2
Coe, James H, 1938, S 14,23:6
Coe, Jessie L, 1942, D 20,44:7

Coe, John A, 1948, Ag 5,21:4
Coe, John A Sr Mrs, 1956, Ap 17,31:1
Coe, John P, 1961, Je 25,77:2
Coe, John P Mrs, 1959, Jl 13,27:5
Coe, Kersey F, 1954, D 21,27:3
Coe, Levi E, 1903, N 3,7:6
Coe, Louis S, 1939, O 27,23:6
Coe, Nathan, 1943, D 7,27:3
Coe, Norman L, 1913, F 10,11:4
Coe, R E, 1872, N 16,1:6
Coe, Richard S, 1961, Mr 2,27:2
Coe, Robert L, 1965, F 7,92:2
Coe, Roland R, 1954, F 22,19:2
Coe, Sage, 1945, F 17,13:5
Coe, Samuel J T, 1947, Ag 13,23:3
Coe, Samuel J T Mrs, 1958, D 4,39:3
Coe, Sayers, 1945, My 20,32:5
Coe, Sherman Page, 1925, Ja 3,13:5
Coe, Sidney, 1945, F 25,37:2
Coe, Theodore I, 1960, N 13,88:4
Coe, Walter E Mrs, 1950, Ag 5,15:3
Coe, Wesley R, 1960, S 23,29:5
Coe, William E, 1956, N 13,37:1
Coe, William O, 1960, Je 29,33:5
Coe, William R, 1955, Mr 16,33:1
Coe, William R Mrs, 1924, D 30,17:6; 1960, O 13,37:1
Coe, William Rogers Mrs, 1924, D 31,13:5
Coe, William V, 1941, O 22,23:4
Coe-Kells, Eleanor Mrs, 1958, D 11,13:5
Coefield, John, 1940, F 9,19:3
Coello, Augusto G, 1941, S 10,23:4
Coelos, Roger M, 1956, N 15,35:1
Coen, Arthur F, 1968, F 2,35:4
Coen, Ida R Mrs, 1948, Ja 24,15:4
Coen, John F, 1958, S 25,33:3
Coen, John J, 1943, F 23,21:5
Coene, Edgar R, 1959, My 11,27:4
Coene, Edgar T Mrs, 1953, Ag 1,11:6
Coene, Emile Sr, 1950, S 25,23:2
Coenen, Frank, 1958, F 8,19:5
Coenen, Joseph P, 1958, S 11,33:2
Coenen, Wilhelm, 1924, Je 3,17:3
Coerne, Louis Adolphe Prof, 1922, S 12,21:6
Coerr, Charles T Rev, 1922, Je 2,17:6
Coerr, J Morris, 1945, O 18,23:2
Coes, Harold V, 1958, D 5,32:1
Coester, Charles F Mrs, 1950, D 28,25:2
Coester, Emil H, 1968, Ap 3,51:1
Coester, William F, 1949, S 18,95:3
Coetiogon, Rene de Countess, 1922, Jl 20,17:3
Coey, J Smiley, 1942, Ja 17,17:2
Cofer, Leland E Mrs (will, Je 1,25:4), 1956, My 23, 31:5
Coffee, Andrew, 1944, Ag 25,13:2
Coffee, Ercy Mrs, 1954, F 13,13:4
Coffee, J Walter, 1968, Mr 13,53:1
Coffee, John F, 1949, Mr 8,25:2
Coffee, Rudolph I, 1955, My 12,29:4
Coffeen, Frank H, 1957, My 14,35:4
Coffeen, Nettie E, 1938, Ap 12,23:5
Coffenberg, Peter, 1944, My 13,19:3
Coffer, Leland E, 1948, F 18,27:4
Coffer, Rooney, 1965, Ag 10,29:3
Coffey, Albert J, 1958, S 14,84:2
Coffey, Barton H, 1937, My 16,II,8:7
Coffey, Charles J, 1954, Ag 29,89:3
Coffey, Christopher J, 1950, N 23,35:2
Coffey, Christopher J Mrs, 1944, My 22,19:6
Coffey, Denis J, 1945, Ap 5,23:4
Coffey, Francis V, 1947, S 13,11:4
Coffey, George R, 1948, Ap 27,25:3
Coffey, George W, 1950, Jl 6,27:6
Coffey, Gerald P, 1950, Ag 18,21:5
Coffey, Jack (Jno F), 1966, F 15,39:3
Coffey, James H, 1964, Mr 20,33:2
Coffey, James J, 1947, D 20,17:3
Coffey, James R, 1950, Ap 1,15:3
Coffey, James V, 1937, Ap 25,II,8:3
Coffey, Jim, 1959, D 23,27:3
Coffey, John, 1944, Mr 26,42:1
Coffey, John A, 1944, Ag 5,11:6; 1945, Ap 2,19:5
Coffey, John A Mrs, 1943, Ag 1,39:2
Coffey, John J, 1948, F 13,21:1; 1964, Je 24,37:2
Coffey, John J P, 1949, Mr 14,19:4
Coffey, John T, 1941, S 19,23:1
Coffey, John W, 1951, Mr 10,4:8
Coffey, Joseph M, 1947, Mr 4,25:5
Coffey, Katherine, 1952, O 17,27:2
Coffey, Margaret, 1955, My 13,25:4
Coffey, Michael J, 1907, Mr 23,9:5
Coffey, Michael J (funl, Mr 26,9:4), 1907, Mr 24,9:5
Coffey, Michael J, 1957, Je 7,23:2
Coffey, Patrick, 1945, N 17,17:6
Coffey, Patrick J, 1947, F 28,23:5
Coffey, Phil G, 1954, N 23,33:1
Coffey, Raymond, 1954, Ag 15,85:2
Coffey, Reuben B, 1959, F 22,88:4
Coffey, Robert A, 1951, D 26,25:4
Coffey, Robert J, 1939, N 3,21:4
Coffey, Robert L Jr, 1949, Ap 21,50:6
Coffey, Samuel, 1963, D 14,27:4
Coffey, T J, 1922, D 23,13:6
Coffey, Vincent, 1937, O 6,25:5

Coffey, Vincent J, 1941, Je 15,36:6
Coffey, Walter B, 1944, Mr 27,19:4
Coffey, Walter C, 1956, F 2,25:1
Coffey, William, 1951, D 10,29:2
Coffey, William S, 1958, D 27,2:8
Coffey, William S Mrs, 1954, Mr 21,89:1
Coffey, William Samuel Rev (funl, Ja 25,9:4), 1909, Ja 22,7:5
Coffin, Albert R, 1945, D 14,27:3
Coffin, Alfred R, 1962, Ap 23,29:4
Coffin, Anna D Mrs, 1940, S 4,23:2
Coffin, Arlyn W, 1947, Mr 15,13:4
Coffin, C A, 1926, Jl 15,23:3
Coffin, C H, 1935, D 9,21:4
Coffin, C W Floyd Mrs, 1944, My 2,19:2
Coffin, Caleb, 1953, Ja 16,24:4
Coffin, Charles F Jr, 1954, Je 18,23:2
Coffin, Charles H, 1916, F 25,11:4
Coffin, Charles H (funl, Ja 17,13:2), 1918, Ja 15,13:2
Coffin, Charles L, 1957, My 31,19:5
Coffin, Charles M, 1956, Jl 23,23:4
Coffin, Charles P, 1940, O 15,23:3
Coffin, D, 1940, N 22,23:5
Coffin, Daniel M, 1943, Mr 23,19:1
Coffin, Dexter D, 1966, Ag 19,33:6
Coffin, Dexter D Sr Mrs, 1963, Ag 20,33:4
Coffin, E, 1884, D 23,5:3
Coffin, Edward Russell, 1907, S 3,9:6
Coffin, Edwin F, 1946, D 25,29:4
Coffin, Eugene Maj, 1907, Jl 24,7:6
Coffin, Fielder J, 1948, Je 3,25:3
Coffin, Fletcher B, 1944, Mr 27,19:6
Coffin, Francis H, 1955, N 15,29:3
Coffin, Francis J H, 1953, Jl 4,11:4
Coffin, George, 1941, Jl 13,29:2
Coffin, George A, 1947, Jl 3,21:3
Coffin, George Albert Capt, 1922, F 4,13:4
Coffin, George F Sr, 1937, O 26,23:4
Coffin, George H, 1946, Je 25,21:5
Coffin, George L Mrs, 1948, D 28,21:1
Coffin, H E Mrs, 1932, F 27,17:2
Coffin, Harold P, 1951, Je 17,86:3
Coffin, Harriet D Mrs, 1939, N 25,17:3
Coffin, Henry S, 1954, N 26,29:1
Coffin, Henry W, 1940, F 20,21:3
Coffin, Herbert H, 1955, D 19,27:2
Coffin, Herbert L Mrs, 1960, F 14,84:1
Coffin, Herbert R, 1958, Ag 30,15:6
Coffin, Howard, 1937, N 24,23:5
Coffin, Howard A Mrs, 1959, Ag 19,30:1
Coffin, Jacob M, 1941, Ap 19,15:2
Coffin, James Henry, 1873, F 7,8:6
Coffin, James P, 1948, F 2,19:4
Coffin, Joel S Jr, 1941, Ag 9,15:5
Coffin, John D, 1961, Je 1,35:1
Coffin, John G, 1923, Ag 2,15:6
Coffin, John R, 1956, N 17,21:4
Coffin, John W, 1952, My 27,27:5
Coffin, Kenneth Ford, 1968, O 23,47:3
Coffin, L, 1877, S 17,4:7
Coffin, Leland V, 1956, O 4,33:5
Coffin, Lester W, 1952, Ag 30,13:4
Coffin, Lonnie A, 1959, Ap 29,33:3
Coffin, Marian C, 1957, F 4,19:3
Coffin, Nelson Perley, 1923, Mr 8,17:4
Coffin, O Vincent Ex-Gov, 1921, Ja 4,13:3
Coffin, Oscar J, 1956, O 31,33:4
Coffin, Otis L, 1944, N 30,23:6
Coffin, Phil L, 1941, D 13,21:5
Coffin, Phil O, 1957, My 18,19:3
Coffin, Philip L, 1947, S 24,23:5
Coffin, Ralston H Mrs, 1952, Mr 15,13:6
Coffin, Ralston Roberts, 1909, S 6,7:6
Coffin, Reuben G, 1951, My 16,35:3
Coffin, Robert P T, 1955, Ja 21,1:2
Coffin, Samuel B, 1955, Ag 11,21:2
Coffin, Seward V, 1949, O 30,86:2
Coffin, T C, 1934, Je 9,15:2
Coffin, Thomas R, 1940, Ja 13,15:4
Coffin, Tristram, 1924, Ja 31,15:4
Coffin, W, 1927, F 15,5:6
Coffin, W Floyd, 1968, Ag 3,25:3
Coffin, W Gregory, 1966, Ja 29,27:2
Coffin, W H, 1955, O 30,88:4
Coffin, W J, 1877, S 9,12:4
Coffin, W S, 1933, D 17,1:5
Coffin, Willets, 1953, Ja 18,93:2
Coffin, William Anderson, 1925, O 27,23:4
Coffin, William C, 1944, D 5,23:4
Coffin, William Edwin, 1953, Ag 15,15:6
Coffin, William H Col, 1912, Ag 3,7:4
Coffin, William Mrs, 1956, O 29,29:4
Coffin, William S (will), 1937, Je 11,2:6
Coffin, William T, 1961, D 11,31:5
Coffin, Winthrop, 1938, D 6,23:5
Coffman, Eugene, 1942, D 11,23:2
Coffman, George R, 1958, Ja 28,27:5
Coffman, Hal, 1958, S 1,13:4
Coffman, Lotus D (por), 1938, S 23,27:5
Coffman, Nellie Mrs, 1950, Je 11,92:2
Coffman, Willie, 1869, F 16,8:4
Coffrain, Edward V B, 1947, D 7,76:4
Coffroth, James W (will, F 11,22:1), 1943, F 7,49:1
Coffroth, James W Prof, 1872, O 18,1:7
Coffyn, Frank, 1960, D 11,88:6
Cofield, Robert B, 1950, Jl 16,68:6
Cofino, Pedro G, 1953, F 11,29:6
Cofner, William B, 1946, F 26,26:2
Cogan, Alma, 1966, O 27,47:1
Cogan, Arthur W, 1941, N 4,26:3
Cogan, Bernard S, 1953, Jl 9,25:5
Cogan, Charles A, 1951, Ap 23,25:2
Cogan, Claire I (Sister Mary de Paul), 1953, N 19, 31:5
Cogan, Constance, 1955, Je 28,27:4
Cogan, Denis, 1950, Jl 19,31:2
Cogan, Francis C, 1914, D 19,13:4
Cogan, Henry, 1950, Jl 18,29:4
Cogan, Henry M, 1947, My 11,60:3
Cogan, James A, 1946, Ap 26,21:2
Cogan, John F, 1938, D 26,24:4
Cogan, John J Sr, 1957, Mr 4,27:2
Cogan, Joseph M, 1938, Ap 12,23:4
Cogan, Joseph M Mrs, 1958, Jl 5,17:4
Cogan, M Stanley, 1965, N 14,89:1
Cogan, Richard, 1939, My 4,23:1
Cogan, Samuel, 1963, S 11,43:5
Cogan, Thomas E, 1951, F 18,76:4
Cogan, William B, 1963, My 16,35:2
Cogan, William F, 1945, F 5,15:4
Cogan, William J, 1959, Jl 14,29:4
Cogan, William M, 1958, Mr 2,89:2
Cogan, William N, 1943, O 6,23:6
Cogan, William P Mrs, 1948, N 23,29:1
Coggan, Linus C, 1952, Jl 11,17:2
Coggeshall, Arthur S, 1958, Ag 16,17:6
Coggeshall, Clayton S, 1961, S 25,33:2
Coggeshall, Freeborn, 1950, Ag 27,89:3
Coggeshall, Freeborn Rev, 1876, N 16,5:1
Coggeshall, G H, 1885, F 22,7:4
Coggeshall, George B, 1907, Ja 10,9:5
Coggeshall, George W, 1944, N 20,21:6
Coggeshall, Harvie B, 1949, Ag 26,20:2
Coggeshall, Helen (Mrs A Chanler), 1966, S 27,47:1
Coggeshall, Henry J, 1907, Jl 15,7:7
Coggeshall, Hooker I, 1943, Ja 22,19:4
Coggeshall, Howard W, 1949, Jl 31,60:2
Coggeshall, James, 1943, Je 28,22:3
Coggeshall, Lowell T Mrs, 1966, Jl 18,27:2
Coggeshall, Murray C Sr Mrs, 1961, Ja 1,49:2
Coggeshall, Murray H, 1960, Je 6,29:1
Coggeshall, Reginald, 1958, S 5,27:1
Coggeshall, Robert F Mrs, 1942, N 5,25:4
Coggeshall, W T, 1867, S 9,2:6
Coggey, J V, 1928, Ag 26,II,12:1
Coggey, John V, 1957, S 9,25:4
Coggey, M J, 1881, Ap 22,5:1
Coggill, George, 1867, Ja 13,5:5; 1940, Ag 5,13:4
Coggins, Calvin L, 1949, F 9,27:3
Coggins, John W, 1940, N 2,15:3
Coggins, M O, 1906, Ja 27,1:6
Coggins, Patrick F Mrs, 1952, Je 5,31:3
Coggshall, Frank B, 1950, Mr 16,32:3
Coggswell, Charles F, 1948, S 18,17:1
Coggswell, John F, 1942, S 3,19:4
Coggswell, William, 1903, D 26,7:7; 1942, D 13,75:4
Coghill, Edith D Mrs, 1939, Jl 29,15:6
Coghill, George E, 1941, Jl 24,17:4
Coghill, Kenneth R, 1948, O 8,25:3
Coghill, Vincent J, 1947, Ja 20,25:4
Coghlan, Charles, 1899, N 28,7:3
Coghlan, Guede, 1955, N 15,33:4
Coghlan, J W, 1879, Mr 27,2:4
Coghlan, Jasper, 1955, O 5,35:3
Coghlan, Joseph M Mrs, 1949, Je 13,19:4
Coghlan, Lillian C, 1947, Jl 23,23:4
Coghlan, Malachy J, 1950, Ag 26,13:3
Coghlan, R, 1932, Ap 5,23:1
Coghlan, Ralph, 1965, O 19,43:3
Coghlan, Thomas F, 1952, Ag 19,23:4
Coghlan, Vincent A, 1961, S 3,60:4
Coghland, Byron K, 1940, O 29,25:6
Cogill, Lida S, 1943, Ap 19,19:6
Cogliolo, Pietro, 1940, D 17,25:2
Cogmard, Theodore, 1872, My 27,5:2
Cogne, Francois, 1952, Ap 16,27:5
Cognetta, James J, 1964, Ag 9,76:4
Cogniard, Hippolyte, 1882, F 9,5:6
Cogniet, L, 1880, N 24,5:2
Cogny, Rene Gen, 1968, S 12,20:3
Cogshall, Wilbur A, 1951, O 6,19:3
Cogswell, Arthur Mrs, 1924, Ap 26,15:4
Cogswell, Charles N, 1941, D 7,77:1
Cogswell, Colwort K P, 1954, Je 14,21:2
Cogswell, Cullen V, 1940, Ja 18,23:2
Cogswell, E B, 1875, My 8,4:7
Cogswell, Francis, 1939, S 23,17:7
Cogswell, Frank A, 1953, Ag 19,29:4
Cogswell, Frederick B, 1951, D 10,29:5
Cogswell, Frederick Hull, 1907, My 17,9:5
Cogswell, George E, 1957, Je 20,29:4
Cogswell, George F Mrs, 1967, Mr 31,37:3
Cogswell, Henry B, 1939, Ja 7,15:3
Cogswell, Henry P, 1944, Je 30,21:5
Cogswell, James K Rear-Adm, 1908, Ag 19,7:6
Cogswell, James Kelsey Rear-Adm, 1908, Ag 13,7:4
Cogswell, Ledyard Jr, 1954, Jl 31,13:6
Cogswell, Leonard W, 1941, Mr 16,45:3
Cogswell, M Col, 1882, N 21,5:2
Cogswell, Richard W, 1938, S 17,17:2
Cogswell, William, 1962, Je 27,35:1
Cogswell, William Brown, 1921, Je 8,17:5
Cogswell, William F, 1963, Jl 31,29:2
Cogswell, William Mrs, 1949, Ja 30,60:5
Cogswell, William S, 1915, Ap 27,13:4
Cogswell, W L, 1879, N 6,4:7
Coha, Charles P, 1946, Ap 24,25:4
Cohalan, Conn, 1950, Jl 1,18:4
Cohalan, Conn Mrs, 1957, Mr 22,23:2
Cohalan, Daniel, 1952, Ag 25,17:2
Cohalan, Daniel F, 1946, N 13,27:1
Cohalan, Daniel F Mrs, 1911, Je 27,9:4; 1923, My 5, 11:4; 1959, D 18,29:3
Cohalan, Denis O, 1957, Ap 11,31:1
Cohalan, Denis O Mrs, 1954, Je 9,31:5
Cohalan, Dermott O'Leary, 1915, Ap 3,9:6
Cohalan, John A, 1952, O 17,27:3
Cohalan, John P, 1950, Mr 20,21:1
Cohalan, John P Mrs, 1964, My 29,29:5
Cohalan, Neil, 1968, Ja 23,43:4
Cohalan, Timothy (funl, D 11,11:4), 1909, D 9,11:5
Cohan, Alex, 1954, Je 7,23:5
Cohan, Arnold, 1967, S 8,39:1
Cohan, Charles A, 1956, Ja 9,13:2
Cohan, Daniel G, 1944, Jl 19,19:5
Cohan, Edward J, 1960, Je 21,33:3
Cohan, George M, 1942, N 6,20:1
Cohan, H C Mrs, 1928, Ag 27,19:3
Cohan, Harris K, 1965, Ag 5,29:4
Cohan, Harry A Mrs, 1963, My 11,25:2
Cohan, Jere J (funl, Ag 3,9:2), 1917, Ag 2,9:5
Cohan, Josephine, 1916, Jl 13,11:6
Cohan, Morris R, 1947, Jl 31,21:6
Cohan, Sydney A, 1956, Ap 3,35:2
Cohan, Will H, 1950, S 21,32:2
Cohane, Jeremiah J, 1943, Mr 11,21:2
Cohane, Sylvester T, 1963, S 29,87:1
Cohane, Timothy, 1949, S 8,29:3
Cohe, Ben, 1951, Jl 5,25:4
Cohe, De Witt C Mrs, 1951, Je 24,72:6
Cohen, A Broderick, 1956, F 28,31:2
Cohen, A Burton, 1956, F 12,88:5
Cohen, A J, 1949, D 31,15:4
Cohen, A S, 1867, D 29,6:5
Cohen, Aaron, 1944, My 23,23:3; 1946, Ap 10,27:3 1950, S 8,32:2
Cohen, Aaron I Mrs, 1949, Ag 4,23:2
Cohen, Aaron Mrs, 1950, S 8,32:2
Cohen, Aaron N Mrs, 1920, Je 24,13:4
Cohen, Abe, 1966, S 4,64:5
Cohen, Abraham, 1937, F 14,II,9:2; 1940, F 8,23:6
Cohen, Abraham (GB), 1957, My 31,19:1
Cohen, Abraham (NYC), 1957, Je 25,29:2
Cohen, Abraham B, 1960, Ap 29,31:5
Cohen, Abraham H Mrs, 1966, Ap 22,41:4
Cohen, Abraham Mrs, 1960, Ja 1,19:4; 1965, N 24
Cohen, Abraham S, 1953, F 8,89:1
Cohen, Abram B, 1967, My 19,39:1
Cohen, Abram H, 1954, Mr 4,25:1
Cohen, Albert B, 1964, D 5,31:3
Cohen, Albert M, 1967, Ag 26,28:4
Cohen, Albert P, 1966, F 24,37:3
Cohen, Alex, 1941, F 20,15:3
Cohen, Alex Mrs, 1959, Ap 15,33:1
Cohen, Alfred M, 1949, Mr 10,27:3
Cohen, Andrew Sir, 1968, Je 19,47:4
Cohen, Anna Mrs, 1938, Ja 17,19:1
Cohen, Arthur, 1968, Jl 24,50:4
Cohen, Arthur J, 1965, Ap 15,33:3
Cohen, Arthur R, 1963, Jl 11,29:4
Cohen, Barnet, 1948, Ja 10,15:4; 1952, S 2,23:4
Cohen, Barnett Dr, 1952, O 25,17:5
Cohen, Barney, 1955, Mr 10,27:4
Cohen, Benjamin, 1939, N 2,7:1; 1943, Je 21,17: 1947, F 3,19:4; 1950, Mr 18,14:2
Cohen, Benjamin A (funl, Mr 16,37:2), 1960, M 86:1
Cohen, Benjamin B, 1905, Ap 3,9:4
Cohen, Benjamin D, 1951, F 28,28:7
Cohen, Benjamin F, 1947, My 6,29:7; 1953, My
Cohen, Benjamin M, 1947, Ja 8,23:1; 1953, F 2
Cohen, Benjamin N, 1962, S 2,57:1
Cohen, Benni, 1957, D 22,41:1
Cohen, Benno, 1942, F 3,19:5
Cohen, Bernard, 1955, S 25,92:6
Cohen, Bernard W, 1955, D 7,39:3
Cohen, Bernhardt, 1966, O 15,29:1
Cohen, Bertha E, 1965, F 3,35:1
Cohen, Bertram, 1955, Jl 18,21:5
Cohen, Betty, 1964, Ap 15,39:5
Cohen, Boaz Dr, 1968, D 12,47:2
Cohen, Boaz Mrs, 1956, D 18,31:4
Cohen, Brunel, 1965, My 12,47:4
Cohen, Charles, 1915, Ja 11,9:5; 1938, Mr 26, 1941, Jl 14,13:5
Cohen, Charles (por), 1949, My 19,29:3
Cohen, Charles, 1951, O 14,88:4; 1953, Mr 26 1955, Mr 16,33:2
Cohen, Charles J, 1944, O 8,42:7

Cohen, Charles Mrs, 1959, O 1,35:2
Cohen, Charles N, 1955, Ag 30,27:1
Cohen, David, 1911, Ap 19,11:5; 1958, F 26,27:4
Cohen, David H, 1964, Mr 3,35:2
Cohen, David I, 1960, Ag 4,25:2
Cohen, David L, 1949, Je 2,27:4
Cohen, David Mrs, 1946, Ap 8,27:4; 1950, Mr 23,29:5
Cohen, David Sr, 1947, Ja 21,24:2
Cohen, David Sr Mrs, 1949, My 19,29:5
Cohen, De Witt C, 1949, Je 4,13:3
Cohen, Edgar F, 1957, Je 13,32:1
Cohen, Edward, 1956, Mr 26,29:4; 1960, D 5,31:5; 1964, Ja 15,31:4
Cohen, Edward E, 1956, O 19,27:3
Cohen, Edward F, 1941, Mr 22,15:3
Cohen, Eleanor, 1937, Ag 8,II,6:3
Cohen, Elias, 1951, N 22,31:2
Cohen, Elias A, 1952, Jl 3,25:4
Cohen, Elias D, 1956, Jl 27,21:5
Cohen, Elias D Mrs, 1966, Jl 19,39:2
Cohen, Elizabeth, 1902, D 17,3:4
Cohen, Elliot E (had plastic bag over head), 1959, Mr 29,8:7
Cohen, Emanuel B, 1959, Ag 14,21:5
Cohen, Emma C Mrs, 1950, O 30,27:4
Cohen, Esdaile P Dr (funl, S 22,19:6), 1924, S 19,23:5
Cohen, Eva S Mrs, 1939, N 2,23:7
Cohen, Evans D, 1966, F 18,33:3
Cohen, Ezra, 1960, Je 14,37:4
Cohen, Ezra Mrs, 1967, Ap 19,45:1
Cohen, Felix S, 1953, O 20,29:1
Cohen, Frances, 1947, Ap 20,60:4
Cohen, Frank, 1959, My 3,86:5
Cohen, Frank A, 1965, Mr 8,29:1
Cohen, Frank I, 1918, Ap 2,13:5
Cohen, Frank J, 1966, S 21,47:3
Cohen, Frank L, 1964, Mr 19,34:1
Cohen, Frank L Mrs, 1968, S 1,53:1
Cohen, Frank Mrs, 1952, Ag 10,60:6
Cohen, Frederic, 1967, Mr 13,37:3
Cohen, Frederick W, 1950, Ja 28,13:4
Cohen, Frederick W Mrs, 1941, My 11,44:5
Cohen, George H, 1949, F 25,23:3; 1950, N 3,27:2
Cohen, George L, 1945, D 9,44:2
Cohen, George R, 1950, N 25,30:6
Cohen, Gustave, 1958, Je 12,31:3
Cohen, H Bernard, 1961, Jl 5,33:3
Cohen, H Howard, 1943, N 5,19:3
Cohen, Hannah F, 1946, N 23,15:5
Cohen, Harold, 1946, O 30,27:4; 1953, D 10,47:3
Cohen, Harold M, 1962, My 31,27:4
Cohen, Harriet, 1967, N 14,43:2
Cohen, Harry, 1922, Mr 13,15:4; 1941, My 26,19:4; 1944, Jl 19,19:3; 1948, My 4,26:2; 1951, F 15,31:5; 1963, O 24,33:3; 1966, F 13,84:8
Cohen, Harry A, 1956, N 1,39:5
Cohen, Harry B, 1967, Mr 11,29:2
Cohen, Harry D, 1959, Je 28,69:2
Cohen, Harry G, 1952, Je 10,27:4
Cohen, Harry H, 1948, Ap 17,15:5
Cohen, Harry M, 1958, N 7,27:3
Cohen, Harry V, 1957, O 21,25:1
Cohen, Harry W, 1918, My 31,13:6
Cohen, Harry Z, 1949, N 27,104:8
Cohen, Hayman H, 1952, O 6,25:5
Cohen, Helen L (Mrs W R Stockwell), 1957, Jl 20, 15:4
Cohen, Henry, 1939, My 23,23:3; 1943, Ag 25,19:4; 1947, Je 30,19:1; 1952, Je 13,23:4
Cohen, Henry (cor, Ag 4,25:5), 1960, Ag 2,29:4
Cohen, Henry A, 1938, Mr 11,19:4
Cohen, Henry E, 1961, D 31,48:5
Cohen, Henry H, 1955, D 6,37:4
Cohen, Henry L, 1925, My 7,19:5
Cohen, Henry N Mrs, 1959, N 25,29:3
Cohen, Herbert S, 1961, Mr 29,33:3
Cohen, Hirsch, 1950, N 18,15:4
Cohen, Hyman, 1941, Mr 20,21:3; 1950, Je 30,23:2; 1968, Ap 13,25:4
Cohen, Hyman H, 1960, S 11,81:5
Cohen, I David, 1953, My 24,89:1
Cohen, I Elvin, 1964, N 5,45:2
Cohen, Ida Mrs, 1953, Jl 12,65:3
Cohen, Irving Dr, 1968, D 28,27:5
Cohen, Irving Mrs, 1963, S 16,35:1; 1966, Ja 13,25:5; 1967, Ja 9,36:8
Cohen, Irwin N, 1967, O 6,39:4
Cohen, Isaac, 1871, S 7,1:6; 1937, Ap 22,23:4; 1943, F 20,13:5; 1947, F 26,25:5; 1947, Ap 22,27:5; 1953, Je 16,27:3; 1963, N 8,31:3
Cohen, Isaac F, 1948, Ap 12,21:3
Cohen, Isadore, 1963, Jl 28,64:8
Cohen, Iser P, 1953, Jl 18,13:4
Cohen, Isidor, 1941, Ag 27,19:5
Cohen, Isidore, 1959, Ap 12,86:5
Cohen, Israel (Mickey), 1952, My 21,27:4
Cohen, Israel, 1952, Ag 15,15:3; 1961, N 27,29:2
Cohen, Israel B, 1940, D 15,62:4
Cohen, Israel Mrs (Mickey), 1952, Je 26,29:1
Cohen, Israel Mrs, 1967, Jl 19,39:3
Cohen, J S, 1935, My 14,21:3
Cohen, J X, 1955, Ap 25,23:4
Cohen, Jack (N Y C), 1960, Ap 14,31:1
Cohen, Jack (Long Beach, NY), 1960, Jl 9,19:6
Cohen, Jack, 1965, O 25,37:2
Cohen, Jack B Mrs, 1947, Ja 25,17:4
Cohen, Jack E, 1957, O 1,33:3
Cohen, Jack E Mrs (R Lewis), 1963, Ap 24,35:4
Cohen, Jacob, 1948, Ja 7,25:4; 1951, Ja 21,76:8; 1954, My 30,45:2; 1957, Ja 19,15:2; 1961, My 23,39:2
Cohen, Jacob D Mrs, 1957, Ja 31,27:4
Cohen, Jacob H, 1964, Jl 7,35:3
Cohen, Jacob M, 1958, Ja 27,27:1
Cohen, Jacob Mrs, 1951, Je 21,27:5; 1953, Ap 16,29:5
Cohen, Jacob R, 1949, Ja 27,23:3
Cohen, Jerome F, 1955, F 15,55:3
Cohen, Jessie, 1945, Ag 17,17:4
Cohen, Jocob D, 1948, S 11,15:6
Cohen, John Mrs, 1954, F 26,20:3
Cohen, John S Jr, 1940, Je 8,15:4
Cohen, Joseph, 1915, N 20,13:6; 1945, Je 4,19:5
Cohen, Joseph Dr, 1937, F 11,23:1
Cohen, Joseph E, 1946, F 1,23:2; 1950, Je 15,31:2
Cohen, Joseph H, 1961, D 3,88:2; 1963, My 13,29:3
Cohen, Joseph Mrs, 1955, N 10,35:4
Cohen, Joseph S, 1951, D 1,13:4
Cohen, Joshua H, 1938, N 25,23:5
Cohen, Josiah Mrs, 1947, Je 7,13:4
Cohen, Julia C Mrs, 1940, D 30,17:4
Cohen, Julius, 1944, Ja 21,17:5; 1947, Ja 21,23:4; 1955, Je 7,33:4
Cohen, Julius H (will, O 17,37:6), 1950, O 7,19:5
Cohen, Julius H Mrs, 1947, D 11,34:2
Cohen, Kathryn H, 1960, Ja 5,31:3
Cohen, L Broderick, 1961, My 20,23:6
Cohen, Lawrence B, 1957, My 4,21:5
Cohen, Lazer H, 1949, D 19,27:1
Cohen, Leah, 1919, S 1,7:4
Cohen, Lee, 1944, Ja 1,13:2
Cohen, Leo, 1943, Je 20,34:6
Cohen, Leonard J, 1947, D 8,25:4
Cohen, Leonard L, 1938, Ap 11,15:3
Cohen, Leroy G, 1954, F 8,23:5
Cohen, Leroy S, 1941, O 16,21:5
Cohen, Lester, 1963, Jl 19,25:3
Cohen, Lewis, 1915, Ag 5,11:5
Cohen, Lewis L, 1946, O 26,17:2
Cohen, Liber, 1951, Ap 18,31:2
Cohen, Louis, 1921, Ja 13,13:5; 1938, My 13,19:3; 1946, Mr 25,25:5; 1948, S 29,29:4; 1950, O 10,31:3; 1951, S 18,31:2; 1952, F 24,86:2; 1953, My 27,31:5; 1956, My 6,86:5; 1958, O 12,87:1; 1963, N 7,37:4; 1965, D 18,30:2; 1966, Ap 22,41:1
Cohen, Louis E, 1955, Jl 29,17:4
Cohen, Louis H, 1955, D 31,13:3; 1967, Jl 1,23:5
Cohen, Louis M, 1950, Je 28,27:4; 1968, Je 12,47:4
Cohen, Lyon, 1937, Ag 16,19:4
Cohen, Margaret Mrs, 1948, Ag 6,2:8
Cohen, Marion Y, 1955, F 14,19:3
Cohen, Maurice, 1956, F 29,31:5
Cohen, Maurice A, 1958, N 26,29:4
Cohen, Maurice Dr, 1968, N 28,37:4
Cohen, Maurice M, 1949, S 18,95:3
Cohen, Max, 1922, Ag 18,13:4; 1941, Je 14,17:4; 1941, N 11,23:5; 1942, O 14,25:1; 1947, Mr 28,24:2; 1950, My 23,29:1; 1950, S 14,31:3; 1951, Jl 28,11:6; 1954, Jl 16,1:1; 1968, Je 14,47:2
Cohen, Max Mrs, 1948, Je 10,25:5
Cohen, Maxwell Mrs, 1947, S 11,27:4
Cohen, Mayer H, 1960, N 5,23:4
Cohen, Melvin B, 1966, D 28,37:3
Cohen, Merrill M, 1963, Je 21,29:3
Cohen, Michael, 1960, Ag 25,29:3
Cohen, Milton, 1942, Jl 26,31:2
Cohen, Milton Sr, 1950, Jl 21,19:2
Cohen, Miriam, 1939, Jl 7,17:5
Cohen, Moe, 1950, Ag 13,76:1
Cohen, Moise K, 1948, Ag 26,22:2
Cohen, Mordecai, 1938, D 22,21:3; 1955, Ja 15,13:5
Cohen, Morris, 1943, S 23,21:2; 1945, O 13,15:1; 1952, Jl 13,61:2; 1954, Jl 20,19:4; 1959, S 27,86:5
Cohen, Morris L, 1965, N 11,50:7
Cohen, Morris P, 1965, F 15,27:3
Cohen, Morris R, 1947, Ja 30,25:1
Cohen, Morris R Mrs, 1942, Je 13,15:3
Cohen, Moses, 1939, S 16,17:2; 1950, N 14,32:3; 1964, Ja 15,31:4
Cohen, Moses S, 1879, F 6,5:4
Cohen, Mouray I, 1964, F 18,35:5
Cohen, Murray, 1962, Mr 20,37:2; 1963, N 1,33:1
Cohen, Murray M, 1948, Jl 7,46:1
Cohen, Nathan, 1940, My 6,17:5; 1942, D 12,17:5; 1955, Ap 10,88:1; 1956, My 9,33:1
Cohen, Nathan B, 1965, D 21,37:3
Cohen, Nathan M, 1958, Ag 17,87:1
Cohen, Nathaniel, 1947, Mr 22,13:3
Cohen, Nissan, 1949, Ap 20,27:2
Cohen, Norman, 1956, Ja 2,21:5
Cohen, Norman M, 1955, O 4,35:2
Cohen, Norman R, 1957, Mr 15,25:4
Cohen, Octavus R, 1959, Ja 7,30:6
Cohen, Paul, 1968, Ap 26,47:1
Cohen, Percy, 1950, My 25,29:4
Cohen, Phil, 1939, Ap 27,25:6; 1949, Mr 23,27:3
Cohen, Phil H, 1957, N 9,27:1
Cohen, Phil Mrs (Lena), 1952, My 22,27:5
Cohen, Phil Mrs (Sadie Isaac), 1952, O 21,29:2
Cohen, Philip, 1963, Jl 25,25:3
Cohen, Philip Mrs, 1945, Ap 21,13:6
Cohen, Phillip, 1946, Je 30,38:3
Cohen, Rebecca, 1908, D 22,9:2
Cohen, Rebecca Mrs, 1938, N 18,21:2
Cohen, Robert W, 1952, N 29,17:2
Cohen, Rose, 1952, Ag 13,21:3
Cohen, Rose Mrs, 1940, Jl 20,15:4
Cohen, Roy M, 1958, O 21,33:2
Cohen, S Howard, 1954, Jl 10,13:3
Cohen, Samuel, 1922, S 17,30:3; 1947, Ag 12,23:3; 1948, Ja 18,60:1; 1948, N 14,76:4; 1953, Ja 16,23:4; 1953, F 26,25:4; 1953, S 2,25:1; 1956, Jl 24,25:5
Cohen, Samuel (Paterson, NJ), 1957, Je 8,19:5
Cohen, Samuel (NYC), 1957, S 12,31:2
Cohen, Samuel (Bklyn), 1957, D 29,49:1
Cohen, Samuel, 1964, Ag 18,31:4; 1965, My 23,84:4; 1965, S 16,47:1
Cohen, Samuel B, 1952, Jl 1,23:5
Cohen, Samuel B Mrs, 1956, N 1,39:3
Cohen, Samuel C, 1946, My 4,15:1; 1965, D 11,33:4
Cohen, Samuel I, 1950, S 3,38:3; 1965, S 6,15:5
Cohen, Samuel J (cor, F 3,23:3), 1955, Ja 31,19:1
Cohen, Samuel J, 1960, Jl 14,27:5
Cohen, Samuel J Mrs, 1957, Je 1,17:5
Cohen, Samuel Jr, 1938, Ap 16,13:3
Cohen, Samuel M, 1945, Ag 30,21:3
Cohen, Samuel Mrs, 1955, Jl 17,61:2
Cohen, Samuel S, 1913, D 30,9:5; 1942, O 26,15:4; 1944, Ap 18,21:1
Cohen, Samuel W, 1956, D 19,31:3
Cohen, Sanford H, 1958, D 10,39:3
Cohen, Saul, 1962, O 15,29:4
Cohen, Sid, 1948, S 9,27:5
Cohen, Siegfried, 1944, Ag 20,33:3
Cohen, Simeon, 1947, N 4,26:3
Cohen, Simon A, 1949, Ja 17,19:6
Cohen, Simon J, 1960, Ja 17,86:5
Cohen, Simon R, 1942, S 17,25:4
Cohen, Sol, 1945, F 19,17:4; 1966, Mr 8,30:4
Cohen, Solomon, 1952, Je 8,86:8
Cohen, Theodore, 1946, Jl 9,22:3; 1954, F 13,13:2
Cohen, Thomas, 1951, Ja 20,15:4
Cohen, Wilbert, 1921, Ag 16,15:2
Cohen, William, 1955, O 30,88:4
Cohen, William N (will, Mr 4,26:8), 1938, F 28,15:1
Cohen, William W, 1940, O 13,49:3; 1940, N 30,19:3
Cohen, William W Mrs, 1959, S 25,29:2
Cohen, Zelig, 1948, Jl 16,19:4
Cohill, David Y, 1949, Ap 10,76:4
Cohill, Edmund P, 1943, Mr 6,13:6
Cohill, Edward, 1967, Je 9,45:3
Cohill, Edward Mrs, 1953, Je 20,17:5
Cohill, William J Rev, 1925, D 21,21:3
Cohl, Emile, 1938, Ja 22,15:3
Cohn, Adolph J, 1952, Mr 7,24:3
Cohn, Albert (funl, Ja 10,17:6), 1959, Ja 9,27:1
Cohn, Albert C Mrs (funl, Je 8,47:3), 1967, Je 6,47:2
Cohn, Alfred E (will, Ag 10,25:3), 1957, Jl 23,25:1
Cohn, Alfred S, 1951, F 5,23:5
Cohn, Aline, 1968, Jl 13,27:5
Cohn, Archie, 1953, Mr 30,21:4
Cohn, Arthur, 1967, Jl 20,37:4
Cohn, Arthur J, 1942, D 29,21:4
Cohn, Bernard L, 1952, Ja 23,27:2
Cohn, Bernard Mrs, 1943, O 22,17:2
Cohn, Catherine M, 1914, D 15,13:7
Cohn, Charles, 1949, N 22,29:3; 1952, N 11,29:4
Cohn, Charles H Mrs, 1950, O 10,31:2
Cohn, Charles M, 1946, D 6,23:3
Cohn, Charles S, 1955, Mr 20,88:6
Cohn, D L, 1880, F 15,7:4
Cohn, David, 1945, O 12,23:4
Cohn, David I, 1960, D 10,2:4
Cohn, David L, 1960, S 13,37:5
Cohn, Edward, 1955, Ag 9,25:3
Cohn, Edwin J, 1953, O 3,17:5
Cohn, Elias A, 1959, Je 29,29:2
Cohn, Ernst, 1956, My 7,27:4
Cohn, Felix, 1939, Je 4,49:1
Cohn, Fred, 1959, Jl 26,68:1
Cohn, Frederick, 1940, Mr 7,23:5
Cohn, Garrison D Mrs, 1960, Ag 8,21:2
Cohn, Harry (funl plans, Mr 1,17:5; funl, Mr 3,27:2), 1958, F 28,21:1
Cohn, Harry L (will), 1956, D 1,35:2
Cohn, Henry I, 1957, O 1,33:4
Cohn, Herman C, 1941, S 5,21:5
Cohn, Herman Mrs, 1948, Jl 23,19:1
Cohn, Irving, 1956, Ja 12,27:5
Cohn, Isidor, 1948, My 16,70:2; 1964, Jl 11,25:3
Cohn, Jack, 1952, Jl 16,25:1
Cohn, Jack (funl, D 12,39:1), 1956, D 10,31:3
Cohn, Jack Mrs, 1958, S 3,33:4
Cohn, Jacob, 1946, My 1,25:3
Cohn, Jacob I Mrs, 1946, Ag 14,26:2
Cohn, Jefferson D, 1951, F 21,28:2
Cohn, Joseph, 1947, My 26,21:1; 1954, Ap 10,15:3; 1962, N 6,33:5; 1966, Ja 22,29:6
Cohn, Joseph E, 1958, F 1,19:5
Cohn, Joseph H, 1953, O 7,29:2
Cohn, Joseph J, 1962, Ag 6,25:4

Cohn, Joseph J Mrs, 1956, O 12,29:3
Cohn, Joseph L, 1954, Ag 25,27:2
Cohn, Joseph L Mrs, 1949, F 19,15:6
Cohn, Julian J, 1918, N 27,13:3
Cohn, Julian M Mrs, 1960, D 3,23:6
Cohn, Leo L Mrs, 1945, D 8,17:5
Cohn, Leon, 1949, N 17,29:1
Cohn, Leonard A, 1944, My 14,46:3
Cohn, Leonard H, 1965, F 20,25:4
Cohn, Leopold Dr, 1937, D 20,27:2
Cohn, Lester D, 1945, My 20,32:2
Cohn, Lester F, 1958, F 1,19:5
Cohn, Louis, 1947, Ja 22,23:2
Cohn, Louis B, 1916, Je 20,11:6
Cohn, Louis Henry, 1953, Ag 28,17:4
Cohn, Louis M, 1958, Ag 20,27:3
Cohn, Louis M Mrs, 1952, Ja 4,23:2
Cohn, M Metz, 1949, My 5,28:4
Cohn, Manuel M, 1948, Je 6,72:5
Cohn, Marcus, 1939, My 19,21:5
Cohn, Marcus M, 1953, N 21,13:5
Cohn, Marjorie, 1920, Jl 8,11:3
Cohn, Max, 1957, Ap 23,31:3; 1959, F 8,86:1
Cohn, Max L, 1943, O 31,48:5
Cohn, Mike, 1949, Ag 16,23:2
Cohn, Milton S, 1937, Mr 20,19:5
Cohn, Morris, 1950, N 8,29:4
Cohn, Morris H, 1950, N 30,34:4
Cohn, Morris Mrs, 1956, Ap 14,17:4
Cohn, Nathan, 1954, Jl 7,31:3
Cohn, Nathan J, 1963, D 27,25:2
Cohn, Nathan L, 1951, S 24,27:2
Cohn, Peter, 1952, Mr 11,27:4
Cohn, Ralph M, 1959, Ag 2,81:1
Cohn, Raymond H, 1955, Ag 26,19:6
Cohn, Robert J, 1924, Ja 30,19:3
Cohn, Samuel, 1947, Jl 8,23:1; 1949, N 8,31:1; 1953, Ap 24,23:5
Cohn, Samuel (SI), 1959, My 6,39:1
Cohn, Samuel (Bklyn), 1959, D 2,43:3
Cohn, Samuel, 1960, Jl 17,61:1; 1962, Jl 22,64:5; 1966, Jl 12,43:5
Cohn, Samuel Mrs, 1952, Je 26,29:5
Cohn, Samuel R, 1945, Mr 22,23:1
Cohn, Saul, 1954, Je 6,86:1
Cohn, Seymour, 1947, Jl 2,23:2
Cohn, Sidney, 1955, S 1,23:4
Cohn, Sigismund Dr, 1915, My 19,13:4
Cohn, Theodore L, 1964, Ag 4,30:1
Cohn, Tobias, 1942, Ja 1,25:6
Cohn, Tobias Mrs, 1955, N 15,33:4
Cohn, Wilhelm Mrs, 1962, F 19,31:4
Cohn, Wolf Mrs, 1945, Je 20,23:1
Cohn-Wiener, E, 1941, Ap 14,17:4
Cohnstaedt, Wilhelm Dr, 1937, O 12,25:5
Coho, Eugene P, 1953, Ag 7,19:1
Coho, Herbert B, 1942, My 20,19:2
Coho, Herbert B Mrs, 1945, Mr 21,24:2
Cohoe, Albert B, 1966, O 19,47:4
Cohoe, Awrey W, 1948, F 13,21:2
Cohoe, Wallace P, 1966, N 12,30:2
Cohoe, Wallace P Mrs, 1956, F 14,29:2
Cohoes, Orlando S, 1957, F 12,27:3
Coholan, Grace M Mrs, 1941, Ap 22,21:1
Coholan, Jeremiah, 1958, Ap 24,31:5
Cohon, Irwin J, 1960, Jl 22,23:3
Cohon, Samuel S, 1959, Ag 23,92:5
Cohron, George E Mrs, 1957, S 7,19:2
Cohu, H S, 1883, My 6,2:7
Coil, Everet J, 1950, O 13,29:5
Coile, Simon V, 1903, N 27,9:5
Coiley, John J, 1958, F 13,29:2
Coimbra, Jose J, 1950, O 6,27:1
Coing, Isaac E, 1940, Ag 8,19:6
Cointe, George L, 1961, Mr 12,86:8
Coit, A B, 1902, Mr 28,9:6
Coit, Alfred, 1947, Je 1,60:5
Coit, Burnettie P, 1940, Ag 1,21:4
Coit, C T, 1881, D 12,1:6
Coit, Carl S, 1943, My 18,23:2
Coit, G, 1881, Ap 22,1:2
Coit, George M, 1903, O 26,7:6
Coit, Henry, 1876, My 19,2:2
Coit, Henry Augustus, 1916, Ag 9,11:6
Coit, Henry Leber Dr, 1917, Mr 14,9:3
Coit, James Milnor Dr, 1922, Ja 7,13:6
Coit, John C, 1947, Ag 12,24:2
Coit, John T Mrs, 1943, N 7,56:6
Coit, John T Rev, 1863, Ja 28,2:3
Coit, Louise V Mrs, 1947, Ja 8,23:2
Coit, Norman H, 1947, S 4,25:6
Coit, Ralph B Mrs, 1948, Jl 20,23:3
Coit, Stanton, 1944, F 17,19:1
Coit, T W Rev, 1885, Je 23,5:6
Coke, John A Jr, 1939, Ap 27,25:1
Coke, Thomas William (Earl of Leicester), 1909, Ja 25,9:5
Coke-Jephcott, Norman, 1962, Mr 15,32:1
Cokefair, I W, 1933, N 26,33:1
Cokeley, W A, 1932, Mr 6,II,7:3
Coker, David R, 1938, N 29,23:4
Coker, Francis B Jr, 1962, Je 29,27:1
Coker, Francis W, 1963, My 27,29:4
Coker, George M Mrs, 1951, Jl 12,25:4
Coker, James L Jr Mrs, 1952, Ag 26,25:3
Coker, William C, 1953, Je 30,23:2
Cokhale, Gopal Krishna, 1915, F 21,3:5
Colac, Frank, 1951, N 10,17:3
Colaci, James, 1937, Mr 23,24:2
Colaco, Jorge, 1942, Ag 25,23:6
Colacurcio, John Sr, 1948, My 21,23:2
Colahan, Arthur C, 1948, Mr 9,23:1
Colahan, Arthur N W, 1952, S 11,31:2
Colahan, Stephen J, 1874, D 11,8:3
Colahan, Walter S, 1957, F 5,23:3
Colahan, Wayne J Sr, 1954, F 19,34:2
Colaneri, Augustine M, 1943, Ja 27,21:2
Colantoni, Amelio, 1960, Ag 17,31:5
Colantoni, John, 1951, N 21,25:2
Colantuano, Romeo C, 1947, Ag 21,23:3
Colaprico, Constantino, 1960, Ja 3,88:2
Colarossi, Allesandro G, 1953, Ag 4,21:2
Colarossi, Angelo, 1949, F 5,15:5
Colasacco, Ernest, 1952, Jl 9,27:3
Colasurdo, P Anthony Sr, 1956, Ag 3,19:5
Colasurdo, P Anthony Sr Mrs, 1943, Jl 19,15:5
Colbath, James A, 1948, F 5,23:5
Colberg, Wilson P, 1951, Je 13,29:4
Colbern, William H, 1959, My 2,23:6
Colbert, Carl Cato, 1968, Jl 7,53:3
Colbert, Charles R Mrs, 1962, Ap 25,39:4
Colbert, Edward V Dr, 1937, Mr 3,23:3
Colbert, Frank O, 1953, Mr 24,31:5
Colbert, Henry, 1962, S 1,19:3
Colbert, Holmes Col, 1872, Mr 26,1:4
Colbert, Irving, 1961, Ja 8,86:6
Colbert, John T, 1952, Ag 15,16:7
Colbert, Joseph R Rev, 1903, O 28,9:5
Colbert, Leo Otis Rear-Adm, 1968, D 25,31:3
Colbert, Thomas J, 1955, Mr 31,27:1
Colbert, William J, 1937, F 17,22:1; 1954, D 29,23:3
Colborn, William T, 1937, Ap 5,19:3
Colbron, Alma D Mrs, 1962, My 12,23:5
Colbron, Grace I, 1943, S 9,25:4
Colburn, Albert P, 1944, My 27,15:4
Colburn, Allan P, 1955, F 8,27:4
Colburn, Cora C, 1939, O 3,23:6
Colburn, Frank H, 1947, My 8,25:3
Colburn, Frederick, 1946, Je 11,23:3
Colburn, Frederick H, 1937, N 25,31:4
Colburn, Frederick W, 1944, Ap 10,19:2
Colburn, H S, 1934, Mr 11,31:1
Colburn, J E, 1879, Ja 2,5:6
Colburn, John N, 1950, N 5,92:4
Colburn, Mary F Mrs, 1943, Ap 5,19:4
Colburn, W G, 1875, S 11,4:7
Colburn, Walter H Mrs, 1968, N 11,47:1
Colburn, Zerah, 1870, My 2,4:7
Colburne, J E, 1878, D 18,4:7
Colby, Albert Ladd, 1924, My 3,15:4
Colby, Aleander G, 1943, Jl 7,19:3
Colby, Arthur, 1904, Ja 21,9:6
Colby, Averill C, 1949, Ap 12,29:4
Colby, Bainbridge, 1950, Ap 12,27:1
Colby, Bainbridge Mrs, 1963, Je 4,39:1
Colby, Barrett C Mrs, 1952, O 13,21:2
Colby, C D W, 1941, S 24,23:5
Colby, Charles C, 1965, Jl 18,68:4
Colby, Charles W, 1955, D 13,40:1
Colby, Edward B, 1953, Jl 25,11:5
Colby, Emanuel M, 1956, N 18,89:3
Colby, Everett, 1943, Je 20,35:1
Colby, Everett Mrs, 1962, Mr 24,25:3
Colby, Ex-Gov, 1873, Jl 22,5:3
Colby, Florence H Mrs, 1940, Mr 16,15:4
Colby, Forrest H Mrs, 1949, Ap 26,26:2
Colby, Francis T (will, Ag 8,13:5), 1953, Jl 31,19:5
Colby, Frank H, 1940, F 17,13:3
Colby, Frank Moore Prof, 1925, Mr 4,19:6
Colby, Frank O, 1951, F 26,23:2
Colby, Frank O Sr Mrs, 1950, Jl 5,32:3
Colby, Franklin G, 1941, Je 6,21:5
Colby, G H Capt, 1903, F 6,1:6
Colby, George L, 1939, Ag 3,19:6
Colby, Gertrude K, 1960, F 3,33:4
Colby, Grace M Mrs (will), 1940, Mr 23,8:1
Colby, H A, 1928, Ag 14,23:4
Colby, H G O Adm, 1926, N 4,27:2
Colby, Harry J, 1952, My 17,19:6
Colby, Helen, 1956, Ag 23,53:1
Colby, Howard B, 1962, Ap 20,28:8
Colby, James A, 1957, Je 11,35:2
Colby, James F (will, N 2,21:2), 1939, O 22,41:1
Colby, Jessie C, 1957, Ap 6,19:5
Colby, John M, 1967, N 24,43:2
Colby, June R, 1941, My 12,17:4
Colby, Kimball G Mrs, 1961, Ap 7,31:2
Colby, Leon S, 1961, Ag 21,23:5
Colby, Louis S, 1947, Mr 24,25:2
Colby, M C Mrs, 1873, D 17,8:4
Colby, Mary C, 1942, My 30,15:5
Colby, Maxwell, 1949, D 19,27:2
Colby, Merrill Maj Gen, 1884, Jl 19,4:7
Colby, Nathalie S, 1945, Je 11,15:5
Colby, Nathalie S Mrs, 1942, Je 11,23:1
Colby, Robert, 1904, N 16,2:2
Colby, Safford K, 1947, Ag 5,23:4
Colby, Stoddard B, 1965, My 13,37:3
Colby, T Edward Mrs, 1948, S 12,74:4
Colby, Walter E, 1945, Ap 19,27:2
Colby, Whitney C, 1963, O 2,42:1
Colby, William H, 1947, D 5,25:3
Colby, William W, 1944, Jl 12,19:3
Colcher, Abraham E, 1959, Je 30,31:4
Colcleugh, Emma S Mrs, 1940, Ja 31,19:5
Colcord, Bradford C, 1953, Ag 17,15:5
Colcord, Frank F, 1952, Mr 22,13:2
Colcord, Harvard F, 1941, N 1,15:6
Colcord, Jane S Mrs, 1939, D 12,27:5
Colcord, Joanna C (Mrs F J Bruno), 1960, Ap 9,23:3
Colcord, Lincoln, 1947, N 17,21:1
Colcord, Roswell K, 1939, O 31,23:6
Colcord, Samuel, 1938, S 24,17:2
Colden, Charles C, 1956, Ag 17,19:3
Colden, Charles J, 1938, Ap 16,13:5
Colden, Charles S, 1943, Ja 14,18:2; 1960, S 15,37:1
Colden, Josephine D Mrs, 1940, Je 19,23:5
Coldren, Clifton C, 1949, Ag 14,68:1
Coldwell, Elias F, 1947, Je 12,25:5
Coldwell, Joseph M, 1949, Ap 5,29:3; 1949, Je 26,60:1
Coldwell, Milton W, 1951, N 26,25:1
Cole, A Eric, 1960, Ja 22,25:1
Cole, Aaron Hodgman, 1914, Ja 1,15:4
Cole, Adda G Mrs, 1941, Jl 23,19:4
Cole, Albert A, 1938, Ag 13,13:6
Cole, Albert L, 1908, Mr 7,7:5
Cole, Albert L Mrs, 1968, Jl 24,50:4
Cole, Alice K, 1954, My 28,23:3; 1962, Ag 25,22:2
Cole, Alice S (est appr), 1961, N 7,35:8
Cole, Allan, 1909, Ap 6,9:5
Cole, Almeron H, 1939, D 28,21:5
Cole, Alphaeus P Mrs, 1962, Ja 1,23:3
Cole, Amos T, 1953, F 2,21:1
Cole, Annie A Mrs, 1913, Ja 4,9:3
Cole, Arthur B, 1950, Ja 29,69:1
Cole, Arthur J, 1940, Je 12,25:4
Cole, Arthur S, 1947, F 16,57:1
Cole, Arthur S Mrs, 1943, N 25,25:4
Cole, Arthur W, 1948, F 10,23:4; 1948, D 24,18:4
Cole, Arthur W Mrs, 1938, Ja 14,23:5
Cole, Asa Judge, 1907, N 30,7:5
Cole, Ashley T, 1965, F 24,42:1
Cole, Ashley W Col, 1920, D 25,7:6
Cole, Augustus, 1940, Ag 7,19:2
Cole, Augustus J, 1953, Je 4,29:1
Cole, Belle, 1905, Ja 6,9:3
Cole, Ben E, 1956, N 25,88:6
Cole, Benjamin E, 1903, D 1,9:5
Cole, Benjamin H, 1954, Ap 11,87:1
Cole, Bert Mrs, 1950, Ag 12,13:6
Cole, Bessie C Mrs, 1948, F 3,25:2
Cole, Blase Dr, 1937, O 4,21:5
Cole, Blase Mrs, 1961, Ja 28,19:1
Cole, Buddy, 1964, N 7,27:1
Cole, C Alfred, 1963, Ap 13,19:6
Cole, C S, 1931, D 30,22:6
Cole, C S Capt, 1906, Je 22,7:6
Cole, Carleton G, 1944, Ap 20,19:3
Cole, Carlton, 1959, O 29,30:4
Cole, Carter S, 1949, N 18,29:4
Cole, Charles, 1942, Jl 9,21:3
Cole, Charles B, 1951, Jl 25,23:3
Cole, Charles B Mrs, 1953, Ja 8,27:3
Cole, Charles Buckingham, 1925, D 14,21:4
Cole, Charles C, 1905, Mr 18,11:5
Cole, Charles D M, 1943, Ja 23,13:3
Cole, Charles E, 1938, Ja 7,20:1; 1948, Ja 23,23:4
Cole, Charles G, 1952, My 17,19:4
Cole, Charles G Mrs, 1957, O 3,29:1
Cole, Charles H, 1952, N 15,17:1
Cole, Charles K Dr, 1920, Mr 3,11:4
Cole, Charles N, 1941, Mr 4,23:5
Cole, Charles P, 1948, F 12,24:3
Cole, Charles Wadsworth, 1912, Ag 28,9:6
Cole, Chauncey E, 1952, Ag 8,17:2
Cole, Chester A, 1958, Mr 23,89:1
Cole, Clarence, 1950, Mr 6,21:4
Cole, Clarence A, 1967, Ap 22,31:5
Cole, Clarence L, 1943, Ja 3,43:1
Cole, Clarence Leroy Lt-Col, 1918, Ag 10,7:5
Cole, Claude W, 1938, My 14,15:6
Cole, Clifford, 1946, Je 5,23:1
Cole, Clifford D, 1951, Ap 28,15:3
Cole, Clifford E, 1949, Ag 1,17:4
Cole, Cornelius (funl, N 5,19:5), 1924, N 4,21:
Cole, Cyrenus, 1939, N 15,23:2
Cole, Cyrus H, 1940, O 15,23:3
Cole, Daniel W, 1958, Je 5,31:5
Cole, David Rev Dr, 1903, D 21,9:6
Cole, Don, 1938, Je 20,15:3
Cole, Donald R, 1943, Ag 22,36:4
Cole, Dora I Mrs, 1939, Ag 9,17:5
Cole, E W, 1928, F 25,14:7
Cole, Earle R, 1944, Mr 8,19:3
Cole, Edward E, 1909, F 6,9:3
Cole, Edward R, 1944, F 24,15:1
Cole, Edward S, 1950, Mr 19,95:3
Cole, Edwin J, 1941, D 21,40:6
Cole, Elwood P R, 1955, N 8,31:1

Cole, Emma J Mrs, 1951, Jl 2,23:3
Cole, Ernest C, 1943, My 27,25:4
Cole, Ernest E (por), 1949, N 20,92:3
Cole, Ernest E Mrs, 1954, O 20,30:1
Cole, F O, 1930, O 8,25:1
Cole, F Robert, 1964, D 19,29:5
Cole, Fay-Cooper, 1961, S 5,35:2
Cole, Felix Mrs, 1939, Ag 28,19:5
Cole, Florence Frances, 1872, Ap 30,1:6
Cole, Floyd R, 1953, O 25,88:5
Cole, Frances M Mrs, 1960, N 23,29:1
Cole, Francis J, 1923, Ja 12,15:5
Cole, Francis T, 1943, Ja 27,21:3
Cole, Francis W, 1966, D 8,47:4
Cole, Frank, 1950, N 22,25:3; 1952, Ja 4,23:3; 1954, Ja 1,23:3
Cole, Frank C, 1949, Ap 2,15:2
Cole, Frank H, 1952, Jl 31,23:3
Cole, Frank L, 1950, D 2,13:5
Cole, Franklin, 1968, Ap 10,43:4
Cole, Fred, 1964, S 21,31:3
Cole, Fred V, 1948, My 10,22:3
Cole, Frederick B, 1938, D 28,26:3
Cole, Frederick E M, 1960, N 24,29:3
Cole, Frederick L, 1941, Jl 2,21:5
Cole, Frederick W, 1914, My 24,IV,7:5; 1945, O 6,13:2
Cole, George, 1882, N 22,5:4; 1952, Ag 17,77:1
Cole, George A, 1959, N 15,86:5
Cole, George C, 1940, Ja 12,17:6; 1947, Ag 3,53:1
Cole, George D, 1951, Je 22,25:2
Cole, George D H, 1959, Ja 15,33:1
Cole, George H, 1943, D 15,27:2
Cole, George Jr Mrs, 1951, Je 24,72:7
Cole, George T, 1937, O 5,25:4
Cole, George W, 1939, O 11,27:4; 1941, D 17,27:5; 1953, N 6,28:4
Cole, George W Justice, 1923, Mr 31,13:5
Cole, George W Mrs (M Kirmse), 1954, D 13,27:2
Cole, Glen W, 1955, O 20,35:2
Cole, Harold E, 1960, Mr 6,86:6
Cole, Harry D, 1961, N 19,89:1
Cole, Harry E, 1937, Jl 2,21:4
Cole, Harry J, 1943, Ap 5,19:5
Cole, Harry O, 1950, F 14,25:2
Cole, Harvey T, 1941, My 22,21:2
Cole, Haydn, 1939, F 14,20:1
Cole, Henry, 1959, F 16,29:3
Cole, Henry G Maj, 1912, O 15,15:6
Cole, Henry Sir, 1882, Ap 20,5:2
Cole, Henry T, 1938, Je 8,23:4
Cole, Herbert E, 1952, Ag 26,25:1
Cole, Herbert M, 1943, Ag 7,11:3
Cole, Hobart A, 1941, O 4,15:4
Cole, Howard, 1947, Je 12,25:2; 1964, S 9,43:1
Cole, Howard A, 1941, Ja 9,21:5
Cole, Howard E, 1950, Ap 29,15:4
Cole, Howard J Sr, 1943, Ja 11,15:4
Cole, Ira E, 1968, O 22,47:4
Cole, Irwin, 1948, O 20,29:3
Cole, J Allen, 1939, D 31,19:1
Cole, J J, 1925, Ag 8,11:6
Cole, J Soley, 1952, Ja 17,27:3
Cole, J Wyckoff, 1940, My 1,23:4
Cole, J Y, 1934, My 22,23:3
Cole, Jackson L, 1945, O 16,23:1
Cole, Jacob A, 1942, O 23,21:2
Cole, Jacob Mrs, 1947, F 3,19:4
Cole, James (Catfish), 1967, Jl 29,9:2
Cole, James L, 1961, N 12,86:6
Cole, James W, 1941, Ag 18,13:2
Cole, Jean, 1939, Ap 24,17:3
Cole, Jeremiah, 1921, Jl 26,15:5
Cole, Jessie D S Mrs, 1940, O 28,17:5
Cole, John C Jr, 1950, O 3,31:5
Cole, John D, 1956, N 15,35:2
Cole, John G, 1950, N 22,25:1; 1962, Je 7,35:4
Cole, John Gully, 1924, S 22,19:5
Cole, John H, 1951, My 19,15:4
Cole, John Leonard, 1943, Ag 1,38:6
Cole, John M, 1956, Ag 25,15:3
Cole, John N, 1922, O 19,21:5; 1961, Ap 7,31:1
Cole, John N Mrs, 1967, D 21,37:1
Cole, John O, 1961, Je 2,31:2
Cole, John P, 1947, Je 10,22:2
Cole, John S, 1968, My 4,39:3
Cole, John S Mrs, 1958, Je 16,23:4
Cole, John W, 1966, N 20,88:8
Cole, Johnny (J L Kowalski), 1961, Jl 29,19:6
Cole, Joseph A Mrs, 1938, S 11,II,11:1
Cole, Joseph H, 1939, Je 20,21:4
Cole, Joseph J, 1925, Ag 9,5:4
Cole, Judson, 1943, O 4,17:5
Cole, Laurence T, 1955, D 19,27:3
Cole, Lester W, 1962, My 6,89:1
Cole, Lewis G, 1954, O 17,86:3
Cole, Lewis G Mrs, 1951, Ap 25,29:2
Cole, Llewellyn, 1942, Mr 29,44:4
Cole, Llewellyn R, 1949, Ja 2,63:3
Cole, Louis A Mrs, 1950, Ja 6,21:4
Cole, Lucius A (mem, S 11,11:5), 1910, Ag 27,7:6
Cole, Mabel H, 1964, Mr 14,23:5
Cole, Maggie P, 1942, Je 17,23:4
Cole, Martin, 1939, F 27,15:4
Cole, Merritt C, 1953, N 2,25:6
Cole, Michael G L Viscount, 1956, Ag 27,19:4
Cole, Nat King (Nathaniel A Coles),(funl plans, F 17,43:4), 1965, F 16,1:2
Cole, Nehemiah T, 1947, Je 6,23:3
Cole, Norman G, 1942, F 26,19:5
Cole, Norvin G, 1952, Ag 22,21:3
Cole, Page E, 1954, Je 18,23:2
Cole, Palmer C Dr, 1906, Jl 6,7:5
Cole, Paul J, 1961, D 2,23:4
Cole, Percival R, 1948, Ag 10,22:3
Cole, Phil G, 1941, Jl 1,23:1
Cole, Philip H, 1944, Je 26,15:5
Cole, Ralph W E, 1949, S 19,23:3
Cole, Rex, 1967, Jl 25,35:1
Cole, Richard C, 1964, O 31,29:4
Cole, Richard J, 1968, O 8,47:1
Cole, Robert (funl), 1911, Ag 5,7:6
Cole, Robert A, 1917, S 22,11:6
Cole, Robert A (funl, Ag 1,23:4), 1956, Jl 28,17:7
Cole, Robert E, 1955, D 6,37:3
Cole, Robert L, 1948, Ja 20,24:3
Cole, Robert M Mrs, 1959, Ja 3,17:5
Cole, Roy E, 1950, Ap 21,23:4
Cole, Rufus, 1966, Ap 22,41:1
Cole, Rufus Mrs, 1951, S 29,17:1
Cole, Rufus S, 1954, My 26,29:2
Cole, Russel T, 1959, O 16,31:3
Cole, S Edgar Mrs, 1952, N 4,29:4
Cole, Samuel V Mrs, 1965, O 24,86:7
Cole, Samuel Valentine Dr, 1925, My 7,19:6
Cole, Seth Toby, 1953, Jl 31,19:6
Cole, Seymour G Mrs, 1948, O 23,15:3
Cole, Sidney, 1961, Jl 12,23:1
Cole, Silas G, 1947, Ag 16,13:3
Cole, Sol E, 1938, Ap 8,19:3
Cole, Sophie, 1947, F 13,23:2
Cole, T, 1931, My 18,17:3
Cole, Thomas A, 1956, My 30,21:4
Cole, Thomas H, 1950, Jl 17,21:5
Cole, Tom, 1953, Je 14,V,4:8
Cole, Truman W, 1960, Ja 21,31:2
Cole, Tulie, 1955, F 19,15:4
Cole, Vera, 1947, O 28,25:3
Cole, Viott M, 1957, Je 7,23:4
Cole, Voranus M, 1949, Ja 23,68:5
Cole, W Arthur, 1961, Jl 15,19:5
Cole, W Bundy, 1939, My 17,23:2
Cole, W Graham, 1953, Ap 13,28:3
Cole, W H D, 1936, Mr 1,II,10:1
Cole, Wallace H, 1949, S 8,29:3
Cole, Walter H Sr Mrs, 1967, F 28,37:3
Cole, Walton A, 1963, Ja 26,7:4
Cole, Wesley H, 1949, O 25,27:2
Cole, Willard G, 1965, My 29,27:4
Cole, William, 1914, Jl 13,9:7
Cole, William A, 1943, Mr 3,23:1
Cole, William B, 1923, Ag 20,11:4
Cole, William G, 1948, Ap 18,72:1
Cole, William H, 1938, O 17,15:4; 1967, F 8,31:1
Cole, William I, 1942, S 12,13:4
Cole, William J, 1939, Je 10,17:4
Cole, William M, 1909, Mr 7,11:5; 1960, D 17,23:4
Cole, William P Jr, 1957, S 23,27:2
Cole, William R, 1952, Ap 12,11:2
Cole, William T Mrs, 1961, Ap 3,30:2
Cole, William V, 1945, Je 20,23:1
Cole, William W, 1939, D 29,15:5
Cole, Willis W Mrs, 1956, O 4,33:3
Cole, Wilmot Lawrence Capt, 1922, Ja 27,15:5
Cole-Hamilton, J B, 1945, Ag 25,11:4
Colean, James R, 1962, N 14,40:1
Colebaugh, Charles H, 1944, My 11,19:3
Colebourne, Rudolph G, 1940, Je 3,15:4
Colebrook, Leslie Mrs, 1950, D 21,26:4
Colebrooke, Lord, 1939, Mr 1,21:4
Colegrove, Charles H, 1943, D 29,17:3
Colegrove, Edward H Mrs, 1937, Je 25,21:3
Colegrove, Ernest L Mrs, 1946, Je 24,31:1
Colehower, Harry H, 1940, F 2,17:3
Coleman, A du P Prof, 1926, Je 16,25:5
Coleman, Alexander W, 1947, Je 11,27:6
Coleman, Algernon, 1939, Ag 9,17:3
Coleman, Archibald, 1966, My 2,37:3
Coleman, Arthur J S, 1947, O 8,25:4
Coleman, Arthur P, 1939, F 27,15:3
Coleman, Bernard F, 1925, O 17,15:4
Coleman, Blake W Capt, 1908, O 23,9:4
Coleman, Bob, 1959, Jl 17,21:3
Coleman, C C, 1928, D 6,31:3
Coleman, C P, 1929, Ap 14,29:3
Coleman, Charles, 1951, Mr 9,25:5; 1954, Ap 26,25:3
Coleman, Charles C, 1953, D 29,23:1
Coleman, Charles C Mrs, 1955, O 21,27:2
Coleman, Charles H, 1945, Jl 28,11:2
Coleman, Charles P, 1957, My 20,25:4
Coleman, Chester R, 1944, D 24,26:6
Coleman, Christopher B, 1944, Je 27,19:2
Coleman, Clarence W, 1949, Ap 23,13:4
Coleman, Claude C, 1953, Ja 10,17:5
Coleman, Clinton B Mrs, 1957, Mr 26,33:2
Coleman, Clyde, 1942, N 8,51:2
Coleman, Cornelius E Sr, 1968, D 13,47:2
Coleman, Cornelius V, 1946, F 20,25:4
Coleman, Cyril, 1958, S 21,86:6
Coleman, D'Alton C, 1956, O 18,33:3
Coleman, Daniel E S, 1941, F 28,19:5
Coleman, Daniel R, 1938, Je 17,21:3
Coleman, David, 1961, N 23,31:2
Coleman, David F, 1944, D 17,38:2
Coleman, David Mrs, 1966, Ag 1,27:3
Coleman, Dawson, 1951, F 9,25:3
Coleman, Donald L, 1947, F 22,13:6
Coleman, Edward D, 1939, S 6,23:3
Coleman, Edward J, 1941, Mr 15,17:1; 1942, F 28,17:4
Coleman, Eleanor G, 1946, Ja 4,22:2
Coleman, Ellen G, 1954, Ap 22,29:4
Coleman, Elliott d'E, 1963, My 28,28:4
Coleman, Emil, 1965, Ja 28,29:1
Coleman, Ephraim H, 1961, D 5,43:3
Coleman, Eugene J F, 1953, Ap 29,29:4
Coleman, Frances, 1967, Ag 5,21:1
Coleman, Francis Col, 1904, Ap 22,9:7
Coleman, Frank J, 1934, Mr 15,23:3
Coleman, Frederick A, 1962, Ja 19,31:3
Coleman, Frederick H, 1953, D 9,11:5
Coleman, Frederick W, 1945, Ja 6,11:4
Coleman, Frederick W B, 1947, Ap 3,25:5
Coleman, G O, 1932, My 9,15:1
Coleman, George A, 1959, F 18,33:1
Coleman, George B, 1903, N 25,9:5
Coleman, George E, 1953, Ap 20,25:2
Coleman, George H, 1963, Je 11,37:3
Coleman, George L, 1946, Mr 23,13:5
Coleman, George R, 1960, Ja 20,31:1
Coleman, George V, 1947, D 12,27:1
Coleman, George W, 1950, Ag 2,25:3
Coleman, Georgia, 1940, S 15,48:2
Coleman, H Roger, 1956, N 30,24:1
Coleman, Harry, 1952, Ja 22,29:2
Coleman, Harry (Private Shorty), 1952, F 24,85:2
Coleman, Harry J, 1957, F 24,85:2
Coleman, Henry, 1903, D 8,9:5; 1949, Ja 1,13:4
Coleman, Henry R, 1967, Mr 22,47:4
Coleman, Herbert L, 1946, Ja 22,27:3
Coleman, Howard B, 1944, Ag 27,33:1
Coleman, Hubert D, 1954, Ja 1,23:3
Coleman, J B Dr, 1877, D 21,4:7
Coleman, J Pressley, 1949, My 24,28:2
Coleman, James, 1943, S 15,27:3
Coleman, James A, 1946, D 30,22:2
Coleman, James H, 1954, F 18,31:5
Coleman, James J, 1954, Ap 27,29:4
Coleman, James J Sr Mrs, 1950, Jl 18,29:4
Coleman, James M Sr, 1958, Ap 13,84:7
Coleman, James S, 1906, D 18,7:2
Coleman, James W, 1962, Jl 8,64:6
Coleman, Jennie H Mrs, 1939, My 18,25:5
Coleman, John, 1904, Ap 22,9:7; 1941, S 26,23:6
Coleman, John (Lake Forest, Ill), 1961, N 28,32:2
Coleman, John (Drexel Hill, Pa), 1961, D 1,33:3
Coleman, John B (Walden, NY), 1951, Mr 31,15:3
Coleman, John B (Calif), 1951, My 26,17:3
Coleman, John B (NYC), 1951, O 23,29:2
Coleman, John B Jr, 1960, N 7,35:5
Coleman, John Caldwell, 1917, F 18,17:2
Coleman, John D, 1958, Ag 23,15:5
Coleman, John F, 1948, O 20,29:2
Coleman, John J, 1924, O 6,19:5; 1942, Ja 19,20:2
Coleman, John L V, 1953, Ja 29,27:4
Coleman, John M, 1961, D 31,48:4
Coleman, John Mrs, 1961, D 1,33:3
Coleman, John S, 1958, Ap 15,33:3
Coleman, John W, 1940, Mr 20,27:3
Coleman, Joseph A Dr, 1968, Mr 21,53:1
Coleman, Joseph E, 1947, Jl 30,21:5
Coleman, Joseph P, 1943, N 17,25:5; 1951, D 8,11:4; 1965, D 26,68:8
Coleman, Julia C, 1951, Ag 4,15:5
Coleman, Lawrence A (por), 1938, F 11,24:2
Coleman, Leander W T, 1954, N 22,23:3
Coleman, Leighton Bp (por), 1907, D 15,13:3
Coleman, Leighton H Jr Mrs, 1968, Je 12,44:6
Coleman, Leonard W, 1938, Jl 5,17:2
Coleman, Les, 1960, N 28,31:5
Coleman, Lindley G, 1940, Ag 25,35:1
Coleman, Luther E, 1952, Ag 3,60:2
Coleman, Lyman, 1882, Mr 17,5:2
Coleman, Maria Jewell, 1878, Je 27,5:4
Coleman, Marian A, 1945, Jl 23,19:5
Coleman, Martin, 1947, Jl 22,23:1
Coleman, Mary, 1941, My 21,23:4
Coleman, McAlister (mem ser, My 27,17:2), 1950, My 19,27:3
Coleman, Melville C, 1941, D 20,19:2
Coleman, Melvin E, 1939, My 20,15:5
Coleman, Mildred T Mrs, 1951, D 8,11:4
Coleman, Mortimer H, 1968, F 23,34:1
Coleman, Nicholas P, 1963, Jl 23,29:4
Coleman, Oliver S, 1950, D 20,31:2
Coleman, Otis W, 1948, My 18,23:5
Coleman, Percy, 1946, D 25,29:4
Coleman, Phil Mrs, 1957, Ag 30,19:3
Coleman, R B, 1881, N 2,5:1
Coleman, Ralph Pallen Sr, 1968, Ap 5,47:3
Coleman, Richard A, 1910, Je 23,7:4

Coleman, Richard H Mrs, 1964, Ja 23,31:1
Coleman, Robert F, 1943, Jl 5,15:3
Coleman, Robert H, 1946, F 14,25:3
Coleman, Robert L Jr, 1950, My 6,15:4
Coleman, Robert M, 1938, Mr 26,15:3
Coleman, Roy V Mrs (cor, My 3,23:1), 1938, Ap 24, II,7:2
Coleman, Samuel J, 1951, Jl 13,21:5
Coleman, Sheldon T, 1964, Je 7,86:6
Coleman, Stewart M, 1960, N 19,21:6
Coleman, Sydney H, 1955, Mr 24,31:3
Coleman, Thomas E, 1964, F 5,35:3
Coleman, Thomas J, 1944, My 20,15:3
Coleman, W A, 1921, S 2,13:2
Coleman, W C, 1904, Ap 1,9:6
Coleman, Walter A Mrs, 1965, Ap 6,39:1
Coleman, Walter C, 1947, O 20,23:4
Coleman, Walter J, 1948, N 11,27:5
Coleman, Walter M Mrs (Satis N), 1961, Ap 19,39:5
Coleman, Warren, 1948, F 14,13:5
Coleman, Warren R, 1968, Ja 16,39:3
Coleman, Wilbur F, 1962, Je 7,35:4
Coleman, William A, 1937, Mr 5,21:1
Coleman, William B, 1940, Je 18,23:3; 1956, O 2,35:3
Coleman, William C, 1948, Je 16,29:2; 1957, N 3,89:1
Coleman, William C Ex-Judge, 1968, Ja 14,84:2
Coleman, William H, 1943, Je 5,15:1; 1946, D 15,77:3; 1951, Je 13,29:5; 1964, Ja 25,23:1
Coleman, William H Mrs, 1958, Ap 1,31:5
Coleman, William J, 1944, F 14,17:4; 1944, D 15,19:3; 1965, O 23,31:3
Coleman, William L Dr, 1904, N 29,9:2
Coleman, William M, 1965, Ja 3,84:5
Coleman, William O, 1939, Mr 16,23:6
Coleman, William T, 1941, D 14,69:1
Coleman, William W, 1965, D 26,68:3
Colen, Bernard D, 1944, Mr 9,17:5
Colen, Bernard D Mrs, 1965, Mr 27,27:5
Colen, Lester R, 1952, F 19,29:2
Colenbrander, Johann W Col, 1918, Mr 5,11:5
Colenso, Bishop, 1883, Jl 6,3:3
Colenso, J W Bishop, 1883, Je 21,4:7
Coler, Bird S, 1941, Je 14,17:1
Coler, Emily M Mrs, 1941, Ag 24,36:3
Coler, Eugene S, 1953, S 2,25:5
Coleridge, Baron, 1955, Mr 28,27:2
Coleridge, John Taylor, 1876, F 12,2:4
Coleridge, Lord (Sir Jno Duke) (por), 1894, Je 15,5:3
Coleridge-Taylor, Samuel, 1912, S 2,9:5
Colerus, Egmont, 1939, Ap 12,23:2
Coles, B J, 1907, My 10,7:4
Coles, Blaine B, 1939, Je 14,23:4
Coles, Cornelia Mrs, 1905, My 24,9:6
Coles, Cyril H, 1965, O 15,45:1
Coles, E J Mrs, 1955, F 24,27:4
Coles, Edward, 1954, Ap 3,15:5; 1965, F 2,33:1
Coles, Floy S Mrs, 1961, Ja 10,47:4
Coles, Franklin, 1943, Ag 11,19:2
Coles, George W Mrs, 1949, N 15,25:1
Coles, H Finlay, 1953, Jl 6,17:4
Coles, Howard L Mrs, 1952, Ja 12,13:4
Coles, Isaac R, 1937, Je 24,25:5
Coles, J Ackerman Dr, 1925, D 17,23:4; 1925, D 20, 11:1
Coles, Jacob V, 1946, S 6,21:3
Coles, James M Mrs, 1960, F 20,23:2
Coles, John E, 1962, Mr 21,39:4
Coles, John L, 1940, N 1,25:5
Coles, Julia W, 1954, Mr 10,25:3
Coles, L Dudley, 1951, N 3,17:4
Coles, Langdon M, 1952, D 27,9:5
Coles, Lohretta B, 1943, Mr 15,14:2
Coles, Marie B, 1956, My 29,27:4
Coles, Mary F, 1947, Ja 8,24:3
Coles, Nathaniel A (Nat King Cole),(funl plans, F 17,43:4), 1965, F 16,1:2
Coles, Nicey Ann Mrs, 1911, S 26,9:5
Coles, Robert L, 1941, Jl 8,19:1
Coles, Robert M, 1957, N 19,33:2
Coles, Ross, 1956, Jl 17,23:5
Coles, Roy H, 1938, Ja 3,21:6
Coles, Sally P Mrs, 1937, My 7,25:3
Coles, Samuel B, 1957, Mr 14,29:2
Coles, Stephen L, 1937, My 8,19:3
Coles, Stricker Dr, 1937, Je 21,19:6
Coles, W Chauncey, 1942, My 21,19:2
Coles, W Chauncey Mrs, 1949, Ap 4,23:2
Coles, Wilbur G, 1940, D 13,23:1
Coles, Willett H Mrs, 1953, O 13,29:5
Coles, William D Mrs, 1919, Ag 9,9:7
Coles, William E, 1941, Ja 22,21:2
Coles, William J, 1937, N 6,17:6
Colesberry, Jean, 1940, My 22,23:5
Colescott, James A, 1950, Ja 13,24:2
Colesworthy, Daniel C, 1955, Je 25,15:5
Colesworthy, William Gibson, 1907, Ap 27,9:6
Colet, C T, 1883, D 1,5:4
Colet, Louise, 1876, Mr 26,7:1
Colet, Philibert, 1945, Ap 17,23:4
Colette, Frederic P, 1951, Ap 2,20:4
Colette, Jean, 1945, Ja 25,19:4
Colette, Sidonie G (funl, Ag 8,85:3), 1954, Ag 4,21:4
Coletti, Andrea D, 1945, D 5,25:6
Coletti, Edward, 1960, F 24,37:4
Coletti, Vincent J, 1954, O 28,35:5
Coley, Bradley L, 1961, Je 2,31:3
Coley, Carl Y, 1946, My 24,19:4
Coley, Clarence T, 1965, My 6,39:1
Coley, Edward H, 1949, Je 7,31:1
Coley, Edward H Mrs, 1940, Mr 4,15:2
Coley, George E Capt, 1906, Ja 20,9:5
Coley, George K Mrs, 1943, Ja 25,13:2
Coley, Thomas L, 1945, Ja 12,15:2
Coley, W B, 1936, Ap 17,21:1
Colfax, Albert Eben, 1925, S 29,27:4
Colfax, Harriet E, 1905, Ap 18,6:3
Colfax, Schulyer Mrs, 1911, Mr 5,II,13:3
Colfax, Schuyler, 1885, Ja 14,1:5
Colfax, Schuyler Jr, 1925, Mr 30,17:5
Colfax, Sibil Lady, 1950, S 26,31:4
Colfax, William S, 1938, Ja 18,23:5
Colfelt, Arthur L, 1946, Ag 31,15:5
Colford, Edith, 1915, Ag 14,7:5
Colford, George W, 1966, F 15,36:4
Colford, Joseph E Sr, 1968, N 20,47:3
Colford, S Jr Mrs, 1927, Je 4,17:5
Colford, Sidney J, 1951, My 26,17:3
Colford, Sidney Jones, 1916, N 26,21:5
Colgan, Andrew A, 1957, D 4,39:2
Colgan, Charles C, 1962, My 22,37:3
Colgan, Delia D Mrs, 1937, F 8,17:4
Colgan, Donald F (funl plans), 1955, Mr 11,25:3
Colgan, Eleanor G, 1938, S 19,19:4
Colgan, F X, 1940, Ap 19,21:2
Colgan, Frank J Dr, 1937, O 13,23:4
Colgan, George A, 1954, Mr 27,17:5
Colgan, George J, 1952, D 12,29:2
Colgan, Helen G, 1953, Je 18,29:4
Colgan, Joseph A, 1963, Je 26,39:3
Colgan, Joseph B, 1956, Ap 27,28:1
Colgan, Joseph S, 1938, Ag 13,13:6
Colgan, Thomas L, 1951, Ap 15,92:1
Colgan, William D Sr, 1961, Ap 26,39:4
Colgate, A Col, 1927, S 6,25:5
Colgate, A W, 1904, Mr 22,9:4
Colgate, Adele S, 1962, My 3,33:4
Colgate, Bowles, 1902, Ap 22,3:6
Colgate, C E, 1880, Ja 9,5:2
Colgate, Caroline B D Mrs, 1940, O 6,48:1
Colgate, Craig Mrs, 1912, O 19,11:5
Colgate, Eugene, 1906, O 17,9:4
Colgate, Gilbert, 1965, O 11,39:1
Colgate, Graig, 1953, Ag 4,21:7
Colgate, Henry A, 1957, O 17,33:1
Colgate, Henry A Mrs, 1953, Ag 28,17:1
Colgate, J S, 1884, D 5,5:5
Colgate, James B Mrs, 1919, Mr 23,20:4
Colgate, James Boorman, 1904, F 8,9:5
Colgate, James C (will, Mr 15,21:8), 1944, F 27,37:2
Colgate, James C Mrs, 1955, D 28,23:4
Colgate, Richard M, 1919, S 18,13:5
Colgate, Robert, 1923, Ja 21,6:3
Colgate, Russell (will, Ag 15,15:4), 1941, Ag 1,15:5
Colgate, S Bayard, 1963, O 9,43:1
Colgate, S M, 1930, N 11,25:1
Colgate, William, 1909, Jl 12,7:5
Colgrain, Lord (C F Campbell), 1954, N 5,21:4
Colgrove, Russell, 1904, D 29,7:6
Colhoon, Carl W, 1944, Ap 11,19:2
Colie, Dayton, 1950, Ag 29,27:4
Colie, Edward N Jr, 1949, O 23,87:3
Colie, Runyon, 1947, Jl 9,23:2
Colijn, Hendrik Mrs, 1947, N 15,17:1
Colijn, Hendrikus, 1944, N 13,19:1
Colin, Albert H, 1968, My 13,43:1
Colin, Alexander, 1875, N 24,1:5
Colin, Gustav, 1910, D 30,11:4
Colin, Herman H, 1954, My 14,23:5
Colin, Samuel, 1966, Ja 18,37:2
Colin, Saul, 1967, Ap 23,92:6
Colish, Abraham, 1963, Ap 11,33:4
Colket, C, 1883, Ap 6,4:7
Colket, G Hamilton Mrs, 1967, O 31,45:1
Colket, George H, 1905, Mr 31,9:6
Colket, Heredith B Sr, 1947, Je 9,21:4
Colket, James H, 1941, Ap 3,23:6
Colket, Tristram C Mrs, 1965, S 15,47:2
Coll, Charles A, 1939, F 25,15:3
Coll, Charles H Jr, 1949, Ja 19,27:3
Coll, D H, 1881, N 9,2:1
Coll, J, 1877, Jl 10,4:6
Coll, James F, 1959, Mr 10,35:4
Coll, Joseph, 1951, D 18,31:3
Coll, Joseph A Mrs, 1947, D 28,40:6
Coll, Joseph Clement, 1921, O 21,15:5
Coll, Michael J, 1948, S 19,76:5
Coll, Owen G, 1960, F 8,29:4
Coll, Patrick, 1938, My 26,25:4
Coll, Raymond S, 1962, Ap 11,43:5
Coll Cuchi, Cayetano, 1961, F 6,23:3
Colla, Ettore, 1968, D 31,27:2
Colladay, Edward F, 1961, N 11,23:4
Colladay, Samuel R, 1945, Mr 22,23:4
Collamer, Charles M, 1942, Jl 14,20:4
Collamer, Eugene E, 1945, Ja 26,21:3
Collamer, Jacob, 1865, N 11,8:1
Collamore, Bertha, 1951, Je 1,47:8
Collamore, Gilman, 1939, O 17,25:2
Collamore, Jerome Mrs (Claire Benedict), 1954, Jl 20,19:4
Collard, James L Mrs, 1966, Jl 9,27:3
Collard, Norman S, 1949, D 6,31:5
Collard, William, 1943, D 21,27:2
Collardet, Brig-Gen, 1921, Jl 5,15:2
Collari, Anthony, 1951, N 29,33:1
Collbran, Harry, 1925, F 16,19:4
Colle, Bernard, 1960, Ap 9,23:4
Colle, Nicolas, 1954, Ag 3,19:3
Colleano, Bonar, 1958, Ag 17,19:5
Colleano, James B (E J Sullivan), 1957, Mr 8,21:1
Colledge, George L, 1965, Ja 3,84:8
Colledge, Kingman, 1944, Je 26,15:3
Collen, George P, 1951, Ag 19,84:6
Collenburg, Monroe H, 1963, Je 15,23:6
Collens, William L Mrs, 1957, My 22,33:4
Coller, Adolph H, 1944, Ag 20,33:2
Coller, Frederick A, 1964, N 6,37:2
Coller, Jasper W, 1938, D 31,15:6
Coller, John H, 1954, N 28,87:1
Colleran, John J, 1925, O 18,5:1
Colleran, Michael J, 1940, N 19,23:2
Colles, Henry C, 1943, Mr 6,13:3
Collester, Donald G Mrs, 1964, Jl 15,35:1
Collet, John C, 1955, D 7,39:2
Collet, Mark Sir, 1905, Ap 27,11:5
Collet, Mark W, 1942, F 27,17:5
Collet, Paul A, 1947, S 28,60:6
Collett, Adah F Mrs, 1943, D 15,27:4
Collett, Charles H Rev, 1937, N 12,21:3
Collett, Gene, 1953, N 4,33:3
Collett, George R, 1942, Jl 6,15:3
Collett, J D, 1942, Ja 23,19:2
Collett, Sister, 1937, Jl 18,II,7:2
Collett, William R, 1938, Je 19,29:2
Colletta, Carol S Mrs, 1945, S 6,25:3
Collette, Maurice, 1956, Ap 4,29:3
Collette, Paul E, 1950, My 18,29:4
Colley, Arthur E, 1949, D 22,23:5
Colley, Edward T, 1956, S 5,27:5
Colley, Frank M, 1953, Je 13,15:4
Colley, G P Gen Sir, 1881, F 28,1:5
Colley, H G Mrs, 1952, Jl 4,13:5
Colley, William, 1949, S 8,29:4
Colleye, Julie, 1951, Jl 7,13:6
Colli, Carlo, 1947, F 4,25:1
Collie, G Norman, 1967, My 26,39:1
Collie, George L, 1954, D 29,23:1
Collie, Ruffin V, 1951, Ja 6,15:2
Collie-MacNeill, Douglas A, 1938, Mr 8,19:1
Collier, Abraham Mrs, 1948, O 27,27:2
Collier, Alfred H Mrs, 1948, Ap 12,21:5
Collier, Barron (will, Ap 6,29:1), 1939, Mr 14,21:
Collier, Bryan W, 1959, D 19,27:3
Collier, Bryan W Mrs, 1947, Ja 7,27:1
Collier, Charles Myles, 1908, S 15,9:6
Collier, Chester W, 1964, Jl 29,33:2
Collier, Clifton B, 1941, My 4,53:2
Collier, Constance (funl plans, Ap 27,31:4), 1955 Ap 26,29:4
Collier, Daniel M, 1961, F 7,34:1
Collier, Daniel R Gen, 1904, Ja 25,7:6
Collier, De Witt M, 1942, Jl 24,20:2
Collier, Edward Augustus Rev, 1920, D 5,22:4
Collier, Elizabeth, 1968, D 1,86:5
Collier, Frank, 1947, Ap 19,15:4
Collier, Frank E, 1950, Ag 27,89:2
Collier, Frederick H, 1941, Jl 8,19:3
Collier, G Kirby, 1954, Je 20,85:1
Collier, George W, 1944, F 26,13:1; 1944, Mr 1,1
Collier, George W Mrs, 1953, Je 14,85:1
Collier, George Z, 1946, Ja 14,19:1
Collier, Gerard A, 1968, N 27,47:4
Collier, Harry C, 1950, N 18,15:6
Collier, Harry D, 1959, F 1,84:3
Collier, J, 1934, Ap 12,24:3
Collier, J P, 1883, S 19,4:7
Collier, J W, 1933, S 29,19:3
Collier, J W P Sr Mrs, 1948, Ja 27,25:4
Collier, J Walter, 1920, Ag 21,7:5
Collier, James Col, 1873, F 4,1:6
Collier, John A, 1873, Mr 25,1:6
Collier, John C, 1912, N 14,11:4
Collier, John E, 1968, My 9,47:1
Collier, John H, 1955, Jl 28,23:3
Collier, John W P Mrs, 1960, O 14,33:4
Collier, Joseph H, 1911, My 4,11:5
Collier, Lizzie Hudson, 1924, O 26,7:3
Collier, Martin H, 1961, F 12,87:1
Collier, Maurice Dwight (funl), 1906, Ja 14,9:
Collier, Miles, 1954, Ap 6,30:5
Collier, Milton, 1945, O 14,44:4
Collier, Paul R, 1951, Jl 15,60:4
Collier, Price (funl, N 6,11:7), 1913, N 4,9:6
Collier, Price Mrs, 1953, O 2,21:4
Collier, Richard G, 1948, Mr 6,13:3
Collier, Robert (Lord Monkswell), 1909, D 2
Collier, Robert J, 1918, N 9,13:1
Collier, Sam, 1950, S 24,V,2:8
Collier, Sargent F, 1968, S 11,47:2

Collier, Theodore, 1963, Ap 10,39:3
Collier, Thomas, 1941, My 17,15:5
Collier, W Armistead, 1947, O 10,25:5
Collier, William B, 1951, Ag 12,79:5
Collier, William D, 1950, Mr 16,31:3
Collier, William M, 1956, Ap 17,31:4
Collier, William M Mrs, 1952, D 27,10:3
Collier, William Mrs, 1909, N 11,9:5
Collier, William Mrs (est), 1910, My 24,9:5
Collier, William Mrs, 1959, Jl 7,33:4
Collier, William S, 1940, S 28,17:4
Collier, William Sr, 1944, Ja 14,19:1
Colligan, Arthur B, 1949, F 26,15:4
Colligan, Eugene A, 1959, O 17,23:1
Colligan, Gilbert F, 1955, O 4,24:3
Colligan, James G, 1952, F 15,26:2
Colligan, John J, 1947, D 30,25:7
Colligan, Lawrence L, 1942, Je 3,24:5
Colligan, Walter E Mrs, 1938, Ag 17,19:5
Collin, Edward, 1866, My 8,5:3
Collin, Frank M, 1944, Ja 3,22:3
Collin, Frederick, 1939, N 27,17:1
Collin, Grace Lathrop, 1913, N 7,9:3
Collin, Louis, 1947, My 1,25:5
Collin, Raphael, 1916, O 22,23:3
Collinet, Henri, 1949, Mr 12,17:6
Colling, Arthur F, 1957, S 22,86:5
Collinge, C, 1936, Ja 16,21:3
Collinge, F Channon Mrs, 1952, Mr 16,90:6
Collinge, Francis V, 1966, Jl 21,33:4
Collinge, Henry J, 1937, Jl 16,19:3
Collings, C T, 1924, D 26,15:5
Collings, Carolina Mrs, 1947, Ag 2,13:2
Collings, Crittenden T Mrs, 1921, Ap 15,15:4
Collings, Karl, 1942, Mr 10,19:2
Collings, Lewis D, 1944, Je 16,19:5
Collings, Lewis E, 1948, D 19,76:6
Collings, Richard T, 1950, Ja 17,27:1
Collings, Thomas C, 1943, D 6,23:5
Collings, Walter N Sr, 1949, S 6,27:4
Collings, William H, 1925, S 22,25:4
Collingwood, Arthur, 1952, Ja 23,27:4
Collingwood, C Gilbert, 1958, N 10,29:2
Collingwood, Charles B, 1937, F 26,22:2
Collingwood, Francis, 1911, Ag 19,7:6
Collingwood, G Harris, 1958, Ap 4,21:2
Collingwood, George H Mrs, 1960, Ja 6,35:2
Collingwood, Helen A Mrs, 1949, Ja 23,68:5
Collingwood, Herbert W Mrs, 1957, Ja 22,29:3
Collingwood, Jennie, 1956, S 8,17:5
Collingwood, John C Jr, 1958, S 17,37:2
Collingwood, Marshall S, 1938, D 26,23:3
Collingwood, Morton, 1945, My 27,26:1
Collingwood, R G, 1943, Ja 12,23:2
Collins, Adison B, 1952, F 22,21:3
Collins, Adm (funl), 1875, S 3,2:5
Collins, Al (Elias B), 1958, Mr 4,29:5
Collins, Alan Copeland, 1968, Ja 7,84:6
Collins, Albert J Sr, 1949, D 25,26:6
Collins, Alfred C, 1941, Je 28,15:2
Collins, Alfred H Mrs, 1941, Mr 3,15:1
Collins, Alfred M, 1951, My 19,15:2
Collins, Alfred Quenton, 1903, Jl 23,7:6
Collins, Alice C, 1949, Ag 5,19:5
Collins, Alice T, 1939, Mr 2,21:2
Collins, Allen G, 1937, Ap 27,23:2
Collins, Alva N, 1940, My 24,19:5
Collins, Andrew J, 1941, S 17,23:5; 1951, D 11,33:3
Collins, Arthur (corr, Je 18,33:3), 1958, Je 17,29:3
Collins, Arthur L, 1950, N 20,25:4
Collins, Arthur Mrs, 1938, Ap 15,20:2
Collins, Aubrey J, 1951, O 4,33:3
Collins, Augustus F W, 1939, Jl 29,15:3
Collins, Austin J, 1952, Ap 7,25:6
Collins, Bart A, 1959, Je 5,27:4
Collins, Bartholomew J, 1951, F 13,31:2
Collins, Benjamin W, 1953, S 19,15:5
Collins, Bernard J, 1948, F 7,15:1
Collins, Bertha W Mrs, 1940, F 6,22:2
Collins, Bertram C Mrs, 1947, Ja 19,53:2
Collins, Burnett C, 1953, N 18,31:1
Collins, Burnett C Mrs, 1939, D 12,27:4
Collins, C B, 1903, Ap 28,9:6
Collins, C C, 1950, F 12,84:5
Collins, C F G, 1883, D 19,5:1
Collins, C Walter, 1948, O 19,28:2
Collins, Calvin Mrs, 1952, Ja 21,15:2
Collins, Charles, 1873, Ap 26,1:5
Collins, Charles A, 1955, Mr 9,27:3; 1958, S 29,27:4
Collins, Charles B, 1958, Ap 6,88:5
Collins, Charles Bonner, 1920, Jl 13,11:5
Collins, Charles C, 1951, Mr 19,27:4
Collins, Charles E, 1952, D 9,33:4
Collins, Charles F, 1953, Mr 1,92:7
Collins, Charles G, 1939, S 22,23:2
Collins, Charles J, 1951, D 1,13:2
Collins, Charles M, 1904, Jl 22,7:2; 1946, Je 28,21:3
Collins, Charles R, 1950, F 4,15:4
Collins, Charles Rev Dr, 1875, Jl 20,4:6
Collins, Charles W, 1941, Ja 22,21:2
Collins, Charles W (est acctg), 1964, Jl 30,25:2
Collins, Clarence H Jr, 1938, Mr 2,19:4
Collins, Clarence L, 1922, S 30,13:6
Collins, Claude R, 1958, Ag 19,27:4
Collins, Cornelius F (por), 1947, F 24,19:1
Collins, Cornelius F Jr, 1965, D 14,43:3
Collins, Cornelius F Mrs, 1942, D 1,25:4
Collins, Cyril, 1943, Jl 26,19:6
Collins, Daniel, 1944, Je 20,19:2
Collins, Daniel C, 1961, Je 14,19:4
Collins, Daniel J, 1941, Ag 26,19:3
Collins, Daniel J Jr, 1946, Ap 21,45:1
Collins, Daniel J Mrs, 1947, My 14,25:3
Collins, Daniel P, 1942, Ag 19,19:2
Collins, Daniel W, 1943, Ja 9,13:4
Collins, Dapper Dan (R A Tourbillon), 1950, Je 21, 38:7
Collins, David J, 1941, F 4,21:2
Collins, Dennis F Mrs, 1951, Je 26,29:5
Collins, Dewey, 1944, O 13,19:5
Collins, Dick, 1953, F 14,17:3
Collins, Dwight M Mrs, 1952, Ja 8,27:2
Collins, E, 1880, Ap 9,5:5
Collins, E K (see also Ja 23), 1878, Ja 27,12:4
Collins, E Pinckney, 1940, Ja 25,21:2
Collins, E T, 1933, F 11,15:1
Collins, Earl K, 1952, Ap 18,25:2
Collins, Earl Mrs, 1955, Ja 13,27:5
Collins, Eddie, 1939, Je 5,17:1; 1940, S 4,23:6
Collins, Eddie Mrs, 1943, F 25,21:5
Collins, Edgar F, 1943, Jl 21,15:2
Collins, Edmund C, 1956, Ag 10,17:3
Collins, Edward, 1951, D 2,89:2
Collins, Edward C, 1958, Ag 25,21:2
Collins, Edward D, 1940, Ja 2,19:1
Collins, Edward E, 1951, Ag 12,77:3
Collins, Edward H, 1944, Ag 15,17:5
Collins, Edward H (trb lrs, Mr 16,36:6), 1961, Mr 9, 29:1
Collins, Edward M, 1903, S 6,7:6; 1938, Ap 22,19:1
Collins, Edward T (Eddie), 1951, Mr 26,23:1
Collins, Edwin F, 1950, Ag 2,25:4
Collins, Elias B Mrs, 1957, F 8,23:3
Collins, Ellen (will), 1913, Je 19,11:6
Collins, Elliott T, 1942, N 15,58:1
Collins, Elmer, 1948, D 29,21:6
Collins, Emily Mrs, 1945, O 21,46:2
Collins, Emily P Mrs, 1909, Ap 30,9:4
Collins, Ernest W, 1944, O 19,23:5
Collins, Eugene R, 1957, Ja 8,31:1
Collins, Everett, 1941, Jl 29,15:1
Collins, Francis A, 1957, N 1,23:5
Collins, Francis D, 1947, F 28,24:2
Collins, Francis W, 1960, Je 12,86:4
Collins, Frank, 1938, F 13,II,6:7; 1963, Je 11,37:2
Collins, Frank A, 1924, Ag 30,9:6
Collins, Frank A (Merion, Pa), 1964, Jl 1,35:3
Collins, Frank A (New Rochelle, NY), 1964, Jl 23, 27:3
Collins, Frank B, 1950, Ag 16,29:2
Collins, Frank M, 1948, N 19,27:1
Collins, Frank W, 1940, Je 28,19:4
Collins, Franklin W, 1943, O 26,23:3
Collins, Frederic Mrs, 1957, My 6,29:5
Collins, Frederic N, 1947, Ja 23,23:5
Collins, Frederick A, 1967, Mr 15,47:3
Collins, Frederick J, 1957, O 4,23:2
Collins, Frederick L, 1950, Jl 26,25:3
Collins, Frederick W, 1948, D 25,17:2
Collins, G Allen, 1957, D 30,23:5
Collins, G P, 1936, O 14,25:1
Collins, Genevieve Mrs, 1953, Ag 14,19:2
Collins, George F, 1966, Ag 29,29:4
Collins, George J Rev, 1968, D 19,47:4
Collins, George L, 1940, Je 18,23:4
Collins, George M Sr, 1950, Jl 1,15:4
Collins, George Mrs, 1948, Jl 28,23:5
Collins, George R N, 1958, Ap 17,31:5
Collins, George Rowland, 1968, O 11,47:3
Collins, George S, 1944, My 31,19:5
Collins, George W, 1955, Ap 7,27:2
Collins, George W Dr, 1924, D 16,25:4
Collins, Gilbert, 1920, Ja 30,15:4
Collins, Gilbert Ex-Justice, 1920, F 2,13:4
Collins, Grellet, 1939, Ap 17,17:5
Collins, Guy N (cor, Ag 18,19:1), 1938, Ag 16,19:1
Collins, H S, 1927, S 12,23:5
Collins, Harold D, 1947, D 23,24:3
Collins, Harold M, 1942, S 25,21:4
Collins, Harry, 1908, Je 21,11:7
Collins, Harry C, 1942, Ag 29,15:1
Collins, Harry E, 1949, My 24,28:3
Collins, Harry S, 1952, Ap 17,29:3
Collins, Harvey S, 1966, F 25,31:5
Collins, Henry D, 1938, Je 10,21:4
Collins, Henry H, 1957, Ja 5,17:5
Collins, Henry H Jr, 1961, My 27,23:4
Collins, Henry J, 1952, D 6,21:3; 1954, Ja 29,19:1
Collins, Henry L Jr, 1961, D 24,36:5
Collins, Herman L, 1940, O 8,25:3
Collins, Horace B, 1942, Ja 18,42:2
Collins, Howard A, 1968, My 18,34:2
Collins, Howard D, 1947, O 10,25:2
Collins, Irving J, 1939, My 23,23:3
Collins, J, 1935, Je 5,19:1
Collins, J A, 1902, N 9,1:3
Collins, J C, 1948, Ja 30,23:3
Collins, J Dillard, 1959, Ja 13,47:3
Collins, J Edwards, 1947, Mr 14,23:4
Collins, J H Judge, 1904, Ja 10,7:6
Collins, J L (will), 1953, D 25,15:6
Collins, J Palmer, 1921, Je 24,15:6
Collins, J Raymond, 1951, Ja 11,26:3
Collins, J Ross, 1943, Ag 16,15:3
Collins, J Walter, 1953, My 17,88:7; 1956, Ag 19,92:3
Collins, Jacob R, 1947, S 18,25:3
Collins, James, 1942, Mr 7,17:5; 1950, F 23,27:3
Collins, James A, 1946, D 5,31:4
Collins, James C, 1950, Ja 23,23:2
Collins, James E Mrs, 1937, S 18,19:4
Collins, James F, 1940, My 2,23:3
Collins, James G, 1920, Ap 9,13:3
Collins, James J, 1923, F 2,15:4; 1943, Mr 7,39:1; 1951, S 6,31:5
Collins, James J Mrs, 1953, Je 26,19:2
Collins, James L, 1954, Ja 10,86:1; 1963, Jl 1,29:3
Collins, James M, 1950, Je 2,23:3
Collins, James Mrs, 1952, Ja 5,11:2
Collins, James P, 1939, Ap 16,III,7:3
Collins, James R, 1957, O 10,33:4
Collins, James S, 1949, D 18,90:4
Collins, James S Mrs (P Drant), 1955, O 5,35:4
Collins, James T, 1947, Je 21,17:1; 1955, Ag 7,73:3
Collins, James W, 1944, Jl 23,35:2
Collins, Jennie T Mrs, 1940, Jl 21,28:8
Collins, Jeremiah, 1939, Mr 11,17:6
Collins, Jeremiah J, 1958, Ap 14,25:3
Collins, Jerome T, 1950, Ag 10,25:1
Collins, Jesse, 1920, N 22,15:4
Collins, John, 1874, Ag 15,4:7; 1914, My 16,11:7; 1964, Ap 26,88:5
Collins, John A, 1947, Ap 7,23:4
Collins, John B, 1941, Ja 31,19:3
Collins, John Bartholomew Com, 1917, Ap 14,13:6
Collins, John Churton Prof, 1908, S 16,9:7
Collins, John Commodore, 1865, S 5,8:2
Collins, John D, 1945, Ja 21,40:3; 1963, Je 13,33:1
Collins, John F, 1944, Jl 4,19:5; 1955, S 11,84:6; 1958, S 10,33:3
Collins, John G, 1944, Ja 12,24:3
Collins, John H, 1943, Ag 7,11:4; 1944, F 3,19:5; 1959, Ap 1,37:2
Collins, John J, 1940, Jl 9,21:2; 1947, Ag 6,23:3; 1951, My 17,31:6; 1952, Jl 16,25:6; 1965, Mr 4,31:1
Collins, John J Mrs, 1944, N 26,53:6
Collins, John M, 1939, F 10,23:2; 1952, My 23,21:3
Collins, John P, 1941, Mr 26,23:4; 1954, Ja 3,88:4
Collins, John R, 1943, N 15,19:4; 1950, F 7,27:1
Collins, John T, 1949, S 30,23:2; 1965, O 20,47:5
Collins, John T Mrs, 1951, Ja 2,18:1
Collins, Jordan Jackson, 1912, F 26,11:4
Collins, Jose (Josephine), 1958, D 7,88:8
Collins, Joseph (will, Je 18,53:3), 1950, Je 13,28:2
Collins, Joseph A, 1938, Ja 8,15:1; 1959, Je 1,27:4
Collins, Joseph C, 1940, F 1,21:4
Collins, Joseph D, 1959, O 29,30:3
Collins, Joseph F, 1956, Ja 27,23:4
Collins, Joseph H, 1948, Ap 6,23:2; 1967, Ja 11,25:3
Collins, Joseph J, 1937, Ap 23,21:1
Collins, Joseph M, 1957, S 20,25:2; 1962, O 30,35:4
Collins, Joseph R, 1937, Ag 25,21:2
Collins, Joseph V Mrs, 1952, My 1,29:6
Collins, Joseph W, 1951, My 18,27:3
Collins, Josiah Sr, 1949, Jl 3,26:4
Collins, Kenneth, 1962, Mr 30,33:1
Collins, Kenneth B, 1916, Ap 16,21:4
Collins, Kenneth Mrs, 1938, N 30,24:1
Collins, L Preston, 1952, S 21,88:6
Collins, Lawrence, 1901, Je 8,3:4
Collins, Lawrence M Jr, 1950, D 6,33:1
Collins, Lawrence S, 1962, D 4,41:1
Collins, Leonard H, 1962, N 29,38:8
Collins, Leroy M Mrs, 1950, N 22,25:3
Collins, Lester, 1957, F 9,19:6
Collins, Lester Mrs, 1967, D 20,45:3
Collins, Lewis, 1904, Ja 11,7:5
Collins, Lewis M, 1938, Jl 10,29:2
Collins, Lorin C, 1940, O 20,50:2
Collins, Lottie (Mrs Jas W Tate), 1910, My 3,13:6
Collins, Lucy B, 1948, F 12,23:2
Collins, M F, 1928, D 23,17:2
Collins, M H, 1943, Ap 3,15:3
Collins, Malcolm G Mrs, 1938, O 11,25:5
Collins, Marguerite (est inventory), 1956, Ja 22,87:8
Collins, Marietta Mrs, 1937, S 1,19:2
Collins, Martha W Mrs, 1941, O 5,48:1
Collins, Martin K, 1958, Jl 28,23:5
Collins, Martin L, 1949, D 27,23:2
Collins, Marvin H, 1961, N 5,88:3
Collins, Mary, 1945, F 2,19:1
Collins, Mary D, 1949, O 4,27:4
Collins, Mary E, 1950, S 16,19:2
Collins, Mary Mrs, 1938, My 24,19:2; 1951, O 12,39:5
Collins, Mary T Mrs, 1941, My 17,15:6
Collins, Matthew G (funl, Je 28,5:3), 1925, Je 27,11:4
Collins, Michael J, 1937, Je 7,19:2; 1937, Ag 26,21:3; 1941, S 7,49:2
Collins, Minturn P, 1957, Mr 30,19:5
Collins, Morgan A, 1946, Mr 22,21:4

Collins, Nan M, 1954, My 14,23:5
Collins, Napoleon Rear Adm, 1875, Ag 21,4:6
Collins, Nur J, 1940, Ap 29,15:6
Collins, Oliver B, 1907, Ja 20,7:6
Collins, Oliver C, 1949, Mr 8,25:4
Collins, P, 1878, Je 25,5:5
Collins, P D, 1883, N 5,4:7
Collins, P H, 1943, D 12,68:1
Collins, Paddy, 1881, Jl 22,8:2
Collins, Pat, 1960, My 21,23:6
Collins, Patrick A, 1905, S 15,9:5; 1953, Jl 20,17:2
Collins, Patrick H, 1943, Je 4,21:2
Collins, Patrick J, 1947, Ag 17,54:3; 1951, Mr 17,15:6
Collins, Patrick K, 1945, Ap 22,36:1
Collins, Patrick L, 1939, D 19,23:3
Collins, Paul A, 1952, Ag 14,23:6
Collins, Paul D, 1967, Mr 29,45:1
Collins, Paul L, 1955, N 1,31:4
Collins, Percy, 1954, Ap 28,31:1
Collins, Peter, 1958, Ag 4,27:3
Collins, Phelps, 1918, Mr 30,13:4
Collins, Phil, 1948, Ag 15,60:5
Collins, Phil S Mrs, 1948, Ja 29,23:4
Collins, Philip S, 1943, S 30,21:1
Collins, Ralph A, 1950, Jl 25,27:4
Collins, Ray, 1965, Jl 12,27:4
Collins, Richard, 1938, D 12,19:6; 1948, Ap 10,13:4
Collins, Richard H, 1945, Mr 28,23:4; 1951, F 5,24:2
Collins, Richard J, 1943, O 9,13:5
Collins, Robert M, 1937, Mr 31,23:1
Collins, Robert O, 1951, Jl 27,19:5
Collins, Roderic G 3d, 1955, Je 14,29:3
Collins, Ross A, 1968, Jl 15,31:5
Collins, Rosser G, 1953, Ja 30,21:4
Collins, Roy H, 1949, Ag 8,15:2
Collins, Russell, 1965, N 15,37:1
Collins, S C, 1883, Jl 14,5:3
Collins, S P, 1903, My 31,2:5
Collins, Sarah J, 1947, N 26,23:1
Collins, Seward B, 1952, D 9,33:3
Collins, Simon, 1948, F 14,13:4
Collins, Stacy B, 1873, Je 27,8:5
Collins, Stephen V, 1953, Je 26,19:5
Collins, Stephen W, 1950, Mr 17,23:2
Collins, T D, 1914, Ap 17,11:6
Collins, Ted (Jos M),(funl plans, My 29,29:1), 1964, My 28,37:4
Collins, Thomas, 1945, Ag 3,17:5; 1948, D 12,92:5
Collins, Thomas A, 1958, Je 3,31:1
Collins, Thomas E, 1950, D 6,33:2
Collins, Thomas E Mrs, 1963, Ap 6,19:6
Collins, Thomas H Mrs, 1962, Ja 5,29:4
Collins, Thomas J, 1942, O 21,21:4; 1954, Ag 23,17:5
Collins, Thomas S, 1951, N 3,17:3
Collins, Timothy S Mrs, 1949, O 25,27:2
Collins, Treve, 1939, Jl 8,15:6
Collins, Truman W, 1964, F 24,25:4
Collins, Ullainee, 1953, Ag 5,23:2
Collins, Ulric B, 1939, Ag 19,15:5
Collins, Vaughan S, 1939, Jl 9,31:1
Collins, Victor F, 1956, O 26,29:2
Collins, W Rowland, 1944, S 28,19:6
Collins, Walter H, 1959, Mr 14,23:4
Collins, Walter T, 1949, Ag 11,23:4
Collins, Walter T Mrs (A Wheaton), 1961, D 27,27:4
Collins, Ward, 1939, Ja 1,24:8
Collins, Whitley C, 1959, My 13,37:3
Collins, Wilkie, 1889, S 24,4:7
Collins, William, 1940, O 4,23:1; 1952, Ap 10,29:4; 1965, Mr 7,82:8
Collins, William A, 1948, My 30,34:4
Collins, William C, 1949, Je 9,31:3
Collins, William E P, 1949, Ja 13,24:3
Collins, William F, 1939, N 19,39:3; 1940, Ja 13,15:5; 1949, Mr 8,25:5
Collins, William F Sr, 1956, N 6,35:3
Collins, William G, 1915, Je 21,9:6
Collins, William H, 1939, Mr 12,III,6:6; 1947, D 1, 21:4; 1948, Ja 17,17:5
Collins, William H Dr, 1937, Ja 15,21:4
Collins, William H Mrs, 1938, Ag 30,17:3; 1948, N 24, 23:5; 1958, Ag 23,15:2
Collins, William Herschel, 1953, F 13,21:2
Collins, William J, 1940, Ag 29,19:6; 1945, D 21,21:3; 1947, S 14,60:2; 1957, Mr 3,84:8; 1959, O 17,23:5; 1960, N 27,86:4
Collins, William K Sr, 1949, Ap 15,23:2
Collins, William M, 1942, Ja 19,20:1; 1946, F 28,23:1
Collins, William Mrs, 1950, S 28,31:2
Collins, William Mrs (Ruth W), 1965, Ja 23,25:5
Collins, William Mrs (Emma M), 1965, N 29,35:5
Collins, William P, 1950, Ap 8,13:6; 1955, O 3,27:4
Collins, William R, 1938, Mr 7,17:1; 1944, F 29,17:3; 1950, Ja 29,69:2; 1961, My 15,31:4
Collins, William T (funl, S 9,19:4), 1961, S 6,37:1
Collins, William T Mrs, 1960, Ap 23,23:4
Collinson, Benjamin Jr, 1938, Jl 19,22:1
Collinson, Harold F, 1955, My 12,29:3
Collinson, Joseph B, 1951, Ap 4,29:5
Collinson, Richard Sir, 1883, S 14,4:6
Collinson, William, 1941, F 1,17:3; 1959, O 21,43:2
Collip, James B, 1965, Je 21,29:1
Collis, C H T Gen, 1902, My 12,2:4
Collis, C H T Mrs, 1917, Jl 29,15:2
Collis, Janette H, 1956, Je 4,29:5
Collis, Joseph R, 1952, D 8,41:2
Collis, Lloyd, 1942, Ja 3,19:6
Collis, William P, 1955, Je 7,33:5
Collison, A Vernon, 1947, Ja 11,19:2
Collison, Perce B, 1966, Ag 21,93:1
Collison, Wilson, 1941, My 26,19:6
Colliss, Shirley, 1941, O 5,49:2
Collisson, Charles S Mrs, 1940, Ap 3,23:1
Collisson, N Harvey, 1966, N 1,41:1
Collister, Edwin B, 1939, S 2,17:7
Collitz, Herman Mrs, 1944, N 24,23:3
Collivadino, Pio, 1945, Ag 27,19:4
Colliver, Donald B, 1944, S 12,19:6
Collman, Charles A, 1952, Ap 18,25:2
Collmar, Charles, 1942, N 22,52:4
Collmer, Carl W, 1951, Ja 12,27:4
Collmus, Charles C Jr, 1937, S 9,23:3
Collom, Andrew H, 1940, Ap 16,23:3
Collom, Samuel H, 1939, Ag 16,23:6
Collopy, Carl J, 1951, Je 18,23:5
Collopy, Ernest C, 1951, S 26,31:2
Collopy, John W Jr, 1964, Ap 12,86:7
Collorbon, Cuthbert, 1945, S 29,15:2
Collord, George W, 1914, Mr 17,11:4
Collord, George W Mrs, 1908, Ja 24,7:5
Colloredo-Mannsfeld, Ferdinand, 1967, D 20,49:1
Colloredo-Mannsfield, Countess, 1939, F 26,28:6
Colloredo-Mansfeld, Countess (M Bradley), 1965, Mr 28,92:3
Colloton, J Edmund, 1961, N 12,86:6
Colloton, John E Mrs, 1953, Ap 27,23:5
Collum, Francis L, 1955, Ag 4,25:4
Collver, Leon L W, 1949, My 16,21:5
Collyer, Bert E, 1938, Jl 29,17:4
Collyer, Frank Sr, 1944, F 23,19:5
Collyer, Herman L Dr, 1923, Ag 16,15:5
Collyer, Homer, 1947, Mr 22,1:5
Collyer, June (Mrs Stuart Erwin), 1968, Mr 19,47:1
Collyer, Langley, 1947, Ap 9,1:2
Collyer, Moses W, 1942, S 23,25:3
Collyer, R N, 1932, Ag 2,17:6
Collyer, Robert Rev Dr (funl, D 3,15:5), 1912, D 2, 11:4
Collyer, Robert T, 1943, F 9,23:4
Collyer, Thomas L, 1949, My 5,27:3
Collyer, William I, 1956, Mr 29,27:4
Colm, Gerhard Dr, 1968, D 27,30:4
Colm, Gerhard Mrs (Hanna), 1965, Mr 22,33:4
Colman, Charles Rev, 1924, Je 4,23:5
Colman, Earl S, 1955, Ja 25,25:2
Colman, Edward A, 1956, Mr 22,35:3
Colman, Ethal M, 1948, N 24,24:3
Colman, Harry A Mrs, 1951, Jl 23,17:5
Colman, Howell Mrs, 1938, O 27,23:6
Colman, Irving S, 1961, Ap 22,25:6
Colman, Jeremiah, 1942, Ja 17,17:3; 1961, Ja 10,47:2
Colman, John D, 1945, S 26,23:5
Colman, John L Mrs, 1944, Ap 25,25:7
Colman, Julia, 1909, Ja 11,9:6
Colman, Leonard M, 1960, N 29,37:3
Colman, Norman J, 1911, N 4,13:6
Colman, Ronald (funl, My 22,29:2; will, My 29,22:1), 1958, My 20,33:2
Colman, Royal C, 1939, Jl 5,17:5
Colman, Russell J, 1946, Mr 23,13:2
Colman, Samuel, 1920, Mr 30,11:3
Colman, Samuel Mrs, 1954, N 16,29:5
Colman, Thomas H, 1940, Mr 19,26:2
Colman, William E, 1953, Mr 9,29:3
Colmas Stanislaus, Bro (E Gagnier), 1955, D 6,37:2
Colmers, Franz A, 1960, Ap 13,40:1
Colmery, Walter S, 1943, N 4,23:3
Colmey, John, 1941, O 18,19:6
Colmo, A, 1934, Jl 7,13:6
Colmore, Charles B, 1950, Je 30,23:2
Colnaghi, Dominic Ellis Sir, 1908, Mr 2,9:5
Colne, William W, 1919, N 10,13:2
Colnes, Thomas H, 1955, Ag 30,27:4
Colnon, Aaron, 1950, N 14,31:2
Colnon, Phil, 1952, Je 13,23:3
Colomb, John, 1909, My 28,9:6
Colomb, Vice Adm, 1899, O 15,7:5
Colombier, Marie, 1910, Ag 31,9:6
Colombo, Emilio, 1937, N 25,31:5
Colombo, John C Mrs, 1951, D 14,31:3
Colombo, Leopold, 1956, Ap 13,25:3
Colombo, Louis J, 1959, Mr 30,31:2
Colombo, Louis J Mrs, 1941, F 28,19:3
Colombo, Nicola, 1942, My 11,15:2
Colombo, Paul, 1951, Jl 16,21:6
Colon, Salvador, 1953, S 8,26:5
Colonel, James P, 1954, F 13,13:6
Coloney, Leslie H, 1950, Ap 11,31:4
Colonna, Fabrizio Prince, 1923, Ag 9,13:5
Colonna, Marc Antonio Prince (Duke of Paliano), 1912, Ja 30,9:5
Colonna, Marcantonio, 1947, Mr 11,27:1
Colonna, Piero Prince, 1939, Ag 25,15:4
Colonna, Princess (Maria Massimo), 1916, N 11,9:2
Colonna, Princess (Evelyn Bryant Mackay), 1919, Mr 31,13:4
Colonne, de Mme, 1880, Jl 25,9:2
Colonsay, Baron, 1874, F 3,1:5
Colony, Alfred T Mrs, 1961, Ap 18,37:1
Colony, Don A, 1950, F 20,25:3
Colony, John J, 1955, F 2,27:2
Colony, Roy J Mrs, 1947, S 25,29:6
Colorado, Rafael, 1959, F 11,39:5
Colpitts, Charles B, 1961, Ja 8,86:7
Colpitts, Edwin H (por), 1949, Mr 7,21:4
Colpitts, Edwin H Mrs, 1940, Mr 13,23:6
Colpitts, Walter W, 1951, D 24,13:1
Colpitts, Walter W Mrs, 1952, Ag 28,23:2
Colpus, Henry H, 1939, N 29,6:5
Colquhoun, Alister C, 1945, D 12,27:5
Colquhoun, Archibald Ross, 1914, D 19,13:5
Colquhoun, Iain, 1948, N 13,15:1
Colquhoun, William, 1938, S 30,21:4
Colquitt, A H Sen, 1894, Mr 27,2:5
Colquitt, O B, 1940, Mr 9,15:1
Colquitt, Oscar B Mrs, 1949, Jl 1,19:6
Colquitt, Walter, 1937, Mr 17,19:4
Colrick, John T, 1948, F 16,21:5
Colsen, Aud C, 1938, My 19,21:1
Colsey, Arthur, 1939, S 16,17:5
Colson, Chester S, 1939, D 6,25:3
Colson, David G Col, 1904, O 2,1:6
Colson, Ellen E A Mrs, 1947, D 12,27:1
Colson, Everett A, 1937, F 24,24:1
Colson, Louis A, 1951, Mr 10,13:5
Colson, William H, 1942, Ja 16,21:4
Colston, A Vaughn, 1949, My 19,29:2
Colston, Albert L, 1949, Mr 9,25:4
Colston, R Semmes, 1925, F 24,19:5
Colston, Robert W Mrs, 1939, Jl 26,19:4
Colt, Alex, 1962, D 4,41:3
Colt, Beatrice, 1914, N 19,11:7
Colt, Don S Dr, 1937, Ja 15,22:1
Colt, Elisha, 1874, F 5,1:7
Colt, Francis S, 1938, My 16,17:2
Colt, Frederick A, 1941, F 2,43:5
Colt, Harris D, 1959, S 29,36:2
Colt, James J, 1967, Ja 19,35:2
Colt, James W, 1941, F 18,23:6
Colt, James W Mrs, 1942, S 25,21:6
Colt, John, 1945, My 23,19:3
Colt, Judson Boardman, 1921, Jl 27,15:6
Colt, Le Baron Bradford Sen, 1924, Ag 19,15:3
Colt, Le Baron D Mrs, 1922, Jl 3,13:7
Colt, Mary E S Mrs, 1947, Je 10,27:5
Colt, Richard C, 1938, N 12,15:6
Colt, Richard C Mrs, 1954, S 4,11:4
Colt, Roslyn E, 1954, My 23,89:2
Colt, Roswell L, 1914, Ja 16,9:4
Colt, Russell G, 1960, Jl 10,72:1
Colt, Samuel Col, 1862, Ja 11,5:2
Colt, Samuel G, 1955, Mr 10,27:3
Colt, Samuel G Mrs, 1947, Ja 14,25:1
Colt, Samuel Mrs (will), 1905, Ag 31,7:7
Colt, Samuel P Col, 1921, Ag 14,22:4
Colt, Samuel S, 1942, D 1,25:4
Colt, Stockton, 1937, Je 23,25:5
Colt, Teresa S Mrs, 1955, My 26,31:4
Colt, Thomas C, 1937, Ap 21,23:3
Colt, William A, 1955, Mr 6,88:4
Colt, William L, 1941, Mr 27,23:5
Colten, Bernard (Feb 16), 1963, Ap 1,35:3
Colter, Alice D, 1947, O 10,25:5
Colter, Carter R, 1939, D 30,15:5
Colthup, James F, 1968, Mr 1,43:6
Colthurst, George O, 1951, Mr 1,27:1
Colthurst, George O (will), 1952, Ap 3,37:6
Colthurst, George Sir, 1925, D 27,7:1
Colthurst, Richard S J, 1955, F 19,15:4
Coltman, Charles L, 1966, Jl 23,25:1
Coltman, Robert W, 1950, Jl 11,31:4
Coltman, Thomas J, 1949, N 29,29:1
Colton, A John, 1968, Ap 10,47:2
Colton, Adelaide Belle Mrs, 1924, My 15,19:4
Colton, Albert J, 1949, Je 19,68:4
Colton, Arthur N, 1963, N 14,35:1
Colton, Arthur W, 1943, D 29,18:3
Colton, Billy, 1878, N 11,5:3
Colton, Charles A, 1956, O 24,37:3
Colton, Charles Henry Bp, 1915, My 10,15:3
Colton, Charles M, 1949, Ja 19,27:3
Colton, Cullen B, 1953, Mr 17,35:5
Colton, D D Gen, 1878, O 11,5:4
Colton, Edwin F, 1965, My 14,37:1
Colton, Eric, 1956, S 2,56:4
Colton, Ferry B, 1954, Ag 11,25:4
Colton, Francis, 1913, Mr 10,9:4
Colton, Frederick T Sr, 1942, D 13,75:5
Colton, Frederick W, 1941, N 25,25:4
Colton, G Q, 1898, Ag 12,7:5
Colton, George R, 1916, Ap 8,15:6
Colton, George W, 1916, Je 23,11:4
Colton, Henry E, 1942, N 3,24:2
Colton, Henry E Mrs, 1937, Ja 21,24:1
Colton, James, 1911, O 5,11:2
Colton, John, 1958, Ap 11,26:1
Colton, John B, 1946, D 29,35:6
Colton, John W, 1950, My 25,29:5
Colton, Joseph K, 1950, Ap 10,19:1

Colton, Lee A, 1942, Mr 25,21:2
Colton, Marjorie A, 1962, Mr 28,39:2
Colton, Richard B, 1952, F 14,27:4
Colton, Thomas J, 1945, O 1,19:5
Colton, Walter E, 1949, Mr 28,21:4
Colton, Wendell P, 1958, Je 22,76:5
Colton, William Francis, 1921, Ja 8,11:5
Colton, William N, 1951, Je 19,29:2
Colton, William R, 1963, D 11,47:1
Colton, 1878, N 3,10:5
Coltorti, Bismarck Mrs, 1952, O 24,23:4
Coltrane, Daniel B, 1937, Ja 18,17:3
Coltrane, John (funl plans, Jl 19,39:3; funl, Jl 22,13:1), 1967, Jl 18,37:2
Coltrin, Bobby, 1945, O 2,17:3
Coltrin, Gilbert S, 1961, S 16,19:4
Colucci, Sabato, 1949, D 31,15:4
Colucci, William V, 1958, Ag 13,27:3
Colum, Mary, 1957, O 23,33:1
Columba, Bro (P J Reilly), 1961, Ag 15,29:2
Columba, Sister (Sisters of St Joseph), 1915, S 9,11:5
Columbo, Giuseppe Sen, 1921, Ja 18,11:4
Columbo, Nicholas Mrs, 1944, S 1,15:5
Columbus, Premo J, 1955, O 4,35:2
Columbus, William F, 1959, My 4,29:5
Colvan, Zeke B, 1945, O 10,36:2
Colvell, George W, 1952, Ap 29,27:5
Colver, W B, 1926, My 29,15:5
Colver, William B Mrs, 1964, D 28,29:3
Colvert, wm R, 1957, Je 4,35:1
Colvig, Pinto, 1967, O 6,39:4
Colvile, Henry Sir, 1907, N 26,9:4
Colvill, A, 1878, D 7,2:4
Colvill, Arthur, 1939, F 12,44:7
Colville, Elizabeth V Mrs, 1941, Ja 14,21:5
Colville, Hugh C, 1940, Ja 23,21:2
Colville, Hugh P, 1953, Mr 22,86:8
Colville, J W Sir, 1880, D 7,2:3
Colville, John (Lord Clydesmuir), 1954, N 2,27:5
Colville, Kenneth H, 1968, D 13,42:1
Colville, Kenneth I, 1965, Ag 27,29:3
Colville, Lord of Culross, 1903, Jl 2,9:6
Colville, Stanley Adm Sir, 1939, Ap 11,24:4
Colville, William Col, 1905, Je 14,9:6
Colville, William J Sir, 1903, O 17,9:6
Colvin, Addison B, 1939, Je 21,23:3
Colvin, Allan D, 1950, Mr 12,92:2
Colvin, Andrew, 1921, Ap 2,11:4
Colvin, Charles A, 1939, Mr 11,17:5
Colvin, Charles H, 1946, Jl 23,25:3
Colvin, D Leigh, 1959, S 8,35:1
Colvin, Darwin Dr, 1911, Ja 9,13:5
Colvin, David L Mrs, 1955, O 31,25:3
Colvin, Edwin R, 1966, Je 16,47:3
Colvin, Eugene T H, 1954, Jl 28,23:3
Colvin, Flora M, 1944, D 16,15:6
Colvin, Fred H, 1965, D 3,39:1
Colvin, Fred H Mrs, 1955, Mr 18,27:4
Colvin, Herbert A, 1949, O 11,31:4
Colvin, Ian D, 1938, My 12,23:2
Colvin, James E, 1956, Je 17,92:3
Colvin, James G, 1968, F 20,47:1
Colvin, Jerome Mrs, 1943, Ag 17,17:4
Colvin, Leon E, 1956, Ag 28,27:3
Colvin, Merrill A, 1946, Je 1,13:4
Colvin, Norman B, 1961, Ap 5,37:1
Colvin, Stephen Sheldon, 1923, Jl 16,11:6
Colvin, Thomas J, 1950, Ap 9,85:1
Colvin, William H, 1949, S 26,25:4
Colvin, William M, 1963, Jl 25,25:4
Colvin, William S, 1922, O 7,15:6
Colvin, Woolf Mrs, 1959, Ja 23,25:2
Colvocoresses, G P, 1932, S 12,15:1
Colwell, Daniel, 1922, S 20,21:5
Colwell, Edwin G, 1945, O 1,19:3
Colwell, Frederick L Sr, 1947, Ja 23,23:1
Colwell, Harris, 1940, Ag 13,19:4
Colwell, Harry E, 1951, Jl 4,17:1
Colwell, James H, 1941, Ja 13,15:4
Colwell, Joseph, 1882, My 20,4:7
Colwell, May L Mrs, 1946, S 18,31:4
Colwell, Paul A Mrs, 1953, F 26,25:3
Colwell, Robert C, 1957, F 4,19:3
Colwell, Robert T, 1967, Je 27,39:3
Colwell, Samuel L Mrs, 1960, My 16,31:4
Colwell, Thomas A, 1953, Jl 8,27:3
Colwell, W H, 1882, Jl 23,12:2
Colwell, Winfield S, 1944, Ja 12,23:5
Colwin, Edward M, 1909, S 19,11:3
Colwin, Martin B, 1967, F 14,43:1
Colwin, Martin B Jr, 1948, F 18,27:4
Colwyn, Lord, 1946, Ja 28,19:5
Colyar, A S Col, 1907, D 14,9:5
Colyer, C Washington, 1918, Je 29,11:5
Colyer, Charles B Mrs, 1944, S 12,19:6
Colyer, Ernest, 1941, My 18,45:1
Colyer, George, 1938, N 16,23:2
Colyer, George D, 1948, D 17,27:4
Colyer, Morrison C, 1939, N 7,28:5
Colyer, Paul H, 1939, Ja 11,19:3
Colyer, Vincent Mrs, 1872, N 2,5:4
Colyer, William J, 1949, Mr 24,27:3
Comacho, Justo, 1954, O 8,34:6

Coman, Francis D, 1952, Ja 31,28:2
Coman, Henry Benjamin Justice, 1912, Ja 11,13:4
Coman, James A Mrs, 1948, F 5,24:2
Coman, John F, 1954, Je 16,31:3
Coman, Katherine Prof, 1915, Ja 12,9:4
Coman, Lawrence H, 1968, D 7,47:2
Coman, Lucien D, 1948, Je 7,19:2
Coman, Martha, 1959, N 29,86:8
Coman, Robert G Mrs, 1941, O 15,21:4
Coman, Teresa, 1960, Jl 22,23:2
Coman, Thomas, 1909, O 24,13:2
Coman, Tine L Mrs, 1941, S 29,17:5
Coman, Wilber E, 1939, Je 11,44:6
Comar, Charlotte Buell Mrs, 1924, N 13,21:4
Comaskey, James, 1903, N 29,7:6
Comba, Richard Brig-Gen, 1907, Mr 31,9:7
Comber, John Mrs, 1960, N 17,37:3
Comber, Robert W, 1945, My 25,19:5
Combermere, Field-Marshal Lord, 1865, Mr 12,6:2
Combes, A C Sr, 1927, Mr 18,21:5
Combes, Abbott C Jr, 1959, Mr 2,27:5
Combes, C W, 1884, F 14,5:2
Combes, Clinton D, 1953, Jl 11,11:5
Combes, Edgar, 1907, Ap 11,11:6
Combes, Frank C Sr Mrs, 1943, Je 9,21:1
Combes, George D A, 1941, S 21,45:2
Combes, Helen M Mrs, 1949, D 18,90:3
Combes, Marie C Mrs, 1961, Ag 21,23:4
Combes, Phoebe A, 1962, Ja 18,29:1
Combes, Rodney C F Mrs, 1956, D 5,39:4
Combes, William H Mrs, 1951, Mr 27,29:1
Combet, Gilbert, 1945, N 16,19:4
Combier, Philibert, 1950, Ap 6,29:3
Combiths, John E, 1953, Mr 18,31:3
Combs, Benjamin, 1940, D 11,27:3
Combs, C J, 1939, Jl 20,19:6
Combs, Daniel, 1953, Ja 4,78:5
Combs, Earle M, 1937, N 28,II,9:3
Combs, Elston, 1951, O 11,37:4
Combs, Elvan, 1942, O 21,21:2
Combs, Emile, 1921, My 26,13:3
Combs, Everett R, 1957, Ja 7,25:4
Combs, Floyd M, 1941, Ja 29,17:4
Combs, Frank B, 1944, Ja 20,19:2
Combs, Frederick A Sr, 1955, Jl 1,21:4
Combs, George Mrs, 1947, F 1,15:5
Combs, George W, 1958, D 7,88:1
Combs, Gilbert W T, 1952, F 28,27:2
Combs, Harry P, 1956, Ag 20,21:4
Combs, J W T, 1903, Ap 2,9:5
Combs, Jess M, 1953, Ag 23,89:3
Combs, John M, 1947, Ap 13,60:4
Combs, Laura L, 1949, Jl 20,25:4
Combs, Leslie, 1940, N 19,24:3
Combs, Mahlon A, 1960, S 8,35:2
Combs, Mary A Mrs, 1938, Mr 1,21:5
Combs, Morgan L, 1955, O 27,33:1
Combs, Roy D, 1944, N 22,19:6
Combs, Roy H, 1941, Ap 26,15:4
Combs, Sidney Mrs, 1958, Jl 5,17:5
Combs, Stephen Mrs, 1942, Ap 8,19:5
Combs, Thomas, 1964, D 11,39:4
Combs, William H, 1951, Jl 24,26:3
Combs, William H Mrs, 1958, Jl 12,15:4
Come, Annie Mrs, 1874, My 6,2:3
Come, Charles J, 1954, N 5,21:3
Come, Charles J Mrs, 1945, O 27,15:5
Comeau, Joseph W, 1966, Ja 12,21:4
Comeaux, Albin D, 1961, Ag 28,25:4
Comeaux, C Stewart, 1954, D 12,89:1
Comee, Frederick R, 1909, Ap 17,9:5
Comeford, Walter (Bro Matthias), 1952, S 30,31:2
Comegys, Cornelius, 1938, Mr 20,II,8:6
Comegys, Elinor F Mrs, 1946, Ap 17,25:1
Comegys, William Henry Col, 1919, Ap 1,11:4
Comella, Guido, 1952, S 28,77:1
Comello, Anthony J, 1949, D 16,31:1
Comen, Louis M, 1944, Ja 8,13:3
Comenetz, Meyer M, 1942, N 17,25:2
Comer, Clifford E, 1968, My 2,48:1
Comer, Donald, 1963, Je 2,84:4
Comer, Edward T Mrs, 1948, Ap 14,27:3
Comer, Eva A Mrs, 1953, Je 4,29:5
Comer, George Capt, 1937, Ap 30,21:5
Comer, Guy W, 1953, S 7,19:5
Comer, Harry, 1922, Ja 5,15:4
Comer, Harry D, 1966, Ap 26,46:1
Comer, Hugh M, 1962, S 19,39:5
Comer, John Preston Mrs, 1968, Ja 24,42:2
Comerford, Eva Mrs, 1941, Je 18,21:2
Comerford, Frank D, 1941, N 25,25:3
Comerford, Helen M, 1956, S 10,27:1
Comerford, Jean C Mrs, 1948, Jl 17,15:4
Comerford, Marie L Mrs, 1941, F 17,15:2
Comerford, Michael E (will, F 17,16:3), 1939, F 2, 19:2
Comerford, Michael J, 1949, Mr 29,25:1
Comerford, William A, 1955, Ag 10,25:5
Comes, Donald A, 1957, Jl 16,26:1
Comes, Emma F, 1952, S 18,29:1
Comes, Washington Irving, 1925, N 25,21:4
Comes, William G, 1948, Jl 29,21:2
Comey, George B, 1938, Ja 26,23:3

Comey, John W (will, Ag 22,19:5), 1952, Ag 9,13:6
Comey, Morris L Mrs, 1957, Jl 23,27:1
Comfort, A M, 1931, Ja 13,27:3
Comfort, Benjamin F, 1941, Je 21,17:2
Comfort, C Ranson Mrs, 1958, Ap 22,33:1
Comfort, Charles W Jr, 1957, My 7,35:3
Comfort, Frank J, 1955, N 3,31:1
Comfort, G Lloyd, 1959, Ag 28,23:2
Comfort, George, 1952, Jl 25,17:5
Comfort, George F Dr, 1910, My 6,9:5
Comfort, Guy, 1938, Mr 9,23:5
Comfort, James A Sr, 1948, N 16,29:2
Comfort, Lucy Randall, 1914, D 12,15:6
Comfort, Mandred W, 1957, Ag 9,19:2
Comfort, Melvin G, 1949, Je 10,27:2
Comfort, Randall, 1959, N 30,31:5
Comfort, William R, 1951, Ag 26,76:5
Comfort, William W, 1955, D 25,48:5
Comfort, William W Mrs, 1965, My 11,39:4
Comin, Robert, 1959, O 9,29:2
Comingore, Edward G Mrs, 1959, Ag 25,31:2
Comings, George F, 1942, Je 12,21:2
Comings, Harry E, 1950, F 19,76:2
Comings, Herbert B, 1945, Mr 14,19:5
Comings, Herbert C, 1948, F 23,25:6
Comins, Joseph S, 1960, O 12,43:2
Cominsky, Jacob Robert (mem ser set, Ag 6,25:2), 1968, Ag 4,68:3
Cominsky, Rebecca M Mrs, 1938, O 7,23:2
Comiskey, C A, 1931, O 26,25:5
Comiskey, Daniel, 1945, Mr 18,42:1
Comiskey, Dennis J, 1946, Jl 7,36:4
Comiskey, Grace L, 1952, Je 16,17:5
Comiskey, J Louis, 1939, Jl 19,19:4
Comiskey, J Louis Mrs (funl, D 14,29:5), 1956, D 11,39:3
Comiskey, J Louis Mrs (will), 1957, Ja 4,21:6
Comiskey, James, 1943, Ap 15,25:5
Comiskey, Martin A, 1948, Ap 13,27:1
Comley, James H, 1959, S 30,29:6
Comley, William H, 1955, Ap 30,17:5
Comly, Catherine F Mrs, 1941, Mr 11,23:1
Comly, Garrard Mrs, 1965, Mr 9,35:3
Comly, Guy S, 1915, O 21,11:5
Comly, James V, 1946, Mr 30,15:1
Comly, Samuel, 1957, N 3,88:7
Comly, Walter S Mrs, 1953, Je 22,21:4
Commager, Henry Steele Mrs, 1968, Mr 29,41:4
Commanday, Frank, 1956, Ag 16,25:4
Commander, Charles C, 1953, Je 21,85:1
Commentry, Andre, 1961, N 19,89:1
Commerford, John Edward, 1922, Jl 17,13:5
Commette, Albert R, 1951, Ap 21,17:3
Commin, Pierre, 1958, Je 25,29:1
Commington, Ellen F, 1956, Mr 21,37:2
Commins, Saxe, 1958, Jl 18,21:1
Commiskey, Arch H, 1948, S 30,27:2
Committee, Louis S, 1958, Mr 8,17:2
Common, James A Mrs, 1950, Ja 24,31:1
Common, Lawrence A, 1953, Ap 7,29:2
Common, Renwick G, 1942, Je 30,21:3
Commons, John R, 1945, My 13,20:5
Commons, Richard H, 1942, N 14,16:2
Commons, William H, 1937, D 21,23:1
Commselman, H E, 1954, O 4,27:4
Comnene, Nicola, 1958, D 9,41:3
Como, Pietro Mrs, 1961, Ap 22,25:1
Comorosky, Adam, 1951, Mr 4,93:1
Compain, Pierre P, 1940, My 2,23:3
Comparette, Thomas Louis, 1922, Jl 5,19:6
Compher, Frederic M, 1966, Ag 18,35:2
Compris, Maurice, 1939, O 21,15:2
Compston, Archie, 1962, Ag 9,25:3
Compton, Alfred D (por), 1949, Ja 29,13:1
Compton, Alfred G Prof, 1913, D 13,13:6
Compton, Alfred S Mrs, 1945, Jl 12,11:5
Compton, Alwyn Lord, 1906, Ap 5,9:6
Compton, Arthur, 1951, Mr 13,31:5
Compton, Arthur H, 1962, Mr 16,1:4
Compton, Beacher W, 1942, Je 22,15:1
Compton, Betty (will, Jl 27,19:6), 1944, Jl 13,17:5
Compton, Charles W, 1952, Ja 18,27:5
Compton, Cy, 1944, Je 20,19:6
Compton, Edgar M, 1950, Ag 30,31:1
Compton, Edward C, 1944, Ap 2,40:2
Compton, Edward Mrs (V Bateman), 1940, My 5, 52:3
Compton, Elias, 1938, My 3,23:4
Compton, Emma L Mrs, 1937, Ja 20,21:5
Compton, Floyd H, 1953, S 26,17:2
Compton, Francis, 1964, S 19,27:4
Compton, Frank E, 1950, My 14,106:4
Compton, Frederick N Mrs, 1949, Ja 18,23:5
Compton, George, 1939, Mr 18,17:4; 1942, F 11,21:5
Compton, George B (por), 1938, Mr 25,19:1
Compton, Glenn C, 1963, My 14,39:5
Compton, H (see also S 17), 1877, S 30,7:3
Compton, Halstead C, 1915, N 22,15:5
Compton, Harry M, 1944, O 13,19:2
Compton, James A, 1955, N 13,87:6
Compton, Joseph, 1937, Ja 19,24:2
Compton, Joseph H, 1957, Jl 3,23:4
Compton, Karl T (mem ser, Je 26,13:5; trb lr, Jl 4,-IV,6:7), 1954, Je 23,1:4

Compton, Leslie I, 1960, O 10,31:3
Compton, Lewis, 1942, O 25,45:1
Compton, Merrill E, 1954, Ja 1,23:4
Compton, Orville C, 1958, Je 3,31:4
Compton, Paul D, 1958, D 3,37:4
Compton, Randall, 1965, O 16,27:5
Compton, Richard J, 1951, F 8,33:3
Compton, Sumner H, 1951, My 10,31:5
Compton, Walter A, 1959, D 11,33:2
Compton, William, 1955, Mr 22,31:4
Compton, William A, 1963, Jl 8,29:5
Compton, William C, 1944, Ag 29,17:4; 1948, My 12, 28:3
Compton, William D, 1955, Ap 2,17:6
Compton, William George, 1968, Mr 18,5:5
Compton, William N, 1939, Ap 11,23:5
Compton, William R, 1957, Jl 13,17:4
Compton, Wilson M, 1967, Mr 8,45:4
Compton, Wilson M Jr, 1964, Jl 14,33:2
Comrie, Alex, 1953, Jl 4,11:5
Comroe, Bernard I, 1945, S 16,44:3
Comstedt, Josef F A, 1965, Jl 17,25:4
Comstock, A, 1877, Je 1,4:6
Comstock, A Barr, 1956, Ap 3,29:4
Comstock, A Barr Mrs, 1953, Ja 26,19:3
Comstock, Albert, 1943, Mr 25,21:2
Comstock, Albert E, 1953, Mr 6,23:2
Comstock, Alexander, 1909, D 23,9:3
Comstock, Alzada, 1960, Ja 16,21:5
Comstock, Amy, 1944, Jl 22,15:6
Comstock, Archie A, 1950, Jl 19,31:3
Comstock, Boyd L, 1950, D 15,31:2
Comstock, C Arthur Mrs, 1954, Ag 28,15:5
Comstock, Charles E, 1953, Ja 14,32:5
Comstock, Charles Mrs, 1957, F 10,85:5
Comstock, Clara B, 1963, S 13,30:1
Comstock, Clarence A, 1939, D 28,21:4
Comstock, Craig F, 1962, O 25,39:4
Comstock, Curtis A, 1943, N 6,13:1
Comstock, Cyrus B Gen, 1910, My 30,11:6
Comstock, Cyrus W Mrs, 1959, O 4,86:2
Comstock, Daniel V, 1917, My 20,23:3
Comstock, David C, 1942, My 21,19:6
Comstock, Earl H, 1942, F 3,19:3
Comstock, Edward H, 1957, Ja 8,31:2
Comstock, Edwin G Mrs, 1943, Mr 9,23:4
Comstock, Elon, 1865, Mr 18,6:1
Comstock, Enos B, 1945, Mr 21,23:1
Comstock, F Ray, 1949, O 16,88:3
Comstock, Fred S, 1948, Je 14,23:5
Comstock, Frederic R, 1942, O 23,21:2
Comstock, Frederick B, 1962, O 22,29:1
Comstock, Frederick W Dr, 1937, Jl 18,23:1
Comstock, George C, 1963, N 18,33:3
Comstock, George S, 1950, Je 26,27:2
Comstock, Gilbert H, 1874, S 9,2:2
Comstock, Harry, 1954, Mr 4,25:3; 1955, Je 25,15:6
Comstock, Henry Mrs, 1950, Ja 30,17:4
Comstock, Herbert C, 1945, F 22,27:2
Comstock, Howard W, 1938, My 29,II,6:8
Comstock, J H, 1931, Mr 21,17:3
Comstock, J J Maj, 1903, Mr 20,9:6
Comstock, John L Dr, 1858, N 24,1:5
Comstock, Joseph A Capt, 1868, Ag 18,4:6
Comstock, Laura, 1948, Ag 8,57:2
Comstock, Laura M, 1954, D 5,61:3
Comstock, Louis K, 1964, Ja 3,23:3
Comstock, Louis K Mrs, 1952, F 2,13:5
Comstock, Marc W, 1948, F 16,21:3
Comstock, Myrtle E, 1945, N 16,19:3
Comstock, Nanette, 1942, Je 24,19:3
Comstock, Oscar F, 1944, Ja 6,23:1
Comstock, Otis Wheeler, 1916, Ag 26,7:5
Comstock, Paul Mrs, 1951, Jl 2,23:5
Comstock, Robert K, 1950, S 2,15:4
Comstock, S R, 1882, S 24,13:2
Comstock, Sara S Mrs, 1937, Jl 30,19:6
Comstock, Sarah, 1960, Ja 24,88:2
Comstock, Walter Coutant, 1912, Jl 21,II,11:4
Comstock, Walter E, 1937, F 25,23:4
Comstock, Willard L, 1943, N 27,13:4
Comstock, William A (por), 1949, Je 17,23:4
Comstock, William H Judge, 1907, O 9,11:5
Comstock, William I, 1958, Je 3,31:2
Comte De Chasseloup-Laudat, 1873, Ap 1,5:5
Comtesse, Robert, 1922, N 18,15:5
Comtois, George W, 1955, O 12,31:4
Comtois, Paul F (more details, F 22,10:3; funl, F 25,31:3), 1966, F 21,3:5
Comunale, Fortunato, 1950, O 5,31:4
Comuni, Luigi, 1942, Je 23,19:1
Comyns, John H, 1943, Ag 7,11:5
Comyns, Raymond J, 1949, Jl 7,25:1
Comyns-Carr, Arthur, 1965, Ap 22,33:2
Conable, Barber B Sr, 1967, Je 22,39:3
Conacher, Ben Mrs, 1955, Ja 3,27:1
Conacher, John, 1947, D 15,25:1
Conacher, Lionel (rites, My 30,45:2), 1954, My 27, 27:1
Conaghan, Bernard F, 1951, N 30,23:5
Conant, Alban J, 1915, F 4,9:6
Conant, Caroline M Mrs, 1937, N 27,17:3
Conant, Charles A, 1915, Jl 7,11:3
Conant, Charles C, 1938, O 21,23:2
Conant, Charles C Mrs, 1944, Ap 8,13:3
Conant, Charles H, 1939, Ap 18,23:5; 1940, My 30, 18:3
Conant, Clarence M Rev Dr, 1917, Ag 27,9:7
Conant, Edith W, 1968, O 11,47:2
Conant, Ernest L, 1948, N 30,27:5
Conant, Francis O, 1943, Jl 23,17:2
Conant, George D, 1953, Ja 3,15:3
Conant, George F, 1938, Je 21,19:4
Conant, H C Mrs, 1865, F 20,4:5
Conant, Henry J, 1948, F 16,21:4
Conant, Howard, 1959, Ap 12,86:5
Conant, James M, 1949, D 31,15:4
Conant, James S Mrs, 1943, Ap 29,21:2
Conant, James Wallace, 1906, Mr 16,9:4
Conant, Leonard H, 1945, Je 11,15:5
Conant, Osmyn P Mrs, 1910, O 13,11:4
Conant, Ralph H, 1939, N 29,23:4
Conant, Robert L, 1921, S 9,15:4
Conant, William A, 1942, Ag 15,11:3
Conant, William G, 1949, Ag 31,23:5
Conant, William Horace, 1968, F 25,77:1
Conant, William M Dr, 1937, F 20,17:5
Conant, William W, 1952, Ag 13,21:3
Conard, Clarence K, 1947, My 19,21:2
Conard, Frederick U, 1954, Mr 15,25:5
Conard, Helen M Mrs, 1942, Jl 26,31:2
Conard, Jane L, 1955, Ap 12,29:1
Conard, Joseph W, 1965, Ap 7,43:4
Conard, Otway M, 1948, Je 12,15:5
Conard, Philip A, 1958, Jl 18,21:1
Conard, William R, 1946, My 2,21:1
Conarro, Harry W, 1967, D 22,31:4
Conarroe, Elvin H, 1953, O 16,27:3
Conarroe, George W, 1882, Ap 13,5:3
Conason, Arnold, 1957, Ja 12,19:5
Conason, Emil G, 1966, Ap 2,29:2
Conaty, Arnold p, 1963, Jl 3,25:4
Conaty, Bernard S, 1940, Ap 10,25:5
Conaty, John J, 1941, My 7,25:1
Conaty, Peter P, 1949, My 18,27:4
Conaty, Terence P, 1953, F 3,25:4
Conaty, Thomas J Bp, 1915, S 19,15:5
Conaty, Thomas Mrs, 1945, Ag 30,21:4
Conaway, Alfred B, 1951, N 10,17:4
Conaway, John L, 1911, Ag 8,9:4
Conaway, Mary Mrs, 1942, S 1,20:2
Conawy, E A, 1940, F 20,21:5
Conboy, Albert J, 1951, Je 16,15:6
Conboy, Francis J, 1942, Je 15,19:3
Conboy, John, 1951, Jl 26,21:3
Conboy, Martin, 1944, Mr 6,19:1
Conboy, Richard K, 1950, Ap 8,31:2
Conboy, S A Mrs, 1928, Ja 9,23:5
Conboy, Thomas G, 1962, Mr 24,25:3
Conby, Joseph A, 1923, N 15,19:3
Concannon, Charles C, 1957, Ag 11,80:7
Concannon, George T, 1960, Mr 23,37:1
Concannon, Henry Col, 1926, S 19,II,7:1
Concannon, Matthias, 1953, Je 30,23:4
Concannon, Patrick J, 1958, Ap 30,33:3; 1966, Jl 9,27:4
Concas y Palau, Vice-Adm, 1916, S 27,11:7
Concepcion de Gracia, Gilberto Dr, 1968, Mr 16,31:1
Concha, Carlos, 1944, D 18,19:5
Concha, Malaquias Sen, 1921, Ag 7,22:5
Concha, Marshal, 1874, Ag 30,1:5
Concha, Marshal Manuel De La, 1874, Je 30,1:5
Concha de Tamayo, Esther, 1924, Je 8,26:1
Conchar, Belden L, 1950, F 22,29:4
Concheso Valdes, Aurelio F, 1955, N 12,19:4
Conchita, M de la C C B S (Mrs Shaw), 1940, Je 16, 38:5
Concistre, Marie J, 1965, Je 30,37:5
Concklin, Jonas F, 1952, N 2,88:2
Concklin, W W, 1883, My 9,4:7
Conde, Bertha, 1944, Ag 20,33:3
Conde, Charles, 1945, O 16,23:5
Conde, Edwin G, 1953, F 6,20:7
Conde, Frederic, 1924, S 15,21:2
Conde, H C, 1901, Ag 4,5:6
Conde, Swits, 1902, Ja 22,7:4
Conde de Aguilar de Inestrillas, Augustin, 1941, Je 10,23:3
Condell, H A, 1951, N 7,29:2
Condell, Herbert T, 1939, Mr 17,22:2
Condell, Lucy, 1954, D 13,27:5
Condello, Michael Mrs, 1953, S 9,29:3
Conder, Raymond C, 1951, Mr 17,15:5
Conderman, Grace E Mrs, 1942, S 25,21:2
Condict, Anna H Mrs, 1938, Mr 2,19:5
Condict, Caroline E, 1949, Ap 12,30:4
Condict, Emmeline H Mrs, 1942, Jl 29,17:3
Condict, Fred G, 1949, Jl 15,19:4
Condict, Phil K, 1949, S 2,17:1
Condie, Robert, 1945, F 22,27:4
Condit, Abbie H, 1948, Ap 20,27:4
Condit, Albert E, 1954, N 11,31:3
Condit, Albert J, 1941, N 27,23:4
Condit, Alice P, 1949, Je 4,13:5
Condit, Augustus Wilson, 1907, Jl 26,7:6
Condit, C Brookfield, 1942, Je 13,15:5
Condit, Charles B, 1950, My 1,25:5
Condit, Charles L, 1924, D 28,5:2
Condit, D Dale, 1955, My 7,17:4
Condit, Edward A, 1959, Ag 9,89:3
Condit, Edward A Jr, 1964, F 13,31:4
Condit, Elizabeth C, 1964, Ja 17,43:3
Condit, Fillmore, 1939, Ja 7,15:3
Condit, Frederick P, 1955, D 20,31:4
Condit, Harry, 1942, F 11,21:2
Condit, Harry H, 1941, Je 20,21:4
Condit, Henry J, 1952, D 24,17:3
Condit, Henry L, 1950, D 23,16:2
Condit, Howard M, 1946, My 17,22:2
Condit, Ira H, 1944, Ja 27,19:3
Condit, J A, 1881, N 9,2:5; 1885, My 26,5:4
Condit, J B Rev Dr, 1876, Ja 5,5:6
Condit, Jabez Pierson, 1903, Jl 22,7:6
Condit, Jotham Halsey, 1909, Ag 8,9:5
Condit, Kenneth H Mrs, 1963, Ag 8,27:4
Condit, Louis O, 1938, Jl 26,19:3
Condit, Louis O Mrs, 1962, Je 26,33:2
Condit, Martha A P Mrs, 1942, O 30,19:4
Condit, Oscar H, 1951, O 29,23:3
Condit, Ralph E, 1945, F 18,34:1
Condit, Roland S, 1938, F 17,21:4
Condit, Sam P, 1904, F 23,7:6
Condit, Sears B, 1951, N 1,29:1
Condit, Walter, 1910, O 8,11:5
Condit, William A, 1943, O 22,17:4
Condit, William H, 1939, Mr 3,24:2
Condit, William R, 1961, Ag 3,23:5
Condle, Willard D, 1941, D 7,77:1
Condlon, Edward J, 1944, Ag 5,11:5
Condom, Juan S, 1937, Ap 8,23:2
Condon, Albert P, 1939, My 28,III,7:3
Condon, Andrew A, 1956, Je 8,25:5
Condon, Anna Mrs, 1938, Ja 19,23:5
Condon, Charles J, 1939, Ap 4,25:2
Condon, Clarence Melville Capt, 1916, Jl 23,17:5
Condon, Daniel J, 1938, Ag 20,15:5
Condon, David, 1939, O 26,23:3
Condon, David A, 1950, Jl 13,25:5
Condon, David A (cor, S 30,47:1), 1966, S 29,47:4
Condon, David A Mrs, 1947, Ja 21,23:2
Condon, David P, 1939, S 4,19:5
Condon, Edmund, 1943, My 30,26:3
Condon, Edward B, 1942, Ap 9,19:3
Condon, Edward B Mrs, 1943, Ag 19,19:4
Condon, Edward F, 1939, Ja 22,35:2
Condon, Edward O'Meagher Capt, 1915, D 16,15:4; 1915, D 19,17:5
Condon, Ellen Mrs, 1941, My 9,21:6
Condon, Francis B, 1965, N 24,39:1
Condon, Frank, 1940, D 20,25:4
Condon, Hamilton, 1947, D 18,29:4
Condon, Harry L, 1946, O 4,23:2
Condon, Henri, 1950, N 1,35:4
Condon, Howard M, 1956, Ja 9,25:1
Condon, James, 1941, F 1,9:3
Condon, James G, 1941, O 16,21:4
Condon, James H, 1958, S 9,35:4
Condon, John, 1915, Ag 10,11:5; 1920, Mr 22,15:4; 1922, N 6,15:2; 1968, S 15,85:1
Condon, John A, 1937, D 21,23:2
Condon, John E Rev, 1925, Je 27,11:6
Condon, John F, 1939, D 9,15:3; 1945, Ja 3,19:6; 1 Ag 23,93:2
Condon, John T, 1940, Jl 14,30:8
Condon, John W, 1960, S 27,13:1
Condon, Joseph F, 1940, Mr 23,13:2
Condon, Kate, 1941, My 28,25:5
Condon, Katherine A, 1924, Ag 28,17:5
Condon, Lawrence R, 1908, F 13,9:6
Condon, Martin J, 1940, F 25,38:5
Condon, Mary J Mrs, 1957, Jl 11,25:5
Condon, Mary M (will), 1941, Ap 27,34:5
Condon, Maurice L, 1953, Ja 25,86:5
Condon, Nellie, 1953, S 25,21:4
Condon, Patrick J, 1937, Ja 20,21:4
Condon, Richard A, 1967, S 28,47:4
Condon, Richard J, 1944, N 15,27:3
Condon, Richard Lawrence, 1910, N 9,9:2
Condon, Thomas, 1941, Jl 5,11:5
Condon, Thomas F Sr, 1946, Mr 22,21:3
Condon, William F, 1942, S 4,24:2
Condon, William J, 1968, Mr 8,39:5
Condon, William S, 1956, D 3,29:2
Condona, Abelardo, 1951, O 15,25:1
Condra, George E, 1958, Ag 9,13:4
Condra, George Mrs, 1950, D 23,15:5
Condran, Jeremiah J, 1952, Ag 3,60:4
Condran, John A, 1956, Mr 26,29:1
Condren, Daniel M, 1943, Mr 13,13:3
Condren, John, 1944, Ag 4,13:2
Condrillo, Michael J, 1968, O 10,47:5
Condron, John J, 1944, D 16,15:2
Condron, Lydia A, 1948, Ap 1,25:4
Condron, Michael, 1955, Mr 28,27:4
Condron, Michael L, 1955, N 22,35:4
Condron, Theodore L, 1955, Ap 14,29:3
Condron, William A, 1944, Ap 13,19:6
Condy, Joseph, 1953, Mr 28,17:5
Cone, Andrew, 1922, F 7,17:3

Cone, Ashley B, 1962, O 21,88:7
Cone, Bernard M, 1956, My 22,33:1
Cone, Caesar, 1917, Mr 3,9:2
Cone, Clarence, 1947, Jl 20,44:2
Cone, Daisy N Dr, 1937, Ag 28,15:6
Cone, E Payson, 1905, Ja 24,6:5
Cone, Earl H, 1942, S 4,24:2
Cone, Edwin F, 1952, Mr 20,29:4
Cone, Frances H, 1954, Ja 4,19:1
Cone, Fred P, 1948, Jl 29,21:5
Cone, Frederick H, 1942, S 6,31:1; 1945, D 28,16:2
Cone, G Herbert, 1945, N 16,19:2
Cone, George C, 1942, Mr 3,23:4
Cone, Gertrude, 1952, F 21,27:3
Cone, Harold M, 1960, D 16,33:1
Cone, Henry H Jr, 1950, O 21,17:7
Cone, Henry S, 1954, Mr 12,14:1
Cone, Herbert A, 1948, F 5,23:4
Cone, Herbert D, 1940, O 31,23:3
Cone, Herman M, 1953, O 1,29:4
Cone, Herman por, 1955, D 11,88:7
Cone, Hutchinson I, 1941, F 13,19:1
Cone, J A, 1883, O 28,12:7
Cone, J L, 1957, Jl 28,61:2
Cone, James F, 1946, Jl 18,25:5
Cone, John E, 1956, Ap 18,31:1
Cone, John J, 1937, Ja 15,21:3
Cone, Michael J, 1956, Ag 24,19:5
Cone, Morris H, 1949, N 28,27:6
Cone, Newell K, 1950, N 25,13:6
Cone, Orello Rev Dr, 1905, Je 25,7:2
Cone, Owen S M, 1909, N 15,9:3
Cone, Peter, 1866, Ja 11,5:1
Cone, R C, 1879, D 21,5:2
Cone, Raymond C, 1947, D 8,27:7
Cone, Robert, 1946, S 20,31:3
Cone, Robert T, 1944, Ja 11,19:2
Cone, Russell G, 1961, Ja 22,84:4
Cone, Spencer H, 1962, O 10,51:4
Cone, Thomas E, 1955, Ag 4,25:4
Cone, William, 1959, My 5,33:2
Conefrey, Frank A Mrs, 1962, My 9,43:4
Coneley, Raymond D, 1959, Je 16,35:3
Conelly, Michael, 1938, O 26,23:3
Coner, Samuel L, 1948, F 19,23:1
Coner, Winfield A, 1943, Ap 29,21:1
Conerty, John E, 1949, Mr 5,17:3
Conerty, Mary F Mrs, 1937, Mr 28,II,8:7
Conerty, Thomas I, 1963, Ag 14,33:1
Conerty, Thomas J, 1946, Ja 22,27:3
Coney, Aims C, 1965, N 7,88:7
Coney, Edward A, 1944, Ja 13,21:4
Coney, Elvira J West Mrs, 1925, N 7,15:6
Coney, Harriot R Mrs, 1941, Mr 26,23:4
Coney, John C, 1944, N 2,19:4
Coney, W D Lt, 1921, Mr 31,13:4
Coneybear, John F, 1961, O 4,45:1
Confesor, Thomas, 1951, Je 8,27:3
Conforti, James, 1963, N 23,29:4
Confrey, Chris W, 1939, Ag 29,21:2
Congalton, William, 1937, Ag 20,17:3
Congar, Isabella Mrs, 1905, Mr 7,9:6
Congdon, Carey, 1949, Jl 21,25:4
Congdon, Chester A, 1916, N 22,13:6
Congdon, Clement H, 1953, F 14,17:2
Congdon, Frank E, 1956, S 12,37:1
Congdon, G Maurice, 1961, My 16,43:1
Congdon, Henry B, 1955, O 1,19:6
Congdon, Henry Martyn, 1922, Mr 2,21:5
Congdon, Herbert W, 1965, Ag 16,27:6
Congdon, James E, 1943, F 6,13:4
Congdon, John B, 1952, N 14,23:1
Congdon, Joseph W Col, 1914, My 2,9:5
Congdon, Richard C, 1937, S 10,24:2
Congdon, Robert E, 1951, Je 24,72:7
Congdon, Roy V Mrs, 1953, Jl 6,17:6
Congdon, Thomas O B, 1914, S 22,11:6
Congdon, William H, 1937, Je 15,23:4
Congedo, Joseph M, 1954, N 2,27:3
Congelton, Earle, 1961, S 1,17:1
Conger, Ben, 1922, Mr 1,5:5
Conger, Charles O, 1949, O 20,29:4
Conger, Dorothy M, 1939, Ap 16,III,6:8
Conger, Edward A, 1963, Ag 8,27:3
Conger, Edward A Mrs, 1953, S 14,27:4
Conger, Edwin H, 1907, My 19,7:4
Conger, Eugene D, 1952, Je 25,29:4
Conger, Everett L Dr, 1914, N 18,11:6
Conger, Frederic P M, 1960, N 5,23:5
Conger, Frederick W, 1950, Je 25,69:1
Conger, Henry C, 1951, Ap 26,29:1
Conger, John, 1951, D 4,33:2
Conger, John H B, 1943, My 19,25:4
Conger, Kenyon B, 1939, Ja 19,19:2
Conger, Laura D, 1962, Jl 25,33:5
Conger, Norman B, 1937, Ag 18,19:4
Conger, Ralph, 1941, N 21,25:2
Conger, Robert A, 1963, Ag 2,27:3
Conger, Stephen C Mrs, 1942, Mr 17,21:3
Conger, W F, 1880, Ap 13,5:2
Conger, William A Mrs, 1955, O 12,31:2
Conger, William H, 1950, D 23,15:2
Congleton, Elmer E, 1954, Ja 17,92:3
Congleton, Eugene, 1946, Mr 15,21:4
Congleton, J T, 1936, D 11,27:3
Congreve, C M, 1878, F 28,4:7
Congreve, William Latouche Maj, 1916, Ag 8,9:7
Conhaim, Herbert J, 1949, Ja 10,25:5
Conhaim, Milton B, 1959, O 1,35:3
Conheim, H, 1927, My 3,27:3
Conheim, Richard J, 1947, Ag 16,13:2
Conhurst, William F, 1960, Je 9,33:5
Conibear, Hiram, 1917, S 11,13:3
Conick, Charles B, 1947, Ag 10,53:2
Conick, Harold C, 1962, Ap 27,35:3
Conick, Harold C Mrs, 1957, F 8,23:5
Coniff, John B, 1947, O 9,25:4
Coniff, Paul R, 1940, Ag 6,20:4
Coniker, Paul E, 1951, Ag 26,77:2
Conill, Mary L Mrs, 1941, Ap 1,23:5
Conine, Joseph E, 1940, My 5,53:2
Coniston, Ralph A, 1955, O 30,88:4
Coniston, Ralph Mrs, 1952, Mr 31,19:5
Conk, Arthur F, 1957, Ap 24,33:3
Conk, John H, 1921, My 4,10:5; 1921, My 7,11:4
Conkey, Charles Mrs, 1964, Ja 1,25:3
Conkey, Fred C, 1945, N 11,41:1
Conkey, Guy E, 1948, Ag 10,21:1
Conkey, Henry Marks, 1915, Jl 25,15:4
Conkey, Henry P, 1953, F 11,29:5
Conkey, Mary, 1949, Mr 22,25:2
Conkey, Ogden F, 1958, Je 3,31:5
Conkey, Walter M, 1872, D 3,1:3; 1873, Ja 4,1:5
Conking, George W, 1917, My 3,11:6
Conkle, E T Mrs, 1959, Ja 25,94:1
Conklin, Agnes M, 1952, F 4,17:3
Conklin, Albert J, 1947, S 1,19:4
Conklin, Albert L, 1953, O 17,15:3
Conklin, Alfred R, 1952, O 23,31:3
Conklin, Arnold A, 1953, Je 16,27:3
Conklin, Arthur C, 1951, Je 12,29:5
Conklin, Arthur S, 1960, My 19,37:4
Conklin, Bernard, 1939, O 6,25:4
Conklin, Bert, 1946, Mr 20,23:1
Conklin, Bert P, 1949, Ap 2,15:1
Conklin, Bogart T, 1944, Je 30,21:4
Conklin, C Edward, 1960, S 29,35:4
Conklin, C Oscar, 1943, Mr 19,19:3
Conklin, Calvin, 1948, N 8,21:4
Conklin, Charles J, 1964, Ja 13,35:1
Conklin, Charles R (por), 1947, Jl 8,23:1
Conklin, Charles S, 1951, Ja 24,27:5
Conklin, Charles S Mrs, 1951, Ja 10,27:4
Conklin, Chester A, 1941, Jl 21,15:4
Conklin, Chester Mrs, 1937, My 16,II,8:5
Conklin, Clara D Mrs, 1942, Mr 22,49:1
Conklin, Clarence J, 1952, Jl 16,25:1
Conklin, Clarence W, 1943, Ap 13,25:3
Conklin, Claude C, 1957, Je 14,25:3
Conklin, Clifford T Sr, 1956, Ap 9,27:1
Conklin, Daniel E, 1910, Ag 2,7:5
Conklin, Daniel P, 1966, O 6,47:4
Conklin, David, 1946, O 9,27:2
Conklin, De Witt, 1954, N 5,15:1
Conklin, Dewitt Mrs, 1941, My 11,44:6
Conklin, Douglass, 1944, N 20,21:4
Conklin, Dumont Rev, 1925, D 24,13:5
Conklin, Edmund S, 1942, O 7,25:3
Conklin, Edward, 1940, Jl 16,20:4
Conklin, Edward L, 1912, Mr 5,11:4
Conklin, Edwin D, 1955, O 18,37:4
Conklin, Edwin G, 1952, N 22,23:1
Conklin, Edwin G Mrs, 1940, Mr 8,22:4
Conklin, Eleanor B, 1954, Ja 21,31:1
Conklin, Eugene H, 1919, Mr 16,20:4
Conklin, F Colwell, 1956, Mr 1,34:6
Conklin, Fanny D, 1946, Je 20,23:6
Conklin, Floyd W, 1952, N 18,31:1
Conklin, Frank A Maj, 1937, Ja 28,25:4
Conklin, Frank J, 1946, Ap 8,27:1
Conklin, Franklin, 1943, Ap 8,23:3
Conklin, Franklin Jr, 1966, Jl 30,25:1
Conklin, Franklin Jr Mrs, 1964, O 19,33:2
Conklin, Fred H, 1941, Ap 30,19:3
Conklin, Frederick (Dr), 1967, O 31,45:2
Conklin, Frederick D, 1945, F 28,23:5
Conklin, Frederick L, 1949, F 4,23:4
Conklin, George, 1924, F 27,17:4
Conklin, George W, 1947, N 5,27:4
Conklin, Gordon R, 1967, Ag 25,35:4
Conklin, Groff, 1968, Jl 20,27:4
Conklin, Harold S, 1948, Ag 30,25:1
Conklin, Harry H, 1938, Ap 4,17:6
Conklin, Harry T, 1942, S 19,15:1
Conklin, Hazen, 1942, Ap 30,19:1
Conklin, Henry J Mrs, 1945, S 23,44:4
Conklin, Howard, 1938, S 8,23:4
Conklin, Howard S Sr Mrs, 1950, Jl 12,29:5
Conklin, Isaac D, 1938, Ag 28,32:8
Conklin, James C, 1937, Ag 25,21:5
Conklin, James H, 1949, N 5,14:2
Conklin, Jean, 1957, N 5,31:3
Conklin, John C, 1945, My 13,20:1
Conklin, John H, 1946, Ap 9,27:4
Conklin, John H Mrs, 1955, Mr 15,29:1
Conklin, John J Mrs, 1966, N 13,89:2
Conklin, John W Rev, 1909, S 13,9:6
Conklin, Joseph, 1944, N 11,13:6
Conklin, Joseph M, 1940, N 25,17:6
Conklin, Joseph P Mrs, 1944, O 21,17:6
Conklin, Joseph W, 1960, Ja 13,47:1
Conklin, Katherine F, 1940, N 6,23:3
Conklin, Leander H, 1963, Ag 10,17:5
Conklin, Lewis R, 1947, S 17,25:3
Conklin, Louisa M Mrs, 1941, Mr 5,21:4
Conklin, Ludolph H Sr, 1952, N 4,30:4
Conklin, Mary Mrs, 1923, Ja 8,17:6
Conklin, Melville G, 1954, Jl 28,23:1
Conklin, Nathan H, 1952, O 11,19:5
Conklin, Paul S, 1961, Ap 30,86:6
Conklin, Peter, 1924, Ja 2,17:3
Conklin, Peter H, 1951, D 28,21:3
Conklin, Platt, 1921, Je 25,11:4
Conklin, R S, 1931, Je 5,23:3
Conklin, Randall W, 1954, S 28,29:4
Conklin, Reginald D, 1964, D 6,88:3
Conklin, Robert, 1937, My 4,25:4
Conklin, Rochester A, 1966, O 25,48:2
Conklin, Roland R, 1938, Ja 3,21:1
Conklin, Roscoe C, 1949, Ja 14,23:3
Conklin, Roscoe L, 1956, Ja 20,23:2
Conklin, Russell F, 1964, Ja 23,31:4
Conklin, Sarah L, 1944, Ja 7,17:5
Conklin, Theodore B, 1966, Mr 11,33:3
Conklin, Theodore E (funl, My 7,21:2), 1924, My 7, 21:3
Conklin, Walter A, 1953, F 7,15:3
Conklin, Wendell Mrs, 1954, Jl 10,28:5
Conklin, Wilford W, 1947, Je 26,23:6
Conklin, William, 1952, Mr 19,29:4
Conklin, William C, 1949, Ag 21,68:8
Conklin, William E Mrs, 1945, N 18,44:1
Conklin, William J Dr, 1921, S 28,19:6
Conklin, William P, 1958, Je 1,86:7
Conklin, William R, 1940, My 21,23:2; 1960, Jl 3,32:4; 1962, O 14,86:1
Conklin, William S, 1949, Je 7,31:3
Conklin, William T, 1943, N 1,17:2
Conkling, Alfred Judge, 1874, F 6,5:5
Conkling, Alfred R, 1917, S 26,13:5
Conkling, Almira, 1961, Je 8,35:2
Conkling, Benjamin H, 1937, S 27,21:5
Conkling, Charles E, 1954, Ap 2,27:2
Conkling, Charles R, 1963, O 8,43:3
Conkling, Edward B, 1950, Ag 23,29:6
Conkling, Edward D G, 1947, N 7,23:3
Conkling, Edward D Mrs, 1945, My 9,23:4
Conkling, Emma G, 1883, Mr 20,5:1
Conkling, F G, 1871, Ap 4,5:5
Conkling, Frank W, 1955, N 8,29:1
Conkling, Grace H Mrs (funl, N 20,35:5), 1958, N 16,88:7
Conkling, Hazid C, 1956, S 29,19:2
Conkling, Ida Z, 1951, Ag 14,23:2
Conkling, Lawrence, 1960, Ap 2,23:6
Conkling, Mabel H Mrs, 1966, O 13,45:1
Conkling, Mary T, 1938, Ap 16,13:1
Conkling, Roscoe, 1888, Ap 18,1:7
Conkling, Roscoe P, 1949, My 24,29:8; 1954, O 29,21:2
Conkling, Roscoe S, 1956, S 16,84:5
Conkwright, Douglas D, 1958, Ag 20,27:2
Conlan, Frank, 1955, Ag 26,19:3
Conlan, Henry J, 1941, O 5,48:7
Conlan, Hugh, 1903, Ap 25,9:5
Conlan, James Dr, 1903, My 3,9:6
Conlan, Lewis J Ex-Judge, 1919, Ap 5,15:4
Conlan, Mary A, 1949, Ja 1,13:2
Conlan, Raymond J, 1964, F 29,21:3
Conlan, Thomas F, 1959, Ap 22,33:2
Conland, Henry H, 1944, Ap 16,42:2
Conland, Thomas, 1867, S 9,8:3
Conlen, J Harry, 1939, O 8,49:2
Conlen, Timothy J, 1942, My 23,13:4
Conlen, William J, 1956, Ap 14,17:6
Conless, Joseph P, 1939, Ja 7,15:2
Conley, Clarence E, 1945, D 20,23:3
Conley, Claude S, 1958, N 22,21:6
Conley, David L, 1950, S 19,29:6
Conley, David Van B, 1961, N 26,87:7
Conley, Donald J, 1949, O 5,43:1
Conley, Edgar T, 1956, Ag 22,29:1
Conley, Edward, 1945, D 3,21:3
Conley, Edward Mrs, 1951, D 28,21:1
Conley, Edwin J, 1958, My 8,29:5
Conley, Evah, 1953, Ag 18,31:8
Conley, Francis L Sr, 1949, Je 3,25:3
Conley, Frankie, 1952, Ag 22,21:3
Conley, George L, 1961, F 15,35:2
Conley, Gordon L, 1943, O 9,13:5
Conley, Herbert J, 1947, Ag 13,23:2
Conley, James G, 1960, Jl 18,27:3
Conley, James H, 1959, My 7,33:4
Conley, James Mrs, 1950, F 15,27:3
Conley, John, 1941, Ap 16,23:4
Conley, John B, 1959, Ag 30,82:5
Conley, L D, 1930, S 8,21:3
Conley, Lawrence A, 1947, D 1,21:2
Conley, Lawrence P Dr, 1937, My 11,25:2
Conley, Louis D Mrs, 1955, O 16,86:2

Conley, Mary Mrs, 1939, Ja 8,42:8
Conley, Michael J, 1961, Ja 13,27:1
Conley, Richard B, 1950, F 8,19:1
Conley, Robert F, 1950, N 8,29:2
Conley, Robert F Mrs, 1949, My 10,25:2
Conley, Samuel D, 1961, Je 17,21:4
Conley, Thomas E, 1949, My 5,27:6
Conley, Walter H, 1946, Ja 10,23:2
Conley, Walter J, 1963, O 31,34:1
Conley, Willard V, 1960, Je 9,33:2
Conley, William, 1941, Je 3,21:4
Conley, William G, 1940, O 22,23:3
Conley, William H, 1951, D 22,15:2
Conley, William J Jr, 1962, O 21,88:6
Conley, William M, 1954, Mr 9,27:2
Conley, William T, 1958, Jl 27,60:7
Conlin, Alan B, 1959, Ap 29,33:3
Conlin, Bernard J, 1963, N 16,27:4
Conlin, Charlotte D Mrs, 1949, Mr 5,18:2
Conlin, Claude A, 1954, Ag 6,17:3
Conlin, Ed C, 1939, Ag 22,19:5
Conlin, Edward, 1954, D 7,33:2
Conlin, Edward F, 1956, N 14,35:3
Conlin, Frank W, 1964, Je 9,35:5
Conlin, James J, 1944, Ag 29,17:4
Conlin, Jimmy Mrs, 1945, My 15,19:4
Conlin, John F, 1954, Je 1,27:5
Conlin, John J, 1960, Ag 5,23:4
Conlin, Patrick J, 1941, Ag 28,19:4
Conlin, Peter, 1905, O 24,9:6
Conlogue, John A, 1959, Ag 29,17:4
Conlon, Charles W, 1953, O 21,24:5
Conlon, Colgan, 1951, O 11,37:1
Conlon, Francis X, 1968, Jl 30,39:1
Conlon, Frank A Dr, 1937, Je 24,25:4
Conlon, Frank J, 1916, Je 30,11:7
Conlon, G I Rev, 1926, Jl 21,19:2
Conlon, Irene M, 1965, Ag 18,35:5
Conlon, James, 1955, Ja 6,27:3
Conlon, John, 1951, S 5,31:4; 1955, Ap 7,10:6
Conlon, John F, 1942, S 4,23:4
Conlon, John Sr, 1951, Ap 11,29:5
Conlon, Joseph E, 1955, D 22,23:3
Conlon, Joseph G, 1948, D 6,25:5
Conlon, Joseph T, 1944, Ja 12,23:4
Conlon, Lawrence J, 1945, Jl 2,15:4
Conlon, Leo F, 1944, Jl 15,13:3
Conlon, M A, 1936, N 17,27:3
Conlon, Malachi, 1950, Mr 28,31:1
Conlon, Michael F, 1950, Je 18,76:8
Conlon, Thomas E, 1943, O 30,15:2
Conlon, William T, 1947, Mr 13,27:2
Conlon (Mother Mary Emmanuel), 1964, F 15,23:3
Conly, Daniel F, 1939, Ag 26,15:4
Conly, Leslie M, 1955, Ag 23,23:3
Conly, Martin F, 1942, Mr 9,19:2
Conly, Q Pius Father, 1904, Ja 23,9:4
Conn, Carl E, 1941, Jl 7,15:3
Conn, Charles B, 1947, Ja 15,25:5
Conn, Donald D, 1954, Ag 14,15:6
Conn, Edward, 1942, Jl 17,15:2
Conn, Edwin H, 1953, My 17,89:1
Conn, Emanuel H, 1953, S 3,21:2
Conn, Frank William, 1918, Jl 13,9:5
Conn, George F, 1945, D 30,14:2
Conn, Granville Priest Dr, 1916, Mr 25,13:4
Conn, Herbert William Prof, 1917, Ap 19,15:7
Conn, Irving, 1961, Jl 13,29:2
Conn, J Wesley, 1941, F 28,19:3
Conn, Jack D, 1966, Ja 28,47:3
Conn, James K Mrs, 1968, Je 8,31:1
Conn, L C, 1941, D 23,21:2
Conn, Margaret M Mrs, 1941, Je 28,15:2
Conn, Whitman P, 1937, Ja 4,29:2
Connable, Frank L, 1947, Mr 16,60:3
Connable, Ralph, 1939, Ap 20,23:4
Connah, Douglas J, 1941, Ag 25,15:1
Connally, Frank, 1948, Jl 19,19:3
Connally, Marvin G, 1960, D 27,29:4
Connally, Tom (cor, O 30,39:2; funl, O 31,34:1), 1963, O 29,1:5
Connard, Philip, 1958, D 9,41:1
Connaught, Duchess of, 1917, Mr 15,11:5
Connaught, Duke of, 1943, Ap 27,23:4
Connaught and Strathearn, Duke of, 1942, Ja 17,8:1
Connaughton, Francis J, 1966, N 20,89:1
Connaughton, George H, 1965, Mr 30,47:4
Connaughton, James, 1914, Mr 25,11:6; 1954, Ag 17, 21:3
Connaughton, William J, 1939, Mr 16,23:2
Conne, P, 1927, S 15,29:3
Conneau, Dr, 1877, S 2,7:3
Conneely, Emmett K, 1942, Jl 12,36:4
Conneen, Andrew M Jr, 1958, N 6,37:1
Connell, Alec, 1958, My 11,86:7
Connell, Andrew J, 1942, My 12,19:4
Connell, Archibald G, 1945, O 6,13:5
Connell, Charles A, 1951, Ap 18,31:3
Connell, Charles R, 1922, S 27,19:3
Connell, Christopher E, 1960, My 30,17:2
Connell, Daniel J, 1937, Je 25,21:2
Connell, Edgar W Mrs, 1948, Ja 3,14:3
Connell, Francis J, 1967, My 13,33:1
Connell, George, 1955, O 24,27:4
Connell, George L, 1947, Ja 28,23:1; 1960, O 16,88:7
Connell, Gerald, 1938, N 24,33:3
Connell, Grant, 1950, My 14,106:4
Connell, Grover C, 1950, Mr 2,28:4
Connell, Herbert S, 1946, Ap 12,27:1
Connell, Hugh G, 1924, Je 17,19:4
Connell, J Carl, 1947, Ja 1,33:6
Connell, James F, 1948, My 12,27:4
Connell, James P, 1909, S 24,11:6
Connell, James S, 1912, Ap 1,13:5
Connell, John, 1946, Je 4,23:4; 1954, My 17,23:4
Connell, John (Sept 16), 1965, O 11,61:1
Connell, John F, 1937, F 19,19:5
Connell, John J, 1946, Jl 27,17:6
Connell, John J A, 1950, O 9,25:1
Connell, John T, 1947, Ag 19,23:5
Connell, Karl, 1941, O 19,45:3
Connell, Malcolm R, 1939, Jl 11,19:6
Connell, Mary M Mrs, 1937, Jl 22,19:6
Connell, Owen J, 1942, Je 17,23:5
Connell, Richard, 1949, N 24,31:1
Connell, Robert Mrs, 1956, Ag 24,19:5
Connell, W E Jr, 1947, Ap 19,15:5
Connell, William, 1909, Mr 22,7:5; 1954, My 28,4:8
Connell, William B, 1954, N 13,15:4
Connell, William H, 1943, Ag 5,15:4
Connell, William J, 1947, Ap 25,21:2
Connell, William L Mrs, 1954, Ag 25,27:5
Connell, William M, 1938, Jl 27,17:6
Connellan, John J Dr, 1937, N 13,19:4
Connelley, Earl J, 1957, Jl 21,60:3
Connelly, Annie T, 1939, My 19,21:5
Connelly, Bobby, 1922, Jl 7,17:6
Connelly, Brian, 1963, Ag 15,29:4
Connelly, Catherine A Mrs, 1947, Mr 30,56:4
Connelly, Charles T, 1944, N 21,25:6
Connelly, Charles W, 1949, Jl 1,19:2
Connelly, Edmond J, 1953, Ja 2,15:2
Connelly, Edward A, 1951, Ja 8,17:5
Connelly, Edward H, 1953, Ag 31,17:2
Connelly, Edward J, 1964, Ap 13,29:5
Connelly, Edward M, 1947, S 2,21:2
Connelly, Eugene L, 1942, Ja 19,17:4
Connelly, Francis P, 1966, Ap 8,28:7
Connelly, Frank H, 1944, Je 17,13:5
Connelly, Frank J, 1959, Ap 22,33:1
Connelly, Garth G, 1950, Mr 23,29:4
Connelly, Henry C, 1946, Ag 10,13:3
Connelly, Henry C Ex-Sen, 1912, O 10,11:4
Connelly, Henry Mrs, 1910, Mr 27,II,11:3
Connelly, Herbert L, 1960, F 24,37:5
Connelly, Hugh J, 1959, My 21,31:3
Connelly, J H, 1903, Mr 16,9:5
Connelly, James, 1942, Jl 11,13:3
Connelly, James A, 1952, O 26,88:6
Connelly, James A Jr, 1944, F 2,21:4
Connelly, James J, 1940, O 1,23:3
Connelly, James L (One-Eyed), 1953, D 22,31:4
Connelly, Jeremiah R, 1943, Mr 1,19:4
Connelly, John A, 1944, O 27,23:6
Connelly, John E, 1949, O 8,13:1
Connelly, John J, 1963, D 17,39:3
Connelly, John M, 1947, Ag 21,23:4
Connelly, John P, 1948, Ap 10,13:6
Connelly, Joseph F, 1958, N 22,21:5
Connelly, Joseph J, 1943, O 21,27:4
Connelly, Joseph T, 1959, Ag 19,29:3
Connelly, Kathleen A, 1956, D 5,39:2
Connelly, Leo A Mrs, 1950, My 10,31:2
Connelly, Leo E, 1943, Je 15,21:2
Connelly, Lincoln C G, 1946, Ja 12,15:3
Connelly, M Joseph, 1956, Ap 26,33:3
Connelly, Margaret M, 1952, O 15,31:2
Connelly, Mary, 1942, O 22,21:3
Connelly, Milton E, 1950, My 22,21:1
Connelly, Nicholas, 1949, Mr 30,25:1
Connelly, Patrick C, 1953, Mr 29,93:1
Connelly, Paul, 1940, Jl 12,15:1
Connelly, Pauline Mrs, 1954, Ag 10,19:4
Connelly, Raphael, 1968, Mr 12,43:1
Connelly, Raymond, 1949, My 5,28:2
Connelly, Reg, 1963, S 24,39:2
Connelly, Thomas H, 1957, D 9,35:2
Connelly, Thomas J, 1951, Ag 21,27:2
Connelly, W C Jr Col, 1912, Jl 10,9:4
Connelly, W M, 1885, Ja 18,2:4
Connelly, Walt W, 1952, D 7,88:6
Connelly, William B, 1953, S 2,25:5
Connelly, William L, 1964, Ap 18,29:5
Connelly, William P, 1950, Ja 8,76:6
Connely, Emmett F, 1960, F 4,31:1
Connely, Laurel L Mrs, 1957, F 8,23:1
Connely, Willard, 1967, Mr 28,45:4
Conner, A V, 1882, Ap 4,5:2
Conner, Arthur, 1965, F 23,33:2
Conner, Arthur Burdette Capt, 1924, My 7,21:3
Conner, Atvill, 1946, Mr 25,25:5
Conner, Ben, 1948, Ap 12,21:4
Conner, Benjamin H Mrs, 1950, D 13,35:4
Conner, Benjamin Howe, 1953, F 9,27:3
Conner, Charles A, 1950, Ap 4,29:1
Conner, Clifford E Mrs, 1967, Ag 8,39:4
Conner, Don R, 1943, S 6,17:4
Conner, Earl Dr, 1925, Je 9,21:5
Conner, Eli T, 1938, Ja 4,24:3
Conner, Emma E (will), 1937, Ag 24,19:6
Conner, F Dwight, 1950, S 30,17:6
Conner, Fox Mrs, 1960, My 15,86:8
Conner, Francis W, 1938, Ag 24,21:5
Conner, Frederick S, 1938, F 23,23:5
Conner, Henry Patridge Capt, 1919, S 11,15:2
Conner, J Barratt, 1956, Mr 22,35:1
Conner, J Verser, 1949, My 9,25:4
Conner, James, 1883, Je 27,4:6
Conner, James D Jr, 1940, O 27,45:2
Conner, John G, 1959, Jl 16,27:4
Conner, Laila C, 1956, Jl 4,19:1
Conner, Lewis A, 1950, D 4,29:1
Conner, Lorenzo, 1938, My 1,II,6:6
Conner, Martin S, 1950, S 18,23:6
Conner, Mary C Mrs, 1941, Ja 1,23:2
Conner, Michael J Rev, 1937, Jl 27,21:1
Conner, Ned, 1958, N 18,37:5
Conner, Owen A, 1940, N 30,17:2
Conner, R Pearce, 1942, D 25,17:5
Conner, Stanley H, 1950, Jl 26,25:3
Conner, W C, 1881, Ap 27,8:2
Conner, W Norman, 1951, Ap 29,89:2
Conner, Warren C, 1955, F 15,27:3
Conner, William, 1952, D 11,33:1
Conner, William (Cassandra), 1967, Ap 7,37:1
Conner, William B, 1941, My 15,23:4
Conner, William Mrs, 1925, O 25,9:1
Conners, Arthur, 1959, Ag 15,17:5
Conners, Arthur Mrs, 1948, F 21,13:1
Conners, Harry, 1951, Ag 14,23:2
Conners, Harry R, 1954, Ja 7,31:5
Conners, J T (Jack), 1952, Jl 6,49:1
Conners, John Ex-Sen, 1909, Ja 11,9:7
Conners, John J Jr, 1949, S 12,21:2
Conners, Lawrence, 1942, F 24,21:1
Conners, Thomas, 1947, S 13,11:3
Conners, W V, 1929, O 6,II,6:1
Conners, William H, 1938, Mr 15,23:3
Conners, William J Jr, 1951, F 4,77:1
Conners, William J Jr Mrs, 1956, O 30,37:3
Conners, William J Mrs, 1924, Mr 27,19:6
Connerty, Frank J, 1953, Mr 22,86:2
Connery, David P, 1956, My 15,32:5
Connery, Henry J Rev, 1937, O 9,19:4
Connery, John F, 1964, S 7,19:5
Connery, John T, 1937, Je 7,19:6
Connery, Julia M, 1950, N 28,31:2
Connery, Lawrence J, 1941, O 20,17:4
Connery, Paul R, 1953, Ja 25,84:5
Connery, Thomas B, 1923, F 11,6:2
Connery, Timothy, 1953, F 4,27:4
Connery, William P Jr Repr, 1937, Je 16,23:1
Conness, Hugh E, 1939, Ja 24,19:3
Conness, John Mrs, 1922, D 25,13:4
Conness, Leland S, 1942, Ap 9,19:4
Conness, Robert, 1941, Ja 17,17:4
Connet, Hugh I, 1946, Je 27,21:3
Connett, Albert N Mrs, 1960, N 5,23:6
Connett, Albert Sr Mrs, 1949, My 14,13:6
Connett, Eugene V, 1905, Je 30,9:4; 1937, Jl 3,15:5
Connett, Frank S, 1962, O 18,39:1
Connett, George T, 1944, O 29,43:1
Connett, Mary C Mrs, 1937, Ja 25,19:4
Connett, May B Mrs, 1937, Jl 10,15:1
Connett, Thomas O, 1938, Ap 26,21:2
Connett, William B, 1961, O 12,29:5
Connette, E G, 1930, D 31,17:1
Conney, Andrew B, 1937, My 1,19:2
Connfelt, Charles M, 1957, Ap 11,31:2
Connick, Andrew J, 1919, Mr 12,11:3; 1947, My 2 25:3
Connick, Charles J, 1945, D 29,13:1
Connick, Louis, 1952, Ag 19,23:5
Conniff, Andrew W, 1955, Ja 2,77:2
Conniff, Andrew W Mrs, 1954, My 24,27:2
Conniff, Thaddeus M, 1938, O 16,44:6
Conning, John S, 1946, Je 21,23:1
Conning, John S Mrs, 1943, D 7,27:5
Conning, William S, 1949, Mr 27,76:6
Connington, Frank, 1964, Ap 5,86:6
Connole, Joseph V, 1950, O 17,31:4
Connole, Martha, 1957, Mr 13,31:4
Connolly, Andrew, 1941, Je 7,17:2
Connolly, Andrew J Mrs, 1947, My 2,21:3
Connolly, Anselm, 1947, My 28,25:4
Connolly, B, 1880, Je 11,5:1
Connolly, Bartley J, 1962, My 5,27:2
Connolly, Bridget Mrs, 1950, Ja 3,25:3
Connolly, Carroll, 1959, Ag 30,82:8
Connolly, Catherine M, 1939, D 10,68:6
Connolly, Charles F, 1939, Ap 4,25:3; 1958, Ja 1958, S 28,88:2
Connolly, Cornelius J, 1954, Ap 7,31:3
Connolly, Daniel, 1941, O 16,21:6
Connolly, Daniel G, 1963, O 3,35:2
Connolly, David J, 1961, S 5,35:3
Connolly, E E, 1926, Jl 26,15:5
Connolly, Edward, 1951, Jl 9,25:4
Connolly, Edward J, 1942, S 21,15:3

Connolly, Ernest V Mrs, 1949, Ja 7,22:2
Connolly, F F Msgr, 1915, Ja 5,15:4
Connolly, Francis J, 1946, Ja 16,23:4
Connolly, Francis X, 1965, N 18,47:4
Connolly, Frank J, 1954, O 6,25:1
Connolly, Frank X, 1966, Ag 7,80:5
Connolly, George, 1953, Jl 4,11:5
Connolly, George E, 1952, O 18,19:4
Connolly, Gerald C, 1949, Je 7,32:2
Connolly, Gregory, 1959, O 14,43:2
Connolly, Harry F, 1950, Ag 5,15:6
Connolly, Henry D, 1940, Jl 15,15:4
Connolly, Hugh, 1946, D 3,31:4
Connolly, J A, 1931, N 28,7:6
Connolly, James, 1957, O 23,33:4
Connolly, James B, 1957, Ja 21,25:5
Connolly, James F, 1917, F 3,13:4
Connolly, James J, 1949, My 15,90:5; 1952, D 12,29:4
Connolly, James J Sr, 1961, Ag 5,17:2
Connolly, James P Sr Mrs, 1950, S 2,15:5
Connolly, James T, 1967, O 3,47:2
Connolly, James V, 1957, Je 20,29:1
Connolly, James W, 1957, Je 29,17:6
Connolly, Jane, 1937, S 13,21:1
Connolly, John A, 1942, S 14,15:6
Connolly, John Aloysuis, 1918, Je 4,13:4
Connolly, John C, 1948, D 25,17:2
Connolly, John F, 1941, Ag 10,37:1
Connolly, John J, 1941, S 26,24:2
Connolly, John S, 1960, D 27,29:4
Connolly, Joseph, 1945, Ag 10,15:3; 1948, My 8,15:6
Connolly, Joseph A, 1943, S 2,19:3
Connolly, Joseph A Msgr, 1922, S 30,13:5
Connolly, Joseph E F, 1939, O 3,23:4
Connolly, Joseph P, 1947, O 9,25:5
Connolly, Joseph V, 1945, Ap 18,23:3
Connolly, M, 1935, N 25,19:1
Connolly, M S Mrs, 1879, Mr 14,2:7
Connolly, Martin, 1937, Ap 1,23:1
Connolly, Maurice Mrs, 1920, Je 9,11:4
Connolly, Michael (see also Jl 16), 1876, Jl 19,8:1
Connolly, Michael, 1939, N 23,27:1
Connolly, Michael P, 1950, O 5,31:4
Connolly, Michael R, 1947, F 14,21:1
Connolly, Michael T, 1946, Je 22,19:2
Connolly, Michael W, 1921, Ja 10,11:5
Connolly, Mike, 1966, N 19,33:2
Connolly, Myles, 1964, Jl 17,27:3
Connolly, P Joseph, 1962, Ag 25,22:1
Connolly, Patrick A, 1946, My 23,21:2
Connolly, Patrick J (Packy), 1961, Ag 20,87:1
Connolly, Patrick Joseph, 1961, Jl 1,17:5
Connolly, Paul T, 1966, Je 17,45:4
Connolly, Paul V, 1952, O 3,23:2
Connolly, Peter F, 1959, N 4,41:3
Connolly, Peter J, 1956, F 28,31:4
Connolly, R B, 1880, Je 1,5:4
Connolly, R B Mrs (funl), 1879, Ap 13,10:6
Connolly, Raymond, 1956, Ap 13,25:2; 1961, Je 2,31:2
Connolly, Richard F, 1940, My 7,25:2
Connolly, Robert E, 1950, O 13,29:4
Connolly, Roger A, 1953, Jl 6,17:3
Connolly, Stephen W, 1938, Jl 1,19:6
Connolly, Sylvester G, 1955, Ag 30,27:3
Connolly, T C, 1878, Mr 19,4:7
Connolly, T Vincent, 1943, O 22,17:5
Connolly, Terrence L, 1961, Mr 26,92:8
Connolly, Thomas, 1903, D 30,7:2
Connolly, Thomas D, 1957, Ja 16,31:1
Connolly, Thomas F J, 1956, Ap 14,17:3
Connolly, Thomas F J Mrs, 1944, Ag 16,19:6
Connolly, Thomas H Sr, 1961, Ap 29,23:4
Connolly, Thomas J, 1949, N 20,92:4; 1950, D 11,25:1
Connolly, Vera (Mrs V C Manning), 1964, O 14,45:2
Connolly, Vincent T, 1937, F 28,II,8:7
Connolly, Walter, 1940, My 29,23:1
Connolly, William F, 1942, N 7,15:3; 1947, Ag 2,13:2
Connolly, William H (Bobby), 1944, Mr 9,17:3
Connolly, William N, 1961, Jl 11,31:3
Connolly, William P Mrs, 1937, My 12,23:5
Connolly, Willmot C, 1944, Mr 1,19:3
Connoly, Ralph A, 1940, F 21,19:1
Connoly, Theodore, 1913, My 7,11:5
Connor, Alfred, 1948, F 23,25:4
Connor, Arthur F, 1961, Ja 21,21:3
Connor, Ben A, 1952, S 2,23:3
Connor, Benjamin C Rev, 1921, Ag 20,7:6
Connor, Bernard L, 1951, Ja 4,29:3
Connor, Brevard M (will), 1953, Ap 14,23:5
Connor, Carleton S, 1961, Ja 14,23:5
Connor, Charles A, 1946, Ag 23,19:2
Connor, Charles A Mrs, 1948, Je 1,23:2
Connor, Charles F, 1956, D 16,87:1
Connor, Clarence H, 1958, Ja 28,27:4
Connor, Cornelius M, 1951, D 30,24:8
Connor, Daniel Francis, 1914, D 11,13:5
Connor, Edward E Mrs, 1943, Ja 14,21:4
Connor, Edward H, 1949, D 30,20:3; 1950, Ja 23,23:2
Connor, Edward J, 1943, My 22,13:3; 1948, N 3,27:2
Connor, Edwin I, 1954, Ja 19,25:3
Connor, Ex-Alderman (funl), 1871, Mr 13,12:7
Connor, Francis J, 1945, F 14,20:2; 1957, Ja 24,29:4
Connor, Francis X, 1944, My 25,21:5
Connor, Frank E, 1948, O 11,23:5
Connor, Frank M, 1942, D 28,19:3
Connor, George J, 1948, Ap 19,23:2
Connor, George L, 1921, S 6,15:5
Connor, George R, 1962, My 22,37:2
Connor, George S L, 1962, Je 28,31:5
Connor, Guy L, 1943, Ap 20,23:1
Connor, Hamilton C Jr, 1964, Ag 1,21:6
Connor, Harry A, 1947, Mr 4,25:2
Connor, Harry P M, 1959, O 31,23:3
Connor, Henry I, 1939, O 24,23:4
Connor, Hugh, 1925, S 10,25:4
Connor, J L, 1946, O 2,29:3
Connor, J T Mrs, 1927, Je 11,19:1
Connor, James D, 1956, Ja 4,27:1
Connor, James F, 1941, S 4,21:5
Connor, James H, 1941, Ag 5,19:4
Connor, James J, 1944, My 4,19:4
Connor, James R, 1958, Jl 13,68:7
Connor, James S, 1946, Ja 9,23:1
Connor, Jeremiah F, 1949, Ap 4,23:6
Connor, Jerome, 1943, Ag 22,36:7
Connor, John H, 1937, N 23,23:5
Connor, John H F, 1945, Mr 9,19:1
Connor, John J, 1953, Ag 16,77:2; 1964, F 22,21:1
Connor, John L, 1951, Mr 9,25:2
Connor, Joseph E, 1961, Je 12,29:5
Connor, Joseph G, 1946, N 1,23:3
Connor, Joseph P, 1942, My 19,19:3; 1952, Ap 2,33:3
Connor, Joseph T, 1940, D 27,19:4
Connor, M Henry, 1950, Jl 20,25:2
Connor, Mabel, 1962, Jl 22,64:5
Connor, Madelyn F, 1944, D 28,19:2
Connor, Marie P Mrs, 1953, Ap 27,23:4
Connor, Martin C, 1950, D 7,33:2
Connor, Maurice E, 1954, My 10,23:6
Connor, Mel, 1961, Ja 30,23:3
Connor, Michael A, 1937, Mr 7,II,8:5; 1947, Ap 27, 60:7
Connor, Michael E, 1941, S 8,15:4
Connor, Michael F, 1956, My 25,23:4
Connor, N L, 1942, Ja 8,22:2
Connor, Nicholas J, 1939, O 29,3:2
Connor, Owen, 1945, Je 7,19:4
Connor, Patrick, 1938, Ag 17,19:5; 1963, Ag 5,29:4
Connor, Patrick J, 1945, D 10,21:1; 1956, F 11,17:6
Connor, Ralph Mrs, 1954, D 17,31:5
Connor, Richard D, 1950, N 17,27:2
Connor, Robert D W, 1950, F 26,76:5
Connor, Robert G Msgr, 1937, Je 1,23:3
Connor, Robert W Mrs, 1944, Mr 6,19:2
Connor, Roland C, 1946, O 6,56:5
Connor, Samuel P, 1945, My 28,19:4
Connor, Thomas F, 1947, S 7,60:7
Connor, Thomas Maj, 1883, Ag 21,2:6
Connor, Washington E Mrs, 1911, N 4,13:6
Connor, Wayne E, 1949, Je 10,27:4
Connor, William, 1948, S 16,29:5
Connor, William A, 1923, F 9,15:2
Connor, William D, 1944, N 22,19:6; 1960, Je 18,23:5
Connor, William D Mrs, 1961, Je 28,35:2
Connor, William F, 1952, Ap 23,29:4
Connor, William J, 1955, O 8,19:4
Connor, William M, 1949, Je 26,60:4
Connor, William R, 1948, Ja 24,15:5; 1954, Jl 27,21:4
Connor, William T, 1945, Mr 23,19:3; 1956, Ap 9,27:4
Connor, William T Mrs, 1961, Ap 22,25:3
Connors, Andrew, 1944, Jl 24,15:5
Connors, Arthur E Sr, 1948, F 12,24:2
Connors, Brigid Mrs, 1948, O 6,29:1
Connors, C J, 1948, D 23,20:2
Connors, Charles F, 1951, N 27,31:2
Connors, Charles J (Chuck), 1962, Ag 19,89:1
Connors, Charles J Mrs, 1960, F 21,92:8
Connors, Edward, 1942, My 16,13:4; 1959, Je 3,35:3
Connors, Edward A, 1946, Jl 11,23:3; 1963, Ag 1,27:5
Connors, Edward D, 1941, N 20,27:1
Connors, Edward J, 1953, Mr 4,27:5; 1964, Ja 29,33:1
Connors, F (see also S 24), 1877, S 25,8:5
Connors, Florence V, 1959, Ja 26,29:4
Connors, Francis J, 1939, F 4,15:2
Connors, Fred, 1951, Je 1,33:4
Connors, George R Mrs, 1959, Ap 16,33:4
Connors, George S, 1941, Ja 19,41:1
Connors, George W, 1943, Je 5,15:2
Connors, James B, 1951, S 30,73:1
Connors, James F, 1951, Jl 7,13:5
Connors, James H, 1941, Jl 12,13:4
Connors, James I, 1944, Jl 6,15:4
Connors, James J, 1951, Ja 27,13:4
Connors, James J Sr, 1952, Ag 30,13:3
Connors, James W, 1958, Ag 16,17:1
Connors, John, 1939, O 7,17:6; 1943, Ag 30,15:5; 1947, Mr 21,21:2
Connors, John A, 1954, Ap 16,21:4
Connors, John A Mrs, 1950, Ag 14,17:4
Connors, John J, 1950, Je 2,23:4; 1959, O 4,86:2
Connors, John M, 1946, Mr 4,23:1
Connors, John T, 1952, D 11,33:2
Connors, Joseph J, 1950, F 20,25:2
Connors, Joseph M, 1948, O 3,64:5; 1967, D 12,47:2
Connors, Leo H Sr, 1957, O 12,19:5
Connors, Martin L Dr, 1937, Mr 10,23:1
Connors, Martin M, 1966, O 11,47:2
Connors, Maurice S, 1940, F 6,22:2
Connors, Michael J, 1945, N 16,19:4; 1948, Ag 13,15:5
Connors, Myles F, 1946, Ja 2,19:4
Connors, Philip Mrs, 1958, N 5,35:3
Connors, Raymond P, 1961, Mr 10,27:4
Connors, Richard, 1938, S 14,23:5
Connors, Thomas F, 1937, Jl 29,19:5
Connors, Thomas J, 1946, Ap 2,27:5; 1958, Ag 18,19:3
Connors, Thomas P, 1965, Je 8,37:1
Connors, W Bradley (funl, F 25,3:3), 1959, F 21,21:1
Connors, William, 1960, Ag 4,25:3
Connors, William F, 1965, F 25,31:3
Connors, William J, 1961, Je 25,76:5
Connorton, Luke J, 1910, D 25,9:3
Conolly, James, 1944, Ap 18,21:4
Conolly, Joseph B, 1957, S 14,19:4
Conolly, Richard L (funl plans, Mr 3,45:1; funl, Mr 6,32:5), 1962, Mr 2,15:1
Conolly, Richard L Mrs (funl plans, Mr 3,45:1; funl, Mr 6,32:5), 1962, Mr 2,15:2
Conolly, Thomas, 1876, Ag 13,6:7; 1945, Je 4,19:4
Conor, Alan B, 1954, Ja 3,89:2
Conor, John W, 1954, Jl 4,31:2
Conor, Lewis S, 1945, Mr 25,38:2
Conor, Lewis S Mrs, 1951, Mr 31,15:1
Conord, Edmund J, 1949, Ja 19,27:5
Conord, Ralph C, 1939, My 10,23:5
Conover, A W Maj (see also S 25), 1901, S 28,9:6
Conover, Alice B P, 1955, Ja 27,23:4
Conover, Augustus H, 1914, Mr 4,11:6
Conover, Charles A, 1941, Ja 20,17:5
Conover, Charles H, 1915, N 5,13:6
Conover, Chriney S, 1951, Mr 16,31:3
Conover, Clara E, 1947, F 15,15:3
Conover, Claude A, 1949, N 24,31:6
Conover, D Lane, 1907, O 17,9:5
Conover, Elbert M, 1952, N 18,31:2
Conover, Elbert M Mrs, 1952, Jl 9,27:5
Conover, Elisha Jr, 1944, D 15,19:4
Conover, George C, 1947, Ag 31,36:3
Conover, George H (corr, Ag 13,36:2), 1944, Ag 12, 11:2
Conover, Harold L, 1956, O 21,86:6
Conover, Harry, 1925, D 5,19:4
Conover, Harry S, 1965, Jl 25,68:2
Conover, Henry A, 1924, Ag 25,13:4
Conover, Hezekiah J, 1941, Ja 15,23:4
Conover, Irene M Mrs, 1937, D 8,25:5
Conover, J Fred, 1948, Ja 21,25:2
Conover, J S Mrs, 1941, O 24,23:2
Conover, John C, 1940, N 5,34:2; 1957, Mr 3,84:4
Conover, John C Mrs, 1947, F 9,61:4
Conover, John L, 1954, Ja 16,15:6
Conover, John S, 1942, Ag 24,15:3
Conover, John W Capt, 1937, F 14,II,8:7
Conover, Joseph L, 1938, Jl 23,13:6
Conover, Joseph P, 1937, F 24,23:2
Conover, Laurus L, 1958, O 12,86:1
Conover, Lawrence P, 1938, S 3,13:2
Conover, Lyburn, 1941, Ap 29,19:5
Conover, Lydia, 1953, Ap 5,76:5
Conover, Nelson D, 1959, O 8,39:4
Conover, Peter S, 1939, My 23,23:2
Conover, Richard S Mrs, 1949, My 20,27:3
Conover, Samuel S, 1938, F 18,19:4; 1962, Ap 12,36:1
Conover, Samuel S Mrs, 1944, S 6,19:6
Conover, Sidney, 1913, S 1,5:4
Conover, T A Commodore, 1864, S 30,5:1
Conover, Thomas A, 1943, O 1,19:2
Conover, Warren Archer, 1915, Ap 22,13:4
Conover, William G, 1955, Ag 16,23:5
Conover, William R, 1941, O 17,23:3; 1942, N 21,13:5
Conovitz, Michael, 1956, O 26,29:3
Conquest, Arthur, 1945, D 7,22:3
Conquest, Ida (Mrs R Bertelli), 1937, Jl 13,19:1
Conquest, Joan, 1941, O 24,23:5
Conquest, Pleasanton L Jr, 1938, N 6,49:1
Conrad, Albert, 1951, S 28,31:2
Conrad, Alex, 1948, Mr 18,27:4
Conrad, Anthony L, 1938, Ap 8,19:5
Conrad, Arcturus Z Rev, 1937, Ja 24,II,8:4
Conrad, Arthur Bruce, 1907, N 6,9:2
Conrad, Basil W, 1953, N 4,33:4
Conrad, Benjamin B, 1955, Jl 17,60:4
Conrad, Bertram B, 1943, Ja 25,14:2
Conrad, Bro (P Hoffman), 1956, Ja 13,23:3
Conrad, C M, 1878, F 12,5:3
Conrad, C P, 1956, Ja 26,29:3
Conrad, Cal W, 1922, O 27,17:4
Conrad, Charles, 1953, S 21,25:4
Conrad, Charles A, 1943, O 14,21:4
Conrad, Charles W, 1957, O 25,27:1
Conrad, Christie Bro, 1957, Jl 19,19:3
Conrad, Clyde K, 1957, Ag 23,19:2
Conrad, Dorothea B, 1949, Je 10,27:2
Conrad, Earl L, 1945, Je 5,19:3
Conrad, Earl O, 1940, Je 27,23:5
Conrad, Edith U, 1960, Jl 30,17:2
Conrad, Edward, 1941, Ap 29,19:2
Conrad, Elbert H, 1942, Ag 9,42:5
Conrad, Eugene J, 1964, Ja 30,29:1
Conrad, Frank, 1941, D 12,25:1

Conrad, Frank L, 1949, O 23,86:3
Conrad, Fred A, 1947, F 27,21:1
Conrad, Frederick Mrs, 1951, Jl 12,25:2
Conrad, Frowin Rev, 1923, Mr 25,6:3
Conrad, G Miles, 1964, S 11,33:4
Conrad, George, 1967, Ja 10,43:1
Conrad, George E, 1949, D 15,35:2
Conrad, George Mrs, 1961, Ag 16,31:2
Conrad, George P, 1939, S 11,19:6
Conrad, George W B, 1947, D 12,27:2
Conrad, Harold, 1953, F 11,29:1
Conrad, Holmes Maj, 1915, S 5,11:4
Conrad, J Mrs, 1936, D 7,23:3
Conrad, Jacob W, 1939, Ap 9,III,6:7
Conrad, Jane L, 1958, O 1,37:4
Conrad, John Mrs, 1957, O 20,86:8
Conrad, Joseph L, 1950, S 1,21:2
Conrad, Kindman L, 1945, Ap 6,15:2
Conrad, Lilly, 1957, Mr 22,23:3
Conrad, Marcus E, 1961, S 22,33:3
Conrad, Marie A Mrs, 1941, S 20,17:4
Conrad, Minnie Mrs, 1940, Ag 2,15:2
Conrad, Owen M, 1960, Je 13,27:2
Conrad, Philip A Mrs, 1945, S 28,21:2; 1964, My 30, 17:6
Conrad, Robert D, 1949, Jl 27,23:5
Conrad, Sidney S, 1947, Jl 11,15:4
Conrad, Stephen D, 1949, My 15,90:2
Conrad, Stephen D Mrs, 1948, D 14,29:4
Conrad, T A Prof, 1877, Ag 10,2:7
Conrad, Will, 1951, Mr 9,52:4
Conrad, William, 1937, Ap 9,21:3
Conrad, William G, 1914, Mr 7,11:5
Conrad, William N, 1968, D 3,47:2
Conrad, William Y, 1949, O 4,27:3
Conrad (Bro K Roukey), 1963, N 23,29:1
Conrad Con (C K Dober), 1938, S 29,25:2
Conrad Edward, Bro (E Fleming), 1951, D 17,31:4
Conradi, Edward, 1944, D 2,13:1
Conradi, Fred G, 1950, S 12,27:3
Conradi, Gabriel K, 1949, D 18,89:1
Conradi, Karl, 1966, D 13,47:5
Conrads, Ernest Sr, 1951, O 25,29:1
Conradson, Conrad M, 1940, My 21,23:3
Conradson, Pontus H, 1938, Ja 22,18:2
Conradt-Eberlin, Viggo, 1939, Je 4,49:3
Conrady, Charles A Ex-Justice, 1919, Mr 18,11:2
Conrady, Howard Conrad, 1916, My 21,19:4
Conran, Eugene Justice, 1917, Ja 5,9:4
Conran, James J, 1964, F 3,27:1
Conran, Philip S, 1957, Jl 13,17:5
Conran, William H B, 1945, Ja 25,19:3
Conried, Heinrich (funl, My 6,9:3), 1909, Ap 30,9:5
Conried, Heinrich Mrs, 1911, Ja 21,13:5
Conried, Richard G, 1968, Ja 31,41:4
Conro, Charles B, 1957, Mr 7,29:4
Conro, Charles B Mrs, 1954, Ja 19,25:1
Conron, John J, 1949, My 1,89:1
Conron, Marie, 1885, Je 7,14:2
Conron, William M, 1964, S 7,19:2
Conrow, A Chester Mrs, 1942, My 26,21:2
Conrow, Harry W, 1946, S 23,23:4
Conrow, Herman Mrs, 1951, N 25,86:4
Conrow, John F, 1949, Ja 14,24:3
Conrow, Leon W, 1943, D 19,48:8
Conrow, Theodore, 1925, Ja 21,21:5
Conrow, Wilford S, 1957, N 26,30:2
Conrow, William C, 1951, D 14,31:1
Conroy, A M, 1951, D 8,11:5
Conroy, Andrew J, 1937, D 24,17:1
Conroy, Bernard P, 1937, N 29,23:4
Conroy, Daniel J Sr, 1958, O 19,87:1
Conroy, David F, 1948, Jl 26,17:4
Conroy, Edmund M, 1948, Je 16,29:2
Conroy, Edward A, 1950, My 18,29:3; 1951, S 9,90:4
Conroy, Edward E, 1956, F 3,23:1
Conroy, Edwin J Mrs, 1944, F 24,15:5
Conroy, Eugene F, 1960, S 13,37:3
Conroy, Frank, 1964, F 25,31:2
Conroy, Frank D, 1953, N 22,89:1
Conroy, Frederick J, 1944, Ag 16,19:6
Conroy, Gardiner Mrs, 1957, My 24,25:2
Conroy, James A, 1954, N 21,87:2
Conroy, James H, 1939, Ap 15,19:3
Conroy, James J Sr, 1938, O 15,17:4
Conroy, John, 1953, N 15,89:1
Conroy, John F, 1956, D 29,15:5
Conroy, John F Jr, 1944, F 17,19:6
Conroy, John H (cor, N 30,47:1), 1966, N 28,39:2
Conroy, John I, 1958, Ja 26,88:4
Conroy, John J, 1957, My 25,21:6
Conroy, John J E Mrs, 1943, Jl 29,19:1
Conroy, John P, 1941, S 14,50:1
Conroy, Joseph E, 1954, Mr 24,27:2
Conroy, Joseph H, 1939, Mr 21,23:1
Conroy, Joseph P, 1941, Je 13,19:5
Conroy, Laurence J, 1951, Mr 9,25:4
Conroy, Lawrence A, 1949, S 29,29:2
Conroy, Marcus D, 1947, Ag 29,17:4
Conroy, Margaret R, 1953, My 28,23:4
Conroy, Mary A C Mrs, 1953, F 6,20:7
Conroy, Mary Mrs, 1957, D 27,20:3
Conroy, Mary Sister, 1903, Jl 11,7:5
Conroy, Michael, 1948, F 23,25:4
Conroy, Michael A, 1961, Mr 30,29:3
Conroy, Perry J, 1950, D 11,25:5
Conroy, Peter J, 1955, Je 19,93:1
Conroy, Stephen J, 1945, D 30,14:4
Conroy, Thomas F, 1953, My 16,19:4
Conroy, Thomas M Lt, 1924, S 11,23:7
Conroy, Vincent F, 1967, Mr 25,3:4
Conroy, Walter A, 1960, N 2,39:3
Conroy, William E (Wid), 1959, D 7,31:5
Conroy, William H, 1961, D 12,43:2
Conroy, William J, 1940, Je 5,25:5; 1940, D 25,27:4
Conroy, William S, 1955, Ap 23,19:5
Conry, Joseph A, 1943, Je 23,21:2
Conry, Michael F (funl, Mr 8,11:5), 1917, Mr 3,9:3
Conry, Thomas, 1947, Je 30,19:2
Cons, Louis, 1942, Ap 21,23:4
Consago, Frank N, 1950, Ja 31,15:2
Consaulas, William B, 1905, Je 20,9:4
Conscience, H, 1883, S 12,4:7
Conselman, William M, 1940, My 26,35:1
Conser, C C, 1939, Mr 22,23:5
Consett, Montagu W W P, 1945, Mr 10,17:1
Considine, George B, 1952, Je 30,19:4
Considine, George F, 1916, Ag 8,9:6
Considine, James P, 1946, Je 15,21:4
Considine, John M, 1941, O 6,17:3
Considine, John R, 1909, Je 27,7:5
Considine, John W Jr, 1961, Mr 23,33:3
Considine, John W Sr, 1943, F 13,11:3
Considine, Mary Mrs, 1914, Ag 3,11:4
Considine, Sophie Mrs, 1957, Je 21,25:2
Considine, William J, 1945, S 25,25:1
Consior, Frank J, 1967, S 12,47:4
Conso, Eleandio, 1941, Jl 7,15:3
Consodine, Charles R, 1952, My 3,21:4
Consodine, William A Mrs, 1961, Ja 28,19:4
Consolbe, Giuseppina Mrs, 1925, N 9,19:5
Consoli, Achille, 1948, My 8,15:5
Consoli, Innocenzo, 1951, O 26,23:1
Consolvo, Charles H, 1947, O 25,19:3
Constabile, Michael, 1954, S 9,31:5
Constable, A G, 1882, O 26,4:7
Constable, Albert 3d, 1945, D 25,23:5
Constable, F A, 1905, Ap 11,1:2
Constable, Howard, 1940, O 17,26:3
Constable, Marie, 1951, S 27,31:6
Constable, Marie L (est tax appr), 1954, S 15,26:4
Constable, T, 1881, Je 19,6:7
Constable, William, 1952, S 27,17:3
Constable, William J, 1959, Ap 22,33:1
Constable, 1881, F 18,2:5
Constable-Maxwell, Marmaduke, 1908, O 6,9:6
Constant, Benjamin, 1902, My 27,9:4
Constant, D'Estournelles Baron, 1924, My 16,19:3
Constant, Frank H, 1950, Mr 17,23:2
Constant, S S, 1885, Ja 12,5:3
Constant, Walter E, 1953, Ag 15,15:4
Constantian, Raphael, 1942, S 12,13:2
Constantine, Albert, 1948, Ja 28,23:5
Constantine, Earl G, 1952, Ja 4,23:3
Constantine, Ex-King of Greece, 1923, Ja 13,13:5
Constantine, Frederick, 1942, Mr 30,17:4
Constantine, George J, 1968, Ja 9,43:2
Constantine, James, 1960, Ja 7,30:1
Constantine, Joseph E, 1961, Ag 6,85:2
Constantine, Roy, 1962, Je 11,31:5
Constantine, Wells W, 1942, My 14,19:2
Constantine, William J, 1912, Mr 16,13:4
Constantinescu, Mititza, 1946, S 21,15:4
Constantini, Celso (funl, O 22,17:4), 1958, O 18,1:1
Constantini, Giovanni, 1956, My 19,19:5
Constantinides, Vladimir, 1964, Jl 8,35:3
Constantino, Florencio, 1919, N 20,13:2
Constantino, John, 1952, Jl 23,23:5
Constantino, Luigi, 1942, Jl 21,19:4
Constantino, Luiz, 1948, D 25,17:1
Constantinou, Lazarus, 1938, Ag 9,19:4
Constantinovitch, Constantine Grand Duke, 1915, Je 17,11:7
Constantinovitch, Vladimir de, 1921, N 19,13:5
Constantius, Paul Bro, 1937, Je 3,28:2
Constanz, Charles E, 1945, My 3,23:3
Constien, Edward T, 1949, O 12,29:2
Conston, Harry Mrs, 1956, S 1,15:6
Consuelo, Duchess of Manchester, 1909, N 20,11:1
Consulich, Giuseppe, 1960, S 25,88:4
Contant, Marinus, 1940, S 19,23:1
Contarini, Salvatore, 1945, S 19,25:5
Conte, Harry A, 1961, Ap 19,39:2
Conte, Italo, 1953, Mr 16,27:6
Conte, Rocco, 1960, Ja 18,27:5
Conte Mayolino, Pepe, 1957, Mr 28,31:5
Content, Harold A, 1944, F 9,19:5
Content, Harry, 1941, Ag 15,17:1
Content, Noah Mrs, 1910, Je 10,9:4
Conterno, Louis, 1910, D 25,9:5
Conterno, Othello Charles, 1921, O 15,13:7
Contessa, Clemence J, 1946, N 2,15:3
Contessa, Emma F, 1952, Ag 6,21:3
Contesse, Susan, 1943, Ja 17,45:1
Contey, Frank Jr, 1962, Ap 4,43:1
Contey, Frank Sr, 1940, D 13,26:6
Conti, August Mrs, 1961, D 28,27:2
Conti, Charles Etienne, 1872, F 17,3:6
Conti, Gaetano T, 1941, S 1,15:3
Conti, Italia, 1946, F 9,13:3
Conti, Joseph A, 1960, D 18,84:1
Conti, Maria, 1953, F 24,25:4
Conti, Pete, 1937, Je 6,II,9:2
Conti, Phil, 1949, N 19,17:5
Conti-Sinibaldi, Ugo, 1942, N 6,23:1
Continho, Adolfo, 1950, Ja 9,26:4
Contini, Attilio J, 1960, Ap 29,31:4
Contis, Richard J, 1910, N 28,9:5
Contle, William, 1910, D 27,9:4
Conto, Armando F, 1964, Ja 25,23:5
Contogeorge, Christopher, 1950, S 1,21:2
Contoit, J H (funl), 1875, O 6,8:4
Contratto, Andrew W, 1961, F 23,27:4
Contreiras, Jose M, 1961, F 20,27:3
Contrell, Frances W Mrs, 1942, Mr 8,42:4
Contrell, Robert G, 1941, N 27,23:4
Contreras, Felipe Dr, 1937, N 7,II,9:2
Contreras, Jose, 1955, My 10,34:3
Conus, Adrien, 1947, O 29,27:1
Conus, Boris Mme, 1961, Ag 6,84:3
Conus, Leon, 1944, Ja 19,19:6
Conver, Harry L, 1950, My 31,29:3
Convers, Ebenezer Buckingham, 1905, Mr 11,9:4
Converse, Alfred L Mrs, 1947, Ja 19,52:1
Converse, Allan D, 1959, S 28,31:5
Converse, Blair, 1939, My 19,21:5
Converse, Charles A, 1940, Ap 15,17:3
Converse, Charles B Dr, 1912, Mr 5,11:5
Converse, Charles Mrs, 1949, O 31,25:2
Converse, Clarence C, 1952, N 14,23:4
Converse, Clarence L, 1953, Jl 24,13:6
Converse, Edmund C, 1912, S 4,11:3
Converse, Edmund Cogswell, 1921, Ap 5,19:1
Converse, Frank B, 1948, Ap 5,21:4
Converse, Frederick S, 1940, Je 9,44:1
Converse, George Albert Rear-Adm, 1909, Mr 30,9:7
Converse, George M, 1962, My 17,37:5
Converse, George P, 1963, Je 13,33:4
Converse, H M Mrs, 1903, N 20,16:1
Converse, Harry E Col, 1920, D 9,13:3
Converse, Harry P, 1960, Mr 2,37:4
Converse, Hugh, 1937, N 14,II,10:5
Converse, John H, 1910, My 4,11:4
Converse, John H Mrs, 1925, Je 27,11:6
Converse, John W, 1944, O 2,19:2
Converse, Lily S Mrs, 1961, S 20,29:3
Converse, Mary E, 1944, Ap 12,21:2
Converse, Mary P, 1961, Jl 3,15:3
Converse, Myron F, 1950, N 13,27:4
Converse, Paul H, 1952, Mr 15,13:5
Converse, R R M Mrs, 1947, Je 27,22:3
Converse, Roger W Jr, 1949, S 25,92:7
Converse, Samuel R, 1944, Jl 3,11:5
Converse, W M, 1872, Jl 27,5:5
Converse, Warren, 1866, Ja 22,5:4
Converse, William A, 1940, Ag 12,15:2
Converse, William F, 1943, Jl 9,17:5
Convery, Frank R, 1952, F 17,84:2
Convery, John A, 1959, Mr 8,87:1
Convery, John M, 1965, Mr 5,30:1
Convery, Neil J, 1966, N 1,41:2
Convery, Walter E Mrs, 1958, D 29,15:6
Convery, William J Msgr, 1937, Ag 21,15:4
Convetse, Edmund Coggswell (Baron von Romberg) 1914, S 30,9:6
Convey, Bridget Mary Mrs, 1922, N 4,13:6
Convey, James E, 1966, My 25,47:3
Convey, James M, 1961, Mr 1,33:3
Convey, Maurice J, 1937, O 17,II,9:3
Conville, William T, 1947, Ja 1,34:2
Conway, Alfred A, 1952, O 14,31:1
Conway, Barret, 1949, D 8,33:2
Conway, Bernard P, 1948, N 7,88:5
Conway, Bertie, 1942, Ja 20,20:4
Conway, Bertrand L, 1959, D 9,45:3
Conway, Carle C, 1959, Ag 20,25:1
Conway, Carle C Mrs, 1966, Ap 22,41:2
Conway, Cecelia A Mrs, 1940, Mr 29,22:3
Conway, Charles, 1949, Mr 2,26:3
Conway, Charles P, 1938, D 1,23:1
Conway, Clarence J, 1948, Ap 13,27:5
Conway, Daniel F, 1907, Je 27,7:6
Conway, Daniel H, 1956, N 3,23:4
Conway, Dennis F, 1945, S 24,19:3
Conway, E H Mrs, 1918, D 23,11:3
Conway, EDmund H, 1960, Jl 14,27:5
Conway, Edward A, 1965, My 25,42:1
Conway, Eustace, 1937, Ag 5,23:5
Conway, Francis J, 1939, S 18,19:5
Conway, Francis M, 1958, F 22,17:1
Conway, Frank J, 1940, O 22,23:6; 1962, Ag 30,2
Conway, Frankie, 1961, Jl 20,27:4
Conway, Fred B, 1874, S 8,4:7
Conway, Fred C, 1947, D 8,25:2
Conway, George, 1939, Ja 11,19:4; 1956, D 23,3
Conway, George E, 1967, D 26,33:2
Conway, George E Mrs, 1957, S 14,19:4
Conway, George H, 1939, Je 21,23:4
Conway, Harry G, 1956, Ja 10,88:4

Conway, Hart, 1919, Je 2,15:6
Conway, Harvey H, 1937, Ja 31,II,9:1
Conway, Henry A, 1951, O 17,31:4
Conway, Henry T, 1940, Ap 2,25:4
Conway, Horace L, 1945, O 2,23:4
Conway, Howard B, 1947, Je 9,21:5
Conway, Hugh Mrs, 1949, My 24,27:4
Conway, J Capt, 1884, Ja 3,5:1
Conway, Jack, 1952, O 13,21:3
Conway, James, 1916, F 24,13:4
Conway, James A, 1941, O 6,17:5
Conway, James F, 1949, S 10,17:6
Conway, James G, 1950, Je 13,27:2
Conway, James J, 1962, O 9,41:2
Conway, James J Mrs, 1950, Ag 1,23:3
Conway, James L, 1938, Ag 4,17:4
Conway, James M, 1949, Ja 4,19:4
Conway, James V, 1956, Ap 17,31:5
Conway, Jases, 1905, Ag 14,7:6
Conway, John, 1950, F 2,27:4
Conway, John A, 1949, Jl 29,21:5; 1954, N 12,21:5
Conway, John A Rev, 1915, O 9,9:3
Conway, John C, 1942, Mr 23,15:5
Conway, John F, 1918, Mr 5,11:5; 1957, Ja 1,23:3
Conway, John J, 1948, F 13,21:2; 1956, Ap 19,31:3
Conway, John P, 1957, F 19,31:3
Conway, John S, 1948, Ap 29,23:2
Conway, John S Mrs, 1945, Je 21,19:5
Conway, John T, 1953, Mr 15,93:3
Conway, John W, 1938, Ag 5,17:4; 1956, O 5,25:5
Conway, Joseph F, 1947, Ag 10,53:3
Conway, Joseph P Mrs, 1945, N 30,23:1
Conway, Joseph Severinus, 1925, D 25,17:5
Conway, Katherine (Sister Philomena), 1952, My 24,16:8
Conway, Leo I S, 1939, Ag 29,21:6
Conway, Lillian F, 1957, Je 28,23:3
Conway, Lord, 1937, Ap 20,25:5
Conway, M F, 1882, F 18,2:4
Conway, M J, 1946, Jl 25,21:5
Conway, Martin J, 1948, My 27,25:2; 1954, My 1,15:4
Conway, Mary E, 1903, S 10,7:6; 1939, Ja 22,34:6
Conway, Michael F, 1940, Jl 6,15:2
Conway, Michael H, 1955, Jl 5,29:1
Conway, Michael J, 1946, Mr 27,27:2
Conway, Michael Mrs, 1944, My 19,19:6
Conway, Michael W, 1903, Ag 10,7:6; 1937, Ag 16, 19:4
Conway, Moncure D, 1907, N 19,9:5; 1907, D 14,9:6
Conway, Nell B Mrs, 1939, D 24,14:8
Conway, Patrick J, 1962, Je 4,29:3
Conway, Raymond E, 1948, My 22,15:4
Conway, Raymond P, 1953, Mr 17,35:8
Conway, Richard, 1951, Je 30,10:5
Conway, Richard J, 1951, N 10,17:3
Conway, Sara G Mrs (funl), 1875, My 3,5:1
Conway, Sarah B Mrs, 1875, Ap 29,7:2
Conway, Theobold E, 1955, Ap 22,25:4
Conway, Thomas F, 1945, N 10,15:4
Conway, Thomas J, 1938, F 10,21:4
Conway, Thomas J Mrs, 1959, Ag 23,93:1
Conway, Thomas Jr, 1962, Ja 5,29:4
Conway, Tom, 1967, Ap 25,43:5
Conway, Walt P, 1945, Ja 13,11:6
Conway, William, 1950, F 11,15:4
Conway, William A, 1939, Ap 9,III,7:2
Conway, William F Sr, 1944, Mr 23,19:1
Conway, William J, 1942, Ap 19,43:1; 1949, F 28,19:2; 1952, F 20,30:4
Conway, William P Mrs, 1964, D 30,25:1
Conway, William W, 1937, N 29,23:6
Conwell, Arthur W, 1942, Ap 10,18:3
Conwell, Edward V, 1944, O 31,19:5
Conwell, Fred C Mrs, 1948, Ja 29,24:3
Conwell, J Frank, 1950, S 22,31:1
Conwell, Joseph J Jr, 1953, Jl 26,69:2
Conwell, Leon M, 1953, Ag 20,27:5
Conwell, Rollin N, 1945, Ap 15,13:1
Conwell, Russell H Rev Dr (funl, D 10,25:5), 1925, D 7,21:5
Conwell, Samuel H, 1952, Ap 4,25:4
Conwell, Walter L, 1948, My 29,15:4
Conwell, Walter L Mrs, 1937, Ap 16,23:4
Conwell, William R, 1942, My 16,13:4
Cony, J E S, 1903, Je 3,9:6
Cony, Robert A, 1945, Ja 2,19:2
Conybeare, George R, 1946, Ap 10,27:4
Conybeare, S E, 1938, Je 2,23:1
Conyers, Joseph, 1920, Je 26,11:6
Conyers, Reginald J, 1948, Jl 27,25:2
Conyngham, Marquis (see also Jl 18), 1876, Jl 19,5:4
Conyngham, William H, 1943, Ap 26,19:5
Conyngton, Hugh R, 1951, N 1,29:3
Conyngton, Thomas, 1937, Mr 21,II,8:5
Conyngton, Thomas Mrs, 1958, Ap 10,29:2
Conze, Godfrey H, 1966, Ja 16,82:6
Conze, Godfrey H Mrs, 1950, Ja 31,23:1
Conzen, Frederick J, 1940, My 18,15:5
Conzett, John V, 1944, N 15,27:1
Cooch, Francis A, 1949, D 14,31:2
Cooder, Clement M Sr, 1949, O 31,25:2
Cooder, Clement M Sr Mrs, 1965, Ag 20,29:2
Cooey, Hubert, 1958, O 6,31:4
Coogan, Bernard A, 1945, Je 28,19:2
Coogan, Clement F, 1942, Ja 14,21:2
Coogan, Danny, 1942, O 29,23:2
Coogan, Edward F, 1960, N 14,31:2
Coogan, Francis M, 1951, Ap 1,92:4
Coogan, Fred, 1959, Jl 13,27:6
Coogan, Gardiner, 1965, Mr 26,35:4
Coogan, James, 1962, Ap 14,25:3
Coogan, James J Mrs, 1947, D 19,26:2
Coogan, James Jay (funl, O 28,11:5), 1915, O 25,9:4
Coogan, John, 1959, N 27,58:1
Coogan, John F Sr, 1947, Je 5,25:1
Coogan, John J Rev, 1924, Ag 26,11:3; 1924, Ag 27, 17:6
Coogan, Mary B Mrs, 1937, N 25,31:3
Coogan, Mel, 1958, Ja 1,25:2
Coogan, Melvin Mrs, 1939, S 22,23:5
Coogan, Peter F Sr, 1944, Ag 31,17:4
Coogan, Thomas H, 1955, Ap 27,31:2
Coogan, W Gordon Jr, 1953, N 9,35:2
Coogan, William C, 1945, Ap 25,23:5
Coogan, William J Dr, 1923, Jl 10,19:6
Cook, A Bruce Mrs, 1960, S 15,37:1
Cook, A J, 1931, N 2,19:3
Cook, A L, 1874, Mr 11,8:5
Cook, Agnes, 1883, Jl 29,1:7
Cook, Albert, 1951, Ap 25,29:2
Cook, Albert C, 1961, Mr 8,33:3
Cook, Albert John Prof, 1916, O 1,23:5
Cook, Albert N, 1958, S 8,29:4
Cook, Albert S, 1952, Mr 12,27:4
Cook, Alex, 1902, Ap 28,9:5
Cook, Alex N, 1942, D 5,15:4
Cook, Alexander B Sr, 1946, Ag 30,17:3
Cook, Alexander Mrs, 1916, Ap 1,13:7
Cook, Alfred A, 1950, Ja 3,25:1
Cook, Alfred A Mrs, 1967, My 28,61:1
Cook, Alfred W, 1958, D 10,39:2
Cook, Allan B, 1967, Ap 23,93:1
Cook, Alonzo B, 1956, D 23,30:8
Cook, Alton F, 1967, Ag 16,41:4
Cook, Andrew J, 1958, F 19,27:5
Cook, Anna H Mrs, 1937, O 15,23:6
Cook, Arthur, 1959, Ja 17,19:5
Cook, Arthur B Mrs, 1944, Mr 17,17:4
Cook, Arthur E, 1938, Je 19,28:6
Cook, Arthur F, 1950, N 11,15:5
Cook, Arthur L, 1965, Mr 21,86:8
Cook, Arthur P, 1948, F 15,60:4
Cook, Barton B, 1964, Ap 14,34:7
Cook, Benjamin A, 1938, Ag 30,17:5
Cook, Benjamin Ladd, 1968, Ap 13,25:1
Cook, Bridget H Mrs, 1947, Je 29,48:3
Cook, C Carroll, 1947, Ja 23,26:1
Cook, Carlotta Church, 1924, D 30,17:6
Cook, Charles A, 1940, Ap 3,23:5
Cook, Charles B, 1948, N 8,21:6; 1955, D 15,37:5
Cook, Charles C, 1940, N 26,23:5; 1953, Mr 3,27:1; 1957, Ag 25,86:5
Cook, Charles C Mrs, 1949, D 1,31:1
Cook, Charles D Dr, 1912, S 6,9:6
Cook, Charles E, 1941, Je 9,19:6; 1947, Ja 3,22:3; 1950, Ag 11,19:4
Cook, Charles F (trb lr, S 6,34:5; mem ser set, S 23,29:3), 1960, Ag 29,25:1
Cook, Charles F Maj, 1919, Ja 4,11:4
Cook, Charles H, 1952, F 1,21:4
Cook, Charles M, 1949, Mr 16,28:2
Cook, Charles S, 1939, F 10,23:2
Cook, Charles T, 1907, Ja 27,7:6; 1947, Mr 5,25:4
Cook, Charley, 1948, Jl 10,15:2
Cook, Chauncey W, 1949, Ag 6,17:7
Cook, Chester A, 1953, Ag 1,11:5
Cook, Clarence H, 1947, Ag 16,13:6
Cook, Clarence J, 1949, Ja 5,26:2
Cook, Clarence J Mrs, 1956, D 20,29:4
Cook, Claude E, 1958, Je 19,31:4
Cook, Clifford A, 1944, Mr 14,19:5
Cook, Clifford F, 1945, Ag 25,11:2
Cook, Constant, 1874, F 25,5:6
Cook, Cyrus Mrs, 1962, Ag 16,27:5
Cook, Daniel, 1955, D 27,23:1
Cook, Daniel Mrs, 1949, Ap 26,25:4
Cook, David, 1903, D 5,9:4
Cook, Delbert, 1959, Je 6,21:5
Cook, Donald, 1961, O 2,31:1
Cook, Dudley H, 1954, Je 3,27:5
Cook, Dutton, 1883, S 14,4:6
Cook, Edgar L, 1942, Ag 1,11:3
Cook, Edmond F, 1908, N 19,9:5
Cook, Edmund J, 1952, Jl 12,13:6
Cook, Edward, 1955, Ag 9,25:4
Cook, Edward F, 1939, N 26,42:8
Cook, Edward G, 1937, Ja 1,23:2
Cook, Edward H, 1953, Mr 20,23:2
Cook, Edward J, 1958, O 18,21:5
Cook, Edward M, 1944, My 22,19:6
Cook, Edward T Sir, 1919, O 2,17:7
Cook, Elisha W Rev, 1904, Ja 5,9:5
Cook, Eliza, 1947, O 4,17:5
Cook, Elizabeth C, 1938, Mr 2,19:5
Cook, Ella Mrs, 1940, Mr 21,26:4
Cook, Elmer J, 1959, O 3,19:7
Cook, Emery I, 1964, Jl 13,29:3
Cook, Enos Foster, 1909, Mr 4,9:5
Cook, Ernest E (will), 1955, Je 7,20:6
Cook, Ernest F, 1961, Mr 4,23:4
Cook, Ernest H, 1961, Je 11,86:6
Cook, Essie, 1956, Je 25,23:1
Cook, Eugene B, 1915, Mr 20,13:4
Cook, Eugene Mrs, 1954, N 14,88:8
Cook, Exter A, 1958, My 14,33:3
Cook, F G Alletson, 1960, Ja 14,33:2
Cook, F H, 1931, D 27,28:3
Cook, Fannie Mrs (por), 1949, Ag 26,20:2
Cook, Finley R Dr, 1937, My 6,25:3
Cook, Francis A Rear-Adm, 1916, O 9,11:6
Cook, Francis K, 1955, F 19,15:5
Cook, Francis Lady, 1923, Ja 20,13:5
Cook, Frank, 1947, D 14,76:5
Cook, Frank A, 1937, Ja 12,23:4
Cook, Frank E, 1923, Ja 23,21:4
Cook, Frank F Dr, 1937, Mr 13,19:3
Cook, Frank R, 1941, O 16,21:5
Cook, Frank W, 1957, Mr 30,19:2
Cook, Frank W Mrs, 1946, My 28,21:1
Cook, Franklin, 1943, Ap 15,25:2
Cook, Fred, 1905, F 18,9:3; 1943, Jl 17,13:6
Cook, Fred P, 1947, Jl 29,21:3
Cook, Frederic, 1961, Jl 11,31:2
Cook, Frederic W, 1944, Je 16,19:2; 1951, N 17,17:4
Cook, Frederic W Mrs, 1947, My 1,25:6
Cook, Frederick, 1945, Je 20,23:3
Cook, Frederick A, 1915, D 17,11:5
Cook, Frederick A (will, S 19,21:3), 1940, Ag 6,19:1
Cook, Frederick A, 1952, O 6,25:4
Cook, Frederick A Mrs, 1922, N 16,19:5
Cook, Frederick M Mrs, 1953, Jl 15,25:5
Cook, Frederick R, 1956, My 1,33:4
Cook, Frederick W Mrs, 1957, Ag 10,15:4
Cook, G L Dr, 1902, N 4,1:6
Cook, George, 1943, O 9,13:3; 1944, Ja 30,38:4
Cook, George C, 1960, Ja 2,31:4
Cook, George D, 1920, D 14,17:4
Cook, George Jr, 1943, D 3,23:3; 1953, D 12,19:5
Cook, George L, 1941, S 28,49:1
Cook, George M, 1943, D 2,27:2
Cook, George Mrs, 1943, Mr 24,23:1
Cook, George S, 1944, S 8,19:4
Cook, George W, 1865, Ap 24,4:6; 1940, D 18,23:5; 1944, Ja 23,38:3
Cook, Gilbert R, 1963, S 21,21:5
Cook, Gordon, 1968, O 30,47:4
Cook, Grant R, 1943, N 15,19:3
Cook, Gustavus W, 1940, Je 5,25:3
Cook, Hal B Mrs, 1964, Je 5,31:4
Cook, Harold A W, 1946, O 4,23:3
Cook, Harold J Mrs, 1955, Ap 15,23:3
Cook, Harold L, 1960, My 23,29:3
Cook, Harrison, 1956, My 21,25:5
Cook, Harry, 1956, Ja 11,31:3
Cook, Harry B, 1950, Jl 11,31:2
Cook, Harry E, 1942, Ja 11,45:1
Cook, Harry L, 1952, Ja 11,21:4
Cook, Harry M Mrs, 1955, Jl 26,25:5
Cook, Harvey R Mrs, 1957, Mr 13,31:5
Cook, Helen, 1953, Mr 25,31:2
Cook, Henry, 1949, My 24,28:3
Cook, Henry A, 1960, D 31,17:3
Cook, Henry C, 1940, Ja 21,34:4
Cook, Henry Clay Gen, 1916, F 23,13:6
Cook, Henry D, 1967, Jl 11,37:3
Cook, Henry H (will), 1905, O 25,9:5
Cook, Henry R Jr, 1955, Ag 15,15:6
Cook, Henry W, 1964, N 9,33:4
Cook, Herbert Sir, 1939, My 5,23:1
Cook, Herman A, 1949, F 17,23:4; 1950, N 23,35:4
Cook, Herman J, 1945, D 13,29:1
Cook, Hermon J, 1956, Ja 21,21:5
Cook, Horace T, 1965, Mr 30,47:3
Cook, Howard B, 1954, S 8,31:4
Cook, Howard B Mrs, 1938, Ja 3,21:4; 1968, Mr 7,43:5
Cook, Howard E, 1957, Ag 17,15:6
Cook, Howard W, 1959, D 9,42:4
Cook, Hugh F, 1952, N 15,17:4
Cook, Ida O Mrs, 1942, Ap 25,13:6
Cook, Irving W, 1958, S 6,17:5
Cook, Ivan E, 1958, Jl 25,19:3
Cook, J Bruce, 1945, Je 30,17:3
Cook, J M, 1899, Mr 5,7:2
Cook, Jacob H, 1950, N 10,27:5
Cook, James A, 1946, Ap 19,30:3
Cook, James H, 1942, Ja 28,19:2
Cook, James J Mrs, 1958, My 17,19:6
Cook, James M Mrs, 1940, O 19,17:2
Cook, James O, 1949, D 24,15:6
Cook, Jenny S, 1954, Jl 17,13:2
Cook, Job W Mrs, 1958, Jl 21,21:3
Cook, Joe, 1959, My 17,84:1
Cook, Joel, 1910, D 16,11:5
Cook, John C B, 1958, N 10,29:3
Cook, John G, 1951, Ag 12,77:2
Cook, John P, 1946, My 10,19:2
Cook, John P Brig-Gen, 1910, O 13,11:4
Cook, John Swinburne, 1915, N 14,19:5
Cook, Joseph, 1901, Je 26,7:5; 1937, Ag 25,21:5; 1947, Jl 31,21:2; 1958, Ja 1,25:1

Cook, Joseph F, 1962, Ag 30,29:2
Cook, Katherine I, 1961, Ap 9,86:5
Cook, Kathryn Mrs, 1939, N 8,23:5
Cook, Kenneth A, 1945, F 7,21:5
Cook, L Haywood, 1938, Ja 25,22:2
Cook, Laurens, 1912, Ap 24,13:4
Cook, Lawyer, 1872, Ja 3,8:3
Cook, Lora H Mrs, 1946, F 11,29:4
Cook, Louis B, 1923, Mr 20,21:4
Cook, Louis J, 1959, N 9,31:4
Cook, Louisa De Windt Whittemore, 1908, Ja 25,9:6
Cook, Lucius, 1952, Ja 4,23:3
Cook, Lucy E Mrs, 1938, Je 18,15:5
Cook, Madeleine R, 1946, Ap 1,27:3
Cook, Manuel M, 1937, O 23,15:5
Cook, Marguerite M Mrs, 1941, Jl 6,27:3
Cook, Martha Mrs, 1952, F 24,84:4
Cook, Mary S Mrs, 1937, Je 24,25:4
Cook, Matthew, 1925, Ja 3,13:5
Cook, Melville T, 1952, Ag 12,19:2
Cook, Milton C, 1961, Ja 16,27:4
Cook, Morgan Mrs, 1943, O 16,13:5
Cook, Morris, 1956, Ja 23,25:2
Cook, Nancy, 1962, Ag 17,23:3
Cook, Nathan J, 1941, My 16,23:1
Cook, Nathan W, 1954, N 20,17:4
Cook, Norman W, 1948, Ag 29,56:5
Cook, Norville W, 1950, Ja 31,24:2
Cook, Oscar, 1947, Mr 31,23:3
Cook, Oscar Sr, 1960, Mr 17,33:2
Cook, P Walter, 1957, Jl 26,19:5
Cook, Peter (Bro Julian), 1952, F 24,86:2
Cook, Phil (por), 1938, Mr 25,20:1
Cook, Phil, 1958, S 19,27:1
Cook, Phil W, 1955, Ja 1,13:6
Cook, Philip, 1912, Ja 8,13:4
Cook, Philip S Mrs, 1960, O 24,29:5
Cook, Pierre F, 1943, Je 17,21:4
Cook, R, 1881, Je 1,5:4
Cook, R F Mrs, 1947, Je 8,60:2
Cook, R Harvey, 1949, N 26,15:4
Cook, Ralph W, 1940, O 30,23:3
Cook, Randolph, 1960, Ap 20,33:6
Cook, Richard C, 1964, S 12,25:5
Cook, Richard F, 1966, Je 22,47:2
Cook, Richard J, 1957, Jl 9,29:3
Cook, Richard W, 1948, My 11,26:2
Cook, Robert B M, 1939, S 28,25:3
Cook, Robert C, 1903, Je 18,9:6
Cook, Robert E, 1945, D 30,14:5
Cook, Robert G, 1940, O 26,15:2
Cook, Robert G Mrs, 1944, N 22,19:1
Cook, Robert J, 1922, D 4,17:4; 1951, O 5,27:1
Cook, Robert P, 1964, Mr 11,39:3
Cook, Roland, 1916, Jl 24,9:6
Cook, Roland M, 1939, Je 16,23:4
Cook, Roy B, 1961, N 24,28:4
Cook, Roy H, 1964, Ag 1,21:4
Cook, Russell A, 1955, Mr 24,31:4
Cook, Russell M, 1949, D 23,22:3
Cook, Russell T Rev, 1864, S 8,5:4
Cook, Samuel (Last Revolutionary Veteran), 1866, My 23,5:3
Cook, Samuel H, 1944, N 9,27:5
Cook, Sanford R Mrs, 1950, My 13,17:6
Cook, Sarah Mrs, 1905, My 2,11:6; 1957, S 12,31:4
Cook, Seabury, 1944, D 8,21:4
Cook, Simon Com, 1907, S 11,9:6
Cook, Smith, 1921, F 24,13:6
Cook, Stanley A, 1949, S 28,27:3
Cook, Stephen G Dr, 1910, N 23,9:5
Cook, Stewart, 1942, My 7,19:2
Cook, Stewart S, 1941, Mr 8,19:5
Cook, Sylvester Rev, 1878, Mr 24,5:4
Cook, Tasker Sir, 1937, S 26,II,9:4
Cook, Thomas, 1892, Jl 20,9:3
Cook, Thomas A, 1940, Ag 21,19:6; 1945, My 23,19:1
Cook, Thomas D, 1940, D 29,24:5
Cook, Thomas F, 1952, Je 2,3:1
Cook, Thomas J, 1950, My 17,29:4; 1952, Je 20,23:6; 1960, Je 19,88:2
Cook, Thomas Mrs, 1939, Mr 10,23:2
Cook, Thomas R, 1958, Mr 1,17:6
Cook, W W, 1883, D 8,2:6
Cook, Waldo L, 1951, S 18,64:2
Cook, Wallace L, 1958, Ap 28,23:4
Cook, Walter (funl, Mr 29,11:3), 1916, Mr 26,21:3
Cook, Walter M, 1959, Jl 24,25:5
Cook, Walter W, 1943, N 9,21:3
Cook, Walter W S, 1962, S 22,25:3
Cook, Ward H, 1961, Ja 20,29:3
Cook, Warren, 1939, My 4,23:2
Cook, Welling T, 1952, Ja 17,27:4
Cook, Wells W, 1916, Mr 31,1:5
Cook, Will A Mrs (A Mitchell), 1960, Mr 20,86:4
Cook, Will M, 1944, Jl 21,19:4
Cook, Willard B, 1952, F 22,21:4
Cook, William, 1924, Ap 5,15:1; 1942, My 18,15:4; 1944, F 5,15:2
Cook, William A, 1944, Ja 9,43:2; 1947, Ja 20,25:4
Cook, William A A, 1957, Mr 5,31:2
Cook, William A Mrs, 1947, N 27,31:1
Cook, William E, 1942, F 24,21:2
Cook, William H, 1949, Ja 8,15:4; 1958, Jl 23,27:4
Cook, William H Col, 1915, Mr 17,11:5
Cook, William J, 1941, N 22,19:6; 1953, Je 12,27:3
Cook, William L, 1942, Mr 6,22:3; 1954, D 16,37:4
Cook, William M, 1949, O 11,34:6
Cook, William N, 1956, O 28,89:2
Cook, William W Mrs, 1943, Ag 10,19:3
Cook, Willis A, 1952, D 4,35:5
Cook, Willis C, 1942, Ja 8,21:5
Cooke, A Hamilton, 1946, Ag 20,28:3
Cooke, A P, 1952, N 11,30:3
Cooke, Alex J, 1963, Ap 24,35:4
Cooke, Alex J Jr, 1958, Ag 8,19:1
Cooke, Alexander J Mrs, 1943, Jl 21,15:1
Cooke, Alice R, 1956, Ja 17,33:4
Cooke, Almon H, 1946, Ag 2,19:5
Cooke, Arthur H, 1950, My 18,29:2
Cooke, Bella Mrs, 1908, N 16,9:7
Cooke, Ben D, 1965, Ja 7,31:4
Cooke, Bennett W, 1956, My 6,86:8
Cooke, Burton A, 1952, Ag 8,17:5
Cooke, C Berkley Jr, 1966, D 20,43:4
Cooke, Carleton S, 1957, Ap 2,31:3
Cooke, Charles H, 1914, Ag 3,11:6
Cooke, Charles L, 1937, Mr 19,23:1
Cooke, Charles M, 1909, Ag 28,7:6; 1947, D 14,78:6
Cooke, Charles Mrs, 1946, Ja 17,23:1
Cooke, Charles S, 1943, Mr 12,17:2
Cooke, Charles W, 1965, D 29,29:2
Cooke, D B, 1884, O 23,5:6
Cooke, D W, 1931, F 11,25:3
Cooke, Delbert V, 1945, S 26,23:2
Cooke, Douglas H, 1948, F 19,23:3
Cooke, E W, 1880, Ja 7,4:7
Cooke, Edward E Mrs, 1949, D 4,108:3
Cooke, Edward G, 1942, Ja 17,17:2
Cooke, Edwin T Gen, 1867, S 12,4:7
Cooke, Elmer B, 1955, Ap 15,23:4
Cooke, Erastus, 1885, Je 21,5:4
Cooke, Flora J, 1953, F 22,63:4
Cooke, Francis C, 1940, Ap 2,25:4
Cooke, Francis W Mrs, 1949, F 15,23:2
Cooke, Frank S, 1945, Ap 26,23:3
Cooke, Frederick Hale, 1912, Ja 14,II,16:2
Cooke, Frederick P, 1941, Ja 20,12:1
Cooke, Frederika, 1944, Ap 11,19:3
Cooke, George, 1908, Ag 7,5:4; 1959, S 5,15:6
Cooke, George A, 1938, D 7,23:5
Cooke, George B, 1939, My 13,15:4
Cooke, George E, 1950, O 2,23:2
Cooke, George J Mrs, 1959, My 13,37:1
Cooke, George Kissam, 1916, Mr 31,1:5
Cooke, George L Mrs, 1943, F 3,19:6
Cooke, George Mrs, 1946, Ja 27,42:7
Cooke, George R Jr, 1966, Ja 10,25:3
Cooke, George W, 1951, O 23,29:2
Cooke, Gerold F, 1959, F 8,86:3
Cooke, Giles B Rev, 1937, F 5,21:1
Cooke, Gordon C, 1954, Jl 21,27:5
Cooke, Gordon D, 1944, Mr 24,19:1
Cooke, Grace, 1951, O 17,31:4
Cooke, Grace E, 1951, Ja 25,25:3
Cooke, H D ex-Gov, 1881, F 25,5:3
Cooke, Harold G, 1958, Mr 18,29:6
Cooke, Harriet N F Dr, 1906, Ja 9,9:4
Cooke, Harris L, 1941, D 11,27:4
Cooke, Harry M, 1958, Mr 24,27:5
Cooke, Harte, 1942, D 15,27:3
Cooke, Harvey M, 1951, N 5,31:6
Cooke, Hedley V Mrs, 1946, D 4,31:5
Cooke, Helen T, 1955, Ap 13,29:5
Cooke, Henry D, 1914, F 19,9:4; 1914, O 10,11:5; 1958, Jl 8,28:1
Cooke, Hereward L, 1946, O 1,23:5
Cooke, Homer, 1923, D 7,21:5
Cooke, Howard J, 1959, N 3,31:1
Cooke, J, 1880, Ap 29,8:3; 1932, N 23,19:1
Cooke, J Joseph, 1941, Ag 16,15:4
Cooke, J Leo, 1961, D 15,37:4
Cooke, James F, 1959, Jl 24,25:1; 1960, Mr 5,19:4
Cooke, James F Mrs, 1954, D 20,29:4
Cooke, James N Mrs, 1949, Jl 1,19:5
Cooke, Jay, 1905, F 17,2:3; 1963, Jl 11,29:1
Cooke, Jay Mrs, 1871, Jl 24,1:6; 1953, Je 18,29:2
Cooke, John, 1882, F 19,7:2
Cooke, John A Sr, 1951, D 1,13:2
Cooke, John B, 1939, Ja 15,39:2
Cooke, John C, 1937, Mr 7,II,8:4; 1961, Ag 5,17:6
Cooke, John L S, 1939, Jl 31,13:4
Cooke, John P, 1946, Ja 19,13:2
Cooke, John S, 1961, Mr 23,33:2
Cooke, John W Mrs, 1948, N 25,31:1
Cooke, Joseph, 1946, Je 24,31:2
Cooke, Joseph F, 1938, Je 26,27:3
Cooke, Josiah Mrs (Mrs Mary Huntington Cooke), 1911, My 22,11:4
Cooke, Juan I, 1957, Je 25,29:1
Cooke, L, 1932, D 26,23:3
Cooke, L A ex-Gov, 1902, Ag 12,1:6
Cooke, L J, 1943, Ag 20,15:4
Cooke, Leland G, 1953, Mr 23,23:3
Cooke, Leslie E, 1967, F 23,35:2
Cooke, Louis H, 1941, Je 26,23:4
Cooke, Louis J, 1937, O 19,25:4
Cooke, Marjorie Benton, 1920, Ap 27,9:3
Cooke, Martin, 1944, Ag 1,15:5
Cooke, Mary M, 1951, N 2,23:1
Cooke, Merle Mrs, 1963, My 24,31:2
Cooke, Michael J, 1961, My 28,64:5
Cooke, Morris L, 1960, Mr 6,86:4
Cooke, Morris L Mrs, 1958, Ag 31,57:2
Cooke, Oakley W, 1946, Mr 10,46:4
Cooke, Oakley W Mrs, 1948, Ag 24,23:3
Cooke, Oliver P, 1938, My 8,II,7:2
Cooke, Ray A, 1949, Mr 22,25:3
Cooke, Richard C, 1950, My 11,30:4
Cooke, Richard H, 1959, My 4,29:6
Cooke, Richard T, 1956, F 29,28:6
Cooke, Robert A (will, Jl 13,24:5), 1960, My 8,87:4
Cooke, Robert Grier (funl, O 22,21:4), 1924, O 19,7:2
Cooke, Robert L, 1955, Jl 26,25:4
Cooke, Robert P, 1952, O 28,31:4
Cooke, Robert S Maj, 1919, Jl 26,9:6
Cooke, Russell, 1958, My 13,29:5
Cooke, Rutherford B, 1939, N 24,23:3
Cooke, S Beach Mrs, 1960, Je 26,72:8
Cooke, Samuel, 1965, My 23,84:5
Cooke, Samuel Rev, 1903, O 29,9:4
Cooke, Samuel Walden, 1865, Ja 8,5:4
Cooke, Sidney T, 1951, Mr 13,31:2
Cooke, Stenson, 1942, N 21,13:3
Cooke, Thomas B, 1954, Jl 18,57:2
Cooke, Thomas C, 1939, Je 11,45:2
Cooke, Thomas L, 1946, My 28,21:2
Cooke, Thomas Mossman, 1921, Ag 3,13:5
Cooke, Thomas N, 1948, My 11,25:4
Cooke, Thomas T, 1965, My 2,88:6
Cooke, Vernon W, 1955, Jl 19,27:3
Cooke, Vincent Stairs, 1917, Ja 5,9:4
Cooke, W F Sir, 1879, Jl 1,5:4
Cooke, W P, 1931, Ag 5,19:1
Cooke, Walter E, 1939, O 10,23:5
Cooke, Walter H, 1939, Mr 29,23:5
Cooke, Walter P Mrs, 1948, N 29,23:4
Cooke, Wesley E, 1946, D 19,29:5
Cooke, William E H, 1955, Mr 4,23:2
Cooke, William H, 1944, Je 7,19:2
Cooke Adams, George Mrs, 1960, Mr 29,38:1
Cooke-Collis, James, 1941, Ap 15,23:5
Cooker, J G, 1903, Ja 22,9:5
Cookingham, Frederick H, 1942, Mr 14,15:2
Cookingham, Henry J Jr, 1940, My 23,23:4
Cookingham, Mary L Mrs, 1940, Je 14,21:1
Cookinham, Richard S, 1947, Ja 25,17:2
Cooklyn, Barnett, 1943, D 17,27:2
Cookman, Alfred Rev, 1871, N 15,1:6
Cookman, Anthony V (trb, Je 10,II,3:5), 1962, Ap 30,27:1
Cookman, Arthur S, 1953, Ja 30,21:4
Cookman, Arthur S Mrs, 1966, My 12,45:3
Cookman, Charles Howland Rev, 1921, D 6,19:5
Cookman, Earl C, 1952, Ag 6,21:2
Cookman, Joseph, 1944, Ag 13,36:2
Cookman, Robert R Mrs, 1951, F 4,76:5
Cooks, Carlos A, 1966, My 7,31:4
Cooksey, Paul, 1940, My 24,19:5
Cooksey, Paul Mrs, 1940, My 24,19:5
Cookson, Henry, 1937, Mr 31,24:3
Cookson, Henry A, 1949, My 25,29:4
Cookson, Thomas K, 1962, S 24,29:2
Cool, Byron E, 1943, D 16,28:3
Cool, Ernest W, 1940, D 8,71:3
Cool, Gerard H, 1949, O 1,13:3
Coolahan, James A Mrs, 1957, My 6,29:1
Coolbrith, I, 1928, Mr 1,25:5
Coolbroth, Harriet N, 1953, S 2,25:2
Cooledge, F S, 1906, Je 9,9:4
Coolen, Charles E, 1953, Ap 3,23:4
Cooley, Alford W Justice, 1913, Jl 21,7:6
Cooley, Anna M, 1955, My 8,89:1
Cooley, Arthur N, 1924, Ag 7,15:5
Cooley, Arthur W, 1953, O 16,27:1
Cooley, Austin C, 1952, Ag 28,23:3
Cooley, Benjamin P, 1941, Ja 25,15:5
Cooley, Charles, 1960, N 16,41:3
Cooley, Charles P Sr, 1954, Ja 20,27:2
Cooley, Charles S, 1950, F 1,29:1
Cooley, Charles S Mrs, 1953, Ja 19,23:1
Cooley, Chauncey H, 1949, O 25,27:1
Cooley, D C, 1937, Ag 10,19:3
Cooley, Earl, 1940, My 7,25:4
Cooley, Emma B Mrs, 1942, F 26,19:6
Cooley, Fannie T Mrs, 1952, My 9,23:4
Cooley, Frank D, 1948, O 19,27:2
Cooley, Frank E, 1945, O 16,23:3
Cooley, Frank Gideon, 1953, F 18,31:2
Cooley, Frederic C Mrs, 1954, Ja 18,23:4
Cooley, George H, 1946, N 1,23:4
Cooley, Halsey E, 1951, N 28,31:5
Cooley, Herbert D, 1939, N 2,23:6
Cooley, Hollis E, 1918, Ag 3,9:5
Cooley, I E, 1944, Jl 14,13:3
Cooley, J C, 1903, Ag 17,7:5
Cooley, Jacob H, 1937, My 11,25:4; 1942, Jl 20,13:
Cooley, Jacob J, 1963, Je 24,27:2

Cooley, James C, 1948, N 23,29:6
Cooley, James Colvin, 1903, Ag 16,7:6
Cooley, James R, 1948, N 7,88:5
Cooley, James S Dr, 1923, O 21,23:2
Cooley, Johanna, 1963, Ag 1,27:4
Cooley, John, 1874, Ag 6,4:6
Cooley, John Clark, 1903, S 6,7:6
Cooley, John J, 1951, Ja 10,27:3
Cooley, John W, 1950, My 23,29:1
Cooley, Justus H, 1944, Ja 1,13:1
Cooley, Justus Mrs, 1954, N 12,21:1
Cooley, Kenneth E Mrs, 1944, Jl 9,35:3
Cooley, Le Roy, 1948, My 14,23:4
Cooley, Leroy C Jr, 1949, My 27,21:2
Cooley, Maxwell S, 1949, N 12,15:1
Cooley, Mortimer E, 1944, Ag 26,11:3
Cooley, Robert Allen Dr, 1968, N 20,57:8
Cooley, Robert L, 1944, My 20,15:4
Cooley, Rossa B, 1949, S 26,25:3
Cooley, Roy O, 1945, O 5,23:4
Cooley, S Morton, 1943, S 19,48:3
Cooley, Stephen P, 1958, S 21,86:8
Cooley, Stuart W Sr, 1959, S 10,35:3
Cooley, Sylvester M, 1940, S 18,23:3
Cooley, T M, 1898, S 13,7:5
Cooley, Thomas, 1943, F 25,21:3
Cooley, Thomas B, 1945, O 15,17:4
Cooley, Thomas R (funl plans, N 30,31:2), 1959, N 29,86:2
Cooley, Thomas R Mrs, 1958, N 24,29:5
Cooley, Walter K, 1956, Je 29,21:6
Cooley, Walter K Mrs, 1953, Ja 30,21:2
Cooley, William T, 1948, Je 6,72:3
Coolican, Louisa (Sister M Hubertine), 1959, O 13, 39:4
Coolidge, A C, 1928, Ja 15,II,7:1
Coolidge, Algernon Jr Dr, 1912, Ja 5,13:4
Coolidge, Alison R, 1952, F 23,26:6
Coolidge, Almon W, 1925, N 4,23:4
Coolidge, Amory, 1952, Ap 3,35:2
Coolidge, Arthur W, 1952, Ja 23,27:5
Coolidge, C, 1933, Ja 6,1:8
Coolidge, C A, 1936, Ap 2,25:1
Coolidge, C A Brig Gen, 1926, Je 3,25:3
Coolidge, Calvin Jr, 1924, Jl 9,19:4
Coolidge, Calvin Mrs (funl, Jl 11,25:2; burial, Jl 13,17:6), 1957, Jl 9,1:4
Coolidge, Cole, 1953, Jl 12,65:1
Coolidge, Dane, 1940, Ag 9,15:4
Coolidge, David H, 1938, My 4,23:4
Coolidge, Elizabeth E Mrs, 1938, Je 22,23:5
Coolidge, Elizabeth S Mrs, 1953, N 5,31:1
Coolidge, Ellen W, 1954, My 1,15:6
Coolidge, Emelyn L, 1949, Ap 16,15:2
Coolidge, Ernest H, 1946, Mr 12,25:5
Coolidge, Francis L, 1942, S 3,19:4
Coolidge, Frank E, 1943, Je 26,13:3
Coolidge, Frederick S Dr, 1915, My 16,16:5
Coolidge, G Greer, 1954, N 3,29:2
Coolidge, H King, 1953, O 24,15:4
Coolidge, H Mountford, 1954, Ag 28,15:3
Coolidge, Henry, 1915, My 13,15:5
Coolidge, J G, 1936, F 29,15:4
Coolidge, J I T Rev, 1913, Je 19,11:5
Coolidge, J Randolph, 1925, N 11,23:4
Coolidge, John E, 1954, D 23,19:4
Coolidge, John S, 1957, O 6,84:7
Coolidge, John T, 1945, N 18,44:1
Coolidge, Julian L, 1954, Mr 6,15:4
oolidge, Lawrence, 1950, Ja 4,35:1
oolidge, Louis A, 1925, Je 1,15:3; 1925, Je 6,15:4
oolidge, Marcus (por), 1947, Ja 24,21:3
oolidge, Marcus A Mrs, 1955, Ag 1,19:5
oolidge, Maria B, 1952, D 29,19:2
oolidge, Marshall H, 1925, My 12,23:5
oolidge, Mary L, 1958, O 10,32:1
oolidge, Philip, 1967, My 25,47:3
oolidge, Richard H Mrs, 1912, N 12,13:6
oolidge, Robert T, 1955, S 26,23:5
olidge, Russell, 1951, F 27,27:3
olidge, Sumner A, 1945, Mr 12,19:5
olidge, Sumner Mrs, 1940, Ap 2,26:2
olidge, Thomas J, 1920, N 18,15:4
olidge, Thomas Jefferson, 1912, Ap 16,13:5
oligan, Peter T, 1952, S 30,31:3
oling, H Lowery, 1949, Ag 11,24:3
oling, R Boyd, 1947, Je 28,13:4
oling, Willis, 1945, Ja 16,19:2
olman, De Witt C, 1915, My 21,13:4
ols, G Victor, 1952, S 13,17:4
ols, Mildred D Mrs, 1958, O 31,29:3
omans, Diana, 1952, Je 19,27:5
omaraswamy, Ananda K, 1947, S 10,27:1
ombe, Andrew P, 1944, Ap 28,19:4
ombe, Charles Palmer Knight Rev, 1908, Mr 29,9:6
mbe, Harry H, 1948, Jl 10,15:2
mbe, Henry B, 1948, Mr 31,26:2
mbe, Thomas Mrs, 1952, S 14,86:1
ombs, Charles W, 1940, Ja 25,21:2
mbs, Christopher F, 1937, O 20,23:4
mbs, Clarence B, 1944, F 27,38:1
mbs, Edward F, 1961, Jl 24,23:2
mbs, Frederick, 1874, Ap 11,12:3

Coombs, Frederick J, 1956, N 20,37:5
Coombs, George H, 1948, N 22,21:2
Coombs, George W, 1945, N 18,43:1
Coombs, Harold E, 1959, Mr 16,31:5
Coombs, Harry E, 1958, Mr 15,17:5
Coombs, Helen C, 1944, Mr 5,36:1
Coombs, Jack (Colby Jack), 1957, Ap 16,33:1
Coombs, Jerome W, 1917, S 15,11:4
Coombs, Jerome W Mrs, 1949, N 30,27:3
Coombs, John H, 1947, Ag 2,13:6
Coombs, Leslie Gen, 1881, Ag 23,2:1
Coombs, Mary A Mrs, 1964, Ap 18,29:4
Coombs, Melville M, 1956, S 1,15:4
Coombs, Richard H, 1960, Ap 20,14:4
Coombs, Robert D Mrs, 1963, Ag 5,29:4
Coombs, S E, 1936, My 23,15:5
Coombs, Sylvan, 1943, Ap 11,48:2
Coombs, William J, 1922, Ja 13,15:3
Coombs, Zelotes W, 1946, Ap 25,21:4
Coon, Abraham J, 1939, Ag 2,19:2
Coon, Anna M Mrs, 1951, N 21,25:2
Coon, Charles Hamilton Rev, 1909, Ja 29,9:6
Coon, Daniel W, 1937, Je 10,23:1
Coon, Edith M, 1939, Je 6,23:4
Coon, Edwin L, 1940, Jl 16,17:3
Coon, Elmer, 1949, Ag 2,19:4
Coon, G Edward, 1941, Ja 20,12:1
Coon, George B, 1941, Ja 20,17:1
Coon, George H, 1965, Mr 23,39:2
Coon, Harold J Mrs, 1952, My 28,29:1
Coon, Harry W, 1951, Jl 23,17:7
Coon, Hesse D, 1954, O 1,23:4
Coon, Homer A, 1945, Ap 9,19:5
Coon, Horace C, 1961, D 12,43:1
Coon, James R, 1961, N 7,33:4
Coon, John H, 1941, S 16,23:5
Coon, John Henry, 1916, Ja 18,11:5
Coon, John L, 1941, O 5,49:2
Coon, Levi, 1949, Ap 27,27:1
Coon, Owen L, 1948, Ag 4,22:2
Coon, Raymond A, 1954, S 13,23:4
Coon, Richard E Jr, 1946, D 7,21:3
Coon, Robert, 1940, My 24,19:2
Coon, Robert W Mrs, 1946, F 15,25:2
Coon, Silas D, 1950, Mr 29,29:1
Coon, W W, 1943, Je 15,21:6
Coon, William H, 1968, Ag 4,69:1
Coon, William H Mrs, 1942, O 18,55:3
Coon, William T, 1952, F 17,85:1
Coonahan, Daniel S, 1957, My 27,31:5
Coonan, John A, 1939, F 14,20:1
Coonan, Julia T, 1938, O 25,23:4
Coonan, William Rev, 1915, N 8,13:5
Cooney, Benjamin J, 1963, D 18,41:2
Cooney, Bruce B, 1945, O 28,43:1
Cooney, Carroll T, 1947, Ag 16,13:6
Cooney, Daniel J, 1965, O 26,45:1
Cooney, Edward, 1947, Ap 2,27:5
Cooney, Edward E, 1953, Ja 2,15:3
Cooney, Edward J, 1967, Ja 22,76:6
Cooney, Edward J Sr, 1952, N 6,29:2
Cooney, Edwin W, 1957, Jl 18,25:2
Cooney, F H, 1935, D 16,27:1
Cooney, Frank D, 1964, Mr 4,37:1
Cooney, Frank D Mrs, 1954, Mr 13,15:3
Cooney, Frank H, 1925, D 27,7:2
Cooney, Frank H Mrs, 1953, Mr 12,25:1
Cooney, James, 1903, Je 12,9:6
Cooney, John, 1945, S 12,25:4
Cooney, John A, 1958, O 13,29:5
Cooney, John D, 1963, Je 26,39:5
Cooney, John M, 1945, O 16,23:4
Cooney, John Mrs, 1944, F 8,15:5
Cooney, John R, 1947, Ja 16,25:3; 1958, F 16,85:1
Cooney, John R Mrs, 1953, Ja 12,27:1
Cooney, Joseph F, 1938, S 23,27:4
Cooney, Joseph H, 1952, S 3,30:4
Cooney, Joseph V Mrs, 1953, Mr 17,35:6
Cooney, Leroy J, 1966, Je 6,41:1
Cooney, Margaret M, 1966, O 11,47:1
Cooney, Marion J, 1955, Ag 14,81:3
Cooney, Philip H, 1967, Jl 25,32:4
Cooney, Ralph B, 1956, F 23,27:4
Cooney, Russell C, 1965, Ja 17,88:7
Cooney, Russell S, 1945, F 18,34:2
Cooney, Thomas F, 1940, Ja 1,23:4; 1949, O 20,29:4
Cooney, Thomas J, 1957, D 15,86:3
Cooney, Vincent T, 1968, Ag 6,37:3
Coonley, Avery Mrs, 1958, Jl 11,23:2
Coonley, Edgar D Dr, 1916, F 10,11:4
Coonley, Frederick, 1955, D 5,31:1
Coonley, Henry E, 1942, Ag 17,15:5
Coonley, Howard, 1966, F 26,25:1
Coonley, Prentiss L Mrs, 1944, Jl 5,17:6; 1961, N 21, 39:4
Coonrad, Lester G, 1945, Ap 10,19:5
Coonrad, Ralph E, 1958, Ja 29,27:3
Coonradt, Arthur C, 1949, Ag 10,22:6
Coonradt, Frank A, 1943, Ap 7,26:2
Coonradt, Leon H Mrs, 1949, S 8,29:5
Coonrod, Charles H, 1948, Ap 27,25:2
Coons, Ada Marr, 1914, Je 20,9:5
Coons, Albert, 1959, Ag 26,29:3

Coons, Arthur G Dr, 1968, Jl 28,65:1
Coons, Bernard (Barney), 1960, Ja 28,22:7
Coons, Clifford J, 1964, F 29,21:6
Coons, David J, 1953, Je 22,21:1
Coons, Edward T, 1943, O 7,23:1
Coons, Edward T Mrs, 1941, N 6,23:5
Coons, Emmett, 1949, F 18,23:1
Coons, Frederick, 1947, D 10,31:4
Coons, Gustav C, 1949, Ap 23,13:5
Coons, Gustav Mrs, 1947, Ag 17,54:5
Coons, Henry R, 1952, My 21,27:2
Coons, Heth G, 1943, Ja 26,19:3
Coons, Horace W, 1957, O 3,29:2
Coons, Merrick E, 1947, Je 21,17:5
Coons, Mervin Mrs, 1951, Jl 12,25:5
Coons, Perry T, 1959, O 19,29:3
Coons, Robbin, 1949, S 21,31:3
Coons, Theresa E C Mrs, 1951, D 24,13:3
Coons, Waldo M Mrs, 1942, Je 13,15:6
Coontz, R E, 1935, Ja 27,26:1
Coop, Squire, 1945, S 11,23:2
Coope, John, 1961, Ja 11,47:3
Cooper, A W, 1950, Jl 24,17:4
Cooper, Ada W Mrs, 1941, S 2,17:3
Cooper, Adista T Mrs, 1941, Mr 3,17:7
Cooper, Alan N, 1960, Ja 17,86:3
Cooper, Alfred, 1952, Je 15,84:2
Cooper, Alfred D (Lord Norwich),(funl, Ja 7,31:1), 1954, Ja 2,11:1
Cooper, Allen R, 1945, S 8,15:6
Cooper, Alvah, 1945, Ag 22,23:3
Cooper, Anna L Mrs, 1944, N 17,19:1
Cooper, Anna P, 1952, Ag 25,17:4
Cooper, Archibald C, 1946, Ag 28,27:3
Cooper, Arthur B, 1959, D 20,60:7
Cooper, Arthur V, 1959, Ap 2,31:4
Cooper, Asa, 1950, Mr 10,27:1
Cooper, Ashley, 1952, Ja 4,23:3
Cooper, Ashley W Mrs, 1949, Ap 6,29:2
Cooper, Ashton B, 1954, S 16,29:2
Cooper, Avery J, 1944, O 26,23:2
Cooper, Avery J Mrs, 1967, Ap 6,39:3
Cooper, Benjamin, 1943, S 11,13:6
Cooper, Benjamin F, 1956, D 31,13:5
Cooper, Bernard, 1956, Ap 3,35:3
Cooper, Bernetta M, 1943, D 8,23:4
Cooper, Bert, 1945, D 7,21:5
Cooper, Bertha Mrs, 1961, Ap 18,37:4
Cooper, Bessie C, 1948, Jl 17,15:2
Cooper, Blucher H Jr, 1947, Ja 9,24:2
Cooper, Brainerd, 1967, F 18,29:3
Cooper, Carl G, 1961, My 30,17:2
Cooper, Carson, 1955, Ap 8,21:3
Cooper, Charles, 1956, S 29,19:3
Cooper, Charles Alfred, 1916, Ap 16,21:4
Cooper, Charles F, 1939, Mr 25,15:5
Cooper, Charles H, 1946, S 18,31:5
Cooper, Charles J, 1910, D 10,11:3
Cooper, Charles K, 1957, Jl 9,29:3
Cooper, Charles Lawrence Gen, 1919, O 2,17:6
Cooper, Charles M, 1951, Jl 10,27:2
Cooper, Charles P, 1950, N 10,27:3; 1959, Mr 15,88:1; 1966, F 6,93:1
Cooper, Charles P Mrs, 1944, S 9,15:4
Cooper, Charles S, 1949, Ag 8,15:5
Cooper, Charles W, 1903, My 27,2:6; 1960, Ag 10,31:2
Cooper, Clarence, 1939, S 7,25:5
Cooper, Clarence E, 1953, O 27,27:2
Cooper, Claude K, 1947, F 6,23:3
Cooper, Colin C, 1937, N 7,II,9:1
Cooper, Colin Campbell, 1920, Ag 21,7:6
Cooper, Crawford J, 1945, N 3,15:2
Cooper, Curtis C, 1948, Ja 2,23:2
Cooper, Dan, 1965, Mr 11,33:1
Cooper, Daniel, 1940, Je 19,23:2
Cooper, Daniel C, 1952, Ag 14,23:4
Cooper, Daniel Mrs, 1946, Jl 27,17:4
Cooper, David, 1945, Mr 20,19:3
Cooper, David B, 1952, D 8,41:1
Cooper, David S, 1967, Ja 4,43:2
Cooper, David Y, 1953, My 15,23:4
Cooper, Dennis A, 1948, My 11,26:3
Cooper, Dexter P (por),(cor, F 4,21:1), 1938, F 3,23:1
Cooper, Drury W, 1957, S 11,33:3
Cooper, Drury W Mrs, 1947, S 16,24:3
Cooper, E James, 1964, Ap 7,35:3
Cooper, Earl J, 1945, Ap 26,23:1
Cooper, Earl P, 1965, O 24,86:4
Cooper, Edward, 1905, F 26,1:1; 1939, Ap 28,25:4; 1951, Je 11,25:3
Cooper, Edward C, 1941, N 15,17:2
Cooper, Edward E, 1942, O 11,56:6
Cooper, Edward W, 1922, Ag 17,13:4; 1948, Ja 14, 26:3; 1956, My 16,35:5
Cooper, Edwin, 1942, Je 25,23:6
Cooper, Edwin N, 1957, Ag 5,21:6
Cooper, Eleanor E, 1943, O 16,13:1
Cooper, Elisha H, 1947, Ja 6,23:2
Cooper, Elisha H Mrs, 1965, My 19,47:3
Cooper, Eliza, 1877, D 31,8:3
Cooper, Eliza Mrs, 1919, My 28,15:3
Cooper, Elizabeth M, 1967, My 20,35:5
Cooper, Emil, 1960, N 17,37:1

Cooper, Emil Mrs, 1952, S 4,27:6
Cooper, Emily B Mrs, 1947, N 24,23:2
Cooper, Emily H Mrs, 1937, Ap 8,23:4
Cooper, Ernest, 1962, S 8,19:6
Cooper, Eugene J, 1940, Ag 10,13:5; 1951, Ja 6,15:3
Cooper, F Warren, 1958, Ag 18,19:4
Cooper, Fletcher E, 1955, F 21,21:5
Cooper, Fletcher E Mrs, 1949, Je 13,19:5
Cooper, Floyd F Mrs, 1952, Je 20,23:5
Cooper, Frances T, 1945, F 23,17:4
Cooper, Francis D, 1941, D 19,25:3
Cooper, Frank, 1946, Jl 17,23:5; 1958, Mr 22,17:1
Cooper, Frank A, 1944, Je 25,30:2; 1949, Je 5,92:7
Cooper, Frank C, 1937, My 17,19:4
Cooper, Frank G, 1952, Mr 6,31:2
Cooper, Frank H Mrs, 1907, Ja 18,7:6
Cooper, Frank Kemble, 1918, D 31,11:4
Cooper, Frank L, 1944, F 26,13:1
Cooper, Frank W, 1963, Ap 27,25:3
Cooper, Fred, 1955, Ja 8,13:6
Cooper, Fred G, 1961, N 16,39:3
Cooper, Fred G Mrs, 1951, O 4,33:4
Cooper, Fred J, 1941, O 22,23:2
Cooper, Fred N, 1947, Je 10,27:5
Cooper, Fred R, 1954, Ja 3,89:3
Cooper, Frederic T Dr, 1937, My 21,21:4
Cooper, Frederick, 1951, O 27,19:6
Cooper, Frederick M, 1946, Ag 13,27:6
Cooper, Frederick T, 1953, My 20,29:2
Cooper, Frederick W, 1944, F 5,15:4
Cooper, Gary (funl plans; trb, My 15,31:4; funl, My 17,37:3), 1961, My 14,1:4
Cooper, George, 1943, D 12,68:4; 1948, D 21,31:2; 1958, O 25,21:5; 1959, Jl 29,29:4; 1960, My 22,87:1
Cooper, George H, 1944, Ag 18,13:1; 1955, My 1,88:5
Cooper, George L, 1937, Ag 11,24:3; 1952, Ap 3,35:2
Cooper, George S, 1940, F 28,21:5; 1946, Ja 28,19:1
Cooper, George T, 1942, Ja 4,48:2
Cooper, George W, 1922, Jl 24,15:4; 1953, Ja 5,21:4
Cooper, Gordon D, 1949, Je 15,29:4
Cooper, Grant, 1918, D 9,13:3
Cooper, Griffith M Mrs, 1940, S 27,23:3
Cooper, Guy D, 1961, O 13,35:2
Cooper, Guy E, 1951, Ag 5,73:1
Cooper, H A, 1931, Mr 2,4:2
Cooper, H W Denness, 1949, N 6,92:1
Cooper, Harry, 1937, O 23,17:2; 1939, My 19,21:6; 1951, F 17,15:2
Cooper, Harry (details, My 30,17:3), 1964, My 28, 37:4
Cooper, Harry H, 1919, My 12,13:4
Cooper, Harvey R, 1943, My 23,43:2
Cooper, Henry C, 1944, Ap 15,11:5
Cooper, Henry D, 1938, Ag 31,15:6
Cooper, Henry E, 1958, Jl 4,19:6
Cooper, Henry E (est tax appr), 1961, Mr 28,22:2
Cooper, Henry H, 1939, Ag 13,29:3
Cooper, Henry J Col, 1925, O 19,21:3
Cooper, Henry R Mrs, 1949, O 8,13:2
Cooper, Henry W, 1948, N 30,27:1
Cooper, Herbert E, 1956, O 2,35:4
Cooper, Herbert F, 1948, My 24,19:2
Cooper, Homer H, 1939, Ja 29,32:8
Cooper, Howard, 1952, Je 28,20:8
Cooper, Howard J Sr, 1953, Je 29,21:3
Cooper, Howard N, 1953, Jl 23,23:1
Cooper, Hugh E, 1945, Ap 24,19:4
Cooper, Hugh E Sr Mrs, 1949, Ag 30,27:1
Cooper, Hugh L Col, 1937, Je 25,21:1
Cooper, Hyman, 1962, Ag 20,23:3
Cooper, Irving, 1952, D 26,15:5
Cooper, Irving B, 1954, Mr 23,27:4
Cooper, J Craig, 1955, Ag 30,15:7
Cooper, J Crossan, 1938, Jl 2,13:6
Cooper, J D Mrs, 1938, Ja 19,23:4
Cooper, J Frank, 1943, O 5,25:3
Cooper, J Nelson, 1959, F 10,33:3
Cooper, J Van Cleft, 1961, My 28,64:4
Cooper, Jack (Red), 1953, S 24,33:2
Cooper, Jacob H (corr, Mr 21,29:8), 1946, Mr 20,25:6
Cooper, Jacob Mrs, 1910, Je 26,II,9:4
Cooper, Jacob Rev Dr, 1904, F 1,7:3
Cooper, James A, 1945, D 25,23:1; 1951, Je 14,27:5
Cooper, James B, 1907, F 26,11:6; 1940, My 31,19:5
Cooper, James E, 1923, Ja 30,17:4; 1943, Ap 8,23:2
Cooper, James F (will, My 7,2:8), 1938, My 4,23:2
Cooper, James F, 1945, Ap 10,19:1
Cooper, James G Jr Mrs, 1945, S 19,25:3
Cooper, James L, 1956, Ja 2,8:8
Cooper, James O Mrs, 1949, N 8,31:5
Cooper, Jay T Mrs, 1954, Ag 30,17:3
Cooper, Jean L Mrs, 1940, Ap 2,25:1
Cooper, Jehu P, 1968, Ja 16,39:2
Cooper, Jere (funl plans, D 20,27:2), 1957, D 19,31:1
Cooper, John A, 1956, Ja 20,23:2
Cooper, John C, 1967, Jl 24,27:1
Cooper, John C Mrs, 1962, F 12,23:1
Cooper, John G, 1956, N 20,37:4
Cooper, John H Mrs, 1952, D 28,49:1
Cooper, John M, 1950, My 29,17:5
Cooper, John S, 1948, Ap 12,21:5
Cooper, John V, 1955, My 4,29:3
Cooper, John W, 1938, Jl 7,19:2
Cooper, Joseph D, 1949, Ja 8,15:5
Cooper, Joseph H Dr, 1968, My 24,47:1
Cooper, Joseph R W, 1923, Ag 2,15:6
Cooper, Joseph T, 1958, Jl 13,68:8
Cooper, Joseph V, 1950, S 24,104:5
Cooper, Katherine Fenimore, 1925, Je 5,17:5
Cooper, Kenneth, 1960, F 24,37:3
Cooper, Kenneth F, 1954, My 25,21:7
Cooper, Kent (funl plans, F 1,23:2; funl, F 4,31:3), 1965, Ja 31,1:6
Cooper, Lane, 1959, N 29,86:6
Cooper, Laura H, 1913, F 22,11:6
Cooper, Leo J Mrs, 1960, N 24,29:5
Cooper, Leon, 1962, Ja 15,27:3
Cooper, Leroy G, 1960, Mr 31,33:1
Cooper, Lew, 1955, My 4,29:5
Cooper, Linn F, 1959, N 15,86:3
Cooper, Llewellyn Capt, 1878, N 12,5:2
Cooper, Lloyd N, 1952, F 16,13:1
Cooper, Louis, 1958, O 24,33:3
Cooper, Louis Dr, 1968, Ag 28,47:2
Cooper, Madison, 1946, Jl 9,22:2; 1956, S 29,19:6
Cooper, Margaret W Mrs, 1950, Mr 21,32:3
Cooper, Marie F Mrs, 1938, F 5,15:5
Cooper, Martin, 1946, My 23,21:5
Cooper, Mary, 1911, Je 28,11:5; 1964, Je 17,43:3
Cooper, Mary H Mrs, 1908, My 16,7:6
Cooper, Mathlena A, 1946, Je 30,38:3
Cooper, Max E, 1960, Je 21,21:2
Cooper, Melville Mrs (E Sutherland), 1960, Mr 1, 33:5
Cooper, Melvin A, 1947, S 19,23:2
Cooper, Michael S, 1947, Ja 1,34:3
Cooper, Morris B, 1954, O 9,17:6
Cooper, Morris Jr, 1943, Je 19,13:2
Cooper, Morris Mrs, 1964, O 14,45:3
Cooper, Morton (funl, N 21,29:4), 1958, N 18,37:1
Cooper, Myers Y, 1958, D 7,88:3
Cooper, Nicholas, 1909, Mr 24,9:3
Cooper, Norma C, 1952, My 28,29:2
Cooper, Oscar F, 1948, O 18,23:3
Cooper, Oscar H, 1945, D 19,25:4
Cooper, Osceola, 1877, Ag 3,8:4
Cooper, Oswald B, 1940, D 18,25:4
Cooper, Otto, 1958, F 13,29:2
Cooper, Page, 1958, Ja 6,39:3
Cooper, Patrick A, 1961, Mr 23,33:2
Cooper, Paul H, 1941, Jl 13,29:1
Cooper, Perrine J, 1944, Ja 18,19:1
Cooper, Peter, 1883, Ap 5,1:7
Cooper, Peter D Mrs, 1953, N 3,31:4
Cooper, Philip Henry Adm, 1912, D 31,7:4
Cooper, Ralph E, 1957, N 10,86:5
Cooper, Ralph S, 1941, Jl 14,13:2
Cooper, Richard, 1925, Ap 24,19:5
Cooper, Richard Jr, 1953, F 4,27:3
Cooper, Richard Powell Sir, 1913, Jl 31,7:6
Cooper, Robert A, 1953, Ag 8,11:2
Cooper, Robert E, 1946, S 22,62:8
Cooper, Robert J, 1939, Ag 18,19:3; 1961, F 8,28:1
Cooper, Robert L, 1966, Ap 2,29:5
Cooper, Robert P, 1951, Ap 30,8:6
Cooper, Roswell D, 1954, N 24,23:5
Cooper, Roy C, 1954, My 12,31:4
Cooper, Rudolf, 1968, D 8,86:6
Cooper, S Ira, 1952, Jl 9,27:5
Cooper, Sam Bronson, 1918, Ag 22,11:3
Cooper, Sam Hawes Mrs, 1904, Ja 2,9:4
Cooper, Samuel, 1908, Ap 24,9:4; 1963, O 10,41:4
Cooper, Samuel E, 1957, Ja 20,92:6
Cooper, Samuel S Mrs, 1958, Je 10,33:3
Cooper, Samuel W, 1939, Ja 14,17:6
Cooper, Simon W, 1943, N 22,19:5
Cooper, Sophie Mrs, 1942, S 29,24:2
Cooper, T E St Paul, 1949, Jl 19,30:3
Cooper, T Frederick, 1954, N 26,29:2
Cooper, T S, 1902, F 8,9:5
Cooper, Tex Mrs (Lady Dolly), 1953, S 9,29:3
Cooper, Theodore, 1919, Ag 25,11:5
Cooper, Theodore Polhemus, 1919, Jl 30,9:3
Cooper, Thomas J, 1949, O 11,31:1
Cooper, Thomas M, 1950, My 24,29:3
Cooper, Thomas M Lord, 1955, Jl 16,15:4
Cooper, Thomas P, 1958, F 20,25:6
Cooper, Thomas S, 1903, My 1,9:5
Cooper, Thurston G, 1956, Je 1,23:4
Cooper, Valentine J, 1940, Ag 11,31:2
Cooper, Viola I, 1951, Mr 23,21:5
Cooper, Violet K (Mrs W Ferris), 1961, Ag 19,17:6
Cooper, Walter B, 1961, My 13,19:6
Cooper, Walter E Mrs, 1965, My 12,47:4
Cooper, Walter I, 1948, D 11,15:4
Cooper, Walter S, 1960, Je 22,35:2
Cooper, Washington Lafeyette, 1911, Mr 11,13:5
Cooper, William, 1880, F 4,3:3; 1949, Ap 5,29:3
Cooper, William F, 1952, N 30,89:1
Cooper, William F Judge, 1909, My 8,7:4
Cooper, William G Mrs, 1960, F 8,29:3
Cooper, William H, 1938, N 18,21:1; 1955, F 3,23:5
Cooper, William M, 1959, F 18,33:2
Cooper, Wyllis, 1955, Je 23,29:1
Cooper-Ellis, Katharine M (K Murdoch), 1962, Jl 4, 21:3
Cooperman, Bernard, 1961, Mr 4,23:3
Cooperman, Herman G (cor, My 26,29:4), 1958, My 25,86:3
Cooperman, Morris B, 1948, Je 27,52:5
Cooperman, Nathan, 1958, Jl 6,56:8
Coopersmith, Asriel, 1943, Ag 2,15:2
Coopersmith, William, 1924, N 30,7:2
Cooperstein, Abram, 1948, Ja 27,26:2
Coops, Helen L, 1953, N 16,25:4
Coor, Thomas Mrs, 1962, S 10,29:4
Coords, Jack, 1943, Jl 17,13:4
Coors, D Stanley, 1960, Mr 7,29:1
Coote, Bert, 1938, S 4,16:5
Coote, Henry, 1949, Je 15,29:1
Coote, Patrick, 1938, Je 21,19:2
Coote, Ralph, 1941, Jl 5,11:3
Coote, William, 1942, Jl 9,21:3
Cootes, F Graham, 1960, D 1,35:1
Coots, J Kenneth, 1953, F 28,17:3
Coots, James Mrs (E Preston), 1960, Ag 20,19:3
Coover, John E, 1938, F 20,II,9:1
Coover, Oscar, 1950, My 4,27:5
Copans, David, 1964, My 13,47:3
Copcutt, Vincent W, 1950, Ja 25,27:2
Cope, Anthony, 1966, My 14,15:5
Cope, Arthur C, 1966, Je 6,41:2
Cope, Arthur S, 1940, Jl 6,15:6
Cope, Elmer F, 1965, My 26,47:3
Cope, Francis Jr Mrs, 1947, Jl 24,21:6
Cope, Harvey D, 1949, Ja 9,72:1
Cope, Herman, 1945, Ag 31,17:2
Cope, John W, 1924, S 27,16:4
Cope, Lord, 1946, Jl 16,24:2
Cope, Louis, 1953, D 14,31:2
Cope, Mary Mrs, 1903, Ap 25,9:5
Cope, Millard, 1964, Ja 5,93:1
Cope, Otis M, 1950, Ja 29,69:1
Cope, Otis M Mrs, 1950, Mr 9,29:2
Cope, Porter F, 1950, D 21,29:2
Cope, Porter F Mrs, 1954, Ja 20,27:4
Cope, Thomas A Jr, 1959, O 31,23:5
Cope, Walter Mrs, 1952, N 16,87:2
Cope, William E Jr, 1968, Ja 24,42:3
Copeau, Jacques (por), 1949, O 22,17:1
Copelan, Sheila, 1966, Ap 20,47:1
Copelan, William Mrs, 1949, Ag 3,23:2
Copeland, Adolph, 1939, Mr 15,23:3
Copeland, Adolph Mrs, 1938, Je 12,39:3
Copeland, Al Mrs, 1943, Ag 9,13:6
Copeland, Benjamin, 1940, D 2,23:2
Copeland, Bruce, 1951, D 28,27:7
Copeland, Charles, 1944, F 4,15:3
Copeland, Charles D, 1937, O 28,23:3
Copeland, Charles E, 1947, Jl 4,13:6
Copeland, Charles Mrs, 1951, Mr 25,72:3
Copeland, Charles T, 1952, Jl 25,18:3
Copeland, Clarence S, 1948, Jl 10,15:3
Copeland, Clem A, 1944, Ag 21,15:5
Copeland, David, 1949, My 13,23:3
Copeland, Edward, 1951, Ja 4,29:3
Copeland, Edward L, 1939, Ap 21,23:2
Copeland, Francis T (cor, N 19,23:4), 1954, N 1 33:1
Copeland, Frederic L, 1955, Ja 10,23:3
Copeland, George, 1953, N 5,31:3
Copeland, Gertrude G, 1949, My 15,90:5
Copeland, Guild, 1964, F 24,25:1
Copeland, Guild Mrs (Stutterin' Sam), 1963, Ap 39:2
Copeland, Harold Mrs, 1958, Ja 18,15:6
Copeland, Harriet R Mrs, 1942, Ap 7,22:4
Copeland, Henry F, 1956, Ja 28,17:3
Copeland, Henry H, 1943, My 14,19:2
Copeland, Howard G, 1951, D 1,13:6
Copeland, Hugh M Mrs, 1944, O 27,23:5
Copeland, Hugh Montgomery, 1922, O 22,30:3
Copeland, Ira, 1941, My 2,21:3
Copeland, Irwin H, 1944, Mr 1,19:1
Copeland, J Frank, 1957, F 20,33:2
Copeland, Lennie P, 1951, Ja 13,15:5
Copeland, Lewis, 1949, N 30,4:2
Copeland, Lillian, 1964, Jl 8,35:1
Copeland, Manton Jr Mrs, 1956, D 30,33:1
Copeland, Mary A, 1952, Ja 5,11:4
Copeland, Morris C Mrs, 1948, N 9,27:2
Copeland, N Newall, 1957, My 24,25:4
Copeland, Oren S, 1958, Ap 12,19:4
Copeland, Pauline Mrs, 1951, N 20,31:1
Copeland, Ralph O, 1958, Je 18,33:5
Copeland, Richard W, 1961, Ap 24,29:4
Copeland, Roscoe P Mrs, 1925, Ag 17,15:5
Copeland, Rosetta A C Mrs, 1940, Ap 21,42:3
Copeland, Royal S Mrs, 1943, D 25,13:6
Copeland, Royal S Sen, 1938, Je 18,1:1
Copeland, Samuel Mrs, 1959, F 12,27:2
Copeland, Stewart Mrs, 1950, Ag 30,32:2
Copeland, Thomas J Mrs, 1938, Ap 22,19:2
Copeland, Walter F, 1951, My 10,31:3
Copeland, Warren E, 1950, F 5,84:4
Copeland, William I, 1942, Mr 15,42:1
Copeland, William J, 1948, Ap 10,13:5
Copeley, Louis H, 1966, Mr 17,43:5
Copello, Enrico Col, 1920, Ap 4,22:3

Copello, Santiago L Cardinal (cor, Fe 11,29:5), 1967, F 10,35:2
Copely, William, 1944, Ja 18,19:5
Copeman, Edward S, 1914, D 22,13:5
Copeman, Lloyd G, 1956, Jl 7,13:5
Copenhaver, Laura Mrs, 1940, D 19,25:1
Copestake, Harry S, 1943, S 8,23:2
Copete Avendano, Hernan, 1954, Ja 23,13:2
Copinger, May I, 1941, Je 29,32:8
Copiola, Aristide, 1949, F 15,23:1
Copithorn, Francis S Mrs, 1954, Ag 5,23:4
Copithorn, Frank H, 1954, My 19,31:3
Copland, Al, 1940, Je 30,32:8
Copland, George R, 1941, Ap 25,19:3
Copland, Milton Mrs, 1949, Ag 14,69:2
Copland, Ralph, 1952, Mr 25,15:4
Copley, Charles F, 1944, My 31,19:1
Copley, Charles H, 1957, N 23,19:5
Copley, Ira C (will, N 9,33:5), 1947, N 3,23:1
Copley, Ira C Mrs (will, Ag 18,19:6), 1949, Ag 2,19:3
Copley, Richard, 1939, Mr 1,21:1
Copley, S Emily Sister (Shaker), 1911, S 12,11:5
Coplin, W M L, 1928, My 31,23:5
Coplon, Harry G, 1952, N 16,88:7
Coplon, Percy, 1949, N 26,10:1
Coplon, Samuel M, 1949, Mr 30,9:1
Copman, Julius William, 1921, F 12,13:5
Copp, A P, 1949, D 6,31:5
Copp, Alfred F Mrs, 1956, O 4,33:4
Copp, Arthur W, 1917, Je 13,13:4; 1962, O 2,39:2
Copp, Charles W Sr, 1939, F 7,19:2
Copp, George V, 1950, Ap 5,31:1
Copp, Theodore B, 1945, Ja 3,17:4
Copp, Tracy, 1955, Mr 26,15:4
Copp, William, 1950, F 28,29:1
Copp, William M, 1940, Mr 17,49:2
Copp, Zed H, 1952, O 4,17:3
Coppard, Alfred E, 1957, Ja 19,15:3
Coppedge, Robert W, 1948, D 23,20:4
Coppee, Evence Baron, 1925, Je 26,17:5
Coppee, Francois, 1908, My 24,9:4
Coppell, Arthur Mrs, 1960, N 2,39:3
Coppen, Charles B, 1950, N 26,90:4
Copper, Joseph B, 1968, My 24,47:2
Copper, Lee E, 1950, Ag 29,27:2
Copperberg, Julius Mrs, 1908, N 15,9:5
Coppernail, George P Mrs, 1939, Je 6,23:6
Coppers, George H, 1960, D 29,25:1
Coppersmith, Clarence W, 1952, Ja 8,27:1
Copperthwaite, Harrier C Mrs, 1952, D 12,29:5
Copperthwaite, Kenyon, 1949, F 11,23:3
Coppes, Frank, 1939, S 24,43:2
Coppet, Andre de, 1953, Ag 21,17:3
Coppet, Frederick de, 1914, O 19,9:6
Coppi, Fausto, 1960, Ja 5,35:3
Coppicus, Francis C, 1966, Je 9,47:1
Coppin, Leon A, 1950, O 28,17:5
Coppinger, Arthur Philip Capt, 1922, D 15,19:4
Coppinger, Boies P, 1961, Ja 6,27:1
Coppinger, John J, 1957, My 4,21:5
Coppinger, John J Brig-Gen, 1909, N 7,13:5
Coppinger, Joseph F Msgr, 1940, Mr 25,15:2
Coppinger, Joseph L, 1952, My 8,31:5
Coppinger, Mary E, 1952, N 27,31:4
Coppinger, Michael M, 1951, F 23,27:3
Coppinger, Vincent, 1949, Mr 16,27:1
Coppini, Pompeo, 1957, S 28,17:6
Coppins, Charles D, 1945, Ap 19,27:4
Coppins, Matilda Mrs, 1951, D 23,22:7
Copplestone, John R, 1939, Je 11,44:7
Coppo, Ernest, 1949, Ja 5,25:3
Coppock, Grace L, 1921, O 19,19:5
Coppock, Walter J, 1958, D 30,35:4
Coppola, Angelo, 1940, Mr 7,23:5
Coppola, Doris, 1948, My 19,48:2
Coppola, Michael J, 1959, D 12,23:1
Coppola, Nicholas J, 1954, F 6,31:3
Coppolino, Carmela M, 1965, Ag 31,33:6
Coppridge, William M, 1959, Ag 30,82:1
Copps, Joseph C, 1966, My 27,43:1
Coppus, Frans H, 1941, Ap 23,21:6
Copsy, Harmon, 1909, Ag 4,7:6
Copulsky, Louis, 1956, D 16,87:1
Copus, Albert E, 1950, O 10,31:6
Copus, John E Father, 1915, Je 13,15:5
Coputt, F (see also D 6 and 7), 1877, D 11,8:4
Coquelin, Benoit Constant (trb, Ja 30,9:5), 1909, Ja 28,9:1
Coquelin, Jean Mrs, 1909, Ag 28,7:5
Coquillot, Jean, 1949, Ag 31,23:4
Cora Maria, Sister, 1945, F 16,23:2
Corack, Via, 1914, Ap 25,15:5
Coralnink, Berl, 1959, Mr 6,25:5
Coralnik, Abram, 1937, Jl 17,15:1
Coranell, Jean J, 1947, Mr 19,25:5
Corap, Andre-Georges, 1953, Ag 18,23:5
Coray, Elisha A Sr, 1909, S 1,9:7
orbaley, Gordon C, 1964, Ag 29,21:4
orbaley, Kate Mrs, 1938, S 24,17:2
orbalis, James J, 1955, Ap 7,27:6
orbalis, William F, 1938, My 29,II,7:2
orballis, Edward R L, 1967, F 3,31:4
orballis, Helen B Mrs, 1961, Ag 26,17:5

Corbally, Thomas J, 1940, My 9,23:3; 1943, Ja 21,21:2
Corbe, Zenan M Mrs, 1947, F 28,23:3
Corbeau, Emanuel, 1947, O 18,16:2
Corbell, Robert T, 1952, Je 14,15:3
Corbet, Alex, 1948, My 18,23:3
Corbet, Charles A, 1952, Jl 17,23:3
Corbet, John, 1939, Ja 15,39:1
Corbet, John H R, 1940, Ja 9,24:2
Corbet, Nelus M, 1938, F 22,21:4
Corbet, William J, 1942, F 4,19:6
Corbet, William J Sr Mrs, 1950, Ap 20,29:2
Corbett, Austin J, 1946, O 23,27:2
Corbett, Boston, 1872, F 24,1:6
Corbett, Charles Clarence, 1919, F 5,11:1
Corbett, Charles H, 1963, Je 25,33:4
Corbett, Charles H Mrs, 1958, S 25,33:4
Corbett, Charles S, 1942, S 3,19:4
Corbett, Clara Mrs (will), 1944, S 8,20:3
Corbett, David J, 1937, My 13,25:6
Corbett, David W, 1943, S 17,21:2
Corbett, Denis A, 1956, S 8,17:4
Corbett, Dennis, 1948, S 11,16:8
Corbett, E A Rev, 1926, O 16,17:5
Corbett, Edward A, 1964, N 30,33:5
Corbett, Edward L, 1952, Mr 18,27:4
Corbett, Edward M, 1938, F 26,15:4
Corbett, Elizabeth Wiley Dr, 1916, Je 7,13:5
Corbett, Frank, 1949, N 7,27:2
Corbett, Geoffrey L Sir, 1937, N 3,23:2
Corbett, George J, 1951, Ag 1,23:3
Corbett, H W, 1903, Ap 1,9:5
Corbett, Harry, 1907, F 17,9:6
Corbett, Harvey W, 1954, Ap 22,29:1
Corbett, Harvey W Mrs, 1952, Ag 28,23:3
Corbett, Howard N, 1938, Ag 23,17:2
Corbett, Hunter Dr, 1920, Ja 13,13:3
Corbett, J Quincy, 1949, N 30,4:6
Corbett, J Wilson Mrs, 1945, Ag 9,21:3
Corbett, James C, 1939, Jl 21,19:3
Corbett, James H, 1953, Mr 26,31:2
Corbett, James J, 1951, N 26,25:2; 1967, Ja 30,26:3
Corbett, James J Mrs, 1959, S 11,27:1
Corbett, James M, 1949, S 8,29:5
Corbett, Jane M Mrs, 1942, O 7,25:5
Corbett, Jim, 1955, Ap 21,29:5
Corbett, John, 1947, F 22,13:3
Corbett, Joseph F, 1949, F 3,23:2
Corbett, Joseph F Mrs, 1942, Mr 22,48:6
Corbett, Joseph J, 1949, O 9,93:1
Corbett, Lambert S, 1945, F 10,11:3
Corbett, Larry, 1947, F 1,15:5
Corbett, Lawrence A, 1964, Je 22,27:4
Corbett, Leonora (will, N 1,47:1), 1960, Ag 2,29:2
Corbett, Margaret, 1957, My 20,25:3
Corbett, Melvin C, 1966, N 5,31:1
Corbett, Michael Mrs, 1943, N 20,13:6
Corbett, Mitchell, 1956, Mr 1,33:4
Corbett, R A, 1942, Ja 17,17:2
Corbett, Ralph E, 1955, O 25,33:3
Corbett, Robert S, 1952, Ag 16,15:1
Corbett, Samuel J, 1947, D 23,23:2
Corbett, Theodore, 1941, N 26,23:3
Corbett, Thomas J, 1945, O 28,43:1
Corbett, Timothy J, 1952, My 24,19:6
Corbett, Walter E, 1954, N 6,17:5
Corbett, William J (will), 1942, Mr 1,49:3
Corbett, William J, 1942, O 12,17:2
Corbett, William P, 1949, Ag 12,17:4; 1951, Ja 19,25:2
Corbetta, Roger H Mrs, 1955, D 30,19:6
Corbin, A R, 1880, Mr 29,5:4
Corbin, Abel Rathbone Mrs, 1913, Jl 1,9:4
Corbin, Albert F, 1942, D 28,19:4
Corbin, Alfred G, 1945, Ag 25,11:3
Corbin, Alfred O, 1941, Ja 19,40:6
Corbin, Arthur E, 1958, Je 7,19:2
Corbin, Arthur L, 1967, My 10,47:3
Corbin, Austin, 1896, Je 5,1:5; 1938, Ag 8,13:5
Corbin, Charles, 1949, Ag 18,21:1
Corbin, Charles A, 1966, N 14,41:6
Corbin, Charles R, 1950, F 20,25:2
Corbin, Clifford L, 1966, Ja 22,29:3
Corbin, Floyd S (funl, Ja 24,17:4), 1924, Ja 22,17:2
Corbin, Floyd S Mrs, 1937, S 4,15:5
Corbin, Frank A, 1956, S 24,27:4
Corbin, H C Gen, 1903, F 24,9:6
Corbin, Harold E, 1947, Ap 21,21:4
Corbin, Harold Harlow Mrs, 1968, S 12,47:4
Corbin, Harold S, 1947, My 8,25:5
Corbin, Henry C Lt-Gen (funl, S 10,9:6), 1909, S 9,9:3
Corbin, Henry P, 1922, F 21,17:3
Corbin, Horace K, 1960, F 6,19:3
Corbin, Horace K Mrs, 1953, Jl 30,23:4
Corbin, J Benjamin, 1948, N 7,88:4
Corbin, Job Dr, 1915, Je 16,11:5
Corbin, John, 1959, Ag 31,21:1
Corbin, Lena H Mrs, 1941, O 10,23:4
Corbin, Lyman, 1952, Jl 1,23:4
Corbin, Phil Mrs, 1937, F 5,21:1
Corbin, R Beverly Mrs, 1948, Ag 25,25:4
Corbin, Ralph A, 1954, Je 18,23:5
Corbin, Richard B, 1960, O 15,23:6
Corbin, Richard Washington, 1922, F 23,15:5
Corbin, William H, 1912, S 26,11:4; 1945, Ap 16,23:3; 1966, Ag 6,23:2
Corbino, Jon, 1964, Jl 11,25:1
Corbit, Lewis H, 1952, S 30,31:1
Corbit, W F, 1881, My 21,2:6
Corbitt, James J Mrs, 1954, Ap 26,25:5
Corbitt, Kenneth F, 1953, Mr 5,27:1
Corbitt, Samuel J, 1950, Ag 10,25:4
Corbitt, William H Mrs (will), 1959, Mr 21,1:7
Corbley, Thomas P, 1942, D 30,23:2
Corbly, Walter S, 1952, N 26,23:4
Corbman, Joseph, 1955, Je 23,29:4
Corbusier, Harold D, 1950, S 1,21:1
Corby, Arthur E, 1954, F 17,31:3
Corby, Augustus C, 1921, Jl 27,15:7
Corby, Charles T, 1948, Ap 10,13:3
Corby, Henry, 1917, Ap 25,11:7
Corby, Israel Mrs, 1946, D 10,31:1
Corby, James F, 1940, Ja 16,23:3
Corby, John E, 1942, Ap 28,21:1
Corby, Karl W, 1937, F 5,21:5
Corby, Lloyd C, 1961, Ap 21,33:6
Corby, Mary E Mrs, 1941, Ja 5,44:4
Corby, Richard L, 1955, Je 3,23:3
Corby, Robert E, 1960, Jl 22,23:3
Corby, Robert L, 1937, N 1,21:4
Corby, Thomas A, 1961, Mr 25,25:3
Corbyn, Sheridan, 1904, Ja 9,9:2
Corcacas, Manoussos, 1957, F 14,27:5
Corchin, Max, 1949, Ja 4,40:2
Corcoran, A Rev, 1904, Ja 30,9:5
Corcoran, Arthur C, 1965, Jl 7,38:1
Corcoran, Brig Gen, 1863, D 23,6:6
Corcoran, Charles A Mrs, 1963, My 9,37:4
Corcoran, Charles R, 1954, My 27,27:2
Corcoran, Cornelius A, 1953, Je 10,29:1
Corcoran, Daniel Lawrence, 1924, Ja 29,19:3
Corcoran, David, 1938, F 21,19:4; 1967, N 5,86:6
Corcoran, Edward B, 1949, Je 29,27:2
Corcoran, Edward T, 1937, N 26,21:5
Corcoran, Ellen (Mrs S P Hill), 1879, My 17,2:6
Corcoran, Francis V, 1939, Ja 30,13:5
Corcoran, George J, 1947, Mr 5,25:2
Corcoran, Henry J, 1950, Je 22,27:3
Corcoran, Henry W, 1924, Mr 3,17:4
Corcoran, James A, 1949, Ja 11,31:2
Corcoran, James A (Jackpine Jim), 1953, D 13,87:1
Corcoran, James A, 1964, D 29,27:4
Corcoran, James A Jr, 1966, Ja 19,41:3
Corcoran, James A Mrs, 1952, Ap 12,11:4; 1964, My 7,37:2
Corcoran, James J, 1938, S 27,21:3
Corcoran, Jennie E Mrs, 1937, Jl 20,23:2
Corcoran, Jeremiah J Mrs, 1949, Ja 14,23:2
Corcoran, Jimmy, 1944, F 4,15:3
Corcoran, John A, 1941, My 23,21:4
Corcoran, John F Mrs, 1948, Mr 17,25:1
Corcoran, John H, 1945, D 29,14:2
Corcoran, John J, 1947, My 1,25:5
Corcoran, John J Sr, 1945, N 17,17:5
Corcoran, John P Mrs, 1963, Jl 10,35:1
Corcoran, John W, 1952, Mr 2,92:3
Corcoran, John W V, 1940, F 14,21:3
Corcoran, Joseph A, 1942, Je 11,23:2
Corcoran, L R, 1949, Ja 4,19:2
Corcoran, Lloyd F, 1950, Ap 20,29:1
Corcoran, Loretta Mother, 1954, Ap 21,29:4
Corcoran, Mary Mrs, 1942, Je 26,21:5
Corcoran, Mickey, 1950, D 10,104:3
Corcoran, Patrick Mrs, 1954, Ja 25,19:3
Corcoran, Peter J, 1951, Ag 11,11:3
Corcoran, Richard F, 1939, Ja 8,42:6
Corcoran, Robert J, 1944, Je 11,45:1
Corcoran, Sanford W, 1946, Mr 19,27:4
Corcoran, Thomas F, 1943, Je 24,21:3
Corcoran, Thomas J, 1956, Ja 11,31:1
Corcoran, Thomas J Mrs, 1955, Jl 23,17:5
Corcoran, Thomas L J (funl, F 25,21:4), 1955, F 22, 21:1
Corcoran, Thomas L J (est tax appr filed), 1956, O 10,41:3
Corcoran, Thomas Mrs, 1957, S 1,56:5
Corcoran, Thomas P, 1959, Ag 25,31:2
Corcoran, Tommy, 1960, Je 27,25:5
Corcoran, W W, 1888, F 25,5:1
Corcoran, William B, 1913, Mr 22,13:5
Corcoran, William H, 1944, N 15,27:3
Corcoran, William H Rev, 1937, My 23,II,10:7
Corcoran, William L, 1958, Ja 19,87:2
Corcoran, William W, 1962, S 10,29:3
Corcos, Joseph Mrs, 1952, S 27,17:5
Corday, Jerome C, 1961, O 25,37:1
Corday, Theodore, 1966, Jl 25,27:5
Corddry, Newell W, 1939, Ag 2,19:3
Cordeaux, Harry, 1943, Jl 3,13:5
Cordeaux, Maud, 1949, Jl 17,58:3
Cordelia, Sister (E Lehman), 1958, Jl 29,23:2
Cordell, Harry B, 1937, Ja 11,19:2
Corden, Joseph A, 1960, O 29,23:6
Corder, Arthur E, 1958, Ap 13,84:1
Corder, Leeta (Mrs J F Murray), 1956, Ag 13,19:5
Cordero, Emilio P Col, 1924, Ja 3,17:3
Cordero, Juan C, 1965, Jl 22,10:7
Cordero, Wilford, 1949, My 7,28:8

Cordes, Amy B, 1937, Je 5,17:2
Cordes, Charles C Mrs, 1912, S 6,9:5
Cordes, Edward C, 1938, F 17,21:5
Cordes, Frank, 1952, O 22,27:6
Cordes, Frank H, 1967, D 3,84:7
Cordes, George H, 1955, Ap 15,23:1
Cordes, John H, 1952, Ja 2,25:3
Cordes, John H F, 1966, Ap 20,47:3
Cordes, John Mrs, 1959, O 20,40:1
Cordes, William, 1937, Ja 8,19:4
Cordes, William Jr, 1956, Ja 17,27:2
Cordey, Paul J, 1941, My 28,25:2
Cordial, Catherine M Mrs, 1940, Ja 24,21:3
Cordial, Edward J, 1946, Je 21,23:3
Cordial, Edward J Mrs, 1941, S 26,23:5
Cordier, Auguste J, 1949, Jl 21,26:5
Cordier, Constant, 1940, F 25,39:3
Cordier, Felix J, 1948, D 8,32:2
Cordilione, Rafaele, 1946, Ag 9,17:3
Cordiner, Jean, 1967, O 24,47:1
Cordingley, Nora, 1951, Mr 15,29:3
Cordler, Theodore A, 1960, Ap 6,41:4
Cordner, A B, 1927, S 8,29:5
Cordner, Arthur B, 1938, Ja 10,17:5
Cordner, Frank, 1946, N 24,78:5
Cordner, Martha N Mrs, 1942, D 3,25:5
Cordner, Robert, 1940, D 1,49:4
Cordner, Robert R, 1940, N 30,17:1
Cordo, Henry A Rev Dr, 1906, N 26,9:5
Cordoba, Gonzalo, 1955, F 9,27:1
Cordon, Norman, 1964, Mr 2,27:3
Cordon, Robert W, 1963, Ap 21,86:7
Cordova, Cyril de, 1943, Ap 17,17:2
Cordova, Eustace de, 1911, S 26,9:5
Cordova, Mathilde de, 1942, Jl 6,15:5
Cordova Davila, Felix, 1938, D 4,60:7
Cordovani, Mariano, 1950, Ap 7,25:2
Cordrey, Hester Mrs, 1910, Je 24,9:5
Cordrey, John A, 1949, O 6,31:1
Cords, Charles D, 1964, Mr 8,86:6
Cordts, Charles, 1947, Ap 20,60:7
Cordts, John N Ex-Sen, 1913, Jl 3,9:4
Corduan, Arthur L, 1950, D 31,43:1
Corduan, Malcolm, 1942, F 8,49:3
Corduke, M J Father, 1903, My 10,7:6
Cordwell, Stephen E, 1948, Ja 16,21:4
Cordy, Henry, 1965, N 29,35:3
Core, Charles B, 1947, Ap 8,27:4
Core, Jennie A H Mrs, 1940, My 6,17:4
Core, Oliver C, 1942, S 20,39:3
Corea, Claude, 1962, S 8,19:1
Corell, Ludwig, 1952, F 2,13:3
Corell, Vernon, 1955, O 20,36:1
Corey, Albert B, 1963, N 10,86:3
Corey, Alfred Adam, 1910, D 30,11:4
Corey, Benjamin, 1907, Jl 15,7:6
Corey, Cecil O, 1951, Ag 17,18:2
Corey, Charles P, 1945, N 24,20:2
Corey, Clara A, 1940, Mr 8,22:3
Corey, Clarence Thurston, 1924, Mr 31,17:2
Corey, Edward L, 1961, My 1,15:1
Corey, Eva D, 1943, S 8,23:2
Corey, Fred B, 1953, Jl 20,17:4
Corey, Fred B Mrs, 1952, N 6,29:4
Corey, Fred D Mrs, 1961, Je 9,33:2
Corey, George H, 1946, S 28,17:4; 1958, N 12,37:1
Corey, George J, 1921, Ja 21,15:6; 1956, My 2,31:5
Corey, Guy E, 1947, Ag 3,52:2
Corey, H H, 1966, Ag 3,37:3
Corey, Henry Thomas Lowry, 1873, Mr 8,7:4
Corey, Herbert, 1954, D 29,23:1
Corey, J B, 1875, S 5,12:2
Corey, J H Capt, 1903, Ag 18,7:6
Corey, John A, 1873, My 1,1:5
Corey, John W, 1953, My 20,29:1
Corey, Joseph W, 1944, Ap 28,19:4
Corey, Lewis, 1953, S 17,29:1
Corey, Madison W, 1952, Ag 11,15:4
Corey, Milton, 1951, O 25,29:3
Corey, Paris V, 1954, D 11,13:5
Corey, Russell B, 1954, My 4,29:4
Corey, S A Dr, 1884, F 28,5:3
Corey, W E, 1934, My 12,15:1
Corey, Wendell (funl plans, N 10,88:5), 1968, N 9, 33:1
Corey, William K, 1941, Jl 12,13:6
Corey and Cushing (Sad Case), 1872, O 31,2:3
Corfield, George H, 1910, Mr 6,II,11:3
Corfield, John E, 1944, F 12,13:3
Corgan, Michael H, 1951, Ag 28,23:3
Corgan, William, 1954, Ja 29,19:2
Cori, Gerty T, 1957, O 27,86:6
Coria, Walter P, 1949, Ja 19,27:5
Coriat, Isador H, 1943, My 27,25:2
Coriell, Abner S Mrs, 1947, Mr 29,15:5
Coriell, Frank A, 1957, F 6,25:5
Coriell, Frederick, 1946, F 4,25:4
Coriell, John H B, 1946, My 29,23:5
Coriell, William McDowell, 1904, F 25,9:5
Coriell, William W, 1937, Jl 26,19:6
Coriell, William W Mrs, 1960, Je 5,86:5
Corin, Isaac, 1925, S 13,5:1
Corin, Max, 1940, Jl 9,21:5
Corin, William H, 1944, N 9,27:2
Coring, William P, 1951, Ja 29,19:3
Corinth, Lovis Mrs, 1967, Ja 11,25:2
Corio, Joseph A, 1944, N 9,27:4
Corish, John L, 1945, S 29,15:3
Cork, J Milton, 1957, Ap 22,25:2
Cork and Orrery, Earl of (Wm H D Boyle), 1967, Ap 20,43:2
Corkan, Lloyd A, 1952, N 17,47:3
Corke, Nelson J, 1951, Ja 5,22:2
Corkery, Cornelius, 1937, Ag 12,19:4
Corkery, Daniel, 1965, Ja 2,19:3
Corkery, Edmund Q, 1950, Ja 21,18:2
Corkery, John A, 1956, N 25,88:4
Corkhill, G B, 1886, Jl 7,1:6
Corkhill, James Edmund Capt, 1919, Ap 20,22:2
Corkhill, Nelson G (est appr), 1962, Jl 18,12:1
Corkill, James F, 1964, D 12,31:2
Corkill, William H, 1945, Ap 24,19:5
Corkin, Joseph Z, 1962, Ja 6,19:4
Corkran, Anna M Mrs, 1937, S 10,23:4
Corkran, Sewell H, 1963, S 27,29:1
Corkran, Wilbur F, 1939, My 12,21:4
Corkum, George H, 1959, N 14,21:5
Corlambert, Louis, 1881, Mr 30,5:3
Corle, Deborah J L, 1963, Ag 26,27:4
Corle, Edwin, 1956, Je 12,35:5
Corlett, Edward, 1951, D 6,33:2
Corlett, Will G, 1954, O 29,21:1
Corlett, William T, 1948, Je 12,15:3
Corlett, William W, 1955, Je 5,84:5
Corley, Benjamin R, 1948, O 4,23:4
Corley, Charles R Msgr, 1914, S 18,9:4
Corley, Dewitt, 1940, Ap 15,17:3
Corley, Donald, 1955, D 14,39:5
Corley, Frank A, 1947, Mr 8,13:3
Corley, Frederick D, 1960, My 9,29:2
Corley, John G, 1938, F 26,15:3
Corley, Judith A, 1965, D 25,10:2
Corley, Ralph A, 1947, Ag 15,17:5
Corley, William F, 1940, Jl 17,21:6
Corlies, Arthur, 1941, Je 16,15:5
Corlies, Benjamin F, 1914, Ja 27,9:6
Corlies, Edmund W Mrs, 1925, Ag 12,21:5
Corlies, J Arch, 1941, D 5,23:2
Corlies, Laura B Mrs, 1937, Ap 10,19:1
Corlies, William P, 1910, Ap 26,11:5
Corliss, Augustus W Brig-Gen, 1908, S 5,7:4
Corliss, Edward P, 1947, D 5,25:4
Corliss, Edward P Mrs, 1942, Je 29,15:2
Corliss, Floyd H, 1956, Mr 26,29:1
Corliss, G W Maj, 1903, My 17,3:2
Corliss, George M, 1949, N 15,26:4
Corliss, Guy C H, 1937, N 25,31:2
Corliss, Julia P Mrs, 1939, D 21,23:3
Corliss, Lorin F, 1940, Ag 22,19:4
Corliss, Samuel T, 1941, O 28,23:2
Corliss, William, 1954, Mr 28,88:4
Corliss, William F, 1960, Jl 3,33:1
Corliss, William V, 1945, S 13,23:5
Cormack, Bartlett, 1942, S 18,21:5
Cormack, Donald G, 1956, F 9,32:2
Cormack, George A, 1938, Je 29,19:6
Cormack, George S, 1951, O 6,19:4
Cormack, John Mrs, 1943, My 18,23:5
Cormack, Leslie S, 1942, Jl 28,17:2
Cormack, Robert W, 1948, N 24,23:5
Corman, Ellis H, 1956, Ag 11,13:3
Corman, Joseph A, 1946, Je 3,21:4
Corman, S Wilbur, 1938, O 10,19:5
Cormia, Frank E Dr, 1968, Ag 27,42:1
Cormican, Patrick J, 1945, F 22,27:1
Cormier, E Alfred, 1951, Je 25,19:5
Cormier, Joseph H, 1950, Jl 20,25:4
Cormis, Louis de Rev, 1916, Mr 5,21:5
Corn, Belmont, 1956, Jl 1,57:2
Corn, Harry, 1960, Ag 24,29:1
Corn, Herbert F, 1966, Ap 30,31:1
Corn, Joseph J (por), 1947, Jl 5,11:5
Corn, Joseph J, 1950, N 27,25:3
Corn, Joseph J Mrs, 1966, O 15,29:4
Corn, Max, 1948, Ag 15,60:2
Corn, Philip A, 1964, Je 25,33:1
Corn, William A, 1957, Je 16,84:6
Cornack, John, 1912, Ap 1,13:5
Cornaire, Jasper W, 1937, Ag 16,19:5
Cornalla, Chris, 1943, Ja 11,15:5
Cornbill, William M G, 1940, Je 12,25:3
Cornbrooks, Ernest I, 1939, Jl 5,17:4
Cornbrooks, Thomas M, 1944, Ap 20,19:4
Corneal, George D, 1944, D 30,11:5
Corneau, Arthur E, 1942, Ag 1,11:5
Corneau, Jeanne Mother Superior, 1955, D 20,31:4
Cornehl, George H, 1941, Je 24,19:4
Cornehlsen, Christian H, 1961, Ja 15,86:7
Corneil, Lincoln, 1948, My 24,19:2
Corneille, James E, 1942, D 19,19:4
Cornejo, Abraham, 1941, D 2,24:2
Corneli, Frank, 1913, S 12,11:2
Cornelia, Mary Mother, 1924, N 27,19:3
Cornelia, William B, 1955, Jl 6,27:2
Cornelis, Edward J, 1964, Jl 2,31:5
Cornelis, Edward J Mrs, 1960, O 27,37:4
Cornelison, John M Dr, 1875, My 25,6:7
Cornelison, Robert W, 1946, Ap 2,27:5
Cornelison, Robert W Mrs, 1962, N 11,88:8
Cornelissen, Arnold Mrs, 1948, Ag 18,25:4
Cornelius, Adam E, 1953, D 12,19:5
Cornelius, Adam E (est tax appr), 1957, N 5,35:8
Cornelius, Arthur Jr (more details, Ag 5,23:4), 1967, Ag 4,29:1
Cornelius, Charles O, 1937, Jl 15,19:5
Cornelius, E Livingston, 1947, Jl 15,23:4
Cornelius, German Painter, 1867, Ap 1,1:5
Cornelius, Harmon V, 1942, N 10,28:2
Cornelius, Harry L Sr, 1948, My 14,23:2
Cornelius, Henry, 1958, My 3,19:4
Cornelius, Henry B, 1965, My 10,33:3
Cornelius, J Cox, 1952, Je 18,27:5
Cornelius, John Mrs (Baroness Gevers), 1908, O 20 9:6
Cornelius, Sarah Jane, 1915, Mr 8,9:5
Cornelius, Stephen G, 1948, S 21,27:5
Cornelius, Willard M Sr, 1957, D 20,27:2
Cornelius, William, 1951, My 26,17:5
Cornelius, William T Mrs, 1950, S 3,38:3
Cornelius Peter, Bro (Lynch), 1961, D 3,88:3
Corneliussen, Elias, 1951, Ap 7,15:4
Cornell, A Boyd, 1949, N 8,31:1
Cornell, Abby G, 1956, S 2,56:3
Cornell, Albert C, 1941, Je 30,17:3
Cornell, Alfred Y, 1937, N 22,19:6
Cornell, Alonzo ex-Gov, 1904, O 16,9:6
Cornell, Alvin S Mrs, 1941, Mr 7,21:2
Cornell, Arthur B Mrs, 1944, Ap 25,23:4
Cornell, Burton H, 1952, N 19,29:5
Cornell, Charles A, 1939, Ag 3,19:6
Cornell, Charles E, 1947, Ja 31,23:3; 1948, Mr 17,2
Cornell, Charles E Mrs, 1946, Mr 19,27:5
Cornell, Charles L, 1942, Jl 20,13:4
Cornell, Charles R, 1958, Je 25,29:4
Cornell, Clarence H, 1916, F 15,11:6
Cornell, Daniel T, 1916, My 30,9:6
Cornell, David W, 1938, S 27,21:2
Cornell, E L, 1903, Je 20,7:6
Cornell, Edward, 1942, N 18,25:4
Cornell, Edward L, 1950, F 2,27:4
Cornell, Edward S, 1944, O 13,19:2
Cornell, Edward S Mrs, 1946, Ja 8,23:2
Cornell, Edwin, 1962, Ap 24,37:3
Cornell, Ethel L, 1963, D 9,35:1
Cornell, Ezra, 1874, D 10,4:7
Cornell, Ferris D, 1945, Jl 8,11:5
Cornell, Frank E, 1941, Ja 22,21:4
Cornell, Frank T, 1952, Je 14,15:4
Cornell, Franklin C, 1945, Ap 3,19:2
Cornell, Fred D, 1942, Ag 12,19:2
Cornell, Fred H Mrs, 1961, O 16,29:4
Cornell, Frederick W Rev, 1937, Ag 22,II,7:4
Cornell, George, 1942, Ja 4,49:1
Cornell, George B, 1946, O 14,29:4
Cornell, George Boardman Dr, 1920, Je 19,13:6
Cornell, George F, 1957, Je 3,27:6
Cornell, George F Mrs, 1949, Ag 14,69:1
Cornell, George W Mrs, 1963, Jl 2,26:5
Cornell, Gertrude, 1948, D 21,28:5
Cornell, Henry B, 1942, S 19,15:3
Cornell, Henry T Mrs, 1945, D 27,19:4
Cornell, Henry W, 1957, Mr 14,29:6
Cornell, Herbert J, 1951, Jl 14,13:2
Cornell, Howard E, 1939, Mr 25,15:6
Cornell, Irwin H, 1963, O 6,88:8
Cornell, Isaac Mrs, 1943, Je 27,32:3
Cornell, J M, 1934, Mr 11,31:5
Cornell, James, 1946, N 26,29:3
Cornell, James W, 1948, Ap 9,23:2
Cornell, Jeannie O M Mrs, 1938, O 6,23:5
Cornell, John A, 1956, Ja 7,17:3
Cornell, John B, 1963, N 6,41:1
Cornell, John E, 1938, Ag 10,19:4
Cornell, Julius M, 1954, Ja 19,26:3
Cornell, Letitia C Mrs, 1937, O 10,II,9:1
Cornell, Lewis F, 1956, Je 28,29:1
Cornell, Mabel K Mrs (will), 1965, My 18,24:5
Cornell, Marguerite E, 1940, Ap 17,23:3
Cornell, Mary E, 1963, F 5,4:6
Cornell, Mary E Mrs, 1940, Mr 28,23:4
Cornell, Maude Mrs, 1942, Ap 12,44:3
Cornell, Milton L, 1958, N 6,37:1
Cornell, Peter C (will, S 29,35:4), 1948, S 25,1
Cornell, Peter J O, 1940, N 30,17:4
Cornell, Peter M, 1946, Ag 24,11:4
Cornell, Richard J, 1957, O 13,85:5
Cornell, Richard L, 1949, Ja 7,21:4
Cornell, Robert, 1938, S 17,17:2
Cornell, Robert Clifford (funl, N 9,13:5), 1918 15:2
Cornell, Rodman M Sr, 1950, My 1,25:5
Cornell, Ross C, 1953, F 28,17:5
Cornell, Russell T, 1957, F 17,93:2
Cornell, Russell T Mrs, 1940, My 20,17:5
Cornell, S Douglas Mrs, 1959, Mr 21,21:3
Cornell, Sidney, 1939, Jl 26,19:3
Cornell, Stephen B, 1948, F 2,19:3
Cornell, T F, 1880, O 25,5:2
Cornell, Theodore S, 1940, Ag 11,31:2

Cornell, Van A H, 1956, O 25,33:5
Cornell, Vincent W, 1942, Mr 24,19:5
Cornell, Virgil H, 1954, Je 7,23:4
Cornell, W M, 1864, Ag 18,5:3
Cornell, Walter C, 1945, Jl 25,23:4
Cornell, Walter G, 1963, O 2,41:4
Cornell, Walter R, 1950, My 29,17:4
Cornell, Warren D Mrs, 1946, Ja 14,19:1
Cornell, Warren M, 1950, Ap 18,31:5
Cornell, William, 1947, Jl 13,44:2
Cornell, William A, 1937, S 5,II,6:6; 1951, O 6,19:3
Cornell, William B, 1957, N 24,87:1
Cornell, William E, 1959, N 14,21:6
Cornell, William F, 1947, F 24,19:5
Cornell, William S, 1962, Je 7,35:3
Cornell, X H, 1937, Ap 29,21:2
Cornella, Albert P, 1965, D 27,25:2
Cornely, Jean Joseph, 1907, D 27,7:7
Cornely, Paul J, 1953, Ap 1,29:4
Corner, Charles Potts Rev, 1921, Mr 20,22:2
Corner, Clarence F, 1955, O 17,27:4
Corner, George W Jr, 1938, S 21,25:5
Corner, Thomas C, 1938, S 5,15:5
Cornero, Tony (A C Stralla), 1955, Ag 1,38:3
Cornet, George A, 1949, O 15,15:2
Cornet, William, 1967, Ag 17,37:2
Cornett, Denver B, 1949, N 24,31:5
Cornetta, George, 1967, My 14,87:2
Corney, Henry S, 1948, D 14,29:5
Corney, Richard, 1904, Ja 24,5:6
Corney, William B, 1951, Ap 16,25:2
Cornfield, Harry I, 1950, D 31,42:8
Cornforth, Clarence G, 1940, N 14,23:4
Cornick, George B, 1947, Ag 30,15:3
Cornick, Joe, 1938, F 3,23:2
Corniglion-Milinier, Edouard, 1963, My 10,33:4
Corning, A Elwood, 1954, Je 13,88:4
Corning, Albert J, 1938, Ap 9,17:2
Corning, C H, 1879, Jl 13,7:2
Corning, Christopher R, 1924, Jl 4,13:5
Corning, Dudley T, 1952, Je 19,27:3
Corning, Edward P, 1965, My 5,47:3
Corning, Edwin, 1964, F 1,23:3
Corning, Erastus, 1872, Ap 10,8:4; 1897, Ag 31,7:4; 1942, N 12,25:5
Corning, Frederick G, 1937, Jl 13,19:4
Corning, George M Mrs, 1947, F 28,23:3
Corning, Hanson K, 1951, F 9,25:5
Corning, Hanson K Mrs, 1960, Mr 16,37:3
Corning, Henry W, 1946, F 2,13:5
Corning, Howard, 1956, F 15,31:3
Corning, J Leonard Dr, 1923, Ag 26,26:4
Corning, James L Rev, 1903, S 2,7:6
Corning, Karen A Mrs, 1966, Ag 12,31:1
Corning, Merritt Sherman, 1914, Jl 9,7:6
Corning, Parker, 1943, My 25,23:1
Corning, Parker Mrs, 1943, Ap 4,40:4
Cornish, Abraham S, 1941, Mr 23,45:1
Cornish, Albert C (cor, F 14,43:3), 1967, F 11,29:4
Cornish, Edward J Mrs (will, Je 5,2:7), 1938, My 19, 21:2
Cornish, Edward R Mrs, 1958, Ap 16,33:1
Cornish, Floyd L, 1950, Jl 7,19:5
Cornish, Frank G Mrs, 1955, D 3,17:5
Cornish, George D, 1945, S 8,15:4
Cornish, Gilbert M, 1939, Je 24,17:2
Cornish, Grube B, 1950, Ja 3,25:4
Cornish, Guy S, 1962, Jl 21,19:4
Cornish, Hubert R, 1944, D 16,15:3
Cornish, Johnston, 1920, Je 27,18:2
Cornish, Leslie C, 1925, Je 25,21:5
Cornish, Louis C, 1950, Ja 8,76:4
Cornish, Mary E Mrs, 1940, F 20,21:5
Cornish, Richard V, 1961, Mr 3,27:3
Cornish, Robert, 1963, Mr 8,12:2
Cornish, Royal G Capt, 1937, F 24,23:3
Cornish, Samuel G, 1937, O 16,19:4
Cornish, Thomas E, 1924, N 3,17:4
Cornish, Vaughan, 1948, My 3,21:1
Cornish, William D, 1908, N 8,11:5
Cornish, Worthen C, 1954, F 27,13:4
Cornman, O P, 1883, Ap 19,5:4
Cornock, Sidney Mrs, 1957, Ag 28,27:4
Cornock, Sidney W (Billy Curtis), 1954, Ap 29,31:4
Cornog, Elwood C, 1962, Jl 4,21:3
Cornoyer, Paul, 1923, Je 18,13:6
Cornplanter, Edward, 1918, Je 19,11:7
Corns, Orja G Sr, 1955, O 5,35:3
Cornthwaite, Miles J, 1955, Ag 27,15:3
Cornue, Arthur W Mrs, 1960, Ap 19,37:4
Cornwall, Barry (Bryon Walter Proctor), 1874, O 6, 5:6
Cornwall, Clift, 1961, D 29,23:3
Cornwall, Edward E, 1940, O 8,25:6
Cornwall, Franklin W, 1938, Ap 16,13:5
Cornwall, George A, 1951, Je 30,15:5
Cornwall, George I, 1947, Mr 7,25:3
Cornwall, George Mrs, 1909, S 2,9:6
Cornwall, George Rev, 1909, S 2,9:6
Cornwall, Harold D Mrs, 1957, Ap 6,19:6
Cornwall, Harvey A, 1942, O 30,19:1
Cornwall, Henry B Prof, 1917, Ap 3,13:6
Cornwall, Leon H, 1949, Mr 5,17:6
Cornwall, N E Rev Dr, 1879, Ag 29,5:4
Cornwallis, Kinahan, 1917, Ag 17,9:6; 1959, Je 6,21:3
Cornwallis-West, William Col, 1917, Jl 5,9:6
Cornwallis-West, William Mrs, 1920, Jl 23,15:3
Cornwell, Alfred, 1948, My 29,15:5
Cornwell, Alfred L Mrs, 1947, My 10,13:6
Cornwell, Alfred Lester, 1968, Ag 6,37:3
Cornwell, Billy, 1949, Mr 31,34:5
Cornwell, Charles C Capt, 1904, F 4,7:6
Cornwell, Charles W, 1947, Ap 25,22:2
Cornwell, Clifford C Rev, 1937, O 21,24:1
Cornwell, Dean, 1960, D 6,41:1
Cornwell, Eugene, 1949, D 20,32:3
Cornwell, George F, 1921, Ja 16,22:4
Cornwell, George R, 1924, O 5,31:1
Cornwell, Harold B, 1953, Ap 28,27:1
Cornwell, John J, 1953, S 9,29:3
Cornwell, John W Jr, 1959, Je 26,25:3
Cornwell, Jorge S del, 1955, Je 30,25:4
Cornwell, Martha J, 1955, My 24,31:1
Cornwell, Mary R, 1948, Jl 24,15:6
Cornwell, Robert H Mrs, 1966, S 28,47:4
Cornyn, John H, 1941, D 25,25:2
Coromilas, Lambros A, 1923, N 15,19:4
Coron, Henry W, 1938, N 16,23:2
Corona, Alphonse A, 1966, My 3,44:8
Corona, Juana, 1910, Ja 25,9:4
Coronas, Jose, 1938, Je 6,17:3
Coronati, Edwin P, 1956, D 20,29:1
Corot, Jean B C, 1875, F 24,5:1
Corporale, Christopher, 1959, Je 7,1:3
Corporale, Roslyn, 1959, Je 7,1:3
Corps, Millicent, 1940, My 2,23:1
Corput, Francois van den, 1948, Ja 20,23:2
Corput, Rex Van D Jr, 1960, Mr 16,37:2
Corr, Bernard, 1912, D 28,7:4
Corr, Frank, 1939, S 13,25:5
Corr, John H, 1942, O 15,23:5
Corr, John J, 1954, O 1,23:1
Corr, Joseph P, 1948, Mr 9,23:4
Corr, Marie V Sister, 1957, S 11,33:1
Corr, May E T, 1966, Jl 1,35:2
Corr, Michael J, 1966, O 31,35:2
Corr, Thomas R Rev, 1914, O 12,9:4
Corr, William E, 1940, O 28,17:5
Corradi, Simon Mrs, 1903, S 3,7:6
Corrado, Peter J, 1945, Ag 11,13:6
Corral, Manuel, 1938, D 1,23:4
Corral, Ramon, 1912, N 11,11:4
Corran, Alex, 1940, O 26,15:2
Corran, James M, 1963, F 8,18:2
Corrao, C S, 1934, O 10,29:3
Corrao, Frank P, 1962, My 16,41:5
Correa, Aquino, 1956, Mr 24,19:5
Correa, David A, 1949, O 31,25:3
Correa, Emanuel H A, 1912, O 25,13:2
Correa, Jose M S, 1942, N 19,25:6
Correa, Luis, 1946, Mr 31,46:3
Correa, Mathias F, 1963, D 6,35:1
Correa, Rodolfo A, 1941, My 30,15:2
Correa, Vduveduviges Mrs, 1948, Ja 15,23:4
Correa da Sa, Carolina M C H, 1954, S 10,23:3
Correale, Anthony, 1964, Ap 5,86:5
Correale, Frank, 1952, Ap 8,29:2
Corregan, Charles H, 1946, Je 20,23:3
Correia, Joao da Silva Dr, 1937, Je 2,23:6
Correia, Jose G, 1954, Ap 27,29:2
Correia da Silva, Jose A, 1957, D 5,35:5
Correia e Castro, Pedro L, 1953, N 18,31:1
Correjolles, Theodore, 1946, N 7,31:5
Correll, Harold A, 1965, Ag 9,25:3
Correll, I H, 1926, Je 18,23:5
Correll, John J, 1954, Jl 6,23:4
Correll, Paul R, 1946, Mr 2,13:2
Correll, Robert G, 1953, D 22,31:5
Correll, S J Mrs, 1933, N 10,21:3
Correoso, A Bravo, 1944, Ja 3,21:4
Correoso, Buenaventura Gen, 1911, Ja 14,11:6
Corretjer, Antonio Jr, 1945, S 18,24:2
Correvon, Henri, 1939, My 12,21:4
Corri, E, 1933, D 22,22:5
Corrican, M Gertrude, 1940, Je 11,25:5
Corrican, Oswald A, 1939, Ag 1,19:6
Corrick, Charles R, 1952, Ag 5,19:2
Corridan, James E Rev, 1937, S 25,17:5
Corridan, Michael F Mrs, 1954, Jl 19,19:6
Corriden, John M, 1959, S 30,29:5
Corrie, John, 1943, My 23,42:7
Corrie, Oliver W, 1956, Ap 5,29:1
Corriell, W L, 1903, O 10,9:6
Corrigan, Archibishop, 1902, My 6,1:7
Corrigan, D J Sir, 1880, F 2,5:3
Corrigan, Douglas Mrs, 1966, My 11,47:3
Corrigan, Emmett, 1950, O 22,92:3
Corrigan, Francis P, 1961, Ap 2,2:4
Corrigan, Frank P Dr, 1968, Ja 23,39:1
Corrigan, Frank P Mrs, 1947, My 30,21:2
Corrigan, George F, 1947, Mr 7,25:3
Corrigan, George W Rev, 1915, My 26,13:7
Corrigan, Harry B, 1954, D 17,31:1
Corrigan, J E, 1935, Ja 10,19:1
Corrigan, J F, 1933, My 29,13:3
Corrigan, J F Dr, 1903, My 13,9:5
Corrigan, J J Msgr, 1927, Mr 3,23:5
Corrigan, J William Mrs, 1940, O 24,25:3
Corrigan, James, 1908, D 26,7:6
Corrigan, James E, 1954, D 10,27:3
Corrigan, James P Rev, 1908, Je 4,7:7
Corrigan, James W, 1948, Ag 28,15:5
Corrigan, James W Mrs (will, F 18,56:1), 1948, Ja 24,15:3
Corrigan, John, 1959, Jl 19,68:2
Corrigan, John D, 1939, Ja 6,21:4
Corrigan, John J, 1922, O 19,21:6; 1949, N 13,94:3; 1954, N 10,33:1
Corrigan, John P, 1943, Je 25,17:4 ; 1966, Ap 15,39:4
Corrigan, Joseph E Mrs, 1958, D 7,88:7
Corrigan, Joseph F Dr, 1918, N 30,11:4
Corrigan, Joseph M, 1942, Je 10,21:1
Corrigan, Mary, 1963, Ap 1,41:1
Corrigan, Maurice J, 1964, My 11,31:4
Corrigan, Michael, 1944, Ag 18,13:2
Corrigan, Michael H, 1937, Ja 17,II,8:7
Corrigan, Patrick J Mrs, 1950, Ap 17,23:4
Corrigan, Patrick T, 1950, Ap 16,105:1
Corrigan, Thomas F, 1960, Jl 26,29:4
Corrigan, Thomas F Mrs, 1945, S 1,11:5
Corrigan, Thomas V, 1948, My 19,27:4
Corrigan, Walter E, 1947, Jl 23,23:6
Corrigan, William J, 1961, Ag 1,31:5
Corrigill, Alex S, 1961, Je 18,89:1
Corriston, Terence, 1945, D 19,25:1
Corriveau, Joseph U, 1946, Ja 15,23:3
Corroon, Catherine L Mrs, 1953, Ag 17,15:3
Corroon, James A, 1940, My 2,23:3
Corroon, James F, 1957, Ag 26,23:2
Corroon, Richard A, 1946, N 15,24:2
Corroon, Richard A Mrs, 1962, Jl 9,31:5
Corrothers, Sylvester L, 1948, Ag 20,17:4
Corrou, John Mrs, 1940, Mr 5,23:5
Corry, Frank B, 1951, O 27,19:5
Corry, Frank M, 1941, Je 7,17:5
Corry, George A, 1943, D 12,68:1
Corry, George Mrs, 1947, Mr 13,27:1
Corry, John J, 1966, Je 24,37:1
Corry, Matthew, 1952, Ja 31,28:2
Corry, Patrick M, 1962, O 1,31:5
Corry, Sarah Morris, 1915, F 23,13:4
Corry, W Sir, 1926, Je 10,25:3
Corry, William Merrill Lt-Col (funl, O 10,22:4), 1920, O 8,13:2
Corsa, George B, 1947, D 2,30:3
Corsall, Gerald, 1958, O 19,83:1
Corsbie, Robert L, 1967, Ja 8,91:4
Corsbie, Robert L Jr, 1967, Ja 8,91:4
Corsbie, Robert L Mrs, 1967, Ja 8,91:4
Corscadden, Felix, 1948, Mr 26,21:4
Corscadden, Felix Mrs, 1939, Jl 19,19:5
Corscaden, James A, 1964, D 13,87:2
Corscaden, James A Mrs, 1956, Mr 22,35:1
Corse, George F, 1956, F 25,19:5
Corse, Henry, 1949, Ag 13,12:2
Corse, William M, 1944, Je 4,42:4
Corser, Charles B, 1954, Mr 4,25:5
Corsi, Alberto, 1941, Jl 18,19:5
Corsi, Antonio, 1924, D 6,15:7
Corsi, Edward (funl, D 18,29:1), 1965, D 14,43:1
Corsi, Mario, 1954, Ap 5,25:4
Corso, Andrew J, 1914, My 7,11:6
Corso, John, 1943, S 8,24:3
Corson, Alan, 1943, Ap 5,19:5
Corson, Bayard W, 1953, Ja 19,23:3
Corson, Benjamin H, 1965, Ag 4,35:4
Corson, D Herman, 1947, Mr 27,27:3
Corson, Edwin C Sr, 1966, Ap 23,31:6
Corson, Edwin T, 1950, My 31,29:5
Corson, Egbert D, 1959, D 13,86:4
Corson, Elton S, 1941, Ja 7,23:3
Corson, George H, 1952, F 2,13:4
Corson, Harry M, 1949, Ap 19,25:5
Corson, Hiram Prof, 1911, Je 16,9:6
Corson, J Griffith, 1964, Ja 26,80:8
Corson, John A, 1946, Ap 4,25:5
Corson, Joshua D, 1953, Ja 29,27:3
Corson, Juliet, 1897, Je 20,5:6
Corson, Louis, 1955, Je 20,21:6
Corson, O T, 1928, Ap 15,II,7:1
Corson, Percy H, 1949, Je 29,28:3
Corson, Robert B, 1943, Ja 25,14:3
Corson, Robert W, 1949, Mr 10,28:3
Corson, St Clair T, 1950, Mr 17,23:2
Corson, T J, 1879, My 11,2:2
Corson, Thomas A, 1944, D 18,19:4
Corson, William R C, 1945, O 3,19:2
Corson, William R C Mrs, 1941, Ja 3,19:3
Corson, William W, 1956, Ap 12,13:1
Corston, George L, 1946, S 26,25:5
Corsuti, Carlo, 1961, F 2,29:3
Cort, Ambrose, 1956, Jl 24,25:3
Cort, Edwin C, 1950, Ja 12,28:5
Cort, Edwin C Mrs, 1955, Mr 18,27:4
Cort, Harry L, 1937, My 7,25:2
Cort, Howard R, 1946, N 20,31:2
Cort, Lottie A, 1939, F 17,19:5
Cort, Nicholas, 1875, My 11,6:7

Cort, Parker M, 1951, S 29,17:6
Cort, Stewart J, 1958, S 24,27:3
Cort, Walter W, 1947, Jl 31,21:6
Cortas, George N, 1943, Jl 2,19:3
Corte, Charles, 1961, Jl 14,47:5
Corte, Fausta M Mrs, 1952, Ag 14,23:4
Cortejarena, Jose Dr, 1921, Jl 26,15:6
Cortell, Robert Mrs, 1958, N 2,88:4
Cortelyou, Charles V, 1940, My 13,17:2
Cortelyou, David Mrs, 1947, Mr 30,56:1
Cortelyou, George B, 1940, O 24,25:1
Cortelyou, George B Mrs, 1947, My 25,62:2
Cortelyou, J T, 1927, Ap 16,15:4
Cortelyou, L H, 1884, S 28,7:1
Cortelyou, Raymond P, 1965, D 19,84:3
Cortelyou, Raymond V, 1961, N 10,35:5
Cortelyou, Rose Seary Mrs, 1925, D 22,21:4
Cortelyou, Spencer V, 1962, Ag 11,17:5
Cortelyou, Theodore C, 1966, My 1,87:6
Cortes, Felix, 1940, Mr 16,15:4
Cortes, Geraldo M, 1962, O 31,19:3
Cortes, Park, 1948, Ap 30,23:2
Cortes, Victor M, 1947, Ag 11,23:5
Cortes, William P, 1943, Ap 20,24:2
Cortes Castro, Leon, 1946, Mr 4,23:5
Cortes Gonzales, Ramon Gen, 1946, Je 22,9:5
Cortese, Anthony J, 1959, S 19,23:6
Cortese, Guido, 1964, S 5,19:6
Cortesi, Arnaldo, 1966, N 27,86:7
Cortesi, Filippo, 1947, F 2,57:2
Cortesi, Roger Mrs, 1958, Ag 3,81:2
Cortesi, Salvatore, 1947, Mr 4,25:1
Corthell, Elmer L Dr, 1916, My 17,11:5
Corthell, Herbert, 1947, Ja 24,21:3
Corthis, Andre Mrs, 1952, Ag 10,60:6
Cortie, Aloysius Laurence Rev, 1925, My 18,15:4
Cortilet, Michael P, 1955, Ag 28,84:3
Cortilli, Leon, 1963, Jl 3,25:3
Cortis, Antonio, 1952, Ap 4,25:2
Cortiss, Harry W, 1951, S 16,85:2
Cortissoz, Royal, 1948, O 18,23:1
Cortizas, Anthony, 1956, Ap 27,27:2
Cortizas, Michael, 1951, Mr 30,24:2
Cortner, Bob, 1959, My 20,45:1
Cortot, Alfred, 1962, Je 16,19:3
Cortright, E E Mrs, 1941, Mr 10,17:4
Cortright, Edgar M, 1954, Ag 25,27:5
Cortright, Fred L, 1941, Ja 10,19:5
Cortright, John B, 1941, D 25,25:5
Cortright, L D, 1880, N 30,5:3
Corum, Bill, 1958, D 17,2:6
Corum, William Mrs, 1953, Ap 7,29:1
Corvallis, Bill, 1950, Ja 5,4:4
Corvinus, Bernard, 1945, D 15,17:4
Corvisart, Lucien, 1882, D 26,5:4
Corwey, Fred, 1959, Jl 4,15:6
Corwin, Alfred H, 1955, O 26,31:2
Corwin, Allen W, 1941, Mr 2,42:7
Corwin, Ambrose D, 1965, Je 10,35:1
Corwin, Arthur F, 1957, Mr 15,25:4
Corwin, Arthur F Mrs, 1941, My 29,19:4
Corwin, B Ryder, 1909, D 27,7:7
Corwin, Charles A, 1938, Ja 28,21:3
Corwin, Charles E, 1958, Je 10,33:5
Corwin, Charles H, 1946, S 23,23:2
Corwin, Charles L Mrs, 1945, Je 4,19:5
Corwin, D Stanley, 1938, Ja 10,17:5
Corwin, David W, 1944, My 24,19:6
Corwin, Dwight T, 1960, Ja 24,88:3
Corwin, Edward A, 1954, D 10,28:3
Corwin, Edward H, 1953, My 9,19:1
Corwin, Edward H Mrs, 1965, My 24,31:5
Corwin, Edward S, 1963, Ap 30,35:1
Corwin, Edward Tanjore, 1914, Je 24,11:6
Corwin, Elizabeth B Mrs, 1939, O 8,49:1
Corwin, Elizabeth E Mrs, 1937, Ag 12,19:3
Corwin, Elmer G Mrs, 1947, D 9,29:2
Corwin, Elmer N Sr, 1951, O 20,15:4
Corwin, F, 1879, Je 19,5:6
Corwin, Frances W, 1953, Ja 7,31:4
Corwin, Frank H, 1938, Ja 16,II,9:2
Corwin, Fred M Mrs, 1943, Ap 9,21:6
Corwin, George E Mrs, 1949, Jl 20,25:5
Corwin, George Mrs, 1950, Jl 18,29:4
Corwin, George W, 1955, F 26,15:5
Corwin, George W Mrs, 1953, N 13,27:2
Corwin, H Garfield, 1950, D 5,31:4
Corwin, Halsey, 1939, Jl 4,13:5
Corwin, Hamilton Stewart, 1922, Jl 20,17:3
Corwin, I Seymour, 1920, F 22,20:4
Corwin, Ibey Mrs, 1959, Jl 25,17:3
Corwin, Isaac L, 1949, Je 8,30:2
Corwin, John A, 1923, Ja 23,21:5
Corwin, John A Sr, 1944, F 15,17:3
Corwin, John E, 1913, S 19,9:4
Corwin, Joseph W, 1961, Jl 14,23:3
Corwin, Lulu M, 1949, Ag 30,27:3
Corwin, Mary E Mrs, 1941, D 6,17:6
Corwin, Nathaniel S, 1952, D 21,52:8
Corwin, Norman L Sr, 1947, N 15,17:5
Corwin, Rachel J Mrs, 1940, Je 12,25:3
Corwin, Raymond R, 1952, Je 27,23:3
Corwin, Robert N, 1944, O 15,44:5
Corwin, Robert N Mrs, 1952, Je 15,84:2
Corwin, Sarah E Mrs, 1940, Ag 3,15:5
Corwin, Selah R, 1909, S 7,9:6
Corwin, Thomas, 1865, D 19,4:5
Corwin, Walter E (por), 1947, D 19,25:3
Corwine, A B, 1880, Je 14,2:5
Corwine, Thomas R, 1952, O 25,17:3
Corwith, Frank H, 1949, F 18,23:1
Corwith, Howard P, 1962, Je 12,37:1
Corwith, J Carlton, 1966, D 8,47:3
Corwith, Lester F, 1946, Jl 3,25:5
Corwther, Frank, 1955, Jl 21,23:4
Cory, Abram E, 1952, Mr 22,13:6
Cory, Abram E Mrs, 1947, Ag 4,17:5
Cory, Albert Mrs, 1964, D 15,44:1
Cory, Allen, 1942, Jl 19,30:7
Cory, Charles B, 1954, Ja 24,85:2
Cory, Clifford J, 1941, F 4,21:4
Cory, David, 1966, Jl 6,45:2
Cory, E Ray, 1962, S 2,59:5
Cory, F E Mrs, 1902, Mr 23,7:7
Cory, Florence A, 1954, My 9,88:5
Cory, Frederick N, 1947, Ag 16,13:5
Cory, George R, 1948, Ja 19,23:1; 1966, D 20,43:4
Cory, Harvey E, 1939, Je 30,19:1
Cory, Harvey E Mrs (will, S 14,16:7), 1939, Mr 13, 17:3
Cory, Ira W Capt, 1904, Mr 4,9:6
Cory, John C, 1952, My 3,21:2
Cory, John M, 1942, Mr 15,43:2
Cory, Kathleen S, 1961, Je 8,35:3
Cory, Ralph J, 1951, O 18,29:3
Cory, Robert H (por), 1947, Mr 17,23:4
Cory, Russell G, 1946, My 28,21:3
Cory, Thomas J, 1965, S 16,47:4
Coryell, Charles N, 1946, Jl 16,23:1
Coryell, Clarence C, 1962, O 24,39:4
Coryell, George H Mrs, 1944, Ja 16,43:2
Coryell, Horace N, 1965, Je 26,29:5
Coryell, James B Maj-Gen, 1924, F 8,19:4
Coryell, John P, 1937, Ap 13,25:2
Coryell, John R, 1924, Jl 17,15:6
Coryell, John R Mrs, 1957, Ja 14,23:4
Coryell, Lillian F Mrs, 1940, Ap 24,23:3
Coryell, Roland S, 1957, Je 14,25:3
Coryell, Russell M, 1941, O 17,23:5
Coryell, William H, 1953, Ja 22,23:3
Coryllos, Polyvious N, 1938, Jl 28,19:6
Coryndon, Robert Sir, 1925, F 11,21:4
Corzen, Arthur S, 1961, Ja 17,37:3
Cos, Jose, 1923, Ag 9,13:5
Cos y Macho, Cardinal, 1919, D 18,13:3
Cosand, Charles E, 1952, Ja 22,29:5
Cosby, Arthur F, 1957, F 27,27:4
Cosby, Edwin T, 1962, N 7,39:4
Cosby, Joseph T, 1943, F 16,19:4
Cosby, Joseph T Mrs, 1958, Mr 16,86:8
Cosby, Spencer, 1962, Mr 28,39:3
Cosby, W C Dr, 1937, S 24,21:3
Cosby, Wilmoth R Mrs, 1939, Jl 4,13:3
Coscarello, Joseph A, 1949, O 18,28:2
Coscia, Phil Mrs, 1961, My 10,45:5
Cosden, Alfred E, 1962, Ap 9,29:4
Cosden, Alfred H Mrs, 1950, Ja 17,27:3
Cosden, Joshua S, 1940, N 18,19:5
Cosden, Samuel G, 1944, S 25,17:3
Cosden, William, 1953, My 1,21:1
Cose, George B, 1947, Ja 1,33:4
Cose, John H, 1948, F 15,60:4
Cose, John H Jr, 1944, O 25,21:4
Cosentino, Anthony J, 1956, Ag 12,84:6
Cosentino, Sylvester, 1964, F 6,29:1
Cosentino, Ubaldo, 1951, Ap 3,27:5
Cosenza, Gaetano, 1951, S 13,31:5
Cosenza, Mario E, 1966, O 25,45:2
Cosgrave, Jessica G Mrs, 1949, N 1,27:1
Cosgrave, John O (por), 1947, S 20,15:1
Cosgrave, John O Mrs, 1952, Je 27,23:5
Cosgrave, John O'Hara 2d, 1968, My 11,35:2
Cosgrave, John S, 1940, Jl 14,31:4
Cosgrave, M, 1931, My 1,27:3
Cosgrave, Millicent, 1939, Je 26,15:4
Cosgrave, Percival J, 1944, N 30,23:2
Cosgrave, Wallace B, 1939, Mr 1,21:6
Cosgrave, William T, 1965, N 17,47:2
Cosgriff, Catherine, 1953, O 21,29:3
Cosgriff, George W, 1951, Ag 7,25:2
Cosgriff, Walter E, 1961, S 28,49:1
Cosgro, Daniel J, 1946, Jl 20,13:3
Cosgrove, E J (Ned), 1950, S 6,58:3
Cosgrove, Edward B, 1962, Ja 7,88:2
Cosgrove, Edward J, 1950, Mr 12,92:2
Cosgrove, Edwin F, 1961, Mr 11,21:5
Cosgrove, Gerard, 1949, O 25,27:1
Cosgrove, James A, 1943, Je 29,20:3
Cosgrove, James C Capt, 1908, D 1,9:5
Cosgrove, James E, 1910, D 26,7:5
Cosgrove, James F, 1938, Mr 23,23:2
Cosgrove, James J, 1939, Ap 26,23:3; 1960, Ag 24,29:1
Cosgrove, John D, 1959, My 14,33:5
Cosgrove, John D Mrs, 1951, Ja 25,25:3
Cosgrove, John J, 1945, Ag 30,21:3; 1955, Mr 29,29:2
Cosgrove, John P, 1951, D 15,13:7
Cosgrove, John S Mrs, 1955, D 23,17:1
Cosgrove, John T, 1948, N 4,30:3
Cosgrove, Joseph E, 1952, Ag 31,44:4
Cosgrove, Joseph F, 1959, F 23,23:3
Cosgrove, Michael J, 1948, D 7,31:2
Cosgrove, Philip, 1923, O 23,21:4
Cosgrove, Raymond, 1942, Ja 3,10:7
Cosgrove, Robert E, 1954, Ja 5,27:2
Cosgrove, Samuel A, 1960, F 29,27:5
Cosgrove, Walter E, 1945, F 28,23:4
Cosgrove, Warner G, 1946, Ja 11,21:1
Coshburn, Henry S, 1965, F 15,27:2
Coshland, Leopold B, 1943, Ag 11,19:4
Cosimini, Roland F, 1945, Jl 12,11:6
Cosine, C S, 1877, D 23,5:5
Cosinuke, John A, 1940, Ap 15,17:5
Cosio, Ricardo, 1943, N 2,25:2
Coskey, Frank S, 1964, Ag 22,21:6
Cosler, Moses C, 1937, Mr 27,15:3
Cosman, Edgar, 1949, Ag 9,25:1
Cosmany, Nicholas, 1946, Je 20,23:4
Cosmas Joseph, Bro (Christian Bros), 1964, My 11, 31:3
Cosmos, Alex, 1962, Jl 25,33:5
Cosmos y Sola, Jose Prof, 1937, D 3,23:3
Cosmus, Richard, 1952, Ag 2,15:4
Cosner, Bayless H, 1944, Mr 28,19:5
Coss, Harold T, 1952, Mr 14,23:1
Coss, John J, 1940, Ap 29,15:3
Cossa, P, 1881, S 18,7:1
Cossaart, Mollie M, 1964, My 20,43:4
Cossar, Walter L, 1937, S 28,23:2
Cossart, Ernest, 1951, Ja 22,17:3
Cossart, Mary E, 1954, Jl 30,17:5
Cossey, Harry Douglas, 1919, D 10,13:3
Cossiera, Emil, 1910, N 2,11:4
Cossman, Max (M Weber), 1960, Ag 21,80:6
Cost, Edward F, 1910, Mr 13,II,11:2
Costa, Alfonso De, 1915, Jl 14,9:6
Costa, Alfonso de, 1937, My 12,23:1
Costa, Bernardo da, 1947, Je 17,25:2
Costa, David, 1873, My 21,1:7
Costa, Edwin J (Eddie), 1962, Jl 31,17:2
Costa, Euclydes Z da, 1963, O 30,39:1
Costa, Frank, 1924, Je 28,13:4
Costa, Frederico A, 1961, N 13,31:4
Costa, Isabel (Mrs Frank X Gallagher), 1967, Je 2 68:5
Costa, Issac Col, 1937, Je 8,25:3
Costa, John J, 1954, Jl 15,27:6
Costa, Joseph, 1953, D 15,39:2
Costa, Leon de, 1951, My 11,27:2
Costa, Luigi, 1939, Je 22,23:6
Costa, M Sir, 1884, Ap 30,5:3
Costa, Michael J, 1940, My 4,17:6
Costa, Vicente, 1943, S 6,17:2
Costa, William G, 1968, My 6,47:2
Costa Ferreira, Eduardo, 1951, Ja 28,76:3
Costa Rego, Pedro, 1954, Jl 7,31:5
Costabile, Arnold A, 1965, F 1,23:4
Costabile, Michael Mrs, 1949, N 7,27:1
Costagini, Filippo, 1904, Ap 16,1:2
Costain, Ernest A, 1951, Mr 1,27:3
Costain, Richard, 1966, Mr 27,86:8
Costain, Thomas B (will, O 23,13:6), 1965, O 9,2
Costales, Jose de J, 1924, Ap 24,19:4
Costan, Ernest A Mrs, 1966, Mr 2,41:1
Costantini, D, 1936, Ja 11,15:3
Costantino, Arturo E, 1944, O 26,23:3
Costanza, Emil L, 1958, Jl 26,15:5
Costanza, John R, 1963, My 29,33:4
Costanza, Samuel, 1945, Ag 7,23:1
Costanzi, Victor J, 1953, Jl 25,11:2
Costanzo, Joseph, 1953, O 28,29:4
Costanzo, Ralph E, 1946, D 28,15:5
Costarelli, Luigi, 1963, Ag 1,27:4
Costberg, Henri E, 1959, Je 2,35:5
Coste, Eugene, 1940, Ja 25,21:5
Coste, Jean J M C V, 1873, S 24,5:5
Costellessa, Joseph C, 1948, S 22,31:4
Costello, Arthur H, 1953, F 6,19:4
Costello, Atkinson, 1939, Mr 31,21:4
Costello, Bartley C, 1941, Ja 16,21:5
Costello, Bernard J Sr, 1965, D 11,33:5
Costello, Charles, 1955, Mr 22,31:4
Costello, Charles A, 1942, S 13,53:3; 1954, Ja 15
Costello, Charles W, 1963, S 27,29:1
Costello, Clarence V, 1947, Je 2,25:6
Costello, Colman K, 1960, Jl 20,29:4
Costello, Daniel W, 1955, Ag 2,23:2
Costello, Dora, 1938, Mr 23,23:4
Costello, Edward H, 1944, S 25,17:3
Costello, Edward J, 1948, Ja 9,21:2
Costello, Edward P, 1939, Ja 10,19:5
Costello, Edward T, 1964, N 10,44:1
Costello, Frank (of Conn), 1966, D 22,33:3
Costello, H M M, 1947, Ag 12,23:3
Costello, Helene, 1957, Ja 29,31:3
Costello, J J, 1883, My 26,5:2
Costello, James B, 1954, N 7,88:1
Costello, James M (will, F 28,8:4), 1941, F 23,
Costello, James M, 1947, F 8,17:2
Costello, James P, 1947, O 1,29:3

Costello, James P Sr, 1945, Jl 23,19:4
Costello, James T, 1942, Ag 27,19:3
Costello, James W, 1943, F 15,15:3
Costello, John A Mrs, 1956, Ap 21,17:5
Costello, John F, 1938, N 21,19:5
Costello, John H Sr, 1949, N 1,27:3
Costello, John J, 1943, Mr 22,19:3
Costello, John M, 1941, Ag 16,15:6
Costello, John Mrs, 1938, Mr 26,15:3
Costello, John P, 1954, O 26,27:1
Costello, Lillian M, 1939, Jl 22,15:2
Costello, Lou (funl plans, Mr 6,25:4; funl, Mr 8,86:7), 1959, Mr 4,31:2
Costello, Lou Mrs, 1959, D 6,86:2
Costello, Louis B, 1959, My 7,33:5
Costello, Margaret C, 1953, Ag 12,31:5
Costello, Maurice, 1950, O 30,27:1
Costello, Maurice J, 1963, D 5,45:4
Costello, Maurice J Mrs, 1957, Ja 18,21:1
Costello, Michael J, 1938, Jl 17,27:3; 1945, D 6,27:3; 1949, Ja 8,15:2
Costello, Michael J Mrs, 1958, N 16,48:1
Costello, Patrick F, 1944, Mr 7,17:2
Costello, Peter M, 1940, S 23,17:1
Costello, Raymond J A, 1948, S 18,17:1
Costello, Thomas F, 1956, Ja 31,29:1
Costello, Thomas F Mrs, 1955, Mr 13,86:1
Costello, Thomas Mrs, 1951, My 29,25:4
Costello, Tim, 1962, N 8,39:2
Costello, Timothy A Mrs, 1968, Ag 28,47:3
Costello, Vincent, 1951, D 3,31:4
Costello, Walter, 1940, N 18,19:4
Costello, William F, 1945, Jl 27,15:4; 1947, Je 19,21:2
Costello, William H Jr, 1945, F 8,19:4
Costello, William J, 1945, Jl 12,13:6; 1952, O 28,31:3
Costello, William N Mrs, 1948, Ja 20,24:2
Costelloe, William H, 1937, Jl 29,19:2
Costelo, David, 1939, D 6,25:5
Costenbader, Charles, 1941, Mr 2,42:2
Costenla, Manuel, 1952, Jl 3,25:3
Coster, Charles G, 1956, S 19,37:3
Coster, Cornelius H P, 1965, My 2,88:2
Coster, Edward L Mrs, 1952, F 20,29:3
Coster, Eric H, 1937, Ja 30,17:3
Coster, Frank Mrs, 1953, Ag 10,23:5
Coster, Maurice, 1937, S 2,21:4
Coster, Maurice Mrs, 1957, Mr 13,31:4
Coster, Oliver D, 1947, Jl 12,13:2
Coster, Oliver D Mrs, 1937, Ap 24,9:4
Coster, William B, 1945, My 16,19:1
Coster, William B Mrs, 1947, Jl 24,21:5
Costerella, Dominick Mrs, 1954, O 15,23:3
Costerella, Flavius N, 1964, Ja 31,27:5
Costermans, Maurice, 1947, Ag 27,23:5
Costetti, Giovanni, 1949, S 5,17:3
Costi, Gaetano M, 1942, Ap 14,21:5
Costich, Emmett R, 1944, Jl 26,19:2
Costigan, Daniel E, 1949, Ap 25,23:1
Costigan, Dennis, 1907, N 19,9:5
Costigan, Edward P, 1939, Ja 18,19:3
Costigan, Edward P Mrs, 1951, S 23,86:3
Costigan, James J, 1954, S 1,27:3
Costigan, L Hubert, 1954, Jl 22,23:3
Costigan, Lucius R, 1952, Ap 20,93:2
Costigan, Lucius R Mrs, 1951, Je 5,31:1
Costigan, Philip J, 1964, Je 25,33:3
Costigan, T P, 1902, Mr 5,9:5
Costigan, Thomas, 1962, Ag 23,29:4
Costigan, William J, 1944, O 21,17:6
Costigan, William J Mrs, 1945, S 15,15:5
Costikyan, Kent R, 1963, Ap 14,92:7
Costikyan, Mihran N, 1964, Ap 7,35:2
Costikyan, S Kent (por), 1949, Jl 4,13:1
Costin, James M, 1949, My 9,25:2
Costine, David A, 1943, Ag 16,15:5
Costoff, Socrates, 1955, Mr 29,30:3
Costolow, Thomas A, 1952, S 3,29:3
Costolow, William E, 1959, N 23,31:6
Coston, Patrick W, 1948, Ap 21,27:2
Coston, William B F, 1954, S 22,29:4
Costopoulos, Stavros, 1968, Je 24,37:3
Costuma, David B, 1956, O 29,29:4
Costuma, Louis F, 1964, O 23,39:3
Cosulich, Guido, 1962, O 27,25:2
Cosulich, Letizia A Mrs, 1961, Ag 24,29:5
Cosulich, Simon J, 1951, Mr 27,29:2
Cot, P A, 1883, Ag 5,7:6
Cotarelo Valledor, Armando, 1950, D 9,15:3
Cotchett, Walter V, 1944, F 24,15:5
Cote, Alcide, 1955, Ag 8,21:4
Cote, Aubert, 1938, My 29,II,7:2
Cote, Henry J, 1940, Ap 29,15:3
Cote, Leon C, 1944, S 29,21:2
Cote, Pierre-Emile, 1950, Ag 4,21:4
Cote, Thomas, 1918, Ja 17,13:3
Cote, William L, 1939, Mr 2,21:2
Cotenoff, Harry, 1946, O 8,23:4
Cotes, Merton Russell Sir, 1921, Ja 29,11:5
Cotey, Frank A, 1954, Ap 24,17:3
Cotey, James A, 1964, N 5,45:2
Coth, Peter A, 1951, Mr 6,27:4
Cothran, Perrin C, 1959, D 23,27:3
Cotignold, Baron (Jochmus), 1881, S 25,5:4
Cotillo, Francis, 1938, N 7,19:5
Cotillo, Salvatore A, 1939, Jl 28,17:1
Cotillo, Salvatore A (will), 1940, Jl 23,19:1
Cotnareanu, Leon Mrs, 1966, Ja 7,29:2
Cotner, Winfield S, 1949, Ja 6,23:5
Cotnoir, Arthur B, 1948, Ag 27,12:8
Cotnran, Frank H, 1948, S 3,19:4
Cotopouli, Marika, 1954, S 12,84:1
Cotrell, Elizabeth L, 1941, Ja 23,21:5
Cotsworth, Albert, 1944, Je 15,19:5
Cotsworth, Moses B, 1943, Je 6,42:4
Cotsworth, Staats J, 1938, Mr 20,II,9:1
Cott, Belton N, 1955, My 7,17:4
Cott, Harry Mrs, 1957, Ag 9,19:3
Cott, Lewis P, 1963, O 20,88:7
Cott, William N, 1938, Ag 7,33:1
Cotta, Anthony, 1957, Ap 30,29:2
Cotta, D, 1879, S 17,5:4
Cottam, George W, 1944, Mr 11,13:6
Cottam, Herbert G, 1954, Ja 30,17:3
Cottar, Mike, 1941, O 23,23:3
Cotten, Henry, 1925, O 3,15:4
Cotten, Joseph Mrs, 1960, Ja 7,29:5
Cottenet, Fannie M, 1956, F 13,27:2
Cottenet, Francis, 1884, Ag 9,4:7
Cottenet, Rawlins L, 1951, Mr 31,15:4
Cottenham, Earl of (Keneim Chas Edw Pepys), 1919, Ap 23,17:2
Cottenham, Earl of, 1943, Jl 21,15:4
Cotter, Arundel, 1952, O 28,31:3
Cotter, Augustine, 1948, Ag 4,21:2
Cotter, Avis M, 1938, My 19,21:3
Cotter, Carrie E, 1948, N 22,21:3
Cotter, Charles F, 1949, Ag 28,75:3
Cotter, Daniel F, 1958, N 11,30:5
Cotter, Daniel J, 1941, Ag 12,19:2; 1956, Je 17,92:5
Cotter, Edward J, 1951, Ja 12,27:2
Cotter, Eugene, 1952, Ag 22,21:4
Cotter, Francis J, 1946, Je 9,40:5; 1964, O 3,29:4
Cotter, Garrett W, 1953, Ap 28,27:1
Cotter, George P, 1946, Ja 29,25:5
Cotter, Harold J, 1949, S 8,29:2
Cotter, Harry A, 1947, Je 11,27:2; 1967, Mr 9,39:1
Cotter, Henry C, 1948, Jl 7,23:1
Cotter, Henry M, 1940, S 22,49:2
Cotter, J William, 1964, Je 16,39:2
Cotter, James H, 1947, D 11,33:3
Cotter, James M, 1954, Mr 17,31:2
Cotter, Jesse A, 1939, S 11,19:6
Cotter, John, 1905, Mr 16,5:3
Cotter, John A, 1950, Jl 19,31:5
Cotter, John F, 1954, Ja 24,84:8
Cotter, John J, 1942, S 7,19:5
Cotter, John J Dr, 1925, F 12,19:3
Cotter, John Mrs, 1943, Je 14,17:3
Cotter, John W Mrs, 1950, S 13,28:2
Cotter, L Edward, 1953, D 27,61:1
Cotter, Lawrence Mrs, 1962, S 3,15:5
Cotter, Leo, 1955, Ag 7,73:2
Cotter, Raymond J, 1961, Jl 3,15:4
Cotter, Richard N, 1949, O 23,84:4
Cotter, Stephen E, 1946, Ja 17,23:2
Cotter, Thomas M, 1944, O 16,19:5
Cotter, Timothy J, 1938, S 20,2:7
Cotter, William Andre, 1918, Ap 4,13:4
Cotter, William E, 1920, Ag 23,11:5; 1947, My 1,25:2; 1957, Ag 17,15:3
Cotter, William E Mrs, 1950, O 24,29:5; 1962, S 17, 31:1
Cotter, William F, 1945, N 17,17:4; 1950, Je 18,76:1
Cotter, William H, 1946, F 12,28:2
Cotter, William L, 1952, Ja 6,93:1
Cotter, William M, 1937, Ap 24,19:3
Cotter, William T, 1940, O 25,21:5
Cotteral, J H, 1933, Ap 23,28:1
Cotterel, William D, 1951, Ja 16,29:4
Cotterell, Edward D, 1949, My 19,29:2
Cotterell, Wesley, 1965, Jl 8,28:3
Cotterill, Albert R, 1954, Je 22,27:5
Cotterill, Charles E, 1947, D 16,33:4
Cotterill, Ernest, 1909, N 4,11:5
Cotterill, George F Mrs, 1954, Ja 5,27:2
Cotters, John Mrs, 1943, S 4,13:6
Cottet, Richard, 1946, Ag 20,27:4
Cottier, Phil S, 1949, N 12,15:4
Cottier, Walter E, 1954, N 7,89:1
Cottin, Diantha W G Mrs, 1940, Mr 17,48:6
Cottine, E Bertram, 1947, N 28,27:1
Cotting, Addison G, 1944, Ap 27,23:4
Cotting, Jameson, 1946, F 8,19:3
Cottingham, George W, 1948, Ap 13,28:2
Cottingham, Isham E, 1943, Jl 12,15:5
Cottis, George W, 1950, O 23,23:1
Cottle, Cassius C, 1949, My 2,25:5
Cottle, William E, 1955, Je 30,25:5
Cottler, Zachary R, 1966, Jl 26,32:1
Cottman, J Hough, 1919, N 18,13:1
Cottman, Samuel J, 1941, Ag 10,37:2
Cottman, Vincendon L Rear-Adm, 1917, Mr 17,13:5
Cottom, Thomas I, 1950, D 7,33:5
Cotton, Aime Mrs, 1967, Je 17,31:4
Cotton, Arthur Cleveland Dr, 1916, Jl 13,11:6
Cotton, Arthur N, 1958, Mr 28,25:3
Cotton, Arthur N Mrs, 1949, Ap 21,25:2
Cotton, Charles H, 1938, Mr 17,21:2
Cotton, Charles M, 1951, S 5,31:5
Cotton, Charles Stanhope, 1909, F 20,7:4
Cotton, Donald R, 1951, Jl 18,29:2
Cotton, Edgar, 1948, My 13,25:2
Cotton, Edward B, 1957, My 24,25:2
Cotton, Elizabeth B Mrs, 1959, Ap 25,21:2
Cotton, Elizabeth Mrs, 1951, Ap 19,31:2
Cotton, Evan, 1939, Mr 8,21:3
Cotton, Francis R, 1960, S 26,33:1
Cotton, Frank A, 1964, Ag 19,37:3
Cotton, Frank B, 1907, My 14,11:7
Cotton, Fred A, 1964, Ja 30,29:4
Cotton, Frederick J, 1938, Ap 15,20:1
Cotton, H A, 1933, My 9,15:1
Cotton, Hamilton H, 1952, Ag 22,21:5
Cotton, J P, 1931, Mr 11,1:2
Cotton, Jack (details, Mr 23,29:1), 1964, Mr 22,76:5
Cotton, John M Mrs, 1961, D 19,33:2
Cotton, Joseph B, 1940, Ag 7,19:3
Cotton, Joseph D, 1949, S 24,13:3
Cotton, Joseph P, 1945, Ja 10,23:4
Cotton, Joseph P Mrs, 1944, N 16,23:4
Cotton, Lester R Mrs, 1952, Ag 23,13:6
Cotton, Lillian (Mrs A E Impey), 1962, O 10,47:4
Cotton, Margaret Mrs, 1939, Ja 11,19:5
Cotton, Maurice, 1944, F 3,19:4
Cotton, N Hugh Mrs, 1943, Je 23,21:1
Cotton, Norman T, 1953, N 20,23:4
Cotton, Paul W, 1948, Ja 15,23:5
Cotton, Richards W (cor, Jl 17,61:2), 1955, Jl 13,25:2
Cotton, Ruth C E Mrs, 1942, O 9,21:3
Cotton, Thomas L, 1964, My 26,39:3
Cotton, Walter G, 1907, S 10,7:6
Cotton, Will, 1958, Ja 6,39:4
Cotton, Willard R, 1949, Ap 9,17:6
Cotton, William D, 1949, Ag 29,17:4
Cotton, William H, 1909, N 8,7:4
Cotton, William H Maj-Gen, 1914, Ap 21,11:5
Cotton, William Sr Mrs, 1951, Ag 25,11:3
Cottor, Timothy, 1910, Je 24,9:6
Cottrell, Abram, 1944, Mr 5,21:3
Cottrell, Benjamin S Mrs, 1945, Mr 30,15:2
Cottrell, Burtis, 1948, D 25,18:3
Cottrell, Donald C, 1956, S 17,27:2
Cottrell, Edgar H, 1922, Mr 9,17:5
Cottrell, Edwin A, 1953, F 11,29:3
Cottrell, Elias Rev, 1937, D 7,25:5
Cottrell, Ella M, 1955, Je 7,33:1
Cottrell, Ensign S, 1947, F 28,23:4
Cottrell, Florance E, 1953, D 27,60:5
Cottrell, Frank, 1944, Jl 2,19:3
Cottrell, Fred C, 1948, D 7,64:5
Cottrell, Frederick G, 1948, N 17,27:1
Cottrell, George T, 1951, F 6,27:1
Cottrell, George Whitcomb, 1923, Ja 21,6:3
Cottrell, H Louise, 1957, Ap 24,33:3
Cottrell, Herbert Sr, 1957, Ag 28,27:3
Cottrell, J Case, 1958, My 14,33:2
Cottrell, James E, 1949, Ag 7,61:2
Cottrell, Jesse Mrs, 1952, N 30,87:4
Cottrell, Jesse S, 1944, Mr 25,15:3
Cottrell, John B, 1952, D 11,33:5
Cottrell, John C Mrs, 1948, My 27,25:4
Cottrell, John W, 1916, N 3,13:5
Cottrell, Judson G, 1956, F 12,89:2
Cottrell, Lew W, 1951, Jl 27,21:7
Cottrell, Myron, 1937, Jl 5,17:2
Cottrell, Nathan R, 1948, S 3,19:5
Cottrell, Osceola P, 1962, S 10,29:2
Cottrell, Robert J, 1953, My 28,23:2
Cottrell, Sylvester V Mrs, 1966, Jl 25,27:2
Cottrell, Willard M, 1939, Je 27,23:5
Cottrell, Williard, 1946, Jl 26,21:3
Cottrelly, M, 1933, Je 17,13:4
Cotts, Gerritt, 1947, My 15,25:2
Cotty, Kathleen Mary, 1925, Mr 23,17:4
Coty, F, 1934, Jl 26,19:1
Coty, Rene (funl plans, N 24,23:3; funl, N 28,39:4), 1962, N 23,29:1
Coty, Rene Mme (funl, N 17,35:3), 1955, N 12,19:3
Cotzhausen, Louis V, 1938, Ap 25,15:2
Coubertin, Marie de, 1963, My 7,43:2
Coubertin, Pierre de Baron, 1937, S 3,17:1
Couceiro, Henrique P, 1944, F 12,13:5
Couch, Arthur C, 1950, N 20,25:5
Couch, Arthur S, 1943, N 18,23:4
Couch, Asa Stone Dr, 1917, F 2,11:5
Couch, Benjamin W, 1945, N 5,19:3
Couch, Bradford M, 1937, Ap 24,19:4
Couch, Clifford, 1955, O 4,28:8
Couch, Daniel L, 1954, Ja 19,25:4
Couch, David W Rev, 1916, Je 25,18:5
Couch, Elbert L, 1937, O 9,19:1
Couch, Franklin Mrs, 1954, O 13,31:2
Couch, Frederick M, 1937, Ja 3,II,8:2
Couch, Harvey C, 1941, Jl 31,17:3
Couch, Herbert N, 1959, Je 7,86:5
Couch, Ira J, 1948, N 28,92:6
Couch, Isabelle C, 1955, Ag 14,81:2
Couch, James F, 1951, Ag 11,11:7
Couch, John R, 1909, My 28,9:6

Couch, Llewellyn H Jr, 1948, Ag 30,17:2
Couch, Louis Bradford Dr, 1921, Ap 21,13:5
Couch, Mathew R, 1959, My 31,76:5
Couch, Ralph F, 1948, F 24,25:4
Couch, Samuel Sr, 1944, Ja 3,22:2
Couch, Sarah M, 1946, Mr 21,25:5
Couch, Virgil L Mrs, 1949, Mr 16,27:4
Couch, Walter C, 1950, D 24,34:8
Couch, Walter D Mrs, 1944, Ag 22,17:5
Couch, William Mrs, 1961, Je 13,35:4
Couch, William S, 1914, Ja 12,9:6
Couchman, Albert R, 1957, D 11,31:1
Couden, Henry N Rev Dr, 1922, Ag 23,13:6
Coudenhove-Kalergi, Countess, 1951, Mr 29,27:4
Couderc, 1875, My 3,1:5
Coudert, C (see also 4a 2), 1880, Ja 3,8:4
Coudert, Charles Mrs, 1903, S 14,7:5
Coudert, Charles Mrs (Duchess de Choiseul), 1919, Mr 14,13:3
Coudert, Frederic R, 1955, Ap 2,17:1
Coudert, Frederic R Mrs, 1962, O 29,29:2
Coudert, Jeanne C Mrs, 1955, Ag 7,73:2
Coudert, L L, 1882, S 15,2:7
Coudert, Philippe G, 1944, F 14,17:4
Coudert, Victor R, 1966, Je 27,35:5
Coudrauz, Henri F V, 1952, Ap 17,4:3
Coue, P E, 1926, Jl 3,13:3
Coues, Elliott Mrs, 1925, Ja 31,13:5
Coues, Robert W, 1943, D 20,23:4
Coues, Samuel F Rear-Adm, 1916, My 2,13:7
Couey, Fred, 1964, N 20,37:2
Coughlan, Arthur, 1943, My 28,21:1
Coughlan, Edward A, 1959, Ag 21,21:4
Coughlan, Emmet P, 1942, My 8,21:4
Coughlan, George R, 1951, D 5,35:1
Coughlan, Harry O, 1954, Mr 3,27:4
Coughlan, John S, 1957, Mr 10,88:6
Coughlan, Michael J, 1950, My 16,31:2
Coughlan, Ted Mrs, 1947, Je 27,21:4
Coughlan, Thomas G, 1939, Je 3,15:5
Coughlan, Timothy M Col, 1937, N 24,23:4
Coughlan, William M, 1952, Jl 6,48:6
Coughlin, Alfred A, 1968, F 10,34:1
Coughlin, Ann B, 1953, O 18,86:3
Coughlin, Arthur M, 1954, F 10,29:1
Coughlin, Clarence D, 1946, D 16,23:3
Coughlin, Dennis J, 1946, Ag 7,27:4
Coughlin, Edward J, 1940, O 6,48:2; 1945, O 11,23:5
Coughlin, Edward M, 1953, O 25,89:2
Coughlin, Elizabeth H, 1949, Ja 11,31:2
Coughlin, Ellen T Mrs, 1948, Ja 7,25:1
Coughlin, Emory A, 1957, Je 4,35:5
Coughlin, Emory A Mrs, 1956, S 23,84:1
Coughlin, Francis J, 1955, Ap 19,31:3
Coughlin, Frank E, 1951, S 10,21:2
Coughlin, Frederick A, 1948, Ap 22,27:2
Coughlin, George F Sr, 1951, Ja 5,21:3
Coughlin, Gerald F, 1950, D 11,25:3
Coughlin, Hale S, 1956, O 3,33:2
Coughlin, Harry J Sr, 1949, D 13,38:1
Coughlin, Henry W, 1968, O 31,47:1
Coughlin, Herbert V, 1957, O 4,23:4
Coughlin, James A, 1953, Ap 21,27:4
Coughlin, James J, 1950, Mr 1,27:3
Coughlin, James L, 1958, Mr 19,31:4
Coughlin, James M, 1952, N 29,17:2
Coughlin, Jeremiah J, 1950, S 20,31:5
Coughlin, John C, 1944, N 6,19:3
Coughlin, John D, 1951, O 1,23:4; 1954, D 9,33:2
Coughlin, John F, 1952, Je 12,33:1
Coughlin, John G, 1952, My 11,92:6
Coughlin, John H F, 1956, O 21,87:2
Coughlin, John J, 1938, N 12,15:3; 1949, O 29,15:5
Coughlin, John P, 1959, O 26,29:4
Coughlin, John W Dr, 1920, D 4,13:4
Coughlin, Joseph A, 1962, N 4,88:5
Coughlin, Joseph D, 1951, S 21,23:3
Coughlin, Joseph F, 1941, Je 14,17:5
Coughlin, Joseph J, 1948, Ap 12,21:4
Coughlin, Joseph T, 1965, Je 25,33:4
Coughlin, Joseph W, 1942, Ag 25,23:3
Coughlin, Margaret C, 1945, Ap 18,23:4
Coughlin, Mary, 1921, My 8,22:2
Coughlin, Mary G, 1964, O 8,43:3
Coughlin, Maurice A, 1942, Ag 11,19:4
Coughlin, Maurice A Mrs, 1950, My 8,23:3
Coughlin, Michael J, 1956, O 22,29:4
Coughlin, Michael J Mrs, 1949, Je 29,28:3
Coughlin, Patrick B Mrs, 1959, My 3,86:4
Coughlin, Robert G, 1951, F 25,85:1
Coughlin, Thomas, 1912, F 1,13:4
Coughlin, Thomas J, 1948, F 27,21:1
Coughlin, Thomas P, 1965, Ap 10,30:1
Coughlin, Timothy J, 1951, F 15,31:5
Coughlin, Walter J, 1951, Mr 22,31:3
Coughlin, William, 1948, Ap 18,71:1
Coughlin, William F Mrs, 1950, Ja 3,25:5
Coughlin, William J, 1966, Mr 21,33:3
Coughlin, William Mrs, 1947, Ja 20,25:3
Coughlin, William P, 1943, My 8,15:2
Coughlin, William S, 1958, Ag 8,19:4
Coughtry, Frank G, 1958, N 4,27:1
Coughtry, William J, 1946, Mr 16,13:3

Cougle, Mary Mrs, 1940, F 7,21:5
Cougle, William H, 1956, Je 28,29:2
Cougnenc, Augustin L, 1945, S 4,23:2
Couig, J Dalton, 1964, D 20,68:7
Coul, Sherwood L, 1948, Ag 31,23:3
Coulborn, Rushton Dr, 1968, Ap 18,47:3
Coulbourn, John I, 1941, F 25,23:4
Coulby, Frank R, 1951, Ag 6,21:5
Coulby, Frank R Mrs, 1952, Je 4,27:4
Couldock, C W, 1898, N 28,7:1
Couldon, Joseph, 1940, F 20,21:2
Couldrey, Frank, 1946, Ap 22,21:4
Coules, Allan H, 1937, O 1,21:6
Coulhart, Eva R Mrs, 1937, Ap 6,23:2
Coulhart, Frazer, 1937, Ja 27,21:3
Coulin, Rogue F, 1945, N 23,23:2
Coull, J, 1880, O 29,2:7
Coull, Margaret A, 1950, Jl 15,13:3
Coull, William, 1942, My 10,42:5
Coulle, Peter Hercules Cardinal, 1912, S 12,11:5
Coulomb, Harry R, 1955, F 16,29:4
Coulon, Emile F, 1947, Ap 2,28:3
Coulon, Ernest J, 1951, Ag 15,27:4
Coulondre, Robert, 1959, Mr 12,31:3
Coulsen, G J A, 1882, O 29,9:2
Coulson, Elizabeth, 1941, Ja 11,17:2
Coulson, James, 1873, Ag 1,5:6
Coulson, W Lee, 1954, O 16,17:4
Coulson, William, 1947, Mr 26,25:3
Coulson, William H, 1960, Ap 8,31:1
Coulson, William H Mrs, 1963, O 31,33:1
Coulson, William J Mrs, 1947, Ag 22,15:6
Coulston, John W, 1952, Ja 15,27:4
Coulston, William J, 1959, Ja 18,88:4
Coult, Joseph, 1924, Mr 13,17:5; 1953, Mr 2,23:4
Coultaus, Charles B, 1950, Ja 18,31:3
Coulter, A Barklie, 1949, D 9,31:1
Coulter, A Capt, 1879, O 28,5:4
Coulter, Calvin B, 1940, My 11,19:5
Coulter, Calvin B Mrs, 1945, Ag 3,17:5
Coulter, Charles J, 1966, Mr 26,29:5
Coulter, Charles P, 1940, Ja 25,21:3
Coulter, Clarence, 1945, Ap 6,15:1
Coulter, Cornelia, 1960, Ap 29,31:1
Coulter, David, 1951, S 1,11:5
Coulter, Douglas, 1953, Ja 22,23:1
Coulter, Elmer D, 1943, D 12,68:5
Coulter, Ernest K, 1952, My 3,21:5
Coulter, Frazer Mrs, 1916, F 23,13:5
Coulter, H Roy, 1940, Je 5,25:4
Coulter, Harry C Mrs, 1946, Ja 8,23:4
Coulter, J Edgar, 1957, Ag 4,80:8
Coulter, J M, 1928, D 24,13:5
Coulter, J Ray, 1962, Jl 28,19:5
Coulter, James T, 1946, Mr 27,27:2
Coulter, John L, 1959, Ap 19,86:2
Coulter, John S, 1949, D 17,17:5
Coulter, John T Mrs (C Bennett),(funl, Jl 28,35:4), 1965, Jl 26,23:1
Coulter, John W, 1967, D 9,47:2
Coulter, Lelia E Mrs, 1942, Mr 23,15:5
Coulter, Leo, 1952, Je 8,87:1
Coulter, Merle C, 1958, Mr 19,31:2
Coulter, Sam, 1880, D 30,2:2
Coulter, Stanley E, 1943, Je 28,21:5
Coulter, Thomas B, 1938, S 28,25:3
Coulter, Thomas D, 1953, Mr 8,90:3
Coulter, Thomas J, 1948, Ap 1,25:5
Coulter, William A, 1955, O 14,27:3
Coulter, William C, 1956, F 26,88:6
Coulter, William J, 1960, Ag 15,23:1
Coulthard, Howard, 1950, O 26,31:1
Coulthard, John C, 1924, F 26,17:2
Coulthwaite, Tom, 1948, Ja 14,26:2
Coulton, Frederick, 1946, Jl 12,17:3
Coulton, George C, 1947, Mr 5,25:1
Coulton, Thomas E, 1965, Ja 23,25:1
Coultrap, McKendree W, 1938, Jl 12,20:2
Coulver, Gladys, 1921, O 7,17:3
Coumbe, Clement W, 1939, Jl 22,15:6
Coumont, Ogareff C, 1950, F 16,23:4
Coumoundouros, Grecian Premier, 1883, Mr 11,9:4
Counahan, James J, 1955, F 6,88:4
Councill, William Hooper Prof, 1909, Ap 18,11:5
Councilor, James A, 1945, F 15,19:3
Coundouriotis, Theodor, 1953, O 12,27:3
Couney, Martin A, 1950, Mr 2,27:2
Couniham, George E, 1947, Ap 15,25:3
Count Alessandro Manzoni, 1873, My 24,7:3
Count De Pourtales, 1874, S 6,1:7
Count De Verneuil, 1873, Je 5,5:6
Count Manderstroem, 1873, Ag 29,4:7
Countant, Alida, 1952, Jl 18,19:4
Countee, Samuel A, 1959, S 13,83:3
Countess Alice De Ferussac, 1874, N 24,8:3
Countess Brunnow, 1874, Mr 15,5:5
Countess of Kenmare, 1873, S 8,1:6
Countess of Paris (Isabelle de Montpensier), 1919, Ap 25,15:4
Countiss, Frederick N, 1953, D 20,77:1
Countryman, Edwin, 1914, Je 14,15:5
Countryman, Sol, 1948, Mr 4,25:4
Countryman, William A, 1943, Ap 26,19:2

Counts, Gerald A, 1964, Jl 31,23:4
Countway, David L, 1949, Je 18,13:3
Countway, Francis A, 1955, S 20,31:4
County, A J, 1944, Ag 22,17:3
Coupal, J F, 1935, Ja 4,22:1
Coupe, Frank H, 1957, O 7,27:5
Coupe, Henry F, 1952, Je 25,29:5
Coupe, Thomas L, 1944, Ap 3,42:6
Coupe, William H, 1923, Mr 31,13:5; 1946, Mr 18,21:3
Couper, Newton, 1907, O 22,9:4
Couper, Richard Hamilton, 1918, Mr 21,13:5
Couper, Victor A, 1938, My 17,24:4
Couper, William, 1942, Je 25,23:2
Couper, William A Mrs, 1939, Jl 21,19:5
Couperthwait, John, 1955, Je 9,29:1
Couperus, Louis, 1923, Jl 17,19:6
Coupland, John W, 1944, Jl 20,19:4
Coupland, Reginald, 1952, N 7,23:4
Courage, William R, 1949, Ap 2,15:5
Courain, Daniel J Sr, 1953, Je 25,27:5
Courbet, Adm, 1885, Je 16,5:1
Courbet, G, 1878, Ja 1,5:2
Courcel, Alphonse de Baron, 1919, Je 18,17:4
Courchesne, Georges, 1950, N 16,31:4
Couri, Arthur N, 1954, N 25,29:5
Courland, Maurice, 1957, N 18,31:2
Courlis, Ira Moore Rev, 1903, Jl 21,9:6
Cournand, Andre F Mrs, 1959, N 23,31:2
Courneen, Frank D, 1958, S 14,84:4
Cournos, Alex, 1948, Jl 16,19:1
Cournos, John, 1966, Ag 28,93:1
Cournos, John Mrs (S Norton), 1959, Ag 16,31:4
Courreges, Pierre Mrs, 1948, Ag 12,21:2
Coursen, Edward I, 1951, N 21,25:4
Coursen, Frederick W, 1940, Jl 21,28:7
Coursen, H Preston, 1954, Jl 2,19:2
Coursen, Hampton Aaron, 1908, D 20,11:5
Coursen, Robert L, 1917, D 11,15:6
Coursen, W Melville, 1961, F 5,80:2
Coursen, Walter L, 1941, Je 26,23:2
Courser, Fitts H, 1937, F 28,II,9:1
Coursey, Thomas H, 1968, Ja 5,24:1
Coursol, Frank, 1951, Ja 15,17:4
Court, George H, 1940, Mr 1,21:3
Court, James F, 1948, Je 24,26:3
Court, Josiah, 1938, F 9,19:4
Court, Nathan Altshiller Dr, 1968, Jl 25,33:4
Court, Raymond A, 1947, Ag 11,23:5
Courtade, Joseph N Mrs, 1947, Mr 27,27:5
Courtade, Pierre, 1963, My 15,40:2
Courtauld, Augustine, 1959, Mr 4,31:1
Courtauld, John S, 1942, Ap 21,23:4
Courtauld, Samuel, 1947, D 3,29:6
Courtauld, Samuel A, 1953, Ja 30,22:3
Courtauld-Thomson, Courtauld G, 1954, N 2,27:4
Courteen, Louis de Count, 1937, Mr 7,II,9:2
Courteen, Sidney G Mrs, 1947, S 23,25:5
Courten, Henry C, 1940, O 16,23:6
Courtenay, Adrian H, 1939, N 27,17:5
Courtenay, W, 1933, Ap 21,17:1
Courtenay, William, 1960, Je 9,33:3
Courteney, Fay, 1943, Jl 23,17:2
Courter, Claude V, 1964, Je 29,27:3
Courter, Edward A, 1958, Jl 6,56:6
Courter, George H, 1948, Jl 20,23:2
Courter, James E Mrs, 1950, D 12,33:3
Courter, Walter S, 1961, Jl 14,23:1
Courtessis, Alexander N, 1967, Ap 3,33:2
Courth-Maler, Hedwig, 1950, N 28,31:1
Courthope, Loyd G Lord, 1955, S 4,56:2
Courtial, Eve, 1954, Ap 19,23:4
Courtial, Gabriel, 1960, Ja 11,45:4
Courtis, Frank Rear-Adm, 1908, Ja 21,7:6
Courtleigh, W, 1930, D 28,26:8
Courtneidge, Robert, 1939, Ap 7,21:4
Courtney, Arthur J, 1950, O 17,31:4
Courtney, Arthur W, 1961, Jl 6,29:4
Courtney, Basil S, 1955, My 29,45:1
Courtney, Caroline Louisa Mrs, 1909, S 9,9:6
Courtney, Carrie C F Mrs, 1940, Ap 11,25:2
Courtney, Charles, 1947, D 30,23:1
Courtney, D G Mrs, 1954, S 18,15:7
Courtney, Ellen Mrs, 1939, D 12,27:3
Courtney, Frances, 1943, Ja 18,15:2
Courtney, Frederick Bp, 1919, Ja 2,9:3
Courtney, Frederick Rev, 1918, D 31,11:4
Courtney, George, 1915, Jl 3,7:4
Courtney, George J, 1952, Ap 28,19:4
Courtney, Giles L, 1942, Mr 2,19:2
Courtney, Harry U, 1950, Jl 25,27:4
Courtney, Hugh M, 1937, Jl 8,23:5
Courtney, J E, 1948, My 31,19:4
Courtney, J M, 1881, Je 22,2:1
Courtney, Jack P, 1937, F 26,21:3
Courtney, James Mrs, 1947, Jl 8,23:5
Courtney, Jeremiah J, 1948, D 12,92:8
Courtney, John, 1905, D 15,9:5; 1957, Ja 29,31:5
Courtney, John H, 1941, O 23,23:2
Courtney, Paul G, 1945, N 6,19:2
Courtney, Ralph (trb lr, Jl 17,24:6), 1965, Jl 2,2
Courtney, Robert W Rev, 1937, Ja 10,II,10:8
Courtney, S G, 1885, F 11,5:5
Courtney, Thomas J, 1942, Mr 24,19:4

Courtney, Thomas James, 1953, F 16,21:4
Courtney, Wilbur E, 1962, Jl 17,25:4
Courtney, William, 1903, O 3,9:6
Courtney, William A, 1948, Ag 31,24:2
Courtney, William H, 1954, D 12,88:3
Courtown, Earl of (J R N Stopford), 1957, Ja 26,3:1
Courtrade, George N, 1962, Jl 21,19:2
Courtright, B Frank, 1947, O 18,15:4
Courtright, Junior A, 1956, N 10,19:4
Courtright, Raymond D, 1965, Mr 24,46:4
Courts, Malon C, 1957, Jl 1,23:5
Courtsounis, John, 1959, Mr 21,23:1
Coury, Joseph M, 1951, Jl 1,1:1
Cousart, James B, 1959, Ag 22,17:5
Couse, Clarence M, 1953, Ap 14,27:5
Couse, Joseph M, 1959, F 14,21:3
Couse, William J, 1953, Je 8,29:2
Couse, William J Mrs, 1952, D 16,31:3
Cousens, John A, 1937, Jl 3,15:5
Cousens, Lyman A, 1941, Je 16,15:1
Couser, Walter J Sr, 1955, Ja 1,13:2
Cousin, Edward J Mrs, 1956, My 9,33:3
Cousin, Victor, 1867, Ja 27,5:1
Cousineau, Edward T, 1951, Jl 16,21:5
Cousino, Adriana, 1948, Je 2,29:1
Cousins, Adelaide M, 1952, Mr 24,25:5
Cousins, Arthur G, 1949, S 26,25:4
Cousins, Christopher C, 1947, D 18,29:4
Cousins, Edward L, 1961, F 11,23:4
Cousins, Edward O, 1944, N 3,21:3
Cousins, Fred W, 1953, My 24,88:4
Cousins, H Gordon, 1965, D 1,47:3
Cousins, Joseph, 1947, Je 15,60:3
Cousins, Joseph A, 1949, O 17,23:1
Cousins, Ralph P, 1964, Mr 16,31:1
Cousins, Wilfred S, 1944, My 10,19:4
Cousins, William L, 1952, F 17,84:7
Cousins, William M, 1953, Ja 16,23:2
Cousley, Stanley W, 1958, My 7,35:2
Coussa, Gabriele A, 1962, Jl 30,23:1
Coussell, E E, 1947, D 30,23:4
Coussens, Penrhyn W, 1944, Ap 27,23:4
Coutan, Jules, 1939, F 24,19:3
Coutant, Augustus, 1951, Ja 9,29:4
Coutant, Homer O, 1944, Je 29,23:5
Coutant, Richard, 1921, S 14,19:5
Coutant, Robert B, 1949, Je 2,28:5
Coutant, Robert G, 1940, Ag 8,19:4
Coutant, Russel S, 1966, My 5,47:5
Coutant, Simon, 1948, S 23,29:5
Coutard, Henri, 1950, Mr 20,21:5
Couter, George S, 1960, F 9,31:4
Coutermarsh, Joseph A, 1939, Ag 20,32:2
Couthoui, Florence Mrs, 1937, Je 12,15:4
Coutinho, Carlos V G, 1959, F 19,31:2
Coutinho, Manuel R, 1957, Ag 14,25:2
Coutlee, Douglas W, 1961, F 18,19:5
Coutlee, George H Mrs, 1948, Je 17,25:2
Coutney, Ada Mrs, 1948, O 6,29:1
Couto, J F de (see also Jl 4), 1877, Jl 6,8:3
Couts, John F, 1944, F 16,17:5
Couttet, Alfred, 1925, S 3,25:4
Coutts, Alan, 1963, O 16,45:4
Coutts, C R V, 1938, O 18,25:3
Coutts, Frances H, 1951, D 23,22:5
Coutts, Frederick Mrs, 1967, D 14,47:3
Coutts, J H, 1904, Ja 9,9:6
Coutts-Bain, Catherine, 1939, Ag 29,21:5
Couture, Joseph, 1949, Mr 6,72:1
Couture, Louis V Mrs, 1923, Je 23,11:5
Couture, Thomas, 1879, Ap 1,2:4
Couturier, Ernst A, 1950, Mr 2,27:2
Couturier, Felix, 1941, Jl 28,13:5
Couturier, Pierre M, 1954, F 11,29:2
Couvreur, A J L, 1944, D 15,19:4
Couza, Alexander John Prince, 1873, My 2,3:7
Couzens, Frank, 1950, N 1,35:1
Couzens, Gerald S Mrs, 1949, O 23,86:3
Couzens, Homer J, 1951, D 3,33:6
Couzens, J, 1936, O 23,1:4
Couzens, James J, 1937, Ja 31,II,8:5
Couzens, James Mrs, 1961, My 23,39:3
Couzens, John C, 1947, S 23,25:4
Couzins, Phoebe (funl, D 9,11:4), 1913, D 7,19:3
Covarrciblas, Miguel, 1924, Jl 8,19:4
Covarrubias, Miguel, 1957, F 6,25:1
Covart, Frank J Sr, 1946, O 17,23:3
Covas, Coralie R, 1947, Ja 2,27:3
Covas, John S, 1945, Ap 18,23:2
Covas, S, 1881, S 17,5:5
Cove, Harry D, 1955, S 23,50:8
Covel, Borden, 1959, Mr 14,23:4
Coveleskie, Harry, 1950, Ag 5,15:6
Covell, C Herbert Mrs, 1951, Ap 27,23:3
Covell, Carrie L, 1946, Mr 25,25:3
Covell, Charles H, 1915, O 23,11:5; 1954, Ja 1,23:5
Covell, F Clyde, 1948, F 4,23:4
Covell, Grant A Mrs, 1948, N 21,88:3
Covell, Henry H, 1950, Ap 8,13:2
Covell, Henry H Mrs, 1961, N 11,23:4
Covell, Leon C, 1960, N 26,21:4
Covell, Otis D, 1965, N 13,29:4
Covelli, Vito Mrs, 1955, Ja 22,11:1
Covello, Oscar, 1942, F 18,19:4
Coven, E Robert, 1952, F 29,23:2
Coven, Gerald, 1962, Ja 7,88:8
Coveney, Charles C, 1945, D 21,21:2
Coveney, James A, 1968, Jl 24,50:3
Coveney, Phil P, 1940, Ja 30,19:3
Coventry, Florence, 1939, N 23,27:4
Coventry, Frederick J, 1949, Mr 4,21:3
Coveos, Dimitrie C, 1920, D 28,11:4
Cover, Berkey E Sr, 1946, D 16,23:4
Cover, George, 1947, Ja 30,27:4
Cover, Howell T, 1960, Ag 6,41:1
Cover, J C, 1872, Jl 17,1:6
Cover, Rodney A, 1964, N 1,89:1
Cover, Thomas Jr, 1937, S 24,21:2
Coverdale, David Mrs, 1952, Je 6,23:2
Coverdale, William H (por), 1949, Ag 11,23:1
Coverdale, William H Mrs, 1955, Je 15,31:4
Coverley, Dudley C, 1957, Jl 18,25:5
Coverly, John Henderson Dr, 1908, F 25,7:4
Coverly, William, 1917, D 27,11:6
Covert, Adrian V, 1938, Ag 24,21:5
Covert, Alfred M, 1965, Ja 6,39:1
Covert, Charles N, 1950, N 21,31:5
Covert, Earl B, 1940, Ja 27,13:5
Covert, James W, 1910, My 18,11:4
Covert, John C, 1919, Ja 15,11:2
Covert, John R, 1942, N 29,64:6
Covert, Manton F, 1950, N 9,33:5
Covert, Marshall H, 1964, D 4,39:3
Covert, Nathaniel, 1951, Ja 19,25:3
Covert, Walter H, 1949, Ag 22,21:5
Covert, William C, 1942, F 5,21:3
Covert, William C Mrs, 1954, S 3,17:4
Covery, Fred B, 1957, F 15,23:4
Covey, Arthur S, 1960, F 6,19:5
Covey, Earl W, 1952, Ag 24,89:2
Covey, George H, 1943, My 25,23:5
Covici, Pascal, 1964, O 15,39:4
Coville, Charles R, 1950, Mr 24,26:3
Coville, Edward G, 1943, Je 1,23:1
Coville, Frederick V Dr, 1937, Ja 10,II,10:4
Coville, Mark F, 1950, Jl 16,69:2
Covington, Caroline W, 1965, Ap 7,43:1
Covington, G B, 1927, F 16,23:5
Covington, G W Jr, 1949, Jl 13,27:4
Covington, George W, 1953, D 31,19:5
Covington, Henry B, 1962, My 8,39:2
Covington, J Harry, 1942, F 6,19:1
Covington, John C Mrs, 1937, D 4,17:5
Covington, John R Mrs, 1955, Je 4,15:3
Covington, Platt W, 1940, Ap 21,42:3
Covington, Robert W, 1949, Mr 22,25:5
Covington, Tom, 1966, My 30,10:5
Covington, William W, 1946, S 1,36:1
Covino, Charles, 1959, F 28,19:6
Covner, Albert H, 1951, O 28,1:2
Covo, Jose M, 1951, Mr 25,72:4
Covode, James Henry, 1909, O 10,13:6
Covode, John, 1871, Ja 12,1:2
Cowan, Alex, 1941, Ja 19,40:2
Cowan, Alexander B, 1947, N 14,23:4
Cowan, Andrew Col, 1919, Ag 24,22:4
Cowan, Bernard M, 1947, Ja 31,15:4
Cowan, David Mrs, 1945, O 30,19:4
Cowan, Edwin A, 1941, Jl 29,15:2
Cowan, Elizabeth C Mrs, 1953, Ag 22,15:4
Cowan, Elmer S, 1950, Ap 17,23:4
Cowan, Fletcher, 1938, N 18,22:3
Cowan, Frank A, 1957, Je 22,15:5
Cowan, Frank B, 1939, Ag 30,17:3
Cowan, Frank Dr, 1905, F 13,7:6
Cowan, Frank I, 1948, F 24,25:2
Cowan, Frank M, 1954, N 29,25:4
Cowan, Frederick W, 1949, Ja 28,21:4
Cowan, George I, 1945, Ja 4,19:1
Cowan, George T, 1967, F 22,29:4
Cowan, Harrison J, 1967, Je 6,47:3
Cowan, Harry W, 1941, N 25,27:7
Cowan, Harry W Mrs, 1952, N 7,23:3
Cowan, Hector W, 1941, O 21,23:6
Cowan, Henry B Sr, 1963, O 20,88:8
Cowan, Henry F, 1951, Mr 4,92:3
Cowan, I Newton, 1960, F 29,27:4
Cowan, Isabel, 1951, Ja 3,25:2
Cowan, James, 1884, N 22,5:3
Cowan, James K, 1943, Mr 9,23:3
Cowan, James R, 1940, Mr 27,24:2
Cowan, Joseph M, 1961, O 27,33:3
Cowan, Louis, 1961, Je 13,35:3
Cowan, Marcy H Mrs, 1968, Ap 26,47:5
Cowan, Maurice, 1966, Je 27,35:2
Cowan, Oliver T, 1962, D 5,47:2
Cowan, Perez Dickinson Rev, 1923, F 11,6:2
Cowan, Phil, 1967, D 20,45:2
Cowan, Royden G, 1945, Ag 10,15:3
Cowan, Rubey, 1957, Jl 30,23:1
Cowan, Sada, 1943, Ag 3,19:3
Cowan, Samuel, 1959, My 17,83:1
Cowan, Sarah E, 1958, Ja 17,25:2
Cowan, Stuart D, 1956, My 3,31:6
Cowan, Thomas, 1948, Ja 27,25:4
Cowan, Thomas H, 1942, N 4,23:1
Cowan, W C Mrs, 1949, Mr 22,25:1
Cowan, Walter H, 1956, F 15,31:2
Cowan, Walter J, 1967, Ap 28,41:2
Cowan, William A, 1939, O 28,15:2; 1952, Je 14,15:3
Cowan, William G, 1948, N 25,31:5
Cowan, William J, 1944, F 13,42:1; 1953, Ja 31,15:5
Cowan, William Leighton, 1909, N 27,9:4
Cowan, William T Sr, 1964, Mr 3,35:3
Cowan, William W, 1937, Ja 5,23:3
Cowanlock, Andrew K, 1919, F 26,11:3
Cowanova, Mary E, 1939, F 26,38:6
Cowans, John Steven Sir, 1921, Ap 17,23:4
Cowans, William, 1947, Ap 3,25:4
Cowap, Charles R, 1939, Jl 28,17:5
Coward, Arthur, 1937, S 14,23:6
Coward, Arthur Mrs, 1954, Jl 1,25:3
Coward, Barry G, 1968, Ap 20,33:4
Coward, Cecil A, 1938, Jl 30,13:6
Coward, Edwin H, 1942, Je 11,23:3
Coward, Harold W, 1961, Ag 13,89:2
Coward, Henry, 1944, Je 12,19:6
Coward, J M, 1928, Mr 6,27:3
Coward, Jacob M, 1943, Ap 4,40:8
Coward, James Moore, 1925, D 11,23:3
Coward, James S, 1923, Mr 13,22:5
Coward, Jesse G, 1963, My 22,41:4
Coward, John Mortimer, 1925, D 10,25:5
Coward, Joseph, 1944, Je 18,35:2
Coward, Joseph B, 1907, Jl 26,7:6
Coward, Mary Mrs, 1939, My 10,23:4
Coward, Matt R, 1955, Ja 29,15:5
Coward, Minnie V Mrs, 1940, Ap 1,19:4
Coward, R A, 1950, Mr 20,21:5
Coward, Raymond A, 1963, Ap 4,47:1
Coward, Thomas R, 1957, Ja 13,84:3
Cowardin, Frank P, 1957, Mr 11,25:5
Cowardin, J A, 1882, N 22,5:4
Cowart, Samuel C, 1943, Ap 24,13:3
Cowden, Thaddeus, 1937, S 23,27:3
Cowdery, Bess H Mrs, 1947, F 15,15:5
Cowdery, Frank D, 1949, Ag 26,20:8
Cowdery, Frank M, 1947, D 4,31:5
Cowdin, E C, 1880, Ap 13,5:2
Cowdin, Elliott Channing, 1917, Ap 29,19:5
Cowdin, J Cheever, 1960, S 16,31:1
Cowdin, John E, 1941, Ja 8,19:1
Cowdin, John E Mrs, 1908, My 6,7:5
Cowdin, Robert Gen, 1874, Jl 10,4:6
Cowdin, Winthrop Mrs, 1938, Mr 3,21:1
Cowdray, Viscount, 1927, My 2,21:1; 1933, O 6,17:3
Cowdray, Viscountess, 1948, F 20,28:3
Cowdrey, Loren M, 1945, O 28,44:2
Cowdrick, Edward S, 1951, My 25,27:2
Cowdrick, William D, 1951, N 14,31:3
Cowee, George F, 1950, D 27,27:3
Cowell, Eugene J, 1954, My 31,13:1
Cowell, Henry, 1965, D 11,33:1
Cowell, John M Sr, 1950, F 5,84:4
Cowell, Lambert M, 1964, Mr 25,41:4
Cowell, Mark, 1939, D 4,23:4
Cowell, Richard N, 1953, Ja 9,21:4
Cowell, Samuel, 1864, Ap 3,2:4
Cowell, William H, 1940, Ag 29,19:5
Cowels, Emil, 1954, N 10,33:4
Cowen, Arthur S, 1963, Ag 27,31:3
Cowen, Benjamin Rush, 1908, Ja 30,7:5
Cowen, Charles A, 1909, D 27,7:7; 1953, Ja 15,27:6
Cowen, David J, 1937, Je 12,15:3
Cowen, Donald D, 1967, Je 23,39:1
Cowen, Dora T Mrs, 1949, D 27,23:4
Cowen, F H, 1935, O 7,15:5
Cowen, Harry G, 1957, F 22,21:2
Cowen, Isaac, 1907, My 29,7:6
Cowen, J K, 1904, Ap 26,1:4
Cowen, Joseph Sir, 1873, D 22,5:4
Cowen, Joshua L, 1965, S 9,41:3
Cowen, Julius A Mrs, 1959, My 15,30:1
Cowen, Max, 1952, Ap 23,54:5
Cowen, Myron M, 1965, N 3,39:1
Cowen, Myron M Mrs, 1967, Jl 28,31:2
Cowen, Newman, 1912, Ja 16,13:3
Cowen, Phil Mrs, 1939, S 29,23:2
Cowen, Philip, 1943, Ap 21,25:1
Cowen, Tracy Mrs, 1953, D 26,13:4
Cowenhoven, Charles T Ex-Judge, 1921, Mr 10,13:4
Cowenhoven, Gerett, 1903, Ag 1,7:6
Cowenhoven, Nicholas R, 1949, O 29,15:3
Cowger, David L, 1967, My 15,43:2
Cowgill, Edna P Mrs, 1938, N 15,23:4
Cowgill, Henry G, 1965, Je 28,29:3
Cowgill, James S Mayor, 1922, Ja 21,13:4
Cowgill, Thomas W Prof, 1911, Ag 13,II,9:6
Cowgill, William, 1949, Ag 19,17:4
Cowgill, William V, 1952, Ap 17,29:4
Cowgill, William W Mrs, 1947, D 20,17:6
Cowham, Frederick E, 1945, Je 5,19:3
Cowham, Joseph H Mrs, 1945, O 11,23:2
Cowham, Robert N, 1957, Ap 12,25:1
Cowherd, William B, 1938, Mr 10,21:2
Cowhey, Joseph L, 1967, Ag 22,39:3
Cowie, Alex H, 1948, Jl 7,46:3
Cowie, David M, 1940, Ja 28,32:5
Cowie, Effie W Mrs, 1939, F 23,23:3

Cowie, George H, 1938, Ap 5,21:4
Cowie, George H Mrs, 1953, Ja 15,27:5
Cowie, Jack B, 1966, My 18,47:3
Cowie, Percy, 1950, Ja 2,23:2
Cowie, R E M, 1934, Je 23,13:4
Cowie, William R Mrs, 1950, Jl 20,25:3
Cowin, John C, 1918, D 23,11:5
Cowing, Edward K, 1946, O 12,19:2
Cowing, H K (see also Ap 23), 1878, Ap 28,8:5
Cowing, Marguerite L Mrs, 1941, Mr 17,17:4
Cowing, Raymond H, 1952, S 25,31:6
Cowing, Rufus B Ex-Judge, 1920, My 8,15:4
Cowing, Rufus B Jr, 1938, Jl 3,13:2
Cowing, Rufus Mrs, 1949, Jl 14,28:2
Cowing, Susan E Mrs, 1951, N 21,25:4
Cowl, Clarkson, 1940, O 30,23:3
Cowl, Clarkson Mrs, 1944, N 27,23:3
Cowl, Donald H, 1957, Ag 25,86:3
Cowl, Jane, 1950, Je 23,25:1
Cowl, Jane (est tax appr), 1954, S 22,40:7
Cowl, William Henry, 1917, F 19,11:5
Cowles, A H, 1929, Ag 15,23:5
Cowles, A R Mrs, 1931, Ag 26,19:1
Cowles, Alfred, 1939, Ja 16,15:1
Cowles, Alfred Abernethy, 1916, D 9,11:5
Cowles, Alice M Mrs, 1922, S 7,17:5
Cowles, Arthur W, 1938, Jl 22,17:2
Cowles, Augustus W Rev, 1913, Mr 16,IV,7:4
Cowles, Beecher M, 1948, Ag 6,17:4
Cowles, Calvin D Col, 1937, Je 23,25:4
Cowles, Charles H, 1941, Mr 22,15:4
Cowles, Charles P, 1920, S 18,9:2
Cowles, Daniel H, 1946, My 1,25:3
Cowles, David C, 1911, N 7,13:4
Cowles, E P Judge (trb), 1875, Ja 5,2:6
Cowles, Edward S (cor, N 19,23:5), 1954, N 17,31:2
Cowles, Edward W Dr, 1919, Jl 26,9:7
Cowles, Edwin, 1968, F 7,47:4
Cowles, Elizabeth Mrs, 1923, Mr 31,13:5
Cowles, Eugene C, 1948, S 24,25:3
Cowles, Francis R, 1952, Je 2,21:6
Cowles, Frank H, 1947, O 2,27:5
Cowles, Frank L, 1944, D 3,57:3
Cowles, Fred G, 1949, O 15,15:2
Cowles, Gardner, 1946, Mr 1,21:1
Cowles, Gardner Sr Mrs (will, My 27,34:4), 1950, Mr 24,25:1
Cowles, George P, 1957, Ap 25,31:1
Cowles, Harriet S Mrs, 1941, Ja 31,19:1
Cowles, Henry C, 1939, S 13,25:6
Cowles, Henry c, 1951, S 11,29:3
Cowles, J Proctor Maj, 1921, Ag 20,7:7
Cowles, James Lewis, 1922, O 23,15:3
Cowles, John H, 1954, Je 19,15:6
Cowles, Joseph G, 1953, Ja 13,27:1
Cowles, Josiah E Mrs, 1940, Jl 6,15:7
Cowles, Julia Darrow, 1919, S 8,13:4
Cowles, Justus A B (will, F 29,42:1), 1940, F 7,21:1
Cowles, Leroy E, 1957, Ja 3,31:3
Cowles, Louise F, 1924, My 7,21:3
Cowles, Mary Hitchcock Mrs, 1906, N 13,9:4
Cowles, Matilda P Mrs, 1937, S 10,23:1
Cowles, Noble P, 1965, S 7,39:4
Cowles, Rheinart P, 1948, N 17,27:2
Cowles, Robert R, 1957, D 31,18:1
Cowles, Russel A Mrs, 1925, Ja 8,25:5
Cowles, Russell A, 1953, N 17,31:2
Cowles, Torris Z, 1919, D 5,15:2
Cowles, W H Mrs, 1938, Ap 11,15:4
Cowles, Walter Cleveland, 1917, N 27,13:3
Cowles, Walter G, 1942, My 31,38:6
Cowles, Walter G Mrs, 1940, O 25,21:4
Cowles, Walter R, 1959, D 10,39:3
Cowles, Wendell H, 1963, Jl 28,64:2
Cowles, William B, 1942, F 12,23:5
Cowles, William H, 1946, Ja 16,23:1; 1951, O 29,23:5
Cowles, William O, 1953, N 17,31:1
Cowles, William Sheffield Rear-Adm, 1923, My 2,19:3
Cowley, C Frank, 1943, Ja 19,20:3
Cowley, Clare Countess, 1949, My 9,27:6
Cowley, Countess, 1946, Je 6,21:4
Cowley, G Spencer, 1947, My 16,23:2
Cowley, Greer W, 1949, F 19,15:4
Cowley, H R C W, 1884, Jl 16,2:7
Cowley, Horace A, 1954, D 10,27:3
Cowley, J Paul, 1956, F 5,86:5
Cowley, James P, 1965, My 18,39:4
Cowley, John, 1944, O 30,19:2
Cowley, Lord (Hy Arth Mornington Wellesley), 1919, Ja 16,13:3
Cowley, Matthew, 1953, D 14,31:3
Cowley, William, 1939, D 21,23:5
Cowley, William F Mrs, 1952, Ag 17,76:3
Cowlin, Edward J, 1945, F 21,19:4
Cowling, Donald J, 1965, N 29,35:3
Cowling, William C, 1956, N 11,86:4
Cowlson, James, 1873, Jl 31,8:5
Cownie, Charles T, 1949, D 25,16:2
Cowper, Francis Thomas de Grey Earl, 1905, Jl 20,7:5
Cowper, George Mrs, 1965, Ap 6,39:2
Cowper, John M, 1943, Ag 9,13:7
Cowper, John W, 1944, Je 8,21:3
Cowperthwait, Charles T, 1940, Ja 28,33:2
Cowperthwait, William D, 1949, Jl 15,19:4
Cowperthwaite, Charles C, 1948, S 17,25:1
Cowperthwaite, Charles C Mrs, 1948, Mr 5,21:4
Cowperthwaite, Henry W, 1947, My 13,25:1
Cowperthwaite, J Fred, 1938, Mr 7,17:4
Cowperthwaite, J Howard, 1938, F 12,15:6
Cowperthwaite, John K Mrs, 1916, F 27,17:5
Cowperthwaite, Nathalie W Mrs, 1938, D 25,15:2
Cowperthwaite, Walter, 1944, Je 16,19:3
Cowpland, C Connor, 1944, F 14,17:2
Cox, A Robert, 1949, Jl 5,23:4
Cox, Abraham B, 1959, N 11,35:5
Cox, Agnes E, 1954, Ap 28,31:5
Cox, Albert L, 1965, Ap 17,19:6
Cox, Albert V, 1944, Ap 10,19:3
Cox, Alice, 1939, Mr 24,19:4
Cox, Allen H, 1944, Jl 7,15:3
Cox, Althea Mrs, 1909, Ag 7,9:6
Cox, Amariah G, 1941, O 19,45:2
Cox, Andrew J, 1942, O 29,23:2
Cox, Arthur M, 1951, Jl 16,21:5
Cox, Atilla Col, 1909, Jl 8,7:4
Cox, Blanche B, 1940, Mr 22,19:2
Cox, C C, 1882, N 27,5:3
Cox, C H, 1901, Ag 9,7:6
Cox, C Ray Mrs, 1941, Mr 19,21:2
Cox, Calvin Mrs (A Ellerman), 1960, Je 6,29:2
Cox, Catherine G Mrs, 1950, Jl 17,21:6
Cox, Channing H, 1968, Ag 21,45:4
Cox, Charles C, 1949, Mr 8,26:3
Cox, Charles Edson Mrs, 1925, F 9,17:4
Cox, Charles Epperson, 1924, Je 22,25:1
Cox, Charles Finney, 1912, Ja 25,11:5
Cox, Charles H, 1924, My 31,15:4
Cox, Charles J, 1963, Je 8,25:5
Cox, Charles M, 1944, Je 14,19:5
Cox, Charles Newton, 1925, O 9,23:4
Cox, Charles R, 1944, Ap 18,21:2; 1962, Ja 19,26:6
Cox, Charles R Mrs, 1962, Mr 30,33:1
Cox, Charles W, 1951, O 24,31:3
Cox, Coleman, 1940, N 27,23:4
Cox, Cyrus L, 1958, Je 25,29:4
Cox, Dale, 1958, My 15,29:4
Cox, Daniel H, 1955, S 2,17:3
Cox, David C, 1947, O 24,23:7
Cox, David H, 1943, Ap 25,34:3
Cox, David W, 1942, S 30,23:3
Cox, De Los L, 1941, F 3,17:1
Cox, Dellilah Garretson Mrs, 1920, F 3,15:2
Cox, Douglas F, 1940, Ap 10,25:1
Cox, E C, 1879, N 26,2:3
Cox, E Eugene, 1952, D 25,29:1
Cox, E J, 1937, N 12,21:4
Cox, E T Mrs, 1885, Ap 4,5:2
Cox, E W, 1914, Je 28,15:5
Cox, Earl A, 1937, S 28,23:2
Cox, Edmund, 1946, Ag 10,13:4
Cox, Edmund V, 1938, Ap 14,23:4
Cox, Edward C, 1948, N 21,88:6
Cox, Edward G, 1939, My 6,17:2; 1950, Je 20,27:5
Cox, Edward L, 1954, S 16,29:4
Cox, Edward T, 1951, F 4,76:5
Cox, Edward V, 1949, D 9,31:3
Cox, Edward V Mrs, 1942, Ap 3,21:4
Cox, Edward W, 1943, Ap 24,13:2
Cox, Edwin, 1968, F 8,43:1
Cox, Edwin L, 1960, Ag 5,23:4
Cox, Edwin P, 1938, Mr 12,17:5
Cox, Edwin R, 1959, Ja 9,27:2
Cox, Edwin R Mrs, 1939, N 12,49:1
Cox, Elizabeth R, 1950, N 10,28:2
Cox, Ernest F, 1950, My 15,21:4; 1959, F 18,33:1
Cox, Eugene R, 1921, My 17,17:6
Cox, Florence T, 1940, My 10,24:4
Cox, Forrest B, 1962, My 23,45:4
Cox, Francis C, 1954, D 25,11:5
Cox, Francis M, 1942, My 20,19:3
Cox, Frank E, 1940, D 12,27:3
Cox, Frank P, 1939, D 2,17:5; 1950, Ag 30,31:4
Cox, Fred J, 1958, F 11,31:4
Cox, Frederick I, 1962, Ap 2,31:5
Cox, George, 1903, D 27,7:6
Cox, George Alburtus, 1914, Ja 17,9:5
Cox, George B (funl), 1916, My 23,11:5
Cox, George B Mrs, 1938, Ag 18,19:1
Cox, George C, 1943, D 18,16:2
Cox, George E, 1944, Jl 21,19:6
Cox, George E Mrs, 1953, My 14,29:2
Cox, George F, 1905, Mr 6,7:2
Cox, George H, 1938, Jl 24,29:4
Cox, George T, 1955, O 29,19:5
Cox, George W, 1961, Ja 19,29:1
Cox, Gilbert R, 1959, D 13,86:4
Cox, Guy W, 1955, D 10,21:4
Cox, H G Dr (funl, Je 1,2:6), 1866, My 30,8:2
Cox, H H, 1950, O 23,23:1
Cox, Harold C, 1939, Ag 27,35:3
Cox, Harry C Jr, 1954, N 6,17:5
Cox, Harry E, 1904, Ag 3,7:6
Cox, Harry W, 1947, F 14,21:3; 1950, Mr 12,93:1
Cox, Harvey W, 1944, Jl 29,13:3
Cox, Helen M, 1946, Ja 19,13:2
Cox, Henry C, 1954, Ap 2,27:3
Cox, Henry L, 1949, Mr 2,26:2
Cox, Herbert C, 1947, S 19,23:4
Cox, Herbert F, 1950, N 18,15:7
Cox, Horace G, 1943, F 3,19:3
Cox, Hugh M, 1958, Ja 7,47:5
Cox, Ida, 1967, N 12,87:1
Cox, Ignatius W, 1965, F 12,29:3
Cox, J Harry, 1942, Ap 30,19:2
Cox, J Hobart, 1939, Je 27,23:4
Cox, J T, 1948, N 6,13:2
Cox, Jacob D, 1953, F 17,34:2
Cox, James A Jr, 1955, N 15,29:1
Cox, James A Mrs, 1950, My 4,27:5
Cox, James C, 1957, Jl 29,19:6
Cox, James Capt, 1925, D 5,19:5
Cox, James F, 1941, F 17,15:1; 1941, Ap 6,48:6
Cox, James J, 1943, Ja 11,15:4
Cox, James L, 1960, F 16,40:1
Cox, James M, 1948, Ja 4,52:8; 1950, O 25,35:4; 1956, Je 3,86:7
Cox, James M Mrs, 1960, N 7,15:3
Cox, James M Sr (funl, Jl 18,25:4; will, Jl 31,23:2), 1957, Jl 16,25:1
Cox, James R, 1951, Mr 20,29:5
Cox, Jay F Sr, 1952, O 20,23:5
Cox, Jennings B Jr, 1913, S 2,7:8
Cox, Jennings S, 1913, O 22,9:6
Cox, Joe, 1938, Jl 7,19:2
Cox, John, 1903, D 20,7:6
Cox, John B, 1903, Jl 31,1:5
Cox, John C Capt, 1872, Ap 1,1:6
Cox, John F, 1942, N 16,20:3
Cox, John Fremont, 1911, N 7,13:5
Cox, John H, 1945, N 24,19:4
Cox, John I, 1946, S 6,21:3
Cox, John J Mrs, 1946, D 22,41:5
Cox, John Jr, 1951, Ap 11,29:4
Cox, John Jr Mrs, 1951, O 3,33:1
Cox, John L, 1955, F 17,27:2
Cox, Joseph, 1904, Ja 7,9:5; 1941, F 11,23:1
Cox, Joseph A, 1940, Ap 24,23:2
Cox, Joseph E, 1952, My 22,27:4
Cox, Joseph F, 1957, Ap 12,25:2
Cox, Joseph G, 1959, S 11,27:2
Cox, Kenneth B, 1968, Ja 11,37:2
Cox, Kenyon, 1919, Mr 18,11:3
Cox, Kenyon Mrs, 1945, D 12,27:5
Cox, L G Mrs, 1953, My 30,15:6
Cox, L H, 1949, Jl 30,15:2
Cox, L Raymond, 1948, S 29,29:5
Cox, Le Moyne F, 1945, S 27,21:4
Cox, Leland G, 1959, Ag 3,27:3
Cox, Leo M, 1957, F 28,27:3
Cox, Leonard, 1963, Ag 19,25:5
Cox, Leslie R Sr, 1952, Ja 29,25:4
Cox, Letchworth, 1907, Mr 15,9:6
Cox, Lewis J, 1939, Mr 29,23:5
Cox, Lydia (Sister Mary of St Veronica), 1960, O 25,35:1
Cox, Maria McIntosh Mrs, 1910, F 23,9:4
Cox, Marie C Mrs, 1944, Jl 5,17:5
Cox, Mark T (funl, Mr 28,13:6), 1909, Mr 24,9:3
Cox, Martin L, 1949, N 5,13:2
Cox, Mary A, 1958, Jl 14,21:2
Cox, Mary E, 1944, Mr 2,17:3
Cox, Mary K Mrs, 1947, D 11,33:2
Cox, Mary S Mrs, 1946, Jl 8,29:2
Cox, Merle D, 1945, Je 14,19:4
Cox, Merle V, 1937, Je 8,25:4
Cox, Michael A, 1944, Je 9,15:5
Cox, Michael P, 1939, Ja 5,23:5
Cox, Milton A, 1947, My 26,22:2
Cox, Oscar F, 1945, Je 5,19:5
Cox, Oscar L (por), 1948, Ag 10,21:4
Cox, Oscar S, 1966, O 6,47:1
Cox, Palmer, 1924, Jl 25,13:5
Cox, Patrick T, 1943, F 15,15:5
Cox, Paul F, 1947, Jl 7,17:5
Cox, Percy Z Maj Gen Sir, 1937, F 21,II,10:8
Cox, Phil, 1939, S 13,25:1
Cox, Preston W, 1962, Jl 16,23:3
Cox, Ralph A, 1948, F 29,60:3
Cox, Raymond B, 1948, Je 28,19:4
Cox, Robert F Mrs, 1939, Je 29,23:5
Cox, Robert H, 1961, Ag 16,31:5
Cox, Robert J, 1967, Ja 7,27:6
Cox, Rosslyn M, 1940, Mr 30,15:2
Cox, Rowland Jr Dr, 1916, Ag 5,9:5
Cox, S Morris, 1952, Mr 1,15:1
Cox, S S (funl), 1889, S 10,4:7
Cox, Samuel Rev Dr, 1903, Jl 22,7:7
Cox, Scott W, 1949, Ag 29,18:2
Cox, Sgt, 1879, D 8,2:1
Cox, Sidney, 1952, Ja 5,11:5
Cox, Stanley C, 1942, Je 8,15:2
Cox, Stanley M, 1955, Mr 19,15:5
Cox, Stephen J, 1952, N 25,29:4
Cox, Theodore, 1908, Ap 4,9:7
Cox, Theodore J, 1942, N 19,25:3
Cox, Theodore M, 1945, S 16,43:2
Cox, Theodore S, 1947, My 11,63:3
Cox, Theron D, 1949, N 9,27:4
Cox, Thomas A, 1939, Mr 4,15:4; 1948, N 13,15

Cox, Thomas H, 1956, F 10,21:5
Cox, Thomas J, 1952, N 18,32:3
Cox, Townsend, 1905, F 28,9:5
Cox, W H, 1875, Ap 15,1:3
Cox, W H Jr, 1882, S 26,8:5
Cox, W Ralph, 1941, Je 11,21:6
Cox, W Rowland, 1946, D 26,25:4
Cox, W S Judge, 1902, Je 26,9:7
Cox, Walter, 1905, D 1,9:6
Cox, Walter C, 1965, Ja 24,81:1
Cox, Walter M, 1940, N 4,19:3
Cox, Walter P, 1937, S 7,21:2
Cox, Walter R, 1941, D 16,27:5
Cox, Walter S, 1956, N 12,29:1
Cox, Walter Y, 1950, F 12,84:1
Cox, William, 1878, My 4,2:5; 1952, D 29,1:2; 1955, F 20,88:6
Cox, William B, 1942, Je 21,36:8
Cox, William E, 1921, Jl 22,11:6
Cox, William F, 1939, Mr 11,17:4
Cox, William H D Mrs, 1951, My 7,25:6
Cox, William J, 1958, My 5,29:2; 1963, Jl 2,30:1
Cox, William J Mrs, 1950, Jl 11,32:3
Cox, William L, 1949, Ap 28,13:3
Cox, William R, 1957, Ja 20,92:3
Cox, William R Mrs, 1925, D 29,23:4
Cox, William S, 1959, S 10,35:5
Cox, William T, 1939, F 17,20:2; 1950, O 19,31:4; 1951, Je 11,25:3
Cox, William T Mrs, 1949, D 2,29:2
Cox, William Van Zandt, 1923, Jl 25,11:7
Cox, William W, 1948, O 30,15:3; 1967, S 2,25:6
Cox, Wilmot T, 1945, D 29,13:1
Cox, Wilmot Townsend Mrs, 1915, D 18,11:5
Coxe, Alexander Brinton Mrs, 1924, S 6,11:7
Coxe, Alfred C, 1957, D 22,40:3
Coxe, Alfred C Mrs, 1947, Ap 14,27:3
Coxe, Davies Dr, 1908, N 12,9:6
Coxe, Frank Col, 1903, Je 3,9:6
Coxe, George 3d, 1951, Jl 28,9:5
Coxe, H O, 1881, Jl 9,5:3
Coxe, Henry B Jr, 1961, Ja 21,21:6
Coxe, Henry Brinton, 1907, Jl 27,7:6
Coxe, Henry M, 1946, Jl 21,40:1
Coxe, Howard C, 1940, N 25,17:3
Coxe, Joseph W, 1937, F 11,23:3
Coxe, McGrane, 1923, Ap 21,11:5
Coxe, Richard C, 1865, S 12,8:2
Coxen, Walter A, 1949, D 17,17:3
Coxen, William, 1946, Ap 8,27:5
Coxey, Jacob S, 1951, My 19,15:1
Coxey, Jacob S Jr, 1957, Mr 21,31:1
Coxey, Jacob S Mrs, 1951, Ja 15,17:4
Coxey, William D, 1943, Ag 10,19:2
Coxhead, John H, 1943, My 26,23:6
Coxhead, John H Mrs, 1938, O 2,49:1
Coxhead, Ralph C, 1951, F 8,33:1
Coxhead, Stuart P Mrs, 1958, Ja 29,27:2
Coxon, Annie F, 1950, F 10,24:3
Coxon, James R, 1944, Jl 11,15:2
Coy, Charles E Mrs, 1953, Ap 14,27:6
Coy, David D, 1959, Ja 1,31:1
Coy, E H, 1935, S 9,19:1
Coy, E W Prof, 1915, Mr 30,11:4
Coy, Eber Mrs, 1950, Ag 1,23:5
Coy, Harold H, 1959, Jl 14,29:5
Coy, James J, 1948, Ag 21,15:3
Coy, John L, 1951, Mr 5,21:4
Coy, Raymond Mrs, 1943, N 28,68:3
Coy, Robert H, 1942, My 25,15:5
Coy, Wayne, 1957, S 25,29:2
Coyan, Robert L, 1955, S 26,23:4
Coykendall, Edward, 1949, F 8,25:6
Coykendall, Frederick (funl, N 23,35:3), 1954, N 19, 23:1
Coykendall, John F, 1924, My 10,13:4
Coykendall, Louis K Mrs, 1957, Ap 12,23:1
Coykendall, Louis T, 1945, My 18,19:4
Coykendall, Ralf, 1968, Mr 18,45:1
Coykendall, Russell A, 1946, O 16,27:1
Coykendall, Samuel D, 1913, Ja 15,13:5
Coykendall, William E, 1963, Jl 27,17:3
Coyle, Anna E, 1947, Ja 28,24:2
Coyle, Catherine L Mrs, 1939, N 18,17:4
Coyle, Charles E, 1951, O 24,31:4
Coyle, Charles J, 1937, Ag 13,15:1
Coyle, Daniel A, 1959, Ap 9,31:2
Coyle, David C Mrs, 1940, O 4,23:5
Coyle, Dean G, 1959, O 4,86:6
Coyle, Edward M, 1941, Ag 24,35:2
Coyle, Edward T, 1938, O 30,41:3
Coyle, Farrell D, 1952, F 2,13:3
Coyle, Francis T, 1963, Je 19,37:1
Coyle, Frank, 1946, S 10,7:4
Coyle, Frank B, 1953, O 25,88:4
Coyle, Frank Dowson, 1909, D 18,13:2
Coyle, Frank J, 1938, Je 23,21:5
Coyle, George A, 1951, N 6,29:3
Coyle, Grace L, 1962, Mr 10,22:1
Coyle, Harold J, 1965, Mr 8,29:4
Coyle, Harry Mrs, 1950, S 10,92:4
Coyle, Henrietta Mrs, 1937, N 27,21:1
Coyle, Hugh, 1908, S 15,9:6
Coyle, Hugh F, 1916, Je 1,11:5
Coyle, Hugh J, 1941, Ap 11,21:4
Coyle, J B, 1934, O 14,32:1
Coyle, James A, 1948, Ag 21,15:4; 1955, Jl 5,29:3
Coyle, James B, 1942, Je 21,36:6
Coyle, James F, 1942, Mr 20,19:3; 1943, Mr 30,26:5; 1950, D 9,15:3
Coyle, James M Jr, 1959, F 21,21:5
Coyle, John, 1869, Jl 20,3:2
Coyle, John B Mrs, 1950, Ag 1,23:2
Coyle, John F, 1951, Ag 28,23:1; 1963, Ap 13,19:5
Coyle, John H, 1913, O 19,IV,15:5
Coyle, John J, 1951, F 8,23:8
Coyle, John L, 1963, Je 14,29:2
Coyle, John P, 1950, Ap 26,29:4
Coyle, Joseph A, 1941, Ap 17,23:6
Coyle, Joseph B, 1947, Ja 22,23:5
Coyle, Kathleen, 1952, Mr 29,15:3
Coyle, L Stanley Mrs, 1956, S 22,17:2
Coyle, Leonidas Col, 1937, N 3,24:1
Coyle, Martin A, 1958, N 29,21:5
Coyle, Marvin E, 1961, S 28,41:1
Coyle, Matthew A, 1957, Ja 23,29:3
Coyle, Michael A, 1957, My 23,33:2
Coyle, Patrick, 1865, My 31,8:5
Coyle, Peter A, 1944, Ag 17,17:5
Coyle, Raymond J Mrs, 1946, D 5,31:2
Coyle, Rita Sister, 1954, D 5,89:1
Coyle, Robert B, 1958, My 9,23:3
Coyle, Stanley, 1918, Je 5,11:5
Coyle, Thomas, 1960, Jl 25,23:5
Coyle, Thomas F, 1942, Ag 12,19:7; 1952, Je 4,27:2
Coyle, Thomas G, 1910, S 1,9:6
Coyle, Thomas L, 1955, Ja 3,27:2
Coyle, Thomas P, 1962, S 2,56:8
Coyle, Walter H, 1950, Ap 9,84:4
Coyle, Walter V, 1948, Ag 9,19:6
Coyle, William A, 1941, Je 15,37:2
Coyle, William E, 1952, Mr 20,29:3
Coyle, William H, 1940, O 18,21:5
Coyle, William R, 1962, F 1,31:5
Coyne, Alex, 1948, Ag 20,17:3
Coyne, Andre, 1960, Jl 22,23:3
Coyne, Arthur, 1951, S 17,21:2
Coyne, Bartholomew B (por), 1938, Ja 8,15:1
Coyne, Bartholomew B Mrs, 1948, N 14,76:2
Coyne, Charles F, 1937, Ap 15,23:5
Coyne, Christopher, 1909, F 2,9:5
Coyne, Edward J, 1944, S 8,19:5; 1958, My 31,15:4
Coyne, Edwin C Mrs, 1951, Ap 1,94:1
Coyne, Eugene H, 1952, Je 2,21:3
Coyne, Ferdinand, 1944, S 21,19:3
Coyne, Frank H, 1966, Ja 17,47:5
Coyne, Frederick E, 1948, N 26,23:4
Coyne, Frederick W, 1946, My 3,21:3
Coyne, H G, 1931, D 10,23:3
Coyne, John H, 1924, Ja 15,19:4; 1964, Ap 7,35:3
Coyne, John J, 1948, N 27,17:2
Coyne, John L, 1941, Jl 24,17:3
Coyne, John Mrs, 1945, Ag 16,19:5
Coyne, John T, 1951, S 24,27:4
Coyne, Joseph, 1941, F 21,19:5
Coyne, Kathleen, 1938, O 8,17:5
Coyne, Patrick Mrs, 1945, Ja 24,21:3; 1945, O 16,23:3
Coyne, Phil M, 1942, N 10,27:3
Coyne, Phoebe (Mrs Frank Smithson), 1942, Ap 9, 19:4
Coyne, Sterling, 1868, Ag 2,5:3
Coyne, Thomas J, 1960, O 28,31:5
Coyne, Vaughan M, 1953, D 27,60:4
Coyne, Vaughn M Mrs, 1948, Je 8,26:3
Coyner, Claude L, 1950, D 8,29:2
Coyte, Reuben, 1941, Ja 31,19:5
Coyula Llaguno, Miguel, 1948, N 24,23:6
Cozens, Frederick W, 1954, Ja 4,19:4
Cozens, John F, 1946, Je 26,25:3
Cozine, Victor E Mrs, 1945, O 5,23:4
Cozine, William H, 1951, My 8,31:5
Cozzens, Charles O, 1947, F 12,25:3
Cozzens, Horatio G, 1944, D 22,17:4
Cozzens, J W Sr Mrs, 1952, O 31,25:4
Cozzens, James W, 1955, N 4,29:3
Cozzens, John H, 1945, Ag 22,23:3
Cozzens, P Robert, 1955, Ag 27,15:4
Cozzens, Samuel, 1924, Ag 13,15:3
Cozzens, Sarah C H Mrs, 1937, Ag 27,19:4
Cozzolino, Constance Mrs, 1941, S 9,23:2
Cozzolino, H Henry, 1958, O 2,37:4
Crabb, Charles F, 1907, S 11,9:5
Crabb, E L, 1882, Mr 28,5:5
Crabb, Ernest D, 1957, S 18,33:1
Crabb, Frank H, 1948, Je 30,25:2
Crabb, John S, 1945, Mr 21,23:1
Crabb, Stephen G, 1937, Ag 27,19:5
Crabb, William W, 1950, Jl 30,60:2
Crabbe, Caren L, 1957, Ap 12,51:2
Crabbe, Edward, 1953, Ag 17,15:4
Crabbe, George N, 1950, F 11,15:6
Crabbe, George W, 1951, S 5,31:1
Crabbe, John Grant Dr, 1924, Ja 31,15:4
Crabbe, Samuel F, 1949, O 17,23:5
Crabbe, Thomas M, 1947, F 17,19:4
Crabbe, Thomas Rear-Adm, 1872, Jl 2,8:6
Crabbs, George D, 1948, S 30,27:5
Crabites, Pierre, 1943, O 11,19:1
Crabtree, Albert E, 1915, D 10,13:6
Crabtree, E Granville Dr, 1947, Je 1,60:4
Crabtree, Edgar E, 1946, Ap 1,27:3
Crabtree, G, 1932, O 26,17:1
Crabtree, Harold, 1956, F 19,92:5
Crabtree, James A, 1966, N 12,29:3
Crabtree, James B, 1966, F 23,39:2
Crabtree, James W, 1945, Je 11,15:3
Crabtree, John H, 1949, S 8,29:3
Crabtree, Joseph C, 1952, D 20,17:5
Crabtree, Loren H, 1956, Je 22,23:6
Crabtree, Lotta, 1924, S 26,21:3
Crabtree, Mary A Mrs, 1905, Ap 12,9:4
Crabtree, Nate L, 1965, F 1,23:2
Crabtree, Paul B, 1953, Ap 6,19:5
Crabtree, Paul L, 1959, Je 3,35:4
Crabtree, William, 1903, Je 9,9:7
Crachi, Domenico, 1958, N 29,21:3
Crackanthorpe, Dayrell, 1950, F 11,15:2
Craco, Louis J, 1966, S 18,84:7
Cracowaner, Samuel W, 1951, Mr 10,13:1
Cracraft, Tom A, 1963, O 10,41:4
Craddock, George Mrs, 1949, D 9,8:4
Craddock, Jack A, 1967, O 14,27:4
Craddock, John F, 1943, D 25,13:4
Craddock, Reginald H Sir, 1937, F 11,23:6
Craddock, Thomas J, 1940, Jl 5,13:5
Craddock, Thomas L, 1937, My 8,17:6
Craford, Robert J, 1955, Ag 22,21:5
Craft, A, 1883, S 22,4:7
Craft, Alton L, 1960, D 26,23:5
Craft, Charles E, 1948, Mr 25,27:2
Craft, Daniel, 1943, Je 28,22:3
Craft, Donald R, 1958, O 8,35:3
Craft, E A, 1954, D 22,23:3
Craft, Elijah R, 1916, F 6,15:5
Craft, Elmer J Mrs, 1948, My 30,34:2
Craft, George G, 1942, O 30,19:5
Craft, George W, 1943, Mr 26,19:2
Craft, George W Mrs, 1961, Ap 12,41:3
Craft, Harvey C, 1938, Ag 7,33:3
Craft, Henry Clay, 1914, D 21,9:4
Craft, Henry K Mrs, 1959, Jl 9,27:5
Craft, Henry L, 1942, F 26,19:2
Craft, Henry S, 1942, S 4,24:3
Craft, Henry S Mrs, 1953, S 23,31:1
Craft, Herbert C, 1948, N 9,27:4
Craft, Ida A, 1947, S 16,23:4
Craft, J Howard, 1941, N 4,23:3
Craft, James H, 1938, S 10,17:5; 1941, Ap 29,19:2
Craft, James N, 1953, N 16,25:3
Craft, John W Mrs, 1949, Ja 28,22:2
Craft, La Verne R, 1938, Ja 26,23:3
Craft, Lafayette A, 1938, Jl 21,21:4
Craft, Marcella, 1959, D 13,86:7
Craft, Otto Henry, 1903, Ag 23,7:5
Craft, Warren M Sr, 1954, Ja 14,29:1
Craft, Warren W, 1947, Ag 7,21:5
Craft, William H, 1954, Ag 28,15:4
Crafts, Andrew F, 1962, Ap 21,20:8
Crafts, Andrew F Mrs, 1952, Ja 13,89:2
Crafts, Arthur A, 1940, Ja 21,35:1
Crafts, George B, 1947, D 28,40:4
Crafts, George P, 1939, Ja 20,19:2
Crafts, Leland Whitney, 1968, Ja 24,42:2
Crafts, Norris P (will), 1959, F 8,19:8
Crafts, Thomas Y, 1951, F 11,88:6
Crafts, Walter J, 1938, D 16,25:2
Crafts, Wilbur F Dr, 1922, D 28,17:4
Cragan, Frank P, 1950, Ag 31,25:4
Cragan, Robert L, 1955, Je 5,84:5
Cragg, Kenneth C, 1948, F 17,25:5
Cragg, Samuel H, 1922, Ja 6,17:5
Cragie, Chester F, 1949, N 4,27:3
Cragin, Adele C, 1940, N 29,21:4
Cragin, Chauncey B, 1940, N 4,19:5
Cragin, Edward Franklin, 1917, Ag 20,9:5
Cragin, Edward Stuart, 1925, D 19,17:5
Cragin, Edwin Bradford Dr, 1918, O 23,13:1
Cragin, Herbert E Sr, 1951, O 22,23:3
Crago, Thomas S Col, 1925, S 14,19:4
Crahan, Lawrence A, 1952, Ap 1,29:1
Craib, B S Mrs, 1937, O 4,21:5
Craib, Balfour S, 1949, N 17,29:3
Craig, A Crawford 6th, 1960, N 18,31:1
Craig, Agnes H, 1962, Mr 8,31:4
Craig, Albert E, 1955, N 30,33:1
Craig, Alec, 1945, Je 27,19:5
Craig, Alex M, 1937, Ag 2,19:5
Craig, Alexander M Mrs, 1946, Ag 29,27:5
Craig, Alfred E, 1953, D 28,21:1
Craig, Alick C Sr, 1951, Ap 15,93:1
Craig, Allan M Jr, 1955, S 17,15:5
Craig, B D K, 1879, My 9,3:3
Craig, Britt, 1919, Mr 19,11:3
Craig, C B, 1936, F 25,19:3
Craig, C C, 1940, Mr 27,21:6
Craig, C Henry, 1946, Ag 25,46:4
Craig, C Henry Mrs, 1939, Jl 9,31:3
Craig, C L, 1935, Ag 7,19:1
Craig, Charles F, 1950, D 10,105:2

Craig, Charles S, 1943, Ag 16,15:1
Craig, Charles S Mrs, 1941, Ja 4,13:5
Craig, Clara E, 1943, Ja 25,13:4
Craig, Clarence T, 1953, Ag 21,17:1
Craig, Cornelius A, 1957, Mr 20,37:4
Craig, David, 1950, S 20,31:2
Craig, David M, 1942, Mr 27,23:5
Craig, David Mrs, 1941, F 24,15:4
Craig, David R, 1960, S 10,21:4
Craig, E M, 1951, Ap 11,29:1
Craig, Earl B, 1944, D 19,21:4
Craig, Edith, 1947, Mr 28,23:2
Craig, Edward, 1940, Ja 2,19:2
Craig, Edward G, 1966, Jl 30,25:2
Craig, Edward J, 1952, O 26,88:5; 1960, N 3,39:3
Craig, Edward M, 1943, Ja 16,13:3
Craig, Elizabeth H, 1947, N 20,30:3
Craig, Elliot, 1941, Mr 16,45:1
Craig, Emmett J, 1939, D 31,18:6
Craig, Eugene, 1939, Ap 11,24:2
Craig, Eugene F, 1947, Ag 16,13:6
Craig, Fay E, 1950, D 18,31:4
Craig, Frances, 1949, F 11,23:2
Craig, Francis, 1966, N 21,45:2
Craig, Frank A, 1953, My 28,23:5; 1959, My 14,33:5
Craig, Frederick P, 1966, O 29,29:4
Craig, Frederick P Mrs, 1947, Mr 19,26:2
Craig, George A, 1956, Ja 31,29:3
Craig, George B Mrs, 1955, Ja 20,31:1
Craig, George L, 1944, F 21,15:3
Craig, George M (Lefty), 1911, Ap 24,9:4
Craig, George W, 1942, N 6,23:5
Craig, Godfrey, 1941, My 28,25:5
Craig, H B J Mrs, 1948, N 6,13:3
Craig, Hardin, 1968, O 17,47:2
Craig, Harry A Sr, 1949, Je 28,27:3
Craig, Harry R, 1941, S 23,23:4
Craig, Hugh, 1962, Ag 15,31:5
Craig, Ida M Mrs, 1953, Mr 3,27:4
Craig, Isaac B Judge, 1925, Ag 5,17:6
Craig, J, 1932, Ag 24,17:3
Craig, J B, 1879, O 30,5:2
Craig, J Frank, 1952, N 7,23:3
Craig, J Reah Jr, 1938, Je 14,21:4
Craig, J William, 1966, Ap 17,87:1
Craig, James, 1903, Ap 26,7:6; 1951, D 11,33:3
Craig, James A, 1940, O 5,15:4; 1942, D 30,23:4
Craig, James B, 1941, D 10,25:4
Craig, James C, 1954, Ap 11,86:4
Craig, James D, 1940, My 28,23:6; 1950, My 14,108:1
Craig, James H, 1945, Mr 10,17:4
Craig, James H Mrs, 1948, My 4,25:3
Craig, James M, 1922, Ja 21,13:4
Craig, James P, 1939, D 24,14:7
Craig, James Y, 1958, Ap 19,21:1
Craig, Jeremiah J, 1904, Ja 17,7:6
Craig, Jerome, 1959, S 21,31:4
Craig, John, 1950, F 1,29:3; 1950, My 20,15:4; 1957, F 2,19:4
Craig, John C, 1953, My 9,19:6
Craig, John D, 1953, Je 19,21:3
Craig, John F, 1944, Jl 18,19:4; 1952, Ja 7,19:4; 1966, O 30,89:1
Craig, John G, 1949, Ja 6,23:2
Craig, John Jr, 1945, D 6,27:3
Craig, John L, 1957, Ag 23,19:4
Craig, John Prof, 1912, Ag 13,9:5
Craig, Joseph A, 1959, Ja 1,31:2
Craig, Joseph E Rear-Adm, 1925, Je 23,19:4
Craig, Laura G Mrs, 1946, O 13,59:5
Craig, Lawrence B Sr, 1950, My 25,29:2
Craig, Malin, 1945, Jl 26,19:1
Craig, Malin Mrs, 1941, My 30,15:3
Craig, Margaret, 1951, N 15,29:3
Craig, Mary C, 1951, Ja 18,27:1
Craig, May M Mrs, 1941, Ap 12,15:7
Craig, Moses A, 1954, N 23,35:2
Craig, Moses A Mrs, 1941, Ap 18,21:2
Craig, Norman E, 1968, O 26,37:3
Craig, Oliver N, 1951, Je 1,26:1
Craig, Patrick F, 1943, F 21,32:5
Craig, Patrick T, 1918, Ag 23,9:6
Craig, Percy G, 1962, N 11,88:7
Craig, R Jr, 1933, N 29,20:1
Craig, R Sewell, 1939, S 5,23:5
Craig, Robert, 1947, My 23,23:3; 1952, Je 5,31:2
Craig, Robert A, 1939, O 13,23:1
Craig, Robert E, 1954, Mr 14,89:2
Craig, Robert H, 1944, Je 19,19:3
Craig, Robert Jr, 1939, Je 21,23:2
Craig, Robert R, 1954, Ap 11,87:2
Craig, Robert S, 1953, Ja 30,22:4
Craig, Roland T, 1960, Mr 17,33:3
Craig, Ruth E, 1962, Mr 24,25:4
Craig, Samuel G, 1960, O 8,23:3
Craig, Samuel G Mrs, 1950, D 16,17:6
Craig, Samuel L, 1953, S 24,33:4
Craig, Samuel R, 1903, S 15,9:6
Craig, Seth C, 1951, Ag 20,19:4
Craig, Stephen W, 1947, Ap 4,23:1
Craig, Thomas, 1946, N 11,27:5
Craig, Thomas Bigalow, 1924, S 2,19:3
Craig, Thomas Canby Dr, 1921, D 15,19:4
Craig, Thomas J, 1951, Jl 13,21:1
Craig, Vivian H, 1944, F 16,17:2
Craig, W Burrows, 1954, F 10,29:2
Craig, W Emerson, 1954, Jl 3,11:6
Craig, Wales B Mrs, 1945, D 5,25:4
Craig, Walter A, 1950, Ag 26,13:6
Craig, Walter F, 1952, D 28,48:8
Craig, Walter G, 1945, S 6,25:5
Craig, Walter G Jr, 1953, N 22,88:3
Craig, Walter G Mrs, 1952, F 26,27:4
Craig, Walter H, 1937, N 26,26:3
Craig, Walter J, 1962, Ag 13,25:5
Craig, William, 1937, Je 30,23:3; 1943, D 3,23:1
Craig, William B, 1925, N 28,15:6; 1938, F 17,21:3; 1948, Ja 20,23:1; 1959, Ja 28,31:1
Craig, William Bayard Dr, 1916, S 17,19:3
Craig, William C, 1943, Ap 13,25:4; 1962, N 16,32:1
Craig, William C Jr, 1968, F 9,27:1
Craig, William R, 1946, Je 2,44:6
Craig, William W, 1952, Ag 24,89:2
Craig, Winchell M, 1960, F 14,84:1
Craigavon, Viscount, 1940, N 25,17:1
Craige, Burton, 1876, Ja 2,6:7
Craige, John H, 1954, Ag 17,21:2
Craige, Ker, 1904, S 2,7:6
Craigen, Maida, 1942, Ap 5,41:3
Craighead, Alex, 1949, S 29,29:5
Craighead, Don C, 1942, Ag 19,19:5
Craighill, Maurice L Mrs, 1947, Ap 28,23:4
Craigie, A M, 1937, Mr 31,24:2
Craigie, Charles, 1943, S 29,21:5
Craigie, David J Brig-Gen, 1913, D 16,11:5
Craigie, Frederic E, 1937, Jl 10,15:5
Craigie, Julia A, 1940, Ja 17,21:4
Craigie, Pearl Mary Teresa Mrs, 1906, Ag 14,7:1
Craigie, Robert, 1959, My 17,84:6
Craigie, William A Sir, 1957, S 3,28:1
Craigmyle, Lord, 1937, Je 30,24:2; 1944, S 30,13:6
Craigner, Sherman M Mrs, 1946, Jl 23,25:2
Craik, Dinah M, 1887, O 14,5:3
Craik, Elizabeth M, 1942, N 6,23:4
Craik, Henry D, 1955, Mr 28,27:2
Crail, Joe (por), 1938, Mr 3,21:4
Crain, Catherine (corr, S 4,19:4), 1944, S 3,27:2
Crain, Davida C, 1956, Ag 27,19:5
Crain, Dunham Jones, 1908, My 18,7:4
Crain, Dunham Jones Mrs, 1914, Ag 21,9:6
Crain, Edmund C, 1940, Ag 30,19:3
Crain, Eli C, 1865, Mr 27,4:1
Crain, Fred M, 1941, N 9,53:1
Crain, J Dean, 1955, Ja 11,25:4
Crain, Thomas C T, 1942, My 30,15:1
Crain, Thomas C T (will, Je 9,15:2), 1942, Je 2,23:3
Crain, Thomas C T Mrs, 1914, S 24,11:6
Crain, William Baker Dr, 1907, Mr 10,9:6
Craine, Benjamin H, 1943, My 10,19:1
Crall, Howard E Col, 1923, F 27,19:3
Crall, Leander H, 1911, Mr 8,11:4
Cram, Arthur B, 1953, Je 2,29:2
Cram, Edward J Judge, 1906, Ja 24,9:6
Cram, Ernest R, 1951, S 4,27:1
Cram, G C Maj, 1869, Ag 26,5:5
Cram, George E, 1965, S 2,31:5
Cram, George Taylor Capt, 1908, Ja 8,9:6
Cram, Harold F, 1948, N 22,21:2
Cram, Harward W, 1950, Mr 29,29:4
Cram, Henry A Mrs, 1910, F 21,9:5
Cram, Henry S Mrs, 1949, N 8,31:1
Cram, J S, 1936, Ja 19,II,9:1
Cram, J Sergeant Mrs, 1960, F 29,27:3
Cram, Jacob, 1869, Jl 8,5:2
Cram, Paul H, 1944, Ag 12,11:5
Cram, Paul P, 1963, S 25,43:5
Cram, Peter H Mrs, 1944, My 3,19:6
Cram, Ralph A, 1942, S 23,25:1
Cram, Ralph A Mrs, 1943, O 2,13:5
Cram, Ralph W, 1952, My 9,23:2
Cram, T J, 1883, D 21,1:5
Cram, W Winston, 1965, N 12,47:1
Cram, Wingate F, 1952, O 5,88:5
Cramer, Arnold W, 1964, Je 22,27:3
Cramer, Austin L (cor, Jl 6,28:2), 1950, Jl 5,31:4
Cramer, Boris, 1945, Mr 11,40:1
Cramer, Charles A, 1942, Je 24,19:6
Cramer, Christian, 1937, D 14,25:2
Cramer, Clarence C, 1946, F 7,23:2
Cramer, Edward Mrs, 1945, Je 21,19:2
Cramer, Edwin S, 1949, Ap 6,29:4
Cramer, Frederick H, 1954, S 5,26:7
Cramer, George B M, 1950, S 27,31:4
Cramer, H Hudson Jr Mrs, 1944, Ag 16,19:5
Cramer, Hiram, 1903, N 13,9:6
Cramer, Jeremiah, 1925, O 1,27:5
Cramer, John B, 1963, S 16,29:7
Cramer, Joseph, 1946, D 17,38:8
Cramer, Keller L, 1942, Je 16,23:3
Cramer, Kenneth F (funl plans, F 22,19:5), 1954, F 21,69:1
Cramer, Ludwig, 1951, O 18,29:4
Cramer, Mary Grant Mrs, 1905, Ap 6,1:4
Cramer, Morgan J, 1943, N 5,19:4
Cramer, Myron C, 1966, Mr 26,29:4
Cramer, Paul G, 1953, D 18,29:4
Cramer, Ralph Mrs, 1965, N 22,37:3
Cramer, Ray P, 1950, S 22,31:4
Cramer, Raymond H, 1954, Mr 29,19:6
Cramer, Raymond V, 1938, D 20,25:5
Cramer, Robert, 1939, Ag 4,13:6
Cramer, Sterling B, 1955, My 27,23:4
Cramer, Stuart W, 1940, Jl 4,15:1
Cramer, Stuart W Jr, 1957, Ja 7,25:1
Cramer, Walter H, 1966, Ja 30,84:5
Cramer, William, 1945, Ag 13,19:3
Cramer, William A, 1952, S 23,33:5
Cramer, William B, 1945, N 21,21:3
Cramer, William E, 1905, My 22,7:5
Cramer, William L, 1947, Ag 30,15:5
Cramer, William Mrs, 1954, S 19,89:2
Cramer-Klett, Theodor von, 1938, Je 1,23:4
Cramm, Walter D, 1950, My 30,18:3
Crammer, Howard S, 1951, My 30,21:5
Crammond, Harold A, 1956, Mr 6,31:1
Cramp, Charles D, 1907, D 30,7:6
Cramp, Charles H, 1913, Je 7,11:3
Cramp, Edwin S, 1913, Je 21,9:6
Cramp, Francis L, 1940, Mr 5,24:3
Cramp, H W, 1901, O 4,7:6
Cramp, Jessie T Mrs, 1938, Ag 9,19:4
Cramp, Louise M Mrs, 1942, N 24,26:2
Cramp, Norman W, 1951, S 1,11:5
Cramp, Ralph E, 1951, O 4,33:1
Cramp, Samuel A, 1912, N 4,11:6
Cramp, Theodore, 1925, Ja 10,13:4
Cramp, Theodore W, 1923, D 25,17:3
Cramp, Theodore W Mrs, 1947, Je 23,23:5
Cramp, Walter C (will, F 22,13:3), 1941, F 19,21:3
Cramp, Walter H, 1950, D 6,33:3
Cramp, Walter S Mrs, 1913, F 24,11:5
Cramp, William, 1879, Jl 7,1:5
Crampton, Albert M, 1953, Mr 14,15:6
Crampton, C Ward, 1964, O 22,35:1
Crampton, C Ward Jr, 1958, O 29,35:3
Crampton, Charles Mrs, 1950, My 4,27:4
Crampton, Charlotte Mrs, 1875, O 9,2:3
Crampton, David, 1955, Ag 30,27:5
Crampton, Ellen M Mrs, 1940, Ja 28,32:2
Crampton, George E, 1945, O 19,23:3
Crampton, Guy C, 1951, N 1,29:3
Crampton, Henry E, 1956, F 27,23:5
Crampton, Henry E Mrs, 1960, Ag 24,29:2
Crampton, James E, 1950, Mr 15,29:2
Crampton, James E Mrs, 1940, Ja 16,23:6
Crampton, John F, 1966, Jl 18,27:3
Crampton, Miriam E Mrs, 1942, O 20,21:6
Crampton, Warren, 1945, Ag 11,13:5
Crampton, William D, 1952, Mr 11,27:2
Cramton, Louis C Mrs, 1950, Ja 21,17:5
Cran, Henry A Mrs, 1910, F 21,9:5
Cranbrook, Earl of (G Gathorne-Hardy), 1906, O 31,9:6
Cranby, George A, 1949, Jl 6,27:5
Cranch, A Girard, 1967, N 11,33:2
Cranch, Eugene T Mrs, 1948, S 21,27:5
Crandale, Karl T, 1942, N 19,25:2
Crandall, Alex W, 1938, Ap 23,15:4
Crandall, Allston J, 1951, My 16,35:2
Crandall, Arthur F, 1951, S 29,17:5
Crandall, Bert F, 1943, F 7,49:2
Crandall, C S, 1924, My 21,19:2
Crandall, Carl H, 1965, Jl 31,21:4
Crandall, Carolyn W Mrs, 1940, Ag 17,15:4
Crandall, Charles E, 1956, N 21,27:4; 1962, Je 7,3[illegible]
Crandall, Charles F, 1963, N 8,31:2
Crandall, Charles F Mrs, 1953, Mr 26,31:4
Crandall, Charles T, 1944, Ap 24,19:3
Crandall, David R Mrs, 1955, Ja 20,31:1
Crandall, Donald P, 1958, Je 20,23:4
Crandall, Edward, 1968, My 10,47:3
Crandall, Edward H, 1944, Ja 20,19:5
Crandall, Edwin J, 1937, Mr 31,24:2
Crandall, Elbert, 1907, O 6,11:6
Crandall, Erie R, 1965, N 21,87:2
Crandall, Florence I, 1937, Ja 1,23:5
Crandall, Floyd J, 1949, My 12,31:1
Crandall, Francis A, 1946, Jl 12,17:4
Crandall, Frank W, 1948, F 23,25:5
Crandall, George, 1964, N 28,22:2
Crandall, George S, 1959, Ag 18,29:2
Crandall, Harley S, 1946, D 20,23:3
Crandall, Harry R Jr, 1939, Je 21,23:2
Crandall, Henry S, 1909, Je 29,7:5
Crandall, Henry Vaughn, 1911, S 7,9:5
Crandall, I B, 1927, Ap 24,30:4
Crandall, Jesse Armour, 1920, Ag 14,7:5
Crandall, Jesse Mrs, 1942, Je 13,15:1
Crandall, John P, 1945, Je 25,17:3
Crandall, John W, 1962, Ja 19,31:1
Crandall, Lewis A, 1956, D 4,39:5
Crandall, Lillian Mrs, 1946, O 16,27:1
Crandall, Louis E, 1950, D 26,23:2
Crandall, Noble, 1943, Ag 16,15:2
Crandall, Orrin P rev, 1914, S 5,7:6
Crandall, Otis Doc, 1951, Ag 18,11:5
Crandall, Phineas L, 1946, N 11,27:3
Crandall, Rand P (por),(cor, D 11,61:2), 1938, [illegible] 25:3

Crandall, Regina K, 1962, Je 6,41:2
Crandall, Rhoba E Mrs, 1957, Jl 19,19:4
Crandall, Richard C, 1953, F 21,13:6
Crandall, Roy, 1938, N 13,45:1
Crandall, Vaughn J, 1963, O 2,41:4
Crandall, Willard R, 1960, My 29,56:2
Crandall, William, 1943, Je 28,21:4
Crandall, William T, 1959, N 4,41:4
Crandell, Arthur R, 1938, Mr 19,15:5
Crandell, Bradshaw, 1966, Ja 26,37:4
Crandell, Charles L Sr, 1963, S 6,29:4
Crandell, Hubert L, 1954, O 5,27:5
Crandell, John L, 1953, My 29,25:4
Crandell, Paul M Mrs, 1953, Ja 30,28:2
Crandell, Walter S, 1950, Mr 21,32:4
Crandell, Walter S Mrs, 1949, Jl 11,17:4
Cranden, Joseph, 1949, Mr 22,25:4
Crandon, Le Roi G, 1939, D 28,22:3
Crandon, Mina S Mrs, 1941, N 2,52:3
Crane, A B, 1930, Ap 17,27:1
Crane, A Bruce, 1962, Ag 29,30:1
Crane, A Bruce Mrs, 1951, My 27,69:1
Crane, Aaron D, 1963, N 8,31:1
Crane, Aaron D Mrs, 1949, D 18,88:3
Crane, Abigail D Mrs, 1941, Je 18,21:5
Crane, Albert S, 1946, Ag 27,27:1
Crane, Alex, 1953, Jl 15,25:4
Crane, Alfred, 1955, F 21,21:4
Crane, Alfred T, 1951, D 15,13:6
Crane, Alna, 1953, Mr 11,29:2
Crane, Amanda A Mrs, 1942, Ap 26,39:1
Crane, Arthur, 1945, Ja 7,38:3
Crane, Arthur G, 1955, Ag 13,13:6
Crane, Arthur M Mrs, 1951, Jl 19,23:4
Crane, Arthur S, 1942, Ja 11,44:4
Crane, Augustus S, 1923, Ja 11,21:6
Crane, Augustus W Dr, 1937, F 21,II,11:1
Crane, Aurelia B, 1953, Mr 12,27:2
Crane, Bayard T Dr, 1937, Ag 15,II,6:6
Crane, Benjamin Mrs, 1951, N 23,29:2
Crane, Bruce, 1937, O 30,19:1
Crane, Bruce Mrs, 1948, Ja 27,25:2
Crane, Burton, 1963, F 4,8:1
Crane, C H, 1883, O 11,4:6
Crane, C Howard, 1952, Ag 17,76:7
Crane, Caroline E, 1956, O 3,33:2
Crane, Charles, 1960, Mr 27,86:4
Crane, Charles D, 1943, S 28,25:2
Crane, Charles E, 1960, S 9,30:1
Crane, Charles L, 1953, N 13,27:3
Crane, Charles R (will, Mr 9,3:4), 1939, F 16,21:1
Crane, Charles R 2d, 1955, N 22,35:4
Crane, Charles S Mrs, 1951, O 28,85:1
Crane, Charlotte A W Mrs, 1938, D 13,25:4
Crane, Charlton W, 1941, Je 6,21:2
Crane, Clara K Mrs, 1940, Ja 21,34:5
Crane, Clara L (will, Jl 16,11:8), 1938, Jl 11,17:3
Crane, Clarence B, 1949, O 13,27:3
Crane, Clarence P, 1947, N 16,77:1
Crane, Claude G, 1938, F 28,15:3
Crane, Clinton H, 1958, D 2,37:1
Crane, Cornelia W S Mrs, 1941, N 18,25:4
Crane, Cornelius, 1962, Jl 10,33:3
Crane, Daniel B, 1943, N 10,23:6
Crane, De Witt, 1950, F 4,15:4
Crane, DeWitt Mrs, 1949, D 16,31:3
Crane, Donald F, 1953, Mr 4,27:5
Crane, Durries, 1956, S 28,27:2
Crane, Edgar H, 1944, Ja 17,19:3
Crane, Edith (Mrs Tyrone Power), 1912, Ja 4,13:6
Crane, Edmund F, 1957, S 19,29:3
Crane, Edward B, 1939, F 12,45:1
Crane, Edward M, 1964, Ap 15,25:6
Crane, Edward Mrs, 1949, F 11,23:3
Crane, Edward P Rev Dr, 1905, Mr 22,9:6
Crane, Elizabeth K, 1960, S 12,29:5
Crane, Ella E, 1945, Mr 6,21:5
Crane, Elno C, 1952, Ag 2,15:6
Crane, Elvin Williamson, 1909, Ja 10,13:4
Crane, Emery L, 1941, Ja 19,41:1
Crane, Ephraim H, 1944, S 20,23:5
Crane, Esther M, 1943, O 26,23:4
Crane, Evan J, 1967, Ja 1,52:1
Crane, F, 1928, N 7,25:5
Crane, Ferrel H, 1950, My 25,29:5
Crane, Fletcher C, 1946, N 19,31:3
Crane, Floyd H, 1911, Ap 27,9:5
Crane, Frances A, 1954, Ag 11,26:3
Crane, Frank, 1917, O 27,17:5
Crane, Frank H, 1948, S 4,15:2; 1954, Mr 9,27:2
Crane, Frank W, 1953, Ja 11,91:1
Crane, Frank W Mrs, 1947, O 4,17:4
Crane, Fred F, 1949, D 26,29:4
Crane, Fred L (por), 1949, Ag 17,24:2
Crane, Frederick, 1903, S 13,7:5; 1915, Ja 27,9:6
Crane, Frederick E, 1947, N 22,15:1
Crane, Frederick Goodrich, 1923, Mr 16,17:4
Crane, Frederick R, 1941, Ja 27,15:1
Crane, Frederick W H, 1925, Ap 28,21:4
Crane, Frederick W H Justice, 1912, N 22,13:3
Crane, George F Mrs, 1961, S 16,19:5
Crane, George J, 1966, Ja 24,35:5
Crane, George M, 1963, Jl 13,17:5
Crane, George W, 1937, Je 21,19:3; 1949, Ja 22,13:5
Crane, Harry A, 1959, N 3,31:3
Crane, Harry W, 1939, Jl 22,15:3; 1944, N 9,27:3; 1964, Mr 23,29:5
Crane, Helen B, 1953, S 29,29:4
Crane, Helen M, 1942, Ja 30,19:2
Crane, Henry L, 1937, Ap 25,II,8:8
Crane, Henry M, 1956, Ja 22,89:1
Crane, Henry W Mrs, 1951, D 19,31:1
Crane, Hilda A, 1951, D 27,21:1
Crane, Howard R, 1967, Mr 25,23:1
Crane, J Irving, 1947, Jl 23,23:5
Crane, J Rev, 1877, D 26,4:7
Crane, J T, 1880, F 17,5:2
Crane, James B, 1949, Jl 17,56:8
Crane, James C, 1952, N 2,88:3
Crane, James H, 1944, Ap 27,23:4
Crane, James R, 1938, My 12,23:2
Crane, James T, 1938, O 14,23:3
Crane, Jason G, 1942, Je 19,23:2
Crane, Jefferson D, 1952, Ja 22,29:4
Crane, Job Mrs, 1943, N 17,25:1
Crane, Joe, 1968, F 25,76:5
Crane, John, 1908, Ap 10,9:5
Crane, John B, 1950, F 26,78:1
Crane, John C, 1940, F 1,21:5
Crane, John M, 1904, D 31,9:7
Crane, John R Mrs, 1951, O 28,84:6
Crane, Jonathan A, 1911, O 1,13:5
Crane, Joseph B, 1946, Mr 10,46:5
Crane, Joseph G, 1941, Ap 24,21:6
Crane, Joseph W, 1949, Mr 19,15:5
Crane, Joshua, 1964, D 8,45:2
Crane, Julius, 1950, F 7,27:1
Crane, Kenneth F, 1943, F 5,21:2
Crane, Kent, 1966, D 9,47:3
Crane, Leander H Mrs, 1952, Mr 24,25:3
Crane, Leroy Bowers, 1916, My 16,13:6
Crane, Lewis, 1949, D 17,17:2
Crane, Louis B Mrs, 1953, Ja 22,23:1
Crane, Louis W, 1938, D 3,19:3
Crane, Lucy, 1882, Ap 25,4:7
Crane, Lydia Hale Mrs, 1918, Mr 2,13:2
Crane, M J, 1928, D 27,23:1
Crane, Michael, 1947, Je 11,27:2
Crane, Montgomery S, 1959, Ap 28,35:3
Crane, Moses M Mrs, 1947, Jl 4,13:5
Crane, Ogden Mrs, 1914, Ja 5,9:6
Crane, Paul E, 1955, Je 9,29:1
Crane, Percy W, 1964, Mr 21,25:5
Crane, Rachel A Mrs, 1937, Ag 8,II,6:7
Crane, Ralph T (por), 1938, My 11,19:4
Crane, Ralph W, 1951, S 10,21:5; 1952, Ap 2,33:4
Crane, Richard Mrs, 1948, Mr 8,23:2; 1952, Je 11,29:3
Crane, Richard T, 1912, Ja 9,13:4
Crane, Richard T Jr Mrs, 1949, Jl 29,21:1
Crane, Robert B, 1967, My 29,25:4
Crane, Robert B Mrs, 1961, Ap 12,41:4
Crane, Robert C, 1962, Ap 25,39:1
Crane, Robert D, 1962, O 25,39:4
Crane, Robert E, 1960, My 13,31:2
Crane, Robert J, 1956, D 28,21:4
Crane, Ronald S, 1967, Ag 29,40:1
Crane, Rosella Mrs, 1912, Ag 20,9:1
Crane, Roy E, 1962, My 16,41:2
Crane, Samuel B, 1941, Mr 2,42:3; 1944, Je 20,19:3
Crane, Samuel J, 1952, Je 11,29:4
Crane, Spencer, 1952, Ja 30,26:5
Crane, Stephen, 1900, Je 6,6:5
Crane, T F, 1927, D 11,31:4
Crane, Theodore, 1951, Je 6,31:4; 1961, My 25,37:4
Crane, Thomas, 1954, F 11,29:4
Crane, Timothy J, 1954, F 12,25:5
Crane, Utley H, 1938, My 7,15:3
Crane, W, 1903, Ap 29,9:6
Crane, W H, 1928, Mr 8,25:3
Crane, W Murray, 1920, O 3,22:2
Crane, W N Mrs, 1880, Mr 12,5:3
Crane, Walter, 1915, Mr 16,11:3
Crane, Walter D, 1951, Ja 2,23:2
Crane, Walter Mrs, 1944, Je 21,19:5
Crane, Walter P, 1949, D 4,108:5
Crane, Walter S, 1940, Mr 10,49:1
Crane, Warren C Mrs, 1924, N 24,17:4
Crane, William C, 1948, S 24,25:3
Crane, William E Jr, 1954, Mr 15,25:5
Crane, William E Mrs, 1946, O 22,25:3
Crane, William F, 1913, D 15,9:4
Crane, William G, 1960, F 19,27:1
Crane, William H, 1944, Ag 25,13:4; 1955, Ap 9,13:5; 1957, Ja 23,29:5
Crane, William J, 1938, Ag 24,21:4
Crane, William M, 1958, O 8,35:2
Crane, William N, 1910, S 15,9:5
Crane, William W, 1946, D 3,32:3; 1961, D 4,37:2
Crane, Winthrop Murray Jr, 1968, Mr 29,45:4
Crane, Z Marshall Mrs, 1916, O 7,11:4
Crane, Z S, 1884, My 25,3:3
Crane, Zenas, 1917, D 18,15:4
Crane, Zenas G, 1949, O 5,29:3
Crane-Baker, John, 1956, Mr 8,29:5
Craner, Lawrence M, 1968, Ja 4,37:2
Cranfield, Arthur L, 1957, O 11,27:3
Cranford, Frederick L, 1940, Mr 30,15:1
Cranford, Frederick L Mrs, 1959, Ja 15,33:2
Cranford, Walter V Mrs, 1960, Je 10,31:2
Crange, Franklin Mrs, 1937, My 20,21:1
Crangle, Roland, 1945, Je 21,19:2
Crangle, William H, 1959, Mr 10,35:2
Crank, Cornelius V, 1955, Mr 13,87:1
Crankshaw, Charles W, 1960, F 7,85:1
Cranley, James D, 1941, Jl 28,13:6
Cranley, Thomas F, 1955, S 21,33:2
Cranmer, Clarkson A, 1954, D 15,31:5
Cranmer, Clarkson Mrs, 1948, O 15,24:2
Cranmer, Clarkson Mrs (Mary Beckman), 1968, F 13,43:3
Cranmer, George T, 1939, Jl 11,19:3
Cranmer, John Mrs, 1944, Ap 16,41:2
Cranmer, Nathan P, 1951, Mr 16,31:3
Cranmer, William H H, 1967, My 3,45:1
Cranmer, William S, 1944, Ap 4,21:6
Cranmer, William S Mrs, 1939, My 23,23:1
Cranmore, George F, 1953, F 13,12:3
Crannage, J Norman, 1950, F 24,24:1
Crannell, Clarke W, 1910, N 15,11:4
Crannell, William W, 1941, Je 17,21:2
Cranor, Donald F, 1948, Jl 9,19:4
Cranor, John R, 1959, Je 14,86:4
Crans, Walter F, 1949, Ap 21,25:1
Cranska, Floyd, 1920, F 5,9:3
Cranston, Claudia, 1947, Je 28,14:3
Cranston, Earl Mrs, 1903, F 9,2:2
Cranston, Frederick L, 1960, Ag 27,19:5
Cranston, George C, 1963, My 1,39:2
Cranston, H (see also S 18), 1877, S 20,8:2
Cranston, Harry D, 1956, S 21,25:4
Cranston, James H, 1952, D 19,31:1
Cranston, Leslie A Mrs, 1947, D 9,29:5
Cranston, Paul F, 1951, My 5,17:4
Cranston, Robert A G, 1953, F 7,15:1
Cranston, Robert B, 1873, Ja 28,1:5
Cranston, Ruth Mrs, 1956, Ap 4,29:3
Cranston, W H, 1871, O 11,4:1
Cranstoun, William D, 1952, F 2,13:4
Cranwell, Edward H, 1946, My 13,21:5
Cranwell, Edward H Jr, 1957, N 24,87:2
Cranwell, James H, 1940, My 17,19:6
Cranwell, James L, 1963, O 31,33:2
Cranworth, Lord, 1868, Jl 28,5:2
Cranworth, Lord (B F Gurdon), 1964, Ja 5,92:2
Crapa, Philip M, 1903, S 22,7:4
Crapo, H A Ex-Gov, 1869, Jl 25,4:7
Crapo, Henry N, 1951, N 28,31:4
Crapo, Herbert L, 1960, O 6,41:6
Crapo, Stanford T, 1939, Ja 28,15:4
Crapser, John C, 1956, F 15,31:2
Crapsey, A S, 1928, Ja 1,19:1
Crapsey, Arthur H, 1955, My 25,33:3
Crapsey, Robert C, 1953, F 12,27:1
Crapster, Thaddeus G, 1941, Jl 27,30:3
Crapullo, George A, 1952, Ag 14,23:5
Crary, Arthur V, 1949, Ag 28,75:3
Crary, George W Dr, 1925, N 17,25:5
Crary, Gordon B Sr, 1959, N 9,31:5
Crary, James H Mrs, 1948, Ja 24,15:5
Crary, John C, 1961, Ag 22,29:5
Crary, Joseph Dayton, 1916, N 2,13:6
Crary, Miner D, 1956, Ap 23,27:4
Crary, Robert Fulton Rev Dr, 1914, N 16,9:5
Crary, Roscoe, 1937, Ap 4,11:3
Crary, W H Dr, 1918, My 25,13:5
Craske, Leonard, 1950, Ag 30,32:2
Crasper, John C Mrs, 1945, F 26,19:4
Crass, Milton, 1950, N 13,28:2
Crasson, Louis F, 1951, S 10,21:5
Craster, Charles V, 1953, D 9,11:6
Crasto, Franklin P, 1940, Je 7,23:4
Crasto, Franklin P Jr, 1945, Ja 8,17:4
Crate, Albert E, 1956, D 14,29:4
Crater, Allen M Mrs, 1924, F 16,13:6
Crater, Annie C Mrs, 1938, N 23,21:3
Crater, Charles T, 1965, N 28,88:8
Crater, David J Mrs, 1950, My 10,31:5
Crater, Douglas Montague, 1922, Mr 23,13:3
Crater, Ellis Dr, 1923, F 23,13:4
Crater, Frank E, 1941, My 10,15:6
Crater, Frank R Sr, 1953, D 11,31:2
Crater, John L Dr, 1915, D 10,13:6
Crater, Lelia M Mrs, 1951, Ap 21,17:4
Crater, Robert M, 1946, My 19,42:6
Crater, Walter K, 1943, My 3,17:4
Crater, Warren, 1951, Ap 26,29:1
Cratt, Arthur D, 1941, S 17,23:3
Cratty, Alfred R, 1954, My 2,89:1
Cratty, John M Mrs, 1950, O 30,27:4
Cratty, M, 1928, F 28,25:3
Craufurd, Lawrence, 1961, Ap 11,37:3
Crautter, Frederick W, 1937, My 8,19:3
Cravath, Alice M Mrs, 1941, Mr 25,23:3
Cravath, Erastus M, 1938, Jl 26,19:6
Cravath, Gavvy (Clifford C), 1963, My 24,31:5
Cravath, Newell J (Jeff), 1953, D 11,31:1
Cravath, Paul D Mrs, 1922, Ap 13,19:6; 1953, Mr 11, 29:1
Cravath, Paul E (will, Jl 12,13:4), 1940, Jl 2,21:1

Crave, Adolph G, 1941, Ap 3,23:4
Craveiro Lopes, Francisco H, 1964, S 3,29:3
Craveiro Lopes, Francisco H Mrs, 1958, Jl 6,56:3
Craveiro Lopes, Joao C Mrs, 1955, N 25,28:5
Craven, A, 1926, O 1,23:3
Craven, A W, 1879, Mr 29,5:2
Craven, Alex, 1961, Ap 3,33:3
Craven, Charles E, 1944, D 18,19:3
Craven, Charles W, 1944, N 19,49:1
Craven, Cornelia, 1961, My 24,41:5
Craven, D Stewart (por), 1949, Je 25,13:5
Craven, Earl E, 1956, Ja 10,31:2
Craven, Earl of, 1883, D 9,2:6
Craven, Edgar M, 1960, Ja 27,30:7
Craven, Edith H Mrs, 1942, Mr 22,48:6
Craven, Frank, 1945, S 2,31:1
Craven, H T, 1905, Ap 14,9:6
Craven, Harry J B, 1966, Mr 10,33:4
Craven, Henry T, 1958, O 14,37:3
Craven, J P, 1968, O 22,47:1
Craven, John, 1947, Ja 1,25:2
Craven, John C, 1941, O 21,23:4
Craven, John T, 1905, F 27,7:5
Craven, Joseph (Bro Patrick), 1955, O 16,86:1
Craven, Leonard, 1948, Je 17,25:3
Craven, Leslie, 1955, Jl 24,65:3
Craven, Macdonough, 1919, F 11,11:3
Craven, Marie Louise Mrs, 1905, Ap 28,9:2
Craven, Milton G Jr, 1947, S 20,15:6
Craven, Nettie Mrs, 1905, My 3,11:1
Craven, T A M Capt, 1864, Ag 16,5:1
Craven, Thomas J, 1967, Jl 15,25:2
Craven, Thomas T, 1950, Ap 7,25:1
Craven, Thomas T Mrs, 1955, S 30,25:3
Craven, Walter Mrs, 1943, D 15,27:3
Craven, William A, 1947, Mr 30,56:2
Craven, William A Jr, 1944, Ja 22,13:6
Cravener, Edward K, 1941, Mr 28,23:2
Cravens, Ben, 1939, Ja 14,17:2
Cravens, J R Mrs, 1903, Je 25,7:5
Cravens, John S, 1946, My 18,19:5
Cravens, John S Mrs, 1943, Jl 14,19:5
Cravens, John W, 1937, Ag 11,24:3
Cravens, Joseph M, 1939, Jl 1,17:6
Craver, Forrest E, 1958, O 19,87:1
Craver, Harrison W, 1951, Jl 29,68:4
Craver, Harry, 1939, Ag 26,15:4
Craver, John W, 1942, Ja 6,24:2
Cravis, Israel S, 1948, S 17,25:1
Cravis, William B, 1949, Je 18,13:3
Craw, Nelson A, 1962, Mr 21,39:1
Craw, Russell E, 1961, O 7,23:1
Crawell, Luther Bornell Capt, 1925, F 17,23:4
Crawfis, Ewing, 1965, D 20,35:4
Crawford, A J, 1903, Jl 20,2:6
Crawford, A William, 1929, Je 28,23:5
Crawford, Adrian H, 1942, My 14,19:1
Crawford, Agnes, 1941, Ja 25,15:5
Crawford, Albert W, 1951, S 22,17:4
Crawford, Alex, 1954, Ag 16,17:2
Crawford, Alfred G, 1947, Ap 22,27:2
Crawford, Alfred P Mrs, 1949, D 7,31:4
Crawford, Alfred R, 1966, Mr 12,27:2
Crawford, Alice E, 1955, Ap 2,13:8
Crawford, Andrew W Mrs, 1943, N 1,17:2
Crawford, Andrew Wylie, 1968, N 29,45:5
Crawford, Anne, 1956, O 18,33:2
Crawford, Arch R, 1965, D 2,41:3
Crawford, Arthur B, 1962, N 7,39:4
Crawford, Arthur J, 1938, Jl 1,19:5
Crawford, Arthur Mrs, 1939, D 10,68:4
Crawford, Arthur W, 1946, Mr 12,25:2
Crawford, Barbara, 1951, Ap 13,24:2
Crawford, Baxter L, 1940, Ja 5,19:1
Crawford, Benjamin J, 1941, S 16,23:5
Crawford, Benjamin J Col, 1910, S 3,7:6
Crawford, Benjamin O, 1946, Ag 29,27:1
Crawford, Bennie Mrs, 1951, My 8,31:2
Crawford, Berta M, 1937, My 28,21:2
Crawford, C Frank (por), 1949, Ag 29,17:5
Crawford, C Scott, 1949, Ja 12,27:2
Crawford, Charles, 1939, O 3,23:3
Crawford, Charles A, 1941, Mr 21,21:4
Crawford, Charles C, 1943, Ap 12,23:5
Crawford, Charles E, 1942, My 21,19:2
Crawford, Charles P, 1940, N 19,24:2
Crawford, Charles W, 1957, S 16,31:3
Crawford, Chauncey A, 1964, Je 24,37:2
Crawford, Chester W, 1959, Je 5,27:4
Crawford, Cliff R, 1958, F 1,19:2
Crawford, Clifton, 1920, Je 6,22:3
Crawford, Coe I, 1944, Ap 26,19:5
Crawford, Daniel Sr, 1937, D 10,26:3
Crawford, David, 1957, Jl 23,27:2; 1964, My 8,33:2
Crawford, David E, 1948, Je 6,72:4
Crawford, Dean B, 1949, Ag 14,69:2
Crawford, Don A, 1951, N 20,31:5
Crawford, Dorothy Mrs, 1950, N 22,25:2
Crawford, Douglas G Mrs, 1959, Ap 6,27:3
Crawford, Douglas J, 1945, Ja 28,37:1
Crawford, E Stetson Mrs, 1956, Je 2,19:2
Crawford, Earl, 1954, N 12,15:1
Crawford, Earl of, 1880, D 16,2:7; 1913, F 1,13:4
Crawford, Earl of (D A E Lindsay), 1940, Mr 9,15:3
Crawford, Edna A, 1955, F 2,27:1
Crawford, Edward, 1964, N 6,37:4
Crawford, Edward C, 1948, S 4,15:5
Crawford, Edward H, 1955, Ap 9,13:5
Crawford, Edward L, 1942, S 5,13:3
Crawford, Etta, 1946, Je 29,19:2
Crawford, Eugene M, 1949, Ag 20,11:3
Crawford, Everett L, 1960, My 2,29:3
Crawford, F Marion (funl), 1909, Ap 11,11:3
Crawford, Francis H, 1949, N 21,25:2
Crawford, Francis X, 1944, Ag 21,15:6
Crawford, Frank, 1941, S 15,17:5
Crawford, Frank H, 1945, Mr 26,19:5
Crawford, Frank Mrs, 1943, S 29,21:5; 1954, My 24, 27:3
Crawford, Fred D, 1942, Jl 25,13:6; 1959, S 29,36:2
Crawford, Fred L, 1957, Ap 14,86:3
Crawford, Frederick R, 1948, Je 14,23:1
Crawford, George, 1948, D 4,19:1
Crawford, George Chappell Dr, 1903, Jl 14,7:6
Crawford, George E, 1949, Ja 18,23:4
Crawford, Gilbert H, 1964, F 28,29:1
Crawford, Gilbert Holmes, 1915, O 14,11:6
Crawford, Gladys Mrs, 1951, Ap 13,24:2
Crawford, Greatest, 1966, N 19,42:2
Crawford, Gustavus C, 1944, Je 30,21:5
Crawford, Gustavus Mrs, 1959, F 4,33:5
Crawford, Harper G, 1940, Jl 16,17:4
Crawford, Harry B, 1948, F 25,23:3
Crawford, Harry J (will, N 14,14:1), 1953, N 4,33:4
Crawford, Henry E, 1944, Ap 3,21:6
Crawford, Homer C, 1942, D 29,21:2
Crawford, Horace M, 1944, Ja 19,19:5
Crawford, Hugh A, 1946, Je 14,21:3
Crawford, Hugh W, 1951, Mr 4,92:3
Crawford, J L, 1946, S 3,19:2
Crawford, J P Wickersham, 1939, S 23,17:6
Crawford, J S, 1903, Je 18,9:6
Crawford, Jack Randall, 1968, Ag 9,35:4
Crawford, James C Col, 1953, F 8,89:2
Crawford, James C Jr, 1960, Mr 3,29:2
Crawford, James D, 1950, My 25,29:5
Crawford, James G, 1952, My 16,23:5
Crawford, James J, 1954, Mr 31,27:2
Crawford, James M, 1960, S 25,88:8; 1963, Je 12,43:3
Crawford, James S, 1939, Mr 18,17:5
Crawford, Jay F, 1938, Je 12,39:3
Crawford, Jesse, 1962, My 30,19:3
Crawford, Jesse Mrs, 1943, Ja 16,13:5
Crawford, John, 1941, Ap 27,38:5; 1949, D 24,16:2
Crawford, John A, 1941, O 31,23:5
Crawford, John F, 1940, S 6,21:2; 1946, Ap 28,44:3
Crawford, John H, 1942, N 13,23:5; 1957, F 13,35:4
Crawford, John L, 1945, Ag 5,37:2
Crawford, John M, 1950, Jl 21,19:4
Crawford, John Mrs (por), 1949, Ag 10,21:5
Crawford, John R, 1951, My 6,92:7
Crawford, John S, 1954, Jl 23,17:4
Crawford, John W, 1939, Jl 31,13:6
Crawford, John W Mrs, 1962, Ja 22,23:3
Crawford, John W R, 1939, Jl 7,17:4
Crawford, Joseph Ury, 1924, N 22,15:6
Crawford, Juliette F, 1938, F 26,15:6
Crawford, Kenneth, 1961, Mr 8,33:1
Crawford, Kenneth B, 1959, D 3,37:4
Crawford, L Burdsall, 1938, Jl 14,21:2
Crawford, Lawrence C, 1949, Ag 27,13:5
Crawford, Lee, 1942, My 2,13:3
Crawford, Lemuel, 1937, D 19,II,9:1
Crawford, Leona M Mrs (will), 1957, Ja 26,11:2
Crawford, Lesley B, 1963, S 26,35:3
Crawford, Lester J, 1946, N 12,29:4
Crawford, Lester Mrs (H Broderick),(funl plans, S 28,31:5), 1959, S 27,86:1
Crawford, Lindsay, 1945, Je 4,19:5
Crawford, Lindsay Mrs, 1951, D 12,37:2
Crawford, Louis C, 1925, Je 17,21:4
Crawford, Lt-Gov, 1875, My 15,10:2
Crawford, Malcolm M Dr, 1937, My 15,19:6
Crawford, Margaret, 1950, N 2,31:4
Crawford, Mary C Mrs, 1939, O 18,25:5
Crawford, Matthew J, 1914, Mr 11,11:6
Crawford, Merrit, 1945, Ag 13,19:5
Crawford, Mimi (Dowager Countess of Suffolk and Berkshire), 1966, F 24,37:4
Crawford, Morris B, 1940, O 10,25:7
Crawford, Morris B Mrs, 1954, F 2,27:6
Crawford, Morris D (por), 1949, Je 25,13:3
Crawford, Nelson A, 1963, Jl 2,26:7
Crawford, O C, 1939, Jl 26,19:5
Crawford, Osbert G S, 1957, N 30,21:5
Crawford, Percy, 1960, N 1,40:1
Crawford, Porter J, 1946, D 28,15:4
Crawford, R, 1934, Ja 25,19:5
Crawford, Raymond, 1938, Mr 10,21:5
Crawford, Raymond S Mrs, 1946, Ap 25,21:1
Crawford, Rheba (Mrs L Lambert), 1966, Ja 8,26:1
Crawford, Richard Sir, 1919, Ag 28,11:4
Crawford, Robert, 1941, S 21,42:1; 1952, S 27,17:1
Crawford, Robert H, 1942, Jl 27,15:4
Crawford, Robert L Mrs, 1962, F 22,25:2
Crawford, Robert Leighton, 1921, S 10,11:5
Crawford, Robert M, 1961, Mr 13,29:2
Crawford, Robert W (will), 1943, S 25,12:1
Crawford, Robert W, 1943, O 17,48:7; 1963, Jl 27,17:2
Crawford, Russell T, 1958, D 29,15:3
Crawford, Ruth M, 1957, Ag 14,25:5
Crawford, Ruth W Mrs, 1959, Mr 28,17:4
Crawford, S E, 1907, S 27,9:5
Crawford, Samuel Earl (Wahoo Sam), 1968, Je 17, 39:3
Crawford, Samuel J Gen, 1913, O 22,9:6
Crawford, Samuel Oakley (Rev Arth Worthington), 1917, D 14,13:4
Crawford, Sarah J, 1907, Ag 3,7:6
Crawford, Sarah M Mrs, 1937, F 16,23:2
Crawford, Seth T, 1943, S 18,17:5
Crawford, Sidney G, 1925, O 22,25:4
Crawford, Stanton C, 1966, Ja 27,33:2
Crawford, Stuart L, 1942, S 3,19:6
Crawford, Thomas B, 1957, S 23,27:6
Crawford, Thomas F, 1940, Mr 15,23:1
Crawford, Thomas J, 1966, Jl 5,37:2; 1968, S 15,84:4
Crawford, W, 1929, Ja 6,7:1
Crawford, W E, 1950, Je 28,27:5
Crawford, W Gordon, 1938, S 9,21:3
Crawford, W H Mrs, 1952, S 26,21:5
Crawford, W S, 1883, F 25,7:4
Crawford, W V, 1938, Mr 23,17:2
Crawford, Walter W, 1952, Jl 1,23:4
Crawford, Warren, 1946, Ja 25,23:1
Crawford, West James, 1923, N 10,13:5
Crawford, Will, 1944, Mr 9,17:3
Crawford, Will C, 1955, Je 1,33:2
Crawford, William, 1913, N 13,11:5; 1940, Mr 14,23: 1951, F 8,33:1
Crawford, William A, 1951, Ap 29,89:2; 1954, O 18, 25:4
Crawford, William C, 1938, Ap 29,21:1
Crawford, William H, 1944, Mr 7,17:1
Crawford, William H Mrs, 1949, S 24,13:4
Crawford, William L, 1950, Je 21,27:5
Crawford, William Mrs, 1962, N 16,31:2
Crawford, William R, 1938, D 7,23:2
Crawford, William R Mrs, 1943, F 18,23:4
Crawford, William S, 1948, Jl 18,54:3; 1948, S 24,25 1950, N 21,32:2
Crawford, William T, 1960, Ag 2,29:3
Crawford, William W, 1941, F 20,19:4
Crawford, Winfield W, 1950, O 17,31:5
Crawford and Balcarres, Countess of, 1947, Ja 10,21
Crawley, Arthur S, 1948, O 9,19:5
Crawley, Charles E, 1954, N 27,13:1
Crawley, Charles H, 1954, S 18,15:2
Crawley, Edward D, 1960, N 12,21:1
Crawley, F M, 1963, My 23,37:2
Crawley, J J, 1959, Jl 9,27:5
Crawley, J Sayre Mrs (M Ward), 1966, My 4,47:4
Crawley, Joseph (funl, Ja 17,15:3), 1925, Ja 13,19
Crawley, Joseph, 1942, My 23,13:2
Crawley, Josiah T, 1943, Mr 19,19:5
Crawley, Mabel, 1912, Ja 11,13:5
Crawley, Matthew J, 1938, D 19,23:3
Crawley, P S, 1956, O 17,35:4
Crawley, Sayre, 1948, Mr 8,23:1
Crawofrd, Thomas F, 1949, Je 12,76:1
Crawofrd, Walter W, 1949, My 21,13:2
Crawshaw, Alfred G, 1950, D 13,35:2
Crawshaw, Odell W, 1942, My 16,13:4
Crawshaw, William H, 1940, Jl 3,17:5
Crawshaw, William H Mrs, 1939, Ja 23,13:4
Crawshay, R (Iron King), 1879, My 27,7:1
Cray, Eugene F, 1953, Ja 5,21:3
Cray, James R, 1937, D 12,II,8:7
Cray, John J (funl, S 17,23:6), 1925, S 16,25:5
Cray, Margaret V Mrs, 1938, My 3,23:4
Cray, Patrick J, 1923, Ap 30,15:5
Cray, William L, 1958, Je 1,86:5
Craycraft, Frederick L, 1923, Mr 16,17:5
Crayzer, Herbert R (Lord Rotherwick), 1958, M 29:4
Crazy Horse, Joe, 1945, D 23,18:4
Crazy Nora, 1865, F 26,3:6
Crazy Snake, Chief, 1912, Ap 6,11:5
Creadick, A Nowell, 1956, Jl 25,29:5
Creadick, Florence N Mrs, 1937, Ja 25,19:2
Creager, John O, 1943, Ja 6,25:4
Creager, Marvin H, 1954, D 5,88:3
Creager, Marvin H Mrs, 1943, O 21,27:3
Creager, R B, 1950, O 29,92:5
Creagh, Edward F, 1959, Jl 17,21:5
Creagh, John J, 1944, Mr 21,20:3
Creagh, John T, 1951, D 11,33:1
Creaghan, John S, 1960, Je 4,23:5
Creaghead, Thomas J, 1950, Mr 5,92:5
Creal, Edward W (cor, O 15,19:4), 1943, O 14,
Creal, Harold L Mrs, 1954, N 17,31:4
Creamer, Benjamin F, 1944, Ag 10,17:5
Creamer, Carroll M, 1963, S 20,33:3
Creamer, Francis A, 1938, S 20,23:4
Creamer, Francis D, 1946, Ap 13,17:2
Creamer, Frank D, 1913, Jl 20,II,11:4
Creamer, Frank D Mrs, 1912, F 5,9:6
Creamer, Harold S, 1944, Mr 13,15:2
Creamer, Harry W, 1947, Ag 20,21:4

Creamer, John F, 1967, Je 29,43:3
Creamer, John F Mrs, 1949, O 13,27:2
Creamer, John L Mrs, 1948, Je 25,24:3
Creamer, Joseph M, 1955, Ap 5,29:2
Creamer, Joseph M Dr, 1918, Jl 30,11:6
Creamer, Mary Mrs, 1945, Ag 5,38:3
Creamer, Patrick L, 1944, F 13,42:1
Creamer, Richard L, 1951, S 2,V,3:6
Creamer, Thomas J, 1914, Ag 5,13:7
Creamer, Wallace A, 1952, My 7,27:4
Creamer, William G, 1953, Ag 26,27:4
Creamer, William H, 1951, S 2,48:8
Creamer, William H Jr, 1962, Ap 17,35:4
Crean, Jeremiah H, 1944, Jl 19,19:1
Crean, John E Mrs, 1961, Je 1,35:3
Crean, Maurice J, 1946, F 1,23:4
Crean, Patrick J, 1949, Ag 5,19:2
Crean, Richard T, 1956, Mr 15,1:3
Crean, Thomas A Jr, 1951, My 4,19:4
Crean, William J Sr, 1950, Ag 28,17:2
Creange, Henry, 1945, Ag 15,19:4
Creary, Daniel F, 1942, F 6,19:4
Creary, James R, 1941, F 28,19:2
Crease, Henry Lady, 1922, D 13,21:5
Creaser, Isaiah, 1952, D 22,25:5
Creasey, Hannah M, 1949, Ag 16,23:4
Creasy, George H, 1959, F 26,31:5
Creasy, Harryette, 1952, Ap 3,36:3
Creasy, John B, 1943, F 8,19:3
Creasy, Raymond C, 1955, Ja 25,25:4
Creasy, William T, 1920, F 17,9:4
Creaton, Thomas M, 1942, Mr 23,15:5
Creatore, Giuseppe, 1952, Ag 16,15:5
Crecca, Rae L Mrs, 1953, Ag 22,15:2
Crecca, William J, 1959, Je 1,27:4
Crecke, Roger Mrs, 1945, D 18,27:3
Crecraft, Earl W, 1950, Ap 1,15:6
Crecraft, Gordon R, 1948, O 24,78:5
Cree, Albert A Mrs, 1952, My 10,21:2
Cree, Charles Mrs, 1948, Ja 16,21:3
Cree, Virginia C Mrs, 1941, F 16,40:7
Cree, William F, 1942, N 10,27:5
Creech, Arabella R, 1957, Mr 19,37:4
Creech, Harris, 1941, My 19,17:5
Creech, James H, 1948, Mr 12,23:2
Creech, Oscar Jr, 1967, D 23,23:4
Creech, Samuel Walley, 1903, Jl 2,9:6
Creed, Charles, 1966, Jl 19,39:1
Creed, Frederick G, 1957, D 13,27:4
Creed, Georges, 1939, Ap 16,III,7:1
Creed, Jason S, 1949, N 30,27:2
Creed, William R, 1903, N 10,9:5
Creed, Williams R Mrs, 1947, Ap 5,19:6
Creede, Gardner, 1942, Ja 8,21:5
Creeden, Daniel W, 1953, Jl 30,23:5
Creeden, John J, 1939, Jl 13,19:4
Creeden, Joseph D, 1944, O 3,23:4
Creedon, John B, 1948, F 27,21:3
Creedon, John W, 1952, Jl 30,23:4
Creedon, Michael, 1939, Ag 5,15:6
Creegan, Charles C, 1939, Ja 5,23:1
Creekmore, Alex, 1952, Jl 2,25:1
Creekmore, Hubert, 1966, My 25,47:2
Creekpaum, Charles C, 1940, Mr 3,45:1
Creel, E C, 1931, Ag 19,21:5
Creel, George, 1953, O 3,17:1
Creel, George Mrs, 1948, Ja 18,60:6
Creel, Julia M Mrs, 1911, S 27,13:5
Creelman, David W, 1952, Ja 6,92:5
Creelman, George W, 1951, D 4,33:1
Creelman, Harlan, 1950, My 27,17:2
Creelman, Harlan Mrs, 1940, S 18,23:2
Creelman, James, 1915, F 13,9:5
Creelman, James (funl), 1915, Mr 5,9:6
Creelman, John A, 1940, S 29,43:2
Creelman, William A, 1946, Ja 29,25:3
Creelman, William J, 1939, Je 3,15:5
Creely, Daniel, 1923, My 21,15:5
Creem, Thomas F, 1943, O 17,49:2
Creer, Frances Kelly Mrs, 1953, F 14,17:3
Creese, James, 1966, F 10,37:3
Creese, Myron, 1945, Jl 31,19:2
Creevey, George M, 1945, My 1,23:4
Creevey, John Kennedy, 1921, Mr 27,22:3
Cregan, Cornelius J, 1959, Ja 26,29:5
Cregan, David J, 1966, Jl 30,25:5
Cregan, Nicholas R, 1939, O 10,23:5
Cregar, Laird, 1944, D 10,54:2
Cregar, Luther, 1953, Ag 12,31:4
Cregar, Peter B, 1959, Ap 10,29:3
Creger, Frank, 1951, My 1,29:4
Cregg, Frank J, 1963, S 6,29:1
Cregg, Paul L, 1955, S 25,93:2
Creghorn, Odie, 1956, Jl 15,61:2
Cregier, Harry E, 1949, My 7,13:4
Cregin, William F, 1940, D 17,26:2
Crego, Martin H, 1955, My 10,29:5
Crehan, Frederic J, 1951, S 2,49:2
Crehan, William J, 1962, My 16,41:5
Crehore, Austen B, 1962, Ag 22,34:1
Crehore, Frank H, 1937, Jl 18,II,7:2
Crehore, William W Mrs, 1952, O 8,31:3
Crehore, William Williams, 1918, S 14,11:3

Creifelds, Richard, 1939, My 5,23:4
Creig, John H, 1938, Mr 29,21:4
Creigh, Frederick T, 1954, F 26,19:2
Creighton, Bertram D, 1945, O 6,13:2
Creighton, David C, 1964, F 23,85:1
Creighton, Edward B, 1939, D 6,25:2
Creighton, Frank W, 1948, D 25,17:4
Creighton, Gordon K, 1960, D 28,27:4
Creighton, J B, 1883, N 14,2:1; 1913, Ag 22,9:6
Creighton, James, 1903, Je 9,9:6
Creighton, James Edwin, 1924, O 9,23:5
Creighton, John A Count, 1907, F 8,9:6
Creighton, John M, 1957, D 17,35:1
Creighton, John T, 1941, My 14,21:5
Creighton, Joseph, 1904, F 23,2:4
Creighton, Kenelm, 1963, Mr 1,4:6
Creighton, Miller R Jr, 1937, F 20,17:6
Creighton, Ralph L, 1948, Ja 4,52:4
Creighton, Robert, 1947, Je 19,21:5
Creighton, Roy L, 1956, Ap 1,88:1
Creighton, Thomas, 1952, Mr 8,13:2
Creighton, Tom, 1949, Ap 7,30:2
Creighton, W Rev, 1865, Ap 25,8:5
Creighton, William J, 1955, Jl 29,17:6
Creixell, Joseph, 1941, Ja 18,15:3
Crelin, Wilbur C, 1954, Mr 10,25:4
Crelley, William D, 1960, Jl 24,64:6
Crellin, Edward, 1948, My 18,23:1
Crellin, Thomas, 1940, Ag 8,39:1
Crellin, Thomas A, 1942, Ag 4,19:6
Cremeans, Henderson, 1909, Ja 30,9:5
Cremen, John F, 1951, Ap 13,23:2
Cremens, John F, 1958, N 14,27:3
Cremer, George, 1907, D 23,9:5
Cremer, Harriet H, 1944, Jl 9,36:2
Cremer, Harry R, 1942, D 6,77:2
Cremer, Herbert, 1951, Ap 4,29:4
Cremer, J T, 1923, Ag 15,17:6
Cremer, Marc A, 1958, Je 7,19:4
Cremer, Mathias, 1938, Jl 29,17:4
Cremers, William, 1949, Ja 18,23:3
Cremieux, J A, 1880, F 11,5:5
Cremin, Bernard L, 1937, Ja 21,23:2
Cremin, Eugene F, 1938, F 20,II,9:2
Cremin, Wallace L, 1952, Je 12,33:2
Cremins, J Henry, 1949, Ja 11,31:4
Cremins, Margot M, 1949, Mr 15,27:4
Cremins, Thomas E, 1948, Ag 28,15:3
Cremona, Mario Mrs, 1953, Ja 6,29:2
Cremonesi, Carlo, 1943, N 26,23:3
Cremonesi, Filippo, 1942, My 19,19:2
Cremonini, 1903, My 31,7:5
Creney, James, 1882, Mr 3,2:6
Crenier, Henri, 1948, O 3,66:1
Crennan, Charles H, 1955, F 18,22:1
Crennan, Thomas A Mrs, 1959, My 21,31:1
Crennan, Vincent de P, 1961, My 25,37:3
Crenny, John J, 1942, F 19,19:1
Crenshaw, A D, 1966, Jl 8,35:2
Crenshaw, James L, 1950, N 24,36:4
Crenshaw, John B, 1942, Jl 20,13:3
Crenshaw, Lewis D, 1947, Ja 16,25:4
Crenshaw, Miriam, 1959, Mr 14,48:8
Crenshaw, Payton C, 1939, Ja 19,19:1
Crenshaw, Richard P Mrs, 1951, N 8,29:3
Crenshaw, S Dabney, 1940, F 6,21:2
Crenshaw, Vaden D, 1950, O 28,17:4
Creore, Alvin W Mrs, 1958, Jl 11,23:4
Creque, Edward, 1941, D 10,25:2
Cresap, Mark W, 1942, My 31,38:4
Cresap, Mark W Jr, 1963, Jl 29,19:2
Cresap, T C, 1901, Ag 8,7:6
Crescenzi, Thomas L, 1950, My 1,25:2
Creshull, Albert T, 1940, Je 27,23:2
Creskoff, Adolph J, 1959, Ja 24,19:3
Cresmer, William T, 1959, My 6,39:2
Crespi, Silvio, 1944, Ja 19,19:2
Crespigny, C de, 1935, Je 27,21:1
Crespo, Concepcion De C Y, 1871, Je 8,2:4
Crespo, J Gen, 1898, Ap 19,3:2
Crespo-Ordonez, Manuel, 1954, N 7,86:1
Cress, G Clifford, 1951, Ja 27,13:4
Cress, G Clifford Mrs, 1954, F 19,27:2
Cress, George O, 1954, My 10,23:4
Cress, John D, 1940, D 21,17:5
Cresse, Charles L B, 1939, N 3,21:5
Cresse, Lewis N, 1914, Ag 11,9:5
Cresse, Wadsworth Sr Mrs, 1953, Ja 28,27:2
Cressey, George B, 1963, O 22,37:1
Cressey, John T, 1943, Jl 21,15:2
Cressey, Paul G, 1955, Jl 8,23:2
Cressman, Henry M, 1941, Jl 27,30:2
Cressman, John C, 1947, Ap 23,26:3
Cresson, Benjamin F Jr, 1923, Ja 26,17:4
Cresson, Caleb Mrs, 1942, Ap 23,23:2
Cresson, Charles C Mrs (Mary Jordan), 1961, My 16,43:1
Cresson, Jack, 1958, O 13,29:4
Cresson, W A, 1948, D 28,22:3
Cresson, W P, 1932, My 13,16:1
Cresswell, Charles T Brig-Gen, 1920, Ag 30,9:6
Cresswell, Cresswell Sir, 1863, Ag 13,5:2
Cresswell, Robert, 1943, S 14,23:1

Cressy, W F Sr Mrs, 1947, Ap 17,27:5
Cressy, Warren F, 1952, Mr 12,28:5
Cressy, Will M Mrs, 1944, Je 29,23:2
Cressy, William H, 1947, Ja 13,21:4
Creswell, Helen, 1949, F 8,25:4
Creswell, J A, 1891, D 24,5:2
Cret, Paul P (will, S 22,32:4), 1945, S 9,47:3
Cret, Paul Philippe Prof, 1914, N 11,13:6
Cretin, Nestor A, 1939, Mr 5,48:5
Cretoni, Serafino Cardinal, 1909, F 4,9:4
Cretty, William B Sr, 1949, Ap 6,29:2
Creutz, Emil C, 1952, Jl 28,15:2
Creveling, Emerson, 1959, O 9,21:3
Creveling, Guy F, 1944, O 13,19:4
Creveling, John L, 1950, F 25,17:4
Crevelling, Peter C Rev, 1911, O 18,11:4
Crew, Ernest G, 1942, Mr 10,19:5
Crew, Henry Dr, 1953, F 18,31:4
Crew, John E, 1948, Je 15,27:3
Crew, William B Ex-Justice, 1912, Ja 25,11:3
Crewe, Marquess of, 1945, Je 21,19:3
Crews, A Douglas, 1957, S 1,56:2
Crews, Albert, 1959, My 12,35:4
Crews, Floyd H, 1964, Ap 6,31:3
Crews, Grasty, 1951, N 2,23:4
Crews, Laura H, 1942, N 14,15:1
Crews, Monte, 1946, O 7,31:4
Crews, R, 1926, S 8,25:1
Crews, Robert J, 1968, Ag 3,25:2
Creyk, R H, 1928, Ag 17,19:5
Creyke, Rolf Mrs, 1921, Jl 31,22:4
Criado, Alfred F, 1957, Ap 18,29:2
Cribari, Angelo, 1942, Je 26,21:6
Cribari, Wolfgang E, 1966, D 13,47:1
Cribb, Ira P, 1943, Je 11,19:2
Cribben, Leo T, 1953, My 3,88:2
Cribbett, George, 1964, My 25,33:4
Cribbin, Michael Mrs, 1956, Ap 14,17:5
Cribbons, John P, 1943, Je 29,19:3
Cribbs, Hyatt M, 1942, Ap 13,15:2
Cribier, Edward, 1956, D 2,87:1
Cribley, John L, 1944, Je 22,19:5
Crichton, Andrew B, 1952, Jl 10,31:3
Crichton, Charles Julian Maitland-Makgill, 1915, N 9, 13:3
Crichton, Harry A, 1967, Ag 7,29:4
Crichton, Hiram N, 1951, Ap 23,25:4
Crichton, John Henry (Earl of Eine), 1914, D 4,11:6
Crichton, Kyle S, 1960, N 25,27:2
Crichton, Leslie N, 1941, S 8,15:5
Crichton, Marshall, 1960, Mr 2,37:4
Crichton, Powell, 1962, N 17,25:4
Crichton, Thomas A, 1954, Je 16,31:5
Crichton, William, 1875, D 29,4:5
Crichton-Browne, H W A F, 1937, O 2,21:4
Crichton-Browne, James (por), 1938, F 1,21:3
Crichton-Stuart, Colum, 1957, Ag 19,19:5
Crichton-Stuart, John Marquess of Bute, 1956, Ag 16, 25:5
Crick, Philip C T Rt Rev, 1937, Jl 14,22:3
Crick, Stanley S, 1955, Ag 11,21:3
Crickard, John, 1882, O 8,5:2
Crickboom, Mathieve, 1947, N 2,73:1
Crickenberger, Robert L, 1946, Ag 7,27:4
Crickmore, Henry G, 1908, N 4,11:6
Crider, James L, 1945, N 28,27:2
Crider, James L Mrs, 1958, N 24,29:5
Crider, John H, 1966, Jl 9,27:4
Crider, John M, 1950, Mr 15,29:3
Crider, John S, 1952, Ja 20,84:5
Crider, Mark B, 1950, S 19,31:3
Crider, Richard S Mrs, 1959, Ag 3,25:4
Cridland, Robert B, 1945, Je 19,19:4
Cridler, Thomas W Mrs, 1946, Ja 8,23:2
Cridler, Thomas Wilbur, 1914, F 25,9:5
Crier, Douglas R, 1950, D 9,15:4
Crighton, Carrie G Mrs, 1946, N 20,31:3
Crighton, R Capt, 1882, D 17,2:6
Crigler, Lewis W, 1938, My 1,II,6:6
Crihfield, Roy, 1939, O 23,19:6
Crile, George Mrs, 1948, Ag 24,23:4
Crile, George W, 1943, Ja 8,19:3
Crilley, Albert C, 1951, D 24,1:1
Crilley, Frank, 1947, N 25,29:3
Crilly, Gerald S, 1924, Jl 13,22:4
Crilly, Joseph, 1947, F 7,23:3
Crilly, William T, 1951, O 11,37:3
Crim, Adelaide, 1938, Ag 2,19:3
Crim, Cal D, 1953, D 20,V,5:6
Crim, Caspar R Maj, 1937, Ja 23,18:6
Crim, Howell G, 1959, My 12,35:3
Crim, J W H, 1933, Jl 3,11:6
Crim, Leroy C, 1947, Ag 14,23:5
Crim, W H Dr, 1902, N 16,7:5
Crimi, Giulio, 1939, O 30,17:6
Crimmen, George A, 1946, My 24,19:2
Crimmings, John J, 1950, S 20,31:4
Crimmins, Harry B, 1960, Je 15,41:1
Crimmins, John, 1954, Ja 28,27:5
Crimmins, John A, 1954, Jl 14,27:2
Crimmins, John D, 1917, N 10,13:1; 1919, F 20,13:2
Crimmins, John F, 1948, Ag 20,17:2
Crimmins, John J, 1954, Je 5,17:5

Crimmins, John J Jr, 1958, Ap 20,85:1; 1961, Mr 4,23:4
Crimmins, John J Mrs, 1950, Jl 13,25:3; 1957, Mr 10, 89:2
Crimmins, Martin L, 1955, F 8,28:4
Crimmins, Robert E, 1947, O 14,27:5
Crimmins, Thomas (see also S 8,10), 1901, S 11,7:6
Crimmins, Thomas, 1968, D 19,47:3
Crimmins, Thomas E, 1911, S 9,9:6
Crimmons, Rose A M, 1967, F 2,10:5
Crimont, Joseph R, 1945, My 22,19:4
Crincoli, Michael, 1949, Ap 21,26:2
Crine, Harriet P Mrs, 1945, Ja 8,17:4
Crinkley, Matthew S, 1967, Jl 4,19:3
Crinnon, Edward T, 1965, Ap 24,29:4
Crippa, E D, 1960, O 21,33:3
Crippen, Alonzo Mrs, 1907, Ag 8,7:6
Crippen, Edward, 1949, F 14,19:4
Crippen, F Alton, 1961, Ag 6,84:4
Crippen, Guy, 1952, S 22,23:4
Crippen, Henry M Jr, 1952, D 10,35:2
Crippen, John W, 1952, D 21,53:1
Crippen, Layton W, 1916, F 19,11:6
Crippen, Layton W (funl, F 21,11:5), 1916, F 20,15:4
Crippen, Le Grande, 1953, O 18,86:6
Crippen, Lee F, 1949, D 30,20:2
Crippen, Maggie M, 1947, Mr 8,13:4
Crippen, Ralph H, 1968, D 17,50:2
Crippen, Schuyler Ex-Judge, 1872, Mr 3,1:6
Cripps, Arthur S, 1952, Ag 3,60:5
Cripps, Stafford, 1952, Ap 22,1:2
Cripps, Walter T, 1950, S 26,31:5
Crique, Pierre A Rev, 1925, N 24,25:3
Criqui, Charles A, 1948, Ap 10,13:4
Crisafulli, Salvatore L, 1958, Je 28,17:4
Crisanti, John, 1949, Jl 7,26:2
Criscuolo, Luigi, 1957, D 11,31:1
Crisfield, George C, 1948, Je 7,19:4
Crisfield, Richard W, 1958, Jl 23,27:3
Crisi, Renato, 1958, N 5,35:1
Crisjolo, Louis, 1945, F 12,19:3
Crisler, Albert, 1958, My 26,29:5
Crisona, Frank J Mrs, 1960, Ag 4,25:5
Crisonino, Dante G, 1943, Jl 30,15:5
Crisp, C F, 1896, O 24,5:4
Crisp, Charles B, 1958, N 9,88:7
Crisp, Charles F Mrs, 1907, Ap 24,9:5
Crisp, Charles R, 1937, F 8,17:1
Crisp, Harry, 1882, Ap 30,2:3
Crisp, Herbert G, 1939, Jl 14,19:2
Crisp, Jane F Mrs, 1955, Ag 12,19:3
Crisp, VanDevanter, 1963, N 25,20:4
Crisp, W T, 1903, My 9,9:6
Crisp, William Benton, 1921, Ja 29,11:4
Crispano, Anthony, 1951, S 12,31:1
Crispano, Phil, 1941, Ag 28,19:5
Crispell, Frank B Mrs, 1952, Jl 31,23:3
Crispell, Frank H, 1949, Ag 23,23:3
Crispell, Peter, 1879, Ja 2,4:7; 1938, S 10,17:4
Crispell, Reuben B, 1967, D 2,39:4
Crispi, Francesco, 1901, Ag 12,7:6
Crispi, Francesco Mrs, 1912, N 26,15:4
Crispi, Mrs (Repudiated wife of Premier Crispi), 1904, N 11,9:2
Crispin, Antonio M, 1949, S 10,17:5
Crispin, Clarence G Mrs, 1955, Ja 1,13:4
Crispin, Franklin M, 1937, F 10,23:3
Crispin, M Jackson, 1953, Jl 4,11:5
Criss, C C, 1952, Mr 10,21:6
Criss, Hugh Ferguson, 1919, Ja 26,20:4
Criss, Martha Mrs, 1914, Jl 10,9:6
Criss, Neil L, 1966, Ap 25,31:4
Criss, Thomas B, 1913, D 9,11:4
Crissey, Edwin Capt, 1912, F 19,9:6
Crissey, Forrest, 1943, N 6,13:5
Crissey, George D, 1952, Ag 31,45:2
Crissinger, Daniel R, 1942, Jl 14,19:3
Crisson, Lincoln, 1954, Ap 30,23:5
Crist, Allan G Mrs, 1945, Ap 25,23:6
Crist, Allen H, 1946, S 7,15:5
Crist, Charles Sr, 1948, D 2,29:5
Crist, Francis N, 1948, My 16,68:5
Crist, George W, 1942, Jl 9,21:6; 1948, N 13,15:2
Crist, Haldy M Mrs, 1942, My 8,21:5
Crist, Harry M, 1946, Ja 20,42:2
Crist, Ira H, 1945, Ap 16,23:5
Crist, James A, 1960, F 4,32:1
Crist, John D, 1957, Mr 6,25:1
Crist, John H, 1919, Mr 31,13:3
Crist, Otto Mrs, 1957, N 23,19:5
Cristani, Serafino, 1943, Ag 19,19:3
Cristea, Miron, 1939, Mr 7,22:1
Cristiancy, I P, 1890, S 9,5:3
Cristillo, Sebastian, 1947, My 10,13:2
Cristman, George W Mrs, 1946, F 9,13:1
Cristo-Loveanu, Elie, 1964, Ap 29,41:2
Cristy, Albert M, 1949, Jl 14,28:2
Criswell, E W, 1944, Ja 29,13:6
Criswell, Edgar G, 1950, D 24,34:1
Criswell, Nancy J, 1947, Ag 13,23:2
Criswell, Robert W, 1905, Ag 4,1:5
Critchett, George Anderson Sir, 1925, F 10,23:3
Critchett, James H, 1957, D 20,27:3
Critchfield, Howard E, 1962, Jl 3,23:5
Critchfield, Leonard, 1951, Ag 11,11:6
Critchley, Alfred C, 1963, F 11,7:5
Critchley, J Vernon, 1948, Je 3,25:5
Critchlow, Frank L, 1945, N 10,15:3
Critchlow, Ray, 1948, N 13,15:6
Criticos, George (George of the Ritz), 1961, Jl 18, 29:4
Crittenberg, George D, 1965, Mr 13,25:3
Crittenberger, Dale J, 1938, Ap 4,17:4
Crittenden, Alonzo, 1883, Ja 24,5:4
Crittenden, Butler P, 1949, Je 17,23:4
Crittenden, Ella M, 1957, S 5,29:4
Crittenden, Eugene C, 1956, Mr 29,27:2
Crittenden, Eugene W Maj, 1874, Ag 6,4:6
Crittenden, G B, 1880, N 30,5:3
Crittenden, Jerome P, 1960, Ja 5,31:2
Crittenden, John J, 1863, Jl 28,1:4
Crittenden, Ray, 1949, Je 6,19:3
Crittenden, Raymond E, 1949, O 9,93:1
Crittenden, Rupert G, 1966, My 9,39:2
Crittenden, Samuel W, 1949, Mr 28,21:5
Crittenden, Walter H, 1919, My 30,9:6; 1947, O 24, 23:3
Crittenden, William Butler, 1921, Jl 28,13:4
Crittenden, William C, 1967, Ag 26,27:3
Crittenden, William H, 1959, N 12,35:4
Crittenden, William J, 1955, My 24,31:2
Crittenton, Charles N, 1909, N 17,9:4
Crittenton, Lawrence A, 1940, N 28,23:2
Critz, Hugh M, 1939, Ja 29,33:1
Critz, Robert Mrs, 1953, Jl 19,57:2
Critzas, Constantine J, 1962, S 4,33:2
Croak, J Edward, 1945, Ag 8,23:5
Croak, Thomas J, 1937, My 25,56:6
Croake, Lawrence E, 1946, D 14,15:4
Croall, David B, 1944, Ja 11,20:2
Croan, Clarence L, 1944, S 29,21:4
Croasdale, Jack F, 1959, Je 20,21:6
Croasdale, S, 1934, O 3,21:4
Crobaugh, Frank L, 1947, D 2,29:3
Crocco, Albert R, 1967, F 4,27:4
Crocco, Anthony E, 1947, N 11,27:4
Crocco, Edward A, 1964, Ap 25,29:3
Crocco, Edward A Mrs, 1950, Jl 28,21:4
Croce, Alfonso, 1948, F 15,61:1
Croce, Benedetto, 1952, N 21,25:1
Croce, Benedetto Mrs, 1964, Mr 1,47:4
Croce, Louis P, 1947, My 16,23:1
Crocetti, Guido M, 1943, O 19,19:5
Crocetti, Guy, 1967, Ag 31,33:2
Crocheron, Bertram H, 1948, Jl 9,19:4
Crocheron, Clarence P, 1959, Mr 20,31:3
Crocheron, D G, 1880, Mr 11,3:2
Crocheron, Irving G, 1949, Mr 24,28:3
Crocheron, Willard E Jr, 1948, Ag 30,17:2
Crockard, Frank H, 1955, Mr 4,23:2
Crockard, William L, 1955, Ja 25,25:3
Crocker, Aimee (Aimee C Galatzine Princess), 1941, F 8,17:6
Crocker, Allen S Mrs (will), 1962, My 22,33:5
Crocker, Alvah, 1874, D 28,1:2
Crocker, C, 1888, Ag 15,5:3
Crocker, Calvin I, 1951, F 17,15:3
Crocker, Caroline, 1941, My 28,25:5
Crocker, Charles, 1961, Mr 14,35:2
Crocker, Charles T, 1948, D 13,23:2; 1954, Ja 30,17:5
Crocker, Charles T Mrs, 1956, Ap 28,17:3
Crocker, Clarence P, 1957, Ap 23,31:3
Crocker, Clifton A, 1939, D 15,25:2
Crocker, Courtnay, 1944, D 17,38:3
Crocker, David H, 1956, Mr 29,27:4
Crocker, E B Mrs, 1901, D 3,9:4
Crocker, Edward S, 1968, Ap 7,92:1
Crocker, Edwin M, 1914, D 16,15:6
Crocker, Francis Bacon Prof, 1921, Jl 11,11:5
Crocker, Frank L, 1945, Je 18,19:1
Crocker, Frederic S, 1956, S 15,17:5
Crocker, George, 1909, D 5,13:5
Crocker, George A Mrs, 1937, D 26,II,6:8
Crocker, George G, 1913, My 27,11:6
Crocker, George H, 1948, Jl 10,15:2
Crocker, George Mrs, 1904, Jl 27,7:6
Crocker, George O, 1944, N 29,23:4
Crocker, Glyndon H, 1945, Ag 3,17:2
Crocker, Harry, 1958, My 25,86:5
Crocker, Harry C, 1943, F 8,19:2
Crocker, Henry, 1883, O 30,5:3
Crocker, Henry Horace, 1904, S 26,9:6
Crocker, James N Mrs, 1943, Ag 18,19:2
Crocker, Jim, 1955, Jl 27,23:5
Crocker, John, 1963, Mr 11,9:3
Crocker, Jonathan W Capt, 1924, Je 5,21:5
Crocker, Joseph N, 1943, D 29,17:5
Crocker, Percy K, 1938, My 7,15:5
Crocker, Philander R, 1955, Ag 10,25:2
Crocker, S L, 1883, F 11,7:3
Crocker, S L E, 1904, My 28,3:2
Crocker, Samuel S, 1964, N 29,86:3
Crocker, Stuart M (mem ser set, S 6,25:4; ser, S 11,35:3), 1956, S 4,29:3
Crocker, Theodore D, 1947, Je 30,19:2
Crocker, Vladimir K, 1961, Ja 2,25:5
Crocker, Walter J, 1947, My 16,23:4
Crocker, William, 1950, F 12,84:1
Crocker, William Blodgett, 1925, Ja 25,7:2
Crocker, William F, 1945, Jl 5,13:7; 1953, My 9,19:4
Crocker, William H (will, O 3,11,8:2), 1937, S 26,3
Crocker, William Mrs, 1948, Jl 3,15:2
Crocker, William T, 1939, My 1,23:3
Crocker, William W Mrs, 1958, S 28,89:1
Crocker, Winthrop N Mrs, 1951, S 10,21:5
Crocket, Charles E, 1946, Jl 6,15:4
Crocket, Oswald S, 1945, Mr 3,13:4
Crocket, Roderick M, 1952, N 14,24:4
Crockett, A F, 1903, O 4,7:6
Crockett, C John, 1959, S 25,24:1
Crockett, Clarence Mrs, 1943, D 18,16:3
Crockett, Earl G, 1950, Ap 18,31:4
Crockett, Elmer, 1924, Je 5,21:5
Crockett, Eugene A Mrs, 1959, Ap 2,31:4
Crockett, Harrison U, 1949, F 14,19:3
Crockett, Horace G, 1966, Ag 17,39:2
Crockett, J Henry, 1947, Ag 19,23:4
Crockett, Janet M, 1943, S 18,17:1
Crockett, John G, 1952, Je 8,87:1
Crockett, John W, 1920, Ap 10,15:4
Crockett, Josephine D, 1946, Ja 25,23:2
Crockett, Lora C Mrs, 1947, D 22,21:2
Crockett, Louise Anderson, 1918, N 11,15:6
Crockett, Newkirk Sr, 1968, Ja 9,43:3
Crockett, Oren D, 1942, F 9,15:4
Crockett, Rob Col, 1902, F 19,9:6
Crockett, Robert L, 1946, My 29,23:4
Crockett, Stuart Rev Dr, 1917, Mr 13,11:5
Crockett, Theodore L, 1966, Je 10,45:2
Crockett, Walter E, 1957, Ja 22,29:1
Crockett, Walter M Sr, 1944, Jl 2,19:4
Crockett, William G, 1940, O 31,23:1
Crockwell, Douglass, 1968, D 2,47:2
Crofford, C Paul, 1950, F 6,25:4
Croffut, William A Dr, 1915, Ag 2,9:6
Crofoot, A Burdet, 1955, N 16,35:2
Crofoot, Charles M, 1959, Ag 25,31:1
Crofoot, Clarence E, 1950, Jl 30,61:2
Crofoot, Inez D, 1957, Je 29,17:6
Croft, Alfred J, 1957, Ap 14,86:4
Croft, Arthur S Mrs, 1959, S 21,31:4
Croft, Charles E, 1945, Ap 1,36:4
Croft, Delmer Eugene Dr, 1925, Ag 16,5:2
Croft, Dudley J, 1966, D 1,47:5
Croft, Edward (por), 1938, Ja 29,15:3
Croft, Frank, 1954, Ja 9,15:1
Croft, George W, 1904, Mr 11,3:2
Croft, H W Mrs, 1949, N 16,29:1
Croft, Harry W, 1947, F 26,26:2
Croft, Lord, 1947, D 9,29:5
Croft, M Olin, 1941, D 11,27:6
Croft, Percy Mrs, 1949, My 7,13:3
Croft, Robert, 1954, D 24,9:6
Croft, S C, 1902, Ap 12,2:3
Croft, Samuel G, 1941, Jl 30,17:1
Croft, William H, 1949, My 15,90:2
Croft, William I, 1940, My 18,15:5
Croftan, Alfred C, 1938, Ag 24,21:6
Crofton, Charles B, 1961, Ag 16,31:2
Crofton, Harry J, 1944, Mr 31,21:5
Crofton, Thomas J, 1967, My 20,35:4
Crofton, William M, 1960, Jl 13,35:5
Crofts, Ernest, 1911, Mr 20,9:4
Crofts, Frederick S, 1951, S 17,21:4
Crofts, Freeman W, 1957, Ap 13,19:3
Crofts, George D, 1954, F 16,25:2
Crofts, James M, 1917, Je 21,13:4
Crofut, Frank V, 1944, D 14,23:4
Crofut, William E, 1940, Mr 10,51:1
Crofutt, Frank, 1956, Ja 17,33:2
Crofwell, Eunice H Mrs, 1959, Jl 21,30:5
Crogan, Frank J, 1941, D 9,31:5
Crogan, George M, 1939, Je 21,23:6
Croghan, Bridget (Sister Mary Zita), 1953, F 8,
Crohan, Frank J, 1940, My 2,23:5
Crohan, Frank J Mrs, 1964, Je 1,29:3
Crohn, Joshua S, 1957, S 9,25:5
Crohn, Marcus Mrs, 1949, Je 8,30:6
Croil, George M, 1959, Ap 11,21:5
Croisetiere, Arthur J, 1940, My 4,6:4
Croisic, Marquis de (Richd de Logerot), 1907, Mr 14,7:5
Croissant, G Frank, 1956, D 8,19:6
Croisset, Francis de, 1937, N 9,23:5
Croisset, Philippe de, 1965, Mr 24,43:1
Croix, Elvia, 1911, Ja 12,13:4
Croizat, Ambrose, 1951, F 12,23:3
Crokat, William Lt-Gen, 1879, N 27,2:6
Croke, Archbishop, 1902, Jl 23,9:5
Croke, Thomas E, 1948, Ap 20,27:4
Croke, William A Sr, 1942, S 2,23:3
Croker, Edward F (trb lr, F 24,12:7), 1951, F 1
Croker, Edward F Mrs, 1955, Ja 16,92:2
Croker, Frank, 1905, Ja 22,1:5
Croker, Herbert, 1905, My 13,1:5
Croker, Howard, 1956, Ja 9,25:1
Croker, John Mrs, 1920, O 22,15:6
Croker, Richard, 1907, Ap 7,9:5
Croker, Richard (funl), 1922, My 5,17:6
Croker, Richard C Mrs (B B Edmonson), 1957, Mr 17,87:1

Croker, Richard Mrs, 1914, S 8,11:6; 1914, O 5,11:2
Croley, Alfred J, 1943, Ag 15,38:4
Crolius, Albert, 1939, D 2,17:3
Crolius, Clinton J, 1953, Mr 26,31:3
Crolius, Fred J, 1960, Ag 30,29:2
Crolius, Olive P Mrs, 1958, Ap 24,31:4
Crolius, William C Jr, 1959, Ja 3,17:1
Croll, Andrew G, 1943, Ja 14,21:4
Croll, Andrew Mrs, 1958, S 20,19:2
Croll, Charles L, 1959, F 5,31:3
Croll, David, 1957, Je 9,88:4
Croll, Edward E, 1954, D 21,27:5
Croll, George B, 1966, Ag 1,27:4
Croll, George M, 1961, Je 7,41:1
Croll, Henry L, 1938, My 20,19:2
Croll, James S, 1950, Jl 25,27:5
Croll, Morris W, 1947, Ag 18,17:3
Croll, Perry B, 1952, F 7,27:4
Croll, Phil C, 1949, Mr 15,27:1
Croll, Samuel H, 1945, S 25,25:2
Croll, Samuel W, 1957, F 28,27:4
Crollius, B Roest, 1947, Je 10,27:4
Croly, Herbert Mrs, 1945, O 1,19:1
Croly, J C Mrs (Jennie June), 1901, D 24,3:4
Cromartie, George G, 1953, Mr 11,29:1
Cromarty, Arthur H, 1948, Ja 6,23:3
Crombie, Arthur C, 1949, Ap 30,13:2
Crombie, Walter C, 1942, N 25,23:4
Crombie, William M, 1939, My 5,23:1
Cromer, C Otis, 1962, My 16,41:2
Cromer, Earl of (R T Baring), 1953, My 14,29:5
Cromer, Joseph L, 1956, Ja 3,31:4
Cromer, Lord (Evelyn Baring), 1917, Ja 30,9:3
Cromer, Margaret E Mrs, 1937, S 12,II,7:4
Cromey, E Warren, 1964, O 13,39:2
Cromie, Robert C Mrs, 1950, Je 1,27:1
Cromie, William J, 1962, Ag 11,17:6
Cromien, Connal C, 1965, Ag 16,27:6
Crommelin, Alfred M, 1903, S 10,7:7
Crommelin, Andrew C, 1939, S 21,23:5
Crommelin, Jacob P, 1923, Ap 10,21:4
Crommelin, John G, 1945, D 25,23:4
Crommie, William P, 1962, S 3,11:1
Crompton, David H, 1946, Jl 9,21:1
Crompton, Lewis M, 1957, O 5,17:5
Crompton, Randolph, 1955, Mr 30,29:4
Crompton, Robert H Sr, 1953, My 9,19:6
Crompton, Rookes E B, 1940, F 16,19:3
Crompton, William J, 1953, Ap 17,25:2
Cromwell, Albert, 1908, Ja 1,9:5
Cromwell, Anna C, 1954, D 28,23:4
Cromwell, Charles, 1938, D 20,25:6
Cromwell, David, 1925, F 13,17:4
Cromwell, David W, 1915, S 12,17:4
Cromwell, Dean B, 1962, Ag 4,19:4
Cromwell, Drexel Mrs, 1966, S 8,47:4
Cromwell, Edward, 1908, F 1,9:5
Cromwell, Ellis, 1912, F 12,11:5
Cromwell, Fannie T, 1946, N 5,25:4
Cromwell, Frederic, 1914, Je 23,11:5
Cromwell, G, 1934, S 18,21:1
Cromwell, H, 1884, O 26,2:3
Cromwell, H B, 1864, Ap 6,1:4
Cromwell, Helen J Mrs, 1942, F 7,17:4
Cromwell, Henry A Mrs, 1950, N 8,29:4
Cromwell, Ida K Mrs, 1942, Ag 20,19:1
Cromwell, Isabella H Mrs, 1937, S 11,17:4
Cromwell, James H R Mrs, 1968, Jl 8,39:5
Cromwell, Jarvis Mrs, 1968, My 13,43:3
Cromwell, John H, 1937, N 29,23:5
Cromwell, Lincoln, 1952, F 10,93:1
Cromwell, Lincoln Mrs, 1963, My 13,29:3
Cromwell, Marguerite C Mrs, 1961, N 26,87:6
Cromwell, Oliver Eaton, 1909, D 22,11:5
Cromwell, Oliver J, 1949, F 25,23:3
Cromwell, Richard (R Radabaugh), 1960, O 13,37:4
Cromwell, Robert H, 1964, Ja 8,34:8
Cromwell, Robert L, 1941, O 12,52:1
Cromwell, Saul Sr, 1947, N 4,25:4
Cromwell, Seymour, 1925, S 17,23:5
Cromwell, Seymour L Mrs, 1959, My 16,23:4
Cromwell, Thomas B, 1957, Mr 26,33:2
Cromwell, William Mrs, 1952, Jl 21,19:4
Cromwell, William N (will noted, Ag 5,23:4), 1948, Jl 20,23:1
Cron, Frederick G Mrs, 1952, S 19,23:3
Cron, George P, 1966, My 18,47:1
Cron, Herman, 1946, N 26,29:4
Cron, James A Mrs, 1948, D 22,23:3
Cron, John F, 1950, O 26,31:4
Cronan, George D, 1939, O 20,23:2
Cronan, Harry C, 1963, Ag 11,84:3
Cronan, Joseph D, 1966, Je 11,31:4
Cronan, Joseph F, 1953, O 9,27:5
Cronan, Thomas D L, 1956, Mr 20,23:1
Cronau, Rudolf, 1939, O 28,15:5
Cronbach, Abraham, 1965, Ap 3,29:4
Cronce, Ira Mrs, 1952, Je 4,27:4
Crone, Arthur E, 1942, Ja 19,17:2
Crone, Edward M, 1938, Je 21,19:5
Crone, Frederick W, 1962, Je 5,41:1
Crone, Frederick W Mrs, 1959, F 13,27:2
Crone, George J, 1957, D 21,19:6
Crone, Kennedy, 1949, Je 21,25:5
Crone, Robert H, 1960, D 23,19:1
Cronecker, G Fred, 1950, N 14,31:1
Cronecker, Gustave P, 1955, F 7,21:2
Cronell, Walter Mrs, 1947, My 21,25:4
Cronell, William, 1941, F 16,41:2
Cronell, William Jr, 1946, F 15,25:4
Cronell, William Mrs, 1951, Ap 28,15:5
Cronely, Frank A, 1938, N 21,19:4
Croney, P Alfred, 1956, D 9,88:1
Cronhardt, Albert F, 1938, Ap 21,19:3
Cronheim, David, 1959, O 20,40:1
Cronin, Anna G Mrs, 1942, Mr 7,17:3
Cronin, Arthur C, 1950, Ag 11,19:4
Cronin, B S, 1933, F 16,19:1
Cronin, Charles H, 1948, F 8,60:4
Cronin, Cornelius F, 1915, Ap 23,13:4
Cronin, Cornelius M, 1947, F 21,19:4
Cronin, Daniel (Bro Benedict Victor), 1966, Ja 20, 30:4
Cronin, David C Rev, 1968, D 11,41:2
Cronin, Denis J, 1943, N 5,19:5
Cronin, Dennis J, 1908, Ja 26,9:5
Cronin, E A, 1878, O 14,5:6
Cronin, E M, 1903, Ag 17,7:5
Cronin, Edmund W Rev, 1911, My 2,11:4
Cronin, Edward J, 1946, Mr 13,29:1; 1958, N 25,33:3
Cronin, Edward T, 1954, Ja 7,31:2
Cronin, Edward V, 1948, Ja 27,25:4
Cronin, Edwin L, 1960, Jl 6,33:1
Cronin, Elizabeth A S, 1954, Ap 9,24:3
Cronin, Evyleen Mrs, 1953, My 15,15:1
Cronin, Francis J, 1944, Je 16,19:2; 1951, S 21,23:2
Cronin, Francis P, 1956, F 13,27:4
Cronin, Francis X, 1953, Ja 31,15:1
Cronin, Frank Q, 1924, Ap 14,17:3
Cronin, Fred W, 1940, N 5,25:4
Cronin, George, 1957, My 18,19:4
Cronin, George D, 1950, N 11,15:1
Cronin, Grover J, 1953, Mr 12,25:1
Cronin, Harold R, 1958, My 7,35:5
Cronin, Henry C, 1941, N 20,27:3
Cronin, James, 1946, N 6,5:5
Cronin, James A, 1937, Jl 8,23:2
Cronin, James J, 1946, Je 8,21:2
Cronin, James T, 1952, Ja 15,27:1
Cronin, Jere J, 1944, Ja 10,17:4
Cronin, Jere M, 1949, Jl 29,21:1
Cronin, Jeremiah, 1949, F 8,25:1
Cronin, Jeremiah J, 1944, F 15,17:4
Cronin, Jeremiah K, 1942, N 27,23:1
Cronin, John A Mrs, 1943, O 15,19:2
Cronin, John F, 1964, Jl 22,33:5
Cronin, John Francis, 1912, Je 14,11:5
Cronin, John H, 1947, O 23,25:5
Cronin, John J, 1941, Ag 24,34:7; 1943, S 29,21:4
Cronin, John J Dr, 1925, Ja 31,13:5
Cronin, John J Jr, 1968, Ap 9,48:1
Cronin, John J Mrs, 1945, Ja 4,19:4
Cronin, John M, 1956, Je 14,33:2
Cronin, John W, 1943, Ja 28,19:3; 1958, Mr 27,33:3
Cronin, Joseph J, 1948, F 7,15:2
Cronin, M D, 1936, Ag 14,17:2
Cronin, Marie, 1951, Jl 26,21:2
Cronin, Matthew A, 1952, Mr 13,30:3
Cronin, Maurice J, 1942, Je 26,21:1
Cronin, Michael J, 1951, Je 27,29:3
Cronin, Michael P, 1957, Mr 8,25:4
Cronin, Ned, 1958, Ag 20,27:3
Cronin, Neil A, 1943, Mr 20,15:2
Cronin, Patrick, 1903, Jl 3,9:6
Cronin, Richard J, 1942, D 24,15:5; 1957, Mr 18,27:5
Cronin, Robert A, 1937, Ag 14,13:2
Cronin, Robert T, 1942, Jl 2,21:2
Cronin, Sarah E, 1958, O 4,21:2
Cronin, Theodore F, 1944, Mr 3,15:2
Cronin, Timothy J, 1967, Ap 18,41:1
Cronin, Timothy J Mrs, 1952, Je 22,68:2
Cronin, Timothy T, 1955, S 21,33:4
Cronin, W Vaughn, 1955, O 14,27:4
Cronin, William, 1965, Mr 11,33:2
Cronin, William F, 1942, S 30,23:4; 1965, O 31,86:8
Cronin, William J, 1956, Jl 13,19:3
Cronin, William L, 1946, O 3,27:6
Cronin, William P, 1968, Jl 23,36:4
Croninger, C A, 1904, Mr 23,1:6
Cronjager, Edwin, 1960, Je 17,38:2
Cronje, Piet A Gen, 1911, F 5,II,11:5
Cronk, Claude B, 1942, O 20,21:2
Cronk, D James, 1946, D 27,19:1
Cronk, Edwin I, 1946, Jl 21,40:4
Cronk, Harrison T, 1945, Ag 19,39:1
Cronk, Harry A, 1952, Mr 27,29:2
Cronk, Henry T, 1947, D 4,31:2
Cronk, Hiram, 1905, My 14,9:6
Cronk, John H Mrs, 1943, D 3,23:3
Cronk, Silas F, 1948, O 17,76:1
Cronk, Walter A, 1950, Ap 29,15:4
Cronkhite, Adelbert Maj Gen, 1937, Je 16,23:5
Cronkhite, Adelbert Mrs, 1954, F 4,25:4
Cronkhite, Arthur B, 1955, N 24,29:3
Cronkhite, E P, 1927, Ap 25,23:3
Cronkhite, Frank C, 1946, Ja 2,19:2
Cronkhite, Henry M Col, 1919, Je 16,13:6
Cronkite, Henry, 1949, D 28,25:2
Cronkite, Joseph Lt-Col, 1903, Je 18,9:6
Cronkrite, William G, 1949, F 16,25:1
Cronley, Elizabeth M, 1951, My 18,27:2
Cronley, John W Sr, 1950, Mr 28,31:2
Cronly, A James, 1937, Ag 3,23:2
Cronon, James, 1937, Je 22,23:5
Cronson, Bernard, 1916, F 3,9:4
Cronson, Berthold, 1937, D 24,17:3
Cronson, Reuben Mrs, 1946, N 30,15:4
Cronthall, Victor C, 1949, S 27,27:1
Crony-Chanel, Prince of, 1873, S 29,2:2
Cronyn, Ben Rev, 1871, S 23,7:1
Cronyn, Theodore, 1967, My 20,35:5
Cronyn, Theodore 2d Mrs, 1968, My 17,44:2
Cronyn, Thoreau, 1943, My 3,17:3
Cronyn, Thoreau Mrs, 1953, Mr 28,17:1
Croohe, Maxwell A, 1953, Ag 22,15:2
Crook, Agnes A Mrs, 1948, O 6,29:2
Crook, Alice M, 1940, F 15,19:4
Crook, Carolina, 1944, Jl 1,15:5
Crook, Charles E, 1955, Jl 20,27:4
Crook, Frank, 1948, S 27,23:1
Crook, Fred H, 1941, Ap 13,38:4
Crook, G Gen, 1890, Mr 22,1:3
Crook, Harry Sr, 1952, O 28,31:1
Crook, John G Mrs, 1947, Ap 9,25:5
Crook, Joseph W, 1938, Mr 1,22:2
Crook, Lawrence, 1943, Mr 14,24:6
Crook, Louis H, 1952, N 20,31:4
Crook, Montgomery P, 1955, Ap 23,19:6
Crook, Wilbur Floyd, 1953, Ag 20,27:4
Crook, Wilfred H, 1963, Ap 17,41:3
Crook, William, 1959, Ap 1,37:1
Crook, William P, 1955, Ag 21,93:1
Crooke, Edward, 1907, Ag 25,7:5
Crooke, Harry A, 1963, Jl 1,29:1
Crooke, P S (see also Mr 16), 1881, Mr 18,5:3
Crooke, William, 1918, F 13,13:8
Crooker, Conrad W, 1947, O 21,23:4
Crooker, Edwin L, 1954, D 30,17:4
Crooker, Frederick F, 1944, N 17,19:3
Crooker, George L, 1946, S 26,25:6
Crooker, Herbert, 1960, Ja 22,27:3
Crooker, Leon T, 1947, My 15,25:4
Crooker, Leon T Mrs, 1949, O 27,27:3
Crooker, Robert H, 1955, Jl 9,15:1
Crooks, C H, 1946, Ja 28,19:4
Crooks, Charles H, 1949, Ja 21,21:2
Crooks, Elliott A, 1958, Ja 9,36:2
Crooks, Esther J, 1949, Jl 29,21:4
Crooks, Ezra B, 1941, Mr 10,17:2
Crooks, Ivan, 1953, My 7,31:2
Crooks, John, 1950, D 11,25:4
Crooks, John R, 1959, Ag 15,17:1
Crooks, John S, 1937, Je 29,21:5
Crooks, John W, 1948, D 6,25:2
Crooks, John W Mrs, 1955, F 2,27:5
Crooks, Sammy, 1965, Ag 31,33:1
Crooks, Samuel, 1918, Ja 17,13:3
Crooks, Taylor W, 1949, N 29,29:4
Crooks, Thomas H Mrs, 1944, Je 9,15:3
Crooks, Thomas L R, 1959, Je 16,35:5
Crooks, William, 1921, Je 6,13:6
Crooks, William P Mrs, 1950, My 30,18:2
Crooks, William Sir, 1919, Ap 6,22:3
Crookshank, Harry F C, 1961, O 18,43:4
Crookshank, Harry Maule Dr, 1914, Mr 26,11:6
Crookston, William J Col, 1937, Ag 10,19:5
Croom-Johnson, Austen H, 1964, My 18,26:4
Croom-Johnson, Reginald, 1957, D 31,17:4
Croop, Arthur M, 1954, N 27,13:2
Croot, John R, 1938, Ja 16,II,8:6
Croot, Samuel, 1963, Ap 4,47:3
Cropley, Charles E, 1952, Je 18,27:3
Cropley, Ralph E, 1959, N 17,35:4
Cropp, David B, 1950, Ag 17,27:4
Cropper, Charles W, 1938, Ag 9,19:6
Cropper, Harry J, 1954, My 24,27:2
Cropper, John, 1906, D 8,11:6
Cropper, Ralph, 1960, O 8,23:1
Cropper, Ross C, 1950, Ja 20,25:2
Cropper, Roy N, 1954, My 15,15:1
Cropsey, Charles D, 1962, S 15,25:3
Cropsey, James C Justice, 1937, Je 17,23:4
Cropsey, James C Mrs, 1957, Ja 1,23:5
Cropsey, James L, 1954, Je 2,31:2
Cropsey, Nebraska, 1916, Mr 11,11:4
Cropsey, William J Col, 1912, Mr 26,13:4
Crosbie, Arthur H, 1946, Ag 24,11:2
Crosbie, George H, 1956, O 25,33:2
Crosbie, John C Mrs Lady, 1953, My 24,89:1
Crosbie, Laurence M, 1954, O 26,27:4
Crosbie, Paul P, 1949, Ag 2,19:5
Crosbie-Roles, Margaretta B N Mrs, 1938, O 8,17:6
Crosby, A B Dr, 1877, Ag 10,2:7
Crosby, A Dixi, 1956, Ag 17,19:1
Crosby, Adam B Sen, 1921, Mr 11,15:6
Crosby, Albert W, 1938, N 12,15:6
Crosby, Alonzo E, 1942, Ag 24,15:6
Crosby, Alpheus Prof, 1874, Ap 19,1:2

Crosby, Bing Mrs (D Lee), 1952, N 2,89:1
Crosby, Bing Mrs (est acctg), 1954, N 9,31:8
Crosby, Byran M, 1949, D 20,6:6
Crosby, C Fred, 1923, F 8,19:5
Crosby, Carroll P, 1952, Ag 28,23:1
Crosby, Catherine H H Mrs, 1964, Ja 8,34:8
Crosby, Charles E, 1942, D 26,11:5
Crosby, Charles N, 1951, Ja 27,13:2
Crosby, Clarence F S, 1953, Ag 23,84:1
Crosby, Cornelia T, 1946, N 12,29:6
Crosby, Cyrus R Prof, 1937, Ja 13,23:1
Crosby, Dixi Dr, 1873, S 30,5:2
Crosby, Edward B, 1905, Ap 30,7:6
Crosby, Edwin S, 1958, My 9,23:4
Crosby, Edwin S Mrs, 1968, N 3,89:1
Crosby, Ernest B, 1948, My 30,34:3
Crosby, Ernest Howard, 1907, Ja 4,7:5
Crosby, Everett (funl, Jl 19,39:4), 1966, Jl 14,35:3
Crosby, Everett U, 1960, Je 5,87:1
Crosby, Fannie I H Mrs, 1951, My 29,25:3
Crosby, Fanny, 1915, F 13,9:3
Crosby, Francis D, 1955, D 20,31:1
Crosby, Francis W, 1950, S 20,31:5
Crosby, Francis W Capt, 1909, D 23,9:3
Crosby, Frank, 1944, Mr 25,15:4
Crosby, Franklin M, 1947, Je 30,19:3
Crosby, Fred G, 1966, Mr 21,33:1
Crosby, Frederic V S Mrs, 1952, Mr 28,23:5
Crosby, Frederick Van Schoonhovern, 1920, D 3,15:2
Crosby, George, 1924, Ja 15,19:2
Crosby, George H, 1941, S 30,23:5
Crosby, George R, 1968, Jl 2,26:6
Crosby, H Lamar, 1954, Mr 21,88:5
Crosby, Harley N, 1955, Ap 27,31:5
Crosby, Harry L, 1950, O 5,31:5
Crosby, Haydn W, 1950, O 14,19:3
Crosby, Henry Ashton, 1917, Ja 11,15:4
Crosby, Henry B, 1910, S 27,13:5
Crosby, Horace, 1914, Jl 25,7:5
Crosby, Howard Dr, 1891, Mr 30,1:5
Crosby, Howard H, 1944, D 6,23:2
Crosby, J P, 1876, S 21,4:7
Crosby, James B, 1942, Jl 1,25:4
Crosby, James H, 1925, O 20,25:4
Crosby, James L, 1939, F 13,15:5
Crosby, John, 1962, Mr 2,29:3
Crosby, John C, 1943, O 15,19:3
Crosby, John F, 1940, Ja 3,21:1
Crosby, John H, 1944, N 16,23:4
Crosby, John P, 1953, F 17,27:2
Crosby, John R Rev Dr, 1937, Ja 30,17:5
Crosby, John Schuyler Col, 1914, Ag 9,15:5
Crosby, John Scuyler Mrs, 1911, D 18,11:4
Crosby, John Sherwin, 1914, F 25,9:5
Crosby, John Sherwin Mrs, 1924, Ja 31,15:6
Crosby, Joseph P, 1938, N 15,23:5
Crosby, Joshua W Capt, 1910, Ap 7,11:4
Crosby, L O, 1948, N 25,31:5
Crosby, Lawrence J, 1944, S 9,15:6
Crosby, Livingston, 1919, My 17,13:7
Crosby, Lt, 1872, O 12,10:5
Crosby, Margaret Mrs, 1949, Ag 8,15:2
Crosby, Mary J, 1883, S 9,9:5
Crosby, Molly, 1953, Ag 27,25:3
Crosby, Nancy (Mrs Romaine H), 1958, Jl 16,29:4
Crosby, Ogden E Sr, 1952, Je 19,27:4
Crosby, Oscar T, 1947, Ja 3,21:1
Crosby, Patrick H, 1953, Ja 28,27:4
Crosby, Percy L, 1964, D 14,35:1
Crosby, Phil W Rev, 1937, Ja 23,18:4
Crosby, Raymond M, 1945, D 15,17:1
Crosby, Robert A, 1946, Je 19,21:2
Crosby, Robert H, 1941, My 13,23:3
Crosby, Robert R, 1938, Je 12,39:4; 1952, Ag 13,21:4
Crosby, Robert Raiston, 1911, My 26,13:4
Crosby, Samuel McCullen, 1923, Jl 31,17:5
Crosby, Samuel Mrs, 1949, My 13,23:1
Crosby, Stephen Moody Col, 1909, S 2,9:5
Crosby, Stephen Van R, 1959, Ja 4,87:1
Crosby, Thomas J, 1941, Jl 14,13:3
Crosby, Thomas Jr, 1947, Ag 24,58:3
Crosby, Thomas Russell Prof, 1872, Mr 3,1:6
Crosby, Thomas W, 1950, S 26,31:3
Crosby, W Clive, 1937, Ja 30,17:2
Crosby, W G, 1881, Mr 22,2:2
Crosby, Walter Floyd, 1915, Ap 6,11:5
Crosby, Walter W, 1946, D 22,41:4
Crosby, Willard B, 1957, Ag 26,23:3
Crosby, William F, 1950, Ag 1,23:4; 1953, Ag 18,23:3
Crosby, William H, 1944, Je 27,19:1
Crosby, William Mrs, 1954, F 1,16:8
Crosby, William R, 1939, N 13,19:4
Crosby, Willis B, 1951, O 6,19:2
Crose, Virgil V, 1952, Mr 3,21:4
Croselmire, Frederick A, 1937, Mr 21,II,8:1
Crosfield, Bertram M, 1951, Ag 24,15:5
Croshier, Ralph, 1955, Ap 13,29:5
Crosier, E Neil, 1956, S 23,84:6
Crosier, Herbt C Rev, 1937, Jl 16,19:4
Crosier, Lillie V Mrs, 1938, Jl 11,17:4
Croskey, John W, 1951, Jl 31,21:4
Croskey, Knowles, 1938, Ja 23,II,8:7
Crosland, D W, 1933, F 4,15:3
Crosland, Edward S, 1940, D 20,25:2
Crosley, Charlotte W Mrs, 1949, Ja 15,17:4
Crosley, E B, 1921, Ap 4,13:4
Crosley, Powel Jr (will, Mr 30,33:5), 1961, Mr 29, 33:2
Crosley, Powel Jr Mrs, 1939, F 27,15:3; 1955, Jl 6,27:2
Crosley, Powel 3d, 1948, Je 15,28:3
Crosley, Walter S, 1939, Ja 8,43:1
Crosman, Charles N, 1941, N 20,27:4
Crosman, G H Gen, 1882, My 30,5:5
Crosman, Henrietta, 1944, N 1,23:1
Crosman, J Heron, 1942, Ap 11,13:6
Crosman, Judson, 1915, D 25,7:5
Crosman, Loring P, 1954, Ap 13,31:2
Crosnoe, Don, 1945, Ag 26,43:2
Cross, Abraham, 1948, Ap 26,23:2
Cross, Alexander, 1924, S 9,19:3
Cross, Allen E, 1943, Ap 24,13:2
Cross, Ambler B, 1950, Ap 9,84:2
Cross, Andrew Jay Dr, 1925, Ap 10,19:4
Cross, Annie F H Mrs, 1938, D 23,19:4
Cross, Anson K, 1944, Je 18,36:2
Cross, Arthur B, 1957, Jl 14,72:6; 1967, Jl 28,31:2
Cross, Arthur L, 1940, Je 22,15:2
Cross, Arthur W, 1951, N 12,25:3
Cross, Austin J, 1937, Je 24,25:2
Cross, Belle Gold Mrs, 1953, F 28,17:3
Cross, Benjamin F, 1950, N 13,27:2
Cross, C V, 1902, Mr 17,9:6
Cross, Carl, 1966, Je 9,1:6
Cross, Carl P, 1953, S 11,21:1
Cross, Cecil M P Mrs, 1947, Jl 15,23:4
Cross, Charles A, 1945, D 12,27:1
Cross, Charles C, 1951, F 26,23:4
Cross, Charles H, 1941, S 21,42:3
Cross, Charles R, 1921, N 17,17:4
Cross, Clarence E, 1951, Mr 2,25:1; 1957, Jl 28,61:3; 1962, Je 2,19:4
Cross, Clarence E Mrs, 1952, F 13,29:3
Cross, Cleaveland R, 1956, Ap 18,31:1
Cross, Clifford, 1958, Ja 6,39:5
Cross, Clifford T, 1950, F 3,24:3
Cross, Clifton V, 1944, Ja 18,19:5
Cross, Earle B, 1946, D 2,25:2
Cross, Edward M, 1965, D 9,47:3
Cross, Edward W, 1939, N 3,21:4
Cross, Eliot (por), 1949, Ja 24,19:1
Cross, Eliot Mrs, 1957, N 10,86:4
Cross, Emily R, 1955, S 22,31:1
Cross, Frank, 1946, N 26,29:1
Cross, Frank B, 1938, F 9,19:1; 1958, F 27,27:1
Cross, Frank L, 1943, Jl 3,13:1
Cross, Fred G, 1941, S 11,23:1
Cross, Fred W, 1950, Mr 9,29:4
Cross, George H Mrs, 1947, My 16,23:2
Cross, George I, 1947, D 5,25:4
Cross, Guernsey T, 1945, N 2,20:2
Cross, Hamilton, 1944, Ap 8,14:8
Cross, Hardy, 1959, F 12,28:1
Cross, Harold L, 1959, Ag 10,27:3
Cross, Harry, 1946, Ap 4,25:3
Cross, Harry D Sr (por), 1949, Ag 2,20:2
Cross, Harry P, 1955, Mr 13,86:7
Cross, Hartley W, 1948, Ap 10,13:3
Cross, Henry, 1964, Je 6,23:4
Cross, Henry H, 1939, O 8,50:4; 1944, F 9,19:4
Cross, Herbert R (Feb 10), 1963, Ap 1,35:3
Cross, Howard B Dr, 1921, D 28,15:5
Cross, J M Mrs, 1878, Jl 3,5:4
Cross, J Theodore, 1956, Ap 13,25:3
Cross, J W Mrs (George Eliot), 1880, D 24,1:7
Cross, J W Rev, 1906, Ag 19,9:6
Cross, James A, 1952, Mr 2,92:3
Cross, James T, 1948, Ag 9,19:4
Cross, Jerome O, 1908, O 7,9:5
Cross, Jesse E, 1953, O 3,17:4
Cross, John B, 1941, Jl 11,15:4
Cross, John H, 1949, Jl 27,23:4
Cross, John H Mrs, 1953, F 8,89:2
Cross, John J, 1946, N 12,29:6
Cross, John L, 1944, N 7,27:1
Cross, John W, 1921, D 20,17:5; 1924, N 4,21:1; 1951, Jl 26,21:3
Cross, John W Mrs (funl, Mr 19,13:5), 1920, Mr 17, 11:4
Cross, Joseph Judge, 1913, O 30,9:3
Cross, Judson L, 1947, O 21,23:2
Cross, L Leslie, 1944, D 18,19:6
Cross, Lavern L, 1953, Mr 24,42:3
Cross, Leach, 1957, S 8,84:1
Cross, Leslie C, 1960, F 12,27:3
Cross, Lewis L, 1953, Ja 30,21:4
Cross, Mae H Mrs, 1944, D 11,23:4
Cross, Marvin, 1908, O 7,9:5
Cross, Mary R, 1942, S 10,28:3
Cross, Miles E, 1947, Ap 17,27:5
Cross, Miller, 1957, F 1,25:3
Cross, Milton A, 1954, S 27,21:2
Cross, Morton R, 1959, My 15,29:3
Cross, Nathaniel, 1866, D 26,1:6
Cross, Norman, 1907, Jl 19,7:6
Cross, Osborn, 1876, Jl 17,5:2
Cross, Randall E, 1941, Jl 22,19:3
Cross, Raymond, 1953, Je 3,31:4
Cross, Richard Assheton Viscount, 1914, Ja 9,11:6
Cross, Richard F Sr, 1949, Mr 5,17:5
Cross, Robert Mrs, 1962, O 1,31:2
Cross, Robert Sr, 1956, O 21,86:6
Cross, S Avery Mrs, 1955, Ja 8,13:5
Cross, Samuel H, 1946, O 15,25:4
Cross, Spencer K, 1951, Ja 6,15:1
Cross, Sumner H, 1955, Ap 24,86:5
Cross, Sumner M, 1937, D 2,25:4
Cross, Thomas E, 1937, N 25,31:6
Cross, Thomas J, 1963, Jl 14,61:1
Cross, Tom P, 1951, D 26,25:3
Cross, W Redmond, 1940, N 17,49:3
Cross, Walter D, 1955, Ap 8,21:3
Cross, Ward, 1947, Ag 23,13:2
Cross, Washington M, 1964, My 30,17:3
Cross, Weimar, 1961, O 27,33:1
Cross, Wellington Mrs, 1955, Je 6,27:2
Cross, Wendell L, 1953, Ap 18,19:1
Cross, Wilbur L, 1948, O 5,1:5
Cross, William D Jr Mrs (G A Andre), 1959, F 7, 12:1
Cross, William E, 1947, D 24,22:3
Cross, William F Mrs, 1962, N 11,87:7
Cross, William H, 1950, F 10,23:4
Cross, William J, 1952, O 28,31:4
Cross, William P Mrs, 1950, N 29,33:2
Cross, William T, 1942, D 29,21:5
Cross, Wilson, 1947, Ja 25,17:5
Cross-the-River, Frank, 1939, My 30,17:4
Crossan, Clarence K, 1960, S 27,38:1
Crossan, William L, 1941, My 25,36:6
Crossbe, Francis Sir, 1872, Ja 6,5:4
Crosse, Charles W, 1951, Ap 23,25:2
Crossen, Harry s, 1951, Mr 12,25:2
Crossen, Leo a, 1951, Ap 11,29:5
Crosser, John R Rev, 1937, D 19,II,8:7
Crosser, Robert, 1957, Je 4,35:2
Crosser, Robert Mrs, 1945, N 21,21:1
Crossett, Edward C, 1955, Ag 1,19:2
Crossett, Harry S, 1963, D 19,33:1
Crossett, Henry B, 1914, Jl 28,7:4
Crossett, W, 1883, Jl 24,8:4
Crossey, John J Rev, 1912, O 26,11:6
Crossfield, Richard H, 1951, Ag 1,23:7
Crossic, Marquise De (Mrs Richd De Logerot), 1913, Mr 14,9:1
Crossin, Franklin S, 1938, Ap 2,15:3
Crossin, John F, 1957, D 9,35:3
Crossland, Edgar, 1941, Je 14,17:3
Crossland, James H, 1939, N 27,17:6
Crossland, Weldon F, 1961, O 8,87:2
Crossley, Arthur L, 1948, Je 8,25:4
Crossley, Duane W Mrs, 1953, Mr 17,35:7
Crossley, Elijah R, 1953, Ja 24,15:4
Crossley, Frank, 1937, O 26,23:1
Crossley, G Reginald Mrs, 1938, Je 15,23:5
Crossley, George C, 1951, Je 11,25:2
Crossley, Joseph, 1942, Ja 8,21:5
Crossley, Julia H Mrs, 1947, F 27,21:2
Crossley, Kenneth, 1957, N 24,87:3
Crossley, Robert H, 1968, S 11,47:1
Crossley, Robert J, 1960, Mr 20,87:1
Crossley, Sarah Mrs, 1915, Ap 27,13:4
Crossley, W T Capt, 1921, Jl 15,11:5
Crossley, William, 1939, Ag 10,19:5
Crossley, William John Sir, 1911, O 13,11:5
Crossly, James, 1883, Ag 17,3:2
Crossman, Charles S, 1941, Ja 4,13:6
Crossman, Edgar G, 1967, Ja 30,29:3
Crossman, Edwina B Mrs, 1938, D 26,23:2
Crossman, Francis M, 1953, S 18,23:2
Crossman, Frank F Mrs, 1941, S 16,23:6
Crossman, Frank M, 1965, Ag 7,21:3
Crossman, George L, 1945, D 31,17:2
Crossman, Henry, 1881, Ja 8,2:4
Crossman, I Booth, 1920, S 10,11:3
Crossman, Ralph L, 1948, My 4,25:2
Crossman, Raymond M, 1963, My 19,86:5
Crossman, Richard H S Mrs, 1952, Jl 7,21:6
Crossman, William H, 1907, D 26,7:5
Crossnay, Miguel K, 1954, Ap 7,31:4
Crosson, C R Father, 1883, Ag 2,4:7
Crosson, Joe (por), 1949, Je 22,31:1
Crosson, John, 1953, Ag 28,17:3; 1958, S 21,86:
Crosson, Margaret M, 1950, Ag 23,29:5
Crosson, Robert, 1946, Ag 25,46:2
Crosswaith, Frank R, 1965, Je 18,35:1
Crosswell, William J, 1947, Ag 16,13:4
Crossy, John Stewart, 1905, My 24,9:4
Crosthwait, Eugene L, 1955, Ja 20,31:2
Crosthwaite, Burwell M, 1938, Je 25,15:6
Crosthwaite, J L Maj, 1919, S 7,23:5
Crosthwaite, John N (funl), 1961, F 9,31:3
Crosthwaite, William Sir, 1968, My 15,47:2
Crostic, Edward A, 1939, Ap 11,23:1
Croswell, Edwin, 1871, Je 16,5:4
Croswell, James Greenleaf Prof (funl, Mr 17,1 1915, Mr 15,11:5
Croswell, Noel, 1960, D 5,31:6
Crotchfelt, William Jr, 1947, O 23,25:6
Croteau, Louis J, 1948, Mr 25,27:3

Crothers, Austin Lane, 1912, My 25,13:5
Crothers, Bronson, 1959, Jl 19,69:1
Crothers, Edna McN, 1966, F 22,23:4
Crothers, George E, 1957, My 17,26:2
Crothers, Lulu M, 1940, D 24,15:3
Crothers, Rachel (trb lr, Jl 12,14:6), 1958, Jl 6,57:1
Crothers, Robert A, 1945, F 8,19:3
Crothers, Thomas D Dr, 1918, Ja 14,11:4
Crothers, Thomas W Sen, 1921, D 12,15:3
Crothers, William F, 1951, Je 11,25:5
Crotti, Andre, 1958, F 1,19:3
Crotti, Jean, 1958, F 1,19:3
Crotty, James J, 1967, S 9,31:3
Crotty, Joseph J, 1960, N 26,21:5
Crotty, Margaret (Sister Mary Evangelist), 1940, O 19,17:6
Crotty, Martin F, 1948, Je 6,72:2
Crotty, Michael C, 1951, S 13,25:1
Crotty, T G, 1956, Ag 17,19:2
Crotty, Thomas T, 1942, Ja 15,19:5
Crotty, William A, 1942, D 15,27:4
Crotzer, Thomas M, 1957, O 16,32:7
Crouch, Albert W, 1954, S 27,21:4
Crouch, Arthur S, 1948, O 24,76:2
Crouch, Carolyn Mrs, 1946, D 23,23:3
Crouch, Charles, 1957, D 13,27:2
Crouch, Charles T, 1949, Je 14,32:4
Crouch, F W N, 1896, Ag 20,9:7
Crouch, Frances K, 1966, D 17,33:4
Crouch, George F, 1959, Je 6,21:3
Crouch, George I, 1959, Mr 3,33:4
Crouch, H Chester, 1903, O 30,9:6
Crouch, Henry S, 1953, D 13,87:1
Crouch, Joel E, 1957, Ag 16,19:5
Crouch, John P, 1955, Ag 31,25:4
Crouch, Leonard C, 1953, Jl 3,19:1
Crouch, Martin, 1957, Ag 30,37:2
Crouch, Paul, 1955, N 19,19:4
Crouch, Robert F, 1957, My 8,37:4
Crouch, Robert G, 1947, My 14,25:3
Crouch, Robert T, 1958, F 20,25:1
Crouch, Rosa, 1949, Jl 3,26:6
Crouch, Sidney, 1959, Ag 25,1:2
Crouch, Walter C, 1943, Mr 11,21:1
Crouch, William Greanleaf, 1872, Ja 29,1:2
Croucher, Thomas, 1939, Mr 7,21:4
Croudle, Peter J, 1955, Ap 23,19:2
Crough, Helen G Mrs, 1966, Mr 28,33:5
Crough, Herbert T, 1951, O 4,33:1
Crough, William H, 1963, S 10,39:4
Crough, William H Mrs, 1952, Ja 5,11:2
Croughton, Amy H, 1951, Ap 11,29:2
Croughwell, Michael, 1944, F 22,24:3
Croul, Julia J Mrs, 1940, Ap 20,17:2
Crounse, Charles R Sr, 1948, Ap 15,25:5
Crounse, Frederick Dr, 1937, Ag 10,19:3
Crounse, William Mrs, 1949, D 5,23:4
Croup, B B, 1950, Ag 23,29:4
Crouse, Albert S, 1953, Mr 3,27:2
Crouse, Carl C, 1942, N 26,27:3
Crouse, Charles L, 1942, D 15,27:5
Crouse, Charles W, 1946, Ap 24,25:5
Crouse, Daniel N Mrs, 1941, My 1,23:2
Crouse, George E, 1945, Jl 8,11:6
Crouse, Huntingdon B Jr, 1951, My 15,26:6
Crouse, Huntingdon B Jr Mrs, 1951, My 15,26:6
Crouse, Huntington B, 1943, Je 12,13:3
Crouse, Ira R, 1939, N 22,21:1
Crouse, John J, 1949, Mr 27,76:4
Crouse, Kenneth C Mrs, 1967, Jl 28,31:2
Crouse, Kenneth C Sr, 1961, Ja 6,27:2
Crouse, Russel (cor, Ap 5,39:2; will, Ap 13,23:1), 1966, Ap 4,1:2
Crouse, Wilford J, 1944, Jl 18,19:1
Crout, E T, 1875, N 29,2:3
Crout, William J, 1952, S 25,31:6
Crouter, Errol E, 1951, Jl 31,21:5
Crouthamel, Edgar C Mrs, 1953, Jl 14,27:2
Croutz, Carl A, 1941, Mr 14,21:1
Crouze, Herman, 1940, Mr 25,2:4
Crow, Allen B Mrs, 1961, N 17,35:1
Crow, Alwyn, 1965, F 6,25:5
Crow, Arthur E, 1939, Je 4,49:3
Crow, C Fred, 1942, S 17,25:5
Crow, Carl, 1945, Je 10,32:1
Crow, Charles S, 1960, Je 1,39:5
Crow, Edmund B, 1945, Mr 1,21:1
Crow, Floyd W, 1949, Je 16,29:4
Crow, Fred, 1952, My 6,29:3
Crow, George Busk, 1912, Jl 3,11:6
Crow, Harker A, 1939, My 15,17:3
Crow, Helen Mrs, 1941, N 25,25:2
Crow, J T, 1881, Mr 24,2:7
Crow, James, 1942, Ap 10,17:1
Crow, James L, 1945, My 26,17:1
Crow, Lester D Mrs, 1966, Ja 24,35:5
Crow, Orin F, 1955, S 23,25:2
Crow, W, 1885, My 11,5:6
Crow, William E, 1922, Ap 13,19:6
Crow, William E Sen, 1922, Ja 2,17:4
Crow, William E Sen (funl, Ag 4,15:5), 1922, Ag 3, 3:6
Crow, William H, 1963, Ap 12,27:4

Crowder, E H, 1932, My 8,II,5:1
Crowder, F W, 1932, S 28,19:3
Crowder, Harry L, 1947, Je 30,19:3
Crowder, Samuel R, 1952, Mr 6,31:1
Crowder, William S, 1968, Mr 19,47:2
Crowdy, Mary N P Mrs, 1942, N 13,23:4
Crowe, Albert M, 1958, My 24,21:5
Crowe, Earl, 1952, Ja 24,27:4
Crowe, Earle R, 1947, Ja 29,25:5
Crowe, Edwin R, 1939, D 18,23:4
Crowe, Eric E, 1952, Je 24,29:4
Crowe, Eric Sir, 1925, Ap 29,21:6
Crowe, Frank, 1944, My 11,19:3
Crowe, Frank A, 1940, Je 1,15:4
Crowe, Frank C, 1941, My 2,21:2
Crowe, Frank T, 1946, F 28,23:1
Crowe, Henry D, 1952, My 13,17:3
Crowe, James J, 1948, S 14,29:4
Crowe, James N Mrs, 1951, O 18,29:6
Crowe, John A, 1961, F 14,37:4
Crowe, John C, 1959, Je 18,31:5
Crowe, John E, 1956, N 25,88:6
Crowe, Margaret K, 1951, Ap 26,29:5
Crowe, Marty, 1951, Mr 30,23:4
Crowe, Mary M E, 1943, S 8,23:3
Crowe, Pat, 1938, O 30,40:6
Crowe, Robert E, 1958, Ja 20,23:1
Crowe, Robert E Sr, 1944, Jl 11,15:1
Crowe, Robert T, 1937, O 19,26:2
Crowe, Robert T Mrs, 1959, O 12,19:5
Crowe, S W Dr, 1904, Ja 26,3:2
Crowe, Samuel J, 1955, N 14,27:2
Crowe, Thomas B, 1940, N 14,23:5
Crowe, Thomas J Mrs, 1953, My 14,29:3
Crowe, Walter G, 1947, N 11,28:2
Crowe, William H Mrs, 1948, Ap 10,13:3
Crowe, William J, 1952, O 25,17:2; 1960, F 25,29:5
Crowe, William M, 1951, My 19,15:5
Crowell, Arthur H, 1940, Mr 28,23:3
Crowell, Benedict, 1952, S 9,31:4
Crowell, Bowman C, 1951, Ap 27,23:3
Crowell, Cedric R, 1955, Je 26,76:4
Crowell, Cedric R Mrs, 1968, S 17,47:2
Crowell, Charles, 1914, Ag 28,9:6
Crowell, Charles B, 1959, Ap 4,19:3
Crowell, Charles E, 1921, Je 13,13:4
Crowell, Chester T, 1941, D 27,19:3
Crowell, Chester T Mrs (Evelyn M), 1960, S 19,31:2
Crowell, Clarence P, 1942, O 5,19:6
Crowell, De Witt G, 1951, Ja 3,27:4
Crowell, Edith H, 1963, N 9,25:2
Crowell, Edward Payson Rev Dr, 1911, Mr 26,II,15:4
Crowell, Evelyn, 1947, Ag 1,17:5
Crowell, Florence P Mrs, 1938, My 12,23:5
Crowell, George C, 1951, My 22,31:4
Crowell, George W, 1946, O 8,24:2
Crowell, Gilmore Mrs, 1948, Je 3,25:3
Crowell, Grace W Mrs, 1951, D 1,13:5
Crowell, H Dayton Jr, 1954, O 8,23:4
Crowell, H Ramsay, 1961, Ja 24,29:2
Crowell, Harry C (por), 1938, Jl 30,13:3
Crowell, Henry C, 1965, N 26,37:3
Crowell, Henry K, 1955, Mr 31,27:4
Crowell, Henry P, 1944, O 24,23:1
Crowell, Herbert H, 1941, S 7,51:6
Crowell, J Addison Mrs, 1953, Ap 13,27:4
Crowell, J Dexter, 1938, Ja 5,21:5
Crowell, J F, 1931, Ag 7,17:5
Crowell, J Foster, 1915, Mr 30,11:5
Crowell, J Gen, 1883, Mr 9,5:6
Crowell, J S, 1921, Ag 18,11:6
Crowell, James Hedges, 1908, Ag 13,7:4
Crowell, James M Rev, 1908, Ja 6,7:4
Crowell, James Mrs, 1944, F 28,17:5
Crowell, James R, 1948, Ja 19,23:3
Crowell, James R Mrs, 1955, Ja 23,85:2
Crowell, John E Mrs, 1945, N 4,43:1
Crowell, John F, 1939, Ja 8,42:7
Crowell, John G, 1939, Mr 26,III,6:8
Crowell, John Rev, 1909, Mr 30,9:4
Crowell, Joseph A, 1952, Ap 3,35:2
Crowell, Joseph E, 1968, Jl 18,33:5
Crowell, Joseph Edgar, 1919, O 17,17:5
Crowell, M L, 1884, Ap 8,5:5
Crowell, Mary F B Mrs, 1964, Ag 8,19:6
Crowell, Merle, 1956, Ag 15,29:3
Crowell, Merle Mrs (D Walworth), 1953, N 7,17:4
Crowell, Nelson J, 1958, F 28,21:3
Crowell, Paul Mrs, 1966, Ja 15,27:2
Crowell, Robert E, 1962, Ap 13,35:4
Crowell, Robert R, 1938, O 28,23:3
Crowell, Robert W, 1951, My 1,29:4
Crowell, T Irving, 1942, Ja 13,19:4
Crowell, Theodore Mrs, 1952, My 9,23:4
Crowell, Thomas I Jr, 1960, Jl 23,19:1
Crowell, Thomas L Jr, 1962, N 22,29:2
Crowell, Thomas Y, 1915, Jl 30,9:6
Crowell, Walter Mrs, 1962, Ag 8,31:3
Crowell, Wilbur S, 1948, D 11,15:5
Crowell, William B, 1940, Ag 20,19:2; 1948, Jl 2,21:4
Crowell, William R, 1948, My 4,26:3
Crowell, William W, 1956, Jl 30,21:4
Crowell, Wilmer G, 1943, Ag 24,19:1

Crowely, Leo F, 1948, D 10,25:1
Crowen, Edward F Rev, 1915, Je 11,15:6
Crowforth, Anderson, 1948, Mr 15,23:2
Crowhurst, A James, 1943, Jl 20,19:4
Crowhurst, Ernest H, 1941, O 17,23:5
Crowinshield, A S Rear-Adm, 1908, My 28,7:5
Crowinshield, Francis B, 1950, My 20,15:2
Crowinshield, Frederic Mrs, 1924, Je 25,23:5
Crowley, Aleister, 1947, D 2,29:3
Crowley, Andrew J, 1937, O 13,23:6
Crowley, Arthur F, 1947, S 26,23:3
Crowley, Arthur J, 1937, N 27,17:4; 1959, S 18,32:1
Crowley, Arthur J Jr, 1954, My 21,27:1
Crowley, Arthur L, 1943, Ja 10,50:3
Crowley, Benjamin F, 1961, Mr 15,39:4
Crowley, C K (1812), 1880, Ja 10,3:3
Crowley, Charles A, 1951, N 12,25:2
Crowley, Charles D, 1947, D 1,21:2
Crowley, Charles F, 1951, Jl 20,21:3
Crowley, Charles H, 1961, Ap 26,39:3
Crowley, Charles J, 1943, O 13,23:6
Crowley, Cornelius, 1920, Ag 12,9:2
Crowley, Cornelius D, 1960, Je 18,23:5
Crowley, Cornelius F Msgr, 1937, Jl 2,21:1
Crowley, Cornelius J, 1946, D 9,25:4; 1957, Ja 1,23:5
Crowley, Cornelius J Mrs, 1958, Je 2,27:2
Crowley, Cornelius P, 1949, N 30,27:2
Crowley, Daniel, 1954, My 7,23:2
Crowley, Dennis R, 1939, Ag 18,19:5
Crowley, Elmer E, 1944, Je 12,19:4
Crowley, Elmer E Mrs, 1964, Ag 4,29:3
Crowley, Fintan, 1954, F 27,13:3
Crowley, Flouence, 1956, Jl 3,25:5
Crowley, Francis A, 1959, Ag 3,25:5
Crowley, Francis B, 1939, Mr 8,21:3
Crowley, Fred J Mrs, 1957, Ap 15,29:1
Crowley, G C, 1931, My 19,23:2
Crowley, George, 1945, Ja 17,21:5
Crowley, George B Mrs, 1967, Ap 12,47:2
Crowley, George C Sr Mrs, 1959, N 22,87:1
Crowley, George R, 1921, D 24,11:6
Crowley, Harry T, 1951, O 1,23:6
Crowley, Helen G, 1946, N 22,23:2
Crowley, Hugh A, 1939, My 10,23:5
Crowley, James, 1958, Ag 1,21:3
Crowley, James A, 1942, N 14,16:3
Crowley, James E, 1950, Mr 9,29:3
Crowley, James F, 1968, Jl 5,25:3
Crowley, James F Rev Father, 1916, My 23,11:5
Crowley, James K, 1952, D 10,35:5
Crowley, James S, 1942, D 26,11:5
Crowley, Jeremiah P, 1950, Ja 15,84:2
Crowley, Jerome B, 1964, Ap 16,37:4
Crowley, Jerome J Mrs, 1949, Ag 8,15:3
Crowley, John, 1908, Je 22,7:2; 1949, D 16,31:4
Crowley, John G Capt, 1921, Ap 1,13:3
Crowley, John H, 1916, Ja 3,13:2
Crowley, John J, 1948, My 15,15:3
Crowley, John T, 1955, My 25,33:5
Crowley, Joseph F, 1947, Ja 21,23:2; 1957, N 21,30:1
Crowley, Joseph G, 1964, O 18,89:2
Crowley, Joseph P, 1957, N 18,31:4
Crowley, Joseph P Mrs, 1962, My 19,41:8
Crowley, Karl A, 1948, Mr 31,26:3
Crowley, M H, 1933, Ag 22,17:3
Crowley, Margaret E, 1937, S 16,25:3
Crowley, Marshall, 1967, S 1,28:8
Crowley, Marshall O Mrs, 1966, Je 14,48:1
Crowley, Mary, 1937, F 17,22:2
Crowley, Mary M, 1943, Ja 27,21:2
Crowley, Maud, 1884, My 28,2:7
Crowley, Milton W, 1950, Ja 17,27:4
Crowley, Patrick E, 1953, O 2,21:3
Crowley, Patrick E Mrs, 1959, My 2,23:3
Crowley, Raymond L Mrs, 1956, D 4,39:3
Crowley, Stewart W, 1947, Mr 21,21:3
Crowley, T J, 1945, O 3,19:3
Crowley, Thomas E J, 1968, F 6,43:4
Crowley, Thomas J, 1964, Mr 11,39:3
Crowley, Thomas M, 1903, D 2,9:5
Crowley, Timothy F Sr, 1943, My 8,15:4
Crowley, Timothy J, 1948, My 1,15:3
Crowley, Ward F, 1959, S 13,84:8
Crowley, William, 1961, Jl 25,27:1
Crowley, William J Mrs, 1955, Jl 20,27:4
Crowley, William S, 1947, Mr 4,26:3
Crowley, William S Rev, 1875, Ja 17,1:4
Crowley, Xavier, 1958, Je 17,29:2
Crown, Abraham, 1956, F 25,19:5
Crown, Gordon T, 1947, N 18,29:4
Crown, James E, 1945, Ja 11,23:4
Crown, John R, 1940, N 15,21:5
Crown, William H Sr, 1942, Jl 7,20:4
Crownfield, David, 1940, F 9,19:4
Crownfield, Gertrude, 1945, Je 3,32:2
Crownhart, J George, 1941, Je 6,21:4
Crowninshield, Anne D Mrs, 1955, S 21,33:5
Crowninshield, Bowdoin B, 1948, Ag 13,15:1
Crowninshield, Casper S, 1910, S 27,13:6
Crowninshield, Edward A, 1938, Ag 27,13:6
Crowninshield, F B, 1877, My 9,4:6
Crowninshield, Francis B Mrs, 1958, Jl 12,15:3
Crowninshield, Frank, 1947, D 29,17:1

Crowninshield, Frederic, 1918, S 15,23:1
Crowninshield, George H Mrs, 1944, Mr 17,17:2
Crowninshield, Jacob, 1907, N 16,9:5
Crowther, Cyril I, 1968, O 29,47:1
Crowther, Elizabeth, 1941, Mr 24,17:4
Crowther, F Bosley Mrs, 1960, Ap 12,33:5
Crowther, Florence, 1943, F 21,32:4
Crowther, Henry, 1937, Ap 30,22:3
Crowther, Herbert S, 1962, Je 24,68:7
Crowther, Herbert S Mrs, 1965, Ag 3,31:2
Crowther, John, 1937, O 24,II,9:2
Crowther, John H, 1939, F 3,15:2
Crowther, John W, 1941, D 23,21:5
Crowther, Kenneth V Mrs, 1957, Ja 6,89:1
Crowther, Mary I Mrs, 1941, My 30,15:4
Crowther, Neil, 1946, Jl 11,23:4
Crowther, Samuel, 1947, O 28,25:4
Crowther, Samuel 3d, 1967, F 2,35:3
Crowthers, Dorothy, 1965, D 28,27:4
Croxall, Catherine, 1939, My 20,15:5
Croxier, William P, 1944, Ap 17,23:2
Croxton, Frederick C, 1960, Ap 4,29:3
Croxton, John Capt, 1913, F 4,11:6
Croxton, Lillian S Mrs, 1949, Ap 8,25:3
Croxton, Philip, 1953, Mr 8,90:4
Croxton, William N, 1944, S 21,19:6
Croy, C C, 1903, S 1,1:6
Croy, Homer, 1965, My 25,41:3
Croy, James R Jr, 1956, My 15,31:2
Croy, Ralph C, 1947, D 20,17:3
Croy, Reginald de, 1961, Ap 15,21:5
Crozer, Edward, 1942, Ap 24,17:1
Crozer, George K, 1921, Je 8,17:5
Crozier, Alfred O, 1939, S 27,25:3
Crozier, Bernard L, 1938, Jl 25,15:4
Crozier, Frank P Gen, 1937, S 1,19:1
Crozier, James R Mrs, 1942, Jl 19,30:8
Crozier, John Baptist Archbishop, 1920, Ap 13,9:3
Crozier, John Beattie, 1921, Ja 10,11:6
Crozier, John J, 1940, My 30,17:4
Crozier, John R, 1943, Je 23,21:2
Crozier, Robert, 1948, My 13,25:4
Crozier, Ronald G, 1963, Ap 21,86:6
Crozier, William, 1942, N 11,25:1
Crozier, William J, 1955, N 3,31:2
Cru, Albert L, 1949, S 13,29:3
Cru, Jean N, 1949, Je 25,13:4
Cruchaga, Miguel, 1949, My 4,29:5
Crucy, Francois, 1958, Jl 28,23:3
Crudelle, Albert P Mrs, 1960, Ap 29,31:2
Cruden, William N, 1950, Ap 21,23:1
Cruea, Davis E, 1947, Ap 21,27:6
Crueger, Gustaf A, 1954, My 16,86:2
Cruess, Charles E, 1948, O 9,19:4
Cruess, Leigh, 1959, Ja 14,27:3
Cruff, Frederick E, 1948, Ja 20,23:3
Cruft, Charles, 1938, S 11,II,11:1
Cruft, Charles Mrs, 1950, S 6,29:2
Cruger, Albert E, 1949, Mr 20,76:8
Cruger, Bernard W, 1961, Jl 24,23:1
Cruger, Bertram, 1952, Jl 20,53:1
Cruger, Catherine Church, 1914, My 9,11:6
Cruger, Dorothy A, 1960, N 19,21:4
Cruger, Frederic H, 1965, Ap 14,41:3
Cruger, Harold, 1939, F 24,19:4
Cruger, J, 1879, N 20,8:6
Cruger, Mary, 1908, N 20,9:3
Cruger, S V R, 1898, Je 29,7:5
Cruger, S Van Rensselaer Mrs (Julien Gordon), 1920, Jl 13,11:4
Cruger, Violet D Mrs, 1944, Je 20,19:2
Crugom, James, 1948, Je 1,23:4
Cruice, Mary Z, 1945, S 5,23:1
Cruickshank, A J, 1945, Ag 1,19:4
Cruickshank, James, 1912, D 24,9:4
Cruickshank, James H, 1949, O 19,29:1
Cruickshank, William C, 1940, O 5,15:6
Cruikshank, Clarence D Mrs, 1943, My 12,25:4
Cruikshank, Cornell, 1968, Ap 11,45:3
Cruikshank, Dwight P, 1954, O 21,27:1
Cruikshank, Edwin Allen, 1921, Ap 15,15:4
Cruikshank, Ernest A, 1939, Je 25,37:2
Cruikshank, Ernest Mrs, 1955, D 27,24:4
Cruikshank, G, 1878, F 2,2:4
Cruikshank, Harold T Sr, 1956, Mr 14,33:1
Cruikshank, Helen Mrs, 1947, Jl 8,23:3
Cruikshank, Herbert K, 1939, S 28,25:5
Cruikshank, J Henry, 1955, Ag 20,17:6
Cruikshank, James A, 1957, Jl 22,19:3
Cruikshank, James Harper, 1968, S 26,55:1
Cruikshank, John M, 1912, D 14,15:3
Cruikshank, Robert J, 1956, My 15,31:4
Cruikshank, Russell V, 1965, S 9,41:5
Cruikshank, Russell V Mrs, 1964, F 19,36:1
Cruikshank, W D, 1950, F 7,27:4
Cruikshank, Warren, 1947, F 12,25:6
Cruikshank, William J Dr, 1925, Mr 4,19:5
Cruikshank, William M, 1963, My 27,29:5
Cruise, Edwin, 1937, F 17,22:1
Cruise, Fred A, 1949, N 24,31:5
Cruise, Gerald J Mrs, 1954, Ja 18,23:4
Cruise, Gerald V, 1952, D 10,35:6
Cruise, Michael J, 1946, Ap 19,29:1
Cruise, Michael J Mrs, 1941, O 28,23:5
Cruise, Peter, 1946, Ag 28,27:5
Crum, Bartley C (left no will, D 24,12:8), 1959, D 11,33:1
Crum, Charles W, 1942, Ja 31,17:6
Crum, Earl L, 1961, Jl 31,19:3
Crum, Earl W, 1941, D 10,25:2
Crum, Frederick Mrs, 1949, Ag 2,19:3
Crum, George F, 1953, S 4,34:2
Crum, George Latham, 1914, My 2,9:6
Crum, Harry E, 1955, Ap 2,17:5
Crum, Jay, 1955, N 5,19:5
Crum, Ralph W Mrs, 1946, My 17,22:2
Crum, Roy W, 1951, My 15,31:6
Crum, William D, 1912, D 8,17:5
Crum, William L, 1967, My 31,43:1
Crumb, Frank A, 1953, Ap 2,27:2
Crumb, Julius R, 1939, O 22,41:2
Crumb, Kittridge B, 1952, O 24,23:5
Crumb, Leverett F Mrs, 1944, O 18,21:2
Crumbaugh, Lucius B, 1939, My 4,23:1
Crumbie, Frank R Sr, 1948, F 1,60:7
Crumbine, Samuel J, 1954, Jl 14,28:3
Crumbley, Thomas R, 1944, O 6,23:2
Crumblin, Thomas C, 1949, Ap 26,25:1
Crumbly, Peter, 1944, D 24,26:2
Crume, James M, 1951, Ag 1,23:3
Crumit, Frank, 1943, S 8,23:1
Crumley, Newton, 1962, F 12,20:6
Crumley, William H, 1939, Ap 7,21:2
Crumlish, James C, 1957, N 22,26:1
Crumm, Martin J Jr, 1949, N 29,29:4
Crumm, William J (death ruling, Jl 26,7:3), 1967, Jl 8,3:5
Crummenauer, Louis, 1957, Ja 5,17:7
Crummey, Edward J, 1968, Ja 3,40:5
Crummey, Safford A, 1946, Mr 17,43:1
Crump, A H, 1942, Je 25,23:1
Crump, Armistead C, 1966, F 17,33:2
Crump, Charles, 1939, My 2,23:4; 1952, Ja 25,22:3
Crump, Edward H (funl, O 19,27:6), 1954, O 17,1:8
Crump, Edward H Mrs, 1956, D 23,30:6
Crump, Edward S Dr, 1923, F 3,13:5
Crump, George A, 1918, Ja 25,11:8
Crump, Henry A, 1941, S 17,23:2
Crump, Jack, 1966, Ap 16,33:5
Crump, James L, 1960, Mr 19,21:4
Crump, P R, 1952, Ja 2,25:2
Crump, W Leslie, 1962, O 11,39:2
Crump, Walter G, 1945, My 2,23:5
Crump, Walter G Jr, 1956, My 10,31:3
Crump, William R, 1946, D 6,23:1
Crumpacker, Edgar Dean, 1920, My 21,15:4
Crumrine, Chester W, 1952, F 8,23:2
Crunden, Allan B, 1968, Jl 3,35:2
Crunden, Robert H, 1940, Jl 28,27:1
Crunelle, Leonard, 1944, S 12,19:3
Crupper, Joseph L, 1940, Mr 30,15:5
Cruse, Bernard A Sr, 1962, S 22,25:5
Cruse, Donald, 1948, Ja 19,24:3
Cruse, Fred T, 1949, Ag 6,17:6
Cruse, Howard R, 1949, Jl 2,15:2
Cruse, James F, 1907, Jl 22,7:5
Cruse, William A, 1962, F 15,29:2
Crusellas, Ramon, 1960, D 18,84:1
Cruser, Frederick V D, 1941, F 4,21:3
Cruser, William C, 1942, Ap 24,17:5
Cruset, Sebastian, 1943, D 29,17:1
Crusinberry, James, 1960, Jl 2,17:6
Crusius, Malcolm A, 1968, O 5,35:6
Cruso, Bash, 1950, S 14,32:3
Crussol, Duchess de, 1947, D 11,33:2
Crutcher, Albert Mrs, 1954, O 30,17:3
Crutcher, Jack R, 1958, O 27,27:2
Crutcher, Richard L, 1952, Je 21,15:4
Crutchfield, Charles E, 1957, Jl 29,19:2
Crutchfield, Charles N, 1952, D 19,31:4
Crutchfield, James S, 1954, Ap 17,13:5
Crutchley, Fenton E Mrs, 1958, Jl 21,21:2
Cruthers, Thomas, 1952, Jl 28,15:4
Cruthers, Torrey A, 1957, Mr 23,19:6
Cruttenden, Harry L, 1941, Ja 20,17:5
Cruttenden, Walter B, 1949, S 6,27:2
Cruz, Anibal (funl, D 22,13:5), 1910, D 19,9:5
Cruz, Carlos B, 1958, S 2,25:1
Cruz, Martina de la, 1949, Ap 26,25:2
Cruze, James (will, S 3,22:5), 1942, Ag 5,19:3
Cryan, James A, 1906, Mr 1,9:6
Cryder, Duncan, 1913, Ag 29,9:6
Cryer, George, 1949, Ja 14,23:4
Cryer, George E, 1961, My 25,37:2
Cryer, John F, 1947, S 14,60:2
Cryer, Matthew Mrs, 1948, N 30,27:4
Crygotis, Dominick, 1952, N 29,17:2
Crystal, David, 1962, Ja 29,25:1
Crystal, George, 1939, O 28,15:5
Crystal, Grace I, 1957, S 4,33:2
Crystal, Jack (correction, O 18,31:1), 1963, O 17,32:6
Crystal, Jacob, 1949, Jl 17,57:2
Crystal, James Rev, 1908, N 13,9:3
Crystal, Leon, 1959, Ag 23,93:1
Crystal, Moses, 1922, Ja 28,13:4
Crystal, Sydney O, 1967, F 22,29:5
Cuadra, Heliodoro, 1941, Ja 16,21:2
Cuadra Chamorro, Pedro J, 1955, D 24,13:5
Cualli, Clara, 1921, Ja 7,13:2
Cuba, Isidore, 1958, Ap 8,29:4
Cuba, Isidore Mrs, 1958, O 9,37:5
Cubas, Jose de, 1957, Ag 11,80:3
Cubas Urquijo, Francisco (Count of Almudena), 1950, Ap 26,29:5
Cubberley, Charles W, 1952, Mr 26,29:5
Cubberley, Ellwood P, 1941, S 15,17:3
Cubberley, John B, 1957, F 28,27:2
Cubberley, Raymond, 1912, Je 3,9:4
Cubberly, John A, 1944, Ap 10,19:2
Cubbon, Miles H, 1958, My 7,35:4
Cubbon, William R, 1947, Ag 2,13:4
Cubert, Ina Mrs, 1947, Ap 1,19:6
Cubeta, Paul, 1944, Ja 2,38:4
Cubeta, Salvatore T, 1952, Je 26,29:5
Cubitt, Thomas A Sir, 1939, My 21,III,6:4
Cuchie, Thomas F, 1950, D 24,36:1
Cuci, Valentine, 1951, S 18,32:4
Cucinell, Samuel A, 1948, Ag 31,26:2
Cucinello, Nicholas G, 1964, Je 23,33:3
Cucolo, Anthony Mrs, 1951, S 11,29:2
Cudahy, Alice D P Mrs, 1942, F 17,21:5
Cudahy, Clara A, 1938, N 29,23:4
Cudahy, Edward A Jr, 1966, Ja 9,56:5
Cudahy, Edward A Sr, 1941, O 19,45:1
Cudahy, Edward A Sr Mrs, 1937, My 4,25:6
Cudahy, John, 1915, Ap 24,11:6
Cudahy, John J Mrs, 1945, O 23,17:4
Cudahy, John Mrs, 1924, Ag 12,11:4
Cudahy, Joseph M, 1947, O 26,68:4
Cudahy, Joseph M Mrs (will, Ap 21,29:4), 1953, Ap 8,29:3
Cudahy, Margaret C Mrs, 1942, Je 15,19:5
Cudahy, Mary T, 1957, Ag 18,83:3
Cudahy, Michael, 1910, N 28,9:5; 1947, F 16,57:2
Cudahy, Michael Mrs, 1919, S 1,7:4
Cudahy, Patrick, 1919, Jl 26,9:7
Cuddeback, A J, 1881, S 1,2:3
Cuddeback, Allan W, 1938, D 5,23:2
Cuddeback, Alva, 1941, Ja 17,17:2
Cuddeback, Caroline, 1952, Ja 18,27:3
Cuddeback, Charles Haynes, 1968, Mr 14,43:3
Cuddeback, Christie E, 1953, Je 25,27:4
Cuddeback, E Gordon, 1944, F 11,19:5
Cuddeback, Eli, 1879, D 7,8:2
Cuddeback, George, 1948, Mr 23,25:5
Cuddeback, Harold M Mrs, 1950, Mr 20,21:4
Cuddeback, Samuel M, 1950, S 1,21:3
Cuddeback, William Herman Judge (funl, Ag 20,15 1919, Ag 17,22:4
Cuddehy, Lucy A Mrs, 1871, D 19,2:3
Cuddihy, Charles F Sr, 1967, S 17,84:8
Cuddihy, Edward J, 1919, S 30,19:2
Cuddihy, H Lester, 1953, Jl 5,49:3
Cuddihy, Joseph A, 1952, Je 29,56:5
Cuddihy, Marguerite Mrs, 1941, Ag 15,17:5
Cuddihy, Robert A, 1957, Jl 7,53:7
Cuddihy, Robert J, 1952, D 23,23:1
Cuddihy, Robert J Mrs, 1944, Je 3,13:2
Cuddy, Edward J, 1942, Ap 24,17:1
Cuddy, James A Mrs, 1962, F 9,26:5
Cuddy, John E, 1953, Mr 27,23:3
Cuddy, Matthew J, 1940, Ag 25,36:5
Cuddy, Raymond J, 1954, Jl 2,19:2
Cuddy, Thomas, 1952, My 31,17:1
Cude, Harold E, 1937, My 11,25:2
Cudebec, Albert B, 1950, Ja 29,69:1
Cudenet, Gabriel, 1948, D 20,25:4
Cudlipp, Chandler, 1967, D 23,23:3
Cudlipp, Edwin, 1946, Ag 19,25:5
Cudlipp, Edwin F, 1943, S 14,23:1
Cudlipp, Joseph, 1917, S 19,13:6
Cudlipp, Percy, 1962, N 6,33:3
Cudlipp, William C, 1940, S 7,15:5
Cudmore, John H Mrs, 1967, F 28,37:2
Cudner, Albert A, 1960, Ap 5,37:4
Cudney, Harry E, 1957, Ap 24,33:5
Cudney, Jay D, 1942, Ap 2,21:5
Cudroff, Henry, 1950, Jl 20,25:5
Cudworth, Henry H, 1944, My 16,21:5
Cudworth, W H Rev, 1883, N 30,1:6
Cue, Pedro, 1950, Jl 14,21:3
Cueman, Claude C, 1941, D 30,19:4
Cueman, J Bentley, 1950, O 18,33:4
Cueman, J Bently Mrs, 1962, Jl 10,33:3
Cuenot, Henri, 1937, Jl 6,14:3
Cuenot, Lucien, 1951, Ja 9,30:5
Cuervo, Luis A, 1954, My 14,23:3
Cuervo Barda, Carlos, 1952, Ja 22,29:1
Cuesta, A L Mrs, 1946, Ja 18,19:2
Cueto, Agusto, 1938, D 28,21:3
Cuett, Franklyn N, 1948, Je 18,23:5
Cuevas, George de, 1961, F 23,27:2
Cuevas Cancino, Francisco Mrs, 1966, F 18,33
Cuff, Albert L, 1968, Ja 21,76:6
Cuff, Charles L, 1938, N 7,19:5
Cuff, Elizabeth A Mrs, 1937, Mr 13,19:5
Cuff, Frank B, 1967, Mr 6,33:5
Cuff, George F, 1953, O 24,15:5
Cuff, James E, 1948, Je 24,25:5

Cuff, James I, 1955, Je 9,29:1
Cuff, James J, 1947, D 27,14:2
Cuff, Leonard, 1940, Ap 22,17:3
Cuff, Margaret G, 1959, Ap 18,23:4
Cuff, Samuel H, 1960, Ag 26,25:3
Cuff, Thomas J, 1953, S 7,19:3
Cuff, William L Mrs, 1943, Ja 10,50:4
Cuffe, F W, 1943, D 23,19:1
Cuffe, Matthew J, 1961, Je 9,33:5
Cuffe, Thomas E, 1959, D 23,27:2
Cuffman, Milton, 1946, F 12,44:6
Cuffney, William, 1939, Jl 16,31:1
Cuffy, Jerry (Jerry Woodhull), 1910, Ja 21,11:5
Cugell Abel G, 1944, O 31,19:4
Cugia, Gen, 1872, Mr 18,1:4
Cugle, Philip M, 1945, My 3,23:2
Cui, Cesar, 1918, Mr 15,13:5
Cuineen, John W, 1952, S 30,31:4
Cuinet, L A, 1933, N 22,19:4
Cuite, Francis A, 1951, Ap 27,23:5
Cuite, Thomas F, 1953, My 10,88:1
Cuite, Thomas F Mrs, 1967, D 29,27:3
Cukela, Louis, 1956, Mr 22,35:2
Cukor, Morris, 1957, D 8,88:1
Culberson, Charles A Gen, 1925, Mr 20,19:3
Culbert, Alma Mrs (will), 1958, S 17,25:6
Culbert, J, 1957, S 28,6:7
Culbert, Jane F, 1962, S 30,86:2
Culbert, Robert W, 1967, S 8,39:2
Culbert, William L, 1946, N 19,31:2
Culbert, William M, 1952, S 30,31:4
Culbertson, A J Owen, 1939, Je 10,11:2
Culbertson, Arthur L, 1963, Jl 22,23:4
Culbertson, Carey, 1942, O 11,56:4
Culbertson, D Franklin, 1942, O 18,52:6
Culbertson, Ely (funl plans, D 29,23:2; funl, D 31,-13:2), 1955, D 28,1:5
Culbertson, Harry E, 1959, Ag 2,81:2
Culbertson, John, 1951, S 7,29:4
Culbertson, John Dickey, 1912, Mr 14,11:4
Culbertson, Josephine M Mrs, 1956, Mr 24,19:3
Culbertson, Lawrence B, 1952, Mr 26,29:3
Culbertson, Peter, 1950, F 9,31:6
Culbertson, Samuel A, 1948, D 12,92:6
Culbertson, Sasha, 1944, Ap 17,23:4
Culbertson, William L, 1958, O 4,21:2
Culbertson, William R, 1952, O 30,31:1
Culbertson, William S, 1966, Ag 14,89:1
Culbreath, Harry C, 1958, Ag 24,86:7
Culbreath, Mildred R, 1951, F 9,25:3
Culbreth, David M R, 1943, O 21,27:3
Culbreth, Henry B, 1943, O 27,23:3
Culbreth, James M, 1949, Mr 31,25:1
Culen, Konstanin, 1964, Ap 8,43:3
Culhane, Edward T, 1937, Ag 28,15:6
Culhane, George T, 1941, My 15,23:3
Culhane, John Herbert, 1922, S 26,17:5
Culhane, Patrick J, 1950, O 21,17:6
Culhane, Peter M, 1947, Ap 13,60:3
Culhane, Robert J, 1939, Ag 27,35:1
Culhane, Thomas J, 1956, O 11,39:4
Culhane, William F, 1964, Jl 3,21:1
Culick, Albert M, 1955, Jl 22,23:4
Culin, Curtis G Sr Mrs, 1949, S 27,27:2
Culin, Curtis G 3d, 1963, N 22,37:3
Culin, Frank L Jr, 1968, Ja 4,34:5
Culin, Stewart Mrs, 1950, Ag 10,25:5
Culkin, Charles M (funl, Ap 12,35:3), 1962, Ap 8,87:1
Culkin, Charles W Mrs, 1963, N 28,39:2
Culkin, Edward F Mrs, 1958, F 25,27:3
Culkin, Francis D, 1943, Ag 5,15:5
Culkin, Joseph, 1940, O 4,23:2
Culkin, Phil R, 1940, Mr 16,15:3
Culkin, Robert L, 1949, Je 14,31:2
Culkin, Thomas J (cor, Ap 13,31:1), 1959, Ap 12,86:6
Culkin, Tom B Capt, 1904, O 7,9:5
Cull, Dan B, 1949, Ag 9,25:2
Cull, Edwin E, 1956, Mr 22,35:4
Cull, Joseph H, 1941, Je 22,32:2
Cull, Louis D Mrs, 1951, O 12,27:2
Cull, Rev Father, 1873, Mr 4,1:4
Cull, Richard W, 1947, N 4,25:5
Cull, Roger W, 1922, Jl 31,11:7
Culle, Frederick John Dr, 1968, Je 11,47:1
Cullem, James M, 1961, F 28,33:5
Cullen, Bernard A, 1960, S 4,68:6
Cullen, Charles W, 1948, Jl 11,50:8
Cullen, Clarence L, 1922, Je 30,17:6
Cullen, Countee, 1946, Ja 10,23:1
Cullen, Dorsey, 1938, Mr 8,19:1
Cullen, Edgar M Ex-Justice, 1922, My 24,19:5
Cullen, Edward J (por), 1949, Je 9,31:4
Cullen, Francis E, 1937, Ag 2,19:4
Cullen, Frederick A, 1946, My 27,23:1
Cullen, George J, 1950, Ja 15,84:6
Cullen, George W Sr, 1961, Ap 1,17:5
Cullen, Glenn E, 1940, Ap 12,23:3
Cullen, Gregory, 1946, Ja 19,13:4
Cullen, Harold, 1915, Jl 3,7:4
Cullen, Harry B, 1940, Ag 28,19:5
Cullen, Harry J, 1946, Ag 1,23:5; 1968, Ag 12,35:1
Cullen, Harry L, 1941, Ja 2,23:3
Cullen, Hugh R, 1957, Jl 5,1:2
Cullen, Hugh R Mrs, 1959, N 17,35:2
Cullen, James F, 1961, My 13,19:3
Cullen, James H, 1950, Mr 24,25:3
Cullen, James J Mrs, 1950, D 15,31:2
Cullen, Jeremiah F, 1948, Jl 12,19:5
Cullen, John, 1915, Ag 10,11:7
Cullen, John A, 1943, Mr 4,19:2
Cullen, John E, 1953, N 18,32:3
Cullen, John F, 1945, Je 12,19:4
Cullen, John J Mrs, 1952, Je 30,19:3
Cullen, John J rev, 1918, My 3,15:5
Cullen, John P, 1940, My 11,19:4
Cullen, Joseph C, 1946, D 31,18:3
Cullen, Joseph W Lt, 1919, Je 29,22:4
Cullen, Kathryn S, 1939, D 14,27:5
Cullen, Lord, 1941, Je 21,17:6
Cullen, Michael J, 1954, Ja 28,27:2
Cullen, Mollie, 1951, O 24,31:4
Cullen, Mortimer A, 1954, Je 27,69:1
Cullen, Patrick J, 1941, My 26,19:2
Cullen, Paul Cardinal, 1878, O 25,3:2
Cullen, Paul J Mrs, 1963, Je 22,23:5
Cullen, Peter J, 1943, S 21,23:2
Cullen, Richard J, 1948, N 14,76:3; 1955, Ag 10,25:6
Cullen, Richard J Mrs, 1946, S 6,22:2
Cullen, Robert E, 1955, Jl 9,15:4
Cullen, Sylvester T, 1942, O 1,23:6
Cullen, T J, 1939, N 25,17:5
Cullen, Thomas, 1916, My 25,13:5
Cullen, Thomas F, 1945, Jl 27,15:6; 1949, S 29,29:4; 1956, Mr 4,88:3
Cullen, Thomas H, 1944, Mr 1,19:1
Cullen, Thomas H Mrs, 1955, Je 23,29:3; 1963, Je 15, 23:3
Cullen, Thomas H Sen, 1913, Ja 30,11:5
Cullen, Thomas J, 1946, Mr 22,21:4; 1953, O 7,29:2; 1954, N 30,29:4
Cullen, Thomas J V Sr, 1966, My 23,41:5
Cullen, Thomas O, 1944, N 10,19:4
Cullen, Thomas P, 1946, Jl 21,40:1; 1968, Ja 25,37:3
Cullen, Thomas R, 1959, Ap 27,27:4
Cullen, Thomas S, 1953, Mr 5,27:4
Cullen, Tracey, 1950, Mr 4,17:3
Cullen, Victor F, 1949, Mr 10,27:2
Cullen, Vincent, 1962, Ja 11,33:4
Cullen, Walter J, 1943, Jl 17,13:6
Cullen, William H, 1951, F 3,15:2
Cullen, William J, 1951, D 30,25:1
Cullen, William T, 1951, S 29,17:2
Cullenbine, Roy Sr, 1947, D 26,15:1
Culler, Arthur M, 1960, O 28,31:1
Culler, Joseph A Dr, 1937, My 19,23:6
Cullerton, Edward F, 1920, F 2,13:4
Cullerton, John A, 1961, Ag 29,31:3
Cullerton, John F, 1937, Je 27,II,7:3
Cullerton, John M, 1965, Ja 10,92:4
Culley, Edward A, 1960, Je 22,35:1
Culley, Fred, 1966, S 21,47:3
Culley, Harry R, 1949, F 12,18:2
Culley, Mabelle R, 1952, Ja 24,27:1
Culligan, James, 1943, Ap 8,23:4
Culligan, William J, 1943, Ap 11,49:2
Cullimore, Allan R, 1956, S 22,17:3
Cullin, James R, 1941, O 22,23:5
Cullinan, Catherine (Sister Mary Coralita), 1956, F 5,86:4
Cullinan, Craig F Mrs, 1949, D 1,31:2
Cullinan, Eustace Jr, 1959, Ag 15,17:4
Cullinan, George E, 1941, Jl 26,15:3
Cullinan, J S, 1937, Mr 12,23:5
Cullinan, John E, 1954, Je 13,89:1
Cullinan, John F, 1945, Ag 9,21:5
Cullinan, John J, 1952, N 19,29:1
Cullinan, Paul A, 1943, Je 26,13:4
Cullinan, Ralph, 1950, Ap 5,31:3
Cullinan, Richard A, 1961, Mr 13,29:4
Cullinan, Thomas H, 1943, Jl 27,21:5
Cullinane, Charles M, 1947, D 25,21:4
Cullinane, James J, 1949, N 19,17:2
Cullinane, Jeremiah J, 1951, Jl 8,61:1
Culliney, James L, 1944, S 7,23:4
Culliney, John J, 1954, Je 15,29:4
Culliney, Michael A, 1944, Ap 28,19:5
Cullings, Clarence A, 1943, Ja 28,19:1
Cullington, James J Mrs, 1948, Ag 31,23:3
Cullingworth, F Janvier, 1957, D 16,29:3
Cullis, Alfred W, 1953, O 17,15:5
Cullis, G Harry, 1962, Mr 17,25:2
Cullis, Winifred C, 1956, N 15,35:3
Cullison, Douglas L, 1958, O 19,87:3
Cullivan, Richard G, 1937, Jl 1,27:4
Cullman, Ferdinand, 1903, D 1,9:6
Cullman, Joseph F (will, Ag 6,14:7), 1938, Ag 2,19:4
Cullman, Joseph F Jr (funl, Mr 21,25:2), 1955, Mr 19,15:1
Cullman, Joseph F Mrs, 1959, Jl 24,25:3
Cullo, James, 1961, Ja 24,29:5
Cullom, Shelby M Mrs (funl, Ag 22,9:6), 1909, Ag 20,7:3
Cullom, Shelby Moore Ex-Sen (funl, F 2,7:5), 1914, Ja 29,9:5
Culloo, Joseph B, 1962, N 14,39:3
Culloo, Michael, 1947, D 6,15:4
Cullum, G W Gen, 1892, Je 29,5:4
Cullum, George, 1947, D 18,29:3
Cullum, George Mrs, 1944, O 25,21:4
Cullum, Hugh P, 1938, Je 2,23:4
Cullum, Norman E, 1951, Ap 26,29:2
Cullum, Paul F, 1962, S 15,25:6
Cullum, Paul F Mrs, 1945, My 21,19:3
Cullum, Rudolph L, 1950, My 11,29:3
Cully, Hiram H, 1953, Mr 22,86:1
Cully, John Mrs, 1961, Mr 7,17:1
Culman, Carl W, 1943, Je 4,21:5
Culman, Otto, 1948, Je 4,23:4
Culman, William, 1941, S 21,45:3
Culme-Seymour, Michael, 1925, Ap 3,19:6
Culmer, Henry L A, 1914, F 11,11:6
Culmo, Joseph, 1949, N 22,29:6
Culmore, March (will), 1952, D 17,46:6
Culnan, Thomas J (Babe), 1962, N 13,37:4
Culp, Cordie J, 1952, Je 1,84:4
Culp, Frank, 1944, D 23,13:4
Culp, Harvey W, 1959, My 12,35:2
Culp, I W Mrs, 1959, S 3,27:3
Culp, Simon, 1946, Mr 31,46:3
Culp, William C, 1953, Mr 19,29:3
Culpeper, Charles E (will, Mr 20,29:6), 1940, F 2, 17:4
Culpepper, Calvin K, 1917, Ag 27,9:7
Culpepper, Henry L, 1966, Ag 16,39:4
Culpepper, James D, 1959, O 23,17:6
Culter, Bloodgood H, 1906, S 27,1:6
Culter, J G, 1927, Ap 22,21:3
Culver, Abraham E Capt, 1909, Je 25,9:4
Culver, Alva, 1952, Ag 3,60:1
Culver, Andrew N, 1906, Jl 11,1:4
Culver, Austin H, 1944, Mr 4,13:4
Culver, B Frank, 1947, N 4,26:2
Culver, Bernard M, 1951, Jl 20,21:1
Culver, Charles H, 1937, Ja 14,21:2
Culver, Charles H Mrs, 1944, Mr 11,13:6
Culver, Charles M, 1938, My 9,17:5
Culver, David Jay, 1968, Mr 23,31:3
Culver, Dudley D, 1944, S 27,21:6
Culver, Edward P, 1940, Ag 22,19:1
Culver, Florence E Mrs, 1957, Ap 28,86:1
Culver, Florence L Mrs, 1937, N 21,II,9:1
Culver, Frank R, 1946, D 1,76:2
Culver, George, 1944, N 7,27:3; 1956, O 31,25:4
Culver, George M, 1939, O 20,23:4
Culver, Gordon M, 1946, My 17,21:1
Culver, H Eugene, 1948, O 10,76:2
Culver, Harry H, 1946, Ag 18,47:8
Culver, Helen, 1925, Ag 20,19:6
Culver, Henry B, 1946, N 29,25:1
Culver, James D, 1866, N 15,2:5
Culver, John S, 1947, Je 15,62:4
Culver, Knight K Sr, 1953, F 5,23:5
Culver, Louisa Bellamy, 1903, Ag 12,9:6
Culver, Ralph F, 1960, Ap 17,39:1
Culver, Rudolph C Mrs, 1945, F 23,17:2
Culver, Sidney Mrs, 1961, Mr 13,29:2
Culver, William H, 1939, S 21,23:3
Culverhouse, Thomas D, 1940, Jl 9,21:6
Culveyhouse, Jack E, 1947, Mr 3,21:5
Culviner, Samuel Jr, 1966, D 7,47:1
Culyer, Frank, 1941, Mr 24,17:3
Culyer, William, 1915, O 9,9:4
Cumann, Otto H, 1955, N 28,31:4
Cumberbatch, Elkin P, 1939, Mr 27,15:4
Cumberland, Roger C, 1938, Je 15,23:5
Cumberland, William W, 1955, F 21,21:3
Cumberledge, Sydney, 1943, Ap 11,48:2
Cumberworth, F W, 1948, N 28,96:5
Cumbler, George W, 1958, N 16,88:4
Cumbler, George W Mrs, 1957, Ja 5,17:6
Cumfer, Donald A, 1946, F 19,25:6
Cumin, Gustavo, 1956, Ag 8,25:4
Cuming, Arthur H, 1941, F 18,23:1
Cuming, Charles S, 1964, F 15,23:2
Cuming, Elizabeth L Mrs, 1954, S 11,17:4
Cuming, Henry F, 1951, Ap 1,93:1
Cuming, Mari A, 1917, D 22,11:5
Cuming, Rochester, 1909, My 20,9:4
Cumings, A P, 1871, N 30,3:2
Cumings, John B, 1937, Mr 15,24:1
Cumings, Pierce A, 1946, Ap 29,21:5
Cumings, Schuyler F, 1967, Ap 2,93:1
Cumino, Charles, 1950, Ap 22,19:5
Cumins, Sigmund J, 1962, My 7,31:3
Cumisky, Eugene, 1938, N 22,24:3
Cummer, Arthur G Mrs, 1958, My 26,29:4
Cummer, Franklin R, 1942, N 23,23:5
Cummer, William E, 1942, My 16,13:5
Cummin, Gaylord C, 1943, O 10,48:8
Cummin, Hart, 1948, Je 3,25:6
Cummin, John W, 1954, Jl 17,13:5
Cummin, Joseph W, 1950, Jl 13,25:5
Cumming, A Irving Mrs, 1955, Ja 27,23:1
Cumming, Alex, 1952, D 10,28:6
Cumming, Alex L, 1954, S 3,17:2
Cumming, Alex Mrs, 1950, Ap 25,31:3
Cumming, Burnett Mrs, 1937, Ag 7,15:3
Cumming, Duncan Mrs, 1950, Ja 25,27:4
Cumming, Frederick H, 1941, Ja 19,40:4

Cumming, George, 1904, Ja 10,7:5; 1950, Mr 27,23:3
Cumming, George R, 1960, Mr 24,33:3
Cumming, Gordon, 1866, Ap 17,5:3
Cumming, Harry, 1952, Ap 3,35:3
Cumming, Henry H, 1945, Jl 19,23:4
Cumming, Hugh S, 1948, D 21,25:5
Cumming, J Rev, 1881, Jl 7,5:1
Cumming, Kenneth N, 1948, Mr 14,72:3
Cumming, Lucy G Mrs, 1959, Jl 1,31:1
Cumming, Peter, 1907, Ap 24,9:5
Cumming, Phil E, 1942, Ap 22,23:2
Cumming, Richard S Jr, 1944, My 16,21:5
Cumming, Robert B, 1953, Je 25,27:5
Cumming, Robert C, 1956, My 16,35:2
Cumming, Robert S, 1942, Je 14,45:1
Cumming, Robert W, 1943, Ja 10,50:2
Cumming, Roger J, 1967, My 1,37:3
Cumming, Rose Mrs, 1939, Mr 9,21:3
Cumming, Rose Stuart, 1968, Mr 23,31:1
Cumming, Ruth (Mrs J C Rodis), 1967, Ag 14,31:4
Cumming, Samuel G Mrs, 1963, N 12,41:3
Cumming, Sarah T F Mrs, 1939, Ja 28,13:6
Cummingham, Margaret F, 1949, Jl 3,26:4
Cummings, A J, 1902, My 3,1:3; 1957, Jl 6,15:5
Cummings, Alan F, 1960, My 23,21:7
Cummings, Alan F Mrs, 1960, My 23,21:7
Cummings, Albert E, 1955, Jl 21,23:3
Cummings, Alex, 1957, N 27,31:4
Cummings, Alexander, 1945, D 13,29:4
Cummings, Alexander M, 1947, Ap 25,22:3
Cummings, Andrew C, 1964, Mr 21,25:6
Cummings, Andrew J, 1937, Jl 10,15:5
Cummings, Arthur R, 1944, My 26,19:4
Cummings, B Ray, 1949, N 25,31:2
Cummings, C P, 1879, Ag 20,5:2
Cummings, Carl E, 1964, Ag 24,27:6
Cummings, Caroline A Mrs, 1941, N 20,27:2
Cummings, Charles, 1914, S 24,11:6; 1947, Ja 9,23:2
Cummings, Charles D, 1957, Je 27,25:2
Cummings, Charles G Mrs, 1950, N 10,28:2
Cummings, Charles M, 1941, D 3,25:4
Cummings, Charles R, 1945, N 27,23:4
Cummings, Charles W, 1865, O 23,5:3
Cummings, Clarence E, 1939, N 12,48:7
Cummings, Clark W, 1950, Ja 15,84:6
Cummings, Cora S Mrs, 1942, Ap 1,21:5
Cummings, D Mark Mrs, 1959, Je 25,29:1
Cummings, David F, 1946, O 17,23:5
Cummings, David Mrs, 1966, Je 6,41:6
Cummings, Earl, 1952, Je 21,15:5
Cummings, Earle R, 1955, Jl 5,29:4
Cummings, Edmund S, 1939, N 18,17:6
Cummings, Edward C, 1960, F 7,60:3
Cummings, Edward E (will, S 22,16:7), 1962, S 4,1:3
Cummings, Edward J, 1943, N 25,25:3
Cummings, Edwin H Mrs, 1956, Ag 1,23:5
Cummings, Ernest E, 1960, My 4,45:3
Cummings, Ernest F, 1951, N 16,25:2
Cummings, Eugene B, 1949, D 17,17:3
Cummings, Eva Mrs, 1941, Jl 26,16:5
Cummings, Everett D, 1940, Je 27,23:3
Cummings, Evlyn D, 1914, Jl 3,9:6
Cummings, Frances W, 1965, Ja 4,29:3
Cummings, Francis B, 1964, Mr 12,35:4
Cummings, Francis Mrs, 1946, Ja 13,43:1; 1950, Mr 14,25:1
Cummings, Francis P, 1939, S 23,17:6
Cummings, Francis P J Rev, 1922, Je 11,30:2
Cummings, Francis V, 1949, Jl 12,27:4
Cummings, Frank A, 1951, Jl 15,60:3
Cummings, Frank C, 1939, D 31,18:7
Cummings, Frank W, 1946, O 23,27:2
Cummings, Frederick, 1952, Mr 4,27:2
Cummings, Frederick A, 1949, Jl 21,25:4
Cummings, George E, 1938, Ap 22,19:2
Cummings, George F, 1910, S 11,II,11:5
Cummings, George W, 1904, Ag 30,7:6
Cummings, Glenn M, 1951, Je 10,93:1
Cummings, Harold F Mrs, 1968, My 23,47:4
Cummings, Harold H, 1945, S 15,15:4
Cummings, Harold N, 1962, Mr 16,31:4
Cummings, Henry M, 1940, My 17,19:2
Cummings, Henry R, 1873, Je 29,8:5
Cummings, Homer S (funl, S 14,23:2; will, S 20,24:5), 1956, S 11,35:1
Cummings, Homer S Mrs (will, S 24,31:3), 1939, Ag 10,19:3
Cummings, Homer S Mrs, 1955, F 14,19:5
Cummings, Irving, 1959, Ap 19,86:1
Cummings, J, 1936, Je 27,17:6
Cummings, J Howell Jr, 1941, D 6,17:7
Cummings, J Howell Jr Mrs, 1952, My 30,15:2
Cummings, J Raymond, 1939, N 7,25:3
Cummings, J W Rev (funl, Ja 9,8:3), 1866, Ja 5,8:5
Cummings, James A, 1946, Ap 28,44:3
Cummings, James A Jr, 1942, N 1,52:3
Cummings, James D, 1967, Jl 25,32:5
Cummings, James E, 1956, F 22,27:2
Cummings, James H, 1966, Jl 5,27:4
Cummings, James J, 1937, Jl 31,15:4
Cummings, James Mrs, 1960, Ag 8,21:5
Cummings, John, 1937, Ag 13,17:2; 1953, Ja 2,15:1; 1953, Je 29,21:3
Cummings, John E, 1946, Ap 2,27:4; 1951, Ja 17,27:2; 1957, Je 29,17:5
Cummings, John E Mrs, 1944, Ag 2,15:3
Cummings, John F, 1953, N 17,31:2
Cummings, John G, 1962, Jl 4,21:3
Cummings, John J, 1951, S 17,21:3; 1963, D 8,86:6
Cummings, John J Mrs, 1951, My 9,33:1
Cummings, John J Sr, 1945, Ja 6,11:3
Cummings, John O, 1959, Ap 21,32:6
Cummings, John P, 1949, O 15,15:1
Cummings, Joseph A, 1918, Mr 13,11:8; 1937, Ap 27, 23:2
Cummings, Joseph L, 1952, My 30,15:4
Cummings, Katherine A Mrs, 1948, Jl 13,28:2
Cummings, Laura, 1947, Ag 26,23:2
Cummings, Lawrence B, 1947, O 21,23:1
Cummings, Lew A, 1959, Ag 9,88:3
Cummings, Mary A Mrs, 1940, Jl 23,19:2
Cummings, Matthew, 1939, F 10,23:4
Cummings, Michael J Col, 1918, Ja 4,11:4
Cummings, Minnie L Mrs, 1924, Ap 18,19:4
Cummings, Mrs, 1867, Ap 13,1:5
Cummings, N Florence, 1949, Ag 17,23:4
Cummings, Noah, 1939, F 14,19:4
Cummings, Paul J, 1951, Je 16,15:6
Cummings, Peter F, 1945, Ja 13,11:2
Cummings, Raymond K, 1957, Ja 24,29:2
Cummings, Richard H, 1938, D 27,17:4
Cummings, Robert A, 1962, O 23,37:4
Cummings, Samuel N, 1955, O 1,19:4
Cummings, Stanley J, 1968, O 6,85:1
Cummings, Thomas, 1941, Je 25,21:5
Cummings, Thomas F, 1938, Ap 12,24:1; 1942, F 12, 23:5; 1955, F 21,21:4
Cummings, Thomas J B, 1957, N 28,31:4
Cummings, Thomas P, 1961, Ja 29,85:2
Cummings, W A E Dr, 1937, My 6,25:1
Cummings, W Barton, 1967, O 14,27:2
Cummings, W Ray, 1954, Je 2,31:4
Cummings, W Walter, 1952, Ag 6,21:2
Cummings, Walter J, 1967, Ag 21,31:3
Cummings, Walter J Jr Mrs, 1968, N 28,37:2
Cummings, Walter P Mrs, 1949, Ag 22,21:3
Cummings, William, 1945, O 6,13:4
Cummings, William A, 1944, Mr 30,21:6
Cummings, William C, 1945, Je 8,19:2
Cummings, William F, 1942, Ap 10,17:1; 1955, D 24, 13:1
Cummings, William H Mrs, 1944, Jl 1,15:6
Cummings, William Heyman, 1915, Je 9,13:5
Cummings, William P, 1940, Jl 5,13:3
Cummins, Albert D, 1939, Je 13,23:5
Cummins, Alden C, 1947, Jl 11,15:3
Cummins, Alexander G, 1946, S 23,23:1
Cummins, Alva M, 1946, Ag 10,13:1
Cummins, Arthur J, 1949, Ja 16,68:4
Cummins, Benjamin F, 1941, O 8,23:3
Cummins, Charles A, 1955, D 22,23:4
Cummins, Claude, 1960, Je 7,35:2
Cummins, Claude Mrs, 1957, Mr 28,31:2
Cummins, Clessie L, 1968, Ag 20,41:3
Cummins, Denis H J, 1947, O 11,17:6
Cummins, Earl E, 1938, Je 8,23:3
Cummins, Edward W, 1941, F 17,15:1
Cummins, G D (see also Je 27 and 28), 1876, Je 29, 10:4
Cummins, G Wyckoff Mrs, 1952, Mr 23,94:4
Cummins, George W, 1965, Jl 17,25:5
Cummins, Henry A, 1939, Ja 2,24:3
Cummins, J Elmer, 1949, N 27,104:5
Cummins, Jack A, 1954, Ap 20,29:2
Cummins, James D, 1965, Jl 16,27:3
Cummins, James F, 1955, O 27,33:1
Cummins, John B, 1959, Ja 2,25:1
Cummins, Joseph M, 1959, O 19,29:4
Cummins, Mantom M, 1966, N 25,37:2
Cummins, Maria S, 1866, O 3,1:7
Cummins, Mary C, 1943, Ag 22,36:8
Cummins, Michael J, 1948, Ja 6,23:2
Cummins, Ralph Mrs, 1953, Mr 21,22:7
Cummins, Richard, 1940, S 4,23:2
Cummins, Samuel, 1967, D 16,41:5
Cummins, Sarah Mrs, 1941, Je 11,21:5
Cummins, Stephen Mrs, 1952, N 18,31:4
Cummins, T J Mrs, 1903, D 23,9:6
Cummins, Thomas C, 1948, My 30,34:7
Cummins, Thomas J, 1951, S 16,83:5
Cummins, Thomas K, 1937, Je 4,23:6
Cummins, William G, 1954, Ag 29,89:3
Cummins, William T, 1953, My 6,31:3
Cumminskey, Thomas L, 1952, Ap 19,15:6
Cummiskey, Charles A, 1942, Jl 4,17:4
Cummiskey, Charles J, 1953, Je 20,17:4
Cummiskey, Frank J, 1943, Je 15,21:6
Cummiskey, J P Rev, 1885, Mr 30,5:6
Cummiskey, Joseph F, 1960, S 4,68:4
Cummiskey, Mary, 1947, Ag 29,17:3
Cummiskey, Mary E, 1942, N 7,15:2
Cumnock, Eva F, 1937, N 10,25:2
Cumont, Franz, 1947, Ag 26,23:3
Cumpanas, Ana Mrs, 1947, Ap 29,19:6
Cumpston, Amy E, 1925, D 30,17:4
Cunard, Anthony G, 1950, Ap 28,21:4
Cunard, Bache Sir, 1925, N 4,23:4
Cunard, E, 1877, S 1,4:7
Cunard, Edward Sir, 1869, Ap 8,5:5
Cunard, Grace (Mrs G Shannon), 1967, Ja 24,37:2
Cunard, Lady, 1948, Jl 11,52:7
Cunard, Nancy, 1965, Mr 18,33:4
Cunard, Samuel Sir, 1865, My 11,1:5
Cunard, William, 1906, Ja 12,9:6
Cuncannon, John, 1951, Ap 28,15:5
Cundall, Frank, 1937, N 16,23:2
Cundall, Herbert M, 1940, My 31,19:3
Cundari, Dominic A, 1962, N 2,31:4
Cundell, Nora, 1948, Ag 4,21:4
Cundy, Percival, 1947, My 22,27:4
Cuneen, Alexis B, 1946, Ja 28,19:2
Cunehan, John A, 1938, N 10,27:4
Cuneo, Charles M, 1957, S 4,34:3
Cuneo, Clarence P, 1952, Mr 23,92:2
Cuneo, Frank, 1942, S 18,21:2
Cuneo, John, 1942, F 28,17:2
Cuneo, Natale J, 1953, Jl 25,11:5
Cuneo, Nicholas, 1925, Ap 10,19:5
Cuneo, Sherman A, 1923, D 13,21:5
Cuniberti, Vittorio Maj-Gen, 1913, D 20,13:6
Cuniff, James H, 1938, Ag 14,33:4
Cuniff, T J Mrs, 1954, Mr 22,27:2
Cuniffe, Joachim, 1938, D 13,26:2
Cuningham, A F, 1871, Je 17,1:4
Cunley, Ella C, 1947, Mr 1,15:3
Cunley, Frank G Mrs, 1945, My 16,19:5
Cunley, Fred M, 1952, Jl 9,27:5
Cunliffe, Guy S, 1959, My 22,27:2
Cunliffe, John J, 1958, S 1,13:6
Cunliffe, John W, 1946, Mr 19,27:1
Cunliffe, Thurlow W, 1960, N 10,47:4
Cunliffe, Thurlow W Mrs, 1946, S 21,15:4
Cunliffe, Walter Lord, 1920, Ja 7,19:3
Cunliffe-Owen, F, 1926, Jl 1,23:1
Cunliffe-Owen, Hugo, 1947, D 15,25:2
Cunliffe-Owen, Hugo (will), 1948, F 6,12:5
Cunliffe-Owen, M, 1927, Ag 29,17:5
Cunnane, John A, 1958, Mr 17,29:3
Cunnane, Joseph A, 1939, D 14,27:3
Cunneen, Arthur J Rev, 1968, Mr 11,41:4
Cunneen, James M, 1965, F 7,92:1
Cunneen, John, 1907, F 22,9:5
Cunneen, John J, 1958, My 29,27:2
Cunneen, Joseph F, 1941, F 19,21:2
Cunneen, Patrick, 1939, Ap 23,III,7:2
Cunneen, Terence F, 1958, Je 12,31:3
Cunneen, Timothy J, 1946, O 17,23:2
Cunneen, William F Sr, 1953, Ag 11,27:3
Cunnick, William R, 1949, S 20,29:1
Cunnie, Edward F, 1957, My 29,27:5
Cunnie, James H D, 1956, Ap 7,19:5
Cunniff, Frank, 1951, S 1,11:4
Cunniff, George E Jr (funl plans), 1955, Mr 18,2
Cunniff, Michael Glen, 1914, D 25,11:4
Cunniff, Vincent D, 1942, F 4,19:5
Cunniffe, Edward Mrs, 1950, F 5,84:7
Cunniffe, Edward R, 1956, Mr 13,27:5
Cunnigham, Robert M, 1954, My 30,44:8
Cunning, Daniel S, 1960, Mr 26,21:5
Cunning, John, 1953, Je 28,60:8
Cunningham, A, 1883, My 17,5:6
Cunningham, A J, 1946, Ag 21,27:5
Cunningham, Alan, 1924, Ap 12,15:4
Cunningham, Albert B Col, 1915, S 30,11:7
Cunningham, Alex M Mrs, 1953, Mr 20,23:4
Cunningham, Alexander M, 1943, S 9,25:2
Cunningham, Alexander T, 1944, O 6,23:3
Cunningham, Alfred G, 1951, Ag 26,77:2
Cunningham, Alfred G Mrs, 1951, Ja 10,27:5
Cunningham, Alfred J, 1945, My 2,23:3
Cunningham, Andrew, 1881, D 8,5:3
Cunningham, Andrew B, 1963, Je 13,33:4
Cunningham, Ann E, 1955, D 3,17:2
Cunningham, Ann Pamelia, 1875, My 10,3:7
Cunningham, Anna C Mrs, 1949, O 29,15:4
Cunningham, Annie M Mrs, 1938, Jl 1,19:3
Cunningham, Arthur G, 1944, Je 5,19:5
Cunningham, Arthur J, 1951, N 13,29:3
Cunningham, Augustine J, 1957, Ag 1,25:5
Cunningham, B J Mrs, 1964, D 12,31:5
Cunningham, Benjamin B, 1946, Ja 3,20:2
Cunningham, Bernard, 1949, N 5,13:5
Cunningham, Bernard Mrs, 1959, Mr 7,22:1
Cunningham, Bert, 1943, S 28,25:5
Cunningham, Bertha Mrs, 1950, O 3,31:2
Cunningham, Bill, 1963, D 15,86:1
Cunningham, Bob, 1944, N 26,58:5
Cunningham, Charles, 1949, S 30,23:3
Cunningham, Charles C Mrs, 1948, Ja 12,19:4
Cunningham, Charles C Mrs (will, My 30,6:7), My 23,39:2
Cunningham, Charles J, 1942, F 5,21:2; 1950, I
Cunningham, Charles Mrs, 1946, S 27,23:5
Cunningham, Chris, 1939, F 2,19:4
Cunningham, Christopher R, 1947, Ap 29,27:4
Cunningham, Clement R H, 1943, D 7,27:1
Cunningham, Cyril E, 1958, N 27,29:5
Cunningham, Daniel F Mrs, 1938, Je 1,23:6
Cunningham, Daniel W, 1942, F 6,19:5

Cunningham, David E, 1941, O 24,23:5
Cunningham, Dode, 1958, Ap 11,25:4
Cunningham, Donald M, 1955, Mr 18,28:5
Cunningham, Edward A, 1937, Ag 16,2:6
Cunningham, Edward B, 1953, D 17,37:4
Cunningham, Edward D, 1953, S 11,21:3
Cunningham, Edward F, 1945, O 30,19:2
Cunningham, Edward J, 1941, N 20,27:4; 1963, D 6, 36:2
Cunningham, Edward P, 1950, Jl 29,13:3
Cunningham, Edwin S, 1953, Ja 23,20:3
Cunningham, Elijah W (Bill), 1960, Ap 18,29:3
Cunningham, Emily B Mrs, 1949, D 5,23:2; 1953, D 28,21:3
Cunningham, Emily P Mrs, 1939, Mr 13,17:2
Cunningham, Eugene, 1957, O 20,86:7
Cunningham, Eugene M Lt-Col, 1968, Je 8,31:3
Cunningham, F Albert, 1947, Jl 30,21:4
Cunningham, Francis J, 1961, N 15,43:5
Cunningham, Frank A, 1948, Ja 21,25:3
Cunningham, Frank J, 1953, N 25,23:2
Cunningham, Frank M, 1943, Mr 16,19:4
Cunningham, Frank S, 1941, D 2,23:3
Cunningham, Fred G, 1941, Ja 28,19:5
Cunningham, Frederick J, 1947, My 20,25:4
Cunningham, George F, 1911, O 15,II,15:4; 1945, O 17,19:4
Cunningham, George M, 1963, Jl 26,25:3
Cunningham, George T, 1955, Ag 9,25:4
Cunningham, George W, 1958, Ja 8,47:4
Cunningham, Gerald, 1944, F 2,21:1
Cunningham, Gilbert C, 1949, N 26,15:3
Cunningham, H N Rev, 1915, My 15,13:6
Cunningham, Harold A, 1945, S 3,23:3
Cunningham, Harold F, 1947, O 12,76:6
Cunningham, Harold P, 1964, Jl 26,57:2
Cunningham, Harry (see also My 19), 1878, My 20, 8:1
Cunningham, Harry, 1938, Ag 26,17:6; 1946, My 11, 27:1
Cunningham, Harry A, 1955, S 17,15:5
Cunningham, Harry C, 1955, My 9,23:4
Cunningham, Henry F, 1959, Jl 31,23:2
Cunningham, Henry P, 1955, Ag 1,19:5
Cunningham, Herbert L, 1950, O 31,27:1
Cunningham, Howell C, 1954, D 29,23:2
Cunningham, Hugh T, 1958, My 22,29:5
Cunningham, J, 1883, Je 10,7:3
Cunningham, Jack, 1941, O 5,49:3
Cunningham, James, 1943, Jl 5,15:5; 1944, Ag 20,32:4
Cunningham, James A, 1961, Mr 22,41:4
Cunningham, James D, 1946, My 30,21:3; 1963, Jl 27, 17:4
Cunningham, James G, 1965, Mr 8,29:2; 1966, My 27, 43:1
Cunningham, James J, 1943, My 21,20:3
Cunningham, James M, 1948, Mr 19,23:3
Cunningham, James T, 1942, My 2,13:2; 1951, D 31, 13:5
Cunningham, James W, 1961, My 23,39:1
Cunningham, Jesse B, 1942, D 7,27:6
Cunningham, John, 1950, F 16,23:2; 1950, D 22,23:5; 1962, D 14,16:5
Cunningham, John B, 1963, Ag 15,29:5
Cunningham, John E, 1963, My 16,35:2
Cunningham, John F, 1948, My 27,25:5; 1953, Ap 30, 31:3
Cunningham, John H, 1937, O 28,25:4
Cunningham, John J, 1960, N 2,39:2; 1938, Ap 21,19:3
Cunningham, John L, 1924, O 16,25:4
Cunningham, John M, 1939, Jl 18,19:1
Cunningham, John Mrs, 1945, Ap 20,19:5
Cunningham, John Sr, 1951, Ag 8,25:4
Cunningham, Joseph A, 1943, Ap 5,19:2
Cunningham, Joseph B, 1919, My 28,15:3
Cunningham, Joseph M, 1968, N 4,47:2
Cunningham, Leo A, 1955, Ag 22,21:5
Cunningham, Leo S, 1950, My 27,17:1
Cunningham, Leslie C, 1944, Ap 29,15:2
Cunningham, Levi S, 1943, My 22,13:4
Cunningham, Louis A, 1954, Je 14,21:1
Cunningham, Louis W, 1939, Ap 22,17:4
Cunningham, Lyman H Lt, 1918, Ja 17,13:3
Cunningham, M F, 1943, D 31,16:6
Cunningham, Margaret C Mrs, 1941, Mr 23,44:8
Cunningham, Margaret I, 1965, Ap 24,29:1
Cunningham, Marta, 1937, Je 26,17:6
Cunningham, Martin J, 1956, Ag 29,29:4
Cunningham, Mary E Mrs, 1943, Ap 19,19:2
Cunningham, Mary Moffat, 1912, Ag 8,9:6
Cunningham, Matthew H Mrs, 1937, Ap 21,23:2
Cunningham, Michael J, 1952, S 10,29:3
Cunningham, Mildred, 1939, Ja 22,34:7
Cunningham, Mrs, 1869, Ag 31,8:4
Cunningham, Myles A, 1938, F 3,23:3
Cunningham, Owen A, 1945, F 14,19:4
Cunningham, Patrick, 1948, Ap 27,25:5
Cunningham, Patrick F, 1937, Mr 14,II,8:4
Cunningham, Patrick J, 1941, Ja 31,19:2; 1941, S 17, 3:4; 1948, My 12,27:2
Cunningham, Paul, 1960, Ag 15,23:2
Cunningham, Paul E, 1950, F 11,15:3
Cunningham, Paul H, 1961, Jl 17,21:2
Cunningham, Paul J, 1952, Jl 17,23:5
Cunningham, Ralph S, 1939, S 2,17:5
Cunningham, Raymond, 1950, N 13,27:2
Cunningham, Raymond G, 1954, S 22,29:3
Cunningham, Richard A, 1959, F 5,31:2
Cunningham, Richard H Dr, 1937, F 26,22:1
Cunningham, Robert, 1874, Jl 14,4:7
Cunningham, Robert D Mrs, 1958, Je 26,27:6
Cunningham, Robert E, 1950, S 20,31:5
Cunningham, Robert H, 1949, N 24,31:6; 1959, S 12, 21:6
Cunningham, Robert L, 1956, F 19,92:5
Cunningham, Ruth, 1956, Jl 4,19:4
Cunningham, Samuel, 1946, Ag 24,11:6
Cunningham, Samuel A, 1918, Mr 29,11:8
Cunningham, Sarah Mrs, 1910, Ja 16,II,11:5
Cunningham, Secor Mrs, 1953, D 25,17:4
Cunningham, Stanley, 1907, N 30,7:5
Cunningham, Sumner A, 1913, D 21,IV,5:5
Cunningham, T W, 1931, Ag 14,17:1
Cunningham, Thomas, 1903, Ag 28,7:6; 1914, Jl 20, 7:2; 1944, F 7,15:3
Cunningham, Thomas A, 1956, F 24,25:3
Cunningham, Thomas C Mrs, 1948, D 1,29:3
Cunningham, Thomas F, 1908, My 28,7:6
Cunningham, Thomas J, 1943, D 28,22:8; 1961, Je 7, 41:2
Cunningham, Thomas M, 1953, O 17,15:5
Cunningham, Thomas O, 1939, D 28,21:2
Cunningham, Thomas Sr, 1942, Mr 1,45:3
Cunningham, Thomas W Jr, 1950, Ap 3,23:1
Cunningham, Tom, 1959, S 5,15:3
Cunningham, W A, 1934, My 6,1:1
Cunningham, Wallace M, 1945, N 15,19:3
Cunningham, Walter H, 1949, Ag 16,23:5
Cunningham, Ward, 1957, N 12,37:3
Cunningham, Ward Mrs, 1962, N 28,39:5
Cunningham, Warren E, 1959, N 20,31:3
Cunningham, Warren E Mrs, 1940, Ag 11,31:4
Cunningham, Warren W, 1953, N 11,31:2
Cunningham, Warren W Mrs, 1955, Je 23,29:1
Cunningham, Wilfred H, 1950, Ja 5,26:3
Cunningham, William, 1879, Je 4,5:2; 1946, F 23,13:1; 1967, F 21,47:4
Cunningham, William A, 1953, S 28,25:4
Cunningham, William D, 1943, O 17,49:1
Cunningham, William D Mrs, 1938, Mr 28,15:5
Cunningham, William F, 1940, N 20,21:4; 1941, D 21, 40:6; 1943, Ja 3,42:2; 1961, Ja 20,29:5
Cunningham, William J, 1950, Jl 11,31:5; 1962, Je 26, 28:8
Cunningham, William J Mrs, 1947, F 16,57:3
Cunningham, William Jr, 1917, Jl 21,11:4
Cunningham, William L, 1944, O 3,23:5
Cunningham, William Lee Rev, 1917, Ap 19,15:5
Cunningham, William W, 1937, N 10,25:3
Cunningham, Zamah, 1967, Je 4,87:1
Cunninghame, Samuel T, 1952, My 4,91:1
Cunnion, Arthur, 1968, D 25,31:3
Cunnion, Daniel C, 1942, Ap 26,40:2
Cunnion, Francis P, 1925, Jl 9,19:4
Cunnion, James, 1908, Ag 31,7:5
Cunnuff, J, 1933, Ja 15,24:2
Cunnyngham, Bertram, 1946, Je 8,21:5
Cuno, Roelants, 1938, Jl 20,19:5
Cuno, W, 1933, Ja 4,19:3
Cunradi, Charles Mrs, 1955, Je 13,23:5
Cuntz, William Cooper, 1916, N 3,13:5
Cuny, Fernand, 1937, Je 1,23:4
Cuomo, Frank, 1957, Mr 12,33:4
Cuomo, Giovanni, 1948, Mr 27,13:5
Cuozzo, Carmine, 1951, D 9,91:1
Cuozzo, Donato, 1940, My 30,17:5
Cuozzo, Michael J, 1940, F 11,48:1
Cupler, Ralph C, 1944, O 26,23:5
Cupp, Garrett, 1951, D 8,11:4
Cuppers, Charles P, 1946, Ap 23,21:4
Cuppia, Jerome C, 1966, S 21,47:4
Cupples, Victor W, 1941, Jl 30,17:5
Cupples, William, 1950, O 26,31:3
Cuppy, Hazlitt Alva Mrs, 1916, Ag 3,11:6
Cuppy, Will, 1949, S 20,29:5
Cuprien, Frank W, 1948, Je 22,25:4
Curati, Peter, 1947, Ap 22,35:7
Curatola, Lorenzo, 1952, My 18,93:2
Curchin, Alex B, 1948, F 15,60:3
Curchin, George Mrs, 1958, N 10,29:3
Curci, Gennaro M, 1955, Ap 15,23:5
Curcio, Michael, 1945, Ag 7,23:1
Curcio, Ralph C, 1958, Jl 9,27:5
Cure, Antonio, 1955, D 19,34:8
Cure, John, 1940, Ja 14,42:8
Curell, Conrad O, 1962, F 3,21:5
Curelop, Isaac, 1967, Ja 21,31:3
Cureton, C M, 1940, Ap 9,23:3
Cureton, H O, 1858, S 20,1:6
Cureton, Lamar, 1951, Ag 6,21:1
Cureton, LaMar Mrs, 1963, My 23,37:5
Cureton, William H, 1949, Mr 2,26:3
Curfman, Floyd G, 1939, N 6,23:6
Curie, Jacques, 1941, F 21,19:3
Curie, M Mme, 1934, Jl 5,1:3
Curie, Pierre Prof (funl, Ap 22,9:2), 1906, Ap 20,11:3
Curlee, Shelby H, 1944, F 2,21:3
Curlee, Zora B, 1939, My 4,23:5
Curlett, A S, 1914, F 24,11:4
Curlett, Aleck, 1942, S 7,19:6
Curlett, J Howard, 1946, My 23,21:2
Curlett, Walter S, 1948, Jl 14,24:3
Curlew, Samuel, 1952, Mr 18,27:5
Curley, Alfred, 1950, Jl 1,15:1
Curley, Catherine (Mother Marie Malachy), 1968, N 11,47:1
Curley, D J (por), 1932, Ag 4,19:1
Curley, David J, 1920, My 25,11:3
Curley, David J Mrs, 1949, Je 21,25:3
Curley, Dick, 1949, N 23,29:6
Curley, Dorothea, 1925, Ja 30,17:4
Curley, Edmund J, 1950, D 4,29:6
Curley, Edward F, 1949, F 2,27:2
Curley, Edward W, 1940, Ja 7,48:3
Curley, Francis X, 1960, Ag 9,27:5
Curley, Frank Mrs, 1940, Ap 5,22:3
Curley, Guy N, 1956, Ja 15,92:3
Curley, Jack (will, Jl 17,13:3), 1937, Jl 12,17:3
Curley, Jack (H Saltzman), 1958, Ag 27,29:3
Curley, James F, 1958, Jl 7,27:2
Curley, James M (funl, N 16,88:5), 1958, N 13,1:4
Curley, James M (estate acctg), 1963, Ag 30,12:1
Curley, James N, 1950, F 25,17:5
Curley, John, 1911, Ag 1,9:5
Curley, John H, 1943, O 13,23:3
Curley, John J, 1915, My 25,15:5; 1940, F 17,13:4; 1944, Jl 27,17:1; 1958, Ag 28,27:3
Curley, John L, 1946, D 2,25:5
Curley, John W, 1958, Ap 6,90:1
Curley, Leo, 1950, F 12,85:1
Curley, Michael J, 1947, My 17,15:5
Curley, Ned, 1967, Ap 5,44:5
Curley, Paul A, 1955, F 23,27:3
Curley, Paul G, 1945, O 15,17:6
Curley, Robert E, 1957, S 20,25:1
Curley, Spencer P, 1962, O 13,25:2
Curley, Thomas A, 1948, Mr 20,13:3
Curley, Thomas F, 1940, My 15,25:3
Curley, Thomas J, 1949, D 29,25:4; 1957, Ap 11,31:3
Curley, William A (funl, O 27,33:2), 1955, O 24,27:3
Curley, William A Jr, 1945, Je 15,19:5
Curley, William H, 1956, Ja 19,33:1
Curls, William, 1943, Ja 19,20:2
Curme, Arthur A, 1944, Jl 16,31:2
Curme, George O, 1948, Ap 30,23:1
Curnen, Edward C Jr Mrs, 1967, My 30,21:1
Curnow, Glenn N, 1944, D 29,15:4
Curnow, Harry R, 1952, Mr 1,15:2
Curon, Francis N, 1941, Je 10,23:3
Curphey, Aldington, 1958, D 1,29:5
Curr, Alfred J Sr, 1943, Je 18,21:4
Currall, Frank J, 1959, Ap 24,27:4
Currall, Frank J Mrs, 1961, Ja 6,27:4
Curran, Albert, 1943, Ag 29,39:1
Curran, Arthur B, 1950, F 23,27:1
Curran, Basil J, 1956, Jl 26,25:2
Curran, Basil J Mrs, 1925, Ag 28,13:5
Curran, Charles C, 1942, N 10,28:4
Curran, Charles J, 1949, Jl 6,30:3
Curran, Charles L Mrs, 1945, My 16,19:4
Curran, Daniel D, 1938, Je 8,23:6
Curran, Daniel J Mrs, 1943, Ap 11,48:2
Curran, David, 1948, Jl 13,27:4
Curran, Delia Mrs, 1941, Ja 30,21:4
Curran, Donald E, 1949, Ag 9,25:4
Curran, Edmund F, 1959, Mr 2,27:5
Curran, Edward, 1943, Mr 8,15:4
Curran, Edward A Mrs, 1960, My 5,35:4
Curran, Edward H, 1945, D 24,15:1
Curran, Edward J, 1956, My 19,19:3
Curran, Edward M Mrs, 1950, Ag 1,23:2
Curran, Edward T, 1945, Mr 30,15:2
Curran, Frank E, 1943, D 11,15:3; 1949, Ag 11,24:7
Curran, Frank Mrs, 1940, Je 30,33:2
Curran, Frederick R, 1953, Je 4,29:3
Curran, G Edward, 1949, F 20,60:3
Curran, George W, 1961, Mr 28,35:2
Curran, Guernsey, 1950, Ap 25,31:6
Curran, Guernsey Jr Mrs, 1954, Je 10,31:2
Curran, Guernsey Mrs, 1966, My 30,19:4
Curran, Harry E, 1949, My 12,31:3
Curran, Helen M, 1957, Jl 31,23:4
Curran, Henry B, 1907, My 5,9:6
Curran, Henry H, 1966, Ap 9,25:1
Curran, Homer F, 1952, Jl 19,15:1
Curran, Hugh G, 1945, N 7,23:3
Curran, Hugh G Mrs, 1941, Ap 17,23:5
Curran, J J, 1936, N 8,II,9:1
Curran, James A, 1949, N 12,15:1
Curran, James E (Bro Calixtus), 1952, S 7,87:1
Curran, James E, 1966, Mr 1,37:2
Curran, James E Mrs, 1954, F 16,25:4
Curran, James M Mrs, 1955, Jl 20,27:3
Curran, James R, 1923, Ag 14,15:4
Curran, James Ross, 1910, Jl 27,9:5
Curran, James T Rev, 1916, Ja 24,11:2
Curran, James W, 1952, F 21,27:2
Curran, Jerry P, 1937, Jl 25,II,8:3

Curran, John C, 1944, Je 25,29:2
Curran, John C Mrs, 1913, S 20,11:5
Curran, John F, 1941, Ja 11,17:4; 1948, D 12,92:4
Curran, John M Mrs, 1937, D 5,II,8:8
Curran, John P Mrs, 1944, Ag 25,13:3
Curran, John W, 1938, N 2,23:2
Curran, Joseph, 1942, F 23,23:6
Curran, Joseph A, 1942, Ap 29,21:5
Curran, Joseph B Sr, 1956, S 20,33:4
Curran, Joseph F, 1946, Jl 17,23:5
Curran, Joseph F Sr, 1963, Ap 18,35:5
Curran, Joseph Mrs, 1963, N 22,37:4
Curran, Kate D Mrs, 1941, Ag 21,17:5
Curran, Louis F, 1943, Jl 29,19:5
Curran, Luke J, 1942, Je 20,13:3
Curran, M Rev, 1880, Je 29,8:2
Curran, Margaret Mrs, 1950, S 27,31:3
Curran, Martin J, 1940, Ap 18,23:3
Curran, Maurice J, 1938, Je 27,17:6
Curran, Maurice W, 1940, Ap 24,23:6
Curran, Michael B, 1955, Mr 9,27:2
Curran, Michael Mrs, 1942, Jl 15,19:5
Curran, Paul A, 1953, S 25,21:4
Curran, Peter B, 1956, N 29,35:5
Curran, Peter F, 1910, F 16,9:4
Curran, Peter J, 1943, Je 26,15:2
Curran, Raymond J, 1952, My 7,27:5
Curran, Richard B, 1959, D 2,43:1
Curran, Robert E, 1964, Jl 11,25:5
Curran, Robert F, 1955, Ap 15,23:1
Curran, Robert I, 1942, My 2,13:5
Curran, Robert W, 1957, Mr 8,25:3
Curran, Samuel J, 1948, Ap 10,13:5
Curran, Sherwood S, 1943, My 16,42:7
Curran, Stephen J Mrs, 1958, My 12,29:4
Curran, Thomas E, 1944, S 22,19:2
Curran, Thomas J, 1954, F 8,23:4
Curran, Thomas J (funl, Ag 2,17:2), 1958, Jl 30,1:2
Curran, Thomas J Mrs, 1966, My 9,39:3
Curran, William A, 1939, F 12,44:8
Curran, William F, 1954, Ja 6,31:1
Curran, William G, 1963, Ap 19,43:2
Curran, William H, 1949, D 30,19:2
Currell, William S, 1943, Jl 18,34:7
Curren, Arthur G, 1961, Jl 17,21:5
Curren, Hector M, 1939, Mr 13,17:2
Curren, Henry H, 1948, Ja 1,23:3
Curren, John J, 1962, F 16,29:3
Curren, Leo J, 1954, S 14,27:2
Curren, Peter Jerome Dr, 1916, Ja 30,17:6
Curren, Robert Col, 1916, S 10,17:4
Curren, Robert G, 1941, Mr 4,23:1
Currence, John P, 1952, O 21,29:2
Currens, Turner F, 1945, My 25,19:3
Currey, Brownlee O, 1952, F 22,21:1
Currey, Clarence E, 1958, S 1,13:6
Currey, Frederick B, 1959, D 1,39:3
Currey, Jonathan B, 1924, Ag 27,17:6
Currey, Leander, 1944, N 15,27:5
Currey, Margery, 1959, Ag 17,23:1
Currey, Martha J Mrs, 1937, O 20,23:3
Currick, Max C, 1947, My 24,15:4
Curriden, Harold B, 1951, F 3,15:4
Currie, A W Sir, 1933, D 1,19:1
Currie, Barton W, 1962, My 9,43:5
Currie, Cameron, 1942, S 17,25:2
Currie, Charles A Dr, 1937, Je 3,25:5
Currie, Charles Paddock, 1903, N 10,9:5
Currie, Chester W Y, 1948, Je 21,21:4
Currie, Clarence A, 1958, O 26,88:4
Currie, D Angus, 1955, Je 27,21:5
Currie, David P, 1967, Ag 28,31:2
Currie, Donald F, 1964, F 4,33:3
Currie, Donald K, 1938, Mr 17,21:5
Currie, Donald Sir, 1909, Ap 14,11:3
Currie, Earl S, 1955, N 8,31:1
Currie, Finlay, 1968, My 11,35:3
Currie, Finlay Mrs, 1959, Jl 29,29:4
Currie, Francis J Mrs, 1946, My 23,21:2
Currie, George, 1953, Ja 10,17:3
Currie, Henry A, 1942, O 11,56:7
Currie, Herbert Mrs, 1945, O 16,23:3
Currie, James C Jr, 1968, My 28,47:3
Currie, James Sir, 1937, Mr 18,25:2
Currie, James T, 1943, F 6,13:6
Currie, John P, 1963, Je 24,27:3
Currie, John S, 1956, D 15,25:4
Currie, John W, 1905, Ap 27,11:6
Currie, Joseph W, 1949, Je 19,68:2
Currie, Julia Mrs, 1948, N 30,27:2
Currie, Marie C, 1949, F 23,27:4
Currie, Norman W, 1943, Ag 2,15:4
Currie, Robert A, 1948, Ja 6,23:5
Currie, Robert J, 1950, Jl 6,27:6
Currie, Robert J Mrs, 1948, N 21,88:7
Currie, Thomas B, 1951, Mr 28,29:2
Currie, Thomas D, 1960, Ap 18,29:4
Currie, Thomas H, 1952, Ja 9,29:5
Currie, Thomas W, 1943, Ap 24,13:5
Currie, Walter Jewett, 1912, My 2,11:5
Currie, William, 1938, Ap 8,19:6; 1940, S 16,19:5
Currie, William C, 1961, Jl 4,19:4
Currie, William H, 1949, Je 13,19:3
Currie, William Mrs, 1955, Ap 16,19:2
Currie-Bell, Thomas Mrs, 1964, Je 17,43:4
Currier, Albert, 1912, My 13,9:6
Currier, Alice Mrs, 1946, Ja 12,15:4
Currier, Andrew F Dr, 1937, Mr 5,21:4
Currier, Benson F, 1948, Ag 13,15:4
Currier, Charles H, 1952, D 23,23:5
Currier, Clinton H, 1943, Ja 7,19:5
Currier, Edward A, 1909, Jl 3,7:4
Currier, Edward P, 1946, Ja 21,23:2
Currier, Edward P Mrs, 1948, O 16,15:4
Currier, Everett R, 1954, My 21,27:2
Currier, Ezra M, 1940, D 24,15:4
Currier, F Nathaniel, 1938, Je 20,15:4
Currier, Francis M, 1948, F 12,24:2
Currier, Frank D, 1921, N 26,13:6
Currier, Frank E, 1946, D 1,76:4
Currier, Frank E Mrs, 1954, Jl 8,23:5
Currier, George B, 1958, Je 23,23:5
Currier, George E, 1954, Ap 3,15:4
Currier, Gilman S, 1954, My 3,25:5
Currier, Harry G Sr, 1937, Ap 12,18:1
Currier, Herbert A, 1941, F 7,19:3
Currier, James P, 1937, Ag 21,15:5
Currier, Leland B, 1954, N 6,17:3
Currier, Leland B Mrs, 1946, Mr 18,21:4
Currier, Mary A, 1957, Mr 28,31:3
Currier, Moody Mrs, 1915, Je 26,9:5
Currier, Richard D, 1947, Je 3,25:4
Currier, Stuart D, 1956, Ja 5,34:1
Currier, Stuart E, 1962, Ja 16,33:1
Currier, Thomas F, 1946, S 16,5:4
Currier, Warren Bp, 1918, S 24,13:4
Currin, Eugene P, 1937, Ag 15,II,7:1
Currin, Francis W, 1966, Jl 24,60:5
Currivan, Donald, 1956, My 18,25:2
Currivan, John J, 1947, Mr 1,15:3
Currivan, John Mrs, 1957, Ja 26,19:5
Curry, Albert B, 1939, D 4,23:2
Curry, Ann J Mrs, 1919, Ja 27,13:4
Curry, Arthur M Mrs, 1954, Ap 15,29:2
Curry, Charles A, 1944, O 11,21:5
Curry, Charles H, 1937, Jl 29,19:5; 1946, Ag 20,27:5
Curry, Charles M, 1944, Mr 15,19:4
Curry, Clement V, 1945, My 26,15:5
Curry, Cornelius A, 1941, Mr 1,15:1
Curry, David, 1941, Ap 10,24:3
Curry, Duncan, 1941, S 2,17:4
Curry, Edward, 1909, N 19,11:4
Curry, Ethelwyn, 1944, F 8,15:1
Curry, Ezra Mrs, 1948, Je 25,24:2
Curry, Francis (Bro Angelus), 1952, Ag 31,45:1
Curry, Francis E, 1945, Ap 29,37:2
Curry, Frank A, 1937, O 3,II,8:6
Curry, Frank H, 1943, D 16,27:4
Curry, Frederick G (cor, F 25,38:8), 1940, F 24,13:3
Curry, George W Mrs, 1947, Jl 30,21:5
Curry, Grove P M, 1946, My 14,21:2
Curry, H Ida, 1964, N 29,86:5
Curry, Harry C, 1949, Jl 8,19:5
Curry, Henry J, 1951, N 7,29:2
Curry, Howard L, 1949, Ja 29,14:2
Curry, J B, 1932, Je 26,30:1
Curry, J L M Dr, 1903, F 13,1:6
Curry, J L Mrs, 1903, My 23,9:3
Curry, James, 1938, Ag 4,17:3
Curry, James E, 1942, Jl 14,20:3
Curry, James J, 1938, Ja 20,23:2
Curry, James Rowland Dr, 1968, Ap 7,92:8
Curry, Jerry Mrs, 1937, D 13,27:4
Curry, John A, 1942, Ap 30,19:4
Curry, John A Sr, 1958, Ag 21,25:4
Curry, John F (funl, Ap 30,29:5), 1957, Ap 26,25:1
Curry, John F Jr, 1966, F 14,29:1
Curry, John H Mrs, 1942, Je 28,32:8
Curry, John J, 1943, Je 3,21:2; 1952, O 5,88:2
Curry, John Mrs, 1944, F 4,15:2
Curry, John P Mrs, 1961, Ap 1,17:5
Curry, John S, 1946, Ag 30,17:1; 1951, Mr 12,25:3
Curry, Joseph E, 1947, S 22,23:3
Curry, Lee Sr, 1952, Ja 3,46:4
Curry, Leslie S, 1958, N 15,16:6
Curry, Lewis H, 1950, O 8,104:4
Curry, Malcolm, 1963, Je 16,84:4
Curry, Marcus A, 1952, N 12,27:1
Curry, Marie C, 1956, Jl 8,64:6
Curry, Marion L, 1954, Mr 31,27:4
Curry, Michael J, 1954, Jl 22,23:1
Curry, Neil J, 1965, Jl 21,37:3
Curry, P H, 1959, Ja 28,31:4
Curry, Patrick, 1952, D 12,29:3
Curry, Patrick J, 1947, My 28,25:2
Curry, Peter B, 1939, S 2,17:7
Curry, Phil J, 1955, Jl 2,15:4
Curry, Philip, 1919, Jl 21,11:2
Curry, Raymond J, 1951, D 11,33:5
Curry, Reginald D, 1948, O 29,25:2
Curry, Rowland A, 1947, Ja 17,23:1
Curry, Samuel P, 1944, N 7,27:3
Curry, Samuel Silas, 1921, D 25,20:3
Curry, Sara, 1940, Mr 13,23:3
Curry, Seldon H, 1950, D 5,32:6
Curry, Stanton, 1949, Mr 27,76:8
Curry, Thomas A, 1947, Je 24,23:6
Curry, Thomas M, 1947, O 5,68:3
Curry, Thomas S Mrs, 1959, Ja 4,88:3
Curry, Truman M, 1945, Ag 31,17:4
Curry, Vincent, 1940, Ap 2,25:2
Curry, Vincent J, 1958, Ag 25,21:1
Curry, Walter, 1962, S 11,34:1
Curry, Walter A (date not given), 1965, O 11,61:1
Curry, Wick, 1951, N 14,31:3
Curry, William, 1945, F 12,19:3
Curry, William J, 1951, Ap 17,29:2; 1960, Je 3,31:4
Curson, Edward J, 1947, S 3,25:3
Curtayne, Daniel J, 1957, Ja 10,29:2
Curtayne, Daniel J Mrs, 1956, Ap 29,86:3
Curtenius, F W, 1883, Jl 14,5:3
Curti, Victor P, 1951, Jl 14,13:5
Curtice, Cooper, 1939, Ag 9,17:3
Curtice, Harlow H, 1962, N 4,88:1
Curtin, A G, 1894, O 8,5:3
Curtin, Andrew G Mrs, 1903, D 8,9:4
Curtin, Charles A, 1948, F 23,25:2
Curtin, Charles C, 1961, N 30,34:3
Curtin, Charles J, 1941, N 18,25:2
Curtin, Charles W, 1941, D 3,25:1
Curtin, Cornelius J Sr, 1953, Mr 12,25:1
Curtin, Cornelius Jr, 1952, D 5,27:4
Curtin, Daniel J, 1938, O 22,17:5
Curtin, Dennis J, 1957, Jl 24,25:1
Curtin, Henry A, 1945, D 4,29:5
Curtin, James C Mrs, 1943, S 27,19:5
Curtin, James H, 1947, My 9,21:4
Curtin, Jeremiah, 1906, D 15,1:4
Curtin, John, 1945, Jl 5,1:3
Curtin, John C, 1945, Je 29,15:3
Curtin, John E, 1959, O 13,39:1
Curtin, John F, 1954, Jl 20,19:2
Curtin, John I Gen, 1911, Ja 2,9:5
Curtin, John J, 1940, D 17,25:1
Curtin, John J Mrs, 1966, Ag 16,39:4
Curtin, Julia F Mrs, 1959, Je 2,35:3
Curtin, Leo E, 1952, Ag 23,13:5
Curtin, Mary F Mrs, 1940, Mr 29,22:3
Curtin, P Rogers, 1937, Mr 28,II,8:8
Curtin, Patrick A, 1951, Ap 22,89:1
Curtin, Raymond, 1945, Mr 31,19:2
Curtin, Raymond F, 1955, Ja 20,31:3
Curtin, Roland G, 1913, Mr 15,13:3
Curtin, Thomas F, 1952, O 17,27:4
Curtin, Thomas H, 1953, Je 5,27:6
Curtin, Thomas J, 1950, My 27,17:6
Curtin, William A, 1941, D 6,17:1
Curtin, William D Mrs, 1955, Mr 31,27:3
Curtin, William L, 1942, O 16,19:5
Curtis, Alan, 1953, F 2,21:4
Curtis, Alfred A Rev, 1908, Jl 12,9:6
Curtis, Angeline S Mrs, 1940, D 2,23:5
Curtis, Annabella Mrs (will), 1938, N 18,22:5
Curtis, Anne E (will), 1937, D 17,23:2
Curtis, Annie N W Mrs, 1940, Ag 14,19:3
Curtis, Anthony de (Toto), 1967, Ap 16,83:1
Curtis, Arthur F, 1920, O 6,15:6; 1951, Ja 30,25:
Curtis, Arthur F Mrs, 1950, Ja 26,27:5
Curtis, Arthur M, 1949, Jl 20,25:6
Curtis, Arthur R, 1952, Ja 18,27:5
Curtis, Arthur R Brig-Gen, 1925, Ap 9,23:4
Curtis, Austen M, 1945, D 24,15:1
Curtis, B Farquhar Dr, 1924, Ag 6,13:4
Curtis, Barton O Mrs, 1946, Ag 15,25:4
Curtis, Benjamin Robbins Judge, 1874, S 16,4:7
Curtis, Billy (S W Cornock), 1954, Ap 29,31:4
Curtis, Bridgham, 1952, F 19,29:3
Curtis, C, 1936, F 9,1:3
Curtis, C H K, 1933, Je 7,1:5
Curtis, C H K Mrs, 1932, Je 1,23:1
Curtis, C Locke, 1940, F 16,19:4
Curtis, Carlton C, 1945, Ap 12,23:1
Curtis, Carrie O Mrs, 1946, Jl 28,40:8
Curtis, Carroll P, 1946, F 13,23:3
Curtis, Caryl M, 1967, Jl 17,29:3
Curtis, Charles A Capt, 1907, My 27,7:6
Curtis, Charles B, 1905, Mr 27,9:2; 1962, Je 26
Curtis, Charles B Mrs, 1959, N 10,47:2
Curtis, Charles C, 1960, Je 25,21:2
Curtis, Charles Densmore Prof, 1925, Je 9,21:5
Curtis, Charles G, 1951, Je 16,15:6; 1953, Mr
1964, N 30,33:2
Curtis, Charles H, 1953, O 23,23:4
Curtis, Charles M, 1945, Ap 16,23:5
Curtis, Charles Mrs, 1924, Je 21,13:5
Curtis, Charles N, 1938, Ap 14,23:1
Curtis, Charles P, 1948, Ap 28,27:6
Curtis, Charles P (trb lr, D 29,24:6), 1959, D
Curtis, Charles P Mrs, 1961, Ap 26,39:4
Curtis, Charles S Mrs, 1951, S 8,17:1
Curtis, Clifford B, 1948, Mr 7,68:5
Curtis, Clifton G, 1943, Ap 24,13:6
Curtis, Coleman R, 1959, N 28,21:4
Curtis, Constance, 1959, N 27,29:4
Curtis, Cornella O Walkup Mrs, 1921, My 1,
Curtis, D Corbit, 1954, Ap 17,13:5
Curtis, Darwin Mrs, 1940, Je 14,21:6
Curtis, David A, 1923, My 24,19:6
Curtis, David Mrs, 1951, O 4,33:1

Curtis, Dick, 1952, Ja 4,40:4
Curtis, E J, 1951, Mr 2,25:1
Curtis, Edith, 1960, Ap 11,31:3
Curtis, Edward, 1961, My 15,31:4
Curtis, Edward Dr, 1912, N 29,15:3
Curtis, Edward L Prof, 1911, Ag 28,7:6
Curtis, Edward S, 1952, O 20,23:3
Curtis, Edwin, 1943, Ap 25,34:8
Curtis, Edwin Upton, 1922, Mr 29,17:5
Curtis, Elbert A, 1948, D 3,25:4
Curtis, Elizabeth, 1946, Jl 23,25:2
Curtis, Elizabeth G Mrs, 1946, F 13,23:3
Curtis, Ellicott D, 1944, S 1,13:3
Curtis, Elroy, 1943, My 26,23:1
Curtis, Elwood A, 1954, Ag 1,85:2
Curtis, Ernest W, 1949, Ag 28,74:4
Curtis, Ernesto de, 1938, Mr 13,XI,7:4
Curtis, Eugene J, 1949, Mr 19,15:1
Curtis, Eugene N, 1944, Ap 21,19:3
Curtis, Everitt P, 1946, Ag 29,27:3
Curtis, F K, 1936, Mr 5,21:3
Curtis, F Kingsbury Mrs, 1965, O 22,43:1
Curtis, F S, 1929, F 16,17:3; 1938, F 8,9:1
Curtis, Fannie B, 1943, N 16,23:4
Curtis, Francis J, 1960, Ap 22,31:1
Curtis, Frank L, 1949, Ap 22,23:2
Curtis, Frank R Col, 1937, Mr 15,23:2
Curtis, Frank S, 1951, N 16,25:4
Curtis, Frazier, 1940, Ja 28,32:4
Curtis, Frederick L, 1952, S 21,89:2
Curtis, G M Jr, 1932, S 1,19:1
Curtis, G T, 1894, Mr 29,5:2
Curtis, G W, 1892, S 1,5:1
Curtis, George F, 1946, Ap 4,25:4
Curtis, George L Rev, 1917, Jl 12,11:3
Curtis, George M, 1915, My 15,13:5; 1915, Ag 29, 15:7; 1965, D 24,17:4
Curtis, George S, 1940, Jl 16,17:2; 1948, Je 4,23:4
Curtis, George V, 1943, Ag 23,15:5
Curtis, George V Mrs, 1960, O 16,88:6
Curtis, George William, 1923, Ag 24,11:6
Curtis, Grant P, 1940, Ag 29,19:5
Curtis, Greely S, 1947, D 16,34:3
Curtis, Gurney T, 1950, N 23,35:3
Curtis, Guy H, 1941, Mr 3,15:4
Curtis, H Holbrook, 1920, My 15,15:3
Curtis, Hale, 1955, N 15,29:1
Curtis, Harland G, 1952, D 6,21:3
Curtis, Harlow H Sr, 1951, Mr 30,23:3
Curtis, Harry A, 1943, Ja 26,19:2; 1963, Jl 2,29:3
Curtis, Harry K, 1946, My 31,23:2
Curtis, Harry M, 1965, Ap 18,80:6
Curtis, Harry Sgt, 1937, Ja 20,21:4
Curtis, Harvey J, 1954, D 29,23:1
Curtis, Harvey L, 1956, Ap 18,31:2
Curtis, Heber D, 1942, Ja 10,15:6
Curtis, Helen P Mrs, 1937, Jl 7,23:6
Curtis, Henry, 1939, Jl 23,29:1
Curtis, Henry D Mrs, 1903, Ag 11,7:7
Curtis, Henry J, 1941, S 24,23:1
Curtis, Henry S, 1954, Ja 10,87:2
Curtis, Henry S Mrs, 1948, O 4,23:1
'urtis, Henry Sanford, 1954, Jl 29,23:2
'urtis, Horace K, 1944, D 19,21:4
urtis, Howard C, 1949, Ap 8,26:3
urtis, Irving B, 1945, F 16,23:4
urtis, Isaac H, 1903, Ap 28,9:6
urtis, Ishmael W, 1949, Ap 10,76:8
urtis, J C, 1881, F 25,5:3
urtis, Jack, 1949, Ap 8,25:4
urtis, James, 1942, Je 30,21:6
urtis, James B, 1922, Ap 28,17:5
urtis, James B Mrs, 1947, N 7,23:4
urtis, James E Mrs, 1956, Jl 19,27:3
urtis, James F, 1952, N 25,29:1
urtis, James L Mrs, 1961, D 6,47:5
urtis, James Langdon, 1903, N 13,9:6
urtis, Jere, 1883, Mr 25,2:2
urtis, Joe, 1958, O 26,88:6
rtis, John D, 1955, O 9,87:1
rtis, John G, 1939, Mr 9,22:2
rtis, John J Mrs, 1953, My 20,29:1
rtis, John L (por), 1955, Je 6,27:5
rtis, John L Mrs, 1957, S 9,25:6
rtis, John T, 1937, O 9,19:4; 1958, My 22,29:4
rtis, John W, 1959, Ja 8,29:2
rtis, John W Mrs, 1942, F 25,20:2
rtis, Joseph, 1944, My 13,19:4
rtis, Joseph H, 1954, Ag 2,17:4
tis, Laurence A, 1939, My 28,III,7:2
tis, Lawrence, 1957, Je 11,35:3
tis, Lebbeus, 1964, F 8,23:2
tis, Leonard E, 1923, Jl 2,15:6
tis, Leslie V, 1944, Ja 25,19:2
tis, Lewis, 1883, Ja 31,5:5
tis, Lewis B (will, O 30,2:2), 1938, O 26,23:5
tis, Lewis B (will), 1939, Ja 17,12:6
tis, Linn W, 1954, O 17,86:6
is, Lionel G, 1955, N 25,27:1
is, Lorne C, 1946, N 8,23:4
is, Louis J, 1942, Ap 13,16:2
is, Loyal B, 1947, F 23,53:3
is, Lucius F, 1954, My 26,29:3

Curtis, Margaret, 1965, D 28,27:3
Curtis, Margaret M W Mrs, 1939, F 11,15:4
Curtis, Marilyn D, 1947, Jl 25,36:6
Curtis, Mary A, 1937, Ap 8,23:2; 1941, Jl 3,19:3
Curtis, Melville G, 1950, My 24,29:1
Curtis, Michael, 1957, Ag 6,10:6
Curtis, Mitchell A, 1949, Mr 11,25:2
Curtis, N Willard, 1919, Ag 24,22:4
Curtis, Nanson B, 1957, N 8,29:4
Curtis, Nelson, 1937, O 3,II,8:5
Curtis, Newton M, 1947, My 9,21:4
Curtis, Newton Martin Gen, 1910, Ja 9,9:3
Curtis, Oakley C Gov, 1924, F 22,15:4
Curtis, Olin Alfred Dr, 1918, Ja 10,13:3
Curtis, Osborn M, 1941, Ap 12,15:5
Curtis, Oscar Henry, 1903, D 29,9:6
Curtis, Otis F, 1949, Jl 6,27:3
Curtis, Paul Allan, 1925, Je 18,21:6
Curtis, Paul R, 1950, D 3,88:5
Curtis, Peter J, 1944, N 27,23:5
Curtis, Ralph T, 1946, S 4,23:4
Curtis, Richard C, 1951, Ja 21,78:2
Curtis, Ritchie A, 1948, Ag 15,60:7
Curtis, Robert D, 1946, Ag 23,19:2
Curtis, Robert W, 1939, F 21,19:3; 1952, S 30,31:6
Curtis, Robert W Mrs, 1938, F 3,23:4
Curtis, Roy E, 1947, Jl 21,17:2
Curtis, Ruth Mrs, 1903, S 19,3:2
Curtis, Sam, 1968, Ag 18,88:3
Curtis, Samuel C Col, 1920, Mr 4,11:5
Curtis, Samuel Ives Rev, 1904, S 24,9:6
Curtis, Samuel J, 1951, Je 26,29:4
Curtis, Sidney B, 1950, My 27,17:4
Curtis, Stanley, 1951, S 30,72:5
Curtis, Stephanie M Mrs, 1954, D 2,31:1
Curtis, Stephen, 1882, Mr 24,3:1
Curtis, Theodore J, 1950, Jl 15,13:5
Curtis, Thomas E H, 1915, S 1,9:5
Curtis, Thomas F, 1958, Jl 29,23:5
Curtis, Thomas Mrs, 1962, F 15,29:3
Curtis, Thomas P, 1944, Je 1,19:4
Curtis, Tyler Mrs, 1875, Mr 19,5:7
Curtis, Varnum P, 1945, F 18,34:4
Curtis, Vera, 1962, F 7,37:2
Curtis, W D, 1937, F 28,II,9:2
Curtis, W E (mem meeting, O 27,8:3), 1880, Jl 7,5:2
Curtis, W J, 1927, O 9,II,9:3
Curtis, Walter F, 1955, S 15,33:4
Curtis, Ward R, 1951, N 16,25:2
Curtis, Warren, 1913, N 4,9:6
Curtis, Wendall J Mrs, 1955, F 20,89:1
Curtis, Wendell J, 1943, O 4,17:4
Curtis, Willard A, 1937, Je 1,23:4
Curtis, William B, 1948, My 14,23:2
Curtis, William D, 1917, Je 30,11:7; 1941, O 4,15:6
Curtis, William E, 1911, O 9,11:5; 1923, Ag 21,17:3; 1944, Mr 7,17:3
Curtis, William F, 1941, My 6,21:2
Curtis, William H, 1962, D 4,41:5
Curtis, William M, 1950, Mr 9,29:1
Curtis, William P, 1943, F 11,19:2
Curtis, William W Sr, 1960, Jl 12,35:4
Curtis, Zay B, 1946, S 2,7:2
Curtis-Bennett, Derek, 1956, Jl 4,2:4
Curtis-Bennett, Noel, 1950, D 3,89:1
Curtis-Brown, Anne (Mrs B Moon), 1965, D 8,47:2
Curtiss, A Parker, 1940, Ap 30,21:4
Curtiss, Alfred L, 1942, Je 30,21:6
Curtiss, Arthur P, 1940, Jl 24,21:4
Curtiss, Benjamin De Forest, 1922, O 21,13:4
Curtiss, C A Rev, 1879, Jl 18,3:6
Curtiss, Charles A, 1949, Ja 24,19:5
Curtiss, Charles F, 1947, Jl 31,21:3
Curtiss, Clayton J, 1938, N 8,23:5
Curtiss, Cyrus, 1879, Je 26,5:2
Curtiss, Donald L Mrs, 1954, Ap 21,29:3
Curtiss, Elisha Prof, 1914, Jl 15,9:7
Curtiss, Elmer L, 1943, Jl 21,15:4
Curtiss, Frederic H, 1967, My 27,31:1
Curtiss, G H, 1930, Jl 24,1:6
Curtiss, George E, 1960, D 17,23:5
Curtiss, George R, 1944, S 5,19:5
Curtiss, Henry S, 1965, Ja 23,25:3
Curtiss, John E, 1960, My 23,29:5
Curtiss, John H, 1940, Je 6,25:2
Curtiss, Julian W, 1944, F 18,17:3
Curtiss, Julian W Mrs, 1944, Jl 14,13:5
Curtiss, LeRoy Mrs, 1953, N 9,35:4
Curtiss, Lloyd, 1954, Jl 23,17:2
Curtiss, N T, 1865, S 5,8:4
Curtiss, Philip E, 1964, My 25,33:2
Curtiss, Richard P, 1957, Je 23,85:1
Curtiss, Samuel S, 1908, S 25,7:5
Curtiss, Thomas H, 1951, Ag 7,25:5
Curtiss, William B, 1945, My 8,19:2
Curtiss, William H, 1960, Ja 18,27:2
Curtiss, William M, 1943, Ag 23,15:4
Curtiss, William Mrs, 1956, F 7,31:1
Curtiss, William P, 1948, Mr 12,23:5
Curtius, Ernst R, 1956, Ap 20,25:1
Curtius, Julius, 1948, N 14,77:1
Curtius, Ludwig, 1954, Ap 12,29:3
Curtiz, Michael, 1962, Ap 12,35:1

Curtman, Louis J, 1958, Ag 31,57:2
Curto, Delphine Mrs, 1870, D 29,2:3
Curtoni, Lillian de, 1938, Ja 14,23:5
Curtze, Frederick F, 1941, My 8,23:2
Curwen, Henry D, 1967, Ag 19,25:5
Curwen, Henry R, 1954, O 1,23:1
Curwen, J, 1880, My 28,5:6
Curwen, W H, 1964, My 27,39:2
Curwood, J O, 1927, Ag 14,28:5
Curwood, Viola Mrs, 1940, D 8,71:4
Curzon, Alfred Rev (Baron Scarsdale), 1916, Mr 24, 11:6
Curzon, Charles E Bishop, 1954, Ag 24,21:5
Curzon, Francis R H P (Earl Howe), 1964, Jl 27,31:2
Curzon, George Mrs, 1942, Ja 4,48:5
Curzon, Marchioness (G E Hinds), 1958, Jl 1,31:4
Curzon, Mary Victoria Lady (funl, Jl 24,3:1), 1906, Jl 19,1:3
Curzon-Howe, Leicester C A S, 1941, F 26,21:2
Cusack, Annette L, 1945, Ap 28,15:5
Cusack, Christopher, 1949, Mr 10,28:2
Cusack, Delia M Mrs, 1941, O 21,23:1
Cusack, Dennis, 1939, Je 14,16:3
Cusack, Edward J, 1954, Je 16,31:3
Cusack, Edwin D, 1950, Ag 27,89:2
Cusack, G Harry, 1952, My 22,27:3
Cusack, George J, 1940, S 11,25:4
Cusack, George R, 1953, S 20,87:3
Cusack, James J, 1949, Jl 21,25:3
Cusack, John F, 1945, O 6,13:1
Cusack, Louis M, 1939, Ja 24,19:2
Cusack, Thomas C, 1961, My 2,37:1
Cusack, Thomas F Bp, 1918, Jl 18,9:4
Cusack, Thomas Francis Bp, 1918, Jl 13,9:5
Cusack, Thomas S, 1958, Ap 15,33:2
Cusano, Paul, 1963, Ag 1,27:2
Cuscaden, Fred A, 1967, Je 23,39:3
Cushamn, Frank H, 1946, Mr 2,13:2
Cushendun, Lady, 1939, D 12,27:1
Cushendun, Lord, 1934, O 13,13:4
Cushing, Albert D, 1940, My 8,23:2
Cushing, Alvin A, 1948, F 19,23:4
Cushing, Alvin Matthew Dr, 1912, D 3,15:4
Cushing, Bradbury F, 1941, Ag 19,21:2
Cushing, Caleb, 1879, Ja 3,5:3
Cushing, Charles, 1944, My 13,19:6
Cushing, Charles C S, 1941, Mr 7,21:3
Cushing, Charles G, 1958, Mr 25,33:5
Cushing, Edward T F, 1956, My 12,19:2
Cushing, Ernest W Dr, 1916, Ag 29,9:5
Cushing, Francis W, 1949, Mr 22,25:2
Cushing, George H Mrs, 1956, O 12,29:3
Cushing, Grafton D, 1939, Je 1,25:1
Cushing, H Dwight, 1954, Ja 25,19:2
Cushing, Harold B, 1947, N 1,15:4
Cushing, Harry A, 1955, S 7,31:4
Cushing, Harry C, 1960, N 26,21:4
Cushing, Harvey M, 1945, F 1,23:6
Cushing, Harvey Mrs, 1949, My 9,25:4
Cushing, Harvey W, 1939, O 8,50:1
Cushing, Henry H Mrs, 1952, O 21,29:5
Cushing, Henry Platt Prof, 1921, Ap 15,15:4
Cushing, Howard B, 1964, Ag 15,21:5
Cushing, Howard Gardiner, 1916, Ap 27,13:4
Cushing, J Col, 1884, Mr 4,5:2
Cushing, J E, 1938, Jl 18,13:6
Cushing, J Stearns, 1913, N 19,9:6
Cushing, James, 1963, Ag 30,21:3
Cushing, James Jr Com, 1873, Jl 19,8:4
Cushing, Jennie W Mrs (will), 1937, D 29,13:3
Cushing, John E, 1956, Ap 24,31:4
Cushing, John M, 1950, Ag 22,27:4
Cushing, John P, 1941, Ap 8,25:5
Cushing, John P Mrs, 1922, Ag 25,13:6
Cushing, John T, 1938, S 26,17:2
Cushing, Livingston, 1916, N 26,21:1
Cushing, M Gertrude, 1945, Mr 8,23:5
Cushing, Margaret W, 1955, Ag 1,19:2
Cushing, Marshall, 1915, My 13,15:5
Cushing, Matthew Mrs, 1943, O 8,19:2
Cushing, Max P, 1951, Ja 14,85:2
Cushing, Michael Mrs, 1951, Je 30,15:6
Cushing, Morgan B, 1956, Ap 23,27:1
Cushing, Nathan, 1903, Ag 11,7:7
Cushing, Nicholas C, 1945, N 23,23:3
Cushing, Oscar K, 1948, O 8,25:3
Cushing, Otho, 1942, O 15,23:1
Cushing, Palmer, 1948, Ap 13,27:3
Cushing, Percy M, 1951, Ap 17,29:1
Cushing, Percy M Mrs, 1958, Ap 24,31:5
Cushing, Prentice, 1948, Ja 11,58:6
Cushing, Robert M, 1907, Ja 11,9:5
Cushing, Royal B, 1950, Ag 24,27:3
Cushing, S B, 1873, Jl 18,5:4
Cushing, S T, 1901, Jl 22,7:7
Cushing, Samuel T, 1960, Ap 18,29:2
Cushing, Samuel T Mrs, 1938, Ap 15,19:1
Cushing, Susanna Y Mrs, 1948, Mr 8,23:1
Cushing, T F, 1902, Je 7,9:5
Cushing, Wade, 1938, N 29,24:1
Cushing, William, 1942, Ag 28,19:5
Cushing, William B Com, 1874, D 19,2:6
Cushing, William C, 1940, Ja 13,15:5

Cushing, William E Mrs, 1945, F 26,19:5
Cushing and Corey (Sad Case), 1872, O 31,2:3
Cushion, Mary J, 1941, Ag 26,19:5
Cushion, Richard B, 1948, My 23,69:1
Cushman, Alvan A, 1948, F 21,13:5
Cushman, Austin Sprague Maj, 1907, Ja 31,9:6
Cushman, B Alden Mrs, 1963, S 29,87:3
Cushman, Benjamin G W Mrs, 1952, Je 7,19:2
Cushman, Burritt A, 1945, D 4,29:2
Cushman, Burritt A Mrs, 1952, S 22,23:2
Cushman, C H, 1883, N 12,5:2
Cushman, C Leslie, 1954, Ja 6,31:3
Cushman, C W, 1903, Ag 20,9:6
Cushman, Charles E Dr, 1951, Jl 21,13:6
Cushman, Charles H, 1957, Ja 6,88:1
Cushman, Charles H Mrs, 1944, Ap 27,23:5
Cushman, Charles P, 1915, S 30,11:7
Cushman, Charlotte, 1876, N 19,4:7
Cushman, Don Alonzo, 1875, My 2,6:6
Cushman, E D, 1931, Ja 3.17:1
Cushman, E H, 1903, F 1,7:5
Cushman, Earl L, 1962, Mr 17,25:3
Cushman, Edwin C, 1909, Mr 7,11:5
Cushman, Elizabeth B Mrs, 1948, Ja 12,25:3
Cushman, Francis W, 1909, Jl 7,4:3
Cushman, Gertrude R (will, O 20,22:3), 1942, S 30, 23:4
Cushman, Hampton P, 1949, F 15,23:3
Cushman, Herbert E, 1944, D 18,19:5
Cushman, Horatio Benzil, 1918, Jl 10,13:5
Cushman, J Clydesdale (por), 1955, Je 30,25:3
Cushman, J T, 1903, Jl 4,7:6
Cushman, James S, 1952, Mr 20,29:1
Cushman, James S Mrs, 1946, F 2,13:6
Cushman, John H, 1963, D 27,23:1
Cushman, Joseph A, 1949, Ap 18,25:4; 1953, Jl 6,17:5
Cushman, L Arthur, 1963, Ja 9,8:2
Cushman, Larimer A, 1940, My 15,25:3
Cushman, Leslie H, 1954, Ag 29,89:2
Cushman, Mary I (Sept 25), 1965, O 11,61:1
Cushman, Merton L, 1940, Ja 29,15:2
Cushman, Nathan A, 1952, Je 11,29:1
Cushman, Olive R Mrs, 1941, F 3,17:4
Cushman, Paul Mrs (will, O 17,26:3), 1960, S 5,15:6
Cushman, Ralph S, 1960, Ag 11,27:4
Cushman, Robert, 1946, Ag 24,11:6
Cushman, Robert E Mrs (C Flowerton), 1965, D 22, 31:2
Cushman, Wells S Mrs, 1948, O 10,76:4
Cushman, William C, 1948, D 24,17:2
Cushman, William C H, 1950, Ag 30,31:2
Cushman, William C Mrs, 1948, Ja 27,26:3
Cushman, William F, 1959, My 9,21:6
Cushmeyer, Martin J, 1950, Ag 31,25:2
Cushmore, Charles L Sr, 1958, Ag 29,23:3
Cushny, Alex O, 1959, D 19,27:3
Cushwa, Charles B Sr, 1951, D 9,90:4
Cushwa, George, 1937, My 8,19:2
Cusick, Eugene A Sr, 1966, Mr 30,45:3
Cusick, James H, 1950, Je 8,31:4
Cusick, Joseph F, 1948, O 15,23:4
Cusick, Leslie P, 1950, D 21,29:2
Cusick, Patrick F, 1958, N 9,88:7
Cusick, Peter J, 1939, F 9,21:6
Cusick, Webster N, 1949, Ja 11,31:1
Cusimano, Peter, 1948, N 26,23:4
Cusmano, John, 1955, My 16,23:4
Cussani, G, 1934, Je 3,31:1
Cussler, Edward, 1949, F 3,23:3
Cussler, Edward Mrs, 1955, O 29,19:1
Cussler, Robert C, 1965, Je 14,33:2
Cust, Aleen, 1937, Ja 30,17:5
Custance, Wilfred N, 1939, D 27,21:1
Custer, Dallas E, 1951, D 5,35:4
Custer, David D, 1941, Ja 15,23:2
Custer, E L, 1881, Ja 10,5:5
Custer, Edward, 1919, My 20,17:6
Custer, Edward A, 1937, S 26,II,8:4
Custer, Ella B, 1948, N 9,27:2
Custer, G A Gen (funl), 1877, O 11,8:1
Custer, G A Mrs, 1933, Ap 5,19:1
Custer, Joe J, 1965, Je 22,21:3
Custer, Lewis B, 1960, Mr 26,21:5
Custer, Omer N, 1942, O 18,52:6
Custer, Omer N Mrs, 1956, D 10,31:4
Custer, Ralph L, 1950, Mr 25,11:8
Custer, Ralph L Mrs, 1950, Ag 4,21:4
Custer, William B, 1940, Mr 18,17:2
Custer, William V, 1962, F 2,29:1
Custis, James B G, 1949, Mr 2,25:2
Custis, John T, 1944, D 4,23:6
Custis, Vanderveer, 1961, Je 18,88:5
Custos, Geoffrey G, 1961, S 18,29:3
Cusworth, William J, 1939, Ap 3,17:2
Cutbill, Catherine, 1941, D 4,25:4
Cutbill, Charles, 1952, Mr 22,13:1
Cutbill, Herbert W, 1952, Je 24,29:3
Cutcheon, Byron M Gen, 1908, Ap 13,7:4
Cutcheon, Franklin W M Mrs, 1947, Je 19,21:5
Cutchins, William S Mrs, 1960, Je 28,31:6
Cutelli, Gaetano, 1944, Jl 17,15:5
Cuthbert, Alison R Mrs, 1940, N 29,21:4
Cuthbert, Father, 1939, Mr 24,21:5
Cuthbert, Frank, 1949, Ja 28,22:3
Cuthbert, J Harper, 1903, Ap 3,9:6
Cuthbert, James B, 1947, Mr 14,23:3
Cuthbert, Lucius M, 1915, D 12,9:3
Cuthbert, Margaret, 1968, Jl 26,31:1
Cuthbert, Percy T, 1944, Ap 27,23:5
Cuthbert, Peter Mrs (J Derby), 1965, Ag 9,25:1
Cuthbert, Thomas N, 1918, F 9,15:8
Cuthbert, Tom, 1950, Ag 3,23:4
Cuthbert, William S, 1957, D 19,29:8
Cuthbert Harry J, 1949, O 13,27:4
Cuthbertson, Francis, 1951, O 7,85:6
Cuthbertson, Harry K Jr, 1954, N 3,29:2
Cuthbertson, Walter A, 1950, My 24,29:1
Cuthbertson Fredk J, 1963, Ap 28,88:2
Cuthell, Chester W, 1942, D 12,17:1
Cuthrell, Hugh H, 1953, S 2,25:1
Cuthrell, Hugh H Jr, 1960, D 23,39:3
Cutler, A L, 1941, Ap 10,24:3
Cutler, Aaron S, 1959, Je 15,27:3
Cutler, Abraham, 1940, My 5,53:1
Cutler, Albert G, 1939, Ag 3,19:6
Cutler, Arthur, 1951, Ap 10,27:1
Cutler, Arthur D, 1953, S 6,52:4
Cutler, Arthur H Dr, 1918, Je 22,11:6
Cutler, Arthur H Mrs, 1918, Ja 2,11:6
Cutler, Bertram, 1952, F 15,25:1
Cutler, Carl C, 1966, F 22,23:4
Cutler, Carl G, 1945, Mr 3,13:3
Cutler, Charles, 1952, D 26,15:4
Cutler, Charles E, 1962, O 2,39:1
Cutler, Charles E Mrs, 1947, F 18,25:3
Cutler, Charles F, 1907, My 20,9:6
Cutler, Charles P, 1953, Ap 25,15:5
Cutler, Charles S, 1958, My 21,33:2
Cutler, Condict W Jr, 1958, Jl 7,27:3
Cutler, Condict W Mrs, 1961, N 8,35:4
Cutler, David A, 1943, N 11,23:5
Cutler, Earle N, 1960, Jl 8,21:1
Cutler, Edward J, 1961, Mr 10,27:1
Cutler, Ella G Mrs, 1939, Ja 4,21:5
Cutler, Elliott C, 1947, Ag 17,52:3
Cutler, George B Mrs, 1951, Ja 19,25:5
Cutler, George C, 1956, Ap 23,27:5
Cutler, George Mrs, 1945, D 14,28:2
Cutler, George V Mrs, 1953, S 15,31:2
Cutler, H S, 1902, D 6,9:5
Cutler, Harry Col, 1920, F 2,13:4; 1920, Ag 29,20:3; 1920, S 3,9:6; 1920, S 17,11:6
Cutler, Henry E, 1959, Jl 9,27:3
Cutler, Henry F, 1945, O 9,21:4
Cutler, Henry W, 1955, Ag 14,81:3
Cutler, Howard W, 1948, D 21,31:2
Cutler, J C Prof, 1870, D 28,1:2
Cutler, J Warren Mrs (will), 1961, Ja 11,12:1
Cutler, Jacob W Mrs, 1946, Ap 6,17:4
Cutler, James E, 1961, Ja 6,27:2
Cutler, John, 1939, F 20,17:3
Cutler, John L Mrs, 1957, Mr 11,25:4
Cutler, John M, 1960, Ap 16,17:5
Cutler, John S, 1949, D 13,31:2
Cutler, John W, 1950, Mr 19,92:3
Cutler, Julia Walker, 1908, O 14,9:5
Cutler, L A Rev, 1903, N 26,7:6
Cutler, Leland W, 1959, N 15,86:6
Cutler, Marshall, 1944, S 26,23:3
Cutler, Martha H, 1951, O 17,31:2
Cutler, Maxwell E, 1959, Ja 26,29:4
Cutler, Otis H (funl, Mr 8,15:6), 1922, Mr 5,26:4
Cutler, Pratt, 1951, F 8,23:6
Cutler, Ralph D, 1960, Ag 12,19:4
Cutler, Ralph D Mrs, 1945, Je 7,19:4
Cutler, Raymond F, 1942, Ja 1,25:4
Cutler, Rev Dr (funl), 1863, F 14,2:4
Cutler, Robert W Mrs, 1954, Ja 11,25:2
Cutler, Sidney, 1952, Jl 1,23:1
Cutler, Sidney J, 1941, Jl 12,13:6
Cutler, Sol, 1941, Jl 23,19:5
Cutler, Thomas D, 1957, Je 16,84:1
Cutler, Thomas J, 1941, Mr 23,45:2
Cutler, W E Prof, 1925, S 3,25:6
Cutler, Walter P, 1947, F 25,25:5
Cutler, Willard W Mrs, 1963, Je 22,23:5
Cutler, William C, 1952, Jl 21,19:4
Cutler, William F, 1957, Ap 7,88:6
Cutley, George E, 1944, N 1,23:3
Cutliffe, John M Mrs, 1907, D 8,11:5
Cutlip, James E, 1959, My 11,27:6
Cutright, Harold G, 1967, Mr 22,47:2
Cutro, Nicholas Mrs, 1951, Ap 10,27:4
Cutshall, Cutty (Robt D Cutshall), 1968, Ag 22,37:3
Cutshall, H Walton Jr, 1963, Je 10,31:2
Cutten, A W, 1936, Je 25,21:3
Cutten, George B (will, D 7,41:2), 1962, N 4,88:4
Cutten, Lionel F, 1938, Ag 22,13:2
Cutten, Ruloff E, 1961, Je 21,37:4
Cutter, Annie E Mrs, 1938, Mr 7,17:2
Cutter, Annie S, 1957, Mr 28,31:2
Cutter, B H, 1880, Ag 9,8:6
Cutter, Charles, 1938, Ap 22,19:1
Cutter, Charles Ammi, 1903, S 11,7:7
Cutter, Charles S, 1939, D 21,26:3
Cutter, Edgar T, 1955, N 12,19:1
Cutter, Edward A Mrs, 1957, Ag 19,19:5
Cutter, Ephraim Dr, 1917, Ap 26,13:6
Cutter, Fred B, 1951, Ag 16,27:5; 1952, Je 7,19:5
Cutter, George W Capt, 1865, D 28,4:6
Cutter, Hampton, 1947, O 25,19:1
Cutter, Henry T, 1914, Ja 22,11:6
Cutter, Irving S, 1945, F 3,11:3
Cutter, John A, 1944, F 19,13:4
Cutter, John Dicks, 1916, O 20,9:3
Cutter, John F, 1956, S 16,84:8
Cutter, John M, 1907, Mr 16,9:6
Cutter, John W, 1951, S 5,31:3
Cutter, Learned R, 1947, F 9,61:2
Cutter, Lewis M, 1940, F 29,19:1
Cutter, Nehemiah Dr, 1859, Mr 26,4:6
Cutter, Ralph B, 1947, Ap 15,25:5
Cutter, Royal, 1955, S 16,23:1
Cutter, Victor M, 1952, D 26,8:3
Cutter, William D, 1942, Ja 23,19:1
Cutti, Berta Mrs, 1948, Ap 24,15:5
Cutting, Aaron B, 1954, O 3,86:2
Cutting, Almond J, 1942, Mr 7,17:4
Cutting, B M, 1935, My 7,1:4
Cutting, Brockhoist Mrs, 1912, S 2,9:5
Cutting, C Surdam Mrs, 1961, Jl 22,21:5
Cutting, Churchill Hunter, 1924, Ap 24,19:4
Cutting, Elisabeth B, 1946, Ag 14,26:3
Cutting, Ellis H, 1924, D 8,19:4
Cutting, Flora L, 1942, Ja 24,17:3
Cutting, Francis B, 1870, Je 28,2:7
Cutting, Fulton, 1967, D 5,50:6
Cutting, George W Jr, 1942, F 6,19:5
Cutting, H, 1926, Je 7,1:6
Cutting, H S, 1884, Ap 26,5:2
Cutting, Haward Mrs, 1917, S 15,11:4
Cutting, Henry D Capt, 1869, Mr 6,2:2
Cutting, Heyward Mrs, 1946, N 6,23:2
Cutting, Hurlbut B, 1950, Mr 2,27:4; 1963, S 26,36:
Cutting, James De Wolf, 1917, Ap 18,13:5
Cutting, John Tyler, 1911, N 26,15:5
Cutting, Juliana, 1944, Je 12,19:2
Cutting, Mary Stewart, 1924, Ag 11,13:5
Cutting, R F, 1934, S 22,15:1
Cutting, R M, 1932, N 22,21:1
Cutting, Robert Bayard, 1918, Ap 5,15:5
Cutting, Robert L, 1910, My 10,9:5
Cutting, Robert Livingston Mrs, 1915, Jl 3,7:7
Cutting, Roy E, 1950, Ag 15,29:3
Cutting, S S, 1882, F 8,5:5
Cutting, Victor W, 1943, D 24,14:7
Cutting, Walter Col, 1907, Jl 24,7:6
Cutting, Walter Mrs, 1925, N 19,25:5
Cutting, William B, 1910, Mr 11,9:3
Cutting, William Bayard (funl, Mr 7,13:5), 1912, Mr 3,15:3
Cutting, William Brockholst Jr, 1911, Jl 1,11:5
Cuttle, Allan M, 1962, F 25,88:6
Cuttler, Harry J, 1961, My 14,86:5
Cuttler, Louis F, 1945, Je 28,19:5
Cuttner, William R, 1963, D 29,42:5
Cuttrell, Florence E, 1965, Jl 1,28:5
Cutts, Henry E, 1946, My 22,21:2
Cutts, M E, 1883, S 2,2:3
Cutts, Oliver F, 1939, Ag 8,17:2
Cutts, Richard M Mrs, 1946, Jl 5,19:3
Cutts, Susan R, 1958, Jl 1,31:1
Cutty, Thomas, 1952, Ap 5,15:5
Cutty, William, 1949, Ja 13,24:3
Cutujian, Avac, 1949, My 21,13:3
Cuvelier, Marcel, 1959, S 16,39:3
Cuverville, Jules Marie de Cavlier de Vice-Adm, 1912, Mr 15,9:4
Cuvillier, James R, 1947, Je 4,27:4
Cuvillier, L A, 1935, My 19,1:3
Cuxton, John L Gen, 1874, My 26,4:6
Cuyler, Anna R Mrs, 1949, Ap 17,76:3
Cuyler, Cornelius C, 1909, Ag 13,7:5
Cuyler, Edward C, 1943, Mr 3,23:3
Cuyler, Edward C Mrs, 1942, Mr 7,17:4
Cuyler, Frances L Mrs, 1941, Mr 1,15:5
Cuyler, George A, 1943, F 6,13:1
Cuyler, Hazen (Kiki), 1950, F 12,84:5
Cuyler, J W, 1883, Ap 18,4:7
Cuyler, John P Mrs, 1947, D 10,31:3
Cuyler, Theodore Ledyard Rev Dr, 1909, F 27,
Cuyler, Thomas De Witt, 1922, N 3,17:3
Cuzanian, A, 1927, S 2,17:3
Cvetic, Matt, 1962, Jl 27,25:3
Cybick, Joseph S, 1965, S 1,37:5
Cyborowski, Martin F, 1941, N 20,27:6
Cybulski, Zbigniew, 1967, Ja 9,36:6
Cyester, Lewis H, 1937, Je 30,23:5
Cyman, Lawrence, 1949, F 24,23:2
Cypher, Henry C, 1937, Je 3,25:3
Cyphers, Abraham F, 1946, Ap 27,17:1
Cyphers, Harry S, 1957, Je 14,25:4
Cyphers, Perry W, 1960, Mr 20,86:7
Cypiot, Onesime C, 1949, Ag 6,17:5
Cypress, Sidney, 1951, Ap 20,29:2
Cyprian, A Bro, 1944, Jl 16,31:1
Cyr, Alfred A, 1954, D 26,61:2
Cyr, Mario S, 1942, Jl 18,13:6
Cyr, Paul N, 1946, Ag 25,46:4

Cyr, William J, 1949, Jl 15,19:6
Cyran, Joseph, 1953, F 21,13:4
Cyrankiewtcz, Jerzy, 1960, D 25,42:1
Cyril, Amba, 1950, O 27,29:6
Cyril, Grand Duchess, 1936, Mr 3,21:1
Cyril Leo, Bro, 1945, Je 1,15:6
Cyril Paul, Brother (J A Crowley), 1950, Je 15,31:4
Cyril Vladimirovitch, Grand Duke, 1938, O 13,23:1
Cyril 2d, Lord, 1949, O 29,15:1
Cyrille, Monsignor, 1947, S 9,31:3
Cyrus, John W, 1954, F 22,19:2
Czachorowski, Matthew A, 1966, My 20,44:1
Czachowski, Kazimiers, 1948, Ag 20,17:3
Czacka (Mother Elizabeth), 1961, My 18,35:4
Czaja, Leo M, 1957, My 10,27:4
Czajkowski, Casimir J Dr, 1968, Jl 5,25:1
Czajkowski, Wladyslaw, 1947, S 8,21:5
Czapak, Andrew S, 1950, Jl 11,31:4
Czapek, Emil, 1960, Ja 1,19:5
Czapik, Gyula, 1956, Ap 27,27:3
Czaplenski, Thomas W, 1951, N 21,25:3
Czarnecki, Anthony, 1952, My 6,29:3
Czarnecki, John, 1955, Ap 1,27:5
Czarnikow, Caesar, 1909, Ap 18,11:4
Czarnogorski, James P, 1949, My 8,76:7
Czarnomska, Marie E, 1938, My 23,17:4
Czarnowski, Vincent Mrs (Marta), 1965, Ja 9,25:4
Czartoriski, Prinse Auguste A, 1946, Jl 2,25:2
Czaster, Stanley A, 1953, Je 15,29:4
Czech, Ludwig, 1942, O 30,4:7
Czeisler, Andor, 1957, Je 15,17:4
Czermak, Wilhelm, 1953, Mr 14,15:3
Czernin, Ferdinand, 1965, D 4,31:1
Czerny, Adalbert, 1941, O 5,48:3
Czerwiec, Joseph H, 1955, Ja 15,13:2
Czerwonky, Richard R, 1949, Ap 17,76:4
Czvitkovicz, A F Rev, 1883, Ag 4,1:2

D

Daab, Frederick F, 1960, Ja 19,35:1
Daane, J Dewey Mrs, 1961, D 11,31:5
Daar, Philip Mrs, 1947, Ag 1,17:4
Da Baca, E C Gov, 1917, F 19,11:4
Dabb, Albert H Sr, 1945, Jl 10,11:7
Dabczynski, Andrew, 1949, Je 15,29:4
Dabe, William H, 1949, Ja 27,23:1
Dabelstein, Donald H, 1958, O 9,37:2
D'Abernon, Viscount, 1941, N 2,53:1
D'Abernon, Viscountess, 1954, My 18,30:3
Dabney, C H, 1879, D 16,4:7
Dabney, Charles W, 1945, Je 16,13:3
Dabney, Ellen P Mrs, 1937, F 1,19:4
Dabney, Ford Mrs, 1961, D 12,43:3
Dabney, Ford T Sr, 1958, Je 23,23:2
Dabney, George B, 1939, S 9,17:4
Dabney, Joseph B Mrs, 1945, Ap 29,37:2
Dabney, Lewis M Mrs, 1946, O 19,21:2
Dabney, Lucy H Mrs, 1937, Je 8,25:5
Dabney, Richard H, 1947, My 17,15:2
Dabney, T S Dr, 1923, D 30,20:1
Dabney, Thomas T Mrs, 1953, F 10,27:3
Dabney, Wendell P, 1952, Je 5,31:2
Dabo, Leon, 1960, N 9,35:1
Daboll, C L, 1866, O 19,1:6
Daboll, Sheridan, 1941, N 1,15:6
Dabour, John, 1905, Mr 26,9:4
Dabrowska, Maria Mrs, 1965, My 21,35:1
Dabrowski, Stefan, 1947, Mr 26,25:1
Dacey, Michael F, 1940, Jl 25,17:5
Dacey, Thomas, 1940, S 5,23:4
Dach, Felix Mrs, 1957, F 28,27:3
Dach, Joseph Mrs, 1959, F 27,52:5
Dach, Sidonia (will), 1944, F 15,19:6
Dachauer, Louis, 1878, Ag 18,7:6
d'Ache, Caran (Emmanuel Poire), 1909, F 27,9:4
Dachenhausen, Friedrich W Von, 1942, Ag 7,17:4
Dachowitz, Hirsh, 1953, N 18,31:3
Dachtera, Paul J, 1907, Je 6,7:6
Dacian Stephen, Bro, 1952, Ja 2,25:2
Dacie, Abbie Wade G Mrs, 1911, Ja 8,13:5
Dacier, William J, 1940, O 11,21:4
D'Acierno, Pellegrino A, 1950, Mr 4,17:4
Dackerman, Henry F, 1944, D 16,15:4
Da Costa, Albert, 1967, N 9,47:1
daCosta, Fred M, 1939, Mr 11,17:6
Da Costa, Harold F Dr, 1937, My 24,19:4
DaCosta, J Chalmers Mrs, 1951, Ja 29,19:4
Da Costa, John A, 1960, Ja 8,25:1
Da Costa, John C Dr, 1910, D 7,13:4
Dacres, Sidney Sir, 1884, Mr 10,5:4
Da Cunha, George W, 1917, My 11,11:1
Dacyshyn, Andrew, 1950, Je 20,27:2
Dadabhoy, Maneckji B, 1953, D 16,35:2
Dadakis, Sophocles, 1954, F 12,25:3
D'Addario, Anthony R, 1960, D 22,23:4
D'Addario, Nicholas, 1951, My 9,33:4
D'Addario, Thomas, 1955, Ja 11,25:2
Daddo, George W, 1913, Ag 8,7:5
Daddow, Benjamin S, 1940, Jl 26,17:5
Dade, Charles Townsend Dr, 1915, D 28,11:4
Dade, Harry E Mrs, 1943, D 16,27:2
Dade, Isaiah C, 1954, F 21,69:2
Dadelsen, Jean-Paul De, 1957, Je 26,31:5
d'Adhermar, Marguerite Countess, 1925, Je 27,11:6
Dadiani, Shalva, 1959, Mr 20,31:2
Dadirran, Markar Dr, 1912, N 25,13:4
Dadmun, George E, 1942, Je 19,23:3
D'Adolf, Oscar, 1952, Ap 2,33:4
Dadolle, Msgr Bp of Dijon, 1911, My 23,11:5
Dadson, Bertram I, 1948, Ag 2,21:1
Dady, Herbert A, 1958, Je 12,31:2
Dady, Ralph J Sr, 1961, Jl 5,33:5
Dady, Timothy J, 1924, My 23,19:5
Dae, Frank, 1959, Ag 30,82:8
Daenzer, Bernhardt, 1951, S 1,11:4
Daenzer, Carl, 1906, S 23,9:6
Daeschner, E, 1928, D 14,29:2
Daffinee, Ralph W, 1959, Je 22,25:4
Daffron, Thomas A, 1957, Je 24,23:4
Dafoe, Allan Roy (will, Ag 6,17:5), 1943, Je 3,21:1
Dafoe, John W, 1944, Ja 10,17:5
Dafour, Jean, 1942, O 15,23:5
Dafrosa, Sister, 1941, Jl 18,19:5
Daftari, Abdullah, 1953, N 1,87:2
Daftary, Ali A, 1946, Ap 23,21:6
Dafter, William, 1953, F 3,25:1
Dagadu, Peter K, 1960, Jl 17,61:2
Da Gama, Domicio (por), 1925, N 10,25:4
Da Gama, Jose T, 1941, F 23,39:6
d'Agata, Guiseppe, 1955, D 3,17:5
Dager, Mary E Mrs, 1941, F 28,19:2
Daggar, George, 1950, O 15,105:1
Daggers, John R, 1906, Ja 7,7:6
Daggert, Charley, 1953, Jl 2,23:5
Daggert, Josiah Taber Col, 1909, S 14,9:5
Daggett, Aaron S (por), 1938, My 15,II,6:3
Daggett, Albert, 1903, D 20,7:5
Daggett, Clark L, 1943, O 22,17:5
Daggett, George F, 1944, My 14,45:2
Daggett, Griswold T, 1941, Jl 22,19:5
Daggett, Herbert M Mrs, 1945, Ja 16,19:2
Daggett, Hiram C, 1951, My 11,27:4
Daggett, Leonard M, 1949, Mr 4,21:5
Daggett, Leonard M Mrs, 1947, Je 9,21:2
Daggett, Lydia J, 1941, Je 7,17:2
Daggett, Mable C, 1955, Ja 12,27:3
Daggett, O E, 1880, S 2,4:7
Daggett, Parker H, 1964, Je 8,29:4
Daggett, Philander Capt, 1875, Ap 23,6:7
Daggett, Robert F, 1955, S 8,31:1
Daggett, V Chapin, 1943, D 10,27:4
Daggett, Volney C Mrs, 1941, Ap 26,15:6
Daggett, Warren C, 1948, Ag 23,17:1
Daggett, William F, 1948, S 4,15:1
Daggett, William Gibbons Dr, 1910, S 19,7:6
Daggett, Windsor P, 1958, Jl 2,29:1
Daggy, A Smith, 1942, Je 17,23:2
Daggy, J Gentry, 1952, My 3,21:1
Dagmar, Princess of Denmark, 1961, O 12,29:2
D'Agnese, Victor J, 1959, Ap 9,31:1
Dagon, Dennis, 1939, O 1,53:3
D'Agostino, Dewey, 1963, O 29,35:1
D'Agostino, Pasquale, 1960, Jl 27,29:3
Da Grosa, Christiana D Mrs, 1947, D 19,25:2
Da Grosa, John, 1953, Ap 24,24:3
D'Aguiar, L H Fereira, 1875, Ag 17,4:6
Dagwell, Benjamin D, 1963, Je 4,39:5
Dahigren, Paul Mrs, 1911, D 28,9:5
Dahl, Esther J E, 1946, Ap 17,25:4
Dahl, George, 1962, Ag 1,31:4
Dahl, Gerhard M, 1953, D 30,23:1
Dahl, Gerhard M Mrs, 1949, Ap 22,23:1
Dahl, John O, 1951, O 17,31:2
Dahl, Joseph O, 1942, Ag 5,19:5
Dahl, Louis, 1952, Je 18,27:2
Dahl, Walter H Jr, 1949, O 29,30:7
Dahl, Warren L, 1965, F 15,27:4
Dahl, Warren L Mrs, 1938, D 17,15:7
Dahlbender, Joseph, 1938, S 15,25:3
Dahlberg, Bror G, 1954, F 22,19:3
Dahlberg, Carl F, 1942, Jl 28,17:5
Dahle, Isak, 1937, N 26,21:5
Dahlen, Carl F, 1954, S 16,29:2
Dahlen, William, 1950, D 6,33:5
Dahlerup, Joost, 1944, Ag 23,19:4
Dahlerus, Birger, 1957, Mr 9,19:3
Dahlgren, Bror E, 1961, D 18,35:5
Dahlgren, Charles Bunker Capt, 1912, Ja 11,13:5
Dahlgren, Eric Bernard, 1922, N 22,21:4
Dahlgren, Joseph D, 1950, Je 30,23:4
Dahlgren, Lucy D Mrs, 1944, Ja 1,13:3
Dahlgren, Paul (see also Mr 24), 1876, Mr 28,5:4
Dahlgren, Rear-Adm, 1870, Jl 13,5:2
Dahlgren, Romolo, 1944, O 11,21:3
Dahlgren, Ulric, 1946, My 31,23:2
Dahlhaus, Edward Mrs, 1950, Ja 27,23:2
Dahlhjelm, Roger C, 1950, My 23,29:3
Dahling, Albert F, 1949, My 4,29:4
Dahlinger, Adolph L, 1939, S 8,23:3
Dahlinger, Adolph L Mrs, 1954, Ja 12,23:2
Dahlinger, Edward P Sr, 1961, My 8,35:2
Dahlman, Julius, 1925, S 23,25:3
Dahlman, Louis A, 1948, Jl 21,23:4
Dahlman, Louis Mrs, 1956, D 11,39:1
Dahlman, Richard C, 1965, My 19,47:3
Dahlstrom, William R, 1952, Mr 10,21:4
Dahm, Frank C, 1960, N 18,31:1
Dahm, James H, 1938, N 10,27:2
Dahmen, Ernest A Jr, 1968, Je 28,41:1
Dahmen, Lloyd C, 1956, O 17,35:5
Dahmen, Raquel, 1947, D 7,77:1
Dahmer, Charles H, 1941, Mr 31,15:3
Dahmer, John S, 1944, Ap 21,19:4
Dahms, John Mrs, 1943, Je 3,21:4
Dahn, Albert A, 1940, Ap 18,23:3
Dahn, Felix S, 1912, Ja 4,13:5
Dahn, Georg, 1957, Jl 14,73:1
Dahn, Gustav A, 1955, F 10,31:4
Dahoney, Lawrence, 1945, Jl 20,19:5
Dahut, Julius, 1957, S 5,29:4
Dahut, William (funl, F 22,21:5), 1955, F 18,21:2
Daiber, Jules, 1948, Jl 7,46:4
Daiger, Matthias L, 1959, Ag 1,17:4
Daigle, Archie A, 1952, Ja 14,19:4
Daigle, Clifton C, 1952, Je 13,23:3
Daignault, Elphege J, 1937, My 26,25:4
Daigneau, Kenneth, 1948, Je 12,8:6
Daikeler, Josef, 1952, D 30,19:3
Dail, Harry W, 1960, Mr 3,29:4
Dailey, Abraham H, 1907, N 3,9:6
Dailey, Adam R, 1940, Je 2,44:7
Dailey, Albert D, 1952, Mr 21,23:3
Dailey, Clara T, 1949, N 2,27:3
Dailey, Clarence J, 1941, F 8,15:2
Dailey, Clarke G, 1964, Ag 4,29:3
Dailey, Daniel J, 1960, Ja 1,19:2
Dailey, Dennis M, 1940, My 21,23:2
Dailey, Edward J, 1950, Je 22,27:3
Dailey, Esther L, 1952, F 11,25:4
Dailey, Florence M (will), 1966, N 16,30:3
Dailey, Frank, 1956, F 28,31:1
Dailey, Frank J Sr, 1957, Ag 28,27:4
Dailey, Guy, 1940, Mr 7,23:6
Dailey, Helen S Mrs, 1940, Mr 1,21:2
Dailey, Herbert, 1961, Jl 15,19:6
Dailey, Hugh F, 1939, O 31,23:6
Dailey, James E, 1954, Jl 15,27:3
Dailey, James F Mrs, 1951, O 23,29:4
Dailey, Jeremiah P, 1957, N 9,27:2
Dailey, John, 1949, Ja 15,17:3
Dailey, John A, 1961, O 22,86:4
Dailey, John F Sr, 1949, Ag 30,27:4
Dailey, John H, 1940, Ja 16,23:2
Dailey, John J, 1941, N 10,17:4
Dailey, Joseph, 1940, S 24,23:5; 1959, Ag 15,17:5
Dailey, L B, 1932, F 18,21:1
Dailey, Oswald, 1937, Ap 30,22:3
Dailey, Peter F (por),(funl, My 26,7:6), 1908, My 24,9:5
Dailey, Peter F (est), 1914, Ag 20,11:5
Dailey, Ralph C, 1950, Je 16,25:3
Dailey, Stewart J, 1960, Jl 22,23:2
Dailey, Ulysses G, 1961, Ap 23,86:6
Dailey, Vincent F X, 1952, S 5,27:2
Dailey, Vincent J, 1956, D 15,25:5
Dailey, W J F, 1939, D 11,23:3
Dailey, W Murray Mrs, 1947, Ja 2,27:1
Dailey, Walter H, 1944, My 15,19:6
Dailey, Walter L, 1905, Je 6,9:5
Dailey, Washington, 1940, Je 19,23:4
Dailey, Wilbur M Dr, 1937, Mr 1,19:4
Dailey, William F, 1940, Ap 27,15:6
Dailey, William G, 1950, O 17,31:3
Dailey, William L, 1949, My 31,23:3
Dailey, William S Mrs, 1938, Jl 22,17:3
Dailinger, John, 1948, Ja 30,23:1
Daily, C Raymond, 1954, S 9,31:4
Daily, Charles S, 1943, Mr 2,19:1
Daily, Cornelius M, 1938, N 26,16:3
Daily, Henry A N, 1948, Jl 14,23:4
Daily, Henry L, 1951, Ag 23,23:4
Daily, James H, 1939, Ja 27,20:2
Daily, John B Rev, 1920, Jl 3,15:6
Daily, John T, 1937, Ap 17,17:2
Daily, Joseph E, 1965, Jl 3,19:3
Daily, Margaret, 1939, F 15,23:2
Daily, Mary T Mrs, 1937, S 1,19:2
Daily, William B, 1938, F 25,17:1
Daily, William J, 1942, Jl 3,17:5
Dain, Clarence F, 1948, Ag 12,21:1
Dain, Donald, 1954, My 23,88:4
Dain, Frank M Jr, 1954, Ja 14,29:2
Dain, Frank McLellan, 1925, Ap 1,23:4
Dain, Henry P Jr, 1955, Ap 11,23:4
Dain, Henry P Mrs, 1950, F 12,84:4
Dain, John W, 1964, Ja 2,27:2
Dain, Thomas A, 1957, N 28,31:3
Daine, Robert L, 1957, Ap 9,33:2
Daines, Lee A, 1946, Mr 30,15:3
Daines, Percy, 1957, Mr 6,31:4
Daines, Robert C, 1948, Mr 12,23:2
Daingerfield, Algernon, 1941, Je 11,21:3
Daingerfield, Anna G Mrs, 1939, N 17,21:3
Daingerfield, Elizabeth, 1951, D 11,33:1
Daingerfield, Elizabeth W Q Mrs, 1944, O 23,19:5
Daingerfield, Lawrence H, 1952, Ja 7,19:3
Daingerfield, W P, 1880, My 6,2:2
Dains, Frank B, 1948, Ja 6,23:3
Dainton, Marie, 1938, F 2,19:2
Dainty, Ernest, 1947, O 31,23:4
Dainty, George W, 1951, Mr 25,74:5
Daire, Francis W, 1949, Jl 13,28:3
Daisey, John D, 1959, N 8,88:7
Daisley, Brooke, 1966, Je 26,73:2
Daiss, Carlton J, 1949, D 24,15:3
Daitch, Lewis, 1964, Jl 2,63:5
Daitch, Paul H, 1963, Je 23,84:8
Daitz, Elliott A, 1960, D 11,88:3
Daix, Augustus 3d, 1952, O 20,23:4
Daix, Daisy, 1950, Ag 17,4:5
Daizell, Lloyd Hunter, 1925, Ap 15,19:3
Dake, Abram M, 1948, Ja 28,23:5
Dake, Charles M, 1957, Jl 27,17:6
Dake, George E, 1947, Ap 5,19:2
Dake, Marie Mrs, 1925, D 13,13:1
Dake, Robert E, 1958, Jl 30,29:5
Dakin, Arthur H Mrs, 1948, Jl 24,15:3
Dakin, Arthur W, 1937, S 11,17:3
Dakin, Burton C, 1947, Ag 1,17:4
Dakin, C Ernest, 1965, Ap 21,45:4
Dakin, Clyde B, 1953, My 6,31:4
Dakin, De Witt C Mrs, 1937, D 1,23:3
Dakin, Henry D, 1952, F 11,25:3
Dakin, Robert W, 1949, Mr 16,27:5
Dakin, T S Gen (see also My 14), 1878, My 1
Dakin, Walter E, 1955, F 16,29:1

Dakins, J Gordon (funl, Mr 15,31:4), 1965, Mr 4,31:1
Dakins, Wellington, 1951, D 11,33:2
Daklugie, Asa, 1955, Ap 9,13:2
Dakowski, Frederick V, 1942, F 15,44:8
Dal Piaz, Francoise, 1967, Mr 28,45:2
Dal Piaz, J H, 1928, Je 19,27:3
Dalacour, Reginald B, 1948, Mr 22,23:5
Dalafield, Frederick P, 1951, Jl 15,60:6
Dalagur, Sol, 1952, Jl 1,23:5
Dalai Lama, 1933, D 20,22:1
Dalal, Ardeshir, 1949, O 9,92:6
Daland, Frederick H, 1937, N 22,19:4
Daland, George G, 1945, Je 17,26:3
Daland, Grace S, 1958, F 18,28:4
Daland, Judson Dr, 1937, Ag 16,19:4
Dalberg, Melvin H, 1947, N 23,76:1
Dalberg, Walter J, 1951, My 16,35:2
Dalbey, Allan K, 1945, D 29,13:4
D'Albiac, John, 1963, Ag 21,33:1
D'Albora, Felix Mrs, 1951, Je 21,27:5
D'Albora, John B, 1962, F 27,33:4
Dale, A, 1928, My 22,27:3
Dale, Albert E, 1954, N 22,23:4
Dale, Alfred G, 1941, Jl 11,15:6
Dale, Alfred Sir, 1921, Ag 16,15:4
Dale, Arnold H, 1939, My 3,23:4
Dale, Benjamin B, 1938, Ag 17,19:3
Dale, Benjamin J, 1943, Jl 31,13:2
Dale, Benjamin M, 1951, Jl 14,13:2
Dale, Charles G Mrs, 1908, S 1,7:5
Dale, Charles H (will, Ag 4,7:5), 1908, Jl 19,7:6
Dale, Charles Mrs, 1968, O 10,47:4
Dale, Chester, 1962, D 18,4:8
Dale, Chester (will), 1966, My 25,44:2
Dale, Chester Mrs, 1953, Ag 6,21:6
Dale, Dora S, 1884, My 5,4:7
Dale, Edward A, 1957, N 10,85:6
Dale, Edward C, 1947, Jl 17,19:5
Dale, Edwin L, 1967, D 3,84:6
Dale, Esther (Mrs A Beckhard), 1961, Jl 24,23:4
Dale, Frederick A, 1943, Ap 18,49:1
Dale, George Jr, 1965, Ag 9,25:1
Dale, George N, 1962, Je 30,19:6
Dale, Harry S, 1962, O 26,31:3
Dale, Henry Sir, 1968, Jl 24,41:1
Dale, J G, 1883, Mr 24,5:3
Dale, J Lowry, 1952, Je 25,29:6
Dale, J Michael, 1959, My 3,87:1
Dale, James F, 1945, Ja 28,38:4
Dale, John G, 1954, Ap 15,29:2
Dale, John G Mrs, 1948, N 1,23:5
Dale, John W, 1903, O 1,9:5
Dale, Joseph, 1941, O 5,49:3
Dale, Louise B Mrs, 1967, D 18,47:1
Dale, M Gilmour, 1948, D 9,34:2
Dale, Martin B, 1962, Jl 5,25:2
Dale, Murray, 1959, D 7,31:2
Dale, Nelson C, 1962, S 17,31:5
Dale, Nelson C Jr, 1946, Ap 24,25:4
Dale, Oswald, 1953, Jl 23,23:4
Dale, Otis G, 1938, D 28,26:3
Dale, P M, 1903, Je 13,9:6
Dale, Richard, 1912, S 19,11:6
Dale, Richard C, 1904, My 23,9:6
Dale, Richard I, 1967, Ag 23,51:5
Dale, Saul H, 1871, D 18,1:4
Dale, T N, 1879, Jl 14,4:7
Dale, T Nelson Prof, 1937, N 17,23:5
Dale, Thomas H, 1912, Ag 22,9:5
Dale, Virginia (Mrs H Shirk-Johnstone), 1957, S 6, 21:1
Dale, William J, 1946, Ja 25,23:3
Dale, William Johnson Dr, 1903, O 8,9:5
Dale, William P Mrs, 1956, Mr 27,35:5
D'Alecy, Anthony J, 1960, O 8,23:3
Dalen, Nils G Dr, 1937, D 10,25:5
D'Alencon, Emilienne, 1945, F 15,19:4
Dales, Frederick, 1961, Ag 25,25:5
Dales, Frederick Mrs, 1957, Mr 11,25:3
D'Alesandro, Thomas Sr, 1952, S 13,17:3
Dalesio, Carmine (cor, Ag 29,17:6), 1959, Ag 28,23:1
Dalessandro, Antonio, 1925, Mr 22,7:1
D'Alessandro, Felix, 1937, N 22,19:4
D'Alessandro, George J, 1952, Mr 26,29:2
D'Alessio, Tommaso, 1948, F 28,15:2
Daley, Bob, 1948, O 12,25:3
Daley, Daniel F Dr, 1937, Ap 25,II,9:2
Daley, Daniel M, 1960, Ap 12,33:5
Daley, Daniel Mrs, 1945, Mr 1,21:2
Daley, Daniel V, 1940, My 5,52:5
Daley, Edward W, 1952, Ja 20,84:4
Daley, Elena A, 1949, O 12,29:2
Daley, Frank P Mrs, 1951, O 10,23:5
Daley, George (por), 1938, F 8,22:1
Daley, George, 1949, Ap 13,29:5
Daley, George Henry, 1909, N 27,9:6
Daley, George M, 1953, Je 11,29:5
Daley, Jacob (cor, F 19,27:3), 1954, F 18,31:3
Daley, James M, 1939, Je 18,37:3
Daley, John F, 1967, D 18,47:2
Daley, John H, 1925, Ag 29,11:5; 1954, N 14,89:2; 1959, Jl 15,29:4
Daley, John Henry, 1954, S 21,27:4
Daley, John J, 1941, Ja 3,19:4
Daley, John P, 1950, S 16,19:2; 1963, Jl 22,23:4
Daley, Joseph, 1950, My 3,29:3
Daley, Joseph F, 1962, Jl 23,21:1
Daley, Joseph K, 1953, Ag 6,21:5
Daley, Leo F Mrs, 1954, Ja 1,23:3
Daley, Leonard J, 1964, Ag 15,21:5
Daley, Loretta Mrs, 1951, Ja 20,15:4
Daley, Mabel Mrs, 1942, Jl 20,13:3
Daley, Margaret N Mrs, 1942, Ja 27,21:4
Daley, Mark J, 1955, Ap 12,29:3
Daley, Mary W Mrs, 1941, O 10,23:2
Daley, Matthew A, 1944, My 2,19:5
Daley, Nelson B, 1952, S 28,78:6
Daley, Owen B, 1904, F 25,9:5
Daley, P T, 1938, Je 13,1:5
Daley, Raymond A, 1951, My 30,21:6
Daley, Robert M, 1950, Je 4,92:3
Daley, Robert M Mrs, 1956, F 2,25:4
Daley, T W, 1879, D 5,1:4
Daley, Thomas V, 1966, Ja 11,29:2
Daley, Timothy, 1918, F 27,11:5
Daley, William B, 1947, F 4,25:3
Daley, William E, 1961, Jl 28,21:5
Dalgazio, Concetta Mrs, 1941, F 1,34:3
Dalgetty, Herbert, 1905, Ap 18,7:1
Dalgin, Ben, 1968, My 17,47:1
Dalgin, Ben Mrs, 1963, S 23,29:5
Dalgleish, Oakley H, 1963, Ag 18,80:8
Dalglish, John, 1946, Je 28,21:4
Dalglish, John Mrs, 1962, Jl 10,33:1
Dalhart, Pecos, 1945, Mr 25,38:4
Dalhart, Vernon, 1948, S 17,25:5
Dalhgren, Gordon A, 1948, F 27,21:3
Dalhousie, Earl, 1880, Jl 21,5:6
Dalhousie, Earl of, 1874, Jl 7,4:7
Dalia, Anthony, 1946, Ap 29,22:2
Dalia, Michael, 1949, Je 7,31:1
Dalis, Samuel, 1960, My 2,29:2
Dall, Jes J Jr, 1942, Je 30,21:5
Dall, Justin M, 1954, Jl 15,27:4
Dall, Louis A, 1949, Ap 23,13:5
Dall, Mary B Mrs, 1942, Ag 4,19:4
Dall, Peter, 1915, Ag 26,9:3
Dall, W H, 1927, Mr 28,21:3
Dall, William H Mrs, 1943, N 12,21:1
Dalla-Chiara, Guiseppe Dr, 1919, D 19,15:2
Dalla Costa, Elia Cardinal (funl plans, D 23,23:1), 1961, D 22,23:1
Dall'Acqua, Robert, 1964, Je 17,43:1
Dallam, Frank B, 1925, N 10,25:5
Dallas, Andrew C Mrs, 1960, Mr 19,21:2
Dallas, C Donald, 1959, Ap 12,86:3
Dallas, C Donald Mrs, 1960, O 21,33:4
Dallas, George M, 1865, Ja 1,8:2
Dallas, George S, 1951, D 25,31:4
Dallas, Harold H Mrs, 1941, Ag 4,13:5
Dallas, Herbert A, 1952, D 9,33:5
Dallas, Hughes, 1958, S 19,27:1
Dallas, John G, 1949, Ag 13,11:5
Dallas, John T, 1961, D 5,43:2
Dallas, Trevanion B, 1938, F 4,21:1
Dallas, Vincent D, 1951, Ag 23,23:3
Dallas, William, 1960, D 15,44:1
Dallas, William J, 1946, Ag 18,47:7
Dalle Torre de Tempio, Giuseppe (Count), 1967, O 19,42:3
Dallek, Robert Mrs, 1962, O 19,26:5
Dallenbach, Eloise S, 1953, N 11,31:4
Dallett, John, 1904, Mr 29,9:6; 1949, N 10,31:5
Dalley, A H Charles, 1958, O 18,21:6
Dalley, J Alden R, 1961, N 11,23:4
Dalley, Maria S, 1947, Je 5,25:3
Dalliba, William S, 1921, Jl 28,13:6; 1962, D 7,39:2
Dalliba, William S Mrs, 1946, My 3,21:2
d'Alligri, Marchesa (Blanch Roosevelt), 1898, S 11, 7:6
Dallin, Cyrus E, 1944, N 15,27:1
Dallin, David J, 1962, F 22,25:1
Dallinger, Frederick W, 1955, S 7,31:4
Dallis, Ernest E, 1942, N 3,23:2
Dallman, V Y Sr Mrs, 1959, Ag 4,27:3
Dallmann, Albert H, 1939, Mr 10,23:4
Dall'Olio, Alfredo (trb lr, N 3,26:7), 1952, S 21,89:1
Dallow, Walter R, 1954, Ja 3,88:3
Dally, Addison B, 1957, My 9,31:1
Dally, Charles M, 1911, Ja 28,11:5
Dally, Philippe, 1945, Jl 7,13:7
Dalmani, William Mrs, 1967, Mr 13,37:1
Dalmann, Rudolph, 1915, Ag 22,13:4
Dalmasse, Louis J, 1941, Je 25,21:1
Dalmatius Francis Jollivet, Bro, 1968, O 13,85:1
Dalmatofsky, Morris (Morris the Peddler), 1965, D 21,37:2
Dalmores, Charles, 1939, D 7,27:2
D'Aloia, J Victor, 1945, My 7,17:4
Dalon, Jules, 1902, Ap 16,9:5
Dalon, William, 1958, F 9,88:7
D'Alonzo, Henry E, 1962, Ja 5,29:2
Dalrymple, Alfred N, 1916, My 25,13:6
Dalrymple, Alfred V (por), 1938, Jl 27,17:1
Dalrymple, Byron W Mrs, 1947, N 9,74:4
Dalrymple, Charles O, 1960, Ag 19,23:4
Dalrymple, Clarence L, 1938, F 5,15:2
Dalrymple, David Mrs, 1946, Ap 8,27:4
Dalrymple, Fitzwilliam, 1940, Ja 4,23:1
Dalrymple, Francis W, 1954, F 4,25:4
Dalrymple, Frank C, 1961, Ag 14,25:4
Dalrymple, George E, 1948, O 10,76:6
Dalrymple, George H, 1959, My 4,29:2
Dalrymple, Harold A, 1952, N 13,31:4
Dalrymple, Henry M, 1904, F 1,7:3
Dalrymple, Hew H, 1945, Jl 13,11:6
Dalrymple, John Charles Mrs, 1968, Je 26,47:4
Dalrymple, Lew M, 1948, Je 9,29:4
Dalrymple, Lewis, 1950, Je 7,29:5
Dalrymple, P A, 1881, N 1,5:3
Dalrymple, Sherman, 1962, Mr 19,29:2
Dalsen, James J Mrs, 1946, Ja 16,23:2
Dalsey, Harry I, 1940, Mr 20,27:4
Dalsheimer, Simon, 1948, Ap 8,25:5
Dalsimer, Allan F, 1963, Jl 4,17:1
Dalsimer, Herbert, 1950, My 10,31:2
Dalsimer, Milton, 1950, S 7,31:4
Dalsimer, Steven P, 1962, Je 25,29:3
Dalsimer, Steven P Mrs, 1943, Je 9,21:3
Dalsimer, Walter D, 1952, Ag 3,61:2
D'Alte, Joseph F Mrs, 1949, O 14,27:2
Dalton, A, 1953, Jl 25,11:6
Dalton, A Gerald, 1959, D 4,32:1
Dalton, Albert P, 1951, D 7,27:3
Dalton, Alice K, 1968, Jl 15,31:3
Dalton, Anne M, 1959, Ag 27,27:4
Dalton, Annie G Mrs, 1938, D 26,23:3
Dalton, Arthur J, 1953, Je 8,29:4
Dalton, Charles, 1933, D 10,II,8:5; 1942, Je 12,22:2
Dalton, Charles H, 1908, F 25,7:4; 1942, F 13,22:2
Dalton, Charles Mrs, 1960, Mr 8,33:3
Dalton, Christopher J, 1937, Ap 6,23:2
Dalton, E, 1937, Jl 14,3:2
Dalton, Edith, 1940, My 28,23:4
Dalton, Edward A, 1953, F 9,27:2; 1960, Jl 26,29:5
Dalton, Edward F, 1945, Ap 6,15:2; 1956, Ja 5,33:4
Dalton, Edward H J N, 1962, F 14,35:3
Dalton, Edward N, 1937, Ag 3,23:5
Dalton, Edward R, 1923, Je 21,19:5
Dalton, Eugene S Dr, 1937, Ap 22,23:2
Dalton, Frank A, 1940, Je 20,23:4
Dalton, Frederick B Mrs, 1958, F 6,27:5
Dalton, George C J, 1961, Jl 18,29:3
Dalton, Grover W, 1959, D 23,27:3
Dalton, Harry F, 1940, Je 30,32:5
Dalton, Helen T, 1968, My 27,47:2
Dalton, Henry G, 1939, D 28,22:2
Dalton, Henry R, 1943, Mr 28,25:1
Dalton, Howard H, 1959, My 10,87:1
Dalton, Howard V, 1955, My 31,27:1
Dalton, Hugh A, 1950, N 16,31:4
Dalton, J C, 1889, F 13,2:6
Dalton, J F, 1876, Ag 4,4:7
Dalton, J Frank, 1951, Ag 17,18:2
Dalton, James, 1942, Ja 31,17:6; 1948, Jl 5,15:4
Dalton, James F Mrs, 1953, Mr 10,29:3
Dalton, James J, 1952, Mr 3,21:1
Dalton, James L, 1952, D 1,23:4
Dalton, Jeremiah J, 1944, D 21,21:5
Dalton, Jeremiah J Mrs, 1945, S 8,15:5
Dalton, John, 1937, Je 6,II,9:2
Dalton, John A (Jack), 1954, Ap 14,29:5
Dalton, John F, 1949, N 16,29:5
D'Alton, John F (Cardinal, funeral, F 7,7:3), 1963, F 2,8:6
Dalton, John H, 1945, My 28,19:3
Dalton, John P, 1919, Mr 11,11:2; 1923, O 18,19:2
Dalton, John R, 1938, Jl 16,13:4
Dalton, John W, 1920, My 25,11:4
Dalton, Joseph (Bro Lawrence Sixtus), 1953, Mr 10, 29:1
Dalton, Joseph N, 1961, N 25,23:5
Dalton, Leo, 1943, Je 2,25:2
Dalton, Leo A, 1948, Mr 21,60:7
Dalton, Liam F, 1965, D 7,47:1
Dalton, Luke A, 1924, Ag 13,15:3; 1953, F 20,19:2
D'Alton, M C, 1947, My 14,25:3
Dalton, Martin, 1960, Mr 24,18:4
Dalton, Michael A, 1954, Ja 3,89:2
Dalton, Michael P, 1946, Ap 1,27:5
Dalton, N N, 1953, Ap 28,27:3
Dalton, Napoleon, 1919, Ap 19,17:2
Dalton, Patrick J, 1939, Ag 20,33:4
Dalton, Peter W, 1948, My 25,27:4
Dalton, Phil S, 1940, D 27,20:2
Dalton, Test, 1945, D 11,25:4
Dalton, Thomas, 1945, My 28,19:3
Dalton, Thomas J, 1937, O 5,25:3
Dalton, W H, 1950, D 14,35:3
Dalton, Walter, 1952, F 19,29:1
Dalton, William, 1923, Ja 28,6:3
Dalton, William A, 1949, My 13,24:2
Dalton, William B Mrs, 1956, N 18,88:4
Dalton, William E, 1938, Jl 16,13:6
Dalton, William F, 1949, My 12,31:4
Dalton, William H, 1947, Ap 6,60:6
Dalton, William J, 1947, S 14,60:3; 1953, O 18,86:4; 1961, Ag 10,27:3
Dalton, William L, 1948, N 2,25:1

Dalton, William P, 1942, N 11,25:3
Daltry, Joseph S, 1967, S 29,47:2
D'Alvarez, Marguerite, 1953, O 21,29:5
Daly, Agnes M Mrs, 1941, Ja 14,21:2
Daly, Alan F, 1967, Jl 11,37:1
Daly, Albert F, 1951, My 1,29:4
Daly, Aloysius A, 1950, F 19,79:3
Daly, Andrew B, 1940, S 10,23:4
Daly, Anne C Mrs, 1947, S 28,60:4
Daly, Arthur C, 1949, Mr 20,76:4
Daly, Arthur J, 1958, O 3,29:4
Daly, Augustin, 1899, Je 8,1:7
Daly, Augustin Mrs (funl, N 13,9:4), 1907, N 11,7:5
Daly, Augustine J, 1938, D 18,49:1
Daly, B, 1933, Ag 19,11:3
Daly, Benjamin F Commodore, 1914, D 30,11:6
Daly, Bernard J, 1948, N 13,15:4
Daly, Bert J, 1952, S 4,27:5
Daly, Bert Mrs, 1946, Ja 17,23:4
Daly, C, 1926, N 21,31:1
Daly, Carroll, 1946, My 28,21:5
Daly, Carroll J, 1958, Ja 17,25:3
Daly, Charles, 1952, D 14,90:4
Daly, Charles D, 1959, F 14,21:3
Daly, Charles F, 1958, Ag 31,56:1
Daly, Charles F Mrs, 1948, Ap 25,69:1
Daly, Charles Howard, 1924, N 19,21:3
Daly, Charles P, 1899, S 20,14:4
Daly, Dan, 1904, Mr 27,7:5
Daly, Dan F (New Brunswick, NJ), 1951, Jl 18,29:3
Daly, Dan Mrs, 1904, Mr 14,9:6
Daly, Daniel, 1937, Ap 28,23:5
Daly, Daniel A, 1944, S 13,19:4
Daly, Daniel C, 1954, Ap 16,21:2
Daly, Daniel F (Hawthorne, NY), 1951, S 14,26:2
Daly, Daniel J, 1945, F 11,40:6
Daly, David J, 1938, Je 7,23:3
Daly, David Mrs, 1948, Ag 21,16:3
Daly, Dennis, 1961, N 7,33:1
Daly, Dennis W, 1939, Mr 16,23:2
Daly, Edmond E, 1948, O 7,29:3
Daly, Edward A, 1937, Je 24,25:5
Daly, Edward C, 1964, N 24,27:5
Daly, Edward F, 1948, Ap 27,25:4
Daly, Edward H, 1938, N 8,23:2
Daly, Edward J, 1959, Jl 21,29:1
Daly, Edward S, 1953, D 30,23:4
Daly, Edwin A, 1951, Ap 25,29:4
Daly, Edwin K, 1960, Mr 29,37:1
Daly, Edwin K Mrs, 1961, Ap 15,21:6
Daly, Elizabeth H Mrs, 1937, My 21,21:4
Daly, Elizabeth T, 1967, S 3,52:8
Daly, Eugene, 1922, Ap 21,13:4
Daly, Eugene V, 1937, Ap 24,19:5
Daly, F A, 1885, Ja 7,5:6
Daly, Frances M, 1959, Jl 16,27:4
Daly, Francis A, 1950, O 1,104:8
Daly, Francis A Mrs, 1949, Jl 25,15:3
Daly, Francis I, 1937, Ag 12,19:3
Daly, Francis J, 1960, Jl 15,23:2
Daly, Frank, 1940, O 13,49:1
Daly, Frank P, 1952, Ag 9,13:6
Daly, George A, 1939, D 17,49:2
Daly, George F, 1940, S 1,21:2
Daly, Gerald H, 1967, Jl 9,61:1
Daly, Gerald V, 1946, Mr 27,27:3
Daly, Helen, 1949, O 8,13:4
Daly, Helen B Mrs, 1946, Jl 3,25:3
Daly, Henry E, 1949, N 26,15:6
Daly, Herbert T, 1924, Je 10,11:4
Daly, Hugh J Father, 1924, D 26,15:5
Daly, J Burrwood, 1939, Mr 14,21:3
Daly, J C W, 1903, N 13,7:6
Daly, J J, 1930, S 21,2:2
Daly, James A, 1953, Ja 26,19:3; 1966, D 29,28:8
Daly, James B, 1959, My 29,23:1
Daly, James F, 1950, Jl 30,60:2
Daly, James Francis Ex-Justice (funl, Ag 10,9:5), 1916, Ag 7,9:6
Daly, James G, 1938, F 6,II,8:2
Daly, James J, 1943, D 1,21:3; 1953, Ag 20,27:6; 1959, Mr 13,29:1
Daly, James J Sr, 1956, F 14,29:4
Daly, James M, 1937, Ap 3,19:4
Daly, James P, 1938, S 9,21:3; 1958, S 13,19:2
Daly, Jeremiah S, 1950, My 9,29:1
Daly, John, 1905, Ap 26,11:1
Daly, John (will, My 17,2:4), 1906, Ap 27,11:4
Daly, John, 1921, S 6,15:5; 1938, S 10,17:4; 1949, Ap 27,27:5
Daly, John A, 1944, Mr 8,19:6; 1949, Ja 13,23:4
Daly, John C, 1950, My 25,29:2
Daly, John F, 1948, F 28,15:6; 1964, F 9,88:6
Daly, John H, 1939, Mr 29,23:6
Daly, John J, 1939, O 17,25:4; 1944, Ap 7,19:4; 1948, Je 26,17:2
Daly, John J Mrs, 1949, F 26,15:5
Daly, John L, 1949, Ag 18,21:2
Daly, John M Mrs, 1946, Jl 26,21:1
Daly, John P, 1954, Ja 5,27:2
Daly, John T, 1950, S 3,38:4; 1952, Ap 3,35:4
Daly, John W, 1921, Ja 13,13:4; 1947, Ja 29,26:2
Daly, Joseph A, 1938, Mr 6,II,9:3; 1947, Ag 10,52:6; 1949, Ap 7,30:3; 1957, Ap 3,31:1
Daly, Joseph D, 1938, F 1,21:5
Daly, Joseph H, 1952, Ag 15,15:2
Daly, Joseph J, 1920, F 24,13:6
Daly, Joseph J (NYC), 1960, Ja 27,33:4
Daly, Joseph J (NJ), 1960, O 4,43:3
Daly, Joseph L, 1941, Ag 7,17:3; 1950, Mr 3,25:1
Daly, Joseph O, 1942, N 4,24:2
Daly, Joseph P, 1937, F 21,II,10:4
Daly, Katherine C, 1940, N 16,17:5
Daly, Kathyrn, 1962, Ap 3,39:4
Daly, L J, 1885, Ja 7,5:6
Daly, Lady, 1939, Ag 12,13:5
Daly, Lawrence A, 1954, My 31,13:1
Daly, Lawrence E, 1966, Ag 21,93:2
Daly, Lawrence R, 1946, Mr 30,15:4
Daly, Leo A, 1952, Ag 7,21:4
Daly, Louis J, 1940, Ag 29,19:2
Daly, M, 1932, Jl 1,21:1
Daly, Mae E, 1954, D 30,17:3
Daly, Marcus, 1900, N 13,2:3
Daly, Marcus Mrs, 1941, Jl 15,20:3
Daly, Margaret E, 1940, F 13,23:2
Daly, Margaret N Mrs, 1967, Jl 6,29:5
Daly, Mark A, 1953, Ag 14,19:4
Daly, Mary H Mrs, 1940, Je 13,23:6
Daly, Matt A, 1937, N 25,31:4
Daly, Matthias, 1949, O 26,29:2
Daly, Maurice F, 1945, S 7,5:6
Daly, Michael J, 1941, My 23,21:6; 1952, O 9,31:2
Daly, Michael L, 1952, Ap 13,76:4
Daly, Michael T, 1913, N 6,11:6
Daly, Owen, 1937, My 15,19:3
Daly, P F, 1932, Ap 22,19:1
Daly, Patrick J, 1940, O 5,15:6; 1953, Ap 25,15:2
Daly, Patrick Mrs, 1943, Mr 13,13:1
Daly, Peter J, 1960, Jl 25,23:2
Daly, Peter M, 1967, Ja 14,31:3
Daly, Peter P, 1951, S 5,31:6
Daly, Peter S, 1917, Ag 17,9:6
Daly, Regina Mrs, 1946, N 1,23:4
Daly, Reginald A, 1957, S 20,23:5
Daly, Richard F Judge, 1968, O 10,47:4
Daly, Richard J, 1967, Ja 18,43:3
Daly, Robert J Maj, 1923, Ja 24,13:6
Daly, Robert R, 1963, Jl 3,25:4
Daly, Sheridan P, 1952, Ap 18,25:3
Daly, T J, 1903, Ja 6,5:2
Daly, Thaddeus M Jr, 1946, Mr 23,13:3
Daly, Thomas, 1924, S 11,23:7; 1941, O 5,V,8:4; 1953, Ja 19,23:2
Daly, Thomas A, 1941, Ja 9,21:5; 1948, O 5,25:1
Daly, Thomas D, 1946, N 8,23:2
Daly, Thomas F, 1939, Mr 11,17:2
Daly, Thomas R, 1962, Ag 5,81:1
Daly, Tom, 1904, Mr 29,6:2
Daly, W, 1936, D 5,19:5
Daly, Walter J Sr, 1954, Jl 16,21:1
Daly, Warren C, 1943, My 3,17:4
Daly, William A, 1947, Je 25,25:4
Daly, William C, 1938, Je 24,19:3
Daly, William Capt, 1912, Ap 5,13:4
Daly, William E, 1939, N 24,23:2
Daly, William J, 1942, F 2,15:2; 1952, Mr 11,27:5
Daly, William J (funl, Je 1,35:4), 1961, My 28,65:1
Daly, William J B, 1949, Jl 23,11:1
Daly, William J Mrs, 1950, My 30,17:3
Daly, William L, 1947, Mr 14,23:4
Daly, William Mrs, 1959, O 12,19:4
Daly, William Y, 1964, My 21,35:5
Dalzell, Arthur A, 1958, S 18,31:2
Dalzell, Charles J, 1948, Ja 27,25:2
Dalzell, David W, 1946, F 14,26:3
Dalzell, Fred B, 1916, Jl 17,11:7; 1948, F 18,27:5
Dalzell, George, 1945, My 22,19:5
Dalzell, George H, 1939, Je 22,23:5
Dalzell, Harry J, 1944, F 25,17:5
Dalzell, Hugh, 1904, F 14,7:6
Dalzell, J, 1927, O 4,29:1
Dalzell, James, 1955, Ap 17,86:6
Dalzell, James M, 1924, Ja 31,15:4
Dalzell, Lloyd H, 1968, F 25,77:1
Dalzell, Mary L Mrs, 1909, My 11,9:7
Dalzell, Robert, 1945, N 23,19:2
Dalzell, Robert S, 1941, O 6,17:2
Dalzell, Russell J, 1945, Ap 4,21:3
Dalzell, William, 1950, My 23,29:1
Dalzell, William C Mrs, 1944, Je 1,19:6
Dalziel, Baron of Wooler, 1928, Ap 19,25:5
Dalziel, Frederick Y, 1960, O 15,23:5
Dalziel, John S, 1937, Ag 21,15:4
Dalziel, Lord, 1935, Jl 17,19:1
Dalziel, Murray, 1942, Ag 29,15:2
Dalziel, Robert, 1966, F 10,34:2
Dalziel, William Mrs, 1952, Je 1,84:5
Dam, A J, 1885, My 17,9:2
Daman, Archbishop of (Rev Pereira), 1925, Ag 25, 17:5
Daman, Max A, 1949, D 13,38:1
Daman, Stephanie Mrs, 1954, S 1,27:5
D'Amanda, Christopher H, 1949, N 17,29:3
Damaskinos, Archbishop, 1949, My 21,13:1
Dambach, Victor, 1944, Mr 1,19:6
Dambly, Harold A, 1953, Ja 17,15:2
D'Ambola, Alfonso, 1959, Mr 20,31:1
D'Ambra, Lucio, 1940, Ja 1,24:2
D'Ambrosa, John P, 1951, S 19,31:4
D'Ambrosia, Nicolas, 1957, Jl 3,23:3
D'Ambrosio, Antonio, 1951, Ag 13,11:3
D'Ambrosio, Edmund, 1952, Je 18,27:4
D'Ambrosio, Virgil, 1943, My 9,40:3
Dame, Charles M Mrs, 1955, O 29,19:5
Dame, Donald, 1952, Ja 22,29:1
Dame, Edward L, 1956, S 30,86:3
Dame, F L, 1933, D 30,13:1
Dame, Lester D, 1942, D 28,19:3
Dame, Lydia M, 1939, My 21,III,7:1
Dame, M Elma, 1952, F 21,27:5
Dame, Nelson P, 1945, D 31,17:3
Dame, Randolph N, 1949, F 20,60:3
Dame, William M Dr, 1923, Ja 29,15:5
Dame, William P Rev Dr, 1937, Ja 19,23:3
D'Amelo, Benjamin A, 1952, Ja 16,25:1
Damerel, William G, 1907, Jl 9,7:6
Damerell, Stanley, 1951, D 13,34:3
Dameron, Alice, 1953, F 28,17:6
Dameron, Tadd (Tadley G),(funl, Mr 12,29:4), 1965, Mr 9,35:2
Damerow, Frank, 1954, D 21,39:5
Damiani, Phil G, 1957, S 12,31:2
Damiano, Celestine J, 1967, O 3,47:2
Damiano, Phil, 1951, Jl 1,51:2
Damiano, Vito Mrs, 1962, Ap 21,19:4
Damico, John, 1920, Jl 29,9:1
Damico, Joseph R, 1956, Ap 24,31:1
Damico, Silvio, 1955, Ap 2,17:1
Damin, Joseph A, 1952, Jl 3,25:4
Damino, Harry O, 1968, Je 19,47:1
Damisch, Heinrich, 1961, Je 9,33:3
Damm, Adam J, 1942, Ap 19,44:5
Damm, Aug, 1942, F 23,21:1
Damm, Charles Mrs, 1944, Jl 10,15:4
Damm, Curtis, 1951, Ap 29,89:1
Damm, Edward J, 1952, Ap 16,27:2
Damm, Eugene, 1925, S 8,21:6
Damm, Walter J, 1962, Je 16,19:2
Dammann, Grace C Mother, 1945, F 14,19:3
Dammann, Leonard, 1961, Je 10,23:5
Dammann, Milton, 1962, Ja 16,33:2
Dammann, Pierre H E, 1954, My 27,27:5
Dammann, Theodore, 1946, Ja 18,19:5
Dammann, W D, 1948, D 8,31:5
Dammenhayn, Alfred F, 1951, Jl 1,51:2
Dammeyer, Albert, 1952, S 24,33:6
Dammon, Clarence E, 1957, Je 11,35:2
Damon, A Willard, 1924, Ja 8,23:2
Damon, Albert F Jr, 1954, S 10,23:2
Damon, Albert H, 1948, Je 20,62:2
Damon, Alex M Mrs (por), 1949, Mr 1,25:3
Damon, Alexander M, 1947, N 27,31:4
Damon, Charlotte E Mrs, 1911, S 5,7:5
Damon, Christopher, 1871, Mr 31,1:3
Damon, Elmer P, 1951, Ja 13,15:3
Damon, Frank J, 1956, F 18,19:2
Damon, Gustavus A, 1903, Ag 3,7:6
Damon, Harry E, 1941, N 13,27:2
Damon, Joseph A, 1962, Ja 10,47:1
Damon, Kenneth F, 1957, Ja 1,23:3
Damon, Les, 1962, Jl 22,64:2
Damon, Lester R Mrs, 1938, Ja 9,42:7
Damon, Lindsay T, 1940, My 7,25:6
Damon, Phil A, 1950, O 13,29:3
Damon, R Hosken, 1960, Ja 19,35:3
Damon, Ralph S (funl, Ja 7,17:2), 1956, Ja 5,33:1
Damon, Samuel, 1924, Jl 3,15:5
Damon, Silas T Dr, 1904, Ja 2,9:4
Damon, Theron J Mrs, 1960, F 24,37:4
Damon, William C Mrs, 1953, N 7,17:5
Damon, William R, 1951, O 18,29:3
Damon, William S, 1950, Ag 24,27:3
Damour, Maurice, 1953, N 16,25:2
Damour, William H Mrs (G Bamonte), 1961, F 23:3
Dampeer, James W, 1947, My 24,15:4
Dampman, Charles, 1947, Ja 23,23:2
Dampman, David B, 1951, Ap 24,29:4
Dampsey, Elsie, 1967, Ja 21,31:5
Damron, Columbia L Mrs, 1941, F 9,49:2
Damrosch, Frank H, 1937, O 23,17:3
Damrosch, Frank H Mrs, 1952, Mr 16,91:1
Damrosch, L Dr (funl, F 16,5:1), 1885, F 16,1:7
Damrosch, Leo Mrs, 1904, N 20,7:5
Damrosch, Leopold (mem), 1910, F 12,9:4
Damrosch, Walter, 1950, D 23,1:2
Damrosch, Walter Mrs, 1949, Jl 29,21:3
Damsel, William H, 1943, Ja 5,20:3
Damski, Paul, 1965, Je 20,73:1
Damsky, Benjamin, 1941, Ap 25,19:5
Damstrom, Algot B, 1950, Ag 8,29:4
Damthu, Tsarong D D, 1959, S 7,4:3
Damude, Arthur B, 1941, S 16,23:5
Damuth, Lester B Dr, 1937, N 4,25:3
Damyanov, Georgi, 1958, N 28,30:8
Dan, Fedor Mrs (Lydia), 1963, Ap 3,47:3
Dan, Samuel L, 1966, O 6,47:5
Dan, Theodore I, 1947, Ja 23,23:4

Dana, A Carroll Mrs, 1915, Mr 24,11:4
Dana, A D, 1928, My 26,17:5
Dana, Abbott G Mrs, 1940, N 20,21:2
Dana, Alan S, 1967, My 2,47:1
Dana, Alice A Mrs, 1950, S 12,27:5
Dana, Allston, 1952, My 13,23:1
Dana, Arnold G, 1947, Ag 24,58:4
Dana, Arnold G Mrs, 1946, O 15,25:1
Dana, C A, 1897, O 18,1:7
Dana, C A Mrs, 1903, Jl 2,9:6
Dana, C L, 1935, D 13,25:3
Dana, Charles, 1906, Je 6,9:6; 1946, Ja 4,21:3
Dana, Charles B, 1948, D 3,25:5
Dana, Charles C, 1937, Mr 16,23:5
Dana, Charles Edmond, 1914, F 3,11:6
Dana, Charles M, 1905, Ag 4,1:6
Dana, Daniel S, 1904, Ja 20,9:6
Dana, David T Mrs, 1947, My 1,25:3
Dana, David T Sr, 1951, Ja 20,15:2
Dana, Deane, 1952, N 5,27:4
Dana, Donald M, 1959, D 11,34:1
Dana, Edmund Trowbridge, 1869, Je 10,5:3
Dana, Elizabeth E, 1939, F 16,21:4
Dana, Elizabeth Opdyke, 1909, Mr 9,9:5
Dana, Everett V, 1958, O 16,37:3
Dana, Florence F Mrs, 1939, Jl 29,15:4
Dana, Frances L, 1941, F 21,19:4
Dana, Francis E, 1910, Je 25,9:5
Dana, Harold S, 1937, Mr 25,25:5
Dana, Harold W, 1943, My 10,19:5
Dana, Henry, 1921, S 6,15:5
Dana, Henry W L, 1950, Ap 28,21:1
Dana, J C, 1929, Jl 22,19:1
Dana, J D Prof, 1895, Ap 15,1:4
Dana, J W (funl, S 5,2:2), 1875, S 4,5:2
Dana, J W Ex-Gov, 1868, Mr 2,5:5
Dana, James D, 1951, D 3,31:2
Dana, Julius, 1906, N 1,9:4
Dana, Leslie, 1955, Ja 5,23:1
Dana, Lucien B, 1956, S 15,17:4
Dana, Mabel B, 1949, S 13,29:2
Dana, Mabelle A, 1949, Je 8,29:2
Dana, Malcolm, 1940, Ag 18,37:2
Dana, Marie L, 1946, D 12,29:2
Dana, Myer, 1944, Je 10,15:3
Dana, Norman P, 1949, Je 14,31:2
Dana, P, 1930, Ap 8,29:1
Dana, Paul Mrs, 1922, F 17,15:5
Dana, Phil, 1954, F 8,23:5
Dana, R Bingham, 1961, Ap 19,39:4
Dana, R Bingham Mrs, 1968, Ja 28,76:4
Dana, R H, 1879, F 4,4:7; 1931, D 17,23:3; 1933, N 30,33:5
Dana, R H Jr, 1882, Ja 8,7:3
Dana, Richard, 1940, S 17,23:3
Dana, Richard C, 1948, O 12,25:4
Dana, Richard Henry, 1917, Ag 9,7:2
Dana, Richard Henry Mrs, 1907, N 27,7:6; 1915, Jl 22,9:5
Dana, Richard Starr, 1904, Ja 20,9:5
Dana, Richard T Mrs, 1943, Ag 15,39:1
Dana, Ripley L, 1939, D 20,25:4
Dana, Robert K Mrs, 1945, D 27,19:4
Dana, S W, 1883, Ja 9,5:4
Dana, Samuel W Dr, 1915, S 2,9:4
Dana, Sylvester, 1910, Ja 5,11:4
Dana, William B, 1910, O 11,11:6; 1945, Ag 25,11:4
Dana, William D, 1965, Je 18,35:4
Dana, William E, 1924, My 1,19:5
Dana, William S (will, F 9,22:4), 1939, Ja 3,17:4
Dana, William S B, 1945, Jl 24,23:5
Danaher, Alice, 1955, Ja 27,23:4
Danaher, Cornelius J, 1958, Ag 2,17:4
Danaher, James E, 1947, S 5,19:2
Danaher, John T, 1951, S 22,17:3
Danaher, Mary L Mrs, 1937, O 2,21:6
Danahy, C Joseph, 1967, D 18,47:1
Danahy, Daniel J, 1952, D 11,33:2
Danahy, James W Mrs, 1954, Ag 7,13:6
Danahy, Mary J, 1949, Ag 2,19:2
Danahy, Philip V, 1911, Mr 26,II,15:4
Danahy, Raymond G, 1951, Ja 31,26:4
Danbe, Felix, 1921, Jl 17,22:4
Danbury, Frank J, 1952, Mr 7,23:3
Danbury, George, 1908, Ja 17,9:6
Danby, Frank, 1916, Mr 18,11:3
Danby, Grover Cleveland, 1919, Mr 15,15:2
Dancak, Michael J Mrs, 1954, O 13,31:4
Dance, Jack, 1959, Ap 13,31:5
Dance, Jane Mrs, 1955, F 27,87:2
Dancer, H M, 1958, N 25,33:3
Dancer, Herbert A, 1959, Je 21,92:7
Dancey, Charles E, 1955, Ap 11,23:5
Dancey, Stanley N, 1945, Je 28,19:4
Danchenko, Mikhail, 1956, Ap 13,25:5
Dancig, Edward, 1948, Ap 21,27:4
Danco, Pierre, 1946, S 20,31:4
D'Ancona, Edward N, 1937, D 20,27:3
D'Ancre, Alfred, 1874, Ag 10,1:3
Dancy, Jasper, 1947, Jl 29,21:3
Dancy, Samuel, 1938, D 23,19:3
Dandaneau, George E, 1952, F 11,25:4
Dandelet, Thomas E, 1950, Mr 31,31:4
Dando, Frederick L, 1958, Jl 13,68:7
Dando, William S, 1953, Jl 16,21:2
Dandolos, Nicholas A (Nick the Greek), 1966, D 27, 35:1
D'Andrade, Joseph, 1949, Ag 2,20:6
D'Andre, Victor, 1944, F 8,15:2
D'Andrea, Cecile, 1953, Ag 27,25:4
D'Andrea, Daniel, 1945, S 8,15:6
D'Andrea, Mark, 1967, Ap 13,43:4
Dandreau, John L Mrs, 1964, Je 14,84:6
D'Andria, Carlo C, 1952, N 11,29:1
Dandridge, Dorothy (will, O 21,58:1), 1965, S 9,41:1
Dandridge, Edmund P, 1961, F 2,29:2
Dandridge, Edmund P Mrs, 1951, D 12,37:3
Dandridge, Philip Mrs, 1909, Jl 26,7:6
Dandrow, C George Mrs, 1961, S 3,61:1
Dandurand, Damase Father, 1921, Ap 14,13:4
Dandurand, Francis X Mrs, 1940, Ap 1,19:3
Dandurand, Leo, 1964, Je 27,25:3
Dandurand, Raoul, 1942, Mr 12,19:5
Dandurand, Thomas L, 1943, F 16,19:4
Dandy, George B Gen, 1911, Ja 15,13:4
Dandy, Jess (funl, Ap 19,19:5), 1923, Ap 16,17:5
Dandy, Walter E, 1946, Ap 20,13:1
Dane, Charles, 1962, O 10,47:1
Dane, Charles W, 1944, Jl 4,19:3
Dane, Chester L, 1953, O 31,17:3
Dane, Chester L Mrs, 1961, Jl 28,21:2
Dane, Clemence, 1965, Mr 29,33:2
Dane, Earl B, 1948, Ap 18,68:4
Dane, Eli, 1951, Je 29,21:3
Dane, Ernest B, 1942, Ap 6,15:3
Dane, Ernest B Mrs, 1949, D 23,22:2
Dane, Essex, 1962, Jl 23,21:3
Dane, Fabian, 1966, My 9,39:2
Dane, John, 1966, Je 27,35:3
Dane, John Jr, 1916, S 2,7:3
Dane, William F, 1949, Ja 9,73:2
Dane, William H 3d, 1961, Jl 13,29:4
Dane, William Mrs, 1924, Ap 29,17:2
Dane-Dworecki, Walter H, 1955, My 21,17:3
Danecour, Pierre, 1940, Jl 29,13:4
Danehy, Paul E, 1950, Ap 17,23:4
Danehy, Thomas J, 1942, Je 1,13:5; 1959, O 10,21:2
Danekind, A C, 1961, S 11,27:1
Danenhower, Mary S Mrs, 1962, Mr 31,25:5
Danenhower, Sloan (cor, N 9,47:4), 1967, N 2,47:2
Daner, William A, 1940, Ap 30,21:4
Danes, Clarence W, 1956, Ja 3,31:1
Danes, Gibson A Mrs, 1964, Ja 8,37:3
Daneski, Teofil T, 1961, D 21,27:1
Danford, Faw W, 1937, Je 22,23:5
Danford, Joseph W Mrs, 1938, Mr 3,21:2
Danford, William B, 1951, Je 10,92:4
Danfort, Ralph E, 1961, S 10,87:1
Danforth, Charles, 1876, Mr 23,2:4; 1914, Ag 10,7:4
Danforth, Charles E, 1923, Mr 29,19:5
Danforth, Charles R, 1956, N 17,21:3
Danforth, Ed, 1962, D 6,43:1
Danforth, Edward, 1964, O 27,39:4
Danforth, Edward M, 1953, O 14,29:5
Danforth, Elliot, 1906, Ja 8,9:3
Danforth, Francis J, 1950, My 3,29:5
Danforth, G E, 1881, Ap 23,5:4
Danforth, George Henry, 1923, Je 29,17:2
Danforth, Harold R, 1961, O 2,31:2
Danforth, Henry G, 1918, Ap 9,13:4
Danforth, Herbert C, 1953, S 10,25:3
Danforth, Herman W, 1949, O 9,92:4
Danforth, Joseph W, 1942, Mr 29,45:2
Danforth, Kate Black Mrs, 1920, Jl 16,11:4
Danforth, Loomis Le Grand Dr, 1921, N 9,15:5
Danforth, Mary S Dr, 1937, Ag 8,II,6:3
Danforth, Murray S, 1943, Je 6,42:7
Danforth, Nicholas, 1959, D 8,45:1
Danforth, Richard E, 1945, Je 6,21:4
Danforth, Richard S, 1962, Mr 29,33:3
Danforth, Stuart T, 1938, N 27,48:6
Danforth, Walter A, 1948, Jl 5,15:2
Danforth, William, 1941, Ap 17,23:1
Danforth, William C, 1949, N 13,92:7
Danforth, William E, 1942, My 25,15:5
Danforth, William H, 1955, D 25,48:7; 1964, O 27,39:3
Dangan, Annette Viscountess, 1959, O 30,2:8
D'Angelico, John, 1964, S 3,29:2
d'Angelo, Aristide, 1960, D 17,23:5
D'Angelo, Caroline Mrs, 1944, Ja 20,19:2
D'Angelo, Louis, 1958, Ag 10,94:1
D'Angelo, Louis Mrs, 1956, Ag 28,27:1
D'Angelo, Mark, 1951, Je 12,29:4
Dangerfield, Benjamin M, 1968, Je 18,47:2
Dangerfield, E, 1932, O 23,37:1
Dangerfield, James, 1941, Ap 24,21:3
D'Angiola, Domenico, 1956, Mr 17,19:5
Danglade, Frank J, 1959, My 26,35:4
Dangler, Benjamin F, 1943, D 31,16:6
Dangler, David E, 1939, N 18,17:5
Dangler, Edward, 1962, Ja 26,31:2
Dangler, Jacob, 1939, F 12,45:2
Dangler, Katie Mrs, 1949, Ag 21,69:2
Danglis, Panyotis Gen, 1924, Mr 10,15:4
Danglow, Jacob, 1962, My 24,35:3
Dangremond, Arthur C V, 1945, D 14,28:2
Dangremond, George C, 1950, Mr 26,92:8
Danguy, Jean L, 1940, Mr 21,25:4
Danhauer, Edward, 1953, Ja 30,17:2
Danheiser, Benjamin, 1946, O 23,27:1
Danheiser, Theodore, 1943, N 16,23:1
Danhof, Ralph H, 1942, F 25,19:1
Daniel, Annie S, 1944, Ag 11,15:6
Daniel, Augustus M, 1950, N 10,28:4
Daniel, Billy, 1962, My 18,31:2
Daniel, Channing W, 1950, Ja 10,29:4
Daniel, Charles D, 1943, F 19,19:2
Daniel, Charles E, 1964, S 14,33:2
Daniel, David R, 1967, Mr 24,31:5
Daniel, Elbert Clifton, 1968, My 1,47:3
Daniel, Eve B Mrs, 1965, N 21,87:1
Daniel, Frank J, 1949, O 26,27:4
Daniel, George, 1961, Ja 19,29:5
Daniel, Greta, 1962, Je 10,86:6
Daniel, Hector, 1953, D 29,6:3
Daniel, Herman, 1959, Je 1,27:5
Daniel, J M, 1865, Ap 7,4:5
Daniel, John, 1938, N 2,23:3; 1950, Mr 3,25:3
Daniel, John F, 1942, N 3,23:2
Daniel, John F 3d, 1948, D 19,76:3
Daniel, John W Sen, 1910, Je 30,7:5
Daniel, Leon Mrs, 1964, N 24,39:1
Daniel, Lewis C, 1952, Jl 20,39:3
Daniel, Nannie P Mrs, 1955, N 28,31:1
Daniel, R T, 1877, Ag 17,4:6
Daniel, Richard T, 1949, Ap 20,27:3
Daniel, Robert Prentiss Dr, 1968, Ja 9,43:3
Daniel, Robert W, 1940, D 21,17:3
Daniel, Royal, 1939, Je 19,15:6
Daniel, Royal Mrs, 1958, Ap 18,23:3
Daniel, Samuel Dr, 1937, Jl 21,21:4
Daniel, Thomas H, 1952, Ja 18,27:5
Daniel, Todd, 1953, Ag 18,23:2
Daniel, Victor (Chief Thundercloud), 1955, D 3,17:6
Daniel-Rops, Henri (H J C Petiot), 1965, Jl 28,35:1
Daniele, Anthony H, 1961, My 19,31:2
Daniell, George J, 1908, Je 26,7:5
Daniell, George J Jr, 1956, Ja 9,25:1
Daniell, George J Mrs, 1941, F 11,23:5
Daniell, George Sr Mrs, 1945, Ap 24,19:6
Daniell, Griswold B, 1957, N 3,88:3
Daniell, Henry, 1963, N 1,33:1
Daniell, John, 1902, Mr 7,9:5
Daniell, John F, 1950, Mr 8,27:2
Daniell, John R, 1961, F 26,92:8
Daniell, Lucetta, 1943, N 6,13:4
Daniell, Madge, 1950, Ap 2,93:1
Daniell, Russell, 1911, Je 25,11:4
Daniell, Theodore F, 1960, O 15,23:6
Daniell, W J Rev, 1881, Je 15,5:2
Daniells, E S, 1960, Jl 20,29:5
Daniels, Aaron W, 1959, Je 4,31:5
Daniels, Abe, 1954, Je 26,13:6
Daniels, Alfred C, 1947, S 5,19:4
Daniels, Allan J, 1961, F 15,35:4
Daniels, Amy L, 1965, F 2,33:3
Daniels, Archibald L, 1962, F 11,87:1
Daniels, Arthur B, 1938, Mr 6,II,8:3
Daniels, Arthur H, 1940, Ap 3,23:3
Daniels, Arthur M, 1961, D 7,43:3
Daniels, Benjamin, 1957, Jl 4,19:1
Daniels, Bertram E, 1958, Je 8,88:8
Daniels, Bolivia B Judge, 1874, Mr 2,5:3
Daniels, Carroll S, 1949, Ag 29,17:4
Daniels, Charles C, 1951, Mr 21,33:2
Daniels, Charles F, 1954, D 9,33:1
Daniels, Charles H, 1942, Mr 5,23:2
Daniels, Charles N, 1943, Ja 24,42:3
Daniels, Charles W, 1959, F 1,85:1
Daniels, Clarence E, 1949, O 15,15:1
Daniels, David Mrs, 1952, O 23,31:5
Daniels, De W C, 1878, S 2,8:2
Daniels, Earle M, 1959, Je 25,29:1
Daniels, Edward G, 1946, D 30,19:5
Daniels, Edwin N, 1943, Mr 27,14:7
Daniels, Effie S Mrs, 1937, My 29,17:2
Daniels, Ellen H Mrs, 1962, Mr 4,86:8
Daniels, Elliott L, 1963, S 24,27:5
Daniels, Eugene Delos Mrs, 1904, N 27,7:6
Daniels, Flora M, 1953, N 28,15:5
Daniels, Forrest L, 1967, Jl 18,37:4
Daniels, Frank A, 1939, Ap 16,III,7:1
Daniels, Frank Herbert Dr, 1915, O 31,7:4
Daniels, Fred C, 1960, Je 4,23:5
Daniels, Fred H, 1913, S 1,5:4
Daniels, Frederick H, 1959, Ag 30,82:6
Daniels, George A, 1948, My 8,15:6
Daniels, George E, 1954, Mr 26,22:3
Daniels, George H, 1908, Jl 2,9:6; 1908, Jl 3,7:4
Daniels, George H Jr, 1953, S 15,31:3
Daniels, George P Mrs, 1949, N 23,29:4
Daniels, George W, 1943, Je 30,21:5
Daniels, Harold E, 1964, F 9,89:1
Daniels, Harold G, 1952, My 24,19:6
Daniels, Harold P, 1946, Jl 3,25:5
Daniels, Harriet McD, 1959, Je 4,31:4
Daniels, Harry, 1946, D 20,23:2
Daniels, Harry C, 1955, O 26,31:5; 1965, F 22,21:4
Daniels, Henry H, 1958, Mr 7,24:1

Daniels, Henry Mrs, 1952, My 12,25:4; 1958, Ag 28, 27:2
Daniels, Isaac, 1864, Jl 1,8:4
Daniels, James Mrs, 1949, D 9,31:2
Daniels, James R, 1961, Je 20,33:4
Daniels, James T, 1953, Ja 3,15:5
Daniels, Jay M, 1957, N 15,27:3
Daniels, John, 1953, F 19,23:1
Daniels, John Horton Jr, 1968, Je 27,43:4
Daniels, John T, 1948, F 1,60:5
Daniels, Johnny, 1952, My 8,31:2
Daniels, Josephus, 1948, Ja 16,17:1
Daniels, Josephus Jr, 1964, F 16,92:5
Daniels, Josephus Mrs, 1943, D 20,23:1
Daniels, Josiah R Rev Dr, 1908, Ag 23,9:6
Daniels, Lee H, 1949, N 22,29:5
Daniels, Leon E, 1945, Mr 17,13:6
Daniels, Lester, 1942, D 27,19:2
Daniels, Lewis J, 1939, S 21,23:1
Daniels, Lloyd C, 1948, Ap 23,23:3
Daniels, Lorenzo Mrs, 1925, D 19,17:5
Daniels, Louis, 1961, Je 7,41:3
Daniels, Marc, 1953, Mr 5,27:2
Daniels, Maria L, 1945, My 8,19:3
Daniels, Mary S, 1950, S 21,31:4
Daniels, Milton B, 1942, D 14,23:2
Daniels, Monroe H Mrs, 1960, D 2,29:4
Daniels, Morris S Jr, 1938, Ag 11,17:3
Daniels, Oscar, 1939, Ap 15,19:4
Daniels, Percy, 1951, Ja 19,25:4
Daniels, Phyllis Mrs, 1959, F 22,88:3
Daniels, Ruel E, 1956, N 13,37:2
Daniels, Rupert B, 1958, N 15,23:5
Daniels, Sarah A Mrs, 1938, Jl 24,29:3
Daniels, Stanley A, 1952, Jl 10,31:3
Daniels, Theodore L, 1965, F 9,37:3
Daniels, Thomas C, 1946, N 5,25:3
Daniels, Vincent, 1945, D 7,21:4
Daniels, Vincent H, 1963, S 6,30:1
Daniels, Walter M, 1958, Ap 5,15:3
Daniels, Warren, 1963, Jl 22,23:4
Daniels, William, 1939, Ag 11,15:3
Daniels, William Cook, 1918, Mr 19,11:7
Daniels, William S, 1949, Ap 26,25:5
Daniels, William T, 1947, My 1,25:3
Daniels, Winfield Mrs, 1959, Je 23,33:1
Daniels, Winthrop M, 1944, Ja 4,17:1
Daniels, Wylie J, 1951, O 5,28:2
Danielson, Adolph, 1940, My 5,52:2
Danielson, Charles E, 1965, Ag 7,21:4
Danielson, Christian P, 1918, Je 10,11:8
Danielson, Clarence H, 1952, My 23,21:2
Danielson, De Forest, 1909, O 19,9:4
Danielson, G Anton, 1939, D 10,68:2
Danielson, G W, 1884, Mr 26,5:4
Danielson, Jacques (est tax appr filed), 1956, Mr 1, 22:6
Danielson, Jacques S, 1952, Mr 4,27:4
Danielson, John P, 1940, O 25,21:2
Danielson, John Weaver, 1913, Ag 10,II,11:5
Danielson, Paul A, 1966, My 21,31:4
Danielson, Reuben G, 1950, Ap 17,23:4
Danielson, Richard E, 1957, My 25,21:3
Danielson, Whitman, 1952, Ja 20,85:2
Danielson, Wilmot A, 1966, Mr 5,27:3
Danihy, John Mrs, 1947, O 16,27:3
Danilchenko, Nicholas, 1957, Ap 8,23:4
Danill, Robert T Judge, 1915, My 28,13:6
Daniloff, Alex, 1960, O 31,31:5
Daniloff, Serge Mrs, 1959, D 10,39:4
Danilov, Nikolai, 1966, S 15,43:6
Danilow, Abraham, 1948, Je 6,19:5
Daniman, Boris R, 1957, O 9,8:4
Danin, Victoria, 1967, O 16,45:2
Daning, Maurice J, 1954, Je 30,27:4
Danish, Hyman, 1967, My 20,35:4
Danish, Max D, 1964, Ja 12,92:6
Danjon, Andre, 1967, Ap 22,31:6
Danjou, Henri, 1954, Ja 11,25:1
Dank, David, 1951, Ag 24,15:4
Dank, Hart Pease, 1903, N 21,1:4
Dankel, Harold C, 1955, Jl 20,27:3
Dankel, Nathaniel S, 1945, Mr 13,23:5
Dankel, Roy E, 1953, F 8,88:2
Danker, Daniel, 1944, Jl 7,15:2
Danker, Frederick H Mrs, 1944, Je 2,15:3
Danker, George, 1957, Ag 30,19:5
Danker, Harry T, 1967, S 25,45:1
Dankmeyer, C L, 1946, Jl 27,17:6
Danks, Alden J, 1946, S 22,63:4
Danly, Ernest E, 1950, S 30,17:6
Danmeyer, Henry B, 1963, My 7,43:4
Dann, Edward H, 1938, Mr 21,15:4
Dann, George J, 1954, F 8,23:3
Dann, George L, 1943, N 19,19:2
Dann, George Mrs, 1949, Ap 5,29:4
Dann, Hollis E, 1939, Ja 4,21:1
Dann, James E, 1951, Ag 28,23:3
Dann, James E Mrs, 1943, Je 15,21:4
Dann, Mary A Mrs, 1940, O 12,17:5
Dann, Mary E Mrs, 1938, My 31,19:4
Dann, Nicholas Robert Dr, 1925, Je 23,19:4
Dann, Percy George, 1968, Mr 24,92:8
Dann, Robert H, 1967, N 24,46:8
Dann, Roger L, 1953, D 14,31:5
Dann, W Carlton, 1947, Jl 4,13:4
Dann, William J, 1948, D 6,25:4
D'Anna, Carmine A, 1950, O 5,31:4
Dannals, Pier, 1944, D 20,23:2
Dannals, Susan M, 1947, F 25,25:4
Dannay, Frederick Mrs, 1945, Jl 5,13:5
Danne, Frederick M D, 1905, Mr 28,9:6
Dannefelser, John P, 1944, Ap 8,13:5
Danneman, Joseph, 1947, Mr 22,13:4
Dannemiller, Augustus F, 1952, N 23,88:4
Dannemiller, Edward, 1939, F 28,19:4
Dannenbaum, Alex W, 1954, D 23,19:3
Dannenbaum, Alexander W Jr Mrs, 1965, N 25,35:4
Dannenbaum, Edwin M, 1940, F 18,41:3
Dannenbaum, Edwin M Mrs, 1948, Ag 26,21:4
Dannenbaum, Harry M, 1938, S 18,44:8
Dannenbaum, Walter, 1967, My 13,33:3
Dannenberg, Frederick M, 1966, S 7,41:3
Dannenberg, Mannie, 1937, My 15,19:5
Dannenberg, Max, 1960, Jl 1,25:5
Dannenberg, Oscar A H, 1950, Mr 9,29:4
Dannenberg, William C, 1955, Ag 11,21:5
Dannenfelser, Phil H, 1956, S 25,33:4
Dannenhauer, Christian W, 1947, D 18,30:3
Danner, Aaron Mrs, 1938, Je 6,17:3
Danner, Edgar W, 1951, O 6,19:5
Danner, Harry E Mrs, 1945, O 10,36:3
Danner, Joseph H, 1941, My 7,25:3
Danner, Louis R Mrs, 1943, S 28,25:1
Danner, Paul R, 1957, F 8,23:3
Danner, Paul R Mrs, 1955, N 9,33:5
Danner, William M, 1952, N 15,17:5
Danner, William M Jr, 1946, D 21,19:2
Dannreuther, Walter T, 1960, Ja 28,31:5
D'Annunzio, Gabriel, 1945, D 9,44:6
D'Annunzio, Gabriele Mrs, 1954, Ja 19,25:1
D'Annunzio, Lola (trb lr, Je 10,II,3:7), 1956, Je 5,39:2
D'Annunzio, Ugo V, 1945, Ja 18,19:3
Danowski, Charles, 1946, D 12,29:3
Danquah, Joseph B, 1965, F 5,31:4
Dansen, Benjamin, 1938, My 28,15:4
Danser, Benedictus H, 1943, N 9,21:1
Danser, Frank C, 1942, Jl 23,19:6
Danser, Jacob S, 1951, Ag 15,27:3
Danser, John, 1949, Ap 7,30:2
Dansereau, J Honore, 1962, My 18,31:5
Dansey, Claude E M, 1947, Je 13,23:4
Dansey, Herbert, 1917, My 31,11:6
Dant, Charles, 1945, My 22,19:6
Dant, George W, 1943, Ap 26,19:6
Dant, Joseph B, 1939, D 3,60:4
D'Antalffy, Dezso, 1945, My 2,23:3
Dantas, Francisco San T, 1964, S 7,19:4
Dantas, Julio, 1962, My 26,25:4
Dantas, Orlando R, 1953, F 2,21:6
Dante, Enrico (Cardinal), 1967, Ap 24,33:4
Dante, Frank, 1954, Ja 30,29:8
Dante, James J, 1951, S 26,31:2
Danton, George H, 1962, Mr 14,39:1
D'Antoni, Salvador, 1957, Ja 4,23:2
Dantz, Nicholas, 1953, N 27,27:1
Dantzig, Eli, 1968, Jl 10,39:4
Dantzig, Tobias, 1956, Ag 11,13:6
Dantzscher, Walter F, 1956, Jl 14,15:4
Danucci, Henry, 1943, My 28,21:4
Danvier, John Mrs, 1947, Ja 9,23:4
Danyovsky, Stephen J, 1947, Je 10,27:5
Danz, Arnold P, 1957, N 24,86:4
Danz, Robert A, 1949, D 14,31:3
Danzak, Andrew, 1957, O 30,29:2
Danzberger, G Harris Mrs, 1961, O 24,37:2
Danze, Michael, 1956, Je 10,89:1
Danzenbaker, William H, 1948, O 19,27:3
Danzer, Charles S, 1950, Ja 20,25:2
Danzer, Mortimer, 1956, S 7,23:4
Danzig, Aaron L Mrs, 1954, Mr 13,15:6
Danzig, Alfred, 1956, Ag 18,17:2
Danzig, George H, 1940, Je 18,23:4
Danzig, Jerome J, 1946, Ja 13,44:2
Danzig, Jerome J Mrs, 1941, D 15,19:4
Danzig, Louis, 1951, Ja 25,25:3
Danzig, Morris, 1940, D 8,69:2
Danzig, Morris Mrs, 1957, D 31,17:1
Danziger, Abraham L, 1949, Ag 28,75:3
Danziger, Arthur W, 1937, Ag 8,II,7:2
Danziger, Berthold Mrs, 1967, O 10,47:2
Danziger, Charles, 1940, Jl 31,17:2
Danziger, Charles W, 1944, F 27,38:4
Danziger, Juliet, 1948, Je 25,23:4
Danziger, Leroy, 1966, Ja 1,17:5
Danziger, Max, 1905, N 15,13:6
Danziger, Seamon, 1940, S 2,15:4
Danzis, Max, 1953, O 22,29:3
Danzis, Max Mrs, 1946, Mr 14,25:3
Danzis, Mordecia, 1952, Ag 16,16:3
Daoud, Pasha, 1873, N 10,1:3
Daouphars, Lucie, 1963, Jl 18,27:5
Daoust, Joseph, 1946, Ag 8,21:5
D'Apolito, Alfred, 1965, N 19,39:4
Dapp, Charles, 1956, Ap 18,31:5
Dapp, Charles F, 1952, S 10,29:5
Dapples, Louis Dr, 1937, Ag 4,19:3
Daragon, Michael, 1953, N 8,88:5
Darahona, Luis Alonzo Gen, 1915, O 21,11:5
Daraji, Abdel L, 1966, Ap 14,1:1
Daranyi, Koloman, 1939, N 2,23:4
Darb, James R, 1943, Mr 25,21:4
Darbaker, Isaac K, 1941, Mr 2,9:1
Darbee, Edgar, 1907, Jl 25,7:6
Darbee, Robert S Mrs, 1944, Ja 14,19:4
Darbee, William, 1958, My 23,23:1
Darbelles, Julio, 1948, N 24,76:1
Darber, Robert S, 1947, Je 17,28:3
Darbey, William J Dr, 1913, Jl 28,7:6
Darblay, N F A, 1873, S 18,4:6
Darbois, Paul, 1943, Je 24,21:1
Darboy, Archbishop, 1871, My 29,1:6
Darby, Ada C, 1953, D 23,25:5
Darby, Arleigh L, 1956, My 6,86:6
Darby, Arthur E, 1942, S 12,13:6
Darby, Azel H, 1959, O 13,39:1
Darby, Benjamin E, 1939, O 12,25:5
Darby, David M, 1940, Mr 21,25:6
Darby, Elston Mrs, 1952, Je 11,29:2
Darby, Francis M, 1903, N 11,9:6
Darby, George A, 1940, S 2,15:6
Darby, George D B, 1947, N 7,23:4
Darby, George Mrs, 1963, N 23,29:2
Darby, Harry B, 1951, Ja 6,15:5
Darby, Henry R, 1946, Ap 23,21:4
Darby, Henry S, 1940, Ap 25,23:5
Darby, J Branch Mrs, 1944, Ap 28,19:2
Darby, J G, 1881, Ap 27,5:5
Darby, J T, 1879, Je 11,5:3
Darby, James B, 1950, N 18,15:6
Darby, John B, 1952, O 24,23:1
Darby, John F, 1953, Mr 1,92:8
Darby, John H, 1947, Ja 3,22:3
Darby, Lambert, 1951, Mr 28,29:2
Darby, Louis Mrs, 1961, Ja 3,29:3
Darby, Michael, 1958, Ag 8,19:1
Darby, Myron G, 1963, S 26,35:1
Darby, Norman A, 1947, O 8,25:4
Darby, Raymond V, 1953, Mr 6,30:4
Darby, Samuel E Jr, 1947, D 7,76:5
Darby, Thomas A, 1908, Jl 11,7:6
Darby, Walter G, 1946, Jl 30,23:4
Darby, Walter R Mrs, 1953, My 24,89:1
Darby, William, 1955, My 15,86:5
Darby, William D, 1947, O 21,24:3; 1950, O 23,23:4; 1966, Jl 30,25:3
Darby, William J, 1953, Mr 17,29:2
Darby, William Mrs, 1950, Je 3,15:5
Darbyshire, James, 1959, F 10,26:4
Darbyshire, John R, 1948, Jl 1,23:5
Darcey, James H, 1964, F 14,29:2
Darcey, Joe (Jos D O'Donnell), 1963, Ag 23,25:1
Darch, Herbert, 1954, F 5,19:3
Darch, John F, 1947, My 27,25:1
Darche, Harris A Dr, 1937, Ap 17,17:1
Darche, Irving, 1940, My 19,42:4
D'Arcis, Clara G Mrs, 1937, My 14,23:1
D'Arcus, Horace Mrs, 1962, Ag 25,19:4
D'Arcy, Augustine F, 1953, Ja 9,21:2
D'Arcy, Charles F (por), 1938, F 2,19:4
D'Arcy, Hugh Antoine, 1925, N 12,25:5
d'Arcy, Jack Lewis, 1922, Jl 8,11:6
Darcy, James S, 1938, My 13,19:6; 1947, F 25,25:3
Darcy, John, 1943, N 5,19:1
D'Arcy, John M, 1939, D 25,23:2
Darcy, Joseph W, 1949, O 22,17:1
D'Arcy, Kathleen M, 1963, D 23,25:2
Darcy, Lucie L, 1961, Je 30,25:2
D'Arcy, Mark, 1938, Mr 7,17:2
Darcy, Patrick J, 1951, Mr 24,13:3; 1967, O 17,15:1
Darcy, Rowland W, 1955, D 7,39:4
D'Arcy, Ruth, 1948, N 11,27:5
D'Arcy, Thomas, 1941, D 18,27:5; 1953, Mr 24,31:2
Darcy, Thomas F Capt, 1911, D 7,13:4
Darcy, Thomas F Jr Capt, 1968, My 20,47:3
D'Arcy, Thomas J Mrs, 1945, O 18,23:6
D'Arcy, William C, 1948, Jl 22,23:6
Darcy, William J, 1948, Ja 1,23:2; 1959, D 20,60:7
Dardel, Nils de, 1943, My 26,23:5
Darden, Colgate W Sr, 1945, My 8,34:5
Darden, J M, 1937, Je 1,23:6
Darden, Lawrence E, 1925, Jl 29,21:6
Darden, Thomas F, 1943, F 26,19:3
Dardenne, Victor H, 1968, Jl 18,33:4
Dardier, Henri Mrs (E Chapel), 1964, Ap 25,29:4
Dare, Clarence E, 1952, N 26,23:5
Dare, Frank R, 1951, Ap 28,15:6
Dare, Helen, 1943, Mr 16,19:2
Dare, Henry M B, 1942, Mr 23,15:1
Dare, Leona, 1922, My 25,19:4
Dare, Maurice E, 1968, S 7,29:3
Dare, Rebecca G Mrs, 1939, N 17,21:4
Dare, William H Capt, 1909, Mr 17,9:2
Daresbury, Baron, 1938, O 25,23:3
Darewski, Edouard, 1920, N 7,22:5
Darewski, Herman, 1947, Je 3,26:2
Dargan, Edwin P, 1940, D 14,17:3
Dargan, James A, 1945, S 11,23:6
Dargan, Olive Tilford, 1968, Ja 24,45:1

Dargan, William R, 1939, O 24,23:5
Dargel, Edward, 1954, Ja 15,19:2
Dargis, Andrew J Sr, 1948, Ja 27,25:3
Dargue, Herbert A Mrs, 1943, S 21,24:2
Dariff, George, 1967, N 28,47:1
Dario, Ruben, 1916, F 8,11:3
Darius, Charles A, 1957, Jl 5,17:1
Darius, Henry A (cor, Ja 31,27:2), 1964, Ja 24,27:4
Dark, Daniel Mrs, 1946, My 1,25:3
Dark, Sidney, 1947, O 12,76:7
Darkcloud, Bessie, 1909, S 18,9:5
Darke, B Danby, 1942, O 15,23:2
Darkenwald, Gordon G, 1961, Jl 6,29:4
Darlan, John L X F Mme, 1950, Mr 5,92:5
Darley, Grace, 1903, Ag 14,7:6
Darling, A B Mrs, 1903, Mr 1,7:5
Darling, Alex P Mrs, 1957, F 13,35:3
Darling, C L, 1878, S 12,8:4
Darling, C W Gen, 1905, Je 23,7:6
Darling, Carolyn, 1959, Jl 5,56:1
Darling, Charles, 1942, My 6,19:1
Darling, Charles B, 1948, Ap 20,27:5
Darling, Charles E, 1941, F 15,15:2
Darling, Charles H, 1944, N 1,23:4
Darling, Chester A, 1937, F 22,17:5
Darling, Dore H Mrs, 1948, Je 14,23:2
Darling, Edward V, 1951, Jl 30,17:3
Darling, Everett F, 1938, My 11,19:2
Darling, F J, 1878, Mr 11,8:6
Darling, Flora Adams Mrs, 1910, Ja 7,9:3
Darling, Fred, 1953, Je 10,32:2
Darling, Frederick R, 1942, S 11,21:1
Darling, George, 1948, S 12,74:3
Darling, Grace, 1955, Jl 19,27:4
Darling, Hale K, 1940, S 19,23:4
Darling, Harold, 1950, Ja 27,23:3
Darling, Harry R, 1952, Ap 10,29:4
Darling, Henry M, 1960, O 19,45:1
Darling, Ira A, 1941, O 12,53:2
Darling, Ivan L, 1961, Ap 9,86:5
Darling, Ivan L Mrs, 1952, Mr 26,29:1
Darling, James, 1958, My 31,15:4
Darling, James J, 1952, N 11,29:3
Darling, James J Mrs, 1960, F 17,35:1
Darling, James S, 1951, D 27,21:5
Darling, Jay N (Ding), 1962, F 13,27:2
Darling, John A, 1948, Ag 29,56:4
Darling, John A Lt-Col, 1912, D 5,17:5
Darling, Joseph R, 1957, S 7,19:4
Darling, Joseph R M Mrs, 1949, My 9,25:3
Darling, L, 1878, Ap 30,5:2
Darling, Leon I, 1947, Mr 6,25:1
Darling, Lonnie, 1951, Ap 20,30:8
Darling, Lord, 1936, My 30,15:2
Darling, Nelson J, 1942, O 27,25:5
Darling, Robert E, 1948, D 16,29:3
Darling, Robert J, 1956, Mr 11,88:3
Darling, Ruel S, 1940, O 28,17:3
Darling, Samuel B, 1948, Je 3,25:3
Darling, Samuel Taylor, 1925, Jl 1,23:4
Darling, Samuel Taylor Dr, 1925, My 23,15:6
Darling, Theodore S, 1913, Je 15,IV,5:5
Darling, Thomas, 1909, Ja 24,11:5
Darling, Thomas E D, 1951, O 20,15:7
Darling, Verne E, 1950, N 25,13:3
Darling, Willard S, 1943, Ap 9,21:2
Darling, William, 1943, Ap 25,35:2
Darling, William B, 1950, O 31,27:2
Darling, William C, 1938, Jl 24,29:4
arling, William Dr, 1884, D 26,5:4
arling, William W, 1951, Ag 19,85:2
arlington, Charles F, 1938, D 29,20:3; 1939, Ja 1,25:2
arlington, Charles G, 1960, N 6,88:6
arlington, Clinton P, 1952, F 21,27:1
arlington, Dorothea, 1947, My 13,25:2
arlington, E L B Mrs, 1933, Je 3,13:4
arlington, Elliott C B, 1950, My 3,29:4
arlington, Emlen, 1950, Ag 12,13:3
arlington, Emlen Mrs, 1951, D 28,21:3
arlington, Frederic W, 1947, Jl 25,18:2
arlington, Frederick, 1943, O 28,23:3
arlington, Gustavus C, 1943, Jl 29,19:5
arlington, Harry, 1914, S 28,9:3
arlington, Hart, 1966, O 23,88:2
arlington, Henry V B, 1955, D 21,29:1
arlington, Herbert S Mrs, 1967, S 2,25:6
arlington, Horace H, 1947, D 18,30:3
arlington, Isaac G, 1956, O 12,29:4
arlington, Isabel, 1950, Je 25,70:1
rlington, J H, 1930, Ag 15,17:1
rlington, Joseph G, 1908, Mr 19,7:5
rlington, Letitia C Mrs, 1944, S 21,19:4
rlington, Mary W B Mrs, 1940, F 20,21:4
rlington, Morton P, 1945, N 4,44:2
rlington, Percy S, 1949, My 17,25:5
rlington, Richard, 1954, Mr 3,27:1
rlington, Thomas, 1903, My 20,9:4; 1945, Ag 24,
9:1
rlington, Thomas D Mrs, 1946, N 29,25:4
rlington, U V W, 1954, O 2,17:3
rlington, Walter, 1955, Ja 4,21:2
rlington, Wayne, 1942, O 22,21:2
rlow, Tom, 1939, N 11,15:5

Darmasetiawan, Dr, 1953, Mr 10,29:4
Darmour, L J, 1942, Mr 18,23:5
Darmstadt, Louis J Mrs, 1960, Ja 15,5:2
Darmstadt, Louis Mrs, 1956, Ag 3,19:3
Darmstatter, Norman D, 1937, Mr 24,25:1
Darnall, Carl R, 1941, Ja 19,40:3
Darnall, John P, 1952, Jl 7,21:3
Darnall, William E Dr, 1937, D 28,21:2
Darnbacher, Fritz, 1958, Jl 3,25:5
Darnbrough, Arthur, 1939, My 9,24:4
Darnell, Albert H, 1952, Ag 26,25:4
Darnell, Grace L, 1953, Je 4,29:2
Darnell, Howard H, 1939, Je 20,21:1
Darnell, Linda (will, My 29,27:1), 1965, Ap 11,92:5
Darnell, William J, 1951, Ja 5,21:3
Darnell, William L, 1923, S 7,15:3
Darney, Daniel, 1910, Ag 4,7:6
Darnley, C C Capt, 1865, O 22,4:2
Darnley, Earl of (E I Bligh), 1955, My 30,13:1
Darnstaedt, Louis F, 1952, Ja 30,26:3
Darnton, Byron Mrs (Eleanor), 1968, My 16,47:1
Darnton, Charles, 1950, My 21,104:4
Daroff, Charles, 1957, S 21,19:2
Daroff, Samuel H, 1967, F 15,41:1
Daron, Don M, 1960, D 26,23:5
Darosa, Jose F, 1950, N 15,31:1
Daroux, G, 1928, S 30,30:5
Darr, Earl A, 1963, O 18,31:3
Darr, Edward A, 1958, O 9,37:4
Darr, George W, 1911, Jl 6,9:5
Darr, Joseph Gen, 1904, Ja 29,9:6
Darr, Mary S Mrs, 1941, F 11,23:1
Darrach, James A, 1912, Jl 7,II,11:5
Darrach, May Dr, 1917, O 19,13:6
Darrach, William, 1948, My 25,27:1
Darragh, John H, 1950, Ja 26,28:3
Darrah, G Blaine (Oct 1), 1965, O 11,61:1
Darrah, Leon C, 1957, S 8,84:6
Darrah, Patrick, 1954, My 8,17:2
Darrah, Thomas W, 1955, Ja 22,11:1
Darraulet, Francois, 1940, Ap 24,23:5
Darre, Richard W, 1953, D 6,50:1
Darrell, Claudia, 1949, Ag 30,27:4
Darrell, Edward F, 1941, Ja 23,21:2
Darrell, John H, 1960, Ap 6,41:2
Darrigrand, Charles D, 1954, D 25,11:4
Darrin, Anthon F, 1943, Mr 28,24:6
Darrin, I G, 1931, S 10,25:5
Darrin, Laurence T, 1949, N 29,29:5
Darroch, William, 1959, Ap 25,21:1
Darrow, Ben H Mrs, 1968, Ap 2,47:4
Darrow, Benjamin H, 1950, Ja 30,17:3
Darrow, Charles B, 1967, Ag 29,37:2
Darrow, Clarence, 1938, Mr 14,15:1
Darrow, Clarence Mrs, 1957, Jl 7,61:1
Darrow, Daniel, 1953, Ja 6,29:4
Darrow, Daniel C, 1965, Je 24,35:4
Darrow, Frank T, 1950, F 28,29:2
Darrow, Frederick R, 1960, D 15,43:1
Darrow, George, 1949, S 26,25:2
Darrow, George A, 1938, O 9,44:7
Darrow, George P, 1943, Je 8,21:2
Darrow, Grover C, 1939, O 27,23:3
Darrow, Helen K Mrs, 1954, D 21,27:4
Darrow, James A, 1963, Je 9,87:2
Darrow, Jane, 1947, N 20,29:2
Darrow, John A, 1947, Ap 1,28:3
Darrow, Paul, 1956, D 21,23:3
Darrow, Whitney Mrs, 1941, Ja 3,20:2
Darrow, William D, 1956, My 11,27:1
Darrow, Wirt E, 1955, Mr 16,33:5
D'Arschot, Wlihelmina Countess, 1912, F 22,9:4
Darsie, Charles, 1948, S 25,17:2
Darsie, Darsie L, 1960, N 1,39:2
Darsie, Hugh D, 1962, Ag 9,25:2
Darsie, James A, 1957, My 14,35:3
D'Arsonval, Jacques A, 1941, Ja 1,23:1
Darst, James E Sr, 1960, Ap 27,37:2
Darst, Joseph M, 1953, Je 9,27:4
Darst, Thomas C, 1948, S 2,24:3
Dart, Anson L Mrs, 1944, Ap 20,19:6
Dart, Edward Mrs, 1913, Jl 27,II,9:4
Dart, Edward N, 1952, D 19,31:4
Dart, Frederick B, 1949, Ap 25,23:4
Dart, Frederick H, 1939, My 14,III,6:8
Dart, George W, 1951, D 12,37:3
Dart, Guy J Mrs, 1951, S 30,72:5
Dart, Harry G, 1938, N 17,25:2
Dart, John Bp, 1910, Ap 17,II,11:4
Dart, Joseph A, 1942, F 6,19:5
Dart, Joseph Mrs, 1955, Ap 11,23:5
Dart, Robert F, 1961, D 5,43:1
Dart, William A, 1942, Ap 12,45:3
Dart, William C, 1946, N 19,21:1
Darte, George L Maj, 1937, O 9,19:4
Darte, George L Mrs, 1937, Jl 23,19:5
Darton, Nelson H, 1948, Mr 4,25:5
Darts, John A, 1959, N 16,31:3
Dartt, Harry H, 1960, F 18,33:2
Dartt, James G, 1962, Ap 9,29:3
Daru, Leon, 1943, O 2,13:2
Daru, Robert, 1967, Ap 22,31:1
Darvas, Alexander Mrs, 1946, Mr 23,13:1

Darveris, N, 1946, N 27,13:5
D'Arville, C, 1932, S 11,30:3
D'Arville, Colette, 1944, D 17,38:4
Darwell, Jane, 1967, Ag 15,39:1
Darwin, Bernard, 1961, O 20,33:2
Darwin, Charles, 1963, Ja 2,4:8
Darwin, Charles R, 1882, Ap 21,5:1
Darwin, Erasmus, 1881, S 12,2:7
Darwin, Francis Sir, 1925, S 20,7:3
Darwin, George H Sir, 1912, D 8,17:5
Darwin, Joseph A O, 1955, F 24,27:3
Darwin, Lady, 1947, F 7,23:5
Darwin, Leonard, 1943, Mr 28,24:8
Darwood, William McKendree Rev Dr, 1914, Ap 28, 13:5
Daryington, Lord (H P Peas), 1949, My 11,30:7
Darzens, Rodolphe, 1938, D 30,15:3
Das, Andrew T, 1964, Je 16,39:5
Das, C R, 1925, Je 17,21:4
Das, Taraknath, 1958, D 30,35:2
Das, Taraknath (trb lr), 1959, Ja 24,18:5
Das, Taraknath Mrs, 1948, Ja 11,56:2
Das Gupta, Kedarnath, 1942, D 7,27:5
D'Ascenzo, Nicola (will, S 11,32:4), 1954, Ap 14,29:6
D'Ascenzo, Nicola Mrs, 1954, N 2,27:5
Dasch, George, 1955, Ap 14,29:4
Dascher, Louis F, 1942, My 23,13:7
Dascomb, Mary P, 1917, N 20,13:4
Dascombe, Colin H, 1952, Ap 7,25:5
Dasey, James J, 1953, Ap 12,89:2
Dash, Hugh, 1960, Je 28,31:2
Dash, William R, 1964, Ag 18,31:1
Dasheff, Nathan Mrs, 1963, O 28,27:5
Dashefsky, Joseph, 1941, Ap 18,21:4
D'Ashemar, Raoul, 1939, Ja 29,32:8
Dashew, Leon, 1943, F 1,15:1
Dashiell, A H, 1881, Mr 19,2:7
Dashiell, Alfred H Rev, 1908, F 16,11:4
Dashiell, James L, 1950, Ap 30,102:8
Dashiell, John F Mrs, 1948, My 22,15:6
Dashiell, Lefferts M, 1938, Mr 1,21:3
Dashiell, Martie Mrs, 1940, N 14,23:4
Dashiell, Paul J Capt, 1937, Jl 7,23:1
Dashiell, R L, 1880, Mr 10,5:6
Dashiell, Sam, 1949, Je 27,27:5
Dashiell, Willard, 1943, Ap 20,23:6
Dashiell, William R, 1939, Mr 17,21:3
Dashiell, William W, 1947, Ag 4,17:4
Dashowitz, Max, 1949, N 3,29:3
Dashwood, Gulian Ludlow, 1907, Ap 30,9:6
Dashwood, Henry T A, 1959, My 26,35:4
Dashwood, Robert, 1943, Ja 7,19:4
Da Silva, Alfredo, 1942, Ag 23,42:1
Da Silva, Alfredo B, 1943, Jl 31,13:4
Daskalos, Charles, 1949, O 19,17:7
Daskam, W, 1932, Ja 23,15:3
Dassau, John, 1946, Ag 27,27:4
Dassett, Myron R, 1968, Je 17,39:1
D'Assisi, ex-King of Spain, 1902, Ap 18,9:2
Dassler, Henry W, 1941, Ja 28,19:4
Dassler, William E, 1949, Ja 12,27:3
Dasso, David, 1952, My 21,27:5
D'Asson, Marquis de Baudry, 1915, My 14,13:5
Dastagir, Sabu (funeral plans, D 4,47:4), 1963, D 3, 43:2
Dastich, Frantisek, 1964, F 18,35:3
d'Astier de la Vigerie, Francois-Pierre-Raoul, 1956, O 11,39:2
D'Atalie, 1873, My 20,1:7
Datar, Balwant N, 1963, F 15,9:8
Dater, Alfred W, 1938, F 22,21:3
Dater, Henry M, 1921, Ap 12,17:5
Dater, Henry Mrs, 1914, Ap 16,9:4; 1940, Je 18,23:5
Dater, Mary C S, 1915, S 4,7:5
Dates, Donald, 1957, Je 27,25:4
Dates, Ralph W, 1952, Ja 23,27:4
Dates, Walter H, 1951, Ja 7,76:3
Datesman, Clarence Mrs, 1959, D 19,27:6
Dath, Hubert, 1945, Ap 25,23:5
Datig, Fred A, 1951, D 13,33:3
Datlow, Joseph, 1964, D 26,17:5
Dato, Eduardo, 1921, Mr 11,15:4
Datre, Cono J, 1958, My 13,29:5
D'Atri, Ralph W, 1964, D 17,41:1
Dattelbaum, William, 1939, S 17,49:1
Datter, Frederick F, 1947, Ag 14,23:5
Datter, Frederick F Mrs, 1950, Mr 16,31:4
Datter, Joseph, 1939, D 13,27:3
Dattner, Bernhard, 1952, Ag 12,19:4
Dattoli, Paul, 1953, Mr 5,27:1
Dattolo, Canelio A, 1960, Ja 20,31:1
Datz, Charles F, 1941, Ap 22,21:4
Datz, Emil E, 1943, Je 10,21:4
Dau, William H T, 1944, Ap 2,15:6
Daub, Albert A Sr, 1946, N 16,19:4
Daub, Henry Mrs, 1948, Jl 2,21:6
Daub, Michael, 1958, N 29,21:4
Dauban, Jeanne A Mrs (Mrs Jeanne A C D Rieffel), 1942, Je 27,13:4
Daube, Jessica Mrs, 1967, N 5,87:1
Daubel, Joseph A, 1951, S 23,87:1
Daubenspeck, Phil, 1951, Mr 7,33:4
Dauber, Samuel, 1965, My 13,37:2

Daubert, C E, 1941, F 27,19:5
Daubert, Ellsworth W Mrs, 1952, Ja 26,13:6
Daubert, William H, 1960, Je 11,21:6
Daubert, William Mrs, 1953, N 21,13:5
D'Aubigne, Jean Henri, 1872, O 22,4:7
D'Aubigne, Ophelia Geer Mrs, 1879, Jl 7,8:4
Daubigny, C F, 1878, F 22,4:7
Daubin, Freland A, 1959, O 25,86:6
Daubner, Margaret M, 1950, Je 28,27:6
Dauby, Nathan L, 1964, My 18,29:2
Daudelin, S Alphonse, 1943, Ag 29,38:2
Daudet, A, 1897, D 17,7:4
Daudet, Alphonse Mrs, 1940, Ap 24,23:4
Daudet, Leon, 1942, Jl 2,21:1
Dauenhauer, Katherin L Mrs, 1946, D 5,32:2
Dauenhauer. Jno J, 1954, Ja 10,86:6
Dauenheimer, John C, 1946, Jl 5,19:2
Dauer, John Paul, 1914, F 5,9:5
Daufkirch, Henry, 1942, Je 2,23:3
Daugaard-Jensen, Jens, 1938, N 28,15:2
Daugette, Clarence D, 1942, Ag 10,19:4
Daugherty, C Lloyd Jr, 1961, Je 17,21:2
Daugherty, Charles S, 1937, N 13,19:2
Daugherty, George H, 1950, Je 6,29:1
Daugherty, George S, 1950, D 8,29:1
Daugherty, Harry K, 1945, N 25,50:3
Daugherty, Harry K Mrs, 1956, D 2,86:3
Daugherty, Harry M, 1941, O 13,17:1
Daugherty, Harry M Mrs, 1924, N 25,23:3
Daugherty, Horace H, 1955, F 5,15:5
Daugherty, James H, 1965, Ja 19,33:3
Daugherty, Jerome Rev, 1914, My 25,11:5
Daugherty, John E Dr, 1937, D 13,27:4
Daugherty, Joseph M, 1946, Mr 14,25:3
Daugherty, Mal S, 1948, D 16,29:5
Daugherty, Mary W Mrs, 1940, My 16,23:5
Daugherty, Silas D, 1939, Je 20,21:6
Daughters, Raymond E, 1967, S 18,47:3
Daughtrey, Lewis, 1948, Jl 23,19:4
Dauhenhauer, Charles, 1938, Ap 13,25:3
D'Aulby, Edward M, 1954, F 6,19:4
Daulton, Agnes W, 1944, Je 6,17:6
Daum, Arnold R, 1964, O 2,37:4
Daum, Irving I, 1942, F 20,17:3
Daum, T J H, 1882, D 16,4:7
D'Aumale, Duc, 1897, My 8,7:4
Daume, Charles, 1958, D 27,2:8
Daumerie, Hector, 1947, Jl 13,44:6
Daumesnil, Baronne, 1884, My 11,4:6
Daumier, H, 1879, Mr 3,4:7
Daumig, Ernest, 1922, Jl 6,19:6
D'Aunay, Count, 1918, O 11,11:3
D'Aunoy, Rigney, 1941, S 18,25:5
Daunt, Robert P, 1956, Ja 20,23:2
Dauphinot, Clarence J, 1961, S 15,33:1
Dauphinot, Emile, 1937, My 25,28:1
Daur, Jacob, 1948, F 7,15:2
D'Auria, Alphonse J, 1959, Ja 7,33:3
Daus, Charles N, 1954, F 2,27:3
Daus, Felix, 1923, Mr 28,19:3
Daus, R L, 1916, O 17,13:5
Dausch, Henry P, 1956, Ja 8,86:7
Dausey, William H Mrs, 1950, My 28,31:4
Dauss, Hooks (Geo A), 1963, Jl 29,19:4
Dausset, Louis, 1940, Ja 24,21:5
Daut, Charles A, 1945, Ap 6,15:4
Daution, Elie P, 1946, Je 29,19:5
Dautrich, Fred L, 1942, N 8,50:5
Dautry, Raoul, 1951, Ag 22,23:5
Dauvray, Helen (Mrs Alb Winterhalter), 1923, D 7, 21:5
Dauzat, Albert, 1955, N 2,35:4
Dav, Frederica Gore Mrs, 1916, N 24,13:5
Daval, Alice, 1907, Mr 11,7:4
Davalos, Balbino, 1951, O 4,33:2
Davant, Edward T, 1942, Ja 20,40:2
Davaz, Suad, 1941, Ag 23,13:7
Dave, Magan S, 1968, My 8,44:5
Davega, Abram, 1961, Je 20,33:5
Davega, Harry S, 1968, S 13,47:4
Davega, Isaac, 1921, O 14,17:4
Daveler, Erie V, 1957, N 12,34:1
Daveler, Erle V Mrs, 1947, Ag 12,23:1
Daven, William Mrs, 1950, Jl 27,25:3
Davenport, Alfred, 1937, Je 29,21:4
Davenport, Alva H, 1952, S 29,23:4
Davenport, Annabelle K, 1948, Ap 23,23:1
Davenport, Arthur T, 1940, Je 12,25:3
Davenport, Basil, 1966, Ap 9,25:4
Davenport, Blanche (Mrs F M Taylor), 1957, Jl 31, 23:4
Davenport, Butler, 1958, Ap 8,29:2
Davenport, Capt (funl), 1872, O 12,10:5
Davenport, Charles, 1903, F 17,2:4
Davenport, Charles (Cow-Cow), 1955, D 3,17:3
Davenport, Charles B, 1942, O 7,25:3; 1944, F 19,13:5
Davenport, Charles K, 1955, D 7,39:4
Davenport, Charles M, 1943, Jl 24,13:4
Davenport, Charles Mrs, 1946, Mr 9,13:3
Davenport, Clarence Mrs, 1937, Je 27,II,6:8
Davenport, Daisy B Mrs, 1942, F 10,20:3
Davenport, Deodate S, 1949, My 28,15:3
Davenport, Dolly (funl), 1874, F 20,3:1
Davenport, E Arthur, 1945, My 15,19:3
Davenport, E L, 1877, S 2,6:7
Davenport, Ed J, 1953, Je 25,27:3
Davenport, Edgar Loomis, 1918, Jl 26,11:5
Davenport, Edmund G, 1966, Ag 11,33:2
Davenport, Edward W, 1951, S 19,31:4
Davenport, Ernest W, 1947, N 24,23:2
Davenport, Erwin R, 1967, Jl 5,41:2
Davenport, Erwin R Mrs, 1950, F 12,84:2
Davenport, Eugene, 1941, Ap 1,23:3
Davenport, F O, 1903, Ag 24,7:7
Davenport, Fanny V (Mrs M McDowell), 1898, S 27,1:5
Davenport, Frank, 1943, O 31,48:4
Davenport, Frank E, 1949, F 3,23:4
Davenport, Frederick M, 1956, D 28,21:1
Davenport, Frederick M Mrs, 1967, Ag 5,23:2
Davenport, George B, 1947, D 28,40:2
Davenport, George Edward, 1907, D 1,11:6
Davenport, George W Mrs, 1937, Ag 29,II,7:5
Davenport, Gideon I, 1967, Ja 24,28:3
Davenport, Guiles D, 1966, Je 11,31:3
Davenport, Harry, 1949, Ag 10,22:4
Davenport, Harry B, 1945, Ja 11,23:5
Davenport, Harry C, 1904, O 23,7:5
Davenport, Harry Rev, 1937, Ap 15,23:3
Davenport, Henry, 1941, Ag 3,35:2
Davenport, Henry B, 1955, Mr 5,17:6
Davenport, Henry Benedict, 1920, F 18,11:3
Davenport, Henry D, 1950, O 19,31:2
Davenport, Henry J, 1960, D 20,33:1
Davenport, Homer C, 1912, My 3,11:1
Davenport, Ira, 1904, O 7,9:3
Davenport, Ira E, 1911, Jl 9,11:5
Davenport, Ira N, 1941, Jl 18,19:4
Davenport, Isabel M, 1939, S 18,19:5
Davenport, J I, 1903, Ag 28,7:6
Davenport, James E, 1956, Ja 26,29:3
Davenport, James E Mrs, 1955, My 21,17:5
Davenport, James Le Roy, 1914, Ap 3,11:6
Davenport, James S, 1940, Ja 4,23:3
Davenport, Jean B Mrs, 1941, My 3,15:4
Davenport, John A, 1940, Mr 21,25:2
Davenport, John S Jr, 1946, Ja 2,19:1
Davenport, Julius B Mrs, 1948, N 2,25:3
Davenport, Kenneth, 1941, N 12,23:4
Davenport, Leroy B, 1966, Jl 5,34:1
Davenport, Lily (Mrs F Thorne), 1878, Ja 15,1:5
Davenport, Llewellyn D, 1948, O 12,25:5
Davenport, Lord, 1934, S 6,19:5
Davenport, Mary, 1916, Je 28,11:4
Davenport, Mary Fairfax, 1924, Mr 7,15:4
Davenport, McHarg, 1941, S 13,17:6
Davenport, Peter B, 1942, Mr 10,20:2
Davenport, Ray H, 1951, Mr 3,13:5
Davenport, Ray H Mrs, 1949, F 4,24:2
Davenport, Richard M, 1953, F 12,14:5
Davenport, Robert H, 1950, Ja 9,25:2
Davenport, Russell W, 1954, Ap 20,29:1
Davenport, Russell W Mrs, 1949, D 22,23:1
Davenport, S Ellsworth Jr, 1958, My 27,31:3
Davenport, S Ellsworth 3d, 1960, N 17,37:1
Davenport, Samuel G, 1953, Jl 5,49:1
Davenport, Serena H G Mrs, 1942, Je 5,17:3
Davenport, Sophia Mrs, 1872, Ja 24,5:5
Davenport, Sumner G, 1956, Mr 9,23:4
Davenport, Theodore Mrs, 1952, D 19,31:4
Davenport, William, 1941, My 13,23:5
Davenport, William E, 1944, Ap 30,46:3
Davenport, William John, 1903, N 1,7:6
Davenport, William S Sr, 1938, F 28,15:5
Daver, Abidin, 1954, F 10,29:4
Daverin, Daniel J, 1941, Ag 26,19:2
Davern, Jeremiah S, 1954, O 27,29:1
Davern, Thomas J, 1951, Ag 5,73:1
Daves, John, 1917, Ja 9,13:3
Daves, John C, 1939, N 3,21:1
Davey, Byron T, 1958, N 8,21:2
Davey, C F, 1878, Ag 16,5:4
Davey, Charles A, 1955, Jl 20,27:4
Davey, Edward, 1941, Ja 23,21:5
Davey, Ernest, 1951, Mr 25,73:1
Davey, Frank H, 1951, Je 20,27:2
Davey, Frederick W, 1948, O 7,29:2
Davey, G Venner, 1962, N 14,39:2
Davey, George, 1950, Ja 20,25:3
Davey, Henry G, 1960, Ag 8,21:3
Davey, J Edward, 1964, Ag 26,39:4
Davey, James A G Mrs, 1938, Mr 30,21:5
Davey, James A G Sr, 1951, S 14,26:2
Davey, John, 1923, N 9,17:4
Davey, John F, 1952, Mr 18,27:3
Davey, John J, 1958, My 19,25:1
Davey, Karl W Mrs, 1948, Ap 7,25:4
Davey, Leonard S, 1962, Mr 24,25:4
Davey, Martin L, 1946, Ap 1,27:3
Davey, Randall, 1964, N 10,47:1
Davey, Robert Charles, 1908, D 27,9:6
Davey, Stewart H, 1942, N 25,23:1
Davey, T Nelson, 1943, N 8,19:4
Davey, Thomas J, 1947, O 26,70:6
Davey, Vernon L, 1914, D 31,9:6
Davey, Warren, 1942, F 26,19:5
Davey, Wheeler P, 1959, O 13,39:2
Davey, William H K, 1944, S 10,46:1
Davey, William N, 1954, Je 9,31:3
Davey, William R P, 1940, Ag 5,13:4
Davia, Ralph D, 1953, N 10,31:2
Davico, Jasa, 1960, Ja 9,21:5
David, Abe J, 1942, N 22,52:4
David, Abe J Mrs, 1964, My 2,27:3
David, Arthur E, 1946, O 28,27:3
David, B Edmund, 1940, F 19,17:1
David, David, 1886, Je 27,9:1
David, Edgar R, 1961, N 6,37:1
David, Edmond, 1950, My 27,17:6
David, Edward J Mrs, 1949, Ap 20,27:3
David, Edward W, 1960, F 14,84:7
David, Esther Mrs, 1911, Ap 6,11:4
David, F C, 1876, Ag 31,2:5
David, Ferdinand A, 1948, S 21,27:1
David, Florence D (Sister M Just), 1959, Je 26,25:
David, Forteena Mrs, 1942, F 9,17:1
David, Francis, 1960, Ag 16,29:4
David, Gertrude Virginia Mrs, 1914, N 3,11:6
David, Hans T, 1967, O 31,49:2
David, Harry W, 1951, Jl 5,25:5
David, Heinz E, 1956, Mr 27,35:5
David, Henry P, 1959, Ag 2,81:1
David, Irwin H, 1950, D 13,35:4
David, J F P, 1882, Ja 30,5:1
David, Jerome, 1945, N 23,23:1
David, John (will, N 30,8:4), 1937, N 16,23:1
David, John, 1945, Jl 6,11:3
David, Joseph B, 1938, F 19,15:5
David, Joseph B Sr, 1964, Ag 31,25:2
David, Lena M Mrs, 1938, Ap 23,15:2
David, Leo J, 1954, Mr 19,23:1
David, Levy H, 1950, Ja 14,15:2
David, Lillian H, 1948, Ap 11,72:3
David, Louis A, 1953, Ja 27,25:4
David, Mary H Mrs, 1940, Ap 24,23:3
David, Mary Sister, 1904, Ja 27,9:7
David, Oren J, 1946, D 19,29:4
David, Phil J, 1951, Mr 7,33:3
David, R W, 1912, Jl 6,7:3
David, Samuel, 1958, Ag 13,27:2
David, Vernon C, 1961, N 16,39:1
David, William, 1965, Ap 15,33:4
David John, Bro, 1950, Ag 16,29:2
David-Mennet, Arthur, 1918, N 16,13:4
Davidge, Harry S, 1955, My 9,23:3
Davidge, John W, 1958, O 10,32:1
Davidge, W P, 1888, Ag 8,5:6
Davidian, Hagop, 1957, My 18,19:5
Davidoff, Eugene (cor, Jl 29,64:7), 1956, Jl 24,2
Davidoff, Henry, 1951, My 5,17:3
Davidoff, Isaac (Dave), 1954, Ap 5,25:4
Davidoff, Joseph, 1955, Ja 17,23:3; 1962, F 10,23:
Davidoff, Meyer, 1957, S 25,58:4
Davidonis, Anthony, 1945, Ap 22,36:2
Davidovitch, Ljuba, 1940, F 20,21:4
Davidow, Edward, 1937, F 15,17:1
Davidow, Ethel Mrs, 1941, S 10,23:7
Davidow, Harry A, 1954, O 23,15:5
Davidow, Harry M, 1957, O 13,86:7
Davidow, Leonard W, 1966, Ag 30,36:5
Davidowitz, Eugene, 1944, Mr 18,13:4
Davidowitz, Jacob P, 1956, Ap 4,29:4
Davids, Charles A, 1941, O 26,43:2
Davids, Cortlandt G, 1940, My 2,23:2
Davids, Courtland I, 1945, My 11,19:3
Davids, David F Mrs, 1915, Mr 31,11:4
Davids, Edwin W, 1907, N 16,9:5
Davids, G W, 1883, Ap 5,5:1
Davids, George Mrs, 1965, O 13,47:2
Davids, John A, 1939, Jl 6,24:2
Davids, T W Rhys, 1922, D 28,17:5
Davids, William John Laurence, 1914, Jl 23,9:4
Davidsburg, Ernst, 1951, S 9,90:4
Davidson, A Bates, 1952, Ag 5,19:1
Davidson, A Higbee, 1943, Ag 6,15:5
Davidson, Abraham, 1941, N 1,15:3
Davidson, Abram L, 1947, S 26,23:2
Davidson, Adela B, 1942, N 2,21:3
Davidson, Adeline T, 1956, O 20,21:5
Davidson, Alexander Jr, 1967, My 15,43:1
Davidson, Alexander Rev, 1870, O 10,5:6
Davidson, Alfred, 1952, N 19,29:5; 1956, N 20,
Davidson, Alfred T, 1964, O 3,29:4
Davidson, Alvah E, 1957, D 15,86:3
Davidson, Andrew Col, 1902, N 11,9:4
Davidson, Arol Mrs, 1955, Jl 10,72:5
Davidson, Arthur C, 1941, S 2,17:4
Davidson, Arthur Col, 1922, O 17,19:3
Davidson, Arthur E Mrs, 1949, O 6,31:2
Davidson, Arthur Sr, 1950, D 31,45:4
Davidson, B Palmer Mrs, 1958, Mr 21,21:1
Davidson, B Palmer Sr, 1956, N 14,35:4
Davidson, Ben Prof, 1968, D 22,52:8
Davidson, Benjamin, 1952, Jl 17,23:4
Davidson, Bernard, 1963, N 19,41:3
Davidson, Bruce J, 1959, N 18,41:4
Davidson, Carter, 1965, O 21,47:3; 1968, D 2
Davidson, Charles F, 1967, N 4,33:2
Davidson, Charles H, 1951, Jl 1,15:2

Davidson, Charles L, 1953, Jl 7,27:2
Davidson, Charles M, 1903, N 24,9:5; 1939, Ap 6,52:2
Davidson, Charles R, 1948, My 11,25:2
Davidson, Charles W, 1945, My 9,23:4
Davidson, Clara, 1953, Ag 19,29:6
Davidson, Claude A, 1945, Ja 25,19:2
Davidson, Claude B, 1956, Ap 20,25:2
Davidson, Clinton Jr, 1957, F 14,27:4
Davidson, Cynthia Mrs, 1904, Ja 10,7:6
Davidson, Daniel S, 1952, D 28,48:3
Davidson, David, 1959, Jl 3,17:2; 1961, Je 9,33:1; 1964, S 5,19:1
Davidson, Donald, 1948, Ag 10,21:4; 1968, Ap 27,39:1
Davidson, Donald A, 1944, My 9,19:2
Davidson, Donald Mrs, 1956, Ap 5,89:2
Davidson, Donald O Mrs, 1960, O 30,86:6
Davidson, Dorothea, 1961, Ap 10,31:4
Davidson, Douglas T Jr, 1964, Ag 27,33:5
Davidson, Edgar, 1943, My 9,40:7
Davidson, Edmund Mrs, 1948, S 11,15:4
Davidson, Edward L, 1948, My 12,27:4
Davidson, Edward L B, 1944, O 12,27:2
Davidson, Edward Y, 1958, My 24,21:6
Davidson, Edwin N Mrs, 1946, Je 15,21:3
Davidson, Ellis W, 1948, N 25,31:2
Davidson, Emmett O, 1944, N 23,31:6
Davidson, Ezra, 1951, O 25,29:2
Davidson, Frank E, 1942, Ja 20,19:2; 1947, Mr 21,21:4
Davidson, Fred O, 1951, N 6,29:2
Davidson, Frederick, 1916, O 6,11:4
Davidson, Frederick K, 1963, Ap 5,47:4
Davidson, Frida, 1959, F 28,19:6
Davidson, G S, 1881, Mr 18,2:2
Davidson, Gabriel, 1958, N 9,88:6
Davidson, George, 1917, S 27,13:5; 1950, D 29,20:2; 1965, Je 19,29:3
Davidson, George G Jr Mrs, 1962, O 19,20:5
Davidson, George Prof, 1911, D 3,15:5
Davidson, H Coolidge Jr, 1968, F 13,43:3
Davidson, Hamilton E, 1959, Jl 29,29:4
Davidson, Harold M, 1955, N 18,25:3
Davidson, Harold Mrs, 1952, Mr 29,15:3
Davidson, Harold S, 1960, F 19,27:3
Davidson, Harry, 1924, Ag 12,11:3
Davidson, Hartley C, 1951, My 29,25:3
Davidson, Henry, 1967, D 20,45:1
Davidson, Henry F, 1961, N 5,88:6
Davidson, Herbert A, 1940, Ja 27,13:5
Davidson, Herman B Mrs, 1954, D 17,31:5
Davidson, Herman P, 1955, O 11,39:4
Davidson, Homer, 1948, Jl 27,25:4
Davidson, Irville F, 1940, D 29,24:8
Davidson, Isobel, 1938, Ag 30,17:6
Davidson, Israel, 1939, Je 28,21:3
Davidson, Israel Mrs, 1953, D 19,15:4
Davidson, J Brownlee, 1957, My 11,21:6
Davidson, J E, 1903, Ag 1,7:6
Davidson, J Edgar, 1965, Ja 23,35:2
Davidson, J Milton Mrs, 1951, Mr 21,33:4
Davidson, J W, 1881, Je 23,5:2
Davidson, J William, 1954, N 8,21:3
Davidson, James, 1942, O 3,15:5
Davidson, James A, 1958, Je 25,29:2
Davidson, James B, 1957, O 3,29:1; 1965, Jl 19,21:7
Davidson, James C, 1940, S 8,49:2
Davidson, James E, 1947, Jl 26,13:7
Davidson, James E (por), 1949, N 13,92:5
Davidson, James E Mrs, 1966, O 9,86:1
Davidson, James H, 1918, Ag 8,11:6; 1948, N 13,15:2
Davidson, James Mackenzie, 1919, Ap 3,11:3
Davidson, James O, 1922, D 17,6:4
Davidson, Jennie M Mrs, 1943, My 8,15:4
Davidson, Jo, 1952, Ja 3,1:2
Davidson, Jo (est tax appr), 1955, O 1,17:1
Davidson, Jo Mrs, 1962, Ag 8,31:4
Davidson, John C Mrs, 1952, My 29,27:5
Davidson, John H, 1954, D 12,88:5
Davidson, John Jr, 1955, D 4,88:2
Davidson, John M Mrs, 1944, My 8,19:4
Davidson, John R, 1949, Mr 26,17:4
Davidson, John R Rev, 1937, My 1,19:3
Davidson, John W E, 1942, S 19,15:2
Davidson, Jon M, 1954, Je 4,23:2
Davidson, Joseph, 1944, Mr 31,21:5; 1945, My 30, 19:5; 1948, Jl 16,19:4; 1949, D 2,29:3
Davidson, Joseph C, 1947, D 11,33:2
Davidson, Joseph E, 1951, Ag 12,76:6
Davidson, Joshua J Mrs, 1951, S 27,31:3
Davidson, Julius, 1943, Mr 24,23:3
Davidson, Julius (Feb 7), 1963, Ap 1,35:4
Davidson, Julius Mrs, 1957, Ag 12,19:3
Davidson, Kenneth R, 1954, D 26,25:1
Davidson, Kenneth S M (rites set, Ap 9,33:3), 1958, Mr 20,29:5
Davidson, L Henry, 1948, O 19,27:2
Davidson, L Herbert, 1965, My 24,31:4
Davidson, Lady, 1936, Je 27,17:3
Davidson, Lafayette Mrs, 1957, Ag 21,27:4
Davidson, Leonidas Herbert, 1925, My 5,21:4
Davidson, Lord, 1930, My 25,28:1
Davidson, Louis B, 1964, My 31,76:3
Davidson, Louis R, 1941, Ag 29,17:2
Davidson, Louis R Mrs, 1951, Ja 20,15:1
Davidson, Luther J, 1951, Ja 5,22:2
Davidson, Luther J Jr, 1948, Ja 22,27:2
Davidson, Lyal A, 1950, D 31,43:1
Davidson, Mary, 1941, D 10,25:1
Davidson, Mary E, 1965, S 14,39:1
Davidson, Matthew, 1958, My 26,29:5
Davidson, Matthew Mrs, 1957, Ap 12,23:1
Davidson, Maurice P, 1956, Jl 17,23:1
Davidson, Milton L, 1939, S 18,19:4
Davidson, Moritz, 1919, N 2,22:3
Davidson, Morris M, 1948, Ja 23,24:3
Davidson, Morris M Mrs, 1941, N 5,23:2
Davidson, Morton, 1938, N 2,23:4
Davidson, Norman, 1950, Ja 1,43:1
Davidson, Norman W Mrs, 1955, F 9,27:3
Davidson, Ogden, 1955, Jl 30,17:2
Davidson, Peers Lt-Col, 1920, Jl 21,13:5
Davidson, Ray, 1941, O 8,23:2
Davidson, Richard P Mrs, 1943, Ap 10,17:4
Davidson, Robert H, 1961, My 10,45:2
Davidson, Robert J, 1943, S 14,23:3
Davidson, Robert Mrs, 1921, Jl 12,13:4
Davidson, Robert P, 1963, O 26,27:3
Davidson, Robert P Mrs, 1951, O 22,23:4
Davidson, Robert W, 1967, S 27,47:3
Davidson, Robert W Mrs, 1944, N 23,31:1
Davidson, Rolland A Mrs, 1946, Ag 23,19:4
Davidson, Roy E (funl, Jl 9,33:2), 1964, Jl 7,35:1
Davidson, S G Mrs, 1945, Mr 8,23:4
Davidson, Samuel G, 1940, My 23,23:2
Davidson, Samuel Sir, 1921, Ag 19,13:4
Davidson, Sarah, 1944, D 18,19:2
Davidson, Saul, 1942, S 28,17:5
Davidson, Sidney, 1965, Ag 10,29:3
Davidson, T G, 1883, S 13,5:3
Davidson, T O, 1940, My 1,24:3
Davidson, Talmadge O Mrs, 1948, Je 29,23:3
Davidson, Tyler, 1866, Ja 20,5:2
Davidson, Victor H, 1958, F 14,24:3
Davidson, Walter, 1942, F 8,48:3
Davidson, Walter R, 1959, Jl 11,19:4
Davidson, Walter V, 1941, Mr 9,41:3
Davidson, Ward F, 1960, Jl 13,35:3
Davidson, William, 1938, O 14,23:1
Davidson, William A, 1937, Ap 22,23:6; 1952, S 16, 29:5; 1957, Jl 26,19:2
Davidson, William A Mrs, 1959, O 13,39:3
Davidson, William B, 1949, F 27,69:2
Davidson, William G, 1941, Ja 11,17:4
Davidson, William J, 1950, S 5,27:2
Davidson, William L, 1951, Jl 8,60:2
Davidson, William T Capt, 1937, N 2,25:6
Davidson, William W, 1942, Ja 29,19:6
Davidson, William W Sr, 1956, Mr 4,88:5
Davie, Fred G, 1940, Ap 11,26:3
Davie, Gordon D, 1937, Ap 6,23:3
Davie, Harold W, 1961, My 1,29:5
Davie, John S B (por), 1943, N 4,23:2
Davie, Maurice R, 1964, N 2,39:1
Davie, Preston, 1967, My 22,43:1
Davies, A Edgar, 1968, My 23,47:3
Davies, A Gardner, 1939, Je 11,44:8
Davies, Abner J, 1948, Mr 2,23:2
Davies, Acton, 1916, Je 13,11:5
Davies, Albert B, 1952, S 25,31:5
Davies, Albert E, 1950, Jl 20,25:2; 1953, Ja 21,31:3
Davies, Alfred, 1941, N 17,19:2; 1949, Ap 28,31:4
Davies, Alfred E, 1911, Jl 17,9:6
Davies, Anna F, 1942, N 20,24:3
Davies, Arthur D, 1946, My 4,15:4
Davies, Arthur M, 1953, Ap 14,27:3
Davies, Arthur P, 1957, S 27,19:3
Davies, B Paul, 1946, Jl 11,23:4
Davies, Ben, 1943, Mr 30,21:2
Davies, Benjamin Rev Dr, 1875, Ag 5,4:7
Davies, Betty A, 1955, My 15,86:6
Davies, Charles, 1876, S 19,4:7
Davies, Charles P, 1939, Ap 18,23:2
Davies, Chester Mrs, 1963, N 3,89:2
Davies, Clara N Mrs, 1943, F 8,20:2
Davies, Clem, 1951, D 23,22:3
Davies, Clement, 1962, Mr 24,25:1
Davies, Daniel, 1966, My 19,47:5
Davies, Daniel J, 1946, Ap 3,25:2; 1959, Ja 29,27:2
Davies, Daniel R, 1944, My 7,46:1
Davies, David, 1921, S 21,15:5; 1944, Je 17,13:4
Davies, David L, 1937, N 26,21:4
Davies, David Mrs (M Kennedy), 1967, Ag 1,33:3
Davies, David P, 1946, O 16,27:3
Davies, E Gordon, 1955, Mr 2,27:1
Davies, Edgar F, 1949, D 23,22:2
Davies, Edward, 1951, Mr 25,73:1
Davies, Edward L, 1951, Ap 17,29:4
Davies, Ellis W, 1939, Ap 30,45:2
Davies, Elmer D, 1957, Ja 8,31:3
Davies, Ernest, 1952, S 4,27:4
Davies, Evan M Mrs, 1941, D 2,23:1
Davies, Fanny E, 1950, Jl 13,25:2
Davies, Francis, 1948, Mr 19,23:2
Davies, Frank B, 1940, Jl 24,21:5
Davies, Frederick B Mrs, 1953, My 26,29:5
Davies, Frederick L, 1939, Ja 17,22:3
Davies, Frederick Martin, 1915, My 3,11:2
Davies, Frederick T, 1958, Ag 30,15:7
Davies, G W, 1953, My 26,29:4
Davies, George, 1955, Ap 15,23:4
Davies, George C Mrs, 1956, Jl 22,61:3
Davies, George O, 1963, My 7,43:4
Davies, Gilbert William, 1910, Jl 27,9:5
Davies, Glyn, 1964, N 2,39:1
Davies, Godfrey, 1957, My 31,19:1
Davies, H E, 1881, D 18,2:1
Davies, Harriet, 1952, Mr 7,24:3
Davies, Harry, 1925, Ja 22,19:4
Davies, Harry H, 1957, S 2,13:6
Davies, Harry W, 1956, D 6,37:2
Davies, Henry Rees, 1917, S 21,9:6
Davies, Henry W, 1941, Mr 12,21:3
Davies, Herbert, 1949, Jl 8,19:1
Davies, Herbert A, 1957, S 14,19:2
Davies, Hubert, 1953, S 1,23:2
Davies, I Newton, 1941, O 17,23:3
Davies, J Clarence Mrs, 1961, Mr 27,31:3
Davies, J Mansfield Col, 1908, O 13,9:4
Davies, J Vipond, 1939, O 5,23:3
Davies, James, 1940, Ja 8,15:4
Davies, James R, 1903, D 11,9:4
Davies, Jenkins H, 1957, My 26,93:1
Davies, John A Com, 1865, S 28,8:3
Davies, John C, 1925, Ja 11,5:2
Davies, John C Mrs, 1953, My 26,29:6
Davies, John E, 1939, Ja 31,21:4; 1940, D 13,26:5
Davies, John H (Jack), 1960, F 16,37:4
Davies, John J, 1946, F 27,25:2
Davies, John M, 1955, S 15,33:1
Davies, John P, 1958, O 14,37:2
Davies, John P Mrs, 1962, My 25,33:3
Davies, John R, 1947, Ag 12,23:6; 1951, F 14,29:3
Davies, John R Jr, 1948, Ap 23,23:1
Davies, John Rumsey Rev Dr, 1919, Mr 16,20:4
Davies, John T, 1938, Ap 2,15:1
Davies, John W, 1955, Je 25,15:2
Davies, Joseph E (funl, My 13,29:2; will, My 14,6:5), 1958, My 10,21:1
Davies, Julien Tappan, 1920, My 7,11:2
Davies, Julien Townsend, 1917, Mr 9,7:6
Davies, Len, 1945, N 25,50:4
Davies, Lew, 1968, D 13,47:3
Davies, Llewellyn J, 1950, D 29,19:3
Davies, Louis Sir, 1924, My 2,19:6
Davies, Mabel, 1960, D 21,31:3
Davies, Marion, 1940, Jl 20,9:1
Davies, Marion (Mrs H G Brown),(funl plans, S 24,87:1), 1961, S 23,19:2
Davies, Marion S, 1940, Ja 14,42:6
Davies, Meurig L, 1940, D 19,25:5
Davies, Natalie R Mrs, 1955, D 13,39:4
Davies, Orville, 1950, Je 12,27:4
Davies, Oscar G, 1949, Jl 13,27:2
Davies, P L Rev (mem ser), 1875, Ag 13,2:3
Davies, Peter L, 1960, Ap 7,37:2
Davies, Phoebe, 1912, D 5,17:5
Davies, Reine, 1938, Ap 3,II,7:3
Davies, Rhys J, 1954, N 2,27:6
Davies, Richard P Mrs, 1938, Ag 3,19:4
Davies, Richard T, 1920, S 4,9:4
Davies, Robert, 1912, F 11,II,13:3; 1937, S 26,II,8:8
Davies, Robert Mrs, 1937, S 26,II,8:8
Davies, Roger M Mrs, 1951, Jl 17,27:1
Davies, Roland C, 1964, S 16,31:6
Davies, Rufus C, 1950, Mr 6,21:4
Davies, Samuel, 1940, My 11,19:4
Davies, Sara, 1950, F 12,86:5
Davies, Shadrach, 1913, F 10,11:4
Davies, Stanley, 1953, S 7,19:5
Davies, Stanley B, 1957, S 28,17:5
Davies, Sylvanus S, 1955, Ap 1,27:3
Davies, T F, 1936, Ag 26,22:1
Davies, Taleasin H, 1943, Mr 26,19:3
Davies, Thurston J, 1961, Ag 15,29:5
Davies, Virginia M (por), 1949, Ap 22,23:2
Davies, W, 1935, Mr 18,17:6
Davies, W Rupert Mrs, 1948, D 21,25:4
Davies, W Sander, 1940, Je 21,21:5
Davies, Walter R, 1937, O 15,23:3
Davies, William E, 1910, Mr 17,9:5; 1948, O 25,23:4
Davies, William H, 1940, S 27,23:4; 1947, N 11,28:2
Davies, William P, 1944, My 20,15:2; 1958, Mr 21, 21:4
Davies, William R, 1939, Ap 15,19:6
Davies, William W, 1953, F 24,25:4
Daviess, Maria Thompson, 1924, S 4,19:5
Daviet, William C, 1938, S 19,19:3
D'Avigdor-Goldsmid, Osmond, 1940, Ap 15,17:3
D'Avignon, F J Mrs, 1942, Mr 18,23:5
D'Avignon, Francis, 1949, N 5,13:6
Davignon, Francis J Dr, 1921, Jl 11,11:4
Davignon, J, 1916, Mr 14,11:3
D'Avignon, John, 1949, O 9,93:1
Davila, Carlos (funl plans, O 21,27:4; funl, O 25,-33:1), 1955, O 20,35:1
Davila, Carlos D Mrs, 1941, Mr 13,21:3
Davila, Charles, 1963, Mr 8,12:1
Davila, Fidel, 1962, Mr 23,33:2
Davilla, Antonio Mrs, 1938, Ja 6,19:4
Davin, Denis W, 1946, Ap 20,13:5

Davin, Edward J, 1948, D 7,31:4
Davin, John, 1950, D 4,29:4
Davin, John P Dr, 1923, S 3,13:4
Davin, John W (will, D 21,49:2), 1949, Ja 8,15:4
Davin, Thomas J, 1961, Je 21,37:5
Da Vinna, Clyde, 1953, Jl 29,23:3
Daviot, Gordon (E Mackintosh), 1952, F 14,27:2
Davis, A, 1933, Ja 20,13:1
Davis, A K, 1884, N 22,5:3
Davis, A P, 1933, Ag 8,17:1
Davis, Aaron, 1903, N 8,7:6
Davis, Abe S, 1949, O 30,84:4
Davis, Abel Gen, 1937, Ja 8,19:3
Davis, Abial B, 1938, O 31,15:2
Davis, Abial B Mrs, 1943, Je 30,21:5
Davis, Abiel Franklin, 1916, Jl 4,11:4
Davis, Abraham, 1943, O 6,23:5; 1965, N 4,47:4
Davis, Abraham Mrs, 1958, Jl 19,15:4
Davis, Abraham N, 1966, O 27,47:2
Davis, Achilles Dr, 1920, My 4,11:1
Davis, Achilles E, 1941, Ja 18,15:4; 1950, N 9,33:6
Davis, Adam C, 1942, Mr 19,21:6
Davis, Adams R Mrs, 1957, Jl 23,27:2
Davis, Adeline C Mrs, 1942, S 17,25:3
Davis, Albert, 1939, Ap 26,23:3; 1942, Ap 23,23:4
Davis, Albert A Dr, 1905, My 7,7:3
Davis, Albert E, 1948, Je 4,23:1
Davis, Albert G, 1957, S 22,86:6
Davis, Albert G Mrs, 1948, N 24,23:4; 1957, S 24,35:4
Davis, Albert S Sr, 1963, Jl 9,31:2
Davis, Albert T, 1961, S 15,30:6
Davis, Alberta E, 1951, N 11,90:5
Davis, Alex H, 1942, D 10,25:3
Davis, Alexander Henry Maj, 1910, O 23,II,13:4
Davis, Alfred, 1948, Jl 1,23:6
Davis, Alfred C, 1946, My 19,42:7
Davis, Alfred E, 1907, Ja 8,9:2
Davis, Alfred H, 1954, Ap 7,31:6
Davis, Alger, 1951, O 16,31:1
Davis, Alice B Mrs, 1942, Je 29,15:5
Davis, Allan, 1949, Ag 31,23:3
Davis, Alys L, 1951, Ja 16,29:2
Davis, Amos, 1947, D 26,15:3
Davis, Andrew J, 1956, Ja 5,34:1
Davis, Andrew J Dr (Poughkeepsie Seer), 1910, Ja 14,9:4
Davis, Ann, 1961, S 5,35:4
Davis, Annie H Mrs, 1937, Ap 3,19:3
Davis, Anthony Mrs, 1953, Ap 11,17:5
Davis, Archibald M, 1943, D 11,15:4
Davis, Arnold L, 1940, S 12,25:5
Davis, Arthur C, 1965, F 11,39:1
Davis, Arthur E, 1943, My 3,17:5; 1951, D 8,11:4; 1954, Je 14,21:1
Davis, Arthur G, 1949, F 22,23:4; 1956, O 9,35:1
Davis, Arthur J, 1951, Jl 24,25:2
Davis, Arthur L Mrs, 1944, My 31,19:4
Davis, Arthur Pattison, 1968, Ap 22,47:1
Davis, Arthur S, 1947, Ja 18,15:2
Davis, Arthur T, 1948, D 19,76:7
Davis, Arthur V (will, N 27,43:7), 1962, N 18,86:1
Davis, Arthur V (est acctg), 1964, My 9,28:6
Davis, Arthur V (est fees total nearly $6-million), 1967, Jl 8,25:4
Davis, Arthur W, 1943, S 11,13:3; 1949, Jl 17,30:1; 1954, Mr 31,27:4
Davis, Augustus Sr, 1946, D 8,77:8
Davis, B Colwell Jr, 1968, Ja 19,44:4
Davis, B Frank, 1955, Ag 12,19:4
Davis, B N, 1950, N 25,13:5
Davis, Bancroft G, 1947, O 23,25:3
Davis, Bancroft G Mrs, 1967, Jl 6,29:4
Davis, Barnet Henry, 1916, N 2,13:4
Davis, Ben, 1942, O 22,21:5; 1956, S 19,37:4
Davis, Ben G, 1946, O 21,31:5
Davis, Benjamin B, 1952, S 16,29:4
Davis, Benjamin F, 1937, N 16,23:4
Davis, Benjamin J, 1964, Ag 24,27:4
Davis, Benjamin J Sr, 1945, O 29,19:3
Davis, Benjamin M, 1953, Je 19,21:4
Davis, Benjamin O Mrs, 1966, O 27,47:3
Davis, Benjamin S, 1940, Ag 7,19:3
Davis, Bennett F, 1957, Ag 27,29:2
Davis, Bergen, 1958, Jl 2,29:2
Davis, Bergen Mrs, 1965, Ja 14,35:3
Davis, Bernard, 1961, O 10,43:3
Davis, Bert A, 1942, F 21,19:2
Davis, Bert F, 1944, Ap 26,19:3
Davis, Bette Mrs, 1959, F 8,75:2
Davis, Blakslee G Mrs, 1946, F 6,23:3
Davis, Blevins Mrs (will, Ap 7,17:6), 1948, Mr 19, 23:3
Davis, Boothe C, 1942, Ja 17,17:1
Davis, Boothe C Mrs, 1939, Mr 16,23:3
Davis, Brett C, 1942, D 27,34:3
Davis, Brett C Mrs, 1942, D 27,34:3
Davis, Brode B, 1943, My 20,21:1
Davis, Burnard S, 1907, Jl 7,7:6
Davis, Burnett A, 1965, Ag 17,33:4
Davis, Burr, 1903, My 4,7:6
Davis, Burt L, 1941, Ag 31,22:2
Davis, C B, 1926, D 10,25:1
Davis, C Edgar, 1944, Mr 31,21:5
Davis, C H, 1877, F 19,5:5; 1933, Ag 6,24:1
Davis, C Olden, 1960, Mr 9,33:4
Davis, C Rexford, 1957, Ag 7,27:4
Davis, Cameron J, 1952, Je 8,86:3
Davis, Carl L, 1959, O 15,39:4
Davis, Carl R, 1956, Ja 17,33:3
Davis, Carleton E, 1957, Ja 30,29:4
Davis, Carol M S Mrs, 1967, Jl 23,60:5
Davis, Carroll P, 1943, Mr 24,24:2
Davis, Catherine B, 1908, Mr 3,7:6
Davis, Cecil, 1953, Ap 13,27:3
Davis, Cecil C Mrs, 1955, S 14,35:3
Davis, Cecil H Mrs, 1941, Jl 19,13:6
Davis, Chandler, 1949, O 30,84:7
Davis, Charles, 1950, O 31,27:2; 1952, F 27,27:5; 1967, My 3,45:2
Davis, Charles A, 1907, F 19,9:6; 1953, S 9,29:1; 1955, Je 6,27:4
Davis, Charles A Prof, 1916, Ap 11,13:6
Davis, Charles B (por), 1943, Mr 4,20:1
Davis, Charles B, 1943, O 24,44:4; 1967, My 1,37:1
Davis, Charles C, 1940, S 6,21:2
Davis, Charles D, 1952, S 6,17:3
Davis, Charles D Mrs, 1947, Mr 25,26:3
Davis, Charles E, 1937, Je 26,17:4; 1940, S 8,49:1; 1946, Mr 3,46:4; 1949, Jl 30,15:6; 1953, S 28,25:3; 1958, S 13,19:3; 1968, F 11,92:2
Davis, Charles E Dr, 1937, S 29,23:4
Davis, Charles E Gen, 1925, Je 2,23:3
Davis, Charles E Jr, 1937, O 20,23:3
Davis, Charles E Rev, 1925, S 11,23:6
Davis, Charles F, 1943, D 21,27:2
Davis, Charles G, 1959, Ja 26,29:3
Davis, Charles G Judge, 1903, Jl 4,7:6
Davis, Charles G Mrs, 1948, My 16,71:1
Davis, Charles H, 1938, D 21,23:1; 1941, Jl 7,15:4; 1945, My 25,19:4; 1951, Je 4,27:6; 1957, Ja 25,21:4
Davis, Charles Henry Rear-Adm, 1921, D 28,15:6
Davis, Charles I, 1954, D 3,17:4
Davis, Charles J Mrs, 1955, F 20,88:6
Davis, Charles Krum, 1968, Ja 10,43:1
Davis, Charles L, 1957, Ja 6,89:1
Davis, Charles Mrs, 1949, Ja 12,28:2
Davis, Charles Mrs (Beatrice), 1966, D 15,47:1
Davis, Charles N, 1939, O 22,41:2; 1941, N 15,17:6
Davis, Charles O Col, 1922, My 24,19:5
Davis, Charles P, 1939, Ja 26,21:6
Davis, Charles P Mrs, 1956, Ja 19,33:2
Davis, Charles R, 1873, Jl 21,1:7; 1939, Mr 23,23:2; 1947, Ag 30,15:6
Davis, Charles S, 1945, N 23,23:5; 1954, Jl 3,11:3
Davis, Charles T (por), 1938, Ja 3,21:2
Davis, Charles T, 1945, D 22,19:4
Davis, Charles W, 1953, Mr 14,15:5; 1956, S 4,29:4
Davis, Charlie, 1952, S 5,16:3
Davis, Chester A (funl), 1965, Ja 27,35:4
Davis, Clara B Mrs, 1938, F 9,20:2
Davis, Clarence, 1944, S 24,46:2
Davis, Clarence G, 1952, D 9,33:3
Davis, Clarence J, 1937, Jl 2,21:3
Davis, Clarence P, 1938, F 9,19:5
Davis, Clark B, 1948, O 17,77:1
Davis, Claude B, 1949, Ag 16,23:2
Davis, Clayton B, 1960, O 22,23:6
Davis, Clayton C, 1965, Ag 25,88:6
Davis, Clyde B, 1962, Jl 20,25:2
Davis, Clyde B Mrs (W Van Arsdale), 1952, Ja 16, 25:5
Davis, Collis H Mrs, 1955, D 12,31:2
Davis, Curt, 1965, O 14,47:4
Davis, Cushman K Sen, 1900, N 28,1:5
Davis, D Dexter, 1958, F 17,23:1
Davis, D Harry, 1947, Ap 23,25:1
Davis, D Harry Mrs, 1948, O 9,17:3
Davis, D Leslie, 1940, Jl 22,17:2
Davis, D Raymond, 1950, S 14,31:1
Davis, Daisy J, 1960, F 7,84:3
Davis, Daniel A, 1915, S 26,15:4
Davis, Daniel R, 1944, Mr 17,17:5
Davis, Danny, 1938, Je 28,19:6
Davis, David, 1946, My 7,21:4; 1947, N 10,29:4; 1951, Ja 20,15:4
Davis, David D, 1954, F 16,25:1
Davis, David D Mrs, 1937, Ag 7,15:2
Davis, David F Mrs, 1960, F 21,92:4
Davis, David G, 1956, N 12,29:2
Davis, David J, 1938, D 8,27:3; 1942, N 20,23:2; 1954, D 20,29:2
Davis, David L Mrs, 1949, Mr 12,17:4
Davis, David Mrs, 1946, F 20,25:4; 1948, Mr 7,68:4
Davis, David T, 1920, Ap 26,13:4
Davis, Dean C Mrs, 1951, Mr 10,13:5
Davis, Dean W, 1953, F 1,88:6
Davis, Delmar L, 1942, Je 20,13:4
Davis, Don R, 1951, S 3,13:3
Davis, Donald D, 1950, Je 8,32:4
Davis, Donald H, 1957, N 3,88:4
Davis, Donald W, 1950, Jl 2,24:5; 1959, Jl 1,31:1
Davis, Douglas M, 1950, Je 2,23:2
Davis, Dowdal H, 1957, Je 22,15:5
Davis, Dudley, 1965, F 6,25:3
Davis, Dudley Mrs, 1941, Ja 27,15:3
Davis, Dwight F, 1945, N 29,23:1
Davis, Dwight F Mrs, 1955, D 29,23:1
Davis, E A, 1903, Je 6,7:6
Davis, E Asbury, 1955, Mr 16,33:2
Davis, E Asbury Mrs, 1946, N 8,23:4
Davis, E Cleland, 1940, Ja 3,22:2
Davis, E Everett, 1943, Mr 31,19:1
Davis, E Steuart, 1955, N 19,19:5
Davis, E William Mrs, 1966, Je 16,47:1
Davis, Earl R, 1957, Ag 11,80:2
Davis, Earle F, 1960, D 5,31:5
Davis, Eaton G, 1958, Ap 15,33:3
Davis, Ebenezer G Jr, 1939, Je 27,23:3
Davis, Eddie, 1956, F 28,31:1
Davis, Eddie (corr, Ag 1,21:1), 1958, Jl 31,23:3
Davis, Edgar, 1940, O 15,23:2
Davis, Edgar B, 1951, O 15,25:2
Davis, Edgar M, 1947, O 10,25:2
Davis, Edmund, 1939, F 21,19:2
Davis, Edward, 1940, F 24,13:5; 1946, Ap 21,47:3; 1951, N 3,17:2; 1964, O 20,37:4
Davis, Edward A, 1940, F 29,19:2
Davis, Edward B, 1942, N 8,51:4
Davis, Edward C, 1940, Je 12,25:5
Davis, Edward H Mrs, 1959, Ap 9,31:4
Davis, Edward K, 1955, Mr 11,25:1
Davis, Edward L, 1948, Je 15,28:3
Davis, Edward M, 1943, Ap 2,21:4
Davis, Edward W Mrs, 1965, O 24,86:8
Davis, Edwin, 1958, F 5,28:1
Davis, Edwin B, 1957, Jl 25,23:2
Davis, Edwin J, 1943, Ag 25,19:5
Davis, Elam H Mrs, 1945, S 4,23:2
Davis, Elias, 1939, D 15,25:1
Davis, Eliza Bancroft Mrs, 1872, Ja 26,5:4
Davis, Eliza Mrs, 1903, N 29,7:6
Davis, Elizabeth, 1947, Je 23,23:4
Davis, Elizabeth S Mrs, 1942, S 25,21:5
Davis, Ella F, 1943, Mr 31,19:1
Davis, Ellabelle, 1960, N 16,41:1
Davis, Elmer (funl plans, My 21,33:4; funl, My 23, 12:2), 1958, My 19,1:6
Davis, Elmer F, 1948, Ag 27,19:2
Davis, Elrick B, 1960, Jl 13,35:5
Davis, Elvert M, 1942, My 1,19:3
Davis, Elwood M, 1949, Ap 17,76:8
Davis, Emanuel, 1946, Mr 8,21:4
Davis, Emerson F, 1961, O 1,86:4
Davis, Emerson Rev, 1866, Ag 24,2:6
Davis, Emily C, 1941, Ap 20,42:2
Davis, Emma C Mrs, 1942, Mr 30,19:4
Davis, Emma J, 1943, F 2,19:5
Davis, Emma M Mrs, 1937, Jl 22,19:6
Davis, Emma P Mrs, 1941, Ap 17,23:4
Davis, Ennis, 1953, My 9,19:2
Davis, Erastus C, 1956, Jl 2,21:4
Davis, Eric G, 1956, D 19,31:2
Davis, Ernest A, 1968, N 19,40:1
Davis, Ernest S, 1938, My 17,23:3
Davis, Ernie (tribute, My 22,47:4; funeral, My 23, 37:4), 1963, My 19,87:1
Davis, Esme, 1960, Ap 21,31:2
Davis, Estelle H Mrs, 1950, Mr 12,92:3
Davis, Etola, 1960, My 5,35:2
Davis, Eugene A, 1944, F 2,21:1
Davis, Evelyn A Mrs, 1938, Ap 1,23:1
Davis, Everett R, 1946, O 5,17:3
Davis, Everett R Mrs, 1950, Ja 29,68:5
Davis, Ewin L (por), 1949, O 24,23:1
Davis, F A J, 1953, Mr 20,23:2
Davis, F Jr, 1934, S 6,19:3
Davis, F Whitney, 1948, Ag 1,59:3
Davis, Fay, 1945, F 27,19:1
Davis, Fellowes, 1920, S 7,15:2
Davis, Ferdinand S, 1939, Ap 27,25:3
Davis, Floyd, 1966, O 27,47:5
Davis, Floyd M Mrs, 1967, F 17,37:4
Davis, Forrest E, 1962, My 5,18:5
Davis, Forrest F, 1960, Jl 12,35:4
Davis, Foster B, 1950, Mr 26,96:1
Davis, Frances, 1945, My 3,23:5
Davis, Francis B, 1940, D 23,19:4
Davis, Francis H, 1947, S 14,60:3
Davis, Francis P, 1953, Jl 17,17:6
Davis, Francis W, 1944, Je 13,19:4; 1950, Ja 30,
Davis, Frank A Mrs, 1942, F 5,22:3
Davis, Frank C S, 1958, Mr 11,29:2
Davis, Frank E, 1946, Jl 27,17:2
Davis, Frank E Mrs, 1944, Mr 7,17:4
Davis, Frank F, 1956, Jl 8,65:2
Davis, Frank G, 1957, O 23,33:5
Davis, Frank H, 1921, My 3,17:4; 1943, S 25,15
Davis, Frank J, 1947, O 6,21:5; 1949, Ja 28,21: 1960, F 13,19:4
Davis, FRank Jr, 1960, Ag 12,19:4
Davis, Frank M, 1945, Ap 28,15:6; 1947, D 12,
Davis, Frank M Mrs, 1951, Ap 6,25:1
Davis, Frank R, 1948, S 18,17:2; 1951, Ap 29,8
Davis, Frank S, 1946, Ag 17,13:2; 1949, My 20 1953, D 17,37:4
Davis, Frank T, 1944, F 5,15:2
Davis, Frank W, 1937, Ag 25,21:4
Davis, Franklin D, 1945, F 16,24:2
Davis, Franklin Hayes, 1905, Je 24,9:5

Davis, Franklin W, 1955, Ap 9,13:4
Davis, Fred, 1938, F 14,17:2; 1963, My 29,33:5
Davis, Fred B, 1943, Ag 14,11:6; 1944, F 17,19:1
Davis, Fred H Justice, 1937, Je 21,19:4
Davis, Fred R, 1940, D 27,19:4
Davis, Fred S, 1949, S 7,29:3
Davis, Frederick C, 1953, Je 6,17:6
Davis, Frederick E, 1953, Jl 18,13:5
Davis, Frederick H, 1950, Mr 15,29:2
Davis, Frederick H Jr Mrs, 1958, Mr 15,17:4
Davis, Frederick J, 1944, Jl 4,19:2
Davis, Frederick W, 1961, Mr 14,35:1
Davis, Frederick W Rev, 1923, Ja 23,21:5
Davis, G L, 1884, D 4,2:4
Davis, G Richard, 1962, Ap 8,86:4
Davis, G Richard Mrs, 1951, My 23,35:3
Davis, G S, 1931, Ja 9,23:1
Davis, Garret Sen, 1872, S 23,1:5
Davis, George, 1937, My 30,13:4; 1939, Jl 6,23:3; 1943, D 4,13:2; 1957, N 26,33:4; 1961, Ja 1,48:8
Davis, George A, 1920, F 13,11:3; 1956, O 11,39:4
Davis, George A Jr, 1961, Je 5,31:1
Davis, George Breckenridge Maj-Gen, 1914, D 17,13:6
Davis, George E, 1951, Mr 25,74:1; 1952, Ag 21,19:2; 1955, Je 17,23:3
Davis, George E Jr Mrs, 1950, N 27,25:4
Davis, George H, 1945, Ap 18,23:4; 1952, Mr 11,27:4; 1953, Ja 28,27:4; 1954, My 28,23:1; 1955, My 6,23:1; 1957, My 4,21:2
Davis, George H Mrs, 1944, Mr 14,19:4
Davis, George J, 1958, D 4,39:1
Davis, George K, 1943, Mr 29,16:3
Davis, George L, 1939, O 28,15:6; 1951, Ja 8,17:2
Davis, George M, 1940, D 30,17:5
Davis, George Mrs, 1939, Ja 2,23:2
Davis, George N, 1948, Ja 7,25:2
Davis, George R Rev, 1904, Ja 5,9:5
Davis, George Ritchie Dr, 1925, Je 26,17:5
Davis, George T, 1944, Je 29,23:1; 1947, D 12,28:3
Davis, George W, 1941, F 25,23:1; 1941, My 8,23:5; 1945, O 14,42:2; 1948, Ap 25,72:2; 1953, N 26,31:3; 1958, D 9,41:4; 1960, Mr 31,33:3
Davis, George W Mrs, 1904, Ag 6,7:6
Davis, Gherardi (will, Mr 19,18:2), 1941, Mr 10,17:5
Davis, Gilbert F, 1882, Jl 11,8:4; 1938, My 7,15:2
Davis, Glenmore W, 1958, Ag 24,87:2
Davis, Glenn B Mrs, 1955, O 5,36:7
Davis, Godfrey, 1961, Ag 22,29:1
Davis, Gomer C, 1941, O 29,23:3
Davis, Grace E, 1955, Ap 16,19:5
Davis, Graham, 1945, D 25,23:3
Davis, Graham L, 1958, Jl 6,56:8
Davis, Grover D, 1939, Jl 4,13:5
Davis, Gunnis, 1937, Mr 24,25:2
Davis, H A, 1953, Ap 21,27:1
Davis, H G Mrs, 1902, D 7,7:5
Davis, H K, 1934, Jl 26,19:4
Davis, H O, 1964, Ag 29,21:5
Davis, H P, 1931, S 11,21:1
Davis, H T, 1905, Ja 29,7:6
Davis, Hal S, 1959, Je 11,33:4
Davis, Harlow M, 1938, Ja 2,42:1
Davis, Harold, 1958, Ja 18,15:4
Davis, Harold A, 1955, Ja 9,87:3
Davis, Harold H, 1961, N 2,37:3
Davis, Harold L, 1960, N 1,39:1
Davis, Harold M, 1957, S 19,29:3
Davis, Harold S, 1965, O 13,47:4
Davis, Harold W, 1967, Ag 4,29:2
Davis, Harold W Mrs, 1951, O 2,28:3
Davis, Harrie Capt, 1920, Ja 15,11:3
Davis, Harriet Tubman, 1913, Mr 14,9:2
Davis, Harry, 1940, Ja 3,21:1; 1965, F 20,25:1
Davis, Harry B, 1937, Je 27,II,7:2
Davis, Harry C, 1948, D 28,21:4; 1956, My 5,19:5
Davis, Harry C Mrs, 1949, Ap 29,23:1
Davis, Harry E, 1948, Mr 29,21:6; 1952, O 21,29:5
Davis, Harry F, 1946, Ag 4,45:1; 1947, Mr 14,23:3; 1955, Jl 7,27:1
Davis, Harry G, 1941, F 23,41:1
Davis, Harry H, 1947, Ag 13,23:3
Davis, Harry J, 1958, S 3,33:6
Davis, Harry L, 1948, F 27,21:4; 1950, My 22,21:2
Davis, Harry T, 1959, F 14,21:5
Davis, Harry T Jr, 1964, Ag 5,33:5
Davis, Hartley C, 1938, Mr 31,23:5
Davis, Harvey N, 1952, D 5,27:1
Davis, Harvey N Mrs (Helen), 1968, D 28,27:1
Davis, Hassoldt, 1959, S 12,21:3
Davis, Henry, 1958, F 4,29:2; 1960, Jl 2,17:4
Davis, Henry A, 1939, Ag 4,13:2
Davis, Henry C, 1910, D 15,9:4; 1939, F 21,19:5; 1939, Jl 8,15:1
Davis, Henry C Mrs, 1916, Jl 23,17:5
Davis, Henry E, 1962, My 27,93:1
Davis, Henry G, 1942, N 4,23:6
Davis, Henry Gassaway, 1916, Mr 11,11:3
Davis, Henry H, 1944, Jl 1,15:3
Davis, Henry J, 1939, Mr 19,III,6:7
Davis, Henry K B, 1941, Mr 24,17:3
Davis, Henry L, 1943, Ap 12,23:5; 1944, Ag 18,13:4
Davis, Henry M, 1941, Mr 4,23:2
Davis, Henry P, 1948, Mr 9,23:4
Davis, Henry Richard, 1920, F 2,13:4
Davis, Henry S, 1948, F 21,13:2
Davis, Henry T, 1946, Ap 28,44:2
Davis, Henry William Banks, 1914, D 3,13:3
Davis, Henry Winter, 1865, D 31,4:4
Davis, Herbert E, 1941, Ag 28,19:5; 1947, My 28,25:4
Davis, Herbert J, 1967, Mr 30,45:1
Davis, Herbert J Judge, 1903, S 29,9:5
Davis, Herman, 1953, D 16,35:4
Davis, Homer C Sr, 1943, Ag 31,17:2
Davis, Horace, 1916, Jl 14,11:6
Davis, Horace A, 1957, O 6,84:8
Davis, Horace L, 1953, My 17,88:8
Davis, Horace N, 1948, O 4,23:5
Davis, Horace W, 1942, Ja 30,19:5
Davis, Howard, 1965, O 18,35:3
Davis, Howard A, 1941, S 22,15:3
Davis, Howard A Mrs, 1946, S 10,7:5
Davis, Howard B, 1955, S 13,31:1
Davis, Howard C, 1938, S 24,17:3; 1962, Mr 31,25:5
Davis, Howard C Sr, 1961, D 6,48:1
Davis, Howard E, 1947, S 14,60:3
Davis, Howard H, 1945, My 30,19:5
Davis, Howard L, 1963, My 11,25:5
Davis, Howard P, 1951, S 13,31:1
Davis, Howard R, 1962, My 3,33:1
Davis, Howard W, 1947, D 30,24:2
Davis, Howland Mrs, 1945, D 4,29:3
Davis, Hugh G, 1942, My 12,19:4
Davis, Hugh L, 1951, Ag 19,84:4
Davis, I L Mrs, 1945, O 21,46:1
Davis, Irving, 1963, My 15,39:1
Davis, Irving G, 1939, Mr 16,23:6
Davis, Irving J, 1956, Ap 18,31:2
Davis, Irving K, 1965, N 9,43:3
Davis, Isabelle, 1949, Ag 12,17:1
Davis, Isador W, 1952, O 9,31:3
Davis, Israel, 1943, Mr 17,21:1
Davis, J, 1878, N 9,8:3
Davis, J Bradford, 1955, F 13,86:3
Davis, J Charles, 1919, Ap 10,11:2
Davis, J Dr, 1883, Ap 10,5:5
Davis, J Frank, 1942, Ap 7,22:2
Davis, J G, 1866, F 4,3:3
Davis, J H Kelso, 1956, My 31,27:6
Davis, J Harry, 1945, O 12,24:2
Davis, J Herbert, 1924, Ap 26,15:4
Davis, J Lionberger Mrs, 1955, F 23,27:4
Davis, J M, 1902, My 3,9:6
Davis, J O, 1954, N 1,27:4
Davis, J Richard, 1964, S 21,31:4
Davis, J Stanley, 1939, Ap 15,19:5; 1951, My 1,29:3
Davis, J W, 1885, F 15,2:2
Davis, J W Mrs, 1902, F 1,9:1
Davis, Jack R, 1968, D 2,47:3
Davis, Jackson, 1947, Ap 16,25:1
Davis, Jackson Mrs, 1941, D 2,23:2
Davis, Jacob C, 1943, D 25,13:4
Davis, Jacob S, 1942, Jl 11,13:2
Davis, James, 1876, Ap 8,2:2; 1945, Ap 21,13:4
Davis, James A, 1966, Mr 23,48:1
Davis, James C, 1937, S 1,19:4; 1947, Ja 8,24:2
Davis, James E, 1949, Je 22,31:5
Davis, James J, 1925, Ag 10,13:4; 1947, N 22,15:3; 1967, F 3,31:2
Davis, James J Jr, 1962, Ap 10,43:2
Davis, James J Mrs, 1940, Jl 25,17:5
Davis, James M, 1942, D 25,17:3
Davis, Jeff, 1952, N 12,27:3
Davis, Jefferson, 1889, D 6,1:7; 1953, O 13,29:3
Davis, Jefferson (Jeff), 1968, Ap 6,40:5
Davis, Jefferson C Gen, 1879, D 2,5:5
Davis, Jefferson Jr, 1878, O 21,2:6
Davis, Jefferson Mrs (funl ser, O 19,9:6; burial, O 20,7:3), 1906, O 17,1:3
Davis, Jefferson Mrs, 1909, Ap 11,11:3
Davis, Jefferson W, 1963, Ap 10,39:4
Davis, Jennie M, 1942, D 25,17:4
Davis, Jennie P Mrs, 1949, Ja 7,21:2
Davis, Jeremiah P Mrs, 1968, Ap 2,47:2
Davis, Jerome D Rev Dr, 1910, N 6,II,13:3
Davis, Jesse B, 1955, N 3,31:4
Davis, Jesse C, 1940, D 26,19:4; 1944, Ap 2,40:1
Davis, Jessica K, 1948, S 10,23:5
Davis, Jessie Ballston, 1904, S 20,7:4
Davis, Jessie Bartlett, 1905, My 15,9:2
Davis, Jimmie H Mrs, 1967, Jl 30,65:1
Davis, Jimmy, 1958, Je 30,27:2
Davis, Joan, 1961, My 24,41:4
Davis, Joe, 1960, D 16,25:6
Davis, Joel Mrs, 1924, N 11,23:2
Davis, John, 1875, Ap 14,7:3; 1948, Ag 12,21:3; 1950, My 28,34:5
Davis, John A, 1941, Jl 5,11:4; 1947, My 29,22:3
Davis, John C, 1944, F 10,15:4; 1946, Mr 11,25:4; 1954, Ag 15,84:6; 1959, S 2,29:2
Davis, John C F, 1937, O 2,21:6
Davis, John Chanler Bancroft, 1907, D 28,7:6
Davis, John D, 1951, Mr 20,29:3
Davis, John E, 1964, Je 10,45:1; 1966, Mr 26,29:5
Davis, John E Sr, 1952, S 9,31:3
Davis, John F, 1943, My 20,21:2; 1944, Jl 24,15:4
Davis, John F Mrs, 1941, Ja 4,13:1
Davis, John H, 1918, F 8,11:8; 1937, O 15,16:3
Davis, John H Jr, 1955, Ag 6,15:6
Davis, John J, 1916, Mr 20,11:4; 1946, Je 25,21:5; 1965, Jl 15,29:3
Davis, John K, 1957, F 23,17:6
Davis, John L, 1949, Jl 29,21:6; 1951, Ja 19,25:5
Davis, John L Mrs, 1939, Ap 6,25:6
Davis, John M, 1938, Je 28,19:2; 1943, N 22,19:5; 1944, Mr 3,15:3; 1960, Je 22,35:5; 1961, Ap 7,31:1
Davis, John M K Gen, 1920, My 21,15:3
Davis, John P, 1947, Jl 18,17:5
Davis, John S, 1944, Ap 23,41:1; 1946, D 25,29:3; 1950, N 19,92:8
Davis, John S Mrs, 1948, Ja 7,25:4
Davis, John Steeple, 1917, D 8,15:5
Davis, John T (will), 1938, Mr 22,16:7
Davis, John T Mrs, 1946, Mr 30,15:4
Davis, John V, 1907, Mr 4,9:5
Davis, John W, 1938, O 5,23:3; 1951, Ag 29,25:1; 1952, Ja 26,13:2
Davis, John W (funl, Mr 29,29:1; will, Ap 1,28:6), 1955, Mr 26,15:4
Davis, John W, 1957, My 29,27:2; 1961, Mr 24,31:2
Davis, John W Ex-Gov, 1907, Ja 26,9:6
Davis, John W Mrs (por), 1943, Jl 14,19:6
Davis, John W Sr, 1945, F 22,27:5
Davis, Jonathan M, 1943, Je 28,21:3
Davis, Jonathan R, 1939, Ag 14,15:5
Davis, Joseph, 1944, Ja 10,17:1; 1949, My 26,29:1
Davis, Joseph A, 1938, Je 16,23:5; 1958, Mr 5,31:1
Davis, Joseph D, 1950, Ap 4,29:2
Davis, Joseph E, 1864, My 12,9:1; 1955, My 18,31:1; 1968, My 8,47:2
Davis, Joseph G, 1942, Ap 4,13:3
Davis, Joseph H Sr, 1954, Jl 19,19:6
Davis, Joseph I, 1955, Jl 31,69:2
Davis, Joseph Mrs, 1948, Je 10,25:4; 1958, Ap 14,25:4
Davis, Joseph P, 1940, N 8,17:5
Davis, Joseph W S, 1959, Ja 7,33:4
Davis, Josephine Mrs, 1942, Ja 1,19:1
Davis, Judson R, 1945, D 25,23:4
Davis, Judson W, 1951, Ag 7,25:2
Davis, Julia B A Mrs, 1952, Jl 5,15:3
Davis, Juliet M Mrs, 1937, Ja 20,21:5
Davis, Julius, 1953, Ja 30,21:3
Davis, Julius M, 1957, Ja 4,23:1
Davis, K B, 1935, D 11,23:1
Davis, Karl E, 1946, Ap 17,25:2
Davis, Kenneth, 1956, Jl 11,29:4
Davis, Kingsbury H, 1954, Ag 8,85:4
Davis, Kirke E, 1944, N 3,21:1
Davis, L C, 1940, Mr 9,15:4
Davis, L Clarke, 1904, D 15,9:3
Davis, L Clarke Mrs (est, O 7,11:4), 1910, S 30,13:3
Davis, L H Dr, 1922, Mr 16,17:5
Davis, L Howell, 1946, Ag 9,17:6
Davis, L L, 1933, My 15,13:6
Davis, Laurence B Mrs, 1959, D 24,19:3
Davis, Lawrence R, 1961, Ag 2,29:1
Davis, Lee I, 1950, F 2,27:2
Davis, Lee P, 1961, N 24,31:2
Davis, Lee P Jr Mrs, 1944, Jl 22,15:6
Davis, Lee P Mrs, 1940, Jl 22,17:4
Davis, Lena O Mrs, 1938, Ap 10,II,6:6
Davis, Leo, 1967, D 6,51:3
Davis, Leonard H, 1946, F 20,25:3
Davis, Leonard M, 1938, My 7,15:6
Davis, Leroy, 1937, Jl 11,II,4:6
Davis, Leslie, 1967, Ja 19,31:5
Davis, Leslie G, 1939, My 7,III,7:1
Davis, Lester F, 1940, Ja 27,13:4
Davis, Levi W, 1952, Ag 15,15:2
Davis, Lewis K, 1939, My 13,15:5
Davis, Lincoln, 1952, Jl 30,24:7
Davis, Lloyd A, 1953, Ag 8,11:5
Davis, Louis, 1922, Je 11,30:2; 1945, O 6,13:2; 1952, My 18,92:6; 1960, Je 29,33:5; 1964, Ag 21,29:3
Davis, Louis A, 1939, Ja 2,24:3
Davis, Louis L, 1948, Ag 14,13:2
Davis, Louis Mrs, 1948, Ap 3,15:5
Davis, Louise D Mrs (funl), 1957, D 5,35:6
Davis, Lyman H Sr, 1941, Je 17,21:3
Davis, M B Sir, 1928, Mr 23,21:5
Davis, Mabelle W Mrs, 1941, Ja 6,15:5
Davis, Madison, 1913, Ag 1,7:6
Davis, Malvin E, 1966, Ag 28,92:1
Davis, Malvin E Mrs, 1959, D 19,27:5
Davis, Manton, 1957, Jl 3,23:6
Davis, Manvel H, 1959, F 12,27:5
Davis, Margaret H, 1948, Ag 27,19:2
Davis, Marih, 1948, S 21,27:5
Davis, Martha C Mrs, 1938, Ap 27,23:5
Davis, Martha W, 1955, D 3,17:5
Davis, Mary G, 1956, Ap 16,27:3
Davis, Mary J, 1948, D 22,23:4
Davis, Mathias H, 1963, Ag 19,25:2
Davis, Max, 1951, S 7,29:2
Davis, Max T Mrs, 1964, Jl 4,13:5
Davis, Maxwell K, 1954, Mr 18,31:3
Davis, Maynard N, 1949, My 14,13:2
Davis, Mead, 1946, Jl 4,19:4
Davis, Merrill B, 1952, Jl 21,19:5
Davis, Merrill N, 1943, Mr 8,15:3

Davis, Mervyn, 1962, My 1,37:2
Davis, Michael, 1940, Ja 31,8:4
Davis, Michael B, 1951, Ja 14,84:4
Davis, Michael M Mrs, 1923, Ap 2,17:4
Davis, Michael T, 1953, Ap 29,29:4
Davis, Michael Van B, 1904, Ap 20,9:6
Davis, Millard, 1957, S 17,35:4
Davis, Milton E, 1963, My 15,39:1
Davis, Milton F (por), 1938, Je 1,23:3
Davis, Minerva M, 1942, Mr 20,19:6
Davis, Minnie L, 1958, F 21,23:1
Davis, Monnett B, 1953, D 27,60:1
Davis, Monnett B (body arrives US), 1954, Ja 1,23:2
Davis, Morgan, 1958, Je 26,27:6
Davis, Morris Mrs, 1912, Ag 5,9:5
Davis, Morton I, 1955, D 16,29:2
Davis, Moses, 1962, F 18,92:4
Davis, Mrs (Equestrienne), 1874, Jl 7,8:5
Davis, Muriel, 1957, N 7,35:4
Davis, Myra, 1909, O 23,11:1
Davis, N Evans, 1944, Ja 18,19:5
Davis, Nathan, 1943, O 30,15:3
Davis, Nathan S 3d, 1956, Ap 21,17:6
Davis, Nathan Smith Dr, 1904, Je 17,9:7
Davis, Nelson F, 1939, N 13,19:6
Davis, Nelson R, 1942, Jl 17,15:6
Davis, Nestor W, 1939, Je 24,17:2
Davis, Newlin S Sr, 1944, S 2,11:2
Davis, Newton B, 1953, Ag 22,15:2
Davis, Nicholas Harper Col, 1917, N 29,13:5
Davis, Nina, 1925, F 26,21:4
Davis, Noah Judge, 1902, Mr 21,9:5
Davis, Noah Mrs, 1903, N 20,9:6
Davis, Noble T, 1966, O 2,86:4
Davis, Norman, 1950, Ag 11,19:4
Davis, Norman A, 1958, Je 28,17:5
Davis, Norman H, 1944, Jl 2,1:2
Davis, Norman H Mrs, 1942, Mr 8,42:2
Davis, Norman P, 1964, Ag 24,27:2
Davis, O K, 1932, Je 4,15:3
Davis, Obadiah E Sr, 1941, F 8,15:5
Davis, Oliver C, 1912, Je 4,11:4
Davis, Oliver L, 1956, D 29,15:2
Davis, Ora G, 1941, My 24,15:6
Davis, Orville L, 1960, S 5,15:3
Davis, Oscar B, 1948, Jl 9,19:3
Davis, Oscar H, 1950, Ap 15,15:4
Davis, Oscar K Mrs, 1960, Je 26,72:6
Davis, Owen, 1920, O 10,22:2
Davis, Owen (trb lr, O 21,II,3:8), 1956, O 15,25:3
Davis, Owen Mrs, 1958, My 25,87:1
Davis, Owen V, 1950, Ap 8,13:5
Davis, Owen V Mrs, 1941, O 25,17:1
Davis, Ozora S Mrs, 1945, S 25,25:2
Davis, P, 1934, Je 6,21:4
Davis, P S Col, 1864, Jl 17,3:6
Davis, Park H, 1950, O 25,35:2
Davis, Park W, 1961, D 12,43:3
Davis, Parke H Mrs, 1952, Je 26,29:1
Davis, Patricia, 1950, Ap 10,19:5
Davis, Paul A 3d, 1948, N 26,23:2
Davis, Paul A 4th Mrs, 1938, N 13,26:3
Davis, Paul E, 1963, Je 26,39:4
Davis, Paul K, 1956, Ja 22,88:7
Davis, Paul Mrs (A Pearce), 1966, Mr 4,33:3
Davis, Paulina Wright, 1876, Ag 25,1:3
Davis, Perry J, 1954, O 14,29:1
Davis, Peter Mrs, 1950, F 17,23:2
Davis, Phil, 1951, N 21,25:3; 1964, D 18,33:3
Davis, Phil D, 1953, My 10,88:2
Davis, Phil H, 1940, F 21,19:3
Davis, Philip Mrs, 1945, Ag 18,11:5
Davis, Pierpont, 1942, Ja 27,21:4
Davis, Price M Sr, 1947, S 23,25:5
Davis, R H Mrs, 1931, Ag 19,21:3
Davis, R M, 1961, Je 28,35:2
Davis, Ralph E Mrs, 1947, Je 20,20:2; 1962, Jl 2,29:4
Davis, Ralph L, 1951, Mr 5,21:3
Davis, Ralph W, 1951, S 16,85:2
Davis, Raymond T, 1953, Jl 4,11:7
Davis, Reese P, 1942, Je 10,21:1
Davis, Reginald L, 1949, Ag 3,23:5
Davis, Richard D, 1871, Je 19,1:7
Davis, Richard H, 1963, S 25,43:4
Davis, Richard Harding, 1916, Ap 15,13:6
Davis, Richard M, 1966, Ap 2,29:4
Davis, Richard N, 1949, Jl 10,56:4
Davis, Richard S, 1956, Je 14,33:2; 1963, Jl 24,31:4
Davis, Richmond P Maj Gen, 1937, S 17,25:3
Davis, Robert, 1908, Jl 19,7:6
Davis, Robert (funl, Ja 12,13:3), 1911, Ja 10,11:3
Davis, Robert, 1949, S 26,25:3; 1951, D 22,16:2
Davis, Robert B Mrs, 1950, D 28,25:3
Davis, Robert Benson, 1920, F 10,9:1
Davis, Robert Benson Mrs, 1915, D 16,15:4
Davis, Robert G, 1948, N 9,30:3; 1949, N 13,94:4
Davis, Robert H, 1942, O 12,17:1; 1958, N 3,37:5; 1965, Mr 31,39:2
Davis, Robert H Mrs, 1967, Mr 19,92:6
Davis, Robert L, 1961, Mr 28,35:5
Davis, Robert M, 1948, O 20,29:5
Davis, Robert Vernon, 1913, Mr 8,15:4
Davis, Robin H Jr Mrs, 1946, Ja 27,42:3
Davis, Rodney, 1946, Ag 4,46:1
Davis, Roger W Sr, 1959, Ap 14,35:3
Davis, Roland L Jr, 1967, N 15,47:3
Davis, Roland M, 1945, O 27,15:4
Davis, Roscoe E, 1948, Mr 31,25:3
Davis, Ross B, 1946, Mr 13,29:5
Davis, Roswell, 1924, O 29,21:2; 1953, Ap 21,27:5
Davis, Rowland F, 1968, Ag 17,27:4
Davis, Rowland L, 1954, F 2,27:1
Davis, Roy, 1953, F 27,21:5
Davis, Roy B, 1947, F 28,23:4
Davis, Roy E, 1951, O 21,92:3
Davis, Roy H, 1956, Je 25,23:3
Davis, Roy M, 1943, S 1,19:4
Davis, Roy T, 1948, S 29,29:5
Davis, Royall O E, 1949, N 1,28:2
Davis, Rufus, 1950, Je 13,27:4
Davis, Russell G, 1950, My 15,21:4
Davis, S Austin, 1924, Ap 9,21:3; 1924, Je 15,23:1
Davis, S B, 1933, F 25,15:1
Davis, S H, 1903, My 9,9:5
Davis, Sada, 1963, Ag 22,27:4
Davis, Sally, 1961, Ag 1,31:5
Davis, Sam, 1945, O 25,21:5; 1949, Ag 23,23:5
Davis, Samuel, 1937, N 14,II,10:5; 1946, N 15,24:2
Davis, Samuel A, 1952, My 15,31:3
Davis, Samuel B, 1958, N 23,88:6
Davis, Samuel G, 1943, Ap 22,23:2
Davis, Samuel J, 1949, O 1,13:2; 1967, Mr 22,47:3
Davis, Samuel L, 1945, D 7,21:2
Davis, Samuel Mrs, 1951, Jl 28,11:6
Davis, Samuel Sheppard, 1924, Ap 13,27:4
Davis, Samuel T Jr, 1915, S 2,9:6
Davis, Samuel T Jr Mrs, 1952, Je 22,69:1
Davis, Sereno P, 1961, O 16,29:1
Davis, Seward, 1941, S 2,17:3
Davis, Sherlock, 1959, Ap 24,27:1
Davis, Sherman L, 1940, F 2,17:3
Davis, Sidney, 1954, My 12,31:2
Davis, Solomon, 1947, N 3,23:2
Davis, Stanleigh C, 1952, N 16,87:2
Davis, Stella B Mrs, 1953, Ja 21,31:1
Davis, Steve Nicholas, 1951, Jl 15,61:2
Davis, Stewart A, 1925, N 7,15:5
Davis, Stuart, 1954, Ja 15,20:3; 1964, Je 26,26:1
Davis, Sydney, 1960, Ja 2,13:5
Davis, T B, 1942, S 29,23:2
Davis, T C, 1884, Ja 22,5:2
Davis, T Carroll, 1953, Mr 7,15:3
Davis, T Lawrence, 1953, O 18,86:7
Davis, T Preston, 1942, F 18,19:4
Davis, T R, 1875, O 22,10:4
Davis, T Rice, 1947, Ag 13,23:1
Davis, T Wallis, 1955, N 25,27:2
Davis, Tenny L, 1949, Ja 27,23:2
Davis, Theodore H, 1941, Mr 19,21:4
Davis, Theodore M, 1915, F 24,9:5
Davis, Thomas, 1872, Je 13,4:7; 1939, O 13,23:4
Davis, Thomas A, 1945, Je 13,23:3
Davis, Thomas A Mrs, 1947, My 5,23:3
Davis, Thomas B, 1948, Jl 4,27:1
Davis, Thomas B Col, 1911, N 27,11:5
Davis, Thomas Bishop, 1871, D 4,1:7
Davis, Thomas C, 1960, Ja 22,27:2; 1964, F 1,23:2
Davis, Thomas D, 1953, Ap 1,29:3
Davis, Thomas E, 1948, S 30,27:5
Davis, Thomas F Jr, 1955, Jl 25,19:2
Davis, Thomas G, 1966, My 28,27:2
Davis, Thomas H, 1911, Je 9,13:4
Davis, Thomas J, 1909, Ag 21,7:2; 1952, Ja 9,29:2; 1953, O 24,15:6
Davis, Thomas L, 1955, Ja 28,19:1
Davis, Thomas S Dr, 1937, S 13,21:2
Davis, Thomas S Mrs, 1946, Ap 2,27:5
Davis, Thomas T, 1872, My 3,5:2
Davis, Thomas W, 1943, S 10,23:3
Davis, Thurber P, 1956, D 1,21:2
Davis, Tobe C Mrs (Dec 25), 1963, Ap 1,35:4
Davis, Ulysses S, 1950, Ap 19,29:4
Davis, V A (Winnie), 1898, S 19,4:6
Davis, V M, 1931, Ap 18,19:1
Davis, Vernon E, 1949, S 29,29:3
Davis, Vernon M Mrs, 1920, Mr 24,9:5
Davis, Victor, 1945, Je 29,15:2
Davis, Victor S, 1940, Mr 26,21:1
Davis, W B, 1956, Jl 2,21:3
Davis, W Earle, 1950, Jl 30,60:6
Davis, W L Y, 1941, My 31,11:2
Davis, W O, 1938, Mr 14,16:2
Davis, W T, 1907, D 4,9:5
Davis, W W, 1941, F 12,21:5
Davis, W W Mrs, 1923, N 29,21:4
Davis, Walter, 1959, F 12,27:1
Davis, Walter A, 1952, O 10,25:1
Davis, Walter Alan, 1968, Jl 21,56:8
Davis, Walter B, 1948, F 29,61:1
Davis, Walter J, 1961, Jl 4,19:4
Davis, Walter Juan, 1921, D 5,17:3
Davis, Walter N, 1958, D 30,35:2
Davis, Walter S, 1940, F 14,21:3; 1958, N 16,88:8
Davis, Walter V, 1953, F 21,13:5
Davis, Walter W, 1947, O 16,27:3
Davis, Walton P, 1951, Ag 16,27:3
Davis, Warren B, 1939, S 2,17:6; 1944, S 16,13:3; 1947, Jl 8,23:3
Davis, Warren H, 1950, Mr 5,92:6
Davis, Warren T, 1960, F 4,31:4
Davis, Watson, 1967, Je 28,45:3
Davis, Watson Mrs, 1957, Ja 27,84:3
Davis, Webster, 1923, F 23,13:5
Davis, Webster B, 1952, F 28,27:4
Davis, Wendell Mrs (W Farmer), 1961, Ag 15,29:3
Davis, Westmoreland, 1942, S 3,19:3
Davis, Westmoreland Mrs, 1963, Jl 15,29:4
Davis, Wilbert, 1943, Ja 30,15:3
Davis, Wilbur B, 1953, Je 5,27:4; 1959, Ja 26,29:5
Davis, Wilbur B Mrs, 1948, My 9,68:5
Davis, Will B, 1962, My 30,19:4
Davis, Will J, 1919, My 17,13:5
Davis, Will L, 1946, My 12,44:4
Davis, Will L Mrs, 1954, Ag 12,25:4
Davis, Willard H, 1949, F 24,23:2
Davis, William (Son of Jeff Davis), 1872, O 17,1:6
Davis, William, 1915, S 17,7:5; 1944, Ja 27,12:2; 194 O 18,23:1
Davis, William A, 1945, Mr 10,17:3; 1949, Je 6,19:4
Davis, William A Mrs, 1958, S 13,19:4
Davis, William B, 1955, F 3,23:3
Davis, William C, 1947, Ja 22,23:4; 1949, Ja 19,27:5; 1949, Ap 19,25:4; 1956, Je 10,88:3
Davis, William C Prof, 1968, Ag 16,33:1
Davis, William C T, 1957, F 3,77:3
Davis, William Dean, 1903, O 20,9:6
Davis, William E, 1937, F 3,24:2; 1953, Ap 10,21:2; 1960, D 26,23:2
Davis, William F, 1946, F 10,40:8; 1967, Ap 24,33:5
Davis, William F Mrs, 1952, S 1,17:6
Davis, William F Rev, 1946, Mr 18,21:5
Davis, William H, 1904, D 8,5:4; 1937, D 31,16:2; 1943, Jl 9,17:2; 1948, Mr 21,60:6; 1948, Ap 16,23:2 1951, Jl 31,22:3; 1955, D 6,38:1; 1962, D 6,43:1; 1964, Ag 15,21:2; 1967, My 9,47:3
Davis, William H K Dr, 1913, S 25,13:3
Davis, William H Mrs, 1956, Ja 14,19:6
Davis, William J, 1961, Jl 27,31:4
Davis, William J Jr, 1944, F 19,13:1
Davis, William J L, 1956, F 19,92:2
Davis, William J Mrs, 1949, Ja 3,23:2
Davis, William J Sr, 1954, Ag 3,19:2
Davis, William L, 1950, Ap 13,29:2
DAvis, William Leonard, 1912, My 26,15:5
Davis, William M, 1905, Mr 28,9:4; 1942, Je 13,15: 1947, Jl 28,15:1
Davis, William Mrs, 1948, Jl 19,19:3; 1960, N 14,3
Davis, William N, 1949, D 6,31:1
Davis, William O, 1938, F 1,21:4
Davis, William P, 1962, S 12,39:1
Davis, William P L, 1941, Mr 21,21:4
Davis, William R, 1941, Ag 2,15:3
Davis, William R Mrs, 1951, D 22,15:3
Davis, William S, 1961, F 23,27:2; 1962, S 22,25:5
Davis, William S Mrs, 1965, Ja 22,43:4
Davis, William Sr, 1948, F 12,23:2
Davis, William T, 1944, Je 17,13:6; 1945, Ja 23,19: 1958, S 24,27:2; 1959, O 28,37:3
Davis, William W, 1937, Ja 13,23:4; 1941, S 23,23:
Davis, Willis A, 1943, Ag 11,19:6
Davis, Willis D Mrs, 1957, O 5,17:2
Davis, Winnifred P, 1951, F 19,23:4
Davis, Wirt Brig-Gen, 1914, F 12,9:4
Davis, Woodbury, 1871, Ag 14,1:1
Davis, Zachariah, 1937, Mr 21,II,3:6
Davis, Zachary T, 1946, D 17,31:5
Davis-Hayes, Margaret Howell Jefferson Mrs, 190 Jl 22,7:6
Davison, Alvah E Mrs, 1945, D 5,25:1
Davison, Amelia, 1937, Jl 13,20:2
Davison, Andrew B, 1955, Ja 4,21:1
Davison, Archibald T, 1961, F 8,31:1
Davison, Arthur B, 1953, Ag 7,19:5
Davison, C Herbert, 1958, O 16,37:4
Davison, Charles, 1921, Ja 9,23:1; 1940, Ap 29,15 1942, Ja 21,18:2
Davison, Charles S, 1942, N 24,25:1
Davison, Charles Stewart Rev, 1920, My 20,13:5
Davison, Charles W, 1941, Ap 21,19:4
Davison, Christopher C, 1950, Ag 1,23:4
Davison, Clarence B, 1938, Jl 18,13:6
Davison, Clarence M, 1964, D 5,31:4
Davison, Danny, 1924, Jl 29,15:5
Davison, David H, 1941, N 23,53:1
Davison, E F, 1879, Ap 1,2:4
Davison, E Mora Mrs, 1948, Ag 30,17:1
Davison, Edward Mrs, 1959, S 25,24:1
Davison, Ellsworth R, 1909, Ap 17,9:5
Davison, Ethelbert L, 1951, Ja 16,29:5
Davison, F Trubee Sr, 1937, S 10,23:2
Davison, Frank E, 1960, Je 30,29:5
Davison, Frederick T 2d, 1954, Mr 2,32:1
Davison, George, 1950, Ja 18,31:5
Davison, George B, 1909, Mr 15,9:6
Davison, George M, 1943, O 2,13:6
Davison, George S, 1942, O 4,52:1
Davison, George T, 1950, Mr 18,14:2
Davison, George W, 1953, Je 17,27:5
Davison, Gregory C Mrs, 1955, F 5,15:6

Davison, Hal M, 1958, Ap 27,87:1
Davison, Harold J Com, 1922, N 29,17:4
Davison, Harold M, 1968, N 16,37:2
Davison, Henry C, 1940, Jl 31,17:5
Davison, Henry J, 1947, Ap 29,27:3
Davison, Henry P (funl, My 9,19:1), 1922, My 8,17:1
Davison, Henry P, 1961, Jl 3,15:2
Davison, Henry P Mrs, 1962, F 1,31:2
Davison, J R, 1871, My 4,2:2
Davison, John A, 1947, Je 28,13:3
Davison, John A Mrs, 1962, Ag 4,19:5
Davison, John L, 1951, My 11,27:1
Davison, Leon A, 1939, D 14,27:4
Davison, Lewis J, 1947, D 30,23:2
Davison, Lorenzo P Col, 1917, Ap 14,13:5
Davison, Mabel, 1939, Ag 24,19:3
Davison, Matthew, 1942, My 20,20:3
Davison, Peter W Brig-Gen, 1920, F 14,11:4
Davison, Philip S, 1965, My 19,47:2
Davison, Sanford A, 1967, My 8,41:4
Davison, Sanford A Mrs, 1957, Jl 22,19:6
Davison, Thomas E, 1966, Je 4,29:2
Davison, W F, 1944, Ja 11,20:3
Davison, Walter S, 1960, Ja 20,31:1
Davison, Walter S Mrs, 1967, F 26,84:6
Davison, William A, 1904, F 12,9:6
Davison, William H (Lord Broughshane), 1953, Ja 20,25:4
Davison, William H, 1955, F 2,27:5
Davison, William J, 1944, Mr 16,19:6
Davison, William M Jr, 1948, Ja 11,56:6
Davisson, Augustus, 1940, Ja 5,19:2
Davisson, Clinton J, 1958, F 3,23:3
Davisson, Elizabeth L D Mrs, 1965, Ap 6,39:4
Davisson, Richard L, 1968, N 25,47:3
Davitch, David H, 1952, S 4,27:1
Davitt, Lawrence J Rev, 1937, F 23,27:2
Davitt, Michael (will, Je 1,7:1), 1906, My 31,7:3
Davitt, Michael E, 1945, O 23,17:5
Davitto, Bernard, 1953, S 12,17:6
Davlin, William R, 1961, O 22,86:2
Davol, Charles J C, 1937, Ap 12,17:3
Davol, Stephen B Mrs, 1939, D 26,19:5
Davol, William C, 1925, My 1,19:5
Davray, Henry D, 1944, Ja 26,19:3
Davren, John W, 1940, Mr 7,23:4
Davson, Edward Sir, 1937, Ag 8,II,7:2
Davson, Ivan B, 1947, Ja 29,25:4
Davy, Bertram H Mrs, 1943, Ag 5,15:5
Davy, Charles F, 1938, S 18,44:5
Davy, Charles G, 1957, Jl 23,27:2
Davy, David A, 1954, Je 14,21:3
Davy, Frederick, 1949, F 26,15:6
Davy, Henry Sir, 1922, My 11,17:5
Davy, James B, 1947, Je 17,25:5
Davy, John M Ex-Judge, 1909, Ap 22,9:4
Davy, Ralph B, 1947, F 19,25:4
Davy, Ruby, 1949, Jl 14,27:3
Davydorf, O Count, 1882, Ag 27,6:7
Davydov, Alex, 1950, Ag 30,32:2
Davydovsky, Ippolit V Prof, 1968, Je 14,47:3
Daw, Charles, 1947, Ja 19,52:1
Daw, Glen, 1949, My 31,25:7
Dawant, Albert, 1923, Ap 19,19:5
Dawbarn, Robert Hugh McKay, 1915, Jl 19,9:5
Dawber, Guy, 1938, Ap 26,15:4
Dawe, Arthur J, 1950, Jl 16,68:7
Dawe, Dorothy A, 1947, O 5,68:4
Dawe, George, 1939, F 10,23:1
Dawe, George G, 1948, S 15,31:5
Dawe, Harry P, 1949, S 29,29:4
Dawe, James Mrs, 1946, Je 15,21:3
Dawe, Norman, 1948, Ja 5,19:4
Dawe, Richard C, 1948, My 11,25:1
Dawes, A Sidney, 1968, Mr 4,37:4
Dawes, Abby N Mrs, 1942, Mr 31,21:1
Dawes, Ada L Mrs, 1939, S 20,27:3
Dawes, Anna L, 1938, S 26,17:3
Dawes, Arthur W, 1950, O 12,31:4
Dawes, Bemen G, 1953, My 17,88:4
Dawes, Catherine P Mrs (will, Ap 30,15:5), 1937, Ap 12,17:1
Dawes, Charles C Mrs, 1966, Ag 12,31:1
Dawes, Charles G, 1951, Ap 24,1:2
Dawes, Charles G Mrs, 1957, O 4,23:3
Dawes, David H, 1952, N 8,17:4
Dawes, Dexter B, 1957, Ap 26,25:2
Dawes, Edward L, 1944, N 21,25:5
Dawes, Edwin M, 1945, Mr 27,19:3
Dawes, Frederick C, 1947, Ap 17,27:2
Dawes, Frederick F Mrs, 1955, Ag 5,19:6
Dawes, George N, 1938, Ap 8,19:4
Dawes, H L Ex-Sen, 1903, F 6,9:5
Dawes, Hamilton M, 1940, My 16,23:2
Dawes, Henry M (will, O 8,14:4), 1952, S 30,31:1
Dawes, James H Sr, 1947, Ja 15,26:3
Dawes, Norman J, 1967, Ap 15,31:1
Dawes, Rufus C, 1940, Ja 9,23:1
Dawes, Spencer L, 1944, Jl 14,13:6
Dawes, William, 1948, O 26,31:1
Dawes, William A, 1950, My 19,27:1
Dawes, William R, 1951, S 22,17:3
Dawkins, Clinton Edward, 1905, D 3,7:6
Dawkins, Richard M, 1955, My 6,23:5
Dawkins, W B Sir, 1929, Ja 16,25:3
Dawkins, William A, 1951, D 18,31:1
Dawless, Frank S, 1939, D 5,27:2
Dawley, Almena, 1956, D 13,37:5
Dawley, Harry R, 1952, Ap 11,23:4
Dawley, J Searle, 1949, Mr 30,25:4
Dawley, T R Jr, 1930, Je 3,31:5
Dawley, T Robinson, 1950, Ag 15,29:2
Dawn, Isabel, 1966, Je 30,39:4
Dawnay, Alan G, 1938, S 29,25:5
Daws, George, 1939, O 2,17:2
Daws, Theodore B, 1956, D 4,39:4
Daws, Van Zandt, 1875, S 5,12:2
Dawson, A O, 1940, Ja 11,23:6
Dawson, Albert F, 1949, Mr 10,27:4
Dawson, Alden B, 1968, N 20,47:4
Dawson, Allan (funl, Je 26,19:5), 1923, Je 25,13:4
Dawson, Allan, 1949, O 16,9:1
Dawson, Allan Mrs (funl, Ap 26,19:5), 1923, Ap 24, 21:4
Dawson, Allan W, 1949, N 14,27:2
Dawson, Archie O (funl plans, Ag 5,33:4; funl, Ag 7,29:5), 1964, Ag 4,29:1
Dawson, Arthur, 1922, Ag 29,15:6; 1961, Jl 6,29:1
Dawson, Arthur E, 1949, F 16,25:1
Dawson, Benjamin S, 1948, Jl 22,23:3
Dawson, C C, 1945, O 18,23:3
Dawson, C Preston, 1947, N 22,15:2
Dawson, Cecil F, 1960, Ag 1,23:4
Dawson, Charles F, 1941, Ja 7,23:5
Dawson, Clifford H, 1944, O 28,15:2
Dawson, Coningsby, 1959, Ag 11,27:2
Dawson, D, 1933, Ja 21,15:3
Dawson, Dana, 1964, My 3,87:1
Dawson, Dennis S, 1941, Ja 15,23:3
Dawson, Dudley, 1937, My 25,28:3
Dawson, Edgar, 1946, My 1,25:4
Dawson, Edward, 1947, O 26,68:6
Dawson, Elizabeth C Mrs, 1937, D 24,19:2
Dawson, Elmer E, 1937, Ja 10,II,10:8
Dawson, Ernest B, 1957, Mr 21,31:1
Dawson, Eugene, 1950, Mr 15,29:2
Dawson, Francis W, 1909, My 6,9:7
Dawson, Frank, 1949, Ap 26,25:4
Dawson, Fred A, 1964, N 19,39:5
Dawson, Fred T, 1965, Ag 19,31:4
Dawson, Frederick F, 1949, F 4,24:2
Dawson, Frederick G, 1954, Mr 9,27:5
Dawson, Geoffrey, 1944, N 8,17:3
Dawson, George (see also D 1), 1876, D 3,10:4
Dawson, George, 1883, F 18,2:1
Dawson, George C, 1957, D 29,49:1
Dawson, George W, 1938, F 6,II,8:6; 1946, D 24,17:2
Dawson, H Alan, 1949, Ag 28,75:4
Dawson, Harry R Mrs, 1941, Ag 26,19:3
Dawson, Henry H, 1937, S 19,II,6:6
Dawson, Henry S, 1949, F 23,27:5
Dawson, Herbert F, 1963, Ap 6,19:3
Dawson, Herbert H, 1958, My 15,29:2
Dawson, J L, 1879, Ja 19,2:3
Dawson, J W, 1951, Jl 22,60:2
Dawson, Jackson Thornton, 1916, Ag 4,9:5
Dawson, James A Mrs, 1968, Ap 25,47:4
Dawson, James F, 1941, Ap 25,19:3; 1941, O 23,23:5
Dawson, James H, 1951, S 4,27:4
Dawson, James L, 1952, D 13,21:4
Dawson, James P, 1953, Mr 7,15:1
Dawson, Jerome, 1945, Je 26,19:5
Dawson, John B, 1956, My 10,31:4
Dawson, John P Rev, 1922, Ap 6,17:4
Dawson, John R, 1948, Mr 21,60:2; 1952, D 21,53:1
Dawson, Joseph, 1946, Je 19,21:2
Dawson, Joseph L, 1947, Jl 1,25:3
Dawson, Joseph W, 1937, Ag 31,23:4
Dawson, Julia G Mrs, 1939, D 27,24:5
Dawson, Julian, 1955, My 7,17:3
Dawson, Kenneth D, 1947, Ja 28,24:3
Dawson, Kenneth L, 1954, N 20,17:4
Dawson, Leslie M, 1948, Ap 24,15:2
Dawson, Lionel M, 1950, Ag 10,25:2
Dawson, Lord, 1945, Mr 8,23:3
Dawson, Lucy H, 1938, My 24,19:1
Dawson, Martin H, 1945, Ap 28,15:4
Dawson, Martin Henry Mrs, 1968, F 14,51:1
Dawson, May, 1952, O 22,27:2
Dawson, Miles M, 1942, Mr 29,45:1
Dawson, Peter (J Glidden), 1957, Jl 23,25:3
Dawson, Phil, 1938, S 25,39:3
Dawson, Ralph, 1948, N 4,29:4; 1962, N 18,86:8
Dawson, Ralph R, 1954, Je 16,31:5
Dawson, Raymond, 1947, O 4,17:5
Dawson, Richard, 1955, S 17,15:4
Dawson, Robert, 1949, N 8,31:5
Dawson, Robert Q, 1943, Ag 11,19:1
Dawson, Robert W, 1958, Jl 17,27:4
Dawson, S K Mrs, 1879, Ag 27,5:5
Dawson, Samuel, 1944, D 27,19:2
Dawson, Samuel H, 1949, Ja 25,23:5
Dawson, Thomas, 1961, D 6,47:3
Dawson, Thomas A, 1952, Mr 13,29:3
Dawson, Thomas C, 1912, My 2,11:3
Dawson, Thomas H Jr, 1959, O 13,39:1
Dawson, W J, 1928, Ag 24,10:6
Dawson, Walter L, 1955, Ag 20,17:6
Dawson, Walter M Mrs, 1962, Mr 21,39:1
Dawson, Warrington, 1962, S 27,37:3
Dawson, Wesley M, 1946, Jl 24,27:5
Dawson, William, 1950, F 24,23:1
Dawson, William A, 1951, F 10,13:3
Dawson, William D, 1966, Ap 29,47:1
Dawson, William O Ex-Gov, 1916, Mr 13,9:5
Dawson, William Sir, 1899, N 20,7:6
Dawson, William W, 1943, O 26,23:5; 1947, F 12,25:3
Dawson-Watson, Dawson, 1939, S 6,23:2
Dawydoff, Alex, 1965, Ag 3,31:1
Day, A J, 1873, Ap 1,5:5
Day, Addison B, 1939, N 30,21:4
Day, Albert A (funl, S 4,7:5), 1911, S 3,II,9:4
Day, Albert R, 1924, Ja 22,17:2
Day, Albert S, 1948, N 11,27:6
Day, Allan C, 1943, D 9,28:3
Day, Anna V, 1945, My 10,23:4
Day, Arthur E Mrs, 1953, Ja 1,23:4
Day, Arthur F, 1953, Jl 15,25:2
Day, Arthur L, 1960, Mr 11,25:1
Day, Arthur M, 1942, Mr 8,42:4
Day, Arthur P, 1952, Ag 27,27:3
Day, Benjamin, 1916, Ag 31,9:3; 1937, N 14,II,10:8
Day, Bernard P, 1967, Ap 13,43:1
Day, C Maj, 1884, Je 12,2:4
Day, C S, 1927, Ja 8,17:4
Day, Cassius M, 1940, Ag 20,19:4
Day, Charles B, 1949, Ja 29,13:1
Day, Charles B Mrs, 1946, Ja 20,42:3
Day, Charles H, 1939, Ja 25,22:1
Day, Charles H (por), 1955, My 28,15:3
Day, Charles I, 1950, Je 23,25:2
Day, Charles J, 1950, Jl 25,27:5
Day, Charles M, 1945, S 8,15:5
Day, Charles O, 1938, F 25,17:3
Day, Charles Orrin Dr, 1910, Ap 6,11:4
Day, Charles P, 1955, Je 16,37:1
Day, Charles R, 1965, Ap 9,33:3
Day, Charles V Mrs, 1950, Ja 6,21:2
Day, Charles W, 1938, Ja 21,20:2
Day, Chris C, 1939, Jl 15,15:6
Day, Clarence R, 1938, S 14,23:4
Day, Clifford L, 1964, F 18,35:4
Day, Clive, 1951, Jl 28,11:1
Day, Clive C, 1958, My 12,29:5
Day, Clive C Mrs, 1965, F 25,31:1
Day, Clyde L, 1938, Jl 21,21:4
Day, Cushman Dr, 1907, O 27,9:5
Day, Cyrus L Prof, 1968, Jl 10,40:1
Day, D Ralph, 1945, Ag 29,23:4
Day, David A, 1954, S 8,31:2
Day, David S, 1962, S 13,37:3
Day, David T, 1925, Ap 17,21:5
Day, Doris Mrs, 1953, S 14,27:4
Day, Dudley M, 1965, F 23,33:3
Day, Dwight H Mrs, 1950, F 20,25:5
Day, Edith H, 1959, Ap 28,35:4
Day, Edmund, 1912, Ja 23,11:5
Day, Edmund E, 1951, Mr 24,13:1
Day, Edward A Mrs, 1944, N 4,15:2
Day, Edward C, 1940, F 27,21:3
Day, Edward L, 1908, Mr 15,9:4; 1952, Ag 14,23:2
Day, Edward M, 1947, My 4,60:7
Day, Edward Parsons, 1906, Je 9,9:4
Day, Edwin B, 1939, S 26,23:3
Day, Elbridge C Day, 1923, F 14,17:5
Day, Elmer W Mrs, 1948, O 15,24:2
Day, Emie S, 1962, Ap 18,39:2
Day, Erastus S, 1921, S 1,15:4
Day, Ernest B, 1945, Mr 1,21:1
Day, Ernest H, 1946, Ag 20,27:2
Day, Everett, 1963, Ag 3,45:2
Day, Ewing W, 1942, N 26,27:5
Day, F Wilson, 1943, D 7,27:1
Day, Fessenden L, 1950, Ja 5,26:7
Day, Flora R, 1958, Ap 24,31:5
Day, Florence R, 1957, Ag 16,19:2
Day, Francis E, 1924, My 4,23:2
Day, Frank J, 1967, Je 1,43:2
Day, Frank M Mrs, 1952, Je 23,19:2
Day, Frank Miles, 1918, Je 18,13:6
Day, Frank P, 1950, Ag 1,23:6
Day, Frank S, 1948, Ap 2,24:2
Day, George A, 1962, My 27,93:2
Day, George C, 1940, N 4,19:5
Day, George H, 1907, N 22,9:5
Day, George P, 1959, O 25,86:1
Day, George P Mrs, 1962, D 4,41:2
Day, George S, 1957, Ja 15,30:4
Day, Georgie W, 1951, Jl 8,60:4
Day, Godfrey M, 1961, O 17,39:2
Day, Grafton E, 1946, My 4,15:4
Day, Gustavus L, 1955, Je 7,33:1
Day, H Frederick, 1942, Ag 10,19:5
Day, H H, 1878, Ag 27,4:7
Day, H Kent, 1925, O 30,21:5
Day, Harold B, 1960, Ap 16,17:6
Day, Harold H, 1953, O 10,17:3
Day, Harold R, 1938, Ja 13,21:1
Day, Harold S, 1953, Ja 10,17:1

Day, Harrison J, 1949, Ag 22,21:2
Day, Harry, 1939, S 17,48:8
Day, Harry A Mrs, 1953, F 24,25:2
Day, Harry B, 1944, N 10,19:1
Day, Harry Brooks, 1921, Jl 6,15:6
Day, Harry D, 1942, F 11,21:1
Day, Harry E Mrs, 1948, Mr 22,23:4
Day, Harry L, 1942, N 19,25:3
Day, Harry V, 1943, Ja 17,44:5
Day, Harvey B, 1951, N 25,86:5
Day, Helen A, 1962, My 13,88:5
Day, Helen Mrs, 1910, S 24,11:5
Day, Henry B, 1941, D 2,23:2
Day, Henry M, 1957, Jl 14,73:1
Day, Herbert J, 1954, Ap 11,86:4
Day, Hilbert F, 1947, My 18,60:2
Day, Hiram B, 1940, Mr 23,13:4
Day, Homer, 1922, Ap 8,15:4
Day, Horace L, 1938, F 5,15:4
Day, Horace T Mrs, 1956, Ap 4,29:2
Day, Howard, 1956, N 20,37:4
Day, Howard Mrs, 1953, Mr 27,23:3
Day, Hugh E, 1947, N 15,17:2
Day, Isaac L Mrs, 1948, F 5,23:2
Day, Ishmael, 1873, D 30,4:7
Day, J, 1931, Ap 4,17:1
Day, J Francis, 1941, Ja 13,15:5
Day, J Walter, 1945, Ap 9,19:5
Day, James C, 1955, N 18,25:1
Day, James E, 1949, N 17,29:5; 1967, N 9,47:1
Day, James F, 1942, Je 13,15:6
Day, James G Mrs, 1955, Jl 29,17:5
Day, James R, 1962, Jl 29,60:8
Day, James R Dr (por), 1923, Mr 14,19:3
Day, Jeremiah (funl, Ag 29,2:6), 1867, Ag 24,1:6
Day, Jerome Mrs (L Lane), 1963, Jl 27,17:3
Day, Jessie A Mrs, 1945, Jl 20,19:4
Day, John, 1961, D 29,23:1
Day, John C, 1954, O 7,23:3
Day, John D, 1956, Je 29,21:2
Day, John F Mrs (V Koch), 1961, N 30,37:4
Day, John G F, 1938, S 27,21:5
Day, John H, 1946, Ja 23,27:4
Day, John I, 1939, My 18,25:4
Day, John L, 1940, N 28,23:3
Day, John P, 1942, S 29,23:2
Day, Joseph L, 1903, S 22,7:5
Day, Joseph P Mrs, 1956, Ja 16,21:4
Day, Josiah F, 1907, Je 4,7:6
Day, Julian, 1947, Je 17,25:5
Day, Katherine E, 1957, My 19,88:3
Day, Katherine S, 1964, Je 6,23:5
Day, Kathyrn, 1963, Ap 18,35:6
Day, L B, 1938, N 23,21:2
Day, L Enos, 1939, My 20,15:6
Day, L Freeman, 1914, N 14,11:6
Day, Lee G Jr, 1966, S 25,84:6
Day, Lee G Mrs, 1964, O 24,29:1
Day, Lee Garnett, 1968, My 25,35:3
Day, Lena L, 1953, Mr 9,29:4
Day, Leroy E, 1955, Ap 19,31:3
Day, Lina A Mrs, 1941, Mr 4,23:3
Day, Louis D, 1952, O 2,29:3
Day, Louisa B Mrs, 1941, Je 7,17:2
Day, Luther, 1965, F 9,37:2
Day, Luther Mrs, 1944, F 24,15:4
Day, M C Mrs (funl), 1876, F 17,7:4
Day, Marie L, 1939, N 10,23:4
Day, Marion M Mrs, 1957, N 22,25:1
Day, Marshall M, 1955, O 30,88:7
Day, Martin C, 1908, Je 2,7:6
Day, Mary A, 1964, Mr 1,83:3
Day, Mary E, 1943, Jl 10,13:7
Day, Mary L, 1954, Jl 8,23:5
Day, Maxwell W, 1950, S 27,32:3
Day, Melville C, 1913, D 30,9:5
Day, Minor H, 1943, My 26,23:6
Day, Nicholas Wyckoff Gen, 1916, Mr 8,11:5
Day, Normal L, 1941, F 12,21:6
Day, Orville E, 1951, My 17,31:4
Day, Osborne A, 1950, Ja 31,23:3
Day, Rachel Brookfield Mrs, 1906, D 21,9:4
Day, Rachel C B Mrs, 1937, F 21,II,11:1
Day, Ralph L, 1947, N 23,72:5
Day, Ralph R, 1947, N 2,72:6
Day, Raymond M, 1951, N 3,17:2
Day, Richard Mrs (D V Vane), 1966, D 18,84:8
Day, Robert B, 1965, Ag 17,19:2
Day, Robert L, 1903, Jl 8,9:7; 1947, Mr 26,25:3
Day, Roby F, 1964, Jl 29,33:4
Day, Rodney D, 1962, Je 17,81:1
Day, Roger S, 1947, My 16,24:2
Day, S Sherwood, 1940, Ap 2,26:3
Day, S Walton, 1946, D 15,77:2
Day, Samuel Winfield Rev, 1921, S 6,15:5
Day, Sarah A Mrs, 1941, N 29,17:5
Day, Sarah J, 1940, My 12,48:1
Day, Schuyler E, 1954, O 22,27:5
Day, Sherman, 1944, D 19,21:4
Day, Stephen A, 1950, Ja 6,22:4
Day, Stephen A Mrs, 1939, Ag 20,32:2
Day, Stephen J, 1963, Je 2,85:1
Day, Susie L L Mrs, 1947, O 22,29:1
Day, T F, 1927, Ag 20,15:5
Day, Theodore, 1952, Ag 22,21:5
Day, Thomas B, 1942, F 21,19:5
Day, Thomas D, 1938, Mr 23,23:2
Day, Thomas E, 1960, F 16,31:3
Day, Thomas E Mrs, 1967, Jl 8,25:6
Day, Thomas M, 1947, D 28,43:3
Day, Thomas M Jr, 1953, S 14,27:4
Day, Tommy, 1906, N 25,3:2
Day, Verne R, 1945, Ag 20,19:5
Day, Vince A, 1945, Ap 28,15:6
Day, W F Rev, 1882, O 24,5:3
Day, Walter L Mrs, 1960, Ja 10,86:5
Day, Walter L Sr, 1942, O 23,21:5
Day, Walter T, 1950, My 28,45:1
Day, Watson B Mrs, 1956, O 20,21:2
Day, Wilbur F, 1959, F 13,27:4
Day, Willard E, 1925, Ag 8,11:6
Day, William A, 1928, Ap 10,29:5; 1941, S 4,21:3; 1949, D 12,33:4
Day, William B, 1938, D 11,60:6; 1956, Jl 9,23:4
Day, William C Mrs, 1943, D 14,27:4
Day, William E Jr, 1962, My 10,37:4
Day, William F, 1942, D 22,25:2; 1944, D 21,21:3
Day, William H, 1941, Mr 4,23:4; 1942, Mr 17,21:6
Day, William H Mrs, 1948, My 16,70:2
Day, William Harrison Maj, 1921, F 13,22:3
Day, William I, 1946, Ja 19,13:1
Day, William J, 1951, Ja 5,21:2
Day, William L, 1938, S 8,23:4; 1953, Mr 7,15:3
Day, William M, 1948, Jl 15,23:2
Day, William P, 1955, N 7,29:3
Day, William R, 1915, F 8,7:4; 1923, Jl 10,19:4
Day, William R Ex-Justice, 1923, Jl 13,15:5
Day, William R Mrs (trb, Ja 9,13:6), 1912, Ja 6,13:3
Day, William S, 1944, F 25,17:5
Day, William W, 1942, Mr 30,17:1
Day, Willis B, 1962, F 21,45:1
Day, Winsor B Mrs, 1938, D 6,23:3
Dayal, Har, 1939, Mr 7,22:3
Dayal, Harishwar, 1964, My 21,35:2
Dayan, Samuel, 1968, Ag 12,35:4
Daye, John F, 1957, Mr 19,37:4
D'Aygalliers, Alfred W, 1943, Ag 6,15:3
Daykin, T Reginald, 1949, D 24,15:2
Dayle, Dennis, 1964, F 16,40:1
Dayley, Anna G W, 1945, Ja 25,19:3
Daynes, Michael, 1960, F 8,29:3
Dayrell, Harry G B, 1956, O 11,39:5
Dayton, Alex V, 1939, N 23,27:5
Dayton, Alfred B, 1950, D 3,88:5
Dayton, Charles Willoughby (funl, D 11,17:4), 1910, D 8,13:3
Dayton, Charles Willoughby Mrs, 1916, Ap 12,13:3
Dayton, Daniel G, 1940, Je 17,15:4
Dayton, Edward C, 1942, Ag 12,19:6
Dayton, Edward T, 1961, Ap 14,29:4
Dayton, Edwin W, 1946, N 6,23:5
Dayton, Elizabeth D Mrs, 1937, O 14,25:1
Dayton, Everett E, 1944, Ap 13,19:6
Dayton, Flora P Mrs, 1941, F 2,44:7
Dayton, Fred E, 1954, O 30,17:2
Dayton, Fred E Mrs, 1960, F 23,31:1
Dayton, Fred W, 1950, D 18,31:4
Dayton, G Nelson, 1950, Ap 2,92:4
Dayton, George F, 1953, S 23,32:3
Dayton, George H, 1906, N 30,9:6
Dayton, George S, 1939, My 8,17:4
Dayton, Grant A, 1950, N 14,31:1
Dayton, Harry A, 1924, D 9,25:3
Dayton, Harry L, 1962, Ja 7,88:6
Dayton, Harry T, 1941, Ja 7,23:4
Dayton, Harry T Mrs, 1943, Ag 15,38:5
Dayton, Harry W, 1944, S 20,23:6
Dayton, Howard B, 1950, Ja 14,15:5
Dayton, Howard S, 1948, S 3,19:3
Dayton, Hughes, 1944, D 4,23:2
Dayton, J Wilson, 1965, F 1,23:3
Dayton, James, 1875, N 2,4:7
Dayton, James A, 1948, Jl 2,21:5
Dayton, James C, 1939, S 14,23:6
Dayton, James H, 1938, N 17,25:3
Dayton, Jay Parmelee Capt, 1968, Jl 5,25:2
Dayton, John, 1908, Ag 19,7:5
Dayton, John H, 1944, Mr 12,38:3; 1950, S 16,19:5; 1953, S 8,31:2
Dayton, John W Mrs, 1959, F 12,27:3
Dayton, Josiah Mrs, 1951, N 21,25:4
Dayton, Katherine, 1945, Mr 6,21:3
Dayton, Kenneth, 1958, D 7,89:1
Dayton, Lewis A, 1948, Ja 30,24:3
Dayton, Lewis S, 1950, Je 25,68:5
Dayton, Logan M, 1956, D 28,21:4
Dayton, Marta S Mrs, 1937, N 30,23:4
Dayton, Mary L, 1956, N 10,19:4
Dayton, Monteath T Mrs, 1946, Ja 29,25:2
Dayton, Nathan H Mrs, 1951, Ja 30,25:4
Dayton, Ralph E, 1948, S 16,29:2
Dayton, Ralph H, 1955, O 23,86:8
Dayton, Rensselaer Williams, 1907, Mr 17,9:6
Dayton, Robert, 1951, Ja 7,77:1
Dayton, Roy, 1955, D 27,23:2
Dayton, Samuel, 1885, F 16,2:5; 1937, F 27,17:4
Dayton, Samuel H, 1940, My 26,34:4
Dayton, W B, 1881, Ap 1,5:4
Dayton, W L, 1864, D 21,5:6
Dayton, W L (funl), 1865, Ja 1,1:2
Dayton, William T, 1950, Je 19,21:4
Da Zara, Alberto, 1951, Je 6,31:3
D'Azevedo, Jacob C, 1938, Ag 10,19:3
Dazey, Charles T, 1938, F 10,21:2
Dazian, Henry (will, My 12,3:2), 1937, My 5,25:1
Dazian, Philip, 1907, O 1,11:6
Deachman, Robert J, 1955, F 18,21:1
Deacon, Arthur P, 1948, N 28,92:5
Deacon, C Clarence, 1962, N 21,33:1
Deacon, C Clarence Mrs, 1956, D 21,23:2
Deacon, David B, 1964, Je 9,35:3
Deacon, E P, 1901, Jl 7,5:4
Deacon, Edward Parker Mrs, 1918, Jl 18,9:6
Deacon, George H, 1947, N 2,72:4
Deacon, George H Mrs, 1954, O 9,17:3
Deacon, Ida, 1904, Mr 24,9:6
Deacon, J Byron, 1958, My 4,88:6
Deacon, John R, 1946, Ja 27,42:3
Deacon, Ralph W, 1946, Mr 27,27:2
Deacon, William, 1947, O 14,28:3
Deacon, William Budd, 1904, Ja 5,9:6
Deacon, William Jr, 1949, Ag 20,11:2
De Acosta, Henry J, 1911, O 19,13:5
de Acosta, Mercedes, 1968, My 10,44:2
de Acosta, Ricardo (funl, Ag 28,7:5), 1907, Ag 26,7:
De Acosta, Ricardo M, 1945, Mr 19,19:3
de Acosta, Ricardo Mrs, 1921, D 6,19:6
Deacy, Leroy T, 1950, Mr 28,32:3
Deacy, William H, 1967, Mr 7,41:3
Deacy, William H Mrs, 1962, Ap 7,25:5
Deady, Owen F, 1952, Mr 29,15:1
Deahy, Matthew F, 1961, N 28,37:1
Deak, Francis, 1876, Ja 29,5:2
Deakin, Alfred, 1919, O 8,19:3
Deakin, Arthur, 1955, My 2,21:3
Deakin, Henry, 1908, D 13,13:5
Deakin, J Augustus, 1961, Mr 13,29:5
Deakin, John Mrs, 1944, N 7,27:4
Deakin, Ralph, 1952, D 20,17:4
Deakins, Frank R, 1958, N 6,37:4
Deakyne, Walter C, 1948, F 13,21:3
Deakyne, Walter L, 1945, D 5,25:5
Deal, Barbara Y Mrs, 1943, Ja 31,44:2
Deal, Edward L, 1943, D 1,21:5
Deal, Elvin A, 1938, D 4,61:1
Deal, Erastus C, 1952, Je 19,27:3
Deal, Erastus C Mrs, 1962, O 18,39:4
Deal, Frank H, 1954, Ag 26,27:5
Deal, Herbert L, 1955, My 12,29:5
Deal, J Colton, 1942, Mr 13,19:2
Deal, Jean, 1959, Ag 8,36:6
Deal, John P, 1946, Je 6,21:4
Deal, John W, 1944, My 10,19:3
Deal, Joseph T, 1942, Mr 8,43:1
Deal, Spencer E, 1959, Ag 8,36:6
Dealaman, Adam, 1903, Ap 25,9:4
Dealaman, Adam T, 1955, F 1,29:2
Deale, J Warren, 1944, S 16,13:5
Dealey, George B, 1946, F 27,25:1
Dealey, George B Mrs, 1960, Ja 29,25:4
Dealey, James Q Dr, 1937, Ja 23,18:3
Dealing, Eleanore, 1946, F 7,23:3
Dealing, William H, 1904, O 20,7:4
De Almeida, James M, 1942, Jl 21,19:5
De Almeida, Petro M, 1948, D 28,21:5
De Alvear, Marcelo T, 1942, Mr 24,19:2
Dealy, D Edmund, 1917, Ap 19,15:5
Dealy, Frank N, 1965, O 15,45:4
Dealy, James H Mrs, 1957, N 1,23:4
Deam, Charles C, 1953, My 31,72:2
Deamer, Pierce H, 1942, N 17,26:2
Dean, Aaron Mrs, 1947, My 23,24:2
Dean, Albert M, 1956, Ap 5,29:1
Dean, Alex, 1939, Jl 29,15:3
Dean, Alfred E, 1967, D 10,87:2
Dean, Archie L, 1962, Mr 28,39:4
Dean, Arthur D, 1949, N 20,92:5
Dean, Arthur D Mrs, 1948, O 29,25:1
Dean, Arthur J, 1942, Je 27,13:4
Dean, Arthur L, 1952, Mr 3,21:1
Dean, Arthur R, 1949, N 12,15:1
Dean, Arthur W, 1952, O 1,33:2
Dean, Arthur Warren, 1952, Mr 21,23:4
Dean, B, 1928, D 8,19:1
Dean, Barney, 1954, S 1,27:5
Dean, Bartholomew, 1954, D 24,13:1
Dean, Bashford Mrs, 1950, My 16,31:3
Dean, Calvin B, 1905, Ap 14,5:5
Dean, Charles, 1925, N 5,23:5
Dean, Charles A, 1947, D 8,25:2
Dean, Charles Augustus, 1908, S 1,7:5
Dean, Charles E, 1937, F 12,23:4
Dean, Charles L, 1909, Jl 30,7:7
Dean, Charles M, 1947, S 21,60:2
Dean, Charles S Mrs, 1949, Ap 12,30:4
Dean, Cliff B, 1937, Je 3,28:1
Dean, Cora (will), 1946, Mr 26,31:4
Dean, Cora Mrs, 1949, N 4,27:2
Dean, Curtis, 1947, N 25,29:2

Dean, D J, 1897, Ja 12,12:4
Dean, David C, 1922, O 18,19:4
Dean, Dayton, 1960, Ja 20,9:3
Dean, Dion K, 1957, F 8,23:3
Dean, Dorothea L Mrs, 1965, Ap 8,39:3
Dean, Dudley S, 1950, S 27,32:2
Dean, Dwight E, 1945, S 25,25:1
Dean, Edward E, 1949, S 29,29:5
Dean, Edwin H, 1946, My 5,44:2
Dean, Elmer, 1940, F 14,21:5
Dean, Elmer M, 1956, S 25,33:3
Dean, Elwood M, 1962, Ap 15,80:7
Dean, Emma Frances, 1919, Mr 16,20:5
Dean, Ernest J, 1953, D 31,19:4
Dean, Ernest W, 1959, O 20,39:2
Dean, Evelina B, 1942, Mr 6,21:3
Dean, Fay S, 1947, Ap 28,23:4
Dean, Francis, 1965, D 24,17:1
Dean, Francis B, 1950, Jl 7,20:3
Dean, Francis M, 1967, D 19,47:3
Dean, Francis Mrs, 1952, My 8,31:5
Dean, Francis N, 1949, Je 30,23:5
Dean, Francis W, 1940, My 26,34:3
Dean, Frank A, 1923, Jl 28,7:6
Dean, Frank E, 1958, My 14,33:5
Dean, Frank K, 1941, Ag 15,17:4
Dean, Frank N, 1944, S 8,19:3
Dean, Frank V, 1958, My 10,21:7
Dean, Franklin, 1947, S 21,60:4
Dean, G Vincent Mrs, 1943, Mr 9,23:4
Dean, George C, 1940, My 22,23:6
Dean, George E, 1948, D 15,33:1
Dean, George F Rev, 1919, Mr 27,13:2
Dean, George W, 1925, S 18,23:6; 1954, Mr 30,27:2; 1955, Ja 31,19:2
Dean, Gerald J, 1966, Mr 19,29:5
Dean, Gilbert B (Jno Lawrence Deanheart), 1921, Jl 23,7:5
Dean, Gordon E (funl plans, Ag 19,27:3; will, Ag 29,15:1), 1958, Ag 16,1:8
Dean, H Trendley, 1962, My 15,39:3
Dean, Harold R, 1945, O 10,36:2
Dean, Harriet, 1905, Ap 19,11:4; 1943, Mr 26,19:2
Dean, Harry C, 1942, Ja 21,17:2
Dean, Harry N, 1943, Ag 3,19:4
Dean, Harry N Mrs, 1952, Je 16,17:6
Dean, Henry E, 1939, F 13,15:6
Dean, Henry Martin Capt, 1903, O 4,7:6
Dean, Herbert D, 1955, S 5,11:5
Dean, Herbert H, 1943, Ja 2,11:4
Dean, Horace M Mrs, 1956, My 5,19:4
Dean, Howard A, 1951, O 15,25:5
Dean, Howard B, 1950, Mr 23,29:5
Dean, J Marshall, 1950, D 20,31:1
Dean, Ja E, 1904, Ja 23,9:5
Dean, James, 1942, Mr 2,20:2
Dean, James (funl, O 9,87:2), 1955, O 1,10:3
Dean, James E, 1940, Mr 17,48:6
Dean, James Mrs, 1953, Jl 8,27:5
Dean, James T, 1939, Je 16,23:3
Dean, James W, 1941, Ag 15,17:4
Dean, John M, 1950, F 7,27:5
Dean, John P, 1948, Jl 24,15:5; 1959, Je 12,27:1
Dean, John W, 1950, Je 24,13:4
Dean, Joseph A, 1902, O 18,9:3
Dean, Joseph L, 1964, Jl 31,23:1
Dean, Josiah S, 1941, N 25,25:3
Dean, Judie Mrs, 1925, Ja 20,21:4
Dean, Julia, 1868, Mr 7,4:6; 1952, O 19,89:1
Dean, Kenneth, 1967, F 9,39:4
Dean, Laurence C, 1949, S 14,31:4
Dean, Lee W, 1944, F 10,15:3
Dean, Louise Mrs, 1948, Je 25,23:1
Dean, M Bertha, 1951, D 28,21:3
Dean, Man Mountain (F S Leavitt), 1953, My 30, 15:4
Dean, Marguerite T, 1952, Ap 23,29:5
Dean, Mary Mrs, 1908, Je 24,7:4
Dean, Mathew, 1924, Ag 15,13:7
Dean, May (Mrs R Bernard), 1937, S 2,21:3
Dean, Morrill K, 1950, Mr 23,29:3
Dean, Paul D, 1938, Je 30,23:5
Dean, Percy T, 1939, Mr 21,23:2
Dean, Phil S, 1941, Jl 6,27:2
Dean, R B, 1884, F 1,5:6
Dean, Raymond S, 1943, Ag 23,15:5
Dean, Reginald S, 1961, My 27,23:6
Dean, Richard P Mrs, 1956, Ja 24,31:2
Dean, Richmond, 1940, S 6,21:4
Dean, Robert J, 1949, Ja 28,21:3
Dean, Robert L, 1938, N 9,23:6
Dean, Robert P, 1951, Ag 4,15:7
Dean, Ruth, 1957, Jl 25,23:3
Dean, S Bobo, 1945, Mr 25,38:2
Dean, Samuel A, 1903, O 30,9:6
Dean, Samuel M, 1949, Je 1,32:6
Dean, Samuel R Mrs, 1964, O 19,33:2
Dean, Samuel W, 1950, S 10,92:4
Dean, Sarah M, 1937, Ja 7,21:5
Dean, Sidney W, 1952, Mr 6,31:5
Dean, Stanley I W, 1955, S 28,35:3
Dean, Thomas M Mrs, 1948, Jl 26,17:5
Dean, Tunis, 1939, Ap 22,17:4
Dean, W B, 1885, F 21,2:2
Dean, W E, 1879, Je 17,5:2
Dean, W N D Rev, 1907, F 5,9:6
Dean, Walter, 1949, Jl 15,19:3
Dean, Walter Lafthouse, 1912, Mr 15,9:4
Dean, Walter N, 1953, Ap 24,23:4
Dean, Walter R, 1954, O 21,27:4
Dean, William, 1905, Ap 24,9:6; 1919, Ja 18,11:4
Dean, William C, 1938, Ag 23,17:5
Dean, William C Mrs, 1958, Jl 31,23:3
Dean, William F, 1905, Je 21,7:7; 1954, Je 17,29:5
Dean, William F Sr, 1956, Jl 30,21:5
Dean, William J, 1913, O 10,11:6
Dean, William Mrs, 1939, Ap 5,25:4
Dean, William S, 1951, O 19,27:5
Dean, William W, 1964, Ja 27,23:3
Dean, Willis L, 1942, D 21,23:4
De Andria, Alcide, 1946, Mr 29,23:4
Deane, Charles J, 1966, Ap 18,29:2
Deane, Ezekiel D, 1944, Jl 2,19:3
Deane, Florence A Mrs, 1952, Mr 17,21:2
Deane, George B, 1903, D 30,7:2
Deane, Harry T, 1939, D 31,19:1
Deane, Helen W (Mrs G F Markham), 1966, Jl 22, 28:5
Deane, J Henry, 1938, Jl 23,13:4
Deane, J Steven, 1944, Mr 11,13:4
Deane, James C Mrs, 1944, S 2,11:5
Deane, John Hall, 1923, Je 21,19:5
Deane, John P, 1951, Je 28,25:3
Deane, Julia F, 1937, O 22,24:3
Deane, Julian S, 1951, Jl 7,13:4
Deane, Percy E, 1946, Ag 18,47:6
Deane, Raymond B Jr, 1949, N 2,12:3
Deane, Sidney N, 1943, My 5,27:4
Deane, Warren C, 1952, Mr 14,23:3
Deaner, Frances Mrs, 1944, N 23,31:5
De Angelis, Angelo C, 1959, Je 13,21:5
DeAngelis, Carmelo E, 1967, My 31,43:1
DeAngelis, Charles L, 1962, Mr 10,21:3
De Angelis, Charlotte E Mrs, 1938, D 24,15:2
de Angelis, Emanuel, 1956, Je 16,19:4
De Angelis, J, 1933, Mr 21,17:1
De Angelis, Phil, 1939, Je 30,19:5
DeAngelis, Thomas, 1965, Ag 2,29:4
De Angell, John F, 1961, Mr 6,25:5
De Angelo, Carlo, 1962, Ja 4,34:1
Deanheart, John Lawrence (Gilbert B Dean), 1921, Jl 23,7:5
De Anquinos, Lawrence L, 1948, O 13,25:2
Deans, Agnes G, 1948, Mr 15,23:5
Deans, David, 1884, O 28,8:3
Deans, John, 1950, Jl 17,21:3
Deans, Malcolm A, 1942, O 10,15:4
Deans, Parks P, 1947, Ja 8,23:1
Deans, Robert S Jr, 1944, S 30,13:6
Dear, Albert Mrs, 1940, My 12,49:2
Dear, Arthur T Sr, 1960, Je 1,39:5
Dear, Brock M, 1946, Ag 11,45:1
Dear, Bryan B, 1950, S 21,31:2
Dear, J Albert, 1959, S 20,86:8
Dear, Joseph A, 1908, D 11,11:4; 1947, Jl 18,17:3; 1967, F 8,28:7
Dear, Richard, 1956, S 8,17:6
Dear, Robert F, 1939, Ag 9,17:4
Dear, Walter M, 1962, Je 3,88:1
Dear, William Y, 1952, O 23,31:1
Dear, William Y Mrs, 1955, N 9,33:2
Dearborn, Ambrose Collyer, 1920, S 20,15:5
Dearborn, Arthur K, 1941, Ag 29,17:5
Dearborn, Bessie D Mrs, 1942, F 14,15:4
Dearborn, David B, 1942, My 4,19:4
Dearborn, Donald C, 1967, N 12,87:1
Dearborn, Emma W, 1937, Jl 29,20:2
Dearborn, Frederick M, 1960, Ja 28,31:4
Dearborn, Frederick M Jr, 1958, F 27,27:1
Dearborn, George B, 1952, Ap 18,25:2
Dearborn, George S (funl, Je 1,15:1), 1920, My 30, 22:3
Dearborn, George V, 1938, D 13,25:2
Dearborn, George V Mrs, 1950, Ja 24,31:1
Dearborn, Henry M Dr, 1904, F 18,9:6
Dearborn, J F, 1903, Je 4,9:7
Dearborn, Karl B, 1952, Ja 27,77:2
Dearborn, Ned H, 1962, Ag 2,25:1
Dearborn, Phil C, 1952, Ap 10,29:3
Dearborn, Richard J Mrs, 1955, Je 11,15:3
Dearborn, Thomas H Mrs, 1957, Ja 28,23:3
Dearborn, Walter F, 1955, Je 22,29:4
Dearden, Arthur, 1944, Je 19,19:5
Dearden, Charles I, 1941, Mr 1,15:2
Dearden, Clarence J, 1950, Jl 18,29:2
Dearden, Edward C, 1954, Ap 15,29:3
Dearden, Edward C Jr, 1945, Ja 29,14:3
Dearden, Edward C Mrs, 1951, S 3,13:5
Dearden, John, 1907, F 24,7:6
Dearden, John E, 1938, D 11,60:5
Dearden, Robert R Jr, 1938, S 23,27:3
Dearden, Robert R Jr Mrs, 1938, Je 10,21:5
Deardoff, Joseph T, 1938, Ja 20,23:5
Deardorff, Harvey A, 1946, My 9,21:3
Deardorff, Jacob, 1939, Je 30,19:1
Deardorff, Louis A, 1961, F 3,25:1
Deardorff, Neva R, 1958, Ag 23,15:3
Deardorff, Ross R, 1951, Ap 29,88:6
Deardourff, Charles C, 1952, Je 26,29:2
Dearholt, Hoyt E, 1939, Jl 14,19:4
Dearie, James A, 1964, Jl 9,33:5
Dearing, Jessie M Mrs, 1941, S 19,23:4
Dearly, Max, 1943, Je 5,15:5
Dearman, Charles, 1964, F 20,29:3
Dearman, Clarence D, 1949, Je 28,28:2
DeArmit, Lillian S, 1952, Jl 7,21:4
Dearmont, Nelson S, 1950, Je 10,17:5
Dearmont, Nelson S Mrs, 1960, O 24,29:4
Dearmont, Russell L, 1967, Ja 13,23:1
Dearmont, Washington S, 1944, Jl 18,19:2
Dearness, Donald F, 1947, Jl 24,21:5
Dearness, John, 1954, D 7,33:3
De Arnoux, Leonie, 1875, F 1,8:2
Dearolf, Walter S, 1949, My 24,28:5
Dearstyne, Edmund C, 1940, Ag 3,15:6
Dearstyne, Frank S, 1939, Je 30,19:3
Dearstyne, James E, 1951, Je 24,72:5
Dearth, Henry Golden, 1918, Mr 28,11:5
Dearth, Walter A, 1946, F 22,25:3
Deary, Louis E, 1941, My 6,21:5
Deas, Arthur W, 1950, D 5,31:3
Deas, Arthur W Jr, 1956, N 27,37:2
Deas, Henri M, 1967, Ja 20,43:5
Deas, Z C Gen, 1882, Mr 7,2:3
Deasey, John E, 1964, O 13,39:1
Deasley, Thomas, 1943, Ap 3,15:4
Deasy, Bichard, 1883, My 7,5:1
Deasy, James J, 1954, Ag 14,15:6
Deasy, John E, 1945, Ap 21,13:4
Deasy, John F, 1953, D 29,23:3
Deasy, Luere B, 1940, Mr 14,23:6
Deat, Marcel, 1955, Mr 31,10:5
Deatly, Robert N Mrs, 1966, O 20,43:4
Deaton, Harry P, 1945, O 26,19:3
Deaver, Bascom S, 1944, O 14,13:6
Deaver, Elmer R, 1953, Jl 9,25:6
Deaver, J B, 1931, S 26,19:1
Deaver, James N, 1950, F 16,23:3
Deaver, Quentin K, 1948, N 12,24:3
Deavitt, Henry M, 1949, My 17,25:4
de Bacourt, Pierre, 1924, Mr 30,X,8:2
De Baecke, Harry L, 1961, N 8,35:3
De Baer, Herbert, 1966, D 30,25:1
Debaets, Gerard, 1959, Ap 28,35:2
De Baize, Abbe, 1880, Ja 31,2:6
De Bakesy, Cornelius, 1947, S 17,25:5
De Bal, Jenny White Singer, 1867, O 31,2:5
Debalta, Stephen L, 1960, N 11,31:3
De Balzac, Mme, 1882, Ap 13,5:3
De Bar, Ben (see also Ag 5 and 29), 1877, Ag 31,1:2
De Bar, Ben, 1878, Ag 29,5:5
Debard, Davis M, 1960, Ap 24,88:2
DeBardeleben, Henry F, 1964, Ap 9,31:4
De Bartolome, Charles M, 1941, My 29,19:2
de Bary, Jerry, 1964, Ja 28,33:8
DeBary, Mildred Mrs, 1950, My 21,104:6
de Bassan, Giorgio, 1956, D 27,25:4
Debaugh, Dan, 1946, Je 4,23:3
De Baun, C J, 1893, My 2,1:2
De Baun, Harold J, 1950, S 22,31:1
Debaun, Harvey, 1950, F 26,76:6
De Baun, Roscoe W, 1958, F 16,86:3
de Baun, Stephen J Mrs, 1967, N 17,47:2
de Bayeux, Robert P Mrs, 1957, D 20,27:4
Debayle, Luis Mrs, 1953, Je 29,21:2
Debayle, Roberto, 1949, O 26,27:4
Debeau, James F, 1925, O 9,23:4
Debeaubien, J William, 1942, Je 3,23:2
De Beaumont, The, 1874, S 24,6:7
de Beaumont, Victor E, 1954, Je 26,13:3
Debeaux, Otto T, 1944, Je 29,13:3
De Bebian, Joseph Mrs, 1950, D 9,15:4
De Beck, William M, 1942, N 12,25:1
de Beer, Edwin J C, 1959, O 28,37:2
De Beer, Jacob S, 1951, Jl 17,27:4
de Beixedon, Daniel Kingsland, 1919, S 9,17:6
De Bekker, L J, 1931, Ja 27,19:3
DeBekker, Leander Mrs, 1951, Ag 11,11:4
Debele, William G, 1941, Ap 8,25:1
De Belleroche, Albert, 1944, Jl 15,13:3
De Belleville, Frederic, 1923, F 27,19:3
De Benedictis, Albert, 1940, My 8,23:2
Debeney, Marie-Eugen (por), 1943, N 11,23:3
Debenham, Frank, 1965, N 25,35:5
Deberard, Fred J, 1956, Ag 3,19:5
De Berenguer, Emilia C Mrs, 1942, My 24,43:1
De Berg, Walter G, 1948, Ja 1,23:2
De Beriot, Charles Auguste, 1870, Ap 14,5:4
de Bermingham, Ferdinand H Mrs, 1965, Mr 23,39:4
de Bermingham, Gertrude K B Mrs, 1959, Je 15,27:3
De Bermingham, Henry Viscount, 1882, F 21,3:1
DeBerry, James H (Hank), 1951, S 11,29:4
DeBerry, John W, 1946, Ap 29,21:2
DeBerry, William N, 1948, Ja 21,25:5
Debes, Roman, 1941, S 21,45:2
Debevec, James, 1952, Mr 7,23:4
Debevoise, Anthony W Mrs, 1957, F 28,27:5
De Bevoise, Charles I, 1958, D 11,13:1
Debevoise, Elliott, 1948, Ja 28,23:5

DeBevoise, Elmer E, 1951, D 22,30:4
De Bevoise, Emma Mrs, 1937, S 22,27:4
De Bevoise, H S, 1897, Mr 20,7:5
De Bevoise, Herbert R, 1952, N 10,25:2
DeBevoise, J Rapelye Mrs, 1947, Je 11,27:2
Debevoise, Katherine P, 1953, Jl 1,29:2
DeBevoise, P L, 1961, S 11,27:3
DeBevoise, P Leroy, 1954, N 10,33:5
Debevoise, Thomas M, 1958, D 22,2:8
de Beylie, Gen, 1910, Jl 19,7:5
De Biase, John S, 1954, Mr 18,31:5
De Bisschop, Charles J, 1945, D 30,14:6
DeBisschop, Frank J, 1955, Mr 8,27:1
De Blacam, Aodh, 1951, Ja 15,17:2
Deblanc, A Gen, 1883, N 10,5:2
De Blanck, Armando R, 1954, Mr 26,22:3
DeBlanco, Anthony C, 1968, My 15,47:2
Debler, Edmund O, 1955, Mr 8,27:3
De Bliek, J Rev, 1883, My 31,5:5
De Bloch, Jean, 1902, Ja 8,7:7
De Blois, Austin K, 1945, Ag 11,13:6
De Blois, George L, 1939, My 5,23:1
De Blois, Lewis A, 1967, F 27,29:1
De Blois, Teresita T C, 1951, Mr 7,33:5
De Blois, William A, 1937, F 3,23:6
Debo, Howard J, 1951, S 14,25:3
De Board, Elmer H, 1953, Jl 10,19:3
Deboben, John R, 1961, Je 11,86:1
De Bobes, Joseph, 1953, Mr 12,25:1
de Bocki, Joseph M, 1913, Ap 22,11:6
De Bodisco (see also Ag 2), 1878, Ag 5,3:6
de Bodo, Richard C, 1965, Ap 24,29:3
De Boe, John F, 1945, Ag 11,13:4
De Boer, Wilke van de Schoor, 1952, O 17,27:3
De Bogart, Edward H, 1951, Mr 10,13:2
De Bogory, Natalie, 1939, S 7,25:5
De Boissy, C Perry, 1944, Ap 13,19:3
De Bold, Robert L, 1952, F 6,22:6
de Bon, Ferdinand Jean Adm, 1923, Jl 7,11:5
de Bonay, Anzela, 1908, Ja 1,9:5
de Bondy, Fred, 1959, My 23,25:5
de Bonneval, Henri A Mrs, 1968, N 13,47:2
Deboo, Michael Mrs, 1943, Ap 9,21:3
De Booy, Theodore Capt, 1919, F 19,13:1
Debord, Sara H Mrs, 1950, Mr 15,29:1
De Borst, Charles F, 1874, S 28,8:2
DeBost, William L, 1951, Ja 19,25:3
Debost, William L Mrs, 1948, Ag 14,13:3
de Both, Jesse (Mrs C Dreutzer), 1959, Ag 31,21:3
de Bothezat, George Mrs, 1963, Ap 1,27:5
de Bourbon, Filiberto, 1968, Mr 5,41:1
de Bourbon, Fulco, 1962, O 26,31:1
De Bout, Clarence C, 1949, N 22,29:4
De Bouzon, Marcel R, 1952, D 20,17:5
De Bow, Albert R, 1938, S 12,17:4
Debow, Fred, 1916, Jl 10,11:4
De Bow, Jacob H Mrs, 1966, O 2,86:8
DeBow, James D B, 1867, Mr 1,5:4
De Bower, Herbert F, 1940, Mr 18,17:2
De Boyler, Laurence, 1940, Je 3,15:3
De Bozoky, Barbara, 1937, N 30,23:2
De Bra, Arthur H, 1958, O 16,37:2
De Brabant, Mary C Mrs, 1939, D 20,25:2
De Bragga, Joseph H, 1939, Ja 28,15:3; 1956, S 2,57:1
Debran, Merrick B, 1944, Ja 19,19:2
de Bresson, Chauncey D, 1961, Ag 28,25:4
de Breteuil, Henri Marquis, 1916, N 5,23:4
De Broglie, Duc, 1901, Ja 20,8:2
Debroglie, Joseph, 1942, F 4,19:5
de Broke, W Lord, 1902, D 26,7:6
DeBronkart, Eugene H, 1968, O 17,47:4
Debrosky, Leopold, 1944, S 24,46:1
Debrot, Jean J Jr, 1963, O 6,88:7
Debrow, Ollie, 1937, Ja 6,23:3
DeBrower, Ernestina L, 1951, S 4,27:3
De Brule, J P, 1909, My 9,11:6
De Brun, Harry C W, 1957, Jl 17,27:4
De Brun, John W S Mrs, 1950, Je 16,25:5
De Bruyn, Marinus, 1953, Ap 5,76:3
Debry, Paul C, 1960, F 14,84:1
Debs, E V, 1926, O 21,25:1
Debs, George S, 1961, Ag 13,89:1
Debs, Theodore, 1945, Ap 14,15:4
Debuchi, Katsuji, 1947, Ag 21,23:6
Debucourt, Jean, 1958, Mr 24,27:1
DeBuis, Daniel, 1951, F 24,13:3
De Buono, Frank, 1940, My 25,17:6
DeBurchardt, Joseph A, 1952, O 6,25:5
DeBurlo, C Russell, 1951, Ap 14,15:2
Debus, Carl, 1955, Je 29,29:4
Debus, William H, 1941, My 12,17:2
De Bussiere, Baroness (see also D 17), 1877, D 19, 4:7
Debussy, Achille Claude, 1918, Mr 27,13:3
Debussy, Adele, 1952, Je 8,87:1
De Bussy, Wales L, 1942, Ja 13,19:1
De Butts, Cary E, 1946, My 21,23:1
Debutts, Clarence E, 1939, O 14,19:4
Debye, Peter W, 1966, N 3,39:2
Debytter, Alphonse, 1937, My 18,23:5
de Cabro Frio, Viscount, 1907, Ja 16,7:4
Decaisne, Joseph, 1882, F 10,5:5
De Calluwe, Emile, 1940, Ag 15,19:5
De Camp, Abram L, 1955, Mr 15,26:8
De Camp, Clarence A, 1948, Ap 15,25:4
De Camp, E O, 1938, My 18,21:1
DeCamp, Evans L, 1951, N 12,25:1
De Camp, George, 1938, Mr 1,21:1
DeCamp, Horace S, 1954, Jl 17,13:7
DeCamp, Ira L, 1960, O 31,31:2
Decamp, J W Maj, 1901, O 15,9:6
De Camp, John A, 1953, Mr 4,27:1
De Camp, John Rear Adm, 1875, Je 25,6:5
De Camp, Joseph M, 1942, Ja 1,25:1
De Camp, Joseph R, 1923, F 13,21:4
De Camp, Lyon, 1945, Ja 4,19:6
De Camp, Ralph D, 1939, My 21,III,7:3
De Camp, Robert L, 1952, Je 15,84:2
De Camp, William Scott, 1905, Ap 7,9:6
deCampi, Willella (Mrs J W O'Mcaley), 1963, S 11, 43:1
Decant, Lincoln G, 1919, D 27,9:4
De Cantillon, Patrick J, 1942, My 1,19:1
De Capite, Michael, 1958, Ja 22,8:6
Decare, Hector, 1954, Jl 2,19:3
Decarli, Nora, 1912, Ag 18,II,11:6
De Carlo, Antonio, 1967, O 3,47:2
De Carlo, Frank, 1951, Ag 4,15:4
DeCarlo, John, 1950, D 14,35:4
De Carlo, Vincent C, 1947, My 23,23:4
de Caro, Frank A, 1955, Mr 20,89:2
de Caro, Frank A Mrs, 1962, Mr 5,23:2
De Carron, Louise, 1937, Je 11,23:5
de Carteret, Samuel L, 1956, Jl 28,17:6
De Casali, G F S, 1885, Je 11,2:2
De Casalis, Jeanne, 1966, Ag 20,25:1
De Casanova, Louis, 1949, Ja 2,63:4
De Cassagnac, Adolphe, 1880, F 2,5:3
De Casseres, Benjamin, 1945, D 7,22:2
De Castro, Allen J, 1947, F 4,26:3
Decastro, Elmer J, 1953, Je 14,36:2
De Castro, Hector, 1909, Ja 31,11:6
De Castro, Morris F, 1966, D 10,38:3
Decatur, Jay R, 1937, O 13,23:4
Decatur, Leroy, 1948, F 28,10:1
Decatur, Stephen, 1964, Mr 10,34:4
Decatur, Stephen Commodore, 1876, Ja 12,4:7
De Caux, Marquis (denial, Ap 26,1:2), 1875, Ap 25, 2:7
Decazes, Duc, 1912, S 1,II,9:4
Decazes, Duchess Dowager, 1873, S 7,1:2
Decazes, Duke (L C E Amanien), 1886, S 18,5:4
Decell, J Lloyd, 1946, Ja 11,22:2
Decent, John J, 1942, Ap 7,21:5
de Cerkey, Edward Demetre, 1907, N 26,9:6
De Cernea, Edward, 1946, Je 10,21:5
Decesare, John, 1943, Ap 18,48:3
De Cesare, John Mrs, 1953, Jl 2,23:2
Decesare, Loreto, 1948, Ja 22,27:1
De Cew, Judson A, 1964, Ap 25,29:5
Dech, Alfred J, 1947, Jl 18,17:3
Dechaene, Jacques R, 1954, Je 13,88:4
de Chair, Dudley R S, 1958, Ag 19,27:4
De Chant, Clement W, 1952, Jl 12,13:4
Dechant, Ernest R, 1947, F 6,23:4
de Chelminski, Leonie Mme, 1956, Je 2,19:2
De Chern, Peter M, 1953, Ag 22,15:6
Dechert, Daniel Orville Mrs, 1968, Mr 22,44:3
Dechert, Henry T Mrs, 1951, Ja 6,15:3
Dechert, Henry Taylor Col, 1915, O 16,11:5
Dechert, Robert Mrs, 1950, O 24,29:3
De Chilly, M, 1872, Je 26,1:6
De Cholnoky, Tibor Mrs, 1948, S 19,76:4
de Chopites, J I Sen, 1923, My 19,13:5
De Christopher, Frederick, 1942, My 8,21:5
DeCicco, Benedict, 1951, F 20,25:3
De Cicco, Michael, 1967, Mr 17,41:3
De Cicco, Michael Mrs, 1948, D 19,76:3
De Cicco, Pasquale, 1945, D 23,18:3
Decies, Dowager Lady, 1941, F 28,19:3
Decies, Lady, 1931, F 3,1:2; 1944, Je 14,19:3; 1945, Ap 5,23:6
Decies, Lord, 1944, F 2,21:1
De Cissy, E L O C, 1882, Je 17,5:2
Deck, Emil M, 1943, Ja 11,15:1
Deck, Howard S, 1962, F 2,29:1
Deckelman, Theresa Mrs, 1955, Mr 27,87:1
Deckenbach, Louis W, 1950, My 13,17:6
Decker, Albert F, 1956, Ja 19,33:1
Decker, Alex D, 1938, My 14,15:2
Decker, Alex S, 1939, Mr 20,17:4
Decker, Alfred, 1942, O 9,21:1; 1948, Jl 24,15:4
Decker, Alfred F, 1948, Mr 23,25:3
Decker, Alonzo G, 1956, Mr 19,31:3
Decker, Alvin J, 1938, Jl 2,13:3
Decker, Alvin W, 1944, Ag 10,17:5
Decker, Ammiel F, 1957, S 29,86:4
Decker, Ansoleum B, 1940, Ap 7,45:3
Decker, Arthur F Mrs, 1962, Ap 12,36:1
Decker, B C, 1933, Mr 23,17:4
Decker, Benjamin F, 1950, Ap 26,29:2
Decker, Blanche R, 1950, N 5,92:5
Decker, Burnet B Sr, 1944, Ap 12,21:4
Decker, Burr E, 1947, Mr 24,25:5
Decker, C Edgar, 1951, Ap 10,27:1
Decker, Casper G, 1942, Ja 26,15:1
Decker, Charles, 1951, D 11,33:5
Decker, Charles J F, 1953, Ja 11,90:6
Decker, Charles M, 1920, Ag 29,20:4
Decker, Charles Mrs, 1908, O 12,9:6
Decker, Charles Sr, 1955, Ja 9,87:3
Decker, Chauncey H, 1944, D 15,19:3
Decker, Clair V, 1950, Ag 9,29:4
Decker, Clarence C, 1941, Ap 17,23:6
Decker, Clarence R Mrs, 1964, Ap 2,33:2
Decker, Clarence S, 1961, Je 30,25:2
Decker, Clarence W, 1939, Jl 29,15:6
Decker, David B, 1919, D 23,9:2
Decker, Del L, 1954, Ap 19,23:3
Decker, Delbert S, 1944, Je 14,19:6
Decker, Duane, 1964, Ag 22,21:2
Decker, Edmund C, 1955, Ja 5,23:3
Decker, Edward A, 1945, N 6,19:6
Decker, Edward E, 1945, Mr 13,23:3
Decker, Edward N, 1958, Mr 31,27:5
Decker, Ellsworth W Mrs (por), 1949, Je 7,31:4
Decker, Eugene M, 1922, Ag 19,11:5
Decker, Everett D, 1952, Jl 1,23:1
Decker, Foster, 1952, S 12,21:3
Decker, Francis W, 1950, Ap 18,31:4
Decker, Fred C Mrs, 1961, D 11,31:4
Decker, Fred L, 1953, S 2,25:2
Decker, Frederick C, 1958, My 20,34:6
Decker, George E, 1939, N 5,49:2
Decker, George F, 1941, Ap 14,17:2
Decker, George W, 1916, Ja 29,9:4; 1937, My 2,II,9:
Decker, Harrison M, 1949, Ap 12,29:2
Decker, Harry, 1951, N 25,86:2
Decker, Harry J, 1940, Ap 16,23:3
Decker, Henry V, 1963, O 1,39:1
Decker, Howard Mrs, 1950, Ja 4,46:3
Decker, Ira, 1948, Je 19,15:1
Decker, J Howard, 1939, N 19,38:8
Decker, James, 1946, D 15,77:6
Decker, James W, 1961, Ap 24,29:5
Decker, John, 1947, Je 9,21:1
Decker, John C, 1941, Jl 30,18:2
Decker, John E Mrs, 1944, Je 6,17:4
Decker, John J, 1951, F 26,23:1
Decker, John P, 1951, Je 29,21:2
Decker, John W, 1950, My 3,29:4
Decker, Johnson, 1944, O 17,23:2
Decker, Joseph L, 1952, Jl 2,25:5
Decker, Joseph S, 1911, Ja 29,11:2
Decker, Karl, 1941, D 5,24:2
Decker, Kathryn Browne, 1919, F 13,15:5
Decker, Lawrence, 1941, Mr 14,21:5
Decker, Leland P, 1958, Mr 16,86:7
Decker, Leroy L, 1950, D 22,23:4
Decker, Lewis F, 1949, Ap 14,25:3
Decker, Louis E, 1944, N 21,25:4
Decker, Mansir B, 1952, S 17,31:5
Decker, Mark H, 1942, Ag 26,19:4
Decker, Mark R, 1948, Jl 8,23:1
Decker, Martin C, 1949, My 24,27:2
Decker, Martin S, 1922, Jl 2,16:4
Decker, Maurice S, 1906, Ja 5,11:3; 1960, Ag 13,1
Decker, Moses J, 1950, Ap 25,31:1
Decker, Oliver J, 1943, My 19,25:2
Decker, Peter S, 1905, Ap 15,11:5
Decker, Petronella W Mrs, 1941, D 24,17:4
Decker, Randall H, 1955, My 25,33:1
Decker, Reuben H, 1942, Mr 21,17:3
Decker, Richard J, 1943, Mr 3,23:1
Decker, Richard M, 1937, My 17,19:4
Decker, Rickcliffe, 1966, Mr 3,33:5
Decker, Robert A, 1954, D 29,23:2
Decker, Robert C, 1966, Je 23,39:4
Decker, Robert H, 1954, O 24,88:7
Decker, Royal C, 1958, Jl 2,29:4
Decker, Russell W Sr, 1958, Ag 5,27:4
Decker, Sarah Platt Mrs, 1912, Jl 8,9:5
Decker, Sydney Jr Mrs, 1943, F 24,21:4
Decker, Walter, 1950, N 1,35:4
Decker, Wellington E, 1937, Ag 18,19:5
Decker, Willard R, 1955, S 20,31:2
Decker, William E, 1950, Ag 5,15:4
Decker, William F (will, N 5,25:6), 1937, O 29,
Decker, William H, 1939, Mr 22,23:2; 1947, Je 2
Decker, William J, 1950, F 22,30:2
Decker, William S Sr, 1961, N 26,88:6
Decker, Wilmer G, 1955, Ja 7,21:1
Deckert, William, 1939, Jl 28,17:4
Deckhut, Frederic, 1951, My 26,17:5
Deckman, John E, 1950, S 26,31:5
Decks, Alfred, 1925, Ap 21,21:6
De Clercq, Gustave, 1942, O 24,15:1
DeClouet, Irene Stewart Dr, 1968, F 7,47:4
De Coe, Harold D, 1952, Mr 25,27:4
de Coligny, Calvert G, 1956, Je 29,21:5
de Comarmond, Joseph H M, 1957, My 31,19:4
de Constant, Paul D, 1955, D 21,29:4
De Coppet, Andre, 1953, Ag 4,21:3
Decoppet, Camille, 1925, Ja 16,17:4
De Coppet, Edward J, 1916, My 2,13:6
De Coppet, Ernest H, 1937, Jl 18,II,7:2
de Coppet, Gertrude, 1960, F 8,29:3
de Coppet, Henry, 1920, O 8,13:1
De Coppet, Robert F, 1952, Jl 21,19:2

De Coppet, Theakston, 1937, N 9,24:1
De Cora, Albert J, 1950, D 26,23:1
Decora, Winnebago Chief, 1865, My 5,4:2
De Cordoba, Pedro, 1950, S 18,23:3
De Cordova, Alfred, 1907, Ap 7,9:6
De Cordova, Arthur E, 1939, F 26,38:7
DeCordova, Julian, 1945, N 24,20:2
De Cordova, Rudolph, 1941, Ja 14,21:2
De Cordova S, 1877, D 1,4:7
De Costa, B F Rev, 1904, N 5,9:2
DeCosta, Eugene, 1947, Jl 10,21:1
De Costa, H S Mrs, 1901, Ap 7,7:6
De Coste, William B (Bro Berard Jos), 1956, F 20, 23:3
Decoster, Atwood L, 1944, S 22,19:2
De Coster, S Ella, 1952, Ag 11,15:3
Decot, Valentine A, 1951, D 20,31:2
Decoto, Ezra W, 1948, Ap 7,25:1
De Cou, Branson, 1941, D 13,21:6
De Courcey, William Henry Dr, 1911, Ap 7,13:4
DeCourcy, Carroll, 1961, Ja 22,85:1
De Courcy, Charles A Justice, 1924, Ag 23,9:4
De Courcy, Ferdinand E Lt-Col, 1912, Mr 29,13:4
deCourcy, Frank R, 1958, F 14,24:1
De Courcy, Harold L, 1944, Je 7,19:1
DeCourcy, Joseph L, 1960, Ja 22,27:2
De Courcy, Stephen Mrs, 1950, Ap 8,13:2
Decoursey, Ethel Mrs, 1937, D 23,21:4
DeCoursey, James J Mrs, 1954, D 3,27:3
De Coursey, S G, 1903, Ja 28,9:6
De Court, Julian, 1942, Ja 9,21:5
de Courville, Albert Mrs, 1960, D 13,31:3
Decoux, Jean, 1963, O 22,37:3
De Cozen, Albert, 1957, Ja 22,29:5
DeCozen, Alfred, 1959, Je 14,86:3
De Cram, Anton Mrs, 1952, O 11,19:4
DeCrescenzo, Vincenzo, 1964, O 14,45:3
De Crette, Paul M, 1938, F 12,15:3
De Cristofalo, Amerigo, 1951, Ap 6,25:3
de Csepel, Edith W, 1967, Ag 8,39:3
de Csipkes, Edward Z, 1956, O 2,35:4
Decter, Jacob, 1946, N 13,27:5
Deddens, William Sr Mrs, 1951, Ap 19,31:1
Dedeck-Hery, Ernestine, 1953, Ag 10,23:5
Dedeck-Hery, Louis V, 1945, D 28,16:2
Dedekind, E H William, 1941, O 28,23:1
Dedekind, J Wilhelm Richard Dr, 1916, F 13,15:4
Dedell, Harry C, 1945, N 13,21:5
Dedell, Robert E, 1940, Ap 14,44:8
Dedell, Thomas C, 1947, My 19,21:6
Dederer, George F, 1947, N 5,27:3
Dederer, George H, 1938, D 22,21:4
Dederer, George H Mrs, 1951, D 20,31:5
Dederick, Allan D, 1956, F 2,25:4
Dederick, Charles P Mrs, 1964, Mr 8,86:5
Dederick, Henry M, 1940, Ap 16,23:2
Dederick, Ransom D, 1944, F 14,17:4
Dederick, William Kells, 1911, Ja 19,9:4
DeDerky, David T, 1938, D 14,25:5
De Derux, Edward C, 1940, Mr 14,23:2
De Dino, Duchess, 1912, Jl 20,7:5
De Dombrowski, Francesco Mrs (est tax appr), 1955, N 8,25:1
Dedon, Walter L, 1949, Ap 9,17:6
Dedona, Frederick, 1950, N 12,93:2
De Dreux, William F Mrs, 1950, F 25,17:6
Dedrick, Benjamin W, 1946, F 19,25:2
Dedrick, Phil J Sr, 1954, Ap 6,29:3
Dee, Agnes C, 1948, Jl 9,19:2
Dee, George W, 1954, Jl 8,23:5
Dee, Jeremiah, 1937, Jl 15,15:1
Dee, Michael, 1937, O 25,19:3
Dee, Michael F, 1953, D 31,19:5
Dee, Michael F Mrs, 1952, O 10,25:4
Dee, Michael L, 1946, O 5,17:6
Dee, Nellie, 1949, Ja 11,31:6
Dee, Sylvia, 1967, Je 13,64:1
Dee, Thomas J Mrs, 1952, Ag 15,15:2
Dee, William, 1937, Jl 21,21:6
Dee, William F, 1953, D 30,23:1
Deedes, Wyndham, 1956, S 4,29:4
Deedman, Donald F, 1963, My 28,75:4
Deeds, Edward A, 1960, Jl 2,17:3
Deeds, Edward A Mrs, 1949, F 10,28:2
Deeds, Joseph B, 1946, Ag 27,27:4
Deegan, Charlotte, 1960, D 21,31:2
Deegan, Cornelius S, 1951, Jl 27,19:6
Deegan, Deirdre-Gael, 1949, My 24,33:1
Deegan, Edward J, 1949, S 26,25:5
Deegan, J P, 1954, S 6,15:6
Deegan, James D, 1961, D 9,56:6
Deegan, James J, 1942, D 8,25:4
Deegan, John G, 1950, O 12,31:6
Deegan, Joseph F Mrs, 1966, Ap 2,29:4
Deegan, Joseph P, 1943, Ap 22,23:5
Deegan, Oswald J, 1950, Ap 27,29:3
Deegan, Patrick J, 1952, Ja 1,25:4
Deegan, Thomas J, 1924, Ap 24,19:3; 1964, D 8,45:4
Deegan, Thomas J Sr, 1966, Ap 16,33:3
Deegan, W F, 1932, Ap 4,17:1
Deegan, William J, 1947, Ja 8,23:2
Deeks, Hiram C J, 1952, N 15,17:1
Deel, George A, 1947, Je 8,60:6
Deel, George A Mrs, 1948, Ap 30,23:5
Deemer, Frank J, 1946, Je 21,23:3
Deemer, Harold D, 1946, D 16,24:2
Deems, C F Rev Dr, 1893, N 19,10:7
Deems, Charles P, 1955, Mr 14,23:3
Deems, Edward M Mrs, 1949, Je 7,31:3
Deems, Walter A, 1959, Jl 7,33:3
Deems, Walter A Mrs, 1962, Ag 31,21:1
Deen, Charles C, 1937, N 17,23:1
Deen, Edward, 1948, Mr 11,27:4
Deen, J Lee, 1951, Ap 26,29:6
Deeping, Warwick, 1950, Ap 21,23:1
Deer, James, 1939, Jl 12,19:5; 1956, Je 20,31:3
Deer, James Mrs, 1959, Jl 15,29:4
de Erdely, Francis, 1959, N 30,31:3
Deere, Charles H, 1907, O 30,9:5
Deere, Charles H Mrs, 1913, Ap 29,9:4
Deerhurst, Viscount, 1927, Ag 9,23:3
Deericks, Julia M Mrs, 1952, Mr 26,29:2
Deerin, James B, 1942, My 30,15:4
Deering, Arthur, 1961, Ja 22,84:3
Deering, C, 1927, F 6,2:4
Deering, Charles Mrs (will, D 23,21:5), 1943, D 1, 21:3
Deering, Charles William Case, 1924, My 13,21:5
Deering, Emil J, 1945, D 8,17:3
Deering, James, 1925, S 22,25:2
Deering, James A (est, Jl 17,7:4), 1915, Jl 9,11:5
Deering, James A, 1956, Jl 29,64:6
Deering, James C, 1938, Ja 23,II,8:3
Deering, James R, 1967, D 12,48:1
Deering, John P, 1947, Ja 6,23:4
Deering, Joseph H, 1939, Jl 27,19:4
Deering, Lawrence A Mrs, 1951, O 11,37:3
Deering, Mary E N Mrs, 1948, N 21,88:4
Deering, N, 1881, Mr 28,5:6
Deering, Phil J Jr, 1949, Ja 31,19:2
Deering, Raymond C, 1965, Je 4,35:3
Deering, William Alloway, 1911, Ag 11,9:6
Deering, William Mrs, 1918, My 27,13:5
Deery, Arthur, 1957, F 1,25:1
Deery, Edwin M G, 1950, Ja 31,23:4
Deery, James, 1950, O 18,33:3
Deery, Robert H (funl, Ap 24,15:4), 1920, Ap 17,15:3
Deery, William A E, 1950, D 30,13:5
DeEsso, Charles, 1950, F 15,21:3
Deesz, Louis, 1950, Ap 20,29:5
Deeter, Sarah M Mrs, 1942, O 23,21:3
Deetjen, Christian, 1940, D 29,23:2
Deetjen, Luis A, 1941, O 29,23:2
Deetjen, Rudolph H, 1967, Jl 8,25:1
Deetjen, Werner, 1939, My 23,23:4
Deeves, Richard, 1919, O 19,22:3
Deeves, Richard A, 1948, Ag 16,19:3
De Fabinyi, Tihamer I, 1953, Je 12,27:5
deFabry, Harold L, 1961, Ag 22,29:3
Defandorf, Francis M, 1963, Ag 20,33:3
Defandorf, Jason F, 1940, S 5,23:5
Defandorf, John A, 1939, N 12,49:2
Defauw, Desire, 1960, Jl 26,30:1
De Fazio, Joseph, 1964, Ap 6,31:3
De Fazio, Samuel, 1951, Ag 5,73:2
Defea, Thomas, 1942, Ag 21,19:4
De Felice, Joseph, 1944, Jl 14,13:3
DeFelice, Louis G, 1961, D 5,43:3
Defenbacher, Herbert D, 1954, D 28,23:2
Defenbaugh, James Elliott, 1909, N 22,9:7
Defenbaugh, Walter, 1940, My 6,17:4
Defendant, Felix Bro (G J Marquart), 1955, Ja 16, 93:1
De Fere, Paul E, 1952, D 11,33:3
de Fermon, Elizabeth C G Mrs, 1940, Ag 13,19:4
Deferrari, John, 1950, My 3,29:3
De Ferussac, Alice Countess, 1874, N 24,8:3
De Fillippie, Maria Giovanna Mrs, 1912, O 17,11:5
De Fillips, Ernest, 1955, N 29,29:4
Defillo, Fernando, 1949, O 31,25:2
De Finganiere, J C Signor, 1866, D 15,4:5
De Flavigny, Marquis, 1873, O 26,1:3
de Florez, Luis, 1962, D 6,43:2
De Florez, Pedro R Mrs, 1947, N 12,27:1
De Foe, Annette (G M Aucoin), 1960, Ag 8,21:2
DeFoe, Frederick W, 1958, D 6,23:5
Defoe, Harry, 1957, Mr 22,23:1
De Foe, Louis V, 1922, Mr 13,15:5
De Ford, Frances A Dr, 1937, Ja 10,II,10:8
De Forest, Alfred V, 1945, Ap 6,15:1
De Forest, Alonzo A, 1903, D 29,9:6
DeForest, Annie J, 1951, Ag 13,17:4
De Forest, Augusta, 1901, O 21,9:4
De Forest, C O, 1901, O 7,1:4
De Forest, Charles D, 1951, N 29,33:2
De Forest, Charles M, 1947, Ap 13,60:1
De Forest, Clarissa B Mrs, 1938, S 30,21:3
De Forest, E T, 1879, Ap 17,2:7
De Forest, Emily J Mrs, 1942, Je 14,45:1
Deforest, Ezra, 1921, Ap 6,15:6
De Forest, Ezra Mrs, 1944, N 21,25:3
De Forest, F Bowden, 1938, Ag 31,15:1
De Forest, Frank V, 1940, Jl 10,19:4
De Forest, Genevieve (Josephine Gerbel), 1911, S 5, 7:6
De Forest, George V, 1912, O 28,11:4
De Forest, Henry L, 1954, Mr 20,15:2
DeForest, Henry P, 1948, Je 14,23:3
de Forest, Henry P, 1958, Ja 4,15:5
De Forest, Henry W (por), 1938, My 29,II,7:1
De Forest, Howard (cor, Ap 7,46:1), 1946, Ap 5,25:2
De Forest, J, 1932, O 13,19:1
De Forest, James, 1903, Je 10,9:7
DeForest, James G, 1942, Je 19,23:5
De Forest, John H Rev, 1911, My 9,11:5
De Forest, Johnston, 1952, N 26,23:4
De Forest, Johnston Mrs, 1940, Jl 30,19:2
De Forest, Julia, 1949, S 10,17:5
DeForest, Kate R MRs, 1948, S 23,29:6
De Forest, Lee (funl plans, Jl 3,15:5;est acctg, Ag 18,6:5), 1961, Jl 2,1:2
De Forest, Lockwood Jr, 1949, Mr 21,25:3
De Forest, Louis E, 1952, My 22,27:2
de Forest, Louis S, 1938, Ag 5,18:4
De Forest, R W, 1931, My 7,1:3
De Forest, Sarah E Mrs, 1915, D 25,7:6
De Forest, W W, 1866, Ja 20,2:3
De Forest, William, 1956, D 24,13:5
de Forge, Abraham, 1925, O 31,17:3
De Forge, Joseph T, 1946, Ja 13,44:2
Deforge, Louis M, 1947, F 5,23:5
De Fornaro, Carlo, 1949, Ag 26,20:3
De Forrest, Lena W Mrs, 1941, Ag 7,17:4
Deforth, Peter, 1944, Je 1,19:1
de Francesco, Italo L, 1967, My 26,47:1
De Francheville, Andree, 1944, S 4,19:5
de Francisci, Anthony, 1964, O 21,47:4
Defrates, Antonio F, 1948, Mr 8,23:1
De Freece, A B, 1903, Ja 10,9:5
Defrees, John D, 1882, O 20,5:5
Defrees, Joseph R, 1958, Ag 7,25:2
De Freest, C R, 1901, My 12,7:6
De Freitas, Anthony, 1940, S 23,17:4
Defrere, Desire, 1964, S 2,37:3
De Freyne, Lord (Arth French), 1913, S 11,11:6
De Frias, Duke, 1874, O 8,6:7
De Friese, L H, 1928, Je 19,27:1
De Friest, Albertus, 1953, Jl 27,19:5
Defriest, Seth, 1939, Ag 22,19:4
De Friest, Sophie B Mrs, 1942, D 4,25:3
De Frino, Catherine Mrs, 1942, F 4,21:7
De Frise, Henry H (corr, Je 13,35:2), 1961, My 28, 64:2
De Frise, Henry H Mrs, 1949, Ag 30,27:2
De Fronzo, Morando, 1965, N 18,47:3
DeFuccio, Charles P, 1955, O 11,39:5
Defuentes, Sidney J, 1940, F 25,38:6
De Funiak, Ernest A, 1945, O 4,23:1
De Funiak, F Col, 1905, Mr 30,9:6
De Gaetano, N Thomas, 1955, Jl 6,27:3
De Gallatin, Charles, 1915, Jl 16,9:3
Degan, Edward J, 1954, Mr 29,19:5
Degan, James J Mrs, 1944, My 12,19:4
de Ganahl, Carl, 1968, Mr 25,41:3
De Ganahl, Charles F, 1939, My 15,17:4
De Ganahl, Mary Mrs, 1950, F 18,15:5
De Garden, Count, 1872, Ag 15,2:6
DeGaris, Frederick Mrs, 1950, Jl 15,13:2
De Garis, Lucy H Mrs, 1939, N 13,19:5
de Garmendia, Carlos G Mrs, 1919, N 12,13:3
De Garmendia, Carlos M, 1939, Jl 11,19:5
De Garmo, Frank Mrs, 1953, S 26,17:4
Degarmo, Harry Mrs, 1949, F 13,76:6
de Garmo, Leon B, 1959, N 30,31:5
de Garmo, Louis, 1959, S 23,39:3
DeGarmo, Phil W, 1954, Mr 31,27:1
Degas, Hilaire Germain Edgard, 1917, S 28,11:7
De Gatur, Gerald T, 1945, Ja 9,19:3
Degelleke, Frank E, 1948, N 5,25:1
De Gelleke, Peter, 1965, Ag 7,21:5
Degelmann, John, 1938, S 7,25:2
Degen, Albert G Mrs, 1943, Mr 6,13:2
Degen, Charles J, 1948, Ja 13,25:5
Degen, Edward A, 1941, F 1,17:3
Degen, George C, 1939, F 25,15:1
Degen, Robert F, 1961, Mr 18,23:5
Degen, Robert F Mrs, 1945, D 18,27:3
Degen, Willard G Mrs, 1960, D 25,29:5
Degenaar, Christopher B, 1962, O 28,88:2
De Genahl, Charles F Mrs, 1952, Jl 14,17:4
Degener, Charles H, 1957, My 23,33:4
Degener, John F, 1924, Ap 17,19:4
Degener, John F Jr, 1956, F 7,31:1
Degener, Lyda M, 1948, S 12,72:4
Degener, Rudolph, 1937, Mr 5,21:4
Degenhardt, George A, 1947, Je 9,21:5
Degenhardt, Martin, 1943, Je 17,21:4
Degenhardt, Peter, 1940, My 5,52:7
Degenhart, Frederick M Sr, 1956, Ja 25,31:1
DeGennaro, Alfred, 1968, My 13,43:2
De Genouilly, Charles R Adm, 1873, My 6,4:7
Degenring, Adolph, 1947, S 7,60:2
Degenring, Anna B, 1959, Ag 29,17:5
Degenring, Gustav, 1960, Mr 10,32:1
De Geofroy, George, 1954, N 27,13:4
De George, Robert F, 1948, Ja 3,13:4
De Gerard, Victor, 1945, Mr 23,20:2
De Gersdorff, Carl A, 1944, Ja 23,37:1
De Gersdorff, Carl A Mrs, 1941, Je 15,36:8

Degetana, Anthony A, 1950, Mr 29,29:3
De Geulard, M, 1874, Jl 5,1:7
de Girolamo, James H, 1956, Mr 4,88:3
De Glehn, Wilfrid, 1951, My 18,27:2
de Glehn, Wilfrid Mrs, 1961, F 21,35:4
Degman, William, 1947, Jl 6,40:8
Degnan, Bernard M, 1967, F 4,27:3
Degnan, Bryan J, 1946, Je 3,21:3
Degnan, Daniel D, 1964, Jl 25,19:6
Degnan, Don, 1951, O 14,88:4
Degnan, John E, 1951, Jl 27,19:4
Degnan, Martin L, 1956, Je 15,25:4
Degnan, Phil A, 1949, O 2,82:7
Degnan, Robert, 1959, F 2,20:2
Degnan, Thomas M Mrs, 1954, N 13,15:2
Degnen, Francis X, 1958, N 1,19:5
Degnen, Thomas J Mrs, 1961, My 28,64:4
Degnon, Michael J, 1925, Ap 23,21:3
de Goencz, Denis, 1956, O 17,35:5
De Gogorz, Emilio, 1949, My 11,29:6
Degogorza, Ernest L, 1952, My 13,23:2
de'Gogorza, Flora Mrs, 1960, Je 17,32:1
De Gogorza, Maitland, 1941, Je 22,32:4
Degolier, Ralph J, 1961, F 20,27:4
De Goll, Clarence A, 1940, Ap 12,23:5
DeGooyer, John G, 1955, Mr 27,87:1
Degoutte, Jean M J, 1938, N 1,23:1
De Gouy, Louis P, 1947, N 15,17:2
De Graaf, George, 1964, Mr 31,35:1
De Grab, Herman, 1949, Ag 3,23:4
De Graff, Alice A, 1939, O 26,23:6
De Graff, Alonzo H, 1940, My 17,19:4
De Graff, Edward T, 1942, Ap 22,23:6
Degraff, Frank C, 1954, Mr 20,15:5
Degraff, George W, 1941, Ag 22,15:4
deGraff, Hendrik, 1965, F 18,33:3
Degraff, James H, 1907, N 28,7:4
De Graff, James W, 1956, Ag 17,19:4
De Graff, James W Mrs, 1951, Jl 18,29:3
Degraff, LeGrand S, 1960, Ap 3,86:7
De Graff, Ralph M, 1944, D 14,23:2
De Graffenried, Gertrude, 1944, Ja 28,17:5
De Graffenried, R C, 1902, Ag 30,9:6
deGraffenried, Ryan, 1966, F 11,20:2
De Gramont, Duke, 1880, Ja 19,5:6
De Grande, Joseph, 1911, My 22,11:4
De Grandval, Leo, 1902, Je 6,7:2
DeGrange, McQuilkin, 1953, D 30,24:3
Degrass, F Maj, 1883, Ja 5,5:4
De Grasse, Joseph, 1940, My 26,35:2
DeGrasse-Fowler, Silvie A M (will), 1941, Ja 17,19:2
de Grassky, Samuel, 1922, Ag 1,19:4
De Grave, Jean J, 1947, Mr 23,60:6
de Gravenhoff, Vladimir, 1960, F 23,31:4
De Graves, William A, 1950, Ja 21,17:2
DeGraw, Frederick D, 1943, Mr 11,21:3
DeGraw, Hamilton Bro, 1937, O 30,19:1
De Graw, John, 1941, Ag 21,17:4
DeGraw, John Mrs, 1963, O 25,31:4
De Graw, Lincoln H, 1955, My 4,29:5
De Graw, Peter Voorhees, 1914, Ag 23,13:6
De Gray, Frederick W, 1942, Je 11,23:4
Degray, Richard, 1909, Jl 3,7:4
DeGray, Robert, 1968, My 29,41:3
DeGrazia, Joseph, 1955, Ja 24,15:5
Degrazio, Joseph N, 1947, N 24,23:3
De Greck, Alfred J, 1945, O 17,19:4
De Grego, Ricardo, 1949, Mr 10,28:3
de Gregori, Giorgio T, 1956, F 8,33:2
De Gress, Francis, 1949, Ja 25,23:4
De Greve, Arthur F, 1957, O 22,33:4
De Grief, P, 1894, Ja 8,5:3
Degroat, Clarence W, 1951, F 6,27:5
De Groat, H Everett, 1958, Ap 10,29:5
DeGroat, Harry DeW, 1959, O 22,37:5
Degroff, Carrie A Mrs, 1942, My 26,21:5
Degroff, Jerome S, 1948, D 13,23:4
DeGroff, Lloyd E, 1946, Ag 26,23:5
De Grofft, Vernon, 1940, Mr 13,23:3
De Groot, A W, 1884, S 20,4:7
de Groot, Adelaide M, 1967, Je 24,29:3
De Groot, Adriaan M, 1942, Ja 19,20:1
De Groot, C P, 1883, N 9,2:2
De Groot, Giles C, 1940, Mr 31,44:4
De Groot, Hugh I, 1948, D 11,15:1
DeGroot, John, 1950, S 19,29:2; 1955, Jl 5,29:1
De Groot, John F (por), 1949, S 7,29:1
Degroot, Katherine Mrs, 1941, Ja 23,21:1
DeGroot, L J, 1942, D 9,27:2
De Groot, Lester A, 1938, O 9,45:2
De Groot, Mortimer, 1953, My 14,29:4
de Groot, Nanno F, 1963, D 28,23:1
De Groot, W A, 1932, Mr 2,19:1
Degroote, John F, 1946, O 17,23:4
De Grouchy, William, 1954, D 1,31:6
De Grove, Edward Ritzema, 1911, Jl 18,9:6
De Grove, Quincy D, 1905, Ag 23,7:5
DeGruchy, John, 1940, Ja 24,21:4
de Grunwald, Anatole, 1967, Ja 14,31:3
Degryse, Henry, 1942, D 8,25:5
Degtyarev, Vassily A, 1949, Ja 18,24:3
de Guichard, Basil, 1958, My 30,21:5
De Guire, George N, 1941, Ja 27,15:4

de Gumoens, George B Mrs, 1956, Jl 13,10:4
De Gunther, Edward J, 1940, Ag 6,22:5
De Gunzburg, Theodore, 1945, My 13,20:4
De Gurio, Michael V, 1953, Jl 3,19:4
De Gurse, T E, 1949, Ag 17,23:3
De Haan, John, 1945, S 12,25:3
DeHaan, Roland L, 1951, F 12,23:1
de Haas, J Anton, 1963, O 9,40:4
De Haas, Jacob J A, 1937, Mr 22,23:4
De Haas, W F, 1880, Ag 26,5:5
De Hallebranth, John, 1949, My 30,13:3
Dehan, Leroy M Mrs, 1954, D 18,15:7
Deharau, French Clown, 1874, Ja 12,8:5
de Hart, Alden, 1955, Je 20,21:3
DeHart, Clarence, 1941, Jl 22,19:4
de Hart, Clarence E, 1955, Ap 24,86:4
De Hart, Emma B Mrs (left no will, Je 16,69:3), 1957, Je 15,1:3
De Hart, Harold, 1952, My 13,30:2
DeHart, John, 1948, Jl 19,19:5
De Hart, John S Jr, 1937, D 25,15:4
Dehart, John W, 1940, D 11,27:6
De Hart, Louis O, 1951, D 27,21:3
De Hart, Madana Fuller Dr, 1911, Je 24,9:6
De Hart, Phoebe A Mrs, 1937, Je 8,25:4
De Hart, Pierson, 1920, Je 20,18:4
De Hart, Raymond C, 1946, N 19,31:3
De Hart, Samuel, 1946, Ap 10,27:4
De Hart, William H Rev Dr, 1916, F 15,11:6
DeHart, William O, 1948, F 29,60:3
De Hart, Winfield S, 1905, D 15,10:2
de Hartmann, Thomas, 1956, Mr 28,31:2
De Hass, Wills Dr, 1910, Ja 26,9:5
De Haven, Albert, 1943, O 16,13:1
De Haven, Alexander H, 1912, Ap 17,13:5
DeHaven, Alexander M, 1946, Jl 26,21:2
DeHaven, Charles, 1954, N 18,33:3
De Haven, David W, 1943, Je 5,15:1
De Haven, E J Lt, 1865, My 6,2:4
De Haven, Edward, 1950, O 18,33:3
De Haven, Flora P Mrs, 1950, S 11,23:4
De Haven, John B, 1945, Je 26,19:2
De Haven, Walter B, 1943, Ap 17,17:4
de Havilland, Geoffrey, 1965, My 22,31:2
De Havilland, Geoffrey Mrs, 1949, Jl 13,28:4
Dehe, William, 1942, F 9,15:4
De Heredia, Georgie B C Mrs, 1946, D 15,76:1
De Hernandez, Francisca M Mrs, 1941, Jl 21,15:5
Dehey, Peter A, 1954, Je 12,15:2
Dehler, Thomas (funl, Jl 26,2:4), 1967, Jl 22,26:4
Dehlgren, Sten, 1947, N 23,74:3
Dehli, Arne, 1942, Ag 13,19:2
Dehls, Frederick, 1958, F 9,88:4
Dehma, Francis X, 1947, S 16,24:3
Dehmel, Richard, 1920, F 12,11:4
Dehmer, George, 1946, D 15,77:7
Dehn, Adolf, 1968, My 20,47:2
Dehn, Amiel O, 1949, N 29,29:3
Dehnert, Elizabeth, 1938, Ag 17,19:1
De Hoan, Israel, 1924, Jl 2,19:4
De Hoff, Hugh C, 1954, F 24,25:1
De Hoffmann, Alexandre Mrs, 1952, D 23,23:4
De Horsey, Algernon Adm, 1922, O 23,15:4
De Horsey, Spencer Victor Yorks Adm, 1937, Mr 22, 23:2
de Horsey, William Henry Beaumont Lt-Gen, 1915, My 8,15:5
de Hospodar, Stephen, 1959, O 14,43:1
De Hosson, Bernard U, 1952, O 1,33:3
De Housszu, Martin, 1953, N 26,32:3
De Hoyos, Luis, 1951, My 9,33:5
De Huff, Henry, 1946, Ag 25,46:1
De Huff, Thomas M, 1963, N 13,41:1
Deibel, Albert T, 1950, D 5,32:2
Deibel, Charles A, 1951, Je 12,29:5
Deibel, Cyril P, 1945, Ja 23,19:3
Deibel, John I, 1943, Ag 21,11:5
Deibel, Joseph, 1953, Ap 1,29:5
Deibel, Rudolph, 1959, Mr 22,86:8
Deibert, Alfred D, 1939, My 28,III,7:2
Deibert, Irwin E, 1967, Ja 7,27:4
Deibler, Anatole, 1939, F 3,3:7
Deibler, Louis, 1904, S 9,7:7
Deichert, Walter H, 1966, N 26,35:3
Deiches, Jacob Mrs, 1946, Jl 18,25:5
Deiches, Maurice (will, N 30,20:5), 1938, F 16,21:1
Deiches, Walter H, 1964, Mr 31,35:2
Deichman, Frank R, 1947, Ap 10,25:3
Deichsel, Albert F, 1956, Je 26,29:1
Deicke, Gertrude, 1952, Ja 9,29:1
Deidling, Rudolph F, 1950, S 17,105:2
Deierlein, Edward, 1946, Ag 22,27:3
Deierlein, Josephine, 1946, Je 11,23:4
Deighan, John P, 1952, Ja 1,25:4
Deignan, John H, 1950, Ap 9,84:4
Deignan, John J, 1946, Ag 31,15:7
Deignan, Patrick I, 1956, My 8,33:4
Deihl, John Mrs, 1939, Ag 29,21:5
Deihl, Joseph A, 1948, N 3,27:5
Deike, F William, 1940, Ag 21,19:3
Deike, George H, 1963, Jl 19,25:4
Deimel, Richard F (por), 1955, S 30,25:3
Deimel, Simon, 1916, F 5,11:4

Deimling, Berthold von, 1944, Mr 3,16:2
Deimling, Joseph A, 1960, D 29,25:1
Dein, Charles W, 1941, Mr 28,23:5
Deindorfer, John C, 1952, D 10,35:1
Deindorfer, John W, 1964, O 21,43:3
Deininger, Charles F, 1953, D 15,44:7
Deininger, Daniel M, 1945, My 22,19:5
Deininger, Dorothea D, 1952, Mr 28,23:1
Deininger, Henry G, 1951, D 22,15:6
Deininger, Herbert O, 1951, Jl 6,23:5
Deininger, Samuel W, 1955, Ag 16,23:4
Deininger, William C (will, S 25,26:4), 1941, S 8,15:
Deininger, William C, 1944, My 8,19:6
Deins, George F, 1967, Ja 19,31:5
Deiro, Pietro, 1954, N 4,31:4
Deis, Charles, 1951, Mr 20,29:1
Deis, William F, 1959, Je 1,27:2
Deisel, Jake, 1951, My 5,17:5
Deisher, Walter N, 1956, F 8,33:1
Deisler, Clemens A Mrs, 1958, Jl 13,69:2
Deisler, William W, 1943, Mr 17,21:4
Deisroth, William H, 1939, Ag 27,35:3
Deiss, Charles F, 1959, Je 15,27:5
Deisseroth, Albert L, 1939, Ag 13,29:2
Deissinger, George B, 1942, My 21,19:1
Deissmann, Adolf, 1937, Ap 6,23:1
Deist, Heinrich, 1964, Mr 8,86:4
Deitch, George, 1937, Ag 7,15:2
Deitch, M Mal, 1966, Mr 17,39:1
Deitch, Phil Mrs, 1949, Je 28,27:3
Deitchman, Louis S, 1946, S 6,21:1
Deitrick, Jacob W, 1946, F 11,29:3
Deitrick, Sarah S, 1963, S 29,86:6
Deitsch, Alan B, 1957, Je 21,25:2
Deitsch, Ph Col, 1903, Ja 28,9:6
Deitsch, Samuel L, 1966, Ap 11,35:1
Deitschman, Nathan, 1912, Ag 6,9:2
Deitz, Herbert J Mrs, 1960, Ap 16,17:5
Deitz, Karl S, 1960, Ag 13,15:4
Deitzer, C, 1882, Ap 1,5:2
deJaive, Edmond M Sr, 1958, N 2,89:2
De Jan, Henri, 1937, Ag 18,19:4
De Janon, Louis, 1906, Ja 24,9:6
De Jara Almonte, Juan, 1945, My 21,19:6
De Jarnac, Count, 1875, Mr 24,7:2
De Jarnette, D C, 1881, Ag 26,5:1
Dejazet, Eugene, 1871, Mr 12,5:1
Dejazet, P V, 1875, D 2,1:3
Dejeau, M, 1879, N 3,2:7
De Jelsi, Joseph, 1942, S 8,23:4
Dejerine, Jules, 1917, F 28,11:4
Dejianne, James, 1940, Jl 2,22:3
De John, Philomena Mrs, 1949, N 8,31:4
Dejon, Edward R, 1940, Ag 6,19:4
de Jong, Cornelis M, 1963, My 3,32:1
DeJong, David C, 1967, S 6,44:6
de Jong, H Holland, 1956, F 17,23:2
De Jong, Matilda Mrs, 1942, F 4,31:4
Dejonge, Alfred, 1939, S 15,23:3
Dejonge, C Edward, 1914, Ag 16,15:6
de Jonge, Solomon, 1938, Ag 4,17:5
De Jonghe, Jules Mrs, 1940, Ja 28,33:1
De Josika-Herczeg, Imre Mrs, 1947, Mr 13,27:5
De Jurenev, Nicholas, 1954, Ap 30,23:5
de Kallay, Nicholas Mrs, 1962, F 6,32:6
De Kay, C, 1935, My 24,21:4
De Kay, Charles Mrs, 1949, N 13,92:6
De Kay, John W, 1938, O 6,23:4
De Kay, Sidney G (por), 1949, Je 24,23:1
de Kay, Sidney G Mrs, 1966, My 23,41:5
De Kay, Willard Mrs, 1948, My 26,25:4
de Kerekjarto, Duci, 1962, Ja 5,29:4
De Keyser, Julius S, 1968, D 17,47:3
de Kiewiet, Christine A, 1960, D 11,88:8
Dekker, Albert, 1968, My 7,47:3
Dekker, Cornelius Mrs, 1937, O 11,21:2
Dekker, John, 1957, Ap 19,15:1
Dekker, Maurice, 1949, O 17,23:1
De Kleine, William, 1957, S 22,86:4
De Klyn, Charles C, 1948, S 9,27:4
De Klyn, Frank B, 1944, Jl 11,15:4
Deknatel, Frank H, 1954, Ag 1,85:2
de Komlosy, Charlotte Walker Mrs, 1919, Ag 5,9
De Koning, John J, 1950, O 25,35:3
DeKoning, William C Sr (will, D 20,20:5), 1957 O 20,86:1
De Korver, Cornelis, 1942, S 27,49:3
De Koster, Bessie, 1953, My 11,27:5
DeKoven, Bernard, 1940, Ag 12,15:2
De Koven, J Rev Dr, 1879, Mr 20,4:6
de Koven, Reginald (funl, Ja 18,22:4), 1920, Ja 11:5
De Koven, Reginald Mrs, 1953, Ja 13,27:3
deKrafft, William, 1963, O 18,31:3
De Kraft, F, 1936, D 26,11:5
De Kraft, Henry G Dr, 1925, My 5,21:4
de Kresz, Geza, 1959, O 3,19:6
De Kruif, Henricka Mrs, 1948, S 12,72:3
de Kupsa, Alfred, 1968, Ap 22,50:8
Delaage, Henri, 1882, Ag 28,1:7
De la Barra, Francisco L, 1939, S 24,43:3
Delabarre, Edmund B, 1945, Mr 17,13:4
Delabarre, Frank L, 1938, Ap 17,II,7:2

De La Bat, B J G, 1942, Ag 22,13:2
De Labilliere, Paul (por), 1946, Ap 29,21:3
De Lacey, E, 1879, Mr 11,2:2
De Lacey, Jules, 1955, Mr 5,17:2
De Lacey, Robert E, 1906, Je 24,9:6
De La Chapelle, Henry, 1947, N 19,27:2
De La Chapelle, Jean P, 1952, D 18,29:2
Delacorte, George Jr Mrs, 1956, Ag 19,92:1
De La Cour, J Carl, 1952, Jl 16,25:3
Delacroix, Anne E, 1949, D 28,25:1
Delacroix (Painter), 1863, Ag 30,6:5
de la Cruz, Tomas, 1958, S 8,29:5
De Lacy, George C, 1919, Jl 2,13:3
De Lacy, Peter, 1915, N 15,11:5
Deladrier, Clovis, 1948, Ja 25,56:3
De Lae, Cornelius, 1953, Ja 21,31:4
Delafield, A Floyd, 1904, Jl 19,7:6
Delafield, Anne O B Mrs, 1941, D 27,19:1
Delafield, E, 1884, N 30,9:2
Delafield, Edward Dr, 1875, F 15,4:7
Delafield, Edward H, 1955, D 2,27:2
Delafield, Elizabeth M, 1943, D 3,23:3
Delafield, Elizabeth M Mrs, 1939, Ap 20,23:4
Delafield, Elizabeth Ray, 1923, My 6,11:1
Delafield, Emma, 1938, D 3,19:2
Delafield, Francis Dr, 1915, Jl 18,15:5
Delafield, Frederick P, 1924, D 15,17:1
Delafield, Frederick P Mrs, 1967, Jl 18,37:4
Delafield, George S, 1942, Mr 27,23:6
Delafield, Henry, 1875, F 16,7:5
Delafield, Herbert A, 1944, D 13,23:4
Delafield, John R, 1964, Ap 9,31:4
Delafield, John T Mrs, 1949, My 3,25:4
Delafield, Joseph, 1875, F 14,7:2
Delafield, Joseph L, 1922, N 21,19:5
Delafield, Joseph L Mrs, 1964, Jl 24,27:5
Delafield, Julia E Mrs, 1937, F 16,23:2
Delafield, Julia Livingston, 1914, N 11,13:4
Delafield, L L, 1883, Mr 29,5:5
Delafield, Lewis L, 1944, S 28,19:5; 1957, Ag 20,27:4
Delafield, Lewis L Mrs, 1947, Ap 25,21:4
Delafield, Maturin Delafield Mrs, 1922, My 28,22:3
Delafield, Maturin L, 1945, Ag 16,19:1
Delafield, Maturin Livingston, 1917, N 6,13:7
Delafield, R, 1930, Ag 5,23:3
Delafield, Richard Maj-Gen, 1873, N 6,5:2
Delafield, Richard Mrs, 1909, S 7,9:5; 1925, Ag 13, 19:6
Delafield, Robert H, 1945, F 13,23:1
Delafield, Robert H Mrs, 1959, Ag 7,23:5
Delafield, Rufus Y, 1874, F 8,3:6
Delafield, Tallmadge P, 1940, My 27,19:4
De La Figaniere, L F, 1885, Ja 26,2:4
Delafleur, Frederick J, 1943, O 5,25:5
Delagi, Michael N, 1957, O 8,36:1
Delagi, Michael N Mrs, 1956, Ja 27,23:3
De Lagrange, Frederic Count, 1883, N 23,2:2
De La Grangerie Dardenne, 1873, S 1,4:7
de la Guardia, Ernesto Mrs, 1959, F 21,1:2
De la Guerra, Delfina, 1953, Ap 26,87:1
Delahant, Raymond F, 1942, D 31,15:2
Delahanty, James, 1953, O 20,29:4; 1954, Ap 24,17:6
Delahanty, Robert J, 1958, My 8,29:3
Delahanty, Thomas, 1951, Ja 12,27:4
Delahanty, Thomas F, 1921, F 23,13:6
Delahanty, William, 1940, Jl 25,17:6
Delahay, William A Mrs, 1944, My 31,19:2
de la Huerta, Adolfo, 1955, Jl 10,74:1
Delahunt, William, 1968, My 15,47:4
Delahunty, John, 1922, S 25,15:4
Delahunty, Thomas Lawrence, 1919, D 16,13:3
De Lai, Gaetans Cardinal, 1928, O 25,29:5
Delaire, Alvin J, 1968, Ap 9,47:2
Delaire, Thomas H, 1952, Ja 4,40:2
Delait, Clementine Mrs, 1939, Ap 21,5:4
De La Jarrie, Gustave Viscount, 1925, Je 16,21:5
Delamain, Henry I, 1914, Jl 29,9:5
De Lamar, Joseph Raphael Capt, 1918, D 2,13:4
De La Mare, A T Mrs, 1938, D 8,27:2
De La Mare, James C, 1910, Mr 4,9:4
de la Mare, Walter (funl, Je 29,21:5), 1956, Je 23, 17:4
Delamarre, Louis Dr, 1918, N 25,13:7
Delamarre, Lucy S Mrs, 1940, Jl 2,21:3
DeLamarter, Eric, 1953, My 19,29:3
Delamater, B W, 1881, Je 22,2:1
Delamater, Clarence, 1943, Ja 31,45:2
Delamater, Frederick R, 1949, F 5,15:2
Delamater, George D, 1947, My 28,25:5
Delamater, Horace S, 1943, Mr 16,19:2
Delamater, Howard, 1946, Jl 22,21:5
De Lamater, J, 1877, D 23,6:7
Delamater, Jane, 1952, Jl 28,15:6
De Lamater, Jessie, 1947, Jl 29,22:2
De Lamater, John S, 1941, Ag 4,13:3
Delamater, Nancy G Mrs, 1953, Ag 27,25:5
De Lamater, Walter A Mrs, 1940, Ap 1,19:5
De La Mater, William D, 1948, Ag 31,26:1
Delamater, Willis, 1947, O 14,27:2
Delamere, Lady, 1914, My 19,9:5; 1943, F 23,21:2
Delameter, William, 1905, F 24,7:6
Del Amo, Gregorio, 1941, S 11,23:2
De La Montaigne, Charles H, 1948, Mr 31,25:2
De La Montaigne, George F, 1924, My 1,19:4
de la Montanye, Marie, 1964, Ja 5,92:7
de la Motte, James F, 1956, Mr 13,27:3
De La Motte, Luke, 1945, F 9,15:2
De La Motte, Marguerite, 1950, Mr 11,15:2
Delan, James E, 1948, Je 25,23:4
Delanay, Michael F, 1946, D 25,29:6
De Lancastro, Count, 1873, O 13,4:7
De Lancey, Bill, 1946, N 29,25:4
Delancey, Bishop, 1865, Ap 6,1:6
De Lancey, Charles H, 1942, F 13,22:2
De Lancey, Edward Floyd, 1905, Ap 9,9:6
De Lancy, Darragh, 1937, N 16,23:2
De Land, C V Col, 1903, S 22,7:4
Deland, Charles A, 1953, Ap 28,27:4
DeLand, Charles J, 1943, Ja 11,15:3
De Land, Clyde O, 1947, Mr 29,15:3
DeLand, Daniel B (por), 1949, N 16,29:2
Deland, Lorin F, 1917, My 3,15:4
Deland, Lorin F Mrs (will, F 2,32:1), 1945, Ja 14, 40:1
Deland, Paul S, 1965, Mr 24,43:1
Delane, J T, 1879, N 25,5:1
Delaney, Andrew J, 1962, D 2,89:1
Delaney, Bernard A Rev, 1915, S 8,13:6
Delaney, Bill, 1944, Je 4,42:3
Delaney, Charles, 1945, Jl 24,23:4
Delaney, Daniel J, 1949, Ja 7,22:7
Delaney, Edward J, 1945, O 5,23:3; 1949, Ag 14,68:2
Delaney, Florence G, 1949, Ja 30,61:1
Delaney, Francis A, 1959, Ag 16,83:1
Delaney, Frederick J (Bro Ambrose of Jesus), 1956, Ag 16,25:4
Delaney, George R, 1944, D 8,21:1
Delaney, Harold J (Cal), 1954, S 22,29:4
Delaney, Henry A, 1949, F 6,76:6
Delaney, Jack, 1948, N 28,94:3; 1966, Ja 16,83:1
Delaney, James A Sr, 1949, Ap 27,27:5
Delaney, James J, 1942, My 10,43:2; 1950, Mr 21,32:2
Delaney, Jere A, 1954, Ja 2,11:2
Delaney, Jeremiah D, 1951, Je 13,29:3
Delaney, John, 1953, F 6,20:6
Delaney, John A, 1950, N 17,27:3
Delaney, John A Sr, 1953, Mr 10,29:4
Delaney, John H, 1952, Ag 15,16:3
Delaney, John H Mrs, 1944, Je 20,19:6
Delaney, John J, 1938, Ja 9,42:3; 1947, O 31,23:3; 1948, N 19,27:1; 1951, S 29,17:2
Delaney, John P, 1956, Ja 13,23:3; 1959, Ap 12,87:1
Delaney, John V, 1958, S 11,33:3
Delaney, John W, 1938, Mr 24,23:2
Delaney, Joseph A, 1951, D 14,31:3
Delaney, Joseph J, 1962, S 10,29:2
Delaney, Joseph L, 1945, F 10,11:2; 1961, My 5,29:1
Delaney, Joseph P, 1938, Ja 4,23:1; 1947, D 18,30:3
Delaney, M A, 1936, N 3,25:1
Delaney, Margaret F Mrs, 1953, Mr 11,29:3
Delaney, Mary, 1942, Ag 23,43:4
Delaney, Matthew, 1946, D 20,24:3
Delaney, Maureen (Mrs P O'Neill), 1961, My 28, 35:2
Delaney, Michael, 1942, Jl 16,19:2
Delaney, Michael J, 1947, D 15,25:4
Delaney, Myron E, 1954, N 4,31:5
Delaney, Patrick J, 1937, Mr 13,19:5
De Laney, Paul, 1946, Ja 4,21:4
Delaney, Peter J, 1951, Ag 28,23:5
Delaney, Robert M, 1956, S 26,33:4
Delaney, Thomas, 1949, My 11,29:2
Delaney, Thomas H, 1957, S 20,6:1
Delaney, Thomas J, 1962, Mr 5,23:4
Delaney, Thomas J Capt, 1937, Ag 11,23:3
Delaney, Tom, 1940, S 19,25:1
Delaney, W F, 1933, Ag 25,15:4
Delaney, Walter J, 1959, S 29,36:3
Delaney, William A, 1966, Jl 26,32:2
Delaney, William E, 1963, Ap 14,92:5
Delaney, William F, 1941, Mr 13,21:5; 1946, F 3,40:3
Delaney, William J, 1941, O 7,24:3; 1942, Mr 28,17:3; 1962, Ag 10,19:4
Delaney, William M, 1950, O 1,104:4
De Lang, Marie Charlotte Mrs, 1914, Mr 28,13:3
De Lange, Eddie, 1949, Jl 16,13:6
de Lange, Louis (Louis de Lange Moss), 1906, Mr 14,2:4
de Lange, Samuel, 1965, N 14,89:1
De Langis, Pierre, 1942, Ag 16,45:4
de Langley, Leland H L G, 1955, O 5,36:6
DeLano, Agnes, 1963, Ap 14,93:1
Delano, Albert, 1904, F 24,9:6
Delano, Alice D, 1948, Ag 25,25:4
Delano, Alonzo, 1874, S 23,4:7
Delano, Arthur H, 1949, Ap 1,26:2
Delano, B F, 1882, My 1,5:1
Delano, Charles, 1883, Ja 24,5:5
Delano, Charles F, 1964, O 10,29:6
Delano, Charles H, 1918, Ap 20,13:8
Delano, Edith B, 1946, S 9,9:2
Delano, Edwin F, 1948, S 18,17:2
Delano, Eugene, 1920, Ap 3,13:5
Delano, Eugene Jr, 1913, F 1,13:5
Delano, Frank Mrs, 1902, Je 17,9:5
Delano, Frederic A (will, Ap 21,24:2), 1953, Mr 29, 94:2
Delano, Frederic A Mrs, 1943, Je 1,23:4
Delano, Frederic M, 1942, Ap 17,17:4
Delano, Frederick H, 1950, F 24,23:3
Delano, Frederick M, 1942, Ja 14,21:2
Delano, George, 1949, Mr 6,72:2
De Lano, George R, 1944, Jl 25,19:4
Delano, Gwen, 1954, N 22,23:1
Delano, Harvey, 1955, Ap 14,29:5
Delano, Harvey Mrs, 1957, O 16,35:2
Delano, Horace H, 1951, Je 8,27:4
Delano, James K, 1960, F 23,32:1
Delano, Jane, 1919, Ap 17,11:3
Delano, Jane A, 1920, S 19,22:2
Delano, John S, 1956, My 1,33:2
Delano, John W, 1945, Ag 24,19:4
Delano, Lyman, 1944, Jl 24,15:5
De Lano, Mary, 1937, Ag 9,20:1
Delano, Mortimer, 1920, S 16,9:2
Delano, Natalie A, 1949, S 9,25:5
Delano, Preston, 1961, S 1,17:3
Delano, Robert Graham Mrs, 1912, Jl 27,7:5
De Lano, Safford S, 1924, D 28,5:2
Delano, Sarah S B Mrs, 1941, D 25,25:4
De Lano, Sterling P, 1945, Je 9,13:5
Delano, Thomas Edwin, 1918, Mr 24,13:1
Delano, Thomas H, 1904, Ja 9,9:6
Delano, Warren, 1920, S 11,13:5
Delano, Warren Mrs, 1922, D 3,5:2
Delano, William A, 1960, Ja 13,48:1
Delano, William A Mrs, 1962, S 19,39:4
Delano, William H C, 1903, N 10,9:5
Delano, William J, 1938, D 28,26:4
De Lano, William R, 1942, Je 9,23:1
Delano, William R Mrs, 1951, Ap 17,29:4
De Lanoie, Herbert M, 1942, O 4,52:1
De Lanoy, Allen A, 1950, F 26,76:6
Delanoy, Charles H, 1952, Ja 19,15:4
Delanoy, George W, 1938, Jl 22,18:4
Delanoy, John A, 1903, Jl 1,9:5
De Lanoy, William C, 1944, Ja 17,19:3
Delanta, Frank, 1911, O 9,11:5
Delanty, Thomas W, 1949, F 27,68:7
Delany, Arthur G, 1947, Jl 6,40:3
Delany, Charles, 1937, S 21,25:4
DeLany, Dorothy, 1960, My 12,35:5
Delany, Edmund J, 1959, F 17,31:2
De Lany, Francis R, 1940, Ag 5,13:5
Delany, Francis X, 1956, Ap 26,33:4
Delany, Fred J V, 1951, Ja 12,27:2
Delany, Frederic J, 1962, O 7,69:4
Delany, G Edmund, 1937, F 17,21:1
Delany, George J, 1959, Ap 8,37:3
Delany, Henry B Mrs, 1956, Je 4,29:6
Delany, Howard S, 1945, Ja 16,19:3
Delany, John A, 1944, Jl 4,19:4
Delany, John J Justice (funl, Jl 17,7:7), 1915, Jl 15, 9:5
Delany, John J Sr, 1938, Je 28,19:6
Delany, Joseph F, 1943, Mr 7,38:6
Delany, Joseph Msgr, 1953, Ja 6,29:3
Delany, Patrick B, 1924, O 21,23:3
Delany, S P, 1935, Jl 6,13:1
De Lap, George, 1941, Jl 30,18:5
Delap, William Mrs, 1959, Mr 11,35:1
De La Parra, Johan, 1946, S 18,31:4
Delapenha, R U (por), 1949, D 17,17:5
Delapenha, Rodolph U Mrs, 1959, Jl 16,27:3
Delapine, Frank, 1948, Jl 19,19:5
Delaplaine, C E, 1885, My 12,5:4
Delaplaine, Capt, 1883, F 23,8:4
Delaplaine, J F, 1885, F 15,2:2
Delaplaine, James H, 1958, O 18,21:5
Delaplaine, Roy W, 1948, F 14,13:6
Delaplante, Arthur W, 1950, O 20,27:5
Delaporte, Edward, 1940, Ap 3,23:5
Delaporte, Edward C, 1944, D 22,17:1
Delaporte, Leo A, 1944, Ja 29,13:6
Delapp, Michael T, 1950, Mr 25,13:5
de la Presilla, Roman, 1958, N 11,30:2
De la Puente y Lopez, Juan M, 1953, Ja 9,22:4
De Lara, David C, 1942, Jl 24,19:5
de Lara, Ramon, 1956, S 21,25:4
De La Reusille, Leon Sr, 1942, Ag 29,15:5
De Larnie, Auguste, 1873, N 29,1:7
de la Roche, Mazo, 1961, Jl 13,29:4
Delaroff, Mishel, 1965, Ap 30,35:3
De La Roie, Francis Jules, 1872, Ap 9,5:3
De Lasala, R P, 1967, My 27,31:1
DeLasho, Vincenzo, 1953, F 18,31:4
Delatour, Albert J, 1940, N 15,21:2
Delatour, Beeckman J Mrs, 1968, Je 17,39:4
De Latour, Louis, 1949, D 16,31:2
Delatour, Samuel P, 1943, N 24,21:5
De La Tour d'Auvergne, Prince, 1871, My 10,1:7
Delattre, Andre, 1952, S 2,23:3
De Lauer, Michael, 1947, S 3,25:4
de Laugier-Villars, Countess, 1925, Mr 23,17:5
Delaunay, Louis, 1937, My 15,19:6
Delaunay-Belleville, Louis, 1912, F 11,II,13:3
Delauney, John B Rev, 1953, F 17,27:4
Delaup, F, 1878, Jl 3,3:2
DeLaura, Catherine A, 1957, Je 19,35:1

De Laurentis, Anthony, 1943, My 19,25:1
de Laurentis, Joseph Mrs (A Ciolli), 1967, F 3,31:2
Delavan, B H Mrs, 1943, O 13,23:4
Delavan, Byron H, 1944, F 12,13:1
Delavan, Charles P, 1947, O 9,25:6
Delavan, D Bryson Mrs, 1938, D 22,21:5
Delavan, Daniel E, 1870, Ap 2,8:3
Delavan, David B (por), 1942, My 24,43:1
Delavan, Edward C, 1939, D 9,15:2
Delavan, Paul T, 1949, F 14,19:4
De Lave, Edwin, 1953, Ag 8,11:3
DeLavel-Crow, Thomas C, 1947, Je 29,48:6
De La Verge, Charles H, 1945, Je 5,19:1
De la Vergne, Abigail C Mrs, 1938, My 24,19:4
Delavigne, Albert, 1947, Ja 2,27:1
Delavigne, Catherine Mrs, 1943, Ap 25,34:3
Delavigne, Theodore, 1937, D 22,25:6
Delavina, Frederick V, 1945, N 8,19:2
Delawder, Walter G, 1947, Je 10,27:6
Delay, Maurice F, 1942, Mr 24,19:2
DeLay, Melville P, 1947, Mr 5,25:3
Del Balso, Frank, 1947, O 16,27:2
Del Balso, Michael, 1947, Jl 15,23:4
Del Bello, Gaetano Mrs, 1946, Je 12,27:4
Delbene, Anthony, 1920, Ja 17,11:3
Delbene, Paul, 1920, Ja 17,11:3
Del Bianco, Oscar, 1945, D 12,27:4
Delbos, Yvon, 1956, N 16,27:1
Delbridge, Thomas G, 1965, Ag 19,31:4
Delbruck, M F von, 1903, F 2,8:6
Delbrueck, H G L, 1929, Jl 16,25:3
Delbrueck, Ludwig, 1913, Mr 15,13:4
Delcamp, S G J Surgeon, 1871, S 15,1:6
Delcamp, Sarah, 1954, S 15,33:1
Del Campo, Conrado, 1953, Mr 18,31:5
Delcasse, Theophile, 1923, F 23,13:4
Del Castillo, Francisco, 1954, Je 19,15:4
Delcher, Dorothy, 1941, Ap 22,21:5
Delco, Willie Mrs, 1950, S 3,32:5
del Collado, Juan M, 1955, O 3,27:4
Del Colliano, Donna, 1953, S 8,16:2
Del Conte, Emidio, 1950, Jl 7,19:2
Delcure, C B T Mrs, 1947, S 26,23:5
Del Drago, Eleanor, 1905, Mr 18,8:2
Del Duca, Angelo M, 1956, S 20,33:4
De Lea, Michael, 1954, S 2,21:4
De Leath, Vaughn (por), 1943, My 29,13:3
Deledda, G, 1936, Ag 17,19:3
DeLee, Joseph B, 1942, Ap 3,21:1
Delee, William S, 1951, Mr 26,23:1
De Leeuw, Adolph L (por), 1942, D 6,77:1
De Leeuw, Peter Jr, 1957, O 20,87:1
Delefield, Tallmadge, 1911, O 17,11:5
Delehanty, Andrew L, 1943, N 20,13:6
Delehanty, Daniel Capt, 1918, F 3,15:2
Delehanty, Harold Mrs, 1966, Je 2,43:3
Delehanty, J Bradley W Mrs, 1962, F 20,36:1
Delehanty, J W Bradley, 1965, Je 9,47:3
Delehanty, James A, 1960, Ap 27,37:2
Delehanty, James A Mrs, 1963, Jl 2,29:1
Delehanty, James T, 1940, Ag 10,13:2
Delehanty, Michael J, 1964, Ap 13,29:2
Delehanty, Michael J Mrs, 1961, N 4,19:3
Delehanty, Patrick H Mrs, 1946, Je 11,23:4
Delehanty, Richard J, 1947, D 30,24:2
Delehanty, Thomas S, 1964, S 20,89:1
Delehanty, Thornton W Mrs, 1951, Jl 28,11:4
Delehanty, William F, 1954, N 17,31:4
Delehey, Charles J, 1951, Ja 11,25:1
De Lello, Carmello Mrs, 1951, S 23,87:1
De Lemos, Adolfo K, 1937, Ag 26,21:6
de Lemos, Arturo, 1920, Ja 12,9:1
de Lemos, Arturo Mrs, 1920, Ja 12,9:1
De Lemos, Frederick F, 1952, Jl 31,23:4
De Lemos, Theodore, 1909, Ap 12,7:5
De Lens, Adrien Mrs, 1942, Ag 19,19:3
Deleo, Joseph, 1951, Mr 29,27:6
De Leon, Aristides, 1954, Jl 26,17:2
de Leon, Daniel (mem , My 14,11:4), 1914, My 12, 11:5
Deleon, F Carrera, 1943, S 12,53:1
De Leon, Gustave, 1952, Ja 14,19:2
DeLeon, Miguel A, 1950, My 21,104:7
De Leon, Thomas Cooper, 1914, Mr 20,11:4
De Leon, Walter, 1947, Ag 2,13:6
De Leone, Francesco B, 1948, D 11,15:6
Delepierre, Octave, 1879, Ag 22,5:3
Deletraz, Lucien E, 1943, S 18,17:4
De Lette, Bruce T, 1956, N 27,37:1
Delevsky, Jacob L, 1957, Ja 6,88:2
Delf, Harry, 1964, F 8,23:3
Delf, Juliet, 1962, Mr 25,88:7
Delfina, Mother (Grazioli), 1967, N 25,39:4
Delfino, Joseph, 1955, Ja 8,13:6
Delfino, Liborio Mrs, 1937, Je 8,25:2
Delfino, Louis Gen, 1968, Je 12,44:5
Delfino, Matthew J, 1948, D 1,29:2
Delfino, Michael, 1938, My 16,17:3
Del Forno, Felice, 1954, Mr 12,21:2
Del Forno, Felice Mrs, 1963, O 12,23:3
Delfosse, Edward, 1906, Ja 22,7:6
Delfosse, Georges, 1939, D 24,14:6
Delfs, Edwin R, 1950, Jl 13,25:2

Delgado, Charles Mrs, 1965, Je 24,35:4
Delgado, Domingo E, 1937, N 12,22:2
Delgado, Enrique C, 1965, Ja 3,84:6
Delgado, Rodriquez Emilio, 1967, N 23,33:2
Del Garcia, Lester M, 1944, N 23,31:1
Del Garcia, Lester M Mrs, 1944, D 2,13:5
Delgardo, Antonio M, 1937, Ja 12,8:6
Del Gaudio, Albert, 1962, Mr 7,35:1
Del Gaudio, Carmine Mrs, 1955, My 27,23:3
Del Gaudio, Matthew W, 1960, S 18,85:3
del Giudice, Guy R M, 1959, Ja 24,19:3
Del Giudici, Alfonso, 1953, Ap 1,29:3
Del Guercio, Joseph, 1953, D 30,23:1
DelGuercio, Vincent R, 1960, Ja 21,31:2
Del Guidice, Edward, 1941, Ag 22,15:4
Delhauer, William H Mrs, 1946, My 16,21:4
De Lherbe, Emil J Mrs, 1951, Mr 29,27:2
de Liagre, Alfred, 1961, Ja 1,48:2
de Liagre, Alfred Sr Mrs, 1960, Mr 17,33:5
Delibero, Joseph, 1966, F 28,27:4
Delibes, Leo, 1891, Ja 17,5:4
Deliduka, John, 1953, Jl 4,11:4
De Liebing, Myra L Mrs, 1950, Je 19,21:4
Deligne, Maurice, 1939, Je 12,17:3
Deligny, Henri V, 1938, Ja 5,21:4
Deligny, Leon A, 1952, F 21,27:4
De Ligter, Harry, 1947, F 27,21:1
Deligtisch, Emanuel, 1962, N 22,29:3
Delile, Paul R, 1955, S 13,31:1
De Lima, Charles A, 1954, Ag 9,17:5
De Lima, Charles A Mrs, 1952, N 19,29:1
de Lima, Edward A, 1964, S 21,31:5
De Lima, Ernest A, 1953, S 22,31:2
de Limur, Andre Mrs, 1964, Jl 1,35:5
Deline, Edward, 1947, Ag 3,52:5
Deline, James E, 1962, N 4,88:4
De Lisle, Agnes R Mrs, 1940, O 13,49:3
De Lisle, Benjamin, 1866, Ag 24,2:6
de L'Isle, Jacqueline C Y Lady, 1962, N 16,32:1
Delisle, Leopold Vietor, 1910, Jl 24,II,7:5
DeLisle, Louis C, 1956, Mr 17,19:5
De L'Isle and Dudley, Lord, 1945, Ap 19,27:2
Delisser, Herbert G, 1944, My 19,19:2
De Lisser, Horace, 1923, Je 28,15:5
Delitzsch, Friedrich Prof, 1922, D 24,20:4
Delius, F, 1934, Je 11,17:1
Delius, W H, 1905, Ap 5,1:6
Delk, Charles R, 1958, Je 18,33:4
Delk, Edwin H, 1940, F 10,15:5
Delker, Thomas B, 1949, Jl 25,15:5
Delkin, E Mrs (Celeste Yeandle), 1916, Ap 21,11:6
Dell, Burnham N, 1963, S 17,35:1
Dell, Charles, 1924, Ag 23,9:3; 1943, O 11,19:5
Dell, Christian N, 1963, D 24,17:4
Dell, Ernest F, 1959, D 2,44:1
Dell, Ethel M, 1939, S 18,19:6
Dell, Frederick C J, 1964, F 6,29:1
Dell, Robert, 1940, Jl 21,29:2
Dell, Rupert L, 1945, O 27,15:4
Dell Isola, Alphonso F, 1958, Ja 26,88:5
Della Casa, Mother Antonietta, 1955, Ja 13,27:5
Della Chiesa, Ettore, 1953, S 5,15:3
Della Chiesa, John Anthony Marquis, 1920, D 11,13:5
della Fazia, Nicholas, 1966, Ap 10,79:5
Della Monica, Alphonse, 1950, F 24,23:3
Della Pietra, Giovanni B, 1940, Ag 29,19:3
Della Rocca, Michael, 1963, D 18,41:2
Della Sorte, Giuseppe, 1950, Ap 27,29:4
Della Torretta, Pietro, 1962, D 6,43:3
Della Volpe, Francis Cardinal, 1916, N 5,23:4
Dellale, Charles, 1941, Ag 12,21:5
Dellapiane, Carlos, 1946, N 13,27:5
Dellar, Ernest Mrs, 1950, Ap 29,15:4
Dellar, Ernest W, 1937, D 19,II,8:7
Dellara, Riccardo, 1940, My 26,34:4
Dellehunt, Charles, 1945, Ag 4,11:6
Dellenbaugh, F S, 1935, Ja 30,19:4
Dellenbaugh, Frederick S Jr, 1952, Ap 18,25:3
Dellepiane, Giovanni, 1961, Ag 14,25:4
Deller, Franklin Mrs, 1951, Ja 11,25:2
Deller, George, 1949, F 8,25:5
Deller, Russel A, 1966, F 19,27:3
Dell'Era, Oliver P, 1948, My 18,23:4
Dellert, Charles F, 1941, Ag 29,17:6
Dellert, John W, 1939, O 17,25:5
Dellevie, Ralph, 1952, F 4,17:5
Dellfant, Max, 1944, Ja 27,19:2
Dellidione, Donato, 1924, Ag 8,13:4
Dellioacono, Felice Mrs, 1949, D 7,31:3
Dell'Isola, Frank Mrs, 1958, Jl 25,19:1
Dell'Isola, Vincenzo, 1949, N 7,27:4
Dello Joio, Casimiro, 1963, Jl 18,27:2
Dello Joio, Casimiro Mrs, 1952, My 13,30:1
Dell'Orefice, Antonio Mrs, 1954, My 22,15:3
Dellplain, Morse O, 1968, F 6,44:1
Dellworth, Emma V, 1959, Ap 4,19:4
Dellworth, Thomas D, 1948, Ap 18,72:5
Delman, David, 1968, My 24,47:1
Delman, Herman B, 1955, O 13,31:6
Delman, Morris R, 1955, Ag 19,19:2
Del Manzo, Milton C (Feb 15), 1963, Ap 1,35:4
Delmar, Charles (estate acctg, S 10,41:8), 1963, Ag 19,25:3

Delmar, Eugene, 1909, F 23,9:2
Delmar, Florence M Mrs, 1941, Mr 28,23:5
Del Mar, Frances, 1957, My 8,37:3
Delmar, Jacob, 1865, D 9,2:7
Del Mar, Walter, 1944, Ap 11,19:3
Delmarsh, Arch, 1948, O 6,29:5
Delmas, D M, 1928, Ag 2,21:5
Delme-Radcliffe, Charles Brig Gen Sir, 1937, D 14, 25:4
Delmhorst, Arthur E, 1951, F 14,30:4
Delmonico, C C (funl, S 26,9:6), 1901, S 21,7:1
Delmonico, Charles, 1884, Ja 15,1:7
Delmonico, Charles C, 1957, Ja 25,21:4
Delmonico, Lorenzo, 1881, S 4,7:5
Delmonico, Lorenzo C, 1947, F 20,25:4
Delmonico, Louis Mrs, 1959, Je 30,31:2
Delmonico, Marie Josephine, 1907, Mr 12,9:6
Delmonico, Rose, 1904, Mr 26,9:6
Delmonico, Siro, 1881, D 20,8:2
Delmont, Al, 1947, Ag 3,52:3
Del Monte, Jacques D, 1964, D 14,36:1
Delmonte, Joaquin, 1882, O 27,5:3
Del Monte, John, 1946, Ap 22,21:1
del Monte, Leon Aldama, 1924, My 22,17:5
Del Monte, Leonard, 1951, N 9,27:1
Del Montenegro, Militza J Princess, 1946, F 18,25:1
Delmoore, Catherine, 1939, Ag 7,2:5
Delmore, George E, 1947, N 24,23:4
Delmore, Ralph, 1923, N 22,19:4
Delmore, Walter, 1920, Jl 17,7:6
Del Morel, Arthur, 1947, Ag 12,23:4
Delmour, L A Mrs, 1902, N 24,5:4
Delmour, Laurence (funl, D 28,7:5), 1907, D 26,7:
De Loach, Asa G, 1944, Mr 17,17:4
Deloach, Josiah, 1880, D 21,5:2
De Lodzia, Julien, 1951, My 3,29:2
De Loes, H, 1942, Mr 17,21:2
Delom, Cyril E, 1948, O 1,25:3
Delom, Cyril E Mrs, 1948, N 2,25:3
Deloncle, Eugene, 1944, Ja 9,42:1
Delone, Lewis A, 1922, Jl 18,11:4
De Long, C E (see also O 27), 1876, N 5,9:2
Delong, Calvin M, 1958, S 7,87:1
De Long, Charles E, 1958, Ja 11,17:4
De Long, Charles F, 1945, D 7,21:2
De Long, Emma W Mrs, 1940, N 26,23:5
De Long, Frank B, 1949, My 30,13:6
De Long, Frank E, 1939, F 16,3:3
De Long, George, 1882, My 10,8:3; 1942, Ja 14,23
De Long, James C, 1952, D 11,33:3
Delong, James F Sr, 1950, D 28,25:1
De Long, James H, 1947, Mr 22,13:5
De Long, James L, 1948, D 22,24:3
De Long, James L Mrs, 1939, O 2,17:3
De Long, Joseph, 1915, My 12,13:4
Delong, Joshua J, 1949, Ap 23,13:3
Delong, Joshua J Mrs, 1949, Ap 23,13:3
Delong, Karl C, 1937, D 4,17:3
De Long, Mary Mrs, 1907, Ap 8,9:6
De Long, Samuel R, 1947, My 18,60:2
DeLong, Walter, 1954, Je 10,31:4
DeLong, Walter M, 1951, S 13,31:3
de Long, William A, 1939, Ja 1,24:7
De Long, William A Dr, 1919, O 4,11:3
De Long, William F, 1946, D 15,77:2
de Longpre, Paul, 1911, Jl 1,11:5
Delooze, Lottie R Mrs, 1955, F 2,12:6
Delore, Louis N Dr, 1937, O 5,25:2
DeLorenzi, Roccolewis, 1946, Jl 6,15:3
DeLorenzo, Frank (Biffo), 1953, Ja 8,30:6
de Lorenzo, Salvatore (Society Kid Hogan), 196 Ap 11,43:4
De Lorenzo, Theresa Mrs, 1946, D 31,17:3
DeLoretto, John, 1950, Je 22,27:1
de Lorimer, Charles C Judge, 1919, My 27,15:5
Delorno, Malteo Mrs, 1944, Ag 23,19:6
De Louisa, John, 1951, Mr 31,15:5
De Lozier, Minette, 1939, N 16,24:2
del Papa, Dante, 1923, F 26,13:5
Del Peso, Robert J, 1958, Ja 22,36:2
Delpezzo, Gennaro, 1911, Ja 6,9:2
Delph, Walter I, 1960, My 30,17:5
Del Prado, R, 1879, Mr 2,5:6
Delprat, John C, 1944, Mr 4,13:2
Del Prete, Thomas A, 1949, S 27,27:1
Del Prete, Vincent, 1952, Jl 3,25:5
Del Principe, Vincent, 1956, Jl 16,21:4
del Puente, Helen, 1924, Ja 31,15:5
del Rio, Angel, 1962, Mr 26,31:3
Del Rio, German W, 1953, O 3,17:2
del Rio, Pablo Martinez, 1907, N 19,9:5
Del Ruth, Hampton, 1958, My 18,87:1
Del Ruth, Roy, 1961, Ap 28,31:2
Delsandro, Dominick J, 1959, Jl 13,27:6
Delsarte, Francois Alexandre Nicholas Chev, 18 Ag 3,1:7
Delson, Isidore, 1954, D 21,27:5
Delson, Isidore Mrs, 1961, N 9,35:2
del Toro Cuevas, Emilio, 1955, N 11,25:6
Del Tufo, Anthony D, 1949, F 17,23:5
DelTufo, Gerardo, 1951, My 13,88:7
Del Turco, Angelo, 1946, N 13,27:3
Deltz, Carl, 1948, Ap 29,23:1

De Luca, Frank, 1947, D 27,13:1
De Luca, Giuseppe, 1940, O 19,17:2; 1950, Ag 28,17:1
De Luca, H Anthony, 1958, Ag 3,80:7
De Luca, Horatio R, 1953, Mr 5,27:3
DeLuca, Louis J, 1966, Je 23,39:2
De Luca, Olympia Mrs, 1918, O 30,11:2
De Luca, Rocco Mrs, 1949, Ag 15,17:5
DeLuca, Tony, 1953, O 17,15:4
De Luca, Vito, 1964, D 9,47:2
Delucci, Joseph, 1921, Mr 7,11:2
De Luce, Percival, 1914, F 22,IV,5:5
de Lucia, Fernando, 1925, F 24,19:4
De Luco, Pasquale, 1910, Je 17,7:2
de Luna, George H, 1962, Jl 9,31:1
deLuna, John M, 1957, Jl 11,25:3
De Lussan, Zelie, 1949, D 19,28:2
De Lutke, F, 1882, Ag 22,5:1
De Luze, Louis P, 1937, Ap 7,25:4
de Luze, Raymond Mrs Baroness, 1956, D 9,89:2
De Luze, Sarah F, 1940, F 27,21:5
Del Val, Josephine Merry, 1925, My 2,15:5
Del Val, Rafael Merry, 1917, Ag 31,7:4
Del Valle, R F, 1938, S 22,23:3
Del Valle Jose A, 1908, Ap 22,9:5
Delvalle Pijem, Rafael, 1938, N 16,23:3
Del Vasto, Nicodemo, 1940, F 2,17:3
Delvaux, Adrian, 1954, Ja 16,15:5
Delveaux, Ignatius M Father, 1905, Je 9,9:7
Del Vecchio, Alex, 1948, Jl 22,23:2
Del Vecchio, Christianziano Mrs, 1959, D 9,45:4
Del Vecchio, Mary, 1959, Jl 3,17:2
Del Vecchio, Thomas Mrs, 1952, Mr 14,20:6
Delventhal, Fred, 1956, Ap 9,27:2
Delville, Elie, 1963, Je 19,37:1
Delvina, Hiqmet, 1958, F 1,19:6
Delvincourt, Claude, 1954, Ap 7,31:4
Delwiche, E J, 1950, Ja 21,17:3
de Lys, Edith (E Ely), 1961, Jl 4,19:2
De Macchi, Clemente, 1942, O 5,19:3
De Macedo, Alfred, 1951, N 6,29:4
De Magnin, Henri, 1938, Mr 18,19:5
DeMaio, James Mrs, 1961, Ap 20,33:4
De Maio, Salvatore, 1960, F 11,35:4
De Malcorra, Jose Camarero, 1944, Ja 31,17:3
De Malignon, F, 1882, Ap 6,2:2
De Malignon, Herman W, 1940, Je 11,25:2
Deman, Joseph, 1952, Ag 28,5:1
De Mance, Henri (cor, O 6,29:4), 1948, O 5,25:2
De Mandato, Arcangelo, 1952, N 15,17:2
Demange, Edgard, 1925, F 12,19:4
De Mange, George J, 1939, S 20,28:2
Demange, Maxine, 1941, Jl 7,6:8
Demann, Franziskus, 1957, Mr 28,31:3
De Many, David B, 1957, Mr 14,29:1
Demar, Caro A Mrs, 1940, Ap 25,23:3
De Mar, Clarence, 1958, Je 12,31:1
Demaray, Arthur E, 1958, Ag 22,21:2
Demaray, Julia Ann Mrs, 1912, Je 8,11:4
Demarchi, Rutilio, 1939, O 11,30:2
DeMarco, Antonio (Tony), 1965, N 16,43:3
De Marco, Joseph Mrs, 1945, O 6,13:5
De Marco, Nicholas, 1963, My 9,37:1
Demarco, Patrick S, 1959, D 2,43:2
De Marco, Samuel A, 1947, Ja 30,25:3
De Mare, Baltzer E L, 1947, Ap 19,15:1
de Mare, Marie Mrs, 1958, Je 24,31:4
Demaree, Albert L, 1964, Ja 16,26:1
Demaree, Albert W, 1962, My 3,33:4
Demaree, Frank, 1958, S 2,25:4
Demarest, A T, 1908, Jl 14,5:6
Demarest, Annie E, 1942, S 4,24:4
Demarest, Benjamin G, 1950, My 31,29:5
Demarest, C Agnew, 1959, My 21,31:2
Demarest, Charles H, 1957, Mr 4,27:5
Demarest, Charles S, 1924, O 8,19:4
Demarest, Clayton, 1940, My 2,23:4
Demarest, Clifford, 1946, My 14,21:1
Demarest, Daniel, 1924, Je 8,26:1; 1937, Ag 24,21:4
Demarest, Daniel Mrs, 1957, Ag 25,87:1
Demarest, David H, 1945, D 5,25:6
Demarest, David P, 1965, N 7,89:3
Demarest, Edward J, 1953, Ag 19,29:3
Demarest, F F, 1931, Mr 31,27:2
Demarest, Frank P, 1925, S 3,25:5
Demarest, Frank S, 1949, Ap 5,29:1
Demarest, Frederick, 1951, My 4,27:3
Demarest, Frederick A, 1962, My 4,34:1
Demarest, Frederick R, 1968, D 13,42:2
Demarest, Garret L, 1947, My 25,62:3
Demarest, George E, 1958, Jl 12,15:1
Demarest, George F Mrs, 1961, Jl 10,21:2
Demarest, George H, 1940, F 7,21:3
Demarest, George H Mrs, 1959, O 5,31:5
Demarest, George L, 1952, N 13,31:4
Demarest, Guilliam B, 1952, Mr 18,27:4
Demarest, Harry M, 1960, D 1,35:3
Demarest, Helen, 1946, Ag 3,15:4
Demarest, Henry S, 1937, Jl 13,19:3
Demarest, Herbert, 1952, Mr 23,92:2
Demarest, Ida A, 1947, Mr 9,60:8
Demarest, Irving V, 1962, F 4,82:3
Demarest, J C, 1927, F 4,19:4
Demarest, J Willis, 1947, N 19,27:2
Demarest, J Woodbridge, 1909, S 19,11:3
Demarest, James, 1921, Mr 28,11:6; 1941, F 12,21:3
Demarest, James A, 1959, Ag 28,23:1
Demarest, James V, 1946, Jl 4,19:4
Demarest, John G, 1940, My 10,23:2
Demarest, John H Dr, 1918, S 17,13:4
Demarest, Kenneth L, 1961, Ap 4,37:1
Demarest, L McGregor, 1959, S 9,41:2
Demarest, L McGregor Mrs, 1962, Ja 25,31:2
Demarest, Margretta, 1941, Ag 20,19:4
Demarest, Mary A, 1946, S 10,7:2
Demarest, Nathan H Rev, 1917, F 18,17:3
Demarest, Peter E, 1942, D 8,26:2
Demarest, Robert K, 1952, Ja 18,17:1
Demarest, William, 1945, O 16,23:3
Demarest, William G, 1953, Je 16,27:3
Demarest, William H S, 1956, Je 24,76:5
Demarest, William J Mrs, 1945, Ap 7,15:3
Demaret, John O, 1941, Je 2,17:3
Demaret, John O Mrs, 1952, Ap 27,90:3
de Margoulies, Vladimir, 1962, F 8,32:1
De Maria, Sebastian, 1939, Ap 6,25:5
DeMaria, Sebastian, 1944, Ag 14,24:3
De Marigny de Mandeville, M B X, 1868, F 16,1:7
De Marinis, Leopold, 1959, Mr 9,29:4
De Marinis, Reginald W, 1957, D 29,49:2
De Maris, Furman A, 1956, Ap 17,31:4
De Maris, Walter, 1947, F 1,15:2
Demarmon, Andrew P, 1952, N 21,25:2
Demarquay, Dr, 1875, Jl 11,6:7
De Marrais, Arthur J, 1937, N 12,26:8
DeMars, Alfred P, 1946, Mr 28,25:1
Demars, Leon P, 1925, Mr 19,21:3
De Mars, Richard, 1962, Jl 18,29:3
De Mars, Theodore E, 1958, O 3,29:4
Demarsh, Leroy E Rev, 1937, D 14,25:3
De Martini, Felix, 1962, O 15,29:3
De Martini, Ferdinand C, 1949, Je 23,27:3
De Martini, Henry, 1940, D 17,25:3
De Martini, Stephan A, 1944, D 25,19:4
De Martino, Raphael M, 1951, Ag 9,21:1
de Martins, Frederick Prof, 1909, Je 21,7:4
Demask, Emil, 1941, O 4,15:6
De Mattia, Barthold, 1944, Mr 4,13:4
De Mattos, Francisco, 1939, F 23,23:4
De Mauriac, Henry D, 1952, D 16,31:5
De Mauro, Pasquale, 1944, F 12,28:2
De Mave, Jack, 1968, Je 22,33:4
De May, Anthony J Jr, 1966, Ag 1,27:3
deMay, Charles F, 1955, Mr 1,25:5
DeMay, Gabriel, 1952, Mr 18,27:3
Dembe, Harry B, 1949, O 24,23:2
Dembeck, Joseph, 1954, Ja 12,23:2
Dember, Harry L, 1943, Mr 23,19:2
Demberg, Joseph, 1966, F 3,31:3
Dembinski, Col, 1864, Jl 3,3:5
Dembitz, Arthur A, 1940, Je 27,23:3
Dembitz, Jacob, 1946, Mr 26,29:4
Dembling, Gus, 1955, My 2,21:4
Dembling, Hyman, 1946, N 14,29:3
Dembling, Samuel, 1954, N 9,27:3
Dembling, William C, 1941, F 3,17:1
Dembo, Boris J, 1952, S 23,33:5
Demboski, William, 1952, Mr 8,13:5
Dembrow, Sam Jr, 1968, S 13,47:1
Demby, Edward T, 1957, O 16,32:3
Demby, Max, 1940, Mr 31,44:4
Demchar, Michael, 1945, O 10,36:3
Demcott, Orey M, 1952, S 4,27:3
De Medeull, Henry C, 1907, S 29,9:6
de Meissner, Sophie R Mme, 1957, Ap 20,17:2
De Meli, Henry Anthony, 1915, Jl 22,9:4
De Melik, Arthur, 1955, Je 17,23:2
De Mello, Adm, 1902, Mr 19,9:6
De Melman, Walter Mrs, 1944, Je 24,13:4
Demelt, Howard C, 1953, My 5,29:5
Demelt, W Eugene, 1954, S 15,33:4
De Mena, Luis, 1942, D 8,25:4
De Menasce, Jacques, 1960, F 1,27:3
De Menkini, Peter E, 1946, Mr 30,15:3
De Menkini, Peter Mrs, 1952, Ap 30,27:2
de Menocal, Daniel Mrs, 1962, Mr 3,21:2
Dement, John J, 1944, S 3,28:8
Demeo, Alfonso, 1951, Je 10,93:1
De Meo, Victor A, 1947, My 19,21:4
de Mercado, Frank E, 1959, Ja 13,47:2
de Mercado, Frank Mrs, 1962, F 17,19:1
De Mere, Raymond, 1953, My 23,15:4
Demerec, Milislav, 1966, Ap 14,35:4
Demeritt, Bertrand R, 1943, D 24,13:2
Demeritt, Daniel Chesley, 1916, Ja 29,9:4
DeMerritt, Charles L, 1957, Je 6,31:4
Demerritt, John E Jr, 1952, Je 28,19:2
Demers, Albert F, 1943, Ja 24,42:7
Demers, L A, 1938, Jl 11,17:5
Demers, Marie J, 1940, Jl 29,13:5
Demers, P P, 1946, Ag 7,27:1
De Mesquita, Jules Bueno, 1954, Ag 30,17:5
Demester, George D, 1946, F 6,23:3
Demetre, Andrew, 1925, S 19,15:5
Demetre, P G, 1945, Jl 18,27:3
Demetria, Sister (Anna Kelly), 1958, My 12,29:4
Demetrios, George Mrs (Virginia Lee Burton), 1968, O 16,47:2
Demetrius, Menelas, 1939, F 25,15:2
DeMetropolis, George Rear-Adm (funl plans), 1968, D 5,47:2
De Metz, Fred A, 1873, N 25,3:1
Demianoff, Paul Mrs, 1962, F 22,25:4
De Micco, Christeropher C, 1957, O 20,87:1
De Michele, Angelo, 1952, Ap 18,25:4
Demidov, Alex P, 1961, My 19,31:4
Demidov, Sophia Princess, 1953, Ap 18,19:2
Demilhau, Louis J, 1967, D 29,27:3
De Milhau, Zella, 1954, Mr 5,19:1
De Mille, Anna G Mrs, 1947, Mr 18,27:2
deMille, Cecil B (funl, Ja 24,19:5; will, Ja 28,31:1), 1959, Ja 22,1:4
de Mille, Cecil B Mrs (funl, Jl 20,29:1), 1960, Jl 18, 27:1
de Mille, Henry C Mrs, 1923, O 9,21:5
DeMille, John B, 1950, Mr 17,23:3
de Mille, William C (funl, Mr 9,27:2), 1955, Mr 6, 89:1
De Mille, William C Mrs, 1956, S 12,37:2
De Milly, Adolphe, 1955, S 13,31:3
Demilt, Irving F, 1951, S 21,23:3
De Milt, James, 1949, Ag 5,19:2
De Milt, Joseph, 1938, Ap 17,II,6:6
De Milt, Samuel T, 1953, F 8,89:1
Deminatus, Agustus Mrs, 1942, Ap 15,21:5
Deming, Adelaide, 1956, F 26,89:2
Deming, Arthur R, 1952, Ja 29,25:5
Deming, C Woodford, 1942, S 10,27:3
Deming, Charles C, 1924, Jl 24,13:4
Deming, Charles K, 1958, F 22,17:4
Deming, Dudley B, 1946, Jl 8,31:3
Deming, Edward Mrs, 1938, S 1,23:3
Deming, Edward W Mrs, 1945, Jl 16,11:6
Deming, Edwin D, 1907, Je 2,7:6
Deming, Edwin W (por), 1942, O 16,19:3
Deming, Eleanor, 1961, Ag 31,27:5
Deming, George E, 1943, Ap 16,22:2
Deming, George M, 1946, Mr 19,27:6
Deming, Harold S, 1954, Mr 8,27:6
Deming, Henry C, 1872, O 10,5:2
Deming, Homer P, 1952, Ap 22,29:4
Deming, James, 1943, D 3,23:4
Deming, John M, 1944, Jl 9,36:1
Deming, Julia Dr, 1968, Mr 9,29:2
Deming, Laurent C, 1945, O 13,15:1
Deming, Lucius F, 1937, S 15,23:7
Deming, Nelson L Mrs, 1937, Ja 14,22:1
Deming, Philander, 1915, F 11,9:4
Deming, Raymond A, 1939, Je 17,15:5
Deming, Richard, 1937, Mr 5,21:4
Deming, Robert M, 1942, Ja 29,19:3
Deming, Sylvester, 1925, Jl 31,15:6
Deming, Thomas H, 1949, O 21,25:3
Deming, William C, 1949, Ap 10,78:5; 1954, Ja 17,92:6
De Miranda, Benjamin H, 1963, Je 18,41:7
Demler, Douglas W, 1954, O 20,29:3
Demler, William M Mrs, 1952, Mr 17,21:5
Demma, Anthony P, 1958, O 4,21:5
Demmary, Arthur J, 1942, F 27,17:4
Demme, Herman C Sr, 1961, Jl 13,29:5
Demmer, Charles C MRs, 1944, My 31,19:6
Demmers, Alfred J, 1949, F 9,28:3
Demmert, Howard H, 1958, Jl 17,27:1
Demmler, Walter R, 1951, Jl 26,21:2
Demmon, Roy E, 1944, F 16,17:3
Demmons, Leonard, 1961, Je 28,35:3
Demmy, Avery S, 1941, D 25,25:2
Demmy, Christian C Jr, 1944, Ag 25,13:4
D'Emo, Basil, 1953, My 5,29:2
Demo, Benjamin H, 1945, Jl 4,13:6
De Moe, William, 1874, S 28,4:7
de Mohrenschildt, Ferdinand, 1919, Mr 5,11:4
De Mole, Lancelot, 1950, My 10,31:4
de Moleyns, Francis A E R, 1964, My 2,27:1
de Moleyns, Francis Mrs, 1957, D 1,88:7
De Molinari, Gustave, 1871, Jl 20,2:4
De Moll, Carl, 1958, Ja 4,15:3
Demond, Charles T, 1939, Mr 7,21:2
Demond, Fred C, 1939, Ja 17,21:5
Demond, Maurice, 1942, Jl 27,15:3
Demond, William J, 1942, Je 11,23:3
DeMonde, George A, 1947, Je 23,23:4
Demonds, Alonzo N, 1943, D 15,27:3
Demonet, Eugene A Sr, 1950, D 28,25:3
de Monocal, Daniel A, 1968, Mr 18,45:1
DeMonseigle, Edmond F, 1950, My 18,29:1
de Mont, Josef Neven Dr, 1915, N 2,11:6
De Montalvo, Marie, 1950, N 3,27:2
De Monteverde, George, 1951, Mr 19,46:6
de Montmorency, Geoffrey, 1955, F 27,87:1
de Montmorency, Raymond H, 1938, D 20,25:3
De Montpensier, Duke Son of, 1873, D 5,1:7
De Montreville, Walter, 1938, F 6,II,9:1
De Montrice, Paul, 1954, My 4,29:1
De Montrouge, Jules A, 1938, F 21,19:4
De Monzie, Anatole, 1947, Ja 13,21:3
De Moos, Charles, 1959, O 29,30:3
Demopoulous, James, 1937, Jl 18,14:3
De Mora, Jose E, 1940, N 27,23:1
Demorest, Alice G Mrs, 1939, Ap 10,17:5

Demorest, Byron P, 1955, F 21,21:1
Demorest, Charlotte K, 1953, Ag 19,29:4
Demorest, George A, 1948, Je 16,29:3
Demorest, Max H, 1942, D 11,23:3
Demorest, Nelson H, 1938, D 19,23:4
Demorest, W C, 1933, N 7,28:2
De Morgan, William Frend, 1917, Ja 18,11:3
Demos, Raphael, 1968, Ag 10,27:1
De Moss, Charles Mrs, 1946, Ag 26,23:1
DeMoss, Madame (Mrs F D Lyon), 1960, Ag 24, 29:3
De Mott, Benjamin R, 1948, O 8,26:2
De Mott, Clifford Monroe, 1918, Ag 29,7:3
De Mott, Daniel V, 1947, Ap 10,25:4
De Mott, Emma C Mrs, 1942, Je 12,21:3
De Mott, F A Col, 1879, S 3,2:5
De Mott, Howard, 1945, My 27,26:1
De Mott, James L Mrs, 1944, O 1,45:1
De Mott, John, 1940, Jl 18,19:5
DeMott, John T, 1950, S 16,19:2
Demott, Raymond F, 1947, Ja 15,25:5
DeMott, Raymond Mrs, 1946, Jl 23,25:3
DeMott, Richard H, 1968, S 1,53:1
Demott, William A, 1945, F 4,38:3
De Mott, William S, 1942, O 6,23:3
de Motte, Helen (Mrs C M Ward), 1955, Jl 10,72:3
De Motte, Laurance W, 1950, O 1,105:1
Dempewolff, Augustus F, 1961, S 21,35:4
Dempsey, A P Mrs, 1941, Ag 11,6:4
Dempsey, Bernard W, 1960, Jl 24,64:3
Dempsey, Cecile Mrs, 1946, Ag 16,21:3
Dempsey, Charles A, 1941, Je 5,23:4; 1955, Mr 29,29:2
Dempsey, Charles E, 1953, O 25,89:1
Dempsey, Charles J, 1951, D 10,29:5
Dempsey, Clifford, 1938, S 7,25:4
Dempsey, Daniel C Mrs, 1952, Mr 6,31:1
Dempsey, David, 1952, Je 14,15:5
Dempsey, Edmund C, 1951, F 17,15:5
Dempsey, Edward F, 1943, D 17,28:2
Dempsey, Edward J, 1947, Ap 12,17:2
Dempsey, Edward Mrs, 1967, Ag 12,25:6
Dempsey, Edward T, 1943, F 14,49:2
Dempsey, Fred J, 1937, Ag 16,19:2
Dempsey, Harold H, 1952, F 20,29:5
Dempsey, J Sr, 1932, Jl 26,15:3
Dempsey, James H Mrs, 1948, O 7,30:3
Dempsey, James Mrs, 1949, N 26,15:6; 1955, F 9,27:1
Dempsey, James S, 1955, O 25,33:2
Dempsey, James V Mrs, 1952, Jl 2,25:1
Dempsey, Jeremiah, 1941, N 19,23:1
Dempsey, Jeremiah Mrs, 1950, F 26,77:1
Dempsey, John C, 1920, Ap 18,22:3; 1950, My 15,21:5
Dempsey, John C Mrs, 1938, S 25,39:1
Dempsey, John E, 1956, Je 16,19:3; 1957, Mr 20,37:4
Dempsey, John J, 1944, Mr 19,41:1; 1946, Ap 7,46:2
Dempsey, John J (funl, Mr 16,86:2), 1958, Mr 12,31:1
Dempsey, John J Mrs, 1950, O 10,31:3
Dempsey, John M, 1953, Ag 7,19:5
Dempsey, John P, 1912, F 5,9:4
Dempsey, Joseph, 1963, My 16,35:3
Dempsey, Joseph F, 1950, Jl 22,15:1
Dempsey, Joseph H, 1963, O 21,31:1
Dempsey, L Walter, 1961, O 16,29:1
Dempsey, Lawrence, 1917, Mr 15,11:4
Dempsey, Louis, 1946, D 12,29:3
Dempsey, Malcolm J Sr, 1944, F 12,13:2
Dempsey, Marcus T, 1965, Ap 25,87:4
Dempsey, Margaret A, 1952, O 3,23:1
Dempsey, Martin F Rev, 1968, D 5,47:4
Dempsey, Maude M, 1960, Je 16,33:5
Dempsey, Michael, 1913, Mr 31,13:5
Dempsey, Michael J Mrs, 1953, N 6,27:3
Dempsey, Neil, 1958, N 3,37:1
Dempsey, Norman P, 1952, Ja 20,84:5
Dempsey, Richard B, 1960, D 14,39:2
Dempsey, Richard H, 1947, Ap 16,25:2
Dempsey, Robert J, 1960, N 2,39:4
Dempsey, Robert S Mrs, 1943, S 30,21:5
Dempsey, Roy S, 1949, My 16,21:3
Dempsey, Roy S Mrs, 1952, D 21,41:3
Dempsey, S Wallace, 1949, Mr 3,25:6
Dempsey, Stanley H, 1951, O 13,17:6
Dempsey, Thomas A, 1938, My 10,21:5
Dempsey, Thomas F, 1904, Ag 25,6:7; 1953, F 14,17:1
Dempsey, Thomas H, 1937, Je 17,23:3
Dempsey, Tom, 1947, N 5,27:2
Dempsey, W Clifford, 1954, Je 27,69:2
Dempsey, Walter A, 1940, My 1,23:1
Dempsey, Walter A Mrs, 1946, F 23,13:3
Dempsey, William A, 1949, O 9,94:3; 1956, N 16,27:2
Dempsey, William E Mrs, 1952, Mr 20,12:2
Dempsey, William J, 1942, Ag 2,38:8; 1956, Je 22, 23:3; 1959, Ag 30,82:7
Dempsey, William T, 1937, Ja 12,23:4; 1940, Ag 22, 19:4
Dempsey, William T Dr, 1937, O 21,23:2
Dempster, Alexander, 1915, Ag 3,9:5
Dempster, Alexander Mrs, 1915, Ag 3,9:5
Dempster, Arthur J, 1950, Mr 12,94:3
Dempster, George R, 1964, S 19,27:5
Dempster, Harry L, 1946, D 9,25:3
Dempster, James H, 1951, Ag 6,21:6
Dempster, John, 1958, My 31,15:5
Dempster, John T H, 1953, Ap 7,29:2
Dempster, Robert B, 1966, O 27,47:4
Dempster, William R, 1871, Mr 26,5:5
Demski, Peter, 1950, N 24,36:3
Demun, Millard F, 1944, N 14,23:4
De Muro, A Theodore, 1967, Je 19,35:2
DeMuro, Paul G, 1968, S 1,53:3
De Musset, Paul, 1880, My 20,1:6
De Muth, Frank, 1942, Ja 22,17:2
Demyer, Harry M, 1953, Ap 9,27:5
Den, Dona Y A Mrs, 1942, Ag 23,42:3
Den, Eleanor, 1946, Ja 12,15:5
Denaci, Edward, 1956, Jl 3,25:2
De Nagy, Laszlo, 1944, Je 17,13:2
Denain, Victor Gen, 1953, Ja 1,23:2
De Nancrede, Charles B G Dr, 1921, Ap 14,13:4
De Naouley, Thomas F, 1961, Jl 22,21:4
De Naouley, Thomas F Mrs, 1941, My 6,21:5
Denari, Andrew, 1958, My 3,19:2
Denarie, Andrew J, 1939, Ap 24,17:5
De Natale, Frederick J, 1952, Ag 5,19:4
de Naucave, Anna, 1924, N 14,19:5
de Navarro, Jose Mrs, 1910, Mr 22,11:2
Denbigh, Dowager Countess of, 1952, F 18,19:3
Denbigh, Earl of, 1939, N 26,43:2
Denbigh, John H (por), 1943, Jl 26,19:3
Denby, Arnold M, 1966, My 23,41:2
Denby, Charles, 1938, F 15,26:1
Denby, Charles Col, 1904, Ja 14,9:5
Denby, E, 1929, F 9,17:1
Denby, Edwin H, 1957, Ja 18,21:3
Denby, G, 1933, S 17,37:1
Denby, Harry J, 1950, D 3,88:4
Denby, William, 1948, Je 18,23:2
Dences, Frederick W, 1955, F 13,86:3
Denchfield, Arthur L, 1955, My 14,19:6
Denckla, C Paul, 1958, Ag 8,19:4
Denckla, Nelsine P S Mrs, 1953, Ja 31,15:3
Dendel, Ernest H, 1957, O 13,86:4
Dendramis, Vassili, 1956, My 10,31:1
Dene, Shafto H, 1956, Ap 16,27:5
Deneau, Rene O, 1942, D 7,27:5
Deneau, Richard Mrs, 1968, Jl 25,33:3
Denecke, Charles J, 1953, Ap 14,27:3
Denecke, John A, 1940, Ag 28,19:2
Denee, John E, 1947, Ag 17,53:1
Deneefe, Robert E, 1956, O 20,21:4
Deneen, Charles S, 1940, F 6,21:1
Deneen, Charles S Mrs, 1950, O 31,27:1
Denegar, Arthur M, 1950, Mr 13,21:2
Denegar, William H, 1946, Jl 21,40:1
Deneholz, Aaron, 1938, D 2,23:2
Denehy, Daniel J, 1962, Jl 3,23:4
Denehy, John A, 1948, D 8,31:2
Denehy, John A Mrs, 1944, O 17,23:4
Denemark, Edward J, 1943, D 24,13:1
Denemark, Emil, 1963, My 9,37:4
Denempont, Louis, 1944, Ap 2,39:1
Deneroy, Martin J, 1946, N 14,29:1
Deneus, Stig, 1960, D 3,23:6
Denfert, Rochereau Col, 1878, My 14,5:3
Dengel, Joseph B, 1943, Ap 17,17:5
Dengg, Louis Mrs, 1950, O 11,33:3
Dengler, Calvin F, 1954, N 4,31:3
Dengler, Franz, 1939, N 29,23:4
Dengler, Henry P, 1955, F 13,86:8
Dengler, Horace W, 1957, Ag 5,21:3
Dengler, Joseph G, 1946, Jl 22,21:4
Dengler, Robert H, 1939, Jl 21,19:4
Dengler, Theobold, 1965, Jl 26,23:4
Denham, Austin, 1948, Je 5,15:2
Denham, Edward B, 1938, Je 3,21:5
Denham, Edwin A Mrs, 1953, Jl 4,11:6
Denham, Edwin J, 1945, F 19,17:5
Denham, George W, 1907, F 4,9:5
Denham, James S, 1959, S 13,84:6
Denham, Lord, 1948, D 1,29:3
Denham, Robert N, 1954, Je 20,86:1
Denham, Thomas A, 1943, My 4,23:2
Denham, William Richard, 1915, S 23,13:5
Denhard, Augustus M, 1942, Jl 18,13:1
Denhardt, Edward L, 1950, Ag 3,23:1
Denhof, Ernst, 1937, F 21,X,8:4
Denholm, Charles E, 1907, S 10,7:4
Denholm, William J, 1955, Jl 30,17:5
Denholm, William Mrs, 1948, S 1,23:1
Denholme, R M, 1914, O 1,11:5
Denholtz, Emanuel, 1959, N 15,86:8
Denicke, George, 1965, Ja 1,19:5
Denier, Tony, 1917, Mr 11,21:4
Denig, Jacob C, 1955, O 6,29:2
Denig, Rudolf C R, 1960, Ag 4,25:5
Denigan, James T, 1953, O 17,15:4
Denike, Abraham Col, 1879, S 9,2:3
Denike, Ellen, 1943, D 16,27:2
De Nike, Frank A, 1965, Mr 29,33:1
Denike, George J, 1953, Ja 22,23:2
Denike, J, 1880, N 5,5:5
Denike, Madeline, 1907, Je 24,7:6
Denike, Robert E, 1951, S 29,17:5
Denikine, Anton, 1947, Ag 9,13:7
Denin, Kate (Mrs Jno Wilson), 1907, F 6,9:6
Denin, Susan, 1875, D 7,5:6
Denis, Edward Bro (H Yergens), 1961, Ja 9,39:3
Denis, George J Mrs, 1947, F 3,19:4
Denis, Judge, 1871, N 9,2:6
Denis, Maurice, 1943, N 19,19:2
De Nise, Alfred S, 1946, N 12,29:2
Denise, Anthony J, 1951, N 30,23:3
Denise, Charles M, 1942, Je 13,15:4
Denise, Garret A, 1960, O 19,45:4
Denisenko, M I, 1949, Ap 20,27:2
Denison, A W (see also F 25 and 26), 1877, F 27
Denison, Alice E Mrs, 1940, N 12,23:4
Denison, Amos A, 1948, Ag 24,23:3
Denison, Arthur C, 1942, My 28,17:1
Denison, Charles Halbert, 1911, Jl 13,9:4
Denison, Charles R, 1959, O 8,39:2
Denison, Ellery Dr, 1910, Ja 14,9:4
Denison, Evelyn E Mrs, 1939, My 6,17:1
Denison, Flora MacDonald Mrs, 1921, My 24,15:4
Denison, George Francis William Henry (Earl of Londesborough), 1920, S 14,11:2
Denison, George H, 1944, Jl 20,19:3
Denison, George Taylor Col, 1925, Je 8,15:4
Denison, H Marcus, 1938, Je 19,29:1
Denison, Henry Willard, 1914, Jl 4,7:4
Denison, Herbert G, 1949, F 1,25:5
Denison, Hugh (cor, D 12,27:1), 1940, N 24,51:3
Denison, J Fred, 1950, My 15,21:6
Denison, John, 1939, Mr 10,23:5
Denison, John A, 1948, Mr 8,23:4
Denison, John A Mrs, 1951, Ag 11,11:5
Denison, Jonathan, 1903, N 17,9:6
Denison, L, 1934, Mr 26,17:3
Denison, L Maude Mrs, 1941, D 30,19:5
Denison, Mary Andrews Mrs, 1911, O 18,11:4
Denison, Muriel, 1954, S 23,33:4
Denison, Robert C Mrs, 1943, Ja 13,23:4
Denison, Robert F, 1952, D 13,21:6
Denison, Robert L Mrs, 1961, O 4,45:2
Denison, S D, 1880, S 4,5:2
Denison, Septimus J A Maj Gen, 1937, N 9,23:3
Denison, Ward Mrs, 1953, My 15,23:3
Denison, Warren H, 1956, Ag 29,29:3
Denison, William E, 1905, My 5,9:4
Denison, William Francis Henry (Earl of Londesborough), 1917, N 17,13:4
Denison-Pender, John J (Lord Pender), 1965, A 35:1
De Nisser, J A P, 1881, Ja 19,5:3
Denissoff, Sviatoslav V, 1957, Ap 20,17:1
De Nittis, Painter, 1884, S 21,6:7
Denizot, Victor, 1925, S 15,25:4
Denk, Adam Mrs, 1947, Mr 8,13:5
Denk, Jacob F, 1962, S 30,86:6
Denker, William J, 1951, Jl 4,17:5
Denkinger, Alice M Mrs, 1942, Ag 14,17:4
Denkscherz, Joseph A, 1955, Ag 26,19:5
Denlike, Charles Mrs, 1944, Mr 4,13:5
Denlin, Bernard Joseph, 1909, Ap 15,9:6
Denlinger, Dorothy, 1949, D 2,29:5
Denlinger, Henry K, 1948, Mr 3,23:4
Denlinger, Stanley, 1960, Ja 4,29:1
Denlinger, Sutherland, 1963, O 7,31:2
Denman, Alvan R, 1941, Ag 8,15:2
Denman, Alvin R Mrs, 1953, F 10,27:2
Denman, Arthur R, 1937, Ag 21,15:2
Denman, Benjamin C, 1952, Ag 16,15:5
Denman, Burt J, 1938, Je 26,27:3
Denman, Charles Mrs, 1950, Ja 14,15:4
Denman, Daniel, 1947, D 27,14:3
Denman, Everett, 1937, Ag 4,7:4
Denman, Frank, 1968, Ag 2,33:4
Denman, Frederick H, 1940, Ja 28,32:7
Denman, George, 1937, O 1,21:4
Denman, Helen E, 1968, N 26,53:5
Denman, Julius R, 1916, My 28,17:4
Denman, Katherine C Mrs, 1941, Je 7,17:3
Denman, Lady, 1954, Je 3,27:1
Denman, Lord (Thos), 1954, Je 25,21:3
Denman, MacDonald S, 1965, Je 18,35:4
Denman, Mark A, 1946, D 28,15:3
Denman, Mark A Mrs, 1939, D 23,15:1
Denman, Sadie E, 1959, S 9,41:3
Denman, Thomas C, 1940, O 16,23:6
Denman, William A Mrs, 1948, My 16,68:5
Denman, William J McN, 1874, Mr 17,2:7
Denman, William V, 1950, D 5,31:3
Denmark, Oscar, 1938, Jl 24,29:4
Denmead, Harry R, 1945, Ag 11,13:3
Denn, John J, 1942, N 12,25:2
Denn, Nicholas A, 1954, My 24,27:4
Denn, Samuel J, 1943, Ja 3,42:6
Dennean, James A, 1966, F 7,29:2
Dennee, Charles F, 1946, Ap 30,22:3
Denneen, Francis S, 1953, My 12,27:3
Dennehey, John J, 1937, Ja 16,36:2
Dennehy, Ptk J, 1954, Jl 30,17:5
Dennehy, Thomas C, 1940, Ap 16,23:5
Dennehy, Thomas C Jr, 1960, Jl 19,29:5
Dennehy, Thomas F, 1958, Ap 12,19:3
Dennehy, Thomas P Mrs, 1958, Ap 18,23:3
Dennen, Arthur Wilson, 1922, My 10,19:6
Dennen, Charles E, 1946, F 22,25:1
Dennen, Ernest J Rev Dr, 1937, Ja 23,18:6

Dennen, George E, 1966, O 17,37:3
Dennen, George E Mrs, 1963, My 1,39:2
Dennen, Thomas Mrs, 1947, N 5,28:3
Denneny, George, 1938, Ja 25,21:4
Denneny, James A, 1947, Jl 16,23:5
Denner, Edward F Dr, 1913, N 15,11:6
Denner, Lorimer, 1964, F 1,23:5
Denner, Samuel, 1949, S 3,13:3
Dennerlein, James J, 1939, F 28,19:5
D'Ennery, A P, 1899, Ja 26,1:6
Dennesen, Clarence H, 1944, Mr 17,17:3
Dennessey, James A, 1938, Ap 17,II,7:1
Dennett, Alfred W, 1908, Ja 25,9:6
Dennett, Asa E, 1948, Ja 22,27:5
Dennett, Carl P, 1955, N 18,25:2
Dennett, Devon, 1960, Ap 25,29:2
Dennett, Edward P, 1947, Ja 28,23:2
Dennett, Harlan I, 1950, N 2,31:4
Dennett, John Richard, 1874, N 29,7:3
Dennett, Maria H Mrs, 1942, D 29,21:4
Dennett, Mary W Mrs, 1947, Jl 26,13:3
Dennett, Nathan W, 1949, Ap 18,25:1
Dennett, Raymond, 1961, S 2,15:5
Dennett, Tyler, 1949, D 30,19:1
Dennett, Tyler E, 1950, Ja 6,21:2
Dennett, Tyler Mrs, 1950, Ag 11,19:2
Denney, Charles E, 1965, Ja 19,33:4
Denney, Edwin C Sr, 1939, Mr 8,21:4
Denney, Elliott S, 1959, D 25,21:6
Denney, Freeman A, 1952, N 16,89:1
Denney, James M, 1945, S 20,23:2
Denney, James Rev, 1917, Je 13,13:4
Denney, Leonard J, 1938, Mr 27,II,7:2
Denney, Oscar H, 1945, Ja 8,17:3
Denney, Oswald E, 1944, F 21,15:3
Denney, Reuben E, 1953, Je 16,27:5
Denney, Thomas A, 1938, F 8,22:2
Denney, William H, 1946, O 28,27:2
Denni, Lucien, 1947, Ag 23,13:3
Dennin, Charles P, 1919, Ja 9,11:3
Dennin, John W, 1961, My 26,33:5
Dennin, Joseph W, 1938, Jl 17,27:3
Dennin, Lawrence P, 1963, D 22,34:4
Dennin, Matthew J, 1945, Ag 14,21:2
Dennin, Thomas Mrs, 1948, My 10,21:4
Dennin, William H, 1920, Ja 6,15:1
Denning, Clarence P, 1952, F 2,13:3
Denning, J M Msgr, 1927, Jl 27,23:5
Denning, John J, 1938, N 12,15:4
Denning, John V Mrs, 1946, N 19,31:4
Denning, L B, 1940, F 7,21:5
Denning, Patrick Mrs, 1944, S 12,19:5
Denning, William L, 1951, Mr 16,31:2
Dennington, Arthur, 1959, My 18,27:4
Dennis, A E Forbes Mrs (P Bottome, Ag 23,25:1), 1963, Ag 24,19:2
Dennis, A P, 1931, Ag 30,28:1
Dennis, Albert G, 1957, O 19,21:5
Dennis, Alfred E Mrs, 1950, D 8,29:1
Dennis, Alfred L (will, Jl 20,19:1), 1939, Jl 7,17:3
Dennis, Alfred L P Mrs, 1950, Je 10,17:2
Dennis, C E, 1951, Ag 24,15:2
Dennis, Calvin L, 1958, Jl 11,23:4
Dennis, Caroline A, 1940, N 26,23:6
Dennis, Charles F, 1948, Ap 3,15:6
Dennis, Charles H (will, O 20,23:1), 1943, S 26,49:1
Dennis, Clarence Ashley, 1921, S 3,9:6
Dennis, Clark M, 1968, Ap 30,53:6
Dennis, Daniel F, 1951, My 31,27:2
Dennis, Dave, 1965, Mr 17,45:2
Dennis, Dorothy W, 1967, D 21,37:1
Dennis, E Willard, 1965, F 23,33:4
Dennis, Eugene (F E Waldron),(funl plans, F 2,-29:1;funl, F 6,23:4), 1961, F 1,35:1
Dennis, F S, 1934, Mr 9,20:1
Dennis, Francis L M, 1962, Mr 29,33:2
Dennis, Fred B, 1951, Mr 29,27:2
Dennis, Fred L, 1958, Ja 29,27:1
Dennis, Frederic J, 1945, F 10,11:5
Dennis, G R, 1882, Ag 14,5:6
Dennis, Gabriel L, 1954, Je 24,27:5
Dennis, George P, 1955, Jl 16,15:6
Dennis, George P Mrs, 1965, O 24,86:4
Dennis, George T, 1939, My 2,23:1
Dennis, Graham Barclay, 1923, Ag 20,11:4
Dennis, Harold, 1947, Ap 7,23:2
Dennis, Harry S, 1955, My 21,17:4
Dennis, Herbert G, 1948, N 3,27:3
Dennis, Holmes Jr Mrs, 1948, N 25,31:3
Dennis, Holmes Van M 3d, 1964, Je 5,31:5
Dennis, James S, 1966, Ag 1,27:5
Dennis, James S Mrs, 1946, O 6,57:1
Dennis, James Teackle, 1918, Ap 2,13:5
Dennis, Jane D, 1944, Ja 24,17:4
Dennis, Jefferson R, 1958, F 18,27:4
Dennis, John, 1920, Ja 1,15:2
Dennis, John A, 1940, Je 11,25:5
Dennis, John B, 1947, F 13,23:4
Dennis, John Edward, 1920, S 19,22:2
Dennis, John J, 1958, Ag 6,25:1
Dennis, John R, 1945, Mr 26,19:3
Dennis, John S, 1938, N 27,48:6
Dennis, John Upshur Ex-Justice, 1916, S 13,9:7
Dennis, John W, 1919, S 10,11:1; 1966, S 5,15:6
Dennis, Jonas R, 1950, S 29,27:2
Dennis, Joseph M, 1958, F 3,23:2
Dennis, Jule P, 1953, D 22,31:4
Dennis, L G, 1885, Je 17,5:3
Dennis, Leonard W, 1958, Ag 11,21:2
Dennis, Mary E, 1938, Ag 29,13:6
Dennis, Morgan, 1960, O 25,35:3
Dennis, N F H, 1872, S 6,5:4
Dennis, Oscar J, 1925, S 16,25:4
Dennis, Otis A, 1939, O 4,25:2
Dennis, Paul G, 1957, D 28,17:2
Dennis, Phil C, 1950, Ja 27,24:3
Dennis, Ralph B, 1942, Ag 25,23:6
Dennis, Rodney G, 1967, Ja 1,52:5
Dennis, Rodney Strong, 1904, Mr 8,9:7
Dennis, Royal R, 1952, Ag 22,21:2
Dennis, Russell, 1964, Je 2,37:5
Dennis, Samuel K, 1953, Ja 13,27:4
Dennis, Samuel S Mrs, 1952, Ja 3,27:1
Dennis, Stephen F, 1953, D 20,77:2
Dennis, Victor L, 1918, F 20,9:4
Dennis, Walter Mrs, 1902, O 23,1:4
Dennis, William, 1958, Je 3,31:5
Dennis, William C, 1962, S 16,86:6
Dennis, William H, 1943, S 8,29:3
Dennis, William H (will, Ja 27,14:3), 1954, Ja 20, 27:4
Dennis, William H 3d, 1967, Jl 13,37:3
Dennis, William Mrs, 1947, Ap 22,27:3
Dennison, Charles E, 1948, Je 8,25:4
Dennison, Charles H, 1910, D 26,7:6
Dennison, Charles M, 1924, Ja 3,17:2
Dennison, Clare, 1954, F 16,25:5
Dennison, Edward G, 1940, F 11,48:3
Dennison, Elizabeth White Mrs, 1906, N 22,9:5
Dennison, Ethan A, 1954, O 10,87:1
Dennison, Fred, 1948, Ag 16,19:5
Dennison, George, 1876, F 16,4:7
Dennison, George H, 1938, N 12,15:5
Dennison, Gov (funl), 1882, Je 16,5:4
Dennison, Harold T, 1940, Jl 19,19:4
Dennison, Henry S, 1952, Mr 1,15:3
Dennison, John P, 1937, My 23,II,10:6
Dennison, John Sr Mrs, 1949, O 27,27:2
Dennison, Lindsay Mrs, 1954, Je 1,27:4
Dennison, M Guion, 1949, O 5,29:4
Dennison, Mary, 1882, D 19,2:7
Dennison, Mary R Mrs, 1942, Jl 30,21:5
Dennison, Orville B, 1959, F 15,87:1
Dennison, R V, 1939, S 29,23:2
Dennison, Robert E, 1950, Je 18,77:1
Dennison, Robert S, 1956, My 15,31:1
Dennison, Thomas W, 1939, Je 28,21:3
Dennison, Walter A, 1908, N 7,7:4
Denniston, Adolph L, 1946, S 10,7:2
Denniston, Alfred Mrs, 1949, Mr 17,25:2
Denniston, Benjamin M, 1952, S 20,15:1
Denniston, Emma P Mrs, 1940, D 20,25:3
Denniston, Frank J, 1949, O 11,34:5
Denniston, Grant, 1962, My 14,29:3
Denniston, Harold S, 1949, O 7,31:3
Denniston, Henry Martyn Rear-Adm, 1922, My 24, 19:5
Denniston, Mary, 1937, My 28,21:5; 1938, Ja 3,21:1
Denniston, Reynolds, 1943, Ja 30,15:5
Denniston, Robert, 1867, D 8,6:5
Dennistoun, Robert M, 1952, O 13,21:5
Denno, Willard Dr, 1951, Ag 30,23:3
Denny, Arch M, 1950, Ja 11,23:1
Denny, Charles B, 1938, O 11,25:5
Denny, Charles R 3d, 1964, Mr 31,35:2
Denny, Collins, 1943, My 13,21:3
Denny, Collins Jr, 1964, Ja 16,25:1
Denny, D Sir, 1928, Jl 26,21:5
Denny, Daniel, 1872, F 11,4:6
Denny, Daniel E, 1925, N 18,23:4
Denny, Frank Lee Col, 1914, Jl 9,7:6
Denny, George H, 1955, Ap 3,86:3
Denny, George L, 1958, O 1,37:5
Denny, George Sr, 1951, Mr 3,13:3
Denny, George T, 1940, S 17,23:6
Denny, George V Jr, 1959, N 12,35:1
Denny, Grover C, 1960, Ja 11,45:2
Denny, Harmar D Jr, 1966, Ja 8,25:3
Denny, Harmar Sr Mrs, 1950, F 19,76:6
Denny, Harold, 1945, Jl 4,13:1
Denny, Harold M, 1952, Jl 20,52:5
Denny, Harold N Mrs, 1943, My 19,25:5
Denny, Henry L L, 1953, My 5,29:5
Denny, Henry W, 1953, S 14,27:4
Denny, Jack, 1950, S 17,104:7
Denny, James J, 1940, My 1,23:5
Denny, Jim, 1963, Ag 28,33:4
Denny, Joseph G Jr, 1957, D 22,41:2
Denny, Linna, 1955, My 24,31:1
Denny, Ludwell Mrs, 1953, My 10,89:1
Denny, Maurice, 1955, F 3,23:3
Denny, Nelson C, 1941, S 18,25:3
Denny, O J, 1951, Mr 19,27:3
Denny, Reginald (funl plans, Je 22,39:3), 1967, Je 18,76:1
Denny, Thomas, 1874, O 23,3:5
Denny, Thomas S, 1943, Je 8,21:2
Denny, W B, 1903, Jl 31,1:6
Denny, Walter B Dr, 1937, Je 24,25:2
Denny, Wayne, 1967, N 22,92:5
Denny, William B, 1950, Je 19,21:5
Denny, William Croghan Col, 1923, F 28,17:3
Denny, William D, 1953, N 24,29:1
Denny, William H L, 1915, S 3,9:5
Denomme, John B, 1951, Ap 3,27:1
Denomy, Alexander J, 1957, Jl 20,15:6
Denonn, Aaron Mrs, 1956, D 30,32:8
De Nonno, Daniel, 1940, Je 14,21:6
De Noon, Clara M, 1950, O 22,92:2
deNooyer, Orrie, 1965, Ja 26,34:3
De Nora, Alfredo, 1940, Jl 26,17:4
deNormand, Kingdom, 1961, My 26,67:5
Denormandie, D J E, 1902, Ja 31,9:4
De Normandie, James Rev Dr, 1924, O 7,23:4
De Notto, Matthew I, 1952, F 16,13:6
Denoue, Guillaume Countess, 1939, N 16,23:2
Denove, Jack, 1968, Ap 10,43:6
de Novellis, Antonio, 1924, N 26,19:4
De Noyelles, E Harold, 1955, Mr 21,25:2
Denoyelles, Frank L, 1938, Ap 22,19:2
Denoyer, L Philip, 1964, S 25,41:4
Denoyer, Pierre, 1965, Ag 20,29:3
Densen, Michael, 1950, D 20,31:4
Densham, Frederick W, 1953, Ja 26,19:5
Densing, George H, 1952, Mr 30,92:3
Denslow, Henry C, 1944, Jl 30,36:1
Denslow, Herbert M, 1944, S 9,15:4
Denslow, Leo E, 1948, Ja 1,23:1
Densmore, Carl D, 1950, Ja 26,27:4
Densmore, Charles R, 1950, Mr 22,27:4
Densmore, Emmet Dr, 1911, F 20,7:5
Densmore, Frances, 1957, Je 7,23:4
Densmore, Helen Mrs, 1904, N 27,5:4
Densmore, John H, 1943, S 23,21:4
Denson, Helen V Mrs, 1953, Ag 18,23:4
Denson, Hyman, 1941, Jl 15,19:3
Denson, Samuel, 1952, S 22,23:3
Denson, William F, 1947, N 4,25:5
Dent, Alfred C, 1937, Jl 8,23:3
Dent, Arthur G, 1950, Jl 8,13:5
Dent, Edward J, 1957, Ag 24,15:3
Dent, Elbert Mrs, 1965, D 15,47:3
Dent, Elmer A, 1944, Je 30,21:4
Dent, Emmet Cooper Dr, 1906, Ja 13,9:5
Dent, Fred Mrs (L M Grace), 1957, D 23,23:5
Dent, Frederick Col, 1873, D 17,1:7
Dent, Hawthorne K, 1958, F 1,19:4
Dent, Hugh R, 1938, N 21,19:5
Dent, Jack, 1950, Je 30,23:3
Dent, John Mrs, 1952, Mr 14,20:5
Dent, Joseph D, 1957, Je 21,25:2
Dent, Lester, 1959, Mr 12,31:2
Dent, Lewis Judge, 1874, Mr 23,5:3
Dent, Magruder, 1966, Ag 9,37:2
Dent, Maurice A, 1956, Je 27,31:4
Dent, R Risley Jr, 1964, Je 8,29:2
Dent, Silas, 1952, D 25,29:3
Dent, Stanley H, 1938, O 7,23:3
Dent, T Ashley, 1955, O 12,31:4
Dent, Thomas J, 1962, My 11,31:1
Dent, Thomas Mrs, 1946, D 20,24:2
Dent, William C, 1952, S 23,33:4
Dente, Loretto, 1945, Ja 8,19:7
Dente, Maria Mrs, 1948, Mr 24,27:3
Dentler, C E, 1955, Ap 4,29:4
Denton, Charles B Mrs, 1961, D 22,24:1
Denton, Charles C, 1938, D 7,23:4
Denton, Clarence H, 1945, Ja 5,15:5
Denton, Edward A, 1956, Ja 26,29:4
Denton, Eugene W, 1951, F 11,88:5
Denton, Frances B, 1948, F 28,15:4
Denton, Frank A, 1945, D 17,21:2
Denton, Frank C, 1949, F 8,25:3
Denton, Frank D, 1943, Ag 18,19:4
Denton, Frederick A, 1966, Jl 24,60:5
Denton, George, 1918, Mr 13,11:3
Denton, George W, 1952, My 2,25:1
Denton, Harold L, 1954, Je 9,31:3
Denton, Harry M Mrs, 1949, D 28,32:1
Denton, Helen H Mrs, 1942, N 14,16:2
Denton, Ian S, 1946, My 18,19:4
Denton, James W, 1950, Je 17,15:2
Denton, Jane A, 1923, Ja 12,15:4
Denton, Myron P, 1940, Jl 25,17:5
Denton, Percy, 1913, N 20,11:4
Denton, Richard, 1950, Mr 23,36:5
Denton, Robert, 1903, Jl 24,7:7
Denton, Samuel F Mrs, 1947, D 25,21:2
Denton, Sherman F, 1937, Je 18,21:6
Denton, Van Ness, 1938, Ap 6,23:3
Denton, W S, 1937, D 29,21:3
Denton, William B, 1950, N 20,25:4
Denton, William D, 1944, O 31,19:4
Dentz, Edmund L, 1961, D 16,25:3
Dentz, Henri-Fernand, 1945, D 14,27:3
Dentz, Thomas J, 1940, F 16,19:2
DeNunzio, Frank, 1948, Jl 16,19:1
Denver, Charles O, 1953, O 26,21:4
Denver, Matthew R, 1954, My 15,15:2

Denver, Robert P J, 1961, Ja 25,33:5
Denville, Alfred, 1955, Mr 24,32:1
Denvir, Margaret A, 1937, N 6,17:5
Denworth, Hugh F, 1941, Jl 1,23:2
Denyn, Jef, 1941, O 9,24:3
Denys, Bro, 1944, O 26,23:4
Denyse, Herman F, 1952, Ja 12,13:2
Denyse, William C, 1914, Mr 15,7:4
Denz, Fred A, 1960, D 29,25:1
Denzer, Bernard, 1951, N 16,25:2
Denzer, Norman, 1951, F 1,25:4
Denzler, George S, 1947, Mr 23,60:3
Denzler, Harry L, 1962, N 21,30:2
De Obarrio, Nicanor A, 1941, Ja 18,15:2
De Orchis, Vincenzo, 1966, D 12,47:2
De Oro, Alfred, 1948, Ap 24,15:3
De Oro, Maria Mrs, 1937, Je 29,21:5
De Orsey, C Leo, 1965, My 1,31:4
de Osma, Julio, 1938, Ag 1,13:3
De Otte, D F A Mrs, 1954, N 20,17:5
De Otte, Detlef F, 1939, D 29,15:5
de Ovies, Julian Segundo Count, 1910, Ap 22,9:5
DePace, Bernardo, 1966, Je 17,45:2
De Pace, Joseph, 1958, N 8,21:4
De Pace, Michael, 1949, Je 9,31:2
De Pace, Oliver, 1947, Je 22,52:6
De Pace, Robert, 1964, F 15,23:5
Depage, Antoine Dr, 1925, Je 11,19:4
De Pahkao, C M, 1878, Ja 9,5:2
de Palluel, Roger, 1968, Jl 19,35:1
De Palma, Angelo, 1947, My 7,27:2
De Palma, Edward, 1957, D 27,24:1
De Palma, Ralph (funl plans, Ap 2,23:5), 1956, Ap 1,89:1
De Paoli, Bruno, 1951, Mr 10,13:4
De Paolis, Alessio, 1964, Mr 10,37:3
De Paolo, Victor P, 1945, D 12,27:1
De Paris, M, 1872, Ap 16,5:4
de Paris, Sidney, 1967, S 15,47:1
De Pasquale, Frank A, 1960, Ja 3,88:3
de Pasquale, Oreste, 1956, Ag 5,77:1
De Pasquale, Victor, 1965, Je 30,37:4
De Pasquali, Bernice, 1925, Ap 4,17:6
De Pass, Alfred, 1952, D 11,33:5
De Pass, Faudell L, 1947, Ag 3,53:1
Depasta, Geoorge S, 1945, F 15,19:2
DePatie, Edmond L, 1966, Ag 7,81:3
de Pau, Flavie Mrs (Flavie Van den Hende), 1925, Jl 21,21:3
De Paye, Jean A, 1948, O 1,26:3
De Pencier, A U, 1949, My 31,24:4
De Perigny, Countess, 1942, Ja 10,18:2
Deperon, Paul, 1952, S 8,29:8
De Persigny, Duc (Jean Gilbert Victor Fralin), 1872, Ja 15,1:6
Depetra, Giullo Sen, 1925, Jl 23,19:5
Depew, Anne Mitchell Mrs, 1925, My 21,23:6
Depew, Arthur, 1940, S 25,27:3
Depew, C M, 1928, Ap 5,1:8
Depew, Chauncey M, 1957, Ja 5,17:3
Depew, Claude E, 1954, Jl 24,13:5
Depew, Edward E, 1947, D 2,29:3
Depew, Edward M, 1914, Ap 12,15:4
Depew, Ganson G, 1924, Ap 1,21:2
Depew, George A, 1950, F 22,29:1
Depew, Harold, 1939, O 20,23:1
Depew, Isaac Mrs, 1885, Mr 27,5:2
Depew, John D, 1960, Ag 4,25:2
Depew, Lawrence, 1904, Ja 4,5:2
Depew, May P Mrs (will, S 26,13:2), 1940, Jl 28,27:5
De Pew, Peter, 1948, Ag 6,17:2
De Pew, Pierre H, 1949, Jl 29,21:1
Depew, Richard H, 1942, F 7,17:2
Depew, Richard H Jr, 1948, Ja 29,23:1
Depew, Richard H Mrs, 1954, Ag 13,15:5
Depew, Sherman L, 1924, O 21,23:4
De Pew, Tunis, 1940, Mr 8,21:3
Depew, Warren A, 1953, Mr 22,87:1
Depew, William A Mrs, 1946, My 16,21:2
De Peyster, B, 1903, O 3,9:6
de Peyster, Cortlandt, 1918, Ag 10,7:3
de Peyster, Elizabeth Van Rensselaer, 1905, D 5,9:3
de Peyster, Emily M, 1917, O 4,13:4
De Peyster, Frederic, 1882, Ag 19,5:3; 1905, My 12,9:4
de Peyster, Frederic A Mrs, 1964, Je 15,29:3
De Peyster, Frederic J Mrs, 1911, Ap 5,9:5
De Peyster, Frederick Jr Col, 1874, N 6,5:5
De Peyster, J A, 1878, My 28,4:7
De Peyster, J L, 1903, My 29,9:5
De Peyster, James, 1874, Je 14,6:6; 1876, F 28,8:2
De Peyster, John Watts Gen, 1907, My 6,9:1
De Peyster, John Watts Jr Col, 1873, Ap 14,5:5
De Peyster, Julia A T Mrs, 1937, Mr 13,19:2
de Peyster, Pierre G, 1919, N 29,11:4
de Peyster, Robert Gilbert Livingston, 1908, Je 17,9:5
de Peyster, William M D Mrs, 1956, Ap 11,33:3
de Peyster, Wilson, 1911, Mr 8,11:4
De Peyster Hosmer, Estelle Mrs, 1953, N 15,89:1
Depeza, Lionel, 1965, My 25,41:2
Depfer, Harry A, 1949, Ap 8,26:2
Dephey, Eden Vinson Dr, 1925, O 24,15:6
Depietri, Carlo, 1952, Ap 13,76:4
de Pimentel Brandao, Mario, 1956, O 25,33:2
Depinet, Fred E, 1953, Jl 20,17:3
De Pingparlier, M, 1875, Ap 3,2:2
De Pinna, Antoinette, 1943, Je 28,21:5
De Pinna, Leo S, 1939, D 24,14:6
Depken, Gerhard D, 1955, Ap 26,29:4
Depkiewicz, John, 1959, Je 25,29:4
De Plante, Henry S, 1955, Jl 11,17:3
de Polgary, Geza, 1919, Ja 28,9:2
Deponai, John M, 1917, O 12,11:5
Depont, Louise H B, 1947, O 14,28:2
Depont, Marie T, 1937, Jl 1,27:5
De Pont, Victorine A B, 1942, Ja 4,48:2
de Postels, Robert N, 1964, Ja 9,31:3
De Pourtales, Count, 1874, S 6,1:7
De Poy, Thomas E, 1952, Ja 2,25:4
Depoyan, Jacob M, 1956, D 1,21:1
Deppe, Edward Mrs, 1952, S 11,31:4
Deppe, William P, 1944, Mr 8,19:2
Deppen, Donald H, 1961, O 12,29:3
Deppenschmidt, William H Sr, 1943, Ap 12,23:4
Depperman, Charles E, 1957, My 10,27:2
Deppeu, Joseph H (will), 1963, O 10,31:7
Depretis, Agostino, 1940, Ja 24,21:5
De Prey, Juan, 1962, D 1,25:4
DePrez, John D, 1937, Ag 27,19:4
De Priest, Oscar S, 1951, My 13,88:3
De Primio, Hercules, 1945, F 7,21:3
De Prume, Jules J, 1947, N 13,27:3
Depue, David A Mrs, 1904, Ja 8,7:5
Depue, Frederick A, 1948, N 13,15:1
Depue, L A Judge, 1902, Ap 4,9:7
Depue, Sherred, 1953, My 1,21:3
De Purucker, Gottfried, 1942, S 28,17:4
Deputy, Willard F, 1938, Ag 10,19:2
Depuy, Abram E, 1941, Ja 10,19:5
De Puy, Adelaide G Mrs, 1940, F 9,19:2
Depuy, Alvin B, 1949, D 15,35:4
De Puy, Eli D, 1953, Ja 8,27:1
De Puy, F A, 1927, Ap 6,27:5
Depuy, H W, 1876, F 6,6:7
De Puy, Harriet Adams, 1917, Jl 17,9:5
De Puy, Harry Wilfred, 1920, Jl 5,9:3
De Puy, Henry F, 1924, O 17,21:3
DePuy, Ketchum M, 1957, N 18,31:5
Depuydt, Martha, 1954, N 8,21:5
De Quarles, Jacob, 1945, Ap 10,19:5
Dequer, Henry H, 1945, D 1,23:6
Dequevauviller, George E, 1943, Je 23,21:2
De Quevedo, Manuel G, 1952, Jl 10,31:2
De Quincy, Thomas, 1859, D 23,4:4
Dequine, Louis E, 1966, Je 5,85:1
Der Brucke, Maurice G, 1958, N 16,88:6
Der Hovhanesian, Tirayre (funl, Ap 5,29:3), 1956, Ap 1,89:2
Der-Yeghiaian, Zaven, 1947, Je 11,27:5
de Raasloff, Harold, 1924, My 28,23:4
de Rahm, Casimir, 1968, Mr 3,88:5
de Rahm, Stephen W, 1961, Jl 8,19:6
De Raimes, Martha F, 1882, Jl 31,8:4
Derain, Andre, 1954, S 11,17:3
de Raismes, Francis E, 1959, Ja 12,39:2
De Raismes, Francis J J Mrs, 1945, Mr 24,17:2
De Raismes, Joseph N, 1940, F 5,17:2
De Raismes, Kathleen B M Mrs, 1942, Ja 12,15:3
De Raismes, May B Mrs, 1937, My 24,19:3
De Raismes, Sophie K Mrs, 1940, My 6,17:3
de Raismes, W Embree, 1964, Jl 16,31:1
Derammelaere, Victor, 1952, N 21,25:3
Deramus, William N, 1965, D 4,31:3
De Randich, George M, 1954, Jl 27,21:2
De Rango, Wilfred D, 1940, D 18,25:4
Derbin, Anthony, 1951, Ap 5,29:2
Derburg, Franz von, 1904, Ja 23,9:5
Derby, A L, 1956, D 26,27:2
Derby, A Lee, 1937, N 16,23:1
Derby, Adolph, 1948, S 10,23:5
Derby, Andrew S, 1947, S 15,17:6
Derby, Arthur L, 1961, Ag 25,25:4
Derby, Ashton P, 1944, Ja 7,17:5
Derby, Aubrey H, 1961, Ag 22,29:4
Derby, Augustin, 1954, My 28,23:4
Derby, Charles F, 1950, N 5,93:1
Derby, Dowager Countess of (Sibyl Louise Beatrix), 1957, Jl 25,23:3
Derby, Earl (funl, N 12,5:4), 1869, O 24,5:3
Derby, Earl of, 1893, Ap 22,9:6
Derby, Earl of (Fredk Arth Stanely), 1908, Je 15,7:4
Derby, Edward A, 1954, My 21,27:2
Derby, Edwin T, 1953, Ap 11,17:4
Derby, Frederic B, 1939, Jl 10,19:4
Derby, Frederick W Dr, 1937, S 5,II,7:2
Derby, George C, 1948, F 20,27:1
Derby, George M, 1948, O 26,32:2
Derby, George W, 1952, S 10,29:4
Derby, Harry L Sr Mrs, 1965, Je 6,85:2
Derby, James L (trb lr), 1961, Ap 26,38:5
Derby, Jane (Mrs P Cuthbert), 1965, Ag 9,25:1
Derby, John A L, 1945, Mr 1,21:2
Derby, John J, 1942, F 5,21:3
Derby, Joseph A, 1938, My 3,23:3
Derby, Lord, 1948, F 5,23:1
Derby, Lucius A, 1942, F 16,17:1
Derby, Richard, 1963, Jl 22,23:1
Derby, Richard C, 1923, F 28,17:3
Derby, Richard Jr (funl, O 5,23:3), 1922, O 4,23:4
Derby, Robert M Mrs, 1957, D 26,19:2
Derby, Roger A, 1949, Je 2,28:5
Derby, S Hasket, 1947, Ap 3,25:3
Derby, Samuel C Prof, 1921, Mr 30,13:6
Derby, Sarah M Mrs, 1939, Mr 17,21:2
Derby, Walter E, 1916, F 15,11:5
Derby, Warren E, 1940, S 5,23:2
Derbyshire, Arthur J, 1943, Jl 3,13:1
Derbyshire, Frederick W, 1948, Ap 19,23:4
Derbyshire, John R, 1963, Jl 17,31:5
Derbyshire, Thomas Mrs, 1956, Ag 24,19:5
Derbyshire, Thoms, 1947, Je 17,25:3
D'Erceville, Stanislas P P, 1954, Ap 14,29:4
Derck, James G, 1956, Je 9,17:3
Dercum, Elizabeth C Mrs, 1942, Je 30,21:3
Dercum, F X, 1931, Ap 24,23:1
Dercum, Susanna E, 1943, Je 11,19:3
Derechin, Michael, 1951, Je 2,19:4
de Redon, John E, 1959, Je 18,31:2
Dereme, Tristan, 1941, O 27,17:2
Deremer, Alfred, 1952, O 18,19:4
Deremer, Earl D, 1948, Ap 19,23:4
Deremer, Howard T, 1955, Ag 30,27:2
De Remusat, Count, 1875, Je 7,1:2
De Remusat, Mrs (funl), 1882, Ag 23,2:3
Deren, Maya, 1961, O 14,23:4
Deren, Solomon D, 1943, Ja 7,19:3
De Renne, Wymberley J, 1916, Je 24,11:7
De Renzis, Michael, 1938, My 10,8:3
De Renzo, Anthony, 1947, Je 5,25:4
Derenzo, Fred, 1917, Jl 28,7:4
de Reszke, Jean, 1925, Ap 29,21:6
de Reuter, George Baron, 1909, N 23,9:4
de Reuter, Oliver Baron, 1968, D 31,27:2
De Revere, F Vance P Mrs, 1938, My 17,23:4
De Revere, Irving, 1951, Ag 16,27:2
de Revuelta, Philip J, 1968, Je 13,47:4
Derevyanko, Kuzma, 1954, D 31,14:6
Derfner, Morton H I, 1958, F 5,28:2
Derfner, Samuel, 1958, D 16,2:6
Dergunov, Alexei P, 1952, D 18,29:1
de Rham, Charles Mrs, 1965, D 26,68:2
de Rham, Frederic F, 1938, S 22,18:6
de Rham, H Casimir, 1916, D 16,13:5
De Rham, Henry C, 1947, Mr 24,25:1
De Rham, Henry C Mrs, 1946, My 19,40:5
Derham, James P, 1956, S 25,33:1
Derham, Joseph, 1951, S 5,31:2
Derham, Philip A, 1962, S 18,39:4
de Rham, William, 1957, F 27,27:2
Deri, Emery, 1959, Mr 21,21:4
De Ribaupierre, Andre, 1955, Ja 18,27:5
Derick, Carrie M. 1941, N 11,23:4
Dericks, Gerard C, 1954, O 19,27:4
Derickson, Samuel H, 1951, N 29,33:5
Deridder, Oliver, 1937, My 1,19:3
De Rienzis, Annibale, 1954, F 6,19:6
Derieux, John B, 1948, Mr 20,13:5
DeRiggi, Raffaele, 1952, Mr 5,29:2
Dering, Harry Ray, 1903, D 1,9:6
Dering, Wladyslaw A, 1965, Jl 14,37:1
Deringer, John P, 1956, Jl 25,29:4
De Ripperda, Frederick M, 1950, Jl 16,69:2
De Ritis, Beniamino, 1956, Ag 13,19:5
De Ritter, Andrew, 1955, Mr 13,87:1
Derivan, Joseph F, 1958, N 10,29:3
Derivan, Thomas J, 1958, Ap 21,23:5
de Rivas, Damaso, 1956, My 30,21:3
Derivaux, C Hubert, 1956, Mr 30,19:3
Derivaux, John A, 1938, My 19,21:3
De Rivera, Edward, 1954, Jl 3,11:6
De Rivera, John Mrs, 1943, Mr 31,19:1
DeRivera, Jose, 1962, Mr 22,35:3
d'Erlander, Gerald, 1962, D 17,15:8
D'Erlanger, Emile B Baron, 1939, Jl 25,19:5
D'Erlanger, Frederic A, 1943, Ap 26,19:4
Derleaux, Samuel A, 1922, F 28,19:1
Derleth, Charles Jr, 1956, Je 14,33:5
Derman, Harry, 1952, Ap 19,15:3
Dermansky, Max, 1951, Ja 20,15:1
Dermody, Edward, 1939, O 31,23:3
Dermody, John J, 1924, F 24,21:3; 1949, Ag 1
Dermody, Joseph L, 1961, Ap 2,77:1
Dermody, Lawrence T, 1947, S 20,15:2
Dermody, Patrick J, 1947, Mr 29,15:2
Dermot, Thomas Capt, 1915, Ja 11,9:4
Dermott, Henry S, 1937, O 8,23:3
Dern, Elizabeth I, 1942, D 16,25:5
Dern, G H, 1936, Ag 28,1:2
Dern, George H Mrs, 1952, S 3,29:4
Dern, H C, 1903, S 9,7:6
Dern, John, 1958, My 23,23:2
Dern, William B, 1947, Ag 5,23:4
Dernburg, Bernhard Dr, 1937, O 16,19:3
Derneburg, Prince, 1902, Mr 30,7:4
De Roaldes, George Mrs, 1951, Mr 9,25:1
DeRoberts, Ernest, 1948, Ja 19,23:5
de Rochefort, Nicholas, 1964, Je 7,87:1
De Rochemont, Louis L G, 1940, D 22,31:3
DeRochemont, Louis L G Mrs, 1946, Jl 17,2
De Rochemont, Max Mrs, 1958, Je 21,19:4

de Rohan, Pierre, 1958, Ag 21,25:5
Deroin, William W, 1948, D 17,27:1
De Roman, Remedios C Mrs, 1952, Ja 25,21:3
Derome, Jules A, 1951, Ja 21,77:1
De Ronde, Abram, 1946, Mr 3,46:3
De Ronde, Abram Mrs, 1943, Je 8,21:5
Deronde, Edgar D, 1947, O 15,27:2
De Ronde, Edgar D Jr, 1950, D 21,29:3
De Ronde, Frank S, 1944, O 31,19:3
DeRonde, Frank S Mrs, 1946, Mr 4,23:5
De Ronde, H Melville, 1938, Ja 27,21:2
De Ronde, Phil, 1950, Je 12,27:5
De Ronde, Walter S, 1940, Mr 3,44:1
De Ronge, Louis Mrs, 1912, Mr 11,13:4
De Roo, Isaac, 1943, Jl 7,19:3
De Roode, Albert V, 1949, Ap 13,29:3
de Ros, Baron, 1907, My 1,9:6
De Rosa, Alfonso, 1960, O 16,88:8
De Rosa, Felix V, 1955, My 19,29:4
De Rosa, Jeremiah, 1945, O 2,23:3
De Rosa, Micheli, 1958, O 3,29:4
De Rosa, Salvator, 1968, Ap 10,47:4
De Rose, Charles A, 1952, Mr 18,27:4
DeRose, Charles A Mrs, 1960, S 24,23:5
DeRose, Charles N Mrs, 1966, Jl 21,33:1
DeRose, Ernest A, 1950, Jl 12,29:2
De Rose, Peter, 1953, Ap 24,23:1
De Rosset, Frederick A Rev, 1915, O 13,15:6
De Rosset, James L, 1953, Jl 20,17:2
De Rossett, William G Mrs, 1949, Ja 24,19:2
de Rothschild, Anthony Mrs, 1910, S 23,13:5
De Rouen, Rene L, 1942, Mr 28,17:6
De Rougement, Rene du T Count, 1940, Mr 29,22:2
Derounian, John B, 1954, Ja 7,31:4
Derouville, George S, 1938, Jl 17,26:5
de Rouville, Hertel, 1916, D 10,21:2
Derow, David, 1943, D 26,32:2
Derr, Andrew F Mrs, 1965, Je 27,65:2
Derr, Carl A, 1953, Ap 30,31:4
Derr, Channing P, 1948, F 20,28:2
Derr, Charles H Mrs, 1938, My 16,17:5
Derr, Charles K, 1950, Ja 13,23:1
Derr, Howard H, 1938, S 5,15:2
Derr, Louis Prof, 1923, My 13,8:2
Derr, Thomas D, 1948, Je 2,29:5
Derra, August G, 1954, My 8,17:4
Derrenbacher, Anthony, 1941, Je 14,17:2
Derres, Henry, 1949, S 1,21:2
Derreydt, Louis, 1953, S 23,31:1
Derrick, Calvin, 1938, N 14,19:6
Derrick, Ira M Rev, 1937, S 29,23:6
Derrick, Joseph T, 1946, Ag 16,21:4
Derrick, Reid Mrs, 1957, Jl 21,61:1
Derrick, W Alton, 1923, My 23,21:4
Derrick, William B Bp, 1913, Ap 16,11:4
Derrick, William E, 1957, My 31,19:4
Derrick, William R, 1941, Ja 11,17:5
Derrick-Swindells, Lucy Mrs, 1952, Ag 15,15:4
Derrickson, Howard J, 1949, Ag 18,21:5
Derrickson, Richard B, 1951, Ag 16,27:2
D'Errico, Corrado, 1941, S 4,21:5
Derrig, Phil F, 1950, My 26,23:6
Derringer, Martin, 1953, Jl 20,17:5
Derringer, Samuel P, 1948, D 28,21:3
Derringer, Theodore, 1874, F 15,1:2
Derry, Charles A, 1941, S 29,17:5
Derry, George H, 1949, Ja 20,27:3
Derry, Harold W, 1948, D 22,23:2
Dersch, Charles, 1938, O 16,45:3
Derse, James H, 1944, S 15,19:4
Dershowitz, Louis, 1955, Ap 10,88:8
Dershuck, John R, 1941, N 13,28:2
Dershuck, William C Mrs, 1946, My 21,23:1
Derso, Aloysius, 1964, D 23,27:1
Derthick, John A, 1945, O 26,19:3
Dertinger, Georg, 1968, Ja 22,47:1
Dertinger, Joseph R, 1951, Jl 26,21:3
De Rudio, C C Maj, 1910, N 2,11:4
De Russey, R E Gen, 1865, N 27,4:1
e Russy, Rene A Maj, 1921, Ja 8,11:5
De Ruyter, John L, 1938, Je 12,39:3
Derval, Paul, 1966, My 16,37:3
Dervieux, Francis, 1940, Mr 25,15:4
Dervin, Francis P, 1957, Ja 17,29:3
Dervin, James P, 1960, N 29,37:5
Dervin, John J, 1967, N 22,47:2
Dervin, John M, 1954, F 18,31:1
Dervin, Joseph J, 1947, S 12,21:2
ervin, Matthew J Mrs, 1941, O 2,25:1
erwent, Clarence (trb, Ag 16,11,1:2), 1959, Ag 7, 23:4
erwent, Elfrida, 1958, Jl 7,27:4
erwent, Lord, 1949, Ja 14,23:5
erwin, John M, 1965, N 6,29:5
erx, Frank, 1952, D 20,17:2
erx, Frank Mrs, 1952, D 20,17:2
ery, D George, 1942, Mr 6,21:4
ery, Louis S, 1958, Je 3,31:3
ery, Rudolph, 1964, O 18,89:2
e Ryka, G Robert, 1945, S 3,31:7
erzhavin, Nikolai S, 1953, F 28,17:4
es Essarts, A S L, 1893, My 30,5:7
es Garennes, Louis P, 1952, My 27,27:1

Des Gouttes, Paul, 1943, Je 21,17:5
Des Graz, Charles G, 1953, Mr 3,27:2
Des Graz, Charles L, 1940, O 25,21:6
Des Hons, Gabriel, 1941, D 8,23:4
Des Jardien, Paul, 1956, Mr 9,23:3
Des Marets, Ernest A, 1914, D 25,11:6
Des Portes, Fay A, 1944, S 18,19:6
Des Rochers, L R, 1942, O 10,15:3
de Sabla, Eugene de J, 1956, Ja 19,33:4
Desai, Bhulabhai J, 1946, My 6,21:5
Desai, Shirajlal B, 1951, Mr 22,31:1
De Saint, Felix Jules, 1874, Je 16,5:6
De Saint Amant Fournier, 1872, D 19,4:4
de Saint-Phalle, Andre, 1967, Ag 18,30:6
De Saint Phalle, F, 1932, Mr 17,24:2
de Saint Phalle, Thibaut Mrs, 1960, Ag 11,27:1
Desaix, Herbert W, 1944, F 3,19:6
De Saldapena, Debraus, 1871, Mr 2,8:2
De Sales, Francis, 1948, Ja 15,23:2
De Sales, Francis Mother, 1940, F 19,17:5
De Salis, John E, 1949, Je 17,23:4
De Salis, John F Count, 1939, Ja 15,38:8
De Salles, Bro, 1939, O 31,23:6
De Salvio, Marie R MRs, 1937, Ja 22,21:4
DeSalvo, Arthur Mrs, 1952, Je 19,27:3
De Sanchez, Dorothy G Mrs, 1941, D 3,25:4
De Sanctis, Adolph G, 1966, F 1,31:3
DeSanctis, Joseph, 1953, S 19,15:5
de Sanno, Albert P Jr, 1960, N 18,31:1
De Santi, Joseph, 1954, N 2,27:4
De Santis, Edward A, 1959, Mr 29,80:2
De Santis, Pasquale, 1953, Ja 1,23:3
deSantos, August R, 1964, Mr 20,33:5
DeSapio, Gerard Mrs (cor on next of kin, O 27,47:5), 1965, O 26,45:4
Desapion, Catherine Mrs, 1950, O 11,33:4
Desatnek, Elias B (por), 1946, O 20,60:2
De Saulles, Arthur Brice Maj, 1917, D 25,15:4
De Saulles, Charles A H, 1962, Jl 18,29:2
de Saulles, Louise Mrs, 1923, Ag 21,17:2
Desaulniers, Esdras, 1951, O 2,27:3
Desaulniers, Joseph A, 1952, Jl 22,25:4
Desaulniers, Lucien L, 1952, Ja 19,15:3
De Saumarez, Baron, 1937, Ap 26,19:6
DeSaussure, Charles A, 1959, O 23,29:4
De Saussure, John, 1945, S 2,31:2
de Sauze, Emile B, 1964, Jl 12,68:2
Desborough, Baron (Wm Hy Grenfell), 1920, D 2, 11:3
Desborough, Ethel Lady, 1952, My 30,15:2
Desborough, Lord, 1945, Ja 11,23:3
Desbrisay, Lucretia, 1948, S 23,29:4
Descalzi, Joseph F, 1956, My 1,33:5
Descaves, Lucien (por), 1949, S 7,29:5
Descelles, Zoel, 1942, N 29,65:2
Desch, George C, 1953, My 18,21:4
Desch, John A, 1945, N 2,20:3; 1966, Ag 6,23:4
Desch, Otto G, 1954, F 8,23:4
de Schaeck, Mary (Baroness), 1966, Je 22,47:2
Deschamps, Alphonse E, 1940, Je 24,15:5
Deschamps, Stephen H, 1967, Ja 19,35:4
Deschamps, V A S, 1883, S 30,1:4
Deschanel, Paul, 1922, Ap 29,15:5
Deschaux, George, 1950, Ja 14,15:4
Deschaux, Joseph, 1950, N 13,28:4
Deschenes, Edgar B, 1946, N 25,27:2
Deschenes, Edmund, 1937, S 29,23:3
Deschere, Paul R, 1964, S 1,35:3
De Schoenholz, Alice Baroness, 1942, Mr 9,19:4
De Schweinitz, George E (por), 1938, Ag 23,17:1
de Schweinitz, George L, 1961, My 15,31:5
De Schweinitz, Paul, 1940, F 9,19:5
Desclee, Aimee, 1874, Mr 28,3:6
Descuffi, Ugo, 1950, N 14,31:2
de Segurola, Andres Mrs, 1961, My 14,86:8
Deseilligny, A N P, 1875, My 3,1:5
Desel, John N Mrs, 1943, Jl 18,35:2
Deselding, Edward F, 1950, Ja 20,6:4
de Selding, Joel S, 1922, Jl 30,26:5
De Selincourt, Ernest, 1943, My 25,23:2
De Selincourt, Hugh, 1951, Ja 22,17:2
Desendorf, Ivan, 1952, Ag 6,21:3
Desenger, William, 1875, D 24,4:6
Deserty, Alex S, 1956, Mr 4,88:2
de Sevelinges, Jean Mrs, 1956, D 24,13:5
de Seversky, Alexander P Mrs (death ruled apparent suicide), 1967, Jl 31,27:2
Desey, Jean, 1960, D 20,33:2
Desfourneaux, Jules, 1951, O 3,20:3
Desgranges, Henry, 1940, Ag 18,37:3
Desgrey, Charles H Mrs, 1949, My 14,29:5
Desgrey, Gustave Jr, 1940, N 28,23:2
Desgrey, Gustave Jr Mrs, 1938, O 10,19:3
Desgrey, Louise H, 1944, D 15,19:2
Desha, Mary, 1911, Ja 30,9:3
Deshaies, Charles J, 1946, Ag 10,13:2
Deshaw, Albert J, 1950, F 4,15:4
De Shay, Jack, 1944, D 13,24:2
De Shazo, John E, 1941, O 20,18:2
Deshazor, Stephen D, 1937, F 16,23:4
De Sheim, Charles, 1941, Je 7,17:6
Deshens, L A, 1881, Ap 16,5:4
de Sherbinin, Andrew G, 1962, Mr 9,19:6

De Sherbinin, Michael J, 1941, Ja 16,21:1
de Sherbinin, William N, 1967, Je 27,39:2
Deshler, Charles D, 1943, Ap 16,22:3
Deshler, Charles F, 1947, My 30,21:1
Deshler, Edward R, 1946, Je 29,19:4
Deshler, James (por), 1938, D 4,61:1
Deshon, G H, 1883, Ja 5,1:7
Deshon, George D Col, 1917, Je 25,11:6
Deshon, George Father, 1903, D 30,2:1
Deshon, Harold D, 1946, Jl 19,19:3
Deshon, Robert Mrs, 1966, Ap 23,31:2
Deshon, William H (Duke), 1937, Jl 9,21:6
De Sibour, Jules H (cor, N 11,23:2), 1938, N 5,19:5
Desiderio, Frank, 1962, O 22,29:4
De Siebenthal, William F, 1948, S 20,25:2
DeSiena, Gerald E Mrs, 1962, F 5,31:4
De Silva, George R, 1942, F 19,19:4
De Silver, Albert, 1924, D 11,23:5
De Silver, Albert Mrs, 1962, Je 2,19:5
de Silver, Carll H, 1913, Mr 11,11:5
De Simeo, Alfred J, 1953, Ag 11,27:5
Desimeo, Antonio, 1947, D 6,15:6
Desimone, D Thomas, 1954, Ap 10,15:4
Desing, Robert W, 1953, D 18,29:1
Desio, Vincent, 1945, Ag 12,40:5
Desjardins, Arthur U, 1964, Ja 18,23:4
Desjardins, Victoria D Mrs, 1941, S 24,23:5
Deslauriers, Anthony, 1956, Ag 20,21:4
Deslauriers, Hermas, 1941, My 29,19:4
Desloge, Firmin V, 1952, My 20,25:3
De Sloovere, Frederick J, 1945, Je 17,26:2
Deslovitsky, dlasimir Maj Gen, 1937, Ja 21,23:2
Deslys, Gaby, 1920, F 12,11:5
De Smedt, Albert, 1950, O 29,93:1
DeSmedt, Frank, 1951, Ja 20,15:5
Desmedt, Joseph P Rev, 1937, Je 29,21:2
deSmitt, Vladimir P, 1965, Jl 20,20:8
Desmond, Arthur W, 1950, D 12,33:5
Desmond, Daniel F, 1945, S 12,25:2
Desmond, Earl D, 1958, My 27,31:4
Desmond, Eleanor, 1949, S 29,29:3
Desmond, Frank B, 1939, O 6,25:5
Desmond, Frank J, 1957, S 29,86:7
Desmond, Helene, 1948, Je 2,29:1
Desmond, James, 1968, Jl 28,64:6
Desmond, James E Mrs, 1958, O 4,21:1
Desmond, James Mrs, 1966, Jl 2,23:5
Desmond, John A, 1950, Ja 10,29:3
Desmond, John J, 1955, N 19,19:4
Desmond, John K, 1952, O 29,29:5
Desmond, John W Mrs, 1964, Ja 13,35:1
Desmond, Joseph G, 1941, D 15,19:3
Desmond, Joseph J, 1942, Je 4,19:2
Desmond, Martin F, 1953, N 6,27:2
Desmond, Mary M Mrs, 1953, S 7,19:2
Desmond, Matthew, 1943, Ag 31,17:6
Desmond, Nora L, 1954, S 3,17:5
Desmond, Patrick, 1942, Jl 2,21:4
Desmond, Robert J (por), 1949, O 5,29:4
Desmond, Shaw, 1960, D 24,15:2
Desmond, Thomas A, 1903, N 26,7:6; 1948, S 20,25:1
Desmond, Walter P Mrs, 1939, S 3,19:1
Desmond, William (por), 1949, N 4,27:3
Desmond, William H, 1941, Ag 19,21:5
Desmond, William J, 1958, Ja 31,22:3
Desmond, William Mrs, 1941, Mr 1,15:3
Desnoes, Alfred M, 1962, Ag 1,31:4
De Sola, B Edward, 1946, My 20,23:4
De Sola, Frederick, 1940, Jl 29,13:5
De Sola, J Charles, 1942, Ag 1,11:6
De Sola, Soloman G Mrs, 1950, Jl 18,30:2
De Sola, Solomon, 1958, Mr 2,89:1
De Solla, J M Rabbi, 1901, Jl 6,7:5
De Somma, Frank L, 1956, S 4,29:3
Desorcy, George O, 1955, F 27,86:4
De Sosiour, Pearl, 1953, Ag 3,17:5
De Sostoa, Carlos, 1941, Jl 29,15:5
De Souchet, A L Dr, 1921, S 22,17:5
DeSousa, George, 1961, My 14,86:5
De Sousa, May. 1948, Ag 12,16:7
De Souza, Barretto Count, 1940, My 14,23:4
Desoye, George, 1905, Ap 22,11:7
Despacher, Jules, 1906, Ja 30,9:6
Despaigne Rivery, Manuel, 1944, Ap 4,21:5
Despard, C J, 1879, My 23,2:7
Despard, Charlotte Mrs, 1939, N 10,23:1
Despard, Clement L, 1957, O 12,19:5
Despard, Douglas C, 1954, Ap 19,23:3
Despard, Frank F, 1952, D 7,88:3
Despard, Walter D, 1923, N 28,17:2
Despau, Sophie Mme, 1867, O 2,2:4
Despecher, Felix J, 1940, Je 11,25:4
Despencer-Robertson, James A, 1942, My 7,19:1
Despiau, Charles, 1946, O 31,25:2
D'Espies, Charles Mrs, 1947, N 2,73:2
D'Espies, James D, 1955, S 12,25:1
Despommiers, E, 1878, Ag 1,3:1
D'Esposito, Joshua, 1954, N 18,33:2
Despradelle, Constant Desire, 1912, S 4,11:3
Despreaux, Frank, 1942, F 14,15:6
Despres, Azarie E C, 1939, D 10,68:4
Despres, Maurice S, 1954, My 3,25:3
Desprez, Mae M Mrs, 1945, S 13,23:3

Despujols, Jean, 1965, Ja 27,35:4
Desrochers, Arthur E, 1951, My 1,29:2
Desrosiers, Francis I, 1956, Jl 22,61:1
Desrosiers, Joseph H, 1909, Ap 25,11:5
Desrosiers, Louis-Delard, 1953, Je 18,29:3
Dessain, A (Canon), 1951, Ag 24,15:5
Dessar, Louis P, 1952, F 16,13:1
Dessar, William Mrs, 1940, N 27,23:4
Dessatoff, Lt (funl), 1871, N 4,8:1
Dessau, Alvin H, 1946, N 24,78:6
Dessau, Alvin H Mrs, 1955, O 11,39:4
Dessau, Benny, 1937, Jl 4,II,7:3
Dessau, F Maude, 1945, Je 30,17:4
Dessau, Frank, 1952, My 7,27:3
Dessau, Frederick I, 1959, F 24,29:2
Dessau, S Henry Dr, 1921, Je 12,22:2
Dessau, Simon, 1904, Ja 12,7:5
Dessauer, Friedrich, 1963, F 18,17:7
Dessauer, Max, 1944, Mr 3,15:5
Dessauer, Norman, 1939, F 18,15:5
Dessauer, S George Mrs, 1942, Je 13,15:3
Dessauer, William, 1943, D 17,27:3
Desseaux, L P, 1881, Ap 4,1:6
D'Essen, Bernard, 1967, My 12,47:2
Dessen, Louis A, 1945, Jl 11,11:5
Dessez, Lester A Mrs, 1956, Ja 9,25:3
Dessez, Paul T, 1940, Ag 30,19:6
Dessino, Constantine, 1940, F 13,23:5
Dession, George H, 1955, Je 21,31:5
D'Essipri, Michael W, 1949, Ag 26,19:4
d'Essling, Prince (Victor Massena), 1910, O 29,11:6
Dessloch, John C, 1955, S 9,23:3
Dessner, Albert L, 1946, Jl 6,15:3
Dessoff, Margarete, 1944, D 2,13:5
Dessoir, Max, 1947, Jl 23,23:6
Dessot, Nathan, 1960, Jl 10,72:4
Dessureault, Masseuire P, 1947, Mr 19,25:3
de St Aubin, Ovide Jr, 1967, N 20,47:2
De St Aubin, Percival, 1940, N 2,15:1
De St. Marcel, E B, 1878, Ja 12,4:7
De Stafani, Joseph Mrs, 1938, Ja 9,42:8
De Stanley, Perce, 1944, S 12,19:4
D'Este, Charles, 1948, Ag 8,56:7
d'Este, Diana, 1955, Ja 26,25:3
d'Este, Julian L, 1964, N 8,88:4
De Stefani, Rafael Esteva, 1922, D 13,21:5
De Stefanis, John, 1949, Je 15,29:3
Destefano, Anthony, 1948, O 26,31:3
De Stefano, Ettore, 1967, Ag 5,23:4
De Stefano, George, 1946, F 16,13:4
Destefano, John, 1959, Jl 9,27:1
De Stefano, Michael, 1944, Mr 9,17:3
DeStefano, Peter A, 1960, N 22,35:5
De Stefano, Thomas A, 1946, Ap 6,17:4
De Stephan, Joseph L, 1959, Ap 20,31:3
De Stephan, Joseph L Mrs, 1961, S 23,19:5
De Stephano, Matthew, 1937, Ja 10,II,10:8
Dester, Thomas R, 1937, Ap 22,23:2
D'Esterhazy, Paul O, 1965, Mr 11,33:1
Desti, Basilio, 1938, D 3,19:3
Destinn, E, 1930, Ja 30,23:1
Destino, Ralph, 1962, Ag 13,25:4
de Stojowska, Marie Jordan, 1925, Ap 5,5:1
Destremps, Victor I, 1937, N 7,II,9:2
Desurney, Frank, 1948, O 6,29:2
Desvarannes, Giorgio P M B, 1943, Je 2,25:1
Desvernine, Eduardo, 1938, Ja 26,23:3
Desvernine, Raoul E, 1966, Je 3,39:4
Desvernine, Raoul F, 1943, N 10,23:2
de Swaan, Abraham, 1955, Ap 4,29:4
de Sylva, Elena D, 1955, Je 16,31:4
DeSylva, George G (Buddy), 1950, Jl 12,29:1
de Szunyogh, Andre, 1960, D 16,33:2
Detaille, Jean Baptiste Edouard, 1912, D 25,11:5
De Tarnowsky, George, 1942, Ja 22,17:4
Detchon, Seymour, 1938, N 18,21:2
De Tegettoff, Vice-Adm (mem ser), 1871, My 2,6:1
Deter, Harry R, 1949, S 4,41:1
Deterding, Henri (will, Je 20,19:3), 1939, F 5,41:1
Detering, Edward F, 1950, S 16,19:5
de Thebes, A Mrs, 1916, D 27,9:3
Dethier, Edouard, 1962, F 21,41:3
Dethloff, Edward C, 1948, My 11,25:4
Dethloff, Walter J, 1949, Mr 26,17:5
De Thulstrup, T de, 1930, Je 10,27:1
De Thygeson, M, 1905, Ap 1,2:2
Detierre, Elmer F, 1947, F 17,19:4
De Tillancourt, Marquis, 1880, D 28,5:4
de Tirrio Tarter, Mary Mrs, 1956, Je 6,33:3
Detjen, William E, 1951, Je 17,84:3
Detjens, John, 1947, Jl 30,21:2
Detlef, William C, 1968, S 14,28:3
Detlef, William Mrs, 1964, Ja 19,76:7
Detlefsen, Enevold O, 1954, Jl 5,11:5
Detlefsen, George A, 1954, S 16,29:2
Detlor, William E, 1947, N 4,25:4
Detmer, Howard F, 1954, Ap 24,17:6
Detmer, Julian F, 1958, N 27,29:2
Detmold, George J Mrs, 1964, Jl 7,35:2
de Transehe, Nicholas A, 1960, D 29,25:4
d'Etreillis, Jeanne B Mrs, 1957, Je 26,31:5
Detreville, Davis D, 1939, Ja 20,19:1
De Treville, Yvonne, 1954, Ja 27,27:5
Detrich, A Nevin, 1946, Ap 30,21:2
Detrick, Charles R, 1954, Ja 10,86:1
Detrick, Christian H, 1950, N 23,35:3
Detrick, E, 1884, Mr 1,2:1
Detrick, Myron H, 1951, S 29,17:4
de Trobriant, Baron, 1885, My 27,5:5
Detroit, J, 1878, S 23,5:4
Detroyat, Michel, 1956, O 6,21:3
Dett, Robert N, 1943, O 4,17:2
Dette, William, 1924, D 4,21:4; 1924, D 7,7:2
Dettelbach, Morris, 1922, Je 12,15:6
Detterer, Ernest F, 1947, N 11,27:2
Dettinger, Elfrieda von E Mrs, 1960, Jl 2,17:3
Dettloff, Adolph M, 1961, S 2,15:4
Dettmer, John, 1940, F 10,15:3
Dettmer, Justus G, 1940, Jl 17,21:5
Dettmers, Frederick O, 1956, Ag 8,25:4
De Turo, Patrick J Jr, 1959, Jl 9,27:4
Detweiler, Charles S, 1962, S 26,39:1
Detweiler, Charles W, 1963, My 12,86:1
Detweiler, Frederick G, 1960, Ap 2,23:5
Detweiler, George H, 1953, Mr 8,91:2
Detweiler, Oscar L, 1939, S 30,17:5
Detweiler, W H, 1903, S 1,1:3
Detwiler, Benjamin H, 1956, Je 8,25:4
Detwiler, Charles H, 1950, D 5,32:6
Detwiler, Howard J, 1951, Jl 9,25:6
Detwiler, Paul B, 1940, Ap 4,23:5
Detwiler, Samuel R, 1957, My 5,21:6
Detwiler, W Sanderson, 1947, O 26,68:4
Detwiler, William F, 1950, S 6,29:5
Detwiller, Charles H, 1940, Mr 23,13:5
Detwiller, Frederick K, 1953, S 21,25:3
Detwyler, William H Mrs, 1944, S 17,42:1
Detzer, Laura Mrs, 1954, Ap 18,89:2
d'Eu, Count, 1922, Ag 30,15:5
d'Eu, Isabel Countess, 1921, N 15,19:4
Deubert, George T, 1960, Mr 20,86:7
Deubert, John G, 1918, Jl 23,13:5
Deuchar, Edwin R, 1964, O 22,35:4
Deuchler, Conrad, 1943, O 23,13:5
d'Eudeville, Alain Count, 1956, Jl 10,31:1
Deuel, Alanson C (will, O 23,10:6), 1954, O 2,30:1
Deuel, Earl Sr, 1949, N 10,32:2
Deuel, Harry J Jr, 1956, Ap 18,31:5
Deuel, Jacob B, 1950, Je 1,27:1
Deuel, Joseph M, 1920, D 5,22:4
Deuel, Kenneth P, 1948, S 23,39:4
Deuel, Samuel, 1949, D 2,29:3
Deuell, Harvey V, 1939, O 30,17:3
Deuerlein, Frederick F, 1946, My 7,21:6
Deuerling, Harry, 1951, N 13,29:2
D'Eufemia, Thomas, 1946, Jl 8,29:4
Deupree, William J, 1953, S 2,25:3
Deuscher, Theodore J, 1939, Je 15,23:3
Deussen, Paul Prof, 1919, Jl 10,15:3
Deuster, Oscar V, 1944, S 26,23:5
Deutch, Jay W, 1965, Je 27,64:6
Deutch, Samuel, 1948, O 20,29:1
Deutch, Zola G, 1965, My 6,39:2
Deute, Arthur H, 1946, F 4,25:3
Deuterman, Joel E, 1955, Ag 8,21:1
Deuth, Eugene Mrs Baroness, 1955, O 13,32:1
Deutsch, Adolph Mrs, 1951, Ag 1,23:5
Deutsch, Albert (funl Je 26,31:2), 1961, Je 19,27:4
Deutsch, Albert, 1966, Ag 27,29:4
Deutsch, Albert L Dr, 1968, N 18,47:4
Deutsch, Alcuin, 1951, My 14,25:6
Deutsch, Allan, 1938, Mr 19,15:2
Deutsch, B S, 1935, N 22,1:8
Deutsch, Bernard S (will), 1938, D 22,2:8
Deutsch, Edward, 1967, F 16,39:1
Deutsch, Emil, 1959, D 21,27:3
Deutsch, Eric H, 1956, D 4,17:4
Deutsch, Estelle, 1937, D 10,26:1
Deutsch, F, 1928, My 20,25:1
Deutsch, Fritz, 1958, My 18,87:2
Deutsch, George M, 1944, Ja 14,19:5
Deutsch, Gotthard (funl, O 16,22:3), 1921, O 15,13:5
Deutsch, Harry S, 1939, F 2,19:3
Deutsch, Henry de la Meurthe, 1919, N 25,11:4
Deutsch, Herman, 1961, O 27,33:1
Deutsch, Herschel Z, 1962, Ja 29,25:4
Deutsch, John T, 1950, Mr 11,7:8
Deutsch, Joseph, 1954, Mr 13,15:5
Deutsch, Joseph J, 1952, Mr 11,27:2
Deutsch, Joseph Mrs, 1958, Mr 8,17:5
Deutsch, Julius, 1968, Ja 19,44:1
Deutsch, Lee, 1959, D 19,27:4
Deutsch, Leonard, 1952, F 25,21:2
Deutsch, Martin M, 1962, F 3,21:2
Deutsch, Maurice, 1957, Je 21,25:2
Deutsch, Max, 1948, D 16,29:3
Deutsch, Milton, 1966, Ap 17,87:1
Deutsch, Monroe E, 1955, O 22,19:5
Deutsch, Morris, 1951, Ap 5,29:5
Deutsch, Oscar, 1941, D 6,17:6
Deutsch, Paul A, 1947, D 13,15:2
Deutsch, Raymond I, 1955, Mr 1,25:2
Deutsch, Rudolph, 1944, Ap 25,23:2
Deutsch, Samuel, 1925, Jl 27,13:4
Deutsch, Sidney D, 1961, O 21,21:2
Deutsch, Sylvan D, 1949, Ag 9,26:2
Deutsch, Viola, 1949, D 6,32:4
Deutsch de la Meurthe, Suzanne Mlle, 1937, N 30,23:1
Deutschbein, Harry J, 1942, F 9,15:2
Deutschberger, Leopold, 1941, Jl 10,19:3
Deutscher, Isaac, 1967, Ag 20,88:1
Deutschman, David, 1957, O 21,25:4
Deutschmann, Paul J, 1963, My 4,25:1
Deutsher, Louis, 1954, F 26,19:5
Deutz, Arthur, 1968, O 19,37:2
Deutz, Herbert J, 1947, Je 5,25:2
Deva, Narendra, 1956, F 20,23:6
DeVadder, Emil, 1965, Je 20,72:5
De Vadder, Henry, 1953, F 4,27:5
Devahastin, Phya, 1951, Jl 8,61:3
De Valera, Vivion Mrs, 1951, Je 20,27:5
De Valin, Hugh, 1942, F 4,20:2
De Vallant, Francis L, 1958, Je 7,19:3
De Valles, John B Rev, 1920, My 13,11:4
de Vallombrosa, Louis M, 1959, Mr 19,34:1
De Valmont, Mme, 1873, O 12,5:3
De Valstedt, John M, 1951, S 1,11:4
Devambez, Andre, 1944, Mr 29,21:4
Devan, Samuel A, 1951, My 5,17:1
Devan, Spencer C Mrs, 1949, Je 13,19:5
Devan, William Capt, 1911, My 7,II,11:4
De Van, William T, 1942, Mr 14,15:2
DeVane, William C, 1965, Ag 17,33:4
Devaney, Ann Mrs, 1939, Ap 25,23:2
Devaney, Helen (Sister Mary Veronica), 1951, N 4, 87:2
Devaney, Howard J Mrs, 1950, Jl 11,31:3
Devaney, James, 1949, N 2,27:4
Devaney, John J, 1955, Ja 8,13:6
Devaney, John P, 1941, S 22,15:1
Devaney, Leo M, 1951, Mr 28,29:1
Devaney, Thomas F, 1941, O 15,21:1
Devanney, Mary M, 1956, Jl 29,65:1
De Vanny, David A Dr, 1937, S 5,II,7:1
Devanny, Earl H, 1962, Ap 24,37:2
Devanny, W Ernest, 1947, O 16,27:2
Devans, Edward J, 1950, F 24,23:2
Devant, David, 1941, O 14,23:5
Devany, John A, 1943, O 7,23:1; 1966, S 11,86:8
Devany, John E, 1938, N 4,23:5
Devare, Carl Pricelius, 1913, Ja 1,17:4
Devau, Jean, 1950, Ja 23,23:2
De Vaugrigneus, Baroness A, 1904, Ap 23,9:5
Devaul, John N, 1946, My 7,21:6
Devault, Margaretta Mrs, 1942, Ja 27,21:4
De Vausney, Clifford, 1947, Ap 29,27:3
de Vausney, Louis N, 1967, N 14,47:1
de Vausney, Louis N Mrs, 1957, N 19,33:3
Devaux, J Walter, 1952, Jl 27,57:1
Deveau, Frederic J, 1958, Ap 20,84:2
De Veau, John G, 1949, F 24,23:2
De Veau, John G Mrs, 1948, O 28,29:2
De Veau, Samuel Mrs, 1950, D 13,35:1
De Veaux, Edward F, 1946, Je 14,21:3
De Veaux, Lyle, 1964, Ag 7,29:2
De Vecchi, Margherita, 1965, Mr 24,43:4
De Vecchi, P, 1931, My 31,25:5
De Vecchi, Paola Mrs, 1954, My 15,15:5
DeVecchi, Robert, 1967, N 20,47:3
Devecmon, William C, 1939, My 25,25:4
de Vegh, Geza Mrs, 1966, N 23,39:3
de Vegh, Imrie, 1962, F 4,82:1
de Vegvar, Alfred N Mrs, 1956, Ag 25,15:2
Develin, J E, 1888, F 24,8:3
Develle, Jules, 1919, N 1,11:5
Devendorf, Earl, 1960, D 29,25:3
Devendorf, Frederick C, 1946, My 6,21:4
Devendorf, Ralph M, 1940, Mr 27,21:3
Deveneau, George A, 1939, F 4,15:3
Deveney, James J, 1956, Ag 6,23:5
Devens, Arthur L, 1957, Ap 15,29:3
Devens, W George, 1946, Jl 14,38:4
Deveny, Thomas, 1953, Ja 23,19:3
Dever, Bernard F, 1951, Ja 15,17:4
Dever, Edward J, 1955, Mr 8,27:4
Dever, Edward J Jr, 1961, N 23,31:5
Dever, Francis J, 1944, D 31,25:2
Dever, George M Sr, 1954, N 15,27:4
Dever, James E, 1937, F 14,II,9:1
Dever, James J, 1942, S 9,23:2
Dever, John B, 1950, D 31,43:1
Dever, John F, 1960, F 7,84:6
Dever, Joseph P, 1952, Ag 20,25:5
Dever, Katherine C Mrs, 1939, Ag 31,19:3
Dever, Marie, 1959, F 15,86:4
Dever, Patrick H, 1944, Jl 19,19:4
Dever, Paul A, 1958, Ap 12,19:1
Dever, Roger, 1948, My 20,29:1
Dever, William E, 1929, S 4,29:3
Devera, Udo (U Lindeman), 1949, Ap 1,50:8
Deverall, Frank A, 1953, O 17,15:2
Deverall, William A, 1960, Mr 1,33:3
Deverall, William G, 1961, S 28,41:2
Deveraux, May (Mrs Edw McEwen), 1925,
21:3
De Vere, Aubrey, 1902, Ja 22,9:3
Devere, Frederick H Mrs, 1953, My 23,15:5
De Vere, James J Mrs, 1951, Mr 11,92:1
Devere, Mildred (Mrs T Terriss), 1964, Ja 4,

Devere, Samuel, 1907, Mr 2,9:6
Devereaux, Eugene, 1955, Ag 13,13:1
Devereaux, Horace K, 1937, Ag 25,21:2
Devereaux, J French Maj, 1920, F 20,15:4
Devereaux, Jack, 1958, Ja 20,23:2
Devereaux, Jack Mrs, 1954, Ap 25,87:4
Devereaux, Thomas G, 1961, Mr 28,35:1
Devereaux, Walter Bourchier, 1923, Ag 10,11:3
Devereaux, William C, 1941, Jl 7,15:4
Deverell, Anthony S, 1940, D 29,24:5
Deverell, Cyril, 1947, My 13,25:4
Devereux, Anthony J A, 1940, D 20,25:1
Devereux, Anthony J A (will), 1941, Ja 28,21:7
Devereux, Charles W, 1951, N 22,31:3
Devereux, Charles W Mrs, 1958, Ag 22,21:4
Devereux, Edward M, 1938, Ja 16,II,8:7
Devereux, F Ramsay, 1963, N 15,32:5
Devereux, George F, 1951, Ja 26,23:2
Devereux, Harvey C, 1958, My 14,33:4
Devereux, James A, 1950, Jl 23,56:2
Devereux, James P S Mrs (por), 1942, Jl 24,19:1
Devereux, John R Mrs, 1944, O 28,15:2
Devereux, Marion, 1948, O 12,25:3
Devereux, Michael F, 1950, D 3,89:1
Devereux, Nicholas E, 1943, My 10,19:4
Devereux, Thomas J, 1942, Ag 12,19:5
Devereux, W K, 1927, D 19,23:5
Devereux, Walter B Mrs, 1959, My 6,39:4
Devereux, William, 1951, Ja 3,27:2
Devereux, William G, 1955, S 17,15:5
Deverman, Harry, 1964, Ja 28,31:3
De Vernon, Frank, 1923, O 20,15:4
De Vernon, Gustave D, 1875, Ap 7,2:3
Devery, James J, 1964, D 13,86:6
Devery, John J Sgt, 1937, Ja 21,35:3
Devery, John J Sr, 1940, O 12,17:6
Devery, Joseph A, 1961, Je 17,21:3
Devery, William S (funl, Je 23,13:4), 1919, Je 22,15:4
Devestern, George A, 1943, D 8,23:2
De Veze, Camille, 1945, D 20,23:4
Devi, Ratan (Mrs F Bitter), 1958, Jl 15,25:5
De Viana, Marquis, 1927, Ap 6,27:3
De Victor, Oliver J, 1962, S 2,56:7
Devienne, 1883, Jl 27,3:7
Devigne, Henri, 1942, D 14,23:2
De Vilbiss, Jess C, 1946, N 30,15:2
Deville, Etienne S, 1944, Mr 29,21:5
Deville, S G C, 1881, Jl 2,5:2
De Villeneuve, M, 1874, My 11,1:5
De Villeroy, Nicholas, 1949, D 25,26:4
De Villers, Rod C, 1950, Ap 17,23:1
de Villiers, Rudolph R, 1955, Ja 22,11:3
De Villon, Blanche, 1914, S 15,11:5
Devin, Edward T (funl), 1962, Ja 6,19:5
Devin, Francis A, 1958, Jl 17,27:1
Devin, H Gen (see also Ap 5), 1878, Ap 7,12:2
Devin, William A, 1959, F 19,31:5
Devine, Andrew, 1909, My 5,11:6
Devine, Bessie O, 1946, O 11,23:4
Devine, Charles E, 1937, Mr 30,23:5
Devine, Charles F, 1945, Je 24,22:3
Devine, Christopher J, 1963, My 11,25:2
Devine, Dennis J, 1949, Mr 13,76:5
Devine, Edward T, 1948, F 28,15:3
Devine, Edwin K, 1950, Ap 13,29:4
Devine, Eugene J Sr, 1967, S 20,47:3
Devine, Francis E, 1961, Ap 20,33:3
Devine, Frank, 1957, N 19,33:4
Devine, Frank L, 1937, N 2,25:4
Devine, George, 1966, Ja 21,47:2
Devine, George S, 1943, Mr 1,19:2
Devine, Georgia P, 1955, F 17,27:3
Devine, Grace, 1937, O 6,25:2
Devine, Harry J, 1942, Ap 28,21:4
Devine, Henry, 1940, My 4,17:4
Devine, James, 1941, Ag 5,19:2
Devine, James A, 1948, My 11,25:5
Devine, James J, 1958, N 18,37:3
Devine, James Rev, 1918, Je 11,11:5
Devine, Joe, 1951, S 23,87:1
Devine, John B, 1941, O 11,17:3
Devine, John C A, 1940, F 22,23:4
Devine, John F, 1940, Mr 8,21:3; 1952, Ap 11,23:1; 1967, O 19,47:1
Devine, John J, 1943, My 4,23:5; 1948, S 25,17:4
Devine, John M, 1959, Mr 2,27:2
Devine, John M Mrs, 1953, Ja 15,27:4
Devine, John P Sr, 1949, Ja 10,25:5
Devine, John T, 1914, Ag 11,9:6
Devine, Joseph, 1948, Ag 5,21:6; 1956, Je 23,17:5
Devine, Leo A, 1964, D 7,35:3
Devine, Lester B, 1951, D 9,90:5
Devine, Luke J, 1941, Ja 6,15:1
Devine, Margaret Mrs, 1945, D 2,46:2
Devine, Mark A Jr, 1950, O 26,31:3
Devine, Michael A, 1941, S 24,23:5
Devine, Michael P Mrs, 1950, Je 9,23:2
De Vine, Nelson R D Mrs, 1949, F 1,25:5
Devine, Patrick F, 1949, My 31,23:5
Devine, Patrick J, 1947, Ja 25,17:5
Devine, Patrick Mrs, 1944, D 28,19:1
Devine, Peter J, 1948, Jl 17,16:3
Devine, Robert F, 1946, My 22,21:1
Devine, Robert L, 1948, F 22,49:1
Devine, Roger L, 1948, D 27,21:2
Devine, Sarah Q Mrs, 1938, Ag 27,13:4
Devine, Thomas, 1957, Ap 3,31:1
Devine, William A, 1962, Ja 8,39:4
Devine, William E, 1954, N 10,33:2
Devine, William J, 1940, S 6,21:3; 1958, O 12,86:4
Devine, William M, 1948, My 1,15:4
Devine, William P, 1937, O 2,21:1
De Vinne, Charles D, 1951, Ag 11,11:4
De Vinne, Daniel Dr, 1883, F 15,8:4
De Vinne, Jessie A, 1953, My 26,29:5
De Vinne, Theodore, 1914, F 17,11:5
Devinney, Albert N, 1952, F 1,21:2
Devins, James F, 1941, Mr 31,15:5
Devins, John B Rev Dr (mem, O 7,13:6), 1911, Ag 27,II,9:5
Deviny, John J, 1955, F 11,23:1
De Virgin, Eric, 1950, My 14,106:5
Devisser, Eugene Mrs, 1960, F 11,29:1
De Visser, Simon, 1875, Ja 18,4:7
de Visser, William M, 1923, D 5,19:4
de Vitalis, Attillio Prof, 1925, D 16,25:4
De Vitis, Italo, 1956, Ap 8,84:3
Devito, A Alfred, 1943, Ag 1,39:2
Devito, Anthony, 1949, D 7,31:3
De Vito, Dominick, 1952, Ap 14,19:4
De Vito, James J, 1951, Je 23,15:6
De Vito, Joseph, 1949, Je 28,27:1
Devito, Joseph, 1950, N 25,13:5
de Vitre, Barbara D, 1960, Ag 12,19:5
Devitt, Alan, 1955, Ja 30,85:2
Devitt, Cornelius F Mrs, 1952, Jl 12,13:3
Devitt, E Eugene, 1903, Jl 29,3:1
Devitt, Edward I Rev, 1920, Ja 27,15:3
Devitt, Ellis K, 1958, N 6,75:4
Devitt, Marion E, 1944, Ja 11,19:1
DeVitt, William, 1948, My 22,15:5
Devitt, William H, 1946, D 1,76:2
DeVitte, Leopold, 1952, My 9,23:5
De Vivo, Henry J M, 1953, F 20,19:3
De Vlieg, Ray A, 1953, O 17,15:1
Devlin, Albert Sr Mrs, 1967, Ag 10,37:4
Devlin, Arthur, 1948, S 19,76:5
Devlin, Arthur Mrs, 1948, Ag 17,22:3
Devlin, Charles, 1881, F 2,8:4
Devlin, Charles A, 1961, Jl 25,28:1
Devlin, Charles F Sr, 1952, O 21,29:4
Devlin, Daniel, 1867, F 23,3:3
Devlin, Denis, 1959, Ag 22,17:1
Devlin, Edward A, 1938, Je 28,19:6
Devlin, Edward I, 1952, Ja 24,27:5; 1959, Ag 14,21:4
Devlin, Edward J, 1949, Jl 17,58:3
Devlin, Francis M, 1953, F 13,21:2
Devlin, Frank, 1940, F 24,13:6
Devlin, Frank B, 1957, N 14,33:3
Devlin, Fred E, 1946, Mr 14,25:5
Devlin, George M, 1959, N 5,35:3
Devlin, Gerald A, 1964, Mr 19,33:1
Devlin, J, 1934, Ja 19,19:3
Devlin, J H Dr, 1864, Ap 6,1:4
Devlin, James, 1924, Ag 6,13:4
Devlin, James E Jr, 1964, My 7,37:4
Devlin, James J, 1954, Ag 1,84:2; 1965, My 28,33:2
Devlin, James L, 1943, Ja 12,23:2
Devlin, James M, 1952, Ag 14,23:3
Devlin, James M Mrs, 1952, D 22,25:2
Devlin, James V, 1948, Je 5,15:3
Devlin, John A, 1941, Ag 1,15:2
Devlin, John C, 1954, D 23,19:4; 1965, Ag 28,17:3
Devlin, John F Mrs, 1940, N 12,23:2; 1964, Mr 16,25:2
Devlin, John H, 1967, Jl 21,31:4
Devlin, Joseph A, 1949, N 5,14:3
Devlin, Joseph C, 1959, Ap 11,21:4
Devlin, Joseph S J, 1946, D 29,37:5
Devlin, Louis T, 1958, Mr 28,25:2
Devlin, M Virginia, 1954, N 7,89:1
Devlin, Margaret E, 1957, O 16,35:3
Devlin, Matthew J, 1960, F 27,19:6
Devlin, Robert J, 1912, Je 27,13:5
Devlin, Ruth, 1947, Jl 15,23:5
Devlin, Samuel J, 1941, O 15,21:2
Devlin, Thomas F, 1952, Jl 2,25:3
Devlin, William (funl, S 28,9:5), 1911, S 25,9:5
Devlin, William, 1938, Jl 22,17:4
Devlin, William A Mrs, 1947, S 28,61:2
Devlin, William F, 1949, S 16,27:2
Devlin, William J, 1954, N 7,88:1; 1961, Ja 9,39:4
Devlin, William T, 1952, Jl 10,31:4
Devoe, A N, 1881, My 10,5:3
Devoe, Alan, 1955, Ag 19,19:1
Devoe, Albert E, 1954, N 28,87:2
De Voe, Andrew Jackson (funl, Ja 27,13:3), 1925, Ja 26,17:3
Devoe, Clifford A, 1945, Ja 29,13:5
De Voe, Fred W, 1966, O 11,47:2
Devoe, Frederick William, 1913, Mr 22,13:5
De Voe, George W, 1944, Ja 21,17:2
De Voe, Harold S, 1952, Jl 12,13:5
De Voe, Harry A, 1945, S 27,21:4
De Voe, J Herbert Mrs, 1944, F 8,15:4
De Voe, John H, 1941, O 17,23:3
Devoe, John J Mrs, 1951, O 30,29:4
De Voe, John M, 1946, Ja 21,23:5
DeVoe, Mary A Mrs, 1940, Ag 31,13:3
DeVoe, Ralph G, 1966, Jl 30,25:1
Devoe, Robert W, 1957, D 2,27:3
DeVoe, Stephen J, 1951, Ag 31,15:4
Devoe, William B, 1951, Je 12,29:5
Devoe, Zeno J, 1938, F 24,19:5
Devoge, John D, 1951, F 20,25:3
De Vogue, Marquis, 1916, N 11,9:3
Devol, Edmund, 1956, Ag 28,27:2
De Voll, Frederick V, 1946, N 30,15:5
Devon, Earl of Rev, 1904, Ja 30,9:5
DeVoney, John B, 1944, Ag 6,38:2
Devons, Ely, 1967, D 30,23:4
Devonshire, Dogwager Duchess of, 1960, Ap 4,29:1
Devonshire, Dowager Duchess (Louise Frederika Augusta von Alten), 1911, Jl 16,II,9:1
Devonshire, Duke of, 1938, My 7,15:4
Devonshire, Duke of (E W S Cavendish), 1950, N 27,25:1
Devoore, Ann (Mrs R P Walden), 1962, My 26,25:5
Devore, Charles A, 1958, Ja 14,30:5
DeVore, Harry S, 1947, O 16,28:2
Devore, Helen S Mrs (will), 1960, Jl 30,13:8
Devore, Hugh J Mrs, 1945, N 2,20:2
Devore, Hugh J Sr, 1952, N 13,31:3
Devore, John H, 1951, O 9,29:4
Devore, Josh, 1954, O 7,23:4
Devore, Leland S, 1939, Ja 17,22:2
Devore, Sy, 1966, Jl 12,43:1
Devorin, Robert M, 1967, My 3,45:3
De Vos, Augustus R, 1956, N 1,39:3
De Vos, Emmanuel, 1921, F 24,13:6
DeVos, Leon, 1960, Jl 6,33:2
De Voto, Bernard A (funl, N 16,35:1), 1955, N 14,1:1
Devou, William P, 1937, D 9,25:1
Devoy, C S, 1933, Ag 2,13:3
Devoy, Harold E, 1951, Ag 21,27:4
Devoy, J, 1928, S 30,II,8:3; 1928, O 3,31:5
De Voy, John J Mrs, 1945, F 23,18:2
Devoy, John William, 1918, Ag 20,9:5
Devoy, Joseph M, 1956, D 19,31:2
Devraigne, Louis, 1946, Mr 24,46:2
Devree, Howard, 1966, F 10,37:1
De Vries, Enrico M, 1953, Ja 24,15:2
de Vries, Hendrick, 1957, D 3,35:2
De Vries, Hendrik Pieter, 1919, D 16,13:3
Devries, Herman, 1949, Ag 25,23:1
De Vries, John H, 1939, F 5,41:3
De Vries, John L, 1951, S 7,29:4
DeVries, Joseph C, 1941, Jl 30,17:3
De Vries, Marion, 1939, S 13,25:3
Devries, Theodore, 1949, Mr 16,27:3
De Vries, Tobias Mrs, 1956, Jl 8,64:4
De Vries, Van Buren W, 1968, Ap 11,45:1
De Vries, William L Rev, 1937, Mr 15,23:1
De Vry, Herman, 1941, Mr 24,17:2
Dew, Caroline W Mrs, 1946, Mr 20,23:3
Dew, Frederick W, 1941, Mr 11,23:3
Dew, J Harry, 1951, D 25,31:2
Dew, James Harvie Dr, 1914, Ja 27,9:6
Dew, Robert W, 1948, My 13,25:3
Dew, Thomas R Sr, 1961, Ag 12,17:5
Dew, W Braxton, 1962, Je 13,41:3
Dew, Walter, 1947, D 17,30:3
Dewaal, Janie T Mrs, 1951, Ap 30,21:4
De Waele, Jules Jr, 1939, Ag 1,19:4
De Wagstaffe, William, 1925, D 19,17:5
de Wahl, Anders, 1956, Mr 10,17:3
De Wailly, Jules, 1875, Mr 15,2:1
DeWald, Bertha, 1953, Ap 10,21:3
De Wald, Charles E, 1950, Ap 22,19:4
De Wald, Ernest T Dr, 1968, O 7,47:4
De Walden, Lord, 1946, N 6,23:3
De Walden, T B, 1873, S 27,4:7
De Walsh, Charles F, 1958, Ap 22,33:4
Dewalt, Charles R Sr, 1953, Ja 21,31:3
De Walt, Raymond E, 1961, My 9,39:1
De Waltoff, Dayve B, 1947, Je 20,19:4
Dewan, Edmond M, 1952, D 20,17:3
De Wan, Martin F, 1947, Ag 23,13:3
Dewan, Philip Gerald (cor, N 10,88:7), 1968, N 9, 33:5
Dewane, William A, 1937, O 10,II,8:3
Dewar, Alec M, 1949, Ag 19,17:1
Dewar, Alex C, 1938, N 20,39:3
Dewar, Arnold, 1951, Mr 15,29:2
Dewar, Charles E, 1944, D 16,15:5
Dewar, Charles V, 1945, Ja 26,21:4
Dewar, George K, 1949, F 19,15:6
Dewar, Harry B, 1945, Ap 14,15:4
Dewar, James Sir, 1923, Mr 28,19:4
Dewar, John A, 1954, Ag 18,29:4
Dewar, Lord, 1930, Ap 12,19:5
Dewar, Michael U, 1950, D 24,35:1
Dewar, Peter M (will, Ag 9,11:1), 1947, Je 5,25:1
De Ward, Dolores B Mrs, 1939, N 6,23:5
Dewart, Clement V, 1954, F 1,23:4
Dewart, Herbert Hartley, 1924, Jl 8,19:4
Dewart, Hugh (por), 1949, Mr 14,19:4
Dewart, William, 1914, Mr 31,11:4
Dewart, William H, 1941, Mr 29,15:4
Dewart, William H Mrs, 1944, F 24,15:1

Dewart, William T, 1944, Ja 28,1:2
Dewart, William T Jr Mrs, 1946, My 8,25:6
Dewart, William T Mrs, 1958, Ap 8,29:4
De Waters, George M, 1943, Mr 2,19:4
de Watteville, Roland A, 1959, Je 24,31:4
Dewees, Lovett, 1965, Ja 17,88:3
Dewees, Theodore J, 1942, F 4,19:4
De Weese, Archibald Prewitt, 1968, Ag 2,33:2
Deweese, Charles E Mrs, 1953, Je 29,29:5
Deweese, Truman A Mrs, 1953, Je 9,27:1
De Weir, Frank H, 1940, My 10,23:5
Deweke, August, 1945, O 9,21:2
Dewell, Burdette G, 1943, Ja 13,23:4
Dewell, John H, 1961, My 31,33:2
Dewer, William H Mrs, 1946, N 10,63:5
De Wet, Christian Rudolf Gen, 1922, F 6,13:4
de Wet, Nicolaas J, 1960, Mr 17,33:2
De Wetter, Herman, 1950, Je 27,29:3
Dewey, Albert B Sr, 1967, F 17,37:2
Dewey, Alex G, 1953, My 5,29:6
Dewey, Arthur Waldo, 1917, Ja 27,9:3
Dewey, Charles A, 1946, D 15,77:6; 1958, Mr 3,27:3
Dewey, Charles A Judge, 1866, Ag 26,5:5; 1908, Mr 23,7:7
Dewey, Charles M, 1937, Ja 19,23:5
Dewey, Charles Mrs, 1905, O 5,1:6
Dewey, Charles Oliver Dr, 1914, Ag 18,9:6
Dewey, Charles S Mrs, 1957, D 14,21:3
Dewey, Davis R (por), 1942, D 14,23:1
Dewey, Diantha L, 1951, Ja 17,27:3
Dewey, E W, 1903, Ja 17,9:4
Dewey, Edward H, 1945, Ja 3,17:4
Dewey, Elvera, 1950, D 20,31:3
Dewey, F H, 1933, Ap 21,18:1
Dewey, Fred S, 1945, My 28,19:3
Dewey, Frederick, 1944, Je 21,19:2
Dewey, Frederick A, 1967, Jl 29,25:5
Dewey, Frederick Hall, 1925, Ja 15,21:6
Dewey, G Mrs, 1931, F 22,19:1
Dewey, George A Jr, 1957, My 1,37:5
Dewey, George A Mrs, 1949, N 4,27:4
Dewey, George F, 1950, Jl 28,21:6
Dewey, George G, 1963, F 13,9:3
Dewey, George M Mrs (funl, N 27,13:5), 1954, N 25,29:1
Dewey, George W, 1951, F 18,76:4
Dewey, H H, 1933, O 26,19:1
Dewey, Harriet M, 1937, S 19,II,6:6
Dewey, Hartley F Mrs, 1946, Ag 27,27:5
Dewey, Haywood G, 1943, O 18,15:4
Dewey, Henry A, 1938, Ja 13,22:1
Dewey, Henry C, 1955, F 6,88:8
Dewey, James F, 1950, Ag 2,25:1
Dewey, James F Mrs, 1946, Ap 16,25:4
Dewey, Joel A, 1873, Je 18,1:5
Dewey, John, 1952, Je 2,1:2
Dewey, John H, 1942, N 14,15:3
Dewey, Joshua, 1864, Mr 6,5:3
Dewey, Katherine B, 1957, D 16,29:2
Dewey, Kenneth, 1947, My 28,26:3
Dewey, Lloyd E, 1960, Mr 25,27:3
Dewey, Lyster H, 1944, N 29,23:6
Dewey, M, 1931, D 27,II,6:1; 1933, My 15,13:4
Dewey, Maurice W, 1944, Ja 23,37:2
Dewey, Orville, 1882, Mr 22,5:5
Dewey, P, 1867, D 17,4:6
Dewey, Phil H, 1939, Ag 11,15:4
Dewey, Ralph C, 1952, Mr 8,30:5
Dewey, Robert T, 1951, S 22,17:5
Dewey, Russell T, 1949, My 14,13:7
Dewey, S, 1933, Jl 31,13:6
Dewey, Sabino Mrs, 1957, Ja 23,29:5
Dewey, Seth B, 1938, Ag 27,13:6
Dewey, Stanley M Mrs, 1948, My 5,25:5
Dewey, Walter E, 1958, Ap 11,25:2
Dewey, William H, 1951, D 14,31:3
Dewey, William M, 1954, My 15,15:2
Dewey, William P, 1917, O 15,13:4
Dewey, Willis A, 1938, Ap 3,II,6:6
Dewhurst, Edward B, 1941, F 26,22:2
Dewhurst, J Frederic, 1967, My 30,21:1
Dewhurst, J Frederic Mrs (M Grant), 1967, Ap 3, 33:3
Dewhurst, James B, 1952, Ag 30,13:4
Dewhurst, John A, 1964, O 17,29:5
Dewhurst, Robert (Bro Basil Jerome), 1957, N 22, 25:4
Dewhurst, William, 1946, D 10,32:2
de Wiart, Adrian C, 1963, Je 6,35:2
Dewick, Charles L, 1937, F 20,17:3
Dewick, Nelson Capt, 1910, D 28,9:4
De Wilde, Cornelis, 1942, Jl 16,19:4
De Windt, Delano, 1953, N 11,31:4
De Windt, Garrett S, 1937, Je 23,25:2
De Windt, H, 1933, D 2,13:4
Dewing, Elizabeth, 1956, N 27,37:1
Dewing, Henry B, 1956, S 6,25:1
Dewing, Hiram E, 1941, Ag 25,15:6
Dewing, Thomas W, 1938, N 5,19:4
de Winter, Alphonse Mrs (requim mass set, Je 4,37:4), 1964, Je 1,29:4
De Winton, Francis Sir, 1901, D 18,9:4
Dewire, Phil K, 1939, O 24,23:4
Dewis, Edwin G, 1958, N 11,29:2
De Witt, Augusta, 1939, F 11,15:3
Dewitt, Benjamin C, 1957, Ap 8,23:4
DeWitt, Benjamin P, 1965, Je 24,35:2
De Witt, Carroll L Mrs, 1941, Ag 1,15:4
De Witt, Charles I, 1952, Ap 29,27:4
DeWitt, Charles W, 1967, Ap 13,43:3
De Witt, Clarence F, 1940, D 8,69:3
De Witt, Clyde A, 1956, N 5,31:1
De Witt, Daniel M, 1948, N 12,23:2
De Witt, David Miller, 1912, Je 25,11:4
De Witt, Edward, 1872, O 2,5:3
DeWitt, Edward, 1940, N 15,21:4
DeWitt, Edward T, 1964, Ap 7,35:4
DeWitt, Edwin D, 1963, Jl 3,25:3
Dewitt, Elmore J Mrs, 1948, Ag 15,61:1
Dewitt, Eugene N, 1947, Je 24,23:5
De Witt, George G, 1912, Ja 13,13:3
De Witt, Grace, 1924, S 16,23:4
De Witt, Grace M, 1949, Mr 30,25:1
Dewitt, Harvey S, 1951, My 23,35:1
Dewitt, Harvey S Mrs, 1945, My 24,19:3
DeWitt, Henry R Mrs, 1945, O 29,19:1
De Witt, J R, 1930, Jl 29,21:3
De Witt, Jerome P, 1940, D 3,25:1
Dewitt, John H, 1937, Mr 8,19:1
De Witt, John L, 1962, Je 21,31:2
De Witt, John Rev Dr, 1923, N 20,19:4
De Witt, Joseph E Mrs, 1949, F 23,27:4
DeWitt, Lillian G Mrs, 1942, Ap 1,21:2
DeWitt, Lulu M Mrs, 1958, N 2,88:3
De Witt, Lydia A, 1953, O 6,29:2
DeWitt, Macdonald Mrs, 1957, Ja 17,29:2
De Witt, Marguerite E, 1962, Je 9,25:4
DeWitt, Norman W, 1958, S 22,31:2
DeWitt, Perry G, 1957, Ja 12,19:4
De Witt, Peter, 1915, F 3,11:6
De Witt, R M, 1877, Ap 17,8:2
DeWitt, Raymond L, 1951, Je 26,29:2
Dewitt, Richard, 1944, O 22,46:2
De Witt, Theodore, 1924, Ap 12,15:4; 1944, Jl 4,19:1
De Witt, Thomas C, 1875, Jl 16,4:6
De Witt, Thomas Dr, 1874, My 21,5:5
De Witt, Wallace, 1949, D 16,31:3
De Witt, Wallace G, 1947, D 30,23:2
DeWitt, William A, 1968, Je 12,47:2
De Witt, William C, 1913, D 5,11:7
Dewitt, William C, 1951, F 6,27:5
Dewitt, William C Mrs, 1938, Je 26,27:4
DeWitt, William F, 1949, Jl 16,13:5
Dewitt, William H, 1939, Ap 11,24:3; 1954, Ap 16,21:2
DeWitt, William P, 1944, Ja 5,17:4
De Witt, William Percival, 1907, F 19,9:6
de Wohl, Louis, 1961, Je 4,86:4
De Wolf, Edward P Mrs, 1920, Je 5,15:4
De Wolf, Eric, 1945, Mr 4,38:2
de Wolf, Halsey Mrs, 1958, My 26,29:3
De Wolf, Henry, 1945, Ap 2,19:4
De Wolf, John, 1913, N 24,11:5
De Wolf, John E, 1964, Je 20,25:3
De Wolf, John W, 1949, My 27,21:5
De Wolf, Joseph C, 1950, Ag 14,17:5
De Wolf, Louis Mrs, 1949, Ag 16,23:1
De Wolf, Melville W, 1911, F 9,7:6
De Wolf, Roger D, 1946, F 5,23:1
De Wolf, Rose R Mrs, 1942, Jl 15,19:3
DeWolf, William A Mrs, 1960, N 22,35:2
DeWolfe, Alfred B, 1954, N 19,32:2
de Wolfe, Edgar S, 1955, S 21,26:4
de Wolfe, Edgar S Mrs, 1957, Je 2,86:1
De Wolfe, Fred C, 1953, S 18,29:1
DeWolfe, George E, 1951, Ja 8,17:1
De Wolfe, George E Mrs, 1941, S 28,49:3
DeWolfe, Harry G, 1952, S 3,29:4
De Wolfe, James P (requiem mass, F 10,34:1), 1966, F 8,39:1
Dewolfe, Joel P, 1940, F 25,38:6
De Wolfe, Tensard, 1945, F 20,19:3
De Wolfe, William T, 1948, F 10,23:3
De Wolff, Otto, 1955, My 25,33:2
De Woody, Charles, 1940, N 29,21:3
Dewsnap, Charles H, 1953, Jl 1,29:2
Dewson, George B, 1939, Ap 27,25:3
Dewson, James H, 1940, O 24,25:5
Dewson, Mary W, 1962, O 25,39:1
Dewstoe, Harley E, 1950, F 15,27:5
De Wyrall, Cyril, 1947, Je 30,19:2
Dexter, Albert F Mrs, 1944, Mr 2,17:5
Dexter, Allen T, 1945, Ag 13,19:4
Dexter, Anna Mrs, 1956, Ag 18,17:6
Dexter, Augustus Charles, 1913, Mr 22,13:4
Dexter, Charles J, 1945, Jl 12,11:7
Dexter, Chauncey, 1872, Ap 5,1:3
Dexter, Daniel S, 1956, O 20,21:4
Dexter, Duncan, 1923, Jl 25,11:7
Dexter, Edith W Mrs, 1942, F 18,19:1
Dexter, Elizabeth G, 1950, Mr 16,31:2
Dexter, Elliott, 1941, Je 24,19:2
Dexter, Fenwick T, 1955, Jl 6,27:1
Dexter, Francis H, 1940, O 25,21:1
Dexter, Franklin Bowditch Prof, 1920, Ag 14,7:7
Dexter, Frederick G, 1937, Ag 1,II,7:3
Dexter, George, 1910, Jl 4,7:6
Dexter, George M, 1951, F 24,13:2
Dexter, Gordon, 1937, Mr 11,23:4
Dexter, Gordon Mrs, 1968, D 16,47:1
Dexter, Grant, 1961, D 14,43:5
Dexter, Henry, 1910, Jl 12,7:5
Dexter, Howard W Jr, 1948, Ja 19,23:5
Dexter, James P, 1951, Mr 1,27:2
Dexter, John H, 1949, My 16,21:5
Dexter, Malcolm, 1948, Jl 5,15:6
Dexter, Orel A, 1951, O 24,31:4
Dexter, Professor, 1869, Ag 19,5:2
Dexter, Raymond C, 1955, Jl 3,33:1
Dexter, Robert C, 1955, O 13,31:2
Dexter, Smith O, 1939, N 28,25:2
Dexter, Stanley Walker, 1918, Mr 25,13:8
Dexter, Thomas A, 1946, My 6,21:2
Dexter, Wallace D Jr, 1939, D 27,21:6
Dexter, Walter, 1944, My 17,19:6
Dexter, Walter E, 1944, S 9,15:6
Dexter, Walter F, 1945, O 22,17:4
Dexter, Wilbur B, 1952, Jl 15,21:3
Dexter, William, 1943, F 9,23:3
Dexter, William E Mrs, 1946, N 20,31:3
Dexter, William H, 1912, Ja 21,II,13:2
Dexter, William Hart Rev, 1925, Ja 28,17:3
Dey, Albert, 1916, Ag 9,11:4
Dey, Anthony, 1912, O 13,17:4
Dey, Ben C, 1952, N 26,23:5
Dey, Donald, 1946, F 26,25:5
Dey, Elwood R, 1943, F 26,19:3
Dey, George E T, 1943, My 18,23:2
Dey, George M, 1942, N 17,26:2
Dey, Henry E, 1942, O 30,19:2
Dey, Henry E Mrs, 1956, Ja 11,29:1
Dey, James, 1946, Je 13,27:3
Dey, John H, 1906, Mr 20,9:6
Dey, Marvin H, 1953, O 30,23:1
Dey, Richard Henry, 1916, Ja 25,9:5
Dey, Richard Mrs, 1944, Je 5,19:5
Dey, Richard Varick, 1925, O 22,25:4
Dey, William F, 1938, S 18,44:7
Dey, William S, 1946, N 10,64:2
Dey, Wyckoff I, 1955, My 6,23:2
Deye, Clarence J, 1945, Ag 4,11:6
Deye, Robert E, 1923, S 17,15:3
Deyette, Dwight C, 1958, Ja 5,86:8
Deym, Franz von Count, 1903, S 5,7:1
Deyo, Alvin, 1950, S 6,29:1
Deyo, Andrew B, 1948, O 10,76:8
Deyo, Bessie H Mrs, 1944, S 22,19:3
Deyo, C W Mrs, 1948, Mr 6,13:5
Deyo, Charles W, 1952, D 20,17:3
Deyo, Erastus Mrs, 1951, F 23,27:4
Deyo, Eugene, 1950, O 2,23:2
Deyo, Felix Le C, 1959, Je 23,33:5
Deyo, Hiram W, 1948, My 14,23:2
Deyo, Israel T, 1953, O 7,29:4
Deyo, J Albert, 1958, Je 25,29:4
Deyo, John E Mrs, 1952, S 6,17:4
Deyo, John H, 1945, F 8,19:1
Deyo, Jonathan N, 1943, Je 13,44:8
Deyo, Katherine Mrs, 1939, Jl 6,23:4
Deyo, Leib, 1946, N 1,23:2
Deyo, Martin W, 1951, O 21,93:1
Deyo, Milo Mrs, 1947, D 4,31:1
Deyo, Norman L, 1946, My 17,21:3
Deyo, Perry, 1937, Mr 24,25:1
Deyo, Raymond S, 1942, O 11,56:8
Deyo, Reuben B, 1944, My 12,19:5
Deyo, Robert, 1951, Ag 4,15:4
Deyo, Solomon Lefevre, 1922, Ag 20,26:5
Deyo, Warren, 1948, N 3,27:3
De Yoe, Edgar A, 1963, O 19,25:4
De Yoe, J Willard, 1956, My 11,27:1
De Yoe, Luther, 1947, Ja 9,23:6
De Young, Benjamin A, 1956, Ap 5,29:4
De Young, Charles, 1913, S 19,9:5
De Young, Jacob, 1940, Mr 15,23:2
De Young, James, 1940, N 13,23:2
De Young, Joseph, 1947, N 18,24:1
De Young, Meichel H (funl, F 19,19:5), 1925, 19:1
Deyrup, Dorothy J, 1961, N 5,88:2
Deys, Jonathan, 1914, N 6,11:5
Deysher, Ellwood H, 1938, D 3,19:2
De Yturbide Augustin, 1925, Mr 4,19:4
de Zafra, Carlos Maj, 1925, N 1,9:2
Dezanneau, M, 1875, O 10,1:7
de Zavala, Adina, 1955, Mr 3,27:3
De Zavala, Mary, 1950, O 3,31:4
Dezell, John F, 1937, O 18,17:2
DeZemler, Charles, 1964, Ag 8,19:6
Dezendorf, Albert S Mrs, 1947, S 27,15:6
Dezendorf, Franklyn B, 1949, N 5,13:5
Dezengremel, Estelle R, 1949, F 12,17:3
Dezer, Charles N, 1966, D 12,47:1
DeZutter, Michel L, 1963, D 26,27:2
Dezzi, Louis, 1939, F 21,19:4
Dhalmar, Augusto, 1950, Ja 28,13:4
d'Harnoncourt, Rene, 1968, Ag 14,43:1
D'Haussonville, Bernard Gabriel Count, 1924,
D'Haussonville, Countess, 1882, My 8,4:7
D'Hermillon, Lucien E, 1947, D 10,31:4

D'Hervilly, A B de St, 1919, Ap 8,11:1
D'Hondt, Jules C, 1947, O 10,25:4
Dhuleep Singh, Maharajah, 1893, O 24,5:6
d'Humy, Fernand E, 1955, D 23,17:1
di Benedetto, Lawrence Sr, 1958, N 11,29:2
di Bergolo, Vittorio Calvi, 1924, Jl 24,13:4
di Bonaventura, Fred, 1964, My 23,23:2
Di Brienza, Frank Sr, 1942, Ag 16,44:8
Di Brienza, Vincent, 1955, My 5,33:2
Di Capiro, Joseph, 1953, Ja 27,25:4
Di Cicco, Luigina Mrs (will), 1943, Je 24,23:2
Di Corcia, Victor Mrs, 1944, Mr 23,19:2
di Cosmo, Pasquale V, 1956, Je 27,31:2
Di Fabio, Felix, 1955, F 15,27:3
Di Falco, Saverio, 1950, Je 2,23:3
Di Fate, John, 1952, F 13,29:3
Di Frasso, Dorothy Countess (will, Ja 7,29:6), 1954, Ja 5,9:2
Di Gesare, Louis A, 1968, D 29,53:1
Di Giacomo, James C, 1968, D 4,47:1
Di Giacomo, Louis, 1946, O 29,25:2
Di Giorgio, Joseph, 1951, F 26,24:2
Di Giorgio, Rosario, 1955, Jl 1,21:4
Di Giorgio, Salvatore, 1960, F 19,27:3
Di Giorgio Salvatore, 1922, D 27,17:5
Di Girolamo, Mario, 1952, S 28,77:2
Di Giulio, Antonio Mrs, 1949, Ja 23,68:6
Di Jiacomo, Francisco Mrs, 1943, Ap 19,19:3
Di Lascia, Anthony, 1967, My 5,39:2
Di Lauro, Thomas, 1965, D 30,23:1
Di Lelio, Alfredo, 1959, Mr 31,30:4
Di Leo, Angelo Mrs, 1966, Jl 30,25:4
Di Leo, Frank G, 1965, D 29,29:3
Di Leo, Joseph A, 1945, Ag 10,15:3
Di Lorenzo, Pasquale, 1954, N 8,21:3
Di Louie, James A, 1960, Ap 11,31:4
Di Lustro, Vito F, 1967, Ja 3,34:2
Di Maggio, Rosario, 1954, Jl 4,30:6
Di Marco, Joseph, 1955, Ag 21,93:3
Di Masi, Fioravanti, 1953, F 28,17:4
Di Metro, Louis, 1938, Jl 18,30:4
Di Minni, Thomas D, 1953, Ja 18,92:5
Di Nardo, Antonio, 1948, Je 30,25:6
Di Neri, P Charles, 1947, Ja 24,21:1
Di Nicola, Joseph, 1961, D 18,35:4
Di Nizo, Philip, 1946, Je 9,40:5
Di Palma, Dominic, 1940, O 10,25:7
Di Paolo, Frederick, 1940, S 29,44:2
Di Pasquale, Antonia, 1954, O 15,23:1
Di Persia, Felix, 1940, N 26,23:3
Di Pesa, Joseph A, 1948, S 1,23:1
Di Pietro, Carmela, 1950, S 18,23:2
di Pietro, James, 1965, S 13,35:4
Di Pirro, Mario G, 1959, O 27,37:3
Di Re, Pasquelle Mrs, 1947, Ag 4,17:5
Di Renzo, Dominic, 1951, Ag 3,21:4
Di San Secondo, Pier M R, 1956, N 23,27:2
di Sciarra, Mofeo Barberini Prince, 1925, Mr 14,13:5
di Silvestro, John M, 1958, O 11,23:4
Di Simone, Vincent, 1949, Jl 13,27:3
Di Spirito, Anthony D, 1951, Ja 4,30:2
Di Stefano, Stefano, 1965, Je 4,35:5
Di Vault, M T, 1922, Je 25,26:2
Di Veroli, Giorgio, 1952, N 20,31:2
Di Vincenzo, Guido, 1954, O 2,17:4
Diab, Najeeb Mrs, 1960, Ag 26,25:2
Diachenko, Alex, 1951, O 24,32:3
Diack, Thomas F, 1952, N 4,29:2
Diack, Walter T, 1955, My 3,31:2
Diaghileff, S, 1929, Ag 20,27:1
Dial, John W, 1952, S 6,17:2
Dial, Nathaniel B, 1940, D 12,27:4
Dialogue, John H, 1924, Ap 21,17:5
Diamant, Arthur H, 1956, Ag 15,29:2
Diamant, David S, 1912, Jl 20,7:7
Diamant, Edward M, 1953, O 12,27:6
Diamant, Solomon, 1923, F 12,13:5
Diamantopoulos, Cimon, 1946, D 7,1:6
Diamare, Gregory, 1945, S 9,45:2
Diament, Albert L, 1938, Mr 3,21:2
Diament, Robert, 1959, Je 25,29:5
Diamente, Gabriel, 1948, O 9,19:2
Diamond, Abraham, 1949, N 11,25:3
Diamond, Arnold, 1955, F 27,86:5
Diamond, Charles L, 1956, My 25,23:2
Diamond, Harry, 1948, Je 22,25:3
Diamond, Henry D, 1962, Ap 19,31:2
Diamond, Henry D Mrs, 1960, Ja 5,31:4
Diamond, Herman, 1950, O 5,31:1
Diamond, Herman M, 1962, Mr 13,32:1
Diamond, Isidor, 1954, Je 29,27:6
Diamond, Jennie, 1944, Je 5,19:4
Diamond, Jerome D Mrs, 1964, Mr 30,29:4
Diamond, Jim (Jas Buchanan Brady), 1917, Ap 14, 13:1
Diamond, John J, 1947, D 6,15:7
Diamond, Joseph, 1943, S 3,19:4; 1950, Je 20,27:4
Diamond, Joseph P, 1947, Ap 26,13:4
Diamond, Joseph S, 1953, My 1,22:3
Diamond, Leon, 1952, Ap 29,27:4
Diamond, Leonard, 1955, N 3,31:1
Diamond, Lou, 1951, S 22,17:4
Diamond, Louis, 1945, D 14,27:5
Diamond, Louis S, 1940, Ap 6,17:2
Diamond, Marcus, 1946, Ap 3,25:1
Diamond, Mary (Sister Mary Eymard), 1965, My 7, 41:2
Diamond, Milton, 1955, O 21,27:4
Diamond, Morris, 1944, N 16,23:3; 1958, Mr 22,17:4
Diamond, Moses, 1949, O 7,27:4
Diamond, Nat, 1967, Mr 13,37:1
Diamond, Patrick J, 1941, Je 6,21:4
Diamond, Paul, 1954, My 29,15:5
Diamond, Phil H, 1956, S 12,37:4
Diamond, Philip, 1962, O 16,47:3
Diamond, Robert, 1957, Mr 24,86:5
Diamond, Samuel, 1937, Jl 28,19:5; 1956, D 20,29:1
Diamond, Simon, 1966, N 27,86:7
Diamond, William, 1961, D 9,27:5
Diamond, William S, 1946, Ja 26,13:3
Diamond, Zalman N, 1950, Ap 25,31:3
Diamond, Zanville, 1968, O 7,47:4
Diana, Stanley A, 1966, S 20,47:2
Dianetti, Louis, 1950, Mr 7,27:2
Diange, Lester, 1937, Jl 25,II,7:4
Dias, Carlos M, 1941, O 20,17:4
Diat, Louis, 1957, Ag 30,19:2
Diaz, A, 1928, Mr 1,1:2
Diaz, Adolfo, 1964, Ja 29,30:1
Diaz, Agustin, 1955, Je 21,31:1
Diaz, Domingo Gen, 1912, D 23,9:4
Diaz, Jose T Msgr, 1937, S 16,25:4
Diaz, Julian L, 1955, Mr 29,29:4
Diaz, Mary Mrs, 1952, Jl 19,15:3
Diaz, Porfirio, 1946, D 29,37:4
Diaz, Porfirio Gen, 1915, Jl 4,11:6
Diaz, Porfirio Mrs, 1944, Je 26,15:5
Diaz, Rafaelo, 1943, D 13,23:3
Diaz, Ramon R Y, 1942, N 25,23:3
Diaz, Temistocles Jr, 1954, S 9,31:2
Diaz Arosemena, Domingo Pres, 1949, Ag 24,25:1
Diaz Barreto, P, 1936, My 20,21:1
Diaz Hidalgo, Luiz A, 1949, Ap 13,29:1
Diaz Redonnet, Ramon, 1968, F 6,43:1
Diaz y Gomara, Miguel, 1949, N 8,31:3
Dibbell, Edwin A Capt, 1907, Ag 30,7:6
Dibbern, George, 1962, S 12,39:2
Dibble, A B Mrs, 1905, D 25,1:4
Dibble, Adelbert, 1940, Ap 20,17:4
Dibble, Alonzo, 1943, My 1,15:4
Dibble, Anna M, 1954, N 11,31:1
Dibble, Charles C, 1948, Ap 6,23:2
Dibble, Charles L, 1940, O 31,23:4
Dibble, Clara M, 1957, Je 4,35:2
Dibble, Edgar J, 1954, Ag 21,17:4; 1965, F 4,31:1
Dibble, Fred A, 1945, Ja 12,15:1
Dibble, George, 1951, S 22,17:2
Dibble, John P, 1943, F 16,20:3
Dibble, Lauretta A, 1952, Ja 25,21:2
Dibble, Lewis A, 1967, Jl 3,17:4
Dibble, Thomas R Mrs, 1952, N 12,27:3
Dibblee, Benjamin H, 1945, N 12,21:4
Dibblee, Harold J, 1943, My 17,15:6
Dibblee, Henry Mrs, 1921, Ag 26,13:4
Dibblee, Thomas W, 1951, D 20,31:4
Dibbs, William A, 1942, Je 3,23:4
Dibdin, Lewis, 1938, Je 13,19:4
Dibelius, Martin, 1947, N 19,27:2
Dibelius, Otto, 1967, F 1,39:1
Dibelius, Otto Mrs, 1952, D 3,33:2
DiBella, August J, 1967, D 31,44:2
Dibert, Herbert M, 1945, Ap 8,36:2
Dibert, John Mrs, 1938, Ag 30,17:4
DiBiasi, Joseph, 1957, S 22,86:6
DiBlanda, Harry A, 1961, Jl 24,23:1
Dibner, Charles W, 1943, My 3,17:2
Dibney, William E, 1952, Mr 19,29:3
Diboll, William J, 1954, Mr 3,27:5
Dibos, Luis, 1955, O 9,86:5
Dibrell, Louis N, 1956, O 10,39:4
Dice, A T, 1932, Mr 26,13:1
Dice, Agnew T Jr, 1944, F 22,24:3
Dicey, Alfred Venn, 1922, Ap 8,15:4
Dicey, Edward, 1911, Jl 8,9:4
Dichman, Ernst Lt-Com, 1916, Ap 23,19:5
Dichter, Charles L, 1962, My 18,31:4
Dichter, Irving S, 1957, Ag 30,19:1
Dichter, Samuel Mrs, 1966, S 4,65:2
Dick, Albert B Jr (will, N 5,8:7), 1954, O 26,27:3
Dick, Albert B Mrs, 1944, S 27,21:3
Dick, Alexander, 1923, Ap 13,17:4
Dick, Andrew A, 1956, N 5,31:3
Dick, Archibald H, 1954, Ja 17,92:6
Dick, Bruce T, 1940, N 9,17:2
Dick, Charles, 1945, Mr 14,20:2
Dick, Christian, 1954, D 24,13:2
Dick, Clyde, 1949, Ag 22,21:5
Dick, Courter, 1941, O 22,23:5
Dick, Elizabeth T Mrs, 1937, N 30,23:3
Dick, Everette W, 1952, O 6,25:3
Dick, Gavin R, 1904, Ja 31,10:2
Dick, George A, 1948, O 17,78:5
Dick, George F, 1967, O 14,27:3
Dick, George F Gen, 1914, N 13,11:6
Dick, H Leonard H, 1940, S 12,25:3
Dick, Henry C, 1946, D 5,31:4
Dick, Henry K, 1953, Je 15,29:4
Dick, Henry Mrs, 1954, F 20,17:3
Dick, Irwin, 1924, Ja 3,17:2
Dick, J B Sen, 1890, My 4,1:3
Dick, J Henry (funl, O 3,15:5), 1925, O 1,27:5
Dick, John, 1942, Mr 7,17:6
Dick, John D, 1954, Je 18,23:3
Dick, Julian, 1921, Ja 6,11:4
Dick, Leon M, 1959, D 28,23:1
Dick, Leon S, 1939, Ap 15,19:4
Dick, Lew Mrs, 1962, F 3,21:4
Dick, Lewis C, 1957, Ap 12,25:4
Dick, Max, 1937, Ja 24,II,8:5
Dick, Percival B, 1949, My 14,13:5
Dick, R McCulloch, 1960, S 17,23:5
Dick, Ralph H, 1950, Ja 1,42:5
Dick, Rebecca, 1919, S 22,11:3
Dick, Samuel, 1865, Ja 31,8:5
Dick, Theodore G Jr, 1957, Mr 2,21:6
Dick, Thomas C Sr, 1952, Mr 29,15:6
Dick, William, 1912, Ap 6,11:6
Dick, William F, 1961, D 5,43:2
Dick, William H, 1951, Ja 13,15:2
Dick, William K, 1953, S 6,52:5
Dick, William R, 1961, O 2,31:4
Dickel, Albert M, 1946, N 16,19:4
Dickel, George C, 1955, D 20,31:5
Dickel, William L, 1948, F 28,15:3
Dickel C W, 1905, My 8,1:1
Dickely, George, 1955, D 24,13:5
Dickens, Alfred Tennyson (funl plans; funl, Ja 5,13:4), 1912, Ja 4,13:4
Dickens, Andrew G Mrs, 1960, Ap 27,37:3
Dickens, C Stafford, 1967, O 14,27:4
Dickens, Charles A, 1955, Ag 24,27:3
Dickens, Charles F Mrs, 1939, O 2,17:5
Dickens, Charles Mrs, 1879, N 23,7:2; 1951, Ag 28, 23:2
Dickens, Fred D, 1947, F 26,25:5
Dickens, Gerald C, 1962, N 22,29:1
Dickens, H F Sir, 1933, D 22,22:1
Dickens, Henry C, 1966, N 7,47:5
Dickens, Homer J, 1948, S 5,40:5
Dickens, John A, 1954, O 24,89:1
Dickens, Marie Lady, 1940, Ja 5,20:3
Dickens, Philip C, 1964, O 6,43:7
Dickenson, Donald M Jr, 1951, Je 14,27:4
Dickenson, Edwin A, 1952, Ap 2,33:3
Dickenson, Edwin C, 1956, N 20,37:5
Dickenson, Ernest H, 1960, Je 10,31:4
Dickenson, Harry, 1949, Ag 26,19:5
Dickenson, Harry A Mrs, 1949, D 28,32:1
Dickenson, Harry G, 1946, O 18,23:2
Dickenson, Harry G Mrs, 1952, Ag 26,25:1
Dickenson, J S, 1876, Mr 26,7:5
Dickenson, James Rea Dr, 1968, O 16,47:1
Dickenson, Melville P, 1968, Ap 18,47:2
Dickenson, Samuel S, 1910, D 25,9:2
Dickenson, William Noble, 1908, D 7,9:4
Dicker, John B, 1949, O 18,27:3
Dicker, Reuben M, 1962, Ja 1,23:2
Dicker, Rosa Mrs, 1943, Jl 18,34:2
Dicker, Samuel B, 1960, F 10,37:4
Dickerman, Charles H, 1937, Ja 12,24:2
Dickerman, Charles Heber, 1915, D 19,17:5
Dickerman, Emma H, 1942, Ap 19,43:2
Dickerman, Frederick W, 1940, S 19,23:1
Dickerman, George S Rev, 1937, Ag 3,23:4
Dickerman, Harrie E, 1942, D 8,25:3
Dickerman, J Henry, 1940, My 21,23:6
Dickerman, Sherwood O Mrs (Maude B), 1965, Mr 19,35:5
Dickerman, Watson B, 1955, Jl 28,23:5
Dickerman, Watson B Mrs, 1908, N 26,9:6
Dickerman, Watson Bradley, 1923, Ap 6,17:4
Dickerman, William C (por), 1946, Ap 26,21:1
Dickerman, William C Mrs, 1959, D 28,23:3
Dickerman, William D Mrs, 1937, O 20,23:2
Dickermann, J S Gen, 1885, Ja 22,5:3
Dickerson, Agnes Mrs, 1953, Ap 21,27:3
Dickerson, Albert T, 1939, N 13,19:4
Dickerson, Albert T Mrs, 1943, Je 18,21:1
Dickerson, Arthur N, 1952, Jl 23,23:4
Dickerson, Benjamin G, 1953, S 4,15:1
Dickerson, Charles E, 1939, Ja 17,22:2
Dickerson, Charles E Mrs, 1947, O 12,76:4
Dickerson, Denver S, 1925, N 29,13:2
Dickerson, E J, 1921, Jl 13,9:4
Dickerson, E N, 1889, D 13,5:5
Dickerson, Edwin H, 1950, N 19,93:1
Dickerson, Emerson W, 1940, Je 25,23:4
Dickerson, Fred T, 1947, Ag 4,17:6
Dickerson, Fred T Jr, 1941, Jl 28,13:2
Dickerson, George B, 1941, Ja 28,19:3
Dickerson, Harry C, 1937, My 5,25:5
Dickerson, Harry L, 1941, Ag 17,38:1
Dickerson, J P Mrs, 1937, S 23,27:4
Dickerson, J S, 1904, Jl 6,9:6
Dickerson, John D, 1944, Ag 31,17:2
Dickerson, John J, 1966, Ag 22,33:4
Dickerson, John S, 1949, Ag 11,23:5
Dickerson, Mervin L, 1942, N 19,25:4
Dickerson, Rolling P, 1938, N 19,17:3

Dickerson, Roy E, 1944, F 25,17:3
Dickerson, S Paul Mrs, 1943, Jl 31,13:1
Dickerson, W F Bishop (funl), 1884, D 26,8:2
Dickerson, Walter T, 1952, Mr 23,94:4
Dickerson, William H Jr, 1954, Ja 24,84:4
Dickerson, William K, 1948, My 21,23:5
Dickerson, William T, 1950, Mr 17,23:1
Dickert, Frank Mrs, 1952, S 10,29:3
Dickert, John G, 1947, Mr 15,13:5
Dickey, Adam H, 1925, F 9,17:4
Dickey, Alvin O, 1946, S 26,25:4
Dickey, Charles D, 1919, F 5,11:1
Dickey, Charles D Mrs, 1962, My 31,27:3
Dickey, Charles E, 1959, O 11,86:5
Dickey, Frank Alexander, 1920, F 7,11:3
Dickey, Halley K, 1956, D 6,38:1
Dickey, Herbert S, 1948, N 4,29:1
Dickey, James, 1953, Jl 10,19:2
Dickey, James A, 1943, N 21,56:5
Dickey, James B (mem ser, N 19,52:4), 1964, O 13, 39:6
Dickey, James B Mrs, 1925, S 2,23:5
Dickey, John Jr, 1937, S 11,17:4
Dickey, John Jr Mrs, 1952, Jl 23,23:2
Dickey, John R, 1937, Ap 3,19:2
Dickey, Joseph M Col, 1925, Ap 14,23:3
Dickey, Lincoln G, 1940, O 26,15:5
Dickey, M W, 1931, Ja 6,27:5
Dickey, Margaret Mrs, 1947, Ap 9,25:2
Dickey, O J, 1876, Ap 22,1:4
Dickey, P, 1933, Ja 9,19:3
Dickey, R E, 1949, Ap 23,13:5
Dickey, Robert L, 1944, O 22,46:5
Dickey, Robert R Sr, 1947, My 1,25:4
Dickey, Samuel, 1944, Je 29,23:4
Dickey, Samuel Mrs, 1959, My 4,29:5
Dickey, William C, 1959, Jl 23,27:3
Dickey, William D Ex-Justice, 1924, My 16,19:2
Dickey, William D Mrs, 1919, Jl 15,11:2
Dickey, William H, 1945, Ja 27,11:4
Dickey, William P, 1950, F 19,76:7
Dickhaut, Benjamin E Mrs, 1954, D 24,13:1
Dickhaut, Charles W Jr, 1956, S 17,27:1
Dickhaut, Chester A, 1947, Ap 10,25:4
Dickhout, Benjamin E, 1911, D 28,9:5
Dickhuth, H Eugene, 1964, Ja 21,29:3
Dickie, George S, 1950, Ag 22,27:5
Dickie, J F, 1933, My 30,15:3
Dickie, John, 1945, F 25,38:1
Dickie, John J, 1947, N 21,27:2
Dickie, Joseph F Mrs, 1943, My 4,23:3
Dickie, Luke B, 1937, S 24,21:3
Dickie, Perry, 1942, Ja 21,18:2
Dickie, Samuel Dr, 1925, N 6,23:6
Dickin, Maria E Mrs, 1951, Mr 3,13:1
Dickins, Curtis H, 1966, Ag 27,30:2
Dickins, Curtis H Mrs, 1945, Je 15,19:4
Dickins, Francis William Adm, 1910, S 16,9:5
Dickinson, A E, 1932, O 25,19:1
Dickinson, A G Mrs, 1917, My 20,23:3
Dickinson, Albert M, 1946, O 6,58:2
Dickinson, Andrew Glassel Col, 1906, Je 6,9:6
Dickinson, Arnold C, 1964, F 29,21:4
Dickinson, Arthur Col, 1914, D 28,9:1
Dickinson, Arthur M, 1941, Ap 5,17:3
Dickinson, Asa D, 1903, N 1,7:6; 1960, N 15,39:3
Dickinson, Ashley W, 1954, My 11,29:3
Dickinson, Baxter Rev Dr, 1875, D 8,6:6
Dickinson, Betty G, 1948, Ja 4,52:1
Dickinson, Bruce, 1954, Je 15,29:3
Dickinson, Charles A, 1954, Ja 26,27:4
Dickinson, Charles E B, 1951, F 19,23:4
Dickinson, Charles H, 1938, Ap 15,20:3
Dickinson, Charles M, 1924, Jl 4,13:5
Dickinson, Charles V, 1957, O 4,21:1
Dickinson, Charles W, 1937, O 6,25:2
Dickinson, chas, 1925, D 8,25:4
Dickinson, Chester G, 1941, S 7,49:2
Dickinson, Clarence C, 1957, O 6,84:5
Dickinson, Clarence C Mrs, 1965, O 14,47:3
Dickinson, Clarence Mrs, 1957, Ag 26,23:2
Dickinson, Clarence W, 1960, My 29,57:1
Dickinson, Clement C (por), 1938, Ja 15,15:1
Dickinson, Clinton G, 1952, O 31,25:3
Dickinson, Clinton R, 1943, F 24,21:1
Dickinson, Daniel S, 1866, Ap 14,4:6
Dickinson, David B, 1914, Mr 11,11:5
Dickinson, Don M, 1917, O 16,19:7
Dickinson, Ed S, 1872, Ap 18,4:5
Dickinson, Edna, 1954, S 18,15:4
Dickinson, Edward, 1874, Je 18,5:4; 1917, Ag 10,9:4
Dickinson, Edward E Jr, 1968, N 23,47:4
Dickinson, Edward M, 1939, Jl 7,17:2
Dickinson, Edward Perry, 1922, Jl 20,17:3
Dickinson, Edwin, 1951, Je 11,25:4
Dickinson, Edwin D, 1961, Mr 27,31:2
Dickinson, Ella S Mrs, 1942, Jl 13,15:3
Dickinson, Emma M Mrs, 1942, S 25,21:2
Dickinson, Fairleigh S, 1948, Je 24,25:3
Dickinson, Frances L Mrs, 1939, F 10,23:3
Dickinson, Frank, 1920, D 4,13:3; 1967, S 24,84:2
Dickinson, Frederick S, 1938, O 12,27:2
Dickinson, Frederick Z, 1924, Ap 8,19:3
Dickinson, G K, 1930, Je 26,23:4
Dickinson, G L, 1932, Ag 4,19:4
Dickinson, George, 1948, D 24,17:3
Dickinson, George H, 1938, Jl 18,13:3
Dickinson, George Mrs, 1967, Mr 22,47:1
Dickinson, George S, 1964, N 8,88:5
Dickinson, Grant Mrs, 1952, Ag 24,89:2
Dickinson, Haiden T Lt Comdr, 1937, Ja 2,11:3
Dickinson, Harold T, 1953, O 6,29:3
Dickinson, Harry B, 1943, D 1,21:2
Dickinson, Helen T, 1960, Mr 16,37:5
Dickinson, Hobart C, 1949, N 29,29:3
Dickinson, Howard C, 1944, Mr 21,19:2
Dickinson, Howard W, 1956, N 12,29:5
Dickinson, Hugh W, 1960, Je 25,21:4
Dickinson, Hunt T, 1967, Mr 11,29:1
Dickinson, Irving Mrs, 1946, Jl 24,27:2
Dickinson, J M, 1928, D 14,29:1
Dickinson, J T Rev, 1884, Jl 24,5:3
Dickinson, James R, 1917, Ag 2,9:4
Dickinson, James W, 1942, Ap 27,15:2
Dickinson, John, 1952, Ap 11,23:1; 1960, O 5,41:2
Dickinson, John B, 1875, Mr 18,7:2; 1941, F 17,15:2
Dickinson, John Mrs, 1955, Jl 14,23:5
Dickinson, John W, 1951, Mr 31,15:2
Dickinson, Joseph Gen, 1904, Ap 27,9:6
Dickinson, Julian A, 1959, Ag 5,27:4
Dickinson, La Fell, 1950, Je 7,29:3
Dickinson, Lawrence S, 1965, Ap 23,35:6
Dickinson, Le Roy, 1951, D 17,31:3
Dickinson, Legh Rev Dr, 1913, Ja 11,11:4
Dickinson, Lester Jesse, 1968, Je 6,47:3
Dickinson, Louis V, 1955, My 31,27:4
Dickinson, Luren D, 1943, Ap 23,17:1
Dickinson, Luren D Mrs, 1940, Ag 9,15:5
Dickinson, Marquis F, 1915, S 19,15:5
Dickinson, Maud Mrs, 1949, N 19,17:3
Dickinson, Maurice G, 1942, D 9,27:5
Dickinson, Melville D, 1940, F 1,21:1
Dickinson, O B, 1873, My 20,1:7
Dickinson, Oliver B, 1939, S 16,17:1
Dickinson, Overton, 1910, N 25,11:5
Dickinson, P P, 1895, O 6,8:5
Dickinson, Paul W, 1951, Mr 18,88:6
Dickinson, Percy R, 1952, Ja 27,77:1
Dickinson, Philemon, 1948, Mr 15,23:6
Dickinson, Philemon O, 1905, Je 20,9:4
Dickinson, Philip L, 1961, My 26,33:1
Dickinson, Prescott R, 1952, D 24,17:3
Dickinson, Quintin T, 1952, Je 3,29:3
Dickinson, Robert B, 1955, F 27,86:3
Dickinson, Robert E, 1950, N 12,92:2
Dickinson, Robert L (trb lr, D 12,32:6), 1950, N 30, 33:5
Dickinson, Robert L Mrs (por), 1938, O 1,17:4
Dickinson, Roscoe G, 1945, Jl 15,15:5
Dickinson, Sackett M, 1955, My 16,23:2
Dickinson, Samuel D Col, 1921, Ap 7,15:5
Dickinson, Samuel W, 1940, S 14,17:6
Dickinson, Sidney, 1919, F 8,15:5
Dickinson, Spencer E, 1952, Mr 31,19:4
Dickinson, Susan E, 1915, N 17,11:5
Dickinson, Thomas H Mrs, 1943, Mr 22,19:3
Dickinson, W F, 1940, O 10,25:3
Dickinson, W L, 1883, N 4,2:4
Dickinson, W Meredith, 1940, N 12,23:1
Dickinson, Walter, 1943, My 7,19:1
Dickinson, Wharton Mrs, 1909, Ap 13,9:5
Dickinson, William F, 1942, Ap 23,23:3
Dickinson, William H, 1950, Ja 20,25:1
Dickinson, Willoughby H, 1943, Je 2,25:3
Dickison, Andrew D, 1951, Ap 17,29:1
Dickle, Edward P, 1912, Ap 11,11:5
Dickman, Emil, 1938, My 6,21:4
Dickman, Franklin J, 1908, F 13,9:6
Dickman, J T, 1927, O 24,21:5
Dickman, John, 1953, Ag 19,30:6
Dickman, Michael, 1962, S 29,23:5
Dickman, Morris, 1953, D 19,15:1
Dickman, Robert N Mrs, 1943, O 29,19:3
Dickmann, Enrique, 1955, D 31,13:4
Dicks, Thomas A, 1944, O 3,23:3
Dickson, Ada Mrs, 1951, S 4,27:5
Dickson, Alex K, 1938, N 6,48:8
Dickson, Alfred B, 1952, Mr 20,29:1
Dickson, Arthur, 1962, My 22,37:2
Dickson, Bertram Capt, 1913, S 30,13:4
Dickson, Byron S, 1938, Ag 7,33:1
Dickson, Charles F, 1948, Jl 25,48:4
Dickson, Charles H, 1961, Jl 24,23:5
Dickson, Charles R, 1938, Jl 10,29:6
Dickson, Daruis M, 1912, Ag 21,9:6
Dickson, David M, 1964, My 7,37:1
Dickson, Dawson D, 1938, Ja 21,19:2
Dickson, Dick, 1962, Jl 16,23:5
Dickson, Donald W, 1955, Ap 12,29:3
Dickson, Dr, 1873, S 3,5:6
Dickson, Earle E, 1961, S 22,33:3
Dickson, Edward A, 1956, F 23,27:3
Dickson, Eleanor, 1919, My 6,15:5
Dickson, Elizabeth Mrs, 1942, My 31,39:2
Dickson, Emmett L, 1949, Ja 7,21:1
Dickson, Ernest C, 1939, Ag 25,15:4
Dickson, Francis, 1942, Ap 25,13:3
Dickson, Frank D, 1964, Ja 20,43:3
Dickson, Frank S, 1953, F 25,27:4
Dickson, Frederick S, 1940, Ja 5,19:4
Dickson, Frederick Stoever, 1925, D 3,25:3
Dickson, G A, 1903, Jl 26,7:6
Dickson, George E Mrs, 1955, My 14,19:5
Dickson, George M, 1957, Ap 10,33:5
Dickson, H R (see also Mr 10), 1877, Mr 12,8:1
Dickson, Henry, 1910, Ja 2,II,13:5
Dickson, J F (see also S 13), 1880, S 15,8:4
Dickson, James, 1906, N 21,9:6; 1945, Mr 22,23:2
Dickson, James B Mrs, 1953, Mr 4,27:6
Dickson, James M Rev, 1913, Ja 30,11:5
Dickson, James Stuart Rev, 1909, Ap 2,9:6
Dickson, Joe L, 1958, My 5,29:4
Dickson, John, 1947, Jl 10,21:2; 1950, Ap 11,31:4
Dickson, John B, 1957, Je 26,31:3
Dickson, John Jr, 1957, Je 4,35:4
Dickson, John Mrs, 1945, Jl 29,40:3
Dickson, Joseph Benjamin, 1919, D 13,13:4
Dickson, Leonard E, 1954, Ja 19,25:4
Dickson, Leslie R Mrs, 1952, Ap 25,23:4
Dickson, Mabel E, 1949, N 16,29:4
Dickson, Marguerite Mrs, 1953, O 12,27:4
Dickson, Marie, 1956, Je 11,31:6
Dickson, Matthew R, 1939, Jl 16,31:4
Dickson, Murray S, 1961, D 19,33:3
Dickson, Philip S, 1962, Ap 29,86:6
Dickson, Richard C, 1948, Ja 15,23:3
Dickson, Robert, 1909, Jl 16,7:6
Dickson, Robert B, 1950, Ap 10,19:3
Dickson, Robert E, 1947, D 13,15:5
Dickson, Robert K, 1952, S 20,15:5
Dickson, Robert L, 1963, S 26,35:3
Dickson, Robert R, 1939, S 29,23:2
Dickson, Ross H, 1954, Jl 10,13:6
Dickson, Samuel, 1915, My 29,11:7
Dickson, Sarah E, 1965, N 23,45:1
Dickson, Sarah J, 1941, O 29,23:1
Dickson, T, 1884, Ag 1,5:3
Dickson, Thomas, 1956, S 15,17:2
Dickson, Thomas H, 1944, F 13,41:1
Dickson, William B, 1942, Ja 28,19:4; 1951, S 7,29
Dickson, William L, 1957, My 26,93:1
Dickson, William T, 1956, D 17,31:5
Dickstein, Alex, 1955, F 14,19:2
Dickstein, Irwin J, 1961, Ag 1,31:3
Dickstein, Moishe, 1956, F 27,23:5
Dickstein, Samuel (trb, Ap 28,54:4; will, My 12,25
1954, Ap 23,27:1
DiCuitiis, James, 1953, Jl 6,17:5
Dicus, George A, 1955, Je 10,25:2
Didanoff, John, 1946, My 4,10:3
Didi, Amin, 1954, Ja 20,2:6
DiDiego, Louis, 1951, N 23,30:2
Didier, Edmund Father, 1903, My 19,9:5
Didier, Eugene L, 1913, S 10,9:6
Didier, Rosa, 1871, Mr 12,5:1
Didoardo, Domenic E, 1962, N 16,31:2
Didot, A F, 1876, F 24,1:5
Didriksen, Joshua M, 1960, Jl 28,27:4
Didrikson, Mildred (Babe),(Mrs M D Zaharias), 1956, S 28,1:2
Didsbury, Chester H, 1941, Je 30,17:4
Didur, Adamo, 1946, Ja 11,21:1
Diebert, Walter S Mrs, 1955, Jl 23,17:5
Diebitsch, Emil, 1949, S 24,13:5
Diebold, Albert H, 1964, F 18,35:1
Diebold, Charles H, 1943, D 26,32:8
Diebold, Charles Jr, 1960, S 11,82:1
Diebold, Paul F, 1953, O 19,21:6
Diebold, William, 1962, My 30,19:4
Dieboldt, Albert, 1951, Je 7,33:3
Dieck, Augustus H, 1910, F 18,7:4
Dieck, Henry W Sr, 1958, N 19,37:2
Dieck, Herman L, 1943, O 23,13:5
Dieck, Richard, 1939, Mr 12,III,6:7
Dieckhoff, Hans H, 1952, Mr 22,13:5
Dieckman, Charles J, 1946, Ag 14,26:3
Dieckman, George E, 1958, My 18,86:7
Dieckman, John G, 1954, Mr 1,25:4
Dieckmann, August H, 1951, Je 15,24:2
Dieckmann, Frederick, 1967, Jl 2,35:2
Dieckmann, Frederick Mrs, 1963, Ap 6,19:4
Dieckmann, John, 1952, Ap 9,31:2
Dieckmann, Otto, 1950, F 5,84:4
Diederich, William H, 1953, My 16,19:3
Diederichs, Herman Prof, 1937, S 1,19:6
Diederichs, Von Vice-Adm, 1918, Mr 11,11:6
Diederik, Jan H, 1948, Ag 7,15:3
Diedrichs, Edward Mrs, 1950, Je 2,24:3
Diefenbach, Elmer G (por), 1949, F 28,19:5
Diefenbach, Ralph J, 1959, Je 12,2:2
Diefenbach, Rich D L Mrs (Johanna Rotter-Diefenbach), 1909, Jl 27,7:3
Diefenbaker, William T Mrs, 1961, F 22,25:2
Diefendafer, A P, 1944, My 17,19:5
Diefenderfer, Frank L, 1942, F 20,17:2
Diefendorf, Allen R, 1943, Jl 31,13:1
Diefendorf, Allen R Mrs, 1939, O 26,23:1
Diefendorf, Burke, 1957, My 8,37:1
Diefendorf, Dorr F, 1953, D 15,44:8

Diefendorf, Elizabeth, 1909, Jl 25,7:6
Diefendorf, Frank, 1940, Mr 8,22:3
Diefendorf, John E Mrs, 1945, Je 30,17:6
Diefendorf, John Jacob, 1909, F 27,9:5
Diefendorf, W T, 1931, N 8,II,7:3
Diefendorf, Will J Mrs, 1947, O 22,29:3
Diefenthaeler, Fleetwood A Sr, 1952, Ap 24,31:3
Diefenthal, Clements C, 1939, My 9,23:3
Diefenthaler, Adalene Mrs, 1948, Jl 16,19:2
Diefenthaler, George E, 1945, Ap 22,36:1
Diefenthaler, John, 1946, Je 11,23:4
Dieffenbach, Albert C, 1963, O 8,43:2
Dieffenbach, Emil E, 1941, D 5,23:3
Dieffenbach, Richard H, 1959, Ja 4,87:1
Dieffenbach, William H Dr, 1937, Ja 14,21:3
Diega, Samuel C, 1939, O 15,49:2
Diegel, Leo, 1951, My 9,33:3
Dieges, Charles J, 1953, S 15,31:2
Diegman, James Mrs, 1948, Je 7,19:5
Diego, Carlos de, 1947, D 14,79:2
Dieguez, Manuel, 1922, Ja 12,17:5
Diehl, Adolph F, 1949, Ja 21,21:4
Diehl, Albrecht, 1938, F 21,36:6
Diehl, Ambrose N, 1940, Ja 5,20:2
Diehl, Charles, 1943, F 2,20:2
Diehl, Charles A, 1945, S 26,23:3
Diehl, Charles S, 1946, Ag 20,27:1
Diehl, Charles S Mrs, 1937, My 22,15:3
Diehl, E Katherine, 1950, O 25,35:2
Diehl, Edith, 1953, My 13,29:1
Diehl, Edwin S, 1962, Ag 4,19:5
Diehl, Erwin D Mrs, 1950, Ag 22,27:4
Diehl, Frederick, 1959, Jl 16,27:6
Diehl, Frederick Mrs, 1944, N 13,19:6
Diehl, George C, 1956, My 27,88:3
Diehl, Hannah Mrs, 1937, Ja 4,29:4
Diehl, Israel S Mrs, 1909, D 2,9:4
Diehl, Jacob, 1946, My 20,24:2
Diehl, John J, 1959, Ap 3,27:2
Diehl, John W, 1944, Ap 9,33:2
Diehl, Martin, 1908, My 4,7:2
Diehl, Miriam E, 1959, F 21,21:5
Diehl, Otto F, 1945, Jl 6,11:5
Diehl, Paul, 1948, My 7,23:2
Diehl, Pauline, 1949, Mr 1,25:4
Diehl, Phil, 1940, S 20,23:6
Diehl, Phil Mrs, 1950, O 3,31:3
Diehl, Philip, 1945, N 14,19:2
Diehl, S Ervin, 1946, S 21,15:4
Diehl, Samuel W B Capt, 1909, Je 16,7:5
Diehl, William, 1937, D 6,27:4
Diehl, William B Mrs, 1946, My 21,23:3
Diehl, William L, 1954, Ag 1,84:2
Diehl, William Rev, 1916, Jl 17,11:5
Diehlenn, W Alfred, 1948, F 11,27:2
Diehm, Charles L, 1956, Mr 22,35:4
Diekamn, Herman J, 1937, F 6,17:5
Diekamp, Maurus, 1942, N 21,13:5
Dieke, Gerhard H, 1965, Ag 26,33:1
Diekman, George C Dr, 1937, Ja 31,II,9:2
Diekneit, William F Sr, 1946, My 24,19:1
Diel, Carl J Mrs, 1965, My 11,39:2
Diels, Ludwig, 1945, D 7,22:3
Diels, Otto P, 1954, Mr 9,27:4
Diels, Rudolf, 1957, N 19,7:2
Diem, Oscar, 1950, D 2,13:3
Diemer, Charles F Mrs, 1952, F 9,13:5
Diemer, George W, 1956, Ag 15,29:2
Diemer, Hugo, 1939, Mr 5,49:1
Diemer, Joseph, 1941, D 17,27:2
Diemer, Louis J, 1919, D 24,13:4
Diemer, Louis M, 1946, D 22,41:3
Diemer, Peter J, 1943, F 25,21:2
Diender, Richard, 1938, Ag 29,13:5
Diener, Fred P, 1960, Ja 14,33:4
Diener, Herbert J Jr, 1966, Ag 4,33:4
Diener, Nathan, 1956, Ag 9,25:2
Diener, William L, 1964, Ag 3,25:3
Diener, William S, 1951, Je 26,29:5
Diener, William W, 1967, Ap 4,43:3
Dienhart, Walter Mrs, 1938, F 2,19:5
Dienst, Ernest J, 1955, Mr 11,25:2
Dienst, Herbert C, 1962, Ja 5,29:2
Dienst, Louis J, 1950, Jl 6,27:1
Dienst, Richard C, 1947, S 30,25:3
Dienst, Robert J, 1959, Ag 21,21:5
Diepen, H G K F, 1946, S 15,9:6
Diepenbrock, Alfons, 1921, Ap 6,15:5
Diephuis, James, 1962, Ap 19,31:1
ierckx, Jules, 1948, My 23,68:4
ierickx, Edward A, 1968, Ap 4,47:3
ierker, Gerard J, 1964, O 6,43:7
ierks, DeVere, 1957, My 23,33:4
ierks, Henry, 1960, F 22,17:1
es, Martin, 1922, Jl 14,13:5
escher, Alfred J, 1946, My 16,21:1
esel, Harrison N, 1956, Je 26,35:6
esel, Rudolf Mrs, 1944, Ap 25,23:2
esel, William F, 1939, O 11,27:1
eseldorff, Erwin P, 1940, N 5,25:6
esenbacher, George, 1944, Jl 30,35:2
esendruck, Zevi, 1940, Je 5,25:2
eserud, Juul, 1947, N 13,27:3

Diesheimer, Oscar, 1907, F 6,9:6
Diessl, Gustav, 1948, Mr 21,60:3
Dieste, Eduardo, 1954, S 3,17:3
Diestel, Arnold Dr, 1924, Ja 4,13:4
Diestelmeir, Aug, 1938, Ap 7,23:4
Dieter, Frederick J, 1944, N 29,23:6
Dieter, Harold E, 1948, S 7,25:1
Dieter, Harry Eugene, 1968, N 19,40:1
Dieter, Paul W, 1937, Ap 7,25:4
Dieterich, C F, 1927, O 7,27:5
Dieterich, F Semler, 1953, Je 21,85:2
Dieterich, Frederick A, 1960, Ap 14,31:3
Dieterich, Frederick H, 1944, F 17,19:3
Dieterich, Frederick J, 1939, Ap 8,15:4
Dieterich, Neil B, 1949, Mr 17,25:3
Dieterle, J George, 1940, Mr 19,25:5
Dieterle, Max, 1949, Je 1,31:3
Dieterle, Max Mrs, 1940, F 14,21:3
Dieterlen, Charles T E, 1952, My 24,19:5
Diethelm, Andre, 1954, Ja 12,23:4
Dietl, John S, 1956, O 20,21:2
Dietman, Herman F Mrs, 1942, Mr 13,19:4
Dietrich, Albert E, 1948, Mr 25,27:4
Dietrich, Amandus M, 1939, Mr 19,III,6:6
Dietrich, Arthur, 1967, Mr 22,47:2
Dietrich, Arthur M, 1949, Ja 12,28:2
Dietrich, August F, 1954, Ag 4,21:5
Dietrich, Byron J, 1954, N 12,21:1
Dietrich, Carl M, 1953, F 1,88:3
Dietrich, Charles H Ex-Gov, 1924, Ap 12,15:4
Dietrich, Charles W, 1941, F 10,20:1
Dietrich, Daniel W (will, Je 2,10:3), 1956, My 6,87:1
Dietrich, Edward J Sr, 1954, Jl 30,17:3
Dietrich, Edward N, 1951, F 7,29:2
Dietrich, Frederick, 1960, O 11,45:3
Dietrich, Georg, 1955, Ag 2,23:4
Dietrich, George, 1947, N 28,27:4
Dietrich, George J, 1954, Ja 17,92:2
Dietrich, Gilbert A, 1962, My 13,88:4
Dietrich, Gustave F, 1956, S 1,15:6
Dietrich, H Richard, 1962, Ag 27,23:6
Dietrich, Henry, 1939, O 17,25:3
Dietrich, Henry D, 1950, Je 2,23:3
Dietrich, Henry E, 1954, F 18,31:1
Dietrich, Hermann, 1954, Mr 8,27:4
Dietrich, Howard H, 1954, Ap 25,86:4
Dietrich, Howard H Mrs, 1956, S 13,35:4
Dietrich, John M, 1939, Ag 6,36:7
Dietrich, Joseph M, 1958, Ap 10,29:2
Dietrich, Marion C, 1948, Mr 4,25:3
Dietrich, Otto, 1952, N 23,89:1
Dietrich, Otto F, 1956, Ja 7,17:5
Dietrich, Ralph, 1961, D 4,37:1
Dietrich, Robert J, 1956, Je 9,41:3
Dietrich, Sepp, 1966, Ap 23,31:3
Dietrich, Tadeusz, 1960, Jl 29,25:1
Dietrich, Walter H, 1949, O 8,13:4
Dietrich, William, 1953, O 5,27:3
Dietrich, William F, 1959, Jl 2,25:2
Dietrich, William H, 1940, O 13,48:8
Dietrichs, Michael Gen, 1937, O 9,19:3
Dietrick, Chad, 1946, Ap 22,21:6
Diettel, Arthur A Capt, 1918, Ag 7,9:3
Dietz, Archibald E, 1965, N 16,43:4
Dietz, Arthur O, 1967, N 29,47:1
Dietz, Aug A Jr, 1954, N 13,15:3
Dietz, August, 1914, Mr 4,11:5
Dietz, Carl F, 1948, My 24,19:3; 1957, O 6,84:8
Dietz, Carla, 1967, Ag 3,33:5
Dietz, Charles R, 1957, My 1,37:3
Dietz, Charles W, 1942, My 7,19:1
Dietz, Daniel L, 1938, Ap 23,15:2
Dietz, Frederick, 1915, Ap 1,15:4
Dietz, Frederick C Rev, 1968, My 17,47:3
Dietz, George, 1872, Ap 9,5:1
Dietz, Gould, 1948, Je 30,25:5
Dietz, Gustave H, 1937, Jl 31,15:3
Dietz, Hannah Mrs, 1950, N 22,25:2
Dietz, Harold F, 1965, Je 16,44:3
Dietz, Harry F, 1954, S 8,31:4
Dietz, Herman J Mrs, 1950, Ag 26,13:3
Dietz, Howard James, 1922, My 5,17:6
Dietz, Johannes B, 1959, D 12,23:2
Dietz, John A, 1939, O 13,23:2
Dietz, John J, 1938, My 5,23:3
Dietz, John J Mrs, 1955, Je 7,33:5
Dietz, Joseph B, 1904, Ja 4,9:6
Dietz, Joseph F, 1962, Jl 5,25:3
Dietz, Joseph J, 1943, Je 18,21:5
Dietz, Lawrence J, 1960, Je 19,88:2
Dietz, Linda, 1920, S 9,11:2
Dietz, Lorna, 1964, Ja 31,27:4
Dietz, Martin J, 1953, S 17,29:6
Dietz, Nicholas, 1938, Mr 24,23:3
Dietz, Nicholas J, 1945, O 31,23:3
Dietz, Olga S Mrs, 1938, N 27,48:7
Dietz, Otto A, 1939, Mr 15,23:3
Dietz, Otto L, 1966, O 20,43:5
Dietz, Ottomar A, 1959, Mr 12,31:4
Dietz, Peter E, 1947, O 13,23:4
Dietz, Reginald W, 1960, Mr 9,33:4
Dietz, Royal O, 1947, Ja 30,25:5
Dietz, Solomon I, 1956, Ap 20,25:3

Dietz, W C F Mrs, 1955, My 11,31:4
Dietz, Walter H, 1960, S 18,86:4
Dietz, William F J, 1964, My 23,23:5
Dietze, Eginhard, 1951, F 27,27:3
Dietzel, Simon, 1938, Mr 23,23:5
Dietzman, Richard P, 1943, D 23,19:1
Dietzold, Herman Mrs, 1943, D 3,23:4
Dietzsch, Edna, 1945, D 11,25:1
Dieuaide, Thomas M, 1923, Ap 15,6:2
Dieulafoy, Jane, 1916, My 28,17:4
Dieulafoy, Marcel A, 1920, F 27,13:5
Dievenkorn, Henry E, 1939, F 15,23:1
Diez, Luise M, 1942, Ap 13,15:6
Difalco, Michael, 1943, F 3,19:5
Difenderfer, Robert E, 1923, Ap 26,19:4
Diffany, Henry, 1949, F 2,56:6
Diffany, Henry Mrs, 1949, F 2,56:6
Diffenderfer, George M Sr, 1943, My 18,23:3
Diffenderffer, Charles H, 1956, Mr 2,23:1
Diffendorfer, Ralph E, 1951, F 1,25:5
Diffendorfer, Ralph E Mrs, 1957, Ja 29,31:2
Diffin, Frank G, 1948, Ja 24,15:5
Difiore, Gabriel, 1945, Je 8,19:1
Digan, Thomas J, 1949, Jl 2,15:6
Digby, Edward K, 1964, Ja 30,29:4
Digby, Fred, 1958, N 4,27:2
Digby, John N, 1959, S 10,35:2
Digby, Lady, 1881, O 9,6:7
Digby, N S, 1876, Ja 13,5:3
Digges, Dudley, 1947, O 25,19:1
Digges, Dudley Mrs, 1947, Ag 22,15:6
Digges, Isaac W, 1953, Jl 10,19:1
Digges, Isaac W Mrs, 1941, Jl 1,23:6
Digges, William J, 1960, Ja 4,29:6
Diggin, Myron B, 1962, Ag 21,33:3
Diggins, Joseph L, 1949, N 22,29:2
Diggins, Paul F Sr, 1957, Ap 17,31:1
Diggins, Ralph C, 1959, My 15,30:1
Diggles, George L, 1953, Je 18,29:4
Diggs, Albert, 1944, D 8,21:4
Diggs, Edward S, 1961, D 5,39:5
Diggs, Gladys D Mrs, 1958, Je 24,31:4
Diggs, J Daniel, 1968, D 12,47:3
Diggs, John Marshall, 1968, My 24,47:4
Dight, Herman H, 1959, Mr 15,89:2
Dight, Sidney R, 1948, Ja 3,13:4
Dighton, George F, 1951, S 13,31:4
DiGiacomo, Vincent, 1962, Ap 8,86:7
Digilio, James, 1943, Je 23,21:4
DiGiovanna, John, 1957, S 29,87:1
Digman, Ralph, 1953, D 22,31:3
Dignam, Mary E W Mrs, 1938, S 7,36:6
Dignan, John, 1953, Ap 14,27:2
Dignan, Thomas G, 1960, Jl 30,17:3
Dignan, Thomas H, 1945, N 21,21:2
Digneffe, Emile, 1937, Je 17,24:1
Digney, Catherine Mrs, 1951, Ag 17,19:7
Digney, Charles E, 1951, Ag 17,19:7
Digney, Frank, 1948, Jl 14,23:2
Digney, Harold P, 1941, S 14,48:2
Digney, R Emmett, 1960, Je 25,21:5
Dignum, Charles J, 1942, Mr 9,19:6
Dignum, Fannie R Mrs, 1942, My 13,19:5
Dihigo, Juan M, 1952, F 16,13:2
Dihlmann, Andreas, 1941, F 8,15:4
DiJanni, Albino, 1955, F 21,21:6
DiJanni, Joseph, 1946, Ag 29,27:5
Dijkstra, L, 1964, Ap 26,34:7
Dijour, Ilja M Mrs, 1956, Jl 3,25:3
Dijxhoorn, Adriaan, 1953, Ja 25,84:4
Dika, Juliette, 1954, S 1,27:3
Dike, Camden C Mrs, 1920, Ja 31,11:3
Dike, John Capt, 1871, Ap 29,1:3
Dike, Norman S, 1953, Ap 16,29:1
Dike, Oscar D, 1940, N 12,23:4
Dike, Paul H, 1956, Je 27,31:1
Dike, Samuel Warren Rev, 1913, D 5,11:6
Dikeman, John, 1879, Ag 26,5:4
Dikeman, Ralph J Sr, 1961, Ap 29,23:1
Diki, Diki, 1925, Jl 22,19:5
Dikijian, Diradour, 1937, D 18,21:6
Dikovics, John, 1963, Ap 10,39:2
Dilberger, Henry J Dr, 1925, Je 24,17:4
Dilbert, Charles, 1953, O 23,23:6
Dilbert, Harry, 1951, O 11,37:1
Dilbert, Louis, 1960, My 10,37:2
Dilday, Virginia, 1953, Ja 25,85:2
Dildine, William H, 1946, Ja 15,23:6
Dilello, Thomas P, 1949, Ap 15,23:1
Dileo, Daniel A, 1947, Ja 10,22:2
Dileo, Joseph C, 1955, Ja 28,20:1
Dilg, W H, 1927, Mr 29,25:3
Dilke, A W, 1883, Mr 13,5:4
Dilke, C W, 1864, Ag 24,2:4
Dilke, Charles Lady, 1904, O 25,9:6
Dilke, Charles Sir, 1911, Ja 27,11:3
Dilke, Fisher W, 1944, Mr 29,21:4
Dilkes, Frank W, 1948, Ag 29,56:4
Dilkes, George R (por), 1938, Ap 6,23:3
Dilkes, George R, 1948, O 9,17:3
Dilks, Charles F, 1945, D 28,15:4
Dilks, John Milton, 1903, O 22,9:6
Dilks, Sampson A Mrs, 1955, Ap 13,29:4

Dilks, W Howard Jr, 1965, Jl 24,21:5
Dill, Andrew H, 1940, Je 19,23:4
Dill, Anna C, 1937, Ag 6,36:1
Dill, Augustus G, 1956, Mr 10,17:4
Dill, B F Col, 1866, Ja 15,4:2
Dill, Chester A, 1951, Mr 21,33:1
Dill, Edmund M Mrs, 1959, Ap 24,27:2
Dill, Elliott C Sr, 1952, F 17,86:3
Dill, Elliott C Sr Mrs, 1953, D 17,37:3
Dill, George B, 1937, My 19,23:4
Dill, Harry, 1948, Ap 22,27:4
Dill, Harry F, 1946, O 29,26:2
Dill, Henry E, 1950, N 22,25:1
Dill, James B Mrs, 1959, Ap 14,35:5
Dill, James Brooks Ex-Judge, 1910, D 3,11:3
Dill, John G, 1944, N 5,54:1
Dill, John W, 1945, Ap 3,19:5
Dill, Joseph H, 1940, Ja 25,21:3
Dill, Lady, 1940, D 25,27:5
Dill, Leonard C Mrs, 1940, Jl 13,14:8
Dill, Leonard C Sr, 1952, Mr 21,23:1
Dill, Max M, 1949, N 23,29:2
Dill, Nettie Mrs, 1938, Jl 21,21:5
Dill, Russell E, 1951, S 28,31:1
Dill, Russell E Mrs, 1964, Je 30,33:1
Dill, Samuel Sir, 1924, My 27,21:4
Dill, William A, 1939, F 9,21:2
Dill, William J, 1952, Ja 15,27:4
Dill, William L, 1952, Ja 16,25:5
Dill, William L Mrs, 1955, N 8,31:4
Dilla, Ralph, 1948, Ag 25,25:1
Dillane, William Mrs, 1946, F 18,21:4
Dillard, Alexander Maj, 1919, My 5,13:2
Dillard, J E, 1953, Jl 11,11:7
Dillard, James B, 1941, O 1,21:6
Dillard, James H, 1940, Ag 3,15:2
Dillard, Paul, 1938, N 11,25:5
Dillaway, C Warren, 1944, F 4,15:4
Dillaway, Rebecca Mrs, 1903, S 18,7:3
Dille, John F, 1957, S 12,31:5
Dillemuth, Charles, 1954, N 6,17:1
Dillenback, Hiram Irving, 1923, Mr 29,19:4
Dillenbeck, Arthur O, 1947, Ap 22,28:3
Dillenbeck, Clark, 1948, O 10,76:4
Dillenberg, D Alan, 1951, My 24,35:5
Dillenberg, Joseph Dr, 1968, Jl 1,33:1
Diller, Alfred W, 1959, Ja 6,33:2
Diller, Alfred W Mrs, 1967, Ja 30,29:3
Diller, Angela, 1968, My 2,47:4
Diller, Burgoyne, 1965, Ja 31,89:1
Diller, Burgoyne Mrs, 1954, F 3,23:3
Diller, Helen E, 1952, D 5,28:3
Dilley, A Urbane, 1956, S 7,24:2
Dilley, Arthur U, 1959, O 13,39:1
Dilley, Charles H, 1942, Mr 26,23:3
Dilley, Oscar H, 1949, Ag 12,17:2
Dilley, Otho Herbert, 1909, Ap 2,9:6
Dilley, Sylvester W, 1950, N 26,90:4
Dillinger, John W, 1943, N 4,23:1
Dillingham, Albert C Mrs, 1953, Jl 27,19:4
Dillingham, Albert Caldwell Adm, 1925, D 7,21:3
Dillingham, Albert R Col, 1937, D 15,25:3
Dillingham, Alex, 1960, Ap 27,37:3
Dillingham, C B, 1934, Ag 31,17:1
Dillingham, C P Capt, 1883, N 15,8:1
Dillingham, Edwin K, 1959, Ag 14,21:4
Dillingham, Frank A, 1941, Ag 22,15:3
Dillingham, Frederic William, 1918, Mr 2,13:2
Dillingham, Frederick H, 1944, Ag 31,17:3
Dillingham, Frederick H Mrs, 1938, D 24,15:5
Dillingham, Harley C, 1965, Jl 19,27:4
Dillingham, Herbert H, 1940, Ag 22,19:3
Dillingham, Herman L, 1958, O 1,37:4
Dillingham, Howard I Mrs, 1962, Mr 22,35:3
Dillingham, James B, 1946, Ag 29,27:2
Dillingham, James D, 1939, Ag 4,13:3
Dillingham, Louise B, 1965, Ja 16,27:5
Dillingham, Louise G Mrs, 1942, Ja 16,21:1
Dillingham, Paul, 1952, My 5,23:5
Dillingham, W A P Rev, 1871, Ap 24,1:3
Dillingham, W S Dr, 1885, Mr 1,2:6
Dillingham, Walter F, 1963, O 23,41:4
Dillingham, William P Sen, 1923, Jl 14,11:4
Dillistin, William H, 1964, Je 14,85:1
Dillistin, William H Mrs, 1961, S 25,33:3
Dillman, Edward L, 1940, My 30,17:5
Dillman, John, 1917, Jl 6,9:6
Dillman, Willard, 1949, O 12,30:3
Dillmeier, William M, 1957, Ja 16,31:5
Dillon, Agnes L, 1948, N 3,27:1
Dillon, Anna H, 1946, Ap 5,25:2
Dillon, Arthur, 1937, Je 7,19:2
Dillon, Arthur J, 1942, Mr 18,23:4
Dillon, Asabel S Mrs, 1960, F 24,37:2
Dillon, Bernard J, 1942, Ap 5,42:2
Dillon, Blanche M, 1942, Jl 3,17:5
Dillon, Charles A, 1941, Ja 19,40:7
Dillon, Charles F, 1957, My 20,25:4
Dillon, Charles J, 1949, N 5,13:6
Dillon, Charles J Mrs, 1944, Je 16,19:2
Dillon, Charles Mrs, 1865, D 14,8:5
Dillon, Charles P, 1914, My 17,IV,7:6
Dillon, Chester A, 1960, N 4,33:2
Dillon, Clarence Mrs, 1961, N 9,35:5
Dillon, D Bruce, 1950, S 18,23:4
Dillon, Daniel J, 1960, N 8,29:2
Dillon, Daniel L, 1948, D 8,31:1
Dillon, David D, 1945, N 9,20:2
Dillon, David F, 1948, Jl 7,23:3
Dillon, Dennis, 1948, F 7,15:4
Dillon, Dennis D, 1964, D 14,35:3
Dillon, E J, 1933, Je 10,13:2
Dillon, Edward H, 1937, Ja 5,23:3
Dillon, Edward J, 1939, O 24,23:5; 1948, F 19,23:1; 1951, O 21,92:4; 1953, Ja 17,15:2
Dillon, Edward N Mrs, 1958, F 18,27:1
Dillon, Edward S, 1959, O 11,86:5
Dillon, Edward S Mrs, 1954, My 16,87:1
Dillon, Edward T, 1955, O 9,86:5
Dillon, Edwin C, 1958, Jl 24,25:2
Dillon, Enrica C, 1946, O 10,27:4
Dillon, Esther Mrs, 1940, My 9,23:4
Dillon, Frank J M, 1961, Ap 23,86:4
Dillon, Frederick J, 1954, Jl 28,23:5
Dillon, Frederick P (Sept 18), 1965, O 11,61:1
Dillon, George F, 1951, Mr 27,29:5
Dillon, George Hill, 1968, My 12,85:1
Dillon, Gregory T, 1957, Je 4,35:1
Dillon, Harry A, 1943, Ja 5,20:2
Dillon, Harry J, 1946, Jl 23,25:3
Dillon, Helen T, 1943, D 20,23:2
Dillon, Henry, 1920, Jl 2,11:5
Dillon, Herbert L, 1968, Ja 9,32:1
Dillon, Isidore (Sotcha), 1961, S 21,35:3
Dillon, J, 1927, Ag 5,17:5
Dillon, J A, 1902, O 16,9:4
Dillon, J Clifford, 1960, Mr 17,33:2
Dillon, Jack, 1942, Ag 9,42:5
Dillon, James, 1941, Jl 2,21:1; 1948, Ap 20,27:5; 1962, My 22,37:2
Dillon, James E, 1925, O 15,23:4
Dillon, James J, 1944, Mr 12,38:4
Dillon, John, 1959, Ag 22,17:5
Dillon, John A, 1959, S 2,29:5
Dillon, John C, 1940, Ja 4,23:4
Dillon, John C Jr Mrs, 1945, Jl 19,23:3
Dillon, John D, 1962, S 3,15:6
Dillon, John Forrest Ex-Judge, 1914, My 6,11:5
Dillon, John I, 1938, Ap 13,25:4
Dillon, John J, 1938, My 2,17:5; 1939, N 29,23:3; 1944, D 2,13:3; 1947, Je 12,25:4; 1950, Mr 23,36:6; 1960, Ag 9,27:5; 1966, Ap 28,43:1
Dillon, John J Mrs, 1953, Ap 24,23:2
Dillon, John J Sr, 1943, D 24,13:4
Dillon, John P, 1948, S 27,23:3
Dillon, John R, 1940, Mr 8,21:4; 1948, S 22,31:5; 1952, Je 17,27:1
Dillon, John T, 1937, D 30,19:6; 1945, S 28,21:2
Dillon, Joseph, 1914, My 20,13:6; 1943, S 28,25:1; 1946, F 25,25:3; 1955, S 30,25:5
Dillon, Joseph A, 1939, My 4,23:1
Dillon, Joseph E, 1951, F 27,27:3
Dillon, Joseph F, 1942, Ja 31,17:6
Dillon, Joseph H, 1938, O 29,19:3
Dillon, Joseph M, 1937, Mr 21,II,8:2
Dillon, Julia A, 1952, Mr 24,25:4
Dillon, L, 1930, Ja 8,27:1
Dillon, Martin F, 1961, F 6,21:1
Dillon, Michael, 1944, Mr 29,21:5
Dillon, Milton S, 1939, F 23,23:3
Dillon, Myrtle J Mrs, 1958, Mr 31,27:4
Dillon, Nicholas F, 1904, Ja 6,9:5
Dillon, Patrick H, 1947, Jl 8,23:3
Dillon, Paul J, 1952, D 8,41:4
Dillon, Paul R, 1950, Je 17,15:5
Dillon, Philip R, 1964, My 3,87:2
Dillon, Philip R Mrs, 1946, Ja 2,19:4
Dillon, Richard C, 1966, Ja 6,27:3
Dillon, Richard J, 1951, O 5,27:1; 1952, D 6,21:3
Dillon, Robert A, 1944, D 1,23:4
Dillon, Robert E, 1952, O 18,19:6
Dillon, Robert F, 1957, N 28,31:1
Dillon, Robert James, 1872, N 27,2:6
Dillon, Schuyler, 1949, F 27,69:2
Dillon, Sean Mrs, 1961, N 21,39:3
Dillon, Sidney, 1892, Je 10,9:3
Dillon, Stephen E, 1938, Mr 13,II,9:3
Dillon, Theodore H, 1961, Jl 12,32:1
Dillon, Thomas A, 1942, Ja 3,19:3
Dillon, Thomas C Mrs, 1964, My 18,29:2
Dillon, Thomas J (por), 1942, Mr 22,49:1
Dillon, Thomas J, 1949, Ja 29,13:5; 1961, D 29,23:2
Dillon, Thomas J Mrs, 1951, Ag 12,77:2
Dillon, Thomas Mrs, 1949, Ja 9,72:3
Dillon, Thomas S, 1937, Jl 21,21:7
Dillon, Walter D, 1940, F 16,19:2
Dillon, Walter E, 1968, F 20,44:1
Dillon, Will A, 1966, F 11,33:1
Dillon, William A, 1925, My 2,15:6; 1953, S 5,15:5
Dillon, William F, 1945, Je 20,23:3; 1956, S 16,84:7
Dillon, William I, 1940, Ja 19,19:5
Dillon, William J, 1945, Mr 4,38:5; 1949, S 20,29:1
Dillon, William T, 1964, O 13,43:2
Dillon, William W, 1957, Mr 4,27:2
Dillont, J Frank, 1915, Mr 8,9:4
Dillow, George M Dr, 1915, Jl 14,9:6
Dills, Duane R, 1952, Jl 26,13:5
Dills, J H, 1882, S 7,5:2
Dills, John F, 1961, S 28,41:4
Dillworth, David, 1939, S 1,17:5
Dillworth, Joseph D, 1944, Je 9,15:4
Dilmore, George S Jr, 1952, Ag 30,13:5
Dilnot, Frank, 1946, Jl 29,21:6
Dilnot, Frank Mrs, 1959, D 31,21:1
Dilon, Robert, 1882, Ap 20,8:1
Dilowa Hutukhtu (several hundred visit bier, Ap 9,14:7), 1965, Ap 8,1:5
Dilthey, William J, 1940, S 21,19:3
Dilts, Alstyne B, 1959, D 31,21:1
Dilts, Asa R, 1947, F 8,17:3
Dilts, Hyacinth, 1951, O 6,19:3
Dilts, J Dothard, 1937, F 15,17:5
Dilts, J Howard, 1952, Je 22,68:2
Dilts, J Howard Mrs, 1959, Jl 19,69:1
Dilts, John C, 1950, N 20,25:5
Dilts, L William, 1958, F 3,23:4
Dilts, Seba A, 1959, Je 13,21:6
Dilts, Seba Mrs, 1950, Ja 26,28:2
Dilts, Theodore H, 1947, S 24,23:4
Diluna, Albert E, 1941, My 25,36:7
Dilworth, Albert C, 1943, F 5,21:3
Dilworth, Annie W Mrs, 1941, Mr 27,23:4
Dilworth, Dewees W, 1958, N 5,39:2
Dilworth, Frank T, 1937, Ja 10,II,9:3
Dilworth, J Dale, 1949, Ap 10,78:4
Dilworth, J Dale Mrs, 1965, Mr 9,35:2
Dilworth, John Robert, 1968, Ja 25,40:1
Dilworth, Joseph, 1967, N 6,47:1
Dilworth, Lawrence Mrs, 1903, D 6,1:6
Dilworth, Read G Mrs, 1922, Mr 26,27:2
Dilworth, William S, 1920, S 24,15:4
DiMaggio, Joseph, 1949, My 4,29:6
DiMaggio, Joseph Mrs, 1951, Je 19,30:3
DiMaggio, Joseph Mrs (will), 1952, Mr 9,V,2:4
DiMaggio, Mike, 1953, My 31,54:1
Dimai, Antonio, 1948, O 6,30:3
Diman, Byron, 1865, Ag 7,3:3
Diman, J L, 1881, F 4,4:7
Diman, John H (por), 1949, Mr 19,15:1
DiMattina, Vincent J, 1966, O 9,86:8
Dimbleby, Richard, 1965, D 23,27:3
Dime, Eric Adolphus, 1924, Ag 1,11:5
Dime, Jimmy, 1939, O 6,25:5
DiMenna, Nicholas, 1966, My 9,39:3
DiMiceli, Joseph, 1942, Ap 25,13:2
Dimick, Justin Gen, 1871, O 15,5:3
Dimick, Stephen W, 1941, Ag 7,17:6
Dimin, Harry, 1948, O 26,31:5
Dimitriew, Kyra B Mrs, 1946, Ap 27,17:6
Dimitriew, Vladimir P, 1964, S 5,19:2
Dimitriyevich, Alex, 1963, S 5,31:1
Dimitroff, George Z, 1968, Ja 3,47:2
Dimitrov, Alex, 1956, Jl 8,2:1
Dimitrov, Georgi Mme, 1958, Jl 6,56:6
Dimitrov, Georgi Premier (por), 1949, Jl 3,1:6
Dimitry, Alexander, 1883, Ja 31,5:5
Dimkin, B T Judge, 1874, D 13,2:6
Dimling, John, 1939, Ag 29,21:4
Dimm, Ira L, 1957, F 4,19:5
Dimmer, Frank J, 1941, O 18,19:1
Dimmick, Clinton M, 1962, O 10,51:6
Dimmick, Frank H Mrs, 1945, S 14,23:3
Dimmick, Frank M Mrs, 1948, Ja 15,23:2
Dimmick, Harry L, 1947, S 7,60:4
Dimmick, Harry L Mrs, 1956, My 10,31:1
Dimmick, J Benjamin, 1920, Ja 16,9:5
Dimmick, O S, 1877, O 9,2:3
Dimmick, S O, 1903, Mr 31,9:6
Dimmick, Samuel O, 1937, S 23,27:5
Dimmit, Charles E, 1939, Ag 16,23:5
Dimmitt, Patterson D, 1948, F 12,23:4
Dimmittz, Arthur L (D B Allen), 1966, Je 11,3
Dimmock, Frank L, 1941, My 29,19:2
Dimmock, W R Prof, 1878, Ap 2,5:6
Dimnet, Ernest, 1954, D 16,37:1
Dimock, A V, 1872, My 29,2:7
Dimock, Anthony W Mrs, 1946, N 10,64:3
Dimock, Anthony Weston, 1918, S 13,11:1
Dimock, Clarence V, 1948, N 9,27:3
Dimock, Ernest K, 1949, Ap 22,24:6
Dimock, George E, 1966, Ja 13,25:2
Dimock, Hedley S, 1958, O 5,86:6
Dimock, Henry F (funl, Ap 13,13:4), 1911, A 11:4
Dimock, Henry F Mrs, 1939, S 13,25:2
Dimock, Julian A, 1945, S 25,25:4
Dimock, Otis K, 1913, S 27,13:5
Dimon, Harry, 1953, N 11,31:3
Dimon, Howard P, 1942, Ag 5,19:3
Dimon, John F Capt, 1912, Mr 20,13:4
Dimona, John R, 1958, S 16,27:1
Dimond, Abraham J, 1956, Ag 5,76:6
Dimond, Anthony J, 1953, My 30,15:3
Dimond, Anthony J Mrs, 1949, S 26,25:2
Dimond, Douglas M, 1962, O 22,29:4
Dimond, E W, 1876, Jl 10,4:6
Dimond, George M, 1951, O 21,93:1
Dimond, James, 1944, Ap 20,19:4
Dimond, James Judge, 1904, D 4,4:5

Dimond, John H, 1943, Ja 14,21:2
Dimond, Joseph H, 1938, Ap 5,21:5
Dimond, Philip, 1968, O 25,47:4
Dimond, Thomas, 1918, Ap 24,13:5; 1938, F 24,19:4
Dimont, C T, 1953, N 7,17:2
D'Imperio, Alexander G, 1964, D 5,31:3
Dimperio, Joseph A Mrs, 1949, Mr 20,76:6
Dimperio, Michael, 1960, Jl 16,19:1
Dimpfl, John, 1946, Jl 15,25:6
Dimsey, John P, 1948, Mr 3,23:2
Dina, A, 1928, Jl 1,II,5:2
Dinahan, Peter Q Father, 1904, Ja 23,9:4
Dinan, Daniel W, 1947, My 9,21:5
Dinan, Francis L, 1950, F 11,15:3
Dinan, Michael T, 1941, F 22,15:2
Dinan, Patrick J, 1942, Ap 5,41:1
Dinand, Augustine A, 1939, Ag 5,15:5
Dinand, John F, 1946, Ja 21,23:4
Dinand, Joseph N, 1943, Jl 30,15:5
Dince, Arthur, 1961, D 28,27:1
Dindas, George, 1968, Ag 1,31:3
Dindorf, William, 1883, Ag 10,5:5
Dineen, Aloysius Msgr, 1968, N 29,45:4
Dineen, Benedict D (funl, Ap 8,29:1), 1958, Ap 4,21:1
Dineen, F George, 1944, S 14,23:5
Dineen, Frank M, 1943, My 7,19:2
Dineen, George A (Feb 21), 1963, Ap 1,35:4
Dineen, George F, 1952, Mr 13,29:1
Dineen, John J, 1937, Ag 1,II,7:3
Dineen, John W, 1952, N 23,88:1
Dineen, Joseph F, 1964, My 1,35:3
Dineen, Joseph P Msgr, 1923, My 12,15:5
Dineen, Leo E, 1940, F 6,21:5
Dineen, Margaret L Mrs, 1920, O 12,15:3
Dineen, Paul, 1948, S 21,27:5
Dineen, William F, 1939, N 12,48:8
Dinehart, Alan, 1944, Jl 18,19:6; 1944, Ag 19,11:6
Dinell, Monroe L, 1956, O 14,86:1
Dinenberg, Leah H, 1954, N 30,29:3
Dinenson, Jacob, 1919, S 3,13:5
Diner, Jacob Dr, 1937, Jl 27,21:5
Diner, Jacob Mrs, 1958, Je 4,33:1
Diner, Milton A, 1959, Je 4,31:5
Dinerman, Benjamin Dr, 1968, Ag 17,27:3
Dinerstein, William, 1938, Ag 8,13:5
Dines, Alta E, 1965, Ap 5,31:4
Dines, Anna A, 1953, O 31,17:6
Dinesen, Isak (Baroness Blixen-Finecke), 1962, S 8, 1:5
Dinesen, Mads J, 1946, Ag 3,15:6
Dingee, Frank A, 1945, Je 28,19:3
Dingee, Mary Mrs, 1914, N 23,11:4
Dingee, Miles B, 1944, Mr 11,13:6
Dingee, Raymond A, 1954, Ap 30,23:2
Dingeldein, William, 1948, Ja 16,21:4
Dingell, John D (funl plans, S 21,33:3), 1955, S 20, 31:1
Dingell, John D Mrs, 1962, Ap 8,87:2
Dingelstedt, Richard M, 1938, Ap 23,15:6
Dingeman, Harry J, 1949, Je 17,23:2
Dinger, Frederick J, 1949, Ag 29,17:5
Dinger, Henry C, 1960, O 16,88:2
Dinger, Jesse E, 1949, Jl 10,57:2
Dinger, Paul, 1948, N 3,27:1
Dingfelder, Carl I, 1944, D 28,19:3
Dingham, C W Dr, 1951, Jl 1,29:2
Dingle, Charles W, 1956, Ja 21,21:3
Dingledine, Raymond C, 1941, F 27,19:2
Dingler, David, 1939, N 18,17:6
Dingley, Anna L, 1954, Jl 16,21:4
Dingley, Arthur H, 1903, S 3,7:7
Dingley, Nelson, 1899, Ja 14,1:5
Dingman, Charles F, 1952, Mr 6,32:3
Dingman, Harry W, 1957, O 3,29:4
Dingman, Herbert A, 1954, O 20,29:3
Dingman, Hiram J, 1947, Jl 12,13:4
Dingman, Jane, 1954, Ag 31,21:6
Dingman, John H, 1912, Ja 29,11:6
Dingman, Lewis H, 1952, Jl 6,49:2
Dingman, Mary A, 1961, Mr 22,41:2
Dingman, Norman M, 1961, O 20,33:2
Dingman, Norman M Mrs, 1955, O 26,31:1
Dingman, Raymond F, 1954, Ap 9,24:6
Dingman, Robert, 1943, O 15,19:4
Dingman, Thomas A Mrs, 1955, Jl 11,23:2
Dingol, Solomon, 1961, Je 14,19:5
Dings, Peter, 1938, O 2,49:2
Dings, Ralph E, 1960, Je 24,27:4
Dingwall, Alexander W, 1918, Jl 29,11:6
Dingwall, Andrew Mrs (Ariel), 1968, Ag 3,25:3
Dingwall, Charles E, 1941, Ap 26,15:4
Dingwall, Harrie R, 1940, Jl 25,17:3
Dingwall, Herbert A Mrs, 1960, My 20,29:1
Dingwall, Robert H, 1968, N 13,47:2
Dinhofer, Julius, 1943, Ag 18,19:6
Dinichert, Paul, 1954, F 15,23:5
Dinkel, Christian, 1903, Ap 18,9:5
Dinkel, Edmund, 1948, Je 3,25:4
Dinkel, Edward, 1952, My 11,92:6
Dinkelacker, Paul F, 1955, Je 6,27:3
Dinkelman Betsey (will), 1938, D 1,21:2
Dinkelspiel, David, 1948, Ap 6,23:2
Dinkelspiel, Lloyd W, 1959, My 16,23:2
Dinkelspiel, Moses, 1916, Je 1,11:6
Dinkey, A C, 1931, Ag 12,19:1
Dinkey, Alva C Jr, 1952, O 28,31:3
Dinkin, Leon Mrs, 1956, Ap 25,35:4
Dinkins, James, 1939, Jl 20,19:4
Dinkins, Tyre J, 1951, Ag 9,21:3
Dinkins, William T, 1949, S 23,23:3
Dinkmeyer, Henry W, 1957, F 17,92:3
Dinn, Louis, 1966, S 23,37:2
Dinneeen, William H Mrs, 1948, Ag 25,25:2
Dinneen, Daniel Mrs, 1949, S 10,17:5
Dinneen, Michael F, 1941, Ag 30,13:2
Dinneen, Rich D, 1960, Je 1,39:5
Dinneen, William H, 1955, Ja 15,13:1
Dinnen, James M, 1945, Ag 16,19:5
Dinney, Henry C, 1958, My 31,15:3
Dinnyes, Lajos, 1961, My 5,29:1
Dino, Duke de (Chas Maurice Talleyrand-Perigord), 1917, Ja 6,13:4
Dinochan, 1872, Ja 2,2:6
Dinoffer, Joseph Mrs, 1948, Ja 21,25:3
Dinsdale, Robert, 1943, N 16,23:4
Dinse, Henry, 1924, My 17,15:5
Dinsen, Hans N, 1949, Ag 23,23:4
Dinsmoor, Alice, 1941, Je 16,15:3
Dinsmoor, Theodore E, 1961, Ag 20,87:1
Dinsmoor, William B Mrs, 1960, S 30,27:2
Dinsmore, Andrew Rev Dr, 1920, S 30,9:5
Dinsmore, Campbell, 1959, S 13,84:2
Dinsmore, Charles A, 1941, Ag 15,17:6
Dinsmore, Clarence Gray (will), 1905, D 29,6:4
Dinsmore, Clifford E, 1960, Jl 20,29:4
Dinsmore, Ed, 1954, D 20,29:3
Dinsmore, Frank, 1948, Jl 7,23:4
Dinsmore, Frank W, 1946, Ap 11,25:6
Dinsmore, James T, 1965, Ja 2,19:2
Dinsmore, John, 1945, D 21,21:1
Dinsmore, John C, 1947, F 20,25:5
Dinsmore, Madelain I, 1948, Ag 14,13:1
Dinsmore, Marion de P C Mrs, 1941, D 20,20:4
Dinsmore, Mary E C Mrs, 1941, S 11,23:6
Dinsmore, Robert S, 1957, S 26,25:3
Dinsmore, S P, 1882, Mr 24,5:4
Dinsmore, Walter, 1965, My 21,71:4
Dinsmore, William B, 1906, Mr 16,9:5
Dinsmore, William B Mrs, 1922, D 23,13:6
Dinstman, Isidor, 1967, Jl 8,25:5
DiNunzio, Ralph Sr, 1958, My 3,19:6
Dinwiddie, Courtenay, 1943, S 14,23:3
Dinwiddie, E C, 1935, My 6,19:1
Dinwiddie, Emily W, 1949, Mr 13,76:8
Dinwiddie, George S, 1968, Jl 24,41:2
Dinwiddie, Marcus W, 1951, Mr 21,33:3
Dinwiddie, W, 1934, Je 18,17:3
Dinwiddie, William C, 1964, O 2,37:5
Dinwoodie, Clara L, 1949, My 10,25:4
Dioda, Peter P Sr, 1959, Jl 20,25:5
Diodine, Frank, 1937, Ap 23,21:4
Dioguardi, Orestes, 1965, D 23,28:2
Diomedes, Alex, 1950, N 13,28:3
Dion, Alfred H, 1958, My 22,29:4
Dion, Countess, 1881, My 24,5:2
Dion, Cyrille, 1878, O 3,8:4
Dion, Edward H, 1959, Ap 15,33:2
Dion, Frederic L, 1943, D 10,28:2
Dion, Hormisdas, 1924, Ap 28,15:4
Dion, Jules P F A de, 1946, Ag 21,28:2
Dionne, Emilie (funl, Ag 9,5:1), 1954, Ag 7,1:3
Dionne, Emilie (est appr), 1955, Ag 19,4:5
Dionne, Fereol E, 1941, D 19,27:6
Dionne, Oliver, 1944, N 28,23:5
Dior, Christian (funl plans, O 26,21:4; funl, O 29,-31:4), 1957, O 24,1:8
Diorio, Anthony, 1947, S 29,21:2
Diossy, G S, 1882, Ap 29,5:1
Diou, Charles J, 1961, My 3,37:4
Diouf, Galandou, 1941, Ag 7,17:5
Dipaolo, Philip, 1943, Ap 24,13:6
Dipizzo, Daniel A, 1955, My 24,31:1
Diplock, Marcus E Mrs, 1955, N 4,29:3
Dipman, Carl W, 1954, Jl 24,13:3
Dippe, Frances M Mrs, 1950, S 14,31:4
Dippel, A, 1932, My 14,15:3
Dippel, Daniel Mrs, 1953, Ja 1,23:5
Dippel, Michael W Mrs, 1944, D 22,17:3
Dippel, Walter H, 1956, Mr 21,38:3
Dippel, William J, 1942, O 9,21:2
Dipple, John W, 1955, Jl 31,68:4
Dippold, George C, 1957, S 9,25:2
Dippold, Herman C, 1962, O 16,47:5
Dippold, Paul A, 1962, S 22,25:4
D'Ippolito, Angelo B, 1956, Ag 9,25:4
Dipson, Nikitas D, 1961, My 5,29:4
Diradourian, Dikran A, 1954, S 19,89:3
Dircks, Walter D, 1945, O 26,19:5
Direnga, Otto G, 1963, Je 3,29:5
Diringshofen, Heinz von, 1967, My 9,40:6
Dirk, Nathaniel, 1961, Ja 5,31:1
Dirkes, Howard J Mrs, 1950, O 23,23:2
Dirks, John F Mrs, 1962, O 25,39:2
Dirks, Leonard R, 1957, D 15,86:3
Dirks, Rudolph, 1968, Ap 22,47:2
Dirksen, Herbert von, 1955, D 21,29:3
Dirksen, Mechteld D, 1957, N 16,19:4
Dirksend, Henry, 1874, Ag 17,1:6
Dirlam, Harry F Mrs, 1949, Ag 17,23:4
Dirmoser, Oswald, 1938, F 8,21:5
Dirr, Peter A, 1961, Ap 20,33:4
Dirr, Peter G, 1967, N 4,33:3
Dirvin, Vincent A Mrs, 1964, Jl 4,13:6
Disbrow, Charles R, 1954, F 16,25:4
Disbrow, Chester H, 1960, O 15,23:5
Disbrow, George Mrs, 1947, My 28,25:5
Disbrow, Gordon V R Mrs, 1958, S 20,19:5
Disbrow, Griffin B, 1943, Je 22,19:1
Disbrow, Hamilton T, 1942, Jl 26,30:8
Disbrow, Joseph P, 1941, S 19,24:3
Disbrow, Leslie C, 1953, Ap 19,90:6
Disbrow, Livingston, 1908, N 15,9:5
Disbrow, Louis, 1939, Jl 11,19:3
Disbrow, Nelson H Mrs, 1956, F 8,33:5
Disbrow, Robert L, 1937, My 5,25:5
Disbrow, Robert Newton Dr, 1923, O 25,19:5
Disbrow, Vanderhoef M, 1938, Ja 7,20:1
Disbrow, William H B, 1952, Mr 26,29:4
Disch, William J, 1953, F 4,27:3
Dischert, William H, 1951, Ap 21,17:4
D'Isere, Guy, 1939, Jl 20,20:4
Diserens, Marcell H, 1964, F 16,92:5
Diserens, Paul, 1958, O 8,35:4
Diserens, Robert C, 1940, Jl 18,19:3
Diserio, John M, 1962, Je 15,27:4
Diserio, Matthew J, 1960, Jl 16,19:1
Diserio, Matthew J Jr, 1941, Jl 12,13:3
Disessa, Louis, 1951, N 5,31:5
Disette, Andrew P, 1948, Ag 2,21:1
Dishart, George, 1937, Jl 17,15:6
Disick, Sol, 1951, O 30,29:5
Disken, Henry J, 1950, My 18,29:1
Diskin, Carlton F, 1967, Ja 28,27:3
Diskin, James, 1949, Ap 21,25:3
Diskin, James A, 1951, Mr 9,25:6
Diskin, Thomas F Mrs, 1957, F 1,25:1
Disler, Louis, 1940, O 9,25:1
Dismond, H Binga, 1956, N 22,33:6
Dismore, Frederick, 1940, F 18,41:2
Dismukes, Douglas E, 1949, D 4,110:3
Dismukes, John T, 1925, D 10,25:5
Disney, Albert E, 1954, O 19,27:3
Disney, E E, 1884, Je 7,5:1
Disney, Elias, 1941, S 14,50:4
Disney, Robert S, 1953, Jl 31,19:3
Disney, Walt (Walter E),(funl, D 17,33:1), 1966, D 16,1:6
Disney, Wesley E, 1961, Mr 27,31:3
Disosway, W W Lt, 1863, O 29,2:5
Disoway, J D, 1878, Je 27,5:5
Disque, Brice P, 1960, Mr 3,29:1
Disque, Robert C, 1968, My 9,47:1
Disque, Robert W, 1946, O 18,23:3
Disque, William, 1948, Ag 12,22:3
Disraeli, Mrs (Countess of Beaconsfield), 1872, D 31,1:2
Diss, Albert B, 1946, F 8,19:4
Diss, Daniel B, 1963, Ap 20,27:4
D'Issertelle, Henry G, 1946, Ag 9,17:6
Dissez, P F Rev Dr, 1908, Ja 26,9:2
Dissinger, Lawrence, 1947, D 3,30:2
Dissinger, Solomon N, 1965, Ja 11,45:4
Dissman, George A, 1947, F 14,22:3
Dissman, George A Mrs, 1947, Ja 30,25:4
Disston, Effie Mrs, 1941, My 27,23:4
Disston, Frank, 1937, Jl 5,17:6
Disston, Harry C, 1916, Ag 19,9:5
Disston, Harry Mrs, 1951, Ja 17,27:2
Disston, Henry, 1945, Ag 30,21:6
Disston, Jacob S, 1938, Mr 1,21:2
Disston, William D, 1950, My 24,29:1
Distelhurst, Heber D, 1956, F 19,93:1
Distillator, Abner Mrs, 1949, Ja 11,31:6
Distin, Charles E, 1949, Ap 15,24:3
Distin, Henry, 1903, O 18,9:5
Distin, William H, 1907, Jl 24,7:6
Distler, Daniel H, 1962, Jl 11,36:1
Distler, Frank C, 1954, My 12,31:5
Distler, John C, 1944, D 12,23:3
Distler, Marion H, 1964, Ja 26,81:1
Distler, Richard W, 1956, F 16,29:4
Distler, Walter G, 1949, O 7,27:4
Ditchburn, John Mrs, 1950, Ag 23,29:3
Ditchett, Samuel H, 1938, Ja 13,21:3
Ditchett, William L, 1948, Mr 21,60:3
Ditchy, Clair W, 1967, Ag 3,33:3
Ditenfass, Henry, 1953, Ag 26,27:5
Dithmar, Edward A (por),(funl, O 18,15:3), 1917, O 17,13:1
Dithmar, Edward A Mrs, 1925, Ja 11,5:2
Dithmar, Henry Mrs, 1907, D 29,9:4
Dithrich, W Heber, 1953, Ap 19,91:1
Dithridge, William I, 1942, F 9,15:3
Ditman, Norman E, 1944, D 16,15:5
Ditmars, Chauncey L C, 1939, O 12,25:4
Ditmars, Edna R Mrs, 1940, Ap 26,21:5
Ditmars, Edward W, 1924, Ja 24,17:4
Ditmars, Frank N, 1944, My 6,15:4
Ditmars, George F, 1942, Mr 25,21:5

Ditmars, Harold E, 1952, Jl 1,23:5
Ditmars, James P, 1941, D 26,13:4
Ditmars, Jessie H, 1940, Jl 8,17:6
Ditmars, John R Mrs (M Olivette), 1959, Mr 18,17:4
Ditmars, Raymond L (por), 1942, My 13,19:6
Ditmars, Raymond Mrs, 1956, Ag 8,25:1
Ditmars, Roy E, 1952, O 28,31:3
Ditmas, Andrew, 1923, Mr 25,6:2
Ditmas, Charles A (por), 1938, Ag 1,13:4
Ditmas, Holmes V, 1940, My 12,49:1
Ditmas, John H, 1914, Je 11,11:6
Ditmas, Mary K, 1940, Mr 24,31:2
Ditmer, Merlin A, 1950, Mr 5,92:6
Ditmore, Frank W Mrs, 1950, N 14,31:2
DiTolla, Robert J, 1958, O 23,32:1
Diton, Carl Mrs, 1953, D 18,29:2
Diton, Carl R, 1962, Ja 27,21:3
Ditore, Michael, 1944, O 8,43:1
Ditoro, William E, 1952, Ja 10,29:4
Ditrichstein, Josephine Mrs, 1939, O 26,23:2
Ditrichstein, L, 1928, Je 30,17:3
Ditson, Alice M Mrs, 1940, My 1,24:3
Dittemore, John V, 1937, My 11,26:2
Dittenhoefer, Abraham Jesse Judge, 1919, F 24,13:2
Dittenhoefer, Myer, 1919, Ap 3,11:4
Ditter, Anna E Mrs, 1944, Ja 23,37:2
Ditter, G Harry, 1958, Jl 17,27:4
Dittler, Herbert, 1951, D 20,31:2
Dittman, Frank W, 1959, Ap 30,31:3
Dittman, J Harry, 1946, S 24,30:2
Dittman, Joseph F, 1960, Jl 7,31:4
Dittman, Louis F Inspector, 1937, My 3,19:3
Dittmann, John A, 1948, O 19,27:3
Dittmar, Anthony J, 1946, O 10,27:5
Dittmar, Carl H, 1950, Mr 12,94:6
Dittmar, Carl H Mrs, 1958, Mr 19,31:5
Dittmar, George C, 1947, D 13,15:3
Dittmar, Henry L, 1953, F 3,25:1
Dittmar, Herman H, 1950, O 31,27:3
Dittmar, Moritz A, 1960, Je 22,35:2
Dittmar, Richard A, 1946, D 30,22:3
Dittmer, Clarence G, 1950, Mr 7,27:5
Dittmer, E G, 1938, Mr 16,23:1
Dittmer, Herbert G, 1964, S 10,35:2
Dittrich, Albert E Mrs, 1947, N 1,15:5
Dittrich, Emil C, 1941, Jl 12,13:4
Dittrich, H Joseph Mrs, 1960, Ja 10,86:3
Dittrich, Joseph A, 1963, Ag 26,27:3
Dittrich, Paul, 1957, N 1,23:1
Dittrich, William F, 1938, Je 22,23:3
Dittrick, Alva R, 1943, F 28,48:2
Dittrick, Charles R, 1945, O 14,44:5
Dittrick, Howard, 1954, Jl 13,23:2
Dittus, Charles H, 1950, D 26,23:3
Ditzel, Augustus H, 1952, Ja 11,21:3
Ditzel, Edward J Sr, 1948, My 5,25:3
Ditzel, Emil A, 1949, Ja 23,68:8
Ditzel, George, 1937, Jl 7,7:7; 1948, Ap 16,23:4
Ditzel, Louis A, 1949, Jl 8,19:3
Ditzel, Oscar M, 1963, S 15,86:3
Ditzler, Hugh, 1949, O 5,29:3
Diven, Alex S, 1952, Jl 25,18:8
Diver, Maud Mrs, 1945, N 11,42:2
Diver, Walter T, 1940, Ap 12,23:3
Divine, Alice, 1950, Je 30,23:6
Divine, Charles H, 1950, My 9,30:3
Divine, Father (Geo Baker),(funl plans, S 12,86:8), 1965, S 11,1:5
Divine, Frank H, 1941, Ap 2,23:5
Divine, Frank J, 1941, O 30,23:2
Divine, Harry M, 1947, Jl 10,21:4
Divine, Jane S, 1942, Je 19,23:4
Divine, John H, 1943, N 13,13:3
Diviney, Frederick P, 1961, Ja 12,29:5
Diviney, Joseph, 1945, Je 27,19:3
Diviny, Mary G, 1953, F 1,88:6
Diviovanni, Marco Mrs, 1954, D 18,15:6
Divler, Alva P, 1943, Mr 28,24:8
Divver, Joseph G, 1948, Ag 2,21:5
Divver, Patrick, 1903, Ja 29,9:5
Diween, Joseph Sir, 1908, N 10,9:4
Dix, Alfred Perkins, 1920, Jl 12,9:4
Dix, Alvah J, 1944, D 20,23:4
Dix, Arthur A, 1948, Ap 7,25:5
Dix, Charles B, 1939, S 17,49:2
Dix, Col, 1873, Ap 5,3:7
Dix, Dorothy, 1951, D 17,31:1
Dix, E C, 1953, My 15,23:3
Dix, E C Mrs, 1947, Ja 18,15:4
Dix, Edgar H Jr, 1963, Ja 29,7:4
Dix, Edward A, 1911, Ag 26,9:5
Dix, Edward S, 1947, D 2,29:2
Dix, Elise W Mrs, 1938, Jl 9,13:5
Dix, Eulabee Mrs, 1961, Je 16,33:3
Dix, Frank W, 1941, Ag 22,15:6
Dix, George E, 1954, F 7,88:2
Dix, George S, 1956, D 24,13:4
Dix, H A, 1933, Je 21,18:2
Dix, Harry, 1968, Mr 8,39:4
Dix, Howard W, 1956, S 16,85:1
Dix, Irving W, 1947, Ja 20,25:3
Dix, J A (funl, Ap 25,8:1), 1879, Ap 20,1:4
Dix, J A, 1928, Ap 10,29:3
Dix, J A Mrs, 1884, F 7,2:4
Dix, J Ross (G S Phillips), 1865, N 10,4:6
Dix, J W (see also Ap 22), 1877, Ap 24,8:2
Dix, Jacob J, 1948, F 8,60:3
Dix, James A, 1865, O 12,4:1
Dix, John A, 1945, O 2,23:6
Dix, John A Mrs, 1923, D 19,19:4
Dix, Lester, 1961, Je 26,31:3
Dix, Lester Mrs, 1938, F 7,15:3
Dix, Lillian, 1922, O 12,19:5
Dix, Maurice J, 1963, My 22,41:5
Dix, Monroe L, 1958, S 1,13:5
Dix, Morgan Dr, 1913, Je 21,9:5
Dix, Morgan Mrs, 1921, My 18,17:4
Dix, Morgan Rev Dr (funl, My 3,11:5), 1908, My 1, 8:3
Dix, Richard (will, S 24,13:2), 1949, S 21,31:1
Dix, Richard (will), 1949, O 19,2:3
Dix, Walter S, 1958, Ja 27,27:1
Dix, Walter S Mrs, 1946, My 23,21:1
Dix, Warren R Mrs, 1915, Ja 11,9:4; 1960, Jl 3,32:4
Dix, William F, 1945, S 12,25:4
Dixey, Henry E, 1943, F 26,19:1
Dixey, Joseph H, 1947, Ja 28,23:1
Dixey, Richard C Mrs, 1924, Ap 4,19:5
Dixey, William B, 1953, Ap 4,13:1
Dixie, Florence Lady, 1905, N 8,9:6
Dixie, George D, 1948, D 28,21:3
Dixie, John, 1956, Jl 25,29:1
Dixien, Jean Marie Leon Bp, 1915, Mr 29,9:5
Dixon, Albert Firman Capt, 1909, Mr 11,9:5
Dixon, Alex B, 1949, My 11,29:5
Dixon, Alex J D, 1948, Je 10,25:3
Dixon, Alexander B Mrs, 1945, Ap 6,15:1
Dixon, Alfred Herbert Sir, 1920, D 11,13:4
Dixon, Alfred M Mrs, 1949, Ag 9,25:5
Dixon, Allan R, 1964, F 20,29:3
Dixon, Amory A, 1952, N 4,29:1
Dixon, Amos F, 1965, My 3,33:4
Dixon, Archibald, 1876, Ap 25,5:5
Dixon, Arthur W Sr, 1962, Jl 10,33:4
Dixon, Augusta P, 1959, F 18,33:1
Dixon, Brandt Van B, 1941, S 8,15:2
Dixon, C Madeleine, 1945, D 24,15:5
Dixon, C P, 1883, Je 6,4:7
Dixon, Campbell, 1958, Ag 2,17:5
Dixon, Carl S, 1950, Ap 30,102:5
Dixon, Charles, 1943, S 30,21:4
Dixon, Charles H, 1940, N 1,25:2
Dixon, Charles J B, 1957, Je 21,25:2
Dixon, Charles M, 1958, O 4,21:1
Dixon, Charles Mrs, 1951, Ja 30,25:1
Dixon, Charles P, 1939, My 1,23:4
Dixon, Clement L, 1964, S 8,29:2
Dixon, Clement L Mrs, 1968, Mr 12,43:1
Dixon, Courtland P, 1943, Mr 18,19:4
Dixon, Courtlandt P, 1921, O 25,17:5
Dixon, Cyrus B, 1939, O 14,19:6
Dixon, Daniel Sir, 1907, Mr 11,7:7
Dixon, DeForest H, 1956, My 8,33:4
Dixon, E H, 1880, D 8,5:1
Dixon, Edgar H, 1962, Ag 3,23:4
Dixon, Edmund J, 1947, O 31,23:4
Dixon, Edward, 1949, Ap 7,30:2
Dixon, Edwin M, 1956, Mr 29,27:5
Dixon, Eleanor S Mrs, 1955, Mr 9,11:3
Dixon, Eleanor W Mrs, 1966, Ja 14,39:2
Dixon, Elizabeth K, 1964, D 12,31:1
Dixon, Elizabeth S, 1943, My 24,15:6
Dixon, Florence, 1943, Ja 15,17:3
Dixon, Frances S Mrs, 1942, F 5,22:3
Dixon, Francis S, 1967, Ja 7,27:4
Dixon, Frank, 1965, O 12,47:2
Dixon, Frank E, 1947, Ja 2,27:2
Dixon, Frank H, 1944, Ja 28,17:3
Dixon, Frank H Mrs, 1955, N 17,35:3
Dixon, Fred J, 1944, N 2,19:4
Dixon, Frederick, 1923, N 25,23:2
Dixon, G A, 1933, O 15,36:3
Dixon, G Arthur, 1957, N 3,88:5
Dixon, G Gale, 1958, D 10,39:2
Dixon, G T, 1933, Mr 28,19:3
Dixon, George, 1965, D 21,37:2
Dixon, George A, 1956, Jl 25,29:5
Dixon, George A Mrs, 1925, O 8,27:3
Dixon, George D (will, Jl 18,II,8:8), 1937, Je 6,II,9:1
Dixon, George D Mrs, 1946, Jl 8,29:3
Dixon, George G, 1939, D 29,15:2
Dixon, George Mrs, 1967, Ja 17,39:2
Dixon, George P, 1956, Jl 11,29:3
Dixon, George S, 1944, O 10,23:3
Dixon, George W, 1938, S 9,21:1
Dixon, Harry J, 1954, Ap 19,23:3
Dixon, Hattie Mrs, 1946, N 29,25:4
Dixon, Helen F Mrs, 1911, S 7,9:5
Dixon, Homer L, 1950, O 2,23:4
Dixon, Hume Mrs, 1955, Jl 31,69:2
Dixon, Irene E, 1911, Je 15,9:5
Dixon, J M, 1934, My 23,19:2
Dixon, J N, 1883, D 20,4:7
Dixon, J Newton Capt, 1875, Mr 14,1:6
Dixon, J Shipley, 1960, Ag 10,31:3
Dixon, J Shipley Mrs, 1954, O 6,25:2
Dixon, J W, 1926, Jl 24,11:3
Dixon, James, 1946, Ap 19,29:3; 1961, S 28,41:4
Dixon, James A, 1953, Jl 9,25:4
Dixon, James B, 1949, Ap 25,23:2
Dixon, James Ex-Sen, 1873, Mr 28,5:5
Dixon, James Jr, 1961, Ag 1,31:2
Dixon, James L, 1960, My 20,29:1
Dixon, Jane (Mrs W H Wells), 1960, O 23,88:7
Dixon, John, 1876, Jl 7,4:6
Dixon, John E, 1961, F 27,27:2
Dixon, John F, 1957, Je 29,17:5
Dixon, John J, 1946, O 25,23:5; 1959, Ap 12,86:3
Dixon, John J Mrs, 1944, N 11,13:6
Dixon, Jonathan Justice (est, Jl 4,7:3), 1906, My 22 9:6
Dixon, Joseph, 1915, My 26,13:5
Dixon, Joseph W, 1962, Ja 29,25:2
Dixon, Joseph W Mrs, 1957, Jl 10,27:5
Dixon, Karl H, 1946, Ap 18,27:4
Dixon, L F, 1956, Je 8,25:5
Dixon, Lee, 1953, Ja 11,91:2
Dixon, Leonard L, 1944, Ag 30,17:4
Dixon, Lewis M, 1961, O 14,23:4
Dixon, Marcella B Mrs, 1950, N 30,33:4
Dixon, Margaret R Mrs, 1938, Ja 19,23:4
Dixon, Maynard, 1946, N 15,23:2
Dixon, Morton, 1956, Mr 24,19:2
Dixon, Morton W, 1959, D 24,19:2
Dixon, Mrs Ex-Sen, 1871, Je 19,1:6
Dixon, N F, 1881, Ap 12,5:3
Dixon, Orloff O, 1940, Jl 27,13:2
Dixon, Pierson J, 1965, Ap 23,35:4
Dixon, R Herbert, 1955, Jl 2,15:5
Dixon, Robert B, 1942, D 17,29:3
Dixon, Robert L, 1951, S 25,29:3
Dixon, Robert P, 1948, N 6,13:2
Dixon, Russell F, 1962, O 13,25:1
Dixon, Samuel G Dr, 1918, F 27,11:5
Dixon, Susan H, 1947, D 11,33:4
Dixon, Theodore P, 1959, Jl 30,27:3
Dixon, Thomas, 1946, Ap 4,25:1
Dixon, Thomas D, 1943, F 17,21:5
Dixon, Thomas F, 1949, Mr 23,27:3
Dixon, Thomas J, 1955, F 27,87:2
Dixon, Thomas Jr, 1953, O 17,15:4
Dixon, Thomas Mrs, 1937, D 30,19:4
Dixon, W E, 1931, Ag 17,15:1
Dixon, W Palmer, 1968, Jl 27,27:3
Dixon, Walter L, 1961, Ja 2,25:4
Dixon, Warren Jr Mrs, 1962, My 2,37:2
Dixon, Wesley M Mrs, 1958, O 19,86:8
Dixon, Wilbur J, 1956, O 24,37:5
Dixon, William A, 1938, Ja 23,II,8:1
Dixon, William D, 1952, Jl 2,25:5
Dixon, William J, 1944, Jl 10,15:6
Dixon, William L, 1954, Mr 1,25:5
Dixon, William T Rev, 1909, Je 4,7:4
Dixon, 1879, N 3,5:1
Dizer, Wright C, 1949, Je 18,13:4
Dizinno, Michael, 1964, Je 16,39:1
Djajadiningrat, Raden L, 1944, Jl 23,35:3
Djanghindin, Alibi, 1953, Ag 17,5:2
Djeneef, Ivan, 1955, Je 14,29:4
Djerf, Ero K, 1968, Ap 24,47:3
D'Jimas, Demetrius E, 1951, Mr 13,31:3
Djojosukarto, Sidik, 1955, S 10,17:6
Djouri el Kihal Mohamed, 1955, F 25,21:2
Djuanda, Kartawidjaja, 1963, N 7,37:4
Djugashvili, Ekaterina G Mrs, 1937, Je 10,23:6
Djukic, Pane, 1952, Jl 4,5:3
D'Korsakoff, Simon Mrs, 1937, D 15,25:4
Dlhos, Philip, 1947, Je 14,15:4
Dlouhy, Charles Frederick, 1907, S 8,7:6
Dlugasch, Morris, 1943, F 20,13:4
Dlugasch, Morris Mrs, 1947, Ja 16,25:1
D'Lugoff, Ralph Mrs, 1964, S 23,47:5
Dmentiev, Nikolai I, 1954, Ag 19,23:3
Dmitri, Ivan (Levon West), 1968, Ap 26,47:3
Dmokhovsky, Vladimir, 1952, My 29,27:3
Dmowski, Roman, 1939, Ja 3,17:3
Dneprov, Ivan, 1943, N 15,19:6
Do Rego Barros, Sebastiao, 1946, O 23,27:3
Doak, Charles G, 1956, Ap 23,27:1
Doak, Eleanor C, 1942, Ag 29,15:4
Doak, James J, 1938, N 7,19:5
Doak, John Y, 1941, My 19,17:4
Doak, W N, 1933, O 24,21:1
Doak, William L, 1954, N 27,13:2
Doak, William N Mrs, 1951, N 14,31:2
Doame, Benjamin H Mrs, 1956, Jl 14,15:5
Doan, Augustus Chasey, 1919, Jl 6,20:4
Doan, Murray M, 1939, N 7,28:3
Doane, Adelaide L Mrs, 1940, Je 3,15:3
Doane, Aloysius S Mrs, 1952, Mr 22,13:1
Doane, Benjamin, 1916, Jl 18,9:7
Doane, Benjamin H (por), 1947, Ag 16,13:3
Doane, Burnett O, 1956, Mr 2,23:4
Doane, C H Dr, 1884, Je 10,5:3
Doane, Charles E, 1937, Ja 29,19:2
Doane, Clarence E, 1947, My 29,21:4
Doane, Eugene P Mrs, 1947, Ag 12,23:4
Doane, Frances H, 1941, D 9,31:2
Doane, Francis A, 1950, O 9,25:5

Doane, G Hobart Msgr, 1905, Ja 21,1:2
Doane, G W, 1928, My 29,25:3
Doane, George W Mrs, 1954, O 19,27:4
Doane, George Washington, 1859, Ap 28,1:6
Doane, Harry, 1937, O 26,23:5
Doane, J Hervey Mrs, 1938, N 11,25:1
Doane, J W, 1901, Mr 24,7:6
Doane, Kendric P, 1956, D 8,19:6
Doane, Leon L, 1952, N 21,25:3
Doane, Luigi Galvani Dr, 1909, Ap 7,11:6
Doane, Percy G, 1945, Mr 29,23:2
Doane, Phil S, 1940, Ap 28,36:3
Doane, Ralph H, 1941, N 8,19:6
Doane, Robert R, 1961, O 21,21:6
Doane, Robert R Mrs, 1966, Ag 2,33:3
Doane, Samuel E, 1952, D 11,33:5
Doane, Timothy N, 1949, N 16,30:2
Doane, W Brad, 1945, O 11,23:2
Doane, Warren F, 1940, Je 14,21:2
Doane, William C Dr, 1909, Ag 3,7:4
Doane, William Croswell Mrs, 1907, N 10,9:5; 1907, N 14,9:6
Doane, William Crowell Bp (funl, My 20,11:5), 1913, My 18,IV,7:6
Doane, William Howard Dr, 1915, D 25,7:5
Dobbelaar, Edward M Mrs, 1959, Ja 29,27:5
Dobbelsteen, Ambrose L, 1947, N 19,28:3
Dobben, Gerard B, 1951, S 8,17:3
Dobberstein, P M, 1954, Jl 27,16:4
Dobbie, Charles, 1956, S 4,29:2
Dobbie, George A, 1951, My 25,27:3
Dobbie, George H, 1944, Ja 20,19:5
Dobbie, John M, 1945, Mr 24,17:6
Dobbie, William, 1950, Ja 21,17:3; 1964, O 4,88:7
Dobbin, Harold L, 1948, Je 9,29:5
Dobbin, Lester B, 1953, S 23,31:2
Dobbin, William E, 1943, Ag 22,36:4
Dobbin, William J Mrs, 1958, N 4,27:1
Dobbins, Donald C, 1943, F 15,15:3
Dobbins, Edgar Y, 1955, Mr 1,25:1
Dobbins, Edward L Col, 1916, Je 7,13:7
Dobbins, Francis V Mrs, 1961, Je 24,21:5
Dobbins, Harry T, 1953, O 16,27:1
Dobbins, James B (will), 1938, N 19,5:2
Dobbins, James M, 1960, F 2,35:2
Dobbins, John W, 1956, My 24,31:4
Dobbins, Langford B, 1958, My 4,89:1
Dobbins, Matthew J, 1923, Ja 30,17:4
Dobbins, Raymond A, 1950, N 5,92:5
Dobbins, T Munroe (will, F 1,10:3), 1952, Ja 25,21:3
Dobbins, Walter C, 1953, Jl 17,17:4
Dobbins, Walter C Mrs, 1965, Je 26,29:5
Dobbins, Walter E, 1954, Ag 10,19:5
Dobbins, William F, 1951, Mr 22,31:2
Dobbrow, Charles, 1937, D 8,25:5
Dobbs, Caroline C Mrs, 1945, S 17,19:3
Dobbs, Charles E W, 1960, F 12,14:5
Dobbs, Clara Mrs, 1937, Mr 9,23:1
Dobbs, Edward W, 1950, Je 4,92:4
Dobbs, George W Jr, 1952, Ap 22,29:4
Dobbs, George W Sr, 1940, O 2,23:3
Dobbs, Gilbert W Mrs, 1945, Jl 6,11:4
Dobbs, Hoyt M, 1954, D 10,27:3
Dobbs, James K, 1960, S 5,15:1
Dobbs, John F, 1949, S 21,31:2
Dobbs, John M, 1966, Ag 28,92:3
Dobbs, John W, 1961, S 1,17:3
Dobbs, Peter, 1954, Mr 23,27:3
Dobbs, Samuel C, 1950, N 2,31:1
Dobbs, William F, 1956, F 2,25:2
Dobbs, William H, 1967, Mr 26,68:8
Dobbyn, Charles R, 1942, Mr 10,19:2
Dobbyn, William, 1939, Ag 6,37:4
Dobecki, Theodore F, 1937, S 9,23:2
Dobell, Charles, 1954, O 20,30:2
Dobell, Howard A, 1944, D 10,53:2
Dobell, Sydney, 1874, Ag 25,4:7
Dober, Conrad K (Con Conard), 1938, S 29,25:2
Doberstein, John W, 1965, O 16,27:5
Doberstine, John N, 1951, Ag 18,11:2
Dobert, Harry, 1948, Ja 30,23:2
Dobes, O P Capt, 1937, Mr 2,21:3
Dobi, Istvan, 1968, N 25,47:1
Dobie, Alonozo S, 1943, Ja 28,19:3
Dobie, Armistead M, 1962, Ag 8,32:1
Dobie, Charles C, 1943, Ja 13,23:4
Dobie, Duncan A, 1939, O 24,23:4
Dobie, Gilmour, 1948, D 25,17:1
Dobie, J Frank, 1964, S 19,27:1
Dobier, Claude A, 1959, N 2,31:1
Dobkin, Alex Mrs, 1963, Ag 9,23:5
Dobkin, Dmitry, 1953, D 26,13:2
Dobkin, Julius, 1962, Ap 19,31:4
Dobkin, Nicholas, 1948, Ap 22,27:3
Dobkins, Francis E, 1949, O 6,31:5
Doblado, Gen, 1865, Je 20,5:4
Doble, Arthur R, 1942, Ja 7,20:3
Doble, Budd, 1919, S 4,13:2
Doble, Eugene H, 1960, Jl 1,25:4
Doble, William H, 1950, O 31,27:3
Dobler, George, 1945, S 24,19:2
Dobler, Gustave A, 1903, S 5,7:7
Dobler, Martin G, 1963, My 19,86:4
Dobler, Martin L, 1955, Ja 23,85:1
Doblin, Alfred, 1957, Je 27,26:1
Doblin, Ernest M, 1951, Jl 16,21:3
Doblin, Joseph W, 1958, Ja 11,17:6
Doblin, L L, 1927, My 18,25:4
Dobner, Joseph S, 1948, S 11,15:2
Doborotvorsky, Yuri A, 1959, F 11,39:2
Dobrecic, Nikola, 1955, N 15,29:4
Dobree, Alfred, 1937, Ja 27,21:4
Dobrim, Abraham E, 1957, Je 13,31:4
Dobrin, Harry, 1952, O 27,27:4
Dobrin, Moritz, 1951, My 25,27:2
Dobriner, Konrad, 1952, Mr 11,27:1
Dobris, M Michel, 1957, N 6,35:3
Dobrish, Joseph, 1962, Jl 20,25:2
Dobrosky, Victor, 1950, Jl 6,27:2
Dobrow, Hyman, 1961, Jl 15,19:1
Dobrowen, Issay A, 1953, D 10,47:1
Dobrski, Julian A, 1968, F 5,35:4
Dobrzinsky, Aaron, 1940, Ja 24,21:6
Dobson, Alfred H, 1951, Mr 20,29:4
Dobson, Charles C, 1940, Je 27,23:4
Dobson, Charles E, 1910, Ja 19,9:5
Dobson, Edward Clarendon, 1919, S 5,11:1
Dobson, Edward S, 1958, O 8,35:2
Dobson, Edward W G, 1955, N 18,85:2
Dobson, Frank, 1963, Jl 23,29:2
Dobson, Frank M, 1956, D 2,87:2
Dobson, George, 1938, O 14,23:2; 1950, Je 24,13:5
Dobson, George A, 1945, Ag 24,19:3
Dobson, George F, 1954, O 30,17:4
Dobson, Gertrude, 1942, Mr 6,21:3
Dobson, Graham C, 1943, Ap 2,21:5
Dobson, Henry Austin, 1921, S 3,9:7
Dobson, Henry C, 1908, My 29,7:3
Dobson, Henry W, 1967, Ag 14,31:2
Dobson, Howard, 1950, F 11,15:3
Dobson, James, 1942, Ja 4,49:2
Dobson, John, 1911, Je 30,9:5
Dobson, Mason H, 1952, D 10,35:5
Dobson, Meade C, 1961, Ag 30,33:1
Dobson, Mollie, 1948, Mr 7,68:5
Dobson, Robert, 1942, Ja 7,20:4
Dobson, Roy Sir, 1968, Jl 9,35:4
Dobson, Thomas, 1953, O 2,21:2
Dobson, Thomas R, 1949, S 20,29:5
Dobson, William A, 1943, Je 4,21:5
Dobujinsky, Mstislav, 1957, N 22,25:3
Dobyns, Ashbel W, 1950, Mr 28,31:3
Dobyns, Daniel T, 1944, S 5,19:6
Docharty, Augustus Thorne, 1917, Ap 22,21:2
Docherty, Bernard E, 1967, Je 9,45:3
Dochez, A Raymond, 1964, Jl 1,35:4
Dock, George, 1951, Je 1,23:3
Dock, John, 1958, Ag 20,27:1
Dock, Lavinia L, 1956, Ap 18,31:3
Dockendorff, J E, 1934, Ap 3,21:3
Docker, Walter H, 1948, Ag 31,23:2
Dockerty, Michael O, 1952, Ag 26,25:1
Dockery, A M, 1926, D 27,15:2
Dockery, Claudius Sr Mrs, 1951, N 30,23:3
Dockery, Mrs (Wife of Gov), 1903, Ja 2,9:3
Dockery, Octavia, 1949, Ap 23,13:5
Docking, George, 1964, Ja 21,29:1
Dockman, John H, 1937, Ap 28,23:1
Dockray, Edward L, 1939, F 7,19:2
Dockstader, Lew, 1924, O 27,19:4
Dockter, Charles, 1956, Ja 25,31:2
Dockwiler, John F, 1943, F 1,15:3
Dockwiller, Lidwina (Sister Mary Louisa), 1954, Jl 17,13:5
Docter, Joseph, 1960, F 7,84:1
Docter, Joseph Mrs, 1954, F 27,13:2
Doctor, August Van A, 1959, N 25,29:2
Doctor, August Van A Mrs, 1960, Ja 24,88:7
Doctor, Charles D, 1946, D 6,23:2
Doctor, Karl (por),(cor on por, O 20,29:2), 1949, O 19,29:3
Doctor, Peter W, 1942, Mr 20,19:4
Doctorow, Jarvis Mrs (Cath), 1968, S 22,88:6
Dod, James Potter, 1917, D 7,13:5
Dod, Joseph Potter, 1917, D 7,13:5
Dod, Lottie (Charlotte), 1960, Je 28,31:2
Dod, Samuel B, 1907, Ap 21,9:4
Dodd, Allison, 1949, Jl 9,13:3
Dodd, Allison Mrs, 1944, F 5,15:3
Dodd, Alvin E, 1951, Je 3,92:3
Dodd, Amzi, 1913, Ja 23,11:5
Dodd, Amzi S, 1940, D 27,20:3
Dodd, Anna R, 1940, Ja 7,48:5
Dodd, Anne B, 1952, F 25,21:3
Dodd, Arthur J, 1955, Ap 29,23:1
Dodd, Arthur W Mrs, 1950, Je 12,27:3
Dodd, Arthur Wright Capt, 1916, Ap 1,13:7
Dodd, Benton G, 1948, O 2,15:3
Dodd, Charles F, 1939, O 24,23:6
Dodd, Charles J (por), 1947, Jl 25,17:1
Dodd, Charles T, 1917, Jl 2,9:5
Dodd, Chauncey Y, 1952, Ja 17,28:3
Dodd, David, 1905, Mr 27,9:2
Dodd, David H, 1953, Jl 16,21:2
Dodd, E Davey, 1956, Je 21,31:2
Dodd, Edward, 1960, Jl 5,31:4
Dodd, Edward A Rev Dr, 1937, My 25,28:2
Dodd, Edward H, 1965, Je 21,29:4
Dodd, Edward L, 1946, F 21,21:2
Dodd, Edward M, 1967, Jl 3,17:5
Dodd, Edward Rev, 1865, S 23,1:6
Dodd, Edward Williams, 1909, S 8,9:4; 1909, O 1,9:4
Dodd, Edwin M Jr, 1951, N 5,54:3
Dodd, Edwin M Jr Mrs, 1951, N 5,54:3
Dodd, Emily, 1944, S 22,19:5
Dodd, Ethel, 1940, Ap 18,23:3
Dodd, Eugene E, 1939, O 5,23:5
Dodd, Fannie M Mrs, 1942, Jl 1,25:6
Dodd, Francis, 1949, Mr 10,27:3
Dodd, Francis J, 1962, N 10,25:6
Dodd, Frank C, 1968, Ja 5,35:1
Dodd, Frank C Mrs, 1952, D 19,31:2
Dodd, Frank Howard, 1916, Ja 11,11:5
Dodd, Frank N, 1943, Ja 11,15:1
Dodd, Frank S, 1937, F 27,17:4
Dodd, Frederic H, 1947, Mr 14,23:1
Dodd, George, 1951, My 3,29:3
Dodd, George A Gen, 1925, Jl 1,23:4
Dodd, George D, 1955, S 10,17:2
Dodd, George L, 1948, D 22,24:2
Dodd, George W, 1945, D 18,27:2; 1947, O 1,29:1
Dodd, Gertrude, 1944, Ja 10,17:3
Dodd, Gertrude Ward Mrs, 1905, Je 14,9:6
Dodd, Harry K, 1957, My 19,88:2
Dodd, Helen C Mrs, 1954, Ag 26,27:3
Dodd, Helen N, 1953, D 9,11:6
Dodd, Horace, 1952, S 14,86:2
Dodd, Howard A, 1955, O 28,25:3
Dodd, I L, 1903, Ag 26,7:6
Dodd, Ira S Mrs, 1919, N 22,13:2
Dodd, Ira S Rev, 1922, Ag 4,15:7
Dodd, Isaac S, 1948, Ja 31,19:6
Dodd, Isabela F, 1943, F 26,19:5
Dodd, Isabella R E Mrs, 1937, Jl 11,II,5:2
Dodd, J Parke, 1903, Ag 6,7:3
Dodd, James (funl), 1875, Jl 9,8:6
Dodd, James M Mrs, 1946, Ag 7,27:4
Dodd, James M Sr, 1949, N 21,25:5
Dodd, Jimmie, 1964, N 11,43:4
Dodd, John A, 1955, N 21,29:6
Dodd, John D, 1941, S 6,15:6
Dodd, John J, 1946, Jl 15,25:5
Dodd, John P, 1943, Je 29,19:4
Dodd, Joseph Col, 1874, N 30,5:2
Dodd, L W, 1933, My 17,17:4
Dodd, Lawrence V, 1958, F 10,23:4
Dodd, Lee W Mrs, 1953, S 8,31:1
Dodd, Lewis K, 1940, Je 16,39:2
Dodd, M Estelle, 1951, O 16,31:4
Dodd, Marion E, 1961, Mr 17,24:1
Dodd, Martin B, 1944, Jl 27,17:1
Dodd, Marvin J, 1944, D 28,19:3
Dodd, Maynard, 1938, Ap 12,24:2
Dodd, Monroe E, 1952, Ag 8,17:5
Dodd, N E Mrs, 1948, Mr 8,23:3
Dodd, Norris Edward, 1968, Je 24,37:3
Dodd, Peter, 1945, D 17,21:3
Dodd, Raymond A, 1954, My 17,24:5
Dodd, Raymond C, 1962, Jl 8,64:5
Dodd, Robert C, 1939, Jl 4,13:2; 1955, O 25,33:4
Dodd, Samuel, 1906, D 13,9:5
Dodd, Samuel H, 1953, Je 10,29:1
Dodd, Samuel L, 1944, Ja 15,13:4
Dodd, T Louis, 1946, N 21,31:2
Dodd, Thomas J Sr, 1953, My 25,25:6
Dodd, Thomas W Capt, 1907, Ja 14,7:6
Dodd, Tommy, 1874, Jl 8,5:6
Dodd, Walter F, 1960, Ap 16,17:3
Dodd, Walter J Dr, 1916, D 19,11:3
Dodd, William E, 1938, My 29,II,7:3; 1940, F 10,15:1; 1940, Mr 4,15:2
Dodd, William E Jr, 1952, O 19,87:6
Dodd, William H Jr, 1954, Ag 26,27:6
Dodds, Bernice L, 1959, Mr 24,39:5
Dodds, Carl J Mrs, 1966, Jl 27,39:2
Dodds, Charles B, 1938, Jl 9,13:6
Dodds, Clarence L, 1946, My 17,44:3
Dodds, Ethan I, 1943, F 26,19:6
Dodds, Francis H, 1940, D 24,15:3
Dodds, Frank J Mrs, 1946, D 25,29:2
Dodds, Frank P, 1959, Mr 14,23:2
Dodds, George F, 1958, O 5,87:1
Dodds, Grant C, 1952, Ag 6,21:2
Dodds, J Isabella, 1954, F 24,25:4
Dodds, J S, 1950, N 5,92:6
Dodds, Jackson, 1961, Ap 9,86:3
Dodds, Jackson Mrs, 1951, My 2,31:2
Dodds, James E, 1952, N 20,31:1
Dodds, John C, 1937, Ja 18,17:1
Dodds, John H, 1948, S 11,15:2
Dodds, Katherine B, 1947, F 22,13:4
Dodds, Norman, 1965, Ag 23,8:4
Dodds, Richard P, 1954, Ap 25,87:2
Dodds, Robert C Mrs, 1951, Ja 31,25:3
Dodds, Robert M, 1967, Mr 26,68:8
Dodds, Samuel, 1947, D 28,40:5
Dodds, Samuel Mrs, 1938, Ag 27,13:5
Dodds, Thomas H, 1942, D 5,15:4
Dodds, Timothy, 1876, Ja 3,4:5

Dodds, Vincent G, 1946, Ag 14,25:6
Dodds, Warren (Baby), 1959, F 15,85:5
Dodelin, Fred A, 1951, Mr 15,29:4
Doderer, Heimito von, 1966, D 24,19:4
Dodero, Alberto, 1951, Mr 3,13:1
Dodes, Morris, 1953, Ap 9,27:4
Dodge, A Douglas, 1963, N 23,29:3
Dodge, Abigail (Gail Hamilton), 1896, Ag 18,5:5
Dodge, Albert L, 1925, S 7,11:5
Dodge, Amos H, 1940, Je 1,15:2
Dodge, Arthur B, 1952, Je 12,33:2
Dodge, Arthur J, 1943, D 7,27:6
Dodge, Arthur Pillsbury, 1915, O 13,15:6
Dodge, Arthur Sr, 1945, Je 14,19:6
Dodge, Avery, 1959, O 4,86:2
Dodge, Bernard O, 1960, Ag 11,27:3
Dodge, Bert E, 1953, Ag 19,29:3
Dodge, C H, 1926, Je 25,1:2
Dodge, Charles C Gen, 1910, N 5,7:4
Dodge, Charles C Mrs, 1910, Mr 29,11:4
Dodge, Charles M, 1940, Je 12,25:6
Dodge, Charles S, 1948, Mr 23,25:3
Dodge, Chester L, 1950, My 16,31:4
Dodge, Chester P Mrs, 1953, Je 18,29:2
Dodge, Clara T Mrs, 1964, Ap 5,86:8
Dodge, Clarence P (will, Ag 24,17:5), 1939, Jl 30, 29:1
Dodge, Cleon C, 1959, Ja 7,33:2
Dodge, D G, 1877, D 31,5:2
Dodge, David Stuart Rev Dr, 1921, D 18,22:4
Dodge, David W, 1959, N 13,29:2
Dodge, Dora I M C Mrs, 1950, Je 19,21:7
Dodge, E A D Mrs, 1927, S 17,17:5
Dodge, E W, 1869, Je 9,4:7
Dodge, Edward L, 1938, Jl 5,17:2
Dodge, Ernest R, 1961, Ag 31,25:4
Dodge, F Clyde, 1948, F 4,23:3
Dodge, Francis S Brig-Gen, 1908, F 21,7:6
Dodge, Frank, 1952, Ap 26,23:6
Dodge, Frank E, 1950, F 18,15:6
Dodge, Frank F, 1938, Je 14,21:2
Dodge, Frank S, 1948, S 19,76:4
Dodge, Frederick Warren, 1915, N 11,13:4
Dodge, Geoffrey, 1941, Ja 22,21:6
Dodge, George A, 1922, S 21,17:5
Dodge, George C, 1942, O 8,27:2
Dodge, George Eggleston, 1904, Ap 15,9:6
Dodge, Gerald C, 1954, My 16,89:6
Dodge, Grace Headley, 1914, D 28,9:5
Dodge, Grenville M Gen, 1916, Ja 4,13:8
Dodge, Guy Phelps, 1923, O 9,21:5
Dodge, H Percival Mrs, 1953, F 21,13:2
Dodge, Harrington, 1881, F 7,5:5
Dodge, Harris T, 1960, Jl 30,17:5
Dodge, Harrison H Col, 1937, My 21,21:5
Dodge, Harry P, 1937, Je 2,23:3
Dodge, Henry E, 1954, F 9,27:2
Dodge, Henry G, 1968, Ag 3,25:3
Dodge, Henry N Dr, 1937, Jl 25,II,7:3
Dodge, Henry T, 1943, Ap 9,21:1
Dodge, Herbert A, 1939, Jl 16,31:2
Dodge, Herbert K, 1962, O 4,39:5
Dodge, Homer, 1960, My 4,45:1
Dodge, Horace E, 1920, D 11,13:5
Dodge, Horace E Jr (will, D 25,30:2), 1963, D 23, 25:4
Dodge, Iola V, 1951, F 21,27:3
Dodge, J A, 1881, N 30,5:4
Dodge, J H P, 1904, F 21,7:6
Dodge, James M Mrs, 1953, Ap 18,19:3
Dodge, John B, 1960, N 3,39:2
Dodge, John F, 1920, Ja 15,11:1
Dodge, John L, 1940, Ap 7,44:7
Dodge, Joseph G, 1965, Jl 17,25:6
Dodge, Joseph H, 1946, S 23,23:2
Dodge, Joseph M (trb, D 4,39:2), 1964, D 3,45:3
Dodge, Joseph Smith Rev Dr, 1921, Ap 14,13:4
Dodge, Kern, 1958, N 7,27:1
Dodge, Kern Mrs, 1943, Jl 14,19:4
Dodge, Leo S, 1952, D 9,33:1
Dodge, Mabel F, 1953, Jl 5,49:1
Dodge, Magdalen T Mrs, 1941, Mr 20,21:2
Dodge, Marcellus H (funeral, D 29,42:5), 1963, D 26,27:2
Dodge, Marcellus H (will), 1964, Ja 17,40:7
Dodge, Marshall J, 1949, My 16,21:6
Dodge, Martin, 1956, N 26,27:3
Dodge, Mary E, 1959, My 24,88:2
Dodge, Mary Mapes Mrs, 1905, Ag 22,7:6
Dodge, Melvin G, 1952, F 12,27:4
Dodge, Murray W, 1937, D 7,25:3
Dodge, Murray W (will), 1938, F 15,23:2
Dodge, Norman, 1953, Mr 21,17:6
Dodge, O E, 1876, N 4,5:2
Dodge, Omenzo G Mrs, 1925, Ag 22,11:6
Dodge, Ozias, 1925, Je 30,19:4
Dodge, Ozias Mrs, 1963, N 26,37:2
Dodge, P T, 1931, Ag 10,15:3
Dodge, Paul, 1937, Je 10,23:1
Dodge, Philip T Mrs, 1961, Mr 17,31:2
Dodge, R J Mrs, 1903, My 15,9:6
Dodge, Raymond (por), 1942, Ap 9,19:1
Dodge, Richard, 1948, Ap 19,23:3
Dodge, Richard Charles Mrs, 1925, O 31,17:4
Dodge, Richard Despard, 1914, Mr 6,11:4
Dodge, Richard E, 1952, Ap 3,35:3
Dodge, Richard E Mrs, 1961, F 4,19:6
Dodge, Robert G, 1964, F 16,92:7
Dodge, Robert H, 1937, N 29,23:6
Dodge, Robert L, 1940, Jl 17,21:4
Dodge, Robert L Mrs, 1960, Jl 19,29:1
Dodge, Samuel D, 1941, D 12,25:3
Dodge, Sherwood, 1968, Jl 7,52:8
Dodge, Stanley D, 1966, Ap 23,31:3
Dodge, Theodore Ayrault Col, 1909, O 27,11:5
Dodge, Uriah Capt, 1907, N 13,9:7
Dodge, Van H Mrs, 1948, Mr 16,27:1
Dodge, Villars A, 1964, F 4,33:4
Dodge, W E (see also F 10), 1883, F 13,8:1
Dodge, W E, 1927, My 5,27:3
Dodge, W E Sr Mrs, 1903, Mr 16,9:6
Dodge, Walter P, 1954, Mr 7,91:2
Dodge, Wendell P Jr, 1947, My 29,21:1
Dodge, Wilbur C, 1952, Je 8,85:1
Dodge, William A, 1945, D 30,14:3; 1946, Ja 1,27:3
Dodge, William D Mrs, 1947, Mr 21,22:3
Dodge, William E Mrs, 1909, Ja 12,9:5
Dodge, William H, 1912, Ja 29,11:6; 1948, O 17,76:4; 1958, O 17,29:2
Dodge, William J, 1940, Ja 21,35:2
Dodge, William T, 1940, Mr 27,21:1
Dodge, Willis E, 1958, Je 12,31:4
Dodge, Zenas U, 1942, Ag 10,19:6
Dodgson, C L Rev (Lewis Carroll), 1898, Ja 16,7:4
Dodgson, Harry J, 1954, F 18,31:2
Dodick, John, 1945, D 27,20:3
Dodin, Edward J, 1953, My 6,31:4
Dodo, Masao, 1944, Mr 30,21:5
Dods, John W, 1950, Jl 22,15:6
Dodshan, Joseph H Mrs, 1939, F 6,13:4
Dodshon, Joseph H, 1948, Jl 24,15:7
Dodson, Alan C, 1946, Ag 25,45:1
Dodson, Albert J, 1940, My 24,19:4
Dodson, Arthur, 1939, N 29,23:1
Dodson, Boyd, 1948, Mr 20,13:2
Dodson, Ezra Newton, 1917, F 6,9:4
Dodson, George J Mrs, 1949, Jl 1,19:1
Dodson, Gerald, 1966, N 5,31:3
Dodson, J E, 1931, D 10,23:1
Dodson, James M, 1954, Jl 21,27:2
Dodson, John R, 1954, Je 7,23:5
Dodson, Joseph H, 1949, O 28,23:4
Dodson, Lamott Mrs, 1951, Mr 10,15:1
Dodson, Lavere A Mrs, 1953, My 22,27:2
Dodson, Louis W, 1945, Ja 10,23:4
Dodson, Louise W Mrs, 1944, My 17,19:5
Dodson, Mary W Mrs, 1942, Jl 27,15:4
Dodson, Richard S Col, 1937, O 7,27:3
Dodson, Robert B (will, S 11,48:1), 1938, Ag 22,13:5
Dodson, Truman M 2d, 1941, Ap 15,23:5
Dodson, Victor L, 1945, Ja 28,37:1
Dodsworth, Alice A, 1953, Je 2,29:6
Dodsworth, J W, 1936, Jl 1,25:1
Dodsworth, Michael J, 1920, F 7,11:3
Dodsworth, T George, 1922, F 26,26:3
Dodsworth, William, 1910, F 9,7:4; 1943, Mr 12,17:3
Dodu, Juliette, 1909, N 6,9:5
Dodwell, Katherine Mrs, 1948, Ja 30,24:2
Dody, Daniel, 1952, My 28,29:6
Dody, Michael J, 1921, Je 3,15:7
Doe, Bert P, 1950, My 16,31:1
Doe, Charles L, 1946, F 19,25:4
Doe, Dudley W, 1944, Ap 27,23:3
Doe, Frank A, 1958, Je 20,23:4
Doe, Howard L, 1944, Ag 28,11:5
Doe, Imogene Mrs, 1951, Jl 5,25:4
Doe, Richard T, 1962, My 5,27:4
Doe, Thomas B, 1966, D 10,37:5
Doe, William H Mrs, 1950, My 28,44:8; 1957, Ap 17, 31:1
Doebler, Belden P Mrs, 1961, Ja 15,86:5
Doebler, Errol W Mrs, 1960, N 13,88:6
Doederlein, Theodore J Mrs, 1950, Ja 8,76:5
Doege, Herman E, 1941, O 26,43:1
Doehler, Charles W, 1938, Ag 4,17:4
Doehler, Herman H, 1964, O 19,33:3
Doehler, Paul A, 1939, Ag 27,35:4
Doehler, William C, 1960, N 14,31:5
Doelbor, Fred M, 1937, Jl 29,19:3
Doeleman, Herman F, 1944, My 31,19:3
Doelger, Anthony, 1904, F 29,7:6
Doelger, Carl P 3d Mrs, 1960, Ap 5,37:1
Doelger, Charles A Mrs, 1947, Mr 5,25:4
Doelger, Charles P, 1946, Ja 1,27:2
Doelger, Edna L Mrs, 1937, O 17,II,8:6
Doelger, Frank G, 1943, O 29,19:2
Doelger, J, 1882, Ag 8,3:2
Doelger, P, 1936, N 16,19:3
Doelger, Pater Mrs, 1925, Ja 3,13:4
Doelger, Peter, 1912, D 16,13:4
Doelger, Peter Mrs, 1962, Mr 27,37:2
Doelker, Fred L, 1958, Ja 10,26:1
Doelker, William G, 1954, My 3,25:4
Doelling, C Ernest, 1947, My 20,25:5
Doemoetoer, Ferenc, 1954, My 9,89:1
D'Oench, Albert F, 1918, Jl 22,11:6
D'Oench, Carrie E, 1925, S 10,25:5
D'Oench, Russell G, 1959, D 19,27:5
Doenecke, Justus D, 1953, S 2,25:4
Doepker, Robert R, 1953, Je 3,31:2
Doerflein, William F Sr, 1951, Ap 15,92:2
Doerflinger, William F, 1957, S 25,29:1
Doerhoefer, Frank J Mrs, 1950, Ja 8,77:1
Doerhoefer, John, 1903, Ag 5,7:6
Doering, Anthony, 1945, Jl 8,11:6
Doering, C Frederick, 1957, O 31,31:5
Doering, Edmund J, 1943, Mr 2,19:3
Doering, Frederick C, 1951, Ja 24,27:4
Doering, Henry A Mrs, 1940, Jl 3,17:6
Doering, Otto C, 1955, Ap 4,29:4
Doering, William Mrs, 1948, F 21,13:2
Doering, Wolfgang, 1963, Ja 18,9:1
Doeringer, Russell C, 1966, D 5,45:2
Doerken, Edward, 1938, D 30,15:2
Doermann, H J, 1932, N 21,17:1
Doermer, Frederick H, 1954, Je 18,23:2
Doern, Peter, 1941, Ja 26,36:2
Doern, William G, 1946, N 4,25:5
Doernberg, Dudley D, 1951, O 9,29:5
Doernberg, Dudley D Mrs, 1939, My 16,23:5
Doerner, Herman, 1949, Je 19,68:6
Doerr, Albert, 1948, O 20,29:2
Doerr, Carl F, 1942, Jl 17,15:4
Doerr, Charles, 1951, Ag 31,15:4
Doerr, George V, 1967, S 2,25:5
Doerr, Harold J, 1943, Mr 25,21:1
Doerr, J B, 1901, Jl 27,7:6
Doerrer, William, 1937, D 11,19:3
Doerries, George W Mrs, 1959, F 25,31:1
Doerrler, Charles J Mrs, 1962, Mr 17,25:3
Doersam, Charles H (por), 1942, Jl 15,19:1
Doersam, Charles Mrs, 1951, Ag 23,23:2
Doerschuck, Richard W, 1964, My 28,37:5
Doerschuck, Walter J, 1961, N 23,31:2
Doerschuk, Margaret W, 1965, F 15,27:4
Doesberg, Frank E, 1939, D 3,60:6
Doescher, Arthur H, 1958, Je 8,88:8
Doessing, Thomas, 1947, Ap 19,15:5
Doetsch, James F, 1967, O 17,47:2
Doft, Benjamin J, 1968, Mr 31,81:2
Doggett, Clinton L, 1941, S 11,23:5
Doggett, D S, 1880, O 28,2:3
Doggett, Herbert O, 1938, Ap 30,15:5
Doggett, John L, 1959, Mr 19,34:1
Doggett, Laurence L, 1957, N 14,33:5
Doggett, Reginald L, 1946, Jl 11,23:3
Doggett, Sidney H Sr, 1952, Ag 17,77:1
Doggett, Walton H Mrs, 1952, Ja 21,15:5
Doggett, William Elkana, 1915, Je 6,17:5
Doggett, William L, 1943, Ap 5,19:4
Dogliotti, A Mario, 1966, Je 4,29:3
Dogole, Irving M, 1954, My 24,27:5
Dogole, Jacob, 1954, Jl 2,19:2
d'Ogries, Valentine, 1959, Ag 30,83:2
Dogro, Francis A, 1939, O 19,23:5
Dohan, Edith H, 1943, Jl 15,21:6
Doheny, Clarence W, 1951, Ja 23,27:4
Doheny, E L, 1935, S 9,1:2
Doheny, Edward L Mrs (will, N 7,23:5), 1958, O 29:2
Doheny, Ellen, 1937, Ag 20,17:4
Doheny, John J, 1939, Ap 12,24:3
Doheny, Morgan Capt, 1871, Ap 4,8:3
Doheny, Richard F, 1951, N 21,25:2
Doherr, John B, 1944, My 19,19:6
Dohert, Michael, 1909, N 15,9:3
Doherty, Adrian C, 1940, Ag 30,19:3
Doherty, Charles Sr, 1962, Mr 31,25:2
Doherty, Daniel L, 1964, Ap 21,33:3
Doherty, Edward F, 1944, N 3,21:2
Doherty, Edward S, 1950, Ja 3,25:5
Doherty, Elizabeth F, 1939, Mr 28,23:5
Doherty, Ellen Mrs, 1947, O 16,27:3
Doherty, Francis R, 1960, Mr 10,31:2
Doherty, Frank J, 1967, Mr 30,45:1
Doherty, George F, 1944, O 24,23:3
Doherty, H M, 1945, S 20,23:4
Doherty, Henry, 1915, F 2,7:6
Doherty, Henry L, 1939, D 27,1:2
Doherty, Henry L Jr, 1941, N 28,23:5
Doherty, Henry L Mrs, 1949, My 30,13:3
Doherty, Hugh F, 1962, My 15,39:4
Doherty, hugh L, 1919, Ag 24,22:4
Doherty, J Edmund, 1960, Ja 10,87:2
Doherty, J P, 1941, S 29,17:3
Doherty, James T, 1956, Ap 1,88:8
Doherty, John H, 1941, O 2,25:1
Doherty, John J, 1951, My 20,89:2; 1955, S 17,1
Doherty, John P, 1937, Je 30,24:2; 1952, F 24,8
Doherty, John R, 1964, O 16,39:5
Doherty, John Sen, 1859, Ap 22,4:5
Doherty, John W, 1961, F 2,29:1
Doherty, John W Dr, 1916, Mr 28,13:6
Doherty, L A W, 1953, Mr 17,29:2
Doherty, Liguoria A, 1940, Ag 26,15:3
Doherty, Manning, 1938, S 27,21:2
Doherty, Mary H, 1948, Ag 20,17:5
Doherty, Michael, 1941, Je 20,21:4
Doherty, Michael J, 1909, O 23,11:2

Doherty, Michael J Mrs, 1954, Ja 7,31:3
Doherty, Michael W, 1943, D 6,23:5
Doherty, Mother Anna, 1950, S 14,31:1
Doherty, P J, 1928, Ap 14,19:3
Doherty, Patrick, 1954, Ap 22,29:4
Doherty, Patrick J, 1963, Ag 27,31:4
Doherty, Paul E, 1967, Jl 24,27:3
Doherty, Peter, 1947, S 22,23:5
Doherty, Peter J, 1963, S 23,29:5
Doherty, Phil A Mrs, 1938, Ja 29,15:7
Doherty, Phil A Sr, 1942, N 22,52:3
Doherty, Ralph E, 1967, O 18,47:3
Doherty, Reginald F, 1910, D 30,11:4
Doherty, Richard, 1941, N 1,15:5
Doherty, Robert E, 1950, O 20,28:2
Doherty, Robert J, 1941, S 21,42:2
Doherty, Robert W, 1949, N 29,29:5
Doherty, Rosaleen (Mrs T J O'Gorman), 1950, D 22,23:2
Doherty, Sarah J, 1938, S 24,17:5
Doherty, Stephen J, 1967, Mr 9,39:3
Doherty, Thomas F, 1937, Ja 27,21:6; 1937, F 26,21:6; 1956, Ap 14,17:4
Doherty, Thomas J, 1945, Mr 2,19:4
Doherty, William, 1951, Mr 7,30:4; 1952, Ja 25,21:2
Doherty, William E, 1954, Mr 19,23:4; 1966, D 20,44:1
Doherty, William H, 1965, Mr 24,43:4
Doherty, William J, 1946, My 17,21:4; 1951, D 16,90:2
Doherty, William T, 1949, O 10,23:4
Dohme, Adolph F, 1942, My 24,43:3
Dohme, Alfred R L, 1952, Je 11,29:3
Dohme, Ida S Mrs, 1937, D 17,25:4
Dohmen, William F, 1938, My 11,19:1
Dohn, Albert F, 1948, Jl 31,15:3
Dohnanyi, Ernst von, 1960, F 11,35:1
Dohner, Harold B, 1963, My 28,28:3
Dohr, James L, 1961, N 25,24:3
Dohrenwend, Gustav J, 1962, Ag 16,27:3
Dohring, Gustav F, 1956, S 28,27:3
Dohrmann, William, 1943, F 17,21:1
Dohrn, Anthon Dr, 1909, O 1,9:5
Doidge, Frederick W, 1954, My 27,27:3
Doig, Arthur H Mrs, 1962, Mr 11,87:1
Doig, James P, 1938, F 4,21:1
Doig, Robert, 1965, O 28,43:5
Doig, Stephen G, 1957, F 25,25:3
Doig, Stephen G Jr Mrs, 1968, D 8,86:5
Doig, Thomas W, 1955, D 23,17:4
Doing, Mahlon B, 1960, Ap 22,31:3
D'Oisly, Maurice, 1949, Jl 20,25:3
Doke, George E, 1951, D 7,27:2
Dokhtouroff, Russian Gen, 1905, Mr 28,2:4
Doktor, Esther B Mrs, 1940, Mr 23,26:3
Dolak, Michael C, 1955, Jl 8,23:2
Dolamore, William H, 1938, Ap 25,15:3
Dolan, Albert H, 1951, Ja 23,27:3
Dolan, Alvin J (Cosy), 1958, D 11,13:4
Dolan, Arthur J, 1938, D 28,26:5
Dolan, Arthur W, 1949, S 30,24:3
Dolan, Bernard J Sr, 1953, My 25,25:5
Dolan, Brooke 2d, 1945, Ag 24,20:3
Dolan, Charles A, 1950, Je 4,92:4
Dolan, Charles E, 1941, S 26,23:4
Dolan, Charles F, 1958, S 8,29:3
Dolan, Clarence W (will, Ap 4,35:1), 1937, Mr 29, 19:4
Dolan, Clarence W Mrs, 1957, O 25,27:3
Dolan, Cyril J, 1945, Ag 5,38:5
Dolan, David J, 1942, Ag 8,11:6
Dolan, David L, 1938, Jl 26,19:3
Dolan, Edward G, 1956, Mr 23,28:2
Dolan, Edward J, 1925, F 9,17:4; 1925, F 12,19:4
Dolan, Edward J Mrs, 1962, Jl 14,21:3
Dolan, Edward J Sr, 1961, Je 29,33:4
Dolan, Edward P, 1965, Je 5,31:5
Dolan, Flora Mrs, 1954, Mr 3,27:3
Dolan, Francis J Rev, 1939, S 7,25:3
Dolan, Francis M, 1949, D 10,17:2
Dolan, Francis X, 1944, My 25,21:3
Dolan, Frank, 1943, Ja 14,21:5
Dolan, Frank A, 1922, S 14,21:6; 1949, S 19,23:4
Dolan, Frank E Mrs, 1945, Je 30,17:5
Dolan, Frank J, 1942, Ag 8,11:2; 1948, O 14,30:2
Dolan, Frankie, 1945, N 14,19:4
Dolan, Frederick J, 1939, N 23,27:6
Dolan, George A, 1954, My 21,27:5
Dolan, George W, 1948, Jl 25,48:7
Dolan, Gerald J, 1939, Mr 4,15:5
Dolan, H Yale, 1949, Jl 28,23:5
Dolan, Henry, 1901, Ag 22,7:6
Dolan, Henry R Mrs, 1951, Je 16,15:4
Dolan, Hugh Francis, 1903, Ag 9,7:6
Dolan, Hugh T, 1956, N 3,23:4
Dolan, J, 1880, F 21,1:2
Dolan, J Frank, 1947, Ap 4,23:4
Dolan, J Vincent Sr, 1940, D 13,23:4
Dolan, James, 1939, Jl 8,15:2
Dolan, James C, 1937, O 27,31:1
Dolan, James F, 1942, Ap 21,23:5
Dolan, James H, 1947, N 20,29:5
Dolan, James M, 1957, My 16,31:4
Dolan, James P, 1942, Mr 5,24:3
Dolan, James R, 1943, Ag 19,19:4
Dolan, James T, 1949, My 26,30:2
Dolan, Joe, 1938, Mr 25,19:2
Dolan, John, 1924, Ag 19,15:4; 1956, O 12,29:4
Dolan, John A, 1963, Je 30,56:4
Dolan, John B, 1954, S 24,23:5
Dolan, John E, 1949, Jl 26,27:2
Dolan, John F, 1959, D 5,23:2
Dolan, John H, 1944, Ag 10,17:5
Dolan, John J, 1957, S 7,19:6
Dolan, John P, 1945, Jl 10,11:4
Dolan, John Rev, 1915, Ap 6,11:5
Dolan, John S, 1958, S 20,19:6
Dolan, Joseph F, 1959, Ja 14,27:4
Dolan, Joseph F Rev Father, 1912, O 31,13:5
Dolan, Joseph T, 1937, F 13,13:5
Dolan, Ken, 1951, Mr 3,13:3
Dolan, Leo P, 1952, Je 18,27:3
Dolan, Margaret H, 1961, S 9,19:6
Dolan, Marguerite, 1949, My 4,29:1
Dolan, Mary R, 1956, N 21,27:4
Dolan, Mary Rose Mother, 1924, Jl 24,13:5
Dolan, Nathan Brooke, 1908, My 4,7:4
Dolan, Owen C, 1951, Ag 31,15:2
Dolan, Patrick, 1903, S 14,7:5
Dolan, Patrick J, 1948, S 23,29:4
Dolan, Patrick L, 1957, Jl 12,21:5
Dolan, Peter A, 1960, Ap 16,17:2
Dolan, Peter H, 1950, F 11,15:1
Dolan, Richard V, 1959, O 14,43:5
Dolan, Sam, 1944, D 31,26:8
Dolan, T Frank, 1946, Je 7,19:4
Dolan, T J, 1905, F 6,5:5
Dolan, Thomas, 1914, Je 13,9:3
Dolan, Thomas A, 1960, Mr 19,21:6
Dolan, Thomas F, 1957, D 14,21:5
Dolan, Thomas H (cor, F 6,23:5), 1947, F 5,26:1
Dolan, Thomas Mrs, 1953, N 12,31:2
Dolan, Vincent Jr, 1957, F 27,11:5
Dolan, Walter R, 1946, O 23,27:5
Dolan, William, 1956, Ja 7,9:3
Dolan, William A, 1952, O 29,29:7
Dolan, William G, 1965, My 29,27:3
Dolan, William J, 1947, O 19,64:2; 1952, Ja 29,25:5
Dolan, William S F, 1946, Mr 21,25:5
Doland, James J, 1960, D 24,15:6
Doland, Lewis M, 1955, F 27,86:1
Dolbear, Amos E Prof, 1910, F 24,9:3
Dolbear, James T, 1958, Ja 20,23:3
Dolbeare, Frederic R, 1962, Jl 18,29:2
Dolbeare, Guy B, 1951, Ja 13,15:3
Dolbeare, Harris M, 1938, Ja 23,II,8:7
Dolbeck, George Nelson Dr, 1919, Ja 22,11:3
Dolberg, Glenn R Mrs, 1957, Ag 15,21:6
Dolbey, Harry S, 1951, D 28,21:2
Dolbey, Mark S, 1962, Ja 11,33:1
Dolbier, Frank W Mrs, 1937, Ag 15,II,7:3
Dolby, George H, 1952, Ja 17,27:3
Dolby, Joseph G, 1945, Je 7,19:5
Dolci, Alessandro, 1954, S 19,89:1
Dolci, Angelo M (Card), 1939, S 15,23:2
Dold, Bruce W, 1958, N 8,21:3
Dold, Jacob C Mrs, 1945, Ja 2,19:4
Dold, Jacob P, 1948, O 13,25:4
Dold, William E, 1942, N 11,25:2
Dole, Alexander, 1922, D 22,15:5
Dole, Andrew R, 1940, Ag 21,19:1
Dole, Andrew R Mrs, 1949, D 11,92:4
Dole, Edward E, 1944, Ag 27,33:1
Dole, Edward E Jr, 1939, Ag 9,17:2
Dole, Frank F, 1939, My 23,23:1
Dole, Frank F Mrs, 1944, Je 22,19:7
Dole, Frederick J, 1952, Mr 26,29:4
Dole, George H, 1942, O 18,52:7
Dole, James D, 1958, My 16,25:1
Dole, Nathan H Mrs, 1944, Je 10,15:3
Dole, Paul L Mrs, 1955, F 10,31:4
Dole, S B, 1926, Je 10,25:3
Dole, Stanley F, 1962, O 8,23:5
Dole, W Herbert, 1953, Mr 11,29:1
Dole, William T, 1945, S 29,15:3
Dolechek, Joseph Mrs, 1960, Je 10,31:5
Dolehide, John T, 1955, Ag 21,93:3
Dolen, William F, 1966, Ap 30,31:4
Dolenz, George (Feb 8), 1963, Ap 1,35:5
Dolezal, Benedict J, 1950, Ja 21,17:1
Dolezal, Charles T, 1951, Mr 21,33:3
Dolfinger, Henry, 1939, Je 11,44:7
Dolfini, Frank L, 1938, Mr 21,15:4
Dolge, Karl A, 1964, D 30,25:1
Dolgenas, Jacob A, 1959, Jl 26,68:2
Dolgin, Kalmon, 1940, Ag 26,15:3
Dolgin, Morris, 1968, Ja 30,41:1
Dolgoroukoff, Prince, 1891, Jl 3,4:7
Dolgorouky, Stephanie Princess, 1954, Je 3,27:2
Dolgov, Peter I, 1962, N 4,2:3
Dolhan, Leo, 1951, Ap 4,29:5
Dolhon, William, 1950, Jl 5,31:4
D'Olier, Alice C, 1937, O 17,II,9:1
D'Olier, Franklin, 1953, D 11,31:3
D'Olier, Franklin Mrs, 1950, Mr 8,27:3
D'Olier, James, 1913, Mr 6,11:3
Doliker, George J, 1948, D 6,25:2
Dolin, Peter J, 1957, Mr 11,25:4
Dolinsky, Herman M, 1954, N 4,31:5
Dolinsky, Hyman, 1916, Je 23,11:4
Dolinsky, Hyman Mrs, 1948, F 9,17:4
Dolinsky, John, 1948, D 22,23:2
Dolivet, Willard W S, 1952, S 8,21:1
Doll, Alfred W, 1957, D 24,15:4
Doll, Anthony H, 1937, S 18,19:4
Doll, Clarence E, 1949, F 9,28:2
Doll, Edgar A Dr, 1968, N 2,37:5
Doll, Elizabeth, 1952, O 22,27:5
Doll, Emily F Mrs, 1938, Ja 18,23:6
Doll, Henry, 1947, F 9,61:2
Doll, Hubert A, 1947, Mr 15,13:1
Doll, Jacob, 1911, N 14,13:5
Doll, Jacob H, 1959, F 24,29:1
Doll, Jacob V, 1952, Ap 16,27:5
Doll, Karl L, 1953, My 27,31:5
Doll, Myron G, 1941, N 12,23:5
Doll, William E, 1943, Jl 23,17:4
Doll, William Hunter Mrs, 1908, D 14,9:5
Dollar, Agnes B Mrs, 1940, D 5,25:2
Dollar, E H, 1914, Jl 23,9:3
Dollar, Margaret Mrs, 1941, F 16,40:1
Dollar, R, 1932, My 17,21:1
Dollar, R Stanley, 1958, S 25,33:1
Dollard, James, 1941, Ja 4,13:6
Dollard, John A, 1945, N 14,19:3
Dollard, John T, 1963, Ag 16,27:4
Dollard, Paul M, 1965, Jl 16,27:4
Dollard, Thomas A, 1937, F 26,21:5
Dollenberg, Frederick P, 1965, My 17,35:5
Dollendorf, Edward L, 1961, Ap 6,33:4
Dollenmayer, Stacy Mrs, 1951, Je 18,23:5
Dollens, Burl A, 1952, F 10,92:3
Doller, Mikhail, 1952, Mr 23,92:1
Dolleway, Duane, 1951, S 30,V,6:5
Dolley, Charles S, 1948, Jl 11,52:7
Dolley, Frank S, 1961, F 27,27:1
Dolley, Sarah Read Adamson Dr, 1909, D 28,9:4
Dolley, Stephen B, 1951, Ja 16,29:1
Dollfus, Edmund Mrs, 1966, F 26,25:1
Dollfuss, Engelbert, 1934, Jl 26,1:8
Dolling, Otto, 1913, S 6,7:2
Dollinger, Aaron, 1937, Je 28,19:6
Dollinger, Lewis L, 1963, Jl 29,19:1
Dollinger, William F (est appr), 1966, N 26,38:8
Dolliver, Charles M, 1962, Mr 8,31:4
Dolliver, James M, 1942, Ap 28,21:5
Dolliver, James P, 1905, Ap 29,11:6
Dolliver, Margaret G, 1938, Ja 19,23:1
Dolliver, Sen, 1910, O 17,9:4
Dolliver, Victor B, 1907, F 25,9:7
Dollnig, Bernice M, 1961, S 16,19:5
Dolloff, Charles H, 1947, Ag 20,21:4
Dolloff, David E, 1948, N 28,94:5
Dolly, Edward T, 1956, Ja 31,29:4
Dolly, Lady (Mrs T Cooper), 1953, S 9,29:3
Dolman, D H, 1949, Ap 19,25:1
Dolman, John Jr, 1952, Jl 10,31:5
Dolman, John Jr Mrs, 1937, Ap 27,23:4
Dolmetsch, Arnold, 1940, Mr 1,21:5
Dolmetsch, Richard Mrs, 1952, D 28,48:3
Dolnick, Max A, 1951, Ap 21,17:5
Doloff, Albert S, 1949, Mr 7,21:2
Dolores, Marie Sister (Euphemia Van Rensselaer), 1914, My 30,11:6
Dolowit, Maurice A, 1958, Jl 22,27:2
Dolp, John H, 1903, S 29,9:4
Dolph, John C, 1937, F 7,II,9:2
Dolphin, Benjamin E Dr, 1915, Ag 22,13:5
Dolphin, John L, 1956, D 25,29:3
Dolphin, Louis J, 1956, Ag 5,77:3
Dolson, Clifford B, 1953, N 18,31:3
Dolson, Corris M, 1945, O 16,23:1
Dolson, George H, 1948, Ap 14,27:3
Dolson, Guy Mrs, 1953, S 19,15:6
Dolson, Josiah W, 1924, O 20,17:6
Dolt, William C, 1953, Jl 27,19:4
Dolton, George W, 1948, N 21,88:3
Doltz, Paul, 1943, F 7,49:1
Dolz, Carlos T, 1948, Jl 14,23:4
Dolz y Arango, Ricardo Sen, 1937, Jl 6,19:5
Dolzen, Charles J, 1951, D 21,27:1
Domachowski, Joseph A, 1942, Jl 3,17:2
Domachowski, Michael J, 1940, F 9,19:3
Domagk, Gerhard, 1964, Ap 26,89:1
Doman, Herman C, 1938, Je 5,44:8
Doman, Robert S, 1950, F 10,23:1
Domashev, Maria P, 1952, My 18,92:4
Domatilla, Mother, 1944, D 29,15:1
Domato, James, 1921, D 11,22:3
Dombek, Michael A, 1950, Jl 9,69:1
Dombek, Samuel, 1955, Ja 7,21:2
Dombroff, Harry B, 1958, S 4,29:1
Dombroff, Joseph G, 1955, Mr 13,86:4
Dombroski, Adam, 1942, Ja 31,30:6
Dombrowski, Adam Mrs, 1959, Ag 23,93:2
Dombrowski, Arthur S, 1942, Jl 25,13:3
Dombrowski, Father, 1903, F 16,1:5
Domecq Garcia, Manuel, 1951, Ja 12,27:3
Domenec, Bishop (see also F 3 and 10), 1878, F 12, 2:4
Domenech, Manuel V, 1942, Mr 16,15:2

Domenjos, John, 1952, F 29,23:3
Domergue, Jean-Gabriel, 1962, N 17,25:4
Domers, G W, 1870, My 26,5:6
Domett, E J, 1903, Ag 1,7:6
Domidion, G A, 1921, Je 11,13:6
Domidion, Gerard P, 1950, Ap 9,70:3
Domin, James A, 1954, N 20,17:4
Domina, Frank E, 1948, Je 21,21:4
Doming, Elinor Mrs (will), 1939, Ag 29,12:6
Domingeuz, Jose L, 1911, O 19,13:5
Domingo, Brignardello Juan, 1950, O 8,104:8
Domingo, Marcelino, 1939, Mr 3,23:3
Domingo, Roberto, 1956, Ag 7,27:1
Domingos dos Santos, Jose, 1958, Ag 17,85:4
Dominguez, Alisiano, 1941, D 21,41:1
Dominguez, Don Gregorio, 1870, Ja 13,1:5
Dominguez, Ramon, 1909, Ap 26,7:5
Dominguez, Robert, 1947, Mr 24,25:2
Dominguez, Vincente J, 1916, Je 29,11:6
Dominiak, Francis X, 1957, S 4,34:1
Dominian, Leon Mrs, 1967, Mr 17,41:4
Dominic, Bro, 1907, S 15,9:6
Dominic, Bro (S W Taylor), 1960, Je 24,27:1
Dominic, Father (A Rapp), 1960, Ja 31,92:8
Dominic Augustine (Bro P J McCaffrey), 1963, D 6, 36:2
Dominica Maria, Sister (Anna Rochford), 1940, My 14,23:3
Dominici, Ernesto, 1954, Ja 18,23:5
Dominick, Bayard, 1914, Je 23,11:4; 1941, My 2,21:5
Dominick, Bayard Mrs, 1955, Mr 14,23:3
Dominick, Gayer G, 1961, Ag 19,18:1
Dominick, Gayer G Mrs, 1964, Ja 31,27:2
Dominick, George C Dr, 1916, O 3,11:4
Dominick, George F, 1944, D 20,23:2
Dominick, George F Mrs, 1919, N 9,22:2
Dominick, George Francis, 1923, Mr 30,17:5
Dominick, H B, 1928, D 24,13:3
Dominick, J W, 1880, Ja 23,8:7
Dominick, Lamont, 1956, Ja 11,31:1
Dominick, William F, 1945, Ja 17,21:2
Dominics, Bertrande de, 1945, N 5,20:2
Dominioni, Camillo C, 1946, N 13,27:4
Dominique, 1877, Ag 10,5:3
Dominquez, Anita, 1959, D 4,32:2
Dominquez, Vincent L, 1965, D 11,33:5
Dominy, Alonson T, 1908, S 10,9:5
Dominy, J M Mrs, 1937, My 3,19:1
Dominy, Jeremiah M, 1943, My 23,42:6
Dominy, Mary E Mrs, 1940, F 21,19:1
Dominy, W Tyson, 1940, Ag 8,19:2
Dominy, Washington T Mrs, 1956, Mr 1,33:2
Dommerich, Louis F, 1912, Jl 23,9:5
Dommerich, Louis W, 1952, D 15,25:4
Dommerich, Otto L, 1938, Mr 9,23:1
Dommerich, Otto L Mrs, 1943, D 31,16:6
Domovs, Joseph, 1944, Ag 10,19:5
Don, Alan C, 1966, My 4,47:4
Don, Carlos, 1909, Jl 19,7:5
Don, David L, 1949, O 28,23:3
Don Carlos, Henry C, 1941, Mr 31,15:4
Don Miguel, 1866, N 23,2:3
Donachie (Sister Miriam Vincetta), 1964, Ap 25,29:5
Donachy, Clarence R, 1948, Ja 17,17:5
Donado, Juan A, 1941, Ag 24,35:2
Donaghey, Frederick, 1937, N 9,23:2
Donaghey, George W, 1937, D 16,27:4
Donaghue, Leo A, 1951, Ag 1,23:5
Donaghue, Michael J, 1948, Je 19,15:4
Donaghy, Harry J, 1949, Je 3,25:4
Donaghy, William H, 1952, F 21,27:3
Donah, Frank H, 1943, Ja 6,27:1
Donahay, Joseph L, 1944, My 25,21:3
Donahey, Ada M, 1950, D 31,43:1
Donahey, Alvin V, 1946, Ap 9,27:1
Donahey, James H, 1949, Je 2,27:2
Donahey, John W, 1947, Je 1,60:6
Donahey, Louis S, 1946, D 6,24:2
Donahey, Louis S Mrs, 1948, Ja 1,23:5
Donahey, Susan G, 1945, Ag 1,19:5
Donahey, William Mrs, 1962, Ap 2,31:1
Donahoe, Dorothy M, 1960, Ap 6,41:2
Donahoe, Edward (Bro Clementian), 1959, Mr 6,25:4
Donahoe, John A, 1942, Ap 3,21:2
Donahoe, John T, 1958, Ja 12,86:7
Donahoe, Margaret L, 1954, D 2,31:5
Donahoe, Michael J, 1920, N 24,17:3
Donahoe, William E, 1946, O 29,25:3
Donahue, Alphonsus J (por), 1949, Jl 3,27:1
Donahue, Ann Mrs, 1937, O 20,23:4
Donahue, Ann T (Sister Maria Cordes), 1956, Jl 17, 23:4
Donahue, Anna L, 1940, Jl 4,15:2
Donahue, Bertin, 1957, Ag 5,21:4
Donahue, Charles H, 1952, N 6,29:4
Donahue, Charles V, 1953, My 3,88:1
Donahue, Claude C, 1937, Ag 18,19:5
Donahue, Cornelius C, 1940, Ap 9,23:2
Donahue, Cornelius F Mrs, 1950, D 19,29:3
Donahue, Daniel A, 1946, Ja 10,23:2
Donahue, Edward J, 1939, Jl 14,19:1; 1946, O 21,31:6
Donahue, Edward J Mrs, 1948, My 11,25:4
Donahue, F Joseph, 1961, Mr 22,41:1
Donahue, George S, 1944, Ag 31,17:1
Donahue, Gilbert Jr, 1951, Ag 9,21:5
Donahue, Guy W, 1954, Jl 3,11:6
Donahue, Harry J, 1964, S 9,43:4
Donahue, Henry, 1949, Ap 7,29:2
Donahue, J, 1930, O 2,25:3
Donahue, James (more details, D 8,47:1), 1966, D 7, 47:2
Donahue, James B Rev, 1937, Je 6,II,9:2
Donahue, James J, 1937, My 30,18:7
Donahue, James M, 1948, My 6,25:4; 1960, Ap 19,37:3
Donahue, James P Mrs, 1956, D 2,86:3
Donahue, James W, 1943, Jl 1,19:5
Donahue, John A Mrs, 1952, D 2,36:6
Donahue, John A Sr, 1939, Ja 25,21:4
Donahue, John E, 1954, Ag 21,17:6
Donahue, John E Mrs, 1958, Je 4,33:1
Donahue, John F, 1949, O 5,29:5
Donahue, John H, 1940, My 5,52:6
Donahue, John J, 1938, Ap 19,21:3; 1944, S 27,21:4
Donahue, John L, 1944, Ag 15,17:2
Donahue, John V, 1943, Mr 6,13:5
Donahue, John W, 1942, Ap 28,21:1
Donahue, Joseph, 1955, N 16,35:1
Donahue, Joseph P (funl, My 1,29:4), 1959, Ap 27, 27:1
Donahue, Lawrence Jr, 1943, O 28,23:3
Donahue, Lester B, 1941, N 3,19:5
Donahue, Martin K, 1941, Ap 23,21:4
Donahue, Michael, 1922, F 2,17:4; 1952, S 18,29:5
Donahue, Michael H, 1937, Ap 11,II,8:5
Donahue, Michael J, 1944, Je 3,13:2; 1950, S 13,27:2
Donahue, Patrick H, 1949, Ag 7,60:4
Donahue, Patrick J, 1950, Je 15,31:2
Donahue, Patrick James Bp, 1922, O 5,23:3
Donahue, Phil D, 1950, N 28,31:3
Donahue, Richard G 3d Mrs, 1953, S 21,25:5
Donahue, Robert F, 1948, S 20,25:1
Donahue, S J, 1934, Mr 3,14:1
Donahue, Sarah, 1952, My 20,25:3
Donahue, Stephen G, 1958, N 2,88:6
Donahue, Stephen J, 1939, Ag 28,19:6
Donahue, Thomas, 1938, Ag 26,17:4
Donahue, Thomas E, 1939, Je 7,23:4
Donahue, Thomas I, 1943, N 3,25:6
Donahue, Thomas J, 1949, D 24,15:1
Donahue, Thomas L, 1959, D 13,86:3
Donahue, Thomas P, 1954, Ag 26,27:2
Donahue, William E, 1942, Ag 13,19:2
Donahue, William H, 1948, N 5,26:3
Donahue, William J, 1953, F 21,14:3
Donahue, William P Sr, 1945, Ap 11,23:3
Donahy, Edgar, 1957, Je 19,35:4
Donal, John S, 1949, Ap 8,26:5
Donald, Ann E, 1950, Ap 20,29:1
Donald, D Sir, 1933, F 18,15:3
Donald, Dick, 1953, S 6,50:1
Donald, Douglas, 1943, Jl 5,15:5
Donald, Graeme Mrs, 1962, S 1,19:3
Donald, James, 1881, Mr 8,5:2
Donald, James M, 1918, S 24,13:5
Donald, Louis, 1948, Ja 29,23:3
Donald, Malcolm, 1949, S 12,21:4
Donald, Marcus M, 1953, D 25,17:2
Donald, Nellie Mrs, 1943, O 19,19:4
Donald, Peter Sr, 1952, O 25,17:4
Donald, William, 1954, Ja 18,23:4
Donald, William H, 1946, N 9,17:3
Donald, William J, 1958, Ap 8,29:1; 1962, Ag 13,18:6
Donald, William Milne, 1912, Mr 9,13:6
Donaldson, Alex, 1948, O 17,78:4
Donaldson, Alfred Lee, 1923, N 8,19:5
Donaldson, Allan W S, 1957, D 27,19:1
Donaldson, Andrew, 1904, Ja 12,7:5
Donaldson, Anna M Mrs, 1939, S 27,25:5
Donaldson, Arthur, 1955, S 30,25:1
Donaldson, Arthur O, 1954, N 6,17:5
Donaldson, Austin S, 1950, Ag 10,25:5
Donaldson, Bertram, 1943, N 2,25:5
Donaldson, Blake F, 1966, F 21,39:1
Donaldson, Charles, 1938, D 8,27:6
Donaldson, Charles D, 1942, N 26,27:2
Donaldson, David, 1943, D 12,69:1
Donaldson, Dorothy Mills, 1968, Ap 27,39:5
Donaldson, E L, 1901, N 13,3:2
Donaldson, Edward B, 1955, Ap 22,25:1
Donaldson, Edward Mrs, 1945, F 4,38:1
Donaldson, Edward V, 1945, Jl 31,19:1
Donaldson, Elma, 1939, Jl 22,15:2
Donaldson, Florence W Mrs, 1937, Jl 2,21:5
Donaldson, Frank, 1945, D 16,40:2
Donaldson, Fred E, 1952, Jl 16,25:3
Donaldson, Frederick L, 1953, O 8,29:4
Donaldson, Frederick N Mrs, 1961, N 14,36:3
Donaldson, G Russell, 1937, N 2,28:3
Donaldson, George H, 1938, Mr 3,21:4
Donaldson, George R Rev, 1937, Ja 26,21:5
Donaldson, Gerald E, 1963, N 30,27:3
Donaldson, Glen, 1967, Mr 2,35:3
Donaldson, Harnett B, 1961, Ag 30,33:4
Donaldson, Harvey J, 1912, Ja 3,13:4
Donaldson, Henry H (por; will, Ap 2,19:3), 1938, Ja 24,23:3
Donaldson, Henry H Mrs, 1952, Ja 10,29:2
Donaldson, Henry S, 1944, Ap 4,21:3
Donaldson, J E, 1948, Ap 7,51:2
Donaldson, James, 1959, Ag 1,17:2
Donaldson, James A, 1956, O 10,39:2
Donaldson, James H, 1957, My 1,37:2
Donaldson, James Sir, 1915, Mr 10,13:6
Donaldson, James Sr, 1943, Ag 17,17:3
Donaldson, John, 1951, F 18,78:4; 1955, Je 10,25:4
Donaldson, John C Mrs, 1955, O 4,35:4
Donaldson, John M, 1941, D 23,21:5
Donaldson, Joseph E, 1948, Mr 21,60:3
Donaldson, Kenneth H, 1953, S 4,34:7
Donaldson, Leonard E, 1951, Ap 7,15:3
Donaldson, Lewis H, 1960, Jl 27,29:1
Donaldson, Lindsay M, 1944, D 23,13:5
Donaldson, Malcolm D, 1958, Jl 12,15:2
Donaldson, McPherrin H, 1945, Ag 23,23:2
Donaldson, Norman V, 1964, Ja 19,76:5
Donaldson, Norman V Mrs, 1946, My 2,21:3
Donaldson, Oliver D (por), 1943, D 5,65:1
Donaldson, Paul, 1952, N 13,31:2
Donaldson, Percy, 1954, My 28,23:1
Donaldson, Robert M, 1923, S 17,15:3
Donaldson, Scott W, 1960, Ja 9,21:1
Donaldson, Starr, 1948, F 19,23:4
Donaldson, Story Mrs, 1945, D 5,25:1
Donaldson, T Q, 1934, O 28,33:1
Donaldson, Thomas B, 1947, My 16,23:1
Donaldson, Thomas Q Jr, 1954, N 25,29:3
Donaldson, Thomas Q Mrs, 1959, N 8,88:2
Donaldson, Wallace, 1911, Je 22,11:6
Donaldson, Walter, 1947, Jl 16,23:1
Donaldson, Walter J, 1952, My 15,31:3
Donaldson, Will, 1954, D 21,27:4
Donaldson, William H, 1948, D 9,33:5
Donaldson, William H Mrs, 1949, Ja 14,24:3
Donaldson, William H sr, 1952, My 23,21:4
Donaldson, William J Rev Dr, 1917, Mr 23,9:5
Donaldson, William R, 1967, Je 29,43:2
Donaldson, Wilson E, 1943, S 20,21:4
Donally, Alvin J, 1940, My 25,17:6
Donaly, James L, 1937, Je 30,24:1
Donan, James A, 1941, F 5,19:3
Donat, Ernest, 1939, Ag 29,21:5
Donat, Ernest Mrs, 1964, D 21,29:2
Donat, Robert (mem ser, Jl 11,23:2), 1958, Je 9,23:
Donat, Winfield, 1953, Mr 20,23:3
Donatella, Joseph, 1939, Ap 2,III,7:3
Donatelli, Phil, 1954, Ap 7,31:1
Donath, Kurt, 1947, D 19,25:1
Donath, Ludwig, 1967, O 2,47:1
Donati, David J Jr, 1941, Mr 18,23:2
Donati, Umberto, 1943, Ja 9,13:5
Donatian, Brother (E M Leport), 1943, S 24,23:4
Donato, Carmine, 1944, My 4,19:4
Donato, Giuseppe, 1965, Ap 12,35:2
Donato, Mitchell F, 1967, S 9,31:4
Donato, Patrick J, 1948, My 1,15:4
Donavan, James G, 1951, O 29,23:5
Donavan, Jerry F, 1938, Je 28,19:2
Donavan, Joseph, 1917, Ag 9,7:2
Donavan, Mike Prof, 1918, Mr 25,13:8
Donavin, Carolyn Mrs, 1938, Ja 5,21:5
Donchi, Mendel, 1942, Ap 26,39:2
Doncourt, Carlton L, 1938, My 20,19:3
Doncourt, Joseph Mrs, 1946, Ja 27,41:1
Donder, Joseph A, 1948, O 29,25:1
Dondero, Angelo L, 1959, Ja 25,92:4
Dondero, Charles A Mrs, 1960, Mr 25,27:3
Dondero, George A, 1968, Ja 30,38:2
Dondero, John A, 1957, Ag 25,87:1
Dondero, Peter, 1949, Jl 31,61:2
Donecker, John C, 1967, Mr 16,40:3
Donegall, Marquis, 1904, My 16,9:6
Donegan, Arthur B, 1954, Ja 25,19:4
Donegan, Christopher E, 1953, S 17,29:2
Donegan, Daniel M Jr, 1943, Mr 29,15:4
Donegan, Denis J, 1965, Je 24,35:2
Donegan, Edmund J, 1959, Ja 6,33:3
Donegan, H George Mrs, 1963, Je 15,23:5
Donegan, Harold H, 1967, Je 6,47:4
Donegan, James A, 1938, N 17,25:3
Donegan, James F, 1952, Ap 18,25:2
Donegan, James J Mrs, 1938, Ap 5,21:4
Donegan, John T, 1948, Jl 1,23:2
Donegan, Justin M, 1956, Mr 9,23:4
Donegan, Mary E Mrs, 1942, O 2,25:4
Donegan, Maurice F, 1950, Mr 26,96:2
Donegan, Thomas J Sr Mrs, 1949, D 18,88:6
Donegan, William J, 1949, Ap 10,76:3
Donegani, Guido, 1947, Ap 18,21:4
Doneger, Abraham L, 1946, Jl 17,23:5
Donehoo, Jane P Mrs, 1941, Ag 31,23:2
Donehoo, Paul T, 1940, D 23,19:2
Donehue, Edward Sr, 1951, S 9,90:1
Donehue, Vincent J, 1966, Ja 18,37:1
Donelian, Ohannes, 1967, My 8,41:3
Donellan, James I Mrs, 1949, Ap 13,29:1
Donellan, Michael A, 1942, Je 28,32:1
Donelli, Alfredo, 1966, Mr 13,86:8
Donelli, Malinda Mrs, 1953, Mr 23,23:2
Donelon, George C, 1960, Ja 4,29:6

Donelson, Andrew, 1915, F 6,11:6
Donelson, Andrew Jackson Maj, 1871, Je 27,1:3
Donelson, Clarence C, 1940, Mr 5,24:3
Donelson, Elizabeth A Mrs, 1871, S 7,3:1
Donelson, John F, 1954, Ap 22,29:2
Donely, George A Mrs, 1953, Ja 5,21:2
Donenfeld, Harry, 1965, F 28,89:1
Donenfeld, Harry Mrs, 1961, F 17,24:6
Doneraile, Viscount, 1941, S 9,23:1
Dones, James A, 1949, Jl 26,27:4
Doneski, Bernard J Jr, 1968, Mr 5,41:3
Donet, Elizabeth D, 1942, D 13,75:4
Doney, Andrew A, 1960, Jl 12,35:1
Doney, Carl G, 1955, N 7,29:4
Doney, Edward D, 1937, O 6,25:3
Doney, Paul H Mrs, 1958, Jl 6,56:5
Dongen, Kees van (Cornelius Theodorus Marie van Dongen), 1968, My 29,39:1
Donges, Eben, 1968, Ja 11,37:1
Donges, Ralph W E Mrs, 1941, D 31,17:2
Donges, Raymond R, 1937, Ap 9,21:4
Donham, George A, 1964, S 25,41:1
Donham, Harold G, 1946, Ap 15,27:3
Donham, Wallace B, 1954, N 30,29:1
Donhauser, Joseph L, 1964, D 4,40:3
Donhauser, Joseph L Mrs, 1944, N 25,13:5
Doniat, Thecla, 1955, Jl 29,17:4
Donichy, Earl A, 1955, Ag 4,25:1
Doniger, David D, 1949, D 5,23:4
Doniger, David D Mrs, 1965, Ja 2,19:4
Doniger, Harry E, 1961, Ja 4,33:3
Donihee, Vincent P, 1937, S 15,23:4
Donihee, W B, 1903, My 13,9:5
Donihee, William B, 1909, O 5,9:5
Donilon, Charles E, 1958, Ag 1,21:3
Donington, Joseph A, 1950, Je 21,27:3
Doniphan, John V, 1946, D 13,23:2
Donk, Augustus Mrs, 1953, Je 30,23:1
Donk, Peter J, 1943, Ag 21,11:4
Donkelberger, Chauncey E, 1937, Ag 25,21:3
Donker, Arie E, 1963, D 28,23:2
Donker, Leendert A, 1956, F 4,19:4
Donkin, McKay, 1968, Mr 19,47:1
Donlan, Edward Jr, 1946, S 30,25:5
Donlan, Francis A, 1945, F 7,21:2
Donlan, George S, 1963, My 30,17:5
Donlan, John J Rev Dr, 1937, F 28,II,8:8
Donle, Charles B, 1937, Je 9,25:1
Donleavy, John J, 1959, Ap 17,25:1
Donley, Charles, 1964, O 1,35:3
Donley, George W, 1939, Ap 9,III,6:6
Donley, Rosser A, 1960, Ap 26,37:1
Donley, Ruth, 1943, Ag 30,17:1
Donlin, E J, 1933, S 24,36:3
Donlin, John H, 1952, Ja 26,13:2
Donlin, M, 1933, S 25,15:3
Donlon, Alphonsus J Rev, 1923, S 5,15:4
Donlon, Cornelius, 1944, Je 1,19:5
Donlon, Francis L, 1943, Mr 25,21:6
Donlon, James F, 1946, N 24,79:5
onlon, John P, 1946, N 3,62:1
onlon, Joseph S, 1965, Jl 9,29:4
onlon, Patrick, 1960, Ap 22,31:2
onlon, Stephen E, 1947, Ja 8,23:2
onlon, Thomas J, 1946, Je 7,19:3
onn, Alfred C, 1955, F 20,88:7
onn, Richard, 1965, D 15,47:2
onna, Joseph P, 1937, Je 25,21:4
onnahoe, Jefferson D, 1937, Ag 27,10:4
onnally, Ada, 1942, Jl 2,21:2
onnally, Harry H, 1947, My 24,15:4
onnan, Elizabeth, 1955, Mr 17,45:3
onnan, John W, 1952, Ag 23,13:1
onnatin, Charles F, 1944, F 24,15:2
onnatin, Louis N, 1948, F 11,27:4
onnatin, Louis N Jr, 1938, Ap 3,II,7:1
onnay, Maurice, 1945, Ap 1,36:2
onnedieu de Bavres, Felix A H, 1952, F 16,13:5
onnel, Charles A, 1943, O 30,15:1
onnel, Philip Sr, 1947, Jl 3,21:4
onnelan, John J F Rev, 1915, Ag 15,13:5
onnell, Barbara, 1951, O 6,19:5
onnell, Ben D, 1952, Mr 29,15:2
onnell, James D, 1907, F 6,9:6
onnell, John C Mrs, 1948, Mr 10,27:4
onnell, John F, 1945, Ja 2,19:2
onnell, Lucy W, 1942, Mr 20,19:4
onnell, Otto D, 1961, Ap 10,31:3
onnell, Philip S, 1962, D 27,7:3
onnell, Webb Mrs, 1943, Mr 4,19:4
onnell, William A, 1947, Mr 28,23:4
onnell, William F, 1949, Ja 21,21:2
onnell, William H, 1938, D 29,19:5
onnellan, Andrew Mrs, 1956, Ja 18,31:4
onnellan, George L, 1953, Ag 31,17:1
nnelley, Naomi, 1951, Jl 4,17:2
nnelley, Richard R 2d, 1950, Ap 29,15:2
nnelley, Thomas E, 1955, F 8,27:5
nnellon, James P, 1957, Ap 10,33:4
nnellon, John A, 1954, D 22,23:3
nnellon, Thomas A, 1948, My 2,76:6
nnelly, Andrew, 1955, Jl 7,27:2
nnelly, Andrew J, 1956, Ap 11,33:2

Donnelly, Antoinette, 1964, N 16,31:5
Donnelly, Arthur J, 1956, Je 1,23:1
Donnelly, Arthur L Mrs, 1961, N 12,86:8
Donnelly, Charles, 1906, D 6,9:4; 1939, S 5,23:3
Donnelly, Charles A, 1959, Ag 2,80:3
Donnelly, Charles B, 1947, Ap 30,25:2
Donnelly, Charles F, 1950, Jl 7,19:1
Donnelly, Charles H, 1954, Ag 20,19:2
Donnelly, Charles J, 1946, S 27,23:3
Donnelly, Cyril A, 1950, O 30,27:4
Donnelly, D, 1928, Ja 4,25:1
Donnelly, Daniel, 1909, Je 24,7:4
Donnelly, Daniel J, 1949, D 22,23:4
Donnelly, E Harold, 1950, Je 24,13:4
Donnelly, E L, 1880, S 18,3:7
Donnelly, Edward, 1940, My 23,24:2
Donnelly, Edward C Mrs, 1957, Jl 30,23:2
Donnelly, Edward F, 1959, Mr 11,35:2
Donnelly, Edward J, 1942, Mr 10,20:2
Donnelly, Eleanor C, 1917, My 2,11:5
Donnelly, Eliza, 1953, Je 5,27:5
Donnelly, Eugene F, 1965, O 15,45:4
Donnelly, Francis A, 1938, My 18,21:4
Donnelly, Francis E, 1951, F 7,29:4
Donnelly, Francis F, 1944, Ap 21,19:4
Donnelly, Francis J, 1940, Ag 2,15:2; 1951, D 16,90:8
Donnelly, Francis X, 1939, N 7,28:3
Donnelly, Frank A, 1962, Ja 14,84:8
Donnelly, George C, 1964, Mr 25,41:1
Donnelly, George C Mrs, 1943, My 5,27:2
Donnelly, George J, 1951, D 9,90:3
Donnelly, Gerard B, 1950, Jl 13,25:5
Donnelly, Harold I Rev, 1937, Jl 11,II,4:6
Donnelly, Harold W Sr, 1959, Ja 24,19:4
Donnelly, Harry, 1955, N 11,25:3
Donnelly, Harry F, 1954, D 2,31:3
Donnelly, Harry L, 1956, Mr 22,35:2
Donnelly, Helen (Sister St Stanislaus), 1958, Jl 31, 23:1
Donnelly, Henry V, 1909, N 15,9:3
Donnelly, Ignatius, 1901, Ja 2,5:2
Donnelly, J J, 1948, O 21,27:3
Donnelly, J Louis Mrs, 1968, Ag 19,37:2
Donnelly, J T, 1883, D 6,2:6
Donnelly, James, 1916, N 18,11:6; 1947, Mr 11,27:1; 1958, My 20,33:3
Donnelly, James A, 1952, Ap 14,19:3
Donnelly, James H, 1953, Ag 27,25:5
Donnelly, James J, 1941, Je 3,21:2; 1957, S 4,33:3
Donnelly, James J Jr, 1945, S 4,23:5
Donnelly, James T, 1956, Je 8,25:2
Donnelly, James T Jr, 1958, Mr 25,33:1
Donnelly, James W, 1945, Jl 2,15:4
Donnelly, Jere F, 1916, D 21,11:2
Donnelly, John, 1947, Jl 12,13:3; 1959, Je 15,27:4
Donnelly, John D, 1952, F 11,25:5
Donnelly, John E, 1946, Jl 12,17:2; 1948, Ap 27,25:3
Donnelly, John H, 1954, F 7,88:2
Donnelly, John J, 1938, Mr 15,23:2; 1944, Ag 23,19:5
Donnelly, John M Mrs, 1957, Ap 7,88:7
Donnelly, John Mrs, 1952, My 14,27:2
Donnelly, John P, 1955, S 8,31:2
Donnelly, John S, 1953, Ag 18,23:2
Donnelly, John T, 1952, S 5,27:4
Donnelly, Joseph, 1962, Je 20,35:3
Donnelly, Joseph A, 1945, My 14,17:5
Donnelly, Joseph E, 1956, Jl 29,12:6
Donnelly, Joseph F, 1954, Ag 18,29:4
Donnelly, Joseph L, 1967, My 3,42:7
Donnelly, Joseph P, 1939, My 27,15:6; 1950, My 12, 27:2
Donnelly, Leo F, 1937, My 21,22:2
Donnelly, Lewis W A, 1950, Ag 15,29:3
Donnelly, M T, 1930, Jl 1,29:5
Donnelly, Mabel C, 1959, Ap 5,86:6
Donnelly, Martin I, 1956, Jl 15,61:1
Donnelly, Mary C Mrs, 1950, F 12,85:1
Donnelly, McClellan J, 1959, Ap 18,23:6
Donnelly, Michael F, 1955, O 29,19:4
Donnelly, Michael J, 1949, Ap 17,76:4; 1950, Mr 3, 25:1
Donnelly, Minerva, 1945, N 9,19:3
Donnelly, Patrick F, 1948, S 30,28:2
Donnelly, Patrick J, 1959, O 26,29:6
Donnelly, Paul D, 1937, F 17,22:1
Donnelly, Peter H, 1950, S 20,31:1
Donnelly, Phil F, 1941, Ag 9,15:4
Donnelly, Phil M, 1961, S 13,45:1
Donnelly, Philenia Mrs, 1938, O 5,23:1
Donnelly, Philip H, 1945, Jl 1,18:1
Donnelly, R G A Gen, 1905, F 28,9:5
Donnelly, Richard C, 1966, Je 25,31:5
Donnelly, Richard J, 1958, F 16,86:7
Donnelly, Rose T, 1946, O 7,31:5
Donnelly, Sadie H, 1948, Ag 3,25:5
Donnelly, Samuel B, 1946, Ja 28,19:1
Donnelly, T L, 1880, Jl 4,7:2
Donnelly, Thomas F Justice, 1924, N 2,7:1
Donnelly, Thomas H Mrs, 1948, S 16,29:4
Donnelly, Thomas J, 1937, O 3,II,8:8; 1952, Je 20, 23:5; 1963, O 3,35:4
Donnelly, Thomas P, 1953, Mr 19,29:3
Donnelly, Thorne, 1963, Ap 25,33:2

Donnelly, Timothy F, 1937, Je 1,23:5
Donnelly, Warren C, 1946, Ja 4,21:3
Donnelly, William A, 1952, D 2,31:3
Donnelly, William A Mrs, 1950, Je 10,17:4
Donnelly, William C, 1938, D 5,23:4
Donnelly, William E, 1960, F 19,27:1
Donnelly, William H, 1940, Je 25,23:4; 1966, My 19, 47:2
Donnelly (Sister Mary Francis), 1960, Jl 24,65:2
Donnelly (Sister Marianette), 1963, D 4,47:3
Donnely, Henry C, 1942, D 20,44:8
Donnenfeld, Morris Mrs, 1956, F 9,31:5
Donnenfield, Joseph, 1965, S 4,21:6
Donner, Alex H, 1964, Je 23,33:4
Donner, Armand R, 1959, Ja 4,88:4
Donner, Arthur, 1922, Jl 8,11:7
Donner, Ben, 1955, Ag 1,19:5
Donner, Eliot M, 1965, Ag 28,21:6
Donner, Herman J, 1954, S 27,21:2
Donner, Michael, 1938, Ap 12,23:5
Donner, Samuel, 1962, S 15,25:1
Donner, Vyvyan, 1965, Je 29,32:5
Donner, Willard H, 1947, My 17,15:1
Donner, William H, 1953, N 4,33:3
Donner, William H Mrs, 1952, N 22,23:6
Donnersmarck, Henckel von Prince, 1916, D 20,13:4
Donnet, Cardinal, 1883, Ja 13,4:6
Donnett, George L, 1951, O 5,28:2
Donniez, Louis J, 1950, O 27,30:3
Donnolly, Robert J, 1908, F 9,11:5
Donny, W Hugh, 1946, My 4,15:5
Donofri, Andrew E, 1967, Mr 30,45:1
D'Onofrio, Charles Mrs, 1949, Ag 11,23:5
D'Onofrio, Rocco, 1943, Ja 14,21:3
Donoghue, Cornelius F, 1947, O 14,27:6
Donoghue, Daniel C, 1939, My 29,15:2
Donoghue, Francis D Dr, 1937, Ja 5,23:5
Donoghue, Francis L, 1948, N 10,29:2
Donoghue, Frank E, 1952, Ja 9,29:4
Donoghue, George T, 1962, N 23,30:4
Donoghue, James A, 1937, Ap 29,21:5
Donoghue, James J, 1954, Ag 9,17:4
Donoghue, James W, 1960, S 24,23:4
Donoghue, James W Mrs, 1950, Mr 3,25:2
Donoghue, Joseph C, 1960, S 29,35:4
Donoghue, Patrick A, 1937, My 31,16:2
Donoghue, Steve, 1945, Mr 24,17:1
Donoghue, Steve Mrs, 1942, F 27,17:5
Donoghue, Terence J, 1956, S 1,15:7
Donoghue, Thomas A, 1950, My 18,29:5
Donoghue, William F, 1950, My 10,31:3
Donoghue, William J, 1952, Ja 27,76:2; 1965, Je 12, 31:2
Donoho, Matilda A Mrs (will, Ag 16,16:1), 1939, Jl 31,13:3
Donoho, Ruger, 1916, Ja 30,17:6
Donohoe, Charles L, 1942, Je 16,23:4
Donohoe, Denis 3d, 1940, N 16,17:2
Donohoe, Frances C Mrs, 1938, Jl 2,13:2
Donohoe, Hugh, 1942, Ap 8,19:4
Donohoe, James A, 1956, F 27,23:1
Donohoe, Joseph A, 1954, Ag 7,13:4
Donohoe, Lucius F, 1951, My 24,35:1
Donohoe, Margaret, 1952, O 5,89:2
Donohoe, Mary J, 1941, Mr 24,17:1
Donohoe, Michael, 1958, Ja 19,86:7
Donohoe, Nellie Mrs, 1941, O 3,23:4
Donohoe, Patrick J, 1952, Ag 7,21:3
Donohoe, Thomas D Mrs, 1952, Je 24,29:5
Donohoe, Thomas F, 1953, F 26,25:1
Donohue, A Jordan, 1947, Ag 27,23:2
Donohue, Arthur J, 1951, Jl 5,25:5
Donohue, Avon A, 1937, My 6,25:3
Donohue, C D, 1928, Mr 6,27:4
Donohue, Charles Ex-Justice, 1910, Ap 19,9:5
Donohue, Charles J, 1951, My 28,21:4
Donohue, Charles J Mrs, 1950, Mr 18,13:2
Donohue, Daniel Mrs, 1947, Je 25,25:4
Donohue, Edward J, 1937, D 24,17:4; 1939, D 6,15:5
Donohue, Edward J Mrs, 1939, D 6,15:5
Donohue, Edward W, 1944, Mr 24,19:2
Donohue, Elizabeth Mrs, 1939, D 16,17:2
Donohue, Ernest, 1959, Ap 25,21:2
Donohue, Florence J, 1953, O 17,15:5
Donohue, Francis B, 1943, Jl 30,15:2
Donohue, Francis J, 1963, Jl 14,61:3
Donohue, Francis J C, 1950, Ap 26,29:5
Donohue, Frank J, 1960, O 1,19:4
Donohue, H Frank, 1941, D 19,25:4
Donohue, James F, 1939, S 22,23:4; 1954, Mr 3,27:4
Donohue, James H, 1938, Je 14,21:3; 1948, O 14,29:3
Donohue, James H Mrs, 1950, D 10,105:1
Donohue, James J, 1963, Ag 28,33:5
Donohue, James M, 1923, Mr 3,13:4
Donohue, James O, 1943, D 19,48:3
Donohue, James Rev Dr, 1918, S 6,13:4
Donohue, Jeremiah J, 1945, Ag 5,38:3
Donohue, Jerry, 1943, Ap 15,25:2
Donohue, John A, 1948, Ag 5,21:4
Donohue, John B, 1956, S 21,25:2
Donohue, John C, 1952, Ag 29,23:1
Donohue, John F, 1950, O 31,27:1; 1950, D 6,33:3
Donohue, John H, 1948, Ap 22,27:4; 1951, F 19,23:1

Donohue, John J, 1939, Ap 7,21:3
Donohue, John S, 1958, Je 24,31:4
Donohue, John W, 1944, F 12,13:4
Donohue, Joseph, 1922, Ag 30,15:5; 1944, My 16,21:5
Donohue, Joseph A, 1959, Ap 7,33:4; 1965, Jl 16,27:2
Donohue, Joseph D, 1945, My 15,19:5
Donohue, Joseph F, 1948, O 26,31:2
Donohue, Katherine M, 1952, O 28,31:4
Donohue, Lawrence P, 1949, My 7,13:5
Donohue, M F, 1932, D 3,17:3
Donohue, Mary H (will, Je 28,22:2), 1938, My 4,23:2
Donohue, Mary V, 1937, O 20,23:5
Donohue, Michael A, 1943, Jl 3,13:7
Donohue, Michael M, 1955, D 15,37:2
Donohue, Patrick J, 1962, F 11,86:5
Donohue, Phil F (will, S 10,24:2), 1937, Ag 17,19:1
Donohue, Thomas A, 1946, Ag 28,27:5
Donohue, Thomas M, 1953, Mr 25,31:5
Donohue, Tim, 1911, S 26,9:3
Donohue, Timothy E, 1953, Ap 11,17:1
Donohue, William F, 1944, N 11,13:4; 1947, S 20,15:2; 1949, Ja 25,24:2
Donohue, William J, 1907, F 4,9:6; 1941, F 15,15:4
Donohue, William T, 1939, Jl 18,19:3
Donohugh, Carol, 1950, Je 18,76:5
Donop, Stanley B von, 1941, O 18,19:5
Donor, John J, 1939, F 23,23:6
Donoughmore, Lady, 1944, F 23,19:5
Donoughmore, Lord, 1948, O 21,27:6
Donovan, Albert D, 1946, Je 22,19:4
Donovan, Alfred E, 1944, Mr 31,21:1
Donovan, Alfred F, 1954, O 27,29:3
Donovan, Andrew T, 1955, O 13,32:1
Donovan, Bernard F, 1959, Ja 25,92:6
Donovan, Catherine (Sister Mary Jerome), 1964, Ap 19,84:8
Donovan, Catherine Mrs, 1906, Ap 18,11:5
Donovan, Charles A, 1909, Ag 24,9:5
Donovan, Clarence W, 1946, Ap 8,27:2
Donovan, Cornelius A Sr, 1953, Mr 11,29:4
Donovan, Cornelius B, 1967, S 21,47:3
Donovan, Cornelius J, 1960, F 27,19:2
Donovan, D J, 1934, My 3,19:2
Donovan, Daniel, 1904, F 10,9:6; 1942, My 28,17:3
Donovan, Daniel J, 1939, Mr 11,17:3; 1955, F 20,89:1
Donovan, Daniel L, 1938, N 9,23:2
Donovan, David B, 1951, N 21,25:3
Donovan, David H, 1963, Ja 15,16:1
Donovan, David R Mrs, 1955, Jl 26,25:2
Donovan, Dennis, 1920, Ag 22,20:5
Donovan, Dennis J, 1948, Je 15,28:2
Donovan, Dennis P, 1966, F 28,27:3
Donovan, Dennis W, 1947, Mr 30,56:2
Donovan, Edward J, 1955, O 22,19:5; 1959, Jl 19,68:4
Donovan, Edwin S, 1957, Mr 3,84:6
Donovan, Elmer W, 1955, Ap 3,87:1
Donovan, Florence F, 1910, D 26,7:5
Donovan, Florence T, 1960, Ap 26,37:1
Donovan, Francis R, 1948, Ag 16,19:2
Donovan, Francis X, 1942, Jl 31,15:6
Donovan, Frank E, 1947, O 17,22:3
Donovan, George H, 1955, Jl 6,27:1
Donovan, George Henry, 1947, Je 2,25:3
Donovan, Gordon I, 1967, Ap 8,31:5
Donovan, H C, 1943, Je 12,13:4
Donovan, Harold J, 1961, My 12,29:3
Donovan, Harry W, 1953, O 9,27:3
Donovan, Herman L, 1964, N 22,86:5
Donovan, J S, 1926, D 8,29:6
Donovan, James, 1944, N 25,13:6
Donovan, James A, 1950, Ja 15,85:2; 1959, S 17,39:4
Donovan, James D, 1944, D 22,17:2; 1958, Je 20,23:2
Donovan, James E, 1948, Ag 27,18:5; 1957, O 22,33:3
Donovan, James J, 1942, O 3,15:6; 1956, Mr 19,31:2
Donovan, Jeremiah, 1938, Ap 5,21:4
Donovan, Jeremiah F, 1951, Ja 9,30:2
Donovan, Jerome F, 1961, S 16,19:4
Donovan, Jerome F Mrs, 1943, Ag 5,15:2
Donovan, John E, 1946, F 13,23:6; 1947, O 23,25:5; 1955, Ap 7,27:4
Donovan, John J, 1937, Ja 11,19:1; 1941, O 12,53:2; 1947, Jl 3,21:4; 1949, Mr 20,76:3; 1950, D 13,35:3; 1967, My 11,54:5
Donovan, John J Jr (funl plans, Mr 14,23:4; funl, Mr 16,33:4), 1955, Mr 13,86:8
Donovan, John J Mrs, 1938, Jl 23,13:3
Donovan, John Mrs, 1959, Ap 15,33:4
Donovan, John R, 1959, S 9,41:2
Donovan, John W Mrs, 1942, F 12,23:4
Donovan, Joseph, 1947, D 20,17:4; 1960, D 5,31:3
Donovan, Joseph A, 1945, Ag 19,39:2
Donovan, Joseph E, 1948, F 27,21:3
Donovan, Joseph F, 1944, Ap 4,21:3; 1952, O 29,29:6
Donovan, Joseph J, 1952, O 24,23:1
Donovan, Joseph J Mrs, 1950, Ag 11,19:1
Donovan, Joseph L, 1938, Ap 21,19:4
Donovan, Joseph O, 1951, Ja 26,23:2
Donovan, Joseph S, 1966, Ap 1,35:5
Donovan, Judith W Mrs, 1957, Ag 24,15:2
Donovan, Katherine B, 1959, S 16,39:2
Donovan, Katherine M Mrs, 1942, Jl 10,17:6
Donovan, Leo, 1950, My 23,30:2; 1957, Ap 7,88:5
Donovan, Leo R, 1949, N 6,94:5

Donovan, Mary A Mrs, 1941, Je 15,37:1
Donovan, Mathew, 1941, Je 3,21:2
Donovan, Maurice A, 1953, D 21,31:5
Donovan, Michael J, 1938, Ap 6,23:4
Donovan, Michael P Mrs, 1963, Ap 1,27:5
Donovan, Mike Prof, 1918, Mr 25,13:8
Donovan, Monica, 1948, D 31,15:3
Donovan, Mrs, 1902, O 23,16:1
Donovan, Patricia, 1940, Ap 10,25:2
Donovan, Patrick, 1911, N 22,13:5; 1941, Jl 27,30:1
Donovan, Patrick A, 1944, F 5,15:4
Donovan, Patrick J (Patsy), 1953, D 26,13:3
Donovan, Paul, 1959, Mr 29,80:6
Donovan, Peter, 1939, My 7,III,6:7
Donovan, Raymond F, 1949, N 4,27:2
Donovan, Richard, 1949, F 8,26:2
Donovan, Richard J, 1965, Ag 22,83:1
Donovan, Richard James, 1920, Je 27,18:1
Donovan, Samuel M, 1955, Jl 22,23:5
Donovan, Sheila, 1952, Ja 2,8:7
Donovan, Thomas F, 1946, N 18,23:2; 1951, Je 26,29:1
Donovan, Thomas J, 1958, Ap 26,19:5
Donovan, Timothy F, 1944, F 4,15:5
Donovan, Timothy M, 1941, N 9,55:6
Donovan, W J, 1928, Ag 22,19:3
Donovan, William A, 1939, O 4,25:2
Donovan, William Edward Henry, 1908, O 31,9:2
Donovan, William F, 1938, Mr 16,23:4; 1942, Jl 4, 17:4; 1945, Mr 6,21:1; 1947, Mr 25,25:2
Donovan, William H, 1943, My 25,23:5
Donovan, William J, 1940, My 2,23:6; 1943, My 10, 19:3
Donovan, William J (Wild Bill),(trb, F 10,33:3; funl, F 12,27:2), 1959, F 9,1:5
Donovan (Sister Mary Genevieve), 1962, Mr 18,86:4
Donsbach, William J, 1966, Ja 20,35:3
Donshea, Frank H, 1954, Je 4,23:4
Donworth, Thomas, 1952, O 8,31:5
Doody, Albert C, 1939, Jl 13,19:4
Doody, Daniel, 1946, S 10,7:3
Doody, Florence, 1956, Ap 28,17:5
Doody, James Mrs, 1945, D 6,27:4
Doody, Leo, 1956, O 6,21:5
Doody, Richard P, 1959, My 10,87:2
Doody, William C, 1951, Mr 1,27:3
Doody, William M, 1956, My 23,31:5
Doody, Willie (Baby Face), 1955, S 30,16:6
D'Ooge, Benjamin L, 1940, Mr 9,15:3
D'ooge, Martin Luther, 1915, S 13,9:6
Dooher, Gerald F P, 1961, O 7,23:2
Dooher, Joseph M, 1966, N 7,47:1
Dooin, Charles, 1952, My 15,31:4
Doolan, John A, 1955, D 1,35:4
Doolan, John M Mrs, 1950, Mr 10,27:1
Doolan, John W, 1950, Ap 12,28:2
Doolan, Leonard W, 1961, S 5,35:4
Doolan, Michael W Mrs, 1949, F 14,19:5
Doolan, Peter B Mrs, 1949, Mr 25,23:3
Dooley, Agnes Mrs, 1964, Ag 20,29:4
Dooley, Arthur H, 1966, Ag 15,27:3
Dooley, Bernard F J, 1939, My 15,17:4
Dooley, Bernard J, 1949, D 29,26:2
Dooley, Channing R, 1956, Je 26,29:1
Dooley, Charles L, 1945, My 7,17:1
Dooley, Daniel A, 1942, N 8,50:4
Dooley, E J, 1927, Ja 17,17:4
Dooley, Edward, 1949, Ag 25,23:2
Dooley, Edward M, 1939, Jl 21,19:4; 1964, Ap 25,12:4
Dooley, Edwin B Mrs, 1952, F 2,13:2; 1962, N 22,29:2
Dooley, Emmett A, 1955, S 26,23:2
Dooley, Francis M, 1958, F 18,27:4
Dooley, Francis Rev, 1915, Jl 8,13:7
Dooley, Frank H Mrs, 1949, Jl 6,30:1
Dooley, H Jordon, 1946, Je 3,21:2
Dooley, H W, 1932, Mr 13,II,6:1
Dooley, Harold J, 1950, F 16,23:4
Dooley, Harry J Mrs, 1952, Je 17,27:1
Dooley, J, 1928, Je 8,25:5
Dooley, J William, 1908, F 28,7:5
Dooley, James, 1950, Ja 3,25:5
Dooley, James A, 1960, Mr 28,29:3
Dooley, James A Rev, 1910, O 22,11:4
Dooley, James C, 1937, Mr 4,23:3
Dooley, James E, 1960, D 11,88:7
Dooley, James F, 1940, Mr 31,2:4; 1949, F 25,23:5
Dooley, James F Jr, 1967, Jl 20,37:5
Dooley, James P, 1946, N 20,31:2
Dooley, James R, 1955, Je 11,15:2
Dooley, John A, 1945, Ap 9,19:2
Dooley, John A Sr, 1967, O 18,47:4
Dooley, John F, 1919, S 13,11:5; 1964, Je 25,33:3
Dooley, John J, 1939, D 19,26:4; 1950, Ap 1,15:3; 1953, Mr 15,93:2
Dooley, John J Mrs, 1944, Ja 14,19:2; 1951, S 27,31:4
Dooley, John M, 1949, O 25,27:1
Dooley, John S, 1939, S 27,25:2
Dooley, Joseph A, 1946, F 9,13:3
Dooley, Joseph C, 1949, Ag 31,23:2
Dooley, Joseph W, 1941, My 3,15:3
Dooley, Margarita Ignatius, 1919, Mr 28,13:8
Dooley, Mark J Mrs, 1952, Ja 3,27:2
Dooley, Mary Mrs, 1939, Jl 8,15:2
Dooley, Matthew E, 1940, Mr 21,25:4

Dooley, Michael F, 1937, O 7,27:4
Dooley, Nellie E Mrs, 1947, Je 9,21:1
Dooley, Nonna (N Naldi), 1961, F 18,19:3
Dooley, R Francis, 1960, F 18,33:3
Dooley, Richard, 1943, Jl 9,17:1
Dooley, Robert E, 1960, Ap 5,37:2
Dooley, Sadie F Mrs, 1941, S 10,23:3
Dooley, Simon F Mrs, 1950, N 18,15:5
Dooley, Thomas A (est acctg), 1964, My 12,37:1
Dooley, Thomas A 3d (funl plans, Ja 20,26:4;trb, Ja 22,85:2), 1961, Ja 19,1:1
Dooley, Thomas F, 1942, Ja 30,19:5
Dooley, Thomas W, 1937, Mr 7,II,9:2
Dooley, Timothy A, 1952, S 21,88:3
Dooley, Tom, 1958, O 13,29:4
Dooley, William, 1921, S 30,15:5
Dooley, William D, 1960, Je 13,27:1
Dooley, William F, 1946, Ag 1,23:4
Dooley, William H, 1944, D 8,21:3
Dooley, William J, 1938, D 16,26:1
Dooley, William M, 1944, O 18,21:2
Dooley, William R, 1954, D 26,61:1
Doolin, Charles E, 1959, Jl 24,25:2
Doolin, John B, 1939, D 31,18:8
Dooling, Eugene E, 1946, O 9,27:3
Dooling, James A, 1949, Je 17,23:3
Dooling, James J, 1937, Jl 27,1:8; 1955, Mr 15,29:1
Dooling, John T, 1949, N 16,29:1
Dooling, John T Mrs, 1946, Ag 1,23:4
Dooling, Thomas J, 1942, Mr 26,23:6
Dooling, Thomas J Mrs, 1955, Ja 19,27:1
Doolittle, Anna H, 1941, D 23,21:5
Doolittle, Charles H Judge, 1874, My 31,6:6
Doolittle, Charles M, 1941, Jl 7,15:3
Doolittle, Dudley Sr, 1957, N 17,87:2
Doolittle, Eben S, 1944, Ap 11,19:2
Doolittle, Edgar J, 1961, O 25,37:3
Doolittle, Edward B, 1949, F 22,23:3
Doolittle, Eric Dr, 1920, S 21,11:6
Doolittle, Florence E, 1945, My 10,23:3
Doolittle, Frank H, 1925, S 28,19:5
Doolittle, Frederick J, 1955, N 22,35:1
Doolittle, Frederick W, 1950, S 14,32:4
Doolittle, Grace Mrs, 1952, Ag 15,16:4
Doolittle, H L, 1903, Je 16,2:4
Doolittle, Herbert S Sr, 1954, O 27,29:3
Doolittle, Hilda (HD), 1961, S 29,35:1
Doolittle, Hooker A, 1966, D 1,47:4
Doolittle, Ida J Mrs, 1937, Je 18,21:3
Doolittle, James H Jr, 1958, Ap 10,15:4
Doolittle, James Ralph, 1918, Jl 27,9:6
Doolittle, Judson A, 1945, Mr 27,19:6
Doolittle, Julia, 1871, S 26,3:1
Doolittle, Julius T A, 1949, Ag 23,23:2
Doolittle, Lewis J, 1939, Jl 15,15:6
Doolittle, Mary E, 1941, D 13,21:6
Doolittle, Mary I, 1938, Ja 8,15:5
Doolittle, Mortimer L, 1950, Ap 18,31:2
Doolittle, Orrin S, 1951, O 30,29:2
Doolittle, Otis Jr, 1948, N 10,29:5
Doolittle, R Edson Mrs, 1942, O 28,23:3
Doolittle, Ralph A, 1957, N 16,19:2
Doolittle, Roy W Mrs, 1955, S 5,11:5
Doolittle, Samuel K Rev, 1917, O 19,13:7
Doolittle, Sylvester, 1881, O 13,5:5
Doolittle, Willard F, 1944, Je 7,19:3
Doolittle, William C J, 1967, Ag 27,89:2
Doolittle, William F, 1948, O 26,31:3
Doolittle, William H, 1947, My 11,60:2
Doolph, Cyrus, 1937, N 26,21:3
Dooly, John Rev, 1915, N 8,13:5
Doom, Robert C, 1957, S 19,15:1
Doon, Caroline C Mrs, 1938, N 16,23:3
Doon, Charles W, 1956, Ja 23,25:5
Doon, John Glasgow, 1918, Jl 28,19:3
Doonan, Henry E, 1953, Ja 8,30:1
Doonan, John B, 1949, F 3,23:4
Doone, Allan, 1948, My 5,25:2
Doone, J J Hayes, 1953, Ap 7,29:3
Dooner, John, 1950, Mr 10,27:3
Dooner, John A, 1917, O 28,21:2
Dooner, Richard T, 1954, S 25,15:7
Doorley, James J, 1948, D 9,33:4
Doorley, William E, 1950, Je 27,29:4
Doorly, Edward, 1950, Ap 6,29:2; 1952, Ja 31,2
Doorly, Henry, 1961, Je 27,33:4
Doorly, John H M, 1949, Ag 6,17:4
Doorly, Nathaniel W, 1945, S 8,15:3
Doorn, Willem van, 1944, Je 29,23:5
Doornbos, Arthur C, 1946, O 23,27:6
Dopking, Al Mrs, 1952, N 26,23:3
Dopp, Arthur J, 1938, F 7,15:4
Dopp, Katherine, 1944, My 15,19:4
Dopper, Cornelius, 1939, S 19,25:2
Dopsloff, Gustav, 1947, F 4,25:4
Doque, Jose Gabriel, 1918, Ja 31,9:5
Dorais, Charles E (Gus),(trb, Ja 5,30:2), 195 19:1
Doran, Adda M Mrs, 1937, Jl 2,21:4
Doran, Alice, 1961, Je 19,27:4
Doran, Charles S, 1954, S 29,31:5
Doran, Charles W, 1954, Mr 18,32:4
Doran, Christopher, 1907, S 19,7:6

Doran, Daniel, 1937, Jl 17,15:3
Doran, Daniel A, 1949, N 15,25:2; 1949, D 22,23:2
Doran, David, 1938, My 31,10:6
Doran, Dr, 1878, F 17,2:2
Doran, Edward B, 1940, S 1,21:1
Doran, Edward W, 1949, Ap 22,23:2
Doran, Eugene, 1953, Jl 2,23:4
Doran, Frank M, 1949, O 25,27:4
Doran, Frank M Mrs, 1953, Ja 28,27:2
Doran, Franklin W Mrs, 1948, Ja 7,26:2
Doran, George, 1912, Ag 16,9:5
Doran, George H, 1956, Ja 8,86:1
Doran, George H Mrs, 1953, Je 17,38:3
Doran, J, 1878, Ja 27,6:7
Doran, J Earl, 1961, Ap 6,33:1
Doran, James M (por), 1942, S 9,23:4
Doran, James P, 1938, Jl 1,19:1
Doran, James R Mrs, 1945, N 13,21:4
Doran, Jessie M Mrs, 1945, Jl 25,23:6
Doran, John D, 1948, S 12,72:4
Doran, John J Mrs, 1953, N 5,31:3
Doran, John Mrs, 1947, My 18,60:1
Doran, John W, 1954, Mr 3,27:2
Doran, Joseph V, 1948, Ja 23,23:2
Doran, Lawrence A, 1939, Mr 11,17:5
Doran, Lawrence T, 1952, F 14,27:2
Doran, Margaret M (Sister Anna Mary), 1942, Ja 30,19:3
Doran, Martha V, 1952, Je 6,23:3; 1953, N 4,33:1
Doran, Mary B Mother, 1953, My 21,31:5
Doran, Michael, 1942, My 4,19:5
Doran, Michael A, 1937, S 10,23:2
Doran, Nicholas Rev, 1903, N 11,9:5
Doran, Ralph K, 1941, Ag 10,36:5
Doran, Robert E Dr, 1911, S 25,9:4
Doran, Robert J, 1945, Ja 31,21:2
Doran, Thomas F Bp, 1916, Ja 3,13:2
Doran, Thomas S, 1943, O 26,23:4
Doran, Wilbur H, 1954, Ja 7,32:3
Doran, William G, 1950, N 2,31:3
Doran, William T Sr, 1956, S 11,35:4
Doranha, Adalberto, 1939, O 10,23:5
Doras, Adam P, 1954, Jl 24,13:5
Dorat, Joseph H Col, 1916, Ja 12,13:4
Dorazio, Arthur T, 1965, Ja 24,80:8
Dorbacker, Henry J Mrs, 1951, N 13,29:1
d'Orbessan, Fernand Mrs, 1960, Jl 24,65:1
Dorbin, William, 1941, D 29,22:7
Dorcas, Herbert C, 1953, O 31,17:5
Dorcet, M Lewis, 1872, F 3,11:6
Dorch, Irwin T Mrs, 1938, Mr 31,23:4
Dorchain, Willy J, 1956, Jl 12,23:3
Dorchester, Daniel, 1944, Ja 13,21:4
Dordelman, Wilbert Mrs, 1967, Mr 29,45:2
Dordick, Jacob R, 1960, Ap 23,23:3
Dore, Arthur G, 1956, My 28,27:4
Dore, Clarence R, 1952, Ap 8,29:5
Dore, Daniel, 1949, O 18,27:6
Dore, Edward S (funl, Ap 8,29:4), 1958, Ap 3,31:5
Dore, Gustave, 1883, Ja 24,5:3
Dore, John F (por), 1938, Ap 19,21:1
Dore, John H, 1950, O 23,23:2
Dore, Victor, 1954, My 28,23:6
Dored, John, 1954, S 24,23:2
Dorelis, Jose, 1967, Ap 4,43:2
Doremus, Alice M Mrs, 1941, Ap 10,23:4
Doremus, Allan N, 1964, S 23,47:3
Doremus, Andrew J, 1946, D 23,23:4
Doremus, Arthur L, 1953, Ap 25,15:5
Doremus, Arthur T, 1940, Je 20,23:6
Doremus, Charles Avery Dr, 1925, D 3,25:4
Doremus, Clarence R, 1955, My 7,17:6
Doremus, Cornelius, 1918, D 14,17:5
Doremus, Cornelius Mrs, 1920, My 6,11:3
Doremus, David H, 1966, N 6,88:8
Doremus, David M, 1909, D 4,11:5
Doremus, Elias Osborn, 1907, My 14,11:4
Doremus, Elizabeth U, 1952, N 2,89:1
Doremus, Estelle E, 1937, Ag 25,21:6
Doremus, Frank C, 1944, Ag 5,11:7
Doremus, Frank C Mrs, 1968, Ap 24,47:2
Doremus, Frank E, 1947, S 5,19:3
Doremus, Frederic S (por), 1949, S 18,92:3
Doremus, Frederick H, 1946, Je 16,40:3
Doremus, George H, 1903, N 15,7:5
Doremus, Harry W, 1942, Ja 17,17:6; 1961, S 12,33:5
Doremus, Henry M, 1921, Ja 18,11:4
Doremus, Henry P, 1907, N 23,9:5
Doremus, James M Mrs, 1937, Ap 4,11:2
Doremus, John, 1940, D 5,25:4
Doremus, Joseph, 1952, My 23,21:3
Doremus, Louis C, 1937, S 24,21:1
Doremus, R Ogden Mrs, 1905, My 22,7:6
Doremus, Raymond H, 1964, S 20,89:2
Doremus, Robert Ogden Dr (funl, Mr 26,7:3), 1906, Mr 23,9:3
Doremus, Rodman B, 1965, Ag 1,76:5
Doremus, Sarah Hall, 1908, Jl 16,7:6
Doremus, T C, 1879, F 18,2:7
Doremus, Thomas E, 1962, S 25,37:1
Doremus, Wallace C, 1940, Jl 8,17:2
Doremus, Walter Lucius, 1916, O 25,11:5
Doremus, William H, 1956, My 23,31:3
Doremus, William R, 1953, Je 24,25:4
Doren, John J, 1940, Jl 26,17:3
Dorer, Engelbert, 1938, My 15,II,7:1
Dorer, George E, 1951, S 22,17:4
Dorer, George P, 1950, O 10,31:5
Dorer, Harry C, 1962, Ja 28,77:1
Dorer, John, 1942, Ap 8,19:5
Dorer, Oscar H, 1956, Ag 18,17:2
Doret, Gustave, 1943, Ap 20,23:5
Doret, Marcel, 1945, F 7,22:2; 1955, S 1,23:5
Dorey, Edward W Sr, 1953, Ag 15,15:2
Dorey, George, 1963, My 14,39:5
Dorey, Hailstead, 1946, Je 20,23:2
Dorey, J Milnor, 1955, Mr 11,25:4
Dorf, Alfred L, 1956, O 6,21:3
Dorf, Harry, 1937, D 8,16:4
Dorf, Joseph, 1938, D 28,26:5
Dorf, Samuel, 1923, F 26,13:5
Dorff, Martin R, 1964, Mr 27,28:1
Dorflinger, Christian, 1915, Ag 12,9:6
Dorflinger, Dwight C, 1944, Mr 1,19:2
Dorflinger, William F Jr, 1944, Jl 7,15:3
Dorfman, Boris W, 1964, Jl 2,31:5
Dorfman, Emanuel, 1949, N 4,27:2
Dorfman, George J, 1952, Mr 4,27:1
Dorfman, Irving, 1961, D 8,42:7
Dorfman, Jacob S, 1959, Ag 6,27:4
Dorfman, Julius, 1962, Jl 28,19:1
Dorfman, Leo B, 1957, F 28,27:4
Dorfman, Max, 1964, My 29,29:3
Dorfman, Nathan, 1960, Je 25,21:6
Dorfman, Ralph I Mrs, 1964, S 9,43:1
Dorfman, Robert I, 1955, My 9,23:5
Dorfman, Samuel D, 1942, Ja 11,44:4
Dorfmann, Henry L Mrs (B Freund), 1963, Ap 30, 35:4
Dorgan, John L, 1960, D 28,27:3
Dorgan, T A, 1929, My 3,25:3
Dorgeval, Harold F, 1940, Ap 8,19:2
Dorgin, Abraham L, 1954, O 16,17:3
Dori, Theodore C, 1939, F 20,17:5
Doria, Fernanda, 1953, My 22,27:4
Doria Pamphili Landi, Gesina Mary Princess, 1955, My 17,29:1
Doria-Pamphilj-Landi, Prince Filippo A, 1958, F 5,27:1
Dorian, Charles P, 1942, O 22,21:4
Dorian, Donald C, 1963, Ap 9,31:1
Dorian, Frank, 1940, Je 15,15:3
Dorigan, Harry W, 1966, My 10,39:3
Dorigny, Leon, 1907, Ag 15,7:6
Dorin, Reuben, 1965, Ap 19,29:3
Doring, Ernest N, 1955, Jl 10,72:7
Dorion, E C E Rev, 1920, Ja 30,15:4
Dorion, Jules, 1939, Mr 15,23:6
Dorion, William J, 1962, Ja 13,21:4
Doris, Charles, 1962, Jl 22,64:3
Doris, Frank J Mrs, 1942, Ja 24,17:1
Doris, James P, 1950, F 18,15:2
Doris, John, 1940, Ag 29,19:4
Doris, John B, 1912, F 7,11:4
Doris, Lillian (Mrs F Mosesco), 1966, Mr 17,43:7
Dority, Frank A, 1953, Je 30,23:5
Dorival, Georges, 1939, Jl 17,19:5
Doriza, Peter G, 1962, N 2,31:2
Dorizas, Michael M, 1957, O 28,27:4
Dorlan, Alfred, 1881, O 27,5:4
Dorland, Frank M, 1950, Ag 4,21:4
Dorland, Gilbert, 1944, My 3,19:2
Dorland, J Vene, 1941, D 15,19:5
Dorland, Joseph O, 1948, N 3,27:5
Dorland, Joseph W, 1965, Je 10,35:2
Dorland, Leroy B, 1958, F 20,25:3
Dorland, Milton M, 1938, Jl 27,17:2
Dorland, Ralph E, 1948, My 15,15:6
Dorland, Ralph E Mrs, 1944, F 22,23:4
Dorland, Raymond P, 1957, Ja 22,29:4
Dorland, Wesley, 1945, Ja 28,38:3
Dorleac, Francoise, 1967, Je 27,39:4
D'Orleans, Henri Prince, 1901, Ag 10,7:6
Dorling, Edward E, 1943, O 28,23:5
Dorlon, Phil S, 1949, Mr 15,27:4
Dorlon, Samuel J Mrs, 1944, D 4,24:3
Dorlon, Sydney, 1873, Jl 29,5:4
Dorman, Arthurina, 1950, Jl 5,1:6
Dorman, Benjamin, 1952, Je 22,69:1
Dorman, Benjamin N, 1966, O 7,43:2
Dorman, Charles A Dr, 1907, D 6,11:4
Dorman, Ebe R, 1948, Jl 17,15:2
Dorman, George A, 1945, O 31,23:3
Dorman, George M, 1940, Ag 29,19:4
Dorman, Gerald D Mrs, 1960, O 23,88:6
Dorman, Harry G, 1943, Ap 24,13:6
Dorman, John C E, 1937, Jl 8,23:5
Dorman, John E, 1945, D 5,25:1
Dorman, John J, 1953, Je 22,21:1; 1960, D 17,23:4
Dorman, John J Mrs, 1940, Ag 17,15:6
Dorman, Orville S, 1916, F 18,11:5
Dorman, Otis, 1950, Jl 5,1:6
Dorman, Richard A, 1903, Jl 1,9:6
Dorman, Robert P, 1958, Mr 6,27:2
Dorman, Roderick A, 1956, O 4,33:1
Dorman, Theodore, 1942, Ja 7,20:2
Dorman, Theodore T Mrs, 1956, Ap 22,86:7
Dorman, William R, 1953, Je 13,15:4
Dormand, Edward M Sr, 1950, Jl 25,27:4
Dormand, Harrold, 1940, My 1,23:3
Dormea, Antonio, 1952, D 29,19:5
Dormer, Daisy, 1947, S 14,60:4
Dormette, Edward H Sr, 1949, O 30,86:1
Dormeyer, Henry A, 1939, O 3,23:5
Dormont, Marc, 1942, Ag 2,39:3
Dorn, Elliot I, 1943, My 27,28:6
Dorn, Frieda E, 1947, O 21,23:4
Dorn, Grace, 1954, Je 22,27:1
Dorn, Harold F, 1963, My 10,33:2
Dorn, John F Sr, 1951, S 18,31:4
Dorn, Lewis C, 1947, Ag 29,17:3
Dorn, Marion V, 1964, Ja 29,33:1
Dorn, Paul, 1947, Je 14,15:6
Dorn, Theodore J, 1950, Ag 21,19:5
Dorn, Walter L, 1961, F 18,19:5
Dornan, John F, 1951, N 16,36:1
Dornan, Robert B, 1943, Ag 4,17:4
Dornay, Louis, 1940, Ag 13,19:2
Dornberger, Herbert E, 1948, Mr 27,13:4
Dornblaser, Harvey A, 1954, Ag 17,21:5
Dornblaser, Thomas F, 1941, D 23,21:2
Dornbrach, F, 1883, F 3,5:4
Dornbrach, Henry Mrs, 1914, Ja 1,15:4
Dornbusch, Sigmund, 1956, D 19,31:3
Dorne, Albert, 1965, D 16,47:1
Dorne, Maurice, 1950, S 26,31:4
Dorner, Alex, 1957, N 5,31:2
Dorner, Fred H, 1942, My 6,19:4
Dorner, I A, 1884, Jl 13,7:1
Dorney, C A, 1903, My 9,9:6
Dorney, James F D Rev, 1937, Ja 3,II,8:3
Dorney, John Francis, 1944, Ap 1,13:4
Dorney, Maurice J Rev, 1914, Mr 16,9:3
Dorney, Richard, 1921, Ja 17,11:4
Dornhoefer, Warren J, 1958, Ag 25,21:5
Dornin, William Coffin, 1916, F 3,9:3
Dorning, John, 1953, Ap 14,27:5
Dorning, Samuel, 1949, Jl 7,25:4
Dornn, Adolph, 1950, Je 28,29:6
Dornstreich, William W, 1946, Ap 27,17:1
Doro, Marie (M K Stewart), 1956, O 10,39:3
Doroghi, Ervin, 1958, O 17,29:2
Dorokhin, Nikolai I, 1954, Ja 11,25:4
Dorokhov, Stepan D, 1966, F 25,31:4
Doroshaw, Jennis M, 1963, S 14,25:6
Dorosz, Walter, 1950, Je 11,92:6
Dorotheos, Archbishop (funl, Ag 4,80:6), 1957, Jl 27, 17:3
Dorotheus, Archbishop, 1921, Mr 19,11:6
Dorothy, Princess of Liechtenstein, 1961, Ap 12,41:1
Dorp, Victor P Capt, 1907, Je 13,7:6
Dorpfeld, Wilhelm, 1940, Ap 27,15:1
Dorr, Alice E, 1961, F 10,24:1
Dorr, Ashton, 1947, S 4,25:4
Dorr, Benjamin Rev, 1869, S 20,5:6
Dorr, Charles H, 1937, D 15,25:1
Dorr, Clinton L, 1955, Ag 15,15:4
Dorr, Dudley H, 1961, D 8,37:3
Dorr, Edward M, 1964, O 27,39:4
Dorr, Herbert R, 1946, Ag 12,21:4
Dorr, John Van N, 1962, Jl 1,57:1
Dorr, Louis L, 1940, Mr 27,21:3
Dorr, Louise B Mrs, 1938, Mr 21,16:1
Dorr, Nancy H Mrs, 1938, S 23,27:5
Dorr, Orin, 1949, O 26,27:5
Dorr, Orlando B, 1949, F 16,25:3
Dorr, Percy O, 1957, My 22,33:4
Dorr, Rheta C, 1948, Ag 9,19:3
Dorr, Roy L Mrs, 1959, Jl 17,21:4
Dorr, Stephen H, 1945, Ja 2,19:2
Dorr, Virginia O, 1941, My 14,21:4
Dorrance, Anne, 1951, Mr 11,96:1
Dorrance, Arthur C, 1946, S 23,23:3
Dorrance, Charles Mrs, 1957, Mr 1,23:3
Dorrance, Daniel J, 1941, Ja 21,22:2
Dorrance, George M, 1949, N 22,29:1
Dorrance, George M Mrs, 1950, Ja 31,23:4
Dorrance, George P, 1963, D 3,43:5
Dorrance, Gordon, 1957, Mr 23,19:5
Dorrance, Harold, 1947, My 23,23:1
Dorrance, J Ford, 1962, Ag 3,15:5
Dorrance, J T, 1930, S 22,19:3
Dorrance, James F, 1961, Ag 7,23:6
Dorrance, John T Mrs (will, Ap 2,17:1), 1953, Mr 11,29:4
Dorrance, Neil H, 1968, Mr 16,31:5
Dorrance, Samuel M, 1957, Ap 13,19:4
Dorrance, Samuel R, 1920, Ap 8,11:4
Dorrance, Sturges Dick, 1968, N 28,37:5
Dorrance, William T, 1953, Ap 8,29:1
Dorregary, Don Antonio, 1882, Mr 24,5:4
Dorrell, Charles E, 1950, Ag 27,88:6
Dorrell, Vernon A, 1949, Je 27,39:5
Dorrell, W Ward, 1968, N 27,47:3
Dorrill, Robert A, 1960, Mr 20,86:7
Dorris, Albert B, 1952, N 6,29:2
Dorris, George P, 1968, N 6,39:2
Dorris, Henry N, 1943, Ag 7,11:4
Dorris, Paul F, 1959, Jl 26,68:2
Dorris, T Ray, 1939, Ag 6,37:1

Dorrothy, Harry S, 1937, N 3,23:4
Dorry, George J, 1956, Mr 24,19:5
D'Ors Rovira, Eugenio, 1954, S 26,87:2
D'Orsay, L, 1931, S 14,17:1
Dorsen, Joseph, 1940, Jl 8,17:5
Dorsenne, Jean Mrs, 1961, O 4,45:1
Dorset, M, 1935, Jl 15,17:6
Dorsett, Andrew A, 1947, Mr 4,25:4
Dorsett, Michael H, 1940, Je 1,15:2
Dorsett, Robert Clarence, 1925, My 6,23:3
Dorsey, Blinn, 1939, S 3,19:3
Dorsey, Catherine M Mrs, 1937, Mr 12,24:2
Dorsey, Daniel A, 1944, S 1,13:3
Dorsey, Dennis B, 1949, Ap 15,23:3
Dorsey, Edmund, 1959, Je 13,21:5
Dorsey, Ernest, 1948, Ap 24,15:5
Dorsey, Frank, 1944, D 17,38:6
Dorsey, Frank G, 1950, Ja 30,17:1
Dorsey, Frank J G, 1949, Jl 14,28:4
Dorsey, Frank Mrs, 1938, Ja 27,21:4
Dorsey, George V, 1950, Je 15,31:5
Dorsey, Grafton D, 1943, D 10,27:4
Dorsey, Harry J, 1945, O 26,19:4
Dorsey, Isabelle E, 1948, Mr 8,23:2
Dorsey, James A, 1962, S 2,57:2
Dorsey, James W, 1966, My 12,14:1
Dorsey, Jimmy (funl, Je 16,84:1), 1957, Je 13,31:1
Dorsey, John G (more details, F 25,32:2), 1966, F 24,25:2
Dorsey, John H, 1941, Ap 13,39:2
Dorsey, John J Sr, 1954, S 11,17:5
Dorsey, John L, 1943, S 16,21:3
Dorsey, Leroy H, 1954, N 10,33:1
Dorsey, Levin L, 1937, Ap 2,23:3
Dorsey, Matthew F, 1958, S 13,19:5
Dorsey, Nicholas W, 1948, Jl 30,18:5
Dorsey, Rebecca L, 1954, Mr 30,27:1
Dorsey, Susan M, 1946, F 6,23:4
Dorsey, Theresa McCarthy Mrs, 1968, F 24,29:5
Dorsey, Thomas F Sr, 1942, Jl 13,15:3
Dorsey, Thomas H, 1955, O 14,27:2
Dorsey, Thomas R, 1950, Mr 10,27:3
Dorsey, Tommy (funl plans, N 28,29:8; funl, N 30,-24:1), 1956, N 27,1:4
Dorsheimer, W, 1888, Mr 28,4:7
Dorsky, Aaron, 1966, My 23,41:3
Dorslinger, Charles H, 1940, Ap 16,23:2
Dorsman, Henri, 1948, Ap 14,27:3
Dorson, Louis J, 1939, D 18,23:3
Dorst, Jacob J, 1940, Je 30,32:6
Dorst, Jacob J Mrs, 1938, F 19,15:3
Dort, J Dallas, 1925, My 21,23:4
Dort, Robert G, 1950, S 22,31:5
D'Orta, Augustine, 1948, Je 18,24:2
Dortch, Elam S, 1943, Ag 31,17:1
Dortch, William P, 1949, F 7,19:5
Dortecos, Carlos, 1946, Jl 26,21:4
Dorting, Emil E, 1953, N 25,23:4
Dorus, Harold J, 1964, Ap 8,43:4
Dorvall, John F, 1945, Je 7,19:6
Dorward, James L, 1947, Je 25,25:5
Dorwart, Harry P, 1964, My 15,36:8
Dorworth, James W, 1949, S 1,21:4
Dory, Pedro von, 1960, Ap 4,42:7
Dos Passos, John R Mrs, 1910, Mr 21,9:5; 1915, My 16,16:4
Dos Passos, Louis H, 1957, D 28,17:5
Dos Passos, Sezefredo, 1941, O 19,44:3
Dos Reis, Jose A, 1955, S 4,56:7
Dosch, E Lloyd, 1960, Ag 23,29:1
Dosch, Joseph P, 1968, Ja 9,43:3
Dosch, Oliver L Mrs, 1948, Ja 24,15:2
Dosch, William, 1954, Mr 28,88:5
Dosch-Fleurot, Arno, 1951, Ap 17,29:3
Doscher, Carl F, 1952, Je 27,23:3
Doscher, Charles, 1922, Mr 9,17:2
Doscher, Charles H, 1944, N 12,49:2
Doscher, George H, 1953, Ja 19,23:3
Doscher, Henry, 1937, Ap 24,19:2
Doscher, J Fred, 1939, N 30,21:4
Doscher, John Mrs, 1956, Jl 28,17:3
Doscher, John N, 1905, Mr 2,9:6
Doscher, William, 1947, D 9,29:2
Doscher, William F, 1963, S 6,29:2
Dosh, Louis P, 1944, Ja 18,19:2
Doshay, Lewis J, 1965, N 7,89:3
Doshna, Joseph, 1952, F 5,29:4
Doskow, Ambrose Mrs, 1946, F 8,19:2
Doskow, Samuel, 1957, Jl 12,21:1
d'Osmoy, Romain, 1920, Je 16,11:3
Doss, H Clay, 1958, My 11,87:2
Doss, Harry, 1950, D 21,29:5
Doss, James M, 1965, Ja 6,39:3
Doss, Roscoe J, 1949, Je 27,27:3
Dossena, Alceo, 1937, O 12,25:3
Dossenbach, Hermann, 1946, Ja 29,25:5
Dossert, Frank G, 1924, Ap 7,17:5
Dost, Theodore O, 1946, F 16,13:2
Dostal, Frank, 1946, N 26,29:5
Dostalik, Henry, 1953, F 11,29:2
Doster, Alexis Mrs, 1945, Ja 28,37:2
Doster, James J (por), 1942, O 22,21:3
Doster, Wadsworth, 1954, Jl 12,19:5
Dostoyevsky, Andrei, 1968, S 20,47:4
Doswald, Hilary M, 1951, Mr 4,92:3
Dot, Adm (Leopold Kahn), 1918, O 26,11:5
Doten, Carroll W, 1942, Je 15,19:6
Doten, Hazel R, 1957, Jl 27,17:2
Dotey, Aaron I, 1946, Je 11,23:1
Dotina, Ralph (J Brennan), 1960, N 3,39:1
Dotson, William I, 1954, S 20,23:4
Dotterer, Amos, 1950, Ap 8,13:3
Dotts, Harry R, 1958, Ap 12,19:5
Doty, A H, 1934, My 28,19:3
Doty, Arthur C, 1958, Ag 3,81:2
Doty, Arthur L, 1949, O 31,25:4
Doty, Augustus F, 1951, My 6,92:1
Doty, Carl Mrs, 1945, N 28,27:3
Doty, Cassius M, 1950, Jl 24,17:3
Doty, Charles W, 1947, F 20,25:2
Doty, Edmund S, 1953, Ag 11,27:3
Doty, Edward N, 1941, Ap 26,15:5
Doty, Ernest C, 1944, N 1,23:2
Doty, Ethan A Mrs, 1949, Je 9,31:6
Doty, Ethan Allen, 1915, Mr 12,11:6
Doty, Foster W, 1958, O 18,21:4
Doty, Frank, 1945, N 28,27:4
Doty, Frank V, 1945, Je 7,19:5
Doty, Frank W, 1941, Ag 5,19:3
Doty, Fred E, 1950, Mr 8,25:1
Doty, Frederick E Mrs, 1947, Jl 18,17:5
Doty, George E, 1940, Je 8,15:2
Doty, Giles S, 1943, O 13,23:4
Doty, Harry E, 1942, Ja 15,19:1
Doty, Henry S, 1963, S 22,87:1
Doty, Howard T, 1951, Ja 23,27:5
Doty, J D Gov, 1865, Jl 8,2:2
Doty, Jessie T, 1952, Ap 9,31:4
Doty, John, 1914, F 13,9:7
Doty, John R, 1963, Je 25,33:3
Doty, John V W, 1904, F 28,7:7
Doty, John W, 1961, Je 24,21:2
Doty, Julia R M Mrs, 1966, Ag 9,37:4
Doty, Katherine S, 1962, Ja 17,33:3
Doty, Kie Mrs, 1941, N 7,24:4
Doty, L L Col, 1873, Ja 20,4:7
Doty, Lawrence F, 1952, Mr 11,27:6
Doty, Lockwood R, 1937, D 17,32:3
Doty, Lockwood W Mrs, 1954, Mr 29,19:5
Doty, Madeleine Z, 1963, O 16,45:5
Doty, Percy C Mrs, 1943, F 10,25:3
Doty, Perry W, 1959, Ag 11,27:1
Doty, Ralph Z, 1943, Jl 6,21:5
Doty, Vernon A, 1940, Ja 3,22:3
Doty, Warren S, 1915, Mr 12,11:6
Doty, William E Mrs, 1943, Ja 9,13:6
Doty, Zina Rev, 1885, Mr 8,2:5
Dotzler, Francis X, 1954, My 22,15:5
Dotzler, Frank J, 1947, My 29,21:2
Dotzler, Theodore Roosevelt, 1923, O 31,15:3
Doub, Albert A Mrs, 1942, Ja 30,19:5
Doubilit, Henry, 1964, Jl 7,35:3
Doubleday, Alan C, 1949, Je 8,29:4
Doubleday, Archilbald, 1954, S 24,23:3
Doubleday, Arthur, 1951, Ja 24,27:4
Doubleday, Charles E, 1943, Ja 15,17:5
Doubleday, Daisy L, 1940, Mr 22,19:2
Doubleday, F N, 1934, Ja 31,17:1
Doubleday, Frank N Mrs, 1918, F 23,13:5; 1946, Ja 2, 19:1
Doubleday, George, 1955, D 8,37:1
Doubleday, George Mrs, 1919, Mr 28,13:2
Doubleday, Harry M Mrs, 1945, My 21,19:5
Doubleday, Nelson, 1949, Ja 12,27:1
Doubleday, Russell, 1949, Je 15,29:1
Doubleday, Theodore D Col, 1864, My 12,4:5
Doubleday, Ulysses F, 1866, Mr 24,4:5
Doublier, Francis, 1948, Ap 4,60:6
Doublier, Francis Mrs, 1953, Mr 16,22:4
Doubman, J Russell, 1951, O 14,88:7
Doubois, Charlotte I, 1948, Ja 12,19:2
Doubrava, Joseph H, 1947, N 11,27:4
D'Oubril, Princess, 1874, Je 30,1:6
Doubs, Richard M, 1949, F 17,23:2
Doucet, Bernard, 1942, S 15,24:2
Doucet, Catherine (Mrs P Doucet), 1958, Je 26,27:4
Doucet, Leon J D, 1942, Mr 4,19:4
Doucett, Frederick L, 1948, Je 21,21:2
Doud, Harriette W Mrs, 1937, Ja 6,23:4
Doud, Ida M, 1960, My 28,21:4
Doud, John S, 1951, Je 24,72:8
Doud, John S Mrs (funl, O 1,19:5; will, O 6,48:6), 1960, S 30,27:4
Doud, Mary L, 1955, O 12,29:1
Doud, Wallace Mrs, 1962, F 12,23:1
Douden, Clarence O, 1938, Ja 18,23:2
Doudge, J R, 1902, Mr 12,9:6
Doudican, Frank J, 1942, D 6,77:2
Doudna, Edward G, 1948, Ap 18,70:1
Douen, William L, 1944, Ag 20,32:1
Dougal, Clarence H, 1958, F 16,86:3
Dougal, Joseph H, 1954, N 19,23:4
Dougall, A Kenneth, 1945, My 23,19:1
Dougall, Arthur Mrs, 1945, My 6,37:1
Dougall, Frederic E, 1952, My 22,27:4
Dougall, Frederick E Mrs, 1949, N 18,29:3
Dougall, J R, 1934, S 19,19:4
Dougall, John B, 1964, Ap 26,89:1
Dougall, John B Mrs, 1946, Mr 7,25:4
Dougall, Keir J Dr, 1937, Ap 14,26:1
Dougan, Arthur T, 1946, Je 19,21:4
Dougan, F Charles, 1954, D 25,11:4
Dougan, Joseph J, 1968, S 5,47:1
Dougan, Robert, 1944, Je 11,45:2
Dougan, Wolston C, 1961, Mr 2,27:2
Doughan, John E, 1943, Jl 31,13:2
Dougher, Edward A, 1949, Ap 18,25:4
Dougher, James E, 1942, O 7,25:5
Dougher, Thomas E, 1944, Je 27,19:6
Dougherty, A Webster, 1958, S 28,88:6
Dougherty, Alfred W, 1946, Ja 31,21:5
Dougherty, Andrew, 1901, Mr 6,9:6
Dougherty, Annie J, 1942, N 4,23:4
Dougherty, Anthony, 1903, D 7,7:3; 1941, O 17,23:4
Dougherty, Charles A, 1940, D 22,30:7
Dougherty, Charles B Gen, 1924, Ag 2,9:6
Dougherty, Charles B Mrs, 1944, F 13,41:2
Dougherty, Charles Mrs, 1952, S 30,31:4
Dougherty, Daniel, 1892, S 6,2:6
Dougherty, Daniel W, 1955, Je 15,31:4
Dougherty, Dennis J, 1951, Je 1,23:1
Dougherty, Donald C, 1940, S 10,23:5
Dougherty, Edward, 1951, D 13,33:5
Dougherty, Edward A, 1952, F 29,23:1
Dougherty, Edward Capt, 1908, Jl 28,5:4
Dougherty, Edward J, 1942, N 12,25:5; 1943, Ja 16 13:2; 1948, O 18,23:4; 1949, Mr 28,21:5
Dougherty, Edwin L Sr, 1949, O 22,17:3
Dougherty, Ella, 1921, O 16,22:4
Dougherty, Francis E, 1961, Jl 22,21:6
Dougherty, Francis Mrs, 1951, Ag 14,23:3
Dougherty, Francis X, 1942, Je 23,19:6
Dougherty, George H, 1959, S 13,84:7
Dougherty, George M, 1943, O 27,23:4
Dougherty, Gerald M, 1952, Ag 7,21:4
Dougherty, Glenn R, 1953, My 6,31:5
Dougherty, Graham Mrs, 1958, Jl 4,19:2
Dougherty, Harry F, 1939, Ag 27,35:1
Dougherty, Helen, 1947, Mr 13,27:2
Dougherty, Helene E, 1963, My 9,37:4
Dougherty, Horace N (por), 1943, Ap 23,17:3
Dougherty, Horace N Mrs, 1942, N 20,23:5
Dougherty, Hugh, 1953, Ag 20,27:5
Dougherty, Isabelle H, 1946, Jl 31,27:2
Dougherty, J Hampden, 1960, Jl 9,19:2
Dougherty, James E, 1914, Mr 11,11:6; 1958, F 2
Dougherty, James E Mrs, 1960, F 7,84:4
Dougherty, James F, 1941, D 7,76:2; 1949, O 6,3
Dougherty, James G, 1948, F 13,21:4
Dougherty, James J (will), 1956, Ja 8,48:1
Dougherty, James J, 1960, Jl 11,29:3; 1964, My 4
Dougherty, James T Rev, 1904, N 19,9:5
Dougherty, Jane, 1951, My 1,29:3
Dougherty, Jeremiah, 1950, Ag 30,31:2
Dougherty, John, 1924, S 2,19:1
Dougherty, John A Mrs, 1955, O 28,26:2
Dougherty, John D, 1946, Mr 2,13:5
Dougherty, John F, 1950, Ja 18,31:3; 1950, N 24
Dougherty, John G, 1949, Ag 7,60:4
Dougherty, John J, 1948, O 9,19:2; 1953, F 24,2 1968, S 17,47:3
Dougherty, John N, 1946, Ap 11,25:4
Dougherty, John P Mrs, 1955, My 7,17:4
Dougherty, John W Mrs, 1950, My 19,27:3
Dougherty, Joseph F, 1951, N 29,33:4; 1963, M 86:3
Dougherty, Joseph M, 1946, O 31,25:6; 1954, S
Dougherty, Joseph R, 1949, D 13,38:1
Dougherty, Lee J, 1947, My 21,25:3
Dougherty, Lottie, 1873, Ap 4,2:6
Dougherty, Louis R, 1948, My 20,29:5
Dougherty, Maurice J, 1913, Jl 17,7:6
Dougherty, Maurice J Mrs, 1913, Jl 17,7:6
Dougherty, Michael J, 1946, F 26,25:1
Dougherty, Michael P, 1949, My 4,29:2
Dougherty, Pat (Mrs G Hunter), 1959, S 3,27
Dougherty, Patrick J, 1940, My 1,23:3
Dougherty, Paul, 1947, Ja 10,21:2
Dougherty, Paul S, 1955, Ja 26,25:1
Dougherty, Phil R, 1937, S 22,27:3
Dougherty, Richard, 1912, Je 11,9:5
Dougherty, Richard E, 1961, O 1,87:1
Dougherty, Romeo L, 1944, D 10,53:2
Dougherty, Searle B, 1946, F 14,25:3
Dougherty, Thomas C, 1946, Je 14,21:6
Dougherty, Thomas F, 1948, Jl 19,19:1; 1960, 92:5
Dougherty, Thomas F Mrs, 1948, Ap 4,60:6
Dougherty, Thomas G, 1964, Ag 21,29:2
Dougherty, Thomas H Jr, 1938, Jl 22,17:3
Dougherty, Vincent J, 1957, Je 13,31:3
Dougherty, W F, 1884, F 3,7:2
Dougherty, William, 1948, Jl 26,17:4; 1949, J
Dougherty, William A, 1946, Jl 18,25:5
Dougherty, William A Mrs, 1950, F 15,27:3
Dougherty, William B Gen, 1915, Jl 15,9:4
Dougherty, William D, 1946, Je 7,19:2
Dougherty, William F, 1944, O 27,23:4
Dougherty, William F Jr, 1958, Ap 24,31:1

Dougherty, William F Rev, 1921, Ap 28,13:3
Dougherty, William J, 1937, D 24,20:2; 1941, F 19, 21:4; 1960, Je 21,33:2
Dougherty, William J Mrs, 1940, D 12,27:1
Dougherty, William R, 1963, O 13,86:7
Doughten, Henry W Jr, 1954, Ag 20,19:2
Doughten, William S, 1957, Ap 10,33:2
Doughton, Isaac, 1948, Ja 26,19:5
Doughton, Joseph A, 1940, F 8,23:5
Doughton, Robert L, 1954, O 2,17:1
Doughton, Robert L Mrs, 1946, F 9,13:2
Doughton, Rufus A, 1945, Ag 18,11:6
Doughton, Rufus A Mrs, 1951, O 30,29:4
Doughty, Addison T, 1950, Je 1,27:1
Doughty, Alla Mrs, 1915, F 14,3:5
Doughty, Dorothy (Susan D), 1962, O 9,41:4
Doughty, Edgar M, 1947, My 26,21:4
Doughty, F Fraley, 1944, O 17,23:5
Doughty, Francis W, 1917, N 1,15:3
Doughty, Frank, 1948, N 9,27:1
Doughty, G W, 1930, S 28,II,8:2
Doughty, George Sir, 1914, Ap 28,13:5
Doughty, Harry J, 1945, Je 20,23:4
Doughty, Henry M Rear-Adm, 1921, My 3,17:2
Doughty, Howard W, 1949, Ja 26,25:1
Doughty, John C, 1967, Ja 20,43:4
Doughty, Lady, 1872, D 14,1:7
Doughty, Mervin P, 1938, S 21,25:2
Doughty, Nathaniel C Sr, 1946, Ag 11,46:3
Doughty, Richard, 1942, N 14,16:2
Doughty, Richard I Sr, 1957, N 17,86:5
Doughty, Robert E, 1952, Ag 5,19:5
Doughty, Roger G, 1950, O 20,27:4
Doughty, Warren P, 1946, Je 7,20:2
Doughty, William E, 1959, Je 20,21:6
Doughty, William F, 1947, Ja 3,21:3
Doughty, William H Jr, 1961, Jl 1,17:3
Doughty-Tichborne, Anthony Sir, 1968, Jl 21,57:1
Douglas, A J Mrs, 1939, Ap 10,17:3
Douglas, Aaron Mrs, 1958, D 30,35:2
Douglas, Alex S, 1949, Je 17,23:5
Douglas, Amanda Minnie, 1916, Jl 19,9:5
Douglas, Amelia, 1940, D 7,17:1
Douglas, Archibald, 1943, D 15,27:2
Douglas, Archibald Jr (Jan 10), 1963, Ap 1,35:5
Douglas, Archibald Lucius Adm, 1913, Mr 14,9:3
Douglas, Archibald Mrs, 1965, Je 18,35:2
Douglas, Arnold Mrs, 1963, O 26,27:1
Douglas, Arthur F, 1956, Mr 10,17:2
Douglas, B B, 1878, D 23,4:7
Douglas, Bernard M, 1944, Mr 17,17:5
Douglas, Carl, 1961, Ja 22,26:8
Douglas, Carleton E, 1948, My 1,15:4
Douglas, Caroline Mrs, 1924, Ag 24,24:4
Douglas, Charles A, 1939, N 2,23:5; 1950, My 28,44:8
Douglas, Charles E, 1937, O 17,II,9:2
Douglas, Charles Gen, 1914, O 26,9:5
Douglas, Charles H, 1947, Ag 31,36:7; 1954, Ap 12, 29:4
Douglas, Charles M, 1942, Mr 16,15:6
Douglas, Charles M Mrs, 1949, Mr 16,28:2
Douglas, Charles Noel, 1920, N 16,15:3
Douglas, Charles W, 1909, Je 3,9:4; 1944, Ja 20,19:4
Douglas, Charles W Mrs, 1952, Ag 30,13:5
Douglas, Chrystie L, 1960, Je 22,35:2
Douglas, Clifford H, 1952, O 1,33:6
Douglas, D'Avignon J Mrs, 1945, Ja 19,19:2
Douglas, Daisy O Mrs, 1957, D 1,88:6
Douglas, Damon G Mrs, 1962, Ap 15,80:3
Douglas, Daniel R, 1949, Jl 26,27:3
Douglas, David, 1916, Ap 6,13:6
Douglas, Donald, 1946, Ja 1,27:4; 1966, Je 19,84:8
Douglas, Dorothy Mrs, 1937, D 9,25:3
Douglas, Dorothy Wolff Dr, 1968, D 11,47:3
Douglas, Duncan Mrs, 1958, S 18,31:5
Douglas, Earl, 1939, O 23,19:4
Douglas, Edgar H Mrs, 1943, My 13,21:1
Douglas, Edward B, 1946, F 8,19:4
Douglas, Edward Donaldson, 1918, Jl 7,21:3
Douglas, Edward M Mrs, 1952, Ja 20,84:3
Douglas, Edward O, 1949, Mr 22,26:4
Douglas, Edward W, 1939, F 8,23:6
Douglas, Ellen, 1923, F 23,13:5
Douglas, Findlay, 1959, Mr 30,31:4
Douglas, Florence Mrs, 1962, Jl 19,57:2
Douglas, Francis, 1947, Mr 7,25:2
Douglas, Francis A K Marquess of Queensberry, 1954, Ap 28,31:1
Douglas, Frank B, 1959, Je 11,33:4
Douglas, Frank L, 1943, O 23,13:2
Douglas, Fred J, 1949, Ja 2,60:6
Douglas, Frederick A, 1940, F 25,38:5
Douglas, G P, 1954, O 19,27:4
Douglas, G W Rev Dr, 1926, O 21,25:2
Douglas, George, 1950, Mr 8,27:3
Douglas, George A, 1952, F 14,27:4
Douglas, George V, 1958, O 11,23:6
Douglas, George W, 1945, F 17,13:6
Douglas, George W Mrs, 1948, Ap 13,27:4
Douglas, Gordon Mrs, 1952, F 14,27:1
Douglas, H L Mrs, 1904, My 14,16:3
Douglas, H T Gen, 1926, Jl 21,19:5
Douglas, Harold F, 1955, Jl 25,19:4
Douglas, Harold Gordon Lt, 1916, D 29,9:4
Douglas, Harriette S, 1956, My 8,33:1
Douglas, Harry, 1938, O 5,23:2
Douglas, Henry B, 1940, N 16,17:4
Douglas, Henry E M, 1939, F 16,21:2
Douglas, Henry Kyd Gen, 1903, D 19,9:4
Douglas, Henry P, 1955, My 6,23:3
Douglas, Henry P Sir, 1939, N 5,49:1
Douglas, Herbert J, 1946, Ag 15,25:6
Douglas, J B Capt, 1908, Je 20,9:6
Douglas, J Sir (see also Ag 4), 1877, Ag 8,2:2
Douglas, James, 1940, S 27,23:2; 1944, My 18,19:2
Douglas, James A, 1909, S 18,9:5
Douglas, James Dr, 1918, Je 26,13:5
Douglas, James F Mrs, 1961, My 20,23:3
Douglas, James Forsythe, 1924, Jl 17,15:5
Douglas, James L, 1950, O 2,23:3
Douglas, James Lady, 1941, F 4,22:3
Douglas, James S (por), 1949, Ja 3,23:1
Douglas, James S Mrs, 1941, Jl 7,15:6
Douglas, Jesse (Oct 7), 1965, O 11,61:2
Douglas, John (por), 1938, D 7,23:1
Douglas, John J, 1939, Ap 7,21:3
Douglas, John M, 1938, Ap 9,17:2
Douglas, John P, 1903, S 21,7:6
Douglas, John S Mrs, 1956, Ag 15,29:4
Douglas, John T, 1940, Je 20,11:2
Douglas, Julia B Mrs, 1941, Jl 7,15:5
Douglas, Kenneth, 1923, O 18,19:3
Douglas, Kenneth R, 1951, S 28,31:1
Douglas, Leon A, 1951, Ag 15,27:3
Douglas, Lloyd C, 1951, F 14,29:1
Douglas, Lloyd C Mrs, 1944, D 31,26:4
Douglas, Lord, 1945, Mr 21,23:3
Douglas, Lowell M Mrs, 1958, Ag 10,92:2
Douglas, M B Mrs, 1932, Mr 11,40:2
Douglas, Malcolm, 1939, F 13,15:3
Douglas, Margaret S Mrs, 1967, N 28,51:3
Douglas, Mary A, 1950, Ag 8,29:2
Douglas, Mary L, 1941, Mr 21,21:5
Douglas, Myron E, 1950, Mr 7,27:4
Douglas, Norman, 1952, F 9,13:3
Douglas, Norval S, 1940, Je 10,17:5
Douglas, Oscar F Jr, 1938, My 10,21:4
Douglas, Paul (funl, S 15,39:2), 1959, S 12,21:1
Douglas, Percy L, 1964, O 22,35:1
Douglas, Phil (Shufflin), 1952, Ag 2,15:4
Douglas, R C, 1941, My 30,15:1
Douglas, Ralph W, 1948, Mr 9,23:3
Douglas, Raymond E, 1940, My 19,43:3
Douglas, Richard S, 1956, Mr 22,35:1
Douglas, Robert C, 1941, Ag 7,38:3
Douglas, Robert Count, 1955, Ag 27,15:6
Douglas, Robert D, 1960, Ja 3,88:8
Douglas, Robert H Mrs, 1964, Ap 8,43:3
Douglas, Robert L, 1951, Ag 16,27:4
Douglas, Robert Martin Ex-Justice, 1917, F 9,11:6
Douglas, Robert P, 1964, Mr 29,60:6
Douglas, Robert S, 1954, Ja 19,25:5; 1959, Ap 10,29:2
Douglas, Robin, 1963, D 23,25:3
Douglas, Sarah K Mrs, 1939, Jl 4,13:6
Douglas, Stanley A, 1948, O 15,23:4
Douglas, Stephen A, 1939, My 2,23:3
Douglas, Stephen A Col, 1937, S 11,17:4
Douglas, Stephen A Sen (funl, Je 8,8:5), 1861, Je 4, 5:1
Douglas, Thomas A, 1938, My 15,II,6:6
Douglas, Walter, 1946, O 4,23:1
Douglas, Walter C, 1960, Ap 7,35:4
Douglas, Walter C Mrs (Helen), 1968, O 2,39:5
Douglas, Walter G, 1966, Mr 31,40:1
Douglas, Walter J, 1941, Jl 3,19:1
Douglas, Walter Mrs, 1963, O 12,23:3
Douglas, William, 1937, Ap 23,21:5; 1941, Mr 23,44:2
Douglas, William A, 1946, N 15,23:1
Douglas, William A S, 1951, Jl 22,61:3
Douglas, William C, 1951, Mr 7,33:5
Douglas, William E, 1958, Mr 16,87:2
Douglas, William H, 1944, Ja 28,18:3; 1949, S 29,29:4
Douglas, William Lewis Ex-Gov, 1924, S 17,23:3
Douglas, William R, 1947, My 20,25:2
Douglas, William Scott, 1908, Ap 24,9:4
Douglas-Hamilton, Malcolm A Lord (mem ser set), 1965, Mr 19,35:2
Douglas-Pennant, Cyril E, 1961, Ap 4,37:4
Douglas-Pennant, Frank (Lord Penrhyn), 1967, F 5, 88:6
Douglass, A E, 1901, O 1,9:5
Douglass, A T, 1884, My 6,5:5
Douglass, Andrew E, 1962, Mr 21,39:1
Douglass, Arthur S, 1942, Mr 8,43:1
Douglass, B F, 1943, My 29,13:3
Douglass, Beaman, 1946, D 6,23:4
Douglass, Beatrice N Mrs, 1942, My 1,19:3
Douglass, Claire, 1960, Ja 11,45:2
Douglass, Clara, 1962, Mr 8,31:1
Douglass, Clarence W, 1951, Jl 14,13:6
Douglass, Earl C, 1942, S 29,23:2
Douglass, Edgar F, 1949, D 12,33:2
Douglass, Edward, 1903, Mr 14,11:1
Douglass, Ella S Mrs, 1939, Ja 8,43:1
Douglass, Ellwoood, 1940, S 9,15:5
Douglass, Fred Mrs, 1903, D 2,9:5
Douglass, Frederick, 1895, F 21,1:5
Douglass, G W, 1928, O 11,27:5
Douglass, George A, 1958, Ap 30,33:3
Douglass, George C, 1940, My 23,23:5
Douglass, George Jr, 1964, N 12,37:1
Douglass, George Mrs, 1937, Ja 10,II,10:7
Douglass, George W, 1956, Je 10,88:4
Douglass, Harlan P, 1953, Ap 15,31:5
Douglass, Howard Justice, 1908, Jl 18,7:6
Douglass, J Emory, 1943, F 6,13:5
Douglass, Jay C, 1943, D 22,23:1
Douglass, John L Mrs, 1945, Je 11,15:3
Douglass, Leon F, 1940, S 8,49:2
Douglass, Leon Mrs, 1943, Ap 30,21:3
Douglass, Louis A, 1950, Je 12,27:2
Douglass, Margaret, 1949, O 26,27:5
Douglass, Ralph E, 1964, Jl 31,24:1
Douglass, Richard W, 1937, O 1,21:4
Douglass, Robert D, 1938, Mr 10,21:1
Douglass, Robert D Mrs, 1940, My 8,23:2
Douglass, Robert Dun, 1904, N 28,7:4
Douglass, Robert R, 1953, O 9,27:1
Douglass, Stephen A, 1967, My 28,60:6
Douglass, T G, 1876, Ag 16,4:7
Douglass, Walter, 1956, My 7,27:2
Douglass, Warren H, 1942, Mr 6,21:4
Douglass, William B, 1947, Jl 9,23:2
Dougrey, George M, 1950, Ag 9,29:4
Doukas, James G, 1953, My 21,31:5
Doulcet (Le), L A (Comte de Pontecoulant), 1885, Ap 3,5:4
Doulens, Edward B, 1956, D 25,25:4
Doulens, Humphrey E, 1964, Ja 1,25:2
Doull, Col, 1865, Ap 8,4:6
Doull, James A, 1963, Ap 9,31:1
Doulton, Harold, 1951, Jl 28,11:4
Doumergue, Gaston, 1937, Je 19,7:1
Doumic, Rene, 1937, D 3,24:2
Dounis, Dimitri, 1954, Ag 14,15:6
Dounoucos, John, 1962, Ag 15,31:1
Dourmashkin, Ralph L, 1956, O 11,39:3
Douropoulos, Constantine Mrs, 1965, Ja 3,84:6
Dousa, Wenzel Sr, 1951, Ja 30,25:4
Dousfield, George, 1943, D 30,17:4
Dousman, Mary E, 1938, D 15,27:4
Dousmanis, George C, 1966, D 13,47:3
Dousmanis, Victor, 1949, Ja 14,23:3
Dousseau, Raymond Mrs, 1964, Je 18,35:5
Douthirt, Walstein F, 1955, Mr 12,29:3
Douthirt, Walstein F Mrs, 1940, S 24,23:5
Douthitt, Frank H, 1950, Mr 19,95:3
Douthitt, John F, 1947, Ja 5,53:4
Douty, Daniel E, 1959, Je 25,29:3
Douty, Nicholas, 1955, My 11,31:1
Douvan, Eugene V, 1956, S 13,35:4
Douw, J De P, 1901, Ja 31,7:5
Dovas, Athanasius C, 1967, D 26,33:2
Dove, Arthur G, 1946, N 24,78:3
Dove, H W, 1879, Ap 6,7:3
Dove, James W, 1954, N 17,31:6
Dove, John S Jr, 1953, Je 27,15:3
Dove, P G (Paddy), 1957, My 26,92:1
Dovell, Ashton (por), 1949, O 29,15:2
Dovell, Ray C, 1968, My 6,47:1
Dovell, Ray C Mrs (Louise), 1966, D 8,47:2
Dover, Elmer, 1940, O 4,23:2
Dover, George T, 1964, N 12,37:1
Dover, Giles L, 1959, Ag 5,27:2
Dover, Lee D, 1964, Je 23,33:4
Dovercourt, Lord (J H Holmes), 1961, Ap 25,35:2
Doverdale, Baron, 1949, Ja 19,27:2
Doverdale, L, 1935, Mr 24,35:5
Dovgalevsky, V, 1934, Jl 15,22:3
D'Ovidio, Francesco Sen, 1925, N 26,23:6
Dovzhenko, Alex P, 1956, N 27,38:3
Dow, Abbot L Mrs, 1962, Ag 12,81:3
Dow, Albert Gallatin, 1908, Je 5,7:4
Dow, Albert N, 1942, N 19,25:4
Dow, Alex (por), 1942, Mr 23,15:1
Dow, Alex Mrs, 1951, S 27,31:2
Dow, Allan W, 1955, D 10,21:2
Dow, Arthur E, 1946, S 18,31:5
Dow, Arthur W, 1945, N 27,23:5
Dow, Arthur W Dr, 1922, D 14,21:3
Dow, Augustus F, 1865, S 11,4:2
Dow, B C, 1937, Ag 29,II,6:6
Dow, C H, 1902, D 5,9:6
Dow, Charles M, 1940, Mr 31,44:2
Dow, Charles R Mrs, 1950, Ag 9,29:2
Dow, Charles W Mrs, 1962, Mr 15,24:2
Dow, Clifford L, 1952, S 2,23:1
Dow, Clinton S, 1944, Je 27,19:4
Dow, David C, 1942, My 28,17:2
Dow, David M, 1953, S 11,21:5
Dow, Dorothy I, 1946, Je 11,23:1
Dow, Edmund L, 1943, D 2,27:1
Dow, Edward A Mrs, 1963, Jl 31,29:1
Dow, Edwin Barlow Col, 1917, Je 30,11:7
Dow, Ervin L, 1945, S 22,17:4
Dow, Ford H Mrs, 1944, Mr 10,15:4
Dow, Harold F, 1941, Ap 26,15:4
Dow, Harold G, 1963, Jl 5,19:4
Dow, Harry G, 1947, S 20,15:6

Dow, Herbert C, 1949, N 7,27:3
Dow, Herbert H Mrs, 1953, Je 30,23:1
Dow, Horace D, 1939, Mr 17,22:3
Dow, Howard M, 1912, Je 13,11:6
Dow, J Arthur, 1954, Jl 10,13:4
Dow, J E, 1878, My 20,2:1
Dow, Joseph P, 1958, D 3,37:2
Dow, Joy W, 1937, F 19,19:4
Dow, Louis H, 1944, Mr 9,17:6
Dow, Mary E Mrs, 1942, N 23,23:4
Dow, Neal Gen, 1897, O 3,13:1
Dow, Oscar C, 1948, Ap 14,27:2
Dow, Paul H, 1950, Mr 25,13:3
Dow, Robert B, 1953, Mr 25,31:2
Dow, Roger, 1967, Jl 18,37:4
Dow, Warren A, 1965, N 23,45:3
Dow, Wilbur E Sr, 1962, D 6,43:2
Dow, Willard H, 1949, Ap 1,26:4
Dow, Willard H Mrs, 1949, Ap 1,26:4
Dow, William H, 1948, F 1,60:5
Dow, William P Jr, 1952, F 28,27:2
Dow, Winthrop N Col, 1903, S 13,7:5
Dow De Witt, C Jr, 1937, Mr 24,25:3
Dowaliby, George M, 1945, Mr 12,19:3
Dowbley, Guillermo J, 1948, S 7,25:2
Dowd, Ambrose F, 1943, N 17,25:1
Dowd, Anna, 1944, D 31,26:5
Dowd, Anna C Mrs, 1937, O 10,II,9:1
Dowd, Bernard W, 1946, Je 8,21:5
Dowd, Ch Ferdinand Rev, 1904, N 14,12:1
Dowd, Charles A, 1959, S 14,29:5
Dowd, Charles J, 1943, D 22,24:3
Dowd, Edward J, 1948, Ja 28,23:6
Dowd, Edward P, 1952, Je 25,29:3
Dowd, Emma C, 1938, D 22,21:4
Dowd, Francis A Jr, 1944, Mr 23,19:6
Dowd, Frank, 1942, N 14,16:3
Dowd, Frederick T, 1962, Je 9,25:3
Dowd, George M, 1960, My 12,35:3
Dowd, H Laurence Dr, 1968, Je 6,47:3
Dowd, Harrison, 1964, D 20,68:8
Dowd, Heman (por), 1939, Ap 22,17:5
Dowd, Homer, 1908, Je 30,7:6
Dowd, James A, 1955, Je 5,84:8
Dowd, James E, 1966, Mr 13,87:2
Dowd, James H, 1949, Ag 12,17:2
Dowd, James Jr Mrs, 1964, D 26,17:6
Dowd, John, 1954, F 27,13:5
Dowd, John H, 1951, Ap 10,27:4
Dowd, John J, 1947, Ap 11,25:1; 1960, F 29,27:4
Dowd, John Mrs, 1939, Ja 1,24:7
Dowd, John R, 1954, N 24,23:3
Dowd, Joseph F, 1954, Je 17,29:5
Dowd, Ledwith H, 1946, Je 4,23:4
Dowd, Margaret L Mrs, 1943, Mr 2,19:4
Dowd, Mary A, 1942, F 6,19:4
Dowd, Mary A (will), 1942, Mr 26,24:3
Dowd, Mary C, 1968, N 19,47:1
Dowd, Mathew, 1952, Ap 11,23:3
Dowd, Michael J, 1960, My 18,41:4
Dowd, Owen J, 1943, D 12,68:4
Dowd, Patrick H, 1939, F 14,20:1
Dowd, Raymond E, 1948, Jl 15,23:3
Dowd, Thomas A Sr, 1954, Jl 30,17:3
Dowd, Thomas F, 1959, F 25,31:3
Dowd, Thomas H, 1953, O 21,29:5; 1959, S 6,72:4
Dowd, Thomas H Mrs, 1937, F 9,23:2
Dowd, Thomas J, 1957, Ag 15,21:4
Dowd, Thomas J Jr, 1945, Ja 17,21:4
Dowd, Thomas Mrs, 1945, Je 29,15:2
Dowd, Thomas V, 1946, F 18,21:5
Dowd, Wallace P, 1962, Ag 23,29:2
Dowd, William, 1899, O 8,7:6
Dowd, William G, 1957, Ap 16,33:5
Dowd, William G Sr, 1949, Ag 28,73:2
Dowd, William J, 1960, O 9,86:8
Dowd, Wyllys E, 1919, Jl 25,11:5
Dowdall, Edward P Mrs, 1951, Ap 26,29:2
Dowdall, Harold J, 1955, Ap 11,23:5
Dowdall, Michael A, 1959, F 22,88:4
Dowdell, Ann D Mrs, 1942, Ja 19,17:5
Dowdell, Hiram L Mrs, 1946, N 25,27:2
Dowdell, James A, 1946, F 3,40:2
Dowdell, William, 1953, S 24,33:3
Dowdell, William F, 1940, S 4,23:4
Dowdell, William S (por), 1938, Ja 1,19:6
Dowden, Benjamin, 1941, Ag 21,17:6
Dowden, Edward C, 1956, Ja 2,21:2
Dowden, Edward Prof, 1913, Ap 5,15:4
Dowden, Percy H, 1950, S 19,29:1
Dowden, Willis G, 1944, F 22,24:2
Dowdey, Clifford S, 1944, N 4,15:1
Dowdle, John J 3d, 1957, N 12,37:1
Dowdney, Daniel J, 1946, Jl 19,19:6
Dowds, Arthur W, 1950, Ag 24,27:5
Dowe, Edgar S Capt, 1912, F 8,11:4
Dowe, Frank L, 1940, N 19,24:3
Dowe, John M, 1946, My 16,21:3
Dowe, Marianna, 1949, Ja 1,13:4
Dowell, Cassius C, 1940, F 5,18:2
Dowell, Clifton A, 1968, My 26,84:3
Dowell, Edwin Mrs (Mrs E Pons), 1950, Ja 4,35:4
Dowell, G, 1881, Je 10,2:7
Dowell, J R, 1876, F 27,2:6
Dowell, W M Berkeley, 1962, F 19,31:5
Dower, James, 1946, D 6,23:1
Dower, James Mrs, 1945, Jl 9,11:6
Dower, Philip J Mrs (I McIntosh), 1963, My 18,27:2
Dowie, A J Gladstone, 1945, Je 5,19:2
Dowie, Horace, 1952, Mr 13,29:4
Dowie, John Alexander, 1907, Mr 15,9:4
Dowie, Robert J, 1954, Ja 2,11:3
Dowis, Solomon F Sr, 1967, N 6,47:1
Dowkontt, Clifford F, 1948, Jl 15,23:1
Dowkontt, George D Dr, 1909, Ag 3,7:5
Dowkontt, George H, 1952, Ag 16,15:5
Dowler, Francis N, 1918, Jl 4,13:2
Dowler, Freeman E, 1950, Ag 26,13:6
Dowley, J E, 1902, D 18,2:6
Dowlin, Clirton, 1944, Ag 2,15:2
Dowling, A, 1930, N 30,30:1
Dowling, Anna M, 1952, F 22,21:3
Dowling, Daniel, 1913, Jl 16,7:7; 1940, D 19,25:2
Dowling, Daniel E, 1915, D 12,19:6
Dowling, Edward, 1912, F 17,11:5; 1960, Ap 4,29:5
Dowling, Edward C Justice, 1908, D 2,9:5
Dowling, Edward D, 1967, D 19,47:3
Dowling, Edward G, 1966, Je 8,47:1
Dowling, Edward J, 1951, Ag 14,23:1
Dowling, Edward J Mrs, 1918, Jl 25,11:5
Dowling, Edward M, 1945, My 21,19:4
Dowling, Elizabeth I, 1940, Ja 25,21:1
Dowling, Ernest, 1964, F 8,23:4
Dowling, Frank L, 1919, S 28,22:4
Dowling, George J S, 1952, Ja 13,88:8
Dowling, Henry P, 1962, Ja 4,33:3
Dowling, Henry T, 1948, N 7,88:8
Dowling, J, 1932, Ag 6,11:4
Dowling, J Edwin, 1966, Jl 5,27:4
Dowling, J Ivimey, 1951, Mr 23,21:6
Dowling, John, 1874, Jl 23,8:5; 1923, Je 26,19:5
Dowling, John C L, 1943, S 20,21:2
Dowling, John F, 1943, S 12,53:1
Dowling, John F Dr, 1937, Jl 21,21:5
Dowling, John G, 1955, Je 17,17:3
Dowling, John J, 1944, Ja 3,21:3; 1945, Je 2,15:2; 1947, Ag 25,17:3; 1949, My 5,28:5
Dowling, John J Sr, 1949, Ja 23,69:1
Dowling, John J Sr Mrs, 1951, Jl 24,25:1
Dowling, John Justice, 1874, Jl 23,8:5
Dowling, John P, 1940, Je 7,23:6; 1947, S 6,17:5
Dowling, John Rev (see also Jl 5), 1878, Jl 8,8:2
Dowling, John W, 1937, Jl 24,15:6; 1949, Mr 25,23:2
Dowling, John William Dr, 1914, My 12,11:7
Dowling, Joseph, 1876, My 17,8:3
Dowling, Joseph F, 1947, Ap 27,60:3
Dowling, Joseph H, 1937, Jl 20,23:1
Dowling, Joseph M, 1954, O 25,27:3
Dowling, Judson D, 1946, N 3,64:3
Dowling, Lee C, 1967, Ja 24,28:6
Dowling, Lyle R, 1964, F 26,35:4
Dowling, Martin J, 1941, Ap 5,17:2
Dowling, Mary B, 1944, My 9,19:6
Dowling, Mary T, 1947, F 14,22:2
Dowling, Michael, 1914, Je 24,11:5
Dowling, Michael J, 1921, Ap 26,15:4
Dowling, Michael T, 1944, Je 26,15:5
Dowling, Otto C, 1946, Ap 15,27:4
Dowling, Patrick A, 1940, Jl 30,19:2
Dowling, Paul T, 1937, D 27,16:3
Dowling, Richard, 1966, Ag 24,51:5
Dowling, Robert E, 1943, Mr 17,21:1
Dowling, Robert L, 1954, Ag 17,21:2
Dowling, Thomas, 1941, S 26,24:2
Dowling, Thomas A, 1912, Je 27,13:3
Dowling, Thomas E, 1949, Ag 3,23:3
Dowling, Thomas J, 1942, Je 3,24:4
Dowling, Thomas J Rev, 1924, Ag 7,15:6
Dowling, V J, 1934, Mr 24,15:1
Dowling, William F, 1937, O 9,19:1; 1948, N 3,27:1
Dowling, William F Sr, 1968, Jl 1,33:3
Dowling, William Lynn, 1913, O 12,15:3
Dowling, William M, 1954, My 22,15:4
Dowling, William P, 1954, S 15,33:3
Down, Emma (will), 1938, F 17,19:2
Downe, Henry S, 1938, D 9,26:1
Downe, Viscount, 1931, D 3,27:3
Downen, John M, 1957, Mr 11,25:4
Downer, Albert E, 1944, Ap 26,19:2
Downer, Charles E, 1943, Je 10,21:3
Downer, Chester S, 1951, Ag 11,11:7
Downer, Delavan B, 1949, My 17,26:3
Downer, George F, 1941, Ap 14,17:2
Downer, Henry E, 1968, S 10,47:2
Downer, Henry E Mrs, 1949, Ap 11,25:5
Downer, Ira R, 1943, My 1,15:4
Downer, J C Rev, 1904, Mr 6,7:6
Downer, Jay, 1949, My 31,23:5
Downer, Kenneth Mrs (C Franke), 1960, My 24,37:1
Downer, Mortimer B Sr Mrs, 1952, F 15,25:3
Downer, Nye Mrs, 1950, Je 12,27:3
Downer, Victor M, 1941, Ag 29,17:4
Downer, W S, 1877, My 10,1:6
Downers, George W, 1951, F 11,88:3
Downes, Albert E, 1955, D 19,27:4
Downes, Alfred M, 1907, D 11,11:4; 1907, D 13,11:4
Downes, Anna R Mrs, 1940, O 30,23:6
Downes, Anne M (Mrs Frank H), 1964, Je 2,37:1
Downes, Arthur H, 1938, Mr 12,17:5
Downes, Brian Francis Rev Bro, 1968, Jl 16,39:3
Downes, Bruce (A J Busch), 1966, Ja 28,47:4
Downes, Carrie B Mrs, 1951, Mr 19,27:2
Downes, Carroll, 1948, Je 3,25:6
Downes, Chauncey B, 1938, Ag 7,33:2
Downes, Edward Ray, 1968, Mr 15,39:2
Downes, Ernest B, 1943, Jl 23,17:3
Downes, Frank H, 1952, D 22,25:2
Downes, Frederick A, 1939, Mr 22,23:4; 1954, F 6,2
Downes, Frederick E Dr, 1937, O 13,23:5
Downes, James R, 1955, F 16,29:3
Downes, John M, 1941, N 14,24:2
Downes, John Mrs, 1938, D 30,16:1; 1944, O 11,21: 1950, Ag 3,23:4
Downes, John R, 1952, F 13,29:4
Downes, John S, 1956, O 21,86:5
Downes, Joseph, 1959, Ag 17,2:7
Downes, Joseph L, 1949, Ap 11,25:6
Downes, Louis H, 1952, Je 16,17:3
Downes, Louis W, 1953, Ap 8,29:5
Downes, Louis W Mrs, 1950, O 29,92:5
Downes, Louise C Mrs, 1940, O 30,19:2
Downes, Marion D Mrs, 1956, D 18,31:5
Downes, Michael T, 1953, N 7,17:1
Downes, Olin (funl, Ag 26,19:4), 1955, Ag 23,23:1
Downes, Robert, 1942, S 9,16:7
Downes, Robert F, 1951, F 6,27:4
Downes, William A, 1948, My 13,25:5
Downes, William H, 1941, F 20,20:3
Downey, Albert H, 1947, Jl 8,23:2
Downey, Bessie O Mrs, 1956, D 12,39:2
Downey, Cairm-Cross, 1938, Je 23,21:2
Downey, Charles J, 1951, N 26,25:3
Downey, Dominick A Sr, 1950, F 17,23:4
Downey, E Kelly, 1948, N 24,23:1
Downey, Edward C, 1947, Ag 27,23:4
Downey, Francis X, 1942, Ap 15,21:5; 1960, Ap 1 83:5
Downey, Frederick W, 1951, Mr 6,27:4
Downey, George A, 1942, Jl 26,31:2
Downey, George B (Jack), 1954, Mr 2,25:5
Downey, George F, 1937, Ja 14,21:4; 1945, N 13,2
Downey, George F Mrs, 1945, O 25,21:4
Downey, Harry A, 1948, N 27,17:3
Downey, Henry A, 1956, N 17,21:2
Downey, Herman H, 1957, Ap 24,33:4
Downey, Hugh C, 1960, F 28,82:3
Downey, Hugh E, 1942, Ap 7,21:5
Downey, Hugh J, 1942, F 1,43:2
Downey, J H Dr, 1937, Ag 29,II,6:7
Downey, James, 1912, My 20,9:4; 1948, D 15,33: 1953, My 31,20:5
Downey, James A, 1959, Je 30,31:2
Downey, James F Jr, 1953, O 6,29:1
Downey, James M, 1948, S 14,29:3
Downey, John F, 1942, S 2,23:4; 1947, Ja 14,26:2
Downey, John I, 1961, Ap 22,25:4
Downey, John I Mrs, 1948, Jl 14,23:3
Downey, John J, 1938, N 24,27:4; 1940, O 31,23
Downey, John M Mrs, 1951, D 27,21:4
Downey, John O, 1943, F 4,23:4
Downey, John V, 1960, Mr 3,30:1
Downey, Joseph, 1925, Ap 13,19:4
Downey, Joseph F Sr, 1958, Ap 25,27:3
Downey, Joseph H, 1949, N 4,27:4
Downey, Leonard S, 1956, Je 24,77:2
Downey, Martin J, 1948, N 29,23:4
Downey, Mary F Mrs, 1954, F 24,25:3
Downey, Maurice, 1939, S 6,23:2
Downey, Morton Mrs, 1964, My 22,35:2
Downey, Nicholas Jr, 1966, Ap 28,43:2
Downey, Norman S, 1968, Ap 27,39:6
Downey, Patrick Mrs, 1949, O 8,13:1
Downey, Peter J Jr, 1961, Ag 11,24:1
Downey, Richard, 1953, Je 17,27:4
Downey, Sheridan, 1961, O 27,33:2
Downey, Thomas, 1943, Mr 8,15:1; 1948, O 10,
Downey, Thomas B, 1951, D 29,11:3
Downey, Thomas J, 1953, D 22,31:2
Downey, Wallace, 1924, Jl 24,13:5; 1967, Mr 15
Downey, Walter E, 1948, D 7,31:4
Downey, Walter F, 1961, Ja 14,23:4
Downey, William, 1945, Ap 5,23:2
Downey, William A, 1954, Mr 31,27:4
Downey, William F, 1914, F 9,7:6
Downey, William H, 1945, D 28,16:2; 1954, Ja
Downey, William H Mrs, 1942, Mr 6,21:3
Downey, William P, 1955, S 10,17:5
Downie, Blanche, 1953, Mr 26,31:3
Downie, Douglas, 1951, Ag 15,27:2
Downie, John M, 1945, D 8,17:2
Downie, John W, 1940, Ag 23,15:4
Downie, Roderick J Mrs, 1945, F 21,19:3
Downie, Thomas P, 1948, Ap 9,23:4
Downing, A E, 1927, S 21,29:3
Downing, Albert E, 1947, S 20,15:4
Downing, B, 1931, My 26,27:1
Downing, Benjamin W, 1948, Ap 22,27:6
Downing, Carl R, 1948, Mr 16,27:5
Downing, Charles Mrs, 1951, S 14,26:2

Downing, Charles T, 1945, Jl 31,19:3
Downing, Edward Mrs, 1950, Mr 8,25:2
Downing, Edward R Mrs, 1961, N 4,19:2
Downing, Flora H W Mrs, 1942, D 24,15:1
Downing, Francis, 1965, Ja 2,19:3
Downing, Frederick C, 1956, My 23,31:4
Downing, George H, 1939, Ag 3,19:5
Downing, George S, 1951, My 7,25:6
Downing, George Shapley, 1923, Mr 1,15:3
Downing, George T, 1903, Jl 22,7:6
Downing, Hardy K, 1960, Jl 11,29:2
Downing, Harold K, 1944, Ap 8,13:6
Downing, Harry J, 1953, S 29,29:5
Downing, Havilah Mrs, 1903, Ap 27,2:4
Downing, J Arthur Mrs, 1945, Mr 7,22:2
Downing, John F, 1961, Jl 23,69:2; 1963, D 1,84:3
Downing, John J, 1955, F 1,29:3
Downing, John P, 1939, Ap 27,25:5
Downing, John R, 1939, Je 26,15:6
Downing, Joseph H, 1961, Mr 22,41:2
Downing, Lefevre W Sr, 1949, N 8,31:5
Downing, Lewis, 1872, N 13,7:6
Downing, Marjorie Mother, 1955, F 6,88:6
Downing, Marshall B, 1945, Ja 24,21:4
Downing, Maurice E, 1965, O 31,86:6
Downing, Mortimer, 1942, D 16,25:5
Downing, Perley E, 1953, Jl 14,27:4
Downing, R F, 1903, My 1,9:4
Downing, Robert F, 1943, F 22,17:4
Downing, Robert L, 1944, O 3,23:6
Downing, Russell V, 1968, Je 29,29:1
Downing, Samuel, 1867, F 20,4:7; 1904, Jl 9,9:6
Downing, Samuel Dr, 1937, Je 16,24:1
Downing, Silas, 1903, Ag 9,7:6
Downing, T Daniel, 1944, F 8,16:3
Downing, Theodore F, 1949, Jl 22,19:4
Downing, Thomas, 1866, Ap 12,5:3
Downing, Thomas H, 1914, Jl 30,9:4
Downing, Virgil L, 1949, Mr 23,27:1
Downing, Walter W, 1941, Ap 4,21:4
Downing, Willard R Mrs, 1957, Je 3,27:5
Downing, Winifred S Mrs, 1941, Ag 26,19:6
Downs, A Sherwin, 1945, D 11,25:4
Downs, Anthony J, 1939, D 22,19:5
Downs, Arthur D, 1942, Mr 10,19:4
Downs, Bernard C, 1955, Ap 17,86:7
Downs, C F, 1945, Ag 22,23:5
Downs, Charles A, 1949, O 10,23:2
Downs, Donald, 1965, Ag 1,76:5
Downs, Elmer, 1941, Jl 9,21:3
Downs, Emma M, 1954, Jl 29,23:3
Downs, Eva Mrs, 1942, F 23,21:5
Downs, Forrest G, 1952, Ag 12,19:4
Downs, Francis, 1939, Jl 8,15:2
Downs, Francis S, 1960, My 18,41:2
Downs, Fred H, 1949, S 19,23:5
Downs, George F, 1943, Mr 2,19:3
Downs, George W Mrs, 1945, F 9,15:2
Downs, Gerald W, 1945, D 30,14:7
Downs, Harry S, 1950, Ja 24,31:5
Downs, Herbert S, 1937, Jl 29,19:4
Downs, J Stanley, 1951, Je 29,21:2
Downs, James C, 1957, D 20,24:7
Downs, Jerome A, 1938, F 6,II,8:2
Downs, John, 1954, F 11,29:4
Downs, John C Mrs, 1957, F 27,27:1
Downs, John M, 1956, N 1,39:6
Downs, John T, 1944, Ap 11,19:4
Downs, Johnny, 1938, S 18,44:7; 1948, N 5,25:4
Downs, Joseph, 1954, S 9,31:5
Downs, Lawrence A, 1940, Ag 11,30:8
Downs, Lawrence A Mrs, 1939, D 23,15:2
Downs, Mary, 1957, Jl 4,19:1
Downs, McCarthy, 1956, S 23,84:8
Downs, Morris, 1961, S 9,19:5
Downs, Nathan, 1944, Ja 4,17:1
Downs, Nichols C Ex-Judge, 1920, N 6,13:2
Downs, Norman, 1946, O 11,23:1
Downs, Richard P, 1946, Ja 30,25:4
Downs, Robert N Jr, 1939, F 10,23:2
Downs, Robert Strawbridge, 1925, My 3,5:2
Downs, Roger S, 1945, F 7,22:2
Downs, Samuel C, 1946, Ag 30,17:2
Downs, Sylvester D Jr, 1957, Ap 24,33:2
Downs, T Nelson, 1938, S 12,17:4
Downs, Thomas, 1952, Mr 7,23:1
Downs, Thomas M, 1960, Ja 31,92:4
Downs, W Findlay, 1967, Ap 28,41:3
Downs, W Findlay Mrs (Felicie), 1968, Ag 24,29:4
Downs, Wallace A Col, 1908, F 14,7:6
Downs, Walter R, 1944, Jl 18,19:1
Downs, William G, 1939, Jl 31,13:4
Downs, William S, 1954, Jl 15,27:3
Downton, Horace W, 1954, My 2,71:4
Dowrie, Alfred D, 1947, D 24,21:4
Dows, David, 1966, Ag 15,27:1
Dows, Mary A Mrs, 1943, D 25,13:4
Dows, Tracy, 1937, Jl 4,II,7:4
Dowse, Edmund Rev, 1905, Ap 28,9:4
Dowsett, Charles W, 1952, Ag 19,23:3
Dowsey, C Malcolm Mrs, 1951, Jl 30,17:5
Dowsey, George H Dr, 1924, Ag 14,15:5
Dowsey, James L, 1961, My 13,19:4
Dowsey, James L Mrs, 1965, Mr 30,47:2
Dowson, James L, 1953, Ap 10,21:5
Dowst, Henry P Mrs, 1941, Ap 17,23:2
Dowst, Henry Payson, 1921, Mr 14,11:5
Dowst, Robert S, 1959, Mr 22,86:7
Dowswell, Harry R, 1955, My 22,89:1
Dox, Charles E, 1968, N 9,33:4
Dox, Hamilton B Gen, 1903, N 14,9:6
Dox, Virginia, 1941, F 15,15:4
Doxey, Wall Sr, 1962, Mr 3,21:4
Doxsee, Charles O, 1965, F 23,33:2
Doxsee, Robert L, 1967, Mr 28,38:3
Doye, Robert W, 1948, Jl 20,24:2
Doyen, Charles Augustus Brig-Gen, 1918, O 8,11:3
Doyen, Eugene Louis Dr, 1916, N 22,13:5
Doying, George E, 1951, My 25,27:2
Doyle, A C Sir, 1930, Jl 8,1:4
Doyle, A P, 1927, N 27,30:1
Doyle, Albert N Mrs, 1952, Ja 21,15:3
Doyle, Alex B, 1964, My 7,37:3
Doyle, Alex I, 1951, F 22,31:3
Doyle, Alexander P Rev, 1912, Ag 10,7:6
Doyle, Alfred L, 1948, Mr 9,23:2
Doyle, Alfred T Mrs, 1964, O 8,43:3
Doyle, Alvin D, 1967, Jl 3,17:3
Doyle, Andrew C, 1952, Ja 5,11:6
Doyle, Andrew S, 1949, D 10,17:2
Doyle, Arthur Conan Mrs, 1906, Jl 5,7:6
Doyle, Bernard F, 1941, N 4,23:3
Doyle, Bernard W, 1949, D 27,23:4
Doyle, Billy, 1945, F 15,19:4
Doyle, Buddy, 1939, N 11,15:5
Doyle, Charles, 1948, Ja 15,23:1
Doyle, Charles E, 1965, D 10,42:4
Doyle, Charles E Mrs, 1949, F 14,19:4
Doyle, Charles J, 1950, F 18,15:4; 1959, N 16,31:4
Doyle, Charles K, 1939, My 21,III,7:1
Doyle, Charles R, 1959, F 15,86:5
Doyle, Clyde, 1963, Mr 15,7:2
Doyle, Daniel P, 1940, F 10,15:5
Doyle, David A, 1939, Ja 20,19:1
Doyle, David B Sr, 1957, Ap 7,89:1
Doyle, David E, 1939, My 25,25:6
Doyle, Denis C, 1955, Mr 10,27:2
Doyle, Dennis Mrs, 1959, Ap 10,29:1
Doyle, Edmund A, 1945, My 6,38:2
Doyle, Edward A, 1960, Je 18,23:6
Doyle, Edward J, 1952, N 13,31:1; 1958, F 1,19:1; 1961, Jl 30,69:1
Doyle, Edward P, 1946, F 6,23:5; 1949, F 15,23:5
Doyle, Eleanor T, 1954, D 15,31:4
Doyle, Ella, 1948, N 27,17:3
Doyle, Ellis E, 1943, Ap 27,24:2
Doyle, Enid T, 1958, Mr 13,29:3
Doyle, Ernest O, 1954, Mr 14,89:1
Doyle, Eugene, 1959, My 8,28:4
Doyle, Eugene J, 1941, Jl 3,19:4
Doyle, Francis B, 1967, N 6,47:2
Doyle, Francis E, 1946, Ja 14,19:4
Doyle, Francis S, 1951, Ag 8,25:5
Doyle, Francis X, 1937, Mr 23,24:2
Doyle, Frank, 1952, O 22,27:3
Doyle, Frank A, 1943, Ag 10,19:3
Doyle, Frank J, 1941, My 29,19:4; 1948, F 10,23:3
Doyle, Frank J Mrs, 1944, Ja 29,13:4
Doyle, Frank P, 1948, Ag 6,17:2
Doyle, George B, 1957, Ap 6,19:5
Doyle, George H Lt, 1921, D 28,15:4
Doyle, George M, 1946, Je 22,19:1
Doyle, Gerald A Mrs, 1954, Ap 4,88:4
Doyle, H R, 1942, F 9,15:1
Doyle, Harold F, 1966, D 21,39:1
Doyle, Harry J, 1964, F 3,27:1
Doyle, Henry G, 1964, N 4,39:1
Doyle, Henry V, 1952, S 9,31:4
Doyle, Howard L, 1954, Ag 12,25:5
Doyle, J Merton, 1953, My 27,31:6
Doyle, Jack, 1944, Ja 31,17:4; 1959, Ja 2,25:1
Doyle, Jacob, 1941, Ag 16,15:4
Doyle, James, 1912, Ag 5,9:6
Doyle, James D, 1938, O 12,27:2
Doyle, James E, 1925, Mr 14,13:4
Doyle, James F, 1956, S 18,35:4
Doyle, James J, 1941, O 25,17:6
Doyle, James R, 1942, Mr 6,22:3
Doyle, James T, 1958, S 5,27:1
Doyle, Jeremiah Mrs, 1951, Jl 19,23:5
Doyle, Johannah E Mrs, 1939, Je 2,23:5
Doyle, John, 1918, O 9,11:3; 1947, My 5,25:7
Doyle, John A, 1939, O 4,25:3
Doyle, John B, 1958, Ja 8,47:3
Doyle, John F, 1911, D 3,II,15:6
Doyle, John F Jr, 1942, Ag 30,42:5
Doyle, John F Mrs, 1945, My 29,15:5
Doyle, John H, 1942, O 27,26:2
Doyle, John J, 1938, My 22,II,7:3; 1944, Ag 20,34:2; 1946, Je 16,40:6; 1949, Ap 21,26:5; 1967, Je 8,47:3
Doyle, John J Mrs, 1938, N 16,23:2; 1948, Mr 17,25:4; 1949, Ag 23,23:1; 1961, Ja 17,37:2
Doyle, John M, 1940, Jl 15,15:6; 1952, My 15,31:4
Doyle, John N, 1944, My 30,21:1
Doyle, John R, 1953, Je 11,29:5
Doyle, John R Mrs, 1963, Je 29,23:2
Doyle, John S, 1950, Jl 15,13:3
Doyle, John T, 1942, My 22,21:1
Doyle, John T (por), 1942, D 10,25:3
Doyle, John T (ed), 1943, Ja 11,14:4
Doyle, John T Mrs, 1951, S 11,29:3
Doyle, Joseph C, 1946, My 9,21:5
Doyle, Joseph E, 1944, Ap 29,15:4; 1946, O 14,29:4
Doyle, Joseph J, 1906, Ja 8,9:6
Doyle, Joseph P, 1947, S 25,29:5
Doyle, Joseph P Mrs, 1951, D 11,33:2
Doyle, Joseph R, 1956, Mr 2,23:4
Doyle, Judd B, 1947, N 23,74:3
Doyle, Judd B Mrs, 1950, S 7,31:3
Doyle, Julia H, 1943, Ag 30,15:6
Doyle, Kate Mrs, 1911, Ap 13,13:6
Doyle, Kathleen, 1952, S 30,31:3
Doyle, Lady, 1940, Je 28,19:5
Doyle, Len, 1959, D 8,45:3
Doyle, Luke C, 1952, Je 17,27:1
Doyle, Lynn (Leslie A Montgomery), 1961, Ag 14, 25:4
Doyle, M Francis, 1938, My 5,23:4
Doyle, Margaret Mrs, 1909, Ap 10,9:5; 1943, F 27,13:5
Doyle, Mary (Sister M Aquinas), 1940, My 24,19:4
Doyle, Mary A, 1944, Ja 10,17:1
Doyle, Mary E, 1949, My 16,21:3
Doyle, Mary U, 1942, D 11,23:4
Doyle, Mary V Sister, 1943, O 31,48:7
Doyle, Michael (por), 1943, N 27,13:4
Doyle, Michael A, 1953, S 15,31:5
Doyle, Michael F (will, Ap 6,26:6), 1960, Mr 28,29:5
Doyle, Michael J, 1945, F 18,33:2; 1950, Ap 25,31:1
Doyle, Miriam, 1962, S 19,39:1
Doyle, Nathaniel, 1910, Ja 16,II,11:4
Doyle, Patrick B, 1961, My 7,86:4
Doyle, Patrick J, 1960, S 23,29:3
Doyle, Pauline M Mrs, 1939, Je 10,17:3
Doyle, Peadar, 1956, Ag 5,77:2
Doyle, Peter, 1946, Mr 13,29:4
Doyle, Philip, 1967, D 1,47:3
Doyle, Ray, 1954, Je 16,31:4; 1960, N 30,37:5
Doyle, Ray T, 1951, Jl 19,23:1
Doyle, Richard, 1883, D 12,4:7
Doyle, Richard H Jr, 1948, Ja 19,23:2
Doyle, Richard Mrs, 1958, Jl 24,25:4
Doyle, Richard S, 1945, S 19,25:1
Doyle, Richard T, 1949, S 17,17:6
Doyle, Robert E, 1951, O 30,29:3
Doyle, Robert Morris Adm, 1925, D 16,25:3
Doyle, Ross A, 1957, Ag 14,25:6
Doyle, Stafford, 1943, Ja 23,13:1
Doyle, Stanley B, 1965, Je 20,72:8
Doyle, T L, 1945, Ag 18,11:4
Doyle, Thomas A, 1941, Ap 7,17:2; 1951, Jl 25,23:4
Doyle, Thomas F, 1940, Jl 8,17:6; 1961, Je 22,31:3
Doyle, Thomas J, 1962, Jl 10,33:2
Doyle, Thomas L, 1955, Ap 9,13:5
Doyle, Thomas Mrs, 1941, Ja 8,19:4
Doyle, Thomas S 2d, 1948, D 4,13:4
Doyle, Thomas W, 1938, Mr 29,21:4
Doyle, Washington D, 1939, O 20,23:2
Doyle, William A Sr, 1967, Ja 25,43:3
Doyle, William B, 1943, N 16,23:1
Doyle, William E, 1944, N 25,13:3; 1953, My 15,23:2
Doyle, William F, 1967, O 11,47:2
Doyle, William H, 1944, Mr 13,15:2; 1947, D 4,31:2
Doyle, William J, 1941, O 14,23:5; 1942, Ap 13,15:5; 1946, Mr 8,21:3
Doyle, William J Sr, 1960, S 4,68:7
Doyle, William M Mrs, 1941, D 9,31:2
Doyle, William Mrs, 1954, My 24,27:3
Doyle, William P, 1954, F 16,25:5
Doyle, William S, 1947, N 7,23:2
Doyle, William T S, 1939, S 25,19:3
Doyle, William T S, 1940, Ja 2,19:4
Doyle, Willie, 1950, Ap 10,19:4
d'Oyley, Marquis (Dr Jno Evans), 1911, Ja 30,9:4
D'Oyly Carte, Rupert, 1948, S 13,21:1
Doyning, Frederick W, 1950, S 9,17:5
Dozer, Harold E, 1947, Ag 24,56:3
Dozier, Lewis D, 1914, My 24,IV,7:5
Dozois, Arthur D Mrs, 1939, F 20,17:1
Dozois, Edmond J Jr, 1955, Je 11,15:5
Dozois, Lucian Mrs, 1953, O 3,17:3
Dozois, Lucien A, 1951, Ap 22,89:2
Drabble, Dorothy, 1925, Ag 21,13:6
Drabek, Peter, 1951, Ag 28,23:3
Drabell, John M, 1954, Ag 10,19:5
Drabkin, Israel E, 1965, Mr 28,92:5
Drabkin, Israel E Mrs, 1938, Mr 22,21:2
Drabkina, F I, 1957, Ja 13,84:2
Drachman, Bernard, 1945, Mr 13,23:5
Drachman, Bernard Mrs, 1925, F 13,17:3; 1960, S 11, 81:4
Drachman, Hyman, 1957, Jl 17,27:2
Drachman, Jerry, 1961, My 22,31:2
Drachman, Morris, 1959, Mr 1,86:4
Drachmann, Holger Henrik Herholdt, 1908, Ja 15,9:4
Drachsler, J, 1927, Jl 23,13:5
Drackett, Harry R, 1948, Mr 6,13:2
Draddy, Daniel A, 1959, N 19,39:4
Draddy, Robert E, 1958, My 6,35:3
Draemel, Milo F Mrs, 1956, Mr 8,29:4

Dragan, Joseph, 1951, O 29,23:6
Drage, Evelyn Mrs, 1957, N 11,29:4
Drager, Frederick W, 1958, F 2,86:8
Drago, Casall del, 1908, Mr 18,7:6
Drago, Charles F, 1954, N 15,27:4
Drago, Dominick, 1950, Mr 3,27:8
Drago, Giovanni del Prince, 1956, My 4,25:5
Drago, Louis A, 1938, My 10,21:6
Drago, Luis Maria Dr, 1921, Je 10,13:6
Dragomiroff, Mikhail Ivanovich, 1905, O 29,9:6
Dragoni, Emilio, 1964, N 6,37:4
Dragoumis, Stephen, 1923, S 19,4:7
Drahos, Janos, 1950, Je 22,27:2
Drain, James A, 1943, My 31,17:3
Drain, Joseph F, 1948, F 10,23:2
Drainard, Clyde, 1953, Ja 7,31:1
Drainard, Clyde Mrs, 1953, Ja 7,31:1
Drake, Albert W, 1944, O 9,23:5
Drake, Alexander W Mrs, 1944, Ja 2,38:3
Drake, Alexander Wilson (funl, F 8,11:4), 1916, F 5, 11:5
Drake, Alfred E, 1955, Ja 2,77:1
Drake, Alva M, 1937, N 25,31:4
Drake, Andrew Jackson Commodore (funl, Ag 10,2:2), 1875, Ag 6,4:6
Drake, Arlington M, 1945, My 10,23:5
Drake, B J Dr, 1916, Jl 13,11:5
Drake, Catherine, 1960, S 3,36:8
Drake, Charles A, 1946, O 24,27:4
Drake, Charles B, 1949, Mr 28,21:4
Drake, Charles E, 1950, Mr 1,27:2
Drake, Charles J, 1953, N 19,31:3
Drake, Charles T, 1949, Ap 23,13:3
Drake, Charles W, 1923, My 11,17:4
Drake, Col, 1864, Je 10,2:2
Drake, Daniel E, 1951, Jl 21,13:6
Drake, Daniel X, 1942, Jl 10,17:4
Drake, Dorson S, 1940, N 26,23:4
Drake, E A, 1948, Ag 17,21:5
Drake, E L, 1880, N 10,5:3
Drake, Elizabeth H Mrs, 1940, O 31,23:5
Drake, Ernest B, 1941, O 24,23:5
Drake, Eugene H, 1958, O 6,31:4
Drake, Francis, 1940, My 3,21:4
Drake, Francis Cornelius D, 1922, F 18,13:3
Drake, Francis E, 1957, Ag 7,27:5; 1960, F 14,84:3
Drake, Francis Marion Gen, 1903, N 21,9:5
Drake, Frank, 1943, Je 18,21:4
Drake, Frank B, 1908, F 3,9:5
Drake, Frank Mrs, 1950, Jl 20,25:5
Drake, Frank O, 1947, D 16,33:3
Drake, Frank V, 1954, Je 7,23:3
Drake, Frederic N, 1965, Ap 16,29:3
Drake, Frederick, 1882, Ap 8,5:4
Drake, Frederick A, 1941, S 18,25:4
Drake, Frederick J Mrs, 1946, Ap 13,17:4
Drake, George W Mrs, 1951, Ja 19,25:4
Drake, Grace B, 1951, Jl 19,23:4
Drake, Grace F Mrs, 1951, Ja 28,76:1
Drake, Harold W Mrs, 1954, Je 8,27:4
Drake, Harry M, 1950, Ja 12,27:2
Drake, Harvey A, 1943, My 7,19:3
Drake, Henry E Mrs, 1925, O 27,23:3
Drake, Henry J, 1963, O 6,88:6
Drake, Henry L Sr, 1952, D 16,31:3
Drake, Herbert F, 1954, Je 7,23:2
Drake, Herbert Mrs, 1955, Ja 5,23:5
Drake, Hervey J Mrs, 1944, S 2,11:4
Drake, Howard E, 1966, My 11,34:5
Drake, Howard W, 1941, O 6,17:2
Drake, J F, 1933, S 1,17:3
Drake, J Frank Mrs, 1954, Ag 11,25:3
Drake, J Madison, 1948, Ag 3,25:5
Drake, J Walter, 1941, N 28,23:4
Drake, James H, 1965, My 19,47:4
Drake, James M, 1906, N 24,11:4
Drake, James Madison Gen, 1913, N 29,13:5
Drake, John, 1885, Mr 29,7:3; 1948, N 3,27:5
Drake, John A Mrs, 1937, D 23,22:4
Drake, John B, 1964, Mr 18,41:2
Drake, John H, 1938, D 28,26:3
Drake, John J, 1954, O 31,89:2
Drake, John J Mrs, 1952, Jl 11,17:5
Drake, John Jacob, 1904, My 11,9:6
Drake, John L, 1951, Je 20,27:4
Drake, John R, 1942, Ap 4,13:1
Drake, Joseph A, 1944, Ag 27,33:2
Drake, Joseph H, 1947, Ag 6,23:4
Drake, Joseph J, 1938, Jl 8,17:2
Drake, Joseph M, 1909, Mr 7,11:7
Drake, Judson C, 1937, Ag 22,II,7:3
Drake, Lauren J, 1918, O 12,13:3
Drake, Lawrence, 1913, S 18,11:5
Drake, Lawrence F, 1953, Ag 6,21:6
Drake, Leonard A, 1961, N 25,24:6
Drake, Manning E, 1941, Mr 27,23:2
Drake, Marcus H Capt, 1907, S 29,9:6
Drake, Marston E, 1966, F 12,27:3
Drake, Milton J, 1966, Ja 13,22:5
Drake, Nathaniel M, 1946, Ag 10,13:5
Drake, Newman H, 1962, Ag 27,23:5
Drake, Phil B, 1938, D 16,25:2
Drake, R R, 1944, D 11,23:4
Drake, Robert A, 1957, Mr 10,88:7
Drake, Roy Stannard, 1916, Ja 30,17:4
Drake, Ruth W, 1948, O 6,29:3
Drake, Samuel Adams, 1905, D 5,9:3
Drake, Silas Dewey, 1908, Jl 17,7:5
Drake, Simeon J, 1914, O 7,9:5; 1925, Ag 21,13:6
Drake, Theodore G H, 1959, O 31,23:5
Drake, Tracy C, 1939, Mr 4,15:3
Drake, Walter E, 1954, Je 15,29:5
Drake, Walter E Mrs, 1946, My 20,23:3
Drake, Warren C Mrs, 1943, My 7,19:1
Drake, Whitford (por), 1938, Ag 25,19:4
Drake, William, 1948, Ja 1,23:2
Drake, William J, 1964, Je 19,31:2
Drake, William W, 1946, Ap 29,22:3
Drake-Smith, Daniel, 1957, Ap 16,33:4
Drake-Smith, Laura, 1948, My 16,69:1
Drakeford, Arthur S, 1957, Je 10,27:2
Drakos, Soter P, 1938, Ap 26,21:4
Drandorff, William F, 1954, Mr 19,24:5
Drandreau, John L Dr, 1968, Jl 20,27:3
Drane, Agnes K, 1954, F 16,25:3
Drane, Brent S, 1948, N 24,23:3
Drane, Frederick L, 1951, Ap 11,29:5
Drane, George Canning Judge, 1922, D 4,17:4
Drane, Herbert J, 1947, Ag 13,23:4
Drane, Malcolm G, 1950, N 8,29:4
Drane, Paul S, 1952, Jl 29,22:3
Draney, John F, 1951, Jl 9,25:4
Draney, John P, 1938, Mr 27,II,7:3
Drange, Carl E, 1956, Je 13,37:5
Dransfield, Jane (Mrs C D Stone), 1957, Jl 19,19:2
Drant, Patricia (Mrs J S Collins), 1955, O 5,35:4
Drapeau, Benjamin L, 1959, Ja 27,33:3
Drapeau, George, 1952, Je 4,27:4
Drapeau, Richard L, 1949, N 22,29:1
Draper, A Wetherell, 1908, D 14,9:6
Draper, Amos G Mrs, 1937, O 13,23:3
Draper, Andrew L, 1948, Ag 13,15:3
Draper, Andrew Sloan (funl, My 1,11:4), 1913, Ap 28,11:3
Draper, Anna C, 1901, D 11,9:4
Draper, Arthur G, 1960, O 16,88:1
Draper, Arthur S, 1963, O 26,27:3
Draper, Arthur S Mrs, 1960, Ap 14,31:2
Draper, B H Bristow, 1944, Je 5,19:6
Draper, B H Bristow Jr, 1957, My 30,19:5
Draper, B H Bristow Mrs, 1949, Ag 14,68:6
Draper, Charles, 1946, Ag 27,27:4
Draper, Charles D, 1947, F 9,61:4
Draper, Charles D Mrs, 1954, S 27,21:4
Draper, Claude L, 1958, My 1,31:5
Draper, D S, 1885, Ap 5,9:3
Draper, David S, 1925, F 9,17:3
Draper, Dexter W, 1961, Ag 24,29:3
Draper, Eben S, 1959, Ap 19,87:1
Draper, Eben S Ex-Gov (funl, Ap 13,11:4), 1914, Ap 10,13:5
Draper, Eben S Mrs, 1913, S 25,13:4
Draper, Ebenezer, 1915, Jl 28,9:6
Draper, Ella, 1944, Ag 16,19:4
Draper, Ernest G, 1954, My 1,15:6
Draper, Ernest G Mrs, 1959, D 1,39:5
Draper, Estella, 1955, Ja 18,17:5
Draper, Frank B Mrs, 1955, Jl 23,17:3
Draper, Frederick E, 1951, S 9,89:2
Draper, Frederick G, 1914, Je 28,15:4
Draper, G B, 1876, S 26,8:2
Draper, G G, 1876, Ap 20,8:4
Draper, George, 1959, Jl 2,25:2
Draper, George A, 1923, F 8,19:5
Draper, George H, 1910, My 14,9:4
Draper, George O, 1938, O 22,17:4
Draper, George W E, 1949, Ap 3,77:1
Draper, Henry, 1882, N 21,1:7
Draper, Henry C, 1960, Jl 30,17:6
Draper, Henry Mrs, 1914, D 9,13:6
Draper, Ida M Mrs, 1942, Ag 5,19:3
Draper, J C Prof, 1885, D 21,5:4
Draper, J Sumner, 1951, F 2,24:2
Draper, J W Prof (see also Ja 5), 1882, Ja 11,8:1
Draper, Jacob S Mrs, 1907, Ag 10,7:5
Draper, James, 1907, Mr 14,7:6
Draper, Jean M (will filed), 1954, O 2,22:2
Draper, Jennie Thompson, 1923, Ag 14,15:4
Draper, Jesse S, 1944, Mr 6,19:6
Draper, John C, 1941, Ja 17,17:2
Draper, John H, 1948, D 19,76:2
Draper, John W Dr, 1911, D 5,13:4
Draper, John W Mrs, 1956, Ja 29,92:6
Draper, Joseph, 1962, Jl 2,29:5
Draper, Martha L, 1943, Je 30,21:3
Draper, Miriam S, 1938, F 9,20:2
Draper, Morris B Mrs, 1951, Ap 3,27:5
Draper, N C, 1883, S 14,4:6
Draper, Patrick M, 1943, N 24,21:1
Draper, Paul, 1925, F 16,19:5
Draper, Paul Sr Mrs, 1952, Ag 27,27:6
Draper, Ruth, 1956, D 31,13:3
Draper, Samuel W F, 1939, D 31,18:8
Draper, Simeon, 1866, N 7,4:5
Draper, T Wain-Morgan Col, 1915, N 9,13:3
Draper, Theodore S, 1959, Jl 12,72:6
Draper, Thomas Bailey, 1917, Ag 15,9:5
Draper, W B, 1885, Ap 18,2:5
Draper, W H, 1877, N 3,1:6
Draper, W H Dr, 1901, Ap 27,9:5
Draper, W Levell, 1940, Ja 27,13:6
Draper, Walter A, 1964, My 10,83:3
Draper, William F Gen, 1910, Ja 29,9:4
Draper, William Franklin Gen, 1919, Je 24,13:4
Draper, William Franklin Jr, 1909, Mr 20,9:4
Draper, William H, 1921, D 8,19:5
Draper, William H Jr Mrs, 1942, N 1,53:1
Draper, William H Mrs, 1914, Ag 17,7:4
Draper, William K Mrs, 1951, Ja 3,25:1
Drapier, William H Jr, 1924, S 4,19:6
Drapkin, Jacob, 1961, D 2,23:5
Drash, John C, 1957, Jl 21,61:1
Drasler, Frank R, 1949, F 16,25:4
Drastier, Franz Mrs, 1910, Ag 1,7:2
Dratler, Jay, 1968, O 16,47:2
Dratty, Robert E Mrs, 1956, Jl 15,61:1
Dratvin, Mikhail I, 1953, D 17,37:5
Draughon, Ralph B Dr, 1968, Ag 15,37:3
Draus, Edward J, 1957, O 16,32:3
Draut, George, 1965, N 22,37:4
Dravo, Charles A, 1958, Je 4,30:1
Drawbaugh, Daniel F, 1911, N 4,13:6
Dray, Harry, 1940, D 9,19:4
Draycott, Wilfred, 1938, O 3,15:4
Drayton, Albert I, 1953, Ap 9,27:1
Drayton, Alfred (por), 1949, Ap 27,27:1
Drayton, Frederick R Jr, 1954, S 19,89:1
Drayton, G G, 1936, F 2,II,9:3
Drayton, Harley (Harold C), 1966, Ap 9,25:3
Drayton, Henri, 1872, Ag 1,8:3
Drayton, Henry, 1950, Ag 29,27:2
Drayton, Henry C, 1942, Mr 23,15:6
Drayton, Henry S, 1923, Ap 10,21:3
Drayton, Joan B Mrs, 1966, Ag 1,27:3
Drayton, John B, 1903, S 4,1:6
Drayton, John W, 1942, S 24,27:6
Drayton, Lady, 1938, Ja 4,24:3
Drayton, Newbold, 1937, S 5,II,6:6
Drayton, P Capt, 1865, Ag 7,8:2
Drayton, Rev, 1865, Ap 9,2:6
Drayton, Robert, 1963, F 22,3:1
Drayton, Robert M, 1939, D 17,49:2
Drayton, Samuel, 1949, Ja 17,19:4
Drayton, William H 3d, 1937, Ja 22,21:2
Drayton, William Jr, 1953, Mr 19,29:5
Drayton, William R Mrs, 1941, F 8,15:3
Dreape, Anthony, 1948, Je 28,19:4
Dreben, Sam, 1925, Mr 16,19:5
Drebinger, John Sr, 1925, My 28,21:5
Drebinger, John Sr Mrs, 1951, D 19,31:5
Drecher, Louis Dr, 1904, My 2,14:3
Drechsler, David, 1955, Ag 31,25:3
Dreckmeier, F W L, 1953, N 19,31:2
Drecq, Henri, 1938, My 26,25:2
Drees, Charles W Mrs, 1947, S 26,23:1
Drefahl, Louis C, 1946, O 31,25:3
Drefus, Carl, 1951, Mr 30,24:4
Drefus, Ferdinand, 1915, Jl 16,9:4
Dreger, Alexander, 1946, Jl 6,15:4
Dreher, Carl E, 1953, My 7,31:4
Dreher, Charles E, 1949, D 26,29:5
Dreher, Ernest A, 1954, Ap 18,88:4
Dreher, George C, 1956, D 19,31:4
Dreher, Gustave F E, 1951, D 24,13:3
Dreher, Gustave F Mrs, 1953, F 2,21:2
Dreher, J Frank, 1959, N 18,41:3
Dreher, Julius D Dr, 1937, O 10,II,8:6
Dreher, LeRoy H, 1965, Ag 12,27:5
Dreher, Walter A, 1962, F 7,34:3
Drehs, Theodore, 1950, Je 11,92:7
Dreibelbis, Carl C, 1947, Ap 8,27:2
Dreicer, Jacob, 1921, Ag 15,13:7
Dreicer, Michael (funl, Jl 29,13:4), 1921, Jl 27,1
Dreicer, Walter, 1938, O 5,23:4
Dreier, C N, 1926, My 17,21:5
Dreier, Dorothea A, 1923, S 16,8:3
Dreier, Henry E, 1955, N 25,28:3
Dreier, John C L, 1938, D 5,23:5
Dreier, Katherine S, 1952, Mr 30,92:1
Dreier, Mary E, 1963, Ag 17,19:1
Dreier, William Y, 1940, D 29,25:1
Dreifoos, Byron G, 1966, S 25,84:6
Dreifoos, Henry Mrs, 1950, Je 20,27:3
Dreifus, Charles, 1952, S 30,31:3
Dreifus, William, 1958, Je 12,31:3
Dreis, Walter H, 1955, D 10,21:5
Dreis, Walter H Mrs, 1965, Ja 23,25:1
Dreisbach, John M, 1958, N 11,29:3
Dreisbach, Paul J, 1953, Jl 11,11:7
Dreisbach, Paul W, 1947, Jl 6,41:3
Dreisbach, Robert R, 1964, Je 26,29:4
Dreiser, Edward M, 1958, Ja 31,22:1
Dreiser, Edward Mrs, 1955, Je 12,86:8
Dreiser, Theodore, 1945, D 29,1:2
Dreiser, Theodore Mrs, 1942, O 3,15:2; 1955, S
Dreisoerner (Sister Mary Chaminade), 1958, A 25:2
Dreissigacker, Philip H, 1954, Jl 17,13:3
Drellich, Samuel B, 1956, Ja 7,17:1

Dreman, John, 1945, Ap 28,15:6
Dremen, Edward F, 1947, Jl 9,23:2
Dremin, D F, 1953, D 11,34:2
Drenk, Lester A, 1961, My 14,87:1
Drennan, Elizabeth, 1951, Mr 3,13:4
Drennan, Jeannie G, 1946, N 5,25:5
Drennan, Michael A, 1941, Ja 10,19:2
Drennan, T J, 1928, Jl 16,19:3
Drennan, William, 1941, F 14,18:2; 1945, D 9,44:3
Drennen, Michael F, 1944, Je 14,19:4
Drennen, Thomas F, 1959, Je 8,27:2
Drepperd, Carl, 1956, Mr 15,31:2
Dresbach, Glenn Ward, 1968, Je 28,41:2
Dresbach, Melvin, 1946, O 19,21:1
Dresbach, Philip P, 1965, Je 5,31:5
Dresbach, Robert Mrs, 1955, Ap 5,19:5
Drescher, A S, 1928, O 21,31:4
Drescher, August F, 1907, D 9,7:4
Drescher, Frank A, 1964, S 15,37:2
Drescher, Theodore B, 1953, F 23,25:2
Dreschler, Anton, 1942, F 27,17:3
Dresden, Arnold, 1954, Ap 13,31:3
Dresden, Sem, 1957, Jl 31,23:6
Dresdner, Karl G, 1953, Ja 25,84:4
Dresel, Alger, 1953, Mr 12,27:4
Dresel, Ellis Loring, 1925, S 21,19:5
Dresel, Fred, 1948, Mr 12,48:4
Dresel, Kurt M, 1951, O 31,29:4
Dresen, John, 1941, N 3,27:2
Dresher, Harry, 1960, O 20,35:2
Dreshman, Christian H, 1955, Ap 5,26:7
Dreshner, Henry, 1965, My 29,1:8
Dreskol, Michael J, 1948, Ap 14,27:5
Dreslin, Margaret Y Mrs, 1939, Jl 18,19:2
Dresner, Jack (Jay), 1959, S 10,35:3
Dress, Alphonse J, 1941, N 9,53:3
Dress, George, 1957, N 11,29:6
Dress, Harry C, 1948, Ja 12,19:2
Dress, William H, 1949, N 11,25:3
Dressel, Albert J, 1948, Ja 17,26:2
Dressel, Edwin C, 1960, N 7,35:5
Dressel, Joseph H, 1958, N 26,12:1
Dressen, Chuck (Chas W),(funl, Ag 14,V,2:6), 1966, Ag 11,33:1
Dresser, Archie E, 1909, N 30,9:4
Dresser, C E, 1903, S 30,9:6
Dresser, Ellen D, 1940, Mr 31,44:6
Dresser, Elliott L Mrs, 1947, Jl 20,44:4
Dresser, Ernest W, 1954, Ag 6,17:2
Dresser, F J C Mrs, 1952, Ap 24,32:3
Dresser, Frank F, 1924, S 10,21:3
Dresser, G W Col (see also My 28), 1883, My 31,5:4
Dresser, George H, 1938, Ja 12,21:3
Dresser, George L, 1957, Mr 1,23:2
Dresser, Henry A, 1946, N 17,68:3
Dresser, Horace, 1877, Je 29,5:2
Dresser, Horatio W, 1954, Mr 31,27:5
Dresser, Horatio W Mrs, 1961, Ag 24,29:2
Dresser, Ivan C, 1956, D 28,21:2
Dresser, John O, 1951, Ja 3,27:1
Dresser, Louise (Mrs J Gardner), 1965, Ap 25,87:3
Dresser, Paul, 1906, Ja 31,11:6
Dresser, Virginia, 1943, N 2,25:3
Dresser, William A, 1954, Ap 22,29:5
Dressin-LeBlanc, Eli A, 1946, Je 6,21:4
Dressler, Agnes M, 1922, D 25,13:4
Dressler, Carroll, 1947, F 26,25:5
Dressler, Cary C Mrs, 1963, Ap 24,35:2
Dressler, George, 1944, Ap 27,23:4
Dressler, Joseph Jr, 1938, D 29,8:3
Dressler, M, 1934, Jl 29,1:6
Dressler, Margaret, 1947, F 26,25:2
Dressler, Oscar Mrs, 1952, My 22,27:6
Dressler, William Prof, 1914, Jl 3,9:5
Dressman, Joseph H, 1962, F 9,29:2
Dressner, Eugene E Mrs, 1950, Je 6,29:5
Dreusicke, Albert, 1949, Ja 11,31:7
Dreutzer, Carl, 1958, My 17,19:4
Dreutzer, Carl Mrs (J de Both), 1959, Ag 31,21:3
Dreux, Edmond, 1946, O 10,27:4
Drevenstedt, Harry E, 1943, F 11,19:4
Drever, Constance, 1948, S 22,31:4
Drever, Peter, 1940, Je 16,39:1
Drever, Thomas, 1965, My 9,87:1
Drew, Albert H Mrs, 1942, Je 5,19:1
Drew, Alden G, 1956, Jl 5,25:4
Drew, Alfred A, 1941, My 13,23:1
Drew, Arthur L, 1940, Ja 23,21:6
Drew, Aurilla V, 1937, Jl 24,15:5
Drew, Benjamin, 1903, Jl 21,9:6
Drew, Charles B, 1961, Ap 1,17:5
Drew, Charles F, 1940, Ag 6,19:4
Drew, Charles H, 1907, N 16,9:5; 1959, F 25,31:3
Drew, Charles R, 1950, Ap 2,76:4
Drew, Charles V, 1937, S 27,21:5
Drew, Cornelius J, 1962, Je 27,32:8
Drew, D, 1879, S 20,8:2
Drew, E Wright, 1952, S 4,27:5
Drew, Edward Bangs, 1924, Ag 18,13:4
Drew, Edward F, 1943, Ap 25,34:4
Drew, Elizabeth, 1965, Ap 9,33:3
Drew, Emma L Mrs, 1942, Ap 2,22:2
Drew, Emmet T, 1960, Ag 19,23:1
Drew, Forrest, 1940, Ag 12,15:6
Drew, Frances W L, 1938, Mr 14,15:5
Drew, Francis W Mrs, 1953, Jl 23,23:3
Drew, Fred, 1939, Je 24,17:2
Drew, Frederic E, 1957, Je 2,86:2
Drew, Frederick M, 1939, Jl 6,23:4
Drew, George, 1937, O 27,31:6
Drew, George Mrs, 1965, Mr 10,41:1
Drew, Gladys Rankin, 1914, Ja 10,9:5
Drew, Groves W, 1939, D 15,25:5
Drew, Harlon W, 1963, Jl 5,16:8
Drew, Harold W, 1949, S 24,13:3
Drew, Harrison R, 1945, S 15,15:3
Drew, Harry Rev, 1910, Ap 1,11:4
Drew, Herbert F, 1947, Ap 10,25:3
Drew, Howard A Mrs, 1952, D 24,17:5
Drew, Howard P, 1957, F 22,21:4
Drew, Howard S, 1941, Je 19,21:5
Drew, Irving Webster Ex-Sen, 1922, Ap 11,19:4
Drew, J, 1927, Jl 10,1:3
Drew, J Mrs, 1897, S 1,7:4
Drew, James B, 1953, S 6,52:3
Drew, James F, 1961, My 19,32:7
Drew, Jeremiah, 1885, Ap 5,9:3
Drew, John, 1953, Je 21,84:7
Drew, John E, 1942, S 6,30:7
Drew, John Mrs, 1918, D 5,13:3
Drew, John T, 1950, S 21,31:4
Drew, Leslie L, 1961, Jl 16,69:1
Drew, Robert N, 1916, N 22,13:5
Drew, Roxanna, 1876, Ja 28,5:2
Drew, Samuel, 1910, O 8,11:6
Drew, Sidney, 1919, Ap 10,11:1
Drew, Sidney Mrs (funl, N 6,23:5), 1925, N 4,23:4
Drew, Walter, 1961, D 27,25:6
Drew, Walter W, 1941, Je 24,19:4
Drew, William, 1943, N 19,19:3
Drew, William A, 1937, F 26,21:3
Drew, William T, 1957, Ja 30,29:2
Drew, William T Mrs, 1951, Ap 24,29:1
Drew, Willis A, 1948, D 24,17:3
Drewery, Mary C Mrs, 1941, O 16,21:6
Drewes, Alfred H, 1967, Je 7,47:3
Drewes, Augusta Mrs, 1945, D 21,36:1
Drewes, Barry H, 1958, N 24,29:2
Drewes, William K, 1960, My 6,31:4
Drewitz, Emil O, 1948, Mr 28,48:5
Drewry, Arthur, 1961, Mr 26,92:5
Drewry, Henry, 1963, Je 13,20:8
Drewry, Herbert R Dr, 1937, D 3,23:5
Drewry, Patrick H, 1947, D 22,22:3
Drewry, Raymond G, 1953, My 7,31:1
Drewry, William Powell, 1912, Jl 18,9:4
Drewry, William W, 1963, Ag 26,27:2
Drews, Charles E, 1944, S 6,19:6
Drews, John F, 1963, N 9,25:5
Drews, Karl, 1963, Ag 16,28:2
Drexel, A J, 1893, Jl 1,1:5; 1934, D 15,13:1
Drexel, Anthony J, 1946, F 26,25:1
Drexel, Anthony J Jr Mrs, 1955, N 30,33:4
Drexel, Constance, 1956, Ag 29,29:2
Drexel, F A, 1885, F 16,2:5
Drexel, George W (will, S 23,13:1), 1944, S 10,46:1
Drexel, George W C Mrs, 1948, D 17,27:1
Drexel, J R, 1935, My 19,33:1
Drexel, J W, 1888, Mr 26,1:7
Drexel, John R Jr, 1921, D 8,19:4
Drexel, John R Jr Mrs, 1943, Ja 28,19:4
Drexel, John R Mrs, 1947, D 10,31:2
Drexel, Joseph W Mrs, 1912, Ja 26,11:5
Drexel, Mary Katherine Rev Mother (will, Ap 5,-34:3), 1955, Mr 4,23:1
Drexel, Victor L Mrs, 1946, Ag 2,19:2
Drexelius, Peter J, 1941, Jl 8,19:2
Drexler, Samuel, 1949, S 28,27:5; 1953, F 27,21:2
Drexler, William F Mrs, 1948, Mr 2,23:2
Drexler, William F Sr, 1949, Ja 11,31:5
Drey, Arthur, 1965, Jl 3,19:3
Drey, Morris (will), 1938, Ja 26,15:4
Drey, Paul, 1953, Mr 20,23:6
Dreyer, Alphonso M, 1939, N 14,23:5
Dreyer, Aug C, 1938, D 30,15:3
Dreyer, August (por), 1943, My 11,21:1
Dreyer, Carl Theodor, 1968, Mr 21,47:1
Dreyer, Dave, 1967, Mr 3,35:4
Dreyer, Eugene R Jr, 1944, Ja 23,38:3
Dreyer, F C H, 1953, N 21,13:3
Dreyer, Felix S, 1958, O 12,83:4
Dreyer, Frank H A, 1945, My 13,20:8
Dreyer, Frederic, 1956, D 12,39:5
Dreyer, Frederick C, 1943, Jl 6,21:3
Dreyer, George, 1937, My 9,II,10:1
Dreyer, Gerhard, 1961, O 17,39:1
Dreyer, H James, 1947, S 25,29:4
Dreyer, Hattie L Mrs, 1937, Ja 15,22:2
Dreyer, Henry W, 1937, My 10,19:3
Dreyer, Herman, 1955, Ag 13,13:6
Dreyer, J Henry Sr, 1948, D 10,25:2
Dreyer, J L E Dr, 1926, S 15,29:3
Dreyer, Jacob S, 1941, My 27,23:3
Dreyer, John F, 1943, Ap 25,35:2
Dreyer, Joseph J, 1949, F 12,18:2
Dreyer, Leslie E, 1960, N 5,23:5
Dreyer, Samuel, 1962, Mr 30,33:3
Dreyer, Samuel J, 1967, Ja 31,31:2
Dreyer, T F, 1954, Jl 14,27:5
Dreyfoos, Alex W, 1951, N 23,29:4
Dreyfoos, W Wallace, 1939, Mr 30,23:4
Dreyfus, A, 1935, Jl 13,1:2
Dreyfus, Armand, 1942, S 3,19:2
Dreyfus, Camille E, 1956, S 28,27:3
Dreyfus, Carl Mrs, 1942, S 15,23:2
Dreyfus, Emil, 1961, Ja 16,27:2
Dreyfus, Eugene G, 1961, Je 4,86:1
Dreyfus, Frederick J, 1950, S 6,23:2
Dreyfus, Gaston, 1915, S 15,9:4
Dreyfus, Henry, 1945, Ja 1,21:4
Dreyfus, Herbert M, 1959, S 12,21:5
Dreyfus, Isaac, 1903, D 30,2:7
Dreyfus, Isidor, 1903, Jl 10,7:6; 1949, Je 5,92:3
Dreyfus, Joseph Mrs, 1952, Je 5,31:1
Dreyfus, Louis (will, D 9,3:7), 1967, My 5,39:3
Dreyfus, Louis A Mrs (por), 1943, Ag 18,19:3
Dreyfus, Louis L, 1940, N 12,23:5
Dreyfus, Max, 1964, My 16,25:4
Dreyfus, Milton D, 1962, Mr 8,31:2
Dreyfus, Paul, 1941, D 24,17:2
Dreyfus, Valerie J, 1956, N 19,31:1
Dreyfus, William, 1946, Mr 14,25:5
Dreyfuss, Barney Mrs, 1950, My 14,108:2
Dreyfuss, Elsie G Mrs, 1937, Ja 24,II,8:1
Dreyfuss, Isaac, 1905, Ap 18,11:4
Dreyfuss, Joseph, 1910, N 4,9:3; 1943, Jl 24,13:1
Dreyfuss, Julius, 1925, My 9,15:3
Dreyfuss, Julius Mrs, 1951, Jl 29,68:3
Dreyfuss, Ludwig, 1918, Mr 7,11:4
Dreyfuss, Michael, 1960, Ap 1,33:2
Dreyfuss, Robert, 1939, Je 19,15:5
Dreystadt, Nicholas, 1948, S 4,15:3
Dribben, Samuel, 1962, F 19,31:5
Dribben, Saul F, 1957, Jl 23,27:1
Drickler, Julius, 1955, O 2,86:7
Dries, Louis, 1956, Je 3,85:1
Dries, Wirt A, 1955, Ap 4,29:1
Dries, Worth A, 1952, D 22,25:4
Driesbach, Fred R, 1949, Ap 26,25:5
Driesbach, Herr, 1877, D 7,5:3
Driesch, Hans A E, 1941, Ap 18,21:1
Driggs, Edmund H, 1946, S 29,62:3
Driggs, Edmund H Jr, 1957, Ag 16,19:5
Driggs, Emily L Mrs, 1940, O 16,23:5
Driggs, Houston H, 1940, My 29,23:5
Driggs, Howard R, 1963, F 19,8:7
Driggs, Ivan H, 1955, My 10,29:4
Driggs, J F, 1877, D 18,4:7
Driggs, Laurence L, 1945, My 27,26:2
Driggs, Laurence L Mrs, 1947, Ap 20,60:3
Driggs, Louis L, 1942, D 25,17:4
Driggs, Marshall S, 1910, S 16,9:6
Driggs, William K Sr, 1965, Ap 8,39:2
Drimer, Henry, 1957, F 22,21:4
Dring, John F, 1948, My 11,26:3
Dring, Robert L, 1953, D 14,31:3
Drinker, Cecil K, 1956, Ap 16,27:2
Drinker, Frederick E, 1944, Ap 7,19:2
Drinker, Henry S, 1965, Mr 12,33:3
Drinker, Henry S Dr, 1937, Jl 28,19:5
Drinker, Henry S Mrs, 1967, S 10,82:3
Drinker, Henry S Sr Mrs, 1939, O 24,23:5
Drinker, Judge, 1864, Ap 8,4:6
Drinker, Katherine R, 1956, Mr 16,23:5
Drinker, Maria G, 1953, Ap 17,26:3
Drinkhard, Gerald A, 1948, O 6,29:3
Drinkhouse, E J Rev, 1903, Ap 20,7:5
Drinkwater, Alexander, 1954, Ap 14,29:5
Drinkwater, Alpheus W, 1962, S 25,37:1
Drinkwater, Edward C, 1950, Ag 20,77:2
Drinkwater, John, 1937, Mr 26,21:1
Drinkwater, Millard F, 1943, My 21,19:3
Drinnen, Frank J, 1962, Ag 10,19:2
Drioton, Etienne, 1961, Ja 20,29:2
Dripps, John H Dr, 1937, D 21,23:1
Dripps, Robert D, 1938, Je 12,39:3
Driscoll, Alfred R Mrs, 1959, O 14,43:4
Driscoll, Allan V, 1944, Je 9,15:4
Driscoll, Arthur, 1941, Ap 28,15:3
Driscoll, Arthur F, 1967, My 5,39:1
Driscoll, Arthur W, 1942, Jl 13,15:3
Driscoll, Augustine B, 1950, F 21,26:2
Driscoll, Bennet, 1941, F 9,48:1
Driscoll, Charles, 1948, Ag 31,23:2
Driscoll, Charles B, 1951, Ja 16,29:1
Driscoll, Charles E, 1950, N 22,26:2
Driscoll, Chrysostom, 1950, Jl 28,21:3
Driscoll, Clara Mrs, 1945, Jl 19,23:6
Driscoll, Clarence J, 1952, My 13,23:3
Driscoll, Clement J, 1939, Mr 25,15:3
Driscoll, Daniel J, 1958, Ag 26,29:1
Driscoll, Daniel W, 1925, Ag 5,17:6
Driscoll, David F, 1951, Ja 25,25:1
Driscoll, Denis J, 1958, Ja 20,23:2
Driscoll, Dennis F, 1937, Jl 12,17:2
Driscoll, Dennis P, 1925, My 24,7:2
Driscoll, Edmund F, 1952, Je 8,85:1
Driscoll, Edward A, 1946, Ja 9,24:2
Driscoll, Eugene J, 1937, Ja 12,23:2

Driscoll, Fannie, 1883, F 24,5:3
Driscoll, Florence O, 1939, Ja 7,15:2
Driscoll, Francis, 1904, S 21,1:4
Driscoll, Francis A, 1945, F 7,21:4
Driscoll, Francis G Mrs, 1940, F 12,17:6
Driscoll, Francis J, 1940, Mr 29,21:4
Driscoll, Frank J, 1940, Ag 27,21:3
Driscoll, George F, 1941, F 26,21:4
Driscoll, Harry O, 1947, Jl 25,17:5
Driscoll, Houston D, 1940, N 5,25:1
Driscoll, James C Sr, 1958, N 1,19:3
Driscoll, James F Rev Dr, 1922, Jl 6,19:6
Driscoll, James G, 1941, Ja 12,44:5
Driscoll, James J, 1949, Ag 26,20:5; 1956, Ag 15,29:4
Driscoll, James M, 1937, O 24,II,8:6
Driscoll, James P, 1948, Mr 18,27:2
Driscoll, James W (Jake), 1954, N 14,88:7
Driscoll, John, 1925, O 26,19:5
Driscoll, John F Jr, 1941, D 28,28:6
Driscoll, John J, 1943, Ap 19,19:1; 1947, Ag 3,52:2
Driscoll, John J Jr, 1950, Mr 3,25:4
Driscoll, John L, 1941, Ja 3,19:3
Driscoll, John O, 1952, Jl 14,17:3
Driscoll, Joseph, 1944, Ap 2,39:2; 1954, My 8,17:1
Driscoll, Joseph A, 1952, Ja 14,19:4
Driscoll, Joseph E, 1948, Mr 24,25:4
Driscoll, Leo B, 1941, Mr 6,21:4
Driscoll, Leo C, 1961, Mr 5,86:6
Driscoll, Margaret (Sister Cecilia Monica), 1954, Mr 30,27:5
Driscoll, Margaret T, 1959, Ja 16,27:2
Driscoll, Mary, 1952, O 6,33:6
Driscoll, Mary E, 1958, Ja 15,39:1
Driscoll, Michael A, 1949, Mr 11,25:1
Driscoll, Michael P, 1941, Mr 23,44:3
Driscoll, Paddy (Jno Leo Driscoll), 1968, Je 30,52:5
Driscoll, Paul, 1968, Jl 23,36:3
Driscoll, Timothy Jr, 1952, F 22,21:3
Driscoll, William H, 1940, Mr 17,49:2; 1950, S 8,31:1
Driscoll, William P, 1950, F 19,76:8
Driscoll, William T, 1960, Je 5,86:6
Driscoll, William V, 1957, Je 17,23:2
Driskill, Edna M Mrs, 1952, Ag 23,13:5
Drisko, Ralph B, 1948, O 8,25:2
Drisler, Mary, 1940, N 14,23:2
Drisler, W Arthur, 1960, F 16,40:1
Drittel, Julius, 1953, F 6,20:4
Dritz, John, 1965, Jl 5,17:5
Drivdahl, Frank L, 1938, D 30,15:2
Driver, Andrew H, 1952, S 10,29:3
Driver, Cecil H, 1958, O 21,33:1
Driver, Frank L Mrs, 1948, Ja 25,56:3
Driver, Harold B, 1941, F 15,15:5
Driver, Samuel Rolles Rev, 1914, F 27,11:3
Driver, W J Mrs, 1941, D 2,23:3
Driver, Wilbur B, 1949, Ag 24,26:4
Driver, Wilbur B Mrs, 1949, O 8,13:2
Driver, William S Mrs, 1957, Ja 19,15:3
Drob, Max, 1959, Je 5,27:2
Drobach, Peter Sr, 1947, N 25,32:4
Drobner, Boleslaw, 1968, Mr 23,31:4
Droege, John A, 1961, Mr 6,25:4
Droesch, Frank Sr, 1951, Mr 1,27:2
Droescher, Robert Jr, 1958, Jl 29,23:2
Droescher, Severin Mrs, 1950, F 21,25:1
Droge, Joseph, 1958, O 6,31:4
Drogheda, Earl of (H C P Moore), 1957, N 23,19:7
Drohan, Edward A, 1942, Mr 7,17:3
Drohan, John P, 1957, F 26,29:3
Drohan, Thomas D, 1952, D 23,23:5
Drohan, William F, 1959, Jl 26,69:1
Droit, Felix, 1911, Ap 8,13:4
Droke, Maxwell S, 1959, N 10,47:1
Drolet, Bernard J, 1944, F 7,15:6
Drolet, Godias J, 1968, Mr 10,93:1
Drolet, Marie J Mrs, 1937, S 26,II,8:7
Dromeshauser, George, 1946, Mr 18,21:3
Dromgoole, Anna F Mrs, 1939, Je 6,23:6
Dromgoole, Frank, 1920, S 23,13:4
Drone, Eaton Sylvester, 1917, F 3,13:4
Droogan, Joseph W, 1940, Ag 28,19:5
Droogan, Phil M, 1951, Mr 10,13:4
Drooz, Irma G, 1964, S 13,86:8
Dropkin, Celia Mrs, 1956, Ag 19,92:8
Dropkin, John J Mrs, 1956, O 1,27:4
Droppers, G, 1927, Jl 8,19:5
Droppers, Garrett Mrs, 1939, Ja 15,38:5
Drosey, Hugh M Sr, 1948, Je 12,15:5
Droshnicop, Samuel, 1937, N 12,21:2
Drosin, Louis, 1958, Ap 19,21:6
Drosnes, Abraham J, 1963, D 26,27:3
Drossaerts, Arthur J, 1940, S 9,15:6
Drossman, Ethel D Mrs, 1948, S 20,25:3
Drossopoulos, John, 1939, Jl 29,15:4
Drost, George T, 1951, N 6,29:6
Droste, Charles F, 1944, O 30,19:5
Droste, Harry C, 1963, My 4,25:3
Drotar, John, 1947, My 26,22:3
Drotar, John Sr Mrs, 1951, O 16,31:3
Drouant, Alphonse, 1938, D 30,16:1
Drouant, Jean, 1949, Je 29,27:4
Drouet, Felix P, 1944, My 27,15:5
Drouet, Henry, 1942, Ag 12,19:1
Drouet, Henry Mrs, 1940, Ag 29,19:6; 1967, F 22,29:3
Drouet, Robert, 1914, Ag 18,9:6
Drought, David H, 1949, O 14,28:6
Drought, James M, 1943, My 2,44:7
Drought, James T Sr, 1944, Je 16,19:2
Drought, Thomas W, 1943, Ja 28,19:3
Drouin, Alphonse E, 1946, S 20,31:4
Drouin, Edward, 1905, Ag 12,7:4
Drouin, Wilfred G, 1958, Ag 28,27:3
Droutman, Ben, 1959, Ag 12,29:4
Drouyn-de-Lhuys, Edward, 1881, Mr 3,5:3
Drown, Edward S Mrs, 1959, My 18,27:1
Drown, Henry C, 1943, Ja 14,21:5
Drown, John H, 1943, O 9,13:6
Drown, T M, 1904, N 17,9:4
Drown, W A, 1879, D 16,4:7
Drowne, H Russell Jr Brig-Gen, 1968, Ap 9,47:1
Drowne, Henry B, 1948, D 28,21:2
Drowne, Sarah A, 1906, Ja 29,9:4
Droysen, J G, 1884, Je 20,2:2
Droz, Lucien Father, 1951, N 21,5:8
Drozdoff, Vladimir, 1960, Mr 12,21:6
Drozdov, Nicolai, 1954, Ja 6,31:4
Drozniak, Edward, 1966, N 2,45:1
Druce, Arthur, 1946, My 9,21:2
Druce, G Sir, 1932, Mr 1,23:1
Druce, H, 1931, Ap 7,27:1
Druck, David, 1943, Je 18,21:4
Druck, Sam, 1959, Ap 14,35:3
Druckenmiller, Barton W, 1964, N 11,43:3
Drucker, Adolphus, 1903, D 11,9:7
Drucker, Isadore J, 1960, O 30,86:4
Drucker, Jack, 1962, Ja 24,21:6
Drucker, Joseph, 1948, Ap 8,25:1
Drucker, Lewis, 1952, Ag 12,19:2
Drucker, Max, 1965, F 4,31:1
Drucker, Oscar, 1945, F 14,19:4
Drucker, Philip A, 1966, F 6,92:6
Drucker, Wilhelmina, 1925, D 8,25:5
Druckerman, Leonard J, 1956, Jl 31,23:4
Drucklieb, Charles A, 1914, F 20,9:4
Druckman, Jacob, 1962, Je 18,25:4
Druckman, Max, 1966, Je 10,45:2
Druckman, Max Mrs, 1965, N 28,88:5
Drudy, George T, 1925, F 6,17:5
Drueck, Charles J, 1945, Jl 1,18:3
Drueding, Albert J, 1948, O 18,23:4
Drueding, Caspar F, 1963, Je 7,31:1
Drueding, Charles C, 1939, S 28,25:5
Drueding, Harry C, 1945, S 25,26:2
Drueding, Henry G, 1939, My 19,21:5
Drueding, Walter F, 1950, Ag 13,76:2
Druehl, Amanda Mrs, 1956, N 5,31:5
Druehl, Fred H, 1950, Mr 9,30:5
Druffel, John H, 1967, My 17,47:4
Druge, Beatrice M, 1943, O 13,23:1
Druhan, Thomas L, 1925, Je 18,21:6
Druie, Richard, 1951, N 20,31:3
Druitt, T Harry, 1944, Je 21,19:1
Drukenbrod, Arthur B, 1947, Mr 20,27:1
Drukenbrod, Millard F, 1958, F 18,27:4
Drukenbrod, Sterling S, 1946, My 21,23:3
Drukker, Dow H, 1963, Ja 12,14:8
Drukker, Millie D Mrs, 1941, S 9,23:4
Drull, L C Mrs, 1941, Jl 31,13:3
Drum, Andrew B, 1955, Ja 24,23:4
Drum, George E, 1938, Mr 18,19:4
Drum, Hugh A, 1951, O 4,1:2
Drum, Hugh A Mrs, 1960, Je 13,27:5
Drum, John D, 1952, F 26,27:3
Drum, Redmond J, 1946, My 19,40:6
Drum, Richard C Brig-Gen, 1909, O 16,9:4
Drum, Walter Rev, 1921, D 11,22:3
Drumgould, John J, 1947, Jl 23,23:5
Drumheller, Allen Sr, 1955, O 2,87:3
Drumheller, Clarence W, 1950, S 27,31:1
Drumheller, Jack V, 1949, F 26,15:5
Drumheller, Leon, 1944, Ap 21,19:3
Drumm, Elizabeth Mrs, 1940, Jl 22,17:1
Drumm, George, 1959, D 18,29:2
Drumm, James H, 1964, N 28,21:5
Drumm, John J, 1937, Ag 13,17:3
Drumm, John M, 1956, N 1,39:5
Drumm, Thomas Porter, 1952, D 28,51:4
Drummer, Charles H, 1904, Ja 5,9:5
Drummon, Chester W Mrs, 1943, F 8,19:4
Drummond, Albert A, 1945, N 4,43:2
Drummond, Alex M, 1956, N 30,23:2
Drummond, Alfred J, 1950, Ap 15,15:6
Drummond, Andrew L, 1921, F 13,22:3
Drummond, Aubrey J, 1960, Mr 5,19:3
Drummond, Edmund J, 1938, D 15,27:5
Drummond, Flora Mrs, 1949, Ja 18,23:1
Drummond, Florence, 1954, F 19,34:1
Drummond, Frances M, 1947, Ja 17,24:2
Drummond, Fred Lindsey, 1904, Ja 25,7:7
Drummond, Frederic L Mrs, 1909, Mr 9,9:5
Drummond, Geoffrey H, 1941, Ap 23,21:3
Drummond, George Edward Gen, 1919, F 19,13:5
Drummond, H Prof, 1897, Mr 12,7:1
Drummond, Harry R, 1948, N 26,23:4
Drummond, Henry, 1961, Ja 22,V,13:2
Drummond, Howard, 1947, My 6,27:1
Drummond, Hugh, 1950, N 19,92:6
Drummond, Huntly R, 1957, D 11,31:4
Drummond, Isaac R, 1950, Mr 31,32:6
Drummond, J H, 1902, O 26,7:5
Drummond, James H, 1938, N 7,6:6
Drummond, John L, 1905, N 13,9:5
Drummond, John N, 1904, Ja 20,9:6
Drummond, John P, 1950, Ap 21,23:2
Drummond, Lady, 1942, Je 11,23:5
Drummond, Laura W, 1961, F 6,21:1
Drummond, Maldwin Mrs, 1915, S 20,9:5
Drummond, Mary J Mrs, 1944, Ap 16,35:3
Drummond, Michael J, 1916, Ja 23,17:3
Drummond, Nelson L, 1951, Ja 25,25:1
Drummond, Robert J, 1951, Jl 24,25:2
Drummond, Robert R, 1946, My 12,44:3
Drummond, Thomas J, 1916, Ag 7,9:6
Drummond, Thomas S, 1939, F 7,19:4
Drummond, Victor Arthur Wellington Mrs, 1912, Mr 27,13:5
Drummond, W H Dr, 1907, Ap 7,9:6
Drummond, William J, 1938, N 28,15:3
Drummond, Winslow, 1956, Jl 11,29:3
Drummond-Grant, Ann, 1959, S 12,21:4
Drummond-Hay, Grace M H, 1946, F 13,23:1
Drumont, Edouard A, 1917, F 6,9:2
Drury, Alfred, 1944, D 25,19:3
Drury, Aubrey, 1959, O 25,87:1
Drury, Charles Carter Adm, 1914, My 19,9:6
Drury, Charles K Mrs, 1947, O 27,21:3
Drury, Charles M, 1941, My 18,45:2
Drury, Daunbeney D, 1946, Ap 19,29:3
Drury, Deborah S Dr, 1915, Ag 24,11:6
Drury, F S E Mrs, 1930, O 14,29:2
Drury, Francis E Mrs, 1943, Ap 17,17:5
Drury, Francis K, 1954, S 4,11:3
Drury, Francis S E, 1941, N 2,55:5
Drury, Frederick W Mrs, 1950, O 19,31:1
Drury, George Dr, 1913, O 21,9:6
Drury, Gerald B, 1950, Ap 6,29:1
Drury, Harold M, 1950, Ap 16,105:1
Drury, Henry G, 1941, Ja 31,19:3
Drury, James C (Prof), 1967, Ap 11,47:1
Drury, James Creighton, 1967, Ap 19,45:4
Drury, James V, 1950, Ja 18,32:2
Drury, John, 1941, O 12,52:2
Drury, John D Rev, 1909, Mr 22,7:5
Drury, John E, 1955, S 17,15:2
Drury, Joseph A, 1961, F 28,33:3
Drury, Joseph F, 1958, Je 20,23:2
Drury, Martin J, 1961, F 27,27:3
Drury, Maynard K, 1966, D 13,47:2
Drury, Michael F, 1944, Ja 3,21:2
Drury, Percy R Mrs, 1956, Jl 16,21:4
Drury, R B, 1933, Ag 20,26:1
Drury, Robert H Mrs, 1950, D 26,23:1
Drury, Samuel S (por), 1938, F 21,19:2
Drury, Samuel S Mrs, 1956, Ja 23,25:5
Drury, T Capt, 1881, S 29,5:2
Drury, Theodore F, 1953, My 11,27:3
Drury, Vincent K, 1966, D 31,19:2
Drury, Walter J, 1959, O 27,37:4
Drury, Walter M, 1946, Jl 18,25:5
Drury, William H, 1960, D 5,31:3
Druscovich (Detective), 1881, D 31,1:3
Drushel, Andrew, 1940, Je 21,21:2
Druskin, Sidney, 1962, Ap 4,43:2
Druss, Harry, 1958, N 10,29:2
Druss, Louis J, 1968, S 15,84:5
Drutzu, Serban T, 1953, Jl 10,19:3
Druva, Julys, 1950, Ag 4,21:3
Druxbury, George H, 1956, Ap 28,17:6
Drwal, Matthew, 1962, Jl 7,17:3
Dry, Morris E Mrs, 1967, Mr 12,86:8
Dryander, Ernest Dr, 1922, S 5,17:6
Dryden, Ethelyn, 1966, Ag 10,41:1
Dryden, F F, 1932, Jl 20,15:1
Dryden, George B, 1959, S 10,35:6
Dryden, George B Mrs, 1950, Ja 23,23:5
Dryden, Hugh L, 1965, D 3,35:4
Dryden, I Thurston, 1947, Ag 1,17:3
Dryden, John F (funl, N 28,13:5), 1911, N 26,
Dryden, John F, 1947, Mr 18,27:4
Dryden, John F Mrs, 1916, Ja 17,11:4
Dryden, Joshua, 1879, F 18,5:1
Dryden, Leo, 1939, Ap 22,17:3
Dryden, William G, 1962, O 26,31:5
Dryer, Edwin J, 1947, Je 18,25:5
Dryer, Edwin J Mrs, 1957, Je 26,31:3
Dryer, H James, 1947, S 25,29:4
Dryer, Joseph H, 1961, My 18,35:5
Dryer, Rufus K, 1937, O 28,23:3
Dryfoos, Henry Jr, 1952, Ag 27,27:2
Dryfoos, Jack A, 1937, Jl 19,15:5
Dryfoos, Millie S Mrs, 1939, F 3,15:3
Dryfoos, Nathan I, 1949, Mr 24,28:2
Dryfoos, O E, 1928, N 4,II,7:2
Dryfoos, Orvil E (funl plans;trb, My 27,29:1), My 26,1:4
Dryfoos, Sidney J, 1962, Ja 3,33:3
Dryfoos, Sidney O E, 1957, S 21,19:1
Dryfoos, Stephen M, 1961, O 22,86:6
Dryfuss, Barney J, 1950, O 15,104:3

Drymon, Ira Mrs, 1952, F 23,11:3
Drynan, Darrel P, 1947, F 3,19:3
Drynan, William R, 1949, Ap 15,23:2
Drysdale, Harry H, 1945, O 7,44:2
Drysdale, Hugh P Mrs, 1953, Ja 5,21:1
Drysdale, John, 1922, Ag 28,11:6
Drysdale, Robert A Jr, 1965, Ja 23,25:4
Drysdale, Robert A Sr, 1964, My 24,92:5
Drysdale, Ronald S, 1955, F 22,21:1
Drysdale, W S Rev, 1882, Ap 7,5:2
Drysdale, William, 1901, S 21,7:3
Drysdale, William F, 1947, Jl 5,11:4
Drysdale, William N, 1953, Ja 15,27:6
Dryshpel, John, 1951, Ja 31,25:4
Dsincsics, Desider Mrs, 1951, My 4,27:4
D'Spain, H Glenn, 1948, Ja 16,21:1
Dua, David (cor, Ag 25,37:3), 1966, Ag 24,45:2
Dua, Octave, 1922, Mr 14,15:3
Duane, A Dr, 1926, Je 12,15:5
Duane, Bob, 1950, Ap 22,19:4
Duane, Charles W Rev, 1915, Je 20,15:6
Duane, F, 1928, Je 17,II,7:1
Duane, J C Gen, 1897, N 9,7:6
Duane, James C, 1953, Mr 2,23:5
Duane, John, 1950, D 27,27:1
Duane, Joseph M, 1912, D 3,15:4
Duane, Leon E, 1952, N 30,88:4
Duane, Patrick J, 1949, My 31,24:3
Duane, Russell, 1938, Ja 20,24:3
Duane, Russell Mrs, 1959, O 27,37:2
Duane, W, 1935, Mr 8,22:2
Duane, William J, 1865, S 28,4:3; 1947, Je 28,13:4
Duane, William J Mrs, 1961, N 23,31:5
Duane, William Mrs, 1953, F 28,17:3
Duane, William N, 1944, Jl 7,15:5
Duane, William N Mrs, 1942, Jl 24,19:1
Duarte Costa, Carlos, 1961, Mr 28,35:3
Dubail, Y, 1934, Ja 8,17:1
Dubaki, Henrietta Mrs, 1917, Jl 21,11:2
Du Barail, Gen, 1902, F 1,9:6
Du Barry, Joseph N, 1961, D 27,27:3
DuBarry, William H, 1958, F 7,21:3
Dubb, Thomas, 1944, Je 18,36:1
Dubbels, Benjamin F, 1953, My 20,29:2
Dubbs, Carbon P, 1962, Ag 25,19:4
Dubbs, Harry, 1953, Je 21,84:7
Dubbs, Henry A, 1939, N 12,48:7
Dubbs, Joseph H Dr, 1910, Ap 10,13:2
Dube, John, 1946, F 14,26:2
Dube, Lionel C, 1951, D 3,31:3
Dube, Morris, 1938, N 6,49:2
Dube, Newman, 1966, N 10,47:4
Dube, Richard C Sr, 1963, S 27,29:3
Dubelbeiss, Eugene J, 1939, Ap 14,23:1
Dubell, Charles B, 1952, Ap 1,29:1
Dubensky, Arcady, 1966, O 15,29:5
Duberstein, Morris Mrs, 1957, N 28,31:3
Dubert, Frank E, 1957, D 6,29:3
Dubetsky, Michael F, 1937, Mr 9,23:4
Dubin, Al, 1945, F 12,19:1
Dubin, David, 1959, Jl 18,15:4
Dubin, Henry, 1963, Ap 23,37:2
Dubin, Ida F, 1964, Ag 30,92:8
Dubin, Julius, 1947, Je 11,27:2
Dubin, Michael S, 1967, My 5,39:1
Dubini, Carlos, 1949, Je 3,25:2
Dubins, Louis, 1953, Mr 14,15:4
Dubins, Louis Mrs, 1949, N 29,29:4
Dubinsky, David, 1960, N 29,37:5
Dubinsky, Hyman, 1955, Mr 20,88:4
Dubinsky, Jacob, 1947, N 25,32:2
Dubinsky, Vladimir, 1938, Ja 11,23:6
Dubiny, Ernest P, 1944, Ap 16,41:1
Dubkovetsky, Fyodor I, 1960, Mr 7,29:5
Dublan, John M, 1957, Ja 9,31:3
Duble, Lawrence A, 1948, F 19,23:5
Dublin, Louis I Mrs (mem ser set, S 2,23:2), 1960, Ag 21,84:4
Dublirer, Samuel, 1947, S 3,25:2
Dubois, A Ford, 1948, Jl 14,24:2
Dubois, Albert, 1944, F 15,17:6
DuBois, Allen Corson Mrs, 1968, Je 8,31:4
Du Bois, Alvan Preston, 1907, N 12,9:5
Dubois, Anatole, 1958, N 11,30:4
Du Bois, Anson Rev Dr, 1905, My 2,11:6
Du Bois, Arthur, 1949, F 6,76:6
DuBois, Arthur Mrs, 1955, F 17,27:5
DuBois, Arthur W Sr, 1957, F 20,33:4
Du Bois, Augustus J, 1915, O 20,11:4
Dubois, Austin, 1943, Ap 17,17:5
Dubois, Benjamin, 1904, Ja 6,2:2
Du Bois, Charles A, 1950, F 19,77:1
Du Bois, Charles A Mrs, 1945, Mr 16,15:2
DuBois, Charles B, 1942, Je 11,23:4
DuBois, Charles B Mrs, 1942, Je 11,23:4
Dubois, Charles F, 1940, Mr 31,46:3
DuBois, Charles F, 1954, F 6,19:3
Du Bois, Charles G, 1940, D 24,15:1
DuBois, Charles Mrs, 1950, Ja 23,23:5
Dubois, Charles W Mrs, 1948, Je 18,23:4
Du Bois, Clarence M, 1939, Jl 4,13:4
DuBois, Clinton D, 1948, F 27,22:3
Du Bois, Coert, 1960, Mr 7,29:1
Du Bois, Cornelius, 1880, F 13,4:7; 1882, My 6,2:5
Du Bois, Cornelius D, 1915, Jl 28,9:4
DuBois, Daniel E, 1949, Je 8,29:2
DuBois, David K, 1944, My 25,21:2
DuBois, Delafield, 1965, Ja 8,29:5
DuBois, Durwood C, 1967, S 9,31:4
DuBois, E Lounsbery, 1956, D 31,13:5
Du Bois, Edward R, 1944, Jl 5,17:5
Du Bois, Edwin W Mrs, 1958, My 24,21:3
DuBois, Eli Mrs, 1953, N 13,27:4
Du Bois, Elizabeth P Mrs, 1953, Ag 25,21:1
Dubois, Emilie, 1871, N 13,5:2
Du Bois, Emma P Mrs, 1939, S 6,23:3
Dubois, Eugene, 1941, Mr 27,23:1
Dubois, Eugene F, 1941, Ja 18,15:1
DuBois, Eugene F, 1959, F 13,27:3
DuBois, Eugene Mrs, 1950, My 26,23:4
Dubois, Evan C, 1945, F 18,34:2
Dubois, F T, 1930, F 15,17:3
DuBois, Floyd R, 1952, O 24,23:4
Dubois, Francis E, 1953, F 2,21:3
DuBois, Frank, 1952, Mr 12,27:3
DuBois, Frank A, 1953, F 4,27:4
DuBois, Frank R, 1941, Ap 2,23:3
DuBois, Franklin S, 1961, Je 25,76:2
Du Bois, Fred, 1950, F 21,25:3
DuBois, Gaston F (will, N 10,15:2), 1953, N 2,25:3
Du Bois, George S, 1948, D 24,17:4
Dubois, George W, 1949, Mr 21,23:5
Du Bois, Gertrude A (will), 1938, Ap 13,45:2
du Bois, Guy P (corr, Jl 21,21:5), 1958, Jl 19,15:4
Du Bois, Guy P Mrs, 1950, S 11,23:6
Du Bois, H A, 1884, Ja 14,2:4
Du Bois, Henri Pene, 1906, Jl 21,7:4
Du Bois, Henry C, 1951, N 4,87:1
Dubois, Henry D C, 1942, My 24,43:2
DuBois, Henry I, 1943, N 28,68:4
Du Bois, Henry Joseph Church, 1924, Ag 8,13:6
Du Bois, Henry P, 1938, Ja 9,42:4
DuBois, Horace A, 1952, Jl 20,52:8
Dubois, J Bourdon Mrs, 1940, S 10,23:1
Du Bois, J V, 1879, Ag 1,5:2
Du Bois, J Van Wyck, 1946, S 28,17:5
Dubois, Jack V, 1966, Ag 18,35:2
Du Bois, James T, 1920, My 28,13:4
duBois, Jean M F, 1957, O 29,31:2
Dubois, John, 1947, Je 27,21:4
Dubois, John E, 1952, O 21,29:1
Dubois, Joseph, 1955, Ja 4,21:4
Du Bois, Joseph L, 1943, O 13,23:3
Dubois, Jules (funl plans, Ag 19,33:3), 1966, Ag 17, 39:3
Dubois, L E, 1929, S 24,31:3
Dubois, Lemuel E, 1952, F 17,84:6
DuBois, Leo C, 1941, Ja 11,17:4
DuBois, Leon Mrs, 1952, F 12,27:3
DuBois, Lester W, 1951, D 5,35:3
Dubois, Lewis W, 1952, Mr 22,13:5
Dubois, Louis, 1946, Ja 26,13:1
DuBois, Malcolm T, 1951, S 9,89:2
Du Bois, Marie, 1938, F 5,15:5
Dubois, Marie A, 1943, Ap 23,17:3
Du Bois, Mary, 1942, Ja 8,21:3
DuBois, Mary C, 1959, Je 21,92:7
Du Bois, Mary S, 1938, F 1,21:4
Dubois, Matthew H, 1943, Ag 11,19:4
Dubois, Odillon, 1954, My 31,13:3
Du Bois, Orin B, 1950, Mr 7,27:4
Dubois, Paul, 1905, My 24,9:6
Dubois, Ralph N, 1954, Ag 16,17:3
DuBois, Richard, 1965, Mr 26,35:2
DuBois, Robert C, 1947, N 15,17:5
Dubois, Samuel W, 1951, D 22,15:4
Du Bois, Sol E Mrs, 1946, Ag 15,25:4
DuBois, Theodore, 1874, D 14,1:6
DuBois, Thomas R, 1962, Ja 1,23:4
Du Bois, Thomas T, 1955, Ag 4,25:1
DuBois, Wallace, 1951, D 27,21:2
DuBois, William E B (funeral, Ag 30,21:4), 1963, Ag 28,33:1
Dubois, William H, 1942, F 11,21:3
Dubonnet, Marius Mrs, 1945, Mr 10,17:4
Du Bos, Charles M, 1939, Ag 18,19:2
DuBose, Beverly M, 1953, Ap 2,27:2
DuBose, Henry W, 1960, F 12,27:4
Dubose, Horace M, 1941, Ja 16,21:2
Du Bose, Joshua H, 1939, N 20,19:5
DuBose, Lucille, 1952, F 27,27:4
Du Bose, William Porcher Rev Dr, 1918, Ag 22,11:5
Du Bosque, Francis L, 1940, Ap 14,44:7
DuBosque, Steele, 1967, N 11,33:1
Dubost, Antonin, 1921, Ap 16,11:4
Dubourg, Cardinal, 1921, S 24,11:2
Dubov, Leopold, 1955, O 16,35:5
Dubov, Martin H, 1951, Ja 2,23:3
Dubovsky, Benjamin, 1963, S 13,30:1
Dubowy, Joseph, 1955, Mr 2,27:3
Dubreuil, Paul B, 1950, S 22,31:1
Dubreul, Amedee, 1885, Mr 23,5:4
Dubreul, J P Rev, 1878, Ap 21,7:1
Dubrevil, Walter N, 1955, My 3,31:1
Dubrey, Elmer, 1951, N 3,6:4
Dubroff, Nathan, 1962, Je 24,68:6
Dubrow, Benjamin, 1958, Jl 22,27:1
Dubrow, Harry, 1948, My 14,23:4
Dubrow, Isidor M, 1966, N 10,47:3
Dubrowsky, David H, 1950, Je 24,13:4
Dubrul, Ernest F, 1954, Mr 10,25:3
DuBrul, Stephen Mrs, 1959, N 17,35:6
Dubsky, Joseph P, 1953, Mr 31,31:3
Dubuc, Jean, 1958, Ag 29,23:2
Dubufe, Edouard, 1883, Ag 14,2:4
Dubufe, Guillaume, 1909, My 28,9:6
DuBuque, Jean H, 1960, Jl 17,62:2
Dubusc, Arthur L, 1956, Mr 11,88:4
Dubwe, Joseph Sir, 1914, Ja 8,11:4
Duc de Giuise (funl, Ag 11,6:3), 1872, Ag 8,5:3
Duca, Cino del, 1967, My 25,47:5
Ducachet, H W Rev Dr, 1865, D 17,5:5
Du Cane, John, 1947, Ap 7,24:3
Ducas, Benjamin P, 1921, Je 26,22:4
Ducasse, Roger, 1954, Jl 21,27:3
Ducassi, Juan E, 1939, Mr 26,III,6:6
Ducceschi, Virgilio, 1952, Je 23,19:5
Duce, James T, 1965, Ag 17,33:1
Ducey, Brian J, 1958, My 21,33:2
Ducey, John, 1956, Jl 10,31:3
Ducey, Julia F Mrs, 1958, Ja 19,86:5
Ducey, Michael J Mrs, 1947, F 22,13:1
Ducey, Patrick A, 1903, Jl 13,7:5
Du Chaillu, Paul, 1903, My 1,9:4
Duchaine, Joseph P, 1961, Mr 25,25:3
Duchamp, Gaston E (J Villon), 1963, Je 10,31:1
Duchamp, Marcel, 1968, O 3,1:5
Ducharme, Andre L C, 1948, Mr 27,13:6
Ducharne, Pedro, 1940, Mr 10,48:2
Duchatel, Mme, 1878, Mr 31,10:3
Duchemin, Henry P, 1950, My 22,21:5
Duchemin, L (Fervacques), 1876, S 9,4:7
Duchemin, Nicholas M, 1965, My 18,39:4
du Chene-de Vere, Aroldo, 1961, F 13,27:5
Duchesne, Elizabeth Mrs, 1952, D 19,31:3
Duchesne, Ernest, 1946, Ag 26,23:1
Duchess Dowager Decazes, 1873, S 7,1:2
Duchess of Aosta, Ex-Queen of Spain, 1876, N 9,4:7
Duchess of Inverness, 1873, Ag 4,4:6
Duchess of Leeds, 1874, Ap 26,10:4
Duchich, Mitchell M, 1960, N 16,41:1
Duchich, Y Ovan, 1943, Ap 8,23:1
Duchin, Eddy, 1951, F 10,13:4
Duchin, Edward F Mrs, 1937, Ag 4,19:1
Duchin, Maurice, 1957, Ag 24,15:1
Duchinsky, John, 1952, Ap 8,29:4
Duchmann, Charles, 1941, My 25,37:1
Duchon, Vladimir A, 1959, O 18,86:3
Duchovny, Moshe, 1960, N 3,39:4
Duchscherer, George, 1941, Ap 19,15:1
Ducie, Earl of (Hy Jno Moreton), 1921, O 29,13:6
Ducie, Earl of (C H B Moreton), 1952, Je 19,27:2
Duck, Frank J G, 1955, N 16,35:5
Duck, William B Sr, 1952, Je 22,68:4
Duckart, Henry F, 1958, Jl 6,56:6
Duckat, Lipman Mrs, 1954, D 28,23:2
Duckat, Rose E, 1950, My 30,18:3
Ducker, Harry, 1937, N 18,23:4
Ducker, Harry T, 1939, Ap 26,23:3
Ducker, Henry, 1942, O 19,19:5
Ducker, Rae (Mrs E B Weiskopf), 1961, Mr 8,33:2
Duckett, Henry, 1940, S 4,23:2
Duckham, Alexander, 1945, F 3,11:4
Duckler, Henry E, 1946, Mr 8,21:2
Duckman, Leonard, 1963, Je 18,37:4
Duckrey, Tanner G, 1958, Ja 11,17:2
Duckwall, Herbert R, 1950, O 2,23:3
Duckwall, J McCarty Mrs, 1953, Jl 29,23:1
Duckworth, Frances, 1940, S 27,16:3
Duckworth, James Sir, 1915, Ja 2,9:6
Duckworth, James W, 1945, D 27,19:3
Duckworth, Milton, 1955, Ag 28,85:2
Duckworth, Willard D, 1940, N 12,23:5
Duclos, David E, 1941, Ag 4,13:2
Duclos, Frederic N, 1951, N 19,23:5
Duclos, Vivian G (Sister Charles), 1953, N 16,25:3
Ducoff, Isidore, 1959, Jl 17,21:4
Ducore, Fannie Mrs, 1937, D 11,19:4
Du Costal, Guy R, 1945, My 29,15:4
Ducote, Richard J, 1937, Mr 27,15:5
DuCoty, Joseph, 1949, N 15,25:4
Du Couedic, Robert V, 1939, Mr 6,48:5
du Cros, Arthur P, 1955, O 30,89:1
Ducrot, A A Gen, 1882, Ag 18,5:5
Ducrot, Frank (T F Fritz), 1939, My 25,25:5
Ducuing, Francois, 1875, O 20,1:6
Duda, Michael, 1968, N 14,47:4
Duda, Wilfred J, 1953, Je 9,27:4
Dudden, Frederick H, 1955, Je 23,29:3
Dudding, Horatio N Adm, 1917, S 12,11:3
Duddington, Joseph, 1953, Ap 6,19:4
Duddy, George R, 1955, F 16,29:3
Duddy, James J, 1943, My 15,15:5
Duddy, James P, 1968, Ap 12,35:3
Duddy, John J, 1946, S 24,29:2
Dudensing, Frank, 1940, N 17,48:3
Dudensing, Richard 3d, 1958, Je 18,33:3
Duder, J Douglas, 1961, N 17,35:2
Duderstadt, August P, 1955, Jl 14,23:5

Dudevant, Baron, 1871, Ap 12,1:2
Dudey, Harry E Mrs, 1949, Ag 5,19:2
Dudgeon, Edward H, 1940, Mr 24,31:2
Dudley, Albert H, 1945, O 6,13:6
Dudley, Albertus T, 1955, F 12,15:3
Dudley, Alfred L, 1944, Ag 8,17:5
Dudley, Benjamin W, 1965, N 12,48:1
Dudley, Blandina Mrs, 1863, Mr 19,8:2
Dudley, Boyd Jr, 1948, D 3,25:2
Dudley, Bruce, 1964, Je 25,33:4
Dudley, Burton R, 1949, F 11,23:1
Dudley, Charles, 1952, Mr 13,29:4
Dudley, Charles B Dr, 1909, D 22,11:5
Dudley, Charles B Mrs, 1940, Ag 27,21:5
Dudley, Charles E, 1938, Ap 2,15:5
Dudley, Charles M, 1957, Ap 6,19:2
Dudley, E Lawrence, 1947, Je 24,23:4
Dudley, Earl of, 1932, Je 30,23:1
Dudley, Earle B, 1955, Je 7,33:5
Dudley, Ed (Edw B), 1963, O 27,89:1
Dudley, Edith S, 1967, Jl 11,37:1
Dudley, Edward B Jr, 1950, N 24,27:1
Dudley, Elbridge G, 1960, Ag 23,30:1
Dudley, Eric, 1947, My 22,27:5
Dudley, Frank A, 1945, S 22,17:6
Dudley, Frank H, 1938, O 29,19:6
Dudley, George, 1960, My 9,29:1
Dudley, George F, 1940, N 20,21:4
Dudley, Gertrude, 1945, Je 21,19:2
Dudley, Gladys, 1961, S 4,15:6
Dudley, Guilford S, 1961, My 1,29:3
Dudley, H F Rev, 1884, My 5,4:7
Dudley, Halwood, 1915, O 11,9:6
Dudley, Harry C, 1968, Je 21,41:2
Dudley, Harry H, 1952, Jl 2,25:1
Dudley, Harry J, 1945, Ag 10,15:5
Dudley, Henry L Mrs, 1941, F 6,21:5; 1949, Ag 3,23:4
Dudley, Hugh R Jr, 1961, S 12,33:1
Dudley, Ian, 1956, My 24,36:5
Dudley, Irving B, 1911, N 28,13:4
Dudley, Irving B Mrs, 1960, Ja 27,33:5
Dudley, Ivan R, 1961, D 27,27:1
Dudley, James P, 1952, Ap 28,19:1
Dudley, John, 1942, S 23,25:2; 1961, F 24,21:8
Dudley, John H M, 1954, Ag 25,27:5
Dudley, John H M Mrs, 1943, Jl 13,22:2
Dudley, John Leonard, 1911, Ag 20,II,9:6
Dudley, John S, 1966, My 3,47:1
Dudley, Joseph P, 1907, F 15,11:4
Dudley, Lyman O, 1963, My 7,43:2
Dudley, Lyman P, 1960, Mr 19,21:4
Dudley, M B, 1946, Jl 18,25:2
Dudley, Nathan A M Brig-Gen, 1910, Ap 30,9:5
Dudley, Oscar A, 1944, O 29,43:2
Dudley, Paul, 1959, My 19,33:3
Dudley, Pemberton, 1945, Mr 10,17:5
Dudley, Pemberton Dr, 1907, Mr 26,9:6
Dudley, Pendleton (mem ser, D 20,43:1), 1966, D 12,47:2
Dudley, Pendleton Mrs, 1954, Ja 29,19:3
Dudley, Peter Mrs, 1948, D 13,23:2
Dudley, Phil E, 1953, D 19,15:6
Dudley, Plimmon Henry Dr (funl, F 27,17:4), 1924, F 26,17:3
Dudley, Ralph, 1952, Je 8,86:8
Dudley, Robert Y, 1955, N 16,35:4
Dudley, Samuel W, 1963, D 25,33:4
Dudley, Samuel W Mrs, 1940, Je 4,23:2
Dudley, T U Bp, 1904, Ja 23,2:4
Dudley, Thomas V Bp, 1919, D 26,11:5
Dudley, Tom, 1950, Mr 4,17:3
Dudley, Walter B, 1944, Ja 5,17:3
Dudley, Walter W, 1945, Ag 22,23:3
Dudley, Warren S Rev, 1925, Mr 25,21:4; 1925, Mr 26,23:5
Dudley, Wesley C, 1938, F 11,23:2
Dudley, Willem E, 1938, My 9,17:5
Dudley, William, 1949, Ag 7,61:2
Dudley, William A, 1953, Ag 8,11:3
Dudley, William A Mrs, 1943, Ja 16,13:4
Dudley, William Frederick Dr, 1912, O 23,13:5
Dudley, William H Mrs, 1961, D 21,27:1
Dudley, William L Dr, 1914, S 10,9:5
Dudley, William R Prof, 1911, Je 5,11:6
Dudley, William Wade Gen, 1909, D 16,9:3
Dudrap, Charles W, 1949, D 16,31:4
Dudrey, John J, 1937, Ja 17,II,9:2
Dudukaloff, Andrew A Mrs, 1953, Ap 24,23:2
Dudziak, Ignatius, 1952, Jl 2,25:6
Duebi, Henri, 1942, Ja 25,40:7
Duechler, Harold C, 1958, O 5,87:2
Dueck, Gernhart Mrs, 1958, Mr 11,29:4
Duel, A B, 1936, Ap 12,II,10:1
Duel, Arthur B Mrs, 1963, N 23,29:5
Duel, Frederick H, 1952, My 15,31:3
Duel, Martha E, 1944, D 1,24:2
Dueland, Rudolf, 1949, N 9,27:2
Duell, Charles H, 1920, Ja 30,15:4
Duell, Holland S, 1942, N 26,27:3
Duell, Holland S Mrs, 1965, Ap 18,80:7
Duell, James C, 1939, My 9,23:2
Duell, Prentice, 1960, Ap 20,39:1
Duell, William C, 1959, Jl 19,68:4
Duell, William C Mrs, 1959, Jl 29,29:4
Duemling, Enno A, 1946, O 23,27:3
Duenas y Argumendo, Juan A, 1941, Jl 5,11:6
Duer, Alexander, 1943, D 16,27:1
Duer, Beverly C Mrs, 1949, O 2,81:2
Duer, Bruce W, 1919, F 16,20:2
Duer, Caroline K, 1956, Ja 23,25:2
Duer, Catherine A, 1903, Ja 24,9:5
Duer, Edward A, 1944, Mr 31,21:3
Duer, Henrietta, 1950, Je 22,27:4
Duer, Henry L Mrs, 1940, O 8,25:4
Duer, Henry Lay Mrs, 1914, F 24,11:5
Duer, James Gore King, 1907, My 28,9:5
Duer, James Gore King Mrs, 1908, Mr 27,9:4
Duer, John, 1901, Ag 15,7:6
Duer, John Beverly, 1910, S 3,7:6
Duer, John Beverly Mrs, 1924, Ja 13,23:1
Duer, Leland B, 1958, Je 17,29:2
Duer, Leo H, 1949, S 11,96:6
Duer, S Naudain Mrs, 1952, F 26,27:3
Duer, W A Mrs, 1903, Mr 23,9:6
Duer, William, 1879, Ag 27,5:5
Duer, William A (will, N 2,9:5), 1905, O 28,9:4
Duerden, John, 1953, Mr 7,15:5
Duernberger, William T Mrs, 1948, O 21,27:3
Duerr, Albert F, 1948, N 10,29:3
Duerr, Alvan E, 1947, N 19,27:3
Duerr, Arthur E, 1958, Mr 7,23:2
Duerr, Ludwig, 1956, Ja 3,31:2
Duerr, Raymond F Mrs, 1949, S 19,23:4
Duerriemann, Freddy, 1944, Ja 29,4:4
Duerriemann, Valdo, 1944, Ja 29,4:4
Duers, Harry, 1948, Ag 31,26:3
Duers, Henry E, 1940, Je 25,23:5
Duesenberg, August S, 1955, Ja 19,27:5
Duesenberg, F S, 1932, Jl 27,17:3
Duesenberry, J P, 1953, Ap 13,27:4
Duessel, Otto, 1939, N 11,15:6
Duessol, Hubert, 1945, S 25,26:2
Duetzman, Lawrence F, 1952, My 12,25:4
Du Faur, Adolph Capt, 1918, Ag 19,9:8
Dufaure, J A S, 1881, Je 28,5:3
Duff, A Adm Sir, 1933, N 23,21:1
Duff, A H (see also Ap 11), 1877, Ap 22,1:5
Duff, A Rev, 1878, F 13,4:7
Duff, A Wilmer, 1951, F 25,84:5
Duff, Adrian, 1920, Mr 8,9:5
Duff, Alex D, 1957, Jl 5,17:4
Duff, Anna C, 1947, Mr 22,13:2
Duff, Arthur, 1952, Ap 6,88:1
Duff, Benjamin J, 1946, Jl 10,23:4
Duff, Clementine F Mrs (will), 1937, F 22,19:2
Duff, Donald, 1941, D 8,23:2
Duff, Donald A, 1952, N 16,88:4
Duff, Edward A, 1943, F 13,11:5
Duff, Edward J, 1939, N 14,23:2
Duff, Elmo, 1951, Mr 12,25:1
Duff, Eugene F, 1958, Mr 13,29:4
Duff, Frederick, 1941, F 2,43:4
Duff, G Lyman, 1956, N 2,27:4
Duff, George, 1946, Ag 28,42:5
Duff, George M, 1953, Ap 20,25:5
Duff, Henry K, 1948, O 17,76:6
Duff, Hezekiah N, 1947, Ap 30,25:5
Duff, J A, 1928, S 2,17:5
Duff, James, 1940, Ap 26,21:2
Duff, James G, 1941, Mr 11,23:1
Duff, James H, 1965, N 5,37:2
Duff, James M, 1956, Ja 29,92:2
Duff, James P, 1948, Ag 14,13:3
Duff, James P Mrs, 1961, Jl 2,32:1
Duff, James S, 1916, N 18,11:5
Duff, Jay R, 1959, Ap 24,27:4
Duff, John, 1943, Je 10,21:2; 1950, S 19,31:2; 1958, Ap 22,33:2
Duff, John D, 1957, Ag 31,15:6
Duff, John J, 1961, Mr 26,92:7
Duff, John T Mrs, 1956, Ja 17,33:1
Duff, Joseph C, 1948, Ja 18,60:5
Duff, Joseph R Mrs, 1945, N 28,27:5
Duff, Leo, 1938, F 22,18:2
Duff, Levi B Col, 1916, Ja 22,9:3
Duff, Louis B, 1959, Ag 30,83:1
Duff, Lyman P, 1955, Ap 27,31:1
Duff, Mary E, 1947, O 6,21:3
Duff, Mary L Mrs, 1937, Jl 18,II,7:3
Duff, Mountstuart Grant Sir, 1906, Ja 13,9:3
Duff, N, 1877, Mr 29,2:2
Duff, Nathan T Mrs, 1952, F 15,25:4
Duff, R J, 1878, Mr 4,8:3
Duff, Ralph L, 1957, Ja 10,29:4
Duff, Richard K, 1953, Ag 16,76:4
Duff, Samuel, 1908, Je 16,9:6
Duff, Thomas, 1963, Jl 26,25:3
Duff, Thomas B Mrs, 1951, Ja 11,25:2
Duff, William, 1953, Ap 27,23:4
Duff, William E, 1953, Je 3,31:3
Duff, William H, 1909, Mr 22,7:5
Duff, William R, 1945, Mr 30,15:3
Duffee, Peter B, 1957, N 8,29:3
Duffee, Warren S, 1967, D 13,47:2
Duffell, R E, 1948, Ag 24,23:2
Dufferin, Lord, 1902, F 13,9:6
Duffett, William H, 1940, Ja 2,19:2
Duffey, Caroline K Mrs, 1940, S 27,23:4
Duffey, Francis J Dr, 1919, Ap 1,11:3
Duffey, Hugh J, 1964, Je 23,33:4
Duffey, Ike W, 1967, Ap 6,39:4
Duffey, William B, 1941, S 25,25:6
Duffey, William J, 1907, F 20,11:6
Duffie, Arch B, 1937, Ja 23,17:1
Duffie, Daniel P, 1943, Ap 25,34:4
Duffield, Edward D (por),(will, O 4,15:5), 1938, S 18,45:1
Duffield, Edward D Mrs, 1945, Jl 27,15:3
Duffield, Eliza, 1953, D 23,26:3
Duffield, Helen K, 1946, Mr 16,13:5
Duffield, Henry G, 1950, F 24,23:1
Duffield, Henry G Mrs, 1953, O 18,86:5
Duffield, Henry M Gen, 1912, Jl 14,II,11:5
Duffield, Howard, 1941, Ja 6,15:3
Duffield, Hugh K, 1968, F 7,47:3
Duffield, J T, 1901, Ap 11,9:5
Duffield, John R Rev, 1937, Ag 16,19:5
Duffield, John T Mrs, 1920, N 25,15:5
Duffield, Norman, 1955, Mr 24,32:2
Duffield, Orville S, 1949, Ap 22,23:1
Duffield, Pitts, 1938, Ag 13,13:6
Duffield, Raymond, 1941, Ap 11,21:5
Duffield, Rev Dr, 1868, Je 27,5:4
Duffield, Roy F, 1940, D 23,19:2
Duffield, Sarah G, 1942, My 1,19:5
Duffield, Sargent D, 1955, Ja 31,19:5
Duffield, Thomas J, 1946, My 16,21:4; 1950, My 9, 29:3
Duffield, William W, 1907, Je 24,7:6
Duffin, Earle C (por), 1949, Ap 20,27:3
Duffin, Harold J, 1947, N 25,32:4
Duffin, J P, 1880, My 13,5:6
Duffin, Simon E Mrs, 1941, Je 8,48:4
Duffle, A M, 1880, D 9,5:4
Duffner, Gaudens, 1948, Ja 10,15:2
Dufford, Frank, 1955, Mr 9,27:4
Dufford, George S, 1945, Ag 29,23:1
Dufford, Lewis A, 1940, Jl 26,17:5
Dufft, Carl Elias Dr, 1920, Ja 10,11:4
Duffus, Charles Z, 1947, Mr 20,27:4
Duffus, Joseph J, 1957, F 8,23:2
Duffus, William M, 1966, Mr 25,41:1
Duffy, Al, 1947, Je 12,25:4
Duffy, Alan, 1943, Je 27,32:6
Duffy, Albert E, 1922, Ag 6,28:5
Duffy, Andrew R, 1940, Je 17,15:4
Duffy, Arthur, 1955, Ja 26,25:4
Duffy, Arthur F, 1960, O 4,43:4
Duffy, Arthur W, 1946, Ag 10,13:3
Duffy, Austin F, 1943, Ja 11,15:2
Duffy, Barney A, 1962, F 11,86:3
Duffy, Catherine H, 1962, My 10,37:2
Duffy, Charles A, 1957, My 8,37:6; 1967, Ag 13,8
Duffy, Charles B, 1941, Ja 4,13:4
Duffy, Charles E, 1942, Ag 9,43:2
Duffy, Charles E Mrs, 1946, S 1,35:1
Duffy, Charles G, 1947, O 28,25:1; 1952, D 11,33
Duffy, Charles J, 1946, F 12,28:2; 1951, N 5,31:5
Duffy, Christopher, 1944, Ag 22,19:2
Duffy, Christopher R, 1949, Mr 6,72:6
Duffy, Daniel P, 1942, N 8,51:4
Duffy, E C, 1939, Mr 18,17:3
Duffy, E L, 1927, N 29,27:2
Duffy, Edmund, 1962, S 13,37:1
Duffy, Edward, 1946, Jl 27,17:5
Duffy, Edward J, 1937, Mr 27,15:1; 1937, N 2,25 1947, Je 26,24:3
Duffy, Edward J Mrs, 1944, O 19,23:4
Duffy, Edward P, 1952, Jl 29,21:3; 1963, Ap 5,48
Duffy, Elizabeth, 1952, F 10,92:5
Duffy, F P, 1932, Je 27,1:2
Duffy, Felix A, 1937, Jl 26,19:5
Duffy, Francis T, 1961, S 7,35:3
Duffy, Frank, 1955, Jl 12,25:5
Duffy, Frank H, 1950, My 22,21:5
Duffy, Frank J, 1917, Ag 3,9:2
Duffy, Frederick P, 1956, D 3,29:5
Duffy, G C Sir, 1903, F 10,9:5
Duffy, Gavan, 1951, Je 11,25:1
Duffy, George F, 1948, Ap 17,15:5
Duffy, George L, 1955, Mr 18,27:2
Duffy, Gerald V, 1954, Ag 20,19:5
Duffy, H T, 1903, Jl 4,7:6
Duffy, Harry T, 1950, N 25,13:2
Duffy, Harry V, 1958, Jl 22,27:2
Duffy, Henry, 1948, N 27,17:2; 1961, N 21,39:5
Duffy, Hugh, 1954, O 20,29:1
Duffy, Hugh B, 1939, D 9,15:4
Duffy, Hugh V, 1965, D 6,37:2
Duffy, J Frank, 1944, F 8,15:1
Duffy, J Frank Mrs, 1951, O 11,37:5
Duffy, J Hamilton, 1955, Ja 5,23:3
Duffy, Jack, 1939, Jl 27,19:2; 1949, D 20,28:6
Duffy, James A Mrs, 1957, My 1,37:5
Duffy, James J, 1941, D 14,68:1; 1945, S 17,19: 1946, F 3,40:1; 1961, F 25,21:1
Duffy, James J Sr, 1964, Ag 29,21:5
Duffy, James K Mrs, 1955, Jl 2,15:6
Duffy, James S Msgr, 1918, F 15,9:4

Duffy, Jimmy, 1960, My 2,29:5
Duffy, John, 1924, My 15,19:3; 1939, Mr 15,17:3
Duffy, John A, 1958, Ag 27,29:2
Duffy, John E, 1958, Je 5,31:3; 1966, Ja 19,41:5
Duffy, John E Mrs, 1956, F 7,31:2
Duffy, John F, 1962, Jl 4,21:5
Duffy, John G Mrs, 1957, Ja 22,29:2
Duffy, John J, 1938, O 8,17:5; 1945, Je 15,19:2; 1951, My 28,21:6; 1952, Mr 16,90:6; 1959, D 12,23:3
Duffy, John J Mrs, 1953, D 22,31:4
Duffy, John L, 1959, Ag 22,17:1
Duffy, John P, 1947, Ag 18,17:5; 1955, O 15,15:1
Duffy, John Q, 1967, F 8,31:1
Duffy, Joseph A, 1956, D 23,31:1
Duffy, Joseph F, 1954, Mr 14,88:5; 1960, D 7,44:3
Duffy, Joseph F Mrs, 1938, Je 8,23:1
Duffy, Joseph M, 1960, D 6,41:2
Duffy, Joseph Mrs, 1947, Ag 18,12:1
Duffy, M J, 1903, Ja 5,14:2
Duffy, Mark J, 1948, S 17,25:4
Duffy, Martin J, 1952, Je 10,27:3
Duffy, Mary C, 1962, S 26,39:2
Duffy, Matthew P, 1940, D 20,25:3
Duffy, Michael, 1941, F 8,15:5; 1944, Ag 16,1:2
Duffy, Michael J Rev, 1937, My 21,21:5
Duffy, Michael P, 1940, Ja 18,23:4
Duffy, Neil G Mrs, 1955, Je 10,25:3
Duffy, Nicholas (will, Je 16,21:5), 1937, My 29,17:4
Duffy, Nicholas P, 1943, Ap 11,48:2
Duffy, P G, 1895, Ag 29,16:1
Duffy, Patrick, 1920, Ja 1,15:2
Duffy, Patrick J Msgr, 1919, Jl 3,10:2
Duffy, Paul, 1948, Ag 6,17:5
Duffy, Paul J Mrs, 1950, My 2,29:3
Duffy, Peter H, 1949, F 21,23:5
Duffy, Peter J, 1940, D 25,27:6
Duffy, Peter L, 1938, Ja 15,15:4
Duffy, Peter Mrs, 1944, O 1,45:2; 1960, Jl 5,31:1
Duffy, Ralph C, 1940, N 22,23:1
Duffy, Richard H, 1953, Ag 22,15:2
Duffy, Robert, 1958, S 6,7:2
Duffy, Robert R, 1964, Jl 16,31:2
Duffy, Rose, 1944, Ag 15,17:2
Duffy, Sarah Mrs, 1923, Ag 31,15:6
Duffy, Stephen E, 1944, Je 7,19:5
Duffy, Stephen V, 1944, Jl 21,19:3
Duffy, Susan C (Sister Marie Paula Duffy), 1940, My 6,17:4
Duffy, Terrence J, 1946, Je 6,21:2
Duffy, Theodore F, 1959, Ap 11,21:5
Duffy, Thomas, 1954, Mr 18,31:2
Duffy, Thomas F Rev, 1922, F 8,17:5
Duffy, Thomas J, 1950, Ja 12,28:3
Duffy, Thomas J Mrs, 1952, Mr 22,13:5
Duffy, W J, 1930, O 6,23:3
Duffy, Walter B, 1911, Ja 15,13:3
Duffy, Walter J Rev, 1937, Je 21,19:5
Duffy, Ward E, 1961, Ap 17,29:5
Duffy, William, 1917, S 10,13:6
Duffy, William C, 1943, O 8,19:4; 1956, My 6,87:2
Duffy, William F P, 1942, Mr 22,49:2
Duffy, William H, 1951, Jl 25,23:5
Duffy, William J, 1913, My 6,11:3
Duffy, William J (Big Bill), 1952, My 26,18:1
Duffy, William J, 1955, Ap 11;23:5
Duffy, William J Mrs, 1917, Mr 23,9:4
Duffy, William J Sr, 1967, S 1,31:4
Duffy, William P, 1938, F 18,19:2
Duffy, William R, 1963, Ap 25,33:4
Du Flon, Alex M, 1949, F 10,27:4
Du Flon, Mrs, 1878, Jl 9,8:5
Du Flon, Pierre Vitalis, 1882, Ap 29,5:1
Du Flon, Thaddeus A Van Z, 1963, O 16,45:4
Duflong, Alfred E, 1950, N 12,92:4
Duflos, Raphael, 1946, Ja 23,27:2
Dufner, Ilka H Mrs, 1942, Ja 1,25:2
Dufor, Ragtt R, 1964, Ag 28,35:4
Dufort, Leo J, 1956, My 9,33:1
Dufour, Guillaume Henri Gen, 1875, Jl 15,4:4
DuFour, Robert M, 1957, Jl 22,19:5
Dufrain, Charles H, 1956, Ap 9,27:4
Du Frenne, Martin F, 1950, D 15,31:5
Dufresne, Candide, 1947, F 14,21:2
Du Fresne, Jeanne, 1922, F 25,13:3
Dufresne, Marcel, 1965, Ag 4,35:5
Dufresne, Marie Mrs, 1953, My 16,19:2
Dufton, Leslie B, 1951, Ag 10,15:5
Dufton, Roberta B Mrs, 1967, My 18,47:1
Dufty, George, 1955, O 11,39:5
Dufy, Jean, 1964, My 17,87:1
Dufy, Raoul, 1953, Mr 24,31:1
Dufy, Raoul Mrs, 1962, Jl 11,35:1
Dugale, Nigel, 1955, S 7,31:4
Dugan, A G, 1943, Je 13,45:1
Dugan, Arthur N, 1962, Ja 6,19:5
Dugan, Bernard D, 1943, Mr 29,15:5
Dugan, Daniel A, 1938, F 19,15:5; 1949, Mr 23,28:2
Dugan, Daniel A Mrs, 1944, My 8,19:4
Dugan, Daniel J, 1946, D 7,21:5
Dugan, Daniel J Sr, 1956, F 5,86:1
Dugan, Daniel S Jr Mrs, 1949, Ja 28,22:3
Dugan, David H, 1940, Ag 1,21:4
Dugan, David H Mrs, 1948, Mr 10,28:3
Dugan, Edward J, 1943, Jl 20,19:1
Dugan, Edward J Mrs, 1955, My 26,31:2
Dugan, Edward P, 1961, S 9,19:4
Dugan, Emmet J, 1952, Mr 27,29:2
Dugan, Eugene O, 1939, Jl 10,19:5
Dugan, Francis, 1945, Ag 25,11:5
Dugan, Francis H, 1941, F 22,15:4
Dugan, George A, 1948, Jl 18,52:5
Dugan, George L, 1956, Ja 9,25:1
Dugan, George Rev, 1921, O 15,13:5
Dugan, Howard F, 1964, Jl 4,13:3
Dugan, James, 1967, Je 2,46:5
Dugan, James A, 1957, S 19,29:2; 1961, Ja 7,19:6
Dugan, James A Dr, 1925, Ap 15,19:4
Dugan, James H, 1958, My 12,29:1
Dugan, John, 1948, N 14,78:6
Dugan, John E, 1953, D 29,23:2; 1960, N 22,35:5
Dugan, John F, 1943, Mr 31,19:4
Dugan, John I, 1948, Ag 10,21:3
Dugan, John J Mrs, 1965, D 18,30:4
Dugan, John M, 1949, My 3,25:2
Dugan, John P, 1942, D 29,21:1
Dugan, Lord (Former W Dugan), 1951, Ag 19,84:5
Dugan, Margaret P, 1947, Ja 4,15:5
Dugan, Matilda M, 1939, D 22,19:4
Dugan, Maurice K, 1955, N 23,23:2
Dugan, Patrick C, 1957, Ag 18,83:2
Dugan, Patrick F, 1945, S 12,25:5
Dugan, Raymond S, 1940, S 1,21:1
Dugan, Robert J, 1947, Ap 21,27:2
Dugan, Robert P, 1946, Jl 21,39:1
Dugan, Thomas B, 1940, Ap 29,15:6
Dugan, Thomas F, 1957, F 24,84:1; 1958, Je 17,29:3
Dugan, Thomas J, 1944, S 23,13:4
Dugan, Thomas L, 1957, My 19,88:4
Dugan, Thomas M (funl, Ja 16,27:2), 1965, Ja 12, 37:1
Dugan, Timothy J, 1957, Mr 7,29:5
Dugan, Walkerman D, 1959, Ag 18,29:1
Dugan, Walter J, 1945, Ag 29,25:6
Dugan, William E, 1924, S 5,17:4; 1953, F 10,27:3
Dugan, William F, 1947, S 29,21:5
Dugan, William J, 1937, My 7,30:3; 1942, Ja 10,15:4
Duganne, A J H, 1884, O 22,5:6
Dugas, Alex Mrs, 1958, Ag 27,29:2
Dugas, Graham C, 1955, F 2,27:4
Dugas, Jean J, 1937, D 8,25:1
Dugas, L A Dr, 1884, O 20,5:4
du Gast, Crespin Mrs, 1942, Ap 29,21:6
Dugdale, Blanche, 1948, My 17,19:5
Dugdale, Charles H, 1964, Ja 8,37:3
Dugdale, Gene, 1942, Mr 2,19:3
Dugdale, George, 1940, F 13,23:1
Dugdale, John, 1963, Mr 13,7:1
Dugdale, R J, 1882, Mr 30,8:2
Dugdale, R L, 1883, Jl 24,5:5
Dugdale, Ralph E, 1964, Ag 20,29:4
Dugdale, Thomas C, 1952, N 14,23:2
Dugdale, William, 1958, Ap 1,31:3
Duge, George W, 1954, O 7,23:4
Duge, Matthew Mrs, 1939, My 19,21:3
Duggan, Alfred, 1964, Ap 5,86:4
Duggan, Charlotte, 1941, N 11,24:2
Duggan, Dana J (will, Ag 17,63:5), 1952, My 15,31:5
Duggan, Dennis J Msgr, 1925, O 27,23:2
Duggan, Ed, 1950, O 18,33:3
Duggan, Edward J, 1968, O 21,47:1
Duggan, Edward L, 1950, Ag 29,27:3
Duggan, Edward N J, 1941, S 7,49:2
Duggan, Edward W, 1945, Ja 3,17:4
Duggan, Eileen M, 1952, Ja 15,27:1
Duggan, Elizabeth A, 1924, O 16,25:4
Duggan, Elizabeth Mrs, 1949, My 17,25:2
Duggan, Frank A, 1937, Ap 11,II,9:1
Duggan, Frank J, 1944, Je 22,19:5
Duggan, Frank L, 1946, Je 23,40:5
Duggan, Frederic L, 1948, Ag 5,21:5
Duggan, Henry, 1921, D 28,15:5
Duggan, Hubert J, 1943, O 26,23:4
Duggan, Jeremiah J, 1944, My 18,19:7
Duggan, John B, 1872, F 18,5:5
Duggan, John J, 1945, Ja 11,23:3; 1954, N 6,17:6
Duggan, Joseph B, 1952, Je 22,69:1
Duggan, Laurence, 1948, D 21,1:8
Duggan, Leo T, 1950, S 23,17:5
Duggan, Matthew J, 1959, Jl 29,29:1
Duggan, Patrick F Sr, 1947, Je 14,15:1
Duggan, Peter F, 1937, Je 19,15:4
Duggan, Ruth A, 1951, O 11,37:3
Duggan, Stephen P (trb Ag 29,26:6), 1950, Ag 19, 13:1
Duggan, Stephen P Mrs, 1966, F 16,43:4
Duggan, Stephen P Prof, 1916, O 9,11:6
Duggan, Thomas, 1953, Ja 25,85:2; 1961, D 3,88:3
Duggan, Thomas S, 1945, N 3,15:4
Duggan, William, 1946, Ag 5,21:6; 1950, N 19,92:3
Duggan, William J F, 1962, Ap 27,35:1
Duggan, William P, 1943, Ag 12,19:5
Duggar, Benjamin M, 1956, S 11,35:4
Duggin, Allen F, 1949, O 12,29:3
Duggin, Charles, 1916, N 12,23:2
Duggins, Hillis, 1954, F 16,25:2
Duggleby, William J, 1944, S 2,11:1
du Ghan, Alfred J, 1957, Ag 9,19:3
Dugliss, Bruce S, 1955, Mr 30,29:2
Dugmore, Lilla B G Mrs, 1939, Je 30,19:2
Dugo, Andre S, 1957, Ja 8,31:3
Dugre, Joseph, 1955, N 5,24:2
Dugro, Philip Henry (funl, Mr 4,11:6), 1920, Mr 2, 11:3
Duguerry, Abbe, 1871, My 29,1:6
Duguet, Alfred, 1916, My 22,11:5
Duguid, James Mrs, 1948, N 10,30:3
Dugundji, Basile D, 1943, My 29,13:5
Duhamel, Georges, 1966, Ap 14,35:7
Duhamel, Joseph Thomas, 1909, Je 7,7:6
Duhan, Eliot, 1963, N 6,36:3
Duhan, John, 1961, My 31,33:5
Duhig, James, 1965, Ap 11,92:3
Duhig, Stanley W, 1964, Jl 4,13:2
Duhigg, Thomas F, 1954, My 27,27:4
Duhigg, Thomas S Rev, 1925, Je 10,23:4
Duhring, Fannie L, 1958, Ap 17,31:1
Duhring, H Louis Mrs, 1938, F 6,II,8:2
Duhring, Herman L Jr, 1953, Jl 20,17:4
Duigan, John, 1950, Ja 10,29:2
Duisberg, C, 1935, Mr 20,21:1
Duisberg, Walter H, 1964, My 26,39:1
Duisenberg, Edward Mrs, 1940, N 30,17:6
Dujardin-Beaumetz, Henri Charles, 1913, S 28,IV,7:5
Dujat, Joseph F, 1964, O 24,29:5
Dukas, Julius J, 1940, S 8,49:1
Duke, Angier B (funl, Ag 6,15:4), 1923, S 5,15:4
Duke, Angier B Mrs (funl plans, Jl 20,55:2;funl, Jl 22,21:4), 1961, Jl 19,1:3
Duke, B N (por), 1929, Ja 9,31:3
Duke, Benjamin N, 1917, F 21,11:5
Duke, Charles J Jr, 1953, S 27,85:7
Duke, Charles W, 1956, Ag 8,25:5
Duke, Emma, 1940, Ag 2,15:4
Duke, Francis V, 1965, Mr 24,46:4
Duke, George, 1945, N 19,21:3
Duke, George A, 1941, S 16,23:5
Duke, Haydn O, 1937, Mr 3,23:1
Duke, James B (funl, O 13,23:4), 1925, O 12,21:4
Duke, James B, 1925, O 14,25:3
Duke, James B Mrs, 1925, O 28,25:4; 1962, Ap 14,25:2
Duke, James Sir, 1873, My 29,5:6
Duke, John G, 1942, Mr 18,23:5
Duke, John Mrs, 1945, D 18,27:4
Duke, Josephine G, 1941, F 18,23:4
Duke, Milton I Mrs, 1951, My 8,31:5
Duke, Robert D, 1960, D 20,33:1
Duke, Thomas S, 1966, Je 4,29:5
Duke, W Bernard Sr, 1946, S 23,23:6
Duke, William D, 1951, O 11,37:2
Duke, William Jr, 1956, Jl 22,61:2
Duke, William Jr Mrs, 1952, Ja 16,25:4
Duke, William R, 1960, Ja 27,30:5
Duke, William Sr Mrs, 1953, Ag 25,21:1
Duke, William W, 1946, Ap 12,27:5; 1953, S 22,31:3
Duke De Broglie, 1870, Ja 28,5:2
Duke De Frias, 1874, O 8,6:7
Duke De Montpensier, Son of, 1873, D 5,1:7
Duke of Bedford (Wm Russell), 1872, My 28,1:5
Duke of Brunswick, 1873, Ag 20,4:7
Duke of Leinster, 1874, O 12,4:7
Duke of Montebello, 1874, Jl 21,5:3
Duke of Rianzores, 1873, S 29,5:3
Dukehart, J Cyril, 1960, Jl 18,27:1
Dukehart, John M Capt, 1872, D 18,1:6
Dukek, William G, 1957, N 28,31:3
Dukelow, Peter J, 1940, Ja 5,19:5
Dukes, Ann R Mrs, 1946, S 14,7:5
Dukes, Ashley, 1959, My 5,33:2
Dukes, Howard R, 1966, F 28,27:4
Dukes, Joseph H, 1875, Ja 17,12:3
Dukes, Paul, 1967, Ag 28,31:5
Dukes, Richard, 1950, Ag 14,17:2
Dukes, Richard Mrs, 1950, Ag 14,17:2
Dukesston of Warrington, Baron, 1948, My 15,15:2
Dukhov, Nikolai L, 1964, My 5,43:2
Dukinfield, Charles Mrs, 1938, Ja 22,15:5
Dula, Grover C, 1946, S 30,25:3
Dula, Julia W Mrs (will, Ag 16,16:1), 1939, Ag 13, 29:2
Dula, R B, 1926, Ap 28,25:3
Dulac, Edmund, 1953, My 30,15:4
Dulac, Germaine, 1942, Jl 23,19:1
Dulaney, Eleanor A Mrs, 1938, F 27,13:1
Dulaney, George W, 1959, My 16,23:4
Dulaney, Henry R Jr, 1948, N 3,27:2
Dulanto, Pedro, 1952, N 20,31:2
Dulanty, John W, 1955, F 12,15:3
Dulany, Joseph Brinkley, 1925, D 17,23:4
Dulany, Richard Hunter, 1917, Ja 2,11:3
Du Lay, George D Sr, 1949, O 17,23:2
Dulberg, Meyer, 1957, Je 20,29:1
Dulcan, Charles B, 1957, Ja 8,31:4
Dulce, Gen, 1869, N 25,1:3
Duld, Samuel, 1949, N 16,29:5
Duleepsinhji, Shri, 1959, D 6,86:8
Duley, Eleanor I, 1942, N 28,13:4
Duley, Frank L, 1937, D 27,15:2
Dulgharu, Ilie, 1953, Je 28,21:2
Duling, J Lawrence, 1954, My 11,29:1

Dulk, William H, 1950, My 14,108:1
Dull, Charles E, 1947, D 21,52:6
Dull, Charles E Mrs, 1945, Mr 5,19:3
Dull, Floyd N, 1957, Mr 14,29:2
Dull, John J, 1949, Ja 19,27:1
Dull, M Eva Mrs, 1942, Ag 20,19:4
Dull, Mark R Jr, 1956, O 18,33:4
Dull, Robert J, 1960, Ja 24,88:3
Dullaghan, Dorothy V, 1954, Je 22,27:2
Dullard, John P, 1957, O 9,35:3
Dullea, Charles B, 1953, F 20,19:1
Dullea, Edward William Rev, 1921, Ja 25,11:5
Dulles, Edith F Mrs, 1941, Je 9,19:5
Dulles, Heatly C, 1956, F 7,31:4
Dulles, John F (funl, My 28,1:3; will, My 29,7:5), 1959, My 25,1:8
Dulles, Joseph H Rev, 1937, Mr 9,23:4
Dulles, L Harrison, 1921, Jl 28,13:5
Dulles, William, 1915, S 15,9:5
Dulles, William W, 1963, My 15,39:3
Dulligan, James F, 1968, Je 9,84:3
Dulligan, Peter J Sr, 1955, Jl 30,17:5
Dullin, Charles, 1949, D 12,33:2
Dullzell, Paul, 1961, D 22,24:1
Dulmage, Marcus B, 1947, My 7,30:5
Dulmage, Mark B Mrs, 1957, Ag 15,21:2
Dulmage, Will E, 1953, F 14,17:3
Dulman, Joseph, 1956, Ag 4,15:4
Dultgen, Arthur, 1956, S 2,57:2
Dulverton, Lord (G A H Wills), 1956, D 2,86:2
Dulyn, Theodore A, 1942, O 18,52:5
Dumahut, Claudius H Rev, 1918, N 28,17:1
Dumaine, Frederic C, 1951, My 28,21:3
Dumaine, Jacques C, 1953, My 13,29:4
Dumaresq, Herbert, 1955, Mr 24,31:1
Dumars, Fabian R, 1919, S 25,15:5
Dumars, Gerald Mrs, 1942, O 6,24:2
Dumary, Henry Mrs, 1947, Ag 15,17:6
Dumas, Alex, 1939, D 20,25:4
Dumas, Alexander, 1895, N 28,5:3
Dumas, Andre, 1943, My 22,13:2
Dumas, George H, 1957, Jl 29,19:6
Dumas, Gustave, 1958, My 29,27:1
Dumas, Hugh C S, 1940, N 6,23:5
Dumas, J B, 1884, Ap 15,5:3
Dumas, Marie A, 1878, O 23,2:7
Dumas, Mary N Mrs, 1938, Ja 1,19:4
Dumas, Walter A, 1952, S 13,17:5
Du Maurier, G, 1934, Ap 12,24:1
Du Maurier, G L P B, 1896, O 9,9:1
Du Maurier, Lady, 1957, N 30,21:6
Dumbadze, Vasili, 1943, Ap 17,17:1
Dumbar, Joseph, 1955, Je 7,33:6
Dumbauld, Charles D Prof, 1922, Je 22,15:6
Dumbauld, George L, 1944, F 5,15:1
Dumbell, George W, 1957, D 7,21:4
Dumbell, George William Rev Dr, 1913, Mr 3,9:4
Dumbell, Henry T, 1947, D 28,40:6
Dumbell, Katherine, 1948, Ag 30,17:2
Dumble, E T, 1927, Ja 28,17:5
Dumbrille, H Hilton, 1957, D 5,35:1
Dumesnil, Charles, 1946, D 30,19:2
Dumesnil, Jacques-Louis, 1956, Je 17,92:5
Dumey, Saul A, 1961, N 20,31:4
Du Mez, Andrew G, 1948, S 28,27:5
Dumini, Amerigo, 1967, D 29,28:1
Dumke, Ralph, 1964, Ja 6,47:4
Dumler, Martin G, 1958, O 22,35:4
Dummer, H Boylston, 1945, N 4,43:1
Dummer, Joseph N, 1942, Ap 11,13:5
Dummer, P C, 1875, S 15,4:6
Dummer, William F Mrs, 1954, F 27,13:2
Dummett, Robert E, 1941, O 19,47:2
Dumonceau, Sepeh H F Count, 1952, Je 30,19:2
Dumond, Cornelius, 1937, S 26,II,8:6
Du Mond, F M, 1927, My 26,25:3
Dumond, Frank V, 1951, F 7,29:3
DuMond, Frank Vincent Mrs, 1968, D 9,47:2
Dumond, Ida K, 1949, S 13,29:4
Dumond, Laurence A Mrs, 1960, S 9,29:1
Du Mond, Marcia A, 1953, N 28,15:6
Du Mond, Nathan Mrs, 1944, F 11,19:4
Dumond, Roscoe C Mrs, 1952, Jl 21,19:2
Dumond, Stephen W, 1946, Ja 16,23:3
Du Mont, Allen B, 1965, N 16,1:3
Dumont, Allen H, 1945, Je 9,13:5
Dumont, C A A E, 1884, Ag 14,5:3
Dumont, Charles, 1939, Ap 23,III,7:2
Dumont, Corinne Mrs, 1942, Mr 24,19:4
Dumont, F Gen, 1871, Ap 17,1:5
Dumont, F M L Rev, 1915, My 12,13:4
Du Mont, Francis M, 1951, D 21,27:2
Dumont, Frederick F Mrs, 1938, D 2,23:5
Dumont, Frederick T, 1939, Je 6,23:6
Dumont, Gabrielle, 1944, Ja 19,19:1
Dumont, George L, 1953, O 5,27:5
Dumont, George W, 1953, Ja 28,27:1
Dumont, J B, 1928, Ap 11,29:3
Dumont, John B Mrs, 1945, Mr 31,19:6
Dumont, Louis W, 1944, Ag 12,11:5
Dumont, Margaret, 1965, Mr 7,83:1
Dumont, Nellie Mrs, 1939, My 26,23:2
Dumont, R Duval, 1940, F 29,19:5
DuMont, Randolph E, 1961, Jl 10,21:1
Dumont, Robert, 1884, Ja 6,5:2
Du Mont, Walter, 1949, O 22,17:5
Dumont, William A, 1955, Ap 9,13:4
DuMont, William H B, 1946, N 4,25:5
Dumont, William Henry, 1914, Jl 26,5:5
Dumortier, Bishop, 1940, F 19,17:2
Du Motay, C M Tessie, 1880, Je 7,2:4
Du Moulin, Frank, 1947, Jl 11,15:1
Du Moulin, John Philip Bp, 1911, Mr 30,11:6
Du Moulin-Eckart, Richard, 1938, Ap 6,23:5
Dumper, Arthur, 1957, Ja 18,21:3
Dumproff, Jacob, 1963, O 24,33:4
Dumser, John S, 1949, D 10,17:3
Dun, Henry W, 1964, O 28,45:2
Dun, Robert G Mrs, 1910, N 7,7:4
Dun, U San, 1949, Jl 12,27:4
Dun-Waters, James C, 1939, O 17,25:2
Dunachie, Russell J, 1962, S 10,29:1
Dunaeff, Ray (R Weston), 1967, Ap 25,43:1
Dunand, Edward L, 1947, Ag 26,23:4
Dunand, Jean, 1942, Je 10,21:4
Dunant, Henri, 1910, N 1,9:5
Dunavan, Alfred W, 1951, S 5,31:5
Dunavan, Louis W, 1943, Ap 20,23:4
Dunaway, Carlyle M Mrs, 1963, Ag 24,19:6
Dunaway, Philip H, 1957, S 15,83:1
Dunaway, Ray S, 1956, Jl 22,61:1
Dunaway, S Judson Mrs, 1947, My 23,24:3
Dunayevsky, Isaak, 1955, Jl 27,23:5
Dunbabin, Thomas J, 1955, Ap 1,27:4
Dunbach, Carl J, 1957, N 28,31:4
Dunbar, Alex, 1955, O 16,86:2
Dunbar, Alex P, 1952, D 3,33:4
Dunbar, Alex P Mrs, 1958, Mr 8,17:5
Dunbar, Anstruther, 1953, N 3,31:4
Dunbar, Arthur E, 1956, My 10,31:1
Dunbar, Arthur W, 1953, N 7,17:3
Dunbar, Brooks, 1961, F 7,33:1
Dunbar, Bruce C, 1968, Jl 23,39:2
Dunbar, C W Harold, 1968, D 18,47:2
Dunbar, Caroline R Mrs, 1939, Ap 26,23:3
Dunbar, Charles, 1939, My 10,23:4
Dunbar, Charles R, 1943, Mr 28,24:7
Dunbar, Charles W, 1941, My 20,23:2
Dunbar, Clarence M, 1949, O 6,31:6
Dunbar, David O, 1947, F 22,13:4
Dunbar, E Helen (Mrs Chas H McClellan), 1964, Je 21,84:6
Dunbar, Ernest W, 1959, Mr 4,31:5
Dunbar, Flanders, 1959, Ag 23,95:4
Dunbar, Frederick W, 1938, F 24,19:5
Dunbar, Guy S, 1954, Ag 9,17:5
Dunbar, Harold C, 1953, S 19,15:4
Dunbar, Harris T, 1943, Ja 16,13:3
Dunbar, Herman G, 1953, S 20,86:4
Dunbar, Howard, 1964, Mr 11,39:4
Dunbar, Humphrey, 1946, Mr 26,29:2
Dunbar, James G, 1948, Ag 6,17:1
Dunbar, James G H R, 1953, Ja 30,4:4
Dunbar, James H Jr, 1962, N 17,25:2
Dunbar, James J, 1939, My 14,III,6:7
Dunbar, James Robert Ex-Justice, 1915, Ag 21,7:7
Dunbar, James V, 1956, F 2,25:3
Dunbar, Jerome, 1957, N 11,29:3
Dunbar, John J, 1946, Ap 23,21:4
Dunbar, John W, 1955, Ja 18,27:5
Dunbar, Lawrence (J F Parsons), 1942, Jl 20,13:4
Dunbar, Margaret E, 1940, Je 18,23:4
Dunbar, Matthew H, 1944, S 13,19:3
Dunbar, Noel, 1953, Je 9,27:2
Dunbar, Oscar H, 1959, Jl 26,68:4
Dunbar, Paul B Dr, 1968, Ag 25,88:6
Dunbar, Paul L, 1906, F 10,1:4
Dunbar, Ralph C, 1948, Mr 14,72:3
Dunbar, Ralph O Justice, 1912, S 20,11:6
Dunbar, Richard S, 1953, F 1,10:1
Dunbar, Robert Mrs, 1952, D 7,89:1
Dunbar, Seymour, 1947, Ap 19,15:3
Dunbar, Stuart B, 1941, My 5,17:5
Dunbar, William F, 1939, Mr 25,15:4; 1940, Je 15,15:5
Dunbar, William K, 1963, My 26,92:5
Dunbar, William K Mrs, 1940, Mr 20,27:1
Dunbar, William L, 1951, F 5,23:5
Dunbar-Nasmith, Martin, 1965, Je 30,37:5
Dunbaugh, Clarence C, 1953, Jl 5,49:2
Dunbaugh, Frank M, 1939, F 23,23:3
Dunboyne, Lord, 1945, My 11,19:2
Duncam, Pat (Louis B), 1960, Jl 19,29:3
Duncan, A Butler Mrs, 1951, D 21,27:5
Duncan, Alec, 1946, Ap 27,17:4
Duncan, Alexander, 1947, Ag 5,23:5
Duncan, Alexander Butler, 1920, My 19,11:5
Duncan, Alfred E Jr, 1963, Ag 2,27:5
Duncan, Allen C, 1959, S 20,86:5
Duncan, Andrew R, 1952, Mr 31,19:5
Duncan, Augustin (trb lr, F 28,II,3:4), 1954, F 22,19:1
Duncan, Augustin Mrs (M Sargent), 1964, S 11,33:2
Duncan, Bertram C, 1961, Ja 20,26:1
Duncan, Bruce R, 1948, N 5,26:2
Duncan, C Arthur, 1939, S 13,25:3
Duncan, C E Oliver, 1964, S 26,23:4
Duncan, C W, 1963, N 23,29:4
Duncan, C William, 1967, Ap 29,35:3
Duncan, Cameron, 1956, Mr 5,23:3
Duncan, Carson S, 1958, O 2,37:5
Duncan, Charles G, 1957, Mr 2,21:3
Duncan, Charles M, 1960, S 2,23:1
Duncan, Charles S, 1952, Je 8,86:7; 1954, O 6,25:1
Duncan, Claudius D, 1961, S 2,15:5
Duncan, Daniel B, 1945, Jl 21,11:2
Duncan, Daniel D, 1950, Mr 21,32:3
Duncan, David D, 1907, Ag 29,7:4
Duncan, David J, 1904, Ja 16,9:6
Duncan, David Prof, 1923, My 22,19:5
Duncan, David S, 1941, Mr 8,19:2
Duncan, Donald, 1965, My 14,37:2
Duncan, Donald L, 1942, Ap 2,22:3
Duncan, Elizabeth, 1948, D 15,33:6
Duncan, Elmer, 1953, N 1,86:7
Duncan, Ethel, 1956, S 26,33:3
Duncan, Florence W Mrs, 1944, My 22,19:6
Duncan, Floyd A, 1937, Ap 19,21:3
Duncan, Frank C Mrs, 1949, S 27,27:4
Duncan, Frank I, 1946, My 13,21:4
Duncan, Fred F, 1950, My 12,27:3
Duncan, Frederick B, 1948, N 23,29:4
Duncan, Frederick S, 1953, Mr 22,86:2
Duncan, Frederick S Mrs, 1945, O 4,23:4
Duncan, G M, 1928, Jl 28,13:5
Duncan, George, 1944, N 22,19:3; 1952, F 20,29:3; 1964, Ja 16,25:2
Duncan, George B, 1950, Mr 17,24:6
Duncan, George H, 1943, Ja 25,14:3
Duncan, George S, 1946, Jl 11,23:5
Duncan, Gertrude P, 1951, Ja 18,27:4
Duncan, H L, 1954, Ag 19,23:4
Duncan, H S, 1907, N 9,9:4
Duncan, Hamilton P, 1951, S 23,86:4
Duncan, Hank (Hy Jas Duncan), 1968, Je 13,47:4
Duncan, Hannibal G, 1950, Mr 5,94:4
Duncan, Harold R, 1946, Mr 20,23:1
Duncan, Harriet M, 1940, S 18,23:1
Duncan, Harrison B, 1949, Mr 8,25:4
Duncan, Harry C, 1952, S 6,17:3
Duncan, Harvey, 1946, S 24,29:2
Duncan, Henry B, 1959, D 20,60:8
Duncan, I, 1927, S 15,1:3
Duncan, Isabella Mrs, 1958, D 10,39:2
Duncan, J, 1928, S 15,19:5
Duncan, J Donald, 1963, My 29,33:2
Duncan, J P, 1901, Ap 8,7:6
Duncan, James B, 1948, My 20,29:5
Duncan, James E Jr, 1939, D 25,23:5
Duncan, John, 1937, O 3,II,8:4
Duncan, John C, 1942, N 23,23:4; 1953, D 13,86:6
Duncan, John C Jr, 1958, My 10,21:5
Duncan, John D, 1942, Jl 21,20:2
Duncan, John P, 1948, F 11,27:5
Duncan, Joseph A Gen, 1912, My 15,11:6
Duncan, K J Maj, 1914, O 22,11:5
Duncan, Lee, 1960, S 21,32:3
Duncan, Lois Mrs, 1953, My 15,11:4
Duncan, Lorne D, 1959, Jl 29,29:2
Duncan, Louis, 1916, F 14,13:5
Duncan, Louis Mrs, 1946, Mr 5,25:5
Duncan, Luther N, 1947, Jl 27,44:6
Duncan, Mabel H, 1955, D 1,35:4
Duncan, Malcolm, 1942, My 3,52:4
Duncan, Marvin W Sr, 1949, S 27,28:3
Duncan, Mary, 1965, Mr 14,20:5
Duncan, Michael S, 1962, My 24,35:4
Duncan, Norman, 1916, O 19,9:1
Duncan, Oscar D (por), 1947, Je 14,15:5
Duncan, Patrick (por), 1943, Jl 18,35:1
Duncan, Patrick B, 1967, Je 6,47:3
Duncan, Paul J, 1947, Ap 29,28:3
Duncan, Raymond, 1966, Ag 17,39:1
Duncan, Rebecca L, 1908, S 20,9:5
Duncan, Rex D, 1949, Jl 25,15:6
Duncan, Richard H, 1948, Mr 5,21:3
Duncan, Robert, 1940, S 15,48:3
Duncan, Robert Kennedy Dr, 1914, F 19,9:5
Duncan, Rosetta, 1959, D 5,23:1
Duncan, S B Irwin, 1946, Ag 23,19:1
Duncan, Samuel, 1945, D 28,15:2
Duncan, Samuel Capt, 1912, Mr 29,13:4
Duncan, Samuel E Dr, 1968, Jl 12,31:5
Duncan, Samuel M, 1939, Mr 19,III,7:1
Duncan, Sarah, 1883, Ap 10,1:4
Duncan, Sebastian Capt, 1915, S 5,11:4
Duncan, Stuart, 1956, My 26,17:6; 1957, Jl 29,1
Duncan, Susan S, 1958, S 24,27:1
Duncan, Thomas E, 1959, F 23,23:4
Duncan, W A, 1884, N 15,2:4
Duncan, W A Dr, 1916, N 2,13:4
Duncan, W B, 1933, Mr 31,19:1
Duncan, W Butler Mrs, 1905, D 12,9:4
Duncan, W W Bp, 1908, Mr 3,7:6
Duncan, W Woffort T, 1945, Ag 4,11:1
Duncan, Walter, 1943, Jl 5,15:2
Duncan, Walter E, 1937, F 3,24:2
Duncan, Walter H, 1949, Jl 4,13:3
Duncan, Walter J, 1941, Ap 12,15:1
Duncan, Warren W, 1938, Ap 12,23:2
Duncan, Washington C, 1953, O 6,29:6

Duncan, William A, 1950, Ap 26,29:5
Duncan, William B Mrs, 1958, Ap 7,21:2
Duncan, William Butler (funl, Je 25,11:4), 1912, Je 21,13:5
Duncan, William C, 1945, N 22,36:3; 1961, Jl 25,27:2
Duncan, William C Mrs, 1953, My 15,11:4
Duncan, William D Mrs, 1937, Ap 14,25:2
Duncan, William M, 1958, Ag 19,27:2
Duncan, Winthrop H, 1943, Jl 21,15:2
Duncan-Clark, Henry B, 1938, S 12,17:3
Duncan-Clark, Samuel J, 1938, Je 13,19:6
Duncan-Jones, A S, 1955, Ja 20,31:3
Duncanson, John, 1939, O 18,26:2
Duncanson, Walter E, 1949, S 6,27:3
Dunckel, Walter A, 1950, N 20,25:3
Dunckel, Walter A Mrs, 1955, Mr 3,27:2
Duncker, Dora, 1916, O 12,11:7
Duncklee, Henry H, 1939, D 30,15:6
Duncklee, Henry H Mrs, 1945, Ag 7,23:1
Duncomb, D S, 1883, Mr 20,5:1
Duncombe, Alfred, 1944, F 4,15:5
Duncombe, David S, 1963, N 26,37:2
Duncombe, Herbert S, 1950, Ja 17,27:3
Duncombe, Raynor S, 1948, N 3,27:3
Duncombe, William, 1945, F 15,19:5
Dundas, Charles, 1956, F 11,17:5
Dundas, Henry, 1950, F 13,21:2
Dundas, Henry Mrs, 1956, Jl 28,17:5
Dundas, Isabella, 1908, Ja 14,7:7
Dundas, James F, 1951, D 28,21:4
Dundas, John G L, 1952, Mr 27,29:2
Dundas, Lawrence J L (Marquess of Zetland), 1961, F 7,33:2
Dundas, Lord, 1922, F 17,15:5
Dundee, Johnny (J Carrora), 1965, Ap 23,35:1
Dundee, Vince (V Lazzaro), 1949, Jl 28,23:4
Dundon, Arthur H, 1939, Je 21,23:3
Dundon, Augustus J, 1940, S 3,17:5
Dundon, Gerald A, 1960, O 31,31:5
Dundon, John A, 1954, N 30,29:2
Dundon, Roscoe C, 1946, Je 19,21:4
Dundon, Tom, 1965, Ag 27,29:5
Dundonald, Earl of, 1935, Ap 13,15:4
Dundore, Raymond D, 1949, Je 23,27:3
Dundr, Vojtech, 1952, Ag 21,19:5
Dundy, Elmer Scipio (funl, F 8,9:5), 1907, F 6,9:5
Dunedin, Viscount, 1942, Ag 23,42:3
Dunegan, Catherine M, 1967, S 18,47:4
Duneka, Frederick A, 1919, Ja 25,11:4
Dunfee, J Mrs, 1942, Mr 18,23:4
Dunford, Honora, 1940, Je 4,23:3
Dungan, Albert W, 1964, N 12,37:2
Dungan, Clyde C, 1946, S 18,31:4
Dungan, David L, 1948, Ja 28,23:4
Dungan, Paul B, 1941, N 28,23:3
Dungan, William W Com, 1904, Ja 15,9:6
Dunglison, R J Dr, 1901, Mr 6,9:5
Dunglison, Robert, 1869, Ap 4,3:5
Dunham, Arthur, 1938, Ja 25,21:5
Dunham, Arthur H, 1946, F 18,21:2
Dunham, C, 1877, F 21,8:4
Dunham, Carroll, 1948, My 26,27:2
Dunham, Carroll Mrs, 1951, S 20,31:6
Dunham, Clarence M, 1940, O 29,25:3
Dunham, Corydon B, 1966, N 11,43:5
Dunham, Daisy E Mrs, 1941, O 3,23:4
Dunham, Durward B, 1949, My 17,25:2
Dunham, Earl F, 1955, Je 9,29:3
Dunham, Edward B Mrs, 1959, Ap 3,27:2
Dunham, Edward K, 1951, Je 12,29:3
Dunham, Edward Kellogg Dr, 1922, Ap 16,28:3
Dunham, Edward Mrs, 1944, Jl 4,19:5
Dunham, Edwin Lewis, 1968, Ja 9,43:3
Dunham, Franklin, 1961, O 29,88:2
Dunham, Fred H, 1948, Ag 12,21:6
Dunham, Frederic G (por), 1943, D 25,13:1
Dunham, Frederic W, 1937, My 16,II,8:7
Dunham, Frederick C, 1946, Ja 16,24:3
Dunham, Gardner C, 1965, Ag 27,29:1
Dunham, George, 1938, Ag 12,17:2
Dunham, George A Jr, 1921, N 1,19:4
Dunham, George C, 1954, N 7,87:5
Dunham, George E, 1922, O 30,15:4
Dunham, George W, 1965, F 19,35:3
Dunham, Grover C, 1955, F 18,21:4
Dunham, Harry H Mrs, 1951, Ag 24,15:4
Dunham, Heber, 1964, Ap 30,35:2
Dunham, Henry B, 1965, Ap 21,45:1
Dunham, Henry V, 1946, My 31,21:1
Dunham, J H, 1901, Ap 29,7:6
Dunham, J Lawrence, 1918, Jl 27,9:6
Dunham, James H, 1942, Ap 22,24:2; 1953, O 22,29:2
Dunham, James H Mrs, 1958, Ag 7,25:2
Dunham, James W, 1963, S 9,27:2
Dunham, Jennie C, 1944, Ja 15,13:5
Dunham, John A, 1948, Ja 21,26:2
Dunham, John F, 1914, D 1,13:6
Dunham, John H, 1943, Je 21,17:4
Dunham, Julia P Mrs, 1940, Jl 20,15:5
Dunham, Laurence, 1918, My 6,13:8
Dunham, Lawrence B, 1959, Ag 9,88:3
Dunham, Lawrence H, 1944, Ja 20,19:4
Dunham, Lawrence Mrs, 1947, Jl 6,40:8
Dunham, Lindsay Sr, 1948, My 20,29:5
Dunham, M, 1931, S 28,19:5
Dunham, Otis E, 1950, O 20,28:3
Dunham, Otis M, 1954, N 10,33:1
Dunham, Raymond L, 1942, N 1,52:6
Dunham, Robert J, 1948, F 4,24:1
Dunham, Robert J Mrs, 1941, Mr 15,17:3
Dunham, Royal W, 1958, Je 18,33:2
Dunham, Russell H, 1958, F 3,23:2
Dunham, Samuel F, 1907, O 8,11:5
Dunham, Sturges S, 1944, S 12,19:2
Dunham, Sturges S Mrs, 1953, Jl 15,25:3
Dunham, Sylvester C, 1915, O 27,11:7
Dunham, Theodore Mrs, 1939, S 14,23:4
Dunham, Theodore N, 1951, N 12,25:4
Dunham, Theodore W Jr (cor, F 16,37:1), 1960, F 13,19:4
Dunham, Theodore W Mrs, 1952, Ap 17,29:1
Dunham, Thomas C, 1909, Je 21,7:6; 1955, O 22,19:6
Dunham, V C, 1918, Ja 22,11:4
Dunham, Warren B, 1941, S 4,21:5
Dunham, William V, 1954, Ap 9,24:4
Dunhill, Alfred, 1959, Ja 5,29:4
Dunhill, Herbert E, 1950, N 9,33:2
Dunhill, Thomas F, 1946, Mr 14,25:6
Dunifer, J Frank, 1950, Mr 22,27:3
Dunifer, J Frank Mrs, 1949, Ag 26,19:3
Dunigan, Bernard Mrs, 1937, D 18,21:5
Dunigan, Jay T, 1954, Jl 8,23:3
Dunigan, Michael, 1940, Ag 16,15:1
Dunigan, Peter F, 1966, F 12,27:5
Dunigan, Raymond I, 1946, Jl 6,15:5
Duning, Raymond W, 1950, Ap 26,29:5
Duniway, Abigail Scott Mrs, 1915, O 12,11:5
Duniway, Clyde A, 1944, D 25,19:1
Duniway, Hubert R, 1938, N 29,23:2
Dunk, Howard W, 1962, S 26,39:3
Dunk, Lewis, 1950, D 1,25:2
Dunkel, Kyle, 1938, Je 6,17:5
Dunkel, Paul A, 1961, Ag 30,33:4
Dunkelberger, William Mrs, 1952, Je 25,29:3
Dunker, Charles H, 1943, Ag 4,17:6
Dunker, Ernest H, 1951, My 4,27:4
Dunkerley, G C, 1959, Ja 26,29:5
Dunkerley, Herbert Mrs, 1962, Mr 17,25:5
Dunkerley, J Raymond, 1958, N 21,29:1
Dunkerly, William, 1952, D 18,29:5
Dunkerton, Thomas H, 1950, O 9,14:3
Dunkle, George H, 1950, Ja 8,76:5
Dunkleberg, C C, 1903, Ag 1,7:6
Dunkley, Ferdinand L, 1956, Ja 7,17:4
Dunklin, Gilbert T, 1945, N 21,21:4
Dunklin, William Wathin Mrs, 1924, Ap 14,17:3
Dunkly, Leonard, 1905, D 28,16:4
Dunlaevy, James B, 1945, F 10,11:6
Dunlap, A K Dr, 1937, Ja 21,23:2
Dunlap, Al, 1946, Ja 29,25:3
Dunlap, Amy, 1940, My 7,25:5
Dunlap, Andrew Rear-Adm, 1914, Ap 12,15:4
Dunlap, Boyce, 1957, Je 20,29:4
Dunlap, C D Mrs, 1953, Ja 8,30:3
Dunlap, Charles E, 1953, Ja 21,31:4; 1966, Mr 10,33:3
Dunlap, Charles J Mrs, 1955, Mr 24,32:1
Dunlap, Charles K, 1940, F 5,18:2
Dunlap, Charles W, 1960, Ap 4,29:3
Dunlap, Clarence E Mrs, 1952, Ag 22,21:5
Dunlap, Cornell Mrs, 1952, Mr 14,20:5
Dunlap, David R, 1968, N 23,47:4
Dunlap, E Lynn Sr, 1963, O 14,29:5
Dunlap, Earl O, 1944, Jl 7,15:4
Dunlap, Edgar B, 1955, O 2,86:6
Dunlap, Edith, 1945, Ag 24,19:4
Dunlap, Esmeralda, 1949, Jl 19,30:4
Dunlap, Frederick L, 1960, O 12,39:3
Dunlap, G M Mrs, 1869, Je 18,1:7
Dunlap, George T, 1956, Je 28,29:3
Dunlap, Harry M, 1960, Ag 24,29:2
Dunlap, Henry Lane, 1914, Ja 12,9:6
Dunlap, Henry M, 1938, Ja 9,43:1
Dunlap, Henry V, 1950, S 17,105:2
Dunlap, Hiram J, 1919, O 27,11:5
Dunlap, Hugh, 1942, Mr 10,19:2
Dunlap, James A, 1938, N 25,23:4
Dunlap, James W, 1941, Ja 1,23:5
Dunlap, Jennings J, 1964, S 24,41:5
Dunlap, John B, 1938, S 25,39:2; 1964, D 8,45:3
Dunlap, John F, 1941, Ja 2,23:4
Dunlap, John H, 1924, Jl 30,13:4
Dunlap, John R, 1937, Je 6,II,8:8; 1955, O 13,31:3
Dunlap, Kenneth J Mrs, 1950, O 24,29:3
Dunlap, Laura C, 1947, Jl 17,19:6
Dunlap, Marshall, 1904, F 5,9:5
Dunlap, Millard F, 1940, F 16,19:1
Dunlap, Orrin E, 1953, Je 15,29:1
Dunlap, Porter, 1957, N 23,19:6
Dunlap, Ralph I, 1948, S 2,24:3
Dunlap, Renick W, 1945, Mr 3,13:5
Dunlap, Richard W, 1955, S 12,25:2
Dunlap, Roy J, 1938, Je 8,23:3
Dunlap, Sallows Mrs, 1912, Jl 7,II,11:5
Dunlap, Samuel Fayles, 1905, Ap 2,9:6
Dunlap, Sophie R, 1953, D 29,23:3
Dunlap, Theodore M, 1964, Je 19,31:4
Dunlap, Thomas Biddle Col, 1916, Ja 26,11:3
Dunlap, Walter F, 1951, Je 26,29:1
Dunlap, Wilbur B, 1952, Je 12,34:3
Dunlap, William H D, 1939, Ag 12,13:3
Dunlap, William P, 1941, Ag 17,39:2
Dunlap, William R, 1940, N 24,51:1
Dunlavy, Edward J, 1955, Mr 25,23:2
Dunlay, Herbert, 1950, Jl 6,27:2
Dunleavy, Christopher B, 1963, D 16,33:5
Dunlevy, David W, 1943, Ag 5,15:5
Dunlevy, John P, 1948, D 15,33:2; 1952, D 28,48:5
Dunlevy, Joseph A, 1950, Ap 18,31:5
Dunlevy, William, 1906, N 15,9:6
Dunlop, August P, 1915, O 9,9:4
Dunlop, Beveridge C, 1961, Jl 3,15:5
Dunlop, Charles, 1944, Mr 18,13:2
Dunlop, David B Mrs (trb), 1950, Ag 11,18:5
Dunlop, G P G, 1949, S 25,92:5
Dunlop, George C Rev, 1937, O 29,21:4
Dunlop, George P, 1955, F 10,31:5
Dunlop, Hugh H, 1956, D 24,13:4
Dunlop, J B, 1921, O 25,17:5
Dunlop, James, 1950, Je 4,92:2; 1957, F 16,17:3
Dunlop, James B, 1953, Ag 8,11:6
Dunlop, James J Rev Dr, 1937, My 25,27:4
Dunlop, John, 1964, Mr 16,31:5
Dunlop, John A, 1954, Ap 20,29:2
Dunlop, John H, 1940, Ag 10,13:5
Dunlop, John Maj, 1907, D 13,11:5
Dunlop, Judson, 1952, S 14,86:2
Dunlop, Margaret A, 1942, Ag 4,19:4
Dunlop, Nathaniel Sir, 1919, N 16,22:4
Dunlop, Robert J, 1950, Jl 1,15:2
Dunlop, Samuel, 1946, Ag 23,19:3
Dunlop, Thomas, 1938, Ja 30,II,8:8
Dunlop, William A Mrs, 1943, Ja 10,50:4
Dunlop, William C, 1945, D 9,45:1
Dunlop, William F, 1938, My 17,23:3
Dunman, Henry, 1939, F 7,19:5
Dunmore, Alex E, 1962, Ja 30,29:5
Dunmore, Earl of, 1907, Ag 28,7:6
Dunmore, Walter T, 1945, Ja 25,19:5
Dunmore, Watson T Mrs, 1938, S 14,23:3
Dunmoyer, Robert J, 1964, My 20,43:2
Dunn, A Arthur, 1955, Mr 5,17:3
Dunn, A W, 1926, N 3,23:5; 1927, N 16,25:3
Dunn, Albert S Mrs, 1967, O 18,47:2
Dunn, Alfred M, 1950, O 16,27:4
Dunn, Allan F, 1956, Jl 20,17:2
Dunn, Andrew J, 1950, Jl 2,25:1
Dunn, Anthony B, 1953, Ja 29,27:2
Dunn, Arch W, 1942, Ap 30,19:6
Dunn, Arthur, 1953, S 17,29:2
Dunn, Arthur D, 1956, S 14,23:2
Dunn, Arthur D Mrs, 1963, My 10,33:5
Dunn, Arthur T, 1956, D 12,39:4
Dunn, Ashton, 1966, Mr 14,31:1
Dunn, B W, 1936, My 11,19:5
Dunn, Bernard, 1940, S 30,17:4
Dunn, Bernard J Sr, 1940, S 30,17:4
Dunn, Bertrand F, 1942, Ap 12,45:2
Dunn, Brian J, 1967, Mr 10,39:1
Dunn, C A, 1903, My 26,9:6
Dunn, Carl S, 1957, S 30,31:6
Dunn, Charles, 1921, Mr 25,15:5
Dunn, Charles A, 1940, My 10,23:1; 1961, Je 14,19:3
Dunn, Charles A Mrs, 1963, Ap 23,37:4
Dunn, Charles E, 1948, N 21,88:4
Dunn, Charles E Mrs, 1951, My 16,35:5
Dunn, Charles G, 1967, D 30,23:1
Dunn, Charles J, 1939, N 11,15:4; 1949, N 30,27:5
Dunn, Charles R, 1949, Ja 22,14:2
Dunn, Charles W, 1951, Ap 4,29:1; 1959, N 3,35:4
Dunn, Chris J, 1942, F 24,21:4
Dunn, Cleveland A, 1956, Jl 23,23:5
Dunn, D Frank, 1942, F 14,15:5
Dunn, Daniel, 1945, S 29,15:5
Dunn, Daniel E Mrs, 1949, D 6,31:5
Dunn, Daniel J, 1940, Ap 3,23:3
Dunn, Daniel O, 1945, N 21,21:1
Dunn, David L, 1949, My 7,13:7
Dunn, David R, 1955, F 18,21:1
Dunn, Donald E, 1964, Je 22,27:2
Dunn, Eddie Mrs, 1962, N 23,30:2
Dunn, Edward, 1943, Je 6,42:5
Dunn, Edward A, 1939, O 4,25:4
Dunn, Edward H C, 1961, Ja 22,85:1
Dunn, Edward J, 1941, F 6,22:2; 1961, My 8,35:4
Dunn, Edward S, 1942, F 16,17:2
Dunn, Edwin C, 1953, Mr 2,23:5
Dunn, Elias B, 1943, Je 5,15:1
Dunn, Ella S Mrs, 1950, Ag 16,29:5
Dunn, Emmett R, 1956, F 14,29:4
Dunn, Ervin S, 1953, F 6,20:5
Dunn, Euphemia C Mrs, 1943, Je 15,21:2
Dunn, F Randolph, 1939, Jl 22,15:4
Dunn, Fannie E Mrs, 1941, Je 14,17:4
Dunn, Fannie W, 1946, Ja 19,13:5
Dunn, Francis X, 1958, Jl 7,27:4
Dunn, Frank A, 1951, Ap 29,88:7; 1959, Je 25,29:5
Dunn, Frank C, 1952, F 26,27:4
Dunn, Frank J, 1948, Ja 13,26:2
Dunn, Frank K, 1940, Ag 9,15:5

Dunn, Frank L, 1947, My 12,21:2
Dunn, Frank M, 1949, Ja 5,25:2; 1950, Ag 17,27:2
Dunn, Frank P, 1965, Jl 8,28:3
Dunn, Franklin J L, 1960, Ap 2,23:6
Dunn, Fred S Mrs, 1951, Je 22,25:3
Dunn, Frederick M, 1937, O 28,25:2
Dunn, Frederick S, 1962, Mr 18,86:1
Dunn, G F, 1929, Ap 1,25:5
Dunn, Gano, 1953, Ap 11,17:1
Dunn, Gano Mrs, 1937, My 13,25:3
Dunn, George A, 1942, F 26,19:3
Dunn, George B, 1942, Jl 29,17:4
Dunn, George D, 1943, F 18,23:2
Dunn, George F, 1951, D 12,37:1
Dunn, George Nelson (Geo D Nelson), 1910, F 21, 9:5
Dunn, George Sr, 1946, Ap 10,27:2
Dunn, George W, 1937, Ap 28,23:2; 1957, Mr 22,23:4
Dunn, George W Mrs, 1951, Ap 28,15:6
Dunn, George Walter, 1914, N 28,13:6
Dunn, Gerald F, 1955, Jl 12,25:5
Dunn, Gordon, 1942, My 4,19:2
Dunn, Harold H, 1953, Je 24,25:4
Dunn, Harris A, 1961, O 9,35:1
Dunn, Harrison M, 1949, Mr 6,72:4
Dunn, Harry, 1946, Jl 19,19:6
Dunn, Harry B, 1956, My 21,25:2
Dunn, Harry B Mrs, 1949, Ja 19,27:1
Dunn, Harry T, 1952, F 21,27:6
Dunn, Harvey, 1952, O 31,25:2
Dunn, Henry (cor, F 14,76:1), 1965, F 13,21:4
Dunn, Henry A Dr, 1917, D 14,13:4
Dunn, Henry E, 1953, My 12,27:3
Dunn, Henry M, 1947, Jl 31,21:1
Dunn, Herbert H, 1941, S 21,44:2
Dunn, Herbert O, 1939, F 14,19:5
Dunn, Homer A Mrs, 1944, Ag 5,11:6
Dunn, Homer E, 1951, O 28,85:2
Dunn, Housten Mrs, 1937, D 21,23:4
Dunn, Houston, 1947, S 19,23:2
Dunn, Hubert E, 1939, Je 23,19:2
Dunn, Ignatius J, 1958, Mr 16,86:7
Dunn, J A, 1941, Mr 26,23:1
Dunn, J J, 1933, S 1,17:1; 1950, My 10,31:2
Dunn, J Malcolm, 1946, O 11,23:6
Dunn, J Reginald, 1952, O 6,25:1
Dunn, Jack, 1938, Jl 16,13:6
Dunn, Jack Mrs (will, F 20,17:4), 1943, F 16,19:3
Dunn, James (Jimmy the Hustler), 1906, N 21,18:3
Dunn, James, 1925, Ag 23,7:3; 1947, D 21,52:7; 1956, Ja 2,21:1; 1967, S 4,21:3
Dunn, James A, 1912, F 9,9:5; 1939, Je 7,23:1
Dunn, James B Rev Dr, 1906, Mr 20,9:6
Dunn, James E, 1955, Ag 20,17:6
Dunn, James F, 1940, D 24,15:2
Dunn, James H, 1903, N 29,7:6; 1937, N 3,24:1
Dunn, James J, 1942, My 9,13:4; 1948, F 10,23:1
Dunn, James L, 1940, Je 20,23:5
Dunn, James M, 1937, Mr 5,21:1; 1943, N 2,25:4; 1956, Ap 12,31:4
Dunn, James P, 1954, Mr 14,88:6
Dunn, James Sir (will), 1956, Ap 10,5:5
Dunn, James V, 1944, S 16,13:5
Dunn, James W, 1917, Ag 13,9:5
Dunn, Jere, 1906, Je 28,7:6
Dunn, Jesse Mrs, 1946, My 31,23:4
Dunn, John, 1913, S 17,9:2
Dunn, John A S, 1966, S 1,35:4
Dunn, John B, 1947, N 26,23:2
Dunn, John E, 1939, Ag 7,15:6
Dunn, John F Sr Mrs, 1944, Ap 22,15:4
Dunn, John H, 1942, Je 3,24:5; 1946, Je 27,22:2; 1954, N 23,35:4
Dunn, John I, 1906, Mr 16,9:5
Dunn, John J, 1948, Je 29,23:2; 1957, D 7,21:1
Dunn, John J Lt (Sir Johnny), 1910, Ja 24,9:1
Dunn, John J Mrs, 1957, N 16,19:3
Dunn, John K, 1951, F 26,23:3; 1959, Ag 27,27:2
Dunn, John L, 1958, Je 26,27:4
Dunn, John R, 1945, N 7,23:1; 1948, D 24,17:4
Dunn, John R Mrs, 1956, Jl 24,25:2
Dunn, John S P, 1950, Ag 3,23:1
Dunn, John T, 1907, F 23,9:6
Dunn, John T Mrs, 1944, D 10,53:2
Dunn, John T Sr, 1951, Ja 11,25:1
Dunn, John W, 1950, Je 7,30:3
Dunn, Joseph, 1951, Ap 10,28:2
Dunn, Joseph A, 1942, Ag 29,15:2; 1957, Ja 16,31:4
Dunn, Joseph A F (por), 1949, Ap 8,26:2
Dunn, Joseph C, 1962, Mr 8,31:3; 1965, Ja 5,33:1
Dunn, Joseph D, 1953, My 6,31:5
Dunn, Joseph F, 1953, Je 13,15:6
Dunn, Lamar J, 1955, Ja 28,19:2
Dunn, Lanier, 1915, Jl 2,11:6
Dunn, Laurence J Mrs, 1950, Ja 17,27:3
Dunn, Lawrence D, 1949, S 27,27:2
Dunn, Lawrence J, 1956, O 30,37:3
Dunn, Leo M Mrs, 1954, Ja 10,87:1
Dunn, Lillian C, 1953, Jl 9,25:3
Dunn, Louis W, 1947, Mr 3,21:4
Dunn, Marine, 1948, N 10,29:2
Dunn, Marshall, 1960, N 22,35:2
Dunn, Marshall Mrs (E McCormick), 1962, Je 18, 25:3
Dunn, Martha Baker (Mrs Reuben Wesley Dunn), 1915, Jl 24,9:7
Dunn, Martin J, 1957, Mr 4,27:5
Dunn, Martin T, 1968, My 28,47:2
Dunn, Martin T Mrs, 1958, Ja 9,33:1
Dunn, Mary, 1921, Ag 4,15:6
Dunn, Mary (Mother Mary Joseph), 1956, Mr 31, 15:5
Dunn, Mary A, 1939, S 23,17:4; 1943, My 3,17:5
Dunn, Mary E Mrs, 1938, My 31,19:4
Dunn, Matthew A, 1942, F 14,15:6
Dunn, Michael F, 1953, Ja 20,25:4
Dunn, Michael J, 1948, D 10,25:4
Dunn, Morley K Mrs, 1962, O 25,39:1
Dunn, Morrill, 1948, Ag 9,19:2
Dunn, Neville, 1957, Mr 13,31:3
Dunn, O J Lt-Gov, 1871, N 23,5:2
Dunn, Peter A, 1958, Ja 26,88:4
Dunn, Philip J, 1945, My 16,19:2
Dunn, Ralph H, 1943, Mr 18,19:5
Dunn, Ramond F, 1942, Jl 22,19:1
Dunn, Reuben Wesley Mrs (Martha Baker Dunn), 1915, Jl 24,9:7
Dunn, Richard F X, 1964, Ag 16,93:2
Dunn, Richard J, 1947, F 3,19:3
Dunn, Richard M, 1950, N 3,28:5
Dunn, Richard T, 1949, Ja 15,17:5
Dunn, Robert (Steed), 1955, D 25,48:1
Dunn, Robert A, 1945, F 22,27:4
Dunn, Robert J, 1958, Ja 11,17:4
Dunn, Robert L, 1953, Mr 21,17:1
Dunn, Robert M, 1943, My 21,19:5; 1948, F 7,15:3
Dunn, Robert R, 1940, Mr 31,46:3
Dunn, Rossell O, 1951, Mr 20,29:4
Dunn, Samuel O Sr, 1958, Ja 6,39:5
Dunn, Stella K Mrs, 1939, My 20,15:2
Dunn, Stephen F, 1944, O 20,19:4
Dunn, Stephen T, 1938, N 19,17:5
Dunn, T Joseph Dr, 1916, N 24,13:5
Dunn, Theodore S, 1947, Je 6,23:2
Dunn, Thomas, 1904, D 29,5:5
Dunn, Thomas A Sr, 1958, Je 21,19:2
Dunn, Thomas B, 1924, Jl 3,15:5
Dunn, Thomas J (funl, D 16,8:2), 1905, D 13,10:1
Dunn, Thomas J, 1914, S 9,9:6
Dunn, Thomas S, 1943, Jl 6,23:7
Dunn, Timothy J, 1942, S 17,25:3
Dunn, Tom J, 1949, Ja 31,19:3
Dunn, Vincent J, 1957, Mr 22,23:2
Dunn, W, 1883, Jl 28,6:1
Dunn, W Frank, 1940, Mr 19,26:2
Dunn, W Sir, 1926, Je 15,25:5
Dunn, Wallace S, 1956, F 27,23:3
Dunn, Walter K, 1957, Ja 1,23:2
Dunn, William, 1941, Jl 1,24:5
Dunn, William B, 1950, Mr 21,29:2
Dunn, William B Sr, 1949, My 8,76:7
Dunn, William D, 1960, Ag 13,15:5
Dunn, William E, 1966, N 20,88:6
Dunn, William H (will, Mr 28,18:1), 1937, Mr 25, 25:4
Dunn, William H, 1955, F 14,19:5
Dunn, William H Jr, 1962, My 12,23:5
Dunn, William J, 1947, Jl 15,23:5; 1952, Mr 24,25:5
Dunn, William J Jr, 1962, F 15,29:1
Dunn, William P, 1942, F 20,17:3; 1951, N 21,25:1
Dunn, William R, 1945, Jl 3,13:2
Dunn, William Rev, 1937, S 8,23:6
Dunn, William S, 1942, Ja 6,24:2
Dunn, William T, 1939, Jl 16,31:2; 1945, D 2,46:4; 1955, N 3,31:3; 1966, D 29,28:5
Dunn, Willis E, 1939, D 2,17:2
Dunn, Wm V, 1954, O 21,27:3
Dunn, Woodbury, 1956, Je 10,78:5
Dunnagan, Mervyn G, 1943, D 31,15:4
Dunnagan, Thomas, 1942, Mr 22,49:3
Dunne, Agnes Mary, 1914, S 17,9:6
Dunne, Arthur J, 1940, D 3,25:2
Dunne, D Rev, 1868, D 26,1:6
Dunne, Desmond, 1922, Je 6,17:4
Dunne, Edward, 1937, Jl 18,II,7:1; 1938, N 10,27:4
Dunne, Edward F, 1937, My 25,27:1; 1948, Ap 2,23:4; 1959, Ag 31,21:4
Dunne, Edward Joseph Bp, 1910, Ag 6,7:6
Dunne, F P, 1936, Ap 25,17:1
Dunne, Finley P (will), 1937, Je 5,15:4
Dunne, Francis F, 1955, Jl 25,19:5
Dunne, Frank H, 1941, Je 18,21:1
Dunne, Frederic M, 1948, Ag 5,21:2
Dunne, Gerald, 1942, N 6,23:5
Dunne, James A (por), 1938, D 25,14:4
Dunne, James A, 1939, F 15,23:4
Dunne, James E, 1942, Mr 1,44:3
Dunne, John J, 1947, O 15,27:4; 1965, Ag 31,33:5
Dunne, John J Sr Mrs, 1957, N 18,31:1
Dunne, John P, 1937, Mr 10,23:5
Dunne, John R, 1950, F 5,85:2
Dunne, John S Mrs, 1947, Jl 31,21:3
Dunne, John V, 1962, Ap 25,39:4
Dunne, John W, 1949, Ag 26,20:4
Dunne, John W Mrs (M Marble), 1965, F 7,92:4
Dunne, Joseph E P, 1962, Ja 13,21:2
Dunne, Leon G, 1945, My 1,23:5
Dunne, M Walter, 1920, Ap 10,15:4
Dunne, M Walter Mrs, 1948, Ag 19,21:1
Dunne, Mary, 1937, S 24,46:4
Dunne, Matthew J, 1953, Jl 11,11:7
Dunne, Michael F, 1945, F 21,19:6
Dunne, Michael J, 1961, Ag 16,31:5
Dunne, Patrick (Bro Pius Patrick), 1956, D 3,29:3
Dunne, Paul J (Bro Bonaventure), 1954, F 16,25:3
Dunne, Peter B, 1949, O 20,29:4
Dunne, Richard A, 1966, Mr 8,39:2
Dunne, Richard E, 1946, My 29,23:5
Dunne, Richard P (Bro Eugene), 1953, Mr 7,16:7
Dunne, Sara C (Mother Mary), 1953, Ap 30,31:5
Dunne, Thomas G, 1959, My 28,31:3
Dunne, Thomas J (trb lr, Ag 16,24:7), 1956, Ag 7, 27:5
Dunne, Ulysses J, 1944, Mr 4,13:6
Dunne, Walter Elliott, 1923, Ja 13,13:5
Dunne, William J, 1961, D 13,43:1
Dunne, William J Rev, 1922, Ag 25,13:7
Dunne, William L Mrs, 1951, O 24,32:2
Dunne, Willis F, 1953, S 24,33:4
Dunnell, E G, 1905, F 4,9:3
Dunnell, John Henry, 1904, Ja 28,9:6
Dunnell, William Nichols Rev Dr, 1921, Mr 15,11:
Dunnells, Clifford G, 1947, Ap 16,25:5
Dunnelly, Austin, 1954, Ag 6,17:5
Dunnett, Frederick, 1958, Je 17,29:6
Dunnette, Alexander, 1920, S 15,9:1
Dunney, Joseph A, 1953, Ag 22,15:6
Dunnico, Herbert, 1953, O 3,17:6
Dunnigan, Ambrose P, 1939, Jl 24,13:7
Dunnigan, James J, 1960, Jl 5,31:2
Dunnigan, John J, 1965, D 12,86:2
Dunnigan, John J Mrs, 1945, Jl 28,11:6
Dunning, Albert E Dr, 1923, N 15,19:4
Dunning, Alex, 1940, Jl 5,13:4
Dunning, Arthur, 1947, N 13,27:4
Dunning, Arthur E, 1945, Je 29,15:4
Dunning, Charles A, 1958, O 3,30:1
Dunning, Charlotte M, 1949, N 1,27:2
Dunning, David M, 1940, Ag 25,36:6
Dunning, Edgar Abram, 1916, Jl 8,9:4
Dunning, Edward R, 1962, S 17,31:6
Dunning, Elizabeth Roe, 1914, F 3,11:6
Dunning, Frank O Sr, 1951, O 6,19:2
Dunning, George A Mrs, 1954, Ap 4,88:5
Dunning, George M (por), 1949, N 18,29:2
Dunning, Halsey Rev, 1869, Ja 14,5:5
Dunning, Harry, 1953, D 23,25:3
Dunning, Helen L Mrs, 1948, Je 4,23:3
Dunning, Henry N Rev, 1916, O 18,11:6
Dunning, Henry S, 1957, F 11,29:3
Dunning, James A, 1925, O 8,27:5
Dunning, James H, 1942, Ja 24,17:5
Dunning, John A, 1962, Ag 14,31:4
Dunning, John E, 1909, My 16,9:6
Dunning, John P, 1907, Ap 18,11:6
Dunning, John W, 1950, D 31,43:2
Dunning, Luta V Mrs, 1941, Jl 3,19:1
Dunning, N Max, 1945, Ap 20,19:5
Dunning, Philip, 1968, Jl 22,41:2
Dunning, Ralph Maj, 1905, My 5,9:4
Dunning, Richard, 1951, Je 23,4:7
Dunning, Robert L, 1949, Je 23,27:1
Dunning, Sarah L, 1941, D 25,25:4
Dunning, Silas Wright, 1924, My 30,15:6
Dunning, Stewart N, 1951, N 24,11:4
Dunning, T Star, 1949, Ag 11,23:2
Dunning, William, 1938, My 25,23:2
Dunning, William A Prof (funl, Ag 28,11:5), 19 Ag 26,11:6
Dunning, William B, 1959, Jl 23,27:3
Dunning, William B Mrs, 1943, Ap 15,25:4
Dunning, William Fullerton, 1907, Ap 2,11:5
Dunning, William M, 1951, My 12,21:6
Dunningham, Jabez E, 1945, Ap 30,19:3
Dunnington, Francis P, 1944, F 4,15:5
Dunnock, Walter O, 1958, Ap 4,21:2
Dunnon, Thomas J, 1957, O 10,33:3
Dunnroy, William Reed, 1921, Mr 30,13:3
Du Nouy, Pierre L, 1947, S 23,25:1
Dunphy, Anne T, 1956, F 26,88:5
Dunphy, Clifford W, 1967, My 2,47:2
Dunphy, Edward J, 1948, My 4,26:3
Dunphy, Herb I, 1952, Ja 25,21:3
Dunphy, John, 1954, F 2,27:4
Dunphy, John F, 1954, Ap 27,29:5
Dunphy, Nicholas, 1955, Ja 26,25:3
Dunphy, Richard J, 1946, S 25,28:2
Dunraven, Earl of, 1926, Je 15,25:3
Dunraven, Earl of (W H WyndhamQuin), 195 O 24,23:1
Dunrossil, Viscount (W S Morrison), 1961, F
Duns, Mary A, 1943, Ja 24,42:2
Dunsany, Lord (E M J M D Plunkett), 1957, 86:1
Dunscomb, Charles E, 1938, N 9,23:4
Dunscomb, Howard, 1942, F 15,44:6
Dunscombe, Duncan, 1965, D 28,27:2
Dunscombe, George E, 1957, Ap 26,25:3
Dunscombe, George E Mrs, 1959, Ag 4,27:5

Dunscombe, Roger, 1961, Ap 4,37:2
Dunscombe, Roger Mrs, 1959, Mr 30,31:1
Dunseith, J Franklin, 1939, Mr 7,22:2
Dunseith, Samuel L, 1958, Ap 9,33:3
Dunsford, W Bevan, 1949, Ap 5,29:2
Dunshee, J, 1881, N 23,2:5
Dunshee, Kenneth H, 1964, S 15,37:4
Dunshee, William Adams, 1925, My 21,23:4
Dunsmore, George H, 1937, F 5,21:2
Dunsmore, John M, 1949, My 17,25:3
Dunsmore, John M Sr, 1951, My 2,31:2
Dunsmore, John W, 1945, O 3,19:3
Dunsmuir, James, 1920, Je 7,15:2
Dunspaugh, William F, 1938, Ap 2,15:4
Dunst, Philip R, 1967, F 16,39:1
Dunstan, Albert A, 1950, Ap 15,15:5
Dunstan, James S, 1962, Ag 18,19:5
Dunstan, Kenneth J, 1938, D 31,15:1
Dunstan, Nelson, 1961, Ja 22,85:1
Dunstan, Richard L, 1949, S 30,24:2
Dunstan, Thomas S, 1960, Ag 4,25:4
Dunstan, William, 1957, Mr 6,31:1
Dunstan, Wyndham, 1949, Ap 21,26:5
Dunstatter, Frank H, 1962, O 28,88:8
Dunster, Charles H, 1948, S 7,25:3
Dunster, James H Mrs, 1940, Ag 28,19:5
Dunsterville, Lionel C, 1946, Mr 20,23:3
Dunston, Irvin, 1959, Ag 23,93:1
Dunston, J, 1927, D 27,19:3
Dunston, Morgan, 1913, My 11,IV,7:6
Dunston, William J Mrs, 1948, D 12,93:1
Dunstone, William H, 1938, D 6,23:5
Dunstone, William H Mrs, 1945, D 30,14:6
Dunton, Harry I, 1939, D 10,69:2
Dunton, John H, 1939, Ap 8,15:3
Dunton, W C, 1884, My 2,5:2
Duntz, Nelson, 1924, Ag 25,13:4
Duntze, John A, 1909, O 25,7:5
Dunvan, Jennie M, 1907, My 28,9:6
Dunville, Robert E, 1963, Mr 1,4:6
Dunwell, Charles T (funl, Je 14,11:5), 1908, Je 13,7:5
Dunwell, James W, 1907, My 23,9:6
Dunwody, Robert Mrs, 1950, Ap 16,106:4
Dunwody, Thomas E, 1959, My 3,86:2
Dunwoody, Charles E, 1905, Mr 14,9:6
Dunwoody, Francis M, 1942, S 22,21:1
Dunwoody, Halsey, 1952, S 3,29:1
Dunwoody, Jesse E, 1946, Ap 29,21:2
Dunwoody, William N, 1954, Mr 12,21:1
Dunworth, Thomas, 1949, F 2,27:2
Dupanloup, F A P Bishop, 1878, O 13,6:7
Du Parc, Adolphe Y M, 1946, My 11,27:6
Du Parcq, Lord, 1949, Ap 28,31:1
Du Pasquier, Claude, 1953, Ja 27,25:1
Du Pavillon, Edmond H, 1946, N 20,31:4
Dupee, Elizabeth N Mrs, 1942, D 26,11:2
Dupee, George P, 1907, S 5,9:5
Dupen, James, 1938, Mr 16,23:4
Dupertuis, S Milton, 1959, Mr 28,17:3
Dupignac, Ebenezer Mrs, 1949, O 4,27:5
Dupire, Jean Mrs, 1951, F 27,27:2
Duplan, John H, 1956, Ag 15,29:4
Duplan, Luis P, 1954, S 25,15:5
Du Plessis, Arthur, 1955, Ap 7,27:5
Du Plessis, Arthur J, 1937, Ja 3,II,9:1
Duplessis, Maurice Le N (funl plans, S 9,41:4; funl, S 11,28:1), 1959, S 7,15:1
du Plessis, Wentzel D, 1957, Ap 1,25:5
Dupong, Pierre, 1953, D 24,15:3
Du Pont, A Felix, 1948, Je 30,25:1
du Pont, A Felix Sr Mrs, 1963, My 9,37:2
Du Pont, A Francis, 1920, My 30,22:4
Du Pont, A J, 1935, Ap 29,15:4
DuPont, Albert J, 1966, N 5,31:2
Dupont, Albert R, 1963, Jl 6,15:5
Du Pont, Alexis I, 1921, My 31,15:4
Du Pont, Alfred C, 1941, Je 1,41:1
du Pont, Alfred I Mrs, 1920, Ja 8,17:1
Du Pont, Alfred L Mrs, 1949, D 14,31:4
u Pont, Alice Mrs (will, Mr 28,13:1), 1937, Mr 20, 19:1
u Pont, Amy E (will, Mr 3,12:2), 1962, F 17,19:1
Du Pont, Arch M L, 1942, Mr 13,19:3
u Pont, Biederman, 1923, O 23,21:4
u Pont, David F, 1955, S 3,31:2
u Pont, E Paul Sr, 1950, S 27,31:3
uPont, Emma C Mrs, 1953, Ja 27,25:2
u Pont, Ernest, 1944, Ag 20,34:5
upont, Eugene, 1902, Ja 29,9:7
u Pont, Eugene, 1954, D 16,37:3
u Pont, Eugene E, 1966, D 18,84:6
u Pont, Eugene Mrs, 1954, N 23,35:2
u Pont, Evelina, 1938, Jl 9,13:3
u Pont, F I, 1942, Mr 17,22:2
Pont, Francis V (will, Je 2,22:7), 1962, My 21,33:1
u Pont, H A, 1927, Ja 1,13:5
u Pont, Henry Belin Mrs, 1953, F 15,93:2
Pont, Henry F Mrs, 1967, N 9,47:4
Pont, Irenee, 1963, D 20,1:7
Pont, Irenee Mrs, 1961, N 30,37:5
u Pont, Lammot, 1952, Jl 25,17:1
Pont, Lammot Jr, 1964, F 24,25:2
Pont, Lammot Mrs, 1968, D 31,27:1

DuPont, Ludger, 1948, Jl 29,21:3
du Pont, Lydia C, 1958, Je 25,25:2
Dupont, Marcel, 1955, Jl 26,25:5
Du Pont, Maurice, 1941, Je 1,40:5
Du Pont, Maurice Mrs, 1951, My 20,88:3
Du Pont, P F, 1928, My 18,23:3
du Pont, Paul, 1957, Ap 21,88:1
du Pont, Philip F Mrs, 1964, Jl 29,33:3
Dupont, Pierre, 1961, My 20,23:4
Dupont, Pierre Mrs, 1938, Mr 6,II,8:2
du Pont, Pierre S, 1954, Ap 6,29:1
du Pont, Pierre S (will), 1955, F 11,8:8
Du Pont, Pierre S Mrs, 1944, Je 24,13:3
Dupont, S F Adm, 1865, Je 24,4:6
du Pont, T C, 1930, N 12,23:1
Du Pont, Victor Sr Mrs, 1943, F 14,49:1
Du Pont, W, 1928, Ja 21,17:3
Du Pont, William K, 1907, D 24,7:6
Du Pont, William K Mrs, 1951, Mr 4,92:5
Du Pont, Zara, 1946, My 3,21:3
Dupont-Hansen, George F, 1954, S 4,11:6
Duprat, Reginald, 1954, F 16,25:1
Dupre, Arthur M, 1949, O 31,25:3
Dupre, Ernest E, 1949, D 8,33:2
Dupre, Ernest Pierre Dr, 1921, S 3,9:6
Dupre, H Edmond, 1941, My 18,44:1
Dupre, Henry Garlan, 1924, F 22,15:5
Dupre, J Huntley Dr, 1968, S 9,47:3
Dupre, John B, 1950, O 3,31:1
Dupre, Marie L Mrs, 1945, Ja 29,14:2
Dupre, Ovide, 1903, Jl 16,7:6
DuPree, C M, 1942, Jl 23,19:4
Dupree, Frank, 1922, F 4,13:4
Dupree, Minnie, 1947, My 24,15:2
Dupree, William F, 1955, F 27,87:2
Dupree, William S Mrs, 1958, O 2,37:6
Dupress, John K, 1967, D 31,44:3
du Prey, Edmond L, 1955, Ja 16,92:2
Duprez, C H, 1902, S 1,7:6
Duprez, Caroline, 1875, My 3,1:5
Duprez, Florence Mrs, 1942, Ja 16,21:5
Duprez, Fred, 1938, O 30,41:2
Du Priest, Robert W, 1952, Ap 22,29:2
Dupriez, Leon H, 1942, O 23,21:4
Dupuis, Charles W, 1961, D 28,27:3
Dupuis, Frank B, 1939, Mr 11,17:3
Dupuy, Charles, 1923, Jl 24,21:4
DuPuy, Charles M Sr, 1961, S 4,15:6
Dupuy, George A, 1943, Jl 7,19:5
Du Puy, H, 1930, Ja 11,17:1
Du Puy, James A, 1948, Mr 19,23:2
Dupuy, James N, 1958, Jl 22,27:3
Dupuy, Jean (funl, Ja 4,23:3), 1920, Ja 1,15:3
Dupuy, L Edward, 1962, Ja 27,21:4
Dupuy, Louis, 1941, N 13,28:3
Dupuy, Louis Mrs, 1949, Ja 1,11:8
Dupuy, Moore, 1910, F 26,7:4
Dupuy, P, 1927, Jl 11,19:4
Dupuy, Paul Mrs, 1951, Ap 14,15:6
Du Puy, William A, 1941, Ag 12,19:3
Dupuy, William A Mrs, 1946, My 16,21:1
Duque, Tomas G, 1965, Ap 2,35:1
Duque y Perdomo, Matias, 1941, F 26,21:5
Duquesne, Frederick J, 1956, My 26,7:1
Duquette, George, 1948, N 23,30:2
Duquette, Herman E, 1948, D 29,22:3
Duran, Carlos Dr, 1924, N 24,17:3
Duran, Facundo Mutis, 1913, Je 22,IV,5:6
Duran, Helen E Mrs, 1953, Mr 16,21:4
Duran, Loborio C, 1952, Ap 5,15:2
Duran-Reynals, Francisco, 1958, Mr 28,25:1
Durand, Auguste, 1909, Je 4,7:5
Durand, Augusto Dr, 1923, Ap 3,23:4
Durand, Cyrus B Rev, 1904, Ag 16,7:6
Durand, E Dana, 1960, Je 7,29:4
Durand, Elias, 1873, Ag 16,1:2
Durand, Elie A, 1939, N 7,25:2
Durand, G H Judge, 1903, Je 9,9:6
Durand, Hamilton H, 1937, F 11,23:2
Durand, Harry S, 1939, Ap 10,18:1
Durand, Herbert, 1944, D 31,26:5
Durand, Howard W Mrs, 1941, F 23,40:2
Durand, J S, 1882, Ag 12,8:4
Durand, John, 1908, O 20,9:5
Durand, Leone, 1945, Mr 28,23:1
Durand, Lionel, 1961, Ja 15,87:1
Durand, Luis, 1954, O 12,27:1
Durand, Maude, 1952, Mr 27,29:4
Durand, Milo A, 1944, My 17,19:3
Durand, Mortimer Sir, 1924, Je 10,11:4
Durand, Nelson C, 1949, Jl 21,25:5
Durand, Pierre, 1951, S 15,15:5
Durand, Pierre-Marie, 1951, Jl 20,21:6
Durand, Scott S Mrs, 1948, F 27,21:2
Durand, Wickliffe B, 1906, D 17,11:5
Durand, William C W, 1954, S 12,84:7
Durand, William F, 1958, Ag 10,92:1
Durand-Ruel, Paul, 1922, F 7,17:3
Durando, Andre, 1946, Ja 1,27:4
Durant, Basil N, 1959, My 10,87:1
Durant, Basil N Mrs, 1945, O 8,15:4
Durant, C W, 1885, Ap 6,5:6
Durant, Charles F, 1873, Mr 4,8:5

Durant, Clara E H Mrs, 1940, Ja 28,32:1
Durant, Clark T Mrs, 1946, O 13,59:3
Durant, Donald, 1941, Ag 12,20:5
Durant, Edward A, 1917, Ap 1,19:3
Durant, Elliot, 1951, D 17,31:1
Durant, Eva (Sister Rose Marit), 1966, Ag 12,31:1
Durant, Frederick C Jr, 1961, D 29,24:7
Durant, H F, 1881, O 5,5:5
Durant, Harold J, 1938, Jl 16,13:8
Durant, Harry R, 1957, Ap 23,31:5
Durant, Harry S, 1941, O 19,19:8
Durant, Harvey L, 1940, Ag 29,19:3
Durant, James W, 1961, Mr 18,23:4
Durant, Joseph, 1943, Mr 28,24:5
Durant, Mary Mrs, 1942, Mr 21,17:5
Durant, Russell C, 1937, N 1,21:2
Durant, W W, 1934, Je 1,23:3
Durant, William A, 1948, Ag 2,21:3
Durant, William C, 1947, Mr 19,25:1
Durant, William W Mrs, 1962, S 17,31:4
Durante, Bartolomeo, 1941, F 28,19:1
Durante, Jimmy Mrs, 1943, F 15,15:4
Durante, Julius J, 1966, My 8,82:1
Durante, Lawrence J, 1963, O 28,27:5
Durante, Mariano, 1952, My 11,66:6
Durante, Oscar, 1945, F 24,11:1
Duranty, Walter, 1957, O 4,23:1
Durban, Charles J, 1954, F 11,29:3
Durban, William T, 1945, O 4,23:4
D'Urbar, Courtois, 1943, F 4,23:5
Durbin, Francis E, 1941, Ja 24,17:4
Durbin, Francis W, 1949, D 11,91:3
Durbin, Harry A, 1954, Ja 23,13:4
Durbin, J B (see also O 20), 1876, O 23,8:2
Durbin, John B, 1952, F 12,27:1
Durbin, John H, 1907, Ap 16,11:6
Durbin, Joseph W 2d, 1953, D 19,15:2
Durbin, Robert H, 1948, Mr 18,27:4
Durbin, Vernon, 1960, Mr 14,30:1
Durbin, W W, 1937, F 6,21:5
Durbin, William O, 1954, F 16,25:3
Durborough, James H, 1939, Mr 4,15:4
Durborow, Charles B, 1938, My 15,II,6:7
Durborow, Le Roy, 1942, Ja 19,17:5
Durborrow, Allen C, 1908, Mr 12,7:6
Durbrow, W, 1879, Je 18,8:3
Durcal, Duke of (Fernando M Baviera y Bourbon),(corr, Ap 7,21:2), 1958, Ap 6,88:2
Durdenevsky, Vsevolod N, 1963, N 16,27:5
Dure, Leon S, 1948, Ja 11,58:4
Dureau, Franklin P, 1924, Ag 20,13:3
Durecut, America, 1953, S 1,23:3
Durell, Fletcher, 1946, Mr 27,27:5
Durell, George B, 1941, O 22,23:3
Duren, George B, 1917, O 25,15:4
Durett, Joseph A, 1948, Mr 4,25:1
Durfee, Abner Mrs, 1950, O 26,31:4
Durfee, Albert R Mrs, 1954, Je 28,19:4
Durfee, Arthur C, 1938, D 27,17:3
Durfee, Arthur J, 1940, My 25,17:5
Durfee, Bradford C, 1964, Je 26,29:2
Durfee, Bradford M C, 1872, S 16,5:6
Durfee, Charles G, 1950, N 14,31:4
Durfee, Charles H, 1964, Ja 21,29:1
Durfee, Charles H Dr, 1968, D 20,47:2
Durfee, Charles H Mrs, 1959, My 4,29:3
Durfee, Herbert A, 1939, S 10,49:2
Durfee, Jim, 1940, F 25,38:4
Durfee, Justin W, 1950, F 3,23:1
Durfee, Nathan, 1948, O 7,29:4
Durfee, Randall N Mrs, 1953, Ja 17,15:4
Durfee, W C, 1901, D 9,9:5
Durfee, Walter H, 1939, Ag 5,15:4
Durfee, Walter H Mrs, 1967, Ag 17,37:3
Durfee, William P, 1941, D 18,27:5
Durgin, Blanche P, 1947, N 27,31:2
Durgin, Calvin T, 1965, Mr 26,35:2
Durgin, Delmer D, 1950, Ag 7,19:5
Durgin, Leonard R, 1946, Ja 4,21:2
Durgin, Russell L, 1956, Ja 14,19:3
Durham, Carl T Mrs, 1953, Ja 11,91:2
Durham, Charles H Mrs, 1951, Mr 18,88:6
Durham, Charles L, 1949, Ap 17,76:8
Durham, Donald B, 1951, S 29,17:4
Durham, Earl of, 1879, N 28,2:2; 1928, S 19,29:5
Durham, Edward A, 1950, Ja 14,15:2
Durham, Edward M Jr, 1954, Je 7,23:2
Durham, Herbert E, 1945, O 26,19:2
Durham, Israel W, 1909, Je 29,7:5
Durham, Jerie, 1916, F 24,13:4
Durham, John W Mrs, 1943, Ap 11,49:2
Durham, Kneeland S, 1937, N 27,17:5
Durham, Knowlton, 1961, D 5,43:4
Durham, Mary E, 1944, N 17,19:3
Durham, Milton J Judge, 1911, F 13,11:5
Durham, Nelson W, 1938, Ap 16,13:2
Durham, Percy J, 1959, Ap 28,35:2
Durham, Plato Capt, 1875, N 14,6:5
Durham, Raymond E, 1939, Ap 3,15:3
Durham, Robert M, 1964, My 21,35:1
Durham, Robert P, 1940, Jl 8,17:5
Durham, Stonewall J, 1950, N 12,93:2
Durham, Thomas F, 1947, Jl 24,21:4

Durham, William L, 1937, S 19,II,7:2
Durham Robt L (por), 1949, Ja 3,23:4
Durhan, George, 1939, S 13,25:5
Durhan, William J, 1963, Je 8,25:5
Durian, William F, 1948, F 3,25:3
Durick, James J Rev, 1912, O 13,17:4
Durick, Jeremiah K, 1960, Jl 29,25:1
Durie, Charles A, 1953, S 20,87:1
Durie, Harrison L, 1965, Ja 15,43:3
Durigan, Hugh M, 1958, N 20,35:4
During, Maurice P, 1967, S 29,47:2
During, Peter, 1952, Mr 9,81:5
Duris, Albert, 1950, Ag 21,23:3
Durivage, F, 1881, F 4,8:4
Durk, Francis L, 1952, N 12,27:2
Durkan, J Ambrose, 1939, Ap 25,23:3
Durkan, John, 1967, S 6,47:1
Durkan, Patrick J, 1939, Ja 3,18:1
Durkee, Albert J, 1951, N 17,17:3
Durkee, Charles A, 1953, O 15,33:2
Durkee, Charles Mrs, 1911, F 23,9:5
Durkee, Chauncey H Mrs (K Clendinning), 1956, Ag 18,17:6
Durkee, Clifford L, 1951, O 17,31:4
Durkee, Emily H Mrs, 1938, Ja 9,43:1
Durkee, Frank W, 1939, My 23,23:5
Durkee, Frank W Mrs, 1946, F 1,24:3
Durkee, Herbert V, 1959, My 26,35:2
Durkee, J Stanley, 1951, O 2,27:3
Durkee, Jeannette Reid Dr, 1907, O 28,9:5
Durkee, Joseph W, 1940, Mr 22,19:4
Durkee, Roland, 1945, Ap 21,13:5
Durkes, Daniel, 1952, Jl 29,21:3
Durkin, Anne G Mrs, 1938, Ag 19,19:2
Durkin, Douglas Mrs (M Ostenso), 1963, N 26,37:3
Durkin, Edmund J, 1949, My 4,29:5
Durkin, Edmund L, 1943, D 21,27:3
Durkin, Frank A, 1961, F 2,29:4
Durkin, James A, 1945, N 15,19:4
Durkin, James F, 1951, N 26,25:5
Durkin, James G, 1940, Ag 21,19:3
Durkin, James M, 1940, Je 24,15:4
Durkin, John, 1939, Ap 15,19:5; 1943, Ap 13,26:2; 1949, D 10,17:4
Durkin, John J, 1950, Jl 3,15:4; 1950, Ag 3,23:1
Durkin, John P, 1938, O 22,17:5
Durkin, John T Sr, 1964, N 24,39:1
Durkin, Joseph, 1942, Ag 23,41:1
Durkin, Joseph A, 1918, Ap 20,13:5
Durkin, Joseph L, 1948, Je 12,15:6
Durkin, Joseph R, 1948, Je 15,27:3
Durkin, Margaret Mrs, 1953, O 10,17:3
Durkin, Martin, 1948, D 5,92:2
Durkin, Martin P (funl, N 19,19:2), 1955, N 14,27:1
Durkin, Mary Antonia (Sister Mary Durkin), 1941, Jl 9,21:5
Durkin, Michael, 1909, Ag 4,7:3
Durkin, P H, 1951, Ja 16,29:5
Durkin, Thomas J, 1949, Je 7,31:2
Durkin, Vincent, 1958, O 16,37:4
Durkin, William J, 1938, Ag 3,19:5
Durlacher, Stanley H, 1957, Mr 25,25:4
Durland, Charles C, 1939, My 29,15:5
Durland, Clarence, 1948, O 21,27:4
Durland, F Col, 1903, O 24,9:6
Durland, Frank, 1946, My 11,27:2
Durland, Frederick L, 1954, Ag 20,19:4
Durland, Frederick L Mrs (will), 1964, Ap 2,35:7
Durland, Leander H Sr Mrs, 1946, N 9,17:4
Durland, Lyda Mrs, 1923, Je 4,15:4
Durland, S L, 1877, Ja 18,5:2
Durland, W, 1929, My 9,29:4
Durland, Wesley G, 1950, S 3,38:3
Durland, Whitman R, 1943, O 2,13:4
Durlewanger, William, 1948, S 15,31:4
Durling, Dwight L, 1961, Mr 18,23:4
Durling, Edgar Mrs, 1948, Jl 20,23:4
Durling, Edgar V, 1957, S 14,19:3
Durling, Grace M, 1953, Mr 10,29:4
Durmashkin, Sara, 1958, Je 3,31:4
Durmer, Florence C Mrs, 1945, O 16,23:4
Durmer, William S, 1945, Je 26,19:4
Durna, Joseph J, 1958, Ja 6,39:5
Durnan, Wesley L, 1955, Ja 22,11:5
Durnell, C E, 1949, F 17,23:4
Durnell, Rudolph H, 1952, My 24,19:5
Durney, Dennis J, 1956, Ja 31,29:4
Durniak, John, 1947, Ja 31,23:2
Durnin, Thomas J, 1955, Jl 2,15:4
Durning, Arthur J, 1940, F 13,23:1
Durning, Bernard J, 1923, Ag 30,13:5
Durning, Harold W Mrs, 1953, Ap 7,29:2
Durning, Harry M, 1958, N 10,29:1
Durning, James G, 1939, My 25,25:5
Durning, Paul A Jr, 1967, Jl 13,37:2
Durning, Peter, 1956, F 5,87:1
Durning, Robert T, 1919, O 10,13:4
Durning, Wilfred J, 1949, Ja 21,22:3
Durning-Lawrence, Edwin Sir, 1914, Ap 22,15:6
Durno, George E, 1957, Ja 28,23:3
Durnovo, Peter Nikolaievich, 1915, S 25,11:4
Durocher, George J, 1938, O 12,27:5
Durocher, George J Mrs (funl, Jl 29,23:2), 1955, Jl 25,19:4
Durocher, William J Sr, 1961, N 14,39:4
Du Roi, Margaret C Mrs, 1940, Jl 29,13:3
Duron, Romulo, 1942, Ag 15,11:6
Duror, Caroline, 1916, Mr 28,13:4
Duross, Charles E, 1950, S 3,39:2
Duross, Charles E Mrs, 1952, F 26,27:3
Duross, James E, 1958, S 1,13:6
Duross, James E Mrs, 1948, Ag 31,23:1
Duross, Mark C, 1968, Jl 5,25:4
Durou y Sure, Luis, 1938, D 19,23:6
Du Roure, Rene, 1940, O 16,23:5
Durr, Charles E, 1949, Mr 26,17:2
Durr, Edward C, 1950, O 11,33:3
Durr, John J, 1964, O 3,29:2
Durr, Louis, 1880, Ap 2,2:5
Durr, Peter W, 1948, F 21,13:4
Durrand, William, 1939, O 8,49:1
Durrant, Arnold S, 1938, Mr 23,23:1
Durrant, William, 1952, S 22,23:2
Durrell, Fletcher B Mrs, 1948, Je 11,23:2
Durrell, Harold F, 1943, Jl 9,17:6
Durrell, Joseph H, 1967, F 23,35:5
Durrell, Robert L, 1947, F 3,19:5
Durrie, Clarence N, 1968, My 13,43:2
Durrie, Horace, 1881, S 15,5:2
Durrie, William A Dr, 1924, D 2,25:4
Durrin, William C, 1965, Mr 8,29:1
Durring, Charles Mrs, 1955, Jl 30,17:6
Durrows, Helen J, 1948, O 18,23:2
Durrschmidt, Lillian M, 1950, S 28,31:2
Durrse, Jacob F, 1958, S 27,21:2
D'Ursel, Robert, 1955, Ap 17,87:1
Durso, Mary A Mrs, 1949, Mr 6,73:2
Durst, Edward, 1945, Mr 12,19:4
Durst, Hugo W, 1963, Je 23,85:1
Durst, Joseph Mrs, 1965, F 18,33:4
Durst, Max, 1952, D 20,17:4
Durst, Seymour B Mrs, 1950, N 10,20:1
Durst, William A, 1940, Ag 21,19:5
Durst, Willis H, 1959, Mr 21,21:6
Durstine, Roy S, 1962, N 29,37:1
Durstine, Roy S Mrs, 1968, D 11,47:2
Durston, Alfred G, 1947, Ap 10,25:4
Durston, Harry, 1950, Je 9,23:5
Durston, Marshall H, 1961, My 5,29:1
Durthaler, J Rev, 1885, My 4,5:6
Durward, Hector F, 1952, Mr 18,27:4
Dury, John H, 1915, Ja 11,9:4
Duryea, Anne S Mrs, 1940, O 12,17:6
Duryea, Charles E (por), 1938, S 29,25:3
Duryea, Charles H, 1957, Ag 14,25:4
Duryea, Charles R, 1943, My 17,15:5
Duryea, Chester B, 1948, Ag 19,44:4
Duryea, Cordelia M Mrs, 1937, Ja 26,21:1
Duryea, Dan, 1968, Je 8,31:1
Duryea, Dan Mrs, 1967, Ja 22,76:6
Duryea, Frank W, 1951, S 25,29:2
Duryea, Frederick B, 1951, Je 19,30:4
Duryea, Frederick R, 1941, Mr 9,41:2
Duryea, Garrett De N, 1966, Ag 18,32:6
Duryea, George (T Keene), 1963, Ag 7,33:2
Duryea, H B, 1884, Ag 28,1:6
Duryea, Herman B, 1916, Ja 26,11:5
Duryea, J F, 1927, Ja 31,17:5
Duryea, J Frank, 1967, F 16,44:5
Duryea, James F, 1949, Mr 30,25:2
Duryea, John, 1907, My 14,11:4
Duryea, John J, 1940, Ja 30,19:5
Duryea, Joseph A, 1944, O 12,27:3
Duryea, Louis T, 1924, Ag 27,17:6
Duryea, Marshall H, 1951, Ap 7,15:6
Duryea, May, 1949, Jl 21,25:5
Duryea, Merle J (Jerry), 1957, My 13,31:4
Duryea, Moses C, 1941, S 2,17:2
Duryea, Nicholas W (funl), 1872, D 22,8:1
Duryea, Nina L S Mrs, 1951, N 3,17:1
Duryea, Oscar, 1952, Mr 8,13:5
Duryea, Otho C, 1941, Ap 29,19:4
Duryea, Perry B Sr, 1968, N 10,89:1
Duryea, Peter, 1944, D 20,23:3
Duryea, Rachel S Mrs, 1942, D 28,20:2
Duryea, Richard A Mrs, 1955, Jl 7,27:2
Duryea, Samuel Bowne Mrs, 1922, Ap 16,28:3
Duryea, Stephen C, 1950, Mr 15,29:5
Duryea, Wallace, 1941, F 19,21:3
Duryea, Walter (est), 1911, Jl 16,II,9:5
Duryea, Walter B, 1954, Mr 11,31:3
Duryea, William, 1907, Ap 28,9:5
Duryea, William F, 1950, N 3,20:5
Duryea, Wright, 1961, O 10,43:2
Duryee, Abraham Rev, 1937, Ag 20,17:3
Duryee, Abram, 1890, S 28,5:3
Duryee, Alice, 1911, F 2,11:4
Duryee, Andrew B, 1948, Je 18,23:5
Duryee, Charles C Dr, 1937, Mr 19,23:1
Duryee, Edward C, 1954, F 25,31:5
Duryee, George Van Wagenen, 1912, Je 29,11:5
Duryee, J A, 1903, My 21,9:4
Duryee, John L, 1944, Je 11,45:1
Duryee, Lily N, 1950, Jl 1,15:5
Duryee, P S, 1877, S 26,4:7
Duryee, Peter S Mrs, 1954, My 23,89:2
Duryee, Ruth M, 1962, N 7,39:3
Duryee, William B, 1964, D 6,88:5
Duryee, William H, 1943, S 12,53:2
Duschnitz, Rudolf, 1964, Je 6,23:4
Duseigneur, Edouard, 1940, Mr 4,15:3
Dusenberry, Charles Jr, 1941, N 28,23:6
Dusenberry, Charles R, 1924, F 9,13:5
Dusenberry, Charles R Mrs, 1920, O 7,15:2
Dusenberry, Elias W, 1947, O 30,25:4
Dusenberry, Frances T Mrs, 1942, S 21,15:4
Dusenberry, Henry, 1958, F 25,27:3
Dusenbury, Arthur N, 1964, Je 24,37:2
Dusenbury, C Coles, 1904, Mr 25,9:5
Dusenbury, Edwin C, 1943, O 19,19:3
Dusenbury, Edwin K, 1949, D 2,29:3
Dusenbury, Edwin K Mrs, 1950, Mr 21,29:1
Dusenbury, Guy M, 1940, Jl 10,19:5
Dusenbury, Harry G, 1915, F 24,9:5
Dusenbury, Joseph Warren, 1904, F 5,3:3
Dusenbury, William A, 1942, Je 11,23:5
Du Shane, Donald, 1947, Mr 13,28:2
Dushanek, Frederick A, 1952, O 26,88:4
Dushinsky, Joseph Z, 1948, O 19,28:3
Dushkind, Charles, 1945, My 30,19:5
Dushman, Saul, 1954, Jl 8,23:2
Dusinberre, George, 1950, Ja 28,13:5
Dusinberre, Isaac, 1952, Ap 3,35:3
Du Souchet, Henry A, 1922, O 28,13:6
Dusovitz, Israel, 1955, D 5,31:1
Dussault, Bona, 1953, Ap 30,31:5
Dussault, Stuart A, 1951, Mr 7,33:5
D'Usseaux, Gustav B, 1948, Mr 17,25:1
Dussel, F E Mrs, 1948, Jl 12,19:5
Dusser de Barenne, Joannes G, 1940, Je 10,17:3
Dussman, Fred, 1953, Je 14,82:5
Dust, John J, 1940, Ja 23,21:3
Dustan, Cyril (por), 1949, Ja 23,68:6
Dustan, Russell M, 1958, O 1,37:5
Duster, Leo J, 1943, Ag 1,38:8
Dustin, Charles E Mrs, 1921, Mr 24,17:6
Dustin, Fred, 1957, My 16,31:4
Dustin, Miles H, 1960, Je 9,33:1
Dustin, Oliver S, 1948, N 16,29:6
Dustman, Rand J, 1955, D 19,27:5
D'Utassy, George, 1953, S 4,34:5
Dutasta, Paul, 1925, D 3,25:4
Dutch, A J, 1876, Jl 8,8:2
Dutch, Charles F, 1953, My 17,89:2
Dutch, Herbert W, 1965, My 22,31:5
Dutcher, Adelia T Mrs, 1941, F 22,17:5
Dutcher, C H, 1903, O 17,9:6
Dutcher, Charles B, 1941, My 9,21:2
Dutcher, Charles Mrs, 1952, Ap 18,25:1
Dutcher, Edith, 1950, My 5,22:3
Dutcher, Edward C Mrs, 1946, D 20,23:4
Dutcher, Edward M, 1943, My 13,21:2
Dutcher, F L, 1932, F 29,17:1
Dutcher, Frank K, 1955, My 26,31:2
Dutcher, Fred D, 1944, Ja 6,23:3
Dutcher, Frederick E, 1942, My 20,19:5
Dutcher, George L, 1937, S 17,25:4
Dutcher, George M, 1959, F 24,30:1
Dutcher, Henry R Sr, 1968, Ja 16,39:2
Dutcher, Howard B, 1944, Ap 24,19:4
Dutcher, Howard J Jr, 1958, Ag 6,25:3
Dutcher, Jessie R, 1963, D 10,43:4
Dutcher, John Bowdish, 1911, Ag 29,7:3
Dutcher, John G Mrs, 1955, O 3,27:4
Dutcher, Malcolm B, 1948, Ap 13,27:4
Dutcher, Merritt, 1952, Ag 27,27:5
Dutcher, R Adams, 1962, Ap 22,80:6
Dutcher, Rodney (por), 1938, N 20,35:2
Dutcher, Russell K, 1958, Je 18,33:5
Dutcher, Silas B, 1909, F 11,7:4
Dutcher, Wallace, 1944, S 20,23:2
Dutcher, William, 1920, Jl 4,21:4
Dutcher, William A Mrs, 1947, D 17,29:2
Dutcher, William E, 1946, D 29,35:4
Dutchick, Harry Mrs, 1944, S 15,19:4
Dutel, George F Mrs, 1947, D 14,80:4
Du Terrail, Ponson, 1871, F 15,2:6
Duthie, Thomas R, 1964, Mr 29,61:1
Duthie, William, 1923, F 17,13:4
Dutkiewicz, Boleslaw, 1946, F 28,23:5
Du Toit, Alexander, 1948, F 26,23:5
du Toit, Daniel, 1967, Ja 16,41:4
Du Toit, Jacob D, 1953, Jl 7,27:5
Du Tot, Walter, 1944, My 10,19:5
DuTot, Walter C, 1944, Je 1,19:1
Dutra, Carmela, 1947, O 9,26:3
Dutrow, Leonard D, 1951, D 16,91:1
Dutschler, Ernest J, 1952, Ag 11,15:5
Dutt, Henry M, 1954, D 12,88:7
Dutt, Paul E, 1958, O 21,33:3
Dutta, Kamini K, 1959, Ja 6,33:1
Dutting, Frances E, 1945, Ap 23,19:3
Dutton, Arthur C, 1945, F 26,19:6
Dutton, Arthur S, 1945, Jl 27,10:6
Dutton, Benjamin A, 1967, Ap 18,41:2
Dutton, Benjamin F, 1915, Je 3,11:5
Dutton, Benjamin Jr Capt, 1937, D 1,23:6
Dutton, Caleb S S, 1958, Ap 18,23:2
Dutton, Charles R, 1946, F 25,25:1

Dutton, Chauncey Noble, 1918, My 14,13:6
Dutton, Clarence E Maj, 1912, Ja 5,13:4
Dutton, E Herbert, 1944, O 6,23:4
Dutton, Edward P (funl, S 11,15:3), 1923, S 7,15:1
Dutton, Emily H, 1947, Je 19,21:2
Dutton, Eugene W, 1956, F 2,25:4
Dutton, Eugene W Mrs, 1953, Mr 14,15:4
Dutton, Frank K, 1947, Je 30,19:1
Dutton, George D, 1953, Jl 27,19:4
Dutton, George E, 1944, Mr 1,19:1
Dutton, George R, 1908, Mr 5,7:4
Dutton, Henry Ex-Gov, 1869, Ap 28,7:2
Dutton, Henry J, 1947, Ap 8,27:2
Dutton, Henry W, 1875, Ap 16,4:7
Dutton, Henry W T, 1942, Ja 10,15:5
Dutton, J, 1931, Mr 27,25:1
Dutton, John A, 1951, Ja 26,24:2
Dutton, Joseph F, 1945, Je 20,23:5
Dutton, Joseph Mrs, 1947, Jl 8,23:3
Dutton, Lewis R, 1948, Ja 5,19:3
Dutton, Martha A L Mrs, 1940, O 10,25:6
Dutton, Norman R, 1959, F 12,27:4
Dutton, Richard, 1948, Ja 27,25:3
Dutton, S W S Rev Dr, 1866, F 4,3:4
Dutton, Samuel Train Dr, 1919, Mr 29,13:3
Dutton, Stephen A, 1944, Ja 12,25:6
Duttweiler, Frederick, 1941, Ap 10,24:2
Duttweiler, Gottlieb, 1962, Je 9,25:2
Dutyee, Peter S, 1954, My 14,23:1
Duval, Ade Mrs, 1956, S 10,27:5
Duval, Alexander, 1922, F 16,15:4
Duval, C Louis, 1925, Jl 12,7:4
Du Val, Clive L Mrs, 1953, Ja 19,23:3
Duval, G L, 1931, Mr 17,60:4
Duval, George S, 1955, Mr 27,86:6
Du Val, Guy (por), 1949, My 2,25:4
Du Val, Guy Mrs, 1948, Ja 15,23:1
Duval, H Reiman Col, 1924, Mr 19,21:5
Duval, Herman, 1961, Je 20,33:5
Du Val, Horace Clark, 1921, S 8,13:4
Du Val, Ida L F Mrs, 1940, Mr 8,22:3
Duval, John H, 1962, F 28,33:3
Duval, John H Lt-Col, 1925, F 15,7:3
Duval, Joseph E, 1958, Je 22,77:1
Du Val, Julia, 1951, Mr 6,27:1
Duval, Laurel, 1952, F 17,84:6
Du Val, Merlin K, 1965, Je 5,31:6
Duval, Raymond-Francis Gen (funl, Ag 25,3:2), 1955, Ag 23,4:3
Duval, Rieman G, 1912, My 11,13:6
Duval, William, 1902, F 13,9:5
Duval-Gozlan, Leon, 1941, O 14,23:4
Duvall, Charles H, 1941, Ja 9,21:4
Duvall, Clair C Mrs, 1954, My 27,27:1
Duvall, E Harold, 1962, O 16,39:3
Du Vall, Edward E, 1956, My 7,27:3
Duvall, Frank B Mrs, 1960, D 22,26:2
DuVall, Frederick W, 1955, Ja 19,27:3
Duvall, Hanson Rawlins, 1925, N 1,9:2
Duvall, Harvey C, 1952, O 22,27:2
Duvall, L R, 1944, S 4,19:1
Duvall, Ralph G, 1941, My 29,19:5
Duvall, Robert W, 1954, Ap 6,30:8
Duvall, Rufus J, 1952, Jl 19,15:3
Duvall, Stanley C, 1957, Ag 15,21:3
Duvall, T W, 1961, Je 15,18:4
Duvan, Hanson R Jr, 1944, N 22,19:3
Duveen, Charles J, 1940, Jl 22,17:1
Duveen, Henry J, 1919, Ja 16,13:3
Duveen, Henry J Mrs, 1925, Ap 18,15:7
Duveen, Joseph Lady, 1922, Je 28,15:7
Duveen, Lord, 1939, My 26,23:1
Duveen, Louis J, 1920, Mr 5,13:5
Duvel, William A, 1965, D 5,89:1
Duveneck, Carl J, 1948, Ag 7,15:5
Duveneck, Frank, 1919, Ja 4,11:4
Du Vernet, F H Rev, 1924, O 23,21:5
Duvernois, Clement, 1879, Jl 10,2:4
Duvernois, Henri, 1937, Ja 30,17:5
Duvernoy, Henry G, 1958, My 13,29:3
Du Vinage, Jacques P, 1939, D 12,27:5
Du Vivier, Edward, 1904, O 16,9:7
Du Vivier, Joseph, 1953, O 19,21:3
Du Vivier, Joseph Mrs, 1962, O 31,37:5
Duvivier, Julien, 1967, O 30,45:3
Duvoisin, Jacques J, 1950, Je 7,29:4
Duvoli, John Sr, 1944, S 12,19:2
Duxbury, Albert, 1952, Ja 2,25:1
Duyckinck, E A, 1878, Ag 15,2:6
Duyckinck, Richard B, 1913, S 21,II,15:4
uys, Gerrit Jr, 1955, Mr 27,86:7
uys, Henry M, 1966, Jl 14,35:4
uys, John H, 1940, Mr 5,23:4
uys, John H Mrs, 1943, N 24,21:3
uyvendak, Jan J, 1954, Jl 10,13:4
uzik, John L, 1949, O 31,25:4
voichenko, Vladimir, 1943, Jl 18,34:7
vorak, Anton, 1904, My 2,9:6
vorak, Antonin, 1956, Je 28,29:3
vorak, Frank J, 1957, Je 26,31:4
vorak, Max Prof, 1921, F 11,11:3
vorak, Richard E, 1964, S 7,19:2
vorak, Rudolph W, 1950, F 19,76:2

Dvorick, Michael Mrs, 1946, F 19,25:3
Dvorkin, Julius, 1947, D 21,52:5
Dvorkin, Julius Mrs, 1956, D 25,25:4
Dvorkin, Moe, 1966, O 10,41:2
Dvorovy, John J, 1949, Ag 28,75:5
D'Vys, George W, 1941, Je 1,40:4
Dwan, Allan Mrs, 1949, Mr 15,27:5
Dwan, John, 1943, O 23,13:2
Dwier, W Kirkland, 1950, My 20,15:5
Dwiggins, Clare V, 1958, O 28,35:5
Dwiggins, William A, 1956, D 26,27:1
Dwight, A T, 1881, F 8,5:5
Dwight, Arthur S, 1946, Ap 22,27:3
Dwight, Benjamin H, 1941, S 2,17:3
Dwight, Benjamin Woodbridge Mrs, 1903, S 16,9:6
Dwight, C C Judge, 1902, Ap 9,9:5
Dwight, Charles A S, 1956, N 4,87:2
Dwight, Cornelia P, 1941, Ap 2,23:4
Dwight, Edmund, 1938, D 17,15:4
Dwight, Edward F Mrs, 1961, O 17,39:3
Dwight, Edward S, 1940, Mr 19,25:4
Dwight, Eliza L M Mrs, 1922, N 28,21:5
Dwight, Ellsworth E, 1955, F 26,15:3
Dwight, Franklin B, 1946, N 21,31:3
Dwight, Harris G, 1959, Mr 26,34:8
Dwight, Harvey H, 1954, S 6,15:3
Dwight, Henry, 1881, Je 28,5:2
Dwight, Henry R, 1948, O 6,29:3
Dwight, J W, 1928, Ja 20,21:5
Dwight, James Dr, 1917, Jl 15,15:3
Dwight, John, 1903, N 26,7:5
Dwight, Jonathan Mrs, 1958, Ja 23,21:4
Dwight, Kirby, 1946, D 5,31:4
Dwight, Kirby Mrs, 1957, Mr 17,87:2
Dwight, Mabel, 1955, S 5,11:6
Dwight, Maitland, 1938, My 23,17:5
Dwight, Marie K Mrs, 1947, Mr 31,23:1
Dwight, Melapiah Everett Rev Dr, 1907, S 15,9:5
Dwight, Richard E, 1951, S 29,17:1
Dwight, S O Rev, 1917, Je 20,11:5
Dwight, Stanley, 1924, Ap 21,17:5
Dwight, T W, 1892, Je 30,8:1
Dwight, Theodore, 1866, O 18,1:7
Dwight, Thomas Dr, 1911, S 9,9:5
Dwight, Timothy, 1916, My 27,11:3
Dwight, Walter J Rev, 1923, F 3,13:5
Dwight, William Buck Prof, 1906, Ag 30,7:5
Dwight, William G Mrs, 1957, Ag 1,25:4
Dwight, Winthrop E, 1944, D 5,23:2
Dwinelle, J W, 1881, F 12,8:1
Dwinnell, Dean N, 1949, S 18,92:4
Dwinnell, George L, 1939, Ap 16,III,7:2
Dwire, Henry R, 1944, Jl 18,19:4
Dworetzky, Julius P, 1942, Ap 21,23:5
Dwork, Edward, 1950, Je 19,21:3
Dwork, Harold K Dr, 1968, Jl 8,39:3
Dwork, Harold K Mrs, 1966, O 30,88:8
Dworkin, Louis H, 1956, Je 28,29:3
Dworkin, Martin, 1961, Jl 10,21:5
Dworkis, Martin B (mem ser, Ag 24,37:1), 1965, Ag 21,21:4
Dworman, Irving, 1962, S 6,31:1
Dworshak, Henry C (funl plans, trb, Jl 25,33:3), 1962, Jl 24,27:4
Dworshak, Henry Sr, 1947, N 27,31:4
Dworsky, Abraham J, 1923, Ja 21,6:3
Dworsky, Bertha Mrs, 1925, N 9,19:4
Dworzak, Joseph C, 1951, F 22,31:4
Dworzanski, Anthony, 1961, O 18,43:1
Dwyer, Albert E, 1940, Mr 22,20:2
Dwyer, Ambrose M Rev, 1937, S 28,23:2
Dwyer, Anna S Mrs, 1953, Mr 13,27:4
Dwyer, Arthur S, 1954, S 22,29:2
Dwyer, Bernard A, 1943, Ag 21,11:6
Dwyer, C Eustace, 1950, Ag 12,13:5
Dwyer, Charles, 1916, Ja 18,11:6
Dwyer, Charles F, 1961, D 9,27:2
Dwyer, Charles G, 1943, Ap 17,17:2
Dwyer, Christopher E, 1958, Ap 20,85:2
Dwyer, Dalton A, 1955, S 19,25:5
Dwyer, Daniel A, 1950, Mr 21,29:2
Dwyer, Daniel Sr Mrs, 1947, D 31,15:1
Dwyer, David J B, 1961, D 8,37:1
Dwyer, Edmund J, 1961, O 18,43:2
Dwyer, Edward, 1950, Ap 12,27:4
Dwyer, Edward Leonard, 1912, S 27,13:5
Dwyer, Edward M, 1957, S 12,31:2
Dwyer, Edwin M, 1951, Jl 12,25:3
Dwyer, Elizabeth, 1946, Jl 11,23:4
Dwyer, Eugene J, 1946, Je 17,21:5
Dwyer, Eugene M Mrs, 1959, N 1,86:3
Dwyer, Francis J, 1952, Mr 17,21:4
Dwyer, Frank, 1943, F 5,21:4
Dwyer, Frank A, 1940, F 23,15:4; 1949, Ja 11,27:3
Dwyer, Geoffrey J Mrs, 1941, N 18,25:5
Dwyer, George F, 1950, Je 14,31:3
Dwyer, Harry W, 1965, Ap 1,35:3
Dwyer, Henry E, 1957, N 12,34:2
Dwyer, Herbert D, 1949, Je 15,29:2
Dwyer, J Edward, 1956, Ap 20,25:4
Dwyer, J J, 1882, Mr 11,5:4
Dwyer, Jack, 1966, Jl 5,27:1
Dwyer, James, 1916, O 8,23:3

Dwyer, James E Jr, 1959, N 28,21:4
Dwyer, James F, 1952, Ap 4,25:3
Dwyer, James G, 1941, Mr 7,21:4; 1947, Ag 4,17:2
Dwyer, James J, 1941, N 30,68:3
Dwyer, James J Mrs, 1945, S 26,23:3
Dwyer, James S, 1961, Ja 14,23:2
Dwyer, Jeremiah, 1940, S 25,29:1
Dwyer, Jeremiah J Sr, 1957, D 20,24:4
Dwyer, John Dr, 1922, N 16,19:4
Dwyer, John E, 1951, Ja 13,15:2
Dwyer, John F, 1939, Ag 19,15:4
Dwyer, John H, 1937, O 14,25:1; 1953, My 3,88:5
Dwyer, John J, 1938, F 10,21:4; 1945, D 8,17:5; 1950, My 10,31:2
Dwyer, John T, 1960, Jl 24,64:3
Dwyer, John T Mrs, 1941, D 14,69:2
Dwyer, John W, 1944, My 19,19:5
Dwyer, Joseph B, 1947, F 15,15:5
Dwyer, Joseph F, 1949, Ja 3,2:6; 1967, O 31,45:1
Dwyer, Joseph F Sr, 1947, Jl 17,19:4
Dwyer, Joseph R, 1966, Ja 10,25:2
Dwyer, Joseph T, 1938, My 11,19:3
Dwyer, Mary D Mrs, 1953, N 17,31:3
Dwyer, Matthew S, 1923, My 11,17:5
Dwyer, Michael, 1953, D 29,23:1
Dwyer, Michael J, 1938, O 4,25:4
Dwyer, Michael Joseph, 1968, N 22,47:1
Dwyer, Michael U Rev, 1924, Ap 9,21:2
Dwyer, P J, 1947, Ja 23,23:3
Dwyer, Patrick, 1964, Ja 13,35:1
Dwyer, Patrick A, 1943, Jl 13,21:5
Dwyer, Patrick C, 1958, Mr 25,31:1
Dwyer, Patrick J, 1943, Ap 20,23:3; 1953, Jl 22,27:3
Dwyer, Paul A, 1953, N 26,31:2
Dwyer, Philip J (est, Je 15,9:6), 1917, Je 11,11:4
Dwyer, R Emmet, 1954, Ap 7,31:2
Dwyer, Redmond J, 1950, D 5,31:4
Dwyer, Robert A, 1960, Mr 10,32:1
Dwyer, Robert E, 1967, Je 28,45:4
Dwyer, Robert E Mrs, 1968, Jl 11,37:2
Dwyer, Robert R, 1961, D 19,33:2
Dwyer, Thomas, 1943, Mr 5,18:3
Dwyer, Thomas A, 1943, Ag 9,13:5; 1964, O 15,39:3
Dwyer, Thomas F, 1944, Ap 19,23:2; 1948, S 26,76:2; 1953, O 14,29:2
Dwyer, Thomas R, 1939, O 22,40:8
Dwyer, Thomas T, 1947, S 24,23:4
Dwyer, William, 1951, N 26,27:8
Dwyer, William A, 1961, N 19,89:2
Dwyer, William G, 1940, Jl 3,17:7; 1962, Mr 4,86:1
Dwyer, William J, 1948, Jl 10,15:5
Dwyer, William Mrs, 1951, Ja 31,25:5; 1953, Mr 14, 15:5
Dwyer, William P, 1954, Ja 12,23:4
Dwyer, William V, 1946, D 11,32:2
Dyaik, John, 1918, Jl 29,11:6
Dyall, Franklin, 1950, My 9,29:2
Dyar, H G, 1929, Ja 22,29:4
Dyas, Ada, 1908, Mr 13,7:4
Dyas, Carl E, 1951, N 22,31:1
Dyas, E, 1877, F 2,4:6
Dyas, Frederick G, 1943, Mr 4,19:5
Dyas, George T, 1951, Ag 28,23:4
Dyas, Thomas C, 1951, Mr 13,31:4
Dyason, Clarence, 1949, O 5,29:5
Dyce, Alexander Rev, 1869, My 22,5:2
Dyce, R A, 1864, Ap 3,2:5
Dyche, Frank B, 1944, F 2,21:2
Dyche, John T, 1953, Jl 21,23:1
Dyche, Louis Lindsay Prof, 1915, Ja 21,9:4
Dyckman, Charles A, 1949, O 18,27:4
Dyckman, Edward I, 1945, O 25,21:2
Dyckman, F Hamilton, 1962, Ap 9,29:4
Dyckman, Francis H, 1904, My 11,9:6
Dyckman, Frank H Mrs, 1945, Mr 8,23:1
Dyckman, Isaac Michael, 1914, D 19,13:4
Dyckman, Laura, 1942, Mr 5,23:2
Dydyk, Sozont, 1950, D 20,31:1
Dye, Alexander V Mrs, 1947, F 15,15:4
Dye, Andrew G, 1952, D 19,31:3
Dye, Burrell T, 1951, My 22,31:4
Dye, Carol F, 1962, Je 12,37:4
Dye, Clair A, 1949, O 11,34:1
Dye, E A, 1960, N 14,31:4
Dye, Edward R, 1961, O 15,88:5
Dye, Fred, 1946, Jl 22,21:4
Dye, Garnett J, 1962, Ja 31,31:3
Dye, George R, 1954, N 20,17:4
Dye, Herbert A, 1950, Ja 31,24:3
Dye, James T, 1947, Ja 21,23:4
Dye, John C, 1956, Ap 27,27:4
Dye, John H, 1911, Je 28,11:5
Dye, John S, 1944, Ag 11,15:2
Dye, Ralph W, 1964, Jl 22,33:1
Dye, Robert E, 1953, Jl 17,17:3
Dye, Sidney, 1958, D 10,11:6
Dye, T Fenton, 1938, F 15,25:5
Dyef, Elmer, 1938, F 20,II,8:3
Dyer, Alex B Gen, 1874, My 21,5:5
Dyer, Alexander Brydie, 1920, Jl 13,11:4
Dyer, Arthur, 1944, Je 15,19:3
Dyer, B Wheeler Mrs, 1965, Jl 24,21:6
Dyer, Bradbury Jr, 1954, O 8,23:5

Dyer, C N, 1878, Ap 25,1:6
Dyer, Charles F, 1951, N 3,17:2
Dyer, D B Col, 1912, D 23,9:4
Dyer, Dan B Mrs, 1956, F 19,92:2
Dyer, David, 1948, N 13,15:3
Dyer, David Patterson, 1924, Ap 30,19:2
Dyer, Eddie (Edwin H), 1964, Ap 21,37:1
Dyer, Edward E, 1957, Ag 18,83:2
Dyer, Edward J, 1942, Ap 30,19:3
Dyer, Edward R Rev, 1925, N 4,23:4
Dyer, Edward Tiffany, 1913, Ja 19,II,17:2
Dyer, Edward Tiffany Mrs, 1919, Jl 10,15:3
Dyer, Elbert H, 1968, Mr 29,45:3
Dyer, Elisha, 1906, N 30,1:4; 1917, Je 3,19:3
Dyer, Elizabeth M Mrs, 1940, D 5,25:5
Dyer, Francis P, 1914, S 7,7:6
Dyer, Frank, 1958, Mr 3,27:3
Dyer, Frank L, 1941, Je 5,23:5
Dyer, Frank Mrs, 1949, S 24,13:6
Dyer, G R, 1934, S 1,13:1
Dyer, George Leland Commodore, 1914, Ap 3,11:6
Dyer, George P Mrs, 1945, Jl 27,15:3
Dyer, George R, 1941, My 6,21:5
Dyer, H Anthony, 1943, Ag 25,19:4
Dyer, Henry Lyman, 1921, N 20,22:2
Dyer, Herman Mrs, 1903, D 21,7:4
Dyer, Horace Edward, 1948, Jl 28,23:6
Dyer, Hugh M, 1938, D 28,26:4
Dyer, Isaac W, 1937, F 14,II,8:7
Dyer, Isadore Dr, 1920, O 13,15:4
Dyer, J L Rev, 1901, Je 17,7:4
Dyer, J Milton, 1957, My 30,19:4
Dyer, J W, 1883, N 20,1:6
Dyer, Jack Mrs, 1955, Ap 9,13:1
Dyer, James E Mrs, 1950, F 20,25:2
Dyer, James J, 1961, Je 30,27:1
Dyer, John E, 1966, Mr 13,87:2
Dyer, John G, 1950, Ag 2,25:3
Dyer, John H, 1952, F 11,25:6
Dyer, John J, 1951, N 22,31:4
Dyer, John N, 1954, Ja 5,27:3
Dyer, John P, 1961, Mr 21,37:4
Dyer, John P Jr, 1956, F 15,31:1
Dyer, Joseph H, 1947, Je 15,60:3
Dyer, Justin, 1937, Ag 27,19:4
Dyer, Leonard H, 1955, N 17,35:4
Dyer, Leonidas C, 1957, D 17,35:1
Dyer, Leonidas C Mrs, 1961, Ap 16,87:1
Dyer, Lorenzo D, 1940, O 28,17:4
Dyer, Louis, 1908, Jl 21,7:5
Dyer, Louisa Mrs, 1944, F 16,17:3
Dyer, Lyman T, 1950, N 28,31:2
Dyer, Lyman T Mrs, 1944, F 5,15:6
Dyer, Martin C, 1947, S 3,27:1
Dyer, Matthew, 1909, S 1,9:4
Dyer, Micah Jr Mrs, 1907, Je 28,7:6
Dyer, Nehemiah Mayo Rear-Adm, 1910, Ja 28,9:4
Dyer, Orville K, 1945, Ja 6,11:4
Dyer, Patrick J, 1953, Ja 10,17:4
Dyer, Paul R, 1949, O 2,82:4
Dyer, Philip S, 1919, Mr 11,11:2
Dyer, R E H, 1927, Jl 25,19:5
Dyer, Thomas B, 1958, F 22,17:2
Dyer, Thomas M, 1958, S 17,37:2
Dyer, Tommy, 1947, F 27,21:1
Dyer, Walter A, 1943, Je 21,17:6
Dyer, Wheeler, 1953, Ag 11,27:1
Dyer, William A Sr, 1944, O 23,19:5
Dyer, William A Sr Mrs, 1954, Je 19,15:3
Dyer, William E, 1952, Ap 20,93:1
Dyer, William E S, 1955, D 10,21:4
Dyer, William J H, 1964, Ap 2,33:1
Dyer, Zeb A, 1904, S 19,7:4
Dyeser, William, 1937, D 20,3:6
Dyett, Herbert T, 1961, My 9,39:4
Dyett, Herbert T Mrs, 1941, Ap 12,15:5
Dygas, Ignacy, 1947, My 21,25:5
Dygert, Emily G Mrs, 1954, Ja 6,31:4
Dygert, Lincoln W, 1949, Ap 16,15:3
Dygert, Warren B Jr, 1941, My 23,21:3
Dygia, Nikolai, 1963, Mr 7,7:3
Dyk, E C W van, 1937, N 12,12:4
Dyk, Solomon, 1944, My 25,21:5
Dyke, A L, 1959, My 18,27:3
Dyke, Chalmers P Mrs, 1957, My 11,21:5
Dyke, Charles, 1871, Ag 3,4:6
Dyke, Cornelius G (por), 1943, Ap 24,13:1
Dyke, Harold D, 1950, Jl 25,27:3
Dyke, Herbert H, 1965, N 6,29:4
Dyke, Nathaniel Jr, 1962, Mr 30,33:3
Dyke, Samuel C, 1924, My 10,13:4
Dyke, W Sir, 1931, Jl 4,13:4
Dykema, Anno C Mrs, 1948, S 8,29:1
Dykema, Martin, 1941, N 17,19:3
Dykema, Peter W, 1951, My 15,31:3
Dykeman, C H, 1966, Jl 4,15:4
Dykeman, Chauncey, 1944, O 14,13:2
Dykeman, Conrad V, 1943, Ja 12,23:5
Dykeman, Conrad V Mrs, 1940, O 5,15:4
Dykeman, James E, 1944, Je 7,19:5
Dykeman, Lester W, 1958, My 14,33:4
Dykeman, Lester W Mrs, 1947, O 27,21:3
Dykeman, Roy L, 1950, Ap 4,29:3
Dykeman, Roy O, 1950, Ag 10,25:3
Dykeman, Walter A, 1941, N 15,17:6
Dykeman, William, 1939, Je 16,23:4
Dykes, Alex, 1957, Ap 21,89:1
Dykes, Andrew H, 1944, D 17,38:4
Dykes, Charles J, 1965, Je 28,29:2
Dykes, Eldon R Dr, 1968, Ag 2,33:1
Dykes, Francis, 1949, S 15,27:2
Dykes, Harlan H, 1940, O 29,25:3
Dykes, James J Mrs, 1959, D 12,23:1
Dykes, Joseph J Mrs, 1950, Mr 10,27:4
Dykes, Margaret T, 1946, Ag 29,27:5
Dykes, William F, 1943, S 18,17:4
Dykman, Ella Cline Mrs, 1905, Mr 1,9:5
Dykman, Henry Trowbridge, 1919, S 29,13:1
Dykman, Isabel A Mrs, 1941, Ap 2,23:4
Dykman, William N, 1937, Jl 21,21:3
Dykstra, Clarence A, 1950, My 7,106:1
Dykstra, Theodore, 1952, Je 24,29:6
Dylewski, Theodore A, 1954, Ap 13,31:2
Dylla, Henry F Sr, 1955, Ja 26,25:4
Dymek, Walenty, 1956, O 24,37:5
Dymling, Carl A, 1961, Je 3,23:5
Dymock, Atkinson, 1959, Mr 24,39:1
Dymoke, Francis S, 1946, Ag 30,4:3
Dymoke, H L, 1876, Ja 16,7:2
Dymow, Ossip, 1959, F 4,26:1
Dymsa, Leopoldas, 1959, Mr 26,31:3
Dynamite, Johnny (Capt Jno O'Brien), 1917, Je 22, 13:3
Dynan, Joseph V, 1951, Ja 25,25:5
Dynan, Thomas W Mrs, 1947, O 10,25:6
Dynes, Donald P, 1953, Ap 15,31:1
Dynes, Oliver W, 1940, My 7,25:5
Dynes, Robert S, 1948, N 9,27:4
Dyniewicyz, Walter, 1947, Mr 16,60:8
Dyniewicz, Leon W, 1946, Jl 4,19:5
Dyonnet, Edmond, 1954, Jl 10,13:6
Dyott, Harold, 1937, S 23,27:5
Dyrenforth, Robert, 1946, D 12,29:3
Dyroff, George M, 1949, My 29,36:5
Dysart, John P Mrs, 1954, O 31,89:2
Dysart, Margaret A, 1949, O 26,27:2
Dysinger, William S, 1947, N 14,23:2
Dyson, Caroline A, 1945, Ap 24,19:3
Dyson, Charles W Mrs, 1944, F 6,41:1
Dyson, Frank Sir, 1939, My 26,23:4
Dyson, George, 1964, S 30,43:4
Dyson, George F, 1951, Jl 11,23:4
Dyson, John R, 1947, N 20,29:2
Dyson, Joseph W, 1965, Jl 16,27:2
Dyson, Robert A, 1959, S 9,41:5
Dyson, Will, 1938, Ja 22,18:2
Dyssord, Jacques (Baron E M de Bellaing), 1952, D 22,25:5
Dzamba, Stephen, 1961, Ap 18,37:1
Dzerzhinsky, F, 1926, Jl 21,19:4
Dzerzhinsky, Felix E Mrs, 1968, Mr 1,43:4
Dzhanashia, Simon, 1947, N 17,21:2
Dziadosz, Joseph, 1944, F 12,13:1
Dziadosz, William V, 1950, Jl 11,32:2
Dziama, Michael G, 1944, S 7,23:6
Dzick, Benjamin J, 1961, Je 20,33:3
Dziewic, Joseph, 1940, N 19,23:2
Dzigan, Albert, 1948, D 11,19:8
Dzijacky, Andrew A, 1958, Ag 12,29:4
Dzikowski, Roman, 1949, Je 28,28:3
Dziomba, Maxim O, 1945, Ja 12,15:5
Dzus, William, 1964, Je 20,25:4
Dzvonchik, Joseph O, 1966, Mr 8,39:1

E

Eacret, Villiers A, 1938, My 13,19:3
Eacrett, Richard J, 1948, Ja 22,27:3
Eadbert, Brother, 1947, N 5,27:2
Eade, Charles, 1964, Ag 28,35:5
Eade, George Jr, 1908, My 18,7:5
Eader, Thomas, 1952, D 15,27:5
Eadie, Alex C, 1951, Mr 28,29:4
Eadie, Colin M, 1945, My 16,19:2
Eadie, D, 1928, Je 11,21:5
Eadie, Edward M, 1961, Je 19,27:3
Eadie, Eleanor O, 1956, Ag 31,17:3
Eadie, James P (por), 1942, My 28,17:5
Eadie, John H, 1908, S 6,9:6
Eadie, John M, 1949, D 14,31:4
Eadie, Noel, 1950, Ap 13,29:2
Eadie, Robert, 1949, Je 11,17:3
Eadon, T Austin Sr, 1952, Mr 26,29:2
Eads, J B, 1887, Mr 11,5:4
Eads, J L, 1951, O 20,15:4
Eads, William J, 1968, Ag 9,35:2
Eady, Wilfrid, 1962, Ja 10,47:4
Eagan, Charles Patrick Brig-Gen, 1919, F 3,15:2
Eagan, Daniel C, 1954, S 1,27:5
Eagan, Eddie (Edw P F Eagan),(funl, Je 17,32:5), 1967, Je 15,47:2
Eagan, Evelyn, 1946, Jl 19,19:4
Eagan, Frank J, 1944, Ag 15,19:2
Eagan, John J, 1937, Ja 5,23:3; 1956, Je 14,33:5; 1957, Ap 13,19:4
Eagan, John J Capt, 1917, D 8,15:4
Eagan, John J Mrs, 1950, My 21,104:4
Eagan, John Maj, 1906, Jl 24,7:2
Eagan, John T, 1941, Ja 25,15:6
Eagan, John T Mrs, 1950, S 28,31:3
Eagan, Joseph D, 1956, Je 5,35:5
Eagan, Marion E, 1964, Mr 13,34:7
Eagan, Vincent A, 1941, My 16,23:2
Eagar, Ansel T Mrs, 1949, Mr 11,26:3
Eagar, Arthur F Mrs, 1943, Ag 5,15:1
Eagar, Robert J, 1949, D 16,31:3
Eagen, Owen, 1920, Mr 3,11:1
Eagen, Thomas S, 1952, Jl 22,25:5
Eager, Edward M, 1964, O 24,29:3
Eager, Frank J, 1943, Mr 1,19:4
Eager, George, 1941, Ag 14,17:1
Eager, George A, 1941, My 20,23:6
Eager, George B, 1942, O 21,21:2
Eager, George M, 1955, O 6,29:4
Eager, George T (funl plans, Je 28,23:4), 1957, Je 27,25:5
Eager, Harold H, 1938, F 16,21:3
Eager, Helen, 1952, O 24,23:4
Eager, John H, 1938, My 8,II,6:4; 1960, Ap 10,86:3
Eager, John M, 1956, N 16,27:1
Eager, John M Dr, 1916, Ag 19,9:5
Eager, John P, 1968, Ag 8,33:1
Eager, Myra E, 1945, Ja 3,17:1
Eager, Phil J, 1942, Ap 10,17:3
Eager, Sarah E Mrs, 1947, My 6,27:4
agle, Barry, 1958, F 1,10:2
agle, Clarence H Mrs, 1952, O 20,23:5
agle, Clarence Henry Maj, 1922, D 28,17:5
agle, Edgar P, 1946, O 12,19:1
agle, Fitch E, 1946, Ag 9,17:4
agle, Frank, 1941, Mr 3,15:3
agle, H Commodore, 1882, N 27,5:3
agle, H H H, 1933, D 6,23:5
agle, Henry, 1949, S 21,32:2
agle, Henry A, 1938, My 4,23:3
agle, Henry Y, 1947, Je 19,21:6
agle, J Frederick, 1961, D 6,47:3
agle, Joe H, 1963, Ja 12,14:8
agle, John H, 1943, Jl 25,31:2
agle, Manny, 1967, My 29,25:3
agle, Oscar Mrs, 1958, Jl 16,29:1
agle, Richard F, 1940, Ja 16,23:2
agles, Frank F, 1940, Je 19,23:6
agles, Reginald H, 1956, N 15,35:5
gles, Richard Mrs, 1954, Ag 19,23:3
agles, Richard P, 1953, My 26,29:6
gles, Thomas, 1903, D 24,9:5
glesfield, Elizabeth Mrs, 1940, Je 25,23:4
glesham, Ross A, 1959, Mr 28,17:1
gleson, John, 1941, F 22,15:6
gleson, William A, 1938, N 3,23:6
gleton, Clyde (trb, F 6,26:7), 1958, Ja 31,21:3
gleton, John T, 1952, D 8,41:4
gleton, Wells P Mrs, 1953, N 24,30:5
gney, Thomas M, 1947, D 11,33:3
kin, Elizabeth B, 1952, My 16,23:2
kin, Frank H, 1954, Ag 24,21:3
kin, J Bryce, 1955, Ap 6,29:3
kin, J Ross, 1946, Je 10,21:3
in, John A Mrs, 1950, Ja 4,46:2
in, John L, 1951, O 6,19:1
in, Malcolm S, 1957, S 28,17:1
in, Mary M Mrs (will), 1955, F 19,19:2
in, Robert E, 1959, O 4,86:1
in, Robert E Mrs, 1965, Ja 5,33:3

Eakin, Thomas A, 1955, D 14,39:4
Eakin, W Boyce, 1957, N 13,32:3
Eakin, W T, 1880, F 1,2:7
Eakin, William B, 1951, Je 5,31:3
Eakin, William B Mrs, 1955, Ja 31,19:3
Eakin, William R, 1955, Je 16,37:1
Eakins, Susan M Mrs, 1938, D 28,26:5
Eakins, William Rev Dr, 1915, N 6,11:7
Ealeley, Charles W, 1940, Ap 5,22:4
Eales, Christopher, 1951, O 5,27:1
Eales, Herbert C, 1949, F 20,60:5
Eales, Irving J, 1953, D 25,17:5
Ealre, David P, 1949, S 19,23:5
Eames, Alfred W, 1948, O 29,25:1
Eames, C, 1930, N 9,31:1
Eames, Charles, 1867, Mr 18,5:1
Eames, Charles H, 1949, Ja 30,61:1
Eames, Edward Everett, 1906, D 9,7:6
Eames, Emma, 1952, Je 14,15:1
Eames, Emma (est tax appr), 1954, Ap 14,26:8
Eames, Francis L, 1912, N 11,11:5
Eames, George H, 1949, Ap 10,76:1
Eames, George M, 1937, S 6,17:3
Eames, Harris G, 1915, N 12,11:6
Eames, Hayden, 1938, N 25,23:6
Eames, Hayden Mrs, 1950, Je 4,92:5
Eames, Henry P, 1950, N 27,25:1
Eames, Jesse J, 1948, O 15,23:1
Eames, Milton H, 1950, My 5,21:5
Eames, Robert D, 1951, S 26,31:4
Eames, Susan Frances, 1953, F 26,25:3
Eames, Thomas B, 1949, S 7,29:1
Eames, W J, 1879, Ja 31,2:2
Eames, Wallace, 1947, Ja 9,24:2
Eames, Wilberforce Dr, 1937, D 7,25:1
Eames, William S, 1915, Mr 6,11:4
Eamon, Sister (M O'Sullivan),(funl, S 2,3:3), 1966, S 1,3:2
Eardley-Wilmot, Lady (A Chapman), 1961, F 23,27:3
Earhart, Edwin S Mrs, 1962, O 31,37:1
Earhart, Herman A, 1949, D 11,93:1
Earing, Harvey M, 1946, F 1,24:3
Earl, Alfred A Mrs, 1949, Ap 17,76:5
Earl, Charles, 1943, Jl 27,17:5
Earl, Charles Jr, 1967, Ja 1,53:1
Earl, Clarence A (por), 1942, S 25,21:3
Earl, Edgar H Mrs, 1937, Jl 16,19:6
Earl, Edward, 1924, Ap 5,15:4
Earl, Elizabeth L, 1944, D 20,23:5
Earl, Frederick C (por), 1938, Ag 16,19:2
Earl, George H, 1919, O 27,11:5; 1951, N 16,36:1
Earl, Harry N, 1937, F 26,22:2
Earl, J Palmer, 1948, D 19,76:2
Earl, Jacob W, 1957, Ja 8,31:4
Earl, John C, 1913, D 3,15:5
Earl, John G Mrs, 1959, Jl 25,17:3
Earl, John R, 1942, Ag 13,19:4
Earl, Joseph D, 1940, O 30,23:5
Earl, M Raymond, 1954, Je 29,27:3
Earl, Mary L, 1951, My 3,19:5
Earl, Maud, 1943, Jl 9,17:4
Earl, Miller C, 1939, O 8,49:2
Earl, Morris Mrs, 1948, Ja 21,25:3
Earl, Mortimer C, 1917, O 17,13:2
Earl, Mortimer Lamson, 1905, S 27,9:1
Earl, Noble C, 1949, Je 1,31:3
Earl, Ralph W, 1964, Ap 27,31:3
Earl, Richard S, 1953, Jl 18,13:1
Earl, Sarah Cecilia, 1904, Ja 6,9:6
Earl, Virginia, 1937, S 23,27:3
Earl, William A, 1938, Je 4,15:4
Earl, William H, 1925, Ap 15,19:3
Earl, William H Mrs (Gertrude), 1965, Je 2,45:2
Earl, William Mrs, 1943, Ja 22,19:2
Earl of Bettand, 1873, My 7,5:4
Earl of Charleville (C W F Bury), 1874, N 3,2:6
Earl of Dalhousie, 1874, Jl 7,4:7
Earl of Galloway, 1873, Ja 4,1:5
Earlcott, Gladys, 1939, My 19,21:2
Earle, A Wilfred, 1958, Ap 20,84:2
Earle, Albert O, 1947, Je 17,25:3
Earle, Alex M, 1940, Ag 29,19:3
Earle, Alice E Mrs, 1911, F 17,9:4
Earle, Amasa H, 1938, Ap 9,17:5
Earle, Arthur P, 1952, F 24,16:1
Earle, Billy, 1946, Je 1,13:3
Earle, Charles, 1940, F 19,17:4
Earle, Clarence E, 1953, N 27,27:3
Earle, E, 1877, My 20,6:7
Earle, Edward, 1945, O 10,21:4
Earle, Edward M, 1954, Je 25,21:1
Earle, Edwin L, 1912, Ap 7,15:3
Earle, Ellis P (will, O 28, 14:3), 1942, O 13,23:1
Earle, Ethel B Mrs, 1940, N 5,25:6
Earle, F P Gen, 1903, Ja 3,3:4
Earle, F P Mrs (funl), 1871, My 16,8:4
Earle, Ferdinand P Mrs, 1918, O 24,13:1
Earle, Florence, 1942, Ap 7,21:3
Earle, Frank Trumbull, 1920, D 5,22:4

Earle, Frederic C, 1951, Mr 16,31:5
Earle, G H Jr, 1928, F 20,21:3
Earle, G Kenneth, 1937, Ja 6,23:2
Earle, Genevieve B Mrs, 1956, Mr 7,35:6
Earle, George F Mrs, 1948, O 2,15:3
Earle, George H Jr Mrs, 1941, N 7,24:3
Earle, Gerald F, 1944, S 17,42:2
Earle, Guyon L C, 1968, My 17,44:2
Earle, Hannah A Mrs, 1941, F 19,21:1
Earle, Henry Mrs, 1954, Ap 15,29:2
Earle, Herbert R, 1941, S 6,15:4
Earle, I Newton, 1938, Je 10,21:3
Earle, J H Sen, 1897, My 21,7:5
Earle, John Milton, 1874, F 9,1:6
Earle, John Walter, 1916, Je 23,11:6
Earle, Michael Mrs, 1951, D 20,32:2
Earle, Octavia M Mrs, 1942, Ag 22,13:5
Earle, Ralph D Jr, 1938, N 15,23:2
Earle, Ralph H, 1939, F 14,19:1
Earle, Raymond B Prof, 1918, N 11,15:6
Earle, Reginald W Mrs, 1965, F 9,37:1
Earle, Richard B, 1945, Ag 14,21:4
Earle, Russell W, 1964, Ag 6,29:3
Earle, Swepson, 1943, N 16,23:4
Earle, Thomas, 1871, My 26,8:3; 1943, Ag 16,15:1
Earle, Thornton, 1946, Je 10,21:2
Earle, Verne A, 1948, Mr 31,25:3
Earle, Victor M, 1966, D 20,43:4
Earle, Walter K Mrs, 1964, O 30,37:5
Earle, Walter O, 1940, Ag 25,35:3
Earle, William C, 1907, D 9,7:4
Earle, William H, 1914, Ag 23,13:6
Earle, William P, 1908, Mr 14,7:6
Earle, William P Jr, 1940, Jl 8,17:3
Earle, William Pitt, 1914, Ag 26,9:6
Earle, Wilton R, 1964, Je 7,86:8
Earle, Winthrop, 1902, Mr 4,9:5
Earles, Henry C, 1925, S 13,5:1
Earley, Adelaide E, 1958, Mr 17,29:1
Earley, Anthony F, 1956, Ag 7,27:2
Earley, Ernest H, 1968, Mr 11,37:1
Earley, Eugene J, 1950, F 7,28:3
Earley, James, 1950, Jl 30,60:2
Earley, Margaret A, 1954, Jl 4,31:3
Earley, May F Mrs, 1937, Jl 17,15:4
Earley, Robert H, 1939, Mr 31,21:4
Earley, Samuel, 1940, My 7,25:2
Earley, Terence J Rev, 1921, Mr 19,11:5
Earley, Thomas J, 1957, Mr 28,31:4
Earley, William, 1871, Jl 6,2:7
Earling, Alfred J, 1925, N 11,23:3
Earling, John J Mrs, 1946, D 6,23:3
Earls, Michael J Rev, 1937, F 2,23:3
Early, Baynard L, 1952, F 23,11:6
Early, Bernard F, 1961, Ap 12,41:3
Early, Daniel J, 1922, Jl 31,11:7
Early, Earl J, 1961, Ag 22,29:5
Early, Ernest R, 1962, Je 20,32:5
Early, Ernest R Mrs, 1939, Ag 4,13:5
Early, Eugene E, 1956, O 22,29:3
Early, Gilbert G, 1943, Mr 9,23:2
Early, J, 1877, S 4,5:5
Early, J A Gen, 1894, Mr 3,1:3
Early, James G, 1943, N 3,25:5
Early, James H, 1953, Jl 4,11:5
Early, John, 1938, Mr 1,22:1
Early, John Bp, 1873, N 7,5:3
Early, John Vinton, 1925, O 7,27:4
Early, Joseph J (por), 1949, O 16,89:1
Early, Joseph J Mrs, 1964, Jl 14,33:2
Early, Joseph N, 1945, D 19,26:2
Early, Margaret E Mrs, 1942, Ag 9,42:4
Early, Martin A, 1925, Ja 13,19:5
Early, Maurice, 1954, F 6,19:4
Early, Melvin A, 1954, Mr 20,15:5
Early, Melvin A Mrs, 1939, O 25,23:5
Early, N B Jr, 1947, Ag 16,13:4
Early, Patrick H, 1944, D 20,23:1
Early, Robert W, 1950, F 2,28:2
Early, Stephen T, 1951, Ag 12,77:1
Earner, John, 1918, Je 5,11:5
Earnest, C Bruce, 1960, Mr 3,30:1
Earnest, Charles W, 1941, F 23,40:1
Earnest, Joel, 1952, Ap 14,19:4
Earnest, John P Jr, 1944, My 9,19:1
Earnest, William D Sr, 1957, D 26,19:1
Earnshaw, Emily C, 1939, F 25,15:4
Earnshaw, Geoffrey S, 1952, S 29,23:3
Earnshaw, George, 1939, D 31,18:6
Earnshaw, George F, 1940, O 2,23:4
Earnshaw, Henry C, 1953, My 23,15:6
Earnshaw, John J W, 1955, Ja 18,27:5
Earnshaw, Joseph C Mrs, 1942, O 10,15:5
Earnshaw, Kirk (por), 1949, Ja 9,72:5
Earnshaw, Ralph, 1940, N 27,23:5
Earnshaw, Warner Gibbs, 1925, S 13,5:1
Earon, Edward D, 1942, Je 20,13:1
Earon, Orville D, 1941, F 20,19:3
Earp, Charles H, 1943, Mr 23,20:3

Earp, Edwin L, 1950, F 5,84:4
Earp, Ernest C Mrs, 1955, Ja 17,23:2
Earp, George W, 1960, D 22,26:2
Earp, J Rosslyn, 1941, My 20,23:2
Earp, Virgil, 1959, N 21,23:5
Earp, Virgil Mrs, 1947, N 18,30:3
Earp, W, 1929, Ja 14,23:3
Earp, W R, 1940, F 6,21:1
Earp, Wyatt Mrs, 1944, D 21,21:5
Earwicker, Charles, 1904, Ja 20,9:6
Easby, Alice R Mrs, 1939, D 31,18:5
Easby, Gertrude E Mrs, 1953, O 10,17:7
Easby, Harriett M, 1922, O 12,19:5
Easby, M Ward, 1949, Je 2,27:4
Easley, George A, 1964, O 3,29:1
Easley, John F, 1956, D 31,13:1
Easley, Phil A, 1952, Je 10,27:2
Easley, Ralph M, 1939, S 8,23:1
Easley, Ralph M Mrs, 1950, F 19,76:5
Easman, George C, 1942, My 20,19:4
Easman, Henry L, 1947, Ap 5,19:5
Easom, Leon H, 1964, Ja 8,37:1
Eason, B Reeves, 1956, Je 13,37:1
Eason, Breezy, 1921, O 27,19:6
Eason, George M, 1965, My 24,31:4
Eason, Isaac W, 1945, D 23,18:6
Eason, J W Capt, 1903, My 5,9:5
Eason, James B, 1949, Jl 13,28:3
Eason, Percival W, 1952, Ja 29,25:1
Easson, Alfred I, 1950, Ap 18,31:2
East, Alfred Sir, 1913, S 29,9:5
East, Arthur Mrs, 1961, F 12,87:1
East, Bion R Mrs, 1962, Ap 3,39:4
East, Charles R Rev, 1915, Jl 24,9:7
East, Ed, 1952, Ja 19,15:2
East, Edward M, 1938, N 10,27:5
East, Ernest E, 1957, N 8,29:2
East, John, 1968, F 28,47:5
East, John L Mrs, 1949, F 27,69:2
East, Russell G, 1943, N 5,19:4
East, William Porter, 1911, D 18,11:5
Eastburn, Charles A Mrs, 1946, Ap 2,27:1
Eastburn, Charles E, 1948, S 2,24:2
Eastburn, Iola K, 1950, My 3,29:1
Eastburn, J Walter, 1953, Jl 6,17:5
Eastburn, Manton Rev, 1872, S 13,5:4
Eastburn, Samuel L, 1946, Jl 28,40:5
Eastburn, Walter N, 1965, Je 16,43:1
Easter, Marguerite, 1946, Mr 21,25:5
Easterbrook, Arthur E, 1952, Jl 31,23:1
Easterbrook, Ervin L, 1937, S 14,23:2
Easterbrook, Helen Francis B, 1866, Jl 4,8:4
Easterday, Susan G Mrs, 1941, Mr 7,21:2
Easterly, Guy, 1963, N 29,37:2
Easterly, Maude M, 1947, N 30,76:4
Easterwood, William E, 1940, Ag 26,15:5
Eastham, Fred C, 1959, D 16,41:3
Eastham, Kenna G, 1944, Ap 21,19:2
Eastham, Melville, 1964, My 8,34:1
Eastin, Bertrand P, 1968, Jl 30,39:2
Eastland, John J, 1939, S 20,27:5
Eastland, Thomas B, 1940, Je 23,30:8
Eastland, W C, 1948, N 18,27:1
Eastland, Woods C Mrs, 1959, D 26,13:5
Eastlund, F Arthur, 1960, Je 13,27:4
Eastlund, John, 1943, D 19,48:8
Eastman, A McA Col, 1877, S 9,6:7
Eastman, Albert S, 1946, N 5,25:4
Eastman, Alex C Dr, 1937, D 24,17:4
Eastman, Alvah, 1939, D 25,23:6
Eastman, Angus, 1943, Ap 2,23:7
Eastman, Cecil, 1959, F 22,88:3
Eastman, Charles A, 1966, Je 18,31:5
Eastman, Charles A Lt Col, 1937, D 17,25:3
Eastman, Charles A Mrs, 1953, D 23,25:3
Eastman, Charles R, 1918, S 30,9:5
Eastman, Clarence W, 1952, Mr 12,27:3
Eastman, Donald, 1962, S 27,34:6
Eastman, Du Bois, 1960, Ag 16,29:5
Eastman, Early C, 1953, Jl 14,27:4
Eastman, Edwin G, 1916, Je 21,11:5
Eastman, Ervin C, 1951, O 8,21:4
Eastman, Francis J, 1947, Ag 26,23:3
Eastman, Frank, 1943, Je 10,21:3
Eastman, Frank L, 1948, D 14,29:5
Eastman, Fred, 1963, Ap 6,19:4
Eastman, Fred E, 1948, Ja 23,23:1
Eastman, Fred W Dr, 1921, Ja 12,15:4
Eastman, G, 1932, Mr 15,1:8
Eastman, Gardner P, 1968, D 8,86:3
Eastman, George P, 1947, Jl 9,23:5
Eastman, George W, 1951, S 27,31:5
Eastman, H Benjamin, 1959, Je 24,31:5
Eastman, H Capt, 1881, Ap 26,5:3
Eastman, H G, 1878, Jl 14,7:5
Eastman, H W, 1882, Ap 1,5:2
Eastman, Hal P (por), 1955, My 6,23:5
Eastman, Harry L, 1963, Jl 8,29:5
Eastman, Herman Mrs, 1950, Ap 7,25:1
Eastman, Horace M, 1951, Mr 3,13:2
Eastman, Irene, 1918, O 25,13:5
Eastman, John, 1951, Jl 12,25:3
Eastman, John C, 1925, Ja 26,17:3
Eastman, John Robie Prof, 1913, S 27,13:4
Eastman, Joseph Mrs, 1903, S 25,7:5
Eastman, Joseph P, 1946, Ja 16,23:1
Eastman, Julia A, 1911, Ja 2,9:4
Eastman, Lawrence R, 1952, Mr 18,27:1
Eastman, Lee J, 1957, Mr 13,31:4
Eastman, Lee J Mrs, 1947, Ap 25,22:2
Eastman, Lucius R, 1943, Mr 15,13:1
Eastman, Lucius R Mrs, 1960, S 6,33:5
Eastman, Marie A, 1946, Ap 18,27:6
Eastman, Max Mrs (E Krylenko), 1956, O 11,39:1
Eastman, Morgan, 1950, Ja 10,29:1
Eastman, Nathaniel, 1956, Ap 24,31:1
Eastman, Nedom A Mrs, 1947, Ag 5,23:1
Eastman, Peter P, 1949, Je 29,27:4
Eastman, Raymond M, 1954, Ag 24,27:2
Eastman, Raymond W, 1956, Mr 30,19:3
Eastman, Rebecca H Mrs, 1937, Je 20,II,6:8
Eastman, Roe S, 1956, N 18,89:1
Eastman, Roe S Mrs, 1957, Je 18,33:2
Eastman, Roger Mrs, 1946, Ja 5,13:1
Eastman, Roy O Mrs, 1950, O 15,104:1
Eastman, Samuel C, 1917, S 1,7:3
Eastman, Samuel E Rev, 1925, F 8,7:1
Eastman, Samuel G, 1947, S 2,21:4
Eastman, Seth Gen, 1875, S 8,4:7
Eastman, William, 1950, Ja 4,35:3
Eastman, William Jr, 1917, N 9,13:5
Eastman, Zebina, 1883, Je 15,5:4
Eastmead, Charles M, 1941, My 7,25:2
Eastmead, George E, 1939, Je 9,21:5
Eastmead, Lewis B, 1956, Ag 28,27:5
Eastment, Percy Mrs, 1948, Ap 27,25:1
Eastmond, Charles Dr (will, D 7,17:1), 1937, N 28, II,8:8
Eastmond, John E, 1953, Ag 21,17:4
Eastmond, Joseph F, 1945, Mr 22,23:2
Easton, Alexander N, 1906, My 23,9:4
Easton, Burton S, 1950, Mr 8,25:2
Easton, Burton S Mrs, 1947, F 8,17:5
Easton, C P Gen, 1885, Mr 5,5:5
Easton, Charles G, 1950, Ap 15,15:3
Easton, Clifford H, 1958, Ag 22,21:4
Easton, Denison Mitchell, 1903, N 4,9:6
Easton, Edward, 1943, S 30,21:6
Easton, Edward D, 1915, My 1,13:6
Easton, Edward Jr, 1964, S 29,43:5
Easton, Edward R, 1950, F 5,84:8
Easton, Edward R Mrs, 1945, Je 28,19:2
Easton, Elwood T, 1943, F 2,19:4
Easton, Emmett E, 1949, D 13,38:1
Easton, Ernest D, 1960, Mr 27,87:1
Easton, Florence, 1955, Ag 14,80:1
Easton, Frederick E Dr, 1921, N 13,22:3
Easton, Gerald, 1961, Je 16,33:3
Easton, Gertrude F Mrs, 1942, Je 25,23:1
Easton, Herbert, 1949, N 3,29:4
Easton, Herbert E, 1919, N 25,11:2
Easton, Irving B, 1948, Ja 26,19:5
Easton, Isabelle, 1916, S 2,7:3
Easton, James I, 1940, F 24,13:4
Easton, Jay A, 1949, Jl 3,26:6
Easton, John, 1949, My 1,88:5
Easton, Kerner, 1965, Mr 10,30:2
Easton, Kerner Mrs, 1956, Ap 25,35:3
Easton, Laird, 1957, Jl 30,23:5
Easton, Lester W, 1960, My 11,39:3
Easton, Mary G Mrs, 1940, Je 18,23:2
Easton, Russell M, 1952, Jl 26,13:5
Easton, S C, 1925, Ap 29,21:5
Easton, S Howard, 1952, Mr 28,23:3
Easton, Thomas Chalmers, 1923, My 25,21:5
Easton, W E, 1941, My 24,15:5
Easton, William H, 1946, Ap 30,21:1
Easton, William J, 1920, Mr 5,13:5; 1948, Ja 5,19:2
Easton, William L, 1865, Mr 23,4:1
Easton, William 2d, 1961, D 2,23:2
Eastvold, Seth C, 1963, F 27,16:1
Eastwick, Abram T, 1948, Jl 13,27:4
Eastwick, Edward P Jr, 1950, Ja 26,28:5
Eastwick, Phil G, 1949, O 11,31:4
Eastwood, Albert B Mrs, 1942, Jl 6,15:6
Eastwood, Alice, 1953, O 31,17:2
Eastwood, Benjamin, 1938, O 15,17:1
Eastwood, Charles W, 1947, F 7,23:3
Eastwood, Elizabeth Howard, 1915, Jl 27,9:6
Eastwood, George A, 1961, Mr 22,41:3
Eastwood, Howard Mrs, 1944, S 30,13:4
Eastwood, James, 1946, My 15,21:2
Eastwood, James Jr, 1960, D 23,19:3
Eastwood, John H Mrs, 1946, D 9,25:3
Eastwood, John Henry, 1921, Ja 13,13:5
Eastwood, Louis, 1949, N 26,8:1
Eastwood, Ralph, 1959, F 20,26:1
Eatherly, Frederick, 1937, My 22,18:1
Eaton, A B, 1877, F 22,5:2
Eaton, Alvah A, 1908, O 2,9:7
Eaton, Amasa M, 1914, O 4,14:4
Eaton, Anna K Mrs, 1955, D 9,27:1
Eaton, Arthur B, 1950, O 11,33:1
Eaton, Arthur H, 1960, Je 12,86:6
Eaton, Arthur T, 1953, Ap 5,77:1
Eaton, Benjamin Allen, 1914, F 19,9:5
Eaton, Benjamin S, 1909, O 11,9:2
Eaton, Bradley L, 1937, Je 11,23:5
Eaton, Charles, 1917, F 10,9:5
Eaton, Charles A, 1953, Ja 24,15:1
Eaton, Charles A Mrs, 1948, N 13,15:5
Eaton, Charles M, 1925, Jl 21,21:5
Eaton, Charles Otis, 1903, O 20,9:6
Eaton, Charles T, 1947, Ja 3,22:3
Eaton, Charles W, 1925, Jl 23,19:6; 1937, S 12,II,6:5
Eaton, Clara, 1954, Ap 4,43:2
Eaton, Clarence E, 1951, Ag 9,21:3
Eaton, Clarence W, 1951, Ja 10,27:4; 1962, Ag 30,29:
Eaton, D Caddy Prof, 1912, My 12,II,17:3
Eaton, Dorman B, 1899, D 24,7:4
Eaton, E H, 1934, Mr 28,23:1
Eaton, E H Rev, 1908, My 12,7:6
Eaton, Earle H, 1950, D 20,31:3
Eaton, Earle H Mrs, 1939, Ag 4,13:5
Eaton, Edith, 1914, Ap 9,11:4
Eaton, Edward A, 1957, Mr 7,29:1
Eaton, Edward B, 1942, D 29,21:5
Eaton, Edward D Mrs, 1937, S 26,II,8:5
Eaton, Edward Lewis, 1914, Jl 5,5:6
Eaton, Eleanor B, 1945, Mr 2,19:3
Eaton, Elizabeth B Mrs, 1940, Ap 25,23:1
Eaton, Elizabeth Harrison Mrs, 1904, My 13,9:6
Eaton, Elliott F, 1956, Ap 25,35:4
Eaton, Elliott F Mrs, 1944, Je 8,21:5
Eaton, Elton R, 1952, Ag 23,13:6
Eaton, Elwyn, 1937, My 4,25:6
Eaton, Emma J Mrs, 1941, My 5,17:5
Eaton, Ernest R, 1963, O 31,33:1
Eaton, Ernest T, 1957, Ag 25,86:3
Eaton, Esther, 1953, Jl 28,19:6
Eaton, Ethel, 1951, Mr 17,15:2
Eaton, Frank, 1958, Ap 9,33:2
Eaton, Frank A, 1944, Jl 28,13:6
Eaton, Frank Herbert Dr, 1908, Ja 14,7:7
Eaton, Frank J, 1943, Jl 11,35:1
Eaton, Frank W, 1940, Mr 18,17:2
Eaton, Fred H, 1948, Ap 29,23:2
Eaton, Frederick C, 1961, N 27,29:4
Eaton, Frederick G, 1954, Ja 23,13:4
Eaton, Frederick H Mrs, 1944, F 1,19:3
Eaton, Frederick Haber (funl, F 1,11:4), 1916, Ja 9:5
Eaton, Frederick W, 1943, S 9,25:2
Eaton, G A Capt, 1924, Ap 24,19:4
Eaton, George E, 1949, F 21,23:5
Eaton, George F, 1949, N 8,31:1; 1956, O 3,33:6
Eaton, George L, 1953, N 12,31:4
Eaton, George L Mrs, 1954, N 2,27:5
Eaton, George T, 1937, Mr 3,23:4
Eaton, Gilbert, 1944, Jl 2,20:2
Eaton, Harold H, 1959, S 22,35:3
Eaton, Harold I, 1951, Ja 15,17:5
Eaton, Harry B, 1943, D 19,48:2
Eaton, Harry N, 1944, Ap 13,19:2
Eaton, Harry T Sr, 1963, My 30,17:2
Eaton, Harvey E, 1938, O 27,23:5
Eaton, Henry, 1941, Ja 28,19:4
Eaton, Henry W, 1950, S 22,31:4
Eaton, Herbert (Lord Cheylesmore), 1925, Jl 30
Eaton, Homer Rev Dr, 1913, F 10,11:4
Eaton, Horace A Mrs, 1949, D 28,25:1
Eaton, Horace Rev, 1883, O 23,5:3
Eaton, Howard, 1953, Ja 1,23:4
Eaton, Hubert L, 1966, S 22,47:4
Eaton, Irving, 1941, O 15,21:5
Eaton, J J, 1940, Ap 5,22:2
Eaton, J Stewart, 1960, Ja 17,86:4
Eaton, Jack, 1968, D 7,47:3
Eaton, James M, 1952, My 2,25:3; 1961, Ja 3,27
Eaton, James W, 1940, Ag 9,15:3
Eaton, James W Mrs, 1945, N 7,23:4
Eaton, Jeanette, 1968, F 21,47:3
Eaton, John Craig Sir, 1922, Mr 31,17:5
Eaton, John Gen, 1906, F 10,9:5
Eaton, John M, 1948, N 10,29:5
Eaton, John P, 1947, My 12,21:3
Eaton, Joll Webster, 1912, O 8,13:5
Eaton, Joseph, 1906, Je 10,9:6
Eaton, Joseph G Rear-Adm, 1913, Mr 9,IV,7:4
Eaton, Joseph Giles Rear-Adm, 1913, Mr 13,11
Eaton, Joseph O, 1875, F 9,5:1; 1949, My 16,21
Eaton, Julian S, 1951, S 18,31:3
Eaton, Lee, 1949, F 14,19:3
Eaton, Lee M, 1958, N 20,35:1
Eaton, Lester, 1948, My 2,77:1
Eaton, Louis D, 1952, Ap 17,29:5
Eaton, Louis E, 1949, Ap 17,76:4
Eaton, Louis W, 1959, S 6,72:7
Eaton, Mabel, 1944, D 7,25:4
Eaton, Marquis G, 1958, F 25,27:2
Eaton, Mary, 1948, O 13,25:3
Eaton, Melvin C, 1966, Ag 3,37:1
Eaton, Oliver K, 1961, S 18,29:5
Eaton, Paul B, 1960, Ap 6,41:2
Eaton, Pearl (Mrs P E Enderly), 1958, S 16,2
Eaton, Percival J, 1938, D 29,19:2
Eaton, R Max, 1944, Mr 27,19:3
Eaton, Robert F, 1962, O 6,25:5
Eaton, Robert Y, 1956, Jl 30,21:5

Eaton, Roy, 1965, My 10,44:8
Eaton, Samuel, 1944, Je 1,19:3
Eaton, Seymour, 1916, Mr 14,11:4
Eaton, Shepherd F, 1940, O 9,25:3
Eaton, Stacey E, 1953, Ag 7,19:2
Eaton, Thomas, 1939, S 17,48:2; 1947, My 13,25:4
Eaton, Thomas H, 1942, N 19,25:5
Eaton, Walter P, 1957, F 27,27:4
Eaton, Walter R, 1939, Mr 15,23:2
Eaton, William E, 1949, N 15,25:1
Eaton, William H, 1952, Ja 13,89:2; 1957, O 10,33:3; 1963, Ap 22,27:5
Eaton, William H Mrs, 1960, S 1,27:2
Eaton, William Mrs, 1951, Ap 15,92:2
Eaton, William O, 1966, Mr 11,18:4
Eaton, William R, 1942, D 17,37:2
Eaton, William S, 1949, Mr 16,28:2
Eaton, William W, 1925, My 1,19:5
Eavenson, Howard N, 1953, F 17,27:3
Eavenson, Marvin S, 1947, Ag 13,23:2
Eavenson, Roland M, 1949, Ja 29,13:4
Eaves, Basil G, 1962, Je 30,19:6
Eaves, George G, 1940, S 22,48:2
Eaves, James, 1950, Jl 4,17:1
Eaves, Lucile, 1953, Ja 21,31:5
Eayrs, Hugh S, 1940, Ap 30,21:4
Eayrs, John H, 1962, Jl 23,21:4
Ebach, Carl A E, 1949, F 28,19:2
Ebann, William B, 1945, S 25,26:2
Ebara, Soroku, 1922, My 21,30:2
Ebbe, Edward, 1964, Je 10,45:4
Ebbe, George P, 1955, My 3,31:4
Ebbe, William T, 1948, N 9,27:2
Ebbers, Frederick Mrs, 1948, S 9,27:3
Ebbert, David W, 1939, D 4,23:2
Ebbert, James M, 1948, Mr 30,23:3
Ebbets, Charles (will), 1944, Je 29,36:5
Ebbets, Charles H (funl, Ap 21,21:6), 1925, Ap 20, 17:4
Ebbets, Charles H Jr, 1944, My 16,21:2
Ebbets, Minnie F A Mrs, 1947, F 1,15:3
Ebbinghousen, Jane A C Mrs, 1942, F 28,17:1
Ebbinghousen, Johanna B, 1950, N 2,31:2
Ebbisham, Lord (R Blades), 1953, My 25,25:2
Ebbitt, Nicholas J Mrs, 1955, D 22,23:5
Ebbutt, Norman, 1968, O 20,86:2
Ebe, R A, 1939, Ap 4,25:3
Ebeid, Makram, 1961, Je 7,38:5
Ebel, Charles, 1942, Jl 25,13:5
Ebel, Edward N, 1951, Ag 8,25:2
Ebel, Henry A, 1950, Je 26,27:3
Ebel, Martin C, 1924, S 20,15:6
Ebel, Martin C Mrs, 1952, My 11,93:1
Ebel, Valentine, 1944, O 18,21:3
Ebeling, Albert H, 1965, Je 28,29:4
Ebeling, George A, 1951, N 15,29:3
Ebeling, Octave P, 1950, Ja 18,31:4
Ebeling, Regina Z Mrs, 1940, Je 27,23:3
Ebeling, Willi H, 1961, D 13,43:4
Ebeling, William G, 1940, Mr 13,23:3
Eben, Harry G, 1938, F 2,19:5
Eben, James G, 1948, N 21,88:8
Eben, Lambert L, 1960, F 22,17:3
Eben, Siegfried N, 1953, F 2,21:2
Eben, Siegfried N Mrs, 1960, Jl 4,15:4
Ebenstein, Aaron, 1957, Ja 13,85:1
Eber, Bobby, 1951, N 2,23:1
Eber, Manuel, 1961, My 13,19:5
Eberach, Nelson F, 1950, My 24,29:3
Eberenz, John, 1957, D 31,17:4
Eberhard, Arnold, 1946, Ap 5,25:4
Eberhard, Engelbert, 1958, O 21,33:4
Eberhard, Ernest G Dr, 1913, Ja 18,13:4
Eberhard, Frederick Nicholas, 1922, My 18,19:6
Eberhard, Harry M, 1962, Je 17,81:1
Eberhard, Konrad, 1859, Ap 16,1:3
Eberhard, Nicholas J, 1957, F 2,19:4
Eberhard, Nicholas J Jr, 1950, Je 18,76:8
Eberhard, Phil J, 1937, Mr 20,19:3
Eberhardt, August, 1952, F 6,29:4
Eberhardt, Frederick G, 1967, F 7,39:1
Eberhardt, Frederick G Mrs, 1951, Ag 8,25:3
Eberhardt, Frederick L, 1946, Jl 19,19:3
Eberhardt, John J, 1937, S 10,23:5
Eberhardt, Louis P A, 1939, Ap 22,17:1
Eberhardt, Magnus von, 1939, Ja 26,21:3
Eberhardt, Maxmillian, 1940, N 13,23:3
Eberhardt, U Seth Sr, 1960, Ja 23,21:3
Eberhardt, Ulrich, 1957, Ag 13,27:4
Eberhardt, William F, 1946, Ap 10,27:3
Eberhart, A O, 1944, D 7,25:5
Eberhart, Charles F, 1948, Ja 4,52:2
Eberhart, John P, 1957, S 6,21:2
Eberhart, Nelle R Mrs, 1944, N 16,23:3
Eberhart, Noble M, 1939, F 11,15:6
Eberhart, Ronald M, 1941, Ap 16,23:4
Eberharter, Herman Mrs, 1955, Ag 6,15:4
Eberharter, Herman P, 1958, S 10,33:1
Eberl, Carl, 1944, N 9,27:2
Eberle, Abastenias, 1942, F 28,17:4
Eberle, David G, 1950, N 7,27:6
Eberle, E A Mrs, 1919, Ag 4,11:4
Eberle, E W, 1929, Jl 7,21:1
Eberle, Eugene A, 1917, O 24,15:5
Eberle, Eugene G, 1942, My 4,19:3
Eberle, George G C, 1955, My 16,23:4
Eberle, Harry L, 1948, Mr 9,23:4
Eberle, James, 1942, F 14,15:3
Eberle, Merab, 1959, N 3,31:3
Eberle, Philip, 1951, Ap 18,31:5
Eberle, Ray Mrs, 1964, F 19,39:3
Eberle, Robert M, 1912, My 25,13:6
Eberle, Warren C Mrs, 1955, S 21,33:3
Eberlein, G Prof, 1926, F 6,15:3
Eberlein, Harold D, 1964, Jl 28,29:3
Eberlein, Jefferson G, 1940, Ag 8,19:6
Eberlein, Nicholas, 1961, Je 25,77:1
Eberlin, George P, 1960, D 24,15:1
Eberling, Christy, 1954, F 23,27:3
Eberling, Herman L, 1945, Ap 4,21:6
Eberly, John A, 1949, Ja 12,27:3
Eberly, Joseph E, 1954, Ag 25,27:3
Eberly, Raymond G, 1941, S 22,15:6
Eberman, C E Rev, 1903, Ap 14,9:6
Ebers, G M, 1898, Ag 9,7:5
Ebers, J James, 1959, Ap 1,37:3
Ebersbach, Alfred, 1955, Je 18,17:5
Ebersole, Amos A, 1943, My 11,21:3
Ebersole, George B, 1953, Ap 5,76:6
Ebersole, Iola R Mrs, 1939, Ap 27,25:2
Ebersole, J Franklin, 1945, Je 25,17:5
Ebersole, J R, 1938, Jl 31,33:4
Ebersole, Newman, 1948, S 24,25:3
Ebersole, Ruel, 1946, F 16,13:2
Ebersole, Russell E Jr Mrs, 1964, N 26,33:4
Eberson, John, 1954, Mr 7,90:4
Eberson, John Mrs, 1954, Jl 16,21:5
Eberstadt, Edward E, 1958, O 4,21:3
Eberstadt, Edward F Mrs, 1957, Ag 11,81:1
Eberstadt, Rudolph, 1961, My 25,37:4
Eberstaller, Alfred, 1956, My 16,35:1
Eberstein, Abraham N, 1914, D 20,15:5
Ebert, Carl Friedrich, 1924, My 24,15:3
Ebert, Charles H, 1959, O 4,86:5
Ebert, Friedrich Mrs, 1955, Ja 20,31:5
Ebert, George, 1959, Mr 29,80:5
Ebert, Henry Clay, 1925, Je 10,23:4
Ebert, John, 1941, O 2,25:1
Ebert, Joseph A, 1955, D 31,13:5
Ebert, Justus, 1946, D 27,19:3
Ebert, Lewis, 1947, N 7,23:3
Ebert, Louis Mrs, 1964, Ap 12,86:2
Ebert, Louis V, 1945, D 20,23:4
Ebert, Peter, 1949, Jl 16,13:4
Ebert, Robert A, 1967, Ag 31,33:4
Ebert, Robert Edwin, 1968, Ag 17,27:5
Ebert, Rudolph, 1938, Ja 22,18:2
Ebert, Rudolph H, 1938, Ag 16,19:3
Ebert, Samuel M, 1949, S 9,26:6
Ebert, St Gemme, 1961, Ja 23,23:2
Eberwein, Howard J Mrs, 1958, Ja 29,27:2
Ebgin, Nachman H, 1943, My 28,21:3
Ebie, A C, 1938, F 27,II,8:3
Ebiger, Walter D, 1945, Jl 26,19:6
Ebin, Ima, 1952, Mr 7,23:2
Ebina, Danjo Dr, 1937, My 23,II,11:2
Ebinger, George D Mrs, 1955, O 22,19:4
Eble, Frank Xavier Z, 1952, D 15,25:4
Ebling, Amana A P Mrs, 1941, Ag 14,17:4
Ebling, Edward E, 1938, F 12,15:4
Ebling, Louis M, 1923, Je 11,13:4
Ebmeyer, Gustav Adolph, 1908, Ag 13,7:4
Ebner, Edward J, 1953, N 26,31:1
Ebner-Eschenbach, Marie von Baroness, 1916, Mr 15, 11:6
Ebner-Rofenstein, Vikter Prof, 1925, Mr 22,7:3
Eborn, William N Mrs, 1968, Je 27,43:4
Eboue, Felix, 1944, My 18,19:4
Ebright, George E, 1954, Je 28,19:4
Ebsary, Frederick G, 1955, Je 8,29:6
Ebsen, Henry L, 1945, Ja 12,15:4
Ebsen, Herman, 1964, Ag 18,31:2
Ebsteen, Frederick H E Maj, 1916, F 9,11:7
Ebury, Lord (R E Grosvenor), 1957, My 6,11:3
Eby, Earl E, 1957, Ag 9,19:2
Eby, Frederick Dr, 1968, F 12,53:8
Eby, Harry K, 1961, Ag 4,21:4
Eby, Isaac Bp, 1910, Je 19,II,11:4
Eby, Jay W, 1952, Ja 26,13:2
Eby, John C Mrs, 1945, Ap 25,23:2
Eby, Joseph D, 1966, Ap 22,29:6
Eby, Kerr, 1946, N 19,31:5
Eby, Louise S, 1948, My 16,68:6
Eby, Samuel C, 1939, F 27,15:5
Eccles, Bernard C, 1942, D 21,23:1
Eccles, David R, 1912, D 6,15:5
Eccles, Ellen S Mrs, 1957, F 27,27:2
Eccles, George W, 1947, Je 24,24:3
Eccles, James A, 1960, Mr 4,25:3
Eccles, John Mrs, 1964, Ja 25,23:3
Eccles, Mary H, 1942, Mr 19,21:3
Eccles, Silas Wright, 1918, Ja 1,17:4
Ecclesine, Adelaide C, 1947, O 24,23:3
Ecclesine, Joseph B Mrs, 1923, Je 4,15:6
Ecclesine, Joseph Brodie, 1909, Mr 14,11:6
Eccleston, Arthur I, 1943, Mr 27,13:5
Eccleston, C Douglas Mrs, 1954, D 29,23:4
Eccleston, J Houston Rev Dr, 1911, Ap 2,II,13:4
Eccleston, John B, 1941, N 4,26:4
Eccleston, John C Mrs, 1946, Ja 29,25:4
Eccleston, William D, 1949, O 25,27:3
Ecclestone, Robert, 1941, Mr 13,21:1
Echandi, Alberto, 1944, S 30,13:6
Echegaray, Jose, 1916, S 16,11:7
Echevarria, Arturo L, 1960, My 10,37:2
Echeverria, Carlos P, 1954, Ag 10,19:6
Echeverria, Charles M, 1948, Ag 18,25:4
Echeverria, Martin J (por), 1947, N 7,23:2
Echlin, Erland, 1951, S 4,27:2
Echmalian, John G, 1946, S 27,23:2
Echols, Angus B, 1967, F 28,34:1
Echols, Angus B Sr Mrs, 1942, Jl 22,19:3
Echols, Francis G, 1942, S 29,24:2
Echols, Oliver P, 1954, My 16,86:1
Echt, Alice B P Von (Baroness), 1959, My 22,27:3
Echtman, Joseph, 1953, Je 28,60:8
Eck, Charles A, 1950, Ag 20,77:2
Eck, Donald R, 1957, O 21,25:4
Eck, E A William, 1942, Mr 31,21:1
Eck, J C van, 1965, F 17,43:4
Eck, Jacob F, 1945, Ag 21,21:5
Eck, Vincent J, 1938, My 22,II,6:7
Eck, William J, 1942, Ag 21,19:6
Eckard, James M L, 1941, Mr 8,19:3
Eckard, Leighton W Rev, 1925, N 18,23:4
Eckardt, Frederick Mrs, 1945, Ap 28,15:1
Eckardt, Max, 1961, O 1,86:2
Eckart, Edward F, 1940, F 19,17:5
Eckart, Frank, 1959, F 26,31:3
Eckburg, Charles A, 1967, D 30,23:3
Eckburg, Charles A Mrs, 1960, F 3,33:2
Eckdahl, Arnold G, 1965, Jl 14,37:4
Ecke, Albert D, 1944, Ap 30,46:3
Eckel, Albert F, 1938, F 20,II,8:8
Eckel, C Richard, 1968, Ap 29,43:4
Eckel, Edwin C, 1941, N 23,51:4
Eckel, George L, 1951, N 3,17:4
Eckel, John C, 1943, D 21,27:3
Eckel, Thomas J, 1962, Mr 18,86:8
Eckelberry, John W, 1957, O 25,27:4
Eckelhoffer, Frederick, 1947, Mr 16,60:2
Eckels, Charles A, 1942, D 22,25:3
Eckels, Charles B, 1940, Ap 29,15:6
Eckels, James H, 1907, Ap 15,9:1
Eckels, James H Mrs, 1924, D 2,25:4
Eckels, Lewis C, 1950, Mr 27,23:4
Eckels, Stanley D, 1940, D 17,26:2
Eckels, Thomas H, 1942, N 22,52:2
Eckenberg, Louis H Mrs, 1951, Ap 13,23:5
Eckenberg, William C Mrs, 1967, F 16,39:2
Eckener, Hugo (funl, Ag 18,29:4), 1954, Ag 15,1:2
Eckenrode, Joseph M, 1954, Ap 27,29:5
Ecker, Frederic W (mem ser set, F 29,21:2), 1964, F 28,29:1
Ecker, Frederick H, 1964, Mr 21,25:1
Ecker, Frederick H Mrs, 1950, N 22,25:3
Ecker, Harry Mrs, 1951, Ja 17,27:3
Ecker, Jacob, 1952, F 20,29:3
Ecker, James A, 1941, Mr 28,23:5
Ecker, Karl, 1879, O 27,4:7
Ecker, William H, 1954, N 4,31:5
Eckerd, J Milton, 1963, My 11,25:2
Eckerdt, A Burton Dr, 1937, Je 20,II,6:7
Eckerle, John, 1945, Ja 26,21:1
Eckerle, John W, 1948, Je 15,28:2
Eckerlein, Alfred N, 1958, Ag 16,17:6
Eckersall, W H, 1930, Mr 25,29:1
Eckersen, George L, 1960, S 27,37:3
Eckersley, Robert N, 1939, Ag 12,13:6
Eckersley, Thomas L, 1959, F 17,32:1
Eckerson, Albert B, 1939, Mr 30,23:4
Eckerson, Albert B Mrs, 1966, Ja 29,27:5
Eckerson, John C R, 1916, O 17,13:5
Eckerson, Lowell B, 1967, Je 10,33:3
Eckerson, Peter Quick, 1904, Ja 13,9:5
Eckerson, William, 1911, Ja 4,9:2
Eckert, Abram D, 1942, Mr 22,48:7
Eckert, Adam E, 1943, O 30,15:5
Eckert, Augustus F, 1954, Ja 27,27:2
Eckert, Bernard H Sr, 1946, Jl 24,27:4
Eckert, Carl J, 1948, My 7,23:2
Eckert, Charles W, 1943, Ja 9,13:2
Eckert, Eddie, 1917, D 26,9:7
Eckert, Edward A, 1951, N 15,29:3
Eckert, Edward G, 1952, My 25,92:6
Eckert, Edward O, 1948, Ag 17,21:3
Eckert, Fred, 1944, Jl 24,15:4
Eckert, George A, 1953, Je 6,17:2
Eckert, George J, 1946, F 16,13:3
Eckert, George M, 1942, My 23,13:6
Eckert, George R, 1942, F 3,19:1
Eckert, Henry J, 1947, D 2,29:3
Eckert, Howard H, 1964, Je 14,84:6
Eckert, J Presper Sr, 1954, Jl 8,23:6
Eckert, Jerome, 1949, D 14,31:2
Eckert, John, 1944, O 24,23:3
Eckert, Lewis P, 1940, Je 13,23:4
Eckert, Louis, 1965, Ag 12,27:4
Eckert, Louis Mrs, 1953, Jl 29,23:4

Eckert, May Belle, 1905, Ap 17,1:3
Eckert, T T Mrs, 1902, Ja 12,7:7
Eckert, Thomas T Gen (funl, O 24,9:6), 1910, O 21, 11:4
Eckert, Thor, 1940, Ja 14,42:5
Eckert, William, 1950, D 27,27:1
Eckert, William A, 1939, Ag 2,19:4
Eckert, William B, 1943, S 9,25:2
Eckert, William H, 1951, O 14,88:5
Eckert, William K, 1950, S 22,31:1
Eckert, William P, 1959, Ag 31,21:4
Eckes, Matthew, 1948, O 25,23:5
Eckes, Peter A, 1961, Ja 3,27:7
Eckes, William P, 1963, My 15,40:2
Eckfeldt, Jacob B, 1938, S 9,21:1
Eckhard, George F, 1945, D 29,14:3
Eckhardt, Albert J, 1957, Je 14,25:4
Eckhardt, Clarence W, 1923, S 18,21:6
Eckhardt, George H, 1963, Je 7,31:5
Eckhardt, George H Mrs, 1937, D 25,15:5
Eckhardt, George J, 1946, S 3,19:5
Eckhardt, George W, 1954, Ja 3,31:1
Eckhardt, Henry, 1942, Jl 14,19:5; 1947, Jl 6,41:1
Eckhardt, Henry P, 1949, My 13,23:5
Eckhardt, Herman W, 1953, F 11,29:3
Eckhardt, John, 1955, D 27,24:4
Eckhardt, Joseph F, 1948, Ag 19,21:2
Eckhardt, Oscar G, 1951, Ap 24,29:2
Eckhardt, Richard D Mrs, 1962, Ap 19,31:2
Eckhardt, Robert E Mrs, 1965, Jl 28,35:5
Eckhardt, Rosa Mrs, 1941, Jl 20,31:3
Eckhardt, William N, 1941, Je 15,36:6
Eckhart, E M, 1948, N 30,27:4
Eckhart, Edmond, 1965, Ap 12,35:3
Eckhart, George, 1948, O 26,31:5
Eckhart, George H (cor, Jl 31,23:6), 1957, Jl 17,27:3
Eckhart, John W 2d, 1938, D 8,27:5
Eckhoff, Alice M Mrs, 1939, O 5,23:5
Eckhoff, Charles L, 1939, My 3,23:3
Eckhoff, Frederick J, 1956, Ap 20,25:5
Eckhouse, Elmer L, 1938, N 22,24:2
Eckhouse, Elmer M Mrs, 1948, Jl 4,26:8
Eckhouse, Joseph L, 1967, Ja 30,26:3
Eckhouse, Lillie R Mrs, 1939, O 4,25:2
Eckl, Joseph A, 1937, My 7,25:1
Eckler, Elmer E, 1959, Ap 1,37:3
Eckler, Harrie D, 1953, N 16,25:3
Eckles, Andrew G, 1946, Ap 4,25:3
Eckles, Elvis L, 1967, Ap 7,37:3
Eckles, Howard S, 1937, Ap 6,23:2
Eckman, Allen R, 1961, My 9,39:3
Eckman, Charles, 1962, F 6,35:3
Eckman, Charles A, 1941, My 23,21:2
Eckman, Charles L, 1950, Ja 2,23:5
Eckman, George Peck Rev Dr, 1920, Je 29,11:5
Eckman, J R, 1929, Ag 3,17:3
Eckman, Julius Rev Dr, 1874, Jl 14,2:7
Eckman, Rena S, 1946, N 10,63:1
Eckman, S W, 1933, Mr 26,30:1
Eckmann, William, 1947, Ja 7,27:4
Eckmeyer, Gustav D, 1906, N 27,9:5
Eckstein, Adolph W, 1963, Je 30,56:6
Eckstein, Alfred, 1947, F 17,19:3
Eckstein, Arthur, 1960, Ag 19,23:4
Eckstein, Clarence L, 1950, Mr 23,29:4
Eckstein, Edward S, 1948, Ag 24,23:1
Eckstein, Helene Mrs, 1949, S 17,17:2
Eckstein, Henry J, 1954, D 7,33:2
Eckstein, J Francis Jr, 1960, N 25,37:1
Eckstein, Louis Mrs, 1950, Ap 28,21:3
Eckstein, Louise Mrs, 1939, Ap 18,23:3
Eckstein, Nathan, 1945, Ag 8,23:3
Eckstein, Nathan Mrs, 1938, Je 24,19:5
Eckstein, Rubin, 1966, O 9,86:3
Eckstein, Samuel, 1922, D 18,17:5; 1945, Jl 16,11:6
Eckstein, Sol W, 1942, Mr 11,19:4
Eckstein, Victor, 1964, Je 3,43:3
Ecksteinn, Albert, 1950, Je 20,27:2
Eckstorm, Jacob Mrs, 1947, Ja 1,33:6
Eckstrom, Lawrence J, 1966, Ap 9,25:1
Eckweiler, Warren J, 1948, Ja 6,23:1
Ecob, James H Rev, 1921, N 7,15:4
Ecoff, Jack, 1963, Jl 4,17:2
Ecoff, Wesley M, 1964, S 9,43:4
Ecton, Zales N, 1961, Mr 5,86:8
Ed, Carl F L, 1959, O 11,86:4
Ed, Eva Mrs, 1939, Ap 12,23:5
Edam, George A, 1943, Ag 28,11:5
Edde, Emile, 1949, S 29,27:4
Eddie, Glenn, 1949, O 30,84:4
Eddine, Sabah Prince, 1915, My 1,13:5
Eddinger, W, 1929, Ja 9,31:2
Eddington, Albin Mrs, 1952, Ap 8,29:4
Eddington, Arthur S, 1944, N 23,31:4
Eddins, Daniel S Mrs, 1965, Ja 14,35:5
Eddins, Thomas K Mrs, 1940, O 6,48:1
Eddison, Lee C, 1954, D 12,88:6
Eddolls, Frank, 1961, Ag 14,25:4
Eddowes, William, 1937, D 9,25:3
Eddy, Alfred U, 1937, O 4,21:4
Eddy, Arch R, 1954, N 16,29:1
Eddy, Arthur, 1941, Ap 27,V,4:8
Eddy, Arthur H, 1937, F 19,19:2
Eddy, Arthur Jerome, 1920, Jl 22,11:5
Eddy, Augustus M Mrs, 1909, Ja 3,11:5
Eddy, Austin W, 1953, Jl 7,27:5
Eddy, Bessie, 1918, My 6,13:1
Eddy, Brayton, 1950, Jl 18,29:5
Eddy, Caleb F, 1951, Mr 2,25:1
Eddy, Cecil E, 1956, Je 28,29:5
Eddy, Charles, 1951, O 25,29:4
Eddy, Charles B, 1951, Ja 11,25:4
Eddy, Charles B Sr, 1941, O 1,21:4
Eddy, Charles F, 1941, Ap 10,24:2
Eddy, Charles H, 1946, O 25,23:4
Eddy, Charles P, 1949, N 2,27:3; 1951, F 1,25:5
Eddy, Charles W, 1943, Jl 12,15:1
Eddy, Clarence, 1937, Ja 11,20:1
Eddy, Clifford R, 1954, Jl 29,23:3
Eddy, D Brewer, 1946, Je 2,44:3
Eddy, E Howard, 1953, Jl 10,19:1
Eddy, Edgar, 1941, Ap 21,19:2
Eddy, Edith S Mrs, 1942, Ag 27,19:4
Eddy, Edward (Masonic funl), 1876, Ja 17,8:4
Eddy, Edward D Mrs, 1957, Ag 27,29:5
Eddy, Elizabeth Mrs, 1925, O 6,27:5
Eddy, Ezekiel E, 1942, My 24,42:4
Eddy, Forrest G, 1939, My 18,25:4
Eddy, Frank, 1944, Jl 20,19:3
Eddy, Frank W, 1914, Je 13,9:5
Eddy, Fred J, 1937, Ag 9,20:1
Eddy, Frederick W, 1941, Jl 27,30:1
Eddy, George A, 1941, Ag 27,19:4
Eddy, George H, 1940, N 2,15:5
Eddy, George W, 1947, Ja 31,23:4; 1954, Jl 25,69:2
Eddy, Harrie A, 1948, Ag 12,21:1
Eddy, Harrison P, 1937, Je 16,24:1
Eddy, Harry C, 1951, Mr 7,33:3
Eddy, Harry Mrs, 1938, Jl 9,13:2
Eddy, Henry S, 1944, Ag 11,15:4
Eddy, Herbert G, 1948, S 12,72:2
Eddy, Isabel K Mrs, 1957, D 20,27:3
Eddy, J Lynn, 1946, Mr 19,27:5
Eddy, James W Mrs, 1950, N 29,33:1
Eddy, Jay E, 1939, Ap 14,23:1
Eddy, Jerome H, 1918, Je 8,11:5
Eddy, Jerome Mrs, 1925, S 23,25:3
Eddy, Jesse G, 1950, Ja 27,24:2
Eddy, John G Brig-Gen, 1925, Ja 31,13:5
Eddy, John L, 1952, F 19,29:3
Eddy, John L Mrs, 1954, Ja 15,19:3
Eddy, Joseph D, 1937, N 7,II,9:2
Eddy, Lillian (Mrs L E Rice), 1966, Ag 27,30:3
Eddy, Manton S, 1962, Ap 11,43:1
Eddy, Martha G Mrs, 1937, Ag 19,19:3
Eddy, Mary Pierson Dr, 1923, S 13,19:3
Eddy, Maxson A, 1958, F 15,17:4
Eddy, Milton W, 1964, Je 16,39:5
Eddy, Montague, 1949, D 23,21:4
Eddy, Nelson, 1967, Mr 7,41:1
Eddy, Richard Rev Dr, 1906, Ag 17,7:6
Eddy, Robert C, 1948, Ag 4,21:2; 1953, S 23,31:3
Eddy, Ruth M, 1955, My 24,31:4
Eddy, S Schuyler, 1944, Ag 22,17:5
Eddy, Samuel A, 1945, S 16,42:3
Eddy, Sarah A, 1945, Mr 31,19:4
Eddy, Sherwood, 1963, Mr 5,16:2
Eddy, Sherwood Mrs, 1945, S 3,23:2
Eddy, Spencer, 1939, O 8,49:1
Eddy, Stanley R, 1958, Ag 18,19:4
Eddy, T M Rev, 1874, O 8,4:7
Eddy, Ulysses D Mrs, 1905, F 3,7:1
Eddy, Ulysses Doubleday, 1917, Ap 3,13:6
Eddy, Vincent L, 1955, S 9,23:3
Eddy, Walter H, 1959, O 1,35:2
Eddy, Walter L, 1954, F 18,13:1
Eddy, William, 1948, F 19,23:4
Eddy, William A, 1909, D 27,7:4; 1962, My 5,27:2
Eddy, William H, 1957, Jl 25,23:5
Eddy, William H Gen, 1911, Ag 10,7:4
Eddy, William H Mrs, 1958, Ja 24,21:1
Eddy, William S, 1942, O 26,15:5; 1943, Mr 31,19:1
Ede, Hubert R, 1961, F 8,28:1
Ede, J Chuter Mrs, 1948, Jl 2,21:4
Ede, Jean C Mrs, 1953, F 17,27:3
Edehohis, George Michael Dr, 1908, Ag 9,9:4
Edeiken, Louis, 1955, Ap 13,29:5
Edeiken, Louis Mrs, 1960, Mr 1,33:2
Edel, Abraham Mrs, 1964, My 24,92:3
Edel, Albert E, 1955, Je 8,29:4
Edel, Alfredo Mrs, 1944, Jl 4,19:2
Edel, George J, 1945, D 31,17:4
Edel, Harold, 1918, N 3,2:1
Edel, Harry T Sr, 1948, Jl 14,23:5
Edel, Richard Mrs, 1949, D 27,23:3
Edelbaum, Saul Mrs, 1960, O 15,23:5
Edelblute, Lucius A, 1953, Ja 15,27:2
Edelbrock, Abbot Alexius Rev, 1908, My 20,7:5
Edelen, James J, 1958, Ag 7,25:5
Edelhertz, Murray, 1961, Je 22,31:3
Edelhoff, Arthur S, 1959, Jl 9,27:5
Edell, Chris L, 1952, D 31,15:2
Edelman, Abram, 1948, F 4,23:1
Edelman, Edward, 1955, F 9,27:2
Edelman, Harry, 1954, S 7,25:2
Edelman, Herman, 1966, F 23,39:3
Edelman, Herman Mrs, 1966, F 23,39:3
Edelman, Joseph S, 1955, O 12,29:1
Edelman, Leo, 1967, Ag 20,89:1
Edelman, Leon, 1949, My 29,36:6
Edelman, Selig Mrs, 1966, Ja 26,37:3
Edelmann, Henry A, 1950, Mr 28,31:4
Edels, Julius, 1941, O 10,23:5
Edelshteyn, Vitaly I, 1965, Ag 4,35:5
Edelson, Joseph D, 1953, N 21,13:1
Edelson, Samuel, 1956, Ja 21,21:4
Edelson, William, 1940, Jl 16,17:5
Edelstadt, Sophia R Mrs, 1962, S 9,84:4
Edelstain, Jacob Mrs, 1950, O 20,28:3; 1954, Ag 19, 23:4
Edelstein, Abraham, 1941, D 1,19:4
Edelstein, Abram Mrs, 1950, Je 26,27:4
Edelstein, E Alexander, 1965, My 3,33:2
Edelstein, Emanuel, 1950, S 30,17:5
Edelstein, Francis J, 1953, Je 8,29:5
Edelstein, Gus, 1951, Ap 24,29:2
Edelstein, Jacob E, 1953, F 12,27:3
Edelstein, John, 1903, Je 20,7:6; 1948, My 17,19:3
Edelstein, John E, 1957, Ja 17,29:2
Edelstein, Julius C C Mrs, 1964, My 15,35:3
Edelstein, Louis Mrs, 1943, O 14,21:4
Edelstein, Ludwig, 1965, Ag 17,33:4
Edelstein, M Michael, 1941, Je 5,24:2
Edelstein, Menahem M, 1954, S 19,88:8
Edelstein, Paul, 1968, F 10,34:1
Edelstein, Simon, 1956, My 13,86:4
Edelstein, Stanley Mrs (Shirley), 1965, S 11,27:3
Edelsten, William, 1951, O 15,25:5
Edelsten, William Mrs, 1911, Ja 20,11:4
Eden, Alfred W A, 1954, D 16,37:5
Eden, Ashley, 1943, Ja 20,19:3
Eden, Beatrice H B Mrs, 1957, Jl 1,23:2
Eden, Charles G, 1939, D 6,25:6
Eden, Cora L Mrs, 1958, My 7,35:5
Eden, Geoffrey M (Lord Auckland), 1955, Je 23
Eden, George A, 1951, O 30,29:2
Eden, John D, 1947, F 4,25:1
Eden, John H, 1943, S 6,17:5
Eden, Marie C Mrs, 1945, Ap 6,15:5
Eden, Muriel T Mrs, 1967, D 9,47:1
Eden, Rob (G H Thomas), 1962, S 17,31:5
Eden, Robert Charles, 1907, Ja 24,9:5
Eden, Sybil, 1945, Je 18,19:3
Eden, Timothy, 1963, My 14,39:2
Eden, William T Mrs, 1944, D 20,23:2
Edenborough, Herbert Mrs, 1958, My 27,31:1
Edens, A Hollis Dr, 1968, Ag 8,33:2
Edens, William G, 1957, N 16,19:6
Eder, Joseph F, 1967, O 20,47:4
Eder, Matthew J, 1966, Je 25,31:5
Eder, Peter J Mrs, 1946, Jl 22,21:5
Eder-Schwyzer, Jeanne Mrs, 1957, O 25,27:2
Ederle, Henry Mrs, 1954, Jl 1,25:2
Edes, H F Rev, 1881, Mr 14,2:7
Edes, Mary E (Mrs S Agnew), 1962, O 27,25:4
Edeson, R, 1931, Mr 25,25:1
Edeson, Robert Mrs (Ellen Berg), 1906, My 3
Edey, Alfred Mrs, 1957, Jl 3,23:5
Edey, Frederick Mrs, 1940, Mr 18,17:3
Edey, Mary W Mrs (will, Ag 18,20:6), 1938, A 17:3
Edey, William Schenck, 1908, Mr 24,7:5
Edgar, Abiel D, 1951, F 25,87:4
Edgar, Andrew J, 1944, Jl 17,15:4
Edgar, Annette D Mrs, 1942, My 27,23:1
Edgar, Archibald, 1958, F 13,29:4
Edgar, C G, 1932, Ag 10,15:1
Edgar, C H Rev, 1884, D 25,5:2
Edgar, C L, 1932, Ap 15,19:3
Edgar, Charles Mrs, 1944, N 14,23:4
Edgar, D A, 1878, Ag 1,5:6
Edgar, David A, 1948, My 22,15:2
Edgar, David E Jr, 1964, Mr 28,19:2
Edgar, David S, 1944, Ag 3,19:3
Edgar, David W, 1949, N 5,13:3
Edgar, Felix F, 1874, Ja 6,4:7
Edgar, Frank C, 1951, Ag 27,19:4
Edgar, George E, 1955, Je 3,23:3
Edgar, George M, 1951, My 16,35:4
Edgar, George S, 1945, F 20,19:2
Edgar, Graham (por), 1955, S 9,23:3
Edgar, Harold T, 1957, Jl 30,23:5
Edgar, Harry W, 1963, Je 19,37:5
Edgar, Henry C, 1963, Je 2,84:1
Edgar, Herman L, 1938, S 6,21:1
Edgar, Herman L Mrs, 1944, Ja 1,13:1
Edgar, J, 1933, My 13,13:4
Edgar, J Augustus, 1955, O 23,86:4
Edgar, James, 1957, Je 9,88:7
Edgar, James A Mrs, 1947, My 21,25:4
Edgar, James C, 1939, Ap 8,15:3
Edgar, John, 1963, Jl 20,6:3
Edgar, Jonathan, 1879, Jl 3,5:3
Edgar, Joseph, 1939, S 12,49:2
Edgar, Joseph A, 1944, Ja 1,13:1
Edgar, Joseph M, 1961, Ag 8,29:3
Edgar, Louis C, 1942, Jl 2,21:3
Edgar, Lucille R, 1948, Ag 29,56:3
Edgar, Margaret, 1951, Ap 17,29:5

Edgar, Mark K, 1951, F 18,77:2
Edgar, Milton Elbert, 1925, Jl 30,19:6
Edgar, Newbold L (funl, Ja 8,23:3), 1924, Ja 7,9:3
Edgar, Newbold Mrs, 1922, O 17,19:4
Edgar, Robert, 1871, Je 11,5:3; 1944, Ap 30,46:4
Edgar, S H, 1902, N 3,9:5
Edgar, Thomas W, 1942, Ag 9,42:8
Edgar, Thomas W Mrs, 1961, Je 7,41:2
Edgar, Walter A, 1955, S 13,31:4
Edgar, Walter S, 1951, Jl 13,21:4
Edgar, William, 1920, O 18,15:1
Edgar, William A, 1914, Mr 6,11:4; 1954, Je 15,29:2; 1961, Ag 28,25:5
Edgar, William Mrs, 1916, F 8,11:3
Edgar, William S, 1941, Mr 28,23:3
Edgar, William S Mrs, 1951, D 24,13:4
Edgarton, Warren P, 1906, Ap 13,9:3
Edgcomb, Ernest I, 1943, Je 9,21:1
Edgcomb, Harry L, 1952, Je 8,86:3
Edgcumbe, Kenelm W E (Earl of Mount Edgcumbe), 1965, F 12,29:1
Edgcumbe, M Lord, 1944, Ap 19,23:5
Edgcumbe, Richard, 1937, N 6,17:6
Edgcumbe, William Henry Lord, 1917, S 26,13:5
Edge, Benjamin Ogden, 1871, Je 13,8:5
Edge, Beulah (will), 1959, Jl 9,2:3
Edge, Charles N, 1944, Je 30,21:3
Edge, Charles N Mrs, 1962, D 1,25:2
Edge, Henry C, 1951, Mr 13,31:3
Edge, Howard H, 1966, Je 22,47:4
Edge, Howard H Mrs, 1956, Mr 11,89:1
Edge, J G, 1883, Mr 12,4:7
Edge, James B D, 1939, O 5,23:2
Edge, John D Maj Gen, 1937, My 3,19:3
Edge, Nelson J 2d, 1947, Ap 1,27:5
Edge, Walter C, 1959, My 14,33:4
Edge, Walter E (funl, N 1,39:2), 1956, O 30,37:1
Edge, Walter S, 1956, D 26,27:5
Edge, Wilfred, 1939, Mr 30,23:4
Edge, William, 1919, Ag 25,11:4
Edge, William S, 1947, N 21,27:4
Edge, Willimina S Mrs, 1944, N 18,13:6
Edgecomb, Daniel W, 1915, My 4,15:3
Edgecomb, Franklin E, 1954, Ap 4,88:3
Edgecombe, Alfred E, 1945, Mr 31,19:2
Edgecombe, Frank O (por), 1947, Ag 7,21:5
Edgecombe, George S, 1957, Ja 24,29:1
Edgecombe, Harry Mrs, 1946, F 6,23:5
Edgecombe, Samuel W, 1959, F 7,19:2
Edgecumbe, Alfred G, 1952, O 4,17:6
Edgecumbe, Joshua C, 1943, S 19,49:1
Edgehill, William D, 1947, Ja 11,19:4
Edgell, Albert J, 1960, D 21,31:4
Edgell, George H, 1954, Je 30,27:3
Edgell, George Stephan, 1915, O 9,9:3
Edgell, Stephen Maurice, 1921, Je 23,17:5
Edgell, William T Jr, 1950, D 24,34:4
Edgell Jean W Mrs, 1953, Ag 16,76:4
Edger, Arthur S, 1958, Jl 5,17:4
Edgerley, Raymond, 1942, Je 6,13:5
Edgerley, William H, 1943, Ja 12,23:4
Edgerly, Edwin L, 1947, N 18,29:5
Edgerly, Jessie F, 1947, D 12,27:2
Edgerly, Seward C, 1943, O 22,10:2
Edgerly, Sherburn E, 1962, Ap 30,27:2
Edgert, Sol, 1951, Ag 10,15:5
dgerton, Charles A, 1945, D 12,27:3
dgerton, Claude D Jr, 1957, Ap 13,19:2
dgerton, Claude H, 1950, O 5,31:4
dgerton, David Morgan Col, 1921, Mr 11,15:4
dgerton, Earle B, 1950, Ap 11,31:4
dgerton, Edne H, 1951, D 18,31:2
dgerton, Fannie I Mrs (will, N 29,2:2), 1938, N 8, 23:4
dgerton, Francis C, 1938, F 20,II,8:6
dgerton, Francis M, 1907, D 20,11:6
dgerton, Franklin, 1963, D 8,86:4
dgerton, Halsey C, 1967, Jl 13,37:2
dgerton, Herbert O, 1942, Ap 22,23:4
dgerton, Hiram H, 1922, Je 19,15:6
dgerton, J I, 1941, My 9,21:4
dgerton, James A, 1938, D 4,61:3
dgerton, Jay B, 1942, O 13,23:2
dgerton, Jedidiah H, 1942, Je 7,41:2
dgerton, John, 1953, S 2,25:4
gerton, John E, 1938, Ag 5,18:3
gerton, John W Jr, 1965, Ag 26,33:3
gerton, John W Prof, 1920, Jl 4,21:1
gerton, Lloyd B, 1942, Mr 16,15:1
gerton, Raymond A, 1940, D 10,25:2
gerton, Robert H, 1956, F 19,92:5
gerton, Walter T, 1959, Ap 2,31:4
gerton, Wright P Col, 1904, Je 25,7:6
gett, Edwin F, 1946, Mr 14,25:2
gett, John G, 1948, Jl 29,21:4
geworth, Richard J, 1951, D 5,35:4
gren, A H Prof, 1903, D 11,9:5
gren, John Alexis, 1908, Ja 28,9:5
gren, Robert W, 1939, S 11,19:1
olm, Charlton L, 1945, S 14,23:2
, Robert Mrs, 1943, Ap 12,23:5
ck, George J, 1952, F 26,27:1
din, Ben M, 1948, Ag 7,15:7

Edie, George S, 1949, Mr 20,76:6
Edie, John R Maj, 1874, O 31,12:3
Edie, Margaret Boyd Mrs, 1915, O 10,17:5
Edie, Raymond L Mrs, 1947, Ap 10,26:2
Edie, Richard Jr Mrs, 1947, O 8,25:3
Edie, Richard Mrs, 1954, S 6,15:5
Edie, William B, 1946, My 29,23:5
Edie, William B Mrs, 1944, Je 26,15:6
Edinburg, William G Mrs, 1939, O 31,23:4
Eding, James H, 1943, N 10,23:3
Edinger, Clarence L, 1937, Ap 13,25:4
Edinger, Cyrus L, 1948, My 7,23:2
Edinger, Herbert L, 1955, Je 28,27:4
Edinger, Irvin B, 1949, D 11,93:2
Edinger, Louis J, 1953, Je 5,27:3
Edinger, Tilly, 1967, My 29,25:2
Edington, Harry E, 1949, Mr 12,17:5
Edington, Ralph, 1950, My 10,31:4
Edison, Abraham, 1953, Jl 25,11:4
Edison, Arthur, 1951, Jl 14,13:6
Edison, Charles Mrs, 1963, Je 29,23:1
Edison, F A Mrs, 1884, Ag 10,2:7
Edison, Harry, 1966, Mr 12,27:1
Edison, Isidore, 1942, D 11,23:4
Edison, Mark A, 1951, Mr 3,13:2
Edison, Richard T, 1950, My 22,21:4
Edison, T A, 1931, O 18,1:4
Edison, T A Jr, 1935, Ag 26,15:3
Edison, Thomas A Jr Mrs, 1950, D 15,31:2
Edison, Thomas A Mrs, 1947, Ag 25,17:1
Edison, William L, 1937, Ag 11,23:1
Edison, William L Mrs, 1946, Ja 4,22:3
Edison, William R (por), 1938, Ap 15,19:2
Edkins, Jay A, 1959, Ap 24,27:2
Edkins, Walter E, 1961, S 3,61:1
Edla, Countess d', 1929, My 22,27:5
Edler, Ignaz, 1908, F 18,7:5
Edleson, Abraham, 1951, Je 14,27:6
Edlich, Theodore J Sr, 1953, Ap 26,86:2
Edlin, George, 1961, My 23,27:4
Edlin, William, 1947, D 1,22:3
Edlin, William S M, 1957, Jl 13,17:3
Edling, Charles G, 1939, Ag 17,21:1
Edlund, C Harold, 1960, Je 23,29:3
Edlund, Claudius Mrs, 1947, Ag 24,57:1
Edlund, Roscoe C Mrs, 1965, Ap 6,39:2
Edman, Irwin, 1954, S 5,51:1
Edman, Solomon, 1937, Ja 5,23:4
Edman, Solomon Mrs, 1953, Ag 6,21:2
Edman, V Raymond, 1967, S 23,31:3
Edmands, Chancy Mrs, 1951, O 12,27:5
Edmands, Isaac R, 1967, D 27,34:3
Edmands, John, 1915, O 18,9:6
Edmands, Samuel S, 1938, My 27,17:2
Edmands, Violet, 1939, Ja 19,42:2
Edminston, Ernest R, 1941, Ag 29,17:5
Edmison, George A, 1961, Ja 20,29:3
Edmiston, Andrew S, 1966, Ag 30,36:5
Edmiston, Hugh C, 1950, O 17,31:2
Edmiston, John R Sr, 1939, S 18,19:4
Edmiston, Robert W, 1965, Jl 18,68:8
Edmond, Sarah, 1953, O 17,15:4
Edmonda, Mary, 1941, F 19,21:4
Edmonds, A V, 1953, Jl 26,40:1
Edmonds, B F Gen, 1874, Ja 25,5:3
Edmonds, C G Mrs, 1946, Je 20,23:4
Edmonds, Charles G, 1949, D 28,32:3
Edmonds, Earl R, 1966, Ag 3,37:2
Edmonds, Franklin S, 1945, O 30,19:5
Edmonds, Gene, 1949, N 21,27:1
Edmonds, George W, 1939, S 29,23:3
Edmonds, Gertrude, 1951, D 8,11:4
Edmonds, Harry C, 1938, Mr 11,19:1
Edmonds, Harry M M, 1945, Ap 6,16:2
Edmonds, Harry Mrs, 1951, Ag 20,19:6
Edmonds, Howard O, 1937, Jl 20,23:6
Edmonds, James E, 1956, Ag 8,25:2
Edmonds, John J, 1947, Jl 23,23:6
Edmonds, John Worth Ex-Judge, 1874, Ap 7,8:3
Edmonds, Leslie, 1947, Je 16,21:5
Edmonds, Rex, 1953, F 7,15:4
Edmonds, Robert K, 1956, S 15,17:3
Edmonds, Samuel M, 1958, Jl 23,27:1
Edmonds, Samuel O Mrs, 1945, Ja 15,19:3
Edmonds, Samuel P, 1943, Je 23,21:5
Edmonds, Walter Dumaux, 1924, My 3,15:4
Edmonds, Walter Mrs, 1956, F 26,88:5
Edmonds, William E, 1946, My 15,21:4
Edmonds, William E Jr, 1956, Mr 12,27:4
Edmonds, William L Jr, 1967, D 31,44:6
Edmonds, William M, 1945, Ja 12,15:3
Edmondson, Earl, 1902, Ja 20,7:2
Edmondson, Ernest F, 1949, Je 2,27:2
Edmondson, Frederick W, 1946, O 5,17:2
Edmondson, George N, 1944, Ag 12,11:3
Edmondson, Thomas W, 1938, N 6,49:1
Edmondson, William, 1951, F 10,13:2
Edmondson, William B, 1937, Ag 4,19:3
Edmondson, William F, 1938, Ag 21,33:4
Edmonson, Edward L, 1959, Ap 25,21:1
Edmonson, Vincent W, 1956, N 29,35:2
Edmonson, William G, 1950, Mr 31,31:3
Edmonston, David B, 1953, Ap 16,29:3

Edmonston, George W, 1953, Mr 8,90:1
Edmonston, Joseph, 1949, O 1,13:4
Edmonstoune-Cranstoune, Charles J, 1950, Jl 8,13:6
Edmster, Willard E (will, Jl 30,17:7), 1940, Jl 11,19:3
Edmund, Brother, 1947, Mr 28,24:2
Edmunds, A Hollis Mrs (Nora), 1968, Mr 28,57:5
Edmunds, Albert J, 1941, D 20,19:5
Edmunds, C Howard, 1951, D 18,31:3
Edmunds, Charles C, 1944, Ap 30,46:2
Edmunds, Charles H, 1921, My 6,13:4
Edmunds, Charles S, 1951, Jl 18,29:5
Edmunds, Charles W, 1941, Mr 2,42:5
Edmunds, Eli D Capt, 1921, Je 24,15:6
Edmunds, Franklin D, 1948, Jl 7,23:2
Edmunds, George L, 1943, S 8,23:2
Edmunds, H Spencer, 1950, Ja 2,23:2
Edmunds, H Spencer Mrs, 1951, Ja 4,29:2
Edmunds, Henry R, 1923, My 7,15:6
Edmunds, J M, 1879, D 15,1:6
Edmunds, J Raynor Prof, 1910, Mr 28,9:3
Edmunds, Jack R, 1950, Ag 20,76:5
Edmunds, James R Jr, 1953, F 5,23:5
Edmunds, Ralph, 1937, Ja 3,II,8:7
Edmunds, Sterling E, 1944, Jl 14,13:4
Edmunds, Sterling E Mrs, 1955, Ja 26,25:3
Edmunds, Thomas F, 1953, Ag 8,11:7
Edmundson, Hec (Clarence S), 1964, Ag 8,19:6
Edney, Florence, 1950, N 26,89:3
Edouin, Willie, 1908, Ap 15,9:6
Edridge-Green, Frederick W, 1953, Ap 19,19:1
Edrop, Percy T, 1945, Ag 25,11:6
Edsall, Carroll A, 1956, D 4,39:1
Edsall, Charles F, 1961, Mr 12,86:7
Edsall, Daniel C, 1952, Ja 17,27:2
Edsall, David L, 1945, Ag 13,19:4
Edsall, Harry L, 1948, Jl 9,19:4
Edsall, J M, 1931, Mr 5,25:5
Edsall, Kennedy Mrs, 1937, Mr 6,17:4
Edsall, Samuel C Rev, 1917, F 18,17:2
Edsall, Warner R, 1953, Mr 27,23:1
Edsall Alb W, 1944, D 15,19:5
Edsberg, Milton E, 1954, Ap 20,29:4
Edschmid, Kasimir, 1966, S 3,23:4
Edsell, Levi P, 1948, N 6,13:2
Edsell, Levi P Mrs, 1960, Mr 21,29:4
Edsell, Royal D, 1944, Ag 14,15:5
Edson, Andrew W Dr, 1924, F 2,13:6
Edson, Bernard F, 1951, F 27,27:4
Edson, Clover Havens, 1924, Mr 6,17:4
Edson, Cyrus Dr, 1903, D 3,1:4
Edson, David Orr Dr, 1923, Mr 1,15:3
Edson, Eleanor, 1965, Ja 13,25:4
Edson, Eugene R, 1946, Ap 4,25:4
Edson, Franklin, 1904, S 25,7:6
Edson, Franklin C, 1952, Mr 2,93:2
Edson, George L, 1942, Ja 3,19:5
Edson, Gus, 1966, S 28,47:1
Edson, Harry A, 1952, S 13,17:5
Edson, J A, 1928, Ag 1,21:5
Edson, J J, 1935, Jl 16,19:3
Edson, Jarvis B, 1911, Ja 27,11:5
Edson, John H Col, 1914, F 12,9:4
Edson, John Tracy Mrs, 1953, F 27,21:3
Edson, Merritt A (funl, Ag 17,27:5), 1955, Ag 15,7:2
Edson, Natalia Mrs, 1939, S 15,23:2
Edson, Newell W, 1959, Jl 6,27:5
Edson, Pearl P, 1947, Je 13,23:2
Edson, Peter Mrs, 1957, Ag 3,15:3
Edson, Ralph, 1958, Je 25,29:2
Edson, Robert C, 1966, O 23,89:1
Edson, Samuel, 1955, Ja 15,13:6
Edson, T R, 1881, N 30,5:4
Edson, William H, 1944, Jl 7,15:1
Edstroem, J Siegfried Mrs, 1944, O 8,42:2
Edstrom, David, 1938, Ag 14,33:3
Edstrom, Edward E, 1955, Ap 29,23:2
Edstrom, J Siegfried, 1964, Mr 19,33:1
Edward, Alexander E, 1947, Ag 21,23:5
Edward, Charles, 1941, F 3,17:5
Edward, Charles H, 1938, Ja 8,15:3
Edward, Clifton V, 1943, O 3,48:5
Edward, David F, 1953, Ap 22,29:5
Edward, Firmus, 1948, Ag 31,24:3
Edward, William K, 1952, Mr 27,29:3
Edwardes, Felix, 1954, F 7,89:1
Edwards, A B, 1905, Mr 8,1:3
Edwards, Aaron T, 1947, O 18,15:3
Edwards, Alan, 1954, My 11,29:3
Edwards, Albert G, 1952, Je 26,29:5
Edwards, Albert Mrs, 1944, Ja 14,19:4
Edwards, Albert R, 1950, Jl 30,61:2
Edwards, Alex, 1938, Je 4,15:5
Edwards, Alfred, 1882, S 10,7:3
Edwards, Alfred A, 1953, Ja 3,15:2
Edwards, Alfred C, 1955, Ap 28,29:5
Edwards, Alfred G Archbishop, 1937, Jl 23,19:4
Edwards, Allan J, 1957, N 1,27:3
Edwards, Allen F, 1948, Ja 15,23:5
Edwards, Allyn, 1968, Jl 12,31:4
Edwards, Amelia B, 1892, Ap 16,1:3
Edwards, Andrew, 1939, Je 12,17:6
Edwards, Arthur E, 1943, My 4,23:1
Edwards, Arthur H, 1943, Ja 14,21:4

Edwards, Arthur J, 1949, D 12,33:3
Edwards, Arthur J M, 1947, Jl 30,21:2
Edwards, Arthur J Mrs, 1943, D 18,15:5
Edwards, Arthur O, 1960, Ag 26,26:1
Edwards, Arthur Rev Dr, 1901, Mr 21,9:5
Edwards, Arthur T, 1946, Ag 27,27:2
Edwards, Arthur W, 1943, My 9,40:5
Edwards, Augustin, 1941, Je 19,21:2
Edwards, Bateman, 1947, S 2,21:5
Edwards, Ben, 1954, Je 18,23:2
Edwards, Bruce V, 1964, Jl 7,35:1
Edwards, C, 1877, S 3,5:4
Edwards, C Fred, 1950, Ap 18,32:3
Edwards, C H, 1903, Ap 27,7:5
Edwards, C Harry, 1942, My 8,21:5
Edwards, C James Mrs, 1942, N 21,28:7
Edwards, C Louis, 1953, Ja 19,23:1
Edwards, C P, 1960, Jl 15,23:3
Edwards, C R, 1931, F 15,29:1
Edwards, Carlo, 1948, Ja 17,18:3
Edwards, Charles, 1947, Ja 14,27:5; 1950, My 17,29:3
Edwards, Charles A, 1951, Jl 23,17:4
Edwards, Charles C, 1956, F 18,19:2
Edwards, Charles E, 1941, Ag 20,19:3
Edwards, Charles F Mrs, 1942, D 14,28:1
Edwards, Charles G, 1942, O 25,44:1
Edwards, Charles J, 1964, Je 28,57:2
Edwards, Charles J Mrs, 1951, Je 18,23:6
Edwards, Charles Jerome, 1925, Ja 25,7:1
Edwards, Charles L Capt, 1923, Ag 10,11:3
Edwards, Charles L Dr, 1937, My 7,25:2
Edwards, Charles S, 1943, D 18,15:3; 1952, Jl 7,21:5
Edwards, Charles T, 1948, O 3,64:5
Edwards, Charles W, 1950, N 11,15:5
Edwards, Clarence, 1937, O 6,25:4
Edwards, Clifford M, 1952, Ag 30,13:4
Edwards, Cornelius S, 1922, Je 5,13:7
Edwards, Daniel M Mrs, 1945, S 15,15:6
Edwards, David, 1952, O 16,29:2; 1964, My 9,27:5
Edwards, David B, 1949, F 4,23:1
Edwards, David Cline, 1919, Je 13,15:5
Edwards, David Mrs, 1961, Ja 9,39:3
Edwards, David Sr, 1950, N 9,33:2
Edwards, David T, 1952, Mr 24,25:5
Edwards, Dean G, 1961, Je 6,37:3
Edwards, Dean G Mrs, 1962, Ja 22,23:4
Edwards, Donald, 1941, Ag 22,15:4
Edwards, Duncan L, 1945, Je 3,32:3
Edwards, Duncan L Mrs, 1967, D 20,45:2
Edwards, E Jay, 1938, O 24,17:4
Edwards, E Jay Jr Mrs (Ethel), 1962, Ap 16,29:3
Edwards, E T, 1954, F 10,29:1
Edwards, E W, 1954, Ag 19,23:5
Edwards, Ed, 1947, F 2,57:6
Edwards, Eddie (Edwin B Sr), 1963, Ap 12,27:3
Edwards, Edmund G, 1906, N 18,7:5
Edwards, Edward B, 1948, F 18,27:1
Edwards, Edward C, 1949, My 11,29:2
Edwards, Edward H, 1942, Ja 12,15:5; 1944, Ja 26, 19:6
Edwards, Edward H Mrs, 1923, S 21,4:7
Edwards, Edward I Jr, 1953, N 18,31:4
Edwards, Edward J, 1949, Mr 21,23:4
Edwards, Edward O, 1953, F 4,27:1
Edwards, Edward S Col, 1921, Ap 1,13:4
Edwards, Eldon L, 1960, Ag 3,29:3
Edwards, Elizabeth, 1944, Ag 21,15:5
Edwards, Elizabeth A, 1954, Je 6,87:1
Edwards, Elvin N, 1946, Jl 17,23:3
Edwards, Ernest A, 1944, D 9,15:5
Edwards, Ernest T, 1918, Ag 5,9:8
Edwards, Everett E, 1952, My 3,21:3
Edwards, Everett J, 1950, Mr 18,13:3
Edwards, F Boyd, 1944, N 11,13:3
Edwards, Fitz B Mrs, 1944, Ap 1,13:5
Edwards, Fleetwood Isher Sir, 1910, Ag 15,7:6
Edwards, Flora L, 1949, Ja 12,28:3
Edwards, Frances R, 1951, Mr 17,15:5
Edwards, Frank, 1967, Je 25,68:6
Edwards, Frank F, 1921, S 3,9:6
Edwards, Frank G Mrs, 1954, D 30,17:5
Edwards, Frank W Sr, 1963, Jl 8,29:5
Edwards, Fred M, 1948, Ja 9,22:2
Edwards, Frederick, 1912, Jl 28,II,11:5; 1948, O 8,25:2
Edwards, Frederick B, 1944, N 7,27:5
Edwards, Frederick W, 1951, Mr 20,16:4
Edwards, Fredericka S Mrs, 1940, My 30,18:3
Edwards, Gabriel B, 1940, Jl 19,19:6
Edwards, George, 1915, O 5,11:5; 1941, F 12,21:3
Edwards, George A, 1942, My 24,43:3
Edwards, George C, 1956, Jl 20,17:4
Edwards, George C Mrs, 1949, Ap 25,23:4
Edwards, George Capt, 1864, D 18,3:5
Edwards, George H, 1941, D 30,19:6; 1946, F 12,28:2
Edwards, George P, 1941, Jl 14,13:4
Edwards, George T, 1963, S 3,33:2
Edwards, George V, 1955, O 8,19:4
Edwards, George V Mrs, 1951, F 22,31:4
Edwards, George W, 1951, Je 21,27:2; 1954, Mr 6,15:3
Edwards, George Walter, 1916, Ap 6,13:5
Edwards, George Y, 1941, Je 11,21:4
Edwards, Gordon L, 1956, Je 15,25:3
Edwards, Grace L, 1942, Ja 9,21:2
Edwards, Gus, 1945, N 8,19:1
Edwards, Gus Mrs, 1959, N 30,31:5
Edwards, H, 1891, Je 10,4:7
Edwards, H L, 1947, O 1,29:3
Edwards, H Nicholas, 1954, Mr 16,29:4
Edwards, Hamilton, 1912, Mr 21,11:4; 1912, Mr 25, 11:6
Edwards, Hamilton Mrs, 1912, Mr 25,11:6
Edwards, Harkness, 1946, My 13,21:5
Edwards, Harold, 1952, F 25,21:5
Edwards, Harold T, 1961, Ag 18,21:2
Edwards, Harrison J, 1957, O 9,35:3
Edwards, Harry, 1924, D 1,17:5; 1939, O 29,40:6; 1942, D 3,25:5
Edwards, Harry M, 1944, N 1,23:3
Edwards, Harry Mrs, 1954, My 3,25:4
Edwards, Harry S, 1938, O 23,41:3
Edwards, Harry T, 1949, My 10,25:5
Edwards, Harry W, 1940, O 1,23:2
Edwards, Henrietta M (will), 1938, D 25,17:6
Edwards, Henry, 1952, N 4,29:4; 1956, D 13,37:2
Edwards, Henry D Mrs, 1948, Mr 20,13:2
Edwards, Henry H, 1944, Je 21,19:4
Edwards, Henry P, 1948, Ag 3,25:1
Edwards, Henry W, 1944, Ja 10,17:2; 1955, Jl 6,27:3
Edwards, Herbert, 1938, D 8,27:2
Edwards, Herbert N, 1941, Jl 14,13:6
Edwards, Howard K, 1959, Ap 21,35:2
Edwards, Ida Floyd, 1922, D 18,17:5
Edwards, Ira, 1943, N 2,25:5
Edwards, Irving E, 1938, Ap 7,23:2
Edwards, Isaac (funl), 1955, Je 8,29:3
Edwards, J Adolph, 1949, Ag 15,17:3
Edwards, J Arthur, 1950, F 21,25:5
Edwards, J Emerson, 1953, Ja 14,31:3
Edwards, J Stanley, 1955, F 12,15:2
Edwards, Jack, 1958, S 18,31:2
Edwards, James, 1947, N 18,29:4
Edwards, James A, 1944, Mr 8,19:3
Edwards, James A Mrs, 1966, Je 15,47:4
Edwards, James F, 1951, D 6,33:3
Edwards, James H, 1952, My 20,25:3
Edwards, James J Mrs, 1937, N 10,25:1
Edwards, James M, 1920, My 25,11:3
Edwards, James M Mrs, 1920, Ja 10,11:4
Edwards, James R, 1954, Mr 20,15:5
Edwards, Jefferson R, 1943, D 4,13:5
Edwards, Jefferson R Mrs, 1959, My 8,27:4
Edwards, Jessie S, 1941, Jl 18,19:5
Edwards, Jody, 1967, O 30,45:1
Edwards, John, 1941, Mr 2,42:6; 1942, Ap 22,23:4; 1959, N 24,37:3
Edwards, John A, 1948, N 22,21:1; 1968, Ja 18,39:3
Edwards, John Couper, 1913, Ja 23,11:4
Edwards, John F, 1939, Ja 21,15:5; 1944, S 2,11:2; 1951, O 13,17:5
Edwards, John G, 1940, Ap 4,23:3
Edwards, John H, 1941, D 2,24:2; 1945, Ag 21,21:5; 1960, Mr 20,87:1; 1962, O 11,39:2
Edwards, John K, 1947, D 23,23:3
Edwards, John O S, 1956, Ja 30,27:5
Edwards, John Passmore, 1911, Ap 23,11:5
Edwards, John R, 1945, F 20,19:3
Edwards, John R Adm, 1922, D 3,5:2
Edwards, John Rev (funl, S 5,17:6), 1922, Ag 31,15:5
Edwards, John W, 1948, S 29,29:3
Edwards, Jonathan, 1875, Ag 24,1:6
Edwards, Jonathan P, 1948, S 14,29:3
Edwards, Joseph B, 1941, F 22,15:5
Edwards, Joseph H W, 1950, Ap 4,30:3
Edwards, Joseph R, 1903, Jl 20,7:6
Edwards, Joshua D, 1915, My 22,11:4
Edwards, Julian, 1910, S 5,7:4
Edwards, Junius D, 1957, Ag 6,27:3
Edwards, Katherine, 1947, N 29,13:2
Edwards, Kenneth, 1947, Mr 10,21:3
Edwards, Kenneth R, 1949, D 18,88:3
Edwards, Kyle P, 1942, N 28,13:2
Edwards, Laura E S Mrs, 1942, Ag 21,19:3
Edwards, Lawrence Stewart Dr, 1903, Jl 26,7:6
Edwards, Leo Mrs, 1940, My 7,25:3
Edwards, Leroy D, 1954, O 31,89:1
Edwards, LeRoy G, 1964, Je 26,29:3
Edwards, Leroy M, 1962, Jl 17,25:1
Edwards, Lewis Dr, 1937, Ap 5,20:1
Edwards, Louis D, 1946, O 12,19:1
Edwards, Louise, 1949, Ag 13,11:5
Edwards, M F, 1942, F 25,19:4
Edwards, M S Mrs, 1929, Ja 15,29:4
Edwards, Maria L, 1941, Ja 11,17:5
Edwards, Mary A Mrs, 1941, Ja 5,45:2
Edwards, Merle M, 1949, O 10,23:4
Edwards, Michael, 1962, S 27,37:4
Edwards, Michael J, 1943, N 21,56:6
Edwards, Milton, 1946, F 18,21:3
Edwards, Minnie Mrs, 1952, Ag 20,25:4
Edwards, Minter, 1925, S 10,25:4
Edwards, Morgan C, 1960, Ja 8,23:2
Edwards, Nan, 1960, Ap 19,37:1
Edwards, Nathan H, 1959, Ja 14,27:3
Edwards, Nathaniel, 1951, Ja 2,23:2
Edwards, Neilson, 1941, Ja 5,45:1
Edwards, Ness, 1968, My 4,39:4
Edwards, Odin, 1945, D 26,19:3
Edwards, Ogden E Mrs (Dorothy R), 1965, Ap 11, 92:2
Edwards, Ogden M Jr, 1940, D 29,25:2
Edwards, Ogden M Jr Mrs, 1946, Ag 31,15:6
Edwards, Oliver S Col, 1921, F 26,11:6
Edwards, Oscar W, 1943, Ja 26,19:3
Edwards, Paul, 1938, Mr 13,II,9:2
Edwards, Paul C, 1962, Jl 25,33:3
Edwards, Paul K, 1959, D 8,45:1
Edwards, Perc, 1950, My 30,17:2
Edwards, Percy N, 1968, N 12,47:2
Edwards, Phil, 1950, N 13,27:2
Edwards, Pierrepont, 1917, S 25,11:5
Edwards, Ralph, 1963, F 5,4:8
Edwards, Ralph S, 1949, Ja 6,23:2
Edwards, Raymond D Rear-Adm, 1968, Ja 15,47:2
Edwards, Reginald T Mrs, 1943, Je 26,13:6
Edwards, Richard F, 1948, S 2,24:3
Edwards, Richard H, 1954, Ap 8,27:5
Edwards, Richard H Jr, 1958, Mr 31,27:2
Edwards, Richard H Mrs, 1955, S 30,25:3
Edwards, Richard S, 1956, Je 3,85:1
Edwards, Richard T Mrs, 1938, Jl 27,17:5
Edwards, Robert, 1948, N 5,25:3; 1949, S 10,17:3
Edwards, Robert C, 1938, Ja 14,23:2
Edwards, Robert C Mrs, 1946, N 3,62:8
Edwards, Robert H, 1952, Ag 15,15:5
Edwards, Robert J Mrs, 1945, Ap 17,23:5
Edwards, Roy R, 1961, Ag 24,29:3
Edwards, S Arlent, 1938, N 5,19:6
Edwards, S Arlent Mrs, 1919, Je 19,13:3
Edwards, Samuel Ex-Justice, 1912, F 17,11:5
Edwards, Samuel H, 1920, Ag 5,7:5
Edwards, Samuel H Mrs, 1945, Jl 21,11:6
Edwards, Sarah A Mrs, 1910, Je 24,9:5
Edwards, Sherman T, 1938, Mr 1,21:4
Edwards, Sol, 1955, Je 9,29:3
Edwards, Sophia Mrs, 1940, S 10,23:1
Edwards, Stephen B, 1942, O 1,23:2
Edwards, T Clyde, 1953, F 25,27:4
Edwards, Thomas M, 1875, My 3,4:7
Edwards, Thomson F, 1955, D 7,39:3
Edwards, Timothy P, 1953, My 20,29:3
Edwards, Tucker C Capt, 1913, Jl 4,7:4
Edwards, Valdemar E, 1946, N 28,27:1
Edwards, Vere B, 1946, My 9,21:6
Edwards, W K, 1878, S 30,5:2
Edwards, W N, 1873, D 19,1:4
Edwards, W P, 1907, N 5,9:5
Edwards, W Rev, 1883, Jl 25,5:3
Edwards, W W, 1876, Mr 12,7:5
Edwards, Walter, 1882, Ap 30,9:4
Edwards, Walter F, 1953, D 31,19:4; 1955, Ap 1
Edwards, Walter J, 1964, O 16,39:5
Edwards, Wardell M, 1949, Mr 3,26:2
Edwards, Warrick R, 1949, Ja 15,17:4
Edwards, William, 1958, Je 1,86:3
Edwards, William A, 1951, N 18,90:2
Edwards, William A Mrs, 1950, Ja 6,21:4
Edwards, William C, 1946, Je 6,21:4
Edwards, William D Mrs, 1925, Ap 22,23:5
Edwards, William Dr, 1905, Ap 27,11:6
Edwards, William E, 1939, Ag 3,19:4
Edwards, William F S, 1941, Je 11,21:2
Edwards, William H, 1907, Ag 13,7:6; 1943, Ja 1952, O 7,29:3; 1959, F 12,27:3
Edwards, William H L, 1937, N 20,17:6
Edwards, William H Mrs, 1942, My 4,19:2; 194 19:3; 1962, Ap 19,31:3
Edwards, William J, 1940, Ja 27,13:1; 1942, Ja
Edwards, William L, 1942, O 4,52:2
Edwards, William Mrs, 1946, D 17,31:5; 1958, 86:3
Edwards, William N, 1955, D 16,29:4
Edwards, William Seymour, 1915, D 27,9:5
Edwards, Winthrop B, 1959, D 30,21:1
Edwards Budge, Agustin, 1956, S 7,24:3
Edwardson, Leonard G, 1941, N 11,23:2
Edwins, A W Dr, 1942, Jl 24,5:5
Edy, John N, 1952, My 11,93:2
Edye, H W O, 1903, My 14,9:6
Eedenburg, Leendert C M van, 1948, Ag 14,13
Eekhout, Bernard Vanderbilt Lt, 1920, Ja 30,1
Eekhout, Willem D H, 1965, My 14,37:4
Eells, Howard P Mrs, 1961, Ag 27,85:2
Eells, Stillman W, 1937, My 13,25:3
Eeskine, James P, 1952, My 26,23:3
Eeustace, Arthur L, 1956, My 22,33:4
Effenberg, Saul, 1958, Je 13,23:2
Effenberger, Paul, 1948, O 15,23:1
Effendi, Suleyman Prince, 1909, Jl 15,7:4
Effinger, Ann H Mrs, 1956, Ja 22,88:6
Effinger, Lawrence E, 1958, Ap 20,85:1
Effinger, William E, 1949, Je 3,25:2
Effrat, Albert G, 1937, F 11,23:4
Effrat, Jacob, 1946, Mr 2,13:5
Effrat, John (funl plans, My 16,88:4; funl, My 47:3), 1965, My 15,31:4
Effrige, Margaret M, 1939, Ap 27,25:1
Effron, Arthur, 1964, Je 26,29:2
Effron, Charles, 1951, N 1,29:5
Effron, Jacob, 1945, F 25,38:1

Effron, Morris L, 1951, D 29,11:2
Effros, Milton, 1967, Je 20,39:2
Effross, Walter Mrs, 1954, Jl 19,19:5
Efird, Jasper W, 1947, O 19,66:4
Efird, John E, 1937, S 7,21:6
Efremov, Nicholas E, 1962, S 15,25:3
Efron, Alex, 1950, D 24,34:2
Efroymson, Gustave A, 1946, N 5,25:3
Efthimiou, Basil, 1953, Je 15,29:3
Egan, Aloysius (Wish), 1951, Ap 14,16:2
Egan, Arthur J, 1956, Je 2,19:6
Egan, Arthur T, 1959, Mr 11,35:2
Egan, Charles E, 1968, N 25,47:1
Egan, Charles F, 1947, O 26,68:6
Egan, Charles M, 1955, N 15,33:5; 1963, Jl 20,19:4
Egan, Charles M Mrs, 1953, My 7,32:3
Egan, Charles R, 1947, N 20,29:3
Egan, Daniel, 1949, Mr 12,17:3
Egan, Daniel W, 1959, Mr 31,21:4
Egan, David, 1958, My 22,29:4
Egan, Edward K, 1963, N 9,25:3
Egan, Edward P, 1951, Jl 28,11:3
Egan, Emily Mrs, 1914, Ag 28,9:5
Egan, Francis (Bro Charles Ambrose), 1952, Jl 17, 23:5
Egan, Francis B, 1949, N 16,29:4
Egan, Frank D, 1945, F 19,17:3
Egan, Frank J, 1925, S 9,25:5; 1939, F 18,15:6
Egan, Frank J Mrs, 1967, My 2,47:3
Egan, Fred F, 1960, Ja 10,86:4
Egan, George F, 1948, Je 12,15:6; 1962, Jl 17,25:2
Egan, Gerald, 1952, Ja 8,27:4
Egan, Gilbert V, 1944, Ap 9,34:4
Egan, H C, 1936, Ap 6,21:3
Egan, Henry K Sir, 1925, O 20,25:5
Egan, James, 1884, S 27,1:1
Egan, James B, 1962, F 3,21:5
Egan, James Bernard Rev, 1924, Mr 10,15:4
Egan, James F, 1945, My 6,37:1; 1966, Mr 18,39:3
Egan, James J, 1948, S 9,27:5
Egan, James W Mrs, 1965, N 25,35:5
Egan, James W Sr, 1949, Ja 19,27:3
Egan, John, 1908, D 2,9:5; 1951, Ap 13,23:2
Egan, John E Mrs, 1957, D 23,23:4
Egan, John H, 1941, S 17,23:2
Egan, John J, 1949, F 2,27:4; 1950, D 24,36:1; 1952, Ag 26,25:5
Egan, John J Mrs, 1950, S 11,23:4
Egan, John P, 1952, O 31,25:3
Egan, John S, 1938, Je 15,23:7
Egan, John T, 1941, Ja 15,23:4
Egan, John W, 1948, Ja 30,24:3
Egan, Joseph, 1953, Ap 27,23:5
Egan, Joseph B, 1937, O 9,19:5
Egan, Joseph E, 1964, Mr 23,29:3
Egan, Joseph F, 1947, Mr 31,23:3; 1957, N 23,19:5
Egan, Joseph L, 1948, D 7,31:1
Egan, Joseph M, 1959, Mr 23,31:4
Egan, Joseph P, 1948, Jl 22,23:1
Egan, Joseph Rev, 1968, Jl 20,27:3
Egan, Joseph V, 1941, O 7,23:4
Egan, L Wallace, 1948, Ag 20,17:5
Egan, Leo (funl plans; trb, N 25,86:8; funl, N 28,39:5), 1962, N 24,23:2
Egan, Louis H, 1950, N 27,25:2
Egan, Marion, 1956, Jl 26,25:5
Egan, Martin (por), 1938, D 8,27:1
Egan, Martin Mrs (funl, Ja 21,21:5), 1925, Ja 19,17:4
Egan, Maurice Francis Dr, 1924, Ja 16,19:3
Egan, Maurice Francis Mrs, 1921, Ja 28,11:4
Egan, Maurice H, 1953, Ap 24,24:4
Egan, Michael, 1956, Jl 28,17:6
Egan, Michael J, 1954, Mr 16,29:3; 1963, D 3,43:5
Egan, Patrick, 1942, D 22,25:5
Egan, Patrick Gen (funl, O 3,15:3), 1919, O 1,17:1
Egan, Patrick J, 1938, N 1,23:4
Egan, Patrick Mrs, 1944, N 16,23:4; 1944, D 1,23:2
Egan, Paul Ex-Mayor, 1968, Ag 22,37:2
Egan, Peter F Rev, 1937, My 11,25:2
Egan, Pierce, 1880, Jl 8,1:6
Egan, Raphael A, 1957, D 24,15:5
Egan, Raymond A, 1957, O 27,87:1
Egan, Raymond B, 1952, O 14,34:2
Egan, Raymond C, 1951, My 22,31:4
Egan, Richard F, 1965, Ja 25,37:4
Egan, Robert M, 1957, My 28,33:1
Egan, Roy J, 1959, N 21,23:4
Egan, Thomas, 1925, Ja 23,19:4; 1940, D 1,62:2; 1945, D 27,20:2
Egan, Thomas A, 1954, D 10,27:2
Egan, Thomas C, 1961, Jl 7,25:4
Egan, Thomas G, 1957, Jl 13,17:3
Egan, Thomas J, 1948, F 17,25:2; 1961, Ja 11,47:5; 1966, S 28,47:2
Egan, Thomas J Mrs, 1957, Ja 24,29:2
Egan, Thomas J Sr, 1951, Mr 6,27:3
Egan, Thomas J Sr Mrs, 1951, O 24,31:2
Egan, Thomas K Jr, 1944, D 26,19:4
Egan, Victor A S, 1956, Jl 22,61:2
Egan, W J Convery, 1957, N 17,86:4
Egan, Walter J, 1954, D 4,17:5
Egan, Wilfred V, 1958, D 1,29:6
Egan, William F, 1961, My 21,87:2
Egan, William H, 1943, S 1,19:1
Egan, William J, 1960, O 12,39:2
Egan, William M, 1952, Mr 14,23:5
Egans, Christopher J, 1943, F 12,19:4
Egar, John Hodson Dr, 1924, Ag 16,11:7
Egas, Camilo, 1962, S 19,40:1
Egas Moniz, Antonio de Abreau Freire, 1955, D 14, 39:2
Egawa, Chuji, 1938, Mr 21,3:6
Egberg, Gustave, 1915, Ap 6,11:5
Egbert, C Mrs (funl, J 9,8:3), 1877, Ja 6,8:2
Egbert, Clothilde D Mrs, 1938, My 5,23:6
Egbert, Frederick W, 1952, Mr 25,27:2
Egbert, George D, 1940, Jl 30,19:1
Egbert, George D Mrs, 1938, D 19,23:3
Egbert, George L, 1957, Ag 7,27:2
Egbert, Harry D Mrs, 1962, Je 15,27:5
Egbert, James B, 1939, Jl 20,19:5
Egbert, James C, 1948, Jl 18,52:3
Egbert, James C Mrs, 1950, Je 30,23:1
Egbert, Leslie F, 1966, Ja 20,30:7
Egbert, Olivia J Mrs, 1947, D 23,24:3
Egbert, Paul S, 1954, O 15,23:3
Egbert, Rae L, 1964, My 14,35:2
Egbert, Seneca, 1939, D 7,27:4
Egbert, W Gordon, 1960, F 9,19:1
Ege, C Robert, 1963, O 6,89:1
Ege, Charles J, 1939, F 15,23:3
Ege, Elizabeth M, 1944, S 11,17:5
Ege, Hettie B, 1942, N 22,52:5
Ege, Otto F, 1951, Je 19,29:3
Egelhof, Adolph J, 1959, Ag 6,27:5
Egelhoff, Albert F, 1949, F 12,17:3
Egelson, Joshua, 1966, F 12,25:2
Egelson, Louis I, 1957, Ap 11,31:5
Egelston, Charles, 1958, N 1,19:1
Egelston, Lewellyn, 1943, S 8,23:2
Egen, David, 1950, Je 20,27:4
Egenolf, Peter, 1925, D 28,15:2
Eger, Paul J, 1947, Jl 20,44:2
Egerer, Aug, 1942, Ja 5,20:2
Egerman, George, 1949, My 19,29:4
Egert, Benjamin J, 1963, Ap 17,41:2
Egert, Jacob, 1948, Ja 22,27:4
Egerton, Edgar C, 1963, D 12,39:2
Egerton, Esther, 1945, Jl 12,11:8
Egerton, Francis Charles Granville (Earl of Ellesmere), 1914, Jl 14,9:7
Egerton, George L, 1940, Ap 3,23:3
Egerton, Granville, 1951, My 5,17:3
Egerton, Jay F Mrs, 1947, Jl 9,23:5
Egerton, Joseph E, 1941, Ag 21,17:1
Egerton, Lady, 1947, Ja 5,53:2
Egerton, Louis Capt, 1917, Ag 9,7:2
Egerton, T R, 1941, My 23,21:4
Egerton, Wallace, 1942, Ag 2,39:2
Egerton, Walter, 1947, Mr 24,25:1
Egerton of Tatton, Baron, 1920, S 10,11:3
Egeth, George, 1966, F 23,39:1
Egg, Oscar, 1961, F 10,27:1
Eggaford, Robert C, 1941, My 4,53:2
Egge, Julius K, 1945, D 21,21:1
Egge, Walter W Mrs, 1961, O 23,29:5
Eggeling, Arthur, 1951, Jl 22,61:2
Eggen, Arne, 1955, O 27,33:4
Eggena, Francis L, 1951, N 27,31:3
Eggena, Gustav, 1942, F 27,17:5
Eggens, John H, 1956, Mr 31,15:4
Eggensperger, Frank C, 1948, Je 23,27:3
Egger, Albert J, 1962, Jl 20,25:5
Egger, Frederick M, 1957, O 22,33:5
Egger, Frederick M Mrs, 1947, Ja 26,53:4
Egger, Toni, 1959, F 15,19:1
Eggers, Alan L, 1968, O 5,35:5
Eggers, Bernard C, 1952, Je 30,19:2
Eggers, Carl, 1956, O 26,29:3
Eggers, Conrad A, 1951, Ag 12,76:8
Eggers, E A, 1903, Ap 9,2:5
Eggers, Edwin W, 1938, Ag 16,19:6
Eggers, Ernest H, 1940, F 9,19:6
Eggers, Frank H (funl, Jl 13,1:2), 1954, Jl 9,17:1
Eggers, Frank H Mrs, 1957, D 6,29:2
Eggers, George, 1939, Ja 2,23:2
Eggers, George W, 1958, S 26,27:2
Eggers, George W N, 1963, My 4,25:6
Eggers, Hermann, 1957, Ja 24,29:1
Eggers, Hermann Mrs, 1945, Ag 4,11:5
Eggers, John W Jr, 1945, Ag 14,21:2
Eggers, Otto R, 1964, Ap 24,34:1
Eggers, Raymond, 1949, My 13,23:2
Eggerstedt, Carl S D, 1958, Ja 11,17:2
Eggerstedt, Fred C, 1965, N 12,47:3
Eggert, F William Sr, 1961, Ja 12,29:5
Eggert, Henry F, 1950, N 21,31:2
Eggert, Herbert F Mrs, 1947, D 21,52:8
Eggert, Paul, 1937, O 8,24:1
Eggimann, Karl J, 1962, Ap 16,29:4
Eggington, Hersey, 1951, Ag 2,21:3
Egginton, Wycliffe, 1951, Je 19,30:3
Egglefield, Percy T, 1948, N 26,23:2
Eggleston, Arthur D, 1959, Ja 20,35:4
Eggleston, Aubrey, 1950, O 2,23:5
Eggleston, Benjamin O, 1937, F 17,21:2
Eggleston, Cary, 1966, N 16,47:1
Eggleston, Charlotte, 1960, Jl 30,17:3
Eggleston, De Witt C, 1950, S 6,30:2
Eggleston, DeWitt C, 1939, D 12,27:4
Eggleston, Edward, 1902, S 4,9:5
Eggleston, Edwin T Mrs, 1944, Mr 25,15:3
Eggleston, Frederick, 1954, N 13,15:4
Eggleston, Fremont, 1948, Ja 4,52:5
Eggleston, George Cary, 1911, Ap 15,13:4
Eggleston, Howard, 1938, Ag 18,20:2
Eggleston, Howard C, 1945, D 3,21:3
Eggleston, Jay Mrs, 1946, D 11,31:4
Eggleston, Leonard, 1947, F 11,27:3
Eggleston, Maitland B, 1949, S 8,29:4
Eggleston, Marjorie E, 1957, Mr 7,29:4
Eggleston, O W Jr Mrs, 1959, N 16,31:4
Eggleston, Orlando W, 1938, Je 10,21:3
Eggleston, William H, 1912, My 26,15:5
Eggley, Emmanuel, 1905, Je 8,1:6
Eggly, Harry J Jr, 1958, Jl 8,28:1
Eggman, Aug M, 1940, Ap 28,36:4
Egidi, Arthur E, 1960, S 17,23:5
Egidi, Guido, 1949, N 2,27:5
Eginton, John W, 1950, Ja 3,25:4
Eglay, Ernest Mrs, 1949, Jl 30,15:3
Egleson, James E A, 1951, D 15,13:6
Egleston, David S, 1908, Ja 2,9:6
Egleston, Gordon H Rev, 1914, Ag 2,15:5
Egleston, Nathaniel Hillyer, 1912, Ag 26,9:6
Egleston, William C, 1907, Mr 26,9:4
Egli, Alfred, 1952, Mr 29,15:5
Eglick, Samuel Dr, 1953, Ja 6,29:4
Eglin, Burdett, 1945, My 24,19:5
Eglin, W C L, 1928, F 8,25:5
Eglington, Frank, 1908, F 6,7:5
Eglington, Robert B Mrs (Marie L), 1960, Je 9,33:1
Egloff, Gustav, 1955, My 1,87:4
Egloff, Max A, 1956, N 29,35:2
Eglowstein, N Harry, 1940, D 10,26:2
Egly, Henry H, 1958, S 4,29:2
Egly, John H, 1960, F 3,33:3
Egmer, L X, 1876, Mr 31,5:4
Egmont, Earl of, 1874, Ag 5,4:6
Egmont, Earl of (Augustua Arth Perceval), 1910, Ag 12,7:6
Egmont, Earl of, 1929, Ja 11,23:2
Egmore, Herbert J, 1954, S 1,27:2
Egnatashvili, A Y, 1949, Ja 3,23:2
Egner, Arthur F, 1943, Je 8,21:1
Egner, Florence M, 1943, Je 11,19:5
Egner, Frank L, 1957, Ag 8,23:3
Egner, Frederick, 1938, S 29,25:4
Egner, Frederick W, 1920, Ja 28,11:4
Egner, Harold F, 1951, N 6,29:4
Egner, Henrietta Mrs, 1947, Ja 14,28:1
Egner, William H, 1942, My 31,39:2
Egnor, Charles Capt, 1903, Ag 8,7:7
Ego, George R, 1949, S 20,29:4
Egolf, James G, 1959, Ja 6,33:2
Egolf, John, 1956, S 7,23:2
Egolf, Willard D, 1964, Ja 9,31:1
Egoroff, N I, 1954, Ja 2,11:2
Egri, Lajos, 1967, F 10,36:2
Eguren, Jose M, 1942, Ap 21,23:2
Ehart, G (Delmonico's George), 1879, Mr 24,5:3
Ehehalt, Arthur J, 1941, F 20,20:2
Ehinger, Paul, 1949, O 3,17:6
Ehle, C E, 1939, My 24,23:3
Ehle, Clarence E, 1948, Mr 3,23:5
Ehleider, Thomas J, 1948, Je 28,19:4
Ehlenberger, Henry, 1944, Ag 16,19:5
Ehlenberger, Walter, 1948, My 28,23:3
Ehler, Adrian A, 1951, N 6,29:5
Ehler, Albert E, 1937, Ag 9,19:5
Ehler, George W (por), 1947, F 16,57:3
Ehler, James T, 1964, Ap 18,29:2
Ehlermann, Carl, 1950, O 18,33:5
Ehlers, Albert, 1941, F 14,17:1
Ehlers, Byron D, 1952, Je 19,27:4
Ehlers, Edgar M L Col, 1917, My 29,13:4
Ehlers, Edward, 1952, S 12,21:3
Ehlers, Edward C, 1938, Ja 19,23:1
Ehlers, F William, 1944, My 24,19:5
Ehlers, Frank, 1923, S 30,7:3
Ehlers, Henry E, 1961, N 28,37:2
Ehlers, Herbert E, 1925, N 13,19:4
Ehlers, Herbert M Sr, 1946, N 13,27:4
Ehlers, Hermann, 1954, O 29,21:2
Ehlers, William J, 1951, Ag 6,21:4
Ehlert, John F, 1960, D 12,29:2
Ehlert, Max H, 1955, Jl 25,19:3
Ehlin, Isidor J, 1949, F 3,24:3
Ehm, William A, 1954, Je 30,27:5
Ehman, Alfred R, 1959, Jl 14,29:3
Ehman, Chris R, 1962, D 2,88:8
Ehman, John, 1953, N 18,32:3
Ehman, Theodora, 1968, Ap 9,48:1
Ehmann, Edward W, 1939, Ja 8,42:6
Ehmann, Edwin W, 1949, Ag 28,72:8
Ehmann, William, 1947, Ap 13,60:2
Ehmke, Howard J, 1959, Mr 18,37:3
Ehmling, Charles J, 1965, Jl 13,33:4
Ehnes, Morris W, 1945, Jl 5,13:6

Ehrbar, Edward, 1968, Ja 31,38:8
Ehrbar, Joseph, 1959, Jl 1,25:7
Ehrbar, Nicholas, 1949, O 22,17:6
Ehrbar, T Vincent, 1949, Mr 26,18:7
Ehrenberg, Frederick, 1910, S 23,13:5
Ehrenberg, Henry, 1954, Jl 8,23:5
Ehrenberg, Herman, 1867, Ja 10,2:4
Ehrenburg, Ilya (funl, S 5,43:1), 1967, S 2,1:3
Ehrenfeld, Abraham, 1959, O 2,27:4
Ehrenfeld, Charles H Dr, 1937, S 27,21:4
Ehrenfeld, Frederick, 1940, Ag 17,15:7
Ehrenfeld, Hugo Mrs, 1959, O 30,27:2
Ehrenfeld, Michael J, 1946, Ap 13,17:1
Ehrenfeld, William, 1955, S 9,23:2
Ehrenfels, H Charles, 1937, F 20,17:4
Ehrengart, Carl, 1949, Mr 16,27:3
Ehrengart, Carl Mrs, 1944, N 16,23:5
Ehrenhaft, Felix, 1952, Mr 6,31:4
Ehrenhaft, Felix Mrs (L Rona), 1958, Ap 3,31:4
Ehrenpreis, Marcus, 1951, Mr 1,28:2
Ehrenreich, Bernard C, 1955, Mr 11,25:1
Ehrenreich, Hirsch, 1953, Je 5,27:3
Ehrenreich, Max M, 1959, D 17,37:4
Ehrenreich, Moritz, 1951, S 21,23:2
Ehrenstein, Maximilian R Dr, 1968, D 30,31:4
Ehrensvaerd, Carl A, 1944, F 18,17:3
Ehrentraut, Walter, 1943, F 16,19:1
Ehrentreu, Samuel J Mrs, 1964, S 4,29:3
Ehrenzweig, Stefen, 1962, O 5,33:2
Ehret, Clement (por), 1949, S 20,29:3
Ehret, Clement Mrs, 1955, N 22,35:3
Ehret, Frank A, 1907, Mr 29,9:6
Ehret, G, 1927, Ja 21,15:1
Ehret, George Jr, 1929, Mr 28,29:3
Ehret, Louis J, 1950, Ap 17,23:2
Ehret, Louis J Mrs, 1960, Jl 9,19:3
Ehrgood, Frederick E, 1952, Ag 5,19:4
Ehrhard, Frederick W, 1955, F 10,31:4
Ehrhardt, Adolph, 1957, Jl 31,23:4
Ehrhardt, Albert, 1947, Jl 8,23:1
Ehrhardt, Donald F, 1949, D 1,44:7
Ehrhardt, George, 1964, Mr 18,41:4
Ehrhardt, George D, 1941, My 13,23:3
Ehrhardt, George Mrs, 1948, O 29,25:2
Ehrhardt, Joseph A, 1949, Jl 17,56:5
Ehrhardt, Peter G, 1951, Je 2,19:5
Ehrhardt, Robert A, 1967, O 18,47:1
Ehrhart, George P, 1960, Je 30,29:1
Ehrhart, John B, 1937, N 7,II,9:2
Ehrhart, Leo J, 1960, Ja 14,33:4
Ehrhart, Raymond N, 1941, My 2,20:5
Ehrhart, Victor H, 1943, O 10,49:3
Ehrhorn, Oscar W, 1957, O 4,23:4
Ehrich, David S, 1965, Mr 14,87:2
Ehrich, Jesse W, 1938, Ap 26,21:3
Ehrich, Manfred W, 1954, Ja 11,25:5
Ehrich, Samuel W, 1919, Ap 19,17:2
Ehrich, W L, 1936, F 3,17:3
Ehrich, Walter L Mrs, 1959, S 9,41:3
Ehrich, William E, 1960, Ag 15,23:2; 1967, D 27,37:3
Ehrich, William J, 1925, Mr 26,23:4
Ehrich, William J Mrs, 1925, F 26,21:4
Ehrick, Fred, 1954, N 28,87:1
Ehrig, Edgar E Sr, 1949, D 1,31:1
Ehringhaus, John C B (por), 1949, Ag 1,17:1
Ehrlich, Arthur Mrs, 1963, My 29,33:4
Ehrlich, Benjamin H, 1964, Jl 21,33:4
Ehrlich, Charles N, 1964, Je 21,84:7
Ehrlich, David P, 1942, Jl 17,15:3
Ehrlich, Frederick W, 1968, Ag 5,39:2
Ehrlich, Godfrey N, 1945, My 26,15:3
Ehrlich, Harry E, 1952, Ag 2,15:2
Ehrlich, Harry L, 1962, N 8,39:1
Ehrlich, Jacob W, 1965, Ag 13,26:7
Ehrlich, Jefferson Mrs, 1960, Ag 21,84:8
Ehrlich, Jerome, 1960, Jl 4,15:5
Ehrlich, John E, 1949, Jl 16,13:6
Ehrlich, Joseph G, 1952, N 11,29:5
Ehrlich, Joseph S, 1942, Ap 12,44:4
Ehrlich, Louis R (funl, O 25,13:5), 1911, O 24,13:5
Ehrlich, Max, 1952, F 16,13:2
Ehrlich, Milton L, 1964, Ap 4,28:3
Ehrlich, Nelson, 1960, Mr 4,25:4
Ehrlich, Paul Dr, 1915, Ag 21,7:5
Ehrlich, Paul Mrs, 1948, D 22,24:3
Ehrlich, Simon, 1958, My 9,23:1
Ehrlich, Simon D, 1957, My 2,31:5
Ehrlich, William, 1955, Je 9,29:2
Ehrlicher, Charlotte T, 1961, Je 11,86:1
Ehrlinger, Charles, 1946, F 21,21:1
Ehrman, Albert L, 1961, Mr 11,21:5
Ehrman, Alfred, 1943, F 28,49:1
Ehrman, Anita L, 1963, Jl 31,26:4
Ehrman, Felix, 1909, Mr 23,9:6
Ehrman, George P, 1958, O 26,88:4
Ehrman, James F, 1968, D 12,47:4
Ehrman, Monroe, 1955, S 26,23:5
Ehrman, Mortimer, 1964, Ja 5,92:3
Ehrman, Samuel, 1949, Ja 3,23:2
Ehrman, William D, 1950, F 22,29:4
Ehrmann, Flora S Mrs, 1939, Jl 14,19:3
Ehrmann, Fredinand B, 1942, S 2,23:5
Ehrmann, Herbert A, 1941, O 18,19:6
Ehrmann, Herman A, 1941, Je 3,21:5
Ehrmann, Max, 1945, S 11,23:4
Ehrmann, Newton, 1942, My 16,13:5
Ehrmann, Robert, 1956, O 13,19:6
Ehrmann, Rudolf, 1963, D 23,25:1
Ehrnman, Frank T, 1951, Jl 25,24:2
Ehrnstrom, George C, 1950, D 15,31:2
Ehrsam, John, 1961, F 24,29:3
Ehrstein, Andrew, 1944, D 21,21:3
Ehrterooth, Gen, 1913, F 7,11:5
Eibel, Jacob I, 1962, F 19,31:4
Eibel, John, 1923, My 13,8:1
Eiben, Conrad, 1954, Ap 7,31:5
Eibschutz, Nathan, 1948, Ag 11,21:3
Eich, Harry A, 1939, My 14,III,7:3
Eich, John, 1940, Mr 28,23:5
Eich, John G, 1943, S 2,11:3
Eichacker, Henry C, 1945, N 6,19:4
Eichberg, Benjamin, 1959, Ag 3,25:4
Eichberg, Frederich, 1941, Jl 31,17:5
Eichberg, Joseph Mrs, 1965, Ja 9,25:2
Eichberg, Louis R Dr, 1937, Jl 8,23:4
Eichberg, Richard, 1952, My 9,23:3
Eichel, Jacob, 1960, Ap 9,17:1
Eichel, Joseph H, 1965, My 8,31:6
Eichel, Leslie P, 1967, Ja 4,41:1
Eichel, Otto R Dr (funl, D 27,9:5), 1924, D 25,17:5
Eichelberger, A W Capt, 1901, Je 14,7:6
Eichelberger, Frank, 1956, O 23,33:2
Eichelberger, George H, 1948, Ag 15,60:7
Eichelberger, George H Mrs, 1959, Ap 2,31:4
Eichelberger, Robert L (funl, S 28,41:4), 1961, S 27, 41:4
Eichelberger, William S, 1951, F 5,23:3
Eichele, Peter J, 1964, Ag 6,29:4
Eichenauer, Julius, 1938, O 24,17:4
Eichenbaum, Samuel, 1951, Jl 13,21:5
Eichenbaum, William W, 1957, My 12,86:2
Eichengreen, Leon B, 1940, N 11,19:3
Eichengreen, Morris, 1937, Mr 15,24:1
Eichenlaub, Camillus, 1947, O 16,27:4
Eichenlaub, Raymond J, 1949, N 10,32:3
Eichenwald, Margaret Mme, 1957, S 13,23:2
Eichheim, Henry, 1942, Ag 24,15:2
Eichholtz, Frederick, 1951, D 21,27:3
Eichholz, Albert H, 1958, F 8,19:2
Eichhorn, Adolph, 1956, Ja 24,32:3
Eichhorn, Charles, 1947, Ap 6,60:4
Eichhorn, Emil, 1925, Jl 28,13:6
Eichhorn, Franklyn H, 1954, F 17,31:3
Eichhorn, Geza, 1954, Je 27,69:1
Eichhorn, William A, 1960, F 29,27:3; 1964, Ap 17, 32:5
Eichi, Marcel, 1956, F 13,27:5
Eichleay, John P, 1940, N 30,17:4
Eichler, Fred H, 1949, Ap 26,25:5
Eichler, George M, 1967, D 17,92:5
Eichler, Henry, 1949, Ag 11,23:6
Eichler, Jules E, 1949, Jl 25,15:4
Eichlin, Edwin E Mrs, 1947, Je 6,23:2
Eichlin, Jonathan R, 1950, My 19,27:2
Eichmann, Andrew E, 1942, Ag 12,19:5
Eichmann, Fred, 1951, Ap 12,33:5
Eichner, Benjamin B (will), 1939, N 14,46:4
Eichner, Charles, 1951, N 22,31:4
Eichner, Clifford E, 1954, D 16,37:1
Eichner, Daniel H, 1967, N 18,37:3
Eichner, Elizabeth, 1938, Ja 22,18:2
Eichner, Floyd L, 1951, Je 17,86:1
Eichner, Laurits C, 1967, Ap 2,93:2
Eichner, Lawrence, 1967, O 31,45:3
Eichner, Moritz, 1947, My 8,25:4
Eichorn, Charles F, 1924, N 3,17:4
Eichorn, Herman, 1948, Mr 29,48:7
Eichwald, Benjamin, 1964, Jl 1,35:6
Eick, Charles W, 1949, F 8,26:2
Eick, Frank I, 1946, Ja 8,23:3
Eick, Wesley C Sr Mrs, 1952, Ap 29,27:5
Eickamnn, Walther, 1948, Jl 25,48:6
Eickelberg, August (funl, My 5,11:4), 1923, My 1, 21:4
Eickelberg, Elliott F S, 1952, My 26,23:4
Eickelberg, Wilbur, 1950, Ag 14,17:5
Eickemeyer, Florence B Mrs (will), 1941, F 5,15:5
Eickemeyer, George, 1958, Jl 28,23:3
Eickemeyer, R, 1932, Ap 26,21:1
Eickhoff, Anthony, 1901, N 7,9:6
Eickhoff, Ludger, 1948, S 22,31:2
Eickwort, John C, 1965, Mr 25,37:3
Eide, Kenneth, 1956, F 2,25:5
Eidelberg, Charles Mrs, 1960, Je 7,35:5
Eidell, Joseph E, 1937, My 17,19:4
Eidelsberg, David, 1963, D 9,35:4
Eidenbenz, Anton Dr, 1904, Ja 1,7:5
Eidenshiem, Louis Mrs, 1942, S 6,30:5
Eidensohn, Samuel, 1960, D 3,23:5
Eidenweil, Charles J, 1946, D 27,20:3
Eidler, Max, 1959, Ja 11,88:2
Eidlitz, Charles L, 1951, Ja 28,76:1
Eidlitz, Cyrus L W, 1921, O 6,17:6
Eidlitz, Ernest, 1937, Ja 11,19:1
Eidlitz, Ernest F, 1959, Mr 23,31:5
Eidlitz, O M, 1928, O 31,31:5
Eidlitz, Otto M Mrs, 1947, Jl 5,11:6
Eidlitz, Robert J Mrs, 1955, S 25,93:3
Eidman, Ferdinand, 1910, My 6,9:6
Eidmann, Frank L, 1941, S 5,21:1
Eidson, Henry, 1949, N 30,4:5
Eidson, Hilda W, 1955, D 23,17:2
Eidt, Charles W, 1956, S 25,33:2
Eidt, Charles W Mrs, 1940, Mr 9,15:2
Eidt, J Wilfred, 1950, F 22,29:2
Eielson, Eiel S, 1949, Jl 11,17:4
Eifert, David Mrs, 1948, Ag 11,21:4
Eiffel, Albert, 1941, Jl 12,13:5
Eiffel, Alexander Gustav, 1923, D 29,13:6
Eiffert, Henry Mrs, 1949, F 22,23:2
Eigenbrodt, D L, 1880, Ja 4,6:7
Eigenbrot, John L, 1956, O 10,39:5
Eigenmann, Carl Mrs, 1947, Ja 14,25:5
Eigo, Joseph M, 1950, O 22,93:1
Eigo, Timothy A, 1957, N 27,31:4
Eikamp, Harold G, 1954, Jl 4,31:1
Eikenberry, William L, 1957, D 22,40:6
Eiker, John T Jr, 1958, My 7,35:1
Eikus, Abram I Mrs, 1953, N 15,88:2
Eilbacher, August J, 1951, F 21,27:2
Eilbacher, John A, 1959, Je 14,86:3
Eilenberg, Hannah M, 1943, My 7,19:1
Eilenberg, Harry, 1949, My 18,27:4
Eilenberger, Clinton B, 1937, Ag 29,II,7:3
Eilenberger, Harry R, 1947, Ap 14,27:5
Eilerman, Robert, 1948, F 8,60:3
Eilers, Arthur E, 1958, Mr 3,27:1
Eilers, Emma, 1951, Mr 29,27:3
Eilers, Frederic Anton, 1917, Ap 24,11:4
Eilers, Karl, 1941, Ag 19,21:4
Eilers, Karl Mrs, 1947, Ja 29,25:2
Eilert, Ernest F, 1943, Je 27,32:8
Eilperin, George, 1963, N 4,35:4
Eilperin, Jacob, 1948, S 1,23:3
Eilperin, Samuel, 1954, Jl 11,73:2
Eilshemius, Henry G, 1940, N 21,29:5
Eilshemius, Louis M, 1941, D 30,19:1
Eiman, John, 1954, D 5,89:1
Eimer, Aug, 1941, Ag 29,17:3
Eimer, August Mrs, 1943, D 26,32:7
Eimer, Henry Mrs, 1944, S 1,13:4
Eimer, John J, 1943, Ja 9,13:3
Eimer, Joseph M, 1949, S 2,17:2
Eimiller, Frank X, 1939, Jl 26,19:1
Ein, Max M, 1959, N 5,35:1
Einaudi, Costanzo, 1953, Ag 20,27:2
Einaudi, Luigi (funl, N 2,37:2), 1961, O 31,31:4
Eine, Earl of (Jno Hy Crichton), 1914, D 4,11:6
Einem, K von, 1934, Ap 8,32:3
Einfeldt, William, 1945, F 26,19:1
Eingold, Aaron H (funl, S 8,31:3), 1954, S 7,25:
Einhaus, Harry M, 1962, Ap 4,43:5
Einhorn, Albert Mrs, 1940, O 19,17:6
Einhorn, Bernard W, 1967, Ag 18,30:8
Einhorn, D Rev, 1879, N 4,5:3
Einhorn, David Rev Dr, 1909, My 18,9:4
Einhorn, Isadore Mrs, 1953, F 5,23:5
Einhorn, Lester J, 1951, Ja 3,27:4
Einhorn, Martin F, 1951, Ap 3,27:5
Einhorn, Max (will, O 8,27:2), 1953, S 26,17:2
Einhorn, Moses, 1966, F 10,37:2
Einiger, Jack H, 1964, S 4,29:3
Einsohn, Israel, 1960, O 27,37:3
Einson, M M, 1936, Ap 17,21:5
Einstein, A Mrs, 1936, D 22,27:1
Einstein, Abe L, 1945, D 15,17:5
Einstein, Adolph K, 1943, F 23,21:2
Einstein, Albert (will pub, Ap 30,17:1; filed, My 5,68:1), 1955, Ap 19,1:2
Einstein, Alfred, 1952, F 17,84:1
Einstein, Benjamin F, 1915, Mr 2,9:4
Einstein, David Lewis (est, My 15,9:3), 1909, My 10,9:4
Einstein, Edwin, 1905, Ja 25,9:4
Einstein, Emanuel, 1909, O 29,9:5
Einstein, Harry (Parkyakarkus), 1958, N 25,6
Einstein, Henry L, 1918, Mr 1,11:5
Einstein, Henry L Mrs, 1943, Je 29,19:3
Einstein, Isaac D Mrs, 1953, O 14,29:4
Einstein, Isadore Mrs, 1949, S 14,31:4
Einstein, Isidore (por), 1938, F 18,19:1
Einstein, Jacob, 1937, Ap 7,25:3
Einstein, Klaus M, 1939, Ja 6,22:2
Einstein, Lewis, 1967, D 5,50:5
Einstein, Max, 1959, Ja 20,35:3
Einstein, Milton I D, 1968, F 1,37:4
Einstein, Pepi (Mrs H Schonberger), 1967, C
Einthoven, W, 1927, S 30,25:3
Einziger, Mortimer Mrs, 1952, Ap 22,29:5
Einziger, William, 1955, O 18,37:3
Einziger, William Mrs, 1965, Mr 21,86:7
Eirineos, Bishop, 1944, My 29,15:6
Eis, Leo, 1961, Ap 28,31:3
Eisaman, Ottice N, 1945, Ap 22,36:1
Eisdell, Hubert M, 1948, Je 1,23:5
Eise, George J, 1950, D 20,32:3
Eisele, Charles F, 1944, N 23,31:3
Eisele, Edward, 1937, N 19,23:5
Eisele, Frank W, 1961, Ap 15,21:5

Eisele, Frederick R, 1950, F 6,25:4
Eisele, Hans, 1967, My 7,13:1
Eisele, J Edward, 1960, Ja 9,21:3
Eisele, John, 1922, N 30,19:5
Eiselen, Frederick C Rev Dr, 1937, My 6,25:3
Eiseline, Daniel A, 1946, D 29,37:3
Eiseman, Aaron, 1964, O 29,35:3
Eiseman, Harry A, 1957, Je 10,27:6
Eiseman, J Jacques Mrs, 1959, N 17,35:5
Eiseman, Jacob B, 1963, Ag 11,84:8
Eiseman, Sigmund, 1940, F 14,21:2
Eisemann, Alex, 1953, Je 28,61:1
Eisemann, Alex Mrs, 1954, Ap 27,29:5
Eisemann, Emil, 1941, Ag 4,13:6
Eisemann, Henry Mrs, 1959, Ag 22,17:6
Eisemann, William, 1953, Ap 3,24:3
Eisen, Carl, 1964, S 26,23:4
Eisen, Gustavus A, 1940, O 30,23:1
Eisen, Isidor, 1961, Je 27,33:2
Eisen, Jacob, 1956, Ag 11,13:6
Eisen, Leo, 1965, Je 3,35:3
Eisen, Leon, 1962, My 24,35:4
Eisen, Philip Mrs, 1959, Jl 3,17:3
Eisenbacher, George, 1950, Ap 4,30:2
Eisenbarth, Emile, 1946, Jl 9,21:5
Eisenbarth, Leonard, 1949, Je 25,13:4
Eisenberg, Aaron, 1964, D 20,68:6
Eisenberg, Abraham, 1956, My 18,25:2
Eisenberg, Abraham D, 1942, My 15,20:2
Eisenberg, Daniel, 1968, O 26,37:2
Eisenberg, David, 1950, S 20,31:4
Eisenberg, David S, 1961, Ap 5,37:4
Eisenberg, Davis Mrs, 1945, D 17,22:3
Eisenberg, George M, 1959, O 28,37:4
Eisenberg, Harold, 1961, Ag 25,25:2
Eisenberg, Harris, 1938, F 6,40:2
Eisenberg, Harry, 1948, Mr 19,23:4; 1951, Mr 22,31:5; 1966, Je 16,47:3
Eisenberg, Henry H, 1949, N 17,29:2
Eisenberg, Irving, 1953, N 25,23:3
Eisenberg, Isaac Mrs, 1965, Ag 23,31:4
Eisenberg, Isidor, 1966, Mr 9,41:3
Eisenberg, Joseph E Mrs, 1964, Mr 25,41:1
Eisenberg, Julius L, 1940, Je 25,23:1
Eisenberg, Louis, 1950, Jl 15,13:3
Eisenberg, Morris, 1958, N 10,29:1
Eisenberg, Murray L, 1964, Jl 10,29:4
Eisenberg, Shlomo, 1959, Jl 15,29:3
Eisenberg, Sidney A, 1964, O 22,35:2
Eisenberger, Frederick, 1949, Ag 13,11:4
Eisenberger, Severin, 1945, D 13,29:4
Eisenbrandt, Frederick B, 1944, F 24,15:4
Eisenbud, Adolph Dr, 1968, Ag 20,41:1
Eisenbud, Kalman, 1954, Ja 20,27:5
Eisendrath, Maurice N Mrs, 1963, Jl 4,17:4
Eisendrath, Sophie Mrs, 1938, Jl 12,19:3
Eisenhand, Henry G, 1937, F 6,17:2
Eisenhardt, Charles A, 1958, Ag 7,25:4
Eisenhardt, Raymond H Sr, 1965, Ag 11,35:1
Eisenhart, Charles M Maj-Gen, 1968, Ja 18,9:1
Eisenhart, Edwin K, 1947, Jl 1,25:2
Eisenhart, Jacob C, 1946, D 9,25:4
Eisenhart, John H, 1948, My 11,25:2
Eisenhart, Karl, 1917, F 10,9:5
Eisenhart, Luther P, 1965, O 29,43:3
Eisenhart, Octava L Mrs, 1953, My 7,31:4
Eisenhart, William S, 1941, N 2,52:2
Eisenhauer, Herbert L, 1959, D 5,23:3
Eisenhaurer, Dan, 1952, Ag 24,89:1
Eisenhower, Abraham L, 1944, D 14,23:1
Eisenhower, Anna Mrs, 1952, O 11,19:5
Eisenhower, Arthur B (funl plans, Ja 28,27:4;funl, Ja 30,10:7), 1958, Ja 27,1:3
Eisenhower, Arthur F, 1942, N 27,23:3
Eisenhower, Earl D, 1968, D 19,47:1
Eisenhower, Edgar N Mrs, 1948, Mr 15,23:3
Eisenhower, George E, 1947, Je 28,14:3
Eisenhower, Ida Mrs, 1946, S 12,7:1
Eisenhower, John F, 1953, N 26,31:5
Eisenhower, Milton S Mrs (funl, Jl 14,24:4), 1954, Jl 11,72:4
Eisenhower, Walter M, 1953, Jl 4,11:3
Eisenhower, William R, 1938, Ap 18,15:2
Eisenlohr, Charles J (will, S 23,23:2), 1947, S 17,25:3
Eisenlohr, Louis H, 1922, Je 9,15:5
Eisenman, Jacob C, 1964, O 25,88:2
Eisenman, Morris, 1948, Ja 20,23:1
Eisenman, William H, 1958, Je 1,86:8
Eisenmann, I Robert, 1968, Ag 21,45:4
Eisenmann, Jacob, 1941, Jl 22,19:3
Eisenmenger, Hugo E, 1950, Ag 29,27:1
Eisenmenger, Karl, 1954, Ag 27,21:2
Eisenoff, Henry M, 1964, Mr 21,26:8
Eisenschiml, Otto, 1963, D 9,35:3
Eisenstadt, Abraham H, 1948, D 3,26:2
Eisenstadt, Benzion, 1951, S 1,11:7
Eisenstadt, Irving Mrs, 1952, O 14,31:3
Eisenstadt, Morris, 1944, Ap 21,19:3
Eisenstadt, Moses, 1943, N 8,19:4
Eisenstadt, Samuel Mrs, 1957, Mr 8,25:1
Eisenstadt, Zvi, 1966, Jl 22,31:2
Eisenstat, Abraham, 1953, D 24,15:5
Eisenstat, Max, 1956, Ag 19,93:1; 1965, Ap 6,39:1
Eisenstein, Albert S, 1953, D 18,29:4
Eisenstein, Alfred, 1949, Ag 19,17:2
Eisenstein, Arthur, 1945, Ja 11,23:5
Eisenstein, Isaac, 1961, Mr 22,41:2
Eisenstein, Judah D, 1956, My 18,25:3
Eisenstein, Louis, 1966, Ja 8,26:3
Eisenstein, Sergei, 1948, F 12,24:2
Eisenstein, Victor, 1957, F 4,19:4
Eiser, Charles Mrs, 1949, O 28,23:4
Eiser, Harry Mrs, 1960, Mr 2,37:4
Eiser, Henry J, 1955, Jl 5,29:1
Eisermann, Ernest J, 1949, Ag 18,21:3
Eisfeldt, Kurt, 1940, My 31,19:5
Eisgrau, Siegfried, 1964, O 22,32:5
Eising, Harry, 1950, D 15,31:5
Eising, Harry Mrs, 1966, S 10,29:5
Eisinga, Krass, 1955, Ap 1,27:3
Eisinger, Ernest F, 1946, O 20,60:6
Eisinger, H Frank Mrs, 1948, N 10,29:5
Eisinger, Jacob S, 1951, Jl 25,23:1
Eisle, Clifford M, 1956, S 20,33:2
Eisler, Armand, 1957, S 18,33:3
Eisler, Arnold, 1947, Ja 29,26:2
Eisler, Bela D (por), 1949, Ag 11,23:5
Eisler, Elfriede (R Fischer), 1961, Mr 16,37:2
Eisler, Fred J, 1955, Ja 21,23:2
Eisler, George J, 1941, Ag 7,17:3
Eisler, Gerhart, 1968, Mr 22,47:1
Eisler, Hanns, 1962, S 7,29:1
Eisler, Nathan A, 1941, N 6,23:5
Eisler, Paul, 1951, O 17,31:4
Eisler, Sol H, 1947, Ja 29,25:2
Eisley, R C, 1940, Je 21,21:1
Eisman, H Seymour, 1956, Ap 11,33:2
Eisman, Max Mrs, 1943, F 17,21:2
Eisman, Paul, 1951, Ag 15,27:2
Eisner, Albert, 1950, Je 11,92:3
Eisner, H Raymond, 1948, O 18,23:3
Eisner, Isadore Mrs, 1966, S 3,23:5
Eisner, J Lester (por), 1955, My 28,15:4
Eisner, Jerome, 1943, Mr 28,24:8
Eisner, Joseph, 1958, My 6,35:1
Eisner, Leopold, 1953, O 28,29:2
Eisner, Mark, 1953, Mr 30,21:3
Eisner, Maurice, 1954, D 17,31:1
Eisner, Max F, 1938, My 29,II,7:2
Eisner, Michael L, 1951, Ag 8,25:6
Eisner, Milford W, 1963, Jl 12,25:3
Eisner, Moritz, 1938, Je 20,15:4
Eisner, Samuel S, 1957, F 27,27:4
Eisner, Sigmund, 1925, Ja 6,25:5
Eisnitz, Louis, 1950, Ja 4,35:4
Eisnitz, William, 1962, Je 3,88:2
Eiss, Stanley, 1967, Ag 7,29:4
Eiss, Wallace H, 1953, Ap 17,25:1
Eissler, Alfred F, 1954, N 21,87:2
Eiswald, George H, 1939, Ag 12,13:7
Eitel, Emil, 1938, F 15,25:5; 1948, Jl 19,19:5
Eitel, Karl, 1954, Mr 10,25:4
Eitel, Robert J, 1948, S 22,31:2
Eiten, Robert B, 1953, O 8,29:4
Eitingon, Max, 1943, Jl 31,13:3
Eitingon, Motty, 1956, Ag 1,23:4
Eitner, Alfred H, 1950, F 23,27:1
Eitner, William Mrs, 1905, Ap 30,1:6
Ek, Peter V, 1945, F 12,19:1
Ekberg, John P, 1960, Jl 22,23:3
Ekblaw, Karl J T, 1947, Mr 20,27:5
Ekblaw, Walter E, 1949, Je 6,19:1
Ekblom, John O, 1966, Mr 24,39:1
Ekelof, Gunnar, 1968, Mr 22,44:3
Ekelund, Harry J, 1958, F 18,22:6
Ekelund, Lucille H, 1960, S 7,37:5
Eken, Andrew J, 1965, Je 12,31:1
Ekenberg, John A, 1951, O 27,19:6
Ekenberg, Leslie J, 1966, F 20,88:5
Ekengren, W A F, 1921, Ja 25,11:4
Ekengren, Wilhelm August F, 1920, N 27,13:5
Ekern, Emil A, 1950, Ja 4,35:1
Ekholm, Alma, 1960, F 28,82:6
Ekins, G H, 1933, N 12,34:3
Ekins, H Roslyn, 1963, O 15,39:4
Ekirch, Arthur A, 1960, D 16,33:1
Ekis, Ludvig, 1943, Jl 8,19:2
Eklund, Carl R, 1962, N 5,31:3
Eklund, Henry Werner Rev, 1920, Ja 8,17:3
Eklund, William, 1940, Ag 17,15:3
Ekman, Carl, 1949, Ag 15,17:5
Ekman, Carl G, 1945, Je 16,13:2
Ekman, Goesta (por), 1938, Ja 13,21:5
Ekroth, Clarence V, 1952, D 3,33:6
Eksergen, Joseph, 1950, Jl 15,13:6
Eksergen, Joseph Mrs, 1949, Mr 18,25:4
Eksergian, Rupen, 1961, D 2,23:4
Ekstrom, Edwin C, 1967, My 8,41:4
Ekswald, Frank L Mrs, 1948, F 14,13:4
Ekwall, William A, 1956, O 18,33:4
Ekwurzel, Mary E Mrs, 1941, Jl 13,29:2
Ela, J H, 1884, Ag 22,5:3
Elam, Annie R Mrs, 1942, Jl 21,15:1
Elam, Elma, 1941, N 14,23:1
Elam, John B, 1916, Mr 28,13:6
Elam, Laura L Mrs, 1940, Ap 23,23:4
Elam, Samuel M, 1963, F 19,8:6
Eland, Mike Mrs (M Carol), 1967, F 7,39:3
Elander, Albin E, 1966, D 7,47:3
El Askari, Tahsin, 1947, S 14,60:3
El-Aswad, Khalil, 1923, Ja 16,21:3
Elba, Marta, 1954, Ap 22,30:4
Elbel, Paul, 1940, Ap 10,25:2
Elbem, Halil E, 1938, N 18,22:2
Elberg, Yehuda Mrs, 1956, Ja 27,23:3
Elbers, Fred O Mrs, 1952, My 13,30:3
Elbert, Augustus Mrs, 1942, Je 12,21:4
Elbert, Charles A, 1944, Ja 9,42:1
Elbert, Henry E, 1945, F 16,23:4
Elbert, John A, 1966, S 12,45:3
Elbert, William, 1950, Ap 23,92:8
Elbinder, David, 1911, N 1,11:5
Elbogen, Ismar, 1943, Ag 2,15:2
Elbow, Charles W Sr, 1958, My 22,29:3
Elbridge, Alfred, 1953, Ag 19,29:3
Elcock, Hoard K, 1952, Mr 6,31:3
Elcock, John J, 1940, S 9,15:3
Elcock, Thomas M, 1948, Ja 5,19:4
Elcock, Thomas R Ex-Judge, 1907, S 6,9:6
Elden, Alfred O, 1946, Jl 3,25:5
Elden, Leonard L, 1943, O 24,45:1
Elden, Samuel J, 1918, Ja 23,9:5
Elden, William R, 1942, S 4,24:4
Elder, Alex H, 1957, Ap 28,86:5
Elder, Alva J, 1940, N 8,21:6
Elder, Andrew, 1940, N 2,15:4
Elder, Andrew Mrs, 1948, Ja 5,19:3
Elder, Arthur A, 1956, Mr 2,23:3
Elder, Bertha F Mrs, 1939, Je 23,19:5
Elder, Bowman, 1954, Je 12,15:3
Elder, Cyrus, 1912, D 16,13:4
Elder, Donald H Mrs, 1953, Ja 8,30:2
Elder, Emma B Mrs, 1938, Jl 14,21:2
Elder, Flint C, 1956, Ja 17,33:4
Elder, Fred G, 1941, Je 11,21:2
Elder, Frederick J, 1959, Je 24,31:5
Elder, George B, 1962, Ap 30,27:1
Elder, George H, 1903, Jl 12,7:6
Elder, George I, 1950, Ag 10,25:1
Elder, George R, 1941, O 17,23:4
Elder, George W, 1954, O 15,23:5
Elder, George W Mrs, 1907, D 7,9:5
Elder, George Waldron, 1916, Je 1,11:7
Elder, Herbert M, 1951, Je 12,29:4
Elder, James, 1946, My 31,23:4
Elder, James A, 1947, N 26,23:4
Elder, James C Mrs, 1959, F 26,31:4
Elder, James F, 1937, Ja 30,17:2
Elder, James W Mrs (L Norris), 1964, Mr 2,27:4
Elder, Jane, 1964, S 19,27:3
Elder, John P, 1941, Ja 27,15:3
Elder, Omar F, 1944, O 26,23:5
Elder, Omar F Jr Mrs, 1961, Je 24,21:1
Elder, Orr J (cor, My 6,29:2), 1957, My 4,21:2
Elder, Orr J Mrs, 1953, Ag 29,17:4
Elder, Paul, 1948, Ja 26,19:4
Elder, Ralph C Mrs, 1948, D 25,17:4
Elder, Rev Mother, 1921, O 2,22:4
Elder, Robert D, 1956, Ja 23,25:5
Elder, Robert H, 1948, Ja 7,25:1
Elder, Robert P, 1941, Ja 26,37:2
Elder, Thomas E, 1948, S 10,23:4
Elder, W H Archbishop, 1904, N 1,1:6
Elder, Walter T, 1953, My 23,15:7
Elder, William J, 1950, My 22,21:3
Elder, William P, 1942, Ag 12,19:2
Elder, William S, 1945, Ag 17,17:5
Elder, William W, 1960, Mr 9,33:3
Elderdice, Hugh L, 1938, My 13,20:4
Elderkin, Ellsworth J Mrs, 1945, N 2,19:1
Elderkin, George W, 1965, D 20,35:2
Elderkin, George W Mrs, 1962, F 17,19:1
Elderman, Gene (H E), 1963, D 25,33:2
Eldert, Albert H, 1940, N 29,21:4
Eldert, Henry C, 1937, F 14,II,9:2
Eldert, John H, 1915, Jl 23,9:7
Elderton, George H, 1951, Ap 16,25:3
Eldh, Carl, 1954, Ja 28,27:4
Eldon, Arthur J, 1962, O 10,51:4
Eldon, Carl W, 1949, Jl 10,56:4
Eldred, A D, 1954, Mr 25,29:2
Eldred, Albert E, 1961, Ag 4,21:5
Eldred, Arthur R, 1951, Ja 6,15:6
Eldred, Burdette P Sr, 1951, Mr 12,25:1
Eldred, Byron E, 1956, My 28,27:3
Eldred, Floyd F, 1957, Je 7,24:2
Eldred, Frank R, 1945, Ap 16,23:2
Eldred, Georgia C, 1948, D 17,27:1
Eldred, Herbert L, 1938, Mr 9,23:2
Eldred, Israel Mrs, 1925, O 1,27:4
Eldred, Percy, 1947, D 10,31:5
Eldred, Raymond B, 1955, My 24,31:2
Eldred, Raymond Mrs, 1949, N 16,29:4
Eldred, Willard H Mrs, 1946, My 19,42:2
Eldred, William T, 1965, N 30,41:1
Eldredge, Charles Q, 1938, F 3,23:2
Eldredge, Clarence G, 1952, Je 21,15:6
Eldredge, Curtis, 1940, Mr 26,21:2
Eldredge, Daniel A, 1952, F 22,22:2

Eldredge, Donald M, 1953, Je 14,84:1
Eldredge, E Irving Jr, 1925, F 9,17:4
Eldredge, Edward H Mrs, 1946, S 15,9:8
Eldredge, Edward I, 1925, F 22,19:2
Eldredge, Elliott M, 1959, O 14,43:1
Eldredge, Elmer D, 1950, Ag 23,29:3
Eldredge, Frank S Mrs, 1950, F 13,21:4
Eldredge, Henry H Mrs, 1954, Mr 19,23:1
Eldredge, Howard D, 1939, Mr 20,17:3
Eldredge, Irving C, 1965, My 23,85:2
Eldredge, J C, 1881, Ag 15,8:2
Eldredge, Loren D, 1939, S 25,19:2
Eldredge, Mary, 1952, F 19,29:3
Eldredge, O Stanley Mrs, 1957, Jl 8,23:4
Eldredge, O Stanley Sr, 1964, Je 26,29:1
Eldredge, Robert, 1938, O 14,23:2
Eldredge, Ruth, 1939, N 4,15:3
Eldredge, Samuel F, 1958, N 22,21:1
Eldredge, Sanford, 1956, N 28,35:3
Eldredge, Stanton, 1942, N 15,56:6
Eldredge, Wilbur H, 1950, F 20,25:3
Eldrid, Gordon H, 1950, Ap 18,31:3
Eldridge, Benjamin F, 1937, Ap 17,17:4
Eldridge, Carleton G, 1960, D 10,23:5
Eldridge, Carleton G Jr Mrs, 1958, Ap 26,19:5
Eldridge, Carleton G Mrs, 1961, Ap 15,21:5
Eldridge, Charles, 1906, Ja 11,9:6; 1947, Jl 2,23:2
Eldridge, Charles H, 1938, Je 11,15:6; 1939, F 9,21:2
Eldridge, Charles Henry Rear-Adm, 1916, Jl 17,11:7
Eldridge, Charles W, 1938, D 18,49:4
Eldridge, Chot, 1941, S 29,17:6
Eldridge, E David, 1943, D 17,28:3
Eldridge, E Warner, 1952, S 20,15:3
Eldridge, Edward H, 1941, Ap 21,19:3
Eldridge, Edwin, 1876, D 18,5:1
Eldridge, Edwin H, 1946, Ag 22,27:6
Eldridge, Everett E, 1948, Ja 31,19:2
Eldridge, Francis H, 1949, Ag 4,23:3
Eldridge, Frank Harold Commodore, 1921, D 6,19:5
Eldridge, Frank T, 1937, Mr 19,23:1
Eldridge, Fred I, 1961, Je 6,37:2
Eldridge, Frederick W, 1937, Ag 11,23:3
Eldridge, Frederick W Mrs, 1951, Mr 24,13:6
Eldridge, George C, 1939, Mr 28,23:5
Eldridge, George W, 1938, Mr 27,II,7:3
Eldridge, Harry E, 1943, D 5,66:6
Eldridge, Henry F, 1924, Ja 15,19:4
Eldridge, Herbert R, 1915, D 23,13:5
Eldridge, Herbert Rucker, 1915, N 23,13:4
Eldridge, Jay G Mrs, 1949, Jl 17,58:3
Eldridge, John D, 1961, S 24,86:1
Eldridge, Joseph B, 1941, D 21,40:8
Eldridge, Lewis Mrs, 1950, My 5,21:4
Eldridge, Linus S, 1957, Ap 29,25:4
Eldridge, Louisa Mrs (funl, D 12,10:2), 1905, D 10, 7:1
Eldridge, Marion, 1939, D 30,15:4
Eldridge, Nemuel, 1946, F 23,13:2
Eldridge, Preston W, 1925, D 15,25:3
Eldridge, Roswell Mrs, 1947, Mr 15,13:6
Eldridge, Samuel D, 1903, Jl 20,7:6
Eldridge, Sarah E, 1939, My 2,24:4
Eldridge, Schuyler T, 1946, S 16,5:6
Eldridge, Thomas P, 1874, D 22,4:6
Eldridge, Watson W Mrs, 1949, Mr 27,78:8
Eldridge, William A, 1953, O 6,29:3
Eldridge, William D, 1950, My 20,15:6
Eldridge, William S, 1956, S 30,87:1
Eldridge, William T, 1944, Ap 24,19:6
Eleanore, Queen, 1917, S 13,13:1
Elebash, Baisley P, 1953, Ja 18,92:4
Elefante, Anthony A, 1946, D 29,35:5
Elemendorf, Peter, 1948, D 31,15:3
Elena, Ex-Queen of Italy, 1952, N 29,17:1
Elenz, Frank, 1957, F 26,29:4
Elesbaan, Felix Bro, 1962, Ap 17,35:4
Eley, John S, 1944, Mr 5,36:1
Eley, W Allan, 1940, Je 30,32:8
Elfenbein, Israel, 1964, S 14,33:2
Elfer, Charles M, 1958, N 23,88:5
Elfers, Herman, 1960, S 10,21:3
Elfers, William R, 1940, O 27,45:1
Elfiein, Frederick, 1941, Ag 28,19:4
Elfin, Alex E, 1952, F 24,85:1
Elfner, Albert H, 1939, Ap 20,23:3
Elfred, Alfred (Freddie Fields), 1952, Ag 25,25:2
Elfreth, Anna E, 1946, Ag 14,25:6
Elfreth, Esther H, 1945, F 14,20:2
Elfreth, John B, 1944, Jl 5,11:2
Elgar, Alfred Q, 1942, Ap 30,19:6
Elgar, B F, 1926, Ja 16,15:5
Elgar, E Sir, 1934, F 23,22:1
Elgar, Francis C, 1938, O 25,23:3
Elgar, Francis C (will), 1940, Mr 1,41:1
Elgar, H Rodger, 1953, Ja 22,23:4
Elgar, H Rodger Mrs, 1967, F 4,27:5
Elgar, Harold B, 1941, My 6,21:3
Elgar, James William, 1908, Ja 3,9:5
Elgart, Abraham, 1953, Ap 5,77:1
Elgart, Harry, 1948, My 14,23:4
Elgart, Samuel, 1949, Je 20,19:6
Elgas, Francis, 1944, Je 6,17:6
Elgas, Matthew J Dr, 1912, S 2,9:6
Elgen, Riley E, 1941, Mr 1,15:5
Elgersma, G J, 1942, S 12,13:1
Elgin, Earl of, 1863, D 27,3:3
Elgin, Earl of (Victor Alexander Bruce), 1917, Ja 19, 7:2
Elgin, Earl of (Edw Jas Bruce), 1968, N 29,45:3
Elgin, Joseph C Mrs, 1959, Ap 27,27:3
Elgin, William F, 1938, Ap 20,23:3
El-Gumail Pasha, Anton, 1948, Ja 14,25:2
Elia, Frank C, 1950, Ja 11,23:4
Elias, Aaron B, 1960, Ja 19,35:2
Elias, Al M, 1939, Ag 2,19:4
Elias, Charles J, 1947, D 28,40:2
Elias, Charles Mrs, 1954, F 23,27:2
Elias, David Mrs, 1954, D 22,23:4
Elias, Don S, 1967, Jl 11,37:1
Elias, Elias D, 1956, F 2,25:2
Elias, Ellis H, 1881, Je 24,5:3
Elias, Harold L, 1956, Jl 21,15:5
Elias, Henry H, 1941, Mr 9,41:3
Elias, Jerome, 1965, Je 20,72:6
Elias, Joseph, 1940, Mr 23,13:3
Elias, Louis J, 1949, S 10,17:3
Elias, Michael A 2d, 1955, S 8,31:3
Elias, Morris, 1924, Jl 15,9:3
Elias, Nathaniel M, 1964, O 17,29:5
Elias, Pearl S Mrs, 1947, Ja 31,23:2
Elias, Percy I Mrs, 1943, F 2,19:5
Elias, Percy L Mrs, 1952, Ap 27,91:1
Elias, Sam, 1955, Ag 16,23:3
Elias, Walter B, 1948, My 20,29:5
Elias, William J, 1949, Je 8,29:4
Elias Ambrose, Bro, 1940, Jl 14,30:8
Eliasberg, Bernard H, 1962, S 13,37:3
Eliasberg, Helene, 1957, D 17,35:4
Eliasberg, Irving Mrs, 1966, My 13,41:3
Eliasberg, Louis, 1954, S 20,23:5
Eliash, Mordecai, 1950, Mr 12,92:1
Eliason, Eldridge L, 1950, Mr 8,27:3
Eliason, James B, 1962, Ja 24,33:3
Eliasoph, Joseph H, 1944, F 5,15:5
Eliasoph, Meyer B, 1959, Ap 18,23:4
Elibank, Viscount, 1951, Mr 13,31:3
Elibank, Viscount (A C Murray), 1962, D 6,43:5
Elichman, Joseph S, 1956, D 15,25:4
Elicker, Paul E, 1967, S 15,44:1
Elicofon, Edward I Mrs, 1965, N 5,37:4
Elie, Rudolph F, 1958, Mr 12,31:1
Elie Justin, Bro (J A Beauregard), 1953, Mr 8,88:4
Eliel, Erwin, 1956, D 18,31:4
Eliel, Paul, 1953, Ag 20,27:2
Eliezer, Edward B, 1958, Ag 2,17:4
Elijah, Alexander, 1945, F 27,19:1
Elin, Herbert W, 1945, F 1,10:2
Elin, Nathaniel, 1960, Ja 24,88:3
Elinson, Iso, 1964, My 9,27:3
Eliot, C N E Sir, 1931, Mr 17,14:4
Eliot, C W Dr, 1926, Ag 23,1:8
Eliot, Charles Mrs, 1946, S 25,27:1
Eliot, Charles W Dr, 1917, Mr 21,11:4
Eliot, Charles W Mrs, 1924, Jl 19,9:5
Eliot, Christopher R, 1945, Je 22,15:3
Eliot, E C, 1940, Ja 3,22:3
Eliot, Edward F W, 1943, Jl 1,19:2
Eliot, Ellsworth Dr, 1912, D 11,13:4
Eliot, Ellsworth Jr (will, N 16,19:1), 1945, N 3,15:3
Eliot, Etienne, 1968, My 18,33:2
Eliot, Frederick M, 1958, F 18,27:1
Eliot, George E, 1943, N 13,13:2
Eliot, Gustavus Mrs, 1951, Je 26,29:2
Eliot, John L, 1947, F 4,25:4
Eliot, Margaret, 1961, N 7,33:4
Eliot, Montague C (Earl of St Germans), 1960, S 20, 39:3
Eliot, Paul M, 1955, Ja 16,92:3
Eliot, Phil, 1948, Je 24,25:2
Eliot, Philip H, 1946, Ap 2,27:2
Eliot, Samuel A, 1950, O 16,27:6
Eliot, Samuel A Mrs, 1954, Ap 27,29:5
Eliot, T S (funl plans, Ja 6,39:3; funl, Ja 8,29:3), 1965, Ja 5,1:2
Eliot, Thomas D Mrs, 1942, Ja 12,15:4
Eliot, W G, 1931, My 4,19:5
Eliot, Walter G Mrs, 1944, Ap 8,13:5
Eliot, William H, 1958, Je 23,23:3
Eliott, Arthur C, 1950, O 29,93:1
Eliott, Gilbert, 1958, Jl 28,23:6
Eliott, Lady, 1945, N 26,21:3
Eliott, Laurence, 1939, S 23,17:3
Eliovson, Moses T, 1966, My 7,31:4
Eliphus, Victor Bro (M E Sullivan), 1962, Ap 1,86:5
Eliphus John, Bro, 1948, Jl 18,54:5
Eliphus Victor, Bro (Jno Jos McConnell), 1913, Jl 28,7:6
Elisabeth, Archduchess of Austria, 1958, F 10,23:4
Elisabeth, Ex-Grand Duchess of Oldenburg, 1955, S 6,25:3
Elisabeth, Princess of Russia, 1940, O 31,23:5
Elisabeth, Queen Mother of the Belgians (funl plans, N 25,35:2), 1965, N 24,1:8
Eliscu, Edward (cor, D 30,21:1), 1959, D 29,25:5
Eliscu, Eugenie R Dr, 1919, Jl 12,9:7
Elish, Karl M, 1962, Jl 28,19:4
Elishewitz, Abraham, 1957, Mr 29,21:2
Elishewitz, Jacob, 1943, Ag 20,15:3
Elisian, Ed, 1959, Ag 31,29:3
Eliz Pierre, Sister (C Schwinden), 1964, D 24,19:1
Elizabeth, Countess, 1944, O 30,19:4
Elizabeth, Dowager Queen of Prussia, 1873, D 16,4:7
Elizabeth, Empress of Austria, 1898, S 11,1:3
Elizabeth, Ex-Queen of Greece, 1956, N 16,27:2
Elizabeth, Mother (Czacka), 1961, My 18,35:4
Elizabeth Amalia, Archduchess of Hapsburg, 1960, Mr 14,29:1
Elizabeth Angela, Sister, 1951, O 16,31:2
Elizabeth Maria, Sister (Sisters of Charity), 1955, D 17,23:5
Elizabeth of Brunswick, Duchess, 1908, Jl 11,7:6
Elizalde, Joaquin J, 1937, O 1,21:3
Elizalde, Joaquin M, 1965, F 10,41:2
Elizega, Enrique A, 1943, Ag 10,19:3
Elkan, Benno, 1960, Ja 11,45:1; 1961, Ja 7,19:6
Elkan, Bruno, 1961, Je 3,23:4
Elkan, Rudolph, 1944, Mr 3,16:3
Elkeles, Samuel Mrs, 1919, Ag 7,7:4
Elkell, Levi Henry Prof, 1916, D 28,9:5
Elkin, Daniel C, 1958, N 4,27:2
Elkin, John P Justice, 1915, O 4,9:5
Elkin, Joseph, 1939, Mr 4,19:4
Elkin, Lewis Mrs, 1907, Ag 29,7:4
Elkin, Mandel, 1962, Ap 23,29:1
Elkin, Meyer Rev Dr, 1915, D 13,13:3
Elkin, Newton, 1942, N 10,27:3
Elkin, William, 1937, N 22,19:3
Elkin, William S, 1944, Ap 25,23:1
Elkind, Abraham H Mrs, 1951, S 6,31:5
Elkind, Joseph Mrs, 1963, Ag 29,29:3
Elkind, Sarah Mrs, 1952, My 12,25:5
Elkins, Blaine, 1924, S 16,23:4
Elkins, Carlisle R, 1949, Ja 11,27:3
Elkins, David, 1945, Ag 27,19:5
Elkins, David Mrs, 1953, F 6,19:2
Elkins, Davis, 1959, Ja 6,34:1
Elkins, Edwin E, 1960, D 22,23:1
Elkins, Felton Mrs, 1953, Ag 29,17:5
Elkins, George W, 1919, O 25,11:4; 1954, My 20,31
Elkins, George W Mrs, 1954, My 15,15:1
Elkins, H A, 1884, Jl 8,2:6
Elkins, Harry, 1952, O 4,17:5
Elkins, Harry S, 1953, Mr 3,27:4
Elkins, Henry O, 1946, Ja 2,19:1
Elkins, Herbert F, 1948, O 31,88:7
Elkins, Higdon B, 1958, N 30,86:8
Elkins, Joseph B, 1956, Je 10,88:4
Elkins, Murray, 1959, Mr 8,86:6
Elkins, Murray M, 1939, My 11,25:3
Elkins, Richard, 1922, Jl 1,13:6
Elkins, Tim, 1957, Je 3,27:5
Elkins, W L, 1902, Mr 14,9:7
Elkins, William J, 1966, Je 6,41:4
Elkins, William L (will), 1939, Ap 25,19:1
Elkins, William M, 1947, Je 6,24:3
Elkins, William M Mrs, 1942, Mr 30,17:5; 1950, Ag 15,30:2
Elkinton, Herbert R, 1966, My 16,37:1
Elkon, Bernard, 1944, O 10,23:3
Elkon, Edmund, 1955, S 7,63:2
El Koury, Daher J, 1948, N 18,27:3
Elkus, James H, 1966, Je 7,47:2
Elkus, Max, 1948, Ag 10,21:2
Elkus, Sarah, 1957, O 9,35:1
Ella Myer, Sister, 1937, D 16,27:5
El Labaidi, Mahmud, 1946, D 27,19:2
Ellam, Alex M, 1952, Ag 31,44:4
Ellam, George E, 1946, F 12,28:2
Ellams, John, 1959, Ag 27,27:1
Elland, Percy, 1960, Mr 4,25:2
Ellard, Charles H, 1959, F 3,31:1
Ellard, Edward J Msgr, 1937, Ag 16,19:3
Ellard, Gerald, 1963, Ap 2,47:1
Ellard, Roscoe B, 1962, Ag 16,27:3
Ellegood, John A, 1961, Jl 1,17:6
Ellegood, Seth G, 1945, D 29,13:5
Ellehammer, Jacob C H, 1946, My 21,23:2
Ellen, Harry A, 1963, S 19,27:3
Ellenbecker, John N, 1939, F 19,39:3
Ellenberg, Louis J, 1951, Je 1,23:4
Ellenberg, Samuel L, 1957, Ag 24,15:5
Ellenberger, A J, 1939, My 24,23:4
Ellenbogen, Eric, 1960, My 30,17:5
Ellenbogen, Fred, 1967, Jl 31,27:3
Ellenbogen, Joseph K, 1945, My 16,19:4
Ellenbogen, Meyer, 1947, Ap 13,60:3
Ellenbogen, Samuel K, 1948, O 30,15:2
Ellenbogen, Thomas F, 1958, D 6,23:1
Ellenbogen, Wilhelm, 1951, F 26,23:3
Ellenborough, Earl of, 1871, D 23,3:7
Ellenborough, Lady, 1873, Ap 12,3:6
Ellenborough, Lord, 1945, My 21,19:4
Ellend, Herbert M, 1967, O 1,84:5
Ellender, Allen J Mrs, 1949, O 1,13:4
Ellender, Joseph H, 1968, Je 28,41:1
Ellender, Wallace R Mrs, 1946, Ag 31,15:6
Ellenstein, Hilda Mrs, 1966, Ap 21,39:4
Ellenstein, Lee M, 1950, Ag 7,19:4
Ellenstein, Meyer C, 1967, F 12,92:5

Ellenwood, Frank O, 1947, S 8,21:5
Ellenwood, Fred A, 1946, D 15,77:4
Ellenwood, James L, 1959, F 20,25:2
Eller, Delabarre M, 1944, N 19,50:6
Eller, Edwin C, 1949, Ag 15,17:5
Eller, Edwin C Mrs, 1944, Ap 4,21:4
Eller, Frank, 1925, S 7,11:5
Eller, Frank E, 1955, My 27,23:1
Eller, Frederick W, 1948, N 5,26:3
Eller, Horace O (Hod), 1961, Jl 19,29:3
Eller, Justina T, 1939, Je 24,17:4
Eller, Max, 1942, Jl 29,17:3
Eller, Oscar Mrs, 1948, S 11,15:3
Eller, Warren H, 1959, O 2,29:2
Eller, William D, 1958, D 10,40:1
Eller, Winn J, 1952, F 28,27:4
Ellerbee, Patricia J, 1956, Mr 19,23:4
Ellerbroek, James D, 1941, N 30,68:3
Ellerhusen, Ulric H, 1957, N 10,86:3
Ellerhusen, Ulric H Mrs, 1950, Ap 21,23:5
Ellerman, Amy (Mrs C Coxe), 1960, Je 6,29:2
Ellerman, Andrew, 1945, My 17,19:4
Ellerman, Dora, 1908, F 11,7:5
Ellerman, Ferdinand, 1940, Mr 21,25:3
Ellerman, Frederick J, 1944, D 12,23:3
Ellerman, J Sir, 1933, Jl 18,17:1
Ellerman, Louis, 1908, F 11,7:5
Ellero, Mary, 1909, Jl 7,4:2
Ellers, Herman H, 1960, S 9,29:1
Ellerson, Henry W, 1941, My 7,25:2
Ellerson, Lawrence B, 1947, F 15,15:5
Ellert, Harry, 1946, Mr 31,46:2
Ellert, Peter J, 1951, Jl 21,13:3
Ellertsen, Johan, 1939, F 4,15:2
Ellery, Arthur, 1945, Ag 30,21:2
Ellery, Channing, 1917, Ap 1,19:2
Ellery, Edward, 1961, Ja 21,21:4
Ellery, Eloise, 1958, Jl 17,27:5
Ellery, George Vallentine, 1916, Ja 14,9:4
Ellery, James, 1964, Ap 12,86:8
Ellery, Joseph Foster, 1916, Ap 18,13:3
Ellery, Nathaniel B, 1956, Mr 1,33:4
Ellery, William H, 1959, Ag 13,27:5
Ellery, William M, 1937, Mr 5,21:1
Elles, Henry, 1925, F 15,7:2
Elles, Hugh, 1945, Jl 13,11:8
Elles, Lady, 1937, D 8,25:5
Ellesmere, Earl of (Francis Chas Granville Egerton), 1914, Jl 14,9:7
Ellesmere, Lord, 1944, Ag 26,11:4
Ellestad, John H, 1965, Mr 6,25:3
Ellet, Elizebeth F, 1877, Je 4,5:2
Ellet, William H Prof, 1859, Je 29,1:3
Ellett, Edward C, 1947, Je 9,21:5
Ellett, Thomas H, 1951, N 25,84:4
Elley, Joseph R, 1942, D 18,27:2
Ellias, Charles J, 1963, Ag 15,29:4
Ellicott, Chanler G, 1944, Ap 12,21:2
Ellicott, Charles E, 1942, Ja 15,19:4
Ellicott, Charles E Mrs, 1945, Ag 28,19:4
Ellicott, Charles R, 1939, Ag 23,21:5; 1957, N 26,33:3
Ellicott, Edward, 1949, F 16,25:6
Ellicott, John M, 1955, S 19,25:4
Ellicott, Joseph J, 1961, Je 24,21:4
Ellicott, William M, 1944, O 5,23:2
Elliffe, Thomas F, 1960, Mr 23,37:3
Elliger, G Dr, 1878, F 24,12:2
Elliman, Albert W Mrs, 1944, Ap 3,21:4
Elliman, Arthur B, 1953, Mr 3,27:4
Elliman, Douglas L Mrs, 1957, D 18,35:5
Elliman, James F Sr, 1955, O 13,31:5
Elliman, Lawrence B, 1954, Jl 25,68:5
Elliman, Lawrence B Jr, 1954, Ap 1,31:5
Elliman, Lawrence B Mrs, 1941, Ag 14,17:2
Elliman, Roland F, 1966, Mr 13,87:1
Elliman, William, 1914, F 22,IV,5:5
Ellin, George R, 1948, Ap 3,15:4
Elling, Walter A, 1950, My 14,106:4
Ellingboe, Jules, 1948, Ap 26,23:2
Ellinger, Albert E, 1944, My 20,15:2
Ellinger, Clifford M, 1951, My 20,89:2
Ellinger, Desiree, 1951, My 1,29:1
Ellinger, Edgar, 1968, S 20,47:1
Ellinger, Edward N, 1937, Ap 29,21:3
Ellinger, Harry O, 1942, F 12,23:3
Ellinger, Louis Mrs, 1967, N 12,86:8
Ellingham, John, 1944, N 1,23:5
Ellingham, Lewis G, 1939, Mr 19,III,6:5
Ellington, Edward L, 1967, Je 16,43:4
Ellington, Jesse T, 1968, Mr 20,47:2
Ellingwood, Charles H, 1949, N 16,29:5
Ellingwood, N D, 1883, Jl 13,4:7
Ellingworth, Clarence, 1943, Je 8,21:3
Ellinwood, Alice J, 1942, F 15,44:1
Ellinwood, E E, 1943, Ag 9,13:5
Ellinwood, Francis Field Rev, 1908, O 1,9:7
Elliot, Arthur D, 1951, D 14,31:4
Elliot, Arthur H, 1962, Ag 26,82:7
Elliot, Augustus G, 1911, My 14,13:4
Elliot, Bob, 1966, My 5,47:3
Elliot, Charles, 1954, F 2,27:2
Elliot, Charles H, 1948, F 26,23:4
Elliot, Daniel Giraud Dr, 1915, D 23,13:5
Elliot, Dr (trb), 1871, Mr 22,2:6
Elliot, Fletcher M, 1946, My 16,21:1
Elliot, Francis, 1940, Ja 21,35:3
Elliot, Frederick H, 1956, S 14,23:2
Elliot, Harriet W, 1946, S 9,9:4
Elliot, Henry Bond Rev, 1912, Ag 26,9:6
Elliot, Henry Rutherford, 1906, Ap 19,13:5
Elliot, Irwin Mrs, 1951, Mr 6,22:2
Elliot, J Mitchell, 1952, O 11,19:3
Elliot, John M, 1958, N 23,89:1
Elliot, John S, 1966, D 22,33:2
Elliot, Laura M Mrs, 1940, Je 10,17:4
Elliot, Louise W Mrs, 1937, Mr 31,24:1
Elliot, Robert, 1941, O 6,17:3
Elliot, Walter, 1958, Ja 9,36:3
Elliot, William A Mrs, 1945, Mr 3,13:2
Elliot, William D, 1941, Je 4,23:1
Elliot-Smith, Grafton Sir, 1937, Ja 2,11:2
Elliott, A Marshall Dr, 1910, N 10,11:4
Elliott, A Roland, 1959, Jl 3,17:3
Elliott, A Wayne, 1951, Mr 10,13:2
Elliott, Albert L, 1939, Ap 25,23:4
Elliott, Albert M, 1958, Jl 12,15:4
Elliott, Alexander Judge, 1904, N 3,7:1
Elliott, Alice H Mrs, 1951, Ag 12,77:2
Elliott, Alonzo, 1909, Ag 21,7:1; 1964, Je 26,29:1
Elliott, Anne R, 1942, O 31,15:2
Elliott, Archer R, 1950, Ag 20,76:3
Elliott, Arthur F, 1948, D 5,92:2
Elliott, Arthur H Dr, 1918, Mr 2,13:5
Elliott, Arthur H Mrs, 1940, Mr 5,24:4
Elliott, Arthur M Rev, 1937, Je 21,19:5
Elliott, Ashbel R, 1937, O 8,23:2
Elliott, Augusta, 1941, N 23,52:4
Elliott, Barnwell, 1948, Jl 13,27:1
Elliott, C Edgar, 1945, Je 16,13:6
Elliott, C L, 1868, S 5,5:2
Elliott, Caroline L, 1940, Ja 15,15:5
Elliott, Charles A, 1939, Je 27,23:2
Elliott, Charles H, 1939, N 17,21:3; 1942, O 10,15:3; 1960, Ag 14,92:6
Elliott, Charles Loring, 1868, Ag 26,4:7
Elliott, Charles T, 1942, Je 21,37:2
Elliott, Charlotte B, 1948, N 16,29:2
Elliott, Clifford Mrs, 1941, Ja 1,23:2
Elliott, Clyde E, 1959, Je 14,86:5
Elliott, Daniel L, 1942, F 11,21:3
Elliott, David J, 1955, Ap 9,27:2
Elliott, Dick, 1961, D 25,23:4
Elliott, Dixon S, 1923, Jl 22,24:5
Elliott, Don W, 1955, O 29,19:4
Elliott, Donald C, 1949, Ag 8,15:2
Elliott, Douglas A, 1944, Ag 2,15:4
Elliott, E J F Mrs, 1949, F 26,15:3
Elliott, Earle E, 1952, Jl 29,21:2
Elliott, Edward C, 1960, Je 17,31:1
Elliott, Edward G, 1947, D 15,28:6
Elliott, Edward L, 1959, O 15,39:3
Elliott, Edward L Mrs, 1946, Jl 25,21:5
Elliott, Edward S, 1967, Mr 21,43:1
Elliott, Elva C Mrs, 1948, My 9,68:3
Elliott, Ernest, 1948, My 22,15:5
Elliott, F Earl, 1951, D 2,89:1
Elliott, Frank L, 1938, D 18,48:7
Elliott, Frank L D, 1939, Mr 27,16:2
Elliott, Frank R, 1961, Jl 20,27:3
Elliott, Frank W, 1949, Je 10,27:2
Elliott, Frederic E, 1963, S 7,19:3
Elliott, Frederick H Mrs, 1939, F 8,23:4
Elliott, G F, 1931, N 5,25:1
Elliott, George A, 1943, O 13,23:2
Elliott, George B (cor, F 21,13:2), 1948, F 20,27:5
Elliott, George C, 1941, Ja 21,21:4
Elliott, George Frederick, 1914, F 27,11:5
Elliott, George H, 1942, Ap 1,21:3; 1962, N 21,33:1
Elliott, George R, 1963, O 19,25:1; 1968, Ap 20,33:4
Elliott, Gertrude (Mrs Johnston-Forbes-Robertson), 1950, D 27,27:2
Elliott, Gilbert, 1944, Ja 8,13:5
Elliott, Guy F, 1940, Mr 5,23:5
Elliott, H, 1928, Jl 9,19:1
Elliott, H A, 1878, Mr 28,5:4
Elliott, Harold C, 1948, Ja 28,23:4
Elliott, Harriet, 1947, Ag 7,21:3
Elliott, Harrison S, 1951, Je 28,25:3
Elliott, Harry, 1948, Jl 9,19:4
Elliott, Harry S, 1967, Ap 14,39:1
Elliott, Harry V, 1960, Ja 21,31:1
Elliott, Henry R, 1947, N 5,27:2
Elliott, Herbert E Sr, 1949, Mr 15,27:5
Elliott, Hiram, 1946, D 19,29:4
Elliott, Homer, 1952, Jl 19,15:4
Elliott, Howard, 1937, D 1,23:2; 1958, Ap 22,33:5
Elliott, Howard Mrs (funl, Ap 26,7:1), 1925, Ap 24, 19:6
Elliott, Howard Mrs, 1925, Ap 28,21:4
Elliott, Huger, 1948, N 15,25:4
Elliott, Huger Mrs, 1954, Je 1,27:4
Elliott, Isaac, 1939, N 4,15:4
Elliott, J, 1946, Ap 17,25:3
Elliott, J D, 1901, Ag 16,7:6
Elliott, J L Rev, 1881, Ap 17,9:4
Elliott, J M, 1901, Ap 29,5:4
Elliott, J Norman, 1959, Ja 22,32:1
Elliott, Jabez H, 1942, D 19,19:5
Elliott, Jackson S, 1942, Mr 11,20:2
Elliott, James, 1952, Ap 15,27:2
Elliott, James A R, 1924, Ag 9,11:6
Elliott, James C Rev Dr, 1915, S 27,9:6
Elliott, James Mrs, 1946, Mr 13,29:4
Elliott, James V, 1965, Ja 19,33:4
Elliott, James W, 1939, F 5,40:2; 1940, Ag 3,15:3; 1953, Jl 22,27:1
Elliott, Jesse M, 1948, Ap 16,23:3
Elliott, Jimmy, 1957, My 6,35:3
Elliott, John (funl, My 28,21:5), 1925, My 27,23:4
Elliott, John, 1938, Jl 8,17:4; 1951, D 19,31:5
Elliott, John C, 1941, D 21,41:2
Elliott, John G, 1910, Mr 4,9:4
Elliott, John H, 1925, Jl 15,17:6; 1925, Jl 17,15:5
Elliott, John J, 1943, D 24,13:3; 1946, Ap 1,27:2; 1963, Je 29,23:1
Elliott, John L, 1942, Ap 13,15:1
Elliott, John S, 1951, F 15,31:2
Elliott, John W Mrs, 1948, Ag 9,19:2
Elliott, Katherine Mrs, 1944, Je 26,15:6
Elliott, Lawrence K, 1957, Jl 29,19:6
Elliott, Lewis G, 1946, O 23,28:2
Elliott, Luella S Mrs, 1939, Ja 8,43:2
Elliott, Madge (Mrs C Ritchard), 1955, Ag 9,26:5
Elliott, Martha Armstrong Mrs, 1925, Mr 9,17:4
Elliott, Matthew, 1942, S 13,53:2
Elliott, Maud H Mrs, 1948, Mr 20,13:1
Elliott, Maxine, 1940, Mr 7,23:1
Elliott, Middleton S, 1952, O 31,25:1
Elliott, Mortimer F, 1920, Ag 8,22:5
Elliott, Newell J, 1937, D 26,II,7:1
Elliott, Nora A K, 1951, Mr 6,27:5
Elliott, Peter A, 1937, Ap 11,II,9:1
Elliott, Phillips P, 1961, Ag 3,23:3
Elliott, Richard H, 1948, Mr 22,23:2
Elliott, Richard T, 1943, Je 12,13:6
Elliott, Richard W, 1938, D 22,22:2
Elliott, Robert, 1950, My 2,29:2
Elliott, Robert C D, 1950, Mr 7,27:3
Elliott, Robert G, 1939, O 11,30:1
Elliott, Robert I Mrs, 1967, F 24,35:4
Elliott, Robert L, 1954, S 2,21:6
Elliott, Robert M, 1945, O 6,13:5
Elliott, Robert W, 1940, F 24,13:6; 1957, Jl 30,23:4
Elliott, Robert W B, 1964, Ag 31,25:4
Elliott, Robert W B Mrs, 1957, My 26,92:4
Elliott, Robert Wallace, 1905, Ap 17,9:7
Elliott, S M Gen, 1875, My 1,7:2
Elliott, Samuel R, 1909, O 27,11:3
Elliott, Seth E, 1958, Je 17,29:4
Elliott, Stella V Mrs, 1941, My 9,21:5
Elliott, Stephen, 1947, Jl 4,13:7
Elliott, Stewart P, 1948, D 13,23:3
Elliott, Thomas Ireland Justice, 1915, D 6,9:4
Elliott, Verl L, 1957, O 26,21:3
Elliott, W, 1928, Ap 19,25:1; 1932, F 6,17:1
Elliott, W Thompson, 1940, Je 21,21:7
Elliott, Wallace H, 1957, Mr 7,29:3
Elliott, Walter A, 1947, Ag 25,17:4
Elliott, Willard H, 1956, O 13,19:2
Elliott, William, 1938, Ag 18,20:3; 1943, Ap 7,25:2
Elliott, William (Wild Bill), 1965, N 28,89:1
Elliott, William A, 1946, Ap 17,25:4
Elliott, William C, 1949, Je 18,13:2
Elliott, William E Capt, 1925, D 29,23:4
Elliott, William H, 1960, Ag 4,25:5
Elliott, William J, 1952, Ja 24,27:2; 1953, Ag 24,23:4; 1960, My 17,37:4
Elliott, William Mrs (funl, Je 8,11:5), 1911, Je 6,9:6
Elliott, William Mrs (Countess Margt Zborowski), 1911, Jl 11,7:5
Elliott, William S, 1957, My 10,27:3
Elliott, William Sr, 1937, Je 20,II,7:1
Elliott, William W, 1950, Ap 5,32:2
Ellis, A C, 1947, My 27,25:2
Ellis, A D, 1881, F 12,1:7
Ellis, A Lee, 1947, S 12,21:3
Ellis, A Leroy, 1938, Ap 30,15:6
Ellis, Albert D, 1948, My 12,28:2
Ellis, Albert H, 1945, N 2,19:5
Ellis, Albert W, 1944, Ap 15,11:5
Ellis, Alder Sr, 1960, D 24,15:3
Ellis, Alex, 1951, N 17,17:4
Ellis, Alston Dr, 1920, N 16,15:4
Ellis, Andrew A, 1948, Mr 11,27:2
Ellis, Angelo J, 1956, F 17,21:1
Ellis, Arthur N, 1955, Je 1,33:5
Ellis, Arthur W, 1955, Je 4,15:5
Ellis, Augustus V Mrs, 1949, N 20,94:1
Ellis, Benjamin P, 1953, O 4,88:6
Ellis, Bowman S Jr, 1948, N 1,23:4
Ellis, Bowman S Sr, 1946, D 9,25:3
Ellis, C Groverman, 1939, My 6,17:6
Ellis, Carleton, 1941, Ja 14,21:1
Ellis, Carlos B, 1963, D 5,62:5
Ellis, Carlyle, 1942, Ap 9,19:5
Ellis, Charles, 1957, D 30,23:5
Ellis, Charles A, 1937, Mr 15,24:1; 1949, Ag 23,23:5
Ellis, Charles B, 1943, My 14,19:4
Ellis, Charles C, 1950, Je 29,29:5

Ellis, Charles E, 1937, Jl 22,19:5
Ellis, Charles E Sir, 1937, F 20,17:5
Ellis, Charles G, 1938, S 19,19:3; 1950, N 14,31:4
Ellis, Charles H, 1940, My 5,53:1; 1954, Mr 28,89:2
Ellis, Charles J, 1964, My 24,93:1
Ellis, Charles L, 1943, S 2,19:3
Ellis, Charles M Mrs, 1955, Jl 15,21:2
Ellis, Charles P, 1914, Ag 10,7:5
Ellis, Charles W, 1940, F 29,19:3
Ellis, Chris, 1950, Je 30,23:2
Ellis, Christ Mrs, 1943, N 13,13:4
Ellis, Claude R, 1945, Ja 6,11:5
Ellis, Clifford A, 1946, Ap 22,21:1
Ellis, Crawford H, 1966, N 13,89:2
Ellis, David M Mrs, 1952, S 17,31:5
Ellis, Degoy B, 1949, Ja 20,27:4
Ellis, Donald A, 1960, Ag 30,29:1
Ellis, E, 1880, My 30,2:7
Ellis, E Huguenin Mrs, 1960, F 13,19:2
Ellis, Edgar C, 1947, Mr 17,23:5
Ellis, Edith (Mrs C B Furness), 1960, D 28,27:4
Ellis, Edward, 1952, Jl 28,15:3
Ellis, Edward C, 1904, S 20,9:6
Ellis, Edward G, 1942, N 20,24:3
Ellis, Edward H Sr, 1957, Ja 20,92:7
Ellis, Edward K, 1946, Je 10,21:2
Ellis, Edward Mrs, 1965, Ag 6,27:2
Ellis, Edward S, 1916, Je 22,11:5
Ellis, Edwin M, 1940, D 21,17:2
Ellis, Elisha Z, 1946, D 22,42:3
Ellis, Elwyn A, 1967, Je 28,45:4
Ellis, Eugene F, 1937, Je 13,II,6:7
Ellis, Evelyn, 1958, Je 6,23:3
Ellis, Everett E, 1964, N 19,39:6
Ellis, Florence E, 1944, Ag 1,15:4
Ellis, Francis B, 1964, Ap 21,37:3
Ellis, Frank B, 1925, F 18,19:3
Ellis, Frank E, 1925, Ap 14,23:3; 1950, S 29,27:4
Ellis, Frank R, 1937, Ap 25,II,8:2
Ellis, Frank W, 1940, Ja 28,32:1
Ellis, Franklin C Sr, 1949, O 14,27:1
Ellis, Fred J, 1953, Je 10,29:2
Ellis, Frederick M, 1937, D 10,25:2; 1967, Jl 20,37:2
Ellis, Frederick W, 1946, Jl 24,27:1
Ellis, Furey, 1957, D 21,19:5
Ellis, Gardner B, 1945, Ja 29,14:5
Ellis, George, 1965, Ja 24,80:7
Ellis, George A, 1942, N 24,25:2; 1952, Je 19,27:1; 1955, O 5,35:3
Ellis, George A Mrs, 1957, Ja 1,23:6
Ellis, George A Sr, 1951, Ag 3,21:5
Ellis, George Albert, 1903, D 28,7:4
Ellis, George D, 1966, Jl 1,35:3
Ellis, George E Mrs, 1941, Ap 30,19:3
Ellis, George W, 1937, O 23,15:5; 1948, Ap 6,24:3; 1951, F 26,23:2
Ellis, Gordon A, 1940, F 1,21:3
Ellis, Griffith O, 1948, F 6,26:7
Ellis, Hannah C, 1962, Ja 31,31:3
Ellis, Harlan M (Hoot), 1953, My 24,89:2
Ellis, Harry, 1944, N 21,25:3
Ellis, Harry P, 1946, Ap 13,17:2
Ellis, Harvey, 1904, Ja 12,1:6
Ellis, Harvey F Sr, 1956, Ag 17,19:2
Ellis, Havelock, 1939, Jl 11,19:1
Ellis, Havelock Mrs, 1916, O 3,11:4
Ellis, Hayne, 1961, My 29,19:2
Ellis, Helen, 1940, N 12,24:2
Ellis, Howard, 1902, D 25,4:2; 1968, F 19,39:4
Ellis, Howard Mrs, 1953, Ap 11,17:4
Ellis, Hubert S, 1959, D 4,31:3
Ellis, Irving L, 1946, My 26,32:2
Ellis, Isaac M, 1946, My 2,21:3
Ellis, J E, 1901, Je 8,2:3
Ellis, J N, 1942, S 30,23:3
Ellis, J William, 1942, Mr 9,19:4
Ellis, James A, 1962, Jl 11,35:1; 1967, S 14,47:1
Ellis, James A Mrs, 1962, Jl 11,35:1
Ellis, James C, 1956, Mr 4,88:8
Ellis, James H S Mrs, 1942, N 8,51:5
Ellis, James J, 1939, My 10,23:5; 1948, Ag 12,21:3
Ellis, James T, 1942, D 10,25:2
Ellis, John, 1948, D 31,15:1
Ellis, John B, 1874, N 23,1:2
Ellis, John D, 1947, S 23,25:5; 1956, Mr 11,88:1
Ellis, John E, 1955, Je 2,29:4
Ellis, John J Mrs, 1949, My 10,25:5
Ellis, John M, 1955, Ap 4,29:4; 1964, F 13,31:2
Ellis, John R, 1945, S 22,17:5; 1960, Ap 28,35:1
Ellis, John W Mrs, 1943, S 4,13:5
Ellis, John Washington, 1910, D 30,11:4
Ellis, Joseph F, 1959, N 3,35:6
Ellis, Kenneth M, 1950, F 14,25:3
Ellis, L Mrs, 1931, Jl 4,13:1
Ellis, Lawrence L, 1964, N 1,89:1
Ellis, Lewis O, 1941, Ap 27,38:3
Ellis, Lilian, 1951, F 22,31:3
Ellis, Lynn W, 1959, S 15,39:3
Ellis, M Robert, 1956, F 28,31:3
Ellis, Margaret Dye Mrs, 1925, Jl 14,21:5
Ellis, Marguerite E, 1950, Mr 28,31:1
Ellis, Marion R, 1939, D 21,23:4
Ellis, Mary G Mrs (will, My 11,19:1), 1940, My 8, 23:1
Ellis, Mary Mrs, 1942, Ap 5,42:1
Ellis, Matt H Col, 1913, D 1,9:4
Ellis, Melville, 1917, Ap 5,13:6
Ellis, Milton, 1947, My 19,22:2
Ellis, Milton A, 1966, Mr 29,41:3
Ellis, Moury I, 1943, D 8,23:1
Ellis, Nathaniel, 1867, My 21,8:5
Ellis, Oscar E, 1951, Mr 10,13:4
Ellis, Oscar E Mrs, 1960, Ap 3,86:5
Ellis, Pauline L Mrs, 1941, Ag 7,17:5
Ellis, R H P Dr, 1925, My 25,17:5
Ellis, Ralph W, 1945, S 30,46:2; 1951, Ja 18,27:1; 1951, N 4,86:8
Ellis, Raymond V, 1955, O 26,31:3
Ellis, Ridsdale, 1955, O 2,86:2
Ellis, Robert A, 1955, My 10,29:3
Ellis, Robert W Mrs, 1954, Jl 9,17:5
Ellis, Robinson Prof, 1913, O 10,11:6
Ellis, Rudolph, 1915, S 23,13:6
Ellis, Rudulph P, 1964, My 9,27:1
Ellis, Ruth H, 1963, O 2,41:3
Ellis, S Moffit, 1963, S 30,29:4
Ellis, Samuel M, 1944, Ap 30,45:1
Ellis, Samuel Mrs, 1952, S 28,54:6
Ellis, Sherman K, 1964, F 29,21:4
Ellis, Sherman K Jr, 1961, Jl 15,19:5
Ellis, Sidney A, 1943, Je 15,21:5; 1949, My 18,27:5
Ellis, Sidney S Mrs, 1967, Ap 22,31:5
Ellis, Steve, 1966, F 17,33:4
Ellis, T G, 1883, Ja 10,5:4
Ellis, T T, 1934, Ja 7,30:1
Ellis, Theodore H, 1945, My 28,19:2
Ellis, Theodore H Mrs, 1949, Jl 14,27:3
Ellis, Theodore S, 1939, S 13,25:4
Ellis, Thomas B, 1953, Jl 18,13:6
Ellis, Thomas B Mrs, 1953, D 25,17:4
Ellis, Victor A, 1954, N 11,31:2
Ellis, Vincent, 1962, My 12,23:1
Ellis, Vincent C, 1967, O 11,47:1
Ellis, W E, 1940, Ap 2,26:3
Ellis, Wade H, 1948, Jl 6,23:4
Ellis, Walter C, 1965, Ap 5,31:3
Ellis, Walter H, 1937, O 30,19:5
Ellis, Warren D, 1940, Ag 23,15:4
Ellis, Wilbur L, 1955, O 14,36:6
Ellis, Willard W, 1946, D 23,23:4
Ellis, William, 1881, F 22,8:3; 1945, Jl 8,11:4
Ellis, William A, 1953, Ap 16,29:5
Ellis, William A Sr, 1951, Je 22,25:2
Ellis, William B, 1940, Ap 27,15:1
Ellis, William C, 1961, D 9,27:3
Ellis, William D, 1918, My 25,13:4
Ellis, William F, 1903, Jl 17,7:6; 1938, S 23,27:3
Ellis, William G, 1959, D 26,13:4
Ellis, William H, 1938, Ja 16,II,9:2; 1948, Ap 15,25:2 1952, Jl 21,19:5
Ellis, William Henry, 1923, S 30,7:3
Ellis, William J, 1940, Ag 12,15:5; 1945, Mr 12,19:3
Ellis, William K, 1950, Mr 30,29:1
Ellis, William M, 1956, Ap 6,26:2
Ellis, William M Mrs, 1947, Jl 1,25:4
Ellis, William Munford Maj, 1921, S 11,21:2
Ellis, William R, 1955, F 1,29:2
Ellis, William S, 1937, N 12,21:5
Ellis, William T, 1950, Ag 16,29:5
Ellis, William V, 1953, Je 13,15:5
Ellis, William W Sr, 1945, Jl 25,23:5
Ellis, Willis A, 1943, My 30,26:2
Ellis, Wilmot E, 1938, Jl 23,13:5
Ellis, Wilson F, 1958, Ap 12,19:4
Ellis, Zenas H, 1943, O 22,17:3; 1945, Ja 7,38:1
Ellish, Abram, 1948, S 24,26:3
Ellish, Alfred J, 1968, S 25,47:2
Ellisher, Frank J, 1968, D 18,47:2
Ellisler, J, 1903, Ag 22,9:6
Ellison, Alanson, 1946, Ja 30,25:1
Ellison, Albert R, 1946, Ap 6,17:3
Ellison, Arthur R, 1946, Jl 15,25:5
Ellison, Benjamin F Sr, 1944, O 14,13:5
Ellison, Benjamin M, 1955, Mr 4,23:1
Ellison, Bennett, 1937, My 14,23:6
Ellison, Charles J, 1918, Ag 12,9:7
Ellison, Charles Ruxton Dr, 1917, F 1,11:4
Ellison, Daniel, 1966, N 7,47:5
Ellison, Edward D, 1957, D 25,32:2
Ellison, Eli A, 1951, Ja 31,25:5
Ellison, Elizabeth W Mrs, 1956, Jl 16,44:5
Ellison, Eugene L, 1916, F 9,11:7
Ellison, F B, 1884, Ja 26,5:2
Ellison, Frank (Biff), 1904, F 27,6:1
Ellison, Frank D Mrs, 1946, Ja 10,23:5
Ellison, Frank T, 1941, Jl 9,21:4
Ellison, Frederick A, 1941, F 20,19:1
Ellison, George C Col, 1924, Ag 17,24:3
Ellison, George H, 1947, My 28,25:4
Ellison, George M, 1942, Mr 10,19:5
Ellison, George R, 1957, Jl 18,25:3
Ellison, H S (Bert), 1955, Ag 13,13:5
Ellison, Henry H, 1937, O 9,19:4
Ellison, Ismar S, 1922, N 13,15:4
Ellison, J B, 1902, D 28,7:6
Ellison, James A, 1946, My 3,22:3
Ellison, John, 1882, N 19,8:7; 1968, Ja 28,77:1
Ellison, Lee A, 1962, Jl 24,28:6
Ellison, Louis, 1958, Je 6,23:2
Ellison, M E, 1882, Mr 7,2:3
Ellison, Max, 1958, Je 6,23:2
Ellison, Millard H, 1958, S 25,33:2
Ellison, Saran R Dr, 1918, Mr 27,13:8
Ellison, Stanley Mrs, 1959, Ap 23,31:2
Ellison, William B, 1924, D 7,7:1
Ellison, William B Mrs, 1951, O 17,31:4
Ellison, William P, 1903, D 21,7:5
Elliston, Grace, 1950, D 15,32:2
Elliston, Harold T, 1941, O 28,23:3
Elliston, Herbert B, 1957, Ja 23,29:4
Ellithorp, John S Jr, 1962, N 28,39:2
Ellithorpe, Raymond, 1945, My 22,19:2
Ellmaker, Lee, 1951, Mr 28,29:1
Ellman, Dave, 1967, D 6,47:1
Ellman, Isadore W, 1957, D 22,40:8
Ellman, Paul M Mrs, 1946, Je 4,23:4
Ellmore, David E, 1946, Ja 2,19:3
Ellms, Evelyn B, 1946, Jl 16,23:5
Ellms, Jay, 1945, Ap 23,19:2
Ellms, Joseph W, 1950, F 9,29:4
Ellner, Samuel H, 1965, F 13,21:1
Ellor, Arthur A, 1949, S 9,26:5
Ellor, Arthur A Mrs, 1949, N 23,29:2
Ellor, Edwin L, 1940, Ag 17,15:4
Ellor, Frederick, 1942, F 14,15:5
Ellor, George B, 1956, My 5,19:6
Ellor, Walter Mrs, 1941, Ap 16,23:3
Elloree, Robert W, 1949, O 27,29:4
Ellrodt, Beauregard, 1938, Ag 6,13:3
Ellrodt, George W, 1944, D 5,23:4
Ellrodt, John C, 1957, Ja 3,33:3
Ellrodt, Louis N, 1940, Mr 2,13:6
Ells, Arthur F, 1963, D 9,35:4
Ells, D P, 1903, Ag 15,7:6
Ells, Frederick A Sr, 1958, F 11,31:1
Ellsen, Helge A F, 1943, S 5,28:8
Ellsler, Effie, 1942, O 10,15:2
Ellsler, George R, 1939, Ag 13,29:3
Ellsler, John A Mrs, 1918, D 13,15:2
Ellson, John V Rev, 1937, My 1,19:3
Ellstein, Abraham, 1963, Mr 25,7:4
Ellstein, Jacob, 1957, Jl 10,27:3
Ellstrom, Victor E, 1943, My 24,15:4
Ellsworth, Albert L, 1950, N 30,33:3
Ellsworth, Alvah D, 1961, Mr 25,25:4
Ellsworth, Arthur T Maj, 1924, Ja 31,15:5
Ellsworth, Bradford, 1950, Ap 17,23:3
Ellsworth, Duncan S, 1967, D 4,47:2
Ellsworth, Duncan S Mrs, 1948, Ap 18,68:7
Ellsworth, Frank E, 1938, My 21,15:5
Ellsworth, Franklin F, 1942, D 25,18:2
Ellsworth, Frederick J, 1937, My 16,II,8:5
Ellsworth, Gleason, 1948, N 20,13:3
Ellsworth, Henry C, 1940, D 1,62:2
Ellsworth, Henry E, 1950, F 22,29:4
Ellsworth, Henry S, 1937, Ja 13,24:8
Ellsworth, Herbert E, 1937, O 5,25:2
Ellsworth, J W, 1914, Mr 11,11:5
Ellsworth, James D, 1940, Je 14,21:4
Ellsworth, James H, 1943, Mr 9,23:3
Ellsworth, James W Mrs, 1921, N 4,17:6
Ellsworth, Jesse F, 1951, S 23,85:5
Ellsworth, John C Mrs, 1957, Ja 29,31:4
Ellsworth, John M, 1921, Ja 25,11:5
Ellsworth, John S Mrs, 1962, S 28,25:7
Ellsworth, Joseph Capt, 1902, Ja 18,9:2
Ellsworth, Lew W, 1947, O 9,25:5
Ellsworth, Lincoln, 1951, My 28,21:1
Ellsworth, Lincoln (est tax appr), 1955, O 29,20:1
Ellsworth, Marc L, 1943, N 14,57:1
Ellsworth, Margaret, 1963, Jl 24,31:3
Ellsworth, Millard F, 1950, F 3,23:1
Ellsworth, Ray, 1966, Je 29,47:3
Ellsworth, Richard C, 1948, S 23,29:5
Ellsworth, Sanford J, 1953, F 24,25:5
Ellsworth, Susan T, 1949, N 8,31:1
Ellsworth, T Gardner, 1925, Jl 16,19:5
Ellsworth, Timothy E, 1904, F 11,9:6
Ellsworth, W W, 1868, Ja 18,1:3; 1936, D 19,19:1
Ellsworth, Wilfred W, 1940, Jl 6,15:4
Ellsworth, William H, 1944, My 1,15:5
Ellsworth, William W Mrs, 1945, S 15,15:4
Ellwanger, William De Lancey, 1913, F 18,13:5
Ellwinge, Louis, 1905, Ap 19,9:5
Ellwood, Arthur, 1949, Jl 22,19:1
Ellwood, Charles A, 1946, S 26,25:4
Ellwood, Edwin A, 1943, Mr 12,17:5
Ellwood, Isaac L, 1910, S 12,9:6
Ellwood, John, 1937, Je 13,36:2
Ellwood, Walter B, 1965, D 10,42:1
Ellyson, J Taylor, 1919, Mr 19,11:2
Ellzey, James M Jr, 1946, S 9,9:2
Elmaleh, Abraham, 1967, Ap 3,33:3
Elman, Mina, 1961, Mr 13,29:4
Elman, Mischa (will, Ap 15,4:6), 1967, Ap 6,1:4
Elman, Murray, 1964, D 8,45:4
Elman, Phil H, 1950, F 13,21:5
Elman, Robert, 1956, D 24,13:2
Elman, Sam, 1968, Ag 14,43:5

Elman, Saul, 1940, My 27,19:4
Elman, Saul Mrs, 1953, Jl 21,23:3
Elman, Ziggy (Harry Elman), 1968, Je 27,43:1
Elmen, Gustaf W, 1957, D 11,31:2
Elmendorf, Charles A, 1950, Ap 8,13:7
Elmendorf, Charles L, 1942, D 16,25:2
Elmendorf, D, 1929, My 8,31:5
Elmendorf, F F, 1883, O 12,4:7
Elmendorf, John B, 1937, F 27,17:4
Elmendorf, John E, 1960, My 27,31:3
Elmendorf, Lester C, 1955, Mr 15,29:1
Elmendorf, Robert H, 1958, O 31,29:3
Elmendorf, Roy C, 1949, S 19,23:4
Elmendorf, Ten Eyck, 1962, Je 4,29:4
Elmendorf, William B, 1943, D 22,24:2
Elmendorf, Wilson D, 1944, D 8,21:1
Elmendorff, Mary Cooke, 1915, Je 14,9:4
Elmer, Anna C Mrs, 1938, Ap 25,15:4
Elmer, Arthur, 1945, Jl 7,13:6
Elmer, Charles B Mrs, 1968, F 28,47:5
Elmer, Charles W, 1954, D 9,33:3
Elmer, Franklin D, 1941, O 3,23:1
Elmer, Harry, 1950, Mr 19,92:4
Elmer, L Q C, 1883, Mr 13,5:4
Elmer, Lucius H, 1942, Mr 27,23:3
Elmer, Matthew K, 1953, Ag 13,25:2
Elmer, Otto C Mrs, 1952, Ag 29,23:1
Elmer, Raymond S, 1947, My 17,15:6
Elmer, Robert P, 1951, Mr 6,27:3
Elmer, Robert S, 1943, Je 6,42:5
Elmer, S Lewis, 1967, Mr 12,86:7
Elmer, Warren P, 1953, D 28,22:3
Elmer, William, 1947, My 9,21:3
Elmer, William P, 1956, My 13,86:4
Elmer, William T Ex-Justice, 1907, N 13,9:6
Elmes, Frank W S, 1939, My 18,25:3
Elmes, Norman J Jr, 1968, Ap 18,47:3
Elmhirst, Leonard K Mrs (Dorothy), 1968, D 16,50:1
Elmiger, George A Sr, 1955, Ja 10,23:4
Elmore, A Robert, 1937, S 13,21:4
Elmore, Alfred, 1881, Ja 27,5:4
Elmore, Barnett N, 1912, S 14,13:6
Elmore, Carl H, 1957, O 22,33:1
Elmore, Cyrus B, 1960, Ja 4,29:4
Elmore, David J, 1948, Je 27,52:7
Elmore, Frank G Mrs, 1947, N 25,32:5
Elmore, George S, 1955, Ja 10,23:3
Elmore, Hurlbert C, 1950, Je 13,27:4
Elmore, J Milton Mrs, 1949, Ja 31,19:4
Elmore, Juan F, 1911, F 26,II,11:3
Elmore, Lewis, 1904, Ag 8,7:6
Elmore, Richard F, 1949, Ag 10,21:1
Elmore, Robert B Mrs, 1958, Ap 12,19:4
Elmore, Thomas L, 1938, F 24,19:3
Elmore, William E, 1952, D 21,52:7
Elmore, William J, 1946, F 10,40:7
lmquist, Anthony F, 1950, Ag 25,21:4
lmquist, Axel L, 1949, N 2,27:5
lms, James C, 1943, My 20,21:3
lms, James C Mrs, 1938, O 9,45:1
lms, Leonard Mrs, 1960, My 5,35:4
lmslie, William G, 1956, My 18,25:4
lmslie, William G Mrs, 1938, Jl 15,17:2
lnick, Abraham, 1948, Ag 26,21:2
lnor, Norman G, 1949, N 19,17:5
lout, C K, 1947, D 5,25:2
lphick, Albert G, 1962, Mr 17,25:2
lphinstone, Lady (Mary F Bowes-Lyons), 1961, F 9,31:3
lphinstone, Reginald C, 1925, Ap 17,21:5
lrick, Charles C, 1939, Ja 18,19:4
lrick, Robert T, 1950, D 21,29:2
lrod, Allen M Mrs, 1950, Je 14,31:6
lroy, Edwin Mrs, 1950, O 5,31:3
lroy, Joseph M, 1947, F 21,19:3
lsa, Princess of Liechtenstein, 1947, S 29,21:5
lsaesser, Armin, 1952, O 30,31:5
lsaesser, George G, 1959, S 29,39:2
lsaesser, Joseph, 1947, N 25,32:6
lsas, Benjamin, 1952, Ag 28,23:2
lsas, Herman, 1938, Ja 15,15:4
sas, William R, 1950, D 11,25:5
sberg, Charles A, 1948, Mr 19,23:1
sberg, Herman A, 1938, S 29,25:5
sberg, Herman A (will), 1940, Mr 1,41:1
sberg, Leon S, 1951, N 30,23:5
sberg, Louis Dr, 1885, F 20,2:4
sberg, N, 1932, Je 5,33:1
sendrath, Julius M, 1955, F 2,27:3
senheimer, Edward E, 1966, Ag 27,30:3
ser, Albert C, 1942, My 16,13:2
ser, F B, 1935, F 2,13:1
ser, Maximilian Jr, 1961, Ja 4,33:2
ser, Maximilian Jr Mrs, 1961, Mr 31,27:3
ser, William J, 1952, Jl 7,21:5
sesser, Morris C, 1949, My 5,27:4
sesser, Paul D Rev, 1937, O 9,19:1
sesser, T Bernard, 1944, Je 2,15:5
ey, Fred T, 1938, Mr 1,21:4
ey, George F, 1947, Ap 3,25:3
ey, Minnie A Mrs, 1947, D 28,40:2
hoff, Bernard E, 1939, Ja 18,20:3
ier, Anastasia Mrs, 1941, Ag 7,19:3

Elskamp, Herman, 1940, Ag 2,15:4
Elsmith, Leonard, 1963, My 16,35:4
Elsmore, Ray T, 1957, F 19,31:5
Elsmore, Thomas, 1937, My 13,25:3
Elsner, Henry Leopold, 1916, F 18,11:6
Elsner, Solomon, 1962, Ap 19,31:1
Elsohn, Eli, 1949, Jl 29,18:7
Elson, Alfred J, 1955, Ja 6,27:3
Elson, Arthur, 1940, F 25,39:2
Elson, Edwin B, 1956, Jl 13,19:4
Elson, Elizabeth C Mrs, 1953, O 2,21:2
Elson, Helen Mrs, 1951, S 1,11:6
Elson, Henry Mrs, 1913, Ag 8,7:6
Elson, Henry W, 1954, Ja 30,17:6
Elson, Joseph P, 1949, Jl 4,13:6
Elson, T Herbert Mrs, 1937, S 4,15:2
Elssler, Fanny, 1884, N 28,3:6
Elst, Leon van der, 1962, F 6,7:7
Elstad, Eivind G, 1960, D 8,35:2
Elstad, Rudolph T, 1959, D 16,41:4
Elste, Louis, 1949, Ag 31,23:3
Elster, Gurden G, 1949, Ja 5,25:5
Elster, Harold H, 1963, S 30,29:1
Elster, Walter, 1938, Mr 7,33:8
Elster, William J, 1947, Je 11,27:5
Elston, Claude P, 1953, O 20,29:4
Elston, Ellsworth D, 1964, My 2,27:5
Elston, Frederick G, 1956, S 23,84:4
Elston, George H, 1948, Ja 27,25:4
Elston, Isaac C Col, 1925, Jl 3,13:6
Elsworth, Alfred D Mrs, 1949, Je 22,31:6
Elsworth, John Watson, 1916, Mr 16,13:4
Elsworth, Philip Capt, 1909, Jl 10,7:3
Elsworth, Randolph M, 1961, Ap 18,37:1
Elterich, Harold N, 1948, Je 3,25:5
Elterich, William O Mrs, 1953, Ag 20,27:2
Elting, Albert A, 1950, Ag 2,25:5
Elting, Arthur W (will, Ja 21,30:2), 1948, Ja 3,13:2
Elting, Carrie D Mrs, 1939, Je 10,17:6
Elting, Cornelius W H, 1903, Ag 23,7:5
Elting, Harold H, 1962, Jl 29,60:8
Elting, Henry Mrs, 1950, D 11,25:2
Elting, Howard, 1954, Mr 25,29:2
Elting, Hubert, 1952, N 13,31:1
Elting, Phil, 1941, Jl 21,15:6
Elting, Victor, 1956, Ag 22,29:3
Eltinge, Isaac B, 1942, Ag 28,19:3
Eltinge, Julian, 1941, Mr 8,19:3
Eltinge, L, 1931, My 15,23:3
Eltinge, William S, 1961, My 21,87:1
Eltisley, Lord, 1942, S 3,19:6
Elton, Charles S, 1947, D 15,25:3
Elton, David H, 1964, Ap 20,29:3
Elton, Fred, 1960, Ap 27,37:2
Elton, James Mrs, 1943, F 21,32:6
Elton, John P, 1864, N 13,2:6; 1948, Mr 9,23:2
Elton, John P Mrs, 1962, Mr 22,35:3
Eltringham, Walter, 1953, Ap 18,2:5
Eltschkner, Antonin, 1961, Mr 5,86:7
Eltz, George J, 1943, Mr 28,24:1; 1958, My 16,25:2
Eluard, Paul, 1952, N 19,29:1
Elvehjem, Conrad A, 1962, Jl 28,19:3
Elverson, J Jr, 1929, Ja 22,29:3
Elverson, James, 1911, F 11,11:6
Elverson, James Mrs, 1923, My 4,17:2
Elverson, John, 1937, Ja 15,22:1
Elvey, Maurice, 1967, Ag 29,37:2
Elvidge, June, 1965, My 3,33:3
Elviken, Andreas, 1950, D 19,29:2
Elvin, Caroline Mrs, 1953, Ap 18,19:5
Elvin, Herbert H, 1949, N 11,26:2
Elving, Bernard Mrs, 1966, Je 17,45:1
Elward, Joseph F, 1943, F 7,48:4
Elward, Joseph P, 1950, Ja 15,85:1
Elwarn, Michael (Bro Christian Bros), 1963, My 2, 35:4
Elwarn Joseph, Brother (P J O'Connor), 1950, Je 27, 29:2
Elwell, Charles F, 1907, Mr 12,9:6
Elwell, D Jerome, 1912, D 29,15:2
Elwell, Dan W, 1941, Ap 14,17:4
Elwell, David, 1958, Je 9,23:5
Elwell, Dwight A, 1948, N 25,31:2
Elwell, Ernest A, 1955, S 11,84:7
Elwell, F Bolton Jr, 1958, D 31,19:1
Elwell, Francis Edwin, 1922, Ja 24,15:4
Elwell, Frederick W, 1958, Ja 4,15:3
Elwell, Harvey J, 1948, My 2,76:7
Elwell, Hector H, 1956, My 11,27:1
Elwell, Helen D Mrs, 1938, F 9,20:3
Elwell, Henry G, 1968, Ag 22,37:4
Elwell, Oliver E, 1948, Ag 17,21:2
Elwell, Royal L, 1938, Ag 11,17:2
Elwell, William, 1882, N 1,4:6
Elwell, William H C, 1943, My 24,15:4
Elwell, Wilmot P, 1945, Jl 31,19:1
Elwes, Frederick, 1956, Mr 29,10:4
Elwes, Henry John, 1922, N 28,21:5
Elwes, Mary F Mrs, 1938, Je 25,15:5
Elwes, Richard Sir, 1968, S 7,29:4
Elwin, Benjamin, 1938, D 7,23:3
Elwin, Verrier, 1964, F 24,25:2
Elwood, Benjamin J, 1965, Je 1,39:2

Elwood, Charles M, 1939, Ja 1,24:7
Elwood, Frederic A Mrs, 1958, F 23,92:2
Elwood, John L, 1943, Ap 16,21:2
Elwood, John W, 1960, Ap 24,88:4
Elwood, Roy L, 1941, Mr 11,23:1
Elwyn, A L, 1884, Mr 16,8:7
Elwyn, Adolph, 1955, Je 11,15:6
Elwyn, Alfred Langdon Rev, 1924, Ag 11,13:6
Elwyn, Emily L, 1951, D 17,31:3
Elwyn, Herman, 1961, S 21,35:2
Elwyn, Larry H, 1942, Ap 19,44:7
Elwyn, Samuel, 1943, N 14,56:5
Elwyn, Thomas L, 1937, My 28,21:3
Elwyn, Thomas L Mrs, 1962, My 12,23:3
Elwyn, William H H, 1942, S 12,13:7
Ely, A H, 1934, Ap 27,21:1
Ely, A M Prof, 1904, D 14,5:6
Ely, Addison Capt, 1920, Ja 31,11:4
Ely, Alan H, 1960, O 15,23:6
Ely, Albert H, 1964, S 30,43:1
Ely, Alfred, 1914, Ag 2,15:4; 1959, O 18,87:1
Ely, Alice Mrs, 1953, D 10,47:5
Ely, Anthony S, 1875, Ap 16,4:7
Ely, Augustus G, 1938, Je 22,23:2
Ely, Austin L, 1951, My 26,17:6
Ely, Carolyn M Mrs, 1954, Jl 25,68:8
Ely, Charles R, 1939, F 24,19:5
Ely, Clarence, 1955, Ap 10,88:1
Ely, D J, 1932, Ag 26,18:1
Ely, D Vaughan, 1948, N 20,13:6
Ely, E T Dr, 1885, Ap 14,2:4
Ely, Edith (E de Lys), 1961, Jl 4,19:2
Ely, Edward C, 1951, Ja 2,10:5
Ely, Edward W, 1941, S 3,23:1
Ely, Elizabeth B, 1953, O 26,21:5
Ely, Elizabeth L, 1941, Jl 1,23:5
Ely, Erastus U, 1942, Je 29,15:5
Ely, Fanny G, 1961, S 14,31:2
Ely, Foster Rev Dr, 1916, Mr 9,13:4
Ely, Francis C Mrs, 1952, Mr 14,23:3
Ely, Franklin, 1939, Jl 10,19:5
Ely, Fred B, 1946, Mr 29,23:4
Ely, Frederick W, 1946, F 22,25:3
Ely, George B Mrs, 1904, Ag 23,7:6
Ely, George P, 1967, D 12,47:4
Ely, George W, 1922, Ag 18,13:3
Ely, Grosvenor, 1959, Ag 24,21:4
Ely, Hanson E, 1958, Ap 29,29:1
Ely, Hanson E Jr, 1938, S 30,21:4
Ely, Harry G, 1955, Jl 13,25:5
Ely, Heman, 1947, Mr 27,27:3
Ely, Henry W, 1942, N 28,13:2
Ely, Herman Mrs, 1938, S 27,21:4
Ely, Hiram B Mrs, 1962, F 17,19:3
Ely, Horace S, 1904, Ap 28,9:6
Ely, James R, 1915, My 24,11:5
Ely, John A, 1967, N 2,47:4
Ely, John Slade Dr, 1906, F 8,12:5
Ely, John T A, 1954, Ja 28,27:4
Ely, John W, 1943, Je 26,13:4
Ely, Joseph B, 1956, Je 14,33:1
Ely, Joseph B Mrs, 1950, Mr 13,21:3
Ely, Joseph Nathaniel, 1922, Ap 16,28:3
Ely, Julia M Mrs, 1937, Je 19,17:4
Ely, Lancelot, 1962, Ap 16,29:4
Ely, Louis B Mrs, 1949, S 22,31:5
Ely, Mary Boies, 1925, Je 6,15:4
Ely, Mary Jerome Rev Mother, 1885, My 2,3:3
Ely, Matthew G, 1964, D 31,19:3
Ely, Matthew G Mrs, 1964, Mr 29,61:1
Ely, Moses, 1884, O 25,2:6; 1944, Jl 16,31:1
Ely, Newbold, 1947, Jl 31,21:6
Ely, Norman S, 1949, Ap 18,25:4
Ely, Richard, 1937, S 13,21:5
Ely, Richard T, 1943, O 5,25:1
Ely, Robert A Mrs, 1945, O 5,23:2
Ely, Robert E, 1948, Jl 14,23:1
Ely, Robert G, 1954, F 22,19:3
Ely, Sarah B Mrs, 1945, N 10,15:5
Ely, Sarah Y, 1937, Je 5,17:1
Ely, Sims, 1954, N 12,21:2
Ely, Smith, 1884, Jl 29,5:3; 1911, Jl 2,9:4
Ely, Sterling, 1961, S 18,29:2
Ely, Theodore N, 1916, O 30,9:2
Ely, Valentine A Mrs, 1948, D 5,92:3
Ely, Van Horn, 1937, D 20,27:3
Ely, W M, 1872, F 7,3:5
Ely, Wilbert B, 1963, Ap 14,92:7
Ely, William, 1949, Je 1,31:5
Ely, William A H, 1943, O 17,48:3
Ely, William Caryl, 1921, D 15,19:6
Ely, William Davis, 1908, Je 12,7:6
Ely, William G Gen, 1906, N 15,9:6
Ely, William H J, 1942, Mr 3,23:4
Ely, William Mrs, 1882, My 8,5:2
Ely, William N, 1942, S 8,23:4
Ely, Wilson C, 1959, Ag 29,17:6
Elyashiv, Shmuel, 1955, Je 21,31:4
Elyea, Dayton M, 1941, Ag 21,17:2
Elzas, Samuel L, 1944, Je 2,15:5
Elzear, Alfred Bro, 1957, S 26,25:2
Elzear Stephen, Bro, 1937, N 29,23:5
Elzy, Ruby, 1943, Je 28,21:4

Emans, Cordelia Mrs, 1921, Ap 21,13:5
Emans, Frederic C, 1950, Ag 19,13:2
Emanuel, Andrew J, 1942, N 8,53:1
Emanuel, Ernest Sayre, 1916, N 15,11:5
Emanuel, John H, 1943, D 28,18:3
Emanuel, Victor, 1960, N 27,87:1
Emanuel, Victor E, 1960, Ap 7,35:4
Emanuel, Victor J, 1937, Ag 15,II,7:3
Emanuel, Walter Lewis, 1915, Ag 6,9:6
Emanuele, Louis, 1952, Mr 29,15:2
Emanuele, Louis Mrs, 1962, My 29,31:5
Emanueli, Luigi, 1959, F 18,33:3
Emard, G Adelbert, 1939, Ag 4,13:4
Ember, A Dr, 1926, Je 2,13:2
Ember, Fernando, 1948, D 1,30:3
Ember, Oscar, 1953, My 22,27:1
Emberson, James W, 1955, Ja 20,31:5
Embery, Joseph R, 1938, N 26,15:1
Embick, F E Col, 1913, S 12,11:4
Embick, Frank F, 1957, Ap 7,88:2
Embler, Albert S, 1941, Ja 26,38:4
Embler, Elizabeth D, 1944, N 30,23:5
Embler, Frank H Mrs, 1949, O 19,29:5
Embler, Wilfred D, 1938, Je 13,19:3
Embleton, Clifford B, 1946, Ap 17,25:5
Emblidge, William R, 1960, Ja 6,35:3
Embly, Thomas W Dr, 1914, Je 30,11:5
Embody, George C, 1939, F 18,15:3
Embree, Claire, 1950, D 23,16:6
Embree, Edwin R, 1950, F 22,29:1
Embree, Harry S, 1954, F 17,31:3
Embree, Ida C Mrs, 1940, D 19,25:1
Embree, John F, 1950, D 23,16:6
Embree, John G, 1921, Je 29,15:3
Embree, William D, 1966, Ap 9,25:5
Embree, William D Mrs, 1962, My 18,31:4
Embres, George W, 1873, S 23,8:1
Embry, Cecil J, 1949, D 19,27:4
Embry, William C, 1959, My 5,33:3
Embury, Augustus, 1943, Mr 17,21:4
Embury, Aymar 2d, 1966, N 15,47:1
Embury, David A, 1960, Jl 8,21:1
Embury, Peter A, 1947, O 26,68:4
Embury, William C, 1943, Je 14,17:4
Emde, Henry C, 1944, Jl 31,13:3
Emden, Frank A, 1954, My 24,27:3
Emden, Fred F, 1947, Ja 8,23:1
Emder, Charles H, 1949, D 31,15:2
Emele, Charles, 1941, Ja 17,36:4
Emely, Walter W, 1959, D 18,29:2
Emens, Henry C, 1952, Je 14,15:6
Emens, Olin E, 1952, My 12,25:4
Emeny, Frank, 1945, O 26,19:2
Emerentia, Mother, 1945, Mr 25,37:1
Emerich, George, 1940, N 25,17:2
Emerich, Leroy E, 1955, My 6,23:2
Emerich, Martin, 1922, S 28,21:4
Emerich, Melvin L, 1943, O 24,44:6
Emerick, Besse, 1939, D 14,27:2
Emerick, Edison J, 1951, F 28,27:4
Emerick, Frederick A, 1946, Mr 22,21:2
Emerick, Harry M, 1938, S 5,15:2
Emerick, John P, 1941, Ag 12,19:7
Emerick, Joseph M, 1948, Ag 14,13:4
Emerling, John J (B Becker), 1954, N 27,13:4
Emerman, Joseph S, 1949, Jl 10,57:1
Emerson, Albert L (will), 1963, Ag 23,27:7
Emerson, Alfred, 1943, O 20,21:1
Emerson, Alfred E Mrs, 1949, S 14,31:5
Emerson, Alfred H, 1947, S 10,27:2
Emerson, B K, 1932, Ap 8,21:3
Emerson, Billy, 1902, F 24,3:4
Emerson, Calvin G, 1957, Ap 17,31:4
Emerson, Carolyn, 1940, D 31,15:4
Emerson, Charles, 1962, F 16,29:2
Emerson, Charles A, 1939, F 7,20:1; 1955, Ag 26,19:2
Emerson, Charles E, 1945, N 9,19:2
Emerson, Charles F Mrs, 1944, Ag 13,35:1
Emerson, Charles Franklin, 1922, D 2,13:4
Emerson, Charles H, 1942, Jl 5,29:3
Emerson, Charles P, 1938, S 28,25:4
Emerson, Cherry L, 1959, O 28,37:4
Emerson, Clay F, 1943, My 12,25:2
Emerson, E C, 1951, O 5,27:3
Emerson, Edgar C Ex-Justice, 1923, D 15,13:3
Emerson, Edward, 1949, My 20,27:2; 1953, N 27,27:2; 1957, O 31,31:2
Emerson, Edward H, 1958, F 27,27:1
Emerson, Edward Randolph, 1925, Ja 4,7:1
Emerson, Edwin, 1959, O 7,43:5
Emerson, Edwin Prof, 1908, N 6,7:3
Emerson, Eileen, 1960, Je 6,29:6
Emerson, Ernest B Sr, 1960, F 7,84:3
Emerson, Fay O Mrs, 1949, Ja 11,31:1
Emerson, Frances W Mrs, 1957, Mr 11,25:2
Emerson, Francis P, 1944, Ja 22,13:6
Emerson, Frank Mrs, 1957, D 6,29:3
Emerson, Frank O, 1952, Jl 4,13:6
Emerson, Frank O Mrs, 1941, Ag 13,17:5
Emerson, Fred L, 1948, S 12,72:3
Emerson, G B, 1881, Mr 6,2:2
Emerson, George B, 1950, Ag 1,23:1
Emerson, George H, 1950, Ja 14,15:3; 1955, O 25,33:2
Emerson, George T, 1952, S 11,31:2
Emerson, George W, 1941, O 15,21:2
Emerson, George W Mrs (Susan), 1965, My 4,43:4
Emerson, Gilbert G, 1962, Ja 3,33:1
Emerson, Guy C, 1942, Jl 4,17:5
Emerson, Gwendolyn T Mrs, 1954, D 20,29:5
Emerson, Harold S, 1951, Jl 7,13:3
Emerson, Haven (trb lr, My 25,20:6; funl, My 25,-21:6), 1957, My 22,33:3
Emerson, Haven Mrs, 1960, Ag 1,23:4
Emerson, Herbert W, 1947, Je 24,23:5; 1962, Ap 14, 25:3
Emerson, Hope, 1960, Ag 26,37:1
Emerson, Howard F, 1947, Ja 3,22:3
Emerson, I E, 1931, Ja 24,17:1
Emerson, Isaac E Mrs, 1946, My 6,21:3
Emerson, J B Dr, 1934, Jl 25,17:6
Emerson, James A Ex-Sen, 1922, F 3,15:4
Emerson, James Jr, 1947, Jl 24,21:5
Emerson, James Mrs, 1949, S 24,13:3
Emerson, Jay N, 1947, Je 13,24:2
Emerson, John, 1956, Mr 9,23:1
Emerson, Josephine, 1964, N 24,39:2
Emerson, Julia T, 1962, S 29,23:6
Emerson, Justin V Mrs, 1950, Ja 24,31:3
Emerson, Kendall Sr, 1962, F 6,35:1
Emerson, L Eugene, 1939, D 18,23:2
Emerson, Leah Mrs, 1961, D 13,43:1
Emerson, Linn, 1951, Ap 18,31:2
Emerson, Louis Woodward, 1924, Je 11,21:5
Emerson, Lowell, 1950, Ja 28,13:3
Emerson, Luther Orlando, 1915, S 30,11:7
Emerson, Margaret C, 1948, S 9,27:6
Emerson, Margaret Mrs (will, Ja 9,43:2), 1960, Ja 3, 88:6
Emerson, Merton J, 1940, Jl 26,17:6
Emerson, Morton L, 1945, F 10,11:5
Emerson, R W, 1882, Ap 28,1:5
Emerson, Ralph, 1914, Ag 20,11:7
Emerson, Ralph W, 1942, Ja 12,15:3; 1946, D 10,31:4; 1956, Mr 23,28:2
Emerson, Robert A, 1966, Mr 15,39:1
Emerson, Robert S, 1937, Ja 24,II,8:2
Emerson, Rollins A, 1947, D 9,33:6
Emerson, Samuel F, 1939, Ap 8,23:8; 1940, N 10,57:2
Emerson, Sara A, 1939, N 4,15:6
Emerson, Sigurd A, 1947, S 11,27:3
Emerson, T M, 1913, N 26,11:5
Emerson, Victor F, 1961, My 20,23:5
Emerson, Victor F Mrs, 1957, F 12,27:5
Emerson, Victor L, 1941, My 7,25:3
Emerson, W Austin, 1966, Jl 21,33:4
Emerson, W W, 1939, Mr 25,15:3
Emerson, Walter H, 1947, Ag 20,21:5
Emerson, Wilbur T, 1962, Ag 21,33:3
Emerson, Willard I, 1966, D 4,88:4
Emerson, William, 1951, Ja 16,29:2; 1957, My 5,89:2
Emerson, William B Mrs, 1952, O 21,29:4
Emerson, William Capt (Bing), 1968, N 27,47:4
Emerson, William R P, 1951, S 6,31:1
Emerson, William Sir, 1924, D 30,17:5
Emerton, Albert, 1948, Mr 10,28:2
Emerton, Phillip W, 1950, O 9,25:3
Emery, A H, 1926, D 3,23:5
Emery, A Hamilton Jr Mrs, 1964, Jl 28,29:4
Emery, Albert C Sr, 1957, Je 29,17:4
Emery, Albert H, 1945, D 13,29:2
Emery, Ald D, 1923, D 10,17:3
Emery, Allan C, 1952, D 19,31:3
Emery, Allan C Mrs, 1963, S 13,29:2
Emery, Ambrose R, 1945, D 1,23:5
Emery, Annie M, 1939, Ap 19,23:2
Emery, Asher B Justice, 1924, Ag 12,11:3
Emery, Charles Goodwin, 1915, Ja 16,9:4
Emery, Charles H, 1950, D 10,105:1
Emery, E Van Norman, 1953, Mr 10,29:4
Emery, Earle C, 1946, N 2,15:6
Emery, Edward, 1938, My 8,II,6:6
Emery, Edward K Justice, 1919, N 13,13:2
Emery, Edward Mrs, 1950, Ja 11,23:5
Emery, Edwin T, 1951, Je 26,29:2
Emery, Edwin W, 1939, Ap 1,19:4
Emery, Ernest William, 1914, Mr 30,9:5
Emery, F L, 1933, F 17,19:5
Emery, Fred A, 1962, Mr 23,33:3
Emery, Frederick W, 1943, Ja 2,11:1
Emery, George M, 1944, N 19,50:1
Emery, George W Mrs, 1948, Ap 25,68:3
Emery, Grover C, 1967, Je 3,31:3
Emery, Henry Crosby Dr, 1924, F 7,17:4
Emery, Henry G, 1956, My 2,31:6
Emery, Hiram W, 1962, My 20,87:2
Emery, Howard, 1941, D 31,17:2
Emery, Ira D, 1958, N 5,39:3
Emery, Jacob, 1943, S 15,27:4
Emery, James A, 1943, F 24,22:2; 1955, S 29,33:2
Emery, James A Mrs, 1951, F 10,13:3
Emery, James H, 1952, My 24,19:4; 1957, N 23,19:1
Emery, Jo Tuttle, 1960, N 15,39:2
Emery, John H, 1947, Ag 25,17:5
Emery, John J, 1908, S 6,9:2
Emery, John M, 1952, Je 12,33:4; 1959, F 2,25:3
Emery, John M Mrs, 1954, F 1,23:2
Emery, John R, 1916, Ja 31,11:4; 1925, S 24,25:5
Emery, John W, 1954, S 14,27:1
Emery, Joseph H, 1941, Mr 3,15:1
Emery, Joseph H Mrs, 1939, O 22,40:7
Emery, Julia C, 1922, Ja 11,21:3
Emery, Katie Putnam Mrs, 1924, My 11,7:1
Emery, Lewis, 1941, N 10,17:6
Emery, Louis Jr, 1924, N 20,23:5
Emery, Manning, 1941, D 7,77:2
Emery, Quincy P, 1944, Jl 21,19:2
Emery, R Edson, 1949, D 30,20:4
Emery, Ralph C, 1943, My 10,19:5
Emery, Raymond G, 1963, Ap 24,35:4
Emery, S A, 1881, Jl 20,5:4
Emery, Theodore, 1939, Ja 1,25:3
Emery, Thomas J, 1906, Ja 17,11:5
Emery, Walter, 1956, Mr 28,31:5
Emery, William C, 1949, Ag 22,21:1
Emery, William M, 1951, Ap 21,17:5
Emery, Z Taylor Dr, 1924, O 8,19:4
Emes, Edward L, 1954, Ap 23,27:3
Emes, William H, 1950, S 22,31:3
Emett, Edward H, 1949, N 1,28:3
Emhardt, William H, 1951, S 23,86:4
Emich, John P Sr, 1944, Mr 23,19:3
Emiet, Cuno, 1961, Jl 19,29:5
Emig, Charles H, 1944, O 7,13:3
Emig, John, 1947, Jl 14,21:5
Emig, Laurence W C Jr, 1950, N 25,13:6
Emigh, William, 1942, Ag 15,11:4
Emilian, Philip Bro, 1957, N 5,31:5
Emin Pasha, 1892, Je 9,8:3
Emison, John C, 1966, Mr 18,39:1
Emlen, John T, 1955, F 11,23:2
Emlen, Samuel 3d, 1966, Ja 12,21:3
Emley, Jay N, 1939, Ja 2,24:2
Emley, Warren E, 1951, Je 6,31:2
Emley, William S, 1946, Mr 9,13:1
Emly, William S Mrs, 1938, S 23,27:3
Emma, Dowager Queen of the Netherlands, 1934, Mr 20,23:1
Emma, Edwin, 1960, N 27,86:5
Emma, Queen Dowager of Sandwich Islands, 188[illegible] My 9,4:6
Emmans, James M, 1942, Jl 30,21:3
Emmanuel, John T, 1966, Ag 25,15:1
Emmanuelli, Felix, 1943, O 22,17:4
Emmel, Randolph, 1946, Ap 19,29:5
Emmeluth, David L, 1950, F 1,29:3
Emmeluth, William W, 1952, Ag 8,17:4
Emmens, Samuel Franklin, 1911, Mr 29,13:5
Emmerich, Charles, 1946, Ja 29,27:6
Emmerich, Hugo, 1961, S 27,41:2
Emmerich, Hugo Mrs, 1963, S 9,27:2
Emmerich, Robert, 1948, N 24,23:6
Emmerich, Rudolf Dr, 1914, N 19,11:7
Emmerson, Henry Robert, 1914, Jl 10,9:4
Emmerson, Louis L, 1941, F 5,20:2
Emmert, Allen R, 1961, Je 15,43:4
Emmert, Fred L Sen, 1937, Jl 12,17:3
Emmert, William B, 1937, N 26,21:1
Emmert, William H, 1945, Ja 8,17:5
Emmerton, C O, 1942, Mr 18,23:2
Emmet, Augustus S, 1952, N 1,21:6
Emmet, Bache M Mrs, 1946, O 15,25:2
Emmet, C Temple, 1957, Jl 25,23:1
Emmet, Cyril William Rev Dr, 1923, Jl 23,13:3
Emmet, Daniel Mrs, 1943, Jl 24,13:2
Emmet, Devereux Mrs, 1943, Je 4,21:1
Emmet, Grenville T, 1937, S 27,1:7
Emmet, Henry C, 1943, F 15,15:2
Emmet, Henry Coster, 1923, Jl 14,11:4
Emmet, J K, 1891, Je 16,2:3
Emmet, Katherine (Mrs A Bement), 1960, Je
Emmet, Lydia F, 1952, Ag 18,17:1
Emmet, Lydia Hubley, 1912, F 15,11:4
Emmet, Margaret (funl), 1883, Mr 4,14:4
Emmet, Patricia, 1959, Ap 14,2:4
Emmet, R S, 1902, N 24,9:5
Emmet, Robert, 1873, F 16,8:5
Emmet, Robert Jr, 1915, N 3,13:6
Emmet, Robert Mrs, 1954, D 15,31:2
Emmet, Robert Temple Mrs, 1920, F 28,11:4
Emmet, Thomas A, 1950, O 6,27:3
Emmet, Thomas Addis Dr, 1919, Mr 2,21:1
Emmet, Watson C, 1940, D 25,27:3
Emmet, William J, 1905, D 23,7:5
Emmet, William J Mrs, 1908, S 27,11:6
Emmet, William L, 1941, S 27,17:1
Emmet, William T Mrs, 1958, Ja 13,29:1
Emmet, William Temple, 1918, F 5,13:5
Emmett, Arthur D, 1947, Je 12,25:3
Emmett, Dan, 1904, Je 30,9:7
Emmett, Gracie, 1940, Je 11,23:6
Emmett, T S, 1880, Ja 15,5:4
Emminger, Erich, 1951, S 2,48:6
Emmitt, J Charles Mrs, 1914, N 26,13:4
Emmons, Abraham S, 1953, N 15,89:2
Emmons, Ann E Mrs, 1958, Mr 4,29:1
Emmons, Arthur B Mrs, 1956, My 2,31:4
Emmons, Arthur B 3d, 1962, Ag 23,29:2
Emmons, B Frank, 1938, N 27,49:1
Emmons, C D, 1933, F 3,17:3

Emmons, Carlton D, 1937, D 31,15:4
Emmons, Charlotte S Mrs, 1956, Ap 1,88:4
Emmons, D W Col, 1905, Ap 20,9:7
Emmons, Delos C (Oct 5), 1965, O 11,61:2
Emmons, Evelyn Mrs, 1938, F 16,21:1
Emmons, Frank R, 1944, F 1,19:1
Emmons, G F Rear Adm, 1884, Jl 24,5:3
Emmons, George D, 1952, Mr 5,29:3
Emmons, George E, 1938, Jl 4,13:5
Emmons, George Foster Rear-Adm, 1908, Mr 22,9:6
Emmons, Grover C, 1944, Ap 15,11:2
Emmons, H H, 1877, My 15,4:7
Emmons, Henry M, 1953, Ja 20,25:2
Emmons, Howard M, 1949, Mr 13,76:3
Emmons, J A Capt, 1878, Jl 6,5:3
Emmons, J Greg, 1940, Ja 11,23:6
Emmons, Kintzing P, 1946, Mr 22,21:2
Emmons, Laura S Mrs, 1948, My 14,23:1
Emmons, Leon, 1958, Ag 30,15:4
Emmons, Lloyd C, 1957, D 10,35:4
Emmons, R W 2d, 1928, Ap 19,25:3
Emmons, Ralph, 1948, Ag 30,18:2
Emmons, Robert Van B (will), 1963, Jl 11,59:1
Emmons, Robert W, 1953, S 22,31:3
Emmons, Roger B, 1954, Mr 25,29:5
Emmons, Walter R Jr, 1957, Ap 29,25:2
Emmons, William T, 1958, My 12,29:5
Emmons, Winfield S, 1950, Ag 2,25:4
Emmott, George Henry, 1916, Mr 11,11:4
Emmott, John Mrs, 1947, Ja 5,53:3
Emonts, Josef F, 1964, Ja 27,23:4
Emory, Burton E, 1941, Jl 21,15:6
Emory, Frederick, 1908, S 22,9:6
Emory, George B Dr, 1937, Ja 15,21:3
Emory, Lloyd S, 1961, Mr 31,27:4
Emory, Orion L, 1952, O 22,27:5
Emory, Percy F Mrs, 1958, Mr 19,31:1
Emory, Robert J, 1940, N 3,56:5
Emory, Samuel T Mrs, 1953, N 24,28:2
Emory, W H Brig Gen, 1887, D 3,4:7
Emory, William Hemsley Rear-Adm, 1917, Jl 16,9:5
Emott, James, 1884, S 12,2:4
Empain, Jean, 1946, F 12,28:2
Empey, Arthur G, 1963, F 27,16:1
Empey, William C, 1954, Ja 27,27:4
Empol, Paul, 1953, Je 27,15:3
Empsall, George H, 1951, D 4,33:1
Emra, Frederick H, 1939, Ap 12,24:3
Emrey, Fred C, 1957, D 20,27:2
Emrey, G Carroll, 1952, O 5,89:2
Emrich, August, 1945, Ap 29,37:1
Emrich, Gustav C, 1943, Ap 6,21:5
Emrich, Louise P Mrs, 1941, Je 17,21:5
Emrich, Richard S Mrs, 1946, My 19,42:3
Emrick, Frederick C, 1948, Ag 11,21:1
Emrick, Melvin, 1958, Jl 2,29:3
Emrick, Robert G, 1955, Ag 7,73:3
Emslie, Robert D, 1943, Ap 27,23:5
Emspak, Julius, 1962, Ap 27,35:2
Emstein, David L, 1909, My 26,9:6
Emswiller, John E, 1940, S 25,27:2
Emy, Sabro, 1958, My 22,29:4
Enami, Masashi, 1958, My 24,8:1
Enander, Fred C, 1948, D 23,19:4
Enander, J J, 1928, D 19,27:6
Enard, Hans E Mrs, 1953, Ap 17,26:4
Enauli, E, 1883, Ag 23,5:7
Enberg, E Russell, 1946, D 5,31:1
Enciso, Philip, 1963, My 10,34:1
Encke, Edith Mrs, 1949, Ja 11,31:4
Encombe, Lady Mary, 1946, D 4,31:4
Endalkatchew, Bitwoded M, 1963, Mr 1,4:6
Endana, Carlos, 1955, S 3,15:7
Ende, Herwegh von Mrs, 1945, F 5,15:3
Endel, Charles W, 1948, My 27,25:2
Endel, Jacob W, 1937, O 2,21:5
Endel, Walter, 1955, F 27,86:2
Endelman, Edward, 1959, My 2,23:5
Endemann, Herman K, 1947, N 5,27:5
Endemann, Hermann Dr, 1909, O 10,13:4
Ender, Otto, 1960, Jl 9,19:4
Enderby, Thomas R, 1939, My 30,17:2
Enderle, A B, 1954, Ag 1,84:3
Enderle, Joseph C, 1959, Jl 24,25:4
Enderle, Max, 1937, My 12,23:3
Enderlin, John G Mrs, 1960, Ja 1,19:3
Enderly, Clifford T, 1958, Ja 7,47:4
Enderly, M B, 1943, D 31,16:5
Enderly, Pearl E Mrs (P Eaton), 1958, S 16,27:2
Enders, Frederick, 1960, Ja 7,29:2
Enders, George W, 1946, O 12,19:5
Enders, Harry H, 1960, Ja 22,27:3
Enders, Harvey T, 1947, Ja 13,21:5
Enders, Henry C, 1948, Ap 2,24:2
Enders, John G Mrs, 1958, S 18,31:4
Enders, John O, 1958, Ap 3,31:2
Enders, Louis, 1952, Jl 23,23:5
Enders, Margaret E, 1951, D 10,29:4
Enders, Thomas B, 1943, Ja 27,21:1
Endersbe, Tracy M, 1966, S 4,64:6
Endersbee, William J, 1962, My 10,37:3
Endfield, Benjamin, 1953, O 7,29:2
Endicott, Allen B Ex-Judge, 1920, N 4,13:3

Endicott, Allen B Jr, 1954, Je 4,23:5
Endicott, Carl E, 1949, O 16,88:2
Endicott, Catherine B, 1925, My 22,19:6
Endicott, George Mrs, 1945, Ap 26,23:2
Endicott, Harry F, 1953, My 14,29:4
Endicott, Henry, 1912, D 15,17:4
Endicott, Henry B, 1920, F 13,11:4
Endicott, Henry W, 1954, Ag 21,29:1
Endicott, James, 1944, Ja 1,13:4
Endicott, James G, 1954, Mr 10,25:2
Endicott, John, 1955, F 8,27:2
Endicott, Mordecai T Mrs, 1955, F 23,27:4
Endicott, Smith H, 1951, N 16,25:5
Endicott, Thomas P, 1947, My 21,25:4
Endicott, Willard N, 1944, Je 8,21:4
Endicott, William, 1941, Ag 26,19:1
Endle, William A, 1949, O 10,23:2
Endler, Aaron D, 1961, Je 30,27:3
Endler, Frank G, 1952, Ag 11,15:5
Endler, Jack, 1954, My 27,27:4
Endler, John J, 1957, O 2,33:2
Endler, Joseph A, 1968, F 15,43:3
Endler, Joseph A Jr, 1944, O 31,19:5
Endler, Jules, 1954, S 23,33:1
Endler, Julian, 1959, S 26,23:3
Endler, Max, 1947, Ja 8,24:3
Endlich, Rubin, 1948, O 21,27:4
Endlich, William M, 1954, F 2,27:1
Endly, W C, 1948, Mr 27,13:2
Endor, Chick, 1941, S 2,17:2
Endres, Alice, 1937, Ag 21,15:4
Endres, Emma Mrs, 1941, Je 25,21:4
Endres, Hubert, 1948, F 2,19:3
Endres, Hugo J, 1955, N 29,29:5
Endres, William A, 1940, Ja 10,21:4
Endress, Frank, 1945, Je 25,17:4
Endress, Fred J, 1942, Jl 10,17:3
Endress, William F Capt, 1915, S 9,11:5
Endrey, Eugene, 1967, Je 27,39:2
Endrich, Felix, 1953, F 1,V,1:2
Endriss, Harry T, 1943, Ja 3,42:5
Endriunas, Vincent, 1964, My 21,35:1
Endrodi, Bela, 1956, My 24,31:3
Endrodi, Cornelius, 1958, O 4,21:1
Ends, Ehrich Marquand, 1918, Mr 22,13:4
Endsley, Harry S Mrs, 1953, S 4,34:2
Endweiss, Jules A, 1944, Ap 21,19:3
Endzweig, Hyman, 1956, D 5,39:5
Ene, Constantin, 1954, My 30,45:2
Enelow, H G, 1934, F 7,19:1
Enequist, John T, 1957, Je 17,23:1
Enequist, William L, 1956, Jl 27,21:6
Enery, Francis L, 1941, S 2,17:1
Enes, Albert W, 1956, Ap 21,17:4
Enesco, Georges, 1955, My 5,33:1
Enestrom, Edgar C A, 1952, N 27,31:1
Eneu, Joseph A, 1947, Ja 26,53:4
Enfield, William L, 1945, Mr 23,19:3
Engalitcheff, Ivan Prince, 1937, O 8,23:5
Engalitcheff, Suzanne B Mrs, 1942, Ag 5,19:5
Engalitcheff, Vladimir N Prince, 1923, Mr 8,17:4
Engart, Charles I, 1960, N 13,88:8
Engberg, A Gov, 1944, Mr 28,19:3
Engbers, John N, 1945, Ap 18,23:5
Engdahl, J L, 1932, N 23,19:3
Enge, Charles G, 1957, My 11,21:3
Engebreth, Gunnard, 1951, Jl 16,21:6
Engel, Adam, 1925, S 2,23:5
Engel, Adam Mrs, 1952, Jl 17,23:4
Engel, Albert, 1954, My 12,31:1
Engel, Albert G, 1952, O 26,88:5
Engel, Albert J, 1959, D 4,31:1
Engel, Alex Mrs, 1951, Je 6,31:3
Engel, Arnold W, 1958, F 22,17:1
Engel, Benjamin, 1956, F 4,19:6
Engel, Bernard Mrs, 1953, O 29,31:4
Engel, Carl, 1944, My 7,45:1
Engel, Charles W Mrs, 1958, S 4,29:5
Engel, Conrad, 1937, S 22,27:5
Engel, Edward F, 1949, F 16,25:2
Engel, Edward J, 1947, Mr 31,23:5
Engel, Edward Mrs, 1943, Mr 5,17:4
Engel, Emma H, 1942, Ag 14,17:2
Engel, Ernest, 1942, Ja 19,17:3
Engel, F Roy, 1968, Je 25,41:3
Engel, Francis X, 1940, S 18,23:2
Engel, Francis X Mrs, 1938, Ag 28,33:4
Engel, Frederick, 1941, Ag 7,17:3
Engel, Fritz F, 1956, N 24,19:3
Engel, Gabriel, 1952, Ag 3,61:1
Engel, George J, 1956, Ap 25,35:3
Engel, Harry M, 1951, Ap 13,23:5
Engel, Henry L, 1949, O 23,84:2
Engel, Herbert D, 1957, Jl 20,15:6
Engel, Herman, 1945, Je 1,15:5
Engel, Howard, 1960, My 2,29:2
Engel, Irving M Mrs, 1957, Mr 31,88:3
Engel, Jacob S, 1946, Mr 19,28:2
Engel, John J, 1957, My 11,21:5
Engel, Joseph, 1937, D 11,19:3; 1940, N 25,17:3; 1950, N 10,27:1
Engel, Joseph F, 1941, Jl 28,13:4
Engel, Joseph W, 1943, Ap 20,24:2

Engel, Katie Mrs, 1937, D 29,22:1
Engel, Kurt, 1942, Ja 23,19:5
Engel, Landolin, 1942, Ag 23,44:1
Engel, Lawrence J, 1956, My 25,23:5
Engel, Leonard, 1964, D 9,47:3
Engel, Leonard Mrs, 1960, F 26,27:1
Engel, Martin (funl, Jl 18,15:6), 1915, Jl 16,9:5
Engel, Maurice K, 1943, Je 21,17:5
Engel, Max Mrs, 1962, S 30,86:3
Engel, Meir, 1964, D 17,41:2
Engel, Minnie Mrs, 1949, S 8,29:5
Engel, Mose, 1941, Ja 22,21:2
Engel, Nicholas (por), 1938, O 12,27:5
Engel, Orlando Mrs, 1950, Ja 15,84:2
Engel, Orlando P, 1949, Je 21,25:5
Engel, Paul J, 1953, O 24,15:6
Engel, Paul J Mrs, 1948, Je 7,19:4
Engel, Peter, 1921, N 29,17:3; 1950, Jl 21,19:3
Engel, Phil, 1950, Ap 10,19:4
Engel, Sigmund, 1956, Ag 2,48:2
Engel, Solton, 1961, Ag 29,31:2
Engel, Walter, 1966, Ap 23,31:6
Engel, Walter F, 1945, O 1,19:4
Engel, Walter R, 1958, D 29,15:4
Engel, William, 1953, Ja 1,23:2
Engel, William H, 1944, Ap 30,46:1
Engel, William M, 1942, O 4,52:1
Engel, William Sr, 1961, Jl 9,77:1
Engelberg, Osias, 1941, F 10,17:2
Engelberger, William V, 1955, Ag 13,13:1
Engelbert, Paul C, 1946, Ag 10,13:2
Engelberth, Jeno, 1943, F 3,19:3
Engelberth, William F Sr, 1947, Ja 10,21:3
Engelbrecht, Curt E, 1957, Ja 9,31:2
Engelbrecht, Helmuth C, 1939, O 10,23:4
Engelbrechten, Max von, 1957, F 15,9:1
Engeldrum, Paul W, 1952, N 8,17:5
Engelen, William J Rev, 1937, Ap 25,II,9:1
Engelhard, Charles, 1950, D 2,13:5
Engelhard, George H, 1945, O 24,21:4
Engelhard, George P, 1968, Mr 30,33:2
Engelhard, John C, 1951, Jl 6,23:1
Engelhard, Max, 1962, My 16,41:3
Engelhardt, Charles A, 1948, Ag 26,21:2
Engelhardt, Charles P, 1952, Ag 7,21:4
Engelhardt, Fred, 1944, F 4,15:4
Engelhardt, George P, 1942, My 25,15:6
Engelhardt, George P Mrs, 1956, Ja 4,27:2
Engelhardt, Henry, 1952, O 3,23:3
Engelhardt, Konrad, 1945, Ag 30,21:5
Engelhardt, Nickolaus L, 1960, F 25,29:4
Engelhardt, Phil, 1948, S 24,25:4
Engelhardt, Theobald H, 1964, O 23,39:1
Engelhardt, William L, 1953, Mr 31,31:4
Engelhart, J A, 1879, F 16,6:7
Engelhorn, John Jr, 1944, Ap 19,23:1
Engelke, Charles B, 1967, Jl 20,37:3
Engelke, Edwin P, 1947, N 8,17:6
Engelke, Frederick E, 1968, Mr 7,43:3
Engelken, Richard C, 1944, Ja 20,19:1
Engelman, Abraham J, 1955, Ap 12,21:3
Engelman, Bernard, 1950, F 8,27:5
Engelman, Charles, 1950, S 26,31:3
Engelman, David, 1962, My 21,33:4
Engelman, Louis R, 1955, Ag 11,21:3
Engelman, Morris, 1948, Je 5,15:3
Engelman, Nelson C, 1949, My 24,28:3
Engelman, William, 1948, D 9,34:2
Engelmann, Frederick W, 1949, O 22,17:6
Engelmann, George J Dr, 1903, N 17,9:6
Engeln, Henry P, 1944, F 9,19:5
Engels, Edward J, 1947, D 31,15:2
Engels, Georg, 1907, N 1,9:5
Engels, George, 1955, My 4,29:4
Engels, William, 1966, Jl 9,27:3
Engelsher, Charles L, 1964, Ag 26,39:2
Engelsher, David J, 1960, My 11,39:4
Engelson, Joseph E, 1946, Mr 18,21:4
Engelstaedter, Julius, 1963, O 27,88:3
Engelsted, Knud, 1954, D 18,15:3
Engeman, William A, 1884, Ja 12,5:3
Engeman Geo H, 1905, Ap 2,9:6
Engemann, John, 1940, Ag 9,15:2
Engen, Hans K, 1966, Ap 7,36:1
Enger, Melvin L, 1956, My 15,32:7
Engert, William K, 1944, Ag 14,15:4
Engert-Colman, Marie S Mrs (will), 1940, Mr 23,8:1
Engesser, Anna Mrs, 1952, N 26,23:4
Engesser, John, 1945, S 1,11:4
Enggren, Arthur D, 1944, Mr 9,17:1
Engisch, Rudolph R, 1944, Ja 30,38:5
Engisch, William, 1937, O 13,23:2
Engl, Josef B, 1942, Ap 9,19:4
England, Alma M Mrs, 1947, F 15,15:4
England, Arthur W Jr, 1949, Mr 24,27:1
England, Charles C S, 1956, D 29,15:3
England, Charles O, 1944, N 25,13:6
England, Clarence A, 1943, Ja 1,23:5
England, Daniel Sr, 1948, F 8,60:5
England, Elizabeth T, 1954, Ap 15,29:6
England, Emily E, 1937, Jl 10,15:2
England, G A, 1936, Je 28,II,8:8
England, George C, 1956, F 18,19:3

England, George S Sr, 1948, N 8,21:5
England, Herbert K, 1952, Jl 14,17:3
England, Herbert K Mrs, 1954, Je 11,23:2
England, I W, 1885, Ap 25,2:2
England, Isaac W, 1942, S 19,15:3
England, J W Capt, 1919, Ap 26,15:4
England, James H, 1950, Mr 21,32:2
England, James Mrs, 1946, Ja 21,23:4
England, John, 1951, D 16,90:4
England, John M, 1965, Je 4,35:4
England, Richard W, 1954, N 13,15:1
England, Robert D, 1954, Ag 8,24:5
England, Simon, 1948, Ap 15,25:4
England, Thomas N, 1943, Jl 24,13:7
England, William H, 1950, My 12,27:3
Englander, Alex J, 1942, N 14,15:3
Englander, Benjamin B, 1954, Mr 2,25:1
Englander, Charles, 1958, Jl 16,29:5
Englander, Henry, 1951, Ap 10,27:1
Englander, James, 1955, D 6,37:3
Englander, Louis, 1954, My 14,23:1; 1966, F 13,84:5
Englander, Louis B Mrs, 1951, Ap 11,29:4
Englander, Louis Mrs, 1951, Mr 18,88:3
Englander, Ludwig, 1914, S 14,9:6
Englander, Max, 1955, D 9,27:4
Englander, Moses, 1968, Ap 15,43:4
Englander, Oskar, 1937, Ja 5,23:3
Englander, Samuel, 1951, N 28,31:1
Englander, Simon, 1951, Mr 7,33:4
Englander, Simon J, 1942, S 6,31:1
Englar, D Roger, 1948, Ja 19,23:5
Englar, S Lee, 1953, Ja 20,25:2
Englar, W C Mrs, 1949, D 4,108:3
Engle, Bessie, 1966, Ap 8,31:4
Engle, Calvin P, 1948, N 10,29:1
Engle, Charles W, 1953, Mr 21,17:1
Engle, Clair, 1964, Jl 31,1:7
Engle, Clyde, 1939, D 27,21:5
Engle, David S, 1949, Ap 4,23:6
Engle, David S Mrs, 1951, D 1,13:6
Engle, Earl T, 1957, D 18,35:2
Engle, Elizabeth J Mrs, 1940, F 19,17:1
Engle, Frank R, 1962, Mr 31,25:4
Engle, Frederick, 1912, Ag 8,9:3
Engle, George, 1943, Ja 16,13:2
Engle, George E Mrs, 1951, F 7,29:1
Engle, George Mrs, 1944, S 12,19:4
Engle, Isaiah G, 1954, Mr 21,88:3
Engle, James L, 1939, My 16,23:3
Engle, Jesse A, 1962, F 15,29:5
Engle, Kenneth, 1956, S 27,35:4
Engle, Martha Mrs, 1944, Ja 31,17:4
Engle, Max, 1950, D 7,33:5
Engle, Morris, 1948, Jl 4,27:2
Engle, Moses, 1910, N 1,9:5
Engle, Rudolph A Mrs, 1958, Ja 13,29:4
Engle, Thomas L, 1950, Mr 17,23:3
Engle, Wallace L (funl), 1966, D 7,5:3
Engle, William C, 1955, D 2,27:1
Englebert, Nicholas J, 1940, N 14,23:1
Englebracht, Charles A, 1940, My 30,17:3
Englebright, Harry L, 1943, My 14,19:1
Englehardt, Charles, 1937, O 15,23:3
Englehardt, George H Mrs, 1952, D 23,23:1
Englehart, Helen, 1941, O 9,23:1
Englehart, Ray Mrs (J Harper), 1965, Ja 1,19:2
Englehart, Robert W, 1965, F 20,25:4
Engleheart, John Sir, 1923, Ap 12,19:5
Engleking, Fred, 1941, D 14,69:3
Engleman, James O, 1943, S 16,21:4
Engleman, Leonard, 1943, Ag 24,19:5
Engleman, Nathan D, 1946, O 10,27:4
Engleman, William P, 1938, O 6,23:2
Englemann, Helmute Mrs, 1954, Jl 4,31:2
Engler, Adolph W, 1909, D 16,9:5
Engler, Ervin W, 1942, O 7,25:5
Engler, Robert F, 1945, My 9,23:5
Englert, Casper, 1949, Ja 22,13:4
Englert, Chris, 1948, S 9,27:3
Englert, George M, 1957, Mr 27,31:6
Englert, John B, 1946, Ag 23,19:3
Englerth, Louis D, 1939, Ag 17,21:4
Englich, Robert B, 1952, N 29,17:2
Englis, John, 1915, Ap 3,9:6; 1953, Jl 9,25:3
Englis, John Mrs, 1914, N 2,9:5
Englisch, Ida P Mrs, 1948, F 11,27:3
English, Abraham L, 1913, Je 20,9:4
English, Allan J, 1946, Je 27,21:5
English, Arthur E, 1947, Jl 25,17:2
English, Benedict, 1955, F 16,29:3
English, Charles H, 1958, Jl 6,56:4
English, Charles R, 1956, N 12,29:4
English, Charles W, 1938, Ja 28,21:2
English, Chester F, 1950, My 30,17:2
English, Conover, 1963, Je 19,37:5
English, Crisp, 1949, Ag 27,13:4
English, David C Dr, 1924, S 20,15:6
English, Douglas L, 1953, Je 14,84:2
English, Earle W, 1966, O 13,45:5
English, Elsa G, 1955, F 11,23:4
English, Eugene M (will), 1940, Ag 23,12:5
English, Frank A, 1959, Ag 6,27:6; 1962, Mr 13,32:2
English, Frederick F, 1952, Ap 30,27:1
English, George, 1957, My 2,31:1
English, George L, 1944, Ja 7,17:3
English, Granville, 1968, S 4,44:4
English, Harold K, 1950, Ja 30,17:2
English, Harold M, 1953, Mr 5,27:4
English, Harry, 1939, Ap 4,25:5; 1951, Je 7,33:3
English, Harry Mrs, 1951, My 23,35:4; 1951, D 29, 11:5
English, Henry F, 1947, N 16,76:6
English, Ida M, 1939, Jl 2,15:2
English, J, 1884, Jl 26,2:3
English, J E, 1890, Mr 3,5:2
English, James, 1937, S 22,27:6
English, James F, 1907, Jl 21,7:6; 1947, Ag 4,17:4
English, James J, 1950, Ja 5,25:4
English, James R Dr, 1937, O 26,23:4
English, Jane P Mrs (Jane Verona), 1941, Jl 23,19:6
English, Jerry I, 1946, My 31,23:4
English, Jerry Mrs, 1955, My 19,29:4
English, Jesse W Mrs, 1938, Ap 4,17:5
English, John, 1960, Ja 4,29:4
English, John J, 1941, N 9,55:5
English, John S, 1950, Mr 21,29:3
English, John T, 1952, D 13,21:7
English, John U, 1940, Je 23,30:6
English, John W, 1955, Ja 1,13:2
English, Judith K Mrs, 1957, My 4,21:3
English, Kate M Mrs, 1949, Mr 8,25:5
English, Lewis H, 1941, F 4,22:2
English, Martha O, 1955, S 14,35:5
English, Martin J, 1958, Ag 9,13:5
English, Melvin L, 1946, D 11,32:3
English, Merle N, 1945, F 6,19:3
English, Mrs Gov, 1874, O 27,6:4
English, Nan T, 1949, S 26,25:1
English, Pennoyer F, 1958, O 9,37:3
English, Phil Jr, 1955, N 1,31:1
English, R E, 1950, D 25,19:5
English, Richard, 1957, O 4,23:2
English, Richard W A, 1964, Jl 25,19:5
English, S S, 1880, O 18,2:5
English, Samuel B, 1949, N 4,27:5
English, Sarah A Mrs, 1940, Je 5,25:4
English, T Dunn, 1902, Ap 2,9:5
English, Thomas, 1961, My 9,39:2
English, Thomas C, 1962, O 3,41:4
English, Thomas F, 1938, Mr 16,23:5; 1941, Ja 13, 15:6; 1955, N 4,30:2
English, Thomas J Sr, 1960, N 26,21:5
English, W D, 1903, Ag 15,7:6
English, W H, 1896, F 8,9:1
English, W M, 1934, Ap 30,15:1
English, Walter C, 1939, Ap 11,23:4
English, William H, 1942, Ap 5,41:1
English, William R, 1953, Mr 6,23:3
English, William T Dr, 1910, F 9,7:4
English Jack (Crawford Notch Hermit), 1912, Ap 30,11:5
Englund, Carl R, 1956, Jl 24,25:2
Engman, Martin F, 1953, O 14,29:2
Engs, Philip W, 1875, My 20,4:7
Engstrand, Stuart, 1955, S 10,36:5
Engstrom, Charles E, 1954, F 1,23:4
Engstrom, Ernest A, 1964, Je 23,33:4
Engstrom, Howard T, 1962, Mr 10,21:5
Engstrom, Malcolm C, 1959, Ap 6,27:3
Engstrom, Sigfrid E, 1955, Ap 30,17:5
Eninger, Joseph C, 1950, My 10,31:5
Enken, Leon, 1964, F 21,29:1
Enkler, Albert, 1942, Mr 10,19:1
Enlind, Knute A, 1941, N 19,23:2
Enloe, Benjamin Augustin Col, 1922, Jl 10,13:5
Enman, William, 1950, Jl 23,56:1
Enna, Aug, 1939, Ag 4,13:4
Enneking, John J, 1916, N 18,11:6
Enneking, Lawrence F Mrs, 1948, D 23,19:4
Enneking, Norbert B, 1952, O 25,17:3
Enners, Edward H Mrs, 1957, Ap 5,25:1
Ennever, William J, 1947, Ag 19,23:3
Enney, Elmer D Mrs, 1953, My 20,29:4
Ennis, Al, 1958, F 9,88:5
Ennis, Anne B, 1958, F 17,23:1
Ennis, Annie W D Mrs, 1938, O 8,17:6
Ennis, Arthur G, 1948, F 18,27:3
Ennis, Arthur I, 1954, S 3,17:3
Ennis, C Frank, 1960, My 3,39:4
Ennis, Charles T, 1940, Ap 12,23:3
Ennis, E Clyde, 1944, N 2,19:2
Ennis, Frank R, 1953, Ag 30,88:6
Ennis, G P, 1936, Ag 29,13:4
Ennis, George H, 1939, F 5,41:4
Ennis, Henry W, 1947, O 14,27:2
Ennis, James Lt, 1918, My 3,15:3
Ennis, jno, 1919, Ag 3,22:5
Ennis, John Y, 1942, Jl 6,15:3
Ennis, John Z, 1961, Je 30,27:1
Ennis, Joseph B, 1955, S 23,26:1
Ennis, Joseph B Mrs, 1942, D 2,25:1
Ennis, Lambert, 1954, D 24,13:5
Ennis, Lawrence, 1938, My 7,15:2
Ennis, Louis A, 1938, F 9,19:5
Ennis, Louis V, 1941, N 19,23:1
Ennis, Merlin W, 1964, Ag 22,21:3
Ennis, Merlin W Mrs, 1961, Je 10,23:6
Ennis, Perry, 1954, Ja 3,89:2
Ennis, Robert B, 1953, F 19,23:5
Ennis, Robert B Col, 1953, My 4,23:5
Ennis, Scott F, 1937, N 11,25:3
Ennis, Skinnay (Edgar C Jr), 1963, Je 4,39:3
Ennis, Thomas L, 1952, O 1,34:5
Ennis, Walter M, 1945, My 11,19:3
Ennis, William, 1938, O 1,17:6
Ennis, William D (por), 1947, O 15,27:1
Ennis, William J, 1952, S 23,33:3
Ennis, William J Rev, 1925, Je 11,19:4
Ennis, William Mrs, 1945, My 17,19:4
Enns, Nicholas F, 1949, Jl 31,61:2
Eno, Amos F, 1915, O 22,11:5
Eno, Amos R, 1898, F 22,1:3
Eno, Charles, 1956, Ja 29,92:8
Eno, Clara R Mrs, 1942, F 27,17:4
Eno, Harry W, 1947, Jl 15,23:2
Eno, Henry Clay Dr, 1914, Jl 17,9:6
Eno, John Chester Mrs, 1912, O 4,13:6
Eno, William P, 1945, D 4,29:3
Eno, William P (will), 1946, F 9,16:5
Enoch, Albert E, 1958, Je 9,23:5
Enoch, Edwin J Jr, 1954, Jl 16,21:1
Enoch, Jacob Mrs, 1952, Ap 21,21:5
Enochs, Herbert A, 1954, Ap 20,29:4
Enochs, J M, 1932, Ap 9,15:5
Enos, A F, 1903, Ag 19,9:6
Enos, Alanson T Jr, 1954, Ja 25,19:2
Enos, Copley, 1939, F 22,21:6
Enos, Frank Mrs, 1962, S 25,37:3
Enos, Laurens, 1944, F 2,21:3
Enos, Marjorie B, 1951, O 16,21:5
Enrica Paleni, Mother, 1943, Je 30,21:4
Enrich, Jules H, 1966, S 13,47:1
Enright, Cornelius J, 1957, Ja 4,23:3
Enright, David B S, 1957, O 18,23:1
Enright, Elizabeth (Mrs Robt Gillham), 1968, Je 45:4
Enright, Emma M Mrs, 1939, Ja 18,19:4
Enright, Frank J, 1942, Ag 23,43:3
Enright, James J, 1944, Mr 2,17:3
Enright, James W, 1941, Ja 19,40:5
Enright, John J (cor, O 2,25:1), 1941, O 1,21:4
Enright, Mary F, 1945, S 23,44:5
Enright, P E, 1941, Mr 20,21:4
Enright, Patrick Rev, 1917, Ap 12,11:4
Enright, Rex, 1960, Ap 7,35:5
Enright, Richard, 1880, D 21,2:3
Enright, Richard E, 1953, S 5,15:1
Enright, Richard E Mrs, 1939, Jl 27,19:5
Enright, Robert J, 1951, S 13,31:2
Enright, Timothy J, 1965, Jl 4,37:4
Enright, William F, 1949, S 18,94:5
Enright, William J, 1944, My 21,43:2
Enright, William K, 1961, F 28,33:4
Enriquez, Alberto, 1962, Jl 14,21:3
Ens, Jewel, 1950, Ja 18,31:2
Enscoe, John J, 1943, Ja 4,15:1
Enselberg, Herman L, 1951, Je 16,15:6
Enser, Edward, 1967, My 30,44:6
Enser, George, 1961, My 15,31:5
Ensey, James B, 1939, My 31,23:4
Ensher, Robert J, 1967, My 8,41:3
Ensign, Amos Merchant, 1909, F 4,9:4
Ensign, Donald, 1964, Ja 25,10:7
Ensign, E W, 1877, O 2,4:7
Ensign, Harry S, 1958, N 18,37:4
Ensign, Herbert Mrs, 1942, Ag 29,15:3
Ensign, Joseph R (will, Mr 25,17:4), 1941, Ja
Ensign, Joseph R Mrs, 1953, O 14,29:3
Ensign, W Grant, 1943, Je 25,17:2
Ensign, William B Mrs, 1945, D 6,27:2
Ensign, William H, 1947, D 2,29:3
Ensinger, Clifford S, 1957, Mr 20,37:2
Ensinger, William M, 1938, My 19,21:2
Enslow, Joseph A, 1937, O 28,25:3
Enslow, Linn H, 1957, N 6,35:3
Ensom, Alfred (G Wilson), 1954, Ag 4,21:3
Ensor, Buddy, 1947, N 15,30:1
Ensor, Issac, 1947, Jl 21,17:4
Ensor, James, 1942, D 19,19:3
Ensor, James (por), 1949, N 20,94:1
Ensor, W Percy A, 1960, Ap 23,23:5
Ensslen, Jack P, 1952, Jl 24,27:3
Enstrom, William N (will, Jl 31,15:4), 1957,
Enteen, Joel, 1959, F 27,25:1
Entenza, Antonio P, 1955, Ag 27,15:5
Enterline, G Dan, 1954, F 26,20:3
Entholt, Daniel, 1925, My 6,23:4
Enthoven, C H Mrs, 1950, Ag 19,13:6
Enthoven, Edward J, 1955, Je 14,29:2
Enthoven, Henri E, 1950, D 28,25:3
Entin, Moses, 1938, My 29,II,7:2
Entmacher, Charles, 1955, D 14,39:2
Entner, Abraham, 1947, Mr 5,25:4
Entratter, Jack Mrs, 1961, My 15,31:3
Entrekin, J O, 1937, S 12,II,6:5
Entriken, Lewis F, 1942, Je 20,13:5
Entriken, Samuel J, 1942, F 21,19:5
Entrikin, Knowles, 1956, D 23,30:5
Entrott, Winfield, 1940, Je 16,38:7

Entwisle, Edward F, 1947, Mr 10,21:3
Entwisle, Frank L, 1915, N 25,13:5
Entwisle, Thomas W, 1914, Je 24,11:5
Entwistle, Adolph R, 1956, O 10,39:5
Entwistle, Edward F Mrs, 1945, S 16,42:4
Entwistle, Frederick T, 1957, Ap 28,87:1
Entwistle, James Rear-Adm, 1910, Mr 24,9:5
Entwistle, Ralph, 1945, My 28,19:3
Entwistle, William J, 1952, Je 17,27:1
Enwright, Frederick W, 1964, Ap 26,88:7
Enz, John H, 1961, F 8,31:5
Enzian, Charles, 1948, D 8,31:3
Enzinger, George, 1959, Mr 17,33:2
Eoff, John R, 1940, Ag 19,17:5
Eolis, Alexander L, 1947, Mr 18,27:5
Eotvos, Baron, 1871, Mr 2,8:1
Epailly, Jules, 1967, My 1,37:2
Epailly, Jules Mrs, 1961, N 22,33:1
Epes, Horace, 1941, Je 20,21:4
Epes, Travis H, 1946, My 7,21:2
Epes, W Perry, 1962, F 4,82:2
Ephraim, Lee, 1953, S 27,86:1
Ephraim, Max, 1942, Ag 27,19:3
Ephrem, Bro, 1940, F 25,38:5
Ephrem Faber, Bro (M Cantwell), 1957, N 30,21:3
Epifanio, Dominic, 1947, Je 5,25:5
Epinger, Isaac, 1905, F 6,7:6
Epler, Curtis D, 1960, N 12,21:4
Epler, William F, 1942, Jl 24,19:5
Epp, Franz R von (por), 1947, F 9,61:2
Eppel, William R, 1951, Ap 20,30:6
Eppelsheimer, Frederick, 1955, Ag 2,23:1
Eppendorff, John G, 1941, S 26,23:1
Eppenstein, Louis A, 1939, O 25,23:4
Eppenstein, Sol C, 1938, Ap 19,22:2
Eppensteiner, William F, 1949, Mr 9,25:5
Epperlein, Paul W, 1959, S 6,73:2
Epperson, Albert W, 1955, Ag 16,49:3
Eppert, Carl, 1961, O 3,36:6
Eppes, Douglas S R, 1940, O 25,21:1
Eppes, Susan B Mrs, 1942, Jl 3,17:4
Eppig, Harry P, 1959, Ag 5,27:2
Eppig, Joseph, 1907, S 30,7:6
Eppig, Theodore C, 1917, Je 29,9:5
Eppig, Theodore C Mrs, 1955, Ja 16,92:5
Eppinger, Hans, 1946, S 29,62:4
Epple, Herman F Mrs, 1947, Ap 19,15:4
Epple, Louis C, 1945, Je 27,19:4
Epple, Rudolf L, 1952, Ap 12,11:5
Eppler, Alex, 1942, My 21,19:3
Eppler, John P, 1950, My 4,27:1
Eppler, Konrad, 1943, Jl 2,19:3
Eppler, William E, 1962, Jl 25,33:1
Eppley, Eugene C, 1958, O 15,39:2
Eppley, Francis M, 1913, O 18,13:4
Eppley, Marion, 1960, N 23,29:5
Eppley, Marion Mrs, 1952, Je 27,23:5
Epps, Lyman, 1942, N 21,13:3
Epps, William A Sr, 1961, Ag 9,33:5
Epps, William R, 1946, D 3,31:4
Epranian, Paul K Mrs, 1953, F 19,23:3
Epstean, Edward, 1945, Ag 10,15:5
Epstein, Abbe, 1951, Jl 28,13:2
Epstein, Abraham, 1942, My 3,53:1; 1952, D 9,33:5; 1955, Jl 18,21:1
Epstein, Adolph, 1937, Ja 10,II,9:3
Epstein, Albert, 1948, D 23,20:2
Epstein, Albert A, 1965, Ja 16,27:5
Epstein, Alfred, 1963, N 12,41:1
Epstein, Alter, 1959, Je 8,27:3
Epstein, Beltzalel, 1938, S 3,13:6
Epstein, Ben, 1958, Ag 26,29:2
Epstein, Benjamin, 1953, F 5,23:2
Epstein, Benjamin L, 1944, Mr 22,19:2
Epstein, Benjamin P, 1952, Mr 15,13:3
Epstein, Bennett, 1962, Mr 20,37:4
Epstein, Bernard, 1952, Je 2,21:5; 1961, Je 19,27:3
Epstein, Brian (funl, Ag 31,33:1; death ruled accidental), 1967, Ag 28,31:4
Epstein, C Joshua, 1939, O 22,40:4
Epstein, Charles, 1957, Ja 28,23:5
Epstein, Charles M, 1949, Ap 30,13:3
Epstein, Charles M Mrs, 1967, Ap 22,31:1
Epstein, Charlotte, 1938, Ag 27,13:4
Epstein, Clifford, 1959, Jl 4,15:5
Epstein, David, 1944, Je 21,19:6
Epstein, Edward Mrs, 1951, Je 29,21:4
Epstein, Ephraim, 1960, Jl 16,19:3
Epstein, Ezriel, 1938, Je 30,23:4
Epstein, Ezriel Mrs, 1944, Je 12,19:2
Epstein, Frank, 1953, Ag 27,25:5
Epstein, Haim F, 1942, Jl 6,15:5
Epstein, Hans L (cor, S 10,82:6), 1967, S 9,31:3
Epstein, Harold, 1961, F 2,29:1
Epstein, Harold B Mrs, 1962, Ja 18,29:5
Epstein, Harry, 1940, Je 8,15:6
Epstein, Harry B, 1952, Mr 9,92:5; 1958, N 23,88:4
Epstein, Harry J, 1956, Jl 11,29:4
Epstein, Henry, 1961, D 31,49:1
Epstein, Henry Mrs, 1966, Ap 28,43:4
Epstein, Hermann, 1939, Ag 8,17:6
Epstein, Hyman, 1966, My 16,37:3
Epstein, Hyman J, 1951, Jl 1,50:2
Epstein, Hyman Mrs, 1963, Ag 8,27:5
Epstein, Irving E, 1954, O 4,27:5
Epstein, Irving M, 1952, Ap 20,92:4
Epstein, Isaac, 1960, My 4,45:1
Epstein, Isaac L, 1938, Ag 6,13:2
Epstein, Isaac L Mrs, 1922, O 7,15:5
Epstein, Isadore, 1961, N 6,37:5
Epstein, Isidore, 1962, Ap 14,25:4
Epstein, Israel G, 1963, Ap 8,47:5
Epstein, Jack, 1957, D 17,35:5
Epstein, Jacob, 1945, D 29,13:2
Epstein, Jacob (funl, Ag 25,31:1; mem ser, N 11,35:2), 1959, Ag 22,1:6
Epstein, Jacob (will), 1960, Jl 20,23:5
Epstein, Jacob J, 1948, Mr 25,27:4
Epstein, Jacob M, 1949, Ja 11,27:3
Epstein, Jacob Mrs, 1950, My 9,29:4
Epstein, Jacob N, 1952, Mr 1,15:3
Epstein, Jean, 1953, Ap 4,13:1
Epstein, Joseph A, 1943, Jl 17,13:6
Epstein, Joseph Sr, 1948, Ag 26,21:4
Epstein, Julius, 1952, My 1,29:5; 1968, Ja 5,35:1
Epstein, Klaus W, 1967, Je 28,45:5
Epstein, Lonny, 1965, Mr 10,41:2
Epstein, Louis, 1947, Jl 8,23:5; 1954, My 16,86:2; 1966, F 23,39:3
Epstein, Louis M, 1949, Mr 23,28:3
Epstein, Martin, 1948, D 20,1:8
Epstein, Maude Mrs, 1917, Jl 25,11:4
Epstein, Maurice Mrs, 1957, S 14,19:6
Epstein, Maurice N, 1943, D 30,17:5
Epstein, Max, 1941, Je 26,23:1; 1949, Je 14,31:3
Epstein, Max (will, S 3,24:7), 1954, Ag 23,17:2
Epstein, May, 1952, Ap 14,19:5
Epstein, Morris, 1948, Ja 24,15:2; 1951, Ag 12,78:7
Epstein, Mortimer, 1946, Je 24,31:2
Epstein, Moses J, 1960, O 11,45:4
Epstein, Moses W, 1937, Ag 24,21:2
Epstein, Nathan, 1956, F 14,29:5
Epstein, Phil G, 1952, F 9,13:4
Epstein, Ralph C, 1959, N 22,87:1
Epstein, Richard (funl, Ag 5,9:3), 1919, Ag 2,7:6
Epstein, Richard I, 1949, Ap 24,76:3
Epstein, Robert, 1953, N 3,31:1
Epstein, Samuel, 1949, D 18,89:2
Epstein, Samuel C, 1945, Ja 29,14:3
Epstein, Samuel E, 1955, Ap 2,17:1
Epstein, Samuel Mrs (funl plans, F 2,29:2), 1961, F 1,35:2
Epstein, Seymour S, 1966, Ag 23,39:4
Epstein, Sidney, 1955, My 6,23:4
Epstein, Sidney S, 1961, O 7,23:1
Epstein, Simon, 1904, F 19,9:5
Epstein, Solomon, 1944, Ap 4,21:4
Epstein, William, 1941, F 10,17:3
Epstein, William G, 1952, Je 17,27:3
Epstein, William N, 1948, D 9,34:3
Epstein, Yetta M Mrs, 1948, Je 1,23:3
Equen, Jonte S, 1950, D 22,23:5
Equen, Murdock, 1964, N 12,37:5
Equi, Marie D, 1952, Jl 15,21:1
Erard, Phil V, 1951, N 28,31:1
Erasmus, Francois C, 1967, Ja 10,40:2
Erath, Charles F Mrs, 1953, S 3,21:2
Erath, Harry, 1939, Ja 4,21:4
Erath, Robert E, 1955, Ap 16,19:1
Erb, Charles F, 1952, Mr 8,31:1
Erb, Donald M, 1943, D 24,13:5
Erb, Edward S Pro, 1937, F 20,17:6
Erb, Frank A Mrs, 1938, S 24,17:3
Erb, Frank C, 1948, Ja 3,14:3
Erb, Frank O, 1950, Ag 28,17:6
Erb, Frederic W, 1946, F 12,25:4
Erb, Jesse S, 1944, O 26,23:5
Erb, Jesse W, 1946, Jl 17,23:2
Erb, John L, 1950, Mr 19,92:3
Erb, John W, 1948, Jl 3,15:5
Erb, Newman (funl, Mr 28,15:5), 1925, Mr 26,23:1
Erb, Paul R, 1942, Jl 30,21:6
Erb, Ray L, 1944, D 28,19:5
Erb, Theobald, 1939, Jl 21,19:5
Erbacher, Herbert A, 1907, Jl 28,7:4
Erbacher, Richard A, 1964, Ja 19,42:5
Erbeck, Arthur, 1942, Ja 15,19:3
Erbeck, Ernest L, 1943, S 14,23:3
Erbeck, Louis A, 1948, O 26,31:3
Erbelding, George, 1907, Ja 15,7:6
Erben, Henry, 1884, My 9,5:3
Erben, Henry Rear-Adm, 1909, O 24,13:1
Erben, Henry V B, 1956, D 27,25:4
Erben, Herman F, 1943, Ap 9,21:3
Erckert, Louis R, 1948, Ja 17,18:2
Erckmann, E, 1899, Mr 15,4:5
Ercolani, Ercolano A, 1941, O 18,19:6
Ercolano, William E, 1966, Ja 13,25:3
Erdahl, Gerald O T, 1961, N 5,88:8
Erdan, J, 1878, S 26,5:6
Erdberg, Samson D, 1962, Jl 13,23:3
Erdel, Edward Mrs, 1946, Ag 2,19:1
Erdelatz, Eddie (Edw J),(more details, N 12,29:4), 1966, N 11,43:2
Erdheim, Max, 1939, D 10,68:2
Erdlitz, Richard J, 1945, D 9,44:6
Erdman, Albert, 1937, Je 15,23:4
Erdman, Ben, 1943, D 15,28:3
Erdman, C J, 1911, Ja 16,11:5
Erdman, Calvin Pardee Mrs, 1925, N 11,23:4
Erdman, Charles R, 1960, My 10,37:3
Erdman, Charles R Sr Mrs, 1960, O 4,43:1
Erdman, Eric, 1950, Ap 12,27:2
Erdman, Frederick C, 1953, F 18,31:4
Erdman, Herbert J, 1959, Mr 13,29:4
Erdman, John P, 1941, Ap 28,15:6
Erdman, Martin (will), 1938, D 1,21:2
Erdman, Seward, 1966, Ja 9,56:7
Erdman, Walter C, 1948, My 19,28:2
Erdman, Walter C Mrs, 1961, Mr 28,35:2
Erdmann, Adolph, 1944, Ja 21,17:5
Erdmann, Albert J (will, Je 28,23:6), 1940, Je 13,23:4
Erdmann, Albert Jr, 1965, Je 12,31:5
Erdmann, Arthur G, 1956, F 18,19:4
Erdmann, Eduard, 1958, Je 23,23:3
Erdmann, John F (funl, Mr 31,27:1; will, Ap 3,19:4), 1954, Mr 28,89:1
Erdmann, John F Mrs, 1952, N 14,24:4
Erdmann, Martin, 1937, Ja 28,25:1
Erdmann, Sturtevant, 1955, My 28,15:5
Erdmann, William (will), 1938, F 17,19:2
Erdmann, William H, 1943, Ap 9,21:3
Erdmann, William L, 1961, Ag 3,23:2
Erdody, Rudolph, 1949, Mr 4,21:4
Erdos, Ivan, 1967, S 27,47:1
Erdwurm, Frank, 1946, Ap 29,21:3
Erdwurm, Max, 1960, Ap 10,86:2
Erenstone, Elize Mrs, 1941, Jl 13,29:1
Erental, Richard F, 1940, Jl 29,13:3
Ergens, Albert A, 1953, Ap 6,19:3
Erhard, Oscar W, 1957, Ag 31,15:6
Erhard, Raymond F (por), 1949, Ap 16,15:4
Erhardt, Bartholamew W, 1937, Je 6,II,8:7
Erhardt, Joel Benedict (funl, S 11,9:5), 1909, S 9,9:5
Erhardt, John G, 1951, F 19,23:1
Erhardt, Pert G Mrs, 1944, O 25,21:5
Erhardt, Stephen, 1944, S 18,19:2
Erhart, W H Mrs, 1902, O 25,9:6
Erhart, William H, 1940, Jl 31,17:2
Erholm, Harry, 1957, Ap 13,19:6
Erhorn, Walter, 1961, Mr 8,33:4
Eric, Howard, 1941, N 29,17:5
Erich, George F, 1947, N 10,29:2
Erich, Rafael W, 1946, F 20,25:1
Erichsen, Hugo, 1944, O 12,27:5
Erichsen, Mylius, 1908, Ag 7,5:4
Erichsen-Brown, Gwehalyn G (G Graham), 1965, N 26,34:4
Erichson, Bright S, 1955, D 8,37:3
Erichson, O Fax, 1937, N 5,23:2
Erick, Murray, 1959, Ag 3,25:4
Erick, Theodore A, 1939, Ja 11,19:6
Ericksen, Andrew, 1955, O 24,27:3
Ericksen, Axel K, 1960, S 28,39:3
Ericksen, Charles F (funl), 1916, F 26,9:5
Ericksen, Emil, 1938, F 4,21:3
Ericksen, Jens E, 1944, D 23,13:1
Ericksen, Peter M, 1955, S 8,31:2
Erickson, A R, 1941, N 10,17:5
Erickson, Abby Mrs, 1905, Mr 7,5:4
Erickson, Alfred W Mrs (will, Je 2,63:3), 1961, F 8, 31:3
Erickson, Arioch W, 1939, D 24,14:8
Erickson, Arvid M, 1960, Ja 9,21:3
Erickson, Betty N Mrs, 1941, Ag 8,15:2
Erickson, Carl, 1951, Ap 20,29:2; 1958, Je 17,29:2
Erickson, Carl E, 1938, S 17,17:5
Erickson, Carl F, 1953, Jl 15,25:4
Erickson, Charles A, 1937, Jl 22,19:6; 1964, F 17,31:3
Erickson, Charles J, 1940, Ja 9,24:2
Erickson, Clarence, 1950, Ap 2,92:4
Erickson, Clifford H, 1966, N 9,40:1
Erickson, Edward L, 1964, Je 6,23:2
Erickson, Edward T, 1941, N 19,23:5
Erickson, Elmer C, 1948, O 30,15:4
Erickson, Elsa Mrs, 1954, Jl 18,56:4
Erickson, Emma Mrs, 1946, Jl 28,14:1
Erickson, Eric R Mrs, 1958, Ag 16,17:5
Erickson, Frank, 1952, Ag 22,21:2
Erickson, Frank A (will, Mr 14,38:4), 1968, Mr 3, 89:1
Erickson, Harry L, 1949, O 29,15:1
Erickson, Henry F, 1952, O 31,21:4
Erickson, John A, 1948, S 25,17:2
Erickson, John E, 1946, My 26,32:2
Erickson, Josiah M, 1967, My 2,47:3
Erickson, Joyce, 1945, D 27,11:4
Erickson, Julius E, 1942, S 26,15:2
Erickson, Julius E Mrs, 1948, Ja 23,24:2
Erickson, Linwood W, 1967, Ja 26,33:2
Erickson, Louis H, 1966, D 5,5:6
Erickson, Martin E, 1950, D 28,25:3
Erickson, Ralph W Mrs, 1951, Ja 31,25:3
Erickson, Samuel E, 1938, D 12,19:2
Erickson, Sven E, 1961, F 9,31:1
Erickson, Swan M, 1946, O 31,25:3
Erickson, Victor M, 1947, S 8,21:3
Erickson, Walfred, 1964, Ag 16,93:1
Ericsen, Carl J, 1957, Ja 1,23:2

Ericson, Arvid C, 1946, S 8,44:4
Ericson, Charles, 1951, Ap 18,31:3
Ericson, Edward A E, 1948, My 30,34:5
Ericson, Elmer, 1964, Ag 20,29:5
Ericson, Eric, 1959, Ag 5,27:1
Ericson, F Eric, 1958, F 7,21:2
Ericson, John H, 1953, Ag 10,23:6
Ericson, Melvin B, 1939, N 9,23:6
Ericson, V A, 1953, Ja 7,31:2
Ericson, Walter, 1947, Je 15,60:4
Ericsson, E Walfrid, 1941, O 14,23:4
Ericsson, Eric Alfred, 1919, O 9,15:4
Ericsson, Frans A, 1952, Mr 13,19:3
Ericsson, Harry G Dr, 1944, Je 19,21:7
Ericsson, Henry, 1947, F 21,19:4
Ericsson, J, 1889, Mr 9,1:7
Ericsson, John M, 1938, Ag 23,17:1
Erik, Prince of Denmark, 1950, S 12,28:2
Eriksen, Anton, 1951, Ag 19,86:1
Eriksen, Edvard, 1959, Ja 14,27:5
Eriksen, Godfrey, 1947, Jl 11,15:5
Eriksen, John, 1953, Mr 19,29:4
Eriksen, Oliver H, 1943, Ap 6,21:2
Erikson, Albin E, 1964, Mr 16,31:2
Erikson, Arman, 1947, Ag 19,23:4
Erikson, Charles J, 1949, Je 7,31:1
Erikson, Gustaf, 1947, S 22,25:6
Erikson, Henry A, 1957, Je 23,85:1
Erikson, John, 1941, F 27,19:5
Erikson, Oscar M, 1948, F 26,23:1
Erikson, Walter W, 1953, Ap 9,27:1
Eriksson, Erik M, 1941, My 23,21:2
Eriksson, Herman G, 1949, F 19,15:6
Eriksson, Nore, 1956, Ja 8,2:6
Eristoff, Alexandre N, 1955, F 12,15:4
Eristoff, Neston Prince, 1961, O 26,35:4
Erk, Edmund F, 1953, D 16,35:4
Erkenback, Eugene P, 1938, F 10,21:4
Erkenbrack, Frederick P, 1943, Mr 3,24:2
Erkins, Henry M, 1938, Mr 31,23:2
Erkkilla, Ernest, 1967, Ja 10,40:2
Erkko, Eljas, 1965, F 22,21:3
Erlach, Gustav F, 1954, Jl 8,23:2
Erlandsen, Oscar, 1943, Ag 18,19:5
Erlanger, A L, 1930, Mr 8,1:5
Erlanger, Camille, 1919, Ap 25,15:4
Erlanger, Emil H, 1941, Ag 15,17:3
Erlanger, Joseph, 1965, D 7,47:2
Erlanger, Julius C, 1957, Ag 11,80:1
Erlanger, Max, 1914, Mr 31,11:2
Erlanger, Mitchell L (will, S 20,25:6), 1940, Ag 31, 13:4
Erlanger, Mitchell L Mrs, 1948, D 11,15:5
Erlanger, Regina Mrs, 1906, O 21,9:7
Erlanger, Sidney C, 1948, Ap 2,23:2
Erlanger, Sydney B, 1945, Je 5,19:5
Erle, W Sir, 1880, Ja 30,5:4
Erlebach, Adolph, 1904, F 7,9:7
Erlenkotter, Charles, 1948, S 28,28:3
Erlenmeyer, Victor E, 1958, N 5,22:8
Erler, Eugene W, 1945, Mr 18,42:2
Erler, Fritz, 1967, F 23,35:1
Erler, William J, 1944, Je 1,19:4
Erles, Leo, 1965, D 6,37:4
Erlich, J, 1938, My 20,13:4
Erlich, Jake, 1952, Jl 20,53:2
Erlich, Nina L Mrs, 1941, Mr 22,15:2
Erlick, Alex H, 1958, Je 26,27:5
Erlick, Sam Mrs, 1943, O 2,13:6
Erlinger, Herman, 1911, Mr 20,9:5
Erm, Jacob, 1948, Jl 17,16:2
Erman, Adolf Prof, 1937, Je 29,21:4
Ermatinger, Peter P, 1954, D 11,13:5
Ermeling, Lewis B, 1953, Je 11,29:2
Ermentrout, Percy, 1952, Ag 15,16:4
Erminger, Howell Jr, 1951, Ag 22,23:2
Ermold, M Atlee, 1952, F 20,29:3
Ernberg, Anna S Mrs, 1940, Ap 2,25:2
Ernberg, Harald, 1944, My 27,15:4
Erne, Frank, 1954, S 18,15:3
Ernenwein, George E, 1960, Ag 6,19:5
Ernest, Alwin C, 1948, My 14,23:1
Ernest, Edward C, 1944, N 5,54:7
Ernest, Grace A, 1943, Jl 20,19:2
Ernest, Harry F, 1950, D 7,33:5
Ernest, Louis, 1947, F 25,25:3
Ernest, Margaretha Mrs, 1925, Ag 27,19:6
Ernest, Roy H, 1941, N 5,23:1
Ernest, William J, 1945, Ja 31,21:3
Ernesta, Sister, 1939, Ap 20,18:3
Erney, Elmer D, 1961, Je 10,23:5
Erney, Miles, 1920, D 7,13:4
Ernhout, John H, 1954, F 14,94:2
Erni, Robert Mrs, 1950, Jl 1,15:4
Ernle, Baron (Rowland Prothero), 1937, Jl 3,15:3
Ernsberger, Millard R, 1940, Ja 26,17:2
Ernst, Alfred F, 1963, O 8,44:1
Ernst, Alfred F Mrs, 1948, Ap 28,27:4
Ernst, Bernard M L, 1938, N 29,23:5
Ernst, Bradford L, 1948, O 20,29:5
Ernst, Carl C, 1961, D 8,42:6
Ernst, Carola L, 1949, S 25,93:1
Ernst, Charles A, 1939, F 2,19:5
Ernst, Charles J A, 1949, Mr 16,27:5
Ernst, Christian, 1950, Ag 9,29:3
Ernst, Clayton H, 1945, O 16,23:2
Ernst, Duke of Saxe-Coburg (funl), 1893, Ag 24,1:5
Ernst, E Herman, 1960, F 15,27:4
Ernst, Eugene C F, 1940, Ag 14,19:4
Ernst, Frank G, 1963, Jl 23,29:4
Ernst, Frank V, 1949, O 20,29:5
Ernst, Frederic, 1953, My 31,73:1
Ernst, Frederick S, 1954, F 15,23:5
Ernst, Fritz B, 1959, F 27,25:2
Ernst, George G, 1944, S 26,23:3
Ernst, Gunther Duke, 1921, F 24,13:6
Ernst, Harold C Dr, 1922, S 8,13:4
Ernst, Henry P, 1946, Ag 4,46:1
Ernst, Hugo, 1954, Jl 23,17:3
Ernst, Irving L (por), 1938, Ap 9,17:1
Ernst, J Henry, 1953, Mr 24,31:4
Ernst, John H Jr, 1950, Ap 19,30:2
Ernst, Milton L, 1942, D 23,19:5
Ernst, Morris L Mrs, 1964, D 4,39:3
Ernst, Myron C, 1941, D 20,19:3
Ernst, Prince (Duke of Saxe-Altenbourg), 1908, F 7, 7:6
Ernst, R P, 1934, Ap 14,15:4
Ernst, Ray T, 1955, Je 23,29:5
Ernst, Walter E, 1950, O 22,93:1
Ernst, William G, 1939, Jl 13,19:6
Ernst, William Mrs, 1952, My 1,29:5
Ernst August, Duke of Brunswick and Lueneburg, 1953, Ja 31,15:2
Ernst II, Duke of Saxony-Altenburg, 1955, Mr 27,86:4
Ernst Ludwig, Former Grand Duke of Hesse, 1937, O 10,II,9:1
Ernster, Adelina, 1963, N 18,33:2
Ernstof, Jacob, 1937, O 27,31:2
Ernstrom, George R Mrs, 1945, Je 26,19:5
Erol, Ralph D, 1924, D 20,15:4
Eron, Francis H Mrs, 1942, S 18,21:2
Eron, Joseph E (por), 1938, S 2,17:6
Eros, Gedeon, 1966, Jl 16,25:5
Eross, John, 1962, Mr 14,39:5
Erpelding, Herbert, 1951, Mr 7,33:4
Erranght, Jeremiah, 1942, Mr 16,17:6
Errante, Guido, 1966, S 9,45:3
Errazuriz, Manuel L, 1966, Je 24,34:4
Errazuriz, Matias, 1953, Ag 13,25:5
Errazuriz, Rafael, 1923, D 28,15:5
Errera, William M, 1954, Ag 28,15:7
Errett, Wade, 1963, Je 27,33:5
Errickson, R Clifford, 1941, N 18,25:3
Errickson, Sarah R, 1937, Ag 22,II,7:3
Errington, Franklin A Mrs, 1952, Ap 13,77:2
Errington, J Frank, 1949, N 8,40:8
Errington, Joseph, 1942, F 10,19:4
Errol, Leon (will, O 21,58:5), 1951, O 13,17:3
Errol, Leon Mrs, 1946, N 9,17:4
Erroll, Earl of, 1928, F 21,25:5
Erskine, Anna G, 1958, Ap 1,31:5
Erskine, Anne L Mrs, 1938, S 1,23:5
Erskine, Arthur W, 1952, D 11,33:3
Erskine, B G, 1945, Je 25,17:1
Erskine, Elizabeth Mrs, 1939, Ag 31,19:2
Erskine, Frank L, 1937, Mr 12,24:2
Erskine, Fred S N, 1957, S 9,25:5
Erskine, George W E J, 1965, Ag 30,25:3
Erskine, Harold P, 1951, Ja 6,15:5
Erskine, Helen, 1961, My 16,37:3
Erskine, Herbert W, 1951, Mr 19,27:2
Erskine, Howard M, 1964, Mr 6,31:2
Erskine, J Douglas, 1957, D 11,31:2
Erskine, James C, 1946, N 16,19:3
Erskine, James H, 1940, Ap 30,21:1
Erskine, John, 1951, Je 3,92:1
Erskine, John F A Lord, 1953, My 4,23:5
Erskine, John K, 1924, O 4,13:3
Erskine, John Mrs, 1949, O 21,25:3
Erskine, Josephine G Mrs, 1938, Ap 11,15:1
Erskine, Michael A, 1943, O 16,13:4
Erskine, Pauline I Mrs, 1960, Ag 16,29:2
Erskine, Ralph C Mrs, 1962, Ja 21,88:8
Erskine, Robert S, 1957, O 16,35:2
Erskine, Wallace, 1943, Ja 7,19:3
Erskine, William Sir, 1952, Jl 18,19:6
Erstein, Benedict, 1952, Mr 16,90:6
Erstein, Jesse H, 1948, Ap 18,68:6
Erstein, Jesse H Mrs, 1950, O 31,27:2
Erstein, Max, 1916, Mr 2,11:5
Erstling, Maurice, 1960, F 19,28:1
Ertl, Edward C, 1961, Ag 26,17:5
Ertl, George, 1939, Mr 15,23:1
Ertle, Eugene E, 1958, Mr 20,29:5
Ertle, Frank J, 1959, S 1,29:4
Ertle, J H, 1932, Je 7,19:3
Ertler, John E, 1952, D 18,29:2
Ertman, E George, 1955, Ap 3,86:3
Ervast, George E, 1956, N 6,35:4
Ervik, Mathias A, 1949, Mr 10,27:4
Ervin, Charles, 1942, O 16,19:3
Ervin, Charles E, 1946, D 17,31:4
Ervin, Charles W (CIO trb), 1953, F 6,20:3
Ervin, Harry, 1940, N 4,19:4
Ervin, James F, 1959, Mr 2,27:4
Ervin, Morris D, 1956, N 3,23:6
Ervin, Ralph W Sr, 1959, D 19,27:5
Ervin, Russell T, 1942, Ja 13,19:1
Ervin, Spencer, 1967, N 2,47:3
Ervin, Spencer Mrs, 1918, D 2,13:7
Ervin, Thomas C, 1950, D 12,33:3
Ervin, William Mrs, 1947, Ja 15,25:1
Erving, Edward V D, 1942, Jl 21,19:3
Erving, Eleanor C, 1950, N 5,92:5
Erving, Henry M, 1946, Je 16,40:3
Erving, Henry W, 1941, Ja 16,21:2
Erving, John, 1917, Mr 8,11:4
Erving, John M, 1903, N 28,9:5
Erving, John Mrs, 1913, O 18,13:2
Erving, Justine B, 1955, N 30,33:5
Erving, William V, 1940, Ag 28,19:5
Erway, Allen D, 1954, N 5,21:3
Erwich, David, 1955, S 19,25:2
Erwin, Alexander S, 1907, Je 8,9:4
Erwin, Amelia, 1905, Je 6,9:3
Erwin, Austin W, 1965, Ag 15,82:7
Erwin, C R, 1926, D 16,27:4
Erwin, Charles R Mrs, 1941, Jl 2,21:1
Erwin, Clyde A, 1952, Jl 20,52:5
Erwin, Frank Jr Mrs, 1967, S 27,47:1
Erwin, Frederick C, 1965, D 2,41:5
Erwin, Henry P, 1920, Ap 25,22:4; 1953, Je 6,17:5
Erwin, Herbert E, 1940, N 17,50:1
Erwin, J N, 1938, Ag 25,19:1
Erwin, James B Brig-Gen, 1924, Jl 11,13:6
Erwin, James R, 1942, N 24,26:2
Erwin, James R Mrs, 1961, Je 4,86:1
Erwin, John N, 1905, D 23,7:5
Erwin, Marcus, 1939, D 20,25:5
Erwin, Marion, 1924, Ap 20,22:1
Erwin, Marion C, 1953, O 9,27:1
Erwin, Ray, 1968, Ja 23,39:1
Erwin, Richard K Justice, 1917, O 6,13:7
Erwin, Robert, 1911, S 8,7:6
Erwin, Robert G, 1906, Ja 14,9:6
Erwin, Ross E, 1953, Ap 6,19:3
Erwin, Staurt, 1967, D 22,31:2
Erwin, Stuart Mrs (June Collyer), 1968, Mr 19,47
Erwin, W A, 1932, F 29,17:5
Erwin, William W, 1940, S 13,23:5
Erwinkisch, Egon, 1948, Ap 2,23:3
Erxleben, Arthur R, 1945, F 7,21:2
Erzinger, William F, 1940, Je 28,19:5
Esbach, Horace W, 1962, Ag 25,22:1
Esberg, Henry (will, S 29,4:5), 1937, S 23,27:2
Esberg, Milton H, 1939, Jl 20,19:5
Esberg, Moses, 1921, N 12,13:5
Escalante, Alonso, 1967, Je 22,39:5
Escalante, Diogenes, 1964, N 15,86:7
Escalante Dellunde, Cesar, 1965, Ap 19,29:3
Escalona, Frank, 1937, Ja 19,23:2
Escandon, Ralph, 1944, Je 27,19:3
Escarre, Aurelio Maria (Dom), 1968, O 23,47:3
Esch, Howard L, 1948, F 9,17:5
Esch, John J, 1941, Ap 28,15:6
Eschelbach, Joseph G, 1945, Je 23,13:5
Eschenberg, Conrad J, 1959, Ag 20,25:4
Escher, Franklin, 1952, My 31,17:6
Escher, G Edward, 1959, Ag 16,82:6
Escher, Henry, 1941, Ja 29,17:3
Escher, James H, 1964, Ap 16,37:5
Escher, John G, 1965, Ag 13,29:3
Escher, Joseph, 1954, D 10,27:5
Eschmann, Joseph T, 1951, N 20,31:1
Eschmann, Peter C, 1966, My 16,37:3
Eschmeyer, R William, 1955, My 23,23:2
Eschwege, Henry T, 1920, Jl 29,9:4
Eschwege, W O, 1903, Je 4,9:6
Eschweiler, Alex C, 1940, Je 13,23:2
Esclangon, Ernest, 1954, Ja 30,17:4
Escobar, Adrian C, 1954, F 17,31:2
Escobar, Francisco, 1942, F 18,19:3
Escobar, Patricio A, 1951, Ja 3,27:4
Escobar de Valde Iglesias, Alfredo Marques, 194 F 25,23:2
Escobosa, Hector, 1963, N 24,22:8
Escoffier, A, 1935, F 13,19:4
Escoffier, Martin E, 1953, O 30,23:4
Escoffier, Paul, 1941, Jl 31,17:2
Escorio, Manuela Senora, 1939, D 1,8:5
Escott, Ivan, 1962, Ap 3,39:4
Esdale, Charles, 1937, Jl 12,17:2
Esdorn, John H, 1940, S 17,23:3
Esenwein, Joseph B, 1946, N 2,15:4
Esh, Barnett Mrs, 1968, F 22,32:6
Eshbach, Horace H, 1962, F 10,23:5
Eshbach, Ovid W, 1958, Mr 5,31:3
Eshbaugh, John O, 1966, Mr 31,39:2
Eshbaugh, William H, 1951, S 13,31:4
Eshel, Arieh Ambassadov, 1968, O 11,47:1
Eshelman, B F Col, 1903, D 18,9:5
Eshelman, Benjamin Mrs, 1952, S 25,31:4
Eshelman, Carrie Mrs, 1955, D 2,27:2
Eshelman, Henry B, 1946, D 3,31:1
Eshelman, Wallace C, 1952, My 15,31:5
Esher, H B, 1903, Mr 30,1:3
Esher, Viscountess, 1940, F 9,19:2
Esherick, Joseph, 1958, N 8,21:4

Eshleman, Charles L, 1951, My 16,35:4
Eshleman, John M Lt-Gov, 1916, F 29,11:3
Eshmont, Len C, 1957, My 13,31:5
Eshner, Augustus A, 1949, D 21,29:3
Eska, Antoni, 1960, Je 26,72:8
Eskanazi, Moses, 1955, Ap 22,11:1
Eskenazi, Solomon, 1960, N 6,43:5
Eskesen, Eckardt V, 1943, D 14,27:4
Eskey, Leonard, 1943, Ja 19,20:2
Eskildsen, Clarence R, 1967, S 26,47:2
Eskin, Israel, 1952, Ap 25,23:3
Eskin, Samuel, 1954, Mr 27,17:5
Eskolsky, Mitchel S, 1959, F 4,33:1
Eskridge, Ladson G Jr, 1960, D 25,42:2
Eskridge, Rich Col, 1903, S 2,7:6
Esleeck, Irving N, 1951, D 8,11:5
Esler, Frederic Brice, 1910, Ag 26,7:5
Esler, Lemist, 1960, N 8,29:4
Esler, Myron, 1955, Ag 30,27:5
Esmarch, Johannes Friedrich August von Dr, 1908, F 24,7:2
Esmay, George K, 1949, Ag 30,27:1
Esmond, Burton D, 1944, Ja 12,23:2
Esmond, E Richard Maj, 1910, N 9,9:2
Esmond, Edward, 1945, My 16,19:3
Esmond, Flora, 1949, My 19,31:6
Esmond, Henry V, 1922, Ap 18,17:4
Esmond, Irwin, 1956, Ag 8,25:6
Esmond, James G, 1948, Je 28,19:4
Esmond, John W, 1951, Mr 7,33:5
Esmond, William G, 1956, N 10,19:2
Esmonde, Anna F Mrs, 1941, Jl 17,19:5
Esmonde, Thomas H Grattan Lady, 1922, D 24,20:3
Esmonds, Fred C, 1904, Je 12,3:2
Espalter, Jose, 1940, Ag 31,13:2
Espana, Jose Count, 1952, Ja 9,29:4
Esparsa, Enrique, 1917, D 22,11:5
Espartero, Dom Baldomero, 1879, Ja 10,5:3
Espartero, 1874, D 30,1:5
Espenscheid, Nicholas, 1945, Ap 4,21:4
Esper, Frederick Mrs, 1943, F 11,19:3
Esperey, Franchet d', 1942, Jl 9,21:1
Esperito, Morris J, 1966, D 3,39:5
Espeut, Kurt W, 1950, Ap 19,30:3
Espie, John P, 1949, D 3,15:5
Espina F Tagle, Concha, 1955, My 20,25:2
Espinal, Louis A, 1944, O 9,23:4
Esping, Paul, 1946, Je 25,21:4
Espinosa, Al, 1957, Ja 5,17:2
Espinosa, Antonio Archbishop, 1923, Ap 9,17:4
Espinosa, Antonio G, 1942, Ja 23,19:1
Espinosa, Edouard, 1950, Mr 24,25:4
Espinosa, Ernest Mrs, 1948, My 22,15:1
Espinosa, Judith, 1949, F 18,23:3
Espinosa, Mariano, 1943, N 3,25:5
Espinosa, Miguel, 1951, N 12,25:3
Espinosa, Rafial De Mrs, 1937, O 24,II,8:8
Espinosa, Raul, 1958, O 21,33:3
Espinosa, Rodolfo, 1944, D 2,13:2
Espinosa de los Monteros, Antonio, 1959, S 21,31:5
Espinosa de Reyes, Manuela, 1945, Mr 1,21:4
Espinosa y Doninquez, William, 1954, O 3,87:2
Espirito Santo, Ricardo, 1955, F 3,23:2
Esposito, Anthony H, 1953, My 28,17:1
Esposito, Anthony L, 1949, O 12,30:3
Esposito, Frank L, 1967, F 9,35:5
Esposito, Joseph R (will, Ag 16,5:2), 1957, Ag 6,27:2
Esposito, Salvatore Sr, 1965, Jl 22,31:5
Esposito, Vincent J, 1965, Je 15,41:4
Espovich, Jacob, 1939, My 17,23:1
Espres, Joseph A, 1968, N 15,47:3
Espy, Arthur Mrs, 1953, D 25,17:5
Espy, Ridgway B, 1952, Ja 5,11:3
Esquenazi, Morris, 1956, Ag 2,25:3
Esquirol, Daniel L, 1938, O 21,23:5
Esquirol, Joseph H, 1944, Jl 1,15:3
Essakow, Hubert, 1956, Mr 22,44:4
Essary, Fred, 1942, Mr 12,19:1
Essayan, Martin, 1939, Jl 16,31:2
Essebaggers, Theodore Mrs, 1963, D 25,33:5
Essefian, Parsegh G, 1957, O 14,27:3
Esselborn, Paul, 1940, My 14,23:5
Esselen, Gustavus J, 1952, O 23,31:5
Esselen, Louis, 1945, Mr 14,20:2
Esselstyn, Everett J, 1938, Ja 6,19:3
Esselstyn, Henry H Mrs, 1956, Mr 7,33:5
Esselstyn, Sherman, 1912, S 23,13:6
Essen, Adm von, 1915, My 22,11:4
Essendon, Lord, 1944, Je 25,29:3
Essenfeld, Abraham M, 1961, My 28,64:5
Essenwanger, Charles L, 1947, S 13,11:2
Esser, Ernst H, 1946, N 23,15:3
Esser, George H, 1956, Mr 29,27:4
Esser, J Henry, 1958, Je 8,88:7
Esser, James H, 1948, D 15,33:2
Esser, Johannes F S, 1946, Ag 10,13:2
Esser, Theodore P, 1942, Ja 6,23:4
Essex, Earl of (Adela Beach Grant Capell), 1916, S 26,11:2
Essex, William Arnold, 1915, S 12,17:4
Essex, William L, 1959, F 27,25:1
Essick, Augustus W, 1945, N 24,19:4
Essick, Charles R (will), 1954, Jl 10,28:3
Essick, Edwin P, 1952, Mr 21,23:2
Essick, Paul J Jr, 1949, Je 18,13:3
Essick, William E, 1951, O 13,17:4
Essick, William W, 1941, Mr 24,17:3
Essig, Albert J, 1947, O 23,25:4
Essig, Norman S, 1952, Jl 6,49:1
Essinger, Bernard, 1946, Je 13,27:2
Essington, George E, 1954, S 13,23:5
Essling, Princess d', 1903, O 4,5:3
Esslinger, Clarence A, 1942, My 21,19:5
Essman, Manual, 1967, Ap 6,39:3
Esson, John, 1953, N 12,31:2
Esson, Louis A, 1939, Ja 4,21:2
Essrig, Julius, 1945, O 11,23:3
Essroger, Charles V, 1939, My 25,25:3
Estabrook, Bailey G, 1952, S 23,33:2
Estabrook, C Maxwell Mrs, 1903, N 21,9:6
Estabrook, Charles M, 1940, S 28,17:4
Estabrook, Charles T, 1905, Je 4,1:4
Estabrook, Curtis G Dr, 1923, Ja 2,13:3
Estabrook, Curtis R Dr, 1923, Ja 4,19:4
Estabrook, E Burk, 1961, S 17,86:5
Estabrook, Fred W, 1939, Ag 20,32:6
Estabrook, George M, 1954, Ag 14,15:4
Estabrook, Henry Dodge, 1917, D 23,15:5
Estabrook, Howard Davies, 1924, D 10,23:2
Estabrook, Leo T, 1937, D 29,22:1
Estabrook, Leon M, 1937, Ag 15,II,7:4
Estabrook, Mansfield, 1950, D 31,42:3
Estabrook, Taylor S, 1903, O 6,9:4
Estabrook, William N, 1939, Ap 9,III,7:2
Estabrooke, Carl B (por), 1938, N 13,44:8
Estabrooke, John H, 1954, Ag 12,25:4
Estabrooke, Kate C Mrs, 1940, F 14,21:4
Estabrooke, William L, 1949, Mr 15,27:2
Estaunie, Edouard, 1942, Ap 4,13:4
Estberg, Edward F, 1944, Mr 5,35:1
Estcourt, T S S, 1876, Ja 7,5:2
Este, D K, 1876, Ap 4,8:4
Este, F, 1926, Ap 27,25:2
Este, J Dickinson, 1961, S 26,39:3
Esteban, Inocencio, 1956, N 12,29:3
Esteban Infantes, Emilio, 1962, S 7,29:3
Estee, Morris M Judge, 1903, O 28,9:5
Estee, Tully C, 1938, My 14,15:3
Estella, Marquis, 1921, My 24,15:4
Estelle, Harry, 1954, N 7,51:6
Estelle, Mary E H Mrs, 1940, Ap 23,23:2
Estelle, R Bruce, 1954, F 11,29:1
Esten, William M, 1943, Ap 17,17:2
Estep, Dana C, 1951, Jl 23,21:5
Estep, Eugene C, 1960, Ap 1,33:4
Estep, Frank L, 1952, D 14,91:2
Estep, Thomas G, 1949, Ag 9,25:5
Esterbrook, Gladys R, 1947, Ag 31,36:6
Esterbrook, O Grant, 1960, S 18,86:6
Esterbrook, O Grant Mrs, 1940, Ag 31,13:4
Esterbrook, Richard, 1960, F 28,83:1
Esterbrook, T G, 1901, My 1,9:2
Esterhazy, Arthur Mrs, 1955, My 7,17:6
Esterhazy, Maj, 1923, Ag 17,13:4
Esterhazy, Moritz Count, 1960, Je 28,31:3
Esterlich Artigues, Juan, 1958, Je 22,76:3
Esterly, Charles J, 1940, S 4,23:2
Esterly, Franklin T, 1947, Mr 21,22:2
Esterman, Marcus, 1925, O 20,25:4
Esternaux, Maximilian F L A, 1941, Ja 4,13:5
Esters, Bernard E, 1966, Jl 19,39:4
Estes, Clarence E, 1937, F 26,21:2
Estes, Frederick R, 1954, F 7,89:1
Estes, George L, 1944, N 13,19:6
Estes, Harry E Jr, 1947, Je 4,27:1
Estes, James F, 1943, Je 7,13:5
Estes, Milo D Capt, 1917, Je 13,13:5
Estes, Ray E, 1937, Ag 11,23:5
Estes, Thomas W, 1962, O 14,85:5
Estes, Wayne, 1965, F 10,38:2
Estes, William L Sr, 1940, O 21,17:5
Estes, Zenas N Mrs, 1939, My 6,17:4
Esteva, Jean, 1951, Ja 13,15:5
Estevenon, Louis Rev, 1912, D 28,7:3
Esteves, Luis R, 1958, Mr 13,29:4
Esteves, Raul, 1955, Jl 4,11:4
Estey, Agnes D Mrs, 1945, D 3,21:4
Estey, Francis W, 1938, Jl 23,13:6
Estey, Frank N, 1953, Jl 3,19:2
Estey, G Howard Mrs, 1942, F 22,26:2
Estey, Henry W, 1949, Ap 10,76:1
Estey, Jacob P, 1952, Ag 17,77:1
Estey, James W, 1956, Ja 23,25:4
Estey, Joseph G, 1946, O 15,26:3
Esther Maria, Sister (E Kenna), 1956, Jl 4,19:4
Estienne, B, 1936, Ap 4,15:5
Estill, H Bramwell Brig, 1968, Ag 17,27:4
Estill, Harry F, 1942, F 13,22:2
Estill, John Holbrook Col, 1907, N 10,9:7
Estill, Joseph G, 1953, My 3,88:3
Estill, Mary A B Mrs, 1942, O 12,34:5
Estill, Reuel C, 1956, S 13,35:2
Estill, Robert C, 1961, N 14,36:2
Estill, T, 1926, O 20,25:4
Estillac Leal, Newton, 1955, My 3,31:3
Estime, Dumarsais, 1953, Jl 21,23:4
Estin, Peter G, 1963, Ap 7,86:3
Estler, Charles E, 1940, Ja 16,23:2
Estler, George Mrs, 1949, Jl 14,27:5
Estony, Frank F, 1951, N 7,29:5
Estopinal, Albert, 1919, Ap 29,15:4
Estrada, Alfonso, 1958, Ja 1,25:2
Estrada, Duke of, 1941, O 6,17:4
Estrada, Enrique, 1942, N 4,23:3
Estrada, Genaro, 1937, S 30,23:5
Estrada, Juan, 1952, Mr 11,27:7
Estrada, Juan J, 1947, Jl 13,44:3
Estrada Menocal, Jose, 1951, N 21,30:2
Estrampes, Jose d' Col, 1923, Mr 23,19:4
Estrich, Willis A, 1939, My 19,21:6
Estrin, Michael, 1960, F 7,84:4
Estrin, Morris M, 1958, Ap 20,84:5
Estroff, Meyer, 1958, Ap 17,31:4
Estrow, Michael, 1960, Ap 15,23:1
Estrup, Jacon Broenum Scavenuis, 1913, D 25,9:4
Estupinian, Baltazar Dr, 1922, Mr 26,27:3
Estwick, Charles F, 1954, O 2,17:6
Esty, Charles A, 1947, Jl 11,15:4
Esty, Edward T, 1942, Jl 6,15:5
Esty, Frederick R, 1939, Jl 2,15:2
Esty, J Russell, 1954, My 1,15:5
Esty, Robert P, 1958, F 25,27:1
Esty, Thomas C Mrs, 1948, N 12,23:3
Esty, William C, 1954, Ja 22,27:5
Esty, William Mrs, 1956, Jl 29,65:2
Esway, Alexandre, 1947, Ag 26,23:1
Etchegoyen, Alcides, 1956, Je 19,29:5
Etchen, Fred R Sr, 1961, N 8,35:4
Etcheverry, Bernard A, 1954, O 28,35:4
Etchingham, John R, 1923, Ap 25,21:4
Etgen, William C, 1964, O 3,29:1
Etgen, William J Mrs, 1947, D 14,76:5
Etgen, William S, 1950, Je 8,32:2
Ethardo, Naomi, 1951, F 16,25:2
Etheredge, S P, 1953, Ja 18,92:6
Etheridge, Adam D, 1940, D 23,19:3
Etheridge, Anton L, 1947, Mr 12,25:1
Etheridge, Harry A, 1957, N 30,21:4
Etheridge, William B, 1957, O 3,29:4
Etherington, Charles K, 1948, Ja 11,56:4
Etherington, Sandford G, 1959, My 16,23:5
Etherington, Sandford G Mrs, 1949, N 27,104:4
Ethridge, Frank K, 1945, F 19,17:2
Ethridge, James M Jr, 1963, S 8,87:1
Ethridge, Martin V B, 1914, Ap 5,15:3
Ethridge, Robert, 1873, Jl 25,4:6
Ethridge, William N Mrs, 1949, Mr 25,23:3
Etling, Henry, 1953, Jl 4,11:6
Etra, Isidor, 1957, N 18,31:2
Etra, William, 1946, N 13,27:2
Etris, Joseph Sr, 1951, D 8,11:3
Etris, Robert, 1956, Ap 6,26:3
Ettari, Francesco Dr, 1925, S 7,11:6
Ettel, Edwin L Mrs, 1944, Je 7,19:6
Ettelson, Henry J, 1952, Jl 5,15:6
Ettelson, Louis, 1949, Ap 12,30:2
Ettelson, Samuel A, 1938, My 9,17:4
Ettenborough, Raymond J, 1947, Ja 3,21:2
Ettenger, Anna, 1957, Ja 24,29:1
Ettenger, Robert L, 1949, My 9,25:2
Ettenson, Frances L Mrs, 1941, Ap 10,23:5
Etter, Forest B, 1950, S 12,27:5
Etter, Harry B, 1940, F 19,17:3
Etter, William K, 1943, Ag 17,17:5; 1953, F 9,27:3
Ettinger, Abraham Mrs, 1966, O 15,29:3
Ettinger, Emanuel, 1941, Ja 2,23:6
Ettinger, Harry, 1946, Jl 25,21:3
Ettinger, Henry, 1949, Jl 24,52:4
Ettinger, Jean A, 1959, F 22,88:4
Ettinger, Louis, 1955, O 8,19:3
Ettinger, Margaret (Mrs R Shattuck), 1967, Ja 14, 31:2
Ettinger, Mark J Mrs, 1950, Mr 17,24:3
Ettinger, Moses, 1943, Jl 6,21:4
Ettinger, Raphael, 1904, Jl 22,7:2
Ettinger, Rose, 1909, My 14,9:5
Ettinger, S Robert Mrs, 1953, O 1,29:3
Ettinger, Virgil P, 1966, D 21,39:4
Ettinger, William L, 1945, D 26,19:1
Ettl, John, 1940, D 24,15:2
Ettl, John Mrs, 1952, D 27,9:2
Ettling, Harry, 1947, Ap 13,60:1
Ettlinger, Albert K, 1960, Ap 27,37:4
Ettlinger, Fred V Mrs, 1953, F 1,88:1
Ettlinger, Harold L, 1944, My 12,19:3
Ettlinger, Katherine Mrs, 1941, F 26,21:5
Ettlinger, Rite B Mrs, 1953, My 1,22:4
Ettman, Eli, 1949, Ap 8,26:2
Ettore, Domenico, 1943, N 10,23:2
Ettridge, James B, 1938, S 20,23:3
Etu, John J, 1955, Je 9,29:4
Etzel, Eugene P Sr, 1964, Jl 12,69:1
Etzel, Frederick J, 1964, My 23,23:4
Etzrodt, Thomas J, 1944, Ap 17,23:3
Euart, William A, 1947, Ja 18,15:4
Eubank, Earl E, 1945, D 19,25:2
Eubank, John A, 1957, Je 20,29:3
Eubank, Marion D, 1940, D 7,17:6
Eubanks, John, 1946, Je 29,19:2

Eubanks, Sam B, 1967, Ja 11,25:1
Eubelacker, Matthew, 1955, My 6,23:3
Euchtritz, Kuno Von, 1908, Jl 30,5:4
Euckon, R C, 1926, S 16,27:4
Eudowe, Harry M, 1946, F 8,19:1
Eudy, Mary C Mrs, 1952, Je 9,23:4
Eugen, Prince, 1947, Ag 18,17:1
Eugene, Archduke of Habsburg, 1954, D 31,13:1
Eugene, Bro (R P Dunne), 1953, Mr 7,16:7
Eugenia Clare, Sister, 1948, Ja 18,60:5
Eugenides, Eugene, 1954, Ap 23,27:4
Eulalia, Infanta of Spain, 1958, Mr 9,86:1
Eulau, Julius, 1952, Ja 3,27:2
Eulenberger, Emil Mrs, 1950, Mr 16,31:1
Eulenburg, Botho Count, 1910, D 4,13:4
Eulenburg, Philip zu, 1921, S 20,17:5
Euler, August, 1957, Jl 3,23:5
Euler, Charles E Mrs, 1951, N 6,29:2
Euler, H L, 1958, F 7,21:5
Euler, W D, 1961, Jl 16,68:1
Euler, William G B, 1958, Mr 13,29:5
Euler, William J, 1949, N 8,31:2
Euler, William J Mrs, 1947, O 16,28:2
Euler-Chelping, Hans von, 1964, N 8,88:3
Eulner, Elmer H, 1957, Ja 19,15:4
Eulner, Florence Mrs, 1948, F 18,27:1
Eulogius, Metropolitan, 1946, Ag 9,17:3
Eumorfopoulosk, George, 1939, D 20,28:2
Eurich, Christian H, 1949, F 3,23:6
Eurich, Conrad F, 1954, Mr 3,27:5
Eurich, Frank 2d, 1942, N 27,23:2
Eurich, Frederick W, 1945, F 21,19:5
Eustace, Alexander C, 1913, Ja 30,11:5
Eustace, Bartholomew J (funl, D 16,86:5), 1956, D 12,39:1
Eustace, Elizabeth Mrs, 1941, Ja 20,17:4
Eustace, Harry J, 1962, Ag 29,29:1
Eustace, Robert B, 1943, O 15,19:3
Eusten, Frank E, 1946, My 5,46:3
Eustice, William H, 1958, S 29,27:6
Eustis, Arthur G Sr, 1959, Ja 29,27:5
Eustis, Celestine, 1921, F 12,13:5
Eustis, Dorothy H Mrs, 1946, S 10,7:1
Eustis, Edith L M Mrs, 1964, N 14,29:4
Eustis, Fred J, 1912, Mr 24,II,15:4
Eustis, George, 1872, Mr 17,1:6
Eustis, George Dexter, 1915, Ap 21,13:6
Eustis, H L Prof, 1885, Ja 13,5:5
Eustis, James B, 1899, S 10,11:3
Eustis, James Biddle, 1915, Jl 9,11:5
Eustis, James W, 1940, Mr 9,15:4
Eustis, John R, 1955, D 10,21:1
Eustis, Newton B, 1914, Ja 7,11:5
Eustis, Percy S, 1937, O 26,23:4
Eustis, W E C Mrs, 1904, Ja 16,9:5
Eustis, W G, 1937, Ja 27,21:2
Eustis, W H, 1928, N 30,23:5
Eustis, William Corcoran, 1921, N 25,15:4
Euston, Countess of, 1903, N 25,1:3
Eutemey, Bert V, 1945, F 24,11:4
Eutsler, D Frank Mrs, 1957, Mr 21,31:1
Euwing, John K Jr Mrs, 1939, Ja 9,15:5
Eva, Harry C, 1956, My 4,25:1
Evald, Emmy C, 1946, D 11,31:2
Evan, Slater, 1940, Ja 7,48:8
Evancy, Gabriel, 1954, O 10,87:2
Evangelides, Timothy, 1949, O 7,27:5
Evangelist, Frank, 1957, N 16,19:4
Evangelist, Louis, 1959, O 27,37:4
Evangelisti, Luigi, 1939, Jl 9,31:1
Evanhoe, Frank N, 1940, Ja 21,35:2
Evans, A O, 1873, S 29,5:2
Evans, A W Gen, 1906, Ap 25,13:6
Evans, Abram, 1907, N 14,9:6
Evans, Adrian C, 1952, Ag 16,5:1
Evans, Albert, 1946, My 1,25:4; 1953, O 23,23:2
Evans, Albert E, 1944, O 3,23:3
Evans, Albert S Col, 1872, N 18,1:7
Evans, Albert W, 1943, My 24,15:4
Evans, Alex W, 1959, D 7,31:6
Evans, Alfred, 1957, S 5,29:4
Evans, Alfred B, 1944, O 14,13:6
Evans, Alfred G, 1921, Ja 11,11:5; 1966, S 20,47:3
Evans, Alfred J, 1944, F 15,17:5
Evans, Alfred W, 1950, S 16,19:7
Evans, Alice P Mrs, 1946, D 27,19:3
Evans, Allen, 1925, Mr 2,17:6; 1960, D 18,84:4
Evans, Alonzo H, 1907, My 28,9:6
Evans, Alvin E, 1953, Je 18,29:3
Evans, Andrew H G, 1956, My 15,31:2
Evans, Anne, 1941, Ja 7,23:1
Evans, Annie L D Mrs, 1961, Mr 6,25:4
Evans, Anson D, 1945, S 11,23:2
Evans, Anthony H, 1942, Ag 30,43:1
Evans, Arch M, 1939, Je 26,15:6
Evans, Arch P, 1948, O 23,15:4
Evans, Archie, 1939, D 31,18:6
Evans, Arlington, 1952, S 9,31:3
Evans, Arthur, 1941, Jl 12,13:6; 1958, S 30,31:4
Evans, Arthur H, 1956, Mr 14,33:4
Evans, Arthur J, 1939, Ag 27,35:2
Evans, Arthur K Mrs, 1953, N 16,25:2
Evans, Arthur L, 1951, D 5,35:5
Evans, Arthur S, 1955, Ag 19,19:4
Evans, Arthur T, 1943, O 7,23:1
Evans, Arthur T Mrs, 1955, Je 13,23:2
Evans, Austin P, 1962, S 22,25:2
Evans, Beatrice R Mrs, 1966, My 24,43:6
Evans, Benjamin D, 1951, Jl 25,23:4
Evans, Benjamin F, 1952, Ag 3,61:1
Evans, Bernard W, 1922, F 28,19:3
Evans, Berne H, 1938, Ap 28,23:3
Evans, Beverly D Judge, 1922, My 8,17:5
Evans, Britton D Dr, 1920, Ja 15,11:2
Evans, C Keith, 1955, Mr 5,17:2
Evans, C Keith Mrs (Betty), 1968, D 29,53:2
Evans, C Todd, 1937, Mr 3,23:2
Evans, C William, 1956, Ag 10,17:2
Evans, Cadwalader, 1880, Ja 21,2:6
Evans, Caradoc, 1945, Ja 13,11:3
Evans, Carl A, 1956, Ja 5,34:1
Evans, Carl A Mrs, 1954, D 19,84:1
Evans, Cecil L, 1967, F 22,29:4
Evans, Charles C, 1941, Jl 12,13:2
Evans, Charles E, 1945, Ap 17,23:5
Evans, Charles H, 1910, Mr 11,9:5; 1963, D 14,27:5
Evans, Charles L, 1943, Je 25,17:4
Evans, Charles N B, 1941, Ja 26,36:2
Evans, Charles S, 1938, O 12,27:1; 1944, N 30,23:1
Evans, Charles T, 1940, My 1,23:3; 1949, My 14,13:6
Evans, Charles W, 1941, Ag 1,15:6; 1964, Ap 1,39:5
Evans, Chris, 1924, N 5,19:3
Evans, Clarence A, 1940, S 6,21:4
Evans, Clarence B, 1947, Mr 30,56:2
Evans, Clement A Gen, 1911, Jl 3,7:5; 1911, Jl 6,9:4
Evans, Clyde W, 1964, Ag 5,33:2
Evans, Curtis A, 1947, My 5,23:1
Evans, Daisy, 1947, Je 21,17:3
Evans, Daniel, 1943, Ap 26,19:5
Evans, Daniel W, 1966, D 16,47:4
Evans, David, 1943, D 4,13:3; 1959, Mr 15,88:5
Evans, David A, 1966, My 22,86:4
Evans, David A Mrs, 1947, Ag 19,23:3
Evans, David G, 1940, S 15,49:2
Evans, David O, 1945, Je 12,19:4
Evans, De Lacy Sir Gen, 1870, Ja 25,5:1
Evans, Deana Mrs (cor; mem service set, N 25,86:4), 1962, N 24,23:4
Evans, Don, 1962, Ja 4,33:4
Evans, Donald, 1921, My 30,9:6
Evans, Donald R, 1948, Ag 11,21:4
Evans, Dorothy, 1944, Ag 29,17:3
Evans, Dr (T Lookup), 1879, Ag 29,2:7
Evans, Dudley Col, 1910, Mr 28,9:5
Evans, Dwight D, 1938, Jl 20,19:4
Evans, E Claude, 1948, Ap 1,25:6
Evans, Earle R Sr, 1955, Ja 5,23:5
Evans, Earle W, 1940, Jl 31,17:1
Evans, Edgar, 1952, Mr 29,15:1
Evans, Edgar H, 1954, Jl 24,13:1
Evans, Edison E, 1942, D 7,27:4
Evans, Edith (Mrs H W Snowden Sr), 1962, O 13, 25:2
Evans, Edith B (C T Merritt), 1964, Je 20,25:2
Evans, Edmund M, 1948, N 14,76:2
Evans, Edward A, 1942, My 26,21:1; 1951, Jl 26,21:2
Evans, Edward M, 1954, Jl 2,19:4
Evans, Edward P, 1944, F 2,21:4
Evans, Edward Payson, 1917, Mr 8,11:4
Evans, Edward Q, 1945, F 22,27:3
Evans, Edward R G R (Lord Mountevans), 1957, Ag 22,27:2
Evans, Edward S, 1945, S 7,23:1
Evans, Edward T, 1945, Ag 26,44:7
Evans, Edward V, 1938, Ag 4,17:2
Evans, Edwin T, 1909, D 21,9:2
Evans, Eleanor G, 1937, Jl 30,19:4
Evans, Elinor V, 1953, Je 7,84:2
Evans, Elizabeth E, 1911, S 15,9:6
Evans, Elmer W, 1951, Ag 24,15:4
Evans, Elmore A, 1942, S 5,13:6
Evans, Elmore Mrs, 1946, Ja 13,43:1
Evans, Elva R Mrs, 1938, Ja 3,21:5
Evans, Elwyn, 1948, S 28,27:4
Evans, Emlyn, 1952, Ap 28,19:1
Evans, Emma Mrs, 1942, F 5,21:4
Evans, Emmett, 1953, D 24,15:4
Evans, Enoch, 1944, D 29,15:2
Evans, Ernestine, 1967, Jl 4,19:2
Evans, Ervin W, 1952, Jl 22,25:1
Evans, Erwin H, 1945, N 26,21:3
Evans, Etelka, 1947, D 15,25:4
Evans, Evan, 1954, Ja 4,19:5
Evans, Evan A, 1948, Jl 8,23:1
Evans, Evan A Mrs, 1940, Ap 7,44:8
Evans, Evan M, 1955, Mr 19,15:2
Evans, Everett I, 1954, Ja 15,19:5
Evans, Fannie E Mrs, 1944, Ja 15,13:6
Evans, Frances I Mrs, 1948, S 9,27:2
Evans, Francis A, 1946, Je 7,19:5
Evans, Francis Henry, 1907, Ja 26,9:5
Evans, Frank A, 1956, D 14,29:4
Evans, Frank B Jr, 1953, Jl 23,23:3
Evans, Frank E, 1941, N 26,23:3
Evans, Frank F, 1937, My 29,17:4
Evans, Frank J, 1946, Ag 20,27:3
Evans, Frank M, 1960, F 8,11:1
Evans, Frank O Mrs, 1948, N 15,25:5
Evans, Frank W, 1955, F 4,19:4
Evans, Franklin B, 1954, S 5,50:2
Evans, Fred E, 1937, Ag 27,19:3
Evans, Fred E Jr, 1937, N 24,23:3
Evans, Fred S, 1948, Ja 1,23:1
Evans, Fred W, 1940, D 20,25:2
Evans, Frederick, 1919, Jl 12,9:7
Evans, Frederick E, 1947, Ja 22,23:4
Evans, Frederick H, 1915, O 11,9:6
Evans, Frederick H Mrs, 1948, My 5,25:2
Evans, Frederick R, 1946, S 17,7:5
Evans, Frederick S, 1954, Ap 5,25:3
Evans, Frederick Sir, 1939, Ag 2,19:5
Evans, G B Gen, 1868, D 9,12:3
Evans, Garfield, 1954, O 20,29:4
Evans, George, 1867, Ap 7,5:4; 1915, Mr 6,11:6; 1942, Ja 13,22:5
Evans, George A Dr, 1925, Jl 15,17:5
Evans, George B, 1943, My 2,44:6; 1950, Ja 27,23:2
Evans, George C, 1940, Jl 29,13:4
Evans, George D, 1942, My 17,46:2
Evans, George E, 1945, Je 9,13:6
Evans, George F, 1908, Ja 11,9:6
Evans, George H, 1916, D 21,11:3; 1948, S 14,29:2; 1954, Ja 8,21:2
Evans, George Mrs, 1941, D 28,28:2
Evans, George R, 1949, Je 1,31:2
Evans, George W, 1940, Je 3,15:4; 1941, Je 6,21:2
Evans, Georgette D Mrs, 1956, Mr 12,27:4
Evans, Gerald G, 1942, Mr 12,19:1
Evans, Geraldine, 1946, My 22,21:3
Evans, Gilbert, 1909, Jl 9,7:6
Evans, Glendower Mrs, 1937, D 13,27:3
Evans, Gomer, 1944, Ag 2,15:5
Evans, Gounod, 1961, N 26,88:5
Evans, Greek H, 1967, Ja 31,31:3
Evans, Gustavus W, 1951, S 27,26:6
Evans, H Clay, 1921, D 13,19:4
Evans, H E, 1951, Ap 25,29:4
Evans, Harold Brown, 1921, S 11,21:1
Evans, Harold W, 1953, S 8,22:1
Evans, Harry D, 1940, Ja 23,21:5
Evans, Harry F, 1949, O 30,84:5
Evans, Harry F Mrs, 1953, Ap 9,27:4
Evans, Harry M, 1947, Ag 5,23:4
Evans, Hartman K, 1942, N 26,28:4
Evans, Haydn, 1964, Mr 31,35:2
Evans, Henry (funl, S 1,13:4), 1924, Ag 30,9:5
Evans, Henry C Rev, 1912, F 5,9:4
Evans, Henry Clay Maj, 1918, O 10,11:2
Evans, Henry F, 1945, S 10,19:5
Evans, Henry G, 1869, Ag 17,4:6
Evans, Henry Mrs, 1944, Jl 16,31:1
Evans, Henry O, 1951, My 3,29:3
Evans, Henry W, 1942, S 28,17:6
Evans, Herbert H, 1946, Mr 19,28:2
Evans, Herbert H Mrs, 1949, Je 26,60:2
Evans, Herbert W Sr, 1964, O 27,39:3
Evans, Hiram K, 1941, Jl 11,15:3
Evans, Homer H Jr, 1968, N 26,47:3
Evans, Homer H Mrs, 1966, Jl 20,41:5
Evans, Horace, 1963, O 27,88:5
Evans, Horace S, 1966, N 6,88:4
Evans, Houston V Maj, 1915, F 12,9:6
Evans, Howard, 1943, Jl 12,15:4
Evans, Howard D, 1950, Ag 7,19:6
Evans, Howard S, 1941, D 15,19:3
Evans, Hoyt B, 1949, N 7,27:5
Evans, Hubert M, 1963, My 23,37:3
Evans, Hubert Mrs, 1954, My 28,23:4
Evans, Hugh I, 1958, Ap 24,31:5
Evans, Hugh P, 1957, D 11,31:4
Evans, Hugo I, 1960, D 22,26:3
Evans, Hwell T, 1950, My 1,25:2
Evans, Ifor L, 1952, Je 1,84:2
Evans, Ira K, 1964, Je 22,27:4
Evans, Irving, 1957, F 8,23:1; 1966, Ag 30,41:2
Evans, Irving L, 1953, O 13,29:6
Evans, Irwin R, 1949, Ap 3,77:2
Evans, Isaac, 1956, Ap 19,31:2
Evans, Isaac Mrs, 1949, F 8,25:3
Evans, Isadore P Mrs, 1942, Ja 30,19:4
Evans, Isobel W, 1954, My 25,27:3
Evans, J A, 1947, Je 25,25:3
Evans, J H, 1928, Mr 15,25:5
Evans, J Harry, 1949, My 4,30:2
Evans, J Morris, 1948, N 23,29:3
Evans, J O, 1881, D 26,8:2
Evans, J P Sr, 1954, Ja 11,5:6
Evans, J Percy, 1916, O 8,23:4
Evans, J Reid, 1942, N 10,27:3
Evans, Jack, 1950, Mr 9,29:1
Evans, Jack M Mrs, 1951, S 7,29:2
Evans, James, 1904, Ja 9,9:6; 1941, Jl 10,40:3
Evans, James A, 1953, Mr 31,31:3
Evans, James D, 1951, S 2,48:6
Evans, James H, 1956, Ap 10,31:1
Evans, James H Mrs, 1948, Ja 1,23:3
Evans, James M, 1959, D 12,23:1
Evans, James Mrs, 1944, Je 4,42:1
Evans, James N, 1937, Ap 11,II,8:2

Evans, James R, 1949, My 11,29:5
Evans, James W, 1956, D 10,31:2
Evans, Jane F S Mrs, 1938, F 4,21:3
Evans, Jay I Mrs, 1947, S 2,21:4
Evans, Jean S Mrs, 1949, S 25,69:3
Evans, Jesse E, 1951, O 4,33:3
Evans, Jessie C, 1956, Ap 15,89:2
Evans, Jocelyn H deG Mrs, 1962, N 13,37:2
Evans, John, 1942, Ap 20,21:6
Evans, John A, 1954, N 12,15:1
Evans, John B, 1951, N 11,91:1; 1956, F 5,87:2
Evans, John C, 1937, Mr 2,21:5; 1942, S 4,24:4; 1946, Ja 14,19:3; 1946, Ap 9,27:3; 1951, S 18,31:5; 1965, S 11,27:1
Evans, John C Rev Dr, 1965, O 16,27:6
Evans, John D, 1964, O 22,32:3
Evans, John Dr (Marquis d'Oyley), 1911, Ja 30,9:4
Evans, John E, 1940, Ag 4,33:2
Evans, John F, 1939, My 5,23:4
Evans, John F Mrs, 1937, D 18,21:3
Evans, John G, 1942, Je 27,13:2
Evans, John H, 1955, Ap 8,21:2
Evans, John J, 1943, D 5,64:3
Evans, John J H, 1949, Je 4,13:5
Evans, John K, 1937, S 5,II,7:2
Evans, John L, 1949, Mr 13,76:5; 1958, Jl 25,19:4
Evans, John M, 1963, N 26,37:2
Evans, John M Mrs, 1956, Jl 15,60:5
Evans, John N, 1953, Ap 9,27:5
Evans, John P, 1939, O 6,25:2; 1941, S 4,21:1; 1947, F 15,15:1
Evans, John R, 1939, Ja 25,21:2; 1946, Ap 20,13:2
Evans, John S, 1939, F 19,39:1
Evans, John W, 1953, Je 17,27:2; 1955, Mr 18,27:2; 1959, Je 25,29:2
Evans, John W H, 1956, N 4,86:5
Evans, Johnnie S, 1958, F 22,17:4
Evans, Joseph A, 1949, Ja 20,27:2
Evans, Joseph B, 1964, Jl 30,27:3
Evans, Joseph D, 1954, D 11,13:4
Evans, Joseph D Mrs, 1950, Ja 13,23:2
Evans, Joseph H, 1948, N 30,27:1
Evans, Joseph Madison, 1922, O 21,13:5
Evans, Joseph O, 1947, N 25,29:1
Evans, Joseph P, 1953, Ag 10,23:4
Evans, Joseph S, 1948, F 4,24:1
Evans, Joseph W, 1954, N 5,15:1
Evans, Katherine F Mrs, 1964, Ag 11,33:3
Evans, Katherine Mrs, 1947, S 22,23:5
Evans, Lanius D, 1953, D 23,25:1
Evans, Lark W Mrs, 1946, F 22,25:2
Evans, Laura F Mrs, 1937, F 13,13:2
Evans, Lawrence Edwards, 1925, My 1,19:5
Evans, Lee L, 1950, Ja 19,28:2
Evans, Lena, 1949, Ja 3,23:4
Evans, Lester J Mrs, 1954, Ap 26,25:4
Evans, Lewis A, 1947, Je 27,21:2
Evans, Lewis M Sr, 1959, N 20,31:3
Evans, Lewis P, 1965, D 25,13:4
Evans, Lidie H Mrs, 1938, Ap 6,23:6
Evans, Lilly Mrs, 1944, Jl 4,24:4
Evans, Linn M A Mrs, 1955, Ap 27,31:1
Evans, Liston P, 1949, Mr 18,25:3
Evans, Lizzie, 1940, F 18,41:2
Evans, Louis, 1956, N 7,31:5
Evans, Louis P Mrs, 1951, O 18,29:5
Evans, Louis R, 1943, D 30,18:3; 1955, My 3,31:4
Evans, Lyall W, 1960, Je 1,39:5
Evans, Malcolm, 1947, D 10,31:1
Evans, Marcellus H, 1953, N 22,88:3
Evans, Margaret L, 1960, Ag 1,23:5
Evans, Margaret Mrs, 1950, Ap 17,23:4
Evans, Marion, 1958, Ja 9,33:1
Evans, Martin Mrs, 1949, D 21,29:3
Evans, Mary J, 1940, N 8,21:4
Evans, Mary S M Mrs, 1940, Mr 26,21:2
Evans, Matilda S, 1953, Ja 11,91:1
Evans, Maurice H Mrs, 1966, Ag 27,29:4
Evans, May G, 1947, Ja 14,25:4
Evans, Milton G, 1939, S 18,19:5
Evans, Miner H A, 1946, My 6,21:5
Evans, Montgomery 2d, 1954, Ap 25,57:6
Evans, Mr, 1874, Ja 2,1:7
Evans, Nelson J, 1940, Mr 2,13:2
Evans, Nelson P, 1952, Mr 23,92:4
Evans, Newton G, 1945, D 21,21:2
Evans, Newton W, 1939, S 27,25:4
Evans, Norris H, 1966, Ja 8,26:1
Evans, Oren W, 1953, Jl 27,19:4
Evans, Orville, 1949, Ap 1,25:4
Evans, Owens D, 1958, Jl 19,15:5
Evans, Phil S Jr Mrs, 1957, Ap 7,89:1
Evans, Philip S Rev Dr, 1913, F 20,11:3
Evans, Powell, 1948, O 29,25:1
Evans, Ralph K, 1960, S 5,15:6
Evans, Ralph L, 1965, Mr 23,39:2
Evans, Ray O Sr, 1954, Ja 19,26:6
Evans, Raymond E, 1959, S 9,41:4
Evans, Reynalds (Chas P R Evans), 1967, Jl 30,64:7
Evans, Richard, 1958, Mr 12,31:3
Evans, Richard B, 1967, Jl 11,37:2
Evans, Richard E, 1964, My 24,92:8
Evans, Richard J, 1914, D 23,13:4; 1947, D 3,29:2
Evans, Richard T, 1940, D 26,19:4
Evans, Robert B, 1961, Ja 4,33:1
Evans, Robert B Jr, 1953, Mr 27,23:2
Evans, Robert D (funl, Jl 10,7:5), 1909, Jl 7,9:5
Evans, Robert D, 1947, My 10,13:4; 1959, N 17,35:4
Evans, Robert D Mrs, 1948, Je 12,15:4
Evans, Robert E Sr, 1958, Jl 9,27:4
Evans, Robert Emory, 1925, Jl 9,19:4
Evans, Robert G, 1941, F 25,23:3
Evans, Robert K, 1960, Jl 31,69:2
Evans, Robert K Mrs, 1956, N 17,21:6
Evans, Robert Mrs, 1956, Je 28,29:3
Evans, Robley D Rear-Adm (funl), 1912, Ja 6,13:5
Evans, Robley D Rear-Adm, 1919, N 25,11:4
Evans, Rosalie Mrs, 1924, Ag 13,15:3
Evans, Ross, 1967, Ag 23,51:1
Evans, Roy A, 1949, S 17,17:3
Evans, Ruby Douglas Mrs, 1968, Je 28,41:1
Evans, Rudolph M (Spike), 1956, N 22,33:1
Evans, Rudulph, 1960, Jl 18,27:5
Evans, Ruth D, 1965, O 29,43:2
Evans, S Howard, 1964, Je 13,23:4
Evans, S Keith, 1955, Je 2,29:3
Evans, Samuel S Sr, 1945, Je 22,15:6
Evans, Samuel Sir, 1918, S 14,11:4
Evans, Scott, 1968, Mr 24,92:8
Evans, Silas, 1959, N 2,31:3
Evans, Silliman (funl, Je 30,25:4; will, Jl 6,55:4), 1955, Je 27,21:3
Evans, Silliman Jr (trb Jl 31,19:1), 1961, Jl 30,69:1
Evans, Stevenson H, 1959, Mr 18,37:1
Evans, Sydney K, 1942, Mr 26,23:4
Evans, T Harland, 1952, N 2,88:2
Evans, T W Dr, 1897, N 16,7:4
Evans, Taliesin, 1907, Ag 12,7:7
Evans, Tallie, 1954, F 8,23:4
Evans, Theodore F, 1961, D 30,19:4
Evans, Thomas, 1940, S 20,23:2; 1950, S 6,29:5; 1955, F 2,27:5
Evans, Thomas E, 1941, Ap 12,15:1
Evans, Thomas G, 1942, Mr 25,21:5
Evans, Thomas H Mrs, 1948, N 5,26:2
Evans, Thomas J, 1947, Ag 26,23:2; 1961, Ap 6,26:1
Evans, Thomas L, 1950, Ag 16,29:3
Evans, Thomas L W, 1950, Mr 3,25:4
Evans, Thomas P, 1950, Ag 9,29:2
Evans, Thomas S, 1945, N 11,42:1
Evans, Timothy Mrs, 1944, D 5,23:4
Evans, Timothy W, 1951, Mr 26,23:3
Evans, Tom, 1943, Mr 14,26:1
Evans, W, 1936, Ap 16,25:2
Evans, W C, 1953, N 9,35:3
Evans, W Smith, 1948, O 2,15:4
Evans, Wallace, 1949, Ag 13,11:1
Evans, Wallace G, 1954, Mr 23,27:4
Evans, Walter, 1952, My 29,27:1
Evans, Walter H Sr, 1959, Jl 14,29:2
Evans, Walter J, 1939, S 2,17:4
Evans, Ward V, 1957, Ag 3,15:3
Evans, Wilfrid M Mrs, 1960, S 11,81:3
Evans, Will, 1941, Mr 9,40:6
Evans, Willet C, 1966, Ja 24,35:4
Evans, William, 1907, Ja 1,9:5; 1950, My 22,21:4; 1956, D 23,30:4
Evans, William A, 1938, O 6,23:5
Evans, William A (will, N 8,27:3), 1939, O 26,23:3
Evans, William A, 1940, Ja 3,21:3; 1940, Je 11,25:2; 1948, N 9,27:5
Evans, William A D, 1956, S 15,17:3
Evans, William B, 1942, F 16,17:1
Evans, William C, 1954, N 27,13:4
Evans, William D, 1950, D 6,33:2
Evans, William D (funl, O 15,15:5), 1955, O 12,31:3
Evans, William D Mrs, 1956, Mr 3,19:3
Evans, William D R, 1944, Mr 30,21:3
Evans, William E, 1937, Mr 22,23:3
Evans, William F, 1939, D 8,25:2; 1950, My 11,29:2
Evans, William G, 1924, O 23,21:5; 1945, O 17,19:4
Evans, William G (Billy),(A Daley on career, Ja 25,40:4), 1956, Ja 24,31:3
Evans, William H, 1940, My 4,17:5; 1945, D 31,17:4; 1947, S 10,27:3; 1949, S 9,25:5; 1953, Ap 18,2:5; 1960, Ag 13,15:6
Evans, William H Mrs, 1954, O 3,86:8
Evans, William J, 1944, S 24,46:3
Evans, William L, 1954, O 19,27:3
Evans, William M, 1939, O 24,23:6; 1944, D 19,21:2
Evans, William M Mrs, 1937, O 29,21:3
Evans, William P, 1958, Ag 18,19:2
Evans, William P Col, 1916, S 30,11:5
Evans, William P Mrs, 1950, Ap 27,29:2
Evans, William R, 1952, Je 23,19:5
Evans, William S, 1954, Je 1,27:1
Evans, William T, 1918, N 26,15:3
Evans, Willis F, 1948, F 16,21:2
Evans, Zack, 1923, F 21,15:4
Evanyke, Andrew H, 1951, N 6,29:5
Evarts, Allen W, 1939, My 31,23:4
Evarts, Benjamin F, 1940, Ag 4,33:2
Evarts, Daniel E, 1968, Ag 29,35:4
Evarts, Daniel E Jr, 1947, Jl 12,13:4
Evarts, Ella M V Mrs, 1937, Mr 20,19:4
Evarts, H G, 1934, O 19,23:1
Evarts, Maxwell, 1913, O 8,11:6
Evarts, Maxwell Mrs, 1937, D 18,21:2
Evarts, Morley K, 1951, N 16,25:4
Evarts, Roy C, 1954, Je 4,23:3
Evarts, W, 1878, Ap 27,2:5
Evarts, William H, 1940, Je 7,23:4
Evarts, William M, 1901, Mr 1,6:6; 1946, N 8,23:4; 1954, Ap 1,32:3
Evarts, William M Mrs, 1903, D 28,7:6
Evatt, Franks G, 1949, F 24,23:5
Evatt, Herbert V, 1965, N 2,33:1
Evaul, Thomas W, 1952, S 5,27:2
Evdokimoff, Nikolai, 1938, Ja 15,32:7
Eve, Arthur S, 1948, Mr 26,21:4
Eve, Duncan Sr Dr, 1937, F 16,23:2
Eve, Edward C, 1960, D 6,41:3
Eve, Harry, 1940, D 11,27:3
Eve (Negress), 1880, D 1,2:4
Evekink, David van Voorst, 1950, Mr 18,13:3
Eveland, Eliza J Mrs, 1903, Ap 22,9:6
Eveleth, Norris P, 1961, Ja 15,86:7
Eveleth C W, 1875, N 25,5:4
Evelyn, Judith, 1967, My 8,41:2
Evelyn, Steven F, 1951, S 29,17:4
Evelyn Marie, Sister (Sisters of Notre Dame de Namur), 1955, O 8,19:3
Evem, Pierre, 1941, Jl 4,13:3
Evemeyer, Edward F, 1950, Ap 15,15:3
Evenden, Edward S, 1957, O 20,86:3
Evens, Allen E, 1953, O 26,21:1
Evens, Jules G, 1950, O 14,10:6
Evensen, J Arthur, 1954, Ag 5,23:6
Everard, James, 1913, Je 1,IV,7:6
Everard, Joseph, 1909, N 25,11:6
Everard, William L, 1949, Mr 13,76:5
Everatt, Charles W Mrs, 1967, F 1,39:4
Everdell, William Col, 1912, N 6,15:5
Everding, Louis C, 1946, Ag 2,19:4
Everest, Barbara, 1968, F 11,92:7
Everest, David C, 1955, O 29,19:6
Everest, Hiram Bond, 1913, Mr 8,15:4
Everest, J G Col, 1924, Ap 19,13:5
Everest, Raymond W, 1939, Ja 27,19:2
Everett, A Leo Mrs, 1921, Jl 15,11:7
Everett, Albert, 1937, D 18,21:2
Everett, Allan F, 1938, Ja 23,II,8:8
Everett, Charles M, 1948, Mr 19,23:4
Everett, Chester M, 1947, Ja 1,33:3
Everett, E H, 1903, Je 12,9:6
Everett, Edith M, 1941, My 19,17:5
Everett, Edward (funl, Ja 20,1:5), 1865, Ja 16,1:3
Everett, Edward, 1903, Jl 28,7:5
Everett, Edward E, 1954, Ja 14,29:4
Everett, Edward Hale, 1925, O 31,17:4
Everett, Edward L, 1948, F 20,27:2
Everett, Edward Mrs, 1859, Jl 6,4:5
Everett, Edward Sr, 1948, Je 16,29:3
Everett, Elizabeth H Mrs, 1940, S 8,49:2
Everett, Evelyn C Mrs, 1960, Ap 21,31:4
Everett, F Dewey Mrs, 1953, N 2,25:4
Everett, Frank D, 1951, Mr 13,31:4
Everett, Frank W, 1941, F 10,17:4
Everett, Franklin T, 1943, Ap 29,21:3
Everett, Fred D, 1940, Je 12,25:6
Everett, Fred M, 1903, Ap 3,9:7; 1955, N 12,19:2
Everett, Guerra, 1944, N 11,13:4
Everett, Harry L, 1940, S 5,23:4
Everett, Harvey L, 1951, N 15,29:5
Everett, Henry A, 1917, Ap 12,11:6
Everett, Henry C, 1963, Jl 17,31:3
Everett, Hiram, 1940, My 4,17:2
Everett, John E, 1952, S 9,31:5
Everett, Josephine P Mrs (will, D 12,53:5), 1937, Jl 6,19:5
Everett, Lemuel, 1918, Jl 30,11:6
Everett, Louella D, 1967, S 28,47:5
Everett, Otis, 1948, Ap 13,27:4
Everett, Percy W, 1952, F 24,84:2
Everett, Ralph Henderson, 1968, S 4,44:4
Everett, Richard M, 1964, Je 17,43:5
Everett, Robert B, 1954, S 9,31:3
Everett, S, 1883, D 19,2:5
Everett, Samuel Harrison, 1914, F 23,9:5
Everett, Samuel Mrs, 1966, F 15,39:2
Everett, Samuel W, 1953, Je 17,27:4
Everett, Silas Kendrick, 1924, S 6,11:7
Everett, T F, 1933, N 26,32:3
Everett, Walker G, 1968, S 17,47:3
Everett, Walter, 1952, Ja 1,25:2
Everett, Walter G Dr, 1937, Jl 30,19:3
Everett, Walter G Mrs, 1955, N 23,23:2
Everett, Wilfred G Sr, 1959, Je 23,33:4
Everett, William H Rear-Adm, 1912, Je 13,11:5
Everett, William J, 1952, F 23,11:4
Everett, William Rev Dr, 1910, F 17,9:5
Everett, William W, 1908, My 30,7:6; 1949, Mr 16,27:1
Everhard, Desmond D, 1925, Ja 6,25:5
Everhart, Ben Matlack, 1904, S 23,9:7
Everhart, William, 1948, F 13,21:5
Everingham, Donald, 1960, N 3,36:4
Everingham, Donald Mrs, 1960, N 3,36:4
Everit, Edward H, 1943, O 7,23:3
Everit, Valentine, 1874, O 28,2:6

Everitt, Benjamin H, 1966, Jl 29,31:3
Everitt, Benjamin H Mrs, 1957, O 3,29:4
Everitt, Byron F, 1940, O 6,49:3
Everitt, C L, 1875, O 18,5:3
Everitt, C Raymond, 1947, My 24,15:5
Everitt, Charles B Mrs, 1950, Mr 8,25:1
Everitt, Charles F, 1940, Mr 5,23:2
Everitt, Charles H, 1944, D 15,19:5
Everitt, Charles P, 1951, Mr 5,21:1
Everitt, Edward, 1911, Ag 20,II,9:6
Everitt, George B, 1941, Ag 3,35:3
Everitt, George T, 1938, My 20,19:5
Everitt, John D, 1940, N 7,25:4
Everitt, John Robert Dr, 1916, My 17,11:5
Everitt, John Rogers, 1919, Mr 1,13:2
Everitt, John T, 1954, N 4,31:4
Everitt, John W, 1949, D 14,31:4
Everitt, Paul, 1955, Ap 27,31:5
Everitt, Samuel A, 1953, N 5,31:1
Everitt, Thomas S, 1937, O 19,26:1
Everitt, William M, 1961, Je 10,23:6
Everleigh, Ada, 1960, Ja 6,21:1
Everleigh, Minna, 1948, S 17,20:3
Everlien, Herman A, 1946, F 22,25:1
Everly, Marvin H, 1948, N 5,25:3
Everman, James, 1941, Ap 9,25:2
Evermann, Phoebe M Mrs, 1940, Mr 31,46:2
Evers, Charles, 1946, Ja 28,19:1
Evers, Edward A, 1954, Ap 5,25:1
Evers, Edwin H Mrs, 1962, Ja 20,21:4
Evers, Francis C, 1945, F 18,34:2
Evers, Frank H, 1943, O 17,III,13:6
Evers, Harry J, 1951, S 2,48:5
Evers, Henry F, 1966, O 1,32:5
Evers, Herbert J, 1962, My 10,37:3
Evers, Herman E, 1955, Je 17,23:4
Evers, Joseph F, 1949, Ja 5,25:2
Evers, Luke J Msgr (funl, Je 28,13:5), 1924, Je 24, 21:3
Evers, Luke J Msgr, 1924, Je 27,19:5
Evers, Merlin, 1950, N 18,15:4
Evers, Owen J, 1948, Ap 25,68:3
Evers, Patrick R, 1953, Ap 26,87:1
Evers, Richard H, 1946, O 11,23:3
Evers, Samuel J, 1965, Mr 22,33:4
Evers, Samuel J Mrs, 1964, Mr 1,83:3
Evers, Thomas, 1874, N 9,8:2
Evers, Thomas J, 1937, S 18,19:3
Evers, William Mrs, 1954, N 27,14:2
Evershed, Francis R (Lord), 1966, O 4,47:1
Evershed, John, 1956, N 19,31:6
Eversley, Baron, 1928, Ap 20,23:4
Eversman, John C, 1953, F 13,21:4
Eversman, Walter A, 1960, Jl 26,30:1
Eversman, Walter Mrs, 1955, Mr 27,87:2
Eversmann, Herbert O, 1958, S 27,21:3
Eversole, George E Mrs, 1955, Mr 13,86:2
Eversole, Julia B Mrs, 1919, Jl 2,13:4
Everson, Arch R, 1948, O 11,23:4
Everson, Charles Severin Rev, 1920, D 9,13:3
Everson, Duane S Mrs, 1950, F 8,28:2
Everson, Edward, 1937, Ja 24,II,9:1
Everson, George Dr, 1937, Mr 7,II,9:3
Everson, George F, 1966, S 2,31:4
Everson, Jesse A, 1939, Ap 10,17:3
Everson, Thomas Mrs, 1944, O 10,23:2
Eversull, Harry K, 1953, S 15,31:6
Evert, William J Mrs, 1949, D 4,108:6
Everts, Arthur G, 1938, My 29,II,6:7
Everts, Harold J Mrs, 1942, Ja 14,21:2
Everts, Lillian (Mrs M Levine), 1960, Je 3,31:4
Everts, Silas E, 1951, D 25,31:3
Everts, William, 1947, Jl 10,21:4
Everts, William Mrs, 1947, Jl 10,21:4
Everwijn, J C A, 1939, Ja 6,21:6
Every, Edward, 1951, O 31,29:2
Eves, Charles K, 1964, Ag 13,29:4
Eves, Curtis C, 1942, S 23,25:6
Eves, Hiram P, 1951, D 28,21:5
Eves, Hubert H, 1961, Jl 28,21:5
Eves, Philmer, 1942, Ja 14,21:5
Eves, Reginald G, 1941, Je 15,37:1
Eves, Richard J, 1947, D 3,29:2
Eves, William H, 1938, O 16,45:4
Eveslage, Lawrence, 1948, Ap 13,27:2
Evesson, Isabelle, 1914, Ag 10,7:4
Evett, Robert, 1949, Ja 17,19:3
Evins, Samuel Holcomb, 1918, N 16,13:4
Evins, Samuel N Sr, 1939, N 21,26:2
Evjen, John O, 1942, Ja 5,20:3
Evjenth, Reinholdt U, 1958, Je 15,77:2
Evjue, William T Mrs, 1957, Jl 27,17:6
Evon, Agnes E, 1959, Jl 18,15:4
Evstifeev, Pavel, 1952, Jl 31,23:4
Evvard, John M, 1948, Ag 1,58:1
Evyan, Miss (Baroness Diana Langer von Langendorff), 1968, Ag 21,42:1
Ewald, Arthur H, 1952, Jl 17,23:3
Ewald, Frank G, 1924, Ap 28,15:5
Ewald, Frederick A, 1958, My 5,29:3
Ewald, Frederick W Mrs, 1945, D 4,29:2
Ewald, George F, 1964, Jl 2,31:3
Ewald, George F Mrs, 1941, Ap 10,23:3; 1963, Ag 2, 27:4
Ewald, Henry George Augustus, 1875, My 6,1:3
Ewald, Henry T, 1953, Ja 10,17:1
Ewald, Herman J, 1939, Ap 11,24:4
Ewald, Louis A, 1958, Ja 17,25:1
Ewald, Rose, 1960, O 30,86:8
Ewald, William G, 1949, Mr 21,23:4
Ewald, William P, 1943, D 7,27:4
Ewan, Frank S, 1954, Mr 22,27:4
Ewan, Josiah W, 1925, S 4,21:6
Ewart, Alfred J Prof, 1937, S 13,21:2
Ewart, Annie B Mrs, 1938, F 9,19:4
Ewart, Frank C, 1942, S 29,23:1
Ewart, Howard, 1912, Jl 7,II,11:1; 1961, F 20,27:5
Ewart, Howard Mrs, 1957, Ag 16,19:4
Ewart, J S, 1933, F 22,19:3
Ewart, Lavens M Sir, 1939, S 23,19:1
Ewart, Matthew J, 1953, My 14,29:2
Ewart, Richard, 1953, Mr 9,2:3
Ewart, Richard Hooker, 1918, O 19,15:1
Ewart, Robert H Sir, 1939, Ag 14,15:2
Ewart, Talbot, 1959, O 24,21:5
Ewaska, Michael M, 1950, Je 7,29:4
Ewbank, Charles C, 1964, Ja 23,31:3
Ewbank, Louis B, 1953, Mr 8,91:2
Ewbanks, William H, 1912, Ap 11,11:5
Ewell, Burt F, 1943, Mr 12,17:1
Ewell, Elliott G, 1965, My 15,31:6
Ewell, J N, 1885, Ja 20,2:6
Ewell, Joseph Emerson, 1924, Je 21,13:6
Ewell, R Stoddard Lt-Gen, 1872, Ja 26,5:4
Ewen, Edward C, 1959, Ag 14,21:4
Ewen, John M Mrs, 1942, Mr 14,15:2
Ewen, Warren L, 1961, S 9,19:5
Ewen, William A C, 1944, Ja 9,42:5
Ewen, William A C Mrs, 1945, Jl 11,11:5
Ewen, William C, 1954, O 18,25:4
Ewer, Arthur C, 1953, O 21,29:2
Ewer, F C Rev, 1883, O 8,1:4
Ewer, Mary A, 1961, N 15,43:3
Ewer, Maurice H, 1944, Ag 6,38:1
Ewers, Ezra Philetus Brig-Gen, 1912, Ja 19,11:6
Ewers, Hans Heinz, 1943, Je 18,21:4
Ewers, Ira L Mrs, 1967, N 19,84:5
Ewertsen, Ernest L, 1961, Ap 16,86:6
Ewertz, Eric H, 1950, Ap 8,13:6
Ewertz, Eric H Mrs, 1951, S 30,72:4
Ewig, Pauline M, 1951, O 9,29:3
Ewin, Hannah J, 1937, O 29,21:4
Ewin, James P Sr, 1948, Ag 9,20:3
Ewin, Myra W, 1952, Je 18,29:7
Ewing, A, 1935, Ja 8,21:1
Ewing, Addison A, 1949, Je 28,28:4
Ewing, Albert E, 1957, Ag 11,80:5
Ewing, Andrew, 1864, Jl 12,2:2
Ewing, Arthur G, 1951, Mr 6,27:1
Ewing, Arthur H Mrs, 1920, Ap 29,13:4
Ewing, Benjamin B, 1952, N 9,91:1
Ewing, Blaine, 1965, D 18,29:5
Ewing, Blaine Mrs, 1943, Ap 5,19:1
Ewing, Caruthers (por), 1947, Ag 21,23:3
Ewing, Charles, 1883, Je 21,4:7
Ewing, Charles A, 1942, Ja 7,20:3
Ewing, Charles H, 1954, Jl 22,23:2
Ewing, Charles H Mrs, 1955, O 26,31:5
Ewing, Charles H Rev Dr, 1937, O 17,II,9:2
Ewing, Charles Mrs, 1937, O 23,15:8
Ewing, Donald H, 1951, F 23,27:3
Ewing, E B, 1873, Je 23,1:6
Ewing, Edward, 1958, Jl 30,29:4
Ewing, Everett, 1942, Ja 12,15:2
Ewing, Fayette C, 1956, Ap 16,27:4
Ewing, Frank, 1968, Ag 13,39:1
Ewing, Frank W, 1943, My 25,23:4
Ewing, Frederic Mrs, 1964, D 19,29:4
Ewing, G E, 1884, Ap 27,9:1
Ewing, George R M, 1967, Je 6,44:4
Ewing, Glenn, 1950, My 14,47:4
Ewing, Guy L, 1951, N 13,29:4
Ewing, H Clay, 1907, Mr 23,9:6
Ewing, Hampton D Mrs, 1953, D 27,60:7
Ewing, Harry C, 1944, F 29,17:3
Ewing, Harvey, 1961, Mr 16,37:1
Ewing, Henry Maj, 1873, Je 14,1:6
Ewing, Isaac P, 1944, My 1,15:3
Ewing, J Cal, 1937, Ja 20,21:2
Ewing, J Franklin Rev, 1968, My 21,47:3
Ewing, James, 1943, My 17,15:3
Ewing, James C R Rev Dr, 1925, Ag 22,11:6
Ewing, James D, 1965, Mr 3,41:2
Ewing, James D Mrs, 1943, F 13,11:2
Ewing, James L, 1954, My 27,27:5
Ewing, Jesse T, 1941, Ag 5,19:2
Ewing, John, 1923, Je 26,19:5
Ewing, John D, 1952, My 18,92:1
Ewing, John E Col, 1907, F 26,11:6
Ewing, John K, 1953, My 3,25:5
Ewing, Joseph A, 1962, My 22,37:4
Ewing, Joseph D, 1958, D 4,39:1
Ewing, Joseph H, 1940, Ja 28,33:2; 1954, Ag 14,15:2
Ewing, Joseph L, 1952, N 29,17:2
Ewing, Mary B, 1938, Ag 29,13:5
Ewing, Mary R, 1949, Jl 8,19:6
Ewing, Neal H, 1953, N 7,17:2
Ewing, Neal H Mrs, 1953, Ja 30,21:1
Ewing, Oscar R Mrs, 1953, Je 21,85:2
Ewing, Paul W, 1955, D 10,21:1
Ewing, R, 1931, Ap 28,27:1
Ewing, Robert, 1947, Je 22,52:6
Ewing, Samuel C Rev Dr, 1908, Ap 6,7:5
Ewing, Samuel Currie Rev Dr, 1908, Ap 8,7:4
Ewing, Samuel E, 1939, N 3,21:2
Ewing, Samuel E Mrs, 1949, F 5,15:7
Ewing, Sister Philemon, 1951, Ap 15,92:1
Ewing, Stella, 1902, D 31,1:2
Ewing, T Gen, 1896, Ja 22,9:6
Ewing, T Jr, 1933, F 9,17:1
Ewing, Thomas, 1871, O 28,4:2; 1942, D 8,25:4
Ewing, Thomas Mrs, 1943, My 5,27:4
Ewing, Thomas 3d, 1962, D 1,12:4
Ewing, Toulmin H, 1938, Ap 28,23:5
Ewing, Walter L, 1950, D 26,23:4
Ewing, William, 1965, My 20,43:4
Ewing, William Alexander Dr, 1918, Ap 23,13:7
Ewing, William B, 1945, Ag 1,19:1; 1947, My 20,25:5
Ewing, William Buckingham (Buck), 1906, O 21,6:2
Ewing, William F, 1943, Ap 2,21:4; 1949, Je 7,32:7
Ewing, William F C, 1965, Ap 26,31:2
Ewing, William Mrs, 1957, Mr 10,89:2
Ewing, William N, 1939, My 29,15:5
Ewing, William Pinckney, 1907, S 8,7:5
Ewing, Wilson, 1952, S 10,19:4
Ewins, Arthur J, 1957, D 31,18:1
Ewins, Frederick J, 1940, My 19,43:1
Ewne, William R E, 1942, D 25,17:5
Ewry, Ray C, 1937, S 30,23:2
Excell, William H, 1950, F 27,19:4
Exelmans, Adm, 1875, Ag 7,1:2
Exeter, Marquis of (W T B Cecil), 1956, Ag 7,27:5
Exley, Gordon R, 1948, Mr 2,23:4
Exley, John O, 1938, Jl 28,19:4
Exmouth, Viscount, 1945, Je 11,15:2
Exmouth, Viscountess (Mrs M G Pellew), 1949, Mr 31,25:5
Exner, Frank G, 1947, F 18,25:4
Exner, Fred Sr, 1949, Mr 22,25:2
Exner, Max J, 1943, O 10,48:8
Expert, Roger-Henri, 1955, Ap 17,87:1
Exposta, Florinda de Jesus, 1953, F 18,31:3
Exselsen, Carl L V, 1964, Ja 9,31:4
Extance, William L, 1918, Je 29,11:5
Exton, Albert L, 1938, Ja 16,II,9:2
Exton, Frederick Mrs, 1945, F 9,15:1
Exton, James A Dr, 1912, Jl 26,9:6
Exton, John Mrs, 1908, Ap 20,7:4
Exton, William G, 1943, Mr 13,13:3
Ey, John A, 1953, O 18,87:1
Eyck, James Ten, 1910, Jl 29,9:5
Eyde, Samuel, 1940, Je 22,15:5
Eydeler, John H, 1956, Ag 14,25:3
Eydenberg, Arnold H, 1963, Ap 16,35:3
Eyer, Elmer S, 1951, F 22,31:3
Eyer, George A, 1961, S 18,29:4
Eyer, Sterling E, 1944, My 10,19:4
Eyerly, Osborne J, 1958, Je 16,23:5
Eyerly, Paul R, 1946, My 28,21:3
Eyerly, R Emmet, 1951, F 14,29:2
Eykmans, J, 1945, Ap 11,23:3
Eylar, M S Mrs, 1950, Je 7,29:5
Eylar, Matthew S, 1948, F 6,26:5
Eyler, Amos L, 1942, My 12,19:1
Eylers, John, 1951, Jl 25,23:3
Eyles, Alfred, 1945, My 20,32:1
Eyles, Arthur H Mrs, 1955, Jl 2,15:4
Eyles, Edward, 1937, My 21,21:1
Eyles, John W Sr, 1937, Ap 25,II,9:2
Eyman, Elmer V, 1955, F 15,27:2
Eymann, Charles A, 1940, Ap 4,23:6
Eynon, Benjamin G, 1952, Jl 9,27:5
Eynon, Edward B Jr, 1955, N 9,33:4
Eynon, William G Dr, 1918, Mr 25,11:4
Eypper, George H, 1942, N 6,23:3
Eyraud, E, 1954, Jl 1,5:7
Eyre, Archbishop, 1902, Mr 28,9:5
Eyre, Beverley M, 1958, F 10,23:1
Eyre, Charles F, 1939, Ja 15,38:3
Eyre, Edgar Ainsworth Mrs, 1921, Jl 15,11:7
Eyre, Edward J, 1962, O 7,82:4
Eyre, Edward L, 1951, S 26,31:5
Eyre, George W, 1942, Ja 7,19:4
Eyre, Henry, 1882, My 5,3:5
Eyre, Henry N, 1967, Ja 31,31:2
Eyre, J W H, 1944, F 22,23:2
Eyre, John, 1905, Ja 26,7:5
Eyre, L, 1928, S 10,23:3
Eyre, Laurence, 1959, Je 8,27:3
Eyre, Lincoln, 1925, O 30,21:5
Eyre, Louisa, 1953, N 11,31:4
Eyre, Maynard Campbell, 1916, My 13,9:5
Eyre, Richard, 1955, S 8,31:3
Eyre, Richard Mrs, 1948, D 2,29:3
Eyre, Samuel A, 1943, F 16,19:1
Eyre, Severn, 1914, Jl 11,7:6
Eyre, Vincent, 1881, O 9,6:7
Eyre, Wilson, 1944, O 24,23:5
Eyrich, George F Jr, 1968, Je 20,45:2

Eyrick, Charles, 1941, F 27,19:3
Eyrick, Charles Mrs, 1941, F 27,19:3
Eysinga, Willem J M van, 1961, Ja 27,23:3
Eysler, Edmund (por), 1949, O 6,31:4
Eysler, James, 1968, Mr 11,41:3
Eysmans, Julien L, 1944, Ja 1,13:4
Eyssell, William Mrs, 1955, S 12,25:3
Eyster, Clarence, 1938, F 13,II,7:1
Eyster, John B Mrs, 1940, Ja 6,13:1
Eytel, Hans Mrs, 1945, S 3,23:2
Eythe, William, 1957, Ja 27,84:1
Eytinge, Pearl, 1914, Mr 10,9:4
Eytinge, Rose (funl, D 22,13:5), 1911, D 21,11:5
Eytle, Julius H, 1948, Ja 16,21:3
Eyton, Charles F, 1941, Jl 3,19:6
Ezekiel, David, 1946, Ap 16,25:3
Ezekiel, Moses, 1917, Mr 28,13:3
Ezekiel, Moses Sir, 1921, Mr 31,13:4
Ezerman, M Sophia Mrs, 1940, N 11,19:2
Ezeta, A Gen, 1897, Mr 9,7:3
Ezickson, Aaron J Mrs, 1951, F 4,77:1
Ezickson, Aaron J Mrs (J Asch), 1963, S 15,87:1
Ezqueta, Gonzalez F, 1949, D 1,31:2
Ezra, Viscount de, 1945, D 29,14:2
Ezra bin Abbas, 1918, N 1,15:3
Ezray, G C Rev, 1903, My 23,9:2
Ezzerman, Werner D, 1940, Mr 19,25:2

F

Faas, Martin F, 1945, My 19,19:1
Faatz, Albert, 1951, Ja 24,27:2
Faatz, Jay S, 1923, Ap 11,21:5
Fabares, Raoul, 1968, D 13,42:3
Fabbi, Allesandro, 1922, F 7,17:4
Fabbri, Augusto, 1940, Ap 1,19:3
Fabbri, E G, 1883, Jl 4,5:2
Fabbri, Edith S Mrs, 1954, D 19,84:6
Fabbri, Ernesto G, 1943, Ap 25,34:6
Fabbri-Muller, Inez, 1909, Ag 31,7:6
Fabbrizi, N Gen, 1885, Ap 25,4:6
Fabbroni, Giuseppe, 1960, O 10,31:3
Fabela, Isidro, 1964, Ag 13,29:4
Fabens, Hannah E, 1937, S 25,17:6
Faber, Alex E Mrs, 1952, F 18,19:4
Faber, Annes, 1943, Jl 23,17:2
Faber, Beryl (Mrs Cosmo Hamilton), 1912, My 3, 11:4
Faber, Charles, 1954, My 29,15:3
Faber, Charles Mrs, 1964, Je 24,37:2
Faber, E, 1879, Mr 4,8:2
Faber, Eberhard, 1946, My 17,21:3
Faber, Eberhard Mrs, 1961, Ap 2,77:1
Faber, Edwin C, 1959, O 22,37:3
Faber, Erwin F, 1939, My 25,25:2
Faber, Franklin G, 1939, Ja 31,21:3
Faber, Geoffrey, 1961, Ap 1,17:4
Faber, Harman, 1913, D 12,11:6
Faber, Henry B, 1938, O 23,40:7
Faber, Henry E, 1915, Je 27,15:5
Faber, Herbert A, 1956, Ap 3,35:3
Faber, John, 1942, My 14,19:3
Faber, John D, 1943, Mr 12,17:2
Faber, Joseph, 1947, Ag 28,23:2
Faber, Leander B, 1950, N 5,94:3
Faber, Leslie, 1918, Ap 19,13:3
Faber, Lester A, 1943, My 21,20:3
Faber, Lothar W, 1943, My 13,21:2
Faber, Otto, 1945, Ag 4,11:2
Faber, Sidney, 1943, D 3,23:2
Faber, Simon, 1925, Jl 26,5:4
Faber, William F, 1967, F 11,29:5
Faber, William M Jr, 1945, F 8,19:5
Faberman, Harris, 1945, Ag 12,39:2
Fabert, Henri, 1941, F 24,15:5
Fabia, John Sr, 1954, Ag 2,10:7
Fabian, Abraham A, 1958, Ja 20,23:2
Fabian, Bela, 1966, D 28,37:1
Fabian, Bela Mrs, 1964, Mr 16,31:1
Fabian, Edward, 1907, Ag 31,7:6
Fabian, Edward S, 1948, Ag 17,22:2
Fabian, Ewald, 1944, F 19,13:3
Fabian, Henry, 1940, F 26,15:4
Fabian, Jacob, 1941, Ap 25,19:4; 1950, Ag 10,25:4
Fabian, Jacob Mrs, 1962, My 2,37:3
Fabian, Richard V, 1957, Ap 7,88:4
Fabian, Simon H Mrs, 1967, F 5,89:1
Fabian, Tracy, 1955, Ap 15,23:3
Fabier, Joseph L, 1948, Mr 18,27:4
Fabini, Eduardo, 1950, My 19,27:2
Fabio, Benjamin, 1958, Ag 3,81:1
Fabius, W J Knockers, 1960, S 2,23:1
Fable, Frederick Jr, 1955, S 13,31:4
Fabler, Harry L, 1944, D 7,25:5
Fables, David G Jr, 1961, F 24,21:3
Fablet, Julian, 1940, N 27,23:3
Fabre, Edouard, 1939, Jl 3,13:5
Fabre, Emile, 1955, S 27,35:3
Fabre, Hector, 1910, S 3,7:6
Fabre, Henri, 1915, O 12,11:4
Fabre, Rene, 1966, O 5,47:2
Fabre, Saturnin, 1961, O 26,35:2
Fabrega, Julio J, 1950, My 23,30:3
Fabregas, Virginia, 1950, N 18,15:3
Fabregue, Casimir Prof, 1908, Jl 24,9:6
Fabres, Oscar, 1960, O 13,37:5
Fabri, Frank F, 1950, O 10,31:3
Fabri, Ludwig S, 1961, Ap 18,37:2
Fabricant, Jacob, 1949, S 6,27:3
Fabricant, Leah K Mrs (cor, D 19,31:4), 1951, D 16, 89:3
Fabricant, Louis (por), 1947, My 15,26:2
Fabricant, Noah D, 1964, My 27,39:2
Fabricant, Rose B, 1954, Jl 30,17:5
Fabricatore, Francis Mrs, 1958, Mr 1,17:5
Fabricius, Herman T, 1949, Jl 22,19:5
Fabricius, J R, 1951, Jl 28,11:4
Fabricius, Jan, 1964, N 25,37:5
Fabrikant, Benjamin, 1965, Ag 11,35:3
Fabrikant, Max, 1967, Ag 23,51:4
Fabrikant, Phil J, 1955, D 6,38:1
Fabrikant, Phil Mrs, 1954, Ja 8,16:1
Fabrique, Charles M, 1940, Ja 20,15:5
Fabrizio, John, 1945, O 9,21:5
Fabry, Alois V, 1954, D 4,17:3
Fabry, Jaro, 1952, F 19,29:3
Fabry, Jean Col, 1968, Je 2,89:1
Fabry, Vladimir, 1961, S 19,14:2
Fabyan, A L, 1902, My 14,9:5
Fabyan, Francis W, 1937, S 5,II,7:3
Fabyan, Nelle Mrs (will), 1939, Ag 2,21:4
Facchinetti, Cipriano, 1952, F 18,19:4
Facchinetti, Vittorino, 1950, D 4,29:5
Faccini, Lazzaro P, 1948, Je 18,23:4
Faccioli, G, 1934, Ja 14,28:3
Facey, J Frank, 1943, O 20,21:2
Facher, Joseph, 1964, Jl 22,33:4
Fachet, Andrew Sr, 1951, My 8,31:5
Fachiri, Alex P, 1939, Mr 28,24:2
Fackelmann, Anton, 1952, Mr 4,27:4
Fackenthal, Frank D Dr, 1968, S 6,43:1
Fackenthal, Joseph D (cor, O 26,47:5), 1967, O 13, 39:2
Fackenthal, Michael, 1938, Mr 24,23:3
Fackenthal, Michael Mrs, 1956, O 12,29:4
Fackler, Clarence, 1953, D 17,37:1
Fackler, David P, 1924, N 1,15:4
Fackler, Edward B, 1952, Ja 10,30:2
Fackler, Edward B Mrs, 1959, Ag 30,82:7
Fackner, Edward Col, 1912, N 18,11:4
Fackner, L E, 1931, D 25,21:3
Fackrell, Fred P, 1941, Ja 26,36:1
Facta, L, 1930, N 6,25:1
Factor, Leah Mrs, 1938, N 11,25:3
Factor, Max (por), 1938, Ag 31,15:1
Factor, Max Mrs, 1949, D 5,23:4
Factor, Samuel, 1949, Ja 12,27:4
Fadden, F A, 1932, My 2,17:2
Fadden, Joseph, 1955, F 13,87:1
Fadders, Louis F, 1942, F 6,19:1
Faddis, Walter S, 1944, Jl 26,19:1
Faddle, J Edward, 1965, Je 27,64:6
Fadem, Charles, 1961, N 6,37:1
Fadem, Joseph, 1961, N 8,35:5
Faden, Jacob Mrs, 1957, N 3,88:3
Fader, C E, 1903, My 23,9:3
Fader, Clementine, 1957, N 18,31:4
Fadiman, Isadore M, 1964, F 27,31:1
Fadum, Chris, 1952, Jl 13,60:3
Faeber, Alfred O, 1949, N 26,30:5
Faede, Edward A Mrs, 1948, D 4,19:2
Faehndrich, Joseph M, 1959, Ag 12,29:4
Faelten, Max R, 1950, F 10,24:3
Faelten, Otto, 1945, Ap 25,23:3
Faelten, Reinhold Mrs, 1938, Ja 8,15:2
Faerber, Louis, 1947, N 19,27:2
Faesch, Ernest E, 1952, Mr 19,29:3
Faeth, Gilbert E, 1957, N 12,37:1
Fafard, Gilbert A, 1945, F 14,19:3
Fafflock, Clara, 1951, Ag 10,17:2
Fafflock, Marie, 1951, S 26,31:1
Fagal, Henry C, 1959, Ag 1,17:2
Fagan, Allen H, 1937, S 18,19:5
Fagan, Arthur L, 1946, Jl 29,21:5
Fagan, Arthur S, 1939, S 29,23:5
Fagan, B J, 1934, S 27,21:3
Fagan, Barney, 1937, Ja 13,23:3
Fagan, Bernard J Mrs, 1951, My 9,33:4
Fagan, Christopher, 1951, Jl 26,23:7
Fagan, E F, 1901, D 8,7:6
Fagan, Edward, 1943, Ja 29,19:5
Fagan, Edward J, 1940, Ja 20,15:2
Fagan, Eleanora (B Holiday),(funl plans, Jl 20,25:3), 1959, Jl 18,15:5
Fagan, F Arthur Sr, 1955, Je 18,17:2
Fagan, Francis M, 1944, My 25,21:3
Fagan, Frank F, 1949, Jl 18,17:5
Fagan, Frank J, 1960, Jl 13,35:3
Fagan, George, 1907, Ag 25,7:5
Fagan, George B, 1955, Ja 28,20:2
Fagan, J B, 1933, F 18,16:2
Fagan, James E, 1955, Mr 14,23:3
Fagan, James L, 1942, Je 5,17:2; 1947, Je 8,60:7
Fagan, James M, 1937, F 14,II,9:3; 1952, My 19,17:4
Fagan, James P Rev, 1906, Ap 29,11:6
Fagan, John A, 1943, Ja 20,19:2
Fagan, John C, 1940, Ja 17,21:4
Fagan, John F, 1942, D 3,25:4
Fagan, John J, 1938, My 3,23:2; 1943, Ag 25,19:2
Fagan, John J P, 1945, O 10,36:2
Fagan, John L, 1937, D 11,19:2
Fagan, John T, 1943, Ja 5,19:2
Fagan, Lawrence, 1921, My 10,17:4
Fagan, Lawrence Mrs, 1959, D 31,21:4
Fagan, Mark, 1948, Ja 1,23:2
Fagan, Mark M, 1955, Jl 17,60:3
Fagan, Matthew F, 1966, Jl 3,35:1
Fagan, Maurice J, 1958, O 15,39:3
Fagan, Mildred E, 1940, Ag 14,19:4
Fagan, Nora Mrs, 1948, O 7,29:3
Fagan, Patrick, 1942, Je 30,21:1
Fagan, Paul I, 1960, D 19,27:2
Fagan, Peter E, 1950, F 19,76:4
Fagan, Peter F, 1956, F 18,19:3
Fagan, Ralph T, 1965, N 7,89:2
Fagan, Robert K, 1956, Ag 29,29:3
Fagan, Thomas F, 1966, My 5,47:3
Fagan, William P, 1952, S 26,21:4
Fagans, Amples, 1949, Mr 13,76:2
Fagans, Ampless Mrs, 1952, S 13,17:2
Fagans, George T, 1951, Je 15,23:2
Fagans, George T Mrs, 1947, Ap 18,21:2
Fagans, James, 1948, Ja 3,13:4
Fagelson, Simon, 1943, Jl 17,13:3
Fagen, Frank J, 1945, S 14,23:1
Fagen, Marguerite E, 1955, Je 19,93:2
Fagen, Michael I, 1940, N 30,17:1
Fagen, William Albert, 1905, Ap 18,2:6
Fageol, Lou, 1961, Ja 18,33:2
Faget, J C Dr, 1884, D 9,2:5
Faget, Julius E Sr, 1947, Ap 4,23:3
Fagg, Fred D Mrs, 1951, D 18,31:4
Fagg, John Gerardus Rev Dr, 1917, My 5,13:6
Fagge, John H L Sir, 1940, Mr 20,34:8
Faggen, Nathan, 1946, N 19,31:5
Faggi, Alfeo, 1966, O 17,37:3
Faggione, William, 1965, S 4,21:7
Fagin, Abraham, 1958, F 24,19:4
Fagin, Albert L, 1953, Mr 28,17:4
Fagin, Isidor, 1946, N 2,15:4
Fagioli, Luigi, 1952, Je 21,15:5
Fagley, Frederick L, 1958, Ag 26,29:4
Fagnani, Alice M L, 1942, Mr 13,19:1
Fagnani, Charles P, 1941, Ja 7,25:6
Fagnani, Joseph, 1873, My 25,5:2
Fagny, Janine (Praline), 1952, Je 25,5:3
Fagot, Eugene, 1919, Ja 11,13:2
Fagundus, Elmer L, 1953, Mr 2,23:6
Fahbrica, Isabella, 1873, Mr 23,1:7
Faherty, Gregory E, 1953, N 2,25:5
Faherty, Mary A S, 1947, Mr 26,25:3
Faherty, Sylvester J, 1951, Mr 7,33:3
Fahey, Aloysius A, 1965, Je 26,29:2
Fahey, Charles J, 1938, D 28,26:2
Fahey, Ferdinand A, 1946, S 8,44:5
Fahey, Francis Mrs, 1948, F 2,19:4
Fahey, Francis R, 1954, Mr 22,27:4
Fahey, Frank J, 1945, F 20,19:5
Fahey, James J, 1941, Mr 7,21:5
Fahey, John H, 1950, N 20,25:1
Fahey, John Mrs, 1944, Je 21,19:6
Fahey, John T, 1941, Ap 30,19:4
Fahey, Joseph F, 1948, F 16,21:2
Fahey, Leo F, 1950, Ap 2,93:2
Fahey, Peter R, 1945, S 15,15:5
Fahey, Ralph P, 1951, Je 26,29:4
Fahey, Thomas A Mrs, 1954, S 25,15:6
Fahey, Thomas J Mrs, 1964, Ja 2,27:4
Fahey, William J, 1940, My 6,17:3
Fahey, William P, 1941, Ap 6,49:1
Fahlberg, Charles Dr, 1910, Ag 17,7:4
Fahmy, A M Mrs, 1961, N 24,31:1
Fahmy, Hussein, 1960, Mr 10,31:1
Fahnestock, A Bruce Sr Mrs, 1954, D 31,13:3
Fahnestock, Albert D, 1939, Ag 3,19:4
Fahnestock, Archer P, 1939, Je 10,17:5
Fahnestock, Camillus S Dr, 1903, Jl 6,7:6
Fahnestock, Carolyn S A Mrs (will, N 7,31:2), 19 O 19,25:3
Fahnestock, Edith, 1956, N 27,37:1
Fahnestock, Ernest Mrs, 1957, My 1,37:4
Fahnestock, Gibson Mrs, 1942, O 9,22:3
Fahnestock, Harris, 1939, O 11,30:4
Fahnestock, Harris Charles, 1914, Je 5,11:5
Fahnestock, James T, 1924, Je 9,17:6
Fahnestock, Louis, 1949, Mr 12,18:6
Fahnestock, Mary M Mrs, 1941, N 7,23:4
Fahnestock, Percival D, 1954, O 10,86:8
Fahnestock, Sheridan (Jno), 1965, Ag 31,33:4
Fahnestock, Snowden A, 1962, N 11,88:7
Fahnestock, Virginia Mrs, 1940, F 27,21:5
Fahnestock, W, 1936, Jl 6,15:4
Fahnestock, William (will), 1940, Je 12,47:1
Fahnestock, William Jr, 1964, Mr 4,34:7
Fahnestock, William Mrs, 1959, My 9,21:6
Fahnstock, Gibson, 1917, Mr 3,9:2
Fahr, Herman, 1939, N 16,23:4
Fahr, John W Jr, 1955, S 24,19:5
Fahremkopf, Nicholas J, 1945, My 6,38:3
Fahrenbruck, William, 1947, F 12,25:4
Fahrion, Frank G Mrs, 1944, S 26,23:5
Fahrney, Milton H, 1941, Mr 27,23:4
Fahs, Charles H, 1948, Jl 16,19:3
Fahs, Louis A, 1939, S 16,17:5
Fahs, Raymond Z Sr Mrs, 1964, Ja 15,31:4
Fahy, Charles H, 1958, Ag 11,21:2
Fahy, Frank P, 1953, Jl 13,25:3; 1956, Mr 27,35:
Fahy, George C, 1948, Ag 3,25:1
Fahy, Jack B, 1947, Jl 2,23:3
Fahy, Lawrence L, 1943, Jl 31,13:5
Fahy, Martin E, 1939, Ap 8,15:4
Fahy, Thomas K, 1949, Je 2,27:4
Fahy, Walter T, 1946, Ja 15,23:4
Fahy, William J, 1943, N 29,19:5
Fahys, George E Mrs, 1952, Je 30,19:3
Faibish, Max M, 1962, O 27,25:4
Faidy, Harriet B Mrs, 1962, N 29,38:5

Faiella, Harry E, 1956, Jl 23,23:6
Faiella, John A A, 1961, Ap 11,37:3
Faiella, Joseph F, 1939, Mr 20,17:4
Faig, John T, 1951, Ap 10,27:2
Faig, Robert, 1962, Jl 31,27:4
Faigle, Carl, 1948, F 17,25:5
Faigle, Eugene, 1951, Jl 4,17:3
Faigle, J Fred, 1938, Ap 3,II,7:3
Faile, Donald S, 1939, Mr 13,17:2
Faile, E Hall, 1947, F 23,53:6
Faile, Edward G Sr, 1961, Ag 6,85:1
Faile, Jane R, 1955, Jl 11,23:3
Faile, Samuel, 1957, Je 30,68:5
Failes, Christopher Mrs, 1943, Ja 16,13:5
Failey, William A, 1939, N 21,26:6
Failing, Arthur B, 1938, Ap 6,23:5
Failing, Edwin T Mrs, 1939, Je 17,15:6
Failing, Frasier M, 1943, Jl 30,15:3
Failing, George Mrs, 1954, Ag 26,27:4
Failing, Marcus, 1952, Ja 25,22:4
Failing, Willis H, 1939, N 24,23:4
Failla, Gioacchino, 1961, D 16,17:4
Faille, Carl A, 1956, Ja 14,19:6
Failoni, Sergio, 1948, Jl 27,25:1
Failor, Clarence W Mrs, 1941, Ag 7,17:4
Fain, Benjamin, 1948, S 7,25:5
Fain, Edmund J, 1950, O 3,31:5
Fain, John R, 1944, Mr 28,19:4
Fain, Simon, 1957, N 18,31:2
Fain, Walter C Mrs, 1962, Jl 21,19:4
Fain, William, 1961, Ap 24,59:5
Fain, William H, 1948, My 30,34:5
Fain, William H Mrs, 1944, O 24,23:5
Fair, Charles M, 1939, Je 8,25:2
Fair, Harry H, 1960, Jl 10,72:1
Fair, James G, 1894, D 30,2:6
Fair, John, 1872, Ja 2,5:6
Fair, John S, 1950, S 1,21:3
Fair, Joseph Brooks, 1907, N 26,9:6
Fair, Nancy Mrs, 1957, Mr 10,89:3
Fair, Simon Col, 1873, Jl 17,4:7
Fair, Virginia, 1948, S 7,26:3
Fair, William Allen Rev, 1903, O 29,9:4
Fairall, Elizabeth, 1966, Ap 26,45:2
Fairand, Charles A, 1941, S 8,15:4
Fairbairn, Agnes, 1953, Ja 7,31:5
Fairbairn, Andrew M Rev Dr, 1912, F 10,11:4
Fairbairn, Edward Sr, 1941, Ja 4,13:1
Fairbairn, Henry Arnold Dr, 1925, Je 12,19:6
Fairbairn, J M R, 1954, My 28,23:4
Fairbairn, James B, 1940, N 15,21:3
Fairbairn, Robert A, 1951, D 20,31:5
Fairbairn, Robert A Mrs, 1941, O 3,23:2
Fairbairn, Stephen, 1938, My 17,23:2
Fairbairn, William Sir, 1874, Ag 19,1:5
Fairbairn, William T, 1949, Ja 2,60:5
Fairbank, Charles W, 1956, Je 29,21:4
Fairbank, Clair W, 1954, My 30,45:1
Fairbank, Clair W Mrs, 1943, Ap 16,22:3
Fairbank, Edward Mrs, 1951, Jl 24,25:2
Fairbank, Janet (por), 1947, S 27,15:3
Fairbank, Kellogg, 1939, F 19,39:4
Fairbank, Kellogg Sr Mrs, 1951, D 29,11:2
Fairbank, Leigh C, 1966, Je 30,39:3
Fairbank, Murry N, 1968, D 31,27:3
Fairbank, N K, 1903, Mr 28,9:5
Fairbank, Robert W, 1966, Ap 2,29:1
Fairbank, Wilson H, 1908, Ja 6,7:4
Fairbanks, Adelaide, 1961, O 25,37:3
Fairbanks, Arthur, 1944, Ja 15,13:2
Fairbanks, Arthur B, 1943, Ja 26,19:3
Fairbanks, Benjamin, 1963, Ap 2,47:2
Fairbanks, C T, 1941, O 14,23:5
Fairbanks, Charles M, 1924, My 30,15:5
Fairbanks, Charles W, 1961, Ag 25,25:4
Fairbanks, Charles Warren, 1918, Je 5,11:2
Fairbanks, Charles Warren Mrs, 1913, O 25,13:6
Fairbanks, David Mrs, 1909, Ag 6,7:2
Fairbanks, Douglas, 1939, D 13,29:8
Fairbanks, Edwin R Jr, 1953, Ap 9,27:3
Fairbanks, Ella Adelaide Mrs, 1916, D 24,15:2
Fairbanks, Frank B, 1947, S 14,60:6
Fairbanks, Frank P, 1939, Ag 10,19:5
Fairbanks, Frederick C, 1940, My 23,24:2
Fairbanks, Frederick C Mrs, 1952, My 31,17:4
Fairbanks, George A, 1949, S 9,26:3
Fairbanks, George Mrs, 1948, Ap 28,27:3
Fairbanks, Gov, 1864, N 23,5:2
Fairbanks, Grant H, 1945, D 28,15:3
Fairbanks, Harold A, 1943, Jl 18,34:8
Fairbanks, Harold W, 1940, S 7,15:4
Fairbanks, Harry B, 1943, Ja 9,13:5
Fairbanks, Henry I, 1944, D 13,23:3
Fairbanks, Henry P, 1946, Ja 26,13:2
Fairbanks, J W, 1903, Je 26,9:6
Fairbanks, John E, 1924, F 25,15:2
Fairbanks, Joseph S, 1939, Mr 21,23:3
Fairbanks, Karl J, 1958, Je 10,33:3
Fairbanks, Kellog Jr, 1963, My 22,41:4
Fairbanks, Laura J Mrs, 1937, F 4,21:1
Fairbanks, Mary Mrs, 1916, O 31,13:6
Fairbanks, Newton H, 1937, Mr 24,25:4
Fairbanks, Ralph, 1951, Je 24,V,4:1
Fairbanks, Ralph W, 1959, F 17,32:1
Fairbanks, Richard M, 1944, Jl 27,17:2
Fairbanks, Robert, 1951, Ag 13,17:5
Fairbanks, Robert P, 1948, F 23,25:4
Fairbanks, Thomas N, 1953, Ag 9,77:1
Fairbanks, Warren C, 1938, Jl 28,19:5
Fairbanks, Warren C Mrs, 1944, O 23,19:3
Fairbanks, Warren E, 1961, Mr 14,35:3
Fairbanks, Warren H, 1941, Ag 7,17:2
Fairbanks, Wilson L, 1953, F 17,27:1
Fairbanks, Wilson L Mrs, 1937, Mr 15,23:3
Fairbourne, Arthur, 1948, S 25,17:3
Fairbrass, George F, 1949, Je 25,13:4
Fairbrook, Alvin J, 1962, Je 6,41:5
Fairbrook, Anthony, 1949, D 27,23:3
Fairbrother, Arthur L, 1922, Ja 4,13:4
Fairbrother, Sydney, 1941, Ja 5,44:4
Fairbrother, William E, 1942, N 6,23:5
Fairburn, William A, 1947, O 3,25:1
Fairburn, William A Mrs, 1962, Ag 5,81:1
Fairchild, Albert C, 1953, Ap 8,29:1
Fairchild, Arthur S, 1951, F 13,31:2
Fairchild, Arthur W, 1956, Ag 3,20:2
Fairchild, Benjamin L, 1946, O 26,17:1
Fairchild, Benjamin T (will), 1939, Ap 6,26:2
Fairchild, Benjamin T, 1957, S 19,29:3
Fairchild, Benjamin T Mrs, 1920, My 18,11:5
Fairchild, Charles, 1910, Jl 8,7:4
Fairchild, Charles B, 1950, Ag 13,77:1
Fairchild, Charles N Mrs (May), 1959, N 30,31:2
Fairchild, Charles Stebbins, 1924, N 25,23:3
Fairchild, Charles W, 1944, N 16,23:3
Fairchild, Clarence A, 1957, Je 28,23:4
Fairchild, Claude W, 1950, D 24,34:4
Fairchild, Daniel, 1938, Ag 9,19:2
Fairchild, David, 1954, Ag 7,13:3
Fairchild, David Mrs, 1962, S 25,37:3
Fairchild, E B, 1877, N 19,5:6
Fairchild, E D, 1922, Je 12,15:1
Fairchild, Edmund W, 1949, D 13,31:1
Fairchild, Edmund W Mrs, 1943, My 22,13:5
Fairchild, Edward Thomson, 1917, Ja 24,9:3
Fairchild, Elmer E Sr, 1954, D 23,19:5
Fairchild, Ernest A, 1941, S 25,25:2
Fairchild, Florence I B Mrs, 1937, My 25,27:4
Fairchild, Frank K, 1945, My 24,19:3
Fairchild, Fred R, 1966, Ap 15,39:1
Fairchild, Frederick P, 1960, Ap 2,23:4
Fairchild, George E, 1950, S 28,31:4
Fairchild, George Mrs, 1962, F 19,31:5
Fairchild, George P, 1955, Ap 18,23:2
Fairchild, George W, 1925, Ja 1,27:3; 1948, S 29,29:2
Fairchild, Henry P, 1956, O 3,33:1
Fairchild, Herbert B, 1962, Jl 16,23:1
Fairchild, Herbert Mrs, 1950, Jl 26,25:5
Fairchild, Herman L, 1943, N 30,27:1
Fairchild, Horace Jones Mrs, 1908, F 2,9:6
Fairchild, Ida G, 1943, F 13,11:5
Fairchild, J D, 1926, F 22,17:2
Fairchild, J H, 1902, Mr 20,2:4
Fairchild, James C, 1946, D 9,25:5
Fairchild, James T, 1947, S 16,23:2
Fairchild, Jarvis R, 1942, Ap 16,21:3
Fairchild, John F, 1943, N 9,21:4
Fairchild, John H, 1873, Ag 20,4:7
Fairchild, Joseph S, 1962, My 3,33:2
Fairchild, L Gen, 1896, My 24,2:5
Fairchild, Lambert, 1959, Ap 26,86:6
Fairchild, Lee, 1910, Mr 20,II,11:2; 1952, My 25,94:4
Fairchild, Louis E, 1950, Jl 26,25:1
Fairchild, Marcus E (cor, My 21,23:1), 1940, My 20, 17:1
Fairchild, May, 1961, S 3,60:4
Fairchild, Muir S, 1950, Mr 18,13:3
Fairchild, Nathan H, 1950, My 13,17:4
Fairchild, P Dexter, 1945, Ap 19,27:2
Fairchild, Paul H Dr, 1937, Je 9,25:3
Fairchild, Roy Mrs (Dallas Tyler), 1953, Jl 28,19:4
Fairchild, S W, 1927, N 14,21:3
Fairchild, Samuel E, 1947, Ja 1,33:3
Fairchild, W D, 1938, Ap 13,25:5
Fairchild, W S, 1880, D 8,5:5
Fairchild, Walter, 1945, My 13,20:2
Fairchild, Walter L, 1940, Ja 8,15:6
Fairchild, Willard, 1946, Ja 5,13:4
Fairchild, William L, 1938, Je 7,23:4
Fairchild, William S, 1940, Jl 11,19:4
Fairchilds, Sydney B, 1904, F 28,5:5
Faircloth, Charles A, 1951, D 4,33:6
Faircloth, Edward C, 1952, Ag 14,23:5
Fairclough, Henry R, 1938, F 13,II,6:8
Fairclough, John H, 1950, My 24,29:1
Fairclough, John H Mrs, 1948, Ap 15,25:2
Fairclough, Napoleon B, 1938, Ap 21,19:4
Fairclough, William W, 1956, My 9,33:4
Fairclough, William W Mrs, 1957, O 29,31:3
Fairey, Richard, 1956, O 1,27:5; 1960, Jl 29,25:2
Fairfax, Albert K Lord, 1939, O 5,23:1
Fairfax, Arthur Percy, 1925, N 30,19:5
Fairfax, Baroness (Mrs Jno Conte Fairfax), 1912, Mr 14,11:5
Fairfax, Beatrice, 1945, N 30,23:1
Fairfax, Charles C, 1944, Je 2,15:4
Fairfax, James, 1961, My 9,39:2
Fairfax, John Col, 1908, Mr 23,7:7
Fairfax, John Conte Mrs (Baroness Fairfax), 1912, Mr 14,11:5
Fairfax, John H, 1950, Je 11,92:1
Fairfax, John W, 1940, F 15,19:6
Fairfax, Lindsay Mrs, 1953, My 7,31:4
Fairfax, M C, 1935, Mr 1,19:1
Fairfax, Wilbur B, 1964, My 18,26:3
Fairfield, Arthur P, 1946, D 16,23:4
Fairfield, E B Dr, 1904, N 19,9:5
Fairfield, Harry S, 1942, Ap 23,24:3
Fairfield, Herbert G, 1958, O 5,87:1
Fairfield, Herbert L Mrs, 1951, Ja 19,25:4
Fairfield, Howard, 1943, D 3,23:2
Fairfield, Lord, 1945, F 6,19:2
Fairfield, Richard Cutts, 1918, Ja 30,9:8
Fairfield, Rufus A, 1939, Ja 2,23:1
Fairfield, Wynn C, 1961, O 18,43:3
Fairgrieve, James T, 1968, Mr 18,45:1
Fairhall, Lawrence T, 1957, Je 19,35:2
Fairhaven, Lady, 1939, Mr 19,III,7:3
Fairhaven, Lord (Urban H R Broughton), 1966, Ag 21,92:8
Fairhead, John E, 1942, Jl 23,19:4
Fairhurst, John T, 1952, F 19,29:1
Fairhurst, William, 1953, O 4,87:1
Fairhurst, William E, 1951, Mr 1,27:4
Fairlamb, Frederick, 1950, D 1,26:3
Fairlamb, James Remington Prof, 1908, Ap 18,9:5
Fairlamb, John F, 1938, O 31,15:3
Fairless, Benjamin F (funl, Ja 5,29:1), 1962, Ja 2,1:3
Fairless, Benjamin F Mrs, 1942, S 30,23:4; 1942, O 1, 23:5
Fairless, David D, 1954, Jl 5,11:4
Fairley, Edwin, 1941, My 17,15:6
Fairley, George E A, 1956, F 16,29:2
Fairley, James, 1940, My 14,23:4
Fairley, James A, 1951, N 11,91:2
Fairley, Samuel C, 1952, Ap 21,21:4
Fairlie, Chester W, 1964, N 12,37:5
Fairlie, John A (por), 1947, Ja 27,23:5
Fairlie, John F, 1966, N 25,37:1
Fairlie, William, 1914, F 18,9:4
Fairlimb, Alex M, 1937, Ap 6,23:2
Fairlis, William, 1953, N 28,15:5
Fairman, C G, 1884, Jl 7,2:4
Fairman, Charles E, 1943, Je 23,21:3
Fairman, E Bruce, 1944, Ag 1,15:2
Fairman, Elizabeth M Mrs, 1952, Mr 28,23:2
Fairman, Francis E Jr, 1958, S 29,27:4
Fairman, Fred W Sr, 1948, N 11,27:3
Fairman, Harry G Jr, 1958, O 21,33:5
Fairman, Hutchinson K, 1949, S 1,21:5
Fairman, James F, 1967, Ap 26,44:5
Fairman, Le G, 1881, F 10,5:6
Fairman, Roy E, 1961, My 30,17:4
Fairman, Roy M, 1951, Ja 29,19:3
Fairman, Seibert, 1961, Je 24,21:1
Fairman, William P, 1950, O 14,19:5
Fairs, Cecil, 1943, S 16,21:6
Fairservis, Thomas, 1942, Ja 19,17:2
Fairservis, Walter A Sr Mrs (E Yeager), 1959, S 5, 15:6
Fairtile, Clarence M, 1947, N 29,13:3
Fairweather, Clement W, 1957, Ap 17,31:1
Fairweather, Earl C, 1946, Je 10,21:5
Fairweather, Frederic H, 1952, Je 25,29:5
Fairweather, George, 1960, S 9,30:1
Fairweather, George M, 1946, Mr 12,25:3
Fairweather, Harold D, 1944, My 14,45:2
Fairweather, James Sr, 1948, N 5,26:3
Fairweather, Tom, 1951, Ja 26,23:4
Fais, Charles C, 1945, Ag 18,11:6
Faison, Elizabeth, 1961, Je 5,9:3
Faison, I W Mrs, 1938, Ap 14,23:1
Faison, John B, 1957, Mr 13,31:4
Faison, John W Mrs, 1963, D 2,37:5
Faison, Samson L, 1940, O 18,21:6
Faison, Samson L Mrs, 1957, N 23,19:4
Faissole, Charles A, 1949, F 8,25:5
Faist, William, 1903, Je 20,7:6
Fait, C W, 1940, My 25,17:2
Faith, Charles A Sgt, 1937, S 5,II,7:1
Faith, Raymond M, 1958, Ja 27,27:3
Faith, William J, 1951, Je 19,29:3
Faithfull, Emily, 1895, Je 4,5:6
Faithfull, Leonard E Mrs, 1937, Ja 29,19:2
Faitlowitz, Jacques, 1955, O 16,86:5
Faitoute, Moses W, 1941, Ag 29,17:5
Faitoute, Moses W Mrs, 1965, Ap 17,19:2
Faivre, Abel, 1945, Ag 16,19:4
Fajans, Irving, 1967, N 5,86:1
Fajans, Irving J, 1964, F 10,27:5
Fajardo, Gabriel J, 1937, Mr 2,21:4
Fajardo, Gabriel J Mrs, 1943, Je 1,23:1
Fajardo, Jose A, 1938, Ja 12,21:4
Fajardo, Pedro P, 1938, My 6,21:5
Fajen, Randolph B, 1960, My 27,31:2
Fake, Edward C, 1945, Je 5,19:2
Fake, Guy L, 1957, S 25,58:2
Fake, Kenneth H, 1963, My 25,25:5
Fake, Lynn B, 1950, O 28,17:4

Fake, Mary L Mrs, 1937, F 17,21:1
Falaguerra, Dominick, 1953, F 6,19:3
Falahee, John J (will, D 19,38:3), 1951, N 14,31:5
Falaleyev, Feodor Y, 1955, Ag 15,15:2
Falanga, Michele, 1942, F 2,15:1
Falardeau, George L Mrs, 1944, My 10,19:2
Falb, Rudolph Prof, 1903, O 1,5:2
Falbo, Italo C, 1946, F 19,26:2
Falbo, Marius P, 1955, Mr 22,31:2
Falcao, Waldemar, 1946, O 4,23:2
Falcao Trigoso, Joao D, 1956, D 24,13:5
Falcaro, Emanuel, 1952, Ag 17,77:1
Falcaro, Emanuel Mrs, 1943, Jl 11,35:1
Falcaro, Joe, 1951, S 9,88:3
Falcetano, Domenico, 1955, Mr 3,27:2
Falcetano, Frank, 1947, O 3,25:1
Falck, Albert, 1951, My 16,35:5
Falck, Alex D, 1950, Ap 6,29:4
Falck, Frederick M, 1951, S 16,85:2
Falck, Harry W, 1940, Ap 27,15:4
Falck, Richard, 1955, Ja 2,76:4
Falco, Charles J, 1923, Ag 25,7:5
Falco, Eugene, 1963, Jl 21,64:4
Falco, Louis A, 1945, Je 22,15:4
Falco, Marie C, 1961, My 10,45:3
Falcon, A R Gen, 1878, Je 25,1:4
Falcon, Alberto, 1919, My 7,15:4
Falcon, Thomas A, 1944, F 2,21:2
Falcone, Maria Mrs, 1925, Je 16,21:6
Falcone, Marie A, 1953, Ag 14,19:1
Falcone, Mario, 1944, Ja 29,13:4
Falconer, Alex, 1956, Je 17,92:6
Falconer, Archibald C, 1944, O 14,13:6
Falconer, Bolivar L, 1953, Ap 27,23:3
Falconer, Bruce M, 1949, Jl 19,29:3
Falconer, Charles E, 1937, Jl 2,21:4
Falconer, Douglas P Jr, 1940, My 20,17:3
Falconer, Ernest H, 1956, Ag 14,25:5
Falconer, Harry W, 1951, O 13,17:3
Falconer, James H, 1938, D 24,15:5
Falconer, John L, 1945, O 16,23:3
Falconer, Joseph H, 1950, Mr 24,25:2
Falconer, Joseph H C Mrs, 1939, O 24,23:4
Falconer, Martha P Mrs, 1941, N 28,23:4
Falconer, Robert, 1943, N 5,19:5; 1957, My 24,26:1
Falconer, Robert C, 1941, F 21,19:1
Falconer, Robert C Mrs, 1939, Ap 17,17:5
Falconer, Stuart A, 1959, Ap 27,27:5
Falconer, William B, 1965, Jl 17,25:5
Falconer, William H, 1921, Je 21,17:4
Falconer-Slater, Katherine E, 1956, F 19,93:1
Falconi, Ariodante F, 1948, Mr 15,23:3
Falconi, Armando, 1954, S 11,17:4
Falconio, Diomede Cardinal, 1917, F 8,13:3
Falda, Joseph, 1963, Ap 23,37:2
Faldini, Julio, 1947, Ja 23,23:3
Faleide, Isak H, 1964, Jl 24,27:1
Fales, A C, 1953, N 26,31:4
Fales, Almon L, 1949, Ag 20,11:5
Fales, Catherine R, 1947, D 2,29:4
Fales, DeCoursey, 1966, Je 20,33:4
Fales, Edward D, 1937, Ap 17,17:4
Fales, Frederick S (por), 1955, S 25,92:6
Fales, Harold A, 1955, O 27,68:5
Fales, Henry H, 1949, Je 5,94:3
Fales, J Winthrop, 1905, Je 20,9:6
Fales, John C, 1964, Ja 5,92:8
Fales, Leroy S, 1944, S 13,19:6
Fales, Mary Mrs, 1959, Mr 22,86:7
Fales, S B, 1880, S 20,3:2
Fales, W Thurber, 1953, My 22,27:3
Fales, Walter, 1953, Ap 22,29:5
Faletti, Anthony L, 1938, Jl 12,20:2
Falhaber, William, 1937, S 11,19:4
Falik, Abraham, 1953, S 30,31:6
Falikman, Moe, 1968, N 5,44:6
Falion, George M, 1938, Jl 19,22:6
Faliski, Herman J, 1948, Ja 14,25:3
Falk, Alfred, 1958, Ag 19,28:7
Falk, Arthur, 1946, Ja 19,14:2
Falk, Arthur Mrs, 1945, O 18,23:5
Falk, Benjamin J, 1925, Mr 21,13:4
Falk, Bernard, 1960, O 11,45:4
Falk, Charles, 1951, Ap 2,25:5
Falk, Clarence R, 1937, O 1,21:3
Falk, Edward, 1955, Je 20,21:2
Falk, Edwin A, 1956, N 15,35:3
Falk, Eliezer, 1938, My 22,II,7:2
Falk, Elliott H, 1956, D 30,33:1
Falk, Elmer W, 1968, Ag 21,42:2
Falk, Frederick W, 1953, Mr 22,86:1; 1965, My 3,33:3
Falk, George K, 1953, N 23,27:1
Falk, George W, 1939, F 1,21:6
Falk, Gilbert, 1965, Ja 23,25:4
Falk, H John, 1941, F 13,19:2
Falk, Harold S, 1957, O 9,35:5
Falk, Henri, 1937, My 7,II,8:4
Falk, Henry L, 1958, F 18,27:4
Falk, Herman W, 1947, F 18,25:3
Falk, Irvin V Sr, 1968, F 13,43:2
Falk, Isaac N, 1955, My 30,13:5
Falk, Isaac N (will), 1956, S 21,20:5
Falk, Jacob, 1949, N 19,17:3
Falk, John H, 1950, Ap 17,23:1
Falk, Joseph, 1942, Ap 18,15:5; 1966, My 29,56:8
Falk, Jules, 1957, D 10,35:2
Falk, Leo J, 1955, S 15,33:4
Falk, Leo J Mrs, 1960, Jl 12,35:1
Falk, Leon Mrs, 1962, F 12,47:3
Falk, Malcolm E, 1937, S 25,17:3
Falk, Maurice (cor, Mr 29,23:1),(will, Ap 2,29:3), 1946, Mr 20,23:1
Falk, Maurice Mrs, 1947, N 5,27:2; 1952, N 12,27:4
Falk, May Dr, 1908, S 11,9:2
Falk, Myron S, 1945, N 27,23:1
Falk, Oscar Mrs, 1966, Ag 25,37:2
Falk, Otto H, 1940, My 22,23:3
Falk, Phil S, 1939, N 19,38:8
Falk, Ralph, 1960, N 3,39:3
Falk, Rudolph, 1960, Ja 2,13:4
Falk, Sawyer, 1961, S 2,15:6
Falke, Charles (Bob Farrall), 1968, Ja 7,36:3
Falke, Fred C, 1948, N 20,13:3
Falke, George A, 1949, Jl 19,29:5
Falkenbach, August, 1953, Jl 15,25:3
Falkenbach, August Mrs, 1944, F 3,19:6
Falkenbach, Charles, 1916, Mr 4,11:7
Falkenbach, Charles H, 1962, Je 9,25:3
Falkenbach, Hedwig Mrs, 1949, Je 6,19:2
Falkenberg, Frantz O, 1951, F 4,77:1
Falkenburg, Charles M, 1951, Ja 14,84:5
Falkenburg, Eugene L, 1944, O 10,23:4
Falkenburg, George G, 1946, Ag 6,25:1
Falkenburg, Herman F, 1957, Je 30,68:8
Falkenbury, Ida M, 1942, Ap 23,24:3
Falkenhain, Frederik F G, 1944, Je 23,19:3
Falkenhausen, Alex von Mrs, 1950, Mr 7,27:4
Falkenhausen, Alexander E von, 1966, Ag 2,31:6
Falkenhayn, Erich von Gen, 1922, Ap 10,15:4
Falkenhorst, Nikolaus von Gen, 1968, Je 27,43:4
Falkiner, George B S, 1961, O 16,29:4
Falkingham, Percival E, 1964, Ag 15,21:3
Falkland, Viscount (Byron Plantagenet Cary), 1922, Ja 11,21:6
Falkland, Viscountess (Mrs Byron Plantagenet Cary), 1920, N 19,15:4
Falkner, Francis H, 1966, D 2,39:5
Falkner, J A, 1880, My 11,2:2
Falkner, Roland P, 1940, N 29,21:1
Falkner, W H, 1909, Je 16,7:6
Falkner, William, 1945, O 19,23:5
Falknor, Frank B, 1963, S 7,19:2
Falkoff, David L, 1967, D 16,41:4
Falky, Joseph J, 1942, N 21,13:2
Fall, Albert B, 1944, D 1,23:1
Fall, Albert B Mrs, 1943, Mr 26,19:1
Fall, Bernard B, 1967, F 22,1:5
Fall, Charles, 1950, D 7,33:4
Fall, Clifford P, 1941, Jl 27,30:1
Fall, Ernest M, 1955, S 23,25:3
Fall, Frank A, 1959, S 8,35:3
Fall, George H, 1937, Je 3,25:3
Fall, Leo, 1925, S 17,23:6
Falla, Fernando Mrs, 1956, Ag 13,19:5
Falla y Mateu, Manuel de, 1946, N 15,23:1
Fallada, Hans, 1947, F 7,23:3
Fallat, Andrew, 1950, Ja 14,15:6
Falle, Samuel Rev, 1937, Jl 24,15:6
Faller, Albert, 1941, Mr 9,41:3
Faller, George Washington Dr, 1923, F 21,15:4
Faller, Jacob (James), 1951, Ag 25,11:5
Faller, John D, 1949, F 7,19:3
Fallert, Berthold C, 1956, O 25,33:6
Fallin, Herbert, 1956, Ap 4,29:1
Falling, Hodgins Capt, 1912, O 17,11:4
Fallis, Edmund T, 1950, Mr 21,32:3
Fallis, Howard T Mrs, 1956, Mr 9,23:2
Fallon, Andrew Judge, 1908, Ap 9,9:4
Fallon, Arthur R Mrs, 1959, S 2,29:3
Fallon, Bernard, 1942, F 13,21:5
Fallon, Bernard J, 1956, D 25,25:4
Fallon, Charles P, 1948, Ag 28,15:4
Fallon, Clarence A, 1937, Mr 26,21:3
Fallon, Clarence G, 1950, Ja 12,27:4
Fallon, Eugene L, 1961, O 30,29:6
Fallon, Francis, 1952, Ap 28,19:3
Fallon, Francis B, 1961, D 18,35:4
Fallon, Francis I, 1939, S 28,25:1
Fallon, Francis X, 1953, N 4,33:3
Fallon, Francis X Mrs, 1949, S 13,29:2
Fallon, Henry H, 1950, Ja 9,26:3
Fallon, Hillman O, 1948, Ja 2,23:1
Fallon, J J Rev, 1903, S 12,9:6
Fallon, James, 1937, Mr 6,17:5; 1952, F 14,27:5
Fallon, James E, 1947, Je 16,21:2
Fallon, James L, 1940, My 25,17:5
Fallon, John C, 1953, Ja 25,84:3
Fallon, John G, 1956, My 12,19:2
Fallon, John J, 1945, F 21,19:3; 1954, Ja 18,23:5; 1962, Je 4,29:4
Fallon, John L, 1953, Ap 9,27:2
Fallon, John M, 1951, Je 23,15:3
Fallon, John Mrs, 1908, Ja 18,9:4; 1947, F 25,25:2
Fallon, John O, 1865, D 19,1:7
Fallon, John P, 1939, Mr 2,21:4; 1951, S 15,15:6; 1958, Ap 17,31:2
Fallon, John P Sr Mrs, 1953, O 18,86:5
Fallon, John V, 1966, Mr 25,41:1
Fallon, Joseph D Mrs, 1941, S 15,17:3
Fallon, Joseph P, 1950, Je 20,27:5; 1950, Jl 6,27:1; 1951, Jl 1,50:5; 1953, N 26,31:2
Fallon, Joseph P Justice, 1915, Jl 19,9:2
Fallon, Mary, 1952, Ja 1,19:4
Fallon, Mary E Mrs, 1938, O 5,23:2
Fallon, Michael J, 1956, Ap 4,29:2
Fallon, Nugent, 1957, Jl 25,23:3
Fallon, Perlie P, 1961, D 7,43:1
Fallon, Peter J Mrs, 1947, N 20,29:1
Fallon, Richard L, 1956, D 1,21:4
Fallon, Stephen J, 1949, Ap 29,23:3
Fallon, Thomas J, 1939, My 13,15:5
Fallon, Tom, 1964, Je 23,33:3
Fallon, W J, 1927, Ap 30,19:3
Fallon, William F, 1941, Ag 1,15:7
Fallon, William H, 1960, D 21,31:1
Fallon, William J, 1943, Ja 26,19:5
Fallon, William W, 1959, F 23,7:6
Fallor, Isaac N, 1925, Ap 3,19:6
Fallot, Eugene, 1940, S 21,19:5
Fallow, W A, 1948, My 4,25:4
Fallows, Edward H, 1940, Ja 13,15:6
Fallows, Samuel Bp, 1922, S 6,15:1
Fallows, Walter J, 1956, O 20,21:4
Falls, Anna E, 1945, F 28,23:2
Falls, Charles B, 1960, Ap 16,17:2
Falls, De Witt Brig Gen, 1937, S 8,23:3
Falls, James G, 1952, Je 11,29:1
Falls, John J, 1948, Ag 19,21:4
Falls, M N, 1876, Ap 9,7:3
Falls, Olivette, 1940, Ap 30,21:4
Falls, W A, 1884, Ag 1,5:3
Faloon, Dalton B, 1952, F 4,17:5
Falorsi, Vittorio, 1953, Ag 26,27:6
Falsey, William J, 1963, D 31,19:4
Falshaw, Thomas Mrs, 1965, Ag 5,29:4
Falter, Alfred, 1954, Jl 15,27:5
Falter, George H Mrs, 1948, Ja 18,61:1
Falter, John F, 1953, Ap 23,29:5
Falter, Nicholas, 1941, N 26,23:2
Falter, Nicholas Mrs, 1946, Ap 16,25:6
Faltermayer, Joseph, 1948, O 5,25:2
Falussy, Aloysius C, 1968, S 8,84:6
Falvello, Nicholas, 1954, Ag 28,15:4
Falvey, Catherine E, 1965, F 8,25:5
Falvey, Daniel J, 1942, Ja 8,22:2
Falvey, Daniel P, 1962, Ap 3,39:3
Falvey, Jerry, 1903, Ap 28,9:5
Falvey, John J, 1949, N 10,31:3
Falvey, Julia F Mrs, 1944, Ag 12,11:3
Falvey, Thomas F, 1944, My 19,19:4
Falvey, Timothy J, 1947, D 3,29:1
Falvey, Wallace, 1958, N 8,21:4
Falzer, G A (Gus), 1953, Ja 28,27:4
Falzone, Michael A, 1967, Ja 27,45:2
Fama, Charles, 1959, Ag 31,21:3
Famel, Sylvain R, 1954, Ag 28,15:3
Familant, Abram S, 1962, Ja 2,30:4
Familton, Robert S, 1957, Ag 30,19:5
Famularo, Thomas, 1968, F 21,47:2
Fanara, Romolo, 1966, Ap 10,79:4
Fanch, Frederick W Mrs, 1944, Ag 29,17:2
Fancher, Albert H, 1950, Mr 24,26:3
Fancher, B H, 1932, Ap 10,II,4:1
Fancher, Charles H, 1906, Ja 29,9:4
Fancher, Charles J, 1955, Je 16,31:5
Fancher, Edward F, 1942, Mr 21,17:4
Fancher, Edwin S, 1963, My 13,29:4
Fancher, Forbes, 1953, Ap 11,17:5
Fancher, Henry W, 1955, Ap 22,25:3
Fancher, Louis, 1944, Mr 5,36:1
Fancher, Mollie, 1916, F 12,11:5
Fancher, Olin H, 1955, Ja 8,13:6
Fancher, Paul A, 1964, My 11,31:1
Fancher, Robert H, 1948, D 2,29:2
Fancher, Samuel H Jr, 1948, My 4,26:2
Fancher, Walter E, 1940, Je 27,23:4
Fanciulli, Francesco (funl, Jl 21,11:5), 1915, Jl 15:6
Fancourt, Darrell, 1953, Ag 30,88:3
Fancourt, Walter F Jr, 1954, Ap 14,29:4
Fancourt, Walter F 3d, 1955, My 21,17:6
Fane, A F S, 1949, N 30,1:8
Fane, James E, 1948, Ja 7,25:2
Fane, Spencer Ponsonby Sir, 1915, D 3,11:6
Fanelli, Frank, 1956, My 19,19:4
Fanelli, Frank A, 1947, F 14,22:2
Fanelli, George C, 1945, Je 2,15:2
Fanelli, George M, 1954, My 26,29:4
Fanelli, George M Mrs, 1952, Mr 11,27:2
Fanelli, John J, 1952, D 23,14:4
Fanelli, Joseph Mrs, 1945, O 3,19:2
Fanelli, Leonardo, 1944, O 1,45:2
Fanelli, Vincent, 1966, Mr 3,33:4
Fanfani, Italo, 1943, S 18,17:1
Fankhauser, Erna Koestler Mrs, 1954, N 7,43:1
Fankuchen, Isidor, 1964, Je 29,27:2
Fannella, Joseph F, 1949, Ja 25,23:3
Fanning, Arch M, 1948, N 11,27:4
Fanning, Clara, 1944, Ja 17,19:3

Fanning, Edward J, 1944, Ja 17,19:4
Fanning, Helen M, 1954, Ja 15,20:3
Fanning, J F Mrs, 1941, Ap 18,21:5
Fanning, J Frank, 1945, Ap 18,23:2
Fanning, J J, 1901, My 14,9:6
Fanning, J T, 1936, D 26,11:1
Fanning, John H, 1954, Mr 7,91:1
Fanning, John R, 1942, N 28,13:6
Fanning, John T, 1954, Jl 16,21:4
Fanning, Joseph T Mrs, 1951, O 30,29:1
Fanning, Leonard M, 1967, D 30,23:3
Fanning, Margaret H Mrs, 1955, F 12,15:3
Fanning, Neuville O, 1958, N 27,29:1
Fanning, Oscar F Mrs, 1942, S 20,41:6
Fanning, Peter, 1964, D 26,17:5
Fanning, Ray N Mrs, 1956, My 3,31:5
Fanning, Raymond J Mrs, 1962, N 21,33:4
Fanning, Richard, 1959, Ja 14,27:4
Fanning, Thomas J, 1953, Ja 12,27:4
Fanning, William J, 1913, My 8,11:6; 1945, Ja 14,40:3; 1948, Ja 22,27:2
Fanning, William N Mrs, 1949, Ja 8,15:3
Fanning, William R, 1951, My 19,15:6
Fanning, William R Mrs, 1944, Je 3,13:2
Fanning, Wilmot E, 1962, N 28,39:1
Fannon, Edgar J, 1949, Jl 19,30:4
Fannon, Frank J, 1950, Mr 28,12:6
Fanon, Franz O, 1961, D 7,43:2
Fanoni, Vincent, 1960, D 21,31:5
Fanos, Anestis, 1961, My 2,37:2
Fanshawe, Ellen H Mrs, 1939, Ap 21,23:2
Fanshawe, John E J, 1938, S 20,23:5
Fanshawe, William S Mrs, 1908, D 11,11:3
Fansler, P E, 1937, N 8,23:2
Fansom, James, 1903, Mr 9,1:5
Fant, David J Sr, 1965, D 4,31:3
Fant, Richard B, 1961, Mr 23,33:3
Fanta, Arthur W, 1963, Jl 12,25:5
Fantham, Harold Dr, 1937, O 27,31:4
Fantilli, Luigi, 1960, D 28,27:4
Fantin-Latour, 1904, Ag 28,9:6
Fantl, A, 1928, Je 2,17:5
Fantle, William J, 1945, S 18,24:2
Fanto, David, 1920, Je 3,11:4
Fanto, Emil C, 1957, F 25,25:6
Fanto, Richard A, 1945, My 19,19:5
Fanton, Sterling H, 1946, Ja 8,23:5
Fantoni, Augusto Count, 1909, O 30,9:5
Fantozzi, Louis, 1958, Je 8,89:1
Fantry, George W, 1963, D 19,33:2
Fantus, Bernard, 1940, Ap 15,17:3
Faour, Dominick J, 1941, O 29,23:2
Fappiano, William, 1945, Ja 24,22:3
Faquet, Emile, 1916, Je 8,13:7
Fara, Charles J, 1948, D 11,15:4
Farabaugh, Charles K, 1952, S 30,31:2
Faraci, Marion C, 1953, Mr 27,23:5
Faraday, Michael Prof, 1867, Ag 28,4:7
Faragher, James L, 1959, F 8,86:1
Faragher, Warren F, 1966, F 2,35:2
Farah, Richard N, 1958, Jl 25,19:2
Faranda, Joseph C Jr, 1961, F 14,37:3
Faranda, Joseph C Sr, 1953, Jl 3,19:3
Faranghi, Ali, 1942, D 1,25:1
Farasey, James K, 1944, Mr 17,17:5
Faravelli, Vice-Adm, 1914, Mr 23,11:4
Farb, Andrew I, 1967, N 21,47:4
Farb, Nathan, 1947, Mr 22,14:3
Farb, Sam Mrs, 1958, Ap 6,88:5
Farber, Alfred J, 1953, Jl 13,25:6
Farber, Alfred J Mrs, 1961, D 19,33:4
Farber, Benjamin, 1954, Ja 16,15:4
Farber, Edwin J, 1939, Mr 31,21:5
Farber, Henry, 1951, Ja 20,15:4
Farber, Ira M, 1964, Ag 15,21:3
Farber, John H, 1943, O 26,23:4
Farber, Max, 1950, Jl 20,25:5
Farber, Ruth S Mrs, 1940, D 18,25:5
Farber, Simon, 1960, F 22,17:2
Farber, Simon Mrs, 1956, Ja 7,17:3
Farber, Simon W, 1947, Ap 5,19:3
Farber, Theodore, 1963, N 17,86:2
Farber, William S, 1963, F 6,4:8
Farbman, Israel, 1954, Ag 12,25:6
Farbstein, W Emanuel, 1960, N 22,35:5
Fardelmann, Adolf V, 1942, F 19,19:5
Fardner, Lawrence F, 1960, Ap 17,92:3
ardon, James L Mrs, 1947, Mr 7,25:2
ardy, James F, 1944, Mr 29,21:2
arenga, Salvatore A, 1965, Ap 7,43:4
arer, Benjamin (will, F 15,23:3), 1952, Ja 29,25:3
arer, Charles H, 1957, S 3,27:3
arer, Samuel Mrs, 1964, Je 28,56:4
arfan, Pedro P, 1945, S 18,23:3
arge, Yves, 1953, Mr 31,32:4
argel, Henry G, 1947, Ag 5,23:3
argo, Alvin W, 1956, Ja 17,33:2
argo, Charles E, 1909, Ja 11,9:6
argo, D G, 1881, Ag 4,5:5
argo, F Miller Jr, 1967, Ap 8,31:3
argo, Frank H, 1950, Je 13,27:4
argo, Frank M, 1942, Jl 18,13:4
argo, Hiram D, 1957, F 13,35:5

Fargo, J F, 1883, Ja 20,2:7
Fargo, James C, 1915, F 10,11:5
Fargo, James Congdel, 1915, F 9,9:3
Fargo, James F (will, Je 29,43:8), 1937, Je 20,II,7:1
Fargo, James F Mrs, 1951, N 26,25:1
Fargo, W G, 1878, Mr 19,4:6
Fargo, William C, 1941, F 4,21:5
Fargo, William P, 1957, My 24,25:4
Farguhar, Arthur B, 1925, Mr 6,19:4
Fargus, William T, 1953, O 13,29:3
Fari, Frederick, 1952, D 13,21:5
Faribault, Joseph E, 1952, Ja 5,11:2
Farid-es-Sultaneh, Doris Princess, 1963, Ag 13,31:2
Faries, Randolph, 1939, Ja 2,24:4
Faries, Robert, 1940, S 10,23:5
Farina, Giovanni, 1957, Ag 19,19:5
Farina, Giulio, 1947, D 28,40:3
Farina, Guiseppe, 1966, Jl 1,26:6
Farina, Luigi L, 1954, D 8,35:2
Farina, Richard, 1966, My 2,15:6
Farinacci, Giuseppe, 1942, Ja 24,15:8
Farinas, Pedro L, 1951, Ag 28,15:5
Farinelli, Arturo, 1948, Ap 24,15:6
Farington, Thomas, 1872, D 3,1:3
Farini, Carlo Luizi, 1866, Ag 6,1:5
Farini, Gilarma, 1929, Ja 22,29:1
Faris, Adeeb, 1957, O 31,31:1
Faris, Barry Mrs, 1956, Ja 9,25:3
Faris, Charles B (por), 1938, D 19,23:1
Faris, Charles B Mrs, 1939, My 8,17:4
Faris, E Barry (funl plans, N 8,39:1; funl, N 10,47:5), 1966, N 7,47:4
Faris, Edgar F, 1945, Jl 7,13:7
Faris, Ellsworth, 1953, D 20,77:2
Faris, John E, 1874, My 30,8:2
Faris, John T, 1949, Ap 14,25:4
Farish, Hunter D, 1945, Ja 18,19:4
Farish, William S (por), 1942, N 30,23:1
Farist, Joel, 1904, N 13,7:6
Farjeon, B L, 1903, Jl 24,7:6
Farjeon, Eleanor, 1965, Je 6,84:6
Farjeon, Harry R, 1957, O 24,33:1
Farjeon, Herbert, 1945, My 5,15:2
Farjeon, Joseph J, 1955, Je 7,33:5
Farkas, Albert, 1956, Je 30,17:4
Farkas, Harold, 1962, Je 20,35:4
Farkas, Mihaly (death confirmed, D 11,33:5), 1965, D 10,47:2
Farkas, Moris, 1948, O 7,17:5
Farkasch, Oscar, 1939, Ap 6,25:6
Farkes, John, 1955, D 8,37:1
Farkington, John S, 1923, Ja 31,19:5
Farkoa, Maurice (funl, Mr 23,11:5), 1916, Mr 22,13:7
Farland, Alfred A, 1954, My 6,33:1
Farlee, George W, 1907, Ag 18,7:5
Farleigh, Henry S, 1954, Ag 26,27:4
Farley, Adrian M, 1945, O 17,19:4
Farley, Anne J, 1947, Ag 6,23:6
Farley, Arthur J Mrs, 1939, Mr 9,21:3
Farley, Bernard, 1952, My 27,27:4; 1968, D 9,47:2
Farley, Cal, 1967, F 20,37:4
Farley, Charles A, 1949, Mr 8,25:3
Farley, Charles G, 1947, S 18,25:2
Farley, Charles J, 1940, Ap 22,17:6
Farley, Charles L, 1942, Ap 25,13:2
Farley, Colvin, 1964, Ag 4,29:2
Farley, David F, 1958, S 22,31:3
Farley, David J, 1949, F 26,15:1
Farley, Edward J, 1947, Ap 25,22:3; 1951, Ja 4,29:2
Farley, Edward P, 1956, Mr 6,31:1
Farley, Eliot, 1952, Ag 2,15:5
Farley, Eliot Jr Mrs (cor, Mr 12,33:4), 1957, Mr 11, 25:5
Farley, Eustace J, 1960, Ag 3,29:6
Farley, Fannie Livingston, 1924, N 14,19:5
Farley, Florence G Mrs, 1962, Mr 25,89:1
Farley, Frank, 1951, Je 1,26:4
Farley, Frank E, 1943, Mr 26,19:5
Farley, Frank J, 1950, Mr 5,92:4
Farley, Frank J Mrs, 1950, Ap 23,95:2
Farley, Frank M, 1958, Mr 18,29:2
Farley, Frank M Mrs, 1958, F 27,27:3
Farley, Franklin, 1960, N 26,21:5
Farley, George H, 1937, Ag 24,21:4
Farley, Hugh D, 1966, D 2,39:2
Farley, J H, 1934, S 22,15:3
Farley, James, 1913, S 11,11:5; 1916, Ja 24,11:2
Farley, James A, 1923, Ag 24,11:7
Farley, James A Mrs (funl, Ja 18,27:5), 1955, Ja 15, 13:2
Farley, James I, 1948, Je 18,23:5
Farley, John, 1916, Ag 21,11:5
Farley, John A Mrs, 1956, Ag 3,19:1
Farley, John Cardinal (funl, S 19,13:1),(por), 1918, S 18,13:1
Farley, John F, 1939, Ja 16,15:4
Farley, John J, 1944, Je 11,46:1; 1953, Ja 4,76:3
Farley, John J Sr, 1957, D 16,29:3
Farley, John T, 1905, Ja 5,7:6
Farley, John V Jr, 1951, Je 10,93:1
Farley, John W, 1959, Mr 14,23:3
Farley, Joseph P Brig-Gen, 1912, Ap 7,II,15:2
Farley, Lehon J, 1949, N 11,25:4

Farley, Lilla, 1965, Jl 5,17:4
Farley, Luke A, 1950, Ag 27,88:2
Farley, Marguerite N Mrs (will), 1956, Ap 21,10:2
Farley, Martin, 1908, Jl 13,7:5
Farley, Mary E Mrs, 1943, Jl 6,21:1
Farley, Mother Katherine, 1955, My 25,33:5
Farley, Olin E, 1941, Ag 6,17:2
Farley, Olin Mrs, 1949, My 31,23:2
Farley, Patrick, 1914, My 21,11:5
Farley, Phil M, 1940, Jl 3,17:6
Farley, Phil R, 1953, F 14,17:7
Farley, Philip, 1882, N 21,5:5
Farley, Philip P, 1958, Ap 20,84:1
Farley, Richard B, 1957, Ag 1,25:2
Farley, Richard H, 1948, My 6,25:4
Farley, Richard S, 1914, O 23,11:5
Farley, Robert H, 1958, Ja 18,15:3
Farley, Robert Mrs, 1943, O 14,21:5
Farley, Simon, 1937, Ap 19,21:3
Farley, T M, 1934, Ap 4,21:1
Farley, Terence, 1925, F 27,17:6
Farley, Thomas, 1940, Ag 14,19:3
Farley, Thomas F, 1948, N 30,28:2
Farley, Thomas J, 1942, Ag 20,19:2
Farley, Thomas L, 1945, F 28,23:3
Farley, Vincent J, 1951, Jl 15,61:3
Farley, Walter L, 1940, Ag 13,19:5
Farley, Walter P, 1951, Ag 24,15:2
Farley, William J, 1956, Mr 6,31:3; 1964, Jl 14,33:3
Farley, William P, 1945, My 7,17:3
Farley, William W, 1952, My 22,27:5
Farlinger, Alexander B, 1947, Mr 1,15:5
Farlow, Albert J, 1953, Jl 26,69:2
Farlow, Arthur C, 1967, F 11,29:5
Farlow, E H Dr, 1937, Jl 8,23:1
Farlow, John W Dr, 1937, S 25,17:6
Farlow, William Gilson Dr, 1919, Je 5,13:4
Farman, Elbert E Mrs, 1946, D 22,41:2; 1951, Ap 30, 21:3
Farman, Elbert Eli Judge, 1912, Ja 1,13:4
Farman, Harold, 1942, N 28,13:1
Farman, Henry, 1958, Jl 19,15:3
Farman, Maurice, 1964, F 28,27:5
Farman, Richard, 1940, F 4,40:5
Farmar, Joseph A, 1944, S 30,13:5
Farmer, Arthur E, 1953, Ja 8,27:1
Farmer, Arthur W, 1952, N 26,23:1
Farmer, Charles H Mrs, 1959, N 7,23:3
Farmer, Charles W Mrs, 1946, Mr 19,27:4
Farmer, Clyde F, 1956, Ag 27,19:6
Farmer, Clyde R, 1945, N 29,23:4
Farmer, Earland M, 1955, Mr 29,30:4
Farmer, Edward I (por), 1942, O 11,56:3
Farmer, Frank E, 1948, Ag 10,21:5
Farmer, Frank W, 1943, N 20,13:4
Farmer, Grosvenor S, 1953, Mr 13,27:4
Farmer, Herbert G, 1948, F 21,13:6
Farmer, Irving G Sr, 1943, S 28,25:3
Farmer, J Leonard Mrs, 1966, Ap 21,40:1
Farmer, Jack, 1950, My 7,108:2
Farmer, James A Mrs, 1938, Ap 20,23:1
Farmer, James L, 1961, My 17,37:3
Farmer, John B, 1944, Ja 27,19:5
Farmer, John J, 1951, F 16,25:5; 1964, Mr 3,35:2
Farmer, John R, 1954, Ja 31,89:2
Farmer, Joseph A, 1950, Je 29,29:2
Farmer, Joseph F Mrs, 1951, My 17,31:6
Farmer, Joseph Mrs, 1949, D 14,31:2
Farmer, Laurence Mrs, 1960, O 26,39:4
Farmer, Leslie P, 1908, My 2,9:4
Farmer, Leslie P Mrs, 1903, Jl 7,7:6
Farmer, Lydia Hoyt, 1903, D 27,3:2
Farmer, Malcolm, 1951, Ap 14,15:2
Farmer, Malcolm Mrs, 1959, D 27,61:2
Farmer, Paul M, 1953, My 8,25:2
Farmer, Richard M, 1945, D 5,25:4
Farmer, Rose, 1910, Jl 5,13:4
Farmer, Seymour J, 1951, Ja 17,27:4
Farmer, Thomas P, 1940, Ap 13,17:1
Farmer, Vincent Mrs, 1943, S 30,21:2
Farmer, Wendell (Mrs W Davis), 1961, Ag 15,29:3
Farmer, William B, 1938, Ja 13,21:3; 1947, O 19,64:5
Farmer, William C, 1946, D 9,25:2
Farmer, William H, 1942, O 11,56:1
Farnam, Elizabeth W, 1939, D 28,21:6
Farnam, Frank W, 1941, Ag 3,35:2
Farnam, H, 1883, O 5,4:7
Farnam, H W, 1933, S 6,17:1
Farnam, Henry Mrs, 1951, My 2,31:5
Farnam, Thomas W, 1943, Ag 4,17:2
Farnam, W L, 1930, N 24,21:3
Farnan, Daniel E, 1961, Je 25,76:7
Farnan, Patrick J, 1940, Ag 26,15:5
Farnan, Thomas C Sr, 1952, S 4,27:2
Farnath, Albert V, 1956, D 7,27:3
Farnau, Earl F, 1954, N 19,23:4
Farndon, Ernest E, 1945, Je 21,19:5
Farndon, Walter, 1964, N 25,37:2
Farnell, Edwin A, 1948, Ap 24,15:4
Farnell, Frederic James Dr, 1968, N 6,39:1
Farnell, Genevieve (Mrs R Bond), 1961, D 4,37:3
Farnell Wm C F, 1947, Jl 22,23:5
Farnham, Alonzo C, 1907, Ag 15,7:6

Farnham, Arthur K Lord, 1957, F 7,27:5
Farnham, Bennett W, 1956, F 26,89:3
Farnham, Bion B, 1944, Ap 2,39:2
Farnham, Charles O, 1947, O 14,27:4
Farnham, Charles W, 1917, O 7,23:2
Farnham, Clinton E, 1949, Ja 9,73:1
Farnham, Dwight T, 1950, S 21,31:3
Farnham, Eliza W Mrs, 1864, D 18,3:5
Farnham, ex-Gov, 1903, Ja 6,9:5
Farnham, Fred H, 1947, S 28,60:5
Farnham, Harry G, 1953, Ag 13,25:6
Farnham, Henry E, 1949, D 4,108:8
Farnham, Hubert J, 1939, My 9,24:4
Farnham, James P, 1945, F 20,19:5
Farnham, James S Mrs, 1946, F 26,25:4
Farnham, John D, 1940, Ap 16,23:4; 1957, O 2,33:3
Farnham, John D Mrs, 1939, Ja 4,21:3
Farnham, Joseph D Mrs, 1943, S 5,28:6
Farnham, Mary F, 1942, N 16,19:2
Farnham, Mateel H Mrs, 1957, My 3,27:3
Farnham, Onsville M, 1948, D 10,25:3
Farnham, Paulding Mrs, 1943, Ap 29,22:2
Farnham, Robert, 1941, Ap 9,25:2
Farnham, Robert Mrs, 1937, S 25,17:5
Farnham, Roger L, 1951, Je 6,31:3
Farnham, William L, 1960, Je 22,35:5
Farnol, John J, 1952, Ag 11,15:3
Farnol, Lynn (funl, Ap 2,47:2; trb lr, Ap 20,26:6), 1963, Ap 1,27:6
Farnon, Mary (Mother Mary Dolorosa), 1952, O 25, 17:3
Farnsworth, A, 1877, Ap 3,4:6
Farnsworth, Albert, 1956, Mr 27,35:5
Farnsworth, Caroline E Mrs, 1913, D 10,13:5
Farnsworth, Charles F, 1952, Je 30,19:4
Farnsworth, Charles H, 1947, My 23,23:2
Farnsworth, Charles H Mrs, 1946, O 24,27:6
Farnsworth, Charles S, 1955, D 21,29:3
Farnsworth, Daniel W, 1958, S 26,28:1
Farnsworth, David C, 1945, Jl 22,38:2
Farnsworth, Don Mrs, 1908, Jl 28,5:4
Farnsworth, Edna A, 1965, Ag 29,85:1
Farnsworth, Edward E Lt Col, 1937, D 20,27:4
Farnsworth, Edward E Mrs, 1950, D 3,88:3
Farnsworth, Ellen, 1957, Je 23,84:6
Farnsworth, Elon, 1877, Mr 26,4:7
Farnsworth, Elon J Brig-Gen, 1863, Jl 8,4:6
Farnsworth, F Crawford, 1947, Ag 9,13:5
Farnsworth, Frank D, 1966, Je 8,47:3
Farnsworth, Frank M, 1949, S 20,29:2
Farnsworth, Frank N, 1965, Mr 25,37:4
Farnsworth, Frederick Dr, 1914, F 24,11:5
Farnsworth, George L, 1963, S 10,39:4
Farnsworth, Harry B Mrs, 1959, S 20,86:4
Farnsworth, Herbert, 1964, Ap 3,33:2
Farnsworth, John G Gen, 1895, Ap 7,5:5
Farnsworth, Kenneth G, 1952, Jl 12,13:4
Farnsworth, Louise M Mrs, 1939, Ag 24,19:6
Farnsworth, Mary E Mrs, 1941, Je 12,23:3
Farnsworth, Paul B, 1947, F 1,15:4
Farnsworth, Robert P, 1940, F 18,43:6
Farnsworth, Ruth Mrs, 1952, D 19,31:1
Farnsworth, Ward, 1946, S 24,30:3
Farnsworth, William C Mrs, 1938, Ja 11,23:4
Farnsworth, Wilson A rev, 1912, Je 7,13:3
Farnsworth, Wilton S, 1945, Jl 11,11:7
Farnsworth, Wilton S Mrs, 1964, Jl 31,23:4
Farnum, Anna S B Mrs, 1940, My 26,34:8
Farnum, D, 1929, Jl 5,17:3
Farnum, Edward S W, 1949, My 6,25:3
Farnum, Frank S, 1954, D 23,19:3
Farnum, Franklyn, 1961, Jl 6,29:4
Farnum, G Dustin, 1912, F 20,11:4
Farnum, H P, 1884, D 4,2:6
Farnum, Henry W, 1943, S 27,19:4; 1965, Ag 8,64:8
Farnum, Howard W Mrs, 1951, Jl 22,60:5
Farnum, Loring N, 1941, N 14,23:5
Farnum, Mark, 1957, Ag 23,19:5
Farnum, Nell, 1945, Mr 3,13:3
Farnum, Peter E, 1948, Ja 2,23:3
Farnum, Ralph, 1860, D 27,5:1
Farnum, Royal B, 1967, Ag 30,43:2
Farnum, Welcome, 1874, My 12,1:3
Farnum, William, 1953, Je 6,17:1
Farnworth, John A, 1956, Jl 16,21:3
Farnworth, T Oliver Mrs, 1949, N 27,105:1
Farnworth, Wilton M, 1961, Ag 25,25:5
Farny, George W, 1941, S 2,17:2
Farny, George W Mrs, 1952, Mr 11,27:4
Farogh, Francis E, 1966, Jl 27,39:2
Faroll, Barnett, 1954, Ja 5,27:3
Faroll, Joseph, 1958, Ja 31,21:2
Faron, Frank A, 1958, Ag 4,21:3
Faron, J Gen, 1881, N 20,2:7
Faron, L B, 1875, O 22,10:4
Farouk Faud, Ex King of Egypt (funl, Mr 20,6:6), 1965, Mr 18,1:7
Faroux, Charles, 1957, F 11,29:4
Farquahar, Dudley, 1946, N 26,29:2
Farquhar, Alice C C Mrs, 1941, Ja 4,13:3
Farquhar, Arthur M Adm Sir, 1937, N 17,23:4
Farquhar, Charlotte B, 1957, Je 6,31:2
Farquhar, Cosmo, 1957, Ja 31,27:5
Farquhar, David, 1958, D 21,2:3
Farquhar, F M, 1883, Jl 6,2:1
Farquhar, Harold B, 1946, O 7,31:3
Farquhar, Jerome G, 1937, Mr 12,23:5
Farquhar, Marion J Mrs, 1965, Mr 16,39:2
Farquhar, Norman Von Heldreich Rear-Adm, 1907, Jl 4,7:6
Farquhar, Percival, 1953, Ag 5,23:5
Farquhar, S Edgar, 1948, Ap 1,25:3
Farquhar, Samuel T, 1949, My 24,27:1
Farquhar, Theodore D, 1939, Je 23,19:2
Farquhar, Thomas L, 1941, F 5,19:3
Farquharson, Arthur, 1947, N 14,23:3
Farquharson, Frank Mrs, 1952, N 4,29:1
Farquharson, Robert Mrs, 1955, F 18,21:3
Farr, Arthur V Mrs, 1958, S 25,33:3
Farr, C B, 1912, Ag 19,9:6
Farr, Charles F W, 1951, Ag 2,21:2
Farr, Charles J, 1959, N 15,86:6
Farr, Charles L, 1954, O 3,86:7
Farr, Charles W, 1944, Jl 13,17:6
Farr, Charlotte C Mrs (will), 1947, D 31,13:7
Farr, Daniel C, 1903, D 17,9:4
Farr, Delano E, 1946, N 1,23:4
Farr, Donald E, 1966, Je 11,31:2
Farr, Doris, 1938, Ja 16,II,8:7
Farr, E W, 1880, D 1,5:1
Farr, Edward Jr, 1967, Ap 10,35:1
Farr, Elizabeth J, 1946, Je 27,21:4
Farr, F Shelton Mrs, 1944, O 5,23:3
Farr, Henry B, 1964, O 3,29:4
Farr, Herman G, 1937, Ag 4,19:3
Farr, Hollon A, 1958, Mr 24,27:3
Farr, J R, 1933, D 12,23:3
Farr, James M, 1953, Ag 7,19:2
Farr, James M 3d, 1961, N 7,33:1
Farr, James S, 1947, S 16,24:3
Farr, John C, 1943, Ja 25,13:2
Farr, John Jr, 1965, S 15,47:1
Farr, John Mrs, 1946, My 25,15:3
Farr, Karl, 1961, S 21,35:1
Farr, Leslie B, 1961, Jl 2,33:1
Farr, Marcus S, 1942, Ag 28,19:3
Farr, Morton, 1955, D 18,92:5
Farr, Orrin H, 1945, Ap 19,27:3
Farr, Otto W B, 1940, F 4,40:6
Farr, Peter R, 1961, Mr 4,23:1
Farr, Phil Mrs, 1948, My 3,21:5
Farr, Richard L, 1963, Je 27,33:4
Farr, Samuel, 1924, F 5,23:3
Farr, Sarah F Mrs, 1941, S 28,49:2
Farr, Shirley, 1955, Ag 26,19:4
Farr, T H Mrs, 1945, Mr 26,19:4
Farr, Thomas H P, 1938, Mr 16,17:6
Farr, W Dr, 1883, Ap 17,5:1
Farr, Walter G, 1950, Ap 11,31:2
Farr, Walter P, 1940, N 19,23:2
Farr, William W, 1940, Ag 20,19:6
Farragher, James, 1949, F 23,27:5
Farragut, D G Adm (funl, Ag 18,1:7), 1870, Ag 15, 5:1
Farragut, Loyall, 1916, O 2,11:6
Farragut, Virginia L, 1884, N 2,3:3
Farrall, Bob (Chas Falke), 1968, Je 7,36:3
Farrall, Frederick O, 1938, Mr 13,II,9:3
Farran, W Capt, 1883, N 12,5:2
Farrand, Charles D, 1951, Je 1,26:2
Farrand, George E, 1954, Je 1,27:5
Farrand, Herbert U Mrs, 1960, Je 1,39:3
Farrand, Hiram A, 1948, Ja 22,27:5
Farrand, Howard P, 1949, Ag 12,17:3
Farrand, Joseph S, 1957, O 29,31:1
Farrand, Livingston, 1939, N 9,23:1
Farrand, Livingston Mrs, 1957, O 12,19:2
Farrand, Max, 1945, Je 18,19:2
Farrand, Max Mrs, 1959, Mr 1,86:3
Farrand, Roy F, 1965, Ag 24,31:3
Farrand, Roy F Mrs, 1943, O 24,44:5
Farrand, Theodore S, 1957, My 15,35:2
Farrand, William, 1941, Ja 14,21:2
Farrand, William H, 1942, S 18,21:5
Farrand, Wilson, 1942, N 5,25:5
Farrant, George A, 1945, Ap 13,17:5
Farrar, Bernard G Gen, 1916, Je 7,13:5
Farrar, Charles E, 1950, S 17,104:8
Farrar, Clarissa P, 1963, N 3,88:5
Farrar, Edward D Mrs, 1948, Jl 26,17:2
Farrar, Edward J, 1951, S 19,31:1
Farrar, Ellen W, 1945, N 10,15:5
Farrar, Eric M, 1947, Ap 12,17:3
Farrar, F Percival, 1946, Mr 12,25:4
Farrar, F S (Ted), 1955, F 10,31:5
Farrar, F W, 1903, Mr 23,9:5
Farrar, Frank C, 1940, Ap 17,23:5
Farrar, Frederick A, 1942, D 19,19:4
Farrar, Geraldine, 1967, Mr 12,1:7
Farrar, Gilbert P, 1957, Ap 5,27:1
Farrar, Gilbert P Mrs, 1950, Jl 28,21:6; 1958, Mr 16, 86:8
Farrar, Gwen, 1944, D 27,19:2
Farrar, H W, 1881, Ap 18,5:5
Farrar, Henrietta Mrs, 1923, Ja 25,19:5
Farrar, Herbert Mrs, 1943, O 16,13:1
Farrar, James M Rev Dr, 1921, Je 24,15:6
Farrar, Jesse L, 1939, O 14,19:5
Farrar, John G, 1950, Ap 27,29:5
Farrar, Judson S Col, 1916, Mr 12,19:5
Farrar, Lilian K P, 1962, Je 24,69:1
Farrar, M Dana, 1959, My 30,17:3
Farrar, Mercer Mrs, 1951, Je 6,31:5
Farrar, Percival Mrs, 1958, Jl 20,65:2
Farrar, Preston C Mrs, 1956, Je 26,29:1
Farrar, Trevor, 1943, Ap 13,25:2
Farrar, Victor C, 1954, F 20,17:4
Farrar, William E Dr, 1925, My 10,6:1
Farrar, William M, 1951, My 9,33:5
Farrar, William M Jr, 1962, Je 5,41:4
Farrel, Franklin Jr, 1967, Je 6,47:1
Farrel, Franklin Sr, 1912, Ja 11,13:4
Farrel, John A Mrs, 1944, D 31,25:1
Farrel, Malcolm, 1952, S 30,31:2
Farrell, Adrian A, 1951, Ap 4,29:3
Farrell, Alex M, 1937, N 25,31:4
Farrell, Andrew A, 1957, My 9,31:5
Farrell, Anna M, 1942, F 11,22:2
Farrell, Arthur A, 1964, Ag 10,31:1
Farrell, Arthur E, 1943, D 5,65:1
Farrell, Arthur M, 1948, D 25,17:5
Farrell, Benjamin P, 1947, D 29,17:4
Farrell, Bernard, 1903, D 7,7:3
Farrell, Bernard A, 1943, Jl 29,19:6
Farrell, Bernard J, 1944, F 5,15:6
Farrell, C A Rev, 1876, F 15,8:6
Farrell, Charles H, 1959, D 31,21:2
Farrell, Charles J, 1943, Jl 10,13:7
Farrell, Charles L, 1940, Ag 26,15:3
Farrell, Charles L Mrs, 1939, Je 10,17:2
Farrell, Charles Mrs (Virginia), 1968, S 26,47:2
Farrell, Charley, 1946, N 26,29:1
Farrell, Chris A, 1939, Ap 24,17:6
Farrell, Clayton S, 1950, O 9,25:2
Farrell, Clinton Pinckney, 1925, Ap 23,21:2
Farrell, Daniel F, 1939, Je 19,15:3
Farrell, Daniel F Jr, 1949, Mr 12,17:4
Farrell, Eddie (Edw S), 1966, D 21,32:5
Farrell, Edgar A, 1953, S 5,15:2
Farrell, Edgar H, 1951, My 29,25:5
Farrell, Edward D, 1924, D 25,17:6
Farrell, Edward J, 1950, Ja 22,78:1
Farrell, Edward L, 1953, Jl 19,57:1
Farrell, Edward M, 1943, F 21,32:7; 1944, O 14,13:5; 1954, Ap 1,31:5
Farrell, Edward P, 1959, O 21,43:4
Farrell, Edward W, 1946, S 6,22:2
Farrell, Eugene, 1948, F 29,60:4
Farrell, Eugene W, 1946, O 15,26:2
Farrell, Eugene W Sr Mrs, 1938, Jl 22,17:2
Farrell, F J, 1926, F 11,21:3
Farrell, Frances J, 1939, O 17,25:1
Farrell, Francis V, 1951, F 14,29:3
Farrell, Frank C, 1942, Jl 8,23:4; 1958, D 2,38:1
Farrell, Frank J, 1937, My 19,23:5; 1954, Jl 22,23:6
Farrell, Frank L, 1942, F 28,17:4; 1947, Ap 23,25:2
Farrell, Frank P, 1937, F 18,21:2; 1945, F 12,20:2
Farrell, Gabriel Rev Dr, 1968, S 21,33:3
Farrell, George E, 1950, Ag 23,29:5
Farrell, Harry J Sr, 1950, Ja 31,23:1
Farrell, Harry T, 1954, O 10,87:2; 1957, D 28,17:2
Farrell, Henry L, 1954, Ap 10,15:6
Farrell, Herbert, 1947, Mr 5,26:2
Farrell, Herbert F Rev, 1924, Ja 19,13:4
Farrell, Hugh, 1960, O 30,86:7
Farrell, J Fletcher (por), 1938, S 27,21:4
Farrell, J H, 1901, F 3,7:6
Farrell, J P, 1902, My 27,9:5
Farrell, James, 1946, Ag 4,45:2
Farrell, James A, 1941, My 29,19:1; 1943, Mr 29,15:1; 1960, N 17,37:3
Farrell, James A Mrs, 1943, O 19,19:2
Farrell, James C, 1939, Ja 12,19:2; 1944, N 14,23:4
Farrell, James C Mrs, 1944, Ag 15,17:5
Farrell, James Charles, 1918, D 29,18:3
Farrell, James E, 1959, D 23,27:2
Farrell, James F, 1937, Ap 6,23:2; 1946, F 18,21:4; 1963, S
Farrell, James J, 1952, D 2,31:5; 1967, Mr 5,87:1
Farrell, James J Jr, 1954, My 30,45:2
Farrell, James J Mrs, 1950, F 26,79:3
Farrell, James P, 1910, D 15,9:4; 1943, S 23,21:2
Farrell, John, 1905, My 3,9:5
Farrell, John B, 1951, My 6,93:1
Farrell, John C, 1953, Jl 29,23:4
Farrell, John F, 1953, Ap 15,31:2; 1963, Ag 29,29:6
Farrell, John H, 1945, My 18,19:5
Farrell, John H Mrs, 1942, Jl 17,15:6
Farrell, John J, 1917, Mr 22,11:3; 1939, Mr 27,15:4; 1942, F 16,17:1; 1943, S 8,23:1; 1946, Ap 21,47:2; 1947, Je 29,48:8; 1947, N 27,32:2; 1948, Mr 16,27:3; 1959, Ja 6,33:4; 1966, Ap 23,31:1
Farrell, John J Mrs, 1954, N 27,13:3; 1955, F 6,88:8
Farrell, John L, 1955, S 13,31:2
Farrell, John M, 1957, N 12,34:1
Farrell, John Mrs, 1916, Je 14,13:6
Farrell, John P, 1954, My 7,23:4
Farrell, John R, 1950, Ap 12,28:2
Farrell, John T, 1943, F 11,19:5
Farrell, John W, 1953, Jl 10,19:5; 1954, Ja 12,23:2
Farrell, Joseph A, 1948, Mr 9,23:2; 1957, O 3,29:3; 1960, Je 14,37:3

Farrell, Joseph E, 1939, Ag 19,15:1
Farrell, Joseph E Sr, 1952, Ap 22,29:3
Farrell, Joseph F, 1942, Ag 7,17:3; 1948, Mr 31,25:1
Farrell, Joseph M, 1952, My 7,27:6
Farrell, Joseph M Mrs, 1950, N 30,33:1
Farrell, Joseph P, 1946, D 8,77:1
Farrell, Joseph W, 1938, Ja 23,II,8:4; 1942, N 5,25:3
Farrell, Leo, 1953, Jl 12,65:2
Farrell, Louis F, 1953, Jl 3,19:6
Farrell, Louis H, 1953, Ja 28,27:4
Farrell, Louis L, 1947, Ag 3,52:5
Farrell, Mark W, 1957, S 14,19:5
Farrell, Mary Elizabeth Mrs, 1909, S 2,9:2
Farrell, Mary F Sister, 1939, Mr 19,III,7:2
Farrell, Mary Mrs, 1946, Ja 10,23:2
Farrell, Matthew J, 1958, N 27,29:5
Farrell, Maurice L, 1939, N 14,23:1
Farrell, Michael H (Bro Maurice), 1955, Jl 13,25:5
Farrell, Michael J, 1953, My 19,29:4
Farrell, Michael J Mrs, 1964, Ag 29,21:5
Farrell, Morgan G, 1941, F 5,20:2
Farrell, Myles A Mrs, 1947, O 7,27:1
Farrell, Patrick J, 1945, O 21,46:2
Farrell, Patrick J H, 1956, D 15,25:4
Farrell, Patrick Mrs, 1958, My 19,25:4
Farrell, Peter J, 1968, O 9,47:4
Farrell, Peter Rev, 1918, N 10,23:1
Farrell, Phil A, 1942, My 1,19:2
Farrell, Porter M, 1959, Mr 21,21:2
Farrell, Ralph G, 1954, O 30,17:5
Farrell, Ralph G Mrs, 1958, O 4,21:5
Farrell, Robert L, 1950, O 5,31:1
Farrell, Ronald L, 1967, F 21,47:1
Farrell, S J, 1933, O 18,19:1
Farrell, Skip (C F Fiedler), 1962, My 10,37:3
Farrell, Sophie H Mrs, 1938, D 30,15:4
Farrell, Stephen A, 1946, Jl 13,15:3
Farrell, Stephen A Mrs, 1942, Ag 17,15:6
Farrell, Sue M P Mrs, 1940, N 28,23:2
Farrell, T, 1880, Jl 24,8:3
Farrell, Taylor W, 1944, Ag 28,11:5
Farrell, Thomas A, 1942, O 10,15:2
Farrell, Thomas A Mrs, 1950, Jl 3,15:3
Farrell, Thomas F, 1946, Jl 30,23:1; 1948, Ja 21,25:1; 1967, Ap 12,47:1
Farrell, Thomas F Mrs, 1966, Ap 4,31:1
Farrell, Thomas J, 1940, Ap 27,15:2; 1945, My 2,23:3; 1947, O 24,23:4
Farrell, Thomas J A, 1941, S 6,15:6
Farrell, Thomas L, 1945, Jl 26,20:2
Farrell, Thomas M, 1942, N 6,23:2; 1959, Ag 29,17:6
Farrell, Thomas R, 1925, N 7,15:5
Farrell, Thomas V, 1950, F 11,15:3
Farrell, Thomas W Capt, 1916, My 4,11:7
Farrell, W J, 1933, F 14,18:4
Farrell, Walter, 1951, N 24,11:5
Farrell, William A, 1956, Mr 20,23:1
Farrell, William C, 1953, Ja 16,23:2
Farrell, William E, 1947, D 31,15:2; 1949, Ag 23,24:2; 1949, N 10,31:5
Farrell, William F, 1943, Mr 23,19:1; 1948, S 20,25:2
Farrell, William H, 1920, Ap 20,9:5
Farrell, William H Jr Mrs, 1943, N 25,25:3
Farrell, William J, 1919, Je 22,15:4; 1950, O 13,29:2; 1951, My 27,68:5
Farrell, William J (por), 1955, Je 28,27:5
Farrell, William J Mrs, 1941, Ap 12,15:4
Farrell, William K, 1958, My 13,29:4
Farrell, William L, 1944, My 24,19:2
Farrell, William Mrs, 1953, Ja 7,31:3
Farrell, William R, 1953, My 21,31:3
Farrell, William W, 1950, N 26,90:4
Farrell, Winifred Mrs, 1912, My 10,11:5
Farrelly, Charles F, 1938, My 8,II,7:3
Farrelly, Felix H, 1882, F 10,5:5
Farrelly, Frances S (Mother M St Jerome), 1942, My 29,17:4
Farrelly, James T Sr, 1948, S 29,29:3
Farrelly, John A, 1945, Mr 30,15:4
Farrelly, John P Rev, 1921, F 13,22:3
Farrelly, Patrick, 1904, Ap 24,7:6
Farrelly, Patrick J, 1942, D 23,19:3
Farrelly, Patrick J Rev, 1914, F 4,9:6
Farrelly, Richard A, 1923, O 27,13:5
Farrelly, S Valentine, 1956, Jl 17,23:3
Farrelly, S Valentine Mrs, 1955, F 5,15:2
Farrelly, Stephen, 1923, Mr 14,19:4
Farrelly, T Charles Mrs, 1952, Je 26,29:5
Farrelly, Theodore S, 1955, Jl 24,64:7
Farrelly, Thomas, 1952, Ag 23,13:1
Farrelly, Thomas P, 1940, S 26,23:3
Farren, Bernard H, 1912, Ja 23,11:3
Farren, David J, 1941, Ja 15,23:3
Farren, George W, 1911, F 4,13:4
Farren, John J, 1940, My 9,23:3
Farren, Joseph A, 1964, F 11,39:4
Farren, Nellie, 1904, Ap 29,9:6
Farren, Nicholas J, 1904, D 11,7:5
Farren, Robert, 1944, O 29,43:1
Farrenc, Jeanne Louise Mme, 1875, S 25,4:6
Farrenkopf, Tobias E, 1942, F 27,18:3
Farrer, Arthur, 1951, N 15,29:5
Farrer, John G Mrs, 1951, Mr 22,31:2
Farrer, Reginald, 1920, N 19,15:5
Farrer, Thomas C, 1940, Ap 13,17:3
Farrere, Claude, 1957, Je 22,15:3
Farrier, Benjamin E, 1945, My 1,23:2
Farrier, Edwin M, 1949, Ap 2,15:1
Farrier, Harry H, 1943, Jl 1,19:4
Farrier, Henry H Mrs, 1951, N 10,17:3
Farrier, J M, 1876, F 16,4:7
Farries, George D, 1941, Ag 21,17:6
Farries, Richard M, 1918, Jl 1,11:6
Farring, George F, 1938, Jl 26,19:3
Farrington, Cecilia M Mrs, 1941, Ja 22,21:2
Farrington, Charles K, 1959, Ag 5,27:5
Farrington, Charlotte G P Mrs, 1938, Mr 25,19:4
Farrington, Delbert G, 1955, D 8,37:3
Farrington, Ernest A Dr, 1937, Ap 7,25:3
Farrington, Florence, 1953, Jl 3,19:4
Farrington, Frank, 1939, Mr 31,21:5
Farrington, Frank E, 1921, O 20,17:5
Farrington, Frederick H, 1941, O 30,23:3
Farrington, G D, 1878, Ja 25,5:2
Farrington, G Lansing Mrs, 1963, Je 10,31:5
Farrington, George B, 1942, D 19,19:1
Farrington, George H, 1941, Jl 30,17:4
Farrington, George W, 1953, F 18,31:1
Farrington, Harold P, 1964, Je 9,35:4
Farrington, Harry F, 1941, F 26,22:2
Farrington, Harry F Mrs, 1949, My 15,90:6
Farrington, Harry J, 1954, D 14,33:3
Farrington, Harvey Mrs, 1950, Ap 17,23:1
Farrington, Herbert N, 1941, Ag 13,17:3
Farrington, Isabelle S Mrs, 1941, Mr 12,21:3
Farrington, James L, 1957, Mr 15,25:5
Farrington, John, 1964, Jl 27,1:1
Farrington, John D, 1961, O 14,23:6
Farrington, John D Mrs, 1954, Ag 26,27:3
Farrington, John G, 1950, Mr 21,29:3
Farrington, Joseph R (funl, Je 24,27:4), 1954, Je 20, 84:3
Farrington, Kate B, 1946, O 13,59:5
Farrington, Louis M, 1940, Ag 31,13:4
Farrington, Ralph Mrs, 1953, My 23,15:5
Farrington, Ralph T, 1968, Mr 26,45:1
Farrington, Raymond F, 1949, F 16,26:2
Farrington, Richard, 1953, F 14,17:5
Farrington, Robert C, 1941, Jl 16,17:3
Farrington, Robert I, 1948, Mr 25,28:3
Farrington, Robert I Mrs, 1951, D 6,33:4
Farrington, Robert J, 1954, Mr 24,27:4
Farrington, Robert W, 1939, N 23,27:1
Farrington, Selwyn K, 1961, F 20,27:3
Farrington, Sidney, 1955, Mr 2,27:2
Farrington, Stephen J Jr, 1957, Je 1,38:1
Farrington, Theodore, 1960, F 25,29:6
Farrington, Thomas T Rev, 1875, Je 6,2:5
Farrington, W R, 1933, O 7,15:1
Farrington, W R Mrs, 1953, Ja 2,15:2
Farrington, Walter, 1945, O 20,11:5
Farrington, William G Rev Dr, 1913, Mr 14,9:1
Farrington, William T Jr, 1961, N 9,35:4
Farris, Charles E, 1950, Mr 27,23:1
Farris, Edmond J, 1961, Ap 15,21:5
Farris, Emil M, 1958, O 21,33:5
Farris, F H Sen, 1926, S 2,21:6
Farris, Ralph W Sr, 1968, Ap 4,47:1
Farris, Wendell B, 1955, Je 18,17:2
Farrisee, William J, 1958, D 2,38:1
Farriss, Charles S, 1938, Ap 15,19:3
Farron, Lucien G, 1951, Ag 2,21:3
Farron, Thomas J, 1923, Ag 9,13:5
Farrow, Campion B, 1944, Ja 22,13:7
Farrow, Clarence Barnett, 1908, Mr 26,7:7
Farrow, Edward S, 1962, Ag 10,19:2
Farrow, Edward S Mrs, 1947, Ja 30,25:2
Farrow, Henry R L, 1957, Jl 14,72:4
Farrow, Hubert M, 1948, F 15,60:6
Farrow, John, 1963, Ja 29,7:6
Farrow, Miles, 1953, Jl 21,23:3
Farrow, Wayne, 1940, Jl 9,42:4
Farrow, William C, 1945, N 27,23:2
Farry, H Earle, 1959, Ag 21,21:4
Farry, P T, 1937, S 24,15:1
Farry, Percy S Sr, 1962, Jl 18,29:4
Farson, Enoch S Mrs, 1950, F 11,15:5
Farson, John, 1910, Ja 19,9:5; 1937, Je 27,II,7:1
Farson, Negley, 1960, D 14,35:1
Farson, William, 1937, O 18,17:1
Farson, William C, 1959, Mr 31,29:2
Farthing, Elizabeth J Mrs, 1944, My 5,19:6
Farthing, John C, 1947, My 7,27:2
Farthing, William J, 1952, Mr 31,19:3
Faruolo, Charles R, 1941, My 23,21:5
Farup, Karl J, 1942, D 27,34:1
Farwell, Arthur, 1952, Ja 21,15:1
Farwell, Arthur L, 1945, Jl 27,15:5
Farwell, Ath L Mrs, 1940, Mr 4,15:2
Farwell, Charles A, 1917, My 18,13:7
Farwell, Charles B, 1903, S 24,9:6
Farwell, Charles S, 1939, Ap 10,17:5
Farwell, Clifford, 1953, Mr 16,25:2
Farwell, Earle, 1947, Je 19,21:3
Farwell, Frank H, 1908, Je 8,7:4
Farwell, Fred M, 1965, Jl 11,69:1
Farwell, George Nicholas, 1923, Ja 1,15:5
Farwell, Granger, 1919, My 17,13:5
Farwell, Grosvenor, 1962, F 23,29:1
Farwell, Harold G, 1963, N 14,35:1
Farwell, Howard L, 1940, F 21,19:5
Farwell, James, 1937, N 27,17:2
Farwell, Jeremiah G, 1904, Ja 30,9:5
Farwell, John L, 1906, D 16,7:6
Farwell, John V (will, Jl 15,16:3), 1944, Je 18,36:1
Farwell, John V Mrs, 1938, D 27,17:5
Farwell, Joseph P Mrs, 1955, Ag 22,21:6
Farwell, Julia H, 1925, N 23,21:4
Farwell, Lorenzo, 1966, Ap 12,39:3
Farwell, Sewell S Maj, 1909, S 22,9:5
Farwell, Simeon, 1911, F 13,11:5
Farwell, Walter, 1943, Ag 1,39:3
Farwell, Walter Mrs, 1941, Ap 7,17:1
Fary, E Wolcott, 1947, Je 24,23:3
Fasanella, Frank F, 1950, Jl 22,15:1
Fasani, Enrico, 1949, F 26,15:5
Fasano, Ernesto, 1944, O 13,19:1
Fasano, Frank, 1953, Ap 9,27:5
Fascetti, Aldo, 1960, S 27,37:1
Fash, Hobart Carson (funl, F 23,17:6), 1925, F 20, 17:4
Fasick, Clyde A, 1951, D 22,15:6
Fasig, W B, 1902, F 20,9:5
Fasola, Ferdinand B, 1939, Ag 30,17:6
Fasolino, Pasquale, 1966, Jl 17,69:1
Fasquelle, Eugene, 1952, F 16,13:5
Fass, Irving, 1960, O 21,33:3
Fass, Jacob J Mrs, 1965, My 17,35:6
Fassberg, Bernard, 1952, Mr 7,23:4
Fassett, Bryant Dr, 1908, Mr 25,9:4
Fassett, Edgar Stewart, 1919, Jl 3,10:2
Fassett, Edwin C, 1949, F 27,68:5
Fassett, Frederick G, 1951, Mr 22,31:5
Fassett, Harvey L, 1941, O 17,23:4
Fassett, Isaac, 1960, Mr 2,37:1
Fassett, James M Mrs, 1961, D 7,43:3
Fassett, Jennie C Mrs, 1939, N 18,17:2
Fassett, John B, 1938, My 18,21:2
Fassett, John J, 1956, Mr 10,17:5
Fassett, Lorenzo J Mrs, 1957, Jl 9,29:5
Fassett, Lyman A, 1950, Mr 3,26:3
Fassett, Norman C, 1954, S 17,27:4
Fassitt, Thomas C, 1951, Mr 14,33:5
Fassitt, William H, 1961, N 10,36:2
Fassler, Samuel, 1958, N 4,27:1
Fassler, Saul, 1953, Mr 8,90:4
Fassnacht, Paul H, 1967, Ag 9,39:1
Fassnacht, Richard C, 1949, Ag 23,23:4
Fasso, Thomas N, 1966, My 20,47:3
Fast, Edward N, 1945, D 17,22:2
Fast, Fred L Mrs, 1947, Jl 10,21:4
Fast, Gustave, 1946, My 11,27:6
Fast, Herman E, 1952, Ag 26,25:4
Fast, John E, 1940, S 25,27:2
Fast, Louis A, 1946, My 7,21:4
Fast, Nathan, 1963, N 10,86:2
Fastenberg, Irving, 1943, O 11,19:3
Fastenberg, Irving Mrs, 1952, My 18,93:2
Fastenberg, Samuel J, 1955, Mr 5,17:6
Fastlich, Adolfo, 1964, Ag 25,33:2
Fastnacht, Mary W Mrs, 1942, Ja 11,44:1
Fastofsky, Stuart, 1964, S 15,37:4
Fasullo, Charles L, 1961, Ja 31,29:3
Fasy, Francis I Mrs, 1961, Je 15,43:5
Faszler, Frederick A Sr, 1951, Ap 24,29:4
Fatch, Edward P, 1942, D 27,35:1
Fater, Anthony J, 1958, Ap 16,33:5
Fater, Cornelius G, 1940, Ap 23,23:4
Fates, Hugh L, 1958, Ap 29,29:5
Fath, Jacques (funl, N 17,31:2), 1954, N 14,89:1
Fath, Mahmoud A, 1958, Ag 17,86:4
Fathauer, Walter H, 1950, D 3,88:4
Fatherley, William E Mrs, 1963, O 27,88:4
Fatman, L, 1883, Mr 23,5:2
Fator, Lester M, 1952, Ja 19,15:3
Fatt, George V, 1954, Jl 22,23:2
Fatta-Rampolia, Baroness, 1947, S 3,25:1
Fattig, P W, 1953, D 10,47:3
Fatula, Andre E, 1947, F 15,15:6
Fatula, Stephen P, 1949, Je 22,31:2
Fatyanov, Alexei, 1959, N 18,41:4
Fatzler, George F, 1949, F 8,26:2
Faubion, Buford P, 1964, D 26,17:3
Faubus, John S, 1966, Ag 25,37:2
Faucett, Elmer J, 1960, Ap 11,31:2
Faucett, James, 1946, D 29,37:4
Faucette, William D, 1947, My 20,25:5
Faucher, Joseph A, 1949, Mr 15,27:1
Faucher, Louis E, 1964, Ap 1,39:3
Faucit, Helen (Lady Martin), 1898, N 1,6:6
Faucon, James P Rev, 1921, N 25,15:4
Faude, John P, 1957, N 9,27:5
Fauerbach, Henry C, 1956, My 29,27:4
Faughnan, John F, 1955, N 2,35:4
Faughnan, John J Mrs, 1962, N 2,31:3
Faughnan, Michael P, 1942, Jl 12,35:1

Faught, Francis A, 1963, Je 8,25:4
Fauks, I Woodruff, 1940, Mr 2,13:6
Faulconer, Oda Mrs, 1943, N 4,23:6
Faulconer, William T, 1951, Ag 20,19:6
Faulconnier, Louis E, 1941, S 16,23:5
Faulds, James W, 1875, F 10,8:5
Faulds, Leslie M, 1955, Ap 14,29:3
Faulds, Mrgt J, 1942, Ag 1,11:7
Fauley, Wilbur F, 1942, D 22,25:4
Fauley, Wilbur F (will), 1943, Ja 7,17:2
Faulhaber, Charles R, 1955, Jl 14,23:5
Faulhaber, Frederick W, 1945, Ag 15,19:4
Faulhaber, George E, 1950, Ap 25,31:5
Faulhaber, Henry J Mrs, 1946, F 28,23:5
Faulhaber, Louis O, 1954, D 8,35:2
Faulhaber, Michael R von, 1952, Je 13,23:1
Faulk, J H Mrs, 1957, F 7,27:4
Faulkenhausen, L von, 1936, My 5,23:3
Faulkner, Anna Florence, 1915, Ja 11,9:4
Faulkner, Barry, 1966, O 28,31:1
Faulkner, C J, 1884, N 2,10:2; 1929, Ja 14,23:4
Faulkner, Charles J, 1953, S 5,15:6
Faulkner, David C, 1949, Ja 9,72:4
Faulkner, David S, 1956, O 14,87:2
Faulkner, Dwight F, 1949, S 17,17:1; 1957, F 19,31:4
Faulkner, E Ross, 1939, My 30,17:3
Faulkner, E Ross Mrs, 1953, Ag 8,11:3
Faulkner, Edna Mrs, 1947, Mr 16,60:2
Faulkner, Edward D Mrs (will, F 8,2:7), 1958, Ja 7, 47:4
Faulkner, Edward H, 1946, Jl 28,40:3
Faulkner, Elizabeth, 1953, F 27,21:4
Faulkner, Ernest P, 1939, Ja 6,21:3
Faulkner, Eunice F, 1958, Ag 23,15:4
Faulkner, Ferris, 1938, N 8,23:5
Faulkner, Frederick E, 1944, Mr 3,15:3
Faulkner, George V, 1955, Mr 26,15:5
Faulkner, Georgene, 1958, Jl 20,65:2
Faulkner, Harold J, 1964, Ap 8,43:1
Faulkner, Harold Underwood Dr, 1968, Je 20,45:3
Faulkner, Harry C, 1963, Jl 8,29:6
Faulkner, Harry M, 1942, My 22,21:4
Faulkner, Henry Clay Dr, 1907, Ja 16,7:4
Faulkner, Herbert K, 1944, S 16,13:4
Faulkner, Herbert W, 1940, Mr 28,23:3
Faulkner, Hilton D, 1952, Ja 23,27:3
Faulkner, J A, 1931, S 7,13:3
Faulkner, J Dr, 1884, O 24,2:3
Faulkner, James C Mrs, 1956, F 26,88:6
Faulkner, James F, 1945, Ja 2,19:4
Faulkner, James W, 1923, My 6,11:2
Faulkner, John A Mrs, 1946, F 7,23:4
Faulkner, John C, 1940, Ap 20,17:4
Faulkner, Katherine, 1943, N 28,68:3
Faulkner, Leon C, 1945, O 30,19:1
Faulkner, Mortimer S, 1945, Ag 10,15:4
Faulkner, Murry C Mrs, 1960, O 17,29:3
Faulkner, Peter J Mrs, 1948, My 24,19:4
Faulkner, Ralph, 1948, Ag 23,17:1
Faulkner, Raymond A, 1950, S 29,27:3
Faulkner, Robert J Mrs, 1952, N 24,23:3
Faulkner, Roy H, 1956, Ag 17,19:1
Faulkner, Rupert E, 1947, Ap 6,60:1
Faulkner, Rupert E Mrs, 1950, Ag 25,21:3
Faulkner, S C Col, 1874, Ag 5,5:2
Faulkner, Samuel, 1919, D 26,11:5
Faulkner, Victor Mrs, 1950, N 27,25:2
Faulkner, Walt, 1956, Ap 23,31:6
Faulkner, Whiting C, 1955, Ja 20,31:4
Faulkner, William (funl, Jl 8,64:1; will, Ag 5,80:2), 1962, Jl 7,1:2
Faulkner, Worthe W, 1959, F 3,27:7
Faulks, Edward A Mrs, 1942, Je 12,21:4
Faulks, F J, 1933, F 20,15:3
Faulks, Frederic J Mrs, 1944, O 10,23:2
Faulks, Nelson W, 1955, Ap 15,23:4
Faulks, Theodore D, 1959, Mr 9,29:3
Faulks, Thomas H Mrs, 1937, S 26,II,8:4
Fauman, Arthur S Dr, 1937, Mr 13,19:3
Faunce, Calvin B, 1948, S 24,25:2
Faunce, Daniel Worcester Rev Dr, 1911, Ja 4,9:4
Faunce, Harold W, 1962, Mr 24,25:5
Faunce, Hiram S, 1939, N 16,24:2
Faunce, James E Mrs, 1955, Jl 26,25:4
Faunce, Kenneth W, 1955, Ag 4,25:4
Faunce, W H P, 1930, F 1,17:3
Faunce, William A, 1940, Ja 6,13:4
Faunce, William H Mrs, 1944, Ap 26,19:2
Faunthorpe, J C, 1929, D 4,31:3
Fauntleroy, Arch M Capt, 1937, Ap 14,25:5
Fauntleroy, Cedric E, 1963, D 6,36:1
Fauntleroy, Thomas, 1939, F 27,15:3
Faure, A J le, 1881, N 24,3:1
Faure, Elie Dr, 1937, N 1,21:4
Faure, Emile, 1940, Mr 19,25:4
Faure, Felix, 1899, F 17,1:2
Faure, Gabriel, 1924, N 5,19:5
Faure, Jean B, 1914, N 11,13:6
Faure, Jean L, 1944, O 27,23:3
Faure, Jeanne, 1950, S 10,92:5
Faure, John P, 1912, Je 20,11:6
Faure, Paul, 1960, N 19,21:3
Faure, Sebastien, 1942, Jl 24,19:5

Faurot, Fred W Sr Mrs, 1951, N 8,29:4
Faurot, Henry, 1948, Je 3,25:1
Faurot, Joseph A, 1942, N 21,13:4
Faurote, Fay L, 1938, S 8,23:2
Faus, Herbert W, 1966, Ap 29,47:2
Fauser, Albert A, 1955, My 4,29:2
Fauset, Crystal B, 1965, Mr 30,47:4
Fauset, Jessie R, 1961, My 3,37:3
Fausher, John, 1938, N 30,46:1
Fauss, Dennis C, 1940, Jl 4,15:4
Faussett, John D, 1939, D 24,21:4
Faust, A W (Bud), 1962, S 23,V,15:1
Faust, Albert B, 1951, F 9,25:3
Faust, Allen K, 1953, S 14,27:4
Faust, Anthony R Mrs, 1916, S 16,11:6
Faust, Arnold, 1961, My 4,37:2
Faust, Christina H, 1943, Ap 26,19:2
Faust, David, 1907, My 10,7:5
Faust, Frederick D Mrs, 1953, N 1,87:1
Faust, Henry N, 1950, O 7,17:2
Faust, J W, 1949, Ap 8,26:3
Faust, Lotta (funl, Ja 27,9:4), 1910, Ja 26,9:5
Faust, Mathias, 1956, Jl 28,17:3
Faust, Otto V, 1953, S 7,19:3
Faust, Paul E, 1952, S 25,31:5
Faust, Richard J Jr, 1951, O 3,33:3
Faust, Roger C, 1949, Jl 22,19:4
Faust, Walter L, 1956, Jl 21,15:4
Faust, William H, 1943, D 24,13:4
Faustmann, Edmund C, 1946, Ag 31,15:6
Fauteux, Aegidius, 1941, Ap 23,21:3
Fauteux, Etherius, 1941, Mr 30,48:7
Fauteux, Guillaume A, 1940, S 11,25:2
Fauteux, Mercier, 1950, Ap 29,15:3
Fauth, Phil, 1941, Ja 7,23:1
Fautrier, Jean, 1964, Jl 23,27:2
Fauver, Clayton K, 1942, Mr 4,19:4
Fauver, Clayton K Mrs, 1939, Mr 13,17:2
Fauver, Edgar, 1946, Ap 4,25:5
Fauver, Edgar L Mrs, 1939, Mr 31,17:2
Fauver, Edwin, 1949, D 18,89:1
Fauver, Frank R, 1954, Ja 10,87:1
Faux, Albert L, 1954, F 3,23:4
Faux, George H, 1960, F 17,35:1
Fava, Phillip V, 1951, D 6,33:5
Fava, Saverio Baron, 1913, O 4,13:4
Faversham, William, 1940, Ap 8,20:2
Faversham, William Mrs, 1945, My 21,19:4
Favier, Bishop, 1905, Ap 5,9:6
Favill, Henry Baird Dr, 1916, F 21,11:4
Favill, John F, 1946, D 23,23:4
Favill, William M, 1908, F 28,7:5
Favino, Anthony J, 1959, Ap 14,35:4
Favor, Edith S Mrs, 1942, N 28,13:5
Favor, Edward P, 1948, Mr 6,13:4
Favor, Gerald, 1947, Mr 10,21:3
Favor, Henry S, 1948, D 31,16:2
Favoreau, Joseph, 1948, My 12,28:2
Favorito, Felix, 1961, Mr 28,35:1
Favorsky, Alexei, 1945, Ag 11,13:4
Favorsky, Vladimir A, 1964, D 31,19:3
Favour, Frank T, 1951, Ap 21,17:4
Favour, Paul G, 1948, My 31,19:6
Favre, Eugene B, 1939, S 28,25:5
Favre, Jules, 1880, Ja 21,2:6
Favreau, Guy, 1967, Jl 12,43:4
Favreau, Walter, 1955, S 13,31:4
Fawcett, Alfred L, 1950, Jl 25,27:3
Fawcett, Claire Mrs, 1960, S 15,37:4
Fawcett, Dame M, 1929, Ag 5,21:5
Fawcett, Deborah, 1950, Ja 2,23:5
Fawcett, Donald N, 1949, D 3,15:3
Fawcett, Edgar, 1904, My 3,9:6
Fawcett, Edward, 1942, S 24,27:4
Fawcett, F, 1877, My 4,8:5
Fawcett, Fred H, 1904, Ja 16,9:5
Fawcett, Genevieve Mrs, 1941, S 23,27:7
Fawcett, George D, 1939, Je 7,23:5
Fawcett, George G, 1955, S 8,31:4
Fawcett, George Mrs, 1945, Je 14,19:6
Fawcett, George W, 1944, F 5,15:6
Fawcett, Henry, 1884, N 7,5:6
Fawcett, Howard S, 1948, D 13,23:3
Fawcett, James M, 1961, S 5,32:4
Fawcett, John C, 1943, Mr 1,19:6
Fawcett, John G Rev, 1920, S 25,13:2
Fawcett, Lewis L, 1952, S 19,23:4
Fawcett, Martin C, 1958, Mr 15,17:1
Fawcett, Mary O, 1938, My 4,23:4
Fawcett, Rebecca, 1950, F 17,23:4
Fawcett, Reginald W, 1963, Jl 19,25:2
Fawcett, Robert, 1967, Ap 14,39:5
Fawcett, Wilford H, 1940, F 8,23:3
Fawcett, William J, 1940, Je 17,15:5
Fawcett, William R, 1958, O 27,27:4
Fawcus, Harold B, 1947, O 27,21:3
Fawkes, Guy, 1957, Jl 4,19:3
Fawkes, Robert, 1948, F 7,15:1
Fawley, William A, 1956, D 22,19:3
Fawls, James F, 1962, Je 29,27:4
Fawsitt, Amy (see also D 28), 1876, D 30,8:3
Fawver, Harry W, 1949, Mr 13,76:1
Fax, Jimmy, 1949, Ag 30,27:2

Faxon, Charles, 1867, Jl 26,2:6
Faxon, Frederick S, 1940, D 12,27:3
Faxon, Huntington P, 1944, Ja 23,38:3
Faxon, John G, 1947, F 5,23:4
Faxon, W, 1883, S 20,5:1
Faxon, Warren E, 1957, N 1,27:3
Faxon, William B, 1941, Ag 14,17:3
Faxon, William O, 1942, N 13,23:2
Faxton, Charles Edward, 1918, F 7,11:8
Faxton, T S, 1881, D 1,4:7
Fay, Alice (Countess di Castangnola), 1963, S 26 35:1
Fay, Alice M Mrs, 1937, Ja 22,21:5
Fay, Aubert J, 1944, D 26,19:2
Fay, August M, 1919, Jl 16,13:3
Fay, B, 1931, S 19,17:4
Fay, Bernard, 1942, Mr 14,15:2
Fay, C Robert, 1959, Jl 20,25:5
Fay, Catherine A, 1953, F 21,13:2
Fay, Charles A, 1948, O 9,19:4
Fay, Charles E, 1957, My 30,19:4
Fay, Charles J Jr, 1940, O 19,17:3
Fay, Charles N, 1944, Ap 9,34:2
Fay, Charles W, 1938, Ja 7,19:4
Fay, Clarence H, 1953, Ja 21,31:6
Fay, Edward, 1904, Je 27,7:3
Fay, Edward A, 1957, Ap 7,88:4
Fay, Edward A Mrs, 1953, Ja 26,19:3
Fay, Edward H, 1946, Je 7,19:1
Fay, Edward P, 1946, D 12,29:3
Fay, Elizabeth T Mrs, 1947, Ja 3,21:2
Fay, Ernest A, 1944, Je 27,19:2
Fay, Eugene, 1941, F 15,15:3
Fay, Everett A, 1967, My 25,47:4
Fay, Frances V Mrs, 1939, O 8,48:8
Fay, Francis B, 1945, Ap 23,19:5
Fay, Frank (Francis A),(will, O 12,33:4), 1961, 41:1
Fay, Frank A, 1937, Jl 7,24:2
Fay, Frank H, 1955, S 23,26:5
Fay, Frank L, 1946, O 11,23:2
Fay, Frankie, 1954, F 16,25:1
Fay, Frederic H, 1944, Je 7,19:4
Fay, Frederick A Mrs, 1945, Mr 7,21:1
Fay, Frederick J, 1911, Je 15,9:5
Fay, George M, 1957, N 18,31:2
Fay, George V, 1940, Je 4,23:5
Fay, Gerard, 1968, Mr 16,31:4
Fay, Henry W, 1959, My 7,33:1
Fay, Horace B, 1951, F 11,88:2
Fay, James A Mrs, 1950, D 16,17:5
Fay, James F, 1940, F 4,41:1
Fay, James H, 1948, S 11,15:3
Fay, James J, 1943, My 14,19:3
Fay, James O, 1944, S 14,23:3
Fay, Jay W, 1945, Mr 3,13:2
Fay, Jean A Sister, 1957, Ag 31,15:6
Fay, John, 1947, D 25,21:5
Fay, John A, 1948, Jl 31,15:4
Fay, John A Mrs, 1943, Jl 19,15:1
Fay, John C, 1913, S 17,9:2
Fay, John J, 1958, My 29,27:1
Fay, John J Mrs, 1947, D 6,15:3
Fay, John L, 1961, Ap 24,29:3
Fay, Joseph M, 1958, D 28,2:7
Fay, Joseph W, 1957, Ja 30,29:4
Fay, L K, 1903, Je 30,7:6
Fay, Leon E, 1944, F 13,14:1
Fay, Lewis G, 1951, D 2,90:4
Fay, Mamie, 1949, Mr 22,25:3
Fay, Margaret H Mrs, 1940, N 26,23:3
Fay, Martin J, 1959, N 27,29:2
Fay, Mary H (Mother Bonaventure), 1966, N
Fay, Mary M, 1957, My 29,27:3
Fay, Michael T, 1949, Ja 2,60:6
Fay, Nancy Mrs, 1921, O 11,19:5
Fay, Owen J, 1954, N 21,87:2
Fay, Patrick J Mrs, 1943, Je 22,20:2
Fay, Paul, 1943, N 10,23:3
Fay, Peter, 1956, Ag 4,15:2
Fay, Phil, 1953, My 14,29:4
Fay, R, 1929, Mr 10,II,8:1
Fay, Ralph O L, 1947, Ja 17,24:3
Fay, Richard, 1952, F 22,21:3
Fay, Russell P Dr, 1903, Ap 1,9:5
Fay, Sam, 1953, Je 1,23:2
Fay, Sidney B, 1967, Ag 30,43:1
Fay, Sigourney W Msgr, 1919, Ja 11,13:5
Fay, Sigourney Webster, 1908, Je 2,7:6
Fay, Thomas A, 1951, Ja 16,29:2
Fay, Thomas E, 1952, D 24,17:5
Fay, Thomas Jr, 1923, Mr 31,13:6
Fay, Thomas M Mrs, 1957, Mr 25,25:3
Fay, Thomas M Sr, 1953, D 14,31:4
Fay, W G Mrs, 1952, D 2,31:2
Fay, Waldo B, 1940, O 17,25:2
Fay, William, 1909, Jl 18,9:6
Fay, William C, 1959, My 12,35:2
Fay, William E, 1939, Ap 26,23:5
Fay, William F, 1956, D 16,87:1
Fay, William G, 1947, O 29,27:3
Fay, William H, 1950, My 17,29:2
Fay, William R, 1954, F 27,13:3

Fay, William W, 1946, Je 2,44:3
Fayant, Frank H Mrs, 1939, S 1,17:4
Faye, Stanley K, 1949, Mr 8,25:2
Faye, Tom J, 1884, My 30,2:7
Fayer, Charles Mrs, 1946, F 21,21:2
Fayer, Mishah Mrs, 1964, Ja 27,23:2
Fayerweather, Charles S, 1942, Ag 26,19:1
Fayerweather, Charles S Mrs, 1958, S 13,19:5
Fayerweather, Frederic M, 1941, Jl 26,15:4
Fayko, George P Jr, 1958, Je 25,29:1
Fayles, George M, 1960, Ja 14,33:4
Fayles, George M Mrs, 1948, Ap 20,27:1
Faymonville, Philip R, 1962, Mr 31,25:4
Fayolle, M E, 1928, Ag 28,23:3
Fayrer, James C S Mrs, 1959, S 13,84:1
Fayrer, Joseph Sir, 1907, My 22,9:4
Fazenda, Louis (Mrs H Wallis),(funl, Ap 21,19:4), 1962, Ap 18,39:3
Fazenda, Nelda T Mrs, 1939, O 31,23:3
Fazio, Anthony, 1950, O 28,17:4
Fazio, Anthony L M Mrs, 1957, Mr 19,37:2
Fazio, Anthony N, 1950, Ja 30,17:3
Fazio, Frank, 1960, F 23,31:1
Fazio, Joseph, 1951, Ap 7,15:3
Fazio, Louis J Mrs, 1950, My 23,29:3
Fazio, Michele de, 1955, F 5,15:5
Fazio, Paolo, 1952, F 6,29:4
Fazlul Hug, A K, 1962, Ap 28,25:5
Fazy, J J, 1878, N 7,5:5
Fead, Louis H, 1943, F 5,21:4
Feagans, Ray F, 1949, O 30,84:4
Feagley, Chester C, 1950, O 5,31:2
Feakes, Alfred C Mrs, 1950, S 12,27:3
Feakes, Edward, 1960, Jl 11,29:3
Feakes, Richard, 1954, O 23,15:5
Feakins, William B, 1946, Mr 26,29:4
Feare, George A, 1954, Je 28,19:4
Fearey, Morton L, 1954, D 14,33:2
Fearey, Morton L Mrs, 1962, Ap 26,33:2
Fearey, Porter, 1942, Ap 2,21:1
Fearing, Albert, 1875, My 25,6:7
Fearing, Albert J, 1950, D 3,88:3
Fearing, B D, 1881, D 11,2:5
Fearing, C F, 1901, Ap 8,7:6
Fearing, Daniel B, 1870, D 1,2:7
Fearing, Daniel B Mrs, 1908, Ap 17,9:6
Fearing, George R, 1920, Ja 27,15:2
Fearing, Joseph L (por), 1945, Jl 30,19:3
Fearing, Joseph L Jr, 1946, D 18,29:4
Fearing, Kenneth, 1961, Je 27,33:3
Fearing, William H, 1904, Ja 25,7:7
Fearis, William E, 1913, D 20,13:6
Fearn, Anne W, 1939, Ap 30,45:3
Fearn, Elmer A, 1953, Jl 21,24:7
Fearn, William R Capt, 1921, S 10,11:4
Fearnley, Samuel, 1951, Ag 4,15:4
Fearnley, Thomas, 1961, Ja 12,29:3
Fearnow, John R, 1951, My 5,17:6
Fearns, John T, 1938, Ap 14,23:4
Fearns, Robert J, 1950, F 11,15:4
Fearns, Robert J Mrs, 1949, O 22,17:6
Fearns, Sylvester J, 1944, F 2,21:2
Fearon, Francis G, 1964, D 4,40:2
Fearon, George R Mrs, 1938, Ja 13,21:2
Fearon, Henry D, 1941, D 14,69:2
Fearon, James Sturgis, 1920, O 29,15:5
Fearon, Percy H, 1948, N 6,13:3
Fearon, William B, 1949, Mr 18,25:2
Fearons, G H, 1930, Je 7,17:3
Fearson, William F, 1937, Jl 31,15:6
Feaster, Frank M, 1950, Mr 21,29:1
Feaster, George L, 1963, O 12,23:4
Feaster, William G Jr, 1950, D 12,33:2
Feather, Arthur R, 1939, Ja 11,19:5
Feather, Norris Mrs, 1947, D 18,30:3
Feather, William, 1951, My 2,31:3
Feathers, Leonard C, 1961, O 23,29:5
Feathers, William C, 1944, Ag 15,17:2
Featherson, Maurice, 1953, D 14,31:1
Featherston, Edward W, 1943, D 10,27:1
Featherstone, Richard, 1948, N 19,27:4
Featherstone, William B, 1951, Ap 14,16:2
Featherstone, William J, 1945, N 20,21:1
Featherstonhaugh, Duane, 1952, O 28,31:3
Feavearyear, Albert, 1953, Ap 25,15:4
Febick, Edward E, 1960, O 2,84:8
Febiger, Christian, 1945, My 13,20:7
Febvre, Lucien, 1956, S 28,27:1
Fechet, Edmund G Lt-Col, 1910, N 17,9:5
Fechet, James E, 1948, F 12,23:1
Fechheimer, A Lincoln, 1954, Jl 30,17:4
Fechheimer, Albert M Mrs, 1966, S 18,84:6
Fechheimer, Alfred, 1957, S 30,31:2
Fechheimer, Lutie H Mrs, 1939, S 26,23:2
Fechheimer, Samuel T, 1948, My 20,29:2
Fechner, Robert, 1940, Ja 1,23:1
Fechteler, Augustus F Rear-Adm, 1921, My 27,17:6
Fechteler, William M, 1967, Jl 5,41:1
Fechter, Charles (funl, Ag 9,2:7), 1879, Ag 6,5:1
Fechtig, Louis R Mrs, 1948, Mr 16,27:2
Fechtig, Robert Y, 1944, Ap 26,19:1
Fechtman, Charles F, 1953, Jl 26,69:3
Fechtman, George A T, 1960, Je 23,29:5
Fechtman, Herman A, 1960, F 7,84:2
Fecke, Charles H, 1956, My 6,86:3
Fecke, Herbert V, 1966, Jl 7,37:3
Fectman, Henry, 1954, Je 23,25:4
Feczko, John H, 1945, Ja 20,11:5
Fedde, Arne S, 1955, Jl 29,17:4
Fedde, G M Nathaniel Sr, 1953, O 10,17:6
Fedden, Romilly, 1939, Ap 3,15:5
Fedder, Herman Mrs, 1925, My 3,5:1
Fedder, Richard L, 1953, D 25,17:6
Fedderke, Fritz W, 1906, D 29,9:5
Fedders, Christ W, 1951, O 3,33:2
Fedders, Theodore C, 1958, Ag 20,27:2
Fedele, Pietro, 1943, Ja 11,15:2
Feder, Daniel, 1956, Ap 11,33:4
Feder, Gottfried, 1941, S 26,24:2
Feder, Isaac, 1924, D 26,15:5
Feder, Isidore A, 1967, Ag 21,31:3
Feder, J Fuller Mrs, 1960, Jl 2,17:2
Feder, Jacob, 1954, Mr 28,88:5
Feder, James L, 1964, Je 29,27:5
Feder, Jean, 1941, Je 4,23:5
Feder, Joseph F, 1944, My 12,19:2
Feder, Marcus Sr, 1942, Jl 26,31:3
Feder, Mark G Mrs, 1950, Ja 6,22:3
Feder, Meyer, 1963, My 22,41:5
Feder, Sid, 1960, F 23,32:1
Feder, William Jr, 1941, Ap 10,23:5
Feder, William L, 1965, My 25,41:4
Federbush, Charles, 1942, O 1,23:3
Federbush, Sender, 1942, Ap 1,21:6
Federbush, Sender Mrs, 1957, Ap 28,87:1
Federer, Anna S Mrs, 1941, Je 2,17:2
Federici, Riccardo B, 1955, Jl 16,15:4
Federighi, Henry, 1960, D 2,29:3
Federlein, Gottfried H, 1952, F 28,27:4
Federman, Harry L, 1952, Ag 29,23:3
Federman, Marcus J, 1942, Je 28,32:8
Federn, Walter, 1967, Ag 3,33:4
Federn, Walther, 1949, F 2,28:3
Federspiel, Peter, 1948, Ag 24,23:5
Fedigan, John J Rev, 1908, Ap 28,9:6
Fediunkin, Ivan F, 1950, F 23,27:2
Fedor, Chester, 1939, Ag 22,19:3
Fedora, Frank, 1947, Ja 3,22:3
Fedorenko, Yacob N, 1947, Mr 28,23:1
Fedorko, Peter, 1944, My 13,19:5
Fedorko, Speridon, 1953, Je 9,27:1
Fedotov, George P, 1951, S 5,31:3
Fedou, R Eaton, 1944, O 10,23:2
Fedter, Bruno, 1949, F 12,17:4
Fedunin, Nikolai A, 1948, F 21,13:3
Fee, B F, 1950, D 15,32:2
Fee, Bernard H, 1947, Mr 7,25:4
Fee, Frank J, 1945, Mr 25,37:1
Fee, Frederick B Sr, 1941, My 14,21:2
Fee, Harry E Jr, 1949, Je 12,25:5
Fee, J G Rev, 1901, Ja 12,1:6
Fee, James A, 1959, Ag 26,29:4
Fee, James Mrs, 1955, O 12,31:3
Fee, John C Mrs, 1943, Jl 5,15:5
Fee, John L, 1941, Ap 22,21:5
Fee, Marguerite C, 1951, Je 5,31:4
Fee, Thomas H, 1943, S 22,23:5
Fee, Thomas J, 1960, Ag 13,15:5
Fee, William, 1949, S 12,21:3
Fee, William E, 1958, D 3,37:1
Fee, William H, 1954, My 24,27:4; 1960, Jl 8,21:4
Feegel, John S, 1944, N 6,19:4
Feehan, Archbishop, 1902, Jl 13,7:5
Feehan, James, 1919, Mr 10,11:4
Feehan, Richard P, 1957, N 3,88:1
Feeherry, Anthony, 1963, D 3,43:1
Feeley, Frank G, 1940, O 21,17:5
Feeley, J J B, 1938, Ap 1,23:3
Feeley, John H, 1938, F 5,15:6
Feeley, Patrick F, 1943, D 7,27:4
Feeley, Paul, 1966, Je 12,86:3
Feeley, Thomas T, 1943, O 12,27:5
Feely, Bernard J, 1938, My 24,19:2
Feely, Edward F, 1964, Ag 31,25:3
Feely, Frank J, 1955, F 23,27:3
Feely, James P, 1962, O 3,41:4
Feely, Joseph A, 1955, Ja 10,23:2
Feely, M M, 1943, O 22,17:2
Feely, Margaret, 1949, O 5,29:3
Feely, Michael, 1883, Je 15,5:4
Feely, Walter F X, 1941, D 5,23:4
Feely, William E, 1964, Mr 22,77:1
Feemster, Robert N, 1963, Ja 16,16:1
Feeney, Albert G, 1950, N 13,27:5
Feeney, C, 1878, Ag 6,1:6
Feeney, Catherine, 1939, F 6,13:3
Feeney, Charles A, 1958, N 14,27:3
Feeney, Edward J, 1957, My 23,33:5
Feeney, Elwood A, 1955, D 25,48:3
Feeney, Emma L, 1947, O 24,23:3
Feeney, Frank, 1938, My 29,II,6:6
Feeney, Frank E, 1948, N 1,23:4
Feeney, Frank L, 1942, Ja 14,21:3
Feeney, Frank L Mrs, 1954, Mr 21,89:1
Feeney, Harry T, 1950, S 20,31:2
Feeney, James, 1941, F 5,19:4
Feeney, James C, 1951, Jl 15,61:2
Feeney, James J, 1956, My 19,19:4
Feeney, James M Mrs, 1954, Mr 5,19:1
Feeney, John, 1960, Ap 12,33:4; 1968, Ja 10,43:1
Feeney, John J, 1937, Jl 16,19:4
Feeney, John M Jr, 1951, Mr 9,25:2
Feeney, John P, 1906, Ja 15,9:6; 1937, My 16,II,8:5
Feeney, John P Mrs, 1943, F 16,19:4
Feeney, Joseph G, 1968, O 21,47:4
Feeney, M Alan, 1959, S 2,29:3
Feeney, Martin J, 1937, N 27,17:2
Feeney, Mary A Mrs, 1958, Je 5,31:4; 1959, N 16,31:3
Feeney, Mary E, 1943, Ap 20,23:1
Feeney, Owen P, 1951, Ja 4,29:3
Feeney, Owen V, 1956, My 19,19:2
Feeney, Patrick J, 1966, O 2,86:7
Feeney, Patrick M, 1966, Je 12,86:6
Feeney, Raphael K W, 1964, Mr 21,26:8
Feeney, Thomas A, 1959, N 18,41:5
Feeney, Thomas A Mrs, 1955, Mr 31,27:1
Feeney, Thomas J, 1955, S 10,17:3
Feeney, William F, 1942, Ja 12,15:5
Feeney, William J, 1939, Mr 10,23:6
Feeny, F L Dr, 1901, Je 1,9:5
Feeny, James Dr, 1916, My 31,13:2
Feeter, J William, 1946, Je 22,19:5
Feeter, John A C, 1955, Ap 2,17:1
Feffer, Herman, 1956, Ag 8,25:2
Feffercorn, Emil Mrs, 1949, Jl 7,25:4
Fegan, Charles G, 1956, Jl 9,23:2
Fegan, Charles P, 1944, N 10,19:2
Fegan, Henry, 1940, Ap 21,43:1
Fegan, Hugh J, 1954, D 21,27:5
Fegan, Joseph C (por), 1949, My 27,21:3
Fegely, Harry C, 1948, S 15,31:3
Fegley, John T, 1959, Mr 31,29:4
Fegley, O George, 1948, D 15,33:3
Fegley, Thomas J, 1939, Mr 2,21:3
Fegtly, Samuel M, 1947, Ag 12,24:3
Fehleisen, Frederick Dr, 1924, Ag 30,9:6
Fehlhaber, Fred N Mrs, 1958, Ag 19,28:5
Fehlhaber, William, 1959, My 24,88:4
Fehliner, Felician M, 1952, Jl 8,27:1
Fehling, C Harry, 1951, Je 20,27:1
Fehling, Edward P, 1966, Je 21,43:3
Fehnel, Sylvanus J, 1948, Je 27,52:4
Fehr, Andrew F, 1940, Mr 31,44:4
Fehr, Frank, 1962, Ag 16,27:5
Fehr, Harry J, 1952, S 17,31:5
Fehr, Herman, 1943, Ja 1,23:6
Fehr, John B, 1937, Ja 17,II,9:2
Fehr, Joseph E, 1944, Ap 21,19:6
Fehr, Louis W, 1957, Mr 26,33:4
Fehr, Thomas, 1945, Jl 20,19:2
Fehrenbach, C, 1926, Mr 27,17:3
Fehrenbacher, Mary, 1946, Ap 7,46:2
Fehrenbacher, William L Mrs, 1946, O 1,23:5
Fehringer, Konrad, 1944, F 1,19:4
Fehrman, Gustav J, 1939, S 24,43:3
Feibelmann, Richard B, 1948, Mr 26,21:5
Feibleman, Bert L, 1939, D 30,15:5
Feibleman, Joseph L, 1941, Jl 6,27:3
Feibleman, Sidney L, 1967, Mr 29,45:2
Feichinger, Franz, 1951, F 14,29:4
Feicht, Russell S, 1949, Ap 23,13:1
Feick, Charles A Mrs, 1953, O 20,29:6
Feickert, Lillian F Mrs, 1945, Ja 22,17:5
Feidelson, A O Mrs, 1957, Mr 21,31:3
Feidelson, Max, 1938, Ap 3,19:6
Feiden, Hyman Mrs, 1965, Ja 4,29:2
Feidt, George G, 1942, Je 29,15:5
Feigelman, Harry, 1953, Jl 30,23:4
Feigen, Arthur P, 1967, Je 10,33:4
Feigenbaum, Dorian Dr, 1937, Ja 3,II,8:5
Feigenbaum, Frank, 1958, F 16,86:1
Feigenbaum, Harry, 1958, Je 21,19:6
Feigenbaum, William M, 1949, Ap 24,76:1
Feigenberg, Leo Mrs, 1955, Ja 18,27:4
Feigenoff, Israel, 1947, O 5,68:2
Feigenspan, Christian W, 1939, F 7,19:3
Feigenspan, Christian W Mrs, 1945, N 9,19:2
Feigenspan, Edwin C, 1953, N 1,86:6
Feigenspan-Stengel, Marie L Mrs, 1940, D 24,15:1
Feighan, John T, 1953, Ag 6,21:4
Feighery, Francis J, 1953, N 4,33:3
Feigin, Anna Mrs, 1942, F 20,17:3
Feigin, Samuel, 1953, Mr 23,23:5
Feigin, Samuel I, 1950, Ja 4,35:2
Feigin, Solomon, 1966, F 17,87:2
Feigl, F, 1933, D 11,19:3
Feigl, George G, 1942, Ag 17,15:4
Feigl, Hugo, 1961, F 6,23:4
Feigley, Howard M, 1955, Ja 18,27:4
Feihl, Frederick, 1946, D 20,23:2
Feiker, Frederick M, 1967, Ja 15,84:5
Feil, Christian G, 1944, Jl 9,35:1
Feil, Leo A, 1946, My 5,46:2
Feilchenfeld, Ernest H, 1956, Mr 26,29:4
Feild, Mrs, 1881, N 14,5:1
Feild, Thomas L, 1937, Ap 7,25:1
Feilden, Hill, 1875, S 7,2:1
Feilding, Viscount, 1937, Ja 11,20:3
Feiler, Arthur, 1942, Jl 12,35:3

Feilitzsch, Louise B von, 1943, My 15,15:5
Feilwel, Berthold Dr, 1937, D 30,19:3
Feimanis, George V, 1962, Mr 1,31:3
Fein, George, 1968, Ja 31,41:2
Fein, Hyman, 1946, Ag 11,45:1
Fein, Jack, 1954, Je 29,27:3
Fein, Jerome H, 1964, Jl 26,56:4
Fein, Lawrence L, 1953, Ag 4,21:2
Fein, Maxwell J, 1955, Jl 15,21:3
Fein, Otto, 1939, D 3,60:5
Fein, Robert, 1944, N 3,21:5
Feinbaum, Israel, 1957, O 28,27:5
Feinberg, Barney, 1963, N 5,28:4
Feinberg, Benjamin F (funl plans, F 8,86:1; trb, F 10,33:3), 1959, F 7,19:4
Feinberg, Benjamin Mrs, 1953, S 27,86:1
Feinberg, Charles, 1962, My 23,45:4
Feinberg, David, 1946, S 21,15:6; 1950, Mr 7,27:3
Feinberg, David Mrs, 1943, F 18,23:3
Feinberg, Davis Mrs, 1952, Jl 16,25:2
Feinberg, Dora, 1943, S 1,19:3
Feinberg, George Mrs (Patricia Jessel), 1968, Je 11, 47:1
Feinberg, Harris, 1951, My 29,25:1
Feinberg, Harry, 1960, My 26,33:1
Feinberg, Harry M, 1953, O 2,21:2
Feinberg, Henry G, 1955, Je 29,29:3
Feinberg, Herman, 1948, My 28,23:4
Feinberg, Israel, 1941, Ap 14,17:2; 1952, S 17,31:3
Feinberg, J George, 1937, Mr 28,II,8:7
Feinberg, Jac Mrs, 1959, S 19,23:4
Feinberg, Jacob N, 1943, F 11,19:2
Feinberg, Jesse, 1949, Ja 25,23:1
Feinberg, Joseph, 1941, F 3,20:3; 1951, S 25,29:3
Feinberg, Leo Mrs, 1949, Jl 9,13:3
Feinberg, Louis, 1949, F 21,23:3; 1953, N 24,29:2; 1965, Je 29,32:8
Feinberg, Meyer, 1951, Jl 4,17:3
Feinberg, Meyer A, 1953, Jl 16,21:5
Feinberg, Michael, 1957, D 8,88:4
Feinberg, Milton, 1954, Jl 4,30:8
Feinberg, Morris, 1951, Mr 27,26:1; 1966, Je 9,47:2
Feinberg, Myron, 1962, My 23,45:4
Feinberg, Phil F, 1949, D 21,29:2
Feinberg, Salmon, 1948, My 30,34:2
Feinberg, Samuel, 1944, Je 27,19:4
Feinberg, Samuel D Rabbi, 1914, D 23,13:3
Feinblatt, Henry M, 1959, D 27,61:1
Feinblum, Sam, 1954, D 21,27:4
Feindt, Aloysia J, 1947, Mr 8,13:1
Feindt, Leo F, 1957, Mr 16,19:1
Feiner, Ben, 1965, Je 8,41:1
Feiner, Benjamin Mrs, 1954, O 12,27:2
Feiner, Philip A, 1961, Ja 15,86:5
Feiner, Samuel, 1946, My 30,21:2
Feinerman, Elias, 1939, S 10,49:2
Feinerman, Harry Mrs, 1960, D 19,27:1
Feinerman, Nathan, 1944, F 16,17:5
Feinfeld, Benjamin B Mrs, 1968, Ja 16,39:1
Feingold, Boris, 1947, S 2,21:4
Feingold, Edward I, 1961, N 19,88:1
Feingold, Gustave A, 1948, Je 26,17:3
Feingold, Louis, 1961, Jl 5,33:3
Feingold, Max, 1955, F 9,25:2
Feininger, Edgar L, 1946, Je 11,23:2
Feininger, Karl, 1922, F 2,17:4
Feininger, Lyonel, 1956, Ja 14,19:3
Feinman, Bessie Mrs, 1948, Ag 18,27:5
Feinne, Theodore I, 1964, Je 8,29:4
Feinson, Isadore Mrs, 1951, Jl 12,25:5
Feinson, Mac B, 1949, Mr 19,15:5
Feinstein, Henry, 1960, Ja 26,33:3
Feinstein, Irving, 1952, Je 29,56:4
Feinstein, Isadore N, 1941, Ja 30,21:5
Feinstein, Jerome T, 1951, S 30,72:5
Feinstein, Leon, 1951, D 27,21:5
Feinstein, Max, 1949, Je 14,32:4; 1951, S 5,31:3
Feinstein, Moses, 1964, S 23,47:1
Feinstein, Myer, 1965, Je 7,37:2
Feinstein, Nathan A, 1958, Ja 6,39:2
Feinstein, Paizor, 1940, Ap 28,37:3
Feinstein, Samuel, 1955, Jl 8,23:4
Feinstone, Morris C, 1943, Ap 29,21:3
Feinswog, David S, 1968, Ag 8,33:2
Feinswog, Jacob, 1950, O 31,27:1
Feinswog, Louis S, 1951, D 6,33:1
Feinswog, Louis S Mrs, 1949, D 9,32:3
Feintuch, Harry, 1967, F 22,29:3
Feintuck, Morris, 1946, Jl 5,7:6
Feiring, Francis C, 1943, S 21,23:2
Feiss, Paul L, 1952, Ja 21,16:4
Feist, Bessie Mrs, 1941, N 28,24:3
Feist, Ernest M, 1965, F 1,23:4
Feist, Felix E, 1965, S 4,21:5
Feist, Hans, 1952, O 1,33:2
Feist, Henry M, 1941, My 7,25:6; 1943, D 19,48:4
Feist, L, 1930, Je 22,25:5
Feist, Louis, 1925, N 4,23:4
Feist, Sigmund, 1943, Ap 9,21:6
Feistel, Harold J, 1961, O 20,33:3
Feit, Abraham, 1961, Ja 19,29:5
Feit, Charles T, 1961, S 27,41:2
Feit, Harold, 1955, Jl 23,17:6

Feit, Harry L Mrs, 1963, My 7,43:3
Feit, Hermann, 1938, Ja 19,23:1
Feitelberg, Adolph S, 1945, O 16,23:3
Feitelberg, Sergei, 1967, S 17,84:5
Feith, Jonkheer R, 1953, Jl 18,13:1
Feith, Joseph A, 1950, S 10,94:2
Feitl, Rudolf, 1956, S 1,15:5
Feitner, Bertha K, 1941, Ag 6,17:3
Feitner, John, 1943, S 3,19:5
Feitner, John F, 1940, N 7,25:4
Feitner, Q F, 1933, F 18,16:1
Feitner, Quentin F, 1962, Ja 2,30:8
Fejer, Joseph, 1950, Jl 23,56:1
Fejos, Paul, 1963, Ap 24,35:4
Feklenko, Nikolao, 1951, O 14,88:5
Fekula, Alex M, 1963, O 22,37:3
Feland, Faris R, 1952, N 15,17:1
Feland, L, 1936, Jl 18,15:1
Felbel, Dore Mrs, 1959, Je 30,31:1
Felbel, Jacob (will, D 17,15:1), 1938, D 14,25:2
Felber, Herman P, 1965, My 12,47:3
Felberbaum, David, 1950, O 28,17:3
Felberbaum, Emil, 1956, Ap 20,25:5
Felch, Grace A Mrs, 1942, F 24,21:5
Felcher, Irving, 1957, Ap 9,33:3
Felcher, John H, 1949, Ap 11,25:4
Feld, David D, 1949, Jl 5,23:2
Feld, Itzik, 1943, O 9,13:6
Feld, Mose M, 1961, Ag 22,29:3
Feld, Samuel L, 1955, Ap 4,29:1
Feld, Ziskind, 1950, My 3,29:5
Feld, Ziskind Mrs, 1951, Ap 20,29:4
Feldamn, Max (Hillside, NJ), 1957, O 1,33:2
Feldan, Herbert, 1960, My 29,56:3
Feldary, Eric, 1968, F 26,32:8
Feldberg, Jacob A Mrs, 1961, Mr 5,86:7
Feldblum, Adolph, 1946, S 10,7:5
Feldblum, Julius, 1967, My 30,19:4
Feldbush, Harry A, 1960, Ag 30,29:3
Felde, Leon (cor, F 4,27:1), 1967, F 3,31:3
Felde, Leon Mrs, 1951, My 5,17:2
Feldenheimer, David E, 1946, My 26,32:2
Felder, Carl S, 1950, My 7,108:3
Felder, David, 1947, Ap 24,25:2
Felder, Jane P Mrs, 1937, Jl 8,23:4
Felder, Paul S, 1942, Ja 23,19:1
Felder, T B, 1926, Mr 13,17:5
Felder, William, 1923, Je 1,19:4
Felderman, Leon, 1945, My 16,19:5
Feldern, Harry, 1944, S 27,23:7
Feldhuhn, Raphael, 1966, N 25,37:2
Feldkamp, Paul C, 1952, F 4,17:2
Feldmahn, Leonty E, 1962, Ja 6,19:4
Feldman, Abe, 1966, Ap 12,35:3
Feldman, Adolph, 1943, My 6,19:4
Feldman, Alex H, 1954, Mr 10,25:2
Feldman, Armand S, 1949, S 3,14:4
Feldman, Benjamin, 1942, Mr 5,23:5
Feldman, Bernard, 1958, Mr 19,31:2
Feldman, Bert, 1945, Mr 27,19:5
Feldman, Bruno J, 1939, Je 28,21:2
Feldman, Charles, 1951, Mr 10,13:4
Feldman, Charles J, 1957, O 25,27:3
Feldman, Charles K, 1968, My 26,84:4
Feldman, Daniel D Dr, 1924, F 12,17:3
Feldman, Daniel D Mrs, 1949, Mr 10,27:1
Feldman, Donald, 1966, Je 31,39:3
Feldman, Dudley, 1964, O 13,43:3
Feldman, George W, 1945, F 22,28:3
Feldman, Harry, 1945, D 13,29:2; 1950, Ap 5,31:3; 1962, Mr 18,86:6
Feldman, Henry, 1952, Ag 28,23:4
Feldman, Herman, 1947, O 17,21:3; 1959, F 22,88:3
Feldman, Hermann, 1947, Ap 7,24:3
Feldman, Hyman, 1948, F 3,26:1; 1957, Ag 17,15:5
Feldman, Irving J, 1965, My 26,47:3
Feldman, Isidore, 1967, Mr 12,45:2
Feldman, Joseph, 1903, D 27,7:5
Feldman, Jules, 1953, Ag 18,23:2
Feldman, Julius, 1953, S 9,33:6
Feldman, Leo M, 1938, F 16,21:5
Feldman, Leon A Mrs, 1955, Mr 22,31:2
Feldman, Louis J, 1953, Ja 22,23:3
Feldman, Louis Mrs, 1947, Ag 26,23:4
Feldman, M Hillel, 1961, Mr 3,27:3
Feldman, Max (Peekskill, NY), 1957, Mr 31,89:2
Feldman, Max, 1962, Ap 24,37:4
Feldman, Melita K (Baroness Kometer), 1957, N 22, 25:2
Feldman, Michael H, 1939, Je 13,23:6
Feldman, Moe M, 1954, F 4,25:5
Feldman, Moe S, 1949, Ap 16,15:4
Feldman, Morris, 1938, Ja 27,21:5
Feldman, Nathan Mrs, 1949, Mr 16,27:5
Feldman, Samuel, 1941, Je 5,24:4; 1947, D 27,13:5; 1954, Ap 8,27:5; 1957, Ag 16,19:3; 1960, S 12,12:7
Feldman, Sol R, 1959, Mr 25,35:4
Feldman, Stanley R, 1953, My 5,29:3
Feldman, Theodore, 1957, Mr 5,31:2
Feldmann, Charles N, 1957, Ag 10,15:4
Feldmann, Markus, 1958, N 4,27:4
Feldmeier, Carl W, 1953, Ap 12,88:4
Feldshon, Samuel D, 1949, Mr 1,25:6

Feldstein, Alfred, 1964, Ap 8,43:4
Feldstein, Bert, 1963, N 29,34:6
Feldstein, Daniel M, 1962, Mr 30,33:5
Feldstein, Zama, 1956, F 14,29:3
Feleky, Charles Mrs, 1950, Ja 27,23:4
Felerski, Adam, 1946, Ja 30,25:5
Feley, Henry N, 1946, N 9,17:5
Felger, Frederick H, 1958, Je 14,21:6
Felger, Glenn F, 1954, Ap 27,29:1
Felhaber, Frank C, 1938, Ag 31,15:2
Felicani, Aldino, 1967, Ap 22,31:5
Felice, Henry C Mrs (Jack), 1958, Ap 2,31:5
Felice, Louis Mrs, 1954, D 13,27:4
Felicetta, Frank, 1948, F 18,27:1
Felici, Alberto, 1950, F 18,15:3
Felici, Ettore, 1951, My 10,31:3
Felician John, Bro, 1940, S 12,25:4
Felician Patrick, Brother, 1945, N 26,21:2
Felin, John J Jr, 1940, Mr 11,15:2
Felin, Mary A, 1949, F 16,26:2
Felin, William E, 1937, My 6,25:3
Felio, Alexander L, 1946, N 5,25:3
Felipe Marques, Hilario, 1952, N 28,25:2
Feliu, Carlos A, 1962, S 25,37:2
Felix, Anthony G, 1958, Ja 22,27:5
Felix, Bro A, 1944, Jl 26,19:6
Felix, Curt, 1939, Ag 22,19:3
Felix, George, 1949, My 15,90:3
Felix, Gus, 1960, My 14,23:6
Felix, Harry, 1942, Mr 31,21:4
Felix, Jose, 1962, Je 30,19:6
Felix, Kanute E Mrs, 1945, Jl 19,23:4
Felix, Leon, 1940, Ja 9,23:3
Felix, S, 1877, F 3,5:1
Felix, Samuel P, 1961, S 9,19:5
Felix, Seymour, 1961, Mr 18,23:2
Felix, William A Mrs, 1951, Jl 16,21:6
Felker, Mary N H, 1924, My 4,23:2
Felker, Walter A, 1946, Ag 17,13:4
Fell, Albert W, 1956, Ap 4,29:1
Fell, Alfred J, 1945, Ag 10,15:4
Fell, Arthur D, 1954, Je 13,89:1
Fell, Baron T, 1939, Ap 18,23:3
Fell, C Lloyd, 1939, N 15,23:6
Fell, Charles E, 1948, F 27,21:4
Fell, D Newlin Ex-Justice, 1919, S 23,17:3
Fell, Daniel A, 1939, N 21,23:4
Fell, David N Jr, 1956, Ap 21,17:3
Fell, E Lawrence, 1943, S 28,25:2
Fell, E Nelson Mrs, 1937, Ja 20,21:3
Fell, Edgar T, 1951, Mr 7,33:2
Fell, Frank J Jr, 1961, D 1,30:3
Fell, George E, 1907, Je 8,9:4; 1954, Jl 9,17:2
Fell, Harold B, 1959, Ja 14,27:4
Fell, Harry M, 1942, F 26,19:3
Fell, Henry L, 1909, F 16,9:5
Fell, Henry R, 1951, Ag 23,23:4
Fell, Herbert G, 1951, S 11,29:2
Fell, Herbert N, 1954, Ag 11,25:5
Fell, Horace R, 1940, Jl 28,27:4
Fell, J Henry Mrs, 1952, N 28,25:1
Fell, J Howard, 1940, F 24,13:2
Fell, John A, 1944, Ja 5,17:5
Fell, John R, 1961, Ap 28,31:1
Fell, L T, 1903, Ap 7,4:5
Fell, Robert G Sr, 1942, Ag 25,23:5
Fell, T Reid, 1937, Jl 4,II,6:7
Fell, Thomas, 1942, Ap 14,22:2
Fell, Walter H, 1937, O 21,24:1
Fell, Winfield S, 1949, N 29,30:6
Felland, O G, 1938, Je 11,15:3
Felleman, Morris, 1904, Ag 14,9:6
Fellenbaum, Sam M, 1949, Jl 3,27:1
Feller, Alex, 1952, N 25,29:5
Feller, Alto E, 1966, Jl 6,42:2
Feller, Edward H, 1943, Ja 7,19:3
Feller, Frank C, 1947, My 12,21:4
Feller, Gordon S, 1948, D 9,33:2
Feller, Harry S, 1954, Ja 19,25:2
Feller, Henry, 1961, Ja 16,27:6
Feller, Henry A, 1943, Je 9,21:1
Feller, John E, 1953, Ja 12,27:3
Feller, Lena Mrs, 1954, D 4,17:4
Feller, Morris, 1956, Jl 17,21:1
Feller, Myrtle M Mrs, 1942, O 4,52:6
Feller, Paul, 1963, Jl 20,6:2
Feller, William, 1943, Ja 11,15:2
Fellers, Carl R, 1960, F 24,37:1
Fellers, John M, 1952, D 16,31:4
Fellers, Robert E, 1961, N 7,33:2
Fellig, Arthur H (Weegee), 1968, D 27,33:1
Fellinger, Frederick, 1948, Jl 30,18:5
Fellitto, Philomena Mrs, 1950, S 18,23:2
Fellman, Emanu-El, 1942, O 25,46:1
Fellman, Morris, 1941, Jl 15,19:6
Fellmeth, William F, 1945, Je 19,19:4
Fellner, Carl, 1956, Je 10,88:5
Fellner, Robert J, 1950, O 16,27:3
Fellner, Sigmund, 1955, Jl 22,23:4
Fellon, Charles, 1937, Je 28,19:3
Fellow, Perry A, 1967, Jl 4,19:4
Fellowes, Cornelius (funl, My 4,9:4), 1909, M
Fellowes, Cornelius, 1957, Ag 24,15:2

Fellowes, Cornelius Mrs, 1922, S 23,15:5; 1952, Ag 14,23:5
Fellowes, E John Mrs, 1951, Je 29,21:4
Fellowes, Manton, 1924, Ja 20,13:2
Fellowes, Rockcliffe, 1950, Ja 29,68:4
Fellows, Albert P, 1940, N 10,57:1
Fellows, Albert W, 1954, Jl 18,57:3
Fellows, Byron M, 1962, S 4,31:5
Fellows, C Gurnee Mrs, 1954, Mr 30,27:2
Fellows, Dexter, 1937, N 27,20:1
Fellows, Edmund H, 1951, D 22,15:5
Fellows, Edward J, 1937, D 10,26:2
Fellows, Edwin R (por), 1945, My 23,19:2
Fellows, Elizabeth H, 1939, F 10,23:2
Fellows, Ernest Thomas Ex-Judge, 1913, Ap 7,9:6
Fellows, Frank J, 1962, Mr 22,35:3
Fellows, Frank Repr, 1951, Ag 28,23:1
Fellows, G B L, 1876, Mr 16,2:2
Fellows, George E, 1942, Ja 15,19:3
Fellows, George Mrs, 1948, D 27,17:5
Fellows, Harold E (funl plans, Mr 10,31:2), 1960, Mr 9,33:2
Fellows, Harry E, 1944, Ap 22,15:6
Fellows, Hubble C, 1956, Jl 13,19:2
Fellows, Isaiah, 1940, O 19,17:3
Fellows, J R Col, 1896, D 8,8:1
Fellows, John Sir, 1913, S 23,11:3
Fellows, Leonard W, 1957, N 4,29:1
Fellows, Lewis F, 1963, S 20,33:4
Fellows, Louis, 1876, O 21,3:5
Fellows, Louisa A Mrs, 1925, Je 3,23:4
Fellows, Otis D Mrs, 1938, D 18,48:7
Fellows, Perry A Mrs, 1954, Ag 23,17:6
Fellows, R S, 1884, Mr 11,2:2
Fellows, William K Mrs (will), 1951, S 5,38:6
Fells, George (G Flevitsky), 1960, My 11,39:1
Fells, John S, 1962, Ag 6,25:3
Felmet, Albert, 1962, F 12,23:2
Felmeth, William G, 1953, S 26,17:6
Felmly, Harry J, 1952, D 1,23:4
Felmly, Lloyd M Mrs, 1968, Je 19,47:3
Fels, Arthur E, 1950, Ja 21,17:5
Fels, Joseph, 1914, F 23,9:5
Fels, Joseph Mrs, 1953, My 17,88:5
Fels, Maurice, 1952, Mr 10,21:5
Fels, Rosena, 1943, S 10,24:3
Fels, Samuel S Mrs, 1943, My 1,15:4
Fels, William C, 1964, N 30,33:1
Felsberg, Arthur P, 1955, D 28,23:6
Felsch, Happy (Oscar E), 1964, Ag 18,31:3
Felsen, Joseph, 1955, Ja 28,19:1
Felsenheld, Arthur, 1951, N 19,23:5
elsenheld, Emanuel (will), 1938, My 13,7:5
elsenthal, Bernhard Rabbi, 1908, Ja 14,7:7
elsenthal, Eli B, 1937, D 3,23:1
elshin, Alvin, 1950, My 5,21:4
elshin, Max, 1960, S 10,21:1
elson, Alfred, 1955, Je 6,27:4
elson, Jacob M, 1962, O 19,31:2
elstad, Rolf, 1955, Ag 1,19:4
elstiner, William, 1968, D 12,43:5
elt, Abraham, 1957, Ag 9,19:1
elt, Benjamin F, 1958, Ag 31,56:5
elt, C M, 1882, N 10,3:4
elt, Carl A, 1953, My 5,29:4
elt, Carl A Mrs, 1966, Ag 12,31:4
elt, E Porter, 1943, D 15,28:2
elt, E Porter Mrs, 1939, Je 24,17:1
elt, Edward W Mrs, 1956, D 24,13:4
elt, Edwin H, 1955, Ag 5,19:3
elt, George Henry, 1906, D 6,9:4
elt, George T, 1939, Ja 23,13:5
elt, Henry W, 1959, O 13,39:5
elt, Jack O, 1953, N 15,89:1
elt, Paul R, 1957, F 7,27:1
elt, Truman T, 1965, Je 29,35:4
eltch, Elbridge S, 1903, O 11,7:6
ltenstein, Moses, 1944, D 23,13:4
lter, D W Col, 1873, D 29,8:2
lter, George W, 1951, Mr 17,15:5
lter, Herbert E, 1951, Ag 1,23:6
lter, John T, 1941, O 8,23:1
lter, Louis R, 1951, N 11,90:5
lter, W L, 1933, Mr 20,15:4
lteroff, Adam H, 1912, D 3,15:5
ltes, Nicholas R, 1958, F 15,17:5
ltes, Norman N, 1948, Je 22,25:4
ltham, Charles F, 1956, My 22,33:2
lthaus, Anthony J, 1944, Je 25,29:2
ltman, Abraham I, 1949, My 4,29:1
ltman, Alfred, 1954, Je 7,23:1
ltman, Charles, 1910, S 21,9:4
tman, Charles H, 1948, Je 27,52:3
tman, Charles L, 1949, Ag 23,23:3
tman, Irving Mrs (G M Freund), 1951, Jl 20,21:4
tner, Charles M, 1954, My 19,31:4
ton, Charles E, 1944, D 12,23:3
ton, Charles N Ex-Sen, 1914, S 15,11:6
ton, Cornelius Conway Prof, 1862, F 28,5:4
ton, Edgar C, 1937, S 19,II,7:3
ton, Francis J, 1957, Ja 20,92:6
ton, Frank, 1909, Jl 9,7:4
ton, Frank P Jr, 1950, S 17,104:4
Felton, George W, 1953, Ag 25,21:3
Felton, Happy (Francis J Jr), 1964, O 22,35:4
Felton, Harold, 1946, D 8,77:2
Felton, Henry E, 1941, N 26,23:6
Felton, Horace S Mrs, 1953, F 28,17:6
Felton, J Jacob, 1947, Je 6,23:2
Felton, J Sibley, 1946, D 3,31:1
Felton, James A Jr, 1959, Ja 24,19:3
Felton, Maria, 1874, Mr 19,8:3
Felton, R L Mrs, 1930, Ja 25,15:3
Felton, S M, 1930, Mr 12,29:1
Felton, Samuel M Mrs, 1923, My 23,21:4
Felton, Verna, 1966, D 16,47:1
Felton, William H, 1909, S 26,13:6
Felton, William M, 1942, My 20,20:3
Felton, William M Mrs, 1955, My 8,89:1
Feltus, Harry J Dr, 1937, N 22,19:3
Feltus, Roy M, 1954, F 24,25:2
Feltz, Firmin, 1945, Ap 8,36:1
Feltz, Leon, 1914, N 23,11:6
Felut, Maurice, 1953, Ag 31,18:3
Fenak, Michael, 1953, O 5,27:5
Fenaughty, Cornelius, 1948, Jl 21,23:2
Fenby, Thomas D, 1956, Ag 5,76:8
Fendall, Richard F, 1944, Mr 15,19:4
Fendell, Morris D, 1961, N 25,23:1
Fender, Frederick Jr, 1959, Ja 24,38:6
Fender, Robert A, 1955, Jl 13,25:3
Fender, William S Mrs, 1945, D 31,17:3
Fenderson, Arthur L, 1953, Ap 16,29:3
Fenderson, George A Mrs, 1949, S 20,29:4
Fenderson, Mark, 1944, D 7,25:1
Fendler, Edvard S Mrs, 1955, Je 28,27:4
Fendrich, Adam E, 1946, Je 4,23:3
Fendrich, John H, 1952, S 20,15:4
Fendrich, Valentine, 1951, S 21,24:3
Fendrick, Edward, 1962, Je 6,41:4
Fendt, John P Mrs, 1959, D 1,39:3
Fenellosa, Ernest F Prof, 1908, S 27,11:7
Fenelon, Martin K, 1941, Mr 16,44:8
Fenerty, Clare G, 1952, Jl 2,25:3
Fenerty, Vincent J Dr, 1937, Ap 17,17:2
Fenety, Edward P, 1946, Ag 2,19:2
Feng Chih-an, 1954, D 18,15:6
Feng Kuo-Chang, 1920, Ja 3,11:3
Feng Kwo-Chang, Mrs, 1917, S 16,18:6
Fenger, Austin B, 1946, D 6,23:4
Fengtantai, 1878, Je 16,7:4
Fenias, Edward, 1958, O 31,26:6
Fenichel, Benjamin, 1964, Jl 2,31:4
Fenichel, Irving M, 1954, S 24,23:4
Fenichel, Saul, 1960, N 2,39:1
Fenichel, Sol Mrs, 1967, Ja 12,39:2
Fenichel, Stanley, 1965, Ag 2,29:1
Fenili, Raphael Mrs, 1953, S 23,32:3
Fenimore, Beulah A, 1951, N 9,27:4
Fenimore, Jason L, 1955, My 27,23:2
Fenimore, Wesley D, 1955, Jl 9,15:5
Fenimore-Cooper, Susan D, 1940, F 26,15:5
Fenley, Edward T, 1958, Jl 25,19:3
Fenley, William H, 1942, N 23,23:5
Fenlon, Edward I, 1965, Mr 19,35:4
Fenlon, John F, 1943, Ag 1,38:7
Fenlon, John T, 1955, Mr 29,29:2
Fenn, A Abner, 1954, My 14,23:6
Fenn, Bessie, 1963, D 15,86:2
Fenn, Bruce, 1943, My 18,23:5
Fenn, Courtenay H, 1953, S 18,24:3
Fenn, Courtnay H Mrs, 1938, F 8,9:1
Fenn, E Hart, 1939, F 24,19:2
Fenn, Edward L, 1949, Ag 2,19:4
Fenn, Francis H, 1947, D 1,21:4
Fenn, Francis R, 1941, Ja 22,21:5
Fenn, George Manville, 1909, Ag 28,7:5
Fenn, Henry, 1911, Ap 23,11:3
Fenn, Herbert K, 1951, Ag 13,17:5
Fenn, Irwin H, 1960, Ja 31,92:8
Fenn, Paul, 1938, Mr 4,23:4
Fenn, Robert H, 1946, Ap 24,25:2
Fenn, Russell S, 1939, Jl 8,15:4
Fenn, Wallace L, 1941, Ja 14,21:5
Fenn, William H Jr, 1946, Ap 15,27:1
Fenn, William H M, 1957, Je 29,17:6
Fenn, William P Mrs, 1964, Je 16,39:2
Fenn, Wilson A, 1947, Jl 19,13:4
Fenna, James M, 1945, Jl 3,13:4
Fennell, Arthur B, 1951, Ap 3,27:2
Fennell, Augustine F, 1948, Ag 10,21:3
Fennell, Benjamin, 1950, S 6,29:3
Fennell, George W, 1937, Jl 28,19:4
Fennell, James A, 1952, Je 5,31:1
Fennell, James R, 1956, Je 16,19:2
Fennell, John P, 1945, My 15,19:4
Fennell, Peter H, 1946, Ap 16,25:4
Fennell, Robert, 1955, Je 8,29:5
Fennell, William F, 1956, D 28,21:1
Fennell, William G, 1967, O 5,39:5
Fennell, William G Rev Dr, 1917, F 28,11:4
Fennelly, Daniel J, 1945, D 22,19:3
Fennelly, Edward J Mrs, 1951, Jl 12,25:3
Fennelly, John B, 1956, O 11,39:5
Fennelly, John J, 1961, Ap 11,37:4
Fennelly, Martin J Mrs, 1955, S 15,33:4
Fennelly, Michael J, 1941, Mr 25,23:5
Fennelly, Richard A, 1950, S 2,15:3
Fennelly, William F, 1960, Ja 23,21:5
Fennelon, Catherine Mrs, 1948, O 18,23:3
Fenneman, Nevin M, 1945, Jl 6,11:3
Fennemore, James, 1941, Ja 27,15:4
Fenner, Charles E, 1963, N 16,27:5
Fenner, David C, 1964, F 2,89:2
Fenner, Edward B Mrs, 1950, My 18,29:4
Fenner, Erasmus D, 1944, Je 8,21:5
Fenner, Frances C Mrs, 1938, Ja 3,22:1
Fenner, Frederick P, 1949, Mr 29,25:3
Fenner, Harvey C, 1952, N 14,23:1
Fenner, Howard A, 1956, N 6,35:4
Fenner, James O, 1952, Je 1,84:5
Fenner, Walter H Mrs, 1955, Ap 8,21:3
Fennessey, John J, 1944, My 5,19:5
Fennessy, James H, 1949, Ap 3,77:1
Fennessy, James H Mrs, 1919, S 12,13:5
Fennessy, James S Col, 1925, S 14,19:4
Fennessy, John, 1948, My 9,68:3
Fenniman, John R, 1939, Ap 22,17:2
Fenning, Frederick H, 1915, F 15,7:3
Fenning, Frederick J, 1943, S 14,23:4
Fenning, James F, 1951, D 18,31:2
Fenningham, John T, 1955, F 11,23:5
Fenno, A W, 1873, F 20,1:5
Fenno, Allen Blanchard, 1918, O 12,13:3
Fenno, Charles C, 1958, O 7,35:2
Fenno, Edward N, 1950, F 25,17:6
Fenno, George F, 1945, Jl 31,19:5
Fenno, H Bradlee, 1941, Jl 28,13:5
Fennselau, Marie F Mrs, 1941, F 20,19:5
Fenollosa, Mary M Mrs (Sidney McCall), 1954, Ja 13,31:4
Fenrich, John N Sr, 1960, D 3,23:6
Fenrich, Joseph S, 1954, O 12,27:4
Fenske, William Mrs, 1960, N 23,29:5
Fensom, Rene, 1953, S 4,34:1
Fenstemaker, Marvin C Mrs, 1954, O 27,29:4
Fenster, Abraham, 1958, Mr 6,27:1
Fenster, Benjamin Mrs, 1965, D 27,25:3
Fenster, Bernard, 1954, N 6,17:5
Fenster, Frederick, 1949, S 19,23:3
Fensterer, Gabriel A Mrs, 1950, Ag 16,29:2
Fensterer, Richard, 1948, Ap 14,27:3
Fenstermacher, Thelma R Mrs, 1955, Ag 21,93:2
Fenston, Earl J, 1958, F 1,19:4
Fenton, A Ward, 1956, Ag 22,29:6
Fenton, Andrew, 1945, Ap 19,27:4
Fenton, Arthur P, 1943, Mr 23,19:1
Fenton, Carrie Mrs, 1940, O 30,23:6
Fenton, Charles W Col, 1918, Ja 16,11:4
Fenton, Chauncey L, 1962, F 9,26:4
Fenton, Clarence M Mrs, 1943, Ap 16,21:1
Fenton, Daniel H, 1956, F 5,87:2
Fenton, Daniel W, 1938, Ja 9,42:3
Fenton, Edward J, 1949, Mr 27,76:2
Fenton, Francis P, 1948, Ag 10,21:1
Fenton, Frank, 1957, Jl 26,19:5
Fenton, Frank P, 1947, Ja 20,25:4
Fenton, Frederick A, 1942, Je 30,21:5
Fenton, Harry C, 1942, Ja 30,19:2
Fenton, Henry E (will), 1941, D 24,14:5
Fenton, Howard W, 1958, Ag 31,56:6
Fenton, James E, 1950, D 5,32:4
Fenton, Jerome D, 1967, N 21,47:4
Fenton, John F Mrs, 1952, D 19,31:2
Fenton, John W, 1939, N 20,19:6
Fenton, Joseph M, 1941, Ap 24,21:3
Fenton, Leon C, 1944, S 13,19:6
Fenton, Lillian A Mrs, 1938, D 31,15:6
Fenton, Louis J, 1952, Jl 1,23:1
Fenton, Mark, 1925, Ag 4,19:4
Fenton, Mark M, 1963, Ap 19,43:1
Fenton, Maurice, 1958, Ap 17,31:2
Fenton, Paul W, 1961, Ag 23,33:4
Fenton, R E, 1885, Ag 26,5:1
Fenton, Rome L, 1946, Ap 4,25:3
Fenton, Samuel P, 1940, Ja 31,19:2
Fenton, Thomas, 1947, Mr 25,26:2
Fenton, W K, 1955, F 25,21:3
Fenton, W T, 1939, F 8,23:3
Fenton, Walter J, 1945, Ap 19,27:1
Fenton, Warren B, 1949, Jl 9,13:2
Fenton, Willard J, 1949, Ag 25,23:2
Fenton, William, 1911, N 9,11:4
Fenton, William M, 1871, My 14,1:5
Fentress, Calvin (will, F 14,28:1), 1957, F 8,23:1
Fentress, E S, 1951, F 15,31:3
Fenwich, Bedford Mrs, 1947, Mr 15,13:2
Fenwick, C P, 1954, Mr 24,27:5
Fenwick, Douglas Mrs, 1947, Ag 14,23:4
Fenwick, Edwin H, 1944, My 10,19:5
Fenwick, Frank F, 1937, N 14,II,10:2
Fenwick, George H, 1945, F 8,19:5
Fenwick, I, 1936, D 25,23:4
Fenwick, James A, 1943, S 12,53:2
Fenwick, John C, 1944, Ap 19,23:5
Fenwick, William, 1946, Jl 12,17:1
Fenwick, William G, 1945, S 6,25:2
Fenwick, William Mrs, 1944, Ap 6,23:6
Fenyes, Ladislas, 1944, Ja 31,17:5

Fenyvessy, Albert A, 1953, Ag 1,11:5
Feo, Ralph, 1944, S 11,17:3
Feodora, Princess of Schleswig-Holstein, 1910, Je 22, 9:5
Feodoroff, Leo, 1949, N 25,31:5
Fequant, Philippe, 1938, D 25,14:5
Ferance, Paul, 1923, Ag 19,26:5
Ferari, Francis Col, 1914, N 12,13:4
Ferari, Joseph G, 1953, My 12,27:2
Feraru, Leon, 1960, O 23,89:1
Ferber, Edna (funl, Ap 19,47:2; will, Ap 24,47:1), 1968, Ap 17,1:2
Ferber, Frederick V Jr, 1950, Jl 12,29:4
Ferber, Jacob, 1946, Ap 18,27:2
Ferber, Jacob C Mrs, 1949, D 1,31:2
Ferber, Jacob J, 1943, Ag 16,15:5
Ferber, Julius Dr, 1953, F 7,15:2
Ferber, Louis Mrs (L Levine), 1965, Ja 11,45:3
Ferber, Martha Mrs, 1954, Ja 9,18:5
Ferber, Nat J, 1945, Je 24,22:3
Ferber, Phil, 1951, Ag 16,27:4
Ferbert, A H, 1948, My 24,19:3
Ferbert, Gustave H, 1943, Ja 16,13:4
Ferbos, Raoul P, 1938, My 26,25:5
Ferchaud, Henry, 1923, Je 18,13:6
Ferciot, J Lloyd, 1953, Ja 24,15:3
Ferderickson, Donald D, 1961, Ja 4,33:3
Ferdinand, Bro, 1948, F 27,22:3
Ferdinand, Charles Archduke of Austria, 1874, N 21, 1:2
Ferdinand, Ex-King of Bulgaria, 1948, S 11,15:1
Ferdinand, John E, 1944, N 28,23:4
Ferdinand Francois Prince, 1924, Ja 31,15:4
Ferdinand I of Austria, 1875, Je 30,4:6
Ferdinand II, King of Naples, 1859, F 9,4:5
Ferdinando Umberto, Prince of Italy, 1963, Je 26,39:2
Ferdon, C Maitland, 1946, S 8,44:6
Ferdon, J W, 1884, Ag 7,5:2
Ferdon, Nora M Mrs, 1947, My 27,25:3
Ferdon, Walter, 1945, D 14,27:2
Ferec, Charles Rev Father, 1874, My 27,1:2
Fereday, Norman Lt, 1937, Je 16,24:2
Ferenbach, Gregory, 1960, O 31,31:4
Ferenbaugh, Louis W, 1939, Ap 30,45:1
Ference, John, 1946, Ap 30,21:5
Ferenchak, Andrew Jr, 1952, Je 6,23:4
Ferenczi, Imre, 1945, Ag 19,39:3
Fereno, Genero Mrs, 1952, S 29,23:4
Ferentzi, Irmfried Mrs, 1964, Ja 15,38:1
Ferg, Frank X, 1950, Ag 25,21:5
Fergus, Corwin A, 1946, Ap 2,27:1
Fergus, George H, 1911, N 26,15:5
Fergus, Robert C, 1952, F 24,84:8
Ferguson, A Capt, 1882, Ag 29,8:4
Ferguson, A Kingsley, 1961, F 22,25:2
Ferguson, A L, 1944, Ja 27,19:4
Ferguson, Alex Mrs, 1949, F 13,77:1
Ferguson, Amelie Mrs, 1917, Mr 15,11:4
Ferguson, Anna G Mrs, 1940, F 24,13:3
Ferguson, Archibald W, 1955, Ag 4,25:4
Ferguson, Arletta E Mrs, 1942, Mr 25,21:1
Ferguson, Armour, 1946, Ja 25,24:3
Ferguson, Benjamin F Mrs, 1951, Mr 6,27:5
Ferguson, Byron D, 1942, Ja 7,19:6
Ferguson, C Vaughan, 1964, Mr 18,41:4
Ferguson, C Vaughan Sr Mrs, 1966, Ja 16,83:1
Ferguson, Catherine S, 1960, Ag 3,29:5
Ferguson, Cecil, 1943, S 6,17:5
Ferguson, Celia M, 1951, Ap 3,27:2
Ferguson, Charles, 1937, Ap 14,25:2; 1944, My 28,33:2
Ferguson, Charles B, 1959, Ja 24,19:4
Ferguson, Charles E, 1951, Je 19,29:4
Ferguson, Charles H, 1951, Jl 9,25:2
Ferguson, Charles H Mrs, 1956, S 7,23:2
Ferguson, Charles J, 1961, Ja 24,29:4
Ferguson, Charles R, 1946, Ap 16,25:1
Ferguson, Charles W, 1954, Ag 28,89:2
Ferguson, Christian W, 1957, Ap 3,31:4
Ferguson, Cornelia P, 1946, Ja 21,23:4
Ferguson, Dave, 1957, S 24,35:5
Ferguson, David, 1920, Je 16,11:4; 1949, S 14,31:5
Ferguson, David Jr, 1946, Ag 21,27:3
Ferguson, Donald R, 1945, Ag 30,21:4
Ferguson, Earl L, 1939, F 9,21:5
Ferguson, Edgar A Jr, 1965, F 27,25:4
Ferguson, Edmund M, 1904, Je 20,9:6
Ferguson, Edward B, 1949, F 7,19:5
Ferguson, Edward J Mrs, 1966, Jl 9,27:3
Ferguson, Edward L, 1915, F 4,9:5
Ferguson, Edwin H, 1959, S 17,39:4
Ferguson, Edwin H Mrs, 1963, My 26,92:8
Ferguson, Elizabeth M (will), 1914, Je 28,15:6
Ferguson, Elsie, 1961, N 16,39:4
Ferguson, Elsie (will), 1962, Ag 28,33:8
Ferguson, Eric, 1967, Je 27,39:2
Ferguson, Francis M, 1910, Je 24,9:5
Ferguson, Frank, 1908, Ap 9,9:4; 1937, S 10,23:3
Ferguson, Frank C, 1964, S 18,35:1
Ferguson, Frank L, 1944, My 29,15:6
Ferguson, Frank L Mrs, 1945, Ap 27,19:4
Ferguson, Franklin A, 1957, Mr 25,87:1
Ferguson, Fred S, 1959, D 7,31:3
Ferguson, G Howard, 1946, F 22,26:2
Ferguson, G Howard Mrs, 1957, O 23,33:5
Ferguson, Garland S Jr, 1963, Ap 13,19:4
Ferguson, Garwood, 1945, Ag 30,21:4
Ferguson, George, 1949, N 11,25:3
Ferguson, George A, 1939, Mr 26,III,6:7
Ferguson, George A Prof, 1917, Mr 29,13:5
Ferguson, George E, 1957, F 24,85:2
Ferguson, George F, 1955, S 30,25:2
Ferguson, George Jr, 1960, N 22,35:1
Ferguson, George M, 1949, Ja 21,22:2
Ferguson, George P, 1952, My 5,23:5
Ferguson, George T, 1964, Jl 25,19:6
Ferguson, George W Mrs, 1949, Ja 3,23:3
Ferguson, Gordon E, 1952, Ag 12,19:4
Ferguson, H Clay, 1940, O 8,25:2
Ferguson, H Clay Mrs, 1946, Jl 10,23:5
Ferguson, Hardy S, 1956, Jl 8,64:7
Ferguson, Harold, 1967, Ap 25,43:5
Ferguson, Harold A, 1964, Je 4,37:5
Ferguson, Harold K, 1943, D 10,27:3
Ferguson, Harriet Mrs, 1946, Jl 17,23:1
Ferguson, Harry, 1960, O 26,39:1
Ferguson, Harry R (will), 1938, Ag 19,7:8
Ferguson, Harry S D, 1948, My 28,23:3
Ferguson, Harvey B, 1915, Je 11,15:5
Ferguson, Helen M F Mrs, 1959, D 25,21:4
Ferguson, Henry A, 1911, Mr 23,9:4; 1954, N 5,15:3
Ferguson, Henry A Mrs, 1943, Ap 18,48:5
Ferguson, Henry L, 1959, F 24,29:4
Ferguson, Henry M, 1945, Ja 20,11:4; 1960, Ja 31,94:3
Ferguson, Henry Prof, 1917, Mr 31,11:6
Ferguson, Herbert L, 1953, D 25,17:3
Ferguson, Homer L, 1953, Mr 15,92:3
Ferguson, Huber Mrs, 1949, N 29,29:3
Ferguson, Hugh F, 1953, Je 10,29:3
Ferguson, Isaac Nelson, 1915, Ja 7,13:4
Ferguson, Isaac S, 1953, Ja 3,15:1
Ferguson, Isabelle, 1942, O 8,27:2
Ferguson, J Albert, 1949, Ag 16,23:2
Ferguson, J De Lancey, 1966, Ag 13,25:2
Ferguson, J Donald, 1964, Je 24,37:1
Ferguson, James, 1955, Ja 16,92:1
Ferguson, James B, 1951, Mr 2,25:1
Ferguson, James E, 1944, S 22,19:3
Ferguson, James Francis Dr, 1904, Ja 8,7:5
Ferguson, James G, 1954, Ag 13,15:6
Ferguson, James J, 1957, O 22,33:1
Ferguson, James L Mrs, 1957, F 26,29:3
Ferguson, James W, 1944, Ap 3,21:5
Ferguson, Jeremiah S, 1939, Jl 1,17:4
Ferguson, Jesse D, 1945, My 22,19:6
Ferguson, John, 1903, Je 26,9:6; 1924, D 30,17:5; 1937, Ja 12,24:2; 1940, O 26,15:5; 1954, F 24,25:3
Ferguson, John A, 1955, Je 11,15:6
Ferguson, John A Mrs, 1937, N 7,II,9:2
Ferguson, John C, 1945, Ag 4,11:1
Ferguson, John C Mrs, 1938, O 7,23:3
Ferguson, John Dr, 1968, Mr 3,88:6
Ferguson, John E, 1957, D 23,23:1
Ferguson, John E J, 1922, My 13,13:6
Ferguson, John F, 1950, Ap 15,15:6
Ferguson, John J, 1917, Jl 24,11:6; 1955, Mr 11,25:2
Ferguson, John J Mrs, 1954, Ja 19,25:2
Ferguson, John M, 1961, D 11,31:2
Ferguson, John R, 1955, Jl 7,27:4
Ferguson, John S, 1954, Je 9,31:3
Ferguson, John W, 1942, F 5,22:2; 1952, Ja 7,19:4; 1957, Ap 28,86:8
Ferguson, Joseph C, 1951, Mr 29,27:5
Ferguson, Joseph C Judge, 1905, Mr 31,9:6
Ferguson, Joseph E, 1948, Ja 20,23:5
Ferguson, Joseph P, 1957, O 24,33:3
Ferguson, Kenneth R, 1954, Je 14,21:1
Ferguson, L Ray, 1963, Ag 17,19:1
Ferguson, Louis, 1941, Ja 7,23:1
Ferguson, Louis A, 1940, Ag 27,21:2
Ferguson, Mae, 1950, Ap 12,27:2
Ferguson, Meade, 1942, Ag 7,17:2
Ferguson, Melville F, 1968, Je 18,47:3
Ferguson, Milton J, 1954, O 24,88:5
Ferguson, Miriam W Mrs ('Ma'), 1961, Je 26,31:2
Ferguson, Neil G, 1958, S 16,27:2
Ferguson, Patrick R Mrs, 1950, Jl 29,13:3
Ferguson, Peter, 1922, My 2,19:6
Ferguson, Peter A, 1964, S 17,43:4
Ferguson, Phebe, 1950, O 12,31:1
Ferguson, Rachel J, 1948, Jl 5,15:1
Ferguson, Ramage, 1939, F 10,23:6
Ferguson, Richard C, 1916, Je 14,13:6
Ferguson, Robert, 1940, O 14,19:2
Ferguson, Robert B, 1916, Ja 12,13:5; 1944, Ap 9,34:3
Ferguson, Robert D, 1945, Je 20,23:1
Ferguson, Robert H, 1945, S 2,32:2
Ferguson, Robert J, 1944, My 16,21:3
Ferguson, Robert M, 1943, F 21,32:6
Ferguson, Robert N, 1950, Mr 26,92:4
Ferguson, Robert R Rev Dr, 1968, Je 1,27:4
Ferguson, Ronald H, 1951, S 13,31:5
Ferguson, Roy E, 1962, S 19,80:1
Ferguson, Russell J, 1955, Ag 22,21:4
Ferguson, Russell S, 1944, Ap 29,15:2
Ferguson, Samuel, 1918, Mr 25,13:4; 1950, F 11,15:3
Ferguson, Samuel A, 1961, F 7,33:3
Ferguson, Samuel D Bp, 1916, Ag 4,9:6
Ferguson, Samuel I, 1952, F 5,29:4
Ferguson, Samuel Jr, 1961, Mr 25,25:6
Ferguson, Samuel Mrs, 1943, S 23,21:4
Ferguson, Sarah B, 1958, O 12,83:2
Ferguson, Smith F, 1950, Jl 23,56:5
Ferguson, Stanley W, 1963, S 19,27:4
Ferguson, Theodore Mrs, 1964, Mr 14,23:6
Ferguson, Thomas, 1916, N 28,13:4; 1948, Ag 22,60:5; 1951, Ag 31,15:5; 1955, Jl 11,23:2
Ferguson, Thomas A, 1951, S 8,17:4
Ferguson, Thomas B, 1921, F 15,9:5
Ferguson, Thomas B Maj, 1922, Ag 12,9:6
Ferguson, Thomas C, 1951, Mr 18,88:3
Ferguson, Thomas E, 1938, O 2,49:1
Ferguson, Thomas W, 1953, F 6,20:5
Ferguson, W J, 1930, My 8,27:3
Ferguson, Walter, 1953, S 12,17:5
Ferguson, Walter E, 1946, D 24,17:4
Ferguson, Walter Mrs, 1962, F 28,19:1
Ferguson, Wilbur E, 1945, F 22,28:2
Ferguson, Willard E, 1943, O 16,13:1
Ferguson, William, 1960, Mr 14,29:4
Ferguson, William A, 1963, N 17,87:1
Ferguson, William B, 1937, O 8,24:2; 1955, Mr 22,31
Ferguson, William C, 1967, Ap 27,45:4
Ferguson, William Dr, 1924, F 5,23:3
Ferguson, William J Jr, 1945, Ap 8,36:2
Ferguson, William Mrs, 1946, Jl 18,25:1; 1959, Jl 9, 27:3
Ferguson, William R, 1961, Mr 19,88:8
Ferguson, William S, 1954, Ap 29,31:3
Ferguson, William T, 1961, S 22,33:2
Ferguson, William W, 1937, F 1,19:2
Ferguson, William W Mrs, 1959, F 10,33:2
Ferguson, Willis S, 1939, D 20,25:2
Fergusson, Arthur G, 1925, Mr 14,13:4
Fergusson, Arthur W, 1908, Ja 31,7:5
Fergusson, Arthur W Mrs, 1922, Ap 27,17:4
Fergusson, Charles, 1951, F 21,27:3
Fergusson, David, 1951, Ap 28,15:4
Fergusson, Frank K Gen, 1937, Jl 19,15:2
Fergusson, George, 1947, Mr 25,26:3
Fergusson, James, 1942, Ap 16,21:5
Fergusson, John D, 1961, Ja 31,29:4
Fergusson, W Neil, 1954, Jl 20,19:2
Fergusson, W Sir, 1877, F 12,4:7
Ferincola, Michele, 1943, Ag 23,17:7
Feringa, John H Rev Dr, 1925, F 2,17:3
Ferkiss, Louis, 1951, O 19,27:1
Ferlaino, Frank R, 1953, S 3,21:3
Ferlaino, John Mrs, 1954, F 14,93:1
Ferlanti, Peter S, 1956, S 20,33:5
Ferleger, Sol, 1951, Mr 27,29:2
Ferlin, Charles R, 1966, Jl 20,41:2
Ferlin, Nils, 1961, O 25,37:2
Ferling, Clarence F, 1948, F 6,23:4
Ferm, Alexis C Mrs, 1944, Ap 13,19:4
Ferman, George F, 1942, D 26,11:4
Ferme, Antonio, 1942, Jl 3,17:6
Fermi, Claudio, 1952, Je 19,27:4
Fermi, Enrico (funl, N 30,29:1; will, D 10,13:6), 1954, N 29,1:4
Fermin, Adelin M C, 1941, My 10,15:1
Fermor-Hesketh, Lady, 1924, S 28,27:3
Fermoy, Baron, 1874, S 18,5:5
Fermoy, Baron (Edmund Fitz-Edmund Roche), S 2,9:2
Fermoy, Lord (Jas Boothby Burke Roche), 1920 N 1,15:6
Fermoy, Lord (E M Burke-Roche), 1955, Jl 9,15
Fern, Edward, 1966, Jl 8,35:2
Fern, Fanny (Mrs Parton), 1872, O 13,5:3
Fern, John P Mrs, 1942, Ag 29,16:7
Fern, Max, 1946, Ja 6,40:4
Fern, Samuel S, 1965, Ap 13,37:3
Fernald, B M Sen, 1926, Ag 24,21:1
Fernald, Bert M Mrs, 1939, Jl 4,13:3
Fernald, Bessie Smith Mrs, 1920, N 7,22:5
Fernald, Charles B, 1944, Ap 25,23:2
Fernald, Charles H, 1921, F 23,13:1
Fernald, Ernest M, 1951, Ja 23,27:2
Fernald, Fred C, 1959, O 24,21:5
Fernald, George B, 1941, Ag 10,37:3
Fernald, Grace M, 1950, Ja 18,32:4
Fernald, Henry B, 1967, F 10,36:1
Fernald, Henry B Mrs, 1950, Ag 26,13:3
Fernald, Henry T, 1952, Jl 16,25:4
Fernald, James Champlain Rev Dr, 1918, N 11,1
Fernald, John M, 1942, Jl 28,17:5
Fernald, Joseph E, 1949, Jl 3,26:4
Fernald, Kenneth G, 1947, Mr 4,25:4
Fernald, Luther D, 1939, D 27,21:3
Fernald, Mabel R, 1952, O 10,25:2
Fernald, Merrit L, 1950, S 24,104:5
Fernald, Merritt C Dr, 1916, Ja 9,17:5
Fernald, Merritt L Mrs, 1957, My 5,88:2
Fernald, O M Prof, 1902, Ap 16,9:5
Fernald, Olga H Mrs, 1957, Je 16,26:6
Fernald, Robert H Dr, 1937, Ap 25,II,8:8
Fernald, Robert L, 1941, O 12,52:2
Fernald, Walter E Dr, 1924, N 28,15:4
Fernalld, Floyd M, 1964, My 19,38:1

Fernan, Katherine M, 1952, S 11,31:3
Fernan, Michael M, 1948, D 28,22:2
Fernandes, Raul, 1968, Ja 7,84:5
Fernandez, Alfonzo J, 1939, O 12,25:5
Fernandez, Anita J, 1938, Ja 19,23:5
Fernandez, Antonio M, 1956, N 8,39:5
Fernandez, Bijou, 1961, N 8,35:5
Fernandez, E L Mrs, 1909, D 22,11:5
Fernandez, Francis Henry, 1903, Jl 23,7:6
Fernandez, Joseph M, 1946, D 13,23:2
Fernandez, Orman B, 1947, D 26,15:2
Fernandez, Oscar L, 1948, Ag 28,15:5
Fernandez, Ricardo W, 1964, Ap 13,29:4
Fernandez, William J, 1957, Jl 31,23:5
Fernandez Crespo, Daniel, 1964, Jl 29,33:2
Fernandez de Cordoba y Salabert, Luis Jesus Duke of Medinaceli, 1956, Jl 15,61:1
Fernandez Ledo, Ramiro, 1952, S 16,29:4
Fernandez y Hernandez, Francisco M Dr, 1937, F 15, 17:4
Fernandini, Eulogio, 1947, D 25,21:1
Fernbach, Henry, 1883, N 13,2:3
Fernberger, Samuel W, 1956, My 4,25:2
Ferneau, David W, 1952, N 29,17:3
Ferneding, Paul, 1945, O 11,23:4
Fernekes, Charles, 1945, My 28,19:4
Fernet, Andre, 1955, D 6,37:4
Fernicola, Paul, 1959, F 21,21:6
Fernicola, Vincent, 1937, Mr 3,23:2
Fernie, Benjamin James Dr, 1908, My 13,7:5
Fernow, Bernhard E Prof, 1923, F 7,15:5
Fernow, Fritz, 1941, Mr 18,23:2
Ferns, James H, 1967, D 26,33:2
Ferns, James R, 1952, Je 12,33:3
Ferns, Robert James, 1919, Ap 8,11:4
Ferns, Robert M, 1963, Jl 19,25:4
Fernschild, George J, 1941, Ag 26,19:2
Fernschild, George J Jr, 1954, Ag 26,27:5
Fernsler, David, 1959, Jl 26,69:2
Fernstermacher, Percy S, 1941, F 21,19:5
Fernstrom, Helma J, 1943, Je 23,21:4
Fernstrom, Karl D, 1953, My 7,31:5
Fero, De Roy S, 1940, Ag 8,19:3
Feron, John C, 1941, O 3,23:4
Feron, Stephen J, 1939, O 21,15:3; 1963, Ap 22,27:1
Ferone, Joseph J, 1964, O 10,29:3
Ferra, Louis, 1949, Ja 18,24:2
Ferragamo, Salvatore, 1960, Ag 9,27:4
Ferragatti, Guido, 1947, Ja 20,25:3
Ferraguzzi, Louis, 1952, N 4,29:2
Ferrall, Benjamin S, 1942, My 5,21:4
Ferrall, Lucy W Mrs, 1942, S 25,21:4
Ferrall, Philip D, 1965, Jl 7,37:3
Ferrand, E S, 1959, Ap 7,33:1
Ferrando, Miguel A, 1947, Mr 11,28:3
Ferrani, Cesira, 1943, My 7,19:2
Ferrante, Gherardo Msgr, 1921, My 6,13:4
Ferranzo, Domeneck, 1940, Ag 3,15:3
Ferrara, Filomeno Rev, 1910, Jl 16,7:6
Ferrara, Frank, 1964, Ag 25,33:2
Ferrara, James, 1949, D 13,38:3
Ferrara, John, 1948, S 30,27:4
Ferrara, Pasquale, 1959, Ag 9,89:1
Ferrari, Andrea Carlo Cardinal, 1921, F 8,7:4
Ferrari, Andrew, 1915, O 27,11:6
Ferrari, Charles, 1953, Ja 11,90:4
Ferrari, Dino, 1943, N 8,19:4
Ferrari, Febo, 1949, Ag 16,23:3
Ferrari, Giuseppe F, 1943, O 31,48:5
Ferrari, Giuseppe M, 1941, Ja 19,40:2
Ferrari, Guillaume, 1955, Ja 5,23:4
Ferrari, Guiseppe, 1876, Jl 22,5:4
Ferrari, Gustave, 1948, S 16,29:5
Ferrari, Guy, 1965, Jl 3,19:6
Ferrari, Italo A, 1951, N 25,87:1
Ferrari, Louis, 1958, My 18,86:2
Ferrari-Fontana, E, 1936, Jl 7,19:3
Ferrari Trecate, Luigi, 1964, Ap 18,29:5
Ferraro, Dominico, 1947, Je 26,9:2
Ferraro, Vincent, 1952, Ag 22,21:4
Ferraro, William A, 1947, O 15,27:2
Ferrary, Leo (cor, D 15,19:4), 1944, D 14,23:2
Ferrata, Domenico Cardinal, 1914, O 11,9:4
Ferraud, Eugene, 1910, Ja 25,9:4
Ferraz, Ivens, 1956, Ap 16,27:2
Ferraz, John F, 1944, N 3,21:4
Ferrazza, John Rev, 1921, O 2,22:4
Ferre, Abel, 1945, Ag 15,19:4
Ferre, Antonio, 1959, N 14,21:2
Ferre, Countess de, 1912, Ag 23,9:6
Ferre, Frans Mrs, 1961, Jl 29,19:6
Ferre, George F, 1959, Mr 21,21:5
Ferre, Gerald F (cor, My 24,89:2), 1953, My 23,15:5
Ferre, Octave, 1875, My 14,2:1
Ferrec, Frank A Mrs, 1949, Jl 15,19:6
Ferree, Barr, 1924, O 15,23:4
Ferree, Eugene H, 1952, Ag 27,27:5
Ferreira, Ellsworth G, 1955, Ja 1,13:3
Ferreira, Virgolino, 1938, Ja 13,7:3
Ferrel, Ralph W, 1960, Ag 28,82:5
Ferrel, Wesley F, 1946, O 6,58:6
Ferrell, Frank W, 1938, Je 28,19:5
Ferrell, Fred C, 1943, My 29,13:5
Ferrell, Horace A, 1938, S 23,27:3
Ferrell, Jane, 1952, Je 5,31:3
Ferrell, John A, 1965, F 20,25:3
Ferrell, Rufus B, 1952, Jl 14,17:3
Ferrer, Carlos M, 1950, O 6,27:5
Ferrer, Jose B, 1941, O 28,23:4
Ferrer, Jose M Dr, 1920, F 24,13:5
Ferrer, Jose M Mrs, 1967, F 21,47:3
Ferrer, Rafael, 1951, F 16,25:1
Ferreri, Vincent J, 1963, Ag 6,31:4
Ferrero, Charles Gen, 1873, My 7,8:5
Ferrero, Gina L, 1944, Ap 1,13:4
Ferrero, Guglielmo, 1942, Ag 5,19:1
Ferrero, Willy, 1954, Mr 25,29:4
Ferrers, Earl, 1937, F 3,23:2
Ferrers, Earl of (R W Shirley), 1954, O 13,31:4
Ferres, Allan J, 1947, N 30,76:3
Ferres, Maria C Mrs, 1941, Ja 13,15:3
Ferretti, Anthony J, 1957, My 21,35:5
Ferretti, Frank D, 1940, Ag 26,15:4
Ferretti, John J, 1967, My 23,47:1
Ferretti, Louis Mrs, 1943, Ja 29,19:5
Ferri, Giuseppe Mrs, 1943, Ag 15,38:6
Ferri, Guido, 1964, Je 26,2:2
Ferri, Pasquale, 1957, O 14,27:3
Ferrick, Michael J, 1942, My 24,42:2
Ferrick, Thomas, 1942, Mr 24,19:5
Ferriday, Edward C, 1945, D 16,40:7
Ferriday, Henry McKeen, 1914, My 7,11:6
Ferrie, David W, 1967, F 23,22:4
Ferrie, G, 1932, F 17,21:3
Ferrie, James H, 1950, Jl 4,17:6
Ferrie, Patrick T, 1949, Ap 13,29:2
Ferrie, Robert B, 1952, Mr 7,23:1
Ferrier, Gabriel, 1914, Je 7,5:6
Ferrier, George I, 1952, Ag 1,18:3
Ferrier, Kathleen (trb, O 25,II,7:2), 1953, O 9,27:3
Ferrier, R Willoughby, 1944, O 31,19:4
Ferrier, Walter F, 1950, N 16,31:4
Ferrier, William W, 1945, Ag 21,21:6
Ferriere, James L, 1903, S 21,1:2
Ferriere, Louis E, 1963, Ag 17,19:3
Ferrigan, Helen M, 1968, Ap 24,47:1
Ferrigni, Joseph P, 1947, Jl 20,44:1
Ferrin, Charles J, 1907, My 31,9:6; 1924, F 29,17:6
Ferrin, Dana H, 1960, Jl 21,27:4
Ferrin, Wesley W, 1941, D 16,27:2
Ferringer, Harry C, 1938, Ag 22,13:6
Ferris, A Fillmore, 1923, D 9,23:2
Ferris, Albert W Dr, 1937, O 5,25:5
Ferris, Alexander, 1917, F 4,19:3
Ferris, Alfred J, 1950, N 8,29:4
Ferris, Anna G, 1955, Mr 24,31:1
Ferris, Bernard J, 1955, N 22,35:5
Ferris, Charles, 1947, F 4,25:3
Ferris, Charles C, 1955, Je 16,31:5
Ferris, Charles J, 1949, Je 4,13:5
Ferris, Charles Mrs, 1948, Mr 1,23:3
Ferris, Charles R, 1952, F 23,11:5
Ferris, Clarence C, 1961, D 21,27:3
Ferris, Cleveland Dr, 1913, Ag 22,9:6
Ferris, Daniel J Mrs, 1960, My 30,17:1
Ferris, David L, 1947, Je 10,27:1
Ferris, David L Mrs, 1943, Mr 1,19:2
Ferris, Edward D, 1951, Ap 6,25:1
Ferris, Edward S, 1956, My 18,25:5
Ferris, Edwin F, 1947, My 2,21:3
Ferris, Elmer E, 1951, My 13,88:8
Ferris, Emery L, 1945, Jl 29,39:2
Ferris, Emma L Mrs, 1940, F 8,23:3
Ferris, Emory L Mrs, 1948, Mr 29,21:3
Ferris, Eugene B Jr, 1957, S 27,19:1
Ferris, Eugene M J, 1939, Ja 31,15:8
Ferris, F, 1877, N 29,5:3
Ferris, Floyd F, 1966, My 26,48:1
Ferris, Francis S, 1952, Jl 30,23:3
Ferris, Frank A, 1918, D 12,15:4; 1946, D 17,38:5
Ferris, Frederick L, 1968, D 28,27:4
Ferris, George A, 1955, Ap 10,88:1
Ferris, George F, 1967, S 21,47:4
Ferris, George Hooper Rev Dr, 1917, S 17,13:3
Ferris, George Newton Dr, 1919, Ja 29,13:5
Ferris, Gilbert B, 1954, O 2,17:4
Ferris, Gilbert H, 1908, O 4,9:4
Ferris, Gordon S, 1938, N 12,15:6
Ferris, Harry B, 1940, O 13,49:1
Ferris, Henry, 1941, Ja 7,23:1
Ferris, Henry A, 1948, Ag 21,15:6
Ferris, Henry C Dr, 1937, N 11,25:6
Ferris, Hobert, 1948, Ap 20,27:4
Ferris, Howard Jr, 1937, Ap 17,17:5
Ferris, Isaac F, 1939, F 16,21:2
Ferris, Isaac Rev, 1873, Je 18,4:7
Ferris, Isabel B Mrs, 1942, D 29,21:3
Ferris, J C, 1876, O 15,2:2
Ferris, Jacob W, 1925, My 29,17:6
Ferris, James, 1869, Ag 14,5:6
Ferris, James J, 1914, My 16,11:6
Ferris, James J Jr, 1961, Ag 28,25:5
Ferris, Jesse S, 1954, N 10,33:3
Ferris, John J, 1924, O 17,21:3
Ferris, John M, 1939, Ag 26,15:5
Ferris, John Mason Rev Dr, 1911, Ja 31,9:5
Ferris, John O, 1942, N 11,25:6
Ferris, Joseph, 1949, Ja 5,25:3
Ferris, Joseph A Mrs, 1950, Ag 12,13:4
Ferris, Joseph J, 1950, D 30,13:3
Ferris, Joseph W, 1961, Mr 30,29:1
Ferris, Lewis F, 1944, Je 28,23:4
Ferris, Lockwood N, 1964, D 9,47:1
Ferris, Louis F, 1952, Je 27,23:6
Ferris, Louis Mrs, 1944, Ja 22,13:4
Ferris, Malcolm, 1937, D 24,20:4
Ferris, Margaret A Mrs, 1939, Mr 21,23:2
Ferris, Mitchell R, 1954, Ja 3,88:1
Ferris, Mortimer Y, 1941, Mr 10,17:2
Ferris, Murray W Mrs, 1948, Ag 22,60:6
Ferris, Murray Whiting, 1920, O 15,13:3
Ferris, Nowell B, 1957, My 2,31:1
Ferris, Paul W Mrs, 1950, S 29,27:4
Ferris, Ralph B, 1938, Ag 5,17:2
Ferris, Ralph J, 1960, O 9,86:7
Ferris, Raymond W, 1945, Mr 4,38:6
Ferris, Richard B, 1911, O 6,13:6
Ferris, Robert, 1907, S 12,7:6
Ferris, Ruth, 1939, Jl 31,13:5
Ferris, S P, 1882, F 5,2:2
Ferris, Scott, 1945, Je 10,32:6
Ferris, Stanley B, 1948, Ap 20,27:3
Ferris, Stephen D, 1953, S 7,19:2
Ferris, Stephen J, 1915, Jl 10,7:5
Ferris, Theodore E, 1953, Je 1,23:4
Ferris, Theodore E Mrs, 1960, O 2,85:1
Ferris, Thomas M, 1941, Ja 13,15:5
Ferris, Thomas T Col, 1874, Ap 8,2:5
Ferris, Vincent J, 1952, S 12,21:3
Ferris, W N, 1928, Mr 24,17:3
Ferris, Walter A (por), 1949, My 16,27:5
Ferris, Walter Mrs, 1952, D 15,25:3
Ferris, Walter Mrs (V K Cooper), 1961, Ag 19,17:6
Ferris, Walton C, 1955, My 10,29:5
Ferris, Warren, 1882, O 6,3:1
Ferris, William E, 1947, Jl 1,25:2
Ferris, William F Mrs, 1965, Mr 26,35:4
Ferris, William Francis, 1968, S 26,55:1
Ferris, William G Maj, 1906, N 25,9:6
Ferris, William H, 1962, Ap 7,25:6
Ferris, William J, 1940, F 11,49:3
Ferris, William J Judge, 1925, F 25,19:2
Ferris, William N Mrs, 1952, Ja 19,15:2
Ferris, William R, 1958, S 7,86:6; 1964, Ap 19,85:2
Ferris, William S, 1946, D 27,19:4
Ferris, William T, 1952, Ap 24,31:2
Ferris, Wolf, 1938, Mr 19,15:5
Ferris, Woodridge N Mrs, 1954, F 6,19:4
Ferriss, Emery N, 1946, Ja 10,23:2
Ferriss, Henry S Mrs, 1942, My 30,15:6
Ferriss, Hugh, 1962, Ja 30,29:4
Ferriss, John M, 1951, Ja 18,27:3
Ferro, Edward, 1968, My 16,47:1
Ferrord, Katie, 1907, Ag 14,7:5
Ferrucci, William, 1954, Je 18,23:3
Ferrulo, Michael J, 1945, Ap 9,19:5
Ferry, Alfred J, 1938, S 28,25:6
Ferry, Charles A, 1924, Ag 2,9:6
Ferry, Charles D, 1961, Ja 10,47:5
Ferry, Charles K, 1940, Ap 14,44:7
Ferry, Charles W, 1950, Mr 6,22:2
Ferry, Dexter M, 1907, N 12,9:6
Ferry, Dexter M Jr, 1959, D 7,31:1
Ferry, E Hayward, 1940, Ap 5,22:2
Ferry, E Hayward Mrs, 1945, Jl 4,13:6
Ferry, Edward W, 1952, O 4,17:2
Ferry, Fairchild N, 1937, Ag 14,13:6
Ferry, Felix, 1953, N 20,24:4
Ferry, Francis J, 1962, Jl 25,33:2
Ferry, Frank Jr, 1947, Ja 10,22:3
Ferry, Frederick C, 1956, Ag 15,29:2
Ferry, George F, 1954, S 26,86:7
Ferry, George J Mrs, 1920, D 31,11:5
Ferry, George Jackson, 1916, O 5,11:3
Ferry, J Milton, 1952, Ag 7,21:6
Ferry, James V, 1949, N 10,31:5
Ferry, John A, 1941, F 18,23:5
Ferry, Joseph J B, 1937, Ja 5,23:6
Ferry, Jules F C, 1893, Mr 18,8:1
Ferry, Louis K, 1957, S 2,13:4
Ferry, Mansfield, 1938, S 5,15:4
Ferry, Mansfield Mrs, 1963, N 11,31:5
Ferry, Margaret K Mrs, 1942, Ja 15,19:3
Ferry, Milton S Rev Dr, 1914, Jl 19,5:6
Ferry, Nelson, 1939, My 25,25:5
Ferry, O S Sen, 1875, N 22,4:7
Ferry, Orlando E, 1940, Ag 6,19:6
Ferry, Ralph M, 1967, My 25,47:3
Ferry, Robert R, 1958, Ap 19,21:2
Ferry, Theodore K Sr, 1961, S 3,60:3
Ferry, Thomas, 1941, My 11,45:2
Ferry, Vernon E, 1952, F 27,27:2
Ferry, W Graham, 1950, Ag 10,25:5
Ferry, Walter T, 1951, D 6,33:3
Ferry, Wesire, 1940, Ja 13,16:8
Ferry, William, 1943, Mr 11,21:3
Ferry, William H, 1947, O 10,25:5
Ferry, William Mrs, 1944, D 19,21:3
Ferschke, Katherine G Mrs, 1939, Mr 5,49:1

Fersman, Alexander, 1945, My 23,19:4
Ferson, Earl B, 1954, D 8,35:2
Ferson, Merton L, 1964, N 23,37:5
Ferstadt, Louis G, 1954, Ag 20,19:5
Fersten, Harry M, 1958, F 18,27:1
Ferster, Andrew J Dr, 1913, Ap 1,11:5
Ferster, James Henry, 1916, F 2,11:5
Ferster, Samuel D, 1961, F 3,23:1
Fertel, Geoffrey F, 1949, Ja 21,13:2
Fertel, Julia D Mrs (will), 1942, F 17,10:4
Fertell, Arthur Mrs, 1965, D 9,47:2
Fertiault, Francois, 1915, O 7,9:7
Fertich, Roscoe, 1938, Mr 21,15:1
Fertig, Alice C Mrs, 1940, Jl 6,15:5
Fertig, Arthur, 1961, O 4,45:4
Fertig, Benjamin Mrs, 1950, Jl 11,31:5
Fertig, David, 1965, Ag 31,33:4
Fertig, Harold I, 1964, Ag 20,29:2
Fertig, Harry, 1953, Ap 3,23:2
Fertig, Jacob, 1964, F 11,40:1
Fertig, John, 1911, Mr 21,11:5
Fertig, John W Mrs, 1955, Je 30,25:1
Fertig, Joseph, 1942, Ag 14,17:2
Fertman, Edward, 1938, N 29,23:2
Ferwerda, H, 1942, D 10,25:4
Feshbach, Hyman, 1942, Je 8,15:3
Feshbach, Tudrus, 1945, My 24,19:1
Fesler, Douglas F, 1940, Jl 24,21:5
Fesler, Mayo, 1945, My 7,17:3
Fess, Charles S, 1955, N 25,27:4
Fess, Joseph Rev Dr, 1920, F 6,13:4
Fess, Leroy E, 1958, Ap 10,29:4
Fess, S D, 1936, D 24,17:1
Fess, Simeon D Mrs, 1925, D 21,21:3
Fessenden, Brig-Gen, 1864, My 5,4:6
Fessenden, Clementina Mrs, 1918, S 15,23:1
Fessenden, Francis Gen, 1906, Ja 3,9:7
Fessenden, Frederick J, 1943, F 25,21:1
Fessenden, Harry Mrs, 1919, Ap 29,15:3
Fessenden, J M Col, 1883, F 10,2:3
Fessenden, James D Mrs (will), 1945, Ja 11,21:6
Fessenden, John S S, 1952, Ap 13,77:3
Fessenden, Joshua A Maj, 1908, Je 25,9:5
Fessenden, Mary A Mrs, 1937, Mr 31,23:2
Fessenden, Maude E Mrs, 1952, Jl 29,21:2
Fessenden, Maynard G, 1952, Ja 2,25:4
Fessenden, Newton H, 1941, Ja 14,21:5
Fessenden, Oliver G, 1921, Jl 22,11:1
Fessenden, R A, 1932, Jl 24,22:1
Fessenden, Reginald A Mrs, 1941, Ap 18,21:4; 1965, Je 12,31:4
Fessenden, Richard W, 1956, Jl 25,29:4
Fessenden, Robert G, 1945, O 11,23:3
Fessenden, Russell G, 1945, F 12,20:2
Fessenden, S C Rev, 1882, Ap 19,5:5
Fessenden, Samuel, 1908, Ja 8,9:6
Fessenden, Samuel Gen, 1869, Mr 21,1:1
Fessenden, Sewall H, 1943, Ap 29,21:5
Fessenden, Stirling, 1944, Ja 17,19:4
Fessenden, William Pitt, 1869, S 9,1:6
Fessler, Carl F, 1947, S 16,23:2
Fessler, Friederike R Sister, 1952, N 9,90:1
Fessler, Laci, 1965, Mr 12,33:3
Fessler, Mitchell Mrs, 1958, Ag 11,21:4
Fessler, William, 1963, N 16,27:2
Fest, Arthur E, 1956, F 19,93:2
Festetics, Gyula de Count, 1922, Ag 31,15:6
Festing, J W Bp, 1902, D 29,7:6
Fetchko, Joseph, 1945, S 28,21:4
Feterson, Ben Mrs, 1964, F 23,84:7
Feth, Charles H, 1951, D 11,33:1
Fetherole, Martin D, 1951, Mr 8,29:4
Fetherolf, James M, 1951, N 27,31:3
Fethers, Alice V Mrs, 1941, F 5,19:1
Fetherston, Charles E, 1955, My 21,17:2
Fetherston, Edgar, 1944, Mr 12,38:4
Fetherston, Gertrude B, 1953, Ag 5,23:4
Fetherston, John J, 1925, D 22,21:3
Fetherston, John T, 1962, O 10,47:1
Fetherston, Mary, 1951, Ap 9,25:5
Fetherston, Thomas C Mrs, 1958, F 8,19:4
Fetherston, Thomas E Mrs, 1951, F 16,25:4
Fetherston, William T, 1959, N 6,29:3
Fetick, George P, 1949, O 5,29:5
Fetick, Henry V, 1938, Mr 13,II,8:6
Fetis, Francis Joseph, 1871, Ap 13,1:6
Fetis, M, 1871, Ap 12,1:2
Fetsch, Henry N (Hen), 1961, Ja 2,25:6
Fetske, Dina M Mrs, 1937, S 14,23:6
Fetske, Edward, 1962, Ag 23,29:4
Fetske, George W, 1945, Ja 22,17:4
Fett, Floyd W, 1956, O 22,29:5
Fett, Harold J, 1942, Jl 2,21:5
Fetten, Robert A, 1949, Ag 3,23:3
Fetter, Dorothy, 1962, Ag 2,25:5
Fetter, Eugene C, 1942, Jl 10,17:4
Fetter, Frank A, 1949, Mr 22,25:1
Fetter, John, 1943, O 2,13:6
Fetter, John H, 1949, Ap 2,15:4
Fetter, Louis H, 1942, D 23,19:5
Fetter, Melvin B, 1951, S 17,21:6
Fetter, Newton C, 1965, D 17,39:1
Fetter, Samuel P, 1921, Mr 19,11:6
Fetterly, Charles H, 1958, My 23,23:2
Fetterly, Charles L, 1959, D 2,43:2
Fetterly, Clarence A, 1951, Jl 28,11:1
Fetterly, Edward, 1953, Ja 4,77:1
Fetterman, George E, 1939, My 7,III,7:1
Fetterman, Joseph L, 1953, Ap 14,35:2
Fetterman, Wilfred B, 1953, Ja 29,27:3
Fetterolf, Andrew C, 1941, Je 24,19:2
Fetterolf, Edwin H, 1941, O 26,43:2
Fetterolf, G, 1932, D 30,17:1
Fetterolf, Horace G, 1937, Mr 22,23:1
Fetterolf, Peter F, 1956, F 8,33:2
Fetteroll, Robert, 1942, Ap 11,13:6
Fettes, David, 1953, O 11,89:2
Fettes, David S Sr, 1942, F 19,19:2
Fettinger, E Forrest, 1942, Ja 29,19:2
Fettinger, Theodore S, 1941, S 5,21:6
Fettretch, Charles S, 1951, Ap 18,31:2
Fetyk, Joseph F Jr, 1950, D 19,29:4
Fetzer, Frank J, 1955, Je 17,23:3
Fetzer, Frank J Mrs, 1955, Mr 8,27:1
Fetzer, Henry H Mrs, 1951, D 30,24:6
Fetzer, John A Mrs, 1952, N 14,23:3
Fetzer, John E, 1966, N 22,41:3
Fetzer, John G, 1951, F 20,25:3
Fetzer, Theodore W, 1945, My 7,17:4
Fetzer, Wade Sr, 1956, S 24,27:6
Feucht, George, 1946, S 21,15:5
Feucht, Otto J, 1956, Jl 27,21:4
Feuchtwanger, Austin J, 1959, Ag 3,25:5
Feuchtwanger, Lion, 1958, D 23,2:6
Feuchtwanger, Maurice, 1943, Ja 10,48:5
Feuer, Abram J, 1966, Ag 1,27:4
Feuer, Edward, 1952, Ja 15,27:4
Feuer, Joseph, 1943, Ja 31,46:1
Feuer, Joseph L, 1946, D 17,38:6
Feuer, Moses A, 1964, My 16,25:3
Feuerbach, Ferdinand L, 1960, Jl 29,25:2
Feuerbach, Joseph J, 1950, Jl 26,25:4
Feuerbach, Louis, 1872, S 18,1:7
Feuerbach, William A, 1951, Ap 8,92:8
Feuerhake, William G, 1961, N 13,31:1
Feuering, Henry F Prof, 1915, Ja 29,9:4
Feuerlicht, Morris M, 1959, D 2,43:1
Feuerlicht, Natalie Dr, 1968, Ja 6,29:2
Feuerstein, Arthur, 1949, Je 4,13:3
Feuerstein, Heinrich, 1942, O 30,8:4
Feuerstein, Henry, 1942, F 2,15:3
Feuerstein, Jacob B, 1943, S 18,17:1
Feuild, Alexander Littlejohn, 1968, O 13,85:1
Feuillerat, Albert G, 1952, N 4,29:3
Feuillet, Octave, 1890, D 30,5:4
Feurer, Hermann, 1954, S 24,23:2
Feustmann, Maurice M, 1943, Ag 28,11:2
Feuz, Eduard, 1944, Je 14,19:3
Fevre, Achille, 1940, Ja 24,21:1
Fevrier, Henri, 1957, Jl 9,29:5
Few, William P, 1940, O 17,25:5
Fewell, Travis M, 1944, S 18,19:4
Fewkes, Ernest E, 1942, Jl 18,13:2
Fewkes, J W, 1930, Je 1,20:3
Fewkes, Vladimir J, 1941, D 13,21:6
Fewlass, Richard A, 1953, S 30,31:5
Fewsmith, Joseph, 1953, Mr 14,15:6
Fewsmith, William L, 1940, Ag 17,15:6
Fewster, Wilson L, 1945, Ap 17,23:4
Fey, Edward C, 1958, F 1,19:2
Fey, Louise Sister, 1954, N 19,32:2
Fey, Philipp A, 1945, D 23,18:3
Fey, Wealth E, 1945, Ja 11,23:3
Feydeau, Georges L, 1921, Je 7,17:4
Feyder, Jacques, 1948, My 26,25:4
Feyen, Harry A Capt, 1937, Je 2,23:1
Feyhl, Horace W, 1960, Ja 22,27:2
Feyl, Albert J, 1953, O 9,27:4
Feyl, Robert R, 1959, N 6,29:3
Feyler, Rodney E, 1950, Jl 30,60:7
Fezandie, Eugene H, 1957, N 11,29:1
Fezandie, Hector, 1943, Ap 28,23:5
Fezier, Charles C, 1952, Ag 12,19:1
Fezzuoglio, Guiseppe, 1940, Ag 1,24:4
Ffolkes, Francis, 1938, O 20,23:2
Ffoulke, Charles M Jr, 1912, N 14,11:5
Ffoulkes, Charles J, 1947, Ap 26,13:6
Ffoulkes, Maud Mrs, 1949, Ap 8,26:4
Ffrench, Charles, 1916, Ag 18,9:6
Fiala, Anthony, 1950, Ap 9,86:3
Fiala, Sigmund N, 1968, Jl 3,35:3
Fialka, Solomon H, 1954, O 20,29:2
Fialkoff, Herman, 1958, D 10,39:4
Fiallo, Fabio, 1942, Ag 29,15:4
Fiallos, Luis, 1947, Ap 19,15:2
Fiancette, Eugene, 1949, Je 8,29:5
Fianey, Charles G, 1875, Ag 17,4:6
Fiaschetti, Michael, 1960, Jl 31,68:5
Fibel, Gertrude L, 1957, Ag 21,27:4
Fibel, Louis H (will, My 12,11:2), 1916, My 3,13:7
Ficalora, Benjamin, 1951, Je 19,29:2
Ficarra, Frank J, 1965, Ja 10,92:1
Fichera, Charles A, 1965, My 1,31:4
Fichlander, Alex, 1955, Mr 1,25:1
Fichter, D Gordon Mrs, 1937, D 13,27:5
Fichter, Daniel A, 1954, F 18,31:3
Fichter, Herman Mrs, 1950, Mr 13,21:3
Fichter, Morris, 1948, Ap 19,23:4
Fichthorn, Emma, 1950, Je 21,22:3
Fichthorn, Walter N, 1951, Jl 20,21:1
Fichtman, L, 1925, Ag 3,15:6
Fichtner, George E, 1937, Ja 30,17:3
Fichtner, Katherine E, 1937, O 10,II,8:5
Fichtner, Oscar P, 1951, My 12,21:5
Fichtner, William, 1941, Mr 25,26:1
Fick, Alex, 1945, Ja 19,19:3
Fick, Carl A, 1960, Ap 28,35:2
Fick, Joseph, 1954, Ja 26,27:2
Fick, Louis F, 1945, O 30,19:2
Fick, Peter J Mrs, 1941, F 16,39:2
Ficke, Arthur D, 1945, D 4,29:4
Ficke, Charles H Mrs, 1961, My 24,41:3
Fickel, Frank L, 1951, My 17,31:4
Fickel, George, 1948, My 22,15:5
Fickel, Jacob E, 1956, Ag 10,17:2
Fickel, James G, 1942, S 14,15:3
Ficken, F R, 1945, Ja 26,21:1
Ficken, George J, 1962, Ja 15,27:3
Fickenscher, Arthur, 1954, Ap 17,13:2
Fickenscher, Elmer W Mrs, 1961, Ag 11,24:1
Ficker, Nicholas T Sr, 1943, My 21,19:1
Fickerssen, Frederick, 1949, Mr 15,27:2
Fickert, Charles M, 1937, O 21,23:3
Fickert, William R, 1952, My 16,23:4
Fickes, Alfred C, 1954, O 5,27:4
Fickes, Edwin S, 1943, D 20,23:5
Fickes, George H Rev Dr, 1937, Ja 7,22:1
Fickes, Robert O Mrs, 1962, My 17,18:8
Fickett, Arthur C Capt, 1920, Ja 28,11:4
Fickett, Homer, 1953, N 3,32:4
Fickett, Kenneth, 1963, D 15,86:2
Fickett, Walter P, 1954, O 29,23:4
Fickinger, Emil H, 1952, Ja 21,15:5
Fickinger, William J, 1940, O 1,23:5
Fickling, Walter J, 1954, F 20,17:5
Fickling, William I, 1947, S 30,25:3
Ficks, E Lincoln, 1944, Je 27,19:3
Fidalgo, Manuel H, 1958, O 2,37:5
Fidanque, Benjamin D, 1937, F 24,23:4
Fidelis, Father, 1921, O 19,19:5; 1937, My 27,2
Fidelis, Mother, 1949, N 25,31:4
Fidelman, Isaac Mrs, 1964, Ag 26,39:6
Fidelman, Isaak, 1958, Ap 30,33:2
Fidelman, Sascha, 1958, Mr 29,17:1
Fidgeon, Arthur J, 1959, Jl 18,15:5
Fidicie Bonnet, Sister, 1942, My 17,47:5
Fidler, Cecil, 1951, O 28,85:2
Fidler, James S, 1960, D 17,23:2
Fidler, William P, 1949, S 17,17:4
Fiducia, Frederick, 1966, My 11,47:3
Fiebeger, Gustav J, 1939, O 19,24:2
Fieber, Moses, 1965, Ap 26,31:3
Fieberg, Paul H Jr, 1950, Jl 24,17:4
Fiebiger, Paul A, 1963, S 16,35:1
Fiebing, John H, 1939, Ap 13,23:2
Fiedelday, J C, 1880, D 5,1:1
Fiedeldey, Louis C, 1945, N 2,19:2
Fiedler, Charles F (Skip Farrell), 1962, My 1(
Fiedler, Ernest, 1913, Mr 1,15:5
Fiedler, George E, 1952, Je 17,27:3
Fiedler, George Judge, 1911, Ag 9,9:5
Fiedler, George L, 1922, My 25,19:4
Fiedler, Henry G, 1953, Jl 13,25:5
Fiedler, Laurence, 1911, Mr 20,9:4
Fiedler, Lulu M, 1947, Mr 23,60:1
Fiedler, Max, 1939, D 9,15:3
Fiedler, Romuald, 1945, Ag 1,19:3
Fiedler, William H F, 1919, Ja 2,9:3
Fiegel, Wesley G, 1948, Je 11,23:2
Fieger, Frederick E, 1942, Ja 19,17:3
Fiegerman, Joseph M, 1954, Ap 30,23:4
Field, A P, 1876, Ag 25,3:4
Field, Abraham L, 1941, D 11,27:4
Field, Albert G, 1941, F 10,17:2
Field, Albert S Jr, 1962, My 15,39:1
Field, Alex J, 1942, Ja 8,21:4
Field, Alfred, 1884, My 28,4:6
Field, Alfred Griffen, 1921, Ap 4,13:5
Field, Archibald D, 1951, Ja 21,77:1
Field, Augustus B Mrs, 1944, Ja 3,21:2
Field, Augustus B Sr, 1948, S 21,27:5
Field, Benjamin, 1876, Ag 17,4:7
Field, Benjamin R Mrs, 1951, Ap 26,29:6
Field, Bryan, 1968, D 15,86:4
Field, C C, 1884, Ap 12,5:2
Field, C M, 1885, F 13,2:2
Field, C W, 1892, Jl 13,5:1
Field, Carter, 1957, O 14,27:2
Field, Charles B, 1957, Ja 2,27:5
Field, Charles C, 1937, My 4,25:2
Field, Charles E, 1947, O 3,25:3
Field, Charles Judge, 1908, S 9,9:5
Field, Charles W, 1959, S 29,36:3
Field, Chester, 1951, N 22,31:5
Field, Clarence E, 1951, Ag 5,72:5
Field, Clifton C, 1968, F 13,43:2
Field, Cornelius J, 1915, S 21,11:6
Field, Cornelius Robbins, 1913, My 30,7:6
Field, Cortlandt de Peyster Mrs, 1922, Je 22,

Field, Crosby Mrs, 1961, Ag 10,27:3
Field, Cyrus Jr Mrs, 1908, S 18,7:4
Field, Cyrus Mrs, 1949, F 27,68:4
Field, Cyrus W, 1946, My 10,19:3; 1948, O 18,23:5
Field, Daniel F, 1937, Ap 27,23:2
Field, Daniel W (will, My 14,46:6), 1944, My 1,15:4
Field, Daniel W Mrs, 1942, Ja 19,17:2
Field, David D (por), 1894, Ap 14,1:7
Field, David D, 1941, O 12,52:3
Field, David E, 1917, Ja 11,15:4
Field, Delia S C Mrs (will, Ag 7,13:4), 1937, Jl 24, 15:5
Field, Dudley, 1880, Ag 11,5:4
Field, E S, 1936, S 22,27:1
Field, Edmund E, 1966, S 2,31:3
Field, Edward, 1876, Je 19,5:2
Field, Edward A, 1957, Ja 28,23:4
Field, Edward D, 1950, Ap 30,102:5
Field, Edward M, 1942, D 18,27:2
Field, Edward M Mrs, 1944, Ap 6,23:3
Field, Edward P, 1963, S 2,15:5
Field, Edward P Jr, 1965, S 16,47:5
Field, Edwin A, 1949, F 16,25:5
Field, Edwin Dr, 1922, O 28,13:6
Field, Elias, 1949, N 16,29:1
Field, Elisha C, 1916, Ap 3,13:5
Field, Eugene, 1895, N 5,16:1
Field, Eugene 2d, 1947, Ja 4,15:5
Field, Francis L, 1938, D 25,14:7; 1966, My 16,37:4
Field, Frank B, 1960, Ap 21,31:3
Field, Frank H, 1943, Jl 9,17:2
Field, Frank H Mrs, 1946, F 19,25:2
Field, Frank W, 1944, Ja 15,13:3
Field, Frank X, 1950, Mr 12,92:8
Field, Franklin L Mrs, 1954, Ag 5,23:1
Field, Fred, 1942, Ap 11,13:1
Field, Fred T, 1950, Jl 24,17:3
Field, Frederick C, 1937, S 24,21:2
Field, Frederick E, 1941, Ja 29,18:2
Field, Frederick L, 1945, O 26,19:3
Field, G Edward, 1944, Jl 4,19:2
Field, G W, 1881, My 8,7:1
Field, George A L, 1938, O 6,23:2
Field, George H, 1945, S 5,23:4
Field, George W, 1937, My 14,23:3; 1938, Ja 20,23:4; 1946, Ag 23,19:2
Field, George W Mrs, 1951, Jl 2,23:5
Field, H H, 1942, Ap 3,21:1
Field, Harold C, 1949, S 23,14:3
Field, Harry E, 1960, My 8,86:5
Field, Harry H, 1948, Mr 1,23:5
Field, Harry N, 1942, S 6,30:6
Field, Harry P, 1953, S 27,87:2
Field, Harry S Sr, 1951, D 28,21:1
Field, Henry, 1917, Jl 9,9:6
Field, Henry (por), 1949, O 18,28:2
Field, Henry A, 1957, Mr 1,23:5
Field, Henry C, 1947, F 22,13:2
Field, Henry M Mrs, 1875, Mr 8,4:6
Field, Henry Martyn Rev, 1907, Ja 27,7:6
Field, Henry P (will, N 4,23:6), 1937, O 1,21:3
Field, Herbert H, 1955, My 30,13:4
Field, Herbert H Mrs, 1960, D 27,29:4
Field, Herbert Haviland Dr, 1921, Ap 7,15:6
Field, Herbert O, 1954, Ap 28,31:4
Field, Herbert P, 1959, S 18,31:4
Field, Herbert W, 1939, S 21,23:3
Field, Hermine, 1944, Ag 20,34:1
Field, Hickson W, 1873, F 18,5:3
Field, Hickson Woodman, 1925, Mr 15,26:4
Field, I Stanton Mrs, 1955, F 16,29:4
Field, Isaac S, 1941, My 13,24:2
Field, J, 1929, Ja 15,29:3
Field, J A, 1927, Jl 17,II,9:3
Field, Jacob, 1960, D 5,31:5
Field, James B, 1937, Ja 26,21:4
Field, John A, 1966, O 23,88:3
Field, John E, 1951, Ap 18,31:2
Field, John H, 1940, My 14,23:2
Field, John H Mrs, 1939, O 1,53:4
Field, John R, 1949, Je 19,68:7
Field, John S, 1921, Ag 18,11:6
Field, Joseph, 1914, Ap 30,11:6; 1947, My 9,21:5; 1948, Ag 17,22:3
Field, Joseph C, 1958, O 20,29:2
Field, Jules R, 1940, Ja 30,19:3
Field, Kate, 1896, My 31,5:3
Field, Lawrence N, 1941, O 26,43:4
Field, Leonard E, 1962, F 7,34:3
Field, Lester, 1937, N 19,23:5
Field, Lewis H, 1940, Je 14,21:4
Field, Lewis L, 1940, My 30,18:4
Field, Lila (L Scholefield), 1954, F 10,29:4
Field, Louise C, 1955, F 22,21:1
Field, Luisa, 1958, N 2,88:3
Field, M A, 1882, Ag 2,5:6
Field, M Augustus, 1907, Jl 23,7:6
Field, M W, 1948, Ap 20,27:5
Field, Margaret E, 1952, Mr 26,21:3
Field, Marshall (funl, Ja 20,9:3; will, Ja 24,1:5), 1906, Ja 17,1:1
Field, Marshall Jr (funl, N 30,9:6), 1905, N 28,1:2
Field, Marshall Jr (est appr, S 29,6:6), 1965, S 20,7:1
Field, Marshall 3d (funl, N 10,19:3; will, N 21,23:1), 1956, N 9,29:1
Field, Martin P, 1938, Mr 1,21:2
Field, Maunsell B Judge, 1875, Ja 25,5:4
Field, Maunsell Bradhurst, 1920, Mr 26,13:4
Field, Michael Mrs, 1960, Jl 28,27:5
Field, Mrs, 1871, My 30,1:3
Field, Norman, 1958, Ja 4,15:3
Field, Otis, 1871, O 26,8:3
Field, Peter, 1949, S 26,25:3
Field, Polly C, 1945, F 24,11:3
Field, Poole, 1948, Ap 25,68:7
Field, R M, 1902, N 12,9:5
Field, R S, 1870, My 27,2:5
Field, Rachel, 1942, Mr 16,15:3
Field, Reamy E, 1945, Ag 17,17:4
Field, Robert M, 1949, N 2,13:3
Field, Robert O, 1948, Jl 15,23:3
Field, Rose Mrs, 1963, N 20,43:1
Field, Roswell Martin, 1919, Ja 11,13:5
Field, Runyon, 1957, Ag 24,15:1
Field, S J, 1899, Ap 10,1:2
Field, Salisbury Mrs, 1953, Je 28,60:6
Field, Samuel, 1944, Jl 4,19:5
Field, Samuel E, 1951, Je 16,15:4
Field, Sarah, 1905, Je 7,6:1
Field, Sid, 1950, F 4,15:1
Field, Stanley, 1964, O 29,35:4
Field, Stanley Mrs, 1962, Je 2,19:3
Field, Stephen D Mrs, 1946, Je 4,23:2
Field, Stephen Dudley, 1913, My 19,9:6
Field, T C, 1885, Ja 26,1:4
Field, T F, 1877, S 14,5:4
Field, T W, 1881, N 26,4:7
Field, Theodore W Mrs, 1920, Ap 10,15:4
Field, Theron R, 1940, Jl 23,19:4
Field, Thorold F, 1960, Je 15,41:1
Field, V Ernest, 1939, My 31,23:1
Field, W Gibson, 1916, O 5,11:6
Field, W R Mason, 1938, F 1,21:3
Field, Walter, 1951, Ag 19,86:2
Field, Walter T, 1939, Ag 19,15:4
Field, Wells L Adm, 1914, N 28,13:6
Field, Wells L Mrs, 1959, S 13,84:6
Field, Wilbur, 1948, Jl 15,23:5
Field, William B, 1949, O 7,28:4
Field, William B O Jr Mrs, 1960, Mr 17,33:6
Field, William J, 1964, Ap 10,35:2
Field, William L W, 1963, Mr 30,7:6
Field, William Pierson Mrs, 1924, My 5,15:3
Fielden, John S C Jr, 1951, S 3,13:4
Fielder, Albert A Sr, 1957, Je 28,23:5
Fielder, Carl J, 1951, My 8,31:2
Fielder, Cecil G, 1937, S 11,17:2
Fielder, Edward C, 1948, Ap 4,60:3
Fielder, Edward M, 1941, S 13,17:1
Fielder, Ernest C, 1953, My 26,29:6
Fielder, Frank Sidney Dr, 1917, Ja 25,9:3
Fielder, George D, 1950, Jl 25,27:6
Fielder, J F, 1879, Ap 8,4:7
Fielder, J W Jr, 1903, S 16,9:5
Fielder, James F (funl, D 6,27:3), 1954, D 3,28:1
Fielder, James Mrs, 1953, N 26,31:1
Fielder, Joseph F, 1948, O 15,23:2
Fielder, Joseph M Mrs, 1946, S 20,32:3
Fielder, Ludwig, 1943, O 19,19:2
Fielder, William C, 1950, Ag 30,31:5
Fielder, William L J, 1942, Je 14,45:2
Fielders, William, 1941, Mr 11,23:5
Fieldhouse, John W, 1938, Je 23,21:4
Fielding, Arthur, 1955, Ap 14,29:4
Fielding, Benjamin, 1953, Je 16,27:1
Fielding, Charles F, 1962, Jl 25,33:3
Fielding, Charles Gale, 1916, Ag 20,15:5
Fielding, Edward, 1945, Ja 11,23:6
Fielding, Edward Gen, 1921, Jl 2,9:7
Fielding, Emily, 1955, D 16,29:1
Fielding, F, 1882, N 11,3:2
Fielding, Fred G Dr, 1937, Ja 10,II,10:4
Fielding, Fred P, 1950, N 21,32:3
Fielding, Frederick W, 1953, O 5,27:6
Fielding, George T, 1960, F 24,37:2
Fielding, Jim, 1950, N 2,31:1
Fielding, Joseph, 1943, N 20,13:4
Fielding, Joseph L, 1945, Ag 16,10:7
Fielding, Loraine, 1966, O 6,47:6
Fielding, Mantle, 1941, Mr 28,23:2
Fielding, Philip H, 1947, S 28,60:5
Fielding, W S, 1929, Je 24,21:3
Fielding, Warren C, 1949, S 17,17:2
Fielding, William H, 1940, O 19,17:2
Fieldman, Harry, 1953, Ap 7,29:1
Fieldman, Isidor, 1959, Ap 24,27:1
Fieldman, Isidor Mrs, 1955, N 27,88:6
Fields, Allan, 1968, Ja 7,84:8
Fields, Andrew C, 1911, F 12,12:3
Fields, Arthur M Jr, 1939, Jl 20,3:7
Fields, Benny (B Geisenfeld), 1959, Ag 17,23:4
Fields, C C, 1945, S 14,23:3
Fields, Charles W, 1952, S 20,15:2
Fields, Ernest S, 1963, Jl 3,27:3
Fields, F Byron, 1953, N 21,13:3
Fields, George, 1937, Ap 26,19:5
Fields, Harold, 1962, Mr 31,25:1
Fields, Harold Mrs, 1961, Je 30,27:3
Fields, Herbert, 1958, Mr 25,33:1
Fields, Isabel Mrs, 1902, S 1,2:5
Fields, J T, 1881, Ap 26,5:3
Fields, Jailer, 1873, Mr 19,1:7
Fields, James T Mrs, 1915, Ja 6,13:5
Fields, Joe M, 1953, Jl 30,23:4
Fields, John H, 1944, S 28,19:6
Fields, John J, 1950, O 15,105:1
Fields, John L, 1948, Jl 14,24:2
Fields, Joice J Mrs, 1940, Mr 19,25:3
Fields, Joseph, 1966, Mr 5,27:1
Fields, Joseph E, 1951, Mr 14,33:1
Fields, Lew, 1941, Jl 22,19:1
Fields, Lew Mrs, 1948, F 19,23:4
Fields, Michael D, 1959, Je 17,35:2
Fields, Mitchell, 1966, O 8,31:2
Fields, N Irving, 1940, Ag 25,35:1
Fields, Solomon, 1911, N 9,11:5
Fields, Stanley, 1941, Ap 24,21:6
Fields, Thomas V, 1946, S 23,23:2
Fields, W C, 1946, D 26,25:1
Fields, W C Mrs, 1963, N 9,25:5
Fields, Wallace D, 1958, Ap 11,25:5
Fields, William, 1961, Ap 25,35:1
Fields, William J, 1954, O 22,28:1
Fieldstein, J Ethan, 1955, Mr 17,45:4
Fielo, Julius Mrs, 1949, Ja 26,25:3
Fien, George F, 1943, Je 29,19:5
Fienburgh, Wilfred, 1958, F 4,3:5
Fiene, Ernest, 1965, Ag 11,35:2
Fiene, Ernest Mrs, 1961, F 18,19:2
Fiene, Paul, 1949, O 31,25:4
Fiennes, Eustace, 1943, F 10,25:2
Fiering, Benjamin, 1953, My 7,31:2
Fiering, I Edward, 1955, D 22,23:1
Fiering, Simon, 1941, S 28,48:1
Fierle, Paul C, 1950, D 26,23:4
Fierman, Maurice M, 1957, F 13,35:4
Fiermonte, Madeleine F A Mrs, 1940, Mr 28,24:2
Fiero, Alfonso Sr, 1960, Ja 14,33:2
Fiero, Ida S Mrs, 1950, Ap 8,13:4
Fiero, J N, 1931, Ap 14,27:1
Fiero, Joshua, 1946, Jl 8,29:5
Fiero, Leo P, 1968, F 16,37:2
Fiero, Raymond H, 1967, Ag 3,33:5
Fiero, William M, 1945, Jl 19,23:3
Fiero, William P, 1912, O 30,13:5
Fierre, Wilhelm A, 1952, Ag 5,19:1
Fierro, Rose Mrs, 1916, Mr 29,11:5
Fiersohn, Sarah Mrs, 1916, Ag 6,17:6
Fierst, Harry P, 1959, D 23,27:2
Fierthaler, George F, 1955, D 18,92:6
Fiesel, Edward A, 1937, S 26,II,9:1
Fiesel, Eva Dr, 1937, My 29,17:5
Fiesel, Joseph, 1925, O 16,21:5
Fiesel, Richard, 1951, O 23,29:4
Fieseler, John A, 1959, Ja 27,33:5
Fieser, James L, 1965, O 21,47:3
Fiester, John L, 1946, Ag 6,25:5
Fiet, Raymond D, 1953, O 7,29:1
Fietta, Giuseppe, 1960, O 2,85:3
Fietz, Werner, 1946, O 29,25:1
Fievez, Alex H J (por), 1949, My 1,88:7
Fife, George B, 1939, Mr 13,17:1
Fife, Harry E, 1951, Ja 15,17:5
Fife, Harry M, 1950, Ja 12,27:4
Fife, Harvey R, 1959, O 24,21:6
Fife, Horace, 1945, My 8,19:3
Fife, Judith, 1966, Jl 28,33:1
Fife, Louis, 1957, S 3,27:1
Fife, Mary L, 1962, Je 13,41:6
Fife, Ray, 1950, My 18,29:4
Fife, Robert H, 1958, Ag 2,17:1
Fife, Robert H Mrs, 1949, My 22,90:7
Fife, William, 1902, Ja 14,9:5; 1944, Ag 12,11:6
Fifer, Joseph W, 1938, Ag 7,33:3
Fifer, Orien W, 1947, S 19,23:3
Fifield, Albert F, 1958, My 22,29:3
Fifield, Edson J, 1967, Je 21,47:1
Fifield, Edward R Mrs, 1947, Mr 3,21:4
Fifield, Emily A Mrs, 1913, Ap 3,9:5
Fifield, Haven G, 1956, Ja 19,33:5
Fifield, Lawrence W, 1964, Jl 24,27:2
Fifield, Stiles R, 1963, D 25,33:4
Figarsky, Abram Mrs, 1960, Mr 2,37:2
Figas, Justin, 1959, O 24,21:6
Figg, E Howard, 1939, F 5,40:3
Figgins, Frank, 1954, N 22,23:2
Figgins, James H B, 1956, D 29,15:4
Figgins, Jesse D, 1944, Je 12,19:1
Figgis, Dudley W, 1964, N 3,31:1
Figgs, John Neville, 1919, Ap 17,11:4
Figl, Leopold (funl, My 15,31:5), 1965, My 10,33:4
Figlymessy, Philip Col, 1907, Jl 26,7:6
Figman, Max, 1952, F 14,27:5
Figner, Vera Mrs, 1942, Je 17,23:3
Figsby, Forrest H, 1938, S 22,23:4
Figueiredo, Fausto de, 1950, Ap 6,29:2
Figueiredo, J Saavedra de, 1943, Je 4,21:5
Figueras, Augustin Gen, 1921, Ja 12,15:4
Figueras, Jose M, 1910, D 3,11:5

Figueras, Mrs, 1873, Ap 23,1:5
Figueras y Moracas, 1882, N 12,9:2
Figueroa, Fernando Gen, 1919, Je 19,13:5
Figueroa, Gilberto, 1962, N 13,37:1
Figueroa y Torres, Alvara de Count, 1950, S 12,27:4
Figueroy, Silas Mrs, 1941, Ap 17,23:3
Figur, Leon, 1958, Je 16,23:4
Fihelly, John W, 1956, S 7,23:4
Fiigon, Austin M, 1954, Ag 29,89:2
Fiji Cannibal, 1872, My 17,5:5
Fike, Charles L, 1950, My 4,27:4
Fike, Henry J, 1939, Ap 5,25:3
Fike, Pierre H, 1943, My 13,21:5
Filak, Dolores M Mrs, 1953, Ap 17,26:4
Filan, Frank, 1952, Jl 24,27:1
Filander, Charles G, 1941, O 19,45:1
Filardi, Basil Mrs, 1946, Ap 18,27:4
Filardi, Basilio, 1953, Je 17,27:3
Filardi, Joseph, 1947, Mr 8,13:2
Filatov, Vladimir P, 1956, N 1,39:4
Filatro, Joseph J, 1956, Mr 18,89:1
Filbert, Edward H, 1950, My 8,23:3
Filbert, John H Mrs, 1954, O 13,31:3
Filbert, Ludwig S Dr, 1903, O 20,9:6
Filbert, William J, 1944, F 5,15:3
Filbig, Albert, 1941, Je 24,19:1
Filchner, Wilhelm, 1957, My 8,37:2
Fildes, L Sir, 1927, F 28,19:1
Fildew, William E, 1943, Jl 20,19:4
Filed, Arthur M, 1946, Ag 1,23:1
Filek, Frank (will), 1940, Ja 7,36:3
Filene, Lincoln (will, S 27,21:8), 1957, Ag 28,27:1
Filene, Lincoln Mrs, 1955, D 8,37:4
Filep, Joseph, 1952, Ja 17,27:5
Filer, Herbert D, 1966, D 27,35:3
Filer, James, 1952, Mr 9,93:1
Filer, William L, 1946, Je 26,25:4
Filerman, Joseph H, 1957, Ag 12,19:5
Files, Charles H, 1943, O 30,15:2
Files, George W, 1939, Ja 4,21:1
Files, Glenn W, 1945, S 13,23:3
Files, Horace R Mrs, 1943, N 4,23:4
Files, J Ray, 1953, O 8,29:2
Files, Ralph E, 1954, Ag 13,15:6
Filfus, Nathaniel, 1944, My 30,21:4
Filho, Joaquim P S, 1950, Ag 1,7:1
Filiberto, Juan de D, 1964, N 12,37:4
Filip, Stanley I, 1938, Je 26,27:2
Filipescu, Grigore, 1938, Ag 26,17:6
Filipovsky, Mikhail S, 1956, Ja 22,88:2
Filipow, Michael, 1950, My 10,31:3
Filipowitz, John J, 1950, D 19,29:4
Filippi, Filippo de, 1938, S 28,25:1
Filipponi, Carlo Mrs, 1949, Ap 6,29:1
Filitti, Bonaventure J, 1963, My 17,33:3
Filitti, Gaetano, 1955, Ag 25,23:4
Filitti, Gaetano Mrs, 1945, My 31,15:4
Filkins, Bertha, 1954, Ja 15,20:3
Filkins, Grace (Mrs A Marix), 1962, S 18,39:1
Fill, John Sr, 1948, D 22,23:3
Filla, Francis J, 1954, S 5,50:2
Fillebrown, Herbert M Mrs, 1942, Ja 13,19:3
Fillebrown, T S, 1884, S 28,9:2
Fillebrown, William Y, 1960, Mr 6,84:8
Filler, George S, 1951, F 1,25:3
Filler, Julius, 1961, S 7,35:2
Filler, Victor W Mrs, 1944, Ap 11,19:3
Filley, Charles C, 1911, F 5,II,11:3
Filley, Everett R, 1958, Mr 22,17:2
Filley, Frederick C, 1951, F 16,25:3
Filley, Oliver D, 1961, Ja 19,29:5
Filley, Richard C, 1948, O 14,30:3
Fillin, Solomon, 1950, Ag 18,21:2
Fillion, Francis, 1943, Ag 12,19:5
Fillipov, Vladimir, 1952, O 20,23:2
Fillman, John W Mrs, 1953, O 15,33:3
Fillmore, Calvin Col, 1865, O 25,2:2
Fillmore, Charles, 1948, Jl 9,19:3
Fillmore, Charles M, 1952, S 20,15:3
Fillmore, Charles W, 1942, Ap 28,21:5
Fillmore, Edward, 1953, Ag 16,76:7
Fillmore, Gleazen Rev, 1875, Ja 27,2:5
Fillmore, Henry, 1956, D 9,88:8
Fillmore, Henry Mrs, 1954, Ap 15,29:4
Fillmore, J A, 1902, F 28,9:5
Fillmore, Margaret S Mrs, 1939, D 24,14:7
Fillmore, Millard Ex-President, 1874, Mr 9,1:5
Fillmore, Millard K, 1941, My 1,23:4
Fillmore, Millard Mrs, 1881, Ag 12,5:2
Fillmore, Parker, 1944, Je 6,17:2
Fillmore, Parker Mrs, 1951, N 26,25:3
Fillo, Nicholas M, 1960, Je 26,73:1
Fillow, A Homer, 1939, Ap 3,15:4
Filman, John H, 1940, Ag 13,19:3
Filmer, Eugene D, 1948, Jl 14,23:2
Filmer, W C T S, 1949, O 13,27:1
Filmer, William P, 1942, N 23,23:2
Filmore, Tommy, 1954, Ja 12,23:5
Filocco, Ralph, 1947, F 13,23:5
Filon, Frederick H, 1952, Jl 12,13:6
Filon, Louis N G Prof, 1937, D 30,19:3
Filosa, Louis A, 1956, My 17,31:3
Filossofoff, Minister, 1907, D 20,11:6
Filou, Antonios J, 1965, S 11,27:1
Filser, Charles C, 1942, Ap 21,23:4
Filsinger, Adam E, 1943, O 1,19:1
Filsinger, Ernst B, 1937, My 27,23:4
Filsinger, Herman C, 1942, O 29,23:3
Filsinger, Raymond H, 1945, Mr 8,23:3
Filtzer, Hyman, 1967, Ja 10,43:3
Finaldi, James V, 1952, S 28,77:2
Finaldi, Richard, 1945, D 5,25:5
Finale, Demitrios (por), 1938, Ap 14,23:4
Finale, Stephen D Mrs, 1956, Je 9,17:3
Finaly, Horace, 1945, My 20,32:3
Finan, Austin L, 1950, My 4,27:2
Finan, Bro, 1944, O 19,23:5
Finan, Charles H, 1947, D 19,25:2
Finan, Edward J, 1960, My 11,39:4
Finan, James Mrs, 1968, Ja 31,41:1
Finan, Joseph B, 1943, Ag 3,19:5
Finan, Joseph V, 1943, S 15,27:3
Finan, Matthew Mrs, 1955, F 8,27:2
Finan, Thomas, 1941, My 18,43:6
Finan, Thomas B, 1939, My 30,17:4
Finarelli, Antoinette Mrs, 1937, Mr 29,II,8:6
Finberg, Martin, 1954, Mr 22,27:2
Finch, Abraham T, 1942, D 28,19:2
Finch, Adelbert, 1942, O 23,21:3
Finch, Benjamin Jr, 1945, Ap 23,19:4
Finch, Burton E, 1957, Ja 18,21:2
Finch, C N, 1944, N 16,23:6
Finch, Charles L, 1939, F 13,15:2
Finch, Charles L Mrs, 1944, Mr 7,17:2
Finch, Chester A, 1949, Je 24,23:4
Finch, Clifton J, 1962, S 5,39:4
Finch, Dick, 1955, N 1,31:1
Finch, Edna S, 1946, Ap 8,27:2
Finch, Edward R, 1965, S 16,47:1
Finch, Edward R Mrs, 1961, Ja 26,29:4
Finch, Edwin (Sept 28), 1965, O 11,61:2
Finch, Effingham S, 1942, Je 25,23:2
Finch, Ellis J, 1941, N 8,19:4
Finch, Emily Mrs, 1953, D 17,37:3
Finch, Flora, 1940, Ja 5,19:3
Finch, Francis Miles, 1907, Ag 1,7:6
Finch, Frank J, 1950, S 3,38:5
Finch, George B, 1961, Ja 23,23:4
Finch, George E, 1942, My 23,13:2
Finch, George H, 1949, O 1,13:4
Finch, George R, 1906, Ja 13,1:1
Finch, George T, 1937, D 20,27:3
Finch, Gordon T, 1937, Je 4,23:1
Finch, H M, 1884, Mr 28,5:3
Finch, H O Rev, 1879, Ag 29,1:6
Finch, Harold E, 1952, F 28,27:5
Finch, Harry B, 1953, O 15,33:4
Finch, Henry A Dr, 1968, O 15,47:3
Finch, Henry L, 1960, F 2,35:1
Finch, Heo Henry, 1907, My 23,9:6
Finch, Hunter J, 1950, N 3,27:2
Finch, Hunter J Mrs, 1950, S 7,31:4
Finch, J Harvey, 1925, Jl 3,13:6
Finch, J R Prof, 1903, My 23,9:3
Finch, James K, 1967, Ap 15,31:1
Finch, James K Mrs, 1964, Je 13,23:4
Finch, James L, 1957, Jl 24,25:3
Finch, James M Mrs, 1965, O 19,43:4
Finch, James Myers, 1968, O 15,47:4
Finch, James O, 1950, Ap 21,23:3
Finch, James W Mrs, 1948, D 11,15:5
Finch, Jeremiah W, 1904, D 17,9:5
Finch, John B, 1948, Ag 19,21:5
Finch, Lyle W, 1945, N 8,19:4
Finch, Miles L, 1949, S 14,31:2
Finch, Miles L Mrs, 1940, N 16,17:6
Finch, Miles S, 1951, S 16,85:1
Finch, Morton E, 1949, O 19,29:1
Finch, Robert, 1963, My 9,28:3
Finch, Robert D, 1946, Mr 8,21:1
Finch, Robert L, 1956, Ap 30,23:5
Finch, Robert Mrs, 1963, My 9,28:3
Finch, Robert V, 1959, F 5,31:3
Finch, Roy G, 1959, Mr 5,31:6
Finch, Rufus C, 1951, Ja 22,17:2
Finch, Sarah Elizabeth Dr, 1921, Je 23,17:5
Finch, William Albert Prof, 1912, Ap 1,13:6
Finch, William E, 1948, Ap 27,25:5
Finch, William E Sr, 1943, Ag 6,15:3
Finch, William R, 1913, Ag 10,II,11:5
Finch, William Y Mrs, 1951, Jl 5,34:3
Fincher, Harry W, 1952, Ja 26,13:3
Fincher, J W, 1948, Ag 31,24:2
Finck, Abbie Mrs, 1940, S 21,19:3
Finck, David H, 1964, Je 6,23:5
Finck, Edward A, 1946, N 23,15:1
Finck, Edward B Mrs, 1955, Jl 19,27:2
Finck, Eugene, 1907, F 3,7:6
Finck, Herman, 1939, Ap 22,17:4
Finck, John, 1951, Ap 28,15:4
Finck, Simon, 1950, O 30,27:2
Finck, Theodore, 1923, Ap 10,21:4
Finck, William C, 1953, Mr 27,23:1
Fincke, Benjamin C, 1948, Mr 24,25:2
Fincke, Clarence M, 1959, Je 20,21:4
Fincke, Clarence M Mrs, 1959, Ja 7,33:4
Fincke, Harry S Dr, 1924, Ja 22,17:4
Fincke, James C, 1957, D 6,29:2
Fincke, Reginald, 1956, My 11,27:2
Fincke, Reginald Mrs, 1966, F 1,35:2
Finckh, Adolph Mrs, 1950, Je 15,31:4
Findahl, Odd, 1955, Ap 9,13:4
Findeisen, Walter L, 1948, O 26,31:1
Finder, Oscar, 1952, N 29,17:1
Findlater, Ramsey, 1955, Jl 26,25:5
Findlater, Stevenson, 1953, N 21,8:6
Findlay, Allan H, 1943, N 17,25:2
Findlay, Andrew, 1957, Jl 28,61:2
Findlay, Andrew D, 1955, Ap 1,27:3
Findlay, E D, 1937, Ag 5,23:2
Findlay, Elizabeth L Mrs, 1941, F 28,19:3
Findlay, Ephraim K, 1950, S 28,31:1
Findlay, Gabriel S Mrs, 1940, Mr 3,44:1
Findlay, Harry L, 1943, S 12,52:2
Findlay, Hugh, 1950, Ag 24,27:3
Findlay, James, 1954, D 27,17:4
Findlay, James N Mrs, 1950, Ap 30,102:7
Findlay, John V L, 1907, Ap 20,9:6
Findlay, John W (cor, Je 3,92:2), 1951, Je 2,19:5
Findlay, L William, 1951, N 9,27:2
Findlay, Louis, 1956, O 30,37:4
Findlay, Merlin C, 1957, Ag 1,25:4
Findlay, Robert C, 1947, Jl 16,23:2
Findlay, Thomas B, 1941, My 30,15:2
Findlay, William, 1953, Je 21,84:7
Findley, A Jr, 1880, My 28,5:6
Findley, Alvin I, 1940, D 13,26:5
Findley, Earl N, 1956, Jl 12,23:6
Findley, Earl N Mrs, 1940, Jl 28,27:3
Findley, Emerson, 1945, F 3,11:3
Findley, George W, 1952, O 23,31:5
Findley, J B, 1941, O 22,23:5
Findley, John H, 1942, O 15,23:3
Findley, Joseph H, 1946, Je 4,23:4
Findley, Palmer, 1964, N 12,37:4
Findley, Paul B, 1962, F 26,27:4
Findley, William M, 1951, Je 12,29:5
Findley, William V B, 1955, Ag 26,19:1
Findling, David P, 1956, Je 15,25:5
Fine, Aaron, 1963, O 23,42:7
Fine, Abraham, 1958, Je 5,31:4
Fine, Andrew M, 1937, Ap 21,23:5
Fine, Andrew M Jr, 1965, Ag 6,27:4
Fine, Bessie Mrs, 1952, Je 24,29:2
Fine, Charles Mrs, 1956, Je 27,31:2
Fine, David Mrs, 1966, F 23,39:4
Fine, Franklin L, 1957, Ap 19,21:2
Fine, George, 1963, O 9,43:4
Fine, H B, 1928, D 23,19:1
Fine, Harry, 1958, Je 30,19:2; 1967, D 30,23:3
Fine, Harry L, 1960, N 29,37:3
Fine, Henry, 1953, Ja 25,84:5
Fine, Irving (trb lr, S 2,II & X,8:5), 1962, Ag 24,22:6
Fine, Isidor, 1959, Jl 1,25:4; 1960, Ag 20,19:2
Fine, James M, 1944, D 18,19:3
Fine, Jarvis, 1950, Je 25,68:8
Fine, John, 1866, Ja 11,2:4
Fine, John Capt, 1922, Jl 14,13:6
Fine, John S Mrs, 1951, Ap 23,25:6
Fine, Joseph Mrs, 1919, Mr 29,13:3
Fine, Julius, 1954, My 1,15:5; 1966, My 15,88:8
Fine, Louis Mrs, 1960, S 24,23:5
Fine, Max, 1958, Jl 19,15:7
Fine, Milton H, 1948, O 13,25:3
Fine, Milton S, 1962, N 14,39:2
Fine, Morris S, 1946, Ag 18,47:2
Fine, Samuel, 1960, S 26,33:3
Fine, Samuel I, 1943, Je 25,17:5
Fine, Seymour H Mrs, 1950, My 5,22:3
Fine, Simon, 1952, Ja 1,25:3
Fine, Theodore, 1956, F 8,33:4
Fine, William A, 1942, My 12,19:5
Fine, William A Mrs, 1952, Ja 6,93:2
Fineberg, Aaron, 1950, D 31,42:6
Fineberg, Abba M, 1957, Mr 22,23:2
Fineberg, Bernard, 1956, Je 30,17:2
Fineberg, Davis, 1945, My 29,15:4
Fineberg, Isaac, 1962, My 25,33:3
Fineberg, Morris, 1949, S 30,16:3; 1949, O 1,8:3
Finegan, Anna M, 1947, F 1,15:1
Finegan, Herbert J, 1952, N 15,17:4
Finegan, James E, 1940, F 11,49:1
Finegan, James V, 1953, Ja 31,15:4
Finegan, John L Jr, 1944, Jl 6,15:5
Finegan, John L Sr, 1944, Ap 26,19:1
Finegan, Rexford W, 1960, Ag 23,29:3
Finegan, T E, 1932, N 26,10:3
Finegan, William J, 1967, Ja 20,43:3
Finegold, Jacob Mrs (will), 1956, Jl 15,51:4
Finehout, Wilbur Mrs, 1951, Ag 9,21:4
Finelite, Abraham C, 1940, S 14,17:3
Fineman, Hayim, 1959, Ap 19,86:3
Fineman, Miriam M Mrs, 1964, O 25,89:1
Finer, Frank J, 1941, Mr 26,23:4
Finer, Harry J, 1946, D 4,31:3
Finer, Joseph J, 1951, Ag 29,25:3
Fineran, Frank, 1915, Ag 19,9:7
Finerty, John F, 1967, Je 6,47:1
Finerty, John J, 1943, S 20,21:4

Finerty, Joseph, 1946, F 19,25:4
Finesilver, Edward M, 1955, D 20,31:3
Finesilver, Harry Mrs, 1957, Mr 23,19:6
Finesilver, Isadore, 1953, Ag 11,27:1
Finesinger, Abraham L Mrs, 1955, Ja 9,87:1
Finesinger, Jacob E, 1959, Je 20,21:5
Fineson, Bernard M, 1967, Je 12,45:2
Finestone, David B, 1940, F 29,19:4
Fingar, Victor J, 1949, Ja 13,23:1
Finger, Charles J, 1941, Ja 8,19:4
Finger, Louis W, 1953, My 8,22:2
Finger, Sarah M, 1943, N 3,25:5
Finger, Sherman W, 1937, Mr 8,19:5
Finger, William L, 1940, Je 13,23:4
Finger, William M, 1945, Je 24,22:5
Fingerhood, Boris, 1946, Ap 28,42:2
Fingerhood, Saul, 1942, O 9,18:7
Fingerhut, Abraham, 1961, Mr 26,93:1
Fingerhut, Alex E, 1952, Mr 22,13:3
Fingerhut, Robert V, 1966, Jl 5,27:1
Fingerle, Josephine Mrs, 1952, N 26,23:1
Fingerman, Henry W, 1963, S 25,43:4
Fingold, George Mrs, 1961, Jl 4,19:1
Fingold, George S (funl plans, S 2,25:4; funl, S 3,33:5), 1958, S 1,13:2
Fingulin, Alfred V, 1947, Ag 8,17:4
Finigan, Rose J Mrs, 1955, O 22,23:3
Finigan, Thomas J, 1947, O 2,27:4
Finizio, Armando G, 1955, Je 11,15:2
Fink, A Elston, 1954, F 2,27:2
Fink, Abraham, 1964, Mr 26,35:3
Fink, Adolph E Mrs, 1942, Ja 29,19:5
Fink, Agustin J, 1944, My 4,19:5
Fink, Albert, 1897, Ap 4,5:4; 1941, Mr 27,23:3; 1942, N 4,23:5
Fink, Amos A, 1937, Mr 26,22:1
Fink, Arthur A, 1949, Ja 11,31:2
Fink, Arthur R, 1946, Je 8,21:4
Fink, August A, 1951, Jl 27,19:5
Fink, Ben W, 1947, Ag 15,17:3
Fink, Charles A, 1955, My 31,27:1
Fink, Clarence M, 1943, Jl 28,15:3
Fink, Colin G, 1953, S 18,23:1
Fink, Daniel, 1952, D 3,33:5
Fink, Denman, 1956, Je 8,25:5
Fink, E C, 1943, Ja 2,11:6
Fink, E Russell, 1941, D 11,27:3
Fink, Elias Dr, 1937, My 2,II,9:2
Fink, Eugene E, 1949, N 12,15:2
Fink, Evert S, 1947, Ja 15,25:1
Fink, Fred C, 1938, F 16,21:1
Fink, Frederick W, 1925, Ja 5,21:4; 1948, Je 29,23:5
Fink, George K, 1963, S 1,57:1
Fink, George R, 1962, Jl 30,23:2
Fink, Grover H, 1952, Ap 20,93:1
Fink, H T, 1926, O 2,19:4
Fink, Hal Mackey, 1924, Je 11,21:4
Fink, Harry, 1951, N 3,17:1
Fink, Henry, 1912, Jl 16,9:5; 1963, D 29,42:6
Fink, Henry A, 1958, N 26,29:2
Fink, Herman A Mrs, 1945, S 16,43:1
Fink, Irving E, 1962, My 25,33:2
Fink, J, 1883, D 28,2:3
Fink, J William Jr, 1959, S 9,41:5
Fink, Jacob D, 1941, Je 13,19:5
Fink, James W Mrs, 1944, Mr 29,21:2
Fink, John, 1943, Ap 15,25:5; 1948, Ja 22,27:3
Fink, Joseph G, 1964, N 13,36:1
Fink, Joseph H, 1961, Mr 29,33:5
Fink, Joseph I, 1939, Jl 18,19:3
Fink, Joseph L, 1964, N 27,36:2
Fink, Kenneth, 1961, Mr 14,35:4
Fink, Lou, 1945, Je 5,19:4
Fink, Louis J, 1965, N 16,47:4
Fink, Mary Margaret Mrs, 1921, Jl 1,13:6
Fink, Nathaniel, 1954, D 5,88:5
Fink, Otto, 1950, F 21,26:2
Fink, Paul, 1947, My 2,22:3
Fink, Paul J, 1958, Jl 4,19:3
Fink, Phil W, 1954, S 22,29:5
Fink, Philip H, 1961, Mr 29,33:5
Fink, Reuben, 1961, F 16,31:3
Fink, Richard, 1966, N 22,45:5
Fink, Samuel M, 1959, N 30,31:4
Fink, Sidney, 1967, D 15,47:1
Fink, Silas, 1937, Ag 4,19:1
Fink, Theodore, 1942, Ap 27,15:5
ink, William, 1940, Mr 23,26:5
ink, William B Mrs, 1948, My 2,76:6
ink, William C, 1912, Ag 5,9:6
ink, William R Mrs (trb, Mr 6,62:7), 1957, F 23,17:5
inkbeiner, Adolph, 1946, Ja 31,21:4
inkbeiner, Edward J, 1946, Mr 25,25:5
inkbeiner, Otto F, 1950, Jl 13,25:2
inke, Charles H, 1961, Ap 26,39:4
inke, Heinrich, 1938, D 22,22:1
nke, John H, 1946, Mr 10,47:1
nkel, Benjamin, 1960, N 12,21:3
nkel, Benjamin Mrs, 1967, Mr 1,43:4
nkel, Emanuel B, 1946, Mr 22,21:2
nkel, Harry A, 1949, Ag 30,27:3
nkel, Henry L, 1938, Mr 9,23:5
nkel, Henry L Mrs, 1948, O 2,15:2

Finkel, Irving, 1965, Je 3,35:5
Finkel, Isadore, 1952, Jl 30,23:2
Finkel, Isadore Z, 1949, D 3,15:1
Finkel, Julius (Elizabeth, N J), 1959, F 2,25:5
Finkel, Julius (Bklyn), 1959, Mr 24,39:3
Finkel, Julius Mrs, 1952, Ag 10,61:3
Finkel, Michael Mrs, 1945, O 13,15:4
Finkel, Morris L, 1950, D 28,26:5
Finkel, Nathan, 1951, N 16,25:4
Finkel, Nathan Mrs, 1946, N 28,27:2
Finkel, Paul B, 1950, Ap 12,27:2
Finkel, Phil Mrs, 1951, F 13,31:4
Finkel, Samuel, 1952, Jl 2,25:2
Finkelbrand, Alex, 1958, Mr 9,86:4
Finkeldey, Frederick F, 1947, Ja 28,23:4
Finkelhoffe, Barney Mrs, 1953, F 26,25:2
Finkell, William T Mrs, 1943, Ap 1,23:1
Finkelpearl, Henry, 1946, Ag 18,47:6
Finkelson, Max Mrs, 1968, My 31,29:2
Finkelstein, Abe Mrs, 1952, Je 7,19:2
Finkelstein, Abraham, 1918, My 31,13:5
Finkelstein, Abraham Mrs, 1950, My 17,29:4
Finkelstein, Alex, 1963, O 9,40:6
Finkelstein, Elliott J, 1954, D 24,13:3
Finkelstein, Herman, 1942, S 13,53:2
Finkelstein, Herman S, 1963, O 11,37:3
Finkelstein, Irving, 1953, S 1,24:4
Finkelstein, Joseph F Mrs, 1952, Jl 13,60:4
Finkelstein, Maurice, 1951, Ja 12,27:3; 1957, F 9,19:3
Finkelstein, Maurice Mrs, 1956, Ja 23,25:6
Finkelstein, Melvin, 1951, Je 21,27:5
Finkelstein, Milton Mrs, 1965, Jl 15,29:3
Finkelstein, Morris, 1962, Jl 30,23:5
Finkelstein, Nathan, 1952, D 9,34:4; 1965, F 27,25:4
Finkelstein, Norma Mrs, 1946, Jl 25,21:2
Finkelstein, Pauline Mrs, 1937, Ag 19,20:1
Finkelstein, Phil, 1954, O 24,89:1
Finkelstein, Sam, 1944, O 24,23:1; 1958, N 9,88:4
Finkelstein, Samuel, 1937, My 16,II,8:7; 1947, Ag 5, 23:4; 1956, N 24,19:1
Finkelstein, Samuel Mrs, 1939, My 15,17:3
Finkelstein, Simon J, 1947, Ap 17,27:3
Finkelstein, Solomon, 1957, O 19,21:2
Finkelstein, William, 1956, F 18,19:4
Finkelstone, Morris, 1946, F 5,24:2
Finkenauer, Charles W, 1953, O 13,29:1
Finkenberg, Adolph Mrs, 1943, Mr 16,19:3
Finkenberg, Alfred J, 1951, Ap 26,32:3
Finkenberg, Edward, 1954, N 26,29:4
Finkenberg, Frederick, 1952, S 28,77:1
Finkenberg, Israel, 1961, Ap 15,21:4
Finkenberg, Sam, 1952, Ag 25,17:4
Finkenbinder, O D, 1954, N 17,31:1
Finkensieper, Adolph, 1959, My 26,35:4
Finkenstaedt, Harry S, 1965, S 25,35:5
Finkenthal, Arnold, 1949, Je 16,29:2
Finkevich, Samuel, 1940, S 13,18:2
Finkle, Abraham, 1957, D 8,88:7
Finkle, Albert, 1968, D 18,47:1
Finkle, Carl, 1951, My 28,21:3
Finkle, Clifford, 1950, Je 9,23:5
Finkle, Frederick C, 1949, Ap 8,26:2
Finkle, Leonard J, 1939, O 3,23:5
Finkle, Phil, 1942, Mr 13,19:3
Finkle, Phil M, 1948, My 29,15:6
Finkle, Samuel, 1951, Je 12,29:4
Finkle, William D, 1951, N 21,25:1
Finkler, Louis, 1943, N 22,19:5
Finkler, Rita Sapiro Dr, 1968, N 9,33:5
Finks, Nelson M, 1964, O 23,39:2
Finks, Robert S, 1944, Je 13,19:6
Finks, Theodora, 1948, O 26,31:2
Finlan, Catherine M, 1946, N 16,19:6
Finlan, Leonard, 1962, My 21,33:3
Finlay, Arthur M Mrs, 1948, D 6,25:5
Finlay, Carlos E, 1944, Mr 12,38:3
Finlay, Charles E, 1940, Jl 11,19:2
Finlay, Charles E Mrs, 1937, Mr 8,19:4
Finlay, Charles J Dr, 1915, Ag 21,7:7
Finlay, Frank, 1955, D 27,26:3
Finlay, George, 1903, O 10,9:6
Finlay, George I, 1961, My 7,87:1
Finlay, Henry J, 1953, Ap 22,29:1
Finlay, J W, 1870, Ag 25,5:3
Finlay, James R, 1951, Ja 3,25:1
Finlay, Kirkman G, 1938, Ag 29,13:5
Finlay, Robert N, 1951, My 29,25:5
Finlay, Thomas, 1923, Mr 1,15:3
Finlay, Viscount, 1929, Mr 10,28:4; 1945, Jl 2,15:5
Finlay, Walter Jr Mrs, 1951, Ap 19,31:3
Finlay, Walter S, 1941, D 19,25:2
Finlay, Walter S Jr, 1953, Je 18,29:1
Finlay, William J, 1938, O 25,23:2
Finlayson, Alex, 1954, F 9,27:4
Finlayson, Alex S Mrs, 1946, Je 8,21:3
Finlayson, Donald J, 1952, Ap 19,15:6
Finlayson, Donald L, 1960, Jl 27,29:2
Finlayson, Edward H Mrs, 1946, Je 10,21:3
Finlayson, James H, 1953, O 10,17:5
Finlayson, John, 1917, Ja 9,13:3
Finlayson, John D, 1950, Je 5,23:2
Finlayson, Murdoch J, 1951, Ag 19,85:2
Finlayson, Robert G, 1956, My 25,23:2

Finletter, Edwin M, 1942, Ag 18,21:6
Finletter, Thomas D, 1947, F 5,23:1
Finletter, Thomas D Mrs, 1938, S 15,25:5
Finletter, Thomas K, 1907, Ap 2,11:5
Finley, Allan, 1925, D 26,15:6
Finley, Charles, 1941, Mr 20,21:5
Finley, Charles M, 1958, Ag 26,29:3
Finley, David C, 1959, Ja 27,33:4
Finley, David E Mrs, 1954, Je 19,15:6
Finley, David R, 1942, D 29,21:1
Finley, Earl E, 1948, D 18,19:4
Finley, Edward, 1941, F 15,15:3
Finley, Edward J, 1965, Ja 23,25:2
Finley, Elizabeth M Mrs, 1941, Mr 27,23:3
Finley, Emmet, 1950, D 14,35:6
Finley, Emmet Mrs, 1955, S 26,23:3
Finley, Ernest L, 1942, O 26,15:5
Finley, Francis J, 1948, My 23,68:3
Finley, Frank, 1903, N 20,9:6
Finley, Frank H, 1939, D 27,24:1
Finley, Garry J, 1948, My 10,21:2
Finley, George W, 1963, N 23,29:1
Finley, Harold M, 1950, Mr 29,29:4
Finley, Harry I, 1940, My 2,24:2
Finley, Henry T, 1940, D 8,69:3
Finley, Homer, 1951, N 18,91:2
Finley, James Alexander Capt, 1907, Ja 25,9:4
Finley, James G, 1911, N 8,13:4
Finley, John H, 1940, Mr 8,1:2; 1942, S 28,17:5
Finley, John H Mrs (funl, N 2,27:2; trb lr, N 6,34:7), 1956, O 31,33:5
Finley, John J, 1940, Mr 19,25:2
Finley, Joseph F, 1951, F 17,15:2
Finley, Joseph F Mrs, 1967, Jl 28,31:3
Finley, Julian, 1965, F 20,25:1
Finley, Lance G, 1951, Ap 24,29:4
Finley, Lester, 1942, D 2,25:2
Finley, Luke A, 1940, Ag 13,19:5
Finley, Martha, 1909, Ja 31,11:6
Finley, Michael J, 1951, D 14,31:3
Finley, P J, 1904, Ap 12,9:7
Finley, Robert, 1940, My 26,34:1
Finley, Sarah E Mrs, 1937, N 16,23:5
Finley, Thomas F, 1950, My 21,104:4
Finley, William, 1952, D 9,33:2
Finley, William L, 1953, Jl 1,29:6
Finley, William W Jr, 1961, Ja 28,19:6
Finley, William W 3d, 1948, Ag 15,60:5
Finley, William Wilson, 1913, N 26,11:5
Finn, Albert E, 1947, Je 10,27:4
Finn, Alex, 1951, D 21,27:2
Finn, Austin, 1905, Ap 10,14:5
Finn, Caesar G, 1949, S 26,27:4
Finn, Catherine L, 1953, F 27,21:1
Finn, Charles G J Dr, 1906, N 4,9:6
Finn, Daniel, 1905, Je 23,1:6
Finn, Daniel E (por), 1949, O 13,27:3
Finn, Daniel E Jr, 1959, F 4,26:2
Finn, Daniel E Mrs, 1952, Ja 3,46:5
Finn, Daniel Magistrate, 1910, Mr 27,II,11:3
Finn, Edward A, 1953, N 6,27:2
Finn, Edward J, 1948, Jl 19,19:3
Finn, Elsie, 1945, N 28,27:1
Finn, F J, 1928, N 3,19:5
Finn, Frank A, 1939, Ja 13,19:1
Finn, George E, 1944, My 7,45:2
Finn, George Thomas, 1916, F 7,11:2
Finn, Harold B, 1955, Mr 14,23:1
Finn, Harry B, 1944, Ap 27,23:6
Finn, Isaac, 1941, N 17,19:5
Finn, J Frank, 1967, N 9,47:1
Finn, James, 1913, Ag 29,9:6; 1915, S 4,7:6
Finn, James A, 1966, My 17,47:4
Finn, James F, 1942, Ag 21,19:6
Finn, James G, 1957, S 18,33:2
Finn, James H, 1952, O 13,21:5
Finn, James J, 1954, Je 13,88:1
Finn, James P, 1952, My 19,17:4
Finn, Jay, 1952, Ap 24,31:3
Finn, Jessie J, 1956, N 30,24:1
Finn, John, 1937, Ap 13,30:2
Finn, John D, 1952, S 18,29:3
Finn, John F X, 1956, S 9,84:1
Finn, John H, 1938, Je 6,17:3
Finn, John J, 1941, Je 9,21:3; 1943, Ja 25,13:2; 1951, O 11,37:4
Finn, Joseph A, 1939, D 10,69:1
Finn, Joseph E, 1952, O 27,27:2
Finn, Joseph H, 1946, O 19,21:4; 1947, Ag 8,17:2
Finn, Joseph Mrs, 1955, Mr 14,23:4
Finn, Mac, 1942, F 3,19:3
Finn, Martin, 1950, Mr 7,27:2
Finn, Michael P, 1943, F 25,21:3
Finn, Patrick W, 1940, D 15,60:3
Finn, Ralph H, 1948, Ap 10,13:5
Finn, Sadie B Mrs (S Borgenicht), 1962, N 22,29:4
Finn, Seymour Mrs, 1946, S 23,23:5
Finn, Theodore A, 1954, My 21,27:4
Finn, Thomas A, 1941, My 29,19:2
Finn, Thomas F, 1938, Ja 7,19:4
Finn, Thomas J, 1948, S 9,27:5
Finn, Vincent E, 1958, Ag 29,23:3; 1967, Jl 15,25:1
Finn, William, 1958, Je 25,1:8

Finn, William H, 1950, Ja 28,13:6
Finn, William J, 1950, O 12,31:6; 1961, Mr 21,37:4
Finnan, Joseph B, 1963, D 21,23:2
Finnan, M T, 1942, My 27,23:2
Finnan, Thomas A, 1953, D 11,34:5
Finnan, Warren G, 1960, Ag 27,19:4
Finne, Carsten H, 1950, Jl 30,60:2
Finnegan, Bro Arcenius, 1964, Je 25,33:1
Finnegan, Charles A, 1947, D 3,29:3
Finnegan, Charles J, 1944, O 18,21:1
Finnegan, Edward, 1945, O 23,17:2
Finnegan, Edward H, 1951, Ja 25,25:3
Finnegan, Edward J, 1959, Ag 29,17:6
Finnegan, Eugene J, 1956, O 3,33:6
Finnegan, Eugene J Mrs, 1964, D 27,65:1
Finnegan, Francis J, 1957, Mr 4,27:5
Finnegan, George P, 1924, S 1,13:4
Finnegan, George W, 1966, S 8,47:2
Finnegan, Gregory V, 1966, Ag 19,33:2
Finnegan, Harry B, 1952, Ja 8,27:4
Finnegan, Herbert B, 1962, Ja 25,31:4
Finnegan, J Francis, 1955, Ag 25,23:2
Finnegan, James, 1937, N 26,13:1
Finnegan, James A (funl plans, Mr 30,88:3; funl, Ap 1,31:3), 1958, Mr 27,33:1
Finnegan, James P, 1941, S 22,15:4; 1967, S 7,53:5
Finnegan, John, 1940, Ag 6,22:6
Finnegan, John A, 1940, Ap 14,44:8
Finnegan, John D, 1949, O 31,25:2
Finnegan, John J, 1954, D 28,23:4
Finnegan, John J Mrs, 1945, Ag 5,38:5
Finnegan, John T, 1945, D 15,17:4; 1961, Je 13,35:3
Finnegan, John T Mrs, 1946, D 25,29:6
Finnegan, Joseph F, 1964, F 13,31:2
Finnegan, Joseph J, 1957, Ap 27,19:5
Finnegan, Joseph M, 1943, Je 22,19:4
Finnegan, Joseph P, 1964, Jl 8,35:2
Finnegan, Patrick J, 1940, Ap 26,21:4
Finnegan, Philip J, 1959, Ja 5,29:5
Finnegan, Richard J, 1955, My 7,17:6
Finnegan, Stephen J, 1965, Ja 8,27:1
Finnegan, Thomas, 1904, Ja 14,9:7; 1939, Jl 23,29:4
Finnell, Carrie (Mrs T J Morris), 1963, N 16,27:1
Finnell, Harry W, 1938, O 2,48:8
Finnell, John F, 1962, Mr 20,37:1
Finnen, Edo, 1942, D 16,25:3
Finneran, Emmett J M, 1942, Jl 5,29:3
Finneran, John A, 1967, Ja 20,43:3
Finneran, John E, 1950, D 29,19:2
Finneran, John P, 1941, S 17,23:6
Finneran, John P Mrs, 1956, N 3,23:4
Finneran, Joseph I, 1942, F 4,19:2
Finneran, Lillian Mrs, 1951, Je 1,26:2
Finneran, Mary A Mrs (M A Timmons),(funl, D 15,25:2), 1956, D 12,39:3
Finneran, Michael J, 1963, Jl 20,19:4
Finnerty, Cyril, 1939, Ag 17,21:5
Finnerty, E Burke, 1956, F 12,88:4
Finnerty, Francis A, 1946, Mr 7,36:6
Finnerty, Jeremiah, 1948, Mr 27,13:3
Finnerty, John B, 1961, Ja 29,85:1
Finnerty, John F, 1950, N 1,35:1
Finnerty, John J, 1949, Mr 29,25:1
Finnerty, John M, 1937, My 18,23:3
Finnerty, John P, 1956, Jl 31,23:3
Finnerty, Joseph, 1955, O 20,35:3
Finnerty, Louis A, 1937, Ag 10,19:3
Finnerty, Michael, 1913, Jl 10,7:3
Finnerty, William F, 1949, D 17,17:3
Finney, B Frank, 1938, Ja 19,23:2
Finney, Benjamin F, 1943, O 22,17:2
Finney, Charles C, 1946, F 17,42:6
Finney, David Craig, 1925, N 13,19:5
Finney, Davida M, 1965, Mr 13,25:2
Finney, Edward C, 1956, S 4,30:3
Finney, Edward W, 1947, N 22,15:5
Finney, Frank, 1957, S 21,19:2
Finney, Frank Mrs, 1959, Ap 9,31:2
Finney, Frederick Norton, 1916, Mr 20,11:4
Finney, George F, 1948, My 10,21:2
Finney, George M, 1949, My 30,13:5
Finney, Harry H Sr, 1965, Ja 27,35:3
Finney, Herbert F, 1961, Ag 28,25:4
Finney, Howard, 1952, Je 23,19:5
Finney, John F, 1907, Mr 15,9:6
Finney, John M T, 1942, My 31,39:1
Finney, John M T Sr Mrs, 1950, Je 18,76:1
Finney, Lyman M, 1939, Mr 6,48:5
Finney, Oswald J, 1942, S 8,23:4
Finney, Peter B, 1948, N 30,27:4
Finney, Ronald T, 1961, O 13,22:2
Finney, William B, 1952, Ja 23,27:3
Finney, William P, 1944, Ag 13,35:3
Finney, William W, 1951, O 15,25:1
Finnie, Haldeman Mrs (I Holt), 1962, Mr 13,32:3
Finnigan, Annette (will, Jl 26,8:6), 1940, Jl 18,19:5
Finnigan, David H, 1964, Je 21,84:8
Finnigan, Edward J, 1941, D 27,19:3
Finnigan, Frederick T, 1956, Ap 7,19:3
Finnigan, Maria Mrs, 1941, Ag 24,35:2
Finnigan, Michael E, 1920, D 1,15:5
Finnin, John H, 1957, F 26,29:4
Finocchiaro, Chevalier Mrs, 1922, Ap 18,17:4
Finogenov, Yakov I, 1968, S 25,43:1
Finran, Wilbur, 1959, D 1,39:6
Finsen, Niels Prof, 1904, S 25,4:1
Finster, John, 1959, D 3,37:3
Finster, Joseph, 1945, Je 23,13:4
Finsterer, Hans, 1955, N 5,19:3
Finsterwald, Adolph, 1942, Je 3,23:5
Finsterwald, Miles, 1961, F 24,29:4
Finsterwald, Russell W, 1962, Je 14,33:5
Finsthwait, William, 1949, D 9,31:1
Finton, Louis, 1951, Mr 25,74:3
Fintz, Morris M, 1945, My 25,19:4
Finucane, Daniel J, 1955, Ap 4,29:2
Finucane, Francis J, 1949, D 12,33:4
Finucane, Peter, 1962, My 8,39:3
Finz, Samuel S Mrs, 1968, Mr 4,37:2
Fiolek, Stanley, 1958, Ja 17,25:2
Fiorato, Noe, 1948, S 25,17:5
Fioravanti, Albert, 1963, Jl 11,29:5
Fiordalisi, George S, 1943, Ja 15,17:5
Fiordalisi, John A, 1962, N 6,33:3
Fiore, Anthony R, 1944, O 22,46:3
Fiore, Autino, 1951, O 23,29:1
Fiore, Carlo, 1953, Ag 12,21:6
Fiore, Frank D, 1961, N 11,23:6
Fiore, Guiseppe, 1937, Ap 22,47:1
Fiore, Michael J, 1961, F 17,24:6
Fiore, Peter, 1955, N 30,33:1
Fiorentino, George, 1962, Jl 24,28:1
Fioretti, Frederico, 1953, Ja 10,17:1
Fiorillo, Joaquin Mrs, 1962, Mr 2,30:1
Fiorito, Angelo (will, O 9,19:3), 1954, S 30,31:5
Fiorito, Ernest, 1960, Ag 24,29:2
Fiorito, Joseph A, 1964, Ap 17,35:2
Fiorito, Louis, 1953, Ag 24,23:6
Fiory, Peter B, 1964, Ja 25,23:5
Fippinger, Henry, 1954, Je 13,89:1
Fippinger, John, 1947, Je 14,15:4
Fippinger, William F, 1957, N 25,19:4
Fique, Katherine N Mrs, 1940, F 10,15:4
Firbank, R, 1926, Je 16,25:4
Firbourg, Rene, 1963, Ja 25,11:4
Fireman, Julius C, 1925, D 12,15:5
Fireman, Peter, 1962, Ap 29,86:8
Firestone, Charles, 1945, My 4,19:4
Firestone, Clark B, 1957, Je 4,35:2
Firestone, Clark B Mrs, 1958, Mr 15,17:3
Firestone, Elmer, 1925, O 22,25:5
Firestone, Harry M, 1960, My 3,39:4
Firestone, Harvey S, 1938, F 8,21:1
Firestone, Harvey S Sr Mrs, 1954, Jl 8,23:3
Firestone, James J, 1942, O 2,25:3
Firestone, John J, 1940, Je 8,15:2
Firestone, Leonard K Mrs, 1965, Ja 11,45:4
Firestone, Raymond C Mrs (will, Ag 2,14:8), 1960, Jl 4,15:2
Firestone, Richard, 1944, S 7,23:2
Firestone, Roger S Mrs, 1943, D 2,27:5
Firestone, Russell A (will, D 18,29:2), 1951, D 13, 33:3
Firestone, Samuel R, 1968, Je 12,47:1
Firgau, Bertha, 1941, F 22,15:6
Firineschi, Ruggero, 1941, Ag 4,13:6
Firkins, Chester, 1915, Mr 2,9:5
Firkins, Neal E, 1941, Mr 28,23:3
Firman, Albert, 1955, O 9,86:2
Firman, Harry, 1958, S 23,33:4
Firmin, Albert B, 1959, Je 9,37:1
Firmin, Antenor Gen, 1911, S 20,13:6
Firmin, Arthur, 1955, My 30,25:5
Firmin, George D, 1948, Mr 2,23:5
Firminger, Walter K, 1940, F 28,22:2
Firnhaber, Emil R, 1942, F 26,19:3
Firnkoess, John E, 1958, Ja 31,21:4
Firor, Frank H Jr, 1961, Jl 24,23:2
Firor, Frank M, 1940, My 28,23:3
Firpo, Luis A (funl, Ag 9,27:4), 1960, Ag 8,21:1
Firsichbaum, Edward M, 1951, My 20,89:1
First, Mahlon E, 1947, F 11,27:4
First, Phil, 1948, My 12,27:3
Firstenberg, Fred, 1965, Ap 6,39:2
Firstenberg, Sol L, 1958, Ja 6,39:5
Firth, Alva B, 1912, Ag 16,9:5
Firth, Edward J, 1865, S 8,2:2
Firth, Eric, 1958, My 29,27:4
Firth, Frederick, 1923, O 20,15:3
Firth, John R, 1948, My 15,15:6
Firth, Lee E, 1954, N 24,23:2
Firth, Margaret K Mrs, 1950, N 22,25:4
Firth, Maurice, 1952, N 23,88:5
Firth, W Francis, 1943, Je 26,13:5
Firth, Walter F, 1951, Ap 19,31:4
Firth, William, 1957, N 12,37:3
Firth, William H, 1942, D 14,23:4
Firuski, Louis J, 1923, S 27,7:3
Fisberg, Jack, 1953, D 14,31:5
Fisch, Abraham M, 1958, Ap 15,34:1
Fisch, Anna, 1966, Mr 1,37:3
Fisch, Fred W, 1957, Ja 29,31:2
Fisch, Gustav G Dr, 1924, Ap 28,15:4
Fisch, Gustav G Mrs, 1967, F 20,37:4
Fisch, Mandel H, 1961, F 16,31:4
Fisch, Moe, 1951, Mr 24,13:4
Fisch, Simon L, 1965, F 13,21:5
Fisch, Simon Mrs, 1958, Jl 17,27:3
Fischbach, Harry Mrs, 1950, S 16,19:4
Fischbach, Howard P, 1951, Ap 24,29:3
Fischbach, Sam, 1956, N 10,19:4
Fischbein, Hyman, 1947, Mr 6,25:2
Fischbein, Louis J, 1953, N 8,88:5
Fischel, Arthur M, 1938, O 21,23:5
Fischel, Dora Mrs, 1938, Jl 31,33:3
Fischel, Ellis Mrs, 1950, Ag 11,19:3
Fischel, Ernest T, 1957, Ja 12,19:2
Fischel, Franz M, 1961, Mr 18,23:6
Fischel, Harold C, 1964, Jl 27,31:5
Fischel, Harry, 1948, Ja 2,23:3
Fischel, Hugo Mrs, 1955, F 17,27:1
Fischel, Jacob, 1939, D 20,25:4
Fischel, Karl, 1939, O 31,23:2
Fischel, Max, 1939, Mr 25,15:1
Fischel, Max I, 1937, S 5,II,6:6
Fischel, Norman F, 1956, Ap 23,27:1
Fischel, Sara G Mrs, 1948, Ag 21,15:6
Fischel, Walter, 1950, Jl 24,17:6
Fischell, Nat, 1962, N 29,37:4
Fischer, Adam E, 1937, My 7,30:3
Fischer, Adelbert H, 1922, Ap 1,15:5
Fischer, Adolph H, 1915, O 23,11:5
Fischer, Albert, 1956, Ag 1,23:5
Fischer, Albert A, 1951, Mr 3,13:2
Fischer, Albert E, 1956, D 24,13:5
Fischer, Albert J, 1962, Mr 24,25:5
Fischer, Albert V, 1951, Je 27,29:3
Fischer, Alfred, 1946, Mr 2,13:5
Fischer, Alice, 1947, Je 26,24:3
Fischer, Alois, 1944, Ap 24,19:2
Fischer, Andor, 1960, F 19,27:2
Fischer, Andrew Jr, 1960, N 14,31:3
Fischer, Anna Mrs, 1946, O 28,27:3
Fischer, Anton, 1957, O 24,33:4
Fischer, Anton O, 1962, Mr 27,37:3
Fischer, Anton O Mrs, 1960, N 6,88:2
Fischer, Arthur C, 1953, Je 23,29:3
Fischer, Arthur E, 1962, N 3,25:4
Fischer, Aug, 1940, Jl 8,17:5
Fischer, Aug Mrs, 1937, My 1,19:5
Fischer, August, 1943, Ag 27,17:3; 1947, Mr 4,25:
Fischer, Benedickt, 1903, Mr 17,9:5
Fischer, Bernard W, 1943, D 31,16:7
Fischer, Bernardo F, 1913, S 16,11:6
Fischer, Bert K, 1947, Ap 17,27:2
Fischer, Burkhardt C Sr, 1953, Jl 7,27:4
Fischer, Carl, 1923, F 16,13:5; 1954, Mr 29,19:5
Fischer, Carl T, 1952, S 22,23:4
Fischer, Carl 3d, 1942, Mr 15,42:5
Fischer, Charles, 1907, D 30,7:5
Fischer, Charles H, 1937, My 5,25:1; 1943, D 10,
Fischer, Charles H Mrs, 1943, D 23,19:4
Fischer, Charles J, 1949, My 14,13:6
Fischer, Charles L, 1948, My 18,23:3
Fischer, Charles S, 1905, N 27,9:4
Fischer, Christian G Rev, 1915, Je 11,15:6
Fischer, Clifford C, 1951, O 12,27:3
Fischer, Conrad A, 1948, N 17,27:3
Fischer, Conrad G, 1948, Je 12,15:1
Fischer, Cornelius C, 1940, D 3,25:2
Fischer, David G, 1939, Ap 23,III,6:8
Fischer, Edmund R, 1940, Jl 19,19:5
Fischer, Edward, 1938, D 31,15:2
Fischer, Edward G, 1966, Jl 19,39:2
Fischer, Edward H, 1950, F 7,27:4
Fischer, Edward J, 1959, My 8,27:1
Fischer, Edward Mrs, 1951, Ja 10,28:2
Fischer, Edwin, 1960, Ja 26,33:4
Fischer, Eli, 1939, Ja 11,19:5
Fischer, Elizabeth P G Mrs, 1940, My 30,17:4
Fischer, Emil Prof, 1919, Jl 17,13:5
Fischer, Emil S, 1945, Mr 27,19:5
Fischer, Ernest W, 1941, Jl 8,19:3
Fischer, Ernst Kuno Prof, 1907, Jl 6,7:4
Fischer, Ernst P, 1956, Jl 13,19:1
Fischer, Eugene, 1955, F 23,27:3
Fischer, Francis G, 1945, O 9,22:2
Fischer, Frank F, 1951, S 19,31:1
Fischer, Frank J, 1941, My 15,23:5; 1949, Mr 1
Fischer, Frederick, 1956, Ap 22,86:3
Fischer, Frederick A, 1941, Ja 28,19:5
Fischer, Frederick B, 1944, Ag 20,33:1
Fischer, Frederick C, 1948, Ap 23,23:2
Fischer, Frederick G (por), 1938, Ap 9,17:5
Fischer, Gabriel, 1947, O 10,25:3
Fischer, George, 1937, N 21,II,9:2; 1941, Ag 2
1947, Jl 3,21:3
Fischer, George A, 1954, My 4,29:1; 1960, My
Fischer, George L, 1948, Je 22,25:3
Fischer, George W, 1964, Ja 14,31:4
Fischer, Gottlob K, 1948, Ap 28,28:3
Fischer, Gustav T Rev, 1937, F 9,23:3
Fischer, Gustave A, 1943, Ja 10,50:2
Fischer, Gustave F, 1957, Jl 27,17:4
Fischer, Gyula, 1944, Mr 8,19:5
Fischer, H Franklin, 1943, Mr 4,19:5
Fischer, H Franklin Mrs, 1954, Je 9,31:1
Fischer, Harold, 1966, My 18,47:4
Fischer, Harry S, 1952, Je 22,68:1

Fischer, Helen F, 1953, Ap 26,85:2
Fischer, Henry, 1949, D 22,23:1; 1950, My 17,29:1; 1958, O 9,37:1
Fischer, Henry J, 1937, O 19,26:1
Fischer, Henry Mrs, 1950, Jl 13,25:4
Fischer, Henry S, 1945, S 23,46:4
Fischer, Hens, 1945, Ap 7,15:4
Fischer, Herbert G M, 1968, My 9,47:3
Fischer, Herman G, 1950, Mr 13,21:5
Fischer, Herman Mrs, 1949, D 1,31:2
Fischer, Herman W, 1952, Jl 19,15:6
Fischer, Hermann, 1942, Mr 6,22:3
Fischer, Hermann L, 1960, Mr 11,26:2
Fischer, Ida, 1956, Ja 23,25:3
Fischer, Irving C, 1962, Jl 29,61:1
Fischer, Israel F, 1940, Mr 17,48:7
Fischer, J C C Mrs, 1949, My 28,15:2
Fischer, Jack C, 1962, My 5,27:2
Fischer, John, 1938, S 8,23:1; 1947, S 11,27:3; 1958, Jl 22,27:1
Fischer, John Augustus, 1917, My 31,11:4
Fischer, John P Sr, 1944, Ap 19,23:1
Fischer, Joseph, 1901, N 26,9:5; 1938, O 16,45:2; 1948, O 19,27:2
Fischer, Joseph A, 1960, O 7,35:2
Fischer, Joseph Mrs, 1925, Ja 21,21:5; 1946, My 30, 21:2
Fischer, Juhan C C, 1951, Ag 17,18:2
Fischer, Kurt, 1950, Je 23,4:8
Fischer, Lawrence F W, 1947, Je 25,25:5
Fischer, Leo J, 1948, Je 23,27:4
Fischer, Leon, 1960, D 8,35:5
Fischer, Leonard E, 1954, F 6,19:2
Fischer, Louis, 1941, O 26,43:1; 1945, Ap 10,19:6
Fischer, Louis A, 1948, Mr 28,48:6
Fischer, Louis E, 1952, F 17,84:6
Fischer, Louis Mrs, 1940, O 2,23:5
Fischer, Luther C, 1953, Ap 30,31:5
Fischer, M Hadwin, 1938, Ag 8,13:2
Fischer, Marie, 1908, Ag 2,7:6
Fischer, Marjorie, 1961, N 3,36:1
Fischer, Martin H, 1962, Ja 21,88:7
Fischer, Mary Mrs, 1921, F 12,13:5; 1944, D 29,15:1
Fischer, Mathias J, 1965, Ag 1,76:5
Fischer, Maurice, 1965, Ag 20,29:2
Fischer, Max, 1954, My 22,15:4
Fischer, Milton H, 1956, My 19,19:5
Fischer, Morris, 1958, Jl 16,29:2
Fischer, Morris R, 1962, O 28,88:7
Fischer, Moses H, 1959, O 31,23:6
Fischer, Nathan, 1942, Je 2,24:2
Fischer, Otto, 1948, Ap 16,23:4
Fischer, Otto G, 1951, N 24,11:3
Fischer, Otto K, 1938, Mr 13,32:6
Fischer, Otto L, 1950, Ap 25,31:5
Fischer, Paul R, 1946, Ag 2,19:1
Fischer, Peter, 1952, F 14,27:3
Fischer, Philipina Mrs, 1941, Mr 10,17:2
Fischer, Raymond H, 1960, D 2,29:2
Fischer, Robert A, 1919, Ap 30,11:4
Fischer, Roy G, 1959, D 24,20:1
Fischer, Rudolph E, 1951, Ap 27,23:2
Fischer, Ruth (E Eisler), 1961, Mr 16,37:2
Fischer, T Tasso, 1945, S 19,25:4
Fischer, Theodore A, 1938, S 25,39:2
Fischer, Theodore C, 1937, N 10,25:6
Fischer, Theodore R, 1943, Ag 17,17:5
Fischer, Thomas F, 1965, F 8,25:1
Fischer, Walter E, 1962, Ag 31,21:5
Fischer, Walter S, 1946, Ap 27,17:4
Fischer, Walter S Mrs, 1965, Ap 12,35:1
Fischer, Wilhelm, 1949, N 15,25:4
Fischer, Will H, 1953, O 5,27:5
Fischer, William, 1901, Je 14,7:6
Fischer, William A, 1922, Jl 18,11:3; 1955, N 6,86:4
Fischer, William C, 1945, Mr 24,17:2
Fischer, William F, 1961, N 16,39:2
Fischer, William G, 1912, Ag 15,9:2
Fischer, William H A Mrs, 1947, Ag 14,23:4
Fischer, William J, 1950, Ap 11,31:2
Fischer, William L, 1939, D 21,26:2
Fischer, William Mrs, 1950, Jl 4,17:1
Fischerauer, Frederick, 1949, D 7,31:6
Fischetti, Charlie, 1951, Ap 12,38:6
Fischetti, Rocco, 1964, Jl 7,42:1
Fischl, Fred L, 1940, Jl 12,15:2
Fischl, Frederick, 1953, Ja 17,15:2
Fischl, Frederick H, 1943, O 31,48:5
Fischl, Ignatius, 1958, Ag 15,22:8
Fischl, Jacques R, 1957, Jl 25,23:4
Fischler, Joseph, 1950, D 1,25:3
Fischler, Peter K Rear Adm, 1950, Jl 15,13:2
Fischman, David, 1948, S 22,31:3
Fischman, Elinor L, 1950, My 16,31:1
Fischman, Isidor, 1955, Ja 23,85:3
Fischman, Murray F, 1963, My 25,25:5
Fischman, Rose J, 1941, O 20,17:3
Fischman, Samuel, 1964, Jl 24,27:3
Fischman, Sanfor, 1949, Ap 7,29:5
Fischman, Simon, 1958, N 23,88:5
Fischman, William, 1959, Ja 18,88:3
Fischmann, Egon W, 1954, Je 14,21:4
Fisdell, Louis, 1959, O 14,43:5
Fiset, Eugene, 1951, Je 9,19:4
Fish, Alfred, 1955, Jl 24,65:3
Fish, Alfred H Mrs, 1940, Ag 1,21:4
Fish, Allan H, 1944, Mr 7,17:6
Fish, Arnold, 1967, S 24,84:4
Fish, Arthur J, 1944, Ag 31,17:1
Fish, Arthur L, 1952, Je 12,33:2
Fish, Azel H, 1949, Ap 2,15:3
Fish, Benjamin, 1880, Je 23,2:7
Fish, Bernice K Mrs, 1953, Ag 28,17:2
Fish, Bert, 1943, Jl 22,19:1
Fish, Cary B, 1941, Ag 14,17:2
Fish, Charles Mrs, 1945, N 11,42:2
Fish, Edmond S, 1966, D 22,33:5
Fish, Edward S Mrs, 1960, D 12,29:3
Fish, Edwards W, 1874, Ag 23,8:1
Fish, Edwin A, 1968, Jl 13,27:1
Fish, Edwin A Mrs, 1938, Je 1,23:5
Fish, Emma W, 1945, My 30,19:1
Fish, Everett W, 1912, Mr 25,11:4
Fish, Fernando T, 1968, O 10,47:2
Fish, Fitz Maurice, 1943, O 15,19:3
Fish, Frederick S Mrs, 1946, Ap 6,17:3
Fish, Gilbert D, 1959, S 8,32:7
Fish, H Andrew, 1950, Ap 8,13:2
Fish, H C Rev, 1877, O 3,4:6
Fish, H Mrs, 1926, O 23,17:3
Fish, H Sr, 1936, Ja 16,21:1
Fish, H Whitney, 1964, Jl 18,19:6
Fish, Hamilton, 1893, S 8,8:1
Fish, Hamilton Mrs, 1960, Jl 4,15:2
Fish, Hamilton W, 1946, S 9,9:5
Fish, Harold W, 1956, Jl 20,17:2
Fish, Harry S, 1960, Ag 1,23:5
Fish, Helen D, 1953, F 7,15:4
Fish, Helen S, 1953, My 22,27:5
Fish, Henry V, 1943, S 27,19:3
Fish, Herbert H, 1948, Ap 9,23:2
Fish, Herbert H Mrs, 1938, Ag 6,13:4
Fish, Hubbard C Capt, 1968, S 29,80:6
Fish, Hyman, 1945, F 9,16:3
Fish, Irving A, 1948, Ap 24,15:4
Fish, Irving D, 1951, N 24,11:3
Fish, J F, 1939, N 14,23:4
Fish, James Dean, 1912, Mr 31,15:3
Fish, John E, 1948, Ap 1,25:3
Fish, John O, 1940, My 25,17:6
Fish, Julian L, 1954, Ap 1,31:4
Fish, Latham A, 1909, S 22,9:3
Fish, Leo Mrs, 1958, Ja 3,21:8
Fish, Leon A, 1965, Ja 30,27:6
Fish, Leon B, 1939, O 7,17:6
Fish, Leonard T, 1951, F 9,25:3
Fish, Melvin L, 1950, Jl 20,25:3
Fish, N J, 1879, My 7,5:3
Fish, Nathaniel L, 1967, S 4,21:1
Fish, Nicholas Mrs, 1908, D 12,11:1
Fish, Paul R, 1948, S 28,27:4
Fish, Paul R Mrs, 1955, Mr 26,15:5
Fish, Pierce L, 1949, My 18,27:2
Fish, Raymond, 1937, Ag 3,42:5
Fish, Richard F Mrs, 1945, Mr 7,21:1
Fish, Robert Capt, 1883, Ja 18,5:5
Fish, Robert N, 1942, O 9,22:2
Fish, Roswell O, 1952, Ja 6,93:1
Fish, Samuel C, 1941, Mr 27,23:3
Fish, Sidney Mrs, 1954, N 27,13:6
Fish, Sidney W, 1950, F 7,27:2
Fish, Sidney W Mrs, 1937, Ap 19,21:4
Fish, Sigmund, 1937, Ap 12,17:2
Fish, Stuyvesant, 1952, Je 27,23:2
Fish, Stuyvesant Jr, 1916, O 2,11:3
Fish, Stuyvesant Mrs (funl, My 29,11:4), 1915, My 27,11:5
Fish, Styvesant (funl), 1923, Ap 13,17:4
Fish, Thomas W Sr, 1946, Jl 24,27:4
Fish, W H, 1880, Jl 9,8:6
Fish, Walter G, 1947, D 22,21:4
Fish, William A, 1944, D 5,23:1
Fish, Williston, 1939, D 20,25:2
Fish, Yeontine M Mrs, 1937, Ja 29,19:4
Fishbach, Aaron Mrs, 1954, N 19,23:3
Fishbach, Alex S, 1952, Ag 12,19:5
Fishback, W M ex-Gov, 1903, F 10,9:5
Fishbeck, Robert A, 1941, D 28,28:4
Fishbeck, Royal B, 1950, Ap 24,25:3
Fishbein, Fannie Mrs, 1947, Jl 16,23:4
Fishbein, Isador, 1957, Ja 17,29:2
Fishberg, Arriga A, 1968, Mr 8,39:4
Fishberg, Arriga A Mrs, 1968, O 22,47:2
Fishberg, Charles, 1960, Mr 2,37:2
Fishberg, Isaac, 1951, F 13,31:2
Fishberg, M, 1934, Ag 31,17:4
Fishberg, Mark, 1952, Ag 20,25:3
Fishbone, Hyman, 1951, Je 17,86:1
Fishburn, Cyrus C Mrs, 1958, S 3,33:4
Fishburn, Junius, 1955, Ap 2,17:4
Fishburn, Junius P, 1954, Mr 25,29:1
Fishburn, Ross W, 1964, Ja 5,92:2
Fishburne, John W Judge, 1937, Je 27,II,6:6
Fishel, Carl M, 1964, F 3,27:4
Fishel, Carl M Mrs, 1937, Ja 13,24:4
Fishel, Edwin D, 1942, Ja 18,42:1
Fishel, Gustave, 1943, Jl 19,15:5
Fishel, Leopold H, 1913, Mr 10,9:4
Fishel, Max, 1961, Je 21,37:5
Fishel, Max Mrs, 1965, Ag 1,77:1
Fishel, Mortimer, 1939, Je 24,17:5
Fishel, Oscar W Mrs, 1950, Jl 27,25:3
Fishel, Philip, 1907, S 19,7:6
Fishel, Theodore K, 1925, O 28,25:5
Fisher, A, 1928, O 23,29:2
Fisher, A J, 1882, Jl 28,5:4
Fisher, A James Jr, 1961, Ag 13,88:3
Fisher, Albert, 1942, Mr 16,15:2; 1945, My 2,23:5
Fisher, Albert E, 1950, Je 26,27:5
Fisher, Albert H, 1948, Mr 27,13:7
Fisher, Albert K, 1948, Je 14,23:1
Fisher, Albert M, 1937, Jl 7,23:2
Fisher, Albert Mrs, 1925, Ag 19,19:7
Fisher, Alfred, 1953, F 10,27:1
Fisher, Alfred J, 1963, O 10,41:1
Fisher, Alva J, 1947, F 18,25:2
Fisher, Andrew, 1914, Jl 23,9:2
Fisher, Andrew J, 1959, Ja 31,19:1
Fisher, Anna, 1942, Mr 20,19:2
Fisher, Anthony Hubert Cardinal, 1912, Jl 31,9:5
Fisher, Arch M, 1948, D 16,29:4
Fisher, Arne, 1944, Ap 9,34:4
Fisher, Arthur E, 1955, D 14,39:4
Fisher, Arthur H, 1947, F 11,27:2
Fisher, Arthur O, 1950, My 5,21:2
Fisher, Benjamin, 1925, Ja 26,17:3
Fisher, Benjamin F Gen, 1915, S 11,9:5
Fisher, Benjamin J, 1946, S 3,19:4
Fisher, Bernice, 1966, My 3,47:4
Fisher, C Edward, 1954, Ja 31,88:1
Fisher, C Elmer, 1943, Jl 24,13:6
Fisher, C H Dr, 1916, D 16,13:4
Fisher, C Irving Dr, 1924, Ap 27,X,8:1
Fisher, C Lloyd, 1960, Jl 1,25:1
Fisher, Carl G (will, Jl 21,21:1), 1939, Jl 16,31:3
Fisher, Carl G, 1950, Je 16,25:2
Fisher, Carl Mrs, 1963, Ag 10,17:2
Fisher, Carrie C B Mrs, 1940, Jl 6,15:2
Fisher, Cecil V Baron, 1955, My 12,29:2
Fisher, Charles, 1891, Je 12,8:1
Fisher, Charles A, 1940, Ja 6,13:2; 1948, Mr 31,25:2; 1950, Jl 31,17:3
Fisher, Charles D, 1906, N 30,1:7
Fisher, Charles E, 1945, Jl 24,23:3
Fisher, Charles E (Gene), 1955, Mr 8,27:4
Fisher, Charles F Dr, 1968, Ap 5,47:2
Fisher, Charles G, 1945, O 6,13:5
Fisher, Charles M, 1949, Ag 23,24:2
Fisher, Charles Mrs, 1946, Jl 9,21:5
Fisher, Charles T, 1963, Ag 9,23:2
Fisher, Charles T Jr, 1958, Ap 15,34:1
Fisher, Chester G, 1965, My 6,39:5
Fisher, Chester H, 1952, Jl 27,56:6
Fisher, Clara, 1940, Ag 8,21:6
Fisher, Clarence E, 1949, Mr 10,28:2
Fisher, Clarence E Mrs, 1966, Mr 14,31:2
Fisher, Clarence F, 1949, Je 27,27:3
Fisher, Clarence I, 1942, S 2,23:3
Fisher, Clarence L, 1959, Ap 16,33:4
Fisher, Clarence P, 1958, Jl 12,15:5
Fisher, Clarence S, 1941, Jl 22,19:4
Fisher, Clark, 1904, Ja 1,7:5
Fisher, Clyde (por), 1949, Ja 8,15:1
Fisher, Clyde Mrs, 1964, F 21,29:2
Fisher, Col, 1874, Ag 17,1:6
Fisher, Col Son of, 1874, Ag 17,1:6
Fisher, Cyril R, 1953, N 9,35:3
Fisher, Cyrus W Col, 1916, My 18,11:5
Fisher, D Warren, 1962, Mr 15,35:1
Fisher, Daniel C, 1961, My 24,36:5
Fisher, Daniel Dwiggins, 1925, S 18,23:5
Fisher, Daniel L, 1940, Ag 9,15:5
Fisher, David, 1942, Jl 2,21:1; 1948, D 16,29:5
Fisher, Dorothie, 1964, My 16,25:3
Fisher, Douglas B, 1963, O 6,88:7
Fisher, Dudley, 1951, Jl 11,23:3
Fisher, Dugald McK, 1964, My 27,39:2
Fisher, Dwight M, 1945, Ja 17,21:2
Fisher, E Boudinot Mrs, 1959, S 25,29:3
Fisher, E F, 1951, Jl 26,21:2
Fisher, E Lynn, 1957, Jl 6,15:3
Fisher, E Monroe, 1958, Mr 19,31:4
Fisher, Earl G, 1953, S 25,21:4
Fisher, Edgar J Dr, 1968, N 20,57:6
Fisher, Edmund D, 1939, My 18,25:5
Fisher, Edmund W, 1939, D 1,23:2
Fisher, Edna M, 1941, O 28,23:1
Fisher, Edson E, 1949, D 6,31:4
Fisher, Edward, 1940, Ja 27,13:2
Fisher, Edward A, 1947, Je 21,17:5; 1950, S 28,31:1
Fisher, Edward C, 1960, Mr 15,39:4
Fisher, Edward F, 1952, Je 11,29:3
Fisher, Edward G, 1950, Ja 26,27:5
Fisher, Edward Sr, 1942, Ag 2,38:7
Fisher, Edward V, 1947, My 6,27:4
Fisher, Edwin, 1947, Ja 29,25:1
Fisher, Edwin A, 1951, Je 17,86:1
Fisher, Edwin G, 1952, Mr 12,27:2
Fisher, Edwin L, 1962, Je 9,25:4

Fisher, Edwin N, 1940, O 29,25:2
Fisher, Elizabeth F, 1941, My 3,15:6
Fisher, Ella W Mrs, 1937, O 12,25:4
Fisher, Elmer E, 1951, Ap 10,27:1
Fisher, Emma C Mrs, 1937, S 18,19:2
Fisher, Eugene H, 1955, F 10,31:2
Fisher, Evan, 1948, S 11,15:1
Fisher, Everett H, 1964, D 2,47:2
Fisher, F B, 1883, Ja 29,5:6
Fisher, F W, 1877, Ja 21,12:6
Fisher, Ferd, 1947, Ja 26,53:4
Fisher, Frances B Mrs, 1959, Ap 23,31:4
Fisher, Frank C, 1967, D 3,84:8
Fisher, Frank C Mrs, 1962, S 30,86:8
Fisher, Frank F Mrs, 1949, Ag 15,17:3
Fisher, Frank Mrs, 1941, S 27,17:5
Fisher, Franklin L, 1953, Ag 13,25:3
Fisher, Franklin S, 1968, F 15,43:4
Fisher, Fred A, 1938, Ja 14,23:3
Fisher, Fred B Mrs, 1921, Je 11,13:4
Fisher, Fred J Mrs, 1952, Ap 16,27:5
Fisher, Fred L, 1948, Ja 27,25:2
Fisher, Frederic, 1943, D 29,17:1
Fisher, Frederic J, 1941, Jl 15,19:1
Fisher, Frederick B (por), 1938, Ap 16,13:3
Fisher, Frederick L, 1952, Ap 7,25:4
Fisher, Frederick S, 1947, Ja 21,24:3
Fisher, Frederick T, 1945, Ap 21,13:2; 1954, Jl 2,19:2
Fisher, Frederick T Mrs, 1945, S 14,23:2
Fisher, G Carl, 1954, F 24,25:2
Fisher, Galen M, 1955, Ja 3,27:4
Fisher, George, 1953, Ja 7,31:2
Fisher, George A, 1947, S 26,23:1
Fisher, George B, 1947, Ja 6,23:3; 1960, Ag 15,23:1
Fisher, George E, 1941, Ja 23,22:2; 1941, Jl 23,19:4
Fisher, George E Mrs (will), 1963, D 27,9:3
Fisher, George E Rev, 1905, Ap 5,9:6
Fisher, George F, 1947, O 31,23:4; 1958, Ja 10,23:2
Fisher, George H, 1910, F 7,9:2; 1953, My 29,25:2
Fisher, George J, 1960, Ap 22,29:1
Fisher, George J Mrs, 1943, F 4,23:3
Fisher, George K, 1940, N 29,21:3
Fisher, George M, 1940, F 26,15:4
Fisher, George O, 1943, Ja 8,20:2
Fisher, George Park, 1909, D 21,9:2
Fisher, Gilbert D, 1943, Mr 12,17:4
Fisher, Gladys, 1959, Jl 16,68:3
Fisher, Gordon, 1945, D 15,17:2
Fisher, Grace D, 1954, Ap 6,29:3
Fisher, H, 1934, Ja 20,15:1
Fisher, H D Rev, 1905, O 31,9:7
Fisher, H Gilman, 1940, Ag 13,19:5
Fisher, H Oscar, 1942, Ap 29,21:2
Fisher, Haldane S, 1953, Ap 29,29:5
Fisher, Hammond E (Ham),(will), 1956, Ja 5,8:6
Fisher, Hannah P Mrs, 1940, My 2,23:2
Fisher, Harold J, 1944, My 2,19:5
Fisher, Harry, 1915, F 24,9:6; 1942, F 28,17:6; 1957, Je 14,25:2
Fisher, Harry A, 1922, N 21,19:4; 1967, D 31,45:1
Fisher, Harry C (Bud),(will, S 16,29:1), 1954, S 8, 31:3
Fisher, Harry G, 1919, F 26,11:4
Fisher, Harry H, 1955, Ja 12,27:4
Fisher, Harry I, 1943, N 4,23:3
Fisher, Harry J, 1965, Mr 21,87:1
Fisher, Harry L, 1961, Mr 21,37:2
Fisher, Harry M, 1958, N 16,88:6
Fisher, Harry S, 1942, My 16,13:4
Fisher, Henry, 1938, My 18,21:5; 1943, S 20,21:4; 1949, Je 24,23:3
Fisher, Henry A, 1945, D 6,27:6
Fisher, Henry J, 1965, Je 26,29:4
Fisher, Henry J Mrs, 1946, D 18,29:2
Fisher, Henry M, 1939, Ap 28,25:4; 1941, Je 25,21:3
Fisher, Henry P, 1967, Ap 5,44:5
Fisher, Henry W, 1937, O 8,23:4
Fisher, Henry W Mrs, 1952, Ap 10,29:2
Fisher, Herbert, 1952, N 10,5:8; 1958, S 28,89:1
Fisher, Herbert A L, 1940, Ap 18,23:3
Fisher, Herbert F Sr, 1958, Ag 9,13:5
Fisher, Herbert P, 1941, Ag 6,17:5
Fisher, Herman E, 1943, Je 14,17:5
Fisher, Howard A, 1942, Ap 1,21:1
Fisher, Howard S Sr, 1959, Jl 12,73:2
Fisher, Howell, 1940, F 11,49:2
Fisher, Irvin H, 1948, Je 27,52:6
Fisher, Irving, 1947, Ap 30,25:1
Fisher, Irving Mrs, 1940, Ja 10,21:5
Fisher, Irving R, 1925, Ja 5,21:4
Fisher, Irwin, 1942, O 29,23:2
Fisher, Ivy C, 1948, Ap 23,23:5
Fisher, J Harding, 1961, My 6,31:6
Fisher, J Wilmer, 1951, D 14,31:2
Fisher, Jaboz F, 1937, O 12,25:2
Fisher, Jacob L Mrs, 1954, Ja 9,15:3
Fisher, Jake, 1951, S 8,17:3
Fisher, James B, 1957, Ap 7,89:1
Fisher, James B Mrs, 1953, F 24,25:3
Fisher, James H, 1951, Mr 16,31:4
Fisher, James T B, 1939, N 25,17:4
Fisher, Jane M Lady, 1955, Ja 31,19:5
Fisher, Jerome B, 1919, Je 19,13:4
Fisher, Joel E, 1966, Ja 7,27:1
Fisher, Joel E Mrs, 1942, Ap 21,23:5
Fisher, John, 1882, Mr 30,5:5; 1902, N 9,10:3
Fisher, John A, 1942, D 27,34:4; 1955, N 1,61:5
Fisher, John Arbutnot (por),(funl, Jl 14,9:4), 1920, Jl 11,22:1
Fisher, John C, 1921, D 19,15:5; 1944, Ap 13,19:5
Fisher, John E Mrs, 1946, Mr 20,23:4
Fisher, John F, 1944, Mr 22,19:2
Fisher, John G, 1950, Jl 10,21:6
Fisher, John L, 1940, Ja 29,15:1
Fisher, John M Dr, 1937, My 22,15:5
Fisher, John R, 1945, Ap 19,27:6; 1959, Je 2,35:1; 1964, My 28,37:3
Fisher, John R Mrs (Dorothy Canfield),(trb lr, N 14,26:5), 1958, N 10,29:4
Fisher, John S, 1940, Je 26,23:3
Fisher, John W, 1939, N 26,42:5; 1954, Ag 4,21:4; 1958, Mr 26,37:2
Fisher, John W Mrs, 1954, Je 13,88:3
Fisher, Joseph, 1952, Mr 6,31:2
Fisher, Joseph G, 1949, Ja 11,27:3
Fisher, Joseph H, 1952, Jl 22,25:4
Fisher, Joseph J Mrs, 1947, Ap 21,21:4
Fisher, Joseph K, 1938, Mr 5,17:3
Fisher, Joseph L, 1956, Jl 30,21:2
Fisher, Judson C, 1956, Ag 26,85:2
Fisher, Julius, 1963, Ap 23,37:3
Fisher, Karl W, 1946, Jl 26,21:2
Fisher, Kate Mrs, 1942, Jl 17,15:4
Fisher, Katherine A, 1958, Mr 17,29:4
Fisher, Katherine E, 1957, S 6,21:2
Fisher, Kenneth V, 1962, F 14,35:4
Fisher, Lamont H, 1941, O 11,34:8
Fisher, Lawrence P, 1961, S 4,15:3
Fisher, Leon E, 1949, Ag 8,15:2
Fisher, Lizette A (will), 1944, N 29,23:1
Fisher, Lizzie Mrs (will), 1940, Jl 2,13:3
Fisher, Lloyd, 1953, F 3,25:4
Fisher, Lloyd W, 1951, Ja 31,25:4
Fisher, Lucius G Mrs, 1910, Ag 7,II,9:4
Fisher, M M Mrs, 1946, Ag 21,27:3
Fisher, Maggie H Mrs, 1938, N 4,23:4
Fisher, Margaret, 1919, N 10,13:1; 1965, Ap 26,31:3
Fisher, Marian, 1951, My 23,35:4
Fisher, Marion N Mrs, 1966, O 30,89:3
Fisher, Mark, 1923, My 1,21:3; 1948, Ja 3,14:2
Fisher, Martin B, 1937, O 19,25:5; 1941, D 18,27:5
Fisher, Martin F Mrs, 1907, Ag 14,7:5
Fisher, Martin L, 1937, My 7,30:2
Fisher, Mary, 1938, Mr 31,23:3
Fisher, Mary C Mrs, 1940, S 15,48:1
Fisher, Mary E Mrs, 1939, Mr 25,15:5; 1941, N 6,23:3
Fisher, Mary J, 1947, O 11,17:5
Fisher, Maurice, 1954, Ag 31,21:2
Fisher, Max, 1943, O 13,23:4; 1964, S 19,27:5
Fisher, Melton, 1939, S 7,25:5
Fisher, Mendel Mrs, 1955, Je 29,29:3
Fisher, Michael, 1964, Je 11,33:5
Fisher, Michael A, 1943, Je 7,13:3
Fisher, Mickey (Meyer Fisher), 1963, Ap 17,41:2
Fisher, Millard, 1962, F 17,19:4
Fisher, Milton M, 1903, Ap 22,9:5
Fisher, Morris, 1956, D 16,86:6
Fisher, Mortimer T, 1960, Je 12,86:6
Fisher, Mulford K, 1955, F 8,27:1
Fisher, Myron I Mrs, 1945, My 20,32:4
Fisher, Myron L, 1948, Ap 24,15:1
Fisher, Nellie G Mrs, 1950, N 2,31:1
Fisher, Norah C, 1952, My 23,21:3
Fisher, Olin, 1920, N 15,15:4
Fisher, Oliver D, 1967, Ja 3,37:2
Fisher, Otis G, 1947, Ap 29,27:2
Fisher, Otto W, 1960, Ag 15,23:4
Fisher, P G, 1953, Ap 11,17:5
Fisher, P Irving Mrs, 1948, Mr 25,27:2
Fisher, Paul M Mrs, 1959, Ap 7,33:4
Fisher, Raymond F, 1952, Jl 5,15:3
Fisher, Raymond G, 1953, Ap 7,29:3
Fisher, Raymond P Mrs, 1951, S 12,31:4
Fisher, Reginald, 1947, F 22,3:3
Fisher, Richard B, 1952, F 9,13:6
Fisher, Richard Fowler, 1968, Je 14,47:1
Fisher, Robert, 1960, Ap 29,31:4
Fisher, Robert C, 1959, Mr 9,29:4; 1962, O 9,41:3
Fisher, Robert D, 1963, My 16,35:1
Fisher, Robert E, 1954, F 14,92:2
Fisher, Robert S, 1948, Ja 23,24:3
Fisher, Robert T, 1942, Jl 8,23:5
Fisher, Robert W, 1960, Jl 3,35:4
Fisher, Rolland R, 1943, F 27,14:8
Fisher, Rollin B, 1948, O 5,25:3
Fisher, Roy G Mrs, 1950, S 24,105:1
Fisher, Russell T, 1951, Ap 25,29:5
Fisher, S Curtis, 1955, S 4,56:7
Fisher, Sallie, 1950, Je 11,92:1
Fisher, Samuel Dr, 1874, Ja 19,1:7
Fisher, Samuel H, 1940, Ja 5,20:3; 1957, Je 8,19:7
Fisher, Samuel J, 1917, Ja 31,11:5; 1938, N 7,19:2
Fisher, Samuel Mrs, 1949, Mr 20,76:4
Fisher, Sara E, 1940, S 10,23:2
Fisher, Sarah Mrs, 1939, S 5,23:4
Fisher, Schuyler, 1956, F 1,31:4
Fisher, Singapore Joe, 1960, Jl 23,19:5
Fisher, Sol, 1951, O 23,29:3
Fisher, Stephen E, 1950, Jl 16,69:2
Fisher, Sydney Sir, 1921, Ap 10,22:3
Fisher, Theodore, 1945, O 8,15:5
Fisher, Theodore C, 1952, F 22,21:2
Fisher, Thomas, 1944, Mr 3,15:3; 1957, F 9,19:6
Fisher, Thomas B Sr, 1942, Jl 19,30:5
Fisher, Thomas G, 1949, Mr 16,27:4
Fisher, Thomas K, 1964, Je 12,35:3
Fisher, Thomas R, 1956, Ap 17,31:2
Fisher, Thomas Sir, 1925, F 23,17:6
Fisher, Urban P, 1947, S 17,25:2
Fisher, Vardis, 1968, Jl 11,37:1
Fisher, Victor S, 1949, Ag 26,19:2
Fisher, W Etherbert, 1939, Mr 20,17:4
Fisher, Waldo E, 1964, My 16,25:1
Fisher, Walter, 1950, My 6,15:6
Fisher, Walter H Mrs, 1955, N 15,33:3
Fisher, Walter I, 1963, N 10,86:4
Fisher, Walter J, 1938, Ja 29,15:5; 1948, Je 6,72:2
Fisher, Walter L Mrs, 1953, Ag 29,27:5
Fisher, Walter M Dr, 1919, D 30,13:3
Fisher, Walter T Mrs, 1961, Ag 14,25:1
Fisher, Wamda Mrs, 1923, Mr 31,13:4
Fisher, Warren, 1948, S 27,23:2
Fisher, William, 1953, Ap 14,27:3; 1959, S 19,23:5; 1962, My 2,37:1
Fisher, William A, 1944, Ag 2,15:3; 1948, D 20,25:2 1954, D 23,19:1
Fisher, William A Mrs, 1958, D 6,23:3
Fisher, William Adm Sir, 1937, Je 26,17:4
Fisher, William C, 1956, Ja 18,31:4
Fisher, William F, 1937, F 14,II,8:7
Fisher, William H, 1946, Ap 6,17:5
Fisher, William H Jr, 1950, Ag 5,15:5
Fisher, William J, 1948, Jl 17,15:2; 1949, S 8,29:5
Fisher, William J Mrs, 1951, Ja 9,29:3
Fisher, William K, 1939, D 30,15:3
Fisher, William L, 1956, Mr 15,31:2
Fisher, William M, 1950, S 21,31:4
Fisher, William P, 1938, S 15,25:4; 1957, Jl 14,73:1
Fisher, William P Sr, 1941, Ap 3,23:2
Fisher, William T, 1948, Ag 21,15:2
Fisher, William W Mrs, 1944, D 30,11:4; 1961, N 2 39:4
Fisher, Willis, 1944, O 12,27:3
Fisher, Willis G, 1948, Mr 27,13:6
Fisher, Winifred, 1967, O 26,47:3
Fisher, Winona Mrs, 1958, O 16,37:2
Fisher, Zenia Mrs, 1942, N 2,21:2
Fisher-Smith, Lady, 1938, Ag 27,13:5
Fishkin, Abraham, 1951, D 25,31:3
Fishkin, Joseph, 1963, N 18,33:3
Fishkind, David, 1954, S 29,31:2
Fishkind, Henry H, 1942, Ag 8,11:6
Fishkind, Joseph S, 1949, Ag 19,17:5
Fishkind, Julius, 1955, Jl 15,21:2
Fishler, Benett H Mrs, 1960, D 22,26:3
Fishler, Franklin, 1943, N 23,26:3
Fishley, William Henry Rev, 1905, Je 8,9:6
Fishman, Abraham, 1948, F 21,13:1
Fishman, Carl, 1956, My 21,25:2
Fishman, David, 1949, N 23,29:5
Fishman, Henoch, 1965, D 8,47:2
Fishman, I Frank, 1962, Ja 4,33:3
Fishman, Jacob, 1946, D 22,41:1
Fishman, Louis, 1952, Mr 11,27:4
Fishman, M H Mrs, 1965, Jl 13,33:2
Fishman, Mary P, 1956, Je 16,19:5
Fishman, Milton J, 1961, Ag 26,17:5
Fishman, Samuel, 1948, F 13,21:3; 1959, Mr 7,21:
Fishman, Samuel B Mrs, 1958, Ap 24,31:4
Fishman, Simon, 1956, My 21,25:2
Fishman, Solomon C, 1966, D 30,25:3
Fishman, William G, 1966, S 3,23:4
Fishon, Irving J, 1962, Jl 5,25:4
Fishpaugh, Jacob A, 1943, Jl 5,15:4
Fishwick, Dwight B, 1956, Mr 7,33:4
Fishwick, Edward T, 1942, Mr 17,21:5
Fishwick, Edward T Mrs, 1944, Jl 8,11:6
Fishwick, John, 1942, S 11,21:4
Fishzohn, Samuel S, 1964, Ag 29,21:5
Fisk, Albert J, 1952, Mr 17,21:6
Fisk, Alexander, 1921, Ag 7,22:4
Fisk, Arthur A, 1947, My 15,25:4
Fisk, Arthur G, 1938, F 26,15:3
Fisk, Bradley, 1962, F 10,23:4
Fisk, C B, 1890, Jl 10,5:4
Fisk, Charles, 1964, O 30,37:1
Fisk, Charles J, 1922, N 28,21:5
Fisk, Charles Wilbur, 1923, O 22,19:4
Fisk, Charles William, 1925, Je 6,15:5
Fisk, Clinton B Mrs, 1912, Ja 3,13:5
Fisk, D W Capt, 1903, Je 10,9:6
Fisk, David S, 1956, Jl 21,15:3
Fisk, Dode, 1941, Ja 1,29:3
Fisk, E L, 1931, Jl 7,23:1
Fisk, Ernest, 1965, Jl 10,25:1
Fisk, F W Prof, 1901, Jl 5,5:7
Fisk, Ford B, 1946, Mr 23,13:3
Fisk, Fred F, 1950, Ap 12,27:3
Fisk, George, 1938, Ja 29,15:4

Fisk, Harry G, 1945, D 1,23:4
Fisk, Harvey E, 1944, O 9,23:3
Fisk, Harvey E Jr, 1951, Ap 3,27:3
Fisk, Harvey E Mrs, 1941, F 5,19:2
Fisk, Herbert W, 1954, My 23,89:3
Fisk, Ira T, 1942, N 24,25:2
Fisk, J Col, 1884, My 24,4:7
Fisk, Jacob C, 1958, Ap 29,29:3
Fisk, James Jr, 1872, Ja 7,1:1
Fisk, John L, 1945, O 30,19:1
Fisk, Kerby H, 1962, Jl 3,23:3
Fisk, Louisa H Mrs, 1955, Mr 21,25:1
Fisk, Louisa Mrs, 1905, Ap 4,11:1
Fisk, Mary C Mrs, 1937, F 10,23:2
Fisk, Mary L, 1962, Jl 30,23:3
Fisk, Miles Rev, 1904, Ja 3,9:5
Fisk, Nelson W, 1923, O 3,15:3
Fisk, Otis H, 1944, Ja 12,23:1
Fisk, Paul R, 1950, F 15,27:5
Fisk, Pliny, 1910, S 8,9:5; 1939, Mr 31,21:1
Fisk, Pliny H, 1948, Ag 18,25:1
Fisk, Pliny Mrs, 1949, Ap 6,29:4
Fisk, Richmond Rev Dr, 1916, Ja 30,17:4
Fisk, Sewall, 1868, Ag 16,5:6
Fisk, W C Col, 1927, Je 17,23:3
Fisk, Walter, 1949, Je 8,29:3
Fiske, A F C, 1931, S 8,25:1
Fiske, A Richard, 1961, Jl 2,32:8
Fiske, Abigall B, 1921, O 15,13:6
Fiske, Alexander Parkhurst, 1922, My 31,15:2
Fiske, Amos Kidder, 1921, S 22,17:5
Fiske, Annette, 1953, Ja 25,85:1
Fiske, Augustus H, 1945, Jl 29,40:4
Fiske, Bradley A, 1942, Ap 7,21:1
Fiske, Burton C, 1942, D 13,74:2
Fiske, Charles, 1876, F 2,4:6
Fiske, Charles Bishop (will, Mr 3,15:4), 1942, Ja 9, 21:1
Fiske, Charles H, 1945, Ja 7,38:3
Fiske, Charles J Mrs, 1937, N 26,21:4
Fiske, Charles P, 1968, Ag 10,27:6
Fiske, Charles P Mrs, 1964, Je 15,29:1
Fiske, Clinton B, 1909, N 29,9:6
Fiske, D Robertson, 1951, S 25,29:2
Fiske, Daniel Ed, 1904, Ja 2,9:4
Fiske, Delancey W, 1948, Mr 9,23:4
Fiske, Dwight, 1959, N 26,37:6
Fiske, E W, 1928, My 31,23:1
Fiske, Edwin H, 1948, Je 17,25:3
Fiske, Edwin W Mrs, 1947, Mr 12,25:4
Fiske, Endicott, 1961, Mr 31,27:1
Fiske, Franklin, 1955, Je 24,21:2
Fiske, G Whitney, 1946, S 27,23:3
Fiske, George, 1953, Ap 9,27:1
Fiske, George F Sr, 1943, O 19,19:1
Fiske, George W, 1945, O 11,23:1
Fiske, H, 1929, Mr 4,1:4
Fiske, Harold C, 1942, Ja 9,21:5
Fiske, Harrison G, 1942, S 4,23:1
Fiske, Henry A, 1949, Jl 26,27:2
Fiske, Henry G, 1942, O 21,17:5
Fiske, Horace S, 1940, Je 4,23:3
iske, Jessie G, 1966, N 16,47:5
iske, John W, 1945, S 18,23:4
iske, Jonathan P B, 1946, N 17,70:5
iske, Joseph W, 1903, O 22,9:6
iske, Laurence H, 1940, Ap 29,15:6
iske, Louis S, 1916, N 12,23:2
iske, Lyman Mrs, 1914, Ja 30,9:5
iske, M M Mrs, 1932, F 17,23:1
iske, Marione C Mrs, 1947, Ja 1,34:3
iske, Mary E Mrs, 1938, Ap 2,15:1
iske, Mary H, 1889, F 5,5:2
iske, Maysie I, 1954, Mr 12,21:2
ske, Redington, 1950, Ap 3,23:5
ske, Redington Mrs, 1960, Ja 31,94:3
ske, Robert N, 1952, Ja 15,27:2
ske, Robert T P, 1903, D 18,9:5
ske, Rodney G Mrs, 1953, Mr 18,31:4
ske, Rogers A, 1947, Ap 17,27:3
ske, Rufus F Mrs, 1950, Jl 13,25:4
ske, S Rev, 1864, My 27,8:1
ske, Stephen, 1916, Ap 28,11:6
ske, Sydney W, 1959, Ap 18,23:5
ske, Thomas S, 1944, Ja 15,13:4
ske, W M L, 1940, O 6,49:2
ske, Warren R, 1967, N 4,33:1
ske, William M L Dr, 1904, D 22,9:4
ske, William Mrs, 1941, Ap 30,19:3
ske, William S F, 1950, Mr 15,29:3
ken, Thomas A, 1950, D 5,31:4
ler, Charles F, 1948, Ap 14,28:3
ler, Harry C, 1942, F 21,19:4
ler, John, 1941, D 23,21:3
sell, Henry G Mrs, 1953, O 12,27:6
son, Henry H Dr, 1914, Mr 30,9:4
ter, Carl H, 1966, O 26,47:1
ter, Paul, 1950, Ap 12,27:3
tere, Charles Mrs, 1947, S 13,11:4
tere, Joseph, 1943, S 20,21:4
tere, Ralph W, 1940, Ja 31,19:5
tere, Robert V, 1949, S 29,29:3
z, Marek, 1963, N 5,31:3

Fitch, A P, 1926, My 22,17:5
Fitch, Abigail H, 1938, S 17,17:4
Fitch, Adelaide L Mrs, 1940, D 25,27:1
Fitch, Albert, 1960, F 14,82:7
Fitch, Albert P, 1944, My 23,23:4
Fitch, Alfred A, 1944, S 30,13:3
Fitch, Amelia M Mrs, 1941, D 29,15:6
Fitch, Ashbel P, 1904, My 5,9:5
Fitch, Benjamin, 1883, N 8,2:5
Fitch, Benjamin F, 1956, My 3,31:1
Fitch, C E Mrs, 1876, Ap 23,12:1
Fitch, C T, 1940, Ja 14,43:3
Fitch, Charles A, 1954, O 24,89:1
Fitch, Charles Elliott, 1918, Ja 14,11:4
Fitch, Charles H, 1964, F 6,29:2
Fitch, Charles W, 1948, Jl 2,21:3; 1964, Mr 7,23:3
Fitch, Charles W Mrs, 1947, S 14,60:5
Fitch, Claude E, 1945, O 26,19:3
Fitch, Clyde, 1909, S 6,7:6
Fitch, Clyde (funl), 1909, S 28,9:4
Fitch, Clyde (est), 1910, N 19,11:3
Fitch, Com, 1875, Ap 19,2:7
Fitch, Cornelia K Mrs, 1943, My 8,15:5
Fitch, Don B, 1950, D 23,16:2
Fitch, Edgar L, 1947, N 17,22:2
Fitch, Edith O, 1937, O 20,23:3
Fitch, Edward, 1946, Ap 16,25:3
Fitch, Edward A, 1967, My 22,43:1
Fitch, Edward A Mrs, 1963, D 16,33:5
Fitch, Edward Mrs, 1940, S 13,23:3
Fitch, Edward P, 1945, O 23,17:4
Fitch, Eleanor S, 1959, Ag 18,29:3
Fitch, Eleazer T Rev, 1871, F 3,5:3
Fitch, Elizabeth R (will), 1940, My 2,26:8
Fitch, Emeline W, 1906, Je 6,9:6
Fitch, Florence M, 1959, Je 4,31:2
Fitch, Frank C, 1956, Ja 31,29:4
Fitch, Frank E, 1940, My 4,17:4
Fitch, Fred F, 1941, F 9,48:2
Fitch, Frederick W, 1951, O 2,27:1
Fitch, G Otis, 1948, D 8,31:2
Fitch, George, 1915, Ag 10,11:6; 1956, S 28,27:3
Fitch, George K, 1906, Je 19,9:6
Fitch, George Mrs, 1949, My 7,13:5
Fitch, Geraldine (Mrs G Morner), 1963, N 22,31:5
Fitch, Gilbert L, 1954, Ag 5,23:4
Fitch, Harry S, 1947, Jl 22,23:1
Fitch, Henry, 1941, Ja 26,38:2
Fitch, Henry S, 1871, My 24,1:6
Fitch, Horace W, 1947, O 26,68:7
Fitch, Iome D Mrs, 1967, My 18,47:5
Fitch, Irving, 1956, My 15,31:3
Fitch, Irving H, 1958, My 6,35:2
Fitch, J Ashley Mrs, 1940, Mr 28,23:4
Fitch, J D, 1881, Jl 21,5:4
Fitch, J W, 1867, Ag 11,5:4
Fitch, J W Gen, 1884, Ap 6,7:2
Fitch, James C, 1939, Ap 23,III,6:6
Fitch, James M, 1942, Ag 21,19:2
Fitch, John A, 1941, S 28,49:2; 1959, Je 17,35:1
Fitch, John B, 1964, Ap 16,37:2
Fitch, Joseph E, 1946, Ag 24,11:2
Fitch, Richard W, 1953, Ja 14,31:3
Fitch, Robert F, 1954, Je 5,17:4
Fitch, Roger S, 1955, S 23,26:6
Fitch, Roy A Mrs, 1946, Ap 16,25:4
Fitch, Theodore, 1923, N 17,13:4
Fitch, Thomas, 1940, Ja 28,32:4
Fitch, Thomas S P Dr, 1909, Ag 25,9:5
Fitch, Thomas W, 1915, Ap 10,11:5
Fitch, Virginia, 1948, Ag 1,56:3
Fitch, Walter, 1914, Jl 17,9:7
Fitch, Wells H, 1955, Ap 15,23:3
Fitch, William A, 1958, F 9,88:8
Fitch, William F, 1915, S 18,9:6
Fitch, William Goodwin, 1914, O 28,13:5
Fitch, William Goodwin Mrs, 1917, My 14,11:3
Fitch, William H Sr, 1945, Jl 4,13:7
Fitch, William J, 1952, F 22,21:4
Fitch, William S, 1875, F 8,5:4
Fitch, Winchester, 1963, My 16,35:3
Fitch, Winchester Mrs, 1941, Ap 30,19:2
Fitchard, Ella M P Mrs, 1942, Je 18,21:2
Fitchen, J Frederick, 1943, Ag 17,17:4
Fitchett, Annie, 1952, N 28,25:3
Fitchett, George H, 1941, My 17,15:3
Fitchett, William A R, 1952, Ag 6,21:4
Fitchie, Robert G, 1946, Jl 11,23:6
Fitchie, Thomas, 1905, S 1,9:6
Fitchner, Harry G, 1938, Ja 5,21:2
Fite, Alonzo S, 1950, O 19,31:4
Fite, Campbell Colwell Dr, 1907, N 10,9:5
Fite, Emerson D, 1953, My 19,29:2
Fite, S M, 1875, O 24,2:7
Fite, Warner, 1955, Je 24,19:1
Fite, William B, 1952, Mr 3,21:5
Fitelberg, Grzegorz, 1953, Je 25,27:2
Fitelberg, Jerzy, 1951, Ap 27,23:2
Fitemeyer, John, 1904, F 18,9:5
Fithian, Benjamin F, 1947, N 7,23:3
Fithian, Edwin Adm, 1908, Ag 30,9:5
Fithian, F J, 1884, Ag 5,5:5
Fithian, George W, 1948, Ag 10,21:2; 1953, Ag 7,19:5

Fithian, Henry H, 1946, Mr 16,13:6
Fithian, Richard B, 1907, Ap 19,9:5
Fitkin, A E, 1933, Mr 19,33:3
Fitkin, A E Mrs, 1951, O 20,15:5
Fitkin, Ralph M, 1962, Jl 18,29:4
Fitler, Edwin H, 1945, S 30,46:6
Fitler, Edwin H 3d Mrs, 1958, N 6,37:5
Fitler, Jane A Mrs, 1942, N 22,52:5
Fitler, Lester D S, 1946, Jl 26,21:1
Fitler, N Myers Mrs (Mary B), 1966, My 17,47:1
Fits Emons, Macy B, 1949, F 17,23:1
Fitspatrick, Edward F Mrs, 1954, F 13,13:3
Fitt, Arthur P, 1947, My 7,31:1
Fitt, Arthur P Mrs, 1942, S 18,21:2
Fitt, Henry C, 1945, Je 6,21:3
Fitter, Euphemia M Mrs, 1956, D 24,13:4
Fitter, Frederick, 1925, Je 25,21:7
Fittin, Joseph G, 1962, Je 26,33:4
Fitts, Ada M, 1943, D 1,21:5
Fitts, Alice E, 1943, Ja 20,19:4
Fitts, Burton T Mrs, 1950, Jl 1,15:4
Fitts, David W, 1944, O 3,17:1
Fitts, Dudley, 1968, Jl 11,37:3
Fitts, Edward B Prof, 1937, S 28,23:4
Fitts, Frederic W, 1945, S 22,17:5
Fitts, George H Justice, 1909, D 18,13:4
Fitts, George R, 1945, Ja 22,17:4
Fitts, Harry W, 1940, Je 22,15:4
Fitts, James L, 1951, Ap 15,92:3
Fitts, William C, 1954, F 28,92:1
Fitts, William C Mrs, 1954, S 25,15:4
Fitts, William W, 1957, Ag 7,27:6
Fitz, Adolph, 1938, Ag 17,19:5
Fitz, Albert H, 1922, My 26,19:6
Fitz, Benjamin John Rev, 1910, Ja 2,II,13:5
Fitz, Frank E, 1938, Mr 8,19:2
Fitz, Grancel, 1963, My 14,39:4
Fitz, Herbert L Mrs, 1954, Je 26,13:5
Fitz, Justin A, 1952, D 10,35:1
Fitz, Reginald, 1953, My 28,23:5
Fitz-Gerald, Arthur S, 1959, Ja 5,29:1
Fitz Gerald, Edward F, 1939, F 16,21:2
Fitz Gerald, Francis V, 1952, N 8,17:4
Fitz-gerald, Gerald Mrs, 1960, My 4,45:1
Fitz-Gerald, James P, 1948, S 21,27:1
Fitz-Gerald, John D, 1946, Je 9,42:3
Fitz Gibbon, Herbert S, 1960, N 6,88:3
Fitz-Gibbon, John J, 1948, Je 5,15:6
Fitz-Gibbon, Michael B, 1956, D 17,31:2
Fitz Hugh, Scribner, 1949, N 2,13:2
Fitz-James, Duke of, 1906, S 26,9:4
Fitz Maurice, Richard J, 1951, Ag 1,23:5
Fitz Maurice, Richard J Mrs, 1950, Ap 16,104:4
Fitz-Randolph, Asa B, 1951, S 17,21:5
Fitz-Randolph, Corliss, 1954, N 7,88:7
Fitz Randolph, Joseph, 1873, Mr 21,5:3
Fitz-Randolph, Mary A Jane Mrs, 1923, F 22,15:4
Fitz Simmons, Edward B Mrs, 1943, Ag 21,11:5
Fitz Simmons, Edward L, 1949, O 30,86:1
Fitz Simon, Andrew R, 1939, Ja 7,15:5
Fitz-Simon, Vincent J, 1950, Ap 12,27:3
Fitz-Simon, William Mrs, 1916, F 8,11:6
Fitz Simons, Ellen T F Mrs, 1948, F 27,21:1
Fitz Simons, Paul Mrs, 1946, Mr 7,25:2
Fitzalan-Howard, Edmund B, 1947, My 19,21:2
Fitzalan-Howard, Henry (Duke of Norfolk), 1917, F 12,9:4
Fitzell, Harry J, 1944, D 27,19:1
Fitzer, Irving E, 1953, Mr 24,42:2
Fitzgerald, A Grover, 1961, D 25,23:4
Fitzgerald, Adolphus L, 1921, S 2,13:2
Fitzgerald, Agnes Mrs, 1924, Ag 19,15:4
Fitzgerald, Alice, 1962, N 11,88:4
Fitzgerald, Anthony W, 1958, F 28,21:2
Fitzgerald, Arthur M, 1957, Jl 17,27:5
Fitzgerald, Austin T Mrs, 1960, Ja 30,21:4
Fitzgerald, Barry (W J Shields),(funl, Ja 8,86:7), 1961, Ja 5,31:2
Fitzgerald, Brinsley Mrs, 1948, F 13,21:2
Fitzgerald, Cabell F, 1943, D 16,27:4
Fitzgerald, Carrol Mrs, 1962, My 31,27:3
Fitzgerald, Charles A, 1960, My 24,37:5
Fitzgerald, Charles F Dr, 1908, F 28,7:5
Fitzgerald, Charles J, 1967, Ag 27,89:1
FitzGerald, Chris J, 1948, D 19,76:1
Fitzgerald, Christopher I, 1947, N 4,25:2
FitzGerald, Christopher J Mrs, 1950, Mr 13,21:2
Fitzgerald, Cissy (Mrs C Tucker), 1941, My 11,44:5
Fitzgerald, Clara P, 1949, N 4,27:4
Fitzgerald, Cora, 1948, O 24,76:1
Fitzgerald, Cornelius E, 1960, S 5,15:5
FitzGerald, D P Mrs, 1903, Je 12,9:6
Fitzgerald, Daniel, 1943, Ag 22,40:3
Fitzgerald, David E, 1942, N 18,25:3
Fitzgerald, David J, 1956, D 31,13:1
Fitzgerald, David J Jr, 1949, N 1,27:3
Fitzgerald, David Mrs, 1955, Je 4,15:3
Fitzgerald, Denis, 1948, Ja 3,13:2
Fitzgerald, Dennis L, 1953, Mr 25,31:3
Fitzgerald, Desmond, 1941, Jl 21,15:4; 1947, Ap 10, 25:1
FitzGerald, Desmond, 1967, Jl 24,27:3
Fitzgerald, E Roy, 1957, Je 16,84:7

Fitzgerald, Edmond, 1960, Mr 8,33:2
Fitzgerald, Edmund, 1911, Jl 6,9:4; 1954, S 25,15:7
Fitzgerald, Edmund J, 1962, Mr 15,32:2
Fitzgerald, Edmund W, 1962, Jl 4,21:6
Fitzgerald, Edward, 1937, Ap 8,23:2; 1941, My 21, 23:4; 1954, O 20,29:5
Fitzgerald, Edward A Mrs, 1945, Mr 27,19:2
Fitzgerald, Edward Bp, 1907, F 22,9:5
Fitzgerald, Edward D, 1940, Jl 13,13:2
Fitzgerald, Edward J, 1948, Je 28,19:1; 1957, Ap 7,89:1
Fitzgerald, Edward J Sr, 1948, My 13,25:5
Fitzgerald, Edward L, 1950, Mr 2,27:5
Fitzgerald, Edward M C, 1912, N 12,13:5
Fitzgerald, Edward P, 1942, My 3,53:2
Fitzgerald, Edward S Msgr, 1911, Ja 31,9:5
Fitzgerald, Egbert, 1947, My 16,23:3
Fitzgerald, Elizabeth Mrs, 1942, Ja 10,15:2
Fitzgerald, Eugene J, 1954, Jl 1,25:5
Fitzgerald, F D, 1939, Mr 17,1:3
Fitzgerald, F Scott, 1940, D 23,19:1
Fitzgerald, F Scott (will), 1941, Ja 22,16:7
Fitzgerald, Francis B, 1961, Mr 23,33:3
Fitzgerald, Frank A, 1951, Mr 30,23:1
Fitzgerald, Frank T, 1907, N 26,9:5
Fitzgerald, Freeman C, 1942, My 7,19:6
Fitzgerald, Genevieve B Mrs, 1940, F 16,19:1
Fitzgerald, George Freeman, 1925, D 9,27:4
Fitzgerald, George R, 1953, Je 9,27:5
Fitzgerald, George T Mrs, 1948, D 6,25:5
Fitzgerald, Harold, 1948, D 9,33:4
Fitzgerald, Henry B, 1943, Ap 20,24:2
Fitzgerald, Howard H, 1944, Ja 3,22:2
Fitzgerald, J F, 1877, Ap 15,10:3
Fitzgerald, J H, 1942, Ap 25,13:1
Fitzgerald, J Henry, 1945, Je 28,19:2
Fitzgerald, J P, 1938, F 13,II,7:1
Fitzgerald, J U P, 1941, F 13,19:2
Fitzgerald, James (funl, D 21,15:4), 1922, D 18,17:5
Fitzgerald, James, 1938, Ap 29,21:2
Fitzgerald, James D, 1910, Jl 3,II,7:4
Fitzgerald, James E Sr Mrs, 1951, D 11,33:4
Fitzgerald, James F, 1946, S 12,7:2
Fitzgerald, James H, 1949, Je 18,13:4
Fitzgerald, James J, 1938, O 11,25:1; 1942, Jl 2,21:4
Fitzgerald, James M, 1939, Ag 18,19:2
Fitzgerald, James Mrs, 1967, O 6,39:2
Fitzgerald, James Newberry Bp, 1907, Ap 5,9:7
Fitzgerald, James P, 1947, Ap 4,24:3
Fitzgerald, James R, 1955, N 17,35:2
Fitzgerald, Jennie B, 1941, Ja 18,15:1
Fitzgerald, Jeremiah B, 1951, Ja 24,27:4
Fitzgerald, Jeremiah T, 1950, My 22,21:6
Fitzgerald, John, 1894, D 31,1:6; 1925, Je 13,15:5
Fitzgerald, John E, 1937, My 14,23:2; 1941, F 22,15:4
Fitzgerald, John F, 1942, Ja 17,17:1; 1943, Jl 8,19:3; 1950, O 3,32:2; 1952, Je 20,23:3
FitzGerald, John F, 1966, Ag 12,31:3
Fitzgerald, John F Dr, 1924, F 6,19:5
Fitzgerald, John F Mrs (Mary J),(funl plans, Ag 11,33:3), 1964, Ag 9,77:1
Fitzgerald, John G, 1939, My 21,III,7:3; 1940, Je 22, 15:4; 1966, Jl 14,35:5
Fitzgerald, John H, 1951, S 13,31:5; 1964, My 20,43:2
Fitzgerald, John J, 1940, Ap 26,21:3; 1941, O 8,23:4; 1942, N 2,21:4; 1945, Ag 31,17:2; 1945, O 13,15:5; 1949, F 17,23:3; 1952, Mr 6,31:1; 1952, My 14,27:1; 1952, Ag 2,15:3; 1953, Je 3,31:5
FitzGerald, John J, 1961, N 12,86:8
Fitzgerald, John J Rev, 1937, F 4,21:3
Fitzgerald, John M, 1952, Ap 2,33:5; 1955, Ap 19,31:2; 1960, F 26,27:1
Fitzgerald, John Mrs, 1943, Jl 15,21:3; 1949, Je 2,27:5; 1955, F 1,29:3
Fitzgerald, John P, 1939, Ag 22,19:4; 1947, D 4,31:4; 1948, Ap 21,27:4
Fitzgerald, John T, 1945, N 15,20:2; 1956, Ja 19,33:2
Fitzgerald, John W, 1937, S 18,19:4; 1942, N 4,23:5; 1967, Jl 18,37:3
Fitzgerald, Joseph, 1943, D 17,27:2
Fitzgerald, Joseph A, 1942, D 24,15:2
Fitzgerald, Joseph F, 1949, My 23,23:2
Fitzgerald, Joseph W, 1954, O 16,17:1
Fitzgerald, Josephine L Mrs, 1942, F 25,19:4
Fitzgerald, Julia J Mrs, 1964, F 3,27:3
Fitzgerald, Julian T, 1957, F 13,35:6
Fitzgerald, Kent, 1958, Ja 1,44:1
Fitzgerald, L R, 1881, O 12,5:6
Fitzgerald, Lawrence J, 1918, Jl 13,9:5
Fitzgerald, Leo D, 1960, Ja 30,21:1
Fitzgerald, Lillian, 1947, Jl 11,15:4
Fitzgerald, Lionel L, 1956, Ag 6,23:4
Fitzgerald, Louis Gen, 1908, O 7,9:4
Fitzgerald, M Eleanor, 1955, Mr 31,27:5
Fitzgerald, Margaret S, 1941, Mr 7,21:3
Fitzgerald, Marguerite, 1940, Ja 21,34:7
Fitzgerald, Mary J, 1950, Mr 7,27:2
Fitzgerald, Mary Mrs, 1938, Mr 2,19:5
Fitzgerald, Matthew W Sr, 1949, S 24,13:4
Fitzgerald, Maurice (Duke of Leinster), 1922, F 5, 22:3
Fitzgerald, Maurice A, 1951, Ag 26,1:2
Fitzgerald, Maurice J Mrs, 1951, O 30,29:5
FitzGerald, Maurice O, 1942, O 16,19:3
Fitzgerald, Maurice P, 1945, Ap 29,38:1
Fitzgerald, Maurice W, 1946, Ja 13,44:2
Fitzgerald, Michael, 1963, O 4,35:3
Fitzgerald, Michael D, 1938, Ap 1,23:1
Fitzgerald, Michael E, 1954, Ap 3,15:1
Fitzgerald, Michael J, 1947, Mr 22,13:5
Fitzgerald, Oscar P, 1959, Jl 12,73:1
Fitzgerald, Oscar Penn Bp, 1911, Ag 6,II,9:6
Fitzgerald, P G Sir, 1880, Ag 10,5:5
Fitzgerald, Patrick J, 1961, Ja 22,84:5
Fitzgerald, Perch H, 1925, N 26,23:6
Fitzgerald, Richard Y, 1942, Je 29,15:5
Fitzgerald, Robert, 1943, Je 20,34:7
Fitzgerald, Robert D, 1940, Ja 22,15:3
Fitzgerald, Robert E, 1941, Ja 19,40:8
Fitzgerald, Robert S, 1961, Ap 7,61:2
Fitzgerald, Robert T, 1952, F 21,27:5
Fitzgerald, Roy G, 1962, N 17,25:3
Fitzgerald, Rufus H, 1966, Ap 13,40:1
Fitzgerald, Sarah A (Mother Mary Hyacinth), 1940, D 20,25:4
Fitzgerald, Sister Mary Catherine, 1964, Ag 29,21:6
Fitzgerald, Stephen E, 1964, Mr 24,33:2
Fitzgerald, T E, 1944, Jl 26,19:6
Fitzgerald, Thomas, 1909, Mr 29,7:4; 1945, Mr 22, 23:3; 1956, Jl 27,21:2
Fitzgerald, Thomas A, 1968, S 9,47:3
Fitzgerald, Thomas A Mrs, 1957, Ja 17,29:1
Fitzgerald, Thomas F, 1920, Ja 31,11:3; 1948, Ap 8, 25:4; 1954, Ap 24,17:6
Fitzgerald, Thomas J, 1948, Ag 8,56:6
Fitzgerald, Thomas J Rev, 1923, D 1,13:3
Fitzgerald, Thomas R Mrs, 1946, Je 12,27:2
Fitzgerald, Thomas W, 1941, F 21,19:2
Fitzgerald, Thomas W Mrs, 1961, Ag 14,25:2
Fitzgerald, Timothy W, 1943, Ap 26,19:2
Fitzgerald, W Rev, 1883, N 25,2:5
Fitzgerald, Walter J, 1947, Jl 20,44:4; 1958, Ja 25,19:5
Fitzgerald, Warren A, 1938, F 9,20:2
Fitzgerald, William, 1903, N 3,7:6; 1942, Jl 21,19:4
Fitzgerald, William A, 1943, My 6,19:2; 1954, Ja 19, 25:5
Fitzgerald, William E, 1960, Ag 13,15:6
Fitzgerald, William F, 1937, N 11,25:2
Fitzgerald, William H Mrs, 1945, Ap 18,23:3; 1957, Ja 1,23:6
Fitzgerald, William J, 1944, My 29,15:5; 1947, My 7, 27:3; 1955, O 19,33:4
Fitzgerald, William P, 1938, S 24,17:5
Fitzgerald, William S, 1937, O 4,21:6
Fitzgerald, William T A, 1948, F 25,23:3
Fitzgerald, William W, 1954, Ap 22,30:4
Fitzgibbon, Gerald, 1909, O 15,11:4
Fitzgibbon, Gerald M P, 1955, Ja 16,93:3
FitzGibbon, James M, 1963, S 20,33:4
Fitzgibbon, Jessie S Mrs, 1941, S 26,23:1
Fitzgibbon, John C, 1946, O 28,27:3
Fitzgibbon, Marion R, 1949, Jl 7,25:3
Fitzgibbon, Mary Irene Sister, 1896, Ag 15,3:3
Fitzgibbon, Maurice, 1949, O 11,31:1
FitzGibbon, Richard E, 1962, Ap 16,29:6
Fitzgibbon, Stephen E, 1954, Ja 19,25:2
FitzGibbon, Thomas O, 1963, O 16,45:3
FitzGibbon, William, 1963, D 6,35:4
Fitzgibbons, John, 1941, Ag 6,17:3
Fitzgibbons, John J, 1966, S 2,31:3
Fitzgibbons, Joseph F, 1943, Jl 17,13:5
Fitzgibbons, Maurice Sr, 1938, F 17,21:4
Fitzgibbons, Thomas B Sr, 1952, Ap 11,23:2
Fitzgibbons, William T, 1954, Ap 24,17:4
Fitzhall, Edward, 1873, N 15,2:6
Fitzharris, Peter J, 1947, My 29,21:5
Fitzharris, Thomas J, 1950, D 12,33:4
Fitzhenry, Daniel, 1944, Ap 19,23:4
Fitzhenry, William, 1952, Mr 15,13:4
Fitzherbert, William, 1920, Ja 17,11:4
Fitzhugh, E C, 1883, D 5,3:6
Fitzhugh, Guston T, 1940, Ja 17,21:2
Fitzhugh, Marion E, 1966, S 23,37:4
Fitzhugh, Percy K, 1950, Jl 7,20:2
Fitzhugh, William B, 1944, D 20,23:2
Fitzhugh, William W, 1966, Ja 30,84:2
Fitzhugh, William W Mrs, 1939, S 19,26:2
Fitziu, Anna, 1967, Ap 22,31:2
Fitzmaurice, Charles B, 1914, S 30,9:5
FitzMaurice, Edmond J, 1962, Jl 25,33:4
Fitzmaurice, George, 1940, Je 14,21:2
Fitzmaurice, James, 1965, S 27,3:5
Fitzmaurice, John H, 1952, Ap 3,36:3
Fitzmaurice, Michael T, 1967, S 2,22:7
Fitzmaurice, Reginald D, 1939, F 22,21:3
Fitzmaurice, Robert M, 1938, Ja 21,19:5
Fitzmaurice-Kely, James, 1923, D 1,13:4
Fitzmorris, Charles C, 1948, Ag 20,17:1
Fitzpatrick, Adolphus Maj, 1907, Ag 10,7:5
Fitzpatrick, Aloysius, 1946, Jl 30,23:2
Fitzpatrick, Aloysius L, 1956, S 14,23:4
Fitzpatrick, Aloysius L Mrs, 1952, Ap 25,23:5
Fitzpatrick, Basil P, 1961, S 13,45:4
Fitzpatrick, Benjamin M, 1940, Jl 29,13:3
Fitzpatrick, Benjamin S L, 1956, F 3,23:1
Fitzpatrick, Bishop, 1866, F 14,5:1
Fitzpatrick, Bridget Mrs, 1945, S 13,23:4
Fitzpatrick, Charles, 1942, Je 18,21:3; 1951, Jl 29,69:3
Fitzpatrick, Charles H, 1945, S 5,23:1
Fitzpatrick, Charles Mrs, 1949, O 31,25:2
Fitzpatrick, Clara C Mrs, 1938, N 26,15:3
Fitzpatrick, Claud S, 1942, My 15,19:5
Fitzpatrick, Cornelius C, 1949, Ag 24,25:4
Fitzpatrick, D F, 1954, Ag 27,21:6
Fitzpatrick, Daniel J, 1950, N 4,17:3; 1960, Je 30,29:2
Fitzpatrick, Daniel L Sr, 1955, N 19,19:4
Fitzpatrick, Dominick, 1944, Ja 20,19:4
Fitzpatrick, Edward A, 1960, S 14,43:3
Fitzpatrick, Edward F, 1947, Ag 20,21:3; 1954, F 21, 68:3
Fitzpatrick, Edward J, 1948, F 26,23:3
Fitzpatrick, Edward J Mrs, 1955, F 4,21:2
Fitzpatrick, Edward T, 1906, My 6,1:5
Fitzpatrick, Ella Mrs, 1937, My 25,28:1
Fitzpatrick, Eugene, 1942, Mr 28,17:4
Fitzpatrick, F F, 1927, N 18,23:4
Fitzpatrick, F Stuart, 1956, Mr 3,19:4
Fitzpatrick, Fenton J, 1954, Mr 12,21:2
Fitzpatrick, Francis J, 1953, Mr 6,23:1
Fitzpatrick, Francis J Mrs, 1953, N 22,88:1
Fitzpatrick, Frank J, 1968, S 17,47:3
Fitzpatrick, Frank R, 1959, O 3,19:5
Fitzpatrick, G A, 1962, D 29,4:6
Fitzpatrick, Geoffrey H J, 1939, Mr 15,23:2
Fitzpatrick, George A, 1941, Ap 29,19:6
Fitzpatrick, George I, 1941, My 6,21:3
Fitzpatrick, George J, 1948, S 19,76:5
Fitzpatrick, George L (por), 1941, Ap 27,39:1
Fitzpatrick, Henry P, 1941, My 15,23:4
Fitzpatrick, Herbert, 1962, Jl 7,17:1
Fitzpatrick, Howard, 1942, F 26,19:4; 1964, Ap 4,27:
Fitzpatrick, Irving, 1948, O 29,25:3
Fitzpatrick, Irving Mrs, 1959, Je 6,21:5
Fitzpatrick, J C, 1942, Ja 28,19:3
Fitzpatrick, James, 1943, Mr 17,21:2
Fitzpatrick, James B O, 1964, F 6,29:4
Fitzpatrick, James E, 1937, D 22,25:5; 1939, My 29, 15:5
Fitzpatrick, James F, 1942, Ap 25,13:3
Fitzpatrick, James F Sr, 1943, O 27,23:3
Fitzpatrick, James M, 1941, Jl 16,17:5; 1947, Ap 16 25:5
Fitzpatrick, James M (por), 1949, Ap 11,25:6
Fitzpatrick, Jeremiah (will), 1940, N 9,19:3
Fitzpatrick, Jesse A, 1945, Je 6,21:4
Fitzpatrick, John, 1946, S 29,60:5; 1950, S 25,23:2; 1958, Ag 23,15:3
Fitzpatrick, John A, 1942, Ja 11,44:3
Fitzpatrick, John B, 1941, Ap 22,21:2
Fitzpatrick, John E, 1961, F 9,31:1
Fitzpatrick, John F, 1960, S 12,29:6
Fitzpatrick, John H, 1946, D 31,18:2; 1952, Ag 25,
Fitzpatrick, John I, 1948, S 25,17:2
Fitzpatrick, John J, 1943, S 1,19:6; 1948, D 14,29:3 1953, My 5,29:4; 1960, S 15,37:2; 1963, Ap 23,37
Fitzpatrick, John M, 1938, Ag 2,19:5
Fitzpatrick, John S, 1962, Je 13,41:4
Fitzpatrick, Joseph A, 1964, Jl 22,33:2
Fitzpatrick, Joseph E, 1939, Ag 1,19:2; 1942, N 19
Fitzpatrick, Joseph F, 1950, O 15,104:2
Fitzpatrick, Julia S Mrs, 1952, F 6,29:5
Fitzpatrick, Keene, 1944, My 23,23:1
Fitzpatrick, Lawrence J, 1942, N 7,15:4
Fitzpatrick, Leo F, 1937, Je 23,25:2
Fitzpatrick, Louis A, 1938, S 29,25:5
Fitzpatrick, M J, 1936, D 4,25:5
Fitzpatrick, Margaret M, 1961, Jl 30,68:4
Fitzpatrick, Martha Mrs, 1948, N 23,29:2
Fitzpatrick, Mary A, 1949, Ag 9,25:2
Fitzpatrick, Mary Mrs, 1956, F 13,27:1
Fitzpatrick, Mary R, 1961, Je 14,19:3
Fitzpatrick, Michael F, 1944, Mr 9,17:6; 1950, D 32:3
Fitzpatrick, Michael J, 1940, S 17,23:2
Fitzpatrick, Ned, 1881, F 20,7:4
Fitzpatrick, Nicholas F Jr, 1943, Ap 21,25:4
Fitzpatrick, Nora M, 1941, S 25,25:3
Fitzpatrick, O Edward, 1948, Mr 13,15:3
Fitzpatrick, P D, 1939, Jl 26,19:5
Fitzpatrick, Paul, 1962, Je 18,25:4
Fitzpatrick, Paul J, 1940, O 29,25:4
Fitzpatrick, Philip A, 1905, N 19,9:6
Fitzpatrick, Richard, 1949, Ag 27,13:6
Fitzpatrick, Richard S, 1964, S 12,25:2
Fitzpatrick, Robert G, 1967, Ag 19,25:2
Fitzpatrick, Thomas, 1940, F 13,23:4
Fitzpatrick, Thomas B, 1919, Ja 16,13:3
Fitzpatrick, Thomas F, 1953, Ap 4,13:2
Fitzpatrick, Thomas L, 1948, Je 10,25:6
Fitzpatrick, Thomas M, 1948, D 2,29:4
Fitzpatrick, Thomas Mrs, 1951, Ja 15,17:2; 1961 Je 18,89:1
Fitzpatrick, Timothy, 1953, Je 30,23:2
Fitzpatrick, W H, 1932, Ja 8,21:3
Fitzpatrick, Walter T, 1948, N 4,30:2; 1951, N 2
Fitzpatrick, William J, 1949, Ap 19,25:5; 1966, 84:6
FitzRandolph, David Berry Rev Dr, 1923, Ap 2,
Fitzrandolph, Emily C Mrs, 1937, Ja 10,II,10:6
Fitzrandolph, Robert S, 1942, Jl 20,13:2

Fitzroy, Adm, 1865, My 15,5:2
Fitzroy, Charles H (Baron Southampton), 1958, D 10,39:3
Fitzroy, Edward A, 1943, Mr 4,19:1
Fitzroy, Herbert W Sr, 1950, Mr 16,31:1
Fitzsimmons, Albert P, 1945, F 24,11:2
Fitzsimmons, Anna, 1907, D 26,7:5
Fitzsimmons, Bob Mrs, 1959, O 19,29:4
Fitzsimmons, Caroline D Mrs, 1956, Mr 26,29:2
Fitzsimmons, Charles J A, 1950, My 31,29:1
Fitzsimmons, Clyde J, 1946, Jl 30,23:3
Fitzsimmons, Cortland, 1949, Jl 27,23:1
Fitzsimmons, E Gayle, 1950, Je 25,70:2
Fitzsimmons, Edgar R, 1953, O 6,29:2
Fitzsimmons, Edwin J Mrs, 1966, Je 30,39:3
Fitzsimmons, Eugene F, 1959, O 19,29:2
Fitzsimmons, Floyd, 1949, Je 22,31:2
Fitzsimmons, Frank, 1966, Jl 5,37:1
Fitzsimmons, George, 1939, Ap 28,25:4
Fitzsimmons, J Charles, 1951, D 12,37:4
Fitzsimmons, James F, 1967, Ap 28,41:2
Fitzsimmons, James M Judge, 1904, Mr 3,9:6
Fitzsimmons, James T, 1937, S 24,21:2
Fitzsimmons, John L, 1942, Ap 3,21:5
Fitzsimmons, John S, 1964, Ap 7,32:3
Fitzsimmons, John W, 1913, O 30,9:3
Fitzsimmons, Laurence J, 1951, Mr 15,31:5
Fitzsimmons, Leslie J, 1965, Mr 16,39:1
Fitzsimmons, Lewis A, 1956, Ap 21,17:6
Fitzsimmons, Mary Mrs, 1940, O 22,23:3
Fitzsimmons, Maurice, 1941, F 28,19:1
Fitzsimmons, Michael A, 1956, D 16,87:1
Fitzsimmons, Robert (funl, O 25,15:5), 1917, O 22, 15:1
Fitzsimmons, Thomas R, 1950, Ag 7,19:5
Fitzsimmons, Thomas S, 1945, O 21,46:7
Fitzsimmons, William E, 1952, Ja 13,88:7
Fitzsimmons, William H, 1945, Jl 1,18:1; 1955, F 22, 21:5
Fitzsimmons, William W, 1941, Ap 29,19:3
Fitzsimon, Cornelius F X, 1940, Mr 5,23:5
FitzSimons, Charles S P Mrs, 1962, Je 28,31:4
Fitzsimons, Curtis, 1942, Ja 31,17:3
Fitzsimons, Edgar M, 1957, Mr 22,23:3
Fitzsimons, Hal P, 1949, Je 26,60:6
Fitzsimons, Lucinda L Mrs, 1942, Jl 1,25:3
Fitzsimons, Terence J Rev, 1968, Mr 7,43:4
Fitzsimons, Thomas Philip, 1914, N 24,13:6
Fitzsimons, Tom L, 1964, O 20,37:4
Fitzwater, Perry B, 1957, D 30,23:2
Fitzwater, Richard L, 1953, Ap 5,76:5
Fitzwilliam, Earl, 1902, F 21,9:5
Fitzwilliam, Earl of, 1943, F 16,20:2
Fitzwilliam, Earl of (E S Wentworth-Fitzwilliam), 1952, Ap 4,25:5
Fitzwilliam, James W, 1953, My 9,19:2
Fiveisky, Michael, 1956, Jl 7,13:3
Fivey, Robert E, 1939, Mr 12,III,7:1
Fix, Alvin F, 1937, Jl 19,15:4
Fix, Frank F, 1945, Ag 28,19:5
Fixell, Abraham H, 1958, Jl 23,27:5
Fixx, Calvin, 1950, Mr 4,17:5
Fizer, John R, 1947, My 28,26:2
Fizzulio, George, 1961, Ap 21,33:5
Fjeld, Erastus I, 1967, Je 27,39:4
Fjeldanger, Kristian, 1953, Ag 4,21:5
Fjellbu, Arne, 1962, O 9,41:1
Flaacke, John F, 1943, N 12,21:3
Flaacke, R Louise Mrs, 1925, Mr 19,21:3
Flaccus, Leonard G, 1942, N 6,23:5
Flaccus, Louis W, 1953, S 17,29:4
Flach, George R, 1965, Jl 16,27:3
Flachs, Adolph, 1963, Jl 3,27:1
Flack, Adelbert W J, 1954, F 17,31:4
Flack, Alonzo, 1958, Jl 2,27:1
Flack, Arthur M, 1941, Ja 26,36:2
Flack, Arthur W, 1943, Mr 18,19:2
Flack, Charles H, 1944, Ap 26,19:2
Flack, Ebenezer, 1962, N 11,88:5
Flack, Edward J Maj, 1914, Je 6,9:4
Flack, Eugene W, 1961, O 13,35:3
Flack, H Earle, 1945, F 27,19:2
Flack, Irvin J, 1938, Jl 7,19:3
Flack, John B, 1952, O 8,31:1
Flack, Joseph (funl plans, My 10,29:1), 1955, My 9, 23:1
Flack, Marjorie (Mrs W R Benet), 1958, Ag 31,56:8
Flack, Murray M, 1951, D 1,13:6
Flack, Priscilla Mrs, 1923, Mr 7,15:4
Flack, Robert W, 1960, My 1,86:8
Flack, Thomas W, 1947, Je 27,22:2
Flack, Walter, 1963, Mr 23,7:1
Flack, William D, 1955, Mr 6,88:1
Flack, William H, 1907, F 3,7:5
Fladd, Dorothea Mrs, 1939, N 15,23:4
Fladness, Severn O, 1953, My 6,31:2
Fladung, August Sr, 1953, Jl 26,69:2
Flaesch, Charles C, 1952, N 16,88:6
Flaesgarten, John, 1948, F 19,23:2
Flager, Henry M (funl, My 24,13:6), 1913, My 23, 13:4
Flagg, A C, 1873, N 26,5:5
Flagg, Alfred G, 1966, Ag 12,31:2
Flagg, Arthur S, 1949, Ap 10,78:7
Flagg, Arthur S Mrs, 1949, N 20,95:1
Flagg, Augustus, 1903, D 1,9:6
Flagg, Caroline K Mrs, 1938, F 11,7:4
Flagg, Charles Noel, 1916, N 11,9:1
Flagg, Daniel S, 1940, Je 17,15:5
Flagg, Dorothy May Mrs, 1968, Jl 20,27:4
Flagg, Edward Octavius Rev Dr, 1911, Ag 24,7:6
Flagg, Elise Mrs, 1916, Ja 20,9:4
Flagg, Elisha, 1948, Mr 11,27:3; 1948, Je 10,25:3
Flagg, Ernest, 1947, Ap 11,25:1
Flagg, Ethan, 1884, O 12,2:5
Flagg, Francis F, 1918, Mr 27,13:7
Flagg, H W, 1948, Je 10,25:2
Flagg, Henry C Mrs, 1903, D 17,9:4
Flagg, Herbert H, 1964, F 2,88:5
Flagg, Herbert J, 1965, Ap 8,39:5
Flagg, Howard W Mrs, 1940, D 7,17:1
Flagg, James M (will, Je 4,16:6), 1960, My 28,21:4
Flagg, John D Dr, 1937, Jl 20,23:5
Flagg, John F, 1919, O 18,13:4
Flagg, John Henry, 1911, My 2,11:4
Flagg, John L, 1874, My 12,5:3; 1954, O 5,27:2
Flagg, Marietta W, 1944, Ja 24,17:5
Flagg, Montague, 1915, D 25,7:6; 1924, Ap 18,19:5
Flagg, Paluel J Mrs, 1943, Ja 19,19:3
Flagg, Phoebe Maria Mrs, 1875, Ap 10,8:2
Flagg, Rufus, 1922, My 19,17:6
Flagg, Stanley G, 1953, S 16,33:4
Flagg, Stewart, 1919, Ja 5,22:4
Flagg, William H Capt, 1874, Jl 24,4:7
Flagg, William Henry, 1918, My 4,15:8
Flagg, Wilson, 1884, My 9,4:6
Flagge, Francis Henry Dr, 1913, N 10,9:4
Flagler, Clement Alexander Finley Col, 1922, My 9, 19:3
Flagler, D W Gen, 1899, Mr 30,3:4
Flagler, Elizabeth Mrs, 1937, Ja 17,II,8:6
Flagler, Harry H, 1952, Jl 1,23:1
Flagler, Harry H Mrs, 1939, D 29,15:6
Flagler, Holland Mrs, 1965, Ja 7,31:4
Flagler, Homer J, 1949, O 29,15:6
Flagler, I A Mrs, 1930, Jl 14,21:4
Flagler, Isaac V Prof, 1909, Mr 18,9:5
Flagler, John H (funl, S 13,21:4), 1922, S 9,13:3
Flagler, John Haldane Mrs (funl, De 29,18:3), 1918, D 26,11:5
Flagler, Phil D, 1941, Ja 10,20:3
Flagler, Zilpha S S Mrs, 1937, Ja 17,II,9:2
Flagstad, Kirsten (death Dec 7 reptd, ed; trb, D 18,5:2), 1962, D 12,6:2
Flagstead, Ira, 1940, Mr 14,23:5
Flahave, Hugh G, 1942, Je 17,23:2
Flaherty, Bernard (Barney Williams), 1876, Ap 26, 5:1
Flaherty, David, 1966, Mr 18,39:2
Flaherty, Dennis, 1943, Jl 23,17:6
Flaherty, Edward, 1950, F 25,17:2
Flaherty, Edward A Mrs, 1947, F 5,26:1
Flaherty, Edward C, 1948, My 29,15:7
Flaherty, Edward D, 1959, Ap 20,31:5
Flaherty, Edward J, 1944, Ja 13,21:5
Flaherty, Francis, 1939, S 3,19:1
Flaherty, Frederick H (por), 1938, S 8,24:1
Flaherty, Hubert W, 1954, Ag 18,29:2
Flaherty, Hugh, 1967, Je 27,39:1
Flaherty, James, 1959, My 27,55:5
Flaherty, James A, 1937, Ja 3,II,9:1
Flaherty, John, 1938, D 20,8:4
Flaherty, John S, 1906, S 26,1:4
Flaherty, John W, 1904, O 27,9:5
Flaherty, Martin J, 1962, Ap 2,31:4
Flaherty, Michael Edward, 1908, Mr 21,9:6
Flaherty, Michael J, 1911, Jl 23,9:5
Flaherty, Michael P, 1941, O 30,23:2
Flaherty, Patrick J, 1948, F 14,13:1
Flaherty, Robert J, 1951, Jl 24,25:3
Flaherty, Sarah (Sister Ann of Jesus), 1913, Ja 26, 17:2
Flaherty, Stephen J, 1947, O 12,76:3
Flaherty, Thomas F Mrs, 1947, Jl 15,23:2
Flaherty, Thomas G, 1943, My 17,15:5
Flaherty, Thomas P Mrs, 1945, Ag 21,13:6
Flaherty, Walter H, 1948, O 27,27:2
Flaherty, William F, 1942, Ag 18,22:3
Flaherty, William J, 1945, Je 23,13:4
Flaherty, William P, 1945, Ap 15,14:3; 1946, S 18,31:2
Flahiff, Edward W, 1954, D 8,35:1
Flahive, Francis B, 1958, Ap 1,31:6
Flaig, Charles A, 1948, S 9,27:4
Flaig, Joseph W, 1959, Je 23,33:5
Flaig, Lula, 1938, D 4,61:1
Flair, Joseph L, 1953, Ag 25,21:1
Flak, Paul P, 1958, Mr 15,17:3
Flake, Albert, 1905, Mr 19,9:4
Flake, Frederick W, 1950, Jl 30,61:1
Flake, Minna M, 1958, F 12,29:3
Flaks, Francis A, 1945, F 1,23:4
Flaks, Jack J, 1965, Ag 6,27:2
Flamand, J C Joseph, 1937, Ap 22,23:5
Flameng, Francois, 1923, Mr 2,15:5
Flameng, Leopold, 1911, S 6,9:5
Flaming, J Emerson, 1948, N 23,29:1
Flamm, George, 1939, N 28,25:5
Flamm, Louis, 1962, N 7,39:2
Flamma, Ario, 1961, Ag 10,27:2
Flamman, John W, 1941, My 17,15:5
Flammarion, Albert, 1937, Mr 16,23:5
Flammarion, Charles, 1967, Mr 30,45:1
Flammer, Charles A, 1937, Je 25,22:1
Flammer, Charles D, 1939, Ja 16,15:4
Flammer, Ernest, 1952, N 11,30:3
Flammer, George A, 1941, Jl 3,19:5
Flammer, Harold, 1939, O 23,19:4
Flammer, William J, 1947, O 11,17:4
Flammer, William J Mrs, 1960, O 28,31:2
Flanagan, Albert S, 1964, O 29,36:1
Flanagan, Anne E, 1941, S 5,22:3
Flanagan, Bud (Robt Winthrop), 1968, O 21,47:1
Flanagan, C Larkin, 1940, Ag 11,30:7
Flanagan, Catherine, 1951, Jl 21,13:6
Flanagan, Charles A, 1937, Je 27,II,6:8; 1948, S 9,27:4
Flanagan, Chris J, 1951, Ap 3,27:5
Flanagan, Edward F, 1955, Jl 12,25:5
Flanagan, Edward J (Father Flanagan), 1948, My 15,15:1
Flanagan, Edward J, 1957, Ja 14,23:5
Flanagan, Eugene, 1940, N 9,17:3
Flanagan, Eugene L, 1962, F 4,82:4
Flanagan, Francis J, 1954, Ap 28,31:5; 1957, D 11,31:1
Flanagan, Francis T, 1963, Jl 25,25:1
Flanagan, Frank J, 1942, O 22,21:5
Flanagan, George A, 1947, D 17,30:3
Flanagan, George P, 1947, N 7,23:1
Flanagan, Harriet Mrs, 1912, Ap 21,II,13:3
Flanagan, Henry E, 1966, F 27,84:5
Flanagan, Henry J, 1957, Ag 13,27:4
Flanagan, Isabella V, 1950, S 22,31:2
Flanagan, J K, 1961, Je 4,86:1
Flanagan, J R, 1884, N 26,8:2
Flanagan, James, 1939, N 6,23:4
Flanagan, James F, 1953, Ja 28,27:5
Flanagan, James G, 1965, S 9,41:4
Flanagan, James J, 1944, O 10,23:2
Flanagan, James S, 1937, Mr 29,19:2
Flanagan, James W, 1949, D 13,31:2; 1950, Jl 25,27:4
Flanagan, Jerome J Rev, 1937, Jl 4,II,7:3
Flanagan, Joanna Mrs, 1916, Je 8,13:7
Flanagan, John, 1938, Je 5,45:1; 1940, D 17,25:2; 1941, Ja 4,13:5; 1952, Mr 29,15:1
Flanagan, John F Mrs, 1949, Ja 21,21:1
Flanagan, John J, 1942, Ja 26,15:2; 1944, F 20,36:3; 1945, Ja 30,19:2; 1954, F 13,13:6; 1959, N 14,21:5
Flanagan, John J Mrs, 1949, O 27,27:4
Flanagan, John J Sr, 1962, My 3,33:1
Flanagan, John R, 1964, D 23,30:4
Flanagan, Joseph A, 1945, Ag 25,11:3
Flanagan, Joseph J Mrs, 1945, Ap 22,36:1
Flanagan, Julia A Mrs, 1940, Mr 13,23:2
Flanagan, Lawrence D, 1966, Ap 5,39:4
Flanagan, Luke, 1950, My 31,29:2
Flanagan, Malachy J, 1955, Ap 11,23:4
Flanagan, Martin F, 1941, N 13,27:4
Flanagan, Martin J, 1942, Ja 21,18:3; 1950, Jl 5,32:4
Flanagan, Mary, 1951, N 7,29:4
Flanagan, Matthew A, 1938, Ag 17,19:4
Flanagan, Oliver L, 1947, Jl 23,23:5
Flanagan, Patrick, 1939, Ja 25,21:1
Flanagan, Patrick J, 1946, Ja 13,44:4
Flanagan, Patrick W, 1955, S 21,33:4
Flanagan, Paul V, 1942, Ap 4,13:4
Flanagan, Peter, 1940, My 14,23:4
Flanagan, Richard, 1958, Ag 1,21:3
Flanagan, Thomas, 1956, N 15,35:1; 1966, Je 10,45:1
Flanagan, Thomas A, 1947, Ag 24,56:2
Flanagan, Thomas C, 1959, My 31,76:4
Flanagan, Thomas E, 1959, Je 6,21:5
Flanagan, Thomas F, 1960, Ja 16,21:5
Flanagan, Thomas H, 1944, N 3,21:4
Flanagan, Thomas J, 1950, O 5,31:3
Flanagan, Thomas Mrs, 1952, O 23,31:4
Flanagan, W L Capt, 1903, Ja 19,2:5
Flanagan, William, 1925, D 25,17:5; 1952, Ja 30,26:5
Flanagan, William E, 1941, My 20,23:5; 1949, Ag 13, 11:1; 1952, D 12,29:2
Flanagan, William F, 1939, F 22,21:5
Flanagan, William J, 1942, O 10,15:3; 1949, O 24,23:6
Flanagan, William K, 1966, Je 6,41:6
Flanagan, William O Mrs, 1957, N 25,31:4
Flanagan, William T, 1939, D 18,23:2
Flanders, Count of, 1905, N 18,9:2
Flanders, Countess of (Princess Marie of Belgium), 1912, N 27,13:5
Flanders, Donald A (death ruled suicide, Jl 24,51:2), 1958, Je 28,38:5
Flanders, Donald A Mrs, 1958, Jl 30,53:4
Flanders, Franklin A, 1952, Je 12,33:1
Flanders, Fred, 1959, Ag 28,23:4
Flanders, George L, 1939, My 26,23:2
Flanders, Ralph B, 1963, Jl 12,25:3
Flanders, Richard W, 1949, Ja 9,72:6
Flanders, Roger H Mrs, 1946, Je 8,21:2
Flanders, Walter C, 1955, Mr 6,88:8
Flanders, Walter C Mrs, 1956, Je 8,25:6
Flandin, Pierre-Etienne, 1958, Je 14,21:2
Flandorf, Walter, 1949, D 9,31:2

Flandrau, Ch E Judge, 1903, S 10,7:6
Flandrau, Charles M, 1938, Mr 31,23:3
Flandrau, J M, 1877, Ja 30,8:1
Flandreau, Ervin S, 1939, Mr 29,23:1
Flandreau, Walter H, 1954, N 16,29:5
Flanigan, C H, 1924, Mr 18,21:5
Flanigan, Clayton H, 1949, Mr 20,76:8
Flanigan, Edmund G, 1960, Ja 2,13:5
Flanigan, Edward J, 1954, My 4,29:5
Flanigan, Francis J Rev, 1937, Ag 26,21:5
Flanigan, Harris Ex-Gov, 1874, O 24,1:5
Flanigan, Howard A, 1967, Mr 31,37:1
Flanigan, James C, 1953, O 27,27:4
Flanigan, John, 1925, N 28,15:5
Flanigan, John G, 1959, Ag 21,21:4
Flanigan, Pierce, 1937, D 18,21:4
Flanley, Hugh F Mrs, 1962, Je 28,31:4
Flann, Wilson H, 1951, N 20,31:4
Flannagan, Dallas S, 1949, O 21,25:4
Flannagan, J J, 1947, F 23,53:5
Flannagan, John W, 1955, Ap 28,29:4
Flannagan, Patrick J, 1912, Je 3,9:5
Flannagan, Roy C, 1952, Ja 28,17:5
Flannagan, Roy K, 1942, Je 19,23:5
Flannelly, James J, 1967, Jl 27,35:1
Flannelly, Joseph F Rev, 1920, O 16,13:4
Flannelly, Mary C Mrs, 1941, Ja 5,44:3
Flanner, Andrew J, 1953, N 20,23:2
Flannery, Edward P, 1948, Ja 28,23:4
Flannery, Frank J, 1950, S 6,29:4
Flannery, George F, 1924, Jl 24,13:4
Flannery, Harriet R Mrs, 1940, D 17,25:2
Flannery, Howard J, 1920, D 25,7:5
Flannery, J Gordon, 1955, F 8,27:1
Flannery, J Harold, 1961, Je 6,37:3
Flannery, J Roger, 1947, D 27,13:2
Flannery, James J, 1920, Mr 9,11:5; 1962, Ap 21,20:3
Flannery, John B, 1951, O 1,23:6
Flannery, John F, 1946, Je 14,21:3
Flannery, John J, 1944, D 1,23:3
Flannery, John J Mrs, 1944, S 15,19:5
Flannery, John Mrs, 1946, My 12,44:1
Flannery, John S, 1954, F 19,27:1
Flannery, John S Mrs, 1948, N 2,25:2
Flannery, Joseph A, 1915, S 21,11:6
Flannery, Joseph F, 1950, Ap 5,31:5
Flannery, Joseph M, 1920, F 19,11:4
Flannery, Margaret M Mrs (will), 1941, D 11,30:3
Flannery, Margaret Mrs, 1952, Ja 8,27:1
Flannery, Michael H, 1955, O 22,19:6
Flannery, Michael Sr, 1949, My 27,21:2
Flannery, Owen M, 1946, F 10,40:5
Flannery, Patrick J, 1937, O 19,25:2; 1956, Ja 14,19:2
Flannery, Patrick J Mrs, 1958, Ja 21,29:2
Flannery, Thomas A, 1957, My 2,31:3
Flannery, Thomas J, 1945, O 25,21:4
Flannery, Vaughn, 1955, D 28,24:1
Flannery, Vincent K, 1966, My 5,48:1
Flannery, W E, 1958, Mr 8,17:4
Flannery, William A, 1941, O 19,44:3
Flannery, William D, 1946, F 15,25:3
Flannery, William E, 1968, Ag 18,88:6
Flannery, William E Mrs, 1956, Mr 6,31:2
Flannery, William J, 1938, Ap 21,19:2; 1944, D 16,15:5
Flannery, William J Mrs, 1958, N 16,89:1
Flannigan, Arthur H, 1948, Ap 4,60:7
Flannigan, Edward T, 1947, Mr 8,13:4
Flannigan, George C 3d, 1943, N 17,25:4
Flannigan, Katherine M (Mrs J P Knox), 1954, Ag 10,19:6
Flannigan, R C, 1928, F 18,17:5
Flannigan, William F, 1943, Ja 27,21:3
Flannigan, William T, 1947, Ag 19,23:4
Flanning, Harriet E B Mrs, 1942, Ja 27,24:4
Flansburgh, Earl A, 1943, Ag 31,17:6
Flanter, Naphtali Mrs, 1955, Ap 4,29:1
Flanymann, August Rev, 1913, Jl 16,7:7
Flarsheim, Edwin S, 1948, Jl 1,23:2
Flartey, George R, 1950, Ag 13,77:2
Flash, Edward, 1944, My 12,19:6
Flashman, Horace W, 1940, My 12,48:2
Flashner, Adolph, 1968, Jl 2,26:3
Flaster, Bernard, 1955, O 18,37:1
Flaster, Karl W, 1965, Ja 29,29:4
Flaster, Leo, 1955, O 18,37:1
Flateau, Georges, 1953, F 14,17:2
Flateau, Henry M, 1944, F 2,21:6
Flath, Harold P, 1946, Jl 16,23:3
Flather, Alice V, 1951, My 15,31:1
Flathmann, Eugene R, 1951, Jl 30,17:5
Flatley, Diarmid J, 1953, O 19,21:6
Flatley, James H, 1958, Jl 10,27:3
Flatley, Sara, 1947, N 30,76:6
Flatley, Thomas R, 1960, O 27,37:5
Flatow, Leon, 1944, F 5,15:5
Flatow, Philip, 1960, My 5,35:1
Flattau, August, 1945, S 19,25:2
Flattery, James F, 1960, Mr 23,37:1
Flatto, Arthur C, 1955, Ag 26,19:5
Flaubert, G, 1880, My 11,2:4
Flaujac, Joseph, 1959, D 14,31:4
Flavelle, Joseph W, 1939, Mr 8,21:1
Flavelle, Orrie W, 1959, Je 24,31:6
Flavia, Sister, 1942, O 23,21:4; 1949, Ja 13,23:4
Flavian, Archbishop, 1960, D 27,29:5
Flavian, Bro, 1948, N 30,27:3
Flavigny, Count, 1873, O 11,4:7
Flavigny, Marie de (Daniel Stern), 1876, Mr 9,5:3
Flavin, Donald F Mrs, 1953, Ja 24,15:1
Flavin, Martin, 1967, D 28,32:2
Flavin, P (Paddy the Painter), 1877, D 27,8:3
Flavin, Walter W, 1940, N 1,25:5
Flax, Azriel N, 1951, F 28,27:4
Flax, Jacob L, 1956, Ja 24,31:5
Flax, Louis Mrs, 1954, Je 13,88:5
Flax, Nathan, 1960, Jl 12,35:1
Flaxbaum, Charles H, 1958, Mr 21,21:3
Fleagle, Edward W Mrs, 1952, Ja 19,15:5
Fleagle, Roy K Mrs, 1953, S 24,33:3
Flechtheim, Julius, 1937, Mr 10,23:4
Fleck, Alexander Lord, 1968, Ag 7,43:2
Fleck, B Walter, 1951, N 25,86:5
Fleck, Carl W, 1955, Mr 5,17:6
Fleck, Christian H, 1947, Ag 25,17:4
Fleck, Eugene M, 1947, F 25,25:3
Fleck, Frederick A, 1961, N 10,35:2
Fleck, Frederick F, 1925, Ag 1,11:5
Fleck, Genevieve Mrs, 1951, O 11,37:1
Fleck, Harold R, 1957, D 22,40:6
Fleck, Henry T, 1937, S 7,21:5
Fleck, Howard, 1944, Ap 1,13:6
Fleck, Jesse W, 1965, N 8,35:5
Fleck, Levan R, 1956, My 15,32:6
Fleck, Paul, 1952, Je 9,1:4
Fleck, Phil H, 1937, Ag 9,20:2
Fleck, Ronald J, 1962, S 11,33:4
Flecke, C (see also O 22), 1877, O 24,8:5
Flecke, Chris, 1939, Ag 18,19:4
Fleckenstein, Henry, 1938, Ja 26,23:3
Fleckenstein, Henry A, 1947, O 28,25:3
Fleckenstein, John J, 1949, O 28,23:1
Fleckenstein, Philip J, 1964, O 7,47:2
Fleckenstine, Nathan L, 1962, Ja 12,35:2
Fleckles, Robert S, 1964, Ag 25,33:4
Fleece, Charles L, 1966, D 11,89:1
Fleer, Henry G, 1957, Ja 13,84:1
Fleer, Robert H A, 1937, Ja 8,19:1
Fleeson, John J, 1940, My 9,23:5
Fleeson, Neville, 1945, S 21,21:2
Fleet, Frank E Mrs, 1960, D 15,44:1
Fleet, William A, 1944, S 20,23:6
Fleetwood, James, 1967, Ap 16,83:2
Flegel, Benjamin F, 1946, N 15,23:4
Flegenheimer, Monroe, 1955, Ag 5,19:3
Fleig, Joseph F, 1948, Ja 21,25:2
Fleischauer, Linda, 1952, S 17,31:6
Fleischer, Abraham, 1957, F 6,25:4
Fleischer, Arthur, 1948, Ap 13,27:1
Fleischer, Benjamin W Mrs, 1942, Ja 15,19:2
Fleischer, C G, 1942, D 22,25:6
Fleischer, Charles, 1942, Jl 3,17:4
Fleischer, Gustave Mrs, 1959, N 12,35:3
Fleischer, Harvey L, 1950, Je 6,29:1
Fleischer, Henry C, 1938, D 20,25:3
Fleischer, Jacob A, 1940, Jl 20,15:4
Fleischer, Joseph, 1948, Mr 30,23:2
Fleischer, Margaret Mrs, 1940, Je 6,25:6
Fleischer, Nat Mrs, 1949, N 20,95:2
Fleischer, Nathan, 1952, My 1,29:4
Fleischer, Richard, 1949, My 9,25:2
Fleischer, Samuel (will, F 10,13:6), 1944, Ja 22,13:3
Fleischer, Samuel Mrs, 1942, Ag 19,19:1
Fleischer, Victor G, 1961, Ja 1,49:2
Fleischer, William F, 1961, Jl 9,77:1
Fleischman, Henry, 1961, Jl 7,25:2
Fleischman, Henry C, 1946, Jl 20,13:6
Fleischman, John, 1963, O 13,86:3
Fleischman, Joseph, 1938, D 14,25:5
Fleischman, Leon S, 1946, Jl 4,19:5
Fleischman, Manny, 1963, D 19,33:4
Fleischman, Samuel, 1924, My 27,21:3
Fleischman, Samuel Mrs, 1953, N 6,27:1
Fleischman, Simon, 1964, O 11,88:5
Fleischman, William, 1922, D 11,17:5
Fleischman, William Mrs, 1945, N 2,20:3
Fleischmann, Charles, 1956, Mr 21,38:3
Fleischmann, Charles R, 1958, S 30,31:3
Fleischmann, E Joseph Mrs, 1946, O 18,23:4
Fleischmann, Edwin M (cor, N 19,31:1), 1953, N 18, 31:1
Fleischmann, Emily Mrs, 1947, S 25,29:4
Fleischmann, Ernest, 1955, N 12,19:2
Fleischmann, Gus, 1950, Jl 2,25:1
Fleischmann, Gustav J, 1941, S 3,23:5
Fleischmann, Harry A, 1905, S 14,9:4
Fleischmann, Julian R, 1967, Mr 5,86:7
Fleischmann, Julius, 1925, F 9,17:4; 1968, O 24,47:4
Fleischmann, Leon, 1956, Ap 18,31:5
Fleischmann, Louis, 1904, S 26,9:7
Fleischmann, Louis Mrs, 1954, Mr 11,31:2
Fleischmann, Maurice, 1937, My 5,25:1
Fleischmann, Max C Mrs, 1960, Jl 5,31:2
Fleischmann, Paul, 1960, Mr 2,37:3
Fleischmann, Paul W, 1957, Je 28,23:5
Fleischmann, Samuel, 1956, Ja 6,24:7
Fleischmann, Udo M, 1952, Mr 3,21:1
Fleischmann, Udo M Mrs, 1962, Mr 18,86:7
Fleischmann, William N, 1945, Jl 3,13:4
Fleischner, Charles, 1960, Ap 27,37:2
Fleischner, Otto, 1939, Mr 26,III,7:2
Fleischut, Joseph F, 1952, O 28,31:3
Fleisher, A W, 1928, D 26,17:3
Fleisher, Alex, 1949, Ag 12,17:5
Fleisher, Arthur A, 1949, Jl 2,15:5
Fleisher, B W, 1946, My 1,25:3
Fleisher, Edwin A (will, Ja 18,84:5), 1959, Ja 11,88:3
Fleisher, Henry C Mrs, 1951, D 31,13:4
Fleisher, Henry H, 1949, N 15,25:2
Fleisher, Horace T, 1964, Ap 14,34:7
Fleisher, Isador Mrs, 1953, F 27,21:4
Fleisher, Louis, 1964, Ap 4,24:3
Fleisher, Nathan, 1920, N 22,15:4
Fleisher, Samuel, 1965, Je 28,29:2
Fleisher, Sidney R (por), 1949, Ag 11,24:2
Fleisher, Walter L, 1959, Ap 20,31:3
Fleisher, Walter L Mrs, 1947, F 16,57:2
Fleishhacker, Herbert Sr, 1957, Ap 3,31:2
Fleishhacker, Mortimer Sr, 1953, Jl 15,25:3
Fleishman, Alvin S, 1943, Ja 27,21:2
Fleiss, Israel, 1965, F 6,25:2
Fleissner, Christian Jr, 1950, F 24,24:2
Fleitas, Joseph, 1951, S 25,29:4
Fleitmann, Frederick T Mrs, 1954, My 22,15:5
Fleitmann, Lida H Mrs, 1939, D 25,23:5
Fleitz, Frederick W, 1916, N 25,13:4
Fleitz, Joseph E, 1943, My 28,21:2
Flelt, Clarence C, 1914, Jl 23,9:4
Flemer, Carl H Sr, 1957, N 30,21:2
Flemer, William, 1925, Ap 17,21:5
Fleming, A Brook Ex-Gov, 1923, O 14,6:2
Fleming, Adrian S, 1940, D 3,25:5
Fleming, Albert M, 1955, Je 28,27:4
Fleming, Alex (burial plans, Mr 16,33:1; funl, Mr 19,15:4), 1955, Mr 12,19:1
Fleming, Alex Mrs Lady, 1949, N 1,28:2
Fleming, Alexander, 1945, Ap 23,19:5
Fleming, Alice, 1952, D 7,89:2
Fleming, Ambrose, 1945, Ap 20,19:3
Fleming, Andrew, 1938, Je 9,23:6
Fleming, Andrew S, 1942, Ag 9,42:7
Fleming, Archibald L, 1953, My 19,29:4
Fleming, Archibald L Mrs, 1941, Mr 26,23:5
Fleming, Archie M, 1948, Ag 23,17:4
Fleming, Aristine Mrs, 1949, My 19,29:2
Fleming, Arthur G S Lt, 1917, S 7,9:4
Fleming, Arthur H, 1940, Ag 12,15:3
Fleming, Arthur P M, 1960, S 15,37:4
Fleming, Bryant F, 1946, S 22,62:5
Fleming, C E, 1904, S 27,9:5
Fleming, C Norris, 1945, Ap 16,23:1
Fleming, Charles A, 1940, O 30,23:2
Fleming, Charles L, 1953, S 16,33:4
Fleming, Clarence C Mrs, 1961, S 12,33:1
Fleming, Clarence C Sr, 1961, Ja 6,27:3
Fleming, Cornelius D, 1946, My 2,22:2
Fleming, Daniel J Mrs, 1955, N 26,19:6
Fleming, David B, 1951, Ag 11,11:5; 1956, Jl 6,21:2
Fleming, David Father, 1915, N 13,11:5
Fleming, David J, 1948, Ap 22,27:1
Fleming, David P, 1955, O 22,19:1
Fleming, Dewey L, 1955, My 19,29:3
Fleming, E L, 1950, F 18,4:2
Fleming, E Morton, 1950, S 1,21:3
Fleming, Edmond K, 1945, S 2,32:2
Fleming, Edward, 1940, My 25,9:2; 1951, Ja 4,31:4
Fleming, Edward (Bro Conrad Edw), 1951, D 17,
Fleming, Edward J, 1943, Mr 25,21:5; 1949, Ap 11,
Fleming, Edward T, 1950, My 17,29:3
Fleming, Edwin, 1923, Ag 14,15:4
Fleming, Eliza A, 1942, Ag 14,17:3
Fleming, Emma E, 1946, Ap 4,25:4
Fleming, Eric, 1966, O 1,31:4
Fleming, Erik, 1954, N 17,31:5
Fleming, Ethel C, 1937, O 18,17:2
Fleming, Eva, 1937, Mr 28,31:4
Fleming, F C, 1882, F 28,3:4
Fleming, Francis P, 1948, Je 28,19:5
Fleming, Frank, 1959, Ap 30,31:5
Fleming, Frank I, 1946, My 9,21:1
Fleming, Frederic S (funl, Je 23,17:3), 1956, Je 2 31:3
Fleming, George N, 1956, Je 2,19:3
Fleming, George W, 1953, Jl 23,23:1
Fleming, Grace S, 1951, N 4,87:1
Fleming, Grant, 1943, Ap 10,17:5
Fleming, Harold S, 1963, D 29,42:2
Fleming, Harry B, 1956, D 23,30:3
Fleming, Harvey B, 1947, O 5,71:1
Fleming, Henry C, 1960, O 13,37:1
Fleming, Henry F, 1940, F 16,19:5
Fleming, Henry S, 1938, O 20,23:3
Fleming, Howard, 1956, Ja 21,21:5
Fleming, Howard W, 1956, Mr 6,31:1
Fleming, Hugh, 1942, Ag 11,19:2
Fleming, Hugh Paul Rev, 1917, Ja 20,11:3
Fleming, Huston, 1913, Jl 19,7:4
Fleming, Ian (will, N 10,56:1), 1964, Ag 13,1:2
Fleming, J C, 1901, Je 29,9:7
Fleming, J Preston, 1957, Je 7,24:2

Fleming, J W, 1928, Ap 28,19:5
Fleming, Jackson Mrs, 1937, S 17,25:4
Fleming, James, 1966, S 1,35:3
Fleming, James A, 1952, Ja 22,29:2
Fleming, James D, 1945, O 9,22:2
Fleming, James H, 1940, Je 29,15:7
Fleming, James J, 1942, S 20,39:2; 1944, Ap 18,21:6; 1953, Jl 9,25:3
Fleming, James L, 1952, Jl 29,21:5
Fleming, James Mrs, 1946, F 23,13:5
Fleming, James Orr Mrs, 1911, My 22,11:4
Fleming, James Pressley, 1903, O 23,7:5
Fleming, James W Dr, 1922, F 8,17:4
Fleming, Joe, 1953, Je 3,31:5
Fleming, John, 1918, Ap 20,13:8; 1918, Ag 20,9:5; 1965, D 17,39:3
Fleming, John A, 1956, Ag 2,25:3
Fleming, John C, 1964, S 13,58:6
Fleming, John C Mrs, 1964, S 13,58:6
Fleming, John J, 1953, O 4,88:2; 1962, Ap 25,39:4
Fleming, John J Mrs, 1947, Ja 27,25:2
Fleming, John L, 1941, D 25,25:4
Fleming, John P, 1947, O 4,17:6
Fleming, John T, 1944, Ap 12,21:2
Fleming, John W Mrs, 1950, O 17,31:5
Fleming, Joseph V, 1951, Je 27,29:3
Fleming, Joseph W, 1967, O 3,47:4
Fleming, Kenneth L, 1940, D 24,15:4
Fleming, Lamar Jr, 1964, Jl 6,29:1
Fleming, Leo R, 1946, Ja 2,19:4
Fleming, Leonard, 1946, D 15,77:6
Fleming, Louis, 1954, Mr 2,25:2
Fleming, Luke J, 1944, Ja 25,19:1
Fleming, M A, 1880, Mr 25,3:4
Fleming, Mark L, 1947, D 8,25:3
Fleming, Mark L Mrs, 1955, Je 16,31:4
Fleming, Martin Dr, 1918, My 11,13:4
Fleming, Martin P, 1941, O 9,23:4
Fleming, Mary E, 1944, F 2,21:5; 1948, Je 3,25:2
Fleming, Matthew C, 1946, F 20,25:6
Fleming, Matthew C Mrs, 1960, O 30,86:1
Fleming, Matthew J, 1961, Ap 16,87:1; 1962, Jl 16,23:5
Fleming, O, 1938, Jl 9,28:2
Fleming, Oscar E, 1944, N 30,23:3
Fleming, Oswald A Mrs (D L Sayers), 1957, D 19, 29:5
Fleming, Phil B, 1955, O 7,25:1
Fleming, Pierce F J, 1940, Ap 20,17:6
Fleming, Richard G, 1962, Mr 29,33:1
Fleming, Robert B Mrs, 1958, F 26,27:4
Fleming, Robert Gen, 1874, My 31,6:6
Fleming, Robert I Col, 1907, S 12,7:6
Fleming, Robert M, 1956, Ag 20,21:3; 1966, Jl 3,35:1
Fleming, Robert V, 1967, N 29,40:5
Fleming, Robins, 1942, N 3,23:1
Fleming, Sanford, 1915, Jl 23,9:5
Fleming, Stephen B, 1961, D 9,27:3
Fleming, T Alfred, 1959, S 22,39:2
Fleming, Thomas, 1951, F 8,23:8
Fleming, Thomas F, 1949, N 22,29:5
Fleming, Thomas J, 1940, N 24,51:2; 1949, My 3,25:5; 1957, N 5,31:3
Fleming, Thomas Jr, 1941, D 4,25:5
Fleming, Thomas W, 1941, F 23,41:2
Fleming, Timothy G, 1958, Je 16,23:4
Fleming, Vic, 1955, O 8,19:6
Fleming, Victor (por), 1949, Ja 7,21:1
Fleming, Vivian M Mrs, 1941, O 13,17:5
Fleming, Walter A, 1961, My 8,35:1
Fleming, Walter G, 1951, N 13,29:2
Fleming, Walter M Dr, 1913, S 10,9:6
Fleming, Walter S, 1938, Ap 7,23:6; 1955, Ap 6,29:3
Fleming, Ward H, 1951, F 23,27:4
Fleming, Warren T, 1949, N 6,92:5
Fleming, William, 1907, D 29,9:5; 1954, O 2,17:2; 1963, My 6,29:4
Fleming, William A, 1906, Ja 3,9:6
Fleming, William H, 1944, Je 11,45:2
Fleming, William J, 1951, O 29,23:2
Flemings, Patrick J, 1950, S 10,92:4
Flemming, Alexander, 1867, F 17,5:5
Flemming, Claude, 1952, Mr 25,27:2
Flemming, Edward A, 1967, N 20,47:2
Flemming, Eric, 1959, Mr 3,35:6
Flemming, Harry H, 1958, Je 16,23:3
Flemming, Harry H Mrs, 1966, Mr 25,41:4
Flemming, Herbert Capt, 1915, My 9,18:4
Flemming, J Ralston Lt Col, 1937, S 27,21:1
Flemming, Jock, 1908, Jl 12,9:6
Flemming, John E, 1940, Je 14,21:3
Flemming, John J, 1948, Ap 2,24:2
Flemming, L L, 1903, Ag 28,7:6
Flemming, Robert L, 1942, F 18,19:4
Flemming, William J, 1941, F 24,15:2
Flemmings, George A, 1938, O 10,19:3
Flers, R de, 1927, Jl 31,24:3
Flesch, Berthold, 1952, D 29,19:3
Flesch, Carl, 1944, N 16,23:4
Flesch, Charles H, 1947, Ja 20,25:3
Flesch, Ella, 1957, Je 7,23:1
Flescher, Abe, 1953, O 15,33:4
Fleschner, Abraham K, 1945, F 12,19:4
Flesh, Leo M Mrs, 1962, Ag 14,32:1
Flesher, Henwood C, 1950, Mr 16,31:3
Fleshman, Arthur C Dr, 1937, F 15,17:3
Fleshner, Isador, 1948, Mr 19,24:2
Flessel, Frank, 1944, F 6,42:3
Fleta, Miguel (por), 1938, My 31,19:2
Fletcher, Aaron J, 1938, S 17,17:5
Fletcher, Albert E Mrs, 1962, Ap 12,35:1
Fletcher, Albert W, 1952, Ag 25,17:3
Fletcher, Alice Mrs, 1945, O 22,17:4
Fletcher, Allen M, 1922, My 12,19:5
Fletcher, Andrew, 1925, N 30,19:5
Fletcher, Angus, 1960, Ag 8,21:5
Fletcher, Ann (Mrs G McAdam), 1958, Jl 1,31:1
Fletcher, Art, 1950, F 7,27:5
Fletcher, Arthur, 1944, S 20,23:4; 1967, Ja 3,34:2
Fletcher, Arthur H, 1952, Ag 25,17:1
Fletcher, Arthur M, 1953, N 13,27:1
Fletcher, Austin Barclay, 1923, Jl 7,11:7
Fletcher, Benjamin H, 1949, Jl 12,27:5
Fletcher, Benjamin K, 1951, D 19,31:3
Fletcher, Bernard, 1941, Jl 30,17:1
Fletcher, C, 1880, Ap 21,4:6
Fletcher, Carmen W, 1954, S 7,25:2
Fletcher, Caroline Rebecca Prof, 1953, F 18,31:4
Fletcher, Cecil B, 1918, N 14,13:1
Fletcher, Cecil G, 1958, Ja 8,47:1
Fletcher, Charles, 1956, My 23,31:3
Fletcher, Charles B, 1946, D 19,29:6
Fletcher, Charles G, 1961, D 16,25:4
Fletcher, Charles H, 1907, My 15,9:6; 1922, Ap 11,19:4
Fletcher, Clarence C, 1962, S 4,31:5
Fletcher, Clarke F Dr, 1925, Ap 1,23:4
Fletcher, Claude B, 1947, S 18,25:4
Fletcher, Clifford J, 1961, Ja 11,47:3
Fletcher, Constance, 1938, Je 11,15:3
Fletcher, Daniel H, 1962, Jl 24,28:5
Fletcher, Duncan U Mrs, 1941, D 24,17:4
Fletcher, Edmund A, 1925, Mr 30,17:5
Fletcher, Edna, 1945, Mr 25,37:1
Fletcher, Edward, 1905, Ja 20,9:3
Fletcher, Edward G, 1948, Jl 24,15:5
Fletcher, Ellen Mrs, 1941, D 4,16:4
Fletcher, Emanuel, 1959, S 8,35:3
Fletcher, Emery A, 1946, D 8,78:5
Fletcher, Esten A (por), 1941, Mr 3,15:3
Fletcher, F F, 1928, N 29,27:3
Fletcher, Frank, 1946, Ap 23,21:5
Fletcher, Frank F Mrs, 1946, O 9,27:3
Fletcher, Frank I, 1963, Je 27,33:2
Fletcher, Frank Mrs, 1946, My 22,21:2
Fletcher, Frank Rev, 1916, Je 30,11:6
Fletcher, George H, 1940, My 28,23:3
Fletcher, Gustavus B, 1941, O 31,23:3
Fletcher, Hal J Mrs, 1938, N 6,49:2
Fletcher, Harley S, 1950, D 18,31:5
Fletcher, Harold H, 1960, S 9,30:1
Fletcher, Harry B, 1948, Ag 30,18:2
Fletcher, Harry W, 1954, Ja 17,92:8
Fletcher, Harvey Mrs, 1967, Ja 3,37:3
Fletcher, Henry (Atty), 1953, Je 7,82:4
Fletcher, Henry, 1953, Ag 27,25:5
Fletcher, Henry B Mrs (will, S 17,21:1), 1941, S 10, 23:6
Fletcher, Henry E, 1916, Mr 8,11:7
Fletcher, Henry Mrs, 1967, My 18,47:3
Fletcher, Henry P (will, Jl 17,5:1; Ag 2,66:5), 1959, Jl 11,19:3
Fletcher, Herbert H, 1941, Ja 6,15:5
Fletcher, Herbert L, 1968, O 4,47:3
Fletcher, Holman, 1939, Jl 4,13:6
Fletcher, Horace, 1919, Ja 14,11:3
Fletcher, Howard C, 1938, Ja 13,21:3
Fletcher, Howard M, 1946, Mr 18,21:4
Fletcher, Isaac Dudley, 1917, Ap 29,19:5
Fletcher, J Gilmore, 1960, D 3,23:4
Fletcher, J S, 1935, F 1,21:3
Fletcher, James M, 1941, Ja 10,19:3
Fletcher, James R Mrs, 1956, Ja 13,23:2
Fletcher, James W, 1941, N 11,23:3
Fletcher, James W Sr, 1949, Ja 23,68:8
Fletcher, Jefferson B, 1946, Ag 18,45:1
Fletcher, John, 1940, Je 12,25:3
Fletcher, John C, 1941, Ag 11,13:5
Fletcher, John D, 1947, O 6,21:2
Fletcher, John G, 1960, Je 26,72:7
Fletcher, John J, 1943, S 7,23:2
Fletcher, John L, 1965, D 7,47:3
Fletcher, John M, 1944, D 13,23:3
Fletcher, John P, 1941, My 11,45:1
Fletcher, John R B, 1950, S 9,17:3
Fletcher, Joseph E, 1924, S 29,15:2
Fletcher, Katherine Mrs, 1910, S 22,9:4
Fletcher, Lazarus Sir, 1921, Ja 10,11:5
Fletcher, Leo C, 1958, Ap 13,84:3
Fletcher, Lindsay Z, 1950, F 23,27:4
Fletcher, Marshall P Mrs, 1954, D 12,89:1
Fletcher, Mary E Mrs, 1942, My 10,42:8
Fletcher, Mary Louise Mrs, 1923, N 5,17:5
Fletcher, May Mrs, 1910, Ja 16,II,11:5
Fletcher, Montgomery Rear-Adm, 1908, F 14,7:4
Fletcher, Moses, 1945, S 16,44:3
Fletcher, Norman C Mrs (Jean B), 1965, S 14,39:3
Fletcher, Norton D L, 1958, Je 22,77:1
Fletcher, Norton D L Mrs, 1955, D 20,31:1
Fletcher, Orlin O Rev Dr, 1937, O 21,24:3
Fletcher, Orville T, 1951, Jl 14,13:5
Fletcher, Percy I, 1961, My 27,23:3
Fletcher, Peter J, 1943, Mr 20,15:5
Fletcher, Peter M, 1949, Ja 7,22:2
Fletcher, Phil K, 1955, Ja 15,13:3
Fletcher, R Leslie, 1958, Ag 12,29:4
Fletcher, Reginald A, 1956, F 24,25:2
Fletcher, Reginald T H (Lord Winster), 1961, Je 9, 33:3
Fletcher, Robert Dr, 1912, N 9,11:5
Fletcher, Robert J, 1952, Ja 3,27:4
Fletcher, Robert S, 1953, Ja 24,15:2; 1956, O 20,21:5
Fletcher, Robert V, 1960, My 17,37:1
Fletcher, Samuel, 1914, Mr 6,11:4
Fletcher, Samuel E, 1943, Je 23,21:3
Fletcher, Samuel R, 1955, Ja 17,23:2
Fletcher, Samuel R Mrs, 1945, Jl 23,19:5
Fletcher, Talmadge E, 1960, S 11,82:6
Fletcher, Tay Mrs, 1940, Mr 10,49:2
Fletcher, Theodore F, 1954, Jl 6,23:5
Fletcher, Thomas, 1954, O 15,23:2
Fletcher, W, 1883, Mr 3,5:3
Fletcher, Walter, 1956, Ap 7,19:4
Fletcher, William, 1947, Ag 26,23:4; 1952, Ja 19,15:4
Fletcher, William A Msgr, 1919, F 22,9:4
Fletcher, William B, 1957, Je 30,68:8
Fletcher, William C D Mrs, 1955, Ap 12,29:2
Fletcher, William D, 1954, Mr 6,15:2
Fletcher, William D C, 1957, Jl 22,19:5
Fletcher, William M, 1943, D 20,23:3
Fletcher, William T, 1937, Jl 23,19:6
Fletcher-Copp, Alfred E Mrs, 1945, Ja 2,19:5
Fletchner, Herman A, 1949, Ja 30,60:4
Flett, John S, 1947, Ja 29,25:4
Flettner, Anton, 1961, D 30,19:3
Fleuchaus, Benjamin J, 1954, Ap 20,29:3
Fleurant, Aram P, 1950, O 12,31:5
Fleuriau, Aime de, 1938, Ja 21,20:5
Fleury, E F Gen, 1884, D 12,6:1
Fleury, Fernando, 1903, D 23,9:6
Fleury, George Arthur, 1920, Je 3,11:5
Fleury, James A, 1945, Ag 21,21:5
Fleury, John, 1947, D 17,30:3
Fleury, Marcel, 1949, Ag 18,21:2
Fleury, Oswald T, 1951, Mr 3,13:3
Fleury, Tony Robert, 1911, D 9,13:4
Flevitsky, Georges (G Fells), 1960, My 11,39:1
Flewellin, George, 1947, F 26,25:4
Flewellin, William, 1941, Mr 5,21:2
Flewelling, Edmund T, 1952, Ja 2,25:4
Flewelling, Ralph T, 1960, Ap 2,23:5
Flewellis, Lester B, 1947, O 17,22:3
Flewwellin, William, 1942, F 21,19:5
Flexer, George A, 1948, O 18,23:5
Flexer, Jacob, 1954, F 3,23:2
Flexner, Abraham, 1959, S 22,1:5
Flexner, Abraham Mrs, 1955, Ja 13,27:5
Flexner, Bernard, 1945, My 4,19:3
Flexner, Carolin A, 1958, Ja 21,29:1
Flexner, Jennie, 1944, N 18,13:4
Flexner, Mary, 1947, Jl 22,23:6
Flexner, Simon Mrs, 1956, Ap 7,19:2
Flexner, Washington, 1943, Ja 1,23:3
Fliashnick, Bernard, 1959, Ag 31,21:2
Flick, Albert L, 1955, N 18,25:1
Flick, Alex C, 1942, Jl 31,15:6
Flick, C Roland, 1940, F 4,40:7
Flick, Clarence N, 1963, O 30,39:3
Flick, George L, 1944, Jl 3,11:4
Flick, Henry E, 1940, Ap 27,15:2
Flick, Howard W, 1958, Je 5,31:3
Flick, John K, 1955, Mr 22,31:3
Flick, Joseph D, 1937, D 15,25:3
Flick, Lawrence F, 1938, Jl 8,17:6
Flick, Lawrence F Jr, 1945, O 3,19:5
Flick, Marshall G, 1941, Ap 18,21:5
Flick, Pat C, 1955, N 6,86:4
Flick, Reuben J, 1940, Ag 25,35:3
Flick, T Walter, 1952, Mr 14,23:3
Flickenger, Henry H, 1947, O 27,21:4
Flicker, Charles, 1968, Jl 4,19:1
Flicker, Edward, 1939, Mr 2,21:1
Flicker, Edward Mrs, 1954, F 27,13:4
Flicker, Sol J, 1958, Mr 31,27:2
Flickinger, Charles L, 1956, O 21,86:4
Flickinger, Harrison W, 1947, O 6,21:2
Flickinger, J Willis, 1939, Ap 9,III,6:8
Flickinger, Jacob F, 1949, My 14,13:3
Flickinger, Lillian A Mrs (Mme L Wiesike), 1960, Ja 31,92:5
Flickinger, Roy C, 1942, Jl 7,20:2
Flickinger, Smith M, 1939, Ap 3,15:3
Fliederblum, Herman J, 1953, O 7,29:1
Fliedner, August C Mrs, 1943, Mr 30,26:3
Fliedner, Eugene B, 1955, O 12,29:1
Fliegel, Otto, 1967, My 1,37:4
Fliehman, Harvey L, 1965, N 7,89:3
Fliesler, Joseph R, 1967, F 24,35:5
Fliess, Robert A, 1875, Ap 1,6:7
Fliess, William M, 1904, Mr 29,9:5
Fliess, Winston S, 1961, Jl 26,31:4

Flight, John W Mrs, 1953, Ap 20,25:4
Flinchbaugh, Frederick L Rev Dr, 1937, Ap 24,19:2
Flindell, Edwin F, 1939, Jl 11,20:4
Flink, Abraham, 1943, F 19,19:1
Flink, Carl, 1944, Ap 7,19:3
Flink, Charles N, 1951, Mr 13,31:5
Flinn, A Rex, 1950, My 30,17:3
Flinn, Alfred D Dr, 1937, Mr 15,23:2
Flinn, Arthur A Mrs, 1950, My 12,27:2
Flinn, Ernest M, 1960, Ja 9,21:1
Flinn, Frederick B, 1957, Ap 16,33:3
Flinn, Henry M, 1942, Je 13,15:1
Flinn, John C, 1946, Mr 3,44:6
Flinn, Mary F, 1958, O 27,27:4
Flinn, Maurice B, 1953, Ja 21,31:3
Flinn, Philip Sheridan, 1909, Mr 29,7:4
Flinn, Ralph E, 1949, Ag 5,19:6
Flinn, Rex Mrs, 1947, Ja 31,23:5
Flinn, Richard O, 1948, Mr 26,21:2
Flinn, Thomas C, 1945, Je 14,19:3
Flinn, Victor, 1941, My 2,21:5
Flinn, William, 1924, F 20,19:5
Flinn, William A, 1964, S 15,37:4
Flinner, Ira A, 1954, My 1,15:3
Flinsch, Rudolf, 1949, Ja 1,13:1
Flint, A Dr, 1886, Mr 14,2:4
Flint, Annie, 1949, D 16,31:3
Flint, Austin, 1955, Jl 21,23:1
Flint, Austin Dr, 1915, S 23,13:5
Flint, Austin Mrs, 1916, My 21,19:4
Flint, Bertram P, 1942, My 18,15:2
Flint, C R, 1934, F 14,22:1
Flint, Charles K, 1968, My 6,47:2
Flint, Charles W, 1964, D 13,86:7
Flint, Clarence B, 1952, F 15,25:5
Flint, Clarence B Mrs, 1959, Ja 12,39:4
Flint, Clifford H, 1947, F 28,23:4
Flint, Clinton M Mrs, 1944, Ag 4,13:2
Flint, David Boardman, 1903, Jl 7,7:5
Flint, Dutee W, 1961, Ap 2,76:1
Flint, Edgar M, 1951, Jl 4,17:2
Flint, Edith F Mrs, 1949, F 24,18:4
Flint, Eliot, 1949, Ja 29,13:3
Flint, Frances E Mrs, 1916, D 27,9:5
Flint, Frank P Mrs, 1955, My 21,17:6
Flint, Frederick, 1908, My 20,7:6
Flint, George E, 1940, D 3,25:1
Flint, George F, 1941, Ja 12,44:1
Flint, George H, 1918, F 26,13:5
Flint, H M, 1876, F 7,5:6
Flint, Harold R, 1944, D 5,23:2
Flint, Harry, 1923, My 24,19:4
Flint, Harry M, 1938, Mr 23,23:4
Flint, Helen C, 1954, Ja 23,13:4
Flint, Henry, 1923, My 23,21:5
Flint, Henry Herrick, 1920, My 9,22:4
Flint, Herbert A, 1938, D 1,23:2
Flint, Isaac C, 1956, Mr 2,23:2
Flint, John, 1937, Ap 11,II,8:2
Flint, Joseph M, 1944, S 24,45:2
Flint, Josiah D Dr, 1908, Ap 1,7:6
Flint, Leland B, 1964, S 24,41:4
Flint, Lester E, 1942, D 14,23:5
Flint, Margaret (Mrs L W Jacobs), 1960, F 28,82:7
Flint, Mary H Mrs, 1937, Mr 6,17:3
Flint, Noel L, 1964, N 23,37:3
Flint, Perley H, 1958, N 12,37:4
Flint, Robert, 1948, O 1,26:2
Flint, Sanford, 1967, Jl 5,39:8
Flint, Seth M, 1941, Mr 19,22:2
Flint, T J S, 1881, Jl 18,8:1
Flint, Wallace B, 1937, Mr 30,23:5
Flint, Walter M, 1957, N 5,31:3
Flint, Wesley P, 1943, Je 4,21:2
Flint, Weston, 1906, Ap 7,9:6
Flint, William W Jr, 1945, N 12,21:4
Flintoft, Robert B, 1946, F 26,26:2
Flipper, Henry O, 1940, My 5,52:2
Flipper, Joseph S, 1944, O 12,27:3
Flippin, James C, 1939, F 17,20:2
Flippin, John R, 1963, D 30,21:5
Flipse, Martin, 1938, Jl 20,19:3
Flirabend, Henry A, 1919, Mr 28,13:2
Flisnick, Thomas, 1949, My 18,27:1
Flitcraft, Clement B, 1950, Ja 16,26:4
Flitcraft, Walter S, 1941, N 18,25:6
Flitcroft, Edward, 1949, Ja 8,15:5
Flite, Miss (of Dickens' Bleak House), 1865, My 5, 2:1
Flitner, Stanwood E, 1944, N 18,13:2
Floasin, Eli, 1952, F 11,25:6
Floberg, Adelbert R, 1937, Ag 29,II,7:4
Floch, Bernard, 1961, Jl 10,21:6
Flock, John W, 1952, D 9,33:1
Flock, John W Mrs, 1943, N 17,25:5
Flock, Joshua Mrs, 1950, Je 25,70:1
Flocke, Carl O, 1938, Mr 11,19:3
Flockhart, James, 1944, Ap 8,13:4
Flockhart, John Mrs, 1948, My 1,15:6
Flockhart, Thomas A, 1955, Jl 2,15:7
Floeckher, Ashton A, 1948, F 25,23:3
Floersh, John A Archbishop, 1968, Je 12,47:4
Floersheimer, Joseph H, 1944, Ag 15,17:2
Floherty, John J, 1964, D 5,31:1
Flohr, Belle, 1945, D 29,13:4
Flohri, Emil, 1938, D 27,17:2
Flomerfelt, James A, 1905, My 24,9:6
Flood, Andrew W, 1948, N 3,27:2
Flood, Anna D Mrs, 1941, Ap 4,21:2
Flood, B A, 1933, My 16,17:3
Flood, Charles A Sr, 1949, Ap 28,31:5
Flood, Charles J, 1956, Ag 2,25:2
Flood, Emmett T, 1942, Ag 9,42:5
Flood, Francis A, 1956, Ag 22,29:3
Flood, Francis W, 1938, Je 1,23:2
Flood, Frank L, 1958, F 16,86:1
Flood, Frederick A, 1944, S 7,23:6
Flood, George B, 1954, N 22,23:2
Flood, Gerald F, 1965, D 27,25:3
Flood, H Carson Mrs, 1945, F 22,28:3
Flood, Henry, 1959, Ap 9,31:1
Flood, Henry D, 1921, D 9,17:5
Flood, Henry G, 1947, Ag 2,13:2
Flood, Henry Jr, 1948, Je 18,23:5
Flood, Henry T, 1945, Ja 7,38:4
Flood, Hugh, 1954, Je 9,19:5
Flood, Ivan, 1953, Ja 16,24:5
Flood, J C, 1889, F 22,5:5
Flood, J Joseph, 1941, Je 6,21:1
Flood, James, 1953, F 6,20:7
Flood, James A, 1962, Ja 3,33:1
Flood, James H Father, 1920, N 18,15:4
Flood, James H Rev, 1920, N 15,15:4
Flood, James J Msgr (funl, Je 28,15:5), 1923, Je 26, 19:1
Flood, James J Rev, 1922, Mr 11,13:5
Flood, John, 1904, Mr 17,7:4; 1924, O 10,19:5
Flood, John A, 1959, My 7,33:1
Flood, John C, 1943, Ja 18,15:2
Flood, John D Sr, 1955, Ag 23,23:5
Flood, John F, 1917, N 17,13:4
Flood, John J, 1944, F 1,19:5
Flood, John P, 1917, Jl 7,9:7
Flood, Katherine, 1945, O 31,23:3
Flood, Kenneth, 1959, Ap 5,86:4
Flood, Mary Mrs, 1920, S 30,9:4
Flood, Mary T, 1943, Ap 14,23:6
Flood, Maurice S Mrs, 1941, Ja 14,21:4
Flood, Ned A (por), 1938, N 9,23:3
Flood, Patrick, 1908, D 29,9:5; 1944, Ag 1,17:6
Flood, Patrick J, 1949, Mr 28,21:2
Flood, Samuel D, 1937, Ja 11,20:1
Flood, T Bromley, 1956, Ap 10,31:3
Flood, Theodore L Rev, 1915, Je 27,15:5
Flood, Thomas, 1941, Ag 15,17:4
Flood, Thomas C, 1948, Ag 21,16:2
Flood, Thomas W, 1941, Jl 11,15:6
Flood, Valentine, 1950, Ag 2,25:1
Flood, W H, 1928, Ag 8,21:4
Flood, Walter H, 1951, Ap 27,23:1
Flood, Walter R Mrs, 1953, S 16,33:3
Flood, Walter V, 1950, N 8,29:5
Flood, William, 1937, Je 17,24:1
Flood, William J, 1945, Ag 8,23:5
Flood, William J Mrs, 1949, N 30,27:4
Flood, William T, 1938, F 19,15:3
Floody, Robert J, 1915, My 20,11:5
Flook, William M, 1962, Ap 6,35:5
Floom, Charles E, 1947, S 16,23:3
Flor, Henry, 1941, N 5,16:6
Flora, Alex N, 1942, Ap 4,13:2
Flora, Snowden D, 1957, Ag 29,27:6
Florance, Eustace L, 1959, Je 28,29:1
Florance, Fred S, 1968, Je 8,31:2
Florance, William E, 1943, Ja 8,19:6
Florant, Lyonel C, 1945, Ja 7,38:2
Florcyk, Joseph F, 1948, Ag 6,17:4
Florczak, Karol, 1946, D 8,77:4
Flore, Edward F, 1945, S 28,21:3
Florea, George G, 1962, Ja 24,33:5
Florea, Jacob, 1956, Ag 26,84:8
Florell, Victor H, 1951, N 2,23:3
Floren, George J, 1940, Jl 10,19:2
Florence, Anna T Mrs, 1906, F 19,9:5
Florence, David W, 1957, My 17,25:4
Florence, Fred F, 1960, D 26,23:6
Florence, Laura, 1957, My 12,86:4
Florence, Thomas B, 1875, Jl 4,7:5
Florence, W J, 1891, N 20,5:1
Florence Hilda, Sister, 1949, Jl 7,25:2
Florence Marie, Sister (F M Scott), 1965, Ag 23,31:3
Florentia, Sister, 1945, Ag 1,19:5
Florentine, M Flora Sister, 1940, Mr 7,23:3
Florentino, Frank G, 1967, Ap 17,37:2
Florentius, Brother, 1941, Ag 5,20:2
Florentius, Rev Brother, 1938, My 2,17:4
Flores, Antonio, 1915, S 1,9:4
Flores, Frederic Mrs, 1953, Ja 24,15:5
Flores, Gen, 1864, N 5,1:2
Flores, George, 1951, S 3,18:6
Flores, Juan, 1921, S 30,15:4
Flores, S F, 1966, F 12,25:4
Flores da Cunha, Jose A, 1959, N 6,30:1
Flores Magon, Enrique, 1954, O 30,17:5
Florey, Frank Mrs, 1943, Ja 4,15:6
Florey of Adelaide, Baron (Howard Walter Florey), 1968, F 23,30:2
Florez, Julio, 1923, Ja 24,13:6
Florian, Walter, 1909, Ap 3,9:5
Florian, William O, 1952, Ag 2,15:3
Florida, James W, 1942, D 13,73:2
Florio, Caryl (Wm Jno Robjohn), 1920, N 22,15:4
Florio, Dan (Dominick), 1965, O 12,48:1
Florio, Edward J, 1962, Je 2,47:3
Florio, Frank J, 1952, Ja 6,93:1
Florio, John D, 1946, D 21,19:6
Florio, Stephen, 1955, O 27,33:4
Florit, Teresa S de, 1960, Ag 19,12:5
Florkowitz, Mendel Mrs, 1949, O 20,29:4
Florman, Arthur M, 1952, O 13,21:4
Florman, Leo, 1955, S 18,86:1
Florman, Morris, 1942, My 17,45:2
Florman, Nils Mrs, 1946, My 24,19:3
Florman, Philip, 1959, Ja 7,33:1
Florschutz, Max, 1938, F 11,24:2
Florsheim, Irving, 1959, O 19,29:2
Florsheim, Irving S (est tax appr), 1961, F 19,54:5
Florsheim, Leonard S, 1964, My 23,23:5
Florsheim, Louis, 1955, O 15,15:1
Florsheim, Milton S (will), 1937, O 9,17:2
Florsheim, Milton S Mrs, 1957, N 17,87:2
Florshein, Stanley C Mrs, 1967, Mr 9,39:1
Florus Lucian, Bro, 1939, Ag 22,19:3
Flory, Arthur C, 1943, Mr 3,24:2
Flory, Burton P, 1941, Ap 30,19:4
Flory, Ezra, 1940, F 17,13:3
Flory, Joseph, 1925, Ap 4,17:5
Flory, Walter L, 1951, Jl 5,25:5
Flosbach, John H, 1953, Ag 29,17:3
Floskins, Maria, 1955, My 3,42:3
Floto, Julius, 1951, Ap 3,27:3
Flotow, H K T Von, 1935, D 21,9:4
Flotow, von-Fredk, 1883, Ja 26,2:6
Flotron, John R, 1939, Ap 26,23:5
Flott, Frederick W, 1967, My 25,47:2
Flotte, Camille J, 1947, Ja 7,28:2
Floud, Francis, 1965, Ap 19,29:4
Floulke, Charles Mather, 1909, Ap 15,9:6
Flouquet, C T, 1896, Ja 19,5:1
Flow, Lucretia Mrs, 1952, Ap 23,29:6
Flower, Anson R, 1909, Ja 7,9:6
Flower, Archibald, 1950, N 23,38:1
Flower, Benjamin O, 1918, D 25,15:4
Flower, Cyril (Baron Battersea), 1907, N 28,7:4
Flower, Fordham, 1966, Jl 11,29:2
Flower, Frank R Mrs, 1939, F 25,15:4
Flower, Frederick, 1961, Ja 29,85:2
Flower, Frederick B, 1937, Mr 7,II,8:8
Flower, Henry C, 1938, Je 21,19:3
Flower, James O Dr, 1906, N 9,9:6
Flower, Leslie J, 1965, Mr 13,25:2
Flower, Mark D Gen, 1907, F 4,9:5
Flower, Nathan M, 1906, D 2,7:6
Flower, Newman, 1964, Mr 13,33:4
Flower, Otis Mrs, 1965, Ap 17,19:2
Flower, Otis P, 1948, S 26,76:4
Flower, Robert E, 1961, Je 13,35:1
Flower, Roswell P (funl), 1899, My 13,1:1
Flower, Roswell P Mrs, 1910, Ag 24,9:5
Flower, Walter, 1938, D 20,26:1
Flower, William G Mrs, 1951, Mr 5,21:1
Flower, William P, 1956, Ag 21,29:3
Flowerman, Samuel H, 1958, Jl 30,29:5
Flowers, Alan E, 1945, D 11,25:2
Flowers, Frank, 1944, S 1,13:5
Flowers, George E, 1954, D 25,11:6
Flowers, George W, 1955, D 3,17:4
Flowers, J G, 1965, F 26,29:1
Flowers, Leslie R, 1950, O 17,31:3
Flowers, Robert L, 1951, Ag 25,11:7
Flowers, William H Jr, 1954, S 21,27:1
Flowers, William R, 1945, Ja 21,40:7
Flowers, William W, 1941, My 2,21:1
Flowerton, Alexander, 1958, F 26,27:1
Flowerton, Consuelo (Mrs R E Cushman), 19 D 22,31:2
Floyd, A L, 1901, Mr 21,9:7
Floyd, Albert N, 1951, Mr 1,27:3
Floyd, Alfred E Sr, 1955, Ap 15,23:2
Floyd, Channing, 1961, S 7,35:3
Floyd, Cora M, 1948, O 6,29:4
Floyd, Dwight E Mrs, 1955, D 13,40:1
Floyd, Edward D, 1917, O 18,15:2
Floyd, Eugene Mrs, 1950, O 4,31:3
Floyd, Evan J, 1945, S 10,19:3
Floyd, J B (por), 1863, S 6,5:3
Floyd, J G, 1881, O 7,5:4
Floyd, J Gelston, 1903, N 28,9:5
Floyd, John B, 1863, Ag 31,1:2
Floyd, Mary, 1963, Ag 11,84:4
Floyd, Nicol Sr Mrs, 1937, S 8,23:5
Floyd, Nicoll, 1950, Mr 23,29:3
Floyd, Nicoll Jr, 1948, Ja 19,23:3
Floyd, Olivia, 1905, D 12,11:2
Floyd, Richard C, 1953, S 17,29:2
Floyd, Robert, 1908, Ja 30,7:5
Floyd, Robert Mitchell, 1912, Je 13,11:4
Floyd, Thomas J L, 1955, Ap 10,88:1
Floyd, W R, 1880, N 25,5:4

Floyd, William, 1943, N 27,13:5
Floyd, William M Jr, 1949, O 6,31:4
Floyd, William Mrs, 1951, N 28,31:5
Floyd-Jones, Elbert, 1946, My 18,19:4
Floyd-Jones, George S, 1941, Ja 17,17:1
Floyd-Jones, Robert Blackwell, 1916, Je 13,11:6
Floyd-Jones, Sarah B Mrs, 1940, Ja 30,19:5
Floyd-Jones, Thomas, 1919, My 12,13:3
Floyd-Jones, Thomas L, 1937, Ja 26,21:5
Floyd-Jones, William Chauncey, 1925, D 7,21:4
Fluck, John J, 1956, Ja 16,21:4
Fluck, Olga E, 1967, S 6,44:6
Flueckiger, Hermann, 1960, Ja 5,31:5
Fluegel, Ewald Dr, 1914, N 16,9:5
Fluegel, Maurice Rev, 1911, F 14,11:5
Fluegelman, Arthur, 1947, O 18,15:6
Fluegelman, Henry, 1949, My 25,29:1
Fluegelman, Max, 1945, Jl 7,13:7
Fluegelman, Max Mrs, 1948, Jl 30,17:4
Fluegelman, Nathan, 1939, Jl 9,31:2
Flues, Hans, 1956, My 25,23:4
Flug, Samuel S, 1962, O 11,39:3
Flugel, John, 1955, Ag 9,25:4
Fluharty, William G, 1943, Mr 30,21:2
Flum, Abe, 1943, My 8,15:4
Flurscheim, Bernard H, 1955, My 27,23:5
Flurscheim, H A Mrs, 1910, Jl 6,7:7
Flurscheim, Hermann A, 1914, Ag 20,11:7
Flusser, Charles W Com, 1864, Ap 26,4:6
Flusser, Joseph, 1947, Ap 20,60:4
Flusser, Nathan, 1964, Ag 4,29:4
Flusser, William W Mrs, 1961, Mr 22,41:4
Flux, Alfred W, 1942, Jl 24,19:6
Fly, James L, 1966, Ja 7,29:1
Fly, Joseph T, 1959, F 15,86:4
Flygare, Carl G, 1939, N 19,38:8
Flygare, Enoch J, 1957, Je 22,15:2
Flyn, Michael J, 1958, F 2,86:4
Flyn, Percival Sir, 1940, Ap 26,21:4
Flynn, Alden S E Mrs, 1946, D 6,23:1
Flynn, Alfred, 1949, S 27,27:1
Flynn, Ann E M Mrs, 1937, Ap 24,19:5
Flynn, Anna C Mrs, 1942, S 20,40:4
Flynn, Anna D Mrs, 1939, F 17,19:3
Flynn, Anna E, 1943, Mr 13,13:6; 1948, Ap 20,27:4
Flynn, Anna K Mrs, 1962, F 25,89:1
Flynn, Anthony J, 1961, My 27,23:3
Flynn, Augustus J, 1949, S 21,31:4
Flynn, Bernard J, 1946, Ag 28,27:4
Flynn, Charles, 1925, Ja 23,19:4
Flynn, Charles A, 1942, My 28,17:1; 1942, D 4,25:4; 1951, Mr 1,27:3
Flynn, Charles A Mrs, 1957, S 3,27:2
Flynn, Charles B, 1952, Je 8,87:1
Flynn, Charles V, 1966, Ag 19,33:3
Flynn, Clair T F, 1962, N 2,31:2
Flynn, Clarence G, 1948, O 24,76:2
Flynn, Cronan, 1961, Ja 15,86:8
Flynn, D, 1934, Ap 11,21:4
Flynn, Daniel, 1942, Je 20,13:5
Flynn, Daniel F, 1937, Je 15,23:2
Flynn, Daniel M, 1945, Ap 3,19:5
Flynn, Daniel V, 1960, O 8,23:2
Flynn, David A, 1945, Je 26,19:3
Flynn, David G, 1957, Je 27,26:7
Flynn, David S, 1953, Ag 21,18:4
Flynn, David X, 1949, S 4,40:6
Flynn, Dennis J Mrs, 1963, N 19,42:2
Flynn, Dennis J Msgr, 1911, Jl 8,9:4
Flynn, Dennis T, 1939, Je 20,21:1
Flynn, Edmund W, 1957, Ap 29,25:3
Flynn, Edward, 1953, O 3,17:4; 1954, Je 6,87:2
Flynn, Edward A, 1958, S 29,27:4
Flynn, Edward F, 1941, Mr 11,23:4
Flynn, Edward J, 1922, Ap 21,13:4; 1938, O 28,23:4; 1939, Mr 3,23:3; 1945, F 25,37:1; 1953, Ag 19,1:1
Flynn, Edward J (est tax appr), 1957, My 1,34:3
Flynn, Edward J Mrs, 1925, Je 29,13:7
Flynn, Edward Mrs, 1943, Ag 30,15:5
Flynn, Edward S, 1950, Mr 10,27:4
Flynn, Edward T, 1904, Jl 8,5:6
Flynn, Edward W, 1938, Ja 4,23:2
Flynn, Elizabeth, 1953, Je 17,27:2
Flynn, Elizabeth G (cremation, S 8,29:4; funl, S 9,3:1), 1964, S 6,1:4
Flynn, Elizabeth L Mrs, 1942, Je 11,23:1
Flynn, Emmet J, 1937, Je 5,17:2
Flynn, Errol (funl plans, O 17,23:3; O 19,29:5; funl, O 20,39:5), 1959, O 15,39:1
Flynn, Fannie V Mrs, 1938, Ja 22,15:3
Flynn, Florence L, 1944, D 2,13:3
Flynn, Francis A, 1944, N 16,23:4
Flynn, Francis A Mrs, 1951, Mr 29,27:3
Flynn, Francis E, 1939, Je 8,25:4
Flynn, Francis E (Bro Cecilian), 1961, My 27,23:3
Flynn, Francis M Mrs, 1967, Mr 14,47:1
Flynn, Francis X, 1954, Ap 24,17:7; 1964, Ja 27,23:4
Flynn, Frank, 1959, Ap 18,23:4
Flynn, Frank H, 1964, My 9,27:1
Flynn, Frank J, 1947, D 1,21:3; 1960, Ap 30,23:6
Flynn, Frank R, 1952, N 29,17:1
Flynn, Frank T, 1956, Ja 13,23:2
Flynn, George F, 1944, Jl 30,36:1
Flynn, George I, 1957, S 26,25:5
Flynn, George W, 1943, Ja 18,15:2
Flynn, Gregory, 1940, Jl 9,21:2
Flynn, H Leonard, 1964, N 16,31:4
Flynn, Hannah, 1922, Ja 29,22:2
Flynn, Harold J, 1959, N 7,23:2
Flynn, Harold L, 1957, Jl 18,25:4
Flynn, Hazel, 1964, My 16,25:1
Flynn, Henry C, 1949, Mr 4,21:2
Flynn, Henry S J, 1946, Mr 6,28:3
Flynn, Howard A, 1948, Je 15,27:4
Flynn, Hugh P, 1949, S 23,23:3
Flynn, J H, 1926, Jl 18,II,7:1
Flynn, J Stephen, 1953, Mr 6,23:2
Flynn, Jack F A (funl plans, N 14,85:5), 1965, N 9, 32:6
Flynn, James, 1912, Ag 12,9:6
Flynn, James B, 1941, My 27,23:5
Flynn, James F, 1944, Je 14,19:7; 1957, Ja 12,19:1
Flynn, James H, 1944, D 6,23:2; 1946, Ja 10,23:4
Flynn, James J, 1948, Jl 5,15:1
Flynn, James J Sr, 1954, F 8,23:2
Flynn, James M, 1946, D 16,24:2
Flynn, James Mrs, 1956, D 26,27:2
Flynn, James P, 1944, Mr 14,19:3; 1950, My 22,21:5
Flynn, James W, 1945, F 23,18:2
Flynn, Jerome B, 1946, D 4,31:2
Flynn, Joe, 1960, Mr 1,33:2
Flynn, John A, 1943, O 31,40:2; 1957, O 26,21:3; 1965, Jl 23,26:5
Flynn, John C, 1940, D 10,25:6; 1942, Ag 9,42:8; 1945, Ja 30,19:1; 1947, N 25,29:2; 1962, Ap 30,27:5; 1964, N 16,31:4
Flynn, John E, 1951, N 25,87:1
Flynn, John F, 1940, S 13,23:4; 1942, Ap 11,13:1; 1942, My 18,15:3; 1951, Ja 16,29:1; 1960, Jl 5,31:2
Flynn, John F Mrs, 1937, O 2,21:2; 1960, Ag 13,15:4
Flynn, John H, 1967, Mr 17,41:2
Flynn, John J, 1946, Mr 4,23:5; 1949, N 7,27:3; 1950, Jl 5,31:3; 1955, Je 20,21:6; 1961, Jl 1,17:4; 1962, N 16,31:1
Flynn, John Lawrence Justice, 1968, N 26,47:1
Flynn, John M, 1941, S 29,17:4; 1942, Ag 18,21:2; 1951, Ja 11,26:2
Flynn, John Mrs, 1960, D 25,42:2
Flynn, John P, 1937, Jl 6,19:5
Flynn, John P Mrs, 1949, Ap 10,76:7
Flynn, John T, 1962, N 22,29:1
Flynn, John T (trb, Ap 29,40:6), 1964, Ap 14,37:3
Flynn, Joseph A, 1943, O 27,23:4
Flynn, Joseph C, 1948, Je 11,23:3
Flynn, Joseph C H, 1941, Je 27,17:3
Flynn, Joseph D, 1939, F 2,19:5
Flynn, Joseph F, 1948, D 24,17:4
Flynn, Joseph J, 1942, N 3,24:3
Flynn, Joseph M Rev, 1910, Ja 6,9:4
Flynn, Joseph P, 1960, Ag 4,25:4; 1964, Ja 26,80:7
Flynn, Joseph R, 1955, N 3,31:2
Flynn, Joseph V, 1940, F 8,23:2
Flynn, L P, 1930, My 20,29:3
Flynn, Lawrence F, 1940, Ja 14,42:6
Flynn, Lawrence J, 1952, F 9,13:2
Flynn, Leo J, 1937, Mr 5,21:2
Flynn, Lisa B, 1967, F 4,27:2
Flynn, Lizzie J F Mrs, 1951, My 8,31:2
Flynn, M B, 1889, Jl 11,5:3
Flynn, Mabel C, 1916, Ap 23,19:4
Flynn, Maria E, 1942, Ja 1,25:3
Flynn, Martin H, 1947, Ap 16,25:4
Flynn, Martin J, 1951, F 17,15:3
Flynn, Mary Mrs, 1940, Ja 13,13:3
Flynn, Matilda C, 1961, My 4,37:4
Flynn, Maurice B, 1959, Mr 6,25:3
Flynn, Maurice J, 1937, O 22,24:2; 1949, Jl 4,13:3
Flynn, May I, 1951, Ja 31,25:4
Flynn, Michael, 1947, Ap 17,27:2; 1956, Ag 12,84:8
Flynn, Michael C Mrs, 1942, Ag 3,15:4
Flynn, Michael F, 1949, O 12,29:3
Flynn, Michael J, 1947, Mr 7,25:2; 1948, O 23,15:6; 1950, Ja 5,26:7; 1952, Ja 1,25:4
Flynn, Michael W, 1939, Mr 8,21:4
Flynn, Molly, 1961, Je 13,35:4
Flynn, Mortimer B, 1948, Ja 23,23:2
Flynn, Nora Langhorne Mrs, 1955, Jl 17,61:3
Flynn, Olney Mrs, 1965, Mr 4,31:4
Flynn, Oscar R, 1952, F 8,23:2
Flynn, Patrick F, 1949, My 22,88:5
Flynn, Patrick J, 1956, O 1,27:4
Flynn, Peter J, 1968, N 9,33:4
Flynn, Peter T Mrs, 1945, Je 19,19:4
Flynn, Ray, 1937, Ap 17,17:5
Flynn, Richard J, 1958, N 7,27:2
Flynn, Richard L, 1940, Ap 14,45:3
Flynn, Robert E, 1945, Je 5,19:3
Flynn, Robin, 1966, D 6,47:3
Flynn, Theodore Thomson Dr, 1968, O 24,47:3
Flynn, Thomas, 1912, Ag 23,9:6; 1937, S 28,23:1
Flynn, Thomas A, 1940, N 26,23:4
Flynn, Thomas Col, 1937, Jl 7,23:2
Flynn, Thomas E, 1959, Mr 23,31:2
Flynn, Thomas F, 1949, My 8,76:4
Flynn, Thomas F (Bro Chronim James), 1954, S 1, 27:5
Flynn, Thomas F, 1964, Je 30,33:4
Flynn, Thomas H, 1942, N 29,64:7
Flynn, Thomas J, 1951, O 21,93:2
Flynn, Thomas P, 1945, N 26,21:2
Flynn, Thomas S Rev, 1917, My 14,11:1
Flynn, Thomas V Mrs, 1963, Je 12,43:5
Flynn, Thomas W, 1940, Mr 21,25:2
Flynn, Vincent E, 1951, My 5,17:1
Flynn, Vincent J, 1956, Jl 8,64:1
Flynn, W J, 1928, O 15,23:5
Flynn, Walter H, 1946, Mr 15,22:3
Flynn, Walter J, 1941, Mr 28,23:5
Flynn, Walter J Mrs, 1956, Ja 28,17:4
Flynn, Walter L, 1959, Mr 27,23:2
Flynn, Walter V, 1942, Ja 27,21:2
Flynn, William, 1910, Je 14,11:4
Flynn, William H, 1946, Je 5,23:2
Flynn, William J, 1941, N 28,24:3; 1947, O 16,27:4; 1948, N 11,27:4; 1961, S 15,30:6
Flynn, William J Mrs, 1961, N 9,35:5
Flynn, William K, 1958, O 10,31:2
Flynn, William L, 1952, O 26,88:4
Flynn, William M, 1951, D 16,89:1
Flynn, William P, 1948, Jl 9,19:3
Flynn, William S, 1945, Ja 28,38:2; 1966, Ap 14,39:3
Flynn, Zittella Mrs, 1938, My 17,23:4
Flynt, Louis W G, 1940, F 21,19:4
Flynt, Robert H, 1955, Ap 22,25:3
Flythe, William P, 1956, Ja 23,25:3
Foan, Henry J, 1947, Je 28,14:2
Foard, John W, 1942, My 25,15:4
Foard, Norval E, 1906, Mr 27,9:5
Foard, Richard W, 1954, Ag 17,21:5
Foard, Robert H, 1944, D 30,11:5
Fobert, Joseph A, 1946, Je 6,21:3
Fobes, Alan C, 1944, Ja 6,23:3
Fobes, Francis H, 1957, S 18,33:2
Fobes, Hiram, 1955, O 23,86:1
Fobes, Joseph H, 1964, My 30,17:3
Fobes, Stanley D, 1942, S 24,27:2
Focacci, Severino A, 1944, N 21,25:5
Focaccio, Pietro E, 1953, Ag 29,17:3
Focarile, James, 1949, N 3,29:5
Foch, Gabriel, 1925, F 11,21:4
Focht, Ben H, 1955, Ja 23,84:4
Focht, Benjamin K Repr, 1937, Mr 28,II,9:2
Focht, Joseph L, 1962, Ap 23,29:4
Focht, Louis, 1944, Je 7,19:3
Fochtmann, Max A, 1949, O 13,27:1
Focillon, Henri, 1943, Mr 4,19:3
Fock, Dirck, 1941, O 19,44:1
Focke, Ferdinand B, 1937, N 5,23:5
Focke, Theodore M, 1949, Mr 3,25:2
Fodder, William L Mrs, 1946, Ag 14,25:1
Foden, Alfred G, 1940, S 23,17:5
Foden, George H, 1950, Ja 11,23:4
Fodor, Alice, 1958, D 5,32:1
Fodor, M W Mrs, 1959, F 11,39:1
Fodor, Nandor, 1964, My 19,37:2
Fodor, Paul, 1954, Ap 6,30:6; 1960, Ja 4,29:3
Fodor, Paul J, 1964, O 8,43:1
Foedisch, Frederick W, 1940, Jl 1,19:3
Foege, Frederick C, 1947, O 12,79:3
Foeldy, Charles, 1954, D 24,13:1
Foelix, Ferdinand C Mrs, 1940, Je 6,25:2
Foeller, Harry W, 1937, Je 30,23:5
Foerderer, Robert H, 1903, Jl 27,7:6
Foerner, George, 1954, D 20,29:5
Foerstel, Gerhard, 1949, S 30,24:2
Foerster, Ferdinand Mrs, 1951, Jl 26,21:3
Foerster, Frederick W, 1959, Je 1,27:2
Foerster, Friedrich, 1966, Ja 22,29:3
Foerster, Henry Rev, 1881, O 21,5:2
Foerster, Josef B, 1951, My 31,27:3
Foerster, Mary C (Rev Mother M Teresa of Jesus), 1959, N 19,39:2
Foerster, Max, 1954, N 12,21:2
Foerster, Richard, 1952, Ap 23,29:4
Foerster, Robert F, 1941, Jl 31,17:6
Foerster, Wilhelm Dr, 1921, Ja 20,9:4
Foerster, Willa, 1946, Je 4,23:3
Foertsch, Hermann, 1961, D 28,27:4
Fogarty, Anna F, 1937, My 3,4:7
Fogarty, Cecil C, 1949, S 25,92:3
Fogarty, Dan G, 1940, O 16,23:6
Fogarty, Edward, 1953, Mr 25,31:3
Fogarty, Edward J, 1948, Jl 6,23:3
Fogarty, Edward Mrs, 1948, D 2,29:4
Fogarty, Edwin B, 1951, Ap 14,15:2
Fogarty, Frank (funl, Ap 9,23:3), 1925, Ap 7,19:4
Fogarty, Frank, 1941, N 10,17:6
Fogarty, George V, 1955, Ag 16,49:3
Fogarty, Hannah E H Mrs, 1942, Ja 25,41:2
Fogarty, Henry W Sr, 1945, Ag 29,23:2
Fogarty, James, 1945, Ag 16,19:2
Fogarty, James F, 1960, Ag 26,25:3
Fogarty, John E, 1941, O 21,23:4
Fogarty, John E (funl plans, Ja 12,39:1; funl, Ja 14,31:2), 1967, Ja 11,25:1
Fogarty, John J, 1954, Ja 3,88:1; 1957, Ja 9,27:3
Fogarty, John J Mrs, 1966, D 7,47:1
Fogarty, John P, 1964, S 1,36:1
Fogarty, Joseph, 1950, Ag 8,30:2

Fogarty, Joseph A, 1958, N 27,29:5
Fogarty, Mae, 1967, Ap 12,47:4
Fogarty, Michael, 1955, O 26,31:4
Fogarty, Sallie S Mrs, 1954, Ja 2,12:3
Fogarty, Thomas, 1938, Ag 12,17:4
Fogarty, Thomas F, 1946, S 30,25:4
Fogarty, Thomas L, 1938, My 11,19:6
Fogarty, Thomas P, 1950, O 5,31:4
Fogarty, Thomas Sr, 1952, O 16,29:4
Fogarty, Walter E, 1946, Mr 23,13:2
Fogarty, William A, 1952, Jl 4,13:5
Fogarty, William J, 1953, Je 26,19:2
Fogarty, William T, 1946, N 5,25:3
Fogarty, William W, 1946, Mr 18,21:2
Fogazzaro, Antonio, 1911, Mr 8,11:4
Fogel, Abraham, 1956, Mr 2,23:2
Fogel, Edwin M, 1949, D 17,17:4
Fogel, Ida Mrs, 1913, Jl 28,7:2
Fogel, Joseph, 1960, O 8,23:4
Fogel, Louis E, 1956, Je 29,21:6
Fogelman, Benjamin H, 1952, Mr 20,29:5
Fogelman, Lazar Mrs, 1964, Ja 1,25:3
Fogelman, Raymond, 1966, Mr 10,33:2
Fogelquist, Tolsten, 1941, Ja 25,15:1
Fogelsanger, Harold E, 1958, Mr 2,88:6
Fogelson, Boris, 1956, Ag 18,17:2
Fogelson, Hirsch, 1957, Ja 21,25:4
Fogerty, Elsie, 1945, Jl 8,11:5
Fogerty, John, 1940, Je 30,33:2
Fogg, Edward C, 1945, Ap 25,23:1
Fogg, Fred T, 1937, Ap 14,25:2
Fogg, George E, 1944, Jl 27,17:3
Fogg, Heman C, 1952, My 6,29:6
Fogg, Isaac, 1962, Ja 10,47:4
Fogg, Joseph G, 1946, D 3,31:2
Fogg, Julius H B, 1951, Ap 29,89:1
Fogg, Sanford L Sr, 1944, D 14,23:3
Fogg, W H, 1884, Mr 25,5:3
Fogg, W S, 1884, D 23,5:3
Fogg, William D, 1949, Ap 28,31:4
Fogg, William R, 1945, Je 17,26:2
Foggin, Frank, 1945, Je 22,15:1
Foggin, Thomas Hedges, 1912, Ja 7,II,15:3
Fogle, J K, 1952, F 22,22:2
Fogle, W H, 1937, Ja 29,19:5
Fogler, John W, 1942, Ja 25,40:4
Fogler, M Farthing Mrs, 1956, S 20,33:3
Fogletto, Benjamin, 1945, Je 3,32:2
Fogo, J Gordon, 1952, Jl 8,27:3
Fohlin, Joseph K, 1951, F 23,27:3
Fohs, Alfred D Prof, 1918, My 15,13:4
Fohs, Charles, 1950, Ja 26,27:5
Fohs, F Julius, 1965, Ja 21,31:2
Fohs, Mother Mary Angela, 1964, S 24,41:1
Foik, Paul J, 1941, Mr 2,43:3
Foil, William A, 1951, Ja 22,17:4
Foisy, J Albert, 1952, Ap 28,19:3
Fokin, Vitaly A, 1964, Ja 25,23:6
Fokina, Michel Mrs, 1958, Jl 30,29:2
Fokine, Michel, 1942, Ag 22,13:1
Fokker, Anthony H G, 1939, D 24,15:1
Foland, Harriet B Mrs, 1937, Ap 28,23:4
Foland, Harry S, 1950, Je 10,17:5
Folcke, Henry C, 1952, Mr 25,27:4
Foldvary, Benjamin Mrs, 1957, S 1,56:5
Folensbee, Bradley J, 1964, Ap 1,39:4
Foley, Adrian L, 1963, Ap 9,31:5
Foley, Anna M, 1960, F 17,35:2
Foley, Arthur, 1962, F 12,23:3
Foley, Arthur J, 1955, S 14,35:3
Foley, Augusta H Mrs, 1956, Ja 17,27:6
Foley, Benjamin J, 1967, O 12,50:2
Foley, Benjamin J Mrs, 1961, Ap 11,37:4
Foley, Bernard H, 1951, Mr 1,28:2
Foley, Cornelius L Mrs, 1949, Ap 15,23:2
Foley, Daniel C, 1949, Je 8,29:2
Foley, Daniel F, 1948, Ja 3,13:3
Foley, Daniel P, 1948, Jl 20,23:2
Foley, Donald G, 1961, S 29,40:6
Foley, Edna L, 1943, Ag 5,15:4
Foley, Edward F, 1922, D 11,17:5; 1950, D 27,27:5; 1954, F 27,13:5
Foley, Edward H Sr, 1950, D 7,33:4
Foley, Edward H Sr Mrs, 1963, Ag 4,80:1
Foley, Edward J, 1939, D 3,61:2; 1950, Ap 8,13:2; 1952, My 2,27:2; 1955, Mr 26,15:1
Foley, Edward J Mrs, 1948, Ja 14,25:1
Foley, Edward M, 1964, Mr 14,50:1
Foley, Edward R, 1942, Ag 24,15:1
Foley, Edward W, 1950, Ja 27,23:4
Foley, Ernest, 1948, N 20,13:6
Foley, Francis C, 1948, My 23,68:5
Foley, Francis E, 1953, O 17,15:6
Foley, Francis J, 1956, Je 11,31:6
Foley, Francis J Mrs, 1959, D 12,23:1
Foley, Frank, 1940, Ja 26,17:2
Foley, Frank A, 1947, Ap 15,25:3
Foley, Frank J, 1949, My 29,36:4; 1963, S 2,15:2
Foley, Frank M, 1959, Ag 7,21:2
Foley, Fred C, 1955, Ag 19,19:4
Foley, George B, 1951, Ap 22,88:1
Foley, George B Mrs, 1947, Jl 6,41:2
Foley, George E, 1938, Je 23,21:1
Foley, George F, 1949, My 27,21:4; 1962, Ja 29,25:3
Foley, George W, 1964, O 7,47:5
Foley, George W Jr, 1962, Mr 16,31:2
Foley, Gerald, 1945, F 27,19:4
Foley, Harry T (por), 1948, D 4,19:3
Foley, J Joseph, 1956, Jl 30,21:1
Foley, James, 1919, Ag 14,9:2
Foley, James A, 1946, F 12,25:1
Foley, James A Mrs (will, Jl 1,27:1), 1954, Je 23,25:5
Foley, James A Mrs (est tax appr), 1956, Jl 25,16:8
Foley, James F, 1958, Ap 16,33:3
Foley, James J, 1945, F 1,23:4; 1949, Mr 15,27:2; 1951, F 22,31:4
Foley, James M, 1941, Je 9,19:1
Foley, James S, 1874, O 5,3:2
Foley, James W, 1939, My 19,21:2
Foley, Jean S, 1948, F 10,23:4
Foley, Jeremiah C, 1920, Ag 1,22:4
Foley, Jerry S, 1941, Ag 11,13:3
Foley, Joe, 1948, O 19,28:2
Foley, John, 1946, My 19,42:4
Foley, John B, 1957, O 6,85:1
Foley, John Burton, 1925, F 5,19:4
Foley, John C, 1955, Ag 13,13:6
Foley, John Capt, 1903, Ag 24,7:6
Foley, John E Mrs, 1962, S 21,30:1
Foley, John F, 1948, Mr 15,23:5
Foley, John G, 1944, N 10,19:2
Foley, John Henry, 1874, Ag 28,1:7
Foley, John J, 1937, F 27,17:5; 1942, Ja 10,15:2; 1946, Mr 24,44:4; 1950, Ja 2,23:4; 1965, N 28,88:7
Foley, John L (trb lr), 1952, Je 21,14:7
Foley, John Mrs, 1946, N 13,27:3
Foley, John P, 1950, N 19,93:2
Foley, John R, 1907, Mr 13,9:6
Foley, John Rev, 1873, O 8,2:4
Foley, John S Bp, 1918, Ja 6,18:5
Foley, John W, 1941, S 11,23:2
Foley, Joseph A, 1950, D 5,31:4
Foley, Joseph B, 1960, Mr 13,86:8
Foley, Joseph F, 1940, Je 29,15:4; 1955, Jl 23,17:2; 1961, F 11,23:4
Foley, Joseph M, 1953, D 15,39:4
Foley, Joseph Mrs, 1956, Ap 15,88:8
Foley, Joseph P, 1953, O 9,27:3
Foley, Kate M, 1940, O 8,25:6
Foley, Kathleen, 1921, F 21,11:5
Foley, Lawrence L, 1949, D 17,17:6
Foley, Leo F X, 1956, My 18,25:2
Foley, Leo Rev, 1937, O 18,17:5
Foley, M Claire, 1959, Jl 23,27:2
Foley, Margaret C, 1959, Jl 28,27:4
Foley, Martin J, 1945, F 10,11:4
Foley, Mary A, 1944, Ap 10,19:5
Foley, Mary E, 1959, O 12,19:3
Foley, Maurice P Bp, 1919, Ag 17,22:4
Foley, Max Henry, 1968, D 9,47:3
Foley, Michael D, 1954, S 18,15:4
Foley, Michael J, 1903, O 27,9:6; 1953, Ag 17,15:2
Foley, Michael J Mrs, 1937, Je 29,21:2
Foley, Michael T, 1944, Jl 9,35:1
Foley, Oscar L, 1949, F 25,23:3
Foley, Owen B, 1947, S 1,19:3
Foley, Owen B Mrs, 1938, My 4,23:6
Foley, Patrick H, 1948, Mr 9,24:3
Foley, Patrick J, 1951, O 6,19:5
Foley, Patrick K, 1937, Ap 14,25:1
Foley, Paul, 1946, S 6,22:2
Foley, Paul A, 1963, O 14,29:2
Foley, Percy G, 1939, Ja 12,19:6
Foley, Peter, 1912, My 7,11:4
Foley, Peter C, 1938, O 10,19:2
Foley, Peter W, 1943, Ag 25,19:6
Foley, Red (Clyde Julian Foley), 1968, S 21,33:1
Foley, Richard Rev, 1907, My 11,7:2
Foley, Roland D, 1946, Ap 1,27:3
Foley, Roy W, 1967, Ap 1,31:4
Foley, Samuel J, 1951, My 15,31:1
Foley, Samuel J Ex-Sen, 1922, Je 27,15:4
Foley, Theodosius, 1951, My 30,22:2
Foley, Thomas, 1958, Mr 4,29:4
Foley, Thomas Bishop, 1879, F 20,2:1
Foley, Thomas F, 1944, Jl 12,19:5; 1954, Ag 11,25:5; 1965, My 31,17:4
Foley, Thomas F Jr, 1939, Mr 31,25:2
Foley, Thomas F Mrs, 1952, My 9,23:5
Foley, Thomas J, 1951, Ap 12,33:1
Foley, Thomas L, 1962, Jl 21,19:3
Foley, Thomas Mrs (funl, Mr 24,23:4), 1925, Mr 23, 17:4
Foley, Thomas P Mrs, 1958, Ag 16,17:5
Foley, Vincent R, 1944, S 12,19:7
Foley, William B, 1951, Ap 13,23:4
Foley, William C, 1953, Ja 8,30:2
Foley, William E, 1951, S 21,23:2; 1960, My 2,29:3
Foley, William G, 1965, D 28,27:4
Foley, William I, 1952, Ag 6,21:3
Foley, William J, 1948, Mr 22,23:4; 1952, D 2,31:4
Foley, William J Sr, 1953, Ap 14,27:1
Foley, William K, 1954, Ja 6,31:2
Foley, William K Mrs, 1951, Ap 21,17:6
Foley, William L, 1937, Je 15,23:2; 1960, O 19,45:3
Folger, Benjamin W, 1941, Ag 9,15:4
Folger, C J (funl), 1884, S 5,1:1
Folger, H C, 1930, Je 12,25:1
Folger, Henry C, 1914, Ja 19,9:5
Folger, John H Mrs (V MacMillan), 1953, D 30,23
Folger, M Glenn, 1946, Ag 5,21:6
Folger, Paul, 1954, O 10,87:1
Folger, Ruth A, 1951, Ja 19,25:2
Folger, Stephen L Mrs, 1961, Jl 13,29:5
Folger, William B, 1965, Ap 16,29:4
Folin, Otto Mrs, 1961, Ja 20,29:4
Foljambe, Cecil George Savile (Earl of Liverpool), 1907, Mr 25,7:5
Folk, Albert A Mrs, 1946, Je 13,27:2
Folk, George E, 1956, Ja 15,92:7
Folk, George E Mrs, 1946, F 23,13:2; 1950, Mr 25,
Folk, Harry S C, 1951, Jl 19,23:2
Folk, Howard N, 1962, N 21,33:4
Folk, J S, 1885, Je 26,2:5
Folk, Joseph W Ex-Gov, 1923, My 29,15:3
Folkart, Harry, 1950, Je 15,31:5
Folke, Bengt E, 1946, Mr 27,27:3
Folkenflik, Bernard, 1959, F 23,23:4
Folkenflik, Max, 1947, O 1,29:3
Folkensen, Claude H, 1948, Jl 7,46:6
Folker, Fred W, 1943, Ap 27,23:5
Folkes, William E Sr, 1951, F 4,76:4
Folkman, Leslie G, 1948, F 17,25:4
Folkman, Nathan, 1956, Ag 10,17:1
Folkner, John H, 1941, My 12,17:6
Folks, Charles W, 1960, My 18,41:2
Folks, Charles W Mrs, 1957, My 18,19:6
Folks, Homer (mem ser plans, Je 5,41:1; ser, Je 11 76:1), 1963, F 14,14:7
Folks, Homer Mrs, 1955, Ag 24,27:3
Folks, Lalitha M, 1915, D 19,17:3
Folks, Ralph, 1940, Mr 18,17:5
Folks, T John, 1962, N 15,37:2
Follamsbee, John G (funl, D 17,13:5), 1914, D 1(15:4
Folland, Henry P, 1954, S 7,26:2
Folland, William H, 1941, Je 6,21:2
Follansbee, Alanson, 1939, S 19,26:3
Follansbee, John, 1957, O 11,27:1
Follansbee, John Mrs, 1947, Ja 14,26:3
Follansbee, Mitchell D, 1941, Ja 27,15:2
Follansbee, Mitchell D Mrs, 1959, N 9,31:6
Follansbee, William U, 1939, D 20,25:4
Follen, Victor J, 1953, S 21,25:4
Follett, Bruce C, 1952, Ap 16,9:5
Follett, Charles, 1952, S 10,29:5
Follett, Charles W, 1952, D 20,17:6
Follett, Foster M, 1937, F 21,II,10:7
Follett, Henry G, 1949, My 13,23:4
Follett, Laura H Mrs, 1937, Ap 14,26:1
Follett, William, 1925, Ag 22,11:6
Follette, Hector Mrs, 1945, F 13,23:3
Follette, Orvis M, 1938, Je 29,19:6
Follette, William H, 1916, F 25,11:5
Folley, Helen V Mrs, 1939, Ag 3,19:5
Folliard, Thomas J, 1951, O 30,29:3
Follick, Mont, 1958, D 11,13:3
Follick, Mont (will), 1959, Ap 9,32:2
Follin, E Dorsey, 1943, F 17,21:1
Folliot, W Charles, 1943, Mr 14,26:3
Follman, Matthew A, 1964, My 28,37:4
Follmer, Charles J, 1950, O 7,19:5
Follmer, Charles P, 1918, Mr 2,13:2
Follmer, Lloyd D, 1948, Ag 5,21:6
Folmer, Mary S Mrs, 1959, Mr 11,35:1
Folmer, William F Mrs, 1946, Mr 8,21:2
Folonie, Robert J, 1941, Ap 12,15:4
Folser, Henry Mrs, 1947, Mr 28,24:2
Folsom, Benjamin, 1922, Ag 24,15:5
Folsom, Charles S, 1954, N 15,27:6
Folsom, Charles S (will), 1955, Mr 3,29:6
Folsom, Charles S Mrs, 1943, Jl 22,19:2
Folsom, Clarence M Sr, 1959, D 4,31:3
Folsom, Clarence S T, 1959, Je 12,27:3
Folsom, Cora M, 1943, Je 2,25:5
Folsom, Donald N B, 1942, O 24,15:6
Folsom, Frank E, 1942, Je 20,13:6
Folsom, Frank Mrs (funl, O 9,35:1), 1956, O 5
Folsom, George, 1869, Ap 11,5:5
Folsom, George Winthrop, 1915, Mr 30,11:4
Folsom, H Lloyd Mrs, 1968, S 29,80:7
Folsom, Harriet Amelia (Mrs Brigham Young), 1910, D 12,9:5
Folsom, Henry L Sr, 1954, O 12,27:1
Folsom, Henry T, 1937, F 28,II,8:8
Folsom, Joseph F, 1939, My 17,23:3
Folsom, Joseph K, 1960, Je 4,23:4
Folsom, Joseph K Mrs, 1950, Jl 18,31:8
Folsom, Lawrence P, 1956, D 8,19:5
Folsom, Leroy R, 1951, Jl 8,61:1
Folsom, Omar, 1943, Ja 11,15:4
Folsom, Oscar Col, 1875, Jl 24,1:4
Folsom, Ralph H, 1918, Mr 24,13:1
Folsom, Ralph P, 1941, My 13,23:1
Folsom, Richard S, 1949, F 22,23:5
Folsom, Thomas W, 1909, Mr 2,9:7
Folsome, Clair E, 1956, Mr 21,37:2
Folson, Edward O, 1946, D 4,31:3
Folster, Frederick W, 1937, D 19,II,8:8

Folster, George T, 1964, Ap 26,88:8
Foltermann, William Jr, 1938, S 13,23:4
Foltis, Constantine C, 1958, My 12,29:2
Folts, Charles G, 1952, O 9,31:4
Foltys, Jan, 1952, Mr 14,23:1
Foltz, Charles J, 1954, N 27,14:2
Foltz, Charles S, 1941, Ja 16,21:5
Foltz, Frederick S, 1952, Ag 29,23:4
Foltz, J M, 1877, Ap 14,2:3
Foltz, James A Jr, 1956, Ap 29,86:3
Foltz, Jonathan C Jr, 1941, Ap 15,23:2
Foltz, Raymond D, 1957, N 3,88:3
Folwell, A Prescott, 1960, Mr 21,29:3
Folwell, Arthur H, 1962, Jl 13,23:1
Folwell, Arthur H Mrs, 1958, My 23,23:2
Folwell, Charles H, 1946, F 20,25:1
Folwell, George H, 1942, O 15,23:5
Folwell, Nathan T, 1938, Mr 16,23:6
Folwell, Phil D, 1955, D 4,88:8
Folwell, William H, 1945, N 15,19:5
Folz, Stanley, 1954, N 4,31:1
Fombona Pachano, Jacinto, 1951, F 8,34:3
Fombrun, Charles, 1961, Jl 7,25:5
Fon Foo Sec, Dr, 1938, O 4,25:4
Fonaroff, Vera, 1962, Jl 24,27:3
Fonarton, Theodore D, 1967, Ap 5,44:5
Foncault, Mlle, 1879, D 31,2:7
Foncin, Pierre, 1916, D 19,11:3
Fonck, Rene, 1953, Je 19,21:1
Fond, Michael, 1951, Jl 27,19:5
Fonda, A P, 1873, Ag 6,8:4
Fonda, Douw H, 1941, Jl 16,17:4
Fonda, George, 1941, F 6,21:3
Fonda, George F, 1951, Ap 22,88:3
Fonda, Harry B, 1941, My 28,25:3
Fonda, Howard B, 1964, Mr 5,30:4
Fonda, James, 1866, Jl 22,5:4
Fonda, John S, 1943, D 23,20:2
Fonda, Nathan C, 1945, N 27,23:1
Fonda, Nathan C Mrs, 1939, D 1,23:5
Fonda, William C, 1938, S 1,23:2
Fondiller, Richard, 1962, Ap 30,27:4
Fondoukis, Michael, 1964, F 25,32:1
Fondren, Walter W Jr, 1961, N 3,70:5
Fones, Alfred C, 1938, Mr 16,23:3
Fong, Lum, 1952, Je 28,19:4
Fongers, Ties, 1944, D 29,15:1
Fonner, James C, 1940, My 29,23:2
Fonseca, Aurelio, 1907, Jl 8,7:6
Fonseca, Hermes Dodrigues Gen, 1923, S 11,15:3
Fonseca, Juan B, 1943, Ag 4,17:6
Fonseca, M D, 1892, Ag 24,1:5
Fonseca, Ricardo, 1949, Jl 23,11:6
Fonss, Christian, 1943, Mr 22,19:2
Font, Mariano, 1952, Mr 4,27:3
Fontaine, Andre C, 1945, Ja 29,14:2
Fontaine, Andre C Prof, 1923, Mr 27,19:4
Fontaine, Arthur B, 1940, D 31,15:4
Fontaine, E Rev, 1884, Ja 21,5:6
Fontaine, Glenn E, 1940, Ja 19,19:4
Fontaine, Harry T, 1965, F 27,25:2
Fontaine, James P, 1943, Je 10,21:2
Fontaine, John B, 1942, Ap 21,23:6
Fontaine, L J Oscar, 1950, Mr 4,17:5
Fontaine, Marie L, 1963, Je 17,25:5
Fontaine, P La, 1935, Jl 10,21:1
Fontaine, S S, 1933, O 17,21:5
Fontaine, Theodore J, 1939, Jl 5,17:3
Fontana, A V Count, 1911, Ja 2,9:5
Fontana, Giovanni B, 1945, Mr 10,17:6
Fontana, Lucio, 1968, S 8,84:1
Fontana, Mark J, 1922, O 21,13:5
Fontana, Stephen, 1950, Ap 23,95:1
Fontanar, Count of, 1960, F 19,27:3
Fontanes, Sylvain, 1955, Jl 30,17:6
Fontanne, Jules, 1942, Je 8,15:2
Fonte, Antonio C, 1943, Mr 28,24:4
Fontenay, Viscount de, 1946, Mr 28,25:1
Fontenelli, Peter Mrs, 1951, O 25,29:2
Fontes, Ernesto, 1956, Je 28,29:4
Fontnouvelle, Charles de Ferry de Count, 1956, 26,33:2
Foote, Charles, 1951, Ag 7,25:6
Fonvielle, Polk K, 1947, Mr 25,25:4
Fonyo, Aladar, 1939, Je 28,21:2
Foo, Ruby, 1950, Mr 16,31:2
Foo, Ping-sheung, 1965, Jl 30,22:5
Foohey, John P, 1940, D 7,17:5
Fookes, Arthur, 1948, Jl 14,24:3
Fooks, Mary, 1939, Jl 19,19:4
Food, Andrew G, 1950, Mr 18,13:2
Food, Emil Mrs, 1950, D 2,13:6
Food, John (por), 1922, Ap 19,19:4
Food, William M, 1959, Mr 29,80:5
Foote, William H, 1954, N 7,88:1
Foote, Malcolm F Mrs, 1951, Je 27,29:2
Foot, Isaac, 1960, D 14,35:3
Foot, Margaret E, 1965, Mr 23,39:3
Foot, Nathan C, 1958, S 6,17:3
Foot, S A, 1878, My 12,7:1
Foot, Solomon, 1866, Mr 29,1:1
Foot, Walter R Mrs, 1959, Ap 1,37:1
Foot, William J, 1950, Mr 23,36:3
Foote, A H Rear-Adm, 1863, Je 27,8:3
Foote, Abram W, 1941, My 15,23:4
Foote, Adrian B, 1958, Ap 30,33:5
Foote, Alex, 1948, Ja 21,26:3
Foote, Amon W, 1943, My 18,23:4
Foote, Andrew H, 1962, D 2,88:6
Foote, Anna E, 1953, Ja 22,23:2
Foote, Arthur E, 1946, Ag 28,27:6
Foote, Arthur W, 1937, Ap 10,19:3
Foote, Bradford Sr, 1947, N 20,29:3
Foote, Carlton A, 1916, Je 10,11:7
Foote, Charles C, 1966, S 12,45:4
Foote, Charles E, 1938, Je 25,15:5; 1939, Ja 1,24:6; 1948, Jl 30,17:3
Foote, Charles J, 1874, F 5,1:6; 1955, Ja 2,76:5
Foote, Charles S, 1939, Ja 14,17:3
Foote, Clayton E, 1947, N 13,28:2
Foote, Edith L, 1940, D 18,25:2
Foote, Edmund W, 1964, F 24,25:4
Foote, Edward M, 1945, F 15,19:4
Foote, Edward M Mrs, 1955, N 23,23:4
Foote, Elisha, 1883, O 27,2:4
Foote, Elizur V, 1945, Ag 8,23:5
Foote, F Stuart, 1954, Jl 9,17:4
Foote, F W, 1879, Mr 20,4:7
Foote, Flora B Mrs, 1950, My 4,27:2
Foote, Frank L, 1964, N 4,39:5
Foote, Frederick D, 1964, D 11,39:5
Foote, G A, 1878, S 7,1:5
Foote, George C, 1943, D 19,49:2
Foote, George P Mrs, 1945, My 5,15:3
Foote, George William, 1915, O 19,11:5
Foote, Gordon R Mrs, 1955, Jl 25,19:5
Foote, Gordon W Mrs, 1953, N 20,23:2
Foote, H S, 1880, My 20,8:1
Foote, Harriet Amanda Mrs, 1923, Mr 31,13:5
Foote, Harry W, 1942, Ja 15,19:6
Foote, Hayden B, 1945, D 27,19:2
Foote, Henry G, 1943, Jl 25,31:1
Foote, Henry L Mrs, 1951, Mr 15,29:3
Foote, Henry W, 1964, Ag 28,35:4
Foote, Horace Allen, 1903, Ap 23,9:5
Foote, J S Dr, 1925, Jl 2,19:5
Foote, John H, 1940, Mr 25,15:4
Foote, John M, 1920, Ap 1,11:4
Foote, John M Mrs, 1947, Ap 1,27:5
Foote, John T, 1950, Ja 31,24:3
Foote, Josephine F, 1937, F 2,23:4
Foote, K L, 1936, Jl 8,21:1
Foote, Lewis N, 1940, My 11,21:4
Foote, Lucius Harwood, 1913, Je 5,11:4
Foote, Margaret R, 1955, Je 12,86:6
Foote, Mark, 1957, Jl 27,17:5
Foote, Morris C Mrs, 1943, Ag 4,17:4
Foote, Nathaniel, 1944, Ja 27,19:2
Foote, Nathaniel F, 1939, Ja 22,35:2
Foote, Nellie K, 1950, Ap 9,84:2
Foote, Norman M, 1957, S 28,17:2
Foote, Patrick J, 1948, S 17,25:3
Foote, Percy W, 1961, Je 24,21:1
Foote, Randal H, 1923, Ja 24,13:5
Foote, Robert B B, 1954, N 10,33:3
Foote, Robert D, 1924, Je 25,23:5
Foote, Sherman K, 1955, F 18,21:1
Foote, Sterling T, 1955, Ja 26,25:4
Foote, Sterling T Mrs, 1947, Jl 23,23:5
Foote, Thomas Jefferson Mrs, 1908, S 6,9:2
Foote, Truman S, 1952, Mr 20,29:4
Foote, Wallace C, 1947, Mr 28,23:3
Foote, Wallace H, 1966, D 28,43:6
Foote, Wallace T Jr, 1910, D 18,13:4
Foote, William L, 1951, F 6,27:3
Footer, Harry, 1945, O 3,19:1
Footer, Joseph W, 1947, Ap 17,27:1
Foothorap, James F, 1966, S 21,47:1
Footner, Hulbert, 1944, N 26,56:4
Forain, J, 1931, Jl 12,II,6:1
Foraker, B, 1935, Mr 30,15:1
Foraker, J B Mrs, 1933, Jl 22,11:1
Foraker, James R, 1907, Ap 28,9:5
Foraker, Joseph B Ex-Sen, 1917, My 11,11:1
Foran, Arthur F, 1961, D 16,25:4; 1967, Ja 31,31:4
Foran, Arthur F Mrs, 1958, F 12,29:3
Foran, George F, 1925, Jl 20,15:6
Foran, John, 1912, N 11,11:5
Foran, John A, 1957, Ja 4,23:4
Foran, John J, 1945, Ja 30,19:5
Foran, William, 1945, D 1,23:1; 1954, Mr 10,25:5
Foras, Max de Count, 1937, Jl 6,19:4
Forastiere, Frank M, 1952, My 3,21:3
Forastiere, Michael, 1959, Jl 4,15:5
Forbath, Albert B, 1962, Mr 29,33:4
Forbell, Charles H, 1946, Ap 16,25:2
Forbell, Leverich Mrs, 1950, Mr 22,27:4
Forbes, A Holland Mrs, 1955, N 5,19:6
Forbes, A P Rev, 1875, O 10,1:6
Forbes, Adele, 1941, Jl 1,23:4
Forbes, Alex Jr, 1957, S 16,31:4
Forbes, Alexander, 1924, O 30,19:4; 1965, Mr 30,39:5
Forbes, Allan, 1955, Jl 10,75:1
Forbes, Allen Boyd, 1923, S 27,7:3
Forbes, Allyn B, 1947, Ja 22,23:1
Forbes, Angus, 1948, My 8,15:3
Forbes, Archibald, 1900, Mr 31,9:3; 1947, Ja 23,26:2
Forbes, Armitage S C Mrs, 1951, S 19,31:2
Forbes, Arthur, 1949, Ap 25,23:3
Forbes, Arthur W, 1946, Mr 19,27:3
Forbes, Atholl L, 1953, N 28,15:4
Forbes, Bertie C, 1954, My 7,24:3
Forbes, C H, 1933, Mr 13,13:3
Forbes, Charles A, 1905, Mr 13,3:6
Forbes, Charles R, 1952, Ap 12,11:3
Forbes, Cyril P, 1956, N 29,35:2
Forbes, David, 1920, Mr 18,11:5
Forbes, Donald, 1957, Ag 29,27:5
Forbes, Dora D Mrs, 1940, Jl 22,17:3
Forbes, Dorothy, 1944, N 20,21:5
Forbes, Douglas, 1950, D 1,25:1
Forbes, Ernest B, 1966, S 10,29:5
Forbes, Esther, 1967, Ag 13,80:4
Forbes, F F, 1933, N 18,15:2
Forbes, F Murray, 1961, N 25,23:4
Forbes, F Preston, 1958, F 4,29:4
Forbes, Francis, 1904, F 19,9:5
Forbes, Francis Blackmore, 1908, My 22,7:6
Forbes, Francis Reginald, 1873, N 24,3:3
Forbes, Frank C, 1962, Jl 18,10:3
Forbes, Frank Mrs, 1947, My 24,15:6
Forbes, Frank P, 1962, Mr 28,39:1
Forbes, G, 1936, O 24,17:3
Forbes, George, 1942, Je 24,19:5
Forbes, George M Mrs, 1945, O 1,19:2; 1950, Ja 7,18:2
Forbes, George O, 1946, D 10,31:2
Forbes, George P Mrs, 1960, Ag 5,23:4
Forbes, George S, 1937, N 4,25:6
Forbes, George Sir, 1940, Ap 19,21:2
Forbes, George W, 1947, My 19,22:2
Forbes, Gilbert, 1954, Mr 9,27:3; 1961, S 19,35:3
Forbes, Gilbert D, 1943, F 12,19:2
Forbes, Gordon C, 1961, Ja 22,84:5
Forbes, Guy, 1938, D 24,15:6
Forbes, H De Courcey, 1920, Jl 17,7:6
Forbes, Harry, 1946, D 20,23:2
Forbes, Harry J Sr, 1943, Jl 16,17:3
Forbes, Harry W, 1950, S 25,23:4
Forbes, Henry H, 1942, O 26,15:5
Forbes, Henry H Mrs, 1941, Mr 15,17:4
Forbes, Henry P Mrs, 1937, Ag 3,23:3
Forbes, Ida, 1941, Je 5,24:4
Forbes, J Grant, 1955, Ap 26,29:2
Forbes, J Malcolm, 1904, F 20,9:4
Forbes, J Murray, 1937, Ap 27,23:6
Forbes, Jack, 1953, Ap 5,76:3
Forbes, James, 1938, My 27,17:5
Forbes, James B, 1948, My 30,34:3
Forbes, James E, 1942, Ja 30,20:2
Forbes, James M Mrs, 1951, O 27,19:2
Forbes, James Mrs, 1959, N 24,37:4
Forbes, Jesse F Mrs, 1943, Ag 3,19:1
Forbes, John Colin, 1925, O 30,21:3
Forbes, John G, 1861, N 22,2:5; 1962, F 3,21:5
Forbes, John H, 1949, Ag 22,21:5; 1966, N 3,39:2
Forbes, John M Mrs, 1947, Ap 8,27:4
Forbes, John Murray, 1921, My 2,15:5
Forbes, John P Rev, 1910, Ap 17,II,11:4
Forbes, John R, 1949, Je 24,23:2
Forbes, Joseph Clement, 1925, Mr 14,13:4
Forbes, Joseph G Abp, 1940, My 23,23:1
Forbes, Josse F Rev Dr, 1922, Jl 9,26:4
Forbes, Kathryn (K F McLean), 1966, My 17,47:1
Forbes, Leighton, 1944, Jl 16,32:4
Forbes, Leslie J, 1949, Jl 14,27:3
Forbes, Malcolm J Mrs, 1952, O 28,31:2
Forbes, Malcolm Mrs (Christine H), 1965, F 20,25:5
Forbes, Mary B, 1962, Ja 15,27:5
Forbes, Montagu O, 1938, O 10,19:3
Forbes, Morris H, 1944, My 14,46:4
Forbes, Phil J Sr Mrs, 1950, O 20,27:5
Forbes, Ralph, 1951, Ap 1,94:1
Forbes, Ralph E (will, D 1,15:5), 1937, Mr 18,25:5
Forbes, Robert F, 1946, N 13,28:3
Forbes, Robert L, 1940, Je 22,15:6
Forbes, Robert L Mrs, 1964, N 4,39:2
Forbes, Robert W, 1947, Jl 7,17:3
Forbes, Russell, 1957, Je 21,28:6
Forbes, T Harold, 1953, Mr 5,27:3
Forbes, Theodore Frelinghuysen Gen, 1917, Mr 11,21:3
Forbes, Thomas F Mrs, 1943, D 19,48:8
Forbes, Thomas L, 1937, Ap 5,19:4
Forbes, Vivian, 1937, D 26,II,6:7
Forbes, W Cameron, 1959, D 26,13:5
Forbes, Waldo E Mrs, 1954, O 15,23:2
Forbes, William H, 1944, Jl 18,19:2
Forbes, William H Maj, 1875, Jl 27,4:6
Forbes, William I Mrs, 1946, Jl 18,25:6
Forbes, William J, 1950, O 5,31:1
Forbes, William O Dr, 1937, N 17,23:6
Forbes, William S Mrs, 1954, F 23,27:3
Forbes, William T Mrs, 1951, O 13,17:4
Forbes-Robertson, Frank, 1947, Mr 17,23:2
Forbes-Robertson, Johnston Sir, 1937, N 7,II,8:1
Forbes-Sempill, Lionel Mrs, 1940, S 6,21:4
Forbes-Trefusis, Charles J R H (Baron Clinton), 1957, Jl 7,60:7
Forbstein, Leo F (por), 1948, Mr 18,27:3
Forbush, Arthur R, 1952, F 26,27:4

Forbush, Charles P, 1910, My 19,9:4
Forbush, Clifton E, 1954, S 28,29:7
Forbush, Gayle T, 1948, Ja 31,19:1
Forbush, S W, 1940, My 19,43:3
Forby, Theodore, 1942, F 6,19:3
Forcade, Alfonso, 1956, F 12,88:7
Forcade, Eugene, 1869, N 22,5:1
Force, Bellmer H, 1939, My 23,23:4
Force, Bellmer H Mrs, 1949, Je 8,29:4
Force, C Warren, 1959, Jl 25,17:5
Force, Catherine T Mrs, 1939, Ag 14,15:4
Force, Dexter C, 1960, Ag 21,84:6
Force, Ephraim S, 1914, Mr 12,9:4
Force, Frances C, 1956, S 13,35:2
Force, Frank B, 1941, Ja 4,13:4
Force, John Campion, 1875, Mr 24,12:4
Force, Juliana Mrs, 1948, Ag 29,56:3
Force, Kenneth O Mrs, 1961, My 18,35:1
Force, Peter Col, 1868, Ja 26,6:5
Force, Raymond C, 1951, N 17,17:3
Force, William F, 1959, Mr 19,33:3
Force, William H, 1917, My 20,23:3
Forcer, Daniel E, 1924, My 31,15:5
Forchelli, Don, 1961, N 24,31:3
Forchheimer, Estelle, 1957, Je 8,19:5
Forchheimer, Frederick, 1945, Je 23,13:4
Forcier, Carl W, 1949, Ap 11,25:3
Forcum, A Linn, 1959, F 25,31:1
Forcum, Jack L, 1953, Ap 17,25:4
Ford, Abraham L, 1941, Mr 2,43:2
Ford, Adrian E, 1947, F 4,26:2
Ford, Agnes, 1944, S 20,23:2
Ford, Albert H, 1940, Ap 21,42:2
Ford, Albert W Dr, 1907, Jl 3,7:6
Ford, Allen P, 1960, F 8,29:2
Ford, Ambrose C Mrs, 1954, D 8,35:4
Ford, Amelia C, 1942, D 10,25:4
Ford, Andrew, 1937, D 30,19:4
Ford, Andrew W Mrs (Nixola Greeley Smith), 1919, Mr 10,11:4
Ford, Andrew W Mrs, 1944, My 26,19:4
Ford, Anne C (Mrs Thos J), 1966, S 8,47:4
Ford, Arthur Rutherford, 1968, Ap 4,47:1
Ford, Austin B, 1944, Ap 2,40:2
Ford, Austin W (por), 1948, My 25,27:5
Ford, Austin W Mrs, 1948, Je 28,20:2
Ford, Benjamin M, 1937, Ap 7,25:2
Ford, Bert, 1949, F 4,24:2
Ford, Blanche C Mrs (por), 1941, Je 8,48:6
Ford, C, 1935, Mr 21,23:6
Ford, C E, 1941, My 1,23:6
Ford, C W, 1873, O 28,2:5
Ford, C W Capt, 1903, Ap 14,9:6
Ford, Cecil, 1951, F 7,29:4
Ford, Charles B Sr, 1946, N 27,25:4
Ford, Charles E, 1942, Ja 19,17:5; 1942, Ag 9,42:7; 1957, O 27,86:3
Ford, Charles H L, 1939, Mr 14,21:5
Ford, Charles J, 1940, Ja 4,23:3
Ford, Charles O, 1956, Ag 8,25:6
Ford, Chris W, 1945, Ap 10,19:3
Ford, Clarence A, 1958, Ag 20,27:3
Ford, Clarence E, 1961, Ap 10,31:5
Ford, Clarence F, 1941, N 25,26:3
Ford, Clement R, 1956, S 26,33:5
Ford, Clyde S, 1953, D 30,23:1
Ford, Cornelius E, 1951, Ap 20,29:2
Ford, D B Rev Dr, 1903, My 5,9:6
Ford, D Rhys, 1946, Mr 13,29:5
Ford, David, 1953, F 4,29:7
Ford, Delos E, 1945, Ja 15,19:4
Ford, Donald, 1964, D 28,29:3
Ford, Dorothy Grant (Mrs Jas P Ford), 1968, N 11, 47:2
Ford, Duane, 1950, Je 17,15:2
Ford, E Kay, 1947, Ja 9,23:2
Ford, E L, 1880, D 18,2:5
Ford, E O, 1901, D 24,7:4
Ford, Eben C, 1948, Ag 30,17:3
Ford, Edmund H, 1947, N 25,32:2
Ford, Edsel B, 1943, My 26,1:7
Ford, Edward, 1920, Je 26,11:6
Ford, Edward A, 1963, Mr 7,7:4
Ford, Edward B, 1957, F 13,35:2
Ford, Edward G, 1958, Ag 24,87:1
Ford, Edward H, 1938, Ap 25,15:3
Ford, Edward H Mrs, 1957, Ja 16,31:4
Ford, Edward J, 1937, Je 29,21:5
Ford, Edward T, 1950, N 28,31:3
Ford, Edwin C, 1949, Ja 23,68:6
Ford, Edwin P, 1962, S 12,39:3
Ford, Elias A, 1912, Ja 21,II,13:2
Ford, Ella E Mrs, 1944, Mr 2,17:5
Ford, Ellen A, 1923, Je 23,11:6
Ford, Ellsworth, 1958, Ap 19,21:1
Ford, Elzie B, 1940, S 17,23:5
Ford, Emery L, 1942, D 21,23:3
Ford, Ethelwyn A Mrs, 1941, Ap 18,21:5
Ford, Eugene A, 1948, S 5,40:7
Ford, Eugene E, 1950, Ja 20,25:3
Ford, Eugene F, 1948, D 13,23:5
Ford, Ford M, 1939, Je 27,23:1
Ford, Frances C, 1950, Mr 9,29:2
Ford, Frances M Mrs, 1956, Je 17,92:3
Ford, Francis, 1953, S 7,19:2
Ford, Francis P, 1959, Je 8,27:6
Ford, Francis W, 1904, F 4,9:6
Ford, Francis X, 1952, S 4,1:4
Ford, Frank B, 1948, Mr 27,13:6
Ford, Frank C, 1941, S 24,23:3
Ford, Frank J, 1950, N 23,35:1
Ford, Frank P, 1937, My 2,II,9:2
Ford, Frank W, 1945, Ja 14,40:1; 1963, S 24,29:1
Ford, Franklin, 1918, Jl 1,11:6
Ford, Frederick L, 1940, D 20,25:4
Ford, Frederick W, 1938, F 19,15:4; 1964, S 14,33:5
Ford, G B, 1930, Ag 15,17:3
Ford, G L, 1891, N 15,16:3
Ford, Garrett N, 1903, Jl 10,7:6
Ford, Gaylord H, 1953, Ja 20,25:5
Ford, George, 1881, Ja 8,2:4
Ford, George A, 1906, D 4,9:5; 1951, O 3,36:3
Ford, George A Mrs, 1960, Ja 24,88:1
Ford, George B Mrs, 1964, F 22,21:5
Ford, George F, 1948, Ap 7,25:5
Ford, George L (will), 1938, Ja 28,42:6
Ford, George M, 1941, Ag 22,15:2
Ford, George Mrs, 1954, Ag 28,89:3
Ford, George R, 1938, S 3,13:2; 1953, S 11,21:2
Ford, Georgie H Mrs, 1940, Jl 10,19:3
Ford, Gerald Sr Mrs, 1967, S 19,51:4
Ford, Gus, 1947, O 8,25:1
Ford, H Clay, 1915, Jl 23,9:7
Ford, H P, 1950, Ap 5,31:4
Ford, Hannibal C, 1955, Mr 14,21:6
Ford, Harold R, 1949, Mr 24,28:2
Ford, Harriet, 1949, D 14,31:1
Ford, Harry C, 1938, My 23,17:2
Ford, Harry Mrs, 1949, Ja 3,23:3
Ford, Harry P, 1937, Ap 10,19:5
Ford, Harry W Capt, 1918, D 19,15:4
Ford, Hazel H Mrs (will), 1962, Ag 17,1:6
Ford, Henry, 1875, F 6,3:6
Ford, Henry H, 1965, Mr 10,30:1
Ford, Henry Jones Dr, 1925, Ag 30,7:3
Ford, Henry Mrs, 1950, S 29,28:2
Ford, Henry P, 1905, Ap 22,11:7
Ford, Hobart, 1965, Mr 2,38:1
Ford, Horatio, 1952, N 30,88:5
Ford, Howard, 1947, D 24,22:2
Ford, Hugh A, 1966, Mr 13,86:7
Ford, Hulda Mrs, 1957, F 23,17:2
Ford, Isaac, 1907, O 9,11:6
Ford, Isaac N, 1912, Ag 9,7:5
Ford, Isaac N (funl), 1912, Ag 11,II,11:5
Ford, J, 1927, S 29,27:3
Ford, J B, 1903, My 2,9:5; 1928, Mr 30,25:2; 1947, Ap 24,25:3
Ford, J Harmon, 1961, Ag 25,25:2
Ford, Jabez Rev, 1912, O 24,11:6
Ford, James, 1944, My 13,19:6
Ford, James A Dr, 1968, F 26,37:4
Ford, James B, 1924, My 18,7:1
Ford, James H, 1944, Jl 24,15:4
Ford, James J Mrs, 1909, F 20,7:4
Ford, James T, 1947, My 31,13:4
Ford, James W, 1957, Je 22,15:4
Ford, Jeremiah A, 1941, Jl 25,15:6
Ford, Jeremiah D, 1958, N 14,27:2
Ford, John, 1908, Mr 6,7:5; 1918, Mr 6,7:1
Ford, John (por), 1941, Jl 26,15:1
Ford, John A, 1938, Ap 18,15:6
Ford, John B, 1940, O 3,25:4
Ford, John B (will), 1941, N 4,25:7
Ford, John B Jr Mrs, 1953, Je 1,23:4
Ford, John D Rear-Adm, 1918, Ap 9,13:8
Ford, John F, 1941, N 4,23:5
Ford, John H, 1949, Ap 2,15:2
Ford, John H Mrs, 1954, Ap 6,29:4
Ford, John Howard, 1914, Mr 4,11:5
Ford, John J Mrs, 1948, S 3,19:5
Ford, John Mrs, 1913, My 10,11:5; 1946, F 15,25:2
Ford, John Mrs (Lois Montross), 1961, S 18,29:2
Ford, John P, 1938, O 12,27:3
Ford, John W Mrs, 1938, Ap 29,21:2
Ford, Joseph, 1939, Je 3,15:6
Ford, Joseph A, 1950, D 6,33:4
Ford, Joseph A Mrs, 1947, Ja 27,23:4
Ford, Joseph B, 1950, D 3,89:1
Ford, Joseph N, 1947, Ap 4,23:2
Ford, Josephine, 1946, F 28,23:3
Ford, L Stanley, 1950, D 23,16:2
Ford, Laurence O Mrs, 1961, Jl 18,29:2
Ford, Leland M, 1965, N 29,35:4
Ford, Louise C Mrs, 1939, Mr 10,23:4
Ford, Lyman H, 1962, My 14,29:3
Ford, Lyndon H, 1944, Ag 3,19:4
Ford, Martin J, 1955, Ap 20,33:3
Ford, Mason F, 1951, Jl 31,21:5
Ford, Mathilde C Mrs, 1941, Jl 4,13:5
Ford, Michael A, 1944, Ag 11,15:1
Ford, Michael J Mrs, 1959, S 13,83:6
Ford, Nancy K Mrs, 1961, My 10,40:3
Ford, Norman J, 1944, Je 10,15:6
Ford, P C, 1947, D 22,23:7
Ford, Patrick, 1911, Ag 28,7:5; 1913, S 24,9:6
Ford, Patrick H, 1958, Je 19,31:4
Ford, Patrick J, 1940, Ja 20,15:6; 1958, O 27,27:2
Ford, Preston Leighton Mrs, 1916, My 16,13:5
Ford, Raedel, 1953, F 14,29:4
Ford, Richard, 1950, Ag 21,19:6; 1961, Ag 22,29:3
Ford, Richard T, 1952, O 14,31:2
Ford, Richard V T, 1949, Ap 15,23:4
Ford, Robert F, 1949, S 3,13:1
Ford, Robert H, 1941, My 28,25:2; 1954, O 22,28:1
Ford, Robert P, 1956, S 24,27:4
Ford, Robert S, 1950, O 30,27:2
Ford, Russell W, 1960, Ja 25,27:5
Ford, S, 1933, Ag 31,17:1
Ford, Sam C, 1961, N 26,88:3
Ford, Sewell, 1946, O 27,63:3
Ford, Sewell Mrs, 1950, D 12,33:4
Ford, Shirley S, 1945, Je 27,19:4
Ford, Stanley B, 1953, N 7,17:5
Ford, Stephen Van Rensselaer, 1910, Je 6,7:4
Ford, Sumner, 1966, F 6,92:6
Ford, Terence L, 1958, N 28,27:3
Ford, Thomas A, 1965, Mr 16,39:5
Ford, Thomas B Jr, 1966, Ag 7,81:3
Ford, Thomas G, 1909, My 26,9:6; 1942, Ap 16,21:4
Ford, Thomas J, 1963, Je 12,43:5
Ford, Timothy P, 1949, Mr 22,25:4
Ford, Townsend Mrs, 1913, N 23,IV,7:5
Ford, Una E, 1953, F 28,17:5
Ford, Vernon O, 1958, N 29,21:4
Ford, W Fred, 1940, S 18,23:3
Ford, Wallace (funl plans, Je 14,47:1), 1966, Je 12 86:4
Ford, Wallace Mrs, 1966, F 10,34:2
Ford, Walter, 1901, Mr 6,9:5
Ford, Walter B, 1948, Ap 9,23:4
Ford, Walter S, 1956, Jl 13,19:2
Ford, Wilbur H, 1946, D 18,29:1
Ford, Willard S, 1951, Mr 13,31:2
Ford, William, 1959, My 7,33:5
Ford, William A Sr, 1948, Ja 27,25:5
Ford, William E, 1939, Mr 24,21:2
Ford, William E Jr, 1940, Ag 16,15:4
Ford, William G, 1919, Je 25,19:6
Ford, William H, 1962, Ag 9,25:4
Ford, William H Jr, 1951, N 17,17:4
Ford, William Hall, 1920, S 25,13:2
Ford, William J, 1949, O 1,13:2
Ford, William J Sr, 1949, N 11,25:4
Ford, William M, 1938, N 28,15:3
Ford, William Mrs, 1940, Jl 20,15:5
Ford, William W, 1937, S 28,23:3; 1941, F 11,23:3
Ford, Willis P, 1942, Ja 1,25:4
Ford, Willis R, 1950, F 5,84:5
Ford, Worthington C, 1941, Mr 8,19:4
Forde, Edna L, 1945, Ap 17,23:6
Forde, Elroy, 1953, N 5,31:5
Forde, Florrie, 1940, Ap 19,21:6
Forde, Hal, 1955, D 6,27:2
Forde, John J, 1958, Mr 18,29:5
Fordham, Fred, 1968, Ap 22,47:4
Fordham, Herbert, 1953, S 12,17:6
Fordham, Lena M Mrs, 1941, S 17,23:2
Fordney, Chester L, 1959, My 27,35:2
Fordney, J W, 1932, Ja 9,17:1
Fordrung, William J Mrs, 1954, O 15,23:2
Fordyce, Alex R Jr, 1959, D 11,34:6
Fordyce, C, 1936, O 1,25:3
Fordyce, Claude P, 1953, Ag 19,29:3
Fordyce, De Lorme T, 1950, N 8,29:5
Fordyce, Edward W Mrs, 1950, N 13,33:4
Fordyce, John Addison Dr, 1925, Je 5,17:4
Fordyce, John R, 1939, Je 11,45:1
Fordyce, Samuel W (por), 1948, Ja 11,56:3
Fore, Sam Jr (funl), 1966, D 27,27:3
Foregger, Richard V, 1960, Ja 20,31:3
Forell, Frederick Joachim Rev, 1968, Ap 5,47:3
Forell, John G, 1961, D 28,12:4
Foreman, Agnes, 1937, Ja 29,19:3
Foreman, Al, 1954, D 24,13:3
Foreman, Albert W, 1950, Ag 15,29:1
Foreman, Alfred K, 1946, D 15,77:4
Foreman, Alvan H, 1958, Mr 25,33:4
Foreman, Avon O, 1944, O 12,27:4
Foreman, Charles J, 1947, O 5,68:4
Foreman, Charles W, 1951, O 30,29:2
Foreman, Edward, 1953, Ja 15,27:2
Foreman, Ernest W, 1944, Mr 5,35:1
Foreman, Estella, 1949, N 7,27:2
Foreman, Francis W, 1957, O 1,33:3
Foreman, Frank, 1957, N 20,35:4
Foreman, Gilbert Mrs, 1946, N 20,31:4
Foreman, Gordon A, 1963, Jl 20,19:3
Foreman, Gus, 1953, F 15,92:3
Foreman, H E, 1964, Ap 15,39:4
Foreman, Harold E, 1958, Jl 14,21:1
Foreman, Harrison W, 1949, Je 4,13:4
Foreman, James F, 1949, S 29,29:2; 1949, O 2,
Foreman, Jules L, 1968, My 24,47:2
Foreman, Loren C, 1945, F 19,17:5
Foreman, M J, 1935, O 17,23:4
Foreman, Walter F, 1951, Mr 7,33:4
Forepaugh, A, 1890, Ja 24,5:4
Forepaugh, J Louis, 1956, Ja 11,31:1

Forepaugh, William F, 1938, S 13,23:5
Forer, Leib, 1948, S 18,17:5
Foresman, Hugh A, 1960, Ja 15,31:3
Foresman, Marcus, 1946, D 30,22:2
Foresman, Robert Mrs, 1954, Ja 3,88:6
Forest, John, 1946, Ap 5,25:4
Forest, John Anthony Bp, 1911, Mr 12,II,13:3
Forestal, Joseph F, 1954, Mr 16,29:3
Forestek, Samuel, 1949, Ap 6,29:1
Forester, Arthur, 1944, Ap 2,40:1
Forester, Arthur W, 1961, Mr 22,41:1
Forester, Cecil S (will, My 11,51:7), 1966, Ap 3,1:7
Forester, Frank, 1948, Ap 28,27:4
Forester, Frank Mrs, 1964, Mr 27,28:1
Forester, Grace M, 1948, S 17,25:1
Forester, Max B, 1960, Ja 26,33:1
Forester, Paul, 1947, D 5,25:1
Forester, Richard A, 1953, N 5,31:2
Foresti, E Felix, 1858, O 8,4:6
Forestieri, Joseph (Mme), 1959, Ja 23,26:1
Forgan, D R, 1931, D 27,28:1
Forgan, David R Jr Mrs, 1937, Ja 10,II,11:1
Forgan, James Berwick (por),(funl, O 30,19:5), 1924, O 29,21:3
Forgan, Robert, 1962, Ja 20,21:5
Forgash, Morris, 1966, O 2,86:2
Forgeng, William A, 1939, F 8,23:4
Forger, Alex, 1962, S 30,87:2
Forger, Alois J, 1960, Ap 28,35:4
Forger, William, 1940, Je 17,15:6
Forgeron, Nelson P, 1950, Ja 6,21:2
Forgerson, Frank A, 1947, Mr 7,26:2
Forgerson, George I, 1947, F 28,23:1
Forget, Anastase, 1955, F 4,19:4
Forget, Joseph David Rodolphe, 1919, F 21,13:6
Forget, Peter, 1938, N 14,12:2
Forgey, Benjamin F, 1960, Mr 21,29:2
Forgey, Chauncey E, 1956, S 7,24:3
Forgey, Frank R, 1951, N 6,29:2
Forgie, James, 1958, Ag 14,29:6
Forgione, Francesco (Padre Pio), 1968, S 24,47:2
Forgione, James C, 1960, Ag 16,29:3
Forgrave, Leslie L, 1953, O 2,21:2
Forhan, Richard J, 1965, D 26,68:6
Forhan, Richard J Mrs, 1954, Jl 7,31:5
Forhead, Harry J, 1963, Ap 2,47:1
Forhecz, Julius M, 1956, Ap 11,33:2
Foringer, Alonzo E, 1948, D 10,26:3
Foris, Julius, 1963, Ap 3,47:2
Forker, Cunningham A, 1947, S 3,25:1
Forker, Eugene, 1948, Ap 26,23:3
Forker, Howard J Justice, 1915, Ap 27,13:5
Forker, J Tyson, 1937, Ap 26,19:4
Forker, John N, 1956, S 22,17:5
Forkins, Marty, 1964, O 6,39:4
Forkner, Allen Mrs, 1954, O 27,29:2
Forlenza, Felix Mrs, 1963, O 18,31:4
Forlenza, John A, 1968, Ag 10,27:4
Forlines, Charles E, 1944, Ag 1,15:3
Forma, Stanley, 1952, Mr 28,23:2
Formad, Marie K, 1944, F 24,15:3
Forman, Addie W Mrs, 1937, D 11,19:1
Forman, Alex A, 1939, Je 16,23:2
Forman, Alfred G, 1950, Ja 4,35:4
Forman, Allan, 1914, Mr 15,7:5
Forman, Benjamin, 1951, Mr 24,13:3
Forman, David, 1960, F 25,29:4; 1966, D 14,47:3
Forman, David S, 1968, Ja 10,43:1
Forman, Douglas N, 1961, S 26,39:2
Forman, Edward G, 1957, D 12,29:1
Forman, Frederick S, 1963, S 30,29:1
Forman, George, 1940, F 6,21:4
Forman, George E, 1962, Mr 24,25:4
Forman, George L Col, 1925, Ja 8,25:4
Forman, Harley G, 1947, Mr 5,25:3
Forman, Henry J, 1966, Ja 4,27:4
Forman, Howard A Mrs, 1955, Je 26,76:4
Forman, Howard S, 1944, S 20,23:2
Forman, Isaac Mrs, 1950, O 18,33:2
Forman, Jack Mrs, 1961, Ap 19,39:4
Forman, John, 1871, S 11,8:5
Forman, John N, 1967, Je 25,68:6
Forman, Josef K (will), 1957, Mr 11,27:6
Forman, Joseph Mrs, 1956, D 8,19:6
Forman, Lawrence, 1968, Ag 18,88:2
Forman, Louis C, 1944, F 16,17:3
Forman, Miles S, 1948, My 24,19:3
Forman, Paul H, 1966, Ap 18,29:5
Forman, Raye G Mrs, 1944, Mr 22,19:5
Forman, Raymond L, 1951, Je 14,27:2
Forman, Robert F, 1960, Mr 13,85:2
Forman, Samuel Mrs, 1958, Ap 28,23:4
Forman, W S, 1908, Je 11,7:3
Forman, Walter Mrs, 1957, Jl 14,73:2
Forman, William, 1956, F 8,33:4
Forman, William S, 1944, My 18,19:3
Formanek, Zdenko, 1962, My 19,27:2
Formanke, Rudolph W, 1948, N 28,92:5
Formato, Louis, 1947, O 10,25:4
Formby, George, 1961, Mr 7,35:2
Formento, Felix Dr, 1907, Je 7,9:5
Formes, Carl, 1874, O 21,4:7; 1889, D 16,5:3; 1954, Jl 12,19:2
Formica, Ignatius, 1957, Je 10,27:5
Formichella, John, 1954, D 28,23:2
Formichella, Michael H, 1967, F 23,35:3
Formichi, Carlo, 1943, D 18,15:3
Formidoni, Richard, 1968, Je 27,43:3
Formon, Henry J Sr, 1959, Ja 14,27:4
Formon, Louis F, 1924, F 22,15:3
Formusa, Vincent, 1942, Jl 10,17:2
Fornabaio, John, 1944, O 17,23:1
Fornaciari, Norma, 1960, N 9,35:1
Fornaro, Antonio, 1910, Je 21,9:4
Fornasero, Aug L, 1953, F 24,25:1
Forne, Theodore, 1949, O 12,29:4
Fornecker, Anton, 1940, Jl 20,15:4
Fornes, C V, 1929, My 23,29:3
Fornes, Charles J, 1917, O 9,11:6
Fornes, Walter F, 1945, F 20,19:5
Forness, Fred W, 1964, N 4,39:4
Forney, Edward H, 1943, My 4,23:1
Forney, J W, 1881, D 10,5:1
Forney, James Brig-Gen, 1921, F 3,7:3
Forney, John H, 1961, Ag 22,29:2
Forney, N Nes, 1957, N 27,31:1
Forney, Stehman, 1916, Ag 9,11:4
Forney, William B, 1943, Jl 15,21:5
Forney, William B Jr, 1958, S 6,17:3
Forni, Louis P, 1947, Ag 21,23:2
Fornia, Rita, 1922, O 28,13:5
Fornier, Charles B, 1948, Ja 9,22:2
Forray, William, 1954, Ap 3,15:2
Forrer, Louis, 1921, S 30,15:5
Forres, Lord (S K G Williamson), 1954, Je 29,27:3
Forrest, A Leland, 1957, My 8,37:1
Forrest, Alfred E, 1940, Ag 29,19:5
Forrest, Alfred E Jr (est tax appr, D 31,18:7), 1955, Je 29,29:4
Forrest, Allan, 1941, Jl 27,30:4
Forrest, Archibald A, 1946, My 8,25:4
Forrest, Archibald A Mrs, 1961, Ap 21,33:1
Forrest, Baron, 1918, S 5,11:6
Forrest, Bedford Gen (see also O 30), 1877, N 1,1:3
Forrest, Belford, 1938, My 2,17:3
Forrest, Charles N, 1946, D 5,32:2
Forrest, Charles Robert, 1912, O 7,11:5
Forrest, Clarence A, 1949, F 10,27:2
Forrest, Edward T, 1951, Jl 11,23:4
Forrest, Edwin, 1872, D 13,5:4
Forrest, Edwin Mrs, 1891, Je 24,5:4
Forrest, Eleanor S Mrs, 1938, Mr 14,15:5
Forrest, Frederick W, 1962, S 19,39:3
Forrest, George, 1938, Je 4,15:2
Forrest, George F, 1952, Jl 31,23:5
Forrest, Henry O, 1946, Ap 16,25:6
Forrest, James G, 1962, S 7,29:2
Forrest, James T, 1947, N 25,29:4
Forrest, Justin H, 1949, Mr 14,19:6
Forrest, Marshall, 1944, Je 24,13:4
Forrest, Maulsby, 1959, Ja 13,47:4
Forrest, Nathan B Gen, 1908, F 9,11:5
Forrest, Sam, 1944, My 1,15:6
Forrest, Wilbur Mrs, 1957, N 22,26:1
Forrest, Wilfred P, 1964, O 2,16:1
Forrest, William O, 1947, My 13,25:4
Forrestal, Frank V, 1959, Ag 16,82:4
Forrestal, William A, 1939, D 30,15:2
Forrestel, John A, 1948, Ag 15,60:6
Forrester, Alexander Rev Dr, 1869, Ap 24,4:5
Forrester, Alfred Day, 1872, Je 13,4:7
Forrester, C Jr, 1881, Je 19,7:5
Forrester, Charles F, 1942, D 6,76:1
Forrester, Claude R G, 1942, Mr 1,45:3
Forrester, Frederick C, 1952, O 15,31:5
Forrester, George R, 1949, Mr 28,21:4
Forrester, Henry, 1882, Ap 11,5:3
Forrester, J C, 1881, Ag 21,7:3
Forrester, James J, 1939, My 2,23:3
Forrester, Malcolm Sr, 1951, D 19,31:4
Forrester, Thomas C, 1945, My 24,19:4
Forrester, W, 1885, F 9,3:4
Forrester, Walter S, 1944, My 24,19:2
Forrester, William A Mrs, 1945, Je 20,23:4
Forrester-Paton, John, 1954, Ag 27,21:2
Forrey, Carl R, 1954, O 9,17:5
Forsalth, William J Justice, 1913, Mr 2,IV,7:4
Forsberg, Conrad E, 1961, N 21,39:1
Forsberg, Edwin F, 1947, My 12,21:4
Forsberg, Gunnar C, 1944, Ag 22,17:6
Forsberg, Lester Mrs, 1948, Ja 21,25:2
Forsch, Albert, 1961, Ag 2,29:2
Forsch, Carl, 1953, Ja 11,90:6
Forsch, Herbert, 1962, Ag 23,29:1
Forsch, James A, 1951, S 6,31:2
Forsch, James A Mrs, 1950, Jl 9,69:2
Forscher, Sidney, 1967, Ja 23,43:2
Forschler, G Elmer, 1944, Ag 12,11:5
Forschner, William A, 1952, O 4,17:4
Forse, Charles T Rear-Adm, 1925, Ap 14,23:3
Forsell, Charles M, 1952, S 30,31:5
Forsell, John, 1941, S 4,22:2
Forselund, Louise (Mrs Carey Waddell), 1910, My 3,13:6
Forshaw, Robert, 1945, S 3,23:2
Forshay, Isaac, 1961, Mr 4,23:3
Forshay, Joseph Burton, 1903, N 23,7:3
Forshay, Ralph H, 1946, My 17,21:2
Forshay, Royce W, 1943, Ap 2,21:6
Forshay, Stewart Mrs, 1957, N 4,29:4
Forshell, Rolf H, 1949, Ag 9,25:2
Forshew, Robert P, 1942, D 11,23:5
Forsht, David, 1907, Ap 20,9:6
Forslund, Jan, 1949, Mr 30,25:3
Forsmith, Albert, 1950, N 23,35:1
Forss, William A, 1954, F 18,31:3
Forssell, Gosta, 1950, N 16,31:1
Forst, Arthur D Mrs, 1952, Je 17,27:1
Forst, Arthur Mrs, 1961, F 8,28:1
Forst, George A, 1942, Jl 19,31:3
Forst, Leo, 1952, N 4,29:2
Forstall, Alfred E, 1952, Jl 3,25:5
Forstall, Alfred E Jr, 1938, Mr 6,II,8:1
Forstall, Armand W, 1948, Ap 22,27:3
Forstall, E J, 1873, N 20,8:4
Forstall, James A, 1949, D 30,19:5
Forstenzer, Harold, 1967, Ap 16,83:1
Forster, Albert A, 1948, Je 3,25:1
Forster, Bernhard D, 1964, N 28,21:4
Forster, Byron R, 1950, S 28,31:2
Forster, Charles, 1908, Ap 5,11:4
Forster, Charles G, 1937, Ag 24,21:3
Forster, Charles W, 1947, S 30,25:1
Forster, Frank J, 1948, Mr 5,22:3
Forster, Frederic J A, 1956, My 11,27:1
Forster, G W, 1961, O 22,86:7
Forster, Guido F, 1946, Ap 16,25:1
Forster, Gustave, 1944, Mr 2,17:1
Forster, H Walter, 1968, My 24,47:4
Forster, Harold J, 1949, N 16,30:3
Forster, Henry R, 1941, F 7,19:2
Forster, Herbert W, 1945, Mr 31,19:4
Forster, I G Gordon, 1953, F 12,27:2
Forster, Isaac, 1938, N 10,27:5
Forster, John (see also F 2 and 6), 1876, F 26,2:5
Forster, John A Mrs, 1942, Mr 1,45:2
Forster, John C, 1943, Je 29,19:2
Forster, John W L, 1938, Ap 26,21:2
Forster, Leon, 1962, Je 10,86:6
Forster, Oscar H, 1947, Jl 24,21:5
Forster, Otto W, 1950, Ag 30,32:2
Forster, Rudolf, 1968, O 28,96:1
Forster, Rudolph, 1943, Jl 8,19:1
Forster, Sam, 1946, S 8,44:2
Forster, Samuel, 1941, Ja 11,17:2
Forster, Samuel D, 1951, Ja 8,17:2
Forster, Tristram Mrs, 1953, D 14,31:3
Forster, W, 1928, Mr 8,25:2
Forster, W E, 1886, Ap 6,2:3
Forster, William J, 1957, Ag 10,15:4
Forster, William W, 1967, S 9,31:3
Forster-Cooper, Clive, 1947, Ag 24,56:2
Forsterer, Bruno A, 1957, Je 13,31:3
Forsthoff, Harry E A, 1962, My 14,29:4
Forstmann, Curt E, 1950, Ja 20,26:3
Forstmann, Julius, 1939, O 28,15:1; 1962, Je 15,27:2
Forstmann, Julius Mrs, 1953, Jl 30,23:6
Forstmann, Reinhold H, 1940, N 9,17:3
Forstner, George G von Baron, 1940, D 11,28:3
Forsyth, Ann E, 1950, F 28,29:4
Forsyth, Cecil, 1941, D 8,23:2
Forsyth, Charles, 1914, N 9,9:5
Forsyth, Charles Col, 1872, Mr 24,1:6
Forsyth, Charles H, 1960, N 4,35:2
Forsyth, Cora A Mrs, 1939, Ag 13,29:2
Forsyth, Daniel W, 1937, O 16,19:2
Forsyth, David, 1941, Ap 15,23:2
Forsyth, David D Mrs, 1944, N 17,19:4
Forsyth, Donald W, 1956, Je 12,35:3
Forsyth, E Avard, 1949, Je 15,29:4
Forsyth, Elizabeth S Mrs, 1940, Ag 23,15:4
Forsyth, Emily V B Mrs, 1942, F 18,19:4
Forsyth, F Norman, 1945, Je 6,21:3
Forsyth, George Alexander Gen, 1915, S 13,9:3
Forsyth, George Wallace, 1918, Je 25,13:7
Forsyth, Harold F Mrs, 1954, Ag 28,89:3
Forsyth, Harry, 1961, Jl 19,29:5
Forsyth, Holmes, 1952, F 4,17:4
Forsyth, J, 1877, My 3,4:7
Forsyth, James C, 1950, My 1,25:1
Forsyth, James McQueen Rear-Adm, 1915, Ag 4,11:5
Forsyth, James W, 1939, N 7,28:4
Forsyth, James W Maj-Gen, 1906, O 25,9:4
Forsyth, John, 1955, My 26,31:5
Forsyth, John A, 1948, My 3,21:3
Forsyth, John B, 1948, F 25,23:4
Forsyth, John D Mrs, 1940, Ag 15,19:4
Forsyth, Joseph C, 1944, Ag 19,11:5
Forsyth, Lionel A, 1957, Ja 2,27:4
Forsyth, Ralph K, 1947, N 12,27:3
Forsyth, Robert, 1922, F 10,15:4
Forsyth, Robert W, 1950, Jl 27,25:2
Forsyth, T Irving, 1950, N 6,27:5
Forsyth, William Mrs, 1947, D 11,33:3; 1950, D 19, 29:3
Forsyth, Winifred, 1942, S 23,25:4
Forsythe, Cephus, 1903, Jl 16,7:6
Forsythe, Clellan S, 1953, S 19,16:5
Forsythe, Edmund M, 1960, D 28,27:3

Forsythe, Fred A, 1939, My 28,III,7:3
Forsythe, Homer J, 1937, Ap 30,22:2
Forsythe, Homer J Mrs, 1965, Jl 4,37:2
Forsythe, John, 1944, F 20,36:2
Forsythe, Joseph M, 1941, Jl 17,19:4
Forsythe, Mary Isabella, 1914, Jl 3,9:5
Forsythe, Mimi, 1952, Ag 22,21:3
Forsythe, Robert S (will, Je 12,24:4), 1941, Je 7,17:1
Forsythe, Timothy J Mrs (Grace S Forsythe), 1922, Jl 22,7:6
Forsythe, Victor C, 1962, My 26,25:5
Forsythe, Wilfred L, 1949, O 7,31:1
Forsythe, William B, 1959, Mr 9,29:4
Fort, Anna E F Mrs, 1937, Ag 26,21:5
Fort, Franklin W (will, Jl 4,6:5), 1937, Je 21,19:3
Fort, Franklin W Mrs, 1952, N 1,21:5
Fort, Fred W Jr, 1947, F 1,15:2
Fort, Frederick W Mrs, 1941, Jl 15,19:5
Fort, G L, 1883, Ja 15,5:3
Fort, George, 1919, Mr 26,15:3
Fort, George A, 1948, Ja 13,26:4
Fort, George C, 1955, Je 26,76:7
Fort, George F Ex-Gov, 1872, Ap 25,8:2
Fort, George Franklin, 1909, Mr 31,11:4
Fort, Gerrit, 1952, S 5,27:3
Fort, Harry S, 1951, N 12,25:2
Fort, J Carter Mrs, 1951, F 20,25:2
Fort, J Irving, 1947, S 1,19:6
Fort, Jardine C, 1962, My 2,46:8
Fort, John Franklin Ex-Gov, 1920, N 18,15:4
Fort, John Franklin Mrs, 1921, N 10,19:5
Fort, John L, 1940, Mr 31,45:2
Fort, John N Jr, 1943, Ja 25,13:5
Fort, John P, 1957, N 5,31:5
Fort, Leslie R, 1945, D 17,21:5
Fort, Margretta, 1956, Ag 5,77:3
Fort, Marion K Jr, 1964, Ag 3,25:3
Fort, Paul, 1960, Ap 22,31:4; 1962, Mr 23,33:2
Fort, Peter, 1875, O 5,6:6
Fort, Randolph L, 1962, F 23,29:3
Fort, Richard, 1959, My 18,28:1
Fort, William E, 1942, Ag 5,19:6
Fort, William L Sr, 1945, Jl 5,13:5
Fortas, William Mrs, 1946, O 11,23:4
Forte, Aldo, 1960, My 25,7:6
Forte, Frank, 1951, Ap 17,29:5
Forte, Gary J, 1957, O 25,27:3
Forte, Irving C, 1939, Ap 17,17:4
Fortenbaugh, Kenneth H Mrs, 1948, D 5,92:6
Fortenbaugh, Samuel B, 1943, F 7,49:2
Fortescue, Earl (H William), 1958, Je 16,23:5
Fortescue, F A, 1942, O 14,25:3
Fortescue, George K, 1914, Ja 14,11:6
Fortescue, George Mrs, 1925, O 3,15:5
Fortescue, Granville R, 1952, Ap 22,29:3
Fortescue, Horace, 1941, Ja 27,15:1
Fortescue, Kenyon, 1939, Mr 17,21:3
Fortescue, Thomas A, 1957, F 24,84:4
Fortescue, Viola, 1953, S 17,29:3
Fortescue, Walter S Prof, 1911, D 30,11:4
Fortesque, Ellen Lady (Emma C Williams), 1885, F 24,1:2
Fortgang, Maurice, 1959, D 7,31:5
Forth, Cleora, 1952, Jl 6,48:6
Forth, Frances G, 1940, Mr 24,31:3
Forth, Frederick Jr, 1945, S 11,23:3
Forthoffer, Frank H Mrs, 1950, Je 17,15:6
Forthuber, Henry L Mrs, 1950, S 2,15:5
Fortier, Anselme, 1959, Je 27,23:3
Fortier, C L Mrs, 1941, O 1,21:3
Fortier, Edward J Prof, 1918, D 26,11:5
Fortier, Joseph A, 1942, N 24,25:3
Fortier, Llewelyn C, 1959, Jl 29,29:3
Fortin, Alexander, 1911, Ap 3,9:4
Fortin, Phil F, 1957, S 11,33:4
Fortinsky, Jacob, 1949, Mr 6,72:4
Fortis, Allesandro, 1909, D 4,11:5
Fortliti, Teresa Mrs, 1947, N 29,13:5
Fortman, Chris J, 1939, F 3,15:4
Fortman, Selig, 1951, F 4,77:1
Fortman, Selig Mrs, 1961, Je 16,33:1
Fortmiller, Paul V, 1941, Ag 19,22:2
Fortnam, Clarence D, 1948, Ap 22,27:1
Fortner, Clark A, 1947, O 18,16:2
Fortner, William G, 1950, D 13,35:5
Fortney, Cliffe D, 1948, Ja 6,23:3
Fortney, John R, 1944, Mr 28,19:3
Fortney, Lorain, 1946, Ja 1,27:3
Fortoul, Jose G, 1943, Je 16,21:5
Fortson, Henry L, 1949, D 11,93:1
Fortson, John L, 1954, Ap 24,17:7
Fortunato, Patrick J, 1959, Jl 1,25:5
Fortunato, Vladimir M, 1938, Je 11,15:3
Fortune, Alonzo W, 1950, D 28,25:1
Fortune, Eulalia Mrs, 1944, S 26,25:2
Fortune, Robert, 1880, Ap 15,5:4
Fortune, Victor M, 1949, Ja 3,23:2
Fortune, William, 1942, Ja 30,19:5
Fortune, William J, 1946, O 16,27:2
Fortunes, James G, 1953, Ja 30,22:5
Fortunoff, Jacob A, 1962, My 10,37:3
Fortuny, the Artist, 1874, N 24,2:2
Fortuny y Madrazo, Mariano Mrs (Henriette N), 1965, Mr 17,45:3
Forward, John, 1949, Ap 30,13:6
Forward, John F, 1955, Jl 30,17:6
Forwood, Harry, 1967, Ja 20,43:2
Forwood, William H Brig-Gen, 1915, My 13,15:5
Fosberg, Gladys, 1921, Ag 19,13:4
Fosbery, George Vincnet Lt-Col, 1907, My 9,9:6
Fosbroke, Hughell Mrs, 1954, Ag 17,21:4
Fosbrook, Howard P, 1953, Je 28,60:7
Foscato, L Vincent, 1966, S 6,47:3
Foscato, Sydney E, 1961, Mr 20,29:4
Foschi, Italo, 1949, Mr 22,25:2
Foschini, Francesco Gen, 1937, D 10,25:5
Foschini, Paul J, 1954, S 24,23:2
Fosdal, Sigbjorn, 1944, Mr 8,19:3
Fosdick, Charles Austin (Harry Castleman), 1915, Ag 23,9:5
Fosdick, Charles H, 1941, My 17,15:5
Fosdick, Clark, 1962, O 13,25:3
Fosdick, Douglas, 1949, Jl 26,27:3
Fosdick, Dudley, 1957, Je 19,35:2
Fosdick, Edith W, 1952, Ap 9,31:3
Fosdick, Frank C, 1945, F 7,21:3
Fosdick, Frank S Mrs, 1950, Jl 11,31:5
Fosdick, Frederick V Judge, 1925, My 12,23:3
Fosdick, Frederick W, 1943, F 25,21:2
Fosdick, Harry E Mrs (mem ser set, N 17,41:1), 1964, N 7,27:2
Fosdick, James W, 1937, S 15,23:5
Fosdick, Willard A, 1958, D 4,39:2
Fosdick G A, 1882, D 26,5:4
Fosgate, Julia F Mrs, 1954, D 1,31:2
Foshag, William F, 1956, My 23,31:3
Foshay, Benjamin S, 1937, O 15,23:5
Foshay, Harold Adams, 1953, F 25,27:2
Foshay, Harry B, 1947, F 10,29:4
Foshay, Harry D Mrs, 1946, My 11,27:3
Foshay, Harry E, 1951, F 14,29:4
Foshay, J Russell, 1947, Je 15,60:7
Foshay, J Russell Mrs, 1949, S 27,27:1
Foshay, Lee, 1960, Je 7,35:4
Foshay, Mary A, 1947, D 31,15:3
Foshay, P Maxwell, 1939, Ja 27,20:3
Foshay, Wilbur B, 1957, S 4,34:1
Foshay, William B, 1939, Jl 3,13:6
Foshay, William F, 1923, Ja 18,15:5
Foshee, Alex M, 1955, Ja 22,11:1
Fosher, Paul L, 1948, N 29,23:4
Foskett, Eben Dr, 1923, Je 15,19:5
Foskett, James H, 1961, My 23,39:3
Foskett, William E, 1939, F 2,19:5
Fosman, Abraham, 1951, O 23,29:2
Fosnot, Harold R, 1965, D 12,87:1
Foss, Anna deB Mrs, 1940, Ag 8,19:3
Foss, Arch C, 1938, N 22,19:3
Foss, Calvin W, 1947, O 24,23:4
Foss, Clifton M, 1951, Mr 29,27:2
Foss, Cyrus D Bp, 1910, Ja 30,II,11:4
Foss, Ernest, 1947, My 31,13:3
Foss, Eugene N, 1939, S 14,23:1
Foss, Florence Winslow, 1968, O 30,47:3
Foss, Frank H, 1947, F 16,57:4; 1948, Ja 4,52:1
Foss, Frank H Mrs, 1949, Jl 8,19:2
Foss, Fred E, 1942, Ja 24,15:8
Foss, Frederic D, 1954, Je 18,23:5
Foss, George E, 1950, Je 30,23:5
Foss, George Edmund, 1912, Je 7,13:4
Foss, H Erwin, 1951, O 14,88:4
Foss, Harold L, 1967, Ag 12,25:3
Foss, Harry C, 1954, O 12,27:2
Foss, Henry J, 1943, My 24,15:2
Foss, Herbert D, 1944, My 18,19:6
Foss, Howard C, 1938, Ja 10,17:6
Foss, Kendall, 1964, Ag 13,32:5
Foss, Lewien B, 1953, Ag 31,17:1
Foss, Martin H, 1949, D 21,29:4
Foss, Martin M, 1953, Ja 14,31:1
Foss, Mary E Mrs, 1962, S 1,19:5
Foss, Oliver R, 1957, F 23,17:3
Foss, Ralph S (por), 1949, S 7,30:2
Foss, Sam Walter, 1911, F 27,9:3
Foss, William L, 1953, Ja 13,27:5
Foss, Wilson P, 1957, N 18,31:1
Fossati, Carlo R Count, 1940, Ja 6,13:5
Fossati, Maurillio Cardinal, 1965, Mr 31,39:4
Fossatti, Ilyana, 1942, F 17,22:3
Fosse, Joseph T, 1937, F 27,33:6
Fossett, Jerry E, 1950, D 15,31:3
Fossume, Flinn L, 1940, Ap 27,15:2
Foster, A B, 1877, N 2,5:3
Foster, A E Manning, 1939, Ag 26,15:4
Foster, A S, 1871, My 3,1:3
Foster, A Volney, 1950, S 5,27:2
Foster, Addison G Ex-Sen, 1917, Ja 18,11:2
Foster, Al Capt, 1911, Jl 8,9:3
Foster, Albert E, 1919, Jl 24,9:1
Foster, Albert Jr, 1948, Mr 7,69:1
Foster, Albert O, 1945, F 1,23:4
Foster, Albt F, 1952, Je 14,15:6
Foster, Alexis C, 1945, My 1,23:5
Foster, Alfred E, 1947, My 30,21:3
Foster, Alfred W, 1962, N 27,37:2
Foster, Alis, 1955, Jl 15,21:3
Foster, Alonzo, 1917, S 8,9:4
Foster, Alrick M, 1952, O 7,29:3
Foster, Amos P, 1952, Ag 8,17:4
Foster, Andrew B, 1963, O 9,43:1
Foster, Andrew W, 1907, F 3,7:6
Foster, Anna B Mrs, 1944, Je 5,19:2
Foster, Annie W, 1951, S 30,72:4
Foster, Asa Lansford, 1904, Ja 14,9:6
Foster, Austin J, 1967, D 12,48:1
Foster, Balthazar S S (Lord Ilkeston), 1952, Ja 5,
Foster, Benjamin F, 1962, N 7,39:4
Foster, Benjamin K, 1949, Mr 3,25:5
Foster, Benjamin O, 1938, Je 23,21:2
Foster, Bert, 1951, F 7,29:2
Foster, Billy, 1967, Ja 21,23:1
Foster, Boutwell H, 1965, D 20,35:4
Foster, C J, 1883, S 8,5:4
Foster, C M, 1901, My 8,9:6
Foster, C W, 1883, Ap 27,5:4
Foster, Carl, 1959, Mr 14,23:4
Foster, Carol H, 1956, O 6,21:5
Foster, Carrie, 1940, Je 27,23:2
Foster, Charles, 1948, Ja 20,24:3
Foster, Charles (Pop),(will, My 16,29:6), 1956, My 6,86:5
Foster, Charles B, 1942, Je 28,33:3
Foster, Charles C, 1942, My 29,17:5; 1943, Mr 23 19:5; 1943, D 4,13:6; 1944, D 2,13:3
Foster, Charles Dr, 1937, D 15,25:5
Foster, Charles E, 1949, D 9,31:5; 1955, D 10,21:
Foster, Charles ex-Gov, 1904, Ja 10,7:3
Foster, Charles F, 1948, S 27,23:1
Foster, Charles G, 1907, O 28,9:5
Foster, Charles H Mrs, 1951, D 8,11:6
Foster, Charles H W, 1955, S 23,26:4
Foster, Charles K, 1945, Jl 29,40:6; 1949, Ja 11,3
Foster, Charles L, 1942, F 16,19:7
Foster, Charles L Mrs, 1947, Ag 7,21:4
Foster, Charles P, 1943, F 10,25:2
Foster, Charles T, 1948, O 22,25:3
Foster, Charles W, 1937, Jl 23,19:4
Foster, Charles W Mrs, 1946, O 11,23:4
Foster, Clarence F, 1944, Ap 18,21:2
Foster, Clark C, 1940, S 25,27:3
Foster, Clark C Jr, 1949, Mr 15,27:2
Foster, Clark H, 1945, S 13,23:2
Foster, Claud H, 1965, Je 22,21:3
Foster, Clayton L, 1960, Ag 26,25:4
Foster, Clifford Mrs, 1961, Ja 21,21:5
Foster, Clyde, 1949, Ap 26,25:4
Foster, Conrad H, 1940, Ap 4,23:5
Foster, D C, 1903, Mr 1,7:5
Foster, David G Mrs, 1943, O 6,23:4
Foster, David Johnson, 1912, Mr 22,9:5
Foster, Dwight E, 1949, N 18,29:4
Foster, E Agate, 1939, S 29,23:4
Foster, Eber F, 1955, Mr 16,33:4
Foster, Eber F Mrs, 1951, My 1,29:4
Foster, Ed F, 1872, Jl 29,1:6
Foster, Edgar H, 1937, Ap 15,23:4
Foster, Edgar K, 1948, Jl 30,17:3
Foster, Edna A, 1945, Jl 12,11:4
Foster, Edward, 1958, Ag 1,21:4
Foster, Edward C, 1950, N 29,36:5; 1964, N 7,2
Foster, Edward K, 1967, N 25,39:3
Foster, Edward P Rev, 1937, Jl 18,II,7:3
Foster, Edward S, 1949, Ja 25,23:2
Foster, Edwin C, 1957, Je 9,88:7
Foster, Edwin H T (por), 1948, Ja 23,23:5
Foster, Elizabeth, 1950, Jl 8,13:4
Foster, Ella W Mrs, 1951, Je 17,86:1
Foster, Emory, 1907, Je 24,7:6
Foster, Ernest H, 1949, Ja 25,23:4
Foster, Esty Mrs, 1957, Jl 24,25:4
Foster, Ethel E P Mrs, 1941, Ap 13,38:4
Foster, Etta, 1954, Mr 24,29:6
Foster, Eugene G, 1938, Jl 17,27:5
Foster, Eugene G Mrs, 1938, N 2,24:2
Foster, Eugene H, 1954, Ap 15,29:5
Foster, F Carlisle, 1968, Mr 7,43:3
Foster, F E, 1876, Mr 10,5:5; 1944, Je 16,19:4
Foster, F Spencer, 1951, F 28,27:4
Foster, Fay, 1960, Ap 19,37:4
Foster, Fernald, 1959, My 28,31:5
Foster, Finlay, 1953, O 31,17:3
Foster, Finley M, 1948, Ja 12,19:3
Foster, Floyd Mrs, 1924, Ag 30,9:6
Foster, Frances M Mrs, 1951, N 6,29:4
Foster, Frank B (will, D 6,26:2), 1940, N 27,
Foster, Frank B, 1957, D 30,23:6
Foster, Frank B Mrs, 1949, S 18,95:3
Foster, Frank J, 1946, Ag 25,45:1
Foster, Frank J Mrs, 1947, Jl 13,44:4
Foster, Frank L, 1961, Je 30,25:2
Foster, Frank L Dr, 1961, F 4,19:4
Foster, Frank M, 1950, O 9,25:4
Foster, Frank P 2d, 1942, Mr 13,19:3
Foster, Frank P 2d Mrs, 1942, Je 14,45:2
Foster, Fred S, 1945, Ap 4,21:5
Foster, Fred W Lt-Col, 1911, Je 30,9:4
Foster, Frederic G, 1965, Je 28,29:2
Foster, Frederick J Mrs, 1946, Jl 9,21:2
Foster, Frederick W, 1908, Mr 15,9:5

Foster, Frederick W C, 1939, F 7,20:1
Foster, G E Sir, 1931, D 31,19:2
Foster, G P, 1879, Mr 23,1:7
Foster, George, 1946, Jl 27,17:3
Foster, George B, 1941, D 30,19:6
Foster, George Burman Dr, 1918, D 23,11:3
Foster, George E, 1938, Jl 24,29:4; 1962, Jl 3,23:1
Foster, George F, 1914, Ag 25,9:6; 1945, Ag 16,19:4
Foster, George G, 1955, Mr 12,19:3
Foster, George G Mrs, 1957, O 26,21:5
Foster, George H, 1940, Je 18,23:3; 1951, Ja 30,25:5
Foster, George I, 1946, Je 25,21:4
Foster, George J, 1942, My 25,15:6
Foster, George S, 1946, Je 9,40:3
Foster, George W, 1937, Ag 15,II,7:3; 1942, F 1,42:6
Foster, Gerard S, 1938, Ap 22,19:4
Foster, Gilbert L, 1940, My 18,15:2
Foster, Giraud, 1945, S 23,44:3
Foster, Glen E, 1962, Ap 30,27:2
Foster, H Alden Mrs, 1955, D 31,13:4
Foster, H Clay Mrs, 1945, Ja 5,15:1
Foster, H D, 1880, O 18,5:5; 1927, D 29,23:2
Foster, H Hastings Jr Mrs, 1952, D 1,23:4
Foster, Hannah J W Mrs, 1940, O 8,25:1
Foster, Harold A, 1953, Ap 6,19:5
Foster, Harrison G, 1940, F 7,21:1
Foster, Harry, 1938, Je 23,21:1
Foster, Harry C, 1917, Mr 7,11:6
Foster, Harry S, 1939, Jl 21,19:1
Foster, Harry V, 1953, Je 10,29:2
Foster, Harry W, 1964, Ag 7,29:4
Foster, Henry C, 1950, Je 2,24:2
Foster, Henry H, 1947, F 23,53:4
Foster, Henry V, 1939, Je 6,23:5
Foster, Henry W Mrs, 1943, Ap 24,13:3
Foster, Herbert H, 1942, D 3,25:6
Foster, Herbert R, 1945, Ag 23,23:6
Foster, Herbert W, 1953, Jl 15,25:4
Foster, Horace W, 1959, Ap 11,21:4
Foster, Horatio A, 1913, Ap 28,11:3
Foster, Howard C, 1941, Mr 26,23:4
Foster, Howell, 1949, Mr 20,76:5
Foster, Hugh M, 1947, My 22,27:6
Foster, I Ira, 1937, Ag 21,15:5
Foster, Inez W, 1965, Jl 3,19:6
Foster, Israel M, 1950, Je 11,92:3
Foster, Ivory Mrs, 1941, S 13,17:3
Foster, J C P Dr, 1910, Ap 2,11:4
Foster, J G Gen Mrs, 1871, Je 7,8:3
Foster, J Hegeman, 1950, D 9,15:3
Foster, J Herbert, 1948, S 17,25:4
Foster, J Herbert Mrs, 1949, D 5,23:3
Foster, J Hugh, 1946, Ap 23,21:4
Foster, J Mansfield, 1943, N 17,25:4
Foster, J R Mrs, 1902, F 23,2:6
Foster, J W, 1873, Jl 1,4:7
Foster, James D, 1938, Ja 6,19:3
Foster, James H, 1938, My 10,21:5; 1943, S 26,48:1
Foster, James K, 1967, Mr 29,45:2
Foster, James L, 1947, Ja 19,53:6
Foster, James P, 1944, Jl 8,11:1
Foster, James W, 1962, My 2,37:1
Foster, Jay Stanley, 1925, Ag 15,11:6
Foster, Jed S, 1962, Je 8,31:3
Foster, Joel Dr, 1884, Je 30,5:4
Foster, John, 1867, N 3,1:2; 1943, N 25,25:3
Foster, John B, 1941, S 30,23:3
Foster, John B Mrs, 1939, O 29,40:8
Foster, John E, 1951, Je 12,29:3; 1963, Jl 6,15:3
Foster, John J, 1943, S 7,23:2
Foster, John M, 1940, D 30,17:2; 1958, Ag 25,21:4
Foster, John M Col, 1920, Ja 8,17:1
Foster, John M Mrs, 1949, Ja 11,31:5
Foster, John S, 1914, Jl 22,9:6; 1943, My 27,25:3; 1960, O 30,86:4; 1964, S 11,33:2
Foster, John S Maj-Gen, 1874, S 3,4:7
Foster, John S Sr Mrs (Flora), 1966, N 19,33:2
Foster, John W, 1917, N 16,11:3; 1944, D 12,23:2; 1957, My 26,93:1; 1966, Mr 23,47:1
Foster, John W Mrs, 1922, Je 19,15:6
Foster, Joseph, 1945, Ag 14,21:3
Foster, Joseph E, 1925, Ap 22,23:5
Foster, Joseph T, 1950, N 23,35:5
Foster, Josephine C Mrs, 1941, Jl 5,11:2
Foster, Josephine G, 1952, D 6,21:3
Foster, Joshua James, 1923, Mr 25,6:2
Foster, Julia M Mrs, 1937, Jl 15,19:1
Foster, Katherine W, 1961, N 8,35:1
Foster, Kenneth, 1955, S 6,25:3; 1964, S 1,36:7
Foster, L S, 1880, S 20,1:7
Foster, L S Mrs, 1903, Ja 21,9:4
Foster, Lady, 1947, Ap 1,27:4
Foster, Lee B, 1965, Ag 8,64:5
Foster, Lillian (por), 1949, My 16,21:4
Foster, Louis Mrs, 1960, Je 5,86:6
Foster, Lucretia Monroe Mrs, 1924, F 12,17:3
Foster, Lucy D, 1955, My 24,31:3
Foster, Luther H, 1949, Jl 7,25:5
Foster, Mack H, 1960, N 7,35:5
Foster, Macomb G, 1938, Je 2,23:4
Foster, Mahlon B, 1944, F 25,17:3
Foster, Maitland P, 1943, D 10,27:3
Foster, Major B, 1958, Jl 6,56:2
Foster, Malcolm C, 1952, Ap 10,29:2
Foster, Manuel, 1946, Je 12,27:5
Foster, Marcellus E, 1942, Ap 2,21:4
Foster, Margaret (Sister Marie Ursulina), 1942, Ja 13,22:4
Foster, Margaret Louise De Milt, 1907, Ag 4,7:6
Foster, Mark P Mrs, 1950, Ja 21,17:4
Foster, Martin D, 1919, O 21,15:3
Foster, Martius D, 1950, Mr 25,11:6
Foster, Mary C, 1951, N 28,31:3
Foster, Mary L, 1959, Mr 17,33:1
Foster, Matthias L Mrs, 1953, F 19,23:3
Foster, Maximillian, 1943, S 22,23:3
Foster, Michael, 1956, Mr 26,29:5
Foster, Michael Sir, 1907, Ja 31,9:6
Foster, Milton W, 1962, Ag 28,31:3
Foster, Morris, 1968, Ag 26,39:3
Foster, Mortimer B, 1957, Jl 7,60:8
Foster, Morton H C, 1943, Ag 21,11:4
Foster, Muriel, 1937, D 24,19:2
Foster, Murphy J, 1921, Je 13,13:4
Foster, Nathaniel G, 1907, Ja 19,7:5
Foster, Nathaniel R, 1952, Ja 27,76:3
Foster, Nathaniel Woodhull, 1910, Ag 18,9:6
Foster, Norman S, 1956, Ap 3,35:3
Foster, Norris A, 1965, Ap 5,31:4
Foster, Orin E, 1946, Ag 31,8:6
Foster, Paul, 1905, Je 24,1:4
Foster, Paul P, 1945, D 23,18:7
Foster, Pell W, 1947, Ap 21,27:6
Foster, Pell W Mrs, 1938, My 17,23:5
Foster, Percy A, 1954, Je 3,27:3
Foster, Percy G, 1947, Ag 12,23:1
Foster, R S Bp, 1903, My 2,9:5
Foster, Reginald, 1944, D 23,13:2; 1960, N 29,37:4
Foster, Reginald C, 1945, Ap 6,15:2
Foster, Reginald L, 1940, Je 14,21:1
Foster, Reginald Mrs (trb lr), 1962, Jl 28,18:5
Foster, Rene, 1960, D 30,19:5
Foster, Reuben Caril, 1908, Ja 28,9:5
Foster, Richard A Mrs, 1943, F 27,13:6
Foster, Richard R, 1955, Mr 28,27:2
Foster, Richard S, 1951, Mr 27,29:5
Foster, Richard V, 1963, D 10,50:8
Foster, Richard W, 1964, S 6,56:4
Foster, Robert A, 1957, Je 27,25:3
Foster, Robert F, 1945, D 27,19:3
Foster, Robert P, 1959, Je 11,33:5
Foster, Roger, 1924, F 22,15:4
Foster, Rufus E, 1942, Ag 24,15:3
Foster, Ruth, 1950, S 30,17:3
Foster, S S, 1881, S 13,3:1
Foster, Sadie Mrs, 1941, N 9,53:3
Foster, Sally R Mrs, 1957, N 8,29:3
Foster, Samuel D, 1944, S 10,45:2
Foster, Samuel G, 1952, Mr 11,27:3
Foster, Sandys B, 1938, Je 10,21:2
Foster, Sara E, 1944, My 1,15:4
Foster, Scott, 1922, Ja 27,15:5
Foster, Stephen C, 1864, Ja 31,3:5
Foster, Stephen M, 1948, N 4,29:5
Foster, Sterling Mrs, 1944, S 25,17:2
Foster, Susan, 1952, O 16,38:6
Foster, T Henry Mrs, 1956, S 30,87:1
Foster, T Jack, 1968, Mr 17,80:8
Foster, T Newton, 1912, N 11,11:6
Foster, Tallmadge Woodward, 1925, Ap 10,19:5
Foster, Thelma H Mrs, 1941, Ag 18,13:5
Foster, Theodore Dr, 1937, F 13,13:4
Foster, Thomas, 1946, Jl 18,25:1
Foster, Thomas B, 1954, Ap 14,29:1
Foster, Thomas G, 1957, My 9,31:6
Foster, Thomas H, 1951, N 15,29:1
Foster, Thomas L, 1945, D 12,27:1
Foster, Thorne, 1954, D 28,23:2
Foster, Vernon W, 1954, D 24,13:6
Foster, Victor A, 1955, N 22,35:5
Foster, Vincent L, 1949, Jl 19,46:3
Foster, Volney W, 1904, Ag 16,7:6
Foster, W Edward, 1940, Ag 9,15:3
Foster, W Edward Mrs, 1946, Jl 26,21:6
Foster, W W, 1954, D 4,17:6
Foster, Walter B, 1871, Ap 2,1:4
Foster, Walter C, 1903, Jl 24,7:6; 1963, Ap 4,47:5
Foster, Walter R, 1944, Jl 19,17:3
Foster, Walter S, 1943, Ja 22,20:3
Foster, Ward G, 1940, Mr 18,17:1
Foster, Warren D, 1961, S 23,19:1
Foster, Warren H, 1947, Ag 31,36:8
Foster, Warren W, 1943, Ag 10,19:3; 1945, My 5,15:4
Foster, Wilbur S Mrs, 1942, My 14,19:2
Foster, Will, 1953, Je 29,21:5
Foster, Will A Mrs, 1964, S 2,37:5
Foster, Willett, 1945, Ag 7,23:2
Foster, William, 1942, Je 16,23:5; 1945, Ag 31,17:4; 1947, D 3,29:2
Foster, William A, 1941, Ap 14,17:2; 1963, Ap 11,33:3
Foster, William B, 1937, D 22,25:5; 1947, D 22,21:1
Foster, William B Mrs, 1939, My 10,23:2
Foster, William D, 1958, Ap 5,15:5
Foster, William E, 1963, My 15,39:2
Foster, William E Mrs, 1951, Je 23,15:3
Foster, William Edward, 1915, Ag 26,9:7
Foster, William F, 1948, S 5,40:4
Foster, William G, 1946, S 27,23:4
Foster, William G Sr, 1961, Ap 2,76:2
Foster, William H, 1938, D 1,23:5; 1941, N 1,15:6; 1945, Mr 1,21:1; 1951, O 19,27:1; 1956, N 3,23:6
Foster, William H Mrs, 1950, My 10,31:5
Foster, William H T, 1949, Jl 9,13:6
Foster, William Henry Col, 1908, Mr 29,9:7
Foster, William J, 1958, D 7,88:1
Foster, William J Jr, 1959, Ja 29,27:5
Foster, William Jr, 1907, F 22,9:5
Foster, William M, 1871, D 8,8:4; 1911, S 28,9:5
Foster, William Mrs, 1951, F 12,23:2
Foster, William Prof, 1937, My 25,28:1
Foster, William S, 1955, N 13,87:4
Foster, William T, 1950, O 9,25:1
Foster, William W, 1940, Jl 2,21:3
Foster, William Z (trb, S 6,37:3;funl, S 7,35:4), 1961, S 2,15:3
Foster, Winifred Y Mrs, 1937, Ag 28,15:4
Foster, Woolston H, 1959, Ja 6,33:4
Foster, Worth W, 1948, Ap 24,15:3
Foster, Zeon L, 1944, D 17,37:2
Foster-Welch, Lucia M Mrs, 1940, Mr 12,23:6
Foth, Benjamin G Mrs, 1952, Ja 10,29:3
Fothergill, John R, 1957, Ag 30,19:1
Fothergill, Philip, 1959, F 1,84:4
Fothergill, Robert R, 1938, Mr 21,15:2
Fothergill, W E Dr, 1926, N 6,17:3
Fotheringham, John T, 1940, My 20,17:5
Fotheringhame, George, 1937, Ap 2,2:2
Foti, Domenico, 1947, Ap 19,15:5
Foti, Frank L, 1960, Ap 11,31:4
Fotitch, Constantin A, 1959, F 15,84:4
Foubleday, Felix D, 1941, My 13,23:2
Foucart, Therese, 1954, Ap 10,15:3
Foucault, Daniel, 1946, Ag 7,20:5
Fouchardiere, George de la, 1946, F 12,25:4
Fouche, Glenn R, 1958, Jl 6,56:1
Foucher, Paul, 1875, F 14,7:3
Fougeray, Louis F, 1955, Ap 29,23:4
Fought, William H, 1942, N 13,23:3
Fougner, Arne, 1965, Mr 15,12:5
Fougner, G Selmer (por), 1941, Ap 3,23:1
Fougner, Robert S Mrs, 1965, Jl 1,31:4
Fouhy, James F, 1951, S 17,21:2
Fouhy, Michael A, 1947, Ap 27,60:3
Foujita, Tsuguji, 1968, Ja 30,38:1
Fouke, George R Jr, 1949, Ap 1,25:2
Fouke, Phil B, 1951, Mr 25,72:4
Fould, M, 1867, O 8,5:2; 1875, F 15,1:7
Foulds, Andrew, 1947, D 3,29:4
Foulds, Colburn S, 1951, Ja 9,29:2
Foulds, Henry T, 1946, Ja 23,27:5
Foulds, Henry W, 1959, Ap 6,27:2
Foulds, Thomas H Mrs (will), 1958, D 5,1:2
Foulds, Thomas H Mrs (est appr revalued), 1960, Mr 25,17:5
Foulds, W C (Billy), 1954, My 15,15:3
Foulis, David, 1903, Mr 18,9:5; 1950, Je 13,27:4
Foulk, Charles T 2d, 1958, N 3,37:1
Foulk, Fred B, 1959, O 29,30:3
Foulk, Lambert J, 1941, Ja 21,22:2
Foulk, Walter L, 1938, F 24,19:4
Foulk, William F, 1965, Ja 9,25:2
Foulk, William H, 1960, D 14,36:1
Foulke, Edward, 1957, Ag 29,27:2
Foulke, F Charles, 1961, My 11,37:2
Foulke, Joseph J Sr, 1942, Ag 31,17:3
Foulke, W D, 1935, My 31,15:3
Foulke, William, 1920, Jl 2,11:4
Foulkes, Bertram T, 1948, Ap 14,27:6
Foulkes, Henry Mrs, 1938, N 13,45:3
Foulkes, Henry Sr, 1945, N 3,15:5
Foulkes, John D, 1941, D 16,27:6
Foulkes, Louis S, 1942, Ap 25,13:6
Foulkes, Rupert Jones, 1912, Mr 2,13:5
Foulkes, William H, 1961, D 10,89:1
Foulkes, William H Mrs, 1943, My 23,43:2
Foulkrod, Collin, 1939, N 18,17:6
Foulkrod, Howard E Sr, 1941, Jl 29,15:2
Foulkrod, John J Jr, 1947, N 19,27:4
Foulkrod, William F, 1910, N 14,9:5
Foulkrod, William W Jr, 1949, Je 7,31:1
Foulks, Dewitt C, 1951, Mr 8,29:4
Foulks, Dewitt C Mrs, 1956, Ap 10,31:1
Foulks, Frank L, 1943, S 19,48:8
Foulks, John A, 1943, Ag 31,17:3
Foulois, Benjamin D (funl, Ap 28,41:3), 1967, Ap 26, 47:1
Found, William A, 1940, Mr 23,26:3
Founder, Curry Mrs, 1948, O 11,23:5
Foune, John, 1923, Jl 10,19:5
Fountain, Alfred H, 1950, N 24,36:3
Fountain, Brainard, 1946, S 10,7:4
Fountain, Charles H, 1956, Je 19,29:2
Fountain, Edward G, 1948, O 18,23:5
Fountain, Edward Perrine, 1903, Ag 16,7:6
Fountain, Frank, 1939, My 11,25:5
Fountain, Frederick O, 1950, O 22,92:1
Fountain, Gerard, 1944, S 29,21:1
Fountain, Gerard Mrs, 1945, S 21,21:2
Fountain, Henry, 1958, Ap 11,25:4

Fountain, James Thaddeus, 1908, Ja 14,7:6
Fountain, Joseph C, 1945, Ag 2,21:8
Fountain, Martha, 1952, Ja 6,95:6
Fountain, Norman C, 1940, O 27,45:2
Fountain, Reginald, 1941, Ap 22,21:2
Fountain, Robert F, 1956, Ja 25,31:3
Fountain, Thomas A Sr, 1949, Ag 20,11:2
Fountain, William A, 1955, Ap 24,87:1
Fountain, William J Dr, 1937, F 23,27:3
Fouques-Durparc, Jacques, 1966, Ag 5,31:1
Fouquet, Louis D, 1942, Ja 21,17:2
Fouquet, Louis D Mrs, 1954, O 7,23:5
Fouquet, Morton, 1943, F 17,21:5
Fouquier, J F H, 1901, D 28,7:6
Fouquieres, Andre B de, 1959, Ja 14,27:5
Fourcade, Jacques, 1959, S 6,55:3
Fourcade, P Louis, 1964, Ag 4,29:4
Fourest, Georges, 1945, Ja 29,13:6
Fourichon, Martin, 1884, N 25,2:6
Fournais, Jacob, 1871, Jl 25,1:6
Fournet, Henri D, 1964, Mr 4,37:3
Fournet, Louis R M C D du, 1940, F 19,17:2
Fournet, Pierre, 1916, My 15,9:6
Fournier, Alfred Prof, 1914, D 25,11:4
Fournier, Alphonse, 1961, O 9,35:2
Fournier, Aurelino, 1956, My 1,39:3
Fournier, Charles A, 1941, O 14,23:4
Fournier, E, 1880, My 11,2:4
Fournier, Eugene, 1949, F 28,19:5
Fournier, Joseph O, 1959, My 6,40:1
Fournier, Josh Capt, 1909, My 11,9:4
Fournier, Leslie T, 1961, Jl 7,25:5
Fournier, Louis, 1948, O 25,23:2
Fournier, N, 1880, Ap 28,2:4
Fournier, Napoleon J, 1948, S 8,29:3
Fournier d'Albe, E E, 1933, Jl 8,11:3
Fouse, Levi Garner, 1914, Ja 17,9:4
Fouse, Winfred E, 1958, Jl 23,27:3
Foussier, Edward, 1882, Mr 17,5:2
Foust, John J Mrs, 1925, D 15,25:4
Foust, Julius I, 1946, F 16,13:5
Foust, William A, 1953, S 3,21:3
Fout, Henry H, 1947, D 6,15:6
Foute, Robert C Rev Dr, 1903, Jl 25,7:6
Fouts, Rupert A, 1947, Je 3,25:2
Fouts, Taylor, 1952, D 13,21:5
Fouts, Theron J, 1954, Ap 29,31:4
Foutts, Ray, 1946, My 27,20:1
Foutz, Edith M Mrs, 1943, Ap 7,25:2
Fouvy, Ellen Mrs, 1953, O 31,17:3
Foville, Alfred de, 1913, My 15,11:6
Fow, Oscar A 2d, 1950, Jl 2,25:1
Fowke, G, 1936, F 9,II,11:3
Fowkes, John T Sr, 1954, O 16,17:5
Fowlds, William Mrs, 1950, Ja 11,23:2
Fowle, Alfred L, 1947, N 22,15:4
Fowle, Arthur E, 1956, Mr 16,23:3
Fowle, Charles W, 1963, F 21,5:6
Fowle, Elizabeth R Mrs, 1912, S 25,13:2
Fowle, Frank F, 1946, Ja 23,27:3
Fowle, James H, 1945, Jl 23,19:4
Fowle, Luther R Mrs, 1949, Mr 2,25:5
Fowler, A Linde, 1956, S 3,13:5
Fowler, Addison (Jack), 1957, Mr 10,89:2
Fowler, Albert Mrs, 1943, Jl 10,13:2
Fowler, Albert N, 1937, Ag 4,19:5; 1954, Je 8,27:3
Fowler, Albert Vann, 1968, D 20,47:1
Fowler, Albert Vann Mrs (Helen), 1968, D 20,47:1
Fowler, Alfred, 1940, Je 25,23:1; 1940, O 29,25:2
Fowler, Alfred L, 1908, Ag 9,9:4
Fowler, Alice L, 1955, Mr 30,29:2
Fowler, Allan P, 1945, My 16,19:4
Fowler, Allen L, 1957, F 3,76:2
Fowler, Amelia Mrs, 1923, Ja 11,21:6
Fowler, Anderson (burial, F 27,9:5), 1906, F 11,7:6
Fowler, Anderson Mrs, 1965, S 15,47:2
Fowler, Angela C Mrs, 1940, My 8,23:3
Fowler, Art, 1953, Ap 10,21:2
Fowler, Arthur, 1949, Je 15,29:1
Fowler, Arthur A Mrs, 1964, Ag 13,32:6
Fowler, Arthur T, 1953, D 19,15:4
Fowler, B Sherman, 1953, Mr 23,23:1
Fowler, B Sherman Mrs, 1937, My 13,16:2
Fowler, Benjamin E, 1937, N 24,23:4
Fowler, Benjamin M, 1937, Mr 20,19:2
Fowler, Berdella K, 1943, Ja 1,23:4
Fowler, Bertha W Mrs, 1941, My 8,23:2
Fowler, Bertrand, 1940, My 21,23:2
Fowler, Brenda (Mrs Jno W Sherman), 1942, O 29, 23:3
Fowler, Burton P, 1963, N 18,33:1
Fowler, C N, 1932, My 28,15:1
Fowler, Carl H, 1942, Mr 31,21:6; 1942, Ap 2,21:5
Fowler, Cedric W, 1968, Ja 24,45:2
Fowler, Charles, 1947, Jl 30,21:4
Fowler, Charles A, 1948, Ag 31,23:1
Fowler, Charles B, 1941, O 29,23:5
Fowler, Charles E Mrs, 1943, Ag 30,15:2
Fowler, Charles F, 1964, Ag 27,33:5
Fowler, Charles F Dr, 1968, Je 11,47:3
Fowler, Charles H, 1953, F 20,20:4
Fowler, Charles Henry Bp, 1908, Mr 24,7:5
Fowler, Charles R, 1949, Ap 10,76:1
Fowler, Charles S, 1949, S 12,21:2
Fowler, Charles S Mrs, 1946, N 23,15:2
Fowler, Charles W Jr, 1948, O 2,15:6
Fowler, Chester C A, 1948, Ap 9,23:4
Fowler, Clarence C, 1938, D 1,23:3
Fowler, Clarence V, 1951, N 20,31:4
Fowler, Clifford K, 1949, O 25,28:3
Fowler, Cutherbert, 1954, D 19,85:1
Fowler, David A, 1865, F 25,5:3
Fowler, David M, 1944, O 5,23:4
Fowler, David O, 1914, Jl 23,9:5
Fowler, Denton, 1904, Ja 13,9:6
Fowler, Dudley F, 1950, S 8,31:4
Fowler, E Dr, 1879, Ap 12,8:1
Fowler, E Frank, 1941, My 15,23:5
Fowler, E Frank Mrs, 1945, Jl 23,19:5
Fowler, Edmund P, 1966, O 8,31:6
Fowler, Edmund P Jr, 1964, Ja 14,31:3
Fowler, Edson B, 1942, Je 23,20:2
Fowler, Edward B, 1940, Je 13,23:5; 1947, Ag 28,23:3
Fowler, Edward Payson Dr, 1914, Ja 30,9:5
Fowler, Edward T, 1953, F 25,27:5
Fowler, Elihu W, 1950, F 1,30:3
Fowler, Elizabeth, 1922, O 31,15:4
Fowler, Elizabeth B Mrs, 1954, Je 18,23:3
Fowler, Elting A, 1916, N 1,11:4
Fowler, Eric Mrs, 1925, O 19,21:5
Fowler, Ernest M, 1950, O 17,31:3
Fowler, Ernest W Mrs, 1948, O 27,27:5
Fowler, Eugene H, 1953, Mr 11,29:3
Fowler, F D, 1884, N 9,9:5
Fowler, Ferdinand S, 1937, S 30,23:5
Fowler, Francis, 1953, Ag 5,23:1
Fowler, Francis J, 1956, Mr 31,15:1
Fowler, Frank, 1910, Ag 20,7:5
Fowler, Frank B, 1951, O 25,29:1; 1955, Mr 2,27:5
Fowler, Frank D, 1951, Ag 27,19:2
Fowler, Frank G, 1961, Ag 24,29:6
Fowler, Frank G Jr Mrs, 1964, Jl 18,19:4
Fowler, Frank M Mrs, 1960, Je 4,23:5
Fowler, Fred H, 1958, F 12,29:4
Fowler, Frederick, 1939, Ap 14,23:5
Fowler, Frederick A Prof, 1910, F 4,7:4
Fowler, Frederick H B, 1958, F 5,27:2
Fowler, Frederick Mrs, 1947, O 10,25:5
Fowler, Frederick P, 1939, N 21,23:2
Fowler, Gene (funl plans, Jl 4,15:2; funl, Jl 7,31:3), 1960, Jl 3,1:6
Fowler, George Bingham Dr, 1907, Mr 7,9:6
Fowler, George D, 1909, O 15,11:5
Fowler, George G, 1948, O 31,88:6
Fowler, George M C, 1951, My 29,25:3
Fowler, George Ryerson Dr, 1906, F 7,9:5
Fowler, George S, 1945, O 22,17:3; 1961, Je 7,41:2
Fowler, Halstead C, 1950, S 8,31:1
Fowler, Halstead P Mrs, 1948, N 4,29:2
Fowler, Harold, 1957, Ja 18,21:1
Fowler, Harry C, 1957, Ja 14,23:2
Fowler, Harry K, 1961, Je 5,31:4
Fowler, Henrietta R Mrs, 1957, Ap 16,33:2
Fowler, Henry, 1938, O 18,25:4; 1944, N 6,19:4
Fowler, Henry Hartley (Viscount Wolverhampton), 1911, F 26,II,11:4
Fowler, Henry M, 1958, Ag 29,23:4
Fowler, Henry W, 1965, Je 23,41:1
Fowler, Herbert L, 1947, Ap 4,23:4
Fowler, Ingles Mrs, 1947, Ap 9,25:1
Fowler, Isaac V, 1869, O 1,5:3
Fowler, J Irving, 1937, Jl 21,21:4
Fowler, J Scott, 1951, Ja 24,27:4
Fowler, Jacob, 1940, Jl 12,15:3; 1943, F 22,17:2
Fowler, Jacob Mrs, 1950, N 12,93:1
Fowler, James A, 1955, N 19,19:3
Fowler, James C, 1947, Ja 9,24:2
Fowler, James H, 1956, My 30,21:6
Fowler, Jessie E, 1943, My 6,19:6
Fowler, John, 1923, D 31,13:4
Fowler, John C, 1947, Jl 12,13:6; 1949, Ag 30,27:2
Fowler, John F Mrs, 1952, Ag 12,19:6
Fowler, John R, 1957, My 19,88:4
Fowler, John S Sir, 1939, S 22,23:2
Fowler, John W, 1946, Jl 16,23:5
Fowler, Joseph G, 1873, Ag 23,8:6
Fowler, Joseph M, 1947, Mr 27,27:1
Fowler, Joseph N (por), 1948, O 6,30:2
Fowler, L C, 1881, S 26,5:6
Fowler, L G Mrs, 1879, F 10,3:5
Fowler, L N Prof, 1896, S 4,10:3
Fowler, Lewis M, 1951, F 8,33:4
Fowler, Lorne R, 1948, F 25,23:2
Fowler, Louisa M, 1960, D 19,27:4
Fowler, Ludlow S, 1961, Ap 13,35:4
Fowler, M V B, 1881, My 10,5:3
Fowler, Martin K, 1950, D 30,13:5
Fowler, Mary W, 1948, F 18,31:3
Fowler, Matthew J, 1942, My 16,13:2
Fowler, Milton A, 1911, N 30,13:5
Fowler, Ned Y, 1953, D 23,25:3
Fowler, Norman H, 1940, Jl 31,17:4
Fowler, O W, 1942, N 13,23:3
Fowler, Orvid S, 1941, Mr 17,17:5
Fowler, Oscar S, 1944, Ja 3,21:3
Fowler, Perry, 1966, Ap 15,39:3
Fowler, Peter H, 1939, Ja 20,19:4
Fowler, Phil D, 1951, D 18,31:1
Fowler, Preston L, 1957, Mr 25,25:2
Fowler, R L, 1936, Jl 14,19:3
Fowler, Ralph H, 1944, Jl 29,13:4
Fowler, Raymond F, 1949, Ja 20,28:2
Fowler, Richard C, 1946, Mr 28,25:2
Fowler, Richard L, 1967, Ja 19,35:2
Fowler, Robert, 1939, Ja 26,21:4
Fowler, Robert A, 1940, Ag 1,21:5
Fowler, Robert G, 1966, Je 16,47:3
Fowler, Robert J, 1960, Ja 22,25:6
Fowler, Robert S, 1954, O 25,27:4
Fowler, Robert S Mrs, 1949, Je 22,31:5
Fowler, Robert W, 1938, Ap 29,21:1
Fowler, Robert W Mrs, 1945, Ap 7,15:5
Fowler, Ross O Mrs, 1960, F 20,23:5
Fowler, Ross O Sr, 1947, Ja 3,21:4
Fowler, Royal H, 1952, S 3,29:5
Fowler, Russell S, 1959, Ja 7,33:3
Fowler, Ruth D, 1960, Ag 12,19:3
Fowler, S Col, 1865, Ja 15,1:3
Fowler, S R, 1903, O 17,9:6
Fowler, Samuel S, 1939, My 2,23:2
Fowler, Samuel W, 1945, Mr 22,23:2
Fowler, Silvie de G, 1940, D 30,17:2
Fowler, Stanley C, 1964, My 8,34:1
Fowler, Stanley C Jr, 1965, Ap 6,39:3
Fowler, Stephen H, 1965, O 27,47:5
Fowler, Stephen W, 1949, Je 12,76:1
Fowler, Susan, 1965, Ja 18,35:1
Fowler, Thomas B, 1945, Ap 3,19:5
Fowler, Thomas N Mrs, 1943, S 26,48:1
Fowler, Thomas P, 1915, O 13,15:5
Fowler, Thomas P Mrs, 1948, Ag 3,25:1
Fowler, Volney B, 1959, O 7,43:2
Fowler, W C, 1881, Ja 17,2:2
Fowler, W S Mrs, 1957, My 17,25:4
Fowler, W W, 1881, S 20,4:7
Fowler, Walter C, 1941, Ja 24,17:2
Fowler, Walter H, 1961, S 7,35:1
Fowler, Will Mrs, 1962, Jl 11,36:1
Fowler, Willard Mrs, 1946, S 20,32:2
Fowler, William, 1938, O 23,41:2
Fowler, William C, 1941, N 28,24:2
Fowler, William E, 1957, Jl 17,27:5
Fowler, William F, 1946, O 22,25:2; 1949, Jl 12,27:
Fowler, William G, 1950, N 5,92:5
Fowler, William H, 1965, N 6,29:4
Fowler, William J, 1948, O 15,23:3; 1960, Ja 23,21:
Fowler, William J Mrs, 1949, Ag 30,27:2
Fowler, William K, 1949, My 1,88:4; 1964, Ja 6,47:
Fowler, William R Sr, 1941, O 27,17:5
Fowler, William S, 1961, Ja 15,87:1
Fowles, E, 1932, D 13,19:1
Fowles, Norman C B Sr, 1939, Ja 22,34:6
Fowley, Hugh D Sr, 1952, O 7,29:5
Fowlie, William H, 1947, Ja 7,27:4
Fowlkes, J Winston Jr, 1949, Ag 10,21:4
Fowlkes, Maynard G, 1952, O 8,31:4
Fowlkes, Vester G, 1965, My 29,27:6
Fownes, Charles K, 1908, S 1,7:5
Fownes, Dorothy D, 1941, Ag 12,19:1
Fownes, Henry G, 1960, Je 12,86:7
Fownes, William C Jr, 1950, Jl 5,31:3
Fox, A M (Abe), 1950, O 17,31:1
Fox, A Manuel, 1942, Je 22,15:6
Fox, Aaron, 1962, Ap 4,43:5
Fox, Abijah C Mrs, 1953, D 10,47:4
Fox, Abraham, 1965, Ja 14,35:4
Fox, Abraham Mrs, 1962, D 4,41:1
Fox, Alan, 1942, Ja 22,17:1
Fox, Alan Mrs, 1916, Mr 12,19:5
Fox, Alanson G, 1951, F 10,13:5
Fox, Alanson J, 1903, O 30,9:6
Fox, Albert C, 1952, F 22,21:4
Fox, Albert M, 1941, My 1,23:3
Fox, Alex K, 1943, My 11,21:1
Fox, Alexander M, 1907, O 7,9:6
Fox, Alfred, 1951, S 3,13:4
Fox, Alfred C, 1955, F 9,27:4
Fox, Alfred C Mrs, 1951, O 13,17:3
Fox, Aline K, 1954, Jl 5,11:7
Fox, Alvin G, 1964, Ap 21,37:1
Fox, Andrew E, 1944, Mr 5,36:1
Fox, Andrew J Mrs, 1940, D 23,19:4
Fox, Ansley H, 1948, Ag 17,21:2
Fox, Anthony Sr, 1946, S 24,29:4
Fox, Arthur E, 1957, Mr 28,31:1
Fox, Arthur L Mrs, 1957, Ja 30,29:3
Fox, Austen G, 1937, My 16,II,8:8
Fox, Austin, 1944, S 15,19:5
Fox, B Frank, 1941, O 21,23:2
Fox, Beauvais B, 1955, Ag 10,25:2
Fox, Bella, 1954, Je 23,25:1
Fox, Benedict, 1965, D 25,13:2
Fox, Benjamin, 1961, Ag 24,29:2; 1968, O 23,47
Fox, Benjamin E, 1948, D 19,76:2
Fox, Bertha A, 1958, Ja 7,47:4
Fox, Betty Mrs, 1960, Ja 3,53:1
Fox, Bradley H, 1955, S 15,33:3
Fox, C, 1879, S 16,5:3
Fox, C F Mrs, 1928, Ag 11,11:5

Fox, C P Father Rev, 1905, Ap 5,9:6
Fox, C V, 1883, O 30,5:3
Fox, Caleb F, 1938, Ag 3,19:5
Fox, Caroline E, 1953, Ap 4,13:1
Fox, Carroll H, 1947, Ag 29,17:5
Fox, Catherine Mrs, 1940, My 24,19:5
Fox, Cecil H, 1963, Ap 3,47:4
Fox, Charles, 1952, S 15,25:3
Fox, Charles B, 1953, F 3,25:3
Fox, Charles D, 1952, Ja 19,15:6
Fox, Charles E (will, Jl 25,21:2), 1937, My 4,25:2
Fox, Charles E, 1945, Ap 6,15:3; 1952, S 28,77:1
Fox, Charles E Mrs, 1945, F 9,16:2
Fox, Charles E Rear-Adm, 1916, F 14,13:4
Fox, Charles H, 1940, Ap 28,36:7; 1950, Ja 28,13:5
Fox, Charles Henry, 1909, F 23,9:2
Fox, Charles J, 1903, D 1,9:6; 1939, O 1,53:3; 1939, O 26,23:1; 1952, Mr 6,31:3
Fox, Charles K, 1875, Ja 24,12:1
Fox, Charles L, 1956, D 13,75:2
Fox, Charles M Rev, 1871, S 5,1:4
Fox, Charles R, 1947, Jl 24,21:6
Fox, Charles Sir, 1874, Je 17,4:6
Fox, Charles T Mrs, 1947, Je 27,22:2
Fox, Charles Y Mrs, 1952, Je 28,20:8
Fox, Chester B, 1945, S 1,11:5
Fox, Christopher G, 1912, S 7,11:5
Fox, Clifford S, 1937, Ap 20,25:5
Fox, Crosby, 1957, My 11,22:2
Fox, Cyril J, 1946, N 17,70:8
Fox, Cyril S, 1951, D 29,11:5
Fox, D Alvin, 1939, Ja 5,23:2
Fox, Daniel E, 1965, F 2,33:4
Fox, Daniel W, 1963, Ap 20,27:5
Fox, David, 1954, D 30,17:1
Fox, David B, 1949, Ag 7,60:2
Fox, David J Mrs, 1942, O 31,15:4
Fox, David P, 1957, Ag 7,27:5
Fox, Delia T Mrs, 1940, N 20,21:3
Fox, Della (Mrs Jno D Levy), 1913, Je 17,11:4
Fox, Dennis R, 1923, Jl 20,13:5
Fox, Dixon R, 1945, Ja 31,21:1
Fox, Dixon R Mrs, 1964, Jl 16,31:2
Fox, Douglas Mrs, 1952, Ag 3,60:1
Fox, E Conrad, 1954, O 12,27:3
Fox, E Tunnicliff, 1967, Ja 9,36:7
Fox, Edward, 1949, F 8,25:2
Fox, Edward J, 1937, F 6,17:2; 1948, N 27,17:2; 1962, Je 2,19:5
Fox, Edward Rowland, 1918, Mr 25,13:4
Fox, Edwin H, 1952, Jl 15,21:3
Fox, Elizabeth G, 1958, N 15,23:3
Fox, Elizabeth Mrs, 1909, Je 23,7:4
Fox, Elizabeth R Mrs, 1941, Je 15,37:1
Fox, Elliott D, 1968, Mr 2,29:4
Fox, Elsie, 1943, Jl 3,13:2
Fox, Emily A R Mrs, 1942, Je 24,19:1
Fox, Emma Mrs, 1948, S 15,31:3
Fox, Emmet, 1951, Ag 18,11:6
Fox, Enoch, 1924, F 26,17:2
Fox, Erbie M, 1952, S 5,27:4
Fox, Ernest F, 1960, D 16,33:2
Fox, Ervin P, 1966, Jl 6,42:4
Fox, F J, 1938, F 18,1:3
Fox, F Sir, 1927, Ja 8,17:5
Fox, Felix, 1947, Mr 26,25:2
Fox, Floyd, 1941, Ja 22,21:5
Fox, Fontaine, 1964, Ag 10,31:4
Fox, Francis S, 1952, D 22,25:5
Fox, Frank A, 1948, Ja 12,19:3
Fox, Frank B, 1941, My 6,21:4
Fox, Frank C, 1960, F 8,29:1
Fox, Frank W, 1948, Ag 6,17:3
Fox, Franklyn, 1967, N 5,86:7
Fox, Fred F, 1951, N 10,17:5
Fox, Fred L, 1924, My 22,17:6
Fox, Frederick J Mrs, 1947, My 21,25:3
Fox, Frederick P, 1958, Mr 17,29:2
Fox, G L (see also O 25), 1877, O 29,1:6
Fox, G Raymond, 1952, O 26,88:2
Fox, Genevieve (Mrs R G Fuller), 1959, O 10,21:6
Fox, George, 1952, D 11,33:3
Fox, George A, 1946, S 25,27:4
Fox, George B, 1948, F 21,13:6
Fox, George E, 1958, My 4,89:1
Fox, George H Dr, 1937, My 4,25:3
Fox, George I, 1952, Ja 24,27:1
Fox, George I Mrs, 1965, Ap 12,35:1
Fox, George L, 1959, Ja 13,47:1
Fox, George L Ex-Judge, 1910, D 7,13:3
Fox, George N, 1950, O 25,38:3
Fox, George P, 1946, S 24,29:4
Fox, George T, 1958, My 11,87:1
Fox, Gordon H, 1953, My 25,25:1
Fox, Grant C, 1939, N 11,15:1
Fox, Guy G, 1949, My 12,31:2
Fox, H Clifford, 1959, N 25,16:6
Fox, Harold R, 1965, F 6,25:4
Fox, Harry (cor, My 7,31:1), 1953, My 6,31:1
Fox, Harry, 1959, Jl 21,29:5
Fox, Harry J, 1941, Jl 11,15:3
Fox, Harry Mrs, 1967, Ja 22,77:1
Fox, Harry P, 1948, Ap 16,23:5
Fox, Harvey, 1951, Mr 24,13:3
Fox, Henrietta, 1938, Je 5,44:6
Fox, Henry, 1951, N 6,29:3
Fox, Henry M, 1942, O 13,24:2
Fox, Henry W, 1953, Ja 25,84:4
Fox, Herbert, 1942, F 28,17:1
Fox, Herbert W, 1953, Ag 16,76:8
Fox, Horace E Mrs, 1953, My 6,31:5
Fox, Howard, 1954, O 20,29:3
Fox, Howard A, 1947, My 11,60:2
Fox, Howard A Mrs, 1964, Jl 9,33:4
Fox, Hugh C, 1944, Ap 16,42:4
Fox, Hugh F, 1940, N 7,25:3
Fox, Hugh F Mrs, 1961, Mr 9,30:1
Fox, I J, 1947, D 18,29:1
Fox, Imro, 1910, Mr 5,9:5
Fox, Irving, 1949, F 18,23:4
Fox, Irving C, 1944, Ag 14,15:3
Fox, Irving Giliss, 1921, S 24,11:2
Fox, Irving J, 1958, N 26,29:3
Fox, Isidore J Mrs, 1964, Ag 21,29:2
Fox, J Bertram, 1946, Ja 25,23:3
Fox, J Bertram Mrs, 1938, Jl 7,19:2
Fox, J D, 1865, Mr 17,4:2
Fox, J E J Mrs, 1946, Ap 5,25:5
Fox, J Edward, 1967, F 22,29:1
Fox, J Francis, 1951, Ag 8,25:3
Fox, J Franklin, 1940, Je 22,15:3
Fox, J M, 1901, Ap 12,9:7
Fox, J Walter, 1948, Ag 24,23:4
Fox, Jabez Ex-Justice, 1923, N 8,19:5
Fox, Jack, 1961, My 16,37:1
Fox, Jack W, 1954, Jl 24,13:3
Fox, James, 1922, N 24,17:4
Fox, James C, 1962, Ag 28,31:4
Fox, James I, 1950, F 20,25:3
Fox, James W, 1942, S 24,27:5
Fox, Jerome, 1957, S 15,83:1
Fox, Jesse W Mrs, 1958, Ap 13,84:3
Fox, John (Requiem Mass), 1875, Ag 13,2:4
Fox, John, 1914, Ja 17,9:5; 1943, Ap 25,34:6
Fox, John F, 1928, D 26,17:4
Fox, John H, 1953, My 13,29:3
Fox, John J (Donna), 1956, Ap 5,29:3
Fox, John L (Tiger Jack), 1954, Ap 7,31:4
Fox, John Lawrence, 1864, D 27,2:3
Fox, John M, 1940, F 16,19:4; 1940, Ap 20,17:4
Fox, John M (will), 1950, Ag 6,56:5
Fox, John Mrs, 1901, D 4,9:4
Fox, John Otis, 1925, O 28,25:5
Fox, John P, 1960, Je 28,31:5
Fox, John R, 1937, S 5,II,2:7
Fox, John Rev Dr, 1924, D 25,17:6
Fox, John V, 1967, My 13,33:2
Fox, John V Mrs, 1966, F 4,31:4
Fox, John Williams Jr, 1919, Jl 9,13:3
Fox, Joseph, 1906, S 1,9:5; 1918, Mr 16,13:3
Fox, Joseph E, 1937, Ja 28,25:3
Fox, Joseph F Mrs, 1950, Ag 23,29:3
Fox, Joseph J, 1955, Ag 25,23:4
Fox, Joseph M, 1949, F 14,19:5
Fox, Josephine, 1953, Ag 4,21:4
Fox, Josephine Bonaparte Mrs, 1925, N 17,25:5
Fox, Lawrence, 1942, D 12,15:4
Fox, Lena S Mrs, 1941, D 5,23:5
Fox, Leo J, 1950, My 27,17:6
Fox, Leo K, 1956, N 29,35:1
Fox, Leon A, 1965, Je 6,84:7
Fox, Lewis P, 1954, Ja 26,27:2
Fox, Lillian G Mrs, 1967, D 10,87:1
Fox, Louis, 1951, Ja 23,27:2
Fox, Louis V, 1959, Jl 12,72:7
Fox, Lyndon E, 1941, Ag 20,19:4
Fox, Marcella, 1956, My 1,33:2
Fox, Martin J, 1961, Ap 5,37:4
Fox, Marvin, 1965, Mr 22,33:3
Fox, Mary E Mrs, 1937, D 8,25:6
Fox, Matthew J, 1952, Je 17,27:1
Fox, Matthew M, 1964, Je 3,43:1
Fox, Matthew Rev, 1925, N 21,17:4
Fox, Michael (funl, Ja 26,17:2), 1913, Ja 23,11:5
Fox, Michael P, 1940, Mr 15,23:3
Fox, Minerva C, 1962, N 10,25:6
Fox, Morris, 1963, Ap 24,35:1; 1967, Jl 10,28:6
Fox, Mortimer J, 1948, My 17,19:1
Fox, Moses, 1938, Ja 14,23:4
Fox, Nicholas I, 1965, O 16,27:3
Fox, Norman A, 1960, Mr 26,21:5
Fox, Oscar E, 1946, Ap 25,21:3
Fox, Oscar J, 1961, Jl 30,69:3
Fox, Owen E, 1951, S 20,31:3
Fox, Owen M, 1953, Ap 2,27:3
Fox, Paddy, 1912, Mr 3,15:3
Fox, Patrick, 1939, Ja 8,42:6; 1949, D 8,33:3
Fox, Patrick D, 1958, Ja 4,15:6
Fox, Patrick F, 1954, Je 10,31:4
Fox, Paul A Sr, 1952, Ap 19,15:4
Fox, Paul L, 1967, F 14,43:2
Fox, Peter H, 1944, Je 14,19:6
Fox, Peter J Jr, 1944, Ap 4,21:3
Fox, Peter W, 1967, O 5,39:4
Fox, Philip, 1944, Jl 23,36:1
Fox, Phillip E, 1959, D 29,16:2
Fox, Ralph, 1937, Ja 5,5:2
Fox, Raymond C, 1949, S 7,29:3
Fox, Raymond H, 1950, Ja 2,23:2
Fox, Raymond J, 1954, Ag 21,17:5
Fox, Raymond M, 1955, My 9,23:2
Fox, Reginald, 1953, Je 26,19:2
Fox, Rhoda A S Mrs, 1940, D 12,27:2
Fox, Richard K (funl, N 21,19:4), 1922, N 15,19:3
Fox, Richard K Mrs, 1949, N 4,27:3
Fox, Richard L, 1946, Ag 6,25:3
Fox, Richard T, 1937, Ap 25,II,8:2
Fox, Robert C, 1942, My 13,19:4
Fox, Robert E, 1955, D 17,23:6
Fox, Roger T, 1940, Je 25,23:4
Fox, Rose E, 1952, Ap 3,35:3
Fox, Roy S, 1955, Je 2,29:4
Fox, Russell R Lt, 1923, Ja 18,15:5
Fox, Samson, 1903, O 25,7:6
Fox, Samuel, 1952, My 31,17:3; 1956, My 11,27:2
Fox, Samuel L, 1937, Ag 17,19:1
Fox, Samuel P, 1951, Mr 29,27:6
Fox, Sarah Allen Mrs, 1953, F 15,92:3
Fox, Stanley W J, 1954, Jl 16,21:1
Fox, Stuart, 1951, Jl 17,27:2
Fox, Theodore T Mrs, 1960, Ja 7,30:1
Fox, Thomas F, 1944, N 21,25:3
Fox, Thomas H Sr, 1953, F 23,25:4
Fox, Thomas J, 1939, Je 2,23:3; 1945, Ja 25,19:4
Fox, Thomas W, 1961, D 25,23:4
Fox, Timothy, 1950, Je 11,92:1
Fox, Vincent B, 1961, Jl 1,17:4
Fox, W Addison, 1947, Ja 3,21:3
Fox, W M, 1880, My 2,1:4
Fox, William, 1939, My 5,23:1; 1952, My 9,23:1
Fox, William A, 1939, Ja 26,21:3; 1950, S 9,17:6
Fox, William A G, 1939, Jl 29,15:5
Fox, William B, 1952, N 14,25:4
Fox, William F, 1963, Ag 5,29:4
Fox, William F Col, 1909, Je 17,7:6
Fox, William F Jr, 1964, My 15,36:6
Fox, William F Sr, 1949, F 5,15:2
Fox, William H, 1952, Ja 19,15:4
Fox, William J, 1937, O 20,23:4; 1947, Ag 28,23:5; 1962, Ja 7,88:6
Fox, William L, 1945, Mr 1,21:4; 1946, D 3,31:4
Fox, William Mrs, 1952, Je 5,31:2
Fox, William R 3d, 1951, N 23,30:2
Fox, William W, 1945, My 28,19:3
Fox, Williams Carleton, 1924, Ja 21,17:5
Fox, Willoughby B, 1941, D 25,25:4
Fox-Strangways, Giles S H (Earl of Ilchester), 1959, O 30,27:1
Foxcroft, Francis A Mrs, 1951, Mr 10,13:6
Foxhall, George, 1953, Je 6,17:6
Foxwell, Herbert E, 1950, O 10,31:1
Foxwell Chas R D, 1944, O 2,19:3
Foxx, Jimmy (Jas E Foxx), 1967, Jl 22,26:1
Foxx, S D Mrs, 1943, Ag 28,11:3
Foy, Anthon L, 1958, S 5,27:2
Foy, Bryan Mrs, 1949, D 6,31:2
Foy, Byron C Mrs, 1957, Ag 21,27:5
Foy, Cyrus C, 1950, Jl 27,25:3
Foy, E, 1928, F 17,21:3
Foy, Eddie Jr Mrs, 1952, F 25,23:5
Foy, Eddie Mrs, 1918, Je 15,11:5
Foy, Eugene T, 1954, F 28,92:2
Foy, Francis A, 1910, D 13,13:5
Foy, Frank M, 1953, O 24,15:3
Foy, Frank W, 1943, D 30,17:1
Foy, Henri, 1954, F 12,25:3
Foy, James J, 1916, Je 14,13:5
Foy, Joel H, 1948, Ja 8,25:2
Foy, John B, 1952, Ja 18,27:4
Foy, John J, 1952, Je 28,19:1
Foy, Johnson, 1943, N 1,17:3
Foy, Michael H Mrs, 1952, Ja 30,25:2
Foy, Richard, 1947, Ap 5,19:3
Foy, Robert A (will), 1942, Ja 14,12:2
Foy, Robert E, 1943, Je 4,21:4
Foy, Thomas F Jr, 1957, F 12,27:4
Foy, Walter F, 1953, Je 5,27:3
Foye, Andrew Jay C, 1905, My 27,9:4
Foye, Fred A Mrs, 1952, O 24,23:3
Foye, Mary E Mrs, 1938, Je 11,15:2
Foyle, William A, 1963, Je 6,35:1
Foytlin, Louis, 1944, Ap 13,19:5
Fozard, Frank, 1950, O 20,27:5
Fraad, Daniel, 1952, O 7,29:3
Fraade, Charles B, 1966, F 17,33:2
Fraatz, Charles J, 1958, F 13,29:3
Frace, J Fred, 1937, Mr 27,15:1
Frack, William A, 1956, O 14,86:8
Frackelton, Will, 1943, D 30,17:4
Frackenpohl, Alex J, 1955, O 7,25:2
Frackenpohl, Roland, 1955, O 12,31:3
Frackman, H David, 1959, D 15,39:6
Fraden, William Dr, 1953, Ag 22,13:4
Fraden, William Mrs, 1953, Ag 22,13:4
Fradkin, Fredric, 1963, O 4,36:3
Fradkin, James J Mrs, 1965, Ja 12,37:5
Frady, Edgar O Mrs, 1922, Mr 3,13:5
Fraenkel, Abraham H, 1965, O 17,86:8
Fraenkel, Bernard Prof, 1911, N 14,13:5

Fraenkel, Joseph Dr, 1920, Ap 25,22:4
Fraenkel, Michael, 1957, My 24,25:3
Fraenkel, Walter H, 1945, Jl 17,13:8
Fraentzel, Gustav, 1965, S 7,39:2
Fraenzel, Albert C, 1956, Mr 18,88:2
Fragner, Albert M, 1908, My 11,7:4
Fragner, David, 1956, Ag 17,19:1
Fragomen, Vincent J, 1950, F 4,15:1
Fraher, Edward F, 1945, Ja 4,19:4; 1945, F 13,23:4
Fraile, Manuel, 1944, Ag 4,13:4
Frailey, Carson P, 1954, Mr 14,88:4
Frailey, J M Commodore, 1877, S 27,5:5
Fraim, Parke B, 1946, Ja 15,23:5
Fraiman, Charles (will), 1959, Mr 17,35:2
Frain, Andy (Andrew T), 1964, Mr 26,35:2
Frain, Cecil M, 1961, D 17,82:3
Frain, Henry Garvey, 1925, F 17,23:4
Fraisse, Gustave P, 1941, My 1,23:6
Fraissinet, Clarence J, 1962, Ap 30,27:4
Fraissinet, Henry L, 1938, O 18,25:4
Frake, Oliver G, 1946, N 13,28:3
Fraker, George W, 1951, My 30,21:5
Fraker, William H, 1950, Mr 11,15:6
Fraleigh, Curtis, 1944, Ja 4,18:2
Fraleigh, Elmer, 1944, My 9,19:1
Fraleigh, George W, 1940, Jl 14,31:3
Fraley, C Bradford Mrs, 1952, F 19,29:3
Fraley, Frederick, 1959, Je 26,25:3
Fralick, Lewis C, 1963, Je 26,39:2
Fralinger, John J, 1938, Je 22,23:5
Fralley, Leonard August Rear-Adm, 1914, Ja 2,9:5
Frame, Alastair M, 1946, O 28,27:5
Frame, Alice, 1903, Ag 6,7:5
Frame, Alice B, 1941, Ag 18,13:4
Frame, Charles Pleasant, 1903, O 23,1:6
Frame, Fred, 1962, Ap 26,33:2
Frame, Gregor M, 1939, D 19,26:4
Frame, J Davidson Mrs, 1939, S 16,17:1
Frame, James Alexander, 1917, Jl 3,9:4
Frame, James E, 1956, D 31,13:6
Frame, John D, 1942, Je 17,23:4
Frame, Nat T, 1948, Mr 23,25:1
Frame, Pemberton P, 1950, O 12,31:4
Frame, T Ellwood, 1955, My 4,29:4
Frame, Thomas C, 1955, Je 9,29:2
Frame, Walter K, 1957, Jl 4,19:1
Frame, Walter R, 1946, F 22,25:1
Frame, William A, 1944, F 21,15:4; 1961, Je 24,21:6
Framer, Mervin, 1960, My 22,86:6
Framer, Sarah J, 1916, N 24,13:3
Frampton, G Sir, 1928, My 22,27:2
Frampton, Mendal G, 1943, N 5,19:4
France, Anatole, 1924, O 16,25:4
France, Charles V, 1949, Ap 15,23:4
France, Clemens J, 1959, Je 10,37:5
France, Clemens J Mrs, 1950, My 6,15:5
France, Edward W, 1952, S 7,87:1
France, Hector, 1908, Ag 20,7:5
France, Henry H Mrs, 1947, S 27,15:5
France, Jacob, 1962, N 13,37:1
France, James, 1940, Ap 11,26:2
France, Joseph I, 1939, Ja 27,19:1
France, Joseph I Mrs, 1944, Ag 18,13:2
France, Melville J, 1955, Jl 23,17:3
France, Melville J Mrs, 1949, F 1,25:3
France, Osman B, 1947, My 4,60:4
France, Rachel Noah Mrs, 1925, Ap 5,5:2
France, Royal W, 1962, Jl 11,35:2
France, Royal W Mrs, 1956, D 12,39:1
France, S H, 1879, Ag 15,5:4
France, Sanford D, 1939, Mr 1,21:4
France, T Jay, 1957, O 10,33:1
France, Thomas J, 1937, Ag 27,19:3
France, Wesley G, 1947, D 5,25:3
France, William Mrs, 1956, Ag 9,25:3
Frances Clare, Sister (M Snyder), 1949, Ap 12,29:3
Frances Elizabeth, Sister, 1940, D 24,15:4
Frances y Sanchez-Heredero, Jose, 1964, S 11,33:2
Franceschetti, Adolphe Dr, 1968, Mr 9,29:3
Franceschi, Gustavo J, 1957, Jl 13,17:5
Franceschi, Vera, 1966, Jl 13,43:1
Franceschini, James, 1960, S 18,86:6
Franceschini, Rocco, 1948, D 28,21:2
Francfort, Henri, 1947, My 10,13:6
Francfort, Maurice, 1944, S 28,19:5
Franch, William C, 1939, O 23,19:3
Francher, William B, 1944, D 8,21:3
Franchetti, Aldo, 1948, F 15,60:5
Franchetti, Anthony, 1947, Jl 20,44:6
Franchetti, F Baron, 1935, Ag 9,1:3
Franchetti, Leopoldo Baroness, 1911, O 23,11:5
Francheville, Andree L de, 1944, S 30,13:5
Franchi, A Cardinal, 1878, Ag 2,5:4
Franchi, Constant A, 1959, F 12,27:2
Franchi, Giovanni, 1907, Ap 14,9:6
Franchimont, Eudere, 1947, Ag 5,23:3
Franchina, S Carl, 1962, Ap 2,31:5
Franchot, Charles P Mrs, 1951, S 2,48:5
Franchot, D W, 1928, S 24,21:5
Franchot, Nicholas V V, 1943, My 8,15:5
Franchot, Nicolas V V 2d, 1938, D 15,27:5
Franchot, Richard, 1875, N 24,5:2
Franchot, Richard H, 1940, D 13,23:3
Franchot, S P Sen, 1908, Mr 25,9:5
Francia-Nava, G, 1928, D 8,19:2
Franciosi, Vincent L, 1962, Ap 7,25:6
Francis, A S Rev, 1882, My 16,5:3
Francis, Ahmed, 1968, S 3,43:3
Francis, Albert H, 1946, Ja 29,25:5
Francis, Albert R Mrs, 1964, S 2,37:4
Francis, Arnold W, 1957, Mr 21,31:2
Francis, Arthur W, 1943, Ap 11,48:4
Francis, Bernard, 1966, Ja 19,38:1
Francis, Borgia Bro, 1942, Ja 30,19:4
Francis, C K, 1940, Mr 26,21:1
Francis, Carleton S, 1941, Mr 15,17:5
Francis, Carleton S Mrs, 1948, Ja 28,23:5
Francis, Charles D, 1967, O 10,47:2
Francis, Charles E, 1942, S 5,13:5
Francis, Charles Joseph, 1878, Mr 9,2:6
Francis, Charles R, 1948, D 27,21:3
Francis, Charles S, 1911, D 2,13:5
Francis, Charlotte A, 1963, O 14,39:3
Francis, Clarence S, 1938, Je 6,17:2
Francis, Cyrus West Rev, 1916, Je 13,11:5
Francis, D R, 1927, Ja 16,30:1
Francis, Dale Mrs, 1961, My 31,33:1
Francis, Dennis L, 1962, Ag 3,23:3
Francis, Donald S, 1951, Je 10,93:1
Francis, Ebenezer, 1858, S 23,4:3
Francis, Edward, 1957, Ap 17,31:2
Francis, Edward W Mrs, 1903, N 25,9:5
Francis, Edwin Alexander, 1914, Ap 14,11:6
Francis, Emily A, 1966, F 15,36:3
Francis, Frederick, 1966, My 18,47:1
Francis, George B, 1940, Ja 7,48:8
Francis, George J, 1942, Jl 10,17:2
Francis, George M Mrs, 1951, O 5,28:2
Francis, Gordon A, 1951, N 15,29:1
Francis, Harris S, 1962, Ag 23,29:1
Francis, Harry P, 1951, Ap 16,25:3
Francis, Henry A, 1939, N 12,48:7
Francis, Henry A Mrs, 1944, D 25,19:6
Francis, Hugh L, 1947, Ja 28,24:3
Francis, Ira A, 1939, F 8,23:3
Francis, J E, 1881, Ag 3,5:4
Francis, Jack, 1951, O 17,32:5
Francis, James, 1913, D 13,13:7
Francis, James D, 1958, Ja 9,33:2
Francis, John, 1882, Ap 25,4:7
Francis, John A, 1937, Ag 27,19:6
Francis, John Jr, 1954, Ja 3,88:2
Francis, John S, 1938, My 15,II,6:4
Francis, John W Dr, 1861, F 11,5:2
Francis, Joseph, 1944, Je 7,19:2
Francis, Joseph H, 1905, D 1,9:6
Francis, Joseph M, 1939, F 14,20:2
Francis, Josiah, 1964, F 23,85:1
Francis, Kay (will, D 17,54:1), 1968, Ag 27,41:2
Francis, Lewis Rev Dr, 1921, N 3,19:6
Francis, Lewis W, 1952, Ja 10,29:3
Francis, Lewis W Mrs, 1962, Je 18,25:1
Francis, Louis, 1874, Je 2,5:5; 1941, S 2,17:5
Francis, Louise W Mrs, 1937, My 30,19:1
Francis, Margaret, 1911, S 12,11:4
Francis, Mary S, 1937, My 11,25:4
Francis, Matthias L, 1948, S 5,40:8
Francis, Medora, 1940, O 4,23:3
Francis, Paul J, 1940, F 9,19:1
Francis, Pearce J, 1942, F 14,15:4
Francis, Percy R, 1950, O 31,27:3
Francis, Philip, 1924, N 3,17:4
Francis, Pomeroy Tucker, 1922, O 29,30:2
Francis, Richard P Dr, 1913, Mr 31,13:6
Francis, Richard S, 1954, O 31,89:3
Francis, Robert C (funl, Ag 4,25:1), 1955, Ag 1,14:2
Francis, Robert T, 1950, Je 11,92:1
Francis, Rollin J, 1954, Ap 24,17:5
Francis, Samuel, 1954, O 19,53:1
Francis, Sidney H, 1954, Ja 28,27:3
Francis, Thayer, 1958, Ja 14,33:4
Francis, Thomas A, 1952, My 25,94:5
Francis, Thomas Mrs, 1915, N 5,13:6
Francis, Valentine Mott Dr, 1907, Je 8,9:4
Francis, William, 1938, Ja 4,23:5
Francis, William A, 1951, D 24,13:3
Francis, William C, 1945, S 9,46:3
Francis, William H, 1962, F 3,21:1
Francis, William H Jr (funl plans, My 26,29:5), 1958, My 25,86:2
Francis, William J, 1949, Ag 9,26:2; 1952, Ag 10,60:4
Francis, William M, 1942, S 3,19:3; 1954, Jl 9,17:4
Francis, William S, 1940, D 13,23:6
Francis, William W, 1959, Ag 12,29:1
Francis Borgia, Mother (Countess De Aldama), 1949, Jl 1,19:5
Francis Charles, Archduke of Austria, 1859, My 24,2:3
Francis de Sales, Mother, 1951, My 9,33:3
Francis II, King of Naples, 1894, D 27,5:1
Francis Joseph Arnolphe, 1907, N 13,9:7
Francis Regis, Bro, 1949, F 25,24:3
Francis V, Duke of Modena, 1875, N 22,5:4
Francis Xavier, Sister, 1956, Jl 10,31:1
Francisco, Betty, 1950, N 27,25:3
Francisco, Charles B, 1940, F 21,19:4
Francisco, Charles M Sr, 1956, Ap 29,86:1
Francisco, Ferris L, 1946, O 12,19:4
Francisco, Frank, 1954, F 25,31:5
Francisco, H M, 1939, Je 3,15:5
Francisco, Harriet F Mrs, 1940, Ag 13,19:3
Francisco, Horace Mrs, 1954, Mr 5,19:1
Francisco, Nial G, 1953, F 16,21:4
Francisco, Taylor L, 1948, Ap 30,23:1
Francisco, Wellington P, 1955, O 18,37:4
Francisco, William H, 1948, D 16,29:4
Franciscus, George C Mrs, 1943, Ja 21,21:4
Franciscus, J A B Capt, 1937, O 9,16:1
Franck, B C, 1932, Ap 7,23:1
Franck, Ben C Mrs, 1946, Ja 10,23:4
Franck, Caroline (Mrs K Downer), 1960, My 24,37
Franck, Charles C, 1938, Ja 5,21:5
Franck, Clarence C, 1963, N 17,86:6
Franck, Fred W, 1939, Mr 29,23:4
Franck, Harry A, 1962, Ap 19,31:5
Franck, Irwin M, 1962, F 21,45:3
Franck, James, 1964, My 22,35:1
Franck, James Mrs, 1942, Ja 12,15:4
Franck, John P, 1947, S 8,21:5
Franck, Louis (por), 1938, Ja 1,19:5
Franck, Lucien, 1942, Jl 3,17:3
Franck, Oscar, 1956, Je 21,31:2
Franck, Russell C, 1959, Jl 28,27:1
Franck, Wolf, 1966, Jl 11,29:3
Francke, Albert, 1945, Mr 16,15:4
Francke, Albert Sr Mrs, 1962, S 11,33:3
Francke, Charles L, 1940, F 4,40:4
Francke, Ernest F, 1959, Jl 26,69:2
Francke, Joseph A, 1956, My 15,31:2
Francke, Luis J, 1938, F 7,15:2; 1950, Jl 6,28:2
Francke, Luis J Mrs, 1953, Je 17,27:3
Francke, Maximilian Mrs, 1962, Ja 10,47:5
Francke, T H Mrs, 1958, Ja 1,25:4
Franckenstein, Clemens von, 1942, Ag 23,43:4
Franckenstein, George, 1953, O 15,14:5
Franckenstein, George Mrs, 1953, O 15,14:5
Franckenstein, Joseph M (widow's lr of cor, O 31,-32:5), 1963, O 8,43:4
Franckenstein, Joseph M (widow's lr of cor, O 31,-32:5), 1963, O 8,43:4
Francklyn, C G, 1929, Ja 12,17:1
Francklyn, Gilbert, 1957, Je 16,84:4
Francklyn, Reginald D Mrs, 1922, Jl 3,13:7
Franco, Cesare, 1937, Jl 26,19:5
Franco, Joseph B, 1946, My 6,21:1
Franco, Manuel Antonio Gen, 1911, O 22,II,15:4
Franco, Martha V Mrs, 1950, S 20,31:3
Franco, Reuben D, 1962, O 28,88:6
Franco, Rocco P, 1957, My 24,25:2
Franco-Ferreira, Edgard C, 1951, Ja 22,17:5
Francoeur, Ida W, 1941, My 25,36:4
Francoeur, Joseph M, 1907, Mr 7,9:6
Francois, Alexander, 1912, Mr 2,13:4
Francois, Camille, 1958, S 16,14:7
Francois, Victor E, 1944, Mr 16,19:3
Francois-Marsal, Frederic, 1958, My 30,21:3
Francoise, Princess of Greece, 1953, F 28,17:3
Francolini, Joseph Nicola, 1920, D 15,15:4
Franconi, Alphonse, 1916, Ja 31,11:2
Franconi-Nief, Leon E, 1951, F 21,27:5
Franconie, Paul Gustave, 1910, Ja 23,II,11:3
Francqui, E, 1935, N 17,II,11:1
Frandsen, J H, 1962, S 22,25:4
Frandsen, Julius Jr Mrs, 1953, Jl 15,25:1
Franey, John, 1877, D 21,4:7
Franey, William, 1940, D 10,25:3
Franges, Oton, 1945, S 7,24:3
Frangioni, Alvaro Mrs, 1946, N 16,19:2
Frank, A Richard, 1952, Jl 10,31:6
Frank, Aaron (funl, My 14,19:2), 1955, My 11,3
Frank, Aaron M, 1968, N 30,39:1
Frank, Aaron Mrs, 1942, S 15,23:3
Frank, Abraham, 1938, Ag 18,19:1; 1951, Ag 14,2
Frank, Abram, 1938, S 11,II,11:2
Frank, Abram T, 1956, D 18,31:1
Frank, Adam Sr, 1956, S 27,35:6
Frank, Adolph R, 1951, Mr 27,29:3
Frank, Albert, 1949, Ja 11,27:2
Frank, Albert R, 1965, Mr 19,35:3
Frank, Alex, 1903, My 8,9:7; 1939, D 16,17:5
Frank, Alfred M, 1949, N 16,29:3
Frank, Alma M M Mrs, 1953, Je 2,29:5
Frank, Amy P, 1962, F 14,35:1
Frank, Armand, 1951, Ag 3,21:4
Frank, Armin C Sr, 1947, Ja 4,15:2
Frank, Arthur, 1941, N 19,23:2; 1944, S 3,28:2
Frank, Arthur G, 1951, S 11,29:3
Frank, Arthur Mrs, 1946, Je 20,23:2
Frank, Arthur W, 1944, Ag 31,17:6
Frank, Barbara W, 1954, Jl 5,11:6
Frank, Ben, 1945, O 18,23:2; 1958, Mr 1,17:2
Frank, Benjamin, 1943, My 26,23:5; 1945, D 28,
Frank, Bernard H, 1954, N 11,31:2
Frank, Bruno (will, Jl 5,11:4), 1945, Je 21,19:4
Frank, Carl H, 1946, Je 11,23:2
Frank, Charles, 1946, F 17,44:6; 1949, F 1,25:4; S 11,29:1
Frank, Charles A, 1951, S 12,31:2; 1964, N 4,39
Frank, Charles A Jr, 1966, O 9,86:2
Frank, Charles A Mrs, 1941, N 17,19:4

Frank, Charlotte, 1951, D 11,29:6
Frank, Christopher H, 1945, Ja 23,19:3
Frank, Claude N, 1939, O 2,17:3
Frank, Clifton I, 1967, F 7,39:2
Frank, Colman D, 1954, F 22,19:2
Frank, Curtiss E Mrs, 1957, N 14,33:3
Frank, Daniel, 1946, F 11,29:4
Frank, David L, 1938, Jl 30,13:5
Frank, David Mrs, 1943, Jl 25,31:2
Frank, Dudley, 1956, F 6,23:5
Frank, E C, 1872, N 30,8:3
Frank, E D, 1955, My 7,17:4
Frank, Edgar, 1961, S 21,35:4
Frank, Edward D, 1967, F 20,37:4
Frank, Edward H, 1953, Ja 5,21:1
Frank, Emil H, 1919, Je 24,13:4
Frank, Eric J, 1965, F 27,25:3
Frank, Erich, 1949, Je 28,27:1
Frank, Ernest G, 1949, Jl 9,13:4
Frank, Ernest M, 1968, D 10,47:1
Frank, Ethel (Mrs Arth W Brigham), 1968, S 28,33:4
Frank, Eugene C, 1914, Ja 12,9:6
Frank, Frederick, 1874, S 8,1:3
Frank, Frederick Mrs, 1946, N 17,31:5
Frank, Fritz J, 1939, D 9,15:3
Frank, George W, 1944, S 16,13:5
Frank, Gertrude (Mrs G Weinstein), 1963, Ag 18, 80:2
Frank, Gilbert, 1967, My 22,43:1
Frank, Glenn A, 1944, Je 28,23:6
Frank, Gustav, 1907, Mr 19,9:5; 1945, Mr 12,19:5
Frank, Harrison J L, 1939, F 15,23:4
Frank, Harry, 1963, My 26,92:5
Frank, Harry H, 1942, Je 18,21:3
Frank, Harry P, 1951, S 20,31:5
Frank, Harry S Mrs, 1946, Ja 29,25:2
Frank, Harry W, 1949, Je 1,31:2
Frank, Hede Mrs, 1961, N 14,27:2
Frank, Henri, 1937, F 2,23:3
Frank, Henry, 1916, N 3,13:5; 1925, N 20,21:4; 1955, Ja 12,27:1
Frank, Henry J, 1949, D 13,31:2
Frank, Henry Mrs, 1910, Ja 7,9:4
Frank, Herman, 1952, Ag 11,15:6; 1957, N 13,32:2
Frank, Herman W, 1941, Ag 23,13:4
Frank, Irving L, 1953, Je 6,17:5
Frank, Isaac, 1939, Ap 11,23:2
Frank, Isaac M, 1921, O 2,22:4
Frank, Isaiah, 1940, S 15,49:1
Frank, Isidore, 1966, O 31,35:5
Frank, J L, 1952, My 5,23:5
Frank, Jack, 1962, Ap 19,31:4
Frank, Jacob, 1945, Mr 5,19:5; 1947, F 12,25:2; 1953, Je 1,23:3
Frank, Jacob C, 1948, Je 16,29:3
Frank, James, 1943, Mr 22,19:3; 1946, S 19,31:2
Frank, James E, 1968, Mr 25,41:4
Frank, Jean M, 1941, Mr 11,24:2
Frank, Jerome N, 1957, Ja 14,23:1
Frank, John J, 1957, N 30,21:4
Frank, John P, 1945, N 24,19:1
Frank, Joseph, 1921, My 24,15:4; 1946, Mr 14,25:5; 1957, D 21,19:5
Frank, Julia H, 1950, Ja 8,76:4
Frank, Julius, 1956, F 13,27:3; 1957, D 3,35:3
Frank, Julius Mrs, 1948, Mr 19,23:2; 1949, Mr 19,15:3
Frank, Karl G, 1940, D 15,62:1
Frank, Laurence B, 1947, Mr 2,61:1
Frank, Lawrence K, 1968, S 24,44:2
Frank, Leo, 1949, F 20,61:1
Frank, Leon, 1955, My 12,29:3
Frank, Leonard, 1942, Ja 11,45:2
Frank, Leonhard, 1961, Ag 19,17:2
Frank, Leslie, 1954, Ag 9,17:6
Frank, Lewis Rev, 1923, My 10,19:5
Frank, Louis, 1941, Mr 23,45:3
Frank, Louis J, 1946, Je 7,20:2
Frank, Louis M, 1910, Ag 5,9:5
Frank, Lucien, 1948, Ag 19,21:2
Frank, Majorie S, 1952, My 27,27:2
Frank, Mark Kenneth Jr, 1968, Ap 17,47:2
Frank, Martin M (funl, My 21,23:4), 1960, My 20, 31:1
Frank, Martin M, 1962, F 28,33:3
Frank, Maurice, 1944, Ag 17,17:2
Frank, Max, 1947, Mr 4,25:2; 1956, F 25,19:4
Frank, Michael, 1946, N 14,29:2
Frank, Mildred, 1967, My 1,37:3
Frank, Milton S, 1959, Ja 8,29:3
Frank, Milton W, 1940, S 18,23:5
Frank, Morris A, 1946, Jl 27,17:5
Frank, Morris H, 1959, Jl 5,56:2
Frank, Morris J, 1954, N 28,87:3
Frank, Morris Mrs, 1952, O 12,89:1
Frank, Morris Rabbi, 1913, N 6,11:6
Frank, Mortimer M Mrs, 1952, F 18,19:4
Frank, Morton E, 1949, N 21,25:4
Frank, Nathan, 1965, D 8,47:2
Frank, Nathan Mrs, 1946, O 6,58:4; 1947, Ap 26,13:6
Frank, Nicholas, 1947, Jl 8,23:5
Frank, Noble L, 1945, S 20,23:4
Frank, P W, 1901, Ap 15,7:6
Frank, Pat (Harry H), 1964, O 13,43:1
Frank, Peter H, 1937, Ap 29,21:2
Frank, Phil F, 1951, Ap 19,31:4
Frank, Phil Mrs, 1953, Je 12,27:2
Frank, Philipp, 1966, Jl 23,25:4
Frank, Ralph O, 1949, S 24,13:5
Frank, Ray Mrs, 1925, Ja 2,15:4; 1925, Ja 3,13:5
Frank, Rene, 1965, Mr 23,39:2
Frank, Robert T (por), 1949, O 16,90:1
Frank, Rosa Mrs, 1943, Ag 17,17:3
Frank, Rose F, 1938, Mr 1,21:2
Frank, Sadie A, 1954, My 30,45:2
Frank, Samuel (will, N 28,II,3:3), 1937, N 17,23:6
Frank, Samuel, 1940, Ap 8,19:6; 1947, N 23,72:5
Frank, Samuel B, 1950, O 19,31:2
Frank, Samuel Leon Dr, 1913, N 23,IV,7:5
Frank, Samuel M, 1943, O 14,21:2
Frank, Samuel Mrs, 1940, S 8,49:2; 1959, Ap 6,27:4
Frank, Sara M Mrs (will), 1937, Ag 10,8:3
Frank, Simon, 1937, Mr 24,25:2
Frank, Simon C Dr, 1968, My 4,39:2
Frank, Tenney, 1939, Ap 4,25:5
Frank, Tessie K Mrs (will), 1938, Je 16,23:2
Frank,Theodore, 1917, S 25,11:5
Frank, Victor H Mrs, 1967, Jl 23,60:8
Frank, Vincent J, 1958, Ja 15,39:1
Frank, Waldo D, 1967, Ja 10,43:1
Frank, Wilfred N, 1950, Ag 22,27:2
Frank, William, 1951, O 10,23:4
Frank, William F, 1938, S 10,17:5
Frank, William H Jr, 1952, S 22,23:4
Frank, William H Sr, 1924, Ap 18,19:5
Frank, William K, 1964, N 23,37:4
Frank, Ulysses M, 1967, Ja 28,27:5
Frankau, Gilbert, 1952, N 5,27:1
Frankau, Pamela, 1967, Je 9,37:3
Frankau, Ronald, 1951, S 12,31:4
Franke, Albert V, 1942, Ap 28,21:2
Franke, Alfred E, 1952, Jl 9,27:3
Franke, Arthur, 1939, F 18,15:3
Franke, Aug C, 1938, D 14,25:1
Franke, Byron J, 1937, My 22,18:2
Franke, Carl, 1942, My 3,54:1
Franke, Charles, 1938, Je 11,15:4
Franke, Elmer E, 1946, Mr 7,25:3
Franke, Emil H, 1941, N 22,19:4
Franke, H Cleveland Mrs, 1952, Ag 10,61:2
Franke, Henry C, 1959, N 4,41:5
Franke, Henry E, 1966, O 30,89:1
Franke, Jay B Mrs, 1949, Mr 30,25:5
Franke, John T, 1968, Ja 18,39:3
Franke, John T Mrs, 1960, F 28,83:1
Frankel, Abraham Mrs, 1960, Jl 15,23:5
Frankel, Albert, 1943, O 20,21:6
Frankel, Andrew H, 1944, My 30,21:2
Frankel, Anton, 1953, Jl 4,5:7
Frankel, Charles, 1942, O 8,27:2; 1964, Je 30,33:2
Frankel, Charles Wilson, 1908, S 18,7:4
Frankel, Edward Dr, 1923, D 17,17:4
Frankel, Edward Jr, 1941, Jl 6,27:1
Frankel, Edward M (cor, N 21,13:1), 1953, N 20,24:3
Frankel, Eli, 1925, Ap 24,19:4
Frankel, Florence H, 1951, D 24,13:5
Frankel, Frederick S, 1954, S 21,27:2
Frankel, Harold, 1958, F 18,27:2
Frankel, Harry, 1948, Je 13,68:6; 1957, Je 4,35:4
Frankel, Henry, 1966, O 25,45:2
Frankel, Henry N, 1941, Je 29,33:2
Frankel, Hyman, 1948, O 14,29:4
Frankel, Isador, 1940, My 2,23:4
Frankel, Jacob, 1905, Mr 12,9:5
Frankel, Jacob M, 1968, Ag 22,37:3
Frankel, Jacob M Mrs, 1942, Ag 30,43:2
Frankel, Jacques, 1952, N 10,25:4
Frankel, John (will), 1939, Mr 7,8:3
Frankel, John R, 1939, Ag 31,19:4
Frankel, Joseph, 1956, Jl 14,15:6
Frankel, Joseph Mrs, 1939, S 15,23:3
Frankel, Joseph W, 1950, Ap 16,104:4
Frankel, Jules, 1939, Ja 7,15:2
Frankel, Julius, 1945, D 8,17:1
Frankel, Kevie, 1968, Ag 15,37:3
Frankel, L K, 1931, Jl 26,18:1
Frankel, Leo P, 1967, Mr 18,29:2
Frankel, Leon, 1951, Ag 17,9:1
Frankel, Louis (will, My 23,5:2), 1937, My 16,II,8:6
Frankel, Louis, 1947, Jl 22,23:5; 1953, Ja 1,23:4
Frankel, Louis H Mrs, 1956, Ag 25,15:2
Frankel, Max, 1939, D 21,23:4
Frankel, Myron, 1966, Je 10,45:1
Frankel, Nathan, 1964, Jl 17,27:1
Frankel, Norman Dr, 1968, Jl 1,33:3
Frankel, Perry Mrs, 1950, F 15,27:2
Frankel, Robert, 1965, Jl 3,19:3
Frankel, Saul S, 1960, Ag 6,19:6
Frankel, Sidney H, 1965, D 7,47:3
Frankel, Simon Mrs, 1946, Jl 8,29:6
Frankel, Walter E, 1945, F 9,16:3
Frankel, William, 1947, N 12,27:2
Frankel, William N, 1961, D 24,36:5
Frankel, William S Sr, 1949, Ap 16,15:5
Frankel, William W, 1962, S 29,23:3
Franken, Bernard J, 1949, Ap 26,25:4
Frankenberg, Jacob H Dr, 1915, Jl 28,9:4
Frankenberg, John H Mrs, 1941, Ap 26,15:3
Frankenberger, Charles H Sr, 1952, O 7,29:4
Frankenberger, Charles L, 1951, Ap 18,31:4
Frankenberger, Joseph E, 1952, Mr 22,13:1
Frankenberger, Joseph E Mrs, 1950, O 10,31:2
Frankenberger, Joseph Mrs, 1950, O 1,104:1
Frankenburg, Walter G, 1957, Jl 5,17:1
Frankenfield, Frederick A, 1949, D 4,108:7
Frankenheimer, Harold S, 1954, Mr 28,88:3
Frankensteen, Louis, 1942, Je 26,21:5
Frankenstein, Anna Countess, 1937, S 11,17:2
Frankenstein, Henry, 1951, Jl 4,17:6
Frankenstein, J, 1881, Ap 17,2:4
Frankenthal, Herman, 1940, Ag 26,15:3
Frankenthal, Hyman, 1950, S 30,17:6
Frankenthaler, Alfred, 1940, Ja 8,15:3
Frankenthaler, Alfred Mrs, 1954, Ap 24,7:5
Frankenthaler, George Mrs, 1961, D 19,33:2
Frankenthurn, Gautsch von Baron, 1918, Ap 23,13:5
Frankfield, Emil, 1912, Je 23,II,17:5
Frankfort, Fred Sr, 1961, Je 28,35:3
Frankfort, Herman, 1937, Ag 20,17:5
Frankfurt, Solomon, 1954, N 20,17:5
Frankfurter, Alfred M, 1965, My 13,37:4
Frankfurter, Arthur, 1957, O 30,29:3
Frankfurter, Felix (trb, F 23,27:1,2; funl plans, F 24,38:4), 1965, F 23,1:6
Frankfurter, Fred S, 1957, Ja 3,33:1
Frankfurter, Moritz Mrs, 1949, F 21,23:3
Frankfurter, Paul, 1943, Ap 23,17:4
Frankfurter, Paul Mrs, 1939, My 26,23:2
Frankfurter, Salomon, 1941, O 23,23:1
Frankhauser, Charles K Jr, 1938, Ja 19,23:4
Frankhauser, Eli I, 1949, S 26,25:4
Frankish, Edgar, 1941, O 25,17:3
Frankl, Oscar B, 1955, D 19,27:3
Frankl, Paul, 1962, Ja 31,31:2
Frankl, Paul T, 1958, Mr 22,17:3
Frankl, Walter, 1963, My 21,37:4
Frankland, Frederick William, 1916, Jl 26,11:6
Frankland, George R, 1905, Mr 29,9:3
Frankland, Samuel M, 1940, F 22,23:3
Frankland, Wilson, 1951, D 25,31:5
Frankle, Arthur C, 1943, Mr 18,19:3
Franklin, Abraham, 1947, My 3,17:4
Franklin, Albert W Sr, 1962, Je 3,88:8
Franklin, Alfred L, 1949, Mr 26,17:5
Franklin, Benjamin, 1951, O 31,29:5
Franklin, Benjamin Sir, 1917, F 18,17:2
Franklin, Benjamin W, 1915, Ap 1,15:4
Franklin, Benjamin W Mrs, 1916, Ja 29,9:4
Franklin, Calvin M, 1941, Jl 24,17:3
Franklin, Charles, 1955, My 29,44:2
Franklin, Charles L Com, 1874, S 20,5:3
Franklin, Chester A (funl, My 12,29:5), 1955, My 8, 88:2
Franklin, Clarence P, 1945, D 14,27:4
Franklin, Clarence P Mrs, 1954, O 12,27:3
Franklin, Cornelius E, 1921, Mr 15,11:4
Franklin, Cornell S, 1959, F 25,31:2
Franklin, Daniel, 1942, O 13,23:6
Franklin, David D, 1945, D 11,25:5
Franklin, David Dr, 1903, O 9,7:4
Franklin, Edward C Dr, 1937, F 14,II,8:4
Franklin, Edward L Mrs, 1956, Jl 21,15:4
Franklin, Esther C, 1965, D 11,33:3
Franklin, F Saxton, 1966, D 8,47:1
Franklin, Fabian, 1939, Ja 9,15:3
Franklin, Frederick S Jr, 1953, Jl 25,11:5
Franklin, G S, 1934, N 15,21:1
Franklin, George B, 1948, F 15,60:4
Franklin, George M, 1965, My 20,43:1
Franklin, George R, 1939, D 24,14:5
Franklin, George S, 1952, Mr 9,93:2
Franklin, George S Mrs, 1967, My 16,45:2
Franklin, George V, 1939, O 11,27:4
Franklin, Harold, 1957, Ja 27,84:3
Franklin, Harold B, 1941, Ap 22,21:6
Franklin, Harris, 1923, Ap 12,19:5; 1923, My 31,15:4
Franklin, Henry J, 1958, Ap 17,31:5
Franklin, Henry T, 1956, Ag 23,27:5
Franklin, Hubert J, 1962, Je 20,35:3
Franklin, Hugo, 1940, Mr 15,23:2
Franklin, Irene, 1941, Je 17,21:1
Franklin, J Clyde, 1948, N 14,76:7
Franklin, J Phillips, 1951, O 22,23:3
Franklin, J R, 1878, Ja 13,6:7
Franklin, James, 1882, F 28,3:4
Franklin, James H, 1961, Mr 24,27:5
Franklin, Jane Lady, 1875, Jl 19,5:6
Franklin, Jean D Mrs, 1941, Ag 28,19:2
Franklin, Jesse B, 1952, Ja 7,19:5
Franklin, John, 1920, O 15,13:4
Franklin, John H, 1950, O 4,31:4
Franklin, John M Jr, 1946, O 24,27:3
Franklin, Joseph, 1947, Ag 5,23:1
Franklin, Joseph A, 1948, F 19,23:3; 1958, Ap 17,31:4; 1959, D 9,45:4
Franklin, Joseph M, 1957, My 21,35:3
Franklin, Joseph P, 1947, Je 17,25:2
Franklin, Leo M, 1948, Ag 9,19:1
Franklin, Lewis B, 1959, Mr 23,31:3
Franklin, Lewis B Mrs, 1962, Ja 19,31:1

Franklin, Lindley M, 1960, Jl 10,72:1
Franklin, Louis, 1938, D 21,23:1
Franklin, Melvin M, 1938, Ag 2,19:3
Franklin, Paul B, 1946, O 31,25:4
Franklin, Pearl, 1958, Jl 12,15:5
Franklin, Peter A, 1914, D 1,13:6
Franklin, Phil, 1951, Ja 10,28:2
Franklin, Phil A S (will, Ag 24,17:5), 1939, Ag 15, 19:1
Franklin, Phil A S Mrs, 1938, O 15,17:4
Franklin, Philip, 1965, Ja 28,30:1
Franklin, Philip A S Jr, 1946, D 3,31:2
Franklin, R L, 1880, S 8,5:4
Franklin, Raymond, 1968, Ag 24,29:4
Franklin, Robert C Mrs, 1947, F 23,53:3
Franklin, Robert M, 1941, D 6,17:4; 1950, Je 5,23:4
Franklin, Rosalind, 1958, Ap 20,85:2
Franklin, Ruford, 1945, Je 20,23:5
Franklin, Rufus C, 1942, D 5,15:4
Franklin, Samuel, 1959, Jl 30,27:3
Franklin, Samuel Mrs, 1943, D 28,17:3
Franklin, Samuel Rhoades, 1909, F 25,7:4
Franklin, Sidney A, 1961, Ag 19,18:1
Franklin, Sidney A Mrs, 1960, O 30,86:5
Franklin, T E, 1884, N 29,2:6
Franklin, Thomas F, 1944, Ap 15,11:5
Franklin, Todd B, 1957, Je 15,17:3
Franklin, W B Gen, 1903, Mr 9,9:5
Franklin, Walter M, 1945, Ap 11,23:3
Franklin, Walter S, 1946, Ja 3,19:3
Franklin, Walter S Mrs, 1962, My 4,34:1
Franklin, Walter Simonds Col, 1911, D 4,13:5
Franklin, Walter T, 1953, D 30,23:3
Franklin, William B, 1942, S 15,23:3
Franklin, William B Mrs, 1946, D 28,16:2
Franklin, William C B, 1951, Jl 12,25:6
Franklin, William M, 1915, N 21,19:4
Franklin, Wirt, 1962, S 26,39:2
Franklin, Yetta, 1965, O 17,86:7
Franklin-Bouillon, Henry, 1937, N 13,19:5
Franklyn, Harold E, 1963, Ap 1,27:5
Franko, Jeannie Mrs, 1940, D 4,27:3
Franko, N, 1930, Je 8,26:1
Franko, Nahan Mrs, 1938, S 13,23:4
Franko, Roberto, 1958, Jl 6,56:3
Franko, Sam Mrs, 1902, D 16,2:4
Franks, Bernard J, 1957, D 5,35:1
Franks, Clem H, 1948, S 21,28:3
Franks, Edward, 1937, Ag 15,II,6:6
Franks, Edward J, 1957, Ag 16,19:2
Franks, George, 1948, Ag 1,56:6
Franks, George C, 1948, O 31,88:5
Franks, Harold, 1949, Ap 19,26:5
Franks, Heyman S, 1960, D 16,33:3
Franks, James B Jr, 1941, N 6,23:1
Franks, James Potter Rev, 1917, Mr 26,11:4
Franks, John B, 1946, N 14,29:4
Franks, Julius F, 1943, D 30,17:4
Franks, Phoenix S, 1940, N 30,17:2
Franks, Robert A Mrs, 1945, Ap 15,14:3
Franosch, Anna, 1947, S 29,21:3
Frans, Fricka, 1952, Mr 11,27:4
Fransen, Rudolf, 1913, F 14,15:2
Fransioli, William J, 1949, O 8,13:4
Fransiosi, James T, 1963, O 19,25:1
Fransson, Linnea, 1939, Jl 25,2:4
Fransson, Sven W, 1938, D 6,23:1
Frant, Samuel, 1961, Jl 31,19:3
Frantz, Alfred J Mrs, 1949, F 4,23:1
Frantz, Corey A, 1945, Ag 3,17:5
Frantz, Dalies E, 1965, D 2,41:2
Frantz, Dolph G, 1953, Jl 8,27:5
Frantz, Frank, 1941, Mr 10,17:3
Frantz, George L C, 1950, Mr 24,25:2
Frantz, Herman C, 1952, S 6,17:2
Frantz, Jacob Frick Dr, 1914, F 8,15:5
Frantz, John T, 1937, Ag 31,23:2
Frantz, Louise (will), 1938, D 18,13:2
Frantz, Nelson A, 1949, My 9,25:4
Frantz, Parcel G, 1949, Je 16,29:3
Frantz, Ralph J Mrs, 1967, Ja 30,29:4
Frantz, Virginia K, 1967, Ag 24,37:1
Frantz, Wilbur M, 1944, Ap 19,23:2
Frantzen, Chell Mrs, 1968, My 27,47:3
Frantzen, John P, 1938, Ag 30,17:4
Frantzen, Peter Mrs, 1955, Ag 24,27:4
Franz, Adolph Sr, 1955, N 23,23:3
Franz, Allen J, 1952, Je 24,29:3
Franz, Barbara, 1952, Jl 19,15:6
Franz, Elmer F, 1968, Je 20,45:1
Franz, Erwin, 1955, O 22,19:6
Franz, Harry P Mrs, 1946, Ap 17,25:5
Franz, John F, 1949, S 27,27:5
Franz, John Mrs, 1945, Ja 13,11:1
Franz, John S, 1945, D 19,26:2
Franz, Joseph, 1959, Je 27,23:6
Franz, Joseph G, 1955, My 18,31:5
Franz, Joseph M, 1964, D 16,46:3
Franz, Walter, 1940, My 5,53:1
Franz I, Prince of Liechtenstein, 1938, Jl 27,17:3
Franz Josef, Duke of Bavaria, 1912, S 25,13:6
Franz Maria Luitpold, Prince of Bavaria, 1957, Ja 27, 84:6

Franzblau, William, 1963, O 2,41:2
Franzell, Gregory A, 1947, Ap 21,21:4
Franzen, Aug R, 1938, S 8,24:1
Franzen, Carl G F, 1966, D 13,47:2
Franzen, Carl J, 1946, Ag 17,13:1
Franzen, Raymond H, 1965, Jl 2,29:2
Franzheim, Kenneth, 1959, Mr 18,37:4
Franzius, G H, 1944, Jl 2,20:2
Franzl, Joseph, 1955, Jl 27,23:2
Franzoni, Geno N, 1955, My 3,31:3
Frapaul, Peter A, 1962, O 18,39:4
Frappier, Ephrem H, 1958, Je 22,76:2
Fraprie, Frank R, 1951, Je 22,25:4
Frapwell, Herbert L, 1964, Je 27,25:4
Frary, Charles J, 1956, My 4,51:1
Frary, Donald, 1919, Ap 8,11:4
Frary, John, 1924, My 22,17:5
Frasca, Armond C, 1955, Ap 3,86:4
Frasca, Kenneth J, 1944, S 23,13:5
Frasca, William R, 1964, Ag 10,31:5
Frascella, Peter (Kid Murphy), 1963, O 30,39:4
Frasch, Herman Mrs, 1924, S 27,16:2
Fraser, A F, 1878, My 25,2:3
Fraser, Agnes, 1940, F 24,13:4
Fraser, Alan C, 1941, S 18,25:4
Fraser, Albert A, 1938, Jl 15,17:3
Fraser, Alex (por), 1938, S 20,23:4
Fraser, Alex A, 1959, Jl 27,25:4
Fraser, Alex Capt, 1937, N 10,25:1
Fraser, Alex G, 1942, S 25,21:3
Fraser, Alex H, 1940, Mr 9,15:2
Fraser, Alex J Mrs, 1961, O 12,29:5
Fraser, Alexander J, 1945, Mr 28,23:2
Fraser, Alexander Mrs, 1968, D 30,31:1
Fraser, Alexander V Capt, 1916, N 9,13:4
Fraser, Alice A Mrs, 1940, O 3,25:6
Fraser, Amorette E Mrs, 1940, Ja 7,49:1
Fraser, Angus M, 1938, Mr 9,23:5; 1957, Mr 31,89:2
Fraser, Anne T, 1966, My 25,5:3
Fraser, Arthur T, 1959, Je 9,37:3
Fraser, Blair, 1968, My 14,47:4
Fraser, C Douglas, 1939, O 29,40:8
Fraser, Carlyle, 1961, S 13,45:1
Fraser, Cecil E, 1947, F 24,19:5
Fraser, Charles, 1952, Ag 10,61:3
Fraser, Charles C, 1940, My 9,23:5
Fraser, Charles Duncan, 1917, My 8,11:5
Fraser, Charles E, 1959, Ag 25,31:3
Fraser, Charles Jr, 1951, O 19,27:3
Fraser, Charles L, 1954, Ap 3,15:3
Fraser, Clarence W, 1968, My 15,47:1
Fraser, Cyrus H, 1951, N 4,86:6
Fraser, Daniel G, 1941, D 16,28:2
Fraser, Donald T, 1954, Jl 22,23:5
Fraser, Duncan, 1939, O 13,23:2
Fraser, Duncan C, 1910, S 28,11:4
Fraser, Duncan W, 1954, D 21,27:3
Fraser, Edward B, 1954, Mr 30,27:3
Fraser, Elijah E, 1940, Ag 8,19:2
Fraser, Eugene B, 1948, Ja 16,21:1
Fraser, Farquhar, 1958, Ja 6,39:2
Fraser, Fenwick W Mrs, 1938, D 21,23:5
Fraser, Florence, 1917, N 26,13:2
Fraser, Forrest L, 1956, Jl 13,19:6
Fraser, Frank L, 1962, Jl 23,21:5
Fraser, Frederick D Mrs, 1960, My 23,29:4
Fraser, G J, 1959, Je 8,6:6
Fraser, George W, 1964, Ja 31,27:4
Fraser, Gilbert, 1924, S 23,23:3
Fraser, Harold W, 1945, Ja 5,15:4
Fraser, Harry G, 1956, Jl 21,15:5
Fraser, Harry W, 1950, My 14,106:3
Fraser, Herbert F, 1953, F 11,29:4
Fraser, Homer E, 1949, F 18,23:3
Fraser, Homer E Mrs, 1944, Je 10,15:3
Fraser, Horatio N, 1942, N 9,23:2
Fraser, Hugh J, 1952, Ag 23,13:5
Fraser, Irene C Mrs, 1938, D 30,15:4
Fraser, J B, 1939, N 3,21:2
Fraser, J F, 1936, Je 8,19:3
Fraser, J Frank, 1943, F 1,15:4
Fraser, J Frederick, 1942, N 5,25:4
Fraser, J H, 1885, F 22,7:4
Fraser, James C Mrs, 1907, Ap 30,9:6
Fraser, James D, 1960, D 14,35:5
Fraser, James D Mrs, 1941, Jl 15,19:4
Fraser, James E, 1950, Ag 30,31:1; 1950, S 2,15:5; 1953, O 12,27:3
Fraser, James E Mrs, 1966, Ag 14,88:2
Fraser, James H, 1964, Mr 6,31:3
Fraser, James W, 1947, D 6,15:6
Fraser, John, 1919, Mr 1,13:4; 1947, D 2,29:4; 1952, Ja 1,25:1; 1962, Jl 6,25:5; 1963, Je 4,39:3
Fraser, John B, 1940, Jl 8,17:4
Fraser, John M (will), 1949, Jl 9,3:5
Fraser, John Mrs, 1911, Ap 20,11:5; 1956, N 23,27:1
Fraser, John R, 1945, D 10,21:2
Fraser, John S, 1953, S 1,23:1; 1959, Je 27,23:3
Fraser, John Sr, 1941, Ag 22,15:6
Fraser, John W, 1941, My 28,25:2
Fraser, Jus, 1923, F 16,13:5
Fraser, Karl C, 1954, S 24,23:3
Fraser, L, 1926, Ap 21,25:4

Fraser, Leon Mrs, 1942, Mr 20,19:2
Fraser, Lewis H, 1956, O 21,86:8
Fraser, Malcolm, 1949, Je 13,19:4
Fraser, Malcolm A, 1948, Ja 7,25:5
Fraser, Margaret L, 1959, Jl 19,9:8
Fraser, Matthew Sir, 1937, D 25,15:6
Fraser, McIntyre, 1949, My 2,25:5
Fraser, Myles A, 1947, O 29,27:5
Fraser, P Verness, 1946, N 12,29:5
Fraser, Peter, 1950, D 12,33:1
Fraser, Peter Mrs, 1945, Mr 8,23:4
Fraser, R F Dr, 1884, Jl 11,5:3
Fraser, Robert, 1957, Ap 12,25:3
Fraser, Robert A, 1945, N 2,19:4
Fraser, Robert W, 1959, Ja 12,39:3
Fraser, Roy M, 1948, N 30,27:1
Fraser, Samuel, 1959, My 18,27:2
Fraser, Samuel W, 1950, My 30,17:2
Fraser, Thomas C, 1950, My 14,106:3
Fraser, Thomas H, 1942, O 11,56:3
Fraser, Thomas Richard, 1920, Ja 6,15:2
Fraser, Thornton, 1940, N 13,18:4
Fraser, W F, 1880, F 22,7:2
Fraser, Walter S Mrs, 1937, Ag 23,19:3
Fraser, William, 1957, Mr 14,29:1
Fraser, William A Jr, 1964, Je 2,37:2
Fraser, William J, 1943, Ja 23,13:5
Fraser, William Mrs, 1966, F 2,35:3
Fraser, William R, 1952, N 6,29:1
Fraser, William W, 1941, Ap 1,23:5
Fraser-Campbell, Arnold, 1958, D 3,37:2
Fraser-Campbell, Evan J Mrs, 1943, Je 10,21:1
Fraser-Campbell, William Baillie Lt, 1918, Ap 5,1
Fraser-Haris, David Dr, 1937, Ja 5,23:3
Fraser-Tytler, William K, 1963, Ag 27,31:4
Frash, Omar T, 1958, My 23,23:2
Frasher, William H, 1945, F 3,11:4
Frasheri, Mehdi, 1963, My 28,28:6
Frasheri, Midhat, 1949, O 4,27:1
Frasier, John E, 1939, Jl 28,17:4
Frasier, Walter G, 1953, O 29,31:5
Frassone, Teresa Mrs, 1952, N 8,17:3
Fratellini, Albert A, 1961, My 16,37:1
Fratellini, Francois, 1951, Je 21,27:3
Fratellini, Paul, 1940, N 7,25:2
Frater, J W Mrs, 1955, O 20,35:4
Fratianne, Pasquale, 1950, Ag 16,29:5
Fratini, Angelini Mrs, 1944, Ap 12,21:2
Fratrits, Eugene, 1961, O 9,35:3
Fratt, George M, 1947, Jl 27,45:2
Frattale, Samuel, 1924, Ag 16,11:6
Fratus, Russell A, 1955, My 25,33:4
Frauehan, August, 1947, Mr 19,25:3
Frauenberger, Carl, 1951, F 27,27:2
Frauenfelder, Emil A, 1958, Mr 23,88:8
Frauenheim, George M, 1968, Ap 7,92:3
Frauenthal, Henry W Mrs, 1943, Mr 31,19:5
Frauenthal, Herman C, 1942, Ag 24,15:3
Frauenzimmer, Otto Mrs, 1948, Jl 15,23:2
Frauson, Arthur W, 1954, Ja 3,88:5
Frauson, Victor, 1942, D 30,23:5
Fravell, James E G, 1950, Je 22,27:4
Frawley, Frank Mrs, 1943, Je 6,42:4
Frawley, Gilbert B J, 1951, O 6,19:1
Frawley, J Edward, 1956, Ag 19,92:1
Frawley, J J, 1926, S 2,1:4
Frawley, James, 1944, Ja 1,13:5
Frawley, James J, 1960, Mr 25,21:2
Frawley, John J, 1911, D 29,11:4
Frawley, Margaret M, 1947, O 16,27:6
Frawley, Mary E, 1939, Je 12,17:4
Frawley, Patrick J, 1967, Ap 19,45:2
Frawley, William, 1966, Mr 4,33:1
Frawley, William J, 1949, F 25,23:4
Fray, E S Mrs, 1903, Ap 25,9:5
Fray, Jacques, 1963, Ja 21,7:4
Fray, John L, 1961, D 3,88:2
Fray, Walter W, 1940, Jl 12,15:2
Frayler, Louis M, 1960, Je 12,86:7
Frayne, Ed, 1944, N 28,23:5
Frayne, Frank I, 1938, S 22,23:2
Frayne, H, 1934, Jl 14,13:4
Frayser, Benjamin H Dr, 1937, Mr 7,II,8:2
Frazar, Everett, 1901, Ja 4,7:5
Frazar, Everett W, 1951, O 15,25:3
Frazar, Lether E, 1960, My 16,31:5
Frazee, Arthur F, 1948, Jl 4,26:7
Frazee, Charles D, 1943, D 12,68:1
Frazee, Ellsworth, 1945, Jl 4,13:7
Frazee, Francis B, 1941, F 23,40:2
Frazee, H H, 1929, Je 5,29:1
Frazee, Harold D, 1964, Ag 6,29:2
Frazee, Harry H Jr, 1956, S 13,35:4
Frazee, Harry P, 1950, O 17,31:4
Frazee, James G, 1941, My 8,23:1
Frazee, James H Mrs, 1957, My 1,37:1
Frazee, Jeremiah S, 1940, Je 4,23:5
Frazee, John Hatfield, 1917, My 6,19:4
Frazee, Milton B, 1942, Ja 1,25:3
Frazee, Percy R, 1937, Jl 9,21:2
Frazee, V, 1881, N 1,5:3
Frazee, Wesley S, 1953, Ag 30,89:2
Frazee, Whitney, 1945, My 28,19:2

Frazer, A D, 1877, Ag 4,1:4
Frazer, Charles B, 1966, My 31,43:3
Frazer, David R Rev, 1916, Ja 25,9:3
Frazer, Elizabeth, 1967, My 16,45:3
Frazer, Emily Mrs, 1946, Mr 7,25:4
Frazer, Fred, 1938, D 14,25:3
Frazer, G Blair, 1922, O 6,23:4
Frazer, George, 1907, Je 9,9:6
Frazer, J Anderson, 1949, Jl 16,13:2
Frazer, J W Prof, 1872, O 14,1:3
Frazer, James C Mrs, 1949, S 23,24:3
Frazer, John, 1964, Je 8,29:1
Frazer, Joseph C W, 1944, Jl 29,13:5
Frazer, Joseph R, 1945, Mr 9,19:2
Frazer, L Mrs, 1928, D 27,23:3
Frazer, Lily Lady, 1941, My 9,21:3
Frazer, Oris Mrs, 1912, F 21,11:4
Frazer, Perry D, 1943, Je 23,21:5
Frazer, Quintan, 1961, Mr 31,27:5
Frazer, Raymond L, 1958, Je 14,21:6
Frazer, Reah Com, 1919, D 31,7:4
Frazer, Spaulding, 1940, Mr 8,21:4
Frazer, William N, 1940, Ap 21,42:3
Frazier, A G H Mrs, 1942, F 22,26:2
Frazier, Alan C, 1951, My 1,29:2
Frazier, C H, 1936, Jl 27,15:5
Frazier, Charles W, 1956, S 26,33:5
Frazier, Charles W Mrs, 1964, Mr 12,35:1
Frazier, E Franklin, 1962, My 22,37:1
Frazier, Earl J, 1957, O 28,27:4
Frazier, Earl J Mrs, 1966, Ap 30,31:4
Frazier, Edwin R, 1951, O 11,37:3
Frazier, Emery L Mrs, 1958, Jl 9,27:5
Frazier, Franklin P, 1923, My 8,17:5
Frazier, Franklin R, 1913, Jl 16,7:6
Frazier, Frederic H, 1939, O 11,27:2
Frazier, George H Mrs, 1958, N 8,21:1
Frazier, Harold S, 1950, Ag 15,30:2
Frazier, J Miller, 1952, Ag 25,17:5
Frazier, James B, 1937, Mr 29,19:5
Frazier, James R, 1951, Mr 22,31:3
Frazier, Kenneth, 1949, S 1,21:5
Frazier, Lynn J, 1947, Ja 12,59:3
Frazier, Marion R, 1945, Mr 21,24:3
Frazier, Robert, 1940, My 20,17:1
Frazier, Robert P, 1914, Ap 20,9:4
Frazier, Royal C, 1951, N 14,31:6
Frazier, Samuel J, 1950, Ag 5,15:3
Frazier, Stanley I, 1951, F 22,31:3
Frazier, Susie, 1952, Ag 2,15:7
Frazier, T McCall, 1950, Mr 30,29:2
Frazier, Thomas M, 1949, Je 9,31:1
Frazier, Victor H, 1954, Ap 10,15:2
Frazier, William, 1882, Ap 16,2:7
Frazier, William F, 1962, S 29,23:1
Frazier, William H, 1946, Ag 28,27:5
Frazier, William W, 1921, Ag 25,13:5; 1939, Ag 26, 15:6
Frazin, Louis, 1954, Mr 6,15:5
Frazin, Louis Mrs, 1955, Ja 28,19:2
Fread, Sidney Mrs, 1966, My 6,47:2
Freake, Charles A M, 1951, N 15,29:5
Frear, Charles W, 1944, My 8,19:1
Frear, Charles Wright Mrs, 1968, O 5,35:5
Frear, Edwin H, 1942, S 8,23:3
Frear, Hugo P, 1955, Ag 22,21:4
Frear, James A, 1939, My 30,18:1
Frear, Robin (Bobby Heath), 1952, Mr 5,29:1
Freas, Henry M, 1938, Je 29,19:4
Freas, Oscar C Sr, 1951, My 3,29:2
Freas, T B, 1928, Mr 17,15:5
Freas, Thomas B Mrs, 1952, O 21,29:5
Freas, William S Rev Dr, 1911, F 15,9:4
Frease, Edwin F, 1938, Ap 23,15:4
Frease, William A Sr, 1947, F 18,25:4
Frech, Franklin, 1952, O 24,23:5
Frech, Frederic F, 1954, Jl 17,13:2
Frech, William O, 1949, Ja 19,28:3
Frechette, George, 1963, S 25,43:5
Frechette, Louis, 1882, Ag 3,2:4
Frechette, Ovide, 1924, Ag 23,9:4
Frechette, Raoul A, 1940, Jl 30,19:5
Frechtel, Harry, 1958, My 16,25:4
Freck, Charles A, 1952, F 13,29:5
Freckleton, T Edward, 1948, F 1,60:4
Freckmann, Henry D, 1967, Ap 9,92:8
Frectman, Bernard, 1967, Mr 29,45:2
Freda, Joseph M, 1952, Jl 21,19:3
Freda, Lester, 1949, Ja 9,72:3
Freda, W Harry, 1961, My 27,23:6
Fredenburgh, Francis D, 1949, F 4,24:3
Freder, Frederick C, 1954, N 16,27:1
Frederic, Harold, 1898, O 20,7:1
Frederich, Hector L, 1949, Je 17,23:4
Frederich, Max, 1962, O 10,47:1
Frederick, Archduke, 1936, D 31,17:1
Frederick, Arthur, 1961, Ja 2,25:1
Frederick, Augustus, 1941, Ja 28,19:3
Frederick, Bro, 1949, Ja 14,23:2
Frederick, Carl A, 1940, My 11,19:6
Frederick, Charles A Mrs, 1946, O 22,25:2
Frederick, Charles H, 1949, Ag 12,18:2
Frederick, Charles L, 1923, My 7,15:6
Frederick, Charles W, 1942, N 30,23:5
Frederick, Claude E, 1944, D 29,15:4
Frederick, David M, 1952, Ja 3,46:2
Frederick, Denver D, 1962, F 3,21:5
Frederick, Donald E, 1937, Jl 7,24:2
Frederick, Edward H, 1941, Jl 2,21:4
Frederick, Edward J, 1941, Mr 11,23:2
Frederick, Eugene, 1944, Je 3,13:4
Frederick, F C, 1952, Je 5,31:6
Frederick, Frank F, 1942, Je 2,23:2
Frederick, George, 1945, Jl 5,13:4
Frederick, George A, 1924, Ag 19,15:5; 1946, Jl 18, 25:1
Frederick, George E, 1951, Ag 8,25:3
Frederick, George R Mrs, 1967, Je 14,47:4
Frederick, Halsey A, 1961, N 27,29:5
Frederick, Henry A, 1947, F 8,17:4
Frederick, J George, 1964, Mr 24,33:1
Frederick, J M H, 1942, Je 11,23:2
Frederick, Leopold Mrs, 1962, Ap 30,27:4
Frederick, Lucille B Mrs, 1942, O 14,25:4
Frederick, Max L, 1949, Jl 8,19:5
Frederick, Paul G, 1947, Ap 2,29:4
Frederick, Pauline (por), 1938, S 20,23:1
Frederick, Peter Mrs, 1948, S 27,23:1
Frederick, Prince of Netherlands, 1881, O 9,6:7
Frederick, Ruth, 1961, F 18,19:4
Frederick, Walter F, 1951, D 2,91:1
Frederick, William, 1950, N 23,35:3
Frederick, William R, 1965, Ja 21,31:2
Frederick, Wilson S, 1946, D 7,21:1
Frederick August, Former King of Saxony, 1932, F 19, 19:1
Frederick Francis IV, Grand Duke, 1945, N 19,21:3
Frederick II, Duke of Anhalt, 1918, Ap 23,13:5
Frederick II, Former Grand Duke, 1928, Ag 10,17:3
Frederick Leopold, Prince, 1931, S 15,25:1
Frederick VIII of Denmark, King, 1912, My 18,13:3
Frederick William III, Emperor of Germany, 1888, Je 16,1:1
Frederick William IV, King of Prussia, 1861, Ja 18,4:6
Fredericks, Harold, 1966, Ap 2,29:3
Fredericks, Harry C, 1952, Ap 18,25:4
Fredericks, Henry Mrs, 1952, Ap 25,23:2
Fredericks, John D Mrs, 1948, S 30,27:4
Fredericks, John J, 1938, Ag 21,33:3
Fredericks, Julius Sgt, 1904, Ja 7,9:4
Fredericks, Karl T, 1963, F 13,9:2
Fredericks, Leonard H, 1943, N 10,23:4
Fredericks, Paul C Jr, 1963, O 28,27:2
Fredericks, Pierce G, 1960, S 27,38:1
Fredericks, Robert T, 1945, Je 10,31:1
Fredericks, Walter, 1959, O 11,86:3
Fredericks, William, 1914, My 20,13:7
Fredericksen, Gordon R, 1962, O 14,85:3
Fredericksen, Julius, 1950, My 8,23:4
Frederickson, Andrew J, 1938, Ag 10,19:3
Frederickson, Charles R, 1955, Je 27,21:5
Frederickson, Harry B, 1950, Jl 13,25:3
Frederickson, Otto A, 1943, Je 7,13:3
Frederickson, William, 1945, My 15,19:4
Frederico, Russell, 1952, Jl 27,56:3
Frederics, John F, 1964, O 25,88:4
Fredette, Joseph A, 1950, D 5,32:3
Fredewest, Joseph, 1875, O 29,5:2
Fredman, J George, 1958, Jl 3,25:5
Fredman, Samuel, 1941, Ap 15,23:1
Fredoux, Rev, 1866, Je 17,4:7
Fredrick, John E, 1943, Mr 4,19:6
Fredrickson, J Simon, 1950, N 15,31:3
Fredrickson, Victor Mrs, 1968, Mr 23,31:3
Fredrikson, Erik, 1954, F 6,19:3
Fredrocko, John, 1919, My 26,15:5
Free, Albert F, 1951, Ag 26,80:1
Free, Albert J, 1939, D 29,15:5
Free, Ardemus R, 1904, D 27,7:6
Free, Arthur M, 1953, Ap 2,27:3
Free, Edward E, 1939, N 26,42:4
Free, Frank A Mrs, 1948, Je 7,19:6
Free, Frank J, 1952, Ap 27,90:4
Free, Harold L, 1949, Ja 13,23:2
Free, J N (Immortal J N), 1906, Je 28,4:2
Free, John E, 1950, Je 1,27:6
Free, Joseph M, 1946, D 24,17:4
Free, Montague, 1965, Ja 29,34:1
Free, Walter H, 1965, D 4,31:2
Free, William H Mrs, 1963, S 12,37:4
Freear, Louie, 1939, Mr 24,21:3
Freear, Walter F, 1948, Ja 24,16:2
Freebairn, Robert, 1966, Ap 15,39:4
Freeble, Benjamin F, 1952, Jl 16,25:2
Freeborn, Cass, 1954, My 11,29:4
Freeborn, George C, 1911, N 3,11:5
Freeborn, J F, 1882, My 10,5:3
Freeborn, James L, 1950, O 18,33:4
Freeborn, Stanley B, 1960, S 18,27:2
Freeborn, W A, 1868, Je 28,5:5
Freeborn, Wilhelmina, 1939, Mr 20,17:2
Freeborne, Sarah, 1906, Je 1,1:3
Freeburg, Victor, 1953, Ja 13,27:2
Freed, Adolph Paul, 1903, Jl 21,16:2
Freed, Alan J, 1965, Ja 21,31:4
Freed, Alexander, 1966, F 22,23:2
Freed, Allie S, 1938, Ja 12,21:6
Freed, Allie S (will), 1939, My 6,20:3
Freed, Cecil F, 1954, Je 15,29:4
Freed, Emerich B, 1955, D 5,31:5
Freed, Frederick S, 1938, D 26,24:3
Freed, Harry, 1943, D 30,17:5
Freed, Isadore, 1960, N 12,21:5
Freed, John E, 1941, My 22,21:2
Freed, Joseph D R, 1941, Ap 19,15:1
Freed, Louis, 1954, My 1,15:5
Freed, Louis Mrs, 1946, Mr 7,25:1
Freed, Meyer, 1947, O 13,23:3
Freed, Ralph Mrs, 1957, N 24,87:2
Freed, Sam, 1941, D 18,27:2
Freed, William A, 1938, Je 10,21:2
Freedgood, Seymour, 1968, Ja 22,47:2
Freedlander, Arthur Mrs, 1946, Ag 15,25:5
Freedlander, Arthur R, 1940, Je 26,23:6
Freedlander, Joseph H, 1943, N 24,21:5
Freedlender, Edward, 1957, Ap 14,86:6
Freedley, George, 1967, S 12,47:3
Freedley, Vinton Mrs, 1955, Mr 1,25:3
Freedman, Abe, 1961, Je 26,31:2
Freedman, Abram S, 1947, N 27,31:5
Freedman, Andrew (funl), 1915, D 7,13:5
Freedman, Barnett, 1958, Ja 7,47:2
Freedman, Benjamin, 1966, Ap 12,39:3
Freedman, Benjamin E, 1968, Jl 30,39:2
Freedman, Bernard, 1962, Jl 6,25:2
Freedman, Charles S, 1964, Ja 7,33:1
Freedman, D, 1936, D 9,30:2
Freedman, Daniel D, 1944, Mr 30,21:5
Freedman, David, 1967, My 12,47:3
Freedman, David A, 1952, Ja 18,27:5
Freedman, David M Mrs, 1967, Ap 17,37:1
Freedman, David S, 1953, My 26,29:4
Freedman, Gilbert, 1937, F 10,23:6
Freedman, Gilbert Mrs, 1949, My 17,25:2
Freedman, Harold, 1966, F 17,33:1
Freedman, Harry A, 1959, Ja 29,27:1
Freedman, Harry J Mrs, 1950, My 18,29:4
Freedman, Isaac A, 1948, O 8,25:2
Freedman, Isaac V, 1953, Ag 4,21:3
Freedman, Isidor, 1951, Ag 4,15:6
Freedman, Jacob, 1950, F 20,25:3
Freedman, Jacob A, 1955, Ap 14,29:3
Freedman, Jake, 1955, N 17,35:2; 1958, Ja 20,23:4
Freedman, James Mrs, 1942, Ja 31,17:5
Freedman, Jaques Mrs (Kath), 1968, O 17,47:2
Freedman, Joseph, 1949, N 20,92:6
Freedman, Joseph B, 1958, F 13,29:5
Freedman, Lou, 1956, F 27,23:1
Freedman, Max, 1967, Ap 14,39:4
Freedman, Max Mrs, 1967, Mr 29,45:1
Freedman, Meyer P, 1967, Ja 4,43:1
Freedman, Michael, 1915, Je 25,11:6
Freedman, Nathan, 1953, Je 25,27:6
Freedman, Samuel P, 1947, Ap 16,25:3
Freedman, Samuel R, 1967, Mr 31,37:3
Freedman, Sanford, 1960, Ja 30,21:3
Freedman, William, 1952, Ja 4,23:3
Freedman, William H, 1938, D 14,25:2
Freedman, Zac, 1968, Ap 26,47:6
Freedman, Zac Mrs (I Thirer), 1964, F 20,29:5
Freedman, Zachary L, 1955, Ag 10,25:2
Freedman Ben Mrs, 1938, My 15,II,6:1
Freedman Isaac, 1938, Ap 25,15:1
Freedman Simcha, 1938, Jl 15,17:5
Freehill, James E, 1963, O 13,87:1
Freehill, Joseph H, 1959, Ja 22,31:4
Freehof, William A, 1950, Ja 25,28:2
Freehoff, Joseph C, 1939, My 2,23:2
Freel, Edward Mrs, 1915, O 14,11:5
Freel, F J, 1884, Ap 6,7:2
Freel, Frank J Dr (will), 1906, Mr 15,2:5
Freel, J Ralph, 1946, Mr 13,29:4
Freel, James J, 1924, Ag 1,11:4
Freel, Thomas F, 1918, My 17,13:8
Freeland, Brad Mrs, 1961, Mr 26,92:6
Freeland, E Y, 1953, Ag 17,15:3
Freeland, George H, 1955, Mr 12,19:2
Freeland, James, 1879, S 24,5:4
Freeland, Theodore H, 1911, Jl 17,9:6
Freeling, Sargent P, 1937, Ap 20,25:5
Freeman, A H, 1883, D 18,5:2
Freeman, Abraham Mrs, 1949, Je 5,92:5
Freeman, Addison B, 1962, Je 16,19:4
Freeman, Albert L, 1941, Mr 14,21:3
Freeman, Albert M, 1938, S 28,25:5
Freeman, Alden, 1937, D 30,19:3
Freeman, Alex, 1967, My 20,35:3
Freeman, Alex Z, 1960, My 10,37:5
Freeman, Alfred, 1942, Mr 15,43:2
Freeman, Alfred G Mrs, 1954, Je 24,27:1; 1958, F 7, 21:1
Freeman, Alfred Mrs, 1965, D 11,33:4
Freeman, Allen W, 1954, Jl 5,11:3
Freeman, Alton A, 1942, S 30,23:3
Freeman, Anthony Mrs, 1951, S 18,31:3
Freeman, Arch, 1948, Ag 17,21:4
Freeman, Arthur C Sr, 1949, Ag 15,17:6
Freeman, B Dexter, 1956, Jl 28,17:4
Freeman, Bartholomew J, 1943, Ja 15,17:2
Freeman, Benjamin, 1944, O 31,19:2; 1956, D 26,27:3

Freeman, Bernard C, 1958, My 10,21:6
Freeman, Bertha A Mrs, 1955, Ag 17,27:5
Freeman, Bruce C, 1940, S 7,15:5
Freeman, C C, 1903, Je 3,9:6
Freeman, C Harold, 1954, Ap 17,13:4
Freeman, Charles D, 1939, Ja 10,19:3
Freeman, Charles H, 1960, Ap 23,23:3
Freeman, Charles K Mrs, 1967, Je 21,47:4
Freeman, Charles M, 1954, F 13,13:5
Freeman, Charles M Dr, 1923, Mr 9,15:4
Freeman, Charles N, 1950, Ag 16,29:1
Freeman, Charles S Mrs, 1943, Ag 18,19:2
Freeman, Charles W, 1960, Je 27,25:5
Freeman, Charles Y Sr, 1964, My 9,27:4
Freeman, Clarence, 1946, Jl 2,25:5
Freeman, Clarence R, 1941, Jl 13,29:2
Freeman, Clayton E, 1959, S 1,29:2
Freeman, Cloye L, 1954, Ag 5,23:5
Freeman, Daniel A Jr, 1968, Ja 8,39:3
Freeman, David B, 1952, D 3,33:6
Freeman, Dillie, 1952, Jl 1,23:3
Freeman, Donald M, 1960, Mr 28,29:5
Freeman, Douglas S, 1953, Je 14,1:4
Freeman, E A Prof, 1892, Mr 17,2:2
Freeman, E W, 1945, Ja 30,19:4
Freeman, Earl A, 1948, D 21,25:4
Freeman, Earle J, 1950, Ja 27,23:1
Freeman, Edward L, 1907, F 25,9:5
Freeman, Edward M, 1954, F 7,89:1; 1958, Ja 23,27:4
Freeman, Edwin R Mrs, 1951, Ap 3,27:4
Freeman, Elizabeth P Mrs, 1907, Mr 6,9:6
Freeman, Elmer B, 1942, D 24,15:2
Freeman, Elsie Garnett, 1903, Jl 7,7:6
Freeman, Emory B, 1961, Je 24,21:1
Freeman, Ernest H, 1955, Je 16,31:5
Freeman, Esther J, 1955, Ap 13,29:5
Freeman, Evert W, 1955, Mr 11,25:3
Freeman, Ezra A, 1948, F 17,25:4
Freeman, F R Rev, 1884, F 11,2:6
Freeman, Fannie E H Mrs, 1938, My 20,19:4
Freeman, Flora M, 1939, Ja 10,19:3
Freeman, Florence H, 1966, Ja 18,37:3
Freeman, Forster W Sr, 1958, Ja 23,27:4
Freeman, Fortunatus Capt, 1874, Jl 24,5:4
Freeman, Frances Schroeder Mrs, 1968, O 7,47:3
Freeman, Francis P, 1948, Je 3,25:2; 1951, S 22,17:1
Freeman, Frank, 1940, O 15,23:5; 1949, O 14,27:4
Freeman, Frank Morgan Gen, 1907, Mr 29,9:6
Freeman, Frank Mrs, 1960, N 14,31:2
Freeman, Fred H, 1943, Mr 13,13:4
Freeman, Frederick, 1944, Ja 17,19:3
Freeman, Frederick C, 1950, N 8,29:4
Freeman, Frederick N, 1941, F 19,21:5
Freeman, Frederick W Mrs, 1958, Ja 19,86:6
Freeman, George, 1946, Ja 14,19:4
Freeman, George F, 1940, Mr 31,46:3; 1955, O 28,25:3
Freeman, George L Sr, 1965, Jl 13,33:3
Freeman, George M, 1958, Jl 29,23:4
Freeman, George S, 1938, Jl 28,19:5; 1948, My 12,27:4
Freeman, George W Mrs, 1948, Jl 7,46:8
Freeman, Gertrude A, 1954, Je 22,27:3
Freeman, Ginevra, 1917, My 16,13:6
Freeman, Grace M, 1967, Ap 21,39:4
Freeman, H Lawrence, 1954, Mr 26,22:3
Freeman, H Lawrence Mrs, 1954, Je 15,29:5
Freeman, Halstead G Mrs, 1957, My 28,33:3
Freeman, Hammer G, 1945, Jl 1,18:3
Freeman, Harrison B, 1942, Ap 10,17:1
Freeman, Harry B, 1939, Ap 9,III,6:7
Freeman, Harry L, 1943, N 24,21:1
Freeman, Harry T, 1942, F 20,17:4
Freeman, Henry Blanchard, 1915, O 17,15:3
Freeman, Henry J, 1940, Mr 23,13:4; 1948, Je 1,23:5
Freeman, Henry O, 1939, My 10,23:5
Freeman, Henry W, 1921, F 24,13:4; 1938, D 2,23:2
Freeman, Herbert C, 1961, S 17,86:6
Freeman, Horace C, 1947, Ap 8,27:3
Freeman, Howard (Co Exec), 1967, S 9,31:2
Freeman, Howard (Actor), 1967, D 13,44:4
Freeman, Howard B, 1937, Ag 22,II,7:1
Freeman, I, 1955, Mr 8,27:3
Freeman, Isabel (Mrs Geo L Norton), 1911, Jl 9,11:5
Freeman, J Douglas, 1944, D 30,11:5
Freeman, J E, 1884, N 30,9:2
Freeman, J Howard Mrs, 1943, F 12,19:5
Freeman, J R, 1932, O 7,17:5
Freeman, Jacob L Mrs, 1944, S 12,19:4
Freeman, James, 1951, N 5,31:1
Freeman, James E, 1943, Je 7,13:1
Freeman, James E Mrs, 1947, F 9,63:5
Freeman, James Mrs, 1945, My 16,19:2
Freeman, Jane, 1963, S 23,29:3
Freeman, Jay C, 1953, Ag 19,29:5
Freeman, John (Bucky), 1949, Je 26,60:7
Freeman, John Francis, 1910, N 18,11:5
Freeman, John J Ex-Justice, 1921, N 1,19:6
Freeman, John M, 1943, O 5,25:2
Freeman, John Mrs, 1952, My 3,21:4; 1968, Jl 14,65:1
Freeman, John P, 1962, N 20,36:1
Freeman, John P Mrs, 1960, F 2,35:4
Freeman, John R, 1961, S 5,35:2
Freeman, John S, 1946, My 11,27:2
Freeman, Joseph, 1945, Ag 19,40:3; 1965, Ag 11,35:1
Freeman, Joseph F, 1948, Ja 19,23:1
Freeman, Joseph J, 1945, N 15,19:3
Freeman, Kathleen Mrs, 1951, D 19,36:4
Freeman, Ladbrook H, 1942, My 16,13:7
Freeman, Leland N, 1937, Mr 24,25:5
Freeman, Leon S, 1966, Ap 15,39:2
Freeman, Leonard B, 1961, F 8,28:1
Freeman, Leslie G, 1961, O 9,35:5
Freeman, Leslie R, 1962, Je 11,31:4
Freeman, Lewis B, 1958, Ja 12,87:1
Freeman, Lewis G, 1949, Ag 25,23:3
Freeman, Louis E, 1952, Je 15,84:4
Freeman, Lucy T S Mrs, 1938, Mr 17,21:2
Freeman, M E W Mrs, 1930, Mr 15,19:3
Freeman, Margaret, 1942, Ag 6,19:6
Freeman, Marilla W, 1961, O 31,31:3
Freeman, Mary Dodd, 1908, N 18,9:2
Freeman, Maurice, 1953, Mr 28,17:2
Freeman, Max, 1949, Jl 10,57:2
Freeman, Max M Dr, 1968, Mr 5,41:3
Freeman, Milton H, 1925, Mr 28,15:4
Freeman, Myron S, 1954, Ap 13,31:5
Freeman, Myron S Mrs, 1954, Ap 13,31:5
Freeman, Nat K, 1949, Ja 5,25:5
Freeman, Nathaniel, 1942, D 24,15:5
Freeman, Orville E (funl, Je 16,11:4), 1962, Je 12, 37:4
Freeman, Otis Dr, 1902, Je 10,9:5
Freeman, Otis M, 1949, Ja 6,23:3
Freeman, Ozias S, 1953, S 26,17:5
Freeman, Pat, 1946, Ap 8,27:2
Freeman, Paul W, 1966, O 3,47:3
Freeman, Perrin N, 1957, My 4,21:4
Freeman, Peter, 1956, My 21,25:4
Freeman, Phil, 1949, Ja 27,24:3
Freeman, Philip Mrs, 1964, N 17,41:2
Freeman, Ralph, 1946, S 3,19:2
Freeman, Ralph H, 1957, Ag 20,27:4
Freeman, Richard, 1939, My 4,23:4; 1943, O 1,19:5
Freeman, Richard D, 1948, O 3,64:6
Freeman, Richard E, 1949, F 9,27:2
Freeman, Richard R, 1940, Mr 30,15:3
Freeman, Robert, 1940, Je 29,15:4
Freeman, Robert H, 1945, Ag 11,13:6
Freeman, Rowland G, 1945, N 15,19:3
Freeman, Samuel, 1920, Ag 31,9:1; 1954, Je 12,15:2
Freeman, Samuel J, 1915, Ag 27,9:7
Freeman, Samuel M, 1958, Je 27,25:1
Freeman, Samuel T 2d, 1954, Ja 3,89:1
Freeman, Sidney J, 1948, O 11,23:5
Freeman, Siler, 1962, S 8,19:5
Freeman, Talbot O (por), 1955, D 8,37:3
Freeman, Theodore B, 1952, O 21,3:1
Freeman, Theodore C (mem ser, N 4,79:1; funl, N 5,16:2), 1964, N 1,46:3
Freeman, Theodore W, 1942, Mr 27,23:1
Freeman, Thomas J A Rev, 1907, O 17,9:5
Freeman, W B, 1935, F 22,25:1
Freeman, W C, 1933, S 14,23:3
Freeman, W Dr, 1880, Ap 7,5:5
Freeman, W Winans Mrs, 1942, Ag 14,17:4
Freeman, Walter, 1951, N 13,29:3
Freeman, Walter C, 1961, Jl 26,31:3
Freeman, Walter S, 1940, My 17,19:6
Freeman, Wilberforce, 1907, Je 20,7:5; 1907, Je 22,7:4
Freeman, Wilfrid R, 1953, My 18,21:5
Freeman, Willard C, 1961, Je 6,37:1
Freeman, William, 1955, Ag 19,19:5
Freeman, William A, 1949, Jl 26,27:2
Freeman, William B, 1963, Jl 17,31:4
Freeman, William H, 1938, Mr 1,21:2; 1946, Ag 6,25:5
Freeman, William P, 1956, Ag 2,25:4
Freeman, William S, 1958, Ag 7,25:4
Freeman, William S Mrs, 1956, D 3,29:2
Freeman, Y Frank Jr, 1962, O 17,39:3
Freeman-Mitford, Algernon Bertram (Baron Redesdale), 1916, Ag 18,9:4
Freeman-Mitford, David B (Lord Redesdale), 1958, Mr 18,29:4
Freeman-Mitford, Rupert, 1939, Ag 9,17:5
Freeman-Mitford, Unity V, 1948, My 31,19:3
Freemantle, A H O, 1951, Ja 13,15:3
Freena, Henry, 1949, Jl 29,18:7
Freer, Arch E Mrs, 1942, D 15,28:2
Freer, Archibald, 1943, N 30,27:5
Freer, Arden, 1963, N 3,88:6
Freer, Charles Lang, 1919, S 26,13:5
Freer, Frederick Warren, 1908, Mr 9,7:4
Freer, Guy Mrs, 1948, Ag 6,17:4
Freer, Harry J, 1941, S 1,15:3
Freer, Harvey J, 1943, Ag 15,38:6
Freer, Henry L, 1953, Ag 5,23:5
Freer, Homer J, 1954, Ap 18,89:1
Freer, Howard M, 1960, Mr 10,31:1
Freer, Hugh M, 1937, F 12,23:1
Freer, J W, 1877, Ap 13,1:6
Freer, Martha A Mrs, 1939, Jl 24,13:5
Freer, Paul G Dr, 1912, Ap 18,13:5
Freer, William D, 1940, O 13,49:2
Freericks, Charles J Mrs, 1956, Ja 24,31:2
Frees, Jacob, 1945, S 25,25:4
Frees, John F, 1950, My 5,21:2
Frees, John F Mrs, 1950, Ag 16,29:1
Freese, Charles F, 1949, F 3,23:2
Freese, Irving C, 1964, S 13,86:3
Freese, Levi F, 1941, My 27,23:2
Freese, William, 1965, F 15,27:3
Freese, William H, 1953, Ap 26,85:4
Freestone, Fred J, 1961, Jl 18,29:3
Freestone, James N, 1938, Ag 2,19:2
Freestone, Jesse H, 1947, Jl 20,44:2
Freestone, Jesse H Mrs, 1949, D 9,31:4
Freet, Frank L, 1942, Mr 14,15:5
Freethy, Frank O, 1945, Jl 14,11:6
Freethy, Frank O Mrs, 1955, Jl 30,17:6
Freeze, Victor J, 1960, Ag 7,84:3
Freezer, Herbert J, 1963, Jl 1,29:4
Freezer, Rose F Mrs, 1938, Ag 31,15:4
Fregeau, Lawrence Mrs, 1950, Ja 27,23:2
Freggens, Carl T, 1952, My 20,25:4
Fregosi, Alessandro Mrs, 1957, Ag 5,21:6
Frei, A C, 1935, Ap 30,17:2
Frei, Charles, 1955, Ap 9,13:2
Frei, Emil Jr, 1967, Ap 8,31:5
Frei, Wilhelm, 1943, Ja 29,19:3
Freiberg, A Julius, 1950, O 17,31:2
Freiberg, Abraham, 1925, O 6,27:5
Freiberg, Bernard, 1938, N 25,23:5
Freiberg, Charles A, 1941, My 6,21:4
Freiberg, Fritz, 1923, F 7,15:5
Freiberg, Leonard, 1954, F 6,19:6
Freiberg, Sol H, 1954, S 2,21:5
Freiberger, David, 1947, Jl 31,21:6
Freid, Isadore, 1959, My 31,76:5
Freid, Max B, 1943, Ja 22,19:3
Freiday, William S, 1961, S 16,19:5
Freidberg, David, 1951, Ja 1,17:2
Freidenberg, David, 1879, N 12,8:4
Freidenberg, Joseph I Mrs, 1953, Ag 6,21:3
Freidenberg, Pauline, 1879, N 12,8:4
Freidenberg, Phil S, 1943, D 21,27:3
Freidin, Jesse, 1968, Jl 19,35:1
Freidin, Jesse Mrs, 1967, Je 7,47:3
Freidinger, William A Mrs, 1959, Jl 11,19:6
Freidlander, Joseph Dr, 1917, Ap 9,13:6
Freidus, A S, 1923, O 4,23:3
Freidus, Eric, 1966, O 28,41:2
Freier, Milton, 1967, Ja 17,39:1
Freifeld, Adolph, 1950, D 30,13:6
Freifeld, George Justice, 1917, N 18,3:4; 1917, N 13:4
Freifelder, Benjamin, 1939, Je 30,19:2
Freihofer, C Albert Mrs, 1953, D 14,31:5
Freihofer, Charles C, 1948, Ag 22,60:4
Freihofer, Charles F, 1942, S 15,23:4
Freihofer, Charles F Mrs, 1947, N 28,27:4
Freihofer, Edwin H, 1947, O 1,29:5
Freihofer, Frank A, 1944, Mr 6,19:2
Freihofer, Stanley H, 1941, Jl 31,17:2
Freihofer, William J, 1939, F 18,15:4
Freil, Raymond A, 1939, My 25,25:5
Freile, William, 1939, Jl 4,13:5
Freilich, Aaron, 1958, Je 3,31:4
Freilinger, Margaret N Mrs, 1937, Mr 16,23:4
Freiman, A J, 1944, Je 5,19:2
Freiman, Lajos, 1937, O 14,25:4
Freiman, Louis, 1967, F 3,28:6
Freiman, Nat, 1956, Ag 16,25:1
Freimann, Aron, 1948, Je 7,19:5
Freimann, Frank, 1968, Ap 1,45:1
Freimark, Harry S, 1958, My 27,31:2
Freimuth, Henry C, 1951, Ag 27,19:4
Freimuth, Rudolph W, 1968, Mr 13,53:1
Frein, John J, 1941, Mr 9,40:8
Freire, Brasiliano A, 1953, Ap 22,29:5
Freire, Carlos M L da S, 1961, N 11,9:6
Freireich, Kal, 1961, Jl 11,31:2
Freirich, Julian, 1958, Ag 16,17:2
Freise, August, 1962, Jl 5,25:3
Freisinger, John M, 1950, S 20,31:1
Freisinger, John Mrs, 1940, N 1,25:5
Freistadt, Harry, 1964, D 17,41:4
Freistadter, Jacob, 1939, O 13,23:5
Freitag, A M, 1882, Jl 28,8:4
Freitag, Erik, 1952, Je 30,19:2
Freitag, Robert J, 1958, Ag 14,29:4
Freitag, Walter, 1958, Je 8,88:4
Freitas, George F, 1948, Mr 30,23:3
Freitas, Jose V de, 1952, S 6,17:3
Freitus, John J, 1947, My 14,25:3
Freiwald, August, 1946, F 21,23:1
Freiystedt, Walter, 1957, Je 3,50:7
Freking, Frank J, 1950, F 23,27:1
Freland, Bram, 1952, S 19,23:2
Frelick, H Victor, 1961, Je 5,31:1
Freligh, Lucia S, 1946, Je 20,23:4
Frelinghuysen, Dumont, 1904, Ja 22,9:6
Frelinghuysen, F T, 1885, My 21,5:3
Frelinghuysen, Frederick, 1924, Ja 2,17:4; 196 My 28,27:3
Frelinghuysen, Joseph S, 1948, F 9,17:4
Frelinghuysen, Joseph S Mrs, 1967, Ap 27,45
Frelinghuysen, Katherine, 1921, Ag 12,13:4
Frelinghuysen, Peter H B Mrs, 1963, Ap 14,9
Frelinghuysen, Peter H B Sr, 1959, Mr 12,31:

Frelinghuysen, Sara B Mrs, 1940, O 19,17:7
Frelinghuysen, Theodore, 1943, F 21,32:6
Frelinghuysen, Theodore Mrs, 1967, Je 13,64:1
Fremantle, E R Sir, 1929, F 12,25:1
Fremantle, Francis E, 1943, Ag 28,11:7
Fremantle, Sydney, 1958, Ap 30,33:3
Fremault, George, 1959, Je 8,27:2
Fremd, Charles, 1943, Je 3,21:2
Fremd, Charles A Sr Mrs, 1961, O 1,87:1
Fremd, Frederick D, 1959, Jl 31,23:4
Fremd, Frederick D Mrs, 1943, S 2,19:4
Fremd, Jonathan E, 1965, Jl 10,25:5
Fremd, Theodore, 1947, Ag 9,13:6
Fremed, George, 1937, Ap 1,23:5
Fremgen, Peter, 1938, F 7,15:3
Fremiet, Emmanuel, 1910, S 11,II,11:5
Fremming, Harvey C, 1947, Mr 2,60:7
Fremont, J C Gen, 1890, Jl 14,1:2
Fremont, J C Gen Mrs, 1902, D 29,7:5
Fremont, John C, 1957, O 14,27:2
Fremont, John C Mrs, 1946, O 24,27:3
Fremont, John C Rear-Adm, 1911, Mr 8,11:5
Fremstad, Olive, 1951, Ap 23,25:3
Frenaye, W E Mrs, 1961, D 6,47:3
Frenaye, William E Jr, 1961, Ap 12,41:4
French, A, 1934, Ja 10,21:3
French, A Milton, 1951, N 5,31:4
French, A P, 1927, My 16,21:5
French, Alice Hayden Mrs, 1923, Jl 31,17:4
French, Allen, 1946, O 7,31:5
French, Amos T Sr, 1941, N 15,17:1
French, Anne C Mrs, 1966, D 21,39:2
French, Anne Warner, 1913, F 4,11:5
French, Arthur (Lord De Freyne), 1913, S 11,11:6
French, Arthur E, 1948, Mr 31,25:4; 1961, Jl 4,19:1
French, Arthur P, 1937, N 19,23:2
French, Arthur W, 1949, My 28,15:4
French, Asa Judge, 1903, Je 24,9:6
French, B B Maj, 1870, Ag 14,1:3
French, Bertrand A, 1947, D 10,31:4
French, Burr J, 1937, F 24,24:1
French, Burton L, 1954, S 13,23:4
French, Byron E, 1925, My 4,19:5
French, Byron Mrs, 1946, My 10,19:4
French, C D, 1954, My 5,31:2
French, Caleb Jay, 1924, F 22,15:4
French, Calvin H, 1940, D 31,15:3
French, Carlos, 1903, Ap 16,9:6
French, Carlos H, 1962, Je 15,27:4
French, Caroline A E Mrs, 1945, D 2,46:6
French, Charles, 1920, Mr 26,13:3
French, Charles A, 1941, Ap 8,25:2
French, Charles E, 1940, N 13,23:3; 1964, N 15,87:1
French, Charles F, 1953, Je 12,27:2
French, Charles G, 1949, Ap 30,13:6
French, Charles Herbert (funl, Ja 29,19:3), 1924, Ja 28,15:4
French, Charles M, 1957, Ag 17,15:4
French, Charles N, 1947, Mr 22,13:5
French, Charles R, 1949, Ag 20,11:4
French, Charles W, 1942, Mr 8,42:7; 1946, O 5,17:2; 1959, My 28,31:3
French, Clayton T A, 1954, Mr 21,89:2
French, Clifford W, 1964, Ja 24,27:3
French, Cyrus E, 1960, Ja 5,31:2
French, D C, 1931, O 8,25:1
French, Daniel, 1874, My 17,2:3
French, Dexter S Mrs, 1967, Ja 7,27:5
French, Earl R, 1967, O 29,84:3
French, Edward Sanborn, 1968, Je 11,47:3
French, Edward Tuck, 1919, Ap 15,11:2
French, Edward V Mrs, 1949, O 26,27:2
French, Edwin Davis, 1906, D 10,7:4
French, Elizabeth Col, 1912, F 3,11:4
French, Elizabeth L Mrs, 1943, S 9,25:5
French, Ella G, 1949, Jl 14,28:2
French, Ellen Tuck Mrs, 1915, D 7,13:5
French, Emmett C, 1947, Je 11,27:4
French, Ernest N, 1958, N 12,37:1
French, Ernest W, 1954, Jl 19,19:3
French, F F, 1936, Ag 31,15:1
French, Ferdinand, 1947, Jl 3,21:4
French, Field Marshall (por), 1925, My 23,15:4
French, Florence Mrs, 1941, O 16,21:3
French, Frances B, 1953, F 26,25:6
French, Francis H Brig-Gen, 1921, Mr 11,15:5
French, Francis J, 1945, O 13,15:1
French, Francis O, 1962, Je 18,25:2
French, Francis O Mrs, 1946, My 18,19:4
French, Frank B (will, F 14,II,2:2), 1937, F 8,17:4
French, Franklin O, 1962, O 6,25:5
French, Fred G Capt, 1937, N 26,21:5
French, Fred W, 1943, Je 1,23:5
French, Frederick C, 1937, Ap 4,II,11:2
French, Frederick E, 1947, Jl 7,17:5
French, Frederick F Mrs, 1960, O 31,31:1
French, Frederick H, 1939, My 13,15:4
French, Garnett B Mrs, 1956, Jl 14,15:2
French, Garrison S, 1937, S 28,23:1
French, George B (will, Ag 3,3:1), 1937, Jl 19,15:3
French, George B Mrs, 1951, S 1,11:4
French, George E, 1965, O 26,45:2
French, George H, 1948, D 7,32:3
French, George L R, 1953, Ja 25,86:4
French, George Leander, 1924, Ja 12,13:2
French, George T, 1939, Mr 8,21:5
French, George W, 1955, Je 30,25:1; 1958, F 4,26:4
French, George W H, 1947, O 13,23:1
French, Georgina G Mrs, 1940, Ja 10,21:2
French, Gertrude H Mrs, 1942, Mr 3,23:1
French, Gladys L, 1961, F 24,21:1
French, Harriet A, 1941, Ap 10,23:5
French, Harry M, 1949, N 7,27:1
French, Harry N, 1959, Ja 6,33:3
French, Henry, 1911, Je 27,9:5
French, Herbert, 1923, Je 14,19:4; 1951, Ja 2,23:1
French, Herbert F, 1938, N 1,23:2
French, Herbert G, 1942, Je 26,21:4
French, Herbert J, 1955, Ag 18,23:6
French, Hollis, 1940, N 22,23:5
French, Howard D, 1955, Ap 24,87:2
French, J Hansell Mrs, 1958, Ja 14,30:4
French, J L, 1936, D 15,25:3
French, J Milton, 1962, Ap 12,35:2
French, J Stewart, 1952, Ap 19,15:3
French, J V, 1879, F 26,8:1
French, J W Col, 1901, N 13,9:6
French, J Wymond, 1952, N 5,27:5
French, James, 1954, Ja 12,23:4
French, James B, 1938, Je 4,15:4
French, James B (por), 1947, D 3,29:4
French, James B Mrs, 1945, Ja 14,39:2
French, James E, 1954, Ja 22,27:4
French, James J, 1941, Mr 7,21:3
French, James M, 1941, F 7,19:5
French, James S, 1941, Mr 6,21:5
French, John, 1966, Jl 23,25:3
French, John C, 1957, N 12,37:3
French, John H, 1947, O 23,25:1; 1952, N 17,25:6
French, John H Mrs, 1958, Jl 22,27:4
French, John J, 1948, N 6,13:1
French, John L, 1941, S 10,23:5
French, John Mrs, 1951, Je 15,23:5
French, John P, 1949, S 27,27:1
French, John R L (Earl of Ypres), 1958, Ap 17,21:3
French, John S, 1945, Je 10,32:2
French, John T Lt-Col, 1909, Ag 14,7:5
French, John W Prof, 1871, Jl 10,1:6
French, Jonas H Col, 1903, F 23,7:7
French, Julius E, 1910, D 3,11:5
French, L V, 1881, Ap 1,5:4
French, Lawrence H, 1942, O 12,34:4; 1951, F 8,23:6
French, Leigh H, 1941, O 13,17:4
French, Leon H, 1960, Ja 12,47:1
French, Leroy A, 1968, N 16,37:2
French, Lester Gray, 1921, Ap 20,13:6
French, Lewis C, 1960, D 19,27:4
French, Lillian Harrington, 1919, Ap 16,13:3
French, Lillie H, 1939, Je 5,17:2
French, Lloyd, 1950, My 25,29:2
French, Lowell L, 1956, F 6,23:2
French, Lyman C, 1943, F 24,21:1
French, Mabel M Mrs, 1937, O 26,23:2
French, Mansfield, 1876, Mr 17,5:5
French, Mansfield J, 1953, Je 6,17:3
French, Marion F, 1957, My 19,88:3
French, Mary F, 1939, Ja 10,19:2
French, Mary M Mrs, 1951, N 5,31:4
French, Mayo L, 1940, Jl 8,17:3
French, Morton B, 1960, Mr 24,33:5
French, Morton B Mrs, 1960, N 30,37:3
French, Moses L, 1943, F 1,15:4
French, Owen B, 1951, F 4,76:3
French, Paul C, 1960, Je 4,23:2
French, Percy W, 1956, Jl 21,15:3
French, Ralph L, 1945, Ap 3,19:5
French, Ralph W, 1942, D 8,25:3
French, Richard Col (funl, Jl 22,8:6), 1872, Jl 18,8:2
French, Robert J, 1943, F 2,19:4
French, Robert T Dr, 1921, Ag 15,13:6
French, Rodney, 1882, My 1,5:1
French, Rolland H, 1966, Mr 5,27:2
French, Rufus T, 1924, Jl 22,15:5
French, Ruth H, 1952, Ag 12,19:3
French, S G Gen (Conferaterate), 1910, Ap 21,11:5
French, Samuel D, 1942, Ja 21,17:3
French, Samuel T Sr, 1956, Je 6,33:3
French, Samuel W, 1943, Mr 15,13:2
French, Sean, 1937, S 13,21:4
French, Seth B, 1961, O 3,39:4
French, Seward H Jr, 1954, S 21,27:3
French, Stuart W, 1946, Ag 8,21:4
French, Sylvester B, 1947, Ap 29,27:1
French, T H, 1902, D 2,9:4
French, T R, 1929, Ja 6,7:2
French, Thomas E, 1944, N 3,21:4
French, Thomas E Dean, 1937, D 17,25:2
French, Thomas M, 1949, D 14,31:3
French, W, 1928, F 2,1:2
French, W H Col, 1881, My 21,2:6
French, W R, 1957, Je 28,23:3
French, Walter B, 1961, F 11,23:3
French, Walter E, 1957, Jl 14,73:2
French, Ward, 1959, Ja 3,35:2
French, William, 1871, O 3,8:2
French, William A, 1947, F 14,21:4
French, William A Mrs, 1949, Je 16,29:1
French, William C, 1950, Je 3,15:5
French, William H, 1938, D 15,27:4
French, William J, 1951, Mr 11,93:1
French, William M R, 1914, Je 4,11:6
French, William W, 1950, My 18,29:2
Frenchman, Alex P, 1940, Mr 21,25:3
Frendberg, William R, 1953, Mr 5,27:4
Frender, Arthur, 1964, Je 28,57:1
Freneau, P L, 1880, D 12,2:3
Frenette, Edward B, 1959, Mr 18,37:4
Frenette, Joseph E, 1953, D 29,23:4
Freney, James J, 1949, My 31,24:6
Freng, Ragnar T, 1952, Jl 11,17:3
Freng, William H, 1950, Je 25,1:6
Frengen, Augustus M, 1940, Mr 7,23:6
Frenier, John H, 1944, Mr 5,36:2
Frenkel, Arthur B, 1963, Ag 28,33:4
Frenkel, Jonas B Mrs, 1937, Ag 19,19:5
Frenkel, Leo S Mrs, 1950, Jl 22,15:1
Frenssen, Gustav, 1945, Ap 20,19:3
Frenville, Max, 1952, D 27,10:3
Frenz, Emil P, 1955, Ja 8,13:3
Frenzel, John P Jr, 1949, D 8,33:5
Frenzel, Theodore, 1965, O 11,39:2
Frere, H B E Sir, 1884, My 30,5:1
Frere, W H, 1938, Ap 4,17:3
Frere, Walter, 1943, Ap 25,35:1
Frerichs, F T, 1885, Mr 15,2:3
Frerichs, Frederich W, 1939, My 2,23:1
Frerichs, Lizzie P Mrs, 1942, Jl 4,17:3
Frerichs, Wilbur E, 1966, F 8,39:3
Freschi, John J, 1944, Jl 30,35:1
Freschl, Carl Mrs, 1943, D 2,27:6
Freschl, Robert, 1949, Ap 19,25:1
Freschl, William F Mrs, 1944, Ap 22,15:5
Frescoln, Elizabeth K, 1941, Ap 13,39:2
Frescoln, Leonard D, 1954, Ja 26,27:4
Frese, George J, 1956, My 18,25:4
Frese, Hans F, 1966, Ag 4,33:5
Fresenius, Henry Mrs, 1940, F 27,21:4
Fresh, Henry, 1939, S 7,25:3
Freshel, Curtis P, 1968, Jl 5,25:2
Freshel, Curtis P Mrs, 1948, Ja 3,13:3
Freshwater, Eagle, 1955, Je 1,33:2
Freshwater, Eagle Mrs, 1938, D 15,27:4
Freshwater, Frank, 1950, Ap 1,15:5
Fresienger, Victor, 1914, Ap 6,9:4
Fresnicks, Andrew Mrs, 1949, D 4,108:4
Freston, Joseph M, 1943, S 12,53:2
Freston, Thomas E, 1951, S 22,17:6
Frete, Edmond Masson, 1903, D 17,9:4
Fretthold, Paul H, 1960, Je 17,31:1
Fretwell, Elbert K, 1962, Ag 23,29:1
Fretz, Frank R, 1948, Mr 4,25:6
Fretz, Herman, 1946, Ap 23,21:4
Fretz, Ida, 1944, Mr 1,19:2
Fretz, James B, 1944, Mr 9,17:5
Fretz, John E, 1950, S 1,21:5
Fretz, Nathan R Mrs, 1954, O 12,27:2
Fretz, Richard, 1946, N 1,23:2
Fretz, William F, 1951, Jl 6,23:2
Freuchen, Peter (mem ser, S 6,21:1), 1957, S 4,33:1
Freud, Alexander, 1943, Ap 23,17:2
Freud, Harry, 1968, O 21,47:3
Freud, Sigmund, 1939, S 24,1:2
Freud, Sigmund Mrs, 1951, N 3,17:4
Freudberg, Leopold, 1948, Mr 21,60:4
Freudemann, Alfred E, 1955, Mr 1,25:4
Freudenberg, Ernest, 1953, Ag 3,17:6
Freudenberger, David E, 1943, S 11,13:2
Freudenberger, John B, 1960, Ja 19,35:1
Freudenberger, Samson Mrs, 1946, Mr 19,27:3
Freudenthal, Alice L Mrs, 1938, Ag 22,13:5
Freudenthal, Elsbeth E, 1953, My 14,29:3
Freudenthal, Josef, 1964, My 6,47:3
Freuler, John, 1954, S 1,27:1
Freund, Abraham Mrs, 1944, Je 14,19:6
Freund, Anton P, 1939, O 16,19:6
Freund, Beth (Mrs Henry L Dorfmann), 1963, Ap 30,35:4
Freund, Charles J, 1949, Ap 15,23:2
Freund, Coenraad, 1949, Ja 29,13:5
Freund, E Martin, 1961, Jl 20,27:4
Freund, Ernst, 1946, Je 7,19:2
Freund, Erwin O, 1947, N 13,27:1
Freund, Eugene, 1949, Jl 18,17:6
Freund, Ferdinand C, 1966, My 14,31:3
Freund, Frederick A, 1956, N 30,24:1
Freund, Gusried V, 1955, Ja 11,25:1
Freund, Harry, 1955, Ja 13,27:4
Freund, Harry D, 1949, Je 15,29:4
Freund, Herman R, 1956, Ag 20,21:5
Freund, Isadore, 1946, Jl 25,21:4
Freund, Jacob A, 1949, Ap 9,17:5
Freund, John C, 1924, Je 4,23:5
Freund, John C Mrs, 1953, Je 12,27:2
Freund, John F, 1932, F 12,21:5
Freund, Joseph A Mrs, 1944, N 11,13:2
Freund, Jules, 1960, Ap 23,23:6
Freund, Jules S, 1951, Ja 14,84:5
Freund, Karl, 1956, F 28,31:3
Freund, Karl Mrs, 1967, Ja 15,67:5

Freund, Leopold, 1944, F 27,38:3
Freund, Louis, 1958, N 13,33:3
Freund, Louis Mrs, 1961, Ja 4,33:2
Freund, Louis R, 1952, Jl 8,27:4
Freund, Marya, 1966, My 24,43:8
Freund, Max, 1909, Ja 8,9:5
Freund, Michael, 1962, N 22,29:3
Freund, Milton B, 1968, Ap 3,51:2
Freund, Moses J, 1938, Ja 23,II,8:7
Freund, Robert, 1952, Ja 31,27:2
Freund, Rudolf, 1960, O 28,31:4
Freund, Sanford H E, 1954, N 30,29:3
Freund, Walter J Mrs, 1948, Ja 16,21:1
Freund, William, 1947, S 27,15:6
Freund-Reisner, Ethel (Mrs D Reisner), 1958, N 17, 31:5
Freundlich, David B, 1958, O 2,37:6
Freundlich, Emmy Mrs, 1948, Mr 18,27:5
Freundlich, Herbert M, 1941, Ap 1,23:4
Freundlich, Julius Mrs, 1962, Mr 10,21:2
Freundlich, Morris, 1943, Ap 26,19:5
Freundt, Edward W, 1949, Jl 6,27:2
Frevert, Bernard T, 1964, Mr 21,25:6
Frevert, Harry L (will, D 25,21:1), 1947, D 14,78:5
Frew, Athol L, 1955, N 9,33:2
Frew, Florence A, 1945, Jl 18,27:4
Frew, Francis, 1962, S 15,25:1
Frew, George H, 1943, Ag 16,15:4
Frew, John, 1901, S 8,7:6
Frew, Walter E, 1941, My 20,23:1
Frew, Walter Edwin Mrs, 1953, F 16,21:3
Frew, William, 1948, F 1,60:4
Frew, William L, 1964, O 27,39:3
Frew, William Nimick, 1915, O 29,13:7
Frewen, Joseph F, 1941, Ja 7,23:3
Frey, A B, 1952, Je 17,27:2
Frey, A J, 1922, Je 14,19:3
Frey, Adalbert, 1941, My 14,21:5
Frey, Adolph, 1938, O 5,23:6; 1949, My 6,25:5
Frey, Adolph O, 1952, S 24,33:5
Frey, Albert J, 1958, My 21,33:4
Frey, Albert Sr, 1948, F 16,22:2
Frey, Albin J, 1961, My 13,19:5
Frey, Azariah M, 1962, Mr 1,31:2
Frey, B Maude, 1960, Ap 2,23:4
Frey, Brice A, 1955, Je 23,29:3
Frey, Brice A Mrs, 1968, Jl 28,64:7
Frey, Calvin A (por), 1947, Ja 2,27:1
Frey, Calvin A Mrs, 1951, Ap 9,25:5
Frey, Carl K, 1937, D 9,25:5
Frey, Carl W, 1955, Ja 15,13:4
Frey, Carrie M, 1955, My 14,19:5
Frey, Carroll, 1955, N 5,19:4
Frey, Charles A, 1955, O 15,15:2
Frey, Charles D, 1959, N 12,35:2
Frey, Charles D Mrs, 1945, Je 3,32:1
Frey, Charles J, 1952, D 7,89:2
Frey, Daniel, 1947, D 5,25:1
Frey, David I, 1949, Jl 26,27:4
Frey, E Ivan, 1948, N 28,96:3
Frey, Edith E Mrs, 1940, My 24,19:5
Frey, Edmund F, 1968, Mr 29,41:3
Frey, Emil, 1922, D 26,13:3; 1951, Ja 12,27:5
Frey, Erwin J, 1946, S 6,21:2
Frey, Ferdinand C, 1961, F 28,33:3
Frey, Ferdinand C Mrs, 1952, Je 4,27:3
Frey, Frank J, 1937, Ap 5,19:1
Frey, Frederick E, 1939, D 19,26:2
Frey, Frederick Mrs, 1949, Ja 12,27:2
Frey, G, 1951, D 1,4:3
Frey, George H, 1965, Je 29,35:4
Frey, George J, 1959, N 14,21:5
Frey, George Mrs, 1952, Mr 27,29:2
Frey, George O Sr, 1951, My 15,31:3
Frey, George W, 1938, Ag 23,17:2
Frey, Granville F, 1948, Je 3,25:3
Frey, Gustave, 1959, Mr 1,86:4
Frey, Harold F, 1948, Ja 10,15:4
Frey, Harry C, 1941, Ja 24,17:3
Frey, Harry W, 1957, Ag 25,86:6
Frey, Henry W, 1958, Je 12,31:4
Frey, Herman C, 1957, D 27,20:1
Frey, Horace, 1903, S 14,7:5
Frey, Hugo, 1952, F 14,27:3
Frey, Isidor, 1939, Je 19,15:5
Frey, J J, 1903, Jl 14,7:6
Frey, J Nelson, 1958, Ja 30,23:4
Frey, Jacob J, 1950, Ap 11,31:1
Frey, John Anthony (Father Bonaventure), 1912, Jl 6,7:4
Frey, John C, 1909, Ag 6,7:4
Frey, John P, 1957, N 30,21:1
Frey, John T Rev, 1914, Mr 31,11:4
Frey, Joseph, 1919, Mr 24,13:3; 1919, Mr 27,13:3
Frey, Joseph A, 1938, Ag 21,31:6
Frey, Joseph M, 1955, Je 3,23:3
Frey, Killian C, 1946, O 28,27:4
Frey, Leo J, 1961, Ag 2,29:5
Frey, Lewis J, 1947, N 1,15:2
Frey, Louis H, 1948, Je 10,25:3
Frey, Louis H Jr, 1944, Mr 17,17:1
Frey, Marie V, 1944, Mr 28,19:6
Frey, Neal D, 1968, My 24,47:3
Frey, Oliver W, 1939, Ag 27,35:1
Frey, Paulus B, 1938, S 18,44:5
Frey, Perry A, 1946, Ag 14,25:4
Frey, Ralph E, 1954, Ja 2,12:3
Frey, Richard K Mrs, 1957, Jl 30,23:4
Frey, Robert L, 1949, D 27,6:2
Frey, Sidney, 1968, Ja 14,84:1
Frey, Timothy S, 1952, My 3,21:1
Frey, Walter F Jr (Sept 20), 1965, O 11,61:2
Frey, Walter G, 1954, F 14,92:3
Frey, Walter Guernsey Mrs, 1916, D 12,11:4
Frey, Walter P Mrs, 1959, O 6,39:2
Frey, William, 1961, F 17,28:1
Frey, William A, 1961, Ag 31,27:4
Frey, William C, 1958, Ag 2,17:6
Freyberg, Bernard C, 1963, Jl 5,19:1
Freycinet, Charles de, 1923, My 16,19:5
Freydberg, Aaron, 1950, N 25,13:4
Freydberg, Eli A Mrs, 1964, Je 5,31:5
Freydberg, George H, 1961, N 28,32:6
Freydberg, Joseph B, 1950, F 25,17:2
Freyer, Bela, 1955, Je 5,85:1
Freyer, Egbert, 1955, N 14,21:6
Freyer, Henry C Mrs, 1957, My 5,88:7
Freyer, Rudolph L, 1965, D 19,84:2
Freyer, Rudolph Mrs, 1947, N 15,17:2
Freyer, William N, 1961, Ap 8,19:3
Freyfogle, Charles F, 1943, Ja 26,19:2
Freyfogle, Edward B, 1937, Jl 20,23:3
Freygang, Gustave G, 1964, D 30,23:2
Freygang, Gustave G Mrs, 1943, Ja 16,13:3
Freyn, Henry J, 1956, Ap 29,86:5
Freyre, D M, 1878, Je 11,5:4
Freytag, Peter D, 1953, Ap 18,34:1
Freytag, Walter, 1959, O 28,37:3
Freyvogel, Charles E C, 1950, Ja 25,27:1
Frezzolini, Ermima, 1884, N 7,5:6
Friant, Charles, 1947, Ap 23,25:1
Friant, Julien N, 1939, O 28,15:2
Friberg, Bernard, 1958, D 9,52:5
Friberger, Harold Mrs, 1951, Jl 7,13:4
Friberger, William W Mrs, 1960, S 23,29:1
Fribourg, Andre, 1948, O 1,25:2
Fribourg, Edwin N, 1939, Je 1,25:3
Fribourg, Jules, 1944, Jl 17,15:5
Fribourg, Jules Mrs, 1968, N 20,57:8
Fribourg, Michel Mrs, 1950, Ap 20,29:2
Fribourg, Rene (Jan 19), 1963, Ap 1,35:6
Fribourg, Victor, 1884, My 9,5:3
Fribourg, Walter A, 1963, My 25,25:3
Fribush, Meyer, 1941, Mr 11,24:2
Frick, Adelaide F, 1956, Ap 1,89:2
Frick, Charles F, 1964, F 9,88:3
Frick, Childs, 1965, My 10,33:1
Frick, Childs Mrs, 1953, Ag 7,19:3
Frick, Elizabeth Mrs, 1905, O 2,1:7
Frick, Ezra, 1942, F 4,19:6
Frick, George, 1946, Ap 25,21:1
Frick, George A, 1941, N 25,25:1
Frick, Henry C, 1919, D 6,11:5
Frick, Henry E, 1960, Ap 1,33:1
Frick, Jacob, 1947, N 13,27:2
Frick, John H, 1952, F 29,23:4
Frick, John Jr, 1961, Jl 23,68:5
Frick, John S, 1941, F 28,21:8
Frick, Mary C D Mrs, 1937, O 10,II,9:3
Frick, Omar T, 1949, O 21,25:3
Frick, Otto F, 1955, F 10,31:3
Frick, Raymond C Mrs, 1953, Jl 14,27:3
Frick, Robert, 1962, N 5,31:5
Frick, Thomas A, 1955, N 27,88:6
Frick, William H, 1947, O 28,25:3
Frick, William H Mrs, 1953, My 4,23:4
Fricke, Charles L Mrs, 1947, D 3,29:1
Fricke, Charles W, 1958, Ja 30,24:1
Fricke, Charles W Mrs, 1950, Je 27,29:4
Fricke, Ernest A, 1946, My 24,19:3
Fricke, Frank R Sr, 1941, Ja 25,15:3
Fricke, George A, 1961, O 7,23:5
Fricke, John, 1951, O 7,87:2
Fricke, Louis P, 1948, My 27,25:4
Fricke, Otto L, 1951, Je 6,31:4
Fricke, Sophie D (est appr), 1959, Ag 28,20:8
Fricke, Wilbur S Mrs, 1953, F 3,25:2
Frickel, John Mrs, 1961, Mr 3,27:1
Fricken, Roy H, 1945, Ja 17,21:5
Fricker, Herbert A, 1943, N 12,21:4
Fricsay, Ferenc, 1963, F 21,9:3
Frid, William G, 1941, N 26,23:3
Frida, Emil, 1912, S 10,9:6
Friday, David, 1945, Mr 17,13:3
Friday, Frederic W, 1950, Ag 9,29:1
Friday, Harry A, 1951, Je 16,15:5
Friday, John A, 1941, S 29,17:5
Friday, William H, 1915, N 5,13:6
Fridel, George J, 1949, Jl 1,19:2
Fridell, Willis S, 1943, D 20,23:2
Fridelt, Jeol, 1962, Ag 13,25:6
Friden, Karl M, 1945, My 2,23:6
Fridenberg, Albert Mrs, 1951, Mr 26,23:5
Fridenberg, Percy H, 1960, Je 4,23:3
Fridenberg, Robert, 1946, Ap 2,27:2
Fridenberger, Alfred, 1952, F 29,23:2
Fridman, William, 1952, S 28,78:8
Fridson, Morris, 1965, F 11,39:1
Friduss, Joseph Z, 1948, D 27,21:2
Friebele, Ella B Mrs, 1951, S 14,25:1
Friebele, Leonard L, 1949, Ag 22,21:2
Friebely, John D, 1966, Ag 25,37:5
Frieber, Joseph, 1962, Ap 7,25:3
Frieber, William, 1957, Ap 4,33:4
Frieberg, J Walter, 1921, Je 10,13:6
Frieberg, Robert, 1963, Je 15,23:5
Frieberg, Stella H Mrs, 1962, Ja 21,88:4
Friebus, Theodore, 1917, D 27,11:6
Fried, Albert V, 1947, O 2,27:3
Fried, Alfred H, 1921, My 7,11:4
Fried, Benjamin, 1958, Ap 5,15:3
Fried, Bernard, 1960, Je 30,29:5
Fried, David Mrs, 1954, Je 22,27:5
Fried, Ethel K, 1949, Mr 9,25:4
Fried, George (por), 1949, Jl 5,23:1
Fried, Harry, 1948, Jl 9,19:2
Fried, Helen Mrs, 1951, Jl 30,11:2
Fried, Isadore, 1959, F 19,31:5
Fried, Isidor, 1950, Mr 29,29:3
Fried, Jack Mrs, 1958, Je 5,31:2
Fried, Joseph, 1956, Ja 11,31:2
Fried, Joseph Mrs, 1953, Ag 2,73:1
Fried, Louis, 1950, My 30,18:3
Fried, Max, 1961, D 22,23:3
Fried, Meyer E, 1957, Ja 20,92:3
Fried, Monte, 1960, Ag 26,25:1
Fried, Morris, 1952, Jl 8,27:5
Fried, Nathan, 1959, N 23,31:3
Fried, Rudolph S, 1951, Je 19,30:2
Fried, Sabina, 1949, N 18,29:1
Fried, Samuel, 1952, Ja 23,27:4; 1956, Ap 14,17:3
Fried, Samuel D, 1953, Ap 4,13:5
Fried, Stanley, 1956, Ag 7,27:2
Friedberg, Annie, 1952, N 21,26:5
Friedberg, Benjamin, 1951, Ag 5,73:2
Friedberg, Billy, 1965, Ap 8,39:4
Friedberg, Carl, 1948, N 26,23:3
Friedberg, Carl (trb lr, O 2,II,9:6), 1955, S 13,31:2
Friedberg, Edward, 1947, N 27,31:3
Friedberg, Eugene, 1966, Jl 9,27:3
Friedberg, Herman, 1957, My 26,92:3
Friedberg, Milton H, 1955, S 2,17:4
Friedberg, Robert M, 1965, Ja 17,88:4
Friedberger, Sanford, 1922, Ap 13,19:6
Friede, Donald, 1965, My 31,17:4
Friede, Frank, 1954, My 5,31:5
Friede, Julian S, 1953, Ag 17,15:6
Friede, Leo, 1959, N 7,23:6
Friede, Sergey, 1920, Jl 22,11:5
Friedeberg, Theodore, 1938, Jl 5,17:5
Friedel, Charles J Jr, 1958, Jl 2,29:2
Friedel, Francis J, 1959, F 14,21:6
Friedel, Herman, 1956, Ja 3,31:2
Friedel, Jacob H, 1946, Ja 22,28:2
Friedel, Jules, 1958, Ja 18,15:5
Friedel, Lee Mrs, 1951, D 5,35:2
Friedell, E F, 1943, O 2,13:4
Friedell, Harold W, 1958, F 18,28:1
Friedemann, Herbert, 1948, Je 7,19:5
Frieden, Alex, 1956, Ap 22,86:3
Frieden, John P Father, 1911, D 3,II,15:6
Frieden, Pierre, 1959, F 24,29:4
Friedenberg, Edward Dr, 1903, D 11,9:5
Friedenberg, Fred S, 1967, N 22,47:2
Friedenberg, Jac, 1952, Ag 27,27:1
Friedenberg, Samuel, 1954, Jl 28,23:4; 1957, My
Friedenheit, Isaac Mrs (will), 1951, Ja 6,16:5
Friedenson, Meyer Mrs, 1957, Mr 21,31:3
Friedenthal, David, 1958, N 14,11:1
Friedenwald, Gilbert A, 1951, Ja 16,29:3
Friedenwald, Harry (cor, Ap 14,23:1), 1950, Ap 31:3
Friedenwald, Jonas S, 1955, N 6,87:1
Friedenwald, Joseph, 1910, D 25,9:2
Friedenwald, Julius, 1941, Je 9,19:5
Frieder, Alex, 1968, Ap 13,25:3
Frieder, Alfred F, 1947, O 21,23:4
Frieder, Charles, 1957, Ap 22,25:6
Frieder, Herman, 1945, F 23,17:4
Frieder, Marcus, 1940, O 14,19:3
Frieder, Morris J, 1958, Jl 10,27:5
Frieder, Phil W, 1948, Jl 26,17:1
Friederich, Max M, 1938, S 18,44:6
Friederika, Princess, 1926, O 17,II,9:1
Friedfeld, Murray M, 1968, D 16,47:1
Friedgen, William G, 1939, F 18,15:4
Friedhaber, George M, 1952, O 28,31:4
Friedheim, A, 1932, O 20,29:6
Friedheim, Arthur Mrs, 1959, Ag 14,21:5
Friedheim, Kate, 1952, Ap 22,29:3
Friedheim, Robert W, 1961, My 23,39:4
Friedigerhead, Max, 1947, Ap 10,25:2
Friedkin, Israel, 1939, Ag 9,17:5
Friedkin, Mayer Joseph, 1916, N 14,11:2
Friedl, John L, 1948, Ap 14,27:5
Friedl, Otto W, 1952, Jl 30,23:2
Friedlaender, Eugen, 1952, Je 18,27:4
Friedlaender, Max Mrs, 1949, Mr 12,17:4
Friedlaender, Pincus, 1937, S 22,27:5

Friedlaender, Walter, 1966, S 8,47:1
Friedland, Abraham H, 1939, Ag 4,13:2
Friedland, Anatol, 1938, Jl 25,15:6
Friedland, Benjamin, 1949, O 29,15:3; 1950, Je 29,29:2
Friedland, Benjamin L, 1946, Mr 31,46:4
Friedland, Henry, 1948, Ap 18,71:4; 1959, Ap 1,37:4
Friedland, Jacob M, 1964, My 30,17:6
Friedland, Joseph, 1965, Ja 2,17:2
Friedland, Morris Mrs, 1950, D 27,27:4
Friedland, Samuel, 1943, Ag 20,15:4
Friedland, Simon, 1954, S 30,31:4
Friedland, Sol, 1945, F 12,19:2
Friedland, Solomon M, 1966, F 7,29:2
Friedlander, Adolph E, 1941, Ag 13,17:6
Friedlander, Al, 1937, My 13,25:5
Friedlander, Albert, 1909, Je 3,9:4
Friedlander, Alex J Mrs, 1940, O 9,25:2
Friedlander, Alex Mrs, 1961, F 18,19:1
Friedlander, Alfred, 1939, My 29,15:2
Friedlander, Alfred J, 1966, O 22,31:1
Friedlander, Bernard, 1951, Ap 26,32:3
Friedlander, Charles, 1959, Je 9,37:4
Friedlander, David Mrs, 1959, My 5,33:1
Friedlander, David W, 1947, Mr 4,25:4
Friedlander, Edgar J, 1959, O 25,87:1
Friedlander, Ettore, 1925, Ag 17,15:5
Friedlander, Henry G, 1965, S 2,31:4
Friedlander, Irving, 1967, Ap 1,32:4
Friedlander, Isac, 1968, Ag 24,29:1
Friedlander, Israel, 1954, Je 20,84:5
Friedlander, J, 1878, Jl 20,2:5
Friedlander, Jacob, 1961, Ap 23,86:5; 1962, S 9,84:3
Friedlander, Jacob H, 1917, S 25,11:7
Friedlander, John, 1921, S 14,19:4
Friedlander, Joseph, 1954, Je 27,68:2
Friedlander, Julius, 1909, My 26,9:6
Friedlander, Leo, 1966, O 25,45:1
Friedlander, Lou, 1952, S 8,21:3
Friedlander, Louis Mrs (will), 1944, S 7,17:6
Friedlander, Marcus, 1944, Ja 11,19:5
Friedlander, Max J, 1958, O 12,83:2
Friedlander, Norman, 1954, Ap 15,29:4
Friedlander, Theodore Sr, 1952, D 4,35:4
Friedlander, Walter J, 1939, Ap 20,23:4
Friedlander, William B, 1968, Ja 3,40:5
Friedler, Julius L Dr, 1914, D 14,11:5
Friedlob, Bert T, 1956, O 8,27:4
Friedman, Aaron, 1939, Jl 15,15:2
Friedman, Abraham, 1939, Jl 28,17:2
Friedman, Abraham I, 1966, N 27,87:1
Friedman, Abraham L Mrs, 1954, Ag 5,23:5
Friedman, Abraham Mrs, 1960, Ja 21,31:1; 1964, Mr 25,41:4
Friedman, Abram, 1945, O 5,23:4
Friedman, Abram Mrs, 1962, Je 29,27:4
Friedman, Alexander Mrs, 1946, Ja 13,43:1
Friedman, Alfred, 1951, Jl 28,11:3
Friedman, Alfred E Mrs, 1944, N 20,21:4
Friedman, Alvin, 1948, F 18,27:1
Friedman, Arnold, 1946, D 30,22:2
Friedman, Arnold L, 1955, Ag 1,19:2
Friedman, Barney L, 1943, Ag 24,19:6
Friedman, Benjamin, 1938, D 13,25:5; 1944, O 26, 23:1; 1955, Mr 29,30:6
Friedman, Benjamin G, 1962, O 8,23:6
Friedman, Benjamin Mrs, 1962, Ja 20,21:6
Friedman, Bernard, 1966, S 14,43:8; 1967, Je 30,37:3
Friedman, Bernard C, 1952, Ag 26,25:1
Friedman, Bernard M, 1964, F 13,31:5
Friedman, Bertha B, 1956, My 18,25:3
Friedman, Conrad Mrs, 1953, Ag 7,19:2
Friedman, D Harry, 1939, N 30,21:5
Friedman, Daniel A, 1961, Ap 16,86:6
Friedman, David, 1943, F 28,49:1; 1945, D 2,45:2; 1953, My 4,23:5
Friedman, David L, 1957, My 17,25:2
Friedman, Deszo Mrs (Mrs J F Capa), 1962, Ja 4, 33:1
Friedman, E David, 1953, Je 8,29:5
Friedman, Edith, 1954, N 18,33:1
Friedman, Edward, 1944, Ja 27,19:4
Friedman, Edward H Mrs, 1947, O 22,29:2
Friedman, Edwin H, 1968, Jl 7,53:2
Friedman, Elisha M, 1951, Mr 26,23:5
Friedman, Ellis O, 1938, Mr 14,16:1
Friedman, Emanuel, 1951, O 9,29:3
Friedman, Fannie Mrs, 1953, Je 16,29:4
Friedman, Fanny Mrs (funl), 1967, My 22,52:1
Friedman, Felix Mrs, 1948, Ag 12,21:1
Friedman, Francis L, 1962, Ag 5,81:2
Friedman, Frank Mrs, 1948, O 17,76:8
Friedman, George, 1941, Ja 28,8:5
Friedman, Harold, 1961, D 14,43:1
Friedman, Harris, 1945, S 5,23:5
Friedman, Harry, 1938, F 4,21:4; 1968, O 20,86:1
Friedman, Harry A, 1950, N 29,33:3
Friedman, Harry G, 1965, N 23,38:1
Friedman, Harry G Mrs, 1960, N 9,35:2
Friedman, Harry J, 1925, O 29,25:6
Friedman, Harry Mrs, 1948, F 1,60:2
Friedman, Henry, 1905, N 13,9:5
Friedman, Henry A, 1955, S 28,35:3; 1958, D 9,41:4
Friedman, Henry G, 1943, S 23,21:5
Friedman, Henry M, 1961, My 5,29:2; 1964, My 28, 37:3
Friedman, Herman, 1965, N 17,48:1
Friedman, Howard, 1959, Jl 18,15:6
Friedman, Hyman, 1945, Ag 3,17:3; 1956, F 28,31:5; 1966, Jl 1,35:3
Friedman, Iganz, 1948, Ja 27,25:5
Friedman, Irving, 1955, D 22,23:1
Friedman, Irving H, 1953, My 17,88:5
Friedman, Irving J, 1965, Ja 27,35:3
Friedman, Irving M Mrs, 1966, Je 24,37:4
Friedman, Irving Mrs, 1952, O 10,25:1
Friedman, Isaac Rabbi, 1924, D 9,25:4
Friedman, Isadore, 1942, Ap 15,21:1; 1950, Jl 30,61:1
Friedman, Isidor, 1947, O 21,23:2; 1962, Ap 9,29:1
Friedman, Isidor H, 1945, Je 3,32:1
Friedman, Israel M, 1945, Je 25,17:3
Friedman, Ivan B, 1962, Je 2,19:5
Friedman, Jacob, 1957, Ja 14,23:4
Friedman, Jacob Mrs, 1966, Ja 30,84:8
Friedman, Jacob P, 1965, Je 10,35:1
Friedman, Jacob S, 1957, Ag 26,23:2
Friedman, Jacob S Mrs, 1960, My 3,39:1
Friedman, Jacob W, 1944, Mr 8,19:2
Friedman, Jeann, 1960, D 21,31:4
Friedman, Jeno Mrs, 1953, Ja 3,15:4
Friedman, John E, 1937, Je 14,23:2
Friedman, Joseph, 1960, Ap 7,35:5
Friedman, Joseph L, 1953, Je 19,21:2
Friedman, Joseph M, 1951, Je 18,23:3
Friedman, Joseph Mrs, 1944, My 19,19:3
Friedman, Joseph S, 1956, My 17,31:2
Friedman, Joshua H, 1962, Ag 20,23:5
Friedman, Julius M Dr, 1937, Ag 28,15:2
Friedman, Leon, 1948, D 16,29:1
Friedman, Leon A, 1963, N 24,23:1
Friedman, Lester, 1957, Mr 5,31:1
Friedman, Lester M, 1955, Ag 18,23:2
Friedman, Louis, 1940, Ag 29,19:2; 1955, Ap 10,89:1; 1961, O 27,33:1
Friedman, Louis A, 1951, Mr 2,25:2
Friedman, Louis L, 1957, My 18,19:5
Friedman, Louis Mrs, 1952, Jl 19,15:5
Friedman, Maurice, 1939, S 8,23:2
Friedman, Max, 1938, Ag 4,17:2; 1949, Je 8,29:2; 1965, Mr 2,35:3
Friedman, Max Mrs, 1947, O 30,26:2
Friedman, Menka, 1903, Je 22,7:6
Friedman, Meyer, 1948, Jl 3,15:6
Friedman, Meyer J, 1951, Je 14,27:2
Friedman, Morris, 1937, N 9,23:5; 1944, N 3,21:4; 1954, O 3,87:1; 1954, D 3,27:1; 1956, Jl 5,25:2
Friedman, Morris Y, 1942, Jl 25,13:5
Friedman, Nathan, 1938, D 23,19:5
Friedman, Nathan (will), 1949, D 10,9:3
Friedman, Nathan, 1958, N 4,27:4
Friedman, Nathan H, 1952, Ja 25,21:4
Friedman, Oliver A, 1957, Ja 14,23:5
Friedman, Oscar J, 1937, Jl 29,19:2
Friedman, Peter, 1960, Je 24,27:3
Friedman, Peter H, 1957, Mr 1,23:2
Friedman, Philip, 1960, F 8,29:1
Friedman, Philippe Mrs, 1962, Jl 27,25:2
Friedman, Pinchas, 1938, Ja 8,15:5
Friedman, Reuben, 1956, F 5,86:2
Friedman, Samuel, 1942, My 3,53:2
Friedman, Samuel (por), 1947, D 15,25:5
Friedman, Samuel B, 1956, D 1,21:3
Friedman, Samuel D, 1951, Ag 17,17:5
Friedman, Samuel D Mrs, 1948, O 7,29:1
Friedman, Samuel G, 1939, N 11,15:5; 1947, Ja 19,53:1
Friedman, Samuel J, 1941, Mr 16,45:2
Friedman, Samuel K Mrs, 1953, Je 29,21:3
Friedman, Samuel Mrs, 1967, F 11,29:4
Friedman, Sheppard, 1921, Mr 25,15:5
Friedman, Sidney T, 1962, Ja 28,77:1
Friedman, Simon S, 1951, F 28,27:4
Friedman, Sol H, 1957, Mr 16,19:6
Friedman, Sol R, 1962, My 17,37:3
Friedman, Stanleigh P, 1960, O 1,19:3
Friedman, Stanley S, 1960, N 25,27:4
Friedman, Theodore, 1950, Mr 15,29:4
Friedman, Victor E, 1964, Mr 9,29:4
Friedman, Walter, 1954, My 24,27:4
Friedman, William, 1937, S 9,23:1; 1968, My 2,48:1
Friedman, William H, 1961, Ap 18,37:2
Friedman, William H Dr, 1925, Je 11,19:3
Friedman, William S, 1944, Ap 27,23:1; 1951, Je 16, 32:6
Friedman, William S Mrs, 1956, Ja 22,88:8
Friedmann, Ahron Mrs, 1958, Jl 30,29:5
Friedmann, Conrad, 1950, Jl 8,13:4
Friedmann, Edward N, 1939, F 4,13:5
Friedmann, Erich, 1959, Je 27,23:5
Friedmann, John M, 1947, S 13,11:6
Friedmann, Joseph, 1960, D 20,33:2
Friedmann, Lionel, 1957, My 22,33:5
Friedmann, Louise K Mrs, 1941, D 3,25:2
Friedmann, Max E, 1954, Ap 1,31:2
Friedmann, Morris Mrs, 1958, D 2,37:1
Friedmann, Nathaniel, 1941, My 11,44:5
Friedmann, Paul G, 1937, Je 9,25:4
Friedmann, Ulrich, 1949, N 16,30:2
Friedner, Mark, 1948, Mr 11,27:1
Friedrich, A Anton, 1961, My 20,23:1
Friedrich, Adolph, 1955, My 19,29:5
Friedrich, August C, 1949, Jl 1,19:2
Friedrich, Charles H, 1966, Ag 2,33:3
Friedrich, Ernst W, 1949, F 25,23:3
Friedrich, Ferdinand A, 1961, Je 23,29:4
Friedrich, Franz II, 1883, Ap 16,5:2
Friedrich, George A, 1957, D 9,35:1
Friedrich, George W, 1952, D 28,48:7
Friedrich, Hans R, 1958, D 7,88:1
Friedrich, James W, 1940, S 15,48:3
Friedrich, John, 1943, Jl 10,13:3
Friedrich, Martin, 1954, O 20,29:4
Friedrich, Prince of Liechtenstein, 1959, O 14,43:1
Friedrich, Prince of Prussia (death ruling, My 3,12:2), 1966, My 2,11:1
Friedrich, Robert H (Strangler Lewis), 1966, Ag 8, 27:1
Friedrich, William, 1953, S 25,21:3
Friedrich, William G, 1963, Ag 19,25:3
Friedrich Karl, Landgrave of Hesse, 1940, Je 2,44:7
Friedrich Wilhelm, Crown Prince, 1951, Jl 21,13:1
Friedrich Wilhelm of Prussia, Prince, 1925, Mr 10,21:3
Friedrichs, Arthur C, 1958, My 3,19:4
Friedrichs, Aug H, 1940, Ja 14,42:5
Friedrichs, Rudolf, 1947, Je 15,62:6
Friedricks, Samuel, 1947, D 1,21:2
Friedricks, Samuel Mrs, 1943, S 18,17:4
Friedriech, Louise, 1911, Jl 25,7:5
Friedsam, M, 1931, Ap 8,1:3
Friedsam, Morris, 1943, Jl 8,19:6
Friedson, Morris (por), 1947, Mr 18,27:6
Friel, Arthur O, 1959, Ja 29,27:5
Friel, Charles F, 1957, Je 13,31:4
Friel, Francis de S, 1964, F 13,31:4
Friel, Henry H Rev, 1925, D 5,19:5
Friel, James E, 1956, F 22,27:3
Friel, Joseph R (Buck), 1940, Ag 18,37:3
Friel, Joseph V, 1961, O 6,35:4
Friel, Richard A, 1943, D 9,27:1
Friele, William Mrs, 1946, Ap 16,25:3
Frieling, Walter, 1957, D 20,24:2
Frielinghaus, Henry, 1967, Ja 12,39:5
Frieman, Alfred E, 1960, Je 30,29:5
Frieman, Edward A Mrs, 1966, My 17,47:3
Frieman, Henry, 1943, Je 17,21:4
Frieman, Hyman, 1955, S 20,31:5
Friend, Al M, 1955, N 28,31:4
Friend, Albert M Jr, 1956, Mr 25,92:1
Friend, Alfred M Mrs, 1958, Ja 11,17:2
Friend, Arthur S (por), 1947, N 18,29:3
Friend, Benjamin M, 1965, F 15,27:1
Friend, Carl E, 1948, F 24,25:3
Friend, Clarence L, 1958, Ja 19,86:1
Friend, David, 1949, N 17,29:5
Friend, David E, 1943, Ja 17,45:2
Friend, Emanuel, 1938, Jl 20,19:5
Friend, Emanuel M, 1904, N 2,9:4
Friend, Emil, 1920, O 3,22:1
Friend, Frederick, 1872, Ja 31,8:5
Friend, Harry M, 1943, Ja 10,48:8; 1945, O 18,23:5
Friend, Hugo M, 1966, My 1,88:3
Friend, James W, 1909, D 28,9:4
Friend, Julia I Mrs, 1941, Je 3,21:1
Friend, Mitchell E, 1960, O 23,88:5
Friend, Mitchell E Mrs, 1953, Ja 1,23:4
Friend, Ralph W, 1949, Jl 27,23:5
Friend, Robert, 1946, Ja 10,23:2
Friend, Robert E, 1962, Jl 15,60:3
Friend, Roger B, 1941, S 21,45:1
Friend, Samuel B, 1913, Ag 31,11:4
Friend, Solomon, 1904, Ap 2,9:6
Friend, Victor A, 1952, Ja 3,46:4
Friend, William, 1937, O 29,21:1
Friendly, Joseph M (por), 1949, O 24,23:5
Friendly, Meyer H, 1938, D 29,20:3
Friendly, Myer, 1937, Mr 9,23:2
Friendly, Myer Mrs, 1923, F 9,15:2
Friendship, W Bruce, 1959, D 23,27:1
Frier, Alex A, 1960, Jl 4,15:6
Frier, James C, 1950, Ag 4,21:2
Frierson, John W, 1959, Ag 15,17:6
Frierson, William L, 1953, My 27,31:5
Fries, Adelaide L, 1949, N 30,27:2
Fries, Albert, 1950, S 17,104:5
Fries, Anna E B Mrs, 1952, Mr 21,23:3
Fries, Charles A, 1940, D 17,25:4; 1948, N 23,29:3
Fries, Charles J V, 1946, My 9,21:6
Fries, Claude S, 1952, F 10,92:4
Fries, Claude S Mrs, 1956, Ja 19,33:1
Fries, Elmer P, 1949, My 20,27:2
Fries, George, 1960, Je 9,33:4
Fries, George Dr, 1866, N 18,3:7
Fries, George G Jr, 1937, Ap 3,19:2
Fries, Harold H, 1946, Jl 1,31:2
Fries, Karl, 1946, O 27,63:3
Fries, Mills M, 1959, O 29,33:1
Fries, Robert G Sr, 1963, O 29,36:4
Fries, William, 1953, F 23,25:6
Friese, Alfred P Mrs, 1965, My 9,87:1
Friese, Elbert D, 1952, S 8,21:4
Frieseke, Frederick C, 1939, Ag 30,17:4

Friesell, H Edmund, 1946, O 28,27:5
Friesen, Abraham P, 1953, Ag 1,11:3
Friesen, Henry J, 1951, Jl 8,60:2
Friesner, Claude R Mrs, 1953, Ja 12,27:3
Friesner, Isidore, 1945, S 9,45:1
Friesner, Isidore Mrs, 1959, Ap 20,31:1
Friesner, Ray C, 1952, D 2,31:2
Friess, Charlotte L, 1960, F 20,23:5
Friestedt, Alice Jacklin Spalding, 1925, N 29,13:2
Friestedt, Arthur A, 1953, Ja 22,23:4
Friesz, Othon (por), 1949, Ja 12,28:2
Frieze, Abraham, 1956, D 27,25:4
Frieze, Lyman B Gen, 1917, S 6,11:5
Frieze, Mary S Mrs, 1941, Jl 31,17:1
Frieze, Savage C Mrs, 1966, S 10,29:3
Friganza, Trixie (funl, Mr 3,27:1), 1955, F 28,19:2
Frigon, Augustin, 1952, Jl 11,17:5
Frigout, Francis W, 1909, Ag 1,9:6
Frijah, Povla (Mrs J Posnanaski), 1960, Jl 11,29:1
Friley, Charles E, 1958, Jl 12,15:6
Friley, Charles E Mrs, 1947, My 28,26:2
Frimpter, George A, 1961, My 24,41:1
Frindel, Samuel Jr, 1956, Je 2,19:3
Frings, Severina, 1925, F 3,13:4
Frink, Alvah C, 1937, Mr 30,24:2
Frink, Charles L, 1937, Ja 27,21:4
Frink, Harrie V N, 1954, F 4,25:5
Frink, Herbert A, 1962, My 19,12:6
Frink, James L Jr, 1959, O 23,29:3
Frink, Joy L, 1946, D 10,31:3
Frink, Ralph A, 1946, Ja 29,25:4
Frink, Theodore W, 1938, S 8,23:3
Frink, William M, 1952, Ap 17,29:2
Frioux, Jean Joseph, 1923, S 2,22:3
Fripp, William J, 1958, F 28,13:3
Fris, Henry H, 1950, D 10,104:3
Fris, Van Henry, 1960, Mr 2,37:4
Frisbee, James, 1956, F 28,31:1
Frisbee, Walter S, 1966, O 28,41:2
Frisbie, C H Capt, 1882, Ap 17,5:1
Frisbie, Joseph P, 1940, O 3,25:4
Frisbie, Owen P, 1963, Je 14,29:2
Frisby, W B Rev, 1902, Je 7,9:5
Frisch, Daniel, 1950, Mr 8,27:1
Frisch, Daniel Mrs, 1959, Ja 2,25:2
Frisch, Ephraim, 1957, D 26,19:1
Frisch, Felix, 1958, Jl 6,57:2
Frisch, Franz, 1950, My 8,23:6
Frisch, Franz Mrs, 1949, Jl 10,57:2
Frisch, Hartvig, 1950, F 12,86:3
Frisch, John A, 1963, My 14,39:4
Frisch, Victor, 1939, O 11,27:1
Frisch, Victor Mrs, 1952, Ag 20,25:5
Frisch, William, 1910, Jl 31,7:5
Frischauer, Edward M, 1964, Ja 17,43:1
Frischauer, Leo Mrs, 1966, Mr 23,47:4
Frischkorn, John C, 1940, Jl 30,19:6
Frischmann, Christian Mrs, 1954, My 9,89:1
Frischwasser, Benjamin F, 1958, Jl 31,23:4
Frischwasser, Benjamin Mrs, 1959, Ap 1,37:1
Frisco, Joe (L W Joseph), 1958, F 18,27:3
Frise, Jimmy, 1948, Je 14,23:2
Frishberg, Israel Z, 1955, O 19,33:3
Frishberg, Naphtali Z, 1960, Ag 10,31:2
Frishkoff, Louis H, 1965, Mr 26,35:1
Friske, Paul W, 1942, Ap 28,21:2
Friskin, James, 1967, Mr 19,92:4
Frison, Theodore H, 1945, D 11,25:1
Friss, Charles E, 1962, D 4,41:4
Frisse, Louis B, 1949, F 1,25:4
Frissell, Frank H, 1945, D 12,27:4
Frissell, Hollis B Mrs, 1948, Je 17,25:4
Frissell, Hollis Burke Dr, 1917, Ag 7,9:4
Frissell, Lewis F, 1943, O 25,15:5
Frissell, Sarah Dr, 1915, Je 21,9:6
Fristoe, John R, 1966, N 9,39:5
Friswell, J H, 1878, Mr 15,5:5
Friswell S H, 1878, Ap 5,2:6
Friszell, Phelps M, 1923, S 13,19:3
Fritch, E H, 1943, Mr 19,20:3
Fritch, Howard F, 1952, O 18,19:5
Fritch, J Scott, 1962, Je 6,41:1
Fritcher, Margaret E Mrs, 1940, Mr 11,15:5
Fritchey, Claygon Mrs, 1942, N 17,25:4
Fritchman, Leon A, 1963, Ag 14,33:4
Frith, Arthur J Prof, 1913, N 12,9:6
Frith, E, 1885, Ap 27,5:3
Frith, Jannie I, 1937, My 6,25:4
Frith, Louis E, 1938, Ap 24,II,7:2
Frith, Vincent, 1944, Je 22,19:3
Frith, William Powell, 1909, N 3,11:4
Fritsch, Alfred, 1965, Mr 20,27:1
Fritsch, Christian, 1924, Ag 17,24:3
Fritsch, Frank M, 1948, Jl 7,23:2
Fritsch, Harry Sr Mrs, 1962, D 8,27:5
Fritsch, Homer C, 1957, Ap 10,33:4
Fritsch, Hugo, 1889, Ja 28,2:4
Fritsch, Joseph Jr, 1954, My 20,31:2
Fritsch, Robert R, 1960, F 20,23:3
Fritsche, Frederic, 1967, D 23,23:3
Fritsche, John, 1947, S 26,23:3
Fritsche, John Jr, 1958, Je 19,31:5
Fritsche, Joseph V, 1947, F 6,23:5
Fritsche, Thorwald, 1902, Ja 19,2:4
Fritschel, George J, 1941, O 7,23:4
Fritscher, Edmund, 1948, Ag 30,18:2
Fritschi, G A, 1948, Ap 16,23:1
Fritts, Calvin E, 1941, D 20,19:4
Fritts, Charles W Rev Dr, 1907, Je 25,7:6
Fritts, Frank, 1962, Mr 3,21:2
Fritts, Frederick B U, 1964, N 21,29:6
Fritts, Howard S, 1948, Je 27,52:5
Fritts, John P, 1948, Je 21,21:6
Fritts, John R, 1968, D 18,47:2
Fritts, Lewis C, 1961, Ap 9,86:3
Fritts, Thomas W, 1938, Mr 29,21:3
Fritts, Wilfred H, 1938, My 6,21:5
Fritz, Agnes M Mrs, 1942, Jl 12,35:2
Fritz, Aime L, 1950, Ja 31,23:2
Fritz, Arthur Z Mrs, 1951, O 16,31:4
Fritz, Carl V Mrs, 1947, Je 12,25:2
Fritz, Charles A, 1964, Ag 17,25:3
Fritz, Charles B, 1944, Mr 17,17:3
Fritz, Charles E, 1957, N 8,29:5
Fritz, Eduard Mrs, 1948, D 26,52:4
Fritz, Edward A Mrs (estate appraisal), 1963, My 1, 57:4
Fritz, Eugene N Jr, 1950, Ap 13,29:1
Fritz, F Herman, 1955, Je 10,25:1
Fritz, George H, 1939, Mr 6,15:5
Fritz, George T, 1956, Jl 12,23:2
Fritz, George W, 1941, S 28,49:2
Fritz, Irving, 1956, F 1,31:4
Fritz, John, 1913, F 14,15:5; 1944, F 11,19:4
Fritz, John H C, 1953, Ap 13,27:3
Fritz, Joseph R, 1950, S 14,31:2
Fritz, Lawrence G Jr, 1945, Je 8,19:5
Fritz, Leo G, 1967, N 26,84:7
Fritz, Mary J, 1952, F 25,21:4
Fritz, Michael D, 1941, Mr 2,42:5
Fritz, T Francis (F Ducrot), 1939, My 25,25:5
Fritz, Victor R, 1956, Jl 24,25:4
Fritz, W Wallace, 1951, N 27,31:4
Fritz, Walter S, 1957, Je 21,25:4
Fritz, William, 1961, Mr 11,21:5
Fritz, William H, 1938, N 1,24:4
Fritzche, Oscar, 1937, N 22,19:4
Fritzell, E Werner, 1945, Jl 12,11:6
Fritzen, Adolf Rev, 1919, S 9,17:2
Fritzinger, Anna C Mrs, 1941, S 13,17:2
Fritzsch, Bernard, 1948, Ja 17,17:5
Fritzsche, Alfred W, 1944, Ja 19,19:1
Fritzsche, Carl F, 1960, O 1,1:1
Fritzsche, Hans, 1953, S 29,29:3
Friz, Clyde N, 1942, N 23,23:2
Frizzell, Addie A Mrs, 1943, Je 26,13:2
Frizzell, Charles F, 1947, Mr 2,60:1
Froat, William T, 1954, Ja 9,15:1
Froats, Esley R, 1954, Mr 24,27:4
Froats, Esley R Mrs, 1956, Jl 12,23:1
Froatz, Frances V, 1951, D 29,11:5
Frobenius, Gustav E, 1951, F 14,29:2
Frobenius, Leo (por), 1938, Ag 10,19:3
Frobisher, Frederick M, 1940, S 13,23:3
Frobisher, Joseph E, 1939, D 28,21:6
Frobisher, Martin Mrs, 1952, Ag 13,15:4
Frocht, Maurice, 1957, My 16,31:4
Frock, Fillmore S, 1954, Mr 1,25:5
Frodel, Alfred C, 1956, Ja 26,29:5
Frodsham, George H Rt Rev, 1937, Mr 7,II,8:2
Froeb, Charles Sr, 1946, O 31,25:6
Froebe, Augustus C, 1962, Ap 9,29:3
Froeber, Lawrence, 1949, My 28,15:4
Froeberg, Peter, 1954, N 18,33:2
Froedtert, Kurtis R, 1951, D 7,27:3
Froehlich, Alfred, 1953, Mr 23,23:3
Froehlich, August, 1949, F 20,60:1
Froehlich, Charles F, 1949, Je 7,31:3
Froehlich, Charles W, 1941, Ap 15,23:4
Froehlich, Elmer W, 1958, S 22,31:5
Froehlich, Ernest Mrs, 1952, Je 28,19:3
Froehlich, Eugene, 1963, N 14,35:4
Froehlich, Francis A, 1949, Jl 7,25:1
Froehlich, George J, 1961, F 24,29:3
Froehlich, Jesse, 1939, My 14,III,7:4
Froehlich, Joseph T, 1942, N 17,25:4
Froehlich, Louis, 1962, Ag 30,29:4
Froehlich, Oscar A, 1958, O 4,21:5
Froehlinger, Richard A, 1955, S 11,84:8
Froelich, Albert Mrs, 1967, D 15,47:2
Froelich, Bellina Mrs, 1920, Ap 1,11:6
Froelich, Carl Prof, 1953, F 14,17:2
Froelich, John, 1948, Ap 30,23:2
Froelich, Michael H, 1961, Ag 26,17:6
Froelich, Myron, 1960, Jl 24,65:1
Froelicher, Otto R, 1961, Mr 20,29:2
Froeliegh, Ella A, 1920, S 26,22:4
Froemel, Rudolph O, 1944, My 5,19:3
Froemming, Bernhard A, 1945, Ag 17,17:4
Froessel, Barbara Mrs, 1942, Mr 20,19:4
Froessel, Charles W Mrs, 1952, Mr 17,21:5
Froessel, Gustave H, 1940, Jl 13,13:1
Froggatt, Joseph, 1940, S 30,17:2
Froggett, Joseph F, 1942, S 13,53:2
Frohlich, Joseph, 1951, Ap 1,93:1
Frohlich, Louis D, 1953, Ap 1,29:2
Frohlich, Louis H, 1947, F 16,57:2
Frohlich, William H, 1939, N 21,26:1
Frohlin, Andrew J, 1943, S 21,23:5
Frohling, Edward A, 1966, O 17,37:4
Frohman, Caryl, 1924, Ja 19,13:4
Frohman, Charles, 1915, My 15,13:5; 1915, My 2 11:5; 1915, Je 3,11:5
Frohman, Daniel, 1940, D 27,14:3
Frohman, Emma, 1937, Ap 16,23:4
Frohman, Emma (will), 1938, Je 22,4:2
Frohman, Etta, 1948, D 26,52:5
Frohman, G, 1930, Ag 17,II,7:3
Frohman, Mae, 1956, Ap 24,31:2
Frohman, Marie H Mrs, 1939, Jl 6,24:2
Frohman, Sidney, 1964, O 31,29:5
Frohne, Henry W Mrs, 1954, Ja 23,13:4
Frohner, Edward H, 1938, Ag 26,17:5
Frohnhoefer, Frederick R M, 1956, Mr 1,34:3
Frohnknecht, Ernst, 1948, Mr 3,23:1
Frohnknecht, Otto O, 1968, N 7,47:2
Frohnmaier, Charles F, 1960, Ja 14,33:2
Frohwein, Ida H, 1956, My 29,27:3
Frolander, Frank C, 1966, My 15,88:2
Froley, Frank L, 1953, Ag 20,27:6
Frolich, Charles A Sr, 1947, Ap 1,27:3
Frolich, Finn H, 1947, S 7,60:6
Frolich, Louis H Sr, 1953, My 17,89:2
Frolich, William F Sr, 1949, O 20,29:2
Frolov, Vasily Mme, 1960, Mr 28,2:4
Frolov-Bagreyev, Anton, 1953, Ag 17,15:4
Frome, A Ransaville, 1955, N 11,25:4
Fromen, Agnes V E, 1956, O 22,29:2
Fromenson, Abraham H Mrs, 1953, Ja 27,25:5
Fromenson, Hillel C, 1941, Jl 23,19:3
Froment, Eugene M, 1954, S 4,11:6
Froment, Frank L, 1917, Ja 30,9:2
Froment, Lydia B Mrs, 1937, N 1,22:2
Fromentin, Charles, 1940, Jl 4,15:3
Fromer, Irving E, 1957, Jl 6,15:4
Fromer, Maurice M Mrs, 1953, N 20,23:1
Fromholz, A Stanley, 1958, Ap 14,25:2
Fromkes, Harry, 1958, F 12,19:1
Fromlet, Victor H, 1939, Ag 29,22:2
Fromm, A Milton Sr, 1958, Ap 30,33:1
Fromm, August H, 1944, My 11,19:4
Fromm, Carl, 1938, N 24,27:5
Fromm, Frederick Mrs, 1949, Jl 26,27:1
Fromm, Harry J, 1949, Ag 16,23:3
Fromm, John F, 1948, Ja 21,26:2
Fromm, Louis, 1944, Ap 13,19:5
Fromm, Nelson K, 1938, Je 23,21:3
Fromm, Otto C, 1942, F 11,21:5
Fromm, Solomon, 1952, S 24,33:4
Fromm, Walter F, 1956, Jl 30,21:6
Fromm-Reichmann, Frieda, 1957, Ap 30,29:2
Fromme, Arthur H, 1956, Ag 26,85:1
Fromme, Henry, 1909, Mr 14,11:5
Fromme, Isaac, 1917, Ag 31,7:4
Fromme, Sophie Mrs, 1940, D 14,17:2
Frommel, Oscar, 1917, My 25,11:4
Frommer, John W, 1962, O 26,31:4
Frommer, William C, 1961, F 26,93:1
Fromuth, Aug G, 1939, D 13,27:2
Fromuth, Charles H, 1937, Je 8,25:5
Fronczak, Francis E, 1955, D 28,23:3
Frondaie, Pierre, 1948, S 28,27:2
Fronefield, W Roger, 1943, D 28,17:3
Froning, Henry B, 1960, O 20,35:5
Fronk, William J, 1962, My 22,37:3
Frontera, Alexander E, 1966, My 14,31:2
Frontera, Stephen, 1948, My 12,28:2
Frontz, Clinton W, 1955, Ag 4,25:2
Frontz, Howard, 1942, O 31,15:7
Froomkin, Joseph, 1950, S 15,26:3
Frosch, Frank J, 1941, My 15,23:3
Frosch, John, 1953, F 21,13:3
Froschauer, Frederick H Mrs, 1949, O 8,13:3
Froscher, Andrew Mrs, 1957, Jl 3,23:2
Frosini, Pietro, 1951, O 2,28:2
Frossard, C A Gen (see also S 4), 1875, S 20,
Frossard, Ludovic O, 1946, F 12,28:1
Frost, A B, 1928, F 24,26:6
Frost, Aaron V, 1907, Mr 23,9:6
Frost, Agnes G Mrs, 1945, Ja 4,19:3
Frost, Albert D, 1953, S 17,29:2
Frost, Albert G, 1968, N 27,47:3
Frost, Alice B Mrs, 1938, D 16,25:5
Frost, Allen, 1946, Ja 11,21:4
Frost, Alvah G, 1954, Ja 24,85:2
Frost, Archie N, 1955, F 12,15:4
Frost, Arlie, 1947, O 28,26:3
Frost, Arthur L, 1942, D 4,25:4
Frost, Augusta S Mrs, 1938, Je 14,21:3
Frost, Austin L, 1958, Ag 19,27:3
Frost, Benjamin DuB Mrs, 1963, S 18,39:1
Frost, Betty A, 1951, D 30,24:2
Frost, C L, 1880, O 27,5:2
Frost, C Stanley Mrs, 1938, F 9,19:3
Frost, Calvin Mrs, 1907, Jl 20,7:6
Frost, Charles F, 1950, F 20,25:3
Frost, Charles S Mrs, 1949, Ag 24,25:2
Frost, Charles W, 1939, Ja 26,21:6; 1951, O 1
Frost, Clyde D, 1941, Jl 6,27:2

Frost, Conway A, 1941, My 12,17:4
Frost, Dan, 1943, My 29,13:1
Frost, David E, 1942, S 29,23:5
Frost, E B, 1935, My 15,21:3
Frost, Edward D Mrs, 1947, D 27,13:4
Frost, Edward I Mrs, 1950, My 22,21:3
Frost, Edward J, 1903, D 16,9:4; 1944, Je 7,19:3
Frost, Edward P, 1950, Jl 29,13:6
Frost, Edwin H, 1952, D 13,21:3
Frost, Edwin H Mrs, 1944, Mr 2,17:2
Frost, Elizabeth H (Mrs W B Blair), 1958, Ap 11, 25:3
Frost, Ellinwood A Mrs, 1943, F 28,49:1
Frost, Eugene, 1943, Ap 21,25:2
Frost, Frances, 1959, F 13,27:2
Frost, Frank A, 1947, S 2,21:4
Frost, Frank J, 1939, Ap 16,III,7:3
Frost, Frank L, 1946, Je 9,40:6
Frost, Frank R, 1944, Je 30,21:6
Frost, Fred, 1944, O 5,23:1
Frost, Fred W, 1946, My 16,21:5
Frost, Frederic W, 1938, O 29,19:3
Frost, Frederick C, 1940, O 14,19:4
Frost, Frederick G, 1966, Jl 31,72:4
Frost, Frederick G Mrs, 1946, O 16,28:2
Frost, Frederick L, 1937, My 18,23:5
Frost, G, 1880, Mr 4,5:6
Frost, G Frederick, 1964, Je 14,84:8
Frost, George A, 1907, N 14,9:5
Frost, George B, 1945, O 2,23:6
Frost, George Henry, 1917, Mr 16,11:5
Frost, George L, 1959, Mr 31,30:4
Frost, George W, 1939, Ag 3,19:6
Frost, Gilman D, 1942, O 9,21:2
Frost, Harold, 1954, O 18,25:2
Frost, Harry L, 1943, O 17,48:6
Frost, Harry T, 1943, D 30,18:2
Frost, Harry W, 1941, F 9,48:2
Frost, Henry, 1964, D 4,39:1
Frost, Henry G, 1951, My 8,31:4
Frost, Henry L, 1951, My 1,29:4
Frost, Henry T Mrs, 1944, Ap 15,11:1
Frost, Herbert H, 1956, S 12,37:4
Frost, Herbert S, 1940, F 22,23:3
Frost, Horace Scott Lt, 1920, Ja 28,11:4
Frost, Horatio T Mrs, 1942, Jl 6,15:4
Frost, Howard A, 1946, D 28,15:2
Frost, Jacob S, 1954, N 17,31:1
Frost, James Marion Dr, 1916, O 31,13:5
Frost, James N, 1949, O 29,15:2
Frost, Jane Mrs, 1908, Ag 15,7:4
Frost, John, 1937, Je 7,19:4
Frost, John W (Jan 19), 1963, Ap 1,35:6
Frost, Jonas M, 1945, F 12,20:3
Frost, Kendall, 1945, S 28,21:2
Frost, Leroy Mrs, 1944, F 9,19:5
Frost, Lorena M, 1952, Jl 30,23:2
Frost, Maxine D Mrs, 1962, Ja 25,31:4
Frost, Meigs O, 1950, Je 10,17:1
Frost, Miriam I, 1957, D 20,24:6
Frost, Owen C, 1967, N 9,61:5
Frost, P F Mrs, 1942, Ag 26,19:7
Frost, Paul R, 1957, Je 23,84:6
Frost, Phoebe W Mrs, 1942, Ja 2,34:3
Frost, Ralph A, 1938, S 23,27:4; 1949, O 4,27:3
Frost, Robert, 1961, Ap 14,29:1
Frost, Robert (trb, Ja 30,5:2; funl set; trb, Ja 31,7:1), 1963, Ja 30,1:2
Frost, Robert J, 1941, N 13,27:1
Frost, Robert Mrs, 1938, Mr 21,15:2
Frost, Rufus W, 1907, Ap 6,7:7
Frost, Russell, 1946, Mr 25,26:3
Frost, S D Rev, 1903, Ja 1,9:4
Frost, Samuel, 1955, Jl 26,25:2
Frost, Samuel H Mrs, 1920, Mr 8,9:6
Frost, Samuel K Mrs, 1943, Ja 3,42:2
Frost, Simeon Taylor Prof, 1923, N 29,21:3
Frost, Stanley, 1942, Je 15,19:6
Frost, Stoel M, 1948, S 8,29:2
Frost, Thomas G, 1948, F 14,13:1
Frost, Thomas G Mrs, 1943, D 10,27:4
Frost, Timothy P Rev, 1937, Jl 6,19:4
Frost, Vincent M, 1949, O 2,81:2
Frost, W E, 1884, Mr 28,3:3
Frost, W H, 1902, Mr 22,9:5
Frost, W L, 1943, O 15,19:5
Frost, W Louis, 1954, N 24,23:2
Frost, Wade H, 1938, My 2,17:3
Frost, Walter A, 1964, Mr 12,35:2
Frost, William A, 1949, O 30,86:2
Frost, William D, 1957, Ja 27,84:8
Frost, William G, 1938, S 13,23:1
Frost, William L Mrs, 1961, D 24,37:1
Frothingham, A L, 1907, Ja 14,7:6
Frothingham, Anna C Mrs, 1939, S 11,19:3
Frothingham, Arthur Lincoln, 1923, Jl 29,6:5
Frothingham, Channing, 1959, Ag 12,29:4
Frothingham, Charles F, 1963, Jl 24,31:6
Frothingham, Charles F Mrs, 1968, Ag 3,25:3
Frothingham, Charles Frederick, 1923, My 18,19:3
Frothingham, Cornelius, 1940, Ja 31,19:6
Frothingham, Edgar V, 1952, O 9,31:6
Frothingham, Edward, 1947, Mr 24,25:2
Frothingham, Edward H, 1950, My 3,29:4
Frothingham, Edward H Mrs, 1957, Mr 23,19:5
Frothingham, Elisabeth W, 1955, F 12,15:1
Frothingham, Francis E, 1954, F 14,92:1
Frothingham, George B, 1915, Ja 20,9:4
Frothingham, Jessie P, 1949, Ja 18,23:5
Frothingham, John B Brig-Gen, 1914, N 22,3:7
Frothingham, John Sewall, 1915, Je 20,15:6
Frothingham, L A, 1928, Ag 24,19:3
Frothingham, Lawrence P, 1953, Jl 7,27:5
Frothingham, Louis A Mrs, 1955, My 6,23:2
Frothingham, P R Rev Dr, 1926, N 29,19:3
Frothingham, Philip, 1918, S 21,9:5
Frothingham, R, 1880, Ja 30,5:4
Frothingham, Robert, 1937, D 9,25:1
Frothingham, Robert Mrs, 1955, Mr 27,87:1
Frothingham, Theodore, 1952, F 10,93:2
Frothingham, Theodore L Mrs, 1937, Ja 23,17:3
Frothingham, Walter D, 1940, Ja 7,48:2
Frothingham, Washington, 1914, O 21,11:6
Frothingham, William I, 1960, My 18,41:1
Froude, J A Prof, 1894, O 21,17:7
Froude, James A Mrs, 1874, F 15,1:7
Frowenfeld, Edward, 1917, Jl 22,15:3
Frowert, Charles G Dr, 1904, Ja 10,2:4
Fruauf, John, 1914, O 16,11:5
Frucht, Arthur, 1962, Ag 16,27:5
Fruchter, Jacob M, 1967, N 1,51:2
Fruchter, Max, 1962, O 22,29:3
Fruchter, Phil Mrs, 1951, Ja 5,21:3
Fruchthandler, Alex, 1967, Ag 4,29:2
Fruchtman, Edward J, 1957, Je 12,35:4
Frueauff, Charles A (will, My 12,29:7), 1950, Ap 24, 25:6
Frueauff, Charles A Mrs, 1944, Ag 16,19:2
Frueauff, Frank W, 1922, Ag 1,19:4; 1922, Ag 6,28:5
Frueauff, Harry D, 1959, Mr 17,33:1
Frueauff, John F Mrs, 1943, Ap 30,21:3
Frueh, Alfred, 1968, S 18,44:1
Fruehauf, Andrew F, 1965, D 6,37:2
Fruehauf, Harry R, 1962, My 2,37:2
Fruehauf, Harvey C, 1968, O 15,47:1
Fruehauf, Roy A, 1965, N 1,41:3
Fruehling, H (Apple John), 1878, S 8,12:3
Fruehwirth, A, 1933, F 10,18:1
Frug, Simon Samuel, 1916, O 6,11:4
Frugoni, Pietro, 1940, S 12,25:4
Fruh, George, 1903, Mr 12,7:4
Fruhauf, Henry, 1945, F 24,11:3
Fruin, Robert H, 1964, Ag 8,19:6
Fruit, John C, 1947, O 30,25:6
Fruithandler, Nancy, 1949, Ja 8,15:1
Fruitman, Sully, 1954, My 27,27:1
Fruits, George, 1876, Ag 10,2:3
Fruitstone, Mitchel, 1941, D 21,40:6
Fruling, Sidney M, 1963, D 23,25:2
Frum, Paul W, 1944, Ap 4,21:2
Frum, Sol, 1947, Jl 20,45:2
Frumberg, Abram M, 1943, S 8,23:5
Frumkes, Irving, 1951, N 26,25:5
Frumkin, Abram, 1942, D 3,25:3
Frumkin, Gad, 1960, Mr 11,25:3
Frumkin, Max, 1965, N 13,29:3
Frutchey, Arthur, 1955, My 26,31:3
Frutchey, George W, 1958, O 17,29:1
Frutchey, William J R, 1951, Je 9,19:2
Fry, Ambrose, 1941, O 23,23:4
Fry, Benjamin H Mrs, 1952, S 25,31:4
Fry, C Luther, 1938, Ap 13,25:3
Fry, Carl H, 1949, F 8,25:3
Fry, Cary H Gen, 1873, Mr 16,5:5
Fry, Charles, 1910, S 4,9:6
Fry, Charles B, 1956, S 8,17:2
Fry, Charles L Rev Dr, 1937, Mr 21,II,8:8
Fry, Charles W, 1937, D 8,25:1; 1960, N 26,21:5
Fry, Charlotte Mrs, 1956, Ap 1,89:1
Fry, Clements C, 1955, N 25,28:1
Fry, Earl C, 1946, My 13,21:4
Fry, Edward J, 1945, Ap 2,19:4
Fry, Edwin S, 1938, My 18,21:1
Fry, Edwin St J, 1958, Mr 15,17:2
Fry, Eileen H Mrs, 1948, My 13,25:4
Fry, F F, 1933, D 14,23:4
Fry, Frank R Dr, 1937, Ja 27,21:5
Fry, Frank S, 1946, My 2,21:5
Fry, Frank S Mrs, 1948, Mr 24,25:5
Fry, Franklin Clark Rev Dr (funl plans, Je 8,31:1), 1968, Je 7,36:4
Fry, Franklin F Mrs, 1961, F 3,25:5
Fry, George B Mrs, 1962, Jl 16,23:2
Fry, George G Comdr, 1937, Ap 2,23:6
Fry, George T, 1943, N 11,23:5
Fry, Grace A, 1948, My 23,70:2
Fry, H Edward, 1946, Jl 17,23:2
Fry, Harry E, 1962, Ja 31,31:4
Fry, Harry M, 1941, My 1,23:4
Fry, Harry S, 1949, My 20,27:4
Fry, Henry J Mrs, 1966, Mr 30,45:4
Fry, Henry S, 1946, S 8,44:4
Fry, Herman D, 1967, Ja 14,31:5
Fry, Horace G, 1958, My 29,27:1
Fry, Horace P, 1950, Ap 25,31:2
Fry, Howard J, 1921, Ap 28,13:3
Fry, Howard M, 1943, O 20,21:2
Fry, Isabelle Mrs, 1952, Ap 2,33:2
Fry, J B Gen, 1894, Jl 12,5:7
Fry, J Gen, 1881, F 5,2:6
Fry, Jacob Rev Dr, 1920, F 20,15:4
Fry, John F, 1946, F 25,25:4
Fry, John Heming Mrs, 1921, S 9,15:4
Fry, John L, 1937, My 7,30:2
Fry, Joseph D, 1948, Ja 2,23:2
Fry, Joseph Storrs, 1913, Jl 8,7:6
Fry, Lawford H, 1948, Jl 12,19:3
Fry, Lewis Cass, 1907, Ag 20,7:5
Fry, Louis, 1940, Mr 24,31:2
Fry, Margery, 1958, Ap 22,33:3
Fry, Mary G, 1947, O 31,33:4
Fry, Nelson B, 1965, F 22,21:2
Fry, Nicholas L, 1938, F 10,21:3
Fry, Paul B, 1955, Ap 13,29:5
Fry, Royce D, 1943, F 23,21:4
Fry, Samuel C, 1941, Ap 29,19:1
Fry, Sydney W, 1913, Ap 20,IV,7:5
Fry, T Dr, 1883, Ag 5,7:6
Fry, T W, 1947, Je 4,27:2
Fry, Thomas C, 1946, Ag 27,27:2; 1956, My 20,86:5
Fry, Varian M, 1967, S 14,47:1
Fry, Vaughn W, 1961, Mr 13,29:5
Fry, W H Col, 1875, Jl 5,4:6
Fry, W Raymond, 1944, N 25,13:5
Fry, W W, 1936, Jl 28,19:1
Fry, Wallace W, 1953, N 25,23:4
Fry, Wilfred Mrs, 1945, D 11,25:5
Fry, Willard C, 1944, D 15,19:5
Fry, William H Dr, 1953, F 14,17:4
Fry, William H Mrs, 1949, F 17,23:4
Fry, William Henry, 1865, Ja 19,4:5
Fry, William J Dr, 1968, Jl 24,50:1
Fry, William L, 1947, N 11,27:4
Fry, William M, 1950, Jl 27,25:6
Fry, William R Jr, 1962, O 22,29:5
Fry, William Sir, 1939, Ag 26,15:6
Fryberg, Francis L, 1964, D 18,33:5
Fryberg, Mart, 1952, O 24,23:3
Fryburg, Charles H, 1956, Ag 2,25:4
Fryburg, L Gertrude, 1948, Je 4,23:4
Frydan, Oscar Mrs, 1949, Je 13,19:3
Fryde, Matthew M, 1965, Mr 17,45:3
Frye, Alburney W, 1950, Ja 23,23:3
Frye, Augusta Mrs, 1937, O 21,8:5
Frye, Ben Mrs, 1961, Jl 28,21:3
Frye, Calvin A, 1917, Ap 25,11:6
Frye, Carl R, 1957, Je 6,31:2
Frye, Charles H, 1940, My 2,23:1
Frye, Dwight, 1943, N 12,22:3
Frye, Edward A, 1937, N 17,23:3
Frye, Ellis B, 1943, D 1,21:4
Frye, Howard, 1967, D 2,39:3
Frye, Howard O, 1963, Je 12,43:2
Frye, J W, 1876, F 22,5:6
Frye, Jack, 1959, F 4,1:8
Frye, John H, 1952, Ap 13,77:1
Frye, John I, 1915, Ap 5,11:4
Frye, Kathryn B, 1952, F 4,17:3
Frye, L Arnold, 1962, O 18,39:2
Frye, Newton P, 1957, My 1,37:5
Frye, Ralph B, 1955, Ag 14,80:2
Frye, Robert P, 1944, D 14,23:4
Frye, Russell H, 1942, My 13,19:4
Frye, William, 1952, Ap 24,32:3
Frye, William (cor, Ap 1,17:5), 1961, Mr 31,27:1
Frye, William Pierce (funl), 1911, Ag 12,9:6
Fryer, Charles E Sir, 1920, N 20,15:4
Fryer, Charles V, 1942, F 23,21:3
Fryer, Douglas H, 1960, D 25,43:1
Fryer, Emily Mrs, 1947, S 27,15:2
Fryer, Eugenie M, 1961, S 20,29:5
Fryer, Gertrude F, 1940, F 7,21:4
Fryer, J Walter, 1942, Mr 10,19:4
Fryer, Julius Mrs, 1952, S 7,87:1
Fryer, Livingston, 1960, Je 26,73:1
Fryer, Robert Livingston, 1915, O 21,11:5
Fryer, Thomas H, 1940, N 7,25:3
Fryer, William, 1960, Ag 30,29:2
Fryer, William J, 1907, Je 5,7:6
Frykman, Andrew T, 1943, N 9,21:4
Fryling, Henry J, 1951, Ag 29,25:3
Frystock, Joseph, 1953, Mr 17,35:6
Fryth, Walter R, 1965, F 9,37:2
Fteley, Alphonse, 1903, Je 13,3:2
Fu Su-nien, 1950, D 21,29:5
Fuad, King of Egypt, 1936, Ap 29,8:2
Fubini, Gino G, 1965, My 8,31:5
Fubini, Guido, 1943, Je 10,21:1
Fubry, William J, 1964, D 12,31:1
Fuch, Adolph, 1950, Ag 26,13:1
Fuch, Frederick Mrs, 1951, O 12,27:5
Fuchs, Alma, 1950, Je 15,31:3
Fuchs, Charles, 1949, Jl 15,21:7
Fuchs, Charles F, 1948, F 24,25:4
Fuchs, Clarence, 1945, Je 9,13:4
Fuchs, E, 1929, Ja 14,1:4
Fuchs, Eduard, 1940, F 7,21:1
Fuchs, Edward A H, 1956, Mr 9,23:3
Fuchs, Edward Mrs, 1953, Je 8,22:5

Fuchs, Emil E, 1961, D 6,47:4
Fuchs, Ephraim, 1958, Ja 4,15:4
Fuchs, Francis J, 1967, S 15,44:7
Fuchs, Frank E, 1964, Ap 18,29:2
Fuchs, Frederick, 1945, My 1,23:1
Fuchs, Henry, 1956, Ap 12,31:4
Fuchs, Herman, 1958, Je 6,23:1
Fuchs, Herman Mrs, 1943, Ja 2,11:6
Fuchs, Hermann, 1917, Je 22,13:6
Fuchs, Hugo, 1946, S 9,9:1
Fuchs, J Hunter, 1957, Je 20,29:4
Fuchs, Jacob, 1940, Ap 25,23:2
Fuchs, Julius, 1953, Ag 17,15:2
Fuchs, Louis, 1960, Ag 3,29:6
Fuchs, Max, 1958, Ja 16,30:1
Fuchs, Max Mrs, 1964, Ja 5,92:6
Fuchs, Morris, 1967, Mr 9,39:3
Fuchs, Nathaniel, 1956, Ja 27,23:5
Fuchs, Nikola J, 1960, N 10,47:4
Fuchs, Otto P, 1965, My 16,87:5
Fuchs, Richard, 1952, My 31,14:7
Fuchs, Sigmund W, 1942, O 21,21:4
Fuchs, Solomon, 1956, F 13,27:5
Fuchs, Theodor, 1956, Je 6,33:3
Fuchs, William W, 1961, Je 2,32:2
Fuchs-Robetin, Herbert von Mrs, 1964, Je 2,37:1
Fucillo, Francis E, 1953, D 28,21:2
Fucini, Renato, 1921, F 27,22:4
Fuden, John J, 1951, Ag 28,23:2
Fudge, H Foster, 1959, Je 11,33:4
Fudge, R B, 1951, F 7,29:2
Fudge, Thomas, 1951, Jl 11,23:3
Fudim, Philip Mrs, 1961, Jl 23,68:1
Fueermann, Emanuel, 1942, My 26,21:4
Fuentes, Alberto, 1954, My 4,29:2
Fuerbringer, Ludwig E, 1947, My 7,31:1
Fuermann, Henry, 1949, Ap 7,29:4
Fuerst, Gene J Mrs, 1950, Ag 26,13:5
Fuerst, John A, 1949, My 21,13:6
Fuerst, Morton S, 1956, D 12,39:5
Fuerst, William F Mrs (will), 1940, Je 28,23:6
Fuerstenberg, C, 1933, F 11,15:3
Fuerstman, H Louis Dr, 1937, F 13,13:1
Fuerstman, Joseph A, 1956, Jl 19,27:4
Fuerth, Gustave J, 1946, F 2,13:5
Fuertinger, Edwin H, 1958, N 16,88:5
Fueslein, Leonie, 1967, Je 3,31:3
Fuess, Billings S Sr, 1960, F 19,27:3
Fuess, Charles J, 1942, My 13,19:2
Fuess, Claude M, 1963, S 11,43:5
Fuess, Claude M Mrs, 1943, Jl 27,17:5; 1956, N 8,39:3
Fuess, Edward, 1953, D 9,11:1
Fuess, Frederick F, 1952, S 18,29:4
Fuess, Frederick W Jr, 1949, F 17,23:3
Fuess, Harold L, 1952, D 14,90:5
Fuess, Louis H, 1942, N 28,13:6
Fuessenich, Frederick F Ex-Sen, 1925, Je 29,13:6
Fuessle, Newton Augustus, 1924, Mr 20,19:6
Fueter, Rudolf, 1950, Ag 11,19:4
Fugazy, Humbert, 1964, Ap 8,43:5
Fugazy, Italo A, 1957, Mr 3,85:2
Fugisawa, Ikunosuke, 1940, Ap 4,23:3
Fugua, H L, 1926, O 12,27:4
Fuguet, Stephen, 1937, Mr 13,19:1
Fuhlenborf, Mathilde (died intestate, O 8,27:3), 1940, S 28,19:3
Fuhlendorf, Edward W, 1943, Je 20,34:7
Fuhr, L Frank, 1945, N 24,19:6
Fuhr, Lewis, 1955, Je 26,76:5
Fuhrer, Mansfred M, 1950, D 6,33:2
Fuhrer, Theodore R, 1956, S 6,25:1
Fuhrman, Abe, 1949, D 17,17:4
Fuhrman, Alex S, 1951, Jl 17,27:3
Fuhrman, Charles F, 1937, F 26,22:1
Fuhrman, George, 1953, S 15,31:5
Fuhrman, Herman, 1955, Ja 13,27:6
Fuhrman, Joseph H, 1949, Ap 15,23:3; 1949, Ap 18, 25:1
Fuhrman, Nathan, 1949, S 29,29:1
Fuhrmann, Barclay S, 1953, Ja 6,29:5
Fuhrmann, Edward, 1939, Ap 29,17:4
Fuhrmann, Frank J, 1949, Ap 16,15:4
Fuhrmann, James P Mrs, 1960, F 14,84:6
Fuhrmann, Joseph W, 1951, D 28,21:4
Fuhrmans, Ernst, 1956, D 2,86:2
Fuji-Ko, Mrs, 1912, D 8,17:5
Fujii, Otowo, 1945, My 25,19:1
Fujikake, Seiya, 1958, Ag 6,25:2
Fujita, Eisuke, 1940, Mr 11,15:5
Fujita, Heitaro, 1940, F 24,13:6
Fujita, Jun, 1963, Jl 13,17:6
Fukatko, Jaroslav, 1956, Jl 14,15:6
Fukuda, Hidesuke, 1955, Je 23,29:4
Fukushima, Gen, 1919, F 21,13:5
Fukushima, Otto, 1952, My 31,17:4
Fulbright, Jack, 1968, Mr 14,43:1
Fulbright, James F, 1948, Ap 7,25:3
Fulbright, Roberta W, 1953, Ja 12,27:3
Fulbright, Rufus C, 1940, Mr 31,45:3
Fulcher, Cornelia M Mrs, 1916, D 24,15:1
Fulcher, William G, 1963, D 31,19:4
Fulchiron, Vincent, 1947, O 7,27:1
Fulco, John, 1958, Mr 13,29:2
Fuld, Annie S Mrs, 1939, Ja 18,19:4
Fuld, Bernhard, 1918, Ja 17,13:2
Fuld, Emanuel I, 1938, Ag 17,19:5
Fuld, F, 1929, Ja 21,21:4
Fuld, Felix Mrs (will, Jl 27,15:3), 1944, Jl 19,19:1
Fuld, Franklin B, 1940, N 30,17:5
Fuld, Fritz von Friedlander, 1917, Jl 18,9:5
Fuld, Gus, 1952, N 19,29:2
Fuld, Herman, 1951, My 2,31:5
Fuld, Isaac, 1939, N 19,38:6
Fuld, J Edward Jr, 1959, Ag 25,31:4
Fuld, Joseph E, 1937, Ja 4,29:1
Fuld, Leonhard F, 1965, S 1,37:1
Fuld, Moe I Mrs, 1957, Ja 5,17:5
Fulda, Clemens F Dr, 1914, F 28,9:4
Fulda, Elisabeth Rungius, 1968, Ja 25,37:3
Fulda, Ludwig, 1939, Ap 18,23:3
Fuldner, Louis Mrs, 1948, N 14,76:1
Fuleihan, Nasri, 1959, Jl 30,27:3
Fulford, Albert E, 1957, Je 17,23:4
Fulford, Natalie, 1954, O 21,27:2
Fulforth, Charles L, 1941, F 27,19:5
Fulgora, Robert, 1947, D 7,76:3
Fulham, Nicholas L, 1942, N 27,23:5
Fulkerson, E Robert, 1940, My 30,17:3
Fulkerson, Elmer C, 1958, N 18,37:3
Fulkerson, Lynn L, 1953, D 31,19:6
Fulkerson, Roe, 1949, Ja 12,27:6
Fulkerson, William N Sr, 1953, Mr 13,27:2
Fulks, Lewis J (V Arden), 1962, Ag 1,31:1
Fullagar, William W, 1942, Jl 12,35:2
Fullam, Dennis F, 1950, Jl 16,68:2
Fullam, Frank L, 1951, Ag 2,21:1
Fullam, James E, 1951, F 24,13:4
Fullam, Joseph P, 1952, D 4,35:2
Fullam, Paul, 1955, Je 23,29:2
Fullam, W F Adm, 1926, S 24,23:5
Fullard-Leo, Leslie, 1950, F 22,29:5
Fullarton, Alan R, 1941, My 21,23:6
Fulle, Charles A, 1944, Ap 10,19:3
Fulle, Fred A, 1964, Ja 24,24:4
Fulle, R Milton, 1943, N 5,19:4
Fullen, Walter, 1944, Je 14,19:4
Fuller, Ada D, 1937, Mr 14,II,8:6
Fuller, Albert C, 1948, Ap 6,23:2
Fuller, Alfred H (funl plans, My 12,35:1), 1959, My 10,52:3
Fuller, Alfred H Mrs (funl plans, My 12,35:1), 1959, My 10,52:3
Fuller, Alfred J, 1939, My 6,17:1
Fuller, Alfred M Mrs, 1948, Jl 4,27:1
Fuller, Alvan T (funl, My 4,89:1), 1958, My 1,31:2
Fuller, Alvan T Mrs, 1959, Ag 5,27:1
Fuller, Anna, 1916, Jl 21,9:8
Fuller, Annie K, 1950, Ja 4,35:1
Fuller, Arthur D, 1966, D 11,89:1
Fuller, Arthur L, 1944, D 8,21:3
Fuller, Arthur W, 1949, Jl 16,13:2
Fuller, Ben H Maj Gen, 1937, Je 9,25:4
Fuller, Benjamin, 1952, Mr 11,27:2
Fuller, Benjamin D Mrs, 1947, Jl 8,23:5
Fuller, Bert S, 1962, My 23,45:4
Fuller, Bradley, 1939, S 21,23:5
Fuller, Burdett D, 1949, D 27,23:1
Fuller, Burnett, 1944, Jl 13,17:6
Fuller, C E US Repr, 1926, Je 26,15:4
Fuller, C N Mrs, 1903, Ja 30,16:2
Fuller, Charles, 1959, S 17,39:2
Fuller, Charles E Col, 1907, O 5,11:6
Fuller, Charles E Rev, 1968, Mr 21,47:3
Fuller, Charles F, 1960, Ja 31,92:3
Fuller, Charles H (por), 1938, D 6,23:1
Fuller, Charles L, 1958, Ag 23,15:4
Fuller, Charles L Mrs, 1960, Ja 14,33:4
Fuller, Charles P G, 1956, My 17,31:4
Fuller, Charles S, 1937, D 23,21:5
Fuller, Clara C, 1940, N 9,17:5
Fuller, Clarence W, 1961, F 19,86:6
Fuller, Claude E, 1957, D 8,87:3
Fuller, Clement A, 1962, Ap 3,39:1
Fuller, Clifford B, 1945, Ja 29,13:1
Fuller, Dean M, 1949, N 24,31:4
Fuller, Dwight B, 1948, My 19,27:2
Fuller, Earl B, 1947, Ag 20,21:1
Fuller, Earl W, 1951, My 18,27:5
Fuller, Edward, 1938, Ap 30,15:4; 1958, Mr 15,17:2
Fuller, Edward C, 1955, Ja 16,92:7
Fuller, Edward Jr, 1951, My 16,35:3
Fuller, Edward L, 1909, Ja 30,9:5
Fuller, Edward M Mrs, 1958, Mr 29,27:1; 1959, D 29, 25:4
Fuller, Edward R, 1964, Mr 5,33:2
Fuller, Edward Y, 1948, Mr 4,25:4
Fuller, Ellis A, 1950, O 30,27:3
Fuller, Elmer D, 1950, Ja 19,27:3
Fuller, Emeline Mrs, 1903, Ag 3,7:6
Fuller, Ernest M, 1937, Je 14,23:4
Fuller, Ernest S, 1946, Ag 1,23:4
Fuller, Ethel R Mrs, 1965, D 14,39:1
Fuller, Eugene F Mrs, 1951, N 25,86:1
Fuller, Ezra B Col, 1925, S 19,15:5
Fuller, Felix D Jr, 1939, F 18,15:4
Fuller, Floyd C, 1937, Mr 8,II,9:2
Fuller, Frances Dr, 1907, Mr 31,9:7
Fuller, Frank C, 1956, My 8,33:3
Fuller, Frank H, 1968, F 16,37:1
Fuller, Frank L, 1952, S 11,31:2
Fuller, Frank W, 1949, My 31,23:4
Fuller, Frederic, 1940, Jl 30,19:6
Fuller, Frederic W, 1940, Ap 20,17:4
Fuller, Frederick L, 1943, Ap 30,21:3
Fuller, Frederick L Mrs, 1937, Je 27,II,7:2
Fuller, Frederick P, 1952, F 22,21:2
Fuller, Frederick T, 1943, My 1,15:5
Fuller, Frederick W, 1947, Mr 26,25:1
Fuller, G, 1884, Mr 22,5:5
Fuller, G A, 1883, Ja 19,5:2; 1931, S 6,20:2
Fuller, G W, 1934, Je 16,15:1
Fuller, George, 1942, D 23,19:2
Fuller, George A Mrs, 1904, Ja 20,2:3
Fuller, George B, 1942, Je 11,23:6
Fuller, George D, 1961, N 23,31:5
Fuller, George E, 1946, Ja 23,27:4
Fuller, George F, 1962, N 11,89:1
Fuller, George L, 1944, Je 10,15:3
Fuller, George S Mrs, 1951, D 28,21:3
Fuller, George V, 1960, O 10,31:4
Fuller, George W, 1939, Mr 18,17:3; 1940, Jl 23,1 1940, O 26,15:2; 1949, F 24,23:4
Fuller, George W Mrs, 1952, Ag 28,23:1
Fuller, George Warren Mrs, 1907, Je 22,7:4
Fuller, Grace M, 1941, D 9,31:4
Fuller, Guerden W Mrs, 1954, N 2,27:4
Fuller, H A, 1931, D 12,19:1
Fuller, H Douglas Mrs, 1946, Je 7,19:3
Fuller, H H, 1954, Ag 10,19:5
Fuller, H Harrison, 1961, Ap 23,86:7
Fuller, Harold, 1954, Mr 18,31:3
Fuller, Harold D, 1957, My 3,27:4
Fuller, Harrison, 1958, S 24,27:2
Fuller, Harvey L, 1959, Je 10,37:4
Fuller, Henry C, 1921, Mr 19,11:6
Fuller, Henry Dean, 1909, Ag 24,9:6
Fuller, Henry J, 1956, Ap 23,27:1
Fuller, Henry M, 1955, S 29,33:5; 1962, Jl 8,18:
Fuller, Henry W, 1911, O 13,11:5
Fuller, Herbert H, 1953, O 1,29:3
Fuller, Homer Taylor, 1908, Ag 16,7:6
Fuller, Horace W, 1925, Mr 24,23:2
Fuller, Howard M, 1944, Ap 1,13:5
Fuller, Hugh N, 1943, D 30,17:4
Fuller, Isabelle P Mrs, 1940, Ag 1,21:3
Fuller, J A, 1903, Mr 22,7:5
Fuller, J Brayton, 1951, Je 30,15:4
Fuller, J E, 1939, Jl 30,29:3
Fuller, J M, 1885, My 26,5:4
Fuller, James A, 1948, F 14,13:4
Fuller, James C, 1940, N 18,19:4
Fuller, James E, 1957, Ja 26,19:1
Fuller, James H, 1907, Ja 16,7:4; 1940, Je 15,1 1968, Ag 3,25:3
Fuller, Jesse, 1921, Ja 27,13:4
Fuller, John F C, 1966, F 11,33:2
Fuller, John T, 1939, My 19,21:1
Fuller, Joseph H Mrs, 1947, Mr 19,25:5
Fuller, L, 1928, Ja 3,25:3
Fuller, Lawrence C, 1952, Jl 29,21:4
Fuller, Lawson N, 1904, Jl 15,7:6
Fuller, Leigh A Mrs, 1937, O 3,II,9:2
Fuller, Leo, 1948, S 21,27:1
Fuller, Leo C Mrs, 1949, D 1,64:1
Fuller, Leon A, 1947, Ja 31,23:4
Fuller, Leonore Byrnes Mrs, 1947, F 14,22:3
Fuller, Leslie, 1948, Ap 25,68:3
Fuller, Levi H, 1939, N 22,21:3
Fuller, Lewis C, 1952, Je 21,15:5
Fuller, Linus E, 1910, N 15,11:4
Fuller, Louis M, 1952, Ag 3,61:3
Fuller, Louis W, 1942, Ag 14,17:2
Fuller, Lucian D, 1941, Je 18,21:4
Fuller, Lucius P, 1954, Ag 31,21:3
Fuller, Luther H, 1938, Ja 16,II,9:1
Fuller, M W Mrs Chief Justice, 1904, Ag 19,
Fuller, Mary C Mrs, 1937, Je 3,25:4
Fuller, Mary V Mrs, 1942, F 27,17:5
Fuller, Mary W, 1943, Jl 8,19:6
Fuller, Max Mrs, 1954, Je 20,84:6
Fuller, Melville, 1924, Je 5,21:5
Fuller, Melville W Chief-Justice (funl, Jl 9,7: 1910, Jl 8,7:5
Fuller, Merton L Mrs, 1941, S 16,23:6
Fuller, Milton A, 1965, Mr 26,35:3
Fuller, Myron, 1949, S 2,17:5
Fuller, Nathan E, 1941, Ja 23,21:2
Fuller, Norman S, 1959, Jl 12,72:8
Fuller, Oliver C, 1942, Ag 19,19:3
Fuller, Patrick N, 1965, Jl 10,25:4
Fuller, Paul Jr, 1948, My 13,25:5
Fuller, Paul M, 1951, Mr 30,23:3
Fuller, Pheobe S Mrs, 1940, S 1,20:7
Fuller, R, 1876, O 23,1:5
Fuller, R O, 1903, Mr 10,9:6
Fuller, Ralph B, 1963, Ag 17,19:5
Fuller, Rathbun, 1937, D 17,32:2
Fuller, Ray W, 1949, Ja 17,19:5
Fuller, Raymond, 1914, Jl 23,9:2

Fuller, Raymond G, 1960, Je 17,32:1
Fuller, Raymond G Mrs (G Fox), 1959, O 10,21:6
Fuller, Raymond T, 1960, Mr 16,37:5
Fuller, Rev Dr (mem ser), 1876, N 24,8:5
Fuller, Richard E, 1964, Ja 9,31:4
Fuller, Robert M Dr, 1919, D 29,9:3
Fuller, Robert O, 1945, O 12,23:2
Fuller, Robert W, 1953, Mr 31,31:2
Fuller, Rudolph C, 1909, Je 23,7:4
Fuller, Samuel L, 1963, N 20,40:1
Fuller, Samuel R Jr, 1966, F 11,33:2
Fuller, Sarah L Mrs, 1924, Mr 30,X,8:2
Fuller, Sidney Thomas, 1912, Je 3,9:6
Fuller, Stuart J, 1941, F 4,21:3
Fuller, T S, 1903, Je 2,9:7
Fuller, Thomas S, 1940, Mr 6,23:2
Fuller, Vincent J, 1945, Jl 24,23:6
Fuller, Vincent S, 1955, F 15,27:2
Fuller, W Brock, 1950, S 20,31:3
Fuller, W E, 1950, F 23,27:4
Fuller, W H, 1878, Ja 8,8:1; 1902, N 27,5:5
Fuller, Warner, 1957, Je 12,35:4
Fuller, Warren E, 1940, My 24,19:3
Fuller, Wesley, 1958, S 14,84:1
Fuller, Wheeler B, 1943, Ag 7,11:6
Fuller, Will S, 1939, N 10,23:2
Fuller, William, 1958, Je 17,29:3
Fuller, William A M, 1952, F 2,13:6
Fuller, William E, 1955, Ag 27,8:6
Fuller, William F, 1948, F 20,27:3
Fuller, William Frank, 1907, F 28,9:6
Fuller, William J, 1944, F 29,17:3; 1951, S 11,29:2
Fuller, William O, 1941, S 22,15:2
Fuller, William O Mrs, 1948, S 26,77:1
Fuller, William S Mrs, 1951, O 25,29:3
Fullerton, A, 1934, My 23,20:2
Fullerton, Arthur, 1948, Ap 1,26:3
Fullerton, C N, 1958, Mr 8,17:6
Fullerton, Charles, 1940, Mr 12,23:5
Fullerton, Charles A, 1945, D 15,17:1
Fullerton, Charles B, 1963, Je 18,37:3
Fullerton, Charles P, 1938, O 6,23:6
Fullerton, D P, 1943, Mr 9,23:2
Fullerton, David, 1947, My 7,27:3
Fullerton, Edward B, 1942, N 1,52:3
Fullerton, Edward D, 1940, Jl 3,17:4
Fullerton, Georgiana Lady, 1885, Ja 21,5:5
Fullerton, Harold O, 1965, Ag 8,65:1
Fullerton, Henry S, 1947, F 21,20:2
Fullerton, Hugh Jr Mrs, 1960, Ap 25,29:4
Fullerton, Hugh S Jr, 1965, S 17,6:1
Fullerton, Hugh S Sr, 1945, D 28,15:1; 1946, Ja 1,27:4
Fullerton, James, 1948, Ag 18,25:3
Fullerton, James Mrs, 1942, O 14,25:2
Fullerton, Martin A, 1948, Mr 4,25:3
Fullerton, Max, 1967, My 6,31:3
Fullerton, Robert, 1945, Ag 25,11:4
Fullerton, Robert M, 1953, D 28,22:3
Fullerton, Robert W, 1950, O 12,31:3
Fullerton, S W Judge, 1902, Ap 5,9:5
Fullerton, Samuel H, 1939, S 19,25:3
Fullerton, William, 1945, Je 24,22:5
Fullerton, William B, 1956, N 29,35:4
Fullerton, William Mrs, 1903, Jl 9,7:6
…lling, Ellis Mrs, 1956, Jl 9,23:3
…llingim, W A Mrs, 1964, Ap 30,35:1
…lis, Charles P, 1946, Mr 29,23:2
…lman, James M G, 1950, S 26,31:5
…llom, Sylvester E, 1951, S 27,31:3
…llum, Matthew J, 1924, Ja 23,17:4
…man, Marian L, 1945, D 27,19:5
…mer, Charley, 1940, F 17,13:5
…mer, Chesta H Mrs, 1957, S 12,31:2
…mer, George H, 1937, D 17,32:2
…mer, George W, 1920, N 19,15:4
…mer, Hampton P, 1944, O 20,19:1
…mer, John C, 1943, S 10,23:3
…mer, Joseph H, 1944, My 16,21:2
…ner, George M, 1948, Mr 20,13:5
…rath, Logan Mrs, 1952, Je 19,27:2
…ton, A C, 1903, O 18,7:6
…ton, Albert C, 1956, F 14,29:2
…ton, Albert W, 1938, Mr 20,II,9:2
…ton, Arch J Jr, 1948, Jl 26,17:3
…ton, Arthur W, 1942, S 18,21:3
…ton, Asa Rev Dr, 1912, Ag 30,9:6
…on, C C, 1883, Je 8,5:2
…on, Chandos, 1904, Ja 12,7:5
…on, Charles H, 1944, Ap 10,19:2
…on, Charles W, 1918, Ja 28,13:5
…on, Chester A, 1951, Ag 18,11:5; 1953, Jl 10,19:2
…on, E, 1878, My 14,5:3
…on, Earl D, 1951, N 2,24:3
…on, Earl D Mrs, 1950, O 27,29:4
…on, Elizabeth (will), 1939, Jl 25,3:6
…on, Florence W, 1957, Mr 19,37:4
…on, Frank, 1954, N 6,17:1
…on, Frank D, 1940, Ap 16,23:5
…n, Frank T, 1961, Ap 12,41:3
…n, Fred A, 1958, Ap 9,33:2
…n, George E, 1953, My 2,15:4
…n, George S, 1937, Ja 5,23:5
…n, Howard C, 1951, Ja 22,17:2

Fulton, Hugh, 1962, O 24,28:1
Fulton, Hugh R, 1940, Ja 5,20:4
Fulton, J D Rev Dr, 1901, Ap 17,9:5
Fulton, J H, 1927, S 26,21:3
Fulton, J T, 1879, S 26,5:2
Fulton, James, 1865, D 15,5:2; 1866, Ja 8,2:4
Fulton, James A, 1950, S 23,17:5
Fulton, James C, 1955, Jl 4,11:2
Fulton, James C Mrs, 1955, F 27,87:2
Fulton, John, 1912, N 3,II,17:4; 1938, Je 30,23:2
Fulton, John A, 1939, O 11,27:4
Fulton, John F, 1960, My 30,17:1
Fulton, John Rev, 1907, Ap 25,9:5
Fulton, Justin D Mrs, 1951, Ja 19,25:4
Fulton, Kerwin H, 1955, D 12,31:2
Fulton, Margaret C Mrs, 1940, O 29,25:6
Fulton, Maude, 1950, N 11,15:1
Fulton, Otho (por), 1938, Mr 2,19:3
Fulton, R Arthur, 1962, Jl 24,39:1
Fulton, Ralph W, 1967, N 21,48:1
Fulton, Robert C Jr, 1960, Ag 31,29:4
Fulton, Robert E, 1938, My 1,II,6:7
Fulton, Robert L, 1945, Jl 7,13:4
Fulton, Robert S, 1954, N 6,17:5
Fulton, Roberta, 1947, Ja 1,33:2
Fulton, Samuel, 1948, S 16,29:3
Fulton, Samuel A, 1954, Ja 5,27:5
Fulton, Samuel C, 1951, F 28,27:1
Fulton, Samuel T, 1919, Mr 29,13:2
Fulton, Thomas, 1947, Ja 20,25:3
Fulton, Thomas Alexander, 1912, Jl 12,9:4
Fulton, Weston M, 1946, My 17,22:3
Fulton, Will H, 1953, O 29,31:5
Fulton, William, 1941, My 14,21:4; 1952, Ag 15,15:3; 1955, Mr 5,17:5
Fulton, William J, 1956, Ap 24,32:1; 1961, Mr 25,25:3
Fulton, William J Mrs, 1947, My 19,21:2; 1961, Ja 18, 33:4
Fulton, William K, 1951, Ja 28,76:2
Fulton, William S, 1964, N 26,33:3
Fulton-Husband, Robert O, 1955, Ap 15,23:2
Fults, Burton J, 1947, Je 8,60:6
Fultz, David L, 1959, N 1,86:4
Fulweiler, John E, 1960, D 23,19:1
Fulweiler, John W Mrs (K C Jones), 1959, Je 6,21:4
Fumasoni Biondi, Leone Count, 1949, Jl 2,15:7
Fumasoni-Biondi, Pietro, 1960, Jl 13,35:4
Fumoleau, Blanche (G Morlay), 1964, Jl 5,43:1
Funaro, Bruno, 1957, Ag 14,25:3
Funaro, Roberto, 1955, Mr 13,86:5
Funaroff, Solomon, 1942, O 31,15:6
Funcannon, Charles, 1950, Je 25,70:1
Funch, Christian F, 1879, D 9,5:3
Funchal, Countess of (M S R de Souza Coutinho), 1961, My 8,35:6
Funck, Emma M Mrs (will), 1940, Ap 2,9:2
Funck-Brentano, Frantz, 1947, Je 14,15:1
Funcke, Walter A, 1958, D 7,88:1
Fundenberg, Walter H Dr, 1937, N 9,23:4
Fung, Paul, 1944, O 17,23:2
Funiack, Mrs, 1912, Ag 31,7:6
Funk, A Col, 1883, O 23,2:6
Funk, Aaron J, 1966, D 11,89:1
Funk, Alphonsus, 1953, Ag 25,21:4
Funk, Antoinette Mrs, 1942, Mr 29,45:2
Funk, August J, 1952, Ja 27,76:6
Funk, Benjamin F, 1914, F 3,11:5
Funk, Carl E, 1961, Je 6,37:1
Funk, Casimir, 1967, N 21,1:8
Funk, Charles E, 1957, Ap 20,17:3
Funk, Charles W, 1937, My 22,15:2
Funk, Clarence S Mrs, 1941, My 15,23:4
Funk, Cynthia E Mrs, 1939, N 20,19:3
Funk, Eugene D Sr, 1944, N 30,23:6
Funk, Frank H, 1940, N 26,23:1
Funk, Frank J, 1958, Ja 6,39:1
Funk, Henry H, 1956, Ja 12,27:3
Funk, Issac K Dr (funl, Ap 9,11:4), 1912, Ap 5,13:3
Funk, J Arthur, 1939, Mr 8,21:5
Funk, J D, 1962, Ap 1,86:8
Funk, John, 1964, Ja 23,31:4
Funk, Joseph, 1942, Jl 11,13:4; 1966, N 27,86:8
Funk, Joseph J, 1942, O 27,26:2
Funk, Oscar F, 1954, N 1,27:3
Funk, Roscoe C, 1950, Ag 6,73:2
Funk, Ross W, 1946, F 19,25:3
Funk, Walter E, 1948, My 12,27:3
Funk, Walther, 1960, Je 4,23:1
Funk, Wilfred J, 1965, Je 2,42:1
Funke, A Edward, 1945, Jl 21,11:5
Funke, Balthaser J, 1946, N 6,23:6
Funke, John Gerhard Rev, 1908, Ja 6,7:4
Funke, Joseph A, 1940, Jl 10,19:4
Funke, Leslie, 1950, O 19,31:2
Funke, Walter H Mrs, 1958, N 12,27:3
Funkhouse, Robert D, 1938, S 1,23:5
Funkhouser, George Mrs, 1945, Je 6,21:5
Funkhouser, H G, 1946, My 30,21:1
Funkhouser, Raymond Joseph, 1968, Mr 11,37:1
Funkhouser, William, 1948, Je 10,25:4
Funn, Arthur L Mrs, 1965, F 15,27:3
Funnell, Frederick C Mrs, 1938, Ja 30,II,8:2
Funnell, Walter S, 1956, Ag 11,13:6

Funsten, James B Mrs, 1948, Ap 2,23:1
Funston, Cornelius, 1944, Jl 11,15:1
Funston, Frederick, 1955, N 5,19:5
Funston, Frederick Maj-Gen (funl, F 25,19:1), 1917, F 24,9:5
Funston, James B Bp, 1918, D 3,15:3
Funston, Thomas C, 1951, D 31,13:5
Funston, William H, 1943, S 17,21:3
Funt, Isidore, 1962, D 8,27:3
Funt, Samuel, 1951, D 16,91:2
Fuqua, Stephen O, 1943, My 13,21:1
Furay, James H, 1955, Jl 21,23:2
Furay, James H Mrs, 1965, Ag 14,23:2
Furay, John B, 1952, Ja 16,25:3
Furbank, Arthur W Mrs, 1958, Mr 17,29:5
Furbeck, George W, 1951, O 20,15:3
Furber, Beverly H Mrs, 1964, N 7,27:5
Furber, Douglas, 1961, F 21,35:4
Furber, Edwin J, 1957, O 18,23:2
Furber, Henry J, 1956, Je 7,31:5
Furber, Montague, 1940, F 9,19:3
Furber, Percy N, 1955, D 16,29:1
Furber, Robert S, 1911, Je 19,9:5
Furber, William A, 1954, Ja 7,31:2
Furbish, George H, 1949, Je 14,31:3
Furbush, Almon J, 1941, Je 30,17:4
Furczynca, U L Mrs, 1903, Ag 30,1:1
Furedi, Nicholas Dr, 1968, D 15,86:1
Furedi, Sandor, 1956, O 7,86:8
Furer, Julius A, 1963, Je 8,25:5
Furey, Charles A, 1951, S 17,21:4
Furey, George F, 1952, Jl 23,23:5
Furey, George W, 1952, O 1,33:2
Furey, Georgianna G Mrs, 1938, My 19,21:5
Furey, John Vincent Gen, 1914, D 18,13:6
Furey, Merwin F, 1960, Jl 20,29:4
Furey, Michael J, 1938, My 27,17:6
Furey, Robert, 1913, Mr 13,11:5
Furey, Warren W, 1958, N 20,35:4
Furey, William B, 1943, Ja 26,19:1
Furgatch, Solomon Mrs, 1954, N 10,33:1
Furgueson, Cornelius, 1938, Mr 8,19:5
Furgueson, Cornelius Jr, 1941, O 2,25:3
Furlan, Boris, 1957, Jl 4,19:4
Furlong, C Wellington, 1967, O 11,47:1
Furlong, Charles E Gen, 1907, S 26,9:6
Furlong, Francis M, 1953, D 17,37:2
Furlong, Frank M, 1943, F 15,15:2
Furlong, Frank P, 1945, Ag 27,19:4
Furlong, Frederick I, 1939, My 20,15:6
Furlong, Gerald, 1954, Mr 15,25:5
Furlong, James T, 1951, Mr 27,29:1
Furlong, John, 1950, O 14,19:1
Furlong, John T, 1944, F 1,19:2
Furlong, May I, 1952, Jl 31,23:1
Furlong, Pauline, 1920, My 27,11:3
Furlong, Phil P, 1940, Ag 28,19:2
Furlong, Raymond B, 1946, Ap 11,25:5
Furlong, William, 1937, Ja 11,19:3
Furlotte, James Mrs, 1955, Jl 20,27:1
Furlow, Floyd Charles, 1923, Ap 27,17:5
Furman, Alfred A, 1940, Ag 16,15:5
Furman, Alice M, 1941, Ja 25,15:2
Furman, Alice Mrs, 1938, Ja 6,19:5
Furman, Anna C R Mrs, 1941, N 15,17:4
Furman, C Mrs, 1942, Je 4,19:5
Furman, Charles, 1957, O 19,21:1
Furman, Charles B Rev, 1937, Ag 12,19:4
Furman, Charles E Mrs, 1948, My 4,25:2
Furman, Charles H Mrs, 1947, My 1,25:4
Furman, Fannie W Mrs, 1948, F 13,21:1
Furman, Franklin D, 1943, N 22,19:1
Furman, George B Mrs, 1938, Ap 17,II,6:5
Furman, George H, 1941, Mr 27,23:3; 1946, Ap 28,42:7
Furman, George W, 1904, Ja 5,9:6
Furman, Harry A, 1943, My 31,17:2; 1943, Je 1,23:2
Furman, Herman C, 1958, My 1,31:1
Furman, Herman D, 1941, Mr 11,23:5
Furman, Horace S, 1952, N 27,31:3
Furman, J M, 1884, D 13,5:2; 1933, Ja 25,12:3
Furman, Job Rockfield, 1925, S 8,21:5
Furman, Joel N Mrs, 1944, O 21,17:5
Furman, John L Mrs, 1948, D 23,19:2
Furman, Lucile, 1961, Ap 3,33:4
Furman, Lucy, 1958, Ag 26,29:4
Furman, M De Witt Mrs, 1949, D 28,32:2
Furman, Martin A, 1962, O 16,47:5
Furman, Mattie V, 1951, Je 21,27:3
Furman, Morton, 1966, My 26,47:2
Furman, Paul N, 1945, N 25,48:6
Furman, Peter N, 1907, D 4,9:5
Furman, Phoebe Mrs, 1924, Je 23,19:3
Furman, Richard W, 1960, Ag 2,29:5
Furman, Robert T, 1951, N 15,29:5
Furman, Theodore B, 1954, Mr 19,23:2
Furman, Vern L, 1954, Je 26,13:4
Furman, Virginia D H, 1942, Ap 13,15:6
Furnald, Francis P Mrs, 1920, F 8,22:2
Furnald, Francis Perkins, 1907, Mr 12,9:6
Furnald, Isaac, 1871, F 28,1:4
Furnald, M Lizzie, 1942, Ja 27,21:5
Furnans, John E, 1953, Ja 25,85:2
Furnas, Charles, 1941, O 16,21:6

Furnas, Miles J, 1954, O 9,17:4
Furnas, Paul J, 1960, S 24,23:5
Furner, Mary S Mrs, 1954, Ja 5,27:1
Furness, C Becher Mrs (E Ellis), 1960, D 28,27:4
Furness, Charles V, 1954, N 1,27:4
Furness, Christopher Lord (Baron Grantley), 1912, N 11,11:4
Furness, Clifton J, 1946, My 28,21:4
Furness, Florence Mrs, 1937, Ag 4,19:4
Furness, George C, 1944, Ap 11,19:5
Furness, H H Jr, 1930, Ap 16,29:3
Furness, Harry S, 1947, F 5,23:3
Furness, Horace Howard Dr, 1912, Ag 14,9:4
Furness, J Wilson, 1953, Mr 5,27:2
Furness, Leo R, 1952, N 9,90:1
Furness, Reginald A, 1951, O 20,15:5
Furness, Stephen Sir, 1914, S 7,7:6
Furness, Viscount, 1940, O 8,25:1
Furniss, Clementina, 1915, Ag 24,11:6
Furniss, Edgar S Jr, 1966, Ag 18,32:4
Furniss, Grace L, 1938, Ap 22,19:1
Furniss, Harry, 1925, Ja 16,17:3
Furniss, Henry D, 1942, Ja 26,15:3
Furniss, Henry D Mrs, 1957, D 16,29:1
Furniss, W P Mrs, 1878, My 6,8:4
Furnival, George A, 1949, Ag 14,70:8
Furnival, James C, 1950, Ag 4,21:4
Furniwall, Frederick J, 1910, Jl 3,II,7:4
Furr, Roger T, 1953, D 29,23:1
Furrer, John A, 1952, F 28,27:1
Furrer, Otto, 1951, Jl 28,3:3
Furrer, Reinhold, 1944, N 19,50:2
Furrer, Rudolph, 1965, Ja 21,31:3
Furrey, Frank W, 1945, Ap 27,19:3
Furrey, Joseph A, 1938, S 1,23:4
Furry, Frank E, 1944, Mr 23,19:5
Furry, Margaret Mrs, 1941, D 28,28:2
Fursch-Madi, Emma, 1894, S 22,4:7
Furse, Katherine, 1952, N 26,23:1
Fursman, Edgar L, 1910, Ap 3,II,11:2
Fursman, Fred Mrs, 1942, My 14,19:2
Fursman, Frederick F, 1943, Je 15,21:5
Furst, Albert, 1959, D 19,27:6
Furst, Breading, 1950, D 21,29:1
Furst, Bruno, 1965, Mr 30,47:1
Furst, C, 1931, Mr 7,19:1
Furst, Charles Sr, 1961, My 11,37:3
Furst, Edward W, 1959, Ag 27,27:2
Furst, F A, 1934, Ja 24,17:3
Furst, George, 1964, Ap 19,85:1
Furst, Henry, 1967, Ag 18,33:3
Furst, Hyman, 1961, Ja 7,19:3
Furst, M, 1934, Je 28,23:4
Furst, Nathan J, 1960, S 16,28:6
Furst, Phil, 1952, Ag 18,17:2
Furst, Sidney J, 1948, S 11,16:6
Furst, Toby, 1952, N 22,23:3
Furst, William, 1917, Jl 12,11:7
Furstenberg, Elizabeth von, 1961, Ja 10,47:3
Furstman, Benjamin, 1951, Jl 29,68:5
Furstman, Jacob C, 1952, Mr 25,27:3
Furth, Albert L, 1962, O 18,39:5
Furth, Carl, 1947, Ja 9,23:2
Furth, Hugo Mrs, 1956, N 27,38:4
Furth, William L, 1955, Ja 15,13:1
Furth, William L Mrs, 1955, Ja 15,13:1
Furthman, Charles A, 1950, My 23,29:2
Furtsch, Amson, 1949, N 5,14:2
Furtwaengler, Wilhelm (funl, D 5,88:4), 1954, D 1, 31:1
Furuhjelm, Ragnar E, 1944, N 21,25:4
Furukawa, Toranosuke Baron, 1940, Mr 31,44:2
Furuseth, Andrew (por), 1938, Ja 23,II,9:1
Fury, Bessie L Mrs, 1950, Je 23,25:4
Fusaro, Samuel J, 1953, Ap 2,27:3
Fuschini, Giuseppe, 1949, Jl 11,17:6
Fusco, Albert, 1943, S 17,21:4
Fusco, Edward F, 1939, Jl 25,19:4
Fusco, Eugenio, 1957, Je 10,27:1
Fusco, Guido, 1964, S 28,29:5
Fusco, James J, 1950, F 11,15:3
Fusco, Matthew P, 1948, Jl 23,19:5
Fusco, Michael, 1961, O 26,35:4
Fusco, Michael J, 1961, Ap 4,37:3
Fusco, Ralph L Mrs, 1961, Mr 30,29:2
Fushimi, Hirouoshi, 1938, O 19,23:5
Fushimi, Hiroyasu Prince, 1946, Ag 17,13:5
Fushimi, Sedanaru Prince, 1923, F 6,19:5
Fushimi, Tsuneko Princess, 1939, Ag 19,15:5
Fushimi, Yorihito Higashi Prince, 1922, Je 27,15:5
Fusi, Siro, 1942, Jl 13,15:2
Fusinata, Eminia, 1876, O 28,2:7
Fusmer, John C, 1943, S 26,49:1
Fuson, Herschel, 1951, Je 16,15:3
Fuson, Samuel D, 1954, N 6,17:4
Fuss, Charles O M, 1944, N 14,23:3
Fussell, Anna E, 1944, S 3,28:8
Fussell, Joseph H, 1942, My 9,13:1
Fussell, Katherine S, 1942, Jl 28,17:1
Fusselman, Paul A, 1949, N 23,29:3
Fusting, F Erwin, 1953, F 26,25:5
Futch, Truman G, 1960, Mr 26,21:1
Futcher, Clifford P, 1948, Mr 3,24:3
Futcher, Mary E, 1948, F 12,23:3
Futcher, Thomas B, 1938, F 26,15:4
Futhey, Bruce, 1964, Jl 16,31:5
Futter, Walter A, 1958, Mr 5,31:4
Futter, Walter A Mrs, 1953, Jl 8,27:2
Futterer, Edward Prof, 1920, F 14,11:3
Futterer, Louis, 1946, My 28,21:3
Futterman, Max J, 1943, My 9,40:7
Futterman, Robert A, 1961, N 13,31:4
Futyma, Frank, 1950, O 29,92:4
Fuxon, Samuel, 1943, F 20,13:1
Fybush, Aaron, 1948, Je 31,19:3
Fybush, Joseph, 1937, S 18,19:4
Fybush, Simon, 1957, My 19,88:3
Fyfe, A M, 1942, Mr 17,21:1
Fyfe, Charles W Mrs, 1957, D 15,86:4
Fyfe, David A, 1944, S 20,23:4
Fyfe, David M (Earl of Kilmuir), 1967, Ja 28,27:1
Fyfe, David T, 1945, Ja 3,17:5
Fyfe, Hamilton, 1951, Je 20,27:3
Fyfe, Howard, 1959, O 25,87:1
Fyfe, John H, 1954, Ja 17,93:2
Fyfe, Louis, 1938, F 9,19:1
Fyfe, Robert, 1950, O 9,25:2
Fyffe, William J, 1961, Ag 26,17:4
Fyke, Frank C, 1952, My 12,25:5
Fyle, George H, 1951, Mr 24,13:4
Fyleman, Rose, 1957, Ag 4,81:3
Fyler, Orsamus R, 1909, N 23,9:4
Fyles, Franklin (funl, My 7,9:6), 1911, Jl 5,11:6
Fyles, Vanderherden, 1915, Ag 11,9:6
Fylstra, John, 1967, My 11,47:3

G

Ga Nun, C Fred, 1944, D 2,13:6
Ga Nun, Gordon M, 1950, Ja 1,42:8
Gaar, James M, 1945, D 2,45:3
Gaarn, Edgar C, 1957, Mr 25,25:1
Gabarine, John, 1950, Mr 14,25:4
Gabarino, Joseph, 1950, Ja 8,76:5
Gabay, Henry R, 1946, Ja 13,44:4
Gabay, Richard L, 1950, O 9,25:4
Gabb, Claude B, 1945, S 8,15:6
Gabbani, Adolph, 1949, Ap 19,25:5
Gabbe, Robert, 1955, Ja 27,23:2
Gabbett, Cecil M, 1940, S 4,23:1
Gabbi, Frederick H, 1958, Ag 10,92:5
Gabel, Alfred, 1962, Jl 3,23:2
Gabel, Harry A, 1948, O 21,27:3
Gabel, Jacob L, 1965, Jl 10,25:4
Gabel, John, 1955, D 25,48:3
Gabel, Kenneth, 1956, O 14,86:6
Gabel, Phil, 1942, O 6,23:3
Gabel, Siegfried G, 1957, Je 15,17:3
Gabel, Siegfried G Mrs, 1964, My 30,17:4
Gabel, Thomas J, 1951, D 25,31:2
Gabeler, William H, 1950, My 1,25:3
Gabell, Columbus W Jr, 1942, D 14,28:1
Gabell, G R, 1942, S 27,49:2
Gabelle, James G, 1940, N 14,23:5
Gabelli, Ottone, 1939, Ja 10,19:4
Gaberson, Avery C, 1952, F 23,11:1
Gabet, Augusto, 1949, F 1,25:4
Gabhard, Karl, 1956, D 11,36:2
Gabhardt, Edward, 1956, Mr 28,31:3
Gable, Bert C, 1946, N 22,23:2
Gable, Charles H, 1954, N 27,13:4
Gable, Clark (funl plans, N 18,31:1; funl, N 20,86:4), 1960, N 17,1:4
Gable, Edwin O, 1941, Ja 12,44:7
Gable, George W, 1940, F 16,19:1
Gable, Gilbert E, 1941, D 3,25:2
Gable, Luther D, 1940, Ja 14,43:1
Gable, Maria F Mrs, 1966, S 26,41:1
Gable, Vivian F, 1937, N 20,17:2
Gable, William H, 1948, Ag 5,21:4
Gableman, Edwin W, 1954, Je 12,15:4
Gabler, George L, 1950, Ag 29,27:6
Gabler, John C, 1957, N 3,88:4
Gabor, Arnold, 1950, Jl 17,21:4
Gabor, Vilmos, 1962, Jl 11,35:2
Gaboury, Joseph A Mrs, 1947, O 2,27:6
Gabovich, Mikhail M, 1965, Jl 16,27:2
Gabrelow, Jacob, 1949, Mr 24,27:4
Gabriac, Marquis de, 1903, N 23,7:3
Gabrick, Clarence A, 1952, Ap 26,23:5
Gabriel, Adolph Mrs (por), 1944, My 10,19:5
Gabriel, Arthur R, 1953, Jl 7,27:3
Gabriel, Barnett, 1955, F 4,21:1
Gabriel, Bertram A, 1955, Mr 12,19:6
Gabriel, Bro (Gabriel Mehler), 1940, Je 1,15:6
Gabriel, Charles L, 1949, S 26,25:5
Gabriel, George, 1950, Ja 24,32:5
Gabriel, Gilbert E (trb, S 7,II,1:5), 1952, S 4,27:3
Gabriel, Gilbert R, 1962, Jl 17,25:1
Gabriel, Grand Duke of Russia, 1955, Mr 2,27:2
Gabriel, Gustavus L, 1941, Ja 1,28:3
Gabriel, Harry S, 1959, Je 15,27:1
Gabriel, Jacob J, 1951, Mr 19,27:1
Gabriel, John M, 1965, Ag 17,33:3
Gabriel, Joseph G, 1944, Mr 28,19:2
Gabriel, Joseph G Mrs, 1946, O 12,19:3
Gabriel, Mother (Mary Redigan), 1916, Ap 1,13:4
Gabriel, Peter Sr, 1948, Je 6,72:6
Gabriel, Samuel, 1920, Ap 30,13:5
Gabriel, Sister, 1938, O 19,23:6
Gabriel, Vivian, 1950, F 22,30:2
Gabriel, William F, 1951, Ja 22,17:2
Gabriele, Spiro D, 1954, Ja 30,17:5
Gabrieli, Francesco P, 1962, Jl 17,25:5
Gabrielidist, Vlassios, 1920, Ap 27,9:3
Gabrielle Delebecque, Mother, 1945, S 29,15:5
Gabrielli, Ralph, 1963, Ag 28,33:4
Gabriels, Henry Bp, 1921, Ap 25,11:4
Gabriels, Henry E Sr, 1943, Mr 8,15:1
Gabrielsen, August Capt, 1919, Je 16,13:5
Gabrielson, Christian, 1958, O 21,33:6
Gabrielson, Gustave E, 1949, N 1,27:2
Gabrielsson, Assar, 1962, My 30,19:5
Gabrilowitsch, Clara Clemens, 1921, D 11,22:3
Gabrilowitsch, Nina C (will, Ja 23,65:3), 1966, Ja 19,41:3
Gabrilowitsch, O, 1936, S 15,29:1
Gabrio, Alfred W, 1946, Jl 7,35:1
Gaccione, Anthony S Mrs, 1956, Ap 19,31:4
Gadboys, Howard L Dr, 1968, Mr 1,43:7
Gadd, Robert F Sr, 1959, N 20,31:5
Gadden, Edward T, 1940, S 27,23:2
Gaddio, Elisha B, 1903, N 27,1:5
Gaddis, David E Col, 1923, Ag 13,13:4
Gaddis, Edgar, 1955, F 2,27:1
Gaddis, George E, 1937, N 26,21:2
Gaddis, Percy A, 1957, F 7,27:6

Gade, Carl J, 1955, Je 20,21:6
Gade, Fredik H J, 1943, Ap 3,15:4
Gade, Herbert, 1964, S 30,43:3
Gade, Herman Mrs, 1938, My 31,19:5
Gade, John, 1943, My 31,17:2; 1952, Je 27,23:1
Gade, John A, 1955, Ag 17,27:6
Gade, Samuel, 1950, O 4,31:4
Gadebusch, Paul, 1943, Je 4,21:4
Gadebusch, Paul H, 1957, D 5,35:5
Gadek, Anthony S, 1955, Ag 28,81:6
Gadek, Joseph A, 1958, Ja 19,86:5
Gaden, Theodore A, 1963, S 17,35:1
Gadeyski, Gerald B, 1948, D 17,28:2
Gadjusek, Karl A, 1946, Ap 30,22:3
Gadlow, David B, 1965, O 31,86:7
Gadol, William N, 1954, Ja 19,25:2
Gadsby, George M, 1960, Mr 30,37:4
Gadsby, Herbert H, 1945, F 19,17:5
Gadsden, Christopher S, 1915, Ja 13,9:5
Gadsden, James Gen, 1858, D 28,4:1
Gadsden, Philip H, 1945, F 28,23:4
Gadski, Berta, 1907, D 21,9:5
Gadski, J Mme, 1932, F 24,21:1
Gaebelein, Arno W, 1952, F 26,27:2
Gaebelin, Arno C Mrs, 1938, N 22,23:5
Gaedcke, Charles, 1942, Ag 18,21:1
Gaedcke, Henry C, 1958, F 24,19:4
Gaede, Henry, 1912, My 9,11:4
Gaede, Henry A, 1942, Ap 9,19:4
Gaede, Henry J, 1959, S 20,86:4
Gaede, William R, 1966, O 14,43:1
Gaedel, Edward, 1961, Je 20,12:6
Gaefsky, Nicholas, 1947, Jl 23,23:5
Gaehr, Paul F, 1955, N 13,88:4
Gael, James, 1913, S 26,11:6
Gaenslen, Frederick J Dr, 1937, Mr 13,19:2
Gaensler, Hugo A, 1951, Ag 15,27:4
Gaertner, Carl F, 1952, N 7,23:2
Gaertner, Clement J, 1967, Ja 29,76:6
Gaertner, Edward C, 1957, N 9,27:5
Gaertner, Frank, 1962, Ag 27,23:2
Gaertner, Fred, 1963, S 8,87:1
Gaertner, Fred Jr, 1961, My 13,19:5
Gaertner, Fred W Jr Mrs, 1950, Mr 28,31:1
Gaertner, William (will), 1948, D 15,36:5
Gaertner, William E Mrs, 1954, N 28,87:2
Gaess, William C Mrs, 1946, Ja 7,20:2
Gaeta, Antonio, 1967, Mr 1,43:2
Gaeta, Basilio, 1962, F 2,29:2
Gaeta, Basilio Mrs, 1962, N 14,39:1
Gaeta, Phil, 1949, Mr 29,26:2
Gaetan, Manuel, 1938, D 1,23:2
Gaetan de Bourbon-Parma, Prince, 1958, Mr 11,29:2
Gaeth, Paul, 1952, N 26,23:2
Gaetjens, Charles F, 1959, O 19,29:1
Gafencu, Grigore, 1957, Ja 31,27:1
Gafencu, Ralou A, 1945, Je 29,15:4
Gaff, Charles, 1907, O 14,9:5
Gaff, Marguerite A, 1953, My 4,23:5
Gaff, Otto, 1941, N 18,27:2
Gaffers, William C, 1946, D 30,19:4
Gaffert, Gustaf A, 1954, My 7,23:3
Gaffey, Francis B, 1944, F 24,15:4
Gaffey, John F, 1946, Je 10,21:5
Gaffey, Michael A, 1961, Mr 5,86:5
Gaffney, Bernard, 1945, N 8,20:2
Gaffney, Cornelia T T, 1940, Jl 16,17:5
Gaffney, Dale V, 1950, Mr 29,29:5
Gaffney, Edward C, 1938, Ap 4,17:5
Gaffney, Edward H, 1947, Mr 15,13:1
Gaffney, Edward J, 1941, Ap 29,19:5; 1948, Jl 22,23:6
Gaffney, Edward R, 1952, N 28,25:4
Gaffney, Eugene M, 1967, O 30,45:2
Gaffney, Francis J, 1949, F 3,24:2
Gaffney, Frank Mrs, 1956, Ja 3,31:2
Gaffney, H Raiford, 1943, Je 10,21:2
Gaffney, Harry B, 1950, Ag 26,13:6
Gaffney, Harry J, 1960, O 10,31:1
Gaffney, J E, 1932, Ag 17,17:3
Gaffney, James, 1950, Jl 5,31:2
Gaffney, James E, 1966, Mr 13,87:2
Gaffney, James Mrs, 1945, N 18,44:2
Gaffney, James T, 1950, Ap 11,31:2
Gaffney, John A, 1949, Je 28,27:5; 1954, D 15,31:1
Gaffney, John Francis Ex-Judge, 1918, F 12,11:2
Gaffney, John J, 1947, N 22,15:4
Gaffney, John L, 1952, F 3,84:4
Gaffney, Joseph J, 1947, N 28,27:4
Gaffney, M Cecilia, 1942, Mr 26,23:5
Gaffney, Matthew P, 1963, Je 2,85:1
Gaffney, Maurice L, 1950, Jl 30,60:2
Gaffney, Michael F, 1938, Ap 4,17:6
Gaffney, Michael G, 1954, N 12,21:3
Gaffney, Patrick G, 1941, Ja 16,21:3
Gaffney, Paul J, 1941, Ag 23,13:5
Gaffney, Ray M, 1952, Jl 23,23:4
Gaffney, Raymond J, 1965, S 8,47:2
Gaffney, T St John (por), 1945, Ja 15,19:3
Gaffney, Thomas, 1953, Mr 23,23:3

Gaffney, Thomas F, 1942, N 5,25:2
Gaffney, Thomas J, 1947, Je 11,27:5
Gaffney, William E, 1946, N 25,27:5
Gaffney, William P, 1960, S 26,33:4
Gaffney (Mother Mary Reginald), 1963, N 27,37:3
Gafford, Jack C, 1964, N 25,37:4
Gafford, James E, 1959, Ja 21,31:4
Gaffre, Louis Albert Msgr, 1914, Jl 8,9:4
Gafner, Samuel W, 1945, Je 23,13:3
Gaft, Max, 1962, Ag 19,89:1
Gag, Wanda (por), 1946, Je 28,21:5
Gagan, Joseph E, 1967, S 8,40:2
Gagan, Thomas F, 1966, Ag 23,39:2
Gagarin, Catherine, 1938, Mr 19,15:3
Gagarin, Gregory A, 1963, Jl 19,25:2
Gagarin, Marie D O Princess, 1946, O 25,23:2
Gagarin, Yuri A Col (funl plans, Mr 29,5:3; funl, Mr 31,21:1), 1968, Mr 28,1:2
Gagarine, Serge N, 1958, O 9,37:1
Gage, Brownell, 1945, F 5,15:5
Gage, Brownell Mrs, 1937, Ja 7,21:3
Gage, Byron Mrs, 1915, Jl 9,11:3
Gage, David V Mrs, 1957, S 24,35:1
Gage, Delia G Mrs, 1942, Ap 20,21:4
Gage, Eugenie A W Mrs (will), 1940, My 17,41:3
Gage, George E, 1948, Mr 9,23:2
Gage, George H, 1943, Ap 10,17:6
Gage, George M, 1940, F 3,13:1
Gage, George R, 1945, Ag 19,39:1
Gage, George W, 1957, Ag 8,23:2
Gage, Harry M, 1961, Mr 21,37:5
Gage, Henry P, 1956, F 11,17:2
Gage, Henry T Ex-Gov, 1924, Ag 30,9:6
Gage, Hilliard R, 1945, F 21,19:2
Gage, Homer (will, Jl 9,14:5), 1938, Jl 4,13:4
Gage, Homer Mrs, 1948, My 17,19:3
Gage, Ina Lady, 1939, Mr 9,21:5
Gage, J Arthur, 1943, N 30,27:4
Gage, J Prescott Mrs, 1946, Ag 3,15:4
Gage, James P, 1955, S 9,23:2
Gage, Jesse W, 1954, Ja 20,27:2
Gage, John H, 1966, Ap 28,43:3
Gage, Joseph G (por), 1945, Ja 4,19:4
Gage, L J, 1927, Ja 27,17:3
Gage, Lyman J Mrs, 1943, Jl 25,30:8
Gage, Moreton Foley Mrs, 1915, Ap 19,9:5
Gage, Nelson W, 1937, O 7,27:2
Gage, Nina D, 1946, O 19,21:5
Gage, Ralph E, 1959, D 10,39:5
Gage, S Capt, 1885, Mr 20,3:7
Gage, Samuel E, 1943, N 1,17:4
Gage, Simon H, 1944, O 21,17:4
Gage, Stephen D, 1939, O 3,23:3
Gage, Thomas H, 1938, Jl 16,13:5
Gage, W Cecil, 1953, Mr 25,31:5
Gage, Walter B Mrs, 1939, My 2,23:4
Gage, Wellesley W, 1924, My 8,19:4; 1925, Je 25,21:5
Gage, William James Sir, 1921, Ja 15,13:4
Gage, William R, 1947, My 16,23:4
Gage, William S, 1941, F 5,19:2
Gage, Wilyton H, 1948, My 18,23:5
Gagel, Paul, 1903, Jl 31,7:6
Gagen, John H, 1943, D 30,17:2
Gagen, Joseph R, 1958, Jl 24,25:4
Gager, C Stuart, 1943, Ag 10,19:5
Gager, C Stuart Mrs, 1956, Ja 14,19:5
Gager, Curtis H, 1962, Mr 21,39:5
Gager, Edwin B, 1922, Ap 29,15:4
Gager, Edwin V Capt, 1914, Jl 14,9:6
Gager, Ernest H, 1944, N 20,21:4
Gager, Estelle C Mrs, 1957, D 28,30:4
Gaggin, T Walker, 1945, O 21,46:1
Gaggion, Clinton J, 1941, Mr 29,15:1
Gaglianello, Joseph, 1952, Ja 11,22:2
Gagliardi, Alex A, 1950, F 6,25:3
Gagliardi, Joseph M, 1944, Mr 28,19:3
Gagliardi, Joseph Mrs, 1944, Ap 8,13:5
Gagliardi, Marian S, 1966, F 14,29:1
Gagne, Ernest, 1948, Jl 31,15:5
Gagne, M, 1876, S 11,5:6
Gagney, Daniel J, 1938, F 4,21:2
Gagnier, Edmund (Bro Colmas Stanislaus), 1955, D 6,37:2
Gagnier, L A, 1944, My 12,19:1
Gagnier, Oliver J, 1941, N 18,25:2
Gagnieur, William Rev, 1937, F 9,23:4
Gagnon, Armand, 1950, S 18,30:2
Gagnon, Arthemise H Mrs, 1953, Ap 7,29:4
Gagnon, Arthur H, 1958, Ja 20,23:2
Gagnon, Blanche, 1951, Mr 15,29:5
Gagnon, Camillien, 1966, Jl 13,19:7
Gagnon, Clarence A, 1942, Ja 6,23:2
Gagnon, Cyrille, 1945, N 2,20:3
Gagnon, Eugenie L R, 1940, Je 13,23:3
Gagnon, Fortunat, 1947, N 18,30:3
Gagnon, Frederick Ernest Amedee, 1915, S 18,9:6
Gagnon, H A Royal, 1947, N 20,29:1
Gagnon, Henri, 1958, S 4,29:5
Gagnon, Henri Mrs, 1959, Ja 28,31:3

Gagnon, Joseph A Mrs, 1955, Ap 13,29:4
Gagnon, Onesime, 1961, O 1,86:3
Gagnon, Wilfrid J T, 1963, Je 11,37:4
Gagua, Illarion, 1951, O 20,15:6
Gaguine, Silvio, 1960, O 18,40:1
Gagziardi, Ernest, 1940, Ja 23,21:6
Gahagan, Fred M, 1943, Jl 8,19:3
Gahagan, Joseph P, 1940, F 17,13:5
Gahagan, Lillian Mrs, 1968, Ap 7,92:2
Gahagan, Tom, 1959, D 22,31:5
Gahagan, Walter H Mrs, 1957, F 8,23:3
Gahagan, Will (por), 1946, Ja 14,19:1
Gahagan, Will Mrs, 1959, Ja 11,88:5
Gahan, Charles J, 1939, Ja 23,13:4
Gahan, Edward F, 1966, Mr 20,87:1
Gahan, John P, 1964, Ag 8,19:4
Gahan, Mary C, 1945, D 27,20:2
Gaherty, Edward T, 1954, Jl 28,23:2
Gahib, Joseph T, 1951, My 25,27:3
Gahm, Joseph, 1937, Je 11,23:3
Gahm, Phil, 1937, Je 10,23:2
Gahnkin, Valentine G, 1962, S 25,37:2
Gahran, Augustus, 1942, Ap 8,19:6
Gahrar, George G, 1949, Ja 23,68:7
Gahs, Harrison M, 1945, Ag 7,23:6
Gahwe, Herman E, 1941, F 20,19:1
Gaido, John, 1968, O 14,47:2
Gaige, Crosby (por), 1949, Mr 9,25:1
Gaige, Frederick H, 1939, N 24,23:2
Gail, George W, 1909, Jl 20,7:6
Gailey, Charles K Jr, 1966, My 23,41:3
Gailey, Robert R, 1950, Ja 21,17:6
Gailey, Watson, 1959, Ja 21,31:1
Gailhard, Pierre, 1918, O 14,11:7
Gailit, August, 1960, N 8,29:1
Gaillard, A Theodore Dr, 1924, D 2,25:5
Gaillard, A Theodore Mrs, 1952, Ja 8,27:5
Gaillard, Charles B, 1948, Jl 20,24:2
Gaillard, Charles B G Mrs, 1952, Mr 22,13:2
Gaillard, David Du Bose (funl, D 9,11:4), 1913, D 6, 11:3
Gaillard, David S Jr, 1951, Je 11,25:2
Gaillard, E S Dr, 1885, F 3,2:3
Gaillard, Edwin S Mrs, 1916, Mr 25,13:7
Gaillard, Elias P, 1957, D 27,20:2
Gaillard, Esther L Mrs, 1939, Ag 11,15:3
Gaillard, George C, 1954, Mr 18,31:3
Gaillard, Gourdin Y Mrs, 1939, N 12,48:7
Gaillard, Jacques, 1941, My 11,44:4
Gaillard, Katherine D Mrs, 1937, D 31,15:3
Gaillard, Marion H, 1946, My 5,45:1
Gaillard, S Palmer Sr, 1959, O 19,29:5
Gaillard, William D, 1959, Ag 19,29:2
Gaillard, William D Mrs, 1946, Mr 9,13:4
Gaillard, William E G, 1939, F 6,13:4
Gaillard, William E G Mrs, 1938, Ja 1,19:3
Gaillardet, F, 1882, Ag 15,5:2
Gaillardin, C J C, 1881, Ja 2,7:1
Gailor, Charles N, 1952, N 30,31:1
Gailor, Chester F, 1942, D 17,29:6
Gailor, Edward, 1924, F 14,17:4
Gailor, Frank H, 1954, Ap 9,24:5
Gailor, T F, 1935, O 3,25:1
Gain, J Cameron, 1952, F 20,29:3
Gainard, Frederic A, 1945, Ag 22,23:6
Gainard, Joseph A, 1943, D 24,14:8
Gainard, Joseph A Mrs, 1949, F 18,24:2
Gainer, Edward, 1948, Ja 13,26:3
Gainer, Henry, 1937, O 5,25:5
Gaines, Ambrose, 1945, F 20,19:2
Gaines, Arthur H, 1963, My 29,33:4
Gaines, Charles (por), 1947, D 5,25:1
Gaines, Charles K, 1944, Ja 4,17:2
Gaines, Clarence M, 1947, Ja 7,27:4
Gaines, Clement C, 1943, Ja 16,13:2
Gaines, Daniel Mrs, 1945, Ja 10,23:3
Gaines, Emma B Mrs, 1942, S 6,31:2
Gaines, Francis P, 1964, Ja 1,25:5
Gaines, Frank, 1939, Ja 4,21:3
Gaines, Frank Rev, 1923, Ap 15,6:2
Gaines, Fred T, 1946, O 20,60:3
Gaines, Henry W, 1938, S 10,17:6
Gaines, I S, 1950, O 9,25:4
Gaines, Jared, 1916, My 26,11:2
Gaines, John S Sr, 1957, Je 25,29:2
Gaines, John S 2d, 1960, O 9,86:5
Gaines, L Ebersole, 1954, Ap 17,13:6
Gaines, Le Grand A Jr, 1937, Ja 26,21:1
Gaines, Lewis M Dr, 1937, My 25,28:3
Gaines, Louis O, 1949, Je 28,27:3
Gaines, Mary, 1949, Mr 20,77:1
Gaines, Morrell W Mrs, 1955, N 7,29:3
Gaines, Myra C, 1885, Ja 10,3:3
Gaines, Owen W, 1944, Ag 30,17:2
Gaines, Richard Kenna Capt, 1968, Ag 5,39:3
Gaines, Sallie P Mrs, 1956, O 10,39:4
Gaines, Samuel L, 1945, Ap 1,36:4
Gaines, Samuel R, 1945, O 11,23:2
Gaines, Sidney Mrs (Rita K), 1965, Jl 8,31:3
Gaines, Thomas P, 1948, F 24,25:3
Gainey, Henry P, 1951, S 21,24:3
Gainford, Lady, 1941, O 28,23:3
Gainford, Lord, 1943, F 16,19:4
Gainfort, James W, 1943, Jl 31,13:5
Gainor, Del C, 1947, Ja 30,25:4
Gainor, Edward J (por), 1947, N 12,27:1
Gainor, James J, 1946, Jl 26,21:3
Gainotti, Luigi, 1940, Je 6,25:1
Gainsborough, Earl, 1881, Ag 14,7:6
Gainsburg, I, 1957, Mr 3,85:1
Gainsburg, I Mrs, 1948, D 5,92:3
Gainsburgh, Edward L Dr, 1968, O 19,37:3
Gainsfort, William F Sr, 1960, Ja 10,87:1
Gainsway, Frederic J, 1954, Ja 9,15:2
Gainsway, Frederick J Mrs, 1953, O 18,86:4
Gainza Castro, Alberto, 1959, Mr 21,21:5
Gainza Castro, Ezequiel, 1960, S 27,37:3
Gainza Paz, Angelica, 1953, Ja 3,15:3
Gair, Emma F, 1961, Ja 27,23:3
Gair, George W, 1940, Jl 22,17:2
Gair, R, 1927, Ag 2,21:3
Gair, Robert, 1937, N 5,23:4
Gairoard, C Mrs, 1942, My 9,13:4
Gairoard, Camille L, 1956, F 25,19:4
Gaisberg, Frederick W, 1951, S 6,31:6
Gaise, Frederick C, 1945, My 25,19:3
Gaisel, Frederick, 1944, Ag 10,17:7
Gaiser, J Harmon Mrs (C Liston), 1964, N 10,47:3
Gaiser, Samuel, 1947, Ap 18,21:4
Gait, Edward, 1950, Mr 16,31:3
Gait, Valentine, 1947, Ag 27,23:4
Gaitan Cortes, Jorge, 1968, Ag 15,37:4
Gaites, George H, 1953, S 3,21:3
Gaites, Joseph M, 1940, D 4,27:6
Gaither, A, 1880, N 26,5:4
Gaither, Frances Mrs, 1955, O 29,19:1
Gaither, H Granger, 1964, S 20,89:2
Gaither, H Granger Mrs, 1954, Jl 10,13:3
Gaither, H R, 1953, F 28,17:5
Gaither, H Rowan Jr, 1961, Ap 8,19:3
Gaither, Harrison N, 1952, Ag 28,23:1
Gaither, Julian O, 1944, Mr 29,21:4
Gaither, Julian O Mrs, 1938, Ja 22,18:1
Gaither, Rice, 1953, D 9,11:1
Gaitree, William B, 1948, My 9,68:3
Gaitskell, Hugh T N (trb, Ja 23,2:4; funl, Ja 24,7:2), 1963, Ja 19,1:2
Gajdamowicz, Peter E, 1949, Mr 3,25:5
Galadzhev, Sergein, 1954, D 26,61:2
Galambos-Brown, Joseph, 1952, F 19,29:4
Galane, George, 1950, Jl 10,21:5
Galantha, Esterhazy De Prince, 1873, S 13,4:6
Galanti, Paul, 1950, O 10,31:3
Galardi, Frederick P, 1959, Ag 29,17:3
Galassi, Theodore V, 1949, Jl 29,21:4
Galassi (Mother Josephine), 1958, N 9,88:8
Galasso, Carl, 1960, Ap 21,31:5
Galati, August, 1952, S 28,77:1
Galatian, Martha E, 1943, Ap 7,25:1
Galatti, John P, 1956, Je 12,35:4
Galatti, Paul Stephen, 1914, Jl 15,9:7
Galatti, Stephen, 1964, Jl 14,33:1
Galatzine, Aimee C Princess (A Crocker), 1941, F 8, 17:6
Galbally, Edward J, 1942, D 7,27:2
Galberry, T Bp, 1878, O 11,5:4
Galbina, Frank J, 1939, Ap 26,23:4
Galbina, Irene D, 1948, Je 8,25:1
Galbraith, Alex T, 1960, O 20,35:3
Galbraith, Clayton S, 1953, Jl 3,19:5
Galbraith, Clinton A, 1923, My 28,15:4
Galbraith, Frederick W Jr Col, 1921, Je 11,13:6
Galbraith, Freeman D, 1938, Ap 19,21:3
Galbraith, Harry, 1942, Jl 21,19:2
Galbraith, James L Dr, 1937, N 5,23:2
Galbraith, Matthew W, 1955, N 6,86:3
Galbraith, P C, 1954, Ja 28,27:2
Galbraith, Peter J Mrs, 1958, O 8,35:4
Galbraith, R Niles, 1959, Mr 20,21:2
Galbraith, Thomas R, 1949, S 3,13:4
Galbraith, W W, 1955, N 16,35:3
Galbraith, Walter J, 1950, O 13,29:1
Galbraith, Walter S, 1939, Jl 18,19:6
Galbraith, William I Mrs, 1952, My 8,31:3
Galbrath, Bert A, 1949, S 24,13:4
Galbreath, Donald L, 1949, N 4,27:4
Galbreath, Otis W, 1938, O 7,23:3
Galbreath, Robert Mrs, 1945, Mr 14,19:2
Galdi, Dante, 1959, D 1,39:4
Galdieri, James J, 1944, Ap 28,19:5
Galdo, Frank, 1955, Mr 19,15:2
Galdos y Belzaguy, Domingo, 1952, Mr 5,29:3
Gale, A Davis, 1952, S 4,27:2
Gale, Alexander B, 1968, Je 27,43:4
Gale, Arthur S, 1964, Jl 7,32:8
Gale, Bertram S Mrs, 1937, F 16,23:1
Gale, Brian O, 1938, My 7,15:1
Gale, Cedric, 1964, S 19,27:3
Gale, Charles A Dr, 1922, O 4,23:5
Gale, Conrad A L, 1955, Mr 4,23:3
Gale, E D, 1882, F 14,8:1
Gale, Ernest L Sr Mrs, 1954, O 27,29:4
Gale, Esson M, 1964, My 16,25:3
Gale, Florence E, 1937, Jl 17,15:3
Gale, Frank A, 1949, Ap 24,76:1
Gale, Frank A Mrs, 1950, My 30,17:5
Gale, frank H, 1954, D 22,23:2
Gale, Frederick R, 1947, Ag 10,53:2
Gale, G William, 1937, My 19,23:5
Gale, George, 1951, D 25,31:4
Gale, George B, 1938, Ag 11,17:4
Gale, George H Mrs, 1950, Je 13,27:3
Gale, George Mrs, 1954, Ap 17,13:4
Gale, George W 3d, 1938, O 6,23:2
Gale, H H, 1877, Ag 2,5:3
Gale, Henry G, 1942, N 17,25:1
Gale, Henry S Mrs, 1957, N 11,29:5
Gale, Hiram R, 1951, Mr 16,31:4
Gale, Hollis P, 1962, O 25,39:2
Gale, Howard C Mrs, 1948, Ag 19,21:2
Gale, Hoyt S, 1952, Jl 8,27:2
Gale, Hoyt W Mrs, 1948, D 17,27:2
Gale, James E Mrs, 1944, N 14,23:3
Gale, James S Rev Dr, 1937, F 3,23:6
Gale, Jennie G Mrs, 1938, O 8,17:7
Gale, John A, 1914, Ag 28,9:6
Gale, L D, 1883, O 25,5:4
Gale, Lynn A E, 1940, Ag 15,19:2
Gale, M F, 1880, My 24,4:7
Gale, Mary V, 1959, Jl 24,25:1
Gale, Maurice Mrs, 1948, F 12,24:2
Gale, Minnie S Mrs, 1940, Ap 20,17:3
Gale, Moe, 1964, S 3,29:1
Gale, Noel, 1920, Ag 18,9:6
Gale, Phil J, 1958, Je 5,31:6
Gale, Philip B, 1945, Jl 26,19:4
Gale, Rodney, 1951, N 24,13:8
Gale, Samuel C, 1961, F 8,31:4
Gale, Sigmund, 1950, S 8,31:2
Gale, T W, 1880, My 16,2:3
Gale, Thomas B Mrs, 1944, Ap 5,19:5
Gale, W M, 1903, My 24,7:3
Gale, Walter, 1940, S 26,23:3
Gale, Walter C (por), 1938, F 26,15:2
Gale, Walter F, 1948, Mr 16,27:3
Gale, William, 1941, Mr 30,49:2
Gale, William M, 1938, Ag 28,33:4; 1943, O 31,48
Gale, Zona Mrs (Mrs Zona Breese), 1938, D 28,
Galeazzi-Lisi, Riccardo Dr, 1968, N 18,47:2
Galeen, Henrik, 1949, Ag 1,17:3
Galeffi, Carlo, 1961, S 23,19:6
Galen, Clemens A von, 1946, Mr 23,13:4
Galen, Daniel, 1951, Ap 7,15:3
Galen, Frank, 1955, Ja 24,23:3
Galen, Franz von, 1961, O 12,29:3
Galen, Joseph L, 1946, N 10,63:7
Galen, Leonard, 1958, N 25,33:3
Galentine, William H, 1945, S 29,15:5
Galento, Frank, 1948, Jl 24,15:6
Galer, Edward P, 1947, My 19,21:3
Gales, Arthur S, 1965, Ja 4,29:4
Gales, George M, 1954, Ag 17,21:5
Gales, Harry D, 1940, Jl 17,21:5
Gales, Joseph, 1860, Jl 27,5:2; 1916, My 2,13:5
Galesco, N, 1877, D 26,1:4
Galewitz, Jacob P, 1950, O 12,31:6
Galewski, Charles, 1942, Ag 12,19:2
Galey, John L, 1949, Ja 22,13:4
Galey, William T Jr, 1963, S 15,86:1
Galfund, Edward, 1950, Ja 17,27:2
Galgano, Frank I, 1942, O 26,15:4
Galiani, Edward, 1940, Ag 6,22:6
Galiano, Basil, 1939, Ag 22,19:5
Galib, George S, 1953, Ag 6,21:3
Galicenstein, Harry R, 1946, S 18,31:2
Galignani, Jean Antoine, 1874, Ja 1,1:7
Galimard, A, 1880, F 7,2:7
Galimore, Willie, 1964, Jl 27,1:1
Galin, Irvin, 1960, N 15,39:4
Galindo, Carlos B, 1943, O 4,17:3
Galindo, Enrique V, 1938, Je 12,38:8
Galinger, George W, 1961, D 12,43:3
Galinger, Solomon Maj, 1909, S 25,11:4
Galinsky, Judas B, 1956, Ja 24,31:5
Galisin, John J, 1949, Mr 25,24:2
Galison, Benjamin, 1960, Ja 1,19:3
Galison, Philip, 1959, O 2,29:2
Galitzen, Michael (M Riley), 1959, Je 12,27:2
Galitzine, Vladimir Prince, 1954, Jl 14,27:5
Galitzyn, Alexandra Princess, 1940, Jl 11,19:3
Gall, Albert W, 1950, Je 3,15:4
Gall, George F, 1959, Ag 7,23:3
Gall, Harold M, 1953, N 22,88:4
Gall, Henry R, 1946, Ja 13,44:2
Gall, Hugh, 1938, My 20,19:4
Gall, John C, 1957, D 15,87:1
Gall, Louis, 1959, Ap 8,37:4
Gall, Lucile von Baroness, 1909, Mr 5,9:4
Gall, Ralf, 1948, Jl 28,23:5
Gall, Stanislaw, 1942, S 19,15:3
Gallacher, William (funl, Ag 22,82:5), 1965, A 26:7
Gallaer, Horace W, 1959, Jl 19,69:2
Gallagan, James H, 1950, D 19,30:2
Gallager, Bernard A, 1951, Je 3,93:1
Gallagher, A Mrs, 1942, Mr 17,21:5
Gallagher, Alfred J, 1951, D 15,13:3
Gallagher, Ambrose W, 1946, D 26,26:2
Gallagher, Anna E H Mrs, 1937, O 12,25:2

Gallagher, Anne, 1942, Mr 2,19:3
Gallagher, Anthony J, 1948, Mr 2,23:3; 1952, Ja 5,11:4
Gallagher, Arthur F, 1944, Je 25,30:1
Gallagher, Bernard, 1947, Mr 24,25:4
Gallagher, Bernard Mrs, 1944, Je 30,21:3
Gallagher, Bessie M, 1939, Mr 5,49:1
Gallagher, C, 1938, Je 20,9:4
Gallagher, Charles, 1949, F 19,15:3
Gallagher, Charles A Sr, 1945, Jl 24,23:5
Gallagher, Charles B, 1964, Je 28,57:2
Gallagher, Charles E, 1944, Mr 15,19:2; 1951, Mr 8, 29:2
Gallagher, Charles H, 1940, Ja 30,19:3
Gallagher, Charles J, 1962, My 23,45:4
Gallagher, Charles P, 1940, F 16,19:4
Gallagher, Charles S, 1940, N 7,25:5
Gallagher, Charles V, 1952, D 29,19:1
Gallagher, Cornelius M, 1968, O 15,47:3
Gallagher, Dan, 1956, My 7,27:1
Gallagher, Dan W, 1949, S 24,13:5
Gallagher, Daniel J Jr, 1949, D 16,31:4
Gallagher, Daniel W, 1947, Je 11,27:5
Gallagher, Dean, 1943, D 21,28:2
Gallagher, Denis F, 1961, O 24,37:1
Gallagher, Dennis D, 1946, D 7,21:4
Gallagher, Edward, 1938, Ap 30,15:4; 1949, Ap 10, 76:1
Gallagher, Edward A, 1940, Ag 10,13:5
Gallagher, Edward C, 1940, Ag 29,19:4
Gallagher, Edward F, 1940, Je 11,25:4
Gallagher, Edward F Mrs, 1950, O 16,27:5
Gallagher, Edward G, 1946, Ja 31,21:3
Gallagher, Edward J, 1941, Ja 30,21:4; 1943, O 27, 23:4; 1949, D 22,23:5
Gallagher, Edward Mrs, 1947, Ag 6,23:5
Gallagher, Edward V, 1954, Ja 26,27:4
Gallagher, Ernest S, 1943, Ap 9,21:2
Gallagher, Eugene A, 1955, Ag 9,25:1
Gallagher, Felix, 1944, N 2,19:1
Gallagher, Francis E, 1950, Mr 25,13:5; 1950, S 10, 92:6
Gallagher, Francis G, 1937, My 17,19:3
Gallagher, Francis H, 1948, Ap 15,25:3
Gallagher, Francis J, 1948, N 27,17:5
Gallagher, Francis P, 1925, D 16,25:4; 1965, Jl 29, 27:5; 1967, Ag 21,31:1
Gallagher, Francis X, 1940, Ja 14,42:7; 1961, D 12, 43:4
Gallagher, Frank, 1962, Jl 18,29:4
Gallagher, Frank J, 1944, Je 25,29:2
Gallagher, Frank P, 1955, Jl 16,15:6
Gallagher, Frank V, 1946, My 25,15:1
Gallagher, Frank X Mrs (I Costa), 1967, Je 25,68:5
Gallagher, George, 1940, F 24,13:1
Gallagher, George E, 1952, N 13,31:4
Gallagher, George G, 1962, N 30,34:5
Gallagher, George W, 1943, Ap 9,21:2
Gallagher, H M Rev, 1903, Mr 17,7:6
Gallagher, Harry S, 1960, Je 16,33:2
Gallagher, Helen D Mrs, 1938, Ag 3,19:5
Gallagher, Henry J, 1955, Je 20,21:2
Gallagher, Herbert R, 1950, Ja 1,42:6
Gallagher, Hugh J, 1948, My 11,25:1
Gallagher, Hugh J Col, 1937, Mr 17,26:2
Gallagher, Hugh W, 1949, S 10,17:1
Gallagher, Isabella Mrs, 1937, My 20,21:5
Gallagher, J Francis, 1957, Jl 12,21:5
Gallagher, J Murray, 1955, F 8,27:2
Gallagher, J Walter, 1941, Ja 5,44:5
Gallagher, James, 1957, D 9,35:2
Gallagher, James A, 1949, Ag 20,11:3
Gallagher, James E, 1939, Jl 16,31:4
Gallagher, James F, 1960, Je 18,23:5
Gallagher, James G, 1942, Ag 2,38:7
Gallagher, James H Mrs, 1957, My 14,35:4
Gallagher, James J, 1940, F 14,21:2; 1946, Ag 22,27:4; 1947, S 10,27:3
Gallagher, James Jr, 1946, Ja 4,21:1
Gallagher, James P, 1952, Ja 13,88:8
Gallagher, James Sr Mrs, 1943, S 28,25:1
Gallagher, James T, 1953, D 16,35:3
Gallagher, John, 1921, Jl 27,15:4; 1941, N 21,17:2; 1946, Ap 26,21:2
Gallagher, John A, 1954, Jl 4,31:2
Gallagher, John C, 1960, Jl 12,35:1
Gallagher, John Dr, 1904, Ja 16,9:3
Gallagher, John E, 1940, Ap 28,37:2
Gallagher, John E Mrs, 1951, Je 19,29:1
Gallagher, John F, 1961, S 9,19:5
Gallagher, John F Mrs, 1958, O 18,21:4
Gallagher, John J, 1941, Ja 11,17:6; 1944, Ag 7,15:2; 1948, Ap 15,25:4; 1948, D 20,25:3; 1950, Ag 16,29:3; 1954, S 17,27:1; 1960, D 25,42:1; 1968, Jl 10,39:3
Gallagher, John J Mrs, 1949, Ja 9,72:2
Gallagher, John M, 1966, D 28,43:1
Gallagher, John P, 1946, Mr 5,26:3; 1946, Je 25,22:3
Gallagher, John T, 1954, S 11,17:4
Gallagher, John V, 1948, S 18,18:2
Gallagher, Joseph A, 1957, Mr 7,29:4; 1958, N 3,37:5
Gallagher, Joseph B, 1952, Ja 29,25:3
Gallagher, Joseph E, 1942, O 23,21:3; 1953, Je 5,27:3
Gallagher, Joseph F, 1949, D 28,32:3
Gallagher, Joseph H, 1943, N 7,57:2
Gallagher, Joseph T, 1946, Mr 20,23:3; 1946, Jl 14, 37:1; 1952, N 27,31:3
Gallagher, Katherine J, 1948, D 10,25:2
Gallagher, Katherine M, 1952, F 22,21:2
Gallagher, Leonard L, 1941, Jl 9,21:6
Gallagher, Leonard L Mrs, 1953, Mr 4,27:5
Gallagher, Lewis E Mrs, 1950, O 11,33:1
Gallagher, Luther C, 1872, O 30,8:5
Gallagher, Manuel C, 1953, My 7,32:3
Gallagher, Manus J, 1959, Mr 29,80:8
Gallagher, Margaret, 1947, Je 27,23:7
Gallagher, Margaret F, 1954, Ap 4,88:1
Gallagher, Margaret L, 1946, Mr 5,25:1
Gallagher, Marie K, 1958, Ap 17,32:6
Gallagher, Mary (Mother Monica), 1953, Ja 13,27:4
Gallagher, Michael, 1943, F 25,21:1; 1957, Ag 28,27:2
Gallagher, Michael B, 1951, S 16,85:2
Gallagher, Michael F, 1939, N 27,17:2
Gallagher, Michael H, 1955, Mr 8,16:5
Gallagher, Michael J, 1943, Ag 13,17:5
Gallagher, Michael J Bp, 1937, Ja 21,23:1
Gallagher, Michael V, 1951, My 19,15:6
Gallagher, Myles J, 1918, F 21,11:3
Gallagher, Neil, 1925, D 28,15:2
Gallagher, Patrick Father, 1919, Ap 4,11:3
Gallagher, Patrick H, 1941, Mr 28,23:2
Gallagher, Patrick J, 1950, Jl 24,17:5; 1952, Je 25,29:4
Gallagher, Patsy, 1953, Je 19,21:4
Gallagher, Paul R, 1940, D 26,19:4
Gallagher, Percy L Mrs, 1950, Jl 9,69:3
Gallagher, Peter E, 1951, N 3,17:2
Gallagher, Phil J, 1951, Mr 4,92:4
Gallagher, Philip B, 1961, Ap 14,10:1
Gallagher, Philip J, 1947, O 2,27:5
Gallagher, Phillip, 1951, D 23,22:6
Gallagher, Ralph W, 1952, Ag 1,17:3
Gallagher, Robert E Msgr, 1968, O 7,47:1
Gallagher, Robert W, 1947, F 20,25:1
Gallagher, Roger J, 1941, N 1,15:3
Gallagher, Sears, 1955, Je 11,15:6
Gallagher, Sister Mary Cornelia, 1962, Ap 19,31:4
Gallagher, Thomas A, 1943, D 7,27:4; 1952, Ja 29,25:3
Gallagher, Thomas Dr, 1925, D 3,25:3
Gallagher, Thomas E, 1951, N 25,86:2
Gallagher, Thomas F, 1907, F 9,9:6; 1941, Jl 6,26:7; 1952, S 4,27:3; 1957, Ag 22,27:6
Gallagher, Thomas J, 1941, Jl 1,23:5; 1949, Je 16,29:4; 1950, F 1,30:3; 1952, N 14,23:3; 1967, Mr 16,47:4
Gallagher, W, 1927, D 17,19:3
Gallagher, W G, 1927, Mr 9,25:1
Gallagher, W N, 1950, N 14,31:2
Gallagher, Walter J, 1957, F 3,76:7
Gallagher, William, 1939, Ag 23,21:5
Gallagher, William F, 1938, Mr 7,17:2; 1946, Mr 26, 29:5
Gallagher, William G, 1937, N 18,23:3
Gallagher, William H, 1956, Jl 12,23:2
Gallagher, William I, 1945, Ap 4,21:5
Gallagher, William J, 1940, Mr 26,21:3; 1944, Ja 4, 17:2; 1946, Ag 14,25:5; 1968, Ag 23,39:2
Gallagher, William M, 1951, D 26,25:5
Gallagher, William P, 1938, My 26,25:2
Gallagher, William Sr Mrs, 1948, N 16,29:1
Gallaher, Albert, 1908, Jl 1,7:5
Gallaher, Edward B, 1953, Ja 10,17:2
Gallaher, Edward B Mrs, 1965, Ap 9,33:2
Gallaher, Ernest Y, 1959, F 26,31:3
Gallaher, Gilbert P, 1955, Mr 24,31:4
Gallaher, Harry P, 1958, O 26,88:7
Gallaher, Hugh, 1956, Ap 3,35:3
Gallaher, J Frank, 1953, Je 23,30:6
Gallaher, Thomas B, 1948, My 22,15:4
Gallahue, Denis, 1941, Ap 1,23:4
Gallaix, Marcel de, 1949, D 8,33:2
Gallalee, John M, 1961, D 5,43:3
Galland, Abram S, 1961, S 20,29:5
Galland, Eugene, 1914, S 12,9:5
Galland, George Mrs, 1944, Ja 18,19:3
Galland, Joseph S, 1947, N 29,13:2
Gallannaugh, Bertram, 1957, Ag 29,27:5
Gallant, Alvin Mrs (Gladys), 1965, N 26,37:1
Gallant, Earl I, 1959, N 9,31:6
Gallant, Frank, 1965, D 29,29:3
Gallant, Frederick C Mrs, 1942, D 31,15:4
Gallant, Joseph, 1957, N 9,27:4
Gallarati-Scotti, Tommaso, 1966, Je 3,39:1
Gallarneau, Hugh Sr, 1952, Je 7,19:1
Gallatin, A H, 1902, Mr 26,9:6
Gallatin, A L, 1880, F 13,4:7
Gallatin, Albert, 1965, S 2,31:3
Gallatin, Albert E, 1952, Je 17,27:3
Gallatin, Albert H Mrs, 1922, D 4,17:4
Gallatin, Albert R, 1939, Mr 14,21:5
Gallatin, Alberta, 1948, Ag 27,19:3
Gallatin, Frederic, 1956, D 2,86:4
Gallatin, Frederick Mrs, 1917, Mr 28,13:5
Gallatin, Goelet, 1962, Ap 30,27:1
Gallatin, James (see also My 30), 1876, Je 27,3:7
Gallatin, James Francis de Comte, 1916, F 21,11:4
Gallatin, James Nicholson, 1916, N 9,13:4
Gallatin, R Horace, 1948, N 2,25:1
Gallaudet, Bern B Mrs, 1949, N 13,92:8
Gallaudet, Edson F, 1945, Jl 3,13:2
Gallaudet, Elizabeth F, 1944, S 4,19:1
Gallaudet, Herbert D, 1944, Je 25,30:1
Gallaudet, Katherine, 1942, D 14,28:3
Gallaudet, Ralph, 1958, Mr 16,87:1
Gallaudet, Thomas Mrs, 1903, Ap 26,7:7
Gallaway, Arthur W, 1938, Ja 15,15:4
Gallaway, George E, 1950, N 21,31:3
Gallaway, George E Mrs, 1953, D 23,25:2
Gallaway, John Macy, 1922, Ja 12,17:6
Gallaway, Mary, 1905, Ap 10,1:3
Gallaway, Merrill W, 1941, My 25,36:7
Gallaway, Robert Macy, 1917, N 14,15:3
Gallaway, William H, 1955, Ag 8,21:1
Gallaway, William S, 1947, Jl 1,25:2
Galle, Edward C Jr, 1960, Mr 24,33:5
Galle, Johann G Prof, 1910, Jl 12,7:5
Galleani, Leoniero Vice-Adm, 1925, Ag 13,19:5
Gallegher, John E, 1949, Ap 6,29:5
Gallegos, Salvador Dr, 1919, Jl 17,13:4
Galleher, George R, 1957, F 1,25:4
Galleher, John K, 1966, Ag 22,33:4
Gallen, Alvin, 1962, Jl 25,33:3
Gallen, Edward J, 1954, Ap 5,25:4
Gallen, Francis J, 1955, Ja 6,27:2
Gallen, James E, 1948, D 8,31:2
Gallen, John C, 1952, S 6,17:1
Gallen, John J, 1955, Ag 9,26:4
Gallen, Leo P, 1953, F 28,17:4
Galler, Charles, 1945, F 18,33:2
Galler, Walter C, 1953, D 31,19:4
Galler, William C, 1958, Mr 22,17:1
Gallert, David J, 1939, Ja 19,19:5
Gallery, Charles, 1945, F 18,33:2; 1945, Ag 3,17:2
Gallery, Daniel V, 1938, My 31,19:5
Gallery, Daniel V Mrs, 1941, Ja 13,15:3
Gallery, J Eugene, 1960, Jl 29,25:2
Galletly, William Mrs, 1943, Mr 1,19:6
Galletti, Antonio, 1949, O 15,15:6
Galley, H W, 1948, Ag 9,20:2
Galley, John V, 1959, D 25,21:2
Galli, Alfredo, 1948, O 1,26:2
Galli, Dina, 1951, Mr 5,21:1
Galli, Enrichetta Mrs, 1923, Ap 14,13:5
Galli, Jose, 1952, N 7,23:5
Galli, Joseph D, 1954, N 21,86:5
Galli, Rosina (por), 1940, My 1,24:2
Galli, Rossi Mrs, 1924, Ja 9,21:3
Galli-Curci, Amelita (will, D 7,30:2), 1963, N 27,1:5
Gallichio, Joseph J, 1961, F 24,21:7
Gallick, Andrew M, 1954, Ag 23,17:5
Gallick, Cuthbert J, 1948, O 20,29:5
Gallico, J Edward, 1952, O 28,31:5
Gallico, Paolo, 1955, Jl 7,27:5
Gallie, Thomas M, 1965, Je 23,41:2
Gallie, William E, 1959, S 27,86:8
Gallien, George B, 1967, Mr 22,47:1
Gallieni, Joseph S Gen, 1916, My 28,17:3
Gallienne, Wilfred H, 1956, Jl 19,27:2
Galliera, Duke de, 1876, D 21,7:6
Gallifet, Gaston Alexandre Auguste Marquis de, 1909, Jl 9,7:5
Galligan, Andrew J, 1949, Ap 10,76:1
Galligan, B F Rev, 1926, N 21,30:4
Galligan, Charles A, 1952, S 7,86:5
Galligan, Charles J, 1948, N 22,21:2
Galligan, Edward M, 1943, Jl 30,15:4
Galligan, J Edward Mrs, 1952, Mr 7,23:4
Galligan, J M Rev, 1901, Ap 4,9:4
Galligan, James, 1968, Je 28,38:1
Galligan, James A, 1945, Ja 19,19:4
Galligan, James F, 1938, F 3,23:4
Galligan, John, 1914, My 11,11:6
Galligan, Michael E, 1944, My 27,15:5
Galligan, Thomas, 1956, Ap 11,33:5
Galligan, William J, 1950, O 13,29:1
Galligan, William J Sr, 1954, D 11,13:1
Galliger, Patrick C, 1945, Mr 26,19:2
Gallimard, Donato, Michel, 1960, Ja 10,86:3
Gallin, Hyman, 1964, Ag 13,29:3
Gallin, Louis, 1958, S 19,28:1
Gallin, Nathan M, 1960, Mr 14,29:2
Gallin, William L H, 1953, Je 18,32:2
Gallinger, George A, 1943, Jl 20,19:4
Gallinger, Herbert P, 1947, F 3,19:5
Gallinger, Jacob H (funl, Ag 20,9:5), 1918, Ag 18, 19:1
Gallingher, Jacob H Mrs, 1907, F 4,9:6
Gallino, Angelo, 1954, Jl 20,19:3
Gallison, Harold H, 1940, Ja 6,13:1
Gallison, Henry Hammond, 1910, O 13,11:4
Gallison, Louis D, 1903, O 18,7:6
Gallivan, J A, 1928, Ap 4,29:4
Gallivan, James F, 1953, My 1,21:2
Gallivan, James J, 1958, N 8,21:1
Gallivan, Michael F, 1939, S 29,23:4
Gallivan, William J Dr, 1921, Jl 14,15:5
Galliver, G A, 1932, Jl 7,17:1
Gallmeyer, Josephine, 1884, F 4,5:3
Gallo, Charles, 1953, Je 9,27:3
Gallo, Charles L, 1968, Ja 16,39:1
Gallo, Donato M Mrs, 1957, N 9,27:6
Gallo, Fortune Mrs, 1948, O 16,15:6
Gallo, Giuseppe, 1950, O 25,38:4

Gallo, Guerino, 1961, Jl 25,27:4
Gallo, John C, 1959, D 23,27:1
Gallo, Lawrence (Larry),(funl, My 22,51:2), 1968, My 19,66:4
Gallo, Michael, 1954, Ap 26,25:4
Gallo Monterrubio, Joaquin, 1965, O 21,47:2
Gallon, Monroe F, 1953, Ja 15,27:5
Gallon, Thomas H, 1945, S 30,46:6
Gallon, Tom, 1914, N 5,11:4
Gallon, William J, 1957, Je 6,31:4
Galloney, Frank H, 1916, Jl 27,9:6
Gallop, H Marcellus, 1943, Ap 11,48:5
Gallori, Emilio, 1924, D 26,15:5
Galloupe, Charles W, 1903, N 29,7:6
Galloway, Bryon S, 1945, Ap 30,19:2
Galloway, Burton M, 1956, My 25,23:2
Galloway, C Douglas 2d, 1960, Ja 5,31:1
Galloway, Charles B Bp, 1909, My 13,7:6
Galloway, Charles F, 1958, S 9,35:1
Galloway, Charles F Mrs, 1958, S 9,35:1
Galloway, Charles M, 1954, S 5,50:7
Galloway, Charles W, 1940, D 15,61:3
Galloway, Clark H, 1961, Ja 3,29:2
Galloway, David B, 1954, Ag 17,21:2
Galloway, David M, 1954, Mr 27,17:3
Galloway, E Frank, 1944, Ap 13,19:5
Galloway, Earl of, 1873, Ja 4,1:5
Galloway, Edward T, 1924, Je 16,15:4; 1963, N 8,31:1
Galloway, Elmer (por), 1948, D 12,92:6
Galloway, Eugene M, 1961, Jl 7,25:2
Galloway, Ewing, 1953, Je 27,15:2
Galloway, Ewing Mrs, 1959, F 15,85:5
Galloway, Floyd E, 1955, S 22,31:3
Galloway, Franklin Mrs, 1949, F 18,23:2
Galloway, George B, 1967, Jl 30,65:1
Galloway, George M, 1965, My 2,88:1
Galloway, H Gordon Mrs, 1937, N 5,23:2
Galloway, Harold H, 1942, Ap 27,15:4
Galloway, Helen L Mrs, 1949, Mr 4,21:3
Galloway, Herbert P H, 1939, Jl 14,19:1
Galloway, James, 1937, F 14,II,9:3
Galloway, Jesse J, 1962, Ap 12,35:3
Galloway, John E, 1940, Ap 30,21:3
Galloway, John H, 1942, Ag 6,19:3
Galloway, John H Mrs, 1944, Mr 23,19:3
Galloway, John W, 1937, N 20,17:5
Galloway, John W Mrs, 1948, My 6,25:4
Galloway, Lee, 1962, F 4,82:5
Galloway, Louise, 1949, O 12,29:5
Galloway, Marguerite, 1957, Jl 1,23:4
Galloway, Richard S, 1938, Jl 4,13:5
Galloway, Samuel, 1872, Ap 6,1:3
Galloway, W S, 1948, Mr 18,27:1
Galloway, William, 1952, N 11,29:3
Galloway, William A, 1909, My 1,9:4
Gallowhur, William G, 1959, My 29,23:4
Gallowhur, William G Mrs, 1952, Mr 8,13:4
Gallozzi, Thomas, 1938, Mr 9,23:1
Gallucci, Arthur, 1967, Ja 24,28:8
Gallucci, Victor E, 1961, Ap 12,41:4
Galludet, Edward Miner Dr, 1917, S 27,13:6
Gallup, Albert Smith, 1906, Mr 22,9:5
Gallup, Anna B, 1956, O 22,29:2
Gallup, Augustus T, 1945, S 15,15:2
Gallup, Burton A, 1959, Ap 22,33:3
Gallup, Charles H, 1942, My 21,19:6
Gallup, Clarence M (por), 1947, Jl 18,17:5
Gallup, Clarence M Mrs, 1953, N 1,87:2
Gallup, Dana G, 1943, O 8,19:6
Gallup, David, 1883, Ag 19,7:2
Gallup, David L, 1924, F 11,15:4
Gallup, Emory L, 1947, N 3,23:5
Gallup, Ernest M, 1950, Je 18,76:7
Gallup, Frank A, 1951, F 16,25:4
Gallup, Fred D, 1949, D 27,23:1
Gallup, George B, 1949, Je 18,13:5
Gallup, George H Sr Mrs, 1953, S 30,31:2
Gallup, Harvey A, 1946, Ag 5,21:6
Gallup, Howard, 1903, Mr 20,9:4
Gallup, Jackson S, 1946, Ag 22,27:5
Gallup, John C Mrs, 1959, O 12,19:6
Gallup, Oren O Mrs, 1961, Jl 5,33:4
Gallup, Sarah M, 1944, Je 24,13:3
Gallupe, H Quimby, 1952, My 30,15:1
Gallwey, Edward H, 1953, Mr 10,29:1
Gallwitz, Max van Gen (por), 1937, Ap 20,25:1
Gally, Merritt, 1916, Mr 10,9:7
Galois, Napoleon, 1874, O 3,3:4
Galos, Ben, 1963, My 20,31:2
Galotti, Primo, 1950, N 5,92:5
Galowit, Andrew Mrs, 1962, Ag 5,81:1
Galowitz, Louis, 1955, Mr 24,31:4
Galperson, Alex, 1950, Ja 5,25:1
Galpin, Barbara Mrs, 1922, Ag 15,11:5
Galpin, Henry L, 1961, Jl 25,28:2
Galpin, Homer K, 1941, Jl 28,13:5
Galpin, Perrin C Mrs, 1965, D 17,39:2
Galschjodt, Harold M, 1955, Ag 5,19:6
Galster, Henry C, 1942, Je 9,23:5
Galston, Clarence G, 1964, Ja 24,27:2
Galston, Clarence G Mrs, 1965, Ja 28,30:4
Galston, Gottfried, 1950, Ap 5,32:2
Galston, Samuel H, 1957, D 25,31:5

Galsworthy, J, 1933, F 1,17:1
Galsworthy, John Mrs, 1956, My 30,21:5
Galt, Annabel, 1938, O 8,17:5
Galt, Caroline M Prof, 1937, Ja 20,21:1
Galt, Carroll Grayson, 1916, N 15,11:5
Galt, Edith J, 1961, My 25,37:6
Galt, Francis L Dr, 1915, N 19,11:5
Galt, Frank A, 1943, Je 18,22:2
Galt, H R, 1926, D 20,21:4
Galt, Howard S Mrs, 1957, Mr 4,27:3
Galt, Hugh A, 1947, F 25,25:1
Galt, John R, 1941, Ag 4,13:3
Galt, Morris, 1955, O 16,87:1
Galt, Morris Mrs, 1948, My 3,21:2
Galt, Roger H Commodore, 1910, Ag 27,7:6
Galt, Russell, 1959, Mr 17,33:3
Galt, Sterling, 1922, D 30,13:5
Galt, T Sir Chief Justice, 1901, Je 30,7:6
Galt, William E, 1955, F 7,21:3
Galter, David J, 1961, O 31,31:4
Galterio, Patrick, 1942, Jl 19,31:3
Galton, Francis Sir, 1911, Ja 19,9:3
Galula, David, 1967, My 12,47:2
Galusha, Irving, 1959, My 31,76:4
Galvagni, Charles, 1939, Ag 22,19:5
Galvan, Manuel de J, 1910, D 16,11:5
Galvani, Ciro, 1956, Ja 30,27:3
Galvez, Jose M, 1950, N 18,15:5
Galvez Suarez, Alfredo, 1946, D 17,31:5
Galvez y Barrenechea, Jose, 1957, F 9,19:5
Galvin, Charles B, 1943, N 21,57:1
Galvin, E J Eustace, 1950, D 8,29:1
Galvin, Edward J (funl, Ja 30,19:4), 1924, Ja 29,19:3
Galvin, Edward J, 1956, F 25,19:4
Galvin, Ellen, 1907, D 11,11:4
Galvin, Elmer W, 1953, Ag 21,18:3
Galvin, Eugene (por), 1948, Mr 30,23:3
Galvin, Eugene G, 1948, N 13,15:2
Galvin, George E, 1950, O 22,94:3
Galvin, Howard E (cor, F 18,21:1), 1955, F 17,27:3
Galvin, J F, 1936, Jl 13,13:1
Galvin, John, 1922, Mr 3,13:5
Galvin, John F Jr, 1966, D 17,33:6
Galvin, John H, 1940, Je 26,23:1
Galvin, John J, 1954, Ja 5,27:1
Galvin, John P, 1949, O 9,95:3
Galvin, John T Jr, 1957, Jl 13,17:5
Galvin, Joseph, 1944, Mr 8,19:4
Galvin, Joseph A, 1954, My 12,31:5
Galvin, Joseph I, 1953, N 17,31:1
Galvin, Leroy S, 1952, Mr 2,92:2
Galvin, Martin E, 1944, Ag 19,11:3
Galvin, Matthew, 1954, Ja 30,17:3
Galvin, Maurice, 1944, Ag 12,11:6
Galvin, Maurice L, 1940, Ag 26,15:4
Galvin, Michael J, 1910, Ag 29,7:6; 1963, D 13,35:3
Galvin, Patrick H, 1944, N 27,23:4
Galvin, Paul V, 1959, N 6,29:2
Galvin, Renaldo J, 1948, O 6,29:2
Galvin, Richard J, 1947, S 27,15:2
Galvin, Stephen L, 1967, O 18,47:1
Galvin, W J, 1953, Jl 1,29:5
Galvin, William, 1942, Ap 9,19:3
Galvin, William E, 1942, S 22,21:5
Galvin, William J, 1951, Ap 14,16:2
Galway, James, 1910, Ap 1,11:5
Galway, Viscount, 1943, Mr 29,15:5
Galzebrook, Otis A 3d, 1966, Jl 22,28:8
Gama, Elizabeth B B da Mrs, 1937, My 10,19:3
Gama Ochoa, Armando H da, 1941, Je 10,23:3
Gamage, Frederick L (por), 1947, S 12,22:2
Gamaleia, Nikolai F, 1949, Mr 30,25:1
Gambara, Gastone Mrs, 1952, O 18,19:5
Gambarelli, Eole, 1958, Mr 24,27:4
Gambarra, Gastone, 1962, F 28,33:2
Gambee, Robert C, 1953, F 6,19:2
Gambee, Wheeler B, 1942, S 25,21:5
Gamber, Clarence, 1941, D 12,25:3
Gamber, John F, 1949, D 28,25:3
Gambert, Nicholas H, 1949, Ap 15,23:3
Gambetta (Biography), 1883, Ja 2,1:7
Gambini, Alberto, 1950, F 27,19:1
Gambino, John, 1956, Jl 9,23:5
Gambino, Pascual, 1960, F 16,40:1
Gambinossi, Dante, 1942, Je 8,15:2
Gamble, Albert A, 1951, D 31,13:3
Gamble, B E Dr, 1937, Jl 10,15:6
Gamble, Bertus D, 1946, Ja 31,21:4
Gamble, Carey Breckenridge Dr, 1921, N 10,19:5
Gamble, Carl H, 1958, Ja 27,27:4
Gamble, Cary B Jr, 1943, Je 2,25:2
Gamble, Cecil H, 1956, Je 20,31:6
Gamble, Cecil H Mrs, 1963, S 13,29:3
Gamble, Charles A, 1939, Jl 21,19:2
Gamble, Charles W, 1943, Ag 8,37:1
Gamble, Chi, 1954, F 14,93:1
Gamble, Clarence J, 1966, Jl 18,27:4
Gamble, David B, 1923, Jl 17,19:6
Gamble, David S, 1945, Ja 10,23:5
Gamble, Edwin P, 1939, Ap 24,17:1
Gamble, Elizabeth, 1947, O 24,23:5
Gamble, Ernest, 1963, Jl 30,29:1
Gamble, George T Mrs, 1949, My 29,36:5

Gamble, Glenn, 1961, N 14,39:1
Gamble, Gov, 1864, F 1,1:2
Gamble, H R, 1931, Ag 10,15:5
Gamble, Henry W, 1939, Jl 26,19:3
Gamble, J Munson, 1942, S 27,48:2
Gamble, J N, 1932, Jl 3,15:1
Gamble, James A, 1957, Ap 20,17:5
Gamble, James L, 1959, My 29,23:2
Gamble, John D, 1952, Mr 9,92:4
Gamble, Josephine Mrs, 1942, Jl 23,19:4
Gamble, Lynn H, 1963, Ap 22,27:4
Gamble, Olivia P, 1961, Ap 13,35:5
Gamble, Paul G Mrs, 1953, N 24,29:2
Gamble, Ralph A, 1959, Mr 5,31:3
Gamble, Ralph A Mrs, 1937, Mr 17,25:2
Gamble, Robert G, 1943, Mr 14,26:2
Gamble, Robert J Mrs, 1947, Je 9,21:4
Gamble, Robert Jackson Ex-Sen, 1924, S 23,23:2
Gamble, Sidney David, 1968, Mr 30,33:3
Gamble, Ted R, 1960, My 19,37:4
Gamble, Thomas, 1945, Jl 15,15:6
Gamble, Thomas F, 1950, Ag 22,27:2
Gamble, Walter W, 1967, Je 6,47:4
Gamble, William, 1922, S 30,13:6
Gamble, William B, 1941, F 16,39:6
Gamble, William O, 1921, Ag 24,11:4
Gamboa, Federico, 1939, Ag 16,23:4
Gambon, Andrew J, 1949, O 17,23:5
Gambone, John H, 1952, N 6,29:3
Gambrell, Enoch P Mrs, 1954, Jl 8,23:3
Gambrell, Fred W Mrs, 1950, N 13,27:5
Gambrill, Chauncey, 1919, Ja 27,13:3
Gambrill, John M, 1953, Ja 16,23:5
Gambrill, Richard V (will), 1953, F 6,21:2
Gambrill, Richard V N, 1952, D 11,33:6
Gambrill, Stephen W (por), 1938, D 20,25:4
Gamburtsev, Alexandrovitch, 1955, Jl 3,32:8
Game, Clyffard, 1955, Jl 20,27:4
Game, William C, 1945, Ag 19,40:3
Gamelin, Maurice G (funl, Ap 25,27:4), 1958, Ap 19,1:6
Gamer, Carl F, 1964, S 4,29:3
Gamer, Helena M, 1966, My 15,88:6
Gamewell, Frank D Mrs, 1906, N 29,9:5; 1947, Ag 17:5
Gamez, Jose D, 1918, Je 12,13:5
Gammack, John Rev, 1937, Ja 3,II,8:6
Gammack, Thomas H (por), 1937, Je 19,17:3
Gammage, Lafayette L, 1955, N 24,29:4
Gammans, David, 1957, F 9,19:5
Gammel, Bert, 1949, F 11,23:4
Gammel, Edith Mrs, 1949, Jl 28,24:2
Gammell, Robert Ives, 1915, Ja 9,11:4
Gammell, William, 1943, N 13,13:4
Gammeter, Harry C, 1937, Ap 12,17:2
Gammie, John, 1968, F 23,34:1
Gammie, John Mrs, 1958, Jl 13,45:2
Gammino, Michael A, 1949, D 3,15:6
Gammon, Edgar G, 1962, My 11,31:2
Gammon, Landon K Mrs, 1954, O 9,17:3
Gammon, Matilda W Mrs, 1955, Mr 6,89:1
Gammon, Robert W Dr, 1948, F 28,15:5
Gammons, Susan L Mrs, 1940, D 13,23:4
Gamon, Robert S Sr, 1953, My 20,29:5
Gamoran, Emanuel, 1962, N 16,31:1
Gamow, George Dr, 1968, Ag 22,37:1
Gampel, Joseph, 1948, O 10,76:4
Gamso, Beatrice, 1952, Mr 10,21:5
Gamso, Joseph J, 1946, Mr 22,21:4
Gamson, Harry L, 1952, N 3,27:5
Gamsu, Charles, 1943, D 10,27:1
Gamwell, Cecil C, 1941, S 21,44:2
Gamwell, Cecil C Jr, 1947, Ap 19,15:3
Gamwell, Charles W, 1943, S 10,23:2
Gamwell Wm W, 1959, Ag 6,27:4
Ganann, Joseph W, 1964, Ap 22,47:2
Ganay, Marquis de, 1948, F 20,27:1
Ganay, Marquise de, 1921, S 19,15:4
Gandara, Antonio, 1917, Jl 3,9:4
Gandara, Jose N, 1954, O 13,31:3
Gandhi, Devadas, 1957, Ag 3,15:5
Gandhi, Feroze, 1960, S 9,29:1
Gandhi, Hiraral M, 1948, Je 28,8:6
Gandhi, Mohandas K Mrs, 1944, F 23,19:3
Gandia, Pedro, 1938, D 28,21:3
Gandino, Adolfo, 1940, Je 8,15:1
Gandolfi, Alfredo, 1963, Je 10,31:2
Gandolfo, Gen (funl, S 3,25:4), 1925, Ag 31,1[illegible]
Gandusio, Antonio, 1951, My 24,35:5
Gandy, Albert L, 1958, Mr 22,17:2
Gandy, Charles M Col, 1937, Ja 11,19:4
Gandy, Curtis Jr, 1950, D 25,19:5
Gandy, George S Sr, 1946, N 27,25:1
Gandy, Lewis C, 1951, Jl 30,17:5
Gandy, Maurice, 1953, Jl 31,19:4
Gandy, Raymond R, 1960, F 22,17:4
Gandz, Solomon, 1954, Ap 1,31:1
Gane, Harold J, 1967, Ja 26,33:1
Ganesky, Peter, 1910, My 27,9:4
Ganey, Helen M, 1950, Je 17,15:3
Ganey, Jeremiah F, 1948, N 3,27:3
Ganfield, William A, 1940, O 19,17:3
Gang, Jane Vorhaus Dr, 1968, O 19,37:4

Gang, Leopold, 1950, Je 17,15:2
Gang, Victor, 1945, S 20,8:4
Gange, Fraser, 1962, Jl 3,23:4
Gange, William J, 1940, Ja 3,21:2
Gangel, Coleman, 1961, N 26,88:2
Ganger, I Arthur (cor, Jl 16,25:2), 1957, Jl 15,19:2
Ganger, Jefferson A, 1954, Jl 5,11:6
Ganghofer, Ludwig Dr, 1920, Jl 27,13:5
Ganiard, Alexander A, 1904, Ja 12,7:6
Ganley, Alice Mrs, 1941, Ja 2,16:6
Ganley, Arthur J, 1959, My 11,27:5
Ganley, Edward H, 1948, Ja 24,15:1
Ganley, Francis L, 1944, Ja 12,23:2
Ganley, James J, 1940, Ag 16,15:4
Ganley, James Vincent, 1923, S 8,13:4
Ganley, Robert S, 1945, O 11,23:5
Ganley, William, 1949, S 4,41:1
Gann, E W (Red), 1954, F 4,25:3
Gann, Edward E Mrs, 1953, Ja 31,15:1
Gann, Thomas (por), 1938, F 25,17:3
Gann, William D, 1955, Je 20,21:1
Gannam, John, 1965, Ja 28,29:4
Gannes, Harry, 1941, Ja 7,10:6
Gannett, Ed Stiles Rev, 1871, Ag 28,4:7
Gannett, Flora M, 1937, My 22,15:6
Gannett, Frank E (funl, D 7,21:5; will, D 10,32:4), 1957, D 4,39:1
Gannett, Frank E (est tax appr), 1960, O 1,16:7
Gannett, Guy P (funl, Ap 28,31:1), 1954, Ap 25,86:1
Gannett, Guy P Mrs, 1951, Mr 23,35:5
Gannett, Henry, 1914, N 6,11:6
Gannett, Herbert I, 1943, Je 13,44:7
Gannett, Howard, 1953, S 4,34:3
Gannett, Joseph K, 1963, Jl 23,29:2
Gannett, William C Mrs, 1952, O 27,27:3
Gannett, William H (por), 1948, Jl 31,15:5
Gannon, Ada K, 1937, S 5,II,7:2
Gannon, Catherine M, 1954, D 23,19:5
Gannon, Charles F, 1957, F 17,92:4
Gannon, Clarence L, 1951, Je 24,72:5
Gannon, Clarence L Mrs, 1940, My 9,23:3
Gannon, E J, 1951, O 12,27:3
Gannon, Edward P, 1963, My 8,39:5
Gannon, Frank G, 1964, O 14,45:2
Gannon, Frank S, 1922, N 9,19:3
Gannon, Gilbert, 1952, D 7,89:2
Gannon, Gov, 1865, Mr 2,4:5
Gannon, Helen, 1959, D 3,37:4
Gannon, James F Jr, 1955, F 15,27:5
Gannon, James J, 1951, My 11,27:2
Gannon, John, 1952, Ja 13,88:3
Gannon, John F, 1940, D 31,15:5
Gannon, John J, 1939, F 12,45:2; 1957, Je 11,35:4; 1964, Jl 2,31:5
Gannon, John J Mrs, 1948, Ag 20,17:1
Gannon, John Mark Archbishop, 1968, S 6,43:4
Gannon, Joseph R, 1939, Ag 28,19:3
Gannon, Joseph W, 1967, Ja 26,33:3
Gannon, Joseph W Mrs, 1942, N 27,23:3
Gannon, Lawrence C, 1952, Ag 8,17:4
Gannon, Marjorie Copeland (Mrs J W Gannon), 1968, N 26,53:6
Gannon, Mary (Mrs Mary A Stevenson),(funl, F 25,4:6), 1868, F 23,4:6
Gannon, Mary (Sister Mary Marion), 1958, Ap 1, 31:1
Gannon, Michael B, 1939, N 22,24:7
Gannon, Patrick J, 1919, D 17,17:2
Gannon, Peter J, 1950, Ja 18,32:2
Gannon, Sabina (Mother Mary Loyola), 1957, My 14,35:4
Gannon, Sinclair, 1948, O 22,25:4
Gannon, Thomas C, 1958, Ja 11,17:1
Gannon, Thomas F, 1948, F 4,23:4
Gannon, Thomas F (por), 1949, Ja 14,23:2
Gannon, Victor T, 1919, My 17,13:7
Gannon, Vincent D, 1956, Ag 29,29:4
Gannon, William A, 1943, Ap 27,23:4
Gannon, William F, 1948, Ja 12,19:1
Gannon, William J, 1943, Ap 26,19:5
Gannon, William P, 1937, Jl 9,21:2; 1950, Jl 4,17:2
Gannone, Peter, 1951, D 27,21:3
Gano, Charles W, 1950, Ja 19,27:3
Gano, D Curtis, 1948, Je 10,25:5
Gano, Edwin E, 1944, N 19,50:2
Gano, Levi M, 1903, N 13,7:6
Gano, Pauline W Mrs, 1950, My 2,29:4
Ganong, A D Mrs, 1958, Jl 10,27:5
Ganong, Frances Mrs, 1947, My 23,23:4
Ganong, J Clair, 1955, My 12,29:4
Ganong, James E, 1944, My 8,19:2
Ganong, Walter S, 1950, Mr 21,29:2
Ganong, Willis A Mrs, 1946, Ja 14,19:3
Ganow, Stacey B, 1947, Je 24,23:5
Gans, Aaron, 1918, Ap 30,13:4
Gans, Albert E, 1957, N 27,31:3
Gans, Anna M F Mrs (will), 1940, Mr 16,15:1
Gans, Charles M, 1964, Ag 3,25:4
Gans, Edgar H, 1914, S 21,7:4
Gans, Edward M, 1942, D 1,25:1; 1958, D 1,29:4
Gans, Henry, 1962, O 21,88:6
Gans, Howard S, 1946, D 13,24:2
Gans, Howard S Mrs, 1944, D 31,26:1
Gans, Isaac, 1940, F 6,21:2
Gans, Joe (Baby),(G Slaughter), 1959, Ap 21,35:4
Gans, Laurence M, 1943, My 2,45:1
Gans, Leonard S, 1958, Jl 30,29:1
Gans, Louis, 1904, F 8,9:5
Gans, Milton H, 1942, S 30,23:6
Gans, Moses J Mrs, 1960, F 26,31:3
Gans, Oscar, 1965, D 7,47:1
Gans, Otto, 1955, F 11,23:2
Gans, Paul F Dr, 1915, Ap 22,13:4
Gans, William A, 1915, Ap 9,11:5
Gansberg, Jacob M Mrs, 1960, N 22,35:2
Gansberg, Murray Mrs, 1967, Ap 15,31:1
Gansbergen, Henry H, 1943, Ja 22,20:3
Ganse, L C, 1880, N 7,2:1
Ganser, Andrew F, 1948, Mr 24,25:4
Ganser, Francis O, 1957, Ap 26,25:4
Gansevoort, Guest Commodore, 1868, Jl 17,5:4
Gansler, Fred H, 1968, My 8,44:2
Gansman, Harry M, 1954, Ja 23,13:3
Ganso, Emil, 1941, Ap 19,15:3
Ganson, Adam M, 1937, D 15,25:5
Ganson, John (trb, Oc 1,1:6), 1874, S 29,5:2
Ganson, Joseph W, 1939, O 25,23:6
Ganss, Jacob Mrs, 1950, F 19,78:1
Ganss, Robert A, 1953, Ja 23,19:3
Ganster, Teresa R Mrs, 1942, Je 5,17:6
Gant, Israel H, 1954, O 5,27:2
Gant, James E, 1940, S 9,15:4
Ganteaume, Henri D A, 1956, O 17,35:5
Ganter, Carl R, 1963, N 11,31:5
Gantert, Frank A, 1940, F 28,21:6
Gantert, Helen Mrs, 1941, S 4,22:2
Gantert, Robert M, 1947, Je 24,23:2
Ganthony, Bonita Mrs, 1939, S 21,23:4
Gantly, Thomas J, 1950, Ja 31,23:4
Gantner, John O, 1951, Ag 2,21:1
Gantner, Otto R, 1967, Ja 16,41:2
Gants, Edward J, 1948, My 9,68:4
Gants, Milfred A, 1945, Mr 20,19:3
Gants, Robert T, 1958, F 18,27:2
Gantt, D Chief Justice, 1878, My 31,1:6
Gantt, Pleasant Mrs, 1944, My 4,19:5
Gantt, Robert Anderson, 1968, Je 25,41:4
Gantvoort, Herman L, 1937, S 18,19:4
Gantz, Aaron, 1938, N 15,23:3
Gantz, Albert Dale, 1968, Ja 25,40:1
Gantz, Charles Sr, 1941, Mr 26,23:3
Gantz, Edwin J, 1942, O 13,23:2
Gantz, Harry, 1949, Ag 12,17:4
Gantz, James W, 1962, D 1,25:4
Gantz, John (Doc), 1954, Mr 30,27:3
Gantz, Joseph, 1945, Ap 27,19:4
Gantz, Joseph Mrs, 1958, Ja 16,29:2
Gantz, William O, 1957, Ag 7,27:4
Gantzer, George, 1916, O 8,23:4
Ganun, Gilbert E, 1940, N 30,17:4
Ganun, Stephen M, 1903, Jl 2,9:6
Ganung, Charles F, 1941, Ag 5,19:2
Ganung, Frederick H, 1967, D 16,41:3
Ganung, George, 1948, Ag 13,15:5
Ganung, Leroy Mrs, 1950, N 3,27:3
Ganz, Albert P Prof, 1917, Jl 28,15:3
Ganz, Isidor, 1959, Mr 6,25:4
Ganz, Louis, 1960, Ap 6,41:4
Ganz, Saul, 1953, O 10,17:4
Ganz, William J, 1968, Je 30,52:7
Ganzel, John H, 1959, Ja 16,27:1
Ganzel, Louis Mrs, 1946, N 9,17:6
Ganzer, Samuel, 1947, My 15,25:1
Ganzlin, Bertha, 1951, N 16,25:2
Gapfert, Randolph, 1965, N 17,47:1
Gapin, William, 1957, D 26,19:2
Gaponovich, Dmitri A, 1952, D 1,23:5
Gapp, Kenneth S, 1966, Jl 6,42:3
Gara, Emmerich, 1963, My 13,29:4
Gara, Max M Mrs, 1953, Jl 20,17:3
Garabed, Joseph (Joe the Turk), 1937, O 12,29:4
Garabedian, Carl A, 1963, Je 13,33:2
Garabedian, N Joseph, 1960, Je 9,33:5
Garabrant, James L, 1960, S 6,35:1
Garabrant, Joseph E, 1963, Ap 17,41:4
Garabrant, Maurice, 1959, O 3,19:3
Garand, Phileas S, 1942, Ap 4,13:7
Garapedian, Vartan, 1951, Ag 31,15:1
Garard, Elzy A, 1939, My 1,23:3
Garat, Henri, 1959, Ag 14,21:2
Garay, Arnold, 1965, My 2,88:2
Garay, Gregory Mrs, 1956, Ja 7,17:4
Garay, Jose de, 1858, S 25,4:5
Garay, Narciso J, 1953, Mr 28,17:2
Garb, John, 1960, Ag 15,23:4
Garba, Peter, 1916, S 8,7:4
Garback, F Phil, 1953, Jl 10,19:5
Garbarino, Joseph J, 1947, Jl 18,17:4
Garbarino, Leon W, 1938, Je 2,23:4
Garbat, Abraham Leon Dr, 1968, Ag 14,39:1
Garbaty, Eugene L, 1966, S 8,47:2
Garbe, Bertha Mrs, 1947, N 13,28:3
Garbe, Ernest M, 1967, D 14,47:2
Garber, D Allyn, 1951, Ag 11,11:2
Garber, Daniel, 1958, Jl 7,15:1
Garber, Daniel A Mrs, 1941, Ag 2,15:6
Garber, Daniel M, 1956, Jl 16,21:5
Garber, David, 1925, My 5,21:4
Garber, Frederick W, 1950, Ag 8,29:5
Garber, John F, 1957, O 29,31:5
Garber, M C, 1948, S 14,29:5
Garber, Martin, 1903, O 29,9:5
Garber, Max, 1960, Ja 4,29:3
Garber, Morris, 1946, S 11,7:2
Garber, Salvini, 1951, Ap 8,92:6
Garbett, Cyril F Archbishop (funl, Ja 5,4:5), 1956, Ja 1,50:1
Garbisch, Henry C Mrs, 1953, Ag 6,21:5
Garbisch, Norbert S, 1967, Ap 24,33:3
Garbo-Zapulla, C Mrs, 1957, Jl 9,33:4
Garborg, Arne, 1924, Ja 15,19:4
Garbow, William J, 1955, Je 19,93:1
Garbutt, Frank A, 1947, N 20,29:5
Garby, Charles E, 1940, D 15,62:6
Garceau, Arthur J, 1942, N 22,52:6
Garceau, Ernest L, 1966, Mr 12,27:4
Garcelon, Alonzo, 1906, D 9,7:6
Garcelon, Harold W, 1943, Ap 19,19:1
Garcelon, William F, 1949, Jl 6,27:4
Garcia, Albert, 1946, Ag 12,21:5
Garcia, Albert R, 1959, Mr 1,86:8
Garcia, Alejandra Mrs, 1937, Ap 10,7:4
Garcia, Alvaro M, 1960, Je 21,34:1
Garcia, Alvaro M Mrs, 1960, My 18,41:4
Garcia, Anthony, 1955, Jl 2,15:6
Garcia, B Fernandez, 1944, Jl 12,19:4
Garcia, Bernardo, 1944, N 1,23:2
Garcia, C Gen, 1898, D 12,1:2
Garcia, Carlos G, 1944, D 20,23:4
Garcia, Domingo, 1921, Je 6,13:6
Garcia, Elie, 1945, D 25,23:6
Garcia, Enrigue Mrs, 1952, Ja 29,3:8
Garcia, Enrique Adm, 1952, Ja 29,3:8
Garcia, Francisco F, 1955, Ja 24,23:5
Garcia, Frank M, 1958, Je 21,19:3
Garcia, Fray S, 1942, O 11,56:1
Garcia, Gregory Maria Aguirrey Cardinal, 1913, O 10,11:6
Garcia, Joseph M, 1945, Ag 12,40:4
Garcia, Joseph S, 1962, F 23,29:3
Garcia, Leon C, 1955, Mr 20,89:1
Garcia, Lisardo, 1939, Je 19,15:3
Garcia, Lizardo, 1937, My 30,19:1
Garcia, M J, 1884, Mr 13,4:7
Garcia, Manuel D, 1940, Ja 27,13:5
Garcia, Mario Madero Mrs, 1911, N 15,11:5
Garcia, Miguel A, 1955, Jl 13,25:4
Garcia, Paulino Dr, 1968, Ag 3,25:1
Garcia, Phil, 1952, Ag 18,17:2
Garcia, Pilar, 1960, O 26,39:4
Garcia, Ramon, 1957, O 12,19:4
Garcia Arias, Rodolfo, 1964, Ag 20,29:3
Garcia-Beltran, Benjamin, 1958, Ap 3,31:2
Garcia Calderon, Ventura, 1959, O 29,33:4
Garcia Canizares, Santiago, 1946, Ap 19,29:2
Garcia Escamez, Francisco, 1951, Je 13,29:3
Garcia Escobar, Luna I S de Mrs, 1945, D 2,46:6
Garcia Gastaneta, Carlos Dr, 1968, Jl 24,50:1
Garcia Granados, Jorge, 1961, My 6,31:3
Garcia Herrera, Manuel, 1958, Ag 28,27:1
Garcia-Lambert, Concha Mrs, 1910, S 8,9:4
Garcia Mansilla, Daniel, 1957, Je 26,31:5
Garcia Monge, Joaquin, 1958, N 1,19:5
Garcia Salazar, Arturo, 1958, Je 9,23:4
Garcia Samudio, Nicolas, 1952, Mr 7,24:3
Garcia Tapia, Antonio, 1950, S 25,23:2
Garcia y Garcia, Antonio, 1953, My 16,19:6
Garcia Zuniga, Eduardo, 1951, Ap 3,27:1
Garcon, Maurice, 1967, D 30,23:4
Gard, Alex, 1948, Je 2,29:5
Gard, Anson A, 1925, Jl 19,7:4
Gard, Homer, 1952, O 9,31:1
Gard, James R M, 1951, My 17,31:3
Gard, Morris H, 1965, O 29,43:4
Gard, William J Jr, 1964, Jl 3,21:2
Garda, Enrico, 1946, Ap 14,46:3
Gardam, William, 1905, Je 30,9:4
Garde, Andrew E, 1946, S 15,9:8
Garde, Walter S, 1947, Ap 2,27:2
Garde, William H, 1907, Ja 29,9:6
Gardella, Adolph J, 1952, Mr 23,92:2
Gardella, Anthony, 1945, Mr 26,19:4
Gardella, Isilius A, 1944, My 9,19:1
Gardella, Louis J Mrs, 1967, S 22,47:1
Gardella, Tess, 1950, Ja 4,46:2
Garden, George, 1950, Ap 10,19:5
Garden, Hugh M C, 1961, O 7,23:6
Garden, John B, 1940, Jl 8,17:3
Garden, John S (mem ser set, Je 18,88:3), 1961, My 22,16:5
Garden, Joseph, 1947, Ag 26,23:2
Garden, Mary (to be cremated, Ja 6,35:3), 1967, Ja 5,1:5
Garden, Robert D, 1939, N 22,21:4
Gardener, Cornelius Mrs, 1940, Ap 20,17:5
Gardenhire, Samuel Maj, 1923, Mr 1,15:3
Gardenier, David, 1965, Ja 17,88:5
Gardenier, John S, 1956, N 29,35:1
Gardenr, Irving J Sr, 1948, O 15,24:3

Gardin, J E, 1926, D 24,15:3
Gardine (Bro Christian Walter), 1961, My 7,87:1
Gardineer, Charles F Mrs, 1951, Ap 3,27:4
Gardiner, Alan H, 1963, D 20,26:6
Gardiner, Alfred G, 1946, Mr 4,23:4
Gardiner, Andrew L, 1910, Ap 25,9:4
Gardiner, Archibald T, 1951, F 25,84:6
Gardiner, Arthur D, 1960, Ja 10,87:2
Gardiner, Asa Bird Gen, 1919, My 29,13:3
Gardiner, Bentley, 1950, Mr 17,23:5
Gardiner, Charles Dr, 1903, S 25,1:6
Gardiner, Charles F, 1947, Ag 1,17:4
Gardiner, Charles H, 1947, Ja 13,21:2
Gardiner, Charles R, 1950, S 23,17:1
Gardiner, Clarence Mrs, 1944, Ap 12,21:5
Gardiner, Curtiss, 1948, F 25,24:3
Gardiner, David L Mrs, 1916, Jl 4,11:4
Gardiner, E Frank, 1941, S 6,15:1
Gardiner, Edith A, 1963, Jl 13,17:4
Gardiner, Edward, 1907, N 5,9:5
Gardiner, Eliza D, 1955, Ja 15,13:5
Gardiner, Elizabeth Coralie Mrs, 1915, Mr 22,9:3
Gardiner, Elizabeth M, 1956, Jl 9,23:6
Gardiner, Frances R P Mrs, 1942, Ap 23,24:2
Gardiner, Frank C, 1947, Jl 9,23:5
Gardiner, Frederick Sir, 1937, Ag 9,19:3
Gardiner, Frederick W, 1964, Jl 9,33:4
Gardiner, G A, 1879, O 6,1:5
Gardiner, G H, 1936, N 11,35:3
Gardiner, George Austin, 1908, Ap 8,7:4
Gardiner, George G, 1954, Mr 23,27:5
Gardiner, George H, 1958, My 23,23:3
Gardiner, George N, 1914, Jl 7,9:6
Gardiner, George N Mrs, 1947, Ap 22,27:2
Gardiner, George Norman Sr, 1937, My 10,19:4
Gardiner, Glenn L, 1962, Ag 8,31:1
Gardiner, Glenn R, 1940, Mr 26,21:3
Gardiner, Harrison W, 1966, Ja 8,47:2
Gardiner, Harry, 1957, Je 26,31:1
Gardiner, Harry M, 1951, Ap 4,29:5
Gardiner, Henry H, 1941, Mr 7,21:5; 1960, Jl 14,27:5
Gardiner, Howard C, 1951, O 3,36:4
Gardiner, Hubert J Jr Mrs, 1942, Ap 18,15:3
Gardiner, Isaac B Mrs, 1954, O 23,15:4
Gardiner, J Stanley, 1946, Mr 3,45:2
Gardiner, J T, 1933, Ag 8,17:3
Gardiner, J W T Col, 1879, O 2,2:3
Gardiner, James G, 1962, Ja 13,21:4
Gardiner, James Terry Mrs, 1912, Ag 1,11:5
Gardiner, John H, 1945, F 23,17:2
Gardiner, John L, 1957, S 19,29:2
Gardiner, John L Mrs, 1967, D 23,23:2
Gardiner, John Lyon, 1910, Ja 22,9:4
Gardiner, John Terry, 1912, S 11,11:6
Gardiner, L, 1936, F 28,22:1
Gardiner, Lillian B Mrs, 1953, D 25,17:6
Gardiner, Lion, 1943, N 3,25:4
Gardiner, Loren F, 1965, Jl 13,33:2
Gardiner, N W, 1871, S 26,8:2
Gardiner, Norman B Mrs, 1956, Mr 31,15:5
Gardiner, Oliver C, 1967, Ja 21,31:3
Gardiner, Oliver C Mrs, 1941, Ap 7,17:4
Gardiner, Percy R, 1965, Jl 3,19:3
Gardiner, Philip P, 1947, O 16,27:5
Gardiner, Raynor M Mrs, 1959, F 17,31:1
Gardiner, Robert A, 1919, Ap 28,15:4
Gardiner, Robert A Mrs, 1955, O 25,33:2
Gardiner, Robert H, 1944, S 17,42:1
Gardiner, Robert Hallowell, 1924, Je 18,19:5
Gardiner, Ruth Kimball, 1924, N 23,7:1
Gardiner, S A, 1902, F 25,9:5
Gardiner, S B, 1882, Ja 6,5:2
Gardiner, Sarah D (will, Ja 13,29:5), 1953, Ja 6,29:3
Gardiner, Sidney, 1952, My 25,94:4
Gardiner, Sidney H Dr, 1914, Je 12,13:6
Gardiner, Theodore L, 1938, Jl 5,17:3
Gardiner, Theophilus M (por), 1941, Ap 9,25:4
Gardiner, Thomas A, 1913, O 31,11:6
Gardiner, William F, 1940, Ja 5,19:4
Gardiner, William F Mrs, 1950, Mr 15,29:2
Gardiner, William H, 1952, Je 22,69:1
Gardiner, William H Mrs, 1947, S 27,15:4
Gardiner, William R, 1951, O 19,27:4
Gardiner, William Tudor, 1953, Ag 3,1:1
Gardner, A C, 1953, O 18,87:1
Gardner, A K, 1876, Ap 9,7:3
Gardner, Addison, 1947, My 11,62:5
Gardner, Alan C, 1963, Ag 9,23:4
Gardner, Albert T, 1967, Jl 13,37:1
Gardner, Alfred A, 1947, Mr 28,23:1
Gardner, Alfred R, 1965, My 16,88:4
Gardner, Alfred T G, 1958, Ag 28,27:1
Gardner, Andrew H, 1947, Je 12,25:4
Gardner, Andrew R, 1942, D 27,34:4
Gardner, Angelina Mrs, 1942, O 14,25:5
Gardner, Anna, 1901, F 22,7:5
Gardner, Arch R, 1939, Je 16,23:3
Gardner, Archibald K, 1962, Ja 22,23:3
Gardner, Arthur, 1967, Ap 12,42:5
Gardner, Arthur H Dr, 1905, Je 13,16:4
Gardner, Arthur T, 1938, F 1,21:2
Gardner, August C, 1951, Mr 4,92:6
Gardner, Augusta S Mrs, 1943, O 5,25:5
Gardner, Augustus F Maj, 1918, Ja 15,13:1
Gardner, Ben, 1956, Ap 7,19:3
Gardner, Bernhard, 1948, Jl 30,17:4
Gardner, Blanchard, 1940, F 6,21:4
Gardner, Carroll H, 1944, My 1,15:4
Gardner, Cassius M Sr, 1942, Ja 3,19:2
Gardner, Charles, 1942, Ag 29,8:2; 1949, Ja 1,13:2
Gardner, Charles E, 1944, Mr 7,17:2
Gardner, Charles G, 1943, F 6,13:5
Gardner, Charles H, 1941, Ag 19,21:5; 1944, Jl 2,19:1
Gardner, Charles Huntington Mrs, 1915, Je 18,11:4
Gardner, Charles Huntington Rev Dr, 1907, Ap 19,9:5
Gardner, Charles K Col, 1869, N 3,2:7
Gardner, Charles S, 1940, F 2,17:4; 1966, D 2,39:3
Gardner, Charles S Mrs, 1948, Jl 26,17:1
Gardner, Chester R, 1950, Ap 12,27:3
Gardner, Clarence, 1946, Jl 9,21:3
Gardner, Clarence Tripp Dr, 1907, My 25,9:4
Gardner, Cyril, 1943, Ja 2,11:3
Gardner, Daniel, 1954, Jl 8,23:4
Gardner, David Pierson, 1908, Ja 18,9:6
Gardner, De Witt Clinton, 1917, O 5,11:6
Gardner, Delmar Y, 1962, N 1,31:4
Gardner, Dock Commissioner, 1874, D 5,1:2
Gardner, E Ervin, 1945, Ap 25,23:5
Gardner, Ed (Edw F),(funl, Ag 21,33:3), 1963, Ag 18,80:5
Gardner, Edmund S, 1942, F 6,8:3
Gardner, Edward, 1964, S 28,29:4
Gardner, Edward H Mrs, 1948, Je 8,25:5
Gardner, Edward J, 1950, D 8,29:1
Gardner, Edward T, 1960, F 23,31:2
Gardner, Emanuel A, 1955, F 18,21:3
Gardner, Emanuel Mrs, 1944, O 23,19:3
Gardner, Ernest T, 1966, My 13,41:4
Gardner, Esmond B Mrs, 1959, Ag 16,82:7
Gardner, Eugene, 1950, N 28,17:1
Gardner, Eugene D, 1937, S 3,17:3
Gardner, Eugene Terry, 1910, Ja 4,13:4
Gardner, Evelyn, 1956, N 24,19:2
Gardner, Ezra Mrs, 1913, Jl 22,7:4
Gardner, F A Dr, 1903, F 14,9:5
Gardner, F D, 1933, D 19,21:1
Gardner, Fletcher, 1952, D 24,17:6
Gardner, Frank A Mrs, 1953, Ja 30,22:3
Gardner, Frank C, 1949, F 19,15:2
Gardner, Frank D, 1963, O 30,39:1
Gardner, Frank H, 1948, F 3,25:1
Gardner, Frank Harris Dr, 1918, F 25,9:5
Gardner, Frank L, 1947, O 29,27:6
Gardner, Frank L Jr, 1957, N 7,35:3
Gardner, Fred, 1943, N 9,21:3
Gardner, Fred C, 1940, Jl 30,19:3
Gardner, Fred W, 1949, D 31,15:6; 1952, Ap 9,31:6
Gardner, Frederick Maj, 1906, F 2,11:6
Gardner, Frederick W, 1950, Mr 2,27:4
Gardner, Gail, 1949, Ap 3,76:3
Gardner, Gary S Mrs (will), 1966, Mr 13,35:1
Gardner, George, 1940, D 12,27:5; 1941, D 24,17:3; 1954, Jl 11,73:3; 1967, S 9,17:5
Gardner, George A, 1906, D 8,11:6; 1958, Ja 22,27:4
Gardner, George C, 1904, Ag 15,7:6
Gardner, George Enos Prof, 1907, D 18,9:5
Gardner, George P, 1939, Je 7,23:1
Gardner, George P Mrs, 1954, My 26,29:1
Gardner, George W, 1946, My 2,21:5; 1950, Mr 19, 92:3; 1964, D 17,41:3
Gardner, George William, 1911, D 19,13:4
Gardner, Guy A, 1959, D 25,21:3
Gardner, H A, 1875, Jl 28,4:6
Gardner, H Rev (funl), 1883, S 3,8:3
Gardner, H Summer, 1963, D 1,47:1
Gardner, Harrison I, 1948, Ag 30,18:2
Gardner, Harry, 1944, Ap 5,19:2
Gardner, Harry E, 1947, S 27,15:4
Gardner, Harry H, 1940, S 18,23:3
Gardner, Hatfield, 1940, Ja 30,19:5
Gardner, Helen, 1946, Je 7,19:4
Gardner, Helen F, 1958, O 14,37:2
Gardner, Helen Hamilton, 1925, Jl 27,13:5
Gardner, Henry A, 1957, Ag 29,27:5
Gardner, Henry B, 1939, Ap 23,III,6:8; 1960, N 22,35:2
Gardner, Henry B Mrs, 1949, Jl 15,19:2
Gardner, Henry F, 1945, D 25,23:1
Gardner, Herbert Coulstoun (Baron Burghclere), 1921, My 8,22:3
Gardner, Herbert L, 1958, N 7,27:3
Gardner, Herbert L Mrs, 1951, Ag 15,27:4
Gardner, Herbert O, 1939, Ja 19,19:2
Gardner, Herbert S, 1955, My 5,33:5
Gardner, Herman, 1947, S 15,17:3
Gardner, Horace L, 1961, N 11,23:3
Gardner, Hubert, 1907, S 15,9:6
Gardner, Hugh, 1884, S 10,5:6
Gardner, Irving I, 1949, O 12,29:1
Gardner, J Howland, 1944, Jl 8,11:2
Gardner, J Howland Mrs, 1950, My 24,29:3
Gardner, J Marc, 1959, D 3,37:5
Gardner, Jack, 1950, O 1,104:8
Gardner, Jack Mrs, 1924, Jl 18,13:5
Gardner, Jack Mrs (L Dresser), 1965, Ap 25,87:3
Gardner, Jacob W, 1941, D 22,17:6
Gardner, James H Mrs, 1948, O 11,23:2
Gardner, James P, 1950, Mr 20,21:2
Gardner, Jane H Mrs, 1940, Mr 23,13:2
Gardner, Jesse, 1942, Ja 28,19:1
Gardner, Joan T, 1963, Ag 4,81:1
Gardner, John, 1939, O 21,15:5; 1943, S 11,13:3; 1945, D 28,15:3; 1954, Ap 29,31:5
Gardner, John C F, 1913, Jl 26,7:6
Gardner, John E, 1940, F 14,21:5
Gardner, John G Mrs, 1922, Ag 2,17:6
Gardner, John H, 1944, O 13,19:2; 1955, O 5,35:4
Gardner, John H Jr, 1967, Ja 22,77:3
Gardner, John H Mrs, 1909, F 3,9:5
Gardner, John J, 1921, F 8,11:4
Gardner, John J Mrs, 1945, Jl 17,13:5
Gardner, John L, 1952, Ag 25,17:1
Gardner, John Mrs, 1957, Jl 20,15:7
Gardner, John R, 1919, N 21,11:3
Gardner, John Stoon Rev, 1923, N 6,19:4
Gardner, Johnny, 1951, Mr 27,29:1
Gardner, Joseph, 1963, Ap 26,36:5
Gardner, Julie, 1960, N 16,41:4
Gardner, K C, 1955, Ap 17,86:5
Gardner, Karl D (por), 1944, F 27,37:1
Gardner, Katherine, 1958, Je 15,77:1
Gardner, Kenneth, 1961, F 14,37:2
Gardner, Kenneth Mrs, 1961, Ja 29,84:8
Gardner, L C (Rube), 1953, Mr 9,29:2
Gardner, Laurence H, 1944, My 20,15:3
Gardner, Lawrence, 1949, O 7,31:1
Gardner, Lawrence Mrs, 1944, F 12,13:6
Gardner, Lee V, 1945, D 14,27:1
Gardner, Lee V Mrs, 1947, Ja 15,25:4
Gardner, Leroy M, 1952, Mr 18,27:1
Gardner, Leroy U (por), 1946, O 25,23:1
Gardner, Lester D, 1956, N 24,19:5
Gardner, Lester D Mrs, 1952, Mr 30,94:2
Gardner, Lindsay C, 1938, Ag 24,21:5
Gardner, Louis B, 1938, Ja 31,19:4
Gardner, Lucien D, 1952, N 3,27:3
Gardner, Mary C Mrs, 1948, Jl 26,17:1
Gardner, Mary M, 1958, D 6,23:5
Gardner, Mat Dr, 1903, Ap 19,7:4
Gardner, Milton, 1954, D 24,13:1
Gardner, Mittie S Mrs, 1939, N 27,17:1
Gardner, Nathaniel P, 1950, My 11,29:3
Gardner, Nellie E, 1962, Jl 11,35:4
Gardner, Nellie T Mrs, 1955, N 4,29:5
Gardner, Norman T, 1954, Mr 16,29:4
Gardner, O Max Jr, 1961, N 11,23:6
Gardner, Obadiah, 1938, Jl 25,15:5
Gardner, Octave E, 1924, Ag 15,13:6
Gardner, Oliver M, 1947, F 7,1:6
Gardner, Paul, 1968, O 8,47:3
Gardner, Paul E, 1938, Ag 21,33:3
Gardner, Percy, 1956, D 11,39:3
Gardner, Percy Dr, 1937, Jl 19,15:6
Gardner, Percy Mrs, 1940, O 12,17:4
Gardner, Percy W, 1955, S 30,25:5
Gardner, Phil, 1950, Jl 29,13:6
Gardner, Prudence Mrs, 1920, Ag 1,22:5
Gardner, Ralph, 1952, Ag 5,19:5
Gardner, Ralph N, 1953, My 26,29:3
Gardner, Richard F, 1952, Ag 19,23:5
Gardner, Richmond P, 1958, O 23,31:2
Gardner, Robert A, 1956, Je 22,23:5
Gardner, Robert H, 1953, Mr 11,29:2
Gardner, Robert S, 1940, My 18,15:6
Gardner, Robert W, 1937, S 9,23:1
Gardner, Roland H, 1960, Je 1,39:4
Gardner, Roy A, 1939, O 1,53:3
Gardner, Russell E, 1938, S 18,44:8
Gardner, Russell W, 1946, O 5,17:4
Gardner, Rutledge, 1923, Mr 20,21:4
Gardner, S Charles, 1957, S 30,31:2
Gardner, S E, 1878, Jl 26,5:4
Gardner, S J, 1864, Jl 19,5:2
Gardner, Samuel H, 1942, F 18,19:5
Gardner, Samuel I, 1959, D 31,21:4
Gardner, Samuel R, 1956, Mr 17,19:6
Gardner, Stella M, 1943, My 6,19:5
Gardner, Susan S, 1943, F 17,21:3
Gardner, Thomas F, 1948, F 21,13:5; 1950, N 3,27
Gardner, Thomas S, 1963, N 12,41:4
Gardner, Trevor, 1963, S 29,86:1
Gardner, W, 1934, My 8,23:1
Gardner, W E, 1947, Ap 12,17:2
Gardner, W H Commodore, 1870, D 20,3:7
Gardner, Wallace M, 1949, Ap 26,25:5
Gardner, Walter A A, 1941, Je 2,17:3
Gardner, Walter C, 1964, My 19,37:3
Gardner, Walter H, 1965, Mr 2,35:4
Gardner, Walter Mrs, 1945, D 1,23:4
Gardner, Walter P (por), 1949, N 14,27:3
Gardner, Warner, 1968, S 10,51:7
Gardner, Warren F Mrs, 1946, N 14,29:3
Gardner, Willetts W, 1952, O 17,27:2
Gardner, William, 1950, F 25,17:6
Gardner, William A, 1941, Mr 25,23:2; 1941, Jl 8 1943, O 10,48:7; 1947, Ja 10,21:1; 1949, Mr 8,2
Gardner, William A Mrs, 1951, Ag 11,11:2
Gardner, William B, 1941, D 16,27:4
Gardner, William D, 1957, Jl 11,22:6
Gardner, William E, 1965, Ap 5,31:3

Gardner, William H, 1937, S 10,23:1; 1942, D 5,15:2
Gardner, William J, 1924, Je 6,17:5
Gardner, William P, 1961, My 12,29:3
Gardner, William S, 1907, My 30,7:6; 1948, F 20,27:3
Gardner, William T Mrs, 1958, Je 9,23:6
Gardner, William Y, 1951, Jl 26,21:5
Gardner, William Y Mrs, 1951, Jl 26,21:5
Gardner, William Z, 1961, F 24,21:5
Gardnier, Elmer D, 1954, F 15,23:4
Gardy, Julian W, 1959, My 2,23:4
Garelick, Phil L, 1953, Je 22,21:2
Garen, David, 1963, Je 8,25:5
Gares, Chester G, 1947, My 14,25:2
Garesche, Claude F, 1962, Jl 31,27:2
Garesche, Edward F, 1960, O 3,31:2
Garets-Bereins, Annie J des Countess, 1941, Ag 9,15:3
Garey, Earl J, 1942, Jl 9,22:4
Garey, Enoch B, 1957, S 26,25:5
Garey, Eugene L, 1953, My 21,31:4
Garey, Eugene L Mrs, 1955, Mr 27,86:4
Garey, Frank S, 1919, D 6,11:5
Garey, James R, 1943, D 3,24:3
Garey, John, 1955, N 26,19:1
Garfall, Joseph Sr, 1948, Ag 10,22:2
Garfield, Abram, 1958, O 17,30:1
Garfield, Abram Mrs, 1945, F 6,19:2
Garfield, Chester A, 1962, Ag 15,31:4
Garfield, David, 1949, Jl 29,21:4
Garfield, Eliza B, 1888, Ja 22,2:6
Garfield, Frederick M, 1964, Ag 19,37:6
Garfield, Gustave B, 1966, Ja 3,27:2
Garfield, Harold J, 1952, O 25,29:4
Garfield, Harry A (por), 1942, D 13,73:1
Garfield, Harry A Mrs, 1944, Je 28,23:2
Garfield, Harry H, 1955, D 16,29:3
Garfield, Herman J, 1955, O 20,36:1
Garfield, Irvin M, 1951, Jl 20,21:5
Garfield, Isidor Z, 1951, N 10,17:6
Garfield, James A Mrs, 1918, Mr 18,13:5
Garfield, James R, 1950, Mr 25,13:3
Garfield, John, 1952, My 22,21:1
Garfield, John (est appr), 1959, Mr 10,40:1
Garfield, John N Mrs, 1959, Mr 8,86:8
Garfield, Julius D, 1941, Ap 8,26:2
Garfield, Julius D Mrs, 1949, D 24,15:2
Garfield, Mason, 1945, S 1,11:5
Garfield, Sylvester S, 1958, Je 4,33:3
Garfield, Walter T Dr, 1947, Je 1,60:8
Garfienkel, Luis M, 1967, Jl 24,27:2
Garfinkel, Bella U Mrs, 1940, Mr 12,23:3
Garfinkel, Cecil Mrs, 1952, Mr 16,90:1
Garfinkel, Harry, 1937, My 28,21:2
Garfinkel, Hyman, 1949, My 9,25:1
Garfinkel, Louis, 1951, N 9,27:1
Garfinkel, Maurice A, 1948, Mr 3,24:3
Garfinkel Nat, 1958, Jl 21,21:4
Garfitt, William, 1946, Ja 23,27:4
Garford, A L, 1933, Ja 24,22:1
Garfunkel, Aaron, 1940, Je 3,15:5
Garfunkel, Aaron Mrs, 1944, D 30,11:6
Garfunkel, Benjamin J, 1960, O 17,29:3
Garfunkel, Charles Mrs, 1952, Jl 3,25:3
Garfunkel, Herman, 1948, Mr 17,25:5
Garfunkel, Max, 1942, F 22,27:3
Garfunkel, Milton, 1961, Je 23,29:2
Garfunkel, Morris, 1942, Ja 12,10:5
Garfunkel, Nathan J, 1943, D 22,23:4
Garfunkel, Norbert, 1940, F 27,21:2
Garfunkel, Sol, 1953, O 6,29:2
Gargan, Edward F, 1964, F 22,21:2
Gargan, Elmer E Mrs, 1953, O 3,17:3
Gargan, J Francis, 1960, Ag 19,23:2
Gargan, Joseph F, 1946, My 23,21:2
Gargan, Patrick F, 1945, O 7,43:1
Gargan, Thomas, 1908, O 16,9:5
Gargan, Thomas J, 1908, Ag 1,7:6
Gargan, William D, 1937, S 23,27:2
Gargani, Eugene G, 1938, Ap 11,15:4
Gargani, William E, 1961, Je 30,27:2
argano, Charles, 1952, D 2,31:4
argano, Giuseppina, 1939, S 19,25:2
argano, Joseph M, 1951, Ap 25,29:3
argano, Pasquale, 1949, Mr 9,26:2
argas, Albert, 1962, My 25,33:5
arges, Milton, 1937, D 23,21:4
arges, William H Mrs, 1947, Je 17,25:2
argill, John T, 1954, Ja 25,19:1
argiulo, Alexander A, 1912, Ja 21,II,13:2
argiulo, Alfredo, 1949, My 13,23:4
aribaldi, Americo, 1938, D 23,19:4
aribaldi, Anita, 1962, Ap 9,29:4
aribaldi, Clelia, 1959, F 3,31:2
aribaldi, Francesca, 1923, Jl 17,19:6
aribaldi, Giuseppe, 1882, Je 3,1:7; 1949, S 22,31:4; 1950, My 20,15:3
aribaldi, Joseph J, 1957, S 16,31:3
aribaldi, Menotti, 1903, Ag 28,5:5
aribaldi, Paul, 1913, Jl 25,7:6
aribaldi, Ricciotti, 1951, S 15,15:4
aribaldi, Ricciotti Capt, 1924, Jl 18,13:5
aribaldi, Teresita, 1903, Ja 6,9:4
aric, Walter J, 1952, Jl 19,15:5
aridel-Thoron, Marquis de, 1938, Ja 1,19:4

Garin, Henry P, 1947, Ja 19,53:2
Garin, Sol, 1955, Ap 5,26:8
Garing, A J, 1961, N 12,86:4
Garis, Charles F F, 1957, Ja 3,31:3
Garis, Charles Mrs, 1958, Ap 6,88:3
Garis, Frank A Dr, 1937, O 16,19:1
Garis, Howard R, 1962, N 6,33:2
Garis, Howard R Mrs, 1954, Ap 21,29:5
Garis, Norman S, 1955, S 17,15:2
Garis, Roger C, 1967, O 4,51:3
Gariss, Fletcher S, 1955, My 5,33:2
Garity, Harold Mrs, 1960, My 27,31:3
Garland, A H, 1899, Ja 27,7:5
Garland, C S, 1923, S 3,13:5
Garland, Charles, 1922, N 24,17:5; 1957, O 11,27:4
Garland, Charles T, 1921, Je 11,13:6
Garland, David S, 1938, Ja 14,23:5
Garland, Frank Milton, 1925, S 9,25:5
Garland, George F, 1947, My 15,25:1
Garland, I S, 1902, S 1,7:6
Garland, J K, 1878, D 24,5:3
Garland, James A, 1906, S 14,7:3
Garland, James P, 1941, Ag 30,13:5
Garland, John, 1950, N 20,25:2
Garland, John R, 1964, Mr 15,87:2
Garland, Joseph E, 1944, My 31,19:2
Garland, L Henry, 1966, N 1,41:2
Garland, Leon, 1941, N 29,17:6
Garland, Mahlen H, 1920, N 22,15:4
Garland, Nathan M, 1943, O 8,19:4
Garland, Nathan M Mrs, 1944, Ja 10,17:1
Garland, Olive R, 1945, Ja 28,38:1
Garland, R Frank, 1962, Je 29,27:4
Garland, Robert (por), 1949, Ap 20,27:1
Garland, Robert (funl, D 31,13:2), 1955, D 28,23:5
Garland, S T, 1903, Ja 4,9:5
Garland, Sanford Mrs, 1962, O 16,39:3
Garland, T J, 1931, Mr 2,21:3
Garland, Thomas W, 1951, Mr 21,33:1
Garland, Thomas W Mrs, 1958, Ag 4,21:3
Garland, William, 1958, D 4,39:4
Garland, William H Maj, 1903, D 16,1:7
Garland, William M, 1948, S 27,23:1
Garland, William M Mrs, 1958, Mr 18,29:4
Garlando, Alexander, 1953, Ja 12,27:4
Garlasco, Frank B, 1960, Ja 26,33:2
Garlen, Charles Mrs, 1967, Ap 16,82:8
Garless, Thomas, 1945, F 15,20:2
Garlich, John H, 1960, My 4,45:3
Garlichs, Charles F, 1955, Je 22,29:4
Garlichs, Frank, 1952, Ag 27,27:2
Garlick, E Earle, 1939, My 20,15:7
Garlick, Frederick J, 1947, Ap 24,25:5
Garlick, George F, 1954, D 2,31:4
Garlick, Herbert E, 1955, O 25,33:1
Garlick, Ralph H Dr, 1968, F 27,39:4
Garlick, William E, 1957, N 9,27:1
Garlock, G F, 1880, D 11,6:3
Garlock, George W, 1952, Mr 15,13:5
Garlock, John H, 1965, Je 8,41:1
Garlock, Olin J, 1942, F 1,43:1
Garlota, G Mrs, 1942, Ja 14,11:1
Garlough, Jay P, 1952, Ag 16,15:3
Garly, Edward, 1938, N 26,16:3
Garman, Cameron, 1959, O 18,87:2
Garman, Charles E Prof, 1907, F 10,7:7
Garman, David, 1907, Ja 5,9:3
Garman, Frederic D, 1955, F 16,29:2
Garman, Harry J, 1953, Ap 23,29:5
Garman, John T, 1950, F 23,27:3
Garman, Theodore, 1954, Ja 23,13:2
Garmany, Jasper J, 1947, Mr 27,27:2
Garmendia, Vice President of Peru, 1873, Ap 17,1:6
Garnar, Arch E, 1956, N 21,27:4
Garnar, George Washington, 1924, Ag 26,11:3
Garneau, Benoit, 1940, Ap 15,17:1
Garneau, Benoit W, 1950, N 29,33:5
Garneau, Edmund J, 1946, N 11,27:3
Garneau, Emile J, 1942, D 9,28:2
Garneau, George E, 1964, Ap 1,39:4
Garneau, J Lucien, 1952, F 1,22:2
Garneau, James F, 1951, O 18,29:4
Garneau, Nemese, 1937, N 17,23:5
Garner, Curtis S (por), 1949, Ap 12,30:2
Garner, D Dickinson, 1963, Ag 24,19:4
Garner, Elmer J, 1944, My 5,21:5
Garner, Gordon, 1953, Je 12,27:4
Garner, Harley, 1952, Jl 3,25:4
Garner, Howard, 1951, Ap 28,15:4
Garner, J N Sr Mrs, 1932, S 21,21:2
Garner, James B, 1960, N 30,37:4
Garner, James W, 1938, D 10,17:6
Garner, Jesse, 1950, Ap 16,104:4
Garner, John M, 1966, Ag 30,41:3
Garner, John N, 1967, N 8,1:5
Garner, John N Mrs, 1948, Ag 18,25:1
Garner, Milfred O, 1945, O 26,19:1
Garner, Richard L Prof, 1920, Ja 24,11:5
Garner, Roy D, 1946, Mr 11,26:2
Garner, Samuel, 1940, Jl 13,13:5
Garner, Tully, 1968, O 3,47:3
Garner, Virginia, 1951, D 18,32:4
Garnes, Paul Scott, 1923, F 14,17:4

Garnet, Clinton L, 1951, Je 6,31:3
Garnet, H H, 1882, Mr 11,5:3
Garnett, Constance Mrs, 1946, D 19,30:2
Garnett, Edward, 1937, F 22,17:5
Garnett, G, 1928, Ap 30,21:5
Garnett, James Mercer Dr, 1916, F 20,15:4
Garnett, Louise A, 1937, N 1,21:2
Garnett, Porter, 1951, Mr 22,31:3
Garnett, Richard Dr, 1906, Ap 14,11:4
Garnett, Theodore S, 1915, Ap 28,13:6
Garnett, Walter J, 1958, Jl 9,27:4
Garnett, William J, 1939, Mr 29,23:2
Garni, Adolf, 1954, Ag 11,25:3
Garni, Adolf Mrs, 1946, D 17,31:3
Garnica, Pablo de, 1959, D 13,86:3
Garnier, Anna M, 1955, Ag 10,25:3
Garnier, Eugene F, 1956, Je 19,29:4
Garnier, Eugene F Mrs, 1952, S 3,29:3
Garnier-Pages, L A, 1878, N 2,3:3
Garnish, Lysle, 1960, D 5,31:4
Garnjost, Alex H, 1937, Jl 3,15:6
Garnjost, Fred A, 1945, F 10,11:4
Garnjost, Paul H, 1941, My 7,25:6
Garnsey, Cyrus Jr, 1955, My 13,25:2
Garnsey, Elmer E (por), 1946, O 29,26:2
Garnsey, Elmer E Mrs, 1949, My 13,23:5
Garnsey, Everett N Mrs, 1946, Ap 19,29:3
Garnsey, G F Sir, 1932, Je 28,21:3
Garnsey, Squire, 1911, Ja 23,7:4
Garnsey, William Smith Dr, 1925, N 16,19:6
Garofalo, Albert Mrs, 1951, Mr 17,15:2
Garofalo, Attilio, 1940, N 8,21:5
Garofalo, Emil R, 1952, My 16,23:4
Garofalo, Frank L, 1941, N 15,17:4
Garofalo, Santo, 1953, Ja 18,93:1
Garofano, James, 1939, Ja 2,23:2
Garr, Eddie, 1956, S 6,25:2
Garr, John H, 1968, My 23,47:5
Garrabrandt, Joseph E Mrs, 1959, Ja 8,29:3
Garrabrant, Bayard T, 1940, S 24,23:3
Garrabrant, Clarence Dr, 1937, O 1,22:1
Garrabrant, George, 1939, Ap 30,44:6
Garrabrant, Joseph J, 1937, Jl 25,II,7:4
Garrabrant, Walter W, 1944, Mr 2,17:4
Garrabrants, William B, 1951, Ja 22,17:5
Garrabrants, William E, 1956, Mr 7,33:2
Garraghan, Gilbert J, 1942, Je 8,15:6
Garrahan, C Justus, 1953, Ag 12,31:2
Garrahan, Charles Mrs, 1957, S 25,29:4
Garrahan, Harold F, 1961, N 4,19:6
Garrahy, George, 1909, Ja 18,9:4
Garrambone, Salvatore, 1944, My 14,46:3
Garramone, Jerry, 1964, S 30,43:5
Garramone, Robert L, 1950, F 15,27:3
Garran, Frank W, 1945, S 19,25:1
Garran, Robert R, 1957, Ja 12,19:3
Garrard, Jeptha Brig-Gen, 1915, D 17,11:5
Garrard, Kenner, 1879, My 16,5:6
Garrard, William, 1962, Ap 15,81:1
Garratt, Geoffrey T, 1942, My 2,13:4
Garratt, Louis W, 1958, Ap 16,33:3
Garraway, George C, 1952, O 27,27:4
Garrecht, Francis A, 1948, Ag 12,21:2
Garredo Canabal, Tomas, 1943, Ap 9,21:2
Garrel, Frank, 1948, O 9,17:3
Garrels, Arthur, 1943, Jl 1,19:4
Garret, Carl M, 1953, Je 15,29:3
Garretson, A B, 1931, F 28,19:3
Garretson, Abram Quick Justice, 1907, Je 11,7:6
Garretson, Bradley, 1937, D 3,24:3
Garretson, Carleton J, 1912, S 3,11:4
Garretson, Ellis Lewis, 1922, Mr 15,19:5
Garretson, F V D Rev, 1919, F 16,20:4
Garretson, Francis M, 1944, Ap 28,19:3
Garretson, Garret J, 1922, Jl 11,15:4
Garretson, Garret J Mrs, 1959, Ap 5,86:6
Garretson, George Mrs, 1948, S 21,27:2
Garretson, George W, 1937, Mr 7,II,8:2
Garretson, Gilbert I, 1941, Jl 4,13:4
Garretson, J C, 1877, Ag 6,8:3
Garretson, James, 1954, O 29,21:1
Garretson, John V D, 1951, O 12,27:4
Garretson, Joseph, 1959, My 21,31:1
Garretson, Josephine B L, 1952, Ap 15,27:4
Garretson, Leland B (por), 1941, Mr 12,21:4
Garretson, LeRoy, 1960, O 27,37:4
Garretson, Luther T, 1957, Mr 31,88:1
Garretson, Martin S, 1955, D 22,23:2
Garretson, Walter B, 1943, F 5,21:3
Garretson, William Channing, 1924, D 13,15:3
Garretson, William V (por), 1948, Je 6,72:2
Garretson, William V, 1961, O 17,39:4
Garretson, William Van P Mrs, 1959, O 15,39:3
Garrett, Alexander C Rev, 1924, F 19,15:3
Garrett, Alfred C, 1946, S 29,62:2
Garrett, Alfred T, 1950, Je 13,27:4
Garrett, Anna C, 1941, F 13,19:6
Garrett, Annette, 1957, N 18,31:3
Garrett, Arthur, 1956, Ja 1,50:4
Garrett, Arthur S, 1955, O 13,31:5
Garrett, Burns, 1958, Jl 6,56:6
Garrett, Campbell D, 1961, F 4,19:5
Garrett, Dyke, 1938, My 31,19:2

Garrett, Edwin, 1954, N 7,89:1
Garrett, Elizabeth, 1877, Jl 18,4:7
Garrett, Finis J, 1956, My 26,17:1
Garrett, Francis W, 1946, S 14,7:5
Garrett, Frank, 1940, S 10,23:4
Garrett, Fred, 1946, S 6,23:7
Garrett, Garet, 1954, N 7,89:1
Garrett, Garet Mrs, 1955, D 31,13:5
Garrett, George J, 1947, S 9,31:2
Garrett, George T Jr, 1947, Ag 28,23:2
Garrett, H Sherid, 1958, Mr 2,89:1
Garrett, Harrison, 1920, Jl 16,11:5
Garrett, Harvey, 1948, Ja 10,15:3
Garrett, Helen S, 1946, N 10,63:6
Garrett, Hugh L Capt, 1925, Jl 13,17:6
Garrett, J C, 1963, Je 23,84:8
Garrett, J T, 1941, Ap 15,23:5
Garrett, J W, 1884, S 26,5:4
Garrett, J W Mrs, 1883, N 18,5:7
Garrett, James R, 1951, Ag 23,23:3
Garrett, John Biddle, 1924, F 17,23:1
Garrett, John S, 1942, O 30,19:3
Garrett, John T, 1938, Ja 9,42:6
Garrett, John W, 1937, Ag 27,19:5
Garrett, John W (por), 1942, Je 27,13:3
Garrett, John W (will), 1942, Jl 6,10:3
Garrett, Kenneth L (funl plans), 1955, D 31,13:6
Garrett, Kent W Mrs, 1948, Jl 23,20:2
Garrett, Legh O Mrs, 1943, Mr 3,23:5
Garrett, Luther D, 1938, N 26,15:4
Garrett, Oliver H P, 1952, F 24,84:3
Garrett, Otis, 1941, My 27,23:2
Garrett, Paul (por), 1940, Mr 20,27:1
Garrett, Paul L, 1955, Mr 1,25:1
Garrett, Paul Mrs (Lillian), 1968, Ag 16,33:3
Garrett, Ralph W, 1960, D 24,15:5
Garrett, Richard M, 1961, Ag 30,33:1
Garrett, Robert, 1896, Jl 30,3:1; 1961, Ap 26,39:1
Garrett, Robert E, 1958, F 9,88:8
Garrett, Robert R, 1959, Ap 20,31:1
Garrett, Samuel K, 1947, Ja 9,24:3
Garrett, Seymour S, 1947, F 15,15:1
Garrett, Theodore S, 1956, Ap 30,23:4
Garrett, Thomas, 1871, Ja 26,5:1; 1884, F 6,4:6
Garrett, Tom, 1944, Ap 30,45:2
Garrett, W Frank Mrs, 1947, O 22,29:1
Garrett, Walter G, 1917, O 21,23:3
Garrett, William, 1903, Jl 16,7:6
Garrett, William A, 1949, N 16,30:2; 1951, Je 24,72:8
Garrett, William A Mrs, 1955, N 28,31:1
Garrett, William Abner, 1924, O 11,15:6
Garrett, William Channing Rev Dr, 1923, D 16,23:3
Garrette, M W Mrs, 1948, Ag 6,17:3
Garrettson, Francis T, 1918, Jl 5,11:4
Garrettson, M R Mrs, 1879, Mr 7,5:3
Garrettson, Marie F Mrs (will, Jl 25,17:6), 1939, Jl 24,13:4
Garrettson, Rutland M, 1917, D 26,9:7
Garrey, Walter E, 1951, Je 17,84:5
Garrick, John Judge, 1901, S 22,7:6
Garrick, Thomas, 1923, N 9,17:4
Garrick, Thomas F, 1947, Je 4,27:2
Garrick, Thomas M, 1955, My 25,33:4
Garrick, Thomas Mrs, 1954, D 12,89:1
Garrick, William, 1949, Ag 3,23:1
Garrido, J, 1956, N 7,42:4
Garriga, Cardinal, 1882, S 27,2:7
Garriga, Mariano S, 1965, F 23,33:4
Garriga y Cuevas, Ramon, 1957, F 3,77:2
Garrigan, Edward J, 1946, Jl 5,19:6
Garrigan, Edward T, 1945, S 28,21:3
Garrigan, James A Rev, 1915, Ap 9,11:5
Garrigan, Philip J Bp, 1919, O 15,17:3
Garrigan, William J, 1939, Ag 7,15:5
Garrigue, Alexander, 1909, Jl 28,9:4
Garrigue, Esperanza, 1941, My 24,15:2
Garrigues, Edwin B Mrs, 1953, Ja 31,15:3
Garrigues, Ellen, 1945, My 12,13:4
Garrigues, H H, 1945, Jl 17,13:7
Garrigues, John S, 1942, F 5,21:1
Garrigues, Leon, 1948, Ap 5,21:5
Garrigues Diaz-Canabate, Antonio Mrs, 1944, N 18, 13:3
Garriott, Edward B, 1910, My 14,9:4
Garriques, Edwin B, 1955, Ag 24,27:5
Garriques, James W, 1948, My 28,23:3
Garris, George D, 1938, Jl 1,19:4
Garris, Williams J, 1948, Ja 4,52:7
Garrish, John P Jr, 1882, Ap 27,7:4
Garrison, A F, 1877, S 2,7:6
Garrison, Addie M Mrs, 1939, Ja 15,38:4
Garrison, Adele (Mrs M White), 1956, D 4,39:2
Garrison, C K Commodore, 1885, My 2,1:5
Garrison, Charles Grant, 1924, Ap 23,21:4
Garrison, Charles J, 1956, My 12,19:4
Garrison, Charles K, 1941, Je 19,21:5
Garrison, Charles O, 1952, S 4,27:5
Garrison, Cornelius K Mrs, 1925, F 7,15:5
Garrison, Cornelius Mrs, 1951, Ja 30,25:3
Garrison, D M, 1927, D 31,17:5
Garrison, E H, 1930, O 29,23:1
Garrison, Edward M, 1950, F 21,25:4
Garrison, F Alfred, 1947, Mr 16,60:8
Garrison, F Lynwood, 1951, Je 11,25:3
Garrison, Flint, 1948, O 22,25:2
Garrison, Francis Jackson, 1916, D 12,11:4
Garrison, Frank W, 1951, Jl 31,21:3
Garrison, Fred S, 1949, N 16,29:4
Garrison, G Harry, 1947, O 5,68:5
Garrison, George, 1948, My 24,19:6
Garrison, George S, 1946, D 29,35:2
Garrison, George Thompson, 1904, Ja 28,9:7
Garrison, Harvey (por), 1939, Jl 24,13:3
Garrison, Homer Jr, 1968, My 8,47:1
Garrison, Ira, 1938, Mr 30,21:2
Garrison, Jacob, 1946, My 6,21:4
Garrison, John, 1937, Mr 2,21:3
Garrison, John B Dr, 1937, My 21,22:1
Garrison, John H, 1939, N 16,23:4
Garrison, John J, 1951, D 26,25:4
Garrison, L M, 1932, O 20,21:1
Garrison, Levi T, 1950, My 7,106:5
Garrison, M Raymond, 1958, S 12,26:1
Garrison, Mabel (Mrs Geo Siemonn), 1963, Ag 22, 27:3
Garrison, Nellie M Mrs, 1938, Ag 28,32:6
Garrison, Otis P, 1950, Ja 2,23:3
Garrison, P Raymond, 1943, S 9,25:4
Garrison, Phil E, 1940, S 24,23:5
Garrison, Roy A, 1951, N 11,91:2
Garrison, S (see also Je 27), 1878, Je 30,12:4
Garrison, Samuel J T, 1940, My 5,53:2
Garrison, Sidney C, 1945, Ja 19,19:2
Garrison, Snapper, 1944, D 14,23:3
Garrison, Theodore T, 1947, Mr 2,60:2
Garrison, Ulysses S Mrs, 1950, Ap 6,29:4
Garrison, W L (funl, My 29,1:5), 1879, My 25,1:7
Garrison, W R, 1882, Jl 2,12:1
Garrison, Wendell Phillips, 1907, Mr 1,9:5
Garrison, William D, 1943, Ap 27,23:4
Garrison, William H, 1907, Ja 18,7:5
Garrison, William Lloyd, 1909, S 13,9:5
Garrison, William Lloyd (mem), 1910, Ja 26,9:5
Garrison, William P, 1946, D 18,29:5
Garrison, William R Mrs, 1923, D 21,17:4
Garrison, William Van S, 1960, O 2,84:7
Garrison, Wyckoff L, 1962, Je 30,19:4
Garritson, Christopher B, 1944, Je 26,15:5
Garritt, Nannie M M Mrs, 1938, Ja 1,19:5
Garritty, Dominic E, 1948, Ag 1,56:2
Garrity, Bernard F, 1951, N 21,25:1
Garrity, Edward C, 1963, Ag 14,33:2
Garrity, Frank, 1945, Ag 5,38:3
Garrity, George F, 1967, Mr 1,43:2
Garrity, Henry Mrs, 1959, Ap 13,31:4
Garrity, James A (por), 1944, Je 10,15:1
Garrity, James Mrs, 1942, My 8,21:4
Garrity, John J, 1950, D 30,13:3; 1961, Jl 19,29:2
Garrity, John J Mrs, 1947, Jl 8,23:3
Garrity, John T Mrs, 1943, N 30,27:3
Garrity, Michael J, 1953, Ja 12,27:4
Garrity, Stephen C, 1943, D 27,19:4
Garrity, Thomas F, 1937, Ap 11,II,9:3
Garrity, William J, 1951, S 13,31:4; 1966, Jl 6,42:2
Garrod, Charles C, 1949, O 25,27:4
Garrod, Heathcote W, 1960, D 28,27:5
Garrod, Joseph H, 1952, Je 12,33:2
Garrod, Rupert C, 1941, Ja 8,19:3
Garros, Roland, 1918, N 1,15:5
Garrow, Louis, 1921, Mr 12,11:6
Garrow, Robert W, 1937, S 9,23:2
Garroway, Dave Mrs, 1961, Ap 29,47:3
Garry, Albert H, 1950, N 30,33:2
Garry, Martin V, 1945, O 28,43:1
Garry, Peter Albert, 1919, Mr 25,13:3
Garry, Thomas J, 1954, Mr 27,17:5
Garsaud, Marcel, 1958, F 13,29:4
Garsia, E C B, 1901, Mr 14,9:6
Garside, Alston H (por), 1946, Ap 27,17:5
Garside, Alston H Mrs, 1937, Jl 28,19:2
Garside, Charles, 1964, N 2,39:4
Garside, Charles Zeh Dr, 1916, Je 3,13:6
Garski, Stanislas, 1923, S 6,15:3
Garson, Byron J, 1965, Jl 24,21:1
Garson, Frank, 1955, S 15,33:2
Garson, Moses L, 1937, N 1,21:2
Garson, Nina S Mrs (will), 1959, F 27,22:3
Garsson, Murray, 1957, Mr 28,32:1
Garsson, Murray W Mrs, 1942, N 13,23:2
Garst, Louis J, 1949, Ap 15,23:1
Garst, Perry, 1939, Ag 30,17:5
Garst, Thomas D Mrs, 1961, Je 8,35:1
Garst, Warren Ex-Gov, 1924, O 7,23:4
Garstin, Dalton V, 1966, N 7,47:1
Garstin, William Edmund Sir, 1925, Ja 9,17:3
Garstka, Andrew S, 1941, Ag 17,38:1
Garte, Paul O, 1952, O 8,31:2
Garten, F Gray, 1956, Ja 9,25:2
Garten, Irving, 1958, Ag 8,19:1
Garten, Nathan, 1962, S 20,33:3
Gartenlaub, Charles, 1960, S 20,39:1
Garter, Charles W, 1903, Je 14,7:6
Garth, David J, 1912, Jl 19,9:5
Garth, Ernest D G, 1962, My 16,41:3
Garth, George, 1949, F 2,27:3
Garth, Horace Everett, 1911, Ag 1,9:5
Garth, Lewis W, 1923, S 6,15:5
Garth, Thomas R, 1939, Ap 21,23:4
Garthe, Louis, 1920, S 9,11:1
Garthwaite, Albert A, 1968, My 20,47:3
Garthwaite, Albert N, 1943, S 24,23:5
Garthwaite, Arthur J, 1946, Mr 5,26:2
Garthwaite, George C, 1954, N 25,29:5
Garthwaite, J C, 1883, F 17,5:4
Garthwaite, J C Dr Mrs, 1903, My 5,9:6
Garthwaite, James H, 1947, Ap 27,60:1
Garthwaite, Jere E, 1951, N 25,87:1
Garthwaite, May E, 1950, Jl 22,15:2
Garthwaite, Oscar B Mrs, 1951, O 23,29:2
Garthwaite, Robert, 1944, Ap 22,15:5
Garthwaite, William, 1956, Je 22,23:2
Gartin, Carroll, 1966, D 20,43:2
Gartlan, Charles T, 1944, My 4,19:3
Gartlan, Eugene B, 1938, My 26,25:2
Gartlan, Fred L Mrs, 1940, Ja 9,24:3
Gartlan, Frederick L, 1944, Ag 19,11:6
Gartlan, George H, 1963, My 13,29:1
Gartland, Arthur J (autopsy rept), 1960, Ja 1,9:1
Gartland, Arthur J Jr, 1959, D 31,37:1
Gartland, Francis J, 1958, Mr 13,29:5
Gartland, Hugh, 1943, Mr 6,13:2
Gartland, John J, 1937, Ja 21,23:4; 1968, D 2,47:2
Gartland, John J Mrs, 1951, O 3,36:3
Gartland, Joseph W, 1954, Ag 16,17:3
Gartland, Ruth, 1946, N 2,15:6
Gartland, Thomas H Rev, 1922, Ap 29,15:4
Gartley, Lillian H, 1943, D 8,23:5
Gartley, William H, 1941, F 14,18:3
Gartling, Charles G, 1960, D 22,23:1
Gartlir, Louis, 1943, Mr 28,24:1
Gartman, Aug, 1948, D 8,31:3
Gartman, Elias, 1955, My 10,29:3
Gartmann, Heinz, 1960, Ag 19,23:2
Gartner, Albert A, 1948, S 10,23:5
Gartner, Edward A, 1938, Ap 2,15:5
Gartner, Louis W, 1953, Je 1,23:4
Gartnes Alzamora, Jose, 1961, Ap 17,8:6
Garton, Catherine Mrs, 1924, F 26,17:2
Garton, Clarence E, 1951, N 16,25:3
Garton, Daniel H, 1922, O 25,19:4
Garton, E C, 1950, Je 3,15:5
Garton, Elam M Rev Dr, 1937, D 14,25:2
Garton, William R, 1939, S 17,49:3
Gartrell, James L, 1948, Ag 31,23:2
Gartz, Kate C Mrs, 1949, My 14,13:4
Gartzide, John L, 1947, Ag 26,23:3
Garvan, Edward J Ex-Judge, 1910, Mr 5,9:5
Garvan, Francis P (por),(will, N 20,20:7), 1937, N 23:1
Garvan, John S, 1954, Mr 20,15:4
Garvan, Patricia, 1918, Ja 23,9:4
Garvan, Patrick, 1912, S 23,13:6
Garver, Danny, 1946, D 30,19:3
Garver, Francis M, 1952, D 10,35:3
Garver, Frank H, 1952, S 25,31:6
Garver, J A, 1936, O 24,17:1
Garver, Jacob C, 1952, D 25,21:5
Garver, Madison M, 1941, My 12,17:2
Garvey, Arthur G, 1944, O 9,23:3
Garvey, Charles B, 1946, Mr 24,44:6
Garvey, Clayton H, 1925, F 8,7:1
Garvey, Dan E Mrs, 1951, Jl 8,61:3
Garvey, E A Rev, 1920, O 23,13:6
Garvey, Francis A, 1942, Jl 23,19:6
Garvey, George A, 1959, Ag 22,17:5
Garvey, J, 1880, O 10,5:3
Garvey, James J Mrs, 1957, F 5,23:4
Garvey, John J Sr, 1956, S 13,35:3
Garvey, John M, 1947, Je 30,19:2
Garvey, John R, 1954, Mr 16,29:4
Garvey, Joseph A, 1941, Je 24,20:2
Garvey, Lawrence R, 1959, Je 24,31:3
Garvey, Marcus, 1940, Je 12,25:4
Garvey, Mary E, 1948, F 28,15:6
Garvey, Mary P Sister, 1951, Ag 25,11:4
Garvey, Michael F, 1965, Ja 14,35:5
Garvey, Ralph J, 1965, O 18,35:2
Garvey, Raymond H, 1959, Jl 2,16:7
Garvey, Russell H Rev, 1968, D 22,53:2
Garvey, Walter A, 1943, My 4,23:2
Garvey, Walter J, 1953, Je 5,27:5
Garvey, William, 1925, N 23,21:4
Garvey, William A, 1966, Ja 8,26:1
Garvey, William H, 1961, S 29,35:4
Garvey, William H Sr, 1960, Mr 2,37:4
Garvey, William J, 1958, Je 7,19:5
Garvice, Charles, 1920, Mr 2,11:3
Garvie, Alfred E, 1945, Mr 10,17:4
Garvie, Edward, 1939, F 18,15:3
Garvin, Albert H, 1952, My 30,15:1
Garvin, Amelia B W Mrs (K Hale), 1956, S 8,
Garvin, Edwin L, 1960, O 11,45:1
Garvin, Frank D, 1960, Mr 26,21:6
Garvin, Frank W, 1959, D 18,29:1
Garvin, Helen M, 1962, Jl 30,23:4
Garvin, Howard L, 1967, Ap 15,31:2
Garvin, Howard M Sr, 1951, N 18,90:3
Garvin, James L, 1947, Ja 24,22:2
Garvin, John A, 1944, My 12,19:5; 1945, D 18,

Garvin, Knox L, 1937, Ag 26,21:5
Garvin, Lester Mrs, 1953, Je 16,27:4
Garvin, Lucius F C, 1922, O 3,21:4
Garvin, Margaret R, 1949, D 6,31:5
Garvin, Michael John, 1918, S 2,9:2
Garvin, S B, 1878, Je 29,5:3; 1878, Jl 2,2:7
Garvin, William C, 1942, Ap 4,13:4
Garvin, William G, 1955, Ap 15,23:3
Garvin, William T, 1966, Ag 12,31:4
Garvy, Peter (por), 1944, F 29,17:2
Garwood, Everett C, 1938, O 25,23:1
Garwood, Samuel, 1963, S 9,27:2
Garwood, Sterling M, 1941, Ja 3,19:5
Gary, Barham R, 1967, Je 28,45:2
Gary, Charles B, 1949, D 31,15:2
Gary, Curtis Case, 1968, Ap 18,47:2
Gary, E H, 1927, Ag 16,1:8
Gary, E T Mrs, 1934, Ap 6,23:4
Gary, Fred E, 1940, F 21,19:4
Gary, Hampson, 1952, Ap 19,15:1
Gary, Hunter L, 1946, D 1,79:3
Gary, Irving C, 1957, N 23,19:6
Gary, J E Judge Mrs, 1902, Je 22,9:6
Gary, James A, 1920, N 1,15:6
Gary, Joseph E Judge, 1906, N 1,9:5
Gary, M W, 1881, Ap 10,1:4
Gary, Robert O, 1948, Ap 10,13:5
Gary, William E, 1937, Ap 19,21:6
Garza, Leopoldo T, 1943, Mr 1,19:2
Garzon, Julia Mrs, 1937, D 23,22:5
Gasbarrini, Antonio, 1963, N 14,35:2
Gascerini, Natale, 1952, F 23,11:3
Gasch, Edna K Mrs, 1944, F 15,17:4
Gascoigne, George, 1953, O 4,89:2
Gascoine, James, 1903, N 28,9:4
Gascon y Marin, Jose, 1962, S 3,15:5
Gascoyne, George P, 1943, S 1,19:5
Gascoyne, William J, 1938, D 28,26:5
Gascoyne-Cecil, W, 1936, Je 23,23:1
Gasdia, Frederick J, 1958, S 6,17:6
Gaselee, Stephen, 1943, Je 17,21:5
Gasewind, Adolph R, 1955, Ja 20,31:5
Gasewind, John R, 1958, O 20,29:4
Gash, Chester A, 1955, N 6,86:8
Gash, Chester A Mrs, 1949, My 11,29:5
Gash, Edward, 1942, Jl 25,13:2
Gaskell, Charles L, 1943, D 11,15:1
Gaskell, Frederic P, 1946, D 27,20:2
Gaskell, Frederic P Mrs, 1938, N 16,23:1
Gaskell, Frederick A, 1949, Ja 9,72:1
Gaskell, Mrs, 1865, D 11,2:3
Gaskell, Peggy Mrs, 1947, Ag 8,17:2
Gaskill, Burton A, 1943, O 1,19:2
Gaskill, Clarence L, 1948, Ap 30,23:3
Gaskill, Edmund C Jr, 1949, D 24,15:6
Gaskill, Frank H, 1937, Ag 23,19:5
Gaskill, George B, 1940, F 2,17:4
Gaskill, I Clayton, 1952, Jl 8,27:3
Gaskill, Joseph G, 1948, Ag 18,25:5
Gaskill, Lois L, 1945, Jl 8,11:7
Gaskill, Loren B, 1944, Mr 14,19:5
Gaskill, Milton, 1952, Je 27,23:4
Gaskill, Palmer D, 1950, D 1,26:3
Gaskill, William F Mrs, 1941, F 19,21:6
Gaskill, William R, 1960, My 31,31:3
Gaskin, Charles, 1951, Ap 28,15:5
Gaskin, Conover, 1939, Ap 20,23:3
Gaskin, Dennis C, 1960, S 13,37:4
Gaskin, George Jefferson, 1920, D 15,15:4
Gaskin, Peter J Col, 1937, Ap 19,21:4
Gaskins, Frederick A, 1948, Mr 17,25:1
Gaskins, Norman, 1955, F 19,15:5
Gaskins, Sidney S, 1954, Ja 6,45:2
Gasner, Joseph F, 1957, Mr 9,19:2
Gasorek, John C Sr, 1951, Mr 11,93:1
Gaspar, Harry, 1940, My 15,23:5
Gaspard, Jules M, 1919, F 19,13:5
Gaspard, Nicholas J, 1942, S 13,53:3
Gaspari, John, 1951, Mr 1,28:2
Gaspari, Joseph, 1964, Ja 13,35:1
Gasparian, Ter, 1949, S 3,13:7
Gasparitsch, Edward Mrs, 1964, O 12,29:1
Gasparoli, Giovanni, 1950, Jl 30,61:1
Gasparotto, Luigi, 1954, Jl 1,25:4
Gasparri, Enrico, 1946, My 21,23:1
Gasparri, P, 1934, N 19,17:1
Gasperi, Alcide De (funl, Ag 24,10:3), 1954, Ag 19, 1:2
Gasperi, Augusto de, 1966, D 14,47:4
Gasperi, Marcella de, 1949, N 15,26:2
Gasq, Paul J B, 1944, N 2,19:2
Gasque, Allard H (por), 1938, Je 18,15:4
Gasquet, Amedee, 1914, My 6,11:6
Gasquet, F A, 1929, Ap 6,17:4
Gass, Charles J, 1951, F 21,27:2
Gass, Florien P, 1958, F 19,27:2
Gass, John, 1951, Ag 15,27:2
Gass, Karl W, 1952, Jl 5,15:5
Gass, Mary A Sister, 1952, Mr 21,23:2
Gass, William E, 1945, Ja 16,19:3
Gassaway, Ellen Mrs, 1948, Ja 13,26:2
Gassaway, Franklin Harrison, 1923, My 23,21:5
Gassaway, James M, 1939, Mr 6,15:4
Gassaway, Louis D, 1940, Mr 31,44:3
Gassaway, Percy L (por), 1937, My 16,II,9:1
Gassenheimer, Walter T, 1958, Ag 18,19:4
Gasser, Herbert S, 1963, My 13,29:4
Gasser, J Lester, 1952, Jl 24,27:5
Gasser, Lorenzo D, 1955, O 31,25:5
Gasser, Lydia E F Mrs, 1941, Jl 15,19:3
Gasser, Roy C, 1961, Ag 17,27:3
Gasser, Roy C Mrs, 1962, O 9,41:2
Gassert, H L, 1902, D 8,9:4
Gassert, Howell Allyn Lt, 1918, My 29,13:5
Gassett, Walter, 1915, Jl 22,9:5
Gassier, Edouard, 1871, D 19,1:6
Gassin, Harry L, 1919, Ap 10,11:2
Gassler, Stephen A, 1944, Jl 19,19:2
Gassman, Joseph N, 1938, F 16,21:6
Gassmann, Jacob F, 1959, D 12,23:1
Gassmann, Michael, 1923, Ap 24,21:5
Gassner, Alfred A, 1959, O 26,29:2
Gassner, John W (trb lr, Ap 16,II,7:3), 1967, Ap 3, 33:1
Gassner, Julius, 1967, Ap 25,43:2
Gassouin, Gaston Gen, 1924, Ja 12,13:3
Gasstrom, Herman, 1956, Ja 27,23:1
Gasstrom, Herman M Mrs, 1960, My 14,23:5
Gast, Alton J Mrs, 1956, F 7,31:5
Gast, George F, 1964, S 6,56:8
Gast, Isidor, 1949, Mr 31,25:5
Gastall, Thomas E Jr (funl, S 30,87:2), 1956, S 26, 17:7
Gastambide, Jules, 1944, Ap 20,19:3
Gasteiger, Albert A, 1946, Jl 19,19:4
Gaster, Emil, 1955, S 9,23:3
Gaster, Hyman Mrs, 1956, S 24,27:5
Gaster, Moses (por), 1939, Mr 6,15:3
Gastman, Joseph L, 1944, N 21,25:2
Gastman, Lodewyk Mrs, 1942, Ag 4,19:6
Gaston, Alex, 1937, S 9,23:1
Gaston, Alex Mrs, 1940, Ap 18,23:1
Gaston, Arthur Lee, 1951, Ag 15,27:5
Gaston, Billy, 1940, D 29,24:5
Gaston, Cecil D, 1940, S 13,23:2
Gaston, Charles R, 1945, N 30,23:2
Gaston, Ernest B, 1937, D 22,25:2
Gaston, Frederick K Jr, 1966, Je 7,47:3
Gaston, Frederick K Mrs, 1949, Ag 7,60:3
Gaston, George, 1937, Ja 15,22:1
Gaston, George A, 1954, Ag 17,21:1
Gaston, George Albert, 1968, F 2,35:4
Gaston, George B, 1942, N 29,64:7
Gaston, George Houston, 1922, Ag 3,13:7
Gaston, Hazle B, 1962, N 22,29:2
Gaston, Henrietta Page Mrs, 1925, Jl 13,17:7
Gaston, Herbert E, 1956, D 9,87:2
Gaston, Hugh K, 1938, Ap 11,15:5
Gaston, Hugh M Mrs, 1914, My 4,9:6
Gaston, James McFadden Dr, 1903, N 13,7:6
Gaston, John, 1949, D 14,31:2
Gaston, John M, 1960, Mr 21,29:6
Gaston, Joseph A Gen, 1937, Ap 2,23:2
Gaston, Lloyd H, 1962, Ag 17,48:1
Gaston, Louis P, 1939, Jl 15,15:1
Gaston, Lucy Page (funl, Ag 22,13:6), 1924, Ag 21, 11:5
Gaston, Mary E, 1956, Ap 21,17:6
Gaston, Raymond E, 1939, Ja 5,23:5
Gaston, W A, 1927, Jl 18,17:3
Gaston, William D, 1948, Mr 23,25:4
Gaston, William G, 1940, Ap 15,17:2
Gastonquay, Thomas A, 1955, F 11,23:3
Gatacre, William Forbes Gen Sir, 1906, Mr 6,9:3
Gatch, Claud, 1939, My 12,21:5
Gatch, Lee, 1968, N 13,47:1
Gatch, Thomas L, 1954, D 18,15:3
Gatchel, Marion H, 1948, Mr 24,25:2
Gatchell, Earle, 1962, O 9,41:2
Gatchell, Evalyn B Mrs, 1955, Mr 2,27:2
Gatchell, George W, 1939, F 5,40:8
Gatchell, William H, 1944, Jl 19,19:3
Gate, Gordon, 1919, Jl 19,9:7
Gate, Simon, 1945, My 17,19:2
Gatelee, John F, 1940, Je 22,15:4
Gately, John F, 1954, Ap 9,23:4
Gately, John J, 1948, Ja 19,24:2
Gately, Joseph A, 1953, Ag 7,19:5; 1967, Ap 9,92:5
Gately, Joseph E, 1940, Jl 23,19:4
Gately, Matthew E Jr, 1964, Je 9,35:3
Gately, Michael A Mrs, 1944, Ag 30,17:3
Gately, Ralph N, 1941, S 25,25:4
Gatenellow, A John, 1949, D 14,31:1
Gatens, Norman E, 1938, Ap 2,15:6
Gatens, Peter R, 1937, D 19,II,9:3
Gates, A A Mrs, 1908, D 15,9:5
Gates, Aaron B, 1948, Jl 10,15:5
Gates, Albert N, 1937, Jl 31,15:3
Gates, Alice C Mrs, 1945, N 23,24:3
Gates, Arthur M, 1945, S 11,23:1
Gates, Asel A, 1905, Ap 19,1:5
Gates, Avery A, 1956, Jl 5,25:4
Gates, Bennett, 1956, D 24,13:4
Gates, Caleb F (por), 1946, Ap 11,25:1
Gates, Caleb F, 1955, D 23,18:2
Gates, Caleb F Mrs, 1937, O 8,23:3
Gates, Calvin F, 1942, D 19,19:3
Gates, Charles A, 1958, Mr 13,29:2
Gates, Charles C, 1961, Ag 30,33:3
Gates, Charles G (funl, O 3,9:4), 1913, N 1,11:5
Gates, Charles Otis Prof, 1906, My 9,9:5
Gates, Charles S Judge, 1937, Jl 21,21:4
Gates, D V, 1879, Ja 3,3:2
Gates, Edward Langdon, 1903, O 6,9:4
Gates, Edwin A, 1950, N 5,93:1
Gates, Eleanor, 1951, Mr 8,29:5
Gates, Elton M Huntington Mrs, 1920, O 24,22:4
Gates, Elwood Mrs, 1948, Ja 11,56:3
Gates, Esther L, 1966, Ja 12,21:1
Gates, Eugene H, 1945, D 30,14:5
Gates, F T, 1929, F 7,27:3
Gates, Francis H, 1925, Jl 7,19:5
Gates, Frank C, 1955, Mr 23,31:4
Gates, Frank L, 1946, Ja 18,19:1
Gates, Franklin H, 1945, N 9,20:2
Gates, Frederick, 1942, S 2,23:1
Gates, Frederick C, 1946, N 19,31:2
Gates, Garret D, 1921, S 11,21:1
Gates, Geoffrey M, 1961, N 3,35:1
Gates, Geoffrey Mrs, 1946, S 12,7:4
Gates, George Augustus, 1912, N 21,13:4
Gates, George N, 1953, O 20,29:5
Gates, H L, 1937, Mr 12,23:4
Gates, Harold A, 1944, N 6,19:6
Gates, Henry L, 1914, O 14,11:6
Gates, Herbert Ellsworth Mrs, 1913, Ag 8,7:6
Gates, Herbert G, 1911, F 18,11:6
Gates, Herbert W, 1948, F 9,17:4
Gates, Horatio H, 1945, Mr 4,37:1
Gates, Horatio H Mrs, 1941, Mr 18,23:5
Gates, Howard E, 1908, N 10,9:5
Gates, Irene, 1962, N 13,37:2
Gates, Isaac E, 1916, F 26,9:4
Gates, J B (see also My 29), 1877, My 30,8:4
Gates, Jack W, 1960, F 27,19:1
Gates, Jay, 1942, My 21,19:3
Gates, John J, 1968, O 12,37:2
Gates, John L Mrs, 1953, Je 23,30:5
Gates, John W, 1911, Ag 9,9:1
Gates, John W (funl), 1911, Ag 13,II,9:6
Gates, John W (funl), 1911, Ag 23,7:5
Gates, John W (est), 1911, D 14,13:4
Gates, L Preston, 1950, F 2,27:1
Gates, Lewis Edwards, 1924, O 2,23:3
Gates, Loren H Mrs, 1949, Mr 29,25:5
Gates, Lorenzo Dr, 1909, F 1,9:6
Gates, Mannie, 1957, Ap 26,25:4
Gates, Marguerite L, 1965, F 20,25:3
Gates, Marvin J Mrs, 1945, F 8,19:2
Gates, McLain, 1939, Ja 1,25:1
Gates, Merrill E, 1922, Ag 12,9:6
Gates, Milo H, 1939, N 28,25:1
Gates, Moody B, 1965, Ja 6,39:5
Gates, Moody B Mrs, 1955, My 6,23:1
Gates, Moore, 1951, Ag 3,21:1
Gates, N J, 1903, Mr 1,9:5
Gates, Owen H, 1940, Ja 20,15:2
Gates, Pauline G Mrs, 1941, F 7,19:6
Gates, Payson G, 1955, F 16,29:4
Gates, Peter Goddard, 1925, Jl 14,21:4
Gates, Ralph L, 1967, Jl 27,35:1
Gates, Raymond F, 1953, Ja 27,25:2
Gates, Reginald G, 1962, Ag 13,25:3
Gates, Richard H Mrs, 1943, Je 6,42:6
Gates, Robert M, 1955, Je 30,25:1; 1962, N 8,39:4
Gates, Russell C, 1964, F 14,29:2
Gates, Ruth, 1966, My 25,47:3
Gates, Samuel, 1947, O 10,25:4
Gates, Stephen, 1953, Je 12,27:1
Gates, Theodore B Gen, 1911, Jl 6,9:4
Gates, Thomas F Capt (por), 1937, N 9,23:4
Gates, Thomas S (por), 1948, Ap 9,23:1
Gates, Wilfred M, 1939, S 29,23:3
Gates, William B, 1942, D 25,17:4
Gates, William Dr (por), 1940, Ap 25,23:1
Gates, William F, 1938, N 25,23:6
Gates, William J, 1954, Ap 19,23:4
Gates, William Jr, 1954, Je 2,31:2
Gates, Willis D Jr, 1947, Ag 18,17:4
Gates, Wilton J, 1942, N 23,23:2
Gateson, Daniel W, 1954, Jl 11,72:3
Gatewood, Dorothea A Mrs, 1948, Je 2,29:3
Gatewood, Dr, 1939, My 23,23:4
Gatewood, Lee C, 1950, Ja 4,35:4
Gatewood, Robert, 1941, S 24,23:6
Gatewood, William Mrs, 1951, Je 19,29:1
Gathany, J Madison, 1957, Mr 9,19:1
Gathergood, Roy, 1949, D 17,17:1
Gathman, Anna M, 1954, F 16,25:3
Gathman, C Henry, 1953, N 22,88:2
Gathman, Herman J, 1959, Ag 25,31:1
Gathman, Herman W, 1955, S 24,19:5
Gathman, John A, 1952, Mr 9,92:6
Gathmann, Emil Sr, 1949, Ag 24,25:5
Gathmann, Louis, 1917, Je 4,11:5
Gathorne-Hardy, Gathorne Earl of Carnbrook, 1906, O 31,9:6
Gathorne-Hardy, John F, 1949, Ag 23,23:4
Gatineau, L A F, 1885, Mr 14,5:2

Gatje, Frederick C, 1948, F 13,21:1
Gatje, George H, 1960, Ja 3,88:3
Gatjen, Charles F A Capt, 1918, D 10,13:2
Gatley, Edward R, 1949, Mr 10,27:2
Gatley, Raymond, 1952, Mr 1,15:4
Gatley, Thomas H, 1950, O 18,33:5
Gatlin, Dana E, 1940, D 1,62:1
Gatling, Norborne P, 1943, D 10,27:4
Gatling, R J Dr, 1903, F 27,1:5
Gatling, Richard H, 1941, Ja 15,23:5
Gatling, Robert B, 1903, D 3,1:6
Gatner, Harold L, 1947, Ja 4,15:2
Gatnow, Hannah Mrs, 1903, D 9,1:2
Gatrell, J William Sr, 1953, Ag 13,25:5
Gatschet, Albert S Dr, 1907, Mr 18,7:5
Gatson, Addison, 1939, D 3,41:3
Gatsopoulos, John K, 1948, D 22,23:4
Gatteaux, J E, 1881, F 12,2:6
Gatter, Herman L, 1951, Je 23,15:5
Gatter, L Stewart, 1953, Ap 6,19:4
Gatti, Orville C, 1956, O 28,89:1
Gatti-Casazza, Giulio (por), 1940, S 3,1:6
Gatti-Casazza, Stedano Sen, 1918, My 1,13:5
Gatti-Casazza, Stefano Mrs, 1922, O 7,15:6
Gattinelli, Angelo, 1941, Mr 22,15:5
Gattis, Raymond T, 1942, My 18,15:1
Gattle, A Caroline A Mrs, 1939, Je 1,25:3
Gattle, Benjamin, 1940, Ja 23,21:5
Gatto, Anthony F, 1950, D 18,31:4
Gatto, Isaac N, 1962, Jl 23,21:5
Gatto, Joseph A, 1965, Ja 15,43:4
Gatto, Victor J, 1965, My 27,37:4
Gattone, Daniel H, 1965, Jl 12,27:5
Gatty, Harold C, 1957, Ag 31,15:1
Gaty, John P, 1963, N 5,31:1
Gaty, Lewis R, 1961, Ag 30,33:3
Gatz, Felix M, 1942, Je 21,37:2
Gatz, Percy W, 1961, F 10,27:2
Gaubart, Phil, 1952, Ja 22,29:2
Gaubert, Philippe, 1941, Jl 10,19:6
Gauch, William, 1945, N 14,19:2
Gauchat, Erich, 1955, N 9,2:5
Gauche, Edward E, 1954, N 3,29:3
Gauche, William J, 1954, D 14,33:3
Gaucher, Albert, 1952, Mr 27,29:2
Gaudaur, Jacob G, 1937, O 12,25:1
Gaudenzi, Edith W, 1942, O 24,15:6
Gaudet, Fernando, 1942, Ap 9,19:5
Gaudet, J Joseph, 1939, Ap 30,45:2
Gaudet, W Arthur, 1961, Mr 2,27:1
Gaudette, Hector L, 1950, Ag 25,21:5
Gaudette, Marie E, 1966, Ap 2,29:2
Gaudiani, Antoine, 1940, O 28,17:3
Gaudiani, Claire H Mrs, 1938, Ap 13,25:5
Gaudiani, Vincent Dr, 1937, O 9,19:2
Gaudielle, Joseph H, 1965, Jl 13,33:4
Gaudineer, Bertrand, 1946, D 20,24:3
Gaudineer, E Frank, 1955, Ag 15,15:5
Gaudineer, William J, 1949, My 8,76:5
Gaudini, Giulio, 1948, Ja 7,25:3
Gaudio, Gaetano (Tony), 1951, Ag 11,11:6
Gaudnier, Ruth M, 1937, S 1,6:4
Gaudreau, William P Rev, 1968, D 1,86:6
Gaudreault, Leo, 1950, Mr 22,27:3
Gaudry, Jean Albert, 1908, N 28,9:5
Gauer, Jack, 1967, Je 27,39:1
Gauff, George K, 1957, D 13,27:4
Gauge, Alex, 1960, Ag 30,18:1
Gauger, Alfred W, 1963, Jl 19,25:5
Gaughan, Richard W, 1944, Ap 7,19:2
Gaughan, Robert A, 1948, S 17,25:2
Gaughey, Rollin, 1925, N 19,25:5
Gaughran, Thomas J, 1947, D 1,21:5
Gaugler, Guy G, 1953, Je 14,84:1
Gaugler, Raymond C, 1952, Ja 12,13:1
Gauguin, Emil, 1955, Ja 21,23:3
Gauhn, Emmett R, 1948, O 19,27:6
Gaul, Christian Mrs, 1943, O 19,19:4
Gaul, Cyril, 1946, F 12,28:2
Gaul, George, 1939, O 7,17:4
Gaul, Gilbert William, 1919, D 22,15:3
Gaul, Herman J, 1949, N 27,104:4
Gaul, J Jr, 1879, Jl 30,2:4
Gaul, John J, 1938, Ja 23,II,8:8
Gaul, Julian A (will), 1958, O 4,23:2
Gaul, Robert D, 1954, My 23,88:4
Gaul, William H, 1944, Ap 10,19:6
Gaule, Margaret (Mrs August T Riedinger), 1910, Je 10,9:4
Gaulin, Alphonse, 1937, Mr 7,1:6
Gaulin, Etienne, 1947, My 15,26:3
Gaulle, Anne de, 1948, F 8,60:2
Gaulle, Jacques de, 1946, F 20,25:1
Gaulle, Pierre de, 1959, D 27,60:3
Gaulle, Xavier de, 1955, F 10,31:3
Gaulois, Paul, 1943, O 18,15:3
Gault, A F, 1903, Jl 9,7:6
Gault, Andrew H, 1958, N 29,21:5
Gault, Arabella S, 1946, Ag 14,25:6
Gault, B M, 1947, D 5,25:2
Gault, Charles N, 1958, Mr 8,17:3
Gault, Edwin S, 1950, Ag 22,27:1; 1958, S 3,33:1
Gaumerais, Jean Mrs, 1941, Ja 23,21:1
Gaumont, Leon, 1946, Ag 12,21:3
Gaunt, Carmen S Mrs, 1940, My 10,23:3
Gaunt, Ernest, 1940, Ap 21,43:3
Gaunt, G W F, 1918, S 25,13:4
Gaunt, George S, 1952, Ja 24,47:3
Gaunt, James, 1916, D 3,23:2
Gaunt, John, 1958, S 25,33:3
Gaunt, Lawrence, 1940, D 29,24:4
Gaunt, Thomas, 1906, Ag 13,7:6
Gaunt, Thomas T Mrs, 1948, S 1,48:6
Gaunt, William C, 1942, D 15,27:6
Gauntlett, Basil D, 1946, S 1,36:1
Gauntlett, Sidney C, 1951, S 23,87:2
Gauntt, Isaiah A, 1938, Ag 4,17:3
Gauntt, Phil L, 1948, D 7,31:4
Gaurnier, Lawrence J, 1955, O 26,31:1
Gaurns, Andrew H, 1944, N 5,54:4
Gaus, Charles H (funl, N 4,11:5), 1909, N 1,11:5
Gaus, Edward A, 1914, N 24,13:6
Gaus, Louis H, 1949, Mr 8,25:3
Gause, Edmund C, 1961, My 24,41:2
Gause, Edmund C Mrs, 1938, Ap 28,23:2; 1949, F 23, 27:2
Gause, Ella T, 1941, F 20,20:3
Gause, Fred C, 1944, F 17,19:2
Gause, Harry Taylor, 1925, Ap 23,21:2
Gause, John R, 1944, O 15,44:7
Gausevoort, Peter (see also Ja 5), 1876, Ja 8,5:2
Gausewitz, Edmund, 1945, Mr 3,13:3
Gausman, George F, 1945, Ap 15,14:6
Gausmann, Margaret V M Mrs, 1939, D 27,21:3
Gauss, Christian, 1951, N 2,1:6
Gauss, Christian Mrs (mem ser plans, O 2,37:3), 1958, S 28,89:1
Gauss, Clarence E (funl plans, Ap 10,86:4), 1960, Ap 9,23:1
Gauss, D Christian Jr, 1955, Je 17,16:1
Gauss, Frank L E, 1925, S 22,25:2
Gauss, Harry B, 1959, Ag 24,21:1
Gaut, Henry, 1945, N 16,19:4
Gaut, Robert Mrs, 1944, S 13,19:3
Gauther, Charles E, 1938, Mr 28,15:2
Gautherot, Gustave, 1948, F 27,21:1
Gauthier, Blanche, 1960, O 9,86:4
Gauthier, Charles Hugh Archbishop, 1922, Ja 20,15:4
Gauthier, Eva, 1958, D 27,2:8
Gauthier, Henry J, 1937, Ja 5,23:4
Gauthier, Joseph A G (por), 1940, S 1,20:7
Gauthier, Joseph C, 1951, S 17,21:5
Gauthier, Robert E, 1966, N 8,39:4
Gautier, Arsene D, 1961, D 17,27:1
Gautier, August E, 1937, Jl 15,19:4
Gautier, Charles A, 1945, Ja 15,19:1
Gautier, Felix C, 1964, Je 16,39:1
Gautier, Harold A, 1957, Mr 7,29:1
Gautier, J A, 1881, D 27,5:1
Gautier, Joseph W, 1939, Ag 19,15:3
Gautier, Leonard H, 1948, F 25,23:5
Gautier, Louis F, 1943, Je 27,32:5
Gautier, Pierre, 1940, D 16,23:2
Gautier, Raoul C, 1947, Ja 23,23:4
Gautier, Theophile, 1872, O 25,4:7
Gautier, William G Mrs, 1947, Mr 17,25:7
Gauvain, E Almore, 1950, Ja 19,27:3
Gauveau, Alphonse Mrs, 1952, Ja 16,25:4
Gauvreau, Emile H, 1956, O 17,35:1
Gava, John, 1908, Je 29,7:5
Gavagan, Edward F, 1952, Ja 11,21:3
Gavagan, Joseph A Justice, 1968, O 19,37:3
Gavagan, Margaret, 1949, Jl 23,11:5
Gavan, Charles J, 1966, Je 1,44:1
Gavazzi, Giuseppe, 1949, N 8,31:5
Gave, Charles N Mrs, 1947, O 20,23:5
Gaveau, Paul, 1943, My 29,13:4
Gavegan, Edward J, 1943, F 7,48:6
Gaven, Helen, 1952, Je 9,23:5
Gaven, Michael, 1958, Mr 12,31:1
Gaver, Floyd W, 1949, N 23,29:4
Gaver, Harry H, 1954, Mr 9,27:4
Gavett, Joseph W, 1941, O 25,17:6; 1942, Ag 29,15:1
Gavey, Eugene M, 1941, F 11,23:2
Gavian, Farkis Mrs, 1959, F 5,31:3
Gavigan, George J, 1946, N 16,19:3
Gavigan, John S, 1957, D 12,29:5
Gavigan, William M, 1952, My 31,17:2
Gavin, Anthony J, 1942, Jl 20,13:3
Gavin, Arthur Mrs, 1949, S 19,23:2
Gavin, David B, 1939, Ag 8,17:5
Gavin, Edward G, 1956, Jl 30,21:4
Gavin, Emma J, 1944, Ag 9,17:4
Gavin, Francis J, 1962, Ap 8,86:3
Gavin, Frank J Mrs, 1945, O 19,23:2
Gavin, Frank S B, 1938, Mr 21,15:5; 1939, Mr 19,III, 6:5
Gavin, George B, 1938, Jl 5,17:1
Gavin, James L, 1945, Ag 7,23:1
Gavin, James T, 1964, Jl 27,31:5
Gavin, John H, 1947, Je 25,25:3
Gavin, John J, 1921, O 12,15:5
Gavin, Joseph P, 1945, O 6,13:3
Gavin, Leon H, 1963, S 16,35:3
Gavin, Mary Lt-Col, 1968, N 14,47:1
Gavin, Michael, 1960, Jl 10,72:2
Gavin, Michael Mrs (will, Ja 18,35:3), 1961, Ja 12, 29:3
Gavin, Stephen A, 1943, O 25,15:4
Gavin, Thomas, 1954, S 18,15:3
Gavin, Thomas F, 1943, D 23,19:2
Gavin, Thomas G, 1941, Ag 11,13:5
Gavin, Thomas Mrs, 1946, Jl 23,25:4
Gavin, W A J, 1948, Ja 7,25:2
Gavin, William E, 1953, Ap 25,15:6
Gavin, William J, 1941, O 13,17:4
Gavit, Bernard C, 1954, Ja 17,93:2
Gavit, E Palmer Mrs, 1937, N 13,19:4
Gavit, John P, 1954, O 28,35:2
Gavit, John P Mrs, 1941, Ja 9,21:4
Gavit, Julia N, 1938, O 3,15:3
Gavitt, Isaac P, 1946, Ag 15,25:5
Gavitt, Jennie C, 1945, D 24,15:4
Gavitt, John E, 1874, Ag 26,4:7
Gavitte, Cortlandt N Mrs, 1950, Je 13,28:3
Gavoille, Clovis A, 1950, F 9,29:2
Gavotti, Guilio Marchese, 1939, O 8,49:2
Gavrilin, Georgii, 1952, Ag 8,17:2
Gavrilov, Vasilii, 1952, Ja 26,13:1
Gaw, Cooper, 1956, N 1,39:6
Gaw, Henry L, 1948, D 11,15:5
Gawales, Michael J, 1947, N 2,72:6
Gawin, August M, 1945, D 10,21:3
Gawkins, John J, 1942, Je 26,21:4
Gawley, Ruby S Mrs, 1944, N 22,19:3
Gawlik, Anthony, 1951, O 12,28:2
Gawling, Joseph, 1964, S 22,39:1
Gawlis, Alex, 1949, D 8,33:3
Gawthrop, Alfred H, 1937, O 23,15:8
Gawthrop, Charles S, 1924, N 1,15:3
Gawthrop, Joseph R, 1942, Ap 22,23:2
Gawthrop, Robert S, 1944, My 18,19:3
Gawthrop, Robert S Mrs, 1949, Jl 19,29:1
Gawthrop, W Ralph, 1943, Mr 31,19:3
Gawtry, Harrison, 1919, Ja 30,13:3
Gawtry, Lewis, 1954, Ap 20,30:3
Gawtry, Lewis Mrs, 1946, Mr 6,27:4
Gaxton, William, 1963, F 4,8:3
Gay, Arturo, 1958, Ap 5,29:2
Gay, Byron, 1945, D 24,15:2
Gay, Charles, 1950, F 24,24:2
Gay, Charles Abram, 1916, N 16,11:4
Gay, Charles M, 1951, D 19,31:5
Gay, Charles R (por), 1946, Mr 24,46:4
Gay, Duncan, 1948, O 11,23:4
Gay, Edward A, 1946, Ap 17,25:5
Gay, Edward J, 1952, D 3,33:5
Gay, Edward R, 1966, Jl 20,41:3
Gay, Edwin F (por), 1946, F 9,13:1
Gay, Ellen S Mrs, 1939, Ja 25,22:1
Gay, F B, 1934, Je 16,15:3
Gay, F Selwyn, 1953, Ap 11,17:3
Gay, Francisque, 1963, O 24,33:3
Gay, Frank W, 1953, Ja 13,27:3
Gay, Fred, 1955, Je 13,23:6
Gay, Frederick P (por), 1939, Jl 15,15:4
Gay, George, 1948, F 16,22:3
Gay, George A (por), 1944, D 15,19:5
Gay, George I, 1964, O 26,31:4
Gay, George W Jr, 1945, N 12,21:4
Gay, H Burton Sr, 1944, My 20,15:1
Gay, H N, 1932, Ag 14,24:3
Gay, Harry S Jr, 1953, Mr 5,27:6
Gay, Herbert S Mrs, 1964, Jl 30,27:4
Gay, Herbert S Sr, 1950, N 3,27:4
Gay, Hershel A, 1954, Ja 11,25:4
Gay, Hobart R Jr, 1952, Ag 12,20:3
Gay, I J, 1938, Ap 8,23:5
Gay, J Edward Jr, 1947, My 27,25:2
Gay, James H, 1955, Je 28,27:5
Gay, Jan, 1960, S 13,37:4
Gay, John D Sr, 1945, S 13,23:1
Gay, John H, 1946, My 31,23:4
Gay, John H Jr, 1947, Mr 9,60:3
Gay, Joseph E, 1914, S 29,11:6
Gay, Joseph H, 1943, F 1,15:2
Gay, Josephine Mrs, 1947, O 6,21:3
Gay, Laura S, 1948, F 16,21:2
Gay, Maisie, 1945, S 15,15:3
Gay, Margaret C (Mrs F Smulders), 1957, S 1[illegible]
Gay, Noel, 1954, Mr 5,19:5
Gay, Norman R, 1966, N 2,45:4
Gay, Patricia, 1965, My 10,33:3
Gay, R V, 1943, D 17,27:2
Gay, Robert Harvey, 1925, N 26,23:5
Gay, Robert M, 1961, Jl 22,21:6
Gay, Sherwood B, 1963, O 6,89:1
Gay, Sophronia Mrs, 1948, Jl 21,23:4
Gay, W A, 1903, My 21,9:4
Gay, Walter, 1937, Jl 15,19:4
Gay, Walter Mrs, 1943, S 16,21:6
Gay, William A Mrs, 1956, Mr 16,23:5
Gay, William D Mrs, 1953, S 22,31:5
Gay, William F, 1950, F 8,27:3
Gay, William H, 1920, My 20,13:5
Gay, William H Mrs, 1945, Ap 20,19:5
Gay, William O, 1946, Je 14,22:2
Gay, William O Mrs, 1949, Ja 7,21:3
Gay, Winckworth Allan, 1910, F 23,9:5

Gaydos, Frank M, 1952, F 13,29:5
Gayer, Arthur D, 1951, N 18,83:4
Gayevsky, Alexander T, 1945, S 3,23:4
Gayfer, Hammond B, 1938, O 15,17:2
Gayford, Oswald R (por), 1945, Ag 12,40:2
Gayk, Andreas, 1954, O 2,17:3
Gayl, Joseph C Mrs, 1962, Ap 23,29:2
Gaylani, Rashid A (funl, ag 31,23:1), 1965, Ag 30, 25:5
Gayle, Ernest L, 1966, O 24,39:3
Gayle, John W, 1941, Ja 8,19:1
Gayle, R Finley Jr, 1957, N 6,35:4
Gayle, William T, 1968, Je 24,37:2
Gayler, Julius F, 1948, F 24,25:2
Gayler, Julius F Mrs, 1950, Je 6,29:5
Gayler, Robert A Mrs, 1939, D 31,18:5
Gayley, James, 1920, F 26,11:3
Gayley, Oliver C, 1916, Ja 10,11:4
Gayley, Samuel A, 1959, Ja 30,27:1
Gayley, Samuel M, 1937, Ag 8,II,6:3
Gaylor, Alfred H, 1949, Ag 16,23:5
Gaylor, Frank C, 1963, Ag 23,25:2
Gaylord, A S, 1877, Je 23,5:4
Gaylord, Augustus, 1901, Mr 31,7:5
Gaylord, Clifford W, 1952, Ja 8,27:5
Gaylord, E Mrs, 1931, O 17,19:7
Gaylord, Edward B Mrs, 1957, Ap 16,33:4
Gaylord, Elston E, 1949, Jl 18,17:6
Gaylord, Frank A, 1944, O 19,23:1
Gaylord, Franklin A, 1943, Ag 15,39:3
Gaylord, George L, 1943, Ja 10,50:2
Gaylord, Harriet E, 1947, D 12,27:1
Gaylord, Harvey R Dr, 1924, Je 23,19:6
Gaylord, Henry J, 1955, Mr 30,29:5
Gaylord, James H, 1953, Jl 22,27:2
Gaylord, James L, 1907, S 9,7:7
Gaylord, Laurence T, 1968, Ja 9,43:4
Gaylord, Melvin S, 1951, F 28,27:1
Gaylord, Mildred I Mrs (will, My 18,15:8), 1954, Ap 11,82:8
Gaylord, Noah H Rev, 1873, Ap 4,8:5
Gaylord, Robert B, 1953, Ag 5,23:3
Gaylord, Samuel W, 1940, S 22,48:2
Gaylord, Seymour A, 1950, D 10,104:6
Gaylord, William S, 1942, Mr 8,42:4
Gayne, C Philip Mrs, 1949, O 4,23:2
Gayne, Edward, 1937, Ja 29,19:3
Gayne, Edward W, 1951, Ag 23,23:3
Gayne, Paul, 1956, O 14,87:1
Gayner, John M, 1952, My 16,23:3
Gaynor, Arthur C, 1953, Je 11,29:3
Gaynor, Edward F, 1946, Ja 16,23:3
Gaynor, Frank, 1961, F 20,27:2
Gaynor, Frank M, 1951, N 24,11:5
Gaynor, Hugh A, 1939, N 30,21:3
Gaynor, James J, 1956, Ap 7,27:3
Gaynor, John E, 1939, F 9,21:5
Gaynor, John F, 1921, D 15,19:6
Gaynor, John M, 1952, Jl 10,31:2
Gaynor, John P, 1958, Je 2,27:5
Gaynor, John S, 1941, My 10,15:7
Gaynor, Leonard Mrs (B Johaneson), 1962, Jl 12, 29:2
Gaynor, Myles B, 1942, N 2,21:5
Gaynor, Norman J, 1964, Ap 30,35:3
Gaynor, Percy J, 1958, Ja 1,25:5
Gaynor, Peter J, 1944, D 20,23:2
Gaynor, Rufus W, 1941, F 15,15:2
Gaynor, T G, 1903, My 15,9:6
Gaynor, W J Mrs, 1926, D 7,27:3
Gaynor, William A, 1913, S 24,9:5
Gaynor, William P, 1959, Ag 30,82:5
Gaynor, William T, 1956, O 7,86:4
Gayron, Paul S, 1954, Jl 12,19:3
Gayton, Loren D, 1951, D 29,11:1
Gaywood, Annie, 1949, D 2,29:1
Gayzur, Frank, 1946, O 24,27:5
Gazagne, Paul Mrs, 1941, O 31,23:4
Gazda, Antoine, 1957, S 24,35:4
Gazdzicki, John C, 1941, Jl 1,23:6
Gazlay, James W, 1874, Je 13,4:7
Gazmuri, Luis, 1940, Jl 25,17:4
Gazulias, Constantine A, 1948, My 24,19:1
Gazzam, Anna Reading Mrs, 1907, Jl 18,7:6
Gazzam, James B, 1909, Ap 1,9:5
Gazzaniga, Marietta, 1884, Ja 4,1:6
Gazzolo, Frank J, 1938, Mr 29,21:3
Gazzoni, Arturo, 1951, F 10,13:6
Geadding, Albert F Ex-Justice, 1922, My 30,13:6
Geaney, John, 1938, Ja 20,23:3
Geaney, Victoria Mrs, 1961, F 27,27:1
Gear, Dale D, 1951, S 25,29:2
Gear, Henry G, 1937, S 25,17:6
Gear, Patrick E, 1952, Ja 22,29:5
Gear, William I, 1939, Ja 11,19:4
Geare, Iltyd H, 1953, Ja 25,85:2
Geare, Norman W, 1960, Mr 12,21:4
Gearhart, Bertrand W, 1955, O 13,31:4
Gearhart, Celestia A Mrs, 1952, D 25,29:2
Gearhart, Edwin W, 1937, F 17,22:1
Gearhart, Fred D, 1941, O 28,23:2
Gearhart, James W, 1958, Jl 25,19:4
Gearie, Alfred, 1938, F 23,23:6
Gearin, George F Mrs, 1953, Mr 27,23:3
Gearin, Michael A Rev, 1968, Je 24,37:3
Gearing, Charles M Mrs, 1950, Ap 18,31:1
Gearing, Henry C Mrs, 1947, My 17,15:3
Gearing, Thomas J, 1952, N 24,23:5
Gearino, Louis J Sr, 1945, D 6,27:4
Gearn, George F, 1948, S 30,27:2
Gearon, Cornelius P, 1947, Ap 16,25:2; 1954, Ap 27, 29:5
Gearon, John J, 1954, S 18,15:6
Gearty, John B, 1939, Jl 11,6:6
Geary, Alex B, 1952, Je 3,29:5
Geary, Alfred H, 1961, O 1,86:3
Geary, Blanche, 1959, Je 21,92:4
Geary, Daniel E, 1950, Je 30,23:6
Geary, Daniel J, 1949, D 23,21:3
Geary, Edward L, 1947, D 1,21:1
Geary, Edwin, 1914, My 9,11:5
Geary, Ethel S Mrs, 1967, Ag 24,37:3
Geary, Gen Ex-Gov, 1873, F 9,5:4
Geary, George R, 1954, My 1,15:2
Geary, H Logan, 1954, Ja 11,25:2
Geary, Harry O, 1959, N 5,35:4
Geary, James B, 1941, S 26,23:5
Geary, James W, 1944, F 27,38:4
Geary, John B Sr, 1952, Mr 7,23:3
Geary, John F, 1951, N 25,84:3
Geary, John H, 1940, Ja 21,35:2
Geary, John W, 1940, F 26,15:5
Geary, John W Jr, 1956, Mr 5,23:5
Geary, John W Mrs, 1952, D 17,33:3
Geary, Joseph P, 1947, O 9,25:3
Geary, Louis J, 1948, O 21,27:3
Geary, Mannis J, 1922, F 27,13:6
Geary, Roy C, 1952, F 17,86:4
Geary, Russell D, 1949, Jl 4,13:5
Geary, Walter F, 1951, O 1,23:5
Geary, William G, 1944, D 2,13:1
Geary, William J, 1946, Jl 21,40:1; 1954, N 11,31:3
Geasey, Robert V, 1953, F 18,31:4
Geaslin, Bon, 1950, Ap 12,27:2
Geatons, James T, 1920, Ap 6,11:4
Geatty, Charles A, 1950, O 11,33:4
Geaty, James A, 1962, Jl 5,25:3
Geb, George F, 1944, Mr 27,19:5
Gebain, Ethel, 1950, Ja 31,23:1
Gebbie, Frederick Sir, 1939, Mr 22,23:4
Gebbie, Marian B, 1949, Ap 5,29:3
Gebby, Elmer R Mrs, 1952, F 2,13:5
Gebel, Sylvan L, 1968, S 23,35:5
Gebelein, Harry A, 1954, Jl 30,17:5
Gebert, Ernst, 1961, N 23,31:6
Gebert, Nicholas J, 1951, Ap 22,88:3
Gebhard, Aug, 1940, Ap 25,23:3
Gebhard, Frederic (funl, S 10,9:6), 1910, S 9,9:4
Gebhard, Heinrich, 1963, My 6,29:5
Gebhard, John G Mrs, 1945, Je 15,19:3
Gebhard, Leonard, 1952, Jl 23,23:2
Gebhardt, Charles, 1962, Ag 30,29:4
Gebhardt, Emile, 1908, Ap 22,9:5
Gebhardt, George F, 1950, Mr 23,36:3
Gebhardt, Henry, 1942, O 1,23:2
Gebhardt, Herbert L, 1956, O 21,86:2
Gebhardt, Raymond L, 1953, Ja 29,27:4
Gebhardt, Richard A, 1938, O 27,23:3
Gebhart, Albert, 1950, Ja 5,25:2
Gechlik, Irving, 1954, Jl 4,1:1
Geck, Fred A, 1952, N 11,29:4
Geddes, Adam E, 1943, Ap 30,21:1
Geddes, Alex, 1904, F 4,9:6
Geddes, Anna B, 1942, S 15,24:3
Geddes, Auckland C, 1954, Ja 9,15:5
Geddes, Charles Paul, 1909, D 18,13:2
Geddes, Charles R 3d, 1951, F 5,23:3
Geddes, Charles Wright, 1914, Jl 19,5:6
Geddes, Donald G, 1949, N 19,17:3
Geddes, Donald G Jr, 1937, My 7,25:2
Geddes, Donald G Mrs, 1961, My 18,35:5
Geddes, Donald P, 1963, F 27,16:1
Geddes, Donald Y, 1954, My 5,31:5
Geddes, Douglas, 1948, F 19,23:5
Geddes, Eric Sir (por), 1937, Je 23,25:3
Geddes, G, 1883, O 9,2:2
Geddes, Hamilton Sr, 1949, My 26,29:3
Geddes, Helen B S Mrs, 1938, My 30,11:5
Geddes, Isabella, 1962, Ja 10,47:4
Geddes, James, 1938, F 17,21:4
Geddes, John, 1946, Mr 31,46:2
Geddes, John G, 1952, O 2,29:4
Geddes, John J, 1950, Ja 31,24:4
Geddes, Norman Bel, 1958, My 9,23:2
Geddes, Norman Bel Mrs, 1943, Ja 18,15:3
Geddes, P Sir, 1932, Ap 18,15:1
Geddes, Sarah I Y Mrs, 1942, O 8,27:1
Geddes, W Roy, 1954, S 15,33:5
Geddes, Walter M, 1915, N 11,13:6
Geddes, William K, 1943, O 22,17:5
Geddes, William L, 1941, Ja 22,21:5
Geddis, Harold J, 1954, Ap 14,29:3
Geddis, W Kenneth, 1959, Ag 1,17:5
Geddy, Vernon M, 1952, O 20,23:4
Gedeon, Joe, 1941, My 21,23:4
Gedney, Elisha H, 1950, Je 8,31:3
Gedney, Elmer E Mrs, 1949, N 10,32:3
Gedney, Eugene V, 1967, Ag 16,41:2
Gedney, George Mrs, 1953, Je 24,25:4
Gedney, George W, 1949, Ag 17,23:6
Gedney, J Harvey, 1940, D 11,27:5
Gedney, John S, 1946, S 11,7:5
Gedney, Stanley Sr, 1947, Jl 29,21:3
Gedney, Walter S, 1953, Ag 18,23:4
Gedney, William Hunt Mrs, 1919, Ag 11,11:4
Gedo, Leopold, 1952, Jl 29,21:6
Gedye, Nicholas G, 1947, My 21,25:4
Gee, Albert, 1947, Jl 22,23:1
Gee, Albert H, 1962, Jl 31,27:2
Gee, Charles, 1956, Je 19,29:4
Gee, Charles Mrs, 1943, Mr 14,26:5
Gee, Edward B, 1903, N 30,2:6
Gee, George, 1959, O 18,86:3
Gee, Horace E, 1950, Jl 29,13:5
Gee, John A, 1944, Ag 6,37:3
Gee, John R, 1946, Mr 19,27:5
Gee, Nathaniel G Dr, 1937, D 19,II,8:4
Gee, Russell F Jr, 1967, My 8,41:3
Gee, Russell F Sr, 1967, My 13,33:5
Gee, Walter S Jr, 1957, O 5,17:2
Gee, William E, 1943, N 14,57:1
Gee, Wilson, 1961, F 3,25:3
Geegan, Seraphin, 1939, Ja 26,21:6
Geel, Howard O, 1950, Mr 20,21:2
Geen, Francois Marie van, 1944, My 4,19:4
Geenzier, Enrique, 1943, S 23,21:5
Geer, Alpheus (por), 1941, Ag 18,13:3
Geer, Alpheus Mrs, 1958, N 29,21:1
Geer, Andrew C, 1957, D 24,15:3
Geer, Bennette E, 1964, D 31,17:2
Geer, Clementine, 1940, My 15,25:1
Geer, Curtis M, 1938, Ag 4,17:2
Geer, Danforth Jr, 1942, N 2,21:2
Geer, Derek J de, 1960, N 29,37:3
Geer, E Harold, 1957, D 25,31:3
Geer, Eleanor P, 1951, Ag 26,77:2
Geer, Enos Throop, 1968, F 20,47:1
Geer, F Joseph, 1925, Ag 26,19:5
Geer, Fayette U, 1948, D 4,19:3
Geer, FRancis H, 1950, Mr 9,29:2
Geer, G J Rev Dr, 1885, Mr 17,5:5
Geer, George J Jr, 1955, Ja 17,23:4
Geer, George J Mrs, 1953, N 13,27:2
Geer, George Jarvis, 1924, N 13,21:4
Geer, Gerard de, 1943, Ag 12,19:3
Geer, Grace W, 1938, Je 28,19:2
Geer, J Eugene, 1940, Mr 19,12:6
Geer, James B, 1950, Ag 18,21:2
Geer, Joseph J, 1940, Mr 22,19:1
Geer, Langdon, 1915, Je 21,9:5
Geer, Laurence P, 1954, Ag 12,25:3
Geer, Noel N Mrs, 1956, F 16,21:7
Geer, Olin P, 1957, O 10,33:2
Geer, Olin P Mrs, 1948, Ap 2,24:2
Geer, Oliver J, 1903, N 14,9:6
Geer, W M, 1935, Mr 10,35:5
Geer, Walter, 1937, F 24,24:2
Geer, William C, 1943, Mr 16,19:1; 1964, S 10,35:3
Geer, William C Mrs, 1949, Ag 18,21:4
Geer, William H, 1925, Ap 3,19:6
Geering, Emil, 1925, My 8,19:4
Geerlofs, John P, 1939, My 13,15:6
Geers, Frederick W, 1955, F 1,29:4
Geers, Lester, 1938, My 28,15:6
Geertz, Allan O, 1950, S 23,17:4
Geertz, Julius F, 1942, O 26,15:4
Geery, John, 1938, Mr 23,23:1
Geery, William B, 1949, D 2,29:2
Gefaell, John E, 1960, Mr 22,38:1
Gefell, Bernard J, 1950, F 10,24:3
Gefell, John B, 1939, N 17,21:2
Geffen, Pauline F Mrs, 1958, D 16,2:4
Geffen, Philip H Mrs, 1947, Je 28,13:3
Geffner, Max, 1956, S 27,42:4
Geffner, Michael M, 1956, My 10,31:1
Geffroy, 1926, Ap 6,29:3
Gegan, Anthony R, 1952, Ap 8,29:2
Gegan, James J Mrs, 1948, F 24,25:3
Gegan, William J, 1949, D 3,15:2
Gegenheimer, Carl, 1966, My 18,47:1
Gegenheimer, Edward C, 1964, Mr 13,34:4
Geggis, William J, 1947, Mr 20,27:3
Gegler, William G, 1952, S 21,88:5
Gegna, Jascha, 1944, S 13,19:4
Gehan, Arthur E, 1945, Ag 14,21:4
Gehan, John F, 1960, Jl 17,61:1
Gehan, Raymond F, 1957, Mr 6,31:2
Gehin, Gustave W, 1943, D 13,23:4
Gehin, Gustave W Mrs, 1941, My 24,15:2
Gehl, Albert A, 1947, S 30,25:4
Gehl, Phil M, 1955, N 18,25:3
Gehle, Conrad H, 1948, Jl 22,23:5
Gehle, Ernest C, 1949, Ap 26,26:3
Gehle, Frederick W, 1960, Ap 26,37:3
Gehle, Robert L, 1952, Ap 11,23:3
Gehle, William A, 1958, Je 8,89:1
Gehlen, Charles W, 1948, D 9,33:3
Gehlert, John E, 1942, Je 16,23:5
Gehlhaus, William A, 1950, Mr 2,27:3

Gehm, Harry J, 1959, Mr 10,36:1
Gehm, John, 1954, Je 24,27:2
Gehm, William H, 1950, Jl 29,13:4
Gehman, William G, 1941, N 27,23:3
Gehres, Loyd F, 1964, My 9,27:3
Gehrig, Anton J Mrs, 1953, Ag 1,11:6
Gehrig, George L, 1949, Jl 24,53:2
Gehrig, George L Mrs, 1963, Jl 24,31:3
Gehrig, Henry L, 1946, Ag 19,25:4
Gehrig, Henry Mrs, 1954, Mr 13,15:2
Gehrig, John A, 1959, N 11,35:1
Gehrig, Lou, 1941, Je 3,1:3
Gehring, C E, 1927, Ja 22,13:3
Gehring, Clifford B, 1946, My 24,19:4
Gehring, Edward H, 1949, O 29,3:2
Gehring, Henry G, 1950, Ja 14,15:5
Gehring, J Arthur, 1953, Jl 19,57:2
Gehring, Lewis C, 1921, Ap 13,15:5
Gehring, Louis Mrs, 1962, Je 19,35:1
Gehring, William C, 1957, Ja 18,22:4; 1964, O 1,35:5
Gehringer, Joseph E, 1943, N 13,13:2
Gehringer, Martin, 1953, S 26,17:2
Gehringer, Theresa Mrs, 1946, Jl 6,15:5
Gehris, Joseph L, 1949, F 13,76:6
Gehrke, Edward H, 1948, S 3,19:1
Gehrlein, Francis J, 1956, Je 23,17:5
Gehrman, Misha Mrs, 1954, My 8,17:3
Gehrmann, Bernard J, 1958, Jl 13,68:7
Gehrmann, Caroline Mrs, 1925, Ap 8,21:4
Gehrmann, Charles F, 1950, Ag 5,15:7
Gehrmann, Felix, 1961, N 17,35:2
Gehrmann, George H, 1959, S 5,15:3
Gehron, William, 1958, N 19,37:1
Gehrs, Augusta M, 1947, Ap 1,27:5
Gehweiler, Adolph A, 1944, Je 4,42:4
Gehweiler, Adolph Mrs, 1947, Jl 2,23:2
Gehweiler, Hugh, 1953, N 10,31:3
Geib, Conrad, 1880, Jl 27,8:3
Geib, Fred, 1950, D 9,15:5
Geib, Henry, 1952, O 10,25:3
Geib, Howell R Sr, 1948, N 5,25:3
Geib, Lester J, 1948, S 9,27:5
Geib, Raymond, 1949, Ap 27,27:3
Geib, William A, 1963, N 10,87:1
Geibel, E, 1884, Ap 7,5:5
Geibel, George Mrs, 1940, Jl 1,19:3
Geibel, Victor B, 1961, Ag 29,31:1
Geibell, George, 1949, F 7,19:1
Geick, George W Ex-Gov, 1911, Ap 14,11:4
Geidel, Christian, 1940, Mr 13,23:4
Geidel, Max, 1940, S 21,19:4
Geier, Charles A, 1947, D 18,30:2
Geier, Fred A Mrs, 1959, Ag 4,27:2
Geier, Oscar A, 1942, N 7,15:2
Geier, Otto P, 1954, Mr 1,25:5
Geier, P A, 1942, N 13,23:4
Geier, Phil O, 1954, Ap 22,30:3
Geiershofer, Henry, 1925, D 29,23:4
Geiffert, Alfred Jr, 1957, Ag 27,29:3
Geigar, William F, 1966, N 23,39:3
Geiger, Adam K, 1959, My 1,29:2
Geiger, Anthony H, 1950, My 9,29:1
Geiger, Bentley J, 1954, S 7,25:2
Geiger, Bernard, 1964, Jl 7,32:6
Geiger, Charles F, 1950, F 25,17:3
Geiger, Charles J, 1959, O 28,37:2
Geiger, Charles Mrs, 1943, F 21,32:8
Geiger, Charles W, 1946, Jl 20,13:5
Geiger, Edgar C, 1961, Ap 11,37:3
Geiger, Edward J, 1949, Ja 12,28:3
Geiger, Ernest, 1957, O 17,33:4
Geiger, Erwin H, 1943, Jl 8,19:2
Geiger, Ferdinand A (por), 1939, Ag 1,19:3
Geiger, Frank A, 1944, N 8,17:5
Geiger, Frank C, 1951, My 22,31:2
Geiger, Frank H, 1941, D 21,41:3
Geiger, Fred W, 1951, Jl 28,11:6
Geiger, Gene, 1963, Ap 12,27:1
Geiger, Harry W, 1946, F 15,25:3
Geiger, Henry Mrs, 1943, S 1,19:4
Geiger, Hermann, 1966, Ag 27,30:1
Geiger, Ivan J, 1955, Ja 14,21:3
Geiger, John J, 1951, Mr 31,15:2
Geiger, John P, 1952, Ag 13,21:2
Geiger, Josephine D S Mrs, 1939, My 11,25:4
Geiger, Leonard R, 1957, Ag 28,19:1
Geiger, Leopold, 1938, Ap 27,23:5
Geiger, Lewis P, 1939, Ja 26,21:5
Geiger, Linwood T, 1945, F 26,19:2
Geiger, Louis F, 1942, Je 11,23:5
Geiger, Marlin G, 1960, My 15,86:1
Geiger, Moritz A Dr, 1937, S 11,17:3
Geiger, Paul H, 1954, Ja 28,27:2
Geiger, Roy S, 1947, Ja 24,21:1
Geiger, Rudolf, 1956, Ag 4,15:6
Geiger, Sylvis G Mrs, 1938, N 12,17:3
Geiger, Valentine Mrs, 1945, My 8,19:4
Geiger, Warren, 1952, D 25,29:5
Geiger, William A, 1952, My 20,25:5
Geiger, William J, 1950, Ja 28,13:2
Geiges, Alexander J Jr, 1944, S 16,13:6
Geikie, Archibald Sir, 1924, N 13,21:5
Geikie, James Prof, 1915, Mr 3,11:7

Geil, William Edgar Dr, 1925, Ap 14,23:5
Geiler, Karl, 1953, S 15,31:1
Geiler, Walter F, 1938, Mr 14,15:5
Geils, Louis C, 1941, Ag 29,17:6
Geiring, Jean, 1962, F 21,41:4
Geirsbach, Stuart F, 1947, Ap 1,27:3
Geis, A James, 1963, S 22,86:7
Geis, John F, 1939, Je 14,23:5
Geis, Joseph A, 1956, Jl 3,25:5
Geis, Norman P (will, Mr 26,16:6), 1938, F 6,II,8:8
Geis, Peter J, 1954, Ag 18,29:3
Geise, Harry, 1953, Je 24,25:3
Geise, Jacob H, 1957, N 1,27:1
Geisel, John, 1944, Je 2,15:6
Geisel, Theodor S Mrs (H Palmer), 1967, O 24,47:3
Geiselman, Austin H, 1945, N 15,20:2
Geiseman, Otto O, 1962, N 9,26:1
Geisenheimer, Morris, 1953, O 15,33:4
Geiser, Albert, 1946, My 10,19:3
Geiser, Arno, 1951, Je 23,15:6
Geiser, Clara Mrs, 1949, Mr 8,25:2
Geiser, Harry, 1953, O 6,29:2
Geiser, Karl F, 1951, Ap 2,25:4
Geisert, Lewis, 1959, Ag 5,27:2
Geisert, William, 1952, F 5,29:4
Geisinger, Joseph F, 1940, Ap 16,23:5
Geisinger, Joseph J, 1945, D 20,23:4
Geisler, Charles F Mrs, 1956, Je 7,31:4
Geisler, David, 1960, S 23,29:5
Geisler, Frederick W, 1950, F 23,27:3
Geisler, Hugo P, 1941, My 9,21:5
Geisler, J Edward, 1947, My 14,25:2
Geisler, Leo W, 1957, Ap 5,27:1
Geisler, Theodore J, 1925, My 23,15:5
Geisler, Walter R E, 1955, Ja 11,25:3
Geismar, Alex H, 1939, My 22,17:2
Geismar, Benjamin, 1938, Ap 29,21:3
Geismar, Herman, 1941, N 5,23:2
Geiss, John, 1942, S 3,20:3
Geiss, John J, 1954, Je 15,29:3
Geissel, Gustav, 1960, O 10,31:4
Geissel, Theodore L Mrs, 1947, Ja 10,21:5
Geissenhainer, D W Rev Dr, 1879, Je 3,5:3
Geissenhainer, Frederick W, 1954, D 9,33:3
Geisser, Lillie J (oct 3), 1965, O 11,61:2
Geissinger, Christian A Mrs, 1953, Ap 23,29:4
Geissler, Arthur D, 1945, Mr 15,23:5
Geissler, Arthur H, 1945, F 20,19:4
Geissler, Edwin H, 1957, My 13,31:2
Geissler, J Henry, 1951, Ja 3,27:1
Geissler, Louis F Mrs, 1965, O 28,43:2
Geissman, John A, 1959, Ja 19,27:5
Geissmar, Berta (por), 1949, N 6,94:4
Geist, A Joseph, 1963, Ag 12,21:3
Geist, A Joseph Mrs, 1966, Jl 23,25:6
Geist, Bernard, 1962, Ap 25,39:4
Geist, Bernard Mrs, 1959, Jl 31,24:1
Geist, Charles, 1955, Mr 9,27:4
Geist, Clarence H, 1938, Je 13,19:3
Geist, Clarence H Mrs, 1959, N 19,39:3
Geist, Gilbert A, 1937, S 14,23:2
Geist, H D Mrs, 1951, D 16,90:2
Geist, Harrison D, 1964, F 21,29:3
Geist, Harry, 1951, Ap 27,23:3
Geist, John L, 1945, S 25,25:4
Geist, Kaufman, 1948, Ap 22,27:1
Geist, Lionel S, 1941, O 11,17:5
Geist, Nathan, 1945, Je 20,23:2
Geist, Samuel H, 1943, D 15,27:3
Geist, Sidney Mrs, 1953, N 8,88:6
Geist, Walter, 1951, Ja 30,25:5
Geister, Janet M, 1964, D 10,58:1
Geistunger, Marie, 1903, O 1,5:2
Geither, Edward C, 1943, N 13,13:2
Geitner, Emil W Mrs, 1947, Jl 24,21:6
Geitz, Albert, 1952, Ap 9,31:3
Geizer, Dr, 1874, N 16,5:1
Gekeler, Henry S, 1950, S 23,17:4
Gelabert, Maria, 1922, Jl 15,9:6
Gelabert, Vincente, 1942, N 15,58:1
Gelardi, Giulio, 1954, Jl 23,17:3
Gelardin, Jacques, 1947, F 11,27:4
Gelarie, Arnold J, 1947, My 9,21:4
Gelas, Jean M, 1954, F 12,25:2
Gelb, Donald, 1968, D 28,27:2
Gelbach, Frederick P, 1946, D 15,76:1
Gelbach, Loring L, 1966, Mr 6,93:3
Gelband, Isidor, 1950, S 26,31:3
Gelband, Manning, 1964, Ag 31,25:3
Gelbart, Gershon, 1959, Ja 9,27:1
Gelbart, Nathan, 1949, N 1,27:3
Gelber, Aaron, 1944, O 26,23:4
Gelber, Ben Mrs, 1951, Jl 13,7:1
Gelber, Charles N, 1938, Mr 4,23:5
Gelber, Frank, 1965, N 28,89:2
Gelber, Herman, 1965, O 14,47:1
Gelber, Isaac, 1963, Jl 4,15:8
Gelber, Isidore B Mrs, 1944, Ap 14,19:4
Gelbert, Charles M, 1967, Ja 14,31:1
Gelder, Alfred, 1941, Ag 27,19:4
Gelderman, Godfrey J, 1948, Je 18,24:2
Geley, Gustave Dr, 1924, Jl 16,11:5
Geleyn, Gaston, 1946, N 17,68:2

Geleyn, Henry L Jr, 1925, Ag 25,17:5
Gelhaus, Fred J, 1955, N 25,27:3
Gelhaus, Henry F, 1952, F 20,29:5
Gelhausen, Herman, 1957, Jl 21,61:3
Gelin, Elsa G, 1947, My 16,23:1
Gelinas, Charles C, 1960, F 17,35:1
Gelinas, Raphael Rev, 1910, Ap 16,11:6
Gelineau, Victor (por), 1938, Ja 22,15:4
Gell, Edith M, 1944, Ap 19,23:2
Gell, Harry J, 1964, N 19,39:4
Gellady, Gerald, 1963, O 7,31:5
Gellatly, W A, 1885, F 14,5:3
Gellen, Aaron, 1937, My 25,27:3
Geller, Abraham, 1941, Ja 29,18:2; 1942, O 9,21:4
Geller, Abraham N Mrs, 1967, Je 20,39:3
Geller, Andrew, 1961, Ag 26,17:4
Geller, Carl, 1942, Je 29,15:2
Geller, David, 1964, F 23,85:1
Geller, Edward, 1948, My 13,25:4
Geller, Frederick Mrs, 1948, Jl 26,17:2
Geller, George, 1953, Mr 18,31:5
Geller, Henry, 1944, Ap 12,21:3
Geller, Herman, 1952, O 13,21:5
Geller, Isadore B, 1966, Ja 24,35:5
Geller, Isidor, 1952, N 27,31:2
Geller, Markel, 1960, Mr 30,37:1
Geller, Markel Mrs, 1957, D 13,27:3
Geller, Morris, 1948, F 13,21:3
Geller, Robert, 1959, Jl 22,27:3
Geller, Sam, 1958, Jl 17,27:4
Geller, Samuel, 1947, N 11,27:1
Geller, Samuel A, 1945, F 28,24:2
Geller, Todros, 1949, F 24,23:2
Gellert, Henry, 1903, N 13,2:3
Gellert, James E, 1967, F 22,29:5
Gellert, Leopold R Mrs, 1950, Jl 11,32:2
Gellert, N Henry Mrs, 1952, D 7,88:4
Gellert, Nathan H, 1959, N 17,35:5
Gellert, Oswald R, 1943, Ap 21,25:4
Gellert, Rosalind, 1952, Je 30,19:3
Gelles, Paul P, 1966, S 25,84:4
Gelles, Samuel, 1949, Je 23,27:2
Gellette, O R (por), 1944, Je 2,15:4
Gellhorn, George Jr, 1968, S 19,47:2
Gellhorn, Maria R, 1964, S 17,43:4
Gellinger, Harry L, 1950, S 29,27:3
Gellis, Isaac, 1906, Mr 21,9:5
Gellis, Sidney N, 1961, N 4,19:4
Gellman, Irving I, 1953, Je 15,29:3
Gellman, Jacob, 1961, Ag 11,24:1
Gellman, Milton B, 1964, Ag 15,21:4
Gellowitz, Sol, 1948, O 1,25:3
Gelm, George E Mrs, 1941, Ap 29,19:5
Gelman, Charles, 1941, Ap 20,42:7
Gelman, Morris, 1946, Ag 17,13:4
Gelnaw, William D, 1944, Ag 5,11:6
Gelo, John, 1957, Ja 14,23:4
Gelo, Salvatore, 1950, Jl 23,56:5
Gelormine, Galvine, 1946, My 13,22:3
Gelrud, Paul R, 1954, O 28,35:2
Gelser, Irvin L, 1942, F 22,26:4
Gelshenen, W H, 1902, Mr 22,9:5
Gelson, David P, 1939, Mr 24,21:2
Gelson, Patrick J, 1904, Ja 3,9:5
Gelst, Carlton, 1925, Ag 26,19:5
Gelston, Arthur W, 1953, N 20,23:3
Gelston, George S 3d, 1940, O 26,15:5
Gelston, Henry M, 1951, Mr 12,25:3
Gelston, James A, 1948, Ag 21,15:2
Gelston, John, 1883, Ja 20,3:2
Gelston, William H, 1953, Ag 12,31:2
Geltser, Ekaterina, 1962, D 14,3:5
Geltzer, Abraham, 1967, S 8,39:2
Geluso, Joseph, 1957, N 29,27:3
Gelvin, Edward H, 1962, F 3,21:4
Gelwicke, Harry R, 1956, My 24,31:1
Gelwicks, H Ellsworth (funl, Je 4,23:1), 1954, J
31:4
Gelwicks, H Ellsworth Mrs, 1951, D 4,33:5
Gelwicks, Harry R Mrs, 1953, O 4,89:2
Gelwicks, Louis E, 1954, D 11,13:5
Gelzenlichter, Charles Mrs, 1944, Je 16,19:3
Gemberling, Joseph B, 1943, O 5,25:4
Gemeiner, William J, 1950, Ag 3,23:3
Gemelli, Agostino, 1959, Jl 16,27:5
Gemier, F, 1933, N 27,17:5
Gemmel, Andrew, 1950, O 30,27:2
Gemmel, Ralph T, 1960, N 27,86:4
Gemmell, Alfred, 1957, My 21,35:2
Gemmell, John Jr, 1962, Ag 1,31:4
Gemmell, John Jr Mrs, 1963, S 8,87:1
Gemmell, Welland S, 1954, Je 19,15:3
Gemmill, Benjamin M, 1940, Mr 6,23:3
Gemmith, W D, 1882, F 28,2:6
Gemora, Charlie, 1961, Ag 20,86:6
Gempler, John O, 1949, N 14,27:3
Gemson, Harry, 1948, Jl 9,19:3
Gemunder, George, 1899, Ja 17,5:4
Gemunder, Oscar A, 1946, Ja 14,19:2
Gemunder, Otto, 1901, Je 13,2:4
Gen, Peanuts, 1902, D 18,9:6
Genard, Gabriel, 1950, Mr 28,31:4
Genaro, David, 1938, Je 6,17:4

Genaro, Frankie, 1966, D 28,43:4
Genauer, Joseph, 1942, Mr 8,42:2
Gendalls, Richard B, 1958, Je 7,19:3
Gendelbien, Olivier Mrs, 1965, Ap 20,4:6
Gendell, David S Jr, 1957, Mr 19,37:4
Gendell, David S 3d, 1963, Ap 20,27:4
Gendell, J Howard, 1910, N 14,9:5
Gendelman, Zachary Mrs, 1949, D 7,31:2
Gendler, Leonard W, 1961, O 31,31:2
Gendre, Francois G, 1939, D 23,15:6
Gendreau, J Ernest, 1949, Je 7,32:2
Gendron, Henri A, 1951, S 19,31:3
Gendron, Joseph E, 1942, N 4,23:6
Gendron, Jules F, 1947, S 13,11:4
Geneau, Alexander, 1907, Mr 24,9:5
Genee, Otley, 1911, N 25,II,13:5
Genee, Rudolf Prof, 1914, Ja 20,9:6
Genel, Samuel, 1961, Ag 6,85:1
General, Levi, 1925, Je 29,13:6
Generales, Demostenes J, 1948, Mr 13,15:4
Genest, Jean C, 1952, Jl 17,23:5
Genest, Sam Dr, 1937, Ap 26,19:3
Genet, Arthur S, 1968, S 20,47:3
Genet, Caroline Mrs, 1938, S 18,44:7
Genet, George Clinton Mrs, 1911, N 27,11:6
Genet, H W, 1889, S 7,8:3
Genet, Louise Henrietta, 1907, My 12,9:5
Genewich, Anthony, 1954, N 20,17:1
Gengenbach, Alfred, 1953, Mr 24,31:1
Gengenbach, Eugene, 1948, O 23,15:5
Gengler, Joseph D, 1959, Jl 29,29:1
Genin, J N, 1878, My 4,2:7
Genin, Thaddeus S, 1937, O 6,25:1
Genina, Augusto, 1957, S 29,86:8
Genis, Leon, 1945, Mr 6,21:4
Genis, Nathan, 1949, D 12,33:3
Genis, Samuel, 1955, S 10,17:3
Genius, Arthur E, 1945, Ja 22,17:4
Genius, Richard M, 1941, S 5,21:2
Genn, Jacob, 1953, Je 29,21:4
Genn, Vernon C, 1953, F 1,88:4
Gennerich, A A, 1936, D 2,22:1
Gennerich, Charles Dr, 1917, S 16,18:7
Gennert, Gustave C, 1951, Ja 26,23:3
Gennert, Gustave C Mrs, 1951, Mr 16,31:1
Gennert, Henry G Mrs, 1944, Ap 27,23:5
Gennes, Jean de Countess, 1951, My 19,15:5
Gennet, Charles W Jr, 1943, O 30,15:6
Genninger, Henry L, 1949, Mr 5,17:5
Genns, Duncan McP, 1958, Ja 23,27:2
Genoa, Duke of, 1931, Ap 16,25:3
Genoe, Hugh P, 1948, Mr 18,27:3
Genovar, William Jr, 1951, N 6,29:5
Genoveffa, M Sister, 1903, D 3,9:5
Genovese, Leonard, 1959, Jl 24,25:5
Genovese, Michael A, 1959, F 12,28:3
Genovese, Philomena Mrs, 1953, Ap 14,35:2
Gens, Charles J, 1941, Ag 18,13:4
Gens, Edward C, 1958, S 9,35:1
Gens, Paul W Mrs, 1958, O 20,29:2
Gensel, Hugo S, 1950, O 19,31:2
Gensemer, Joseph L, 1955, Ja 22,11:5
Gensemer, Ogden D, 1964, D 5,31:2
Gensheimer, Ernest, 1947, O 29,27:4
Gensheimer, John S (por), 1947, N 13,28:3
Gensler, Ray W, 1956, S 18,35:4
Genso, John F, 1950, Jl 18,30:3
Genso, John F Mrs, 1957, Je 30,69:2
Genstein, Samuel J, 1948, My 13,25:3
Gent, Ernest V, 1964, Je 22,27:2
Gent, Ernest V Mrs, 1945, Ag 21,21:4
Gent, H van, 1947, Ap 1,27:6
Gent, Thomas J Jr Mrs, 1964, F 18,21:6
Genter, Chester, 1949, S 23,23:3
Genth, Lillian, 1953, Mr 29,92:3
Genthe, Arnold (por), 1942, Ag 11,19:1
Genthe, Arnold, 1942, O 15,28:3
Genthner, William M, 1957, Ap 8,23:4
Gentil, Eugene B, 1961, Ap 26,39:4
Gentile, Don S, 1951, Ja 29,1:2
Gentile, Felix M (cor, My 15,35:3), 1957, My 13,31:5
Gentile, Joseph, 1959, Je 28,68:7
Gentile, Joseph S, 1918, D 16,15:1
Gentile, Louis, 1955, S 12,25:5
Gentile, Patsy, 1937, Je 5,17:3
Gentile, Ralph Mrs, 1954, Mr 13,15:5
Gentile, Vincent Jr, 1965, Ap 29,35:1
Gentle, Alice (Mrs J Proebstel), 1958, Mr 2,88:5
Gentle, Benedict, 1943, N 2,25:2
Gentle, Catherine M Mrs, 1945, D 29,15:8
Gentle, David, 1945, D 29,15:8
Gentle, William, 1948, S 3,19:1
Gentles, Harry W, 1957, Ag 25,86:1
Gentry, Cyrus S, 1967, N 4,33:5
Gentry, Franklin M, 1957, Ap 19,21:3
Gentry, Guy G, 1954, Mr 29,19:5
Gentry, Henry B, 1940, My 8,23:5
Gentry, James, 1912, Jl 26,9:6
Gentry, Martin B, 1956, Ag 2,25:5
Gentry, Mollie Mrs, 1948, O 26,31:2
Gentry, W T Col, 1885, Je 30,5:2
Gentry, William T, 1925, Ja 12,15:3
Gentsch, Jesse, 1950, N 26,90:4
Gentz, Will T, 1952, My 29,27:5
Gentzel, R E, 1934, Mr 4,30:1
Genuario, Salvatore P, 1959, Ja 8,29:4
Genung, Alfred V C, 1956, Mr 7,33:4
Genung, Ella M, 1964, Ja 8,34:8
Genung, George L, 1959, Ja 8,29:1
Genung, George L Mrs, 1943, S 7,23:3
Genung, James H, 1952, Ag 28,23:5
Genung, John F Prof, 1919, O 2,17:7
Genung, L T, 1942, Jl 15,19:2
Genz, Alex J, 1939, D 7,27:5
Genz, Herta N Mrs, 1951, Ap 23,25:2
Genz, Louis C, 1953, D 22,31:3
Genzer, William, 1952, F 26,28:2
Genzlinger, Jacob Mrs, 1948, Ag 17,21:4
Genzmer, George A, 1943, Je 27,32:2
Geoffrion, Aime, 1946, O 16,27:4
Geoffroy, Actor, 1883, S 9,9:2
Geofroy, M Antoine de, 1946, S 22,63:6
Geoghan, George A, 1946, My 12,44:1
Geoghan, John J, 1942, Ap 4,13:5
Geoghan, John J (cor, Ap 5,27:1), 1957, Ap 4,33:3
Geoghan, William Dr, 1909, N 29,9:5
Geoghan, William F X, 1959, N 25,29:4
Geoghan, William F X Mrs, 1963, O 21,31:2
Geoghegan, A D (por), 1940, Ag 3,15:7
Geoghegan, Anthony V B, 1962, S 14,31:2
Geoghegan, Charles W, 1954, S 23,33:4
Geoghegan, Chris J, 1940, F 28,21:1
Geoghegan, James F, 1963, Je 13,33:4
Geoghegan, John F Mrs, 1940, O 16,23:4
Geoghegan, Kate, 1945, Mr 1,21:4
Geoghegan, Owney (funl, Ja 25,2:3), 1885, Ja 21,8:1
Geoghegan, Stephen J, 1903, S 8,7:6
Geoghegan, Thomas P, 1951, N 19,23:6
Geoghegan, Thomas W, 1959, Ja 11,88:3
Geoghegan, William, 1901, Mr 13,9:7
Geoghegan, William C, 1948, Mr 22,23:5
Geoghegan, William H, 1952, Ja 29,25:5
Geoghegan, William H Sr Mrs, 1945, Ja 30,19:5
Geohegan, William J, 1951, O 1,23:5
Geoly, Charles, 1959, Je 18,31:4
Geonnotti, Antonio, 1952, Ag 6,21:3
Geores, Erik G, 1946, O 5,17:2
Georg, Archduke von Habsburg Lothringen, 1952, Mr 26,29:3
Georg, Duke of Mecklenburg, 1963, Jl 8,29:1
Georg, Heinrich, 1946, N 13,27:2
Georg VII, Catholicos (funl, My 30,45:2), 1954, My 12,31:2
Georgariou, Peter, 1951, Jl 16,21:6
George, Adam G Mrs, 1956, Je 29,21:5
George, Albert D, 1940, Mr 24,30:7
George, Alfred J, 1940, D 4,27:4
George, Almer D, 1940, S 10,23:2
George, Amon L, 1946, D 10,31:5
George, Andrew J, 1907, D 28,7:6
George, Andrew J Mrs, 1939, My 4,23:3
George, Arial W, 1948, D 25,17:5
George, Avery B, 1952, D 9,33:4
George, C W, 1874, Ag 7,1:3
George, Charles, 1960, O 5,41:2
George, Charles A, 1940, Je 29,15:5; 1950, Ag 4,21:5
George, Charles C, 1940, F 19,17:1; 1958, Jl 28,23:6
George, Charles E Col, 1937, Ag 22,II,7:1
George, Charles H, 1942, Jl 31,15:2; 1948, My 16,68:4
George, Charles J Mrs, 1954, O 6,25:2
George, Charles P Mrs, 1955, O 19,33:4
George, Czarowitch, 1899, Jl 11,7:1
George, David G, 1948, Ja 25,56:8
George, David J, 1949, My 18,27:6
George, David Mrs, 1903, D 1,9:6
George, Dorothea A, 1953, F 16,21:5
George, E, 1880, Ag 10,5:2
George, Edward A Rev, 1921, D 23,13:6
George, Edward J, 1950, O 26,31:2
George, Edwin B, 1963, S 15,87:1
George, Edwin J, 1942, S 25,21:2
George, Edwin S Mrs, 1959, Ag 25,31:4
George, Elva A, 1953, Ja 20,25:4
George, Florence Mrs, 1915, Jl 11,15:7
George, Frank D, 1945, Ap 2,19:4
George, Frank X, 1953, Jl 7,27:4
George, Franklin, 1951, F 18,77:1
George, Frederick B, 1943, Jl 6,21:5
George, George K, 1942, My 12,19:3
George, Gladys (funl plans, D 10,28:2), 1954, D 9, 40:7
George, Harold C, 1937, S 24,21:5
George, Harry Capt, 1924, Jl 23,15:3
George, Harry L, 1941, Ja 4,13:3
George, Harry Mrs, 1952, S 23,33:4
George, Harry R, 1948, Mr 24,25:2
George, Helen (Sister Ruth), 1878, S 20,5:4
George, Henry, 1897, O 30,1:7
George, Henry H 3d Mrs, 1956, N 23,27:3
George, Henry Jr, 1916, N 15,11:5
George, Henry L, 1948, F 8,60:7
George, Henry Mrs, 1946, D 7,21:1; 1963, O 3,35:4
George, Henry P, 1941, F 25,23:4
George, Henry W (por), 1945, N 7,23:3
George, J Edward, 1953, Je 20,17:5
George, J Z Sen, 1897, Ag 15,5:5
George, James H, 1950, Ap 17,23:3
George, James R, 1960, Ap 25,29:4; 1961, Ap 24,29:2
George, Jerome R, 1942, D 3,25:2
George, John, 1939, Ap 17,17:3; 1957, Ja 17,29:3
George, John B D Mrs, 1962, S 2,56:8
George, John J, 1961, Mr 1,33:5
George, John M, 1948, My 21,23:3
George, John S, 1916, N 17,9:3
George, John Valance, 1916, Ag 17,11:3
George, King of Hanover, 1878, Je 13,5:3; 1878, Jl 4, 2:1
George, Lewis Bro, 1960, S 10,21:5
George, Louis H, 1951, Mr 17,15:4
George, Louis J, 1952, Ag 6,21:3
George, Louise W, 1949, Jl 2,15:4
George, Madeline (Mrs E L Wertheim), 1960, Ap 6, 41:5
George, Manfred, 1966, Ja 1,17:1
George, Marie, 1955, Jl 16,15:5
George, Melbourne E W, 1959, O 21,43:4
George, Michael, 1925, My 17,6:1
George, Nathan F, 1944, Mr 28,19:4
George, Nathan R, 1941, Mr 27,23:5
George, Nicholas Mrs, 1947, Mr 30,56:4
George, Nugent M, 1948, O 9,19:1
George, Peter G, 1952, S 16,29:3
George, Peter K, 1947, D 6,15:6
George, Prince of Bavaria, 1943, Je 2,25:5
George, Prince of Greece (funl, D 5,35:5), 1957, N 26,33:4
George, Prince of Russia, 1938, N 9,23:1
George, Ralph B, 1944, Jl 23,35:4
George, Ransom G, 1950, F 21,25:2
George, Richard F, 1912, S 29,13:5
George, Robert, 1967, S 15,47:2
George, Robert B, 1960, Ap 20,39:4
George, Robert T, 1948, Je 15,28:2
George, S, 1933, D 5,23:1
George, Samuel, 1903, Ag 8,7:7
George, Samuel E, 1954, Mr 3,29:1
George, Samuel S, 1957, N 9,27:4
George, Theodore Rev, 1914, D 31,9:5
George, Thomas E (Lefty), 1955, My 14,19:2
George, Thomas J, 1947, F 9,61:3
George, Thomas W, 1907, F 5,9:6
George, V, 1936, Ja 21,1:8
George, W L, 1926, Ja 30,15:2
George, W L Mrs, 1920, D 11,13:5
George, W R, 1936, Ap 26,II,10:3
George, W S, 1881, D 30,5:4
George, Walter, 1943, Je 5,15:6
George, Walter F (funl, Ag 6,27:1), 1957, Ag 5,1:6
George, Walter F Mrs, 1958, O 29,35:2
George, William, 1943, Ja 22,19:2
George, William D, 1953, Mr 3,27:1; 1963, F 14,3:3
George, William F, 1938, S 21,21:6; 1964, Jl 28,29:1
George, William H, 1943, Jl 17,13:3; 1946, S 9,9:5
George, William J, 1946, Je 19,21:3
George, William P, 1955, Jl 24,64:1
George, William R G, 1915, S 14,11:5
George, William R Mrs, 1962, Ap 13,35:3
George, William Shaw, 1925, Ap 13,19:4
George Charles, Prince of Hesse, 1881, Mr 5,5:2
George Francis, Bro (G D Byrne), 1953, O 26,21:1
George Francis, Bro (G D Byrne), 1953, O 26,21:1
George II, Duke of Saxe-Meiningen, 1914, Je 26,13:5
George Thomas, Bro, 1955, Jl 30,17:4
George VI, King, 1952, F 7,1:8
Georgen, Vances M, 1944, My 21,43:2
Georges, Alphonse, 1951, Ap 25,29:3
Georges, Christian, 1937, Ja 7,21:5
Georges, Nemer, 1946, Mr 27,27:4
Georges, Stathes T, 1958, O 14,37:3
Georgeson, Lloyd W, 1945, Ap 6,16:2
Georgetti, Aurea B Mrs (will, N 4,5:3), 1938, O 28, 23:3
Georgi, Edwin Mrs, 1958, N 25,33:5
Georgi de Mallerais, William C H M Mrs, 1966, My 25,47:5
Georgia, Elizabeth (Sister M Rosaria), 1958, F 13, 29:3
Georgia Stevens, Mother, 1946, Mr 29,23:2
Georgian, George E, 1949, Ap 14,25:3
Georgie, Leyla, 1945, S 25,25:2
Georgiou, Christodoulos, 1966, O 22,31:5
Georgis, Theodore, 1920, O 22,15:2
Geover, George W, 1915, D 28,11:4
Gephart, George F, 1956, Ap 26,33:4
Gephart, J Russell, 1957, N 26,33:1
Gephart, J Russell Mrs, 1964, Jl 24,27:1
Gephart, Joseph Curtin, 1968, My 14,47:3
Gepp, Henry, 1909, D 21,9:2
Geppelt, Emil Sr, 1939, O 27,23:4
Geppert, William L, 1946, Je 21,23:1
Geraghty, Ben, 1963, Je 19,37:2
Geraghty, Carmelita (Mrs C Wilson), 1966, Jl 8,35:4
Geraghty, Charles M, 1941, Ag 22,15:2
Geraghty, Elihu R, 1959, F 17,62:3
Geraghty, Frank D, 1955, Ag 5,19:4
Geraghty, Frank J, 1944, N 21,25:4
Geraghty, Gerald, 1954, Jl 10,13:4
Geraghty, James, 1949, F 12,17:6
Geraghty, James F, 1955, My 15,86:5

Geraghty, James F Mrs, 1948, F 2,20:2
Geraghty, James J, 1959, Mr 17,33:1
Geraghty, James M, 1942, O 8,27:1
Geraghty, James P, 1950, Je 5,23:6
Geraghty, John B, 1950, F 8,27:1
Geraghty, John T Dr, 1924, Ag 18,13:3
Geraghty, Leo M, 1959, Ag 18,29:1
Geraghty, Martin J Rev, 1914, S 30,9:6
Geraghty, Nora E O Mrs, 1949, Je 22,31:5
Geraghty, Patrick Mrs, 1940, My 14,23:4
Geraghty, Tom C, 1945, Je 6,21:1
Geraghty, William H, 1949, D 19,27:1
Gerald, Ed Fitz, 1904, Ja 23,9:5
Gerald, Florence, 1942, S 9,23:2
Gerald, Ina, 1942, F 28,17:1
Geraldi, Mike, 1949, Ja 29,13:3
Geralds, Stephen W, 1949, Ag 3,23:2
Geran, Carroll V, 1954, Ag 17,21:3
Geran, Elmer H, 1954, Ja 14,29:2
Gerard, Adolphus S, 1943, O 13,23:6
Gerard, Alick S Sr, 1960, Jl 12,35:4
Gerard, Barney, 1962, Jl 1,56:2
Gerard, Barney Mrs, 1950, Mr 24,25:2
Gerard, Bro, 1940, My 27,19:3; 1953, Ja 6,29:3
Gerard, Bro (H F Langland), 1960, Mr 6,84:5
Gerard, Caesar (will), 1938, Je 9,2:3
Gerard, Caroline Mrs, 1937, F 20,17:4
Gerard, Charles, 1961, Jl 1,17:6
Gerard, Eddie, 1937, Ag 8,II,6:8
Gerard, Eric Prof, 1916, Ap 1,13:4
Gerard, George, 1966, Je 15,47:1
Gerard, Gustave L, 1949, Ja 14,23:1
Gerard, Irving V, 1959, Ap 28,35:2
Gerard, James W (trb, F 10,2:5; funl, F 12,9:2), 1874, F 8,5:5
Gerard, James W, 1907, S 21,9:4; 1951, S 7,1:2
Gerard, James W Mrs, 1956, Ja 20,23:1
Gerard, John P, 1945, Ag 29,23:1
Gerard, Julian M, 1944, F 27,38:2
Gerard, Julian M Mrs, 1963, Ap 16,35:2
Gerard, Kenneth C, 1951, Ja 18,27:5
Gerard, Louis, 1961, Ap 1,17:6
Gerard, Louis Mrs, 1938, Ag 30,17:5
Gerard, Margaret, 1954, Ja 13,31:3
Gerard, Mother (M G Phelan), 1960, Mr 23,37:1
Gerard, Nettie T Mrs, 1942, Ag 23,43:2
Gerard, Orie J Mrs, 1952, N 18,32:3
Gerard, Reed H, 1952, N 15,17:5
Gerard, Sanford E, 1950, O 31,27:4
Gerard, Sherman, 1923, Je 2,11:6
Gerard, Sidney N, 1954, F 12,25:4
Gerard, Sumner, 1966, Mr 12,27:1
Gerard, Teddie, 1942, S 2,23:5
Gerard-Varet, Louis A, 1944, D 8,21:3
Gerardet, Karl, 1871, My 20,2:4
Gerardi, Joseph A, 1964, Ap 19,85:1
Gerardo, Dominick, 1965, N 27,31:5
Gerasimov, Aleksandr M, 1963, Jl 25,25:4
Gerasimov, Sergie V, 1964, Ap 21,33:3
Gerassimos, Michael Mrs, 1942, Jl 22,19:2
Gerba, Michael Mrs, 1944, O 18,21:3
Gerbault, Alain J (por), 1944, Ag 22,17:4
Gerbel, Josephine (Genevieve De Forest), 1911, S 5, 7:6
Gerber, Alice A Mrs, 1940, S 6,21:2
Gerber, David, 1922, My 27,13:6
Gerber, Edward D, 1944, Ag 3,19:5
Gerber, Edwin R, 1948, Jl 15,23:4
Gerber, Frank, 1952, O 8,31:1
Gerber, George, 1959, Ap 18,23:5
Gerber, Haim Mrs, 1950, F 6,25:3
Gerber, Harry R Mrs, 1949, Ja 18,23:2
Gerber, Henry A, 1963, My 28,28:3
Gerber, Ida, 1961, N 11,23:5
Gerber, Julius, 1956, Jl 18,27:5
Gerber, Louis, 1937, O 4,21:6; 1955, Mr 3,27:3
Gerber, Mace P, 1948, Je 23,27:3
Gerber, Max, 1953, N 3,32:3; 1968, F 4,80:7
Gerber, Nathan B, 1961, Ap 13,35:3
Gerber, Robert, 1968, Jl 24,50:2
Gerber, Samuel R, 1960, Mr 12,21:5
Gerber, Walter, 1951, Je 20,27:4
Gerber, William M, 1954, S 28,29:6
Gerbereux, Vincent de P, 1965, D 16,47:2
Gerbert, Herman Peter Dr, 1915, D 20,11:5
Gerbi, Giovanni, 1954, My 8,17:2
Gerbrandy, Pieter S, 1961, S 9,19:3
Gerdau, Carl Mrs, 1964, Ja 20,43:3
Gerdau, Otto Mrs, 1960, Mr 15,39:1
Gerdes, Augustus M, 1952, Je 19,27:1
Gerdes, Augustus M Mrs, 1957, Je 18,29:1
Gerdes, Henry T (por), 1948, Ap 1,25:5
Gerdes, John, 1959, D 15,39:3
Gerdes, Theodore R, 1953, D 15,39:3
Gerdsen, William C, 1939, F 7,19:4
Gerdts, Herbert J, 1959, N 19,39:5
Gerdy, Robert S, 1965, D 24,17:3
Gere, Allan F, 1939, Jl 23,29:1
Gere, E Clarence, 1954, S 13,23:5
Gere, James Belden Dr, 1920, N 20,15:4
Gere, James E, 1950, Mr 10,28:2
Gerecke, August, 1916, My 3,13:6
Gerecke, Henry, 1961, O 13,35:2
Geremonte, Anthony Mrs, 1950, Mr 9,29:2
Geren, Harry O, 1942, Jl 18,13:6
Gerenbeck, George, 1949, Je 18,13:2
Gerencser, Joseph, 1949, S 1,21:3
Gerendasy, Julius Mrs, 1963, O 28,27:2
Gerenday, Ladislaus, 1947, O 8,25:3
Gerety, Peter L, 1950, Jl 27,25:1
Gerety, William E, 1946, My 14,21:3
Gerewich, Tibor, 1954, Je 13,89:1
Gerfen, Ernest E, 1944, D 14,23:5
Gergely, John J Mrs, 1943, D 4,13:3
Gergely, Paul, 1950, Ap 25,31:4
Gergely, Tibor Mrs (A Lesznai), 1966, O 5,42:8
Gergen, John J, 1967, Ja 18,43:3
Gerghunoff, Alberto, 1950, Mr 3,25:4
Gerham, Harry M, 1962, S 19,39:4
Gerhan, Arthur C, 1948, Je 19,15:4
Gerhard, Albert P, 1963, N 24,22:8
Gerhard, Arthur H, 1949, Ag 31,23:3
Gerhard, Charles E, 1953, Je 14,84:1
Gerhard, Charles Z, 1941, Jl 2,21:3
Gerhard, George, 1939, D 11,23:5
Gerhard, George A, 1951, Ja 21,77:1
Gerhard, George K, 1959, F 10,33:2
Gerhard, Harry E, 1950, S 20,31:4
Gerhard, Karl, 1964, Ap 25,29:2
Gerhard, Melchior N, 1943, O 12,27:4
Gerhard, Robert H, 1963, Ap 18,35:2
Gerhard, William A, 1964, D 20,68:8
Gerhard, William C, 1955, F 18,21:2
Gerhards, William F, 1951, S 25,29:4
Gerhardt, Charles, 1957, Je 7,23:3
Gerhardt, Elena, 1961, Ja 12,29:1
Gerhardt, Erwin O, 1960, S 27,37:1
Gerhardt, George, 1955, Jl 26,25:3
Gerhardt, Jacob, 1942, Ap 15,21:1
Gerhardt, Jacob H, 1948, D 15,33:4
Gerhardt, Lydia Mrs, 1942, F 11,21:5
Gerhardt, S W, 1924, Mr 3,17:5
Gerhart, Clarence M, 1947, Mr 15,13:1
Gerhart, William H, 1950, F 19,76:1
Gerhauser, William H, 1952, N 24,23:4
Gericke, Paula Mrs, 1940, Je 13,23:3
Gericke, Wilhelm (por), 1925, O 30,21:4
Gerig, John L, 1957, S 21,20:1
Gerig, William, 1944, Ap 4,21:6
Gerihg, Catharina Mrs, 1941, S 12,21:3
Gerin, Leon, 1951, Ja 18,27:1
Gerin-Lajoie, Leon, 1959, F 16,29:4
Gerini, Marchese L, 1947, O 4,17:2
Gerion, Frederick J, 1959, S 10,35:4
Gerity, William H Sr, 1960, My 19,37:4
Gerken, Frederick Jr, 1951, N 20,31:4
Gerken, Henrietta, 1956, Ag 19,92:2
Gerken, John F Mrs, 1952, Je 12,33:4
Gerken, John H, 1949, Jl 16,13:3
Gerken, John Mrs, 1948, F 1,60:6
Gerken, Rudolph A, 1943, Mr 3,23:3
Gerkens, William E, 1958, Ap 4,24:1
Gerkin, Chester J, 1967, Mr 28,39:3
Gerkin, John A, 1951, Jl 31,21:3
Gerlach, Alton M, 1968, O 20,86:6
Gerlach, Charles F, 1941, D 16,27:3
Gerlach, Charles L, 1947, My 5,23:2
Gerlach, Frank C, 1948, F 17,25:5
Gerlach, George W, 1954, Ag 25,27:3
Gerlach, Harry J, 1950, Je 16,25:5
Gerlach, Herbert C (funl, Ag 31,56:5), 1958, Ag 29, 23:1
Gerlach, Joseph, 1955, Ag 10,25:4
Gerlach, Otto F, 1950, S 12,27:2
Gerlach, Peter A, 1961, Je 14,19:2
Gerlach, Theodore A, 1946, Ag 25,46:4
Gerlaird, Peter, 1939, Mr 17,22:2
Gerlein, Eduardo I, 1956, Je 4,29:5
Gerlette, Anne (Mrs G Voskovec), 1958, My 28,31:3
Gerli, Emanuel (will), 1937, S 21,28:5
Gerli, Joseph (por),(will, D 8,51:2), 1940, N 23,17:5
Gerli, Paolino Mrs, 1963, Je 9,86:5
Gerli, Paul Mrs, 1951, Jl 8,61:2
Gerlich, Benjamin, 1951, Ag 5,72:4
Gerlier, Pierre Cardinal, 1965, Ja 17,88:3
Gerling, Jacob, 1937, Mr 21,II,9:3
Gerlinger, George T Mrs, 1960, Ap 7,35:3
Gerloff, Frederic O, 1952, O 3,23:2
Gerloff, Theodore, 1942, Jl 23,19:5
Germain, Auguste, 1915, D 16,15:4
Germain, David P, 1943, N 1,17:5
Germain, Henri, 1905, F 3,7:3
Germain, Herman, 1960, S 24,23:4
Germain, John H, 1950, N 30,33:3
Germain, Louis Jr, 1945, Mr 10,17:4
Germain, Walter, 1962, Je 24,35:4
German, A P, 1953, D 9,11:1
German, Anthony J, 1946, My 10,19:4
German, E, 1936, N 12,27:1
German, F G, 1937, O 14,25:1
German, Frank F, 1942, Ja 5,17:4
German, Harold R, 1964, Mr 6,28:3
German, Misha, 1947, S 27,15:6
German, Oscar W, 1946, Ag 12,21:4
German, W M N, 1933, Ap 1,15:5
German, W P Z, 1953, Je 16,27:2
German, William J Mrs, 1943, Mr 15,13:4
Germann, Charles A, 1940, My 27,19:4
Germann, Ernest, 1956, N 28,35:3
Germann, George B, 1958, My 8,29:4
Germann, Gerhard S, 1956, Jl 28,17:6
Germann, John C, 1946, F 8,19:4
Germanos, Strenopoulos, 1951, Ja 24,27:3
Germer, Adolph, 1966, My 28,27:1
Germer, Herman G M, 1946, Ag 8,21:5
Germogen (Met), 1954, Ag 5,23:3
Germon, Euphemia, 1914, Mr 7,11:5
Germon, Greene Mrs, 1909, Ag 11,7:6
Germon, J D, 1901, My 7,9:7
Germond, Elizabeth, 1942, My 6,19:1
Germond, Henrietta, 1952, Ag 11,15:3
Germond, Henry S, 1950, Jl 14,21:2
Germond, Henry S Mrs, 1954, Je 9,31:3
Germond, Henry Sheldon, 1920, D 16,17:4
Germond, M J, 1948, Jl 30,18:2
Germond, Willis H, 1945, F 8,19:3
Germunder, Rudolph F, 1916, Jl 10,11:7
Gernandt, Herbert L, 1946, N 5,25:2
Gernandt, Jay H, 1947, Je 20,19:1
Gerner, John C, 1945, Jl 31,19:1
Gernerd, Fred B, 1948, Ag 9,20:2
Gernert, Frank N, 1952, My 20,25:2
Gerngross, Leo, 1958, Je 2,27:5
Gernhardt, Caroline L Mrs, 1939, D 16,17:2
Gernhardt, Joseph A, 1955, D 1,35:5
Gernon, Blaine B, 1954, Ap 15,29:1
Gernon, Edward T Mrs, 1940, S 22,49:2
Gernon, Frank E, 1956, D 3,29:3
Gernon, James L, 1946, N 16,19:5
Gernsback, George B, 1953, Ag 7,19:1
Gernsback, George B Mrs, 1954, Mr 13,15:5
Gernsback, Hugo, 1967, Ag 20,88:4
Gernsback, Sidney, 1953, F 20,19:1
Geroe, Josef, 1954, D 29,23:2
Gerofsky, Benjamin L, 1956, Ap 8,84:4
Geroge, Albert L Mrs, 1947, D 20,17:3
Geroge, Grace (Mrs Wm A Brady), 1961, My 20, 23:5
Geroge, Henry W, 1942, Jl 9,21:2
Geroge, Mary, 1947, F 23,21:1
Geroge II, King of Greece, 1947, Ap 2,1:1
Gerolamo, Michael, 1950, Jl 27,25:3
Gerold, John H, 1949, Je 8,29:2
Gerold, John H Mrs, 1946, Mr 21,25:4
Gerome, Jean Leon, 1904, Ja 11,7:4
Geron, Abraham, 1958, S 9,35:2
Geronimo, John, 1939, Mr 9,21:1
Geronimo, Robert, 1966, O 27,47:1
Geronimo, 1909, F 18,7:3
Gerould, Gordon H, 1953, Ap 12,88:3
Gerould, James T, 1951, Je 9,19:3
Gerould, John H, 1961, Jl 16,69:1
Gerow, Benjamin R, 1961, D 18,35:1
Gerow, Clarence H Jr, 1946, My 26,32:2
Gerow, Elsa Mrs, 1937, D 28,7:2
Gerow, Fred, 1948, F 18,27:1
Gerow, Grant W, 1950, Ja 26,28:5
Gerow, Helen Mrs, 1943, Mr 21,19:5
Gerow, John Y, 1944, My 19,19:3
Gerow, Leonard R, 1944, Ja 19,19:4
Gerow, Percy H, 1945, My 31,15:5
Gerow, Wilbur E, 1949, Ja 1,13:6
Gerrans, H Montgomery, 1939, My 14,III,7:3
Gerrard, Alec C, 1943, Je 6,44:1
Gerrard, Charles, 1953, Mr 16,25:2
Gerrard, Douglas, 1950, Je 7,33:1
Gerrard, Francis B, 1937, Ap 29,21:6
Gerrard, Frederick B, 1947, Je 18,25:3
Gerrie, John W, 1949, Mr 10,27:5
Gerriets, Frederick W, 1954, Jl 9,9:4
Gerrin, John, 1919, Jl 8,11:4
Gerring, Frank P, 1950, D 30,13:2
Gerrish, B, 1883, N 5,2:6
Gerrish, Elizabeth W, 1944, My 19,19:5
Gerrish, Frank S, 1944, F 10,15:4
Gerrish, Frederick H Dr, 1920, S 9,11:1
Gerrish, J W, 1958, F 14,23:4
Gerrish, Thornton, 1955, Jl 5,29:2
Gerrish, Thornton Mrs, 1958, N 12,37:1
Gerrish, William C, 1947, Jl 18,17:1
Gerrits, George J, 1952, My 5,23:5
Gerrity, Edward F Sr, 1952, Je 28,19:1
Gerrity, Edward J Mrs, 1965, Je 1,39:3
Gerrity, George J, 1956, My 4,25:4
Gerrity, Gerard, 1947, Jl 16,23:3
Gerrity, Joseph (Bro Benignus), 1953, Ja 28,27:3
Gerrity, Thomas Patrick Gen, 1968, F 25,76:5
Gerrity, William J, 1938, Ap 8,19:4
Gerry, Allston Mrs, 1944, Ag 16,19:2
Gerry, Angelica L, 1960, N 5,23:5
Gerry, Ann, 1883, F 18,7:4
Gerry, David Mrs, 1962, Mr 28,39:3
Gerry, Duncan F, 1951, F 24,13:5
Gerry, E T, 1927, F 19,15:3
Gerry, Elbridge T Mrs, 1920, Mr 27,13:3
Gerry, Henry A, 1960, Ap 18,17:3
Gerry, James, 1873, Jl 28,2:3
Gerry, James Henry, 1907, Ja 3,9:5
Gerry, James L, 1951, N 14,31:3

Gerry, Katherine R, 1954, O 31,89:2
Gerry, Louis C Jr, 1948, Je 23,27:3
Gerry, Louise C, 1962, Je 23,23:1
Gerry, Peter G, 1957, N 1,27:2
Gerry, Peter G Mrs, 1958, D 22,2:5
Gerry, Robert L, 1957, N 1,27:3
Gerry, Robert L Mrs, 1966, My 30,19:4
Gersbach, Edward A, 1955, D 25,48:2
Gersch, Emanuel, 1965, Mr 11,33:1
Gerschefski, Otto J Mrs, 1948, My 27,25:3
Gerschinsky, Teddy, 1922, Je 28,15:6
Gersham, Max, 1955, Mr 20,89:2
Gershberg, Herbert Mrs, 1964, Ag 29,21:4
Gershel, Benjamin J, 1921, Ja 10,11:4
Gershel, Milton A, 1945, S 8,15:5
Gershel, William, 1919, Jl 25,11:5
Gershen, Hyman, 1968, Ap 3,51:2
Gershenson, Harry, 1968, Ja 24,45:2
Gershinskey, Robert M, 1943, O 6,23:4
Gershon, Isaac Rabbi, 1882, My 8,8:3
Gershon, Julius, 1957, Ap 23,31:2
Gershon, Victor P, 1968, S 29,80:1
Gershovitz, Samuel D, 1960, S 6,35:1
Gershwin, Aaron, 1954, D 25,11:2
Gershwin, George, 1937, Jl 12,1:4
Gershwin, Morris Mrs, 1948, D 17,27:3
Gerson, Armand J, 1954, Ag 28,15:7
Gerson, Edmund, 1914, My 22,13:6
Gerson, Edmund Mrs, 1924, Jl 30,13:5
Gerson, Felix N, 1945, D 14,27:4
Gerson, Harry A, 1965, F 18,33:4
Gerson, Henry, 1948, D 24,17:1
Gerson, Jack, 1961, Mr 4,23:6
Gerson, Jacob Mrs, 1952, O 2,29:3
Gerson, James J (cor, O 3,17:5), 1953, S 29,29:5
Gerson, Leonard B, 1960, Ja 26,33:3
Gerson, Max, 1959, Mr 9,29:5
Gerson, Morris, 1947, Ja 30,25:4; 1964, Ja 28,31:2
Gerson, Paul, 1957, Je 8,19:6
Gerson, Virginia, 1951, Ag 5,72:3
Gerson, William Mrs, 1943, F 26,20:2
Gerst, Francis J Rev, 1968, O 2,39:1
Gerst, Frederick, 1940, My 22,23:4
Gerste, Henry S, 1947, Ag 25,17:4
Gerstein, Frank, 1957, F 1,25:2
Gerstein, Solomon, 1948, Je 23,27:6
Gerstein, Solomon Mrs, 1966, Jl 13,43:3
Gerstell, Arnold, 1955, Jl 29,17:2
Gersten, Harry, 1955, F 5,15:4
Gersten, Rebecca Mrs, 1942, S 3,16:8
Gerstenberg, Adolph, 1941, D 6,17:6
Gerstenberg, Charles W (por), 1948, S 16,29:1
Gerstenberg, Erich, 1940, N 4,19:3
Gerstenberg, John E, 1967, N 2,47:1
Gerstenberger, Emil, 1961, N 4,19:5
Gerstenberger, Henry J, 1954, Je 26,13:4
Gerstenberger, Henry L, 1962, F 27,34:1
Gerstenfeld, Norman Rabbi, 1968, Ja 28,76:4
Gerstenfeld, Samuel, 1958, Je 7,19:3
Gerstenfeld, Samuel Mrs, 1963, Je 5,41:4
Gerstenzang, Leo, 1961, F 2,29:1
Gerstenzang, Leon Mrs, 1947, F 8,17:3
Gerstenzang, Samuel, 1947, Ap 7,3:5
Gerster, Arpad G Dr, 1923, Mr 12,15:4
Gerster, Etelka, 1920, S 30,9:5
Gerster-Gardini, Berta, 1951, Ag 8,25:3
Gerstl, Bernard Rev, 1920, Ag 17,13:4
Gerstl, Karl, 1938, Mr 3,21:2
Gerstle, Leo, 1956, Jl 31,23:5
Gerstle, Leopold Mrs, 1925, N 10,25:4
Gerstle, Mark L Sr, 1952, My 16,23:1
Gerstle, William L, 1947, Ag 7,21:2
Gerstley, Isaac, 1951, Ap 4,29:5
Gerstley, Isaac Mrs, 1955, Ap 6,29:4
Gerstman, Felix G, 1967, Ja 12,39:1
Gerstner, Robert R, 1957, O 19,21:6
Gerstung, August, 1949, My 10,25:4
Gerstung, Oscar M, 1957, N 14,33:5
Gertenbach, Theresa Mrs, 1939, Ja 1,24:6
Gerth, Arthur W, 1951, Jl 1,29:1
Gerth, Charles R, 1949, My 13,23:5
Gertner, Herman, 1962, Ja 23,33:4
Gertner, Joseph Mrs, 1939, Mr 8,21:3
Gertner, Michael, 1967, Mr 6,29:8
Gertner, Samuel, 1937, O 24,II,9:2
Gertrude, Countess of Dudley (G Millar), 1952, Ap 26,23:5
Gertrude, Mother, 1940, S 22,49:1
Gertrude, Sister M, 1937, N 2,25:3
Gertrude Elise, Sister, 1947, My 22,27:3
Gertrude Morange, Mother Our Lady of the Retreat in the Cenacle, 1957, Mr 4,27:2
Gertz, Harry, 1954, Ag 19,23:1
Gertz, Harry Mrs, 1957, Ag 10,15:6
Gertz, Louis, 1957, D 6,29:1
Gertz, Max, 1948, Mr 11,27:1
Gertz, Samuel, 1957, O 7,27:3
Gertzen, Frederick W, 1946, My 13,21:2
Gertzloe, Lester C, 1957, Ap 19,21:4
Gerung, Frederick, 1961, My 18,35:1
Gerusky, John, 1959, D 4,31:1
Gervais, Alfred A Vice-Adm, 1921, Mr 18,15:6
Gervais, Arthur J, 1966, S 18,84:8
Gervais, Paul, 1879, F 11,5:5
Gervais, Wilfrid A, 1966, Je 28,45:1
Gervaise, Rev Father (funl), 1872, Jl 27,8:4
Gervase, Bro (Carroll), 1964, Je 25,33:1
Gervasini, Charles F, 1944, F 29,17:5
Gerville-Reache, Jeanne (Mrs Geo Gibier Rambaud), 1915, Ja 6,13:5
Gerville-Reache, Leodore, 1911, Ja 31,9:4
Gervinus, Prof, 1871, Ap 6,2:3
Gerwig, Edgar C, 1943, Mr 28,24:7
Gerwig, George W, 1950, N 13,28:4
Gerwig, Stuart T, 1948, Ap 25,68:4
Gerwiner, Robert C, 1958, D 4,39:5
Gery, Charles G Mrs, 1953, Mr 31,31:5
Gery, William B, 1957, Ja 3,33:3
Gerzog, Bennett G, 1958, Ja 13,29:2
Gesang, Nathan, 1944, F 17,19:4
Gescheidt, Adelaide, 1946, S 20,31:4
Gescheidt, L A, 1876, Ag 22,5:4
Geschick, Emile H, 1942, Mr 23,15:4
Gesecus, Robert W, 1965, Ag 10,29:1
Gesell, Arnold L, 1961, My 30,17:1
Gesell, Arnold L Mrs, 1965, F 4,31:4
Gesell, Charles L, 1958, Ap 1,31:4
Gesell, Herbert R, 1946, Jl 11,23:1
Gesell, Jacques, 1944, Ja 23,37:2
Gesell, Robert, 1954, Ap 21,29:4
Gesell, William H, 1956, Je 8,25:6
Gesell, William H Jr, 1961, Mr 10,27:3
Gesick, Joseph J, 1968, O 13,84:6
Gesin, John H Mrs, 1952, Jl 2,25:1
Gesler, Earl E, 1958, Ag 12,29:3
Gesner, Abram, 1864, My 10,4:5
Gesner, Anthon T, 1939, Ja 15,38:6
Gesner, Anthony T Mrs, 1948, Je 28,19:2
Gesner, Bertram M Dr, 1968, Ag 23,39:3
Gesner, Brewer Dr, 1874, N 13,4:7
Gesner, Graydon T, 1937, Ap 17,17:4
Gesner, Oscar Mrs, 1943, Je 22,19:4
Gessford, Joseph G, 1942, Ap 18,15:4
Gessler, Harry C, 1950, S 21,31:3
Gessler, Otto, 1955, Mr 25,24:6
Gessler, Theodore A K Rev Dr, 1925, D 5,19:5
Gessling, Edmund R, 1954, D 2,31:3
Gessner, David, 1942, D 19,19:4
Gessner, Dean Martin Rev, 1912, N 7,13:5
Gessner, Lawrence G, 1965, Mr 1,27:3
Gessner, Leopold, 1945, D 14,27:2
Gessner, Robert Prof, 1968, Je 17,39:1
Gesswein, Herman G, 1953, N 8,89:3
Gest, Alex P, 1938, Ja 24,23:5
Gest, Emma Mrs, 1943, Mr 12,17:4
Gest, Guy M, 1948, O 27,27:1
Gest, John B, 1907, Mr 2,9:6
Gest, John S, 1947, Mr 28,23:2
Gest, Margaret (will), 1965, O 29,45:4
Gest, Morris (por), 1942, My 17,45:1
Gest, Morris Mrs, 1948, Mr 24,25:4
Gest, William P, 1939, Ja 13,19:1
Gest, William P Mrs, 1954, Ja 7,31:5
Gestefeld, Ursula M Rev, 1921, O 25,17:5
Gestetner, Sigmund, 1956, Ap 20,25:3
Gestido, Oscar D, 1967, D 7,52:1
Gestner, Russell, 1960, My 12,35:4
Getchell, Dana K, 1950, N 4,17:5
Getchell, Edith L Mrs, 1940, S 19,23:4
Getchell, Edward L, 1954, F 24,25:3
Getchell, J Stirling (will), 1941, Ja 23,16:6
Getchell, John B Mrs, 1944, F 1,19:3
Getchell, John S, 1945, My 15,19:3
Getchey, Al, 1954, Mr 7,91:2
Getelman, Ralph E, 1952, Jl 30,24:7
Gethman, Walter W (por), 1938, Jl 9,13:4
Gethoefer, Louis H, 1946, Jl 28,40:5
Getleson, James S, 1956, My 3,31:3
Getman, Albert A, 1940, O 29,25:3
Getman, Anson, 1959, S 17,39:2
Getman, Arthur Kendall Dr, 1968, S 15,85:1
Getman, Edson E, 1967, S 23,31:3
Getman, Frederick H, 1941, D 3,25:6
Getman, Horace G, 1949, D 10,18:2
Getman, Mary, 1922, S 29,19:3
Getschell, J Stirling (por), 1940, D 18,25:1
Gette, O J, 1955, Ja 16,92:3
Gette, William F, 1943, N 5,19:5
Gettelman, Frederick, 1954, Je 25,21:4
Gettelson, Abraham J, 1941, N 8,19:1
Getter, Marcus E, 1949, Ja 18,23:1
Gettey, Boyd C, 1950, Ag 21,19:4
Gettinger, Joseph H, 1948, O 24,76:2
Gettinger, Milton M, 1955, Je 21,31:4
Gettinger, Paul P, 1956, F 23,27:3
Gettinger, William, 1943, Mr 16,19:3
Gettings, Delia, 1948, N 6,13:2
Gettings, Martin F, 1962, My 20,87:1
Gettings, Michael F, 1939, Jl 3,13:5
Gettle, William F, 1941, D 14,68:7
Gettler, Alexander Oscar Dr, 1968, Ag 4,69:1
Gettner, Herman, 1963, S 21,21:5
Getto, M J (Mike), 1960, Ag 28,83:3
Gettrust, Joseph F, 1947, F 13,24:3
Getty, Alice, 1946, Je 13,27:4
Getty, Boyd C Mrs, 1958, F 23,93:1
Getty, Carl H Mrs, 1943, Ap 11,49:1
Getty, Cornelia, 1948, Je 9,29:4
Getty, Emily, 1944, O 10,23:1
Getty, Frank, 1954, My 3,25:3
Getty, Frank D, 1967, S 21,47:1
Getty, G W Gen, 1901, O 4,7:6
Getty, Hugh, 1922, D 5,19:5
Getty, Hugh H, 1947, D 20,17:3
Getty, Innes, 1958, O 21,33:5
Getty, Innes Mrs, 1958, N 17,31:4
Getty, John, 1941, D 11,27:6
Getty, Mary C B Mrs, 1939, My 30,17:5
Getty, Phil B, 1956, O 2,35:2
Getty, Robert J, 1963, O 27,88:2
Getty, Robert N, 1941, Ap 16,23:6
Getty, Robert P, 1939, Ja 21,15:2
Getty, Samuel E, 1924, My 27,21:4; 1952, N 14,23:5
Getty, Timothy C W, 1958, Ag 19,27:2
Getty, Walter B, 1943, Mr 19,19:2
Getty, Walter P, 1958, N 3,37:2
Getty, Walter P Mrs, 1955, Je 9,29:2
Getty, William J T, 1939, N 24,23:3
Gettys, Katherine M Mrs, 1948, Je 16,29:1
Getz, Anthony Mrs, 1966, Ja 13,25:4
Getz, Arthur H, 1962, My 20,86:5
Getz, Charles, 1941, S 7,50:2
Getz, Charles L, 1962, F 22,25:3
Getz, Emery, 1953, Jl 25,11:3
Getz, Forry R Mrs, 1948, F 22,49:1
Getz, George F (por), 1938, F 12,15:4
Getz, Irving, 1956, Jl 28,36:7
Getz, Martin, 1948, Mr 8,23:5
Getz, Matthew, 1956, Jl 23,23:6
Getz, Rabbi, 1902, O 27,6:4
Getzoff, Abraham Mrs, 1964, O 11,88:4
Getzoff, Morey G, 1947, Mr 3,21:4
Getzov, Harry, 1956, D 16,86:6
Geucke, Rudolf, 1947, O 2,27:5
Geuting, Anthony H, 1947, Jl 20,44:3
Geuting, George N, 1945, Ja 4,19:5
Geuting, Joseph T, 1953, My 4,23:4
Gevaert, Joseph, 1959, D 18,29:3
Gevedon, Raney Mrs, 1959, Mr 22,86:5
Gever, Samuel, 1951, Je 26,29:3
Gevers, Baroness (Mrs Jno Cornelius), 1908, O 20, 9:6
Gevers, W A F Mrs, 1952, My 6,29:5
Gevertz, Louis, 1959, Ag 9,88:4
Gevirtz, Abraham Mrs (Oct 3), 1965, O 11,61:2
Gevirtz, Allen, 1950, My 19,27:2
Gevirtz, Charles Mrs, 1950, Ag 13,77:1
Gewecke, John H (por), 1937, My 8,19:4
Gewiss, Harry Mrs (G Layton),(funl), 1965, S 7,39:3
Geyelin, H Rowle Mrs, 1959, Ja 28,31:4
Geyelin, Henry R, 1942, S 8,23:5
Geyer, Andrew Mrs, 1965, Ag 7,21:3
Geyer, Caroline M, 1947, O 28,25:4
Geyer, Clara M Mrs, 1941, My 10,15:2
Geyer, David F, 1941, Ja 21,22:2
Geyer, Ellen M Dr, 1953, F 4,27:5
Geyer, Fred P, 1939, O 24,23:3
Geyer, Friedrich, 1949, Jl 14,6:7
Geyer, George, 1960, Ag 4,25:3
Geyer, George E, 1962, O 16,47:4
Geyer, George H Mrs, 1949, F 15,23:2
Geyer, George W, 1938, Ap 8,19:4
Geyer, Harvey D, 1952, D 23,23:3
Geyer, Karl R, 1956, O 24,37:4
Geyer, Lee E, 1941, O 12,52:1
Geyer, Linwood H, 1961, Ag 1,31:5
Geyer, Orel R, 1959, O 21,43:2
Geyl, Pieter, 1967, Ja 3,37:1
Geyler, John B, 1949, Ag 6,17:4
Geyser, Frank R, 1949, Ap 30,13:6
Geyser, Paul H, 1952, O 14,31:3
Gezo, King of Dahomey, 1859, Ap 9,4:3
Ghavam, Ahmad es Sultaneh (funl, Jl 26,25:6), 1955, Jl 24,65:1
Ghelderode, Michel de (trb lr, Ap 22,VII,p24), 1962, Ap 2,31:3
Ghent, Frank Mrs, 1946, F 20,25:5
Ghent, Raymond C, 1963, Ja 3,15:8
Gheon, Henri, 1944, S 11,17:3
Gheorghiu-Dej, Gheorghe (funl, Mr 25,5:1), 1965, Mr 20,27:1
Gheraldi, Joseph Mrs, 1956, Jl 13,19:4
Gherardi, Bancroft (por), 1941, Ag 16,15:1
Gherardi, Bancroft Adm, 1903, D 11,9:6
Gherardi, Bancroft Mrs, 1963, Je 16,84:4
Gherardi, Gherardo, 1949, Mr 11,25:1
Gherardi, Walter R (por), 1939, Jl 26,19:1
Gherardi, Walter R Mrs, 1951, N 14,31:4
Gherky, William D, 1937, Ja 19,17:5
Gheusi, P B, 1943, F 4,23:2
Ghezzi, Frank, 1958, Mr 21,21:2
Ghezzi, V Frank Mrs, 1960, F 22,17:1
Ghidoni, John J, 1942, Jl 31,15:6
Ghiglia, Anna P Mrs, 1944, Ja 31,17:5
Ghiglione, William J, 1966, Mr 13,86:3
Ghika, Jon Prince, 1881, Ap 4,5:3
Ghika, Matyla, 1965, Jl 16,27:2
Ghika, Vladimir Count, 1954, Ag 20,14:3
Ghiloni, Pietro, 1952, Ap 29,27:5

Ghiloni, Pietro G, 1950, Ap 26,29:4
Ghinelli, Mario, 1946, Ja 31,21:4
Ghione, Franco, 1964, Ja 21,29:3
Ghiosay, Louis, 1940, S 18,23:1
Ghiradelli, Louis L, 1948, Je 26,17:5
Ghirardini, Emilio, 1965, Jl 19,27:3
Ghirla, Peter, 1952, F 25,21:4
Ghiselin, Francis H, 1963, O 17,35:3
Gholson, Edwin, 1949, Ja 8,15:5
Ghoneim, Mohammed Z, 1959, Ja 12,9:5
Ghormley, Ralph K, 1959, Je 7,85:2
Ghormley, Robert L, 1958, Je 22,76:1
Ghosh, Ajoy K, 1962, Ja 14,84:4
Ghosh, P K, 1960, Je 20,2:3
Ghosh, P K Mrs, 1960, Je 20,2:3
Ghosha, Sarath Prince, 1920, F 12,11:4
Ghriskey, Robert D, 1941, Mr 18,23:3
Ghuznavi, Abdelkerim Sir, 1939, Jl 25,19:5
Giacalone, Vitto J, 1966, My 19,47:4
Giacchi, 1913, D 1,9:4
Giacci, Gabrielle, 1956, D 4,39:2
Giachery, Donna M, 1947, Ja 29,26:2
Giacobbi, Paul, 1951, Ap 5,29:3
Giacobini, Genaro, 1954, Mr 11,31:3
Giacometti, Alberto, 1966, Ja 13,22:1
Giacommetti, C P, 1882, S 28,4:7
Giacona, Louis Sr, 1952, S 26,22:5
Giaimo, Charles E, 1964, Jl 29,33:4
Giaimo, Francis P, 1959, Ja 10,17:3
Giambalvo, Nathaniel L, 1965, O 23,31:5
Giamboi, Salvatore, 1958, O 20,29:4
Giammette, Dominick Mrs, 1950, My 26,23:5
Giampietro, Albert V, 1962, Je 13,41:5
Gian-Francheschi, Joseph S, 1945, O 18,23:1
Gianakoulis, Theodore, 1964, Je 16,39:3
Gianakouras, Peter, 1968, Ag 17,27:5
Gianella, Marguerite H Mrs, 1942, Mr 13,19:4
Gianelli, Cardinal, 1881, N 8,5:2
Gianelli, Victor E, 1951, My 31,27:3
Gianelloni, Vivian, 1957, N 15,27:1
Gianfrancheschi, G Rev, 1934, Jl 10,21:3
Gianini, Mario A, 1957, My 2,31:5
Giannatasio, Gennaro, 1947, O 3,25:1
Giannattasio, Luis, 1965, F 8,25:4
Giannelli, William J, 1962, Ja 10,47:3
Giannini, A H, 1943, F 8,19:5
Giannini, A H Mrs, 1959, S 26,23:5
Giannini, A P Mrs, 1941, D 22,17:5
Giannini, Alberto, 1952, Ap 10,29:2
Giannini, Amedeo P, 1949, Je 4,13:1
Giannini, Bernard, 1954, S 11,17:6
Giannini, Eugene J, 1923, Mr 3,13:4
Giannini, Federico Mrs, 1946, Ja 9,23:1
Giannini, Ferruccio, 1948, S 18,17:1
Giannini, Frediano, 1939, O 26,23:4
Giannini, George J, 1957, Jl 12,21:4
Giannini, Guglielmo, 1960, O 15,23:5
Giannini, Joseph, 1953, S 7,19:2
Giannini, Lawrence M, 1952, Ag 21,19:1
Giannini, Mario C, 1952, Ag 25,17:2
Giannini, Virgil D, 1938, My 1,II,7:3
Giannini, Vittorio, 1966, N 29,39:1
Gianniny, Samuel V Sr, 1957, S 26,25:4
Gianoli, Bressler Mrs, 1912, My 14,11:4
Gianotti, Countess, 1915, Je 28,9:6
Giaquinto, Paolo, 1968, Jl 26,31:3
Giarbino, Frank, 1924, My 4,23:1
Giard, Joseph O, 1956, Jl 12,23:5
Giardi, Richard H, 1968, Mr 1,13:7
Giardina, I Paul, 1966, Ag 23,39:1
Giardini, Joseph, 1963, Ag 13,31:1
Giasi, John, 1962, My 26,25:2
Giasson, Venceslas, 1956, O 18,33:2
Giaugue, Florien, 1921, My 11,17:4
Giaugue, Isabella J, 1953, O 31,17:4
Giauque, Charles E Mrs, 1947, F 10,29:2
Gibb, Alex, 1958, Ja 22,27:4
Gibb, Alex Mrs, 1951, Ja 7,77:2
Gibb, Alfred A, 1939, O 19,23:4
Gibb, Anna P Mrs, 1942, Mr 8,43:2
Gibb, Arthur, 1911, Ja 15,13:3
Gibb, Arthur N, 1949, D 26,29:2
Gibb, Claude, 1959, Ja 16,28:1
Gibb, Florence S Mrs (por),(will, Je 15,20:7), 1941, My 18,45:1
Gibb, Frederick William Maj-Gen, 1968, S 9,47:4
Gibb, George C, 1951, O 2,27:1
Gibb, George Stegmann Sir, 1925, D 18,23:4
Gibb, George T L, 1944, Ja 6,23:5
Gibb, George W, 1953, Je 16,27:4
Gibb, H Elmer, 1913, O 31,11:6
Gibb, Howard, 1905, Je 18,7:6
Gibb, John (will, N 18,4:5), 1905, Ag 28,7:4
Gibb, John R, 1944, Je 21,19:3; 1949, Mr 3,25:4
Gibb, Lewis Mills, 1912, Jl 7,II,11:5
Gibb, MacGregor, 1959, Ja 29,27:4
Gibb, Margaret, 1967, Ja 9,39:2
Gibb, Mary, 1967, Ja 9,39:2
Gibb, Robert P, 1960, N 6,88:4
Gibb, T David, 1966, F 28,27:2
Gibb, Thomas B, 1955, F 5,15:6
Gibb, Walter, 1912, Jl 26,9:5
Gibb, Walton, 1951, S 7,29:1
Gibb, William T, 1939, Jl 8,15:5
Gibb, William T Mrs, 1948, Ag 3,25:4
Gibbens, Ray V, 1960, Ja 5,31:4
Gibbert, Daniel T, 1947, D 10,31:3
Gibbes, Jessie B, 1948, Jl 14,23:5
Gibbes, R W Dr, 1866, O 21,1:7
Gibbings, Robert, 1958, Ja 21,26:5
Gibbins, Henry, 1941, Ap 10,23:4
Gibbo, Charles W, 1955, F 23,27:5
Gibbon, Charles O, 1946, F 19,25:4
Gibbon, David J Capt, 1907, Mr 7,9:6
Gibbon, Elwyn, 1942, Ag 24,3:2
Gibbon, James F, 1939, S 28,25:2
Gibbon, John H Sr, 1956, Mr 15,31:3
Gibbon, John H Sr Mrs, 1956, Mr 22,35:1
Gibbon, John M, 1952, Jl 3,25:1
Gibbon, Joseph D, 1962, My 25,33:4
Gibbon, P, 1926, Je 1,25:3
Gibbon, Thecia, 1925, Ja 24,13:4
Gibboney, John, 1903, Ja 25,8:2
Gibboney, Raymond L, 1954, D 2,31:1
Gibboney, Stuart, 1944, Ap 25,3:6
Gibbons, Allan E Mrs, 1952, Ag 23,13:2
Gibbons, Bernard, 1952, My 6,29:5
Gibbons, C E (funl), 1882, Je 1,3:2
Gibbons, Carroll, 1954, My 11,29:5
Gibbons, Cedric, 1960, Jl 27,29:4
Gibbons, Charles, 1968, F 3,29:4
Gibbons, Charles E, 1950, F 1,29:4
Gibbons, Chester H, 1948, Ap 17,15:3
Gibbons, Douglas, 1962, Jl 9,31:4
Gibbons, Douglas Mrs, 1953, O 3,17:3
Gibbons, Edmund F, 1964, Je 20,25:5
Gibbons, Edmund R, 1946, Jl 13,15:5
Gibbons, Edward C, 1966, D 18,84:7
Gibbons, Edward L, 1943, Jl 14,19:3
Gibbons, Floyd P (por), 1939, S 25,19:4
Gibbons, Frank, 1964, S 3,29:5
Gibbons, Frank B, 1940, F 21,19:3
Gibbons, Frank L, 1945, Ja 20,11:7
Gibbons, Freeland J, 1957, Ja 10,29:3
Gibbons, Freeland J Mrs, 1958, Jl 5,17:5
Gibbons, George A, 1949, Ap 24,76:1
Gibbons, George B (por), 1938, O 24,17:4
Gibbons, George B Mrs, 1963, D 21,23:5
Gibbons, George Christie Sir, 1918, Ag 9,11:8
Gibbons, George R, 1950, S 4,17:3
Gibbons, George W, 1925, S 23,25:3
Gibbons, George Washington Col, 1919, Jl 24,9:3
Gibbons, H A, 1934, Ag 8,17:4
Gibbons, Harold S, 1953, S 29,29:2
Gibbons, Harry R, 1921, Ap 20,13:6
Gibbons, Henry J, 1949, F 27,69:2
Gibbons, Herbert A Mrs (Helen D), 1960, S 2,23:2
Gibbons, J J, 1942, F 5,21:3
Gibbons, James Capt, 1916, Ja 26,11:3
Gibbons, James H, 1956, Mr 4,88:1
Gibbons, Jimmy, 1949, O 10,30:7
Gibbons, John, 1947, D 12,27:4
Gibbons, John A, 1941, Ag 31,22:3
Gibbons, John F, 1909, Je 6,9:5
Gibbons, John H, 1944, D 23,13:1; 1949, My 18,27:2
Gibbons, John H Mrs, 1953, Je 3,31:1
Gibbons, John J, 1917, Ja 30,9:2; 1949, N 23,29:1; 1957, Jl 16,25:2
Gibbons, John M, 1945, My 30,19:2; 1959, N 7,23:4
Gibbons, John T, 1924, Mr 15,13:4; 1941, Ja 2,23:3
Gibbons, John W, 1939, Ap 9,III,6:8
Gibbons, Joseph F, 1942, Ap 11,13:5
Gibbons, Joseph F Mrs, 1940, N 13,23:6
Gibbons, Lloyd I, 1955, Ja 23,50:1
Gibbons, Mary, 1920, D 4,13:4
Gibbons, Mary Mrs, 1956, Mr 4,88:1
Gibbons, Maude A Mrs, 1939, F 8,23:3
Gibbons, Mervin J Mrs, 1950, O 15,104:5
Gibbons, Michael T, 1953, Ja 18,93:2
Gibbons, Mike, 1956, S 1,15:4
Gibbons, Miles F, 1939, Je 22,23:2
Gibbons, Milton A Mrs, 1961, Ja 16,27:2
Gibbons, Morton R Sr, 1949, N 10,31:6
Gibbons, Patrick E, 1966, S 10,29:4
Gibbons, Patrick H, 1945, Je 8,19:4
Gibbons, Patrick J, 1959, N 29,86:4
Gibbons, Paul W (por), 1941, Mr 11,24:3
Gibbons, Peter W, 1948, Jl 5,15:1
Gibbons, Philip J, 1946, O 23,28:2
Gibbons, Redmond P, 1957, N 14,33:2
Gibbons, Richard H Dr, 1924, Ap 9,21:2
Gibbons, Rose E, 1937, S 1,19:3
Gibbons, S J Sir, 1876, Ja 14,1:6
Gibbons, Stanley, 1913, F 26,13:4
Gibbons, Stephen B, 1958, My 24,22:6
Gibbons, Theodore M, 1946, F 27,25:5
Gibbons, Tom, 1954, Ja 25,19:4
Gibbons, Tommy (Thos J), 1960, N 20,87:1
Gibbons, William, 1937, O 2,21:1
Gibbons, William A, 1954, Jl 3,11:5
Gibbons, Willis A, 1967, My 31,43:4
Gibbs, A Hamilton, 1964, My 26,39:1
Gibbs, A W, 1922, My 20,15:6
Gibbs, Alphonso, 1948, O 29,26:3
Gibbs, Angeline L, 1951, N 29,33:5
Gibbs, Archie D, 1948, F 17,25:2
Gibbs, Arthur H, 1956, Mr 22,35:4
Gibbs, B F, 1882, S 10,7:4
Gibbs, Benjamin A, 1940, Jl 20,15:2
Gibbs, Burte B, 1944, N 17,20:2
Gibbs, Burton O, 1938, Ag 29,13:5
Gibbs, Caroline, 1965, Mr 3,3:2
Gibbs, Cora, 1966, Ja 25,41:3
Gibbs, Douglas S (por), 1941, Mr 17,17:3
Gibbs, E, 1954, My 13,29:5
Gibbs, E B Capt, 1882, Ap 27,7:4
Gibbs, E Everett, 1938, Jl 17,27:4
Gibbs, Edmund D, 1945, My 21,19:5
Gibbs, Edwin, 1968, Ag 15,37:2
Gibbs, Elvira Mrs, 1961, N 4,19:3
Gibbs, Emily O, 1907, Ap 28,9:5
Gibbs, Fletcher B, 1938, Mr 25,19:2
Gibbs, Francis W, 1944, F 10,15:5
Gibbs, George, 1940, My 21,23:6; 1942, O 11,56:1; 1950, D 21,29:6
Gibbs, George A, 1937, S 2,21:1
Gibbs, George S, 1947, Ja 10,22:2
Gibbs, H L, 1933, My 8,15:3
Gibbs, Harold B, 1956, N 3,23:4
Gibbs, Harry E, 1952, Je 1,84:5
Gibbs, Henry Hucks (Lord Aldenham), 1907, S 15, 9:6
Gibbs, Herbert H, 1946, Mr 26,29:3
Gibbs, James (funl), 1875, Jl 18,7:6
Gibbs, James Church, 1904, Ja 10,7:6
Gibbs, John, 1945, N 3,15:2
Gibbs, John E, 1937, My 28,21:4
Gibbs, John K, 1949, Ja 7,22:3
Gibbs, John M, 1937, O 12,25:4
Gibbs, John Richmond, 1906, Jl 24,7:6
Gibbs, John S Jr, 1953, O 31,17:5
Gibbs, John T, 1960, D 29,25:2
Gibbs, Josiah Prof, 1903, Ap 29,9:5
Gibbs, K Mrs, 1934, My 10,21:1
Gibbs, L D, 1929, Mr 2,17:1
Gibbs, L Shirley, 1954, N 26,29:2
Gibbs, Lady, 1939, O 9,19:5
Gibbs, Leroy M, 1949, N 23,30:5
Gibbs, Lincoln R, 1943, D 15,27:4
Gibbs, Louis D, 1943, Ap 24,14:8
Gibbs, M R, 1881, Mr 13,5:4
Gibbs, Mahaley, 1915, O 9,9:3
Gibbs, Malcolm G, 1944, Ja 28,17:1
Gibbs, Michael P, 1943, N 8,19:4
Gibbs, Milton E, 1940, Ag 22,19:2
Gibbs, Nancy, 1955, O 14,27:5
Gibbs, Norman F, 1951, Ap 29,89:2
Gibbs, Paul W, 1963, O 11,37:2
Gibbs, Philip, 1962, Mr 12,31:1
Gibbs, Raymond B, 1947, Mr 10,22:2
Gibbs, Richard, 1875, Jl 16,4:6
Gibbs, Robert, 1901, My 20,2:4
Gibbs, Robert P, 1941, F 23,41:3
Gibbs, Rufus M Mrs, 1965, Ag 6,27:3
Gibbs, Samuel C, 1956, My 3,31:3
Gibbs, Theodore B, 1909, O 28,9:6
Gibbs, Theodore K Maj, 1909, Ja 17,11:6
Gibbs, W C Gov, 1871, F 22,1:5
Gibbs, W H Maj, 1909, Ag 18,9:5
Gibbs, W Rockwood Mrs, 1947, Je 14,15:2
Gibbs, William D, 1944, Je 28,23:2
Gibbs, William F, 1967, S 7,45:1
Gibbs, William T, 1937, Ja 29,19:5
Gibbs, William Warren, 1924, O 26,7:2
Gibbs, Willis B, 1940, Ag 9,15:6
Gibbs, Wolcott (funl, Ag 21,25:5), 1958, Ag 17,
Gibbs, Wolcott Mrs, 1963, Jl 31,29:3
Gibbs, Zella, 1907, Ag 16,7:6
Gibby, Edgar M, 1968, D 5,47:3
Gibby, Helen B Mrs, 1937, My 12,23:2
Gibby, Herbert B, 1953, Ag 8,11:3
Gibby, Leroy A, 1942, My 8,21:3
Gibby, Mariana R, 1950, O 1,104:4
Gibby, William D, 1940, O 20,50:1
Gibeling, Howard W, 1958, Ja 27,27:2
Giberne, Agnes, 1939, Ag 22,19:4
Giberson, Crawford, 1924, Ap 20,22:1
Giberson, Dudley A, 1938, Ag 29,13:6
Giberson, Harrison T, 1938, N 1,23:4
Gibert, Audinet, 1916, Ap 4,13:7
Giblin, Charles A Mrs, 1949, S 6,27:4
Giblin, James Father, 1904, D 4,7:6
Giblin, John L, 1957, Je 27,25:4
Giblin, Lee F, 1964, D 7,35:3
Giblin, Richard T, 1951, Je 23,15:3
Giblin, V A, 1912, Je 18,11:5
Giblin, Vincent C, 1965, Mr 22,33:4
Giblin, Walter M, 1964, My 2,27:1
Giblin, William, 1944, My 3,19:2
Giblin, William A, 1950, D 30,13:6
Giblon, Harold A Mrs, 1950, S 13,27:3
Giblon, John, 1962, Jl 4,21:5
Giblyn, Leo F, 1960, D 21,31:3
Gibner, Herbert C, 1948, N 15,25:2
Gibney, Albert J, 1948, Ja 21,25:2
Gibney, Charles F (por), 1940, D 10,25:5
Gibney, Edward, 1950, Ja 14,15:4
Gibney, Ernest C, 1951, Ag 7,25:2
Gibney, Frank F (por), 1941, Ja 28,19:2

Gibney, Frank S, 1959, F 9,26:1
Gibney, Grover H, 1946, D 31,17:5
Gibney, Homer Dr, 1915, F 17,11:6
Gibney, Joseph J, 1962, My 10,37:5
Gibney, Robert A, 1957, O 22,33:2
Gibney, Robert A Mrs, 1948, F 27,21:2
Gibney, Terrence V, 1953, S 15,31:2
Gibney, Thomas F, 1956, My 18,25:3
Gibney, Thomas P, 1953, Jl 29,23:2
Gibney, Virbil P Mrs, 1945, Je 14,19:5
Gibouleau, G H, 1949, Ja 11,31:2
Gibson, A B, 1948, Je 8,26:3
Gibson, A Grace, 1939, S 28,25:5
Gibson, Adna W, 1943, My 22,13:4
Gibson, Albert Jr, 1945, Jl 21,24:6
Gibson, Alex D Jr, 1948, Mr 23,25:4
Gibson, Algernon T, 1940, D 15,60:4
Gibson, Alvin, 1952, Je 2,22:4
Gibson, Andrew, 1939, F 3,15:4
Gibson, Ann E Mrs, 1940, Ap 15,17:3
Gibson, Archer, 1952, Jl 16,25:3
Gibson, Archibald, 1881, Ja 27,1:4
Gibson, Arthur F, 1954, S 4,11:3
Gibson, Arthur J, 1943, D 16,27:1
Gibson, Ben J, 1949, Jl 10,56:5
Gibson, Bradford A, 1938, F 26,15:2
Gibson, Breckinridge Stuyvesant, 1920, My 30,22:3
Gibson, C F, 1881, Je 9,5:6
Gibson, C H Capt, 1912, S 25,13:6
Gibson, C Huntley, 1946, Jl 31,27:2
Gibson, Charles D, 1944, D 24,26:1
Gibson, Charles D Mrs, 1956, Ap 21,17:2
Gibson, Charles De Wolf Mrs, 1922, Jl 1,13:5
Gibson, Charles E, 1944, Ap 5,19:2
Gibson, Charles H, 1954, N 20,17:3
Gibson, Charles L (por), 1944, N 25,13:3
Gibson, Charles R, 1955, Mr 10,27:4
Gibson, Charles R Mrs, 1945, O 9,21:3
Gibson, Charles S, 1950, Mr 26,92:5
Gibson, Charles S Mrs, 1943, My 13,21:4
Gibson, Christine A, 1955, Je 1,33:4
Gibson, Christopher D, 1944, Jl 1,15:6
Gibson, Clair J, 1955, Ja 26,25:2
Gibson, Clarence E Mrs, 1952, Jl 27,58:6
Gibson, David, 1945, Jl 7,13:4
Gibson, David E, 1963, D 14,27:3
Gibson, David R, 1960, Jl 17,61:1
Gibson, E A, 1948, Ag 19,18:7
Gibson, E Lacy, 1962, My 3,21:3
Gibson, Edmund R (Hoot), 1962, Ag 24,25:2
Gibson, Edward (Lord Ashbourne), 1913, My 23,13:5
Gibson, Edwin H, 1953, Ap 16,29:5
Gibson, Edwin T, 1959, F 24,29:1
Gibson, Elmer F, 1941, S 16,23:3
Gibson, Ernest W, 1940, Je 21,21:1
Gibson, Ernest W Mrs, 1958, Ag 16,17:1
Gibson, Fannie H Mrs, 1939, N 11,15:3
Gibson, Florence W, 1946, F 15,25:1
Gibson, Francis, 1937, O 9,19:5
Gibson, Francis Marion Capt, 1919, Ja 18,11:3
Gibson, Frank E, 1953, Ag 16,77:1
Gibson, Frank H, 1946, D 30,19:4
Gibson, Frank H Mrs, 1946, Je 10,21:5
Gibson, Frank L Mrs, 1945, Jl 6,11:7
Gibson, Fred, 1953, Ag 25,21:5
Gibson, Frederick J, 1925, F 22,19:3
Gibson, Frederick M, 1952, My 16,23:6
Gibson, Frederick M Mrs, 1947, Je 3,26:3
Gibson, Frederick R Rev, 1968, Mr 7,43:3
Gibson, G G, 1934, Ja 12,23:5
Gibson, George, 1953, F 5,23:4
Gibson, George C, 1948, Ap 21,27:1
Gibson, George E, 1959, Ag 28,23:5
Gibson, George G, 1940, My 8,23:3
Gibson, George H, 1943, Jl 29,19:4; 1955, Jl 23,17:2
Gibson, George M, 1967, Ja 27,45:3
Gibson, George R Mrs (P Ryan), 1949, F 16,4:4
Gibson, George Rutledge, 1907, F 7,9:6
Gibson, George S, 1951, Jl 4,17:4
Gibson, H de B Mrs, 1903, My 27,9:3
Gibson, Hamilton, 1956, O 6,21:4
Gibson, Harold H, 1950, Ja 15,84:2
Gibson, Harold K, 1946, O 26,17:5
Gibson, Harry C, 1954, Jl 12,19:1
Gibson, Harry W, 1948, My 12,27:2
Gibson, Harvey D, 1950, S 12,27:1
Gibson, Henry R, 1938, My 27,17:2
Gibson, Henry W, 1941, Ap 17,23:5
Gibson, Holbrook, 1946, Jl 31,27:1
Gibson, Hopkins Mrs, 1949, Ap 29,23:2
Gibson, Horatio Gates Gen, 1924, Ap 19,13:4
Gibson, Hugh, 1946, O 12,19:2
Gibson, Hugh Mrs, 1950, Mr 20,21:5
Gibson, Hugh S (funl, D 16,37:2), 1954, D 13,1:2
Gibson, Ida A Mrs, 1944, Je 17,13:2
Gibson, J Alan, 1953, Ap 11,17:3
Gibson, J Chester, 1937, D 24,17:3
Gibson, J Hollis, 1904, Mr 31,9:2
Gibson, J L, 1954, N 5,21:2
Gibson, J M, 1902, N 9,7:6
Gibson, J S, 1877, O 21,2:7
Gibson, J Stewart Mrs, 1940, Ap 5,22:2
Gibson, James, 1944, Ja 5,18:2; 1950, D 4,29:3
Gibson, James A, 1943, My 27,25:3; 1944, O 21,17:5
Gibson, James Edgar, 1953, F 11,29:3
Gibson, James J, 1955, S 17,15:5
Gibson, James K, 1939, Ap 10,17:3
Gibson, James M, 1966, Je 1,44:1
Gibson, James S, 1941, Je 22,32:7
Gibson, James T Dr, 1920, S 18,9:1
Gibson, James T Mrs, 1950, Jl 20,25:4
Gibson, John B (cor, N 19,11:8), 1960, N 16,26:4
Gibson, John J, 1939, My 8,17:5; 1943, O 3,49:1
Gibson, John Jr, 1925, Jl 10,17:6
Gibson, John M, 1948, D 23,20:4
Gibson, John Monro Rev, 1921, O 14,17:4
Gibson, John W, 1947, Mr 21,21:5; 1950, My 11,29:1
Gibson, Joseph D, 1963, N 16,27:1
Gibson, Joseph Thompson Rev Dr, 1922, Jl 18,11:3
Gibson, Josh, 1947, Ja 21,19:7
Gibson, Kasson Church Dr, 1925, D 30,17:4
Gibson, Katherine B Mrs, 1941, O 9,23:5
Gibson, Kenneth C, 1956, Ag 19,92:1
Gibson, Kiliaen van R Mrs, 1967, Ja 12,39:1
Gibson, Langdon, 1923, S 6,15:5
Gibson, Lawrence C, 1946, Jl 11,23:5
Gibson, Leon L, 1943, D 28,17:2
Gibson, Lewis T, 1945, Ag 10,15:5
Gibson, Lyman F, 1940, O 18,21:6
Gibson, Margaret, 1939, Ja 1,13:2
Gibson, Marguerite J, 1958, N 29,21:2
Gibson, Millard H, 1945, My 6,38:1
Gibson, Persifor F Jr, 1950, N 22,25:5
Gibson, Peter, 1910, Jl 24,7:6
Gibson, Preston, 1937, F 16,24:1
Gibson, Ralph B, 1962, Ag 4,19:3
Gibson, Ralph H, 1951, My 20,88:4
Gibson, Raymond E, 1959, Ap 29,33:5
Gibson, Raymond E Rev, 1968, Ag 10,27:4
Gibson, Richardson Mrs, 1953, S 3,21:2
Gibson, Robert, 1919, F 18,11:5; 1940, Jl 27,13:3
Gibson, Robert F Sr Mrs, 1967, Jl 20,37:3
Gibson, Robert H, 1960, My 4,45:3
Gibson, Robert J, 1950, Mr 24,26:3
Gibson, Robert M, 1938, Ap 23,6:5; 1949, D 20,31:5
Gibson, Samuel P, 1951, Ap 25,29:3
Gibson, Sidney V, 1922, My 21,30:1
Gibson, Stanford J, 1945, Mr 9,19:4
Gibson, Stanford J Mrs, 1949, S 18,92:2
Gibson, Stanley, 1956, O 25,33:4
Gibson, Sydney C, 1944, D 27,19:6
Gibson, T M, 1884, F 26,2:4
Gibson, Thomas, 1941, Jl 4,13:3
Gibson, Thomas A Lt-Col, 1925, F 2,17:3
Gibson, Thomas J Mrs, 1958, F 1,19:5
Gibson, Thomas S, 1967, Je 3,31:2
Gibson, Vernon D, 1956, Ap 10,31:1
Gibson, W Frazer, 1938, S 10,17:6
Gibson, W H, 1881, Je 25,8:1
Gibson, W V, 1954, S 12,84:6
Gibson, Walter C, 1964, D 9,50:4
Gibson, Wilfred W, 1962, My 27,93:2
Gibson, William, 1914, My 5,11:6; 1943, My 24,15:4
Gibson, William A, 1943, Je 18,21:5
Gibson, William B, 1941, D 31,17:2
Gibson, William C Rear-Adm, 1911, My 11,11:5
Gibson, William D, 1942, Ap 23,23:4
Gibson, William D Mrs, 1951, Je 5,31:5
Gibson, William E, 1950, Ap 5,31:2
Gibson, William H, 1921, Ag 28,22:4; 1948, My 24, 19:4
Gibson, William J, 1922, D 23,13:6; 1939, F 17,19:2
Gibson, William J (will, Jl 26,15:4), 1947, Jl 22,23:1
Gibson, William M, 1951, Jl 9,25:5
Gibson, William Maj, 1903, S 25,7:5
Gibson, William R, 1964, N 24,39:2
Gibson, William R Mrs, 1956, Ja 7,17:4
Gibson, Woolman H col, 1937, D 24,17:4
Gick, William H, 1944, Jl 15,13:5
Giddens, George, 1920, N 22,15:5
Giddens, Zambry P, 1965, N 13,29:4
Giddes, Albert C, 1944, S 2,11:6
Giddes, Elmer A, 1944, D 5,23:2
Giddes, Robert L, 1941, S 7,51:4
Gidding, Jacob M, 1940, My 3,21:5
Gidding, Jesse D, 1953, Ag 13,14:3
Gidding, Louis, 1940, Ja 30,20:3
Giddings, Daniel B, 1937, F 24,24:1
Giddings, Dorothy, 1947, D 19,25:1
Giddings, E Cleveland, 1960, O 1,19:4
Giddings, Edward Fuller, 1920, F 13,11:3
Giddings, Edward L Capt, 1903, Jl 29,2:4
Giddings, Elizabeth H Mrs, 1939, Ap 9,III,7:1
Giddings, Emanuel M (por), 1947, S 26,23:1
Giddings, F H, 1931, Je 12,21:1
Giddings, George W, 1948, Ag 17,21:5
Giddings, Grotius Col, 1867, Je 28,1:7
Giddings, H Starr, 1958, D 10,39:3
Giddings, Harold G, 1949, My 30,13:1
Giddings, Harry, 1949, Je 16,29:4
Giddings, Howard A, 1949, Mr 18,26:3
Giddings, Howard C, 1952, My 30,15:3
Giddings, J Louis, 1964, D 10,47:1
Giddings, J R, 1864, My 28,4:5
Giddings, Joshua R, 1938, Ap 16,13:5
Giddy, Harry D, 1959, D 14,31:2
Gide, Andre, 1951, F 20,25:1
Gideon, Abraham, 1952, D 18,29:2
Gideon, Dave, 1950, Ja 7,18:3
Gideon, Henry J, 1951, Je 26,29:1
Gideon, M J, 1933, N 12,35:5
Gideon, Valentine, 1951, F 12,23:4
Gideon, Valentine G Mrs, 1950, S 24,104:5
Gidley, Everett F, 1959, F 21,21:6
Gidley, James W Mrs, 1956, Ap 29,86:1
Gidley-Lake, Walter H, 1938, Mr 31,23:2
Gie, Stephanus F N, 1945, Ap 10,19:4
Giebel, Helen S (Sister Mary Vincent de Paul), 1955, Je 21,31:3
Giebel, Henry, 1963, Jl 6,15:2
Giebel, Henry W, 1947, Ap 23,25:3
Giebel, Leo, 1943, Je 26,13:6
Giedion, Sigfried Dr, 1968, Ap 12,35:1
Gieg, L Frederick, 1966, My 2,37:2
Giegerich, Arthur, 1924, S 21,29:2
Giegerich, Charles J, 1959, F 24,29:1
Giegerich, L A, 1927, D 21,25:3
Giegerich, Louise Boll Mrs, 1923, S 4,17:2
Gielgud, Frank, 1949, Ap 14,25:1
Gient, Julian, 1949, O 17,23:2
Giere, Margaret, 1952, Ag 25,17:3
Giere, Robert F, 1944, S 30,13:4
Giering, Carl J, 1947, S 26,23:3
Giering, Percival L, 1962, Mr 11,87:1
Gierl, Frederick P, 1943, F 20,13:5
Giers, N C de, 1895, Ja 27,5:1
Gierth, William, 1922, Mr 15,19:6
Gies, Arthur G, 1955, Je 5,85:1
Gies, Louis G, 1941, O 25,17:2
Gies, Paul, 1948, Ja 30,23:1
Gies, William J (cor, My 23,31:5), 1956, My 21,25:2
Gies, William J Mrs, 1963, O 19,25:5
Gies, William J Sr, 1944, Ap 1,13:2
Giese, Carl A, 1939, My 3,23:5
Giese, Ewald F, 1938, Jl 11,17:5
Giese, Frank C, 1940, Jl 23,19:5
Giese, Frederick D, 1957, N 24,87:3
Giese, George E, 1964, Ap 11,25:2
Giese, Henry W, 1939, Ag 5,15:3
Giese, Herman R, 1968, N 6,39:3
Giese, William H, 1952, Ag 13,21:2
Gieseking, Walter, 1956, O 26,1:6
Giesel, Frederick W, 1963, O 29,36:7
Gieselberg, William T, 1957, Ag 16,19:5
Giesemann, George A, 1961, Je 17,21:3
Gieske, Herman E, 1954, F 9,27:6
Giesler, Anton, 1946, Mr 19,27:2
Giesler, Harold L (Jerry),(funl, Ja 5,29:5), 1962, Ja 2,29:1
Giesler, Joseph, 1951, Je 23,15:4
Giesow, William H, 1940, My 15,23:5
Giesseman, Clifford, 1957, S 4,33:2
Giessen, Charles Mrs, 1952, Ap 11,23:3
Giessler, Fritz, 1947, S 6,17:4
Giesting, F A, 1928, Ap 27,25:5
Giesy, Paul M, 1958, Ag 26,29:1
Giffard, George Augustus, 1925, S 25,21:4
Giffard, George J, 1964, N 19,39:6
Giffard, Henri, 1882, Ap 18,5:4
Giffard, Stanley L, 1858, N 24,1:5
Giffen, Charles M Rev, 1909, Ap 22,9:3
Giffen, Elizabeth N Mrs, 1937, My 21,21:3
Giffen, Frank C, 1948, Ap 19,23:2
Giffen, Nathaniel M, 1964, Ap 25,29:1
Giffen, Obed C, 1941, My 7,25:5
Giffen, R L, 1946, Mr 20,24:2
Giffen, Robert Sir, 1910, Ap 13,11:4
Giffin, Henry C, 1961, My 29,19:3
Giffin, Howard, 1948, My 1,15:3
Giffin, James E, 1942, My 22,21:4
Giffin, Lowell C, 1961, Ap 26,39:4
Giffin, Mortimer P Mrs, 1943, N 15,19:2
Giffin, William G, 1939, O 28,15:5
Gifford, A, 1931, S 28,19:1
Gifford, A N, 1873, F 6,8:2
Gifford, Albert L, 1959, Mr 29,80:4
Gifford, Albert L Mrs, 1953, Ap 1,29:2
Gifford, Alexander Sr, 1967, N 8,40:4
Gifford, Alfred G, 1954, S 18,15:4
Gifford, Alice A, 1944, S 17,42:3
Gifford, Archer P, 1948, F 15,60:3
Gifford, Arthur P, 1955, Ag 25,23:2
Gifford, Arthur T, 1949, D 7,31:2
Gifford, Benedict E, 1948, Mr 23,25:3
Gifford, Burt S, 1942, F 5,21:2
Gifford, Charles A, 1937, My 4,25:1
Gifford, Charles C, 1962, S 16,86:4
Gifford, Charles L, 1947, Ap 24,57:1
Gifford, Charles L Mrs, 1951, Ja 27,13:4
Gifford, Delbert F, 1960, Mr 20,86:4
Gifford, E Garfield, 1954, Ag 15,85:1
Gifford, Edward W, 1959, My 18,27:4
Gifford, Frank H, 1951, Ag 7,25:3
Gifford, Franklin K, 1948, N 28,92:7
Gifford, Frederick H Mrs, 1965, Ag 26,33:2
Gifford, George, 1883, Jl 3,4:7; 1951, Jl 20,21:3
Gifford, George B, 1908, F 18,7:5
Gifford, George E, 1937, Ap 25,II,8:7
Gifford, George E Mrs, 1944, Ap 18,21:3

Gifford, George Mrs (Augusta Hall Gifford), 1915, F 10,11:3
Gifford, Glenn J, 1958, Ap 20,84:5
Gifford, Harry, 1960, Ja 10,86:4
Gifford, Harry M, 1952, N 12,27:3
Gifford, Heman, 1954, D 20,29:1
Gifford, Herschel H, 1940, Ap 8,19:2
Gifford, Isaac C, 1940, My 13,17:3
Gifford, James M, 1938, O 21,23:2
Gifford, James N, 1957, Ja 23,29:4
Gifford, James P (trb lr, S 27,40:6), 1961, S 17,87:1
Gifford, James P Jr, 1945, Ag 17,8:3
Gifford, John C, 1949, Je 27,27:5
Gifford, John J Col, 1912, O 5,13:6
Gifford, Kenneth C, 1963, S 27,29:3
Gifford, L M, 1953, S 11,21:1
Gifford, Lester C, 1956, O 19,27:1
Gifford, Livingston, 1937, F 12,23:5
Gifford, Lord, 1937, Ja 31,II,9:2
Gifford, Luther M, 1955, Mr 24,31:1
Gifford, Marie L D Mrs, 1938, Ja 6,19:5
Gifford, Myra D, 1950, Ag 15,29:3
Gifford, Paul, 1944, O 26,23:4
Gifford, Phil C, 1957, S 12,31:4
Gifford, Ralph G, 1959, F 28,19:4
Gifford, Ralph S, 1937, S 20,23:6
Gifford, Ralph W Prof, 1925, D 3,25:3
Gifford, Richard C, 1955, Jl 17,60:8
Gifford, Robert F, 1944, D 4,23:5
Gifford, Robert Swain, 1905, Ja 16,9:3
Gifford, Robert W, 1959, Jl 8,29:3
Gifford, Sanford R, 1944, F 26,13:5
Gifford, Sanford Robinson, 1880, Ag 30,5:4
Gifford, Sarah L P Mrs, 1941, Ap 26,15:6
Gifford, Stanley Pelham, 1917, Ja 2,11:3
Gifford, U Grant, 1949, N 24,31:6
Gifford, Walter S, 1966, My 8,1:7
Gifford, William, 1941, Je 22,32:2; 1961, Jl 20,27:2
Gifford, William F, 1949, Ap 8,25:3
Gifford, William M, 1955, Ja 21,23:1
Giffosway, Martha, 1912, Jl 20,7:6
Gifft, Howard M, 1956, D 21,23:1
Gifkins, John C, 1940, Ap 25,23:3
Gigante, Hugh A, 1967, N 18,37:3
Giger, George J, 1946, F 28,23:6
Giger, Gustav A, 1953, Ag 21,17:1
Giger, H Rudolf, 1964, Ap 23,39:4
Giger, Stephen, 1958, Mr 21,21:3
Gigli, Beniamino (funl plans, D 2,27:4; funl, D 3,35:5), 1957, D 1,89:1
Gigli, Joseph, 1960, Je 17,31:4
Giglio, Clemente, 1943, Jl 16,17:5
Gignilliat, Leigh R, 1952, O 31,25:3
Gignoux, Frederick E, 1956, Mr 25,92:1
Gignoux, Louise Fowler, 1919, O 20,15:6
Gignoux, Maurice, 1955, Ag 23,23:5
Gignoux, Reginald M, 1904, Ag 18,1:6
Gigot, Francis E Dr, 1920, Je 16,11:3
Giguere, Chambord, 1954, Ja 9,15:5
Giguere, Edmour F, 1958, My 6,35:4
Giguere, J E Theodule, 1940, My 11,19:5
Gihon, A L Dr, 1901, N 18,7:4
Gil, Enrique, 1958, O 3,30:6
Gil, Martin, 1955, D 10,21:6
Gil, Matias E, 1953, O 6,29:1
Gil, Raimundo, 1942, D 17,37:5
Gil, Stephen, 1966, Ap 30,31:4
Gil Peres, Jules (Peres-Jalin), 1882, F 26,4:5
Gilady, Raphael D, 1967, Jl 8,25:4
Gilaryi, Lawrence, 1953, My 19,29:4
Gilbane, William H Mrs, 1955, F 13,86:3
Gilber, Charles E, 1951, Je 18,23:6
Gilbert, A, 1929, D 22,II,5:3; 1934, N 5,19:3
Gilbert, A C Jr, 1964, Je 28,57:1
Gilbert, A Frank, 1945, N 26,21:3
Gilbert, Abbey E, 1964, Mr 17,35:2
Gilbert, Abija, 1881, N 27,2:2
Gilbert, Abner W, 1944, N 13,19:4
Gilbert, Abraham S (por), 1946, Jl 1,31:4
Gilbert, Adrienne I Mrs, 1967, D 27,34:8
Gilbert, Albert C, 1948, F 14,13:2; 1952, Mr 16,91:2; 1965, My 10,33:4
Gilbert, Albert M Mrs, 1944, N 9,27:3
Gilbert, Alfred C, 1961, Ja 25,1:2
Gilbert, Allyn T, 1947, Mr 7,25:5
Gilbert, Ann Mrs, 1904, D 3,9:1
Gilbert, Anne S Mrs, 1942, Ap 28,21:2
Gilbert, Archibald F, 1953, Jl 8,27:2
Gilbert, Arthur A (A A Goldberg), 1952, N 29,13:5
Gilbert, Arthur H, 1954, Je 18,23:7
Gilbert, Barry, 1961, N 27,29:4
Gilbert, Benjamin H, 1954, Ap 5,25:4
Gilbert, Bernard E Mrs, 1955, My 8,89:1
Gilbert, Blanche Mrs, 1945, Ap 30,19:3
Gilbert, Bradford L Mrs, 1919, S 20,11:5
Gilbert, Bro, 1947, O 20,23:4
Gilbert, C, 1934, My 18,23:1
Gilbert, C W, 1933, My 18,19:1
Gilbert, Calvin, 1939, S 15,23:5
Gilbert, Caroline M Mrs, 1955, Je 1,33:2
Gilbert, Cass Jr Mrs, 1938, O 18,25:4
Gilbert, Cass Mrs, 1952, S 5,27:4
Gilbert, Charles (funl, O 14,11:6), 1910, O 13,11:5
Gilbert, Charles B, 1913, Ag 28,9:3
Gilbert, Charles D, 1953, Je 19,22:3
Gilbert, Charles E, 1947, F 3,19:2; 1951, N 8,29:4
Gilbert, Charles E Dr, 1917, Je 19,13:5
Gilbert, Charles Edwin, 1925, Ag 2,5:4
Gilbert, Charles K (funl, N 22,21:4), 1958, N 20,35:2
Gilbert, Charles L, 1941, Ag 30,13:2
Gilbert, Charles P H, 1952, O 27,27:3
Gilbert, Charles T Mrs, 1915, Jl 9,11:5
Gilbert, Charles V, 1946, Je 9,40:6
Gilbert, Chauncey M, 1949, O 4,27:1
Gilbert, Clara Bordeon Mrs, 1921, N 11,13:4
Gilbert, Clifford W Dr, 1937, Ja 30,17:5
Gilbert, Clinton (funl), 1871, Jl 20,8:3
Gilbert, Clinton W Mrs (Pauline), 1968, Jl 31,41:1
Gilbert, Clyve Mrs (D Alexander), 1960, Je 23,29:5
Gilbert, Curtis F, 1871, Jl 28,8:4
Gilbert, Dale E, 1949, Mr 24,28:2
Gilbert, Daniel J Sr Mrs, 1959, O 22,37:5
Gilbert, Don O, 1959, F 10,33:4
Gilbert, Donald N, 1965, Ja 17,88:6
Gilbert, Donald W, 1957, Ag 28,27:4
Gilbert, Douglas, 1948, Ja 20,23:4
Gilbert, E Morgan, 1947, S 14,60:4
Gilbert, Edgar V M, 1962, Ag 17,23:2
Gilbert, Edwin (will), 1906, Mr 7,2:5
Gilbert, Edwin C, 1958, Ag 24,87:2
Gilbert, Eliza E, 1961, O 31,31:5
Gilbert, Elmer E, 1945, Ag 29,19:5
Gilbert, Emily F, 1962, Ap 30,27:1
Gilbert, Eugene, 1966, Je 20,33:1
Gilbert, F A, 1901, Ja 19,1:3
Gilbert, F B, 1927, Ag 29,17:4
Gilbert, F E, 1882, My 16,5:3
Gilbert, Felix, 1968, Je 11,47:2
Gilbert, Fenton L, 1953, Ja 9,21:3
Gilbert, Fitch, 1959, Ag 13,27:3
Gilbert, Fitch Mrs, 1962, Ja 16,33:4
Gilbert, Florence A P Mrs, 1940, My 3,21:2
Gilbert, Foster B, 1949, Mr 11,25:2
Gilbert, Francis, 1951, F 16,25:1; 1951, N 11,90:3
Gilbert, Francis W, 1953, Ap 5,76:3
Gilbert, Frank C Mrs, 1940, Ag 27,21:2
Gilbert, Franklin (F Goldberg), 1961, Ja 30,23:5
Gilbert, Fred A, 1938, Ap 7,23:6
Gilbert, Fred H, 1965, Ja 5,33:2
Gilbert, Frederic N (will, Jl 5,21:2), 1962, Je 21,31:3
Gilbert, Frederick L, 1951, Mr 4,93:1
Gilbert, Frederick M Mrs, 1942, Ja 9,21:3
Gilbert, Frederick S Mrs, 1957, Jl 21,61:2
Gilbert, Gama, 1940, S 25,27:4
Gilbert, George, 1943, Mr 25,21:4
Gilbert, George B, 1948, F 21,13:4
Gilbert, George D, 1954, S 7,25:3
Gilbert, George Fred, 1904, Ja 14,9:7
Gilbert, George L M Mrs, 1954, Ag 31,21:5
Gilbert, George R, 1961, Ag 4,21:2
Gilbert, George Y, 1943, Mr 3,23:3
Gilbert, Gerard, 1943, My 8,15:2
Gilbert, Glenn D, 1937, Jl 22,19:4
Gilbert, Grace B Mrs, 1940, D 9,19:3
Gilbert, Guy, 1947, Ag 21,23:4
Gilbert, H F B, 1928, My 20,25:4
Gilbert, H Walter, 1951, Ap 14,15:2
Gilbert, Harold N, 1966, N 18,43:3
Gilbert, Harry, 1953, Ja 28,27:5
Gilbert, Harry B, 1960, D 4,88:6
Gilbert, Harry Bramhall, 1911, Je 20,9:5
Gilbert, Harry M, 1964, O 14,45:1
Gilbert, Henry Sir, 1901, D 24,7:6
Gilbert, Henry W, 1944, D 16,15:6
Gilbert, Herbert T Mrs, 1953, Mr 31,31:3
Gilbert, Hiram T, 1939, N 30,21:3
Gilbert, Horatio N, 1943, Ag 31,17:6
Gilbert, Howard F, 1949, O 19,29:2
Gilbert, Howard W, 1948, Ja 18,60:3
Gilbert, Hubert, 1945, Ap 26,23:1
Gilbert, J, 1936, Ja 10,19:1
Gilbert, J Clark, 1903, N 1,5:2
Gilbert, Jabez Mrs, 1925, Ap 7,19:6
Gilbert, Jacob H, 1966, Ap 9,22:8
Gilbert, James, 1918, Mr 11,11:6
Gilbert, James H, 1948, S 2,23:3; 1958, Je 6,23:2
Gilbert, James Horn, 1918, Ag 1,11:5
Gilbert, James J, 1962, O 14,85:5
Gilbert, James P, 1953, O 18,86:6
Gilbert, James S, 1957, Je 19,35:2
Gilbert, Jasper, 1951, Ap 14,11:7
Gilbert, Jean, 1942, D 21,19:6
Gilbert, Jermima, 1947, Mr 2,52:5
Gilbert, Jesse, 1954, D 13,27:3
Gilbert, John, 1889, Je 18,5:1; 1957, N 30,21:5
Gilbert, John C, 1939, My 31,23:5; 1949, Ja 7,21:4
Gilbert, John F, 1959, Mr 14,23:3
Gilbert, John J (por), 1939, Jl 27,19:3
Gilbert, John J, 1957, N 11,29:2
Gilbert, John M, 1952, O 2,29:4
Gilbert, John P, 1953, D 15,39:3
Gilbert, Joseph, 1944, My 9,19:3; 1956, Ja 16,21:6; 1966, Ag 7,56:1
Gilbert, Joseph E, 1958, Ap 19,21:1
Gilbert, Joseph M, 1949, Ag 24,25:2
Gilbert, Joseph Thomas, 1916, N 14,11:2
Gilbert, Joshua A, 1948, Ap 20,27:2
Gilbert, Katherine E, 1952, Ap 29,27:2
Gilbert, Keller H, 1964, Je 6,23:5
Gilbert, L Rev, 1885, Mr 29,2:4
Gilbert, Lady (Rose Mulholland), 1921, Ap 27,17:4
Gilbert, Larry, 1965, F 18,33:3
Gilbert, Laura M, 1942, Ja 6,23:1
Gilbert, Lawrence M Jr, 1941, Ag 25,15:3
Gilbert, Le Roy, 1937, N 2,25:3
Gilbert, Levi P Dr, 1917, D 25,15:4
Gilbert, Lewis, 1954, Jl 31,13:4
Gilbert, Lewis M, 1950, O 10,31:4
Gilbert, Linus R, 1966, Ja 25,41:3
Gilbert, Lyman D, 1914, My 5,11:6
Gilbert, Lyman D Mrs, 1951, F 27,28:4
Gilbert, Mabelle S, 1951, My 9,33:2
Gilbert, Marvin E, 1954, F 22,19:5
Gilbert, Maude, 1953, Jl 8,27:6
Gilbert, Max M, 1938, Ag 10,19:4
Gilbert, Maxwell C, 1966, Mr 24,39:5
Gilbert, Melvin J, 1968, My 26,84:3
Gilbert, Mercedes, 1952, Mr 6,31:4
Gilbert, Merle, 1951, Ja 14,51:2
Gilbert, Morris Mrs, 1966, F 20,88:5
Gilbert, Nat C, 1940, Ap 20,17:2
Gilbert, Nelson R, 1954, Ag 26,27:5
Gilbert, Newell C, 1953, Ag 3,17:4
Gilbert, Newton W (por), 1939, Jl 6,23:1
Gilbert, Norman, 1961, Mr 23,33:4
Gilbert, Norman Mrs, 1950, F 17,23:4
Gilbert, Paul J, 1950, Mr 9,30:2
Gilbert, Paul N, 1960, Je 1,39:5
Gilbert, Paul T, 1953, Ag 8,11:3
Gilbert, Prentiss B, 1939, F 26,39:1
Gilbert, Ralph, 1939, Jl 31,13:4
Gilbert, Rene, 1914, S 26,11:7
Gilbert, Richard L Mrs, 1954, Jl 9,17:3
Gilbert, Rodney, 1968, Ja 12,34:3
Gilbert, Roland L, 1951, S 22,17:6
Gilbert, Ross K, 1939, Ag 18,19:4
Gilbert, Roy L, 1961, Ap 5,43:1
Gilbert, S C Capt, 1903, O 5,7:6
Gilbert, S Parker, 1938, F 24,1:3
Gilbert, S Price, 1951, Ag 29,25:2
Gilbert, Samuel, 1963, S 20,33:4
Gilbert, Samuel L, 1967, My 22,43:2
Gilbert, Samuel T, 1947, Mr 5,25:3
Gilbert, Sarah E, 1916, Jl 7,11:7
Gilbert, Seymour L, 1958, Je 2,27:5
Gilbert, Seymour P Mrs, 1937, N 16,23:2
Gilbert, Simeon, 1944, Je 28,23:6
Gilbert, Stanley A, 1967, Jl 11,37:2
Gilbert, Stanley E, 1950, Mr 18,14:2
Gilbert, Stanley E Mrs, 1941, F 22,15:2
Gilbert, Stephen F, 1874, Je 15,4:7
Gilbert, T Garwood, 1963, Jl 14,61:1
Gilbert, Thomas B, 1947, Ap 13,60:2
Gilbert, Thomas F Mrs, 1967, My 28,60:8
Gilbert, Tookie (Harold J Gilbert), 1967, Je 25,6
Gilbert, Truman S, 1906, Mr 7,9:4
Gilbert, Victor B Dr, 1937, S 17,25:5
Gilbert, W I, 1940, N 29,21:5
Gilbert, Walter, 1947, Ja 13,21:1
Gilbert, Walter C, 1937, My 30,19:1; 1939, F 17,1
Gilbert, Walter J, 1949, S 12,21:5; 1950, Je 17,15:
Gilbert, William, 1903, F 26,9:6; 1964, Ap 4,27:1
Gilbert, William A, 1940, My 30,17:2
Gilbert, William A Mrs, 1951, N 13,29:1
Gilbert, William E, 1954, D 9,33:3
Gilbert, William E Mrs, 1952, N 22,23:3
Gilbert, William G, 1952, Ag 12,19:3
Gilbert, William J, 1925, Ja 31,13:6; 1925, F 3,13:
Gilbert, William M Mrs, 1953, Jl 30,23:6
Gilbert, William Morris Rev Dr, 1924, D 31,13:5
Gilbert, William S Sir, 1911, My 30,11:3
Gilbert, William T, 1908, Jl 3,7:4
Gilbert, William W, 1953, S 16,33:1
Gilbert, William Wallace, 1925, Ap 21,21:5
Gilbert, Wright L, 1937, Ap 7,25:3
Gilberti, Frank, 1946, Ja 9,23:3
Gilbertie, Salvatore J, 1959, F 11,39:2
Gilbertson, Frank J Jr, 1938, Jl 5,17:4
Gilbertson, George H, 1950, Ap 24,25:5
Gilbertson, J Stewart, 1952, S 14,86:5
Gilbey, Arthur S, 1964, My 29,29:1
Gilbey, Walter (por), 1945, Ap 12,23:2
Gilbey, Walter Sir, 1914, N 13,11:6
Gilbey, William G Mrs (Baroness Vaux of Harrowden), 1958, My 13,3:6
Gilbreath, James R, 1965, Jl 10,25:5
Gilbreth, Frank B Maj, 1924, Je 15,23:1
Gilbride, Francis J, 1957, Ag 23,19:3
Gilbride, Francis J Jr, 1967, O 25,47:2
Gilbride, John J, 1952, Je 14,15:3; 1961, Je 12,29
Gilbride, Mary, 1951, Ja 9,29:1
Gilby, George T, 1951, D 16,91:2
Gilchrest, James D, 1947, N 13,27:4
Gilchrest, John T, 1950, Je 28,27:1
Gilchrest, William Forrest, 1922, N 14,19:4
Gilchrist, Alex Jr, 1948, F 3,25:4
Gilchrist, Alexander Rev Dr, 1907, Ja 28,7:4
Gilchrist, Charles A Brig-Gen, 1906, Ja 24,9:6
Gilchrist, Daniel T, 1950, O 17,31:4

Gilchrist, Donald B, 1939, Ag 5,15:4
Gilchrist, Donald C Mrs, 1956, Je 1,23:1
Gilchrist, Edward L, 1954, Ap 2,27:2
Gilchrist, Elizabeth, 1914, Ap 11,11:6
Gilchrist, Frank H, 1939, Ja 18,19:1
Gilchrist, Fred C, 1950, Mr 11,15:4
Gilchrist, Harry L, 1943, D 28,17:3
Gilchrist, James D, 1903, My 24,7:4
Gilchrist, John A, 1957, N 1,23:6
Gilchrist, John F (por), 1940, Ap 12,23:1
Gilchrist, John F, 1945, Ag 5,37:2
Gilchrist, John M, 1944, N 28,23:4
Gilchrist, John W Mrs, 1950, Mr 24,25:1
Gilchrist, Peter S, 1948, Ja 1,23:1
Gilchrist, Robert M, 1917, Ap 6,13:6
Gilchrist, Thomas B, 1962, Ja 25,31:4
Gilchrist, Thomas B Mrs, 1956, Ja 7,17:2
Gilcrease, Thomas A, 1962, My 7,31:2
Gilcrist, Charles B, 1948, My 12,28:2
Gildart, Emerson D, 1949, Jl 6,27:4
Gilday, John J, 1947, D 24,21:4
Gildea, Charles A, 1944, N 23,31:2
Gildea, Charles A Jr, 1968, N 24,87:2
Gildea, Charles A Mrs, 1964, Je 25,33:2
Gildea, James E, 1946, N 20,31:5
Gildea, James L, 1951, O 19,27:5
Gildea, Mary, 1957, F 20,33:4
Gildea, Patrick, 1951, Jl 2,23:5
Gildea, William A, 1942, Mr 12,19:5
Gildemeester, Peter J, 1943, D 5,66:8
Gildemeester, Peter J Mrs, 1943, Je 23,21:3
Gildemeister, F A, 1955, Ap 19,31:3
Gildemeister, Juan, 1957, S 15,84:7
Gilder, Harry M, 1940, Ja 29,15:1
Gilder, Harwood Mrs, 1946, F 4,25:2
Gilder, J B, 1936, D 10,27:4
Gilder, Jeannette Leonard, 1916, Ja 18,11:3
Gilder, John Francis, 1908, D 3,9:4
Gilder, Richard W, 1909, N 21,13:3; 1910, F 10,7:4
Gilder, Richard Watson Mrs, 1916, My 29,11:6
Gilder, Robert F, 1940, Mr 9,15:2
Gilder, Rodman, 1953, O 1,29:4
Gilder, William Howard (funl), 1913, Je 24,11:5
Gildersleeve, Algar C, 1952, My 5,23:5
Gildersleeve, Alger C Mrs, 1954, Jl 30,17:2
Gildersleeve, Basil Lanneau Dr, 1924, Ja 10,21:5
Gildersleeve, Charles, 1952, F 8,23:2
Gildersleeve, Charles C, 1947, N 3,23:4
Gildersleeve, Charles Edward, 1911, N 5,II,15:5
Gildersleeve, Charles Mrs, 1944, Je 1,19:1
Gildersleeve, Elmer Mrs, 1937, Ap 16,23:1
Gildersleeve, G L, 1879, Mr 12,8:1
Gildersleeve, Gordon H, 1946, F 20,25:3
Gildersleeve, Henry, 1944, Ja 16,43:2
Gildersleeve, Henry Alger, 1923, F 28,17:3
Gildersleeve, Henry Mrs, 1944, Ja 16,43:2
Gildersleeve, John S, 1952, Mr 25,27:1
Gildersleeve, Joseph A, 1960, S 3,17:5
Gildersleeve, Nelson B, 1954, My 13,29:5
Gildersleeve, Oliver, 1912, Jl 28,II,11:6
Gildersleeve, Virginia C, 1965, Jl 9,1:4
Gildersleeve, Virginia C Mrs, 1923, Ag 26,26:4
Gildersleeve, Warren M, 1948, Mr 17,25:1
Gildersleeve, Willetta C Mrs, 1938, Ap 3,II,6:5
Gildersleeve, William, 1950, S 4,17:6
Gildes, Antony, 1941, O 9,23:4
Gildner, Edwin R, 1946, My 2,21:2
Gildroy, Clarence L, 1963, Ag 16,27:3
Gile, Archie B, 1954, S 27,21:5
Gile, Ben C, 1940, My 20,17:4
Gile, John F, 1955, Ja 30,84:6
Gile, John Martin Dr (funl, Jl 19,7:4), 1925, Jl 16, 19:5
Giles, Cecil D, 1939, O 9,19:6
Giles, Charles, 1948, Mr 13,15:1
Giles, Claude W, 1955, Ag 1,19:6
Giles, Dennia A Mrs, 1960, F 26,27:2
Giles, Dennis A, 1962, S 7,30:1
Giles, Dorothy, 1960, D 31,17:5
Giles, Edson R, 1952, Ja 18,27:2
Giles, Edwin M, 1946, S 18,31:3
Giles, Elmer E, 1962, D 1,25:5
Giles, Frank D, 1954, Je 23,26:8
Giles, Frank W Mrs, 1958, N 29,21:4
Giles, H Rev, 1882, Jl 11,2:4
Giles, Hattie M Mrs, 1948, Ja 15,23:1
Giles, Henry S, 1952, Ag 14,23:2
Giles, Howard, 1955, F 1,29:4
Giles, Howard E, 1955, N 1,31:2
Giles, Hugh, 1963, D 8,86:7
Giles, Isabelle Mrs, 1959, F 23,23:4
Giles, J A Rev, 1884, S 26,5:5
Giles, J E, 1880, N 7,2:6; 1928, D 25,23:2
Giles, J H, 1952, N 20,31:3
Giles, J S, 1881, O 29,5:2
Giles, James F, 1941, Mr 15,17:6
Giles, John J Mrs, 1948, Ja 3,13:3
Giles, John W Mrs, 1966, Mr 20,86:4
Giles, Julia R H Mrs (J Hoyt),(will, N 26,12;5), 1955, N 1,31:2
Giles, Katherine Mrs, 1941, Je 29,33:1
Giles, Leon M, 1949, F 13,76:2
Giles, Leroy N, 1946, Ap 28,44:7
Giles, Lucy M, 1950, Ag 23,29:2
Giles, Malcolm R, 1953, O 1,29:6
Giles, Morgan W Mrs, 1956, Ap 9,27:1
Giles, Ray Mrs, 1948, Jl 17,16:2
Giles, Reginald H, 1957, Je 14,25:2
Giles, Reginald H Mrs, 1943, F 4,23:5
Giles, Robert J, 1937, Ja 2,14:3
Giles, Robert Mrs, 1947, Ap 6,60:2
Giles, Roy A, 1942, Ja 1,25:2
Giles, W F, 1879, Mr 23,2:5
Giles, W S, 1939, Ag 16,23:5
Giles, W Warren, 1941, My 11,44:6
Giles, Walter C, 1956, Je 10,88:4
Giles, Warren C Mrs, 1943, Jl 11,35:1
Giles, William H, 1954, Je 5,34:5
Giles, William Ogden, 1907, My 1,9:6
Gilfeather, Michael Mrs, 1943, F 22,17:2
Gilffillan, C Agnes, 1943, D 15,27:4
Gilfilian, G, 1879, F 6,8:1
Gilfillan, Alex B, 1953, Ap 17,26:4
Gilfillan, J Gordon, 1945, Ja 6,11:3
Gilfillan, J Gordon Mrs, 1944, Ap 27,23:4
Gilfillan, Joseph (will, N 11,70:5), 1951, O 27,19:4
Gilfillan, Sennet W, 1961, Mr 6,25:4
Gilfillan, Sherman L, 1939, O 2,17:6
Gilfillan, W Whitehead, 1944, F 12,13:6
Gilfillan, William A, 1945, N 12,22:2
Gilfillas, Joseph A Rev, 1913, N 20,11:4
Gilfoil, Harry, 1918, Ag 11,17:3
Gilford, John P Mrs, 1943, Je 27,32:4
Gilford, Samuel T Mrs, 1950, Mr 30,29:4
Gilfort, Robert Charles, 1914, O 28,13:5
Gilfry, Henry H, 1925, F 9,17:3
Gilg, Alfred J, 1951, O 12,27:1
Gilg, Frank X, 1958, Ja 28,27:4
Gilg, Frank X Mrs, 1958, Ja 28,27:4
Gilgan, Edward A, 1944, O 24,23:6
Gilgannon, William T, 1966, Ag 19,33:5
Gilgar, Edward P Col, 1912, My 31,15:6
Gilgar, Paul A, 1943, Ag 18,19:1
Gilgoff, Max, 1952, Ag 15,15:3
Gilham, Fanny L Mrs, 1942, My 9,13:6
Gilham, George, 1937, Ap 26,19:5
Gilham, George L, 1943, My 3,17:4
Gilhams, Hugh S, 1956, Mr 14,33:5
Gilhooley, Frank P Sr (Flash), 1959, Jl 13,27:3
Gilhooley, James J, 1940, S 20,23:3
Gilhooly, Andrew, 1912, Ja 27,11:5
Gilhooly, Edward J, 1962, Mr 4,86:8
Gilhooly, James Peter, 1916, O 17,13:6
Gilhooly, John J, 1942, Ag 23,43:4
Gilhooly, Thomas A, 1940, Mr 24,30:8
Gilhuly, Edward H, 1961, F 12,86:4
Gilhuly, Holmes R, 1953, Jl 19,57:1
Gilhuly, Stephen, 1952, Mr 6,31:4
Gilien, Ted, 1967, Mr 14,47:4
Gilinsky, Solomon, 1961, S 6,31:3
Gilkey, Arthur K, 1953, Ag 27,1:4
Gilkey, Charles W Mrs, 1955, N 13,89:2
Gilkey, James G, 1964, Jl 16,31:3
Gilkison, Frank E, 1955, F 26,15:4
Gilks, Robert J, 1944, Ag 22,17:5
Gilks, W Roy Mrs, 1953, Je 29,21:5
Gilkyson, Joseph R, 1913, Je 19,11:6
Gill, Alexander C, 1943, Ap 8,25:8
Gill, Andre, 1885, My 3,2:2
Gill, Arthur E, 1939, Ja 9,15:5
Gill, August E, 1967, O 16,45:2
Gill, Benjamin Prof, 1912, F 12,11:5
Gill, Charles A, 1943, F 18,23:1; 1946, My 16,21:4; 1947, F 26,25:2
Gill, Charles C (por), 1948, Ja 14,25:6
Gill, Charles E Mrs, 1945, Ag 2,19:5
Gill, Charles H, 1938, Mr 2,19:4
Gill, Charles O, 1959, Je 3,35:5
Gill, Colin U, 1940, N 27,23:3
Gill, Corrington C, 1946, Jl 14,37:1
Gill, David Sir, 1914, Ja 25,IV,5:5
Gill, Dennis, 1946, Jl 12,17:5
Gill, Dorothy D Mrs, 1953, O 6,59:1
Gill, Edward H, 1941, F 26,21:2
Gill, Elbyrne G, 1966, O 2,86:4
Gill, Eric, 1940, N 19,24:2
Gill, Ernest, 1909, Ap 4,13:4
Gill, Eugene E, 1948, Mr 12,23:5
Gill, Everett Jr, 1954, Ap 26,25:2
Gill, Fletcher L, 1953, Ap 27,23:3
Gill, Fletcher L Mrs, 1948, N 22,21:5
Gill, Francis L Mrs, 1945, Ag 20,19:4
Gill, Frank, 1950, O 28,17:5
Gill, Frank M, 1942, My 9,13:6
Gill, G W, 1882, Ap 14,4:3
Gill, George, 1950, F 9,29:2
Gill, George C, 1955, F 17,27:4
Gill, George H Mrs, 1957, Ja 6,89:2
Gill, George M Sr Mrs, 1952, Ap 10,29:4
Gill, George T, 1960, My 25,39:2
Gill, Hamilton A Sr, 1944, My 3,19:3
Gill, Harry L, 1956, S 2,56:4
Gill, Harry R, 1942, N 26,28:3
Gill, Harvey M, 1951, Jl 7,13:4
Gill, Irving L, 1946, O 21,31:6
Gill, Isaac Mrs, 1949, Ap 23,13:3
Gill, J Goodner, 1959, O 17,23:3
Gill, Jack, 1945, D 29,13:4
Gill, James, 1945, D 5,25:4; 1955, My 31,27:4
Gill, James A, 1942, Ja 25,31:2
Gill, James B, 1951, Ag 3,21:6
Gill, James D, 1937, My 23,II,10:7
Gill, James J, 1949, Ja 31,19:3
Gill, James P, 1961, N 1,43:7
Gill, James P Jr, 1957, Je 1,17:6
Gill, Joe H (por), 1944, Je 17,13:5
Gill, John E Jr, 1944, F 10,15:4
Gill, John F, 1966, D 16,47:4
Gill, John G, 1967, Jl 26,39:4
Gill, John G Jr Mrs, 1941, Mr 20,21:5
Gill, John G Mrs, 1947, Ag 18,17:5
Gill, John Gen, 1912, Jl 3,11:6
Gill, John H, 1951, N 1,29:5
Gill, John J, 1956, N 9,29:4; 1963, D 31,19:2
Gill, John L, 1937, Ag 3,23:4
Gill, John L Mrs, 1937, Ag 3,23:4
Gill, John M, 1952, Ja 15,27:5
Gill, John M Rev Dr, 1937, D 14,25:3
Gill, John T, 1956, Jl 9,23:6
Gill, Joseph B, 1942, S 24,27:5
Gill, Kermore F, 1951, Jl 14,13:4
Gill, Leslie, 1958, Mr 19,31:4
Gill, Martha R Mrs, 1955, My 3,27:1
Gill, Martin, 1948, S 13,21:2
Gill, Martin L Jr, 1959, Je 21,93:1
Gill, Mary E, 1954, Ja 15,20:3
Gill, Mathew Jr, 1909, Jl 20,7:4
Gill, Michael J, 1945, F 8,19:3
Gill, Milton Prof, 1968, O 27,82:1
Gill, Patrick F, 1923, My 22,19:5
Gill, Patrick J, 1948, O 11,23:3
Gill, Paul L, 1938, Je 1,23:4
Gill, Robert O, 1950, S 24,V,3:5
Gill, Robert S, 1943, D 31,16:6
Gill, Roy, 1967, O 15,85:1
Gill, Sarah E Mrs, 1937, N 30,23:4
Gill, Ted G, 1951, Mr 6,27:5
Gill, Thomas P, 1959, Mr 5,31:1
Gill, thos A, 1947, Mr 10,21:4
Gill, W H Noell, 1940, Ag 7,19:3
Gill, W T, 1941, Ja 29,17:1
Gill, Walter A (funl), 1960, N 5,9:1
Gill, Walter H, 1953, Ag 1,11:6
Gill, Walter J, 1940, Ap 4,23:4
Gill, Walter N, 1941, My 28,25:3
Gill, William, 1943, Ja 22,19:4
Gill, William A, 1957, F 12,27:4
Gill, William A Rear-Adm, 1918, O 11,11:3
Gill, William D (see also Ja 2), 1904, Ja 3,9:5
Gill, William F, 1904, Mr 18,9:2; 1947, Je 25,25:4
Gill, William J, 1938, Mr 18,19:1
Gill, William M, 1940, O 15,23:5
Gill, William S, 1965, Je 5,31:5
Gill, Wilson L, 1941, S 14,51:5
Gill, Wilson L Mrs, 1956, D 12,39:5
Gilladette, Harry L, 1956, O 1,27:6
Gillam, Burns, 1954, Je 10,31:5
Gillam, Jonathan, 1924, Je 23,19:6
Gillam, Manly M, 1925, Mr 24,23:3
Gillam, Russell E, 1943, Ap 4,41:2
Gillan, John M, 1945, Ag 9,21:5
Gillan, Margaret (Mrs E Koppel), 1958, D 4,39:5
Gillan, Thomas J Rev, 1937, Ap 9,21:3
Gilland, Nell F Mrs, 1942, N 4,23:5
Gillander, John G, 1946, My 16,21:3
Gillar, Frederick C, 1948, N 13,15:6
Gillard, Edward F, 1960, Mr 14,29:2
Gillard, Robert A, 1953, D 28,22:3
Gillaudeu, William L, 1907, Mr 23,9:5
Gillaume, Eugene, 1905, Mr 1,2:2
Gille, F C Gustave, 1959, Mr 4,31:1
Gille, Henry C, 1948, S 7,26:2
Gilleaudeau, Joseph R, 1950, F 7,27:3
Gilleaudeau, Raymond, 1958, O 14,37:2
Gillece, Joseph F, 1952, F 6,29:5
Gillem, A C Gen, 1875, D 5,2:7
Gillem, Jennings F, 1951, N 12,25:3
Gillen, Alice, 1937, Ja 8,20:2
Gillen, Andrew M (por), 1939, Ag 17,21:4
Gillen, Arthur J, 1943, Ag 26,17:6
Gillen, Charles P, 1956, Jl 1,56:8
Gillen, Dolores (por), 1947, D 10,31:1
Gillen, George M, 1953, Ja 9,21:4
Gillen, Harold W, 1959, D 11,34:5
Gillen, Henry F, 1958, N 17,31:4
Gillen, John J, 1941, N 14,23:4
Gillen, John V (move details, S 10,56:3), 1967, S 9, 17:5
Gillen, Lester J, 1937, Ap 28,23:5
Gillen, Luke Mrs, 1950, Ja 17,27:2
Gillen, Madeline, 1911, Ag 14,7:5
Gillen, Margaret J Mrs, 1944, Ja 24,17:3
Gillen, Martin J, 1943, S 23,21:6
Gillen, Michael J, 1942, F 2,15:5
Gillen, Michael J Mrs, 1963, S 15,86:2
Gillen, Silas L, 1954, N 10,33:3
Gillen, Thomas F, 1941, F 19,21:3
Gillen, Thomas J, 1958, My 18,87:1
Gillen, William J, 1942, Ap 13,15:4

Gilleran, Bernard, 1959, Ag 23,92:5
Gilleran, Edward P, 1967, Mr 29,45:2
Gilles, Albert, 1956, F 14,29:3
Gilles, Clara V, 1955, F 5,15:1
Gilles, Fernando, 1920, My 26,11:4
Gilles, Jean, 1961, Ag 12,17:3
Gillespie, Abraham L, 1950, S 11,23:3
Gillespie, Alex J, 1952, Ja 23,27:5
Gillespie, Anthony, 1924, N 17,19:5
Gillespie, Arthur, 1914, My 12,11:5
Gillespie, Arthur S, 1952, D 29,19:3
Gillespie, Bernard A, 1949, S 14,31:5
Gillespie, Bernarde B, 1939, D 31,18:8
Gillespie, Bindley M, 1966, Je 21,43:2
Gillespie, Charles, 1955, Ap 12,18:4
Gillespie, Darl D, 1950, F 4,15:2
Gillespie, David H M, 1959, Mr 1,87:1
Gillespie, David J, 1952, N 6,29:2
Gillespie, Dean M, 1949, F 3,24:2
Gillespie, E Curtis, 1958, Ja 9,36:3
Gillespie, Edward N, 1947, My 7,27:3
Gillespie, Frances, 1948, N 30,27:4
Gillespie, Francis C, 1937, F 10,23:1
Gillespie, Franklin S, 1940, Jl 30,19:3
Gillespie, G De H, 1884, Ja 25,2:5
Gillespie, George C, 1942, Ap 9,19:1
Gillespie, George D Bp, 1909, Mr 20,9:4
Gillespie, George J Jr, 1967, Ap 10,35:2
Gillespie, George J Sr, 1953, F 18,31:1
Gillespie, George L Maj-Gen, 1921, Ag 27,9:5
Gillespie, George Lewis Maj-Gen, 1913, S 28,7:6
Gillespie, Georgiana B, 1951, Mr 16,31:1
Gillespie, H P, 1903, Ap 21,9:5
Gillespie, Hamilton D, 1951, Ap 21,17:4
Gillespie, Henry L Mrs (C MacDonald), 1962, Jl 27, 25:4
Gillespie, Herbert B Mrs, 1958, Je 1,87:1
Gillespie, Howard L, 1958, F 23,92:4
Gillespie, Isabelle C Mrs, 1942, Ag 23,42:2
Gillespie, J Hamilton Col, 1923, S 8,13:5
Gillespie, J Stuart, 1964, D 29,27:2
Gillespie, J Stuart Mrs, 1954, D 2,31:5
Gillespie, J W, 1881, O 11,4:7
Gillespie, James Capt, 1910, Ap 14,11:4
Gillespie, James E, 1961, D 23,23:3
Gillespie, James J, 1940, My 3,21:5
Gillespie, James Mrs, 1959, N 21,23:1
Gillespie, James P, 1956, Ag 4,15:7
Gillespie, James W, 1954, Ap 28,31:3
Gillespie, Joan, 1959, O 16,31:2
Gillespie, John, 1942, N 28,13:2
Gillespie, John (por), 1948, Ap 11,72:3
Gillespie, John A Mrs, 1958, My 19,25:2
Gillespie, John J, 1963, S 7,19:5
Gillespie, John M, 1946, Ja 19,13:5
Gillespie, John M Mrs, 1938, O 26,23:5
Gillespie, John S Mrs, 1944, Ap 22,15:5
Gillespie, John T Sr, 1960, My 22,86:4
Gillespie, Julian, 1939, Je 24,17:4
Gillespie, Lawrence L (will, Mr 8,23:7), 1940, F 8, 23:1
Gillespie, Louis, 1956, D 2,86:1
Gillespie, Louis H, 1956, Ja 21,21:6
Gillespie, Louis J, 1941, Ja 26,36:1
Gillespie, Louis Packard, 1905, Ap 1,11:5
Gillespie, Marian E, 1946, D 27,20:3
Gillespie, Michael J, 1950, O 21,17:4
Gillespie, Myra B Mrs, 1959, Ap 5,86:8
Gillespie, Patrick J, 1920, N 6,13:2
Gillespie, Richard H, 1941, Ja 16,21:4; 1952, My 23, 21:5; 1957, Mr 2,21:6
Gillespie, Richard H Mrs, 1948, Mr 16,27:4
Gillespie, Robert D, 1945, N 11,41:1
Gillespie, Robert McM Mrs (funl, Ag 25,11:4), 1915, Ag 24,11:5
Gillespie, Samuel H, 1957, D 2,27:4
Gillespie, Schuyler W (por), 1942, Ja 4,49:1
Gillespie, Thaddeus, 1955, Ap 23,19:4
Gillespie, Thomas A 2d, 1924, Jl 12,9:7
Gillespie, W Fulton, 1949, D 4,108:5
Gillespie, Walter H, 1941, D 2,23:4
Gillespie, William, 1947, S 14,60:4
Gillespie, William E, 1967, N 7,39:5
Gillespie, William F, 1952, Mr 18,27:3
Gillespie, William H, 1951, S 12,31:4; 1961, Ap 24,29:1
Gillespie, William J, 1944, Ag 22,17:1
Gillespie, William L, 1949, Ag 19,17:3
Gillespie, William P 3d, 1963, D 25,33:2
Gillespie, William R Mrs, 1949, Ja 27,23:2
Gillespie, William W, 1907, D 31,7:5
Gillespy, Howard, 1938, F 9,19:5
Gillespy, Robert R, 1948, F 18,27:3
Gillet, Charles William, 1909, Ja 1,11:4
Gillet, Joseph, 1904, Jl 22,7:2
Gillet, Joseph E, 1958, Je 6,24:1
Gillet, Lorenzo Minor, 1920, S 13,15:3
Gillet, Louis, 1943, Jl 2,19:4
Gillet, Louis B, 1941, Ap 26,15:5
Gillet, Paul, 1949, N 22,29:1
Gillet, Stanislas M, 1951, S 5,31:1
Gillet, Sully, 1912, Ap 5,13:5
Gillett, Arthur L, 1938, S 10,17:3
Gillett, Arthur L Mrs, 1951, Jl 30,17:6
Gillett, Burt W, 1944, Ap 13,19:2
Gillett, Charles R, 1948, S 5,40:5
Gillett, Clarence S, 1961, Je 20,33:4
Gillett, Darwin L, 1937, Mr 4,23:5
Gillett, E H Rev Dr, 1875, S 3,4:6
Gillett, E Kendall, 1966, Je 25,31:3
Gillett, F H, 1935, Jl 31,17:1
Gillett, Frederick W, 1958, S 6,17:6
Gillett, G W, 1878, O 24,2:5
Gillett, George Sir, 1939, Ag 11,15:2
Gillett, George W, 1937, Ap 21,23:2
Gillett, Henry W, 1943, Mr 13,13:4
Gillett, Horace W, 1950, Mr 5,93:1
Gillett, Howard F, 1943, O 23,13:5
Gillett, J B, 1937, Je 14,23:2
Gillett, James N, 1937, Ap 21,23:3
Gillett, Melville, 1943, Mr 21,26:8
Gillett, Philip L, 1938, N 29,23:4
Gillett, R H, 1876, O 26,4:7
Gillett, Ransom H, 1941, Ja 17,17:3
Gillett, Wilbur Dr, 1908, Ap 3,9:6
Gillett, William Kendall Prof, 1914, S 29,11:5
Gillett, William Maj, 1925, D 6,13:1
Gillette, A D Rev, 1882, Ag 25,5:3
Gillette, Alfred M, 1947, Je 15,62:5
Gillette, Annie Mrs, 1906, Ap 6,11:5
Gillette, C Rev, 1869, Mr 7,5:2
Gillette, Cassius G, 1917, Mr 19,11:4
Gillette, Claude, 1959, S 28,31:5
Gillette, Claude W, 1955, D 23,17:1
Gillette, David F, 1963, S 20,33:3
Gillette, DuBois J, 1965, Ag 21,21:4
Gillette, Elizabeth Van R, 1965, Je 28,29:2
Gillette, George A, 1941, My 4,52:3
Gillette, George H, 1941, F 23,41:2
Gillette, Guy M Mrs, 1956, Ja 4,27:4
Gillette, Halbert P, 1958, Je 21,19:6
Gillette, Harold W, 1954, Je 30,27:4
Gillette, Howard F Mrs, 1942, N 19,25:2
Gillette, Ira P, 1944, Mr 4,13:2
Gillette, J Lt-Col, 1881, N 25,5:2
Gillette, John M, 1949, S 27,27:4
Gillette, John R, 1940, Jl 17,21:3
Gillette, Justin W, 1952, D 10,35:1
Gillette, K C, 1932, Jl 11,13:1
Gillette, Kenelm A Mrs, 1965, Ap 24,29:2
Gillette, King G, 1955, Je 19,93:2
Gillette, Leon M Mrs, 1949, O 25,27:2
Gillette, Leon N, 1945, My 4,20:2
Gillette, Melvin E (por), 1947, S 12,21:3
Gillette, R Sumner, 1944, S 11,17:3
Gillette, Ralph, 1953, Ja 22,23:2
Gillette, Viola P Mrs, 1956, Ap 3,35:2
Gillette, Wallace C, 1960, O 24,29:3
Gillette, Wallace Mrs, 1950, Ja 31,23:3
Gillette, Walter Dr, 1908, N 8,11:6
Gillette, William, 1937, Ap 30,21:1
Gillette, William B, 1937, Ag 3,23:6
Gillette, Willis K, 1946, O 23,27:3
Gillette, Wilson D, 1951, Ag 8,25:1
Gilley, Charles R, 1939, My 19,21:4
Gilley, Franklin William, 1909, Jl 26,7:6
Gilley, W Herbert, 1940, Ja 7,48:5
Gilley, William F, 1874, Jl 10,4:6
Gillham, Robert Mrs (Eliz Enright), 1968, Je 10,45:4
Gillhouse, John C, 1954, S 23,33:2
Gilliam, Don, 1960, Mr 7,29:1
Gilliam, Theodore, 1954, N 3,29:3
Gilliam, Thomas H Mrs, 1947, My 27,25:2
Gilliam, William S, 1946, Ap 10,27:2
Gilliard, E Thomas, 1965, Ja 28,29:3
Gilliat, Charles G Rev Dr, 1910, Ag 29,7:5
Gilliatt, William, 1956, S 28,3:2
Gillice, Jane (Sister M Benigna), 1959, My 5,33:4
Gillich, Stephen Mrs, 1955, My 11,31:2
Gillick, Howard T Mrs, 1954, Ag 10,19:1
Gillick, James T, 1956, D 31,13:1
Gillick, John F, 1945, My 15,19:2
Gillie, Daniel R, 1937, S 9,23:1
Gillie, George B, 1964, Ap 21,37:2
Gillie, George W, 1963, Jl 5,16:8
Gillie, Jean, 1949, F 22,23:4
Gillie, Robert B, 1958, My 14,33:4
Gillies, Alex, 1940, Ja 21,35:1
Gillies, Andrew, 1942, Ap 5,42:3
Gillies, Donald B, 1956, S 30,86:7
Gillies, Edwin J, 1922, O 19,21:5
Gillies, Frank E, 1943, S 15,27:2
Gillies, George C, 1957, Ap 17,31:3
Gillies, Harold D, 1960, S 12,29:4
Gillies, Hugh A, 1940, Ap 25,23:4
Gillies, James A, 1938, My 21,15:3; 1961, S 20,29:5
Gillies, John C, 1949, F 7,19:4
Gillies, John J, 1947, Ag 29,17:2
Gillies, John W, 1942, Ap 1,21:4
Gillies, Martha B, 1951, Ag 19,85:1
Gillies, W King, 1952, N 17,25:4
Gillies, Walter M, 1951, S 26,31:2
Gillies, William R, 1965, O 13,47:2
Gillig, George J, 1958, Ag 30,15:6
Gillig, Henry F, 1917, Ag 31,7:4
Gillig, John, 1882, Mr 6,5:2
Gillig, John G, 1925, Mr 9,17:4
Gillig, Otto, 1948, S 8,29:3
Gilligan, Arthur C, 1943, O 26,23:3
Gilligan, Catherine Mrs, 1907, Ag 2,7:4
Gilligan, Edward A, 1940, D 29,24:7
Gilligan, Eugene F, 1968, Ap 20,33:1
Gilligan, Francis C, 1942, F 6,19:4
Gilligan, James J, 1939, My 18,25:5
Gilligan, James P, 1945, N 28,27:2
Gilligan, James R, 1959, Ja 19,27:4
Gilligan, John A, 1948, S 12,74:4
Gilligan, John A Mrs, 1951, Mr 30,23:1
Gilligan, John J, 1950, O 18,33:3
Gilligan, Michael A, 1943, Je 4,21:3
Gilligan, Paul A, 1954, My 6,33:2
Gilligian, Edward V, 1943, Mr 19,19:1
Gillilan, Lewis W (por), 1942, Ap 21,23:5
Gillilan, Strickland, 1954, Ap 26,25:3
Gilliland, A Raymond, 1952, D 1,23:4
Gilliland, C Ray, 1957, Ja 31,27:2
Gilliland, Ezra T, 1903, My 14,9:2
Gilliland, Frederick H, 1940, S 8,49:1
Gillin, Charles P Rev, 1915, My 28,13:6
Gillin, Edward C Jr, 1967, O 11,47:3
Gillin, John J Jr, 1950, Jl 20,25:4
Gillin, John L, 1958, D 9,41:5
Gillin, Robert F, 1909, Ja 20,9:4
Gillinder, Frederick R, 1939, F 10,23:2
Gillinder, James, 1948, S 23,29:4
Gillingham, Albert V, 1953, Ag 12,31:3
Gillingham, Anna (name spelling cor, Je 1,29:4), 1964, My 31,76:2
Gillingham, Arthur D, 1955, Ja 20,31:2
Gillingham, F C Mrs, 1909, Ag 31,7:5
Gillingham, Harrold E, 1954, Mr 28,88:4
Gillion, Thomas V, 1942, Ag 4,19:5
Gillis, Alexander J, 1943, F 7,48:3
Gillis, Andrew J (Bossy), 1965, N 5,37:1
Gillis, Andrew J Mrs, 1951, Ja 15,17:3
Gillis, Ann (Mrs W J Slocum), 1957, D 17,35:2
Gillis, Bosanquet Wesley, 1915, Ap 15,13:5
Gillis, Eugene J, 1944, My 2,19:3
Gillis, Floyd, 1944, Je 13,19:3
Gillis, Frank D, 1941, Ja 17,17:3
Gillis, Frank D Mrs, 1948, S 26,76:8
Gillis, Harry G, 1958, Ag 12,29:4
Gillis, James M, 1867, Ag 22,3:1
Gillis, James M (funl, Mr 19,37:5), 1957, Mr 15,
Gillis, Katherine E, 1951, N 21,25:3
Gillis, Lee J, 1949, F 4,23:2
Gillis, Linwood C, 1944, O 6,23:1
Gillis, Mack E, 1939, D 22,19:5
Gillis, Meyer, 1940, Ja 6,13:5
Gillis, Roderick A, 1950, My 20,15:5
Gillispie, Frank J, 1949, Mr 24,28:5
Gillispie, Raymond L, 1952, S 21,89:2
Gilliss, Walter, 1925, S 26,17:6
Gillman, Barbara B Mrs (por), 1940, Jl 24,21:4
Gillman, Fred J, 1949, F 20,60:3
Gillman, Jacob, 1962, Mr 21,39:4
Gillman, James E, 1961, Mr 15,39:5
Gillman, Joseph M Dr, 1968, Ap 3,52:1
Gillman, Thomas V Maj, 1953, F 28,17:5
Gillmore, Donald E, 1967, Ag 10,37:4
Gillmore, F E, 1945, Mr 18,42:5
Gillmore, Frank, 1943, Mr 30,21:1; 1943, Ap 1,2
Gillmore, Frank Mrs, 1959, O 22,37:6
Gillmore, Frederick C, 1938, F 12,15:3
Gillmore, Henry Mrs, 1965, Ja 14,35:1
Gillmore, Q A Gen, 1888, Ap 8,1:4
Gillmore, Quincy A, 1956, Ja 6,24:5
Gillmore, Quincy A Mrs, 1956, Mr 23,27:2
Gillmore, Quincy O Mrs, 1945, Ap 10,19:1
Gillmore, Quincy O'Maher Col, 1923, Jl 15,24:4
Gillmore, Reginald E, 1960, F 8,29:4
Gillmore, William E (por), 1948, N 8,21:3
Gillo, Henry C, 1948, S 8,29:2
Gillon, Benedict I, 1946, Jl 17,23:4
Gillon, George L Maj, 1937, Ag 11,24:1
Gillooly, John, 1968, My 18,34:8
Gillott, Samuel Sir, 1913, Je 30,7:4
Gillou, Pierre, 1953, Ja 4,76:7
Gillow, Joseph E, 1959, Ag 2,81:1
Gillpatrick, Wallace, 1925, Ag 31,15:5
Gillroy, James P, 1955, My 21,17:2
Gillroy, John H, 1956, Je 25,23:2
Gillson, Hugh V, 1944, F 19,14:8
Gillule, William J, 1965, N 21,86:3
Gilluly, George Kenneth, 1921, S 13,17:4
Gillum, Henry Col, 1907, Mr 26,9:6
Gilman, Ada, 1921, D 20,17:5
Gilman, Alfred A, 1966, S 15,43:1
Gilman, Arthur, 1909, D 29,9:5
Gilman, Benjamin, 1954, My 30,44:6
Gilman, Bessie A L Mrs, 1937, F 6,21:4
Gilman, C P Mrs, 1935, Ag 20,44:2
Gilman, Charles C, 1938, Jl 1,19:2
Gilman, Charles Sr, 1967, Je 21,47:2
Gilman, Charles W, 1941, Jl 29,15:5
Gilman, Daniel Colt (funl, O 17,9:5), 1908, O
Gilman, Edgar D, 1957, O 23,33:1
Gilman, Edward Robinson Maj, 1911, F 11,11:5
Gilman, Elisabeth, 1950, D 15,31:2
Gilman, Florence, 1947, Ag 2,13:5

Gilman, Frances P, 1938, Mr 27,II,7:4
Gilman, Francis D, 1947, O 25,19:5
Gilman, Fred, 1942, O 29,23:4
Gilman, G F, 1901, Mr 4,1:4
Gilman, George, 1881, O 6,5:3
Gilman, George T, 1948, S 19,76:6
Gilman, Gorham D, 1909, O 4,9:5
Gilman, Gregory, 1949, Ag 22,21:2
Gilman, Herman, 1961, Mr 29,33:1
Gilman, Isaac (por), 1944, Ag 29,17:4
Gilman, J Bruce, 1954, Ap 16,21:3
Gilman, Jay A, 1959, Je 1,27:2
Gilman, Jeremiah H Gen (funl, Jl 29,9:6), 1909, Ag 27,7:5
Gilman, John R, 1958, My 1,31:5
Gilman, Jules V Dr, 1968, F 19,39:2
Gilman, La Selle, 1964, F 29,21:5
Gilman, Laurence C, 1955, N 25,28:5
Gilman, Lawrence, 1939, S 10,49:1
Gilman, Lawrence Mrs, 1964, Jl 28,29:5
Gilman, Louis (por), 1944, Ag 6,37:4
Gilman, Luthene C, 1942, S 9,23:6
Gilman, Mabel I, 1943, Je 29,19:4
Gilman, Margaret, 1958, My 28,31:3
Gilman, Max M, 1965, Mr 3,41:2
Gilman, Miss (Sister Serena), 1871, Ja 11,2:5
Gilman, Phil K, 1948, S 8,30:3
Gilman, Roger, 1964, D 4,40:2
Gilman, Roger Mrs, 1952, Ja 6,92:5
Gilman, Samuel P (por), 1941, Mr 18,23:3
Gilman, Thomas P, 1937, D 18,21:5
Gilman, Virgil C, 1903, Ap 29,9:6
Gilman, W S, 1884, O 5,3:6
Gilman, Walter D, 1948, N 24,23:5
Gilman, Wesley A, 1953, D 7,2:3
Gilman, William C, 1963, My 1,39:1
Gilman, William R, 1946, Mr 20,23:4
Gilman, Zeeb, 1946, Je 8,21:4
Gilmant, Felix Alexandre, 1911, Mr 31,11:4
Gilmarten, Frank, 1951, D 22,15:4
Gilmartin, Daniel T Jr, 1952, Je 18,27:5
Gilmartin, David J, 1949, N 15,25:4
Gilmartin, Edward F, 1939, Jl 25,19:1
Gilmartin, Eugene R, 1961, Mr 5,87:1
Gilmartin, Hugh, 1964, O 7,47:3
Gilmartin, Irene, 1948, N 20,13:5
Gilmartin, James J Rev, 1918, O 25,13:5
Gilmartin, John R, 1958, Ap 13,83:6
Gilmartin, Joseph A, 1954, My 23,88:5
Gilmartin, Lant, 1947, S 1,19:4
Gilmartin, Maurice A, 1961, S 10,86:3
Gilmartin, Michael J, 1944, N 16,23:4
Gilmartin, Patrick J Rev, 1914, My 14,11:5
Gilmartin, Richard T, 1964, S 23,47:2
Gilmartin, Robert D, 1965, Ap 16,29:1
Gilmartin, Robert J, 1964, Ag 7,29:4
Gilmartin, Terence E Rev, 1937, Jl 3,15:2
Gilmartin, Thomas D, 1941, O 6,17:3
Gilmartin, William V, 1952, My 17,19:5
Gilmer, Albert H, 1950, Je 7,29:3
Gilmer, Charles G, 1952, N 25,29:2
Gilmer, G Walker Jr, 1959, S 9,41:2
Gilmer, George O Mrs (D Dix), 1951, D 17,31:1
Gilmer, John H, 1940, S 4,23:5
Gilmer, John T, 1954, D 29,23:3
Gilmer, Ludwell H, 1956, Mr 30,19:5
Gilmor, A H, 1903, Ap 15,9:6
Gilmor, Harry Col, 1883, Mr 5,5:5
Gilmor, Mary S, 1942, O 18,52:7
Gilmor, Robr Mrs, 1954, F 5,20:3
Gilmore, A D Pollock, 1948, My 16,68:5
Gilmore, Albert D, 1961, D 8,37:3
Gilmore, Albert D Mrs, 1953, D 14,31:3
Gilmore, Albert F, 1943, Je 9,21:4
Gilmore, Alex H, 1939, F 7,19:3
Gilmore, Alfred C, 1958, Ja 15,39:2
Gilmore, Alton F, 1960, Je 30,29:3
Gilmore, Arthur, 1952, Je 12,33:3
Gilmore, B Bernard, 1942, N 14,16:3
Gilmore, B R, 1957, N 13,35:2
Gilmore, Byron B, 1943, Ag 3,19:6
Gilmore, Charles J, 1946, Ag 26,23:6
Gilmore, Charles P, 1959, Ag 21,21:4
Gilmore, Charles W, 1945, S 29,15:4
Gilmore, Earl B, 1964, F 27,31:4
Gilmore, Eddy L K, 1967, O 7,30:3
Gilmore, Edward, 1949, Mr 30,25:4
Gilmore, Edward G, 1908, N 6,7:3
Gilmore, Edward V (funl, Ag 16,7:6), 1919, Ag 15, 11:5
Gilmore, Elizabeth Mrs, 1942, Ag 13,19:5
Gilmore, Ethel M Mrs, 1953, Ja 6,22:1
Gilmore, Eugene A, 1953, N 5,31:2
Gilmore, F P Adm, 1904, S 26,9:6
Gilmore, Frank, 1944, Mr 23,19:1
Gilmore, Frank G Mrs, 1947, N 24,23:3
Gilmore, Frank Mrs, 1939, My 28,III,7:1
Gilmore, Goodlatte B, 1952, N 20,31:5
Gilmore, Harry, 1942, S 11,21:2; 1966, Ag 25,37:2
Gilmore, Hazel D Mrs, 1949, Ap 16,15:6
Gilmore, Helen (por), 1947, O 9,25:4
Gilmore, J F Mrs, 1882, Je 14,3:5
Gilmore, J R, 1928, S 17,23:5
Gilmore, James, 1945, My 29,15:4
Gilmore, James A, 1947, Mr 20,28:2
Gilmore, James Mrs, 1952, Ap 9,31:4
Gilmore, John H, 1940, Jl 1,19:3
Gilmore, John W, 1942, Je 26,21:6
Gilmore, Joseph H, 1939, O 6,25:6
Gilmore, Joseph Henry Dr, 1918, Jl 24,11:4
Gilmore, Joseph L, 1948, Ap 9,24:2
Gilmore, Joseph M, 1962, Ap 3,39:2
Gilmore, Joseph V, 1942, Ag 28,19:5
Gilmore, Lyman, 1951, F 19,23:3
Gilmore, Mary Dame (Mrs Wm A), 1962, D 4,41:1
Gilmore, Maurice E, 1957, N 21,33:4
Gilmore, Melvin R, 1940, Jl 27,13:5
Gilmore, Morris D, 1960, O 3,31:1
Gilmore, Muriel, 1962, N 6,33:3
Gilmore, Nathaniel, 1958, F 6,27:1
Gilmore, P J, 1892, S 25,1:6
Gilmore, Park M Dr, 1937, My 14,23:1
Gilmore, Paul W, 1954, Mr 27,19:8
Gilmore, Robert A, 1951, Ja 27,13:4
Gilmore, Samuel Lewis, 1910, Jl 19,7:5
Gilmore, Thomas A, 1953, F 23,25:4
Gilmore, Thomas F, 1959, My 12,35:5
Gilmore, Thomas Mador, 1921, Je 6,13:7
Gilmore, Walter M, 1946, D 21,19:3
Gilmore, William Guy, 1921, N 1,19:6
Gilmore, William P Mrs, 1946, My 16,21:2
Gilmore, William W, 1958, Jl 11,23:4
Gilmour, Andrew, 1941, Mr 10,17:4; 1954, N 11,31:3
Gilmour, Arthur H, 1944, Ap 19,23:5
Gilmour, F Charles, 1954, My 20,31:3
Gilmour, Frederick C, 1950, N 3,27:4
Gilmour, George, 1916, Je 16,13:5
Gilmour, George P, 1963, Jl 14,61:2
Gilmour, Howard C, 1955, Je 13,23:7
Gilmour, James M, 1944, My 6,15:4
Gilmour, James Mrs, 1920, Je 12,13:3
Gilmour, John H, 1922, N 25,13:5
Gilmour, John L, 1938, Jl 13,21:4
Gilmour, John R, 1961, S 7,35:4
Gilmour, John T, 1957, D 24,15:2
Gilmour, Nancy, 1937, N 30,23:1
Gilmour, Robert Brig Gen Sir, 1939, Je 25,36:6
Gilmour, W Ellis, 1956, Ja 25,31:4
Gilmour, William R Mrs (M Roach), 1966, Ja 24, 35:6
Gilmour, William T, 1958, Ap 18,23:5
Gilner, Elias Mrs, 1968, Jl 18,33:3
Gilpatric, Walter H, 1955, O 7,25:5
Gilpatric, Walter J, 1941, Mr 15,17:2
Gilpatrick, Alonzo B, 1941, Ap 1,23:3
Gilpin, C Monteith, 1950, N 4,17:4
Gilpin, Charles, 1874, My 23,1:7; 1874, S 10,6:7
Gilpin, Clinton D, 1948, Ag 27,18:5
Gilpin, E W, 1876, Ap 30,7:1
Gilpin, Ferdinand L Jr, 1953, Je 26,19:3
Gilpin, Francis H, 1939, D 30,15:4
Gilpin, Harold P, 1956, My 25,23:4
Gilpin, Harry, 1950, Jl 25,27:2
Gilpin, Joe C, 1949, Mr 20,76:8
Gilpin, John, 1911, S 11,9:4
Gilpin, Kenneth N, 1947, Je 22,52:8
Gilpin, M Tyson Mrs, 1966, D 31,19:5
Gilpin, Mason C, 1958, N 24,29:2
Gilpin, Richard T Sir, 1882, Ap 25,4:7
Gilpin, Samuel B 2d, 1956, Jl 25,29:3
Gilpin, Sherman F, 1941, F 20,19:5
Gilpin, Vincent, 1962, Ap 17,35:3
Gilpin, Wallace H, 1956, N 17,21:5
Gilpin, William J, 1948, Mr 15,23:5
Gilrain, James M, 1948, S 20,25:2
Gilraine, Winifred, 1955, Mr 22,31:3
Gilreath, Sallie Rohton Mrs, 1953, F 9,27:4
Gilroy, Clarence C, 1957, Ja 22,29:4
Gilroy, E A, 1942, Ag 10,19:6
Gilroy, Edward E, 1952, F 29,23:5
Gilroy, Edward E Mrs, 1942, Ap 5,41:1
Gilroy, Edward M, 1967, Ag 5,21:1
Gilroy, Edward M Mrs, 1952, Ap 5,15:4
Gilroy, Edward N Sr, 1950, My 10,31:1
Gilroy, Eugene C, 1912, Ja 15,13:4
Gilroy, Foster, 1949, Ja 4,19:3
Gilroy, Frank B, 1959, Je 15,27:2
Gilroy, Gerald M, 1961, N 27,29:3
Gilroy, J Herbert Mrs, 1942, Ja 7,19:4
Gilroy, John H, 1937, My 9,II,10:1
Gilroy, John J, 1924, N 11,23:2
Gilroy, Joseph E, 1958, S 23,33:5
Gilroy, Lawrence T, 1946, S 16,5:4
Gilroy, Mame, 1904, Ag 9,7:6
Gilroy, Mary J Mrs, 1941, Mr 19,21:4
Gilroy, Patrick J, 1949, Ap 27,27:4
Gilroy, Peter F, 1941, D 1,19:4
Gilroy, Ralph, 1961, Ag 8,29:2
Gilroy, Ralph C, 1962, Je 15,27:2
Gilroy, Thomas F (funl), 1911, D 3,15:3
Gilroy, Thomas F, 1947, F 5,23:3
Gilroy, Thomas F Jr, 1921, Ag 25,13:5
Gilroy, Thomas J, 1938, Mr 27,II,6:6
Gilroy, Thomas Jr Mrs, 1956, N 5,31:4
Gilroy, William A, 1963, My 23,37:5
Gilroy, William E, 1962, Je 2,19:2
Gilroy, William F, 1952, S 12,21:1; 1961, D 7,43:1
Gilroy, William J, 1938, My 1,II,6:5
Gilsdorf, Frederick J, 1967, Ag 19,25:3
Gilse, J N Van, 1941, N 30,68:1
Gilsenan, James N, 1953, S 13,85:2
Gilsenan, Terence J, 1968, Je 21,41:4
Gilsey, Gardner L, 1950, F 8,27:4
Gilsey, Gardner L Mrs, 1967, O 26,47:2
Gilsey, Peter, 1873, Ap 9,4:7; 1901, N 11,1:1
Gilson, Arthur, 1942, Jl 24,19:1
Gilson, Bernard F, 1946, F 20,25:3
Gilson, F, 1878, Ap 20,8:2
Gilson, James W, 1939, My 13,15:6
Gilson, John A, 1941, Jl 15,19:5
Gilson, John L, 1944, N 25,13:4
Gilson, John T, 1941, Mr 25,23:4
Gilson, Lottie (funl, Je 13,11:4), 1912, Je 11,9:5
Gilson, Morley H, 1957, Ap 25,31:2
Gilson, Orin A, 1959, N 2,63:5
Gilson, R R, 1933, Ag 3,17:3
Gilson, Ray R, 1944, Ag 20,33:3
Gilson, Raymond J, 1947, Je 25,25:2
Gilson, Robert M, 1947, O 28,26:3
Gilson, Roy E, 1956, Jl 31,23:1
Gilt, Carl M, 1959, Mr 24,39:5
Giltner, E E Mrs, 1959, Jl 22,28:1
Gilvarry, James H, 1947, Je 10,27:6
Gilvey, Edward P (Bro Aileran Edw), 1957, F 13, 35:2
Gilyard, A P, 1946, Je 18,25:2
Gilzenberg, Pauline Mrs, 1947, Jl 26,13:6
Gimbel, Benedict Mrs, 1954, Mr 5,19:1
Gimbel, Bernard F (funl, O 3,47:1; will filed, O 15,-27:4), 1966, S 30,1:4
Gimbel, C, 1932, S 10,15:1
Gimbel, Charles Mrs, 1949, Ap 18,25:5
Gimbel, Daniel (por),(will, S 14,17:2), 1939, S 9,17:3
Gimbel, David A (funl, Jl 10,27:2), 1957, Jl 8,23:2
Gimbel, Ellis A, 1950, Mr 18,13:1
Gimbel, Ellis A Jr, 1964, Ja 5,93:1
Gimbel, Ellis A Jr Mrs, 1944, Ag 19,11:3
Gimbel, Ellis A Mrs, 1948, Je 24,25:1
Gimbel, Frederic A, 1966, Je 11,1:8
Gimbel, Isaac Mrs (will, D 9,22:2), 1944, N 28,23:4
Gimbel, Jacob, 1941, Mr 9,41:2; 1943, Ja 30,15:3
Gimbel, John (por), 1922, N 8,15:3
Gimbel, Louis S Mrs, 1943, Mr 13,13:4
Gimbel, Simeon H, 1940, Je 12,25:3
Gimbi, Magdeline Mrs, 1944, F 12,28:2
Gimino, Frank J V, 1967, F 21,44:6
Giminski, John F, 1948, Ag 24,24:3
Gimma, Giovanni B, 1953, F 16,21:5
Gimma, Giovanni B Mrs, 1953, Jl 24,13:4
Gimmestad, Lars M, 1943, S 15,27:4
Gimpel, Ernest, 1907, Ja 9,9:5
Gimpel, Henry Col, 1914, D 31,9:5
Gimson, Rowland K, 1953, S 26,17:1
Gincano, John A, 1945, My 24,19:4
Ginder, A Edwinna, 1956, N 28,35:5
Ginder, Francis G, 1946, Ja 9,23:2
Ginder, Howard D, 1959, My 29,23:4
Ginder, Philip De Witt Maj-Gen (funl plans, N 9,-33:5), 1968, N 8,47:4
Ginder, Samuel P, 1959, Jl 18,15:4
Gindhart, Isaac D Jr, 1964, O 6,43:7
Gindin, Moe, 1941, Ag 13,17:2
Ginex, Charles, 1956, My 2,31:6
Gingell, Charles A, 1956, Ag 4,15:6
Gingenbach, Norman W, 1956, Ap 18,31:2
Gingg, Rudolf C, 1949, Ag 29,17:4
Gingle, Edward F, 1960, Je 21,33:2
Gingold, Aaron M, 1960, Ja 15,31:2
Gingold, David, 1964, Ap 21,33:4
Gingold, David Mrs, 1954, My 29,15:6
Gingold, Joseph R, 1952, F 3,85:1
Gingold, Moe P, 1958, Ap 20,84:6
Gingold, Oliver J, 1966, Mr 9,41:3
Gingold, Philip Mrs (S Udin), 1960, Ap 28,35:4
Gingold, Pinhas M, 1953, S 22,31:2
Gingrich, A N, 1942, Mr 21,17:5
Gingrich, Clara A, 1957, Jl 16,25:2
Gingrich, Curvin H, 1951, Je 18,23:6
Gingrich, H Melvin, 1958, F 8,19:2
Gingrich, Irving, 1941, F 4,21:3
Gingrich, John E, 1960, My 28,21:3
Gingrich, John E Mrs, 1968, Mr 24,92:7
Ginistrelli, Sen, 1920, S 23,13:4
Ginisty, Charles, 1946, Ja 9,24:2
Ginley, Anne, 1948, My 18,24:3
Ginley, Mary A, 1952, Ag 5,19:4
Ginman, A H, 1954, N 9,27:3
Ginman, Ralph G, 1949, F 28,19:3
Ginn, Arthur, 1942, Jl 20,13:5
Ginn, Edwin, 1914, Ja 22,11:5
Ginn, Frank H (por), 1938, F 7,15:5
Ginn, Glenn Mrs (R H Lee), 1964, Mr 27,27:4
Ginn, Lowen E, 1942, D 14,23:4
Ginn, Lowen E Mrs, 1951, Mr 25,72:6
Ginn, Morris, 1958, S 6,17:4
Ginnane, Henry T, 1942, Ag 29,15:2
Ginnell, Laurence, 1923, Ap 20,17:4
Ginner, Isaac C, 1952, Ja 7,19:4
Ginnever, Arthur, 1940, Ja 30,19:4

Ginns, Robert S, 1967, My 6,31:3
Ginocchio, John, 1940, Jl 16,17:2
Ginocchio, Serfina, 1954, D 3,28:1
Ginori-Conti, Piero Prince, 1939, D 4,23:5
Ginorio, Gonzales, 1944, Jl 10,15:5
Ginsberg, A, 1927, Ja 3,19:3
Ginsberg, Abraham, 1951, N 26,25:4
Ginsberg, Abraham J (cor, N 16,31:1), 1962, N 14, 39:3
Ginsberg, Barnet Mrs, 1955, O 25,33:1
Ginsberg, Charles, 1955, Ap 28,29:2; 1957, Ap 3,31:1
Ginsberg, Clara Mrs, 1956, Mr 25,92:5
Ginsberg, David F, 1958, Jl 6,57:3
Ginsberg, David V, 1951, N 13,55:7
Ginsberg, Harry Mrs, 1968, S 21,33:4
Ginsberg, Henry, 1962, Ap 17,35:2
Ginsberg, Henry J, 1912, Ja 4,13:4
Ginsberg, Herbert, 1968, Je 8,31:3
Ginsberg, Irving, 1964, O 5,33:2
Ginsberg, Jacob, 1965, F 1,23:4
Ginsberg, Jacob Mrs, 1959, My 27,35:2
Ginsberg, Joseph H, 1949, Mr 30,25:2; 1957, D 26,19:3
Ginsberg, Joseph H Mrs, 1953, N 13,27:2
Ginsberg, Louis Mrs, 1966, Je 28,45:1
Ginsberg, Maxwell R, 1968, Mr 6,47:3
Ginsberg, Meyer, 1967, Ag 13,80:7
Ginsberg, Milton Mrs, 1953, F 19,23:3
Ginsberg, Morris, 1947, O 21,23:5
Ginsberg, Moses, 1959, Ag 31,21:1
Ginsberg, Myer, 1956, Jl 21,15:4
Ginsberg, Nathan J, 1939, F 12,44:8
Ginsberg, Pauline Mrs, 1950, Jl 19,31:4
Ginsberg, Philip, 1962, Ag 25,22:1
Ginsberg, Ralph Mrs, 1949, Ag 31,23:3
Ginsberg, Robert, 1945, D 13,29:1
Ginsberg, Rose, 1917, N 6,13:2
Ginsberg, Rose Mrs, 1951, O 16,31:3
Ginsberg, Rudolph, 1950, Ag 13,76:3
Ginsberg, Samuel, 1957, S 14,19:2
Ginsberg, Sherman, 1966, Jl 13,43:1
Ginsberg, Stanley, 1944, Jl 26,19:1
Ginsburg, Abraham R, 1953, Ap 3,23:1
Ginsburg, Annie Mrs, 1940, Ap 11,26:2
Ginsburg, Benjamin, 1948, Jl 25,48:7
Ginsburg, Carl, 1952, O 10,25:1
Ginsburg, David Christian, 1914, Mr 10,9:5
Ginsburg, David Mrs, 1946, Ap 2,27:4
Ginsburg, Harry, 1954, Ap 4,89:1
Ginsburg, Jacob, 1944, Jl 11,15:1
Ginsburg, James L, 1963, D 16,33:4
Ginsburg, Jekuthiel, 1957, O 8,35:1
Ginsburg, John, 1953, Ja 4,76:3
Ginsburg, Joseph, 1954, Jl 16,21:4
Ginsburg, Max, 1948, Ag 22,60:6
Ginsburg, Saul, 1940, N 17,49:2
Ginsburg, Saul Mrs, 1951, Mr 24,13:4
Ginsburg, Sol W, 1960, Jl 3,32:8
Ginsburg, Solomon, 1953, D 27,60:8
Ginsburg, William I, 1965, Mr 15,31:4
Ginter, Gustavus A Mrs, 1955, Je 6,27:5
Ginter, Robert M, 1946, Jl 31,27:2
Ginther, Samuel, 1956, Ja 1,51:1
Ginty, Elizabeth B, 1949, N 22,32:3
Ginty, Tommy, 1954, Ja 3,88:1
Gintzler, Morris, 1963, S 29,87:2
Ginzberg, Louis, 1953, N 12,31:5
Ginzberg, Raphael, 1956, Ja 25,31:2
Ginzburg, Isidor, 1947, O 13,23:4
Ginzburg, Joseph, 1942, F 18,40:3
Ginzburg, Moses P, 1938, My 8,II,6:7
Ginzburg, Simon, 1944, Ja 13,21:5
Ginzler, Martin, 1946, Ap 16,25:3
Gioffre, Bruno Mrs, 1965, Ap 1,35:1
Gioia, Alfonso, 1950, Mr 24,25:1
Gioia, Antonio, 1957, F 6,25:6
Giolitti, G, 1928, Jl 17,21:1
Giolitti, Giovanni, 1921, My 12,17:4
Gionataiso, Arthur, 1964, Ja 30,29:3
Giorani, Giorgio, 1940, S 27,23:2
Giordana, Tullio, 1950, Ja 30,17:1
Giordani, Francesco, 1961, Ja 25,33:1
Giordano, Alfred S, 1958, F 16,86:7
Giordano, Amedeo, 1952, Ja 24,28:2
Giordano, Anthony F, 1943, D 2,27:1
Giordano, Antonio Prof, 1925, Mr 14,13:4
Giordano, Bruno Sr, 1968, Je 8,31:3
Giordano, Carmine, 1951, Ag 3,21:3
Giordano, Davide, 1954, F 3,23:4
Giordano, Elizabeth L, 1967, Jl 11,37:1
Giordano, Galeazzo, 1947, Ap 5,19:5
Giordano, Genaro, 1951, Jl 25,23:5
Giordano, Joseph, 1938, F 17,21:3
Giordano, Michael, 1949, My 25,29:1
Giordano, Philip, 1947, Mr 9,60:8
Giordano, Ralph E, 1964, D 3,45:5
Giordano, Robert, 1966, Ap 9,25:3
Giordano, Salvatore, 1937, Ja 12,23:3
Giordano, Thomas, 1953, Ap 14,27:1
Giordano, Umberto, 1948, N 13,15:1
Giorgetti, Eduardo, 1937, N 27,17:5
Giorgi, Oreste Cardinal, 1924, D 31,13:5
Giorgiani, Albert, 1949, Je 26,45:8
Giorgio, Frank, 1944, Ag 16,19:2
Giorni, Linda Mrs, 1937, My 13,25:5
Giovanelli, Felix B, 1962, Jl 28,19:5
Giovannetti, Eugenio, 1951, My 3,29:5
Giovanni, Paolo di, 1948, Ag 17,22:2
Giovannitti, Arturo, 1960, Ja 1,19:4
Giovannossi, Guido R, 1941, Ja 25,21:2
Giovanola, Guido P, 1943, Mr 23,6:6
Giovinco, Paul A, 1961, Ja 4,33:1
Giovine, Richard S, 1967, Ap 6,39:4
Gipe, Carl E Mrs, 1956, Jl 22,61:1
Gipprich, Franz P, 1948, N 20,13:2
Gipprich, John L, 1950, Mr 8,27:2
Gipson, Richard McC, 1962, F 7,37:4
Giragi, George A, 1938, My 10,21:2
Giraldi, Auguste, 1952, O 7,29:4
Giraldi, Marie-Louise Mrs, 1940, Ap 8,19:1
Girard, Albert, 1954, Ja 7,31:4
Girard, Andre, 1968, S 4,44:3
Girard, Armand T, 1952, Ja 21,15:5
Girard, Bettina, 1905, Ja 9,2:5
Girard, Carlo M, 1945, O 7,44:5
Girard, Eddie, 1946, D 11,31:4
Girard, Eugene N S, 1962, S 17,31:5
Girard, Frank, 1949, Je 25,13:3
Girard, Gustave, 1945, Ag 14,21:2
Girard, H E, 1952, N 14,23:3
Girard, Henri R, 1948, My 13,25:6
Girard, Henry E, 1950, D 16,17:4
Girard, Jessie G Mrs, 1941, Ja 28,19:4
Girard, John, 1947, O 8,25:4
Girard, Mary A Mrs, 1941, O 11,17:2
Girard, Prime, 1949, Jl 31,60:6
Girard, Richard A Mrs, 1961, S 18,29:5
Girard, Rodolphe, 1956, Mr 30,19:3
Girard, Theodore Sen, 1918, O 15,13:1
Girard, Victor F, 1952, My 8,31:2
Girard-Clark, Harriet, 1880, Jl 29,5:2
Girard-di Carlo, John J 2d, 1962, F 4,82:4
Girard Majella, Sister (Ledwidge), 1950, S 25,23:4
Girarde, Lagrand Gen, 1924, D 24,15:3
Girardi, Joseph I, 1954, Mr 8,27:1
Girardi, William L, 1965, S 12,87:2
Girardin, E de, 1881, Ap 28,5:1
Girardin, Saint Marc, 1873, Ap 13,5:5
Girardini, Guiseppe, 1923, O 23,21:4
Girardon, Giovanni, 1959, Jl 16,27:2
Girardon, Mario S (funl, S 17,17:3), 1949, S 14,31:3
Girardot, Etienne, 1939, N 11,15:3
Giraud, Charles F, 1954, Ja 25,19:4
Giraud, Henri-Honore, 1949, Mr 12,17:1
Giraud, P F E, 1881, D 30,5:4
Giraud, Stuart A, 1940, D 24,15:3
Giraudoux, Jean (por), 1944, F 1,19:3
Girault, Arsene N Prof, 1874, My 9,4:7
Girbach, Paul Sr, 1953, Ja 15,27:1
Girbovsky, Cornelius, 1942, D 25,17:1
Girdansky, Louis Mrs, 1945, D 19,25:1
Girden, Kenneth, 1947, Jl 19,13:5
Girden, William M, 1966, Ap 6,43:4
Girdler, S Brent, 1941, Mr 5,21:5
Girdler, Tom M, 1965, F 5,31:1
Girdler, Walter H Sr, 1945, Ja 8,17:2
Girdlestone, C Rev, 1881, Ap 30,2:4
Girdlestone, E Rev, 1884, D 5,5:6
Girdwood, Sarah Mrs, 1937, N 27,17:5
Giriat, Dionys, 1940, D 4,27:4
Giriat, John C, 1948, Ag 27,19:2
Girier, Andre, 1967, My 5,39:4
Girjenti, Count of, 1871, N 28,5:4
Girl, Christian, 1946, Je 11,23:5
Girling, Robert S Jr, 1948, My 15,15:2
Girlock, Edward F, 1947, N 14,23:1
Girod, Julius L, 1957, N 28,31:5
Gironda, Elizabeth Mrs, 1925, Jl 14,21:5
Girosi, Cesare, 1954, Ag 8,85:3
Girosi, Marcello, 1965, Ja 15,43:1
Girouard, Desire Justice, 1911, Mr 24,11:4
Girouard, J Alfred, 1952, D 1,23:5
Giroud, Camille A Mrs, 1959, Jl 7,33:4
Giroud, Pierre F, 1944, O 11,21:3
Giroux, Charles H, 1954, Mr 19,23:1
Giroux, Edmond, 1939, Ag 27,34:8
Giroux, Ralph J Mrs, 1945, Ap 30,19:1
Giroux, Wilford J, 1947, My 5,23:5
Girsdansky, Joseph, 1952, F 15,25:1
Girstenlauer, Robert D, 1959, Ja 21,31:4
Girtanner, Jules E, 1943, Jl 9,17:1
Girten, Michael, 1940, Jl 27,13:3
Girton, Evan W, 1964, Ap 22,47:1
Girvan, Andrew, 1950, S 28,31:3
Girvan, Cuthbert G, 1944, D 19,21:4
Girvin, Herbert C, 1947, D 9,29:4
Girvin, John H, 1938, O 24,17:5
Girvin, Willard S, 1954, F 3,23:4
Gisborne, Harry T, 1949, N 11,25:1
Gisborough, Lord, 1938, Ja 24,23:2
Gisburne, Robert, 1904, Ja 1,7:5
Gisel, Eugene S, 1964, F 10,27:3
Gish, Dorothy, 1968, Je 6,47:1
Gish, James A, 1949, N 11,25:2
Gish, Mary R Mrs, 1948, S 18,17:6
Gishler, Abel D, 1952, Ag 29,23:3
Gisiger, Walter, 1955, D 4,89:1
Gisin, Emil A, 1947, Ag 26,23:5
Gisler, Charles P, 1940, D 16,23:4
Gislingham, Walter E, 1949, O 8,13:4
Gisselbrecht, Joseph Mrs, 1950, S 18,23:4
Gissin, Aaron, 1964, D 21,29:3
Gissing, Algernon, 1937, F 9,23:4
Gissing, Charles C, 1950, Ja 26,27:2
Gissing, George, 1903, D 29,9:5
Gissler, Frank E, 1951, Mr 23,21:3
Gist, Arthur S, 1952, O 27,27:6
Gist, James B, 1954, Ap 28,31:5
Gist, Lillian J, 1949, Jl 3,26:5
Gist, Margaret A, 1949, S 25,92:7
Gistintzev, Alex, 1942, S 15,23:2
Gisvold, Erick, 1943, My 4,23:1
Gitelman, Benjamin, 1953, Ap 25,15:4
Gitelman, Louis B, 1964, Ap 3,33:5
Gitelson, M Leo, 1964, Ag 24,27:1
Gitelson, Maxwell, 1965, F 4,31:2
Gitelson, Nehemiah Mrs, 1952, Mr 8,13:2
Gitenstein, Israel, 1960, S 15,37:4
Gitenstein, Israel Mrs, 1947, F 21,19:1
Githens, Horace G, 1943, D 11,15:5
Githens, Horace G Mrs, 1937, Je 27,II,7:2
Gitin, Samuel, 1942, Mr 1,45:1
Gitlan, Charles, 1965, Ag 24,31:1
Gitlin, Benjamin, 1953, O 13,29:5
Gitlin, Henrietta, 1949, D 6,31:3
Gitlin, Irving, 1967, D 13,44:4
Gitlin, Samuel Y, 1954, Ag 26,27:4
Gitlow, Benjamin, 1965, Jl 20,33:1
Gitlow, Kate Mrs, 1940, N 20,21:5
Gitlow, Samuel S, 1954, Ja 10,87:1
Gitman, Harry, 1959, F 24,29:1
Gittelson, Samuel J, 1938, Je 27,17:4
Gitterman, A N, 1940, Je 20,23:6
Gitterman, Henry, 1916, Ja 23,17:4
Gitterman, Joseph L, 1939, N 7,28:3
Gitterman, Joseph L Jr Mrs, 1957, Ap 26,25:3
Gittinger, Henry W, 1953, Ja 28,27:3
Gittinger, William C, 1959, Jl 29,29:4
Gittinger, William F, 1951, N 7,29:5
Gittings, D Sterett, 1948, Ja 10,15:5
Gittings, John C, 1950, Mr 10,28:2
Gittings, Richard, 1882, Ag 3,2:4
Gittings, Robert L, 1948, F 5,24:3
Gittins, Robert H, 1957, D 26,19:2
Gittler, Joseph Mrs, 1966, Je 12,87:3
Gittler, Stephen, 1954, N 20,17:5
Gittlin, Benjamin Mrs, 1957, N 10,85:2
Giudici, Samuel, 1943, Mr 16,19:3
Giuffra, Eleazar, 1939, Ag 19,15:1
Giuffre, Gianbattista, 1964, Je 12,35:2
Giuliana, Robert A, 1958, My 29,27:1
Giuliano, Joseph, 1949, My 12,31:2
Giuliano, Michael, 1946, O 30,27:3
Giuliano, Salvatore, 1955, Ja 5,23:4
Giunta, Joseph, 1942, S 22,21:1
Giuseffi, Jerome, 1968, D 15,86:3
Giustetti, Flippo, 1940, N 14,23:4
Givan, George N, 1945, N 16,19:3
Give, Henry L de, 1948, F 9,17:2
Giveans, Boudewine Mrs, 1945, Ap 23,19:5
Giveans, Bradford W, 1938, O 9,45:3
Given, Anne Mrs, 1953, Ja 27,10:6
Given, Ellis E W, 1939, My 14,III,6:8
Given, Ernest D, 1946, O 16,28:2
Given, Frederick J, 1959, Je 26,25:1
Given, James C, 1951, N 11,91:1
Given, John L, 1957, My 22,33:4
Given, John L Jr, 1957, S 18,33:4
Given, John L Jr (will), 1959, Mr 5,33:5
Given, John L Mrs, 1956, O 6,21:6
Given, John R, 1941, D 6,17:3
Given, Leila I, 1959, F 14,21:2
Given, Ralph H, 1957, My 22,33:5
Given, Robert W, 1959, D 12,23:5
Given, William B Jr, 1968, Ja 31,41:3
Given, William G, 1940, Jl 14,31:3
Givens, Alex C, 1953, Ap 21,27:5
Givens, Amos J Dr, 1919, Jl 8,11:4
Givens, Charles G, 1964, S 29,43:5
Givens, Earl C, 1954, Jl 22,23:2
Givens, Edward G Jr, 1967, Je 7,30:2
Givens, James A, 1957, My 7,35:4
Givens, Jasper Mrs, 1952, Je 25,29:2
Givens, W A, 1946, My 30,21:5
Givens, Webster C, 1968, S 8,84:5
Givens, William H, 1951, My 3,29:4
Givens, William R, 1950, S 19,29:1
Giventer, Martin, 1952, N 29,17:3
Gividen, John H, 1951, Je 4,27:4
Givner, Joseph, 1966, F 26,25:5
Gjertsen, Percy, 1961, S 30,25:4
Gjesdahl, Fredrik L, 1959, Jl 31,23:2
Glab, Lloyd E, 1937, Ja 23,17:3
Glacken, Edward F, 1956, Mr 27,35:2
Glacken, William J, 1955, Ag 22,21:6
Glackens, William J (por), 1938, My 23,17
Glackens, William J Mrs, 1955, O 30,88:3
Glackin, Edward J, 1939, Je 18,37:3
Gladchuk, Chet, 1967, S 6,47:3
Gladding, Daniel H Mrs, 1953, My 21,31:3

Gladding, Edward G, 1948, Ja 3,13:5
Gladding, Samuel Capt, 1910, My 2,9:5
Glade, Richard, 1939, Je 3,15:5
Gladeck, Frederick C, 1948, Ap 28,27:3
Gladfelter, Charles F, 1939, Jl 20,19:6
Gladfelter, Walter S, 1952, Ag 16,16:3
Gladfelter, Wilford S, 1958, O 30,31:2
Gladkov, Fedor, 1958, D 29,15:4
Gladney, Sam Mrs, 1961, O 3,36:7
Gladson, John W, 1966, Ag 15,27:4
Gladstern, Bertha, 1953, Ja 1,23:5
Gladstone, Arnold E, 1947, Ag 12,24:2
Gladstone, B, 1935, D 14,15:1
Gladstone, David, 1964, Je 16,39:1
Gladstone, H N, 1935, Ap 29,15:2
Gladstone, Helen, 1925, Ag 20,19:7
Gladstone, Henry Mrs, 1962, Je 13,41:5
Gladstone, Hugh S, 1949, Ap 6,29:5
Gladstone, Irving R, 1941, F 9,51:6
Gladstone, John E, 1945, F 14,19:4
Gladstone, Peter Mrs, 1961, N 29,41:2
Gladstone, Robert W, 1951, Je 2,19:3
Gladstone, Robertson, 1875, S 24,1:4
Gladstone, Samuel, 1938, D 31,15:4
Gladstone, Sidney A, 1965, Ja 18,35:1
Gladstone, Stephen Rev, 1920, Ap 27,9:3
Gladstone, Viscountess, 1953, Je 23,29:2
Gladstone, W E, 1898, My 19,1:7
Gladstone, W E Mrs, 1900, Je 15,6:7
Gladstone, W H, 1891, Jl 5,1:3
Gladstone, William D (Billy), 1961, O 6,35:2
Gladstone of Hawarden, Lady of, 1941, Jl 25,15:5
Gladwin, Ellis W, 1937, Ag 22,II,7:3
Gladwin, Harrison W, 1942, My 19,19:4
Gladwin, Mary E, 1939, N 23,27:2
Glaenzer, Harry, 1943, My 25,23:6
Glaenzer, Richard B, 1937, Ap 16,23:1
Glaesel, Ernest, 1961, F 9,31:2
Glaeser, Albert J, 1948, F 26,23:6
Glaeser, Carl H, 1960, Ja 12,45:6
Glaeser, Hugo W, 1947, O 15,27:3
Glaeser, Jesse R, 1960, Jl 5,31:5
Glaesser, Karl F, 1937, D 9,25:5
Glaessner, Arthur F, 1941, S 18,25:3
Glaessner, Charles L (por), 1944, F 28,17:3
Glafke, William H, 1956, O 2,35:3
Glagolin, Boris S, 1948, D 13,23:2
Glahn, John von, 1904, F 14,7:5
Glahn, Wilbur A, 1951, F 8,33:3
Glaisher, James F R S, 1903, F 9,9:5
Glaman, Eugenia F Mrs, 1956, O 21,86:5
Glamkowski, Edward F, 1967, Mr 4,27:5
Glamkowski, Joseph V, 1945, Je 21,19:3
Glancy, Alfred A, 1959, Ag 5,27:4
Glancy, Hugh, 1954, Ap 27,29:1
Glancy, Margaret M Mrs, 1941, Ja 17,17:4
Glancy, Virginia V Mrs, 1950, Mr 15,29:1
Glander, Frederic, 1950, D 6,33:1
Glanding, Charles W, 1941, Jl 26,15:4
Glannan, Peter H, 1943, O 21,27:5
Glans, S Walfrid, 1950, Ja 4,35:4
Glant, Abraham, 1957, My 11,21:7
Glantowe, Lord (John Jones Jenkins), 1915, Jl 28,9:5
Glantz, Charles Mrs, 1950, Ag 11,19:5
Glantz, Leib, 1964, Ja 30,29:4
Glanville, Stephen R K, 1956, Ap 28,17:5
Glanz, Hyman, 1943, Ap 16,22:2
Glanz-Leyeless, Aaron, 1966, D 31,19:3
Glaoui, Caid Madni, 1918, Ag 16,7:5
Glaoui, Thami el Mezouari el Pasha of Marakkesh, 1956, Ja 24,31:4
Glardon, Frederic W, 1965, My 6,39:2
Glarner, Andre, 1953, D 14,31:5
Glas, Emil, 1958, My 20,33:4
Glasby, B L, 1866, F 7,5:3
Glasby, Jonathan P Jr, 1966, Ap 28,43:3
Glasby, William Brown, 1910, Ag 25,7:5
Glasco, Benjamin F, 1964, S 12,25:6
Glascock, James, 1950, O 7,19:5
Glascock, Terrell H, 1942, Ag 25,23:6
Glascoff, Donald G, 1963, Jl 30,29:3
Glascott, Annie, 1947, Mr 1,15:5
Glascott, Edward F, 1949, Ap 17,76:6
Glascott, John A, 1966, Ja 29,27:1
Glascott, Phil J, 1938, My 15,II,6:2
Glascow, Boris G, 1940, S 8,49:2
Glase, John O, 1950, D 14,35:2
Glase, Paul E, 1955, S 23,25:3
Glaser, Abraham Mrs, 1959, D 25,21:4
Glaser, Abram, 1958, F 24,19:1
Glaser, Arthur A, 1964, F 18,35:3
Glaser, Edward C, 1948, Jl 13,27:5
Glaser, Frank B, 1949, F 25,24:2
Glaser, Frantisek, 1951, Mr 31,15:4
Glaser, Gustav, 1940, Mr 13,23:5
Glaser, Harry, 1952, Ag 11,15:6
Glaser, John L, 1964, F 29,21:2
Glaser, Joseph M, 1967, Ap 18,41:1
Glaser, Joseph P, 1956, Jl 21,15:6
Glaser, Julius, 1952, Ap 6,89:1
Glaser, Julius G, 1955, Mr 19,15:1
Glaser, Lulu, 1958, S 6,17:5
Glaser, Milton W, 1965, My 15,31:5

Glaser, Otto C, 1951, F 8,33:5
Glaser, Otto P, 1942, S 14,15:3
Glaser, Raymond, 1955, Ap 13,29:5
Glaser, Rudolph H Mrs, 1953, Ja 12,27:4
Glaser, Saul J, 1962, O 27,25:3
Glasgow, Arthur G, 1955, O 29,19:5
Glasgow, Arthur G Mrs, 1952, Ag 25,17:5
Glasgow, David Bayle, 1915, D 14,13:5
Glasgow, Edward L Mrs, 1953, Jl 7,27:3
Glasgow, Ellen A G, 1945, N 22,35:3
Glasgow, Hugh, 1948, Jl 18,52:6
Glasgow, Jacob, 1952, S 4,27:1
Glasgow, James W, 1952, O 7,29:3
Glasgow, Maude, 1955, N 22,35:6
Glasgow, Robert, 1922, Ap 6,17:4
Glasgow, Robert D, 1964, Jl 16,31:1
Glasgow, William, 1955, Jl 5,29:2
Glasgow, William J, 1967, Ag 5,23:4
Glasheen, Edward L, 1948, Ap 16,23:1
Glasheen, John C, 1945, Ap 26,23:3
Glashow, Lewis, 1961, My 27,23:6
Glasier, J Arthur, 1940, My 18,15:7
Glasier, John B Mrs, 1950, Je 15,31:6
Glasman, Arthur, 1953, Ag 16,76:6
Glasmann, William, 1916, My 13,9:5
Glasofer, Joseph, 1959, Je 10,37:2
Glaspell, Susan (por), 1948, Jl 28,23:3
Glass, Alex, 1941, Ap 19,15:4
Glass, Andrew, 1925, N 23,21:5
Glass, Annie Mrs, 1903, Ja 31,6:6
Glass, Bernard, 1940, Ap 7,44:8
Glass, Bertram G, 1960, Je 8,39:2
Glass, Carter, 1946, My 29,1:2
Glass, Carter Jr, 1955, D 2,27:1
Glass, Carter Mrs, 1937, Je 6,II,9:2; 1959, Jl 5,56:5
Glass, Charles H, 1939, Je 25,37:1
Glass, Chester, 1921, Ja 8,11:5
Glass, Clarence, 1959, Ag 13,27:3
Glass, David F, 1942, S 19,15:3
Glass, Dudley, 1943, N 28,68:6
Glass, Edgar T, 1944, Ap 10,19:5
Glass, F P, 1934, Ja 11,21:1
Glass, Francis A, 1944, D 16,15:6
Glass, Gaston J, 1965, N 13,29:6
Glass, George A, 1945, D 30,14:2
Glass, George D, 1944, Ap 22,15:6
Glass, Gordon G, 1946, My 5,46:2
Glass, Harry F, 1942, F 24,21:6
Glass, Henry, 1916, F 28,9:2
Glass, Henry (funl), 1916, Mr 1,11:4
Glass, Henry Rear-Adm, 1908, S 3,7:5
Glass, Irwin M, 1965, Ag 26,33:5
Glass, J Nathaniel, 1937, F 21,II,10:4
Glass, Jacob A, 1962, O 15,29:4
Glass, Jennie Mrs, 1967, F 3,31:3
Glass, John H, 1965, D 20,35:5
Glass, Joseph, 1955, Ja 20,31:1
Glass, Leo M, 1958, Jl 11,23:3
Glass, Leopold C, 1946, My 26,32:7
Glass, Louis, 1924, N 14,19:5; 1948, F 21,13:6
Glass, M M, 1934, F 4,30:1
Glass, Max H, 1950, S 8,32:3
Glass, Max Mrs, 1951, O 5,27:2
Glass, Meta, 1967, Mr 22,47:1
Glass, Michael A W, 1962, My 3,33:1
Glass, Montague Mrs, 1948, Ja 26,19:2
Glass, Morris, 1961, Mr 30,29:4
Glass, Oscar, 1960, My 11,39:1
Glass, Powell, 1945, Jl 9,11:7
Glass, Robert, 1955, My 8,88:3
Glass, Robert C, 1958, Jl 7,27:3
Glass, Robert J, 1962, F 6,32:5
Glass, Robert S, 1946, Jl 5,19:6
Glass, Russell, 1950, Jl 10,13:6
Glass, Simon H, 1955, F 6,88:4
Glass, Veronica G, 1944, Je 20,19:6
Glass, W A, 1879, Ap 26,2:4
Glass, William A, 1955, Je 12,87:1
Glass, William C, 1945, Mr 13,23:2
Glass, William M, 1967, Je 22,39:4
Glass, William P, 1942, Ag 1,11:4
Glassberg, Jack, 1958, Mr 3,27:4
Glassbrook, Grant F, 1941, Ja 31,19:4
Glassbury, John A, 1962, Jl 10,33:3
Glassco, J Grant, 1968, S 21,33:4
Glasscock, Carl B, 1942, N 15,58:2
Glasscock, John W, 1947, F 25,25:2
Glasscock, Mabel S Mrs, 1946, N 20,31:3
Glasscock, William E, 1925, Ap 13,19:3
Glassell, Alfred C, 1966, My 23,41:3
Glassenberg, Charles, 1945, N 20,21:4
Glasser, Benjamin F, 1967, Ja 31,31:3
Glasser, Bernard, 1948, F 17,26:2
Glasser, Harold A, 1948, O 23,15:4
Glasser, Herman, 1955, Ap 21,29:2
Glasser, Joseph J, 1951, S 18,31:2
Glasser, Otto, 1964, D 12,31:5
Glasser, Otto C Mrs, 1952, N 12,27:3
Glasser, Rudolph W, 1947, S 6,18:2
Glasserow, Charles N, 1967, O 12,45:3
Glassey, Frank P S, 1964, F 23,84:6
Glassford, Allie D Mrs, 1937, Ja 10,II,9:2
Glassford, Charles A Mrs, 1949, My 28,15:6

Glassford, David D, 1946, Ja 17,23:4
Glassford, Joseph R, 1946, S 25,27:2
Glassford, Pelham D, 1959, Ag 10,27:3
Glassford, S Robert, 1946, S 22,62:6
Glassford, William A 2d, 1958, Jl 31,23:5
Glassgold, George M, 1956, F 17,21:2
Glassman, Abraham, 1941, S 14,38:4
Glassman, Herman, 1951, Ap 23,25:5
Glassman, Isaac, 1955, My 5,33:6
Glassman, Joseph, 1959, S 11,28:1
Glassman, Leo, 1964, O 31,29:4
Glassman, Leo B, 1956, F 25,19:6
Glassman, Ruth, 1959, My 2,23:5
Glassman, Walter D, 1943, N 7,56:7
Glassmeyer, Edward, 1943, Mr 23,19:2
Glassmire, Albert T, 1952, Je 5,31:4
Glassmire, Augustin J, 1946, Jl 25,21:2
Glassmire, Charles M, 1940, O 8,26:2
Glassner, Frank, 1949, F 11,23:2
Glassner, James J, 1964, Ag 20,29:4
Glasson, David G Mrs, 1948, Jl 16,19:2
Glasson, J J, 1882, Mr 13,5:2
Glasson, Rex F, 1939, Ap 27,25:5
Glasson, T Bath, 1952, D 27,10:4
Glasson, William, 1945, Ja 5,15:3
Glasston, Hyman M, 1947, O 21,23:3
Glassup, Frederick, 1948, F 19,23:1
Glatt, Hulda M, 1950, Ja 1,42:6
Glattauer, Frederick, 1938, F 12,15:6
Glatz, George C, 1947, My 26,22:3
Glatz, Joseph, 1905, Ja 29,4:4
Glatzmayer, Joseph J, 1944, D 27,20:3
Glauber, Gordon, 1947, Je 17,25:3
Glauber, I Peter, 1966, D 11,89:1
Glauber, Moritz, 1943, Jl 23,17:4
Glauber, Moritz Mrs, 1952, N 20,31:3
Glauber, Stanley E, 1946, D 30,19:4
Glauberg, Max, 1937, F 20,17:5
Glaubit, Robert William Dr, 1921, Mr 29,15:5
Glaubitz, Hugh J, 1939, Ja 17,21:4
Glaubman, Joseph, 1954, Jl 28,23:2
Glauser, Jacob, 1947, Ag 8,17:2
Glave, George Y Mrs, 1960, O 17,29:2
Glaver, Joachim Gotsche, 1925, Je 1,15:3
Glavin, David E, 1964, My 29,29:1
Glavin, John F, 1949, Je 28,27:3; 1960, N 8,29:4
Glayser, Edmund D, 1925, Ja 13,19:6
Glazebrook, Francis H, 1956, Mr 12,27:1
Glazebrook, Haslett M, 1962, Mr 1,31:5
Glazebrook, Hugh de T, 1937, My 8,19:6
Glazebrook, Hugh T de, 1937, My 8,19:6
Glazebrook, James R, 1958, Ag 24,86:3
Glazebrook, Otis A Jr, 1954, My 24,27:1
Glazebrook, Otis A Jr Mrs, 1960, O 6,41:4
Glazebrook, R, 1935, D 17,23:2
Glazer, Abraham A, 1943, N 13,13:2
Glazer, Anna Mrs, 1944, O 9,23:5
Glazer, B Benedict, 1952, My 16,23:1
Glazer, Benjamin F (Barney), 1956, Mr 19,31:3
Glazer, Henry G, 1953, N 8,88:6
Glazer, John D, 1948, Mr 8,23:4
Glazer, Nathan, 1957, Ag 28,27:2
Glazer, Simon, 1938, My 23,17:6
Glazier, George M (por), 1938, S 9,21:2
Glazier, Henry S, 1939, O 7,17:4
Glazier, Henry S Mrs, 1959, Ap 16,33:1
Glazier, Irene Mrs, 1940, Ap 30,21:2
Glazier, John B, 1954, D 10,27:3
Glazier, Louis, 1953, S 6,50:4
Glazier, Willard Col, 1905, Ap 27,11:5
Glazier, William S Mrs, 1961, F 25,21:2
Glazunoff, A, 1936, Mr 22,II,10:1
Gleadowe, Reginald, 1944, O 12,27:3
Gleanson, James A, 1944, S 7,23:1
Gleason, Abner C Mrs, 1944, Jl 11,15:4
Gleason, Agnes D Sister, 1940, My 6,17:3
Gleason, Andrew C (will, N 26,25:3), 1952, F 11,25:5
Gleason, Anna, 1959, Mr 4,31:1
Gleason, Anson Rev, 1885, F 25,2:3
Gleason, Arthur Huntington, 1923, D 31,13:4
Gleason, Carlisle J, 1940, My 1,24:4
Gleason, Carlisle J Mrs, 1949, Mr 24,28:3
Gleason, Charles, 1948, Jl 15,23:3
Gleason, Charles A, 1952, Je 17,27:1
Gleason, Charles H, 1945, O 24,21:3
Gleason, Clarence W, 1942, N 5,26:2
Gleason, Cornelius J Sr Mrs, 1947, Ja 25,17:2
Gleason, Daniel J, 1942, My 6,19:5; 1944, Jl 29,13:4
Gleason, Daniel Sr Mrs, 1949, Ap 8,26:4
Gleason, Dennis L, 1953, F 19,23:4
Gleason, E Blakeney (est appr), 1961, My 24,43:3
Gleason, E P, 1901, S 27,7:6
Gleason, Edward J, 1942, S 15,24:2; 1951, O 2,27:3; 1962, O 1,31:1
Gleason, Edwin S, 1937, Ap 15,24:2
Gleason, Edwin S Mrs (Mary), 1968, D 26,37:2
Gleason, Eldon H Sr, 1955, O 15,15:4
Gleason, Emmet B, 1958, N 22,21:4
Gleason, Fred Grant, 1903, D 7,2:4
Gleason, Frederick B, 1952, Ja 3,46:4
Gleason, George A, 1955, N 11,25:2
Gleason, George D, 1939, S 28,25:4
Gleason, George H, 1953, My 26,29:5

Gleason, George J Mrs, 1952, Mr 15,13:6
Gleason, George M Mrs, 1952, F 6,29:2
Gleason, Harvey J, 1950, F 26,78:1
Gleason, Howard S, 1950, Je 1,27:5
Gleason, J B, 1935, My 2,21:3
Gleason, James, 1947, Jl 12,13:4; 1959, Ap 14,35:1
Gleason, James E, 1964, F 13,31:5
Gleason, James F, 1952, Je 19,27:2
Gleason, Joe D, 1959, Mr 11,35:2
Gleason, John A, 1955, Ap 10,89:1
Gleason, John E, 1961, Mr 10,27:2
Gleason, John F, 1949, Jl 7,26:2; 1960, O 9,86:5
Gleason, John J, 1923, Mr 15,19:5; 1950, Ja 24,31:2
Gleason, John J Capt, 1923, Mr 14,19:4
Gleason, John P, 1946, Ag 16,21:3
Gleason, John S, 1946, Mr 26,29:5
Gleason, John T Sr, 1962, S 1,19:4
Gleason, Joseph F, 1940, Ap 17,23:4
Gleason, Joseph F Mrs, 1948, S 17,25:1
Gleason, Joseph M, 1942, O 31,15:6
Gleason, Julia M, 1943, Mr 18,19:2
Gleason, K, 1933, Ja 10,21:1
Gleason, Karl, 1949, My 30,13:3
Gleason, Lafayette B, 1937, O 25,19:1
Gleason, Louise, 1952, Ja 3,46:5
Gleason, Lucile W, 1947, My 19,21:3
Gleason, Lucy Mrs, 1946, Je 28,23:5
Gleason, Mabel Mrs, 1947, S 8,23:6
Gleason, Marshall W, 1955, Jl 26,25:3
Gleason, Martin A, 1945, Ja 4,19:1
Gleason, Mary Felix Sister, 1940, N 15,21:4
Gleason, Michael, 1940, D 28,15:2
Gleason, Michael J, 1951, F 7,29:2
Gleason, Miner, 1958, F 16,64:5
Gleason, Neil J, 1946, Jl 29,21:5
Gleason, Patrick J (funl), 1901, My 21,9:1
Gleason, Paul J, 1954, S 11,17:6
Gleason, Regina, 1940, Mr 26,21:5
Gleason, Richard A, 1939, Jl 4,13:4
Gleason, Richard L, 1949, N 25,31:4
Gleason, Rutherford E, 1949, Jl 9,13:6
Gleason, Sarah L Mrs, 1910, Ag 16,7:4
Gleason, Thomas, 1952, N 9,91:2
Gleason, Thomas A Mrs, 1956, S 30,87:1
Gleason, Thomas C, 1923, Ag 19,26:4
Gleason, Thomas E, 1939, Je 5,17:4
Gleason, Timothy, 1903, Je 24,16:5
Gleason, Vincent D, 1956, Ag 5,77:2
Gleason, W, 1933, Ja 3,18:1
Gleason, William, 1922, My 25,19:5
Gleason, William C, 1952, N 14,23:2
Gleason, William E, 1924, Mr 2,22:3
Gleason, William F, 1937, Ap 27,23:6
Gleason, William H Mrs, 1924, Ja 10,21:5
Gleason, William J, 1950, Mr 10,27:2
Gleason, William P, 1965, Jl 14,37:4
Gleason, William W, 1944, Ja 31,17:6
Gleason, Wulstan, 1959, My 4,29:5
Gleaves, Albert Adm (por), 1937, Ja 7,21:1
Gleaves, Albert Mrs, 1946, S 12,7:2
Gleavy, John W, 1944, Je 15,19:5
Glebocki, Joseph B, 1951, O 5,28:4
Gleckler, Robert P, 1939, F 27,15:5
Gledhill, Alfred, 1968, S 30,47:4
Gledhill, Eli, 1938, Ap 23,15:3
Gledhill, Ernest, 1966, Jl 14,36:1
Gledhill, Henry R, 1944, F 13,41:1
Gledhill, Herbert W Sr, 1946, Mr 3,45:1
Gledhill, Horace, 1948, My 3,21:3
Gledhill, James E, 1940, Mr 21,25:5
Gledhill, John M, 1950, Ja 17,27:2
Gledhill, Reuben L, 1938, D 16,8:2
Gledhill, William Henry, 1920, Ja 9,7:1
Gleeman, David, 1958, Ap 5,15:4
Gleesel, Paul, 1947, N 5,3:1
Gleeson, Art, 1964, N 28,21:5
Gleeson, J Albert, 1950, Ap 8,13:4
Gleeson, James E, 1953, Mr 9,29:3
Gleeson, James J, 1957, S 6,21:3
Gleeson, John A Rev, 1919, Je 24,13:4
Gleeson, John M, 1968, Je 21,41:1
Gleeson, M C, 1927, Ag 10,23:3
Gleeson, Richard A, 1945, D 25,23:4
Gleeson, William A, 1948, Ja 8,25:4
Gleeson, William J Dr, 1968, Ag 31,23:5
Gleich, Frank E, 1949, Mr 28,21:2
Gleich, Louis, 1961, S 26,39:3
Gleichen, Edward Lord Maj-Gen (por), 1937, D 16, 27:1
Gleichen, Feodora Lady, 1922, F 23,15:5
Gleichen, Helena, 1947, Ja 29,25:4
Gleichert, George, 1937, Jl 8,23:2
Gleichmann, August, 1964, Mr 18,41:2
Gleichmann, Henry A, 1940, Mr 5,23:2
Gleim, Charles S, 1957, Mr 11,25:3
Gleim, Russell Mrs, 1947, Ag 7,21:4
Gleises, John Dr, 1903, Ag 15,7:6
Gleisser, J W L, 1928, D 8,19:6
Gleissner, John M, 1941, F 28,19:4
Gleitsman, Louis, 1951, N 7,29:3
Gleitsmann, Joseph William Dr, 1914, Jl 4,7:5
Gleizes, Albert, 1953, Je 25,27:4
Glekel, Jacob S, 1951, F 12,23:5

Glemby, Harry, 1965, Ja 11,45:2
Glen, Charles T, 1908, Ja 20,9:4
Glen, James A, 1950, Je 29,29:5
Glen, Joseph A, 1957, Ag 11,81:1
Glen, Maxwell Mrs, 1952, D 14,91:2
Glen, S R, 1880, My 14,3:4
Glen, Willard A, 1946, N 23,15:2
Glen-Coats, Thomas G, 1954, Mr 13,15:3
Glenconner, Lord (Edw Priaux Tennant), 1920, N 22,15:4
Glendening, Harold, 1958, S 14,84:1
Glendening, Harold Mrs, 1948, O 29,26:2
Glendening, John W, 1966, Je 16,47:5
Glendenning, John (will), 1955, Ja 27,25:8
Glendenning, William W Mrs, 1955, O 8,19:2
Glendining, George R, 1968, F 6,43:2
Glendining, George R Mrs, 1961, My 7,86:8
Glendining, Sherman, 1958, O 25,21:1
Glendinning, Elizabeth R F Mrs, 1942, O 13,23:2
Glendinning, H Percival, 1960, Jl 19,29:5
Glendinning, John, 1916, Jl 18,9:6
Glendinning, John R, 1956, Je 1,23:3
Glendinning, Malcolm C, 1953, D 20,77:1
Glendinning, R, 1936, Ap 20,19:2
Glendinning, Thomas A, 1943, F 19,20:3
Glendon, Harriet, 1950, F 2,27:5
Glendon, John W, 1950, F 15,21:3
Glendon, Richard A, 1956, Jl 10,31:1
Glendon, William M, 1940, O 28,17:4
Glendy, William M Commodore, 1873, Jl 17,4:7
Glenfield, Joan, 1947, Ja 31,25:5
Glenn, Alfred T Sr, 1940, Jl 31,17:5
Glenn, B C, 1952, N 11,30:3
Glenn, C B Mrs, 1938, Ap 22,19:3
Glenn, Donald E, 1958, Mr 13,29:4
Glenn, E F Brig Gen, 1926, Ag 7,11:4
Glenn, E R, 1939, Ja 25,21:3
Glenn, Earl R, 1962, Ag 8,31:3
Glenn, Edgar E, 1955, Mr 11,25:5
Glenn, Elizabeth J M Mrs, 1947, Ag 10,53:2
Glenn, Elliott H, 1952, My 22,27:6
Glenn, Forrest, 1954, Ag 25,27:5
Glenn, Fred Mrs, 1943, F 12,19:3
Glenn, Gaylord Mrs, 1940, Jl 21,28:7
Glenn, George, 1949, O 20,29:3
Glenn, George D, 1954, Jl 7,31:3
Glenn, Gerrard, 1949, Ja 26,25:5
Glenn, Grosvenor K, 1952, N 23,88:4
Glenn, Henry Patterson, 1923, S 14,19:5
Glenn, Howard, 1960, O 10,1:1
Glenn, Howard A, 1947, N 29,13:4
Glenn, Ida M, 1944, Ag 19,11:2
Glenn, J Lyles, 1938, My 3,23:6
Glenn, Jack Mrs, 1955, N 12,19:4
Glenn, James D, 1958, My 10,21:5
Glenn, James W, 1962, O 9,41:4
Glenn, John, 1948, Mr 20,13:3
Glenn, John B, 1962, D 8,27:2
Glenn, John F, 1959, F 1,84:7
Glenn, John F Mrs, 1949, Ag 20,11:4
Glenn, John H Sr, 1966, S 10,29:3
Glenn, John M Mrs (por), 1940, N 5,25:5
Glenn, Joseph W, 1955, Jl 14,23:5
Glenn, L C, 1951, Ja 13,15:3
Glenn, Mary, 1949, Mr 1,25:2
Glenn, Milton W, 1967, D 17,92:7
Glenn, Otis F, 1959, Mr 13,26:4
Glenn, Paul J, 1957, Ap 28,86:8
Glenn, Robert, 1959, Mr 20,32:1
Glenn, Robert B, 1920, My 17,15:1
Glenn, Robert L, 1954, Ja 4,19:3
Glenn, Robert M Mrs, 1938, Ap 8,19:5
Glenn, S W, 1903, F 11,9:6
Glenn, Selmo C, 1951, Ap 25,29:4
Glenn, Thomas F, 1968, Ap 17,32:5
Glenn, Thomas K, 1946, O 12,19:3
Glenn, Toby, 1957, Ag 19,19:3
Glenn, William A, 1954, Jl 23,17:5
Glenn, William L, 1950, O 26,31:4
Glennen, Stephen P, 1955, Ap 16,19:2
Glenney, James A F, 1954, Ag 25,27:3
Glenney, Walter L, 1949, Mr 27,78:5; 1953, D 9,11:1
Glenney, Walter L Mrs, 1952, Ap 1,29:5
Glennie, Alex J, 1937, Ja 9,17:4
Glennon, Bert, 1967, Jl 1,23:6
Glennon, Charles C, 1957, Ap 7,88:1
Glennon, Edward J, 1956, S 7,23:1
Glennon, Harrison R, 1963, Jl 30,29:2
Glennon, James H, 1940, My 31,19:6
Glennon, John, 1946, Mr 10,1:3
Glennon, John E, 1945, Je 14,19:5
Glennon, Joseph A, 1938, Ja 2,40:4
Glennon, Joseph P, 1940, S 18,12:4
Glennon, Martin, 1952, S 6,17:4
Glennon, Mary A, 1940, Jl 28,27:3
Glennon, Michael J Rev, 1937, Je 4,23:4
Glennon, Philip T, 1917, Jl 15,15:3
Glennon, Thomas C, 1952, D 6,21:4
Glennon, Thomas F, 1942, Jl 16,19:4
Glennon, William H, 1946, D 24,17:2
Glennon, William J, 1949, O 13,27:4
Glennon, William Mrs, 1945, O 28,44:2
Glenny, Bryant B Mrs, 1946, N 5,25:3

Glenny, Charles H, 1922, O 2,17:7
Glenny, W Harry, 1942, Jl 27,15:6
Glenravel, Lord, 1937, Je 15,23:5
Glenroy, James Richmond, 1907, Je 2,7:5
Glentoran, Lord (H Dixon), 1950, Jl 21,19:4
Glentworth, Clarence A, 1953, Ag 16,76:4
Glentworth, Marguerite L, 1956, S 4,30:2
Glenz, Christian W, 1952, Ap 21,21:3
Glenz, George, 1960, Je 27,25:5
Glerum, Jay B, 1949, O 11,34:1
Glessner, Albert S, 1942, Ap 5,41:1
Glessner, John G M Mrs, 1943, O 17,49:1
Gleste, George B, 1953, O 29,31:2
Glew, Henry L, 1951, Ap 29,89:1
Gleyre, Gabriel Charles, 1874, My 17,1:7
Gleysteen, William H, 1948, Ja 19,23:4
Glezen, Lee L, 1960, S 28,39:4
Glibert, Joseph, 1948, Je 26,17:2
Glicenstein, Enrico, 1943, Ja 1,23:1
Glick, Bernard, 1948, Ja 30,23:3
Glick, Edward J, 1948, N 19,27:2
Glick, Fred, 1955, Ja 6,27:4
Glick, Hyman, 1948, My 30,34:2
Glick, Jesse, 1947, Ap 18,21:4
Glick, Joseph, 1943, O 18,15:2; 1948, Jl 10,15:2
Glick, Louis, 1961, Mr 8,33:6
Glick, Sara L Mrs, 1940, Ja 8,15:2
Glickenhaus, Jacob S, 1966, D 15,47:2
Glickfeld, Irving B, 1962, My 19,27:5
Glickman, Abraham M Mrs, 1959, Ap 30,31:3
Glickman, Alfred M, 1954, N 3,29:5
Glickman, Allen, 1963, D 22,34:1
Glickman, Benjamin, 1951, Ap 24,29:3
Glickman, Benjamin Mrs, 1952, Je 18,27:4
Glickman, David, 1953, F 27,21:2
Glickman, Harry, 1959, O 8,39:4
Glickman, Louis, 1968, D 6,47:1
Glickman, Moses N, 1959, Ag 18,29:1
Glickman, Philip, 1947, Jl 15,23:1
Glickman, Pincus, 1957, Mr 18,27:4
Glickman, William S, 1951, O 30,29:5
Glicksman, Solomon, 1943, My 20,21:2
Glickson, H, 1939, My 24,23:3
Glickstein, Abraham, 1947, N 1,15:5
Glickstein, Izzo, 1947, Ap 18,21:4
Glidden, Albert G, 1951, Jl 22,60:4
Glidden, C J, 1927, S 12,23:3
Glidden, Carlton, 1937, D 1,23:2
Glidden, Edson W, 1950, Ap 27,33:1
Glidden, Elmer G, 1942, Ag 15,11:4
Glidden, G D B, 1885, Ja 27,5:4
Glidden, Henry L, 1949, F 23,27:5
Glidden, James D, 1960, Ap 30,47:2
Glidden, Jay S, 1940, O 28,17:5
Glidden, John N, 1964, S 18,35:1
Glidden, Jonathan (P Dawson), 1957, Jl 23,25
Glidden, Mae Z Mrs, 1945, D 24,15:5
Glidden, Mary P T Mrs, 1953, Ap 15,31:3
Glidden, Miles A, 1938, Je 19,29:1
Glidden, Minnie M, 1938, D 29,20:3
Glidden, Nathaniel F, 1965, Jl 6,34:2
Glidden, Nathaniel F Mrs, 1964, D 3,49:2
Glidden, Robert G Mrs, 1948, Ja 22,27:3
Glider, Samuel Mrs, 1950, N 23,35:2
Gliedt, Theodore, 1938, D 26,23:4
Gliem, John H, 1939, O 21,15:4
Glienke, Franziska, 1955, Je 11,15:6
Gliere, Reinhold (funl, Je 29,21:6), 1956, Je
Gliet, Albert, 1951, Ja 19,25:4
Gliet, Gustav, 1950, O 20,28:3
Glikin, Samuel, 1942, Mr 1,45:2
Gliksman, Jerzy, 1958, S 15,21:6
Glimm, Clarence E, 1939, Ap 29,17:6
Glines, Earle S, 1963, Ag 31,17:2
Glines, Stephen D, 1938, S 11,II,11:2
Glines, Walter A, 1947, N 17,21:2
Glines, Walter A Mrs, 1951, Ag 28,23:4
Glinka, F N, 1880, F 26,4:6
Glinos, John D, 1959, Ja 8,29:4
Glintenkamp, George W, 1953, Jl 25,11:4
Glintenkamp, Hendrik (por), 1946, Mr 20,2
Glintenkamp, Hendrik Mrs, 1967, D 11,47:3
Glisson, James Y, 1952, Jl 22,25:3
Glisson, John, 1950, Ag 11,25:6
Glitsch, H, 1943, F 23,6:3
Glixon, S Arthur, 1964, Jl 26,57:1
Globus, James, 1950, O 4,31:3
Globus, James Mrs, 1957, O 11,27:4
Globus, Joseph H, 1952, N 21,26:3
Gloeckler, Frederick, 1940, Ag 6,20:3
Gloeckner, Caroline A, 1941, Mr 8,19:5
Gloeckner, Charles F, 1950, O 31,27:4
Gloeckner, Eleanor M, 1965, D 2,41:3
Gloeckner, Karl, 1953, O 4,89:1
Gloeckner, Louis B, 1937, N 26,26:4
Glogau, Emile Mrs, 1951, Mr 9,25:1
Glogau, Jack, 1953, O 31,17:5
Glogovsky, Matthew N, 1951, S 13,31:6
Glogowski, Kurt, 1960, D 12,29:4
Glore, Charles F, 1950, O 7,17:2
Glore, Evins F, 1941, Ap 14,17:4
Glore, Harrison C (por), 1955, Je 8,29:3
Glorieux, Alphonsus J Rev, 1917, Ag 26,19:

Glorieux, Henry, 1916, S 21,11:2
Glorieux, William L, 1924, Ap 19,13:5
Glos, Lucy M Mrs, 1941, Jl 1,23:2
Glose, Adolph, 1939, O 12,25:6
Gloss, George M, 1952, F 7,27:3
Gloss, John A, 1945, Ap 1,36:3
Gloss, Petronella Mrs, 1947, Mr 19,25:4
Gloss, Samuel D, 1941, N 18,25:4
Glosser, David, 1954, Ag 29,88:5
Glosser, David A, 1964, Mr 15,86:4
Glosser, Nathan, 1955, S 11,85:1
Glossinger, John, 1968, Jl 25,33:1
Glossop, Glenn A, 1962, Ag 22,33:1
Glosten, Edward R, 1958, S 6,17:4
Gloster, Robert F, 1954, Jl 15,27:4
Gloth, William C, 1944, D 4,23:4
Glotzbach, Frank L, 1947, Ap 7,23:3
Glotzbach, James M, 1949, Ap 16,15:3
Glover, Albert, 1951, N 19,23:1
Glover, Albert G, 1941, Ag 5,20:2
Glover, Amelia (Mrs Al Laurence), 1910, F 10,7:5
Glover, Arthur J, 1949, My 9,25:4
Glover, Charles C Mrs, 1943, Ap 15,25:2
Glover, Charles L, 1922, O 27,17:4
Glover, Charles P Mrs, 1947, O 3,25:3
Glover, David D, 1952, Ap 7,25:2
Glover, E Elizabeth, 1967, Mr 31,37:4
Glover, Earl F, 1943, Jl 17,13:4
Glover, Frederic S, 1954, Ja 15,19:4
Glover, G Horton, 1941, N 24,17:5
Glover, H Lester Mrs, 1952, Mr 15,13:6
Glover, Hamilton F, 1950, Ja 12,27:3
Glover, Henry L, 1954, Je 19,15:6
Glover, Herbert J, 1959, F 16,29:2
Glover, Herbert J Mrs, 1951, S 1,11:2
Glover, Howard M, 1923, Mr 24,13:5
Glover, Hunter, 1948, D 14,29:4
Glover, J M, 1931, S 9,27:5
Glover, James W, 1941, Jl 16,17:2
Glover, Jesse W Mrs, 1964, N 4,39:2
Glover, John C, 1956, Je 7,13:3
Glover, John E, 1948, Je 12,15:1
Glover, John I Mrs, 1945, F 4,38:1
Glover, Joseph L, 1939, Mr 14,21:5
Glover, Joseph P, 1955, My 13,25:4
Glover, Maxwell H, 1952, My 13,30:1
Glover, Morton L, 1952, D 9,33:5
Glover, Patrick W R, 1957, Ap 27,19:3
Glover, R, 1884, D 25,1:5
Glover, R Mrs, 1884, D 25,1:5
Glover, Ralph J Msgr, 1968, Ja 14,54:4
Glover, Rhoda Mrs, 1920, O 8,13:1
Glover, Rita, 1959, S 5,15:6
Glover, Robert H, 1947, Mr 25,25:5
Glover, Robert H Mrs, 1953, Ja 30,22:3
Glover, Robert P, 1961, F 2,29:2
Glover, Roy N (funl plans; trb, Ap 2,31:4), 1958, Ap 1,31:2
Glover, Samuel L, 1945, Je 28,19:3
Glover, T A, 1878, Ja 7,8:2
Glover, Terrot R, 1943, My 28,21:1
Glover, Thomas B, 1966, N 8,39:2
Glover, Thomas E, 1962, O 6,2:8
Glover, Thomas J, 1939, N 5,49:3
Glover, W Curtis, 1968, Ap 2,47:2
Glover, W Harvey, 1959, N 22,86:5
Glover, W Harvey Mrs, 1954, Mr 31,27:2
Glover, W Irving, 1956, My 1,33:1
Glover, William, 1944, Mr 14,19:1
Glover, William E, 1961, O 28,21:1
Glover, William F, 1917, O 29,13:2
Glover, William H, 1953, F 24,25:4
Glover, William Mrs, 1950, Ag 27,89:2
Glowacki, William, 1953, N 10,31:4
Glowe, John, 1947, F 26,25:4
Glubb, Frederick M, 1938, Ag 2,19:4
Gluchowski, Kaziemierz, 1941, S 17,23:2
Gluchowsky, Meyer S Mrs, 1947, S 4,25:6
Gluck, Alma (por), 1938, O 28,23:1
Gluck, Arnold J (J Arnold), 1962, Je 16,19:2
Gluck, Charles H, 1938, F 17,21:3
Gluck, Charlotte Van N, 1959, Mr 19,33:4
Gluck, David H, 1956, Ap 17,31:3
Gluck, Edwin L, 1953, S 1,23:2
Gluck, Ernest, 1943, F 12,21:2; 1967, Je 25,69:1
Gluck, Frank T, 1952, Mr 29,15:3
Gluck, Henry, 1954, N 18,33:1
Gluck, Henry L, 1950, N 1,35:3
Gluck, Joseph, 1967, S 18,47:3
Gluck, Julius C, 1954, Ja 13,31:5
Gluck, Morton E, 1958, O 2,37:4
Gluck, Nathaniel, 1950, N 1,35:2
Gluck, Samuel, 1957, My 18,19:6
Gluck, Samuel Dr, 1908, D 19,9:4
Gluck, Samuel J, 1943, Ag 13,17:4
Gluck, Themistocles, 1942, Ap 30,19:5
Gluck, Walter, 1957, F 6,25:3
Gluck, William H, 1958, O 6,31:3
Gluckin, Harry, 1951, Ap 9,25:4
Gluckman, Dennis, 1965, D 10,47:3
Gluckman, Herman, 1939, Ap 30,44:6
Gluckman, Saul K, 1966, F 28,27:4
Glucksman, Benjamin L, 1957, S 26,25:4
Glucksman, Charles, 1948, S 2,23:3
Glucksman, Erwin J, 1957, O 18,23:1
Glucksman, Harry L, 1938, F 19,15:1
Gluckson, Isadore, 1966, My 25,47:1
Gluckstadt, Eric J, 1952, Mr 4,27:3
Gluckstein, Alex M, 1952, Mr 15,13:3
Gluckstein, Isidore, 1920, D 13,15:5
Gluckstern, Samuel, 1946, Jl 24,27:2
Glueck, Adolph M, 1948, My 21,23:2
Glueck, Anna Mrs, 1954, S 8,31:4
Glueck, Charles F, 1940, S 6,21:2
Glueck, Ernest Mrs, 1958, Ap 6,88:8
Glueck, Frank J, 1956, Ap 11,33:5
Glueck, Herman Mrs (Gemma), 1962, N 3,25:1
Glueck, Jason R, 1952, F 2,13:6
Gluek, Alvin G, 1952, Je 2,21:1
Gluhareff, Michael E, 1967, S 5,43:1
Gluhareff, Serge E, 1958, Ja 10,26:1
Glunt, Omer, 1963, Je 28,30:1
Glunz, Charles A Mrs, 1950, Je 22,27:5
Glunz, Charles E, 1947, N 28,27:1
Glushak, Joseph, 1939, O 20,23:5
Glushak, Leopold I, 1964, Mr 25,41:3
Glushak, Leopold Mrs, 1962, Ap 17,35:5
Gluskstern, Simon, 1954, F 9,27:2
Glutting, Paul R, 1962, Ap 16,29:4
Glyer, G Arthur, 1944, Ja 22,13:1
Glyn, C Adm, 1884, F 18,5:1
Glyn, Elinor, 1943, S 24,23:1
Glyn, Maurice, 1920, Ag 22,20:5
Glynn, Bernard (funl), 1914, Ap 13,11:4
Glynn, Bridget (Sister Mary Patricia), 1963, My 13, 29:2
Glynn, Cornelius, 1938, Jl 6,9:2
Glynn, Edward L, 1956, O 5,25:4
Glynn, Ella (will), 1941, Ap 8,31:8
Glynn, Francis J, 1938, F 7,15:4
Glynn, Frank L, 1947, Ag 1,17:2
Glynn, G A, 1926, Ag 15,II,7:1
Glynn, George Mrs, 1959, O 28,37:2
Glynn, Gerald T, 1955, Jl 23,17:3
Glynn, Harold C, 1953, Ja 24,15:5
Glynn, Helen C, 1941, N 6,23:1
Glynn, James P, 1942, My 10,42:7
Glynn, James T, 1945, F 10,11:4
Glynn, John E Mrs, 1946, D 13,23:1
Glynn, John J, 1941, Ag 19,21:4; 1942, F 11,21:2; 1946, Jl 24,27:1; 1957, Mr 31,89:2
Glynn, Joseph F, 1948, Ap 15,25:3
Glynn, Margaret D (Sister Mary Edmund), 1942, Je 17,23:6
Glynn, Margaret M (Sister Grace Antonia), 1965, Je 11,31:1
Glynn, Marion Mrs, 1950, S 19,26:3
Glynn, Martin H Ex-Gov, 1924, D 16,25:3
Glynn, Martin H Mrs (will, Mr 6,62:5), 1949, Ja 1, 13:2
Glynn, Matthew A, 1957, Ag 10,15:5
Glynn, Peter J, 1939, O 8,3:6
Glynn, Pierce T, 1965, Ap 26,31:3
Glynn, Thomas J, 1938, My 24,19:3
Glynn, Thomas Mrs, 1950, My 5,21:2
Glynn, Thomas V, 1941, Je 26,23:5
Glynn, Vincent D Mrs, 1942, Ja 6,23:5
Glynn, William J, 1947, Mr 23,60:2
Glynne, Stephen Sir, 1874, Je 18,1:7
Gmeiner, George J, 1956, F 10,21:4
Gmelin, Paul, 1937, N 21,II,8:8
Gmuer, Dorothy R Mrs, 1950, My 11,29:2
Gmur, Beat, 1952, Mr 31,19:1
Gnade, Edward R, 1947, Ag 14,23:3
Gnaedinger, Emil J, 1939, S 30,17:6
Gnesina, Yelena, 1967, Je 6,44:4
Gnessin, Menachem, 1951, Ag 23,23:6
Gnevshin, Afanasiy, 1938, Jl 26,19:4
Gnichtel, William S, 1937, Mr 4,23:2
Gniessin, Mikhail F, 1957, My 10,27:2
Gnocchi, Carlo, 1956, Mr 1,4:5
Goad, Bertram Mrs, 1947, D 1,21:3
Goadby, Clarence, 1916, Ja 8,9:5
Goadby, Eugene, 1918, Ap 17,13:4
Goadie, David R, 1907, Ja 24,9:5
Goan, Orrin S, 1941, O 30,23:4
Goas, Harry J, 1946, D 25,29:3
Goas, Howard L, 1958, Mr 21,21:5
Goate, Edward B, 1962, O 10,47:3
Gobat, Charles Albert, 1914, Mr 17,11:4
Gobbi, Clothilde O, 1960, N 8,29:3
Gobbi, John, 1950, Ap 29,15:3
Gobeille, Harrold L, 1958, Ap 3,31:4
Gobel, Adolph, 1924, Mr 27,19:5
Gobel, Herman, 1964, N 30,33:4
Gobel, R D, 1944, Ja 7,17:5
Goben, George Mrs, 1942, Ag 26,19:4
Gober, Walter D, 1961, Mr 29,33:3
Gobin, Hillary A Dr, 1923, Mr 19,17:5
Gobin, J P S Maj-Gen, 1910, My 2,9:4
Goble, Edward R, 1942, My 7,19:6
Goble, Frank B, 1940, Ag 10,13:3
Goble, George W, 1963, S 22,86:8
Goble, Harry V, 1960, S 17,23:6
Goble, James O, 1943, F 6,13:3
Goble, Luther Spencer, 1905, Ja 21,9:4
Goble, Stanley J (por), 1948, Jl 26,17:3
Goble, William J, 1948, S 8,30:2
Goble, Wilson F, 1963, My 28,28:5
Goblet, Rene, 1905, S 14,9:4
Gobright, S A, 1881, My 15,1:6
Gochenour, Arthur B, 1949, N 13,92:7
Gocher, William H, 1937, N 21,II,8:8
Gock, Alfred J, 1962, Ap 7,25:3
Gockel, Joseph, 1941, Jl 24,17:5
Godard, Aretas A, 1948, S 11,15:4
Godard, C W, 1883, F 21,2:4
Godard, Emile S, 1948, Mr 28,48:3
Godard, Gabrielle, 1942, F 8,50:2
Goday, Jose Senor, 1869, O 9,4:1
Godbeer, George H, 1961, N 17,35:4
Godbeer, George H Mrs, 1953, O 5,27:1
Godbold, Edgar, 1952, N 22,23:2
Godbout, Adelard, 1956, S 19,37:5
Godbout, Eugene, 1943, Mr 27,13:3
Godbout, Oscar, 1967, Je 18,76:4
Godby, Edward J, 1946, Jl 29,21:4
Godby, J Joseph, 1959, Ja 31,19:5
Godby, Joseph P, 1968, N 9,33:5
Godcharles, Frederic A, 1944, D 31,25:2
Godchaux, Charles, 1954, O 24,89:1
Godchaux, Frank A Sr, 1965, Jl 5,17:4
Godchaux, Jules, 1951, Jl 6,23:3
Godchaux, Paul L, 1924, S 30,23:1
Godd, G D, 1933, Ja 8,30:1
Goddard, Alvano C, 1952, Mr 4,28:3
Goddard, Alvin C, 1958, O 12,86:2
Goddard, Arthur E, 1955, Ap 13,29:6
Goddard, Calvin H, 1955, F 23,27:5
Goddard, Charles A, 1965, Mr 15,31:3
Goddard, Charles F, 1946, My 21,23:4; 1954, Ap 9, 23:4
Goddard, Charles F Mrs, 1941, F 28,41:2
Goddard, Charles H, 1962, S 22,25:4
Goddard, Charles H Mrs, 1959, O 6,39:2
Goddard, Charles W, 1951, Ja 12,27:1
Goddard, Clarence W, 1939, Je 29,23:4
Goddard, Convers, 1945, Ja 20,11:5
Goddard, D A, 1882, Ja 11,5:4
Goddard, Dwight, 1939, Jl 9,30:6
Goddard, E Claude, 1941, Ag 7,17:2
Goddard, Edwin C, 1942, Ag 16,44:8
Goddard, Ely Col, 1910, O 20,13:4
Goddard, F Norton, 1905, My 29,1:1
Goddard, F Percy Mrs, 1965, Ap 6,39:3
Goddard, Francis, 1918, My 30,11:4
Goddard, Francis W, 1958, Mr 18,29:2
Goddard, Frederic W, 1953, My 4,23:6
Goddard, Frederick R, 1947, Ap 29,27:3
Goddard, George E, 1942, F 23,21:4
Goddard, George W Jr, 1966, Ag 8,27:5
Goddard, Harold C, 1950, F 28,30:2
Goddard, Harold C Mrs, 1950, Ja 12,27:4
Goddard, Henry, 1955, Ag 27,15:3
Goddard, Henry H, 1957, Je 22,15:3
Goddard, Herbert A, 1944, Ja 15,13:1
Goddard, Herbert M, 1943, N 24,21:5
Goddard, Ira, 1919, Je 6,13:5
Goddard, Irvine, 1955, Ag 4,25:2
Goddard, J F, 1901, My 15,9:6
Goddard, Jacob M, 1968, O 20,86:5
Goddard, John C (por), 1945, Mr 18,41:1
Goddard, John Mrs, 1948, My 5,25:1
Goddard, John N, 1944, Ag 28,11:5; 1948, D 10,25:1
Goddard, John T, 1952, N 28,25:2
Goddard, Joseph, 1943, O 2,13:5
Goddard, Josiah H, 1944, Mr 13,15:4
Goddard, Kingston Rev, 1875, O 26,4:5
Goddard, Leonard M, 1953, Ap 18,19:5
Goddard, Leslie L, 1940, Ap 14,45:1
Goddard, Malcolm D, 1968, D 2,29:1
Goddard, Mark G, 1943, S 28,25:4
Goddard, Mary A, 1941, Ja 19,40:6
Goddard, Morrill (will), 1938, D 31,2:8
Goddard, Morrill G, 1937, Jl 2,21:3
Goddard, Norman O Mrs, 1949, My 13,23:2
Goddard, P E, 1928, Jl 14,13:5
Goddard, Percy S (funl plans, Mr 31,27:2), 1954, Mr 30,27:1
Goddard, Robert H (por), 1945, Ag 11,13:3
Goddard, Robert H I (will, N 29,147:4), 1959, N 21, 23:2
Goddard, Robert Hale Ives Col, 1916, Ap 24,13:4
Goddard, Robert Hale Ives Mrs, 1914, Jl 3,9:6
Goddard, Ruben J, 1939, N 4,15:5
Goddard, Stephen J, 1967, My 22,43:2
Goddard, Thomas J, 1959, Ag 6,27:5
Goddard, Walter E, 1951, N 16,36:1
Goddard, William, 1954, Ja 17,93:2
Goddard, William Col, 1907, S 21,9:4
Goddard, William I Sr, 1944, My 17,19:6
Goddard, William Mrs, 1921, Je 30,17:2
Goddard, William Neale Capt, 1917, Jl 6,9:6
Goddard, William W, 1967, Mr 30,45:4
Godde, Timothy H Mrs (will), 1943, S 28,12:3
Godde, Timothy Mrs, 1943, Je 19,13:6
Godden, Stephen E, 1954, S 22,29:3
Goddin, John M, 1958, Je 22,76:2
Goddin, John M Mrs, 1952, Jl 29,21:1

Goddu, Louis A O Dr, 1937, N 13,19:5
Godebski, Cyprien, 1909, N 27,9:5
Godeffroy, Richard, 1913, N 26,11:6
Godehn, Paul M, 1952, F 1,22:2
Godell, Lavinia, 1880, Ap 2,2:5
Godey, L A, 1878, N 30,2:4
Godfrey, Ada S Mrs, 1952, Je 1,84:4
Godfrey, Alvin K, 1956, Jl 6,21:1
Godfrey, Arthur Hanbury Mrs, 1968, F 28,47:4
Godfrey, C C, 1927, S 1,23:5
Godfrey, C H, 1928, S 25,31:3
Godfrey, Carlos E, 1941, Ja 9,21:2
Godfrey, Charles, 1949, Ag 21,68:7
Godfrey, Charles H, 1940, Ag 9,15:2
Godfrey, Chester N, 1952, My 7,27:6
Godfrey, Dan, 1903, Jl 1,5:1
Godfrey, Dan Sir, 1939, Jl 21,19:4
Godfrey, Daniel C, 1945, Jl 14,11:8
Godfrey, Edward J, 1949, Jl 3,26:4
Godfrey, Edward K, 1958, D 4,39:5
Godfrey, Edward S Jr, 1960, D 14,35:4
Godfrey, Edwin D, 1951, N 3,17:6
Godfrey, Elmer E, 1938, Je 17,21:3
Godfrey, Fletcher, 1962, Mr 19,29:1
Godfrey, Frank M, 1947, My 22,27:3
Godfrey, Fred, 1953, F 23,25:4
Godfrey, George, 1947, Ag 14,23:6
Godfrey, George W Mrs, 1950, Ja 25,25:1
Godfrey, Grace, 1944, Ag 26,11:7
Godfrey, H, 1936, Ja 19,II,8:5
Godfrey, Harry, 1944, O 14,13:5
Godfrey, Harry B, 1951, D 19,31:1
Godfrey, Henry F, 1940, Je 11,25:6
Godfrey, Howard G, 1959, Jl 30,27:2
Godfrey, Ida E Mrs, 1941, F 13,19:4
Godfrey, J Clark, 1948, N 27,17:3
Godfrey, J W, 1901, N 10,13:3
Godfrey, James D, 1950, F 22,29:2
Godfrey, James J, 1942, Ag 30,42:7
Godfrey, James M, 1948, Jl 2,21:4
Godfrey, John E, 1966, Ag 16,39:2
Godfrey, John T, 1958, Je 13,23:4
Godfrey, Jonathan, 1882, Ag 4,5:2
Godfrey, Jonathan Mrs, 1916, N 26,21:1
Godfrey, Lincoln, 1916, F 9,11:6; 1950, Je 27,29:4
Godfrey, Lincoln Jr, 1958, D 20,2:5
Godfrey, Macauley S U, 1941, S 30,23:6
Godfrey, Maurice F, 1941, Jl 6,27:2
Godfrey, Norman L, 1947, Ja 25,17:4
Godfrey, Oscar M, 1941, Mr 17,17:3
Godfrey, Peter T, 1957, Je 2,87:1
Godfrey, Ray A, 1950, N 21,31:3
Godfrey, Robert, 1953, Ap 11,17:2
Godfrey, Samuel, 1956, F 25,19:4
Godfrey, Samuel T, 1949, Ja 19,27:4
Godfrey, Sebastian, 1946, Ap 26,21:2
Godfrey, Spencer K, 1963, Je 28,30:1
Godfrey, Vaughn, 1965, S 4,21:4
Godfrey, Walter E, 1958, Mr 27,33:2
Godfrey, William Cardinal (funl, Ja 30,9:4), 1963, Ja 23,7:2
Godfrey, William T, 1943, S 5,29:2
Godfrey-Faussett, Bryan, 1945, S 23,46:6
Godfroy, Frank, 1938, Je 29,19:5
Godhelp, Jacob C, 1946, D 20,24:2
Godigkeit, John F, 1938, Ag 17,19:1
Godillot, John F Mrs, 1955, O 29,19:2
Godin, Emilie G, 1945, My 31,15:5
Godin, Marcel, 1954, S 13,23:2
Godinez, Sebastian de Mrs, 1943, N 4,23:4
Goding, William, 1949, O 22,17:2
Godkin, E L, 1902, My 22,9:3
Godkin, Edwin Lawrence Mrs, 1907, N 9,9:4
Godknecht, Paul E, 1961, F 25,21:5
Godknecht, Paul E Mrs, 1962, Jl 12,29:2
Godlee, Phil, 1952, S 28,77:1
Godlee, Rickman J Sir, 1925, Ap 21,21:5
Godlewski, Bronislaw, 1954, S 25,15:5
Godlewski, Leon A, 1948, Ag 26,21:3
Godley, Clarence B, 1942, S 14,15:1
Godley, Edwin A, 1948, N 15,25:3
Godley, Frederick A, 1961, F 22,25:2
Godley, Frederick A Mrs, 1962, S 21,30:4
Godley, George M, 1940, Ag 12,15:6
Godley, Henry Sr, 1950, My 6,15:3
Godley, Michael F, 1941, Ag 16,15:5
Godley, Paul F Mrs, 1963, Je 6,35:2
Godlove, Isaac H, 1954, Ag 15,85:1
Godman, Cyril, 1938, Ap 4,17:3
Godnick, Charles S, 1957, My 19,88:3
Godnick, Samuel P, 1958, S 8,29:4
Godnick, William N, 1937, S 8,23:3
Godoff, Harry, 1937, S 9,23:2
Godofsky, Elias I, 1951, N 28,31:1
Godolphin, Francis R, 1965, Ag 24,31:2
Godolphin, Francis R Mrs, 1959, Mr 24,39:4
Godolphin, Thomas, 1962, Ag 2,15:1
Godon, S W Rear-Adm, 1879, My 18,2:5
Godone, J, 1880, F 4,3:3
Godowsky, Leopold (por), 1938, N 22,23:1
Godoy, Mrs, 1940, D 22,30:2
Godoy, Ruperto, 1950, My 31,29:2
Godoy Agostini, Gaston, 1954, F 16,25:3

Godrey, Aaron W, 1943, D 22,23:2
Godron, Mary S Mrs, 1941, Ap 12,15:1
Godron, William E, 1947, Ap 15,25:5
Godsen, Thomas, 1903, Je 13,9:6
Godsey, Susan C, 1873, N 10,5:5
Godshalk, David O, 1911, Ja 30,9:4
Godshalk, Ernest L, 1955, O 12,31:2
Godshall, Wilson L, 1956, Je 2,20:1
Godsho, Albert P, 1955, Ja 9,87:3
Godsoe, Robert U, 1962, N 13,37:2
Godson, Jose Mrs, 1954, Jl 21,27:2
Godson, William F H Jr, 1940, S 14,17:4
Godstrey, William C, 1940, F 21,19:2
Godwin, A H, 1884, Ja 6,5:2
Godwin, Becky (funl), 1968, S 1,18:1
Godwin, Bernard, 1967, F 16,44:2
Godwin, Cortlandt, 1953, Je 4,29:2
Godwin, Cortlandt Mrs, 1953, Ap 10,21:4
Godwin, Daniel, 1884, Ap 17,4:7
Godwin, David P Mrs (T Strabel), 1959, My 29,23:4
Godwin, Earl, 1956, S 25,33:3
Godwin, Francis (Frank), 1959, Ag 6,27:3
Godwin, Frederick M, 1961, Ag 22,29:4
Godwin, Harold Mrs, 1951, D 31,13:5
Godwin, Herbert, 1952, Ag 5,19:1
Godwin, Jack W Mrs, 1942, N 27,23:4
Godwin, Joanne Mrs, 1951, Ja 19,26:2
Godwin, Joseph H, 1903, Ag 10,7:6; 1947, My 29,21:1
Godwin, Parke, 1904, Ja 8,7:4
Godwin, Philander H Mrs, 1960, F 11,26:3
Godwin, R Hugh, 1964, Jl 9,33:4
Godwin, Roy M, 1965, O 21,47:2
Godwin, Stuart, 1944, Mr 21,19:4
Godwin, Thomas M, 1940, My 31,19:4
Godwin, Victor, 1950, Je 18,76:4
Godwin, Victor Mrs, 1952, My 20,25:1
Godwin-Austen, Henry Haversham Lt-Col, 1923, D 5, 19:4
Godzinski, Anne (Sister Mary Eudosia), 1955, N 3, 31:5
Goe, Theodore J, 1939, My 12,21:2
Goebbels, Katharina Mrs, 1953, Ag 12,31:5
Goebbels, Konrad, 1949, Je 13,19:2
Goebel, Albert C, 1950, D 11,25:4
Goebel, Anthony Rev, 1937, D 18,21:4
Goebel, Charles C, 1950, N 22,25:1
Goebel, Frank J, 1962, My 13,88:5
Goebel, George C, 1943, Mr 12,17:4
Goebel, Henry Sr, 1943, D 30,18:2
Goebel, Karl J, 1937, Je 9,25:1
Goebel, Lewis S, 1915, N 4,11:4
Goebel, Oscar, 1953, Ja 3,15:3
Goebel, Sophie F B Mrs, 1938, Ap 13,25:4
Goebel, William, 1940, Mr 15,23:5
Goebel, William Gov, 1900, F 4,1:7
Goebler, Fred A, 1952, My 11,93:2
Goeckel, Henry J, 1960, Je 13,27:4
Goeckel, Henry J Mrs, 1957, O 19,21:5
Goeckler, Frank E, 1960, Ap 12,33:4
Goeddert, Ernst, 1949, N 1,27:3
Goeddert, Karl A, 1945, Ag 14,21:4
Goeddert, William H Jr Mrs, 1953, N 10,31:3
Goedecke, Milton, 1961, D 4,37:2
Goedecke, Oscar A Jr, 1958, Ag 5,27:5
Goedeke, Frank Jr, 1953, Je 22,21:4
Goedel, Herman, 1940, Ja 24,21:3
Goeding, Francis B, 1940, Je 26,23:2
Goedkoop, Daniel, 1947, Mr 5,25:5
Goedrich, Paul, 1948, Mr 16,27:5
Goeghegan, John F, 1945, Ag 8,23:5
Goehler, Olga E, 1940, O 7,17:1
Goehr, Walter, 1960, D 5,31:6
Goehren, George E, 1944, Je 13,19:4
Goehring, Harrison D, 1950, Ja 18,31:3
Goehring, Richard C, 1953, Jl 6,17:5
Goeke, Joseph G, 1949, N 30,27:3
Goeku, Chosho, 1957, Mr 6,31:4
Goelet, Beatrice, 1902, F 12,9:5
Goelet, Henry, 1962, Ag 30,29:1
Goelet, J B, 1882, S 3,2:6
Goelet, M R Mrs, 1929, F 24,30:1
Goelet, Ogden, 1897, Ag 28,7:4
Goelet, Peter, 1879, N 22,1:5
Goelet, Robert, 1879, S 23,8:2; 1899, Ap 28,7:1; 1966, F 7,29:1
Goelet, Robert Mrs (funl, D 21,13:5), 1912, D 5,17:1
Goelet, Robert Mrs, 1914, Ag 1,9:7
Goelet, Robert W (will, Jl 12,15:8), 1941, My 3,15:1
Goelet, Robert W Mrs (por), 1949, Jl 15,19:1
Goelet, Roberta W Mrs, 1949, Jl 17,56:7
Goell, Charles, 1954, O 16,17:6
Goell, Jacob, 1940, N 27,23:4
Goeller, Charles, 1961, Ag 1,31:1
Goeller, Charles L, 1955, Mr 8,27:2
Goeller, Emily, 1958, O 21,33:5
Goeller, Gustave R, 1941, Jl 23,20:5
Goeller, Jacob D, 1956, Ja 4,27:3
Goeller, Robert A Mrs, 1937, Jl 24,15:4
Goeltz, Louis, 1877, N 14,4:7
Goeltz, William S Mrs, 1947, S 9,31:2
Goelz, Albert, 1960, My 26,33:3
Goembel, John E, 1945, D 23,8:1
Goemboes, Julius Mrs, 1939, N 30,21:5

Goemboes de Jakfa, J, 1936, O 7,21:2
Goenaga, Francis R de Dr, 1937, Mr 2,21:3
Goepel, Walter Eugene, 1919, Ag 21,11:5
Goepel, Walter R, 1956, Mr 16,23:3
Goepfert, Charles H, 1937, Ag 11,24:4
Goepp, R Max, 1950, My 19,27:2
Goepp, R Max Jr, 1946, O 12,19:4
Goeppe, Albert, 1946, Je 15,21:5
Goerge, Albert Joseph, 1968, Ja 9,43:3
Goerge, Voya (Djordjevich), 1951, My 12,21:2
Goergei, Arthur Gen, 1916, My 23,11:5
Goergii-Georgenau, Baroness von, 1953, D 2,2:7
Goericke, Henry E, 1948, N 11,27:4
Goering, Adina, 1942, Je 23,19:2
Goering, Bernard, 1949, D 3,15:1
Goering, G Charles, 1953, Ap 3,23:2
Goeringer, Fred J Jr, 1944, Je 10,15:4
Goerke, Oscar J, 1963, D 23,25:3
Goerke, Rudolph J, 1938, Ap 14,23:5
Goerke, Rudolph J Jr, 1964, Mr 4,34:6
Goerner, Friedrich A, 1948, S 28,27:3
Goerss, Richard W, 1941, Ag 20,19:3
Goertner, Francis R, 1964, Ag 16,92:8
Goertner, George S, 1939, Ag 2,19:4
Goes, Charles (Charley Burns), 1944, F 15,17:6
Goes, Louis L, 1946, N 13,27:5
Goessmann, Charles Anthony Dr, 1910, S 2,9:6
Goetchius, Charles W, 1938, Je 4,15:4
Goetchius, Morgan, 1950, Je 15,31:5
Goetchius, Seymour, 1940, My 29,23:5
Goethals, Effie R Mrs, 1942, Ja 2,23:4
Goethals, Frederick C, 1915, Ap 17,11:2
Goethals, G W, 1928, Ja 22,1:2
Goethals, John, 1942, Ag 26,19:5
Goethals, Thomas R, 1962, Mr 25,88:2
Goethe, Joseph A, 1948, Ja 8,25:5
Goethschlus, Benjamin, 1948, Ap 23,23:4
Goetsch, Charles, 1940, My 1,23:3
Goetsch, Emil, 1963, My 24,31:3
Goetsch, F A, 1947, F 17,19:5
Goetsch, Walter R, 1950, My 9,31:4
Goetschius, Garrett A, 1954, N 1,27:5
Goetschius, John M, 1946, Je 5,23:1
Goetschius, Percy, 1943, N 19,19:5
Goett, John J, 1951, S 12,31:2
Goetter, Peter P, 1947, Je 3,25:2
Goetting, Adolph H, 1923, My 2,19:3
Goetting, August H Col, 1920, O 4,13:2
Goetting, Louis C Jr, 1962, O 4,39:5
Goettsche, George, 1947, D 13,15:3
Goetz, Arthur B, 1959, Mr 10,35:1
Goetz, Aug, 1940, S 5,23:4
Goetz, Augustus, 1957, O 1,33:1
Goetz, David, 1965, Ja 22,43:1
Goetz, E Ray, 1954, Je 14,21:1
Goetz, Ferdinand Dr (funl, O 19,11:4), 1915, O 11:5
Goetz, Francis, 1937, Ja 10,II,9:2
Goetz, George, 1961, Je 19,27:5
Goetz, Henry E, 1947, F 21,19:2
Goetz, Herbert C, 1941, Ap 9,25:6
Goetz, Isador, 1952, Ap 19,15:4
Goetz, Jacob H, 1957, My 19,88:5
Goetz, Jennie L Mrs, 1939, D 3,60:8
Goetz, John, 1939, My 13,15:5; 1944, Ag 27,33:2; 1952, My 29,27:3
Goetz, John G Mrs, 1952, Mr 4,27:3
Goetz, John H, 1950, S 26,31:4; 1964, Ap 25,29:
Goetz, Joseph, 1917, My 17,13:6
Goetz, Joseph G, 1956, Ja 3,31:3
Goetz, Lawrence, 1962, N 1,31:4
Goetz, Louis, 1943, Je 11,19:4
Goetz, Marie, 1922, D 18,17:5
Goetz, Marie D, 1949, Ag 23,23:4
Goetz, Morris, 1938, Je 14,21:2
Goetz, Norman S Mrs, 1953, N 3,31:3
Goetz, Oswald H, 1960, O 18,39:2
Goetz, Paul, 1937, O 18,17:5
Goetz, Phil B, 1950, D 2,13:6
Goetz, Richard, 1954, D 11,13:3
Goetz, Richard (will), 1955, Mr 27,118:6
Goetz, Richard K, 1943, F 4,23:1
Goetz, Robert C F, 1965, Ag 3,31:2
Goetz, Wilbur E, 1957, S 26,25:3
Goetz, William, 1938, O 17,3:6; 1942, Ja 18,42; 1951, Ag 15,27:5
Goetze, Frederick A, 1950, Mr 8,25:1
Goetze, Frederick W, 1944, F 1,19:6
Goetze, G A, 1882, Mr 22,5:5
Goetze, Sigismund, 1939, O 25,23:5
Goetzen, Adolph von Count, 1910, D 2,9:5
Goetzen, Engelbert Mrs, 1962, My 9,43:1
Goetzinger, Martin E, 1953, Ja 9,21:2
Goetzman, Alfred M, 1944, My 2,19:4
Goewey, Dwight L, 1955, D 19,27:4
Goff, Almon P, 1949, N 10,31:5
Goff, Byron H, 1962, Je 25,29:1
Goff, Charles A, 1939, N 24,23:4
Goff, D L, 1926, Jl 23,13:5
Goff, Darius, 1938, Ja 7,19:5
Goff, Dora A Mrs, 1958, O 6,31:3
Goff, Frank Dr, 1968, Ag 30,33:2
Goff, Fred H, 1923, Mr 15,19:5

Goff, Fred H Mrs, 1956, Jl 14,15:6
Goff, G Russell, 1942, Mr 15,42:8
Goff, G W, 1876, Mr 5,2:7
Goff, John W (funl, N 11,23:1), 1924, N 10,17:3
Goff, John W, 1944, D 19,21:2
Goff, John W mrs, 1911, Jl 31,7:6
Goff, L B, 1927, Ap 3,28:1
Goff, Mandel B, 1950, Ja 26,27:4
Goff, Nathan, 1920, Ap 24,15:3
Goff, Nathan Gen, 1903, Ap 18,9:4
Goff, Nathan 3d, 1961, F 26,92:8
Goff, Orlo S, 1950, S 1,21:5
Goff, Park Sir (por), 1939, Ag 16,III,7:2
Goff, Samuel, 1947, O 9,25:4
Goff, William A, 1947, Je 11,27:3
Goff, William E, 1942, D 14,23:2
Goff, Winfred, 1907, F 12,9:6
Goffe, Robert H, 1968, D 7,47:2
Goffe, Robert H Sr, 1944, D 8,21:5
Goffe, Robert H Sr Mrs, 1946, F 25,25:4
Goffigan, Page N, 1958, Ap 5,15:5
Goffin, George M, 1950, Ap 9,84:2
Goffio, Joseph L, 1954, Ag 19,23:5
Goffred, Thomas, 1947, O 23,25:5
Goffstein, Ben, 1967, Ag 17,37:4
Goforth, Samaria A Mrs, 1938, Ap 1,23:2
Goga, Octavian, 1938, My 8,II,7:1
Gogarty, Henry A, 1941, Mr 25,23:6
Gogarty, Oliver S, 1957, S 23,27:4
Gogarty, Oliver St J Mrs, 1958, Je 24,31:1
Gogate, Rajaram V, 1955, O 28,25:2
Goge, Osmond, 1947, O 3,25:1
Goge, Sigmond, 1903, Je 18,9:6
Goger, Milton J (cor on cause of death, O 30,34:2), 1956, O 24,37:5
Gogerty, John, 1952, My 10,21:3
Gogerty, John D, 1953, My 7,31:4
Gogerty, John D Mrs, 1956, N 19,31:4
Gogerty, Joseph A, 1960, N 5,23:3
Goggin, James E, 1941, N 1,15:3
Goggin, James H Mrs, 1948, S 2,23:3
Goggin, Jeremiah J Mrs, 1945, D 29,13:2
Goggin, John E, 1950, D 13,35:5
Goggin, John J, 1954, Ag 31,21:6
Goggin, Mabel, 1942, Mr 25,21:4
Goggin, Victor T, 1946, N 18,23:3
Goggin, William A Jr, 1960, Jl 15,18:1
Goggin, William H Rev, 1924, Ap 9,21:2
Goggins, T Joseph, 1950, Ap 26,29:3
Gogoff, Samuel, 1959, My 28,31:5
Gogonues, Roland von, 1943, Ja 2,11:5
Gogszell, Herbert M, 1938, Ja 9,43:1
Goheen, George A, 1948, F 6,26:6
Goheen, John L, 1948, F 4,24:2
Goheen, Kenneth G, 1954, S 15,33:1
Goheen, Robert H H Dr (cor, O 20,86:4), 1968, O 19,37:3
Goheen, Robert Mrs, 1968, D 22,52:5
Gohl, Edgar F, 1958, Ag 12,29:1
Gohl, William, 1949, Mr 11,25:4
Gohler, August, 1943, Ja 7,19:5
Gohn, Herman F, 1948, Ap 7,25:3
Goho, Reuben E, 1952, F 9,13:2
Gohorel, Fernand P, 1960, My 1,86:8
Gohring, Henry M, 1945, F 21,19:2
Goicoechea, Antonio, 1953, F 12,27:4
Goicouria, A V de Mrs, 1904, Ag 19,9:6
Goicouria, Gen, 1870, My 8,1:7
Going, Frederica, 1959, Ap 13,31:1
Going, Seymour Mrs, 1945, Ja 3,17:5
Goitein, David E, 1961, Jl 30,68:4
Gojdic, Peter P, 1960, S 18,86:2
Gokey, William, 1904, D 29,7:6
Golan, Harry G, 1961, S 26,39:2
Golas, George, 1951, Ag 8,25:6
Golat, Phillip, 1958, Mr 20,29:4
Golat, Solomon Mrs, 1966, Ja 12,21:4
Golay, Marcel J E Mrs, 1958, N 27,29:1
Golay, Maurice, 1949, N 23,29:5
Golburgh, Maxwell, 1966, Mr 14,31:1
Golby, Aaron N, 1938, Jl 7,19:4
Gold, Arthur Mrs, 1959, Ja 11,88:5
Gold, Benjamin Mrs, 1957, Ag 30,19:5
Gold, Bernard L, 1965, Jl 6,33:2
old, Charles, 1946, Je 1,13:5
old, Charles E, 1953, Ag 7,19:3
old, Charles L, 1940, Ag 23,15:2
old, David, 1954, D 20,29:3; 1964, Je 6,23:3
old, Dorothy, 1958, Ja 15,29:1
old, Emanuel H, 1958, Mr 8,17:5
old, G Leonard, 1968, S 27,47:3
old, G Leonard Mrs, 1964, Ag 15,21:5
old, Harcourt Sir, 1952, Jl 29,21:5
old, Harold J, 1955, N 18,25:4
old, Harry, 1938, Ap 14,23:2
old, Harry H, 1948, Mr 18,27:3
old, Henry, 1958, S 11,33:2
old, Henry R, 1965, Ja 7,31:2
old, Howard R, 1959, F 20,25:2
old, Irving B, 1953, Mr 4,27:5
old, Irving J, 1956, O 7,86:4
old, Irving W Mrs, 1961, Ag 9,33:3
old, Jack S, 1953, S 5,15:4

Gold, James D, 1956, Ap 16,27:1
Gold, John Mrs, 1954, O 25,27:3
Gold, Joseph, 1953, My 17,89:1
Gold, Louis (por), 1937, D 24,17:3
Gold, Louis T, 1955, O 26,31:1
Gold, Max, 1947, Ag 31,37:1
Gold, Michael, 1938, Ja 13,22:1; 1938, S 9,21:3; 1967, My 16,45:1
Gold, Mitchell A, 1962, F 9,26:6
Gold, Morris R, 1948, Mr 27,13:6
Gold, Moshe M, 1956, S 24,27:1
Gold, Peter, 1958, Jl 16,29:2
Gold, Philip, 1958, N 19,37:5
Gold, Ralph, 1949, Ag 2,19:3
Gold, Samuel, 1945, Ja 21,40:2
Gold, Simon, 1955, Ap 11,23:5
Gold, Sol, 1959, Ap 26,86:7
Gold, W J Rev, 1903, Ja 12,9:6
Gold, Warren Mrs, 1961, Ap 6,26:8
Gold, William, 1957, S 21,19:2
Gold, William B Sr, 1946, D 16,23:4
Gold, William Mrs, 1966, Jl 28,33:3
Gold, Wolf, 1956, Ap 9,27:2
Gold, Zev Mrs, 1961, My 9,39:2
Goldan, S Ormond, 1944, Ap 25,23:6
Goldat, George Prof, 1968, Ap 14,77:2
Goldbacher, Elizabeth H Mrs, 1940, Je 19,23:6
Goldbas, Lena Mrs, 1949, N 6,94:5
Goldbaum, Mose, 1942, Ag 12,19:3
Goldbeck, Cecil, 1958, Jl 3,25:3
Goldbeck, Walter Dean, 1925, O 14,25:2
Goldberg, Abraham (por), 1942, Je 6,13:3
Goldberg, Abraham, 1945, Mr 20,19:1
Goldberg, Abraham I, 1953, My 22,27:4
Goldberg, Abraham M, 1950, Je 6,29:3
Goldberg, Abram, 1942, N 22,52:3
Goldberg, Adolph, 1952, S 22,23:3
Goldberg, Alex, 1949, Mr 7,21:5
Goldberg, Alexander Mrs, 1946, Ja 27,42:4
Goldberg, Alfred R, 1949, Mr 16,27:1
Goldberg, Arthur, 1938, Je 4,15:3
Goldberg, Arthur I, 1953, Jl 3,19:4
Goldberg, Baruch, 1939, My 31,23:3
Goldberg, Benjamin, 1954, Jl 31,13:4
Goldberg, Bernard, 1955, My 13,25:3
Goldberg, Bernard D, 1964, O 7,47:2
Goldberg, Bertram, 1937, Ja 22,23:6
Goldberg, Charles F, 1961, Ag 31,27:2
Goldberg, Charles J, 1955, My 10,29:1
Goldberg, David, 1903, Jl 12,11:2
Goldberg, David (Pop), 1952, My 11,93:1
Goldberg, David, 1966, F 14,29:2
Goldberg, David L, 1959, Jl 17,21:3
Goldberg, Frank, 1945, N 22,35:4
Goldberg, Franklin (F Gilbert), 1961, Ja 30,23:5
Goldberg, Fred, 1961, Ja 27,48:1
Goldberg, George W, 1950, Ag 28,17:3
Goldberg, Gussie Mrs, 1923, My 17,19:6
Goldberg, Harold, 1960, D 25,42:4
Goldberg, Harold S, 1967, D 20,45:1
Goldberg, Harry, 1948, Mr 23,25:5; 1957, S 24,35:1; 1959, S 23,35:3
Goldberg, Harry A, 1950, Jl 10,21:4
Goldberg, Harry N, 1953, Mr 13,27:1
Goldberg, Henry J, 1961, D 2,23:4
Goldberg, Herbert E, 1958, Mr 29,17:6
Goldberg, Herman D Dr, 1968, F 22,31:1
Goldberg, Herman J, 1953, Je 18,29:5
Goldberg, Herman Mrs, 1959, Ag 23,92:6
Goldberg, Hersch, 1937, Jl 18,II,7:1
Goldberg, Hirsch Rabbi, 1911, D 26,9:6
Goldberg, I L, 1935, S 17,23:1
Goldberg, Irving, 1950, O 13,31:1; 1958, Ja 12,86:8; 1962, Mr 4,86:7; 1962, O 10,47:3
Goldberg, Irwin, 1952, O 29,29:6
Goldberg, Isaac, 1938, Jl 15,17:4; 1939, Ap 27,25:2; 1946, Ap 30,21:3
Goldberg, Isadore Mrs, 1960, Ag 25,29:3
Goldberg, Isidor, 1958, S 13,19:4; 1961, N 24,28:3
Goldberg, Israel (R Learsi), 1964, Ag 4,29:2
Goldberg, Jack, 1966, D 3,39:4
Goldberg, Jack Mrs, 1951, N 26,25:4
Goldberg, Jacob, 1950, Ap 18,31:2; 1960, Jl 11,29:2
Goldberg, Jacob A, 1954, D 14,33:4
Goldberg, Jacob B, 1945, Ap 10,19:4
Goldberg, Jacob J, 1956, O 1,27:2
Goldberg, Jacob Mrs, 1949, Ja 25,23:4
Goldberg, Jacob S Mrs, 1944, Ja 12,23:3
Goldberg, James T (J T Ormont), 1962, Ag 30,29:5
Goldberg, Jennie, 1947, O 6,21:2
Goldberg, Jesse L Mrs, 1958, My 29,27:3
Goldberg, Joe, 1954, Ap 3,15:2
Goldberg, Joseph, 1949, Ja 9,72:1; 1953, F 15,93:2
Goldberg, L Chester, 1938, D 23,19:5
Goldberg, Lena Mrs, 1938, My 15,II,6:4
Goldberg, Leon H (funl, D 7,39:5), 1962, D 6,43:1
Goldberg, Leon S Mrs, 1942, N 1,52:3
Goldberg, Lionel M, 1959, N 16,31:5
Goldberg, Louis, 1957, Ja 7,25:5; 1960, Mr 9,33:5
Goldberg, Louis D, 1953, Ja 17,15:4
Goldberg, Louis E, 1956, S 25,33:5
Goldberg, Louis Mrs, 1957, D 31,17:2
Goldberg, Louis P, 1957, D 12,30:1

Goldberg, M, 1926, N 22,23:4
Goldberg, Mark, 1956, Ag 1,23:3
Goldberg, Maurice, 1957, Mr 2,21:5
Goldberg, Maurice Mrs, 1960, N 14,31:3
Goldberg, Max, 1941, N 29,17:2; 1946, D 10,31:4
Goldberg, Max G, 1959, Ja 23,25:2
Goldberg, Meyer, 1922, Ag 1,19:4; 1944, Ja 12,23:2; 1954, F 26,20:3
Goldberg, Morris, 1950, N 18,15:6; 1955, Ja 28,20:1
Goldberg, Morris Mrs, 1947, Ap 10,25:4
Goldberg, Moses W, 1964, F 19,39:3
Goldberg, Nathan, 1961, D 7,43:2
Goldberg, Nathan Mrs, 1966, O 8,31:4
Goldberg, Oscar, 1958, Ag 12,29:4
Goldberg, Philip, 1964, Mr 25,41:2
Goldberg, Reuben, 1948, Ag 1,59:2; 1954, S 27,21:1
Goldberg, Robert, 1941, Je 14,17:6
Goldberg, Samuel, 1905, Je 16,9:6; 1948, Ag 20,17:4; 1955, My 28,15:6
Goldberg, Samuel A, 1964, Ag 30,93:1
Goldberg, Seelig Mrs, 1949, Ap 28,31:3
Goldberg, Shephard J, 1924, Ja 15,19:4
Goldberg, Sidney I, 1952, Jl 14,17:4
Goldberg, Sidney N, 1964, D 19,29:4
Goldberg, Silas, 1947, Ja 18,15:4
Goldberg, Sol, 1958, Ja 3,21:5
Goldberg, Sol H, 1940, Je 6,25:3
Goldberg, Tessie Mrs, 1954, My 8,17:6
Goldberg, William, 1942, Ja 14,21:3
Goldberg, William H, 1957, O 3,29:1
Goldberg, William T, 1967, Je 4,86:4
Goldberger, Arnold J, 1958, Ag 3,80:6
Goldberger, Benjamin M, 1952, Mr 7,23:4
Goldberger, David L, 1957, O 3,29:1
Goldberger, Emanuel, 1963, Je 20,33:5
Goldberger, Isador H, 1967, My 10,47:2
Goldberger, J, 1929, Ja 18,23:1
Goldberger, Jacques, 1947, Je 6,23:5
Goldberger, Joseph Mrs, 1959, S 13,84:7
Goldberger, Leo, 1939, D 26,19:4
Goldberger, Leo J, 1958, F 23,92:6
Goldberger, Leo Mrs, 1956, Mr 19,31:3
Goldberger, Lewis A, 1967, Jl 24,27:3
Goldberger, Ludwig M, 1913, O 23,11:6
Goldberger, Morris B, 1942, Ja 25,31:1
Goldberger, Morris F Mrs, 1953, Ap 30,31:4
Goldberger, Sidney, 1961, D 23,23:5
Goldblatt, Adolph R, 1951, D 1,13:5
Goldblatt, Arthur, 1952, N 30,88:8
Goldblatt, David, 1945, D 11,25:2; 1966, S 8,47:1
Goldblatt, Hannah Mrs, 1941, Jl 7,15:1
Goldblatt, Maurice H, 1962, Mr 3,21:4
Goldblatt, Mose, 1941, O 23,23:3
Goldblatt, Nathan, 1944, N 4,15:4
Goldblatt, Robert, 1964, Mr 27,28:1
Goldblatt, Samuel, 1944, Ag 8,17:5
Goldblatt, Samuel Mrs, 1954, Jl 3,11:5
Goldbloom, A Allen, 1962, D 1,25:1
Goldbloom, Alton, 1968, F 4,80:5
Goldbloom, Simon L, 1954, My 3,25:4
Goldblum, Meyer, 1967, Ag 23,51:4
Goldbogen, Sophie Mrs, 1962, D 20,8:3
Goldbright, L H Jr, 1945, S 2,32:1
Goldburg, Aaron, 1954, O 11,27:3
Goldburg, Hyman, 1954, S 3,17:5
Goldburg, Jack, 1955, Ja 13,27:4
Goldburg, Julius, 1959, Je 24,31:4
Goldburg, Louis, 1966, O 30,89:1
Goldburgh, Harold L, 1962, O 9,41:1
Golde, Eliot S, 1961, Ag 1,31:3
Golde, Louis, 1942, My 28,17:2
Golde, Morris, 1950, Ag 9,29:3
Golde, Morris Mrs, 1950, Ag 17,27:4
Golde, Sydney R, 1968, Je 30,52:7
Golde, Walter H, 1963, S 5,31:5
Golde, Walter H Mrs, 1964, S 28,29:4
Golde, Walton Mrs, 1950, Ag 30,31:3
Golden, A George, 1959, My 13,37:1
Golden, Andrew, 1963, My 16,35:4
Golden, Barry, 1967, O 15,85:3
Golden, Benjamin, 1957, F 6,25:5
Golden, Bert, 1940, N 11,19:2
Golden, Clinton S, 1961, Je 13,35:3
Golden, D V W, 1873, Jl 15,4:7
Golden, Daniel F, 1955, Mr 18,27:4
Golden, Frances M, 1946, Ap 27,17:2
Golden, Francis L, 1952, Ag 6,21:7
Golden, Garrett, 1940, Ag 12,15:3
Golden, George Fuller, 1912, F 18,II,13:4
Golden, George H, 1948, Ap 7,25:1
Golden, Harry, 1954, Jl 24,13:6
Golden, Herbert J, 1956, N 15,35:5
Golden, Issac J K, 1953, My 21,31:5
Golden, Jack R, 1951, F 27,27:3
Golden, James A Mrs, 1943, Jl 13,21:3
Golden, James J, 1944, Je 30,21:2
Golden, James M, 1939, F 23,23:3
Golden, John (funl, Je 11,13:5), 1921, Je 10,13:5
Golden, John, 1953, Ja 30,21:3
Golden, John (funl, Je 20,21:4; will, Jl 24,23:1), 1955, Je 18,17:1
Golden, John A, 1941, Ag 9,15:1
Golden, John E, 1938, F 6,II,9:2

Golden, John Mrs, 1955, O 7,25:2
Golden, John W Sr, 1952, D 28,49:2
Golden, Joseph, 1955, Je 2,29:5; 1967, Je 5,43:2
Golden, Joseph S, 1960, Ap 6,41:5
Golden, Julius J, 1968, D 20,42:3
Golden, Katherine M, 1956, O 6,21:5
Golden, Leo E, 1956, Ja 15,92:5
Golden, Leon, 1966, Ap 20,47:4
Golden, Louis M, 1954, Mr 2,25:5
Golden, Mark, 1958, D 2,37:5
Golden, Mary G, 1950, Jl 30,60:1
Golden, Matthew G, 1946, N 12,29:1
Golden, Matthew J, 1944, F 16,17:2
Golden, Max, 1946, Ja 26,13:5
Golden, Michael, 1938, D 31,15:2
Golden, Patrick A, 1948, S 13,21:3
Golden, Richard (funl, Ag 13,7:6), 1909, Ag 11,7:6
Golden, Richard M, 1949, N 17,32:6
Golden, Robert E, 1941, S 13,17:1
Golden, Ross Mrs, 1957, Mr 22,23:4
Golden, S Herbert, 1941, Ja 2,23:5
Golden, S Herbert Mrs, 1961, O 26,35:3
Golden, Samuel, 1963, Ap 24,35:2
Golden, Samuel H, 1960, D 10,23:3
Golden, Samuel M, 1950, D 29,19:4
Golden, Simon P, 1945, S 22,17:4
Golden, Theodore E, 1937, O 11,27:3
Golden, Thomas J, 1957, Ag 6,27:1
Golden, W N, 1949, Ag 31,23:5
Golden, William, 1959, O 24,21:3
Golden, William A, 1949, O 7,31:1
Golden, William G, 1945, O 30,19:1
Golden, William M, 1966, Mr 3,33:3
Golden, William M Mrs, 1940, My 4,17:3
Goldenberg, Asher, 1954, F 15,23:2
Goldenberg, Franciszek, 1960, D 27,29:3
Goldenberg, Frank, 1950, F 10,23:1
Goldenberg, George, 1960, Ja 30,21:3
Goldenberg, Herman Dr, 1937, Ap 2,23:4
Goldenberg, J G (will), 1901, Ap 20,9:5
Goldenberg, Leon, 1958, Jl 26,15:3
Goldenberg, Louis O, 1945, Ja 9,19:3
Goldenberg, Marcel, 1958, Jl 31,23:2
Goldenberg, Maurice A, 1961, Je 25,76:6
Goldenberg, Max, 1961, S 16,19:1
Goldenberg, Murray W, 1964, Jl 23,27:4
Goldenberg, Philip, 1944, Ap 18,5:4
Goldenberg, Samuel, 1945, N 1,23:1
Goldenberg, Saul, 1952, Je 10,27:5
Goldenberg, Sidney, 1948, Je 28,19:1
Goldenblum, William, 1953, Ap 16,29:3
Goldenburg, Levi, 1884, D 1,2:6
Goldenheim, Jacob, 1967, Mr 13,37:1
Goldenhorn, I Faerber, 1942, Ja 14,21:3
Goldenkranz, Sol Dr, 1937, My 18,23:3
Goldensky, Elias, 1943, Mr 11,21:2
Goldenson, Samuel H, 1962, S 1,19:5
Goldenson, Samuel H Mrs, 1938, Ja 26,23:1
Goldenthal, Carol Dr, 1919, Jl 3,13:3
Goldenweiser, Emanuel A, 1953, Ap 2,27:5
Goldenweizer, Alex B, 1961, N 28,37:2
Golder, Benjamin M, 1946, D 31,18:3
Golder, F A, 1929, Ja 8,31:3
Golder, Fred R, 1953, F 12,27:2
Golder, Henry T Mrs, 1944, D 19,21:5
Golder, William E, 1945, Jl 3,13:4
Golderman, Caspar, 1906, D 16,7:6
Goldey, Jacob, 1953, D 29,23:1
Goldey, William H, 1938, Je 15,23:5
Goldey, William J, 1907, D 5,9:4
Goldfaden, Abraham, 1908, Ja 10,7:5
Goldfader, Phil, 1951, Ag 27,19:4
Goldfarb, Barnett, 1965, Je 14,33:2
Goldfarb, Henryk, 1957, N 13,35:3
Goldfarb, Isadore, 1950, Je 13,27:3
Goldfarb, Israel, 1967, F 14,43:1
Goldfarb, Jack, 1959, Jl 15,30:1
Goldfarb, Louis, 1956, Mr 16,23:3
Goldfarb, Louis E, 1943, Ap 8,23:4
Goldfarb, Mary Mrs, 1938, Je 7,23:4
Goldfarb, Morris, 1938, Ap 22,19:2
Goldfarb, Nathaniel D, 1942, Ap 6,15:5
Goldfarb, Robert S, 1965, Ag 11,39:1
Goldfarb, Samuel J, 1945, Je 30,17:7
Goldfarb, Saul B, 1965, My 27,37:2
Goldfarb, Walter, 1953, Je 5,27:4
Goldfarb, William, 1945, Ag 18,11:5
Goldfeather, Henry, 1954, Ja 9,15:4
Goldfein, Joseph, 1961, N 24,28:7; 1966, Ag 1,27:3
Goldfein, Simon, 1963, Jl 18,27:5
Goldfield, Henry, 1948, My 20,29:4
Goldfield, Ignatz Mrs, 1948, S 8,29:4
Goldfine, Ascher, 1949, D 31,15:3
Goldfine, Bernard, 1967, S 23,31:1
Goldfine, Irving M, 1953, S 28,25:5
Goldfine, Jacob H, 1956, Ag 10,17:4
Goldfine, Joseph F, 1960, Mr 27,86:2
Goldfine, Samuel J, 1960, Ag 28,82:8
Goldfogle, Alex, 1950, Jl 23,56:4
Goldfogle, H M, 1929, Je 2,26:2
Goldforb, Abraham J, 1962, Ap 18,39:4
Goldhaber, Gerson Mrs (Sulamith), 1965, D 14,43:2
Goldhaft, Arthur D, 1960, Ap 3,86:6
Goldhammer, Adolph, 1942, D 28,10:7
Goldhammer, Isidor, 1956, O 21,86:7
Goldhammer, John (por), 1942, D 13,72:1
Goldhill, Walter A, 1960, Jl 19,29:5
Goldhorn, Ludwig B, 1944, N 17,19:4
Goldhuber, Samuel, 1950, Ap 19,32:4
Goldich, Bob, 1957, Mr 24,V,1:5
Goldie, Charles F, 1947, Jl 13,44:1
Goldie, George Taubman Sir, 1925, Ag 23,7:3
Goldie, John (funl), 1871, Jl 17,8:6
Goldie, Matthew R, 1939, Jl 25,19:1
Goldie, William, 1903, S 8,7:6
Goldie, William V, 1953, Ja 29,27:4
Goldin, Harry Mrs, 1960, Jl 20,29:2
Goldin, Horace, 1939, Ag 23,21:6
Goldin, Horace Mrs, 1945, S 15,15:4
Goldin, Jacob, 1948, Ap 19,23:5
Goldin, Mitty, 1956, Je 29,21:3
Goldin, Myron R, 1968, Ag 8,33:4
Goldin, Shepard J, 1952, Ap 11,23:2
Goldin, Sidney M, 1937, S 21,25:2
Golding, Arnold H (por), 1947, Ap 7,23:3
Golding, Barnett S, 1950, Ja 22,78:2
Golding, Bernard, 1961, D 15,37:5
Golding, Claude E, 1947, Ag 28,23:3
Golding, Elaine (Mrs B Tuthill), 1951, Mr 14,33:3
Golding, Ernest A, 1938, Jl 18,13:3
Golding, Ethel, 1904, Mr 2,9:7
Golding, Frank H, 1941, F 5,20:3
Golding, Guyon S, 1940, Je 25,23:6
Golding, Harold H, 1952, N 8,17:6
Golding, Herbert G, 1937, S 20,23:6
Golding, Herbert George Jr, 1968, N 4,47:2
Golding, J F Dr, 1903, Je 9,9:6
Golding, James M (por), 1938, Ag 1,13:3
Golding, Jerrold R, 1967, Ap 8,31:5
Golding, John N, 1919, Ag 11,11:3
Golding, Joseph, 1942, Ag 19,19:2
Golding, Joseph E, 1950, Jl 29,13:5
Golding, Louis, 1958, Ag 10,93:1
Golding, Louis T, 1961, S 12,33:1
Golding, Paul C, 1945, O 26,19:1
Golding, Samuel H Mrs, 1955, Je 1,33:2
Golding, Samuel R, 1957, N 15,27:2
Golding, Simon Mrs, 1953, D 11,31:3
Golding, Thomas, 1941, F 18,23:2
Golding, Thomas J, 1949, Mr 21,23:5
Golding, William C, 1949, Ja 18,23:5
Golding, William H, 1956, Je 24,76:8
Goldkette, Jean, 1962, Mr 25,89:1
Goldlust, James Dr, 1915, Jl 29,9:6
Goldlust, Samuel, 1949, O 16,88:1
Goldman, A Milton, 1955, Ag 27,15:5
Goldman, Abner H, 1952, O 30,31:3
Goldman, Abraham, 1944, Ja 25,19:5
Goldman, Abraham A, 1956, Mr 14,33:2
Goldman, Albert, 1960, My 24,38:1; 1967, My 6,31:1
Goldman, Alex, 1949, Je 16,29:1; 1952, Ap 11,12:3
Goldman, Ben, 1961, Ag 11,23:2
Goldman, Benjamin B, 1955, Ja 10,23:3
Goldman, Benjamin E, 1959, S 23,35:2
Goldman, Bernard, 1914, Mr 19,9:5
Goldman, Bert, 1959, Ja 1,31:3
Goldman, Charles, 1939, F 2,19:2; 1962, My 12,23:5; 1966, F 7,29:3; 1967, Ag 22,34:6
Goldman, Charley, 1968, N 12,43:3
Goldman, David, 1944, S 15,19:5
Goldman, David E, 1958, Jl 28,23:2
Goldman, Edward, 1951, S 20,31:5
Goldman, Edwin F (funl, F 23,27:3), 1956, F 22,27:4
Goldman, Emanuel, 1963, D 8,86:5; 1967, Ap 20,43:2
Goldman, Emil, 1951, Mr 17,15:4
Goldman, Emma, 1940, My 14,23:1
Goldman, F Mrs, 1932, Ja 26,23:3
Goldman, Frank, 1965, Mr 17,45:1
Goldman, G George, 1959, Je 22,25:4
Goldman, George, 1953, Je 25,38:4
Goldman, Harold, 1956, Ja 19,33:1
Goldman, Harold L, 1965, N 20,35:7
Goldman, Harris (will), 1939, Mr 30,25:1
Goldman, Harry, 1941, D 27,19:5; 1947, F 16,57:2; 1947, O 6,21:2; 1949, Jl 20,25:1; 1951, Ap 17,29:3; 1951, Ag 5,72:6
Goldman, Henry (por), 1937, Ap 5,19:1
Goldman, Henry Jr, 1955, Mr 10,27:1
Goldman, Henry Mrs, 1954, O 4,27:5
Goldman, Herbert, 1963, My 20,31:2
Goldman, Herman, 1968, Ja 25,37:1
Goldman, Ira G, 1962, N 30,33:3
Goldman, Irma F, 1960, F 23,31:2
Goldman, Isaac, 1925, My 8,19:4
Goldman, Isadore, 1948, N 18,27:2
Goldman, Isidor Mrs, 1954, My 23,27:5
Goldman, J J Mrs, 1960, Ap 22,31:4
Goldman, Jack, 1967, Jl 31,27:2
Goldman, Jack J, 1965, Mr 11,33:2
Goldman, Jacob, 1940, O 9,25:2; 1948, Ap 19,23:5
Goldman, Jacob S, 1942, Ja 3,19:6
Goldman, Jonas B, 1953, My 16,19:1
Goldman, Joseph, 1951, Ap 26,29:4
Goldman, Joseph Mrs, 1953, Ag 18,23:3
Goldman, Joshua S, 1947, Jl 11,15:1
Goldman, Julian N, 1962, Mr 18,86:7
Goldman, Julius, 1938, D 14,25:4
Goldman, Justus, 1951, Je 11,25:2
Goldman, Lawrence E, 1956, S 4,30:2
Goldman, Leon, 1943, My 3,17:5; 1965, Mr 21,86:4
Goldman, Louis, 1940, My 4,17:4; 1940, N 16,17:4
Goldman, Louis C, 1946, N 25,27:5
Goldman, Louis J, 1921, Ag 25,13:5
Goldman, Marcus, 1904, Jl 21,7:7
Goldman, Martin C, 1961, O 26,35:3
Goldman, Max, 1946, Ja 9,23:1; 1949, Ja 13,23:3; 1966, Ag 25,37:3
Goldman, Maxwell H Mrs, 1954, Jl 10,13:5
Goldman, Mayer C (por), 1939, N 25,17:3
Goldman, Milton, 1947, O 5,68:3
Goldman, Milton E, 1964, Jl 12,69:1
Goldman, Morris (Moe), 1957, Mr 27,31:6
Goldman, Morris, 1962, S 14,31:1; 1968, Mr 12,43:1
Goldman, Morris G Mrs, 1953, F 2,21:4
Goldman, Morris M, 1938, O 3,15:5
Goldman, Mortimer L, 1960, Ag 14,93:1
Goldman, Moses A Dr, 1925, Ap 13,19:4
Goldman, Moses M, 1961, O 5,37:2
Goldman, Ralph H, 1951, N 20,31:3
Goldman, Russell, 1954, Mr 11,31:1
Goldman, Sam, 1965, My 21,35:3
Goldman, Sammy, 1964, Ag 28,29:1
Goldman, Simon, 1948, Mr 31,25:5
Goldman, Solomon, 1953, My 15,24:3
Goldman, Stanley F, 1942, F 25,20:3
Goldman, Sydny, 1958, My 3,19:5
Goldman, Toby Mrs, 1923, Jl 26,15:4
Goldman, Victor, 1959, F 27,52:5
Goldman, William (por), 1938, Ap 10,II,7:1
Goldman, William, 1966, Ap 23,31:2
Goldman, William M, 1955, Je 4,15:6
Goldmann, Fred E, 1961, Je 20,33:5
Goldmann, Samuel, 1956, My 30,21:5
Goldmark, Carl (por), 1942, F 21,19:4
Goldmark, Charles J, 1942, N 5,25:6
Goldmark, Godfrey, 1968, Mr 14,43:2
Goldmark, Godfrey Mrs, 1937, N 6,17:5
Goldmark, J, 1881, Ap 20,5:4
Goldmark, James, 1947, Je 2,25:5
Goldmark, James Mrs, 1943, S 10,24:3
Goldmark, Josephine, 1950, D 16,17:3
Goldmark, Pauline, 1962, O 20,25:6
Goldmark, R, 1936, Mr 7,15:1
Goldmark, Ralph W, 1958, N 5,39:1
Goldmark, Susan, 1941, S 24,23:3
Goldmuntz, Paul, 1940, Mr 20,27:4
Goldmuntz, Romi B, 1960, My 14,23:4
Goldner, Charles M, 1914, N 27,11:4
Goldner, David, 1953, Je 20,17:6
Goldner, Estelle, 1942, My 21,19:3
Goldner, Eugene B, 1952, Ap 28,19:5
Goldner, Eugene B Mrs, 1948, D 20,25:4
Goldner, Herman W, 1959, Je 16,35:4
Goldner, Jacob, 1968, S 30,47:2
Goldner, Max, 1938, S 21,25:4
Goldney, Frederick H, 1940, F 23,15:2
Goldovitz, Samuel, 1949, S 13,29:3
Goldowsky, Harry, 1948, N 22,21:4
Goldowsky, Ira, 1963, My 5,86:4
Goldpaugh, Frederick, 1937, Je 14,23:5
Goldreyer, Boris, 1940, Jl 13,13:6
Goldrich, Clara B Mrs, 1937, O 13,23:2
Goldrich, Jessie Mrs, 1944, Mr 27,21:6
Goldrich, Leon W Dr (por),(funl, Ja 12,23:3), 1 Ja 10,II,10:3
Goldrich, Manny, 1968, My 29,36:3
Goldrick, Thomas F, 1948, O 29,25:1
Goldring, David, 1943, F 9,23:5
Goldring, Ferdinand W, 1961, Ap 19,39:2
Goldring, Joseph G, 1966, F 3,32:1
Goldring, Louis, 1950, S 2,15:4
Goldring, Martin S, 1958, Jl 22,27:3
Goldsand, Bertha, 1966, Ag 7,81:1
Goldsboro, William B, 1937, My 3,19:4
Goldsborough, Andrew J, 1941, Jl 22,19:3
Goldsborough, Charles B, 1959, Ap 14,35:4
Goldsborough, E Lee Jr, 1961, My 27,23:5
Goldsborough, Edmund K Dr, 1912, Mr 15,9:4
Goldsborough, Edmund L, 1953, Je 30,23:4
Goldsborough, J R Commodore (see also Je 23, 1877, Je 26,4:7
Goldsborough, John B, 1943, Mr 27,13:3
Goldsborough, L M, 1877, F 21,5:5
Goldsborough, Laird S, 1950, F 15,1:2
Goldsborough, Phillips I, 1946, O 23,27:1
Goldsborough, Robert G, 1950, My 25,29:2
Goldsborough, T Alan, 1944, Ja 10,17:4; 1951, 84:1
Goldsborough, W T, 1876, Ja 28,5:2
Goldsborough, William W, 1943, Jl 14,19:4
Goldsborough, Winder E, 1957, Ja 14,23:4
Goldsborough, Worthington, 1918, Ap 24,13:5
Goldscheider, Walter F, 1962, Mr 29,33:2
Goldschlag, Nathan, 1938, My 17,2:2
Goldschlag, Oscar, 1948, My 5,25:3
Goldschlag, Paul E, 1956, Ja 4,27:4
Goldschlag, Samuel, 1922, Ag 6,28:4
Goldschmid, Maurice, 1938, Ja 12,21:4

Goldschmidt, Adolph, 1944, Ja 7,17:5
Goldschmidt, Alfons (por), 1940, Ja 23,21:3
Goldschmidt, Bernhard Rev, 1922, Ag 23,13:6
Goldschmidt, Charles, 1951, Mr 23,21:2
Goldschmidt, Daniel, 1950, F 16,23:4
Goldschmidt, David, 1955, Ag 17,27:5
Goldschmidt, Edward E Mrs, 1940, S 17,23:5
Goldschmidt, Edward W, 1960, D 16,33:2
Goldschmidt, Ernest, 1947, D 1,21:2
Goldschmidt, Ernst P, 1954, F 23,27:3
Goldschmidt, George B, 1912, Ap 20,15:6
Goldschmidt, H P, 1923, Mr 17,13:2
Goldschmidt, Hans Dr, 1923, My 25,21:5
Goldschmidt, Harry, 1957, Ja 13,84:5
Goldschmidt, Henriette, 1920, F 17,9:4
Goldschmidt, Herman, 1944, Ap 7,20:2
Goldschmidt, Hyman, 1952, N 28,26:6
Goldschmidt, Jakob, 1955, S 25,92:5
Goldschmidt, Lazarus, 1950, Ap 19,29:4
Goldschmidt, Louis, 1953, Ag 27,25:3
Goldschmidt, Martin, 1944, Ap 9,33:3
Goldschmidt, Michael, 1871, S 17,8:3
Goldschmidt, Oscar A, 1955, Mr 13,86:6
Goldschmidt, Otto E, 1944, Je 30,21:3
Goldschmidt, Otto Mrs (Jenny Lind), 1887, N 3,5:5
Goldschmidt, Richard B, 1958, Ap 26,19:5
Goldschmidt, S A, 1933, Ja 29,24:3
Goldschmidt, Samuel, 1951, Ag 9,21:2
Goldschmidt, Victor M, 1947, Mr 27,28:2
Goldschmidt, Werner, 1958, Jl 25,19:5
Goldschmidt-Hermanns, Alice Mrs, 1959, N 29,86:6
Goldschmidt-Rothschild, Maximilian B Baron, 1940, Mr 31,45:2
Goldschneider, Louis, 1953, S 6,50:1
Goldsmid-Montefiore, Claude J, 1938, Jl 10,29:3
Goldsmid-Montefiore, Leonard N, 1961, D 28,27:4
Goldsmith, Abraham, 1938, Je 23,21:4
Goldsmith, Abraham D, 1955, N 5,19:5
Goldsmith, Alan G, 1961, Ap 1,17:3
Goldsmith, Alfred F, 1947, Jl 30,21:1
Goldsmith, Alva W, 1965, F 27,25:4
Goldsmith, Arthur J, 1964, S 21,31:3
Goldsmith, Basil M, 1957, D 8,88:8
Goldsmith, Benjamin, 1950, F 14,25:4; 1961, Ja 4,33:1
Goldsmith, Benjamin J Mrs, 1943, Mr 29,15:4
Goldsmith, Bernard Mrs, 1946, N 19,31:4
Goldsmith, Berthold Mrs, 1950, Je 29,29:5
Goldsmith, Charles A, 1949, S 13,29:1
Goldsmith, Charles Mrs, 1944, Ap 28,19:4
Goldsmith, Charles N, 1907, Ja 4,7:6
Goldsmith, Clarence H, 1942, F 23,21:5
Goldsmith, Darwin H, 1952, F 9,13:3
Goldsmith, David E, 1947, D 13,15:1
Goldsmith, Dudley H, 1944, Ap 19,23:2
Goldsmith, Edward J, 1911, S 28,9:5
Goldsmith, Emanuel, 1939, F 15,23:4
Goldsmith, Ernest, 1964, Jl 15,32:8
Goldsmith, Eugene, 1956, N 15,35:2
Goldsmith, Evelyn (will, F 17,13:1), 1940, Ja 5,20:3
Goldsmith, Frank, 1958, My 9,23:1
Goldsmith, Fred, 1939, Mr 29,23:4
Goldsmith, Freda Mrs, 1924, S 24,19:2
Goldsmith, Frederick E, 1944, Ag 9,17:6
Goldsmith, Frederick Thomas, 1905, Ap 19,11:4
Goldsmith, George E (cor, F 17,27:2), 1961, F 16, 31:2
Goldsmith, George F, 1950, Mr 17,24:4
Goldsmith, George F Mrs, 1941, Ap 11,21:3
Goldsmith, Glenn W, 1943, O 30,15:5
Goldsmith, Harry B, 1958, My 18,86:7
Goldsmith, Henry, 1938, Ja 22,15:4
Goldsmith, Herbert J, 1956, D 30,32:8
Goldsmith, Herman Mrs, 1955, My 20,25:4
Goldsmith, Hugo, 1950, Je 29,29:3
Goldsmith, Hugo Mrs, 1954, S 3,17:5
Goldsmith, Hyman H, 1949, Ag 9,25:5
Goldsmith, Ingomar, 1939, F 11,15:3
Goldsmith, Irving, 1956, N 17,21:3
Goldsmith, Irving I, 1951, Je 4,27:3
Goldsmith, Isaac S (por), 1947, Mr 23,60:3
Goldsmith, J Wheeler, 1957, F 19,31:4
Goldsmith, James A, 1950, Je 22,27:1
Goldsmith, James Mrs (Patino),(funl, My 19,31:4), 1954, My 15,15:2
Goldsmith, Joel S, 1964, Je 18,35:5
Goldsmith, John F, 1966, Ja 5,31:1
Goldsmith, Joseph, 1953, S 1,23:4; 1958, S 12,25:2
Goldsmith, Kathleen, 1955, Ag 25,23:3
Goldsmith, Ken, 1943, Je 9,21:3
Goldsmith, Lawrence L, 1948, Ap 7,25:2
Goldsmith, Leo, 1952, My 19,17:6
Goldsmith, Leo Mrs, 1963, N 13,41:2
Goldsmith, Leon, 1941, Ja 3,19:1
Goldsmith, Louis, 1955, N 10,35:5
Goldsmith, Louis N, 1962, F 10,23:5
Goldsmith, Louis S, 1958, Ag 1,21:4
Goldsmith, Marc S, 1960, My 4,45:1
Goldsmith, Marcus, 1963, Ag 22,27:5
Goldsmith, Marcus A Mrs, 1958, N 15,23:2
Goldsmith, Markul Mrs, 1961, Je 1,35:1
Goldsmith, Martin H, 1950, F 10,23:2
Goldsmith, Max, 1940, F 7,21:2
Goldsmith, Max Mrs, 1949, D 26,29:4
Goldsmith, Max S, 1949, F 7,19:3
Goldsmith, Milton, 1957, S 23,27:5
Goldsmith, Milton Mrs, 1963, Ap 18,35:6
Goldsmith, Mitchel, 1947, Ap 16,25:3
Goldsmith, Norman R, 1953, O 10,17:7
Goldsmith, Phil, 1940, Ja 24,21:3
Goldsmith, Phil N, 1952, D 31,15:5
Goldsmith, Philip H, 1958, S 20,19:5
Goldsmith, Raymond W Mrs (Selma), 1962, Ap 16, 29:5
Goldsmith, Reuben S, 1958, Ag 22,21:2
Goldsmith, Robert, 1924, F 26,17:2
Goldsmith, Robert Mrs, 1954, D 22,23:1
Goldsmith, Samuel J, 1948, Ja 1,23:2
Goldsmith, Samuel M, 1959, Ja 26,29:6
Goldsmith, Samuel T, 1960, Mr 31,33:3
Goldsmith, Sidney W, 1946, Jl 1,31:2
Goldsmith, Simon, 1949, Mr 1,25:5
Goldsmith, Simon M, 1939, D 19,23:3
Goldsmith, Solomon L, 1958, Jl 7,27:4
Goldsmith, Theodora, 1941, Jl 19,13:4
Goldsmith, Theodore R, 1962, Mr 25,88:5
Goldsmith, Wallace, 1945, Ap 2,19:4
Goldsmith, Walter A, 1949, O 11,34:5
Goldsmith, William, 1947, Je 13,23:3
Goldsmith, William D, 1947, Ap 4,23:2
Goldsmith, William J, 1944, Jl 25,19:4
Goldsmith, William Mrs, 1949, F 23,27:3
Goldspinner, Louis, 1960, My 7,23:5
Goldspinner, Louis Mrs, 1951, My 2,31:5
Goldstandt, Fred S, 1952, F 29,23:3
Goldstein, Aaron M Mrs, 1950, Ag 9,29:5
Goldstein, Abraham, 1938, N 14,19:5; 1953, N 17,31:4
Goldstein, Abraham J, 1944, My 18,19:1
Goldstein, Abraham L, 1943, D 14,27:4
Goldstein, Adele Mrs, 1938, Ap 12,23:2
Goldstein, Adolph O, 1945, My 21,19:3
Goldstein, Albert A, 1952, My 24,19:6
Goldstein, Alex, 1951, Je 14,27:6
Goldstein, Arthur I, 1966, D 7,47:2
Goldstein, Benjamin, 1963, My 11,25:3
Goldstein, Bernard, 1959, D 8,45:4
Goldstein, Bernard I, 1953, O 5,27:4
Goldstein, Charles Mrs, 1966, O 25,45:1
Goldstein, Charles S, 1938, S 29,25:1; 1949, F 11,24:2
Goldstein, David, 1952, Je 15,85:1; 1958, Jl 1,31:2; 1960, Mr 1,33:4
Goldstein, David Mrs, 1963, N 12,41:1
Goldstein, Edgar B, 1949, Ja 30,60:7
Goldstein, Edgar B Mrs, 1948, Mr 3,23:2
Goldstein, Edward Mrs, 1958, S 6,17:5
Goldstein, Edwin S, 1948, Mr 11,27:1
Goldstein, Emanuel M, 1958, Je 21,19:1
Goldstein, Ephraim, 1949, Jl 30,15:4
Goldstein, Ephraim Mrs, 1951, N 13,30:6
Goldstein, Fannie Mrs, 1948, Mr 24,25:5
Goldstein, George A, 1953, S 7,19:5
Goldstein, Gus Mrs, 1954, D 14,33:2
Goldstein, Gustave, 1962, Jl 28,19:4
Goldstein, Harris Mrs, 1959, Je 20,21:5
Goldstein, Harry, 1914, Ag 2,15:4; 1952, F 12,27:4
Goldstein, Harry B Mrs, 1948, D 28,21:4
Goldstein, Harry D, 1968, Je 17,39:2
Goldstein, Henry, 1951, Ap 30,21:4
Goldstein, Henry J, 1964, S 24,41:4
Goldstein, Herbert S Mrs, 1961, Je 5,31:2
Goldstein, Herman Mrs, 1954, Ag 4,21:5
Goldstein, Herman Rev, 1906, N 11,9:6
Goldstein, Hiram, 1947, O 12,76:7; 1953, O 19,21:7
Goldstein, Hyman I, 1954, Mr 18,31:4
Goldstein, Ida Mrs, 1949, My 25,29:4
Goldstein, Irving, 1966, S 28,47:2
Goldstein, Irving I, 1965, Ag 29,84:6
Goldstein, Isadore Dr (por), 1937, D 24,17:5
Goldstein, Israel P, 1960, S 26,33:5
Goldstein, J Walter, 1953, Je 28,61:1
Goldstein, Jacob, 1920, F 13,11:4; 1941, Ag 4,13:4
Goldstein, Jacob M, 1938, Jl 18,13:4
Goldstein, Jennie (Mrs C W Groll), 1960, F 10,37:1
Goldstein, Jesse S, 1959, My 16,23:5
Goldstein, John, 1947, O 1,29:4
Goldstein, Jonah J (funl plans, Jl 24,27:2; funl, Jl 26,36:2), 1967, Jl 23,60:3
Goldstein, Joseph, 1937, Ja 14,21:2; 1952, F 23,11:3; 1959, Jl 2,25:1; 1962, N 15,37:2
Goldstein, Joseph M, 1939, N 1,23:5
Goldstein, Julius M, 1938, Ja 16,II,9:3
Goldstein, Julius Mrs, 1962, Jl 10,33:3
Goldstein, Lena Mrs, 1949, Mr 7,21:5
Goldstein, Leon, 1966, Mr 2,41:5
Goldstein, Leonard, 1954, Jl 24,13:4
Goldstein, Leonard J, 1953, Je 18,29:5
Goldstein, Louis, 1942, My 16,13:3; 1945, F 11,39:1; 1950, Ap 26,29:2; 1950, S 21,31:2; 1951, S 16,84:6; 1951, S 18,31:2; 1957, Mr 19,37:3; 1960, Ap 9,23:5; 1961, Ap 29,23:2; 1961, S 29,35:5; 1965, Ap 16,29:1
Goldstein, Louis F, 1937, Je 3,25:5
Goldstein, Louis W, 1951, Ag 22,23:5
Goldstein, Manning, 1963, S 8,86:8
Goldstein, Maurice, 1954, My 9,89:1
Goldstein, Max, 1942, My 10,42:5
Goldstein, Max Mrs, 1961, Mr 14,35:4
Goldstein, Maxwell, 1939, Je 29,23:4
Goldstein, Meyer A, 1940, Ap 1,19:5
Goldstein, Meyer M, 1960, D 13,31:2
Goldstein, Michael, 1951, Je 22,25:4
Goldstein, Milton J, 1950, Ap 29,15:4
Goldstein, Monroe M, 1960, Ja 3,88:8
Goldstein, Morris, 1951, My 30,21:3
Goldstein, Morris Mrs, 1945, D 13,29:2
Goldstein, Morton Mrs, 1964, Ja 11,23:2
Goldstein, Nathan, 1947, Je 4,27:2
Goldstein, Nathan C, 1953, S 8,31:2
Goldstein, Nathan N, 1946, Ja 18,19:4
Goldstein, Nathan S, 1961, N 5,88:3
Goldstein, Philip, 1964, Je 27,25:5
Goldstein, Samuel, 1925, F 14,13:4; 1941, Ag 14,17:4; 1945, Mr 5,21:4; 1951, S 23,86:2; 1964, O 9,39:1
Goldstein, Samuel B, 1957, Mr 12,33:4
Goldstein, Samuel E, 1940, D 8,68:4; 1951, My 14,25:5
Goldstein, Samuel H, 1939, Jl 18,19:6
Goldstein, Samuel Mrs, 1957, Je 21,25:1
Goldstein, Sidney E, 1955, Mr 21,25:4
Goldstein, Sidney E Mrs, 1937, Ag 18,19:3
Goldstein, Simon, 1958, F 25,27:1
Goldstein, Sol G Mrs, 1941, Jl 3,19:4
Goldstein, Victor, 1948, D 18,19:6
Goldstein, Wallace, 1958, My 1,31:5
Goldstein, William, 1955, Ap 3,87:1
Goldstein, William Mrs, 1968, N 26,53:3
Goldstein, William N Mrs, 1964, N 1,88:8
Goldstine, Harry, 1954, Je 23,26:5
Goldstine, Mark T, 1954, Mr 6,15:5
Goldstine, Samuel J Mrs, 1951, N 2,23:2
Goldston, Will G, 1948, F 25,24:2
Goldstone, Abner, 1956, Ag 17,19:1
Goldstone, Benjamin, 1949, O 14,28:3
Goldstone, Bracton, 1950, S 12,27:3
Goldstone, David K, 1958, My 6,35:3
Goldstone, Edwin G, 1960, O 30,86:2
Goldstone, George A, 1951, Ap 17,29:4
Goldstone, Jacob, 1940, Je 7,23:2
Goldstone, Joe, 1957, D 15,86:5
Goldstone, Joe Mrs, 1958, Ja 31,22:4
Goldstone, Karl H, 1964, Ap 4,27:1
Goldstone, Lafayette A, 1956, Je 23,17:2
Goldstone, Nathan, 1966, My 10,39:6; 1966, Jl 27,39:4
Goldstone, Salo H, 1952, O 8,31:4
Goldstone, Sarah Mrs, 1942, My 12,19:3
Goldstone, William, 1957, D 22,41:2
Goldstrom, David, 1956, F 27,23:3
Goldstucker, Theodore Prof, 1872, Mr 23,2:7
Goldsworthy, Colin, 1949, My 2,25:3
Goldt, John, 1949, F 3,24:2
Goldthorp, Edgar A, 1951, Ap 26,29:4
Goldthwait, Clarence, 1951, N 1,29:2
Goldthwait, Frederick E, 1914, Jl 6,7:5
Goldthwait, James W, 1948, Ja 3,14:2
Goldthwaite, Bradley D, 1945, Mr 16,15:3
Goldthwaite, Dora, 1922, Ag 20,26:4
Goldthwaite, Du Val R, 1954, Ap 28,31:6
Goldthwaite, G, 1879, Mr 18,5:2
Goldthwaite, G G, 1943, Jl 8,19:6
Goldthwaite, G Tarleton, 1941, D 25,25:4
Goldthwaite, George E, 1960, Ja 12,47:2
Goldthwaite, Mary E Mrs, 1925, Jl 29,21:5
Goldthwaite, Steven G, 1946, N 10,62:3
Goldvogel, Louis D, 1951, Ja 2,23:3
Goldwag, Joseph S, 1951, Jl 12,25:3
Goldwaite, Anne (por), 1944, Ja 30,37:2
Goldwasser, David, 1960, Mr 4,25:2
Goldwasser, Murray J, 1964, Mr 10,37:4
Goldwater, Abraham L, 1951, Mr 24,13:2
Goldwater, Baron Mrs, 1966, D 28,37:3
Goldwater, Edward, 1950, S 21,31:1
Goldwater, Harry, 1938, Je 4,15:5
Goldwater, Louis, 1937, Mr 12,23:1
Goldwater, Morris, 1939, Ap 12,23:4
Goldwater, S S Mrs, 1958, Je 27,25:5
Goldwater, Sigismund S, 1942, O 23,21:1
Goldwater, Simon N, 1947, Ap 21,27:5
Goldweber, E William, 1959, Ja 11,88:3
Goldweitz, Phil, 1949, D 28,32:4
Goldworn, Matthew, 1947, O 28,25:3
Goldwyn, Irving D, 1961, Je 1,35:1
Goldwyn, Louis R, 1962, Mr 22,35:4
Goldwyn, Murray, 1959, F 13,27:3
Goldwyn, Solomon S, 1966, Ag 29,29:4
Goldy, Abraham J, 1963, Ag 26,27:2
Goldzier, Charles, 1922, Ja 10,19:3
Goldzier, Morris, 1923, Ja 10,23:5
Golembe, Charles, 1944, N 15,27:3
Golembe, Julius, 1947, Mr 21,21:4
Golembe, Louis, 1960, F 5,27:3
Golemis, Daniel, 1944, N 22,19:6
Golenischev-Kutuzov, Serge Count, 1950, N 15,31:3
Goler, Frank H, 1944, Ag 16,19:4
Goler, George W, 1940, S 19,23:3
Golestan, Stan, 1956, Ap 23,27:3
Golia, Jack Mrs, 1947, S 15,17:4
Golick, Maurice H, 1963, N 14,35:3
Golightly, Joshua R, 1962, Ag 28,31:4
Golin, Irving, 1955, N 6,87:1
Golin, Reuben, 1965, Ag 15,83:2
Golinko, Jerome I, 1959, F 10,33:1
Goll, George, 1941, F 12,21:5

Goll, James F, 1954, My 28,16:4
Goll, John G, 1947, S 24,23:4
Gollan, Campbell, 1916, D 14,15:5
Gollan, Henry C, 1949, Ag 8,15:1
Gollancz, Victor, 1967, F 9,39:1
Golliday, Gail, 1957, Jl 1,23:5
Golling, Carl F, 1940, Ag 15,19:3
Gollmar, Arthur H, 1947, Jl 26,13:5
Gollock, Georgina A, 1940, D 5,25:2
Gollomb, Joe, 1950, My 24,29:2
Gollow, Ellis E Mrs, 1952, Mr 4,28:3
Golluber, Gerald, 1944, Je 1,19:4
Golluber, Otto A, 1951, Mr 12,25:1
Golly, Aloise M, 1951, Ag 7,25:5
Golman, Alex M, 1954, N 27,14:2
Golnick, Charles F, 1949, Ag 6,15:6
Golob, Larry, 1956, N 26,27:2
Golodny, Mikhail, 1949, Ja 22,13:6
Golomb, Albert W, 1967, F 25,28:1
Golomb, Benjamin, 1952, Jl 24,27:2
Golomb, Eliahu, 1945, Je 12,19:3
Golomb, Jacob J, 1951, Ag 25,11:4
Golomshtok, Eugene A, 1950, Je 23,25:2
Golos, Leonard, 1960, Mr 29,37:4
Golovanov, Nikolai, 1953, S 1,23:4
Golovaty, Ferapont P, 1951, Jl 28,11:5
Golovensky, Max, 1956, Mr 24,19:2
Golovensky, Max Mrs, 1942, Je 15,19:4
Golovin, Louis Mrs, 1944, D 6,23:4
Golovko, Arseni G, 1962, My 19,27:4
Golsin, Thomas S, 1940, N 12,23:3
Goltra, Edward F, 1939, Ap 4,25:3
Golub, Jacob J (trb lr, O 10,16:6), 1953, S 23,32:3
Golub, Jacob S, 1959, Mr 28,17:1
Golub, Joseph, 1946, O 6,57:1
Golub, Louis, 1957, F 21,27:5
Golub, Morris, 1967, My 30,21:4
Golub, Solomon, 1952, Je 19,27:2
Golubeff, Natali, 1942, F 14,9:1
Golubev, Konstantin D, 1956, Je 13,37:1
Golubev, Vladimir V, 1954, D 6,27:4
Golubowski, Solomon, 1945, N 21,21:2
Golwynne, Henry A, 1956, Ap 5,29:5
Golze, Richard Mrs, 1955, N 30,33:3
Goma y Thomas, Isidro Card, 1940, Ag 23,15:3
Goman, Henry A, 1945, O 17,19:4
Gomberg, Alex, 1958, Ap 2,31:2
Gomberg, M Robert, 1958, Ap 26,19:4
Gomberg, Moses, 1947, F 13,24:2
Gomberg, Paul Mrs, 1954, Ag 19,31:2
Gombers, Henry B, 1941, D 23,21:5
Gomborow, Jacob H, 1954, O 2,17:6
Gombosi, Otto J, 1955, F 18,21:1
Gomery, John E, 1948, My 30,34:2
Gomes, Teixeira, 1941, O 19,44:1
Gomes, William H Mrs, 1947, Jl 25,18:2
Gomes Machado, Lourival, 1967, Mr 18,29:5
Gomez, Alejandro, 1940, S 20,23:4
Gomez, G, 1933, Mr 6,13:5
Gomez, General (W Zaisser), 1958, Mr 7,23:2
Gomez, Isadore, 1944, Je 22,19:4
Gomez, Joaquin, 1951, O 8,21:4
Gomez, Jose D, 1942, My 8,21:4
Gomez, Jose Miguel Gen, 1921, Je 14,15:3
Gomez, L, 1929, Ja 14,23:4
Gomez, Luis A, 1952, O 19,88:5
Gomez, Mariano, 1951, Mr 26,23:3
Gomez, Maximo Gen, 1905, Je 18,7:1
Gomez, Rafael (El Gallo), 1960, My 26,33:3
Gomez, Roman, 1951, Ag 10,15:6
Gomez, Vincente Dr, 1924, Jl 30,13:4
Gomez de Barry, Mercedes Mrs, 1950, N 21,22:3
Gomez Jaime, Alfredo, 1946, Ag 22,27:5
Gomez-Jordana, Francisco de, 1944, Ag 4,13:5
Gomez Ochoa, Delio, 1959, Jl 23,16:1
Gomez Ruiz, Louis E, 1966, D 21,39:2
Gomez y Arias, Miguel M, 1950, O 27,29:1
Gomikman, Isidore, 1919, N 29,11:4
Gominger, B Frank, 1962, F 28,33:1
Gomme, Maurice S R, 1943, Je 5,15:1
Gommel, Ernest G Mrs, 1958, F 14,24:1
Gommel, Ernest J Mrs, 1952, Ap 27,90:4
Gomori, George, 1957, Mr 1,23:4
Gomory, Andrew L Mrs, 1947, Je 24,24:3
Gompers, Ab, 1903, Ja 30,9:6
Gompers, Alex J Mrs, 1962, O 2,39:2
Gompers, Alexander J, 1947, Ag 30,15:6
Gompers, Lewis, 1920, Mr 24,9:5
Gompers, Sadie J, 1918, N 6,17:3
Gompers, Samuel J, 1946, Mr 13,29:3
Gompers, Samuel Mrs, 1920, My 7,11:1; 1953, Ag 2, 73:3
Gompers, Simon, 1953, S 22,31:5
Gompers, Solomon, 1919, S 9,17:2
Gompers, William, 1915, Ag 16,9:6
Gompert, William H, 1946, My 21,23:5
Gompertz, Edmund, 1954, Ag 26,27:5
Gompertz, Leo, 1968, F 27,43:3
Gomperz, Theodor, 1912, Ag 30,9:6
Gomph, Charles L, 1952, F 19,29:5
Gon Sam Mue, 1959, Mr 8,86:8
Gonard, John L, 1942, N 3,23:3
Gonatas, Stylianos, 1966, Mr 30,45:3
Goncharov, George, 1955, Ja 1,13:5
Gonclaves, Francisco, 1939, Ap 5,25:6
Goncourt, E L A de, 1896, Jl 17,5:1
Goncourt, Joseph H, 1950, D 11,25:3
Gonda, Joseph A, 1951, F 6,27:4
Gonday, Edward, 1949, O 25,28:3
Gonder, Walter B, 1940, Ja 16,23:1
Gondolfo, Joseph H, 1957, N 24,87:4
Gondor, Ferenc, 1954, Je 2,31:5
Gondran, Sophie M Mrs (will, F 5,9:5), 1938, Ja 22, 15:2
Gondree, G O, 1955, F 19,15:5
Gondret, Henri F, 1964, Ap 22,47:2
Gong, Lue Gim, 1925, Je 5,17:5
Gongora, Manuel de, 1953, Mr 12,27:1
Gongwer, Burr, 1948, S 30,27:3
Gongwer, Burr F, 1961, F 27,27:2
Gongwer, Elton A, 1943, Ag 18,19:2
Gonikman, Charles, 1952, Ap 12,11:2
Gonnaud, Edward A, 1951, Je 28,25:3
Gonneau, Georges P, 1947, F 6,23:3
Gonnell, Maurice, 1921, Je 5,22:2
Gonningsater, Anton M, 1968, Je 22,33:2
Gonnoud, Vincent P, 1961, S 26,39:1
Gonsalves, Emidion, 1954, My 28,23:2
Gonterman, Madison G, 1941, O 1,21:2
Gonthier, Charles, 1909, Mr 29,7:4
Gonvierre, Claude, 1964, N 25,37:2
Gonyaw, Charles, 1953, Je 4,29:4
Gonyeau, Matilda Mrs, 1915, My 25,15:5
Gonzaga, Maurizio Prince, 1938, Mr 25,19:2
Gonzales, Alfonse, 1908, Ag 2,7:7
Gonzales, Antonio C, 1921, Ap 27,17:4
Gonzales, Celio, 1946, S 2,17:5
Gonzales, Charles, 1912, Mr 27,13:4
Gonzales, George W, 1943, Ja 26,19:3
Gonzales, Joachim V, 1923, D 22,13:4
Gonzales, Joaquin, 1952, Mr 30,4:1
Gonzales, Mendoza Antonio, 1906, Ja 16,11:5
Gonzales, Miguel, 1951, N 21,30:2
Gonzales, Ricardo, 1960, F 9,31:4
Gonzales, Richard J, 1947, S 20,15:4
Gonzales, Thomas A, 1956, My 15,31:1
Gonzales, Thomas A Mrs, 1957, F 7,27:4
Gonzales, Vincente V, 1942, Mr 31,21:3
Gonzales, Walter G, 1938, Ja 18,23:5
Gonzales, William E, 1937, O 21,24:2
Gonzales Luna, Efrain, 1964, S 12,25:4
Gonzalez, Antonio C, 1965, Ap 18,80:5
Gonzalez, Antonio C Mrs, 1954, Ag 9,17:3
Gonzalez, Carlos, 1966, O 5,47:3
Gonzalez, Elpidio, 1951, O 19,27:4
Gonzalez, Galo, 1958, Mr 10,23:5
Gonzalez, Isaac, 1954, Ap 22,29:4
Gonzalez, Jose I, 1942, S 24,27:2
Gonzalez, Joseph E Sr, 1945, Ag 16,19:4
Gonzalez, Juan N, 1966, D 8,47:2
Gonzalez, Juan N Mrs, 1966, D 8,47:2
Gonzalez, Juan O, 1941, S 7,50:1
Gonzalez, Lodge, 1942, D 25,17:5
Gonzalez, M Gen, 1893, Ap 11,5:1
Gonzalez, Manuel, 1944, O 17,23:4
Gonzalez, Maria, 1951, Je 4,27:5
Gonzalez, Osiris L, 1941, Je 5,23:5
Gonzalez, Raymond, 1962, Je 16,19:6
Gonzalez, Ruf, 1938, Je 7,23:5
Gonzalez Anaya, Salvador, 1955, F 1,29:3
Gonzalez Cabada, Isidoro, 1952, N 10,25:4
Gonzalez Concha, Jose M, 1953, Mr 4,27:5
Gonzalez Del Riego, Luis, 1949, O 17,23:5
Gonzalez Garza, Rogue, 1962, N 14,39:3
Gonzalez Lopez, Luis A, 1965, N 13,29:5
Gonzalez Malo, Jesus, 1965, D 31,21:2
Gonzalez Martinez, Enrique, 1952, F 20,30:4
Gonzalez Ramos, Dominga, 1963, Je 14,29:3
Gonzalez y Rodriguez, Celso, 1940, Mr 6,23:5
Gonzalez y Rodriguez, Miguel, 1950, N 14,31:3
Gonzata, Mother, 1917, S 5,11:3
Gooch, C Joseph, 1954, D 20,29:4
Gooch, Edwin, 1964, Ag 3,25:2
Gooch, George Peabody Dr, 1968, S 2,19:5
Gooch, Joseph L Jr, 1959, O 18,86:6
Gooch, Lady, 1879, N 1,1:5
Gooch, Tom C, 1952, Je 14,15:5
Gooch, William Wallace, 1916, F 19,11:4
Good, Albert E, 1944, S 23,13:5
Good, Arthur J, 1958, S 14,84:3
Good, Arthur M, 1961, Je 29,33:3
Good, Brent, 1915, N 11,13:6
Good, Charles F, 1953, O 17,15:3
Good, Charles Sr, 1949, N 19,17:5
Good, Donald S, 1956, N 6,35:1
Good, Edward J, 1949, Ja 16,68:2
Good, Emmett F, 1954, Ja 14,29:2
Good, Eugene J, 1947, Ag 7,21:2
Good, F A Maj, 1942, Ja 15,19:5
Good, Frances C Mrs, 1942, Ag 31,17:2
Good, Frank, 1951, D 15,13:5
Good, Frederick L, 1962, Ag 9,25:5
Good, George, 1942, Jl 18,13:7
Good, George A, 1951, D 30,24:2
Good, Harry H, 1940, My 29,23:6
Good, Herman B, 1937, D 29,22:2
Good, Howard H, 1963, Ag 15,29:5
Good, James I Rev Dr, 1924, Ja 23,17:4
Good, James W Mrs, 1962, Mr 8,31:4
Good, John, 1908, Mr 25,9:5; 1953, Ap 30,31:2
Good, John A, 1953, Ja 21,31:4
Good, John H, 1954, Mr 3,27:4
Good, John S, 1947, Mr 14,23:2
Good, Lloyd A, 1951, S 8,17:3
Good, Luther O, 1947, Ap 2,27:3
Good, Michael, 1944, S 4,19:5
Good, Percy, 1950, D 5,32:5
Good, Robert C, 1942, Ag 6,19:4
Good, Robert H, 1940, O 15,23:5
Good, Robert V, 1941, S 18,25:5
Good, Thomas J, 1946, F 1,24:2
Good, Walter S, 1948, S 7,26:3
Good, Weston E, 1938, S 4,16:6
Good, William H Mrs (funl, Ja 6,23:4), 1956, Ja 4, 27:2
Good Voice, Chief, 1907, Ag 18,7:4
Goodacre, Clifford M, 1950, My 18,29:5
Goodale, Alfred, 1951, F 17,15:4
Goodale, Benjamin, 1938, D 26,23:2
Goodale, Benjamin E Mrs, 1942, D 8,25:1
Goodale, Charles F, 1950, Ja 13,23:5
Goodale, George Lincoln Prof, 1923, Ap 13,17:4
Goodale, George P, 1919, My 8,17:3
Goodale, Greenleaf A Brig-Gen, 1915, F 18,11:6
Goodale, Helen B Mrs, 1958, Mr 25,33:3
Goodale, J H, 1901, Ap 21,7:6
Goodale, John H, 1943, Ap 4,41:1
Goodale, Robert C, 1957, S 26,25:6
Goodale, Samuel Bushnell, 1916, Ja 18,11:4
Goodale, Walter S, 1941, O 9,23:4
Goodale, William M, 1938, Ag 28,32:7
Goodall, Charles E, 1951, O 3,36:3
Goodall, E F, 1880, My 11,2:5
Goodall, Edwin B, 1947, Ag 8,17:6
Goodall, Elizabeth H Mrs, 1941, My 9,21:6
Goodall, Fred R A, 1904, Jl 30,7:4
Goodall, George, 1905, Ap 6,11:6
Goodall, Henry S, 1951, O 9,29:6
Goodall, Herbert W, 1965, O 27,47:5
Goodall, James R, 1947, S 26,23:4
Goodall, Marian Le Petit Mrs, 1907, Mr 17,9:5
Goodall, Robert A, 1953, O 24,15:2
Goodall, Samuel I Mrs, 1959, D 5,23:4
Goodaly, Frank W, 1948, Ag 27,18:4
Goodan, Roger, 1943, D 15,27:4
Goodbar, Charles L Mrs, 1947, D 21,54:1
Goodbar, Joseph E, 1953, Jl 22,27:4
Goodbody, John L, 1951, Je 4,27:3
Goodbody, Marcus, 1958, My 27,31:2
Goodbody, Robert, 1911, Ap 14,11:6; 1958, Ja 9,3 1967, Ap 26,47:2
Goodbody, Thomas P, 1955, Je 9,29:4
Goodbody, William U, 1949, Ap 19,25:2
Goodbody, William W Mrs, 1953, My 10,89:2
Goodbread, Robert, 1907, Jl 5,7:3
Goodchild, Donald, 1951, S 29,17:3
Goodchild, F M, 1928, F 19,27:5
Goodchild, Frank, 1946, S 30,25:6
Goodchild, Franklin M, 1962, Jl 3,23:2
Goodchild, William, 1940, D 28,15:3
Goode, D Clyde, 1967, D 11,47:5
Goode, Fenimore C, 1960, Je 4,23:6
Goode, Fenimore C Mrs, 1949, Ap 27,27:5
Goode, Gladstone, 1947, Mr 19,25:4
Goode, H W, 1907, Ap 1,9:7
Goode, John, 1909, Jl 15,7:4
Goode, John M, 1952, F 10,92:5
Goode, Kenneth M, 1958, My 20,33:1
Goode, Paul R, 1959, Ja 19,27:5
Goode, Richard, 1953, My 26,29:4
Goode, William A, 1944, D 17,38:2
Goode, William H C Mrs, 1958, Jl 15,25:1
Goodell, A, 1880, Mr 2,5:2
Goodell, Charles L Rev Dr, 1937, Ap 28,23:4
Goodell, David H Ex-Gov, 1915, Ja 23,11:6
Goodell, De Forrest, 1945, N 14,19:5
Goodell, Edwin B, 1942, O 17,15:6
Goodell, Francis Mrs, 1951, O 14,88:4
Goodell, Henry H, 1905, Ap 25,11:8
Goodell, J M, 1927, Je 23,25:5
Goodell, John, 1938, N 1,23:4
Goodell, Phil, 1957, F 23,17:6
Goodell, Raymond B, 1958, O 3,29:2
Goodell, Reginald R, 1944, Ja 25,19:6
Goodell, Roswell Eaton, 1903, O 20,9:6
Goodell, Thomas Prof, 1920, Jl 8,11:4
Goodell, W Rev, 1878, F 17,1:3
Goodell, Walter J, 1953, N 24,29:2
Goodell, William Rev, 1867, F 23,3:1
Goodelle, Grant H Mrs, 1950, D 7,33:3
Goodelman, Harry J, 1967, Ag 8,39:1
Goodelman, Israel M, 1966, N 13,88:8
Goodelman, Leon, 1957, D 23,23:5
Goodelman, Simeon, 1949, Je 23,27:3
Goodelman, Simeon Mrs, 1949, S 27,28:3
Gooden, B Parks, 1950, Ap 4,29:4
Gooden, John S, 1950, Je 10,17:1
Gooden, Robert B Mrs, 1952, My 13,30:2
Goodenough, Arthur H, 1940, O 6,48:1

Goodenough, Arthur H Mrs, 1951, O 26,23:5
Goodenough, Arthur Rev Dr, 1921, F 10,7:5
Goodenough, Claude E, 1955, O 26,31:1
Goodenough, Erwin R, 1965, Mr 21,87:1
Goodenough, Eugenia M Mrs, 1941, Mr 11,23:4
Goodenough, F C, 1934, S 2,14:1
Goodenough, Florence E, 1940, S 10,23:5
Goodenough, Francis, 1940, Ja 13,15:4
Goodenough, Henry J, 1943, My 7,19:3
Goodenough, Louis B, 1965, Je 18,35:3
Goodenough, Luman W, 1947, Ja 8,23:4
Goodenough, William, 1945, Ja 31,21:2
Goodenough, William M, 1951, My 24,35:3
Gooderham, Albert E, 1943, Ja 24,42:4
Gooderham, Albert Lady, 1955, Mr 20,89:2
Gooderham, Edward D, 1950, D 8,30:3
Gooderham, George, 1905, My 2,11:6
Gooderham, George H, 1942, D 23,19:6
Gooderham, Melville R, 1951, N 26,25:3
Gooderham, Norman R, 1940, Je 8,15:5
Gooderson, Frederick W Mrs, 1944, Ja 8,13:3
Gooderson, Hannah, 1940, Ag 28,19:6
Gooderson, Mathias N, 1864, Mr 28,5:2
Goodeve, James, 1880, Ap 30,2:2
Goodeve, Lesley C, 1955, N 13,88:4
Goodeve, Lindsay M, 1955, F 3,23:4
Goodfellow, Arthur N, 1953, Ja 17,15:6
Goodfellow, Charles C, 1964, Mr 22,76:7
Goodfellow, Ferdinand, 1947, Jl 20,45:2
Goodfellow, Frederick J, 1949, Ja 7,21:2
Goodfellow, George R, 1938, O 25,23:5
Goodfellow, Graydon M, 1950, F 8,27:4
Goodfellow, John C, 1939, Ag 8,17:1
Goodfellow, Nancy S, 1950, O 22,94:6
Goodfellow, Raymond C, 1960, My 27,31:3
Goodfellow, Roy, 1958, S 30,31:2
Goodfellow, Wallace W Mrs, 1960, Jl 24,64:4
Goodfield, Arthur G, 1953, Ap 13,27:3
Goodfried, Ignatius L, 1938, O 25,23:1
Goodfriend, Harry, 1966, Je 29,47:4
Goodfriend, Henry B Mrs, 1952, O 11,19:5
Goodfriend, Leonard M, 1940, N 27,23:5
Goodfriend, Nathan, 1942, Ja 18,42:5
Goodfriend, Sidney, 1957, S 25,29:2
Goodfriend, Simon (por), 1939, N 8,23:2
Goodger, Alfred W, 1951, Je 6,31:4
Goodhand, Arthur W Sr, 1949, F 8,25:3
Goodhand, Oscar G, 1948, Ja 12,19:4
Goodhart, Al, 1955, D 2,27:3
Goodhart, Albert E Mrs (will), 1952, Ag 1,8:6
Goodhart, Albert E Mrs (est tax appr), 1955, Ja 15, 30:8
Goodhart, Arnold M Jr, 1962, Mr 18,86:7
Goodhart, Edwin J, 1962, F 26,27:4
Goodhart, Howard L, 1951, Ag 11,11:3
Goodhart, Morris, 1959, My 23,25:1
Goodhart, Phil J Mrs (por), 1948, Jl 14,23:4
Goodhart, Philip J (por), 1944, Ap 27,23:3
Goodhart, S Phil, 1956, D 7,27:3
Goodheart, William R Jr, 1960, Je 29,33:4
Goodheart, William R Jr Mrs, 1960, D 9,31:3
Goodhue, Allan E, 1948, Ap 21,27:6
Goodhue, Andrew J, 1923, Ap 26,19:5
Goodhue, Bertram G (funl, Ap 26,15:5), 1924, Ap 24,19:3
Goodhue, Charles E, 1940, Ja 31,19:2
Goodhue, Everett F, 1953, D 21,31:4
Goodhue, F Abbot, 1963, Je 11,37:3
Goodhue, Frank W, 1941, Mr 8,19:5
Goodhue, Frederick, 1910, S 5,7:5
Goodhue, Isaac W, 1938, Ap 26,21:4
Goodhue, Willis M, 1938, N 24,27:1
Goodier, James H Mrs, 1961, D 25,23:3
Goodier, Louis E Jr Mrs, 1954, Jl 22,23:2
Goodin, Herman R, 1943, Ja 30,15:2
Goodin, Michael H, 1940, Mr 11,15:1
Goodin, Philip T, 1947, Ja 18,15:5
Gooding, E Mrs, 1946, O 31,25:5
Gooding, Edwin Mrs, 1952, N 21,25:2
Gooding, F R, 1928, Je 25,21:5
Gooding, Frank H, 1948, F 29,60:4
Gooding, Gladys, 1963, N 20,43:1
Gooding, J Hunter, 1947, Ap 15,25:3
Gooding, L E Mrs, 1947, S 23,25:3
Gooding, Lee E, 1962, D 18,4:7
Goodis, David, 1967, Ja 10,40:5
Goodison, Fred, 1942, F 17,21:5
Goodison, Herbert E, 1907, Ja 26,9:5
Goodison, John E, 1955, Ag 28,85:2
Goodkind, Aaron, 1956, F 21,33:1
Goodkind, Gilbert E, 1952, Ja 31,17:1
Goodkind, Gilbert E Mrs, 1952, Ja 31,17:1
Goodkind, Herbert K Mrs, 1956, Ja 23,25:3
Goodkind, Lester H, 1940, O 27,45:3
Goodkind, Martin H Mrs, 1962, Ap 20,27:1
Goodkind, Maurice L, 1939, Ja 5,23:6
Goodkind, Morris, 1968, S 7,29:1
Goodking, Nathan Mrs, 1939, S 17,49:1
Goodkowitz, Hyman S, 1953, Mr 6,20:8
Goodland, Walter S, 1947, Mr 13,27:3
Goodlander, Mabel R, 1944, F 29,17:3
Goodlatte, Thomas A R, 1939, Ja 5,23:5
Goodlet, Constantin R Mrs (cor, N 13,33:1), 1958, N 12,37:2
Goodlett, M C Mrs, 1914, O 18,3:6
Goodliffe, J B, 1903, Ag 14,7:6
Goodliffe, Walter T, 1944, Ap 22,15:4
Goodling, Cletus L, 1950, Ja 5,25:3
Goodloe, John D Mrs, 1947, Ag 17,53:1; 1968, Ag 13, 39:3
Goodloe, Robert M, 1952, Jl 25,17:4
Goodlove, Alberta, 1955, Ag 18,23:2
Goodman, Aaron, 1904, My 1,7:3; 1950, N 28,31:2
Goodman, Abraham, 1950, Ag 23,29:6
Goodman, Abraham H, 1951, F 8,34:2
Goodman, Abraham H Dr, 1951, Je 28,25:5
Goodman, Abraham L, 1946, O 11,23:4
Goodman, Abram Mrs, 1962, Jl 19,27:3
Goodman, Al Mrs, 1961, O 15,88:5
Goodman, Albert W Col, 1937, Ag 23,19:4
Goodman, Alex, 1953, S 4,34:2
Goodman, Alpheus M, 1956, My 30,21:4
Goodman, Arthur, 1965, F 7,92:2
Goodman, Arthur D, 1944, Mr 9,17:5
Goodman, Arthur F, 1955, Ag 2,23:2
Goodman, August, 1945, Ap 17,23:1
Goodman, Barnet, 1946, Ag 13,27:6
Goodman, Benjamin, 1941, D 26,14:2; 1964, Jl 2,28:2
Goodman, Benjamin F, 1948, Ag 27,19:2
Goodman, Benjamin Mrs, 1952, O 26,88:1
Goodman, Benjamin S, 1952, Ja 12,13:3
Goodman, Berthold V, 1939, O 12,25:4
Goodman, C Heber, 1959, N 17,35:5
Goodman, Charles (por), 1945, My 24,19:1
Goodman, Charles, 1963, D 5,45:2
Goodman, Charles E, 1952, Jl 19,15:5
Goodman, Charles I, 1950, Ap 5,31:4
Goodman, Charles Mrs, 1958, S 21,87:3
Goodman, Charles S, 1946, S 28,17:6
Goodman, Daniel, 1951, Jl 15,60:4
Goodman, Daniel C, 1957, My 17,25:1
Goodman, David, 1957, Ap 14,86:7
Goodman, David J, 1958, Ag 22,21:3
Goodman, David M, 1948, My 15,15:6
Goodman, Eckert (Jules E Jr), 1964, Je 16,39:2
Goodman, Edmund L, 1953, Ja 3,15:5
Goodman, Edward, 1962, O 4,39:3
Goodman, Edward Harris Maj, 1916, Mr 5,21:6
Goodman, Edwin, 1953, Ag 20,27:1
Goodman, Edwin Mrs, 1961, Ja 16,27:4
Goodman, Elias, 1915, F 24,9:6
Goodman, Elizabeth A, 1967, S 7,45:2
Goodman, Ephraim, 1941, Jl 2,21:4
Goodman, Eugene W, 1962, Ja 1,23:5
Goodman, Frank, 1944, Jl 14,13:3; 1958, S 24,27:5
Goodman, Frank B, 1954, My 9,88:2
Goodman, Frank C, 1958, Jl 12,15:3
Goodman, Frank Sr Mrs, 1949, Mr 24,27:2
Goodman, Frank V, 1956, My 19,19:4
Goodman, Franklin, 1924, F 21,17:6
Goodman, Fred, 1957, Ap 16,33:3
Goodman, Fred S, 1938, Jl 14,21:4
Goodman, Frederick L, 1952, Je 8,86:6
Goodman, Gordon, 1960, D 11,88:7
Goodman, Harry, 1949, Ag 17,23:4; 1968, Mr 19,47:2
Goodman, Harry I, 1958, S 9,35:4
Goodman, Harry S, 1962, Ag 9,25:4
Goodman, Harvey, 1966, Je 17,45:5
Goodman, Helen R Mrs (will), 1954, O 30,18:1
Goodman, Henry J, 1964, O 24,29:3
Goodman, Henry M R (por), 1939, Ja 15,39:2
Goodman, Henry M R Mrs, 1957, F 4,19:4
Goodman, Herbert S, 1956, Ap 10,31:2
Goodman, Herman J Mrs, 1943, Jl 13,21:2
Goodman, Herman S, 1965, Ja 7,31:2
Goodman, Irving R, 1950, Je 20,27:3
Goodman, Isadore, 1962, Ja 29,25:4
Goodman, Jack A, 1957, Jl 23,27:3
Goodman, Jack A Mrs, 1965, My 1,31:5
Goodman, Jack J, 1943, Ag 19,19:2
Goodman, Jacob J Mrs, 1961, Ag 6,84:3
Goodman, James E, 1966, Ja 17,47:3
Goodman, James P, 1951, Ap 29,89:1
Goodman, Job, 1955, D 24,13:6
Goodman, John F, 1947, Mr 7,25:4
Goodman, John H, 1951, Ja 23,27:1
Goodman, John S, 1941, O 20,17:4
Goodman, Joseph, 1916, My 5,11:6; 1941, F 12,21:5
Goodman, Joseph (por), 1941, My 10,15:1
Goodman, Joseph, 1949, Jl 19,29:4
Goodman, Joseph C, 1964, Mr 9,31:8
Goodman, Joseph D, 1958, N 25,33:2
Goodman, Joseph M, 1958, Ag 17,86:8
Goodman, Jules E, 1962, Jl 11,35:1
Goodman, Jules E Mrs, 1959, D 5,23:3
Goodman, Julius, 1959, Ag 29,17:5; 1968, Je 24,37:4
Goodman, Lazure L, 1966, Ja 30,84:5
Goodman, Lester L, 1965, Ag 4,35:3
Goodman, Lester R, 1952, Jl 4,13:4
Goodman, Louis, 1938, Mr 6,II,8:4
Goodman, Louis E, 1961, S 16,19:3
Goodman, M L Mrs, 1945, Ap 9,19:4
Goodman, Mary M Mrs, 1941, F 27,19:5
Goodman, Matthew, 1967, Ag 10,24:5
Goodman, Maurice, 1939, Mr 20,17:4; 1945, Ag 1,19:3
Goodman, Maurice Mrs, 1960, Jl 10,72:3
Goodman, Max, 1949, Mr 10,27:5; 1949, D 27,23:1; 1950, My 11,29:2; 1952, F 3,85:1
Goodman, Max D, 1937, D 28,22:3
Goodman, Max Mrs, 1959, Ag 11,27:1
Goodman, Michael L, 1953, Je 3,31:5
Goodman, Mildred E Mrs, 1940, Mr 19,25:4
Goodman, Morris, 1941, S 29,17:2; 1956, O 13,19:5
Goodman, Morris A, 1966, Ap 11,35:2
Goodman, Morris Mrs, 1951, F 12,23:4; 1960, Ag 3, 29:4
Goodman, Mose, 1953, Ja 25,85:2
Goodman, Nathan, 1953, Ag 23,76:4; 1955, F 25,21:4
Goodman, P C, 1923, F 20,17:3
Goodman, Patrick, 1921, Ja 10,11:5
Goodman, Patrick E Mrs, 1950, O 25,35:4
Goodman, Paul, 1949, Ag 15,17:4; 1949, S 2,17:1
Goodman, Paul H, 1966, N 14,41:5
Goodman, Phil, 1939, F 23,23:6
Goodman, Phil (por), 1940, Jl 21,28:8
Goodman, Richard, 1911, N 8,13:5
Goodman, Robert, 1948, Je 10,25:2
Goodman, Robert B, 1957, S 12,31:3
Goodman, Robert G, 1937, Je 21,19:6; 1939, Mr 13, 17:4
Goodman, Rosalie Cheney, 1925, My 26,21:4
Goodman, Rosamond Mrs, 1968, D 13,47:2
Goodman, S Fabian, 1954, Jl 18,56:6
Goodman, Sam, 1967, My 2,47:1
Goodman, Samuel, 1937, D 17,25:2; 1958, Jl 13,68:5
Goodman, Samuel Col, 1914, Mr 24,9:4
Goodman, Samuel Jr, 1905, Mr 5,9:3
Goodman, Samuel Mrs, 1947, F 2,57:7
Goodman, Seymour, 1966, Ag 6,23:4
Goodman, Sidney S, 1966, Mr 13,87:2
Goodman, Stanford D, 1941, Ag 23,13:5
Goodman, Theodore, 1952, My 16,23:1
Goodman, Walter E Mrs, 1953, My 6,31:5
Goodman, Wesley B, 1965, D 13,39:2
Goodman, William, 1927, Ap 22,21:5; 1954, Ja 16,15:4
Goodman, William E Jr, 1949, Ap 27,27:1
Goodman, William M, 1958, D 30,35:3
Goodman, William O Mrs, 1943, S 25,15:5
Goodman, Yetta Mrs, 1953, Mr 7,15:4
Goodner, Monroe H, 1962, Ag 26,83:1
Goodness, J Edgar, 1942, Mr 20,19:2
Goodney, Benjamin N, 1962, Jl 6,25:5
Goodnight, James Lincoln, 1914, O 3,11:4
Goodnough, C Jay, 1938, Jl 23,13:4
Goodnough, Lynn G, 1965, Ap 29,35:4
Goodnough, Walter S Prof, 1919, Je 11,15:5
Goodnow, Charles Allen, 1918, Jl 28,19:3
Goodnow, David F (por), 1947, O 8,25:6
Goodnow, David F Mrs, 1954, D 18,15:2
Goodnow, Edward A, 1905, F 2,5:5
Goodnow, Frank J (por), 1939, N 16,23:3
Goodnow, John, 1907, D 10,9:4
Goodnow, Josephine Mrs, 1939, S 30,17:5
Goodnow, Nathan B, 1903, N 8,7:6
Goodpasture, Ernest W (cor, S 27,37:2), 1960, S 22, 27:2
Goodrich, Albert W, 1938, Mr 31,23:5
Goodrich, Alice Dougherty Mrs, 1920, O 1,11:5
Goodrich, Annie W, 1955, Ja 1,13:1
Goodrich, Arthur F, 1941, Je 27,18:2
Goodrich, Bernard H, 1945, N 5,19:2
Goodrich, C Lloyd, 1941, D 13,21:4
Goodrich, Caspar F Mrs, 1908, My 30,7:5
Goodrich, Charles H (por), 1939, My 7,III,7:1
Goodrich, Charles H Mrs, 1950, N 1,35:2
Goodrich, Charles Mrs, 1952, Jl 7,21:6
Goodrich, Charles W Mrs, 1952, Mr 22,13:3
Goodrich, Chauncey Allen Prof, 1860, F 28,5:1
Goodrich, Chauncey W, 1956, O 6,21:5
Goodrich, Clarence A, 1946, F 28,23:5
Goodrich, Clark E, 1951, Jl 14,13:6
Goodrich, Cora F Mrs, 1941, N 1,15:6
Goodrich, Cyrus A, 1951, Ap 20,29:1
Goodrich, David M, 1950, My 18,29:1
Goodrich, David M Mrs, 1951, Je 5,31:2
Goodrich, Donald R, 1945, Jl 14,11:3
Goodrich, Dorothy A, 1953, Mr 24,42:2
Goodrich, E Raymond, 1968, Ap 3,52:1
Goodrich, Edson E, 1950, S 11,23:4
Goodrich, Edward B, 1953, Ja 23,19:2
Goodrich, Edward I Mrs, 1951, Ja 28,76:5
Goodrich, Edward S, 1953, N 22,88:6
Goodrich, Edwin S, 1946, Ja 8,23:4
Goodrich, Elizabeth A Mrs, 1941, D 1,19:2
Goodrich, Ernest P (trb lr, O 18,2636), 1955, O 9, 87:2
Goodrich, Evelyn Mrs, 1947, O 16,27:3
Goodrich, Frances L, 1944, F 21,15:3
Goodrich, George B, 1940, Ja 30,19:5
Goodrich, George H, 1954, Mr 24,27:3
Goodrich, Grace, 1939, S 19,26:2
Goodrich, Henry W Mrs, 1958, Jl 25,19:2
Goodrich, Herbert F, 1962, Je 26,33:3
Goodrich, Herbert F Mrs, 1940, F 10,15:6
Goodrich, J Z, 1885, Ap 21,5:4
Goodrich, James P, 1940, Ag 16,15:3
Goodrich, John D Maj, 1937, O 19,25:3
Goodrich, John Ellsworth, 1915, F 26,9:6
Goodrich, John F, 1937, Mr 13,19:3

Goodrich, L Keith, 1968, Ap 19,47:5
Goodrich, Lester A, 1938, D 26,23:5
Goodrich, Louis, 1945, F 1,23:6
Goodrich, Louis C, 1904, Ja 1,7:6
Goodrich, Louis C Mrs, 1943, O 3,48:3
Goodrich, Merritt A, 1944, N 29,23:1
Goodrich, Milan E Mrs, 1951, Ag 19,86:1
Goodrich, Milo, 1881, Ap 16,5:4
Goodrich, Nathaniel L, 1957, My 2,31:4
Goodrich, Pierre E, 1951, Ag 13,17:4
Goodrich, Robert E, 1965, D 4,31:4
Goodrich, Samuel Griswold (funl, My 14,8:3), 1860, My 11,4:5
Goodrich, Thomas F, 1904, N 10,9:4
Goodrich, W H Rev Dr, 1874, Jl 20,4:7
Goodrich, Wallace, 1952, Je 8,86:8
Goodrich, William B, 1954, F 4,25:3
Goodrich, William F Mrs, 1955, F 1,29:4
Goodrich, William Mrs, 1947, O 26,70:6
Goodrich, William W, 1906, N 22,9:5
Goodridge, Edwin A Dr, 1916, Je 1,11:5
Goodridge, Edwin H, 1962, Jl 29,61:1
Goodridge, Ethel I Mrs, 1937, D 15,25:4
Goodridge, Malcolm, 1956, Jl 18,27:1; 1966, F 28,27:4
Goodring, Elias J, 1942, Ag 21,19:3
Goodrow, Ray, 1942, My 12,19:2
Goodsell, Charles T, 1941, N 26,23:1
Goodsell, Daniel Ayres Bd, 1909, D 6,9:3
Goodsell, Frances P Mrs, 1937, O 10,II,8:4
Goodsell, George H Rev Dr, 1907, My 19,7:4
Goodsell, John W, 1949, N 22,29:5
Goodsell, Louis F, 1924, My 28,23:4
Goodsell, Nelson, 1948, Ja 30,24:3
Goodsell, P Hamilton, 1950, My 29,17:5
Goodsell, Percy H Mrs, 1959, Je 4,31:4
Goodsell, Willystine, 1962, Je 1,28:1
Goodsmith, Heber M, 1945, Ap 10,19:1
Goodson, Alfred L, 1940, N 30,17:2
Goodson, James O, 1957, D 17,35:3
Goodson, Katherine (Mrs A Hinton), 1958, My 13, 29:5
Goodson, William C, 1946, Jl 25,21:4
Goodspeed, Arthur W, 1943, Je 7,13:5
Goodspeed, Arthur W Mrs, 1961, O 1,86:2
Goodspeed, B F Schuyler, 1944, My 16,21:4
Goodspeed, Charles B (por), 1947, F 25,25:3
Goodspeed, Charles E, 1950, N 1,35:3
Goodspeed, Charles T, 1949, N 20,95:3
Goodspeed, Edgar J, 1962, Ja 14,84:2
Goodspeed, Frank L, 1941, Jl 23,19:5
Goodspeed, George W, 1946, Ja 25,23:2
Goodspeed, Henry S, 1959, Ap 23,31:3
Goodspeed, James H, 1950, D 1,26:3
Goodspeed, Morton, 1965, Ja 30,27:1
Goodspeed, Morton Mrs, 1962, Jl 24,27:3
Goodspeed, T W, 1927, D 17,19:5
Goodspeed, Thomas H, 1966, My 19,47:4
Goodspeed, Warren M, 1955, Ap 26,29:1
Goodstein, David, 1966, Ap 11,35:2
Goodstein, David M, 1966, Ag 23,39:4
Goodstein, David Mrs, 1949, O 10,23:2
Goodstein, Harris N Mrs, 1966, Ag 5,31:4
Goodstein, Harry, 1942, Je 30,21:4; 1953, Ag 26,27:3
Goodstein, Henry D, 1951, Jl 2,23:5
Goodstein, Herman B, 1966, F 16,43:4
Goodstein, Isaac, 1924, O 15,23:4
Goodstein, Julius, 1953, N 12,31:2
Goodstein, Mark, 1946, O 31,25:3
Goodstein, Samuel, 1909, F 19,9:6
Goodwell, George W, 1946, F 11,29:5
Goodwill, Harry C, 1951, N 6,29:1
Goodwillie, David H, 1952, O 19,88:6
Goodwillie, David H Dr, 1907, My 17,9:5
Goodwillie, Mary, 1949, Je 29,27:4
Goodwillie, Robert H, 1950, D 30,13:6
Goodwillie, Stuart, 1967, F 9,39:2
Goodwillie, Walter S Jr, 1937, D 27,16:3
Goodwin, Abraham, 1966, F 21,39:5
Goodwin, Adolph O, 1943, Je 10,21:1
Goodwin, Albert, 1968, My 7,47:1
Goodwin, Albert C, 1912, Mr 19,11:4; 1937, O 5,25:3
Goodwin, Alice G V, 1949, Je 13,19:4
Goodwin, Allen, 1949, N 22,29:4
Goodwin, Almon, 1905, N 3,9:5
Goodwin, Arthur C, 1947, Ap 21,27:1
Goodwin, Arthur P, 1948, Ap 6,23:5
Goodwin, Austin M, 1945, N 2,19:4
Goodwin, Bill, 1958, My 10,21:4
Goodwin, C L, 1873, Ag 28,2:7
Goodwin, Carl H, 1946, Ja 9,23:4
Goodwin, Caroline L G Mrs, 1941, O 8,24:2
Goodwin, Charles, 1949, D 8,33:2
Goodwin, Charles A, 1954, O 9,17:3
Goodwin, Charles A Mrs, 1952, F 26,27:3
Goodwin, Charles F, 1941, D 13,21:4
Goodwin, Charles H, 1951, Ag 24,15:3
Goodwin, Charles W, 1941, Je 5,24:3
Goodwin, Clarence N, 1956, S 23,84:6
Goodwin, Daniel L, 1948, F 5,23:3
Goodwin, Dexter B Mrs, 1946, Jl 26,21:2
Goodwin, E McK Dr, 1937, Jl 19,15:3
Goodwin, Edward, 1949, Mr 1,1:5
Goodwin, Edward A, 1966, Ja 24,35:4
Goodwin, Edward C, 1948, D 15,33:5
Goodwin, Edward H, 1965, Ag 23,31:4
Goodwin, Edward H Mrs, 1939, N 7,25:3
Goodwin, Edward Hockley Rev, 1911, O 19,13:6
Goodwin, Edward I, 1955, My 21,17:6
Goodwin, Edward J, 1941, Ap 12,15:6
Goodwin, Edward M, 1948, O 4,23:4
Goodwin, Edward N, 1968, F 6,44:1
Goodwin, Eleanor, 1922, Ap 18,17:4
Goodwin, Ernest A, 1953, N 13,27:3
Goodwin, F Spencer, 1953, Jl 9,25:2
Goodwin, Forrest (funl, Je 1,7:6), 1913, My 29,11:6
Goodwin, Francis Dr, 1923, O 6,15:4
Goodwin, Francis M Sr, 1962, My 23,45:3
Goodwin, Frank A, 1947, Je 16,21:4
Goodwin, Frank J (funl, Mr 12,19:4), 1925, Mr 10, 21:4
Goodwin, Fred C, 1942, D 4,25:5
Goodwin, Frederick H, 1968, D 9,55:6
Goodwin, G C, 1869, My 14,2:3
Goodwin, G G, 1933, F 17,19:1
Goodwin, G K, 1882, Ag 2,5:6
Goodwin, George, 1945, Ap 5,23:5
Goodwin, George M (por), 1947, Jl 13,44:1
Goodwin, George W, 1940, Mr 25,15:5
Goodwin, Grenville, 1951, Ag 29,25:2
Goodwin, Hannibal Mrs, 1914, S 23,9:4
Goodwin, Hannibal Rev, 1901, Ja 1,9:6
Goodwin, Harold C, 1942, Mr 2,19:3
Goodwin, Harry, 1942, O 26,15:2; 1956, S 17,27:5; 1961, Je 16,33:3
Goodwin, Harry I, 1940, F 29,19:1
Goodwin, Harry M, 1949, Je 28,27:1
Goodwin, Ichabod, 1882, Jl 5,2:1
Goodwin, J, 1878, Mr 16,5:5
Goodwin, J Cheever, 1912, D 20,15:4
Goodwin, J Pryse, 1959, Ag 29,17:4
Goodwin, Jack C, 1949, My 28,15:2
Goodwin, James J, 1915, Je 24,11:6
Goodwin, James L, 1967, Mr 3,35:2
Goodwin, James L Mrs, 1945, D 6,27:5
Goodwin, James Rev Dr, 1917, Ja 4,11:5
Goodwin, James W, 1959, D 31,21:5
Goodwin, Jasper Tillerous, 1913, Ja 12,II,17:1
Goodwin, John, 1940, Ja 3,21:1
Goodwin, John A, 1925, N 27,17:4; 1940, D 27,19:4; 1950, My 30,17:1
Goodwin, John E, 1948, N 20,13:4
Goodwin, John W, 1937, Ag 24,22:1
Goodwin, Joseph E, 1957, Ja 13,84:2
Goodwin, Josephine S (will), 1940, Mr 1,41:2
Goodwin, Karl H, 1939, F 13,15:3
Goodwin, Katherine R, 1961, S 26,39:3
Goodwin, Kenneth P, 1954, Je 22,27:5
Goodwin, Leo F, 1944, Ag 17,17:6
Goodwin, Leo J (Budd), 1957, My 27,31:2
Goodwin, Leonard, 1948, My 9,68:4
Goodwin, Leonard Mrs, 1951, D 20,31:5
Goodwin, Mark L, 1947, N 24,23:4
Goodwin, N, 1876, Jl 23,12:6
Goodwin, Nat C, 1919, F 1,13:3
Goodwin, Nellie Le Reine, 1968, Ap 28,83:1
Goodwin, Phil A (por), 1937, Je 7,19:3
Goodwin, Phil J, 1941, Ap 28,15:5
Goodwin, Philip L, 1958, F 14,23:1
Goodwin, Ralph E, 1939, D 17,48:8
Goodwin, Richard F (Oct 3), 1965, O 11,61:2
Goodwin, Richard La Barre, 1910, D 11,17:3
Goodwin, Richard V, 1952, Ap 2,33:2
Goodwin, Roy C, 1950, O 30,27:2
Goodwin, Ruth S, 1943, Mr 30,21:3
Goodwin, Sidney, 1947, N 28,27:3
Goodwin, Thomas, 1903, S 12,9:6
Goodwin, Thomas H, 1945, Ap 5,23:4
Goodwin, Thomas J, 1949, Mr 6,72:2
Goodwin, W H Rev Dr, 1876, F 22,5:6
Goodwin, Walter L, 1952, Ja 16,17:4
Goodwin, Wayne M, 1940, F 10,15:3
Goodwin, Wilder, 1955, N 27,88:7
Goodwin, Wilder Mrs, 1947, D 17,29:4
Goodwin, Willard T, 1953, Ag 8,11:1
Goodwin, William A, 1939, S 8,23:3
Goodwin, William A R Mrs, 1954, F 22,19:2
Goodwin, William B, 1940, My 31,19:3; 1950, My 19, 28:4
Goodwin, William C, 1948, Mr 18,27:3
Goodwin, William D, 1947, My 13,25:1
Goodwin, William G, 1958, Ja 23,27:5
Goodwin, William H, 1905, F 20,7:4
Goodwin, William H Dr, 1937, My 24,19:3
Goodwin, William J, 1957, D 16,29:3; 1962, N 21,33:4; 1963, D 22,34:2
Goodwin, William L, 1941, Ja 18,15:5; 1941, N 1,15:6
Goodwin, William Watson Prof, 1912, Je 17,9:7
Goodwine, Lucy, 1959, Je 17,35:1
Goodwyn, A T, 1931, Jl 2,27:5
Goodwyn, P A, 1945, O 23,17:5
Goodwyn, Wilfred L Jr, 1956, Je 10,88:3
Goody, Charles H, 1966, Mr 14,31:1
Goodyear, A Conger, 1964, Ap 24,33:3
Goodyear, A Conger Mrs, 1966, Jl 22,31:5
Goodyear, Caroline, 1962, O 29,29:5
Goodyear, Charles W, 1911, Ap 17,11:4
Goodyear, De Mont, 1946, Ja 26,13:4
Goodyear, E F, 1949, Jl 27,23:2
Goodyear, Ella P Mrs, 1940, S 30,17:1
Goodyear, Ellsworth D Gen, 1910, S 5,7:5
Goodyear, Esther, 1950, Ja 10,29:5
Goodyear, John, 1964, Je 25,33:2
Goodyear, John J, 1939, Jl 12,19:5
Goodyear, Mary B, 1938, My 24,19:2
Goodyear, Nelson, 1917, Mr 10,11:4
Goodyear, Nelson Mrs, 1953, Jl 7,27:2
Goodyear, Robert B Mrs, 1942, F 11,21:5
Goodyear, Ruth E, 1964, Ag 10,31:2
Goodyear, Walter, 1939, Jl 31,13:5
Goodyear, William, 1938, N 2,23:2
Goodyear, William H, 1941, N 22,19:5
Goodyear, William H Prof, 1923, F 20,17:1
Googe, George L, 1961, S 30,25:6
Googins, J B Mrs, 1950, Mr 25,13:4
Gookin, Edward R, 1945, Mr 7,21:5
Gookin, F W, 1936, Ja 19,II,8:4
Gookin, Vincent A, 1959, O 26,29:4
Gookin, Warner F, 1953, Mr 4,27:1
Goold, Edgar H, 1954, Jl 7,31:5
Goold, Gilbert Mrs, 1959, My 31,76:4
Goold, J, 1879, O 2,2:3
Goold, James A, 1962, My 15,39:2
Goold, Paul P, 1925, D 9,27:4
Goold, Samuel, 1966, F 10,34:1
Goold, William D, 1938, F 22,21:5
Goolden, Francis H W, 1950, Je 14,31:3
Goolfby, James, 1948, O 26,31:1
Goolrick, Robert E M, 1946, N 14,29:4
Goolsby, George Mrs, 1944, S 11,17:6
Goolsby, John R, 1950, D 15,32:3
Goomrigian, Leon H, 1946, D 4,31:4
Goon Gee Mah, 1944, Ap 10,19:2
Goos, Julius, 1939, My 30,17:6
Goosey, Thomas, 1954, Ja 23,13:5
Goosmann, J C, 1938, Ja 23,II,8:6
Goossens, Eugene, 1962, Je 14,1:5
Goossens, Eugene Sr, 1958, Ag 1,21:5
Goossens, Eugene Sr Mrs, 1946, S 16,5:6
Gootenberg, Phil, 1942, S 22,21:2
Gopner, Serafima I, 1966, Ap 5,39:3
Gopsill, Carolyn, 1953, Mr 14,15:2
Gopsill, James, 1884, Jl 27,3:2
Gopsill, John G, 1920, Mr 30,11:5
Gorab, Joseph B, 1966, Jl 1,35:4
Goral, John L, 1945, Ap 27,19:1
Goranflo, Jennie E, 1941, S 5,21:3
Gorar, Louis J, 1952, Je 29,56:7
Gorbach, Abraham, 1952, F 3,84:1
Gorbatov, Boris L, 1954, Ja 21,31:2
Gorbold, Raymond P Mrs, 1952, Ja 11,21:1
Gorby, Isaac I, 1942, S 26,15:2
Gorcey, Bernard, 1955, S 13,31:3
Gorcey, Samuel, 1961, Mr 13,29:4
Gorcheck, Frank, 1941, Ap 1,23:2
Gorchickoff, Herman, 1943, S 2,19:4
Gorczyca, Louis F Sr, 1948, My 29,15:6
Gord, Max, 1937, Ag 14,13:7
Gordan, Isaac, 1917, S 23,23:2
Gordan, John D Dr, 1968, Mr 11,41:3
Gordani, Nina (Mrs J B Seldin), 1966, Ja 21,47:4
Gordeau, G C Mrs, 1951, O 2,27:4
Gorden, Thomas A, 1949, O 22,17:3
Gorden, Vincent J, 1960, Jl 7,31:3
Gordiano, Samuel F Rev, 1914, O 23,11:4
Gordich, David, 1952, Ja 4,40:2
Gordich, Leo W, 1951, Ja 30,25:3
Gordillo, Maurizio, 1961, Ap 17,29:4
Gordin, Jacob (trb, Je 14,7:5), 1909, Je 12,7:3
Gordine, Sacha, 1968, Je 9,84:6
Gordineer, Richard C, 1946, My 23,21:1
Gordis, Hyman, 1946, Ag 7,27:5
Gordohn, John N, 1967, My 8,41:5
Gordon, A A, 1931, Je 16,27:1
Gordon, Abraham S, 1957, F 3,76:5
Gordon, Adam R, 1951, Ja 12,27:2
Gordon, Agnes (Mrs Ralph Gordon), 1967, My [illegible] 47:2
Gordon, Albert F, 1948, Mr 18,27:1
Gordon, Albert F Mrs, 1939, F 25,15:6
Gordon, Albert I Rabbi, 1968, N 7,47:1
Gordon, Alex, 1939, F 14,19:5; 1940, My 4,17:2; [illegible] Mr 20,13:2; 1950, Jl 19,31:3; 1957, Mr 30,19:2
Gordon, Alex I, 1952, Jl 1,23:1
Gordon, Alex Mrs, 1948, O 30,15:5; 1950, N 21,3[illegible]
Gordon, Alexander S, 1968, S 24,47:2
Gordon, Alfred, 1942, D 9,27:4; 1953, Ja 14,31:1
Gordon, Allen, 1955, Jl 19,27:6
Gordon, Allison, 1941, D 2,23:5
Gordon, Amos K, 1955, O 9,87:2
Gordon, Anne E, 1959, N 19,39:4
Gordon, Anthony H, 1964, Ap 11,25:1
Gordon, Anthony W, 1942, D 1,25:3
Gordon, Armistead C, 1953, My 14,29:6
Gordon, Arthur, 1966, Ag 13,25:3
Gordon, Arthur H, 1938, D 3,19:5; 1953, My 16,[illegible]
Gordon, Arthur Hamilton (Baron Stanmore), 19[illegible] Ja 31,11:5
Gordon, Basil, 1901, Jl 30,2:5
Gordon, Beirne Jr, 1937, F 20,17:4

Gordon, Ben E, 1954, Jl 29,23:3
Gordon, Benjamin, 1952, S 9,31:3; 1963, Je 19,37:2
Gordon, Benjamin D, 1952, Jl 31,23:5
Gordon, Benjamin L, 1965, Mr 31,39:1
Gordon, Bernard, 1944, O 4,20:2; 1948, Jl 7,46:4
Gordon, Bernard Dr, 1944, Ap 14,19:5
Gordon, Brook, 1951, Je 1,23:3
Gordon, Buford F, 1952, Ja 21,15:4
Gordon, C C Rev, 1883, D 3,5:5
Gordon, C Henry (por), 1940, D 4,27:1
Gordon, Charles, 1938, My 3,23:6
Gordon, Charles (por), 1945, My 5,15:3
Gordon, Charles, 1951, O 9,29:3
Gordon, Charles A, 1958, O 31,26:1; 1966, Je 18,31:2
Gordon, Charles B Sir (por), 1939, Jl 31,13:3
Gordon, Charles D, 1954, My 16,87:1
Gordon, Charles H, 1958, Jl 29,23:3
Gordon, Charles L, 1966, Ja 19,41:4
Gordon, Charles M, 1951, Jl 4,17:4
Gordon, Charles S, 1917, D 18,15:5
Gordon, Charles W, 1939, N 28,25:3; 1943, D 2,27:1
Gordon, Charles William Rev Dr (por), 1937, N 1, 21:5
Gordon, Clarence, 1920, N 27,13:6
Gordon, Clarence E, 1951, Ag 29,25:6
Gordon, Crawford, 1967, Ja 28,27:4
Gordon, Crawford Sr, 1957, Jl 21,60:8
Gordon, D S, 1930, Ja 29,23:4
Gordon, Damon G Mrs, 1949, D 30,20:2
Gordon, Daniel F, 1938, F 11,23:2
Gordon, Daniel Miner Dr, 1925, S 2,23:4
Gordon, Daniel Mrs, 1939, O 27,23:6
Gordon, David B, 1964, F 5,35:5
Gordon, David M, 1962, N 22,19:5
Gordon, David S, 1946, Mr 9,13:3; 1952, Ja 21,15:3
Gordon, David W Mrs, 1964, Ap 3,33:5
Gordon, Delbert V, 1953, Mr 9,29:5
Gordon, Dennis B, 1962, Ja 26,16:3
Gordon, Don O, 1965, Je 11,31:1
Gordon, Donald, 1953, Ag 16,76:4
Gordon, Donald L, 1965, Mr 6,25:2
Gordon, Donald Mrs, 1950, Mr 2,27:2
Gordon, Douglas, 1944, My 4,19:6
Gordon, Douglas Huntley, 1918, Ap 9,13:4
Gordon, Duff Lady, 1869, Jl 29,5:5
Gordon, Earle C, 1938, D 19,23:6
Gordon, Earle C Jr, 1954, Ag 24,21:5
Gordon, Edith H, 1939, D 18,23:3
Gordon, Edward W, 1958, F 10,23:2
Gordon, Edwin C, 1961, S 20,29:2
Gordon, Edwin K Mrs, 1954, Jl 1,25:4
Gordon, Eli, 1954, Ag 26,27:3
Gordon, Elias Mrs, 1960, Ap 28,35:2
Gordon, Ella C, 1948, D 17,27:3
Gordon, Ellen W Mrs, 1956, D 26,27:3
Gordon, Elsie M, 1951, Ja 20,15:5
Gordon, Emanuel L, 1960, Ja 27,30:8
Gordon, Ernest A, 1947, D 11,33:2
Gordon, Ernest B, 1956, F 13,27:4
Gordon, Eugene, 1954, Ap 6,33:7
Gordon, Eugene Corry, 1910, Ja 1,9:5
Gordon, Ezekiel, 1962, F 16,29:1
Gordon, F M, 1932, Ja 19,24:1
Gordon, Ferdinand D, 1954, N 24,23:2
Gordon, Florence, 1956, N 17,21:3
Gordon, Forrest E, 1945, F 8,19:3
Gordon, Francis A, 1960, Mr 8,33:2
Gordon, Frank C, 1960, Ja 16,21:1
Gordon, Frank H, 1953, F 12,27:2
Gordon, Frank H Mrs, 1944, D 12,23:3
Gordon, Frank M, 1946, N 30,15:2
Gordon, Frank S, 1959, Ap 24,27:4
Gordon, Fred G R, 1944, F 24,15:6
Gordon, Fred H, 1951, S 30,72:4
Gordon, Frederic S, 1951, Ag 10,15:1
Gordon, Frederic S Mrs, 1949, Mr 26,17:3
Gordon, Frederick Charles, 1924, Mr 22,15:6
Gordon, Frederick E, 1941, N 18,25:1
Gordon, G B, 1927, S 9,25:3
Gordon, G N, 1949, Mr 23,28:4
Gordon, G P, 1878, Ja 28,4:7
Gordon, G Swayne, 1949, Je 25,13:4
Gordon, George, 1913, Mr 26,11:4; 1942, F 4,19:4
Gordon, George (por), 1949, Ag 28,72:4
Gordon, George, 1966, My 29,56:3
Gordon, George A, 1941, S 25,25:5; 1959, My 12,35:1
Gordon, George A Mrs, 1965, Jl 23,29:1
Gordon, George C, 1964, My 29,29:3
Gordon, George H Jr, 1957, My 23,33:2
Gordon, George Hamilton, 1860, D 27,8:2
Gordon, George M, 1941, Ja 25,15:4; 1961, D 4,37:4
Gordon, George M Mrs, 1961, Ja 31,29:5
Gordon, George S, 1942, Mr 13,19:4
Gordon, George S E, 1940, F 29,19:1
Gordon, George W Gen (funl, Ag 13,9:5), 1911, Ag 10,7:4
Gordon, Gert (Mrs A Rothenberg), 1963, Je 8,25:2
Gordon, Guy W, 1959, Ja 7,33:4
Gordon, Guy W Mrs, 1958, Je 27,25:1
Gordon, Harold, 1952, S 21,89:3
Gordon, Harold Mrs, 1948, O 31,88:6
Gordon, Harris, 1947, Ap 2,27:1
Gordon, Harry, 1950, Je 6,30:2; 1953, N 23,27:1; 1964, Jl 15,35:5
Gordon, Harry A (por), 1947, My 17,15:3
Gordon, Harry C, 1944, O 29,43:1; 1949, Je 18,13:2
Gordon, Harry H, 1951, Mr 6,27:2
Gordon, Harry Mrs, 1949, D 17,17:1
Gordon, Harry W, 1944, O 24,23:2
Gordon, Harvey A (por), 1938, D 16,25:4
Gordon, Henry A, 1948, F 22,48:4
Gordon, Henry A Mrs, 1950, Ap 15,15:2
Gordon, Henry B, 1954, Jl 21,27:4
Gordon, Henry T, 1942, Ja 6,23:3
Gordon, Herbert, 1964, Ag 29,21:5
Gordon, Herbert B, 1959, F 16,29:3
Gordon, Herman, 1957, N 20,32:1
Gordon, Howard, 1948, F 17,25:1
Gordon, Howard H, 1965, Mr 4,31:4
Gordon, Hugh H Maj, 1937, D 12,II,9:2
Gordon, Huntley, 1956, D 10,31:2
Gordon, Hyman, 1956, N 13,37:3
Gordon, Ira H, 1946, Jl 9,22:2
Gordon, Irving G, 1965, D 12,87:1
Gordon, Irwin L, 1954, Jl 22,23:5
Gordon, Isaac, 1938, F 20,II,9:1
Gordon, Isaac L, 1947, D 16,33:1; 1950, Jl 1,15:5
Gordon, J Howard, 1949, F 20,61:1
Gordon, J Lindsay, 1940, Mr 4,15:4
Gordon, J Morton, 1959, F 3,31:1
Gordon, J R, 1961, Ag 1,31:1
Gordon, J R Mrs, 1954, N 7,88:6
Gordon, J Wallace, 1903, Je 14,7:6
Gordon, J Wesley A, 1950, Ja 9,25:1
Gordon, Jacob, 1943, Ag 30,15:6
Gordon, Jacob Mrs, 1937, Je 8,25:2; 1948, Je 17,25:5
Gordon, Jacob N, 1939, Ja 2,24:2
Gordon, Jacques (por), 1948, S 16,29:3
Gordon, James, 1938, Ag 30,17:5; 1941, My 14,21:5
Gordon, James C (will), 1945, Mr 16,11:1
Gordon, James C, 1952, O 1,33:2
Gordon, James Ex-Sen, 1912, N 29,15:5
Gordon, James F, 1942, N 6,23:3
Gordon, James G, 1937, Mr 21,24:1; 1953, Ap 24,23:5
Gordon, James Lindsay, 1904, D 1,9:4
Gordon, James R Mrs, 1951, Ag 23,23:2
Gordon, James T, 1944, Ja 24,17:6
Gordon, Jan, 1944, F 3,19:1
Gordon, Jane, 1953, F 25,27:3
Gordon, Jeanne, 1952, F 23,11:5
Gordon, Jennie Mrs, 1938, Ap 11,15:2
Gordon, Jessie F, 1942, D 12,17:3
Gordon, John, 1950, Ja 22,59:1
Gordon, John B Gen, 1904, Ja 10,7:4
Gordon, John H Mrs, 1951, S 6,31:4
Gordon, John J, 1915, Jl 1,11:5; 1951, Jl 31,21:2; 1954, D 31,14:4; 1956, Jl 9,23:5
Gordon, John J Capt, 1875, My 28,5:4
Gordon, John R, 1948, O 29,25:2
Gordon, John Rev, 1923, F 10,13:5; 1925, Ag 3,15:4
Gordon, John S, 1940, O 14,19:4
Gordon, John T Mrs, 1948, O 7,30:2
Gordon, John W 2d, 1957, Mr 21,31:2
Gordon, Joseph, 1940, O 1,23:1; 1956, My 10,31:2
Gordon, Joseph L, 1964, Mr 13,33:1
Gordon, Joseph W Mrs, 1953, Mr 10,29:3
Gordon, Julien (Mrs S Van Rensselaer Cruger), 1920, Jl 13,11:4
Gordon, Julius, 1938, Jl 16,13:6; 1954, Jl 8,23:5
Gordon, Kenneth, 1943, Ja 9,13:4; 1947, S 11,27:1
Gordon, L B, 1948, Ap 9,23:2
Gordon, Lawrence, 1962, S 5,39:3
Gordon, Lee A C Jr, 1960, Ap 14,37:4
Gordon, Leo, 1957, Je 25,29:4
Gordon, Leon, 1944, Ja 1,13:5; 1960, Ja 5,31:3
Gordon, Leon S, 1950, Jl 26,25:5
Gordon, Leonard J Dr, 1905, Ja 18,9:4
Gordon, Leroy O, 1942, Je 18,21:1
Gordon, Louis, 1949, Ag 7,60:8; 1959, Ag 23,93:3; 1959, O 10,21:2; 1961, S 21,35:2
Gordon, Louis F, 1964, Ja 13,35:4
Gordon, Louis Mrs, 1951, Jl 24,25:2; 1956, N 21,27:3
Gordon, Mack, 1959, Mr 1,86:1
Gordon, Mackenzie, 1943, Je 10,21:4
Gordon, Malcolm K, 1964, N 15,87:1
Gordon, Manya (por), 1945, D 29,13:3
Gordon, Maria O, 1939, Je 26,15:5
Gordon, Mark, 1944, Ag 18,13:5
Gordon, Mary C Mrs, 1942, S 12,13:5
Gordon, Max L, 1948, N 5,26:2
Gordon, May E, 1940, N 21,29:3
Gordon, May Mrs (will), 1952, Je 5,36:5
Gordon, Mervyn H, 1953, Jl 29,23:3
Gordon, Michael, 1949, Ag 3,23:6
Gordon, Michael S, 1951, Ja 11,25:2
Gordon, Miles A Mrs, 1959, F 4,33:4
Gordon, Miller L, 1948, O 19,27:3
Gordon, Morris, 1953, Je 9,27:2
Gordon, Morris Mrs, 1950, O 9,25:4
Gordon, Murray B, 1946, Je 30,38:4
Gordon, Myer M, 1960, My 17,37:4
Gordon, Myron, 1959, Mr 13,26:7
Gordon, Nathan, 1953, My 3,88:3
Gordon, Nathl E, 1948, Je 25,23:3
Gordon, Newell T, 1953, Jl 20,17:3
Gordon, Nick G, 1945, N 17,17:3
Gordon, Norman S Mrs, 1939, My 24,23:6
Gordon, Onslow A, 1948, Jl 9,19:2
Gordon, Onslow A Dr, 1937, Jl 5,17:3
Gordon, Paul V Mrs, 1958, Mr 30,89:2
Gordon, Peyton, 1946, S 18,31:3
Gordon, Phil, 1941, F 7,19:5; 1951, O 25,29:2
Gordon, Phil W, 1951, O 13,17:2
Gordon, Philip W Mrs, 1956, F 3,23:3
Gordon, R, 1880, N 17,5:5
Gordon, Raymond A, 1946, Ag 3,15:2
Gordon, Reginald, 1946, Mr 27,27:1
Gordon, Rena R, 1945, My 29,15:5
Gordon, Richard E, 1960, N 17,37:1
Gordon, Richard H, 1956, S 22,17:3
Gordon, Richard H Capt, 1917, N 22,13:4
Gordon, Robert B, 1923, Ja 4,19:4; 1953, Ja 30,21:2
Gordon, Robert H, 1963, O 15,39:5
Gordon, Robert I Mrs, 1951, S 12,31:3
Gordon, Robert J, 1948, Ja 24,15:5
Gordon, Robert L (por), 1946, F 13,23:3
Gordon, Robert L, 1952, N 21,25:4
Gordon, Roy Mrs, 1944, F 4,15:1
Gordon, Samuel, 1939, Ap 2,III,6:8; 1939, D 5,27:3; 1945, Ap 8,35:2; 1949, Ap 10,76:5; 1951, Je 23,15:4; 1960, Ja 21,31:4; 1966, S 29,47:1; 1967, Mr 16,47:1
Gordon, Samuel F, 1956, Mr 15,31:4
Gordon, Samuel G, 1952, My 18,92:4
Gordon, Samuel J, 1947, O 25,19:5
Gordon, Samuel Mrs, 1943, Ja 29,19:2; 1943, Ag 1,38:7
Gordon, Samuel S, 1964, S 27,85:6
Gordon, Samuel W, 1920, Jl 12,9:4
Gordon, Seth C Dr, 1921, Je 23,17:6
Gordon, Shelby, 1959, N 5,35:5
Gordon, Sherwood R Mrs, 1953, S 13,84:6
Gordon, Spencer, 1950, S 13,27:2
Gordon, T Roy, 1948, Ag 3,25:4
Gordon, Thomas, 1920, Ag 9,9:7; 1937, D 20,27:4
Gordon, Thomas F, 1956, Je 4,29:4
Gordon, Thomas S, 1959, Ja 23,25:2
Gordon, V, 1928, O 7,II,8:2
Gordon, Vera, 1948, My 10,21:4
Gordon, Victor D Mrs, 1941, S 6,15:2
Gordon, Virgil C, 1951, N 9,27:4
Gordon, Walter C Mrs, 1956, Ja 21,21:5
Gordon, Watson M, 1958, Ag 13,27:4
Gordon, Watson M Jr, 1949, Ja 28,22:3
Gordon, Wilfred P, 1947, D 15,25:4
Gordon, Will, 1946, Ja 8,23:2
Gordon, William, 1942, Ja 18,44:4; 1962, Je 10,86:7
Gordon, William A, 1944, D 8,21:2; 1959, Je 24,31:4; 1960, Ja 14,33:3; 1962, O 13,25:4
Gordon, William B, 1938, Ja 12,21:1
Gordon, William D, 1961, N 24,31:4
Gordon, William F, 1955, F 12,15:2
Gordon, William H Mrs, 1950, N 11,15:3
Gordon, William J (funl, Jl 21,11:3), 1915, Jl 17,7:6
Gordon, William J, 1944, Ap 3,21:2; 1956, Ap 3,29:6
Gordon, William J Mrs, 1945, Ja 3,17:2
Gordon, William Mrs, 1941, Je 22,32:5
Gordon, William S, 1944, F 18,17:4; 1952, Mr 15,13:5
Gordon, William S Jr, 1956, Ag 28,27:5
Gordon, William Sr, 1938, Mr 15,23:3
Gordon, William W, 1942, Ja 29,19:2
Gordon, William W Brig-Gen, 1912, S 12,11:5
Gordon-Cumming, Alex P, 1939, F 24,19:1
Gordon-Cumming, Florence Lady, 1922, O 11,19:5
Gordon-Lennox, Lord, 1949, My 6,25:4
Gordon-Smith, Allan, 1951, F 13,31:3
Gordon-Taylor, Gordon, 1960, S 6,35:3
Gordy, William S, 1950, D 6,33:3
Gore, Alfred L, 1962, F 5,31:3
Gore, Arthur R, 1937, Ag 6,17:3
Gore, Ben, 1953, O 5,27:1
Gore, C, 1932, Ja 18,15:3
Gore, C E Mrs, 1912, Ja 8,13:5
Gore, Carribelle P Mrs, 1939, Jl 18,19:3
Gore, Carrol J, 1956, N 20,37:5
Gore, Carrol W, 1950, My 14,108:1
Gore, Carroll W Mrs, 1948, F 23,25:5
Gore, Charles A Mrs, 1861, F 21,5:2
Gore, chas E Mrs, 1950, Ap 15,15:3
Gore, Edward L H, 1954, S 25,15:5
Gore, F Porter, 1960, My 18,41:4
Gore, F Porter Mrs, 1963, O 17,32:5
Gore, George Putnam, 1904, Ja 9,9:2
Gore, Grant P, 1959, O 29,33:1
Gore, Howard M, 1947, Je 21,17:1
Gore, James H, 1939, Je 12,17:3
Gore, John J, 1939, F 22,21:6
Gore, John K, 1943, Je 24,21:2
Gore, John P, 1961, O 19,35:1
Gore, M Elting, 1958, Mr 27,33:4
Gore, Mary B, 1949, Mr 15,27:2
Gore, Michael, 1953, Ag 17,15:2
Gore, Ollie H, 1937, S 8,23:3
Gore, Quentin P, 1967, Mr 29,45:3
Gore, Ralph, 1961, Mr 29,33:4; 1962, S 2,57:1
Gore, Thomas, 1940, Je 30,33:1
Gore, Thomas P (por), 1949, Mr 17,25:1
Gore, Thomas P Mrs, 1963, My 9,37:3
Gore-Kelly, Horace Mrs, 1949, Ap 17,76:4
Gore-Langton, W H P, 1873, D 13,1:7
Gorecki, Charles S, 1966, Ag 16,39:5

Gorecki, Henry J, 1964, Ap 8,43:1
Gorelik, Aaron N, 1960, Jl 18,27:6
Gorelik, Abraham M, 1958, F 8,19:5
Gorelik, Morris, 1951, S 14,25:2
Goren, Oscar, 1947, S 5,19:4
Gores, Paul, 1925, Ag 4,19:4
Goreth, Charles, 1943, S 17,21:2
Goretti, Assunta Mrs, 1954, O 9,17:3
Gorevic, Ferdinand, 1966, My 2,37:3
Gorey, George R, 1942, F 10,19:5
Gorey, Matthew J, 1948, Ja 15,23:4
Gorfinkle, Joseph L, 1950, D 25,19:3
Gorgas, Harry S, 1954, S 24,24:1
Gorgas, Kate F, 1942, Mr 29,45:2
Gorgas, William C (funl, Jl 8,11:4), 1920, Jl 6,15:2
Gorgeous George (G R Wagner),(trb, D 28,23:1), 1963, D 27,25:1
Gorges, Raymond C H, 1943, F 22,17:1
Gorgin, Walter Mrs, 1948, Ja 13,25:4
Gorgolis, John, 1947, F 2,57:8
Gorgoni, Rudolph, 1963, My 16,35:3
Gorham, Andrew L Mrs, 1954, Jl 8,23:5
Gorham, Anthony F, 1957, D 14,21:5
Gorham, Arthur N, 1957, Ja 24,29:5
Gorham, Augustus S, 1907, F 18,9:6
Gorham, Cort W, 1949, Ag 27,13:3
Gorham, Edson B, 1940, S 23,17:5
Gorham, Edwin S, 1960, F 23,31:4
Gorham, Frank A, 1945, Jl 18,27:4
Gorham, Frank H Dr, 1937, S 4,15:3
Gorham, Frederick S Mrs, 1955, My 25,33:2
Gorham, George D, 1957, D 22,40:2
Gorham, Henry Beecher, 1925, N 7,15:5
Gorham, Henry W, 1949, Ag 22,21:6
Gorham, Herbert, 1905, Ap 18,2:6
Gorham, James H Rev, 1937, Ja 9,17:3
Gorham, John, 1945, Ag 29,23:4
Gorham, John E Mrs, 1949, Mr 30,25:3
Gorham, L Whittington Dr, 1968, Jl 29,20:1
Gorham, Leslie W, 1960, F 18,33:3
Gorham, Nehemiah O, 1907, Mr 25,7:6
Gorham, Ralph W, 1940, D 14,17:5
Gorham, Raymond C Mrs, 1939, Ap 15,19:2
Gorham, Robert S, 1913, Je 19,11:5
Gorham, Willis E, 1958, S 15,21:6
Gorham Herbert N, 1959, My 11,27:4
Gori, Michael Rev, 1937, Ja 5,23:2
Gorilowich, John F, 1952, N 28,25:1
Gorin, Abraham, 1961, O 25,37:1
Gorin, Jerome P, 1938, N 29,23:4
Gorin, Joseph H, 1955, Jl 6,27:1
Gorin, Katherine D, 1966, Je 26,72:8
Goring, Howard A Mrs, 1938, F 9,19:5
Goring, Howard C, 1938, Mr 28,15:6
Goring, Mary C Mrs, 1940, O 25,21:4
Gorkiewecz, Walter Mrs, 1956, Je 27,63:2
Gorky, M, 1936, Je 19,21:1
Gorky, Maxim Mrs, 1965, Mr 28,92:3
Gorling, Lars, 1966, Ag 2,33:1
Gorlitzer, Benjamin, 1956, Mr 30,19:4
Gorman, Andrew W, 1943, Mr 10,19:5
Gorman, Arthur J, 1961, Ag 4,21:5
Gorman, Arthur Pue, 1919, S 4,13:3
Gorman, Arthur Pue Sen (funl, Je 8,9:1; est appr, D 16,5:2), 1906, Je 5,9:1
Gorman, Beatrice, 1918, O 25,13:5
Gorman, Bernard J Sr, 1953, My 14,29:2
Gorman, Charles H Jr, 1948, N 19,27:2
Gorman, Charles I, 1940, F 12,17:4
Gorman, Charles J, 1943, D 20,23:2
Gorman, Clarence R, 1942, S 15,23:5
Gorman, Daniel G, 1965, O 19,43:2
Gorman, Daniel J, 1961, O 28,21:3
Gorman, Douglas, 1945, Ja 30,19:2
Gorman, Douglas S Jr, 1959, Ag 6,27:3
Gorman, Edward, 1954, N 24,23:2
Gorman, Edward A, 1948, Jl 22,23:6
Gorman, Edward Capt, 1864, Mr 21,5:1
Gorman, Edward T, 1948, Ja 6,23:5
Gorman, Francis, 1954, Ag 13,15:6; 1955, My 28,15:6
Gorman, Francis R, 1962, F 11,87:1
Gorman, Frank J, 1949, Mr 18,25:3
Gorman, Frank L Sr, 1950, N 9,33:6
Gorman, Gabriel, 1964, Je 28,57:1
Gorman, George A, 1952, Jl 26,13:4
Gorman, George W, 1942, F 1,43:3
Gorman, Gertie Amelia Mrs, 1920, D 19,22:4
Gorman, Gibson E, 1956, Ja 8,86:4
Gorman, Herbert S, 1954, O 29,21:3
Gorman, Horace P, 1953, Ja 14,31:2
Gorman, J E, 1883, Je 5,2:6
Gorman, J Leonard Mrs, 1955, D 8,37:3
Gorman, J Mike Mrs, 1966, O 4,47:2
Gorman, James E (por), 1942, Mr 26,23:3
Gorman, James G, 1944, D 30,11:7
Gorman, James J, 1946, S 26,25:1; 1959, Je 28,69:2
Gorman, James J (Bro Alpheus James), 1961, Mr 10,27:3
Gorman, John, 1950, S 30,17:2
Gorman, John A, 1947, My 6,27:1
Gorman, John J, 1939, Ag 25,15:2; 1941, D 12,25:1
Gorman, John J (por), 1945, D 24,15:4
Gorman, John J, 1953, My 30,15:4
Gorman, John J Sr, 1957, Mr 25,25:2
Gorman, John L, 1961, My 24,41:2
Gorman, Joseph D, 1950, N 19,92:7
Gorman, Julia (Mother Mary Borchmans), 1912, Jl 2,11:3
Gorman, Katherine, 1943, Je 20,34:7
Gorman, Katherine C Mrs, 1938, My 23,17:2
Gorman, Lawrence C, 1952, D 28,49:1
Gorman, Lawrence J, 1953, Ap 26,86:2
Gorman, Leo G, 1947, Ap 24,25:4
Gorman, Leon P, 1951, D 2,90:3
Gorman, Martin J, 1945, My 27,26:2
Gorman, Mary, 1941, S 5,21:3
Gorman, Mary A Mrs, 1940, Mr 3,45:2
Gorman, Mary C Mrs, 1961, Ap 7,31:4
Gorman, Mary M Mrs, 1937, Jl 25,II,7:4
Gorman, Michael, 1924, Mr 10,15:4; 1958, O 12,86:3
Gorman, Michael Mrs, 1942, O 4,53:1
Gorman, Mike Mrs, 1958, Je 5,31:4
Gorman, Owen J Mrs, 1954, O 17,84:4
Gorman, Patrick H, 1946, Jl 22,21:2
Gorman, Patrick J, 1946, Jl 7,36:6
Gorman, Patrick J (Bro Anesius Maurice), 1958, Jl 22,27:3
Gorman, Peter, 1942, S 18,21:2
Gorman, Richard J, 1946, Je 19,21:2
Gorman, Robert, 1962, Jl 2,29:2
Gorman, T P (Tommy), 1961, My 16,37:2
Gorman, Thomas A, 1942, S 9,23:4; 1951, Mr 17,15:4
Gorman, Thomas B, 1949, My 3,25:4
Gorman, Thomas E, 1948, O 11,23:4
Gorman, Thomas F, 1943, Mr 31,19:4; 1952, Mr 4,27:5
Gorman, Thomas H, 1958, N 25,33:1
Gorman, Thomas J, 1943, S 29,21:3; 1945, O 13,15:5
Gorman, W A, 1876, My 22,5:2
Gorman, William B Mrs, 1943, O 10,48:6
Gorman, William H, 1915, Jl 8,13:5; 1954, Jl 21,27:2
Gorman, William J, 1955, Jl 9,15:1
Gorman, Wilredge H, 1950, Ag 20,76:1
Gormanston, Viscount (Jenico Wm Jos Preston), 1907, O 30,9:5
Gormely, Francis P (por), 1944, Jl 14,13:3
Gormier, August J, 1952, Ja 23,27:1
Gormley, James F, 1967, O 1,84:4
Gormley, James J, 1964, N 11,43:4
Gormley, James P, 1968, My 8,47:1
Gormley, James P Mrs, 1960, Ap 1,33:5
Gormley, John J, 1957, Jl 27,17:2
Gormley, John L, 1946, S 25,27:4; 1965, My 31,17:3
Gormley, John V, 1946, Mr 21,25:2
Gormley, Joseph E, 1957, Mr 1,23:4
Gormley, Michael J (por), 1945, O 5,23:1
Gormley, William, 1921, O 31,15:5
Gormley, William E, 1951, My 23,35:5
Gormley, William J, 1964, Ag 5,33:1
Gormly, Charles F, 1943, Je 28,21:3
Gormly, George, 1940, Ap 7,45:1
Gormsen, Harold F, 1958, S 7,86:4
Gormsen, Harold F Mrs, 1951, Ja 28,76:1
Gornes, Martin M Mrs, 1941, Jl 10,19:1
Gornston, Seymour F, 1955, D 13,39:4
Gorny, Valentine Mrs, 1951, N 3,17:4
Gorochow, Isidor, 1953, Ja 12,27:2
Gorodetsky, Nikolai, 1953, O 18,87:1
Gorodetzky, Jac, 1955, N 4,29:3
Gorodn, Phil, 1948, O 2,15:1
Gorodovikov, Oka O, 1960, F 28,82:8
Gorokhoff, Ivan T, 1949, Ja 25,23:2
Gorovitz, Louis, 1951, Ap 22,88:3
Gorozita, Juan Rev, 1937, D 19,II,9:1
Gorr, Thilo, 1951, Mr 2,25:1
Gorra, Aziz S, 1964, My 13,47:4
Gorrell, Adam D, 1948, Ag 8,57:2
Gorrell, Edgar S (por), 1945, Mr 6,21:1
Gorrell, Frank E, 1951, Ja 18,27:4
Gorrell, Henry I, 1958, Ja 7,47:4
Gorrell, Stuart, 1963, Ag 10,17:5
Gorrie, John T, 1942, Ja 27,21:1
Gorrie, Robert H, 1947, Ja 14,26:3
Gorrie, William, 1951, Ja 18,27:2
Gorring, Verna, 1959, N 7,23:5
Gorringe, H H, 1885, Jl 7,5:1
Gorringe, Thomas Mrs, 1945, My 20,32:2
Gorrissen, Hans, 1937, N 5,23:4
Gorrostieta, Liceniado Enrique, 1921, My 10,17:4
Gorry, Edward W, 1942, S 30,23:6
Gorry, George, 1939, Mr 20,17:6
Gorsch, Rudolph V Mrs, 1967, Ag 5,23:2
Gorse, James Calder, 1906, Ja 9,9:4
Gorska, Anna Mrs, 1937, Ja 30,36:6
Gorska, Charlotte, 1949, O 12,29:1
Gorski, Anton Rev, 1937, D 11,19:4
Gorski, Eugenia R Mrs, 1938, Jl 20,19:5
Gorski, Joseph A Sr, 1947, Ja 31,23:3
Gorski, Martin, 1949, D 5,23:3
Gorski, Waclaw O, 1937, Ja 3,II,8:6
Gorsky, Isaac, 1953, S 13,84:5
Gorsline, Charles, 1940, F 4,41:1
Gorsline, Ernest E, 1948, Jl 31,15:3
Gorsline, Frank D, 1957, O 5,17:3
Gorsline, Ralph H, 1937, D 28,22:1
Gorsline, Ralph V M, 1945, S 29,15:3
Gorsline, Tracy F, 1943, Ag 1,39:1
Gorsline, William H Sr, 1942, D 4,25:5
Gorson, Morris M, 1941, S 5,21:2
Gorson, Myer, 1951, My 30,21:2
Gorson, Samuel, 1953, Ag 4,21:3
Gorssman, Albert, 1963, My 31,23:6
Gorst, Harold E, 1950, Ag 15,30:3
Gorst, John Eldon Sir, 1916, Ap 5,13:8
Gorsuch, H Stanley, 1939, Jl 28,17:5
Gorsuch, Harry B, 1964, Ag 8,19:5
Gorsuch, John C, 1938, Je 16,23:6
Gorsuch, John W, 1949, My 27,21:1
Gort, Godfrey, 1948, O 26,31:3
Gort, Viscount, 1946, Ap 1,27:1
Gortatowsky, Jacob D (will, Mr 4,13:1), 1964, Ja 14,31:1
Gorten, Manfred L, 1952, S 3,30:3
Gorter, Evert, 1954, F 18,31:4
Gorthy, Willis C, 1960, D 5,31:2
Gortner, Ross A (por), 1942, O 1,23:1
Gorton, Arthur T, 1952, Ag 3,61:3
Gorton, Arthur T Mrs, 1953, F 18,31:3
Gorton, D D, 1947, Ag 6,23:3
Gorton, David Allyn Dr, 1916, F 23,13:5
Gorton, Eliot Dr, 1917, Mr 4,21:2
Gorton, Elmer E, 1961, O 26,35:4
Gorton, Elmer E Mrs, 1949, N 16,30:2
Gorton, Frank H, 1939, Mr 21,23:3
Gorton, Harrison M, 1949, S 18,92:2
Gorton, Henry H (por), 1940, F 10,15:4
Gorton, Joseph C, 1943, O 6,23:2
Gorton, Neville V, 1955, D 1,35:3
Gorton, Sheridan, 1948, Je 4,23:1
Gorton, Sheridan Mrs, 1957, Ag 29,27:5
Gorton, William S, 1966, Ja 18,34:1
Gorton, William T, 1948, Ap 2,23:1
Gorts, Eldon Sir, 1911, Jl 13,9:5
Gortschakoff, A M Prince, 1883, Mr 12,1:5
Gorven, John, 1951, My 19,15:2
Gos, Albert, 1942, Je 25,23:4
Gosa, Francis D, 1951, Jl 20,17:3
Goscelin, Patrick (Bro Adjutor), 1912, N 19,15:4
Goschen, Charles Hermann, 1915, Mr 23,9:4
Goschen, Edward Sir, 1924, My 21,19:1
Goschen, George Joachim Viscount, 1907, F 8,9:6
Goschen, Harry (por), 1945, Jl 10,11:5
Goschen, Viscount, 1952, Jl 25,17:3
Goschen, William, 1943, Je 16,21:5
Gosden, Leta S Mrs, 1942, Mr 26,23:6
Gosdorfer, Louis C, 1961, Ap 19,39:3
Gose, J Gordon, 1963, Je 19,37:4
Gosfield, Maurice, 1964, O 20,37:4
Gosford, Countess of, 1944, Mr 5,36:2
Gosford, Countess of (Mildred), 1965, S 11,27:5
Gosford, Dowager Countess of, 1967, Ja 27,45:3
Gosford, Earl of (Archibald Brabazon Sparrow Acheson), 1922, Ap 12,21:5
Gosford, Earl of (A C M B Acheson), 1954, Mr 89:1
Goshen, Anne M, 1966, D 13,47:4
Goshen, Elmer I, 1941, D 20,19:4
Goshorn, Clarence B, 1950, D 12,28:3
Goshorn, H Rook, 1950, My 27,17:5
Goshorn, Harry R, 1951, Ap 28,15:6
Goshorn, Robert C, 1953, Ap 16,29:2
Goshorn, William V, 1952, My 13,23:3
Goski, John, 1957, Ja 27,84:6
Goslee, Frederick M Mrs, 1954, O 22,27:2
Goslee, Walter S, 1954, D 15,31:3
Goslin, H Foster, 1944, F 16,17:4
Goslin, Omar P (por), 1942, D 19,19:4
Gosline, William A (por), 1947, F 22,13:5
Gosling, Albert E, 1940, Ja 13,15:5
Gosling, Edward P, 1939, O 29,41:2
Gosling, Ernest P, 1945, Ag 22,23:3
Gosling, Francis E (ed, Mr 2,18:4), 1942, F 23,
Gosling, Joseph W, 1938, Ap 5,21:3
Gosling, Katherine L Mrs, 1942, Ja 24,15:8
Gosling, Louise B Mrs, 1941, D 11,27:6
Gosling, Walter W, 1939, Mr 5,49:2
Gosman, Paul A, 1964, Je 4,37:2
Gosman, W Burnet, 1946, Je 7,19:5
Gosnell, Arthur J, 1949, Ag 31,23:5
Gosnell, Frank L, 1956, N 24,19:4
Gosnell, R Whitney, 1960, S 19,31:2
Gosnell, Stanley E, 1951, Je 5,31:3
Gosner, Howard N, 1952, S 7,83:3
Gosney, Ezra S, 1942, S 16,23:1
Goss, Adeline Mrs, 1943, Ag 22,31:3
Goss, Albert S, 1950, O 26,31:1
Goss, Bailey, 1962, My 2,76:1
Goss, Caroline S Mrs, 1941, Ap 11,22:3
Goss, Charles, 1950, My 8,23:4
Goss, Charles A, 1938, Ag 14,33:5
Goss, Chauncey P, 1918, Jl 20,9:8; 1964, O 29,
Goss, Chauncey P Jr, 1948, D 20,25:6
Goss, Edward O, 1938, Jl 5,17:5
Goss, Elbridge Henry, 1908, O 10,9:5
Goss, Eliot P, 1940, Je 23,30:7
Goss, Elizabeth D, 1953, D 11,34:1
Goss, Elizabeth M Mrs, 1950, F 13,21:4
Goss, Frank, 1911, O 1,13:5
Goss, Frank A, 1939, Ag 27,35:1

Goss, Fred L Mrs, 1907, O 9,11:5
Goss, Frederick Llewellyn, 1914, N 11,13:4
Goss, George A, 1942, O 14,25:4
Goss, Harry H, 1954, Ja 8,21:4
Goss, Harry L, 1942, S 2,19:2
Goss, J Sr, 1880, My 12,4:7
Goss, James H, 1949, O 22,17:2
Goss, John, 1937, N 6,17:6; 1940, Ag 24,13:4
Goss, John H, 1944, O 17,23:6
Goss, Leon H, 1946, Mr 31,46:3
Goss, Leonard W, 1958, Ap 3,31:2
Goss, Otis Mrs, 1967, Jl 16,64:4
Goss, Ralston R, 1947, D 30,23:5
Goss, Samuel, 1938, Mr 14,16:4
Goss, Thomas, 1925, D 31,15:4
Goss, William M, 1962, Jl 5,25:4
Goss, Wright D Jr, 1959, F 10,33:2
Gossard, Harry C, 1954, D 8,35:3
Gosse, E Sir, 1928, My 17,25:3
Gosse, Philip, 1959, O 6,39:3
Gosselin, George A, 1956, N 27,37:3
Gosselin, Jean, 1937, Ag 10,19:3
Gosselin, Leopold C, 1938, Ag 25,19:4
Gosselin, Martin le Merchant Hadsley Sir, 1905, F 27,7:5
Gosselin, Robert T A Mrs, 1945, Mr 9,19:1
Gosselin, Wilfred, 1950, O 8,104:2
Gosselin, William O, 1937, Jl 30,19:4
Gosser, Thomas W Mrs, 1953, My 19,29:4
Gossett, Benjamin B, 1951, N 14,31:6
Gossett, J Edgar Mrs, 1954, D 5,88:4
Gossett, John E, 1939, Je 18,37:2
Gossett, Louis Mrs, 1960, Mr 11,26:3
Gossin, Frank A, 1871, Mr 22,5:3
Gossip, Arthur J, 1954, My 28,23:2
Gossip, George, 1957, Mr 6,31:2
Gossler, Philip G (por), 1945, My 19,19:1
Gossling, John E, 1937, Ap 1,23:1
Gossling, John H, 1947, Mr 4,25:3
Gossman, H Peter, 1968, Ja 2,37:1
Gossman, Jennie, 1951, My 24,35:3
Gossner, John, 1946, Ag 28,27:3
Gossweiler, Ernest D, 1951, F 2,23:2
Gossweiler, Walter, 1949, N 17,29:3
Gosswein, Louis F, 1968, O 8,47:1
Gostin, Myer Mrs, 1956, Ag 28,27:4
Gosts, Frank, 1948, Ag 19,21:4
Gosztony, Adam, 1955, O 6,29:2
Got, F J E, 1901, Mr 21,1:6
Gotch, John A, 1942, Ja 18,44:3
Gotesmani, Carlos Alastaire Raoul (Marquis de Mijana), 1912, Ja 26,11:5
Gotfredson, Lawrence, 1943, F 14,49:2
Gotham, Walter E, 1961, Ja 31,29:2
Gotham, William E H, 1960, F 24,37:1
Gothe, David E, 1966, D 22,33:4
Gothelf, Louis M, 1968, N 16,37:1
Gotland, Samuel, 1937, S 27,5:5
Gotlieb, M H, 1933, Ag 8,17:4
Goto, Count, 1929, Ap 13,7:3
Goto, Yonosuke, 1960, Ap 15,2:7
Gotsch, John, 1942, Je 10,21:3
Gotsch, Joseph, 1916, Ap 22,11:6
Gotschi, Paul, 1950, O 20,28:3
Gotsfeld, Mendel Mrs (Bessie), 1962, Jl 31,30:1
Gotshal, Sylvan, 1968, Ag 12,35:1
Gott, Benjamin Frank Col, 1904, Jl 13,7:6
Gott, Beryl K Mrs, 1941, Jl 2,21:4
Gott, Charles, 1938, F 19,15:2
Gott, Charles C D, 1954, Ag 6,17:2
Gott, Eccles J, 1939, Je 16,23:4
Gott, Edgar N, 1947, Jl 18,17:2
Gott, Edwin, 1940, Jl 26,17:4
Gott, G P, 1903, Ap 28,9:5
Gott, Herbert S (por), 1941, Ja 31,19:3
Gott, John, 1914, Mr 13,9:4
Gott, O Wilson, 1940, Je 16,38:8
Gotta, Ridgeway Mrs, 1940, Jl 10,19:2
Gottermeyer, Anthony, 1950, Ap 11,31:3
Gottesfeld, Chone, 1964, Ja 28,31:4
Gottesfeld, Joseph, 1944, D 24,25:2
Gottesman, Abraham Mrs, 1944, O 22,46:4
Gottesman, Callman Mrs, 1963, S 16,35:4
Gottesman, Charles A, 1960, F 27,19:4
Gottesman, D Samuel, 1956, Ap 22,86:3
Gottesman, D Samuel Mrs, 1942, Jl 29,17:4
Gottesman, Joseph M, 1952, Ap 12,11:4
Gottesman, Julius Dr, 1968, Ag 20,41:3
Gottesman, Leo, 1956, Jl 24,25:1
Gottesman, Mendel (por), 1942, D 17,29:3
Gottesman, Michael, 1958, My 13,29:4
Gottesman, Morris L, 1956, Mr 1,33:3
Gottesman, Sidney M, 1946, S 21,15:2
Gottfried, Benjamin, 1951, Ja 22,17:4
Gottfried, Carl M Mrs, 1956, N 21,27:6
Gottfried, Emil H, 1953, Ap 25,15:3
Gottfried, Felix, 1951, My 2,31:2
Gottfried, George M, 1938, Jl 7,19:5
Gottfried, Joseph Mrs, 1948, Ag 3,25:3
Gottfried, Mary M, 1961, Je 25,76:4
Gottgetreu, Henry, 1946, Ja 22,27:1
Gotthardt, George, 1949, My 4,29:4
Gottheil, Paul, 1915, S 23,13:4
Gottheil, R J H, 1936, My 23,15:1
Gottheil, Richard J H Mrs, 1947, Je 13,23:5
Gotthelf, David, 1943, N 25,25:4
Gotthelf, Maurice, 1954, Ap 24,17:4
Gotthelf, Philip Mrs, 1946, D 28,15:5
Gotthell, William S Dr, 1920, Ja 8,17:3
Gotthold, Arthur F, 1951, N 26,25:1
Gotthold, Isaac, 1882, Ap 12,5:6
Gotthold, Philip H, 1908, Mr 19,7:5
Gotti, Girolamo Maria Cardinal, 1916, Mr 20,11:3
Gottleib, Herman, 1925, O 29,25:5
Gottleib, Leon A (por), 1947, Ja 14,25:3
Gottler, Archie, 1959, Je 25,29:3
Gottlick, Charles E, 1946, O 4,23:3
Gottlick, Francis J Mrs, 1949, Ja 7,21:2
Gottlieb, Aaron, 1956, O 12,29:2
Gottlieb, Albert S, 1942, Ja 15,19:5
Gottlieb, Alfred, 1940, Ag 12,15:4
Gottlieb, Arnold, 1968, N 20,47:3
Gottlieb, Arthur, 1965, Ja 14,35:2
Gottlieb, Arthur M, 1968, F 26,37:3
Gottlieb, Benjamin, 1959, Je 27,23:4
Gottlieb, Benjamin W, 1952, Ap 10,29:2
Gottlieb, Bernard N, 1952, Ja 31,27:4
Gottlieb, Bernhard, 1950, Mr 17,23:4
Gottlieb, Charles, 1960, Je 6,29:2; 1968, Ag 14,43:4
Gottlieb, Charles Mrs, 1962, N 10,25:3
Gottlieb, David R, 1960, S 3,17:6
Gottlieb, Edward, 1961, O 25,37:3
Gottlieb, Emil Mrs, 1958, Ja 14,33:2
Gottlieb, Frank O, 1959, D 21,27:4
Gottlieb, Fred, 1946, My 29,23:5
Gottlieb, George, 1963, Jl 11,29:4
Gottlieb, Harry, 1948, S 1,24:3
Gottlieb, Harry N, 1948, Ap 14,28:2
Gottlieb, Herman, 1947, N 18,29:2
Gottlieb, Herman S, 1967, Ag 25,35:4
Gottlieb, Isaac, 1946, D 12,29:1
Gottlieb, Isidor, 1950, Jl 11,32:2
Gottlieb, Jacob, 1963, Je 6,35:1
Gottlieb, Jacques L, 1946, O 19,21:5
Gottlieb, Joseph, 1960, My 12,35:4; 1960, My 30,17:4
Gottlieb, Joseph W, 1966, D 1,47:5
Gottlieb, Julius, 1953, Mr 29,95:3
Gottlieb, Leo, 1943, N 3,25:3
Gottlieb, Lewis, 1937, F 15,17:2
Gottlieb, Louis J, 1949, N 12,15:2
Gottlieb, Mack L, 1964, D 30,25:2
Gottlieb, Mark J, 1938, D 22,21:4
Gottlieb, Maurice, 1952, N 5,27:2
Gottlieb, Maurice L, 1964, O 26,31:5
Gottlieb, Moritz M, 1952, N 24,23:3
Gottlieb, Phil, 1949, Ja 19,27:4
Gottlieb, R F, 1903, Ag 17,7:5
Gottlieb, Rose, 1951, Mr 9,25:4
Gottlieb, Theodore D, 1939, F 1,21:2
Gottlieb, William, 1946, Ap 19,29:5
Gottlieb, William L Mrs, 1947, Ja 3,21:3
Gottlober, Alexander, 1943, Ja 10,50:3
Gottlober, Sigmund, 1967, Ag 15,36:3
Gotto, Anthony J, 1951, F 3,15:3
Gottreich, Joseph, 1948, O 26,31:3
Gottron, Adolf, 1960, Jl 1,25:3
Gottry, C W, 1956, Jl 30,21:1
Gottsberger, B Britton, 1955, Mr 2,27:3
Gottsch, Frank, 1966, Ap 5,39:3
Gottschalk, Edward B, 1944, F 12,13:5
Gottschalk, Ferdinand (por), 1944, N 17,19:1
Gottschalk, Henry, 1946, S 8,44:3
Gottschalk, Joseph, 1942, N 9,23:5
Gottschalk, Louis, 1915, N 18,9:5
Gottschalk, Louis Moreau, 1870, Ja 21,5:2
Gottschalk, Max W, 1942, Ap 23,24:5
Gottschalk, Oliver A, 1957, My 27,31:3
Gottschalk, Victor, 1952, Ja 20,86:6
Gottschall, Andrew W, 1962, My 23,45:5
Gottschall, Morton Dr, 1968, Jl 31,41:1
Gottschall, Morton Mrs (Frances), 1968, S 14,31:3
Gottschall, Simon, 1943, My 15,15:4
Gottscho, Adolph, 1954, Ag 24,21:3
Gottsegen, Julius J, 1941, Mr 18,23:4
Gottsegen, Leo, 1946, D 7,21:1
Gottsmann, Joseph, 1949, Ja 11,27:4
Gottwald, Klement Mrs, 1953, O 29,31:2
Gottwald, Klement Pres, 1953, Mr 15,1:6
Gottwals, David H, 1950, Ja 5,26:7
Gotwald, Luther A, 1966, My 7,31:1
Gotwals, Clayton K, 1942, Jl 14,19:5
Gotwals, J Elmer, 1958, F 8,19:5
Gouaux, Leon L, 1943, F 14,48:6
Goubeaud, George J, 1943, F 13,11:4
Goubeaud, George J Mrs, 1942, F 25,19:3
Goubeaud, Henry J Sr, 1938, F 3,23:4
Goubert, Harold V, 1957, S 2,13:6
Goucher, John F Dr, 1922, Jl 20,17:4
Goucher, Mary C Mrs, 1902, D 20,9:6
Goud, James T, 1943, Mr 18,19:2
Goude, Leslie G, 1944, Ja 15,13:2
Goudey, E Gordon, 1946, Ap 12,27:3
Goudey, T Eugene, 1938, Ja 23,II,8:7
Goudey, William B, 1956, Ag 13,19:6
Goudge, Henry L, 1939, Ap 25,23:2
Goudie, Peter A, 1966, Jl 20,41:4
Goudiss, C Houston (por), 1945, O 30,19:2
Goudkoff, Paul P, 1955, My 26,31:2
Goudman, Paul L, 1937, Mr 28,II,8:7
Goudy, F W Mrs, 1935, O 22,21:3
Goudy, Frederic W, 1947, My 12,21:1
Goudy, Grocer C, 1951, S 21,23:2
Goudy, William R, 1960, N 19,21:5
Gougar, Helen M, 1907, Je 7,9:7
Gouge, George F, 1948, O 22,25:5
Gouge, Henry A, 1904, O 10,9:3
Gougelman, Pierre E, 1963, Je 3,29:3
Gougeon, Permillie, 1947, Ag 24,58:1
Gougerot, Henri, 1955, Ja 16,93:3
Gouget, William T, 1952, Ja 2,25:4
Gough, Edward C Mrs, 1950, Ap 21,23:1
Gough, Edward J, 1956, D 29,15:3
Gough, Florence, 1958, Ag 3,80:4
Gough, Frank A, 1938, Ag 16,19:3
Gough, Harry Munsell, 1912, Mr 23,13:5
Gough, Herbert J, 1965, Je 4,35:5
Gough, Hubert, 1963, Mr 20,16:1
Gough, Hugh Viscount, 1869, Mr 4,4:7; 1919, O 16, 17:3
Gough, Hugh W Viscount, 1951, D 6,33:4
Gough, J B, 1886, F 19,5:3
Gough, John, 1953, Ag 27,25:2
Gough, John F, 1956, Mr 14,33:5
Gough, John J, 1949, Mr 11,25:3
Gough, Lewis K, 1967, N 14,43:5
Gough, Raymond, 1967, F 10,36:1
Gough, Raymond Mrs, 1960, S 21,32:4
Gough, Robert W, 1953, Ja 9,21:1
Gough, William D, 1955, Ja 1,13:1
Gough-Calthorpe, Augustus (Baron Calthorpe), 1910, Jl 23,7:6
Gough-Calthorpe, Somerset Sir (por), 1937, Jl 28,19:3
Gouin, E A, 1960, My 18,41:2
Gouin, Eugene, 1909, Je 1,9:6
Goulandris, John P, 1950, Jl 11,31:5
Goulandris, Peter Mrs (Chryssi), 1965, Ag 28,21:2
Goulart, Vincentina Mrs, 1963, Jl 10,35:1
Gould, Alan Mrs (funl), 1966, S 9,45:2
Gould, Albert T, 1947, Mr 2,60:5
Gould, Alex C, 1957, F 24,85:1
Gould, Alfred Pearce, 1922, Ap 20,17:4
Gould, Alice B, 1953, Jl 28,19:1
Gould, Anthony, 1921, Mr 1,13:4
Gould, Arch B, 1948, Ag 29,56:4
Gould, Arthur C, 1903, D 16,9:5
Gould, Arthur R, 1946, Jl 25,21:3
Gould, Ashley M Justice, 1921, My 21,13:4
Gould, Augustus A Dr, 1866, S 17,8:5
Gould, Aylmer B, 1956, Ag 14,25:5
Gould, B A Prof, 1896, N 28,1:2
Gould, Barbara A Mrs, 1950, O 16,27:3
Gould, Benjamin A, 1937, Je 25,21:3
Gould, Benjamin Mrs, 1961, Ap 25,35:3
Gould, Billy, 1950, F 2,27:2
Gould, C Carroll, 1954, Mr 5,19:2
Gould, C W, 1931, Mr 20,25:3
Gould, Carl F, 1939, Ja 5,23:3
Gould, Charles A, 1951, Ag 28,23:4
Gould, Charles E, 1955, Ap 3,87:1
Gould, Charles E Mrs, 1949, Ag 17,23:3
Gould, Charles M Mrs, 1946, O 30,27:5
Gould, Charles N, 1949, Ag 15,17:3
Gould, Charles O, 1952, Ap 26,23:4
Gould, Charles W, 1945, Ja 30,19:2
Gould, Chester M, 1952, F 29,23:1
Gould, Clifford A, 1941, Je 12,23:4
Gould, Clifford A Mrs, 1938, S 10,17:6
Gould, David, 1968, Mr 20,47:3
Gould, David E, 1959, Jl 23,27:4
Gould, David L, 1939, Ja 26,21:4
Gould, David M, 1961, Ap 3,30:1
Gould, Dayton R, 1943, Mr 11,21:4
Gould, Douglas A Mrs, 1966, Mr 28,33:3
Gould, Douglas Attwood, 1968, F 20,44:3
Gould, E, 1933, Jl 13,19:1
Gould, E S, 1885, F 20,8:2
Gould, Edgar D, 1945, Ja 30,19:2
Gould, Edward, 1937, Ag 16,19:3
Gould, Edward F, 1953, Mr 8,90:6
Gould, Edward J, 1950, S 6,29:4
Gould, Edward W Mrs, 1954, F 4,25:3
Gould, Edwin M L, 1952, D 28,48:6
Gould, Edwin Mrs, 1951, O 15,25:6
Gould, Elbert W, 1954, Jl 11,72:2
Gould, Elgin R L Dr (funl, Ag 21,7:6), 1915, Ag 19, 9:1
Gould, Elgin R L Mrs, 1955, Ja 23,85:1
Gould, Elizabeth G, 1882, F 16,8:1
Gould, Ellen T, 1937, D 27,15:3
Gould, Emily Mrs, 1875, S 20,8:2
Gould, Emmett, 1954, S 19,89:2
Gould, Ernest G, 1950, D 30,13:4
Gould, Eugene J, 1964, Je 20,25:2
Gould, Everett W Dr, 1937, Ag 19,19:4
Gould, Francis Carruthers Sir, 1925, Ja 2,15:4
Gould, Frank D, 1950, S 5,27:2
Gould, Frank E, 1955, Ap 6,29:1
Gould, Frank Horace, 1918, Ja 27,17:3
Gould, Frank J (funl plans, Ap 3,35:2; funl, Ap 5,-29:3), 1956, Ap 1,88:1

Gould, Frank M (will, Mr 3,26:6), 1945, Ja 14,40:5
Gould, Frank P, 1939, S 26,23:5
Gould, Frank R, 1953, Je 23,29:4
Gould, Franklin F, 1966, F 15,39:3
Gould, Fred J, 1940, Ag 16,15:4
Gould, Frederic A, 1938, Ja 26,23:5
Gould, Frederick L Mrs, 1907, D 17,9:5
Gould, Frederick S Mrs, 1948, Mr 6,13:6
Gould, Frederick T, 1953, F 14,17:5
Gould, George C, 1948, Mr 27,13:4
Gould, George E, 1943, Je 25,17:3
Gould, George H, 1940, S 16,19:4
Gould, George H Mrs, 1945, Ap 5,23:2
Gould, George J, 1923, My 19,13:6; 1963, Je 8,25:4
Gould, George J Mrs (funl), 1921, N 15,19:4
Gould, George Milbry, 1922, Ag 9,11:6
Gould, George R, 1945, D 14,27:1; 1949, Jl 1,19:2
Gould, Gerald B, 1953, Mr 22,86:1
Gould, Gilbert R, 1949, Mr 18,25:2
Gould, Glenn C, 1944, Mr 2,17:1
Gould, Gordias H P, 1919, Je 10,13:4
Gould, Gordon, 1946, Ag 26,23:5
Gould, H Howard, 1939, S 19,25:2
Gould, H Mrs, 1930, D 25,21:1
Gould, H Zinn, 1923, F 8,19:5
Gould, Hannah F, 1865, S 8,4:2
Gould, Harold W, 1948, Mr 22,23:5; 1951, Jl 19,23:4; 1953, Mr 4,27:4
Gould, Harris B Mrs, 1966, D 18,84:4
Gould, Harris P, 1946, O 18,23:4
Gould, Harry (por), 1945, Jl 19,23:3
Gould, Harry E, 1945, O 27,15:5
Gould, Harry H, 1965, O 13,47:4
Gould, Harry Mrs, 1945, Ja 12,15:4
Gould, Harry P, 1938, N 5,19:1
Gould, Henry R, 1943, Ja 5,19:6
Gould, Howard, 1938, F 4,21:3
Gould, Howard (est acctg), 1960, O 20,37:8
Gould, Howard Mrs, 1954, D 25,11:3
Gould, Howard S (petition to probate will filed, D 3,31:3), 1959, S 15,39:1
Gould, Ira, 1872, Jl 12,5:4
Gould, J, 1935, Ja 28,15:1
Gould, J Howard, 1963, My 11,25:4
Gould, J Kingsley, 1962, O 22,29:4
Gould, Jack, 1949, N 30,1:8
Gould, Jack G, 1952, F 7,27:6
Gould, James G, 1944, Jl 7,15:6
Gould, James M, 1943, F 17,21:2
Gould, Jay, 1892, D 3,1:5; 1967, Jl 2,35:2
Gould, Jay Mrs, 1889, Ja 14,5:2
Gould, Jerome F, 1956, D 18,31:2
Gould, John, 1881, F 5,2:6
Gould, John A, 1944, Ag 5,11:5
Gould, John G, 1938, D 3,19:6
Gould, John J, 1964, Ag 8,19:5
Gould, John R, 1944, F 20,36:1; 1948, N 11,27:1
Gould, John W, 1955, Jl 12,25:3
Gould, John W DuB Mrs, 1967, My 11,54:4
Gould, Joseph F (funl plans, Ag 22,27:1; funl, Ag 24,15:4), 1957, Ag 20,27:3
Gould, Joseph R, 1953, O 17,15:3
Gould, Juan, 1965, Je 28,29:4
Gould, Julius Mrs, 1949, F 10,27:2
Gould, Kingdon, 1945, N 8,19:2
Gould, Kingdon Mrs, 1961, F 14,37:4
Gould, Lillian R Mrs, 1940, F 21,19:5
Gould, Loe, 1950, Ap 22,19:3
Gould, Lyttleton B P, 1954, My 22,15:6
Gould, Marshall B, 1955, Je 2,29:3
Gould, Marshall H, 1947, Ja 16,25:4
Gould, Morse, 1965, F 27,25:4
Gould, Morton L, 1949, S 29,29:2
Gould, Myron N, 1958, Je 10,33:2
Gould, Nathan J, 1941, O 28,23:3
Gould, Nathaniel, 1919, Jl 26,9:3
Gould, Nathaniel J, 1962, Mr 13,32:1
Gould, Norman J, 1964, Ag 21,29:3
Gould, Orissa W Dr, 1904, My 5,9:7
Gould, Ormond V, 1962, My 20,86:8
Gould, Peter, 1960, Ja 18,27:2
Gould, Polly, 1957, Ag 20,53:1
Gould, Ralph E, 1954, S 16,29:3
Gould, Raymond N, 1960, Jl 31,69:1
Gould, Richard, 1955, Ap 6,29:5
Gould, Richard N, 1954, D 13,27:2
Gould, Robert H R, 1961, O 5,37:2
Gould, Robert P, 1948, N 22,22:2
Gould, Robert S, 1959, Ap 9,31:4
Gould, Roscoe Hall, 1952, Ag 22,21:4
Gould, Sidney, 1938, N 19,17:1
Gould, Stephen, 1968, Mr 20,47:3
Gould, Sylvester C, 1909, Jl 21,7:6
Gould, Symon, 1963, N 25,19:1
Gould, Symon Mrs, 1962, Mr 30,33:5
Gould, T R, 1881, D 1,4:7
Gould, Theodore J, 1953, My 25,25:3
Gould, Theodore P, 1962, O 4,39:4
Gould, W R, 1884, Ja 1,2:6
Gould, Walter, 1955, S 6,25:2
Gould, William, 1882, Mr 22,5:5
Gould, William H, 1950, Ap 2,92:3
Gould, William J (funl, My 10,6:1), 1925, My 9,15:6
Gould, William J Mrs (trb lr, N 11,28:6), 1958, N 5, 39:3
Gould, William R, 1944, O 8,42:7
Gould, William S, 1955, Ja 4,21:3
Gould, William S Jr, 1964, N 16,31:5
Gould, William Saltonstall, 1921, Ja 20,9:4
Goulded, Peter, 1965, Ap 21,45:2
Goulden, Allen S, 1941, D 25,25:1
Goulden, Howard N, 1957, N 3,88:2
Goulden, Joseph A Col (funl, My 6,13:6), 1915, My 4,15:6
Goulden, William, 1940, O 30,23:2
Goulder, Herbert G (cor, Ag 24,25:1), 1949, Ag 13, 11:1
Goulder, Mortimer K (cor, Ja 6,67:2), 1955, Ja 5,23:2
Goulding, Edmund, 1959, D 25,24:2
Goulding, F R, 1881, Ag 29,4:7
Goulding, Frank C, 1939, N 26,43:2
Goulding, Joseph, 1905, N 26,9:6
Goulding, Phil H, 1957, Mr 30,19:5
Goulding, Walter B, 1950, Ag 31,25:1
Gouldman, William C, 1953, My 16,19:1
Gouldy, Daniel, 1950, S 21,31:1
Gouled, Felix, 1952, Je 4,27:5
Goulet, Arthur, 1945, S 25,25:4
Goulett, Paul R, 1962, N 1,31:2
Gouley, John W S Dr, 1920, Ap 28,11:5
Goulston, Henry P, 1941, S 26,23:6
Goulston, Leopold M, 1954, Ag 6,17:3
Goundorova, Elizabeta P Princess, 1939, Je 16,23:5
Gounod, Bertha, 1937, O 4,23:8
Gounod, C F, 1893, O 18,1:5
Gounot, Charles A, 1953, Je 21,84:6
Goupil, J, 1883, My 1,4:7
Gour, Hari S, 1949, D 26,29:5
Gourary, Jules, 1964, O 24,29:5
Gouraud, Henri J E, 1946, S 17,7:5
Gouraud, Jackson (funl, F 24,9:2), 1910, F 22,9:4
Gouraud, Powers, 1954, S 18,15:6
Gourd, Henry E, 1925, Mr 20,19:5
Gourd, Henry E Mrs, 1952, S 20,15:3
Gourdin, Edward O, 1966, Jl 23,25:6
Gourevitch, Boris, 1964, Ap 6,31:2
Gourevitch, Gregoire, 1959, Ja 22,31:1
Gourevitch, Lazare, 1967, D 14,47:1
Gourgaud, Eva Baroness, 1959, Jl 15,29:1
Gourielli Tchkonia, Artchil Prince, 1955, N 23,23:3
Gourko, Count, 1901, Ja 30,9:5
Gourlay, Lawrence, 1923, Ap 3,23:5
Gourlay, William, 1955, Ap 23,19:6
Gourlay, William Maj, 1911, D 30,11:5
Gourley, Harry B, 1953, D 18,29:1
Gourley, Harry B Mrs, 1942, My 27,23:3
Gourley, John H, 1939, N 8,23:5
Gourley, Joseph H, 1946, O 28,27:2
Gourley, Louis H, 1950, Mr 30,29:1
Gourley, Norman R, 1954, D 8,35:4
Gourlie, John Hamilton, 1904, F 21,7:6
Gouron, Francois, 1951, O 25,29:4
Gousha, Joseph R, 1962, F 17,19:3
Gousha, Joseph R Mrs (D Powell), 1965, N 16,47:1
Gouss, Harold A, 1962, O 23,37:5
Goutches, Charles R, 1941, Mr 21,21:2
Goutell, Carl R Mrs, 1965, Ap 1,35:2
Gouveia, Teodosio C Cardinal, 1962, F 7,37:2
Gouverneur, Maud C, 1947, Mr 31,23:1
Gouverneur, Samuel L Mrs, 1914, Mr 14,11:5
Gouwens, Teunis E, 1960, My 18,41:2
Govaars, Gerrit, 1954, O 24,89:1
Govan, Charles H, 1921, Ap 25,11:4
Govan, Joseph F, 1947, Ag 7,21:3
Gove, Anna M, 1948, F 5,23:6
Gove, Aroline P Mrs, 1939, My 22,17:4
Gove, Arthur E, 1939, O 28,17:4
Gove, David W, 1945, Je 5,19:5
Gove, Edgar A Mrs, 1943, Mr 16,19:1
Gove, Everard, 1949, Je 10,27:5
Gove, George A, 1945, My 24,19:2
Gove, Jay, 1949, Mr 31,25:3
Gove, Lydia P, 1948, F 25,23:2
Gover, George W, 1943, Ap 10,17:4
Govern, Hugh, 1938, S 7,36:3
Govern, William H, 1943, O 30,15:3
Govern, William J, 1945, O 18,23:2
Governale, John, 1950, Mr 28,32:3
Govers, Francis X, 1943, F 12,19:2
Govey, James J, 1941, Ag 7,17:2
Govier, Sheldon, 1948, Jl 25,48:3
Govil, Hari G, 1956, Jl 10,31:2
Govin, R, 1926, F 16,25:3
Govin, Rafael R Mrs, 1960, Ag 17,31:4
Govorov, Leonid A (funl, Mr 22,5:6), 1955, Mr 20, 89:1
Gow, Alex J, 1948, D 7,31:1
Gow, Arthur C, 1951, S 2,49:1
Gow, Charles R, 1949, Jl 30,15:6
Gow, George C (por), 1938, Ja 13,21:4
Gow, George C Mrs, 1947, Je 2,25:4
Gow, James, 1952, F 12,27:4
Gow, Joseph, 1953, Ja 25,85:2
Gow, Leonard Mrs, 1937, Je 26,17:6
Gow, Pauline, 1944, Ap 4,21:1
Gow, Peter, 1958, My 15,29:4
Gow, Robert M, 1937, Ap 26,19:4; 1964, S 20,88:8
Gow, Teddy, 1940, My 11,19:4
Gow, William G, 1964, Ja 9,31:2
Gow-Smith, Francis (por), 1939, N 11,15:1
Gowan, A T Mrs, 1903, Ja 17,4:3
Gowan, Hyde, 1938, Ap 2,15:5
Gowan, William H (funl plans, My 29,16:4), 1957, My 26,12:3
Gowanloch, J Nelson, 1952, My 29,27:2
Gowans, William, 1870, N 30,2:6
Gowdey, Chester A Sr, 1951, S 16,85:1
Gowdy, Frank K, 1951, D 29,11:4
Gowdy, Hank (Hy M), 1966, Ag 2,33:1
Gowdy, John K, 1918, Je 26,13:5
Gowdy, Robert C, 1950, Mr 28,31:3
Gowdy, Robert S, 1955, Ag 3,23:5
Gowen, F B, 1889, D 15,1:7
Gowen, Francis V Mrs, 1963, N 3,88:2
Gowen, George B, 1955, Ag 5,19:5
Gowen, J E, 1885, F 17,2:5
Gowen, James B, 1958, Ag 11,21:5
Gowen, John F, 1949, N 12,15:5
Gowen, John K Jr, 1961, Je 26,31:5
Gowen, Robert F, 1966, Je 3,39:2
Gowens, Henry Jr, 1953, Ja 4,78:3
Gower, Alastair Lord, 1921, Ap 29,15:4
Gower, Fielding, 1937, D 6,27:6
Gower, Frank C, 1947, O 7,27:4
Gower, George L, 1951, Jl 19,23:2
Gower, George W, 1938, Ap 13,13:5
Gower, H Leveson, 1954, F 2,27:2
Gower, Joseph O, 1948, N 28,92:4
Gower, Merritt Melville, 1911, F 4,13:4
Gower, Pauline, 1947, Mr 4,25:3
Gower, Ronald Sutherland Lord, 1916, Mr 10,9:6
Gower, William B, 1937, Ag 31,23:3
Gower, William B Mrs, 1955, N 9,33:4
Gower-Rees, A P, 1956, S 3,13:5
Gowers, Ernest, 1966, Ap 18,29:1
Gowers, William Richard Sir, 1915, My 5,13:6
Gowin, Robert, 1947, My 5,25:7
Gowing, Mary K Mrs, 1947, N 17,21:3
Gowlan, John F, 1950, O 5,33:5
Gowran, Harry C, 1941, N 23,53:1
Gowrie, Earl of (A Hore-Ruthven), 1955, My 4,
Gowrie, Frederick W, 1952, Jl 28,15:3
Gowrie, John L, 1955, Ap 3,86:5
Gowrie, William, 1953, S 9,29:2
Goyanes, Everado, 1955, D 30,19:3
Goyau, Georges, 1939, O 26,23:1
Goyeneche, Arturo, 1940, N 27,23:6
Goyer, Dennis A, 1951, Je 7,33:4
Goyer, Nina, 1944, N 9,14:7
Goyette, John C, 1952, S 27,17:2
Goza, Thelma Mrs, 1952, My 11,92:3
Gozzett, Amy G R Mrs, 1941, Mr 3,15:5
Graad, Douwe jan de, 1948, Ag 10,21:3
Graasman, Samuel, 1907, Ap 24,9:5
Grab, Jacob, 1937, S 5,II,7:1
Grab, Oscar F, 1958, Je 10,33:2
Grabar, Igor, 1960, My 18,41:5
Grabau, Amadeus W, 1946, Mr 27,27:1
Grabau, John, 1947, My 2,22:2
Grabau, John C, 1942, Ag 17,15:5
Grabau, John F, 1948, Je 22,25:1
Grabau, John N, 1940, D 3,25:3
Grabau, John W Mrs, 1915, Mr 23,9:5
Grabau, Mary A (lr), 1949, My 24,26:6
Grabbe, Alexander, 1947, Mr 17,23:5
Grabbe, Marie Countess, 1951, Je 9,19:6
Grabel, Melvin, 1966, Ag 25,37:5
Grabel, Vernon O, 1955, N 20,88:6
Graber, C Lee, 1954, Ja 24,84:3
Graber, Fred A, 1950, Mr 23,29:3
Graber, Fred A Mrs, 1950, Ja 12,27:2
Graber, Irving, 1962, Jl 6,25:3
Grabfelder, Morris, 1920, Ag 6,9:6
Grabfelder, Samuel, 1920, Ap 19,15:5
Grabfelder, Samuel Mrs, 1948, Ja 27,25:3
Grabhorn, Edwin, 1968, D 18,47:2
Grabhorn, Merwyn B, 1963, Jl 28,65:1
Grabill, Ethelbert W, 1951, D 1,13:5
Grabill, John D, 1937, N 21,II,9:2
Grabiner, Harry M (por), 1948, O 25,23:3
Grabish, Josef, 1947, Ag 16,13:6
Grable, Conn, 1954, Ja 26,27:1
Grable, Errett M, 1959, D 30,22:1
Grable, Lillian Mrs, 1965, Ja 1,19:4
Grabner, George, 1944, Jl 9,36:2
Grabo, Carl H, 1955, F 21,21:5
Graboski, Stanislaw, 1947, N 23,72:6
Grabosky, Samuel, 1953, Ag 2,73:2
Grabovsky, Boris, 1966, Ja 30,84:3
Grabowski, Reginald, 1955, Ap 3,86:7
Grabowsky, Ernest F, 1951, O 31,29:1
Grabski, Stanislaw, 1949, My 8,77:1
Graburn, A Lynne Jr, 1965, O 28,43:2
Grace, Allen E, 1947, Jl 10,21:1
Grace, Anna Mrs, 1950, F 14,26:4
Grace, Arthur B, 1943, F 11,19:4
Grace, C B, 1938, Je 7,8:5
Grace, Charity, 1965, D 1,47:2

Grace, Charles M (Daddy),(funl plans, Ja 23,19:5), 1960, Ja 13,47:3
Grace, Cornelius J, 1943, Jl 10,13:6
Grace, Edward F, 1949, Ag 27,13:4
Grace, Edward P, 1952, N 22,23:2
Grace, Eugene G (funl plans, Jl 27,29:4; funl, Jl 28,27:4), 1960, Jl 26,29:1
Grace, Eugene G Mrs, 1956, N 10,19:4
Grace, F J, 1877, Ap 3,8:5
Grace, Frank J, 1948, Ag 1,56:5
Grace, Harvey, 1944, F 17,19:3
Grace, Henry E Adm, 1937, Mr 20,19:4
Grace, Irving P Capt, 1912, Ag 8,9:6
Grace, J D, 1876, N 16,5:2
Grace, James N, 1945, Je 10,32:3
Grace, John, 1955, Mr 9,27:5
Grace, John G, 1950, Ap 27,29:5
Grace, John P, 1940, Je 26,23:2
Grace, John W, 1904, S 20,9:6
Grace, John W Mrs, 1922, Ja 18,17:3
Grace, Joseph J, 1951, Ja 26,23:4
Grace, Joseph P, 1950, Jl 15,13:3
Grace, Joseph P Mrs, 1938, Ja 1,19:2
Grace, Joseph P Sr, 1950, Jl 19,31:5
Grace, Louise N, 1954, F 11,29:1
Grace, Lucille M (Mrs F Dent), 1957, D 23,23:5
Grace, Luke A Rev, 1914, Mr 28,13:5
Grace, Martin J, 1952, Ap 15,27:4
Grace, Michael P, 1920, S 21,11:6
Grace, Morgan H, 1943, Jl 3,13:4
Grace, Morgan H Mrs, 1959, Ap 28,35:1
Grace, Nancy, 1956, Ja 12,27:2
Grace, Nicholas, 1939, N 10,23:2
Grace, Patrick J, 1954, Jl 13,23:4
Grace, Richard P, 1955, Je 24,19:1
Grace, Richard P Mrs, 1948, Ag 4,21:3
Grace, Robert E, 1957, N 13,35:2
Grace, Roderick V, 1954, S 28,29:5
Grace, Thomas, 1952, F 4,17:4
Grace, Thomas Bp, 1921, D 28,15:6
Grace, Thomas G, 1958, Ja 9,33:1
Grace, Thomas L, 1938, F 15,25:4
Grace, Thomas T, 1951, F 16,25:4
Grace, William Gilbert Dr, 1915, O 24,17:4
Grace, William J, 1948, F 9,17:3; 1955, S 22,31:5; 1959, Ap 18,23:4
Grace, William R, 1904, Mr 22,9:3; 1943, Ap 1,23:1
Grace, William R Mrs, 1922, O 25,19:4
Grace, Wrestler, 1883, Ap 6,5:1
Grace Anita, Sister (Boozan), 1949, Ag 2,19:5
Grace Anita, Sister (Molloy), 1957, O 18,23:2
Grace Antonia, Sister (M M Glynn), 1965, Je 11,31:1
Grace C Dammann, Mother, 1945, F 14,19:3
Grace Edna, Sister, 1942, My 30,15:2
Grace Miriam, Sister (Winters), 1965, Mr 4,31:4
Grace Winifred, Sister, 1944, N 2,19:1
Gracey, Burton B, 1960, My 6,31:2
Gracey, Charles S, 1943, Mr 3,23:2
Gracey, Edward J, 1951, S 24,27:4
Gracey, Frances Ida, 1912, F 24,11:5
Gracey, George F H, 1958, Mr 19,31:3
Gracey, John T Rev Dr, 1912, Ja 6,13:3
Gracey, William A, 1944, O 17,23:5
Grachin, Peter, 1945, N 4,43:1
Gracht, Willem A J M van der, 1943, S 4,13:7
Gracida, Gabriel de Sr Mrs, 1946, Ag 28,20:4
Gracie, Adeline, 1948, N 5,25:1
Gracie, Charles R, 1963, Jl 1,29:4
Gracie, Constance S Mrs, 1937, D 13,27:2
Gracie, Cordenia E Mrs, 1937, My 5,25:3
Gracie, James King, 1903, N 24,6:3
Gracy, Leonard R Maj, 1937, Ja 13,23:2
Grad, Frank, 1968, Ja 21,76:8
Grad, Frank Mrs, 1959, Ap 6,27:4
Grad, Herman, 1955, N 8,31:3
Grad, Herman Mrs, 1952, Mr 5,29:2
Grad, Nathan, 1960, Ap 20,39:2
Gradi, Nipoleone L, 1949, Jl 22,19:3
Gradle, Harry S, 1950, My 27,17:4
Gradstein, Alfred, 1954, O 18,25:4
Gradwohl, Meyer H, 1938, Mr 23,23:3
Gradwohl, Rutherford B H, 1959, My 10,87:2
Grady, Clyde, 1939, D 6,25:4
Grady, David V, 1951, My 14,25:5
Grady, Donald H, 1966, D 29,28:7
Grady, Edward M, 1945, Mr 20,19:2
Grady, Edward Mrs, 1950, My 4,27:3
Grady, Elizabeth A Mrs, 1955, Ap 8,21:5
Grady, Ellen, 1952, Je 22,68:1
Grady, Everett J, 1950, Ja 18,32:2
Grady, Francis J, 1959, Ap 14,35:5
Grady, Fred, 1951, Je 23,15:5
Grady, George, 1956, Ja 23,25:5
Grady, H W, 1889, D 24,5:1
Grady, Henry F, 1957, S 15,84:1
Grady, Henry Jr Mrs, 1943, D 13,23:5
Grady, Henry W Jr, 1942, Jl 12,36:2
Grady, Hugh A, 1952, My 28,29:5
Grady, J D, 1880, O 4,5:3
Grady, James A Mrs, 1944, Mr 10,15:5
Grady, James H, 1941, F 18,23:4
Grady, James L, 1942, My 6,19:1
Grady, James T, 1954, N 19,23:2
Grady, James T Mrs, 1944, My 6,15:1
Grady, James W, 1940, Ja 2,19:3
Grady, John, 1956, D 11,36:3
Grady, John J, 1950, Mr 22,27:5
Grady, John P, 1949, My 21,13:5
Grady, John W, 1950, Je 4,92:5
Grady, Leander A, 1946, Je 22,19:1
Grady, Malachy T, 1952, S 16,29:4
Grady, Michael J, 1939, Je 5,17:4
Grady, Michael W, 1943, D 5,65:1
Grady, Ronan C, 1945, Jl 5,13:5
Grady, Steven J, 1943, Mr 18,19:5
Grady, Thomas Francis Gen, 1912, F 6,11:5
Grady, Thomas J, 1956, D 1,21:1
Grady, W O'G Gen Sir, 1878, Mr 23,1:6
Grady, William E (por), 1940, N 8,21:3
Grady, William F, 1942, S 30,23:6; 1946, Mr 27,27:5
Grady, William T, 1953, N 3,31:1
Grady, William T Mrs, 1955, D 29,23:4
Grae, Harris, 1951, D 20,31:2
Graeber, Nicholas J, 1947, Ap 5,19:3
Graebner, Herman C, 1940, D 18,25:2
Graebner, Theodore, 1950, N 15,31:2
Graef, Charles, 1944, F 28,17:2
Graef, Charles F W, 1948, N 30,27:3
Graef, Conrad R, 1966, Je 17,6:6
Graef, Emil A, 1903, D 13,7:6
Graef, George M, 1946, Ja 31,21:5
Graef, Leonard, 1948, Ja 29,23:4
Graef, P Paul, 1944, Ja 29,13:5
Graef, Robert E, 1968, Ap 21,80:3
Graefenecker, Michael A, 1949, Ja 8,15:2
Graeff, C (Masonic Funl), 1878, Ag 3,2:7
Graeff, Frederick J, 1961, F 22,25:4
Graeff, George B Mrs, 1955, Je 25,15:6
Graeff, James M, 1908, F 23,7:6
Graeff, Louis Mrs, 1950, Ja 6,22:2
Graeff, Phil, 1948, N 13,15:5
Graeme, Betty (Mrs H B Peirce), 1963, S 11,43:3
Graeme, Robert Sr, 1944, My 16,21:3
Graeme, William H Sr, 1946, N 5,25:6
Graener, Paul, 1944, N 16,23:5
Graeser, Edward, 1957, My 23,33:3
Graessle, Frederick W, 1961, Mr 7,35:3
Graessner, Karl, 1967, N 22,47:4
Graetle, Emma T, 1942, Ja 19,17:2
Graettinger, Martin A, 1950, O 31,27:2
Graetz, Paul (por), 1937, F 18,21:1
Graetz, Paul, 1966, F 8,39:3
Graeve, Oscar, 1939, N 21,23:5
Graeves, Carolyn, 1958, D 6,23:1
Graf, Alois W, 1957, S 19,29:4
Graf, August, 1946, My 3,21:4
Graf, Carl C, 1947, Ja 30,25:2
Graf, Charles Dr, 1922, N 13,15:4
Graf, Charles E, 1941, N 21,17:3
Graf, Don, 1962, N 9,26:2
Graf, Edwin, 1945, Mr 16,15:3
Graf, Ernest H, 1950, D 21,29:4
Graf, Felix, 1960, F 18,33:4
Graf, Frank, 1953, Ja 11,90:2
Graf, Helen H Mrs, 1937, Jl 9,21:5
Graf, John B, 1967, Je 17,31:4
Graf, John F, 1960, Ag 12,19:4
Graf, Max, 1958, Je 25,29:3
Graf, Milton, 1949, Jl 15,19:6
Graf, Oskar M, 1967, Je 29,43:3
Graf, Oskar M Mrs, 1959, N 13,29:1
Graf, Peter, 1949, O 5,60:6; 1951, O 21,92:4
Graf, Richard A, 1959, Ja 11,88:2
Graf, Robert J (por), 1949, Ja 4,19:3
Graf, Sigmund, 1948, F 10,23:3
Graf, Sonja (Mrs V Stevenson), 1965, Mr 7,82:1
Graf, Will J, 1949, Je 22,31:4
Graf, William I, 1954, F 4,25:4
Graf, William J, 1955, Mr 29,30:4
Graf, William Mrs, 1944, F 9,19:3
Graff, Adolph, 1952, D 14,90:4
Graff, Albert G, 1947, F 23,53:4
Graff, Alvin H Col, 1937, O 30,19:3
Graff, Charles E, 1946, Mr 15,22:2
Graff, Charles Hamilton, 1912, D 13,15:4
Graff, Clarence, 1955, Ag 26,19:2
Graff, Edward C, 1958, F 7,21:4
Graff, Edwin D, 1947, Mr 17,23:2
Graff, Elsie R, 1959, O 16,31:4
Graff, Frank M Mrs, 1952, Je 27,23:5
Graff, Fritz W, 1957, Ap 22,25:4
Graff, George, 1943, Jl 4,21:2
Graff, George E Mrs, 1952, S 4,27:6
Graff, George W, 1922, Ag 22,17:5
Graff, Henry G, 1953, Ag 2,73:1
Graff, Horace M, 1949, Ja 25,23:5
Graff, Howard E, 1948, F 7,15:3
Graff, Howard W, 1961, D 30,19:5
Graff, Jacob L, 1939, Ag 5,15:6
Graff, James Wotherspoon (funl, D 1,15:2), 1919, N 30,22:4
Graff, Leslie Mrs, 1967, O 21,31:2
Graff, Lewis E, 1952, O 11,19:5
Graff, Louis G, 1955, Ap 19,31:2
Graff, Robert U, 1916, Ja 18,11:2
Graff, Theron C, 1937, F 17,21:2
Graff, Walter A, 1937, Ap 22,23:4
Graff, Wesley M, 1937, Je 6,II,8:7; 1964, O 11,88:8
Graff, William R, 1957, My 29,27:1
Graff, Yetta, 1925, Jl 14,21:5
Graffe, Frances L Mrs, 1940, D 29,24:6
Graffenried, Leo de Baron, 1937, Ja 15,21:4
Graffenried-Villars, Emmanuel de, 1964, Je 16,39:3
Graffin, Edward M, 1941, My 29,19:2
Graffin, George Mrs, 1957, N 22,16:7
Grafflin, Charles F, 1925, Ap 5,5:1
Grafflin, Douglas G, 1959, Ag 24,21:2
Grafflin, Samuel W (por), 1941, Mr 21,21:1
Grafftey-Smith, Anthony, 1960, O 15,23:4
Graffunder, James E, 1961, D 25,23:2
Grafner, Emanuel, 1954, Je 3,27:2
Grafner, Emanuel Mrs, 1949, My 4,30:2
Grafner, William, 1949, Jl 24,52:5
Graft, Walton J, 1958, S 7,87:1
Graftio, Genrich O, 1949, My 6,25:3
Grafton, Charles Chapman, 1912, Ag 31,7:4
Grafton, Duke of (Augustus Chas Lennox), 1918, D 6,15:4
Grafton, Dutchess of, 1943, S 12,52:8
Grafton, E C, 1876, Je 25,2:2
Grafton, E R Mrs, 1901, Ap 12,9:6
Grafton, H Kirby (por), 1939, Jl 20,19:5
Grafton, Joseph J, 1947, Ap 23,25:3
Graftstrom, Sven, 1955, Ja 4,7:6
Grafulla, C S, 1880, D 4,3:7
Gragen, William H, 1949, Mr 3,25:2
Gragg, Charles I, 1956, O 31,33:2
Gragnano, Joseph A, 1963, My 4,25:5
Grah, Max, 1951, N 11,90:6
Graham, A B, 1948, Ap 6,23:5
Graham, A H, 1954, Ag 19,23:2
Graham, Agnes, 1947, Ja 16,25:1
Graham, Albert, 1956, Ap 15,89:1
Graham, Albert B, 1960, Ja 15,31:1
Graham, Albert D, 1957, My 17,25:2
Graham, Albert E Mrs, 1948, D 6,25:1
Graham, Albert H, 1954, Ap 19,23:2
Graham, Alex, 1948, Mr 1,23:1
Graham, Alex G Jr, 1954, O 28,35:1
Graham, Alex W, 1949, Ja 31,19:5
Graham, Alvin L, 1961, Ag 12,17:1
Graham, Andrew A, 1950, Ap 2,93:2
Graham, Andrew A Mrs, 1954, Mr 12,21:1
Graham, Andrew T, 1939, Ap 2,III,6:7
Graham, Anna A Mrs, 1937, Jl 7,24:2
Graham, Archibald, 1944, F 22,23:2
Graham, Archibald H, 1943, Je 22,19:4
Graham, Arthur B, 1951, Ag 17,9:7
Graham, Arthur B Mrs, 1962, N 23,29:3
Graham, Athol, 1960, Ag 2,36:2
Graham, Austin A, 1961, Jl 25,27:4
Graham, Ben G, 1942, Mr 21,17:4
Graham, Bernard Mrs, 1953, N 18,32:4
Graham, Bernard W, 1959, S 26,23:3
Graham, Bessie, 1966, S 4,64:6
Graham, Betty, 1951, F 15,31:3
Graham, Boyd B, 1941, Ag 14,17:5
Graham, Bridget T, 1946, My 2,21:4
Graham, C Stewart, 1942, Ja 10,15:5
Graham, Carlisle D Capt, 1909, My 4,9:4
Graham, Carroll B, 1948, Ag 22,63:5
Graham, Charles D, 1938, Mr 1,21:3
Graham, Charles E, 1944, D 29,15:1
Graham, Charles H, 1937, My 22,15:2
Graham, Charles H (por), 1948, Ag 30,17:3
Graham, Charles R, 1956, Jl 22,61:2
Graham, Charles V, 1967, Mr 21,43:2
Graham, Charles W, 1939, Ja 31,21:2
Graham, Chester M, 1952, Ap 18,25:2
Graham, Christopher, 1952, Je 21,15:5
Graham, Clarence R, 1943, Jl 4,21:1
Graham, Conyers B, 1939, N 3,21:2
Graham, Corden T, 1940, N 28,23:5
Graham, Cyrus A, 1941, F 24,15:5
Graham, D Gordon, 1966, S 8,47:4
Graham, Dale J, 1938, O 26,23:3
Graham, David, 1942, Ap 26,39:2
Graham, David B, 1941, N 25,25:1
Graham, David N, 1957, F 7,27:5
Graham, David P, 1948, D 19,76:5
Graham, David W, 1946, S 27,23:5; 1961, Ag 18,21:5
Graham, Diane M Mrs (D Harris), 1960, S 22,54:5
Graham, Dolliver W, 1951, Mr 28,29:1
Graham, Donald D, 1957, Ja 10,29:1
Graham, Donald M, 1947, S 16,24:3
Graham, Dorothy (Mrs J B Bennett), 1959, Je 26, 25:5
Graham, Douglas, 1958, Mr 16,86:6
Graham, Douglas Beresford Malise Ronald (Duke of Montrose), 1925, D 11,23:4
Graham, E R, 1936, N 23,21:1
Graham, Early P P, 1946, F 24,44:3
Graham, Edward H, 1966, Mr 17,47:5
Graham, Edward J, 1915, Ag 23,9:6
Graham, Edward K, 1921, F 20,22:1
Graham, Edwin E, 1953, Je 12,27:3
Graham, Edwin H, 1947, Ag 28,23:6
Graham, Elizabeth, 1859, S 15,1:6
Graham, Elizabeth N Mrs (E Arden),(funl, O 22,31:1; will, O 28,31:4), 1966, O 19,1:2

Graham, Elmer A, 1943, Mr 30,26:5
Graham, Ephraim F, 1962, D 27,7:1
Graham, Eric Clive Lt, 1917, Ja 14,19:1
Graham, Eugene E, 1951, Jl 10,27:2
Graham, Evarts A, 1957, Mr 5,31:1
Graham, F D J, 1949, Ag 22,21:2
Graham, F Ronald, 1963, Ap 8,47:5
Graham, Felix B, 1962, Ap 10,39:4
Graham, Floyd H, 1945, D 13,29:4
Graham, Frances W Mrs, 1940, Ag 20,19:3
Graham, Francis W, 1953, My 20,29:1
Graham, Frank, 1948, O 4,23:5; 1965, Mr 10,41:1
Graham, Frank C Mrs, 1958, S 23,33:3
Graham, Frank D, 1949, S 25,1:2
Graham, Frank H, 1951, Jl 13,21:6
Graham, Frank P Mrs, 1967, Ap 28,41:4
Graham, Frank X, 1940, N 20,21:1
Graham, Fred M, 1959, F 8,86:1
Graham, Frederick B, 1945, Ja 6,11:2
Graham, Frederick W W, 1942, Ja 18,42:5
Graham, G, 1881, Mr 3,5:3
Graham, G S, 1931, Jl 5,14:1
Graham, George (por), 1937, Ap 16,24:1
Graham, George, 1939, N 17,21:4
Graham, George A, 1924, O 7,23:4
Graham, George A Mrs, 1967, O 3,47:1
Graham, George C, 1941, O 8,23:4
Graham, George D, 1949, D 9,31:3
Graham, George M, 1944, N 17,19:2
Graham, George P, 1943, Ja 4,15:3
Graham, George S, 1942, My 4,19:2
Graham, George W, 1939, S 29,23:2; 1965, Ja 9,25:4
Graham, Gladwyn, 1959, N 19,39:3
Graham, Gordon, 1957, N 4,29:4
Graham, Grant R, 1950, Ja 13,23:2
Graham, Guy H, 1950, Jl 27,25:5
Graham, Gwethalyn (G G Erichsen-Brown), 1965, N 26,34:4
Graham, H, 1936, O 31,19:6
Graham, H Montrose, 1944, F 28,17:3
Graham, H Tucker, 1951, Ja 9,29:2
Graham, Harlan L Jr, 1967, Ja 17,39:1
Graham, Harold, 1951, Je 21,27:4; 1965, My 6,39:4
Graham, Harold J, 1963, Ap 18,35:4
Graham, Harold M, 1956, Jl 21,15:4
Graham, Harry, 1952, O 19,87:7
Graham, Harry H, 1937, S 26,II,8:5
Graham, Harry W, 1951, O 6,19:3
Graham, Helen, 1945, Ag 30,21:4
Graham, Henry, 1940, Ja 2,20:1
Graham, Henry F, 1958, Je 23,23:6
Graham, Henry S, 1943, Ap 5,19:4
Graham, Herbert N, 1950, Ja 18,31:1
Graham, Herbert W, 1967, D 20,45:3
Graham, Horace F, 1941, N 25,25:1
Graham, Horace R (will, N 17,26:4), 1954, N 10,33:3
Graham, Howard F, 1960, Ag 13,15:6
Graham, Howard G, 1957, Ap 24,33:3
Graham, Hugh, 1953, S 6,52:6
Graham, Hugh F, 1938, Mr 15,23:4
Graham, Hugh R, 1943, Mr 24,23:2
Graham, Hugh T, 1963, My 12,86:3
Graham, Ida G Mrs, 1957, Ag 30,19:5
Graham, Inez Mrs, 1963, N 1,33:3
Graham, J, 1883, D 20,4:7
Graham, J D Col, 1866, Ja 7,3:3
Graham, J Frank, 1952, Je 6,23:4
Graham, J George R, 1955, N 16,35:3
Graham, J H Commodore, 1878, Mr 17,1:6
Graham, J Howard, 1951, O 6,19:6
Graham, J L (see also Jl 25), 1876, Jl 27,8:4
Graham, J L, 1882, S 1,5:2
Graham, James, 1917, D 12,15:5; 1945, Ap 13,17:5
Graham, James (Lord Montrose), 1954, Ja 21,31:4
Graham, James, 1961, Je 16,33:3
Graham, James A, 1940, Mr 28,23:5; 1946, Jl 10,23:3; 1948, Ag 18,25:2; 1953, Jl 1,29:2
Graham, James F, 1960, Jl 20,29:4
Graham, James Frank, 1910, F 1,9:5
Graham, James G, 1937, O 31,II,11:3
Graham, James H, 1945, S 12,25:4; 1960, Je 26,72:5
Graham, James J, 1948, Mr 11,27:2; 1956, Ap 7,19:5
Graham, James Larmour Dr, 1968, N 2,37:3
Graham, James M, 1945, O 24,21:4; 1962, Ap 6,35:2
Graham, James P, 1942, My 21,19:2
Graham, James R Rev Dr, 1914, Ap 10,13:6
Graham, James Robert George Sir, 1861, N 6,4:5
Graham, James S, 1939, Mr 29,23:5; 1953, Mr 3,27:1
Graham, James S Mrs, 1961, Mr 1,33:4
Graham, James V, 1944, Ap 9,33:1
Graham, James V Mrs, 1957, Ja 2,27:1
Graham, Jay R, 1950, F 19,76:2
Graham, Jean, 1943, Ap 2,21:5
Graham, Jennie W Mrs, 1947, D 22,22:2
Graham, Jesse J, 1957, Mr 31,88:5
Graham, Jessie L, 1952, S 23,33:4
Graham, John, 1894, Ap 10,8:3; 1938, Jl 7,19:6; 1947, Mr 12,25:3; 1955, Je 23,29:2; 1964, S 24,41:3
Graham, John A, 1944, Ap 1,13:5; 1950, N 20,25:5; 1965, Ag 9,25:2
Graham, John C, 1949, N 26,15:6; 1950, Ag 27,88:6; 1956, Ja 20,23:3; 1963, Ag 21,33:1
Graham, John Capt, 1916, D 24,15:1
Graham, John D, 1942, Je 10,21:5
Graham, John F, 1944, My 8,19:2
Graham, John H, 1940, Mr 19,25:4; 1943, My 11,21:5
Graham, John J, 1917, Ag 27,9:5; 1938, Jl 5,17:6; 1941, N 18,25:5; 1950, N 7,27:2
Graham, John L, 1951, Mr 8,29:2
Graham, John M, 1945, Ja 13,11:5
Graham, John R, 1966, Ja 20,30:5
Graham, John S, 1948, Ag 24,23:2
Graham, John W Jr, 1952, F 28,27:4
Graham, Joseph, 1938, Ja 25,21:2
Graham, Joseph A, 1910, Ja 24,9:4
Graham, Joseph M, 1948, Jl 3,15:5
Graham, Joseph Marshall, 1909, F 4,9:4
Graham, Kelley, 1962, My 6,88:6
Graham, Kenneth L, 1961, N 8,35:4
Graham, Letitia V Mrs, 1938, D 18,44:6
Graham, Lillian, 1961, O 2,31:1
Graham, Louis E, 1965, N 12,47:4
Graham, Loyal Y Rev Dr, 1917, S 8,9:4
Graham, Loyal Y 3d, 1961, O 3,36:7
Graham, Lucien Mrs, 1945, Mr 15,23:4
Graham, Ludovia Mrs, 1952, Je 18,27:4
Graham, Ludwig T, 1967, S 18,47:1
Graham, M Col, 1885, Ja 21,5:5
Graham, Malcolm K, 1941, Jl 13,28:7
Graham, Malcolm M, 1956, Ag 11,13:2
Graham, Malcolm Mrs, 1953, My 15,23:3
Graham, Mansfield Mrs, 1947, Ag 6,23:6
Graham, Margaret, 1937, D 5,II,9:2
Graham, Margaret A, 1964, S 26,23:5
Graham, Margaret Mrs, 1944, O 2,19:6
Graham, Marion G Mrs, 1940, S 4,23:3
Graham, Martha Mrs, 1959, Je 26,25:4
Graham, Matthew J, 1947, Ap 13,60:2
Graham, Matthew W, 1944, Ap 25,23:2
Graham, Michael E, 1909, F 16,9:6
Graham, Michael J, 1952, Ap 15,27:5
Graham, Milton D, 1954, Ja 18,23:3
Graham, Milton E, 1949, Jl 21,25:4
Graham, Minnie S, 1962, Ap 3,39:3
Graham, Miriam Lady, 1946, O 22,25:5
Graham, Monroe, 1907, S 2,7:6
Graham, Montrose S, 1939, Ja 15,39:2
Graham, Morland, 1949, Ap 10,76:6
Graham, Nell D, 1948, My 26,25:4
Graham, Norval B, 1944, F 12,13:4
Graham, Otis L, 1947, S 27,15:5
Graham, Otis Mrs, 1952, Je 17,27:4
Graham, Patricia, 1943, O 7,23:3
Graham, Patrick J Capt, 1920, Jl 25,20:5
Graham, Patrick J Mrs, 1962, Ap 22,80:6
Graham, Ralph T, 1954, Ap 2,27:3
Graham, Ray A Mrs, 1941, F 14,18:3
Graham, Robert, 1910, Mr 10,9:4; 1950, F 20,25:2
Graham, Robert C, 1967, O 5,39:3
Graham, Robert D Capt, 1905, Je 28,2:1
Graham, Robert H, 1953, D 27,60:6
Graham, Robert J, 1956, Mr 6,31:4
Graham, Robert L Jr, 1968, Jl 17,43:3
Graham, Robert R, 1943, N 10,23:6; 1957, Je 16,84:6
Graham, Robert S, 1947, D 17,29:4
Graham, Robert Stuart Sir, 1917, My 11,11:2
Graham, Robert T, 1942, Mr 27,23:5
Graham, Robert W, 1950, Ja 3,25:2; 1951, Ja 27,13:4
Graham, Roger, 1938, O 27,23:6
Graham, Ronald, 1949, Ja 27,23:4; 1950, Jl 5,31:6
Graham, Roscoe R, 1948, Ja 19,23:2
Graham, Roy C, 1955, Ag 21,93:2
Graham, Roy W M Mrs, 1968, N 2,37:5
Graham, Sam, 1951, D 21,27:2
Graham, Samuel A, 1958, Jl 23,27:4
Graham, Samuel H, 1937, N 23,23:3; 1952, Jl 29,21:5
Graham, Samuel Jr, 1938, My 31,19:4
Graham, Samuel Lyndsay, 1923, Mr 24,13:5
Graham, Sigsbee, 1945, Je 20,23:3
Graham, T J Dr, 1869, S 19,4:7
Graham, Theodore K Dr, 1968, N 13,47:2
Graham, Thomas A, 1941, D 7,79:1; 1948, D 21,25:1; 1955, My 14,19:6
Graham, Thomas J, 1942, Mr 3,23:4; 1942, My 13, 19:5; 1951, Mr 21,33:4
Graham, Thomas L, 1967, Jl 31,27:2
Graham, Thomas M, 1943, Ap 23,17:2; 1946, Mr 29, 23:1
Graham, Thomas P, 1938, Mr 10,21:2
Graham, Thomas W Mrs, 1958, Ja 17,25:2
Graham, Thompson B, 1946, Jl 25,21:2
Graham, Van Wyck, 1876, Ja 23,6:5
Graham, Virginia (Mrs B G Van Breems), 1964, Jl 26,56:2
Graham, W A, 1952, Mr 30,93:2
Graham, W Frank, 1962, Ag 29,29:4
Graham, W R, 1958, Ja 11,17:2
Graham, W R Maj, 1903, N 13,7:6
Graham, W W, 1913, Ag 31,11:5
Graham, Walter, 1914, Ag 19,9:5
Graham, Walter J, 1946, N 7,31:4
Graham, Walter Mrs, 1937, Ap 20,25:4
Graham, Walter O, 1960, N 19,21:6
Graham, Whidden, 1944, O 28,15:7
Graham, Wilfred Mrs, 1938, My 20,19:2
Graham, Willard J, 1966, N 7,47:5
Graham, Willard Sr, 1958, F 11,31:1
Graham, William, 1946, N 6,23:3; 1947, Ap 16,25:6; 1953, My 26,29:4; 1955, F 24,27:1
Graham, William A, 1875, Ag 12,4:6; 1925, Ag 5,17:6; 1939, N 7,25:4; 1954, O 11,27:4
Graham, William B, 1952, F 20,29:5
Graham, William C, 1955, Ag 1,19:4
Graham, William D Mrs, 1964, Ja 22,37:4
Graham, William E Dr, 1937, D 27,16:3
Graham, William E Mrs, 1946, D 30,19:3
Graham, William G, 1962, Mr 19,29:3
Graham, William H, 1938, Mr 29,21:4; 1941, F 23, 41:1; 1942, D 5,15:5; 1951, Mr 5,3:6; 1962, Ja 15,27
Graham, William H Mrs, 1963, Ag 4,81:1
Graham, William Irving, 1871, Ag 28,5:7
Graham, William J (por), 1937, N 11,25:1
Graham, William J, 1940, Ja 7,48:3; 1944, D 17,37:2; 1954, N 11,31:4
Graham, William J Mrs, 1952, S 19,23:2
Graham, William Jr Mrs, 1954, Je 11,23:4
Graham, William M, 1940, D 15,61:3
Graham, William M Brig-Gen, 1916, Ja 18,11:4
Graham, William P, 1950, Ja 2,23:5; 1962, Ja 12,35:1
Graham, William W Mrs, 1940, D 29,25:1
Graham, Winifred, 1950, F 6,25:6
Graham-Little, Ernest G, 1950, O 10,31:5
Graham-Rogers, Charles T, 1955, S 26,23:2
Grahame, George, 1940, Jl 10,19:5
Grahame, John F Mrs (A Maissel), 1962, F 6,35:3
Grahame, Leopold, 1945, Ag 5,37:1
Grahame, Malcolm R Mrs, 1948, S 2,23:2
Grahame, Thomas E, 1907, Mr 18,7:2
Grahame, Thomas E Mrs, 1907, Mr 18,7:2
Grahame, Thomas J (por), 1938, S 25,39:1
Grahame-White, Claude, 1959, Ag 20,25:4
Grahame-White, Mrs, 1925, D 5,19:5
Grahill, John M, 1950, F 26,76:4
Grahl, Ernest E, 1949, O 21,25:2
Grahlfs, Herman, 1948, Ja 18,60:1
Grahlfs, Lincoln, 1968, Ja 4,34:3
Grahn, K, 1928, S 21,29:3
Graig, Walter J, 1961, N 10,36:1
Graine, Murray R, 1965, Jl 20,33:5
Grainer, John S, 1951, My 26,17:4
Grainer, Stephen W, 1953, Jl 9,25:5
Grainger, Albert A, 1955, N 20,89:2
Grainger, Charles F, 1923, Ap 15,6:3
Grainger, Charles M Capt, 1915, Je 9,13:4
Grainger, George V, 1944, My 6,15:5
Grainger, James Ross, 1968, Ag 15,37:5
Grainger, Percy (will, Ap 15,12:3), 1961, F 21,35:
Grainger, Richard L, 1952, Jl 23,23:2
Grainger, William, 1943, Je 2,25:1
Grakelow, Charles H, 1960, O 12,39:1
Graley, Joseph O'Connor, 1911, D 1,13:5
Gralla, Jacob, 1953, Jl 6,17:6
Grallman, George, 1949, Ja 14,23:4
Gralnick, Isidore, 1953, Ja 15,18:2
Gralnick, Phil, 1952, S 3,30:3
Gram, Edmund, 1947, Ja 28,23:2
Gramann, H F Max, 1943, N 5,19:4
Grambo, Harrison, 1876, Ja 5,5:2
Grambrell, J B Dr, 1921, Je 11,13:5
Grambs, George L, 1965, Ja 22,43:3
Gramer, William A, 1920, Ja 24,11:4
Gramlich, Henry W, 1955, Je 6,27:3
Gramling, Elmer H, 1948, O 10,78:2
Gramling, Robert E, 1939, Ap 16,III,6:8
Gramm, Benjamin A, 1949, Jl 19,30:4
Gramm, Carl H, 1945, O 9,21:2
Gramm, Charles W, 1940, Ap 15,17:3
Gramm, Edward M, 1940, Ap 2,26:2
Gramm, Harris, 1957, Ja 5,17:7
Gramm, Harry F Mrs, 1948, O 13,25:2
Gramm, Parke N, 1951, Ja 15,17:5
Gramm, Walter, 1967, N 24,46:6
Gramme, Hubert, 1937, D 21,23:4
Grammer, Carl E, 1944, Mr 18,13:5
Grammer, Carl E Mrs, 1945, N 22,35:3
Grammer, Frank, 1950, Jl 30,60:2
Grammer, Gottlieb G, 1864, My 15,6:4
Grammer, Percy L, 1944, Ag 26,11:6
Grammont, Joseph M, 1940, O 28,17:4
Gramont, Armand de, 1962, Ag 4,19:5
Gramont, Duke de, 1880, Ja 19,5:6
Grampp, Frederick G Mrs, 1961, Ag 4,21:1
Grampp, Lena R, 1953, Mr 28,17:3
Grampp, William E, 1951, O 2,27:2
Grams, Fred C, 1949, D 12,33:1
Gramsch, A Louis, 1946, F 3,40:3
Gramwell, Sarah W B Mrs, 1941, Ap 17,23:2
Granach, Alexander (por), 1945, Mr 16,15:1
Granados, Niloal, 1942, N 4,23:3
Granady, James T W, 1959, N 13,29:2
Granahan, William T (trb, My 29,27:2), 1956, My 26,17:3
Granard, Earl of, 1948, S 13,21:5
Granary, Lorraine M Mrs, 1953, Jl 26,69:1
Granata, Genserico, 1942, F 23,21:3
Granatoor, Maurice A, 1949, S 17,17:4
Granberg, Henry A T, 1904, F 15,7:6
Granberg, William H, 1918, D 17,13:4

Granberry, D Webb, 1960, S 23,29:1
Granberry, George F, 1956, Jl 12,23:5
Granbery, Alice L, 1938, S 15,25:4
Granbery, E Carleton, 1961, Je 2,31:1
Granbery, E Carlton Mrs, 1939, Ag 31,19:4
Granbery, George P, 1956, D 25,25:4
Granbery, George P Mrs, 1960, F 26,27:3
Granbery, John C Bp, 1907, Ap 2,11:5
Granby, Albert H, 1903, Ag 6,7:6
Grand, Alfred, 1937, Jl 6,19:6
Grand, Gordon, 1950, Ap 19,30:3
Grand, Jennie A Mrs, 1961, D 22,23:2
Grand, Kathleen A, 1946, Jl 25,21:1
Grand, Sarah, 1943, Mr 13,21:6
Grand Central Pete (Peter Lake), 1913, Jl 18,9:6
Grand Duchess Helene Paulovna, 1873, Ja 23,1:7
Grand-Jean, Charles, 1965, Jl 15,29:3
Grandbois, Leo E, 1958, N 8,21:5
Grande, Anthony V, 1951, Jl 25,23:3
Grande, John B Mrs, 1949, Je 24,23:5
Grande, Michael A, 1959, F 11,39:3
Grandgent, Charles H (por), 1939, S 12,25:3
Grandi, Achille, 1946, S 29,61:2
Grandin, Daniel Mrs, 1952, My 4,91:2
Grandin, Edward S Jr, 1949, O 15,15:3
Grandin, Frances, 1959, Jl 22,27:4
Grandjean, Charles A, 1947, Je 25,25:4
Grandland, Leone R, 1950, Ap 3,23:2
Grandlienard, Edward T, 1951, N 28,31:2
Grandmont, Ernest de, 1951, Jl 21,13:5
Grandon, D W Mrs, 1945, D 12,27:5
Grandon, David W, 1943, Ag 13,21:6
Grandpre, Ambrose G, 1938, Ap 27,23:5
Grandspeare, Helene M, 1938, N 7,5:5
Grandy, Alex C, 1956, Jl 7,13:5
Grandy, Lauren H, 1953, D 18,29:3
Grandy, Raymond Jr, 1950, Je 27,30:5
Granelli, Michael S, 1938, D 23,19:5
Graner, Charles, 1951, Mr 12,25:2
Graner, L Peter, 1947, S 25,29:4
Granero, Ulciseno F Maj, 1937, Ap 15,23:5
Granes, Charles, 1913, Ag 3,II,9:4
Granes, Robert Mrs, 1909, My 31,7:6
Granet, Adolph, 1956, Ja 13,23:6
Granet, Guy, 1943, O 13,23:3
Granetz, Abram B, 1944, F 8,15:3
Graney, Charles D, 1956, Mr 20,23:2
Graney, William J, 1913, My 27,11:5
Granfield, William J, 1959, My 30,17:4
Granfield, William T, 1961, S 7,35:4
Grange, Alexander Dickson, 1915, Ja 20,9:4
Grange, Amaury de la, 1953, Je 11,29:4
Grange, Consuelo de la, 1944, Ja 28,17:3
Grange, David E, 1940, Mr 30,15:2
Grange, Ina F, 1953, N 13,27:1
Grange, John N L, 1954, Ja 10,86:5
Grange, William D Mrs, 1955, Ap 2,17:1
Grange, William G, 1940, O 14,19:4
Grange, William J, 1960, D 1,35:3
Granger, Albert R, 1951, F 2,24:3
Granger, Alfred H, 1939, D 4,23:3
Granger, Allen W, 1949, Mr 9,26:2
Granger, Amos P, 1866, Ag 25,3:2
Granger, Arthur, 1947, N 5,27:2
Granger, Arthur H, 1939, F 22,21:6
Granger, Arthur L Mrs, 1951, Ja 24,27:2
Granger, Arthur Otis, 1914, Jl 31,9:5
Granger, Carl V, 1960, My 14,23:5
Granger, Daniel Larned Davis, 1909, F 15,7:4
Granger, David Mrs, 1949, Ag 8,15:1
Granger, Elihu J, 1914, My 10,IV,7:6
Granger, Elizabeth A S Mrs, 1940, D 20,25:2
Granger, Elvin B, 1960, O 14,33:2
Granger, Farley E Sr Mrs, 1959, Mr 28,17:4
Granger, George A (por), 1945, Ag 6,15:6
Granger, Gordon Maj-Gen (see also Ja 12), 1876, Ja 26,8:2
Granger, Henry, 1916, F 14,13:2
Granger, John, 1883, Je 28,4:7
Granger, John Tileson, 1916, Jl 4,11:5
Granger, Laura M, 1966, D 10,37:3
Granger, Leonard R, 1951, Ja 8,17:4
Granger, Lester B Mrs, 1965, Mr 8,29:1
Granger, Marie R Mrs, 1947, Mr 15,13:3
Granger, Orrin L, 1958, N 18,37:4
Granger, Phil, 1952, Mr 3,21:5
Granger, Rene, 1941, Ja 22,21:1
Granger, Richard R Mrs, 1947, Ja 18,15:5
Granger, Robert R, 1940, Mr 29,22:3
Granger, Sherman, 1952, Je 29,56:3
Granger, Walter, 1941, S 8,15:1
Granger, William F, 1938, D 24,15:3
Granger, William J, 1945, Ja 18,19:3
Granger, William L, 1953, Ag 22,15:2
Granges, Baroness des, 1941, Ja 24,17:1
Granich, Louis, 1950, Ja 5,2:4
Granichstaedten, Bruno, 1944, Je 1,19:3
Granick, Herbert, 1961, Je 27,33:2
Granie, Clarissa V, 1949, Ap 1,25:3
Granie, John, 1939, D 15,25:3
Granieri, Charles, 1939, F 26,38:6
Granieri, Louis W, 1951, D 16,91:2
Granirer, Louis W, 1966, Jl 16,25:3
Granirer, Martin, 1964, Ja 29,30:4
Granlund, Nils T, 1957, Ap 22,22:3
Grannan, Joseph H, 1947, D 4,31:4
Grannells, Arthur J, 1945, N 8,19:2
Grannis, Appleton, 1950, S 24,104:4
Grannis, Arthur C, 1960, Jl 5,31:2
Grannis, E B Mrs, 1926, Mr 23,27:1
Grannis, George H, 1909, Jl 5,7:5
Grannis, H (see also Ja 27), 1878, Ja 28,8:1
Grannis, John H D, 1943, N 14,57:2
Grannis, Percy Mrs, 1957, O 29,31:4
Grannis, Winslow, 1937, Mr 27,15:3
Granniss, Anna J, 1947, Jl 2,23:6
Granniss, Irwin, 1965, My 14,37:1
Granniss, Robert A, 1917, D 27,11:6; 1945, Je 8,19:3
Grannum, Hugh Parker, 1968, F 17,26:1
Granott, Abraham, 1962, Jl 22,64:4
Granowitz, Jacob Mrs, 1964, My 8,33:2
Granowitz, Sanford Mrs, 1968, Ja 19,47:2
Granowsky, Alex, 1937, Mr 12,23:4
Granowsky, Reuben, 1943, Ap 23,17:6
Granser, Albert F Jr, 1937, Jl 26,19:5
Gransky, Joseph, 1958, F 10,23:2
Granstedt, Oskar F, 1955, Jl 9,15:4
Grant, A Raymond, 1967, Ag 16,41:3
Grant, A W, 1930, O 2,25:5
Grant, Adolph Mrs, 1937, Je 19,17:2
Grant, Agnes, 1944, N 6,19:3
Grant, Agnes R, 1952, Ag 10,61:1
Grant, Alan M Jr Mrs, 1950, S 14,31:2
Grant, Albert Baron, 1899, Ag 31,7:4
Grant, Albert H, 1955, F 12,15:1
Grant, Albert S, 1957, N 14,33:4
Grant, Alex, 1941, Ag 8,15:6; 1949, Ap 21,26:4
Grant, Alex B, 1958, N 21,29:3
Grant, Alex R, 1940, Mr 28,23:4
Grant, Alex Sir (por), 1937, My 22,15:3
Grant, Alexander, 1912, Jl 20,7:6
Grant, Alexander G, 1946, O 15,25:2
Grant, Alexander Sir, 1884, D 1,2:6
Grant, Alfred T, 1948, N 27,17:1
Grant, Amelia H, 1967, Ag 15,39:3
Grant, America W Mrs, 1942, O 31,15:3
Grant, Arthur, 1943, Je 1,23:4; 1950, Je 27,29:1
Grant, Arthur R, 1945, N 7,23:2; 1949, Ag 25,23:4
Grant, Asahel H, 1952, O 4,17:4
Grant, Basil H, 1947, My 15,25:1
Grant, Bert, 1951, My 11,27:1
Grant, Bethune M Jr, 1939, O 31,23:5
Grant, Bryan M Sr, 1942, Ag 19,19:1
Grant, Byron, 1957, Jl 27,17:6
Grant, Catherine D, 1951, Jl 2,23:3
Grant, Charles C, 1951, D 12,37:2
Grant, Charles H, 1939, Ja 23,13:5; 1939, Je 13,23:3
Grant, Charles J, 1956, My 27,88:6
Grant, Charles S, 1951, Ja 11,25:3; 1961, S 15,33:1
Grant, Charles W, 1949, Jl 26,27:2
Grant, Chauncey Mrs, 1922, N 10,17:2
Grant, Clara, 1865, Ap 16,3:5
Grant, Clarence T, 1960, Jl 12,35:3
Grant, Clinton F, 1958, Jl 4,19:2
Grant, Daniel B (por), 1948, D 28,21:1
Grant, Daniel G, 1953, N 4,33:1
Grant, David E, 1968, Je 12,47:3
Grant, David N W, 1964, Ag 17,25:3
Grant, De Forest, 1960, F 16,37:5
Grant, De Forest Mrs, 1952, Ja 25,21:5
Grant, Douglas Stewart, 1921, N 24,19:6
Grant, E M, 1884, O 26,2:3
Grant, E Virginia, 1954, Jl 1,25:6
Grant, Edward H, 1960, S 29,35:4
Grant, Edward J, 1950, Mr 31,32:2
Grant, Elihu, 1942, N 4,23:1
Grant, Elihu Mrs, 1950, Ja 11,23:3
Grant, Ernest H, 1953, Ag 6,21:5
Grant, Ethel W M Mrs, 1940, My 3,21:6
Grant, F Sir, 1878, O 6,2:2
Grant, Floyd S, 1916, Ag 13,15:6
Grant, Forest, 1957, Je 8,19:4
Grant, Forest T Mrs, 1956, Je 1,23:2
Grant, Francis J, 1953, F 18,31:3
Grant, Francis S, 1949, D 17,17:5
Grant, Frank P, 1947, F 1,15:3
Grant, Fred C, 1955, Jl 19,27:2
Grant, Frederick E, 1946, O 27,62:4
Grant, Frederick L, 1953, O 25,88:5
Grant, Frederick W, 1937, Ja 4,29:3
Grant, Fulton T, 1949, Ja 16,69:1
Grant, G M, 1902, My 11,9:6
Grant, Gabriel Dr, 1909, N 9,9:6
Grant, George, 1942, N 29,64:8
Grant, George D, 1959, Ja 27,33:2
Grant, George De Forest, 1905, Ap 6,11:6
Grant, George E, 1955, Je 20,21:5
Grant, George R, 1940, D 29,24:5
Grant, George T, 1941, Mr 1,15:4
Grant, George W, 1947, Ap 6,60:4
Grant, George W Mrs, 1937, Jl 31,15:6
Grant, Gordon, 1962, My 8,39:1
Grant, H L, 1882, N 15,5:4
Grant, Hamilton Sir, 1937, Ja 25,19:4
Grant, Hannah, 1883, My 12,2:5
Grant, Harold O, 1956, Mr 8,29:6
Grant, Harold T W, 1965, My 9,87:1
Grant, Harry J, 1963, Jl 13,17:1
Grant, Havens Mrs, 1949, My 29,36:5
Grant, Heathcoat, 1938, S 27,21:3
Grant, Heber J (por), 1945, My 15,19:1
Grant, Henry Mrs, 1956, O 7,86:5
Grant, Henry W, 1949, Ap 17,76:4
Grant, Herman, 1940, Mr 17,47:7
Grant, Homer B, 1939, N 21,26:6
Grant, Homer J, 1940, Mr 19,25:3
Grant, Horace R, 1947, F 19,25:4
Grant, Hugh, 1904, Ja 30,9:5; 1910, Jl 13,7:4
Grant, Hugh A, 1940, S 26,23:2
Grant, Hugh J Mrs, 1944, My 8,19:2
Grant, Hunter B, 1954, Je 24,27:2
Grant, Israeli Mrs, 1906, Ap 25,13:2
Grant, J F Gen, 1905, Ap 13,11:5
Grant, J R, 1903, Ag 28,7:6; 1934, Je 9,15:1
Grant, James, 1879, My 27,5:4
Grant, James A Sr, 1964, Ag 1,21:5
Grant, James Alexander, 1920, F 7,11:3
Grant, James Alexander Lady, 1922, Jl 20,17:4
Grant, James B, 1945, D 9,44:2; 1947, My 26,21:5
Grant, James Benton, 1911, N 2,11:5
Grant, James E, 1966, F 21,39:3
Grant, Jean H, 1961, O 4,45:5
Grant, Jennie D Mrs (por), 1941, Je 9,19:4
Grant, Jerome C, 1949, O 19,9:6
Grant, Jesse R, 1873, Je 30,5:6
Grant, Jesse R (funl), 1873, Jl 2,5:6
Grant, Jesse R, 1920, Ag 29,20:5
Grant, Jesse R Mrs, 1945, Mr 2,19:3
Grant, Jesse Root Mrs, 1924, Jl 2,19:5
Grant, John, 1938, Ja 29,15:6
Grant, John A G, 1952, Ja 26,13:6
Grant, John B, 1962, O 18,39:1
Grant, John B Mrs, 1944, Jl 10,15:5
Grant, John Dr, 1904, Je 15,7:7
Grant, John H, 1905, Mr 11,9:4; 1946, O 8,23:4
Grant, John Hudson, 1914, Jl 28,7:4
Grant, John J, 1953, Jl 14,27:1
Grant, John K Mrs, 1953, Jl 28,19:4
Grant, John M, 1941, Mr 26,23:1
Grant, John M de B, 1938, O 19,23:2
Grant, John O, 1924, Je 23,19:3
Grant, John P, 1946, Je 1,13:3
Grant, John W D, 1955, S 24,19:3
Grant, Joseph D, 1942, F 20,17:4
Grant, Kate E, 1954, Mr 30,27:3
Grant, Lawrence, 1952, F 21,27:5
Grant, Lester E, 1965, Je 8,41:2
Grant, Lewis A Maj-Gen, 1918, Mr 21,13:5
Grant, Libbie Y Mrs (will), 1938, Mr 26,16:5
Grant, Lincoln, 1924, O 27,19:5
Grant, Louis Bedell, 1925, Je 18,21:5
Grant, Louis J, 1913, Mr 27,11:5
Grant, Louis N, 1963, Ap 16,35:4
Grant, Louis N Mrs, 1961, D 29,23:4
Grant, Madison (por),(will, Je 5,19:2), 1937, My 31, 15:5
Grant, Margaret (Mrs J F Dewhurst), 1967, Ap 3, 33:3
Grant, Margaret E Mrs, 1938, S 2,17:4
Grant, Marshall, 1957, D 5,35:4
Grant, Mary Mrs, 1941, Ja 26,37:2
Grant, Milton J, 1962, F 5,31:3
Grant, Milton J Mrs, 1955, Je 12,87:1
Grant, Moe Mrs, 1958, Ja 4,15:4
Grant, Nellie, 1922, Ag 31,15:4
Grant, Noel Rear-Adm, 1920, Mr 9,11:5
Grant, O L, 1881, Ag 7,2:2
Grant, Percy, 1952, S 9,31:4
Grant, Peter S, 1950, Mr 22,27:2
Grant, Prof, 1874, S 8,4:7
Grant, Pryor M Rev, 1937, D 17,32:2
Grant, R Snydam, 1912, D 17,15:3
Grant, Raymond A, 1957, Ag 21,27:3
Grant, Richard, 1903, Jl 30,7:6
Grant, Richard F, 1957, My 28,34:2
Grant, Richard R H, 1957, S 25,29:4
Grant, Robert (por), 1940, My 20,17:4
Grant, Robert, 1952, Je 8,86:6; 1952, S 23,33:3; 1964, F 4,33:1
Grant, Robert D, 1946, O 29,25:3
Grant, Robert F (por), 1937, D 16,27:5
Grant, Robert J, 1949, N 25,31:4
Grant, Robert L Mrs, 1938, Ap 29,21:2
Grant, Robert M, 1942, Je 11,23:1; 1943, Ap 14,23:2
Grant, Roderick C, 1951, F 24,13:4
Grant, Roderick M, 1961, Je 8,35:3
Grant, Roland D Rev Dr, 1912, Ag 23,9:6
Grant, Ronald M, 1910, Mr 9,9:3
Grant, Rupert (Lord Invader), 1961, O 18,43:2
Grant, S Hastings, 1910, My 10,9:5
Grant, Stanley H, 1965, Je 26,29:4
Grant, Stephen M, 1948, N 24,23:3
Grant, Sydney, 1953, Jl 14,27:3
Grant, Taylor B, 1956, O 16,33:3
Grant, Theodore E Mrs, 1953, Ja 23,19:2
Grant, Theodore F, 1963, N 13,41:3
Grant, Theresa, 1947, F 15,15:5
Grant, Thomas, 1944, Mr 10,15:2
Grant, U Jr, 1929, S 27,27:3

Grant, U S Gen, 1885, Jl 24,1:1
Grant, U S Jr Mrs, 1909, N 11,9:5
Grant, U W, 1943, Jl 20,19:5
Grant, Ulysses S, 1947, Ja 14,26:3; 1951, D 21,27:4; 1961, Mr 11,21:5
Grant, Ulysses S Mrs, 1920, F 26,11:4
Grant, Ulysses S 3d Maj-Gen, 1968, Ag 30,33:1
Grant, Ulysses S 3d Mrs, 1962, My 24,35:4
Grant, W A, 1903, F 27,2:2; 1940, Jl 29,13:2
Grant, Walter B, 1939, F 16,21:4
Grant, Walter J, 1938, Ag 27,13:4
Grant, Walter M, 1950, Mr 31,32:5
Grant, Walter S, 1956, Mr 5,23:2
Grant, Walter S Dr, 1937, Ap 11,II,9:1
Grant, Wesley, 1952, O 7,29:3
Grant, Wheadon M, 1965, Ap 28,45:2
Grant, William, 1939, My 26,23:5; 1945, F 9,16:3
Grant, William A, 1947, Je 30,19:5; 1948, S 5,40:4; 1954, Mr 17,31:4
Grant, William F, 1954, O 8,23:2
Grant, William H, 1952, Ap 23,29:5
Grant, William S, 1912, Je 20,11:6
Grant, William T Mrs, 1954, F 9,27:3
Grant, William W, 1942, O 26,15:5
Grant, Wilmot B, 1944, N 5,54:4
Grant-Duff, Arthur C, 1948, Ap 14,28:3
Grant-Schafer, George A, 1939, My 13,15:4
Grant-Suttie, Gerald L P, 1949, My 25,29:4
Grantham, Andrew S, 1955, F 1,29:3
Grantham, George F (Boots), 1954, Mr 18,31:5
Grantham, William Sir, 1911, D 1,13:5
Grantland, Charles H, 1940, My 21,23:5
Grantland, Mary, 1947, Ag 29,17:2
Grantley, Lord, 1954, Jl 18,56:5
Grantvoort, Arnold J, 1937, My 20,21:2
Grantz, Walter A H, 1957, S 25,29:2
Granville, Bernard, 1947, My 13,26:2
Granville, Charles N, 1956, Jl 8,64:6
Granville, Earl, 1939, Jl 22,15:7
Granville, George Leveson-Gower Second Earl, 1891, Ap 1,5:4
Granville, Rose Lady, 1967, N 18,37:2
Granville, Sydney, 1959, D 25,21:2
Granville, William A, 1943, F 5,21:3
Granville, 4th Earl (W S Leveson-Gower), 1953, Je 26,19:1
Granville-Barker, Harley, 1946, S 1,36:1
Granville-Barker, Harley Mrs, 1950, F 18,15:2
Granville-Smith, Walter, 1938, D 8,27:4
Granvow, Franklyn A, 1958, F 13,29:4
Grape, Maurice H, 1954, Jl 21,27:2
Grape, Maurice H Mrs, 1944, Jl 18,19:3
Grapes, Edwin E Mrs, 1947, O 21,23:4
Grapes, Wilfred A Jr, 1949, Jl 14,28:2
Grapewin, Charles, 1956, F 3,23:3
Grapewin, Charles Mrs, 1943, S 12,52:6
Gras, Basile Gen, 1901, Ap 16,9:5
Gras, Harold W, 1953, Ap 3,23:4
Gras, Max, 1947, S 4,25:4
Grasbeck, Sune W, 1952, Ja 10,29:5
Graschenkov, Nikolai (date not given), 1965, O 11, 61:2
Grasman, August, 1911, F 20,7:5
Grass, A Irving, 1963, Ag 24,19:4
Grass, Isaac J Mrs, 1953, Mr 14,15:4
Grass, John, 1918, My 15,13:4
Grass, John A, 1943, Ag 31,17:2; 1949, F 1,25:2
Grasse, Arnold, 1949, S 19,23:5
Grasse, Edwin, 1954, Ap 10,15:2
Grasse, Frank, 1953, Ja 13,27:4
Grasse, Gertrude, 1938, D 7,23:5
Grasse, Walter F, 1962, Ag 22,33:3
Grasselini, Gaspard Cardinal, 1875, S 18,1:4
Grassell, John Mrs, 1947, N 15,17:3
Grasselli, Edward, 1949, N 17,29:4
Grasselli, Thomas S, 1942, Ag 23,42:2
Grassett, Bernard, 1955, O 22,19:2
Grassett, John E, 1958, Ja 18,15:3
Grassheim, Kurt M, 1948, N 17,27:2
Grassi, Enzo, 1957, Je 5,35:5
Grassi, Eugene C, 1941, Jl 17,19:2
Grassi, Giovanni Battista, 1925, My 6,23:4
Grassi, Giuseppe, 1950, Ja 26,27:2
Grassi, Harriet M Mrs, 1938, Ap 8,19:4
Grassi, Otto J A (cor, Ag 3,25:5), 1959, Ag 2,81:3
Grassi, Otto J A Jr, 1962, Ag 14,31:3
Grassi, Perry G, 1951, Jl 15,61:1
Grassi, Robert D, 1957, S 18,33:3
Grassi, Waldemar H, 1952, S 11,31:3
Grassman, A F, 1947, Ag 2,13:5
Grassman, Harry A, 1961, F 27,27:2
Grassmann, Edward C, 1966, Jl 7,37:2
Grasso, Frank, 1967, N 11,33:1
Grasson, Robert, 1962, Je 8,31:2
Grasty, Charles H, 1924, Ja 21,17:4; 1924, Ja 23,17:4
Gratacap, Louis P, 1917, D 22,11:5
Gratacap, Thomas B, 1924, Ja 3,17:1
Grate, Augustus Radcliffe, 1903, S 24,9:6
Grateau, M, 1936, Je 4,23:1
Gratke, Charles, 1949, Jl 13,1:8
Graton, Carlos, 1953, Je 12,27:1
Gratry, Abbe A J A, 1872, F 22,5:5
Grattagni, Luigi, 1942, D 23,19:1
Grattan, Ann Mrs, 1925, Ap 10,19:3
Grattan, Catherine M Mrs, 1937, Ag 24,21:2
Grattan, Charles G, 1951, O 18,29:4
Grattan, Domenico Mrs, 1966, My 10,39:4
Grattan, Dominick R, 1955, Je 18,17:6
Grattan, H P Mrs, 1876, D 18,8:2
Grattan, Harry, 1951, S 26,31:6
Grattan, John E (por), 1949, Ag 2,19:3
Grattan, Lawrence, 1941, D 10,25:5
Grattan, Thomas Colley, 1864, Jl 26,2:6
Grattan, William J, 1938, D 6,23:4; 1967, D 10,86:8
Grattan-Doyle, Nicholas, 1941, Jl 15,19:5
Gratton, Walter J, 1949, F 28,19:5
Gratz, Alfred, 1938, Ja 2,41:1
Gratz, Alice S, 1951, D 15,13:1
Gratz, Henry M, 1939, Je 21,23:3
Gratz, Herbert F, 1954, Jl 16,21:1
Gratz, Simon, 1925, Ag 22,11:5
Gratzol, Otto, 1952, D 13,21:4
Grau, Edward, 1946, O 31,25:2
Grau, Herman, 1912, O 28,11:4
Grau, J (see also D 15), 1877, D 17,8:1
Grau, Jacinto, 1958, Ag 16,17:2
Grau, Jules, 1905, S 12,9:6
Grau, Louis Mrs, 1962, F 21,45:3
Grau, Matt, 1952, O 6,25:6
Grau, Maurice, 1907, Mr 15,9:5
Grau, Miguel, 1961, Je 9,33:5
Grau, Robert G, 1944, Ap 13,19:3
Grau, Seymour, 1947, N 20,29:4
Graubard, John (por), 1940, My 16,23:1
Graubard, Meyer D, 1939, Jl 18,19:5
Graubard, Moritz, 1944, Ag 11,15:5
Graubard, Morris Mrs, 1938, D 24,15:7
Graubard, Simon H, 1942, My 14,19:3
Graudan, Nikolai, 1964, Ag 14,27:4
Grauel, Fred M, 1955, My 4,29:3
Grauer, Adolph, 1951, O 2,27:1
Grauer, Albert L, 1946, Ap 24,25:1
Grauer, Bill Jr, 1963, D 17,39:2
Grauer, Carol, 1954, D 5,89:1
Grauer, Christopher G, 1945, My 20,32:6
Grauer, Edward (por), 1942, Jl 2,21:5
Grauer, Edward Mrs, 1941, F 11,23:4
Grauer, Frank, 1945, F 18,34:6
Grauer, Ida Mrs, 1964, Jl 27,31:4
Grauer, Max J, 1954, F 6,19:4
Grauer, Otto C U, 1954, Jl 10,13:7
Graul, Gottlieb, 1910, Je 14,11:5
Graul, Jacob, 1938, F 15,25:5
Graul, Russell Y, 1961, F 8,31:1
Graule, Magdelena M Mrs, 1952, Mr 18,27:2
Grauley, Margaret Mrs, 1939, S 30,17:4
Grauley, S O, 1958, D 7,88:7
Graulich, John P, 1947, N 25,32:3
Grauman, Sid, 1950, Mr 6,21:3
Graumann, Harry, 1938, S 20,23:2
Graupner, Adolphus E, 1947, S 21,60:6
Grausam, Jacob W, 1954, F 20,17:5
Grauten, Charles C Mrs, 1951, Ag 16,27:2
Grauwiller, Frederick E, 1949, D 10,17:5
Graux, Lucien, 1941, My 13,23:3
Gravagna, Fred, 1954, S 15,33:4
Gravalec, Joseph S, 1944, F 17,19:4
Gravany, James J, 1967, S 22,47:3
Gravatt, Phil B, 1953, Ap 14,27:2
Gravatt, Walter H, 1950, O 31,27:3
Gravatt, William F, 1958, Ja 27,27:2
Gravatt, William L, 1942, F 15,45:3
Gravdahl, Ragnvald A, 1955, Ja 7,21:3
Grave, Caswell, 1944, Ja 10,17:5
Grave, Charles, 1941, Ag 28,19:5
Gravel, Elphege Bp, 1904, Ja 29,2:6
Gravel, Emile J, 1952, Mr 2,92:2
Gravel, Eugene O Mrs, 1967, S 5,25:4
Graveley, Richard C Mrs, 1943, Jl 8,19:5
Gravell, J Harvey, 1939, D 9,15:5
Gravell, J Harvey (will), 1940, F 6,16:3
Gravell, Thomas, 1951, O 26,23:4
Gravell, William H, 1953, S 7,19:2
Gravelle, Medos, 1944, D 30,11:3
Gravelle, Phil O, 1955, F 5,15:5
Gravely, Francis W Mrs, 1951, Mr 21,33:1
Gravely, Jules, 1954, Jl 25,69:1
Gravely, William S, 1947, N 11,27:2
Gravely, Willis T, 1953, Ja 25,86:5
Gravendyk, Jacob, 1965, Ja 10,92:6
Gravenor, Percival A, 1957, S 15,84:8
Graver, Andrew E, 1946, S 30,25:3
Graver, Herbert S Sr, 1954, Ag 8,85:1
Graver, Philip S, 1945, Ag 13,19:3
Gravereaux, Claude, 1943, N 25,27:3
Graversat, G A Lt, 1864, Jl 17,3:5
Graves, A, 1936, Jl 16,17:6
Graves, A A, 1903, D 23,9:6
Graves, A B, 1903, O 10,9:7
Graves, A P, 1931, D 28,17:1
Graves, Alden W, 1956, Mr 6,31:5
Graves, Alex, 1950, S 14,31:2
Graves, Alice R, 1951, N 18,90:3
Graves, Allard McG, 1967, Ag 24,37:3
Graves, Allen B, 1957, F 4,19:2
Graves, Alvin C, 1965, Jl 30,25:1
Graves, Andrew B, 1948, F 19,23:4
Graves, Arthur C, 1950, Mr 3,25:4
Graves, Arthur H Mrs, 1938, Ja 30,II,8:3
Graves, Carl F, 1954, Mr 10,25:2
Graves, Carleton H, 1943, Ja 9,13:2
Graves, Charles, 1948, My 13,25:2
Graves, Charles Brazelton, 1909, Mr 25,9:4
Graves, Charles H, 1940, Ag 16,15:3
Graves, Charles H Mrs, 1949, Ap 16,15:1
Graves, Charles L, 1942, Mr 29,44:6; 1944, Ap 19,23:6
Graves, Charles M, 1952, D 27,9:1
Graves, Clara B, 1961, F 18,35:5
Graves, Clifford I Mrs, 1962, N 20,36:1
Graves, Clyde M Mrs, 1945, Mr 23,20:2
Graves, Collins M, 1954, Je 30,27:5
Graves, Collins M Mrs, 1955, D 26,19:4
Graves, Craig, 1955, S 27,35:1
Graves, David B (por), 1942, Mr 15,43:1
Graves, Edwin D Mrs, 1963, Ap 29,31:3
Graves, Edwin J, 1937, D 26,II,6:8
Graves, Elizabeth M Mrs, 1939, Mr 17,22:3
Graves, Ernest, 1953, Je 12,27:2
Graves, Ernest Mrs, 1968, Ap 7,92:8
Graves, Eugene S, 1951, Ja 5,21:2
Graves, Ferdinand, 1950, O 25,35:5
Graves, Floyd H, 1953, N 17,31:3
Graves, Frank H, 1948, Ja 21,26:3
Graves, Frank P, 1956, S 14,23:1
Graves, Frank P Mrs, 1943, F 26,19:3; 1952, Ap 8,29
Graves, Frank Sloan, 1968, N 14,47:3
Graves, Frederick R (por), 1940, My 18,15:3
Graves, Gaylord W, 1952, N 10,25:2
Graves, Gemont Rev Dr, 1915, Ja 29,9:6
Graves, George, 1949, Ap 3,76:5
Graves, George B, 1937, Jl 8,23:3
Graves, George D Mrs, 1946, S 16,5:6
Graves, George J, 1942, Mr 6,21:2
Graves, George K Jr, 1962, Mr 27,37:1
Graves, Gordon R, 1964, Mr 27,27:3
Graves, Harmon S, 1940, S 14,17:6
Graves, Harold C, 1968, My 3,47:1
Graves, Harold N, 1966, N 19,33:4
Graves, Harold T, 1962, Jl 21,19:6
Graves, Henry, 1947, Ag 31,31:8
Graves, Henry C, 1937, S 6,17:3
Graves, Henry S, 1951, Mr 8,29:3
Graves, Henry W, 1953, Ja 22,23:1
Graves, Herbert R, 1947, Mr 23,60:3
Graves, HErman A, 1947, D 23,23:4
Graves, Homer A Mrs, 1949, Mr 27,78:5
Graves, Horace, 1911, Ag 26,9:3
Graves, Horace W, 1941, Je 11,21:6
Graves, Howard T, 1953, Je 3,31:2
Graves, James D Mrs, 1954, Ag 18,29:1
Graves, James W, 1945, Ag 24,19:3; 1950, Ag 24,2
Graves, Jennie M Mrs, 1949, Je 2,27:1
Graves, John C, 1948, Ag 30,17:1
Graves, John H, 1948, Ja 10,15:2
Graves, John L, 1953, Ja 9,21:3
Graves, John R, 1956, Ap 19,31:1
Graves, John T Mrs, 1950, N 13,27:5
Graves, John T 2d, 1961, My 20,23:7
Graves, John Temple, 1925, Ag 9,5:3; 1925, Ag 11
Graves, Joseph C Mrs, 1959, N 21,23:6
Graves, Joseph W, 1962, Je 14,33:5
Graves, Julia C Mrs, 1944, N 10,19:2
Graves, Laura H, 1940, F 1,21:4
Graves, Lester H, 1960, Ja 5,31:4
Graves, Lester H Mrs, 1949, O 5,29:4
Graves, Louis, 1965, Ja 24,80:8
Graves, Lucien C Mrs, 1943, Ag 12,19:1
Graves, Lulu G, 1949, Ag 3,23:6
Graves, M I, 1953, N 21,13:2
Graves, Mark, 1942, Je 2,23:1
Graves, Merle D, 1961, S 11,27:4
Graves, Norman B, 1951, Mr 21,33:3
Graves, Norman W, 1941, Jl 24,17:7
Graves, Otho M, 1954, O 16,17:7
Graves, Perle A, 1953, D 30,23:3
Graves, Perle A Mrs, 1950, Ja 26,28:4
Graves, Phil P, 1953, Je 4,29:5
Graves, Ralph H (por), 1939, D 2,17:1
Graves, Robert A (por), 1949, S 10,17:5
Graves, Robert E Mrs, 1940, D 14,17:5
Graves, Rufus E, 1943, O 15,19:5
Graves, Stanley E, 1950, Mr 28,32:3
Graves, Stuart S, 1940, N 1,25:1
Graves, Thaddeus, 1912, S 12,11:4
Graves, Thomas F, 1940, D 8,69:2
Graves, W P, 1933, Ja 26,20:1
Graves, W Sproull, 1960, Ja 28,31:2
Graves, William, 1906, Jl 1,9:7; 1937, D 30,19:3
Graves, William B, 1944, N 9,27:4
Graves, William B Prof, 1915, My 7,13:5
Graves, William C, 1942, My 9,13:2
Graves, William E, 1944, F 2,21:4
Graves, William Elliott, 1925, O 15,23:4
Graves, William G, 1962, S 12,39:1
Graves, William L, 1940, Mr 14,23:5
Graves, William L Mrs, 1961, Je 27,33:4
Graves, William P, 1947, Ja 10,21:1
Graves, William S, 1922, F 28,19:3
Graves, William S (por), 1940, F 28,21:1

Graves, William W, 1965, D 28,27:2
Graves-Lord, Walter, 1942, Je 20,13:2
Gravesen, Carl J, 1954, Ja 8,21:3
Graveson, William E (por), 1947, F 5,23:4
Gravill, Walter, 1957, Ag 7,27:5
Gravilov, Alex V, 1959, Jl 4,15:1
Grawn, Charles T, 1942, N 14,16:2
Grawoig, Haim, 1948, Ap 19,23:2
Gray, A Freeman, 1957, F 2,19:3
Gray, A G Commodore, 1876, N 11,4:6
Gray, A Prof, 1888, Ja 31,5:1
Gray, Aaron, 1962, F 22,25:4
Gray, Abraham R, 1950, Jl 10,21:4
Gray, Alanson M (por), 1948, S 21,27:1
Gray, Albert E N, 1942, O 29,23:2
Gray, Albert M Mrs, 1943, S 27,19:2
Gray, Albert S, 1960, Ap 23,23:6
Gray, Albert Z, 1964, Ag 30,93:1
Gray, Alden, 1959, D 10,39:3
Gray, Alex C, 1949, My 3,25:5
Gray, Alex Mrs, 1958, Ja 10,26:2
Gray, Alfred Freeman (will), 1914, Je 17,11:4
Gray, Alfred M, 1941, Mr 25,26:1
Gray, Alonzo, 1943, My 21,20:2
Gray, Andrew, 1953, Mr 25,31:4
Gray, Anna Mrs, 1938, Mr 15,23:2
Gray, Arthur, 1940, Ap 15,17:2
Gray, Arthur C Mrs, 1963, Ag 28,33:5
Gray, Arthur W, 1957, Ap 9,33:1
Gray, Ashton W, 1938, Ja 5,21:3
Gray, Augustus B, 1939, S 21,23:4
Gray, Augustus T Sr, 1949, Ja 3,23:4
Gray, Austen, 1954, Je 25,21:5
Gray, Austin K, 1945, D 5,25:4
Gray, Austin K Mrs, 1947, Jl 21,17:5
Gray, Avis, 1956, S 13,38:1
Gray, B D, 1946, N 27,25:5
Gray, Benjamin F, 1949, D 20,31:2
Gray, Benjamin H Mrs, 1966, My 18,47:3
Gray, Bernard A, 1964, My 5,43:5
Gray, Bert R, 1949, Ap 30,13:6
Gray, Billy (C O'Donnell), 1882, N 22,5:2
Gray, Bradley C, 1953, N 19,31:5
Gray, Bromley, 1959, F 5,31:4
Gray, C C Dr, 1884, N 26,2:2
Gray, C L, 1938, Je 9,17:4
Gray, Campbell, 1944, My 17,19:4
Gray, Carl R (por), 1939, My 10,23:3
Gray, Carl R Jr, 1955, D 3,17:3
Gray, Carl R Jr Mrs, 1959, F 24,29:3
Gray, Carl R Mrs, 1956, Je 18,25:1
Gray, Carol E Jr, 1951, N 15,29:4
Gray, Carolyn, 1938, D 30,16:1
Gray, Charles B W, 1945, D 15,17:5
Gray, Charles D, 1941, Ag 23,13:5
Gray, Charles E, 1951, F 27,27:1; 1959, Ag 16,82:8
Gray, Charles H, 1916, F 22,11:5; 1939, Jl 2,15:4; 1948, Mr 18,28:2; 1959, My 15,30:1; 1968, Je 21,41:2
Gray, Charles Mrs, 1952, Mr 1,15:1
Gray, Charles O Jr, 1954, Mr 30,27:5
Gray, Charles P, 1953, D 9,11:4
Gray, Charles W, 1947, My 23,24:2
Gray, Charlotte C F Mrs, 1937, F 3,23:5
Gray, Chester H, 1964, Ap 2,33:4
Gray, Clarence, 1957, Ja 7,25:4
Gray, Clarence H, 1939, Jl 3,13:5
Gray, Clarence H Mrs, 1951, Jl 22,61:1
Gray, Clinton D, 1948, F 22,49:1
Gray, Clyde D, 1944, Mr 30,21:4
Gray, Colman, 1965, S 10,35:2
Gray, Daniel J, 1954, Ag 21,17:4
Gray, David, 1968, Ap 13,25:5
Gray, David E, 1950, Je 16,25:4
Gray, David G, 1953, N 26,31:5
Gray, David L (por), 1941, F 12,21:1
Gray, David Mrs, 1946, S 19,31:3; 1952, O 18,19:6
Gray, David W, 1938, O 23,40:8
Gray, Dean, 1955, O 11,39:3
Gray, Dick, 1954, Mr 26,22:3
Gray, Donald E, 1939, S 29,23:4
Gray, Dwight, 1944, N 1,23:4
Gray, Earl (Hy Gray), 1882, S 11,5:3
Gray, Earl S, 1954, Mr 30,27:5
Gray, Earle V, 1946, Ap 23,21:2
Gray, Edward, 1939, Ap 4,25:4; 1941, Ap 14,17:1
Gray, Edward C, 1949, Ja 28,21:4
Gray, Edward F, 1938, Je 24,19:2
Gray, Edward F Mrs, 1953, F 6,19:4
Gray, Edward G, 1945, Je 16,13:4
Gray, Edward H, 1944, My 30,21:2
Gray, Edward Jr, 1941, Ja 1,23:3
Gray, Edward Mrs, 1903, D 30,7:2; 1906, F 5,4:1
Gray, Edward W (por), 1942, Je 12,21:3
Gray, Elisha Prof, 1901, Ja 22,9:5
Gray, Elizabeth H Mrs, 1942, Ja 22,17:1
Gray, Elmer H, 1939, S 30,17:6
Gray, Emma G Mrs, 1957, Jl 12,21:5
Gray, Ernest A, 1951, F 18,76:5
Gray, Esther Mrs, 1940, N 26,23:2
Gray, Eugene F, 1945, O 5,23:3; 1948, S 10,23:1
Gray, Everett W, 1953, S 6,50:2
Gray, Finly H (por), 1947, My 9,22:2
Gray, Francis A, 1938, Ap 20,23:3
Gray, Frank D Dr, 1916, Je 12,11:4
Gray, Frank E, 1962, Je 16,19:6
Gray, Frank M, 1947, Je 4,27:2
Gray, Frank W, 1951, Ag 13,17:5
Gray, Fred J, 1948, Ja 31,19:5
Gray, G G, 1875, Ag 16,4:7
Gray, G Raymond, 1952, Je 8,87:2
Gray, Genevieve Mrs, 1950, Ap 13,24:5
Gray, George, 1940, Ag 21,19:4; 1961, D 6,47:5
Gray, George E, 1948, S 30,28:2
Gray, George Edward, 1913, Ja 3,9:4
Gray, George Ex-Judge (por), 1925, Ag 8,11:5
Gray, George F, 1923, Mr 24,13:5
Gray, George M, 1946, D 3,31:5
Gray, George R Judge, 1910, N 5,7:4
Gray, George T, 1938, Ja 9,42:5
Gray, George W, 1948, N 19,28:2; 1960, D 30,20:1; 1962, Mr 1,31:2
Gray, Gilda (M Michalski),(funl plans, D 25,21:3), 1959, D 23,27:4
Gray, Glen, 1963, Ag 25,83:1
Gray, Gloria, 1947, N 23,74:4
Gray, Goodwin I, 1954, Ag 18,29:4
Gray, Gordon Mrs, 1953, Jl 16,21:4
Gray, H P, 1877, N 13,4:7
Gray, H Willard, 1950, O 24,29:2
Gray, H Willard Mrs, 1942, Ap 20,21:1
Gray, Hamilton, 1950, O 30,27:5
Gray, Harold, 1968, My 10,47:1
Gray, Harold L, 1961, Mr 2,27:1
Gray, Harry J, 1962, S 30,86:5
Gray, Hedden, 1953, Mr 20,23:2
Gray, Henry (Earl Gray), 1882, S 11,5:3
Gray, Henry, 1938, O 7,23:4; 1948, My 11,25:3
Gray, Henry A, 1939, D 14,27:2
Gray, Henry Dr, 1915, Je 21,9:5
Gray, Henry G, 1954, Jl 16,21:4
Gray, Henry Mrs, 1945, Mr 12,19:2
Gray, Henry W Col, 1907, F 24,7:6
Gray, Herbert, 1947, My 25,60:3
Gray, Herbert L Dr, 1921, Jl 24,22:4
Gray, Horace, 1901, Jl 19,7:6
Gray, Horace A Jr (will), 1959, Ja 10,17:2
Gray, Horace Judge, 1902, S 16,9:5
Gray, Horace Mrs, 1949, Je 6,19:1
Gray, Howard A, 1945, F 27,19:4; 1958, Je 4,31:5
Gray, Howard E, 1957, Ag 11,80:2
Gray, Howard L, 1945, S 16,42:7
Gray, Hugh J, 1943, Mr 5,17:4
Gray, I P, 1895, F 15,1:4
Gray, Ira L Mrs, 1953, Ap 9,27:2
Gray, Irving, 1953, Ap 22,29:4
Gray, Isabel H Mrs, 1946, D 12,29:3
Gray, Isabel S Mrs, 1938, Mr 19,15:1
Gray, J A, 1951, Je 8,27:2
Gray, J Barbour, 1940, Jl 3,17:3
Gray, J Copeland Mrs, 1949, Je 1,31:3
Gray, J Douglas, 1952, Mr 13,29:3
Gray, J F (funl), 1882, Je 9,8:6
Gray, J J, 1947, N 5,27:4
Gray, J J Mrs, 1949, Mr 13,76:5
Gray, J Newton, 1957, O 9,35:1
Gray, Jabez, 1950, Jl 23,57:2
Gray, Jabez Mrs (M O'Shea), 1956, Je 2,19:3
Gray, James, 1904, D 29,7:5; 1951, S 14,26:3; 1956, Je 6,33:2
Gray, James A, 1952, O 30,31:1; 1954, N 20,17:5
Gray, James B, 1967, O 13,36:3
Gray, James E, 1963, O 27,88:3
Gray, James H, 1949, S 16,27:2; 1949, D 13,38:3
Gray, James M, 1942, F 2,15:2
Gray, James R, 1951, S 27,31:4
Gray, James R Mrs, 1940, Ja 7,49:3
Gray, James Richard, 1917, Je 26,13:5
Gray, Jennie L, 1913, Mr 4,13:4
Gray, Jessie, 1948, My 30,34:7
Gray, John, 1883, Ja 22,5:4; 1939, S 6,23:5; 1942, Je 14,46:1
Gray, John A, 1925, My 21,23:6
Gray, John A C, 1967, Jl 16,65:1
Gray, John A C Mrs, 1904, F 19,9:6
Gray, John Cameron, 1914, F 14,11:6
Gray, John Clinton Ex-Judge, 1915, Je 28,9:6
Gray, John Clinton Ex-Judge (funl, Jl 1, 11:5), 1915, Je 29,13:3
Gray, John D Mrs, 1966, My 19,47:3
Gray, John E, 1954, Jl 7,31:1
Gray, John F (por), 1941, Mr 20,21:3
Gray, John G, 1950, D 18,31:3
Gray, John H, 1938, Ag 6,13:6
Gray, John H (por), 1946, Ap 5,25:1
Gray, John H, 1946, My 17,21:1
Gray, John Howard, 1903, N 22,7:6
Gray, John J, 1947, Mr 23,60:2
Gray, John L, 1939, S 30,17:3
Gray, John Mrs, 1952, Ag 31,45:1
Gray, John N, 1871, Mr 22,2:6
Gray, John P, 1939, Ja 8,42:6
Gray, John W, 1950, My 1,25:5; 1966, F 6,92:6
Gray, Joseph, 1949, Jl 16,13:5
Gray, Joseph E Sr, 1954, Ja 10,87:2
Gray, Joseph M M, 1957, Ja 10,29:1
Gray, Joseph P, 1941, F 23,41:2
Gray, Joseph R Jr, 1953, Je 12,27:3
Gray, Joseph S, 1953, N 6,27:2
Gray, Julia Mrs, 1954, D 2,31:3
Gray, Katherine L Mrs, 1947, My 3,17:1
Gray, Lendal G, 1943, Jl 9,17:3
Gray, Leon E, 1948, D 8,31:4
Gray, Leonard, 1957, Jl 18,25:4
Gray, Lincoln, 1941, Ag 29,17:3
Gray, Lizzie Mrs, 1938, Ja 20,23:2
Gray, Louis, 1939, My 16,23:6
Gray, Louis H, 1955, Ag 20,17:6
Gray, Lydia L, 1948, D 10,25:3
Gray, Lyman F, 1938, F 26,15:2
Gray, M, 1878, N 9,8:3
Gray, Marion F Mrs, 1944, Ja 30,38:4
Gray, Mark R, 1947, F 27,21:2
Gray, Mary N Mrs, 1941, My 3,15:5
Gray, Mason H, 1943, My 24,15:2
Gray, Matthew J, 1943, O 6,23:4
Gray, Maurice F (J McGee), 1961, N 21,39:5
Gray, Max, 1952, Mr 22,13:1
Gray, Miller, 1903, S 16,9:6
Gray, Milner, 1943, Ap 11,48:2
Gray, Minnie Mrs, 1952, F 8,23:3
Gray, Neil, 1938, Ja 5,21:1
Gray, Norman, 1952, Ap 30,27:5
Gray, O L, 1956, S 28,27:1
Gray, Olin D, 1938, S 3,13:2
Gray, Olin D Mrs, 1950, Ja 24,31:5
Gray, Percy R Mrs, 1955, My 20,25:3
Gray, Philander Raymond, 1914, S 16,11:7
Gray, Philip H, 1922, N 28,21:5
Gray, Philip P, 1966, Jl 3,35:1
Gray, Ralph G, 1956, Jl 5,25:4
Gray, Ralph S, 1961, O 19,35:2
Gray, Raymond C, 1952, N 15,17:1
Gray, Raymond J, 1945, Jl 22,38:2
Gray, Raymond S, 1952, Mr 9,92:2
Gray, Richard J, 1966, My 3,47:3
Gray, Robert, 1951, D 29,11:4
Gray, Robert B, 1952, O 12,89:1
Gray, Robert Jr, 1905, My 27,9:4; 1918, F 26,13:4; 1925, Ap 25,15:4; 1952, Ap 1,29:1
Gray, Robert L, 1945, O 21,46:2; 1952, Ag 13,21:3
Gray, Robert M, 1953, D 10,48:3
Gray, Roland, 1957, N 24,86:7
Gray, Russell, 1948, D 10,26:3
Gray, S Stanley, 1965, Mr 12,33:3
Gray, Sam, 1953, Ap 17,25:5
Gray, Sarah H, 1877, Ag 5,5:6
Gray, Sherril M, 1937, Je 22,23:5
Gray, Sidney R S, 1940, Ja 14,43:2
Gray, Susan L (will), 1959, Ja 10,17:2
Gray, T T, 1931, Ap 29,25:5
Gray, Temperance, 1951, Jl 19,23:4
Gray, Theodore F N Mrs, 1962, O 21,88:8
Gray, Theodore P, 1951, Ja 28,76:2
Gray, Thomas F, 1951, F 8,33:2; 1957, Jl 11,25:4
Gray, Thomas J, 1924, D 1,17:4; 1964, S 11,33:1
Gray, Thomas Jr, 1963, My 2,35:3
Gray, Thomas N Dr, 1918, Jl 24,11:4
Gray, Trevor G, 1953, Je 4,29:1
Gray, W A, 1946, O 22,25:6
Gray, W C Rev, 1901, S 30,7:6
Gray, W H Mrs, 1909, Ap 14,11:5
Gray, W Leon, 1941, My 11,44:4
Gray, W Malcolm, 1948, D 14,29:3
Gray, Walker I, 1945, N 13,21:2
Gray, Walter S, 1956, Ja 30,27:3
Gray, Weston A, 1954, Ja 15,20:3
Gray, Wilford D, 1939, N 24,23:3
Gray, William, 1938, Ag 15,15:6; 1945, My 17,19:1; 1952, O 8,31:4; 1957, Jl 17,27:5
Gray, William A, 1943, S 9,25:5; 1955, S 29,33:4
Gray, William A Jr, 1937, Mr 7,II,9:2
Gray, William A Mrs, 1961, D 28,27:2
Gray, William B (Mar 11), 1963, Ap 1,35:7
Gray, William D, 1958, O 2,37:5
Gray, William E, 1948, Ap 1,25:5
Gray, William G Mrs, 1954, Jl 10,13:7
Gray, William H, 1940, Mr 4,15:4; 1959, O 3,19:5
Gray, William H Sr, 1952, N 2,88:6
Gray, William J, 1938, Ja 1,19:4; 1942, Ag 11,19:6; 1949, Ag 18,21:3
Gray, William Maj, 1937, Je 26,17:5
Gray, William N Jr Mrs, 1949, Je 16,29:1
Gray, William P, 1962, O 16,47:3
Gray, William R, 1937, Ap 1,23:1
Gray, William R Mrs, 1938, F 21,19:3
Gray, William S, 1947, Jl 3,21:3; 1948, S 1,24:2; 1960, S 9,29:3; 1960, O 21,33:4; 1965, Mr 10,30:3
Gray, William S Mrs, 1947, S 6,17:4
Gray, William T, 1950, My 12,27:2
Graybill, Henry B, 1951, Ap 6,25:2
Graybill, Henry J, 1959, Ap 12,29:1
Graybill, James Edward, 1916, S 4,7:4
Grayburn, Vandeleur M, 1943, S 17,21:2
Graydon, Gordon, 1953, S 20,87:1
Graydon, Samuel, 1962, Mr 31,25:3
Graydon, Thomas, 1949, O 16,75:3
Graydon, Thomas Mrs, 1949, O 16,75:3
Grayhurst, John W, 1962, Mr 5,23:1
Grayot, John L, 1951, Ja 26,23:2

Grayson, Bette, 1954, F 24,25:3
Grayson, Cary T, 1938, F 15,1:4
Grayson, Charles P, 1939, Ag 17,21:6
Grayson, Clifford M, 1951, N 13,29:5
Grayson, Evelyn, 1941, My 12,17:1
Grayson, Frank Y, 1955, F 10,31:2
Grayson, Hal, 1959, O 31,23:7
Grayson, Harry M, 1968, O 1,47:3
Grayson, Helen S, 1962, My 8,39:2
Grayson, Howard M, 1957, Ag 3,15:4
Grayson, John A, 1947, F 10,2:3
Grayson, L A, 1961, My 29,19:5
Grayson, Ralph, 1943, Ap 15,25:5
Grayson, Stewart M, 1950, Je 3,15:6
Grayson, Theodore J, 1937, D 24,20:3
Grayson, Walter, 1955, Ag 15,15:2
Grayson (Moody Merrill), 1903, D 25,7:5
Grayzel, Abraham G, 1965, Mr 27,27:6
Grazi, Enrico, 1953, O 1,29:4
Graziani, Raffaele, 1944, O 29,43:2
Graziani, Rodolfo (funl, Ja 14,8:4), 1955, Ja 12,27:2
Graziano, Anthony W, 1968, Mr 5,41:1
Graziano, Joseph S, 1954, O 30,17:3
Graziano, Salvatore, 1958, Jl 18,21:1
Graziano, Vincent, 1957, Ja 24,29:2
Grazioli (Mother Delfina), 1967, N 25,39:4
Graziosi, Giuseppe, 1942, Jl 4,17:3
Grazzani, Vitaliano, 1952, My 5,27:6
Grdina, Anton, 1957, D 3,35:2
Grdnia, Mathias J, 1951, D 2,90:2
Greacen, Edmund, 1949, O 5,29:2
Greacen, Eleanor M, 1966, Mr 13,86:5
Greacen, Joseph W, 1960, O 13,37:4
Greacen, Robert F, 1964, N 10,47:5
Greacen, Samuel L, 1958, F 4,26:4
Greacen, Walter J, 1956, O 13,19:4
Greacen, Walter S, 1939, Jl 16,31:4
Greagor, Joseph E Sr, 1950, F 28,29:4
Greak, Clayton A, 1947, Ap 16,34:5
Grealer, Gustave, 1941, Jl 14,13:1
Grealy, John J, 1951, My 18,27:4
Grealy, John J Mrs, 1962, Je 21,31:4
Grean, Alexander M Jr, 1968, O 23,47:1
Grean, Alexandre M, 1961, D 5,39:6
Greaney, Thomas E, 1944, F 5,15:4
Greaney, Thomas J, 1940, Ap 10,25:2
Greany, John, 1903, D 25,7:7
Grearson, Chipman E, 1949, Ag 10,21:4
Greason, E Spencer, 1954, D 30,17:5
Greason, Edgar C Mrs, 1960, Je 30,29:5
Greason, Edgar C Sr, 1940, Ja 13,15:4
Greason, John R, 1941, My 31,11:5
Greason, Murray, 1960, Ja 2,6:4
Greason, William, 1948, Mr 25,27:1
Greathouse, Charles H, 1948, My 26,25:5
Greaves, Arthur (funl, O 20,11:3),(por), 1915, O 19, 11:3
Greaves, Arthur Mrs, 1901, Jl 17,7:5; 1920, S 26,22:4
Greaves, Charles, 1942, Je 17,23:2
Greaves, Donald L, 1953, Jl 24,13:2
Greaves, Frederick T, 1953, Ag 24,23:4
Greaves, George E Mrs, 1952, F 16,13:4
Greaves, Harrison A, 1939, D 16,17:3
Greaves, John C Mrs, 1965, Je 18,35:3
Greaves, Mary Lady (Mrs B A Blanger), 1955, F 24,15:1
Greaves, Richard P, 1948, My 1,15:4
Greaves, Valerian E, 1939, Je 4,49:2
Greaves, Victor C Mrs, 1941, Jl 8,19:2
Greaves, Walter, 1943, N 24,21:3
Greaves, William, 1955, D 25,48:3
Greavette, Thomas, 1958, Ag 29,23:1
Greaza, Walter N Mrs (H Ambrose), 1966, N 12, 29:2
Greb, George H, 1953, My 15,23:2
Grebe, Earl C, 1957, Ag 14,25:5
Grebe, Harriett S Mrs, 1948, Je 5,15:4
Grebe, Henry C, 1952, My 26,23:4
Grebenshchikov, Ilya, 1953, F 12,27:3
Grebenstchikoff, George, 1964, Ja 17,43:3
Greber, Pierre, 1968, Je 5,3:4
Grebert, Herbert J, 1946, Ja 9,23:3
Greble, E S J, 1931, O 1,27:3
Greble, Edwin S Jr, 1947, Ja 2,27:4
Greble, Edwin S Mrs, 1947, N 2,73:1
Greble, Sarah, 1880, Jl 30,3:3
Grebneaire, Christophel L, 1958, Ja 4,15:4
Grece, Phil W, 1942, Ag 20,19:2
Grechen, Henri, 1938, O 6,23:2
Greco, Andrew, 1952, Ap 12,11:5
Greco, Egisto del, 1947, Mr 7,25:1
Greco, Gaetano, 1943, Ja 9,13:4
Greco, Johnny (funl, D 16,56:2), 1954, D 13,36:5
Greco, Joseph, 1949, D 20,31:2
Greco, Joseph R, 1958, S 9,35:3
Gredig, John, 1945, Jl 20,19:4
Greechan, Hugh J, 1938, Ja 18,23:3
Greef, Ernest F Mrs, 1952, D 9,33:4
Greeff, Charles A, 1961, My 18,35:4
Greeff, Enno, 1937, F 26,21:4
Greeff, Ernest F, 1921, F 18,11:4
Greeff, J G William, 1954, Jl 29,23:3
Greehy, John Mrs, 1939, O 5,23:2

Greelaw, Frank M, 1955, Ap 6,29:3
Greeley, Agnes R, 1967, S 13,44:4
Greeley, Alwyn W, 1945, Jl 27,15:5
Greeley, Arthur H, 1956, D 25,25:5
Greeley, David, 1911, D 17,II,13:4
Greeley, Eddy H (por), 1938, Ap 12,23:3
Greeley, Edwin S Gen, 1920, Ja 11,22:3
Greeley, Emma, 1940, Ja 7,48:4
Greeley, George E, 1948, S 15,31:1
Greeley, Harold D, 1964, Jl 30,27:4
Greeley, Harold D Mrs, 1965, N 24,39:2
Greeley, Harriett, 1940, D 6,23:3
Greeley, Horace (funl, N 2,4:6, D 5,8:1; trb, D 3,8:3), 1872, N 30,4:6
Greeley, Horace, 1950, Je 11,92:7
Greeley, Horace Mrs, 1872, O 31,6:7
Greeley, James A, 1956, Ap 28,17:5
Greeley, Jean M (Mother Jean Marie), 1957, S 27, 19:4
Greeley, Leslie C, 1950, Jl 31,17:5
Greeley, Samuel A, 1968, F 6,43:2
Greeley, William, 1952, S 18,29:3
Greeley, William B, 1955, D 2,27:2
Greeley, William B Mrs, 1949, O 30,86:1
Greeley, William R, 1966, O 12,43:3
Greely, A W, 1935, O 21,19:1
Greely, Ida (Mrs N Smith), 1882, Ap 12,8:2
Greeman, Louis W, 1949, Ag 4,23:2
Green, A E, 1940, O 3,25:4
Green, A K, 1935, Ap 12,23:4
Green, Aaron S, 1941, S 10,23:5
Green, Abner (A Greenberg), 1959, S 7,13:8
Green, Addison L, 1942, Je 26,21:5
Green, Addison Mrs, 1955, O 21,27:3
Green, Adolf, 1938, Ag 13,13:3
Green, Adolphus W Mrs, 1912, O 19,11:5
Green, Adolphus Williamson (funl, Mr 11,21:4), 1917, Mr 9,7:3
Green, Alanson Harvey Prof, 1914, Jl 16,9:6
Green, Albert, 1943, O 19,19:5
Green, Albert B, 1955, Mr 2,27:2
Green, Albert L, 1957, Je 23,84:7
Green, Alex C, 1949, Je 12,76:4
Green, Alexander, 1907, F 25,9:6
Green, Alfred E, 1960, S 6,33:4
Green, Alfred G, 1937, Mr 3,23:4
Green, Alfred M, 1954, Ap 17,13:6
Green, Alice, 1950, Jl 4,17:3
Green, Alice Mrs, 1929, My 29,31:3
Green, Allen P, 1956, Je 11,31:6
Green, Alonzo P, 1942, S 19,15:3
Green, Alvah, 1943, N 21,56:1
Green, Andrew H, 1947, Ap 18,22:2
Green, Anna M B Mrs, 1940, Mr 29,21:3
Green, Anna R Mrs, 1939, Ag 9,17:3
Green, Anna Van R Mrs, 1937, Mr 16,23:3
Green, Archie C, 1948, Ap 15,25:4
Green, Arthur C, 1950, N 1,35:4
Green, Arthur N, 1957, D 11,31:4
Green, Arthur W, 1939, Ap 29,17:6; 1943, Ja 28,19:2
Green, Ashbel, 1954, Ja 19,25:3
Green, Augustus, 1882, S 22,2:2
Green, B F Mrs, 1949, Ag 28,73:1
Green, Benjamin, 1963, D 23,25:3
Green, Benjamin H, 1937, S 6,17:5
Green, Bernard I, 1951, Ap 10,27:3
Green, Bernard L, 1952, Mr 1,15:3
Green, Bernard W, 1952, Je 19,27:2
Green, Bert, 1948, O 6,29:3
Green, Bertrand W, 1963, N 3,89:3
Green, Bud Mrs, 1965, N 29,35:2
Green, Burton, 1922, N 18,15:5
Green, C Douglass, 1953, Jl 26,69:1
Green, C L, 1884, F 17,3:4
Green, Caleb S Mrs, 1909, Jl 25,7:7
Green, Catherine, 1903, Ag 20,9:6
Green, Cecil, 1951, Jl 30,21:2
Green, Charles, 1942, N 16,19:1; 1955, Ja 17,23:3
Green, Charles A, 1944, My 8,19:6
Green, Charles C, 1965, Jl 18,68:2
Green, Charles E, 1938, F 11,23:4; 1967, D 26,33:2
Green, Charles H, 1907, Ap 29,9:6
Green, Charles Henry, 1908, Jl 20,9:6
Green, Charles P, 1958, Jl 23,27:4
Green, Charles S Sr, 1961, My 23,39:2
Green, Charles T, 1939, Mr 29,23:2
Green, Charles W, 1952, Je 10,27:2
Green, Clark, 1941, O 10,29:4
Green, Clifford F Mrs, 1944, O 28,15:6
Green, Clyde C, 1946, Mr 27,27:4
Green, D C, 1884, O 10,2:4
Green, Daniel C, 1944, Jl 3,11:6
Green, David S, 1952, F 11,25:5
Green, Delon F, 1942, Je 29,15:6
Green, Denis, 1954, N 7,88:2
Green, Doron, 1949, N 1,27:5
Green, Dorothy, 1961, Ja 15,86:7
Green, Dorothy (Mrs N November), 1963, N 18,33:5
Green, Duff Gen, 1875, Je 11,1:7
Green, Dwight H (funl plans, F 23,92:2), 1958, F 21, 23:1
Green, E H R, 1936, Je 9,23:4
Green, E H R Mrs (will, My 2,21:4), 1950, Ap 12, 27:4
Green, Earl W, 1954, Ag 31,21:5
Green, Edgar L, 1953, D 25,17:3
Green, Edward, 1902, Mr 20,9:5; 1951, S 1,11:6
Green, Edward B, 1950, F 13,21:3
Green, Edward E, 1938, Jl 1,19:4
Green, Edward F, 1952, Ag 14,23:2
Green, Edward H, 1963, N 19,41:1
Green, Edward H 2d, 1959, Mr 21,21:2
Green, Edward L, 1937, Mr 14,II,8:4
Green, Edward M, 1944, Ag 13,36:1
Green, Eleanor B, 1954, Ap 14,29:5
Green, Eleanor M (Princess Viggo), 1966, Jl 4,15:1
Green, Elizabeth A, 1941, Mr 11,23:4
Green, Elizabeth C, 1949, Mr 23,27:2
Green, Elmer A, 1940, My 5,52:1
Green, Elmer E, 1944, Ag 4,13:5
Green, Elmer J, 1943, Je 4,21:2
Green, Elmer S, 1947, Ja 23,23:5
Green, Elmore C, 1938, F 9,19:2
Green, Ely, 1968, Ap 29,43:3
Green, Ernest, 1949, Je 17,23:4
Green, Ervine J, 1949, D 2,29:3
Green, Ethelbert, 1962, O 31,37:4
Green, F L, 1930, D 18,25:1
Green, F Warren, 1956, N 18,89:2
Green, Fitzhugh, 1947, D 3,25:3
Green, Francis H, 1951, Ja 24,27:5
Green, Francis S, 1942, Je 25,23:3
Green, Frank, 1949, N 30,27:1
Green, Frank A, 1951, D 23,23:1
Green, Frank B, 1943, F 9,23:4
Green, Frank C, 1949, Mr 13,76:5
Green, Frank D, 1955, Je 14,29:1
Green, Frank K, 1938, Ap 27,23:2
Green, Franklin A, 1914, My 1,13:6
Green, Fred, 1940, Ag 4,33:1
Green, Fred C, 1960, Jl 26,29:4
Green, Fred J, 1963, S 21,21:1
Green, Fred W, 1949, Jl 16,13:5
Green, Frederick, 1953, Ap 19,90:2; 1956, Jl 29,65
Green, Frederick L, 1944, Je 6,17:3; 1953, Ap 16,2
Green, Gay, 1951, Je 10,93:2
Green, George, 1938, Ap 25,15:1
Green, George A, 1923, S 15,15:6; 1949, F 23,27:1
Green, George A L, 1949, Ag 11,23:5
Green, George C, 1947, F 27,21:1
Green, George D, 1940, O 17,25:4
Green, George E, 1917, Ja 17,9:3
Green, George F, 1964, Ag 3,25:2
Green, George G, 1938, Ap 15,20:4; 1951, O 18,2 1958, S 13,19:6
Green, George G Col, 1925, F 22,19:2
Green, George M, 1956, Ja 20,23:1
Green, George R, 1948, D 15,33:5
Green, George S, 1945, Ja 7,38:4
Green, George T Mrs, 1948, My 2,76:5
Green, George W, 1905, Ap 4,11:6; 1937, F 1,19: 1947, O 19,64:4; 1947, O 29,28:3; 1962, Jl 24,2
Green, George Walton, 1903, D 15,9:4
Green, Grafton, 1947, Ja 28,23:3
Green, Griswold, 1961, Ap 5,37:4
Green, H, 1878, Jl 16,2:5
Green, H W, 1876, D 21,4:6
Green, Halcott P, 1949, Ag 3,23:3
Green, Harold A, 1959, Ja 19,27:3
Green, Harold C, 1950, S 3,32:5
Green, Harold L, 1951, Ap 15,92:3
Green, Harold T, 1967, F 27,29:1
Green, Harry, 1958, Je 7,87:1; 1966, Mr 24,39:4
Green, Harry F, 1941, F 28,19:3
Green, Harry J, 1958, Jl 2,27:1
Green, Harry T, 1950, D 21,29:3
Green, Harry T S, 1942, Ag 29,15:3
Green, Heatley, 1947, S 22,23:2
Green, Helen, 1958, N 23,88:2
Green, Henderson M, 1941, Mr 12,21:3
Green, Henry, 1948, Ja 8,25:2
Green, Henry C, 1946, O 2,29:5
Green, Henry L, 1951, Je 8,27:3
Green, Henry W, 1939, N 25,17:6
Green, Herbert G, 1950, S 7,31:5
Green, Herbert P, 1920, Ag 24,9:3
Green, Hetty Mrs (por), 1916, Jl 4,11:3
Green, Homer M, 1948, Mr 8,23:3
Green, Horace, 1943, Ap 21,25:2; 1943, N 15,
Green, Horace Dr, 1866, D 3,4:7
Green, Howard C, 1940, Ap 6,17:5
Green, Howard Mrs, 1945, My 25,19:1
Green, Howard W, 1959, Jl 9,27:2
Green, Hyman, 1968, S 17,94:3
Green, Irving I, 1965, N 15,37:4
Green, Isaac, 1937, S 4,15:6
Green, Isaac H, 1937, Mr 26,21:4
Green, Isadore L Dr, 1937, Jl 15,19:3
Green, J Larned, 1954, F 3,23:3
Green, J R, 1883, Mr 8,5:4
Green, Jackie, 1952, Ag 4,15:4
Green, Jacob, 1947, S 21,60:7
Green, James, 1955, S 1,23:3
Green, James A, 1945, Ap 3,19:4; 1955, F 19,
Green, James B P, 1966, F 20,88:3
Green, James F, 1968, Je 15,35:1

Green, James G Rear-Adm, 1909, F 17,9:4
Green, James H, 1953, Ap 3,23:3
Green, James Hudson, 1903, Jl 27,7:6
Green, James J, 1949, F 2,27:3; 1959, Jl 29,29:4
Green, James L, 1942, N 7,15:4
Green, James Monroe Dr, 1920, N 2,17:5
Green, James Mrs, 1956, Ap 4,29:2
Green, James O Dr, 1924, Mr 11,19:3
Green, James O Jr Maj, 1937, D 15,25:2
Green, James O Mrs, 1922, My 27,13:5
Green, Jesse B Mrs, 1947, Mr 26,25:3
Green, Jesse C Dr, 1920, Jl 27,13:5
Green, jno T, 1960, My 12,35:3
Green, John, 1914, S 15,11:6; 1949, Ap 8,26:2; 1952, My 10,21:4; 1957, F 21,27:2; 1960, Mr 9,33:4
Green, John A Gen, 1872, Je 21,1:7
Green, John Brenner Rev, 1905, Ap 7,9:6
Green, John Dr, 1865, O 22,5:3; 1913, D 9,11:4
Green, John E, 1966, Mr 19,29:5
Green, John E Jr, 1947, N 10,29:1
Green, John English, 1909, S 4,7:5
Green, John F, 1945, Ap 8,35:1
Green, John J, 1942, Ja 21,17:3
Green, John Kneeland, 1922, D 1,17:4
Green, John Mrs, 1956, F 23,27:3
Green, John O J, 1942, O 6,23:2
Green, John P, 1924, Mr 10,15:4
Green, John W, 1947, My 18,60:4; 1950, Jl 29,13:6; 1954, O 4,27:4
Green, Joseph, 1939, O 18,25:1; 1946, Je 13,27:2; 1959, F 23,23:2
Green, Joseph A, 1963, O 30,39:4
Green, Joseph I (por), 1939, Je 1,25:3
Green, Joseph J, 1958, Ap 8,29:4
Green, Joseph M, 1966, O 20,43:3
Green, Joseph P, 1950, S 9,17:6
Green, Joseph R, 1963, S 3,33:1
Green, Kane S, 1957, Ja 30,29:2
Green, Kenneth, 1961, Mr 20,29:2
Green, L Kenneth, 1945, Ja 23,19:4
Green, Laurence H, 1956, Ag 3,17:6
Green, Laurence J, 1938, F 17,21:3
Green, Lawrence E, 1952, Mr 28,24:3
Green, Lemuel B, 1925, Ag 23,7:4
Green, Leo, 1963, D 21,23:1
Green, Leon, 1950, Ag 29,27:2
Green, Levi, 1964, My 2,27:5
Green, Lewis H, 1941, O 27,17:4
Green, Lilian, 1901, Jl 21,3:1
Green, Lincoln, 1940, Je 20,23:4
Green, Lonsdale Jr Mrs, 1954, Mr 30,27:4
Green, Louis, 1945, S 11,23:5; 1946, Ag 29,27:5; 1955, Jl 15,21:5; 1957, Ja 18,22:5
Green, Louis A, 1968, O 25,47:5
Green, Louis Mrs, 1956, D 7,27:1
Green, Lowell, 1946, Jl 5,19:2
Green, Lt-Col, 1864, Je 4,9:4
Green, Lucien B, 1945, F 28,23:3
Green, Lucy M, 1909, F 7,11:7
Green, Mabel D, 1949, D 10,17:2
Green, Manford D, 1938, N 12,15:4
Green, Margaret S Mrs, 1941, My 13,23:1
Green, Martin, 1917, Ag 2,9:4
Green, Martin (por), 1939, D 9,15:5
Green, Mary A Mrs, 1937, O 3,II,8:4
Green, Mary M F Mrs, 1942, Ag 7,17:5
Green, Mary R Mrs, 1941, Jl 20,30:4
Green, Maxwell M, 1941, Jl 30,17:2
Green, Melissa Mrs, 1940, Je 28,19:2
Green, Merrill H Mrs, 1946, Mr 1,21:2
Green, Mildred C, 1951, F 25,87:5
Green, Morris, 1963, My 23,37:5
Green, Myer, 1956, Jl 7,13:6
Green, Nathan W, 1955, Ap 23,19:5
Green, Nathan W Mrs, 1942, Ja 30,19:3
Green, Nathaniel Com, 1873, Mr 24,1:7
Green, Nelson, 1955, N 12,19:4
Green, Norvin Dr, 1893, F 13,1:7
Green, Norvin H (will, Ap 23,8:6), 1955, Ap 13,29:5
Green, Norvin Mrs, 1906, N 7,9:5
Green, O M, 1959, O 4,87:1
Green, Oliver W Mrs, 1951, Ja 6,15:1
Green, Orla R, 1954, My 27,27:1
Green, Oscar, 1966, Je 4,29:4
Green, Oscar Mrs, 1924, Jl 24,13:4
Green, Ottmer J, 1955, Ap 3,86:3
Green, Paul, 1947, Je 14,15:2
Green, Paul C, 1951, Ag 1,23:6
Green, Paul E, 1937, Mr 13,19:2
Green, Percy, 1951, Jl 29,69:2
Green, Percy D, 1939, My 22,17:3
Green, Perry L, 1957, Jl 30,23:1
Green, Peter, 1942, Ja 15,19:4
Green, Phil J, 1948, D 21,25:3
Green, Philip A, 1947, Jl 29,21:4
Green, Polly, 1949, Je 20,19:3
Green, Ralph W, 1946, Je 17,21:5
Green, Rebecca A Mrs (will), 1906, Ja 19,10:6
Green, Robert, 1955, F 11,23:2
Green, Robert C, 1958, S 10,33:4
Green, Robert G, 1947, S 8,21:3
Green, Robert L, 1952, Je 23,19:5
Green, Robert M, 1956, O 24,37:6
Green, Robert R, 1948, Jl 9,19:3; 1959, Ag 27,27:5
Green, Robert W, 1957, F 19,31:4
Green, Ronald C, 1951, Ja 6,15:3
Green, Rosa Mrs, 1914, D 12,15:7
Green, Rosie Silbert Mrs, 1924, Jl 26,9:6
Green, Roy M, 1948, Ja 24,16:2
Green, Rudy, 1949, Mr 23,27:5
Green, S F Dr, 1884, My 30,5:1
Green, Samuel, 1916, Ja 28,9:5; 1949, Ag 19,1:3; 1950, My 26,23:1
Green, Samuel A Dr, 1918, D 6,15:6
Green, Samuel H, 1956, S 27,35:4
Green, Samuel L, 1957, My 3,27:1
Green, Samuel M Mrs, 1948, Jl 6,23:2
Green, Samuel Mrs, 1924, Ap 4,19:3
Green, Samuel T, 1949, Ja 9,73:1
Green, Samuel W, 1941, D 27,19:2
Green, Sarah Mrs, 1955, Ag 19,19:3
Green, Seth, 1888, Ag 20,5:2
Green, Seward T, 1941, Ap 9,25:4
Green, Seward T Mrs, 1954, O 24,89:1
Green, Sheldon R, 1959, O 1,35:2
Green, Sherman D, 1950, My 29,17:4
Green, Signey L, 1966, S 16,37:1
Green, Stanley H, 1955, Ap 28,29:4
Green, Stephen H Rev, 1919, Jl 26,9:6
Green, Stockton, 1956, D 28,21:3
Green, Thad K, 1909, O 10,13:6
Green, Theodore F, 1966, My 20,47:1
Green, Theron Benson Dr, 1923, Jl 24,21:4
Green, Thomas, 1950, My 17,29:2
Green, Thomas D, 1954, My 17,23:5
Green, Thomas F, 1939, Ja 24,19:5
Green, Thomas J, 1947, Jl 20,44:4
Green, Thomas Mrs, 1948, N 13,15:4
Green, Thomas S, 1953, Ja 26,19:2
Green, Tom R, 1950, Jl 12,29:3
Green, Vanderbilt, 1942, S 7,19:3
Green, Vanderbilt T Mrs, 1943, Ja 4,15:4
Green, Vivian, 1940, Ja 5,19:2
Green, W, 1881, O 23,9:2
Green, Wallace, 1957, D 7,21:2
Green, Walter C, 1950, My 28,45:1
Green, Walter J, 1951, Je 19,29:1
Green, Walter J Mrs, 1945, S 28,21:4
Green, Walter Kerr, 1911, N 11,13:5
Green, Walter L, 1962, Mr 27,37:1
Green, Walton A, 1954, D 4,17:6
Green, Ward, 1956, Ja 23,25:4
Green, Warren E, 1945, Ap 28,15:6
Green, Warren K, 1964, F 5,35:4
Green, Warren L (funl, Ag 15,11:4), 1919, Ag 13,11:3
Green, Wendell E, 1959, Ag 24,21:5
Green, Wharton, 1957, Ap 20,17:4
Green, Wharton Col, 1910, Ag 7,II,9:4
Green, Wharton Mrs, 1946, Jl 8,29:2
Green, Wilfred, 1960, Ap 20,39:4
Green, Will J, 1946, N 23,15:5
Green, William, 1925, F 25,19:2; 1952, N 22,1:2
Green, William A Mrs, 1938, N 16,23:1
Green, William B Sr, 1945, Ap 8,36:2
Green, William D, 1938, My 6,21:6; 1953, Ap 11,17:4; 1957, N 18,31:4
Green, William G, 1965, F 24,41:5
Green, William G Mrs, 1954, Je 7,23:2
Green, William H, 1962, F 4,82:3
Green, William J Jr (funl plans, D 24,17:1; funl, D 25,33:1), 1963, D 22,34:2
Green, William Lawrence, 1924, F 9,13:5
Green, William Mrs, 1953, D 14,31:2
Green, William R, 1940, My 25,17:6; 1947, Je 12,25:6
Green, William S, 1947, D 15,25:2; 1949, Je 4,13:6
Green, William T, 1946, F 12,28:1
Greenabaum, Arnold, 1940, My 26,35:1
Greenacre, Isaiah T, 1944, Ap 10,19:5
Greenalch, William H, 1946, My 17,21:4
Greenall, Thomas, 1937, D 23,21:5
Greenan, John T, 1961, F 3,23:1
Greenawald, George C, 1940, Je 19,23:4
Greenawald, John A, 1957, My 11,21:4
Greenawald, Paul B, 1952, S 5,27:1
Greenawalt, David F, 1938, N 13,45:3
Greenawalt, Elmer Ellsworth, 1920, Mr 9,11:5
Greenawalt, John E, 1964, Mr 13,33:2
Greenaway, Francis W, 1953, N 11,31:1
Greenaway, Kate, 1901, N 8,9:5
Greenaway, M Emily, 1961, D 8,37:2
Greenaway, Percy, 1956, N 27,38:7
Greenaway, William F, 1944, Jl 18,19:1
Greenbacker, Charles F, 1965, F 22,21:2
Greenbaum, Abe, 1956, F 29,31:4
Greenbaum, Adolf, 1951, Jl 15,61:1
Greenbaum, Bernard A, 1965, O 28,43:4
Greenbaum, Carl Mrs, 1963, S 18,39:2
Greenbaum, Charles, 1961, Ag 19,18:1
Greenbaum, Charles Mrs, 1947, Ja 29,25:4
Greenbaum, Emmanuel S, 1939, Mr 27,15:4
Greenbaum, Ferdinand, 1907, Ap 19,9:5
Greenbaum, George H Mrs, 1955, S 9,23:2
Greenbaum, Isidor, 1954, D 9,33:1
Greenbaum, Jack, 1944, Je 25,29:2
Greenbaum, Jacob E, 1947, My 18,60:2
Greenbaum, John, 1947, Ag 15,17:5
Greenbaum, Joseph, 1946, S 17,7:3
Greenbaum, Lawrence S, 1951, Ag 29,25:1
Greenbaum, Leo, 1950, Ag 4,21:4
Greenbaum, Louis, 1946, O 7,31:2; 1948, Ag 12,21:1; 1954, Mr 16,29:3
Greenbaum, Max, 1949, D 9,32:4
Greenbaum, Meyer, 1938, Mr 19,15:2
Greenbaum, S, 1930, Ag 27,21:3
Greenbaum, Samuel, 1937, Je 9,25:6
Greenbaum, Samuel Mrs, 1925, Jl 16,19:6
Greenbaum, Sigmund S, 1949, O 4,27:5
Greenbaum, Solomon, 1944, F 25,17:3
Greenbaum, Solomon Mrs, 1948, F 15,60:4
Greenberg, Abraham (por), 1941, My 11,45:2
Greenberg, Abraham (A Green), 1959, S 7,13:8
Greenberg, Abraham, 1962, O 23,37:5
Greenberg, Abraham S, 1951, N 8,29:3
Greenberg, Albert M, 1960, N 5,2:7
Greenberg, Annie Mrs, 1951, My 30,21:3
Greenberg, Archie H, 1961, My 25,37:1
Greenberg, Arnold, 1938, S 2,17:5
Greenberg, Ben, 1943, Je 23,21:6
Greenberg, Benjamin Mrs, 1962, O 6,25:5
Greenberg, Bernard, 1954, Je 15,29:3; 1961, Je 21,37:2
Greenberg, Charles, 1956, F 29,31:4
Greenberg, David, 1944, F 29,17:3; 1959, F 26,31:5; 1959, Jl 25,17:6
Greenberg, David B, 1968, Mr 26,45:1
Greenberg, David Mrs, 1951, Jl 6,23:1
Greenberg, Edward L, 1956, Ap 19,31:2
Greenberg, Emanuel, 1962, O 5,36:4
Greenberg, Emanuel Mrs, 1951, Ap 22,89:2
Greenberg, Emil, 1945, My 12,13:5
Greenberg, George Mrs (Addie Williams), 1968, Jl 26,33:4
Greenberg, Gerson G, 1959, My 24,89:1
Greenberg, Harry, 1951, Ag 10,15:4; 1956, F 15,31:3; 1961, N 2,37:4; 1965, Je 27,64:8
Greenberg, Harry M, 1940, N 18,19:2
Greenberg, Harry Mrs, 1952, Ap 21,21:5
Greenberg, Harry P, 1967, D 18,47:2
Greenberg, Hayim, 1953, Mr 15,93:1
Greenberg, Henry, 1946, Jl 24,27:3; 1956, Ag 15,29:3
Greenberg, Henry C (funl, Mr 12,33:4), 1965, Mr 10, 41:3
Greenberg, Henry D, 1953, O 4,89:2
Greenberg, Henry M, 1919, Je 8,20:5
Greenberg, Herman, 1959, Ap 7,33:1
Greenberg, Herry Mrs, 1966, Ja 10,25:2
Greenberg, Irving, 1951, N 11,90:8
Greenberg, Isaac E, 1939, Jl 23,29:3
Greenberg, Israel, 1951, Ap 16,25:5; 1967, Ap 21,39:1
Greenberg, Jacob, 1949, F 1,25:5; 1963, Mr 22,9:5
Greenberg, Jonas S, 1955, D 6,38:1
Greenberg, Joseph, 1959, Ap 4,19:5; 1962, N 21,33:1
Greenberg, Joseph J, 1963, Je 17,25:2
Greenberg, Joseph L, 1952, Ja 4,23:1
Greenberg, Joseph L Mrs, 1948, N 10,29:4; 1956, Ag 30,25:4
Greenberg, Joseph S, 1964, Ag 20,29:4
Greenberg, Kune, 1942, D 31,15:3
Greenberg, Leo, 1963, Jl 7,52:8
Greenberg, Louis, 1937, O 24,II,9:2; 1949, Ja 19,27:2
Greenberg, Louis A, 1966, Ap 4,31:2
Greenberg, M Bernard, 1953, Ag 20,27:5
Greenberg, Maurice S, 1942, Je 1,13:2
Greenberg, Max, 1947, Ap 18,21:1; 1960, Ja 12,47:4
Greenberg, Max Mrs, 1959, Ja 5,29:6
Greenberg, Morris, 1949, Je 24,23:4; 1957, Jl 5,17:1; 1960, My 26,33:1
Greenberg, Morris L, 1964, Ja 12,92:5
Greenberg, Morris Mrs, 1952, D 4,35:4
Greenberg, Nathan, 1948, Ag 12,22:2
Greenberg, Nathaniel, 1963, Ap 8,47:5
Greenberg, Noah, 1966, Ja 10,25:2
Greenberg, Samuel, 1939, Je 22,23:6; 1952, D 11,33:4; 1954, Jl 29,23:2
Greenberg, Samuel Mrs, 1957, Jl 22,19:4; 1967, Ja 12, 39:2
Greenberg, Saul, 1946, Je 28,21:3
Greenberger, Arthur J, 1964, F 6,30:1
Greenberger, David, 1957, Mr 1,23:4
Greenberger, Jacob, 1951, S 27,31:2
Greenbert, Isaac, 1943, O 15,19:4
Greenbie, Sydney, 1960, Je 10,31:1
Greenblat, Abraham, 1962, S 16,86:6
Greenblatt, Alfred, 1949, Ja 18,23:1
Greenblatt, Isaac Mrs, 1952, Ag 26,25:4
Greenblatt, Martin, 1955, D 1,35:2
Greenblatt, Max, 1951, F 13,31:2
Greenblatt, Oscar, 1953, O 27,27:3
Greenblatt, William, 1938, S 1,23:5
Greenblau, Solomon, 1938, Ag 31,15:1
Greenbrush, Samuel Mrs, 1949, Ag 14,68:3
Greenburg, Albert, 1952, D 13,21:3
Greenburg, Harry, 1956, S 8,17:1
Greenburg, Harry Mrs, 1951, Jl 18,29:4
Greenburg, Rose Mrs, 1953, N 22,88:2
Greendlinger, Leo Mrs, 1958, O 14,37:4
Greendlinger, Samuel, 1968, O 7,47:4
Greendorfer, Sidney Mrs, 1968, Ag 12,35:4
Greene, A Furman, 1960, Ag 3,29:4
Greene, A Lawrence, 1955, Ag 16,49:3

Greene, A Rev, 1881, O 21,8:5
Greene, Abe J Mrs, 1945, Mr 27,19:2
Greene, Adele, 1948, O 5,25:2
Greene, Ainslie W, 1945, O 19,23:5
Greene, Alex, 1954, D 4,17:2
Greene, Alfred D, 1949, O 13,27:4
Greene, Allan R, 1963, My 28,37:1
Greene, Allister, 1923, Mr 10,13:4
Greene, Alliston, 1948, Je 25,23:3
Greene, Amy B, 1938, Mr 3,21:4
Greene, Arthur M Jr, 1953, S 4,15:1
Greene, Arthur M Maj, 1915, My 20,11:5
Greene, Arthur M Mrs, 1949, Ja 12,27:2
Greene, Balcomb Mrs, 1956, N 27,38:1
Greene, Bartlett, 1946, My 17,22:3
Greene, Bella D, 1950, My 12,27:2
Greene, Belle, 1950, Jl 3,14:6
Greene, Burch, 1954, F 2,27:1
Greene, C G, 1886, S 28,5:4
Greene, Carleton, 1942, N 15,58:2
Greene, Caroline B, 1955, D 4,88:3
Greene, Caroline F Mrs, 1937, D 12,II,9:1
Greene, Charles A, 1909, S 28,9:6; 1955, F 23,27:4
Greene, Charles E Prof, 1903, O 18,7:6
Greene, Charles F, 1948, D 9,33:3
Greene, Charles J, 1947, O 29,27:3
Greene, Charles L (will), 1946, Jl 17,28:5
Greene, Charles N, 1925, Jl 8,17:5
Greene, Charles Thurston Maj, 1923, Ag 20,11:4
Greene, Chris, 1944, O 21,17:4
Greene, Clay M Mrs, 1949, Je 28,27:2
Greene, Clayton W (Sept 20), 1965, O 11,61:2
Greene, Cordelia A Dr, 1905, Ja 29,7:4
Greene, Dan, 1946, Ap 3,25:4
Greene, Daniel C, 1941, Ap 6,49:2
Greene, Daniel Crosby Dr, 1913, S 16,11:6
Greene, David, 1960, S 4,68:8
Greene, De Witt C, 1938, N 27,48:7
Greene, Douglass T, 1964, Je 15,29:3
Greene, E W C (see also D 28), 1877, D 30,1:6
Greene, Edward A, 1937, N 28,II,9:2; 1942, Mr 13,19:2
Greene, Edward B, 1957, O 22,33:3
Greene, Edward J, 1941, D 4,25:5; 1957, F 7,27:5
Greene, Edward L, 1950, Mr 16,32:3; 1952, S 29,23:3
Greene, Edward Lee Dr, 1915, N 11,13:4
Greene, Edward M, 1956, Mr 2,23:3
Greene, Edward W, 1967, O 21,31:1
Greene, Edwin D, 1960, Ap 10,86:8
Greene, Edwin F, 1953, D 9,11:1
Greene, Elbridge G, 1946, Jl 20,13:3
Greene, Elbridge G Mrs, 1943, Ag 10,19:2
Greene, Eliza H Mrs, 1906, N 22,6:4
Greene, Ella C, 1945, Ap 4,21:2
Greene, Elmer W Jr, 1964, D 28,29:2
Greene, Emma H Mrs, 1952, Ag 7,21:2
Greene, Emma K, 1951, Ja 7,78:5
Greene, Ernest W, 1967, N 11,33:4
Greene, Eugene L, 1956, Jl 17,23:2
Greene, Eugene L Mrs, 1956, Ap 17,31:4
Greene, Evarts B, 1947, Je 25,26:2
Greene, Evie, 1917, O 5,11:6
Greene, F Harry, 1951, Ap 15,93:1
Greene, Floyd L, 1954, Ap 15,29:3
Greene, Francis Vinton Maj-Gen, 1921, My 16,15:3
Greene, Frank, 1946, O 28,27:4
Greene, Frank C Mrs, 1953, Je 18,29:3
Greene, Frank L Mrs, 1949, D 23,21:4
Greene, Frank Mrs, 1947, F 20,25:2
Greene, Frank N, 1939, F 3,15:4
Greene, Frank R, 1940, Ja 21,34:5
Greene, Frank W Mrs, 1954, O 20,29:2
Greene, Franklin, 1938, Mr 31,23:5
Greene, Fred J, 1948, F 22,48:2
Greene, Fred R, 1937, S 11,17:4
Greene, Fred S, 1946, My 11,27:1
Greene, Frederic S, 1943, Ap 11,49:1
Greene, Frederick, 1948, Je 16,29:2
Greene, Frederick D, 1962, O 19,31:1
Greene, Frederick S, 1939, Mr 27,15:1
Greene, G F Rev Dr, 1926, N 20,17:4
Greene, G W, 1883, F 3,5:4
Greene, Gardiner, 1925, F 11,21:2
Greene, George C Mrs, 1952, Jl 31,23:4
Greene, George D, 1955, Mr 25,23:4
Greene, George E, 1938, F 14,17:4; 1943, Ag 2,15:3
Greene, George J, 1955, Je 5,84:7
Greene, George M, 1948, F 9,17:3; 1961, D 24,36:1
Greene, George M Col, 1912, Ja 17,13:6
Greene, George Mrs, 1957, Ap 20,17:5
Greene, George S Jr, 1922, D 24,20:3
Greene, George T, 1941, Ag 4,13:4
Greene, George W Judge, 1925, Ja 29,19:3
Greene, Gustave, 1960, F 12,28:1
Greene, Guy S, 1942, F 21,19:3
Greene, Guy T, 1947, S 10,27:5
Greene, H A, 1878, Jl 10,1:2; 1903, Je 24,9:6
Greene, Hamilton W, 1966, O 21,41:4
Greene, Harold C, 1950, Mr 4,17:5
Greene, Harris H, 1965, Ap 30,36:6
Greene, Harry, 1950, D 31,42:6; 1959, Jl 11,19:5
Greene, Harry A, 1924, Ja 22,17:4
Greene, Harvey S, 1943, F 21,32:5
Greene, Henry A, 1950, Jl 11,31:3
Greene, Henry A Maj-Gen, 1921, Ag 20,7:5
Greene, Henry C, 1951, D 30,24:3
Greene, Henry F, 1915, D 21,13:4
Greene, Henry Irving, 1919, S 24,17:6
Greene, Herbert E, 1942, S 4,23:5
Greene, Herbert E Mrs, 1944, Je 29,23:3
Greene, Herbert M, 1962, Ap 17,35:2
Greene, Herbert Wilbur, 1924, S 26,21:5
Greene, Homer, 1940, N 27,23:3
Greene, Howard, 1956, Jl 12,23:4
Greene, Howard E, 1924, Je 16,15:4
Greene, Howard T, 1958, D 18,2:5
Greene, Irving, 1961, Ja 27,23:1
Greene, Irving H Mrs, 1953, O 18,87:1
Greene, J J, 1941, Mr 1,15:2
Greene, J Walter, 1948, N 23,29:4
Greene, J Warren, 1917, Mr 27,11:4
Greene, Jacob L Col, 1905, Mr 30,9:6
Greene, James A Mrs, 1961, Mr 1,33:3
Greene, James B Jr, 1968, Je 5,47:1
Greene, James E, 1955, Ag 16,23:4
Greene, James F, 1948, D 27,21:1
Greene, James G, 1954, Ja 19,26:3
Greene, James H, 1943, Mr 31,19:1; 1960, F 5,27:4
Greene, James H Mrs, 1946, F 27,25:4
Greene, James S, 1950, S 18,23:5
Greene, James W, 1939, Je 17,15:3
Greene, James W Mrs, 1949, Ag 10,21:1
Greene, Jerome C, 1961, S 12,33:3
Greene, Jerome D Mrs, 1941, Jl 2,21:1
Greene, John, 1942, S 4,24:3
Greene, John H, 1922, S 18,13:3; 1940, Mr 30,15:5; 1951, O 22,23:5
Greene, John H Rev, 1917, Ja 30,9:2
Greene, John J, 1938, Ag 31,15:5
Greene, John L, 1947, Ag 3,53:2
Greene, John M Rev Dr, 1919, Ap 30,11:4
Greene, John P, 1945, N 6,19:5
Greene, John T, 1945, Ag 9,21:4; 1948, Ap 13,27:1
Greene, John W, 1951, D 23,22:7
Greene, Joseph, 1964, F 7,31:3
Greene, Joseph A, 1940, Ag 12,15:3
Greene, Joseph F, 1956, My 3,31:2
Greene, Joseph I, 1953, Je 27,15:3
Greene, Joseph K Rev Dr, 1917, F 17,11:4
Greene, Joseph W, 1950, Mr 7,28:2
Greene, Joseph W Jr, 1939, Je 15,23:4
Greene, Josiah E (por), 1955, Je 14,29:1
Greene, Katherine S Mrs, 1940, Mr 3,45:1
Greene, Kenneth A, 1961, O 22,86:2
Greene, Kenneth E, 1948, F 5,23:5
Greene, Larry C, 1956, Mr 26,29:2
Greene, Larry Mrs, 1956, Ja 19,33:3
Greene, Laurence (funl), 1955, F 13,86:7
Greene, Leo A, 1954, My 22,15:5
Greene, Leonard Mrs, 1965, O 23,31:4
Greene, Lew A, 1966, D 7,47:4
Greene, Lewis D Mrs, 1944, Ap 5,19:6
Greene, Lonsdale Jr, 1960, N 27,86:3
Greene, Louis A, 1953, Ja 26,19:2
Greene, Louis C, 1948, Ag 19,21:5
Greene, Louis D, 1937, F 5,21:2
Greene, Louis S, 1947, N 13,27:2
Greene, Marc T, 1966, S 16,37:3
Greene, Margaret C, 1946, Ag 31,15:5
Greene, Mark H, 1958, Je 5,31:3
Greene, Marshall Winslow, 1921, Mr 25,15:5
Greene, Martin E, 1907, N 5,9:5
Greene, Mary B, 1949, Ap 23,13:2
Greene, Michael F, 1951, O 21,92:5
Greene, Milbury M, 1937, F 17,22:2
Greene, Morris Mrs, 1954, O 16,17:5
Greene, N, 1877, D 1,4:7
Greene, Nathan, 1964, O 31,29:2
Greene, Nathan Mrs, 1962, Je 20,35:1
Greene, Nelson L, 1947, Ja 31,23:2
Greene, O Roy, 1948, N 15,25:1
Greene, Paul B, 1951, Mr 19,28:4
Greene, Peter J, 1944, Jl 30,35:3; 1945, N 13,21:2
Greene, Philip L, 1944, N 14,23:5
Greene, Phillipse E N, 1949, Jl 15,19:5
Greene, Quincy Shaw, 1918, Ap 13,13:5
Greene, Raleigh W, 1954, Ap 30,23:4
Greene, Ralph C, 1958, Ag 29,23:4
Greene, Ralph N, 1941, Ag 2,15:6
Greene, Ransom, 1949, O 5,29:4
Greene, Raymond A, 1958, Jl 27,61:2
Greene, Raymond Austin Col, 1922, Ja 4,13:5
Greene, Richard, 1950, Ap 28,21:5
Greene, Richard Gleason Rev, 1914, Jl 8,9:6
Greene, Richard R, 1951, Jl 24,25:5
Greene, Richard T (por), 1949, O 31,25:1
Greene, Robert, 1965, Mr 13,25:4
Greene, Robert L Mrs, 1955, N 2,35:2
Greene, Robert Mrs, 1964, Ag 31,25:3
Greene, Robert W, 1922, Ap 19,19:4
Greene, Roger, 1924, Je 21,13:5; 1954, N 3,29:1
Greene, Roger S (por), 1947, Mr 29,15:4
Greene, Roscoe M, 1956, D 14,29:2
Greene, Ryland W, 1949, N 20,92:4
Greene, Ryland W Mrs, 1955, Jl 19,27:4
Greene, S Harold, 1937, N 21,II,9:1
Greene, S S Prof, 1883, Ja 25,5:6
Greene, Samuel A, 1944, Ag 30,17:4
Greene, Sarah E Mrs, 1952, Je 21,15:6
Greene, Stephen A, 1949, D 3,15:5
Greene, Theodore A, 1951, Je 10,92:5
Greene, Thomas B, 1938, F 13,II,7:2
Greene, Thomas C, 1961, Je 17,21:5
Greene, Thomas E, 1944, Mr 27,19:4; 1955, Ap 15,
Greene, Thomas G, 1945, Ap 21,13:3
Greene, Thomas G Mrs, 1957, Mr 23,19:4
Greene, Thomas L, 1904, Mr 29,9:6
Greene, Thomas T Sr, 1949, My 1,88:8
Greene, Thomas W, 1952, N 29,17:4
Greene, Van Rennselaer H, 1964, Jl 27,31:5
Greene, Vernon, 1965, Je 7,37:3
Greene, W B Col, 1878, Je 3,5:3
Greene, W Friese, 1921, My 7,11:4
Greene, W W, 1881, S 15,2:1
Greene, Walter D, 1941, F 21,19:4
Greene, Walter T, 1938, Mr 18,19:2
Greene, Warren J, 1954, Ja 14,29:1
Greene, Wilfred A Lord, 1952, Ap 18,25:1
Greene, Will O, 1950, My 10,31:3
Greene, William, 1940, Jl 15,15:5; 1952, S 4,27:5
Greene, William A, 1948, Mr 3,23:3; 1967, Ja 28,2
Greene, William C, 1963, Ap 30,35:2
Greene, William Cornell Col (funl, Ag 8,9:4), 19 Ag 6,II,9:5
Greene, William G, 1962, O 18,39:2
Greene, William H (will), 1947, Je 26,26:1
Greene, William M Mrs, 1955, My 24,31:2
Greene, William M Sr, 1965, O 16,27:3
Greene, William S, 1924, S 23,23:3
Greene, William V, 1960, My 17,37:4
Greene, Winfield W, 1965, Mr 27,27:5
Greenebaum, Alex, 1942, Jl 22,19:2
Greenebaum, Alexander H, 1968, Ja 16,39:2
Greenebaum, Charles L Mrs, 1952, Mr 17,21:4
Greenebaum, David S, 1919, N 6,13:3
Greenebaum, Elias, 1919, Jl 26,9:6
Greenebaum, Frederic, 1948, S 9,27:3
Greenebaum, James E, 1943, Jl 31,13:3
Greenebaum, Jonas, 1947, O 26,68:5
Greenebaum, Leo, 1967, Ja 20,43:1
Greenebaum, Leon C, 1968, Mr 26,45:4
Greenebaum, M Ernest Jr, 1949, Mr 18,25:1
Greenebaum, Max, 1939, S 13,25:4
Greenebaum, Max A, 1951, Mr 2,25:3
Greenell, William J, 1949, Jl 30,15:2
Greener, Alfred W, 1937, Ag 31,23:2
Greenes, Harry, 1951, My 14,25:3
Greenewald, D Frank, 1908, O 29,9:5
Greenewalt, Frank L Mrs, 1950, N 28,31:5
Greeney, Walter A, 1938, D 8,27:3
Greenfield, A E, 1918, D 8,22:3
Greenfield, Abraham L (por), 1941, Jl 26,15:5
Greenfield, Adolph, 1945, F 2,19:4
Greenfield, Albert M (trb, Ja 7,27:4), 1967, Ja
Greenfield, Albert M Mrs, 1949, My 30,13:6
Greenfield, Benjamin, 1952, Ja 3,46:4
Greenfield, Benjamin S, 1944, Ag 18,13:3
Greenfield, Bernard H, 1962, Jl 3,23:5
Greenfield, E T (the Black Swan), 1876, Ap 2,
Greenfield, E T Mrs, 1915, Jl 22,9:5
Greenfield, Edward L Mrs, 1968, Je 23,73:1
Greenfield, Edwin Truman Col, 1920, Ap 4,22:1
Greenfield, Frederick W, 1967, Mr 18,29:4
Greenfield, George H Mrs, 1953, Ag 21,18:3
Greenfield, George S, 1948, S 7,25:1
Greenfield, Goldye, 1950, Jl 28,21:6
Greenfield, Harry, 1944, Ag 17,17:4; 1951, My
Greenfield, Herbert, 1949, Ag 24,25:2
Greenfield, Herman, 1964, D 26,17:4
Greenfield, Hull, 1946, Ja 19,13:5
Greenfield, Hyman, 1946, Jl 30,23:4
Greenfield, Isaac, 1952, D 22,25:3
Greenfield, Jacob, 1956, Ja 16,21:5
Greenfield, Jacob Mrs, 1947, D 16,33:3
Greenfield, James M, 1915, Jl 22,9:5
Greenfield, Jean, 1944, Ag 17,17:6
Greenfield, Joseph R, 1964, N 8,63:7
Greenfield, Kent R, 1967, Jl 27,35:3
Greenfield, Mannie, 1963, O 4,35:2
Greenfield, Morris, 1948, Mr 11,27:3; 1951, Ja
Greenfield, Nathaniel L, 1957, Ja 13,84:4
Greenfield, Nicholas C, 1954, My 10,23:5
Greenfield, Robert A, 1938, My 18,21:6
Greenfield, Ruth Adelaide (Adelaide Cheire), Ap 4,15:4
Greenfield, Samuel J Rev, 1937, Ap 6,23:1
Greenfield, Samuel Rev, 1937, Jl 12,18:1
Greenfield, Simon, 1946, Jl 10,23:3
Greenfield, William B, 1949, N 14,27:4
Greenfield, William E, 1949, Je 8,29:4
Greenglass, Barnet Mrs, 1958, F 4,26:5
Greengrass, Barney, 1956, Mr 5,23:3
Greenhalgh, Frank L, 1955, F 10,31:4
Greenhalgh, George T, 1949, Mr 6,72:5
Greenhalgh, Howard K, 1952, S 25,31:5
Greenhalgh, Sidney F Mrs, 1950, Ja 18,31:1
Greenhalgh, Sidney N, 1947, N 5,27:2
Greenhalgh, Warren, 1959, D 30,22:1
Greenhall, Frank Mrs, 1952, My 20,25:1
Greenhall, Leonard D, 1955, Ap 2,17:6

Greenhaugh, Mary Harrod Mrs, 1871, Ja 23,2:7
Greenhaus, Abraham M, 1949, Mr 14,19:6
Greenhaus, Benjamin J, 1951, My 27,69:2
Greenhause, Meyer W, 1953, O 31,17:5
Greenhill, David, 1947, Je 6,23:5
Greenhill, Max, 1962, Je 15,27:5
Greenhill, Minerva A C Mrs, 1939, D 3,60:7
Greenhood, Benjamin J, 1948, Mr 14,72:6
Greenhouse, Charles A, 1966, S 17,29:2
Greenhouse, Jacob, 1955, O 19,33:5
Greenhouse, Louis, 1944, F 22,23:3
Greenhouse, Martin E, 1937, Ap 4,II,10:7
Greenhouse, Richard I, 1958, F 9,88:8
Greenhow, Rose Mrs, 1864, O 21,8:2
Greenhut, B J, 1932, Mr 30,19:5
Greenhut, Fanny V, 1937, Ap 22,23:3
Greenhut, John N, 1960, D 16,33:1
Greenhut, Joseph B Capt, 1918, N 18,15:3; 1918, N 21,15:4
Greenidge, Charles A (por), 1941, Ja 24,17:1
Greenig, William F, 1957, D 24,15:4
Greenile, David, 1911, D 18,11:5
Greenin, Edmund L, 1948, Je 19,15:2
Greening, Benjamin J, 1941, Jl 12,13:3
Greening, Charles H, 1951, D 23,22:7
Greening, Charles R, 1957, Mr 30,19:3
Greeninger, Arthur (funl, Je 9,33:1), 1960, Je 8,39:3
Greenland, Henrietta H Mrs, 1946, Ag 11,46:3
Greenland, W B, 1875, Ag 24,4:7
Greenlaw, Albert T, 1959, Ja 24,19:5
Greenlaw, Ralph M, 1951, F 20,25:4
Greenlaw, Ralph W, 1947, Je 27,21:4
Greenlaw, Walter S, 1947, O 17,21:2
Greenlay, James C, 1947, O 28,25:2
Greenleaf, A W (see also Mr 1), 1878, Mr 4,8:3
Greenleaf, Almon E, 1937, S 12,II,7:2
Greenleaf, Arthur R, 1945, D 19,25:3
Greenleaf, Benjamin, 1864, N 10,3:4
Greenleaf, Carl D, 1959, Jl 11,19:3
Greenleaf, Charles, 1924, Ap 11,21:5
Greenleaf, Charles H Brig-Gen, 1911, S 4,7:5
Greenleaf, Charles Howe Lt-Com, 1913, Mr 16,IV,7:4
Greenleaf, Edwin H, 1952, F 8,23:4
Greenleaf, Fred B, 1952, S 15,25:3
Greenleaf, Henry S Col, 1937, N 10,25:2
Greenleaf, J L, 1933, Ap 16,28:1
Greenleaf, John C, 1958, Ja 19,86:7
Greenleaf, Kenneth T, 1966, Mr 6,93:1
Greenleaf, Lewis S, 1947, Ap 29,27:5
Greenleaf, Lewis S Mrs, 1959, Ap 12,86:5
Greenleaf, Patrick Henry Rev, 1869, Je 23,8:2
Greenleaf, Ralph, 1950, Mr 16,31:3
Greenleaf, Ray, 1950, F 15,27:2
Greenleaf, Thomas, 1908, Ja 22,7:5
Greenleaf, William D Mrs, 1947, N 26,23:3
Greenleaf, William E, 1959, Jl 9,27:4
Greenleaf, William M, 1940, O 27,45:2
Greenlee, Richard S, 1965, Mr 2,35:4
Greenlee, Verne, 1967, Ap 11,33:8
Greenlee, Walter, 1953, My 14,29:5
Greenlee, William A, 1952, Jl 8,27:2
Greenleem, William B, 1953, Mr 2,23:4
Greenlees, Mary A Mrs, 1940, Ap 4,23:1
Greenley, Howard, 1963, N 28,39:2
Greenley, James W, 1950, Mr 28,31:2
Greenley, William, 1955, Mr 2,27:3
Greenly, Albert H, 1960, S 14,43:2
Greenly, Cornelia M Mrs, 1914, F 15,5:5
Greenly, John H M, 1951, Ja 1,17:5
Greenly, Russell J, 1953, Je 27,15:2
Greenly, W L, 1883, D 2,13:2
Greenman, Arthur D, 1944, Ap 4,21:4
Greenman, Edward, 1947, Mr 17,23:2
Greenman, Edward W, 1908, Ag 4,7:5
Greenman, Frances H Mrs, 1940, Ap 4,23:6
Greenman, Frederick F, 1961, Je 27,33:1
Greenman, Harry J, 1965, Je 21,29:1
Greenman, Michael E, 1965, F 19,35:4
Greenman, Milton J Dr, 1937, Ap 9,21:1
Greenman, Russell S, 1943, Mr 16,19:4
Greenman, Saul, 1961, Ag 9,33:6
Greenman, Susie H Mrs, 1954, F 6,19:2
Greenman, Walter F, 1945, Jl 27,15:4
Greenman, William G, 1956, F 9,32:1
Greenop, John, 1917, F 24,9:4
Greenop, William H, 1953, Ag 18,23:5
Greenough, Benjamin F Mrs, 1909, Ja 12,9:5
Greenough, Carroll, 1941, Ag 21,17:3
Greenough, Charles E, 1952, My 12,25:3
Greenough, Charles P 2d Mrs, 1952, D 31,15:3
Greenough, Chester N (por), 1938, F 28,15:3
Greenough, Cornelia, 1949, O 6,31:4
Greenough, David S Jr, 1950, D 12,33:2
Greenough, George G Gen, 1912, Je 28,13:6
Greenough, Henry V Mrs, 1953, Jl 18,13:1
Greenough, Henry W Mrs, 1948, O 15,23:5
Greenough, J B, 1901, O 12,9:6
Greenough, James Carruthers, 1924, D 5,21:5
Greenough, John James, 1908, Ag 27,7:6
Greenough, John Mrs, 1947, Ag 22,15:5
Greenough, Malcolm, 1948, My 3,21:1
Greenough, R S, 1880, N 10,5:3
Greenough, Richard S, 1904, Ap 24,4:5
Greenough, Robert B Dr (por), 1937, F 17,21:1
Greenough, Walter C Mrs, 1955, O 10,27:5
Greenough, Walter H, 1955, Ja 8,13:6
Greenough, William B, 1956, N 19,31:2
Greenough, William W Mrs, 1952, Ag 22,21:3
Greenquist, Frank A, 1943, Ja 5,19:5
Greensfelder, Albert P, 1955, Ap 19,31:2
Greenshields, R A E, 1942, S 29,23:5
Greenslade, John H Mrs, 1938, Mr 26,15:1
Greenslade, John W, 1950, Ja 7,17:5
Greenslade, John W Mrs, 1943, Mr 29,15:4
Greenslade, William G, 1958, N 8,21:4
Greenslet, Ferris, 1959, N 20,31:2
Greenslet, George F, 1953, F 21,13:5
Greensmith, Harry G, 1944, D 8,21:4
Greenspahn, Solomon, 1947, N 19,27:1
Greenspan, Benjamin, 1954, Mr 25,29:1
Greenspan, Benjamin E, 1959, My 5,33:5
Greenspan, Benjamin E Mrs, 1966, Je 7,47:3
Greenspan, David H, 1966, Ag 1,27:3
Greenspan, Henry Mrs, 1953, N 18,31:2
Greenspan, Isadore, 1965, D 19,84:6
Greenspan, Isidore, 1955, Mr 21,25:3
Greenspan, Jacob, 1943, Mr 20,15:3; 1955, O 29,19:5
Greenspan, Jacob Mrs, 1952, F 12,27:2
Greenspan, Joseph, 1954, Mr 18,31:2
Greenspan, Joshua, 1957, Je 1,17:5
Greenspan, Phil, 1957, Mr 8,25:1
Greenspan, Sara, 1968, Mr 3,88:7
Greenspoon, Louis, 1962, My 6,88:4
Greenspun, David S, 1964, O 16,39:2
Greenstein, Adolph, 1944, Mr 10,15:4
Greenstein, Ben, 1956, My 3,31:4
Greenstein, Benjamin, 1949, D 21,29:1
Greenstein, Gertrude, 1941, My 15,23:2
Greenstein, Jacob Mrs, 1954, Ap 4,89:1
Greenstein, Jesse P, 1959, F 13,27:1
Greenstein, L Arthur, 1964, F 15,23:4
Greenstein, Max, 1957, My 24,26:1
Greenstein, Meyer L, 1955, Ja 22,11:6
Greenstein, Mollie L Mrs, 1937, F 15,17:2
Greenstein, Morris, 1948, O 16,15:5
Greenstein, Samuel, 1924, Ap 14,17:3; 1946, O 23,30:2
Greenstein, William, 1955, O 23,86:3
Greenstone, Ellison (Al), 1955, Jl 30,17:4
Greenstone, James P, 1968, O 24,47:4
Greenstone, Julius H, 1955, Mr 8,27:3
Greenstone, Leonard, 1944, Mr 25,15:4
Greenstone, Shirley, 1957, My 13,31:3
Greenstreet, Sydney H (est estimated, F 3,25:7), 1954, Ja 20,27:1
Greenthal, David Mrs, 1948, F 11,27:4
Greenthal, Henry Mrs, 1961, O 12,29:5
Greenthal, Jennie, 1952, Jl 24,27:4
Greenthal, Monroe W, 1963, Je 30,56:2
Greenthal, Roy M, 1950, Ja 28,13:2
Greenwald, Abraham, 1947, Jl 16,23:3; 1965, Ap 8, 39:4
Greenwald, Abraham Mrs, 1942, F 8,49:3
Greenwald, Bertram L, 1950, F 13,21:4
Greenwald, Carleton, 1965, F 14,88:8
Greenwald, Daniel, 1954, Ap 1,31:1
Greenwald, Eddie, 1951, N 28,31:1
Greenwald, Edwin W, 1963, O 6,89:1
Greenwald, Eugene L, 1953, D 24,15:3
Greenwald, Harry, 1959, Ap 7,34:1
Greenwald, Hyman Mrs, 1964, S 10,35:3
Greenwald, Irwin T, 1953, Ap 10,21:4
Greenwald, Jay A, 1945, N 7,23:5
Greenwald, Jerome J, 1959, N 18,41:5
Greenwald, Jesse, 1958, Ag 5,27:4
Greenwald, Joseph, 1938, Ap 2,15:5
Greenwald, Joseph H, 1951, Ag 16,27:5
Greenwald, Leon, 1962, Je 2,19:1
Greenwald, Lina S Mrs, 1945, My 11,19:4
Greenwald, Louis, 1956, Ag 29,29:2; 1958, D 6,23:2
Greenwald, Max, 1949, N 27,104:6
Greenwald, Max Mrs, 1951, My 8,31:4
Greenwald, Milton, 1948, F 9,17:1
Greenwald, Nathan, 1945, Mr 9,19:4
Greenwald, Nathan Mrs, 1944, D 12,23:1
Greenwald, Oscar J, 1941, F 18,23:3
Greenwald, Philip, 1944, Ag 3,19:5
Greenwald, Reuben, 1939, Ag 1,19:5
Greenwald, Samuel R Mrs, 1963, Ap 30,35:1
Greenwald, Willard F, 1953, Mr 1,92:3
Greenwaldt, William F, 1955, Ja 6,27:3
Greenwall, Henry W, 1913, N 28,15:6
Greenwalt, Boyd R, 1950, N 30,33:4
Greenway, Cornelius, 1968, Ja 10,43:2
Greenway, Thomas H, 1949, Je 14,31:2
Greenway, Walter B, 1940, D 22,31:3
Greenway, Wilton, 1939, Ja 23,13:4
Greenwell, Albert W, 1965, Mr 7,83:1
Greenwell, Bernice Sister, 1952, Mr 29,15:6
Greenwell, Dan A, 1958, Ag 2,17:6
Greenwood, Allen, 1942, O 25,46:1
Greenwood, Arthur, 1944, F 2,21:1; 1954, Je 10,31:3
Greenwood, Arthur H, 1963, Ap 27,25:1
Greenwood, Burgess, 1913, N 1,11:5
Greenwood, Charles S, 1949, N 2,27:6
Greenwood, Charles T, 1939, D 28,21:1
Greenwood, Charles W, 1951, N 24,11:3
Greenwood, Chester, 1937, Jl 7,24:2
Greenwood, Elizabeth Ward, 1922, N 29,17:4
Greenwood, Ernest, 1955, Je 16,31:2
Greenwood, Ernest Mrs, 1952, Mr 12,27:2
Greenwood, Frederick, 1966, F 7,29:2
Greenwood, Frederick Mrs, 1966, F 7,29:2
Greenwood, Frederick W Sr, 1950, Ap 5,31:2
Greenwood, George C, 1968, Jl 18,33:4
Greenwood, George D, 1956, O 24,37:2
Greenwood, Grace, 1904, Ap 21,1:4
Greenwood, H Paul, 1958, Mr 15,17:3
Greenwood, Harry, 1946, S 6,21:3
Greenwood, Harry D Sr, 1957, F 19,31:4
Greenwood, Harvey E, 1947, Ap 3,25:5
Greenwood, Helen E, 1967, Mr 23,35:2
Greenwood, Henry E Sr, 1952, D 2,36:4
Greenwood, Herbert P, 1962, O 20,25:5
Greenwood, Herbert S, 1951, S 14,25:2
Greenwood, Hugh A Dr, 1937, Je 22,23:5
Greenwood, Ira J, 1950, D 9,15:4
Greenwood, Ivan A, 1947, Mr 11,27:2
Greenwood, James Sr, 1949, Ag 23,23:3
Greenwood, John, 1876, Mr 4,5:2
Greenwood, John E, 1954, My 20,31:3
Greenwood, John M, 1946, N 22,24:2
Greenwood, Joseph G, 1946, Ag 17,13:2
Greenwood, Lord (por), 1948, S 11,15:5
Greenwood, Louis A, 1940, D 8,71:1
Greenwood, Louis W, 1948, F 20,27:3
Greenwood, Major, 1949, O 7,31:3
Greenwood, Marcus J, 1948, Ag 15,60:2
Greenwood, Mary H, 1953, My 23,15:6
Greenwood, Maurice J, 1949, My 21,13:6
Greenwood, Moses, 1941, D 26,13:2
Greenwood, Raymond E, 1949, Ja 10,25:4
Greenwood, Richard B, 1915, Je 9,13:4
Greenwood, Richard F Mrs, 1940, Ap 21,43:1
Greenwood, Sarah I Mrs, 1940, Ag 10,13:4
Greenwood, Stanley, 1962, Ag 10,19:1
Greenwood, Walter E, 1950, N 12,92:3; 1957, Mr 17, 86:3
Greenwood, Wilbur R (por), 1949, N 5,13:5
Greenwood, Wilbur R Jr, 1962, Je 22,64:1
Greenwoood, William, 1939, D 7,27:4
Greer, Anna M O Mrs, 1942, O 19,19:5
Greer, Arthur Lady, 1937, Mr 20,19:5
Greer, Arthur Mrs, 1959, F 18,33:2
Greer, Austin G, 1944, Mr 7,17:4
Greer, Beriah Rev, 1874, My 5,1:6
Greer, Bertrand C Mrs, 1940, My 20,17:2
Greer, C Lester Mrs, 1966, Jl 7,37:1
Greer, Charles, 1922, S 13,21:4
Greer, Charles D Sr, 1948, Mr 1,23:5
Greer, Christopher M Jr, 1960, N 12,21:4
Greer, David Hummell (por), 1919, My 20,17:1
Greer, David Hummell Mrs, 1919, Je 18,17:5
Greer, Frank B, 1943, My 10,19:4
Greer, Frank U, 1949, My 18,27:4
Greer, Fred B, 1944, My 26,19:4
Greer, George E, 1956, Ap 29,86:2
Greer, George H, 1956, Ap 10,31:3
Greer, George W, 1943, My 23,42:6
Greer, Guy E, 1955, Ap 14,29:3
Greer, H C, 1948, Ag 6,17:2
Greer, Harry, 1947, Mr 21,21:3
Greer, Henry K Mrs, 1960, My 22,86:2
Greer, Hilton R, 1949, N 28,27:3
Greer, Howard D, 1937, O 5,25:2
Greer, J Lee, 1950, S 24,104:3
Greer, Jacob, 1919, My 26,15:6
Greer, Jerome, 1959, Ag 5,27:4
Greer, John, 1955, Ag 12,19:5
Greer, John A, 1960, Jl 5,31:4
Greer, John E Col, 1907, S 20,9:6
Greer, John F Mrs, 1956, Ap 18,31:2
Greer, John Mrs, 1943, Je 10,21:4
Greer, Lawrence, 1925, D 15,25:2
Greer, Louis M, 1946, My 30,21:4
Greer, Louis M Mrs (will, S 7,10:5), 1946, Ag 11,45:2
Greer, Philip A, 1946, Ag 15,25:3
Greer, Raymond M, 1955, N 11,25:3
Greer, Raymond M Mrs, 1950, Jl 8,13:6
Greer, Samuel, 1953, Jl 10,19:2
Greer, Samuel E, 1952, Ap 25,23:1
Greer, Samuel M (por), 1948, S 20,25:3
Greer, Samuel M, 1953, Ja 15,27:3
Greer, Thomas S, 1948, Jl 31,15:3
Greer, Tommy, 1949, Ja 7,21:4
Greer, William A, 1939, F 19,39:3
Greer, William J (por), 1941, F 27,19:4
Greer, William K, 1945, O 20,11:4
Greeson, William A, 1942, N 26,27:3
Greet, Clare, 1939, F 15,23:3
Greet, Maurice, 1951, My 31,27:5
Greever, Walton H, 1965, Ap 1,35:3
Gref, Anthony, 1915, Ap 24,11:6
Grefe, Charles H, 1938, S 29,25:4
Greff, Clarence F, 1954, My 20,31:4
Greffly, Frederick (B Rice), 1965, F 14,89:1
Greffuhle, Elisabeth de Countess, 1952, Ag 24,89:3
Greg, Charles J, 1947, Je 27,22:3
Greg, W R, 1881, N 17,5:2
Grega, Charles W Sr, 1949, O 30,86:1

Grega, Samuel Rev, 1968, Mr 11,41:2
Gregerson, Christen P, 1949, O 18,27:1
Gregg, Abel J (por), 1944, Ap 27,23:6
Gregg, Alan, 1957, Je 21,25:1
Gregg, Albert H, 1960, S 1,27:2
Gregg, Alex W, 1958, Je 26,27:5
Gregg, Alfred W, 1950, Je 9,23:4
Gregg, Dacid, 1948, Ja 6,23:2
Gregg, David M, 1951, N 30,23:1
Gregg, David McMurtrie, 1916, Ag 8,9:6
Gregg, David Rev Dr (funl, O 14,17:2), 1919, O 12, 22:3
Gregg, Edith F, 1925, N 13,19:4
Gregg, Frank M, 1937, Ja 7,21:4
Gregg, George, 1942, D 20,44:7
Gregg, Harry W Mrs, 1944, D 3,58:6
Gregg, James E, 1946, F 24,43:1
Gregg, James Jr, 1958, N 24,29:5
Gregg, John A Bishop, 1953, F 19,23:3
Gregg, John A F, 1961, My 3,37:4
Gregg, John H C, 1963, O 9,43:1
Gregg, John P, 1952, O 30,31:3
Gregg, John R, 1948, F 24,25:1
Gregg, Maurice, 1942, Mr 12,19:2
Gregg, Norman McA, 1966, Jl 28,33:2
Gregg, Paul E, 1949, Jl 10,56:6
Gregg, Philip E, 1967, N 9,47:5
Gregg, Prof (A B Jaquitte), 1883, Ap 14,1:3
Gregg, Robert, 1947, Ag 20,21:1
Gregg, Royal J, 1951, S 25,29:1
Gregg, Thomas A, 1944, Ag 25,13:4
Gregg, W M, 1881, S 3,5:5
Gregg, Will R, 1946, Mr 12,25:3
Gregg, William B, 1954, Ag 7,13:6
Gregg, William C, 1946, Ja 24,22:2
Gregg, William H, 1915, Je 22,15:6
Gregg, William S, 1939, S 15,23:5
Gregg, Willis R (por), 1938, S 15,25:1
Gregh, Fernand, 1960, Ja 6,35:2
Grego, Angeline Mrs, 1957, Ap 18,29:3
Grego, Walter J Sr, 1959, D 17,37:1
Gregoire, Raymond, 1942, F 25,19:1
Gregor, David G, 1954, O 18,25:3
Gregor, Elmer R, 1954, Ap 5,25:2
Gregor, Joseph, 1960, O 21,33:4
Gregor, Nora, 1949, Ja 25,24:3
Gregori, Louis A, 1910, O 27,11:4
Gregorieff, Alexander P, 1947, Je 9,21:1
Gregorious, George J, 1956, Ap 6,25:3
Gregorius, Msgr, 1924, N 18,25:3
Gregorius, Ralph F, 1946, Ag 1,23:5
Gregorius, William P, 1944, My 15,19:4
Gregory, Alfred, 1953, Jl 2,23:4
Gregory, Alfred C, 1946, D 1,79:2
Gregory, Alice, 1953, Ap 21,27:1
Gregory, Alyse (Mrs L Powys), 1967, Ag 31,33:3
Gregory, Andrew L Mrs, 1937, Je 14,38:4
Gregory, Anna L, 1945, Mr 18,41:1
Gregory, Annie K Mrs, 1943, D 18,15:3
Gregory, Appleton, 1937, Mr 3,23:4
Gregory, Arthur C Mrs, 1959, D 13,86:3
Gregory, Augusta Lady, 1932, My 24,19:1
Gregory, Benjamin, 1950, Jl 23,56:3
Gregory, Bessie Mrs, 1937, Ja 3,II,8:3
Gregory, Carey E, 1943, Ap 7,25:5
Gregory, Caspar R Mrs, 1948, Ja 19,23:2
Gregory, Casper Rene Dr, 1917, Ap 14,13:5
Gregory, Charles, 1915, My 21,13:4
Gregory, Charles A, 1945, Je 12,19:2
Gregory, Charles E, 1961, D 11,31:4
Gregory, Charles W, 1954, N 19,23:2
Gregory, Chester A, 1956, D 5,39:3
Gregory, Clifford C, 1965, D 2,41:5
Gregory, Clifford D Mrs, 1937, N 12,21:5
Gregory, Clifford V, 1941, N 19,23:4
Gregory, Colin, 1959, Ja 11,88:5
Gregory, Daniel Seelye Rev Dr, 1915, Ap 15,13:5
Gregory, Dora, 1954, Mr 9,27:3
Gregory, Dudley S, 1874, D 9,4:7
Gregory, Duncan, 1951, Ja 30,25:2
Gregory, E M Gen, 1871, N 8,5:4
Gregory, Edgar B, 1947, My 9,22:3
Gregory, Edmund B, 1961, Ja 28,19:4
Gregory, Edward Cooke, 1924, My 18,7:1
Gregory, Edward John, 1909, Je 23,7:4
Gregory, Eliot, 1915, Je 2,13:6
Gregory, Elma C, 1953, Jl 9,25:4
Gregory, Emily R, 1946, Ja 20,42:5
Gregory, Eugene J, 1916, Mr 27,11:4; 1954, D 27,17:4
Gregory, F H Adm, 1866, O 5,8:3
Gregory, Fanny Lady (Mrs E Stirling), 1895, D 31, 5:4
Gregory, Francis F, 1952, Mr 9,93:1
Gregory, Frank G, 1962, N 24,23:5
Gregory, Frederick G, 1961, N 30,37:3
Gregory, Frederick L, 1953, D 15,39:3
Gregory, G E, 1931, Ag 31,15:1
Gregory, George A, 1946, D 2,25:3
Gregory, George D, 1956, Je 23,17:3
Gregory, George E, 1942, My 18,15:3
Gregory, George H, 1942, Ap 8,19:4
Gregory, H Clyde, 1951, My 1,29:3
Gregory, Harry S Mrs, 1960, D 5,31:4
Gregory, Heathe, 1943, N 25,25:5
Gregory, Helen E, 1941, My 31,11:1
Gregory, Henry E (will, F 7,39:7), 1937, Ja 25,19:5
Gregory, Henry W, 1950, Ap 1,15:1
Gregory, Herbert, 1952, Ja 29,25:3
Gregory, Herbert B, 1951, Mr 10,13:5
Gregory, Holman, 1947, My 10,13:3
Gregory, Howard, 1956, Ap 13,25:2
Gregory, Howard C, 1946, Ap 24,25:1
Gregory, Hugh W, 1952, Ap 3,35:5
Gregory, I M, 1901, Mr 10,21:7
Gregory, Ira O, 1943, F 2,19:2
Gregory, Jackson, 1943, Je 15,21:5
Gregory, James A B, 1959, F 20,25:4
Gregory, James R, 1947, My 11,62:3
Gregory, Jerome Bro, 1957, S 1,57:1
Gregory, John (trb lr, Mr 6,26:6), 1958, F 22,17:3
Gregory, John B Mrs, 1951, Ag 3,21:5
Gregory, John G, 1947, Ap 13,60:5
Gregory, John H, 1937, Ja 20,22:2
Gregory, John R B, 1938, Mr 1,21:4
Gregory, Joseph H Sr, 1951, My 5,17:5
Gregory, Josephine Mrs, 1912, Jl 4,7:5
Gregory, Julian A, 1939, Mr 18,17:1
Gregory, Julian A Mrs, 1937, D 21,23:3
Gregory, Julius, 1955, D 6,38:1
Gregory, L W (por), 1946, Jl 30,23:5
Gregory, Lane F, 1949, Ja 29,13:5
Gregory, Lee O, 1941, O 19,47:2
Gregory, Lemuel L Mrs, 1960, Je 29,24:3
Gregory, Lewis, 1910, N 12,9:5
Gregory, Louis B, 1909, F 7,11:4
Gregory, Louise H, 1954, N 2,27:4
Gregory, M C Mrs, 1918, F 10,17:1
Gregory, Martin L, 1967, Ag 1,33:2
Gregory, Maurice C, 1949, O 28,23:2
Gregory, Menas S (por), 1941, N 3,19:1
Gregory, Nicholas P, 1961, O 21,21:4
Gregory, O S, 1882, Jl 8,8:5
Gregory, Percival H Mrs, 1941, N 15,17:2
Gregory, Ralph A, 1951, D 30,24:7
Gregory, Ralph J, 1941, Ap 26,15:5
Gregory, Raymond J, 1942, N 18,25:5
Gregory, Raymond W, 1954, Je 3,27:3
Gregory, Richard, 1952, S 16,29:3
Gregory, Richard H, 1954, Ag 27,21:4
Gregory, Richard H Mrs, 1943, Mr 11,21:1
Gregory, Robert, 1947, Ap 13,60:3
Gregory, Robert B Mrs, 1947, Ap 30,25:4
Gregory, Roger T, 1937, Jl 9,21:4
Gregory, Roy A, 1942, Je 30,21:2
Gregory, Seth, 1959, F 3,31:3
Gregory, Stanley R, 1946, My 16,21:4
Gregory, Stephan, 1944, Ap 2,40:2
Gregory, Stephen S Mrs, 1940, S 30,17:2
Gregory, Stephen Strong, 1920, O 26,17:4
Gregory, T W, 1933, F 26,24:5
Gregory, Tappan, 1961, My 2,37:4
Gregory, Thomas, 1941, Ap 16,23:5
Gregory, Thomas B, 1951, Jl 12,25:1
Gregory, Thomas E, 1955, O 6,29:4
Gregory, Walter L, 1965, N 4,47:4
Gregory, William A, 1906, Ja 15,9:6
Gregory, William A Jr, 1955, Mr 8,27:5
Gregory, William B, 1945, Ja 31,21:6
Gregory, William E, 1956, Mr 15,31:5
Gregory, William Gov, 1901, D 17,9:5
Gregory, William H, 1948, N 16,29:5; 1959, Ja 29,27:3
Gregory, William H Jr, 1962, Je 26,33:4
Gregory, William H Mrs, 1952, Ja 8,27:2; 1968, Ap 28,83:1
Gregory, William S, 1949, Je 14,31:2
Gregory, Willis G Dr, 1937, Mr 22,23:1
Gregory (Met), 1955, N 13,87:5
Gregory Auxilian, Bro (Wall), 1958, Ap 20,84:4
Gregson, Herbert, 1942, Jl 2,21:6
Gregson, Mary W Mrs, 1939, My 15,17:5
Gregurevich, John J, 1955, D 18,92:6
Grehan, Thomas B, 1957, O 29,31:2
Greib, Lawrence F, 1955, N 10,35:4
Greichmann, William, 1939, Jl 1,17:6
Greider, Eugene, 1954, Mr 2,25:4
Greif, Charles, 1937, Ja 17,II,8:5
Greif, Samuel, 1967, S 2,22:8
Greif, Wilfrid Dr (por),(cor, O 31,II,11:1), 1937, O 30,19:4
Greifer, Eli, 1966, S 27,47:1
Greiff, Lotti J, 1949, F 23,27:2
Greiff, Samuel J, 1961, D 22,23:1
Greiff, Sidney, 1964, O 28,45:3
Greiffenstein, Berta von, 1954, N 4,14:7
Greifzu, Theodore A, 1961, Ap 1,17:3
Greig, Alexander, 1906, My 28,9:6
Greig, Gordon J, 1949, F 11,23:1
Greig, James A, 1944, N 15,27:5
Greig, James A (Oct 2), 1965, O 11,61:2
Greig, Louis, 1953, Mr 2,23:3
Greig, Norman, 1957, S 4,34:5
Greig, Robert B, 1947, D 1,21:1
Greig, Rodger B, 1949, Ag 30,27:1
Greig, Stuart O, 1949, N 14,27:4
Greil, Cecile L, 1940, Je 11,25:5
Greim, Emil J, 1942, Jl 1,25:5
Greims, Alice E, 1942, O 7,25:5
Greiner, Adalbert, 1968, Ja 24,42:2
Greiner, Alex W, 1958, Ap 22,33:3
Greiner, August H, 1953, N 5,31:4
Greiner, Edwin D P, 1940, S 12,25:4
Greiner, Ernest O, 1951, Jl 28,11:2
Greiner, Fred, 1922, D 26,13:3
Greiner, Jacob B, 1953, Ap 28,27:3
Greiner, Joseph C, 1949, My 8,76:6
Greiner, Julius W, 1938, Mr 14,15:4
Greiner, Leopold Mrs, 1949, Jl 12,27:4
Greiner, Mary Mrs, 1946, Jl 28,39:1
Greinert, Emil, 1955, My 7,17:4
Greinsky, Jacob Mrs, 1957, Ag 5,19:1
Greiper, Louis P, 1953, My 10,89:1
Greiper, Myron E, 1951, N 24,11:5
Greis, Fred A, 1958, S 12,26:1
Greis, Henry N, 1947, Jl 17,19:5
Greis, V Frank, 1956, Ag 22,29:1
Greischer, Samuel, 1951, Mr 16,31:2
Greisen, H Peter Mrs, 1950, Jl 13,25:4
Greiss, Justin W Mrs, 1942, Ja 5,17:5
Greissman, Jacob, 1968, My 15,47:3
Greist, Henry W, 1955, N 12,19:6
Greist, Walter C, 1944, S 19,21:5
Greiwe, John E Dr, 1937, O 30,19:2
Grekin, Jacob, 1942, Ap 7,21:3
Grekov, Assen K, 1954, Mr 3,27:3
Grekov, David D, 1953, S 10,25:6
Grell, Christian, 1942, Mr 7,17:5
Grell, Gustave, 1939, Je 1,25:5
Grella, Rocco, 1938, D 6,23:4
Greller, George E Sr, 1954, F 24,25:2
Grelling, R, 1929, Ja 17,25:3
Gremer, Charles J, 1943, Mr 24,23:3
Gremillet, Justin M L, 1941, Mr 9,40:8
Greminger, Albert N, 1951, Ag 24,15:4
Gremmels, Charles E, 1965, Ag 31,33:5
Gremminger, Catherine Mrs, 1954, Ja 10,86:6
Grendal, Vladimir, 1940, N 18,19:2
Grendon, Felix, 1965, Je 21,29:5
Grene, Dorothy A Mrs, 1949, S 4,40:8
Grene, Harriet Fisher Mrs, 1923, N 22,19:5
Greneker, Claude P (por), 1949, Ap 8,25:1
Grenelle, Levi Osborn Rev, 1914, Je 19,13:5
Grenet, Auguste J, 1938, Ag 18,20:3
Grenet y Sanchez, Eliseo, 1950, N 5,93:2
Grenfell, David Rhys, 1968, N 27,47:3
Grenfell, Francis Wallace Lord, 1925, Ja 28,17:3
Grenfell, George P, 1946, Ja 2,19:3
Grenfell, Russell, 1954, Jl 9,17:2
Grenfell, Thomas, 1945, Ap 23,19:3
Grenfell, Victoria Lady, 1907, F 5,9:6
Grenfell, Wilfred Lady, 1938, D 10,17:4
Grenfell, Wilfred T, 1940, O 10,1:2
Grenfell, William Henry (Baron Desborough), 1 D 2,11:3
Grenier, Arthur J, 1951, N 27,31:5
Grenier, George G, 1942, F 22,26:2
Grenier, Roy P, 1961, Ap 1,17:3
Grenier, William F, 1948, My 3,21:2
Grening, Paul C, 1962, F 2,29:5
Grenlee, Ole, 1954, Ap 18,52:4
Grennan, John L (por), 1946, Ja 11,21:3
Grennan, Kenneth L, 1940, Ap 16,23:4
Grennan, Stanislaus, 1941, S 27,17:4
Grennell, George, 1877, N 21,4:5
Grenolds, Walter J, 1950, F 20,25:3
Grenon, Peter, 1944, D 13,23:1
Grenough, William, 1949, F 2,28:3
Grenquist, Ernst A, 1940, O 13,48:8
Grente, Georges, 1959, My 4,29:3
Greppi, Count, 1921, My 10,17:4
Greppi, Vittorio, 1907, Jl 3,7:5
Gresham, Herbert, 1921, F 24,13:6
Gresham, Herbert Mrs, 1923, D 30,20:1
Gresham, James W, 1958, Mr 22,17:5
Gresham, Thomas, 1945, Ja 15,19:3
Gresham, W Q, 1895, My 28,1:7
Gresham, William L (trb, S 25,34:6), 1962, S 1
Greshler, Hyman J, 1958, Ag 1,21:4
Greshoff, Henry P, 1947, Je 10,27:3
Gresley, Nigel, 1941, Ap 7,17:1
Gress, Louis, 1939, S 13,25:5
Gress, Louis G, 1943, Ap 19,19:4
Gress, Walter B Sr, 1949, Ag 1,17:3
Gressel, Joseph, 1949, S 29,29:3
Gresser, Albert P, 1952, My 25,93:1
Gresser, David A, 1953, Ap 16,29:4
Gresser, Edward B, 1951, Ap 30,21:4
Gresser, Edward J, 1957, S 2,13:2
Gresser, John S, 1941, Mr 11,23:4
Gresser, L, 1935, Ja 31,19:4
Gresser, Lawrence T, 1955, O 22,19:3
Gresser, Samuel M, 1960, F 11,35:5
Gressick, William W, 1951, S 22,17:5
Gressing, Boniface Mrs, 1949, My 6,25:4
Gressing, Frederick J, 1949, Jl 26,27:1
Gressitt, James F, 1945, N 30,23:5
Gressler, James F, 1960, N 2,39:2
Gressman, H, 1927, Ap 8,23:5
Greswold, Annie Mrs, 1919, Ja 9,11:2
Gretchaninoff, Alexandre Mrs, 1947, Ja 23,23:

Gretchaninoff, Alexandre T, 1956, Ja 5,33:3
Grether, Walter W, 1949, Ag 12,18:2
Gretsch, Frederick, 1952, S 28,77:1
Gretsch, Walter, 1940, My 29,23:2
Gretsch, Walter Mrs, 1956, Mr 6,31:2
Gretsch, William W, 1948, S 11,15:4
Gretsinger, Albert Lindsay, 1908, F 26,7:7
Grett, B, 1936, My 18,17:1
Gretton, F, 1882, N 17,5:4
Gretton, Harry A, 1938, Ja 14,23:5
Gretton, John Lord, 1947, Je 4,27:1
Gretz, Harry C, 1951, Je 28,25:5
Gretz, William Jr, 1952, S 1,17:4
Gretz, William 3d, 1957, N 20,35:5
Greuschow, Ruth Mrs, 1949, O 4,27:1
Grevatt, Edward M, 1964, S 3,29:4
Grevatt, Joseph Curran, 1948, Jl 30,18:2
Grevatt, Peter A, 1938, F 22,21:6
Greve, Louis W, 1942, F 3,19:3
Greven, Carl, 1952, Ap 5,15:3
Grever, Joseph F, 1943, N 11,23:5
Grever, Leo A Mrs, 1951, D 16,90:1
Greverend, Catherine, 1941, Ja 1,23:5
Greves, Phyllis T Mrs, 1951, N 7,29:3
Greves, Selden C, 1950, F 11,15:6
Greville, Charles Beresford Fulke Capt, 1909, D 3,11:4
Greville, Fulke-Southwell Greville Nugent Lord, 1883, Ja 26,2:6
Greville, Henry, 1902, My 27,9:4
Greville, Margaret, 1942, S 16,23:2
Greving, Frank T, 1966, Ap 1,35:2
Grevnell, G Rev, 1883, Je 23,4:7
Grevstad, Nicolay, 1940, F 21,19:4
Grevy, Jules, 1891, S 10,8:1
Grevy, Paul Louis Jules, 1914, My 5,11:6
Grew, Edith Agnes, 1924, Ap 15,21:2
Grew, Edward W, 1945, Ja 26,21:3
Grew, Edward W Mrs, 1956, O 7,86:4
Grew, Henry S, 1953, Jl 21,23:4
Grew, Henry S Jr, 1966, F 21,39:1
Grew, Henry Sturgis, 1910, F 9,7:4
Grew, Joseph C, 1965, My 27,1:8
Grew, Joseph C Mrs, 1959, Ag 17,24:1
Grew, Randolph C, 1947, Je 13,23:3
Grew, William C, 1948, O 5,25:1
Grewen, Frederick J, 1959, Ap 19,86:1
Grey, Albert Henry George Lord, 1917, Ag 30,11:5
Grey, Andrew S, 1938, Ja 25,22:3
Grey, Arthur, 1960, Ja 2,13:5
Grey, Arthur W, 1950, Ap 19,29:2
Grey, Bernard, 1967, Mr 25,23:3
Grey, Bessie Y Mrs, 1954, Je 8,27:3
Grey, Charles F, 1951, O 14,88:5
Grey, Charles Frederick, 1925, My 12,23:4
Grey, Charles G, 1953, D 10,47:1
Grey, Charles M, 1955, Je 23,29:2
Grey, Charles R, 1963, Ap 3,47:2
Grey, Clarence N, 1949, Ja 18,24:3
Grey, Clifford, 1941, S 27,17:6
Grey, Countess, 1944, S 25,17:2
Grey, Emile, 1917, O 4,13:4
Grey, Eva W, 1907, Mr 16,9:5
Grey, Francis T, 1941, Ja 25,15:2
Grey, Frank, 1951, O 5,28:3
Grey, Frank S, 1966, S 1,35:1
Grey, Harold, 1946, Jl 27,17:2
Grey, Harold H, 1953, Mr 28,17:4
Grey, Harry, 1963, O 19,25:2
Grey, Hugh M Sr, 1961, Mr 13,29:4
Grey, Ida C, 1938, S 8,7:7
Grey, J O, 1954, Ja 27,27:1
Grey, Jack S Jr, 1954, Ap 1,31:1
Grey, James C, 1943, S 26,48:2
Grey, Jane, 1944, N 10,19:3
Grey, Joseph W, 1956, Ja 11,31:2
Grey, Katherine, 1950, Mr 22,27:5
Grey, Louis L, 1942, Mr 14,15:1
Grey, Madeline, 1950, Ag 18,21:4
Grey, Robert G, 1962, My 23,45:3
Grey, Samuel H, 1903, D 8,9:3
Grey, W R, 1944, My 11,19:2
Grey, William (Earl of Stamford), 1910, My 25,9:4
Grey, Zane (por), 1939, O 24,23:1
Grey, Zane Mrs (will, Ag 21,55:5), 1957, Jl 27,17:5
Grey de Ruthyn, Lord, 1934, My 23,20:2
Grey Du Ruthyn, Lord (J L W Butler-Bowden), 1963, O 26,27:2
Grey of Falloden, Viscount, 1933, S 7,21:1
Grez, Alfonso, 1966, N 27,86:6
Grez, William F, 1879, O 25,8:2
Gribanovsky, Anastassy (funl, My 26,47:4), 1965, My 24,31:4
Gribayedoff, Valerian, 1908, F 17,7:3
Gribbel, J Bancker, 1947, Ag 27,23:6
Gribbel, John B (will), 1947, O 14,19:3
Gribbel, John B Mrs, 1961, Mr 20,29:4
Gribbin, Eugene J, 1950, Ja 11,23:6
Gribbin, Robert Mrs, 1945, Jl 10,11:3
Gribble, Francis H (por), 1946, O 4,23:5
Gribble, George A, 1942, Ja 4,49:1
Gribbon, Daisy R Mrs, 1938, S 29,25:5
Gribbon, Eddie (Sept 28), 1965, O 11,61:2
Gribbon, Harry (Silk Hat Harry), 1961, Ag 1,31:2
Gribbon, William E, 1941, Je 25,21:1
Gribell, W Griffin, 1946, D 12,29:4
Gribetz, Louis J, 1964, D 28,29:2
Grice, C C, 1876, Jl 27,4:7
Grice, Harold I, 1953, Ap 25,15:5
Grice, John E, 1958, Jl 16,29:4
Grice, Samuel W, 1940, Ja 25,21:3
Grice, Warren, 1945, My 28,19:2
Gridley, Abraham, 1937, Ja 3,II,8:6
Gridley, Charles O, 1966, O 12,43:4
Gridley, Charles O Mrs, 1955, D 12,31:4
Gridley, Edward, 1907, My 6,9:2
Gridley, Elmo L, 1941, O 6,17:2
Gridley, Leon U, 1952, Ja 4,40:2
Gridley, Leonard C, 1952, F 18,19:5
Gridley, Martin M, 1943, Ag 3,19:5
Gridley, Oscar W, 1942, My 29,17:5
Gridley, Philo, 1864, Ag 19,4:4
Grieb, H Norman, 1917, Ag 29,9:4
Grieb, Joseph C, 1947, N 8,17:1
Grieb, Lawrence Mrs, 1952, My 26,42:4
Grieb, Michael G, 1949, Je 1,31:3
Grieb, William G, 1922, Je 15,19:6
Griebe, Robert E Mrs, 1944, Je 23,19:4
Griebel, Louis F, 1946, D 31,18:2
Griebenow, August, 1925, D 24,13:4
Grieco, Christopher, 1924, Ag 18,13:3
Grieco, Fred, 1966, O 7,43:2
Grieco, James, 1945, F 6,19:2
Grieco, Joseph, 1940, My 3,42:1
Grieco, Ruggero, 1955, Jl 24,65:2
Grieder, Daniel Rev, 1937, Ja 12,23:4
Grief, A V, 1938, Ag 18,20:3
Grief, Martin, 1911, Ap 2,II,13:5
Grieff, Joseph N (por), 1941, Je 9,19:3
Grieg, Edvard (funl, S 6,9:5), 1907, S 5,9:5
Grieg, Lillian A Mrs, 1957, D 20,24:4
Grieme, Hans, 1960, Ja 14,33:1
Grieme, Henry F, 1960, O 27,37:1
Grieme, Henry F Mrs, 1959, My 21,31:4
Grier, Albert C, 1941, N 2,53:1
Grier, Albert O H, 1953, Ja 25,86:5
Grier, Charles D, 1948, D 4,13:3
Grier, David P, 1947, D 25,21:2
Grier, Edgar B, 1952, Je 19,27:6
Grier, Edmund W, 1957, D 9,35:5
Grier, Edward R, 1941, F 13,19:2
Grier, F W, 1879, Je 19,5:6
Grier, Francis E, 1959, O 14,43:5
Grier, Frank L Mrs, 1953, S 27,86:4
Grier, Franklin, 1923, Mr 22,19:5
Grier, G Layton, 1944, Mr 18,13:5
Grier, G M, 1878, D 22,2:2
Grier, George W, 1966, Jl 25,27:5
Grier, Harry L, 1942, Ap 13,16:2
Grier, Jimmy, 1959, Je 5,27:4
Grier, John A, 1958, Je 27,25:2
Grier, John C, 1961, Ap 13,35:5
Grier, John P (por), 1939, Ag 10,19:4
Grier, John S, 1966, Jl 2,23:4
Grier, R C Judge, 1870, S 27,5:3
Grier, Ralph H, 1949, F 20,60:3
Grier, Robert, 1944, D 19,21:1
Grier, Rose M, 1947, D 11,34:3
Grier, Samuel M, 1939, My 29,15:2
Grier, William A, 1953, S 12,17:3
Grier, William A W, 1942, Ap 14,21:2
Grier, William T, 1924, Ja 18,17:4
Grierson, Benjamin H, 1911, S 2,7:4
Grierson, Herbert, 1960, F 21,92:4
Grierson, James Moncrieff Gen, 1914, Ag 18,9:5
Grierson, John W, 1944, F 6,42:2
Gries, Aaron, 1925, O 8,27:4
Gries, Arthur J, 1966, Ap 24,86:7
Gries, Bernard, 1948, O 5,25:1
Gries, Herman, 1937, F 3,23:4
Gries, Herman Mrs, 1948, D 16,29:3
Gries, John M, 1953, S 25,21:2
Gries, Moses J Rabbi, 1918, N 2,15:5
Gries, Otto, 1964, Mr 5,33:3
Griesa, Charles A, 1944, Ap 2,39:3
Griesbach, Herman F, 1952, S 21,89:2
Griesbach, W A, 1945, Ja 22,17:4
Griesbeck, Franklin J, 1956, Jl 10,31:4
Griese, Arthur G, 1940, D 22,30:6
Griese, David C, 1950, Jl 22,15:4
Griesedieck, Alvin, 1961, F 1,35:5
Griesedieck, Edward J Sr, 1955, Mr 7,27:3
Griesedieck, Henry L, 1943, D 11,15:1
Griesel, John H, 1913, Ap 28,11:3
Griesel, John H Mrs, 1925, Je 26,17:5
Griesel, Nellie H R Mrs, 1942, Ap 9,20:2
Griesemer, David E, 1958, O 1,37:4
Griesemer, Douglas (por), 1941, Ap 26,15:2
Griesemer, Douglas Mrs, 1955, N 9,33:2
Griesemer, Joseph, 1955, O 20,36:1
Griesemer, Z Lawrence Mrs, 1951, N 1,29:4
Grieser, Arthur K, 1947, N 30,76:3
Grieshaber, Carl F Sr, 1940, D 27,19:2
Grieshaber, Hugo E, 1938, My 23,17:3
Griesmer, Frederick J, 1939, Jl 4,13:7
Griess, Wilmer T, 1948, F 28,15:5
Griessman, Paul, 1940, S 22,49:1
Griest, Maurice, 1964, Ap 11,25:1
Griest, Nathan L, 1946, Ap 14,46:2
Griest, Thomas H, 1947, Ja 10,21:3
Grieumard, Emilie E, 1940, D 5,25:3
Grieve, Alex C Mrs, 1953, Mr 27,23:3
Grieve, Alex J, 1952, S 25,31:4
Grieve, Anna B Mrs, 1938, My 8,II,6:4
Grieve, Douglas H, 1951, Ja 15,17:3
Grieve, E E, 1879, Je 20,5:2
Grieve, Fred, 1959, Jl 17,21:5
Grieve, James, 1946, Ja 29,25:4
Grieve, Kenneth J M, 1942, S 27,48:5
Grieve, Lucia C G, 1946, N 27,25:1
Grieves, Harry B, 1941, Ap 6,49:1
Grieves, James M, 1958, Jl 17,16:1
Grieves, Lorin C, 1951, Ag 6,21:5
Grieves, Roy, 1949, D 6,31:1
Grieves, Walter C, 1960, Je 14,37:1
Grifee, Fred, 1951, N 2,23:3
Grifenhagen, Edward E, 1914, N 27,11:6
Grifenhagen, Herbert M, 1966, Jl 7,37:4
Grifenhagen, Jacob B, 1914, Mr 7,11:6
Grifenhagen, M, 1932, O 30,36:1
Griffel, Jacob, 1962, Mr 15,35:1
Griffel, Roy O Mrs, 1942, Je 8,15:4
Griffen, Ch R Mrs, 1903, D 1,9:6
Griffen, Charles Field, 1919, Ja 21,9:3
Griffen, Edward E Mrs, 1961, N 27,29:2
Griffen, Edward H, 1944, N 12,48:6
Griffen, Edwin C, 1941, Je 12,23:4
Griffen, Eugene Gen (funl, Ap 14,9:6), 1907, Ap 12, 9:6
Griffen, George E, 1911, Ap 17,11:5
Griffen, H Abbott Mrs, 1947, Ja 23,26:2
Griffen, Henry L, 1907, Ag 29,7:4
Griffen, John D Mrs, 1943, Jl 13,21:4
Griffen, Joseph A, 1966, My 9,39:1
Griffen, Lillie A Mrs, 1943, Mr 2,19:3
Griffen, Martin I J, 1911, N 11,13:5
Griffen, Nannie, 1925, Jl 19,7:3
Griffen, Percy, 1921, Mr 16,9:4
Griffen, R A Rev, 1909, Jl 29,7:6
Griffen, Richard F, 1965, F 2,33:4
Griffen, Solomon Bulkley, 1925, D 12,15:5
Griffen, Thomas, 1912, N 4,11:5
Griffen, W P, 1922, Jl 23,21:2
Griffen, William J, 1948, O 4,23:3
Griffes, Charles Tomlinson, 1920, Ap 10,15:5
Griffeth, Arthur V, 1944, S 17,42:2
Griffeth, George B, 1948, Ag 22,62:5
Griffeth, Joshua, 1925, S 7,11:5
Griffeth, Merle R, 1953, N 23,27:3
Griffin, Alex R, 1959, Je 27,23:5
Griffin, Ames O, 1939, F 12,44:7
Griffin, Andrew P, 1937, F 18,21:1
Griffin, Arthur, 1953, F 7,15:6
Griffin, Arthur B, 1946, Ja 7,20:2
Griffin, Arthur J, 1943, Ja 21,21:2
Griffin, Austin K, 1951, Ja 30,25:3
Griffin, Bernard (funl plans, Ag 22,29:4; funl, Ag 29,29:2), 1956, Ag 20,21:1
Griffin, Bulkley S, 1967, My 17,47:2
Griffin, Burns, 1959, Ap 6,27:5
Griffin, Burt W, 1949, Ja 12,27:4
Griffin, Carlton E, 1940, Jl 25,17:2
Griffin, Caroline F Mrs, 1937, Ag 3,23:5
Griffin, Carroll W, 1959, My 6,39:3
Griffin, Ceylon O Maj, 1937, Ag 14,13:5
Griffin, Charles D Mrs, 1963, Ag 11,84:4
Griffin, Charles E, 1949, D 2,29:4
Griffin, Charles F, 1954, Mr 22,27:6
Griffin, Charles L, 1946, Ap 19,29:2
Griffin, Charles Maj-Gen, 1867, S 16,5:2
Griffin, Charles W, 1949, D 24,15:1; 1955, Je 14,29:4
Griffin, Clinton R, 1959, Ap 10,29:2
Griffin, Cornelius J, 1947, D 26,15:3
Griffin, Courtlandt B, 1948, Ap 14,28:3
Griffin, D J, 1926, D 12,II,8:8
Griffin, D S, 1884, S 17,5:3
Griffin, Daniel G, 1943, D 30,17:4
Griffin, Daniel J Mrs, 1958, Ja 7,47:1
Griffin, Daniel S, 1938, Ag 27,13:5
Griffin, Dick, 1950, D 2,13:5
Griffin, Dominic B, 1948, N 6,13:2
Griffin, Don W, 1943, Ap 28,23:3
Griffin, Donald C, 1950, Jl 1,15:5
Griffin, E A, 1901, Ap 13,1:5
Griffin, E H, 1929, Ja 23,23:3
Griffin, Edward C, 1945, Mr 5,19:2
Griffin, Edward G, 1950, N 9,33:1
Griffin, Edward G Mrs, 1943, O 7,23:5
Griffin, Edward J, 1956, My 20,86:6
Griffin, Edward M, 1943, My 2,45:1
Griffin, Edward Payson, 1903, Jl 19,7:6
Griffin, Edward T, 1944, D 14,23:5
Griffin, Edward V, 1941, Ag 17,38:2
Griffin, Edwin A, 1957, D 30,23:5
Griffin, Elizabeth V M Mrs, 1937, Je 17,23:5
Griffin, Eugene A, 1947, O 4,17:1
Griffin, F Stanley, 1955, Ag 4,25:4
Griffin, Francis, 1947, S 28,60:6; 1951, O 14,89:2
Griffin, Francis D, 1965, O 16,27:2
Griffin, Francis E Mrs, 1966, Ja 10,25:1

Griffin, Francis X, 1948, F 20,28:2
Griffin, Frank, 1962, N 2,31:3
Griffin, Frank A, 1951, Mr 30,23:1
Griffin, Frank L, 1953, F 22,63:5
Griffin, Frank R, 1953, Mr 24,31:4
Griffin, Frank R Mrs, 1950, D 7,33:4
Griffin, Franklin D, 1953, D 19,15:4
Griffin, Fred B, 1941, O 4,15:6
Griffin, Frederick, 1946, Ja 16,23:5
Griffin, Frederick R, 1966, Ap 25,31:5
Griffin, Frederick S Rev, 1937, Ag 10,19:2
Griffin, G W H, 1879, Jl 12,5:6
Griffin, George, 1860, My 7,4:5
Griffin, George A, 1950, Ag 1,23:2
Griffin, George B Mrs, 1943, N 21,56:4
Griffin, George C, 1941, D 7,76:2
Griffin, George D J, 1949, Mr 28,21:3
Griffin, George H, 1938, Mr 23,23:2
Griffin, George M, 1941, F 1,17:3
Griffin, George W, 1942, Mr 16,15:1
Griffin, Georgia B, 1937, D 31,15:5
Griffin, Gerald, 1919, Mr 17,15:3; 1962, Ja 13,21:3
Griffin, Gerald J, 1958, F 20,25:4
Griffin, Gerald K, 1960, My 1,87:3
Griffin, Gerald S, 1941, Jl 30,18:5
Griffin, Guy B, 1956, F 13,27:5
Griffin, Gwyn, 1967, O 14,27:1
Griffin, H, 1880, Jl 16,8:3
Griffin, Hancock, 1951, N 26,25:3
Griffin, Hannah V, 1951, O 18,29:5
Griffin, Harry, 1950, Ap 8,13:3
Griffin, Harry M, 1954, My 15,15:6
Griffin, Harry W, 1951, Ap 24,29:4
Griffin, Helen N Mrs, 1950, D 5,31:2
Griffin, Henry J, 1958, Ja 29,27:2
Griffin, Henry K, 1941, D 16,27:3
Griffin, Henry P, 1948, Mr 23,25:2
Griffin, Herbert M Sr Mrs, 1953, Ag 7,19:1
Griffin, Hugh Reed, 1922, My 6,11:5
Griffin, Irving, 1944, N 15,27:4
Griffin, J, 1927, Ja 27,17:5
Griffin, J T Col, 1902, Ja 26,7:5
Griffin, James, 1903, My 3,9:6; 1943, D 15,27:1; 1944, Ag 26,11:3
Griffin, James A, 1948, Ag 6,17:4
Griffin, James A Jr, 1963, D 21,23:2
Griffin, James B, 1947, Jl 27,45:3
Griffin, James F, 1947, S 16,23:2
Griffin, James F Mrs, 1946, Je 8,21:5
Griffin, James G, 1943, N 20,13:6
Griffin, James H, 1950, Mr 22,27:1; 1955, S 18,86:4
Griffin, James T, 1940, Je 28,19:2
Griffin, John, 1939, Mr 17,22:3; 1942, Je 18,21:6
Griffin, John A, 1950, Mr 16,32:2; 1956, Ag 21,29:5; 1960, D 14,39:1
Griffin, John A Mrs, 1955, Jl 9,15:3
Griffin, John F, 1942, Ap 20,21:4; 1952, S 14,86:2
Griffin, John F Mrs, 1952, Ag 24,88:1
Griffin, John G, 1956, D 22,19:4
Griffin, John H, 1944, O 3,23:4; 1948, Ja 22,27:5
Griffin, John H (funl, F 5,20:3), 1954, F 1,23:4
Griffin, John H, 1962, N 30,34:8
Griffin, John J, 1940, Ag 20,19:1; 1944, Je 26,15:5; 1946, S 8,44:5; 1953, S 24,33:2; 1954, Je 19,15:6; 1966, Ap 28,43:2
Griffin, John J Mrs, 1949, Jl 15,19:3
Griffin, John T, 1952, Je 2,21:4
Griffin, John W (por), 1948, Jl 29,21:4
Griffin, John W, 1962, F 17,19:5
Griffin, Joseph, 1947, Je 28,13:4
Griffin, Joseph A, 1937, Jl 10,15:2
Griffin, Joseph B, 1944, N 27,23:4
Griffin, Joseph M, 1947, Ja 30,25:2
Griffin, Joseph P, 1950, F 11,15:4
Griffin, Joseph R, 1954, My 14,23:2
Griffin, Kenneth, 1951, Ja 4,39:5
Griffin, Kenneth J, 1958, Mr 27,33:4
Griffin, L Gilson, 1946, Je 1,13:2
Griffin, Lawrence E, 1949, S 13,29:2
Griffin, Leander, 1944, F 2,21:2
Griffin, Lester B, 1947, My 22,27:2
Griffin, Loren A, 1953, Ag 26,27:6
Griffin, Lyman W, 1941, N 3,19:3
Griffin, Mabel S, 1942, Ja 27,21:2
Griffin, Manley (G Barnett), 1958, Ja 17,25:3
Griffin, Margaret M, 1946, Ja 25,24:2
Griffin, Margaret W Mrs, 1941, O 18,19:4
Griffin, Martin E, 1964, My 20,43:3
Griffin, Martin L, 1942, Ag 31,17:5
Griffin, Matthew F, 1925, N 23,21:5
Griffin, Michael, 1965, N 3,39:2
Griffin, Milo G, 1952, Ap 30,27:3
Griffin, Nathaniel E, 1940, Ag 26,15:2
Griffin, Nelson F, 1950, Ja 8,77:1
Griffin, Oliver C Capt, 1921, Jl 26,15:4
Griffin, Oscar D, 1954, F 8,23:3
Griffin, P R, 1931, Ja 16,21:1
Griffin, Patrick, 1907, D 3,9:6
Griffin, Patrick Francis, 1915, O 27,11:7
Griffin, Percy F, 1938, Ap 6,23:4
Griffin, Phyllis H Mrs, 1956, Jl 5,25:4
Griffin, Prescott, 1941, Jl 19,13:5
Griffin, R S, 1933, F 22,19:1
Griffin, Raphael, 1956, Je 27,31:6
Griffin, Robert, 1959, Ap 29,33:2
Griffin, Robert G, 1968, Mr 23,31:5
Griffin, S G Gen, 1902, Ja 15,9:5
Griffin, Stella G Mrs, 1940, Ja 16,23:1
Griffin, Stephen D, 1925, D 17,23:4
Griffin, Susie A, 1947, N 3,23:4
Griffin, Terrence W, 1953, Je 4,29:2
Griffin, Thomas, 1937, O 27,31:5
Griffin, Thomas A, 1946, Ja 29,25:2
Griffin, Thomas A Rev Dr, 1910, N 8,9:4
Griffin, Thomas B, 1937, F 7,II,8:6
Griffin, Thomas D, 1938, N 12,15:5
Griffin, Thomas H, 1943, Ja 14,21:3
Griffin, Thomas J, 1945, D 3,21:3
Griffin, Timothy E, 1925, S 18,23:5
Griffin, Timothy G, 1955, F 23,27:2
Griffin, Tracy E, 1957, Mr 29,21:4
Griffin, Vincent J, 1962, Ap 22,81:8
Griffin, Virgil C, 1957, Mr 29,21:1
Griffin, Walter H, 1947, Mr 28,24:3
Griffin, Walter T Rev Dr, 1907, D 14,9:5
Griffin, Watson, 1952, Ja 11,21:4
Griffin, Wes, 1956, Jl 28,17:4
Griffin, William (por), 1949, Je 29,27:3
Griffin, William (left no will), 1949, Ag 6,15:3
Griffin, William A, 1942, F 2,15:2; 1944, Mr 20,17:3; 1950, Ja 2,23:1
Griffin, William H, 1947, Mr 1,15:3; 1950, N 13,27:3
Griffin, William J, 1924, O 18,15:6; 1944, My 2,19:5; 1950, Jl 4,17:4; 1957, Jl 6,15:6
Griffin, William J Jr, 1958, O 5,87:1
Griffin, William J Sr, 1959, S 6,72:8
Griffin, William L, 1956, Ap 23,27:3
Griffin, William L J, 1953, O 25,89:1
Griffin, William M, 1965, My 23,85:2
Griffin, William Mrs, 1945, Ag 1,19:2
Griffin, William R, 1945, N 25,50:2
Griffin, William V, 1958, Ja 16,29:3
Griffin, William V Mrs, 1954, Ag 8,85:3
Griffin, Wilmot E, 1925, N 13,19:5
Griffin, Z F, 1938, F 12,15:3
Griffing, Bertrand N, 1949, Ja 27,23:3
Griffing, E C Mrs, 1903, S 2,7:6
Griffing, Edward J, 1965, O 13,47:1
Griffing, Edward S, 1944, S 20,23:3
Griffing, Estelle S Mrs, 1937, N 15,23:6
Griffing, Fred L, 1942, S 1,19:3
Griffing, Fred L Mrs, 1948, Mr 29,21:5
Griffing, J C Capt, 1903, My 21,9:4
Griffing, Joseph, 1939, N 15,23:5
Griffing, Robert P, 1956, Ja 9,25:5
Griffing, Robert P Mrs, 1938, O 25,23:4
Griffing, W Irving, 1941, Ja 13,15:4
Griffis, Dorothy N Mrs, 1942, F 14,15:3
Griffis, Edgar, 1945, F 21,19:4
Griffis, Enid, 1957, Ja 2,27:4
Griffis, Harold, 1961, Jl 2,33:2
Griffis, Joseph K, 1954, My 11,29:3
Griffis, Lawrence W, 1967, Ja 28,27:1
Griffis, W E, 1928, F 6,19:3
Griffis, William E Mrs, 1959, Je 23,33:1
Griffith, Aaron H, 1945, My 11,19:2
Griffith, Alan A, 1963, O 15,39:4
Griffith, Albert L, 1963, Ap 6,19:2
Griffith, Albert T, 1940, O 29,25:3
Griffith, Beatrice Fox Mrs (Mrs Chas F Griffith), 1968, D 7,47:4
Griffith, Benjamin W, 1945, Mr 19,19:5
Griffith, Charles E, 1964, Ag 25,33:4
Griffith, Charles F, 1954, O 19,27:3
Griffith, Charles M, 1939, Ja 13,19:5; 1954, D 20,29:5
Griffith, Charles S Mrs, 1950, Ag 21,19:5
Griffith, Charles T, 1943, S 30,21:3
Griffith, Charles W, 1943, Ag 10,19:5
Griffith, Chauncey H, 1956, O 8,27:5
Griffith, Clark C (funl plans, O 31,33:4; funl, N 1,-31:3), 1955, O 28,25:1
Griffith, Clark Mrs, 1957, O 15,33:2
Griffith, Clinton C, 1966, D 6,47:1
Griffith, D Milton Mrs, 1952, O 5,88:4
Griffith, David W, 1948, Jl 24,15:1
Griffith, De Witt C, 1946, Jl 5,19:4
Griffith, Dickinson E, 1950, Ag 12,13:3
Griffith, Earl, 1940, Mr 31,45:1
Griffith, Earl L, 1966, Je 7,47:1
Griffith, Earl Mrs, 1941, My 25,36:4
Griffith, Edith N R Mrs, 1937, S 4,15:5
Griffith, Edward, 1918, Jl 6,9:5; 1948, D 15,33:1; 1951, O 26,23:3
Griffith, Edwin M, 1946, Mr 15,22:2
Griffith, Eldred, 1937, N 7,II,9:3
Griffith, Eleanor G, 1939, F 7,20:2
Griffith, Elmer C, 1959, Mr 29,80:2
Griffith, Enoch L, 1946, F 1,23:4
Griffith, Eugene C, 1946, My 30,21:4
Griffith, Eugene F, 1956, Jl 7,13:6
Griffith, Eustace B, 1944, My 3,19:6
Griffith, Evan C, 1949, Ap 30,13:5
Griffith, Everett F, 1947, N 27,31:2
Griffith, Frank D, 1945, Ap 21,13:5
Griffith, Fred C Mrs, 1945, O 18,23:2
Griffith, Fred P, 1965, F 9,37:3
Griffith, Frederick J (por), 1949, F 6,76:3
Griffith, George Dr, 1904, My 30,5:6
Griffith, George G, 1940, O 8,25:6
Griffith, George J, 1950, Ap 17,23:2
Griffith, George P, 1947, N 18,29:1
Griffith, George R, 1940, Ag 6,19:5
Griffith, Goldsbrough S, 1904, F 25,9:5
Griffith, Grace, 1949, D 6,31:1
Griffith, Hall M, 1957, Ag 19,19:5
Griffith, Harriet Pomeroy R, 1915, Mr 3,11:5
Griffith, Harry D, 1946, Mr 9,14:2
Griffith, Harry G, 1873, Mr 6,1:6
Griffith, Harry M, 1957, Ag 9,19:3
Griffith, Harry W, 1942, F 23,21:4
Griffith, Heber E Mrs, 1949, Ap 26,25:2
Griffith, Helen S Mrs, 1961, Jl 15,19:6
Griffith, Henry E Mrs, 1960, Jl 16,19:3
Griffith, Henry W (funl plans, Jl 25,29:4), 1956, Jl 24,25:4
Griffith, Horace P, 1941, Ag 14,17:4
Griffith, Howard B, 1942, D 3,25:4
Griffith, Hoyt D, 1947, Ja 6,23:5
Griffith, Hugh W, 1942, O 19,19:4
Griffith, Ivor, 1961, My 17,38:1
Griffith, J E Capt, 1877, Jl 8,6:7
Griffith, J M, 1882, O 24,5:3
Griffith, James, 1951, D 7,29:4
Griffith, James H, 1951, My 15,31:2; 1952, D 10,3
Griffith, Jennie A Mrs, 1949, Je 11,18:8
Griffith, John, 1911, N 26,15:6
Griffith, John F, 1956, Ag 17,19:2
Griffith, John J, 1942, Ap 30,19:2
Griffith, John L (por), 1944, D 8,21:1
Griffith, John P, 1938, O 22,17:5
Griffith, John P C, 1941, Jl 30,17:2
Griffith, John P M, 1953, Je 27,15:5
Griffith, John Q, 1952, O 21,29:2
Griffith, John S, 1951, Ja 22,17:1
Griffith, John S Mrs, 1951, Ag 14,23:5
Griffith, Joseph, 1944, N 30,23:1
Griffith, K L, 1967, D 9,47:2
Griffith, Leo G, 1949, F 2,28:2
Griffith, Lewis D, 1912, O 7,11:5
Griffith, Lewis T Lt-Col, 1919, Ap 20,22:3
Griffith, Maddy (Mrs Jesse Brinker Griffith), 19 Ja 2,37:1
Griffith, Parker O, 1960, Mr 13,86:3
Griffith, Parker O Mrs, 1960, D 9,31:1
Griffith, Patrick, 1946, F 6,23:4
Griffith, Paul A, 1953, Ja 19,23:2
Griffith, Paul M, 1944, Mr 30,21:6
Griffith, Percy L Mrs, 1952, D 30,19:1
Griffith, Percy T, 1950, S 1,21:4
Griffith, Raymond, 1957, N 27,31:4
Griffith, Raymond E, 1956, Mr 31,15:4
Griffith, Richard, 1951, Ja 22,17:3
Griffith, Robert E (funl, Je 11,86:4), 1961, Je 8
Griffith, Robert E Mrs, 1962, Je 10,86:5
Griffith, Robert M, 1944, My 1,15:2
Griffith, Robert M Maj, 1937, Ja 4,7:5
Griffith, Robert Mrs, 1962, Je 21,31:2
Griffith, Rupert E, 1943, N 26,23:5
Griffith, Russell B, 1952, N 14,23:4
Griffith, Ruth M, 1957, S 14,19:2
Griffith, Sam, 1963, Je 27,33:3
Griffith, Samuel H, 1905, Ap 25,11:6
Griffith, Samuel Sir, 1920, Ag 13,9:6
Griffith, Sarah E Mrs, 1942, Jl 22,19:1
Griffith, Stephen C Jr, 1954, S 2,21:5
Griffith, Stephen M, 1956, Jl 7,13:4
Griffith, Susan D (will, O 7,21:4), 1938, S 28,2
Griffith, Thomas F, 1960, F 17,35:3
Griffith, Thomas R, 1942, N 14,16:2; 1948, D 1
Griffith, W C, 1939, Mr 26,III,7:1
Griffith, W H, 1883, Jl 24,3:7
Griffith, W Maben, 1952, Jl 11,17:3
Griffith, W P, 1936, F 18,24:3
Griffith, Walter A, 1937, Ap 27,23:4
Griffith, Walter I, 1951, S 30,74:5
Griffith, Walter S, 1872, N 26,4:7
Griffith, Walter W, 1925, S 22,25:5
Griffith, Walton H, 1966, Je 10,45:4
Griffith, William A, 1940, My 26,34:3
Griffith, William B, 1939, Ja 9,15:2; 1952, Ja 7
Griffith, William D, 1954, N 17,28:2
Griffith, William E Capt, 1925, N 19,25:4
Griffith, William G, 1964, Mr 28,19:3
Griffith, William H, 1905, Ap 15,11:5
Griffith, William J, 1960, F 3,31:2
Griffith, Yeatman, 1939, Je 18,37:2
Griffith-Boscawen, Arthur S T, 1946, Je 2,44:5
Griffith-Davies, John D, 1953, D 19,15:5
Griffiths, Alfred, 1943, D 27,19:2
Griffiths, Arthur C, 1947, N 15,17:4
Griffiths, Arthur F Mrs, 1957, Je 14,25:3
Griffiths, Charles H, 1954, O 26,27:2
Griffiths, Charles H Mrs, 1939, S 16,17:4
Griffiths, David G, 1954, Ap 9,23:2
Griffiths, David R, 1953, D 29,23:1
Griffiths, Eben, 1967, D 14,47:3
Griffiths, Edward M (por), 1939, My 28,III,7
Griffiths, Edward R, 1952, Ja 20,84:6
Griffiths, Elizabeth, 1948, F 18,27:4

Griffiths, Farnham P, 1958, Jl 2,29:4
Griffiths, Frank C, 1939, My 9,23:4
Griffiths, Frederick D, 1967, F 21,44:5
Griffiths, Frederick J, 1951, N 24,11:2
Griffiths, George A, 1945, D 16,40:4; 1949, S 30,23:3
Griffiths, George F, 1957, S 30,31:4
Griffiths, George H (por), 1946, Mr 28,25:3
Griffiths, George H, 1950, Mr 28,32:2
Griffiths, George W, 1947, Ap 7,23:3
Griffiths, Harold D, 1941, Ja 30,21:1
Griffiths, Hugh B, 1960, Ja 17,86:4
Griffiths, Hugh Mrs, 1939, Ag 4,34:7
Griffiths, James H (funl, F 28,29:2), 1964, F 25,31:3
Griffiths, James H Mrs, 1964, Ja 20,43:2
Griffiths, John, 1937, O 8,24:1
Griffiths, John E, 1961, Jl 11,31:1
Griffiths, John J Mrs, 1946, D 2,25:4
Griffiths, John L (funl, My 20,13:6), 1914, My 18,9:3
Griffiths, Lawrence, 1944, F 9,19:4
Griffiths, Leon H Mrs, 1952, Ap 1,30:3
Griffiths, Llewellyn W, 1950, O 22,92:2
Griffiths, Mansel P, 1945, N 6,19:4
Griffiths, Melville O, 1948, Mr 31,25:2
Griffiths, Millard F, 1937, Ja 4,29:4
Griffiths, Norman Mrs, 1952, F 27,27:3
Griffiths, Percy L, 1947, O 5,68:6
Griffiths, Percy L Mrs, 1945, Je 16,13:5
Griffiths, Richard, 1938, O 10,19:5
Griffiths, Richard Sr, 1949, D 15,35:6
Griffiths, Robert, 1941, Ja 29,17:5
Griffiths, Samuel M, 1938, D 26,24:4
Griffiths, Thomas, 1960, Jl 15,23:4
Griffiths, Thomas J, 1924, F 7,17:5
Griffiths, Thomas S, 1939, D 11,23:3
Griffiths, W H, 1885, Mr 24,3:3
Griffiths, William H, 1959, Ja 30,27:2
Griffiths, William T, 1952, Ag 1,18:6; 1962, Mr 11,86:3
Griffiths, William W, 1958, Mr 11,29:4
Griffitts, William F, 1943, O 13,23:3
Grifo, Michael J, 1955, O 20,35:4
Grigaitis, Walter K, 1957, N 17,87:1
Grigg, Edward (Lord Altrincham), 1955, D 2,27:5
Grigg, Eugenie L, 1940, Ja 28,32:1
Grigg, Grace B (por), 1946, Ja 30,25:5
Grigg, Harry K, 1946, Mr 16,13:3
Grigg, James, 1964, My 7,37:1
Grigg, John, 1864, Ag 5,3:1
Grigg, Joseph W Sr, 1951, Ja 16,29:4
Grigg, Walter A, 1945, D 9,45:1
Griggs, Allmond M, 1941, Je 4,23:5
Griggs, Art, 1938, D 20,25:3
Griggs, Charles W Mrs, 1944, N 11,13:5
Griggs, Edward H, 1951, Je 7,33:4
Griggs, Ellsworth W, 1939, My 7,III,7:2
Griggs, Elmer V, 1968, Je 1,27:5
Griggs, Elsie M, 1954, Ag 28,15:5
Griggs, Frederick, 1952, Ag 11,15:5
Griggs, Frederick L M, 1938, Je 8,23:5
Griggs, G Clinton, 1962, Ap 7,25:3
Griggs, G Gresham, 1956, O 23,33:4
Griggs, G Gresham Mrs, 1953, My 27,31:3
Griggs, G M, 1881, Je 15,5:2
Griggs, George, 1939, N 3,21:6
Griggs, George L, 1939, O 9,19:6
Griggs, Harry E, 1942, S 24,27:4
Griggs, Herbert L (por), 1944, S 21,19:3
Griggs, Herbert L Mrs, 1938, Jl 20,19:6
Griggs, J Edgar Mrs, 1947, Jl 4,13:3
Griggs, J W, 1927, N 29,27:3
Griggs, James M, 1910, Ja 6,9:5
Griggs, John, 1967, F 27,29:1
Griggs, John C Mrs, 1947, N 14,23:2
Griggs, John L, 1961, Jl 17,21:5
Griggs, John W 2d Mrs, 1963, Ag 31,17:6
Griggs, Leland, 1964, Je 30,33:4
Griggs, M Y, 1941, F 3,20:2
Griggs, Maitland F, 1943, Jl 26,19:4
Griggs, Maitland F Mrs, 1950, Mr 20,21:4
Griggs, Mary A, 1962, Mr 20,37:1
Griggs, Mary G, 1945, Ja 24,21:4
Griggs, Robert F, 1962, Je 10,86:5
Griggs, Robert F Mrs, 1956, Jl 24,25:3
Griggs, Stephen A, 1937, Ap 3,19:3
Griglio, Lawrence V, 1950, N 18,15:4
Griglio, Pietro, 1947, O 22,29:4
Grignard, Emile E, 1954, N 3,29:2
Grignon, Philias A, 1950, Jl 28,21:4
Grigoriev, Boris, 1939, F 9,21:5
Grigorovich-Barsky, Peter, 1965, N 22,37:3
Grigsby, Bertram J, 1954, S 21,27:5
Grigsby, Braxton, 1916, Mr 19,19:7
Grigsby, Emilie B, 1964, F 14,29:3
Grigsby, H B, 1881, My 6,2:4
Grigsby, Walter B Capt, 1937, Ap 20,25:3
Griliches, Samuel S, 1965, Je 25,33:2
Grill, A Maurice, 1957, Ja 5,17:6
Grill, A Maurice Mrs, 1950, Jl 31,17:2
Grill, John, 1945, Mr 18,42:1
Grill, Larry, 1948, D 4,13:5
Grill, Louis F, 1953, Ag 7,19:4
Grill, Nicholas A, 1942, My 19,20:2
Grill, Ray, 1937, Ja 11,20:2
Grill, Walter, 1956, F 27,23:2
Grillo, Nicholas, 1953, My 10,33:3
Grillo, Salvatore A, 1952, O 16,29:3
Grills, Walter H, 1943, D 17,27:3
Grim, Allan K, 1965, D 9,47:3
Grim, Charles E, 1962, Je 3,88:7
Grim, Charles O, 1937, F 6,17:2
Grim, F R Dr, 1924, My 22,17:6
Grim, George W, 1956, O 17,35:4
Grim, J Nelson Mrs, 1953, Jl 11,11:6
Grim, Joseph, 1939, Ag 20,33:3
Grim, Robert H, 1945, Ag 21,21:5
Grim, Webster, 1947, Jl 26,13:3
Grimal, Raymond, 1955, Ap 6,29:4
Grimaldi, Enrico Prince, 1954, D 20,29:3
Grimaldi, Frederick L, 1962, Ap 14,27:6
Grimaldi, Marquess (Ernest Geo), 1953, F 18,31:1
Grimard, Eloi, 1953, O 7,29:3
Grimault, Jean, 1952, F 15,25:4
Grimball, Elizabeth B, 1953, Ag 31,17:3
Grimberg, Leizer, 1944, N 16,23:2
Grimble, Arthur F Sir, 1956, D 14,29:2
Grimditch, William H, 1966, Jl 29,31:2
Grime, Arthur E, 1938, O 12,27:6
Grime, Joseph, 1938, Je 30,23:1
Grime, Robert T, 1940, Jl 7,25:1
Grimes, Albert C Sr, 1944, Ap 27,23:5
Grimes, Alex V, 1941, D 1,19:5
Grimes, Arthur V, 1952, Ap 22,29:2
Grimes, Big George, 1903, S 6,10:7
Grimes, Carlton O (cor, Ja 17,24:2), 1940, Ja 16,23:5
Grimes, Charles H, 1951, S 3,13:4
Grimes, Charles P, 1957, N 1,23:1
Grimes, Clinton G, 1960, Jl 10,72:2
Grimes, Earnest M, 1961, Ja 21,21:4
Grimes, Edward J, 1952, S 17,31:6
Grimes, Edward L, 1951, Ap 24,29:3
Grimes, Edward T, 1942, F 12,23:5
Grimes, Emma C, 1945, Ja 13,11:3
Grimes, Eugene L, 1957, Jl 19,19:2
Grimes, Frances, 1963, N 11,31:4
Grimes, George A, 1953, Je 23,29:4
Grimes, J Stanley, 1903, S 29,9:5
Grimes, James F, 1944, F 23,19:5
Grimes, James W Ex-Sen, 1872, F 9,8:4
Grimes, John Archbishop, 1922, Ag 2,17:7
Grimes, John F, 1948, N 18,27:4
Grimes, John W, 1946, S 4,23:1
Grimes, Lester A, 1963, N 7,37:3
Grimes, Louis I, 1944, Ja 30,37:2
Grimes, Margaret A, 1944, Jl 1,15:5
Grimes, Marin J, 1948, Ja 2,23:3
Grimes, Oscar R, 1953, My 28,23:3
Grimes, Patrick J Mrs, 1962, Jl 7,17:5
Grimes, Peter A, 1941, Je 13,19:5
Grimes, Robert, 1903, D 9,9:5
Grimes, T Manning, 1950, Ag 19,13:4
Grimes, Virginia, 1944, Ag 26,11:6
Grimes, Willard M, 1960, Ap 13,39:4
Grimes, William A, 1961, N 17,35:1
Grimijser, J C, 1947, D 31,15:4
Grimke, Angelina W, 1958, Je 11,36:1
Grimley, Jennie P Mrs, 1942, Mr 20,19:2
Grimley, John G, 1948, Mr 6,13:5
Grimley, John G Mrs, 1962, Jl 26,27:5
Grimley, John J Mrs, 1949, Ja 19,27:2
Grimley, John M, 1957, F 2,19:3
Grimley, Roy J, 1966, My 7,31:5
Grimley, Thomas H Mrs, 1963, Ap 23,37:2
Grimm, Albert P, 1945, Mr 3,13:1
Grimm, C F Rev, 1903, My 7,9:6
Grimm, Carl W, 1952, F 27,27:3
Grimm, Charles, 1953, Ap 6,19:3
Grimm, Charles K, 1956, Ap 1,89:2
Grimm, Earle D, 1941, Mr 22,15:5
Grimm, Edward L, 1938, N 4,23:6
Grimm, George, 1945, O 20,11:6
Grimm, Hans, 1959, S 28,31:5
Grimm, Herbert L, 1939, S 24,43:1
Grimm, J Henry, 1950, D 23,15:2
Grimm, Jacob, 1863, O 9,2:3
Grimm, John F, 1937, O 13,23:5
Grimm, John J Mrs, 1946, Ag 13,27:2
Grimm, John M, 1943, D 23,19:3
Grimm, John Mrs, 1947, My 11,63:3
Grimm, Karl J, 1954, S 22,29:3
Grimm, Lawrence P, 1946, O 4,23:1
Grimm, Martin, 1947, Ag 22,15:2
Grimm, Paul H, 1925, D 18,23:4; 1925, D 19,17:6
Grimm, Peter Mrs, 1967, D 16,41:4
Grimm, Robert, 1958, Mr 9,87:1
Grimm, Rudolph J, 1962, N 1,31:4
Grimm, Warren O Mrs, 1958, F 15,17:3
Grimm, William C, 1950, My 30,17:4
Grimm, William C H, 1960, O 21,33:2
Grimm, William L, 1943, Ja 15,17:3
Grimm, William Mrs, 1950, My 31,29:3
Grimmell, Julius C Rev, 1921, S 3,9:6
Grimmer, G Skiffington, 1956, My 2,31:5
Grimmer, Otto, 1955, O 9,86:3
Grimmer, Roy D, 1954, F 7,89:1
Grimmer, Walter, 1938, Ap 26,21:3
Grimmer, William F, 1955, My 27,23:5
Grimmett, Leonard G, 1951, My 29,25:4
Grimoldi, Alberto E, 1953, Jl 24,13:6
Grimond, Andrew, 1966, Mr 24,12:6
Grimshaw, Beatrice J, 1953, Jl 1,29:5
Grimshaw, David W, 1951, Jl 15,60:3
Grimshaw, Elliott W, 1961, Ja 18,33:1
Grimshaw, Ira L, 1943, Ja 2,11:2
Grimshaw, John, 1938, F 18,19:3
Grimshaw, John Mrs, 1949, F 20,60:3
Grimshaw, Lamar C, 1950, Jl 30,60:3
Grimshaw, Robert, 1941, Ap 10,23:3
Grimsley, Edgar H, 1965, O 21,47:4
Grimson, Samuel B, 1955, N 30,33:4
Grimston, William Hunter (Wm Hunter Kendal), 1917, N 8,15:4
Grimthorpe, Lord, 1905, Ap 30,7:6
Grimthorpe, Lord (Ernest Wm Beckett), 1917, My 10,13:6
Grimwood, Harry W, 1925, My 2,15:5
Grinager, Alex, 1949, Mr 9,25:2
Grinan, John F, 1957, My 24,25:3
Grinberg, P Irving Mrs, 1945, Je 13,23:3
Grinberg-Vinaver, Leon Mrs, 1964, My 27,39:2
Grindal, Herbert W, 1959, My 31,77:2
Grindal, Herbert W Mrs, 1948, F 20,27:4
Grindel, Louis, 1948, D 8,31:5
Grindell, Gustav, 1950, Ap 12,27:4
Grindell-Matthews, Harry (por), 1941, S 12,21:3
Grinden, William Joseph Maj, 1920, N 27,13:6
Grindley, Arthur R, 1949, My 24,27:2
Grindley, John C, 1961, Ag 3,23:2
Grindol, Herbert White, 1906, F 7,9:5
Griner, George, 1948, My 30,34:4
Gringras, Albert F, 1952, Mr 27,29:6
Grinius, Kazys, 1950, Je 5,23:4
Grinius, Kazys V Jr, 1965, My 31,17:6
Grinman, Daniel, 1940, Ja 2,19:2
Grinn, Frank J, 1942, D 20,44:7
Grinnan, Robert T Mrs, 1955, Je 15,31:2
Grinnel, Frederick, 1905, O 22,9:6
Grinnel, Robert C, 1945, Mr 19,19:4
Grinnell, Ashbel P Dr, 1907, Ap 7,9:5
Grinnell, Ben, 1925, S 29,27:4
Grinnell, C, 1869, Ag 12,5:1
Grinnell, Charles Edward, 1916, F 3,9:3
Grinnell, Edgar, 1937, Ja 11,19:5
Grinnell, Edith W Mrs, 1938, Mr 24,23:6
Grinnell, Edmund, 1948, F 3,25:1
Grinnell, Edmund Mrs, 1956, Jl 12,23:2
Grinnell, Elizabeth M P Mrs, 1945, N 7,23:3
Grinnell, Elmer W, 1941, Mr 15,17:1
Grinnell, Emogyene, 1957, N 17,87:2
Grinnell, Ernest G, 1954, F 7,89:1
Grinnell, Francis B Dr, 1937, N 21,II,8:7
Grinnell, Frank, 1875, S 13,4:7
Grinnell, Frank W, 1964, Mr 14,23:6
Grinnell, G Frank, 1945, Mr 7,22:2
Grinnell, George B (por),(will, Ap 17,27:6), 1938, Ap 12,23:1
Grinnell, Henry, 1874, Jl 2,4:7
Grinnell, Henry W Mrs, 1944, Ap 3,21:6
Grinnell, Henry Walton, 1920, S 4,9:2
Grinnell, Irving, 1921, My 12,17:4
Grinnell, Joseph, 1939, My 30,17:2
Grinnell, Julia Mrs (funl), 1872, Mr 31,5:2
Grinnell, Lawrence, 1950, Mr 2,28:3
Grinnell, Lawrence I Mrs, 1960, N 3,39:3
Grinnell, Lawrence Mrs, 1950, N 4,17:4
Grinnell, M H (see also N 25,26), 1877, N 27,8:2
Grinnell, M J, 1865, Jl 27,8:4
Grinnell, Moses H, 1872, F 27,5:2
Grinnell, Russell, 1948, Jl 3,16:2
Grinnell, Sarah S Mrs, 1941, N 21,17:2
Grinnell, William F, 1912, D 13,15:4; 1918, Ap 25,13:5
Grinnell, William M Mrs, 1944, Ag 12,11:2
Grinold, John W Mrs, 1961, Jl 7,25:1
Grinsfelder, H J, 1967, Ap 4,43:1
Grinstead, Minnie J Mrs, 1925, D 25,17:4
Grinstead, William M, 1952, Ag 3,61:2
Grinsted, A T, 1903, My 22,9:4
Grinsted, W Stanley, 1938, Jl 22,17:4
Grint, Alfred P, 1948, S 20,25:3
Grinton, George W, 1949, Je 14,31:5
Grinton, George W Mrs, 1954, S 28,29:6
Grinwis, John, 1947, D 14,76:6
Griot, George, 1953, S 11,21:3
Griot, George Mrs, 1944, F 25,16:5
Grip, F William, 1966, My 16,37:2
Gripenberg, A Lt (see also Jl 8), 1878, Jl 10,8:2
Gripp, James C, 1958, D 6,23:4
Grippen, William J Mrs, 1943, Je 10,21:4
Grippin, William Avery, 1911, Mr 3,11:4
Grippin, William J, 1950, Jl 27,25:5
Grippo, Anthony T, 1951, Mr 6,27:1
Grisbach, A H R, 1879, My 14,5:3
Grisby, Albert B, 1954, My 26,29:1
Griscom, Clement A Mrs, 1923, Mr 2,15:4; 1958, S 4, 29:1
Griscom, Clement A 3d Mrs, 1955, Je 8,29:2
Griscom, Clement Acton (por), 1912, N 11,11:3
Griscom, Clement Acton, 1918, D 31,11:4
Griscom, I Norwood, 1954, Jl 31,13:4
Griscom, J Milton Mrs, 1967, Jl 1,23:5
Griscom, Leo E, 1956, Ag 18,17:2

Griscom, Lloyd C, 1959, F 9,26:1
Griscom, Lloyd C Mrs, 1914, N 17,13:4
Griscom, Ludlow, 1959, My 29,23:1
Griscom, Mary W, 1946, N 6,23:1
Griscom, Milton, 1943, Je 7,13:4; 1949, F 6,20:5
Griscom, Rodman E Mrs, 1919, Je 16,13:5
Griscom, William B, 1940, Mr 24,30:7
Grisdale, Thomas, 1937, My 12,23:4
Grisell, Thomas O, 1945, N 6,19:2
Griser, John M, 1957, O 16,35:2
Grishaber, William J, 1943, Je 19,13:4
Grishaver, Ira M, 1950, D 23,15:3
Grishin, Ivan, 1951, Je 23,15:5
Grishko, Grigory E, 1959, F 11,39:4
Grisi, Mme, 1869, N 30,1:7
Grisman, Samuel H, 1955, Mr 2,11:4
Grismer, Carey W, 1941, Ja 12,44:2
Grismer, Charles, 1925, Mr 19,21:3
Grismore, Grover C, 1951, Mr 11,94:5
Grissell, Wallace A, 1954, Ap 8,27:3
Grissom, Arthur, 1901, D 4,9:4
Grissom, Virgil I (funl and burial plans, Ja 29,49:2), 1967, Ja 28,1:8
Grist, Frank D, 1960, Ag 25,29:1
Gristede, Charles (por), 1948, O 31,88:3
Gristede, Diedrich B Mrs, 1959, N 15,87:1
Gristock, Frank W, 1942, S 26,15:4
Griston, Harris J, 1952, O 3,23:2
Griswald, Gerrit S, 1938, F 26,15:3
Griswald, M R Dr, 1903, Mr 2,2:2
Griswold, A H (por), 1940, F 25,39:1
Griswold, A Whitney (funl, Ap 23,37:1), 1963, Ap 20,1:4
Griswold, Albert C, 1954, Jl 22,23:4
Griswold, Arthur R, 1957, Jl 1,23:5
Griswold, C W, 1883, Ag 21,2:6
Griswold, Carolyn, 1937, Je 23,25:5
Griswold, Carolyn M Mrs, 1938, My 18,21:2
Griswold, Carroll C, 1949, Jl 22,19:5
Griswold, Chester, 1902, Ja 24,7:5
Griswold, Christiana M MRs, 1947, F 6,23:6
Griswold, Clifford B, 1962, Ja 31,31:2
Griswold, Daniel Paine Mrs, 1922, Jl 27,17:6
Griswold, Dixon B, 1967, F 22,29:4
Griswold, Dwight P (funl, Ap 15,29:4), 1954, Ap 12, 29:1
Griswold, Edna E Mrs, 1937, Je 29,21:3
Griswold, Ella A, 1940, Ja 27,13:6
Griswold, Elmer W, 1916, D 25,9:5
Griswold, Ely, 1960, N 5,23:5
Griswold, Evalyn M, 1951, O 21,93:1
Griswold, Ezra P, 1939, Jl 26,19:3
Griswold, Fanny E, 1953, Jl 22,27:3
Griswold, Florence, 1937, D 7,25:5
Griswold, Francis B Mrs, 1921, Ap 28,13:3
Griswold, Frank G, 1937, Mr 31,23:3
Griswold, Frank G (will), 1938, S 27,24:2
Griswold, Frank J, 1948, O 30,15:4
Griswold, Frederick Jr, 1952, Mr 27,29:5
Griswold, G, 1884, Ap 27,14:5
Griswold, G Edmund, 1943, N 26,23:4
Griswold, George, 1917, Mr 19,11:4; 1964, D 9,50:3
Griswold, George N, 1953, My 2,15:5
Griswold, Glenn, 1940, D 6,23:5; 1950, My 16,31:1
Griswold, H W, 1939, Jl 5,17:3
Griswold, Hal H, 1953, F 8,88:3
Griswold, Harold C, 1950, My 16,31:4
Griswold, Harold E, 1952, Jl 9,27:1
Griswold, Harold H, 1950, Ag 12,13:2
Griswold, Hector C, 1959, S 2,29:4
Griswold, Herman H, 1942, F 27,18:3
Griswold, Herman H Mrs, 1962, O 8,23:3
Griswold, Hervey D, 1945, My 19,19:4
Griswold, Hervey D Mrs, 1944, Ja 21,17:4
Griswold, Hovey H Mrs, 1960, Mr 6,86:5
Griswold, James B Lt, 1917, O 26,15:4
Griswold, James B Mrs, 1959, S 24,37:1
Griswold, John A, 1872, N 1,5:2; 1940, O 11,21:2
Griswold, Joseph L Mrs, 1937, O 26,23:2
Griswold, Josephine H Mrs, 1937, S 30,23:3
Griswold, Laurence W, 1947, S 5,20:2
Griswold, Le Grand, 1916, Mr 12,19:4
Griswold, Lilian, 1937, N 23,23:2
Griswold, Lyman W, 1944, F 1,19:3
Griswold, Merrill, 1962, Ja 9,48:1
Griswold, Merritt W Mrs, 1945, S 27,21:5
Griswold, Merton L, 1951, Mr 29,27:2
Griswold, Morgan B, 1943, Ap 27,23:2
Griswold, Oscar W, 1959, O 7,43:4
Griswold, Paul J, 1951, Ap 18,31:2
Griswold, Putnam, 1914, F 27,11:3
Griswold, Robert G, 1957, My 31,19:1
Griswold, Robert G Mrs, 1960, Jl 21,27:5
Griswold, Robertson, 1958, Ag 30,15:3
Griswold, Roger W, 1944, D 17,38:3
Griswold, S K, 1903, Ag 5,7:6
Griswold, S L, 1882, Ja 25,5:2
Griswold, S M, 1930, N 29,17:1
Griswold, Samuel B, 1921, D 22,15:4
Griswold, Stephen B, 1912, My 5,II,15:5
Griswold, Stephen J, 1952, Ap 28,19:2
Griswold, Stephen M, 1916, Je 3,13:6
Griswold, Victor M, 1945, D 25,23:5
Griswold, Wareham, 1876, Ja 16,2:7
Griswold, Whiting, 1874, O 30,4:6
Griswold, William C, 1947, Jl 12,13:5
Griswold, William Churchill Dr, 1923, Ag 25,7:5
Griswold, William E S, 1964, Ja 21,29:4
Griswold, William E S Mrs, 1944, Mr 31,21:4
Gritschke, Erwin, 1950, Mr 1,27:3
Gritschke, Samuel, 1952, Jl 1,23:4
Gritzmacher, Adolph, 1946, D 31,18:4
Gritzner, Albert, 1958, S 6,17:4
Gritzner, Alexander, 1945, Jl 1,18:2
Grizzley, M, 1946, Jl 19,19:4
Groark, George F, 1944, D 2,13:6
Groark, Patrick, 1954, N 7,89:2
Groark, Thomas J, 1937, Ap 16,23:2; 1940, S 15,48:3
Groat, Carl D, 1953, Jl 27,19:4
Groat, Francis P, 1954, S 5,50:2
Groat, George G, 1951, S 11,29:3
Groat, Ida J Mrs, 1939, Ja 17,21:6
Groat, Robert B, 1959, F 14,21:4
Groat, William A, 1945, S 11,23:4
Groat, William B Sr, 1946, F 10,42:4
Groat, William Mrs, 1946, Ag 13,27:3
Grob, Frederick, 1964, D 18,34:6
Grob, Henry, 1937, Mr 3,23:1
Grobe, Alfred J, 1961, Ag 14,25:1
Grobe, Walter H Mrs, 1951, O 8,21:4
Groben, W Ellis Mrs, 1940, Mr 3,45:2
Grober, Joseph A, 1949, D 22,23:3
Grober, Konrad, 1948, F 16,21:4
Groberg, David, 1963, Jl 3,27:1
Grobert, Henry, 1943, Ap 4,41:1
Grobet, Charles E, 1950, Jl 11,31:4
Grobler, Pieter G W, 1942, Ag 24,15:5
Groboski, John J, 1965, F 17,43:2
Grobow, Edward L, 1956, S 1,15:6
Grobschmidt, John W, 1939, S 7,25:3
Groce, Byron, 1924, O 9,23:5
Groce, Joseph B, 1937, D 12,II,9:1
Groch, Sigmund N, 1961, N 9,35:3
Grochau, Henry R (est acctg), 1964, O 7,47:1
Grock (A Wettach), 1959, Jl 15,29:1
Grocoff, Jacob, 1943, Ap 29,21:1
Grod, Aime G Mrs, 1963, S 21,21:2
Grodecky, Zev, 1968, Je 20,45:4
Groden, Emily C Mrs, 1942, O 30,19:5
Groden, Mary V, 1954, Ap 18,88:8
Groden, Morris, 1951, F 23,27:1
Groden, Morris Mrs, 1949, Ag 26,19:5
Grodfeld, Ludwik, 1955, S 22,31:1
Grodin, J Gerard, 1966, D 4,89:1
Grodin, Thomas Mrs, 1966, O 9,86:1
Grodinsky, Julius, 1962, Jl 11,35:1
Grodsky, Charles, 1948, Ap 2,23:1
Grodzins, Morton M, 1964, Mr 10,34:4
Groeber, Adolf, 1919, N 21,11:3
Groedel, Franz M, 1951, O 13,17:2
Groedel, Harry, 1967, O 10,47:3
Groedel, Max M, 1945, Ja 18,19:5
Groehl, Frederick J, 1961, F 23,27:1
Groehl, Henry M, 1958, F 4,29:2
Groel, Augusta N Mrs, 1947, O 18,15:4
Groell, Dora S Mrs, 1957, D 23,23:4
Groenendaal, Peter J, 1949, S 1,21:6
Groener, Wilhelm (por), 1939, My 5,23:3
Groeninger, William J, 1943, Mr 1,19:6
Groenke, A Robert, 1955, Ja 16,92:4
Groenman, Frans E H, 1943, Je 21,17:4
Groepler, Frederick P, 1945, Jl 1,18:3
Groesbeck, Alex J, 1953, Mr 11,29:3
Groesbeck, Arthur B, 1940, D 1,62:2
Groesbeck, Clarence E, 1948, Ag 22,62:2
Groesbeck, Dan S, 1950, Ag 31,25:3
Groesbeck, Edward, 1942, My 10,43:2
Groesbeck, Edward A Mrs, 1952, Ag 9,13:2
Groesbeck, George S, 1954, Ag 11,25:2
Groesbeck, John H, 1879, My 21,2:6
Groesbeck, Philip, 1959, Je 11,33:3
Groesbeck, Stephen, 1873, Mr 30,5:1
Groesbeck, Stephen Gen, 1904, My 9,9:3
Groeschel, Lesser B, 1943, F 24,21:1
Groessle, Benjamin P, 1950, My 7,106:2
Groessle, Charles, 1945, Ap 10,19:1
Groesz, Josef, 1961, O 4,45:4
Groetken, J J, 1941, Ap 9,25:2
Groetzinger, John, 1962, S 3,15:3
Grof, George N Mrs, 1948, S 30,27:1
Groff, Charles G, 1940, O 26,15:3
Groff, Frank F, 1942, Ja 26,15:2
Groff, Frazier, 1957, S 14,19:5
Groff, Fred D, 1952, Jl 15,21:4
Groff, G Weidman, 1954, D 7,33:1
Groff, Gordon E, 1961, F 17,28:1
Groff, James A, 1952, Mr 2,92:2
Groff, Raymond E, 1961, O 11,47:2
Groff, Russell A, 1958, O 29,35:4
Groff, Sam, 1950, Mr 21,18:5
Groff, Warren W, 1952, My 23,21:2
Grogan, Charles A, 1955, Je 27,21:5
Grogan, Dennis R, 1938, D 28,26:4
Grogan, Edward G Mrs, 1948, Ag 22,60:7
Grogan, Francis J, 1946, Jl 27,17:2
Grogan, Frank M, 1941, Ag 7,17:1
Grogan, George T, 1944, Mr 1,19:4
Grogan, George W, 1940, Jl 14,30:8
Grogan, James A, 1950, N 21,31:3
Grogan, James J, 1949, D 21,29:2
Grogan, John, 1945, S 6,25:2
Grogan, John J, 1968, S 17,47:1
Grogan, Joseph E, 1938, O 21,23:3
Grogan, Nicholas J, 1960, N 18,31:2
Grogan, Patrick, 1950, O 14,19:4
Grogan, William, 1950, O 8,68:2
Groger, Edward, 1950, Ap 5,31:4
Grogin, George, 1954, Jl 16,21:3
Groh, Edward, 1905, Ja 4,9:3
Groh, Heinie, 1968, Ag 24,29:1
Groh, Herman Mrs, 1938, D 12,19:5
Groh, Louis E, 1948, N 8,21:3
Groh, Paul, 1937, Ap 26,19:5
Groh, Theodore J, 1960, S 16,31:2
Grohe, Glenn E, 1956, Ap 16,14:6
Grohmann, H Victor Mrs, 1943, My 3,17:4
Grohmann, Will, 1968, My 8,47:2
Grohmann, William M, 1947, My 5,23:1
Grohn, H Van, 1879, O 6,5:5
Grohusko, David, 1948, Mr 21,61:1
Grol, Milan, 1952, D 4,35:4
Groll, Albert L, 1952, O 3,23:1
Groll, Albert L Mrs, 1937, Mr 9,24:2
Groll, Augustus F, 1950, D 15,31:3
Groll, Charles W, 1949, O 28,23:5
Groll, Charles W Mrs (J Goldstein), 1960, F 10,3
Groll, Mabel B Mrs (will), 1950, Ag 6,48:4
Grolle, Johan, 1956, Je 14,33:1
Grollman, Louis, 1953, D 13,86:5
Grombach, Andre, 1951, S 13,31:4
Grombacher, Irving S, 1950, Ag 4,21:6
Gromer, Irving, 1959, Je 18,31:5
Gromoll, Otho C, 1945, S 9,45:1
Gron, Niels, 1924, Mr 22,15:6
Gronau, Hans von, 1940, F 24,13:5
Gronau, William F, 1924, Ap 12,15:4
Gronbeck, Axel C, 1964, My 15,36:4
Gronbeck, Walter G, 1954, My 1,15:4
Gronberger, Sven Magnus, 1916, Ap 26,13:5
Grondahl, Lars Olai, 1968, Ja 27,29:4
Gronemann, Carl F, 1941, N 6,23:1
Groner, Duncan L, 1957, Jl 20,14:4
Groner, John A C, 1949, D 10,17:4
Groner, Morris L, 1941, Je 11,21:2
Groner, V D Gen, 1903, N 26,7:6
Gronich, Harry, 1954, D 9,33:4
Gronim, Michael, 1955, D 10,21:5
Groninger, Carl H, 1958, Jl 13,68:7
Groninger, Katharina, 1943, N 18,13:3
Gronlund, Theodore O, 1966, D 28,37:2
Gronna, Asle J Ex-Sen, 1922, My 5,17:5
Grono, Joseph F, 1952, Ap 3,37:3
Gronouski, John A Sr, 1964, Je 7,86:8
Groody, Louise (Mrs J Loofbourrow), 1961, S 1
Groom, Edward, 1903, Ap 20,7:4
Groom, John, 1939, Mr 22,23:5
Groom, Maud F, 1955, F 13,86:4
Groom, Robert, 1948, F 20,27:2
Groome, Agnes P R Mrs, 1937, O 6,25:5
Groome, Harry C, 1941, My 21,23:1
Groome, John C Jr, 1955, O 4,35:4
Groomes, William, 1939, N 18,17:6
Groopman, David, 1943, My 10,19:4
Groose, H G, 1939, D 3,60:2
Groothedde, John J, 1952, S 27,17:1
Groothuis, Irving Mrs, 1957, Ap 13,19:2
Groover, Frank C, 1944, Ja 29,13:6
Groover, Paul, 1954, Jl 9,17:1
Gropper, Harry, 1961, D 27,27:4
Gropper, Milton H, 1955, O 29,19:3
Gros, Andrew L Mrs, 1947, Mr 11,27:4
Gros, Edmund L (por), 1942, O 18,53:1
Gros, Louis, 1955, Je 1,33:5
Gros, Raymond Mrs, 1950, O 7,19:4
Grose, Adolph, 1911, D 9,13:4
Grose, Charles H, 1946, Ja 20,42:3
Grose, Clyde L, 1942, My 8,21:6
Grose, Dorothy Mrs, 1951, S 1,17:7
Grose, George R, 1953, My 7,31:3
Grose, Harry, 1938, Ag 3,19:6
Grose, Howard B, 1939, My 20,15:3
Groseclose, Henry C, 1950, Je 5,23:5
Grosenbaugh, Royal A, 1941, Ap 8,26:3
Grosenbeck, John J, 1941, S 28,48:2
Grosenbeck, Louis Mrs, 1944, Ap 6,23:3
Groser, Herbert W, 1940, Ap 29,15:3
Groset, John P, 1957, Jl 19,19:4
Grosfater, Sol, 1961, Ap 21,33:5
Grosjean, Charles J, 1950, Ag 29,27:4
Grosjean, Florian, 1903, Ja 25,8:2
Grosjean, Joseph J, 1952, Ap 19,15:4
Grosjean, Paul, 1957, Jl 3,23:4
Grosman, Robert D, 1955, D 18,93:1
Gross, A, 1928, Ag 12,27:5
Gross, Aaron, 1968, Ja 20,26:7
Gross, Abraham H, 1950, S 26,31:2
Gross, Adolph, 1959, F 14,21:3
Gross, Adolph L, 1958, Ap 24,31:2
Gross, Albert, 1914, D 19,13:5

Gross, Albert B, 1963, Ag 7,33:4
Gross, Albert H, 1948, Ag 18,25:4
Gross, Alex, 1958, Mr 26,37:1
Gross, Alfred, 1957, Mr 2,21:6
Gross, Alfred C, 1940, O 19,17:4
Gross, Andrew, 1882, Ag 20,7:1
Gross, Anna Mrs, 1952, Mr 25,27:2
Gross, Anthony V, 1956, Ja 25,31:4
Gross, Arnold, 1946, Je 1,13:5
Gross, Arthur, 1950, N 27,25:2
Gross, Arthur M, 1951, O 17,31:1
Gross, Bernard, 1950, My 21,104:6
Gross, Charles, 1941, D 7,77:1
Gross, Charles E, 1925, Ja 1,27:3
Gross, Charles Prof, 1909, D 4,11:5
Gross, Charles W, 1957, Ap 1,25:4
Gross, Daniel I, 1945, O 2,23:2
Gross, David, 1958, F 1,19:5; 1967, N 3,45:2
Gross, David Mrs, 1940, Je 1,15:5
Gross, Edward S, 1966, N 19,33:1
Gross, Edward T, 1948, Ap 21,28:2
Gross, Edward V Mrs, 1947, F 9,62:4
Gross, Fabius, 1950, Je 20,27:4
Gross, Francis O, 1938, Ap 25,15:4
Gross, Frank C, 1954, O 3,86:7
Gross, Fred L (por), 1947, Ja 18,15:5
Gross, Fred W, 1952, N 5,27:3
Gross, Frederick E Sr, 1945, D 12,27:3
Gross, Frederick W, 1946, Je 24,31:1
Gross, Frederick W Mrs, 1944, F 6,42:1
Gross, George, 1948, N 12,23:4; 1950, N 2,31:2; 1960, F 28,83:1
Gross, George F, 1951, N 29,33:6; 1954, S 22,29:5
Gross, George I, 1966, O 31,35:1
Gross, George W, 1939, N 8,23:3
Gross, H J, 1927, Ap 4,23:5
Gross, Hans Prof, 1915, D 12,19:6
Gross, Harry, 1945, My 24,19:4
Gross, Harry E, 1958, Je 13,23:2
Gross, Henry, 1940, D 8,68:4; 1941, S 5,22:2; 1945, S 5,23:1; 1951, S 29,17:6
Gross, Henry H, 1947, S 29,21:2
Gross, Henry J, 1951, My 28,21:4
Gross, Henry Mrs, 1946, My 31,23:3; 1953, Mr 10,29:4
Gross, Henry S, 1962, Ag 21,33:1
Gross, Hyman Mrs, 1954, Jl 16,21:5
Gross, Irving, 1960, Jl 16,19:4
Gross, Isaac Mrs, 1948, Mr 28,48:6
Gross, Jack, 1954, Ag 3,19:4
Gross, James H Mrs, 1956, Ag 4,15:6
Gross, John C, 1948, Ag 12,22:2
Gross, John G Mrs, 1949, My 23,23:1
Gross, John H, 1951, Ja 2,12:6
Gross, John I, 1961, Jl 22,21:6
Gross, Joseph, 1951, F 20,25:2
Gross, Joseph W, 1945, O 4,23:4
Gross, Julia Mrs, 1943, D 2,27:5
Gross, Lawrence T, 1952, Ja 27,77:2
Gross, Leopold, 1941, My 8,23:1
Gross, Louis, 1965, Jl 15,29:4
Gross, Louis C, 1951, Ja 10,27:1
Gross, Louis D, 1964, Ja 2,27:4
Gross, Louis H, 1957, O 22,33:5
Gross, Malcolm W, 1944, Ja 22,13:5
Gross, Marcu S, 1948, Jl 9,20:2
Gross, Marcus, 1953, F 24,25:1
Gross, Max, 1953, N 9,35:4; 1967, Ag 4,29:1
Gross, Meyer P, 1964, Ja 12,92:5
Gross, Milt, 1953, D 1,2:8
Gross, Milton, 1961, O 14,23:5
Gross, Miriam Mrs, 1956, Mr 27,70:7
Gross, Moritz, 1947, O 25,19:3
Gross, Morris E, 1954, N 7,87:5
Gross, Moses, 1951, Ja 8,17:4
Gross, Naftoli, 1956, Ap 9,27:3
Gross, Nathan L (Nate), 1960, My 13,31:2
Gross, P Philip, 1959, Ag 28,23:1
Gross, Phil, 1940, D 26,19:4
Gross, Phil G, 1953, Je 26,19:2
Gross, Phil Mrs, 1950, S 27,31:2
Gross, Philip P, 1968, D 21,31:6
Gross, Reuben H, 1956, Mr 30,20:3
Gross, Robert A Mrs, 1959, Ja 11,88:4
Gross, Robert B, 1950, Jl 20,25:3
Gross, Robert E, 1961, S 4,15:4
Gross, Robert H, 1942, D 21,19:7
Gross, Royce L Mrs, 1949, D 23,11:3
Gross, Rudolph, 1944, My 17,19:6
Gross, S D Prof, 1884, My 7,5:3
Gross, Sam, 1944, Ag 15,17:4
Gross, Samuel, 1946, N 19,21:1
Gross, Samuel E, 1913, O 25,13:6
Gross, Samuel H, 1953, D 28,21:2
Gross, Samuel P, 1961, Mr 7,35:4
Gross, Seymour R Sr, 1958, Je 1,86:4
Gross, Simeon F, 1964, Ja 2,27:3
Gross, Simon, 1939, F 7,19:3; 1959, S 19,23:3
Gross, T Arthur, 1960, Mr 4,25:3
Gross, Theodore C, 1951, Mr 13,31:4
Gross, Walter, 1967, N 30,47:4
Gross, Walter W, 1956, F 18,19:2
Gross, William D, 1942, My 8,21:3
Gross, William Sr, 1949, D 1,31:6
Gross, Yanka Mrs, 1962, Jl 15,60:2
Grossarth, Frank D, 1952, N 4,30:5
Grossbeck, John A, 1914, Ap 29,11:6
Grossberg, Adolph, 1952, Je 3,29:5
Grossberg, Jacob G, 1950, Ja 30,17:6
Grossberg, William Mrs, 1963, S 2,15:5
Grossblatt, Phil, 1955, My 28,15:2
Grosscup, Peter S Judge, 1921, O 3,13:4
Grosscup, Raymond C, 1947, Ag 4,17:3
Grosscup, Walter T, 1950, S 25,23:2
Grosse, Ernest G, 1956, Mr 5,23:3
Grosse, Frederick H, 1953, Ap 6,19:4
Grosse, Julius, 1902, My 11,9:5
Grosse, Otto H, 1962, N 10,25:2
Grossegebauer, John, 1946, F 21,21:3
Grossel, Ira (J Chandler),(funl, Je 20,33:1; will, Jl 6,19:1), 1961, Je 18,88:3
Grosselfinger, Frederick H, 1965, Ag 29,84:8
Grossenbach, G W, 1941, N 10,17:2
Grosser, John F, 1951, Ja 20,15:3
Grosset, A, 1934, O 28,32:1
Grosset, Alex D, 1958, O 31,29:1
Grosset, Garnet W, 1962, Ag 31,21:5
Grossfield, Harry, 1944, Mr 20,18:2
Grosshans, Adolph, 1955, O 23,86:8
Grossi, Camillo, 1941, Je 17,21:2
Grossi, Carmine, 1965, Ag 31,33:3
Grossi, Enzo, 1960, Ag 13,15:7
Grossinger, Harry (will, Ag 7,15:1), 1964, Jl 23,27:4
Grossinger, Harry, 1965, Ap 11,92:4
Grossinger, Selig Mrs, 1952, Ag 17,76:5
Grossklaus, Alfred W Mrs, 1959, Jl 18,16:3
Grosskopf, Siegmund Mrs, 1948, Jl 13,28:2
Grossley, Richard S, 1955, N 19,19:2
Grossman, Abraham, 1951, N 4,86:5
Grossman, Abraham L, 1949, Ap 2,15:2
Grossman, Albert M, 1962, Ja 16,33:3
Grossman, Alexander, 1946, N 25,27:3
Grossman, Arthur, 1951, Ap 22,89:1
Grossman, Benjamin, 1954, Ap 23,27:2
Grossman, Bernard L, 1951, O 4,33:4
Grossman, Charles, 1954, Ja 30,17:5
Grossman, Darwin Mrs, 1949, D 21,29:1
Grossman, David D, 1947, Ag 9,13:6
Grossman, David M Mrs, 1949, My 23,23:3
Grossman, David R, 1961, Ag 17,27:2
Grossman, Edward, 1955, Jl 18,21:2
Grossman, Edward N, 1968, Ap 23,47:1
Grossman, Elias M, 1947, S 20,15:2
Grossman, Erwin, 1967, S 25,45:2
Grossman, Frank (por), 1947, Je 17,25:4
Grossman, George, 1957, D 21,19:5
Grossman, George A, 1943, Jl 4,20:5
Grossman, George J, 1939, O 5,23:5
Grossman, George J Mrs, 1939, Mr 24,21:4
Grossman, Harold J, 1967, F 1,39:4
Grossman, Harry, 1951, Jl 17,27:3
Grossman, Helen, 1941, My 30,15:1
Grossman, Herman Mrs, 1943, F 6,13:1
Grossman, Horace M, 1941, Ja 31,19:5
Grossman, Hyman, 1958, Ag 16,17:5
Grossman, Irving, 1918, Jl 29,11:6; 1964, Mr 25,41:2
Grossman, Isaac, 1967, O 17,47:3
Grossman, Isaac Mrs, 1959, Je 15,27:5
Grossman, Isador, 1957, S 30,31:4
Grossman, Isidore, 1946, Ap 10,27:2
Grossman, Isidore Mrs, 1944, Mr 24,19:3
Grossman, Jacob, 1957, Mr 17,86:2
Grossman, Jacob Dr, 1968, D 26,35:1
Grossman, Jacob J, 1953, F 24,25:3
Grossman, Julius Mrs, 1955, O 13,32:1
Grossman, Lawrence R, 1944, F 24,15:5
Grossman, Louis, 1966, Ag 6,23:5
Grossman, Mack, 1965, Je 25,33:1
Grossman, Marc Mrs, 1944, Ja 4,17:4
Grossman, Max, 1940, Ja 6,13:5; 1962, Ja 20,21:6
Grossman, Max Mrs, 1956, Ap 14,17:3
Grossman, Meyer, 1950, My 6,15:6; 1955, Jl 11,23:3
Grossman, Milton, 1960, Jl 5,31:4
Grossman, Milton L, 1956, O 22,29:3
Grossman, Morgan, 1951, Je 22,25:4
Grossman, Morris, 1943, Ja 29,19:2; 1955, D 30,19:5
Grossman, Moses H (por), 1942, Je 8,15:1
Grossman, R Rev, 1927, S 23,27:5
Grossman, Reuben, 1964, Ag 31,25:1
Grossman, Rudolph Mrs, 1947, Ja 22,23:5
Grossman, Sidney Mrs, 1956, F 10,22:1
Grossman, Vasily S, 1964, S 18,32:5
Grossman, Waldemar H, 1942, S 27,49:2
Grossmann, Arpad S, 1907, Ja 8,9:2
Grossmann, George J, 1943, N 5,19:2
Grossmann, Grace, 1958, Ja 14,33:2
Grossmann, Henryk, 1950, N 26,90:5
Grossmith, George, 1880, My 10,5:2; 1912, Mr 2,13:5
Grossmith, George Jr Mrs, 1951, My 26,17:5
Grossmith, Weedon, 1919, Je 15,22:5
Grossmuller, Harry, 1945, Jl 22,38:1
Grosso, Joseph, 1952, Ag 20,25:6
Grosso, Rosa del Mrs, 1955, Ja 16,92:8
Grosulov, Ivan A, 1955, Ap 6,29:1
Grosvener, Thomas W Col, 1871, O 22,1:1
Grosvenor, Charles H Gen, 1917, O 31,13:5
Grosvenor, E A, 1936, S 16,25:3
Grosvenor, E P, 1930, Mr 1,19:5
Grosvenor, Gilbert H, 1966, F 5,29:1
Grosvenor, Gilbert Mrs, 1964, D 27,65:1
Grosvenor, Graham B, 1943, O 29,19:1
Grosvenor, Howard E Mrs, 1954, My 25,27:2
Grosvenor, James B, 1905, S 26,9:6
Grosvenor, James B M Mrs, 1916, S 14,7:6
Grosvenor, Norman Mrs, 1940, Ag 9,15:3
Grosvenor, Robert E (Lord Ebury), 1957, My 6,11:3
Grosvenor, Robert Victor, 1921, N 6,22:4
Grosvenor, Rose A (will, F 25,22:4), 1942, F 16,17:3
Grosvenor, Samuel Conant Dr, 1914, Jl 19,5:6
Grosvenor, Samuel Howe Mrs, 1917, D 9,23:2
Grosvenor, Violet E, 1942, D 10,25:2
Grosvenor, William M (por), 1944, My 31,19:1
Grosvenor, William M Jr, 1968, Je 25,41:4
Grosvenor, William M Mrs, 1951, Ja 31,25:3
Grosvenor, William 3d Duke of Westminster (Feb 22), 1963, Ap 1,36:8
Grosvenor, Willie Lee, 1909, Mr 7,11:5
Groswold, Crawford, 1962, Mr 21,39:5
Groswold, Myron B, 1960, Ja 20,31:4
Grosz, George, 1959, Jl 7,33:1
Grosz, George Mrs, 1960, Ag 2,29:1
Grosz, Viktor, 1956, Ja 10,31:4
Grosz, Wilhelm, 1939, D 11,25:6
Groszberg, Desiderius, 1962, Mr 24,25:3
Groszmann, M P E Dr, 1922, O 4,23:5
Groszmann, Walter P, 1946, O 18,24:2
Grote, Alex Mrs, 1949, O 7,27:3
Grote, Aug D, 1951, Ag 25,11:2
Grote, David J Mrs, 1966, Ja 31,39:3
Grote, F R, 1878, Ap 26,2:5
Grote, Frank C, 1951, Ap 20,29:1
Grote, Frederick A, 1950, Ja 14,15:4
Grote, G Mrs, 1878, D 31,5:4
Grote, George, 1871, Je 20,1:7
Grote, Henry W, 1942, Je 21,36:7
Grote, John, 1947, Je 25,25:3
Grote, John E, 1910, F 8,9:5
Grote, Louis, 1944, Ag 8,17:2
Grote, Mrs, 1879, Ja 27,2:6
Grote, William F (Fatty), 1904, S 29,9:6
Grotefend, Emmett H, 1959, Jl 30,27:2
Grotewahl, Max, 1958, S 9,35:4
Grotewohl, Otto (funl plans, S 23,13:7), 1964, S 22, 1:2
Groth, Christian F, 1943, D 14,27:2
Groth, Christian F Mrs, 1942, S 30,23:4
Groth, Edward, 1961, D 19,29:6
Groth, Louis, 1949, S 21,31:4
Groth, Matilda F Dr, 1937, D 12,II,8:7
Groth, Otto H, 1947, N 12,27:1
Groth, Theodore B, 1949, Je 19,68:3
Grotheer, John D Mrs, 1964, O 19,33:4
Grother, Henry J, 1948, Ja 21,25:1
Grotker, Abraham J, 1964, Ap 25,29:3
Groton, William Mansfield Rev, 1915, My 26,13:7
Grotrian, Augustus D Rev, 1906, D 16,7:6
Grotrian, Walter, 1954, Mr 4,25:3
Grotta, Adele L Mrs, 1937, O 10,II,8:6
Grotta, James L, 1943, Je 28,21:1
Grotta, Joseph E, 1960, F 7,84:2
Grotz, Arthur B, 1958, O 8,35:1
Grouard, George H (will), 1938, Je 28,22:2
Groucher, John W, 1910, S 21,9:4
Grouitch, Slavko Mrs, 1956, Ag 14,25:2
Groulx, Lionel, 1967, My 24,32:5
Ground, Moses, 1912, N 25,13:6
Grounds, Wilbert L, 1963, S 1,57:1
Group, Harold E, 1962, S 10,29:2
Groupe, Ralph, 1947, O 2,27:5
Grouse, John M, 1964, My 12,37:4
Grousset, Paschel, 1909, Ap 11,11:3
Grousset, Rene, 1952, S 13,17:5
Grout, Don, 1943, Jl 23,17:5
Grout, E M, 1931, N 10,25:3
Grout, Edgar H, 1951, Ja 9,30:3
Grout, George H, 1938, Je 19,29:2; 1950, S 13,27:3
Grout, H McIntyre Jr Mrs, 1956, Ag 6,23:6
Grout, Harold M Mrs, 1949, Jl 30,15:4
Grout, Horace G, 1950, O 11,33:5
Grout, Jonathan, 1942, Ap 11,13:1
Grout, Josiah Ex-Gov, 1925, Jl 20,15:5
Grout, Ralph W, 1944, N 24,23:5
Grout, Ralph W Jr, 1960, O 24,29:3
Grout, Thomas J, 1913, Je 17,11:4
Grove, Charles C, 1956, Ja 15,93:2
Grove, De W C, 1884, Mr 18,5:4
Grove, E W, 1927, Ja 28,17:3
Grove, Emma C Mrs, 1959, Ag 7,23:4
Grove, Frederick P, 1948, Ag 21,15:1
Grove, George W, 1950, Je 7,29:5
Grove, James H, 1951, My 3,29:5
Grove, Louis N Sr, 1949, N 30,27:4
Grove, Margaret, 1960, Je 15,41:4
Grove, Max Mrs, 1950, O 31,27:4
Grove, Nelson B, 1951, F 13,31:2
Grove, Robert B, 1954, Jl 25,68:7
Grove, Robert M Mrs, 1960, Ag 17,31:4
Grove, Wallace J, 1963, Ag 9,23:5
Grove, Walter E (funl plans), 1956, S 20,33:3
Grove, William G, 1948, My 29,15:4; 1957, Ap 12,25:2

Grove, William R, 1952, Ag 9,13:5
Grover, Arthur C, 1953, Mr 19,29:4
Grover, Burnard, 1945, Je 16,13:4
Grover, C Gen, 1885, Je 8,5:6
Grover, Charles R, 1942, Ja 24,17:3
Grover, Clayton, 1959, Je 9,37:3
Grover, Clayton D, 1965, Ap 24,29:5
Grover, Delo C, 1955, Ja 27,23:5
Grover, Elijah L, 1946, Ag 22,27:4
Grover, Frederick O, 1964, Je 5,31:2
Grover, George P, 1944, N 8,17:6
Grover, George W, 1950, Jl 27,25:3
Grover, Jerry C Mrs, 1961, My 9,39:3
Grover, Joseph, 1940, O 10,25:2
Grover, Lafayette Ex-Gov, 1911, My 11,11:5
Grover, Leonard, 1947, Mr 26,25:2
Grover, Lewis C, 1939, D 16,17:1
Grover, Lloyd W, 1945, F 4,38:2
Grover, Marion L Mrs, 1951, F 23,27:2
Grover, Martin Judge, 1875, Ag 24,4:7
Grover, Pearley F, 1947, Ap 10,25:3
Grover, Richard J, 1953, Jl 16,21:4
Grover, Scott, 1951, Mr 28,29:3
Grover, William M, 1943, D 25,13:4
Groves, Augustus N, 1949, Jl 25,15:4
Groves, Benjamin F, 1949, O 24,23:2
Groves, Charles, 1909, Jl 10,7:5
Groves, Charles A, 1942, Ag 17,15:3
Groves, Charles S, 1948, N 16,29:4
Groves, Charles W, 1940, S 13,23:4
Groves, Edgar A, 1951, N 27,31:6
Groves, Ernest R (por), 1946, Ag 30,18:2
Groves, Frank A, 1946, D 19,29:2
Groves, Frederick S, 1924, Ag 20,13:4
Groves, George A, 1945, Jl 23,21:2
Groves, George A Mrs, 1945, Jl 23,21:2
Groves, George C, 1941, O 24,24:2; 1948, F 17,25:2
Groves, H Lawrence, 1966, Ag 12,31:1
Groves, Harold L, 1953, Mr 26,31:5
Groves, James S Mrs, 1957, F 13,35:4
Groves, John, 1965, Jl 31,21:2
Groves, Michael D (trb, D 5,32:8), 1963, D 4,18:3
Groves, Robert G, 1949, My 21,13:4
Groves, Samuel N, 1956, D 6,37:4
Groves, Thomas, 1948, Jl 31,15:1
Groves, William D, 1968, F 13,43:2
Grovlez, Gabriel, 1944, O 25,21:5
Grow, Fred A, 1950, D 1,25:3
Grow, Galusha Aaron, 1907, Ap 1,9:6
Grow, Walter L, 1945, Ja 31,21:3
Grow, Walter T, 1953, Ag 14,8:6
Growdon, Laurence A, 1954, Je 28,19:5
Growney, William A, 1950, D 1,26:3
Growoll, Adolf, 1909, D 8,11:5
Groy, John A Mrs, 1947, O 10,25:4
Groza, Petru, 1958, Ja 8,47:4
Grozier, Edwin Atkins, 1924, My 10,13:5
Grozier, Richard, 1946, Je 20,23:4
Grskovic, Nicholas, 1949, Mr 22,25:2
Gru, George (por), 1948, N 17,27:3
Grubart, Harold Mrs, 1967, Ap 11,41:2
Grubb, Charles E, 1954, Ap 15,29:2
Grubb, Charles L, 1944, O 20,19:2
Grubb, E Burd Mrs, 1958, Jl 5,17:3
Grubb, Edward, 1939, Ja 25,22:1
Grubb, Edward Burd Gen (funl, Jl 10,7:4), 1913, Jl 8, 7:5
Grubb, Emma F Mrs, 1944, Je 22,19:6
Grubb, Francis, 1955, Ja 22,11:5
Grubb, George A, 1953, N 3,31:3
Grubb, Henry B, 1919, S 17,13:2
Grubb, Joel E, 1938, Ja 12,21:1
Grubb, Lamar C, 1949, Ja 19,27:4
Grubb, Silas M, 1938, F 8,21:3
Grubb, W Earl, 1937, Jl 27,21:1
Grubb, W I, 1935, O 28,19:3
Grubb, Warner N (por), 1947, F 15,15:3
Grubb, William R, 1966, Ja 27,33:4
Grubbe, Emil H, 1960, Mr 27,86:3
Grube, Albert A, 1963, N 7,34:2
Grube, August J, 1950, Jl 12,29:3
Grube, Charles S, 1964, F 29,21:5
Grube, George W, 1950, D 12,33:3
Gruben, Peter, 1950, Jl 23,56:5
Gruber, Abraham (funl, D 13,13:3), 1915, D 11,13:3
Gruber, Abraham Mrs, 1916, F 6,15:6
Gruber, Benjamin B, 1958, O 18,21:2
Gruber, E L, 1941, My 31,11:6
Gruber, Ellsworth, 1953, Je 1,23:5
Gruber, F Franklin, 1941, D 7,77:3
Gruber, Frank C, 1959, S 9,41:4
Gruber, Fred W, 1963, D 22,34:2
Gruber, George, 1948, Ap 3,15:3
Gruber, Harry, 1958, O 14,37:4
Gruber, Herbert W Mrs, 1961, Ap 30,86:6
Gruber, Isaac, 1923, S 29,7:2
Gruber, Joseph, 1960, D 24,15:6
Gruber, Joshua, 1951, Je 7,33:1
Gruber, Lennox Mrs, 1951, Jl 23,17:4
Gruber, Lewis Mrs, 1949, Ap 17,76:7
Gruber, Mary Mrs, 1953, Ap 6,19:6
Gruber, Max, 1951, D 30,25:1
Gruber, Morris M, 1961, Jl 6,29:3
Gruber, Ralph E, 1953, Ja 31,15:4
Gruberg, Rubin, 1942, Ap 17,17:5
Gruberg, Samuel, 1959, O 12,19:6
Gruberman, Feleceta Mrs, 1957, My 22,13:6
Grubiak, Andrew, 1952, S 12,21:3
Grubin, Maurice Mrs, 1967, O 21,31:5
Grubman, Alex, 1937, O 9,19:6
Grubman, Jacob H, 1944, F 17,19:1
Grudzinski, Stanley J, 1961, O 24,74:6
Gruelle, John, 1938, Ja 10,17:5
Gruelle, Richard, 1914, N 9,9:5
Gruellemeyer, Theodor H (cor, D 10,47:4), 1953, D 9,11:1
Gruen, Ferdinand, 1948, Ag 6,17:2
Gruen, Francis W, 1938, D 27,17:4
Gruen, Frederick G, 1945, S 16,44:4
Gruen, George J, 1952, Je 5,31:3
Gruen, Oscar Mrs, 1962, Ap 9,29:4
Gruen, Victor Mrs, 1962, Jl 18,29:3
Gruenauer, William, 1948, O 26,31:4
Gruenbaum, Arthur S, 1953, Ja 27,25:4
Gruenbaum, Gustave Dr, 1937, F 2,23:1
Gruenberg, Benjamin C, 1965, Je 2,29:3
Gruenberg, Benno, 1962, My 4,34:1
Gruenberg, Elizabeth W (Mrs J Weiss), 1965, Ap 1, 35:4
Gruenberg, Louis (trb lr, Jl 5,II,9:3), 1964, Je 11,33:2
Gruendgens, Gustaf, 1963, O 8,43:2
Gruendler, Ernest W, 1944, F 16,17:1
Gruendler, Herman F, 1946, N 24,76:6
Gruendler, Karl Dr, 1914, My 31,5:5
Gruenebaum, Morris, 1951, My 19,15:2
Gruener, Theodore Lt, 1910, Ag 9,9:4
Gruenert, Paul R Jr, 1967, F 9,35:5
Gruenewald, Edward R H, 1938, My 6,21:6
Gruenewald, George J, 1955, Ag 31,25:2
Gruenewald, Marcellus J, 1946, O 22,25:3
Gruenewald, Nicholas, 1949, Ja 7,21:2
Gruenfeld, Josef Mrs, 1952, D 30,19:4
Gruening, Emil Dr, 1914, My 31,5:5
Gruening, Peter B, 1955, N 6,21:1
Gruening, R, 1934, Ag 1,17:4
Gruenstein, Benjamin M, 1962, Je 16,19:2
Gruenstein, Harry, 1955, D 16,29:3
Gruenstein, Siegfried, 1957, D 9,35:5
Gruenthal, Max, 1962, Ap 29,86:8
Gruenther, Chris M Mrs, 1957, Mr 28,31:4
Gruenwald, Alfred, 1951, F 25,87:5
Gruenwald, Martin G, 1953, Jl 21,23:4
Gruenwald, Otto A C, 1946, My 6,21:4
Gruenwald, William, 1939, F 23,23:5
Gruenwald, William S, 1947, S 6,17:5
Gruerry, Alex, 1948, O 20,29:1
Grueschow, Augustus, 1948, N 28,92:5
Gruess, William M, 1945, O 31,23:2
Gruett, Frederick T R Capt, 1911, Jl 10,7:5
Gruetzner, Eduard Prof, 1925, Ap 4,17:5
Gruetzner, John, 1950, O 1,104:8
Grugan, Frank C Maj, 1917, N 7,13:4
Gruger, Dorothy G, 1957, O 9,35:2
Gruger, Frederic R, 1953, Mr 22,87:1
Gruhl, Edwin, 1933, Ja 23,14:3
Gruhler, William L, 1954, Jl 29,23:5
Gruhnert, Herman C Rev, 1922, Jl 22,7:7
Gruitch, Slavko (por), 1937, Mr 24,25:1
Grulee, Clifford G Sr, 1962, O 26,31:1
Gruler, William J, 1953, Ja 5,21:5
Grumaer, Alfred H, 1945, N 26,21:3
Gruman, Harris, 1952, S 29,23:5
Grumbach, Louis J, 1952, S 20,21:6
Grumbach, Salomon, 1952, Jl 14,17:3
Grumbacher, Stanley, 1961, D 30,19:4
Grumbles, William H, 1966, Mr 21,33:2
Grumet, Jacob, 1962, F 15,29:4
Grumich, Margaret Mrs, 1945, O 24,21:2
Grumm, Arnold H, 1959, S 25,29:3
Grumman, Frederick C, 1942, Je 22,15:4
Grummon, Stuart E, 1960, Je 3,31:2
Grumsfeld, Ernest A Mrs, 1960, N 10,47:5
Grun, Jules A, 1938, Ja 25,21:4
Grunau, Isabel M Mrs, 1952, My 12,25:3
Grunauer, Louis H, 1942, F 6,19:3
Grunauer, Sidney, 1953, Mr 16,19:2
Grund, Ernst, 1907, Mr 30,9:7
Grund, Francis J, 1863, O 2,4:5
Grunder, Charles E Sr, 1958, Ag 2,17:4
Grundfest, Sam, 1955, N 30,33:1
Grundhoffer, John W, 1962, N 18,86:1
Grundle, Joseph Sr, 1947, F 4,25:4
Grundman, Albert J, 1938, Jl 30,13:3
Grundman, Julius, 1941, Jl 27,25:2
Grundmann, Otto, 1966, Ap 13,40:1
Grundner, Joseph, 1960, O 14,33:2
Grundstrom, Erik G, 1953, O 5,27:1
Grundy, Cecil R, 1944, D 13,23:2
Grundy, Cuthbert C, 1946, F 2,13:2
Grundy, Cyrus W, 1955, My 22,88:1
Grundy, Frederick, 1924, Mr 29,15:4
Grundy, G C, 1881, Mr 18,8:5
Grundy, G Edmund, 1960, S 21,32:4
Grundy, George W, 1950, My 16,31:3
Grundy, J Owen Mrs, 1956, N 18,88:8
Grundy, Joseph R (funl, Mr 7,35:1; will, Mr 8,26:4), 1961, Mr 4,23:2
Grundy, Margaret R, 1952, F 2,13:2
Grundy, R C Dr, 1865, Jl 7,2:2
Grundy, Sydney, 1914, Jl 6,7:5
Grundy, Thomas, 1942, Ja 29,19:3
Gruneison, C, 1879, N 4,5:2
Grunenberg, Hubert van, 1944, D 19,21:2
Grunenthal, William F, 1950, N 4,17:3
Gruner, Charles Mrs, 1951, Je 25,19:5
Gruner, George J, 1962, My 7,31:4
Gruner, Oskar C Mrs, 1940, Ap 26,21:3
Gruner, Otto H, 1942, D 18,27:5
Grunert, Robert G, 1940, D 27,19:2
Grunert, Robert W, 1964, Ja 11,23:4
Grunewald, Henry W, 1958, S 26,28:3
Grunewald, Max E Mrs, 1950, Ag 1,23:3
Grunewald, Theodore, 1949, Jl 26,27:3
Grunewald, Theodore J, 1966, My 25,47:5
Grunewald, Walter R, 1949, N 12,15:3
Grunhof, William F Jr, 1950, N 4,17:3
Grunigen, Arnold Jr, 1956, Ja 20,23:3
Gruning, Frank J, 1941, Mr 22,15:2
Gruninger, Henry, 1964, Ap 16,37:1
Gruninger, John Mrs, 1954, F 28,93:1
Grunow, Alfred W, 1954, Je 9,31:3
Grunow, Julius S, 1952, Jl 16,25:1
Grunow, William C, 1951, Jl 7,13:7
Grunsfeld, Hannah N Mrs, 1939, F 22,21:3
Grunski, Joseph P, 1953, Ag 23,89:1
Grunsky, C E, 1934, Je 10,31:5
Gruntal, Benedict H, 1968, D 26,37:2
Gruntal, Clara L, 1964, Ja 21,29:3
Gruntler, Crester E, 1944, O 23,19:2
Grunwald, Alfred Mrs, 1953, D 24,15:1
Grunwald, Hugo, 1956, O 3,33:4
Grunwaldt, Edward M, 1915, N 18,9:5
Gruny, Joseph, 1944, Ag 20,34:4
Grupe, E Raymond, 1939, N 17,21:3
Grupe, Grover R, 1961, Ja 28,19:2
Grupe, Henry J, 1955, Ja 12,27:4
Grupe, S Floyd, 1949, O 20,29:5
Grupp, Morris, 1968, O 22,47:2
Gruppe, Charles P, 1940, O 1,23:6
Gruppe, Hazel M (Mrs O M Hibbard), 1958, Je 3 19:3
Grushlaw, Israel, 1943, D 11,15:6
Gruskin, Benjamin, 1950, D 7,33:4
Grusky, Henry, 1959, Jl 25,17:6
Gruson, Harry, 1956, Jl 9,23:6
Grussner, Albert, 1953, Jl 12,65:2
Grussner, Nicholas H, 1953, Jl 30,23:2
Grutgen, John G, 1947, N 22,15:5
Grutman, Alexander, 1962, Ag 14,31:4
Gruttadurian, Michael J, 1951, Jl 8,V,9:1
Grutzner, Charles Mrs, 1956, Ja 18,31:1
Gruver, Elbert A, 1949, F 7,19:4; 1962, N 12,29:4
Gruver, Esdras L, 1961, F 21,35:5
Gruver, Samuel A, 1948, S 30,27:4
Gruver, W F, 1950, D 1,25:2
Gruzenberg, Michael (M Borodin), 1953, S 3,21:
Gryczka, James E, 1957, Ap 17,31:2
Grygorewicz, Vincent J, 1962, Mr 29,33:4
Grylls, H J Maxwell, 1942, Je 22,15:5
Grymes, Arthur J Jr, 1963, Ap 19,43:1
Grymes, Mason F H, 1944, D 27,19:4
Grymes, Oliver S, 1952, N 15,17:5
Grzesiak, Stephen S, 1952, My 27,27:4
Grzeskinski, Albert C, 1948, Ja 1,23:4
Gsell, Francis X, 1960, Jl 13,35:4
Gseller, Albert H, 1943, Je 1,23:4
Gsovski, Vladimir, 1961, Ja 14,23:1
Guachalla, Fernando, 1908, Jl 28,5:4
Guaico, Joseph, 1920, Je 12,13:3
Guaitioli, Alfio, 1939, S 7,25:3
Gual Villalbi, Pedro Prof, 1968, Ja 13,31:1
Gualino, Riccardo, 1964, Je 10,45:4
Gualtieri, Humberto, 1949, O 26,27:4
Guani, Alberto, 1956, N 26,27:4
Guarando, Ralph, 1921, Mr 23,13:4
Guard, John W, 1939, N 14,23:5
Guard, Kit, 1961, Jl 20,27:2
Guard, Richard J, 1943, Ja 6,25:3
Guard, Samuel Mrs, 1940, Mr 20,27:3
Guard, Shirley R, 1943, N 9,21:2
Guard, W J, 1932, Mr 4,19:1
Guard, William J Mrs (funl, Mr 31,17:3), 1924, Mr 28,17:4
Guardascoine, Ezechiele, 1948, N 25,32:2
Guardia, Clara D, 1937, Je 15,23:2
Guardia, M Gen, 1884, N 28,1:3
Guardia, T, 1882, Jl 26,5:6
Guardia, Tomas Jr, 1964, Mr 14,23:6
Guardia Jaen, German G, 1947, Ap 15,25:3
Guardineer, Frederick R Mrs, 1943, S 29,21:3
Guardini, Romano Rev, 1968, O 2,39:4
Guareschi, Giovanni, 1968, Jl 23,39:3
Guarglia, Albert, 1923, Ap 20,17:3
Guarini, Frank J Sr, 1963, S 6,29:3
Guarino, Anthony, 1959, N 5,35:2
Guarneri, Felice, 1955, Ap 5,29:2
Guarneri, Fernando, 1940, N 21,29:3
Guarnieri, Antonio, 1952, N 26,23:2
Guarnieri, Frank J, 1958, F 3,23:4

Guastavino, Rafael, 1950, O 20,27:4
Guastavino, Raphael, 1908, F 3,9:4
Guay, Alfred L, 1947, My 9,21:2
Guayant, Claude E, 1951, F 18,76:4
Guazzoni, Enrico, 1949, S 25,92:7
Guba, Phil M (por), 1949, Ag 19,17:4
Gubb, J Edward Mrs, 1944, S 25,17:4
Gubb, Larry E, 1966, N 11,43:3
Gubbins, William C, 1938, S 28,25:3
Gubellini, Pietro, 1941, N 16,56:2
Gubelman, Moisei I, 1968, Ja 20,29:2
Gubelman, Oscar L (por), 1940, O 11,21:5
Gubelmann, William S, 1959, S 27,86:4
Gubelmann, William S Mrs, 1956, Jl 10,31:2
Gubergrits, M Moisevich, 1951, My 12,21:1
Guberlet, John E, 1940, D 31,15:5
Guberman, Louis, 1949, S 14,31:4
Gubert, Mary Agnes Sister, 1882, Ag 9,1:6
Gubin, Sidney S, 1955, D 20,31:2
Gubitose, Charles J, 1967, My 15,43:3
Gubkin, Ivan, 1939, Ap 22,17:4
Gubler, Fred C, 1946, Ja 9,23:1
Gubler, Friedrich T, 1965, O 7,3:6
Gubner, Harry, 1941, Je 12,23:4
Gubner, Walter D, 1944, D 21,21:4
Gubner, Walter Mrs, 1951, My 20,89:1
Guchkoff, A I, 1936, F 15,15:3
Guck, Edward C, 1954, O 27,29:3
Guck, Homer, 1949, Je 17,23:2
Guckenberger, George Mrs, 1954, N 24,23:1
Gucker, Henry J, 1965, F 3,35:3
Guckin, James A, 1951, D 23,22:5
Gudakunst, Don W, 1946, Ja 21,23:1
Gudansky, Abraham, 1945, Ag 10,15:2
Gudat, Marvin, 1954, Mr 4,25:5
Gude, Arthur J Jr, 1957, Jl 10,27:5
Gude, Edward C, 1937, S 3,17:5
Gude, Frederick, 1944, My 10,19:4
Gude, O J, 1925, Ag 16,5:3
Gude, O J (funl, S 4,21:6), 1925, S 2,23:5
Gude, O J Jr, 1944, D 27,19:1
Gude, Ove (funl, Jl 5,13:6), 1910, Jl 3,II,7:4
Gudebrod, Charles B, 1945, S 11,23:3
Gudebrod, Charles B Mrs, 1941, Jl 10,19:6
Gudebrod, Louis A, 1961, D 6,47:1
Gudebrod, Morton P, 1965, Ja 24,81:2
Gudefin, Leon J, 1953, D 15,39:4
Guderian, Heinz, 1954, My 17,23:1
Guderman, Jack Mrs, 1963, N 18,33:4
Gudernatsch, J Frederick, 1962, O 30,35:2
Gudgel, John M, 1947, Mr 24,25:5
Gudgeon, Bertrand C, 1948, O 24,76:3
Gudger, Emmett C, 1941, My 11,45:1
Gudger, Eugene W, 1956, F 20,23:4
Gudger, Francis A, 1967, F 10,35:2
Gudger, Hubert B Dr, 1910, O 3,9:4
Gudger, James R Mrs, 1955, Ag 29,19:5
Gudmand, Alex P, 1960, Mr 21,29:1
Gudzi, Nikolai K, 1965, N 3,39:4
Gue, Martha Mrs, 1903, S 6,20:4
Guedalia, Moses, 1916, Mr 18,11:6
Guedalla, Herbert Mrs (Lily Hanbury), 1908, Mr 6, 7:5
Guedalla, Philip, 1944, D 17,37:1
Guedel, John Mrs (H Parrish), 1959, F 23,23:1
Guedin, J, 1878, N 11,8:6
Gueguetchkori, Eugene P, 1954, Je 9,31:4
Guelezian, Lucy E, 1958, My 14,33:3
Guelfi, John V, 1957, Je 18,33:3
Guelich, Heinrich Rev, 1909, F 13,9:6
Guell, Eduardo T, 1941, Ap 27,38:3
Guell, Juan Claudio Count (mem mass set), 1958, My 14,33:5
Guellnitz, Wilbur J, 1947, D 7,76:4
Guelman, Henrietta Mrs, 1941, Mr 25,26:1
Guelman, Henry, 1938, Ap 30,15:5
Guelstroff, Max, 1947, F 10,29:2
Gueniot, A, 1935, Jl 17,19:3
Guenther, Charles F, 1962, Ap 28,25:3
Guenther, Christian E, 1966, Mr 7,27:4
Guenther, Francis L Gen, 1918, D 6,15:4
Guenther, George A, 1940, D 4,27:5
Guenther, George H, 1937, S 8,23:1
Guenther, Henry A, 1953, Ag 26,27:6
Guenther, Ida V J Mrs, 1938, Ap 15,19:4
Guenther, J C Rev, 1903, Je 19,9:5
Guenther, J M Rev, 1901, My 11,9:6
Guenther, Louis, 1953, Mr 12,27:3
Guenther, Louis Mrs, 1961, S 7,35:4
Guenther, Marie, 1950, Jl 13,25:3
Guenther, Otto, 1954, Je 9,31:5
Guenther, Otto O, 1963, Jl 4,17:4
Guenther, P, 1932, Ja 18,15:5
Guenther, Rudolph, 1966, Ja 7,29:4
Guenther, Rudolph Mrs, 1948, Ag 19,21:2
Guenther, Theodore C, 1938, O 31,15:1
Guenzberg, David Baron, 1910, D 24,9:6
Guenzburg, Baron, 1909, Mr 3,9:5
Guenzel, Edward F Mrs, 1958, My 11,86:8
Guenzel, Martin R Mrs, 1958, N 10,29:3
Guepratte, Emile P, 1939, N 22,21:2
Guequierre, Jacques P, 1954, Ja 17,93:2
Guerard, Albert L, 1959, N 14,21:3
Guerazzi, Francesco, 1873, S 25,1:7
Guercken, Paul, 1947, O 13,23:4
Guerdan, Leon, 1949, D 16,31:3
Guerdan, Leon Mrs (funl plans, My 22,35:1), 1964, Mr 21,35:4
Guerin, Anderson Martell, 1921, D 11,22:2
Guerin, Byram C, 1945, F 9,16:2
Guerin, Camille, 1961, Je 10,23:4
Guerin, Charles H, 1938, My 2,17:5
Guerin, Eddie, 1940, D 7,5:1
Guerin, Emmanuel P Mrs, 1957, S 18,33:3
Guerin, John J, 1947, My 25,60:4
Guerin, Joseph, 1923, My 7,15:5
Guerin, Josephine P Mrs, 1940, Mr 10,49:2
Guerin, Jules, 1946, Je 15,21:5
Guerin, Jules Mrs, 1949, Ag 6,17:6
Guerin, Loyola I, 1941, Je 19,21:6
Guerin, Theophile, 1961, My 29,19:5
Guerin, Thomas I, 1956, O 13,19:5
Gueritey, Charles H, 1953, Je 7,83:1
Guerlac, O G, 1933, Ja 18,19:3
Guerlain, Jacques, 1963, My 8,39:3
Guernsey, A H, 1902, Ja 20,7:5
Guernsey, D W Judge, 1902, F 9,7:5
Guernsey, F A, 1941, D 30,20:2
Guernsey, Florence, 1919, Ja 18,11:3
Guernsey, Florence Mrs, 1901, My 21,9:5
Guernsey, Frederick F, 1923, F 23,13:5
Guernsey, George T Mrs, 1939, Mr 2,21:5
Guernsey, Henry William, 1924, Ap 15,21:2
Guernsey, Herbert, 1939, N 24,23:4
Guernsey, Homer W, 1959, Ja 13,47:4
Guernsey, Homer W Mrs, 1946, Jl 8,29:1
Guernsey, James S, 1959, O 29,33:2
Guernsey, Margaret A Mrs, 1941, Ag 13,17:5
Guernsey, Nathaniel T Mrs, 1943, Ap 28,23:2
Guernsey, Raimund T, 1952, D 18,29:5
Guernsey, Raymond G, 1959, My 20,35:4
Guernsey, Roscoe, 1961, Je 15,43:5
Guernsey, S J, 1936, My 23,15:3
Guernut, Henri, 1943, My 31,17:6
Gueronniere, A de la, 1876, Ja 8,1:7
Gueroult, M, 1872, Ag 4,4:7
Guerra, Alirio D, 1940, Ja 16,23:4
Guerra, Frank, 1967, F 17,37:1
Guerra, Leargo, 1963, F 8,18:1
Guerra, Manuel G, 1951, Ja 23,27:2
Guerra, Rafael, 1941, F 22,15:1
Guerra, Virginia Mrs, 1937, Ja 6,21:6
Guerra del Rio, Rafael, 1955, N 4,29:3
Guerra Duval, Adalberto, 1947, Ja 16,25:4
Guerrant, Catherine L Mrs, 1937, Ja 20,22:2
Guerrero, Jose G, 1958, O 28,35:5
Guerrero, M, 1928, Ja 24,29:3
Guerrero, Pastor, 1942, F 7,17:3
Guerrero y Torres, Jacinto (funl, S 17,21:6), 1951, S 16,84:5
Guerrini, Ugo E, 1968, S 13,47:2
Guerrlich, Francis Mrs, 1954, N 20,17:4
Guerry, Legrand, 1947, Ag 15,17:5
Guerry, Salvatore Mrs, 1952, Ag 15,16:4
Guertin, Joseph M, 1946, S 17,7:2
Guertin, Marie P Mrs, 1947, Je 8,60:1
Guertner, Franz (por), 1941, Ja 30,21:3
Guesde, Jules, 1922, Jl 29,7:6
Guese, Theodore, 1951, Ap 10,27:4
Guesfeldt, Paul Prof, 1920, Ja 21,7:2
Gueshoff, Ivan, 1924, Ap 13,27:4
Guess, Harry A, 1946, Ap 12,27:2
Guess, Harry A Mrs, 1940, D 26,19:5
Guess, Harry C, 1953, D 9,11:1
Guest, Bernie, 1956, D 14,29:2
Guest, Carroll M, 1945, Je 15,19:5
Guest, Christian H, 1957, O 11,27:3
Guest, Edgar A (funl, Ag 8,17:6), 1959, Ag 6,27:1
Guest, Edgar A Mrs, 1945, Ag 29,23:4
Guest, Edgar M, 1954, D 17,31:3
Guest, Edward H, 1953, Ag 21,17:2
Guest, Frederick E Capt (por), 1937, Ap 29,21:1
Guest, Frederick E Mrs, 1959, O 8,39:5
Guest, George M, 1943, Ap 7,25:4; 1966, N 27,86:7
Guest, Harry M, 1950, Ja 19,28:2
Guest, Helen, 1952, My 10,21:3
Guest, Ivor Bertie (Baron Wimborne), 1914, F 23,9:5
Guest, James H, 1948, My 30,34:5
Guest, John Commodore, 1879, Ja 13,5:4
Guest, Kenneth J, 1955, F 25,21:3
Guest, Richard P, 1958, O 8,35:4
Gueterbock, Paul, 1954, Mr 11,31:4
Guettel, Matthew, 1966, Ag 25,37:1
Guetter, J Walter, 1937, My 2,9:2
Guevara, Celia de la S Mrs, 1965, My 19,47:2
Guevara, Juan G, 1954, N 27,13:3
Guevara, Pedro, 1938, Ja 19,23:2
Guevremont, Hyacinthe Mrs (Germaine), 1968, Ag 24,29:5
Gueye, Lamine, 1968, Je 11,44:5
Guffey, Albert A Mrs, 1951, Mr 18,89:1
Guffey, Ida V, 1952, Mr 11,27:4
Guffey, J M, 1930, Mr 21,27:1
Guffey, Joseph F, 1959, Mr 7,21:1
Guffey, Pauletta, 1946, N 10,63:7
Guffey, Pauletta (will), 1947, Ja 5,54:3
Guffey, Wesley S, 1914, Ap 24,13:6
Guffey, William H Dr, 1873, My 6,4:7
Guffin, Ross Maj, 1903, S 26,9:4
Gugel, David, 1955, F 13,86:4
Gugenheim, Solomon, 1945, F 23,17:2
Gugert, George, 1958, D 29,15:5
Guggenheim, Adolf Mrs, 1946, Ja 5,13:4
Guggenheim, Arthur S, 1940, Ja 30,19:5
Guggenheim, Bernhard, 1958, S 13,19:3
Guggenheim, D, 1930, S 29,1:4
Guggenheim, Daniel, 1925, F 24,19:4; 1942, D 31,15:2
Guggenheim, Daniel Mrs (por), 1944, My 14,45:1
Guggenheim, Edythe W Mrs, 1942, N 16,20:3
Guggenheim, Emanuel, 1952, Ap 9,31:2
Guggenheim, Florette Mrs (will, D 7,17:1), 1937, N 16,23:4
Guggenheim, George C, 1938, N 2,24:2
Guggenheim, Harry F Mrs (A Patterson),(trb, Jl 4,15:7), 1963, Jl 3,27:1
Guggenheim, Harry L, 1950, Ap 3,23:2
Guggenheim, Isaac (por), 1922, O 11,19:3
Guggenheim, Isaac, 1942, S 15,23:5
Guggenheim, John S, 1922, Ap 27,17:4
Guggenheim, Joseph S, 1955, O 13,32:1
Guggenheim, M Robert, 1959, N 17,35:3
Guggenheim, Max, 1915, O 11,9:6
Guggenheim, Max H, 1948, Ag 9,20:2
Guggenheim, Meyer, 1905, Mr 17,9:3
Guggenheim, Morris, 1950, Jl 15,13:4
Guggenheim, Murry, 1939, N 16,23:1
Guggenheim, Murry Mrs, 1959, F 3,27:4
Guggenheim, Siegfreid E, 1943, Je 9,21:3
Guggenheim, Simon (por), 1941, N 4,23:1
Guggenheim, Solomon R, 1949, N 3,29:1
Guggenheim, Solomon R Mrs, 1954, N 29,25:1
Guggenheim, Solomon R Mrs (est acctg), 1957, N 27,17:1
Guggenheim, William, 1941, Je 28,15:1
Guggenheim, William Mrs, 1957, My 15,35:4
Guggenheimer, Charles, 1952, Jl 18,19:4
Guggenheimer, Charles S, 1953, N 9,35:1
Guggenheimer, Charles S Mrs (Minnie),(funl, My 27,43:2), 1966, My 24,1:5
Guggenheimer, Clarence M, 1944, F 16,17:3
Guggenheimer, Emil, 1925, Je 30,19:5
Guggenheimer, Frederick L, 1956, D 2,86:4
Guggenheimer, Harry R, 1962, Ag 21,33:2
Guggenheimer, Jay C Mrs, 1959, Ag 30,82:4
Guggenheimer, Julius, 1956, Jl 7,13:5
Guggenheimer, Max Jr, 1912, Ag 29,9:5
Guggenheimer, Meyer (est appr), 1905, Ag 1,12:4
Guggenheimer, Randolph (funl, S 16,9:5), 1907, S 13, 7:6
Guggenheimer, Solomon C, 1924, Mr 27,19:5
Gugger, Samuel, 1940, F 21,19:5
Guggiari, Jose P, 1957, O 31,31:3
Gugino, Carmelo, 1946, D 22,41:8
Gugino, Thomas F, 1952, Ja 11,22:2
Gugler, Ralph, 1958, Mr 8,17:2
Guglielmetti, Dr, 1943, F 24,22:2
Guglielmi, Joseph, 1948, Ap 17,15:4
Guglielmi, Osvaldo L, 1956, S 4,29:4
Guglielminetti, Amalia, 1941, D 6,17:6
Guglielmo, Pesco del, 1951, My 5,17:2
Guglieri, Peter N Mrs, 1959, Jl 25,17:5
Gugnoni, Anthony Mrs, 1958, Ap 16,33:1
Guhl, Fred, 1941, S 17,23:5
Guhl, Mary S C Mrs, 1956, D 27,25:4
Guhl, Wendelin Rev, 1917, Ap 6,13:5
Guhse, H Paul, 1964, O 29,36:1
Guibert, Benjamin, 1881, D 10,3:3
Guibert, John C, 1958, Ag 30,15:4
Guicciardi, Vincenzo, 1965, Ja 3,84:7
Guicciardini, Count, 1915, S 2,9:4
Guiccioli, Countess, 1873, Mr 28,5:5
Guichard, Victor, 1884, N 12,2:6
Guichard, Xavier, 1947, Mr 25,25:4
Guida, Joseph, 1942, Mr 10,20:3
Guidano, Albert, 1949, Je 18,13:2
Guidelly, Edward A, 1946, N 12,29:5
Guider, John W, 1968, Ja 20,29:2
Guidet, Alfred V, 1941, Jl 15,19:5
Guidi, Archbishop, 1904, Je 27,7:5
Guidi, Cardinal, 1879, Mr 2,7:3
Guidice, Joseph A, 1954, Ag 17,21:3
Guidicini, M Guiseppe, 1868, Ja 10,5:3
Guido, Andrea Mrs, 1943, Mr 27,13:4
Guido, R Dominick, 1949, N 12,15:3
Guieysse, Pierre Paul, 1914, My 21,11:5
Guifredo, Catherine Mrs, 1950, Jl 23,33:1
Guignard, Alberto da V, 1962, Je 27,32:8
Guignard, Susan R, 1955, Jl 1,21:5
Guignet, Maurice, 1949, My 27,21:3
Guigon, A B, 1878, F 22,5:4
Guihard, Paul L (mem ser NYC; burial, France, noted, O 6,26:3), 1962, O 1,23:6
Guiho, Daniel, 1950, Ap 11,31:1
Guilaine, Louis, 1941, Ag 20,19:3
Guilbeaux, Henri, 1938, Je 19,28:7
Guilbert, Harry, 1945, O 11,23:2
Guilbert, William J, 1942, Jl 21,19:5
Guilbert, Yvette, 1944, F 4,16:2
Guild, Albert O, 1952, Ag 5,19:3

Guild, Annie E Mrs, 1868, Je 8,5:1
Guild, B Thurber, 1958, Je 17,29:4
Guild, Cameron S, 1954, O 19,27:5
Guild, Courtenay, 1946, Ap 25,21:3
Guild, Curtis, 1915, Ap 7,13:3
Guild, Curtis Sr, 1911, Mr 13,9:5
Guild, Frederick T, 1941, My 10,15:6
Guild, G M, 1903, Ag 22,9:6
Guild, Henry J, 1964, S 15,37:3
Guild, J C, 1883, Ja 9,5:4
Guild, Kenneth H, 1959, Ag 16,82:6
Guild, Lewis T, 1943, D 23,19:4
Guild, Ray W, 1956, F 16,29:1
Guild, Roland B, 1965, D 14,39:3
Guild, Roy B, 1945, Ja 14,40:3
Guild, W H, 1948, Jl 30,17:2
Guild, William, 1962, N 21,33:1
Guild, William B, 1909, F 15,7:4
Guilday, Peter, 1947, Ag 1,17:5
Guilden, Morris (por), 1945, Jl 14,11:6
Guile, Elias B, 1945, Mr 30,15:2
Guile, Hubert V, 1955, Ja 31,19:1
Guiler, Henry A, 1938, N 23,21:1
Guiles, Austin P, 1953, N 14,17:2
Guilett, George L, 1944, S 19,21:4
Guilfoil, Edward J, 1948, Ap 30,24:2
Guilfoil, F Kelsey, 1951, Je 6,31:1
Guilfoil, Oscar Mrs, 1955, Ja 1,13:6
Guilfoil, Paul H, 1941, Jl 17,19:6
Guilfoil, Watson M Mrs, 1944, My 6,15:4
Guilfoile, Francis P, 1943, Mr 21,26:5
Guilford, Agnes C Mrs, 1939, Mr 16,23:5
Guilford, George A, 1945, Je 14,19:4
Guilford, Jesse, 1962, D 3,31:2
Guilford, John, 1950, S 3,38:3
Guilford, Julia D Mrs, 1949, Je 8,30:3
Guilford, Nathan, 1907, My 12,9:5
Guilford, William M, 1938, D 11,61:1
Guilfoy, Mary P Mrs, 1942, Ag 28,19:2
Guilfoyle, Daniel T, 1946, Mr 7,25:3
Guilfoyle, Francis J, 1949, Ag 12,19:7
Guilfoyle, James H, 1950, O 1,104:4
Guilfoyle, John, 1958, O 2,37:4
Guilfoyle, John F, 1962, O 16,47:3
Guilfoyle, John T, 1940, D 13,23:2
Guilfoyle, Leo J, 1960, N 16,41:3
Guilfoyle, Paul, 1961, Je 30,27:1
Guilfoyle, Richard T, 1957, Je 12,35:2
Guilfoyle, William E, 1946, Ap 30,21:2
Guilhempe, Nemorin, 1943, Jl 2,19:5
Guiliani, George, 1957, F 5,23:4
Guiliano, Balbino, 1958, Je 16,23:2
Guill, J H Jr, 1959, O 11,86:3
Guillamore, Viscount (O'Grady), 1943, N 29,19:3
Guillaumat, Marie L A (por), 1940, My 19,43:1
Guillaume, Albert, 1942, Ag 14,17:6
Guillemaut-Despecher, Clara Mrs, 1959, Je 21,92:3
Guillemette, Alphonse E, 1950, Ag 24,27:3
Guillermo Castillo, Lucas, 1955, S 11,84:6
Guillet, Cephas, 1948, D 4,13:6
Guilliams, John, 1944, Ag 10,17:4
Guillini, Jean, 1945, N 19,21:1
Guillow, Paul K, 1951, Ag 29,25:2
Guillow y Zavalza, Eulogio Msgr, 1922, My 20,15:6
Guilluim, William H, 1944, Ja 20,19:4
Guilmain, Armand Mrs, 1949, Ag 2,20:2
Guilmette, Charles E Mrs, 1952, Ag 2,15:5
Guimaraes, Anibal M, 1952, My 23,21:4
Guimaraes, Protogenus, 1938, Ja 7,19:3
Guimaraes Rosa, Joao, 1967, N 21,48:1
Guimard, Hector, 1942, My 21,19:1
Guimares, Albert, 1952, S 30,43:6
Guimes, Plato, 1955, Jl 16,15:3
Guimet, Emile, 1918, O 17,15:3
Guimond, Lou F, 1950, My 25,29:4
Guinan, Bessie D Mrs, 1939, My 28,III,7:3
Guinan, Sarah, 1942, F 28,17:5
Guinan, T, 1933, N 6,19:1
Guinan, Tommy (Thos J Guinan), 1967, Je 27,39:4
Guinan, William Mrs, 1946, F 13,23:5
Guinan, William P, 1946, O 5,17:2
Guindon, Elizabeth T Mrs, 1908, D 24,7:5
Guinee, Timothy P, 1962, Ja 14,84:3
Guiness, Algernon, 1954, O 27,29:4
Guiness, George G, 1950, F 14,25:2
Guiney, D Joseph Jr, 1958, Ag 25,21:3
Guiney, David F, 1937, Ap 15,23:3
Guiney, G Franklin, 1954, Ja 10,86:5
Guiney, Irene Mrs, 1964, D 31,17:1
Guiney, John B, 1941, Mr 26,23:5
Guiney, Louise Imogen, 1920, N 4,13:5
Guiney, Margaret B Mrs, 1937, O 6,25:5
Guiney, Timothy P, 1962, Je 4,29:3
Guinle, Arnaldo, 1963, Ag 27,31:2
Guinle, Guilherme, 1960, My 22,86:7
Guinn, Robert J, 1943, Je 12,13:2
Guinn, Thomas W, 1951, Ap 8,92:1
Guinn, W A, 1950, D 28,25:1
Guinnasso, John J, 1953, Ap 29,29:5
Guinness, Arthur E, 1949, Mr 23,28:4
Guinness, Arthur Edward (Lord Ardilaun), 1915, Ja 21,9:5
Guinness, B S Mrs, 1931, Ja 6,27:1
Guinness, Benjamin S, 1947, D 17,29:2
Guinness, Henry S, 1945, Ap 6,15:3
Guinness, Patrick, 1965, O 6,2:4
Guinness, Rupert E C L Earl of Iveagh, 1967, S 15, 47:1
Guinness, William H, 1953, Ja 27,25:3
Guinsburg, Theodore Rev, 1923, O 4,23:3
Guinta, J Edwin, 1959, Jl 13,27:5
Guinther, Laurence O, 1940, D 30,17:4
Guinup, Charlies, 1956, F 28,36:1
Guinzberg, Harry A Mrs (will, F 3,25:2), 1955, Ja 29,15:4
Guinzburg, George K, 1966, Ap 4,31:2
Guinzburg, H A, 1928, N 17,19:3
Guinzburg, Louis A, 1945, Ja 20,11:4
Guinzburg, Ralph K, 1957, Ja 17,29:2
Guinzburg, Ralph K Mrs, 1963, My 27,29:4
Guinzburg, Roland H, 1965, Ag 31,33:3
Guinzburg, Victor Mrs, 1945, Jl 9,11:7
Guion, Alvah Rev, 1872, N 7,8:4
Guion, Clarence C, 1958, O 1,37:2
Guion, Clement, 1882, O 7,5:4
Guion, G W, 1882, Ja 21,5:4
Guion, Gilbert P Mrs, 1942, Jl 15,19:1
Guion, Henry D, 1910, My 20,9:6
Guion, J M Rev Dr, 1878, Jl 24,5:6
Guion, John A, 1948, My 21,23:3
Guion, John A Mrs, 1953, Ap 11,17:4
Guion, Walter, 1941, N 13,27:1
Guirado, Luz Mrs, 1947, D 15,25:2
Guirand, Anne, 1881, O 9,6:7
Guirey, Kadir, 1953, Je 3,31:3
Guirreri, Noel A, 1945, My 26,15:1
Guis, Nicholas, 1957, Jl 18,25:1
Guisan, Henri, 1960, Ap 8,31:2
Guisasola y Menendez, Victorien Cardinal, 1920, S 3, 9:6
Guise, Duchess of (Isabelle of France), 1961, Ap 22, 25:5
Guise, Duke of (por), 1940, Ag 27,21:1
Guise, Elizabeth C Mrs (Florence), 1960, D 12,29:3
Guise, Joseph B, 1950, S 3,38:6
Guise, Philip, 1947, Jl 17,19:5
Guistwhite, Bruce H, 1942, Je 5,17:4
Guitart, Justino, 1940, F 1,21:3
Guiteau, Frederick W, 1903, O 6,9:4
Guiteau, John Wilson, 1916, F 4,9:6
Guiteras, Albert F (por), 1955, My 27,23:3
Guiteras, Juan Dr, 1925, O 29,25:5
Guiteras, Ramon Dr, 1917, D 14,13:4
Guiterman, Arthur, 1943, Ja 12,23:3
Guiterman, Franklin, 1915, My 10,15:4
Guiterman, Katherine M, 1948, My 25,28:3
Guiterman, Kenneth S, 1954, Mr 19,23:2
Guiterman, Milton S, 1944, Mr 15,19:2
Guiterman, Percy L, 1937, My 5,25:3
Guiterman, Rudolph Mrs, 1959, N 27,29:1
Guitry, Jean M, 1941, O 30,23:5
Guitry, Lucien, 1925, Je 2,23:3
Guitry, Sacha (funl, Jl 28,61:3), 1957, Jl 24,26:1
Guizado, Jose R, 1964, N 3,31:3
Guizado, Juan A, 1951, Ja 22,17:2
Guizar y Valencia, Rafael, 1938, Je 7,23:4
Guizot, William, 1874, S 9,5:1
Gulager, D P Mrs, 1877, My 30,5:1
Gulbenkian, Calouste Mrs, 1952, Jl 3,25:1
Gulbenkian, Calouste S (funl plans, Jl 22,23:5), 1955, Jl 21,23:2
Gulbenkian, Gullabi Mrs, 1957, Mr 15,26:1
Gulbenkian, Haroutiune, 1947, O 26,70:3
Gulbenkian, Haroutiune Mrs, 1962, My 3,33:5
Gulbenkian, Krikor Mrs, 1965, My 31,2:5
Gulbenkian, Sylvia, 1965, My 31,2:5
Gulbranson, Clarence, 1947, N 4,25:2
Gulbranssen, Trygve, 1962, O 12,31:2
Gulck, George K, 1946, Jl 26,21:5
Guldahl, Olaf G, 1940, My 13,17:2
Gulde, John K, 1952, Mr 1,29:5
Gulden, Charles, 1916, Ag 16,7:4
Gulden, Charles Mrs, 1941, Jl 22,20:2
Gulden, Frank, 1961, Ja 25,33:4
Gulden, George W, 1940, Ag 9,15:6
Guldin, James H Jr, 1939, Ja 2,23:3
Gulesian, Moses H, 1951, D 31,13:5
Gulgakov, Alex, 1953, F 14,17:1
Gulguski, Bartholomew J, 1913, My 21,11:6
Gulick, Alice Gordon Mrs, 1903, S 15,9:6
Gulick, Ann L Mrs, 1938, N 11,25:5
Gulick, Archibald A, 1959, Jl 12,72:5
Gulick, Bertrand L, 1942, Ja 26,15:4
Gulick, C V Mrs, 1928, Jl 29,25:1
Gulick, Charles B, 1962, My 24,35:2
Gulick, Charles B Mrs, 1948, My 27,25:5
Gulick, Charles L, 1942, D 23,19:5
Gulick, Charles P, 1955, S 6,25:3
Gulick, Charles W Rev, 1937, S 3,17:4
Gulick, Charlton Reading Dr, 1924, O 25,15:6
Gulick, Earl, 1945, D 8,17:3
Gulick, Edward L Mrs, 1951, F 5,23:3
Gulick, Ernestus S, 1913, Ja 7,11:6
Gulick, Horace S, 1949, F 3,23:5
Gulick, John C, 1916, Je 22,11:4
Gulick, John Gilbert Dr, 1916, Ja 20,9:4
Gulick, John H R Mrs, 1958, Mr 16,86:5
Gulick, John W, 1939, Ag 19,15:3
Gulick, Luther Halsey, 1918, Ag 14,9:3
Gulick, Powell M, 1955, Je 9,29:6
Gulick, Richard M, 1911, Ag 7,7:6
Gulick, Sidney L, 1945, D 24,15:3
Gulick, Thomas T Dr, 1923, Ap 17,21:4
Gulick, Walter D, 1946, N 28,27:4
Gulick, Warren S Mrs, 1940, Je 8,15:6
Gulick, William H Mrs, 1943, Ap 27,24:2
Gulik, Robert H van, 1967, S 29,40:1
Gulinelli, Federico, 1954, D 17,31:4
Gull, Cyril, 1923, Ja 10,23:5
Gull, Louis M, 1951, F 22,31:3
Gulland, George L, 1941, My 5,17:2
Gulland, John William, 1920, Ja 29,9:5
Gullberg, Hjalmar, 1961, Jl 20,14:6
Gullen, Henry (por), 1940, My 17,19:5
Guller, Hyman Mrs, 1949, Je 13,19:2
Gullett, Augustus A, 1937, Ag 18,19:2
Gullian, Reuben, 1940, Ag 25,35:2
Gullickson, Francis L, 1944, Ap 16,42:1
Gullion, Allen W, 1946, Je 20,25:1
Gullion, Blair, 1959, Ja 31,19:2
Gullion, Charles, 1941, N 3,19:3
Gullion, Walter, 1940, Ap 25,23:3
Gulliver, Julia H, 1940, Jl 28,27:2
Gulliver, William, 1950, N 21,45:4
Gulliver, William Curtis, 1909, My 26,9:5
Gullo, Charles, 1952, Ap 13,76:4
Gullotta, Patsy, 1968, S 14,28:1
Gullparzer, Franz, 1872, Ja 26,5:4
Gully, Edward Mrs, 1943, Mr 28,25:1
Gully, Henry, 1956, Ap 24,31:3
Gully, Louis D, 1967, Mr 29,45:3
Gully, William Court (Viscount Selby), 1909, N 7, 13:5
Gulmares, Antonio, 1916, Jl 20,11:6
Gulnac, Abram D, 1946, S 28,17:4
Gulnac, Robert E, 1943, Jl 20,19:3
Gulon, George M Gen, 1910, N 10,11:4
Gulotta, Gaspar, 1957, D 31,17:2
Gulotta, Peter F, 1960, F 5,27:3
Gulvin, Reuben H, 1937, Je 16,24:2
Gulyassy, Emil D, 1956, N 10,19:5
Gumaelius, Charles, 1938, Jl 14,21:2
Gumaer, Andrew, 1951, Ja 18,27:4
Gumaer, Lawrence W, 1942, S 30,23:2
Gumaer, William H, 1954, O 7,23:5
Gumauskas, Joseph, 1955, Jl 24,65:3
Gumb, Ernest T Mrs, 1965, Ag 14,23:3
Gumbel, Emil J, 1966, S 13,47:2
Gumbel, Emil J Mrs, 1952, N 4,29:3
Gumbel, Simon, 1909, Ag 15,7:4
Gumberg, Alex, 1939, My 31,23:1
Gumbert, Elizabeth W Mrs, 1939, Ag 20,33:3
Gumbert, Robert F, 1957, Ja 20,93:2
Gumbert, William S, 1946, Ap 14,46:2
Gumbiner, Tobe Mrs, 1940, F 23,15:5
Gumbinsky, Oscar, 1925, F 18,19:4
Gumble, Frank W, 1951, N 2,24:2
Gumble, Mose (por), 1947, S 29,21:1
Gumble, Stella E Mrs, 1950, F 13,22:4
Gumble, Wolcott W, 1957, Ap 10,33:1
Gumbleton, Henry A, 1914, My 26,11:6
Gumbrecht, Alfred C, 1961, S 5,35:4
Gumbs, Robert, 1955, Jl 22,23:1
Gumby, L S Alex, 1961, Mr 18,23:4
Gumey, B Egbert, 1951, N 3,17:6
Gumm, Frederick, 1957, S 14,19:6
Gummere, Amelia M, 1937, O 9,19:2
Gummere, Barker Jr, 1914, Mr 10,9:5
Gummere, Charles E, 1941, Mr 4,23:3
Gummere, Henry V, 1949, F 10,27:5
Gummere, Henry V Mrs, 1956, Mr 11,88:4
Gummere, John W, 1960, Ag 12,19:4
Gummere, Samuel R, 1920, My 29,15:2
Gummey, Charles F, 1955, Ja 6,27:4
Gummey, Chas-Henry, 1965, Ja 14,35:2
Gummick, Charles J, 1952, Je 17,27:2
Gump, A Livingston, 1947, Ag 31,36:6
Gumpel, Morris, 1941, N 28,23:4
Gumpert, Edward A, 1965, My 30,50:8
Gumpert, Martin, 1955, Ap 19,31:1
Gumpertz, Samuel W, 1952, Je 23,19:1
Gumpertz, Samuel W Mrs, 1941, Je 2,17:3
Gumport, Benjamin A, 1952, O 11,19:4
Gumprecht, Otto Dr, 1925, My 13,21:5
Gumprecht, Walter R, 1950, D 17,84:4
Gumtow, Mary K Mrs, 1948, Jl 22,23:3
Gumuchian, Kirkor, 1949, F 14,19:5
Gumucio, Rafael L, 1947, Je 16,21:3
Gumuspala, Ragip, 1964, Je 7,86:5
Gunaltay, Shemsettin, 1961, O 20,33:1
Gunby, Louis W, 1951, F 23,27:1
Gunckel, Lewis B, 1903, O 4,7:6
Gund, George, 1966, N 16,47:4
Gund, George Mrs, 1954, Ap 28,31:2
Gundaker, Charles A, 1908, My 7,7:6
Gundaker, Guy, 1960, Ap 28,83:1
Gundel, Charles J, 1950, S 7,31:4
Gundell, Glenn, 1965, Jl 14,37:5
Gundeman, Charles E, 1954, S 15,33:4

Gunder, Dwight F, 1964, O 22,35:4
Gunder, Norbert, 1937, S 28,23:1
Gunderman, Frederick, 1905, Ap 26,2:3
Gunderman, Peter S, 1910, My 30,11:6
Gundersen, Magnus, 1946, Ja 9,23:4
Gundersen, Reidar E, 1966, Jl 31,72:3
Gundersen, Robert M, 1952, Jl 6,49:2
Gundersen, Rudolf G, 1940, Ja 25,21:5
Gunderson, Alexander F, 1944, Jl 23,35:1
Gunderson, Carroll A, 1956, D 4,39:4
Gunderson, Hendrik Dr, 1925, N 6,23:5
Gunderson, Henry A, 1940, O 8,25:3
Gunderson, Marjorie R Mrs, 1953, S 29,29:2
Gundie, G H, 1877, D 3,5:2
Gundlach, Conrad J Mrs, 1948, Ja 12,19:2
Gundlach, Ernest J, 1942, S 19,15:2
Gundlach, Francis K, 1942, O 14,25:5
Gundlach, Otto H F, 1949, Ap 15,23:4
Gundlach, Walter H, 1964, My 20,43:4
Gundling, George, 1956, Ap 14,17:6
Gundrum, George, 1946, Jl 5,19:5
Gundrum, Joseph B, 1958, F 6,27:2
Gundrum, William A Mrs, 1946, Ag 11,46:1
Gundry, Sydney, 1953, Ag 30,89:1
Gundy, Clyde Mrs, 1959, Ag 10,27:5
Gundy, James H, 1951, N 11,90:7
Gunesoplu, Adil (funl), 1958, My 3,4:4
Gungunhana, Maria J X, 1952, N 20,31:4
Gunion, Philip C Jr, 1962, S 21,30:1
Gunkel, Helen, 1950, My 3,27:4
Gunkel, Woodward W, 1954, Ap 20,29:4
Gunkel Sylvester, 1963, Jl 21,64:7
Gunlocke, William H, 1937, Ag 23,19:3
Gunlogsen, Bertel Hogne, 1918, F 1,9:5
Gunmere, W S, 1933, Ja 27,19:1
Gunn, Aeneas Mrs, 1961, Je 12,29:4
Gunn, Alex S, 1941, Ap 10,23:4
Gunn, Basil H, 1945, F 12,19:4
Gunn, Charles A, 1945, O 20,11:3
Gunn, Charles A Mrs, 1953, S 24,33:1
Gunn, David, 1943, N 12,21:4
Gunn, Donald, 1952, O 25,17:5
Gunn, Edgar C Mrs, 1940, N 5,25:4
Gunn, Edgar G, 1941, Mr 31,15:5
Gunn, Edwin H, 1940, O 11,21:5
Gunn, Elizabeth H, 1956, Ap 15,88:5
Gunn, George C, 1937, F 28,II,9:1
Gunn, Glenn D, 1963, N 25,20:2
Gunn, Grace E Mrs, 1939, Ap 9,III,7:2
Gunn, H C, 1917, S 27,13:6
Gunn, Harry, 1958, Ag 6,25:4
Gunn, Harry E, 1944, D 12,23:1
Gunn, Herbert, 1962, Mr 3,21:5
Gunn, J N, 1927, N 28,21:5
Gunn, James, 1965, Ja 1,19:2
Gunn, Janet Dr, 1924, Ap 2,19:4
Gunn, Jean, 1941, Je 30,17:3
Gunn, John E, 1946, D 19,29:2
Gunn, John Edward Bp, 1924, F 20,19:4
Gunn, John K, 1939, My 30,17:5
Gunn, Lloyd T Sr, 1953, O 28,29:3
Gunn, Reuben V, 1943, Je 4,21:4
Gunn, Ross, 1966, O 16,89:1
Gunn, Selskar M (por), 1944, Ag 3,19:1
Gunn, Sydney A, 1941, O 24,24:3
Gunn, Thomas M, 1943, Ja 19,19:2
Gunn, Thomas P, 1943, D 2,27:5
Gunn, Walter E, 1945, O 25,21:5
Gunn, Walter T, 1956, O 14,87:2
Gunnarson, Arthur B Mrs, 1962, N 7,39:2
Gunnell, Francis M Rear-Adm, 1922, Je 12,15:6
Gunner, Edwin Mrs, 1941, O 2,25:5
Gunner, Frank J Jr, 1955, O 8,19:2
Gunner, John H, 1911, Ag 4,7:6
Gunness, Christian, 1946, D 25,29:2
Gunnett, Stanton C, 1952, Ag 19,23:1
Gunning, John F, 1956, O 24,37:4
Gunning, John S, 1950, S 23,17:5
Gunning, Lina W Mrs, 1942, D 25,17:2
Gunning, William Sr, 1943, My 4,23:4
Gunnison, Alice Mrs, 1903, Ag 4,7:7
Gunnison, Almon Dr, 1917, Jl 1,19:4
Gunnison, Austin, 1915, Ap 4,14:1
Gunnison, Foster, 1961, O 20,33:3
Gunnison, Frederick E, 1922, Ja 11,21:4
Gunnison, H F, 1932, N 25,15:1
Gunnison, Hugh B, 1942, Jl 12,36:6
Gunnison, Stanley E, 1949, My 24,27:2
Gunnison, Walter Balfour Dr, 1916, D 21,11:4
Gunsaulus, Allen C, 1954, Ag 2,17:4
Gunsaulus, Frank W Dr, 1921, Mr 18,15:6
Gunse, Oscar F, 1916, Mr 23,4:7
Gunshanan, Thomas W, 1950, F 7,27:5
Gunson, Joe, 1942, N 16,19:1
Gunst, Emanule H, 1939, My 3,23:2
Gunst, M A, 1928, Je 24,27:3
Gunstead, Clarence N, 1947, Ag 19,23:5
Gunster, Joseph F Mrs, 1964, Mr 15,86:5
Gunter, Archibald C Mrs, 1925, My 22,19:6
Gunter, Archibald Clavering, 1907, F 26,11:6
Gunter, John H, 1949, S 25,92:3
Gunter, Julius, 1940, O 27,44:3
Gunter, Lee C, 1950, D 31,42:3
Gunter, William A, 1940, D 5,25:6
Gunther, Albert E (por), 1942, Mr 12,19:3
Gunther, Alexander, 1966, My 18,47:4
Gunther, Arthur H, 1960, Je 26,72:5
Gunther, Bernard G, 1943, My 2,45:1
Gunther, Blair F, 1966, D 24,19:1
Gunther, C G, 1885, Ja 24,5:4
Gunther, Charles F, 1920, F 12,11:5
Gunther, Charles J, 1949, Mr 17,26:2
Gunther, Charles J Mrs, 1956, F 7,31:3
Gunther, Charles O, 1958, Je 9,23:4
Gunther, Charles O Mrs, 1952, Ap 16,27:4
Gunther, Edward, 1920, Jl 17,7:5
Gunther, Emil A, 1959, F 27,25:2
Gunther, Emma H, 1960, F 20,23:3
Gunther, Ernest L, 1948, Mr 28,48:4
Gunther, Ernest Rudolph, 1923, Ap 16,17:5
Gunther, Frances, 1964, Ap 7,35:4
Gunther, Franklin L Mrs, 1952, N 28,25:2
Gunther, Franklin M, 1941, D 23,21:1
Gunther, Frederick W, 1952, Ap 22,29:3
Gunther, George Jr, 1943, Mr 1,19:3
Gunther, J C, 1876, Mr 7,4:5
Gunther, John F G, 1946, Mr 22,22:3
Gunther, John J, 1916, Jl 23,17:7
Gunther, John Jr, 1947, Jl 2,23:5
Gunther, Joseph J, 1963, D 27,23:3
Gunther, Joseph W, 1960, Jl 19,29:4
Gunther, Richard W, 1913, Ap 6,IV,7:4
Gunther, William H, 1952, F 8,23:4
Gunther, William Mrs, 1947, Jl 29,21:2
Gunther-Mohr, John J, 1942, My 8,21:4
Guntner, Frank G, 1950, N 8,29:5
Gunton, George Prof, 1919, S 13,11:7
Gunton, William, 1950, Ja 31,24:2
Gunzbourg, Jules M, 1950, O 16,27:4
Gunzbourg, M D Mrs, 1946, F 8,19:3
Gunzbourg, Pierre de, 1948, Jl 31,15:7
Gunzbourg, Raoul, 1955, Je 1,33:2
Gunzburger, Norbert, 1916, Jl 6,13:6
Gunzel, George G, 1964, F 28,34:1
Gunzendorfer, Ludwig, 1941, My 25,36:5
Gunzenhauser, Francis J, 1945, My 3,23:2
Gunzenhauser, Frank E, 1940, N 6,23:5
Gunzer, William, 1943, O 23,14:3
Guppy, H B Dr, 1926, My 22,17:4
Guptil, Walter C, 1948, N 11,27:4
Guptill, Arthur L, 1956, Mr 1,33:3
Guptill, Page D, 1958, O 19,87:1
Gupton, Lawrence A, 1948, F 21,13:2
Guranowsky, Abraham Rabbi, 1912, S 21,11:6
Gurdin, Emanuel, 1957, Ja 13,84:6
Gurdjieff, G I (por), 1949, O 31,25:3
Gurdon, Bertram F (Lord Cranworth), 1964, Ja 5, 92:2
Gurdon, Martha Rev, 1920, N 20,15:4
Gureasko, Samuel, 1960, Jl 25,23:3
Gurfein, Louis Mrs, 1938, Jl 30,13:6
Gurge, James V, 1938, Jl 9,13:6
Gurgues, Bishop (funl), 1874, F 13,1:5
Gurian, Irving, 1966, O 14,43:3
Gurian, Max, 1965, N 1,41:3
Gurian, Waldemar, 1954, My 27,27:2
Guridi, Jesus, 1961, Ap 9,86:6
Gurin, Joseph, 1967, Ja 16,41:4
Gurin, Maizie Guss Dr, 1968, Jl 5,25:4
Gurin, Morris, 1961, O 23,29:2
Gurina, Zinaida, 1951, Ja 15,17:2
Gurk, Edward H, 1943, Ja 24,42:2
Gurkin, Samuel S, 1961, N 19,88:3
Gurley, Chester W, 1952, Ja 23,27:1
Gurley, Frank B, 1955, Mr 5,19:2
Gurley, George A, 1939, Ap 30,45:1
Gurley, Melville B, 1962, F 3,21:4
Gurley, Rev Dr, 1868, O 1,7:1
Gurley, Richard H, 1960, O 9,86:8
Gurley, Royal, 1962, Ja 15,27:4
Gurley, William B Mrs, 1943, Je 22,19:5
Gurley, William F, 1915, F 18,11:6
Gurley, William F E, 1943, Je 28,21:2
Gurley, William Wirt, 1923, Mr 12,15:4
Gurlitt, Cornelius, 1901, Je 19,7:6
Gurly, Nancy S, 1883, Ja 10,7:2
Gurman, Stuart I, 1961, Ag 27,84:5
Gurnec, Walter S, 1918, N 28,17:2
Gurnee, Delia E, 1915, D 1,13:4
Gurnee, Eugene A, 1941, Ja 30,21:1
Gurnee, Raymond D, 1954, Ja 22,27:2
Gurnee, Walter S, 1939, F 5,40:4
Gurnee, Walter S Mrs, 1925, S 26,17:5
Gurneee, Walter S (est appr), 1905, S 26,9:6
Gurner, Ronald, 1939, My 18,25:3
Gurnett, Daniel W, 1945, Jl 1,17:3
Gurnett, Edward F, 1954, F 8,23:3
Gurney, Augustus M, 1967, Ap 13,43:2
Gurney, Charles A, 1952, O 24,23:3
Gurney, Charles E, 1945, D 31,17:4
Gurney, Daniel, 1953, F 4,27:4
Gurney, Edmund Mrs, 1948, Ap 7,25:5
Gurney, Henry B, 1956, O 11,39:1
Gurney, Henry B Jr, 1950, Mr 28,31:3
Gurney, Henry High Comr Sir, 1951, O 7,1:6
Gurney, Herbert Reed, 1924, N 15,13:5
Gurney, Herbert S, 1950, Ag 19,13:7
Gurney, Howard F, 1942, Mr 24,19:1
Gurney, Ivor, 1937, D 28,22:4
Gurney, James J, 1963, O 20,88:7
Gurney, Marion F (Mother Marion of Jesus), 1957, F 11,29:4
Gurney, Richard, 1903, My 19,9:6
Gurney, Ronald W, 1953, Ap 15,31:3
Gurney, Russell, 1878, Ja 1,4:7
Gurney, Samuel G, 1956, Ap 12,31:4
Gurney, Samuel Rev, 1924, Ag 14,15:5
Gurney, W H, 1882, Mr 7,2:3
Gurney, William, 1879, F 3,5:3; 1942, Je 1,13:6
Gurock, Louis, 1965, O 19,43:4
Gurock, Nathan B, 1960, N 16,41:1
Gurowski, Adam Count, 1866, My 5,1:3
Gurpide Beope, Pablo Bp, 1968, N 19,47:1
Gurria, J M, 1943, D 25,13:2
Gursel, Cemal (funl plans, S 18,24:3; funl, S 19,43:4), 1966, S 15,43:1
Gurskey, John B, 1951, S 25,29:1
Gurss, Samuel, 1951, O 1,23:6
Gurt, Raymond M, 1962, O 13,25:2
Gurtman, Maurie J, 1965, D 12,86:4
Gurvich, Samuel C, 1942, O 18,52:6
Gurvitch, Samuel M, 1957, O 1,33:2
Gurwitt, Robert I, 1949, F 25,23:2
Gury, Karl E, 1939, N 26,42:4
Gurzeler, Frederick A, 1963, Ap 28,88:2
Gusciora, Stanley, 1956, Jl 10,17:6
Gusev, Dmitri N, 1957, Ag 29,27:2
Gushee, Edward G, 1941, D 6,17:5
Gushee, Edward S, 1954, F 24,25:5
Gushee, Edward T, 1954, D 16,37:4
Gushee, R A, 1933, O 8,39:1
Gushen, Irving, 1963, N 15,35:4
Gushue-Taylor, George Mrs, 1953, S 4,34:1
Gusikoff, Isidor, 1962, O 20,25:4
Guski, John J, 1946, N 3,64:5
Guskin, Reuben, 1951, O 5,27:3
Gusmer, Aage, 1956, My 3,31:1
Guss, Augustino, 1951, Mr 26,23:3
Guss, Henry R Gen, 1907, Ap 26,9:6
Guss, Lazarus, 1965, O 31,86:6
Gussenhoven, George, 1949, F 16,25:4
Gussenhoven, Walter, 1946, Ja 25,23:4
Gussin, Sol D, 1958, Jl 30,29:6
Gussner, Thomas, 1958, Mr 21,21:1
Gussner, William G, 1952, Ja 22,29:3
Gussow, Bernard, 1957, F 10,87:1
Gussow, Bernard Mrs, 1962, Ja 17,33:3
Gussow, Nathan, 1960, D 29,25:2
Gussow, Sam, 1959, Ag 28,23:1
Gussow, Sam Mrs, 1962, S 9,84:8
Gustafson, Andrew, 1955, Jl 23,17:1
Gustafson, Carl O, 1963, O 19,21:8
Gustafson, Carl O Mrs, 1963, O 19,21:8
Gustafson, Charles, 1950, Ap 25,31:3
Gustafson, Clifford A, 1961, F 11,23:5
Gustafson, Edmund R, 1951, Je 7,33:3
Gustafson, Gabriel Dr, 1915, My 2,20:5
Gustafson, Gilbert E, 1958, Ap 26,19:3
Gustafson, Grace M, 1951, Ag 31,15:2
Gustafson, Gustaf, 1953, Ag 3,17:6
Gustafson, Gustaf O, 1955, Mr 11,25:2
Gustafson, Herbert E, 1963, N 11,31:5
Gustafson, Howard, 1966, My 29,56:8
Gustafson, Oscar O, 1959, D 26,13:5
Gustafson, Walter E, 1945, O 19,23:4
Gustafson, Walter G, 1964, Jl 21,33:2
Gustafson, William A, 1958, Ag 27,29:1
Gustav, Charles W, 1949, N 3,29:3
Gustav, Cornelius F, 1959, N 14,21:1
Gustav, Prince, 1944, O 7,13:4
Gustav-Ernst of Erbach-Schoenberg, Prince, 1908, Ja 30,7:5
Gustave Adolph, Crown Princess, 1920, My 2,22:4
Gustavson, Lealand R, 1966, Jl 22,31:4
Gustavson, Marcus N, 1941, N 30,69:2
Gustavson, Victor L, 1951, Ag 10,15:6
Gustin, Albert L, 1943, Ag 30,15:6
Gustin, Byron F Rev, 1951, Jl 13,21:1
Gustin, Don, 1949, Mr 22,25:2
Gustin, Ellen Rev, 1924, My 1,19:4
Gustin, John C, 1964, Jl 13,29:2
Gustine, John S Jr, 1949, Ja 15,17:2
Gustke, Henry G A, 1944, Mr 14,19:4
Gutbrod, Albert Mrs, 1955, Je 15,31:2
Gutbrod, Dr, 1905, Ap 18,11:5
Gutches, George A, 1955, Jl 19,27:3
Gutekunst, Frederick, 1917, Ap 28,13:5
Gutekunst, Leonard Sr, 1954, D 30,17:4
Gutekunst, William A, 1959, Ja 16,28:1
Gutelius, Joseph C, 1953, Mr 7,15:4
Gutelius, William H, 1920, F 11,11:4
Gutenberg, Beno, 1960, Ja 28,31:2
Gutenko, John (Kid Williams), 1963, O 20,88:7
Gutenkunst, Charles A Jr Mrs, 1950, N 27,25:4
Gutentag, George, 1944, My 16,21:6
Gu'eri, Adam, 1948, Ja 7,25:2
Guterl, Gerald Sr, 1968, N 7,47:2
Guterman, Carl E F, 1957, Mr 28,31:4
Guterman, Harry N, 1946, Ap 20,13:5

Guterman, Henry, 1966, O 21,41:4
Guterman, Henry Mrs, 1957, S 12,31:3
Guterman, Henry S, 1953, Ag 7,19:3
Guterman, Hyman, 1962, F 6,35:2
Guterman, Louis, 1959, O 8,39:3
Gutermuth, Charles S, 1948, Jl 15,23:5
Gutero, Walter J, 1947, Ag 16,13:1
Guterson, Mischa, 1951, S 29,17:5
Gutfreund, Fanny Mrs, 1940, Jl 26,17:5
Gutfreund, Sigmund, 1945, N 17,17:3
Gutgemon, Gustave, 1959, My 7,33:4
Gutgsell, E F J, 1903, My 14,9:6
Gutgsell Adolph E, 1944, D 2,13:6
Guth, Charles G, 1948, My 25,27:6
Guth, George W, 1942, D 2,25:2
Guth, John, 1903, Je 9,9:6
Guthe, Karl E Dr, 1915, S 12,17:6
Gutheil, Charles A, 1946, S 24,29:4
Gutheil, Emil A, 1959, Jl 8,29:4
Guthinger, George J, 1953, Ap 27,23:5
Guthlein, John F, 1954, Jl 10,13:5
Guthlein, John F Sr Mrs, 1949, Ap 14,25:5
Guthman, Edwin L, 1953, Ap 26,86:2
Guthman, Sigmund, 1943, Ag 24,19:3
Guthman, William (por), 1941, Jl 10,19:3
Guthmann, Simon, 1938, Je 18,15:4
Guthner, William E, 1951, Ja 25,25:2
Guthrie, A A, 1874, F 16,1:2
Guthrie, A B Sr, 1954, S 3,17:2
Guthrie, Albert N Mrs, 1962, Jl 3,23:1
Guthrie, Alfred, 1882, Ag 18,5:5
Guthrie, Anna N Mrs, 1955, O 30,89:1
Guthrie, Archibald, 1913, My 18,IV,7:6
Guthrie, C E, 1940, Jl 27,13:6
Guthrie, Charles B, 1937, O 17,II,9:2
Guthrie, Charles C, 1963, Je 17,25:2
Guthrie, Charles S, 1906, Ja 5,11:3
Guthrie, Charles S Mrs, 1957, Je 20,29:2
Guthrie, Charles W, 1939, Jl 1,17:3
Guthrie, Connop (por), 1945, O 3,19:3
Guthrie, David F Jr, 1948, O 21,27:5
Guthrie, Donald, 1958, N 1,19:3
Guthrie, Elmer F, 1952, D 19,31:3
Guthrie, Frank V, 1939, F 14,19:2
Guthrie, Frederick P, 1959, F 7,19:6
Guthrie, George G, 1950, My 5,22:2
Guthrie, George W (por), 1917, Mr 9,7:5
Guthrie, Giles F, 1950, Mr 21,29:2
Guthrie, H G, 1881, Ap 19,5:3
Guthrie, Henry B Sr Mrs, 1953, Ag 6,21:4
Guthrie, Hugh (por), 1939, N 4,15:3
Guthrie, J Edward H Mrs, 1959, N 11,35:3
Guthrie, J Gordon, 1961, Je 24,21:5
Guthrie, James, 1869, Mr 14,5:1
Guthrie, James F, 1958, Ag 20,27:4
Guthrie, James K, 1949, D 8,33:4
Guthrie, James R, 1953, Jl 7,27:5
Guthrie, John, 1955, Mr 17,45:4
Guthrie, Joseph A, 1947, Jl 12,13:6
Guthrie, Mortimer J, 1952, D 27,9:5
Guthrie, Norah Mrs, 1956, Jl 7,13:4
Guthrie, Oliver P, 1944, N 7,27:5
Guthrie, Ossian Mrs, 1904, N 30,5:5
Guthrie, P N Gen, 1902, F 25,9:5
Guthrie, Percy A, 1948, Ap 25,71:3
Guthrie, Raymond S, 1950, Ap 30,102:3
Guthrie, Robert P, 1945, F 3,11:6
Guthrie, Robert R, 1968, My 6,47:1
Guthrie, Robert W Col, 1922, Jl 25,11:6
Guthrie, Thomas, 1873, F 25,4:7
Guthrie, Thomas H, 1937, Je 7,19:4
Guthrie, Virgil B, 1968, Je 15,35:4
Guthrie, W D, 1935, D 9,21:1
Guthrie, Walter E, 1941, Je 7,17:5
Guthrie, Walter J, 1940, Mr 3,44:1
Guthrie, Watson A, 1939, Ap 2,III,7:2
Guthrie, William, 1950, Mr 7,27:2
Guthrie, William A, 1916, O 15,21:5
Guthrie, William B (por), 1940, N 7,25:1
Guthrie, William D Mrs, 1958, Mr 28,25:4
Guthrie, William J, 1939, Ag 29,21:5
Guthrie, William L, 1959, N 10,47:3
Guthrie, William L Col, 1918, Ap 9,13:4
Guthrie, William N (por), 1944, D 10,53:1
Guthrie, William N Mrs, 1959, Jl 28,27:4
Guthrie, Woody, 1967, O 4,47:3
Gutierres, Garcia, 1884, S 3,2:3
Gutierrez, Alonzo, 1879, Ag 2,2:2
Gutierrez, Eulalio, 1939, Ag 14,15:6
Gutierrez, Juan M, 1946, Mr 18,21:5
Gutierrez, Marcel, 1947, N 2,73:2
Gutierrez Arancibia, Jose M, 1941, Ja 24,17:1
Gutierrez Colana, Jose, 1945, Je 25,17:2
Gutierrez Solis, Andres, 1952, Ag 23,13:6
Gutkes, Frederick A, 1940, O 19,17:5
Gutkin, Joseph Mrs, 1951, O 14,89:1
Gutkin, Samuel S, 1958, Je 3,31:4
Gutkind, Erwin A Dr, 1968, Ag 10,27:3
Gutkowska, Anna, 1945, My 14,17:3
Gutland, Edward C, 1942, N 15,57:1
Gutleber, Henry W, 1951, D 1,13:3
Gutlohn, Ralph R, 1949, Ag 7,61:1
Gutmacher, Manfred S, 1966, N 8,39:1
Gutman, Abraham L, 1944, Ja 1,13:2
Gutman, Alexander B Mrs, 1946, Mr 7,25:2
Gutman, Arthur, 1945, S 6,25:4
Gutman, David, 1957, Mr 10,88:5
Gutman, Edwin J Mrs, 1938, F 22,21:6; 1943, D 22, 24:3
Gutman, Harry Mrs, 1953, D 10,48:4
Gutman, Ida N Mrs, 1939, Ap 1,19:5
Gutman, Isaac, 1941, Mr 3,15:4; 1941, O 22,23:1
Gutman, Jacob (por), 1944, My 9,19:2
Gutman, Joel, 1950, F 18,15:4
Gutman, Julius, 1921, Ag 27,9:5; 1947, Ag 18,17:5
Gutman, Louis, 1964, Jl 19,65:1
Gutman, Louis Mrs, 1953, N 22,88:3
Gutman, Max, 1944, Ja 30,37:1
Gutman, Nelson, 1955, Ag 18,23:4
Gutman, Selmar, 1960, Ap 19,23:2
Gutman, William R Mrs, 1946, Je 4,23:3
Gutman-Marinel, Adolphe Mrs, 1952, F 11,25:6
Gutmann, Erwin K, 1948, D 23,19:4
Gutmann, Ferdinand, 1954, Ja 25,19:2
Gutmann, Frederick G, 1940, Ja 13,15:3
Gutmann, Harold, 1956, D 26,27:2
Gutmann, Jesse, 1939, S 3,19:3
Gutmann, Julius, 1960, O 23,89:1
Gutmann, Sumner, 1948, Jl 30,18:2
Gutmueller, Robert G, 1940, Ag 8,19:5
Gutner, Saul, 1968, O 24,47:2
Gutnick, Sam S, 1952, S 18,29:3
Gutowski, Bob, 1960, Ag 3,12:3
Gutowski, Walter T (Sept 25), 1965, O 11,61:2
Gutradt, Charles, 1948, N 8,21:5
Gutsell, Hiram S Mrs, 1951, Ag 23,23:3
Gutshall, Simon Mrs, 1943, F 23,21:3
Gutstadt, Richard E, 1954, My 24,27:3
Gutt, Camille Mrs, 1948, Ap 21,27:4
Gutt, Traugott J, 1951, My 5,17:2
Guttag, Henry, 1956, Ap 30,23:5
Guttag, Julius, 1962, Mr 29,33:3
Guttchen, Ralph, 1959, Jl 25,17:4
Guttenberg, John P, 1952, Je 24,29:3
Guttenberg, Samuel, 1953, Ag 5,23:6
Guttenburg, Mitchell, 1954, Ja 11,25:6
Guttentag, Charles A, 1937, S 20,23:4
Gutter, Harry L, 1965, Ag 23,31:5
Gutteridge, Mary V, 1962, Je 23,23:1
Gutteridge, Wesley W, 1953, Mr 25,31:3
Gutterman, Albert, 1957, Ag 2,19:1
Gutterman, Joseph, 1955, S 29,33:1
Gutterman, Morris, 1942, Ag 7,17:6
Gutterman, Morris D, 1953, Ja 12,27:2
Gutterson, Albert L, 1965, Ap 8,39:5
Gutterson, Alburn M, 1946, Ap 21,46:3
Gutterson, Fred S, 1938, S 1,23:5
Gutterson, Herbert L, 1960, Ag 7,84:5
Gutterson, Wilder (cor, Jl 13,25:1), 1950, Jl 12,29:5
Guttery, Arthur Thomas Rev Dr, 1920, D 18,13:4
Guttin, Adolph, 1923, My 1,21:4
Gutting, Adolph, 1948, D 7,32:2
Gutting, Otto J Mrs, 1958, N 2,89:3
Guttman, Edward, 1964, Ag 5,33:2
Guttman, Hudel Mrs, 1954, S 10,23:1
Guttman, Oskar, 1943, S 9,25:2
Guttman, Solomon, 1950, Ja 11,23:4
Guttmann, Louis, 1949, Ja 6,23:2
Guttormsen, Andrew G, 1949, Mr 17,25:3
Guttridge, Emma Mrs, 1939, Mr 6,6:4
Guttridge, Frank, 1945, Jl 21,11:3
Guttzeit, Arthur P Lt, 1919, Je 23,13:4
Guttzeit, Charles W, 1949, Je 8,30:5
Gutwillig, Bernard, 1948, Ja 4,52:3
Gutwirth, Charles, 1963, Jl 26,25:2
Gutwirth, Charles A, 1967, Je 8,47:5
Gutwirth, Gutman, 1953, Ja 26,22:8
Gutwirth, Marc R, 1966, Je 16,47:4
Gutzeit, Louis, 1959, F 6,25:1
Gutzkow, Karl, 1878, D 29,8:5
Guy, Albert E Mrs, 1947, Ja 23,23:3
Guy, Alma I, 1938, S 30,21:3
Guy, Arthur, 1937, Ap 13,25:6
Guy, Arthur S, 1945, My 25,19:3
Guy, Bobby, 1964, My 29,29:2
Guy, C L, 1930, Jl 23,21:1
Guy, Charles C, 1950, S 20,31:1
Guy, Charles E, 1946, F 19,26:2
Guy, Clarence B, 1951, Ap 28,15:4
Guy, David W, 1960, My 29,57:1
Guy, Earl V, 1951, Ag 25,11:5
Guy, Ernest, 1948, Ja 9,21:2
Guy, George D, 1951, O 17,31:2
Guy, George H, 1923, Ap 4,17:5
Guy, George R, 1942, Je 13,15:3
Guy, J H, 1881, Mr 29,4:7
Guy, J Samuel, 1953, Ag 18,23:1
Guy, Mark, 1951, F 24,13:5
Guy, Phil L O, 1952, D 8,41:3
Guy, Raymond, 1947, Mr 30,56:2
Guy, Robert A, 1937, Ja 7,22:1
Guy, Seymour J Mrs, 1907, S 29,9:4
Guy, Thomas J, 1948, N 9,27:4
Guy, W E, 1928, Jl 25,21:5
Guyer, Anthony, 1952, My 30,15:3
Guyer, Arthur W, 1938, Ap 7,23:6
Guyer, Emily Mrs, 1967, Ap 2,80:1
Guyer, Foster E, 1957, N 10,85:6
Guyer, George W, 1945, Ag 13,19:5
Guyer, R G, 1939, Ja 15,38:2
Guyer, Ulysses S, 1943, Je 6,44:1
Guyer, William, 1944, O 4,20:3
Guylee, Ernest J, 1952, Ja 19,15:5
Guyman, Clarence L, 1951, N 26,25:4
Guyn, J White, 1953, Ap 16,29:2
Guynemer, Georges, 1917, O 5,11:5
Guyon, David, 1941, O 21,23:4
Guyon, Henry A, 1908, S 4,7:6
Guyon, Henry A Mrs, 1959, Ap 16,33:2
Guyon, Louis, 1945, My 17,19:5
Guyon, Roy, 1941, Jl 26,18:3
Guyot, A H, 1884, F 9,5:2
Guyott, Louis E, 1942, F 16,17:2
Guysi, Alice V, 1940, Mr 24,31:3
Guzewicz, Walter L, 1962, F 13,35:5
Guzik, Anthony J, 1966, F 5,29:5
Guzik, Jake (Greasy Thumb), 1956, F 22,18:5
Guzik, Mandel L, 1943, O 17,48:5
Guzman, Antonio, 1958, Je 7,19:2
Guzman, Fernando, 1946, F 8,19:3
Guzman, Herman, 1940, D 11,27:4
Guzman, Max, 1963, S 22,86:7
Guzman, Susan Countess, 1911, Ag 6,II,9:6
Guzy, Isaac, 1945, Mr 26,19:5
Guzzoni, Alfredo, 1965, Ap 16,29:3
Guzzy, Anna, 1949, D 16,31:2
Gwalior, Maharaja of (Jiwaji Rao Scindia), 1961, Jl 18,29:1
Gwaltney, Eugene C, 1951, D 1,13:6
Gwaltney, Pembroke Decatur, 1915, F 11,9:5
Gwathmey, Arch B Jr (por), 1937, My 14,23:5
Gwathmey, Archie B, 1956, My 19,19:3
Gwathmey, Gaines, 1959, S 16,39:2
Gwathmey, J Temple, 1924, Je 13,19:6
Gwathmey, James T (por), 1944, F 12,13:3
Gwatkins, Willoughby G Sir, 1925, F 4,21:3
Gwenn, Edmund (funl plans, S 9,41:3), 1959, S
Gwerin, Patrick, 1942, S 29,23:3
Gwilliam, James R, 1939, Ag 16,23:1
Gwilliam, John, 1964, Jl 19,64:2
Gwillim, Stanley S, 1958, Jl 29,23:1
Gwilym, David Y Rev, 1911, D 14,13:3
Gwin, George S Sr, 1955, Jl 10,73:2
Gwinn, Frederick W Jr, 1956, O 17,35:3
Gwinn, Frederick W Mrs, 1954, N 15,27:4
Gwinn, John H (cor, F 16,25:1), 1954, F 14,92:
Gwinn, Ralph W (will, Mr 28,31:6), 1962, F 28
Gwinn, Ralph W Mrs, 1957, O 15,30:1
Gwinn, William P Mrs, 1957, S 19,29:3
Gwinnell, Charles, 1961, Ap 15,21:5
Gwinner, Edward W, 1949, S 2,17:4
Gwinner, Frederick, 1909, S 3,9:5
Gwydyr, Baron (Peter Robt Burrell), 1909, Ap
Gwyer, Charles L, 1956, D 11,39:4
Gwyer, Frederick D Mrs, 1950, Jl 7,19:2
Gwyer, Frederick Dr, 1924, Ja 13,23:1
Gwyer, John, 1945, N 20,21:5
Gwyer, Maurice L, 1952, O 14,31:2
Gwyer, Roy V, 1945, F 5,15:4
Gwyn, Harry M, 1938, F 9,19:5
Gwyn, James Gen, 1906, Jl 19,7:6
Gwyn, Lewis R, 1950, Ag 30,31:5
Gwyn, Lewis R Mrs, 1944, Ja 15,13:5
Gwynn, Frederick L, 1966, Ja 2,72:7
Gwynn, Joseph Kean, 1919, F 26,11:4
Gwynn, Robert B, 1954, D 13,27:2
Gwynn, Stephen, 1950, Je 12,27:3
Gwynn, William C, 1955, F 8,27:1
Gwynne, Abram E, 1905, N 27,9:4
Gwynne, Alice, 1946, Ap 22,21:5
Gwynne, Arthur C, 1952, My 3,21:2
Gwynne, Arthur C Mrs, 1945, Jl 6,11:7
Gwynne, C Allan Mrs, 1952, F 1,22:2
Gwynne, Charles T (por), 1945, F 1,23:3
Gwynne, Edgar A, 1950, Ja 25,27:3
Gwynne, Edward E Mrs, 1958, Ja 6,39:3
Gwynne, Erskine (por), 1948, My 6,25:2
Gwynne, Howell A, 1950, Je 28,27:5
Gwynne, John A, 1906, Mr 13,9:4
Gwynne, John W Mrs, 1956, Ag 25,15:6
Gwynne, Llewelyn H, 1957, D 5,35:4
Gwynne, Walter L, 1955, Ap 9,13:3
Gwynne-Vaughan, Helen F, 1967, Ag 31,33:2
Gwyther, Geoffrey M, 1944, Jl 28,13:2
Gyarmati, Louis, 1956, Ag 17,19:5
Gyde, Praxille, 1946, Ap 12,27:4
Gyderson, Lydia M Mrs, 1941, S 11,23:6
Gye, F, 1878, D 5,2:2
Gye, William E, 1952, O 15,31:5
Gyger, Edgar G, 1941, My 2,21:4
Gymer, Frederick E, 1962, Mr 23,33:1
Gyongyosi, Janos, 1951, O 30,29:4
Gyoreffy-Bengyel, Colben, 1942, Je 15,19:2
Gyori, Cyril, 1945, Mr 4,38:7
Gypsy Queen (Gannie Jeffers), 1884, Ap 16
Gzowski, C S, 1940, S 9,15:5

H

Haab, Robert (por), 1939, O 16,19:3
Haac, Norman N, 1963, My 14,39:5
Haack, Billy, 1954, N 11,31:4
Haacke, Henry, 1903, D 23,9:6
Haacker, Fred C, 1957, Ja 22,29:5
Haag, Alfred H, 1941, Ja 15,23:3
Haag, Carol C, 1942, Jl 14,19:4
Haag, Christian T, 1958, O 8,35:2
Haag, Francis E, 1945, O 1,19:4
Haag, Frederick, 1938, F 8,7:6
Haag, George P, 1938, Jl 7,19:3
Haag, Hans, 1955, D 31,13:3
Haag, Herman E, 1956, Jl 6,21:1
Haag, Jackson D, 1949, F 16,25:2
Haag, Jacob Mrs, 1937, My 9,II,11:1
Haag, John A, 1944, Ag 6,37:2
Haag, John C, 1961, O 9,35:1
Haag, Joseph Jr, 1958, Mr 11,29:1
Haag, M D, 1949, Ja 11,27:2
Haag, Philipp A, 1944, Ja 5,17:2
Haak, P G Mrs, 1953, Mr 16,19:3
Haake, Alfred P, 1961, N 3,36:1
Haake, William, 1945, S 22,17:4
Haakon VII, King of Norway (funl, O 2,11:5), 1957, S 21,1:1
Haan, Bierens de, 1943, S 30,21:2
Haan, George W, 1948, F 10,23:3
Haan, R M, 1932, Jl 6,19:3
Haan, William G Maj-Gen, 1924, O 30,19:5
Haar, Henry M, 1910, S 22,9:4
Haar, Henry P, 1949, Je 30,23:6
Haar, Louis, 1954, N 10,33:3
Haar, Thomas S, 1964, Jl 26,56:4
Haar, William, 1942, F 28,17:4
Haarbleicher, Arthur H, 1946, My 17,21:4
Haarde, William H, 1950, Ja 23,23:4
Haardt, G M, 1932, Mr 17,21:1
Haardt, Gaston, 1937, F 3,23:2
Haardt, Georges, 1939, O 12,25:3
Haaren, Arthur H, 1952, My 4,64:2
Haaren, Edgar J Mrs, 1957, Ja 30,29:3
Haaren, Ernest C, 1953, My 23,15:5
Haaren, John H Dr, 1916, S 24,19:3
Haarer, John W, 1941, Ap 25,19:2
Haarmaan, Walter L, 1958, D 30,32:2
Haarmeyer, H J, 1933, Mr 14,22:5
Haartz, John C, 1941, Ag 4,13:3
Haas, Abraham, 1942, Je 19,23:4
Haas, Abraham Mrs, 1949, Jl 25,15:5
Haas, Albert J, 1950, D 29,19:4
Haas, Alfarata, 1954, S 17,11:6
Haas, Alfred M, 1947, D 21,52:4
Haas, Arthur, 1950, O 24,29:5
Haas, Arthur E, 1941, F 21,19:3
Haas, Benjamin F (cor, Ja 2,13:1), 1960, Ja 1,19:3
Haas, Bruno, 1952, Je 7,19:6
Haas, Charles A, 1962, Ja 18,29:4
Haas, Charles C, 1967, Mr 14,47:2
Haas, Charles J, 1957, S 5,29:2; 1959, D 24,19:2
Haas, Chris N, 1948, Ap 30,23:3
Haas, Christian, 1943, Ap 3,15:4
Haas, Cyril H, 1961, Ja 12,29:2
Haas, David Mrs, 1950, Jl 14,21:4
Haas, Emil M, 1949, D 27,23:2
Haas, Ernestine L Mrs, 1939, My 3,24:2
Haas, Francis J, 1953, Ag 30,88:1
Haas, Fred C, 1952, Ap 9,31:2
Haas, Fred J, 1903, N 12,9:5
Haas, Frederick S, 1955, O 12,31:5
Haas, Frederick S Mrs, 1962, Mr 8,31:4
Haas, George A, 1964, My 30,17:5
Haas, George C, 1963, D 28,23:3
Haas, George J, 1956, My 7,27:4
Haas, George L, 1951, S 28,31:4
Haas, George M, 1943, Ag 3,19:1
Haas, George Mrs, 1966, F 25,31:4
Haas, Harry H Mrs, 1954, Ap 11,86:2
Haas, Harry L, 1953, Mr 21,17:1
Haas, Henry, 1956, O 3,33:5
Haas, Henry L, 1948, O 15,24:2
Haas, Herbert R, 1950, S 13,27:4
Haas, Herman, 1937, Ja 25,19:4; 1943, D 6,23:5
Haas, J A W Dr, 1937, Jl 23,19:6
Haas, J I, 1937, S 9,23:3
Haas, Jacob R, 1947, D 25,21:2
Haas, John E, 1961, N 8,35:4
Haas, John G, 1937, D 21,23:4; 1963, S 29,86:4
Haas, John L, 1938, S 26,17:2
Haas, John Mrs, 1945, Je 10,32:3
Haas, John N Mrs, 1944, Ja 27,19:1
Haas, John R C, 1961, Je 5,31:2
Haas, Joseph, 1958, Jl 22,28:1
Haas, Joseph S, 1962, N 5,31:5
Haas, Julius C, 1955, N 1,31:2
Haas, Leah S Mrs, 1947, D 20,17:4
Haas, Leopold F W Dr, 1917, Ja 20,11:3
Haas, Louis G, 1938, S 27,21:2
Haas, Louis J, 1956, My 20,86:8
Haas, Louis S, 1941, Je 30,17:2
Haas, Lucien L, 1949, Je 14,31:4
Haas, Milton E Mrs, 1937, N 13,19:2
Haas, Otto, 1960, Ja 3,88:3
Haas, Philip L, 1947, N 15,17:4
Haas, Raoul R, 1939, Jl 22,15:5
Haas, Reynold L, 1955, S 21,33:5
Haas, Richard, 1942, F 27,17:4
Haas, Samuel T, 1959, D 23,27:5
Haas, Sidney V, 1964, D 1,41:1
Haas, Solomon, 1909, N 24,9:5
Haas, Stephanie (Mrs E Kronold), 1957, D 9,35:6
Haas, Talfourd N, 1939, F 18,15:6
Haas, William (por), 1949, Mr 4,21:1
Haas, William C, 1943, D 23,19:3
Haas, William E P Rev, 1937, Jl 7,23:5
Haas, William F, 1944, Ja 7,17:4
Haas, William S (cor, Ja 18,31:1), 1956, Ja 4,27:5
Haase, Adolph A, 1948, My 2,76:5
Haase, Adolph Mrs, 1941, O 31,23:3
Haase, C (Baron De Mainey, Dr Carlos), 1880, Mr 15,5:4
Haase, Charles H, 1947, My 25,60:6
Haase, Ernst, 1961, O 12,29:1
Haase, Fred C, 1952, Jl 22,25:2
Haase, Friedrich, 1911, Mr 18,13:6
Haase, George A, 1938, Ja 27,21:5
Haase, Hugo, 1919, N 8,13:3
Haase, John F, 1948, Ja 14,25:2
Haassler, August, 1950, N 26,90:3
Haasted, Clara Mrs, 1954, My 22,7:5
Haasted, Lars, 1948, S 1,23:2
Haatanen, Alfred, 1961, S 26,40:1
Habbert, George L, 1953, My 15,23:2
Habberton, C (Toddie), 1877, F 3,8:5
Habberton, John, 1921, F 26,11:6
Habekotte, George F, 1943, Mr 4,19:2
Habel, A, 1879, Ja 5,7:4
Habel, Clifford A, 1954, O 9,17:3
Habenicht, William, 1952, Je 8,64:5
Haber, Ben, 1949, Je 7,31:2
Haber, Bernard, 1959, F 27,25:1
Haber, Charles L, 1957, S 5,29:2
Haber, David, 1937, F 17,22:1
Haber, Ferdinand I, 1965, N 19,39:1
Haber, Ferdinand I Mrs, 1953, Mr 13,25:5
Haber, Isador, 1960, Ja 16,21:3
Haber, Isidore I Mrs, 1945, My 16,19:1
Haber, John, 1950, Jl 29,13:5
Haber, John S, 1943, Je 16,21:4
Haber, Julius, 1966, S 24,23:2
Haber, Louis I (por), 1947, O 22,29:1
Haber, Mollie T Mrs, 1951, Jl 14,13:1
Haber, Moses W, 1956, F 26,89:3
Haber, P B, 1940, Ja 3,22:4
Haber, Paul J, 1950, Jl 9,69:1
Haber, Phil, 1954, F 16,25:5
Haber, Sam Mrs (Pauline), 1965, Mr 25,37:2
Haber, William M, 1963, Je 13,33:4
Haber, Zigmund, 1950, Jl 15,13:6
Haberacker, Eugene O M Dr, 1925, Ap 6,19:5
Haberer, Charles, 1944, My 5,19:2
Haberer, Herman J, 1953, My 31,74:2
Haberer, Joseph V Dr, 1925, D 8,25:5
Haberkorn, William P, 1944, Ap 24,19:4
Haberland, Ulrich, 1961, S 11,27:6
Haberle, Ernest (por), 1948, My 4,25:4
Haberle, John H, 1951, Ag 2,21:6
Haberle, Norman H, 1960, D 7,44:7
Haberlin, Grover C, 1947, My 27,25:3
Haberlin, James H, 1952, Jl 11,17:5
Haberman, Alex S, 1964, Ap 28,37:2
Haberman, Isser A Mrs, 1961, N 19,89:1
Haberman, Meyer J, 1945, O 5,23:3
Haberman, Morris Mrs, 1955, Ag 28,85:1
Haberman, Phil W, 1953, Ap 20,25:3
Haberman, Roberto, 1962, Mr 5,23:4
Habernicht, August J, 1951, D 24,13:3
Habersack, Nivard H, 1963, Jl 14,61:1
Habersham, Jessie Mrs, 1921, Ag 18,11:6
Haberstick, Charles, 1958, Ja 6,39:3
Haberstick, Fred T, 1955, N 8,31:4
Haberstroh, Fred, 1937, S 10,23:1
Habert, Charles, 1951, N 29,33:5
Habert, Henri, 1946, F 19,25:4
Habib, Fred, 1954, Mr 31,27:4
Habib Lotfallah, Prince, 1949, O 13,27:1
Habich, Louis, 1965, Ag 1,77:1
Habich, Paul J, 1949, Ap 11,25:3
Habicht, C E, 1883, Mr 30,5:4
Habirshaw, W, 1881, Je 11,5:1
Habirshaw, William M Dr, 1908, Ag 17,7:5
Habrich, Emil J, 1957, N 9,27:4
Habsburg, Otto de Bourbon, 1954, N 2,27:4
Haby, Francois, 1938, Ap 27,23:4
Haby, Linus, 1943, N 18,23:2
Hacbang, Soforino Bp, 1937, Ap 5,20:1
Hach, Elizabeth, 1952, O 16,29:3
Hacha, Emil, 1945, Jl 1,17:1
Hachceister, Herman, 1947, My 14,25:5
Hachemeister, Harry, 1946, Ja 11,21:2
Hachemeister, Harry Mrs, 1946, Ja 11,21:2
Hachenburg, Max, 1951, D 4,33:2
Hachette, Louis, 1941, Ap 16,23:5
Hachette, Rene, 1940, Ag 24,13:6
Hachfield, Aug, 1942, S 6,30:5
Hachmeister, Adolph, 1917, Jl 6,9:6
Hachmeister, Harry A, 1960, S 10,21:4
Hachtel, Edward, 1960, F 18,33:1
Hachtmann, Andrew P, 1955, Je 13,23:6
Hack, Charles W, 1923, O 7,6:3
Hack, Frederick C, 1947, Jl 22,23:4
Hack, Frederick F, 1961, Mr 27,31:4
Hack, George, 1952, N 20,31:5
Hack, Henry, 1955, Ja 1,13:4
Hack, Margaret M Mrs, 1947, F 21,19:1
Hack, Oren S Mrs, 1961, Ag 20,86:3
Hack, Otto A, 1942, N 20,23:4
Hack, Otto A Mrs, 1944, My 16,21:2
Hackathorne, George, 1940, Je 27,23:4
Hacke, Count, 1864, Je 10,2:2
Hacke, Erica H von Countess, 1951, Jl 1,51:1
Hacke, Paul H, 1907, S 8,7:6
Hackel, Julius, 1947, My 3,17:5
Hackemann, Louis, 1966, O 18,45:2
Hackenberg, James O, 1950, Je 9,23:2
Hackenburg, Frederick L, 1952, Ja 11,21:5
HacKenley, John, 1943, N 16,23:2
Hackenschmidt, George, 1968, F 20,47:2
Hacker, Arthur H Mrs, 1950, O 8,104:5
Hacker, C W Louis, 1944, Jl 9,36:1
Hacker, Casper W, 1937, Ja 21,23:5
Hacker, Christian G, 1941, S 21,44:2
Hacker, Fred A, 1958, Je 3,31:2
Hacker, Joseph C, 1915, F 18,11:6
Hacker, Louis M Mrs, 1952, Mr 21,23:3
Hacker, Max, 1937, S 7,21:6
Hacker, Ralph G, 1966, Ja 10,25:3
Hackert, Clinton A, 1943, Jl 31,13:4
Hackes, John R Mrs, 1964, S 10,35:1
Hackes, Simon, 1907, N 12,9:7
Hacket, John J, 1938, S 7,36:3
Hacket-Pain, William Gen, 1924, F 15,15:6
Hackett, Charles, 1940, S 18,23:5
Hackett, Charles (por), 1942, Ja 2,23:1
Hackett, Corcellus H, 1917, Ja 28,17:3
Hackett, Corden T, 1941, Ag 1,15:1
Hackett, Earl D, 1949, S 9,26:3
Hackett, Edmond B, 1953, N 12,43:6
Hackett, Edmund F, 1954, N 28,86:4
Hackett, Edward, 1958, Ag 6,25:2
Hackett, Edward J, 1947, F 23,53:4
Hackett, Ernest A, 1949, My 7,13:3
Hackett, Eva S, 1949, Ap 15,23:1
Hackett, Frances M, 1942, F 24,21:2
Hackett, Francis, 1962, Ap 26,33:1
Hackett, Frank D, 1951, S 5,31:1
Hackett, Frank S, 1952, F 7,27:3; 1953, Mr 4,27:5
Hackett, Frank S Mrs, 1937, F 14,II,8:6
Hackett, Frederick, 1963, Mr 20,16:1
Hackett, George, 1942, N 28,13:4
Hackett, H B Rev Dr, 1875, N 3,4:5
Hackett, Harold F, 1963, Je 25,33:3
Hackett, Harold H (will, N 30,8:4), 1937, N 21,II,9:3
Hackett, Harold H Mrs, 1958, N 17,31:2
Hackett, Harold W, 1958, Ja 7,47:2
Hackett, Harry C, 1954, D 9,33:1
Hackett, Henry T, 1951, Ja 11,26:3
Hackett, Horatio B (por), 1941, S 9,23:1
Hackett, J K, 1879, D 27,1:7; 1926, N 9,27:1
Hackett, James F, 1967, Ap 8,31:4
Hackett, James H, 1871, D 29,5:2
Hackett, James H Mrs, 1937, Je 14,23:3
Hackett, James Henry Mrs, 1909, O 28,9:4
Hackett, James J, 1947, Jl 1,25:3
Hackett, James W, 1941, Jl 15,19:6
Hackett, John, 1916, Je 24,11:7
Hackett, John C, 1944, N 6,19:5
Hackett, John H, 1944, N 15,27:1; 1956, S 16,84:2
Hackett, John J, 1946, O 19,21:6
Hackett, John M, 1954, Ja 5,27:1
Hackett, John S, 1940, Jl 6,15:2
Hackett, John T, 1944, My 20,15:2; 1960, Mr 24,33:4
Hackett, John Winthrop Sir, 1916, F 22,11:5
Hackett, Joseph, 1957, F 10,85:3
Hackett, Joseph J, 1944, My 7,46:1
Hackett, Le Roy, 1953, Mr 18,31:2
Hackett, Lewis W, 1962, Ap 30,27:3
Hackett, Maurice J, 1947, S 23,25:4
Hackett, Paul E, 1956, Je 12,35:4
Hackett, Philip, 1961, Ag 14,25:4
Hackett, Raymond, 1958, Jl 8,27:3
Hackett, Raymond E, 1964, Jl 12,69:1
Hackett, Richard, 1949, F 9,27:4
Hackett, Richard Mrs, 1939, F 14,19:3
Hackett, Robert Mrs, 1953, O 5,27:4
Hackett, Stephen, 1937, O 17,II,8:5
Hackett, Theodore (Dody), 1956, Mr 11,88:8
Hackett, Thomas J, 1960, N 23,29:4

Hackett, Thomas M, 1955, D 9,27:3
Hackett, W S, 1926, Mr 5,21:5
Hackett, Waldo N, 1960, Ap 24,88:4
Hackett, Walter (por), 1944, Ja 22,13:1
Hackett, William, 1956, Je 8,25:3
Hackett, William A, 1941, My 3,15:5
Hackett, William H (por), 1938, N 11,25:4
Hackh, Otto Prof, 1917, S 25,11:7
Hacking, Lord, 1950, Jl 31,17:5
Hacking, Mark, 1949, Mr 19,9:4
Hackl, George F, 1954, D 15,32:1
Hackl, Ralph, 1947, S 29,21:2
Hackl, Roderich, 1946, Ag 20,27:5
Hackland, William N, 1945, Mr 3,13:5
Hacklander, F W, 1877, Ag 6,3:3
Hackler, Joy M, 1950, Je 27,29:5
Hackler, Kent C, 1956, Ap 9,51:4
Hackley, Belva Mrs, 1960, Jl 12,35:4
Hackley, Caleb Mrs, 1913, S 5,9:5
Hackley, Charles E Dr, 1925, Je 16,21:5
Hackman, Abe, 1960, Mr 18,25:1
Hackman, Alfred N, 1945, O 17,19:2
Hackman, Bertha, 1949, Mr 30,25:4
Hackman, Murray, 1953, D 19,15:3
Hackman, Murry, 1959, Jl 14,29:4
Hackman, William H, 1950, Ag 11,19:3
Hackney, Charles A, 1937, F 9,23:4
Hackney, Clarence (por), 1939, Ap 28,25:2
Hackney, Clarence W Sr, 1941, Ja 6,18:6
Hackney, Edward, 1952, Jl 3,25:4
Hackney, Ezekial M, 1955, Ja 6,27:2
Hackney, H Eastman, 1967, Jl 5,41:4
Hackney, Harry Mrs, 1944, F 14,17:4
Hackney, Harry W, 1945, Ja 26,21:4
Hackney, James B, 1949, Ja 5,25:1
Hackney, John L, 1948, Jl 18,52:4
Hackney, Leonard J, 1938, O 4,25:3
Hackney, Louise W, 1945, Mr 28,23:4
Hackney, Rachel Ann, 1922, Je 26,13:7
Hackney, Ray, 1965, Mr 12,47:3
Hackney, Thomas, 1946, D 25,29:5
Hackney, William C, 1925, D 10,25:5
Hackstaff, Alexander G, 1912, N 30,13:3
Hackstaff, Frederick, 1940, O 26,15:2
Hackstaff, Frederick W, 1952, F 11,25:4
Hackstaff, J Frank Mrs, 1914, Ja 16,9:5
Hackworth, Earl C, 1946, Je 15,21:4
Hackzell, Anders W A, 1946, Ja 16,23:3
Hacohen, Israel, 1953, Je 1,23:3
Hadad, Nadra, 1950, My 28,32:5
Hadakin, Helen, 1947, Mr 6,25:5
Hadamard, Jacques S, 1963, N 1,33:2
Hadas, Ethel J E Mrs, 1953, Mr 14,15:3
Hadas, Moses (mem ser, O 14,43:2), 1966, Ag 18,1:4
Hadaway, William S, 1953, Ap 14,27:3
Hadayak, Sadek, 1951, Ap 10,14:4
Haddad, Abraham A, 1962, Ap 1,86:6
Haddad, Sam S, 1967, My 3,42:7
Haddaway, George W, 1947, Ag 19,23:3
Hadded, Gregorius, 1928, D 20,27:4
Hadden, Alex, 1957, Mr 31,88:2
Hadden, Alex M (por), 1942, S 3,19:1
Hadden, Alexander Dr, 1912, Mr 18,11:5
Hadden, Alexander Mrs, 1967, Ap 15,31:4
Hadden, Arthur A, 1953, Ag 17,15:5
Hadden, C, 1930, Ag 10,II,8:3
Hadden, C W, 1953, Ap 15,31:3
Hadden, Clarence W, 1966, N 19,33:4
Hadden, Frances, 1943, Jl 13,21:1
Hadden, Frederic, 1955, My 25,9:3
Hadden, Gavin, 1956, Mr 10,17:6
Hadden, George, 1925, F 15,7:3
Hadden, Grace L Mrs, 1942, My 26,21:2
Hadden, Harold F, 1938, Je 15,23:4
Hadden, Harold Farquhar, 1915, Ag 12,9:6
Hadden, Howard S, 1950, My 31,29:4
Hadden, J E Smith, 1914, Ja 5,9:6
Hadden, John B, 1966, F 14,29:2
Hadden, John J, 1941, Ap 12,15:6
Hadden, Samuel C, 1956, My 12,19:5
Hadden, Sarah B Mrs, 1904, F 25,1:3
Hadden, T Irving Mrs, 1949, Je 15,30:3
Hadden, Theodore I, 1948, Mr 23,25:5
Hadden, W A, 1880, Ap 4,2:6
Hadden, William E, 1955, Jl 30,17:1
Haddeus, Johannis Rev, 1913, D 28,II,15:5
Haddington, Earl of (Geo Baillie-Hamilton Arden), 1917, Je 12,13:2
Haddix, M Cornelius, 1950, F 21,25:3
Haddleton, Alfred W, 1957, D 29,49:2
Haddock, Charles, 1907, N 28,7:4
Haddock, Herbert James, 1946, O 6,59:6
Haddock, J Albert, 1918, F 22,11:5
Haddock, John C, 1914, D 21,9:4
Haddock, John C Jr, 1959, N 12,35:2
Haddock, John C Mrs, 1940, Mr 14,23:4
Haddock, Paul F, 1937, D 6,27:5
Haddock, Stewart, 1937, Je 5,17:3
Haddock, William C Jr, 1956, S 10,27:5
Haddon, Alfred C (por), 1940, Ap 22,17:4
Haddon, Henry G, 1944, N 26,58:4
Haddon, William T Mrs, 1950, Je 21,27:2
Haddow, Glenn K, 1955, Je 16,31:2
Haddow, Hugh Jr, 1951, S 19,31:5
Hade, Floyd F, 1947, Jl 10,21:6
Hade, John J Sr, 1946, Ag 6,25:4
Hadel, Selma, 1920, Ja 14,9:1
Haden, Harry Y, 1949, Ja 15,17:6
Haden, James R, 1947, F 26,26:3
Haden, Robert A Mrs, 1955, Jl 29,17:5
Haden, Russell L, 1952, Ap 27,91:2
Haden, William D, 1945, Ap 9,19:3
Haden-Guest, Angela (Mrs O Martinez), 1965, D 1, 47:5
Haden-Guest, Leslie, 1960, Ag 22,25:4
Hadfield, Barnabas B, 1961, Je 25,76:3
Hadfield, Benjamin G, 1938, D 28,26:4
Hadfield, Edward J, 1949, F 27,69:2
Hadfield, Jesse, 1956, Ja 3,31:4
Hadfield, Murray, 1944, Mr 7,17:3
Hadfield, Robert A, 1940, O 2,23:3
Hadfield, Robert Mrs Lady, 1949, N 8,31:1
Hadfield, Seth, 1941, D 9,31:4
Hadfield, William S, 1948, S 22,31:1
Hadi Ghazali, Abdul, 1953, Ap 1,29:2
Hadidian, H M, 1945, My 20,32:2
Hading, Jane, 1941, F 19,21:5
Hadji Tahar ben Mohammed Ibn Saud Wahabi, Prince, 1938, Mr 19,15:4
Hadjikiriakos, Alex, 1956, Mr 26,29:5
Hadjopoulos, Lazaros G, 1952, Je 16,17:5
Hadkins, Frank Mrs, 1952, Ja 4,23:2
Hadler, Otto, 1953, O 4,87:1
Hadley, A T, 1930, Mr 6,1:5
Hadley, Alden H, 1951, F 28,25:4
Hadley, Arlene B, 1947, S 3,25:6
Hadley, Arthur F, 1950, O 28,17:2
Hadley, Bump (Irving D), 1963, F 16,8:8
Hadley, Carleton S, 1945, F 18,33:1
Hadley, Chalmers, 1958, My 13,29:4
Hadley, Charles O, 1947, Ag 31,36:5
Hadley, Charles S, 1941, O 12,52:1
Hadley, Charles W, 1950, Mr 3,6:4
Hadley, Clifton O, 1963, Je 11,37:2
Hadley, Earl J Mrs, 1947, Ja 9,23:5; 1962, O 9,41:3
Hadley, Emerson, 1916, N 12,23:2
Hadley, Ernest E, 1954, Ag 11,25:6
Hadley, Francis E, 1940, D 14,17:4
Hadley, Frank L, 1945, F 28,23:3
Hadley, George, 1960, S 15,37:4
Hadley, George Daniel Rev, 1915, Ag 10,11:6
Hadley, George W Sr, 1950, My 18,29:2
Hadley, H E, 1929, Ja 15,29:5
Hadley, H H Prof, 1864, Ag 5,3:1
Hadley, H S, 1927, D 2,23:3
Hadley, Harold, 1964, Ag 25,33:3
Hadley, Harry W, 1942, Ap 14,21:2
Hadley, Helen M Mrs, 1939, Ap 1,19:5
Hadley, Henry, 1937, S 7,21:3
Hadley, Henry H Col, 1903, D 3,9:4
Hadley, Hermine C R Mrs, 1939, Ja 27,19:4
Hadley, Howard D, 1924, Je 20,19:6
Hadley, J M Maj, 1909, Je 22,7:6
Hadley, John A, 1958, F 13,29:5
Hadley, Josephine W Mrs, 1939, N 9,23:5
Hadley, Lindley H, 1948, N 2,25:2
Hadley, Lindley H Mrs, 1947, My 3,17:3
Hadley, Lindsey S B, 1952, D 18,29:2
Hadley, Nelson B, 1948, Je 4,23:5
Hadley, Samuel H, 1943, O 13,23:3
Hadley, Samuel H Rev (funl), 1906, F 13,3:2
Hadley, Walter E, 1955, D 14,39:2
Hadley, Will B, 1965, Ja 1,19:1
Hadley, Willb Mrs, 1938, Ja 9,42:6
Hadley, William A, 1941, O 4,15:3
Hadley, William B, 1938, O 14,23:2
Hadley, William L, 1967, Ja 3,34:1
Hadley, William W, 1960, D 17,23:4
Hadlock, Albert E, 1952, Ag 7,21:3
Hadlock, Albert E Mrs, 1949, Mr 9,26:2
Hadlock, Harriet F Mrs, 1948, D 28,21:5
Hadlow, Gertrude, 1943, Mr 14,24:6
Hadow, Henry Sir, 1937, Ap 10,19:5
Hadranyi, Paul Mrs, 1950, O 24,29:4
Hadsell, George Arthur Col, 1923, Mr 1,15:3
Hadsell, Irving W, 1967, S 12,47:2
Hadwen, Seymour A, 1947, Ap 21,21:4
Hadwen, William Perry, 1907, S 18,9:6
Hadwin, John D, 1942, Ja 20,19:5
Hadzsits, George D, 1954, Je 10,31:6
Haeberle, Arminius T, 1943, O 29,19:3
Haeberle, Richard Sr, 1955, Ag 14,81:1
Haeberle, Richard Sr Mrs, 1944, Ap 28,19:2
Haeberly, Harry, 1961, Mr 7,35:1
Haebler, Phil E, 1952, Je 9,23:5
Haebler, Theodore, 1952, D 18,29:3
Haebler, William T, 1956, F 8,33:4
Haebler, William T Mrs, 1960, F 12,27:1
Haeckel, Ernest Heinrich Prof, 1919, Ag 10,23:3
Haecker, Carl V, 1955, O 8,19:7
Haedge, Carl, 1947, Mr 26,25:4
Haedrich, Harold W, 1949, O 6,31:6
Haefelein, George, 1938, Je 7,23:3
Haefeli, Walter, 1938, N 19,17:5
Haefelin, Fannie J, 1948, Ap 3,15:6
Haefle, Fred, 1958, My 22,29:3
Haefner, Herbert, 1952, Je 29,59:5
Haefner, Leonard W Mrs, 1950, Ja 7,17:3
Haegele, William A, 1951, F 6,27:1
Haegelen, Marcus-Claude, 1950, My 27,17:4
Haehnlen, Walter L, 1942, Mr 6,22:2
Haelle, Frank Sr, 1943, Je 16,21:5
Haemer, Henry S, 1940, Jl 16,17:3
Haemmerlein, Jean B Mrs, 1949, S 21,31:4
Haendel, Frederick G, 1937, S 22,27:3
Haendel, Stanley S, 1964, N 11,43:1
Haendle, Karl M, 1949, O 15,15:3
Haenens, Antoine d', 1947, F 13,24:3
Haenisch, Konrad Dr, 1925, Ap 29,21:4
Haensel, Fitzhugh, 1944, My 5,19:3
Haentjens, A A, 1884, Ap 12,3:2
Haer, Ernest Mrs, 1959, S 18,31:1
Haering, David W, 1942, N 1,53:1
Haering, George J, 1963, F 5,4:6
Haering, Max A, 1954, Je 18,23:2
Haering, W Dr, 1872, Ja 16,5:2
Haertel, Herman Mrs, 1948, F 19,23:3
Haertl, Paul (por), 1938, F 23,23:3
Haertlein, Albert, 1960, Je 8,39:2
Haertter, Edward D, 1942, Ap 21,23:5
Haeseler, Alice, 1962, S 11,33:2
Haeseler, Gottleib von, 1919, O 28,13:2
Haeseler, Kurt W, 1958, My 20,33:1
Haesener, Eugene A, 1955, O 18,37:3
Haesig, Frank A, 1946, D 21,19:4
Haessig, M C, 1946, My 28,21:4
Haessler, Luise, 1955, Jl 9,15:6
Haeusler, William L, 1953, Jl 26,69:2
Haeussler, Gustave A, 1959, Je 4,31:3
Hafeland, Rudy, 1955, F 20,89:1
Hafele, Jacob, 1944, Mr 23,19:4
Hafeli, Martin, 1947, Jl 30,21:6
Hafely, Alfred C, 1940, Je 2,45:2
Hafemann, Louis M, 1947, Ja 21,23:2
Hafemeiser, Fred F, 1950, Jl 22,15:4
Hafen, Virgil O, 1949, O 7,28:5
Hafer, David S, 1951, O 9,29:2
Hafey, Catherine K Mrs, 1939, Ap 28,25:5
Hafey, Francis X, 1958, F 25,27:1
Hafey, William J, 1954, My 13,29:2
Haff, Albert D, 1954, F 1,23:2
Haff, C Clayton, 1939, F 6,13:5
Haff, Carroll B, 1947, Ap 11,25:5
Haff, Delbert J, 1943, Ag 12,19:5
Haff, Frank Ellsworth, 1922, Ja 4,13:5
Haff, Harry P Capt, 1922, F 2,17:4
Haff, Henrietta Mrs, 1938, Mr 26,15:2
Haff, Henry Capt (funl, Jl 4,7:4), 1906, Jl 1,9:4
Haff, Mary H Mrs, 1937, N 19,23:4
Haff, Stephen Sr, 1944, O 8,43:1
Haff, William P W, 1946, D 18,29:3
Haffa, Albert D, 1908, Ja 7,7:4
Haffa, George J Col, 1924, Ap 10,23:4
Haffelman, John, 1908, Je 8,7:4
Haffen, Henry L, 1959, Ap 28,36:1
Haffen, John, 1910, S 26,13:6
Haffen, L F, 1935, D 26,17:1
Haffenden, Charles R, 1952, D 25,29:6
Haffenreffer, Adolf F Mrs, 1950, Mr 14,25:1
Haffenreffer, Rudolph F (will, O 19,14:6), 1954, O 10,87:2
Haffenreffer, Theodore C Mrs, 1958, Ag 5,27:2
Hafferkamp, Edward L, 1948, S 8,29:1
Haffey, Frank D, 1944, D 15,19:5
Haffey, Robert E, 1948, Ap 26,23:4
Haffkine, W M W, 1930, O 28,25:3
Haffner, Charles A Dr, 1915, D 15,15:5
Haffner, Frederick, 1912, N 22,13:3
Haffner, Jacob H, 1945, S 5,23:3
Haffner, Joseph B, 1944, Mr 24,19:4
Hafford, Augusta Mrs, 1950, Ag 9,29:1
Hafford, George J, 1954, O 6,25:1
Hafid, Moulay, 1937, Ap 5,19:3
Hafley, Charles F, 1940, O 18,21:3
Haflin, Harry J Jr, 1940, N 8,21:4
Hafner, Alfred, 1954, Ap 15,29:4
Hafner, Alfred Mrs, 1947, Ap 16,25:4
Hafner, August G, 1948, Ag 26,21:3
Hafner, Casper A, 1955, N 30,33:2
Hafner, Charles A, 1960, Ag 2,29:3
Hafner, Frank, 1941, S 27,17:1
Hafner, Lawrence C, 1938, D 25,14:7
Hafner, Lloyd K, 1952, N 9,90:1
Hafner, Louis, 1946, O 25,24:2
Hafner, Mark, 1949, D 8,33:5
Hafner, Mary E Mrs, 1937, Jl 4,II,7:2
Hafner, Otto H (funl plans, Jl 30,25:4), 1966, 31:4
Hafner, Victor L, 1947, Ap 28,23:5
Haft, Harry G, 1964, Ja 7,33:2
Haft, Harry G Mrs, 1966, Ap 10,76:6
Haft, Henry H, 1952, Ja 25,21:2
Haft, Isaac, 1941, Je 25,21:5
Haft, Joseph G, 1946, F 5,23:3
Haft, Max H, 1939, F 13,15:5
Haft, Max Mrs, 1937, Je 14,23:5
Haft, Morris W, 1968, My 24,47:1
Haft, Nathan, 1957, S 22,86:4
Haft, Samuel, 1968, My 20,47:1

Hafter, Max, 1954, Jl 1,25:5
Hafter, Robert M, 1955, Ag 11,21:5
Hagadone, Burl C, 1959, D 9,45:3
Hagadorn, Francis, 1903, Jl 6,7:6
Hagadorn, John, 1871, Ja 21,5:3
Hagadus, Peter, 1958, F 15,19:3
Hagaman, Andrew, 1937, F 10,23:6
Hagaman, Charles A, 1952, Ap 2,33:6
Hagaman, Charles A Mrs, 1940, O 20,49:2
Hagaman, Emma A, 1942, Ja 8,21:2
Hagaman, Frederick O Mrs, 1959, Je 1,27:1
Hagaman, Harry T, 1952, Mr 11,27:6
Hagaman, John F, 1962, Je 9,25:2
Hagaman, John J, 1937, Ag 23,19:2
Hagaman, Peter S, 1951, N 10,17:4
Hagan, Charles F, 1947, My 16,23:1
Hagan, David L, 1967, F 19,88:8
Hagan, Eugene P, 1961, Jl 26,31:5
Hagan, J J, 1929, Mr 4,25:3
Hagan, James, 1947, S 3,25:1
Hagan, James J, 1940, Jl 21,28:8; 1946, Ja 7,19:3
Hagan, James J Jr, 1940, Ap 4,23:4
Hagan, John C Jr, 1959, N 11,35:4
Hagan, John F, 1943, Jl 31,13:5
Hagan, John G, 1956, O 6,21:2
Hagan, John R, 1946, S 29,60:4
Hagan, John V, 1967, Ap 5,47:3
Hagan, Joseph, 1937, Mr 16,14:7
Hagan, Joseph F A (Jack O'Brien), 1942, N 12,23:1
Hagan, LeRoy, 1951, O 10,23:6
Hagan, Peter P, 1959, O 6,39:4
Hagan, Robert E, 1948, S 21,19:5
Hagan, Robert P, 1945, Ag 21,17:4
Hagan, Rose, 1948, Jl 30,18:6
Hagan, Walter F, 1949, Ap 19,25:2
Hagan, William A, 1946, F 15,25:2
Hagar, Barbara A Mrs, 1942, N 11,25:2
Hagar, Edward McKim, 1918, Ja 19,11:5
Hagar, Emily S Mrs, 1946, S 9,9:5
Hagar, Frederick W, 1940, Ap 27,15:6
Hagar, George Jotham, 1921, Jl 26,15:3
Hagar, James W Mrs, 1958, Mr 4,29:1
Hagar, Marshall S, 1949, O 20,29:5
Hagarty, Albert C, 1943, N 23,25:3
Hagarty, Frank A, 1940, Ja 13,15:4
Hagarty, William F, 1950, Ja 31,23:2
Hagboldt, Peter, 1943, Ag 5,15:5
Hagearty, William E, 1953, N 15,88:1
Hagedorn, Adolf G, 1939, D 23,15:3
Hagedorn, Alonzo G Mrs, 1921, Mr 15,11:3
Hagedorn, Fred, 1940, S 29,44:4
Hagedorn, George A, 1955, D 25,49:1
Hagedorn, Hermann, 1964, Jl 28,29:1
Hagedorn, Hermann Sr, 1919, N 28,13:1
Hagedorn, Joseph H, 1949, Mr 6,72:4
Hagedorn, Rudolph A, 1960, Jl 24,65:1
Hagedorn, William, 1953, N 18,31:1
Hagell, Edward G, 1953, Ap 16,29:1
Hagelstein, Robert, 1945, O 22,17:4
Hagelston, Charles W, 1950, Je 1,27:2
Hageman, Aaron M, 1956, O 13,19:5
Hageman, Alvin G, 1951, N 23,30:2
Hageman, Andrew Rev Dr, 1924, F 17,23:2
Hageman, Carl E, 1957, S 15,84:6
Hageman, Harry A, 1944, Mr 25,15:6
Hageman, Isaac, 1925, F 20,17:3
Hageman, James W, 1943, Je 6,44:2
Hageman, S M, 1905, Ap 4,11:1
Hageman, William L, 1951, Ja 7,76:4
Hagemann, Florence C, 1944, D 19,21:3
Hagemann, Frederick L, 1957, F 28,27:5
Hagemans, Jacques R A, 1943, S 8,24:3
Hagemeier, Arthur E Mrs, 1945, Je 28,19:1
Hagemeister, Harry J, 1960, Ap 27,37:4
Hagemeister, Homo, 1959, Ap 26,86:8
Hagemeyer, Aug, 1938, Ag 31,15:3
Hagemeyer, Emily Mrs, 1941, S 7,49:1
Hagemeyer, Frank E, 1955, My 8,88:3
Hagemeyer, Frank H, 1958, Ja 4,15:5
Hagemier, Marie Mrs, 1942, D 6,76:4
Hagen, Albert M, 1961, Mr 20,29:5
Hagen, Cecil V Mrs, 1959, Jl 15,30:1
Hagen, Charles, 1942, N 4,23:3
Hagen, Charles F, 1958, Je 15,76:6
Hagen, Charles J, 1942, N 22,52:4; 1947, Mr 1,15:2
Hagen, Charles W Sr Mrs, 1962, Ap 17,35:2
Hagen, Henry C, 1967, O 24,47:1
Hagen, Howard H, 1942, D 15,28:2
Hagen, James O, 1943, O 11,19:5
Hagen, John H, 1948, Je 27,52:3
Hagen, Louis Mrs, 1962, S 18,39:3
Hagen, Mabel T, 1939, Mr 28,24:2
Hagen, Norman R, 1959, Ag 17,24:1
Hagen, Orville R, 1944, Ja 25,19:4
Hagen, Oskar F L Mrs, 1938, O 5,23:4
Hagen, Paul J, 1951, O 28,84:7
Hagen, Sivert N, 1966, F 20,88:7
Hagen, Spencer, 1959, Je 22,25:3
Hagen, Theodore, 1871, D 28,5:5
Hagen, Thomas Capt, 1937, F 5,21:2
Hagen, William E, 1942, Jl 20,13:6
Hagen, William Mrs, 1949, O 22,17:2
Hagen, Winston H, 1966, Je 16,47:6
Hagen, Winston H Mrs, 1955, D 23,17:2
Hagen, Winston Henry, 1918, F 2,11:8
Hagenah, Edward R, 1950, D 8,29:5
Hagenauer, Paul H, 1943, My 12,25:4
Hagenbeck, Carl, 1913, Ap 15,11:6
Hagenbeck, Carl L, 1948, N 29,23:5
Hagenbeck, Heinrich, 1945, F 8,19:3
Hagenbeck, Johann H, 1941, Ja 15,23:1
Hagenbeck, Lorenz, 1956, F 27,23:2
Hagenbuch, Lloyd G, 1947, O 8,25:4
Hagenbucher, John, 1946, Jl 23,25:2
Hagendorn, William V (por), 1942, Jl 28,17:2
Hagenhauer, Ludwig, 1949, Jl 21,25:1
Hagens, Pearl, 1964, F 8,23:3
Hagensick, A Charles, 1940, D 17,25:4
Hager, Albert B, 1960, Mr 31,33:4
Hager, Albert Francis, 1921, Ja 19,11:4
Hager, Charles S, 1944, S 29,21:5
Hager, Clint W, 1944, D 12,23:5
Hager, Clyde, 1944, My 23,23:3
Hager, Edward T, 1956, Mr 3,20:2
Hager, Elizabeth Mrs, 1904, Ja 3,9:5
Hager, Ethel Mrs, 1946, S 3,19:6
Hager, George L, 1951, O 13,17:4
Hager, George W Sr, 1955, Jl 20,27:1
Hager, Hubert A, 1953, Ag 26,27:5
Hager, Israel, 1942, O 14,25:4
Hager, Israel Mrs, 1960, Ap 23,23:5
Hager, Lee, 1944, Ag 13,36:3; 1960, Ap 11,31:1
Hager, Martin, 1938, Je 13,19:3
Hager, Milton O Mrs, 1951, My 4,27:3
Hager, Richard S, 1939, O 20,23:2
Hager, S W Mrs, 1950, Ap 17,23:3
Hager, William H Sr, 1947, Mr 20,27:5
Hager, William M, 1942, Jl 2,21:2
Hager, Willis D, 1903, Jl 16,3:5
Hager, Willis D Mrs, 1946, Ja 21,23:5
Hagerman, Augusta Mrs, 1946, My 23,21:5
Hagerman, Edward A, 1944, Ap 25,23:4
Hagerman, Florence L, 1951, Ap 12,33:5
Hagerman, Henry H, 1940, My 30,17:5
Hagerman, Joseph G, 1946, O 18,23:2
Hagerman, Richard, 1966, Mr 7,27:2
Hagerman, Samuel P Sr, 1952, Ag 30,13:7
Hagerman, Stanley, 1947, O 16,27:5
Hagerstrom, Carl, 1957, My 24,25:1
Hagerstrom, John A, 1946, O 15,25:3
Hagerstrom, John S, 1951, My 15,31:1
Hagerty, Cornelius A, 1920, Ap 20,9:5
Hagerty, Edward R, 1945, Je 21,19:1
Hagerty, Harry (Cherry), 1953, My 30,30:2
Hagerty, Harry C Mrs, 1965, My 12,47:5
Hagerty, Harry J, 1950, Jl 28,21:4
Hagerty, Jack, 1955, Ag 2,23:3
Hagerty, James A (funl trb, N 28,37:2; trb lr, D 2,22:6), 1961, N 25,23:3
Hagerty, James E, 1946, N 11,27:2
Hagerty, John F Dr, 1937, F 2,23:3
Hagerty, John F Mrs, 1954, Ja 9,15:4
Hagerty, Michael H, 1908, F 11,7:6
Hagerty, Patrick, 1940, Jl 13,13:6
Hagerty, Thomas H, 1938, My 3,23:4
Hagerty, William J, 1949, My 21,13:4; 1953, S 1,23:3
Hagerup, George Francis Dr, 1921, F 9,9:4
Hagey, James T, 1942, My 11,15:6
Hagey, John F, 1943, D 13,23:3
Haggard, David A, 1958, Mr 22,17:3
Haggard, George W, 1951, Jl 1,29:1
Haggard, Henry R Mrs, 1943, S 6,17:4
Haggard, Howard W, 1959, Ap 23,31:3
Haggard, Howard W Jr, 1937, Ja 5,23:5
Haggard, Rider, 1925, My 15,19:4
Haggard, William, 1962, F 21,45:2
Haggard, William D (por), 1940, Ja 29,15:1
Haggart, George S, 1950, Mr 12,92:4
Haggart, Harry H, 1958, Jl 15,25:2
Haggarty, Charles J, 1947, Ag 10,52:6
Haggers, Harry, 1950, Mr 27,23:1
Haggerson, Fred H, 1952, O 15,31:3
Haggerson, Fred H Mrs, 1952, F 28,27:5
Haggerty, Anna C Mrs, 1937, Ja 8,19:4
Haggerty, Charles Justice, 1922, D 7,19:6
Haggerty, Charles P, 1915, N 9,13:3
Haggerty, Charles R, 1941, Ap 24,21:5; 1949, D 14, 31:5
Haggerty, Cornelius Jr, 1945, Ag 16,19:4
Haggerty, Daniel A, 1965, N 29,35:3
Haggerty, Daniel P, 1945, D 19,25:2
Haggerty, Dennis J, 1951, My 3,29:2
Haggerty, Donald F, 1956, Ag 10,17:4
Haggerty, Ellen E Mrs, 1937, Mr 14,II,8:3
Haggerty, Frank T, 1951, My 10,31:4
Haggerty, Frederick B, 1965, O 14,47:4
Haggerty, George F, 1956, Mr 25,92:1; 1961, Je 10, 23:5
Haggerty, George V, 1941, Ap 4,21:1
Haggerty, Henry F, 1913, N 28,15:6
Haggerty, James A, 1940, Jl 16,17:5; 1950, S 26,31:3; 1959, S 23,35:5
Haggerty, James D, 1952, Ja 12,13:2
Haggerty, Jeremiah, 1925, Ap 16,21:4
Haggerty, John A, 1962, Je 28,31:3
Haggerty, John B, 1953, Mr 5,27:1
Haggerty, John M, 1954, Ja 24,59:3
Haggerty, Joseph D, 1956, N 21,27:5
Haggerty, Joseph F, 1954, My 8,17:2
Haggerty, Justice, 1873, My 9,8:5
Haggerty, Leo F, 1965, Je 8,41:3
Haggerty, Louis C Sr, 1958, S 7,86:6
Haggerty, M E Dean, 1937, O 7,27:5
Haggerty, Margaret M, 1942, Ja 31,17:5
Haggerty, Martin L, 1960, Ja 11,45:2
Haggerty, Mary A Mrs, 1937, O 29,22:3
Haggerty, Michael F Mrs, 1962, Ja 20,21:5
Haggerty, Michael O Mrs, 1944, Ag 28,11:4
Haggerty, Ogden, 1875, S 1,4:7
Haggerty, Patrick J, 1960, My 10,37:5
Haggerty, Peter J, 1945, Ja 1,21:2
Haggerty, Phil J, 1941, Ag 5,19:2
Haggerty, Robert J Rev, 1937, My 22,15:4
Haggerty, Robert Sr, 1954, Ja 14,29:1
Haggerty, Sara L Mrs, 1937, My 27,23:2
Haggerty, Stephen J, 1949, S 1,21:4
Haggerty, Thomas J, 1956, Ja 16,21:1
Haggerty, Timothy, 1946, Ja 19,13:2
Haggerty, Vincent B, 1943, Jl 28,15:2
Haggerty, Vincent F, 1958, O 7,35:3
Haggerty, William Capt, 1909, Je 28,7:5
Haggerty, William S, 1954, Ja 20,27:5
Haggin, James B, 1914, S 15,11:5
Haggin, James B Mrs, 1965, Je 10,35:3
Haggin, James Ben Ali Jr, 1923, My 16,19:5
Haggins, Ben A, 1951, S 3,13:3
Hagglund, Lorenzo F, 1960, Jl 23,19:6
Haggott, John C, 1964, Ag 21,30:1
Haghe, Louis, 1885, Mr 12,5:6
Hagin, Harry, 1945, My 25,19:2
Hagin, Maurice, 1940, Je 14,21:3
Hagin, William N, 1943, N 16,23:3
Hagle, Anson E, 1942, Je 21,36:8
Hagler, Sam, 1950, Je 29,29:4
Hagman, Benjamin J, 1965, Jl 15,29:3
Hagman, Roy W, 1968, Jl 6,21:4
Hagmann, Frank G, 1955, Mr 8,27:3
Hagmann, Raymond J, 1961, O 4,45:1
Hagmann, William G, 1942, Ap 28,21:1
Hagner, A, 1880, Ap 9,5:5
Hagner, Alexander Buston, 1915, Jl 1,11:7
Hagner, Feodor, 1955, O 22,19:6
Hagner, Francis R, 1940, Jl 8,17:6
Hagner, Randall H, 1937, Jl 27,21:4
Hagodorn, Frank, 1948, Ag 20,17:2
Hagood, James H, 1946, Ja 7,19:1
Hagood, Johnson (por), 1948, D 23,19:5
Hagopian, Jacob H, 1948, Jl 13,27:3
Hagstrom, Carl J, 1946, Ja 22,27:1
Hagstrom, Gustav S, 1950, Je 14,31:3
Hagstrom, Henry T, 1961, D 5,39:4
Hagstrom, John B, 1955, F 17,27:2
Hagstrom, Jules A, 1944, F 10,15:1
Hague, Arnold, 1917, My 15,13:1
Hague, Clair, 1945, F 9,15:2
Hague, Edward W, 1966, N 15,47:1
Hague, Francis B, 1941, F 14,17:1
Hague, Frank (funl plans, Ja 4,27:2; funl, Ja 6,23:1), 1956, Ja 2,1:3
Hague, Frank Jr (will, D 19,63:4), 1967, D 7,52:2
Hague, Frank Mrs (est appr), 1965, F 17,45:1
Hague, George, 1915, Ag 27,9:6; 1925, Je 13,15:6
Hague, George H, 1957, Mr 21,33:3
Hague, George P, 1951, D 25,31:4
Hague, Joseph, 1939, Ag 3,19:5
Hague, Joseph T, 1944, D 27,19:4
Hague, Louis M, 1967, Jl 5,41:2
Hague, Mary, 1946, My 21,23:1
Hague, Robert A, 1953, S 17,29:3
Hague, Robert L (por),(will, Mr 14,18:8), 1939, Mr 9,21:1
Hague, William A, 1954, Jl 3,11:5
Hagy, John, 1956, Ag 22,29:5
Hagy, Joseph H, 1949, O 31,25:5
Hagy, Kenneth H, 1964, Ap 24,34:1
Hagyard, E W, 1951, Ag 23,23:5
Hagyard, John R, 1948, N 29,23:3
Hagyard, William R, 1941, O 16,21:4
Hahm, George Mrs, 1949, Ap 6,29:1
Hahman, Frederick, 1948, D 24,17:4
Hahn, Albert F, 1952, F 3,85:2
Hahn, Alfred, 1937, Je 19,17:3
Hahn, Alice L, 1944, Je 25,29:1
Hahn, Alta R, 1960, Ja 29,25:2
Hahn, Archie, 1955, Ja 23,84:6
Hahn, Arthur W, 1949, Ag 22,21:2
Hahn, Barbara Mrs, 1942, S 1,19:1
Hahn, Beatrice R, 1956, N 5,31:5
Hahn, Bernard (por), 1943, Mr 9,23:3
Hahn, Charles, 1943, Ag 5,15:1; 1957, N 21,41:7
Hahn, Charles G, 1943, Ag 17,17:5
Hahn, Charles W Sr, 1951, Ja 9,29:1
Hahn, Clifford A, 1950, Ag 14,17:3
Hahn, Deldrich Dr, 1918, Ap 12,13:8
Hahn, Dorothy A, 1950, D 12,33:3
Hahn, Douglas Mrs, 1968, Je 21,41:3
Hahn, E Adelaide, 1967, Jl 9,60:8
Hahn, Edgar, 1941, N 30,68:2
Hahn, Edwin F, 1951, O 8,21:2

Hahn, Emmanuel O, 1957, F 16,17:2
Hahn, Frank W, 1939, N 27,17:2
Hahn, Frederick D Mrs, 1961, Ap 20,33:3
Hahn, Frederick E, 1942, N 26,27:5
Hahn, Frederick J, 1957, D 25,31:2
Hahn, Frederick W, 1948, My 27,25:3
Hahn, George, 1946, Ja 28,19:2
Hahn, George H, 1944, Jl 1,15:4; 1952, My 4,91:1
Hahn, George P Judge, 1937, F 13,13:6
Hahn, Gustave M, 1957, Ap 3,31:5
Hahn, Harry, 1952, Jl 11,17:4
Hahn, Helen, 1941, F 1,17:3
Hahn, Henry, 1947, Ja 16,25:1
Hahn, Henry J, 1937, Ja 24,II,8:6
Hahn, Herbert R, 1949, N 22,29:1
Hahn, Herman F, 1954, Ja 29,19:4
Hahn, Herman J (por), 1948, Je 12,15:2
Hahn, Hubert F, 1956, Ag 28,27:3
Hahn, Hugo, 1954, O 29,21:1; 1967, N 8,40:1
Hahn, Irving, 1950, D 24,36:1
Hahn, J Elmer, 1964, Ap 10,39:6
Hahn, J Jerome, 1938, D 7,23:5
Hahn, James E, 1955, S 2,17:4
Hahn, John, 1925, S 27,7:3; 1967, Jl 20,37:1
Hahn, John F, 1937, S 11,17:2; 1945, Ja 25,19:5
Hahn, John W, 1939, My 10,23:2
Hahn, Joseph A, 1953, O 18,86:5
Hahn, Joseph C, 1952, O 17,27:2
Hahn, Joseph R, 1949, My 11,29:4
Hahn, Julius, 1963, Je 25,33:3
Hahn, L Albert Dr, 1968, O 6,84:8
Hahn, Leo L, 1952, N 21,26:3
Hahn, Lew (funl plans, Jl 29,65:1), 1956, Jl 27,21:3
Hahn, Manuel, 1955, Ja 2,77:2
Hahn, Otto Dr (funl, Ag 2,33:3), 1968, Jl 29,1:5
Hahn, Otto Mrs (por), 1944, Jl 26,19:4
Hahn, Otto Mrs, 1968, Ag 15,37:5
Hahn, Paul F, 1967, My 5,39:2
Hahn, Paul M, 1963, Ag 10,17:4
Hahn, Percey E, 1953, Mr 26,31:2
Hahn, Peter W, 1958, Ap 14,25:4
Hahn, Reynaldo, 1947, Ja 29,26:3
Hahn, Rudolph J, 1955, Ja 4,21:2
Hahn, S, 1880, Mr 9,8:1
Hahn, Theodore E, 1944, Ag 6,37:2
Hahn, Valentine J Mrs, 1956, Ja 27,23:2
Hahn, William, 1937, Jl 3,15:4
Hahn, William A, 1954, F 26,20:3
Hahn, William F, 1955, Ag 7,73:1
Hahn, William H, 1937, Ag 28,15:4; 1946, F 28,23:2
Hahn, William P, 1966, N 12,29:1
Hahne, Ernest H, 1952, N 27,31:5
Hahne, Fred, 1952, Mr 20,29:1
Hahne, Max, 1949, Mr 22,25:6
Hahne, Raymond, 1946, Ap 22,21:4
Hahner, Marcella Mrs, 1941, S 2,18:2
Hahnke, Wilhelm von Field Marshall, 1912, F 9,9:5
Hahnlen, Erwin, 1950, Mr 28,32:2
Hahnlen, Robert W, 1965, Ap 13,37:2
Hahnloser, Emil, 1940, F 4,40:3
Hahr, Aug C, 1941, F 26,22:2
Haibach, Philip, 1946, Je 18,25:4
Haible, Gustav, 1939, N 30,21:5
Haid, Leo, 1924, Jl 25,13:4
Haid, Paul L (por), 1942, S 1,19:3
Haidar, S R Min, 1940, Ja 19,4:3
Haidar Pasha, El Ferik Mohammed, 1957, O 2,33:4
Haifleigh, James E, 1956, My 30,21:3
Haig, Alfred R, 1943, N 17,25:4
Haig, Countess, 1939, O 18,25:5
Haig, Emma, 1939, Je 10,17:6
Haig, Frank, 1942, S 9,24:4
Haig, George, 1905, D 28,4:2
Haig, George Ogilvy Mrs, 1920, Jl 31,7:7
Haig, Hamilton H, 1963, Jl 24,31:5
Haig, J T, 1962, O 25,39:3
Haig, James B, 1953, Jl 19,56:8
Haig, John, 1947, My 14,25:5
Haig, Robert, 1953, O 4,88:5
Haig, Robert E Mrs, 1965, Je 25,33:1
Haig, Robert M, 1953, Je 10,29:3
Haig, Robert M Jr, 1965, Ag 24,31:2
Haig, Stevenson B, 1943, N 26,23:3
Haig, Stevenson B Mrs, 1938, Ag 28,33:3
Haigazian, A H Prof, 1922, My 26,19:6
Haigh, Albert M, 1951, S 1,11:5
Haigh, Albert W Mrs, 1948, Je 18,23:3
Haigh, Arthur H Sr, 1950, F 15,27:5
Haigh, B P, 1941, My 4,II,6:2
Haigh, Bernard P, 1941, F 1,18:3
Haigh, Douglas D, 1939, Ja 22,34:6
Haigh, Edward E, 1953, F 16,21:3
Haigh, Edwin V, 1948, D 11,15:4
Haigh, Fred Mrs, 1953, Ag 4,21:6
Haigh, George C, 1956, Mr 20,23:3
Haigh, Harry L, 1943, Mr 2,19:1
Haigh, Henry A, 1942, My 19,19:4
Haigh, Herbert, 1947, O 21,23:2
Haigh, J L Mrs, 1881, Ja 8,5:5
Haigh, Mervyn G, 1962, My 21,33:3
Haigh, Sam L, 1964, Je 12,35:3
Haigh, Susanna (Mrs L H Hardy), 1956, N 9,29:3
Haigh, Thomas D, 1963, O 21,31:3
Haigh, Winthrop Mrs, 1959, O 25,86:4
Haight, Aaron R Mrs, 1944, Ap 21,19:4
Haight, Adelbert, 1945, Je 20,23:1
Haight, Adson J, 1946, D 4,31:4
Haight, Alfred E, 1943, O 25,15:4
Haight, B I, 1879, F 25,8:4
Haight, Benjamin D, 1925, Ja 17,15:4
Haight, C Sidney, 1956, O 20,21:5
Haight, Charles Coolidge, 1917, F 9,11:5
Haight, Charles Mrs, 1937, O 1,21:2
Haight, Charles S (por), 1938, F 21,19:3
Haight, Charles S (cor, Ap 20,33:3), 1968, Ap 19,47:3
Haight, Charles W, 1937, F 14,II,8:8
Haight, D H, 1876, My 1,4:6
Haight, David L Dr, 1918, O 1,13:2
Haight, Edward Col, 1913, S 21,II,15:6
Haight, Elizabeth H, 1964, N 16,31:2
Haight, F M, 1866, F 26,1:7
Haight, F Putney, 1957, O 10,33:1
Haight, Forest A, 1954, D 29,23:4
Haight, Frederick Everest, 1924, Je 15,23:1
Haight, George I, 1955, O 2,86:2
Haight, George S, 1965, F 18,33:4
Haight, H H, 1878, S 3,5:2
Haight, Harry B, 1940, Jl 13,13:2
Haight, J Arthur, 1947, My 2,21:1
Haight, John H, 1955, O 4,35:4; 1968, F 15,43:4
Haight, John H Mrs, 1968, Mr 5,41:2
Haight, John M Mrs, 1947, Mr 5,25:1
Haight, John S, 1961, Ag 17,27:5
Haight, Joseph, 1938, Ap 10,II,6:7
Haight, Julius E, 1953, O 10,17:3
Haight, Julius E Mrs, 1948, Ag 13,15:5
Haight, Leighton G, 1941, D 25,25:1
Haight, Lewis H, 1937, D 26,II,7:1
Haight, Louis, 1944, Ja 10,17:1
Haight, Louis Mrs, 1940, Ap 27,15:1
Haight, Mark H, 1942, Je 9,23:1
Haight, Paul B Mrs, 1962, Jl 17,25:1
Haight, Percy M, 1947, Je 22,52:7
Haight, Raymond, 1947, S 3,25:4
Haight, Robert S, 1950, Ap 5,31:3
Haight, Robert S Mrs, 1959, Ja 11,88:5
Haight, Robert W, 1945, N 18,44:1
Haight, Sherman Mrs, 1945, Je 14,19:2
Haight, Stephen Samuel, 1912, My 3,11:5
Haight, Theodore, 1951, F 8,33:4
Haight, Theodore S, 1938, Ag 5,18:2
Haight, Thomas G, 1942, Ja 27,21:1
Haight, Thomas H, 1959, S 5,15:6
Haight, Walter, 1968, O 4,57:4
Haight, Walter P, 1957, Ap 9,33:1
Haight, William, 1942, Mr 2,19:3
Haight, William T, 1950, F 27,19:5
Haigney, John J, 1941, Mr 27,23:5
Hail, George Mrs, 1948, Je 25,24:3
Hail, Harriet W Mrs, 1942, Mr 1,45:4
Haile, Berard, 1961, O 2,31:3
Haile, C, 1931, N 15,II,7:1
Haile, E S Mrs, 1949, S 15,27:5
Haile, Welby W, 1949, My 16,21:2
Haile, William, 1876, Jl 23,12:6
Hailey, Foster B (trb, Ag 15,26:2; funl plans, S 20,-47:3), 1966, Ag 14,88:3
Hailey, Lady, 1939, Ja 31,21:2
Hailey, William E, 1938, Ap 7,23:3
Hailiman, James D Mrs, 1958, Je 30,19:5
Hailpern, Jacques, 1963, S 22,87:1
Hailsham, Viscount (D M Hogg), 1950, Ag 17,28:2
Hailu Taclehaimenot, Ras, 1951, My 16,35:1
Haim, Albert, 1951, N 30,23:2
Haim, Emil, 1949, Ja 30,60:6
Haim, Matti, 1967, Jl 31,27:2
Haiman, Mieczyslaus, 1949, Ja 17,19:4
Haimbach, John Mrs, 1949, Mr 22,26:2
Haimes, Sandor L Mrs, 1967, F 6,29:1
Haimes, Solomon M, 1961, O 28,21:3
Haimhausen, E H von, 1935, Ja 15,19:1
Hain, Frederick R, 1956, My 15,31:1
Hain, Ira J, 1952, Mr 6,32:3
Hain, Jack, 1949, S 2,17:2
Hainari, Tilma Mrs (por), 1940, Mr 14,23:4
Haine, Horace J, 1940, S 28,17:5
Haine, William Mrs, 1952, Ag 23,13:4
Hainer, Dudley C, 1958, F 4,26:5
Hainer, James A, 1947, My 31,13:2
Hainer, John A, 1941, Ap 10,24:3
Hainer, Raymond M, 1967, Ag 27,89:1
Haines, A Engle, 1949, S 8,29:4
Haines, Albert, 1942, Ja 22,17:3
Haines, Alfred C Jr, 1958, S 30,31:4
Haines, Alfred C 3d, 1962, S 10,29:5
Haines, Ancil F, 1937, My 11,25:3
Haines, Anthony Mrs, 1940, Ag 15,19:4
Haines, Arthur, 1946, My 5,46:1
Haines, Atwell B, 1964, Ap 30,35:2
Haines, Augustine, 1873, Jl 28,5:6
Haines, Benjamin M, 1942, My 28,17:3
Haines, Benjamin W, 1954, Je 21,27:4
Haines, Bertha Mrs, 1957, Ag 6,27:2
Haines, Charles A Dr, 1924, D 13,15:3
Haines, Charles C, 1942, Je 6,13:4
Haines, Charles E Mrs, 1947, Ap 10,25:2
Haines, Charles G, 1948, D 29,22:2
Haines, Charles T, 1938, O 2,49:3
Haines, Charles W, 1940, Ja 18,23:3
Haines, Daniel, 1877, Ja 27,4:6
Haines, Donal H, 1951, Ag 29,25:3
Haines, Donald B, 1965, My 11,3:4
Haines, E Glenn, 1940, Je 7,23:3
Haines, Edgar F, 1943, Jl 23,10:2
Haines, Edward C Mrs, 1950, F 28,29:3
Haines, Edward P, 1937, O 17,II,9:1
Haines, Eleanor Dr, 1924, Ap 24,19:4
Haines, Ellen L, 1937, D 20,27:2
Haines, Ellsworth G, 1942, My 2,13:5
Haines, Elwood L (por), 1949, O 30,84:5
Haines, Ernest L, 1948, Jl 3,15:2
Haines, Florence, 1955, Ag 9,25:4
Haines, Francis S, 1941, My 2,21:4
Haines, Frank D Mrs, 1954, My 22,15:4
Haines, Franklin, 1953, Ag 28,17:2
Haines, Frederick, 1942, Ag 14,17:1
Haines, Frederick S, 1960, N 23,29:4
Haines, George C, 1949, Jl 2,15:5
Haines, George E, 1949, Je 21,25:5
Haines, George E Dr, 1874, Ag 31,8:2
Haines, George H, 1947, D 14,80:6
Haines, George 4th, 1964, Jl 26,57:1
Haines, Gordon W (por), 1938, Je 8,23:4
Haines, Harry L, 1947, Mr 31,23:3
Haines, Helena S, 1942, My 6,19:4
Haines, Henry A, 1950, Jl 16,69:3
Haines, Henry A Mrs, 1951, F 14,29:4
Haines, Henry H, 1957, Mr 28,31:4
Haines, Henry S, 1922, Je 26,13:7
Haines, Henry S Mrs, 1921, D 26,13:2
Haines, Howard L, 1962, Ja 6,19:4
Haines, J Frederick Mrs, 1944, My 5,19:4
Haines, J Kay, 1951, F 15,31:4
Haines, Jane B, 1937, S 23,27:6
Haines, John C, 1942, O 7,25:6
Haines, John F, 1938, F 27,II,9:2
Haines, John P Mrs, 1911, Mr 20,9:4
Haines, John Peter, 1921, Je 28,15:4
Haines, John Taylor Maj, 1911, My 12,11:4
Haines, Joseph E, 1944, Je 13,19:3
Haines, Joshua C, 1953, O 22,29:6
Haines, Lawrence C, 1952, O 1,33:4
Haines, Mahlon N, 1962, N 1,31:1
Haines, Matthias L, 1941, D 24,17:2
Haines, Nat B (N Burns),(funl, N 14,40:1), 1962, N 10,25:1
Haines, Oscar G, 1937, Je 12,15:2
Haines, Patrick J, 1948, D 24,17:1
Haines, Penrose W, 1914, Ap 26,IV,7:6
Haines, Phoebe R, 1949, Je 3,25:4
Haines, Rachel G Mrs, 1942, Ja 20,20:3
Haines, Ray E, 1962, O 13,25:4
Haines, Richard, 1937, Mr 6,17:1
Haines, Risley G, 1964, S 28,29:4
Haines, Robert A, 1964, Ja 5,92:1
Haines, Robert T, 1943, My 7,19:2
Haines, Roy, 1941, D 3,26:2
Haines, Rush T, 1955, N 25,27:1
Haines, Samuel E, 1938, N 29,23:2
Haines, T H Gen, 1883, Ag 16,5:5
Haines, Thomas H, 1951, Mr 3,13:3
Haines, Thomas K Mrs, 1946, O 28,27:2
Haines, Virtus L, 1920, Je 29,11:4
Haines, W A, 1880, Mr 9,8:2
Haines, W Albertson Sr, 1946, S 6,21:1
Haines, W F, 1879, Jl 3,5:3
Haines, Walter A Sr, 1967, Je 13,64:1
Haines, William (por), 1948, N 28,92:6
Haines, William C (Cyclone), 1956, Ap 9,27:1
Haines, William H, 1941, Jl 6,28:2
Haines, William H Jr, 1941, Ja 27,15:3
Haines, William T, 1947, S 28,60:3
Hainfeld, Charles F, 1963, Ap 19,43:4
Haining, Robert H, 1959, S 17,39:3
Hainisch, Michael (por), 1940, Mr 1,21:3
Hains, Augustus V, 1940, Je 27,23:2
Hains, Daniel D, 1937, D 4,17:6
Hains, Douglas, 1955, Je 16,37:1
Hains, Edmont P Sr (will), 1938, D 10,19:7
Hains, Henry Stevens Col, 1923, N 4,23:3
Hains, John P, 1964, Mr 26,35:4
Hains, Peter C Maj-Gen, 1921, N 8,19:5
Hains, Robert P, 1938, Jl 23,13:4
Hainsworth, William R Mrs, 1948, N 10,29:1
Hair, George R, 1951, Mr 29,27:4
Hair, Robert E, 1956, D 14,29:4
Haire, Alphonsus Mrs, 1951, Je 12,29:5
Haire, Andrew J, 1956, S 25,33:1
Haire, Andrew J Mrs, 1963, My 8,39:4
Haire, Anna R, 1941, Ag 7,17:3
Haire, Arthur W, 1948, Ag 29,56:5
Haire, Floyd J, 1951, Ja 7,77:2
Haire, John E, 1940, My 3,21:2
Haire, John E Lord, 1966, O 8,31:1
Haire, Norman, 1952, S 13,17:2
Haire, Peter A Mrs, 1944, Ap 7,19:3
Hairston, Ralph M, 1959, Ap 23,31:4
Hairston, Robert H, 1952, F 17,84:3
Haisch, Elmer L, 1957, My 11,21:3

Haist, George A, 1906, N 13,1:4
Haist, William A, 1944, Ja 21,17:3
Hait, Joseph H, 1946, S 5,27:4
Hait, Louis, 1950, N 21,31:4
Hait, Mortimer H, 1965, F 20,25:5
Haite, William B, 1953, N 8,89:1
Haith, Gordon J, 1952, Ja 27,77:1
Haitowitsch, Abram, 1964, Jl 10,30:1
Haizinger, Amelia, 1884, Ag 13,5:6
Hajek, George J, 1955, Mr 13,87:2
Hajek, Joseph, 1962, O 13,25:2
Hajek, Marcus, 1941, Ap 23,21:6
Hakanson, Walter L, 1963, Jl 18,27:4
Hake, Edward W, 1954, Jl 21,27:5
Hake, Gordon, 1962, Jl 23,21:5
Hake, Henry, 1951, Ap 5,29:4
Hake, John D, 1937, Ap 29,21:2
Hake, Lewis C, 1952, N 1,21:7
Hake, William Augustus Gordon, 1914, Jl 14,9:6
Haken, Josef, 1949, My 4,29:4
Haker, Eugene W, 1952, O 11,19:3
Haker, John, 1942, My 15,19:3
Hakim, Leon H, 1956, Jl 15,60:5
Hakim, Loekman, 1966, Ag 21,77:8
Hakimi, Ibrahim, 1959, O 21,43:5
Haking, Richard, 1945, Je 12,19:6
Hakman, Emanuel A, 1958, Jl 2,29:1
Hakohen, Israel Nussenbaum Stock Mrs, 1968, D 11, 47:1
Hala, William W, 1950, F 12,84:6
Halas, Barbara Mrs, 1951, My 12,21:2
Halas, Walter, 1959, D 21,27:2
Halasz, Henry Mrs, 1951, O 31,29:5
Halbach, Ernest K, 1958, Ja 25,19:4
Halban, Hans, 1964, N 30,33:3
Halban, Joseph Prof, 1937, Ap 24,19:5
Halberstadt, Alexander E, 1962, F 25,88:7
Halberstadt, Isidore, 1943, Jl 31,13:1
Halberstadt, William, 1963, My 15,40:1
Halberstadter, Joseph, 1964, D 29,27:1
Halberstaedter, Ludwig H (por), 1949, Ap 22,24:4
Halbert, Frederick Capt, 1919, My 17,13:5
Halbert, H Lynn, 1943, Ap 8,23:4
Halbert, Leroy A, 1958, Mr 4,29:3
Halbert, Norman, 1948, My 18,23:2
Halbig, Johann, 1882, S 1,5:2
Halbig, John, 1943, O 13,23:4
Halblaub, Henry, 1947, N 6,28:3
Halble, William J, 1962, Ja 22,23:1
Halbleib, Edward A, 1957, N 20,35:3
Halbleib, Joseph C, 1937, Ag 17,19:5
Halbreich, Samuel, 1955, D 16,29:1
Halbrook, Lowell, 1876, Ag 1,5:6
Halcott, Charles H Mrs, 1943, N 8,19:5
Hald, Henry M, 1966, Mr 9,41:2
Hald, Leo Rev, 1924, Jl 27,23:4
Hald, William B Sr Mrs, 1955, My 7,17:3
Haldane, Elizabeth S, 1937, D 28,22:2
Haldane, J S, 1936, Mr 16,17:3
Haldane, J S Mrs, 1961, D 12,57:5
Haldane, James A L, 1950, Ap 22,19:6
Haldane, John B S, 1964, D 2,1:4
Haldane, Mary Elizabeth Mrs, 1925, My 21,23:5
Haldane, Viscount, 1928, Ag 20,17:4
Haldane, William Henry, 1913, N 6,11:7
Haldane-Duncan, Robert Adams (Earl of Camperdown), 1918, Je 7,13:6
Haldeman, Benjamin A, 1955, Mr 5,17:2
Haldeman, Edwin, 1872, Mr 21,1:6
Haldeman, Elizabeth, 1909, Je 17,7:6
Haldeman, I M, 1933, S 28,21:1
Haldeman, Isaac M Mrs, 1947, Ja 22,23:2
Haldeman, John C, 1937, Ja 18,17:3
Haldeman, S S, 1880, S 12,2:4
Haldeman, William B Gen, 1924, O 28,23:3; 1924, O 30,19:5
Haldeman-Julius, E E, 1951, Ag 1,24:2
Haldeman-Julius, Marcet Mrs, 1941, F 14,17:5
Haldemann, Alice Mrs, 1915, Mr 20,13:5
Halden, Alfred A, 1956, Mr 20,23:2
Haldenstein, Herbert W, 1968, Ag 6,37:2
Haldenstein, Herbert W Mrs, 1962, My 30,19:3
Haldenstein, Isidor, 1950, Jl 1,15:4
Haldenstein, Isidor Mrs, 1952, Jl 7,21:3
Haldenstein, Samuel P, 1967, Ap 3,33:2
Haldenstein, Samuel P Mrs, 1954, O 5,27:4
Halderman, Charles F, 1953, Je 25,27:2
Halderman, John Acoming Gen, 1908, S 23,9:5
Haldezyos, Efsectios D, 1951, Ja 14,51:2
Haldin, Phil, 1953, N 10,31:2
Haldon, Lord, 1938, Ag 17,19:6
Hale, Alan, 1950, Ja 23,23:3
Hale, Albert C Dr, 1921, Ap 26,15:4
Hale, Anna W Mrs, 1937, Mr 19,24:3
Hale, Annie R Mrs, 1944, D 28,19:4
Hale, Artemus, 1882, Ag 5,5:2
Hale, Arthur, 1940, Mr 2,13:5
Hale, Arthur A, 1943, F 23,21:4
Hale, Arthur C, 1950, Mr 15,29:2
Hale, Arthur W, 1939, N 6,23:6
Hale, B Rust Rev Dr, 1863, Ja 27,5:3
Hale, Benjamin J, 1951, N 5,31:3
Hale, C, 1934, Ap 10,23:3
Hale, C Arthur, 1949, S 28,27:2
Hale, C K Brig-Gen, 1870, My 31,4:2
Hale, C Wesley Mrs, 1953, O 19,21:4
Hale, Chandler, 1951, My 24,35:5
Hale, Charles, 1882, Mr 3,2:6; 1938, O 7,23:5; 1946, F 7,21:5
Hale, Charles B, 1944, F 4,16:3
Hale, Charles F, 1962, Ja 14,84:6
Hale, Charles R, 1946, F 14,25:4
Hale, Clarence F Dr, 1953, F 1,88:6
Hale, Clayton B Mrs, 1947, Ap 25,22:3
Hale, Creighton, 1965, Ag 12,27:3
Hale, Dean, 1950, F 2,27:4
Hale, Dorothy Q, 1942, Mr 10,19:3
Hale, Dwight E, 1937, D 17,32:3
Hale, E J, 1883, Ja 3,5:4
Hale, E Mrs, 1930, O 10,23:5
Hale, E W Maj, 1905, Ap 22,11:6
Hale, Earl M, 1961, Mr 11,21:5
Hale, Edward E Jr Mrs, 1963, My 26,92:4
Hale, Edward E 3d, 1953, Mr 20,23:2
Hale, Edward Everett Mrs, 1914, My 26,11:5
Hale, Edward Everett Rev Dr, 1909, Je 11,9:3
Hale, Edward J Maj, 1922, F 16,15:4
Hale, Edward L, 1940, Ag 9,15:2
Hale, Edward Rev, 1918, Mr 30,13:4
Hale, Eleanor W Mrs, 1942, Ag 3,15:5
Hale, Ellen D, 1940, F 12,17:3
Hale, Eugene Ex-Sen, 1918, O 28,11:3; 1918, O 31, 13:3
Hale, Eunice Terry Mrs, 1919, D 29,9:3
Hale, F, 1931, O 23,23:3
Hale, Florence, 1959, D 5,23:6
Hale, Floyd O, 1938, Mr 19,15:6
Hale, Francis, 1866, Ag 14,5:3
Hale, Frank G, 1945, S 30,46:5
Hale, Frank L Mrs, 1961, N 8,35:2
Hale, Frank O, 1951, Ja 13,15:6
Hale, Frank Rogers, 1907, Je 4,7:5
Hale, Frank T, 1954, Ap 3,15:3
Hale, Franklin D, 1940, Ap 22,17:5
Hale, Fred S, 1951, D 11,33:3
Hale, Frederick, 1963, S 29,87:1
Hale, George, 1956, Ag 16,25:4
Hale, George C, 1948, N 5,25:3
Hale, George Dr, 1904, Ja 31,7:6
Hale, George E (por), 1938, F 22,21:1
Hale, George H, 1937, N 7,II,9:2
Hale, Girard Van B, 1958, O 31,26:1
Hale, Girard Van B Mrs, 1958, N 28,27:1
Hale, Gordon D, 1947, O 20,23:5
Hale, Harris G, 1945, O 10,21:1
Hale, Harry C, 1946, Mr 23,13:6
Hale, Henry E, 1925, My 16,17:7
Hale, Henry Ewig Dr, 1925, My 15,19:5
Hale, Herbert D, 1954, N 18,33:6
Hale, Herbert Dudley, 1908, N 11,9:6
Hale, Horace C, 1943, F 28,47:8
Hale, Horton, 1957, Je 17,11:6
Hale, Hugh E, 1952, My 2,25:5
Hale, Ira D, 1941, Mr 2,42:8
Hale, Isaiah, 1938, F 15,25:5
Hale, J P, 1883, O 17,4:6
Hale, James E, 1950, N 29,33:3
Hale, James T, 1865, Ap 29,2:2
Hale, John, 1946, F 15,26:3; 1947, My 5,23:6
Hale, John E, 1942, My 9,13:1
Hale, John H, 1944, Mr 29,21:2
Hale, John Howard, 1917, O 13,13:6
Hale, John T, 1960, D 2,29:1
Hale, Jonathan, 1966, Mr 2,41:1
Hale, Joseph A Mrs, 1948, O 18,23:5
Hale, Katherine (Mrs A B W Garvin), 1956, S 8,17:2
Hale, L C, 1933, Jl 27,17:1
Hale, Lincoln B, 1958, Ja 24,21:1
Hale, MacFarland, 1965, N 22,37:4
Hale, Malcolm, 1968, N 2,37:5
Hale, Marshal Mrs, 1948, D 27,22:2
Hale, Marshal Sr, 1945, N 4,44:2
Hale, Matthew, 1925, S 2,23:4
Hale, Michael R, 1945, Mr 30,15:4
Hale, Minnie A Mrs, 1941, Ag 23,13:6
Hale, Nathan, 1863, F 15,3:6; 1871, Ja 11,1:2
Hale, Natt, 1963, O 16,45:5
Hale, Oscar, 1950, D 10,105:1
Hale, P, 1934, D 1,13:4
Hale, Perry, 1948, Ap 8,25:1
Hale, R, 1934, S 19,19:1
Hale, R S, 1881, D 15,5:3
Hale, Reuben B, 1950, N 4,17:3
Hale, Richard K, 1956, S 19,37:1
Hale, Richard K Sr, 1940, Mr 22,19:2
Hale, Richard W, 1943, Mr 6,13:5
Hale, Robert, 1940, Ap 19,21:6
Hale, Robert Rev, 1863, Jl 18,3:4
Hale, Robert S, 1942, Ja 3,19:3
Hale, Roger D, 1963, Ap 25,33:3
Hale, Sarah J B, 1879, My 2,4:6
Hale, Shelton, 1920, S 14,11:2
Hale, Sonnie (J R H Munro), 1959, Je 10,37:3
Hale, Susan, 1910, S 18,II,13:5
Hale, Susan B, 1943, Mr 29,15:4
Hale, Swinburne, 1937, Jl 4,II,6:6
Hale, Sydney A, 1942, Ag 14,17:3
Hale, Thomas, 1919, D 15,15:3
Hale, Titus S, 1957, My 21,35:5
Hale, W G, 1928, Je 24,26:6
Hale, W W (see also My 11,12), 1876, My 14,5:4
Hale, Walter, 1917, D 5,13:5
Hale, William, 1944, F 19,13:2; 1947, Ja 17,23:3; 1954, N 7,88:6
Hale, William B, 1938, D 28,26:2; 1944, Ja 19,19:5
Hale, William B Mrs, 1963, Jl 28,64:7
Hale, William Bayard, 1924, Ap 11,21:5
Hale, William G, 1952, Je 28,19:4
Hale, William Henry Dr, 1919, My 6,15:6
Hale, William I, 1946, Ag 3,15:6
Hale, William J, 1951, Jl 23,17:2; 1955, Ag 9,25:3
Hale, William M, 1952, Ja 25,21:4
Hale, Willis H, 1961, Mr 26,92:3
Hale, Willis W, 1947, Mr 11,27:2
Hale, Winfield B, 1964, S 1,35:1
Hale, Worth, 1961, Ja 17,27:4
Hale-White, William, 1949, F 28,19:6
Halen, John D, 1949, O 11,34:1
Hales, Charles A, 1949, Je 20,19:6
Hales, Elmer A, 1950, Jl 23,56:5
Hales, Elmer A Mrs, 1949, Jl 22,19:1
Hales, Ethelbert Mrs (M Pearson), 1959, Ja 30,27:4
Hales, G Willard, 1954, Ag 16,17:2
Hales, Kenneth A, 1946, N 10,63:5
Halevy, Clarence H, 1954, O 21,27:4
Halevy, Daniel, 1962, F 5,31:2
Halevy, Leon, 1883, S 23,12:5
Halevy, Ludovic, 1908, My 9,7:5
Haley, Abraham Z, 1966, Ja 24,35:5
Haley, Albert C, 1959, Ap 21,35:2
Haley, Andrew G, 1966, S 11,87:1
Haley, Anna M, 1919, F 8,15:5
Haley, Betty Mrs, 1956, Ja 12,27:2
Haley, Delia F, 1949, S 23,23:1
Haley, Dennis M, 1950, Ja 15,85:1
Haley, E J M, 1881, Je 10,5:4
Haley, Eben B Capt, 1905, Ap 5,9:5
Haley, Ed A, 1949, My 21,13:2
Haley, Edwin J, 1943, Ja 26,20:2
Haley, Frank G, 1968, S 13,47:3
Haley, Frank L, 1951, Ap 21,34:5
Haley, G M, 1952, Ag 4,16:3
Haley, George, 1954, Ap 3,15:1
Haley, Honora I, 1955, Ag 7,73:1
Haley, Hugh D, 1952, F 9,13:3
Haley, James M, 1949, Ja 19,27:4
Haley, Jesse H, 1947, Je 29,48:5
Haley, John J, 1942, S 20,39:2; 1950, My 26,23:3
Haley, John P, 1954, Ap 13,31:2
Haley, John R, 1952, Jl 25,18:3
Haley, John T Mrs, 1960, F 10,37:4
Haley, John W, 1963, Ag 1,27:5
Haley, Joseph H, 1950, My 16,31:3
Haley, Leo W, 1949, S 27,27:3
Haley, Margaret A, 1939, Ja 8,43:2
Haley, Norman B, 1951, Jl 10,27:2
Haley, Patsy, 1951, Je 21,27:2
Haley, Paul J, 1953, F 14,17:6
Haley, Peter J, 1954, Je 21,23:5
Haley, Ralph S Mrs, 1951, Ap 19,31:5
Haley, Robert D, 1959, Je 26,25:2
Haley, Roy M Mrs, 1965, Ap 30,35:1
Haley, William J, 1952, O 26,88:3; 1957, S 26,25:3
Haley, William M, 1962, S 29,23:4
Halfeld, Adolf, 1955, N 25,29:3
Halferty, Guy, 1954, F 17,31:1
Halff, G A C, 1950, S 12,27:2
Halff, Hugh, 1957, Ap 15,29:2
Halff, Mayer L, 1950, Je 26,27:4
Halfman, Walter E, 1950, Je 11,92:2
Halfmann, Arthur H, 1938, Ap 20,23:5
Halfmann, E W Luther, 1951, D 2,90:1
Halfmann, William L, 1952, Ja 27,76:8
Halford, A J, 1910, Ap 18,9:5
Halford, Elijah W (por), 1938, F 28,16:1
Halford, Frank, 1955, F 9,25:3
Halford, Frank B, 1955, Ap 18,23:3
Halford, John H, 1968, Jl 10,39:1
Halford, Juliet M, 1966, Mr 27,86:5
Halford, William Lt, 1919, F 15,11:4
Halfpenny, Arthur G, 1964, Jl 13,29:3
Halfpenny, Cornelius, 1941, Ja 11,17:3
Halfpenny, John C, 1945, My 25,19:5
Haliburton, Arthur Laurence Lord, 1907, Ap 22,9:5
Haliburton, hugh, 1922, Je 16,17:7
Haliburton, J D, 1879, Ja 28,1:4
Haliburton, Justice, 1865, S 12,8:2
Haliday, Edwin Mrs, 1951, N 2,23:1
Haliday, Emily M, 1940, D 7,17:2
Haliday, Franklin H, 1941, F 16,40:2
Haliday, George V, 1945, S 19,25:4
Haliday, Harry T, 1956, Ap 3,35:1
Haliday, William J, 1946, Jl 13,15:4
Halide, Edib (Mrs H E Adivar), 1964, Ja 11,23:3
Halifax, Earl of (Edw F L Wood),(trb lr, D 29,24:6), 1959, D 24,1:3
Halifax, Viscount, 1934, Ja 20,15:3
Halim, Mohammed Ali Prince, 1944, Ja 19,19:5
Halit, Pasha, 1873, Je 15,3:6

Halk, Kate (will), 1942, D 15,29:8
Halkais, Vasil, 1941, S 18,25:1
Halkett, Baron H Mrs, 1943, F 8,19:2
Halkett, John (por), 1944, N 3,21:5
Halkett, Walter A, 1955, S 27,35:1
Hall, A C, 1881, S 15,5:2
Hall, A C A, 1930, F 27,24:1
Hall, A Edson, 1951, Ap 9,25:5
Hall, A H, 1867, Jl 14,3:7
Hall, A O, 1898, O 8,1:7
Hall, Aaron Rev, 1912, Je 4,11:5
Hall, Abigall Mrs, 1923, Ja 25,19:5
Hall, Addison B, 1956, D 25,25:6
Hall, Adin A, 1942, Ja 29,19:5
Hall, Agnes L, 1948, F 27,22:3
Hall, Alan D, 1951, Ja 31,26:4
Hall, Albert E, 1953, Ja 1,23:5
Hall, Albert Granger, 1924, Ja 14,17:5
Hall, Albert H, 1940, Ag 13,19:3
Hall, Albert J, 1953, Jl 22,27:3
Hall, Albert K, 1963, My 29,33:3
Hall, Albert L, 1950, D 21,29:1
Hall, Alex, 1951, Mr 8,29:3
Hall, Alexander C, 1968, Ag 1,31:2
Hall, Alfred A, 1952, N 7,23:3
Hall, Alfred A Judge, 1912, Ja 22,9:6
Hall, Alfred E Mrs, 1952, My 25,94:5
Hall, Alfred H, 1943, Ap 22,30:5
Hall, Alfred S, 1940, Ag 2,15:5
Hall, Alice M, 1952, Jl 8,27:3
Hall, Allan E, 1944, Ja 18,19:2
Hall, Allen Garland Prof, 1915, D 6,9:4
Hall, Allen L, 1945, Ja 10,23:5
Hall, Alton P, 1951, S 2,49:1
Hall, Andrew, 1945, Ja 23,19:4
Hall, Anna M, 1881, F 1,5:2
Hall, Anthony D, 1925, S 25,21:5
Hall, Anthony W (por), 1947, D 13,15:3
Hall, Arch S, 1955, Jl 1,21:4
Hall, Arlington C, 1948, D 3,25:4
Hall, Arthur, 1947, Mr 26,25:1
Hall, Arthur F, 1942, N 11,25:2
Hall, Arthur J, 1941, Je 14,17:2
Hall, Arthur S, 1951, Mr 6,27:4
Hall, Arthur W, 1938, Mr 9,23:3
Hall, Aurelia E, 1960, O 26,39:3
Hall, Barton, 1951, S 12,19:4
Hall, Basil, 1951, My 17,31:3
Hall, Beatrice D Mrs, 1942, F 2,15:1
Hall, Benjamin Elihu, 1914, Jl 22,9:5
Hall, Benn, 1962, O 24,39:3
Hall, Bolton, 1938, D 11,61:3
Hall, Bolton (will), 1939, F 7,15:2
Hall, Brooks C, 1958, Ag 15,46:7
Hall, Burton P, 1924, Je 23,19:6
Hall, C G, 1961, Ja 15,86:4
Hall, C H Rev Dr, 1895, S 13,4:6
Hall, C Stuart, 1968, D 24,20:5
Hall, C Stuart Mrs, 1968, Ja 24,42:1
Hall, C W M, 1903, Ag 22,9:7
Hall, Carl S, 1956, Ja 16,21:4
Hall, Caroline D Mrs, 1942, S 3,19:1
Hall, Caroline P, 1903, N 7,9:6
Hall, Chalmers G (por), 1946, Ja 5,13:3
Hall, Channing, 1942, D 16,25:6
Hall, Chapin, 1943, Jl 12,15:4
Hall, Charles, 1937, Ja 3,II,8:4
Hall, Charles A, 1958, D 1,29:1
Hall, Charles A K, 1939, Ag 6,36:7
Hall, Charles B, 1937, Ag 25,21:2
Hall, Charles B Maj-Gen, 1914, My 12,11:6
Hall, Charles B Mrs, 1957, F 3,76:1
Hall, Charles Cuthbert Dr, 1908, Mr 26,7:6
Hall, Charles E, 1947, Ja 21,23:2
Hall, Charles G, 1939, Mr 28,23:2; 1947, N 5,27:2
Hall, Charles H, 1941, Ap 22,21:3; 1948, Je 2,29:5; 1948, N 21,88:2; 1952, Ag 13,21:5; 1959, S 18,31:1; 1963, Je 23,85:1
Hall, Charles H Jr, 1949, Ap 8,26:3
Hall, Charles H Sr Mrs, 1955, Ja 13,27:1
Hall, Charles J G, 1903, O 13,9:5
Hall, Charles L, 1937, Je 5,17:5; 1940, Ap 5,21:1
Hall, Charles M, 1959, O 8,39:4
Hall, Charles Martin Dr, 1914, D 28,9:1
Hall, Charles P, 1953, Ja 28,27:1
Hall, Charles R, 1959, Ap 15,33:3
Hall, Charles S, 1946, Ag 3,15:2
Hall, Charles T, 1938, Jl 23,13:7; 1948, N 15,25:5
Hall, Charley, 1943, D 7,27:1
Hall, Chester I, 1953, D 9,11:1
Hall, Clarence A, 1942, Jl 22,19:6
Hall, Clement O, 1944, Jl 20,19:4
Hall, Clifton R, 1945, Ap 20,19:6
Hall, Cora H Mrs, 1952, N 11,29:3
Hall, Cornelius A, 1953, Mr 6,23:1
Hall, D Donald, 1954, My 30,45:1
Hall, D T, 1881, Je 10,8:4
Hall, Damon E, 1953, D 19,15:2
Hall, Daniel M, 1925, O 20,25:4
Hall, Daniel V, 1944, N 16,23:2
Hall, David C, 1947, N 30,76:3
Hall, David M, 1960, Ja 30,21:4
Hall, David P, 1868, N 29,5:5

Hall, Derrick L, 1937, Ja 1,23:2
Hall, Don C Mrs, 1951, Ag 9,21:3
Hall, Donald A, 1968, Jl 3,35:1
Hall, Dorothy, 1953, F 4,27:5
Hall, Douglas, 1950, Ap 28,21:4
Hall, Douglas P, 1945, Jl 6,11:7
Hall, Duane, 1947, S 20,15:5
Hall, Dudley, 1940, N 16,17:6
Hall, E H, 1936, My 5,23:1
Hall, E K, 1932, N 11,19:1
Hall, E O, 1883, S 23,8:7
Hall, E Rev Dr, 1877, S 10,5:5
Hall, Earl B Mrs, 1948, Jl 3,15:6
Hall, Earle W, 1954, D 7,33:3
Hall, Eben H, 1948, Mr 8,23:4
Hall, Eda L, 1957, D 31,18:1
Hall, Edgar A Mrs, 1947, F 1,15:5
Hall, Edgar H, 1962, S 5,39:3
Hall, Edgar L, 1945, Mr 22,23:1
Hall, Edmond, 1967, F 13,33:4
Hall, Edward C, 1938, Ag 26,17:4
Hall, Edward C M, 1939, F 6,13:4
Hall, Edward Clark, 1947, F 26,25:3
Hall, Edward E, 1946, Ja 29,25:2
Hall, Edward Everett, 1925, Ag 26,19:5
Hall, Edward F, 1957, F 2,19:6
Hall, Edward J, 1914, S 18,9:6
Hall, Edward K Jr, 1961, Ap 24,29:4
Hall, Edward K Mrs (por), 1949, O 16,88:1
Hall, Edward L, 1947, Ap 24,25:2; 1950, Mr 1,27:2
Hall, Edward T, 1962, O 4,39:5
Hall, Edward W Mrs (will), 1943, Ja 8,21:4
Hall, Edwin H, 1938, N 21,19:3
Hall, Edwin L, 1956, Ap 3,29:5
Hall, Edwin S, 1953, Ag 15,15:3
Hall, Egerton E, 1951, O 16,31:3
Hall, Elizabeth, 1952, My 10,21:4
Hall, Elizabeth S, 1950, Jl 27,25:6
Hall, Ella Mrs, 1939, Jl 21,19:2
Hall, Ellsworth Sr, 1945, D 15,17:2
Hall, Elmer C, 1959, O 6,39:3
Hall, Elmer E, 1939, Ap 20,23:4
Hall, Elmer H, 1966, D 1,47:4
Hall, Elsie L, 1884, Ap 4,5:4
Hall, Elwin B, 1949, Ja 21,21:1
Hall, Elwood C, 1945, F 14,19:3
Hall, Elwood C Mrs, 1945, Ap 13,17:3
Hall, Emma J Mrs, 1941, Je 6,21:2
Hall, Emma R, 1949, S 7,30:5
Hall, Ernest Ex-Justice, 1920, Je 14,15:4
Hall, Ernest O W, 1953, Ja 6,29:4
Hall, Ernst von Prof, 1909, Je 29,7:4
Hall, Eugene A, 1923, N 7,17:6
Hall, Eugene Freeman, 1915, Je 14,9:4
Hall, Evangeline R, 1947, D 2,29:1
Hall, Everett J, 1953, My 21,31:2
Hall, Everett J Mrs, 1944, O 24,23:1
Hall, Everett W, 1960, Je 20,31:3
Hall, F C, 1954, Ap 28,31:3
Hall, F J, 1926, O 16,17:4
Hall, Fairfax, 1958, Je 5,31:2
Hall, Fairfax Mrs, 1962, My 21,33:4
Hall, Felix, 1942, Ap 6,8:6
Hall, Ferd L Mrs, 1951, My 19,15:1
Hall, Fitzgerald, 1946, F 8,19:1
Hall, Florence, 1952, Ja 3,46:3
Hall, Florian G Mrs, 1946, Je 10,21:4
Hall, Ford P, 1951, S 23,87:2
Hall, Frances J, 1954, My 29,15:3
Hall, Frances Minturn, 1921, O 24,15:5
Hall, Frances S (por), 1942, D 20,47:3
Hall, Francis B, 1922, Mr 15,19:5
Hall, Francis Bloodgood Rev, 1903, O 5,7:6
Hall, Francis C Mrs, 1965, My 12,33:4
Hall, Francis E, 1950, O 3,31:4
Hall, Frank A, 1919, Jl 19,9:7
Hall, Frank A Jr, 1949, O 14,27:3
Hall, Frank B, 1937, F 2,23:6; 1959, S 15,39:5
Hall, Frank B Mrs, 1949, S 7,29:2
Hall, Frank G, 1944, Ag 1,15:4; 1964, Je 24,37:3; 1967, F 21,47:3
Hall, Frank H, 1943, Mr 24,23:1; 1957, N 3,88:8
Hall, Frank L, 1922, D 14,21:2
Hall, Frank O, 1941, O 19,44:1
Hall, Frank O Mrs, 1950, O 1,105:1
Hall, Fred, 1954, O 11,27:4
Hall, Fred P Jr, 1957, N 30,21:5
Hall, Fred S (por), 1946, F 1,23:4
Hall, Frederic, 1946, Je 16,40:5
Hall, Frederick, 1953, O 20,29:2
Hall, Frederick Aldin Dr, 1925, Mr 25,21:4
Hall, Frederick Byron Justice, 1913, Ja 16,17:4
Hall, Frederick C, 1949, Ap 13,29:1; 1957, Ja 19,15:4
Hall, Frederick E Mrs, 1959, Mr 6,25:5
Hall, Frederick E Sr, 1952, Ag 25,17:1
Hall, Frederick G, 1946, O 18,23:5
Hall, Frederick J, 1943, Ap 8,23:3
Hall, Frederick L, 1949, D 7,31:2
Hall, Frederick P, 1939, Jl 8,15:6
Hall, Frew, 1938, Je 8,23:4
Hall, G Emlen, 1940, S 16,19:5
Hall, G T Capt, 1881, Je 6,2:4
Hall, Gaylord C, 1954, Mr 24,27:2

Hall, Gene W, 1951, D 1,13:2
Hall, George, 1909, My 29,7:4; 1959, F 26,31:5
Hall, George A, 1904, F 23,7:6; 1941, O 6,17:3
Hall, George C Col, 1872, Ap 27,4:6
Hall, George C Jr, 1954, Ap 13,31:3
Hall, George C Mrs, 1960, D 15,44:1
Hall, George E, 1944, F 5,15:2; 1948, Ap 23,23:3
Hall, George F, 1904, Je 9,5:3; 1937, Ja 6,23:5
Hall, George G, 1951, Je 27,29:3
Hall, George H, 1942, Ja 11,44:2
Hall, George M, 1960, Jl 7,31:1
Hall, George R, 1944, Jl 7,15:3
Hall, George S, 1944, Ap 29,15:5
Hall, George W, 1941, Jl 2,21:2; 1941, O 26,42:1; 1949, Ag 16,23:3; 1949, Ag 19,18:2
Hall, George W Viscount, 1965, N 11,50:3
Hall, Gertrude (Mrs W C Brownell), 1961, Mr 1,3
Hall, Glenn, 1939, F 21,19:5; 1953, My 24,88:2
Hall, Gordon R, 1946, Mr 12,25:5
Hall, Gordon Robert Dr, 1923, O 24,19:4
Hall, Granville Stanley Dr, 1924, Ap 25,17:4
Hall, Grover C, 1941, Ja 10,19:3
Hall, Guillermo, 1940, Je 2,44:5
Hall, Gursham A Mrs, 1955, F 25,21:2
Hall, H Arthur, 1948, S 1,23:3
Hall, H B, 1884, Ap 28,8:1
Hall, H C, 1901, O 30,9:5; 1936, N 10,25:3
Hall, H Curtis, 1949, Je 21,25:3
Hall, H Curtis Mrs, 1949, Ag 12,17:1
Hall, H Ivan, 1943, My 21,20:2
Hall, H P, 1907, Ap 10,7:7
Hall, H Rush, 1948, N 24,23:5
Hall, Hal L, 1951, N 19,23:2
Hall, Harlan, 1941, Ja 15,23:2
Hall, Harland M, 1945, O 5,23:3
Hall, Harold (funl, Jl 16,29:3), 1958, Jl 13,69:1
Hall, Harold C, 1946, Ag 30,17:4
Hall, Harold E (por), 1955, Jl 10,72:5
Hall, Harold I, 1963, My 24,32:1
Hall, Harold Mrs, 1962, Mr 21,39:2
Hall, Harold S, 1951, F 10,13:2
Hall, Harold T, 1964, S 17,43:2
Hall, Harrison Mrs, 1943, O 4,17:3
Hall, Harry, 1945, Ag 20,19:4; 1946, O 7,31:1
Hall, Harry A, 1951, F 26,23:2
Hall, Harry C, 1951, My 10,31:3
Hall, Harry D, 1955, S 29,33:1
Hall, Harry L Dr, 1937, Ap 24,19:5
Hall, Harry Mrs, 1948, Ja 15,23:4
Hall, Harry S, 1940, Je 15,15:6
Hall, Harry S Sr, 1949, O 10,23:4
Hall, Harvey M, 1956, F 29,31:2
Hall, Hattie E Mrs, 1923, Jl 9,13:2
Hall, Helen C, 1951, O 26,24:2
Hall, Henry, 1920, F 7,11:3; 1947, Ap 11,25:2
Hall, Henry A, 1948, D 30,22:2
Hall, Henry A L, 1955, My 24,31:3
Hall, Henry Augustus Dr, 1913, Mr 7,11:5
Hall, Henry B, 1953, Mr 16,19:3
Hall, Henry D, 1903, D 17,9:4
Hall, Henry H, 1906, Ap 10,6:5
Hall, Henry J, 1941, F 2,44:1
Hall, Henry J S, 1938, S 13,23:5
Hall, Henry L, 1944, S 1,13:5; 1954, D 15,31:3
Hall, Henry L Mrs, 1939, D 5,27:4
Hall, Henry N, 1949, Mr 27,40:1
Hall, Henry U, 1944, N 4,15:5
Hall, Herbert E, 1963, F 9,8:1
Hall, Herbert H, 1938, Ag 20,15:7
Hall, Herbert H Dr, 1968, My 1,47:4
Hall, Herbert O, 1944, F 28,17:3
Hall, Herbert S, 1963, Ag 10,17:3
Hall, Herbert W, 1945, Je 19,19:3
Hall, Herrie V, 1951, Ja 11,25:3
Hall, Herschel S, 1921, F 7,11:5
Hall, Hiland K, 1947, O 7,27:4
Hall, Hiram S, 1957, My 26,93:1
Hall, Horace L, 1947, Mr 11,28:2
Hall, Howard B Mrs, 1940, S 14,17:3
Hall, Hubert, 1944, Ag 4,13:4
Hall, Hudson E, 1954, O 21,27:4
Hall, Hugh J, 1953, Je 21,85:1
Hall, Irving K, 1952, N 15,17:5
Hall, Isaac Albert Maj, 1915, N 5,13:5
Hall, Isaac S, 1963, O 4,35:3
Hall, Isabel H, 1952, O 6,25:4
Hall, J Andrew, 1960, Ja 19,35:3
Hall, J De Camp Col, 1937, N 24,23:5
Hall, J E, 1941, Ag 3,35:3
Hall, J H Rev, 1878, Ja 6,7:2
Hall, J K P, 1915, Ja 6,13:4
Hall, J P, 1928, Mr 14,25:5
Hall, J Victor, 1955, Jl 7,27:1
Hall, James, 1940, Je 8,15:3; 1959, O 6,39:1
Hall, James A, 1943, Jl 10,13:6; 1946, S 19,3
Hall, James B, 1916, N 12,23:2
Hall, James F, 1950, Ja 24,31:4
Hall, James G, 1952, Ap 20,92:4; 1953, Je 1
Hall, James H, 1942, Je 9,23:5
Hall, James J, 1947, Je 6,23:3
Hall, James J D, 1951, S 7,29:4
Hall, James J Father, 1919, Je 28,9:3
Hall, James K, 1948, S 12,74:2

Hall, James L, 1961, S 1,17:1
Hall, James N, 1951, Jl 7,13:1
Hall, James P, 1919, Je 12,15:5; 1938, D 24,15:6
Hall, Janette M, 1955, Ap 21,29:5
Hall, Jean H, 1959, Ag 4,27:3
Hall, Jeff, 1959, Ap 5,V,6:6
Hall, Jennie, 1955, Ap 5,29:4
Hall, Jn G Mrs, 1948, Ag 29,60:2
Hall, John, 1952, D 24,17:5
Hall, John A, 1908, S 4,7:7
Hall, John Dennin, 1909, Ap 21,7:5
Hall, John F Jr, 1952, Ja 12,13:3
Hall, John Gen, 1872, My 8,1:7
Hall, John H, 1952, Ag 16,15:2; 1953, Ag 6,21:3
Hall, John Hudson Mrs, 1968, Mr 22,44:3
Hall, John I, 1913, Ja 2,11:4
Hall, John J, 1962, Mr 15,35:1; 1967, O 13,39:1
Hall, John J Mrs, 1948, F 18,27:3; 1961, Jl 27,31:3
Hall, John Jr, 1953, O 5,27:6
Hall, John L, 1960, Je 14,34:3
Hall, John L Mrs, 1955, Je 13,23:5
Hall, John M, 1943, Je 8,21:4
Hall, John Manning, 1905, Ja 28,7:4
Hall, John Mrs, 1904, F 14,7:6
Hall, John Parker, 1873, N 20,5:1
Hall, John R, 1951, O 26,23:3
Hall, John Rev Dr, 1898, S 18,1:7
Hall, John S, 1941, Ja 14,21:3; 1946, O 25,23:2
Hall, John S Mrs, 1955, Ja 22,11:2
Hall, John Sir, 1907, Je 26,7:5
Hall, John T, 1955, O 12,29:1
Hall, John W, 1957, Mr 21,31:4
Hall, John Walter, 1916, Ja 16,17:5
Hall, Joseph, 1951, Mr 2,25:2; 1951, Jl 12,25:3
Hall, Joseph A, 1940, Ag 9,15:2
Hall, Joseph J, 1967, Ap 27,45:2
Hall, Joseph J Mrs, 1949, Ap 26,25:4
Hall, Joseph P, 1939, Ap 30,45:3
Hall, Josephine, 1920, D 7,13:3
Hall, Juanita, 1968, Mr 1,37:2
Hall, Julia W Mrs, 1939, Ap 6,25:4
Hall, Kathryn C, 1947, Jl 18,17:3
Hall, L Burton, 1937, Je 7,19:5
Hall, L G (Sister Louise), 1883, Mr 29,8:2
Hall, L Norris, 1952, Je 22,69:1
Hall, Lawson W, 1939, O 13,23:1
Hall, Leighton A, 1949, Ja 19,27:5
Hall, Leland A, 1942, N 21,13:3
Hall, Lemuel C (por), 1946, O 19,21:6
Hall, Leonard, 1947, S 12,21:2
Hall, Leroy A, 1949, O 6,31:4
Hall, Lewis C Mrs, 1948, S 11,15:2
Hall, Lewis E, 1945, Ag 4,11:4
Hall, Lewis H, 1963, Jl 20,19:5
Hall, Lewis W, 1950, S 18,23:4
Hall, Lionel P, 1951, Ap 11,29:2
Hall, Logan, 1956, My 25,23:5
Hall, Lolabel, 1946, Ap 28,44:2
Hall, Loren B, 1954, Ja 5,27:4
Hall, Louie A, 1944, Ag 15,17:4
Hall, Louis B, 1948, N 18,27:2
Hall, Louis F, 1960, Ag 22,25:3
Hall, Louis H, 1949, N 18,29:1
Hall, Louis H Mrs, 1952, Mr 23,92:2
Hall, Louis Jr, 1952, O 18,19:6
Hall, Louis P, 1941, D 20,19:2
Hall, Lyle G, 1958, Ap 30,33:4
Hall, Lyle G Sr Mrs, 1962, Ag 18,19:4
Hall, M Carter, 1941, Ag 12,19:6
Hall, Margaret H, 1966, Ap 29,47:1
Hall, Margaret S Mrs, 1942, My 19,19:1
Hall, Marie F, 1958, S 1,13:2
Hall, Marion, 1954, Ja 3,89:1
Hall, Marjory B Dr (Mrs Barton Hall), 1967, N 30, 47:4
Hall, Marshall R, 1947, Ap 10,25:4
Hall, Marshall W, 1924, D 28,5:2
Hall, Martin J, 1958, F 2,87:1
Hall, Martin T, 1951, O 8,21:5
Hall, Martin V W, 1946, Mr 25,25:5
Hall, Martin W, 1959, N 10,47:1
Hall, Mary A G Mrs, 1939, S 27,25:4
Hall, Mary E, 1956, N 8,39:5
Hall, Mary F, 1956, Je 3,87:1
Hall, Mary G Mrs, 1913, Ja 3,9:4
Hall, Melville P, 1940, D 18,25:2
Hall, Melvin A, 1962, N 25,86:5
Hall, Merchant B, 1944, Ja 18,19:4
Hall, Miles J, 1947, Mr 12,25:4
Hall, Millie, 1946, Ag 16,23:7
Hall, Milton, 1965, Je 5,31:6
Hall, Milton E, 1949, Ag 23,23:2
Hall, Minna B, 1951, Jl 25,23:1
Hall, Mira H, 1937, Ag 27,19:5
Hall, Monica M, 1952, O 25,17:5
Hall, Myers F, 1948, N 8,21:1
Hall, Myron Mrs, 1946, Je 26,25:1
Hall, Myron S, 1963, Jl 24,31:3
Hall, N E Rev, 1875, O 23,4:6
Hall, Nathan K Judge, 1874, Mr 3,4:6
Hall, Nelson L, 1944, Jl 29,13:4
Hall, Newman Rev, 1902, F 19,9:4
Hall, Nichols, 1965, Je 14,33:4
Hall, Noel S E, 1957, N 12,34:1
Hall, Nora B, 1952, My 6,29:4
Hall, Norman B, 1962, Ap 29,87:1
Hall, Norris F, 1962, Ap 28,25:3
Hall, Oliver, 1954, F 16,25:2
Hall, Oliver C Mrs, 1962, Jl 10,33:1
Hall, Oliver L, 1946, N 18,23:5
Hall, Orson L, 1950, Je 13,27:3
Hall, Oscar J, 1940, S 19,23:3
Hall, Owen, 1907, Ap 11,11:6
Hall, Patrick J, 1943, Ap 11,48:3
Hall, Pauline, 1919, D 30,13:3
Hall, Percival, 1953, N 9,35:5
Hall, Percy F, 1950, N 2,31:2
Hall, Percy L, 1948, O 16,15:2
Hall, Percy M, 1947, N 21,27:4
Hall, Perley M, 1946, Ja 22,27:2
Hall, Perry E Sr Mrs, 1961, Ap 30,87:1
Hall, Peter P-G, 1962, Ap 28,25:2
Hall, Phil W, 1952, F 18,19:1
Hall, Philander D Mrs, 1944, S 22,19:3
Hall, Porter, 1953, O 8,29:3
Hall, R H, 1882, Jl 3,8:5
Hall, R M Col, 1874, Jl 20,4:7
Hall, Radclyffe (por), 1943, O 12,27:3
Hall, Radford S, 1959, F 19,31:5
Hall, Rae B, 1959, Mr 28,17:3
Hall, Ralph E Sr, 1961, My 3,37:3
Hall, Ralph M, 1959, My 22,27:1
Hall, Ralph W Mrs, 1965, Ja 13,25:4
Hall, Randall Cooke Rev Dr, 1921, Jl 29,13:4
Hall, Ray L, 1941, D 25,25:2
Hall, Raymond G, 1961, Ja 6,27:1
Hall, Raymond L, 1942, Ap 30,19:6
Hall, Reginald, 1943, O 23,13:1
Hall, Reginald W, 1948, Je 2,29:5
Hall, Reinhard, 1947, S 5,19:3
Hall, Richard, 1938, Je 23,14:8
Hall, Richard D, 1924, N 9,7:1
Hall, Richard W, 1873, Jl 5,1:4
Hall, Robert, 1882, Je 13,5:1; 1967, S 26,47:1
Hall, Robert A, 1942, F 3,19:1; 1944, Je 16,19:6
Hall, Robert B, 1941, Ja 1,23:5
Hall, Robert E, 1953, D 9,11:4
Hall, Robert F, 1949, O 17,23:1
Hall, Robert F Jr, 1943, O 8,19:5
Hall, Robert Henry Gen, 1914, D 30,11:6
Hall, Robert I, 1938, O 19,23:3
Hall, Robert P, 1950, D 5,31:3
Hall, Robert S, 1941, Je 12,24:3
Hall, Robert W, 1941, S 7,50:2
Hall, Rodney D, 1948, Ja 14,25:3
Hall, Roland C Mrs, 1946, F 17,42:4
Hall, Rollie B, 1968, N 6,47:1
Hall, Ronald S Mrs, 1956, D 2,50:3
Hall, Rosetta S, 1951, Ap 7,15:5
Hall, Ross C, 1939, F 3,15:2
Hall, Roy F, 1961, F 22,25:4
Hall, Roy M, 1945, F 24,13:2
Hall, Roy S, 1957, N 27,31:1
Hall, Roy S Mrs, 1945, S 19,25:4
Hall, Roy W (Oct 5), 1965, O 11,61:2
Hall, Russ, 1937, Jl 7,23:1
Hall, Ruth J, 1949, Ag 10,21:5
Hall, S Carter, 1956, Ja 9,25:4
Hall, Samuel R, 1940, O 15,23:5
Hall, Samuel W, 1951, S 2,48:6
Hall, Sarah R Mrs, 1940, My 17,19:2
Hall, Selma, 1946, Mr 19,27:1
Hall, Sherman M, 1963, Ag 13,31:3
Hall, Sherwood E, 1961, Mr 27,31:1
Hall, Sidney B, 1946, Ag 13,27:3
Hall, Silas Mrs, 1951, Ja 16,29:3
Hall, Stanley W, 1949, D 3,15:4
Hall, Susie H S Mrs, 1942, Ja 25,41:1
Hall, T C, 1936, My 28,23:3
Hall, T J, 1878, S 28,8:2
Hall, T W, 1901, Jl 6,7:4
Hall, Theodore S Mrs, 1909, Jl 4,7:6
Hall, Thomas, 1911, N 20,11:4
Hall, Thomas B, 1945, My 3,23:4
Hall, Thomas B Mrs, 1942, O 8,27:1
Hall, Thomas F, 1921, Jl 7,11:5
Hall, Thomas G Mrs, 1943, N 27,13:1
Hall, Thomas W, 1913, D 3,15:5; 1955, Ag 3,23:5; 1958, F 4,26:5
Hall, Thompson E, 1954, My 26,29:1
Hall, Thornton Mrs, 1968, My 30,25:4
Hall, Thurston, 1958, F 22,17:5
Hall, Tracy Q, 1949, Ja 30,60:5
Hall, Tyler, 1937, Je 16,23:3
Hall, V G, 1880, O 21,5:4
Hall, Valentine G Mrs, 1919, Ag 16,7:6
Hall, Vernon, 1960, My 5,35:2
Hall, Victor B Dr, 1937, Ja 27,21:1
Hall, Victoria Mrs, 1925, Ap 20,17:5
Hall, W A, 1885, F 9,2:3
Hall, W E, 1880, S 11,2:6
Hall, W H, 1877, S 15,2:4; 1927, Ja 12,25:3; 1935, D 12,25:2
Hall, W H Capt, 1903, Ag 26,14:2
Hall, W L, 1883, Jl 3,4:7
Hall, W P, 1883, S 29,1:5
Hall, W P Lt Col, 1865, O 22,5:3
Hall, W T (Biff), 1903, My 17,7:6
Hall, Walker G, 1962, Je 7,35:1
Hall, Walter, 1963, S 25,43:1
Hall, Walter A, 1950, My 21,108:2
Hall, Walter B, 1948, Mr 16,27:2
Hall, Walter G, 1949, Ap 2,15:3
Hall, Walter H, 1948, Ap 13,27:2
Hall, Walter M, 1951, Mr 21,33:1
Hall, Walter M Mrs, 1945, Mr 31,19:6
Hall, Walter P, 1962, My 4,34:1
Hall, Walter S, 1943, S 1,19:2
Hall, Walter T, 1942, Jl 7,19:5; 1952, Mr 26,29:4
Hall, Warren S, 1939, Ag 3,19:6
Hall, Wells A, 1938, Ap 7,23:5
Hall, Weston B (por), 1948, D 8,31:3
Hall, Wilford, 1937, S 30,23:5
Hall, Wilford F, 1962, Mr 3,21:6
Hall, Willard, 1875, My 12,6:5
Hall, Willard J, 1959, S 19,23:5
Hall, Willard M, 1953, Ap 11,17:4
Hall, Willard Mrs, 1959, My 31,76:5
Hall, William, 1949, Je 1,31:3; 1952, Ja 5,11:1; 1954, Ja 15,20:3; 1957, Ja 6,89:3
Hall, William A, 1964, D 4,40:2
Hall, William B, 1944, Ag 9,17:5
Hall, William C, 1937, Ag 16,19:3
Hall, William Capt, 1908, Ja 7,7:4
Hall, William Cornelius, 1911, Je 7,9:4
Hall, William D W Mrs, 1949, Jl 9,13:4
Hall, William E, 1949, Ja 1,13:5; 1950, Mr 19,95:6; 1953, F 12,28:3; 1961, Ja 24,29:1
Hall, William E Mrs, 1954, Mr 17,31:2
Hall, William E Mrs (M Higgins), 1966, Ja 4,27:1
Hall, William F, 1942, Je 14,45:2
Hall, William G, 1937, N 11,25:6; 1962, O 15,29:4
Hall, William Gen, 1874, My 4,1:7
Hall, William H, 1923, Jl 3,13:5; 1946, O 25,24:2
Hall, William H Mrs, 1941, D 27,19:5
Hall, William Henry Col, 1922, F 16,15:5
Hall, William Hunt Dr, 1918, Jl 10,13:8
Hall, William L, 1940, Ja 31,19:4
Hall, William O, 1954, My 22,15:4
Hall, William P, 1937, Ag 15,II,6:5; 1940, Ag 11,30:8
Hall, William R Mrs, 1946, Ap 16,25:5
Hall, William Ralph, 1953, Ja 9,21:2
Hall, William S, 1921, S 10,11:5; 1948, D 18,19:5; 1950, F 12,84:2
Hall, William T, 1947, O 17,22:4
Hall, William W, 1944, D 1,24:2; 1952, Mr 29,15:5; 1952, S 30,31:4
Hall, Willie, 1967, My 25,47:1
Hall, Willis, 1953, Jl 29,23:3
Hall, Winfield S, 1942, O 4,52:6
Hall-Jones, W Sir, 1936, Je 20,17:4
Hall-Thompson, Percival H, 1950, Jl 8,13:7
Halladay, Arthur J, 1951, D 5,35:4
Halladay, Fletcher J, 1937, Jl 21,21:3
Halladay, John B, 1955, Ja 16,93:2
Halladay, John E, 1903, D 11,9:5
Halladay, Maude E, 1947, My 29,22:3
Halladay, Reg, 1954, Ja 1,23:6
Hallager, Sigurd, 1953, Mr 23,23:4
Hallahan, John F, 1943, N 25,25:4
Hallahan, John William 3d, 1910, Jl 2,7:4
Hallahan, Sarah C Mrs, 1942, S 30,23:5
Hallahan, William F, 1946, N 26,29:2
Hallahan, William L, 1961, N 7,33:2
Hallam, Alfred, 1920, Ja 2,11:2
Hallam, Frederick W, 1954, Mr 31,27:3
Hallam, Henry, 1859, F 17,1:2
Hallam, T Douglas, 1948, D 15,33:4
Hallanan, George H, 1961, D 16,25:2
Hallanan, Walter S Mrs, 1964, N 17,34:8
Hallander, Elvin Emil, 1968, Ap 8,47:3
Hallard, Archibald, 1947, Ap 1,27:3
Hallarman, Harry, 1956, O 11,39:1
Hallas, George, 1948, Je 8,25:4
Hallborg, Henry E, 1958, Je 4,33:3
Halle, Anthime, 1939, Ag 12,13:6
Halle, Arthur J, 1958, Ja 15,29:2
Halle, Charles Joseph, 1921, D 21,19:5
Halle, Eugene S, 1951, O 17,31:1
Halle, Fannina (Mrs Walter Halle), 1963, D 17,39:4
Halle, Hiram J, 1944, My 31,19:5
Halle, Isidore Mrs, 1951, Ap 12,33:4
Halle, Jack S, 1916, D 2,11:4
Halle, Jacques S Mrs, 1962, My 5,27:2
Halle, Joseph, 1939, O 9,19:7
Halle, Lady (Mrs Norman Neruda), 1911, Ap 16,II, 11:4
Halle, Louis (por), 1949, Ja 5,26:3
Halle, Louis J, 1950, N 28,32:3
Halle, Salmon P, 1949, S 14,31:3
Halle, Samuel H, 1954, Ag 12,25:6
Halle, Samuel H Mrs, 1951, N 4,87:2
Halle, Will S Mrs, 1952, Ag 13,21:4
Halle, William W, 1940, Ja 16,23:3
Halleck, Abraham, 1944, S 7,23:3
Halleck, Fitz-Greene, 1867, N 21,5:3
Halleck, Henry W Maj-Gen, 1872, Ja 10,1:4
Hallefas, Frank H Mrs, 1942, D 9,27:3
Halleman, Harvey, 1940, Je 8,15:5

Hallen, Frederick, 1920, F 29,22:5
Hallenback, George, 1915, Ag 21,7:5
Hallenbeck, Berger Q, 1941, O 29,23:4
Hallenbeck, Charles E, 1904, Ja 23,9:5
Hallenbeck, Charles S, 1950, Ja 3,25:4
Hallenbeck, Conrad, 1915, Ja 22,11:4
Hallenbeck, E, 1934, Je 3,31:4
Hallenbeck, Edwin F, 1955, Je 14,29:4
Hallenbeck, Ezra B, 1937, My 19,23:6
Hallenbeck, George W, 1937, Ja 6,23:1
Hallenbeck, Grover, 1952, S 5,27:2
Hallenbeck, Harry C, 1913, Ap 1,11:5; 1918, Ap 13, 13:5
Hallenbeck, Helen R, 1944, S 21,19:3
Hallenbeck, Lloyd M, 1944, Ap 27,23:2
Hallenbeck, Marc G, 1948, S 17,25:3
Hallenbeck, Ward D, 1942, F 9,15:1
Hallene, Oscar R, 1959, Ag 29,17:4
Haller, Albin Dr, 1925, My 1,19:4
Haller, Charles, 1952, Je 11,29:5
Haller, Charles R, 1948, My 24,19:4
Haller, Frank S, 1955, Je 15,31:4
Haller, Franklin P, 1939, O 24,23:5
Haller, Fred C, 1943, Je 29,19:4
Haller, Fred J, 1950, O 25,35:5
Haller, Frederick, 1955, Ap 15,24:3
Haller, George, 1955, S 30,25:3
Haller, George J Sr Mrs, 1953, My 14,29:5
Haller, Herman, 1943, My 8,15:4
Haller, John F Dr, 1910, D 4,13:4
Haller, Josef, 1960, Je 8,39:3
Haller, Karl W, 1950, O 24,29:2
Haller, Paul H Jr, 1950, S 27,31:4
Haller, Paul H Mrs, 1962, Mr 22,35:5
Haller, Paul R, 1949, D 21,29:1
Haller, Richard V, 1948, F 14,13:4
Haller, Roger L, 1954, N 27,13:1
Haller, Rudolph O, 1957, Ap 4,33:4
Haller, Wilford C, 1950, Ap 3,23:4
Halleran, Aloysius G, 1925, Ap 2,21:5
Halleran, Arthur J, 1951, F 4,76:4
Halleran, Cornelius, 1938, F 7,15:3
Halleran, George S, 1963, S 27,29:1
Halleran, John J, 1966, My 12,45:2
Halleran, Laurence B, 1963, Ap 29,31:4
Halleran, William J, 1938, F 12,15:5; 1955, Ap 28,29:4
Hallermeier, John, 1937, F 9,23:2
Hallermeier, Joseph Sr, 1951, N 15,29:4
Halleron, John J, 1946, My 30,21:1
Hallet, Richard M, 1967, S 15,44:3
Hallet, Robert L A, 1947, O 28,26:3
Hallett, Benjamin F, 1862, O 1,4:6
Hallett, Charles W S, 1941, Ag 15,17:2
Hallett, Cordice V, 1961, N 15,43:3
Hallett, Edward M, 1956, Ag 5,77:2
Hallett, Erastus H, 1943, Ja 30,15:4
Hallett, Erwin B, 1966, Ja 28,47:3
Hallett, F Carl, 1939, Ja 31,21:2
Hallett, F Sir, 1933, F 7,19:1
Hallett, Frederick S, 1949, My 20,27:3
Hallett, Frederick T, 1911, Mr 27,11:4
Hallett, George D, 1945, Mr 16,15:4
Hallett, George H, 1947, Ag 14,23:1
Hallett, Horace F, 1959, My 26,35:5
Hallett, J H (see also Ap 23), 1878, Ap 24,5:5
Hallett, John Mrs, 1967, O 11,47:2
Hallett, Louis, 1940, O 1,23:2
Hallett, Lucius F, 1940, Je 5,25:3
Hallett, Lyell T, 1952, My 28,29:5
Hallett, Mabel S, 1943, N 28,68:8
Hallett, Mal, 1952, N 22,23:3
Hallett, Norman, 1959, D 20,60:6
Hallett, Ralph Hubbard, 1953, F 20,19:2
Hallett, Reuben Mrs, 1952, My 13,30:1
Hallett, Richard D, 1966, D 22,33:3
Hallett, Robert, 1959, D 21,27:5
Hallett, Robert L, 1952, My 18,92:3
Hallett, Samuel, 1864, Jl 30,3:2
Hallett, Thomas L, 1957, Mr 17,86:2
Hallett, Thomas L Mrs, 1942, Jl 1,25:6
Hallett, Walter E (will, My 30,4:3), 1937, My 14,23:4
Hallett, Wilmot C, 1944, Je 1,19:2
Hallett, Zenas D B, 1940, Ja 5,19:3
Halley, Benjamin R, 1937, Mr 25,25:1
Halley, Charles H, 1960, Mr 26,21:3
Halley, Eben, 1948, O 17,78:3
Halley, Harold C, 1947, N 2,72:5
Halley, Mary H Mrs, 1938, Je 29,19:3
Halley, Mary J, 1948, Ag 15,61:2
Halley, McClure Mrs, 1924, My 7,21:4
Halley, Rudolph (funl, N 22,33:3), 1956, N 20,37:1
Halley, Rudolph (est tax appr), 1959, D 1,14:6
Halley, Solomon R Dr, 1937, Mr 27,15:2
Halley, Thomas, 1948, S 27,23:6
Halley, William A, 1942, My 14,19:4
Halley, William J, 1966, My 9,39:1
Hallgarten, Adolph, 1885, F 15,2:2
Hallgarten, Charles L, 1908, Ap 21,9:5
Hallgarten, Julius (mem ser), 1884, Ja 9,8:1
Hallgren, Arthur G, 1942, S 3,15:4
Hallgren, Mauritz A, 1956, N 12,29:1
Hallgring, George W, 1947, Ag 23,13:6
Hallheimer, Jonas, 1946, Ap 8,27:1

Halliburton, Erle P Mrs, 1951, D 10,29:3
Halliburton, Erle P Sr, 1957, O 14,27:2
Halliburton, Robert A, 1939, N 30,21:4
Halliburton, Shine S, 1963, D 11,47:3
Halliday, Alfred, 1938, Ag 25,19:5
Halliday, Charles William, 1908, Mr 4,7:7
Halliday, D M Rev, 1884, D 9,2:5
Halliday, Donald A, 1956, Jl 12,23:5
Halliday, Edgar, 1964, Ja 15,32:1
Halliday, Eleanor F, 1955, F 13,86:5
Halliday, Ernest C, 1951, Mr 28,29:2
Halliday, Ernest M, 1961, Ag 25,25:3
Halliday, Fisk D, 1953, D 19,15:5
Halliday, George C, 1941, O 7,23:5
Halliday, Gloria G Mrs, 1957, Ap 19,21:1
Halliday, Harold F, 1949, Mr 27,76:6
Halliday, Harry E, 1950, O 27,29:1
Halliday, Howard T, 1959, Je 15,27:4
Halliday, J Dean, 1960, Ap 16,17:3
Halliday, John, 1947, O 18,15:1
Halliday, John T Mrs, 1961, Jl 13,29:5
Halliday, Lewis, 1966, Mr 11,33:1
Halliday, Malcolm F, 1955, Ja 3,27:5
Halliday, Mary E Mrs, 1903, O 30,1:6
Halliday, Morris S, 1943, My 18,23:3
Halliday, S B Rev Dr, 1897, Jl 10,12:3
Halliday, S D, 1907, O 3,9:4
Halliday, Walter D, 1954, S 9,31:5
Halliday, William E, 1945, S 5,23:4
Halliday, William R, 1946, My 25,15:6
Halligan, Bert L, 1942, N 11,25:5
Halligan, Christopher J, 1937, N 23,23:5
Halligan, Harold J, 1946, Ag 24,11:5
Halligan, Howard A, 1950, Je 19,21:4
Halligan, John J, 1924, Ag 23,9:4
Hallimond, John G Dr, 1924, N 22,15:4
Hallinan, Dominick J, 1967, My 1,37:4
Hallinan, George J, 1950, Mr 26,92:6
Hallinan, John F, 1946, Ag 21,27:3
Hallinan, Joseph F, 1945, Ja 11,23:1
Hallinan, Joseph J, 1956, O 18,33:4
Hallinan, Patrick, 1950, Mr 14,49:7
Hallinan, Paul J Archbishop, 1968, Mr 28,57:3
Hallinan, William J, 1952, Jl 4,13:6
Halline, Allan G, 1951, O 16,31:1
Halling, Bliss O, 1947, Jl 4,13:5
Halling, Jens, 1965, F 8,25:1
Hallinger, Earl S, 1957, My 8,37:1
Hallinger, Nathan, 1964, Ag 5,33:1
Hallisey, Dennis J, 1941, Mr 1,15:5
Hallissey, Charles J, 1946, Je 8,21:6
Halliwell, Charles Eleazer, 1907, My 7,9:6
Halliwell, George W, 1938, D 25,14:5
Halliwell, John, 1938, Ja 2,40:3
Halliwell, Kenneth L, 1967, Ap 10,47:1
Halliwell, Phillips J O, 1889, Ja 5,5:2
Halliwell, R Davis, 1959, O 9,29:1
Halliwell, Richard T Sr, 1942, N 2,21:1
Halliwill, Maynard O, 1952, Ap 2,33:3
Hallman, Alvin D, 1946, Jl 29,21:4
Hallman, David, 1874, D 14,1:6
Hallman, E C, 1948, S 23,29:4
Hallman, Eli S, 1955, Ag 27,15:6
Hallman, Henderson, 1940, Ap 4,23:4
Hallman, John P, 1924, My 3,15:4
Hallman, Linwood L, 1937, Ag 16,19:5
Hallock, A Avery, 1955, My 19,29:3
Hallock, Alice E M Mrs, 1942, F 19,19:5
Hallock, Allen R, 1962, Ap 10,39:3
Hallock, Benjamin T, 1949, Ag 15,17:5
Hallock, Charles P, 1950, Ja 26,27:2
Hallock, Charles S, 1954, S 9,32:4; 1954, S 22,30:1
Hallock, Charles W Mrs, 1942, Ag 21,19:1
Hallock, Constance, 1956, Mr 5,23:4
Hallock, David H, 1939, N 15,23:2
Hallock, Edward F, 1939, F 25,15:2
Hallock, Elizabeth C Mrs, 1940, O 3,25:2
Hallock, Emma C, 1946, N 12,29:5
Hallock, Fannie, 1945, N 29,23:3
Hallock, Frank H, 1944, D 14,23:2
Hallock, Frank K Dr (will, Jl 22,17:6), 1937, Ap 30, 22:2
Hallock, Frank S, 1950, F 2,27:5
Hallock, Frederick B, 1945, F 25,37:1
Hallock, Gen Mrs, 1873, Ap 20,12:4
Hallock, George D, 1925, Je 26,17:6
Hallock, George F, 1937, Mr 26,21:5
Hallock, George Sr, 1944, Ap 19,23:1
Hallock, Gerard, 1866, Ja 5,5:4
Hallock, Grace T, 1967, Ag 19,25:3
Hallock, Harold P Mrs, 1953, My 12,27:5
Hallock, Harry, 1946, Jl 1,31:2
Hallock, Henry A Mrs, 1944, Ap 10,19:5
Hallock, Henry G C, 1951, Ja 19,25:5
Hallock, Henry N, 1956, Ap 30,23:5
Hallock, Henry N Mrs, 1939, Ja 23,13:3
Hallock, Henry P Mrs, 1951, Ja 1,17:5
Hallock, J H, 1875, N 22,8:2
Hallock, James B, 1947, Ag 30,15:3
Hallock, James C, 1918, N 14,13:1
Hallock, James R, 1953, Ag 16,77:1
Hallock, James W, 1943, O 20,21:3
Hallock, John H, 1944, Mr 14,19:1

Hallock, John W Dr, 1937, Jl 18,II,6:8
Hallock, Joseph A, 1903, My 3,9:6
Hallock, Joseph N, 1942, O 3,15:5
Hallock, Joseph Newton Rev Dr, 1913, Mr 25,13:5
Hallock, Lesley W, 1954, Ap 24,17:4
Hallock, Orrin S, 1947, Ja 19,52:2
Hallock, Otto F Mrs, 1947, F 13,23:1
Hallock, R T, 1879, Ja 22,2:5
Hallock, Ruth M, 1945, My 19,19:3
Hallock, Samuel F, 1946, Ja 29,25:3
Hallock, Samuel T, 1952, Mr 25,27:4
Hallock, Silas F, 1949, Ap 25,23:5
Hallock, W A, 1880, O 4,5:4
Hallock, Waverley W, 1943, D 16,27:4
Hallock, William, 1946, Ap 11,25:2
Hallock, William E Mrs, 1939, S 30,17:6
Hallock, William Prof (funl, My 23,13:5), 1913, My 22,11:4
Hallock, Wilmot Y, 1956, Ag 7,27:4
Hallock, Zachariah R, 1954, D 24,13:4
Halloran, Daniel Rev, 1909, N 6,9:5
Halloran, Ennis J, 1946, Jl 6,15:2
Halloran, Frederick J, 1951, Ja 28,77:2; 1952, Jl 10, 31:2
Halloran, James V, 1941, Mr 13,21:3
Halloran, John L, 1944, Ap 7,20:2
Halloran, John V, 1940, Je 2,44:7
Halloran, M W, 1952, O 22,27:4
Halloran, Michael J, 1915, D 6,9:3
Halloran, Peter J, 1951, Ap 25,29:5
Halloran, Roy D, 1943, N 11,23:1
Halloran, Ursula, 1963, N 14,39:4
Halloran, Walter J, 1948, N 15,25:3
Halloran, Walter J Mrs, 1951, F 17,15:1
Halloran, William, 1943, Ja 18,15:1
Halloran, William A, 1937, O 21,23:4
Halloran, William F, 1947, My 12,21:5
Halloran, William M, 1954, Ja 20,27:1
Hallow, Abe, 1955, O 7,25:3
Halloway, Emma, 1943, S 15,27:3
Halloway, Harriette R, 1966, O 15,29:2
Halloway, Henry R Mrs, 1944, Ja 29,13:1
Hallowell, Albert V, 1956, Jl 31,23:4
Hallowell, Anna J F Mrs, 1941, Je 3,21:5
Hallowell, Frederick F, 1945, Ag 19,39:1
Hallowell, G H, 1926, Mr 28,26:3
Hallowell, Guernsey A, 1944, F 29,17:2
Hallowell, H H, 1903, Ag 14,7:7
Hallowell, Israel, 1949, Ag 28,75:3
Hallowell, Jean F, 1938, F 15,25:4
Hallowell, N Penrose, 1961, F 14,37:3
Hallowell, N Penrose Mrs (trb lr, Mr 30,20:7), 195 Mr 28,17:3
Hallowell, Richard P, 1904, Ja 6,9:5
Hallowell, Robert, 1939, Ja 28,15:1
Hallowell, Robert H, 1958, Je 14,21:6
Hallowell, William C L, 1941, Mr 26,23:4
Halls, Thomas E Capt, 1937, Mr 4,23:3
Hallstead, Walter G, 1945, S 21,21:4
Hallstead, William F, 1908, F 24,7:5
Hallstein, Henry A, 1949, Mr 21,23:4
Hallstrom, Alfred L, 1951, Ap 12,77:3
Hallstrom, Samuel W, 1943, Je 15,21:4
Hally, Dora, 1945, D 20,23:2
Hally, E G Capt, 1881, Mr 30,5:3
Hally, Mary C, 1907, Je 16,7:6
Halm, Jules F, 1961, Ja 7,19:4
Halm, William E, 1950, F 21,25:2
Halma, Harold, 1968, Je 18,44:5
Halmi, Arthur L Mrs, 1965, Ag 23,31:5
Halmi, Artur L, 1939, D 5,27:2
Halmos, Eugene E, 1959, F 3,31:3
Halpenny, Annie M, 1953, N 7,17:5
Halper, Louis J, 1957, F 10,86:1
Halper, Louis J Mrs, 1959, S 8,35:2
Halperin, Abraham, 1951, Mr 23,21:2
Halperin, George, 1961, N 8,35:5
Halperin, George P, 1961, My 8,35:4
Halperin, Hal, 1945, Mr 5,19:2
Halperin, Harry J Mrs, 1961, Mr 14,35:3
Halperin, Jacob E, 1946, My 3,21:2
Halperin, Morris Dr, 1937, Ag 20,17:4
Halperin, Moses P, 1957, Ap 23,31:2
Halperin, Simon Mrs, 1952, Jl 26,13:4
Halpern, Alex J, 1956, Jl 10,31:4
Halpern, David, 1956, Mr 13,27:5
Halpern, David Mrs, 1940, Ap 18,23:4
Halpern, George E, 1957, S 11,33:5
Halpern, Harold J, 1946, Ag 18,45:1
Halpern, Harry Mrs, 1956, Ja 10,31:3
Halpern, Irving W, 1966, D 11,88:6
Halpern, Israel, 1950, Jl 16,69:1
Halpern, Jacob, 1964, Ja 1,25:4
Halpern, Joseph, 1957, N 22,25:4
Halpern, Max, 1966, F 27,85:1
Halpern, Max E, 1954, D 12,89:2
Halpern, Michael, 1960, Ag 17,31:1
Halpern, Philip, 1963, Ag 26,27:1
Halpern, Ralph Mrs, 1961, F 18,19:5
Halpern, Sue, 1966, Je 8,47:2
Halpert, James A, 1965, Ja 10,92:4
Halpert, Joseph, 1959, Ja 25,92:1
Halpert, Joseph S, 1955, N 14,27:5

Halpert, Percy, 1966, N 1,41:3
Halpert, William, 1948, Mr 28,48:6
Halpin, Cecilia A, 1947, N 7,23:4
Halpin, Charles A, 1946, Mr 16,13:3
Halpin, Charles B, 1955, Mr 6,88:5
Halpin, Edward P, 1945, Ap 27,19:1
Halpin, Elizabeth, 1948, Ap 1,25:3
Halpin, Eugene Jr, 1962, O 18,39:4
Halpin, Eugene 3d, 1943, Mr 21,27:1
Halpin, Francis, 1925, Jl 6,11:6; 1925, Jl 9,19:5
Halpin, Frederick T, 1948, S 21,28:2
Halpin, George H, 1959, O 21,43:4
Halpin, George V, 1949, Je 22,31:2
Halpin, Henry, 1924, F 14,17:4
Halpin, J Ray, 1956, Je 25,23:1
Halpin, James G, 1961, Je 11,87:1
Halpin, John J, 1960, Mr 21,29:2
Halpin, John J Jr, 1960, Ag 9,27:2
Halpin, John J Mrs, 1950, Ja 26,27:3
Halpin, Martha G Mrs, 1937, F 27,17:5
Halpin, Michael C, 1955, Jl 19,27:5
Halpin, Michael J, 1941, S 11,23:6
Halpin, Patrick A Rev, 1920, D 10,15:4
Halpin, T M, 1881, Mr 28,5:6
Halpin, Thomas E, 1954, Mr 23,27:1
Halpin, Thomas F, 1941, Ag 30,13:7
Halpin, Thomas L, 1952, Ap 16,27:4
Halpin, Thomas M, 1958, Jl 15,25:2
Halpin, William, 1937, Ag 23,19:2
Halpin, William (por), 1941, Ag 12,19:5
Halpin, William, 1947, Mr 13,27:2
Halpin, William A, 1938, O 25,23:5
Halpin, Zachariah P, 1948, Mr 21,60:2
Halpine, Charles G Gen (funl, Ag 9,8:2), 1868, Ag 4, 2:4
Halprin, Aaron, 1957, Mr 6,31:3
Halprin, Abraham J, 1949, O 10,23:5
Halprin, Abraham J Mrs, 1968, Ja 25,40:1
Halprin, B M, 1903, F 7,2:6
Halprin, Dorothy Mrs, 1951, S 3,13:5
Halprin, Jacob Mrs, 1947, F 20,25:3
Halprin, Julius, 1968, Ag 7,43:1
Halsall, J Thompson, 1950, Ap 6,29:1
Halsbury, Lord, 1921, D 12,15:3
Halsell, Harold, 1950, S 19,29:3
Halsell, Harry H, 1957, F 5,23:3
Halsey, A Woodruff Mrs, 1945, N 13,21:4
Halsey, A Woodruff Rev Dr, 1921, Ap 21,13:6
Halsey, Alfred D, 1958, S 13,19:4
Halsey, Benjamin G, 1943, Ap 27,24:3
Halsey, Benjamin S, 1956, D 13,37:2
Halsey, C C, 1901, Ja 11,9:5
Halsey, C Van Rensselaer Mrs, 1950, My 30,18:3
Halsey, Charles B, 1944, Ap 14,19:2
Halsey, Charles D, 1923, S 14,19:5
Halsey, Charles D W, 1961, My 28,64:6
Halsey, Charles E Capt, 1913, D 6,11:6
Halsey, Charles Woodruff, 1925, Je 6,15:5
Halsey, Clinton G, 1940, Ap 4,23:6
Halsey, Clinton G Mrs, 1949, Je 5,92:8
Halsey, Cornelia Baldwin, 1903, S 16,9:7
Halsey, Donald P, 1964, Ap 17,35:2
Halsey, Edmund R, 1943, My 21,19:2
Halsey, Edward G (por), 1940, Je 22,15:6
Halsey, Edward G Jr, 1961, Ap 11,37:4
Halsey, Edwin A, 1945, Ja 30,19:1
Halsey, Eldred A, 1960, Mr 9,33:3
Halsey, Fanny Deane, 1859, Je 7,1:1
Halsey, Florence, 1945, Ja 30,19:5
Halsey, Francis Whiting, 1919, N 25,11:3
Halsey, Frank D, 1941, Ap 9,25:2
Halsey, Frederick K, 1945, Ag 10,15:2
Halsey, Frederick R, 1918, S 30,9:6
Halsey, Frederick R Mrs, 1908, O 18,VII,11:5
Halsey, George Albert, 1906, Ap 4,9:7
Halsey, George Moore, 1922, D 5,19:5
Halsey, Hampton H, 1947, D 11,33:2
Halsey, Harriet, 1946, F 13,23:1
Halsey, Harvey R (por), 1937, F 21,II,10:6
Halsey, Harvey R, 1955, D 25,48:4
Halsey, Harvey R Mrs, 1967, My 2,47:1
Halsey, Henry A, 1914, D 23,13:4
Halsey, Henry B, 1909, Ap 4,13:4
Halsey, Herbert D, 1946, S 25,27:2
Halsey, Hugh, 1940, Mr 22,20:2
Halsey, I Y, 1955, O 6,29:3
Halsey, Jesse, 1954, Ja 13,31:2
Halsey, Levi W, 1955, Mr 11,25:1
Halsey, Lionel (por), 1949, O 28,23:1
Halsey, Loring F, 1940, F 29,19:6
Halsey, Lt-Col, 1877, N 20,4:7
Halsey, N Wetmore, 1911, Jl 2,9:5
Halsey, Newcomb G, 1947, Je 3,26:2
Halsey, Norris H, 1925, Mr 12,19:4
Halsey, Ralph W, 1946, S 11,7:5
Halsey, Reinhold H F, 1951, S 4,27:2
Halsey, Robert H, 1955, S 16,23:1
Halsey, Robert L, 1958, Je 18,33:3
Halsey, S R, 1884, Je 18,4:7
Halsey, Samuel A Mrs, 1950, Ap 2,93:1
Halsey, Thomas M, 1938, Ap 2,15:2
Halsey, W Gurden, 1960, Mr 29,37:3
Halsey, W Roy, 1952, D 13,21:2
Halsey, Walter N, 1943, D 23,20:2
Halsey, William D, 1939, Mr 2,21:5
Halsey, William Edward Dr, 1922, N 22,21:4
Halsey, William F (funl plans, Ag 18,30:5; funl, Ag 21,21:1), 1959, Ag 17,1:2
Halsey, William F Mrs, 1947, My 26,21:5; 1968, O 26,37:4
Halsey, William M Jr, 1949, O 29,15:1
Halsey, William W, 1941, Ag 6,16:2
Halsey, Woodruff W, 1967, Ja 23,43:3
Halstead, A Willis, 1946, Ja 8,23:4
Halstead, Albert (por), 1949, My 22,90:3
Halstead, Albert, 1956, Ap 5,29:4
Halstead, Albert Jr Mrs, 1949, Ag 12,17:1
Halstead, Albert Mrs, 1957, F 12,27:5
Halstead, Alex S, 1949, Ag 21,68:4
Halstead, Allen, 1946, O 10,27:6
Halstead, Antoinette, 1943, Mr 14,26:3
Halstead, Benjamin W, 1943, O 20,21:4
Halstead, Benton Col, 1919, F 27,11:2
Halstead, Byron C, 1963, Jl 15,29:3
Halstead, Charles E, 1948, Mr 21,60:3
Halstead, Charles F Dr, 1937, Mr 9,24:2
Halstead, Clarence, 1938, O 15,17:5
Halstead, David H, 1945, Ap 13,17:3
Halstead, Frank M, 1925, Je 25,21:5
Halstead, G, 1884, O 27,5:6
Halstead, George S, 1939, F 5,40:4
Halstead, George W Mrs, 1950, O 3,31:4
Halstead, Harry, 1946, Je 6,21:1
Halstead, Irving H, 1965, F 28,88:5
Halstead, J Henry, 1950, S 23,17:5
Halstead, Jacob, 1915, O 6,11:7
Halstead, John F, 1939, F 12,44:5
Halstead, Joseph Singer Dr, 1925, S 15,25:4
Halstead, Kenneth B, 1967, Ag 16,41:4
Halstead, Marshall, 1908, Ja 30,7:5
Halstead, Murat, 1908, Jl 3,7:3
Halstead, Purdy Mrs, 1951, S 30,72:5
Halstead, Robert, 1925, Jl 11,11:5
Halstead, Robert Mrs, 1925, Jl 7,19:4
Halstead, Samuel B, 1946, Mr 28,25:3
Halstead, Schurman, 1868, O 9,7:1
Halstead, W, 1878, Mr 5,4:6
Halstead, William S Dr, 1922, S 8,13:4
Halsted, Abel H, 1873, Ap 14,5:5
Halsted, Byron David Dr, 1918, Ag 29,7:5
Halsted, C S, 1876, N 18,2:2
Halsted, Cornelius H, 1954, D 20,29:5
Halsted, David Frost, 1903, Jl 12,7:6
Halsted, Douglas Mrs (C H Bloss), 1958, Ap 10,29:3
Halsted, Edward B, 1938, F 5,15:4
Halsted, Gilbert C, 1941, Ja 24,17:4
Halsted, Gilbert C Mrs, 1952, F 25,21:5
Halsted, Hannah Mrs, 1941, Ag 29,17:7
Halsted, Hans O, 1947, Ap 14,27:4
Halsted, Harbeck, 1967, S 25,45:1
Halsted, Harold C Mrs, 1968, Mr 9,29:5
Halsted, Henry M Jr, 1964, Ag 9,76:5
Halsted, Herman G, 1962, My 13,88:7
Halsted, Jacob H Mrs, 1944, Ja 4,17:4
Halsted, James H, 1938, Ag 12,17:2
Halsted, John, 1919, Jl 17,13:5
Halsted, John Fletcher, 1919, N 26,13:1
Halsted, Josephine D Mrs, 1938, O 23,40:8
Halsted, L P Mrs, 1910, Ag 6,7:5
Halsted, N N Gen, 1884, My 7,8:2
Halsted, O S, 1877, Ag 30,2:2
Halsted, Osborne Sr, 1939, O 18,25:5
Halsted, R F Lt-Col, 1881, My 26,5:4
Halsted, Richard Haines, 1925, Ap 30,21:4
Halsted, S Hazard, 1941, My 29,19:3
Halsted, Thomas H, 1956, N 22,33:1
Halsted, William P Maj, 1925, O 14,25:3
Halt, Karl R von, 1964, Ag 7,29:5
Haltenhoff, William C, 1948, Ja 24,15:5
Halter, Anthony P, 1961, F 18,19:3
Halter, Edward J, 1942, Jl 13,15:2
Halter, John J, 1951, D 6,33:1
Halter, Joseph, 1955, Jl 10,72:1
Haltermann, H Henry, 1948, Mr 3,23:2
Haltermann, H Henry Mrs, 1943, S 11,13:5
Haltigan, Patrick J, 1937, Jl 10,16:1
Halton, Bibb D, 1949, D 28,25:3
Halton, Charles, 1959, Ap 18,23:2
Halton, Elizabeth Mrs, 1940, Ap 1,19:2
Halton, Frederick J, 1943, N 6,13:1
Halton, J A, 1928, D 23,17:1
Halton, Mary (por), 1948, Ja 27,25:1
Halton, Matthew H, 1956, D 4,39:2
Halton, William, 1944, Ap 28,19:5
Halton, William Mrs, 1944, Mr 22,19:3
Haltzman, Robert C Mrs, 1951, O 7,87:2
Haluschinski, Theodosius, 1952, S 1,17:5
Halverson, Henry M, 1954, Mr 2,25:1
Halverson, Leslie E, 1953, F 24,25:3
Halverson, Marvin P, 1967, F 27,29:3
Halvorsen, Albert G, 1966, Ja 4,27:3
Halvorsen, Josephine, 1961, Ap 10,31:5
Halvorsen, Oscar, 1941, Mr 19,22:3
Halvorsen, Otto B, 1923, My 24,19:6
Halvorsen, Peter, 1945, Ap 26,23:4
Halvorson, Cromwell A B, 1963, Je 13,33:2
Halvorson, Harlow W, 1966, Ag 21,92:7
Halvorssen, Oeistein L, 1962, F 1,31:5
Halwartz, Carl Mrs, 1943, My 29,13:2
Haly, Joseph F, 1955, D 5,32:1
Haly, Percy, 1937, F 17,22:2
Halyburton, Charles P, 1939, F 21,19:2
Halychyn, Dmytro, 1961, Mr 27,31:3
Ham, Arthur H, 1951, Ap 5,29:5
Ham, Bertram A, 1944, My 7,45:2
Ham, Clifford D, 1950, Ja 12,28:2
Ham, Clifford W, 1939, Je 9,21:4
Ham, Edward B, 1965, D 2,41:2
Ham, Frank B, 1939, Mr 25,15:2
Ham, Frederick C, 1941, F 8,15:1
Ham, Frederick J, 1940, O 24,25:2
Ham, Harry H, 1954, F 21,69:1
Ham, James M, 1918, D 17,13:4
Ham, John, 1948, N 23,29:1
Ham, Mordecai F, 1961, N 2,37:3
Ham, Roscoe J, 1953, D 28,21:4
Ham, Roswell G Jr, 1967, Mr 9,39:4
Ham, Samuel Vinton Col, 1924, Ag 22,13:6
Ham, Thomas J, 1911, F 13,11:5
Ham, William H, 1941, N 10,17:5
Ham, William W, 1943, D 7,27:2
Ham Tai-Young, 1964, O 25,88:2
Hamacher, Edward A, 1954, Mr 27,17:6
Hamada, Kunimatsu (por), 1939, S 8,23:4
Hamaguchi, Y, 1931, Ag 27,17:3
Hamai, Shinzo, 1968, F 27,43:2
Hamaker, William N, 1947, D 10,31:1
Haman, Charles J, 1949, S 26,25:3
Haman, Charles R, 1939, My 30,17:3
Haman, Walter A, 1968, Mr 7,43:4
Haman, William A, 1942, D 21,23:4
Hamann, Valentine, 1951, Mr 5,21:1
Hamann, William A Mrs, 1958, My 22,29:5
Hamaoka, Ituso, 1939, F 25,15:2
Hamar, James L Jr, 1960, D 31,17:4
Hamar, James L Mrs, 1953, Ap 14,35:1
Hamber, Harvey F Mrs, 1961, Ag 23,33:4
Hamberg, Harold, 1954, F 9,27:3
Hamberg, Louis, 1952, F 6,29:4
Hamberg, Richard M, 1923, My 21,15:5
Hamberger, Frank X, 1950, My 23,29:4
Hamberger, William F Lt-Comdr, 1937, S 2,21:3
Hamberry, James L, 1961, F 27,27:5
Hamberry, William L, 1965, N 4,47:2
Hambidge, George W, 1943, Ag 4,17:5
Hambidge, Jay, 1924, Ja 21,17:5
Hambidge, William H, 1939, Ap 17,17:3
Hambleden, Lord (por), 1948, Ap 1,25:4
Hamblen, Kyle S, 1952, O 3,23:4
Hambleton, Anna B C Mrs, 1939, Jl 16,30:7
Hambleton, Frank Sherwood, 1908, Ag 18,9:6
Hambleton, Maurice, 1940, Je 6,25:4
Hambleton, Thomas Edward, 1906, S 22,7:4
Hambley, Walter H, 1947, O 31,23:3
Hambley, William G, 1953, F 5,23:3
Hamblin, Constance, 1910, Ja 21,11:4
Hamblin, David K A Sr, 1959, N 7,23:3
Hamblin, Eliza Mary Ann, 1873, Jl 6,8:4
Hamblin, J E Maj-Gen, 1870, Jl 5,3:4
Hambly, Lydia A, 1942, Ap 27,15:6
Hamborg, Axel, 1950, Ag 25,15:2
Hamborsky, William J Mrs, 1948, Mr 9,24:2
Hambourg, Boris, 1954, N 27,13:2
Hambourg, Mark, 1960, Ag 28,83:2
Hambourg, Michael, 1941, D 18,27:6
Hambrecht, George P, 1943, D 24,13:5
Hambrecht, Henry J, 1949, O 29,15:2
Hambright, Charles M, 1938, O 8,23:1
Hambright, Frank P, 1941, Ag 1,15:3
Hambright, William B, 1964, N 3,31:4
Hambright, William B Mrs, 1968, Jl 12,31:1
Hambro, Carl J, 1964, D 16,43:3
Hambro, Carl J Mrs, 1943, Ag 1,39:2
Hambro, Charles, 1963, Ag 29,29:4
Hambro, Eric, 1947, D 30,23:4
Hambro, John H, 1965, D 6,37:3
Hambro, R Olaf, 1961, Ap 26,39:2
Hambro, Sybil E Mrs, 1942, F 1,42:2
Hambrock, Louis, 1950, D 18,31:4
Hamburg, Augustus V (por), 1940, N 23,17:1
Hamburg, David Dr, 1916, Ja 22,9:5
Hamburg, Edwin C, 1957, Jl 9,27:1
Hamburg, Louis, 1958, O 29,35:3
Hamburger, Adolf, 1962, O 18,39:3
Hamburger, Adolf L, 1959, D 29,25:2
Hamburger, Arthur J, 1962, My 31,27:1
Hamburger, David A, 1944, S 6,19:5
Hamburger, Fred J, 1960, Mr 1,33:1
Hamburger, Gabriel Mrs, 1961, S 16,19:4
Hamburger, Harry, 1966, Ja 18,37:4
Hamburger, Harry H, 1966, S 20,47:3
Hamburger, Harry Mrs, 1954, D 11,13:2
Hamburger, Henry, 1940, Mr 22,19:5
Hamburger, Henry W, 1956, Ap 6,26:3
Hamburger, Hilda, 1942, My 20,19:3
Hamburger, Irving, 1953, Ap 1,29:4
Hamburger, Isaac, 1913, Jl 9,7:6
Hamburger, Jacob, 1958, O 13,29:5
Hamburger, Jacob Mrs, 1952, Ap 18,25:3

Hamburger, Louis, 1903, Ag 13,7:6; 1957, O 29,31:3
Hamburger, Manes I, 1940, Je 23,30:6
Hamburger, Mildred, 1957, Ja 9,31:5
Hamburger, Moritz, 1955, Ap 30,17:2
Hamburger, Nathan, 1910, S 16,9:5
Hamburger, Philip, 1921, Je 9,15:4
Hamburger, S B, 1926, D 29,21:2
Hamburger, Samuel, 1942, Jl 2,21:5
Hamburger, Simpson Capt, 1916, Ag 10,9:5
Hambury, Cecil Sir, 1937, Je 11,23:5
Hamcke, Elmer W, 1955, Ja 8,13:4
Hamcke, Nicolaus Mrs, 1953, F 10,27:2
Hameerslough, Charles R Mrs, 1950, Ap 29,15:2
Hamel, Aime I, 1947, Mr 26,25:1
Hamel, Robert Sr, 1941, Ag 19,21:5
Hamel, S Reginald Mrs, 1961, My 18,35:4
Hamelin, Admiral, 1864, F 6,8:1
Hament, Morris, 1964, Je 5,31:3
Hamer, Alvin C, 1950, My 6,15:3
Hamer, Frank, 1955, Jl 12,25:2
Hamer, Fred B, 1953, D 31,19:5
Hamer, George F, 1945, O 3,19:5
Hamer, J Wesley, 1944, O 23,19:2
Hamerman, Joseph, 1950, Ag 4,21:3
Hamerow, Chiam S (C Schneyer), 1961, Jl 27,31:4
Hamerschlag, A A, 1927, Jl 21,21:5
Hamerschlag, Frank N, 1950, My 15,21:4
Hamerschlag, Royal P, 1951, Jl 27,19:1
Hamerslag, Albert R, 1968, Mr 22,47:1
Hamerslag, Victor, 1953, My 13,29:6
Hamersley, Adrian, 1947, F 20,25:5
Hamersley, Arnold G, 1964, My 10,83:2
Hamersley, Carl S, 1938, Je 7,23:2
Hamersley, J H, 1901, S 17,7:6
Hamersley, James Hooker Mrs, 1904, Ja 6,9:1
Hamersley, Louis G, 1942, Je 3,23:3
Hamersley, Mrs, 1867, F 21,5:3
Hamersley, William Ex-Justice, 1920, S 18,9:2
Hamersly, Lewis R Mrs, 1920, My 19,11:5
Hamersly, Lewis Randolph, 1911, Ja 2,9:4
Hames, C Eugene, 1956, S 13,35:2
Hamid, Abdul, 1918, F 12,11:1
Hamid, Samuel J, 1954, Ap 29,31:5
Hamid Bey, Abdulhak, 1937, Ap 14,26:1
Hamid Bin Thevain, Sultan of Zanzibar, 1896, Ag 26, 5:1
Hamiel, Dorman E, 1950, Ja 31,24:3
Hamil, Ralph E, 1946, Ja 2,19:1
Hamil, Robert, 1880, S 12,2:4
Hamill, Alexander S, 1947, S 1,19:5
Hamill, Alfred E, 1953, Jl 13,25:4
Hamill, Barker G, 1937, D 14,25:3
Hamill, Chalmers, 1954, N 5,21:3
Hamill, Charles H, 1941, Ag 11,13:6
Hamill, E A, 1927, Ja 15,15:3
Hamill, George W, 1940, D 11,27:3
Hamill, Howard M, 1915, Ja 23,11:6
Hamill, Hugh H, 1909, My 15,9:5
Hamill, Ignatius A, 1940, Je 24,15:5
Hamill, James, 1876, Ja 11,5:3
Hamill, James A, 1941, D 16,27:1
Hamill, James F, 1938, Mr 15,24:1
Hamill, James M, 1939, Je 17,15:2
Hamill, James T, 1951, D 20,31:4
Hamill, John F, 1946, S 11,7:5
Hamill, John Francis, 1919, My 22,15:6
Hamill, Margaret C, 1938, Jl 9,13:5
Hamill, Marietta M, 1953, Je 11,29:2
Hamill, P J, 1930, Ja 13,1:4
Hamill, Ralph C, 1961, Jl 6,29:5
Hamill, Samuel H Mrs, 1903, Je 14,7:6
Hamill, Samuel M, 1948, My 4,25:5
Hamill, Samuel R, 1908, Ja 25,9:6
Hamill, William Arthur, 1904, F 4,9:6
Hamilton, A, 1928, Je 4,21:5
Hamilton, A T, 1884, My 3,2:3
Hamilton, Adam, 1952, Ap 29,27:2
Hamilton, Adam B, 1945, Je 3,31:1
Hamilton, Adelaide, 1915, My 10,15:4
Hamilton, Adolphus, 1882, Ag 26,3:2
Hamilton, Albert H (por), 1938, Jl 3,12:8
Hamilton, Alex J, 1940, Ap 25,23:4; 1948, Ag 12,22:3
Hamilton, Alex Mrs, 1951, O 12,27:4; 1952, F 10,93:2
Hamilton, Alex R, 1948, Ap 3,15:2
Hamilton, Alex V, 1960, O 20,35:4
Hamilton, Alex 5th, 1953, My 14,29:6
Hamilton, Alexander, 1875, Ag 3,4:6; 1916, F 5,11:5; 1947, Mr 13,27:3
Hamilton, Alexander Gen, 1907, D 11,11:4
Hamilton, Alexander J Mrs, 1943, D 25,13:2
Hamilton, Alexander Mrs (funl), 1871, Jl 25,8:5
Hamilton, Alfred, 1942, Ap 12,45:1
Hamilton, Alfred S, 1953, S 28,25:4
Hamilton, Alice, 1905, S 18,7:7
Hamilton, Allan McLane Dr, 1919, N 24,15:3
Hamilton, Alston Brig-Gen, 1937, D 21,23:5
Hamilton, Andrew, 1908, Mr 2,9:1
Hamilton, Andrew J, 1943, Ja 10,48:4
Hamilton, Andrew Mrs, 1907, Jl 19,7:6
Hamilton, Andrew T, 1954, Je 20,84:4
Hamilton, Andy, 1953, Jl 29,23:3
Hamilton, Angelo, 1961, F 13,27:6
Hamilton, Angus, 1913, Je 19,11:4
Hamilton, Anthony W P (Patk), 1962, S 25,37:2
Hamilton, Arch Sir, 1939, Mr 19,III,6:8
Hamilton, Archie N Mrs, 1940, Ap 13,17:6
Hamilton, Arthur, 1943, Ja 4,15:6
Hamilton, Arthur de C, 1959, Je 14,87:1
Hamilton, Arthur L, 1947, S 23,25:4
Hamilton, Augustus W, 1940, Ja 24,21:2
Hamilton, B Wallace, 1951, Je 5,31:1
Hamilton, Betty L Mrs, 1939, S 22,23:2
Hamilton, Braddin (funl, Ap 3,15:4), 1922, Ap 2,29:3
Hamilton, Burgoyne (por), 1937, D 27,16:4
Hamilton, C A Judge, 1901, D 1,7:6
Hamilton, C Carter, 1949, Mr 30,25:2
Hamilton, C J Dr, 1937, D 20,27:4
Hamilton, C Lawrence, 1955, F 10,31:2
Hamilton, C Lord, 1884, Je 5,4:6
Hamilton, C Stanley, 1960, Je 18,23:3
Hamilton, Carl L (por), 1946, My 28,21:3
Hamilton, Carl W, 1967, F 5,89:2
Hamilton, Caroline V, 1945, S 20,23:2
Hamilton, Charles A, 1942, Ag 25,23:2; 1943, O 31, 48:6
Hamilton, Charles Alfred, 1919, Ja 23,13:3
Hamilton, Charles D P, 1940, Mr 7,23:3
Hamilton, Charles F, 1938, S 24,17:6
Hamilton, Charles H, 1946, D 3,31:1
Hamilton, Charles K, 1914, Ja 23,11:3; 1967, Je 7,51:5
Hamilton, Charles L, 1940, Je 7,23:3
Hamilton, Charles M, 1942, Ja 4,49:2; 1945, F 23,17:3
Hamilton, Charles R, 1949, N 17,29:1; 1954, Ap 6,29:5
Hamilton, Charles R Mrs, 1938, Ag 26,17:3
Hamilton, Charles T, 1962, Ag 22,33:2
Hamilton, Charles W, 1948, D 30,19:5; 1953, D 15, 39:1
Hamilton, Christie P, 1945, Ap 27,19:5
Hamilton, Christie P Mrs, 1944, S 3,28:8
Hamilton, Claud Lord, 1925, Ja 27,13:3
Hamilton, Claude T, 1941, O 31,23:5
Hamilton, Clayton (por), 1946, S 18,31:1
Hamilton, Clinton P, 1944, My 19,19:2
Hamilton, Clyde C, 1959, D 9,45:4
Hamilton, Colson E, 1950, O 20,27:2
Hamilton, Cosmo (por), 1942, O 15,23:3
Hamilton, Cosmo Mrs (Beryl Faber), 1912, My 3, 11:4
Hamilton, David C, 1948, Ap 6,23:4
Hamilton, David C Sr, 1945, N 14,19:4
Hamilton, David G, 1915, F 17,11:6
Hamilton, David J, 1937, My 18,23:2
Hamilton, David S, 1938, Jl 18,13:3
Hamilton, Don, 1966, D 6,47:1
Hamilton, Don A, 1951, D 20,31:2
Hamilton, Don Sr, 1959, Je 3,35:1
Hamilton, Donald, 1939, Ap 13,23:2
Hamilton, E Paul, 1960, Ag 29,25:2
Hamilton, E Paul Mrs, 1950, D 19,31:7
Hamilton, Earl P, 1968, Je 9,84:7
Hamilton, Edith (trb lr, Je 16,IV,10:6), 1963, Je 1, 21:4
Hamilton, Edna V, 1967, Jl 25,32:3
Hamilton, Edward E, 1944, Ag 30,17:4
Hamilton, Edward H, 1956, D 21,23:3
Hamilton, Edwin L, 1944, Ap 5,19:6
Hamilton, Elise M Mrs, 1952, Mr 16,90:1
Hamilton, Elizabeth B Mrs, 1966, Ap 20,47:4
Hamilton, Elwood (por), 1945, S 20,23:3
Hamilton, Eric K C, 1962, My 22,37:4
Hamilton, Eric S, 1944, Je 28,23:4
Hamilton, Ernest, 1959, O 22,37:3
Hamilton, Ernest A, 1955, Ja 26,25:4
Hamilton, Ernest Lord, 1939, D 15,25:3
Hamilton, Ernest Mrs, 1968, Ap 15,43:4
Hamilton, Euphemia W Mrs, 1953, Ag 24,23:3
Hamilton, Everett R, 1942, F 25,19:4
Hamilton, F H Dr, 1886, Ag 12,5:4
Hamilton, Fay C (por), 1942, Mr 8,43:1
Hamilton, Flora, 1947, Je 27,21:3
Hamilton, Francis J, 1946, Mr 19,27:1
Hamilton, Francis M, 1942, D 8,25:2
Hamilton, Francis M Mrs, 1946, Ap 9,27:2
Hamilton, Francis S Mrs, 1915, Je 6,17:6
Hamilton, Frank, 1946, S 10,7:4; 1947, D 12,28:2; 1952, F 12,27:2
Hamilton, Frank S, 1944, Ja 19,19:5
Hamilton, Frank W Sr, 1948, D 2,29:2
Hamilton, Franklin Elmer Ellsworth Bp, 1918, My 6, 13:8
Hamilton, Frederic H, 1956, Ja 31,29:3
Hamilton, Frederic R, 1952, F 21,27:2
Hamilton, Frederick C Col, 1905, Mr 2,9:6
Hamilton, Frederick G, 1944, Ja 4,18:2
Hamilton, Frederick P, 1942, Ag 13,19:5
Hamilton, Frederick R Mrs, 1942, O 1,23:6
Hamilton, Frederick Tower Adm, 1917, O 25,15:4
Hamilton, Frederick W, 1940, My 23,23:2
Hamilton, G Johnson (por), 1948, N 14,78:3
Hamilton, G Lord, 1927, S 23,27:4
Hamilton, G Powell Mrs, 1948, Ap 1,25:4
Hamilton, Gail (Abigail Dodge), 1896, Ag 18,5:5
Hamilton, Gavin G Lord, 1952, Je 24,29:5
Hamilton, George, 1947, Ja 13,21:5
Hamilton, George Alexander, 1871, S 20,5:4
Hamilton, George B, 1939, Ag 24,19:5
Hamilton, George E, 1916, F 1,11:7; 1946, My 26,32:
Hamilton, George E Mrs, 1944, F 25,17:3
Hamilton, George F Sr, 1942, Ja 13,19:3
Hamilton, George G, 1939, Ja 18,20:4
Hamilton, George H, 1915, F 15,7:5
Hamilton, George L, 1940, S 26,23:6; 1950, O 25,35:
Hamilton, George Leon, 1922, My 2,19:5
Hamilton, George V, 1956, S 26,33:4
Hamilton, George W, 1948, Ag 25,25:3; 1951, N 9, 27:2; 1957, Ap 1,25:3
Hamilton, Gordon, 1967, Mr 11,29:3
Hamilton, Grace L, 1956, Mr 14,33:5
Hamilton, Gustaf A Sr, 1946, N 9,17:4
Hamilton, H Adelbert, 1939, My 24,23:3
Hamilton, H Lester, 1960, F 27,19:3
Hamilton, Hale (por), 1942, My 20,19:1
Hamilton, Harold H, 1925, S 13,5:1
Hamilton, Harry A, 1953, Jl 11,11:4
Hamilton, Harry L, 1952, F 28,27:2
Hamilton, Harry M, 1954, D 10,27:2
Hamilton, Harry S, 1938, My 24,19:2
Hamilton, Harry T (por), 1944, F 7,15:5
Hamilton, Heber J, 1952, Ja 6,93:1
Hamilton, Helen B Mrs, 1937, Ja 23,17:2
Hamilton, Helen E P Mrs, 1940, F 19,17:2
Hamilton, Henry, 1918, S 5,11:5
Hamilton, Henry D, 1942, Ag 19,19:1
Hamilton, Henry H, 1948, Ja 21,25:2
Hamilton, Henry Plevoe, 1918, S 29,21:1
Hamilton, Henry R, 1940, Je 18,23:2
Hamilton, Henry R P, 1943, S 7,23:6
Hamilton, Herbert F, 1959, Jl 18,15:3
Hamilton, Hugh Dr, 1923, O 8,17:3
Hamilton, Hugh F, 1963, Jl 26,25:2
Hamilton, Ian (por), 1947, O 13,23:1
Hamilton, Ida L, 1947, My 7,27:3
Hamilton, Irving B, 1958, F 5,28:1
Hamilton, Isaac, 1940, Jl 10,19:1
Hamilton, J A, 1878, S 26,5:6
Hamilton, J C, 1882, Jl 26,5:6
Hamilton, J Howard, 1955, Ja 10,23:4
Hamilton, J M, 1936, S 12,17:5; 1939, Jl 4,13:6
Hamilton, J Stuart, 1956, O 18,33:3
Hamilton, J W Bishop, 1934, Jl 25,17:4
Hamilton, Jacob, 1904, F 9,9:6
Hamilton, James (Duke of Abercorn), 1913, Ja
Hamilton, James, 1961, Ja 16,27:6
Hamilton, James A, 1941, D 25,25:1; 1950, My 8
Hamilton, James A Mrs, 1937, Je 15,23:4
Hamilton, James C, 1952, O 15,31:2
Hamilton, James D, 1925, O 17,15:4
Hamilton, James H, 1939, F 28,20:3
Hamilton, James J, 1940, Jl 12,15:5
Hamilton, James M, 1938, My 22,II,7:4; 1940, S 27:3; 1943, Je 3,21:6
Hamilton, James R, 1947, Jl 21,17:5
Hamilton, James S, 1953, Je 6,17:3
Hamilton, James T, 1966, D 18,84:7
Hamilton, James W, 1943, D 20,23:5
Hamilton, Jane (Rev Mother Vincent), 1966, N 48:1
Hamilton, Janet, 1873, D 6,10:6
Hamilton, Jerome M, 1958, F 18,27:2
Hamilton, John, 1948, My 4,25:1
Hamilton, John A Sr, 1937, D 31,15:3
Hamilton, John C, 1953, O 1,29:5
Hamilton, John C Sr, 1957, D 21,19:6
Hamilton, John D M Sr Mrs, 1937, D 5,II,9:3
Hamilton, John D Maj, 1937, Mr 11,23:4
Hamilton, John F, 1967, Jl 13,37:1
Hamilton, John H, 1942, Jl 11,13:4
Hamilton, John Hew North Gustav (Earl of Sta 1914, D 3,13:3
Hamilton, John J, 1947, N 12,27:1
Hamilton, John Lyon, 1904, F 12,9:6
Hamilton, John M, 1905, S 24,9:4; 1951, Ag 7,
Hamilton, John Mrs, 1949, Mr 23,27:2
Hamilton, John P, 1946, N 26,29:5
Hamilton, John P (funl), 1954, O 27,29:5
Hamilton, John S, 1951, Je 18,23:5; 1962, F 11
Hamilton, John T, 1939, S 18,19:6; 1951, Ja 30
Hamilton, John W, 1938, N 12,15:5
Hamilton, Joseph G, 1957, F 20,33:6
Hamilton, Joseph G du R, 1961, N 13,29:6
Hamilton, Joseph H, 1941, Ja 8,19:1
Hamilton, Joseph R, 1943, Ja 4,15:5
Hamilton, Joseph S, 1945, Je 26,19:4
Hamilton, Josephine Mrs, 1941, My 10,15:6
Hamilton, Juliette P Mrs, 1952, Ag 6,21:5
Hamilton, Kenneth A, 1966, Ja 8,25:3
Hamilton, Kenneth G, 1961, N 4,19:5
Hamilton, L McLane Capt, 1868, D 6,11:5
Hamilton, L Rev, 1882, Ap 17,5:1
Hamilton, Lauchlan A, 1941, F 12,21:3
Hamilton, Laura J, 1941, My 14,21:5
Hamilton, Leon, 1938, F 26,15:3
Hamilton, Lloyd N, 1945, D 24,16:2
Hamilton, Louis A, 1944, Ap 1,13:6
Hamilton, Louis H K, 1957, Je 24,23:1
Hamilton, Louis McLane, 1911, Ag 31,7:6
Hamilton, M R Col, 1901, Ja 24,9:5
Hamilton, Margaret, 1957, S 12,31:4
Hamilton, Margaret V Mrs, 1940, Jl 29,13:5

Hamilton, Mary, 1945, F 7,21:4
Hamilton, Mary M Mrs, 1953, Ja 24,15:6
Hamilton, Mary Mrs, 1938, Je 19,29:1
Hamilton, Mary S, 1941, My 18,43:4
Hamilton, Maxwell M, 1957, N 13,35:1
Hamilton, May Copeland Mrs, 1924, D 31,13:5
Hamilton, Miller, 1945, Mr 2,19:3
Hamilton, Molly (Mrs Mary A), 1966, F 12,25:2
Hamilton, Morris W, 1955, Ap 21,29:5
Hamilton, Noble, 1903, S 27,7:6
Hamilton, Norman R, 1964, My 27,27:2
Hamilton, Orme R, 1949, N 6,94:5
Hamilton, Patrick J, 1946, D 12,29:1
Hamilton, Patrick L, 1944, Ap 12,21:3
Hamilton, Peggy-Kay, 1959, S 23,35:3
Hamilton, Peter, 1952, Ap 28,19:5
Hamilton, Philip M, 1947, Ap 12,27:1
Hamilton, R, 1878, Mr 15,5:5
Hamilton, R Andrew, 1950, Je 2,23:4
Hamilton, Raymon Mrs, 1967, F 12,92:8
Hamilton, Raymond B, 1956, My 17,31:4
Hamilton, Raymond S, 1966, Ap 8,31:1
Hamilton, Reginald N, 1946, Ag 16,21:6
Hamilton, Richard F (Tody Hamilton), 1916, Ag 17, 11:3
Hamilton, Richard J, 1956, Jl 12,23:4; 1962, F 21,45:2
Hamilton, Richard J Mrs, 1940, My 28,23:5
Hamilton, Robert, 1941, Ja 14,10:4
Hamilton, Robert A Mrs, 1943, Mr 27,13:4
Hamilton, Robert B, 1914, Ja 6,13:6; 1950, O 25,35:3
Hamilton, Robert B Mrs, 1948, My 11,25:2
Hamilton, Robert J Jr, 1945, Ap 2,19:4
Hamilton, Robert Mrs, 1946, Jl 10,23:5
Hamilton, Robert W, 1944, Jl 18,19:3; 1950, Jl 4,17:6
Hamilton, Rolland J, 1962, My 18,31:4
Hamilton, Ronald G, 1957, My 6,29:3
Hamilton, Ruth, 1913, Ag 23,7:3
Hamilton, Samuel H, 1959, D 20,60:6
Hamilton, Samuel L Dr, 1953, F 10,27:5
Hamilton, Samuel W, 1951, Jl 28,11:5
Hamilton, Sanford L, 1940, N 9,17:1
Hamilton, Sarah H, 1944, Je 1,19:2
Hamilton, Sarah M, 1951, D 22,15:4
Hamilton, Schuyler, 1907, F 14,9:6
Hamilton, Schuyler Gen, 1903, Mr 19,9:3
Hamilton, Scott B, 1949, S 7,29:1
Hamilton, Sidney J, 1951, Ja 15,17:3
Hamilton, Spencer C, 1957, Je 17,23:4
Hamilton, Spencer C Jr, 1966, D 11,88:5
Hamilton, Spencer C Mrs, 1943, F 22,17:2
Hamilton, Spencer S, 1963, Jl 4,17:3
Hamilton, Stephen W, 1952, F 3,84:1
Hamilton, Sue C, 1943, D 7,27:1
Hamilton, Theodore, 1916, Je 28,11:4
Hamilton, Theodore F, 1904, D 4,7:6
Hamilton, Theodosia S Mrs, 1941, S 12,22:3
Hamilton, Thomas, 1949, Ja 21,22:3
Hamilton, Thomas A Sr, 1961, D 31,48:4
Hamilton, Thomas B (por), 1939, F 19,39:3
Hamilton, Thomas B, 1940, Mr 5,23:3
Hamilton, Thomas G, 1947, F 25,25:2
Hamilton, Thomas H, 1959, D 11,34:7
Hamilton, Thomas J, 1947, Ap 17,27:5
Hamilton, Thomas J Sr, 1937, S 3,17:2
Hamilton, Thomas J Sr Mrs, 1963, My 28,16:2
Hamilton, Thomas L, 1908, Ag 21,7:4; 1908, Ag 25, 7:6; 1908, Ag 29,9:4
Hamilton, Thomas Mrs, 1950, O 19,31:1
Hamilton, Victor J, 1944, Jl 20,19:5
Hamilton, W B Rev Dr, 1912, Ag 3,7:4
Hamilton, W J, 1884, Mr 4,2:3
Hamilton, Walter, 1961, Ap 21,33:2
Hamilton, Walter A, 1946, Mr 30,15:2; 1958, My 3, 19:5
Hamilton, Walter G, 1948, Ja 6,23:4
Hamilton, Walter M Mrs, 1958, D 11,13:4
Hamilton, Walton H, 1958, O 29,35:3
Hamilton, Ward J, 1948, Ag 1,59:2
Hamilton, Wilbur H, 1964, Jl 23,27:1
Hamilton, Willard I Mrs, 1940, Ag 30,19:4
Hamilton, Willard L, 1955, N 30,33:5
Hamilton, William, 1942, Ag 4,20:2; 1943, Ag 15,38:6; 1948, D 18,19:2
Hamilton, William A, 1952, N 24,23:2; 1953, Je 6,17:2
Hamilton, William B, 1948, Jl 23,20:2
Hamilton, William B Mrs, 1944, Jl 1,15:6
Hamilton, William C, 1911, O 7,13:6
Hamilton, William E, 1960, F 19,28:1
Hamilton, William F, 1948, F 14,13:5; 1964, D 23,30:4
Hamilton, William G, 1940, Ap 12,23:5; 1940, N 25, 17:4
Hamilton, William Gaston, 1913, Ja 24,11:4
Hamilton, William H, 1909, Je 30,7:2; 1937, Jl 21, 21:6; 1945, N 2,19:2; 1950, Ja 4,35:3
Hamilton, William H Mrs, 1942, O 12,34:7
Hamilton, William J, 1943, F 22,17:4; 1948, Ja 29, 23:2; 1952, S 10,29:4
Hamilton, William J Jr, 1956, O 5,25:2
Hamilton, William J Mrs, 1961, Ap 20,33:2
Hamilton, William L, 1950, My 19,27:4
Hamilton, William Mrs, 1914, Ag 21,13:5
Hamilton, William O, 1952, Ja 1,25:2
Hamilton, William P, 1950, My 9,30:4
Hamilton, William P Mrs, 1916, O 4,11:6; 1955, Mr 15,29:2
Hamilton, William R, 1940, D 17,25:5
Hamilton, William Reeve Col, 1914, S 20,15:4
Hamilton, William Rev Dr, 1872, F 10,1:4; 1921, O 18,17:4
Hamilton, William S, 1954, F 20,17:3
Hamilton, William S H, 1962, F 27,33:2
Hamilton, William T, 1903, O 8,9:5; 1942, N 12,25:2
Hamilton, Zachary M, 1950, N 30,33:1
Hamilton and Brandon, Duke of, 1940, Mr 17,49:2
Hamilton-Russell, Gustav L Mrs, 1938, Ap 5,21:2
Hamlen, Fred E, 1939, N 17,22:2
Hamlen, Harry H, 1943, F 16,19:2
Hamlen, Joseph R, 1957, Ja 5,17:4
Hamlen, Paul F, 1965, Jl 5,17:3
Hamlen, Paul M, 1939, Jl 11,20:3
Hamler, William A, 1955, O 11,39:5
Hamlet, Francis P, 1945, Ag 7,24:3
Hamlet, Harry G, 1954, Ja 26,27:1
Hamlet, R William, 1966, S 13,47:2
Hamlet, William H M, 1951, N 21,25:2
Hamlett, Eugene C, 1943, Ja 1,23:5
Hamlett, Horace I, 1961, Mr 28,35:4
Hamley, Arthur J, 1961, F 6,23:4
Hamlin, A D F Dr, 1926, Mr 22,1:7
Hamlin, Abraham, 1958, O 29,35:1
Hamlin, Anna, 1925, Ap 27,17:5
Hamlin, Arthur S, 1945, Mr 9,19:1
Hamlin, C B, 1883, S 4,5:2
Hamlin, Charles E, 1921, Je 28,15:4
Hamlin, Charles Gen, 1911, My 16,13:5
Hamlin, Charles S (por), 1938, Ap 25,15:1
Hamlin, Charles S Mrs, 1964, Mr 8,86:6
Hamlin, Chauncey J, 1963, S 25,43:3
Hamlin, Chauncey J Mrs, 1951, Mr 29,27:2
Hamlin, Christopher R, 1957, F 26,29:4
Hamlin, Cicero J, 1905, F 21,7:6
Hamlin, Clarence C (por), 1940, O 31,23:3
Hamlin, Conde, 1943, Je 22,20:3
Hamlin, Dorothy, 1919, Ja 23,13:3
Hamlin, Edward, 1947, Ag 11,23:3
Hamlin, Edwin W, 1948, Ap 28,28:3
Hamlin, Elijah L, 1872, Jl 18,5:6
Hamlin, Eva S Mrs, 1942, Ag 6,19:6
Hamlin, F H, 1884, N 13,5:5
Hamlin, Francis B, 1955, Ja 29,15:2
Hamlin, Francis P, 1962, S 9,84:6
Hamlin, Frank S, 1953, Je 21,84:4
Hamlin, Fred A, 1959, F 10,33:4
Hamlin, Fred E Dr, 1937, Ja 31,II,8:3
Hamlin, Fred R, 1904, N 28,7:4
Hamlin, Frederick H, 1946, My 4,15:2
Hamlin, Fritz C, 1945, Ag 28,19:5
Hamlin, George E, 1946, Je 6,21:3
Hamlin, George H, 1951, Jl 18,29:4
Hamlin, George J, 1923, Ja 12,15:5
Hamlin, George N, 1943, S 18,17:1
Hamlin, George W, 1941, N 29,17:3; 1947, N 12,27:4
Hamlin, George W Mrs, 1964, Je 27,25:5
Hamlin, Hannibal, 1891, Jl 5,1:7
Hamlin, Hannibal (will, Mr 13,II,3:2), 1938, Mr 7, 17:5
Hamlin, Hannibal Mrs, 1925, F 2,17:3
Hamlin, Harry L Mrs, 1957, D 31,17:3
Hamlin, Herbert, 1954, Ag 12,25:5
Hamlin, Herbert W, 1957, F 24,84:1
Hamlin, Horace P Mrs, 1956, Mr 16,23:2
Hamlin, Isaac, 1967, F 17,37:1
Hamlin, James S, 1960, S 21,32:3
Hamlin, Jane, 1940, Ja 7,49:2
Hamlin, John A, 1908, My 22,7:4
Hamlin, Leslie E, 1952, Ja 28,17:4
Hamlin, Leslie Mrs, 1959, My 14,33:1
Hamlin, Marston A, 1963, Jl 6,15:4
Hamlin, Marston L, 1968, S 14,31:2
Hamlin, Mary E Mrs, 1937, Mr 14,II,8:7
Hamlin, Morrill Mrs, 1947, S 6,18:2
Hamlin, Oscar J Mrs, 1946, F 19,25:2
Hamlin, Paul M, 1968, Ag 26,39:5
Hamlin, Robert P Mrs, 1944, Ap 26,19:4
Hamlin, Scoville, 1951, O 25,29:5
Hamlin, Simon M, 1939, Jl 28,17:6
Hamlin, Talbot F (trb lr, O 14,IV,10:6), 1956, O 8, 27:3
Hamlin, Teunis Slingerland Rev Dr, 1907, Ap 19,9:5
Hamlin, Theodore O, 1941, N 17,19:5
Hamlin, Varney B, 1948, Ap 11,72:2
Hamlin, W Seward, 1937, Ag 29,II,6:6
Hamlin, William H, 1942, My 15,20:4; 1951, S 29,17:2
Hamlin, William O, 1938, My 15,II,7:2
Hamline, John H, 1904, F 15,7:2
Hamlisch, Joseph, 1943, S 26,48:2
Hamm, Anna Mrs, 1941, Ja 5,44:3
Hamm, Arba G, 1952, O 26,89:1
Hamm, Arthur E Mrs (Beth), 1958, N 23,88:8
Hamm, Edson W, 1945, My 14,17:3
Hamm, Frederick I (cor, F 15,27:2), 1955, F 14,19:2
Hamm, Frederick J, 1968, S 4,47:2
Hamm, Judith Anne, 1945, N 30,25:7
Hamm, Stafford L, 1951, My 13,90:1
Hamm, William A, 1959, Mr 23,31:3
Hamma, Floyd L, 1944, D 3,57:2
Hamman, George, 1953, D 20,77:1
Hamman, Louis, 1946, Ap 29,21:3
Hammann, Charles A, 1957, My 9,31:5
Hammann, Ellis C, 1939, N 22,24:8
Hammann, Francis E, 1943, Ja 10,49:1
Hammann, George E, 1940, Mr 19,25:1
Hammann, Valentine B, 1943, N 29,19:5
Hammar, Gustaf W, 1954, Ag 20,19:3
Hammar, Hugo G E, 1947, Ja 9,24:3
Hammar, V C Mrs, 1932, Ag 9,17:5
Hammarlund, Oscar, 1945, Ag 27,19:4
Hammarskjold, Ake W Judge, 1937, Jl 8,23:6
Hammarskjold, Dag (funl plans, S 21,9:6; funl, S 30,1:3), 1961, S 19,1:8
Hammarskjold, Dag (est appr), 1962, Jl 28,5:1
Hammarskjold, Knut H L, 1953, O 13,29:1
Hammarskold, J Gottfried, 1940, My 20,17:5
Hammarstrand, Robert E Dr, 1968, O 24,47:5
Hamme, William R, 1956, Ja 10,34:2
Hammeke, William, 1949, My 21,13:4
Hammeken, Edward F, 1957, Ag 27,29:4
Hammel, Charles C Mrs, 1956, O 3,33:2
Hammel, Frank J, 1966, N 2,45:4
Hammel, George H Mrs, 1947, Mr 1,15:3
Hammel, Harry, 1952, D 11,33:2
Hammel, James Mrs, 1946, F 13,23:2
Hammel, John S Gen, 1873, F 22,2:3
Hammel, Leopold, 1914, My 16,11:7
Hammel, louis, 1904, D 17,9:5
Hammel, Wilbert C, 1960, N 4,33:3
Hammell, Alfred L, 1962, F 9,29:2
Hammell, Alfred L Mrs, 1956, O 11,39:3
Hammell, George W, 1903, Jl 25,7:6
Hammell, John E, 1958, My 10,21:6
Hammer, A Wiese, 1956, D 30,32:4
Hammer, Anna M, 1942, Ap 3,21:2
Hammer, Catherine T Mrs, 1942, Mr 22,48:6
Hammer, E Walter, 1958, Ja 17,25:4
Hammer, Edward T, 1960, My 9,29:1
Hammer, Edwin W, 1951, O 12,28:3
Hammer, Einar, 1954, Mr 17,31:4
Hammer, Elizabeth R, 1966, S 20,47:2
Hammer, Ernest E, 1941, F 28,19:2
Hammer, Fred, 1939, Mr 15,23:5; 1944, Ag 10,17:6
Hammer, G Adolph, 1944, O 14,13:2
Hammer, George A Sr, 1957, Ag 11,81:1
Hammer, Haaken H, 1942, N 9,23:1
Hammer, Harry B, 1949, S 28,27:4
Hammer, Harry Mrs, 1950, My 17,29:1
Hammer, Henry F, 1965, Ag 2,29:3
Hammer, Horace H, 1948, D 27,22:2
Hammer, Isador, 1964, Jl 15,35:1
Hammer, Jacob Dr, 1953, F 26,25:1
Hammer, Joseph J, 1949, Ap 2,15:3
Hammer, Joseph T, 1959, F 7,19:4
Hammer, Josephine, 1940, My 9,23:4
Hammer, Julius, 1948, O 20,29:3
Hammer, Julius Mrs, 1960, F 18,33:4
Hammer, Louis, 1959, Mr 21,21:5; 1963, N 26,38:6
Hammer, Philomena, 1949, Ja 3,23:4
Hammer, Richard A, 1957, N 16,19:4
Hammer, Rolf Mrs, 1947, Ag 12,23:3
Hammer, Samuel, 1954, S 10,23:3
Hammer, Stanley, 1961, Ap 23,86:4
Hammer, Thomas D, 1937, Ap 28,23:3
Hammer, Trygve (por), 1947, Je 29,48:3
Hammer, Victor K, 1967, Jl 11,37:1
Hammer, W J, 1934, Mr 25,29:1
Hammer, William A Mrs, 1910, My 1,II,11:4; 1955, S 20,31:5
Hammer, William C Jr, 1952, Ja 11,21:3
Hammer, William J, 1950, O 14,19:2
Hammer, William Sr, 1938, N 13,44:7
Hammergren, David I, 1944, Ag 14,15:3
Hammerich, Hans, 1952, N 21,25:2
Hammerle, William C, 1965, Je 4,35:2
Hammers, Elizabeth, 1942, N 26,27:4
Hammers, James S, 1953, S 2,25:2
Hammers, Karl R, 1949, S 9,25:5
Hammers, Lilian, 1951, Je 6,31:6
Hammers, Morgan J, 1940, Ap 30,21:6
Hammerschlag, Joseph, 1940, N 26,23:5
Hammerschlag, Max G, 1954, My 25,27:4
Hammerschlag, Max G Mrs, 1965, S 13,35:4
Hammerschlag, Max L, 1967, F 18,29:2
Hammerschlag, Morris, 1949, Ja 29,14:2
Hammersley, Henry, 1919, Ag 21,11:4
Hammersley, Leona A, 1948, Mr 30,23:2
Hammersley, Lester B, 1948, O 22,25:2
Hammersley, William H, 1942, My 16,13:1
Hammersley, William J, 1952, D 14,90:6
Hammersley, William P, 1950, My 23,29:3
Hammerslough, Alexander J, 1966, Ag 15,27:5
Hammerslough, Charles R, 1948, D 15,33:4
Hammerslough, Julius, 1908, Je 20,9:6
Hammerslough, Louis, 1903, Je 23,7:6
Hammerslough, William J, 1963, F 12,4:5
Hammersmith, Paul, 1937, N 13,19:5
Hammerstein, Abraham Lincoln, 1914, F 6,9:5
Hammerstein, Anna N Mrs, 1939, D 24,14:8
Hammerstein, Arthur, 1955, O 13,31:2
Hammerstein, Arthur Mrs, 1921, N 12,13:4
Hammerstein, Augusta W Mrs, 1940, O 22,23:2

Hammerstein, Baron von, 1905, Mr 21,11:5
Hammerstein, Harry (funl, Jl 30,9:6), 1914, Jl 29,9:6
Hammerstein, Oscar Mrs, 1946, Ja 16,23:4
Hammerstein, Oscar 2d (funl plans, Ag 24,29:4; funl, Ag 25,29:4), 1960, Ag 23,1:3
Hammerstein, Reginald K, 1958, Ag 10,94:1
Hammerstein, William, 1914, Je 11,11:3
Hammerstein, William (funl), 1914, Je 12,13:6
Hammerstein, William Mrs, 1910, Ag 21,II,7:5
Hammerstein-Equord, Kurt von, 1943, Ap 28,23:2
Hammerton, John A, 1949, My 13,24:2
Hammes, Fred, 1953, D 9,11:1
Hammes, Henry W, 1938, Ap 25,15:3
Hammes, Phil C, 1949, Mr 19,15:2
Hammesfahr, Alex C C (por), 1941, Jl 12,13:1
Hammett, Alfred L, 1937, Ag 21,15:2
Hammett, Dashiell (funl, Ja 13,29:1; will, F 7,66:1), 1961, Ja 11,47:4
Hammett, Elizabeth B Mrs, 1938, D 14,25:3
Hammett, Francis H, 1957, Je 23,84:8
Hammett, Fred M, 1941, Ag 24,35:2
Hammett, Frederick S, 1953, Ap 15,31:2
Hammett, George H (will), 1937, S 21,10:6
Hammett, John E Dr, 1968, Jl 29,20:8
Hammett, Walter N, 1924, Jl 24,13:4
Hammill, Caleb W, 1921, Jl 19,15:6
Hammill, Hamilton J, 1959, Ja 23,25:3
Hammill, John, 1949, D 10,19:5
Hammill, Joseph F, 1939, Ja 31,21:2
Hammill, Margaret, 1873, S 6,8:4
Hammis, Annette, 1913, Ag 21,9:6
Hammitt, John K, 1942, My 11,15:4
Hammitt, Joseph, 1903, Ag 29,7:5
Hammitt, Joseph O, 1966, Ap 1,35:2
Hammitt, Walter, 1957, S 13,23:4
Hammon, J H, 1944, Je 9,15:5
Hammon, James H, 1944, Ag 30,17:4
Hammona, George, 1907, Jl 24,7:5
Hammond, A B, 1934, Ja 16,21:3
Hammond, Albert H Mrs, 1951, Ja 11,26:3
Hammond, Albert W, 1948, S 4,15:2
Hammond, Alfred D, 1943, Jl 9,17:1
Hammond, Alonzo J, 1944, D 3,58:5
Hammond, Andrew H, 1906, Mr 2,9:6
Hammond, Andrew J, 1949, Ja 29,14:3
Hammond, Aubrey L, 1940, Mr 20,27:5
Hammond, Bray, 1968, Jl 23,39:1
Hammond, C W, 1903, O 31,9:6
Hammond, Caleb D, 1942, My 8,21:6
Hammond, Charles, 1919, Ag 18,11:4
Hammond, Charles F, 1944, D 4,23:4; 1951, Ja 4,29:2
Hammond, Charles F Mrs, 1962, Ap 2,31:4
Hammond, Charles M, 1943, O 1,19:5; 1964, F 17,31:2
Hammond, Charles Mifflin, 1915, Je 16,11:6
Hammond, Charles N, 1941, Je 6,21:3; 1942, Je 28, 32:6
Hammond, Charles R, 1942, Mr 14,15:3
Hammond, Charles S, 1939, O 28,15:5
Hammond, Chauncey B, 1952, F 13,29:4
Hammond, Clarence A Sr, 1942, O 23,21:4
Hammond, Clarence L, 1939, Je 10,17:5
Hammond, Claude R, 1937, Mr 10,23:5
Hammond, Creed C, 1940, Ap 3,23:4
Hammond, David Q, 1964, N 23,37:5
Hammond, Dorothy, 1950, N 26,90:4
Hammond, E Z, 1873, Je 1,1:1
Hammond, Edgar B, 1937, Ag 14,13:4
Hammond, Edward P (por), 1940, My 29,23:5
Hammond, Edward P Rev, 1910, Ag 16,7:6
Hammond, Edward W, 1944, Ja 6,23:2
Hammond, Edwin A, 1912, Ja 5,13:4
Hammond, Eli Shelby, 1904, D 18,7:6
Hammond, Elizabeth L Mrd, 1939, My 10,23:4
Hammond, Eugene I, 1948, N 21,88:7
Hammond, Ezra, 1907, Mr 22,11:6
Hammond, F Carleton, 1938, F 9,19:1
Hammond, F Prescott Jr, 1956, N 17,21:4
Hammond, Frank C, 1941, Ap 13,39:3
Hammond, Fred W (por), 1942, Ja 9,21:3
Hammond, Frederick D, 1952, D 3,33:3
Hammond, Frederick W, 1948, Je 7,19:6
Hammond, Freeman, 1968, Mr 13,53:2
Hammond, G B, 1876, Ap 6,4:6
Hammond, Gardiner G Mrs, 1955, Je 26,77:2
Hammond, George A, 1944, Mr 24,19:3
Hammond, George B, 1940, Ja 28,33:1
Hammond, George B Mrs, 1947, Ag 20,21:3
Hammond, George Mrs, 1950, Jl 10,21:5
Hammond, George U, 1940, Je 3,15:2
Hammond, Grace S Mrs, 1937, Ja 22,21:1
Hammond, Graeme M (por), 1944, O 31,19:1
Hammond, Gustavus A Capt, 1937, Ap 23,21:2
Hammond, Halsey, 1940, Jl 27,13:3
Hammond, Harry L, 1953, Jl 15,25:2
Hammond, Harry P, 1953, O 23,23:5
Hammond, Harry S, 1960, Je 10,31:3
Hammond, Harry W, 1948, Jl 4,26:7
Hammond, Helen G, 1944, O 26,23:3
Hammond, Henry B, 1958, S 24,27:2
Hammond, Henry L, 1925, S 18,23:5
Hammond, Herbert T, 1948, Jl 8,23:3
Hammond, Howard, 1948, S 17,25:2
Hammond, Isaac D, 1947, F 25,25:4
Hammond, J F, 1879, Je 27,5:2
Hammond, J H Mrs, 1931, Je 19,23:1
Hammond, J H Sr, 1936, Je 9,23:1
Hammond, J P Rev Dr, 1884, Ag 10,7:3
Hammond, Jabez Dean, 1968, Ja 24,45:3
Hammond, James, 1940, O 26,15:4; 1951, Ag 4,15:7
Hammond, James B, 1913, Ja 28,11:2
Hammond, James G Mrs, 1945, Ja 20,11:1
Hammond, James W, 1950, Ag 25,21:5
Hammond, Jason E, 1957, O 21,25:4
Hammond, John, 1939, Ag 11,15:5; 1964, Ag 26,39:5
Hammond, John B, 1940, Jl 21,29:4
Hammond, John C, 1940, My 12,48:2; 1948, F 29,60:3
Hammond, John C Mrs, 1966, My 29,56:6
Hammond, John D Rev, 1923, D 12,21:2; 1925, Ja 25, 7:1
Hammond, John F, 1946, S 5,27:3
Hammond, John H, 1949, Je 29,27:1; 1949, Jl 2,15:6
Hammond, John H Jr, 1965, F 14,88:4
Hammond, John H Jr Mrs, 1959, D 13,86:3
Hammond, John Henry Mrs, 1923, My 21,15:4
Hammond, John L L, 1949, Ap 9,17:4
Hammond, John M, 1939, Je 30,19:2
Hammond, John S (por), 1939, F 10,68:3
Hammond, John S Mrs, 1955, F 11,23:2
Hammond, John W, 1962, N 21,33:3
Hammond, John W Mrs, 1962, S 21,30:1
Hammond, Johnson F, 1961, D 6,47:5
Hammond, Karl R, 1951, O 8,21:1
Hammond, Kensey J Dr, 1937, Ag 4,19:3
Hammond, Laurens Mrs (will, Mr 6,15:2), 1954, F 20,4:7
Hammond, Laurie, 1939, Ja 29,33:3
Hammond, Leonard C, 1945, D 22,19:1
Hammond, Lester C, 1957, Je 15,17:4
Hammond, Lester C Mrs, 1943, D 16,27:3
Hammond, Lincoln A, 1945, D 5,25:5
Hammond, Lorimer, 1968, F 27,39:2
Hammond, Lorimer Mrs (Alexandra), 1966, Jl 6,42:2
Hammond, Louis M, 1938, My 22,II,6:8
Hammond, Lowell F, 1951, Ja 2,23:2
Hammond, Luther S, 1947, Jl 1,25:4
Hammond, Lyman P, 1952, N 16,87:1
Hammond, Lyman P Mrs, 1959, Ag 24,21:4
Hammond, M C M, 1876, Ja 28,5:2
Hammond, Mary E, 1943, Ja 14,21:1
Hammond, N LeRoy, 1963, N 12,41:4
Hammond, Nathan B, 1939, Jl 19,19:4
Hammond, Newton, 1945, Je 6,21:5
Hammond, Ogden H, 1956, O 30,37:3
Hammond, Otis G, 1944, O 3,23:2
Hammond, P, 1936, Ap 26,II,10:1
Hammond, Peirce A, 1960, Jl 16,19:1
Hammond, Phil Dr, 1937, F 9,23:2
Hammond, R Noel, 1941, Je 21,17:3
Hammond, Robert B, 1956, Je 2,20:3
Hammond, Robert B Mrs, 1950, D 20,31:4
Hammond, Robert S, 1948, F 16,21:1
Hammond, Roland, 1957, Je 13,31:4
Hammond, Roland B, 1952, Jl 26,13:6
Hammond, Roy E (por), 1949, Ag 18,21:5
Hammond, Russell J, 1948, F 11,27:2
Hammond, S H, 1878, D 1,2:1
Hammond, Samuel, 1911, Je 23,11:6
Hammond, Sarah K Col, 1925, N 26,23:5
Hammond, Sen, 1864, N 20,8:1
Hammond, T W, 1936, S 4,19:1
Hammond, Theron D, 1946, F 23,13:5
Hammond, Thomas, 1909, S 23,11:1
Hammond, Thomas A, 1940, S 8,49:2
Hammond, Thomas J, 1946, Jl 24,27:3
Hammond, Thomas S, 1950, Je 16,25:1
Hammond, Thomas W Mrs, 1943, My 24,15:6; 1961, Ag 24,29:5
Hammond, W Edward C, 1940, S 3,17:5
Hammond, W H, 1905, Mr 30,6:4
Hammond, Walter E, 1941, My 4,53:2
Hammond, Wardlaw M, 1955, N 11,25:1
Hammond, Wilbur K, 1942, Ja 14,21:6
Hammond, Will Jr, 1964, F 18,35:2
Hammond, Willard D Sr, 1961, O 25,37:4
Hammond, William, 1905, My 5,9:4
Hammond, William A, 1900, Ja 6,1:2; 1938, My 10, 21:3
Hammond, William C, 1949, Ap 17,78:1
Hammond, William G, 1945, D 23,18:8
Hammond, William J, 1943, Mr 26,19:4
Hammond, William R, 1909, D 20,9:3
Hammond, William S, 1951, S 25,29:1
Hammond, William T S, 1940, Jl 17,21:2
Hammond, William W, 1939, Ap 15,19:3
Hammond, Winfield Scott Gov, 1915, D 31,9:8
Hammonds, Dorus, 1959, Mr 19,33:1
Hammons, Earle W, 1962, Ag 2,25:3
Hammons, Edwin F, 1955, Jl 6,27:2
Hammons, H George, 1948, N 23,29:3
Hammons, Harry E, 1957, S 4,33:3
Hammons, Samuel, 1968, F 26,33:5
Hammons, Walter S, 1951, Je 29,21:3
Hamner, Charles S, 1953, S 4,34:3
Hamner, Charles S Mrs, 1948, Mr 14,72:2
Hamner, James G, 1938, Jl 21,21:4
Hamner, Patrick H, 1959, Je 5,27:1
Hamner, William Mrs, 1954, Jl 21,27:4
Hamnett, Nina, 1956, D 17,31:4
Hamnett, Whitney S, 1951, My 11,27:1
Hamon, Alfred Mrs, 1955, F 24,27:1
Hamon, Ray L, 1967, F 21,44:5
Hamonneau, Maurice A, 1952, Ap 2,34:3
Hamor, William A, 1961, N 25,23:2
Hamparian, Hampar B, 1954, S 4,11:3
Hampden, Tener, 1916, Ag 3,11:6
Hampden, Walter (cremated, Je 13,23:1), 1955, Je 12,86:1
Hampe, Bela, 1948, O 13,25:3
Hampe, Edward, 1950, Jl 13,25:5
Hampe, William R, 1944, S 12,19:3
Hampel, Edward H, 1951, S 16,84:6
Hampp, Ralph P, 1962, My 8,39:3
Hampshire, Elisabeth Mrs, 1941, Ja 11,6:7
Hampson, Alfred L, 1952, My 13,23:4
Hampson, Arthur C, 1948, F 16,21:3
Hampson, Clara S, 1941, D 20,19:6
Hampson, Fred, 1955, N 26,19:5
Hampson, Helen G, 1947, My 14,25:2
Hampson, James J, 1956, Jl 27,21:1
Hampson, Phil F Mrs, 1954, S 24,23:2
Hampson, Theodore, 1940, Ag 22,19:4
Hampson, William, 1937, O 7,27:4
Hampston, Arthur, 1958, N 18,37:5
Hampton, Aaron B, 1954, F 6,19:3
Hampton, Adam R, 1949, Jl 9,13:3
Hampton, Amelia B Mrs, 1940, Je 14,21:1
Hampton, Arthur S, 1943, F 13,11:2
Hampton, Aubrey O, 1955, Jl 18,21:5
Hampton, Bertha, 1949, D 4,108:3
Hampton, Celwyn E Capt, 1913, D 25,9:4
Hampton, Charles, 1945, Ja 19,19:2
Hampton, Charles H Mrs, 1951, D 27,21:2
Hampton, E Wade, 1963, O 4,35:1
Hampton, Edwin R, 1949, F 11,23:2
Hampton, Elizabeth G, 1956, Ja 11,31:2
Hampton, Ellis Houston, 1953, F 26,25:3
Hampton, Ellsworth K Sr (will), 1937, Jl 21,19
Hampton, Faith, 1949, Ap 2,32:2
Hampton, Frank W, 1946, F 1,24:2
Hampton, George, 1962, Ag 26,82:6
Hampton, George C, 1953, Jl 11,11:6
Hampton, Kensey J, 1942, Je 13,15:2
Hampton, L N, 1955, Mr 6,89:2
Hampton, Lewis M, 1948, N 25,31:2
Hampton, Lord, 1880, Ap 10,5:5
Hampton, Lord (Herbert S Pakington), 1962, N 31:5
Hampton, Louis R, 1955, N 15,29:4
Hampton, Louise, 1954, F 12,25:3
Hampton, Samuel F, 1945, Je 28,19:3
Hampton, Thomas J Rev, 1922, Je 6,17:3
Hampton, Vernon L, 1960, Ag 16,29:1
Hampton, Wade Gen, 1902, Ap 12,9:5
Hampton, Wade Jr, 1879, D 24,5:3
Hampton, William H, 1957, F 28,27:4
Hampton, William M, 1960, F 12,28:1
Hamrah, Elias A, 1953, Mr 6,20:6
Hamrah, Joseph A, 1948, N 30,27:4
Hamric, Darrell H Mrs, 1955, O 4,35:4
Hamrick, Eli, 1945, Ap 3,19:3
Hamrick, Forrest G, 1943, Jl 10,13:5
Hamrick, Hayward R, 1957, Ja 22,29:3
Hamrick, Leland F, 1961, Ja 12,29:3
Hamrick, Waite C, 1963, Ag 19,25:4
Hamrock, Patrick J, 1939, Ag 25,15:5
Hamson, Lucy L, 1944, O 15,44:8
Hamstra, Herman, 1954, O 1,23:1
Hamsun, Knut, 1952, F 20,29:1
Hamtil, Allan, 1948, Je 30,25:4
Hamwi, George J, 1967, F 15,45:1
Hanaburgh, Emory F, 1948, D 25,17:5
Hanafin, jno, 1919, Je 12,15:2
Hanaford, George R, 1948, S 22,31:1
Hanaford, Harry P, 1925, Ag 21,13:5
Hanaford, Harry Prescott Mrs, 1924, Ag 2,9:6
Hanaford, Phebe A Rev, 1921, Je 3,15:3
Hanagan, Daniel M Mrs, 1947, N 4,25:2
Hanak, Edward Sr, 1948, D 5,92:3
Hanamann, Edwin J, 1964, Je 17,43:1
Hanan, Addison G, 1923, Jl 17,19:6
Hanan, Albert P, 1942, S 21,15:6
Hanan, Alfred Partridge, 1919, S 28,22:4
Hanan, Charles Talbot Smith, 1920, Ja 30,15:4
Hanan, James H (funl, Ag 28,7:5), 1920, Ag 2
Hanan, James T, 1950, Ap 26,29:2
Hanan, John H, 1941, F 2,44:1
Hanan, John H Mrs, 1907, Ap 2,11:5; 1920, Ja
Hanan, John Mrs, 1958, N 11,30:1
Hanan, Joseph B, 1950, F 28,29:4
Hanan, Joseph H Mrs, 1951, F 23,27:3
Hanan, Leo F, 1964, Jl 7,35:3
Hanan, Leo F Mrs, 1956, Ap 2,17:3
Hanan, Lucy L, 1955, S 17,10:1
Hanatschek, Herman C, 1963, Jl 27,17:2
Hanau, Agil (por), 1940, Ap 3,23:5
Hanau, Alex N, 1954, D 31,14:6
Hanau, Kenneth J, 1957, Ap 29,25:4
Hanauer, Albert, 1956, Jl 1,56:7
Hanauer, George H, 1942, S 2,23:2

Hanauer, Jerome J (por), 1938, S 4,16:7
Hanauer, Leonard G, 1967, Mr 9,39:4
Hanavan, Elizabeth B Mrs, 1942, Ag 9,42:6
Hanavan, William L, 1966, Ap 30,31:4
Hanawalt, Alva, 1939, F 8,25:3
Hanaway, Joseph, 1939, F 1,21:2
Hanaway, Roy C Mrs, 1964, F 18,35:1
Hanaway, Samuel Prof, 1920, N 9,15:1
Hanberg, John V, 1959, My 14,33:4
Hanburger, Fred W, 1948, Mr 18,27:1
Hanbury, Hugh J, 1965, Ap 9,33:1
Hanbury, Lily (Mrs Herbert Guedalla), 1908, Mr 6, 7:5
Hanbury, Patrick Capt, 1903, S 6,7:6
Hanbury, R W, 1903, Ap 28,2:4
Hanby, Albert T, 1947, Jl 15,23:3
Hanby, Benjamin F, 1946, Ja 25,23:2
Hanby, Benjamin F Mrs, 1949, Jl 12,27:2
Hanby, Walter R, 1952, Mr 29,15:4
Hance, Edward R, 1946, O 15,25:2
Hance, G C, 1884, F 27,5:2
Hance, George C, 1938, O 20,23:2; 1947, Ja 9,23:3
Hance, John A, 1947, F 23,53:7
Hance, John A Mrs, 1947, My 16,23:4
Hance, Joseph L, 1914, O 15,13:6
Hance, Joseph N, 1957, Ap 19,21:4
Hance, Paul Jr, 1957, D 22,40:2
Hance, Spencer W, 1940, O 27,45:2
Hance, Wallace E, 1943, F 6,13:4
Hance, Wendell D, 1962, F 20,36:1
Hancel, Max J Mrs, 1967, Mr 14,47:3
Hancey, Elbridge Ex-Judge, 1925, D 25,17:6
Hanch, Charles C, 1946, O 23,27:6
Hancher, Charles N, 1945, N 25,50:3
Hancher, H Francis Mrs, 1946, Je 12,27:1
Hancher, Mark, 1941, Je 3,21:5
Hancher, Virgil M, 1965, Ja 31,89:1
Hanchett, David S, 1943, Ag 28,11:2
Hanchett, Reuben C, 1944, D 18,19:1
Hancke, Nicolaus, 1948, Ap 28,27:4
Hancock, A S Dr, 1903, Mr 1,7:3
Hancock, Adeline F Mrs, 1948, My 16,68:3
Hancock, Alfred, 1950, F 2,27:4
Hancock, Arthur B Sr, 1957, Ap 2,31:1
Hancock, Carolyn, 1951, Ap 21,17:3
Hancock, Charles B, 1943, S 8,24:3
Hancock, Charles E, 1949, D 20,31:3
Hancock, Charles Mrs, 1949, Ja 21,22:2
Hancock, Charles T Mrs, 1949, D 23,21:2
Hancock, Clarence E, 1948, Ja 4,52:6
Hancock, D P, 1880, My 22,5:3
Hancock, Don, 1951, Ja 7,76:3
Hancock, E Adrian, 1943, N 19,19:5
Hancock, Edmund W, 1957, D 5,35:2
Hancock, Edwin, 1941, Mr 19,22:3
Hancock, Elinor, 1942, Ap 15,21:4
Hancock, Elmer N, 1915, S 10,11:6
Hancock, Fay L, 1955, S 24,19:4
Hancock, Frank, 1938, Ag 16,19:2
Hancock, Frank A D Mrs, 1954, S 27,21:4
Hancock, Frank B, 1938, Ja 19,23:2
Hancock, G Allan, 1965, Je 2,45:4
Hancock, George H, 1947, My 21,25:4
Hancock, George L, 1955, F 10,31:1
Hancock, H Irving, 1922, Mr 13,15:6
Hancock, Harris, 1944, Mr 21,19:5
Hancock, Herbert M, 1959, O 6,39:4
Hancock, James, 1952, Jl 24,27:5
Hancock, James E, 1949, Je 1,31:5
Hancock, Jean P-G, 1955, N 16,35:1
Hancock, John, 1859, Ja 4,1:5; 1953, Ja 19,2:2
Hancock, John C, 1957, Je 22,15:5
Hancock, John Col, 1912, O 27,II,17:2
Hancock, John F, 1951, N 30,23:2
Hancock, John M, 1956, S 26,33:3
Hancock, John S, 1942, D 29,21:2
Hancock, Lillian M Mrs, 1939, Mr 1,21:4
Hancock, Marshall H, 1959, Mr 8,87:2
Hancock, Milton S, 1945, Mr 5,19:5
Hancock, Myrtle J Mrs, 1948, Ag 21,15:5
Hancock, R, 1885, Ja 1,5:4
Hancock, R B, 1884, Mr 18,5:4
Hancock, Ralph, 1950, S 2,15:5
Hancock, Stoddard, 1956, Mr 29,27:4
Hancock, Theodore E, 1916, N 20,13:5
Hancock, Thomas, 1951, O 14,89:2
Hancock, Tony, 1968, Je 25,41:3
Hancock, W S Gen, 1886, F 10,1:7
Hancock, Walter C Mrs, 1958, My 17,19:7
Hancock, William A, 1957, Mr 12,33:3
Hancock, William D, 1948, Ja 30,23:3
Hancock, William F, 1915, My 26,13:6
Hancock, Winfred Scott Mrs (cor, My 11,11:5), 1911, My 8,11:5
Hancock, Witt Mrs, 1950, Ap 25,31:5
Hancox, Frederick B, 1948, Je 28,20:3
Hancox, Fredk-John, 1955, O 30,88:6
Hancox, Gilbert, 1965, Ja 3,84:6
Hancox, Richard G Mrs, 1949, Ja 14,23:1
Hancox, William C, 1943, O 26,23:2
Hancy, Edward J, 1943, S 1,19:6
Hand, Albert H, 1943, Ja 21,21:1
Hand, Alfred, 1949, S 3,13:7
Hand, Allan H, 1961, My 23,39:3
Hand, Arthur C, 1944, O 19,23:3
Hand, Augustus N, 1954, O 29,23:1
Hand, Augustus N Mrs, 1967, Ap 11,47:2
Hand, Benjamin W Mrs, 1948, Ap 3,15:3
Hand, Charles S, 1952, Mr 8,13:3
Hand, Charles Walter, 1915, O 29,13:5
Hand, Chauncey H, 1961, N 21,39:5
Hand, Clarence F Mrs, 1955, Je 1,33:5
Hand, Daniel, 1891, D 18,5:4
Hand, David, 1920, Jl 22,11:5
Hand, Donald D, 1944, S 17,42:2
Hand, Edward, 1865, N 26,6:5; 1939, S 1,17:4; 1956, D 10,31:5
Hand, Edward J, 1948, D 27,21:4
Hand, Edward L, 1950, Je 30,23:5; 1958, Ag 1,21:1
Hand, Edward P, 1949, Ja 5,25:1
Hand, Elbert O 2d, 1960, My 13,31:2
Hand, Ethel J, 1949, Mr 22,25:5
Hand, Frank, 1944, N 26,56:4
Hand, Frank E, 1944, Ap 23,41:2
Hand, Frank Mrs, 1939, F 6,13:3
Hand, George H Mrs, 1955, My 8,88:3
Hand, George T, 1945, My 15,19:5
Hand, Herbert T Jr, 1964, O 7,47:2
Hand, Howard E, 1941, S 29,17:6
Hand, Howard F, 1948, Jl 22,23:2
Hand, Ira, 1949, Ap 27,27:3
Hand, Ira Mrs, 1948, F 15,60:2
Hand, J Edward, 1939, S 30,17:6
Hand, J P, 1933, Ja 14,9:1
Hand, James L, 1939, S 28,25:3
Hand, James L Mrs, 1955, O 21,27:2
Hand, James W, 1962, O 11,39:1
Hand, John, 1948, Je 21,21:5; 1956, O 14,86:4
Hand, John E, 1962, N 9,35:1
Hand, John J, 1952, Ja 10,29:2
Hand, John J Mrs, 1950, My 15,21:3
Hand, John W Mrs, 1957, Ja 9,31:4
Hand, Johnny, 1916, O 19,9:2
Hand, Jonathan, 1943, My 22,13:5
Hand, Joseph P, 1961, Ap 13,35:2
Hand, Kenneth C Mrs, 1950, S 28,31:5; 1964, Ap 4, 28:2
Hand, Lafayette R, 1942, D 8,25:2
Hand, Learned (trb, Ag 20,57:4,5), 1961, Ag 19,1:2
Hand, Learned Mrs, 1963, D 13,36:6
Hand, Leslie L, 1957, Ag 18,83:2
Hand, Matalida B Mrs, 1938, F 25,17:5
Hand, Molly W, 1951, S 7,27:3
Hand, Oliver K, 1941, F 4,22:3
Hand, Richard B (cor, F 15,27:2), 1955, F 14,19:3
Hand, Richard Lockhart, 1914, O 8,11:6
Hand, Robert F (por), 1942, Mr 6,21:3
Hand, Robert F Mrs, 1947, S 21,60:4
Hand, Russel C Lt-Col, 1918, Jl 28,19:3
Hand, Tallmadge S Mrs, 1946, Ja 1,28:2
Hand, Thomas M (funl, D 31,13:5), 1956, D 27,25:3
Hand, William, 1941, N 20,27:2
Hand, William B, 1938, My 26,25:2
Hand, William F, 1948, S 27,23:1
Hand, William H Jr, 1946, My 25,15:1
Handal, Bishara G, 1947, Mr 5,25:5
Handel, George F, 1963, D 24,17:5
Handel, Louis, 1945, Ja 21,40:3
Handel, Samuel, 1964, Ap 18,29:3
Handel, William H, 1952, My 10,21:2
Handelman, Samuel, 1961, Ja 24,29:3
Handelsman, Benjamin, 1948, Je 24,25:4
Handelsman, Benjamin F, 1945, S 26,23:3
Handelsman, Henry, 1952, Je 5,31:2
Handersen, William A Mrs, 1950, Ja 27,24:3
Handerson, David Jr, 1950, S 19,42:6
Handin, Louis, 1964, Je 1,29:4
Handke, Georg, 1962, S 9,84:4
Handke, Paul A, 1944, F 16,17:1
Handle, Morris, 1954, Ja 22,27:1
Handleman, Harry J Dr, 1937, Jl 13,20:3
Handleman, Henry C, 1967, My 20,35:1
Handleman, Joseph E, 1957, S 1,56:7
Handler, Alfred A, 1947, Ap 3,25:3
Handler, Harry, 1965, Ag 18,35:4
Handler, Joshua, 1949, Ag 18,21:4
Handler, Leslie H Mrs, 1960, N 9,35:3
Handler, Milton Mrs, 1953, Ja 5,21:2
Handler, Nathan E, 1964, F 20,29:4
Handler, Ray F Mrs, 1953, Ag 22,15:6
Handley, Carroll A, 1961, Jl 26,31:2
Handley, George, 1939, F 9,21:2
Handley, John J, 1941, O 18,19:4
Handley, John P, 1955, Ag 12,5:1
Handley, Louis D, 1956, D 29,15:3
Handley, M Mailler, 1946, D 17,38:3
Handley, Richard H, 1914, Jl 16,9:6
Handley, Robert D Mrs, 1963, S 27,29:4
Handley, Tommy (por), 1949, Ja 10,15:3
Handley, William E, 1943, Ap 4,40:7
Handley, William S, 1962, Mr 20,37:4
Handley, William W, 1919, S 29,13:2
Handlin, Joseph, 1951, S 18,32:3
Handlin, Joseph Mrs, 1960, O 16,89:1
Handloser, Siegfried, 1954, Jl 4,3:6
Handly, John, 1947, Ap 17,27:3
Handly, Richard J, 1946, Ag 6,25:6
Handmacher, Alvin, 1966, Ap 16,33:2
Handman, Charles W, 1948, O 6,30:2
Handman, Louis A, 1956, D 10,31:5
Handman, Max S, 1939, D 27,21:4
Handorf, August V, 1955, My 21,17:5
Hands, Charles E, 1937, N 3,23:5
Hands, Henry, 1952, D 21,53:1
Hands, William C Dr, 1937, S 9,23:3
Handschin, Charles H, 1964, Ap 23,39:4
Handsfield, Frederick H Mrs, 1956, S 12,37:4
Handshy, C F, 1942, N 20,24:4
Handwright (Sister Ursula Marie), 1967, N 2,47:3
Handy, Albert M, 1956, Ja 20,23:6
Handy, Andrew W, 1942, Ag 21,19:4
Handy, Anson B, 1946, Mr 26,29:3
Handy, Charles M, 1944, Jl 28,13:3
Handy, Clive C, 1946, F 17,44:2
Handy, Daniel N, 1948, O 18,23:4
Handy, E Edward, 1949, O 25,27:1
Handy, Edward A, 1907, N 22,9:5
Handy, Edward H, 1947, Je 2,25:4
Handy, Edward O, 1956, Ap 29,86:2
Handy, Elizabeth V, 1939, Mr 27,15:3
Handy, Harry Mrs, 1964, Je 29,27:5
Handy, Howard R, 1938, My 2,17:5
Handy, James S, 1941, S 29,17:6
Handy, John B U Mrs, 1947, My 10,13:5
Handy, Joseph B, 1960, Ag 7,85:2
Handy, M P Maj, 1898, Ja 9,7:5
Handy, Martin, 1921, F 4,11:3
Handy, Percy, 1965, O 30,35:1
Handy, Percy B Mrs, 1954, O 9,17:1
Handy, Richard Fleming, 1914, My 6,11:6
Handy, Russell H, 1955, S 15,33:4
Handy, Thomas F, 1944, D 24,25:1
Handy, Thomas H, 1951, F 11,88:6
Handy, Wallace S, 1944, Ja 7,17:3
Handy, William C (funl plans, Mr 30,88:5; funl, Ap 3,33:1), 1958, Mr 29,17:4
Handy, William Y, 1956, Ja 10,34:6
Handyside, Blanche S Mrs, 1937, Ap 25,II,9:2
Handyside, George P, 1952, F 9,13:2
Handziuk, John P, 1947, S 6,17:2
Handzlik, Jean, 1963, Jl 12,25:3
Hanecy, John Mrs, 1948, S 13,21:6
Haneda, Toru, 1955, Ap 14,36:1
Hanelin, William B, 1949, Jl 25,15:4
Haneman, Frederick, 1950, My 4,27:5
Haneman, John T, 1960, My 19,37:3
Haneman, Vincent S Mrs, 1965, D 2,41:6
Hanes, Edward L, 1947, Je 16,21:4
Hanes, Harry E, 1966, Mr 3,33:4
Hanes, John W Mrs, 1947, Jl 20,45:2
Hanes, Pleasant H Sr, 1967, S 4,21:5
Hanes, Robert M, 1959, Mr 11,35:4
Hanes, Sam B, 1957, Ap 5,27:2
Haney, Amy C Mrs, 1951, Ja 1,17:2
Haney, Anna, 1942, F 12,24:2
Haney, Carol (trb; funl, My 14,36:1), 1964, My 12, 37:2
Haney, Charles H, 1944, Je 21,19:3
Haney, Cletus G, 1941, O 19,44:1
Haney, Fred S Mrs, 1948, Je 11,23:4
Haney, Frederick S, 1948, Ag 22,60:6
Haney, James M, 1949, Ag 19,17:1
Haney, Jennie M S Mrs, 1940, Ag 18,37:2
Haney, Jennie Pomerene, 1919, Jl 19,9:7
Haney, Jesse, 1901, Ag 6,7:6
Haney, John D, 1950, D 27,27:2
Haney, John D Mrs, 1957, Ag 26,23:5
Haney, John L, 1940, Je 20,23:4; 1959, D 30,21:4
Haney, Joseph A, 1959, Ap 17,25:4
Haney, Karl, 1961, F 27,27:5
Haney, Lewis H Mrs, 1944, Mr 23,19:5
Haney, Rein G, 1948, O 27,27:4
Haney, Thomas G, 1953, Ja 13,27:1
Haney, Thomas M Mrs, 1961, Je 3,23:5
Hanf, Albert, 1925, Je 27,11:6
Hanf, Elmer C, 1954, F 3,23:3
Hanf, George V, 1939, Jl 16,31:4
Hanf, John J, 1950, Mr 5,92:3
Hanf, Noel E, 1944, Ja 4,17:3
Hanff, Joseph A, 1964, Mr 19,33:2
Hanfling, Solomon, 1937, My 14,23:3
Hanford, Benjamin, 1910, Ja 25,9:4
Hanford, Clarence D, 1944, Mr 21,19:5
Hanford, Claude A, 1955, N 5,19:5
Hanford, Ernest J, 1937, N 6,17:4
Hanford, Eugene G, 1940, Ag 28,19:6
Hanford, Florence S Mrs, 1941, Je 14,17:5
Hanford, Frederick W, 1943, D 29,18:2
Hanford, George, 1951, Ap 20,29:5
Hanford, George A, 1949, Ap 6,29:2
Hanford, George Bennett, 1919, Jl 6,20:3
Hanford, George F, 1908, Ja 26,9:4
Hanford, H, 1879, Ag 24,12:1
Hanford, Henry G, 1937, Ja 10,II,10:3
Hanford, J Holly Mrs, 1944, Ja 11,20:2
Hanford, P, 1883, Ap 19,5:4
Hanford, Robert B Mrs, 1947, Ap 7,23:2
Hanford, Robert G, 1964, D 12,31:1
Hanford, Warren Day, 1915, Ap 5,11:4

Hanford, William F, 1949, Jl 3,26:5
Hanford, William H Dr, 1914, Ja 21,9:4
Hanft, David, 1967, Jl 25,32:7
Hanft, J Perry, 1950, Jl 18,29:3
Hanft, Jack Mrs, 1956, Ap 29,86:4
Hanft, Ronald J, 1964, F 8,23:6
Hangarter, Andrew, 1950, Mr 11,15:3
Hangarter, Ernest J, 1942, Ap 4,13:3
Hangarter, Joseph J, 1964, Jl 19,64:8
Hangartner, Otto Mrs, 1960, F 20,23:1
Hangen, Herman C Mrs, 1964, My 6,47:2
Hanger, Frank M, 1941, Je 18,21:2
Hanger, Harry B, 1925, O 19,21:3
Hanger, Hugh H, 1952, O 3,23:4
Hanger, William S, 1947, N 3,23:3
Hangley, Patrick J, 1949, S 7,29:4
Hanham, J Moore Maj, 1924, Ja 1,23:2
Hanhart, William, 1910, D 11,17:3
Hanie, L H, 1947, Mr 24,27:4
Hanify, Edward F, 1954, Ap 24,17:6
Hanigan, John L, 1952, Ag 22,21:3
Hanighen, Frank C, 1964, Ja 11,23:2
Hanihara, Massanao, 1934, D 20,26:2
Hanily, Edmund F (Bro Ambrose), 1952, O 14,31:5
Hanington, C L Maj, 1937, O 2,21:5
Hanisch, Arthur, 1966, D 31,19:5
Hanisch, George K, 1948, D 15,33:5
Hank, Frederick B, 1962, My 1,37:3
Hanke, Paul, 1937, Ja 30,17:4
Hanken, John R, 1937, Ap 16,23:4
Hankerson, Frederick P, 1955, Ap 11,15:5
Hankes, Louis C, 1943, O 2,13:3
Hankin, Ernest H, 1939, Ap 3,15:4
Hankin, Yoshua, 1945, N 12,21:3
Hankins, Abraham, 1963, Ag 13,31:4
Hankins, Charles H, 1945, Jl 13,11:6
Hankins, Edward R, 1954, D 20,29:1
Hankins, Elmer W, 1954, Je 13,89:1
Hankins, Frederick W, 1958, Ag 5,27:4
Hankins, Harry H, 1942, F 12,23:2
Hankins, Juliette C Mrs, 1941, Mr 23,44:3
Hankins, Morrison T, 1962, O 31,37:5
Hankinson, Benjamin, 1950, Ja 18,31:3
Hankinson, Charles R, 1945, Ja 23,19:5
Hankinson, Emerson J, 1937, Jl 30,19:7
Hankinson, Frank, 1946, Jl 12,17:6
Hankinson, Ralph A, 1942, Ag 21,19:4
Hankinson, Ray L, 1966, D 28,43:1
Hankinson, Robert M, 1938, Ja 2,40:4
Hanks, Charles H Jr, 1943, My 19,25:3
Hanks, David W, 1952, N 14,23:2
Hanks, E Gertrude, 1949, O 24,23:1
Hanks, Frederick C, 1939, N 17,21:2
Hanks, Herbert M, 1951, D 25,31:6
Hanks, J T, 1936, N 19,25:4
Hanks, John P, 1949, O 29,15:4
Hanks, Lemba T, 1943, D 26,32:8
Hanks, Louis M, 1950, Ap 30,102:3
Hanks, Lucien S, 1925, D 18,23:4
Hanks, Marshall B, 1948, D 14,29:2
Hanks, Oliver T, 1950, Je 30,23:3
Hanks, Rose E, 1939, D 31,18:8
Hanks, S J, 1950, F 3,23:2
Hanlan, James P, 1961, N 26,88:5
Hanley, Alberta Sister, 1952, F 5,29:2
Hanley, Alfred M, 1956, My 10,31:4
Hanley, Aloysius J, 1938, D 14,26:1
Hanley, C Justin, 1961, Mr 7,35:2
Hanley, Charles P Mrs, 1949, Ag 21,69:1
Hanley, Cyril J, 1951, D 28,21:1
Hanley, Daniel A, 1946, Mr 6,27:3
Hanley, Daniel W, 1956, Ap 2,23:4
Hanley, Earl, 1951, Mr 7,27:5
Hanley, Francis E, 1962, F 8,31:2
Hanley, Francis X, 1949, Mr 18,26:3
Hanley, Frederic P, 1961, Ap 18,37:4
Hanley, George A, 1950, Ag 24,27:6
Hanley, George W, 1962, Ag 20,23:5
Hanley, George W Mrs, 1944, My 13,19:6
Hanley, Gerald T, 1950, Mr 14,25:1
Hanley, Harold C, 1957, Ja 23,29:1
Hanley, Harry, 1950, Ag 12,13:4
Hanley, Harry V, 1966, Mr 25,41:5
Hanley, J M Dr, 1937, Ag 2,19:3
Hanley, J Swift, 1964, N 29,87:2
Hanley, James A, 1954, F 2,27:2
Hanley, James F, 1942, F 9,15:3; 1958, Je 10,33:1
Hanley, James H, 1945, Jl 10,11:6
Hanley, James J, 1950, F 20,25:5
Hanley, James L, 1951, Ap 17,29:3
Hanley, James M, 1944, Je 18,36:1
Hanley, James M Rev, 1920, My 26,11:4
Hanley, James P, 1958, Je 27,25:1
Hanley, James R Mrs, 1946, S 9,9:2
Hanley, Joe R, 1961, S 5,35:1
Hanley, John A, 1958, D 3,37:2
Hanley, John C P, 1950, Jl 24,17:2
Hanley, John J, 1939, Jl 9,31:3; 1950, N 7,27:3; 1954, Je 6,86:4; 1956, D 6,37:3; 1968, O 14,47:4
Hanley, John P, 1959, N 3,31:2
Hanley, Joseph F, 1962, D 8,27:3
Hanley, Kate Rhodes Mrs, 1944, Jl 2,19:2
Hanley, Lawrence, 1905, Ag 29,7:4
Hanley, Lawrence J, 1942, O 2,25:3
Hanley, Lewis E, 1952, N 18,31:2
Hanley, Martha E, 1959, Ap 4,19:3
Hanley, Michael G, 1951, D 23,22:6
Hanley, Michael J, 1948, Mr 23,25:1
Hanley, Michael L, 1954, My 31,13:3
Hanley, Miles, 1954, F 5,19:2
Hanley, Richard H J, 1967, Ap 5,47:2
Hanley, Robert E, 1962, Je 16,19:5
Hanley, Robert J Sr, 1955, F 13,86:4
Hanley, Sarah E, 1958, F 13,29:4
Hanley, Stephen W, 1961, Ap 24,29:5
Hanley, Thomas, 1956, Ag 18,17:5
Hanley, Thomas H, 1964, Ap 11,25:5
Hanley, William, 1915, My 11,15:4; 1941, Ap 23,21:7
Hanley, William A, 1966, N 12,29:3
Hanley, William B Jr, 1959, O 4,86:5
Hanley, William H, 1957, F 27,27:3
Hanley, William J, 1939, N 11,15:2; 1961, N 15,43:4
Hanley, William J Mrs, 1953, F 14,17:6
Hanlin, Fred A, 1947, Ap 20,60:3
Hanlin, Harry R, 1945, Ap 25,23:2
Hanline, Harry G, 1945, Je 26,19:5
Hanline, Simon M, 1938, Ap 12,24:1
Hanlon, Arthur F, 1925, My 3,5:2
Hanlon, Charles, 1953, My 23,16:5
Hanlon, Earl S, 1946, Jl 31,27:5
Hanlon, Edmund, 1949, F 18,23:5
Hanlon, Edward F, 1942, F 24,21:2
Hanlon, Edward G, 1937, Ap 15,23:5
Hanlon, Edward K, 1956, My 3,31:5
Hanlon, Edward L, 1941, O 8,23:4
Hanlon, Edward M, 1952, Ja 15,27:5
Hanlon, F, 1927, Ag 3,23:5
Hanlon, Francis W, 1958, Ja 11,17:6
Hanlon, Frank, 1938, F 16,21:2
Hanlon, Frank J, 1967, My 6,31:4
Hanlon, Frank R, 1956, Ag 24,19:5
Hanlon, Frank T, 1957, Ag 12,19:4
Hanlon, James R, 1943, My 3,17:2
Hanlon, John, 1940, Ap 20,17:5
Hanlon, Joseph T, 1956, S 20,33:1
Hanlon, Leroy M, 1947, O 7,27:4
Hanlon, Louis, 1954, My 6,33:2
Hanlon, Martin J, 1942, Ap 14,21:4
Hanlon, Michael P, 1940, S 25,27:5
Hanlon, Theodore E, 1947, F 20,25:5
Hanlon, Theodore M, 1945, Jl 20,19:5
Hanlon, Thomas, 1868, Ap 6,1:2
Hanlon, Thomas J, 1955, My 28,15:2; 1960, S 8,35:1
Hanlon, William C, 1951, Ap 26,29:2
Hanlu, Lin, 1943, Mr 16,8:4
Hanly, Thomas B, 1941, Ap 15,23:6
Hanmer, Alfred K Jr, 1956, S 11,38:1
Hanmer, Alfred W, 1953, F 22,60:6; 1959, N 12,35:2
Hanmer, Andrew J, 1947, N 4,25:1
Hanmer, J Sir, 1881, Mr 12,2:7
Hanmer, Lee F, 1961, Ap 28,31:3
Hanmer, Willard J, 1962, My 24,35:3
Hanmore, Louis F, 1939, My 25,25:4
Hann, Charles Jr, 1957, Je 6,31:3
Hann, Elmer E, 1937, F 26,21:3
Hann, Julia R Mrs, 1941, Mr 9,40:5
Hann, Le Roy C Mrs, 1949, S 9,25:3
Hann, Richard E, 1946, My 14,21:2
Hann, Thomas E, 1949, S 29,29:4
Hann, Vincent R, 1961, Ja 26,29:5
Hann, Warren D, 1940, F 26,15:2
Hanna, Alexander C, 1942, F 6,19:2
Hanna, Alexi, 1951, Ap 9,25:4
Hanna, Barbara, 1956, S 19,37:2
Hanna, Carl H Mrs, 1950, My 25,29:3
Hanna, Charles A, 1950, My 20,15:6
Hanna, Charles G, 1942, D 17,37:1
Hanna, Clarence C Sr, 1944, Je 20,19:1
Hanna, D Blythe (por), 1938, D 2,23:1
Hanna, Dan R, 1921, N 4,17:5
Hanna, Daniel R Jr, 1962, S 14,31:4
Hanna, Donald J, 1949, Jl 29,21:5
Hanna, E J Archbishop (por), 1944, Jl 11,15:4
Hanna, Eddie, 1949, S 19,29:4
Hanna, Edmund S Dr, 1904, Ja 19,9:6
Hanna, Francis D, 1938, F 9,19:4
Hanna, Frank B, 1941, N 8,19:5
Hanna, Frederick, 1938, Mr 18,19:3
Hanna, George C Jr, 1963, My 1,39:1
Hanna, George T, 1950, Jl 7,19:1
Hanna, Henry G, 1948, S 22,31:3
Hanna, Horace L, 1952, O 4,17:6
Hanna, Howard M, 1945, Mr 18,42:4
Hanna, Hugh Henry, 1920, N 1,15:6
Hanna, J M, 1871, My 4,2:4
Hanna, J Marvin, 1959, Je 10,37:2
Hanna, James, 1872, Ja 16,5:2; 1947, Je 26,23:3
Hanna, James A, 1950, S 7,31:2
Hanna, James Mrs, 1953, Ja 23,19:2
Hanna, Jefferson O, 1951, O 3,36:4
Hanna, John, 1964, Ag 27,33:4
Hanna, John B, 1916, My 10,13:7; 1943, D 4,13:3
Hanna, John C, 1938, S 18,45:2
Hanna, John F Sr, 1949, Ja 29,13:6
Hanna, John M Mrs, 1957, N 10,86:8
Hanna, John Mrs, 1942, Jl 7,20:5
Hanna, Josiah C Mrs, 1940, O 13,49:3
Hanna, Leo R, 1940, O 1,23:5
Hanna, Leonard C, 1919, Mr 25,13:4
Hanna, Leonard C Jr, 1957, O 6,84:1
Hanna, Leonard C Jr (est acctg), 1960, Ap 17,67:5
Hanna, Louis B, 1948, Ap 24,15:4
Hanna, Luther R, 1956, Jl 8,64:1
Hanna, M E, 1936, F 20,20:1
Hanna, Marcus A Mrs, 1921, N 18,17:5
Hanna, Margaret M, 1950, Mr 30,29:4
Hanna, Mark, 1958, Ag 16,17:3
Hanna, Mark A Sen, 1904, F 16,1:2
Hanna, Mark R, 1950, Ap 20,29:5
Hanna, Mary, 1956, My 25,23:3
Hanna, Mary Mrs, 1909, D 14,11:4
Hanna, Matthew E Mrs, 1947, Ag 11,23:5
Hanna, Max R, 1949, My 31,24:4
Hanna, Meredith, 1955, F 13,86:3
Hanna, Michael J, 1943, F 7,48:5
Hanna, Patrick, 1948, Ap 27,26:3
Hanna, Phil T, 1957, Je 2,86:5
Hanna, R Philip, 1957, Jl 21,60:6
Hanna, Robert J, 1953, D 13,86:6
Hanna, Robert K, 1947, Ap 30,25:5
Hanna, Samuel O, 1938, Ag 6,13:5
Hanna, Thomas A, 1952, My 28,29:5
Hanna, Thomas K, 1951, Mr 20,29:1
Hanna, Thomas R Mrs, 1942, Jl 31,15:4
Hanna, Thompson S, 1940, Ja 26,17:3
Hanna, Ulysses S, 1940, F 19,17:6
Hanna, William J, 1946, Ag 3,15:5
Hanna, William J, 1959, O 23,29:2
Hanna, William John, 1919, Mr 21,13:3
Hanna, William T, 1950, S 21,31:2
Hanna, Wylie J, 1957, Ag 9,19:5
Hannafin, John Mrs, 1956, Ag 28,27:4
Hannaford, George Mrs, 1961, D 21,27:1
Hannaford, Joseph, 1947, Ap 26,13:6
Hannagan, Johanna G Mrs, 1950, Ag 28,17:2
Hannagan, Steve, 1953, F 6,19:1
Hannah, Adelaide Mrs, 1941, O 17,23:2
Hannah, Charles C, 1946, Ja 22,27:4
Hannah, Edward I, 1944, D 29,15:5
Hannah, Herbert L, 1949, Je 2,27:3
Hannah, Ian C, 1944, Jl 8,11:4
Hannah, John (por), 1947, Je 8,60:3
Hannah, Mabel A, 1949, O 19,29:4
Hannah, Mabel L, 1960, Je 20,31:4
Hannah, Marta Mrs, 1943, Ap 29,21:3
Hannah, Miles C, 1962, D 6,43:3
Hannah, Thomas A, 1958, Ag 11,21:5
Hannah, William S, 1944, Mr 30,21:5
Hannahs, George C, 1960, My 9,29:1
Hannahs, Mary E, 1939, N 30,21:6
Hannahs, Ray G, 1955, Ag 28,85:1
Hannam, Charles, 1947, Je 5,25:5
Hannam, H H, 1963, Jl 14,61:3
Hannaman, C Park, 1957, N 23,19:1
Hannan, Charles R, 1907, D 25,7:6
Hannan, Charles T, 1950, F 17,24:2
Hannan, Edward A, 1937, D 3,24:3
Hannan, Edward Sr, 1916, S 7,9:4
Hannan, James F, 1951, S 14,25:4
Hannan, John, 1938, O 27,23:4; 1953, Ja 4,76:4
Hannan, John J, 1946, N 24,79:5
Hannan, John L, 1956, N 20,37:4
Hannan, Joseph A Sr, 1956, Je 2,19:3
Hannan, Michael J, 1949, Jl 1,19:6
Hannan, Patrick J, 1966, Je 21,43:3
Hannan, William E, 1937, D 25,15:3
Hannan, William J, 1964, D 22,27:5
Hannan, William J Mrs, 1947, My 1,25:1
Hannant, Morrison E, 1940, F 13,23:1
Hannay, Gerald, 1966, Ag 11,33:2
Hannay, James, 1910, Ja 13,9:5
Hannay, John R R (por), 1938, F 24,19:4
Hannay, Neilson C, 1962, S 22,25:1
Hannay, Robert, 1940, Mr 20,27:1
Hanneford, Edwin, 1967, D 11,47:2
Hannegan, John P Mrs, 1947, N 3,23:4
Hannegan, Robert E, 1949, O 7,27:1
Hannegan, Robert E (est acctg), 1954, Mr 6,1
Hannegan, Robert J, 1951, Ap 15,92:1
Hanneken, George W, 1954, Ag 20,19:6
Hannelly, Charles J, 1945, Ap 27,19:3
Hannen, Lancelot, 1942, Ag 25,23:1
Hannern, R A, 1944, Ja 23,37:3
Hanners, Alva R, 1956, Ag 17,19:1
Hannerty, James J, 1918, Jl 11,11:5
Hannevig, Christopher, 1950, Je 12,27:5
Hannewald, William G, 1960, N 2,39:5
Hanni, Herman, 1953, My 23,15:6
Hannibal, George Henry, 1907, N 11,7:3
Hanniball, Aug, 1940, D 23,19:5
Hanniball, August Jr, 1959, F 25,31:4
Hannigan, Charles B, 1957, Ap 30,30:2
Hannigan, Dennis, 1950, D 27,27:1
Hannigan, Hugh J, 1942, Mr 21,17:2
Hannigan, Hugh L, 1940, Je 23,30:4
Hannigan, James A, 1947, Mr 22,13:1
Hannigan, James W Sr Mrs, 1948, O 2,15:4
Hannigan, John E, 1949, F 27,68:6
Hannigan, Joseph J, 1938, My 9,17:6

Hannigan, Judson, 1959, F 5,31:1
Hannigan, Richard W, 1949, Jl 8,19:1
Hannigan, Stephen I, 1943, Je 15,21:3
Hannigan, Walter J, 1965, Ag 30,25:2
Hannikainen, Tauno, 1968, O 13,84:7
Hannin, Michael P, 1941, Ag 26,19:4
Hanninen, George J, 1953, Jl 28,19:4
Hanning, Helen Mrs, 1942, Ja 20,19:3
Hannington, Walter, 1966, N 19,33:3
Hannon, A Joseph, 1953, Ag 1,11:4
Hannon, Albert H, 1951, My 15,31:2
Hannon, Austin R, 1960, N 17,37:1
Hannon, Francis J, 1944, Ag 6,38:1
Hannon, Frank J Mrs, 1968, Jl 25,33:4
Hannon, George C, 1947, S 30,25:1
Hannon, J M, 1933, Mr 25,15:1
Hannon, J Raymond, 1962, Je 13,41:2
Hannon, J Raymond Mrs, 1946, F 21,21:3
Hannon, John, 1947, Jl 19,13:6
Hannon, John D, 1951, D 2,89:1
Hannon, John J, 1905, S 7,7:6; 1951, S 5,31:5
Hannon, John P, 1954, S 3,17:4
Hannon, John R, 1947, O 16,27:2
Hannon, John W, 1952, S 19,23:2
Hannon, Joseph M, 1945, Ja 10,23:2
Hannon, Patrick J H, 1963, Ja 12,14:5
Hannon, Patrick W, 1952, Mr 29,15:2
Hannon, Robert E Mrs, 1946, My 25,15:2
Hannon, Stephen V, 1965, N 4,47:5
Hannon, Thomas F, 1951, Jl 19,23:5
Hannon, Thomas J, 1957, Je 6,31:2
Hannon, William, 1955, O 4,35:2
Hannong, Lucretia H Mrs, 1951, My 17,31:5
Hannum, Henry O, 1948, Ja 25,56:5
Hannum, John B Jr, 1942, Ja 16,21:2
Hannum, John B Judge, 1937, Ap 21,23:4
Hannum, Joseph, 1903, Je 15,7:6
Hannum, Levi Taylor, 1905, Mr 5,9:4
Hannum, Luther K Rev Dr, 1968, Ap 23,47:1
Hannum, Robert R, 1967, D 21,37:1
Hannweber, Louis, 1940, F 21,19:2
Hannweber, Rose P Mrs, 1940, F 22,23:2
Hanny, William F, 1947, D 21,52:7
Hano, Edward, 1954, O 10,87:1
Hano, Louis C, 1946, Je 12,27:5
Hanold, Frank J, 1938, Ag 15,15:6
Hanold, George C, 1952, Jl 21,26:2
Hanold, William W (por), 1937, My 3,19:4
Hanopole, Jack, 1952, N 12,27:1
Hanotaux, Gabriel (por), 1944, Ap 12,21:3
Hanover, Clinton D Jr, 1965, Jl 9,26:5
Hanover, Clinton D Sr, 1957, Ag 17,15:6
Hanover, Edward A, 1942, Ag 30,42:3
Hanover, Norman, 1953, Ap 11,17:2
Hanrahan, Arthur L, 1951, S 8,17:5
Hanrahan, Daniel A, 1947, N 29,13:1
Hanrahan, David C, 1944, Ja 21,17:6
Hanrahan, Denis A, 1942, Ap 22,23:3
Hanrahan, Edmond M Mrs, 1957, Ja 18,21:1
Hanrahan, Edward M, 1952, O 2,29:5
Hanrahan, Frank R, 1954, S 16,29:5
Hanrahan, James G, 1966, Je 28,42:1
Hanrahan, James M, 1941, S 2,18:2
Hanrahan, John, 1964, Mr 23,29:5
Hanrahan, John E, 1919, Mr 13,11:3
Hanrahan, John H Jr, 1967, Ap 28,41:1
Hanrahan, John H Sr, 1946, Jl 3,25:6
Hanrahan, John T, 1940, Ag 15,19:6
Hanrahan, Joseph P, 1966, Ap 3,84:8
Hanrahan, Michale J, 1955, Ag 9,25:2
Hanrahan, Ralph V, 1951, O 12,27:3
Hanrahan, Raymond L, 1958, N 25,33:2
Hanrahan, Thomas H, 1940, Ja 11,23:4
Hanrahan, William G, 1949, Je 24,23:4
Hanrahan, William M, 1941, Je 18,21:1
Hanratty, Edward J, 1949, Jl 2,15:3
Hanratty, Nathan, 1957, Ja 28,23:3
Hanretty, Francis T, 1940, O 20,49:2
Hanritta, A T, 1952, Ag 25,17:3
Hans, Austin A, 1949, S 4,40:4
Hans, Herman T, 1950, My 7,108:3
Hans, Herman T Mrs, 1951, Jl 31,21:2
Hans, Nicholas W, 1947, N 11,27:4
Hansberry, Lorraine V (funl, Ja 17,88:6; will, Ja 29,25:3), 1965, Ja 13,25:1
Hansbrough, H C, 1933, N 17,19:3
Hanschell, Albert J, 1937, Ag 23,19:3
Hanscom, A J Col, 1907, S 12,7:6
Hanscom, Charles R, 1918, N 1,15:5
Hanscom, Elizabeth D, 1960, F 3,33:4
Hanscom, Howard W Mrs, 1949, O 9,92:4
Hanscom, John Forsyth, 1912, O 1,13:6
Hanscom, M J R, 1882, Jl 17,2:5
Hanscom, Ray P, 1948, Ap 19,23:3
Hanscom, W L, 1881, S 4,2:1
Hanscomb, Charles H, 1949, Ap 26,25:3
Hansel, C, 1936, F 25,23:3
Hansel, Charles F, 1954, F 7,20:3
Hansel, Douglas R, 1968, Ap 24,47:3
Hansel, Herman D, 1956, Mr 27,35:4
Hansel, Howell, 1917, N 6,13:4
Hansel, John, 1957, D 3,35:6
Hansel, Val, 1949, O 27,27:3
Hansell, Charles J, 1951, My 9,33:4
Hansell, Charles L, 1941, O 26,43:2
Hansell, Charles Mrs, 1945, Je 24,22:2
Hansell, Clarence W, 1967, O 24,47:2
Hansell, Elsworth R, 1963, D 27,25:3
Hansell, George B, 1946, My 13,21:3
Hansell, Howard R, 1942, Mr 7,17:4
Hansell, Sven B, 1957, Mr 28,31:1
Hansell, William A, 1943, S 11,13:4
Hanselman, Arthur, 1916, Jl 17,11:2
Hanselman, Fred C, 1948, My 9,70:2
Hanselman, James J Rev, 1920, My 5,11:4
Hanselman, Joseph Francis Father, 1923, Ja 17,17:6
Hanselman, Joseph M Rev, 1911, Jl 26,9:6
Hansen, Abel, 1937, D 15,25:6
Hansen, Agner B, 1948, Jl 6,23:2
Hansen, Albert E, 1951, My 11,27:1
Hansen, Albert Mrs, 1952, O 7,29:4
Hansen, Alfred, 1952, F 13,29:5
Hansen, Alfred Mrs, 1947, S 3,25:5
Hansen, Alice G, 1953, O 20,29:4
Hansen, Allen O (por), 1944, Ja 22,13:5
Hansen, Armin C, 1957, Ap 26,26:1
Hansen, Arthur A, 1942, S 29,24:2
Hansen, August, 1945, Je 11,15:4
Hansen, Axel, 1961, Je 27,33:4
Hansen, Axel W, 1954, N 2,27:6
Hansen, Bjarne G H, 1955, Ja 22,11:1
Hansen, C X, 1941, Ag 16,15:5
Hansen, Canute, 1965, Ap 19,29:4
Hansen, Carl G, 1949, Mr 21,23:4
Hansen, Carl O, 1954, S 2,21:4
Hansen, Carl W, 1961, My 22,31:1
Hansen, Charles A, 1949, O 8,13:1
Hansen, Charles C, 1938, Je 30,23:5
Hansen, Charles C Mrs, 1965, Mr 16,39:2
Hansen, Christian, 1950, N 28,31:3
Hansen, Christian A, 1958, Ja 21,29:4
Hansen, Christian A Mrs, 1957, N 20,32:2
Hansen, Edmond, 1914, Ag 18,9:7
Hansen, Edna J, 1953, N 2,25:5
Hansen, Edward, 1947, O 9,25:1
Hansen, Edward H, 1958, F 22,17:4
Hansen, Ejnar, 1938, My 14,15:2
Hansen, Elwood, 1962, S 5,39:2
Hansen, Eric, 1965, Je 11,31:3
Hansen, Evelyn, 1961, Ag 17,27:5
Hansen, Ferdinand, 1951, D 27,21:5
Hansen, Fred, 1950, S 3,32:5
Hansen, Frederick, 1943, Ap 16,22:2
Hansen, Frederick C, 1942, D 30,23:5
Hansen, Frederick M, 1949, Ag 26,19:4
Hansen, Gerald Mrs, 1948, Je 13,69:1
Hansen, Gottfried Adm, 1937, My 28,21:5
Hansen, H Albert, 1948, O 19,28:2
Hansen, H Emil, 1951, Ja 2,23:3
Hansen, Hans, 1954, Je 6,86:2; 1962, Je 19,35:2
Hansen, Hans C, 1940, Ap 20,17:4; 1953, Mr 15,93:2
Hansen, Hans C (funl, F 29,27:4), 1960, F 20,23:1
Hansen, Hans J, 1937, S 5,II,7:2
Hansen, Hans M K, 1948, O 15,23:2
Hansen, Hans P, 1967, Ja 16,41:2
Hansen, Hans R, 1945, S 20,23:5
Hansen, Harald G, 1946, O 5,17:2
Hansen, Harold, 1962, Jl 16,23:5
Hansen, Harold R, 1966, Ja 26,37:4
Hansen, Harry, 1950, My 8,36:2
Hansen, Harry B, 1956, Ja 16,21:3
Hansen, Harry E, 1954, Jl 12,19:4
Hansen, Hazel D, 1962, D 21,8:6
Hansen, Henry, 1903, Jl 9,7:6; 1925, Jl 18,13:5
Hansen, Henry E, 1961, Jl 3,15:5
Hansen, Henry R, 1944, Ja 7,17:2
Hansen, Herbert V, 1946, S 26,25:5
Hansen, Herman G, 1954, O 27,29:1
Hansen, Howard, 1952, Ap 14,28:2
Hansen, Howard Mrs, 1950, N 25,17:6
Hansen, Howard S, 1949, Ja 23,70:3
Hansen, J M, 1929, D 15,II,7:1
Hansen, J Tofte, 1948, Ja 26,19:3
Hansen, James, 1965, Ap 18,65:6
Hansen, John A, 1954, F 5,20:3
Hansen, John F, 1958, My 28,31:1
Hansen, John G, 1953, O 31,17:4
Hansen, John P, 1965, Ap 12,26:3
Hansen, John V, 1955, My 31,27:4
Hansen, Joseph T, 1950, Mr 11,15:6
Hansen, Juanita, 1961, S 28,41:4
Hansen, Karl J, 1955, N 3,31:3
Hansen, Lewis, 1965, N 19,39:4
Hansen, Louis, 1951, O 27,19:4
Hansen, Marcus L, 1938, My 12,23:5
Hansen, Marius H, 1950, Ap 24,25:4
Hansen, Neils Peter, 1904, Ja 11,2:4
Hansen, Nelson C, 1956, Jl 30,21:3
Hansen, Nicholas, 1945, Ja 24,21:1
Hansen, Niels F, 1949, Jl 24,53:2
Hansen, Ole, 1952, O 1,33:4
Hansen, Ole A, 1949, My 20,27:2
Hansen, Ole M, 1951, Ja 18,27:4
Hansen, Paul F, 1946, My 17,21:2
Hansen, Paul S, 1948, S 27,23:4
Hansen, Peter A, 1937, Mr 12,23:2
Hansen, Peter Andreas, 1874, Ap 2,5:6
Hansen, R E A, 1947, Ag 18,17:3
Hansen, Ralph, 1950, Jl 26,25:3
Hansen, Rasmus, 1949, D 4,108:3; 1952, D 13,15:2
Hansen, Roy L, 1959, Ap 11,21:2
Hansen, Thomas A, 1961, Ja 5,31:4
Hansen, Victor E Mrs, 1944, S 12,19:6
Hansen, William, 1949, O 4,27:5
Hansen, William E, 1963, S 27,29:4
Hansen, William T, 1946, Ap 4,25:4
Hansen, William W, 1949, My 24,27:1
Hansen, William W Mrs, 1949, O 1,28:2
Hanser, Arthur R, 1955, Mr 19,15:5
Hanser, Charles F, 1961, Je 15,43:4
Hanser, Phil, 1949, N 6,92:3
Hansford, Benjamin, 1954, D 3,27:2
Hansford, E S, 1920, O 1,11:3
Hansford, E S Mrs, 1920, O 1,11:3
Hansford, Frank, 1937, Je 16,23:3
Hansford, Monteville M, 1942, Mr 15,42:4
Hansgen, Walter, 1966, Ap 8,21:2
Hansgirg, Fritz J, 1949, Jl 25,15:3
Hansi (J J Waltz), 1951, Je 11,25:4
Hansl, Arthur, 1905, Mr 9,7:6
Hansl, Arthur (cor, Jl 18,25:3), 1946, Jl 17,23:3
Hansl, Raleigh, 1960, Mr 15,39:2
Hanslick, Edward Dr, 1904, Ag 8,7:6
Hansman, William G, 1952, S 11,31:5
Hansmann, Carl A, 1916, Ja 10,11:4
Hansmann, George H, 1949, Ja 30,60:4
Hanson, A Ellis, 1953, F 7,15:2
Hanson, Albert P Mrs, 1962, Ja 13,21:4
Hanson, Alvin E, 1965, N 22,37:3
Hanson, Anton Mrs, 1944, Ap 13,19:3
Hanson, Axel, 1956, Ja 17,33:3
Hanson, Bert, 1938, D 14,25:1
Hanson, Burton, 1922, Ag 6,28:5
Hanson, Burton S Jr, 1959, S 4,21:4
Hanson, Carl F, 1945, Ap 28,15:4
Hanson, Carroll, 1957, D 10,35:3
Hanson, Charles A, 1919, Ap 26,15:4
Hanson, Charles C, 1952, Jl 23,23:5
Hanson, Charles E, 1958, Ag 9,13:7
Hanson, Charles W, 1966, Jl 14,35:2
Hanson, Charles W D, 1959, D 28,23:2
Hanson, Chester P, 1942, Ap 30,19:5
Hanson, Daniel, 1953, Je 13,15:4
Hanson, E Irving, 1955, Ja 17,23:6
Hanson, E Irving Jr, 1943, Ag 18,19:5
Hanson, Edward, 1942, My 16,13:6
Hanson, Edward B, 1952, F 26,27:3
Hanson, Elisha, 1962, Ag 12,81:1
Hanson, Elliott S, 1962, My 8,39:3
Hanson, Ellis M, 1939, Ag 28,19:5
Hanson, Elwood Mrs, 1952, Ap 3,35:1
Hanson, Emil W, 1948, Ag 24,23:4
Hanson, Ernest R, 1959, Ag 15,17:4
Hanson, Ernest W, 1954, D 17,31:1
Hanson, Felix V, 1956, My 26,17:5
Hanson, Florence C Mrs, 1951, F 3,15:5
Hanson, Francis J, 1940, Ja 23,21:3
Hanson, Frank B, 1945, Jl 22,37:2
Hanson, Frank J, 1960, N 9,35:1
Hanson, Frank R, 1964, O 4,89:1
Hanson, Fred J, 1948, F 20,28:2
Hanson, Frederick R, 1964, Jl 5,43:2
Hanson, George J, 1944, Je 29,23:2
Hanson, George McKay, 1924, Ap 6,27:2
Hanson, George W, 1940, N 1,25:6
Hanson, H A Capt, 1937, Ja 20,21:5
Hanson, Halvor C, 1939, D 11,23:6
Hanson, Hans, 1939, My 15,17:6
Hanson, Harry A, 1939, N 20,19:4
Hanson, Harry D, 1944, F 22,23:4
Hanson, Henrietta, 1965, Ja 17,88:4
Hanson, Henry, 1954, O 22,27:2
Hanson, Henry W A, 1962, Jl 3,23:3
Hanson, Herbert C, 1962, Mr 7,35:1
Hanson, Hester, 1952, N 28,25:1
Hanson, Hilding F C, 1952, Mr 11,27:2
Hanson, Horace R, 1942, S 13,53:1
Hanson, Inger-Jo, 1957, D 3,41:2
Hanson, J C M, 1943, N 10,23:3
Hanson, James E, 1966, Mr 15,39:4
Hanson, James W, 1943, O 16,13:3
Hanson, John A, 1961, Ja 27,23:3
Hanson, John E, 1944, My 7,46:1
Hanson, John F Maj, 1910, D 16,11:3
Hanson, John P, 1947, Mr 11,27:1; 1962, Ap 11,43:4
Hanson, Joseph C, 1948, Ag 22,62:6
Hanson, Joseph M, 1963, Jl 9,31:4
Hanson, Joseph Mills, 1921, Ja 12,15:4
Hanson, Joseph W Jr, 1958, Mr 13,29:5
Hanson, Lars, 1965, Ap 9,33:2
Hanson, Leland S, 1966, Ap 4,31:2
Hanson, Leonard G, 1964, O 28,45:1
Hanson, Louis E, 1960, O 25,35:4
Hanson, Louis H, 1954, O 9,17:6
Hanson, Margaret, 1948, F 23,25:4
Hanson, Michael F, 1950, Ja 31,23:1
Hanson, Michael F Mrs, 1940, D 20,25:1
Hanson, Miles, 1948, Je 2,29:3
Hanson, Neils, 1948, Jl 3,15:4

Hanson, Ola Mrs, 1957, Mr 23,19:4
Hanson, Ole (por), 1940, Jl 8,17:4
Hanson, Ole Mrs, 1944, My 14,46:1
Hanson, Oscar B, 1961, S 27,41:3
Hanson, Paul, 1940, O 7,17:2
Hanson, Paul P, 1968, Ap 8,47:1
Hanson, Perry O Mrs, 1951, Ap 10,27:2
Hanson, Peter B, 1965, Ap 16,29:2
Hanson, Peter H, 1953, Ja 26,19:2
Hanson, R D, 1876, Mr 7,5:4
Hanson, R Kent, 1956, Jl 31,23:4
Hanson, R Kent Mrs, 1955, My 11,31:5
Hanson, Raymond O, 1944, Jl 10,15:5
Hanson, Richard B, 1948, Jl 15,23:1
Hanson, Richard L, 1958, Jl 2,29:4
Hanson, Samuel B, 1938, D 5,23:5
Hanson, Stephen H, 1953, Mr 21,17:2
Hanson, Thomas, 1903, Jl 11,7:6
Hanson, Victor H (por), 1945, Mr 8,23:1
Hanson, Virginia L, 1968, Mr 25,41:5
Hanson, Walter P, 1953, Je 12,27:5
Hanson, William, 1954, O 3,86:8
Hanson, William C, 1955, Mr 10,27:2; 1960, N 8,29:3
Hanson, Wyman D, 1950, Ap 13,29:3
Hanssen, Jacob H Mrs, 1953, Mr 21,17:4
Hanssen, Jan M J A, 1958, Je 27,25:1
Hanssen, Klaus Dr, 1915, Ja 4,11:5
Hanssler, John C, 1946, F 10,40:7
Hansson, Kristian G, 1962, Mr 14,39:2
Hansson, Per A, 1946, O 6,59:3
Hanstein, John, 1957, Je 22,15:6
Hanstein, Walter, 1940, Ja 17,21:6
Hanston, Lloyd H Mrs, 1941, S 17,23:3
Hansue, Harris M (por), 1937, Ja 10,II,9:3
Hanszen, Harry, 1950, Ag 27,89:3
Hantke, Arthur, 1955, O 11,39:2
Hantke, Arthur Mrs, 1949, Jl 20,25:1
Hantke, Ernst Dr, 1903, S 14,7:5
Hantman, Harold, 1958, Je 9,23:5
Hanton, Arthur Mrs, 1955, My 22,89:1
Hanton, Carl, 1953, Je 15,29:3
Hanton, Edward L, 1938, My 28,15:7
Hantsche, Albert E, 1951, S 5,31:3
Hantsche, Emil G, 1950, O 4,31:2
Hanus, Josef, 1953, My 23,15:4
Hanus, Paul H, 1941, D 15,19:1
Hanusek, Anton, 1952, Jl 13,61:2
Hanusek, Ernest E, 1952, S 26,21:3
Hanusik, John, 1945, Jl 28,11:6
Hanusovsky, John T, 1960, Ag 14,93:1
Hanvey, James J Sr, 1947, O 13,23:4
Hanway, John, 1962, O 30,35:4
Hanway, P J, 1905, Je 7,9:5
Hanyen, Edward P Mrs, 1944, Ap 11,19:5
Hanzl, William F, 1964, Ap 22,47:4
Hanzlik, Paul J, 1951, F 3,15:3
Hanzsche, Ella B Mrs, 1937, Jl 26,19:6
Hanzsche, William T, 1954, Je 23,26:3
Hapgood, Ernest G, 1953, Ap 4,13:3
Hapgood, Hutchins, 1944, N 19,50:1
Hapgood, Hutchins Mrs, 1951, D 3,31:6
Hapgood, Lyman S, 1950, D 29,19:4
Hapgood, M J, 1926, Je 19,15:4
Hapgood, Norman (por), 1937, Ap 30,22:1
Hapgood, Powers, 1949, F 5,15:1
Hapgood, Thomas L, 1950, S 23,17:2
Hapgood, Walter E, 1949, Ap 13,29:4
Hapgood, William R, 1961, Ja 21,21:3
Happ, Henry, 1947, F 4,25:4
Happ, Lewis, 1953, D 11,31:3
Happ, Lewis H, 1963, Jl 8,29:2
Happer, Andrew P, 1958, D 7,89:1
Happerset, Isaac G, 1907, S 10,7:6
Happich, William F, 1950, D 2,13:4
Happy, Benjamin H, 1938, Jl 11,2:4
Happy, Marvin L, 1960, Jl 4,15:4
Happy, Thirza L, 1953, F 11,29:4
Haps, Henri C, 1960, Je 20,31:4
Hara, Yoshimichi, 1944, Ag 8,17:3
Harada, Tasuku, 1940, F 23,15:3
Haraden, Edward, 1942, Ap 11,13:4
Harahan, James T Jr, 1946, Je 19,21:2
Harahan, William J (por), 1937, D 15,25:1
Harald, Prince of Denmark, 1949, Mr 30,25:2
Haralson, John B (Cap), 1967, Ap 15,31:5
Haralson, Jonathan Justice, 1912, Jl 12,9:4
Haran, Allan T, 1956, N 4,87:3
Harang, Pierre Mrs, 1967, Ag 22,39:1
Harar, Duke of, 1957, My 14,5:3
Harasty, Ernest J, 1968, Je 25,41:2
Harasty, Julius, 1951, S 11,29:3
Haraszthy, Gaza Major, 1879, F 5,3:4
Haray, Joseph Johnston, 1915, My 3,11:2
Harbach, Francis O Mrs, 1954, S 27,21:3
Harbach, Otto A, 1963, Ja 25,11:5
Harbach, Otto Mrs, 1967, S 8,39:2
Harbater, Lester, 1955, O 4,35:5
Harbaugh, Carl, 1960, Mr 1,33:4
Harbaugh, Charles, 1939, Ap 18,23:4
Harbaugh, Corliss E, 1952, D 9,33:1
Harbaugh, Marion D, 1952, Mr 21,23:4
Harbaugh, Thomas C, 1924, O 29,21:2
Harbeck, Eugene R Mrs, 1954, S 23,35:5
Harbeck, Harry S, 1948, Mr 3,23:5
Harbeck, J H, 1878, F 3,6:7
Harbeck, Jervis R, 1939, Mr 2,21:3
Harbeck, John H, 1910, N 9,9:2
Harbeck, Lord, 1876, Jl 16,1:5
Harbeck, W H, 1909, F 17,9:7
Harben, Will N, 1919, Ag 8,9:2
Harbenneau, John C, 1909, Mr 14,11:5
Harber, Giles Bates Adm, 1925, D 31,15:5
Harber, William J, 1952, Ja 16,25:3
Harberger, J S, 1880, O 10,7:5
Harbert, Clarence R, 1951, Je 30,15:4
Harberton, Viscountess, 1911, My 3,13:6
Harbester, Edward Mrs, 1944, Ja 12,23:4
Harbin, Hanson L, 1943, Mr 14,24:4
Harbinson, Alex M, 1958, Ap 10,29:5
Harbison, Andrew B, 1955, Ag 23,23:3
Harbison, Anne, 1938, N 14,19:6
Harbison, Clarence E, 1960, O 3,31:2
Harbison, E Harris, 1964, Jl 15,35:1
Harbison, Frederick, 1941, F 14,18:3
Harbison, Helen D, 1952, O 16,29:4
Harbison, Kitty, 1938, N 14,19:6
Harbison, Robert C, 1937, O 22,19:4
Harbison, Shelby T Mrs, 1923, Ag 14,15:4
Harbison, William A, 1950, S 17,105:1
Harbison, William A Mrs, 1945, D 14,27:3
Harbord, Arthur, 1941, F 25,23:4
Harbord, Frank W, 1943, Ja 3,42:8
Harbord, James G, 1947, Ag 21,23:1
Harbord, James G Mrs (will D 29,13:3), 1937, My 30,18:5
Harbord, John, 1945, Je 27,19:4
Harbottle, Anna Mrs, 1947, Ja 26,53:3
Harbou, James B, 1944, Ap 5,19:2
Harbour, Harry, 1946, Ja 16,23:1
Harbrouck, Harriett, 1947, F 21,19:4
Harburg, E Gordon, 1948, Ag 31,26:1
Harburger, David N, 1905, F 1,5:3
Harburger, George J, 1958, Ja 15,29:1
Harburger, Horace G, 1950, Je 4,92:4
Harburger, Julius, 1914, N 10,11:5
Harburger, Richard L, 1965, Mr 29,33:5
Harbut, Will (por), 1947, O 5,68:4
Harby, Isaac, 1946, O 29,25:1
Harby, Lee Cohen Mrs, 1918, O 22,13:1
Harby, M E Mrs, 1955, S 24,19:5
Harby, Marx E, 1958, Ja 17,25:4
Harcourt, Alfred, 1954, Je 21,23:2
Harcourt, Augustus George Vernon Prof, 1919, S 6, 11:2
Harcourt, Bernard d' Count, 1958, S 7,86:3
Harcourt, Bertram E, 1940, D 10,26:2
Harcourt, C, 1880, O 29,2:3
Harcourt, Cecil, 1959, D 21,27:3
Harcourt, Duke of (Eugene Francois Henrie), 1908, My 18,7:5
Harcourt, Elizabeth Viscountess, 1959, O 31,23:4
Harcourt, Eugene d' Count, 1918, Mr 11,11:6
Harcourt, Frank (S Macnamara), 1955, Ag 4,25:5
Harcourt, George (por), 1947, O 2,27:5
Harcourt, George A, 1939, Je 11,44:7
Harcourt, Herman, 1954, Mr 26,21:4
Harcourt, J T Rev, 1872, Je 1,1:6
Harcourt, Lady (E Suart), 1950, O 26,31:5
Harcourt, Lewis Viscount, 1922, F 25,13:5
Harcourt, Mary E, 1961, Ja 12,29:2
Harcourt, Robert, 1943, Mr 21,26:8
Harcourt, Robert d', 1965, Je 20,72:4
Harcourt, Terence M, 1948, N 4,30:3
Harcourt, Vernon, 1951, Ag 5,73:2
Harcourt, Vivian, 1948, Mr 13,15:4
Harcourt, William Vernon Sir, 1904, O 2,4:3
Harcourt-Smith, Cecil, 1944, Mr 31,21:1
Harcum, O Marvin Mrs, 1958, D 25,2:4
Harcus, A Drummond, 1964, My 11,31:4
Hard, Alfred J (cor, Ag 8,17:3), 1944, Ag 7,15:4
Hard, Anson Wales, 1917, Je 21,13:5
Hard, DeCourcy L, 1966, Jl 13,43:4
Hard, Dudley J, 1950, O 10,31:3
Hard, Fannie B, 1951, Ap 7,15:3
Hard, Frederick H, 1951, Je 20,27:3
Hard, G M, 1926, Je 25,21:5
Hard, James A, 1953, Mr 13,25:4
Hard, James M B, 1943, F 23,21:3
Hard, Melvin, 1880, Ja 9,5:2
Hard, Sherwood M, 1948, D 27,21:1
Hard, Walter, 1946, Ja 9,23:4
Hard, William, 1962, F 1,31:1
Hard, William Mrs, 1961, Ap 14,29:2
Hardacre, Ralph B, 1942, Ja 6,23:2
Hardaloupas, Evangelos T, 1962, Jl 15,61:2
Hardart, Augustin S Mrs, 1940, My 24,19:5
Hardart, Vincent (Bro Altheus Matthew), 1961, N 10,35:4
Hardaway, Joseph B, 1957, F 6,25:4
Hardaway, R Travis, 1961, My 30,17:4
Hardcastle, Corinne B, 1941, Ap 23,21:2
Hardcastle, Edward M Rev, 1909, Ag 16,7:5
Hardcastle, Harry H, 1949, D 4,108:5
Hardcastle, John K Maj, 1937, Ap 22,23:5
Hardcastle, Joseph Prof, 1906, Je 19,9:6
Hardcastle, William B, 1939, Je 2,23:4
Hardcastle, Yellott F, 1951, F 6,27:2
Hardebeck, Carl, 1945, F 12,19:4
Hardee, Cary A, 1957, N 22,25:2
Hardee, Lillian L, 1949, Ag 8,15:2
Hardeen, Theodore (por), 1945, Je 13,23:1
Hardell, John G, 1943, S 29,21:5
Hardell Leonard A, 1960, D 28,27:2
Harden, Archie H, 1949, D 2,29:3
Harden, Arthur, 1940, Je 18,23:2
Harden, Charles H (cor, O 7,29:2), 1967, O 5,39:2
Harden, Edward W, 1952, My 2,25:2
Harden, Edward W Mrs, 1959, Ja 24,19:4
Harden, Grace, 1968, Ag 9,35:5
Harden, Harlan C, 1940, S 21,19:2
Harden, Harry A, 1950, F 15,27:5
Harden, Ivan C, 1940, D 19,25:4
Harden, James, 1914, Ap 7,9:6
Harden, M, 1927, O 31,19:3
Harden, Orville, 1957, Ag 18,44:4
Harden, Ralph C, 1961, Ja 10,47:4
Harden, Robert W, 1961, Ap 19,39:1
Harden, Robert W Mrs, 1967, Ja 18,43:4
Harden, Thomas C, 1925, My 17,6:1
Harden, W Spencer, 1948, Jl 1,23:3
Harden, Walter C, 1950, S 2,15:6
Harden, William H, 1947, N 24,23:4
Hardenberg, Charles L Mrs, 1949, Ja 6,23:2
Hardenbergh, Ambrose, 1966, N 10,47:2
Hardenbergh, Daniel B, 1938, My 8,II,7:2
Hardenbergh, Edmund D Mrs, 1957, Ag 5,21:3
Hardenbergh, Emma A, 1945, Mr 15,23:4
Hardenbergh, George Jr, 1966, S 12,45:4
Hardenbergh, George Rutgers, 1915, Ag 20,11:6
Hardenbergh, Henry, 1955, F 10,31:4
Hardenbergh, Henry Janeway, 1918, Mr 14,13:3
Hardenbergh, J B Dr, 1870, Ja 24,5:5
Hardenbergh, James, 1872, My 1,5:3
Hardenbergh, John Mrs, 1952, N 12,27:5
Hardenbergh, John Warren, 1925, My 20,23:4
Hardenbergh, Raymond W, 1949, F 4,23:4
Hardenbergh, Thomas E, 1957, Ja 11,24:1
Hardenbergh, William P, 1940, D 10,25:2
Hardenbergh, William P Jr, 1948, Je 6,72:5
Hardenbrook, Burt C, 1941, D 22,17:5
Hardenbrook, David L, 1939, Ap 25,23:3
Hardenburg, Earle V, 1950, D 6,33:3
Hardenburg, Reuben H, 1950, Je 17,15:3
Hardenstine, George N, 1951, O 12,27:2
Harder, Charles W, 1956, O 18,33:1
Harder, Edward P, 1947, Je 16,21:6
Harder, George A, 1959, My 30,17:3
Harder, George H, 1947, S 27,15:6
Harder, George N, 1946, My 12,44:1
Harder, Oscar E, 1956, Jl 12,23:4
Harder, Ralph G, 1961, Ap 17,29:4
Harder, Robert L, 1945, O 13,15:2
Harder, Victor A, 1914, Ag 11,9:5
Harder, William H, 1941, Mr 30,49:2
Hardesty, Edmond C, 1940, Mr 5,23:4
Hardesty, Frederick A, 1956, Je 9,17:5
Hardesty, John F, 1953, Je 22,21:1
Hardesty, Medley S, 1940, N 21,30:2
Hardesty, Shortridge, 1956, O 18,33:2
Hardesty, W C, 1962, Ap 20,28:5
Hardgrove, John R, 1947, Ja 12,59:4
Hardgrove, Stewart, 1946, Je 21,23:3
Hardgrove, Thomas E, 1914, S 22,11:6
Hardie, Arthur Mrs, 1916, Jl 14,11:5
Hardie, Francis H Lt-Col, 1912, Ap 27,13:4
Hardie, G W, 1879, Ag 31,6:7
Hardie, George B, 1939, D 11,23:2
Hardie, Harry D, 1953, F 8,88:3
Hardie, J A Gen, 1876, D 16,4:6
Hardie, James B, 1950, Ja 25,28:2
Hardie, James Keir, 1915, S 27,9:5
Hardie, John J, 1943, Ag 26,17:4
Hardie, Joseph P, 1958, Ag 25,21:4
Hardie, R, 1881, Je 29,1:6
Hardie, Robert Gordon, 1904, Ja 10,9:5
Hardie, Thomas M, 1946, Je 3,21:3
Hardie, W J Gen, 1873, N 7,5:3
Hardie, Walter, 1938, Ag 22,30:5
Hardie, William H, 1959, N 2,31:2
Hardigg, Carl A, 1967, F 2,36:1
Hardiman, Alfred F, 1949, Ap 19,25:4
Hardiman, Frank M, 1948, Je 13,68:7
Hardiman, Howard, 1938, Je 11,15:5
Hardiman, James F, 1941, F 6,21:2
Hardiman, James F Mrs, 1945, N 15,19:5
Hardin, Abraham Tracy, 1922, F 23,15:5
Hardin, B Lauriston, 1966, N 5,31:4
Hardin, Charles R, 1951, Je 22,25:1
Hardin, Charles R Mrs (por), 1941, Ap 23,21:5
Hardin, Clara A, 1964, F 22,21:4
Hardin, E B Gen, 1875, N 22,5:3
Hardin, Edel P, 1962, Je 8,31:3
Hardin, Edward J, 1951, Jl 24,25:4
Hardin, Edwin D, 1948, O 14,29:3
Hardin, F Hammond, 1962, Mr 22,35:4
Hardin, John G, 1937, D 17,32:4
Hardin, John H, 1952, S 22,23:4
Hardin, John R (por), 1945, D 8,17:1
Hardin, John R Mrs, 1939, Mr 31,21:4

Hardin, Julia Mrs, 1948, Jl 16,19:2
Hardin, Martin D Brig-Gen, 1923, D 13,21:5
Hardin, Martin D Mrs, 1966, S 7,41:4
Hardin, William B, 1943, D 27,19:1
Harding, Alfred A, 1958, D 4,39:4
Harding, Alfred Bp, 1923, My 1,21:4
Harding, America L M Mrs, 1944, Je 28,23:2
Harding, Arthur E, 1941, Ja 8,19:5
Harding, Arthur H, 1952, F 10,93:2
Harding, Arthur M, 1947, D 26,15:2
Harding, Augustus J, 1967, Ag 30,43:3
Harding, B F Dr, 1923, Mr 25,6:2
Harding, Bertha E, 1958, Ja 8,47:1
Harding, Caroline, 1946, Ja 8,23:1
Harding, Charles, 1939, Mr 1,21:1; 1943, D 11,15:5; 1954, D 24,13:2
Harding, Charles F, 1942, Ap 14,21:6
Harding, Charles F Jr, 1940, Ag 16,15:3
Harding, Charles L, 1944, F 20,36:4; 1953, S 24,33:3
Harding, Charles T, 1939, Mr 27,15:2
Harding, Chester, 1866, Ap 4,1:7
Harding, Chester E, 1945, My 30,19:3
Harding, Clark J Mrs, 1959, Mr 17,30:5
Harding, E (Signor Blitz), 1880, N 18,2:7
Harding, Earl, 1965, Mr 2,38:4
Harding, Earl Mrs, 1964, O 10,29:2
Harding, Edward, 1952, Ja 10,29:3
Harding, Edward J, 1940, O 6,49:2
Harding, Edward Mrs, 1938, Ap 18,15:6; 1953, Jl 7, 27:3
Harding, Edward N, 1938, Ag 29,13:4
Harding, Edwin R, 1943, F 19,19:4
Harding, Elizabeth, 1958, F 19,27:4
Harding, Elizabeth B F Mrs, 1955, N 16,35:4
Harding, Ernest A, 1942, Jl 17,15:5
Harding, Eugene C, 1944, Ag 12,11:5
Harding, Eva Dr, 1920, Jl 28,13:5
Harding, Florence King Mrs (funl, N 24,17:3), 1924, N 23,7:1
Harding, Florence Mrs, 1940, Ap 14,45:2
Harding, Frank, 1939, Jl 19,19:6
Harding, Frank F Capt, 1937, N 21,II,9:1
Harding, Frank W, 1951, O 21,92:7
Harding, Fred C, 1950, O 21,17:2
Harding, G T, 1928, N 20,31:3
Harding, G T Jr, 1934, Ja 19,19:1
Harding, G W Dr, 1903, Ja 15,9:6
Harding, Gardner L (por), 1940, Mr 21,25:1
Harding, Gardner Mrs (Mabel D), 1965, Mr 18,33:5
Harding, George, 1902, N 19,9:6
Harding, George F, 1939, Ap 3,15:2
Harding, George Franklin, 1915, D 28,11:3
Harding, George J 2d, 1951, Ag 26,80:4
Harding, George M, 1959, Mr 28,17:2
Harding, George T Mrs, 1955, Jl 28,23:6; 1964, N 26, 33:2
Harding, George W, 1905, Mr 11,9:4
Harding, Gilbert C, 1960, N 17,37:2
Harding, Goodwin M, 1951, My 13,88:5
Harding, Granville, 1950, Je 15,31:5
Harding, H J, 1928, Mr 21,29:5
Harding, Harold J, 1952, O 27,27:5
Harding, Harry E, 1956, D 20,29:5
Harding, Henry L, 1949, Je 13,19:3
Harding, Horace E, 1963, My 26,92:6
Harding, Horace W, 1965, My 12,47:4
Harding, Hugo, 1948, N 28,92:3
Harding, J H, 1929, Ja 5,19:3
Harding, J Morgan, 1963, O 20,88:3
Harding, Jack, 1968, My 28,47:3
Harding, Jack E, 1954, Ap 18,89:2
Harding, James, 1906, S 17,9:6
Harding, James G, 1951, Jl 10,27:4
Harding, James P, 1953, Ap 23,29:3
Harding, Jasper, 1865, Ag 26,2:5
Harding, John, 1939, F 10,23:5
Harding, John C D, 1937, My 29,17:4
Harding, John P, 1943, Mr 13,13:2; 1958, Ja 28,27:1
Harding, John V, 1961, Ag 21,23:4
Harding, John W, 1953, Mr 12,27:1
Harding, Joseph J, 1937, Jl 23,19:5; 1960, O 25,35:3
Harding, Julia M, 1943, Jl 11,34:6
Harding, Kathleen (Mrs J J Snyder), 1958, F 3,23:2
Harding, Leroy Lawerre, 1953, F 16,21:1
Harding, Lewis M, 1952, F 12,27:1
Harding, Lillie W Mrs, 1948, S 8,29:3
Harding, Louis R, 1949, D 28,32:3
Harding, Lyn, 1952, D 27,10:3
Harding, Malcolm T M, 1949, Ap 22,23:3
Harding, Margaret, 1924, Ja 28,15:3
Harding, Mary E, 1948, Ag 27,18:3
Harding, Michael J, 1946, N 18,23:5
Harding, Nelson (por), 1945, Ja 2,19:3
Harding, Patrick F, 1949, Ap 3,76:8
Harding, Patrick H, 1948, Ap 27,25:3
Harding, Paul C, 1950, N 1,35:5
Harding, Richard, 1943, D 12,45:3
Harding, Richard R, 1947, F 15,15:3
Harding, Richard R Mrs, 1945, Mr 17,13:4
Harding, Richard T, 1952, Ag 6,21:3
Harding, Russell, 1908, Mr 4,7:6
Harding, S Lawrence, 1948, My 19,27:1
Harding, Samuel B, 1955, Ja 8,13:4
Harding, Samuel G Capt, 1937, Ap 13,25:2
Harding, Thomas E W, 1950, Ag 18,21:2
Harding, Thomas J Mrs, 1958, Mr 15,17:1
Harding, Victor, 1954, S 10,23:4
Harding, Victor M, 1945, O 25,21:3
Harding, Walter C, 1956, O 21,86:5
Harding, Walter H, 1950, N 21,31:1
Harding, William B, 1944, Ja 5,17:4
Harding, William B (funl plans, Jl 2,35:1; mem ser set, Jl 3,17:3), 1967, Jl 1,23:5
Harding, William B Mrs, 1955, D 9,27:2
Harding, William H, 1919, Je 10,13:4; 1955, O 1,19:6
Harding, William J, 1952, My 14,27:4
Harding, William J Col, 1918, F 15,9:5
Harding, William Mrs, 1946, Ja 12,15:4
Harding, William N Sr, 1951, N 18,90:2
Harding, William P G, 1930, Ap 8,29:3
Harding, William R, 1949, D 28,32:1
Harding, William T, 1958, S 7,86:3
Hardinge, Hal W (por), 1943, S 16,21:3
Hardinge, Lord, 1944, Ag 3,19:3
Hardinge, Winifred Selina Lady, 1914, Jl 12,5:4
Hardinge of Penhurst, Alex H L Lord, 1960, My 30, 17:3
Hardingham, Walter R H, 1938, N 20,38:8
Hardison, Frank H, 1942, Ap 1,21:5
Hardle, Wainwright, 1911, N 21,9:5
Hardman, Herbert V, 1966, S 5,15:5
Hardman, J B S, 1968, Ja 31,38:7
Hardman, J B S Mrs, 1953, Je 30,23:5
Hardman, James A, 1961, S 14,31:1
Hardman, James A Mrs, 1943, Ja 22,20:2
Hardman, John S Dr, 1922, Jl 5,19:6
Hardman, William H, 1956, My 23,31:3
Hardman Lamartine G Dr (por), 1937, F 19,19:4
Hardon, Cora B Mrs, 1939, D 8,25:4
Hardon, Henry K, 1941, Jl 30,17:2
Hardoon, Liza Mrs, 1941, O 4,15:2
Hardorove, Timothy A, 1953, D 17,37:2
Hards, Ira A, 1938, My 4,23:5
Hardstaff, Joe, 1947, Ap 4,24:3
Hardt, Curt B, 1941, O 17,23:6
Hardt, Ernest, 1947, Ja 10,22:2
Hardt, Frank M (por), 1949, Ja 31,19:1
Hardt, John P Mrs, 1961, Jl 31,19:5
Hardtke, Webster A, 1947, S 27,15:4
Hardwell, Allen, 1910, Ap 30,9:6
Hardwell, James, 1921, Je 22,15:1
Hardwell, Oswald R Mrs, 1946, My 22,21:4
Hardwick, C Z, 1967, My 14,87:1
Hardwick, Charles T Mrs, 1943, My 3,17:2
Hardwick, Gordon A Mrs, 1954, Mr 28,88:4
Hardwick, Hiram B, 1950, D 29,19:3
Hardwick, Huntington R (Tack), 1949, Je 27,28:2
Hardwick, Melbourne H, 1916, O 26,11:5
Hardwick, Thomas W, 1944, F 1,19:6
Hardwick, Thomas W Mrs, 1937, Jl 13,20:2
Hardwick, Watson, 1952, Je 16,17:2
Hardwick, William H, 1955, N 24,29:2
Hardwick Herbert, 1955, Mr 17,45:3
Hardwicke, A H G Maj, 1922, Jl 11,15:3
Hardwicke, Cedric (funl, Ag 11,33:5; will, S 10,29:1), 1964, Ag 7,29:1
Hardwicke, Earl of, 1873, S 18,4:6
Hardwicke, Henry Mrs, 1947, Mr 8,13:5
Hardwicke, Henry S W, 1939, My 13,15:5
Hardwood, James E Sr, 1939, My 6,17:3
Hardy, A B C, 1946, N 24,76:5
Hardy, A H, 1950, Ag 15,30:2
Hardy, Albert S, 1953, My 13,29:5
Hardy, Alpheus S, 1943, Ag 5,15:2
Hardy, Alpheus S Mrs, 1955, N 16,35:5
Hardy, Anna L, 1951, O 6,19:4
Hardy, Arthur S, 1943, Jl 5,15:6
Hardy, Arthur T, 1940, Je 8,15:6
Hardy, Ashley, 1940, Jl 30,19:4
Hardy, Audubon L, 1943, O 18,15:2
Hardy, Benjamin, 1951, D 24,1:1
Hardy, Benjamin H, 1943, Jl 16,17:1
Hardy, C M, 1903, My 3,9:6
Hardy, Caldwell, 1923, Ag 27,11:3
Hardy, Charles, 1945, Je 10,32:5
Hardy, Charles A, 1948, Ap 1,25:4
Hardy, Charles H, 1942, Jl 7,20:3
Hardy, Charles J, 1956, Ja 18,31:1
Hardy, Charles J Mrs, 1956, Ag 13,19:5
Hardy, Charles O, 1948, D 1,29:3
Hardy, Charles S, 1945, Ap 22,36:1
Hardy, Cherry, 1963, D 27,25:1
Hardy, Clarence L, 1950, O 29,93:1
Hardy, Cosmo F, 1964, Ap 21,33:4
Hardy, Cullen B, 1959, N 21,23:3
Hardy, David A, 1940, Ap 23,24:2
Hardy, David P, 1957, S 18,33:4
Hardy, Delphia, 1947, N 1,15:5
Hardy, Don, 1966, Je 6,41:2
Hardy, E A, 1952, N 2,88:2
Hardy, Edward R, 1951, Je 30,15:6
Hardy, Edwin N, 1950, Ag 17,27:6
Hardy, Emma K Mrs, 1938, Je 23,21:5
Hardy, Ernest George Dr, 1925, O 27,23:2
Hardy, Franklin E, 1951, Ap 20,29:2
Hardy, Gaston, 1925, N 24,25:3
Hardy, George, 1937, Mr 20,3:1
Hardy, George C, 1950, Mr 15,29:3
Hardy, George E, 1946, S 8,44:6
Hardy, George E (por), 1949, Jl 1,19:4
Hardy, George F, 1947, O 3,26:2
Hardy, George J, 1943, Je 1,23:3
Hardy, George W, 1950, F 25,17:4
Hardy, Godfrey H, 1947, D 2,29:1
Hardy, Grace A B Mrs, 1940, Je 25,23:6
Hardy, Guy, 1946, My 6,21:3
Hardy, Guy H, 1947, Ja 27,23:2
Hardy, H Reginald, 1959, Je 28,69:1
Hardy, Hippolyte L, 1942, Jl 11,13:2
Hardy, Horace W, 1954, Je 9,31:5
Hardy, J Gordon, 1956, D 15,25:3
Hardy, J Martin, 1957, Ja 28,23:4
Hardy, J Rufus, 1959, S 4,21:2
Hardy, Jack W, 1955, Jl 4,11:5
Hardy, James E, 1939, My 13,15:6
Hardy, James G, 1953, S 8,31:4
Hardy, James H, 1949, Ja 17,19:4
Hardy, James T, 1945, Mr 11,40:3
Hardy, John, 1953, O 10,17:5
Hardy, John A Sr, 1938, F 26,15:3
Hardy, John C, 1938, O 31,15:5
Hardy, John D, 1954, N 22,23:3
Hardy, John F, 1949, F 26,15:1
Hardy, John G, 1943, My 15,6:1; 1952, Mr 6,31:3
Hardy, John Henry Justice, 1917, O 12,11:6
Hardy, Joseph, 1942, Mr 7,17:5
Hardy, Karl J, 1950, Ag 30,31:2
Hardy, Kate, 1940, O 7,17:5
Hardy, Lamar, 1950, Ag 19,13:3
Hardy, LeGrand H, 1954, Ap 15,29:1
Hardy, LeGrand H Mrs (S Haigh), 1956, N 9,29:3
Hardy, Leonard F, 1943, Mr 25,21:3
Hardy, Lowell E, 1951, Ap 15,92:6
Hardy, Marjorie, 1948, Je 22,25:2
Hardy, Mary C, 1960, My 5,35:3
Hardy, Oliver (trb, Ag 9,18:3; funl, Ag 10,15:5), 1957, Ag 8,23:4
Hardy, Oscar J, 1950, Ag 7,19:4
Hardy, R, 1927, Ag 15,17:5
Hardy, Ralph W, 1957, Ag 6,27:4
Hardy, Robert Boyd, 1916, Ja 26,11:3
Hardy, Robert H, 1942, Jl 13,15:4
Hardy, Rodney, 1904, Ja 27,13:1
Hardy, Roger W, 1957, D 13,27:1
Hardy, Roy M, 1953, O 5,27:1
Hardy, Samuel P, 1953, Ja 27,25:3
Hardy, Sarah Abigail Mrs, 1918, S 15,23:1
Hardy, Stanton M Dr, 1968, Mr 1,43:8
Hardy, Theodore E, 1949, F 13,77:1
Hardy, Thomas Mrs (por), 1937, O 18,17:2
Hardy, Toney A Mrs, 1962, Je 7,35:4
Hardy, W H Judge, 1917, F 19,11:4
Hardy, Walter A, 1941, Mr 25,26:1
Hardy, William H, 1919, N 2,22:3
Hardy, William M Mrs, 1956, S 30,86:1
Hardy, William N, 1950, F 28,29:5
Hardyman, Hugh, 1960, Ap 7,35:2
Hare, A J C, 1903, Ja 23,9:2
Hare, Alfred Mrs, 1950, My 2,29:3
Hare, Burton L, 1942, My 23,13:6
Hare, Charles H, 1947, Ja 23,26:1
Hare, Charles W, 1942, D 7,27:3
Hare, Clair G, 1959, Jl 11,19:5
Hare, Dudley, 1957, F 11,35:1
Hare, Emlen S, 1962, Mr 11,86:8
Hare, Ernest (por), 1939, Mr 10,23:1
Hare, H A, 1931, Je 16,27:3
Hare, H B, 1879, Mr 25,5:4
Hare, Herman G Mrs, 1958, My 29,27:2
Hare, Hobart N, 1966, Jl 28,33:1
Hare, Horace B, 1956, Jl 17,23:2
Hare, Hugh F, 1967, Jl 20,37:4
Hare, J Knowles, 1947, F 28,24:2
Hare, J M, 1928, Jl 15,23:1
Hare, J Madison, 1938, O 8,17:6
Hare, James H (por), 1946, Je 25,21:3
Hare, James J Mrs, 1945, Jl 18,27:5
Hare, Jay V, 1953, N 22,88:2
Hare, John C, 1945, My 24,19:3
Hare, John E, 1950, Ag 12,13:3
Hare, John R Mrs, 1956, Ja 21,21:5
Hare, John Sir, 1921, D 29,15:4
Hare, Joseph B, 1947, Je 6,24:2
Hare, Lumsden, 1964, S 1,36:2
Hare, Marmaduke, 1942, D 13,75:5
Hare, Meredith Mrs, 1948, Ag 23,17:3
Hare, Montgomery Mrs, 1962, Je 19,35:3
Hare, Morin S, 1955, N 14,27:5
Hare, N D, 1877, D 11,4:7
Hare, Russell I, 1955, Ap 22,25:3
Hare, S Herbert, 1960, Ap 20,39:4
Hare, Silas, 1908, N 28,9:5
Hare, T Truxtun, 1956, F 4,19:4
Hare, Thomas, 1879, Ap 8,4:7; 1938, F 27,II,8:8
Hare, Thomas W, 1965, D 9,47:3
Hare, Walter B, 1950, Jl 4,17:3
Hare, William C, 1945, Je 23,13:3
Hare, William C Jr, 1955, F 5,15:4
Hare, William E, 1959, Je 8,27:5

Hare, William H, 1960, Ap 14,37:4
Hare, William Hobart Bp, 1909, O 24,13:2
Hare, William S, 1950, Ja 24,31:2
Harer, Frederick W, 1948, Ap 28,27:3
Harer, William B, 1945, O 12,23:4
Harer, William B Mrs, 1942, Mr 25,21:4
Harewood, Earl of, 1947, My 25,60:1
Harewood, J DaCosta, 1957, My 16,31:2
Harewood, Lady, 1943, My 8,15:3
Harff, Frank R, 1940, Je 1,15:4
Harff, Henry, 1946, O 10,27:5
Harfield, W Redett, 1955, S 8,31:4
Harford, Austin, 1944, O 4,19:1
Harford, D William, 1958, N 19,37:4
Harford, David W, 1963, N 3,88:1
Harford, Everett D, 1960, Ap 26,37:3
Harford, Harry, 1925, S 22,25:4
Harford, Lloyd G, 1952, N 23,88:1
Hargadon, Francis B, 1955, Ap 13,29:1
Hargadon, Leo I, 1952, Jl 18,19:5
Hargan, David D, 1958, My 15,29:3
Hargan, Martha M Mrs, 1940, Jl 6,15:6
Hargedon, Joseph M, 1955, F 21,21:1
Harger, Charles M, 1955, Ap 4,29:1
Harger, Edgar B, 1946, F 23,13:4
Harger, George D, 1942, Ja 28,19:4
Harger, Line, 1951, D 27,21:1
Hargest, William M, 1948, F 17,25:4
Hargett, Carol Mrs, 1950, Ja 11,30:5
Hargis, Thomas, 1951, S 24,27:4
Hargous, Robert L, 1905, N 26,9:4
Hargrave, Arthur A, 1957, S 14,19:6
Hargrave, Charles Mrs, 1949, Je 1,31:2
Hargrave, Edward J Mrs, 1951, Jl 25,23:1
Hargrave, Elmer, 1948, N 2,25:3
Hargrave, Frank S, 1942, Mr 12,19:5
Hargrave, Frederic C Mrs, 1950, Ag 16,29:4
Hargrave, Homer P, 1964, F 4,30:8
Hargrave, Thomas J, 1962, F 22,25:4
Hargrave, William, 1942, O 4,53:2
Hargraves, John W, 1945, Mr 12,19:4
Hargraves, Thomas W, 1954, D 8,35:1
Hargreaves, A P L Mrs, 1934, N 17,15:1
Hargreaves, Frederick H, 1941, Jl 24,17:6
Hargreaves, George T (por), 1942, Ap 23,23:3
Hargreaves, Herbert J, 1938, Jl 14,21:4
Hargreaves, James H, 1937, Ap 24,19:2
Hargreaves, John, 1953, Ja 17,16:3
Hargreaves, John M, 1959, Je 7,86:3
Hargreaves, Joseph W, 1912, Je 1,11:4
Hargreaves, R T, 1939, Mr 7,22:3
Hargreaves, Richard L, 1941, N 13,27:2
Hargreaves, William, 1956, My 4,25:3
Hargreaves, William T Mrs, 1950, D 31,42:7
Hargrove, George C, 1964, D 2,50:5
Hargrove, Henry L, 1938, Mr 15,23:1
Hargrove, Pinckney S, 1941, Ap 11,21:4
Hargrove, Reginald H, 1954, Ja 11,5:3
Hargrove, Robert H Jr, 1941, Ja 31,19:4
Hargus, Lee M, 1960, Mr 18,25:1
Harig, John J, 1952, Mr 27,29:2
Hariman O B, 1926, My 2,1:7
Haring, Alex, 1960, Mr 15,39:2
Haring, Charles F, 1960, Ag 28,83:3
Haring, Charles F Mrs, 1952, O 21,29:3
Haring, Charles H, 1939, S 19,26:3
Haring, Clarence H, 1960, S 5,15:6
Haring, Clarence M, 1951, Jl 11,23:3
Haring, David W, 1874, Ja 16,2:6
Haring, Forrest C, 1952, Jl 11,17:6
Haring, George Mrs, 1937, Mr 16,23:5
Haring, Harry, 1948, D 12,92:5
Haring, Harry A, 1937, O 13,23:4
Haring, Horace E, 1957, N 13,32:4
Haring, J Elliott Mrs, 1939, Ja 27,19:6
Haring, J Vreeland, 1954, O 3,86:3
Haring, Malcolm M, 1952, Ja 2,25:2
Haring, William P, 1958, Ja 30,23:4
Harington, Cecilia, 1947, Mr 21,22:3
Harington, Charles H (por), 1940, O 24,25:3
Harington, E C Rev, 1881, Jl 19,5:4
Harinxma Thoe Slooten, Pieter A V van, 1954, Ag 6, 17:5
Harison, Elizabeth, 1956, O 19,27:2
Harison, William, 1948, Ag 26,21:5
Harison, William Benjamin, 1921, Je 8,17:6
Harjes, Charles B, 1952, Mr 20,33:5
Harjes, Fred H, 1947, N 8,17:1
Harjes, H H Col, 1926, Ag 22,1:4
Harjes, John H, 1914, F 16,7:5
Harkavy, Alex, 1939, N 28,26:2
Harkavy, El Hanan Prof, 1916, Ap 29,11:6
Harkavy, Harold J, 1965, N 30,41:1
Harkavy, Irving A, 1952, My 6,29:3
Harkavy, J Bernard, 1956, Mr 26,29:4
Harker, Alfred, 1939, Jl 30,29:2
Harker, Gen, 1864, Ag 3,5:3
Harker, Herbert L, 1940, Jl 20,15:5
Harker, John Mrs, 1950, N 21,31:4
Harker, Joseph, 1902, Ja 7,7:5
Harker, Joseph R, 1938, Jl 9,13:4
Harker, Joseph R Mrs, 1947, Jl 19,13:6
Harker, Lewis Emory, 1918, Ap 13,13:5
Harker, Mason, 1950, Ja 20,25:3
Harker, Nancy E, 1957, D 13,18:3
Harker, Richard F, 1961, N 26,87:5
Harkey, Tula Lake, 1918, D 31,11:3
Harkins, Anne K, 1954, N 16,29:1
Harkins, Bernard F, 1964, F 18,35:3
Harkins, Charles B, 1966, My 4,47:3
Harkins, D H Mrs, 1878, Ag 30,5:5
Harkins, Daniel J, 1947, O 21,23:2
Harkins, Daniel J Sr, 1956, Ja 17,33:4
Harkins, Dixie (Mrs C Carter), 1963, S 2,15:5
Harkins, George Mrs, 1942, N 15,59:3
Harkins, James W, 1943, Jl 10,13:2
Harkins, John, 1940, N 19,24:3; 1944, Mr 22,19:5
Harkins, John J, 1948, Ap 23,23:1
Harkins, Mary E Mrs, 1939, Ja 27,19:2
Harkins, Matthew W Bp, 1921, My 26,13:3
Harkins, P Bertram, 1964, S 15,37:5
Harkins, Percy S, 1953, Mr 17,29:1
Harkins, Phil J, 1937, N 18,23:2
Harkins, Robert, 1950, Mr 1,27:4
Harkins, Susan G, 1937, O 13,23:1
Harkins, Thomas J Mrs, 1957, D 7,21:1
Harkins, William D, 1951, Mr 8,29:2
Harkins, William F, 1951, S 5,31:2
Harkins, William J, 1945, Ag 26,44:5
Harkins, William S, 1945, Jl 3,13:6
Harkless, James H, 1940, Ja 27,13:5
Harkless, John E Sr, 1951, O 7,86:8
Harkness, A M R Mrs, 1926, Mr 28,26:1
Harkness, Alan, 1952, Mr 4,35:8
Harkness, Albert Granger Prof, 1923, Ja 30,17:4
Harkness, Albert Prof, 1907, My 27,7:6
Harkness, Andrew H, 1943, Mr 2,19:1
Harkness, Charles W Mrs, 1916, D 9,11:3
Harkness, Charles William, 1916, My 2,13:5
Harkness, Edward B, 1951, Jl 27,19:6
Harkness, Edward S, 1940, Ja 30,1:2
Harkness, Edward S Mrs, 1950, Je 7,29:1
Harkness, Edward S Mrs (est acctg), 1954, O 16, 19:7
Harkness, Horace L, 1954, Je 26,13:4
Harkness, Isabel, 1941, N 18,25:1
Harkness, J Rev, 1878, Jl 6,5:3
Harkness, James H, 1941, Ap 23,21:4
Harkness, Jeanette Mrs, 1941, My 24,15:3
Harkness, LeRoy T, 1957, Ja 13,84:1
Harkness, Leroy T Mrs, 1956, Mr 9,23:1
Harkness, Loring E, 1941, My 24,15:5
Harkness, Mary A Mrs, 1938, My 12,23:5
Harkness, Norris Worrell, 1910, Ag 11,7:6
Harkness, W J K, 1960, Jl 7,31:6
Harkness, William Adm, 1903, Mr 1,7:4
Harkness, William H, 1937, D 8,25:5; 1954, Ag 14,15:5
Harkness, William H Jr Mrs (por), 1947, Jl 21,17:3
Harkness, William J (Pop), 1965, Ja 24,80:8
Harkness, William L, 1919, My 11,22:5
Harkness, William L Mrs, 1947, Ja 15,25:5
Harkrader, Harry W, 1940, N 20,21:3
Harkrader, Susan W Mrs, 1937, Mr 1,19:2
Harkrader, Tullis T, 1944, F 7,15:5
Harks, Anna (Mother Mary Evarista), 1943, Ag 3, 19:1
Harl, Maple T, 1957, Ap 18,29:1
Harlan, Andrew T Judge, 1907, My 20,9:6
Harlan, Anna S, 1963, Jl 9,31:1
Harlan, B A Judge, 1912, Ja 28,II,13:4
Harlan, Bruce, 1959, Je 23,33:4
Harlan, Byron B, 1949, N 12,15:2
Harlan, Edgar R, 1941, Jl 14,13:2
Harlan, Edwin H W, 1939, Ag 8,17:2
Harlan, George C Dr, 1909, S 26,13:4
Harlan, George S, 1938, Ja 6,19:5
Harlan, Harry V, 1944, N 8,17:2
Harlan, Henry D, 1943, S 7,23:2
Harlan, Homer B Mrs, 1954, D 17,31:1
Harlan, John M Mrs, 1957, O 23,33:3
Harlan, John Marshall Justice (funl, O 18,11:4), 1911, O 16,11:5
Harlan, John Mrs, 1916, O 10,11:6
Harlan, Kenneth, 1967, Mr 8,45:3
Harlan, Laura, 1949, Ja 19,27:4
Harlan, Otis (por), 1940, Ja 21,35:1
Harlan, S Jr, 1883, F 7,5:5
Harlan, Scott P, 1948, Ja 2,23:3
Harlan, Veit, 1964, Ap 14,37:1
Harlan, William H, 1942, Ag 28,19:5
Harland, Edward Brig-Gen, 1915, Mr 11,11:4
Harland, Henry, 1905, D 22,9:5
Harland, John, 1947, F 27,21:2
Harland, Marion, 1922, Je 4,28:3
Harland, Marion (Mrs Edw Payson Terhune), 1922, Je 7,19:5
Harland, W G B Dr, 1907, S 15,9:6
Harlang, Julius, 1940, Je 3,15:3
Harle, Hugh C, 1955, Ag 11,21:6
Harlech, Lady (Mrs David Ormsby Gore),(funl, Je 3,31:3), 1967, My 31,49:1
Harlech, Lord, 1938, My 9,7:1
Harlech, Lord (W G A Ormsby Gore), 1964, F 15, 23:1
Harlem, Herbert, 1952, Ja 17,28:2
Harless, N B, 1939, Ja 4,21:4
Harley, C E, 1903, My 14,9:6
Harley, Edward A, 1941, Jl 10,19:1
Harley, Edward A Father, 1924, D 12,21:3
Harley, Edward J, 1955, N 28,31:4
Harley, Francis L, 1952, My 11,92:6
Harley, George B, 1959, Ja 27,33:3
Harley, George G, 1939, Ap 27,25:2
Harley, Halvor L, 1957, Mr 18,27:2
Harley, Herbert L, 1951, F 14,30:3
Harley, J Harry, 1944, Ja 9,42:1
Harley, J R, 1947, Ap 30,25:3
Harley, James W, 1966, Je 30,39:4
Harley, John D, 1916, F 15,11:6
Harley, John E, 1957, S 8,84:6
Harley, John H, 1947, Ja 12,59:4
Harley, John J, 1923, Jl 26,15:4
Harley, Joseph C, 1942, O 24,15:3
Harley, Joseph E (por), 1942, F 28,17:3
Harley, Joseph Jr, 1951, S 21,12:1
Harley, Michael F, 1925, O 1,27:5; 1925, O 2,23:5; 1925, O 4,5:3
Harley, Richard J, 1952, Ap 4,25:4
Harley, William, 1939, Jl 30,29:3
Harley, William B Jr, 1956, D 11,39:4
Harley, William B Sr, 1939, Ag 25,15:3
Harley, William H, 1947, My 15,26:2
Harlin, H Jacob, 1943, S 15,27:5
Harlin, John, 1966, Mr 23,19:4
Harling, W Franke, 1958, N 23,88:3
Harllee, William C (por), 1944, N 22,19:6
Harloe, Frank J, 1966, Ag 2,31:5
Harloe, William L, 1941, Jl 13,28:8
Harloe, William V, 1957, Jl 29,19:3
Harlow, Alvin F, 1963, N 19,42:2
Harlow, Arthur B, 1951, S 4,27:2
Harlow, Arthur H, 1958, F 21,23:2
Harlow, Arthur H Jr, 1966, Mr 26,29:3
Harlow, August D, 1944, My 24,19:6
Harlow, Augustus D Mrs, 1954, O 24,88:7
Harlow, George A, 1950, My 27,17:6
Harlow, Gertrude C Mrs, 1947, Ag 23,13:4
Harlow, Haddesa Hamilton Mrs, 1907, Je 18,7:5
Harlow, Harry Addison Rev, 1913, Je 29,5:5
Harlow, Jean, 1937, Je 8,1:4
Harlow, John B, 1945, My 17,19:2
Harlow, John M, 1907, My 14,11:6
Harlow, Lloyd N, 1954, Je 1,27:1
Harlow, Louis, 1937, S 20,23:2
Harlow, Mabel, 1940, Ja 14,42:5
Harlow, Maurice, 1925, F 26,21:4
Harlow, Ralph L, 1960, O 11,45:2
Harlow, Ralph V, 1956, O 4,33:5
Harlow, Richard, 1920, F 19,11:4
Harlow, Richard C (Dick), 1962, F 20,35:2
Harlow, Robert E, 1954, N 16,29:1
Harlow, Sarah Mrs, 1953, Ja 1,23:3
Harlow, Skip D, 1947, F 24,19:3
Harlow, William A, 1953, Je 9,27:4
Harlow, William Mrs, 1952, D 15,25:4
Harlow, William P Col, 1904, D 7,1:6
Harman, Albert S, 1952, Ja 9,29:1
Harman, Alpha S, 1947, S 12,21:5
Harman, Archer, 1911, O 10,13:5
Harman, Arthur W, 1958, Ap 3,31:3
Harman, Asher W, 1952, F 16,13:4
Harman, Austin M, 1950, Je 30,23:6
Harman, Bryant, 1945, Mr 9,19:4
Harman, Charles F Mrs, 1940, Ap 5,21:1
Harman, Frank S, 1964, Je 9,35:3
Harman, Frederick M, 1942, S 27,48:7
Harman, George W Mrs, 1954, Ag 13,15:5
Harman, J F, 1936, N 26,31:1
Harman, John N (por), 1939, N 7,25:3
Harman, John W, 1904, Ja 8,7:5
Harman, Martin C King of Lundy Is, 1954, D 7,
Harman, Patrick H, 1958, N 30,86:1
Harman, Pinckney J, 1966, My 14,31:6
Harman, S Willard, 1948, Mr 18,27:1
Harman-Ashley, John Jr, 1949, Mr 3,25:6
Harman-Ashley, Raymond, 1947, D 2,29:4
Harmans, William F, 1942, Ja 8,21:3
Harmati, S, 1936, Ap 6,21:1
Harmatz, Jacob, 1966, Jl 3,34:8
Harmer, Henry R, 1966, Mr 15,39:5
Harmer, Hugh M, 1938, N 21,19:6
Harmer, James T, 1937, F 12,23:3
Harmer, Josiah P, 1950, Ag 10,25:2
Harmer, Sidney F, 1950, O 25,35:1
Harmer, Torr W, 1940, O 4,23:3
Harmer, William J, 1947, S 10,27:4
Harmon, A D, 1952, Ag 8,17:3
Harmon, A Jackson Mrs, 1956, D 24,13:4
Harmon, Ada D, 1943, Je 27,32:4
Harmon, Anna M Mrs, 1960, Ap 2,23:6
Harmon, Archer, 1954, Mr 27,17:5
Harmon, Archibald R Mrs, 1923, Ap 13,17:3
Harmon, Arthur, 1942, My 18,15:4
Harmon, Arthur L, 1958, O 18,21:3
Harmon, Charles, 1956, Ag 18,17:5
Harmon, Charles L, 1942, S 7,19:5
Harmon, Chris W, 1941, S 20,17:5
Harmon, Christopher W, 1962, My 31,27:4
Harmon, Claire G, 1959, Mr 10,35:1

Harmon, Clifford B (will, S 29,30:3), 1945, Jl 3,13:1
Harmon, David J, 1951, Mr 25,74:5
Harmon, E Willard, 1921, S 10,11:5
Harmon, Edward L, 1922, S 14,21:6
Harmon, Frank D Mrs, 1944, D 30,11:7
Harmon, Frank J, 1941, Jl 13,29:2
Harmon, Fred E, 1945, D 9,44:2
Harmon, G, 1926, Ap 16,23:5
Harmon, George M Gen, 1910, N 22,11:4
Harmon, George S, 1944, D 15,19:2
Harmon, Guy E, 1951, S 12,31:1
Harmon, H E, 1967, Ap 1,31:3
Harmon, Hannah P Mrs, 1941, My 6,21:4
Harmon, Harmon P Mrs, 1940, Ja 3,22:3
Harmon, Harry W, 1940, Jl 10,19:3
Harmon, Henry G, 1964, O 6,43:4
Harmon, Herbert W, 1956, S 24,27:3
Harmon, Hubert R, 1957, F 23,17:3
Harmon, I, 1967, Ap 6,39:3
Harmon, J, 1927, F 23,23:3
Harmon, James E, 1946, N 10,63:2
Harmon, John H, 1957, Je 4,35:1
Harmon, John H Mrs, 1949, Ap 7,29:2
Harmon, Joseph, 1947, N 27,31:1
Harmon, Leonard J, 1959, Ja 13,47:3
Harmon, Louis, 1948, O 6,29:2
Harmon, Louis Mrs, 1952, Ja 13,88:8
Harmon, Louise B Mrs, 1944, Mr 8,19:3
Harmon, Peter C, 1962, O 12,31:2
Harmon, Robert L, 1941, S 8,15:3
Harmon, Thomas J Sr, 1950, Ap 20,29:4
Harmon, Tommy (Thos H Harmon Jr), 1967, Jl 19, 39:4
Harmon, Virginia M Mrs, 1958, Ja 27,27:3
Harmon, W Burke, 1950, N 17,27:1
Harmon, W E, 1928, Jl 16,19:1
Harmon, Walter E, 1951, Ag 31,15:4
Harmon, Watson, 1947, F 17,19:5
Harmon, William C Jr Mrs, 1951, O 14,88:6
Harmon, William E Mrs, 1948, O 6,29:1
Harmonay, Mary Mrs, 1938, My 22,II,6:6
Harmonay, Michael J, 1945, N 6,20:2
Harmony, David Butty Rear-Adm, 1917, N 3,15:4
Harms, Henry, 1940, Ag 13,19:1
Harms, Henry T Jr, 1953, O 30,23:1
Harms, J Henry, 1946, Ag 24,11:4
Harms, John D, 1946, F 13,23:1
Harms, Kershaw, 1957, Jl 13,17:4
Harms, Magnus E, 1959, Mr 23,31:4
Harms, Samuel F, 1951, Mr 16,31:2
Harmsworth, Alfred Mrs, 1925, Ag 31,15:6
Harmsworth, Harold, 1952, S 8,21:5
Harmsworth, Lady, 1942, My 5,21:2
Harmsworth, Lord, 1948, Ag 14,13:1
Harmsworth, Robert L Sir, 1937, Ja 20,21:3
Harmsworth, Vyvyan G, 1957, Jl 17,27:2
Harn, Orlando C, 1955, O 12,31:2
Harnack, A von, 1930, Je 11,27:1
Harnden, James H, 1914, Mr 5,9:4
Harned, Albert W Dr, 1937, My 30,18:4
Harned, Asa, 1943, Ja 22,19:3
Harned, Bedell H Mrs, 1964, Mr 12,35:2
Harned, Bedell Holmes, 1968, My 6,47:2
Harned, Charles M, 1948, Jl 21,23:2
Harned, Daniel D, 1939, F 13,15:6
Harned, Florence B Mrs, 1941, Jl 19,13:1
Harned, R H, 1937, Ja 12,23:3
Harned, Samuel A, 1943, Jl 30,15:2
Harned, Virginia, 1946, My 1,25:2
Harned, W Leon, 1947, O 11,17:3
Harner, Herman, 1941, Ap 27,38:4
Harner, Nevin C, 1951, Jl 25,23:3
Harnett, Charles A, 1960, F 12,27:1
Harnett, Daniel J, 1947, Ja 1,34:3
Harnett, E B Capt, 1865, Ja 8,8:4
Harnett, J H, 1884, Ja 12,5:3
Harnett, Jacob H Mrs, 1951, S 15,15:3
Harnett, John C, 1944, Mr 21,20:2
Harnett, John L, 1937, F 15,17:5
Harnett, Joseph P, 1937, My 30,18:6
Harnett, Nora H Mrs, 1954, O 25,14:4
Harnett, William, 1959, Je 7,86:5
Harney, Albt G, 1954, O 20,29:2
Harney, Benjamin R, 1938, Mr 3,21:5
Harney, Harold W, 1940, My 12,48:1
Harney, Jeff, 1923, Jl 15,24:4
Harney, John B, 1957, Mr 30,19:3
Harney, Julia, 1960, Je 10,31:3
Harney, Katherine T (Mother Theresa Vincent), 1954, D 1,31:3
Harney, Matthew F, 1941, Ag 18,13:1
Harney, Thomas P, 1960, Jl 19,29:4
Harnickell, Henri C, 1940, S 28,17:4
Harnisch, Giulio, 1953, Mr 7,15:6
Harnisch, Joseph J, 1941, S 21,45:2
Harnly, Morris H Mrs, 1957, D 28,17:3
Harno, Albert J, 1966, Je 24,37:2
Harns, Burton K, 1948, My 21,28:3
Harnung, Louis C, 1957, D 7,21:5
Harold, Bro, 1947, Ap 18,21:3
Harold, James A Rev, 1903, Jl 10,7:6
Harold, Joseph F X, 1940, Ja 4,23:2
Harolds, Louis R, 1967, Mr 15,47:3
Harole, Ralph E, 1944, Ag 3,19:5
Haroucine, S B, 1954, Mr 17,6:2
Haroutunian, Joseph Dr, 1968, N 17,86:5
Harp, Charles E, 1943, D 23,19:4
Harp, Harry J, 1949, D 6,31:4
Harp, Henry J Dr, 1937, Ap 9,21:5
Harpas, Alex Mrs, 1948, Ap 26,23:3
Harpe, Charles E, 1952, Ag 1,17:2
Harpel, Benjamin F, 1955, Ja 15,13:4
Harpending, A V, 1871, Ap 24,4:7
Harpending, Harry B, 1951, Je 14,27:2
Harpending, Pierre L, 1942, Jl 25,13:2
Harper, A H, 1950, Ja 26,27:4
Harper, Albert M, 1949, Ag 25,23:5
Harper, Alex J, 1940, S 24,23:3
Harper, Andrew, 1937, Je 27,II,7:2; 1959, O 15,39:1
Harper, Arvilla Mrs, 1956, Ag 7,27:4
Harper, Austin C, 1950, F 2,27:3
Harper, Blake, 1950, Ja 29,68:3
Harper, Charles, 1950, N 14,31:1
Harper, Charles F, 1952, My 2,25:3
Harper, Charles N, 1947, N 27,31:5
Harper, Charles W, 1950, O 1,104:6
Harper, Clarence L, 1940, Ja 14,42:8
Harper, Constantine J, 1965, D 9,47:1
Harper, Cornelius A, 1951, Je 28,25:2
Harper, Daniel R, 1960, N 30,37:5
Harper, David E, 1943, Jl 15,21:3
Harper, Donald, 1954, Ap 25,86:3
Harper, Donald L, 1955, Ag 2,23:5
Harper, Donald L Mrs, 1941, Mr 12,21:2
Harper, Donald Mrs, 1965, F 13,21:3
Harper, Edward D, 1948, D 12,92:2
Harper, Elizabeth Mrs, 1907, O 31,9:6; 1941, Ap 9, 25:5
Harper, Emma L Mrs, 1940, Ag 27,21:5
Harper, Ethel, 1961, N 11,23:5
Harper, Eugenia L Mrs, 1940, Jl 6,15:5
Harper, F, 1890, My 23,5:2
Harper, F M, 1881, O 5,5:5
Harper, F R, 1948, Ja 7,25:3
Harper, Fletcher, 1877, My 30,4:7; 1963, N 5,31:2
Harper, Florence H Mrs, 1939, S 3,19:3
Harper, Fowler V, 1965, Ja 9,25:1
Harper, Frank, 1958, Ap 4,21:1
Harper, Frederick J, 1945, My 18,19:5
Harper, George D, 1951, My 15,31:4
Harper, George M, 1947, Jl 15,23:3
Harper, Glenn, 1960, Ag 13,15:6
Harper, Grace S, 1964, F 27,31:2
Harper, Harrison W, 1920, Ag 29,20:4
Harper, Harry B, 1948, Ag 28,15:6
Harper, Harry C, 1963, Ap 24,35:3
Harper, Harry F, 1949, Ag 9,25:2
Harper, Harry G, 1939, N 26,43:2
Harper, Harry L, 1954, Mr 14,88:2
Harper, Harvey W, 1958, N 25,33:1
Harper, Henry H, 1953, Mr 6,20:5
Harper, Henry S, 1944, Mr 2,17:5
Harper, Hubert H, 1957, N 4,29:1
Harper, Hugh D, 1944, D 12,23:4
Harper, I H, 1931, Mr 17,29:2
Harper, J Fletcher, 1959, D 26,13:4
Harper, J Frank, 1937, Ja 18,17:5
Harper, J G, 1881, My 15,2:5
Harper, J Henry, 1938, Ja 26,23:4
Harper, J P, 1881, O 9,7:1
Harper, Jacob C, 1939, Je 1,25:6
Harper, James (funl, Mr 31,4:1), 1869, Mr 29,5:5
Harper, James, 1911, Jl 28,9:6; 1919, Je 17,15:4; 1944, Ja 23,38:2; 1946, Ap 24,25:3
Harper, James Thorne, 1916, Ag 27,17:5
Harper, Jane, 1964, Mr 29,61:1
Harper, Jeane (Mrs R Engelhart), 1965, Ja 1,19:2
Harper, Jeremiah, 1943, S 2,19:4
Harper, Jesse C, 1961, Ap 1,31:3
Harper, John, 1924, Mr 6,17:4
Harper, John B, 1956, My 4,25:5
Harper, John E T, 1949, My 28,15:5
Harper, John F, 1964, Jl 21,33:3
Harper, John G (J London), 1963, D 20,26:7
Harper, John J Mrs, 1954, My 21,27:1
Harper, John K Mrs, 1962, Ap 24,37:2
Harper, John L, 1924, N 29,13:4
Harper, John M Mrs, 1952, Jl 22,25:3
Harper, John Wesley, 1915, Ag 15,13:5
Harper, Joseph A Mrs, 1950, Mr 1,27:3
Harper, Joseph Abner, 1910, O 3,9:5
Harper, Joseph H, 1954, Je 22,27:1
Harper, Joseph W, 1941, O 25,17:4; 1963, S 12,37:4
Harper, Joseph Wesley, 1870, F 15,5:2
Harper, Katherine C Mrs, 1939, Ag 21,13:4
Harper, L Frank Mrs, 1950, Jl 9,69:2
Harper, Lathrop C, 1950, Ag 13,77:3
Harper, Lathrop C Mrs, 1957, Mr 2,21:4
Harper, Lillie H, 1941, S 23,23:2
Harper, Lou Mrs, 1948, N 13,15:2
Harper, Lucius C, 1952, F 11,25:3
Harper, Marion, 1962, N 8,39:4
Harper, Martha M, 1950, Ag 5,15:4
Harper, Merritt W, 1938, My 11,19:6
Harper, Nelson N, 1952, Jl 6,48:8
Harper, Olive, 1915, My 4,15:5
Harper, Oliver J, 1957, Je 10,27:1
Harper, Paul V, 1949, S 17,17:2
Harper, Ralph M, 1955, Jl 5,29:2
Harper, Raymond, 1956, F 15,31:4
Harper, Robert A, 1946, My 13,21:1
Harper, Robert B, 1945, Ag 30,21:5
Harper, Robert D Mrs, 1957, Ap 27,19:2
Harper, Robert N, 1940, S 24,23:2
Harper, Roger Francis Prof, 1914, Ag 7,11:6
Harper, Rosco C, 1948, F 18,27:4
Harper, Russell R, 1948, Ap 3,15:2
Harper, Ruth A, 1937, O 17,II,8:7
Harper, Samuel, 1943, N 7,56:6
Harper, Samuel N (por), 1943, Ja 19,19:1
Harper, Samuel W, 1950, D 12,33:5
Harper, T George, 1953, Mr 18,31:1
Harper, Tacie B M Mrs, 1942, N 8,51:6
Harper, Theodore A, 1942, My 7,19:5
Harper, Thomas B, 1964, My 18,26:4
Harper, Thomas E, 1955, F 24,27:2
Harper, Thomas J, 1946, N 7,31:5
Harper, Thomas R, 1940, Je 9,45:2
Harper, Walter N, 1947, N 22,15:2
Harper, William A, 1911, Ja 15,13:3; 1942, My 13,19:2
Harper, William D (por), 1939, D 3,61:1
Harper, William E, 1940, Je 5,25:2; 1950, D 4,29:1
Harper, William G, 1945, My 22,19:1; 1952, Jl 17,23:5
Harper, William H, 1946, O 26,17:4
Harper, William J, 1942, D 14,28:4; 1956, Mr 4,88:1; 1957, My 19,88:2
Harper, William R, 1953, O 19,21:5
Harper, William R Mrs, 1942, My 30,15:4
Harper, William Rainey Dr (funl, Ja 15,9:1), 1906, Ja 11,9:1
Harper, William S, 1946, O 24,27:4; 1949, O 24,23:5
Harper, William St John, 1910, N 8,9:4
Harper, William T, 1952, N 21,25:2
Harper, William W, 1949, Je 28,27:4
Harpignies, Henri Joseph, 1916, Ag 30,9:6
Harpst, Lamont L, 1945, Ap 25,25:5
Harpster, Walter C, 1960, Ag 5,23:4
Harquail, Raymond J, 1959, N 3,31:3
Harr, Karl G, 1957, F 28,27:5
Harr, Luther A, 1950, Jl 31,17:3
Harraca, Carlos J Commodore, 1953, F 24,25:3
Harraden, Amos F B, 1941, O 15,21:2
Harraden, B, 1936, My 6,23:3
Harragan, George P, 1958, F 15,17:3
Harragin, A E H, 1941, My 22,21:1
Harrah, Ernest, 1950, D 25,19:4
Harrah, Phil J, 1940, D 10,25:2
Harral, George, 1903, Jl 14,7:6
Harral, George S, 1952, F 18,19:2
Harral, Ida B Mrs, 1948, My 26,25:3
Harrap, George G, 1938, O 31,15:5
Harrar, Elwood A, 1953, Jl 28,19:5
Harrat, Frank T, 1941, S 16,23:4
Harre, T Everett, 1948, Jl 28,23:2
Harrell, Alfred D, 1946, D 17,31:4
Harrell, Alfred Mrs, 1954, S 9,31:2
Harrell, David Sir, 1939, My 13,15:3
Harrell, George R, 1953, Ag 10,23:6
Harrell, Guy A, 1960, Je 5,86:8
Harrell, Joel E, 1968, Ap 8,47:2
Harrell, Mack, 1960, Ja 30,21:4
Harrell, William F (por), 1944, Jl 18,19:1
Harrer, Frederick, 1961, S 7,35:4
Harrer, Gustav A, 1943, N 27,13:4
Harrer, William V, 1941, S 25,25:2
Harrickey, Raymond J, 1949, F 25,24:2
Harridge, Will Mrs, 1956, N 7,29:4
Harries, Fred P, 1943, Jl 4,21:1
Harries, G H, 1934, S 30,34:1
Harries, Oscar L, 1948, F 23,25:2
Harries, William H Capt, 1921, Jl 25,13:5
Harriet, Sister of the order of all Saints, 1876, Mr 14, 7:4
Harrigan, Arthur W Sr, 1956, D 22,19:4
Harrigan, Edward (funl, Je 10,13:5), 1911, Je 7,9:3
Harrigan, Edward A, 1948, S 24,25:3
Harrigan, Ellen Mrs, 1945, S 14,17:7
Harrigan, Francis L, 1968, Jl 28,65:1
Harrigan, Frank A, 1939, Ag 8,17:2
Harrigan, George M, 1941, Ag 30,13:6
Harrigan, Henry J, 1940, O 20,47:4
Harrigan, James, 1946, D 21,19:5
Harrigan, James J, 1959, Ap 11,21:2
Harrigan, James T, 1963, My 30,17:3
Harrigan, John Dr, 1918, Ja 1,17:7
Harrigan, John H, 1947, Ja 7,27:2
Harrigan, John J, 1941, Ja 6,15:3
Harrigan, Joseph Mrs, 1925, Jl 23,19:5
Harrigan, Lillian A Mrs, 1938, Ap 7,23:5
Harrigan, Margaret C, 1943, Mr 7,38:3
Harrigan, Ned Mrs, 1918, Mr 25,13:3
Harrigan, Nolan, 1966, Ap 4,31:1
Harrigan, Richard J, 1957, Mr 12,33:3
Harrigan, Thomas F, 1961, N 7,33:3
Harrigan, Thomas H, 1946, N 12,29:3
Harrigan, William, 1920, F 11,11:4; 1966, F 2,32:1
Harrigan, William F Mrs, 1959, Mr 6,25:2
Harrigan, William J, 1952, F 27,27:2
Harrigfeld, Frederick H, 1954, Mr 27,17:5

Harriman, Alice Mrs, 1925, D 25,17:4
Harriman, Alonzo J, 1966, S 11,86:6
Harriman, Archie S, 1941, Ja 10,19:5
Harriman, Arthur, 1957, S 3,27:4
Harriman, Arthur N, 1960, Ag 14,92:5
Harriman, Bernard J, 1956, Jl 27,21:1
Harriman, C, 1878, Mr 13,4:7
Harriman, Charles, 1912, Ap 23,13:4
Harriman, Charles A, 1919, Mr 15,15:4
Harriman, Charles C, 1946, Jl 30,23:4
Harriman, Charles H Mrs, 1909, F 2,9:5
Harriman, Chester K Mrs, 1922, N 16,19:5
Harriman, David E, 1949, Ja 20,28:2
Harriman, E H Mrs, 1932, N 8,21:1
Harriman, E T Mrs. 1934, Mr 6,23:1
Harriman, Edward A, 1955, Jl 18,21:5
Harriman, Edward A Mrs, 1941, O 8,23:6
Harriman, Frank B, 1944, Jl 9,36:1
Harriman, Frederick C, 1958, My 14,33:4
Harriman, Frederick Mrs, 1921, D 16,17:5
Harriman, Frederick W Mrs, 1912, Ap 8,11:5
Harriman, H M, 1933, Ja 4,17:4
Harriman, Henry I, 1950, Jl 6,27:4
Harriman, Henry I Mrs, 1944, D 22,17:5
Harriman, Herbert M Mrs, 1907, O 9,11:6
Harriman, J Borden (funl, D 3,13:4), 1914, D 2,13:5
Harriman, J Borden Mrs (funl plans, S 5,43:3), 1967, S 1,28:6
Harriman, James, 1912, My 15,11:4
Harriman, Jerome T, 1942, D 31,15:1
Harriman, Job, 1925, O 28,25:4
Harriman, John, 1961, Ja 2,25:5
Harriman, John E Sr, 1954, Ap 20,29:2
Harriman, Joseph, 1925, D 3,25:3; 1925, D 6,13:1
Harriman, Joseph W (por), 1949, Ja 24,19:3
Harriman, Joseph W Mrs, 1939, Je 12,17:5
Harriman, M B Mrs, 1930, D 31,17:5
Harriman, Margaret C Mrs, 1966, Ag 8,27:3
Harriman, Norman F, 1949, Jl 1,19:4
Harriman, Oliver, 1904, Mr 13,7:4
Harriman, Oliver (por),(will, Ag 18,39:1), 1940, Ag 15,19:3
Harriman, Oliver Mrs, 1950, Mr 29,29:1
Harriman, Orlando, 1911, D 30,11:4
Harriman, Orlando H, 1945, Jl 3,13:4
Harriman, Orlando H Mrs, 1940, Ja 6,13:3
Harriman, Perley, 1949, Je 18,13:4
Harriman, Philip Lawrence Dr, 1968, Mr 4,37:4
Harriman, Rudolph F Mrs, 1950, Je 9,23:4
Harriman, W, 1884, Jl 26,4:7
Harriman, W M, 1903, Ap 5,7:5
Harriman, Wilmer P, 1942, Ja 20,19:4
Harring, Irving G, 1950, Ag 18,21:3
Harrington, Alan, 1950, Mr 29,1:3
Harrington, Albert A, 1953, Ag 26,27:4
Harrington, Amos T, 1945, O 2,23:5
Harrington, Arthur W, 1964, Jl 1,35:5
Harrington, B J Prof, 1907, N 30,7:4
Harrington, Bertrand J, 1950, F 22,29:3
Harrington, Blaine G, 1952, O 2,29:3
Harrington, Burt D, 1942, Ap 17,17:5
Harrington, C S Mrs, 1952, D 4,35:4
Harrington, Charles A, 1915, Mr 12,11:6; 1955, O 18, 37:5
Harrington, Charles E, 1923, Mr 24,13:5; 1954, Ja 11, 25:2
Harrington, Charles E Mrs, 1910, F 10,7:5
Harrington, Charles H, 1938, O 10,19:2
Harrington, Charles J, 1960, Jl 26,5:4
Harrington, Charles L Mrs, 1947, D 9,33:5
Harrington, Charles M, 1952, N 25,29:3; 1955, S 29, 33:4
Harrington, Charles P Jr, 1962, N 22,29:4
Harrington, Charles Prof, 1908, S 12,7:6
Harrington, Chelsea H, 1951, Ap 26,29:5
Harrington, Clarence M, 1956, O 20,21:5
Harrington, Cornelius J Judge, 1968, Jl 8,39:3
Harrington, D J Rev, 1903, Je 6,7:6
Harrington, Daniel, 1948, S 30,28:3
Harrington, Daniel R, 1959, F 24,29:1
Harrington, David L, 1961, Je 4,87:1
Harrington, Denis A Jr, 1941, Ap 17,23:4
Harrington, Denis J, 1946, F 7,23:1
Harrington, Dennis A, 1940, Ap 30,21:3
Harrington, Dennis J Mrs, 1937, Je 30,24:1
Harrington, Dennis John, 1906, Ap 12,9:5
Harrington, Edward B, 1941, Je 29,33:2; 1954, My 16, 88:4
Harrington, Edward F, 1951, Ja 17,28:5
Harrington, Edward J, 1938, D 2,23:5
Harrington, Edward M Mrs, 1959, Je 11,33:5
Harrington, Edward P, 1942, Jl 27,15:5
Harrington, Edwin D, 1950, Ag 18,21:4
Harrington, Edwin I, 1958, D 4,39:2
Harrington, Edwin L Dr, 1918, F 25,9:5
Harrington, Elizabeth, 1945, Je 8,19:2
Harrington, Elliott D, 1951, Ap 2,25:5
Harrington, Emerson C (por), 1945, D 16,39:1
Harrington, Emerson C Mrs, 1948, Ap 9,23:4
Harrington, Eugene E, 1944, Jl 28,13:5
Harrington, Floreal C, 1947, D 15,25:4
Harrington, Francis Alfred, 1922, Ag 29,15:6
Harrington, Francis C, 1940, O 1,23:1
Harrington, Francis E, 1944, D 2,13:4; 1947, My 10, 13:4
Harrington, Francis J, 1948, Je 9,29:5
Harrington, Fred P (por), 1940, Je 18,23:4
Harrington, George, 1941, Ag 17,39:2
Harrington, George L, 1939, Je 13,23:3
Harrington, George W Mrs, 1957, D 27,19:4
Harrington, Gerald F, 1947, Ag 30,15:4
Harrington, Gertrude P, 1955, D 24,13:5
Harrington, Gordon S, 1943, Jl 5,15:4
Harrington, Guy L, 1943, N 30,27:4
Harrington, Harriet E, 1950, Je 7,29:3
Harrington, Harry N, 1942, S 7,19:4
Harrington, Helen N, 1953, Mr 24,31:2
Harrington, Henry J Mrs, 1953. Ap 5,77:1
Harrington, Henry J W, 1939, Ja 22,34:8
Harrington, Henry L, 1951, Ja 30,25:4
Harrington, Hubert J, 1956, Ag 25,15:5
Harrington, J Morris, 1949, F 22,23:4
Harrington, James A, 1947, S 3,25:4
Harrington, James F, 1942, N 26,27:1
Harrington, James S, 1948, S 13,21:2
Harrington, James T, 1948, F 28,15:5
Harrington, John, 1909, My 25,9:6
Harrington, John J (funl, Je 14,11:3), 1910, Je 11,11:5
Harrington, John J (est), 1913, Je 25,9:5
Harrington, John J sr, 1956, D 16,86:1
Harrington, John L, 1942, My 21,19:3
Harrington, John Maddison, 1925, S 18,23:5
Harrington, John P, 1941, My 29,19:4
Harrington, John T, 1947, My 1,25:2; 1962, S 30,87:1
Harrington, John W, 1952, Je 28,19:1
Harrington, Joseph, 1959, S 8,32:8
Harrington, Joseph E, 1947, My 1,25:3
Harrington, Joseph F, 1958, Je 4,33:2
Harrington, Joseph P, 1950, F 11,15:2
Harrington, Joseph T, 1948, O 14,30:2
Harrington, Karl P, 1953, N 17,31:2
Harrington, Lawrence R, 1947, Ja 5,53:5
Harrington, Lord (Chas Augustus Starhope), 1917, F 6,9:3
Harrington, Lynn J, 1940, Ja 9,23:1
Harrington, Margaret Mrs, 1937, Jl 1,27:2
Harrington, Michael Mrs, 1950, N 29,33:5
Harrington, Milton A, 1942, My 28,17:4
Harrington, Otis W, 1949, N 12,15:5
Harrington, Pat Sr (Danl P), 1965, S 3,27:5
Harrington, Peter, 1956, D 4,39:3
Harrington, Phil (por), 1949, F 13,76:5
Harrington, Preston M, 1942, Ag 21,19:1
Harrington, Purnell F Rear-Adm (por), 1937, O 21, 24:1
Harrington, Randall A Mrs, 1953, D 14,31:4
Harrington, Richard, 1884, N 19,2:3
Harrington, Robert E, 1944, S 29,21:4
Harrington, S M, 1865, D 11,2:3
Harrington, Stanley, 1949, Ag 2,19:1
Harrington, Thomas F (por), 1955, Jl 12,25:3
Harrington, Thomas H, 1956, My 8,33:2
Harrington, Thomas V, 1950, Ap 4,30:3
Harrington, Thomas W, 1951, S 16,84:4
Harrington, Timothy, 1910, Mr 14,7:4
Harrington, Timothy A, 1952, Ap 17,29:3
Harrington, Vernon, 1942, N 20,23:2
Harrington, Victoria Mrs, 1939, Ap 30,45:1
Harrington, Vincent F, 1943, D 9,27:2
Harrington, Virgil D, 1944, Ja 19,19:4
Harrington, Walter, 1962, F 6,35:2
Harrington, Walter E, 1924, D 13,15:3
Harrington, Walter G, 1947, Ag 20,21:3
Harrington, Walter L, 1955, D 22,23:3
Harrington, Wentworth L Mrs, 1942, Je 27,13:4
Harrington, William L, 1962, Ap 7,25:5
Harrington, William P, 1947, Ja 25,17:4
Harrington, William T, 1954, Jl 5,11:6
Harriot, Josephine T Mrs, 1937, Jl 15,19:4
Harriot, Randolph F, 1937, Ag 19,19:4
Harriot, S Carman, 1922, Je 26,13:6
Harriot, Samuel J, 1919, Jl 25,11:5
Harriott, Frederick C, 1914, My 30,11:6
Harriott, R, 1878, N 22,2:2
Harriott, Roscoe, 1950, F 3,24:4
Harris, A H, 1931, N 22,II,7:1
Harris, A I, 1942, O 19,19:4
Harris, Abraham Dupont, 1912, Jl 26,9:5
Harris, Abram L, 1963, N 17,87:1
Harris, Abram M, 1957, Je 29,17:6
Harris, Addison C, 1916, S 3,19:4
Harris, Alan A, 1940, Ag 14,19:5
Harris, Alan H Mrs, 1962, My 26,25:3
Harris, Albert H, 1938, N 16,23:2; 1950, Jl 2,24:6
Harris, Albert M, 1945, Ag 8,23:5; 1948, Ja 29,25:5
Harris, Albert S, 1939, Ja 23,13:2
Harris, Albert W, 1914, Ag 27,11:5
Harris, Albert W (will, N 22,42:5), 1958, N 11,29:3
Harris, Albert W (est acctg), 1959, Mr 31,3:3
Harris, Albert W Mrs, 1961, Mr 25,25:5
Harris, Alexander, 1947, Mr 28,24:2
Harris, Alfred, 1940, Mr 5,23:4
Harris, Alfred F (por), 1943, Je 29,19:3
Harris, Alfred I, 1958, Ja 28,27:5
Harris, Alfred S, 1947, Ag 24,58:1
Harris, Alfred W Sr, 1965, Ap 4,87:3
Harris, Andrew L Ex-Gov, 1915, S 14,11:5
Harris, Archie F, 1965, My 3,33:3
Harris, Arnold Mrs, 1951, Je 28,25:3
Harris, Arthur, 1916, Ag 9,11:4; 1943, My 31,17:4
Harris, Arthur A Sir, 1939, D 11,23:4
Harris, Arthur E, 1954, Mr 9,27:5
Harris, Arthur H, 1938, Mr 3,10:3
Harris, Arthur M, 1941, Mr 29,15:5
Harris, Arthur S, 1946, Jl 18,25:1
Harris, Asa J, 1945, My 2,23:4
Harris, Augustus, 1873, My 12,4:7
Harris, Augustus E, 1968, My 21,47:2
Harris, Augustus Sir, 1896, Je 23,3:1
Harris, Averell, 1966, S 30,47:1
Harris, B Harve, 1962, Jl 30,23:2
Harris, Barnett G, 1960, Ja 29,25:4
Harris, Basil (por), 1948, Je 19,15:1
Harris, Basil Mrs, 1955, D 31,13:3
Harris, Benjamin, 1951, Mr 29,27:6
Harris, Benjamin E, 1957, S 3,27:4
Harris, Benjamin F, 1952, O 17,27:2
Harris, Benjamin W, 1907, F 8,9:6
Harris, Bernard B, 1962, Ja 25,31:1
Harris, Bertha J, 1945, Jl 11,11:6
Harris, Beulah L Mrs, 1959, D 13,86:4
Harris, Beverly D, 1948, Ja 26,19:4
Harris, Bishop, 1874, Mr 17,1:5
Harris, Bravid W, 1965, O 23,31:2
Harris, Burton Dr, 1923, Mr 7,15:4
Harris, C C Chief Justice, 1881, Jl 27,3:5
Harris, C E Mrs, 1903, Je 23,7:6
Harris, C F, 1881, O 6,3:4
Harris, C F Mrs, 1881, O 6,3:4
Harris, C Morgan, 1963, Ap 19,43:3
Harris, C Mrs, 1935, F 10,31:1
Harris, Calvin J B, 1945, O 10,21:4
Harris, Carl C, 1960, Ap 9,23:5
Harris, Carl T, 1945, Ap 18,23:3
Harris, Carl W, 1937, D 19,II,9:2
Harris, Carleton T, 1965, Ag 23,31:3
Harris, Chapman S, 1945, S 4,23:1
Harris, Charles, 1943, S 5,28:5; 1957, My 15,35:3
Harris, Charles A, 1938, N 4,23:3; 1947, D 18,30:2
Harris, Charles B, 1924, Ap 5,15:1; 1964, O 21,47:
Harris, Charles C, 1959, Ap 1,37:4
Harris, Charles E Mrs, 1951, S 17,21:4
Harris, Charles H, 1942, My 29,17:6
Harris, Charles J, 1941, O 14,23:1
Harris, Charles Jr, 1940, My 1,23:5
Harris, Charles L, 1950, Jl 5,31:4
Harris, Charles Mrs, 1955, Ap 30,17:5
Harris, Chauncey Col, 1911, Mr 21,11:5
Harris, Clarence J, 1941, N 29,17:4
Harris, Clement L, 1948, D 6,25:1
Harris, Clifton T Rev, 1937, O 22,23:2
Harris, Clinton L, 1944, N 17,19:1
Harris, Clinton Stanford, 1920, Je 29,11:4
Harris, Clyde K, 1958, Mr 3,27:1
Harris, Constance Mrs, 1951, My 5,17:1
Harris, Cornelius C, 1950, Ja 29,68:5
Harris, Credo F, 1956, Ap 4,29:1
Harris, D L, 1879, Jl 13,7:2
Harris, Daniel, 1943, S 1,19:2
Harris, Daniel (por), 1945, F 9,15:1
Harris, David Sr, 1960, Mr 11,25:2
Harris, David W, 1950, Ap 3,23:4
Harris, Dawson B, 1953, S 27,86:1
Harris, De Lancy P (por), 1949, Mr 2,26:2
Harris, Diane (Mrs D M Graham), 1960, S 22,5
Harris, Don A, 1961, O 14,23:3
Harris, Donald R, 1949, Ja 19,27:4
Harris, Downey L, 1956, D 25,25:2
Harris, Duncan G Mrs, 1968, My 14,47:1
Harris, Dwight Miller, 1903, Jl 25,7:6
Harris, E Dr, 1884, F 1,8:1
Harris, E Knight, 1959, N 11,35:2
Harris, Earl, 1959, O 4,86:6
Harris, Earl B, 1938, D 29,19:5
Harris, Edgar, 1953, My 1,22:3
Harris, Edward H, 1937, O 25,19:6
Harris, Edward J, 1940, O 7,18:2
Harris, Edward M, 1944, F 15,17:4
Harris, Edward Sr, 1948, Ap 10,13:5
Harris, Edward W, 1942, Ag 12,19:5
Harris, Edward W P, 1959, O 28,37:1
Harris, Edwin, 1938, Ag 11,17:4; 1955, D 17,23:
Harris, Edwin A, 1946, D 2,25:2; 1961, Jl 22,21:
Harris, Edwin A Mrs, 1946, Mr 17,44:5
Harris, Edwin A Sr, 1955, O 9,86:2
Harris, Edwin S, 1941, Ja 31,19:1
Harris, Edwin V, 1960, Jl 8,21:4
Harris, Elijah Paddock, 1920, D 11,13:4
Harris, Elmer B, 1966, S 8,47:3
Harris, Elmer Mrs, 1963, S 1,56:8
Harris, Elmore R, 1968, D 9,55:3
Harris, Emanuel, 1951, Jl 7,13:3
Harris, Emerson P, 1937, F 19,20:1
Harris, Emerson P Mrs, 1951, Ag 17,17:2
Harris, Emma, 1941, F 4,22:2
Harris, Emmet Lt, 1919, S 28,22:2

Harris, Ernest L, 1946, F 3,40:2
Harris, Evan B, 1956, Jl 25,29:3
Harris, Evelyn, 1961, S 18,29:5
Harris, Everett R, 1954, My 1,15:4
Harris, F, 1931, Ag 27,17:1
Harris, F Tompkins, 1958, N 8,21:1
Harris, Flagler Mrs, 1966, My 11,47:4
Harris, Frances E, 1958, My 21,33:3
Harris, Francis R, 1943, O 27,23:2
Harris, Frank B, 1955, Je 29,29:2
Harris, Frank C, 1961, Jl 30,69:3
Harris, Frank J, 1946, Mr 12,25:2
Harris, Frank L, 1952, Je 18,27:3
Harris, Frank S, 1951, Ag 4,15:3; 1953, My 3,89:2
Harris, Frank W, 1959, Ap 16,33:4
Harris, Franklin, 1952, N 15,17:1
Harris, Franklin S, 1960, Ap 20,39:1
Harris, Fred H, 1961, Je 9,33:2
Harris, Fred M, 1950, Jl 20,25:4
Harris, Fred Mrs, 1956, Ap 5,29:1
Harris, Fred T, 1925, D 16,25:4
Harris, Frederic R, 1949, Jl 21,25:1
Harris, Frederic R Mrs, 1945, Jl 22,37:1
Harris, Frederick M, 1954, O 22,27:5
Harris, Frederick M Mrs, 1952, O 9,31:5
Harris, G S Beckwith, 1955, Ap 10,88:1
Harris, George, 1875, N 16,2:2; 1915, Mr 17,11:5; 1954, Ap 18,89:2; 1955, F 3,23:4
Harris, George A, 1958, N 24,29:4
Harris, George B, 1940, Jl 6,15:3; 1952, D 25,29:4
Harris, George de L, 1959, Ja 1,31:4
Harris, George Dr, 1922, Mr 2,21:5
Harris, George F Dr, 1911, S 11,9:4
Harris, George H, 1938, Ja 21,19:2; 1942, My 7,19:2; 1951, Jl 29,69:2
Harris, George N, 1937, My 14,23:1
Harris, George R, 1905, Mr 14,9:6
Harris, George S, 1946, Ap 13,17:3; 1950, F 17,24:2; 1957, O 28,27:2
Harris, George Sr, 1949, Je 1,32:4
Harris, George W, 1948, Mr 28,48:4; 1957, Mr 24, 86:2; 1964, Jl 21,33:1
Harris, George W Mrs, 1952, Ja 29,25:5; 1959, Je 14, 86:8
Harris, Gerald W, 1962, Ag 11,17:5
Harris, Gibson W, 1941, Ag 11,13:2
Harris, Gilbert D, 1952, D 5,27:4
Harris, Gilbert McC, 1966, Ag 21,93:2
Harris, Gorham W, 1951, Je 20,27:3
Harris, H Crittenden, 1939, Mr 3,23:2
Harris, H D, 1882, Mr 30,5:5
Harris, H Richard Rev Dr, 1924, Jl 31,13:7
Harris, H V, 1941, F 6,21:2
Harris, Hans, 1960, Ag 1,23:5
Harris, Harold, 1958, F 12,29:2
Harris, Harold E, 1960, D 8,35:2
Harris, Harriet L, 1958, Je 14,21:4
Harris, Harry, 1937, Ap 22,23:1; 1948, O 5,25:3; 1951, Je 26,35:5; 1959, Je 6,21:5; 1967, Ag 24,37:5
Harris, Harry A Mrs, 1945, Mr 13,23:5
Harris, Harry L, 1944, Ag 19,11:6
Harris, Harry Mrs, 1950, Ag 23,29:5
Harris, Harry Mrs (D Lazard), 1960, Jl 16,19:5
Harris, Harvey E, 1941, D 22,17:5
Harris, Hayden B, 1951, O 6,19:4
Harris, Hayden B Mrs, 1958, Ja 23,27:2
Harris, Henry, 1879, Je 14,3:3; 1966, Ja 14,39:3
Harris, Henry A, 1937, D 3,23:3; 1939, Ap 23,III,6:7
Harris, Henry C Mrs, 1946, Ag 10,13:6
Harris, Henry F, 1955, Ag 16,49:2
Harris, Henry G Mrs, 1957, S 12,31:2
Harris, Henry H, 1949, Mr 30,25:4; 1965, Jl 1,31:4
Harris, Henry J, 1963, Ap 29,31:3
Harris, Henry L Col, 1920, Mr 9,11:1
Harris, Henry R, 1939, Je 6,23:4
Harris, Henry S, 1952, D 22,25:3
Harris, Henry S T Col, 1916, D 18,11:4
Harris, Henry Tudor Brownell Rear-Adm, 1920, Jl 14, 9:4
Harris, Henry W, 1955, Ja 13,27:5
Harris, Henry W Mrs, 1948, My 19,27:2
Harris, Herbert A, 1954, S 13,23:5
Harris, Herbert E, 1954, Ag 17,21:5
Harris, Herbert H (por), 1949, Mr 22,25:3
Harris, Herbert H, 1950, Mr 21,32:3
Harris, Herbert I, 1943, Ap 26,19:5
Harris, Herman J, 1960, D 15,43:3
Harris, Herman Mrs, 1942, D 3,15:2
Harris, Homer R, 1945, Mr 15,23:1
Harris, Horace R, 1956, F 5,86:2
Harris, Howard M, 1962, Ag 29,14:4
Harris, Hubert, 1955, Ja 11,27:8
Harris, Hugh C, 1960, Jl 12,35:2
Harris, Hyman, 1948, O 14,29:3
Harris, I G, 1897, Jl 9,10:3
Harris, Ieuan, 1940, Mr 3,44:1
Harris, Ira, 1875, D 3,4:7
Harris, Ira Capt, 1925, Je 23,19:4
Harris, Irving, 1957, D 8,87:4
Harris, Irving A, 1966, My 19,47:2
Harris, Irving D Mrs (Claire McCardell),(funl, Mr 27,33:5), 1958, Mr 23,1:8
Harris, Irwin D, 1945, O 6,13:6

Harris, Isaac, 1907, Ja 31,9:6; 1956, F 14,29:4
Harris, Isaac S, 1940, S 11,26:2
Harris, Isabelle F Mrs, 1946, O 6,26:3
Harris, Isidore, 1944, Ja 20,19:1
Harris, Isidore L, 1958, Ja 1,25:1
Harris, Issac Faust Dr, 1953, F 2,21:1
Harris, J A, 1930, Ap 27,II,8:1
Harris, J Albert, 1950, N 16,31:5
Harris, J Edward, 1953, Ag 22,15:6
Harris, J Victor, 1949, S 16,27:3
Harris, Jack H, 1944, Jl 19,19:6
Harris, Jack P, 1958, N 7,27:2
Harris, Jacob M, 1964, My 17,87:3
Harris, James, 1949, Ja 7,22:2; 1955, D 16,29:3
Harris, James A, 1947, Ap 17,27:4; 1957, Ja 5,17:5
Harris, James E, 1944, Mr 10,15:4; 1949, Ja 7,22:3
Harris, James Fitz, 1910, S 8,9:4
Harris, James H, 1942, F 16,17:4
Harris, James L, 1945, O 22,17:5
Harris, James R, 1941, Mr 2,42:6; 1958, My 3,19:4
Harris, Janet, 1941, Ja 12,44:3
Harris, Jennie L, 1941, My 3,15:4
Harris, Jerome, 1966, Jl 19,39:3
Harris, Jerome Mrs, 1947, Ag 1,17:4
Harris, Joe, 1953, Je 13,15:3
Harris, Joe M, 1951, F 12,16:6
Harris, Joel C Jr, 1964, S 13,86:4
Harris, Joel C Mrs, 1938, O 30,40:7
Harris, Joel Chandler, 1908, Jl 4,5:4
Harris, Joel Smith, 1916, My 4,11:5
Harris, John, 1942, F 24,21:2
Harris, John A Jr, 1940, F 19,17:3
Harris, John B, 1940, N 17,50:1; 1952, F 13,29:4
Harris, John F, 1939, Ja 27,19:5
Harris, John F (will, Ap 30,15:4), 1941, Ap 15,23:4
Harris, John F, 1959, F 19,31:2
Harris, John F Mrs, 1943, Ja 13,23:4
Harris, John H, 1947, S 12,22:3
Harris, John H Dr, 1925, Ap 5,5:1
Harris, John J, 1966, Ja 3,27:3
Harris, John J Mrs, 1955, F 18,21:2
Harris, John J Rev, 1937, Je 9,25:3
Harris, John M, 1942, Ap 24,17:1; 1948, Ag 4,21:3; 1949, O 13,27:3
Harris, John N D, 1946, Ag 3,15:2
Harris, John P Mrs, 1947, S 3,25:3
Harris, John S Gen, 1906, Ja 26,9:5
Harris, John T, 1940, Ja 27,13:2
Harris, John V, 1950, Ap 13,29:1
Harris, John W (por), 1943, F 21,32:4
Harris, Joseph, 1948, Mr 17,25:3; 1956, N 24,19:1; 1959, D 11,33:2
Harris, Joseph H, 1952, O 26,88:4
Harris, Joseph J, 1966, F 22,23:1
Harris, Joseph Mrs (Sylvia), 1966, N 12,29:5
Harris, Joseph P, 1947, D 6,15:5
Harris, Joseph R (cor, My 21,33:1), 1958, My 20, 34:7
Harris, Joseph S, 1910, Je 3,7:4
Harris, Julian LaR (Feb 9), 1963, Ap 1,35:7
Harris, Julius, 1943, Ja 22,20:3
Harris, Katherine W, 1954, O 21,27:6
Harris, Keber R, 1950, Ag 12,13:1
Harris, Lady, 1941, S 25,25:2
Harris, Lancelot M, 1941, Mr 25,23:5
Harris, Laura (cor, Ap 20,25:1), 1956, Ap 15,88:7
Harris, Laura Colver Mrs, 1903, Ag 7,7:7
Harris, Lee W, 1951, Jl 6,23:4
Harris, Leigh, 1956, Ag 11,13:6
Harris, Leon, 1956, D 15,25:5
Harris, Leon Mrs, 1966, Ja 29,27:3
Harris, Leonard B, 1962, N 12,29:5
Harris, Leopold, 1939, Ap 2,III,7:1
Harris, Linden T, 1953, Mr 25,31:4
Harris, Lloyd, 1925, S 28,19:5
Harris, Lloyd C, 1954, Ag 28,15:6
Harris, Lorenzo W, 1946, Je 27,22:2
Harris, Louis, 1940, My 7,25:3; 1961, O 17,39:3
Harris, Louis H, 1952, N 3,27:3; 1962, Ap 26,33:3
Harris, Louis I, 1939, Ja 6,21:1; 1953, Ja 14,31:5
Harris, Louis M, 1938, F 17,21:3; 1949, S 1,21:1; 1955, N 13,88:4
Harris, Louis Mrs (F I Kapp), 1965, Mr 23,39:4
Harris, Lt, 1873, My 15,1:2
Harris, Lucien M Sr, 1939, O 17,25:5
Harris, Luella C, 1953, Ag 21,17:2
Harris, M Anstice, 1956, Ja 16,21:5
Harris, M H, 1930, Je 24,25:1
Harris, M J, 1959, Je 8,6:6
Harris, Mac (por), 1947, Ja 23,25:7
Harris, Marcus N, 1942, D 30,23:4
Harris, Mark, 1938, S 27,21:2; 1946, O 22,25:5
Harris, Mark G, 1941, Mr 22,15:6
Harris, Mark H, 1945, Je 21,19:2
Harris, Mark S, 1964, Ag 1,21:3
Harris, Martin, 1875, S 1,5:3
Harris, Mary B, 1957, F 23,17:2
Harris, Mary H Mrs, 1925, Ag 10,13:7
Harris, Maude, 1939, Je 29,23:3
Harris, Maurice H Mrs, 1939, O 14,19:3
Harris, Max, 1960, S 19,31:3
Harris, Merriman Colbert Bp, 1921, My 9,11:4
Harris, Michael J, 1940, F 3,13:1

Harris, Mildred, 1944, Jl 21,19:2
Harris, Milton, 1955, Mr 15,29:2
Harris, Mily M Mrs, 1939, N 14,23:3
Harris, Mitchell, 1948, N 17,27:2
Harris, Morgan C, 1948, Mr 31,25:1
Harris, Morgan E, 1958, D 9,41:1
Harris, Morris, 1956, Mr 13,27:4
Harris, Morris L, 1946, N 30,15:3
Harris, Mort, 1938, Ap 27,23:4
Harris, Moses J, 1913, Ja 29,11:4
Harris, Murray A Mrs, 1952, Ap 18,25:2
Harris, Myron, 1939, Jl 8,15:1
Harris, Nancy H, 1949, O 20,29:6
Harris, Nanette T Mrs, 1938, Jl 1,19:2
Harris, Natalie P Mrs, 1952, D 18,29:4
Harris, Nathan, 1965, Jl 11,69:2
Harris, Nathan A, 1949, Je 7,31:2
Harris, Newton M, 1953, Ja 5,21:4
Harris, Norman Wall, 1916, Jl 17,11:5
Harris, Norval K, 1959, D 30,19:1
Harris, O T Mrs, 1949, Ja 20,27:3
Harris, Orsamus T Mrs, 1905, My 2,11:6
Harris, Oscar P Mrs, 1955, My 24,31:1
Harris, Otis, 1958, Ag 16,17:3
Harris, Pat Mrs, 1921, S 23,15:7
Harris, Paul P (por), 1947, Ja 28,23:1
Harris, Percy, 1952, Je 29,56:3
Harris, Peter C, 1951, Mr 19,28:4
Harris, Phil H, 1956, Ap 6,25:3
Harris, Philip N, 1965, Ap 22,33:2
Harris, Ralph A Mrs, 1952, Mr 14,23:2
Harris, Ralph S, 1961, Jl 1,17:2
Harris, Randall, 1950, S 22,39:4
Harris, Raymond A, 1945, F 13,23:3
Harris, Raymond F, 1956, Jl 10,31:5
Harris, Richard, 1903, N 24,9:5
Harris, Richard A, 1944, Ja 2,38:4
Harris, Richard G, 1951, F 5,23:1
Harris, Richard J Mrs, 1964, F 22,21:2
Harris, Richard L, 1955, N 24,29:5
Harris, Robert, 1954, Je 30,27:4
Harris, Robert C, 1952, O 13,21:3
Harris, Robert D, 1938, Jl 15,17:5
Harris, Robert H, 1958, Jl 9,27:4
Harris, Robert I, 1966, Je 29,47:2
Harris, Robert J, 1942, D 11,23:2
Harris, Robert L, 1948, F 8,60:7; 1950, My 10,31:4
Harris, Robert V K Jr, 1939, O 11,27:1
Harris, Robert W Mrs, 1961, O 26,35:4
Harris, Ronald, 1942, Mr 12,19:1
Harris, Roscoe E, 1949, S 7,29:3
Harris, Rose B Mrs, 1940, Ap 12,24:2
Harris, Roy J, 1952, My 21,27:2
Harris, Russell, 1957, N 28,31:2
Harris, Sally S, 1951, O 12,28:2
Harris, Sam H, 1941, Jl 4,13:1
Harris, Sam J, 1966, Ap 21,40:1
Harris, Samuel A, 1949, Ag 9,25:4
Harris, Samuel D, 1948, D 24,17:3
Harris, Samuel G, 1940, Je 29,21:6; 1962, S 25,37:3
Harris, Samuel J, 1940, F 1,21:6; 1942, F 8,49:1
Harris, Samuel J Mrs, 1959, Mr 3,33:1
Harris, Samuel W, 1946, Ap 24,25:3
Harris, Seale, 1957, Mr 17,87:2
Harris, Sidney, 1923, F 27,19:3; 1948, My 29,15:7; 1955, O 25,33:4
Harris, Sidney F (trb, O 13,37:1; est acctg, N 6,88:3), 1955, O 4,35:3
Harris, Sidney S Mrs, 1925, Ja 25,7:1
Harris, Siebel C, 1937, Ag 14,13:1
Harris, Simon D Mrs, 1964, Ja 19,76:6
Harris, Simon Rabbi, 1917, Je 3,19:4
Harris, Sol, 1954, N 3,29:3
Harris, Spencer, 1964, D 20,68:8
Harris, Stanley J, 1951, O 13,17:1
Harris, Stephen M, 1966, Jl 29,31:1
Harris, Susan J, 1944, Ap 21,19:5
Harris, Sydney E, 1962, D 1,25:2
Harris, T (see also F 26), 1878, Mr 1,2:2
Harris, Thaddeus W, 1946, Jl 22,21:5
Harris, Thomas A, 1940, Ap 14,45:2
Harris, Thomas D, 1956, Ag 9,25:6
Harris, Thomas J, 1943, Mr 15,13:4
Harris, Thomas J Mrs, 1951, My 24,35:6
Harris, Thomas L, 1941, Ag 24,34:8; 1943, S 28,25:4
Harris, Thomas L Mrs, 1961, Ag 16,31:4
Harris, Thomas R Rev Dr, 1909, Ja 25,9:5
Harris, Tom, 1947, My 8,25:5
Harris, Victor, 1943, F 16,19:5; 1950, Ja 4,35:5; 1965, Jl 1,28:5
Harris, Vincentia Sister, 1952, Ap 8,29:3
Harris, Virginia Mrs, 1952, O 23,31:5
Harris, W A, 1864, Ap 10,3:4; 1912, S 23,13:2
Harris, W Hall, 1938, My 1,II,6:7
Harris, W J, 1932, Ap 19,21:1
Harris, W Randall, 1953, F 22,61:2
Harris, W Rev, 1885, Mr 25,1:6
Harris, W T Mrs, 1948, Ja 6,24:2
Harris, W W, 1932, Ag 7,24:3
Harris, Wade N, 1967, Ag 10,37:1
Harris, Walden, 1954, O 21,27:3
Harris, Walt, 1947, O 6,21:3
Harris, Walter, 1946, O 13,59:7

Harris, Walter B, 1941, N 2,52:1
Harris, Walter C, 1952, F 24,85:1
Harris, Walter E, 1939, N 10,23:3
Harris, Walter J, 1945, Jl 31,19:1
Harris, Walter P, 1945, S 21,21:1
Harris, Walter S, 1940, D 10,25:5; 1945, Je 23,13:2
Harris, Walter W, 1952, F 8,23:4
Harris, Warren, 1938, F 15,25:3
Harris, Whitney F, 1962, F 24,27:4
Harris, Wilfred E Dr, 1916, Jl 26,11:7
Harris, Will J, 1967, D 15,47:2
Harris, William, 1903, S 5,7:6; 1916, N 7,11:5; 1923, O 27,13:5; 1924, Ap 6,27:2; 1953, Ap 8,29:5; 1953, N 8,31:1; 1954, F 25,31:5; 1956, Ap 23,31:6
Harris, William Alexander, 1909, D 21,9:3
Harris, William B, 1952, Mr 5,29:3; 1952, N 13,31:2; 1965, Ap 29,35:3
Harris, William B Mrs, 1937, D 12,II,8:7
Harris, William C, 1953, My 19,29:2
Harris, William D, 1944, Mr 11,13:3
Harris, William E Dr, 1937, Ja 15,21:3
Harris, William F, 1963, N 3,88:8
Harris, William Fenwick Prof, 1923, My 15,19:4
Harris, William H, 1919, N 15,11:3; 1939, Ap 17,17:5; 1959, Ap 29,33:4; 1959, My 10,86:6
Harris, William J, 1904, F 22,5:6; 1943, F 8,20:3
Harris, William J Mrs, 1953, S 3,15:5
Harris, William Jr, 1946, S 3,19:1
Harris, William L, 1951, N 1,29:1
Harris, William Laurel, 1924, Jl 7,15:5
Harris, William M, 1955, Jl 10,73:1
Harris, William Mrs, 1921, Ap 28,13:4
Harris, William R, 1915, Ja 27,9:6; 1948, Mr 15,23:6
Harris, William Sr (funl, N 28,13:4), 1916, N 26,21:1
Harris, William T, 1949, Ag 26,19:3; 1951, N 17,17:4
Harris, William T Mrs, 1958, Ja 10,26:3
Harris, William Torrey, 1909, N 6,9:5
Harris, Wilmot L, 1913, My 8,11:5
Harrison, A, 1930, O 14,25:1
Harrison, Abraham, 1938, D 2,23:5
Harrison, Abraham E, 1958, F 7,21:4
Harrison, Agatha Mrs, 1954, My 11,29:5
Harrison, Albert A, 1946, Ag 31,15:3
Harrison, Alden E, 1942, Je 6,13:1
Harrison, Alex, 1960, N 26,21:6
Harrison, Alfred C, 1950, Ja 28,13:6
Harrison, Alfred Craven Jr, 1925, Jl 10,17:7
Harrison, Alfred F, 1956, S 27,35:4
Harrison, Allan S, 1962, Mr 6,35:1
Harrison, Allrich S, 1958, D 19,2:6
Harrison, Ambrose I, 1910, Ag 26,7:5
Harrison, Anne F Mrs, 1940, My 27,19:5
Harrison, Archibald W, 1946, Ja 9,23:2
Harrison, Arthur H, 1948, F 25,23:5; 1955, My 12,29:4
Harrison, Arthur M, 1955, S 1,23:2
Harrison, Austen S, 1942, F 26,19:3
Harrison, B, 1929, My 12,28:7
Harrison, Benjamin, 1901, Mr 14,1:7
Harrison, Benjamin E, 1942, Je 28,32:8
Harrison, Benjamin Mrs, 1892, O 25,1:7; 1948, Ja 6, 23:1
Harrison, Benjamin S, 1949, S 23,23:2
Harrison, Benjamin V, 1953, N 14,17:2
Harrison, Benjamin V Mrs, 1952, Ag 3,60:2
Harrison, Bernard J, 1941, D 31,17:2
Harrison, Bertram, 1955, Ag 25,23:4
Harrison, Beverly N, 1954, Ag 22,92:2
Harrison, Birge Mrs, 1947, S 9,31:5
Harrison, Burton Mrs, 1920, N 22,15:2
Harrison, Burton N, 1904, Mr 30,9:2
Harrison, Byron L, 1960, N 9,35:4
Harrison, C C, 1929, F 13,23:3
Harrison, C Peer Dr, 1912, S 3,11:4
Harrison, Caleb M, 1904, Mr 13,9:6
Harrison, Carter H, 1952, O 31,23:7; 1953, D 26,13:4
Harrison, Carter H Mrs, 1955, My 24,31:2
Harrison, Carter H 3d, 1964, N 10,47:2
Harrison, Caskie Dr, 1902, N 14,9:5
Harrison, Cecil R, 1940, D 12,27:1
Harrison, Charles A, 1938, Jl 21,21:3; 1955, Je 17,23:2
Harrison, Charles C Jr, 1948, D 23,20:3
Harrison, Charles E, 1939, Mr 12,III,7:2
Harrison, Charles L, 1912, S 15,II,15:5
Harrison, Charles L Mrs, 1949, My 29,36:4
Harrison, Charles V Mrs, 1940, Jl 19,19:3
Harrison, Charles W, 1947, S 13,11:5
Harrison, Charles Y, 1954, Mr 19,23:3
Harrison, Clarence D, 1959, My 23,25:5
Harrison, Clark W, 1958, S 18,31:2
Harrison, Clifford E, 1951, Je 30,15:7
Harrison, Cyril R, 1965, S 3,27:3
Harrison, David, 1964, F 28,29:1
Harrison, David E, 1947, D 5,23:5
Harrison, David J, 1953, Mr 21,17:2
Harrison, Dennis J, 1938, O 7,23:2
Harrison, Dorothy A, 1960, Je 9,33:4
Harrison, Earl G, 1955, Jl 30,17:4
Harrison, Edgar P Sr, 1937, F 25,23:3
Harrison, Edlow Wingate, 1925, N 28,15:6
Harrison, Edward, 1967, O 18,47:2
Harrison, Edward K, 1951, My 30,23:2
Harrison, Edwin M, 1953, Je 25,27:3
Harrison, Ernest H, 1941, D 16,28:2

Harrison, Eveleen, 1949, F 3,23:2
Harrison, F Earle, 1957, Mr 21,31:2
Harrison, Fairfax (por),(cor, F 4,21:1), 1938, F 3,23:5
Harrison, Fannie L Mrs, 1943, Ja 21,21:2
Harrison, Faustino, 1963, Ag 21,33:5
Harrison, Floyd R, 1961, S 26,39:1
Harrison, Fosdick B, 1940, Mr 3,45:1
Harrison, Francis B (funl plans, N 29,27:3; funl, D 5,35:2), 1957, N 22,25:1
Harrison, Francis Burton Mrs (will, D 13,10:2), 1905, N 26,1:5
Harrison, Francis M, 1960, O 19,45:2
Harrison, Francis T Mrs, 1941, Ag 27,19:4
Harrison, Frank H, 1965, Ag 4,35:4
Harrison, Fred R, 1953, Ap 24,23:1
Harrison, Frederick, 1923, Ja 15,15:5
Harrison, G Donald, 1956, Je 16,19:3
Harrison, Gab, 1902, D 16,9:6
Harrison, Geofrey H, 1939, F 17,19:4
Harrison, George, 1937, Ap 24,19:5
Harrison, George A, 1945, Ag 20,19:3
Harrison, George D, 1942, My 10,43:3
Harrison, George L, 1955, N 23,23:2
Harrison, George L (funl plans, Mr 7,23:2; funl, Mr 8,17:4), 1958, Mr 6,27:4
Harrison, George L Mrs, 1914, D 31,9:5; 1951, Jl 7, 13:4; 1961, Ag 10,27:2
Harrison, George M, 1968, D 3,47:1
Harrison, George T, 1942, Ag 27,19:3
Harrison, George Tucker Dr, 1922, N 4,13:6; 1925, O 5,21:4
Harrison, George W Mrs, 1937, O 19,25:4
Harrison, Gilbert W, 1959, O 26,29:5
Harrison, Gordon, 1945, O 12,23:1
Harrison, H S, 1930, Jl 15,23:3
Harrison, Harold, 1948, Mr 23,25:2
Harrison, Harry, 1949, Je 19,71:5
Harrison, Harry E, 1951, Jl 24,25:2
Harrison, Harry L, 1952, F 28,27:6
Harrison, Helen S, 1941, My 7,25:3
Harrison, Henry, 1954, F 22,19:1
Harrison, Henry A Mrs, 1959, My 26,35:3
Harrison, Henry D, 1941, D 18,27:3
Harrison, Henry F, 1954, S 28,29:6
Harrison, Henry H, 1946, D 31,18:2
Harrison, Henry K Mrs, 1939, D 28,6:5
Harrison, Henry R, 1962, F 21,41:3
Harrison, I Carrington Mrs, 1956, S 21,25:3
Harrison, J B, 1881, Mr 27,5:1; 1940, Ag 27,21:2
Harrison, J Henry (por), 1943, Ap 3,15:1
Harrison, J Kearsley M, 1953, Jl 3,19:1
Harrison, J Max, 1966, Ap 6,43:1
Harrison, J S, 1878, My 29,5:5
Harrison, J W Mrs, 1903, N 13,12:1; 1909, F 19,9:6
Harrison, Jack, 1960, N 20,86:5
Harrison, James, 1948, My 7,23:1; 1959, My 3,86:3
Harrison, James A Prof, 1911, F 1,11:5
Harrison, James Findley, 1907, F 15,11:4
Harrison, James R, 1950, F 22,29:2
Harrison, James W, 1947, Ag 5,23:5
Harrison, James W Mrs, 1960, Jl 28,27:4
Harrison, Jared F Mrs, 1909, Ap 16,9:4
Harrison, Jeanne B Mrs, 1956, S 10,27:4
Harrison, Jerome G, 1961, Ag 22,29:4
Harrison, John, 1948, N 12,23:3
Harrison, John A, 1943, Jl 16,17:3
Harrison, John B, 1921, Mr 11,15:4
Harrison, John D (por), 1943, F 9,23:1
Harrison, John F, 1951, Ap 15,92:2
Harrison, John H, 1950, Ja 14,15:5
Harrison, John Jr, 1952, Je 13,23:5
Harrison, John M, 1952, S 20,15:1
Harrison, John Mrs, 1937, Jl 30,19:4
Harrison, John P, 1956, Jl 8,64:3
Harrison, John T, 1960, My 24,37:2
Harrison, John T Sen, 1903, D 19,9:5
Harrison, Joseph, 1944, O 12,27:5
Harrison, Joseph D, 1943, D 25,13:3
Harrison, Joseph F X, 1954, D 2,31:1
Harrison, Joseph Jr, 1874, Mr 28,7:4; 1957, Jl 13,17:4
Harrison, Joseph L, 1950, My 20,15:3; 1960, Mr 29, 37:3
Harrison, Joseph O B, 1903, D 16,9:4
Harrison, Joseph T, 1958, F 19,27:1
Harrison, Joseph W, 1952, O 8,31:1
Harrison, Julian C, 1951, S 20,31:4
Harrison, Julius, 1963, Ap 6,19:2
Harrison, Lee, 1916, O 31,13:7
Harrison, Leigh Mrs, 1951, D 20,31:4
Harrison, Leland, 1951, Je 8,27:1
Harrison, Lewis L, 1946, Je 29,19:5
Harrison, Lora M, 1941, Ag 8,15:4
Harrison, Lottchen P Mrs, 1953, Ag 16,77:2
Harrison, Louis, 1942, Ag 12,19:6
Harrison, Louis H, 1949, Je 9,31:4
Harrison, Louis Mrs, 1909, N 27,9:4
Harrison, Luther, 1959, Ja 18,88:3
Harrison, Lynde, 1906, Je 9,9:4
Harrison, M Hunter Mrs, 1961, S 7,35:2
Harrison, Margaret, 1938, Mr 30,21:3
Harrison, Marion, 1950, Ja 25,27:4
Harrison, Mary L, 1947, Je 30,19:2
Harrison, Maud, 1907, Ap 29,9:5

Harrison, Maurice E Sr, 1951, F 12,23:4
Harrison, Meyer, 1945, Mr 24,17:4
Harrison, Meyer S Mrs, 1956, F 19,92:4
Harrison, Michael B, 1948, S 30,28:2
Harrison, Milton S, 1965, My 31,17:5
Harrison, Milton W (por), 1949, Ag 9,25:3
Harrison, Mortimer A, 1954, N 13,15:6
Harrison, Nancy H, 1963, Ag 8,9:4
Harrison, Neil F, 1959, Ja 2,25:1
Harrison, Neil G, 1956, Ap 25,35:2
Harrison, Oswald, 1947, O 11,17:6
Harrison, Pat, 1941, Je 23,1:2
Harrison, Paul W, 1962, D 1,25:3; 1963, My 28,28:8
Harrison, Pearson, 1945, O 22,17:6
Harrison, Phil H, 1950, Jl 8,13:7
Harrison, Philip N, 1920, Mr 30,11:5
Harrison, R A, 1878, N 2,3:3
Harrison, R B, 1935, Mr 15,21:1; 1936, D 14,23:1
Harrison, R M, 1958, My 14,33:4
Harrison, Ralph W, 1959, D 13,86:8
Harrison, Randolph P, 1940, Ap 12,23:2
Harrison, Ray, 1957, Jl 17,27:4
Harrison, Rex Mrs (K Kendall),(funl plans, S 9,41:4), 1959, S 7,15:5
Harrison, Rex Mrs (K Kendall),(est value set), 1960, Mr 9,5:6
Harrison, Richard B, 1950, F 23,27:4
Harrison, Richard C, 1960, Ja 25,27:4
Harrison, Richard C Mrs, 1941, S 7,51:3
Harrison, Robert, 1953, Ap 4,13:1
Harrison, Robert F, 1948, Jl 18,52:5
Harrison, Robert J, 1946, O 20,60:8
Harrison, Robert T, 1961, O 9,35:5
Harrison, Roland R, 1941, Ja 17,17:4
Harrison, Ronald B, 1967, Je 30,34:3
Harrison, Ross G, 1959, O 1,35:4
Harrison, Ross G Jr, 1965, Ap 21,45:5
Harrison, Ross G Jr Mrs, 1965, Ap 21,45:5
Harrison, Ross R, 1951, D 3,31:3
Harrison, Royal N, 1940, F 28,21:2
Harrison, Royle R, 1956, Ja 9,25:4
Harrison, Rufus Freeman, 1907, Ap 29,9:6
Harrison, Russell B Mrs, 1944, N 29,23:2
Harrison, Sally, 1957, Mr 26,33:1
Harrison, Sam, 1939, O 24,23:3
Harrison, Samuel, 1939, Ja 17,22:3
Harrison, Saul E, 1944, O 15,44:6
Harrison, Stanley, 1950, F 16,23:2
Harrison, Stephen B, 1947, Ag 18,17:2
Harrison, Stephen Mrs, 1947, Je 9,21:2
Harrison, Sumner D, 1962, F 27,33:2
Harrison, Susan R, 1938, My 23,17:1
Harrison, Thomas, 1925, N 4,23:3
Harrison, Thomas Barclay, 1921, Jl 29,13:4
Harrison, Thomas G Mrs, 1946, D 15,77:5
Harrison, Thomas P, 1949, N 2,27:3
Harrison, Thomas W, 1910, My 23,7:6
Harrison, Tilson L, 1947, Ja 19,53:7
Harrison, W G, 1883, N 19,5:1
Harrison, W Henry Mrs, 1951, S 3,13:3
Harrison, Wallace K, 1941, D 8,23:4
Harrison, Walter J, 1952, Jl 1,23:5
Harrison, Walter L, 1958, My 23,89:1
Harrison, Walter M, 1961, S 6,37:2
Harrison, Walter T, 1944, Jl 11,15:3
Harrison, Wayles R, 1949, My 31,23:1
Harrison, Wayne D, 1948, O 6,29:4
Harrison, Will, 1965, N 20,35:4
Harrison, William A, 1949, F 18,23:1; 1951, S 10,2
Harrison, William B, 1940, Je 4,24:2; 1948, Jl 14,2.
Harrison, William E, 1949, Ap 2,15:2
Harrison, William F, 1942, Jl 27,15:5
Harrison, William H, 1943, Mr 10,19:3; 1955, Jl 2(27:4; 1956, Ap 22,87:1; 1962, Ag 3,23:4; 1948, A
Harrison, William H Mrs, 1864, F 28,1:4; 1961, Mr 11,21:5
Harrison, William H 2d, 1956, Ap 7,19:3
Harrison, William J, 1909, Mr 24,9:3
Harrison, William K Mrs, 1949, Mr 30,25:1
Harrison, William L, 1951, My 13,88:3
Harrison, William M, 1965, Ap 17,19:5
Harrison, William P, 1940, Je 29,15:3
Harrison, William R, 1968, Mr 31,81:2
Harrison, William W Mrs, 1907, Ja 19,7:5
Harrison-Berlitz, Victor, 1965, Mr 31,39:1
Harrison-Irvine, Jessamine Mrs, 1956, Ap 3,35:3
Harriss, Charles Langdon, 1925, S 28,19:5
Harriss, H H Sr, 1947, D 28,40:2
Harriss, John A (por),(will, N 19,33:2), 1938, O 23:3
Harriss, Raylis E, 1912, D 15,17:4
Harriss, Robert M Mrs, 1938, Ap 29,21:4
Harriss, W Leslie (por), 1937, Je 2,23:5
Harriss, Wayne E, 1958, My 6,35:3
Harrity, James E, 1946, F 22,25:2
Harrity, Margaretta J, 1941, Ja 27,15:2
Harrity, Richard Mrs, 1967, S 24,84:1
Harrity, William F, 1912, Ap 18,13:5
Harrje, Frederick J, 1944, My 4,19:4
Harrocks, Thomas L, 1961, S 15,30:6
Harrod, Benjamin Morgan Maj, 1912, S 8,II,13:4
Harrod, Clifford L, 1952, Je 10,27:3
Harrod, William A, 1947, Je 13,23:4
Harroff, Fred F, 1955, Mr 29,29:3

Harrold, Anson F, 1907, Ap 19,9:5
Harrold, Charles W, 1956, Mr 19,31:3
Harrold, Ernest W, 1945, O 23,17:6
Harrold, Howard A, 1949, Ja 24,19:4
Harrold, John A, 1942, F 21,20:5
Harrold, John F, 1940, O 19,17:4; 1962, Ag 26,82:6
Harrold, O, 1933, O 24,21:4
Harrold, Sears, 1954, D 28,23:4
Harron, Raymond V, 1965, My 26,47:2
Harron, Robert, 1920, S 6,7:5
Harron, Thomas J, 1957, D 24,15:4
Harrop, George A Jr (por), 1945, Ag 5,38:3
Harrop, Herbert B, 1956, Ap 9,27:5
Harrop, James L, 1937, F 7,II,8:7
Harroun, G K, 1901, S 14,7:5
Harroun, Ray, 1968, Ja 20,29:2
Harrow, Benjamin, 1958, Ja 27,27:3
Harrowby, Earl of (J H D Ryder), 1956, Mr 31,15:6
Harrower, David C, 1940, My 3,21:4
Harrower, David Dr, 1937, Ag 8,II,6:3
Harrower, Pascal (por), 1946, Jl 1,31:5
Harrower, Pascal R, 1965, Ja 3,85:1
Harry, Arthur J, 1948, Ap 23,23:4
Harry, Edward J, 1951, N 18,90:6
Harry, Felix L, 1952, Ag 8,17:3
Harry, J M, 1903, Ag 30,7:6
Harry, Joseph E, 1949, Ag 13,11:3
Harry, Mabel, 1941, Jl 16,17:1
Harry, Myriam M, 1958, Mr 12,31:4
Harry, Rush N, 1938, My 30,11:4
Harryman, William K, 1959, Ja 16,27:1
Harsanyi, Ladislaus, 1968, My 8,44:3
Harsanyi, Paul, 1962, Mr 2,30:1
Harsanyi, Vendel, 1952, Jl 22,25:4
Harsanyi, Zsolt de (por), 1944, F 28,17:4
Harsch, Frank, 1938, Jl 26,19:4
Harsch, John W, 1962, Ja 23,33:1
Harsell, B L, 1882, Je 8,5:4
Harsell, Norman, 1923, My 8,17:5
Harsen, Jacob, 1937, Ap 4,II,10:7
Harsen, Jacob Dr, 1863, Ja 7,2:1
Harsh, Glenn E, 1950, N 21,31:3
Harsha, William T, 1950, D 17,85:1
Harshaw, E B, 1945, S 19,25:4
Harshaw, Frederick T, 1947, Ap 27,60:1
Harshbarger, Ira J, 1940, Jl 13,13:5
Harshe, Robert B Mrs, 1953, D 14,31:5
Harshe, Robert E, 1938, Ja 12,21:3
Harshe, William R, 1950, Ja 8,76:5
Harshman, George, 1940, O 19,17:4
Harshman, Thurman, 1938, Ja 27,21:1
Harson, C Edward, 1949, O 15,15:5
Harson, Harry Mrs, 1949, My 16,21:1
Harstad, Oscar N, 1949, Ap 28,31:6
Harstein, Nathan B, 1946, Ap 19,29:1
Hart, A C, 1935, Jl 25,19:3
Hart, Abraham, 1950, S 6,29:5
Hart, Albert B, 1943, Je 17,21:1
Hart, Albert E, 1957, Ja 18,21:2
Hart, Albert V, 1948, N 12,23:4
Hart, Alex J, 1943, Je 25,17:2
Hart, Alex R, 1938, D 27,17:4
Hart, Alfred (will), 1938, Ap 28,2:5
Hart, Alfred A, 1958, S 19,27:3
Hart, Alfred P, 1954, S 5,51:2
Hart, Alfred Thomas, 1953, F 25,27:3
Hart, Alonzo K Mrs, 1947, Ja 6,23:5
Hart, Annie, 1947, Je 15,60:2
Hart, Artemus Elijah, 1920, F 16,11:5
Hart, Arthur, 1922, Jl 8,11:6; 1943, D 24,14:6
Hart, Arthur D, 1946, My 25,15:4
Hart, Arthur H, 1964, My 9,27:4
Hart, Arthur S, 1938, Mr 5,17:3
Hart, Augustin S, 1947, D 29,17:5
Hart, Augustus B, 1916, Jl 8,9:4
Hart, Austin H, 1937, My 15,19:5
Hart, B J, 1885, Je 30,2:1
Hart, Barnet Mrs, 1937, S 7,21:2
Hart, Bartley, 1940, D 25,27:1
Hart, Bartnett, 1960, O 6,41:4
Hart, Benjamin S, 1949, F 14,19:4
Hart, Benno, 1939, D 3,60:3
Hart, Benno Mrs, 1966, Ag 17,36:3
Hart, Bernard (funl, Ag 21,21:4), 1964, Ag 19,37:2
Hart, Bertha, 1949, O 10,23:5
Hart, Bertrand K Mrs, 1944, Je 20,19:5
Hart, Bloomer, 1880, D 18,2:3
Hart, Boies C (por), 1946, Je 16,40:8
Hart, Boies C Jr, 1960, S 29,35:2
Hart, Carl K, 1952, D 25,29:5
Hart, Cecil, 1940, Jl 17,21:2
Hart, Charles, 1950, My 25,29:5
Hart, Charles A, 1959, Ja 30,28:1
Hart, Charles Aaron, 1914, O 1,11:5
Hart, Charles C, 1956, N 26,27:5
Hart, Charles D, 1951, F 16,25:3
Hart, Charles Edward Rev Dr, 1916, D 17,19:3
Hart, Charles F (por),(funl, D 4,30:2; will, D 12,29:7), 1945, D 2,45:1
Hart, Charles F, 1948, Ag 8,56:7
Hart, Charles F Mrs, 1953, Ja 10,17:3
Hart, Charles H, 1938, Jl 15,17:5; 1940, Ja 7,48:4
Hart, Charles Henry, 1918, Jl 31,9:5
Hart, Charles J, 1943, Jl 15,21:5
Hart, Charles Mansfield, 1968, Ap 16,44:3
Hart, Charles P, 1957, Mr 23,19:6
Hart, Charles S, 1951, Ja 26,23:1
Hart, Charles W, 1949, My 28,15:3
Hart, Charlie, 1950, O 26,31:4; 1954, S 15,33:3
Hart, Claude V, 1938, Ap 12,23:4
Hart, Clayton J, 1952, My 29,27:1
Hart, Cornelius A, 1944, Ja 19,19:3
Hart, Cornelius F, 1949, My 31,23:3
Hart, Cornelius N, 1956, Ap 24,31:4
Hart, Crawford A, 1962, Ja 29,25:4
Hart, Crawford P Mrs, 1946, O 9,27:3
Hart, Dan Seixas, 1904, Mr 25,9:5
Hart, Daniel F X, 1960, Mr 10,31:2
Hart, Daniel P, 1949, O 19,29:4
Hart, David, 1958, Je 4,31:6
Hart, David T, 1951, Je 9,19:3
Hart, Donald P, 1942, Je 28,32:6
Hart, Donald P Mrs, 1948, D 28,21:6
Hart, E Francis, 1948, Ag 15,60:2
Hart, Earl, 1948, O 12,25:5
Hart, Edward, 1939, N 22,21:1; 1959, Je 15,27:4
Hart, Edward A, 1948, Ag 18,25:3
Hart, Edward F, 1937, Jl 9,21:1; 1958, N 8,21:5
Hart, Edward H, 1951, Jl 6,23:3
Hart, Edward J, 1956, N 30,23:3; 1957, Jl 21,60:2; 1960, Je 20,31:4; 1961, Ap 21,33:1
Hart, Edward L Mrs, 1948, Mr 9,23:3
Hart, Edward M, 1938, O 23,40:7
Hart, Edward W, 1924, My 29,19:6; 1951, F 4,76:5
Hart, Edwin B, 1953, Mr 13,25:3
Hart, Edwin C, 1956, N 19,31:5
Hart, Edwin P, 1955, N 9,33:1
Hart, Elmer R, 1950, My 29,29:2
Hart, Ernest, 1944, D 6,23:5
Hart, Ernest F, 1917, O 3,13:5
Hart, Ernest N, 1950, Mr 12,94:3
Hart, Errol E Mrs, 1957, Ja 31,27:4
Hart, Eugene F, 1937, My 11,25:3
Hart, Eugene M, 1965, Jl 7,37:3
Hart, Frances N, 1943, O 26,23:3
Hart, Francis, 1877, Ap 26,10:4
Hart, Francis B, 1949, S 25,92:5
Hart, Francis R (por), 1938, Ja 19,23:1
Hart, Frank, 1954, Ag 6,17:4
Hart, Frank E, 1962, N 15,37:5
Hart, Frank J, 1944, S 10,45:1
Hart, Frank S, 1946, F 16,13:1
Hart, Franklin A, 1967, Je 23,39:2
Hart, Fred A, 1940, Jl 2,21:6
Hart, Frederick H M, 1953, My 25,25:5
Hart, Fritz, 1949, Jl 11,17:5
Hart, G O, 1933, S 10,38:3
Hart, Gardiner T, 1960, Ag 26,25:4
Hart, Gardner O, 1949, D 3,15:1
Hart, George H, 1959, Ag 4,27:5
Hart, George H C, 1943, S 4,13:2
Hart, George Mrs, 1944, Je 2,15:4
Hart, George P, 1951, Jl 15,60:3
Hart, George Spencer, 1913, S 12,11:4
Hart, Gordon J, 1949, Mr 31,25:5
Hart, H Beverly, 1938, Je 16,23:4
Hart, H H, 1932, My 10,21:5
Hart, H Martyn, 1920, Mr 25,11:6
Hart, Harold B, 1943, Ag 19,19:2
Hart, Harold C, 1937, Jl 17,15:5
Hart, Harold G, 1952, S 11,31:2
Hart, Harry, 1951, Ap 3,27:1; 1952, Mr 26,29:4
Hart, Harry B, 1954, Ja 8,21:3
Hart, Harry Mrs, 1949, S 28,27:4
Hart, Harry S, 1960, F 16,37:4
Hart, Harry W Jr, 1964, Mr 20,33:4
Hart, Henry B, 1903, Jl 25,7:2
Hart, Henry B Mrs, 1952, Jl 26,13:6
Hart, Henry C, 1943, Mr 24,23:4
Hart, Henry G, 1958, N 18,37:3
Hart, Henry G Mrs, 1951, My 9,33:5; 1955, O 21,27:2
Hart, Henry J, 1948, My 31,19:5
Hart, Henry W Mrs, 1918, O 18,13:2
Hart, Herbert T Mrs, 1950, S 13,27:2
Hart, Herbert W, 1906, Ag 8,7:4
Hart, Hickson F, 1938, N 8,23:6
Hart, Horace Greeley Mrs, 1919, Jl 20,21:3
Hart, Hornell, 1967, Mr 1,43:3
Hart, Howard S, 1944, Mr 9,17:2
Hart, Hubert C, 1940, Ag 16,15:5
Hart, Ida A, 1946, D 31,17:2
Hart, Israel Dr, 1907, Je 24,7:6
Hart, J Garwood, 1952, S 2,23:4
Hart, J T, 1877, Mr 3,4:7
Hart, Jacob L, 1952, Mr 2,92:1
Hart, James, 1937, Ap 29,21:2; 1951, Ag 10,15:1; 1959, S 21,31:3
Hart, James A, 1960, F 28,82:6
Hart, James A Mrs, 1947, D 29,17:2
Hart, James D, 1924, My 22,17:4
Hart, James E, 1954, Mr 10,25:1
Hart, James F, 1946, Ja 8,24:2; 1947, Je 5,25:1; 1959, F 25,31:5
Hart, James H, 1965, Ja 2,19:4
Hart, James J Mrs, 1944, F 24,15:4
Hart, James Morgan, 1916, Ap 21,11:6
Hart, James P, 1947, Ag 16,13:3
Hart, James S, 1946, D 19,30:2
Hart, Jesse E, 1949, Ja 22,13:5
Hart, Joel C, 1942, Ap 11,13:6
Hart, John, 1940, Jl 4,15:6; 1945, My 4,19:1; 1945, Je 28,19:6; 1949, Jl 2,15:5; 1957, Ap 8,23:5; 1960, Ap 13,39:3
Hart, John C Rev, 1922, Je 25,26:3
Hart, John F, 1948, O 28,29:2
Hart, John G, 1940, My 21,23:3
Hart, John G H, 1954, My 15,15:2
Hart, John J, 1951, My 30,21:3; 1953, Ag 13,25:2; 1954, Ja 6,31:4
Hart, John L, 1938, Ap 5,23:2
Hart, John M, 1957, Ap 8,23:2
Hart, John Mrs, 1958, My 30,21:3
Hart, John W, 1944, O 24,23:3
Hart, Joseph, 1921, O 3,13:2
Hart, Joseph E, 1946, O 1,23:6
Hart, Joseph G, 1942, Je 5,17:3
Hart, Joseph H, 1948, N 3,27:4
Hart, Joseph H Jr, 1954, Ja 23,13:2
Hart, Joseph K, 1949, Mr 12,17:6
Hart, Joseph S, 1963, S 18,39:4
Hart, Joseph T, 1962, Mr 9,19:6
Hart, Joseph W, 1960, Jl 24,64:3
Hart, Josh, 1909, Ag 22,9:6
Hart, Jules Mrs, 1953, Mr 17,29:2
Hart, Julian G, 1949, D 27,23:1
Hart, Julian L, 1963, F 12,4:6
Hart, Kenneth R, 1967, F 2,35:2
Hart, Laurance H Mrs, 1961, S 27,42:1
Hart, Laurence C Mrs, 1948, S 26,76:5
Hart, Lawrence M, 1947, N 20,29:1
Hart, Lemuel H, 1903, My 23,9:3
Hart, Lemuel M, 1917, Ap 25,11:7
Hart, Leo J (por), 1939, S 28,25:4
Hart, Leroy C, 1945, D 5,25:4
Hart, Leslie J, 1952, Je 14,15:3
Hart, Levi, 1874, D 24,5:2
Hart, Lila G, 1943, S 28,25:2
Hart, Lorenz (Larry), 1943, N 23,25:2
Hart, Louis B, 1939, Jl 19,19:6
Hart, Louis L, 1948, D 25,18:2
Hart, Lucille M (por), 1945, D 22,19:1
Hart, Lucy Mrs, 1939, N 9,23:6
Hart, Luke E, 1964, F 20,29:2
Hart, Luke E Mrs, 1951, Je 1,23:3
Hart, M Beth, 1953, D 9,11:6
Hart, Malcolm D, 1950, S 28,31:4
Hart, Mark, 1950, N 28,31:2
Hart, Mary A Mrs, 1942, S 12,13:6
Hart, Mary C Mrs, 1937, S 11,17:3
Hart, Mary F, 1947, O 24,23:4
Hart, Mary Mrs, 1937, Je 8,25:5
Hart, Matilda S Mrs, 1948, My 29,15:5
Hart, Maude, 1943, N 20,13:5
Hart, Max, 1950, My 24,29:1
Hart, Maxwell S, 1948, Mr 15,23:2
Hart, Merwin K, 1962, D 2,88:6
Hart, Michael J, 1948, Jl 14,23:2; 1951, F 15,31:1
Hart, Michael Mrs, 1952, Ag 17,76:4
Hart, Milton, 1937, N 18,23:5
Hart, Mitchell, 1872, Ag 5,8:5
Hart, Morris Washington, 1925, F 28,13:5
Hart, Moss (funl plans, D 22,23:2), 1961, D 21,1:7
Hart, Moss (mem ser), 1962, Ja 10,25:3
Hart, Nathan H, 1938, Mr 6,II,8:6
Hart, Neal, 1949, Ap 4,23:1
Hart, Nettie, 1962, S 27,37:2
Hart, Nona C, 1956, N 11,87:1
Hart, O B Gov, 1874, Mr 19,5:3
Hart, Olive E, 1950, N 19,92:8
Hart, Oliver Mrs, 1944, S 14,23:5
Hart, P H, 1937, S 20,23:2
Hart, Parker E, 1949, My 6,25:1
Hart, Patrick E, 1953, Ap 8,29:2
Hart, Patrick J, 1945, My 17,19:1
Hart, Percy C, 1951, D 23,22:7
Hart, Perry P, 1966, O 4,47:3
Hart, Peter, 1943, Ja 9,13:3
Hart, Peter A, 1947, My 20,25:3
Hart, Peter J, 1949, N 21,25:3
Hart, Phoebe C Mrs, 1941, Ja 29,17:4
Hart, R, 1883, Ap 21,2:6
Hart, R H, 1942, My 6,19:6
Hart, R Sir, 1931, O 20,25:3
Hart, Ray, 1948, D 2,29:4
Hart, Ray H Mrs, 1960, Ap 23,23:4
Hart, Raymund, 1960, Jl 18,27:2
Hart, Richard, 1951, Ja 4,30:2
Hart, Richard J (J Capone), 1952, O 2,29:4
Hart, Robert F Mrs, 1955, N 12,19:2
Hart, Robert Sir, 1911, S 21,13:6
Hart, Roy, 1951, D 29,11:1
Hart, Roy M, 1947, Ja 14,25:6
Hart, Samuel, 1878, S 4,5:6
Hart, Samuel C, 1940, My 23,23:5
Hart, Samuel G, 1942, F 26,19:3
Hart, Samuel W, 1945, Jl 23,19:4
Hart, Sanders W, 1942, O 26,15:4
Hart, Sophie C, 1948, D 5,92:6
Hart, Stanley H, 1944, N 15,27:4

Hart, Stanley M, 1965, Ap 14,41:1
Hart, Stephen F Maj, 1937, F 6,17:4
Hart, T N, 1927, O 5,27:5
Hart, T Russell, 1874, Ag 9,8:3
Hart, Theodore S, 1951, Ja 2,23:5
Hart, Thomas, 1947, Ja 19,53:4
Hart, Thomas C, 1945, Je 19,4:6
Hart, Thomas F Mrs, 1951, Ja 17,27:1
Hart, Thomas R, 1954, D 10,27:2
Hart, Thomas R Jr, 1960, My 10,37:5
Hart, Vincent, 1939, Ja 30,13:4
Hart, Vincent G, 1957, Ag 4,38:4
Hart, Vivian S, 1947, Ap 17,27:5
Hart, W D, 1946, Mr 17,46:5
Hart, W H Maj Gen, 1926, Ja 3,II,9:1
Hart, W Lee, 1957, D 24,15:1
Hart, Walter F, 1945, D 27,20:3
Hart, Walter H, 1956, D 27,25:2
Hart, Walter R Mrs, 1956, Je 7,31:4
Hart, Walter S Mrs, 1952, Ap 21,21:3
Hart, Weldon, 1957, N 21,29:4
Hart, William, 1938, Jl 28,19:5; 1945, F 27,19:3
Hart, William C, 1943, Je 3,21:5
Hart, William D, 1937, Mr 7,II,8:7
Hart, William F, 1939, F 1,21:3
Hart, William G, 1966, Je 17,45:3
Hart, William H Mrs, 1955, Je 7,33:4
Hart, William J, 1918, Ag 10,7:5; 1947, Je 12,25:6
Hart, William M, 1910, Ja 2,II,13:5
Hart, William R, 1954, Ja 12,23:2
Hart, William R Mrs, 1963, N 1,33:4
Hart, William S, 1946, Je 25,21:1; 1947, D 21,54:1
Hartcorn, Albert E, 1940, Je 15,15:4
Hartdegan, Carl, 1963, My 4,25:1
Hartdegen, Joseph Mrs, 1947, N 12,27:2
Harte, Archibald C, 1946, Ap 15,27:4
Harte, Bret, 1902, My 7,9:3
Harte, Charles R, 1956, N 14,35:4
Harte, Dennis J, 1917, F 21,11:5
Harte, Edward S Mrs, 1953, N 12,31:4
Harte, F William, 1940, Mr 16,15:5
Harte, Griswold, 1901, D 14,9:5
Harte, Howard B, 1968, F 21,47:4
Harte, Richard Dr, 1925, N 16,19:5
Harte, Richard T, 1947, Ag 16,13:3
Harte, Thomas J, 1962, S 22,25:5
Harte, William F Mrs, 1961, Jl 9,77:1
Hartel, Alex, 1962, My 15,39:3
Hartel, George H, 1944, F 6,42:4
Hartemann, Andre, 1951, My 2,31:1
Harten, George H Mrs, 1949, O 28,23:2
Harten, James, 1960, Ag 5,23:3
Harten, James A, 1939, F 8,23:3
Harten, Max, 1957, My 26,92:5
Hartenstein, Loie Mrs, 1958, My 2,27:2
Hartenstein, William, 1951, Jl 29,68:5
Hartenstine, Charles J, 1952, Je 15,84:6
Harter, Benedict A, 1963, Ag 3,17:4
Harter, Edward R, 1949, D 16,31:4
Harter, George A, 1943, Jl 24,13:6
Harter, Gorham H, 1938, Mr 28,15:2
Harter, Harry J, 1944, Je 1,19:5
Harter, Harry M, 1957, S 22,86:5
Harter, Isaac, 1957, Ag 23,19:4
Harter, J Francis, 1947, D 20,54:1
Harter, Laura van D Mrs, 1940, D 4,27:3
Harter, Leslie J, 1963, O 22,38:1
Harter, Loren E, 1949, Jl 25,15:4
Harter, Stanley L, 1953, Je 13,15:4
Hartfelder, Frederick, 1953, F 16,21:4
Hartfield, John W, 1957, D 7,21:5
Hartfield, Joseph M, 1964, D 21,29:4
Hartfield, William, 1925, Jl 13,17:7
Hartford, Beldon F Mrs, 1943, D 8,23:3
Hartford, Edward F, 1942, My 31,38:2
Hartford, Edward Vassallo, 1922, Jl 1,13:6
Hartford, Fernando W, 1938, Jl 23,13:6
Hartford, George H, 1917, Ag 30,11:6
Hartford, George L, 1957, S 25,29:1
Hartford, George L Mrs, 1944, My 10,19:4
Hartford, John A, 1951, S 21,23:1
Hartford, John A Mrs, 1948, S 6,13:2
Harth, Joseph, 1952, O 8,31:4
Harth, William, 1960, Ag 15,8:4
Hartich, Estelle Crane Mrs, 1924, S 23,23:2
Hartig, Ernest L, 1948, Mr 29,21:6
Hartig, Henry J, 1939, Ja 27,20:3
Hartig, Hugo Mrs, 1963, Ag 21,33:2
Hartigan, Charles C, 1944, F 26,13:2
Hartigan, Clare, 1937, O 8,23:5
Hartigan, John A, 1952, Jl 19,15:5
Hartigan, John J, 1947, Je 5,26:2
Hartigan, John L, 1965, Ag 22,26:8
Hartigan, Maurice H, 1948, Ap 3,15:3
Hartigan, Richard, 1925, Ag 27,19:5
Hartigan, Thomas L, 1924, O 10,19:5
Hartigan, Thomas P, 1957, D 25,31:2
Hartill, Isaac, 1948, D 30,19:1
Hartill, Rufus M Mrs, 1965, O 31,86:7
Hartin, W F, 1945, Ja 12,15:4
Harting, Hans, 1951, S 26,31:2
Harting, Hugh E, 1961, O 10,43:3
Hartinonoff, Nicholas B, 1944, O 1,45:2
Hartke, J Ward, 1962, My 20,87:1
Hartke, Ruth, 1964, S 2,15:4
Hartkopf, Charles, 1938, Ja 29,15:3
Hartkopf, William H, 1944, S 22,19:4
Hartkorn, August, 1965, Mr 17,45:2
Hartl, Harry J, 1947, Ag 3,52:3
Hartle, Russell P, 1961, N 24,31:1
Hartley, A C, 1960, Ja 29,25:1
Hartley, Albert J, 1937, N 4,25:3
Hartley, Arthur Just, 1968, My 26,84:1
Hartley, Benjamin, 1955, D 28,26:7
Hartley, Charles, 1939, O 31,23:4
Hartley, Charles Sir, 1915, F 22,9:3
Hartley, E Mrs, 1929, N 17,26:1
Hartley, Edith D, 1947, Mr 16,60:4
Hartley, Edward, 1918, My 19,23:2
Hartley, Edward A Mrs, 1949, N 1,27:4
Hartley, Ernest, 1959, D 19,27:5
Hartley, Eugene F, 1961, D 6,47:1
Hartley, Florence, 1954, F 1,23:5
Hartley, Francis Chester Mrs, 1909, Ap 23,9:4
Hartley, Francis 2d, 1962, S 19,40:1
Hartley, Frank Dr, 1913, Je 20,9:4
Hartley, Frank S, 1950, Je 24,13:4
Hartley, G Russell, 1947, Jl 14,21:3
Hartley, George B, 1941, Mr 14,21:2
Hartley, George I, 1949, F 12,18:2
Hartley, George I Mrs, 1956, Ap 3,35:3
Hartley, Gordon C, 1949, Mr 30,25:5
Hartley, Harold, 1964, F 2,89:1
Hartley, Harriet L, 1951, O 19,27:1
Hartley, Henry, 1953, Mr 9,90:2
Hartley, Herbert, 1957, My 10,27:3
Hartley, James J (por), 1943, D 12,68:3
Hartley, James J, 1944, Ja 13,21:3
Hartley, John G, 1951, Ja 5,21:5
Hartley, John Mrs, 1941, My 11,44:4
Hartley, Jonathan Scott, 1912, D 7,15:5
Hartley, Joseph A, 1957, Ag 10,15:6
Hartley, Lyman R Mrs, 1966, Jl 27,39:2
Hartley, Marcellus, 1902, Ja 9,9:1
Hartley, Marda Mrs, 1961, Ja 17,37:4
Hartley, Marsden, 1943, S 3,19:3
Hartley, Richard Rev Dr, 1910, Ja 14,9:4
Hartley, Robert R, 1945, My 12,13:6
Hartley, Roland H, 1952, S 22,23:3
Hartley, Roy J Mrs, 1950, N 4,17:5
Hartley, W S, 1902, Jl 16,9:4
Hartley, Walter S, 1948, Jl 20,23:6
Hartley, William A, 1951, Ap 23,25:3
Hartlieb, J F, 1943, Mr 11,29:7
Hartlieb, J Frederick (por), 1943, Ja 27,21:1
Hartman, Aaron M, 1959, Jl 9,27:5
Hartman, Albert C, 1937, D 31,16:1
Hartman, Allen M, 1955, Mr 17,45:5
Hartman, Anna G Mrs, 1952, Je 22,68:1
Hartman, Arthur J, 1944, O 26,23:1
Hartman, Bertram, 1960, Ag 2,29:3
Hartman, Bertram T, 1942, D 20,45:1
Hartman, C H Rev, 1903, My 19,9:6
Hartman, Carl G Dr, 1968, Mr 2,29:1
Hartman, Charles Frederick, 1922, Mr 2,21:5
Hartman, Charles R, 1942, Ja 23,19:4
Hartman, Charles S, 1945, O 16,23:4
Hartman, Clarence F Mrs, 1955, My 8,89:1
Hartman, Dale A, 1950, Ja 22,78:1
Hartman, Don, 1958, Mr 24,27:1
Hartman, Edward, 1943, N 7,57:2
Hartman, Edward C, 1948, Ap 26,23:3
Hartman, Edwin H, 1947, Je 21,17:2
Hartman, Emanuel M, 1940, Mr 27,21:4
Hartman, Emanuel S, 1962, My 28,29:5
Hartman, Emil A, 1951, D 11,33:4
Hartman, Eral D, 1962, Jl 21,19:2
Hartman, Ernest F, 1942, O 2,25:4
Hartman, Ernest G, 1965, F 2,33:2
Hartman, F M Prof, 1932, Mr 29,19:1
Hartman, Frank, 1944, Ap 5,19:3
Hartman, Frank E, 1952, S 20,15:4
Hartman, Frank M, 1942, Ag 28,19:1
Hartman, Fred S, 1954, N 20,17:4
Hartman, Fritz, 1916, Ag 5,9:4
Hartman, G, 1936, N 3,23:1
Hartman, Galen Mrs, 1946, S 24,29:2
Hartman, George H, 1964, F 4,33:2
Hartman, George W, 1957, D 26,19:3
Hartman, Gertrude, 1955, My 13,25:1
Hartman, Grace (Mrs N Abbott), 1955, Ag 9,25:1
Hartman, Harry B, 1944, Je 14,19:6
Hartman, Harry H, 1950, Ja 29,68:4; 1951, Ja 9,29:2
Hartman, Hartley J, 1955, F 16,29:5
Hartman, Harvey W, 1948, O 9,19:4
Hartman, Henry G, 1952, Ja 5,11:4
Hartman, Herbert H, 1947, D 10,31:3
Hartman, Herbert W, 1945, O 3,19:3
Hartman, Howard R, 1959, O 9,21:3
Hartman, Hugh W, 1940, Je 9,44:1
Hartman, Hugo, 1950, N 21,31:6
Hartman, Jess, 1967, N 4,33:1
Hartman, Joel S, 1965, Je 21,29:4
Hartman, John, 1925, D 29,23:4; 1951, O 29,23:2
Hartman, John A, 1942, My 13,19:2
Hartman, John C, 1941, Ja 4,13:2; 1947, D 16,33:4
Hartman, John D Mrs, 1941, Mr 20,21:5
Hartman, John H, 1945, Ja 10,23:3
Hartman, John M, 1939, Jl 20,19:6
Hartman, John R, 1948, Mr 30,23:5
Hartman, Joseph, 1948, O 27,27:3
Hartman, Joseph A Mrs, 1963, Ap 8,47:4
Hartman, Kalman, 1914, F 18,9:4
Hartman, Kenneth P, 1966, Je 4,29:1
Hartman, Lee F, 1941, S 23,23:3
Hartman, Lee S, 1948, My 30,34:4
Hartman, Lee S Mrs, 1962, F 15,29:2
Hartman, Leon, 1944, Mr 12,37:2
Hartman, Leon W, 1943, Ag 29,39:2
Hartman, Leroy L, 1951, N 4,86:3
Hartman, Lewis O, 1955, Jl 2,15:3
Hartman, Lillian, 1943, Je 20,34:7
Hartman, Louis H, 1964, Jl 10,29:3
Hartman, Louis H Mrs, 1964, O 6,39:2
Hartman, Malcolm J, 1954, Ap 25,86:2
Hartman, Marie E (Mother Mary Carmelita), 195
My 20,25:3
Hartman, Mary B, 1948, N 2,25:3
Hartman, Maurice, 1948, F 9,17:3
Hartman, Maurice P, 1943, D 16,28:3
Hartman, Max E Mrs, 1966, S 13,47:2
Hartman, Myrtle M, 1949, D 24,15:3
Hartman, Oscar F Mrs, 1948, O 26,32:3
Hartman, Otto R, 1924, Ap 19,13:5
Hartman, Pierre, 1946, Mr 26,22:7
Hartman, R N Prof, 1903, My 9,1:4
Hartman, Samuel D Dr, 1918, Ja 31,9:3
Hartman, Samuel I, 1957, Jl 17,27:5
Hartman, Siegfried F, 1953, S 2,26:6
Hartman, Sydney J, 1950, Je 7,29:2
Hartman, W Emory, 1958, Je 6,23:3
Hartman, William H, 1946, My 28,21:1
Hartman, William N, 1960, S 18,86:8
Hartman, William Sr, 1945, Mr 13,23:4
Hartman, Winfield L, 1952, O 13,21:3
Hartman, Winfield L Mrs, 1941, Mr 25,23:4
Hartman, York A, 1940, Jl 3,17:3
Hartmann, Adolph N, 1903, Jl 15,7:6
Hartmann, Albert C, 1941, O 31,23:6
Hartmann, Andrew P, 1945, Ap 20,19:5
Hartmann, Arthur H, 1951, O 14,88:6
Hartmann, Arthur M, 1956, Mr 31,15:2
Hartmann, Carl F, 1961, Jl 18,29:5
Hartmann, Carl F Mrs, 1943, D 18,15:2
Hartmann, Charles F, 1955, Jl 15,21:6
Hartmann, Daniel, 1952, Mr 3,21:4
Hartmann, David, 1925, D 17,23:3
Hartmann, Edward L (por), 1944, Ja 1,13:4
Hartmann, Edward M, 1949, Ap 10,78:3
Hartmann, Eugene, 1905, Je 13,9:6
Hartmann, Felix von Cardinal, 1919, N 12,13:1
Hartmann, George, 1949, D 24,15:4
Hartmann, Georges, 1940, F 11,48:1
Hartmann, Gustave, 1961, Ag 12,17:1
Hartmann, Henri, 1952, Ja 4,23:4
Hartmann, Herman, 1966, My 29,56:6
Hartmann, Ingo F, 1965, Ap 20,39:3
Hartmann, J W, 1934, Ja 5,21:1
Hartmann, John B, 1952, S 17,31:3
Hartmann, John N, 1939, Ap 23,III,7:1
Hartmann, John N Sr Mrs, 1945, Ag 14,21:4
Hartmann, Joseph, 1942, S 5,13:4; 1946, Ja 30,25
Hartmann, Joseph Sr Mrs, 1949, My 9,25:1
Hartmann, Karl, 1954, Ja 8,21:4
Hartmann, Karl A, 1963, D 14,27:3
Hartmann, Karl Robert Eduard von, 1906, Je 7,7:
Hartmann, Louis, 1941, F 10,20:3; 1941, Je 17,2
1950, Jl 18,30:2
Hartmann, Ludo Prof, 1924, N 16,7:2
Hartmann, Rudolph C M, 1943, My 25,23:6
Hartmann, Sadakichi, 1944, N 23,31:3
Hartmann, Thomas Mrs, 1947, Mr 8,13:1
Hartmann, William V, 1947, Ag 25,17:6
Hartmann, Winfield S S, 1955, D 24,13:4
Hartmann, Zoltan, 1964, Jl 7,35:1
Hartneady, Michael J, 1938, Ag 13,13:5
Hartner, John A, 1940, Mr 23,13:4
Hartner, Rudolph, 1944, Jl 7,15:5
Hartnett, Anne C, 1948, Je 10,25:3
Hartnett, Augustus H, 1944, D 4,23:1
Hartnett, Edward F, 1962, Mr 31,25:5
Hartnett, Edward J, 1925, Ap 11,13:4
Hartnett, Edward P, 1946, Jl 27,17:3
Hartnett, Ellen A Mrs, 1947, N 16,76:5
Hartnett, Frank S, 1944, F 1,20:2
Hartnett, Fred, 1941, F 4,25:5
Hartnett, Fred J, 1945, N 29,23:4
Hartnett, Henry E, 1939, N 6,23:4
Hartnett, J A, 1932, Ap 8,21:5
Hartnett, James S, 1939, My 3,23:4
Hartnett, John F, 1963, Je 7,31:2
Hartnett, John L, 1937, F 15,17:5
Hartnett, Josephine J, 1953, My 1,21:3
Hartnett, Matthew H, 1952, F 13,29:5
Hartnett, Maurice M, 1954, Mr 31,27:3
Hartnett, Robert J, 1964, Ap 15,39:4
Hartnett, Thomas F, 1957, My 28,33:1
Hartnett, Thomas R, 1951, S 10,21:4
Hartnett, Thomas Sr, 1950, Ja 19,28:3

Hartney, Edward, 1952, D 11,33:5
Hartney, Frank, 1939, Ag 11,15:2
Hartney, Harold E, 1945, O 6,13:3
Hartney, Joseph J, 1951, D 2,89:1
Hartney, Martin J Mrs, 1948, O 19,27:5
Hartney, Martin J Sr, 1946, O 3,27:5
Hartney, William, 1945, My 11,19:3
Hartog, Jacob, 1962, D 5,47:4
Hartog, Louis N, 1943, Ja 18,15:4
Hartog, Mabel Lady, 1954, Jl 18,9:2
Hartog, Philip, 1947, Je 28,13:5
Hartogensis, Benjamin H, 1939, Jl 14,19:6
Hartogensis, Samuel A, 1939, S 27,25:3
Hartough, William C, 1953, Mr 14,15:4
Hartpence, Alanson Mrs, 1916, Ja 19,11:5
Hartpence, Edgar L, 1948, Ap 17,15:4
Hartpence, John P, 1913, N 17,9:4
Hartpence, Robert W, 1943, Ja 15,17:4
Hartranft, Chester D Rev Dr, 1915, Ja 22,11:4
Hartranft, J F Gen, 1889, O 17,2:5
Hartranft, Linn, 1903, N 23,7:3
Hartranft, Russell, 1945, Jl 12,11:6
Hartranft, Thomas W, 1944, Mr 8,19:3
Hartranft, William F, 1953, F 24,25:1
Hartridge, Clifford W (por), 1937, Ap 11,II,9:1
Hartridge, Emely B (por), 1942, S 26,15:3
Hartridge, J, 1879, Ja 9,5:2
Hartridge, Julian, 1942, Je 9,24:2
Hartroft, Samuel M, 1942, Mr 28,17:1
Harts, William W, 1961, Ap 23,86:5
Hartsell, Harold Mrs, 1960, Je 7,35:2
Hartsell, Harry, 1955, F 16,29:4
Hartsell, Malcolm J M, 1967, F 23,35:2
Hartshorn, Arthur A, 1950, F 23,27:1
Hartshorn, Cora L (will, N 3,39:1), 1958, O 19,87:2
Hartshorn, Edwin A Capt, 1916, Mr 16,13:5
Hartshorn, Edwin S, 1965, Mr 13,25:2
Hartshorn, Elden B, 1961, F 28,33:2
Hartshorn, Emily P, 1942, Ja 28,19:3
Hartshorn, J W Sibley, 1956, S 24,27:1
Hartshorn, John M Sr, 1952, Ag 29,23:5
Hartshorn, Lamott, 1947, S 27,15:6
Hartshorn, Prescott B, 1943, Ja 18,15:1
Hartshorn, Stanford H, 1951, O 24,31:2
Hartshorn, Stewart (por), 1937, Ja 13,23:3
Hartshorn, Stewart H Mrs, 1945, Ap 30,19:4
Hartshorn, V, 1931, Mr 14,1:2
Hartshorn, William S Mrs, 1952, Ap 10,29:5
Hartshorn, Willis E, 1939, Ag 5,15:3
Hartshorn, Winfred M, 1956, Jl 2,21:6
Hartshorne, Charles, 1908, O 31,9:5
Hartshorne, Douglas R, 1950, Ap 23,94:3
Hartshorne, Francis C, 1950, Ap 18,31:4
Hartshorne, Howard M, 1954, F 4,25:5
Hartshorne, Hugh, 1923, Je 29,17:2; 1967, D 15,47:2
Hartshorne, Hugh Sr, 1951, Jl 17,27:5
Hartshorne, Richard, 1948, F 20,27:4
Hartshorne, Robert D, 1949, Jl 19,30:2
Hartshorne, S G, 1903, Ag 14,7:6
Hartsock, J Lewis, 1943, D 30,18:2
Hartsock, Marie, 1957, Ag 21,27:1
Hartson, Charles M, 1953, F 12,27:3
Hartson, Charles M Mrs, 1954, Ja 10,86:1
Hartson, D P, 1953, N 10,31:1
Hartstein, Benjamin A, 1964, F 24,25:3
Hartstein, Edward N, 1938, F 11,23:5
Hartsuff, George Gen, 1874, My 17,7:2
Hartswick, F Gregory, 1948, Jl 12,19:6
Hartswick, Jennie B, 1939, F 5,41:3
Hartt, Charles P, 1872, Je 24,5:4
Hartt, Dudley N, 1950, Je 8,31:5
Hartt, Edward, 1883, S 14,4:6
Hartt, Erastus, 1913, N 14,11:6
Hartt, Geog W, 1965, Ja 7,37:4
Hartt, George Le Baron, 1913, Ja 10,11:4
Hartt, George M, 1954, O 29,23:2
Hartt, H Le B, 1880, F 23,8:4
Hartt, Henry, 1940, Mr 29,21:4
Hartt, J C Dr, 1901, N 26,3:3
Hartt, J Twining, 1937, F 1,19:2
Hartt, Jay S, 1962, Ap 15,80:6
Hartt, Mary B, 1946, Je 30,38:3
Hartt, Mary E Mrs, 1941, N 25,26:2
Hartt, Maurice, 1950, Mr 16,32:2
Hartt, Rollin L, 1946, Je 18,25:3
Hartung, Adolph, 1944, My 30,21:3
Hartung, Albert M, 1958, My 11,86:6
Hartung, Charles, 1914, Ja 24,9:4
Hartung, Charles C, 1953, Je 3,31:1
Hartung, Frederick J, 1952, Ja 4,40:3
Hartung, George A, 1952, Je 24,29:2
Hartung, Harold H, 1942, Jl 31,15:4
Hartung, John, 1945, Je 5,19:4
Hartung, John V, 1954, Jl 3,11:7
Hartung, Ralph C, 1961, Ja 25,33:4
Hartung, Sylvester E, 1950, S 13,27:2
Hartung, Theron A, 1954, Je 12,15:3
Hartung, Walter H, 1961, S 30,25:5
Hartveld, Samuel, 1949, S 3,13:6
Hartweg, Norman E, 1964, F 18,35:2
Hartwell, A S Brig-Gen, 1912, O 31,13:5
Hartwell, Abel W Prof, 1908, D 6,13:6
Hartwell, Albion, 1959, Mr 5,31:5
Hartwell, Alfred Stedman Ex-Justice, 1912, Ag 31,7:4
Hartwell, Bartholomew, 1937, F 12,23:3
Hartwell, C Terence, 1953, My 2,15:3
Hartwell, Charles E Mrs, 1956, Ja 30,27:3
Hartwell, Emily S (trb lr, O 10,22:7), 1951, O 5,27:3
Hartwell, George K, 1949, D 13,31:2
Hartwell, Harold T, 1937, Ja 9,17:4
Hartwell, Harry, 1952, O 10,25:4
Hartwell, Harry A, 1960, Mr 7,29:5
Hartwell, Harry F, 1943, D 9,27:1
Hartwell, Hiram M, 1954, Mr 4,25:3
Hartwell, Howard Mrs, 1944, D 10,53:2
Hartwell, Hugh Nesbitt, 1912, Mr 24,II,15:4
Hartwell, John A (por), 1940, D 1,62:1
Hartwell, John A Mrs, 1947, D 24,21:2
Hartwell, John E, 1939, Je 18,37:2
Hartwell, Mildred, 1951, Ag 27,19:2
Hartwell, Philander W, 1940, D 31,15:2
Hartwell, Reginald W, 1950, F 5,84:5
Hartwell, Stephen W, 1957, Ap 30,30:2
Hartwick, Sophus, 1953, F 4,27:4
Hartwig, Charles C, 1950, S 16,19:5
Hartwig, Frank A, 1940, My 17,19:1
Hartwig, Fred L, 1965, Ja 15,43:1
Hartwig, Otto J Mrs, 1956, Je 25,23:4
Hartwig, Theodore G, 1948, Mr 13,15:6
Hartwig, Walter, 1941, Ja 18,15:6
Hartwig, Walter Mrs, 1961, O 2,31:3
Hartwright, Esau, 1937, S 21,25:2
Harty, Edmund T, 1954, O 5,27:4
Harty, Hamilton (por), 1941, F 20,19:1
Harty, J G Archbishop, 1927, O 30,27:1
Harty, J Patrick, 1959, F 26,31:5
Harty, James J, 1953, Ap 23,29:5
Harty, John M, 1946, S 13,7:6
Harty, William, 1948, F 14,13:2
Hartz, J Frederick, 1944, F 29,17:4
Hartz, Richard A, 1949, Ag 28,73:1
Hartz, William, 1937, Ag 13,17:5
Hartz, William B, 1956, S 29,19:3
Hartzberg, John M, 1954, D 30,17:3
Hartzberg, Louis, 1958, Mr 25,33:4
Hartzel, John H Jr, 1941, My 27,23:4
Hartzel, Walter J, 1951, Je 25,19:5
Hartzeler, Jacob Rev, 1916, Ja 3,13:2
Hartzell, Allen, 1950, Je 25,70:2
Hartzell, Arthur E, 1940, D 4,27:2
Hartzell, E Keith Mrs, 1950, Jl 21,19:4
Hartzell, Edson K, 1954, Jl 19,19:5
Hartzell, George W, 1945, Ag 25,11:3
Hartzell, Harry O, 1940, Ag 22,20:3
Hartzell, James B, 1947, F 26,25:4
Hartzell, Rachel, 1954, F 22,19:3
Hartzell, W Frank, 1940, Mr 9,15:5
Hartzell, W H Rev, 1916, S 4,7:4
Hartzell, Wilson S, 1938, Je 10,21:2
Hartzell Wm K, 1949, Jl 30,15:2
Hartzler, H B Rev Dr, 1920, S 4,9:4
Hartzog, Justin R, 1963, D 24,17:3
Haruta, Yoshitame, 1945, F 16,23:1
Harve, A, 1930, S 26,23:4
Harvell, Adelaide, 1949, F 1,25:2
Harvell, Herman L, 1950, Ag 23,29:6
Harver, Phyllis, 1960, N 21,58:6
Harveson, Carleton B, 1954, Je 30,27:6
Harvey, A T, 1881, My 30,5:4
Harvey, Addie L Mrs, 1938, Ag 1,13:5
Harvey, Albert S, 1941, N 26,23:1
Harvey, Albert W, 1956, Ja 5,33:2
Harvey, Alex, 1949, N 21,25:3
Harvey, Alexander Duer, 1968, Ja 10,43:2
Harvey, Alexander Mrs, 1946, Ja 17,23:4
Harvey, Alfred, 1941, S 22,15:4
Harvey, Allyn F, 1941, O 23,23:4
Harvey, Alvin C, 1942, Ag 24,15:5
Harvey, Andrew M, 1949, Jl 20,25:3
Harvey, Anne L Mrs, 1954, Ja 6,31:4
Harvey, Anson B, 1946, Ap 18,27:5
Harvey, Arlington C, 1943, N 18,23:1
Harvey, Arthur Crosthwaite, 1924, Ap 15,21:2
Harvey, Basil, 1958, F 17,23:3
Harvey, Byron, 1965, Je 8,41:2
Harvey, Byron S, 1954, D 20,29:3
Harvey, C Henry, 1941, N 16,56:4
Harvey, Charles E, 1940, Ja 16,23:5; 1942, Je 23,19:4; 1949, Ja 28,22:3
Harvey, Charles E Mrs, 1952, F 14,27:1
Harvey, Charles J, 1944, F 11,19:5
Harvey, Charles Thompson, 1912, Mr 12,13:4
Harvey, Chester K, 1952, Je 7,19:4
Harvey, Clarence, 1945, My 4,19:5
Harvey, Clarence E, 1945, Ja 2,19:3
Harvey, Clifford V, 1948, F 6,23:2
Harvey, Daniel C, 1939, My 8,17:3
Harvey, Daniel R, 1959, Jl 31,24:1
Harvey, Earl H, 1954, Je 7,17:4
Harvey, Edmund N, 1959, Jl 22,27:1
Harvey, Edna L, 1938, O 11,25:2
Harvey, Edward F, 1951, F 7,29:4
Harvey, Edward H Mrs, 1944, F 2,21:3
Harvey, Edwin L, 1953, Ag 21,17:2
Harvey, Edwin M, 1952, Mr 6,31:2
Harvey, Eli, 1957, F 14,27:3
Harvey, Eli Mrs, 1919, S 4,13:3; 1924, Ja 18,17:5
Harvey, Erwin M, 1945, Jl 17,13:7
Harvey, Ethel B, 1965, S 3,27:4
Harvey, Everett C, 1948, F 24,25:2
Harvey, Ezra J, 1943, My 21,19:3
Harvey, Florence, 1960, Mr 15,39:4
Harvey, Francis M, 1941, Mr 25,23:4
Harvey, Frank H, 1954, Mr 3,27:1
Harvey, Frank W, 1954, Ap 8,27:3
Harvey, Fred, 1960, My 17,37:2
Harvey, Fred A, 1945, Ap 28,15:6; 1951, My 24,35:3
Harvey, Frederick, 1955, Ag 19,19:1
Harvey, Frederick S, 1950, My 7,106:4
Harvey, G B M, 1928, Ag 21,1:5
Harvey, G Mrs, 1931, S 6,II,4:1
Harvey, George E, 1948, Je 4,23:1
Harvey, George H, 1942, Jl 14,19:2; 1960, D 13,31:5
Harvey, George L, 1923, Ag 14,15:4
Harvey, George L (Feb 15), 1963, Ap 1,35:7
Harvey, George Mrs, 1948, F 5,23:5
Harvey, George R, 1952, Ap 10,29:3
Harvey, George S, 1944, S 8,19:5
Harvey, George Sir, 1876, Ja 24,5:4; 1939, Mr 29,23:4
Harvey, George U, 1946, Ap 7,44:1
Harvey, Georgette, 1952, F 18,19:5
Harvey, Georgia, 1960, My 19,37:6
Harvey, Gilbert A Mrs, 1954, S 2,21:3
Harvey, H T Dr, 1925, Jl 31,15:6
Harvey, Hamilton S, 1952, O 7,29:3
Harvey, Harold A, 1955, D 22,23:3
Harvey, Harold B, 1949, D 6,31:3
Harvey, Harold C, 1949, Jl 18,17:4
Harvey, Harry H, 1955, O 16,87:1
Harvey, Henry B Mrs, 1962, Ag 22,33:1
Harvey, Herbert R, 1941, Ag 21,17:3
Harvey, Herbert S, 1951, N 14,31:2
Harvey, Hiland B, 1947, D 11,33:3
Harvey, I J Jr, 1964, O 15,39:1
Harvey, J Harry Mrs, 1954, Mr 1,25:5
Harvey, Jack, 1960, S 20,31:5
Harvey, James, 1953, S 1,23:4; 1954, S 15,33:3
Harvey, James A, 1938, N 6,15:5; 1939, My 25,26:4
Harvey, James Clarence, 1917, S 20,23:2
Harvey, James J, 1946, N 6,23:5; 1954, Ja 1,23:1
Harvey, James J Mrs, 1944, Je 28,23:1
Harvey, James R Mrs, 1955, My 25,33:1
Harvey, James V, 1965, Jl 16,27:3
Harvey, John, 1920, F 10,9:1; 1944, O 14,13:6
Harvey, John A, 1940, N 5,25:3
Harvey, John E, 1944, My 8,19:4
Harvey, John J, 1938, Jl 7,19:5
Harvey, John L, 1943, Mr 29,15:4; 1948, N 21,88:4
Harvey, John S C Mrs, 1957, N 14,33:4
Harvey, Joseph, 1961, Ap 5,37:1
Harvey, Joseph C, 1953, O 3,17:4
Harvey, Joseph R, 1961, Ag 18,21:5
Harvey, Julia M Mrs, 1942, N 14,15:4
Harvey, Julien H, 1960, Mr 3,29:4
Harvey, Julien Mrs, 1954, O 11,27:4
Harvey, Katherine, 1962, O 16,47:7
Harvey, L, 1949, Jl 26,27:1
Harvey, Laning, 1942, Ag 6,19:3
Harvey, Lawson M, 1920, Je 26,11:6
Harvey, Lee F, 1950, Ap 22,19:5
Harvey, Leo B, 1958, Mr 14,15:1
Harvey, Leon A, 1942, Ap 19,44:4
Harvey, Lester M, 1964, Ag 5,33:5
Harvey, Lilian, 1968, Jl 28,65:1
Harvey, Loran J, 1939, Ag 25,15:5
Harvey, Louis, 1943, S 28,25:1
Harvey, Luke F, 1944, Jl 18,19:5
Harvey, Margaret, 1949, O 11,31:2
Harvey, Margaret Doyle, 1912, O 6,II,17:4
Harvey, Mary T, 1966, S 29,47:5
Harvey, Melvin J, 1951, Jl 4,17:6
Harvey, Mervin C, 1947, O 26,70:4
Harvey, Moses Rev, 1901, S 4,7:5
Harvey, N Darrell, 1951, O 15,25:6
Harvey, Olin Frisbee, 1953, F 26,25:1
Harvey, Paul, 1948, Ja 9,22:2; 1955, D 16,30:1
Harvey, Peggy (Mrs Robt J), 1964, N 20,37:4
Harvey, Peter, 1877, Je 28,5:2
Harvey, Phil S Sr, 1951, O 28,85:2
Harvey, Philip Mrs, 1966, My 22,86:5
Harvey, R M, 1959, D 15,39:5
Harvey, Ray F Dr, 1968, F 3,29:2
Harvey, Robert G, 1967, Ag 3,33:4
Harvey, Robert M, 1941, Jl 25,15:6
Harvey, Robert N Maj-Gen, 1937, F 16,23:3
Harvey, Robert R, 1945, F 22,27:1
Harvey, Rodney B, 1945, N 6,19:4
Harvey, Roland B, 1917, N 15,13:4
Harvey, Roland H, 1943, Mr 12,17:2
Harvey, Russell W, 1950, My 15,7:4
Harvey, S L, 1903, Ja 9,9:5
Harvey, Samuel C, 1953, Ag 24,23:3
Harvey, Samuel C Mrs, 1962, Jl 23,21:4
Harvey, Samuel R, 1947, D 18,29:3
Harvey, Spencer G, 1957, Ag 23,19:2
Harvey, Theodore R, 1938, F 2,19:3
Harvey, Thomas, 1949, O 8,13:3
Harvey, Thomas F, 1923, Ag 23,15:4
Harvey, Thomas M Jr, 1939, My 11,25:3

Harvey, Thomas Sr Mrs, 1943, D 27,19:2
Harvey, Thomas W, 1938, Ap 9,17:6
Harvey, Thomas W Jr, 1965, Je 27,64:7
Harvey, Tom Jr, 1938, Jl 15,17:6
Harvey, Turlington Walker, 1909, S 14,9:6
Harvey, Vernon J, 1961, O 1,86:1
Harvey, W Craig Mrs, 1944, Ap 17,23:2
Harvey, W H Mrs, 1948, O 3,64:3
Harvey, W W, 1958, S 28,88:3
Harvey, Wallace P, 1943, My 21,19:2
Harvey, Walter J, 1958, My 20,33:4
Harvey, Walter M, 1945, O 27,15:6
Harvey, Walter Miles, 1968, Mr 10,92:5
Harvey, William, 1952, Ja 24,27:4
Harvey, William A, 1955, Jl 28,23:4
Harvey, William B, 1949, My 30,13:2
Harvey, William C Jr, 1955, Ag 6,15:5
Harvey, William H, 1945, D 31,17:4
Harvey, William H Capt, 1937, Mr 26,22:1
Harvey, William H Mrs, 1951, Mr 22,31:1
Harvey, William J, 1952, F 19,29:5; 1961, Ap 14,29:4
Harvey, William Jr, 1964, Jl 29,33:5
Harvey, William L, 1938, Mr 15,23:1
Harvey, William P, 1940, Ap 28,37:2
Harvey, William R, 1953, My 28,23:6
Harvey-Jellie, Wallace R, 1955, Mr 9,27:3
Harvie, James B, 1964, Je 5,31:2
Harvie, John B, 1941, N 16,57:2
Harvie, Peter L, 1944, F 5,15:6
Harvie, W J, 1933, Mr 24,17:3
Harvier, Cecelia Mrs, 1920, D 5,22:4
Harvison, Louis H, 1963, O 30,39:4
Harward, Henry B, 1944, Ap 17,23:4
Harwell, Henry E, 1961, Ja 23,23:2
Harwi, Solomon J, 1952, Mr 19,29:1
Harwin, Murray E, 1967, My 3,42:8
Harwood, A A, 1884, Ag 29,2:3
Harwood, Addison, 1947, Ap 2,27:1
Harwood, Addison Mrs, 1947, Ap 2,27:1
Harwood, Albert S, 1908, N 1,9:4
Harwood, Basil, 1949, Ap 5,30:7
Harwood, Benjamin, 1968, Je 11,44:3
Harwood, Channing E, 1956, D 30,33:2
Harwood, Charles, 1950, O 24,29:5
Harwood, Charles M, 1954, F 7,88:3
Harwood, Clayton E, 1948, My 15,15:6
Harwood, Ely W, 1920, D 9,13:3
Harwood, F J, 1940, Ag 20,19:1
Harwood, F Maj, 1883, Mr 27,5:4
Harwood, Floyd C Mrs, 1951, Je 2,19:5; 1967, F 12, 92:8
Harwood, Francis L, 1957, Ja 28,23:5
Harwood, Frank H, 1948, D 20,25:5
Harwood, Franklin A, 1940, S 20,23:5
Harwood, George A Mrs, 1962, Jl 17,25:1
Harwood, H Harvey, 1942, Ag 24,15:2
Harwood, H M Mrs (F Tennyson Jesse), 1958, Ag 7,25:3
Harwood, Henry, 1950, Je 13,27:1
Harwood, John G, 1945, F 1,23:1
Harwood, John T, 1937, Jl 25,II,7:4
Harwood, Landry Jr Mrs, 1956, My 29,27:5
Harwood, Louis D, 1948, F 6,23:3
Harwood, Mel, 1948, Mr 8,23:1
Harwood, N B, 1885, My 26,1:6
Harwood, Ralph E, 1951, Mr 1,27:3
Harwood, Robert W, 1939, S 2,17:4
Harwood, Van N, 1933, Je 12,15:5
Harwood, Wallace W Mrs, 1952, S 9,31:3
Harwood, William A, 1943, O 7,23:1
Harza, Leroy F, 1953, N 24,29:4
Harzfeld, Sieg, 1944, Mr 8,19:1
Harzof, Max, 1942, Ja 5,17:4
Hasal, Antonin B, 1960, Ap 24,89:1
Hasberg, Gustave de Mrs, 1937, Ag 1,II,6:3
Hasbrook, Charles E Col, 1920, Ag 19,9:4
Hasbrook, Frank, 1947, Jl 31,21:5
Hasbrouck, A B, 1879, F 25,5:5
Hasbrouck, Alexander C, 1947, Ja 22,23:3
Hasbrouck, Alfred, 1948, O 3,67:2
Hasbrouck, Alfred Col, 1920, Ag 20,9:6
Hasbrouck, Bruyn, 1938, Mr 24,23:3
Hasbrouck, Charles, 1914, N 4,7:5
Hasbrouck, Charles D, 1942, My 23,13:6
Hasbrouck, David S, 1922, Ag 29,15:6
Hasbrouck, Dudley C, 1937, My 15,19:6
Hasbrouck, Edwin M, 1956, My 26,17:6
Hasbrouck, Emily W Mrs, 1940, Mr 27,21:4
Hasbrouck, G S, 1901, Ap 10,9:5
Hasbrouck, Gilbert D B, 1942, Je 6,13:1
Hasbrouck, Hazel W Mrs, 1948, Jl 2,21:3
Hasbrouck, Henry C, 1962, O 23,37:5
Hasbrouck, Henry C Brig-Gen, 1910, D 19,9:4
Hasbrouck, Howard C, 1940, D 29,24:8
Hasbrouck, Isaac Mrs, 1948, Je 5,15:4
Hasbrouck, Isaac N, 1925, Ap 17,21:4
Hasbrouck, Jacob L, 1945, Jl 12,11:6
Hasbrouck, James F, 1945, O 18,23:4
Hasbrouck, John L, 1947, Mr 6,25:4
Hasbrouck, Johnston, 1945, Ja 23,19:1
Hasbrouck, Louis B (por), 1947, Ag 17,53:1
Hasbrouck, Martin, 1940, S 25,27:5
Hasbrouck, Mary E, 1907, My 18,7:4
Hasbrouck, Minnie B Mrs, 1938, S 17,17:2
Hasbrouck, Morton C, 1948, Jl 17,15:6
Hasbrouck, Philip B Prof, 1924, Jl 20,20:4
Hasbrouck, Richard O, 1950, F 20,25:4
Hasbrouck, Stephen, 1881, D 29,2:7
Hasbrouck, Walter, 1945, O 8,15:2
Hasbrouck, Warren G Mrs, 1949, O 7,27:4
Hasbrouck, Webster D, 1940, F 2,17:2
Hascall, Robert C, 1949, F 7,19:2
Hascall, Theodore Frelinghuysen, 1908, Mr 26,7:4
Hascall, Vincent C, 1947, F 20,25:4
Hascall, W H S, 1927, Mr 26,17:6
Hascher, Leopold, 1949, Mr 8,25:4
Haschka, Ferdinand T, 1944, My 16,21:6
Haschke, Theodore A, 1954, O 6,25:2
Haseba, Sumitaka, 1914, Mr 16,9:4
Hasegawa, Sabro, 1957, Mr 13,31:2
Hasegawa, Yoshimichi Viscount, 1924, Ja 29,19:3
Haselden, Kyle Rev, 1968, O 4,57:4
Haselden, W K, 1953, D 29,23:4
Hasell, Lewis Cruger, 1923, O 27,13:4
Hasell, Mason Cruger, 1905, Je 17,9:5; 1905, Je 20,9:4
Haseltine, Chelsea W, 1951, D 17,32:6
Haseltine, Herbert, 1962, Ja 9,47:4
Haseltine, Sherwin L, 1950, Ja 29,69:1
Haselton, Barton, 1939, Je 19,15:3
Haselton, Mark B, 1946, Ag 21,27:6
Haselton, Merton L, 1966, O 19,38:6
Haselton, Page S, 1967, Ap 29,35:2
Haselton, Phil Mrs, 1949, Ap 12,30:3
Haselton, Seneca Ex-Justice, 1921, Jl 22,11:6
Haselwood, Harry, 1920, S 30,9:5
Hasenack, James E (por), 1949, Ap 22,24:5
Hasenauer, Catherine, 1956, Ap 14,17:5
Hasenflug, Henry, 1941, O 21,23:1
Hasenfus, John C, 1943, N 7,57:1
Hasenfuss, George B, 1956, Mr 20,23:1
Hasenpflug, Sophia Mrs, 1950, Ap 6,29:2
Hasenstab, Phil J, 1941, D 29,15:5
Haserodt, Edmund B, 1941, Mr 30,49:1
Haseth, Howard B, 1952, My 15,31:2
Hasey, Fred L, 1949, Ja 8,15:3
Hasford, William F, 1958, Ja 16,29:1
Hashiguchi, Tatsuo, 1945, Je 29,15:2
Hashimoto, Kingoro, 1957, Je 30,69:1
Haskel, Isidore J, 1951, D 27,21:3
Haskel, Samuel E, 1960, Jl 3,33:1
Haskell, A J L, 1962, Ag 4,19:4
Haskell, Amory L, 1966, Ap 13,43:1
Haskell, C N, 1933, Jl 6,21:1
Haskell, Carl C, 1966, Jl 19,39:2
Haskell, Charles Sumner, 1903, Jl 14,7:6
Haskell, Clark, 1950, N 10,27:4
Haskell, Clinton H, 1952, Mr 22,13:6
Haskell, D C, 1883, D 17,1:4
Haskell, D H, 1881, D 21,5:2
Haskell, Daniel H, 1874, N 14,3:6
Haskell, E B Mrs, 1903, My 6,5:3
Haskell, E Dudley, 1955, Je 28,27:3
Haskell, E Dudley Mrs, 1956, Ap 13,25:4
Haskell, E E, 1933, Ja 30,13:3
Haskell, E K, 1941, Ap 7,17:4
Haskell, Edwin Bradbury, 1907, Mr 26,9:6
Haskell, Frank, 1958, F 11,31:4
Haskell, Frank Col, 1864, Je 5,4:5
Haskell, Frederick K, 1950, Ag 22,27:6
Haskell, Frederick T Mrs, 1964, Ag 1,21:6
Haskell, Guy P, 1954, Jl 11,73:3
Haskell, Harold C, 1957, Jl 2,27:5
Haskell, Harry G, 1951, Ja 5,21:5
Haskell, Harry Leland Brig-Gen, 1908, O 27,9:5
Haskell, Henry J, 1952, Ag 21,19:3
Haskell, Henry J Mrs, 1946, F 5,23:5
Haskell, Henry S, 1955, Mr 5,17:4; 1956, My 7,27:4
Haskell, Henry S Mrs, 1949, Ag 10,21:2
Haskell, Henry Wallace Dr, 1917, Jl 28,15:3
Haskell, J Amory, 1923, S 10,17:6
Haskell, John B, 1940, Ja 5,19:2
Haskell, John D, 1962, Ag 5,81:2
Haskell, John G, 1941, My 19,17:3
Haskell, L, 1933, O 21,15:1
Haskell, Langdon C, 1956, Ag 13,19:6
Haskell, Lester A, 1947, D 7,76:4
Haskell, Margaret R Mrs, 1942, S 19,15:6
Haskell, Mellen W, 1948, Ja 16,21:2
Haskell, Michael, 1942, F 4,19:5
Haskell, Murray Mrs, 1957, Je 27,26:6
Haskell, Nelson C, 1952, Jl 6,48:7
Haskell, Norman R, 1942, F 21,19:5
Haskell, Phil G, 1950, S 9,17:3
Haskell, Raymond, 1945, Ap 7,15:2
Haskell, Robert H, 1965, Mr 22,33:3
Haskell, Robert H Mrs, 1953, S 7,19:6
Haskell, Royal J, 1958, D 4,39:3
Haskell, Samuel C L, 1949, O 11,31:1
Haskell, Samuel Spring, 1903, D 16,9:4
Haskell, W C, 1914, My 6,11:5
Haskell, W E, 1933, My 3,17:1
Haskell, Weston B, 1950, S 28,31:4
Haskell, Willabe, 1913, My 8,11:5
Haskell, William E Jr, 1953, Ag 30,89:1
Haskell, William E Jr Mrs, 1961, Je 27,33:1
Haskell, William H, 1938, Ap 14,23:4; 1952, D 16,31:2
Haskell, William N, 1952, Ag 14,23:1
Haskell, William N Mrs, 1964, Ag 5,33:3
Haskell, William S, 1941, Je 29,32:7
Haskell, William S Mrs, 1947, Jl 19,13:4
Haskett, W J (see also D 19), 1876, D 21,6:1
Haskew, George M Mrs, 1950, S 26,31:2
Haskil, Clara, 1960, D 8,35:3
Haskin, Charles J, 1954, S 1,27:3
Haskin, Edward V, 1938, O 22,17:6
Haskin, Estelle, 1940, S 18,23:1
Haskin, Frederic J, 1944, Ap 25,23:1
Haskin, Frederick J Mrs, 1950, F 10,23:4
Haskin, James, 1943, F 7,48:2
Haskin, John D, 1945, D 19,26:2
Haskin, Minerva M, 1964, N 21,29:6
Haskin, Samuel, 1954, Jl 1,25:4
Haskin, W L, 1931, S 25,25:5
Haskin, Walter E, 1959, Ja 19,27:5
Hasking, Arthur P, 1952, My 30,15:3
Hasking, James G, 1916, N 9,13:7
Hasking, James G Mrs, 1944, S 13,19:6
Haskins, C W, 1903, Ja 10,9:6
Haskins, Caryl Davis, 1911, N 19,II,15:4
Haskins, Charles H Prof, 1937, My 15,19:3
Haskins, Charles N, 1942, N 15,58:1
Haskins, Clark Caryl, 1904, S 4,9:6
Haskins, Dennis A, 1956, Ag 30,25:2
Haskins, Edward W, 1938, O 19,23:5
Haskins, Edward W Mrs, 1950, O 25,35:4
Haskins, Franklin Evans, 1920, N 15,15:5
Haskins, George M, 1941, Ag 11,13:2
Haskins, George M Mrs, 1951, D 31,13:3
Haskins, Harold, 1937, Ag 21,15:3
Haskins, Henry S Mrs, 1952, S 3,30:6
Haskins, Kittredge, 1916, Ag 8,9:5
Haskins, Lester W, 1962, Ja 6,19:5
Haskins, Minnie L, 1957, F 6,25:3
Haskins, Robert B, 1937, S 9,23:3
Haskins, Robert Rev, 1903, O 28,9:5
Haskins, Samuel M, 1948, O 27,27:2
Haskins, W Horace, 1921, Ag 12,13:6
Haslam, A Herbert, 1955, F 15,27:4
Haslam, A Sir, 1927, Ja 14,19:5
Haslam, Herbert, 1940, Ja 18,23:2
Haslam, Herbert Mrs, 1958, O 12,83:3
Haslam, J Henry Rev, 1912, S 19,11:6
Haslam, John, 1940, My 22,23:4
Haslam, Robert C, 1954, Ap 19,23:1
Haslam, Robert T, 1961, Ap 5,37:1
Haslam, Samuel Mrs, 1956, Ag 21,29:5
Haslehurst, Mary A Mrs, 1942, S 8,23:3
Hasler, Charles, 1944, N 28,23:6
Hasler, Henry, 1919, D 21,22:4
Hasler, Jacob J, 1946, F 8,19:1
Hasler, Robert T, 1955, Mr 3,27:3
Haslet, Clarence L, 1954, Ja 17,92:7
Haslett, Caroline Dame, 1957, Ja 5,17:6
Haslett, Elmer, 1964, F 2,89:1
Haslett, Harold D, 1953, Mr 9,29:1
Haslett, John W, 1941, My 22,21:4
Haslett, Samuel E, 1920, Ja 17,11:4
Haslin, James H, 1911, Ja 24,9:5
Haslinger, Ferdinand, 1937, Ap 16,24:1
Hasluck, Neville R, 1949, F 7,19:3
Haslun, Joseph Mrs, 1950, Ap 23,95:1
Haslun, Louise, 1951, Mr 6,27:5
Haslund-Christensen, Henning, 1948, S 14,29:3
Hasman, J Henry Mrs, 1948, N 19,27:5
Hason, Anton, 1941, Mr 28,23:2
Haspadar, Frank, 1955, Jl 5,59:2
Haspel, Harry S, 1939, Ap 16,III,6:7
Haspel, Irving M, 1958, N 7,27:2
Haspel, Wilhelm, 1952, Ja 7,19:3
Hass, Adolf, 1940, Mr 24,30:8
Hass, Henry Col, 1907, Je 30,7:6
Hass, Ida E Mrs, 1942, S 7,19:4
Hass, Irving G, 1961, Jl 31,19:2
Hass, Lewis, 1956, Ag 19,92:6
Hass, Louis, 1905, N 30,9:6
Hass, Oscar P, 1957, Ag 25,31:4
Hassall, James H, 1958, F 11,31:1
Hassall, John, 1948, Mr 9,23:2
Hassam, C, 1935, Ag 28,17:1
Hassam, Childe Mrs, 1946, O 14,29:3
Hassam, Walter E Capt, 1925, D 28,15:3
Hassan, Mohammed Prince, 1943, Ja 8,19:5
Hassan, Selim, 1961, O 1,86:1
Hassan Pasha, Mahmud, 1949, Jl 17,58:3
Hassani, M T el, 1943, Ja 19,10:6
Hassard, J R G, 1888, Ap 19,8:4
Hassard-Short, Frederick W, 1953, F 13,21:1
Hassay, Rudolph J, 1954, O 15,23:5
Hasse, Adelaide R, 1953, Jl 30,23:5
Hasse, Charles M, 1904, Ja 23,9:5
Hasse, Kurt, 1943, F 10,25:6
Hasse, William H, 1942, Ap 21,23:1
Hassel, Otto H, 1947, Ag 15,17:3
Hasselback, Robert A, 1914, Mr 18,11:6
Hasselberger, John, 1951, S 26,31:2
Hasselbow, Don Carlos Gen, 1903, S 1,7:6
Hasselhuhn, Charles H, 1962, N 21,33:2
Hassell, Arthur A, 1951, D 8,11:5
Hassell, George, 1937, F 18,21:3

Hassell, Howard W, 1942, My 25,15:3
Hassell, Ira F, 1959, Je 14,87:1
Hassell, Ira F Mrs, 1939, My 23,23:5
Hassell, J Dr, 1884, S 29,4:7
Hassell, Robert F, 1941, D 5,23:4
Hassell, Samuel W Mrs, 1943, F 21,32:6
Hasselmans, Louis, 1957, D 28,18:1
Hasselo, Norman A Mrs, 1966, Ag 3,37:3
Hassemer, Albert F, 1953, Ja 13,32:3
Hassenauer, Leo J, 1951, My 25,27:5
Hassenfeld, Halal, 1943, Mr 4,19:4
Hassenfeld, Henry J, 1960, Ag 5,23:4
Hassenzahl, Kennedy, 1950, Mr 20,21:4
Hassett, Arthur D, 1962, My 22,37:1
Hassett, Francis B, 1942, S 22,21:1
Hassett, George E Jr, 1961, Je 8,35:4
Hassett, J John, 1947, O 19,64:1
Hassett, John J, 1953, F 28,17:6
Hassett, John V Mrs, 1950, Ap 27,29:1
Hassett, Patricia, 1964, D 15,44:1
Hassett, Thomas J, 1945, Ag 27,19:5
Hassett, William D, 1965, Ag 30,25:1
Hassig, William, 1953, My 1,21:2
Hassin, George B, 1951, Ag 16,27:6
Hassinger, Albert H, 1949, My 3,25:1
Hassinger, William Mrs, 1950, F 9,29:3
Hasskark, Paul L G, 1950, F 23,27:2
Hassler, Anthony E, 1947, Ag 26,23:1
Hassler, Henry J, 1952, S 20,15:4
Hassler, Henry J Mrs, 1944, F 27,38:1
Hassler, Isaac, 1940, F 17,13:5
Hassler, John F, 1952, Jl 25,18:5
Hasslocher, John B, 1920, Ja 22,17:2
Hasslocher, Paulo G, 1966, Je 10,45:1
Hasso, Henry, 1957, Ja 16,35:3
Hassold, Carl F R, 1950, Ja 29,68:6
Hassold, Victor C, 1954, My 2,88:4
Hasson, James, 1880, My 29,5:1
Hasson, James H, 1968, Jl 7,53:2
Hasson, John, 1947, Ap 3,25:2
Hasson, John E, 1942, Ag 26,19:4
Hasson, John J Mrs, 1953, F 5,23:2
Hasson, W F C Prof, 1908, F 15,7:6
Hassrick, Emerson Mrs, 1945, Je 1,15:2
Hast, Marcus Rev, 1911, Ag 30,7:5
Haste, Gibson C, 1953, Ap 15,31:4
Haste, Gibson C Mrs, 1956, Ja 26,29:1
Hastie, C Norwood, 1951, Ja 15,17:5
Hastie, Harry, 1952, Ja 10,29:4
Hasting, D H, 1882, S 26,5:3
Hastings, Abner H, 1939, Ja 18,19:1
Hastings, Ada M Mrs, 1951, D 4,33:5
Hastings, Alvin A, 1949, D 22,23:4
Hastings, Anna E B Mrs, 1955, S 20,31:6
Hastings, Anne Mrs, 1921, Ja 30,22:4
Hastings, Arthur C, 1958, My 8,29:4
Hastings, Berthold F, 1944, Ag 12,11:6
Hastings, Charles D, 1940, Ag 8,19:6
Hastings, Charles E, 1942, Je 4,19:3
Hastings, Charles H, 1941, Ja 25,15:4
Hastings, Clarence A, 1954, O 13,31:2
Hastings, Clifford J, 1946, S 29,62:3
Hastings, D H Dr, 1884, Ap 16,4:6
Hastings, D H Ex-Gov, 1903, Ja 10,9:5
Hastings, Daniel G, 1942, Mr 23,15:3
Hastings, Daniel O, 1966, My 11,47:1
Hastings, E P Mrs, 1909, My 26,9:5
Hastings, Earl F, 1961, S 10,86:2
Hastings, Edward Mrs, 1943, S 27,19:3
Hastings, Edwin G, 1965, Jl 21,41:1
Hastings, Elinor I, 1952, Ag 11,15:2
Hastings, Ella Mrs, 1924, O 18,15:6
Hastings, Ernest C, 1942, Mr 2,19:5
Hastings, Eugene H, 1964, Jl 1,35:5
Hastings, Foster, 1952, O 3,23:4
Hastings, Frank J, 1952, Ap 22,29:3
Hastings, Frank S, 1924, Jl 6,21:3
Hastings, Frank W Jr, 1951, D 14,31:1
Hastings, Frederick Rev, 1937, Ja 17,II,8:2
Hastings, George, 1866, S 2,5:3
Hastings, George A, 1956, Mr 31,15:4
Hastings, George B, 1967, Ap 13,43:5
Hastings, George Seymour Col, 1909, Ja 2,9:5
Hastings, George T, 1947, S 17,25:4
Hastings, Glover S, 1948, Ag 1,59:2
Hastings, H J, 1883, S 13,5:3
Hastings, Harold E, 1950, Ag 12,13:5
Hastings, Harold W, 1949, D 10,17:1
Hastings, Henry P, 1942, Ag 19,19:3
Hastings, Herbert S, 1945, Jl 30,19:3
Hastings, Hill, 1948, F 15,60:6
Hastings, Howard L, 1955, Mr 22,31:4
Hastings, Howard R, 1956, Mr 16,23:2
Hastings, Hugh, 1916, Jl 28,11:6
Hastings, Irving F, 1962, Ag 26,82:5
Hastings, J S Mrs, 1876, Je 12,7:5
Hastings, James L, 1949, Jl 26,27:4
Hastings, James Mrs, 1951, Ja 14,84:3
Hastings, James S (Luke McLuke), 1921, Je 4,13:6
Hastings, Jennie R Mrs, 1937, My 4,25:4
Hastings, Jerome Lake, 1924, Ag 1,11:4
Hastings, John A, 1964, D 11,39:3
Hastings, John E Mrs, 1961, Ag 27,85:1
Hastings, John R (por), 1942, Ap 4,13:6
Hastings, John V, 1948, Mr 1,23:4
Hastings, Katherine S, 1950, D 21,29:2
Hastings, Lady (Mrs Geo Chetwynd), 1907, F 4,9:5
Hastings, Lord (A E D Astley), 1956, Ja 19,33:5
Hastings, Lorne E, 1943, N 8,19:5
Hastings, Marquis of, 1868, N 11,5:5
Hastings, May M Mrs, 1938, Jl 30,13:6
Hastings, Milo, 1957, F 26,29:4
Hastings, Morris C, 1961, F 21,35:2
Hastings, Patrick, 1952, F 27,27:4
Hastings, Paul P (por), 1947, S 18,25:5
Hastings, Percival V Sr, 1952, Mr 17,21:2
Hastings, Quincy D, 1949, Ag 4,23:2
Hastings, R Blair, 1949, Mr 9,25:2
Hastings, Richard, 1885, Ja 8,2:4
Hastings, Richard Mrs (M Hay), 1957, Je 5,35:3
Hastings, Robert C, 1952, Mr 22,13:2
Hastings, Russell Gen, 1904, S 20,9:6
Hastings, Samuel D, 1903, Mr 27,9:6
Hastings, Samuel M, 1942, O 24,15:6
Hastings, Stewart E, 1955, N 8,29:4
Hastings, T, 1929, O 23,29:1
Hastings, T James, 1946, Je 26,25:3
Hastings, Theodore M, 1950, O 30,27:6
Hastings, Thomas Nelson, 1907, My 17,9:5
Hastings, Thomas S Rev Dr, 1911, Ap 3,9:5
Hastings, W W, 1938, Ap 9,17:2
Hastings, Walter M, 1943, Je 14,17:5
Hastings, Warren S, 1941, Ag 23,13:4
Hastings, Watson B, 1968, Mr 22,44:5
Hastings, William A, 1950, Jl 31,17:3
Hastings, William A Mrs, 1962, My 27,92:6
Hastings, William G, 1907, Je 29,7:6
Hastings, William H, 1943, Ja 31,46:1
Hastings, William T Mrs, 1953, Ag 2,73:2
Hastings, William W, 1961, Jl 17,21:4
Hastings, Wilmot R Mrs, 1943, S 29,21:3
Hastings, Zed S, 1950, Je 14,31:5
Haston, George E, 1953, Ap 10,21:2
Hastorf, Albert H, 1941, S 29,17:6
Hasty, Percy A, 1948, N 1,23:5
Hasty, Thomas, 1940, Ag 2,15:4
Haswell, Charles H, 1907, My 13,9:6
Haswell, Ernest B, 1965, O 20,47:3
Haswell, John P, 1939, Jl 31,13:4
Haswell, John R, 1949, Jl 31,61:1
Haswell Ernest R L, 1951, S 21,24:3
Haswell Wm D, 1951, Ap 29,89:2
Haszard, Francis L, 1938, Jl 25,15:5
Hata, Hikosaburo, 1959, Mr 21,21:3
Hata, Shunroku, 1962, My 11,31:3
Hatanaka, Takeo, 1963, N 11,31:5
Hatch, A R, 1882, Mr 6,5:2
Hatch, Albert Judson, 1924, O 28,23:4
Hatch, Alfred Smith, 1904, My 14,9:1
Hatch, Arnold S, 1943, O 21,27:2
Hatch, Arthur, 1957, My 8,37:1
Hatch, Arthur Melvin, 1923, Je 9,11:6
Hatch, Azel F, 1965, D 1,47:4
Hatch, Benis W, 1949, Jl 25,15:4
Hatch, Caleb, 1938, Ag 27,13:5
Hatch, Carl A, 1963, S 16,35:1
Hatch, Charles A, 1925, S 24,25:4
Hatch, Charles B, 1941, Ja 25,15:4; 1965, Ja 20,39:4
Hatch, Charles H, 1954, My 12,31:3
Hatch, Charles R, 1941, Ap 15,23:2
Hatch, Daniel B, 1925, Je 22,15:5
Hatch, Darwin S, 1920, Ja 22,17:2
Hatch, David Philips, 1924, Ag 18,13:4
Hatch, E Jr, 1933, Ja 25,17:3
Hatch, E Sanford, 1946, Ap 15,27:3
Hatch, E W Dr, 1874, F 9,4:7
Hatch, Edward P, 1909, S 21,9:5
Hatch, Edward P Mrs, 1906, F 3,9:4
Hatch, Edward Sargent, 1924, Ag 26,11:3
Hatch, Edward W, 1924, Je 2,17:6
Hatch, Emily N, 1959, D 27,60:3
Hatch, Eugene H, 1925, Je 11,19:4
Hatch, Everard E, 1940, My 15,25:1
Hatch, Everett N, 1956, D 31,13:2
Hatch, Fanny C, 1948, D 13,23:4
Hatch, Florence (will), 1959, O 3,39:3
Hatch, Francis March, 1923, Mr 20,21:4
Hatch, Frank, 1938, O 26,23:2
Hatch, Frank L, 1951, Ag 26,79:3
Hatch, Frederic H Mrs, 1952, Je 30,19:2
Hatch, Frederick W, 1953, Mr 3,27:4
Hatch, G Milton, 1947, S 11,27:4
Hatch, George E, 1939, Ag 11,15:4
Hatch, George W, 1941, My 31,11:5
Hatch, H Morgan, 1952, Ja 24,47:3
Hatch, Harry C, 1946, My 9,21:4; 1960, Mr 11,26:1
Hatch, Harry H, 1946, Ja 15,23:3
Hatch, Helena K, 1948, Ja 8,25:5
Hatch, Hezekiah E Mrs (por), 1943, D 11,15:4
Hatch, Horace, 1873, O 30,8:4; 1950, S 2,15:6
Hatch, Howard E, 1952, N 7,23:2
Hatch, Israel T, 1875, S 25,5:2
Hatch, J P Gen, 1901, Ap 14,3:4
Hatch, James A, 1944, Jl 26,19:2
Hatch, James H, 1938, D 23,19:2
Hatch, James Lewis, 1858, S 30,4:6
Hatch, John F, 1953, S 10,25:4
Hatch, John Porter Gen, 1919, Je 28,9:4
Hatch, John R, 1955, O 15,15:2
Hatch, John W, 1959, Ja 28,31:4
Hatch, L Boyd, 1957, S 1,57:1
Hatch, Leonard W, 1958, N 24,29:5
Hatch, Lillian A, 1962, Je 1,27:2
Hatch, Livingston, 1960, My 16,31:4
Hatch, Lorenzo J, 1914, F 7,11:6
Hatch, Olive, 1906, My 15,1:5
Hatch, Prentice H, 1968, Ag 29,35:2
Hatch, Raymond S Mrs, 1959, F 5,31:2
Hatch, Richard D, 1964, Ag 16,93:2
Hatch, Robert L, 1937, D 30,19:5
Hatch, Robert Lee, 1924, My 23,19:5
Hatch, Roger C, 1943, N 26,23:4
Hatch, Roscoe C, 1966, My 7,31:3
Hatch, Roswell D, 1922, Je 8,19:5
Hatch, Roy W, 1955, S 13,31:3
Hatch, Roy W Mrs, 1945, Mr 23,19:2
Hatch, Rufus, 1893, F 24,1:5
Hatch, Rutherfurd L, 1947, Ap 14,27:1
Hatch, S I, 1939, Ag 4,13:1
Hatch, Sarah H Mrs, 1937, F 26,22:1
Hatch, Theodore A, 1946, Ja 2,19:2
Hatch, Vermont, 1959, Ap 5,86:1
Hatch, W B, 1883, Ap 16,5:2
Hatch, Waldo M Mrs, 1946, Ja 10,23:3
Hatch, Waldo Morrison, 1968, Je 30,52:6
Hatch, William, 1925, S 7,11:6; 1948, Ja 15,23:2
Hatch, William J, 1937, Jl 2,21:5
Hatch, William M (Oct 5), 1965, O 11,61:2
Hatchell, John L, 1939, Ap 4,25:4
Hatcher, Arthur B Mrs, 1941, Jl 16,17:2
Hatcher, Eldridge B, 1943, Jl 22,19:4
Hatcher, G S Mrs, 1903, S 18,7:5
Hatcher, George R, 1948, Je 19,15:2
Hatcher, Harry H, 1949, My 26,29:1
Hatcher, Harry K, 1950, Ag 1,23:2
Hatcher, Harry T, 1962, Ja 20,21:3
Hatcher, Julian S, 1963, D 6,35:2
Hatcher, Orie L (por), 1946, Ap 3,25:3
Hatcher, Robert A, 1944, Ap 2,39:2
Hatcher, W H Capt, 1926, D 22,21:2
Hatcher, Warren G, 1952, F 5,29:5
Hatcher, William B, 1947, Ap 4,23:2
Hatcher, William E Dr, 1912, Ag 25,II,11:5
Hater, Harry J, 1960, Ja 11,45:1
Hates, W C, 1934, Jl 27,17:4
Hatfield, Albert D, 1945, Ja 25,19:1
Hatfield, Albert R, 1955, Ja 20,31:5
Hatfield, Amos, 1903, My 22,9:4
Hatfield, Anderson, 1921, Ja 8,11:5
Hatfield, Andrew L Mrs, 1943, Ag 27,17:5
Hatfield, C Alex, 1961, Ja 1,49:2
Hatfield, Charles A S, 1942, Ja 20,19:6
Hatfield, Charles E, 1938, N 12,15:2
Hatfield, Charles F, 1939, Je 23,19:5
Hatfield, Charles J, 1951, Ag 26,77:2
Hatfield, Charles M, 1958, Ap 15,40:3
Hatfield, Charles R, 1941, Ja 9,21:2
Hatfield, Charles S, 1950, F 11,15:2
Hatfield, Chester, 1879, D 16,4:7
Hatfield, E F, 1883, S 23,3:4
Hatfield, Edward R, 1950, N 3,27:1
Hatfield, Edward R Mrs, 1963, Ap 1,27:6
Hatfield, Elizabeth C Mrs, 1941, F 2,44:1
Hatfield, Ellis, 1943, My 31,17:2
Hatfield, Frank C, 1939, Ja 25,22:1
Hatfield, George, 1957, Mr 24,86:2
Hatfield, George B, 1946, Ag 20,27:4
Hatfield, George E, 1953, N 28,15:6
Hatfield, George E Mrs, 1958, Jl 24,25:2
Hatfield, George J, 1953, N 16,25:4
Hatfield, George W, 1941, F 1,17:4
Hatfield, Greenway W, 1943, F 17,21:3
Hatfield, H Glenn Mrs, 1938, S 28,25:5
Hatfield, Harley, 1940, Ap 16,25:6
Hatfield, Harry W, 1953, Ap 26,86:1
Hatfield, Helen, 1950, Ja 10,29:3
Hatfield, Henry R, 1943, Mr 12,17:5
Hatfield, Herbert, 1945, N 30,23:3
Hatfield, Herbert Mrs, 1940, Ja 29,15:2
Hatfield, J A, 1931, Jl 5,14:3
Hatfield, J B Taylor, 1923, S 6,15:4
Hatfield, J Horace, 1956, F 15,31:5
Hatfield, James T, 1945, O 5,23:5
Hatfield, James T Mrs, 1940, Ag 27,21:3
Hatfield, Jay J, 1960, F 2,35:2
Hatfield, John H, 1944, O 15,45:1
Hatfield, John Z, 1944, Ja 23,37:2
Hatfield, Joseph C, 1952, O 7,29:3
Hatfield, Joshua A Mrs, 1946, Ja 15,23:1
Hatfield, Kenneth E, 1942, Jl 2,21:3
Hatfield, Lansing, 1954, Ag 24,21:4
Hatfield, Louis E, 1957, Je 16,84:5
Hatfield, Marcus P, 1939, N 28,25:2
Hatfield, Milton E, 1958, Mr 13,29:3
Hatfield, Oliver R, 1944, S 7,23:5
Hatfield, R G, 1879, F 20,2:1
Hatfield, R M Mrs, 1903, My 30,7:5
Hatfield, Ralph E, 1950, Ag 13,77:2
Hatfield, Richard P, 1962, Je 21,31:1

Hatfield, Samuel J, 1941, Ja 5,45:1
Hatfield, Thomas F, 1925, O 9,23:5
Hatfield, Thomas Mrs, 1965, Ap 18,81:1
Hatfield, Tolbert, 1939, N 1,23:6
Hatfield, W A, 1930, Ag 23,13:3
Hatfield, William B, 1945, Je 7,19:6
Hatfield, William H, 1943, O 18,15:5; 1954, My 27, 27:3
Hathaway, C Henry (por), 1946, O 8,23:3
Hathaway, Carl, 1938, Ja 26,23:2; 1941, F 2,44:7
Hathaway, Charles, 1903, Jl 3,9:6
Hathaway, Charles E, 1941, O 11,17:4
Hathaway, Charles E Sr, 1944, Je 27,19:5
Hathaway, Charles F, 1948, D 23,19:5
Hathaway, Charles Mrs, 1941, O 7,23:4
Hathaway, Charles P, 1925, Ja 17,15:4
Hathaway, Chester F, 1947, Ap 15,25:1
Hathaway, Chester Mrs, 1955, Mr 18,27:1
Hathaway, Clarence, 1963, Ja 25,11:4
Hathaway, Curtis R, 1922, Ap 7,17:5
Hathaway, Dexter C, 1950, Je 13,27:3
Hathaway, Edwin C, 1939, S 25,20:2
Hathaway, Ernest C, 1956, Ja 17,33:2
Hathaway, Esse V, 1939, Mr 25,15:4
Hathaway, Eugene H, 1922, Mr 18,13:4
Hathaway, Forrest Henry Brig-Gen, 1912, Jl 30,9:5
Hathaway, G H, 1931, Ap 8,23:5
Hathaway, George A Mrs, 1954, D 2,31:3
Hathaway, George A Rev, 1968, Je 11,47:3
Hathaway, Guilford C, 1943, N 10,23:4
Hathaway, Harle W, 1945, N 24,19:5
Hathaway, Harry St C, 1960, D 25,42:2
Hathaway, Heath, 1951, Ja 3,27:4
Hathaway, Herbert M, 1944, N 7,27:6
Hathaway, Howard W, 1944, D 5,23:5
Hathaway, I W Rev, 1903, Je 18,9:6
Hathaway, James, 1908, Jl 5,9:3
Hathaway, James B, 1942, D 24,15:3
Hathaway, James L M, 1937, Ja 24,II,8:4
Hathaway, Jane D Mrs, 1949, Jl 3,26:4
Hathaway, Jean Mrs, 1938, Ag 25,19:1
Hathaway, John R, 1942, Ag 1,11:6
Hathaway, John T Mrs, 1937, Je 2,23:5
Hathaway, King, 1944, Je 15,19:2
Hathaway, Les, 1952, D 7,88:3
Hathaway, Levy M Col, 1937, D 15,25:2
Hathaway, Lewis J, 1953, D 30,23:3
Hathaway, Lillie V, 1958, D 5,32:1
Hathaway, Louise P Mrs, 1940, O 7,17:5
Hathaway, Neal, 1963, S 4,39:1
Hathaway, Odell S, 1966, Mr 14,31:1
Hathaway, Robert W (Seigneur of Sark), 1954, D 16,37:2
Hathaway, Russell, 1963, Ap 4,47:2
Hathaway, Russell B, 1965, Je 19,29:5
Hathaway, Savory C, 1947, Ag 15,17:5
Hathaway, Stewart S, 1963, Ag 24,19:7
Hathaway, W A, 1925, D 17,23:5
Hathaway, Warren Sr, 1947, Mr 30,56:2
Hathaway, William A, 1949, Ja 29,13:4
Hathaway, William J Mrs, 1954, D 7,33:3
Hathaway, William Mrs, 1946, Ja 12,15:5
Hathcock, James S Mrs, 1957, Je 15,17:6
Hatherly, Lord, 1881, Jl 11,4:7
Hatheway, C Morris, 1942, Ag 4,19:6
Hatheway, Charles H, 1940, F 13,23:5
Hatheway, Lynn W, 1953, Ag 22,15:1
Hatheway, William E, 1953, Ja 3,15:5
Hathorn, Frank H, 1913, Mr 26,11:3
Hathorne, Edward J, 1923, N 9,17:4
Hathway, Frank J Mrs, 1962, O 6,25:6
Hathway, Marion (Mrs T R Parker), 1955, N 20,88:3
Hatler, Walter, 1944, Je 10,15:5
Hatley, Harold W, 1957, My 13,31:3
Hatlo, Jimmy (Jas C), 1963, D 2,37:3
Hatmaker, Benedict, 1948, O 5,25:1
Hatori, Ayao, 1914, Ap 3,11:6
Hatoyama, Ichiro (funl, Mr 12,31:3), 1959, Mr 7,21:2
Hatrick, Archibald S, 1950, F 3,24:4
Hatrick Edgar B, 1949, S 16,28:2
Hatry, Clarence, 1965, Je 12,31:2
Hatt, George Rev, 1883, N 25,2:5
Hatt, George T, 1941, Ag 16,15:6
Hatt, J William Mrs, 1964, Ja 27,23:3
Hatt, Joel W, 1914, Ag 2,15:5; 1942, Je 29,15:2
Hatt, John E, 1945, Ap 15,14:3
Hatt, Orville L, 1941, Ag 17,38:2
Hatt, Paul J, 1953, Ja 13,27:5
Hattemer, Philipp A, 1960, O 12,43:2
Hattemer, Valentine P, 1958, Ag 10,94:1
Hatten, Anna, 1954, Jl 8,23:1
Hatten, John, 1940, S 28,17:4
Hattenbach, Joseph, 1940, F 3,13:3
Hattenback, Frank J, 1945, Mr 18,42:4
Hattendorf, William H, 1958, Mr 10,23:1
Hatter, Elmer F, 1941, Ag 22,15:7
Hattersley, Carroll G, 1955, F 8,27:1
Hattersley, Charles M, 1953, Ja 1,23:3
Hattersley, Roy A, 1964, Je 26,29:3
Hatting, P A, 1933, Mr 1,17:1
Hatton, Augustus R, 1946, N 14,29:3
Hatton, Catherine Mrs, 1949, Jl 6,27:2
Hatton, E Roy, 1961, My 31,33:5
Hatton, Edward H, 1959, Ag 16,83:1
Hatton, Fanny L Mrs, 1939, N 28,25:5
Hatton, Frank, 1883, Mr 25,1:3; 1894, My 1,5:5
Hatton, Fred J, 1946, D 15,77:3
Hatton, Frederick J, 1941, Ja 5,44:7
Hatton, H Brooks, 1954, O 6,25:4
Hatton, Herbert W Mrs, 1968, Mr 20,47:3
Hatton, James J, 1955, Ag 17,27:5
Hatton, Jennie C H Mrs, 1937, Ag 10,19:2
Hatton, John F, 1954, Jl 25,69:2
Hatton, Joseph, 1907, Ag 1,7:6
Hatton, Oscar P Mrs, 1941, My 23,21:6
Hatton, R Marion, 1943, O 17,48:3
Hatton, William H, 1937, Mr 31,23:3
Hattori, Takushiro, 1960, My 2,29:5
Hattrich, John J, 1942, Mr 22,48:7
Hattstaedt, John J Mrs, 1961, Ag 9,33:5
Hatun, Nene, 1955, My 24,31:1
Hatvany, Lili Mrs, 1967, N 13,47:4
Hatzel, George Grover Dr, 1922, O 6,23:5
Hatzel, Richard J (funl, My 30,22:4), 1920, My 28, 13:3
Hatzfeldt, von Count, 1901, N 23,9:2
Hatzfeldt-Wildenburg, Francis Prince, 1910, N 5,7:4
Hatzfeldt-Wildenburg, von Clara Princess, 1928, D 19,27:5
Hatzler, Elizabeth, 1882, Ja 16,5:5
Hauben, Sol S, 1967, N 5,86:8
Haubennestel, Louis P, 1943, Ja 26,19:4
Haubenstock, Max, 1948, Ag 8,57:2
Haubenstock, Sigmund, 1959, My 28,31:3
Hauber, Joseph G, 1958, S 30,31:2
Hauberg, George D, 1947, Je 24,23:1
Haubert, Charles H Justice, 1937, Je 15,23:5
Haubert, Charles J, 1918, Mr 15,13:8
Haubert, Earl P Sr, 1950, My 16,31:3
Haubert, William J, 1914, O 22,11:5
Haubold, Fred E, 1963, O 9,43:2
Hauburger, Jacob L, 1951, S 15,15:6
Hauch, Edward F, 1953, S 9,29:3
Hauck, Adam, 1944, N 7,27:1
Hauck, Adolph W Sr, 1958, F 21,23:1
Hauck, Charles B, 1937, S 15,23:4
Hauck, Ernest, 1959, My 7,33:1
Hauck, Fred, 1960, Jl 6,33:1
Hauck, George Maj, 1937, My 26,25:3
Hauck, Gustav, 1939, O 19,23:3
Hauck, Henry G, 1960, N 28,31:4
Hauck, Herman Mrs, 1954, O 10,87:1
Hauck, Howard A, 1959, Ag 25,31:3
Hauck, John J Jr, 1944, My 19,19:5
Hauck, Joseph B, 1951, N 13,29:2
Hauck, Joseph F, 1957, F 6,25:6
Hauck, Laurence F, 1948, My 25,27:3
Hauck, Lester F Mrs, 1943, D 11,15:5
Hauck, Louis T, 1940, D 22,30:8
Hauck, Peter Jr, 1922, S 14,21:6
Hauck, Peter Jr Mrs, 1944, D 24,26:4
Hauck, Raymond, 1940, Ag 4,33:3
Hauck, William A, 1950, Jl 29,13:1
Hauenstein, Arthur, 1947, Ap 13,60:2
Hauenstein, Jacob, 1945, O 4,23:6
Hauer, Daniel J, 1943, D 15,27:2
Hauer, Josef M, 1959, S 24,37:4
Hauer, Royal A, 1951, Jl 20,21:4
Haufe, Otto C, 1960, Ag 11,27:5
Hauff, George, 1956, O 13,19:2
Hauff, John J, 1963, Jl 18,27:3
Haug, Charles F, 1968, My 24,47:2
Haug, Emanuel, 1945, F 24,11:5
Haug, Hans, 1967, S 16,33:2
Haug, Herbert E, 1968, Ag 29,35:5
Haug, Jacob C F, 1946, My 31,24:2
Haug, John S, 1961, Ap 22,25:5
Haug, William B Mrs, 1951, Ja 18,27:2
Haugaard, William E, 1948, S 18,17:3
Haugan, Oscar H, 1943, S 8,23:4
Hauge, C, 1907, D 20,11:5
Haugh, Gale, 1955, D 27,23:3
Haugh, Henry A Jr, 1956, N 15,35:5
Haugh, James F, 1950, O 19,31:2
Haugh, James T, 1940, D 17,26:2
Haugh, John Mrs, 1948, Ap 6,24:3
Haugher, Arthur, 1944, Ag 5,11:5
Haughey, Louis C, 1960, S 2,23:1
Haughey, William H, 1939, Ap 15,19:3
Haughney, James V, 1943, D 16,27:2
Haught, Sara H Mrs, 1946, D 19,29:3
Haughton, James Maj, 1912, Ag 25,II,11:6
Haughton, John, 1951, N 13,30:4
Haughton, Mrs (funl), 1871, D 27,5:5
Haughton, Nicholas, 1902, D 31,9:6
Haughton, Richard, 1947, S 3,25:4
Haughwout, Frank G, 1960, F 8,29:3
Haughwout, Irving R, 1945, Ja 23,19:1
Haughwout, James A, 1956, Ag 17,19:2
Haughwout, James M, 1949, S 25,92:3
Haughwout, Lefferd M A, 1952, Ap 21,21:4
Haughwout, William W, 1945, Je 13,23:5
Haugwalder, Rudolf, 1953, Jl 25,11:6
Hauk, Minnie (Baroness von Hesse-Wartegg), 1912, N 19,15:4
Hauk, Minnie, 1929, F 7,27:5
Haukap, John, 1946, My 6,21:1
Haulenbeck, Charles J, 1946, N 13,27:3
Haulenbeck, Garrie B Mrs, 1948, S 28,27:4
Haulenbeek, Garrie B, 1966, Jl 8,35:2
Haulenbeek, John W Sr, 1941, Je 27,17:3
Haulenbeek, P Raymond, 1966, Ja 21,47:3
Haultain, Frederick W G, 1942, Ja 31,17:6
Haultcoeur, Hippolyte (Chef Phillip), 1967, F 15,41
Haun, Elinor A, 1953, F 5,23:3
Haungs, Edward F, 1953, Mr 15,92:1
Haunstein, Wesley, 1949, N 28,27:5
Haupert, Paul S, 1941, O 10,23:2
Haupt, Alma C, 1956, Mr 17,19:4
Haupt, August, 1922, D 30,13:5
Haupt, Charles H, 1937, Ap 11,II,8:3
Haupt, Charles R Mrs, 1960, Mr 26,21:2
Haupt, Hans, 1952, F 20,30:3
Haupt, Herman, 1905, D 15,9:5
Haupt, Ira (funl, Je 15,23:5), 1963, Je 14,31:1
Haupt, Jacob, 1962, N 11,88:6
Haupt, Lewis H, 1956, F 25,19:5
Haupt, Lewis M, 1937, Mr 11,23:3
Haupt, P Dr, 1926, D 16,27:5
Haupt, Raimund W, 1944, S 10,45:2
Haupt, Samuel B, 1913, S 30,13:4
Haupt, Stuart L, 1963, D 3,43:4
Haupt, William, 1953, O 26,21:1
Haupt, William K, 1939, F 23,23:6
Haupt, William M, 1957, S 27,19:1
Hauptfuhrer, Henry, 1943, S 21,23:2
Hauptli, Albert Jr, 1964, O 6,43:7
Hauptman, Anna C Mrs, 1942, Ja 16,21:1
Hauptman, Solomon C, 1925, S 12,15:6
Hauptman, solomon C, 1925, S 14,19:5
Hauptmann, Alfred, 1948, Ap 6,24:3
Hauptmann, Carl, 1921, F 5,11:5
Hauptmann, Gerhart, 1946, Je 12,27:3
Hauptmann, William J, 1967, O 28,31:2
Haurlen, LeRoy Mrs, 1952, O 10,25:3
Haury, Christian, 1947, F 25,25:5
Haury, Otto Sr, 1961, Ap 22,25:3
Haus, Henry Mrs, 1948, Ap 15,25:3
Haus, Phil, 1958, My 25,86:5
Hausamann, Ernest E, 1943, Ag 17,17:4
Hausauer, Robert D, 1945, F 1,23:6
Hauschel, Alphonse R, 1956, Je 23,17:2
Hauschild, Manfred A, 1961, F 10,24:1
Hauschka, Hugo Mrs, 1948, D 24,18:2
Hause, Donald B, 1952, Je 9,23:6
Hause, Frank J, 1957, Ag 31,15:4
Hausegger, Siegmund von, 1948, O 15,24:3
Hauselt, Charles E, 1938, Ag 25,19:5
Hauseman, William C, 1948, My 12,27:1
Hausemann, Adolf von, 1903, D 10,9:4
Hausen, Max Mrs, 1966, Ja 8,26:6
Hausen, Max von Lt-Gen, 1922, Mr 21,19:6
Hauser, A Frank, 1941, Jl 12,13:1
Hauser, Adolph W, 1952, My 23,21:1
Hauser, Alex, 1954, N 26,29:4
Hauser, Andrew M, 1946, F 1,24:2
Hauser, Arthur M, 1948, S 30,27:3
Hauser, Carl, 1915, Ap 16,13:4
Hauser, Charles P, 1958, F 25,27:4
Hauser, Conrad, 1944, Ap 10,19:4
Hauser, Conrad A, 1943, Mr 15,14:2
Hauser, Emil (Wauseka), 1941, My 21,23:4
Hauser, Ernst A, 1956, F 13,27:4
Hauser, George, 1951, My 26,17:6
Hauser, George D Mrs, 1951, Mr 22,31:5
Hauser, George F C, 1941, Jl 2,21:3
Hauser, George H, 1958, My 28,31:1
Hauser, Henry E, 1950, Je 21,27:3
Hauser, Herbert B Sr, 1950, My 29,17:5
Hauser, Israel, 1956, F 8,33:4
Hauser, Julius, 1920, Mr 27,13:3
Hauser, Milton I, 1967, Je 7,47:2
Hauser, Odell, 1941, F 11,23:1
Hauser, Otto Mrs, 1941, O 6,17:3
Hauser, Paul S Mrs, 1961, S 26,39:2
Hauser, Phil, 1938, Je 22,23:1
Hauser, Rudolph, 1947, Ag 5,23:3
Hauser, Walter, 1959, Jl 15,29:2
Hauser, William M Sr, 1959, N 18,41:5
Haushalter, George M, 1943, Ag 8,37:2
Haushalter, Walter M, 1963, Ag 31,17:3
Hausheer, Emil F, 1950, Je 14,31:1
Hausheer, Walter C, 1960, F 27,19:3
Hausknecht, C Edward, 1943, F 28,47:5
Hausler, Fred J, 1949, Ag 24,25:3
Hausler, Frederick O, 1947, Ag 30,15:2
Hausman, Charles G Mrs, 1951, Ja 18,27:4
Hausman, Edward C, 1907, Ap 6,7:7
Hausman, Emanuel, 1952, My 12,25:4
Hausman, Eugene, 1965, F 23,33:3
Hausman, Harris, 1954, O 28,35:3
Hausman, Harris Mrs, 1959, D 3,37:4
Hausman, Isidore Mrs, 1955, S 19,25:4
Hausman, Leon A, 1966, F 4,31:4
Hausman, Marx B, 1957, Ja 3,33:4
Hausman, Maurice A, 1954, Je 29,27:5
Hausman, Morris Mrs, 1945, Ap 26,23:2
Hausman, Samuel W, 1960, Ja 3,88:4
Hausman, Sol, 1939, O 21,15:4

Hausman, W Scott, 1954, S 26,87:1
Hausmann, Anna Mrs, 1937, Ja 19,23:5
Hausmann, Clement M, 1948, O 2,15:3
Hausmann, Erich, 1962, F 23,29:2
Hausmann, George E, 1954, O 25,27:5
Hausmann, J Elmer, 1967, Je 3,31:4
Hausmann, Julius, 1951, O 15,25:1
Hausmann, Theodore Capt, 1911, D 29,11:4
Hausmann, Theodore W, 1960, Ja 27,33:1
Hausrath, Alfred H Mrs, 1958, My 24,21:4
Hauss, Rosetta V Mrs, 1945, Mr 23,19:5
Hausser, John, 1939, D 25,23:4
Haussermann, Charles F, 1960, Ag 10,31:2
Haussermann, John Mrs, 1948, Jl 9,19:1
Haussermann, John W, 1965, Jl 12,27:2
Hausske, Louise H Mrs, 1947, D 16,34:3
Haussler, Edward E, 1960, N 13,88:8
Haussling, Francis R, 1941, Ag 5,20:4
Haussmann, Alfred C, 1963, Ap 1,27:4
Haussmann, Baron, 1869, O 9,3:1
Haussmann, G E Baron, 1891, Ja 13,2:5
Haussmann, William A, 1940, Ap 2,25:2
Haussner, William H, 1963, Je 9,87:1
Haussonville, Comte d (J Othenin), 1884, My 29,5:3
Haust, Jean, 1946, N 27,25:5
Haustetter, Albert, 1938, S 13,23:4
Hauswirth, Louis, 1960, Je 18,23:4
Hauswirth, William L, 1966, Jl 19,39:3
Hauswirth, William L Mrs, 1940, O 16,23:2
Haut, Jules L, 1966, Ap 7,39:1
Hautau, Fred W, 1953, Ja 11,90:1
Hautau, Frederick L, 1959, Je 27,23:3
Hauteclocque, Jean de Count, 1957, S 28,17:3
Hautefort, Louis, 1941, Je 8,49:1
Hauter, Holly L, 1950, Mr 24,26:2
Hauteville, Frederic Sears Grand d' Baron, 1918, Je 17,13:8
Hauvel, Peter van den, 1940, Ag 9,15:3
Hauver, Elwin H, 1955, N 10,35:5
Hauxwell, Amy D Mrs, 1940, Mr 21,25:3
Havala, Paul Sr, 1956, F 16,29:5
Havard, John D, 1942, Mr 11,19:2
Havard, Michel, 1949, My 17,25:1
Havard, William J, 1963, D 30,21:3
Havas, George, 1962, Mr 17,25:2
Havasabian, Peter, 1938, S 7,25:1
Have, Jeanne M Mrs, 1939, Ap 15,19:5
Haveghan, Patrick J, 1946, Jl 12,17:4
Havekotte, Harold, 1941, Mr 18,23:4
Havelka, Edward Sr, 1954, N 13,15:3
Havelka, Rudolph, 1955, O 29,19:1
Havell, George F, 1960, F 29,27:2
Havell, Harry P Mrs, 1958, Mr 7,23:3
Havell, Wesley J, 1944, Jl 13,17:4
Havelock, Lady, 1882, S 11,5:4
Havemeyer, Albert, 1874, Ag 23,8:3
Havemeyer, Arthur, 1955, N 19,19:5
Havemeyer, Augustus H, 1907, Ag 13,7:6
Havemeyer, Charles F, 1960, D 17,23:3
Havemeyer, Frederick C, 1910, Ap 26,11:5; 1948, Je 3,25:4
Havemeyer, H O Mrs, 1929, Ja 7,29:3
Havemeyer, Helen M, 1947, Ag 30,15:3
Havemeyer, Henry O, 1965, F 14,89:1
Havemeyer, Henry O Mrs, 1962, O 11,39:2
Havemeyer, Herbert E, 1943, My 13,21:6
Havemeyer, Horace, 1956, O 26,29:4
Havemeyer, J W Mrs, 1921, Ag 3,13:5
Havemeyer, James, 1912, Ag 19,9:6
Havemeyer, John C, 1922, Je 9,15:5
Havemeyer, John F, 1952, Je 16,17:5
Havemeyer, Raymond, 1925, F 22,19:3
Havemeyer, T A, 1897, Ap 27,12:3
Havemeyer, Theodore A Mrs, 1914, My 4,9:6; 1951, Ja 22,17:2
Havemeyer, Theodore 3d, 1941, Ap 9,25:7
Havemeyer, W A, 1903, Je 30,7:5
Havemeyer, William F (funl, S 12,11:5), 1913, S 11, 11:6
Havemeyer, William F Mayor, 1874, D 1,1:7
Haven, Alfred C, 1968, N 9,33:2
Haven, Alfred Pell, 1923, Je 6,21:4
Haven, E O Bp, 1881, Ag 4,5:6
Haven, George B, 1953, Mr 8,91:1
Haven, George G, 1925, Jl 24,13:7; 1944, S 17,42:3
Haven, George G Mrs, 1923, N 15,19:4
Haven, George Griswold Mrs, 1919, S 21,22:3
Haven, Gilbert, 1880, Ja 4,1:5
Haven, H P, 1876, My 1,4:6
Haven, Henry Cecil Dr, 1915, F 20,11:6
Haven, Howard A, 1907, Mr 18,7:6
Haven, J A, 1875, D 14,5:2
Haven, Joseph E, 1937, My 5,25:2
Haven, Joseph Prof, 1874, My 26,4:6
Haven, L E, 1952, Ag 7,21:5
Haven, Parkman B, 1943, S 4,13:6
Haven, Philo P, 1948, Jl 13,27:5
Haven, Samuel C, 1949, N 22,29:3
Haven, W L F, 1875, My 25,6:7
Haven, William I Mrs, 1952, F 23,11:2
Havender, Joseph Jr, 1963, D 28,23:3
Havender, Joseph Sr, 1952, D 14,91:2
Havender, Lester F, 1952, My 17,19:3
Havenga, Nicholaas C, 1957, Mr 14,29:6
Havenner, Franck R, 1967, Jl 26,39:1
Havens, A C, 1884, Mr 16,8:7
Havens, Abram Vaughn, 1968, Mr 30,33:5
Havens, Anthony M Mrs, 1949, My 20,27:4
Havens, Archibald S, 1951, Ja 24,27:5
Havens, Arthur V, 1949, Ap 29,23:3
Havens, Benjamin F, 1943, S 21,23:4
Havens, Catherine E, 1939, F 20,17:2
Havens, Charles E, 1937, Ag 9,19:4
Havens, Donald, 1959, Mr 26,31:1
Havens, Edward D, 1955, Ja 23,85:2
Havens, Elmer A, 1951, S 6,31:2
Havens, Elmer H Mrs, 1938, Ja 4,23:4
Havens, Frank S, 1942, Ja 24,17:1
Havens, Fred C, 1956, D 18,31:2
Havens, Henry C, 1946, F 23,13:5
Havens, J S, 1903, Ag 18,7:6; 1927, F 28,19:5
Havens, James D, 1960, D 2,29:3
Havens, John G W Ex-Sen, 1912, N 29,15:4
Havens, John L, 1944, Ja 14,19:4
Havens, John L Mrs, 1959, Ap 9,31:1
Havens, Judd W, 1942, D 24,15:1
Havens, Lawrence A, 1944, Jl 28,13:3
Havens, Mary C, 1952, O 15,31:1
Havens, Mary Mrs, 1952, F 1,21:2
Havens, Munson, 1942, Ja 16,21:4
Havens, Samuel M, 1943, N 6,13:2
Havens, Silas H, 1908, Mr 13,7:4
Havens, Valentine, 1944, Je 30,21:5
Havens, Valentine B, 1948, Jl 22,23:1
Havens, Verne L, 1944, Ag 14,15:6
Havenstein, Rudolf E A Dr, 1923, N 21,19:3
Havenstrite, Russell E, 1958, Mr 19,31:2
Haver, Alonzo, 1953, My 5,29:2
Haver, Jennie M, 1956, D 23,30:4
Haver, Thomas T, 1952, Ja 21,15:3
Haver, William E, 1967, D 11,47:3
Haverbeck, Harrison M, 1953, Je 6,17:2
Haverfield, Ralph F Mrs, 1958, Ap 18,23:5
Haverin, Charles B, 1965, Ag 13,26:7
Haverlin, Charles A Mrs, 1958, F 6,27:1
Haverly, Bert, 1908, N 1,9:5
Haverly, Jack, 1901, S 29,9:5
Haverly, Jack Mrs, 1910, Jl 5,13:4
Havermale, Albert G, 1941, O 3,23:1
Haveron, Francis L, 1957, F 6,25:3
Havers, Rebecca Mrs, 1948, F 4,23:2
Haverstick, Charles S, 1950, My 18,29:5
Haverstick, Park W, 1960, O 9,86:7
Haverstick, Washington, 1939, S 19,26:4
Haverstock, Samuel F, 1940, Ag 11,31:3
Haverty, Clarence, 1960, D 24,15:3
Haverty, Frank Mrs, 1937, N 11,25:4
Haverty, Geraldine M, 1939, N 12,48:8
Haverty, James J (por), 1939, O 19,23:3
Haverty, John M, 1944, Ap 23,43:6
Haverty, P M Maj, 1901, S 19,7:6
Haverty, Robert Sr, 1952, F 16,13:3
Havey, Ambrose S, 1955, Jl 9,15:1
Havey, Ambrose S Sr, 1937, Je 13,II,7:1
Havey, Ambrose S Sr Mrs, 1954, Ja 15,19:2
Havey, Francis P, 1945, Mr 14,19:2
Havey, I Malinde, 1938, S 8,24:2
Havey, Joseph J, 1954, Ja 11,25:3
Havey, Lawrence, 1924, D 5,21:5
Havey, Peter H, 1948, My 27,25:1
Havey, Phil J, 1937, Je 9,25:5
Havey, William C, 1959, D 10,39:2
Havez, Jean, 1925, F 13,17:4
Havighurst, Alfred R, 1943, Ja 24,42:4
Havilan, Aaron B, 1954, S 16,29:3
Haviland, Aaron B Mrs, 1953, Ap 9,27:4
Haviland, Amidee T, 1959, S 19,23:5
Haviland, Arden, 1947, Je 8,60:8
Haviland, Arthur, 1919, Je 22,15:4
Haviland, Augusta, 1925, O 27,23:3
Haviland, Bartholomew, 1945, Ap 10,19:4
Haviland, Benjamin C, 1952, Ag 6,24:8
Haviland, C Augustus, 1918, S 21,9:8
Haviland, C E, 1921, Mr 31,13:5
Haviland, C F, 1930, Ja 2,25:1
Haviland, Caroline E, 1949, Ag 23,23:3
Haviland, Carrie S, 1948, N 23,30:2
Haviland, Catherine, 1903, Ap 13,14:2
Haviland, Clark D, 1953, Ap 13,27:6
Haviland, Clifford G, 1946, O 15,25:4
Haviland, David, 1879, D 14,7:1; 1948, Mr 14,73:1
Haviland, Dean A, 1962, Jl 15,60:3
Haviland, Edward C, 1944, Mr 11,13:1
Haviland, Edward C Mrs, 1941, D 18,27:2
Haviland, Edward W, 1944, O 5,23:5
Haviland, Emma C, 1938, D 25,15:1
Haviland, F B, 1932, Mr 31,21:1
Haviland, F Ross, 1954, Je 29,27:2
Haviland, Foster L Mrs, 1948, F 9,17:3
Haviland, Frank B, 1944, Ja 23,38:2
Haviland, Freeman, 1946, Jl 2,25:3
Haviland, George E, 1958, Mr 29,17:4
Haviland, Henry F, 1966, Je 6,41:5
Haviland, Henry M, 1942, D 13,74:3
Haviland, Ida P Mrs, 1938, D 4,60:6
Haviland, J G, 1882, S 6,5:2
Haviland, James A, 1945, Ag 10,15:5
Haviland, James T, 1957, Ap 30,29:4
Haviland, John M, 1948, Ap 24,15:1
Haviland, LeGrand Jr, 1953, Ja 30,21:3
Haviland, Lindsley, 1955, F 4,21:3
Haviland, Louis Mrs, 1957, Mr 19,37:2
Haviland, Norman H Dr, 1937, F 14,II,9:1
Haviland, Phoebe T Mrs (est tax appr), 1954, Mr 25,14:4
Haviland, Reed G, 1955, S 28,35:2
Haviland, Reed G 2d Mrs, 1960, Ja 20,31:4
Haviland, Rena, 1954, F 21,68:1
Haviland, S A, 1877, N 26,5:6
Haviland, Sarah M Mrs, 1910, S 21,9:4
Haviland, Sarah T, 1950, N 23,35:4
Haviland, Thomas F Mrs, 1961, Ag 3,23:5
Haviland, Walter C, 1945, My 15,19:5
Haviland, Walter W, 1955, N 10,35:5
Haviland, William, 1917, S 22,11:6
Haviland, William Kipp, 1921, F 24,13:6
Haviland, Willis B, 1944, D 2,13:7
Haviland-Taylor, Katherine, 1941, N 29,17:6
Havill, Clinton H (trb lr, Ap 9,26:6), 1953, Mr 26, 31:6
Havill, Egbert U, 1942, My 15,19:2
Havlik, Frank V, 1950, Jl 10,21:5
Havlin, John H, 1924, D 18,21:5
Havner, Harrison H, 1957, My 2,31:4
Havnes, John W, 1956, Je 1,23:1
Havranek, Ulrich, 1937, S 19,XI,8:4
Havre, Samuel L Mrs, 1947, Ap 12,17:5
Havrilla, Alois, 1952, D 8,41:2
Havron, John, 1915, Jl 27,9:5
Haward, Harry E, 1953, S 10,25:6
Hawaweeny, Raphael Bp, 1915, Mr 8,9:5
Hawbolt, Hannah P Mrs, 1951, Ap 1,92:1
Haweis, H H Rev, 1901, Ja 30,9:5
Hawes, Alexander C Col, 1913, D 10,13:5
Hawes, Alfred Mrs, 1944, Mr 23,19:2
Hawes, Alfred T, 1949, D 2,29:4
Hawes, B F, 1902, F 10,3:3
Hawes, Belle vs P H, 1884, F 24,5:2
Hawes, C Wesson, 1955, S 23,25:2
Hawes, Carnelius C, 1952, Ag 31,44:1
Hawes, Charles H, 1943, D 15,27:4
Hawes, Charles L, 1947, Jl 22,23:2; 1951, Je 12,29:4
Hawes, Christopher G, 1945, D 27,19:4
Hawes, Edward S, 1942, N 23,23:5
Hawes, Frederic B, 1946, D 1,76:5
Hawes, G W, 1882, Je 24,5:5
Hawes, George R, 1968, D 29,53:1
Hawes, Gilbert Ray, 1923, Ap 17,21:4
Hawes, Granville P Judge, 1907, S 14,9:5
Hawes, Harry B, 1947, Ag 1,17:4
Hawes, Harry B Mrs, 1952, Mr 29,15:5
Hawes, J, 1878, N 9,8:3
Hawes, J A, 1936, Mr 1,II,11:1
Hawes, James William, 1918, S 2,9:2
Hawes, John, 1944, Ap 12,21:4
Hawes, John J, 1905, O 7,9:4
Hawes, John K, 1962, My 21,33:4
Hawes, Kirk Judge, 1904, S 10,9:6
Hawes, Owen S, 1941, Ja 22,21:1
Hawes, Philip T, 1944, Jl 21,19:3
Hawes, Stewart S, 1967, N 11,33:3
Hawes, W Gerald, 1957, S 18,33:5
Hawes, W Gerald Mrs, 1955, N 9,33:4
Hawes, W Gilbert, 1948, N 11,27:2
Hawes, Willard, 1883, N 11,9:5
Hawes, William F, 1947, My 21,25:4
Hawes, William L, 1874, Ap 30,2:5
Hawgood, Arthur H, 1945, Je 24,22:4
Hawgood, Harvey R, 1952, Ja 16,25:1
Hawie, Said, 1950, Jl 11,32:2
Hawk, Earl, 1961, Ap 29,23:4
Hawk, George W, 1955, Je 10,25:2
Hawk, Glenn C, 1952, My 2,25:1
Hawk, James W, 1941, S 15,17:3
Hawk, John C Mrs, 1947, S 5,20:2
Hawk, Jonathan B, 1939, D 5,27:1
Hawk, Phil B Mrs, 1954, D 9,33:2
Hawk, Philip B, 1966, S 15,43:3
Hawk, R M A, 1882, Jl 1,2:7
Hawk, Samuel, 1882, Ag 12,5:2
Hawk, William M, 1938, Mr 20,II,8:2
Hawke, George, 1938, D 29,19:4
Hawke, James A Rear-Adm, 1910, Jl 27,9:5
Hawke, John A (por), 1941, O 31,23:3
Hawke, John D, 1954, O 21,27:1
Hawke, Lord (por), 1938, O 11,25:3
Hawke, Minnie, 1952, Mr 4,27:2
Hawke, William B, 1963, Ja 4,4:1
Hawke, William W, 1940, Ap 5,21:3
Hawken, chas E, 1939, My 31,23:1
Hawkes, Albert W Mrs, 1960, My 25,39:1
Hawkes, Charles, 1903, S 26,9:4
Hawkes, Charles E, 1948, F 2,19:2
Hawkes, Charles R, 1916, Mr 14,11:4
Hawkes, Charles W Mrs, 1949, Ja 26,25:3
Hawkes, Clarence, 1954, Ja 20,27:2
Hawkes, Edward F, 1955, Ja 21,23:4
Hawkes, Edward J, 1947, O 3,25:3
Hawkes, Edward Z, 1960, O 7,35:1

Hawkes, Forbes R (por), 1940, Ag 25,35:1
Hawkes, Geoffrey, 1961, Jl 19,29:4
Hawkes, George B, 1949, Ja 2,60:7
Hawkes, George E, 1954, F 19,27:5
Hawkes, George Mrs, 1947, D 19,25:4
Hawkes, George W, 1954, S 19,89:1
Hawkes, Herbert E, 1943, My 5,27:1
Hawkes, Irving M, 1940, Mr 23,13:5
Hawkes, J G Maj, 1906, Mr 30,9:4
Hawkes, John Mrs, 1954, Je 22,27:4
Hawkes, Kenneth H, 1960, Ja 18,27:2
Hawkes, Lewis A, 1943, Je 30,21:2
Hawkes, Lincoln E, 1948, N 21,88:1
Hawkes, McDougall, 1929, Mr 21,19:2
Hawkes, McDougall Mrs, 1947, D 6,15:4
Hawkes, Nathan W, 1953, Mr 8,90:3
Hawkes, Ralph, 1950, S 10,92:3
Hawkes, Robert Mrs, 1942, Mr 1,45:3
Hawkes, Samuel, 1959, Je 27,23:3
Hawkes, Thomas G, 1949, Mr 10,27:5
Hawkes, Walter F, 1939, Ag 24,19:5
Hawkes, William F, 1950, Jl 13,25:2
Hawkes, William H, 1952, O 13,21:2
Hawkes, William V, 1964, S 9,43:2
Hawkesworth, Edward G, 1949, Ag 15,17:1
Hawkesworth, Robert Wright, 1909, Mr 25,9:4
Hawkey, George H Mrs, 1949, Je 27,27:5
Hawkey, T C Mrs, 1949, N 24,31:6
Hawkin, Robert C, 1939, Ja 11,19:3
Hawkins, A, 1933, Jl 9,20:1
Hawkins, Alfred E Sr, 1945, S 18,23:2
Hawkins, Alma Mrs, 1940, F 6,21:3
Hawkins, Alvin ex-Gov, 1905, Ap 28,9:4
Hawkins, Arthur F, 1939, Je 28,21:3
Hawkins, B Lee, 1952, Ag 9,13:4
Hawkins, Benjamin B, 1946, Ap 25,21:2
Hawkins, C H Dr, 1884, Jl 22,5:2
Hawkins, Charles H, 1940, Mr 22,19:2; 1941, Ja 16, 23:2
Hawkins, Charles W, 1958, Ap 23,33:1
Hawkins, Charles W Mrs, 1941, D 29,15:2
Hawkins, Chester S, 1951, Je 17,84:7
Hawkins, Cornelius S, 1950, F 27,19:5
Hawkins, Crawford W, 1952, Mr 14,20:6
Hawkins, Daniel C, 1941, Mr 3,7:5
Hawkins, David, 1967, My 2,47:3
Hawkins, Delmar E, 1956, My 14,25:5
Hawkins, Dexter T (Sept 22), 1965, O 11,61:2
Hawkins, Dorothy L, 1938, Ag 19,19:3
Hawkins, E Eugene Jr, 1960, Ja 11,45:5
Hawkins, E Rev, 1882, N 21,5:2
Hawkins, Edgar A, 1952, Je 4,27:4
Hawkins, Edward Capt, 1908, Je 11,7:4
Hawkins, Edward J, 1940, Jl 31,17:3
Hawkins, Edward R, 1963, O 20,89:1
Hawkins, Elbert A, 1964, Je 5,31:3
Hawkins, Erastus S, 1961, Ja 19,29:2
Hawkins, Ernest C, 1944, Ja 8,13:2
Hawkins, Ernest G Mrs, 1945, O 10,21:3
Hawkins, Eugene D Mrs, 1964, S 30,43:1
Hawkins, Eugene Dexter, 1919, Jl 11,11:3
Hawkins, Eugene Sr Mrs, 1954, N 18,33:4
Hawkins, Fenner, 1953, D 26,13:2
Hawkins, Florence G, 1951, D 31,13:6
Hawkins, Frank B, 1946, O 19,21:5
Hawkins, Frank D Jr, 1945, O 17,38:6
Hawkins, Frank J, 1951, F 5,23:2
Hawkins, Frederick, 1947, N 3,23:1
Hawkins, Frederick M, 1957, N 29,29:1
Hawkins, G Frederick, 1937, My 29,17:3
Hawkins, G Frederick Mrs, 1964, Ap 2,33:2
Hawkins, George, 1948, Ap 11,72:1
Hawkins, George Henry, 1949, Jl 18,17:5
Hawkins, George K, 1940, F 27,21:3
Hawkins, George W, 1964, Jl 28,29:1
Hawkins, Glenwood, 1948, F 7,15:5
Hawkins, Graham, 1956, Je 6,23:5
Hawkins, Hamilton S, 1950, O 21,17:3
Hawkins, Hamilton S Brig-Gen, 1910, Mr 29,11:3
Hawkins, Harold F Sr, 1959, S 11,27:2
Hawkins, Harry B, 1941, Ag 26,19:3
Hawkins, Harry L, 1955, F 3,23:1
Hawkins, Harry L Mrs, 1954, D 10,27:1
Hawkins, Henry (Lord Brampton), 1907, O 7,9:5
Hawkins, Henry, 1947, S 6,17:4; 1951, Ja 16,29:2
Hawkins, Henry J, 1957, Ap 18,29:4
Hawkins, Herbert H, 1942, F 21,19:1
Hawkins, Horace A, 1937, O 2,21:1
Hawkins, Horace H, 1947, O 4,17:1
Hawkins, Horatio G Mrs, 1943, S 14,23:4
Hawkins, Ira, 1967, My 26,39:1
Hawkins, Irwin E, 1941, Ap 18,21:4
Hawkins, J Earl, 1957, F 15,23:3
Hawkins, James H, 1950, Mr 2,28:5; 1950, D 29,19:3
Hawkins, James W, 1958, N 14,27:3
Hawkins, Joel E Rev, 1918, S 17,13:4
Hawkins, John A, 1941, F 23,40:2; 1947, S 9,31:2
Hawkins, John A Mrs, 1962, My 21,33:4
Hawkins, John J, 1943, Mr 3,23:3
Hawkins, John M, 1959, D 17,37:3
Hawkins, John P, 1909, Jl 3,7:4
Hawkins, John Parker Gen, 1914, F 8,15:6
Hawkins, Jonathan, 1915, Je 16,11:4
Hawkins, Lady, 1946, D 30,19:5
Hawkins, Laurence A, 1958, My 17,19:3
Hawkins, Layton S, 1960, Jl 31,69:3
Hawkins, Lester Mrs, 1953, Je 2,29:4
Hawkins, Lewis E, 1943, F 28,48:2
Hawkins, Lewis E Mrs, 1961, Jl 17,21:1
Hawkins, Maxwell, 1962, O 6,25:5
Hawkins, Michael, 1954, Mr 28,88:5
Hawkins, N A, 1936, Ag 19,21:3
Hawkins, Nancy McComber Mrs, 1907, Ap 3,9:4
Hawkins, Nathan F, 1951, Mr 3,13:5
Hawkins, Nathaniel T, 1955, S 23,25:4
Hawkins, Paul, 1959, Ja 4,88:4
Hawkins, Paul R, 1945, Ag 29,23:6
Hawkins, Phil, 1951, O 31,6:4
Hawkins, Ralph J, 1955, Ag 26,19:2
Hawkins, Raymond, 1944, Mr 31,21:5
Hawkins, Rex W, 1942, Ja 6,24:2
Hawkins, Richard (Mar 15), 1963, Ap 1,35:7
Hawkins, Richard M, 1943, N 2,25:2
Hawkins, Richard Mrs, 1913, Ap 21,11:6
Hawkins, Rush C Brig-Gen, 1920, O 26,17:4
Hawkins, Samuel N, 1955, N 23,23:4
Hawkins, Simeon S, 1906, Ja 23,9:5
Hawkins, T B Capt, 1901, Ap 26,7:6
Hawkins, T H Dr, 1926, Jl 22,19:4
Hawkins, Thomas C, 1937, Mr 3,23:4
Hawkins, Thomas Patrick, 1914, Ap 5,15:2
Hawkins, Victor, 1946, My 6,21:2
Hawkins, Walter M, 1960, O 2,84:6
Hawkins, Warner M, 1960, F 23,32:1
Hawkins, Wesley D, 1942, O 30,19:5
Hawkins, Wesley U, 1949, Ja 28,21:4
Hawkins, Wilford J, 1959, Ap 12,86:5
Hawkins, William E, 1951, Ap 15,92:1
Hawkins, William R, 1949, Ag 31,23:6
Hawkins, William W, 1953, F 20,19:3
Hawkins-Ambler, George A, 1945, O 28,44:2
Hawkinson, Alex, 1956, Mr 4,88:4
Hawkridge, Leslie D, 1952, Ap 22,29:2
Hawks, Alice Mrs, 1937, N 19,23:2
Hawks, Allard Mrs, 1944, O 3,23:3
Hawks, Annie Sherwood Mrs, 1918, Ja 4,11:8
Hawks, Arthur W, 1949, Ap 1,25:2
Hawks, Byron M, 1937, Je 17,24:2
Hawks, Charles Jr, 1960, Ja 7,29:5
Hawks, Erastus L Mrs, 1947, Ag 24,56:1
Hawks, Fannie, 1950, Ap 19,29:3
Hawks, Francis Lister, 1866, S 28,4:6
Hawks, George H Sr, 1953, N 26,31:3
Hawks, George W, 1952, My 5,23:5
Hawks, Richard, 1950, Ja 31,24:2
Hawks, Virginia W Mrs, 1946, D 25,29:5
Hawks, Wayne, 1968, Ap 11,45:1
Hawks, Wells, 1941, D 5,23:1
Hawks, William E (will), 1961, N 15,45:3
Hawks, William W, 1941, S 18,25:4
Hawkseworth, Anna M Mrs, 1938, Jl 8,17:5
Hawksworth, Alfred, 1913, F 17,11:4
Hawksworth, George, 1958, My 24,21:5
Hawkwood, Albert E, 1945, Ag 23,23:2
Hawkwood, Ernest Henry, 1953, Ja 14,31:3
Hawlett, O Holly, 1961, Ja 19,29:5
Hawley, Alan R (por),(will, F 25,9:2), 1938, F 17, 21:1
Hawley, Alan W, 1948, O 21,27:5
Hawley, Alonzo, 1945, F 7,21:5
Hawley, Anna B, 1937, Mr 22,23:4
Hawley, Anna C, 1953, Jl 13,25:6
Hawley, Bostwick Rev, 1910, Jl 30,7:6
Hawley, Charles B, 1915, D 30,13:5
Hawley, Charles C, 1953, F 18,31:4
Hawley, Charles G, 1939, Ap 18,23:2
Hawley, Charles W, 1912, My 13,9:6; 1937, Ap 22, 23:4
Hawley, Clifford B, 1947, Ag 15,17:5
Hawley, Cornell S, 1939, F 26,38:6
Hawley, David, 1903, N 26,7:6
Hawley, David Father, 1876, F 2,4:6
Hawley, Donald P, 1950, Ap 13,29:2
Hawley, Earl, 1957, Je 17,23:1
Hawley, Edmund S Mrs (por), 1945, O 16,23:3
Hawley, Edwin (por),(funl, F 4,13:5), 1912, F 2,9:1
Hawley, Emerson, 1938, S 20,23:5
Hawley, Emily, 1937, Ap 8,23:5
Hawley, Emily A, 1942, N 8,50:6
Hawley, Esther, 1968, D 5,47:2
Hawley, Frances B, 1946, Je 7,19:4
Hawley, Frank, 1949, N 30,27:4
Hawley, Fred F, 1943, F 12,19:1
Hawley, Frederick B Jr, 1949, D 7,31:5
Hawley, George A, 1941, My 17,15:2
Hawley, George M B, 1941, O 6,17:2
Hawley, George S, 1956, O 22,29:5
Hawley, George W, 1940, Ja 2,19:2
Hawley, H Dudley, 1941, Mr 31,15:4
Hawley, Harvey F, 1953, Jl 20,17:4
Hawley, Henry, 1952, O 16,29:4
Hawley, Henry W, 1905, S 22,9:6
Hawley, Henry W Mrs, 1963, O 31,33:4
Hawley, Hiram B, 1946, O 18,23:3
Hawley, Irad, 1865, My 24,2:5
Hawley, J G, 1903, Ap 20,7:5
Hawley, J H, 1929, Ag 4,24:4
Hawley, James L, 1959, O 20,39:1
Hawley, Jess B, 1946, Mr 22,21:3
Hawley, John B, 1941, Ja 10,19:5
Hawley, John G, 1955, F 23,27:5
Hawley, John H (por), 1940, Ap 12,23:6
Hawley, John Mitchell Rear-Adm, 1925, F 11,21:4
Hawley, John S, 1913, D 30,9:5
Hawley, Joseph R Gen, 1905, Mr 18,7:2
Hawley, Joseph R Mrs, 1925, F 10,23:3
Hawley, Joseph Sir, 1875, My 6,10:7
Hawley, Katherine V, 1946, F 27,25:4
Hawley, Margaret F, 1963, D 19,33:5
Hawley, Margarita L, 1940, Je 3,15:3
Hawley, Ormi Mrs, 1942, Je 5,17:5
Hawley, Otis M, 1941, D 2,23:4
Hawley, Paul R, 1965, N 26,37:1
Hawley, R K Mrs, 1909, O 26,9:5
Hawley, R S, 1903, Ja 20,9:5
Hawley, Ralph W, 1949, D 28,32:3
Hawley, Robert Bradley, 1921, N 29,17:3
Hawley, Robert G, 1961, F 23,27:1
Hawley, Roy M, 1954, Mr 22,27:5
Hawley, Royal A, 1941, S 21,44:2
Hawley, S C, 1884, N 11,2:4
Hawley, Samuel B, 1949, S 27,27:5
Hawley, Samuel B Mrs, 1937, Ap 16,23:1
Hawley, Stuart C, 1953, Mr 2,23:3
Hawley, Theodosia R de, 1937, S 22,27:3
Hawley, Thomas J Mrs, 1957, D 4,39:4
Hawley, Thomas P, 1967, F 8,31:3
Hawley, Truman R, 1951, N 17,17:6
Hawley, Walter A, 1952, F 27,27:4
Hawley, Walter A Mrs, 1957, Mr 9,19:1
Hawley, Walter L, 1909, F 10,9:4
Hawley, Walter S, 1937, Je 9,25:6
Hawley, William Dickerman, 1925, N 24,25:5
Hawley, William P, 1946, N 25,27:3
Hawley, William Young, 1919, Jl 28,11:4
Hawley, Willis C, 1941, Jl 25,15:3
Hawley, Willis C Mrs, 1938, F 5,15:6
Hawn, Orra G, 1943, F 5,21:1
Haworth, Joseph, 1903, Ag 29,2:7
Haworth, Lawrence A, 1949, N 30,27:3
Haworth, Lester C, 1954, Ag 17,21:3
Haworth, Norman (Walter), 1950, Mr 20,22:3
Haworth, Paul L, 1938, Mr 25,19:4
Haworth, Peter, 1948, D 21,25:4
Haws, Henry E, 1951, Ag 20,19:5
Haws, Robert T, 1863, Mr 23,4:6
Hawse, Virgil P, 1948, N 30,28:2
Hawthorn, Mike (funl, Ja 29,24:5), 1959, Ja 23,
Hawthorne, Andrew, 1951, My 13,88:4
Hawthorne, Andrew Mrs, 1952, O 14,34:2
Hawthorne, Bayard Mrs, 1938, Ap 3,II,7:1
Hawthorne, C W, 1930, N 30,II,9:1
Hawthorne, Charles W Mrs, 1945, Ap 18,23:4
Hawthorne, Daniel J, 1966, Jl 23,25:1
Hawthorne, Ed, 1951, Je 3,95:3
Hawthorne, F Gerald, 1961, O 17,39:5
Hawthorne, Frank Warren Col, 1911, N 26,15:5
Hawthorne, Fred, 1952, Ag 3,60:2
Hawthorne, George B, 1939, Mr 1,21:4
Hawthorne, Gladys, 1882, S 27,1:7
Hawthorne, Grace, 1922, My 26,19:6
Hawthorne, Harry L, 1948, Ap 10,13:4
Hawthorne, Herbert R Mrs, 1951, S 2,48:5
Hawthorne, Hugh R, 1962, Ja 13,21:2
Hawthorne, J, 1934, Jl 15,22:1
Hawthorne, John F, 1960, Ap 29,31:2
Hawthorne, John R Mrs, 1946, Ap 16,25:3
Hawthorne, Julian, 1957, My 2,31:4
Hawthorne, Julian Mrs, 1949, Ja 7,21:5
Hawthorne, Kenneth C, 1942, N 16,19:5
Hawthorne, Louis, 1958, Ag 12,29:5
Hawthorne, Louise (Mrs Geo Morton), 1876, 4:7
Hawthorne, Louise, 1876, Jl 1,5:5
Hawthorne, Nathaniel, 1864, My 20,4:5
Hawthorne, Nathaniel Mrs, 1871, Mr 2,1:2
Hawthorne, Nell (Mrs R Vernon), 1960, Jl 24
Hawthorne, Paris F, 1942, Ja 28,19:4
Hawthorne, Una, 1877, S 12,5:3
Hawthorne, Walter T, 1950, Ja 3,25:4
Hawthorne, William, 1953, Mr 3,27:3
Hawthorne, William J, 1950, Ap 27,29:2
Hawtin, George Mrs, 1937, Ja 20,21:5
Hawtof, Israel J, 1959, D 6,86:1
Hawtrey, Charles, 1923, Jl 31,17:1
Hawtrey, Henry, 1961, N 18,23:4
Hawtrey, John G, 1954, O 28,35:4
Hawtrey, William, 1914, Ja 8,11:4
Hawxby, Fred G, 1954, Jl 19,19:5
Hawxhurst, Elizabeth, 1922, Ja 18,17:4
Hawxhurst, Harold E, 1947, Ja 31,23:3
Hawxhurst, Harry Mrs, 1956, Ap 4,29:3
Hawxhurst, James H Rev, 1923, Ag 13,13:4
Hawxhurst, Mary K, 1956, My 1,33:1
Hawxhurst, Walter, 1942, Ap 22,24:2
Haxall, Bolling W Mrs, 1958, Mr 12,31:3
Haxall, J Triplett, 1939, Je 7,23:4
Haxall, Milo S Gen, 1904, Ag 31,7:6
Haxthausen, E von, 1914, Jl 14,9:6

Haxton, G Sherwin, 1959, Mr 20,31:1
Haxton, G Sherwin (est acctg), 1961, N 1,61:7
Haxtun, Adelaide, 1941, Je 9,19:4
Hay, A Jr, 1881, Je 6,5:5
Hay, A S, 1901, Je 24,1:1
Hay, Albert E, 1954, N 20,17:1
Hay, Archibald Fitzroy George (Earl of Kinnoull), 1916, F 8,11:2
Hay, Arthur D, 1952, D 20,17:5
Hay, Arthur H, 1937, Ag 21,15:4
Hay, Charles E, 1916, Ja 16,17:5
Hay, Charles M, 1945, Ja 17,21:5
Hay, David, 1941, O 21,23:2
Hay, David Mrs, 1946, Ap 11,25:3
Hay, Davis S, 1940, Ja 3,21:2
Hay, Douglas, 1949, F 25,23:1
Hay, Douglas W, 1922, My 22,15:5
Hay, E G, 1933, F 22,19:5
Hay, Earl D, 1953, Ja 4,76:3
Hay, Eduardo, 1941, D 28,28:2
Hay, Edward, 1921, Jl 12,13:4
Hay, Edward G, 1942, D 17,29:3
Hay, Edward N, 1958, Ag 26,29:1
Hay, Edwin B Jr, 1954, O 29,21:1
Hay, Ellis S, 1943, D 8,23:4
Hay, Esther M, 1966, F 14,29:3
Hay, George D, 1968, My 10,47:2
Hay, George I, 1925, Ap 30,21:3
Hay, H Harvey, 1947, Ag 19,23:6
Hay, Henry G Sr, 1919, Ag 20,15:2
Hay, Henry H, 1941, Ja 9,21:2
Hay, Henry H Mrs (A LeCroix), 1967, Je 22,39:4
Hay, Ian (J H Beith), 1952, S 23,33:3
Hay, J Bevan, 1955, Ja 28,19:3
Hay, J Lewis, 1949, My 29,36:6
Hay, J Lewis Mrs, 1940, Ja 7,48:4
Hay, James, 1950, N 14,32:2
Hay, James B, 1941, S 6,15:5
Hay, James D H Sir, 1873, Jl 31,1:4
Hay, John Baldwin, 1912, Ap 10,13:4
Hay, John G, 1964, My 27,39:4
Hay, John Lord, 1916, My 5,11:6
Hay, John Milton (funl plans, Jl 2,2:7; funl, Jl 6,9:1), 1905, Jl 1,1:5
Hay, Joseph Mrs, 1914, Ap 26,IV,7:5
Hay, Louis C, 1938, Jl 16,13:6
Hay, Louis C Mrs, 1946, Jl 3,25:2
Hay, M E, 1933, N 22,19:1
Hay, M G, 1928, Ag 31,19:3
Hay, Marley F, 1963, O 10,41:2
Hay, Mary (Mrs R Hastings), 1957, Je 5,35:3
Hay, Paul F, 1962, My 24,35:3
Hay, Ralph E, 1944, Jl 30,35:2
Hay, Robert Mrs, 1910, F 2,9:4
Hay, Samuel R, 1944, F 5,15:2
Hay, Silas C, 1913, N 14,11:6
Hay, T H, 1881, D 11,2:6
Hay, Thomas A H Col, 1925, My 29,17:5
Hay, Thomas J, 1954, Jl 23,17:2
Hay, W Oakman Jr, 1965, F 26,29:1
Hay, Walter T, 1950, N 25,13:3
Hay, Wellington B, 1953, F 16,21:6
Hay, Will (por), 1949, Ap 19,25:3
Hay, William B, 1948, My 31,19:4
Hay, William C, 1953, Ja 12,27:4; 1966, My 10,45:3
Hay, William C Mrs, 1949, Mr 19,15:1
Hay, William H, 1940, Jl 20,15:2; 1946, D 18,30:2
Hay, William H Mrs, 1958, Ag 30,15:6
Hay, William I, 1955, N 10,35:3
Hay, William O, 1950, N 5,94:5
Hay, William P, 1947, Ja 28,23:4
Hay, William W Mrs, 1948, Ja 26,19:5
Hay, Woodhull, 1952, N 19,32:3
Hayakawa, Kichiro, 1922, O 17,19:4
Hayakawa, Sessue Mrs, 1961, O 19,35:3
Hayami, S, 1926, S 14,29:3
Hayard, Leon, 1903, S 20,29:7
Hayashi, Gonsuke Baron (por), 1939, Je 28,21:1
Hayashi, Haruyuki, 1944, Je 2,15:6
Hayashi, Itsuro, 1965, F 6,25:2
Hayashi, Joji, 1960, Ap 6,41:4
Hayashi, Senjuro, 1943, F 5,21:3
Haycock, Ernest, 1950, O 14,19:1
Haycock, John, 1966, Ag 13,25:2
Haycock, Joseph L, 1937, N 24,23:3
Haycock, Ormonde B, 1938, Ag 20,15:4
Haycock, Percy R, 1951, N 20,31:4
Hayday, Arthur, 1956, F 29,31:5
Hayden, Adelbert C, 1940, O 17,25:2
Hayden, Adelbert Mrs, 1943, Je 18,21:4
Hayden, Arthur G, 1964, Mr 19,34:1
Hayden, Arthur Hull Mrs, 1968, D 14,45:2
Hayden, Austin A, 1940, Jl 11,19:5
Hayden, Bernard J, 1959, Jl 7,33:2
Hayden, C H, 1901, Ag 5,7:6
Hayden, Carl Mrs, 1961, Je 26,31:3
Hayden, Catherine P, 1939, D 27,24:1
Hayden, Charles, 1937, Ja 9,17:1
Hayden, Charles E, 1948, Ja 26,19:3
Hayden, Charles F, 1943, S 18,17:2
Hayden, Charles H, 1920, Ag 24,9:2
Hayden, Charles S, 1937, D 21,23:4; 1955, Je 16,31:1
Hayden, Claude G, 1948, Jl 10,15:3

Hayden, Edith E, 1909, My 14,9:5
Hayden, Edward D, 1908, N 16,9:5
Hayden, Edward E Mrs, 1951, Mr 13,31:3
Hayden, Edward J, 1953, N 4,33:5
Hayden, Edward T, 1958, Ap 11,25:2
Hayden, Eugene E, 1951, O 30,29:1
Hayden, Eugene T, 1948, F 20,27:1
Hayden, Francis Henry, 1968, Ja 26,44:8
Hayden, Francis S Sir, 1910, Je 2,9:4
Hayden, Frank J, 1937, F 10,23:5
Hayden, Frank S Prof, 1922, O 9,15:6
Hayden, George W, 1959, N 19,39:4
Hayden, Harold P, 1941, Jl 31,17:4
Hayden, Harry, 1955, Jl 25,19:5
Hayden, Harry V Jr, 1949, O 28,23:4
Hayden, Henry I Capt, 1925, Ap 9,23:3
Hayden, Henry Whiting, 1925, Ja 8,25:4
Hayden, Horace, 1955, Ag 23,23:3
Hayden, Horace E Mrs, 1961, My 21,86:4
Hayden, Howard P, 1950, D 13,35:3
Hayden, J L R, 1951, Ag 13,17:6
Hayden, James A, 1943, Ag 24,19:5
Hayden, James Albert, 1907, Ja 24,9:5
Hayden, James B, 1945, Ag 23,10:5
Hayden, James S, 1938, Mr 11,19:2
Hayden, Jay G Mrs, 1950, Ja 31,23:1
Hayden, Joel B, 1950, Ja 11,23:5
Hayden, John, 1948, Ag 24,24:3
Hayden, John C, 1965, Ag 14,23:5
Hayden, John J, 1952, O 30,31:5; 1958, Ag 22,21:1
Hayden, John K, 1952, My 6,29:1
Hayden, John Mrs, 1951, Ag 27,19:2
Hayden, Joseph R, 1945, My 22,19:1
Hayden, Josiah W, 1955, Je 16,31:3
Hayden, Lawrence W, 1962, Je 8,31:1
Hayden, Lloyd F, 1938, My 3,23:1
Hayden, Lucile Siegbert Mrs, 1921, Ap 22,13:4
Hayden, Martin, 1946, Ag 3,15:4
Hayden, Martin J, 1952, D 7,72:6; 1954, Ja 10,87:1
Hayden, Michael J, 1925, Ag 23,7:1
Hayden, Moses, 1944, Ja 28,17:5
Hayden, Percy G, 1948, Ap 16,23:4
Hayden, Perry, 1954, Mr 19,24:3
Hayden, Perry D, 1962, N 10,25:3
Hayden, Philip, 1913, My 16,11:4
Hayden, Philip M, 1959, F 3,31:1
Hayden, Robert, 1960, O 21,33:2
Hayden, Robert P, 1940, Ja 30,20:3
Hayden, Stephen A, 1953, F 4,27:2
Hayden, T Jerome Jr, 1967, Ja 6,35:3
Hayden, Thomas F, 1911, Jl 8,9:4; 1941, Je 20,21:2
Hayden, Thomas J Jr, 1946, Mr 16,13:4
Hayden, W B Col, 1916, Jl 12,11:4
Hayden, William L, 1954, Mr 31,27:3
Haydn, Howell M, 1938, Je 24,19:5
Haydock, Charles, 1951, S 4,27:2
Haydock, Charles E, 1955, F 12,15:2
Haydock, George S, 1957, N 7,35:2
Haydock, Thomas O Jr, 1942, N 14,15:2
Haydon, Albert E Mrs, 1949, S 27,28:3
Haydon, Florence, 1918, Ag 7,9:8
Haydon, Glen, 1966, My 9,39:2
Haydon, Stuart, 1954, Ag 17,21:1
Hayduk, Joseph Mrs, 1942, My 22,21:4
Haye, Alexandre Mrs, 1942, Ja 27,21:2
Haye, Helen, 1957, S 3,27:2
Hayen, Emil Mrs, 1945, Ja 7,38:1
Hayes, A, 1936, O 20,26:3
Hayes, A A, 1882, Je 26,1:2
Hayes, Albert B, 1951, Mr 23,21:1
Hayes, Albert J, 1940, O 25,21:5
Hayes, Alfred Mrs, 1959, F 23,23:5
Hayes, Alice L, 1950, N 24,35:2
Hayes, Allan S, 1961, Je 17,21:6
Hayes, Arthur, 1937, My 6,25:4
Hayes, Arthur M, 1968, D 18,47:3
Hayes, Bartlett H, 1951, Mr 9,25:5
Hayes, Bernard J, 1921, My 25,17:4
Hayes, Bertram F (cor, My 17,15:1), 1941, My 16, 23:3
Hayes, Bruce I, 1953, S 29,29:5
Hayes, Byron, 1952, F 18,19:5
Hayes, C Willard Dr, 1916, F 10,11:3
Hayes, Carlton J H, 1964, S 4,29:1
Hayes, Carroll, 1965, My 17,35:4
Hayes, Carter H, 1952, Jl 16,25:5
Hayes, Charles F, 1941, D 7,76:1
Hayes, Charles H Capt, 1914, Ja 18,5:4
Hayes, Charles Harris Rev Dr, 1910, Ag 18,9:6
Hayes, Charles J, 1946, Ag 29,27:3
Hayes, Charles R, 1955, Mr 8,27:1
Hayes, Charles W, 1918, D 15,22:3
Hayes, Clarence B, 1949, N 12,15:5; 1955, Ap 2,17:3
Hayes, Clyde J, 1949, D 7,33:7
Hayes, Cornelius G, 1947, N 12,28:3
Hayes, Cornelius J, 1938, D 14,25:4
Hayes, Cornelius V, 1964, Ap 12,87:1
Hayes, Dalton, 1950, Ja 15,84:4
Hayes, Daniel M, 1951, O 10,23:6
Hayes, David J A, 1959, Je 18,22:5
Hayes, David V, 1956, N 16,28:1
Hayes, David W, 1948, Je 24,25:4
Hayes, De Witt C, 1947, Mr 11,27:1

Hayes, Dennis A, 1917, Ja 3,11:2
Hayes, E A, 1942, Je 4,19:4
Hayes, E B, 1903, Ap 2,9:5
Hayes, E C (Billy), 1943, D 17,27:4
Hayes, E Donald, 1948, Ap 21,27:3
Hayes, Earl M, 1949, Ag 30,27:3
Hayes, Eben, 1945, Ag 14,21:4
Hayes, Edmund A, 1952, Mr 19,29:1
Hayes, Edmund Gen, 1923, O 20,15:4
Hayes, Edward, 1948, S 19,76:3
Hayes, Edward A, 1952, N 30,88:8; 1955, Ap 2,17:2
Hayes, Edward B, 1909, Mr 20,9:4
Hayes, Edward J, 1961, My 20,23:3
Hayes, Edward Mortimer Gen, 1912, Ag 16,9:6
Hayes, Edward P Mrs, 1964, Jl 22,33:3
Hayes, Edwin Louis Gen, 1917, Ja 2,11:3
Hayes, Edwin P, 1952, Ja 22,29:1
Hayes, Ernest M, 1960, S 7,37:6
Hayes, Eugene J, 1964, Mr 16,31:4
Hayes, Evelyn H Mrs, 1964, Ap 6,31:4
Hayes, F B, 1884, S 21,9:4
Hayes, F Barry, 1937, Je 18,21:4
Hayes, F Clifton Mrs, 1949, D 25,26:4
Hayes, Florence Mrs, 1938, Jl 17,26:8
Hayes, Francis A, 1943, D 1,21:3
Hayes, Francis H, 1947, Ja 19,53:3
Hayes, Francis I Mrs, 1940, N 10,56:2
Hayes, Francis T, 1964, Ja 15,31:1
Hayes, Francis V, 1964, Ja 10,43:1
Hayes, Frank, 1955, Je 23,29:5; 1959, D 8,45:1
Hayes, Frank E Mrs, 1951, D 5,35:4
Hayes, Frank P, 1950, Ja 5,25:2
Hayes, Frederick A, 1966, F 3,31:3
Hayes, Frederick S, 1945, Ja 26,21:2
Hayes, Garland H, 1950, Ja 13,23:5
Hayes, George B Mrs, 1949, D 14,31:3
Hayes, George E C, 1968, D 21,37:4
Hayes, George M, 1941, Ja 4,13:2; 1957, O 11,27:1
Hayes, George S, 1946, My 4,15:4
Hayes, Gerald A, 1938, My 16,17:4
Hayes, H Jay, 1957, Ag 16,19:1
Hayes, Hammond V, 1947, Mr 23,60:2
Hayes, Harold M, 1957, Ag 25,86:5
Hayes, Harry L, 1948, Ag 19,21:2
Hayes, Harry R, 1952, Mr 18,13:3
Hayes, Harvey C Dr, 1968, Jl 16,39:3
Hayes, Helen W, 1945, Je 9,13:4
Hayes, Henry R (por), 1955, Je 30,25:5
Hayes, Herman J, 1951, Je 26,29:3
Hayes, Hiram W, 1939, Jl 2,15:2
Hayes, Howard W, 1903, N 27,9:5; 1954, S 21,27:2
Hayes, I I, 1881, D 18,2:1
Hayes, Ira (funl plans, Ja 26,27:8; funl, F 3,25:6), 1955, Ja 25,7:6
Hayes, Isaac E, 1955, Ja 26,25:3
Hayes, J Arthur, 1948, O 2,15:5
Hayes, J B Dr, 1908, Ja 18,9:6
Hayes, J C Col, 1883, Ap 23,5:4
Hayes, J E, 1904, My 26,7:6
Hayes, J W, 1934, Mr 13,21:1
Hayes, James, 1940, Je 24,15:6
Hayes, James A, 1941, D 5,23:5; 1947, Je 24,23:2; 1954, D 8,35:2
Hayes, James D, 1956, Ja 28,17:5
Hayes, James E, 1873, My 8,5:2; 1948, Ag 7,15:6; 1953, S 20,86:5
Hayes, James G, 1946, D 16,23:4
Hayes, James H, 1949, S 3,13:3
Hayes, James J, 1946, Ap 13,17:3; 1952, My 24,19:4
Hayes, James J Mrs, 1944, Mr 7,17:1
Hayes, James L, 1916, Je 2,11:4; 1942, F 6,19:1; 1956, S 9,85:1
Hayes, James M, 1956, N 21,27:5
Hayes, James Mrs, 1948, Je 14,23:3
Hayes, James P Mrs, 1946, S 20,31:1; 1958, Ap 7,21:3
Hayes, James R 2d, 1945, S 10,19:4
Hayes, James Rev, 1907, My 29,7:7
Hayes, James S, 1937, Ap 3,19:5
Hayes, Jay O, 1948, S 2,24:3
Hayes, Jere R, 1959, Jl 10,25:2
Hayes, John, 1919, Mr 30,22:5
Hayes, John A, 1945, Je 11,15:4
Hayes, John A Mrs, 1950, O 16,27:3
Hayes, John D, 1957, Mr 5,31:3; 1958, O 23,15:4; 1966, Ag 3,33:4
Hayes, John F, 1960, D 18,84:1
Hayes, John F Mrs, 1949, D 6,31:2
Hayes, John G, 1946, Je 7,19:5
Hayes, John H (por), 1941, Ap 27,38:2
Hayes, John H, 1949, F 24,23:3
Hayes, John H (will), 1950, Jl 28,10:7
Hayes, John H, 1965, Jl 11,68:4
Hayes, John J, 1941, Je 20,21:4; 1946, N 12,29:5; 1948, D 17,27:3; 1949, D 14,31:2; 1950, F 22,30:2; 1951, My 12,21:4; 1964, Jl 6,29:3; 1965, Ag 26,33:2
Hayes, John J Mrs, 1943, D 19,48:7; 1954, O 20,29:4; 1958, N 14,27:1
Hayes, John L, 1941, N 11,23:2
Hayes, John M, 1957, Ja 31,27:3
Hayes, John R, 1946, Ja 1,27:4
Hayes, John S, 1949, My 24,27:2
Hayes, John V, 1951, F 22,31:3
Hayes, Joseph E, 1965, My 24,31:2

Hayes, Joseph Gen, 1912, Ag 20,9:6
Hayes, Joseph V H, 1953, F 1,89:1
Hayes, Joseph W Mrs (Mary), 1962, Ap 10,39:3
Hayes, Justin E, 1955, F 3,23:1
Hayes, Lambert K, 1942, Jl 18,13:6
Hayes, Leo D, 1941, D 8,23:4
Hayes, Leroy L F, 1950, F 19,76:2
Hayes, Lewis H, 1947, Ag 19,23:2
Hayes, Lewis J, 1951, Je 23,15:2
Hayes, Louis V, 1953, O 7,29:4
Hayes, Lucy A, 1937, My 15,19:5
Hayes, Lucy P Mrs, 1939, D 5,27:4
Hayes, Lydia Y, 1943, F 10,25:1
Hayes, Margaret D Mrs, 1938, My 3,23:3
Hayes, Martin L (funl, F 14,93:1), 1954, F 11,29:2
Hayes, Mary L Mrs, 1940, Mr 16,15:3
Hayes, Matthew F, 1943, Mr 11,21:2
Hayes, Max E, 1950, Ap 10,19:2
Hayes, Max S, 1945, O 12,23:3
Hayes, May Mrs, 1940, Ag 13,19:2
Hayes, Metz B, 1952, F 23,11:4
Hayes, Michael A, 1962, Ag 27,23:2
Hayes, Michael J Mrs, 1951, O 16,31:2
Hayes, Monard V, 1962, Je 12,37:2
Hayes, Morgan D, 1952, F 24,85:1
Hayes, Myron J, 1956, N 23,27:2
Hayes, N J, 1928, Ja 3,7:3
Hayes, Neil G, 1951, N 19,23:2
Hayes, Nellie K Mrs, 1939, Je 2,23:5
Hayes, Patrick, 1917, N 7,13:2; 1948, Je 4,23:5
Hayes, Patrick J Cardinal, 1938, S 5,1:4
Hayes, Patrick Mrs, 1945, Ag 18,11:6
Hayes, Peter J, 1938, Ap 10,19:3
Hayes, Phil, 1949, N 26,15:4
Hayes, Phil P, 1947, Ja 5,53:1
Hayes, R B Mrs, 1889, Je 22,1:5
Hayes, R S, 1905, Mr 3,9:4
Hayes, Ralph V, 1942, Ja 5,17:5
Hayes, Richard C, 1959, D 9,42:1
Hayes, Richard C Mrs, 1952, D 7,88:6
Hayes, Richard F, 1958, Je 18,33:5
Hayes, Richard F Sr Mrs, 1955, Je 26,76:6
Hayes, Richard S, 1961, S 19,35:4
Hayes, Robert, 1948, Mr 10,27:3
Hayes, Rutherford B, 1893, Ja 18,1:7
Hayes, Rutherford B Mrs, 1946, S 1,36:2
Hayes, Sam, 1958, Jl 29,23:2
Hayes, Samuel P, 1958, My 9,23:1
Hayes, Samuel W, 1941, Mr 16,44:8
Hayes, Sarah Jones, 1909, N 23,9:4
Hayes, Scott, 1943, Ag 3,19:5
Hayes, Scott Russell, 1923, My 7,15:6
Hayes, Selden W, 1937, Ap 28,23:2
Hayes, Stephen Mrs, 1947, Jl 11,15:2
Hayes, T Frank, 1965, Mr 27,27:3
Hayes, Theodore, 1945, My 7,17:1
Hayes, Thomas, 1939, F 27,15:4
Hayes, Thomas F, 1950, Mr 14,25:4
Hayes, Thomas G, 1943, S 4,13:2
Hayes, Thomas Gordon, 1915, Ag 27,9:6
Hayes, Thomas H, 1960, O 1,1:1
Hayes, Thomas H Mrs, 1943, O 1,19:2
Hayes, Thomas J, 1944, Ag 18,13:6
Hayes, Thomas Mrs, 1945, Ap 13,17:4; 1948, Ag 27, 18:4
Hayes, Thomas S, 1959, My 19,33:4
Hayes, Timothy J, 1925, Ag 28,13:6
Hayes, Vincent de P, 1963, O 23,41:4
Hayes, W Kenneth, 1961, Mr 29,33:1
Hayes, Wade H, 1956, S 5,27:2
Hayes, Wade H Mrs, 1939, D 9,15:5
Hayes, Walter F, 1949, F 23,27:2
Hayes, Walter J, 1950, D 4,29:4
Hayes, Walter T, 1948, Ja 25,56:4
Hayes, Watson M, 1944, S 29,21:5
Hayes, Webb C 2d, 1957, Jl 11,25:4
Hayes, Will L, 1946, Jl 9,21:3
Hayes, William, 1960, My 9,29:4
Hayes, William A, 1942, S 14,15:4; 1949, O 30,86:1; 1958, D 29,15:4
Hayes, William A Mrs, 1951, Ja 6,15:4
Hayes, William C, 1963, Jl 11,29:4
Hayes, William C Mrs, 1961, Ag 7,23:4
Hayes, William D, 1941, F 13,19:3
Hayes, William E, 1939, D 16,17:3; 1959, N 22,86:6
Hayes, William F, 1946, Mr 12,25:2; 1953, Ja 31,15:5; 1953, S 11,21:3
Hayes, William F Mrs, 1943, Mr 6,13:3
Hayes, William H, 1961, Jl 11,31:5
Hayes, William J, 1947, Ja 24,22:3
Hayes, William L, 1950, Ag 8,29:5
Hayes, William P, 1963, My 1,39:5
Hayes, William R, 1952, S 12,21:1
Hayes, William Van V, 1958, Je 28,17:4
Hayes, William W, 1948, Jl 30,17:4
Hayfield, William T Sr, 1943, Je 17,22:2
Hayford, F Leslie Mrs, 1965, My 1,31:1
Hayford, John Filmore, 1925, Mr 11,21:3
Hayford, Max F, 1953, Jl 9,25:2
Hayford, Orville, 1945, N 29,23:4
Hayhow, Edgar C, 1957, Ag 24,15:1
Hayhow, Lena C Mrs, 1952, Ap 16,27:2
Hayhurst, Cyril W, 1949, Mr 10,27:2
Hayhurst, Ralph, 1952, N 23,89:2
Hayias, Peter, 1941, D 1,19:3
Hayler, Guy, 1943, S 24,23:5
Hayles, Charles E, 1952, S 4,27:2
Haylon, Dennis J, 1939, N 8,23:5
Hayman, A L, 1956, Ap 8,84:6
Hayman, Adam C, 1945, Jl 11,11:4
Hayman, Al, 1917, F 10,9:2
Hayman, Albert C, 1964, Ag 8,19:2
Hayman, Alfred, 1921, My 15,22:3
Hayman, David, 1901, D 28,7:6
Hayman, E (see also Jl 11), 1901, Jl 12,7:6
Hayman, G M Mrs, 1910, S 23,13:5
Hayman, George T, 1956, Jl 1,56:8
Hayman, George W Sr, 1948, Jl 31,15:6
Hayman, Harold, 1966, F 5,2:6
Hayman, Henry T, 1941, F 9,49:2
Hayman, Joseph M Jr Mrs, 1957, Ja 22,29:2
Hayman, Ralph W, 1961, F 3,25:3
Haymen, Bp of Namur and Luxembourg, 1941, O 31, 23:1
Haymerle, Baron von, 1881, O 11,4:7
Haymond, Thomas S Gen, 1869, Ap 25,5:1
Hayn, H Edward, 1951, My 16,35:3
Hayne, A, 1867, Ja 16,2:4
Hayne, P H, 1886, Jl 8,5:3
Hayne, Sanford A, 1947, Mr 27,27:2
Hayne, Walter, 1945, F 4,38:5
Hayne, Walter E, 1967, Jl 12,43:4
Hayner, Rutherford, 1939, Mr 15,23:5
Haynes, A C, 1951, Ag 3,21:4
Haynes, Alfred D Sr, 1960, F 26,27:3
Haynes, Archibald Cushman, 1912, Je 12,13:6
Haynes, Arthur K, 1951, My 5,17:5
Haynes, Caleb V, 1966, Ap 7,36:2
Haynes, Carlyle B, 1958, Mr 13,29:1
Haynes, Caroline C, 1951, S 7,29:1
Haynes, Charles E, 1953, S 29,29:4
Haynes, Charles R, 1960, N 24,29:4
Haynes, Charles V, 1962, Ag 18,19:5
Haynes, Chester F, 1957, O 5,17:1
Haynes, Chester F Mrs, 1944, S 7,23:3
Haynes, Chester W Mrs, 1954, My 18,29:3
Haynes, Clarence H, 1956, F 26,88:6
Haynes, Daniel, 1954, Jl 30,17:5
Haynes, Daniel H, 1959, Mr 2,27:4
Haynes, Daniel O Mrs, 1954, My 14,23:3
Haynes, David W, 1937, Ja 19,17:4; 1964, My 6,47:4
Haynes, Edgar John, 1919, D 31,7:4
Haynes, Edward, 1944, My 6,15:6
Haynes, Elizabeth, 1948, Jl 2,21:6
Haynes, Elwood, 1925, Ap 14,23:4
Haynes, Emory J Rev, 1915, Ja 1,17:4
Haynes, Eric G, 1959, Mr 15,88:7
Haynes, Evan, 1955, Mr 20,88:6
Haynes, Everett C, 1956, Ap 30,23:4
Haynes, Frederick J, 1940, My 4,17:3
Haynes, Frederick J Mrs, 1953, Ja 19,23:1
Haynes, Frederick R, 1941, F 23,41:3
Haynes, G Alfred, 1944, My 24,19:3
Haynes, George E (trb lr, Ja 16,20:6), 1960, Ja 10, 87:1
Haynes, George E Mrs, 1953, O 27,27:5
Haynes, George H, 1947, O 31,23:5
Haynes, Glenn C, 1942, Je 7,42:1
Haynes, H W, 1907, S 25,9:5
Haynes, Harry Thomas, 1924, Je 27,19:5
Haynes, Henry H, 1939, Ap 18,23:5
Haynes, Henry W, 1946, N 14,29:5; 1950, Mr 16,31:4
Haynes, Henry Williamson Prof, 1912, F 17,11:5
Haynes, Howard, 1954, Ag 16,17:4
Haynes, Irene A Mrs, 1944, Ja 7,17:2
Haynes, Irving S, 1946, O 11,23:2
Haynes, James R, 1966, S 9,45:2
Haynes, John C, 1950, S 23,17:6
Haynes, John H Dr, 1910, Je 30,7:4
Haynes, John H Mrs, 1951, Ag 3,21:5
Haynes, John L, 1945, N 17,17:5; 1945, D 7,21:2
Haynes, John R Dr, 1937, O 31,II,11:4
Haynes, Joseph A, 1943, Ja 27,21:4
Haynes, Julia A, 1951, Ja 17,28:5
Haynes, Lacy C, 1951, Ap 5,29:4
Haynes, Landon C, 1956, D 3,29:5
Haynes, Lou Mae Mrs, 1948, Je 10,25:2
Haynes, Merritt W, 1953, Mr 1,93:2
Haynes, Robert B, 1955, F 27,86:3
Haynes, Rowland, 1963, O 19,25:3
Haynes, Roy A, 1940, O 21,17:4
Haynes, Royal S, 1956, Ja 21,21:6
Haynes, Selden L, 1941, Ag 29,17:6
Haynes, Stephen, 1879, D 30,5:2
Haynes, T C, 1905, Ap 18,1:6
Haynes, Thornwell W, 1951, O 4,33:2
Haynes, Tilly, 1901, Ag 11,5:6
Haynes, Viola A Mrs, 1939, Je 21,23:5
Haynes, William A, 1940, D 6,23:5
Haynes, William D, 1953, Je 9,27:4
Haynes, William F, 1938, Je 4,15:5
Haynes, William H, 1903, N 15,5:4; 1953, Ag 1,11:6
Haynes, William Mrs, 1964, F 2,89:2
Hayness, Charles W, 1925, Je 25,21:5
Haynia, George W, 1937, Ag 1,II,6:3
Haynie, James Henry, 1912, My 16,11:4
Haynie, Raymond L Jr, 1959, Ap 27,27:1
Haynor, George H, 1946, Ap 1,27:4
Hays, A B, 1881, Ja 29,2:4
Hays, A M, 1883, O 16,4:7
Hays, Abram P, 1947, S 19,23:3
Hays, Alexander Gen, 1864, My 10,4:5
Hays, Arthur A, 1959, Je 14,87:1
Hays, Arthur G (funl, D 17,31:3; will, D 28,20: 1954, D 15,31:2
Hays, Arthur G (trb), 1955, Mr 17,30:3
Hays, Arthur G Mrs, 1944, Je 4,42:2
Hays, Austin, 1915, Jl 26,9:6
Hays, C Lansing, 1957, Jl 16,25:2
Hays, Charles, 1879, Jl 2,5:2
Hays, Daniel Peixotto (funl, N 28,17:3), 1923 17:1
Hays, David S, 1939, F 3,15:3
Hays, David S Mrs, 1965, Ap 10,29:3
Hays, Edward C, 1954, Ja 30,17:2
Hays, Edward D, 1941, Jl 26,15:4
Hays, Edwin D, 1959, Jl 22,28:1
Hays, Eugene D, 1938, O 20,23:5
Hays, Frank, 1945, Ap 16,23:5
Hays, Frank C, 1963, S 9,27:3
Hays, Frank Mrs, 1945, Ap 16,23:5
Hays, George A, 1945, Ap 16,23:4
Hays, Harold M (por), 1940, Ag 22,19:3
Hays, Hinkle, 1957, N 29,29:2
Hays, Hiram J Mrs, 1967, Ja 26,33:1
Hays, Hugh Sr, 1956, Je 21,31:5
Hays, I Minis Dr, 1925, Je 6,15:4
Hays, Jacob, 1903, Je 16,7:6
Hays, James B, 1953, O 26,21:3
Hays, Jay W, 1937, D 29,21:5
Hays, Jean C Mrs, 1950, Je 12,30:3
Hays, John C, 1942, Jl 22,19:1
Hays, John T, 1919, Ap 11,11:2
Hays, John W, 1945, S 30,46:3
Hays, L Walter, 1939, Ap 12,23:5
Hays, Lawrence R, 1955, Ap 4,29:5
Hays, Lydia A, 1951, D 12,37:4
Hays, Marion M, 1964, Ap 12,87:1
Hays, Martin, 1952, O 9,31:5
Hays, Mary L Mrs, 1938, O 28,23:5
Hays, Moe M, 1942, My 5,21:4
Hays, Mortimer, 1962, O 1,31:3
Hays, N, 1876, Ag 26,3:1
Hays, Norman P, 1965, Jl 5,17:3
Hays, Oscar C, 1958, S 4,29:2
Hays, Paul H, 1958, Mr 21,21:2
Hays, Raphael S, 1954, My 28,23:3
Hays, Raphael S Mrs, 1954, O 8,23:3
Hays, Rebecca T, 1925, Je 24,17:4
Hays, Robert L, 1959, N 25,29:2
Hays, Rufus P, 1952, F 7,27:4
Hays, Samuel L, 1947, O 6,21:5
Hays, Silas B, 1964, Jl 26,56:8
Hays, Steel, 1959, Je 9,37:5
Hays, Thomas H Maj, 1909, N 10,9:4
Hays, Thomas W, 1966, Je 8,47:4
Hays, Tilly L Mrs, 1942, Mr 28,17:3
Hays, Walter Mrs, 1943, S 27,19:3
Hays, Will H (funl, Mr 11,31:5; will, Mr 21,5 1954, Mr 8,1:4
Hays, Will H Mrs, 1960, Ag 30,29:3
Hays, Will S Col, 1907, Jl 24,7:6
Hays, William H, 1949, Ag 31,23:5
Hays, William H Mrs, 1959, Ap 17,25:2
Hays, William R, 1943, Jl 17,13:4
Hays, Wilson D, 1946, Mr 1,22:2
Hayselden, Alfred N, 1954, Ja 15,19:4
Hayston, John, 1938, Je 23,21:3
Hayt, G, 1879, F 18,1:4
Hayter, Evan W, 1959, Jl 13,27:5
Hayter, Lord, 1946, N 9,17:6
Hayter, W G Sir, 1879, Ja 13,2:5
Haythorn, Charles A Mrs, 1955, My 17,29:4
Haythorn, Samuel R, 1949, D 7,31:5
Haythornthwaite, William Rev, 1921, S 20,1
Hayton, D G Sir, 1878, D 28,4:7
Hayum, Arthur H, 1961, O 1,86:4
Hayunga, George E, 1956, Mr 21,38:3
Hayvoronsky, Michael, 1949, S 13,29:1
Hayward, Alfred E, 1939, Jl 27,19:5
Hayward, Ashton H, 1963, N 21,39:2
Hayward, Bob, 1961, S 11,33:5
Hayward, C A, 1937, Ap 5,20:1
Hayward, Carey S, 1951, Jl 17,27:3
Hayward, Charles B, 1937, O 12,25:2; 1938,
Hayward, Charles E, 1956, Je 30,17:3
Hayward, Clarence B, 1873, O 9,8:5
Hayward, Clyde F, 1955, S 12,25:5
Hayward, Edward F Rev, 1923, D 24,11:6
Hayward, Edward P M D, 1905, Mr 15,9:6
Hayward, Edwin A Mrs, 1952, N 3,27:3
Hayward, Elizabeth, 1937, Ja 3,II,8:5
Hayward, F Harold, 1945, Jl 4,13:8
Hayward, Florence, 1925, Jl 6,11:6
Hayward, Fortune Mrs, 1957, Mr 9,19:1
Hayward, Fred P, 1955, Ja 27,23:1
Hayward, Frederick William, 1953, F 9,27:2
Hayward, G Boynton, 1949, N 4,27:1
Hayward, Harry G, 1941, My 20,23:4

Hayward, Harry L, 1956, F 27,23:1
Hayward, Harry M, 1958, Je 9,23:4
Hayward, Henry G A, 1966, My 8,82:1
Hayward, Henry S Lt, 1919, Ap 3,11:3
Hayward, Henry Selby, 1914, D 16,15:4
Hayward, John, 1869, O 16,7:2
Hayward, John A, 1948, Ja 12,19:4
Hayward, John B, 1966, F 14,29:4
Hayward, John L, 1949, Ag 19,17:4
Hayward, Joseph Ming, 1917, S 14,9:3
Hayward, Lady, 1940, My 26,34:4
Hayward, Margaret, 1907, Ja 13,9:2
Hayward, Marjorie, 1955, D 15,39:6
Hayward, Merton E, 1943, F 5,21:5
Hayward, Nathan, 1944, Je 23,19:6
Hayward, Paul P, 1963, My 7,43:1
Hayward, Ralph A, 1951, Ja 13,15:4
Hayward, Ralph B, 1937, Ag 26,21:2
Hayward, Richard Rev, 1910, N 24,11:2
Hayward, Samuel, 1964, Ag 2,77:1
Hayward, Sarah L Mrs, 1938, N 28,15:4
Hayward, Sidney C, 1965, My 30,51:1
Hayward, Sidney W Mrs, 1952, Jl 20,52:1
Hayward, Sterling P, 1956, Ag 8,84:8
Hayward, Thomas B, 1937, Ap 21,23:3
Hayward, Thomas W, 1939, Jl 20,19:4
Hayward, Vincent S, 1960, Je 13,27:5
Hayward, Walter B (trb lr, Ap 24,32:7), 1957, Ap 17,31:4
Hayward, Walter B Mrs, 1947, Ap 8,27:1
Hayward, Walter F, 1953, S 8,31:3
Hayward, Walter L, 1937, Mr 1,19:2
Hayward, William, 1909, Ap 12,7:4
Hayward, William (por), 1944, O 14,13:3
Hayward, William E, 1942, My 27,23:1
Hayward, William F, 1956, F 19,93:1
Hayward, William H, 1957, S 7,19:2
Hayward, William L, 1937, D 5,II,9:1
Hayward, William R, 1958, F 24,19:5
Haywood, Allan S, 1953, F 22,60:1
Haywood, Dave, 1947, N 22,15:5
Haywood, Frances Dillon, 1968, Ja 4,37:3
Haywood, Frank Earle, 1923, D 6,19:4
Haywood, Frank Sydney, 1925, S 5,13:5
Haywood, Gerald, 1956, Ja 10,34:7
Haywood, Harry L Mrs, 1939, Ja 4,21:5
Haywood, J Maurice Mrs, 1951, Mr 30,23:5
Haywood, Louis A, 1949, F 22,23:3
aywood, Valentine, 1963, Ja 5,8:1
aywood, W D, 1928, My 19,13:3
aywood, William, 1944, Jl 17,15:5
aywood, William R, 1943, Ap 2,21:3
aywood, William T, 1943, N 17,25:6
ayworth, Emma Mrs, 1944, N 4,15:3
azam, John G, 1951, Je 20,27:4
azard, Amos W, 1950, Ag 2,25:1
azard, Arnold W, 1942, Je 19,23:3
azard, Bowdoin, 1957, F 24,50:8
azard, Carl H, 1943, Ag 25,19:2
azard, Caroline, 1945, Mr 20,19:1
azard, Charles, 1938, S 28,25:5
azard, D S, 1903, Ja 6,9:4
azard, Daniel L, 1951, S 23,87:1
azard, Edgerton Mrs, 1943, F 3,19:2
azard, Edward C, 1905, F 3,7:2; 1954, N 7,87:4
zard, Frank A, 1943, My 25,23:2
zard, Frank F, 1947, Jl 13,44:7
zard, Frank F Mrs, 1956, My 26,17:4
zard, Frederick Rowland, 1917, F 28,11:4
zard, G M, 1903, Je 10,9:6
zard, Geoffrey C, 1962, Je 9,25:4
zard, Helen, 1954, Jl 24,13:2
zard, Henry B, 1954, N 29,25:5
zard, John C, 1960, Jl 17,62:2
zard, John D, 1952, Je 24,29:4
zard, Leverett Sr, 1949, N 16,29:4
zard, Rowland, 1945, D 22,19:3
zard, Rowland Gibson, 1918, Ja 24,9:5
zard, Samuel B Mrs, 1944, S 26,23:5
zard, Samuel Maj, 1876, Ja 12,4:7
zard, Schuler Mrs, 1949, Ap 19,26:3
zard, Schuyler, 1948, Ja 10,15:2
zard, Thomas P, 1968, O 15,47:3
zard, Thomas Tilly, 1911, Jl 10,7:5
zard, W Tilden, 1941, Ja 4,30:8
zard, Walter Capt, 1916, Ag 12,9:7
zard, William A (funl, Jl 22,7:5), 1922, Jl 20,17:4
zard, William D, 1948, My 4,25:3
azer, Edgar W, 1946, Mr 2,13:5
e Winkelman, G A W C de, 1946, Ag 30,17:2
el, Homer H, 1968, F 5,35:5
el, John R, 1951, O 14,88:5
el, John R Mrs, 1949, Je 12,76:1
el, R C, 1950, Ag 22,27:3
el, William H, 1939, O 14,19:1
elbaker, Frank A, 1939, Jl 8,16:3
elett, C William, 1956, Mr 18,89:2
elgrove, Guy B, 1950, Ag 4,21:3
elhurst, Charles B, 1947, Jl 21,17:3
elhurst, Robert P, 1958, F 20,25:5
ell, Arthur M, 1949, Ap 15,23:1
ell, Charles R, 1951, N 27,31:3
ell, Frank, 1957, O 8,35:2

Hazell, John W, 1951, Jl 14,13:5
Hazell, William Sr, 1950, N 27,25:4
Hazelrigg, Hal W, 1967, S 29,40:2
Hazeltine, Alice I, 1959, My 31,77:2
Hazeltine, Caroline, 1946, Ja 8,23:2
Hazeltine, Charles W Com, 1921, Ja 29,11:4
Hazeltine, George, 1915, S 10,11:6
Hazeltine, Harold D, 1960, Ja 24,88:3
Hazeltine, Herbert S, 1948, My 13,26:3
Hazeltine, Karl S, 1949, Mr 16,27:4
Hazeltine, L Alan, 1964, My 26,39:3
Hazeltine, Leonard, 1874, Ag 25,4:6
Hazeltine, Mary E, 1949, Je 18,13:5
Hazeltine, Prescott, 1871, O 1,1:6
Hazelton, B T, 1939, S 14,23:4
Hazelton, Bart J, 1948, N 16,29:2
Hazelton, George C, 1921, Je 25,11:6
Hazelton, George G, 1922, S 5,17:6
Hazelton, Herbert H, 1952, Je 29,56:5
Hazelton, Hugh, 1940, Ja 29,15:4
Hazelton, Isaac B, 1943, Ja 28,20:2
Hazelton, John H, 1957, D 22,42:3
Hazelton, John M, 1940, Jl 16,17:4
Hazelton, John T, 1947, Ag 22,15:3
Hazelton, Samuel, 1917, Ja 27,9:3
Hazelwood, Charles F, 1956, Ag 31,17:1
Hazelwood, Craig B, 1953, Je 26,19:2
Hazelwood, Edgar H, 1941, Je 25,21:4
Hazelwood, William B, 1937, Ja 26,21:1
Hazen, A D Gen, 1901, D 5,7:5
Hazen, Allen Dr, 1903, N 19,9:7
Hazen, Carleton T, 1959, Ja 27,33:2
Hazen, Charles A, 1960, O 30,86:5
Hazen, Charles D (por), 1941, S 19,23:1
Hazen, Charles E, 1947, Ag 5,23:2
Hazen, Conrad P, 1918, F 16,11:5
Hazen, Daniel, 1939, Ja 17,21:4
Hazen, Deane S, 1952, Mr 9,92:5
Hazen, Douglas Sir (por), 1937, D 28,21:4
Hazen, Edward H, 1941, Ja 15,23:4
Hazen, Emily Hall Mrs, 1924, Ja 18,17:4
Hazen, Freeman B, 1943, O 13,23:2
Hazen, Gardner, 1960, Ap 13,39:2
Hazen, George W Mrs, 1958, Jl 3,25:4
Hazen, Grace, 1940, Mr 5,23:3
Hazen, Grace L, 1944, Mr 3,15:4
Hazen, Henry H, 1951, My 3,29:6
Hazen, Hervey C Rev, 1914, Jl 28,7:4
Hazen, Horace Clark Mrs, 1920, Ag 27,11:5
Hazen, James R, 1913, N 15,11:6
Hazen, John L, 1946, Ja 12,15:2
Hazen, Joseph C, 1967, Ag 3,33:4
Hazen, Josephine Mrs, 1940, Ag 7,19:2
Hazen, Josiah J, 1948, O 23,15:4
Hazen, Lady (Mrs J D Hazen), 1963, Jl 4,17:1
Hazen, Louise C, 1951, F 11,88:5
Hazen, Melvin C, 1941, Jl 16,17:5
Hazen, Melvin C Mrs, 1939, S 16,17:3
Hazen, Raymond R, 1950, Je 8,31:4
Hazen, Robert C, 1966, D 11,88:5
Hazen, Silas A, 1958, O 27,27:4
Hazen, W B Gen, 1887, Ja 17,5:3
Hazen, Walter L, 1941, My 10,15:1
Hazen, William, 1949, Jl 8,19:2
Hazen, William E, 1940, Ag 22,20:3; 1946, Ja 6,40:4
Hazen, William E Mrs, 1966, My 16,37:2
Hazen, William L (por), 1944, Ap 14,19:4
Hazen, William L Mrs, 1958, Mr 24,27:4
Hazen, William Mrs, 1957, N 6,35:1
Hazen, William N, 1949, S 15,27:4
Hazen, William P, 1923, Ap 13,17:4
Hazenburg, Dorothy, 1924, My 4,23:1
Hazewell, C C, 1883, O 7,2:2
Hazlehurst, Thomas H, 1949, Ap 7,29:5
Hazlerigg, Lord, 1949, My 26,29:3
Hazlett, Everett (Swede),(funl plans, N 5,16:4;funl, N 6,37:1), 1958, N 4,27:1
Hazlett, Harry F, 1960, S 29,35:1
Hazlett, James M (por), 1941, N 9,53:1
Hazlett, John M, 1945, Ag 5,37:1
Hazlett, Samuel M, 1956, Jl 24,25:4
Hazlett, Samuel M Mrs, 1953, Ap 19,90:1
Hazlett, Walter T, 1951, Jl 6,23:3
Hazlitt, William Carew, 1913, S 9,7:4
Hazzard, Charles, 1938, Ag 26,17:5
Hazzard, Charles M, 1952, Jl 17,23:4
Hazzard, Franklin W, 1952, O 30,31:4
Hazzard, Jason, 1954, N 16,31:2
Hazzard, John C, 1955, Ja 31,19:1
Hazzard, Lawrence S, 1958, Mr 2,88:8
Hazzard, Linden S, 1957, D 26,19:3
Hazzard, Marshall P, 1949, Ja 27,23:3
Hazzard, Robert D, 1945, Jl 28,11:4
Hazzard, Robert D Mrs, 1948, D 8,31:1
Hazzard, Robert P Sr, 1948, Ag 23,17:4
Hazzard, William Henry, 1904, Ja 26,9:5
Heacock, Allen D, 1968, N 5,44:8
Heacock, Charles H, 1961, Ja 1,48:2
Heacock, Edward, 1939, Mr 13,17:2
Heacock, Edwin H, 1942, O 25,44:4
Heacock, Frank A, 1966, Je 16,47:5
Heacock, James H, 1953, Mr 8,91:1
Heacox, Frank L, 1953, Ap 24,23:4

Head, A P, 1905, Je 23,2:2
Head, Adrian, 1961, My 3,37:5
Head, Alfred H, 1957, D 27,19:3
Head, Allen H, 1950, S 6,30:3
Head, Barclay Vincent, 1914, Je 13,9:4
Head, Betsy Mrs, 1907, Je 15,9:6
Head, C Bruce, 1945, Jl 18,27:6
Head, C J, 1942, Ap 11,13:3
Head, Cedric Mrs, 1950, Ag 8,29:5
Head, Charles, 1910, Ja 13,9:5
Head, Charles W, 1954, N 11,31:1
Head, Edward L, 1940, D 20,25:3
Head, F Bernard (por), 1947, Jl 1,25:2
Head, Francis, 1859, N 14,2:1; 1947, My 30,21:6
Head, Francis Bond Sir, 1875, Jl 24,4:6
Head, Frank R, 1943, Je 5,15:5
Head, Franklin Harvey, 1914, Je 29,9:6
Head, Frederick W, 1941, D 19,25:5
Head, Henry, 1940, O 10,25:3
Head, Henry Culver, 1925, Ap 17,21:5
Head, Henry W N, 1964, Je 17,43:3
Head, J A, 1902, Mr 21,1:6
Head, James J, 1945, S 16,43:2
Head, James L, 1956, Je 4,29:3
Head, James M Mrs, 1945, S 11,23:3
Head, John W, 1874, N 13,6:4
Head, Joseph, 1950, Je 6,29:2
Head, Leon O, 1961, Mr 16,37:1
Head, Leon O Mrs, 1957, Ap 29,25:5
Head, Mabel, 1963, Je 24,27:2
Head, Malcolm A, 1951, D 28,21:2
Head, Natt, 1883, N 13,2:3
Head, Neil C, 1954, Ja 17,92:1
Head, Richard L, 1962, O 13,25:6
Head, Samuel F, 1946, Ap 8,27:4
Head, Sidney, 1945, N 13,22:3
Head, Thomas, 1938, N 28,15:2
Head, Walter D, 1967, Ja 29,76:6
Head, Walter W, 1954, My 4,29:3
Headden, John, 1909, Ag 2,7:6
Headds, Michael, 1907, Jl 5,7:4
Headfort, Dowager Marchioness of, 1958, Ag 19,27:2
Headings, Donald M, 1955, My 19,29:1
Headlam, Arthur C, 1947, Ja 18,15:2
Headland, Courtenay, 1953, My 27,31:6
Headland, Isaac T, 1942, Ag 3,15:5
Headland, Paul B, 1949, Ja 9,72:5
Headle, Marshall, 1945, My 5,15:6
Headlee, Thomas J, 1946, Je 15,21:2
Headley, Abner, 1951, Je 19,29:3
Headley, Albert J, 1937, Ag 17,19:3
Headley, Arthur B, 1951, N 7,29:2
Headley, Arthur V Mrs, 1946, O 23,27:1
Headley, Clifford, 1948, O 12,25:4
Headley, Frank P, 1937, Mr 4,23:5
Headley, George V, 1940, Ag 10,13:4
Headley, Hal P, 1962, Mr 23,33:4
Headley, Harry, 1950, Ag 26,13:3
Headley, Harry T, 1938, S 30,21:5
Headley, I H Maj, 1914, N 1,17:4
Headley, Joseph A, 1950, Ag 31,25:1
Headley, Joseph E, 1951, D 7,28:2
Headley, Lord, 1935, Je 23,26:1
Headley, P C Rev, 1903, Ja 6,9:5
Headley, Raymond, 1952, N 7,23:4
Headley, Samuel H, 1939, Mr 31,21:5
Headley, Sanford A, 1959, S 29,39:4
Headley, W S, 1883, Ap 1,2:4
Headley, Walter E, 1968, N 17,86:6
Headley, Will C, 1938, Ja 25,22:2
Heady, Elmer E, 1948, Je 4,23:4
Heady, Harold P, 1959, My 13,37:1
Heady, John J, 1951, F 15,31:3
Heady, Morrison, 1915, D 23,13:4
Heady, P Emerson, 1940, Ja 2,19:4
Heady, Robert, 1949, Ja 9,42:5
Heady, Wallace R, 1942, My 10,42:6
Heafner, Clayton, 1961, Ja 1,48:7
Heafy, Edward L, 1948, Mr 21,60:3
Heafy, Francis J, 1959, Ag 15,17:1
Heafy, Patrick E, 1953, Ja 11,90:1
Heagen, Andrew Mrs, 1963, Ap 12,27:1
Heagen, Matthew L, 1951, S 23,86:5
Heagerty, Palmer, 1962, Ja 11,33:3
Heagney, Herbert E, 1955, N 23,23:4
Heagney, William H, 1955, Jl 15,21:5
Heal, Ambrose, 1959, N 17,35:5
Heal, Henry, 1950, Ag 13,76:4
Heal, William S, 1917, Jl 19,11:6
Heald, Charles E, 1923, My 25,21:5
Heald, Charles M, 1939, D 2,17:2
Heald, Daniel A, 1945, Jl 9,11:5
Heald, Edward C, 1942, Ja 3,32:2
Heald, Elvin S, 1947, S 17,25:4
Heald, Frederick D, 1954, Ap 25,87:2
Heald, Samuel W, 1947, Ag 12,24:2
Heald, William H, 1939, Je 5,17:2; 1944, Ag 26,11:4
Heale, Charles J, 1949, D 2,29:6
Healey, Arthur D, 1948, S 17,25:3
Healey, Edward F, 1945, Ja 5,15:5
Healey, Edward J, 1938, My 10,21:5; 1955, Je 14,29:1
Healey, Eugene J, 1953, Ja 14,31:1
Healey, Flora E Mrs, 1941, Je 17,21:3

Healey, Frank H, 1938, Mr 10,21:5
Healey, George A, 1948, Ag 22,63:3
Healey, George C, 1943, D 12,68:4
Healey, Horace G, 1938, D 11,60:5
Healey, J Ward, 1946, O 19,21:6
Healey, James C, 1967, Ja 10,43:3
Healey, James C Mrs, 1956, Ap 19,31:2
Healey, James H, 1949, Ag 30,27:3; 1960, Ja 31,93:1
Healey, John E, 1951, Ag 14,23:4
Healey, John H, 1949, N 14,27:2
Healey, John J, 1947, S 15,17:4; 1954, D 12,88:3
Healey, Joseph, 1939, N 3,21:5
Healey, Julia, 1915, S 13,9:5
Healey, Mary, 1939, F 28,6:2
Healey, Mary Mrs, 1940, Ja 3,22:3
Healey, May, 1915, S 13,9:5
Healey, Philip J, 1959, Je 26,25:3
Healey, Thomas F, 1944, My 11,19:2
Healey, Thomas J, 1944, O 8,44:1
Healey, William J, 1950, S 5,27:3
Healey, William J Mrs, 1944, Ap 17,23:4
Healey, William V (por), 1949, Mr 10,27:2
Healing, George, 1954, S 24,23:2
Healing, James, 1943, Ja 9,13:4
Healy, A Augustus, 1921, S 29,17:4
Healy, A Augustus Mrs, 1912, Jl 17,9:4
Healy, A J Rev, 1875, O 22,10:4
Healy, Angelus, 1953, Ag 23,88:4
Healy, Ann M, 1963, S 28,19:6
Healy, Bernard A, 1963, Ag 30,21:5
Healy, Bernard W, 1938, O 20,23:4
Healy, Catherine, 1955, Ap 25,14:8
Healy, Charles E, 1962, Ag 16,27:4
Healy, Charles P, 1957, Ja 20,92:4
Healy, Clarence, 1944, Mr 29,21:3
Healy, Constance M Mrs, 1944, O 26,23:1
Healy, Dan Mrs (H Kane), 1966, S 27,47:3
Healy, Daniel, 1940, Ja 24,21:5
Healy, David, 1916, Mr 17,11:6
Healy, Eugene A, 1945, My 11,19:5
Healy, Francis J, 1940, D 11,27:6
Healy, Frank, 1923, My 22,19:2
Healy, Frank A, 1950, O 17,31:3
Healy, Frank E, 1945, D 29,14:2
Healy, Frank P Mrs, 1958, Je 16,23:1
Healy, Franklin C, 1959, Ap 13,31:5
Healy, Fred A, 1947, O 12,79:3
Healy, Gabriel Rev, 1911, Jl 4,9:2
Healy, George J, 1950, O 21,17:5
Healy, George P, 1961, S 28,41:3
Healy, Gerald A, 1941, Ap 10,24:3
Healy, Henry W, 1957, Ag 16,19:1
Healy, J E, 1934, My 31,19:4
Healy, J Edward Jr, 1963, N 27,27:2
Healy, James, 1877, Ja 21,7:3; 1940, S 15,48:1; 1961, Jl 14,23:4
Healy, James J, 1944, Ap 26,19:5; 1951, Mr 1,27:3; 1963, Ag 18,81:2
Healy, James P, 1939, Mr 28,23:1
Healy, James Rev, 1915, Je 19,9:7
Healy, Jennie E Mrs, 1940, Mr 19,25:1
Healy, Jeremiah F, 1953, Ag 25,21:2
Healy, Jeremiah Mrs, 1952, Ap 18,25:1
Healy, Jerome F, 1925, D 31,15:4
Healy, John, 1963, Jl 28,64:8
Healy, John A, 1947, S 9,31:6
Healy, John F, 1945, Ap 27,19:2
Healy, John G Col, 1909, Je 7,7:4
Healy, John J, 1948, Je 9,29:4
Healy, John J Mrs, 1947, N 24,23:1
Healy, John Mrs, 1951, Jl 1,51:1
Healy, Joseph D, 1945, Ja 28,37:2
Healy, Joseph L, 1948, O 9,17:4
Healy, Joseph X, 1947, D 29,18:3
Healy, Kerndt M, 1960, S 20,39:2
Healy, Malachi F, 1946, D 13,23:3
Healy, Mark F, 1964, D 17,41:3
Healy, Martin A, 1949, Mr 6,73:1
Healy, Martin J, 1942, Ag 31,17:5
Healy, Matthew G (funl, D 22,23:5), 1954, D 19,85:1
Healy, Maurice, 1923, N 10,13:4
Healy, May A Mrs, 1965, Ag 3,31:3
Healy, Michael J, 1937, Mr 9,23:3; 1937, O 28,25:5; 1961, Jl 9,77:2
Healy, Michael W, 1946, Jl 30,18:2
Healy, Minnie, 1948, Ag 8,57:1
Healy, Morgan J Jr, 1964, F 16,92:8
Healy, Nicholas J Jr, 1942, N 4,23:5
Healy, Nicholas J Mrs, 1945, N 11,42:2
Healy, Nicholas J Sr, 1955, F 14,19:4
Healy, Owen, 1901, Mr 7,9:5
Healy, Owen D, 1950, O 5,31:2
Healy, Patrick, 1947, Jl 29,21:3
Healy, Patrick J Msgr (por), 1937, My 20,21:3
Healy, Patrick Rev, 1910, Ja 11,9:4
Healy, Ralph F, 1952, Ja 9,29:2
Healy, Raymond, 1946, Jl 12,17:3
Healy, Robert E (por), 1946, N 18,23:4
Healy, Robert W Gen, 1912, N 4,11:6
Healy, Stephen J, 1956, Mr 21,38:2
Healy, T, 1930, Jl 21,15:1; 1931, Mr 27,25:3; 1937, D 22,3:4
Healy, T Donald, 1965, My 20,43:1
Healy, T J, 1927, My 10,27:3
Healy, Thomas B, 1941, Ja 21,21:3
Healy, Thomas F, 1947, Mr 10,21:3
Healy, Thomas H Mrs, 1947, Mr 26,25:2
Healy, Thomas J, 1925, O 7,27:5
Healy, Thomas M, 1940, N 24,48:3; 1952, D 24,17:3
Healy, Thomas P (por), 1949, Ag 27,13:3
Healy, Thomas R, 1948, F 26,23:1
Healy, Tim (por), 1947, O 14,27:5
Healy, Timothy Mrs, 1947, Jl 5,11:5
Healy, Walter F, 1958, My 16,23:6
Healy, Wilbert C, 1948, N 8,21:2
Healy, Wilbert C Mrs, 1945, D 18,27:2
Healy, William F, 1910, Je 24,9:6
Healy, William H, 1957, D 14,21:4
Healy, William J, 1924, S 3,17:2; 1954, Ag 17,21:5; 1961, D 15,37:2
Healy, William P, 1954, N 8,21:5
Heaney, Charles N, 1945, Ap 8,36:1
Heaney, Francis J, 1941, D 19,25:3
Heaney, Francis Mrs, 1954, Ap 9,23:2
Heaney, Harry G, 1943, N 26,23:1
Heaney, James A Jr, 1962, Jl 3,50:7
Heaney, John A, 1949, O 29,15:1
Heaney, John J, 1945, Je 18,19:4
Heaney, Joseph A, 1962, Jl 4,21:5
Heaney, Noble S, 1955, S 28,35:4
Heaney, Seamus, 1964, F 8,11:1
Heaney, Thomas M (cor, O 31,29:3), 1958, O 30,31:4
Heany, John A, 1946, S 29,61:1
Heap, David Porter Brig-Gen, 1910, O 26,9:4
Heap, Jane, 1964, Je 23,33:1
Heaphy, Patrick L, 1948, Jl 12,19:5
Heaphy, Thomas M, 1953, F 21,13:5
Heaps, Abraham A, 1954, Ap 5,25:1
Heaps, I W, 1938, O 17,15:4
Heapy, William Mrs, 1940, S 16,19:5
Heard, Arthur M, 1938, N 28,15:1
Heard, Charles C, 1959, O 5,31:4
Heard, Charles H, 1945, F 21,19:3
Heard, Edward C (por), 1947, D 4,31:1
Heard, Fannie B, 1944, N 6,19:2
Heard, John W Mrs, 1943, Ja 16,13:2
Heard, Llewellyn, 1957, S 29,87:1
Heard, Oscar E, 1940, Jl 16,17:2
Heard, Paul F, 1964, F 29,21:4
Heard, Walter S, 1950, Mr 17,23:2
Heard, William A, 1958, Ap 17,31:3
Heard, William E, 1938, Ja 29,15:5
Heard, William H Bp, 1937, S 13,21:2
Heard, William N Sr, 1956, Ag 10,17:5
Heardon, Billy, 1938, Ja 2,42:1
Hearin, James T, 1967, Ja 12,39:2
Hearing, William G, 1967, O 6,39:3
Hearle, Francis T, 1965, S 3,27:5
Hearn, Arthur H (funl, D 29,9:4), 1910, D 26,7:5
Hearn, Arthur J, 1955, N 15,29:5
Hearn, Bunn, 1959, O 12,19:1
Hearn, C C, 1928, F 13,19:3
Hearn, Cornelius, 1950, Jl 20,25:5
Hearn, David W Rev, 1917, S 15,11:4
Hearn, Edward H, 1945, Jl 19,23:4
Hearn, Frederick W, 1940, N 30,17:3
Hearn, George H Maj, 1923, Ja 6,13:4
Hearn, Henry, 1949, Je 24,23:1
Hearn, Henry J, 1950, Ja 5,25:4
Hearn, J Bayard, 1937, S 23,27:1
Hearn, John T Col, 1937, N 16,23:6
Hearn, Joseph C, 1960, Je 22,35:5
Hearn, Joseph R, 1953, D 13,86:7
Hearn, Katherine F, 1950, Ag 13,77:2
Hearn, Lafcadio, 1904, S 29,9:6
Hearn, Marion, 1953, Je 4,29:2
Hearn, Murray, 1954, Mr 12,21:4
Hearn, Paul J, 1938, Ap 6,23:3
Hearn, Raymond E, 1960, D 15,44:1
Hearn, Sam, 1964, O 30,37:3
Hearn, Sanford C, 1959, My 8,27:2
Hearn, Stanley B, 1951, S 8,17:4
Hearn, Theodore J, 1961, Je 14,19:2
Hearn, W K, 1881, Jl 27,5:1
Hearn, Walter, 1940, My 20,17:5
Hearn, William E, 1945, Je 8,19:1
Hearn, William G, 1949, Ag 19,17:6
Hearn, William P Sr, 1953, N 12,43:7
Hearne, Charles S Dr, 1937, Ag 18,19:4
Hearne, Daniel A, 1941, S 21,44:1
Hearne, E L Judge, 1870, Ja 28,2:4
Hearne, Edward W, 1954, My 14,23:4
Hearne, Jonathan D, 1905, Je 19,9:6
Hearne, Robert J, 1951, N 23,29:2
Hearne, Robert J Mrs, 1942, N 12,25:1
Hearon, Charles O, 1959, Ap 13,31:1
Hearon, James P, 1964, Mr 7,23:5
Hearsey, John, 1903, S 8,7:6
Hearst, G Sen, 1891, Mr 1,1:7
Hearst, George Mrs, 1919, Ap 14,13:3
Hearst, Isabelle Lady, 1942, Ap 11,13:3
Hearst, James Mrs, 1951, O 10,23:2
Hearst, John R (funl plans, N 16,88:4; funl, N 18,-37:5), 1958, N 14,27:1
Hearst, William, 1941, S 30,23:4
Hearst, William R, 1951, Ag 15,1:2
Hearst, William R (est acctg), 1956, D 2,55:1
Heart, Herbert L, 1964, D 4,40:1
Heartfield, Frank Rev, 1925, Mr 6,19:4
Heartfield, John, 1968, Ap 30,47:2
Heartman, Charles F, 1953, My 10,88:4
Heartt, Jonas C, 1874, My 2,12:3
Hearty, Edgar W J, 1964, Ag 27,31:4
Heartz, Angelina C, 1960, Mr 17,33:3
Heary, Vincent G, 1958, Ag 21,25:3
Heasley, Harry, 1941, Ap 21,19:4
Heasley, Harry Mrs, 1953, S 26,17:4
Heaslip, Charles T, 1941, O 16,21:7
Heaslip, Frederick J, 1956, My 30,21:4
Heaslip, John W Jr, 1952, Ag 3,60:4
Heaslip, William E Mrs, 1953, Ag 1,11:4
Heater, Guy C, 1947, Ag 27,23:6
Heater, John L, 1953, My 10,89:1
Heater, William, 1949, Ag 26,19:5
Heath, A Fife, 1949, Ap 15,23:2
Heath, Alfred R, 1957, D 11,31:2
Heath, Allen S Dr, 1910, Ja 4,13:5
Heath, Andrea Capt, 1871, Ag 24,8:4
Heath, Andrew M Jr Mrs (L Chapman), 1967, Ja 22,62:3
Heath, Arch B, 1942, D 10,25:5; 1945, Ja 9,19:1
Heath, Armour R Sr, 1958, S 9,35:1
Heath, Baron, 1879, F 9,8:3
Heath, Benjamin W Mrs (A Buckley), 1967, Ja 18 43:2
Heath, Bobby (R Frear), 1952, Mr 5,29:1
Heath, Charles S, 1958, My 16,25:4
Heath, Charles W, 1941, My 20,23:3
Heath, Cuthbert E, 1939, Mr 9,21:2
Heath, Daniel C, 1908, Ja 30,7:5
Heath, E R, 1932, O 28,19:1
Heath, Edward J, 1957, Jl 6,15:5
Heath, Edwin G, 1920, Je 20,18:4
Heath, Edwin J, 1953, O 25,88:3
Heath, Elmer H, 1938, S 25,38:6
Heath, Ernest H, 1951, F 8,34:2
Heath, Ferry K, 1939, My 28,III,6:7
Heath, Forrest A, 1938, Ja 31,19:5
Heath, Frank, 1946, O 7,31:4
Heath, Franklin W, 1937, Je 23,25:5
Heath, Fred H Dr, 1952, Ja 28,17:4
Heath, Fred T, 1938, Ja 26,23:4
Heath, Frederick M, 1949, Ja 31,19:3
Heath, Frederick W, 1938, S 7,36:4
Heath, Gardiner M, 1937, S 11,17:6
Heath, George, 1958, S 13,19:2
Heath, George D Sr, 1948, Mr 21,60:6
Heath, Gertrude A Mrs, 1948, D 15,33:2
Heath, Harley, 1942, Mr 31,21:4
Heath, Henry R, 1908, Ap 21,9:6
Heath, Herbert, 1954, O 26,27:3
Heath, Herbert M, 1912, Ag 19,9:6
Heath, Howard Mrs, 1952, Mr 14,20:8
Heath, Hubert A, 1937, Ag 18,19:6
Heath, Hubert A Mrs, 1960, Mr 18,25:3
Heath, Hugh, 1942, Mr 14,15:1
Heath, J Mott, 1956, S 21,25:3
Heath, James, 1942, D 29,21:2
Heath, James Ewell, 1912, D 9,11:4
Heath, John, 1956, My 3,36:1
Heath, Julien P, 1944, F 3,19:3
Heath, Kate Q Mrs, 1940, Ap 29,15:4
Heath, Lawrence S, 1956, Mr 26,29:4
Heath, Lewis A, 1954, N 20,17:6
Heath, Lewis M, 1954, Ja 13,31:3
Heath, Louanna (Mrs C Martin), 1958, Ag 6,2
Heath, Louis J, 1939, Ja 9,15:2
Heath, Margaret O Mrs, 1941, Ap 18,21:3
Heath, Mary H Mrs, 1942, My 26,21:5
Heath, Otto L, 1944, D 13,23:5
Heath, P S, 1927, Mr 31,23:1
Heath, Ralph C, 1945, Ag 15,19:4
Heath, Raymond D, 1940, D 22,30:7
Heath, Riley H, 1951, S 25,29:3
Heath, Royal V, 1960, Jl 27,29:3
Heath, Russell D, 1967, Je 4,86:3
Heath, Thomas Brig-Gen, 1925, O 20,25:5
Heath, Thomas K (por), 1938, Ag 20,15:3
Heath, Virgil P, 1947, Ja 14,26:2
Heath, Virgil P Mrs, 1941, F 23,41:3
Heath, W Layton, 1960, O 10,31:4
Heath, W Lloyd, 1957, D 17,35:3
Heath, W Lloyd Mrs, 1941, O 23,23:5
Heath, Walter C, 1947, Jl 31,21:4
Heath, Walter H, 1950, Ja 26,28:2; 1965, Ap 4
Heath, Wendelin, 1961, S 10,86:2
Heath, William, 1910, S 19,7:4
Heath, William A, 1940, Jl 14,31:1
Heath, William P, 1950, D 2,13:6
Heathcote, Charles W, 1963, Ag 7,33:4
Heathcote, Clifton, 1939, Ja 20,19:4
Heathcote, Francis C C, 1961, S 13,45:3
Heathcote, W, 1881, S 5,2:1
Heathcote, William E Mrs, 1951, Mr 20,29:3
Heathe, Lester E, 1909, Mr 25,9:4
Heather, Theodore J Mrs, 1938, O 19,23:4
Heatherington, Clark W Mrs, 1940, Ja 9,23:5
Heatherington, James J, 1941, O 30,23:4
Heatherley, Clifford, 1937, S 17,25:4

Heatherton, Daisy J Mrs, 1942, N 17,25:3
Heatherton, Leslie N Mrs, 1942, Je 16,23:3
Heathfield, Mary Mrs, 1937, O 29,22:2
Heatley, Leo T, 1943, Je 18,22:3
Heatley, Robert F, 1943, Ag 4,17:3
Heatley, Thomas, 1938, O 30,41:1
Heaton, Abraham, 1872, Ja 2,5:6
Heaton, Charles, 1906, N 9,6:1
Heaton, Clement J, 1940, Ja 29,15:3
Heaton, Clifton M, 1944, Ag 20,34:4
Heaton, D R Perry, 1954, Je 17,29:5
Heaton, Eugene E Sr, 1950, Ap 11,31:2
Heaton, Frank G, 1942, Ag 23,43:2
Heaton, Frederick, 1949, Ap 28,31:5
Heaton, Harry C, 1950, D 29,19:3
Heaton, J H, 1902, N 5,9:4
Heaton, J L, 1935, F 22,21:1
Heaton, John Clayton, 1915, Je 27,15:5
Heaton, John E Mrs, 1951, Je 8,27:3
Heaton, John H Mrs, 1944, Je 17,13:3
Heaton, John Langdon, 1919, Ja 3,9:1
Heaton, Judge, 1877, D 27,4:7
Heaton, Step B, 1937, D 29,22:3
Heaton, William C, 1943, N 22,19:2
Heaton, William C Mrs, 1964, Ap 28,37:1
Heaton, William D, 1948, Ja 15,23:2
Heaton, William H, 1942, F 12,23:4
Heaton, William P Mrs, 1949, Jl 14,27:6
Heatter, Anna F Mrs, 1941, My 29,19:5
Heatter, Gabriel Mrs, 1966, Ap 12,35:4
Heatwole, C J, 1939, Jl 7,17:5
Heatwole, Joel P Mrs, 1951, O 15,25:3
Heatwole, Timothy O, 1949, Ap 29,23:2
Heavener, James, 1956, S 17,27:4
Heaver, Walter L, 1909, My 27,9:6
Heavey, Christopher J, 1909, Mr 19,9:5
Heavey, Clarence A, 1951, S 13,31:3
Heavey, John T, 1951, F 8,33:3
Heavey, John W, 1941, N 19,23:4
Heavilin, J Seegar, 1957, N 20,35:2
Heaviside, Oliver, 1925, F 5,19:5
Heaviside, Sophia E, 1940, N 9,17:4
Heazelton, Frank K, 1945, D 24,15:1
Hebach, Frank E, 1944, O 24,23:1
Hebald, Selian, 1959, F 18,33:5
Hebard, Arthur F, 1946, Ja 10,23:3
Hebard, Daniel L, 1941, My 15,23:1
Hebard, Edward A, 1937, D 16,27:5
Hebard, George Whiting, 1911, N 18,13:5
Hebard, Morgan, 1946, D 29,37:3
Hebard, Percy J, 1953, My 14,29:5
Hebard, Roy W, 1959, F 6,25:4
Hebb, Arthur, 1944, Ap 25,23:6
Hebb, Clarence A, 1956, O 9,35:2
Hebb, Clarence A Mrs, 1968, Ap 24,47:2
Hebb, George K, 1940, My 17,19:2
Hebb, Richard D, 1951, Mr 2,25:3
Hebb, Thomas C, 1938, Ag 16,19:5
Hebbard, Charles B Mrs, 1952, Mr 7,23:5
Hebbard, Delbert C Judge, 1923, Ag 21,17:2
Hebbard, Edgar C, 1962, O 1,31:1
Hebbard, Franklin, 1938, Mr 19,15:1
Hebbe, Charles, 1953, Ja 30,21:3
Hebbelyn, Henry E, 1962, S 17,31:5
Hebberd, Edgar Z, 1960, My 25,39:3
Hebberd, Gilbert C, 1914, Ap 28,13:5
Hebberd, R W, 1928, N 25,II,8:1
Hebbert, Clarence M, 1967, Ap 4,44:1
Hebble, Amos S, 1948, Ag 17,22:2
Hebble, Howard M, 1952, N 23,88:2
Hebden, Edward Field, 1919, O 1,17:2
Hebden, Edward K, 1945, Jl 13,11:7
Hebel, Oscar, 1946, F 19,25:6
Hebeler, George, 1957, Ag 2,19:6
Hebendahl, John P, 1942, N 15,56:3
Hebendahl, William F, 1952, My 18,92:5
Heberhart, Charles E, 1943, N 19,19:1
Heberle, John J, 1942, N 18,25:3
Heberlein, Georges, 1944, N 3,21:2
Heberlein, Louis H, 1939, F 17,19:2
Heberlein, Rudolf, 1958, Ja 8,47:2
Heberling, Samuel E, 1943, My 29,13:2
Heberman, Alexander G, 1912, S 10,11:4
ebert, Antoine Auguste, 1908, N 6,7:4
ebert, Arnold B, 1951, Mr 19,17:2
ebert, Charles E, 1962, Jl 31,30:1
ebert, Jane P, 1953, Ap 25,15:3
ebert, Joseph, 1952, O 27,27:1
ebert, Joseph D, 1949, Mr 25,23:2
ebert, Robert S Jr, 1963, Ag 7,33:4
ebert, William F, 1962, Je 23,23:6
ebler, William O, 1962, S 23,86:3
ebner, George Jr, 1940, D 10,25:2
ebrew, Joseph S, 1950, F 28,29:3
ebron, James W, 1921, Ag 30,15:4
ebron, John F A, 1955, D 29,23:1
ecard, William A, 1946, My 21,23:2
echanova, Rufino G, 1967, My 9,47:2
echler, Charles H, 1962, My 12,23:2
echler, F George, 1956, D 4,39:1
echt, Alex, 1949, F 6,76:5
echt, Alfred, 1962, Je 21,31:4
echt, Aug C, 1948, Ja 16,21:4

Hecht, Ben (funl, Ap 22,47:4), 1964, Ap 19,1:3
Hecht, Catherine Mrs, 1939, Mr 23,23:6
Hecht, Clinton J, 1937, O 24,II,9:2
Hecht, David S, 1959, Jl 9,27:3
Hecht, Emanuel, 1925, F 16,19:2
Hecht, Emanuel Mrs, 1944, My 11,19:4
Hecht, Emil, 1949, N 1,27:3
Hecht, Henry H, 1937, Ja 8,20:2
Hecht, Howard S, 1962, Ja 8,39:5
Hecht, Irvin S Mrs, 1956, Ap 11,33:5
Hecht, Joseph, 1938, O 7,23:2
Hecht, Joseph A, 1952, D 23,23:2
Hecht, Julius L, 1955, Je 11,15:3
Hecht, Ludwig, 1959, Mr 11,35:4
Hecht, Marie Mrs, 1941, Jl 6,27:1
Hecht, Martin Mrs, 1952, Ja 9,29:4
Hecht, Meyer, 1944, Ap 21,19:1
Hecht, Meyer Mrs, 1947, S 16,23:3
Hecht, Milton Dr, 1968, My 2,47:3
Hecht, Moses, 1937, D 23,22:2
Hecht, Moses S, 1954, Ja 8,21:2
Hecht, Moses S Mrs, 1951, Jl 25,24:2
Hecht, Reuben Mrs, 1940, Mr 23,13:6; 1950, O 3,31:4
Hecht, Robert, 1956, My 14,25:6
Hecht, Robert L, 1943, F 18,23:1
Hecht, Roger, 1957, Je 14,25:2
Hecht, Rudolf S, 1956, Ja 19,33:1
Hecht, Samuel, 1907, F 10,7:6; 1942, S 22,21:4; 1964, F 8,23:6
Hecht, Samuel A, 1965, Je 12,31:3
Hecht, Samuel D Mrs, 1955, Jl 8,23:1
Hecht, Samuel L, 1948, Jl 3,15:6
Hecht, Samuel L Mrs, 1951, Ag 7,25:3
Hecht, Selig, 1947, S 19,23:1
Hecht, Solomon Mrs, 1957, Ap 25,31:1
Hecht, W C, 1930, S 7,II,7:1
Hecht, Walter, 1953, O 6,29:6
Hecht, William, 1949, Ap 22,23:2
Hechtman, Morris, 1943, D 28,17:2
Hechtman, Sam Mrs, 1963, O 21,31:5
Heck, August C, 1917, Ap 24,11:5
Heck, Donald C, 1960, F 24,37:5
Heck, Edson B, 1952, S 27,17:3
Heck, Emile, 1943, Je 30,21:1
Heck, Fred, 1945, Mr 12,19:5
Heck, George C Jr, 1951, O 2,16:5
Heck, Henry H, 1945, D 12,27:4
Heck, John S, 1952, My 4,90:3
Heck, Joseph F, 1952, Ap 5,15:4
Heck, Lew, 1957, Mr 21,31:2
Heck, Lew M Mrs, 1937, My 15,19:4
Heck, Lloyd L, 1948, O 26,31:4
Heck, Louis, 1905, Ap 17,1:3
Heck, Magdalena Mrs, 1950, N 2,31:1
Heck, Myron C, 1947, N 2,72:6
Heck, Nicholas H, 1953, D 23,26:3
Heck, Oswald D (funl plans, My 23,25:1; funl, My 26,35:5), 1959, My 22,1:7
Heck, Oswald D (est acctg), 1960, Mr 19,11:4
Heck, Oswald E (funl, F 8,23:4), 1954, F 5,19:3
Heck, Peter, 1960, Jl 18,15:1
Heck, Rudolph C, 1922, Jl 2,16:3
Heck Geo C, 1959, Mr 27,23:2
Heckathorn, Everett H, 1947, Ag 22,15:2
Hecke, George, 1953, Ja 15,27:4
Heckel, Charles B, 1940, D 25,27:4
Heckel, Charles E, 1943, S 16,21:3
Heckel, Edward G, 1941, N 20,27:6
Heckel, Frederick C, 1943, Je 9,21:2
Heckel, George B, 1941, Ja 21,21:1
Hecker, Anthony Mrs, 1943, Mr 7,38:5
Hecker, Arthur E, 1957, Ja 9,31:4
Hecker, Arthur S, 1943, Jl 29,19:6
Hecker, Earl A, 1942, S 2,23:2
Hecker, Ernest A, 1958, O 9,37:5
Hecker, Eugene A (will), 1960, Ag 20,11:7
Hecker, F K F, 1881, Mr 25,2:3
Hecker, Frances H, 1945, Jl 10,13:3
Hecker, Frederick, 1945, Jl 14,11:3
Hecker, Guy C, 1952, O 11,19:5
Hecker, Guy J, 1938, D 5,23:6
Hecker, John, 1874, My 8,8:4
Hecker, John C, 1950, My 13,17:4
Hecker, John V, 1924, F 20,19:4
Hecker, John W Jr, 1947, Ap 12,17:3
Hecker, Louis M, 1947, F 27,21:3
Heckerman, Howard D, 1950, Ag 31,25:2
Heckert, Charles Girven Rev Dr, 1920, D 8,17:3
Heckert, John W, 1952, Je 8,85:1
Heckett, Robert, 1947, Ap 23,25:1
Heckle, George R, 1949, Ja 18,24:2
Heckle, Joseph F, 1950, D 1,25:1
Heckler, Edwin L, 1964, Je 26,29:2
Heckler, W, 1936, O 26,17:4
Heckman, Bertha C, 1951, My 30,21:5
Heckman, Charles D Sr, 1962, Jl 28,19:3
Heckman, Edward C, 1940, My 5,53:2
Heckman, Frederick T, 1948, S 28,27:5
Heckman, George J, 1951, Ja 17,28:2
Heckman, Louis H, 1946, My 13,21:3
Heckman, Richard S, 1942, My 4,19:5
Heckman, Samuel B, 1957, Jl 28,61:3
Heckman, W, 1927, Mr 8,25:1

Heckman, W H, 1939, Ja 1,24:5
Heckman, William O, 1952, Ap 4,33:7
Heckmann, Jacob, 1939, Ag 15,19:4
Heckmann, William J, 1946, S 25,27:4
Heckscher, Aug (por),(will, My 4,56:1), 1941, Ap 27,1:2
Heckscher, August Mrs, 1924, Ag 15,13:6
Heckscher, James, 1949, Ja 14,24:3
Heckscher, John G (funl, Jl 8,7:5), 1908, Jl 6,7:4
Heckscher, Ledyard, 1951, Ag 18,11:7
Heckscher, Lucretia, 1949, Je 25,13:2
Heckscher, Maurice, 1944, Ap 27,23:2
Heckscher, Stevens Mrs, 1956, Jl 27,21:4
Heckscher, Virginia H C Mrs, 1941, Jl 11,15:3
Hecksher, Richard M, 1949, My 21,13:3
Heckstall-Smith, Brooke, 1944, Mr 7,17:6
Hecox, Arthur D, 1962, Ja 10,47:3
Hecox, James S, 1952, My 9,23:4
Hecsch, Lee F, 1953, Mr 24,31:3
Hector, Annie (Alexander), 1902, Jl 13,7:5
Hector, Eugene, 1940, Mr 16,15:6
Hector, William S, 1942, Jl 20,13:2
Hedayti, Ahmad, 1955, S 19,25:5
Hedberg, Oren, 1946, F 19,25:1
Hedberg, Rangner B, 1956, D 2,86:2
Hedbloom, C A, 1934, Je 7,23:3
Hedden, A Leslie, 1943, Jl 25,30:8
Hedden, Albert H, 1945, N 28,27:4
Hedden, Anna M, 1942, Je 21,36:8
Hedden, Charles L, 1961, Ag 12,17:1
Hedden, Eugene B, 1950, O 31,27:4
Hedden, George P, 1961, Ag 21,23:5
Hedden, Henry, 1945, Jl 31,19:4
Hedden, James S, 1951, Je 19,29:4
Hedden, John S, 1945, Mr 7,21:2
Hedden, Josephine, 1940, Jl 9,21:5
Hedden, Ralph C, 1947, My 18,60:1
Hedden, Samuel, 1903, Ag 3,7:6
Hedden, Samuel S, 1949, Ja 4,19:3
Hedden, William H, 1924, Ap 28,15:4
Heddesheimer, William G, 1954, O 29,21:2
Hedding, Walter D, 1952, Mr 28,24:4
Heddon, Charles, 1941, Je 26,23:4; 1941, N 13,27:5
Heddy, Harold M, 1955, Jl 18,21:2
Heddy, Martha D, 1946, Mr 12,25:4
Hedeman, Helen, 1955, Ja 9,86:7
Hedeman, Will O, 1946, Ap 11,25:4
Hedeman, William H, 1952, Ja 1,25:3
Hedeman Fred H, 1962, Jl 15,60:2
Heden, Ernest, 1944, D 31,26:3
Hedenberg, George W Mrs, 1945, Je 26,19:3
Hedenberg, W A, 1903, Ap 18,9:4
Hedenskoog, Ernest, 1955, N 5,19:5
Hederman, T M Sr, 1948, F 26,23:1
Hedervary, Khuen von Count, 1918, F 19,13:5
Hedgcock, William E (por), 1943, O 28,23:4
Hedge, Charles Gorham, 1921, Mr 8,11:4
HEdge, George W, 1912, Je 24,9:4
Hedge, Herbert T, 1940, Ja 3,22:3
Hedge, Homer Washington Capt, 1909, S 11,9:4
Hedge, William R, 1943, Ap 21,25:2
Hedgecock, Frederick M, 1960, Ja 20,31:4
Hedgeland, Frederick W, 1909, My 31,7:7
Hedgepeth, Levi L, 1958, S 4,29:4
Hedger, Harry L, 1946, N 13,27:2
Hedges, Andres J, 1962, N 17,25:2
Hedges, C Monroe, 1945, Ap 4,21:4
Hedges, Carolyn B Mrs, 1947, O 2,27:2
Hedges, Christine J Mrs, 1940, Jl 31,17:5
Hedges, Claude S, 1957, F 5,23:4
Hedges, Dayton, 1957, Je 8,19:5
Hedges, Fletcher, 1911, My 22,11:4
Hedges, Frank H, 1940, Ap 13,17:2
Hedges, Frank L Mrs, 1959, My 2,23:3
Hedges, George B, 1956, S 13,35:5
Hedges, Henry Pierson Ex-Judge, 1911, S 27,13:6
Hedges, Ida F Mrs, 1938, N 21,19:2
Hedges, James, 1908, Mr 2,9:6; 1962, Jl 17,25:2
Hedges, James B, 1965, O 14,47:5
Hedges, Job E, 1925, Mr 20,19:5
Hedges, John, 1950, D 21,29:2
Hedges, John W Mrs, 1950, F 4,15:2
Hedges, Kenneth, 1957, F 6,25:5
Hedges, Marlon H, 1959, Ja 9,25:1
Hedges, Martha E, 1947, Ja 23,23:2
Hedges, Mertland M, 1964, Je 16,39:2
Hedges, Robert C, 1943, D 18,15:4
Hedges, Robert L Jr, 1950, Ap 30,102:7
Hedges, Robert W, 1950, N 17,27:1
Hedges, Russell E, 1945, Ag 22,23:4
Hedges, S Frank, 1963, My 30,17:4
Hedges, Samuel B Rev, 1916, My 8,11:6
Hedges, Samuel C, 1952, Ap 1,29:3
Hedges, Sidney M Col, 1924, O 24,19:5
Hedges, Stephen, 1942, My 27,23:1
Hedin, Adolph, 1905, S 21,9:7
Hedin, Alma, 1958, My 31,15:6
Hedin, Edith, 1947, My 13,23:2
Hedin, Sven A, 1952, N 27,31:1
Hedley, Edward M, 1951, D 14,31:4
Hedley, Edward M Mrs, 1945, My 4,19:2
Hedley, Edwin, 1947, My 23,23:2
Hedley, Frank, 1955, Jl 17,60:1

Hedley, Frank Mrs, 1944, F 13,41:3
Hedley, J H, 1883, Ag 31,4:7
Hedley, Nellie M, 1951, Ja 3,27:3
Hedley, Robert, 1948, Ag 4,21:1
Hedley, Thomas A, 1937, Je 9,25:4
Hedley, Thomas W Mrs, 1943, Jl 8,19:3
Hedlund, Francis P, 1945, F 9,16:3
Hedlund, Mauritz, 1940, Jl 7,25:2
Hedman, Andrew, 1952, D 16,31:6
Hedman, Carl M, 1924, S 19,23:5
Hedman, Clement Mrs, 1960, N 8,29:3
Hedman, George, 1962, Ag 20,23:4
Hedquist, Art O, 1964, Ag 15,21:6
Hedrick, Charles B, 1943, Ja 13,23:2
Hedrick, Charles E, 1937, My 6,25:2
Hedrick, Earle R, 1943, F 4,23:1
Hedrick, Erland H, 1954, S 21,27:4
Hedrick, Ira G, 1937, D 29,22:1
Hedrick, Lillian Mrs, 1954, D 25,11:2
Hedrick, Lloyd, 1946, F 9,13:5
Hedrick, Orian R, 1943, My 12,25:2
Hedrick, Ulysses P, 1951, N 16,36:1
Hedrick, Walter H, 1962, O 25,39:4
Hedrick, William F, 1956, Je 21,31:5
Hedstrom, C B, 1942, Ap 5,41:2
Hedstrom, Carl O, 1960, Ag 31,29:3
Hedstrom, Charles E, 1943, S 3,19:4
Hedstrom, Charles V Mrs, 1944, D 22,17:4
Hedstrom, Eric L, 1961, F 22,25:1
Hedstrom, O G Rev, 1877, Mr 7,8:4
Hedtler, Robert S, 1944, D 10,54:7
Hedtoft, Hans Premier (funl plans, Ja 31,19:1; funl, F 7,21:3), 1955, Ja 30,85:1
Hedworth, John Mrs, 1949, Jl 20,25:2
Heebner, Charles K, 1938, N 16,23:5
Heebner, Robert C, 1942, Jl 11,13:5
Heed, Charles R, 1954, My 25,27:2
Heed, Edward H, 1937, Ag 25,21:5
Heed, John C, 1908, F 15,7:6
Heed, Ruth B Mrs, 1964, S 2,37:5
Heed, Thomas D, 1957, F 1,25:4
Heede, Christian Prof, 1920, Ag 25,9:2
Heedy, Edward, 1949, Mr 1,1:5
Heedy, Henry W, 1938, Ja 15,15:5
Heefner, Daniel, 1956, My 2,31:4
Heekin, Albert E, 1955, Mr 12,19:6
Heekin, James J, 1959, S 9,41:2
Heekin, James R Sr, 1957, S 19,29:3
Heekin, Walter V, 1954, Ag 30,17:4
Heelan, Dennis J, 1952, Ja 13,88:5
Heelan, Edmond, 1948, S 21,27:3
Heeland, Herman O, 1957, D 28,17:5
Heely, Allan V, 1959, Jl 9,27:1
Heely, Augustus V, 1937, Ja 29,19:2
Heely, Patricia I, 1961, F 7,33:2
Heemsath, George, 1940, O 22,23:2
Heemskerck, W F K Bischoff van, 1946, Jl 11,23:5
Heenan, Denis Col, 1872, Jl 6,1:6
Heenan, Francis C, 1941, Ja 29,17:1
Heenan, John C, 1873, O 27,5:4
Heenan, Joseph W A, 1951, O 11,37:3
Heenan, Peter, 1948, My 13,25:2
Heenehan, James T, 1958, Ja 20,23:4
Heeney, W B, 1955, Ap 15,23:2
Heeney, William (Willie), 1951, Jl 15,60:4
Heep, Robert H, 1951, Ja 31,25:2
Heep, William G, 1943, O 21,27:5
Heer, Fridolin J, 1940, Mr 3,45:2
Heer, Hans, 1959, My 24,88:5
Heer, John F, 1944, Ap 25,23:2
Heeran, Matthew A, 1955, Ap 23,19:3
Heerdt, Allie, 1958, F 5,27:4
Heeren, Adolf A Mrs, 1954, Je 2,31:4
Heeren, Don Pedro Stanley (funl, S 23,13:6), 1915, S 21,11:6
Heeren, Gustav E, 1938, Ag 28,32:5
Heeren, Henry R, 1963, O 3,35:3
Heeren, Reinhard L, 1968, S 1,53:1
Heermance, Clayton J, 1941, O 23,23:2
Heermance, Cuyler Mrs, 1944, My 4,19:5
Heermance, Radcliffe, 1958, O 31,26:4
Heermance, Susie L, 1938, O 11,25:4
Heermann, Emil (ed trb, Ja 17,IV,8:3; trb lr, Ja 20,-26:7), 1954, Ja 14,29:3
Heery, Francis W, 1953, S 29,29:2
Hees, J Ledlie, 1940, Je 29,15:7
Hees, William R (por), 1948, Ja 2,23:4
Hees, William R Mrs, 1952, S 7,85:1
Heeseman, Frederick R Mrs, 1950, S 7,31:2
Heeseman, Henry M, 1938, O 22,17:5
Heesh, William H, 1944, O 29,44:2
Heeter, William F, 1939, My 7,V,8:7
Heeve, William L, 1949, Ag 16,23:4
Hefelbower, Samuel G, 1950, S 13,27:5
Hefele, Edward J, 1960, Jl 29,25:6
Hefele, George H, 1960, Mr 23,37:3
Hefele, John B, 1953, N 14,17:5
Heffelfinger, Frank T, 1959, Jl 12,73:2
Heffelfinger, W W (Pudge), 1954, Ap 3,15:1
Heffer, Jerome, 1958, N 22,21:1
Hefferan, Katherine Mrs, 1909, Jl 30,7:6
Hefferan, William S Jr, 1961, My 13,19:4
Hefferan, William S Mrs, 1953, N 8,89:3
Hefferen, H, 1883, My 22,5:5
Hefferin, John F, 1959, Ap 5,86:5
Heffering, James, 1953, O 31,17:5
Heffering, Russell J, 1957, My 9,31:3
Hefferman, John, 1954, N 4,14:7
Hefferman, William J Mrs, 1944, My 28,34:2
Heffern, Andrew D Mrs, 1959, Jl 9,27:5
Heffern, John J, 1937, N 1,21:4
Heffern, Samuel E, 1951, Ap 17,29:4
Heffern, William C, 1947, N 15,17:2
Heffernan, Agnes, 1967, D 22,31:2
Heffernan, Christopher J, 1959, Ja 13,47:1
Heffernan, Cornelius W, 1947, O 31,23:5
Heffernan, Edward M, 1946, N 12,29:2
Heffernan, Francis J, 1955, Mr 31,27:4
Heffernan, Francis P, 1953, N 20,23:3
Heffernan, Fred T, 1937, Ag 2,19:5
Heffernan, George P, 1953, D 18,29:3
Heffernan, Howard J Mrs, 1944, Ap 26,19:1
Heffernan, James G, 1963, N 28,39:3
Heffernan, James J, 1967, Ja 29,77:2
Heffernan, James M, 1950, F 8,27:2
Heffernan, James Mrs, 1937, D 5,II,9:2
Heffernan, James W, 1943, Je 8,21:4
Heffernan, John, 1952, Ja 27,77:3
Heffernan, John F, 1938, S 9,21:4
Heffernan, John J Mrs, 1959, Mr 20,31:3
Heffernan, John M, 1965, Ja 10,92:6
Heffernan, John V, 1958, Mr 2,89:1
Heffernan, John V Mrs, 1938, N 8,23:5
Heffernan, Joseph R Rev, 1923, Mr 15,19:5
Heffernan, Leo, 1944, Ja 5,17:4
Heffernan, Leo G, 1956, F 12,88:5
Heffernan, P Herbert, 1944, My 14,46:1
Heffernan, Patrick, 1947, N 9,74:4
Heffernan, Richard R Sr, 1951, S 29,17:4
Heffernan, Thomas, 1945, O 19,23:3
Heffernan, Thomas F, 1951, Mr 2,25:1
Heffernan, Thomas J, 1962, Ja 25,31:2
Heffernan, William H, 1937, Ja 7,21:4
Heffernan, William J, 1948, F 2,19:4; 1955, F 9,27:3
Hefferon, John J, 1938, Mr 27,II,6:6
Heffinger, Fred, 1961, Jl 10,21:5
Heffinger, Fred Mrs, 1966, S 10,29:4
Heffley, Eugene Clifton, 1925, Jl 26,5:3
Heffley, N P, 1935, O 19,17:3
Hefflon, Oscar V, 1948, Ap 24,15:4
Heffner, Ed, 1942, Mr 14,15:3
Heffner, Francis L, 1960, Ap 7,35:4
Heffner, Harry E, 1956, Je 1,23:3
Heffner, Wesley E, 1968, O 1,48:1
Heffren, Michael M, 1953, My 10,88:2
Heffron, Caroline B Mrs, 1941, Jl 10,19:5
Heffron, John J, 1937, Ja 24,II,9:2; 1940, Jl 25,17:6
Heffron, Thomas L, 1940, S 5,23:5
Heffron, William J, 1939, Ap 20,23:4
Hefftner, Max, 1946, S 2,17:4
Heflebower, Robert C Mrs, 1937, S 7,21:4
Hefley, Morris J, 1945, O 18,23:4
Heflin, Clyde E, 1958, Jl 9,27:2
Heflin, Hazel B, 1952, Ag 16,3:2
Heflin, Howell T Dr, 1937, Je 19,17:5
Heflin, J Thomas, 1951, Ap 23,25:5
Heflin, Robert D, 1947, Ja 25,17:1
Hefner, Charles, 1945, S 29,15:2
Hefner, Henry, 1941, Mr 16,45:4
Heft, Herb, 1967, Ag 23,51:8
Heft, Nathan Hopkins Col, 1915, F 27,11:5
Heft, Nathan Mrs, 1944, Ap 29,15:3
Hefter, Florence, 1947, Mr 12,25:1
Hefti, Rudolph J, 1964, Je 9,35:4
Heftman, Josef, 1955, Ja 19,27:3
Hefty, Henry Mrs, 1948, D 11,15:5
Hegan, John R Mrs, 1957, F 25,25:1
Hegarty, Daniel A, 1956, O 23,33:5
Hegarty, Daniel M S, 1960, F 19,27:1
Hegarty, Edward F, 1944, Jl 16,31:3
Hegarty, Elizabeth M, 1965, D 27,25:3
Hegarty, Francis J, 1954, D 16,37:1
Hegarty, John, 1950, O 10,31:2
Hegarty, John J, 1954, Jl 12,19:3
Hegarty, John Laurence, 1918, Je 13,13:4
Hegarty, Richard, 1941, My 14,21:2
Hegarty, Timothy Mrs, 1958, Mr 9,86:4
Hegarty, William J, 1961, D 29,24:7
Hegel, Ernest Mrs, 1952, O 17,27:3
Hegel, William A, 1949, Je 9,31:3
Hegel, William E, 1952, N 4,30:4
Hegel, William J Jr, 1961, D 6,48:1
Hegel, William Mrs, 1949, Ja 11,27:1
Hegelman, Peter, 1944, N 10,19:3
Hegeman, A B Mrs, 1880, Ap 26,8:2
Hegeman, A R B Rev, 1920, Mr 1,9:4
Hegeman, A W, 1878, Je 5,1:7
Hegeman, Adrian G, 1921, My 23,13:6
Hegeman, Arthur W, 1958, Ap 14,25:2
Hegeman, Benjamin Arrowsmith, 1903, N 4,9:6
Hegeman, Bertram Mrs, 1962, O 12,22:1
Hegeman, Clarence H, 1950, Ja 6,21:3
Hegeman, Daniel A, 1925, My 29,17:5
Hegeman, Daniel J, 1923, Ja 31,19:6
Hegeman, Daniel Van Brunt, 1919, Mr 26,15:3
Hegeman, Edward A, 1937, Ja 22,21:4
Hegeman, Jaques D Jr, 1950, Mr 22,27:3
Hegeman, John C, 1953, Jl 7,27:4
Hegeman, John G Mrs, 1940, O 15,23:3
Hegeman, John R Maj, 1923, O 26,17:4
Hegeman, John Rogers, 1919, Ap 7,13:3
Hegeman, John W, 1951, Mr 23,21:4
Hegeman, Joseph Mrs, 1903, Ap 19,7:4
Hegeman, Julia De W, 1941, S 21,44:2
Hegeman, M Stewart, 1939, Ap 25,23:5
Hegeman, M Stewart Mrs, 1939, F 1,21:1
Hegeman, Percy S, 1948, Ap 28,27:3
Hegeman, Ruth E, 1944, F 16,17:1
Hegeman, W W, 1876, Jl 11,4:7
Hegeman, Walter E, 1952, O 9,31:4
Hegeman, William, 1875, O 4,4:5
Hegeman, William P Mrs, 1938, D 22,21:4
Hegemann, W, 1936, Ap 13,17:1
Heger, Anthony Brig-Gen, 1908, Ja 26,9:4
Heger, Emil R, 1958, Je 12,31:1
Heger, Paul Prof, 1925, N 10,25:4
Heggarty, A F, 1947, Ag 22,15:3
Heggemeyer, William H Jr Mrs, 1947, My 29,22:2
Heggen, Abner M, 1958, N 27,29:1
Heggie, O P, 1936, F 8,15:3
Heggie, William J, 1958, Mr 16,86:4
Heggvelt, H G, 1924, N 21,19:5
Heglon, Meyriane, 1942, Ja 13,19:4
Hegmann, Marcus, 1961, Je 17,21:3
Hegnenberg-Dux, Frederick Von Count, 1872, Je 17,
Hegner, Bertha H Mrs, 1937, N 15,23:5
Hegner, Robert W, 1942, Mr 12,19:2
Hegney, Christian, 1924, Ag 11,13:5
Hegney, Michael, 1925, S 3,25:4
Hegstrom, Emil, 1940, Ja 27,13:6
Heguy, Jean B, 1946, D 14,15:4
Hegy, Eugene A, 1960, Ja 13,47:2
Hegyi, Alex, 1948, My 10,21:4
Heher, John, 1937, Ag 13,17:3
Hehir, Patrick Maj-Gen, 1937, My 3,19:4
Hehl, Gustave L, 1963, O 24,33:2
Hehman, Lazarus S, 1968, My 23,47:4
Hehmeyer, Alexander Mrs, 1967, Je 3,31:5
Hehmeyer, Frederick W, 1962, Ap 23,29:3
Hehn, Charles G, 1939, S 15,23:4
Hehn, William C, 1947, D 4,31:5
Hehr, John G, 1945, Ag 5,37:3
Hehre, Frederick W, 1941, Jl 28,13:5
Hehre, Frederick W Mrs, 1947, Je 9,21:6
Heib, George R Mrs, 1952, Ja 19,15:6
Heibel, Frederick E, 1951, Jl 24,25:2
Heiber, William P, 1942, N 1,52:6
Heiberg, Charles, 1966, N 26,35:2
Heiberger, Wesley M, 1944, O 28,15:3
Heichelheim, Fritz Moritz Dr, 1968, Ap 24,47:2
Heick, Harry E, 1951, O 14,89:2
Heid, Alex, 1951, O 2,27:4
Heid, Frederick, 1944, My 20,15:2
Heid, Gustav A, 1964, S 12,25:3
Heidal, Jack, 1950, S 9,17:1
Heidbrink, Frederick H, 1944, Je 24,13:6
Heide, Charles R, 1949, Mr 16,27:3
Heide, H, 1931, D 14,19:1
Heide, Henry Jr, 1950, Ap 26,29:3
Heide, Henry Jr Mrs, 1962, Ap 19,31:3
Heide, Herman L, 1968, Ja 29,31:4
Heide, Julius A, 1951, Je 26,29:4
Heide, William F (por), 1947, Ap 28,23:1
Heidel, Alex, 1955, Je 20,21:3
Heidel, Cecil T, 1944, N 15,27:5
Heidel, William A, 1941, Ja 16,21:5
Heidelbach, Alfred S, 1922, F 2,17:1
Heidelbach, John, 1916, Je 28,11:5
Heidelberg, Charles, 1906, Mr 7,9:7
Heidelberg, Michael Mrs, 1946, Jl 2,25:5
Heidelberger, Gustav, 1945, Ap 4,21:2
Heidell, Irving, 1940, My 14,23:5
Heidelman, Mel F, 1952, My 5,23:6
Heideloff, Clayton H, 1949, D 11,92:3
Heideman, George E, 1960, Je 30,29:3
Heiden, Konrad, 1966, Jl 20,41:1
Heiden, Leo R, 1960, F 11,35:4
Heidenreich, Carl, 1965, S 8,47:4
Heidenreich, Carl S, 1954, F 26,19:1
Heidenreich, Frederick J, 1952, Ja 6,95:6
Heidenreich, John F, 1944, Mr 16,19:5
Heidenreich, Theodore E, 1954, My 9,89:2
Heidenstam, Carl G V von, 1940, My 21,23:4
Heidenstam, Rolf von, 1958, Ag 7,25:5
Heidenthal, Warren C Mrs, 1942, Ap 2,21:2
Heiderich, John H, 1958, N 12,37:2
Heidinger, James V, 1945, Mr 23,19:4
Heidner, Dorothea M Mrs, 1940, O 26,15:1
Heidorf, Jacob J, 1950, Ag 8,29:4
Heidrich, Arnost, 1968, F 13,43:1
Heidrich, Arthur J, 1947, Je 9,21:4
Heidrich, Herman C Mrs, 1960, Jl 28,27:3
Heidrick, Frederick V, 1943, F 9,23:2
Heidt, Emil C, 1959, F 26,31:2
Heidt, George J, 1958, Ap 27,86:4
Heidt, John V, 1948, Mr 19,23:2
Heidt, Joseph, 1962, Ag 18,19:4
Heidt, Mary Mrs, 1955, Mr 18,28:4
Heifetz, Haim Mrs, 1955, N 6,87:1

Heifetz, Rubin Mrs, 1947, Ja 11,19:2
Heiges, Jesse S, 1955, Ja 19,27:3
Heighe, Robert H, 1947, Ap 3,25:5
Heighe, Robert H Mrs, 1953, My 29,25:6
Height, Howard, 1942, F 15,44:3
Height, Joseph H, 1952, N 14,23:3
Heikal, Hussein, 1956, D 10,31:1
Heike, Charles R, 1913, Jl 5,9:6
Heike, Henry J, 1953, F 7,15:4
Heike, Mary V, 1951, D 13,33:4
Heikel, Walter, 1954, My 22,15:4
Heiken, Charles A, 1963, Jl 11,29:5
Heikenbroek, Johan C, 1948, Mr 20,13:4
Heikkila, Arthur B, 1950, Ja 15,85:1
Heikkila, William, 1960, My 8,88:4
Heil, Alfred W, 1961, Jl 26,31:4
Heil, C A Jr, 1947, D 30,23:4
Heil, Charles A, 1951, S 9,90:1
Heil, Edward J, 1941, Je 11,21:4
Heil, George L Sr, 1953, Ag 31,18:3
Heil, Henry F, 1948, N 6,13:2
Heil, Joseph S, 1956, Ja 14,19:2
Heil, Joseph S Mrs, 1960, Ap 16,17:5
Heil, Julius P, 1949, D 1,31:3
Heil, Max, 1957, S 18,33:4
Heil, Ralph H, 1950, O 27,30:5
Heil, Walter D Mrs, 1948, Ap 28,30:7
Heil, William A, 1944, N 3,21:2
Heilberg, Milton J Sr, 1960, My 12,35:3
Heilborn, Helge, 1960, S 20,39:1
Heilbron, Ian, 1959, S 15,39:4
Heilbroner, Albert M Mrs, 1939, Je 8,25:5
Heilbroner, Louis, 1924, Je 27,19:5
Heilbroner, Milton D, 1942, My 7,19:2
Heilbroner, Samuel, 1915, F 28,3:4
Heilbronn, Albert, 1938, Ap 24,II,7:3
Heilbronner, Leon C, 1953, S 18,23:3
Heilbronner, Louis, 1949, Ag 21,68:6
Heilbronner, Raoul, 1941, My 14,21:3
Heilbroun, Justus, 1903, S 3,7:7
Heilbrun, David Mrs, 1951, Jl 6,23:3
Heilbrunn, Henry, 1942, Ap 25,13:5
Heilbrunn, Isaac Mrs, 1924, Ag 10,24:4
Heilbrunn, Julius, 1952, Mr 5,29:3
Heilbrunn, Lewis V, 1959, O 30,54:1
Heiles, Carl J, 1961, Ja 4,33:5
Heilferty, Robert S (por), 1942, O 17,15:5
Heilich, Arthur C Mrs, 1953, S 2,25:1
Heilich, William F Mrs, 1950, O 26,31:3
Heilig, Ernest Mrs, 1966, Je 19,84:7
Heilig, Minnie Mrs, 1940, Je 7,23:1
Heilig, Robert, 1961, My 29,19:3
Heilig, Russell F, 1952, Ja 4,40:2
Heiligman, Otto R, 1941, S 27,17:3
Heilman, Adam G, 1943, Ag 13,17:4
Heilman, Charles J Mrs, 1956, D 8,19:2
Heilman, Edgar J, 1945, Ag 27,19:4
Heilman, Ernest D Mrs, 1954, S 21,27:5
Heilman, Herbert W, 1947, Je 4,27:2
Heilman, John R, 1952, Mr 1,15:4
Heilman, Joseph, 1937, My 13,25:4
Heilman, Ralph E Dr, 1937, F 17,22:1
Heilman, Warren B, 1965, D 6,37:3
Heilman, Wesley P, 1967, O 4,51:2
Heilman, William, 1952, Mr 15,13:5
Heilman, William C Mrs, 1950, O 12,31:3
Heilman, William G, 1950, Ap 16,106:5
Heilmann, Harry (funl, Jl 13,21:1), 1951, Jl 10,27:1
Heilmann, William, 1937, Jl 9,21:3
Heilner, George B, 1942, S 19,15:5
Heilner, Jules E, 1946, Je 5,23:3
Heilner, Julius Mrs, 1947, N 26,23:4
Heilner, Lewis Cass Rear-Adm, 1912, Ja 26,11:5
Heilner, Mary V, 1955, S 10,17:7
Heilner, Mortimer M, 1961, S 10,87:1
Heilner, Samuel (por), 1938, My 30,11:5
Heilner, Samuel Mrs, 1950, Je 27,29:3
Heilos, Lawrence C, 1947, Ap 3,25:5
Heilperin, Paul, 1937, Je 8,25:2
Heilprin, Angelo Prof, 1907, Jl 18,7:5
Heilprin, Edgar, 1939, N 3,21:5
Heilprin, Giles E Mrs, 1948, Ag 1,57:1
Heilprin, Giles F, 1943, F 1,15:2
Heilprin, Louis, 1912, F 14,11:3
Heim, Adam H, 1943, S 15,27:6
Heim, Albert M, 1964, F 26,15:6
Heim, Alfred F (will), 1945, Je 26,19:1
Heim, Charles E, 1964, N 30,33:5
Heim, Edward, 1943, Ja 11,15:6
Heim, Emery M, 1946, Ag 2,19:2
Heim, Emmy, 1954, O 14,29:2
Heim, Eugene A, 1951, Ag 24,15:2
Heim, Francis Mrs, 1952, O 27,27:3
Heim, Hugh W, 1952, Jl 3,25:2
Heim, J William, 1949, Ja 16,68:2
Heim, Jacques, 1967, Ja 9,36:4
Heim, John A (will), 1939, N 21,15:2
Heim, John A (will), 1940, Mr 16,15:1
Heim, John F, 1954, F 25,31:3
Heim, Milton M, 1940, Ap 3,23:2
Heim, Oscar B, 1952, Je 11,29:1
Heim, Oscar V, 1957, F 11,29:6
Heim, Siegfried W, 1939, Ap 1,19:3
Heim, William, 1945, My 10,23:4
Heim, William L, 1950, F 18,15:4
Heiman, David, 1949, Je 8,29:3
Heiman, Eugene, 1953, Mr 5,27:1
Heiman, Harry B, 1942, My 23,13:4
Heiman, Henry, 1947, N 18,29:4
Heiman, Jacob H, 1942, N 14,15:5
Heiman, Marcus, 1957, S 10,33:3
Heiman, Mark, 1947, Jl 3,21:4
Heiman, Nathan H, 1948, N 23,29:1
Heiman, Preston J, 1958, O 14,37:4
Heiman, Solomon, 1944, D 4,23:1
Heimann, B H Mrs, 1950, N 20,25:2
Heimann, Heinrich, 1964, Ap 28,37:4
Heimann, Henry H, 1958, S 14,84:1
Heimann, Hugo, 1951, F 24,13:5
Heimann, William, 1939, S 3,19:3
Heimbach, Ernest E, 1968, F 19,39:1
Heimbach, Harry W, 1943, S 21,23:1
Heimbeck, Adolph (will), 1958, Jl 10,19:1
Heimendahl, W Edward Prof, 1910, F 23,9:4
Heimer, Louis B, 1945, Je 23,13:3
Heimerdinger, Berthold, 1961, Je 23,29:3
Heimerdinger, Frederick M, 1950, Mr 21,29:3
Heimerdinger, Harry R, 1966, D 16,47:3
Heimerdinger, Joseph E, 1903, S 25,7:5
Heimerdinger, Joseph E Mrs, 1956, N 10,19:6
Heimerle, Francis W, 1950, N 7,27:4
Heimers, Lili, 1956, D 14,29:2
Heimlich, Gerson, 1941, Je 25,21:5
Heimlich, Gerson Mrs, 1943, Je 12,13:5
Heimlich, Samuel M, 1959, Ag 29,17:4
Heimmel, Edward E Mrs, 1947, Ap 8,27:1
Heimowitz, Joseph, 1943, Jl 1,19:5
Heims, Henry J Mrs, 1950, Mr 12,92:1
Heimsoth, Joseph W, 1955, O 1,19:2
Hein, Carl (por), 1945, F 28,23:5
Hein, Carl C Rev Dr, 1937, My 1,19:6
Hein, Charles, 1910, F 7,9:2
Hein, Erich, 1957, N 30,2:5
Hein, Ernest A, 1939, My 17,23:5
Hein, Harry, 1952, Mr 1,15:4
Hein, Hermann, 1939, O 17,25:3
Hein, Illo (por), 1948, Mr 5,21:4
Hein, Joseph, 1941, F 13,19:5
Hein, Joseph Mrs, 1964, F 18,35:2
Hein, Lionel, 1947, Mr 6,25:2
Hein, S, 1928, D 20,27:3
Heina, Edwin, 1951, Mr 31,15:2
Heinal, William A, 1963, Jl 27,17:5
Heinaman, Edward, 1942, F 28,17:2
Heinbokel, J F, 1944, Ag 23,19:5
Heindel, John E, 1941, Jl 20,31:4
Heindel, Max Mrs, 1949, My 12,31:6
Heindel, Richard H Mrs, 1962, Je 3,73:5
Heindl, Alexander, 1917, S 6,11:4
Heine, Amelie Miltenberger, 1915, My 17,9:4
Heine, Arthur, 1953, Ap 26,86:5
Heine, Carlos F, 1951, S 13,31:1
Heine, Henry, 1950, My 12,27:2
Heine, Henry F, 1950, Ja 23,23:1
Heine, Henry J, 1961, Je 25,77:1
Heine, John A, 1968, D 1,86:8
Heine, John F, 1944, Mr 4,13:4
Heine, Raymond F, 1951, Ja 9,30:2
Heine, Robert M, 1952, Jl 1,23:2
Heine, Thomas T, 1948, F 1,61:1
Heine, Wolfgang, 1944, My 11,19:6
Heine-Geldern, Robert Prof, 1968, My 30,25:2
Heineke, Alfred C, 1951, Ja 18,27:3
Heineken, Gustav, 1951, Jl 4,17:3
Heinelt, Delmar, 1967, S 2,21:2
Heineman, Claude M, 1907, S 17,11:6
Heineman, Clifford, 1950, O 25,35:1
Heineman, Dannie N, 1962, F 2,29:2
Heineman, Henry, 1910, Ja 2,II,13:5
Heineman, Milton J Mrs, 1964, Ja 10,43:1
Heinemann, Adolph, 1941, Jl 11,15:2
Heinemann, Felix, 1955, S 25,93:2
Heinemann, H Newton Dr, 1908, F 12,7:5
Heinemann, Hans, 1967, Jl 30,64:8
Heinemann, Mimi F Mrs, 1940, N 20,21:1
Heinemann, Samuel S, 1959, My 12,35:1
Heinemann, Siegfried, 1912, Mr 6,11:4
Heinemann, William, 1949, N 19,17:2
Heinemeyer, Gustav L, 1949, Je 8,29:1
Heinemeyer, Herman, 1952, Ja 6,93:2
Heinen, Frederick C, 1961, My 10,45:3
Heiner, Gordon G, 1943, D 24,14:7
Heiner, John H Mrs, 1947, My 18,60:5
Heiney, Walter M Mrs, 1946, Jl 3,25:4
Heinhold, William, 1904, Ja 14,9:2
Heinigke, Otto W, 1968, S 21,33:2
Heininger, Henry, 1943, N 4,23:5
Heinisch, R Maj, 1874, Ag 7,4:6
Heinke, Llewellyn H, 1947, Ag 4,17:4
Heinkel, Ernst (funl, F 5,28:1), 1958, Ja 31,21:1
Heinkel, William C, 1953, My 28,23:1
Heinkel, William C Mrs, 1937, S 1,19:5
Heinl, Robert D, 1950, N 27,26:2
Heinlein, Edward, 1949, Ap 20,27:1
Heinlein, George Mrs, 1946, F 11,29:4
Heinlein, Mary V, 1961, D 27,27:3
Heinman, Louis, 1904, Ap 3,20:7
Heinmuller, John P V, 1960, Jl 12,35:1
Heinold, Fred W, 1959, O 21,43:2
Heinrich, Christian, 1954, D 15,31:1
Heinrich, Edward O, 1953, S 30,31:3
Heinrich, Jacob J, 1950, Jl 30,60:8
Heinrich, John A, 1955, Jl 6,27:1
Heinrich, John C, 1945, My 25,19:3
Heinrich, Julia, 1919, S 19,13:4
Heinrich, Julius J F, 1925, Ja 4,7:2
Heinrich, Kurt A, 1961, My 30,17:5
Heinrich, Leonard A, 1966, F 2,35:2
Heinrich, Max, 1916, Ag 10,9:3
Heinrich, Otto, 1948, F 4,23:1
Heinrich, Wilhelm, 1911, D 28,9:5
Heinrich, William, 1965, My 2,88:6
Heinrich Franz Wilhelm, Prince of Bavaria, 1958, F 17,42:1
Heinrichs, Alfred P, 1954, F 19,27:2
Heinrichs, Charles E, 1963, My 4,25:2
Heinrichs, Gustav D Dr, 1923, F 15,19:5
Heinrichs, Harry H, 1955, Je 19,93:2
Heinrichs, Henry A, 1942, Ap 1,21:4
Heinrichs, Herbert W, 1952, Ja 23,27:4
Heinrichs, Jacob, 1947, S 1,19:3
Heinrichs, Jacob Mrs, 1949, Ja 7,22:2
Heinrichs, Leo Father, 1908, Mr 3,7:5
Heinrichs, Otto P Jr, 1948, Mr 28,48:5
Heinrichs, Waldo H, 1959, Je 16,35:2
Heinrichsmeyer, Louis F, 1960, Ja 24,88:4
Heinrici, Max, 1948, Jl 13,27:5
Heinritz, Melvin J, 1951, O 25,29:5
Heinroth, Theodore F, 1964, F 5,35:4
Heins, Bino (Christian Heins), 1963, Je 16,V,1:1
Heins, Carl A, 1943, D 29,17:2
Heins, Donald, 1949, Ja 3,23:1
Heins, Ernest August, 1906, Ja 26,9:5
Heins, George L Mrs, 1938, N 13,45:4
Heins, George Lewis, 1907, S 27,9:6
Heins, Harry E, 1947, Ap 13,60:5
Heins, Henry F, 1948, My 2,77:1
Heins, Isaac Capt, 1883, S 15,8:2
Heins, Raymond A, 1949, S 27,27:3
Heins, W J, 1883, O 3,5:5
Heinselman, Robert E, 1940, Mr 25,16:2
Heinsheimer, A M, 1929, S 1,17:3
Heinsheimer, Charles J, 1910, D 24,9:6
Heinsheimer, Edward L Mrs, 1953, F 21,13:4
Heinsheimer, Louis A, 1909, Ja 3,11:5
Heinsheimer, Norbert (por), 1939, Ap 25,23:4
Heinsius, Jacobus, 1947, My 22,27:4
Heinsohn, Ernst D W, 1944, My 4,19:3
Heintel, Charles H, 1955, Ja 21,23:2
Heintskill, Henry A, 1946, O 25,23:1
Heintz, George Sr, 1915, Je 30,11:6
Heintz, Henry J, 1943, Ag 13,17:6
Heintz, Ida Mrs, 1961, My 1,29:2
Heintz, John E, 1957, S 27,19:4
Heintz, Joseph J, 1958, D 2,37:5
Heintz, Michael G, 1951, Je 23,15:3
Heintz, Philip B, 1943, Jl 30,15:6
Heintze, Richard W Prof, 1937, Mr 24,25:4
Heintzelman, Arthur W, 1965, Ap 6,39:2
Heintzelman, C H, 1960, My 2,29:3
Heintzelman, S P, 1880, My 2,5:4
Heintzemann, George A, 1966, F 14,29:2
Heintzen, Alfred, 1951, My 3,29:6
Heintzleman, B Frank, 1965, Je 25,33:2
Heintzleman, Percival S, 1942, O 24,15:2
Heintzman, Charles T, 1954, S 30,31:4
Heinz, Conrad Sr Mrs, 1944, Je 30,21:4
Heinz, Fannie Mrs, 1954, Ja 30,17:6
Heinz, Frank, 1952, Je 20,23:4
Heinz, Frederick A, 1947, D 2,29:1
Heinz, Frederick C, 1964, S 27,86:6
Heinz, Harry J, 1937, O 15,23:3
Heinz, Henrietta, 1954, Ja 23,13:2
Heinz, Henry J, 1919, My 15,17:5
Heinz, Howard (will, F 18,18:4), 1941, F 10,20:1
Heinz, Howard Mrs, 1952, S 26,22:4
Heinz, John P, 1944, Ap 11,19:5
Heinz, M P, 1947, O 4,17:3
Heinz, Otto F, 1952, S 21,89:2
Heinze, A P, 1931, My 22,25:5
Heinze, F Augustus (est appr, N 7,11:7), 1914, N 5, 11:3
Heinze, F Augustus Mrs, 1913, Ap 3,9:6
Heinze, Otto C, 1948, D 29,22:3
Heinze, Robert F, 1937, D 4,17:6
Heinzelman, Fred, 1962, My 28,29:5
Heinzelman, Paul, 1957, F 15,23:2
Heinzen, Karl A, 1939, Mr 25,15:2
Heinzeroth, Harry L, 1953, My 4,23:5
Heinzmann, Otto J, 1950, Ja 31,24:2
Heipertz, Kuno, 1950, Je 10,17:2
Heipertz, William, 1937, S 28,23:3
Heiremans, Brockmann Oscar, 1944, My 4,13:3
Heirendt, Frank, 1938, Ap 5,21:3
Heironimus, Walter W Mrs, 1966, Je 2,43:3
Heise, Charles G, 1939, N 12,49:1
Heise, Ellen, 1938, Ap 15,20:2
Heise, Frederick H, 1946, Je 9,40:3
Heise, Theodore R, 1948, Ap 18,72:3

Heisel, William W, 1950, Ap 19,29:4
Heiselberg, Andrew C, 1949, Jl 6,30:1
Heisenberg, Karl, 1946, S 30,25:6
Heisenbuttel, Frederick Mrs, 1968, Ja 29,31:3
Heiser, Dan, 1950, F 8,27:3
Heiser, Frederick D, 1952, Mr 18,27:5
Heiser, George W Mrs, 1951, Jl 15,60:3
Heiser, Victor G Mrs, 1965, O 11,39:5
Heiserman, Clarence B (por), 1946, N 25,27:3
Heiserman, Clarence B Mrs, 1948, Je 17,25:5
Heiserman, Robert B, 1951, My 2,31:4
Heiserman, Robert B Mrs, 1961, D 8,42:7
Heisey, E Wilson, 1942, Ja 22,17:4
Heisey, William C, 1939, Je 23,19:5
Heisig, Mary, 1966, Mr 5,27:4
Heising, Raymond A, 1965, Ja 17,88:5
Heiskell, Morgan, 1967, Ap 30,43:4
Heisler, August H, 1943, O 1,19:2
Heisler, John C, 1938, S 11,II,11:3
Heisler, John S, 1953, Je 29,21:6
Heisler, Roger J Sr, 1943, N 14,56:7
Heisley, Frederick A, 1938, Jl 16,13:3
Heislitz, Adolph E, 1940, Ap 15,17:5
Heisman, George, 1938, Ap 7,23:5
Heisman, George E, 1950, S 27,32:3
Heisman, John W Mrs, 1963, N 20,43:1
Heismann, Christian E, 1951, N 21,25:1
Heiss, Charles A, 1962, O 21,89:1
Heiss, Edward A, 1966, Jl 1,35:5
Heiss, Edward Mrs, 1956, O 31,33:6
Heiss, G Roland, 1937, O 8,23:4
Heiss, George, 1952, Ap 23,29:3
Heiss, Henry, 1885, Je 21,2:3
Heiss, Lewis W Sr, 1957, F 14,27:5
Heiss, Marion W, 1959, S 14,29:3
Heiss, Melton H, 1944, Ja 1,13:2
Heisse, J Fred Rev Dr, 1923, N 9,17:4
Heissenbuttel, Frederick F, 1951, Mr 6,27:5
Heissenbuttel, Henry C Mrs, 1948, Ap 14,27:4
Heissenbuttel, Henry D, 1903, Jl 13,7:5
Heissenbuttel, O D, 1913, Jl 17,7:5
Heissenbuttel, William F Mrs, 1961, My 14,86:6
Heist, Jacob (will), 1938, My 8,III,9:2
Heist, Stanley H, 1961, S 1,17:1
Heitfeld, Henry, 1938, O 23,40:8
Heitkamp, Howard S, 1938, F 22,21:1
Heitler, Edward, 1957, My 13,31:4
Heitman, Charles E, 1948, O 3,64:7
Heitman, Edward, 1940, S 27,23:2
Heitman, Harry A Mrs, 1956, F 15,31:2
Heitman, William F, 1945, Ja 11,23:3
Heitmann, Claus, 1952, Je 18,27:3
Heitmann, George H, 1957, O 30,29:3
Heitmann, Louis H, 1938, My 21,15:5
Heitmuller, Alfred, 1951, O 13,6:1
Heitner, J A, 1909, Ag 30,7:5
Heitsch, Hubert M, 1941, S 21,44:1
Heitzler, Herman, 1960, Ag 11,27:4
Heitzman, Donald, 1921, Jl 30,9:5
Heitzman, Edward Mrs, 1921, Jl 30,9:5
Heitzman, George W, 1957, Mr 9,19:5
Heitzman, William H, 1948, N 29,23:4
Heitzmann, Fred L, 1945, My 23,19:2
Heitzmann, Louis, 1939, Jl 10,19:2
Heizer, Lewis W, 1950, Ag 1,23:4
Heizer, Oscar S, 1956, Ag 6,23:4
Heizmann, Charles Mrs, 1950, Ap 19,29:1
Hejduk, William, 1957, Ja 26,19:1
Hekking, Gerard, 1942, Je 9,23:2
Hekking, Martin J, 1937, Ap 17,17:5
Hekma, Jacob (por), 1949, F 18,23:1
Hekman, John, 1951, N 24,11:5
Hektoen, Josef, 1950, N 18,15:4
Hektoen, Ludwig, 1951, Jl 6,24:2
Hektoen, Ludwig Mrs, 1954, My 3,25:2
Helander, Herman S, 1937, Ap 16,24:1
Helbein, William, 1960, Jl 13,35:2
Helbig, Louis, 1956, Jl 11,29:5
Helbling, John A, 1942, Ap 14,21:1
Helbrant, Maurice, 1962, Jl 15,60:2
Helburn, J Willard, 1950, Ap 17,23:3
Helburn, Theresa (Mrs J B Opdycke),(cor, Ag 20,-25:4), 1959, Ag 19,29:3
Helbush, Herman H, 1964, Ja 5,92:2
Helck, Henry J Mrs, 1947, O 3,25:1
Helck, Henry P Mrs, 1955, My 4,29:3
Held, A, 1880, S 18,7:6
Held, Ada J Mrs, 1965, O 23,31:5
Held, Adolph Mrs, 1954, S 21,27:5
Held, Anna (funl, Ag 14,9:4), 1918, Ag 13,9:3
Held, Felix, 1944, S 1,13:4
Held, Frederick G, 1953, Je 30,23:3
Held, Harold, 1964, O 6,39:1
Held, Harry Mrs, 1947, Je 6,23:5
Held, Harry R, 1948, D 30,19:5
Held, Harry R Jr, 1966, D 6,47:2
Held, Heinrich (por), 1938, Ag 5,18:1
Held, Henry, 1939, Ag 7,15:5
Held, Isidore W, 1947, Mr 3,21:3
Held, John Jr, 1958, Mr 3,27:4
Held, John S H, 1952, Ag 19,23:2
Held, Joseph W, 1949, D 19,27:3
Held, Louis J, 1955, S 22,31:4
Held, Omar C, 1966, Je 25,31:5
Held, Samuel Mrs, 1953, Mr 25,31:2
Held, Stanley S, 1942, Ap 5,41:1
Held, Theodore, 1950, Ja 31,23:2
Held, Warren, 1960, Ap 2,23:6
Held, William A, 1945, D 14,28:2
Helde, George G, 1954, S 26,87:1
Heldeman, Bruce, 1948, N 30,27:1
Helder, Ruby, 1938, N 23,21:4
Helder, William B, 1939, Ja 11,19:1
Heldman, A John, 1940, Je 2,45:2
Heldman, Morton J, 1964, Ja 17,40:1
Heldman, Norvin J, 1961, My 23,39:3
Heldman, Warren J, 1966, D 23,25:2
Heldt, Henning, 1950, My 8,23:4
Heldt, Peter M, 1957, Mr 13,31:1
Hele, Thomas S, 1953, Ja 24,15:4
Helein, Jules, 1958, Ja 18,15:5
Helen Grace, Sister (K McFadden), 1955, Ja 15,13:1
Helen Lucas, Mother, 1944, N 5,54:5
Helen Mallon, Mother, 1945, Ja 1,21:5
Helena, Edith Mrs, 1956, N 28,35:2
Helena, Princess of Serbia, 1962, O 17,39:1
Helena Beste, Sister, 1944, O 21,17:5
Helena Victoria, Princess, 1948, Mr 14,73:1
Helene, Charles, 1953, Jl 8,27:4
Helf, J Fred, 1915, N 21,19:5
Helf, Jacob R, 1962, F 24,27:1
Helfand, David, 1947, Ag 5,23:2
Helfand, Samuel B, 1967, O 21,31:3
Helfeldt, Carl, 1882, Ap 17,5:1
Helfenbein, Ladislas Mrs, 1958, My 29,27:4
Helfenstein, Edward T, 1947, D 23,24:2
Helfenstein, James Morris, 1953, F 18,31:2
Helfer, Arthur, 1960, My 18,41:4
Helfer, Henry G, 1961, My 25,37:5
Helfer, Joseph E, 1963, O 13,86:5
Helfer, Philetus M, 1948, F 20,60:6
Helfer, Walter, 1959, Ap 18,23:5
Helferich, Henry F, 1953, Je 23,29:5
Helffrich, Cyril C, 1947, F 27,24:3
Helfgott, George, 1954, Ag 9,17:5
Helfgott, Jack, 1956, D 5,39:2
Helfgott, Moses N, 1966, Ag 28,93:1
Helfgott, Simon, 1957, S 9,25:6
Helfman, Max, 1963, Ag 13,31:4
Helfrich, Charles H, 1946, Je 1,13:1
Helfrich, Charles M, 1947, Ja 5,53:4
Helfrich, Conrad E L, 1962, S 21,30:1
Helfrich, Emma W Mrs, 1942, Ap 15,21:4
Helfrich, Emory W (Ty), 1955, My 20,88:4
Helfrich, Frank J Mrs, 1959, D 21,27:3
Helfrich, George W, 1959, O 9,29:2
Helfrich, Henry W A, 1946, My 17,21:2
Helfrich, John, 1942, N 12,25:4
Helfrich, John H, 1939, S 20,27:3
Helfrich, Theodore H, 1954, Jl 27,21:2
Helg, Arthur, 1955, Ja 14,21:1
Helgans, Edward H Mrs, 1949, Ap 17,76:6
Helgeby, Carsten J, 1951, D 27,21:1
Helgesen, Henry T, 1917, Ap 11,13:6
Helgesen, L Orville, 1964, N 18,47:4
Helgott, Leo B, 1939, Ag 27,35:3
Helick, Chauncey G, 1947, N 21,27:1
Helie, Faustin, 1884, O 26,2:5
Helies, Frank B, 1947, D 14,79:3
Heling, Charles, 1938, Je 22,23:2
Helinski, James J, 1953, O 12,27:6
Heliodoro Valle, Rafael, 1959, Jl 30,27:3
Helis, William G, 1950, Jl 25,27:1
Helitzer, Marcus Mrs, 1956, N 5,31:5
Helker, George C, 1951, Ag 24,15:4
Hellade, James, 1953, Ag 17,15:3
Hellar, Harry, 1912, Jl 15,9:3
Hellard, Richard J, 1954, O 17,84:3
Hellawell, Edwin V, 1948, Ap 25,68:4
Hellberg, Oscar W, 1954, Ag 14,15:7
Helle, Oisten Mrs, 1951, D 15,13:5
Hellen, C E, 1944, O 18,21:1
Hellenbrecht, Charles W, 1946, Mr 2,13:6
Hellencourt, Henry L d', 1940, My 30,17:3
Hellendall Hugo, 1954, Je 14,21:3
Heller, A Gerald, 1957, S 20,25:3
Heller, Abraham, 1951, D 22,15:5
Heller, Adolf, 1954, Jl 3,9:1
Heller, Adolph, 1951, My 20,89:1
Heller, Albert G Sr, 1951, O 3,33:1
Heller, Alex, 1953, F 22,61:2
Heller, Alexander G, 1944, Jl 24,15:5
Heller, Alfred, 1953, Ag 27,25:1; 1957, O 25,27:4
Heller, Alfred L, 1948, Je 15,28:3
Heller, Bert, 1944, O 18,21:2
Heller, C F, 1952, D 17,33:2
Heller, Chaim, 1960, Ap 12,33:1
Heller, Charles Mrs, 1964, O 25,88:3
Heller, Clyde A, 1937, Ja 12,23:2
Heller, David, 1948, My 6,25:4
Heller, David L, 1939, Jl 18,19:2
Heller, Dick D Sr, 1958, Jl 29,23:5
Heller, Edgar W, 1962, N 5,31:4
Heller, Edgar W Jr, 1961, Ja 2,25:2
Heller, Edgar W Mrs, 1942, O 23,21:3
Heller, Edmund (por), 1939, Jl 20,19:3
Heller, Edward E, 1942, N 23,23:3
Heller, Edward H, 1961, D 20,33:4
Heller, Edwin A, 1949, D 27,24:2
Heller, Edwin H, 1950, Ap 15,17:2
Heller, Elizabeth, 1949, D 10,18:2
Heller, Ernest A Mrs, 1949, Ja 19,27:1
Heller, Eugene F, 1940, O 27,44:3
Heller, Eugenie M, 1952, Jl 23,23:2
Heller, Ferdinand, 1942, Jl 31,15:7
Heller, Ferdinand Mrs, 1944, D 14,23:1
Heller, Ferle (Mrs M Hoffman), 1964, Ja 13,35:1
Heller, Florence G Mrs, 1966, Ja 6,27:4
Heller, Frank, 1947, O 17,22:2
Heller, Frank J, 1946, F 26,25:3; 1965, My 12,47:4
Heller, Frank R, 1954, Jl 23,17:3
Heller, Frank W, 1942, Jl 22,19:4
Heller, Frederick G Mrs, 1947, Mr 2,61:1
Heller, G P, 1880, My 11,2:4
Heller, Garson F Sr, 1968, D 8,86:6
Heller, George, 1952, Ap 20,93:1; 1955, D 30,19:4
Heller, George AFTRA exec sec, 1955, My 31,27:1
Heller, George C, 1948, Jl 24,15:5
Heller, Glenn C, 1951, O 16,31:2
Heller, Gustav P, 1966, O 30,89:1
Heller, Hans E, 1966, O 2,86:8
Heller, Harold S, 1954, Jl 2,19:2
Heller, Harry E, 1951, Jl 6,23:2
Heller, Helen W Mrs, 1955, N 30,38:2
Heller, Henry, 1959, Jl 17,21:5; 1964, Mr 2,27:3
Heller, Henry R, 1952, Je 25,29:2
Heller, Herbert, 1953, Je 2,29:5
Heller, Herbert J Mrs, 1953, S 26,17:6
Heller, Hyman L, 1950, Ag 9,29:6
Heller, Irving E, 1966, O 13,45:4
Heller, Isaac M, 1942, Je 7,43:3
Heller, Isaac S Mrs, 1938, My 14,15:4
Heller, Jacob, 1960, Ap 4,29:5
Heller, Jacob Dr, 1953, F 17,27:4
Heller, Jacob J, 1948, S 26,76:7
Heller, Jacob Mrs, 1953, Mr 13,27:2
Heller, John H, 1958, O 18,21:5
Heller, John W, 1948, D 29,21:4
Heller, Joseph, 1953, Mr 27,23:3
Heller, Judah G, 1965, Jl 27,33:2
Heller, Louis B, 1939, Ap 26,23:2
Heller, Louis H, 1938, My 25,23:4
Heller, M, 1929, Mr 31,26:1
Heller, M T, 1949, Ag 22,21:5
Heller, Marcus, 1956, O 27,21:4
Heller, Martin G, 1938, Je 4,15:1
Heller, Martin J, 1958, O 20,29:1
Heller, Matthew, 1962, N 22,29:2
Heller, Max, 1955, My 21,17:3
Heller, Max Mrs, 1939, N 18,17:2; 1949, Mr 18,2
Heller, Maxwell L, 1963, My 16,35:2
Heller, Morris Mrs, 1944, D 20,23:4
Heller, Murray J, 1952, Mr 6,32:3
Heller, Napoleon B, 1951, F 2,23:3
Heller, Nathan Mrs, 1952, Mr 12,27:2; 1954, D 2
Heller, Oscar, 1904, O 11,9:4
Heller, Otto, 1941, Jl 31,17:1
Heller, Otto Mrs, 1947, S 26,23:5
Heller, Paul E, 1948, F 27,21:3
Heller, Preston B, 1954, Ja 8,21:3
Heller, R P, 1878, N 28,1:6
Heller, Reinhold, 1947, O 16,28:3
Heller, Robert F, 1958, O 18,21:6
Heller, Samuel, 1937, Mr 2,21:4; 1950, Jl 21,19:
1967, Mr 7,41:4
Heller, Samuel E, 1937, Mr 7,II,8:7
Heller, Sidney, 1960, Jl 22,23:1
Heller, Sigmund, 1952, F 3,85:2
Heller, Sol, 1944, Ag 28,11:4; 1949, My 28,15:3
Heller, Walter D, 1966, N 14,41:5
Heller, Walter M, 1947, Jl 30,21:4
Heller, William D, 1962, Mr 14,39:3
Heller, William F, 1946, Ap 9,27:5
Hellerman, Allen, 1949, D 5,23:6
Helleu, P, 1927, Mr 25,21:5
Hellick, George F Sr, 1955, S 13,31:1
Hellier, Charles E, 1940, Ap 30,21:4
Hellinger, Charles G, 1937, D 11,19:4
Hellinger, Charles H, 1948, Ap 2,23:3
Hellinger, Joshua, 1960, N 19,21:7
Hellinger, Mark, 1947, D 22,21:3
Hellis, Arch W, 1949, Ja 3,23:2
Helliwell, Charles H, 1955, D 1,35:5
Hellman, Al, 1961, D 21,4:7
Hellman, Alfred M, 1955, Ja 14,21:1
Hellman, Carl R, 1964, F 7,32:5
Hellman, Edgar A, 1948, F 2,19:2
Hellman, Enid, 1942, Ap 5,42:3
Hellman, Eugene A, 1941, Ap 30,19:4
Hellman, George S, 1958, Jl 18,21:3
Hellman, Harry, 1948, S 8,29:5
Hellman, Isaiah W Jr Mrs, 1959, D 4,31:2
Hellman, Isaias W Jr, 1920, My 11,9:4
Hellman, Jacques, 1946, N 28,27:2
Hellman, Leo, 1948, Ap 27,25:2
Hellman, Maurice S, 1943, Ja 18,15:4
Hellman, Max, 1911, Ja 6,9:4
Hellman, Max B, 1949, Ag 5,19:3
Hellman, Milo (por), 1947, My 12,21:4

Hellman, S Raymond, 1958, Ap 16,33:4
Hellman, Sam, 1950, Ag 12,13:1
Hellman, Sidney L (por), 1938, N 4,23:2
Hellmann, Emil, 1944, Je 17,13:4
Hellmann, Fred (por), 1942, Jl 29,17:1
Hellmann, Louis E, 1964, Ja 12,92:5
Hellmayer, Charles E, 1944, Ap 29,15:5
Hellmund, Henry Sr, 1956, Ag 18,17:2
Hellmund, Rudolph E, 1942, My 18,15:6
Hellmuth, James, 1962, Jl 31,24:7
Hellsten, Ernest G, 1956, Mr 13,27:2
Hellstrom, Carl R, 1963, Ap 8,47:1
Hellstrom, Erik G, 1953, Mr 1,92:7
Hellstrom, Victor Mrs, 1950, Ja 10,29:4
Hellstron, C Ivar, 1959, O 8,39:3
Hellweg, Edgar D, 1956, Ja 30,27:6
Hellwig, Edward W, 1940, F 20,21:4
Hellwig, Helena (Mrs W H Pouch), 1960, N 27,86:3
Hellwig, Theodore A, 1961, Mr 2,27:4
Helm, Albert W, 1956, Mr 1,33:2
Helm, Ben H, 1946, My 30,21:1
Helm, Carl, 1959, F 11,39:5
Helm, Carl C, 1962, F 8,31:3
Helm, Carl C Mrs, 1957, O 2,33:2
Helm, Charles W Mrs, 1948, My 18,23:2
Helm, David D Jr, 1955, F 13,87:1
Helm, Edwin M, 1951, Ap 19,31:3
Helm, Eleanor M, 1960, My 3,39:2
Helm, Florence, 1954, Mr 14,88:5
Helm, Frank, 1939, Mr 10,23:5
Helm, George F Sr, 1960, O 29,23:5
Helm, Gov, 1867, S 9,1:3
Helm, Harry S, 1947, My 8,25:2
Helm, Harvey, 1919, Mr 4,11:3
Helm, J I Rev, 1880, O 18,6:6
Helm, James M Mrs (funl, Ag 10,19:1), 1962, Ag 7, 29:1
Helm, James W, 1943, Mr 9,23:3
Helm, Leslie C, 1957, Ag 23,19:3
Helm, Lewis, 1937, Ag 11,23:6
Helm, MacKinley, 1963, Ap 8,47:4
Helm, Mary C, 1938, O 19,23:6
Helm, Rae C, 1949, Ja 4,40:2
Helm, Sallie Mrs, 1922, Ja 4,13:5
Helm, Stephen, 1903, Ag 17,7:5
Helm, Walter D, 1949, Ja 8,15:3
Helm, William L, 1957, N 29,29:2
Helm, William P, 1958, N 1,19:6
Helm, Willis C, 1949, My 21,13:4
Helman, Max, 1960, Jl 7,31:2
Helman, Nathan C, 1961, N 21,39:2
Helmann, Moritz, 1925, S 24,25:4
Helmbold, Elmo P, 1939, S 21,23:4
Helmbold, Gerald H, 1952, D 12,29:1
Helmcken, John Sebastian, 1920, S 3,9:6
Helme, J Burn, 1945, N 14,19:2
Helme, James B, 1952, Ag 28,23:3
Helmecke, August, 1954, F 28,92:3
Helmeister, Henry, 1879, Ja 22,5:6
Helmer, Alfred S H, 1966, O 10,41:2
Helmer, Florence T, 1942, D 27,34:5
Helmer, Frank Ambrose, 1925, O 1,27:5
Helmer, Frederick F Dr, 1937, Mr 20,19:2
Helmer, John J, 1967, Ag 25,35:4
Helmer, Lester G, 1948, D 14,29:4
Helmer, Mulford B Mrs, 1943, D 31,16:7
Helmerick, Amelia Mrs, 1945, D 26,10:8
Helmers, Henry, 1948, Je 11,23:5
Helmers, Nick F (por), 1943, Ja 3,42:7
Helmersen, G, 1885, Mr 6,5:5
Helmetag, Carl Sr, 1943, Ja 4,15:4
Helmholt, Charles von, 1923, Mr 8,17:4
Helmholtz, Hermann von Prof Baron, 1894, S 9,5:2
Helmholz, Henry F, 1958, Ag 20,27:4
Helmich, Edward, 1960, O 15,23:6
Helmick, Eli A, 1945, F 10,11:3
Helmick, Milton J, 1954, O 20,30:2
Helmig, Alphonse H, 1954, My 12,31:2
Helmke, Harry, 1939, N 7,52:2
Helmle, Frank J, 1939, Jl 16,30:6
Helmlinger, Benjamin C, 1939, Ag 28,19:2
Helmrath, Albert, 1952, Mr 22,13:4
Helmrich, Aug G, 1942, Ja 8,21:2
Helms, Arthur T, 1940, S 26,23:6
Helms, Charles, 1947, My 6,27:2
Helms, Charles B, 1953, Mr 13,25:5
Helms, Edgar J, 1942, D 25,17:3
Helms, Elizabeth Mrs, 1946, Ag 29,27:3
Helms, Elmer E, 1955, Mr 2,27:4
Helms, Elmer E Mrs, 1951, N 27,31:3
Helms, Franklin W Sr, 1955, Je 3,23:6
Helms, Fred C, 1945, D 11,25:4
Helms, Henry A, 1952, Jl 17,23:6
Helms, Herman Mrs, 1943, Jl 6,21:2
Helms, Hermann, 1963, Ja 8,8:6
Helms, James K, 1956, O 3,33:3
Helms, John E, 1942, F 17,21:2
Helms, Leon W, 1949, S 12,21:3
Helms, Leslie R, 1948, Mr 13,15:3
Helms, Levi, 1948, D 8,31:2
Helms, Paul H, 1957, Ja 9,88:3
Helmstadter, George, 1951, Ja 13,15:6
Helmstadter, George L, 1941, Jl 24,17:6
Helmstadter, William L B, 1948, D 10,25:2
Helmstetter, Ernest Rt Rev Abbot, 1937, Jl 11,II,4:7
Helmus, Adolph, 1920, N 28,22:4
Helmus, Aug, 1942, D 20,44:7
Helmuth, Louis, 1953, Ap 2,27:2
Helmuth, Osvald, 1966, Mr 19,29:5
Helmuth, Paul M, 1947, Ja 4,15:5
Helmuth, W T Dr, 1902, My 16,9:5
Helmuth, William Tod Mrs, 1918, D 2,13:8
Helner, Alexander, 1947, Ag 21,23:5
Helper, Harold H Mrs, 1943, O 13,23:4
Helpern, Milton Mrs, 1953, Ja 13,27:2
Helprin, Benjamin E Dr, 1937, Je 29,21:2
Helprin, Henry Mrs (Frances Langren), 1968, Ag 9, 35:2
Helps, William J, 1954, Jl 28,23:2
Helpser, S Jack Mrs, 1956, Mr 5,23:1
Helsby, Henry R, 1959, Ag 18,29:2
Helsper, F Jack, 1964, N 24,39:1
Helstadt, Hans C, 1911, Ap 6,11:5
Helstein, Ira, 1946, Ag 7,27:3
Helt, Scott, 1956, Ag 10,17:5
Heltman, Harry J, 1962, Je 13,41:4
Helton, Alfred, 1937, Mr 8,19:4
Helton, Henry Dwight Dr, 1917, F 13,11:4
Helvanar, Anasbos, 1907, Ag 20,7:7
Helvering, Guy T, 1946, Jl 4,19:3
Helwick, Edward C Sr, 1959, S 16,39:1
Helwig, Adolphus L, 1946, D 30,19:4
Helwig, Alfred, 1947, Ap 22,27:3
Helwig, Charles, 1944, Mr 24,19:2
Helwig, Harry G, 1941, Ap 24,21:4
Helwig, Jacob E, 1944, Ap 9,33:2
Helwitz, Aaron, 1964, S 13,86:6
Hely, Joseph W, 1941, O 8,23:1
Hely-Hutchinson, Victor, 1947, Mr 12,25:5
Hely-Hutchinson, Walter Francis Sir, 1913, S 24,9:5
Helyar, Frank G, 1963, Ap 17,41:1
Helyar, James E, 1945, Ja 13,11:4
Hem, Halvor O, 1952, N 12,27:2
Hem, Lawrence, 1962, Ag 29,30:1
Hemachandra, Balatunga Mrs, 1953, Ap 26,87:1
Hemans, Charles, 1876, N 25,3:7
Hemans, Lawton T, 1916, N 18,11:4
Hemberger, Theodor, 1956, F 16,29:4
Hemel, Peter W, 1957, Ap 24,33:5
Hemelrijck, Maurice van, 1964, O 11,88:4
Hemelt, Francis J, 1948, F 11,27:5
Hemen, Frank J, 1939, Ja 15,38:7
Hemens, Rollin D, 1968, Je 22,33:4
Hemenway, Charles Clifton, 1968, D 29,52:3
Hemenway, Charles D, 1945, My 23,19:3
Hemenway, Charles R, 1947, O 17,22:5
Hemenway, Ida S Mrs, 1940, O 15,23:3
Hemenway, John, 1954, N 23,13:3
Hemenway, Kenneth H, 1957, Ap 16,33:1
Hemenway, Myles, 1947, Jl 7,17:4
Hemenway, Ralph W, 1952, Ap 2,33:4
Hemenway, Rufus N, 1947, F 10,29:4
Hemenway, Thomas S, 1947, My 26,21:5
Hemes, Edward C, 1965, F 26,29:2
Hemhauser, Robert H, 1955, Ap 11,23:5
Heming, Arthur, 1940, O 31,23:5
Heming, Charles W, 1954, D 18,15:3
Heming, William S, 1938, Mr 9,23:2
Heminger, Isaac N, 1941, Mr 9,40:7
Hemingford, Lord, 1947, D 11,33:3
Hemingwag, Elbert S, 1949, D 7,31:4
Hemingway, C E Mrs, 1951, Je 29,21:2
Hemingway, Courtland G, 1948, F 26,23:4
Hemingway, Donald H, 1941, D 12,25:4
Hemingway, Edith A, 1960, Jl 31,69:1
Hemingway, Ernest (funl plans, Jl 4,9:2; funl, Jl 7,13:1), 1961, Jl 3,1:5
Hemingway, Ernest (est acctg), 1964, F 22,1:7
Hemingway, Frank, 1874, O 19,8:4
Hemingway, Frank G, 1940, Ag 28,19:2
Hemingway, G H, 1951, N 17,17:5
Hemingway, Harold E Mrs, 1950, F 24,23:3
Hemingway, Harry J, 1965, Je 18,15:7
Hemingway, Hughey S, 1940, O 2,23:5
Hemingway, Isabel A, 1941, Mr 4,23:6
Hemingway, James S, 1961, F 21,35:2
Hemingway, Pauline P Mrs, 1951, O 2,27:2
Hemingway, Samuel, 1882, Ja 1,7:4
Hemingway, Samuel B, 1958, D 31,19:1
Hemingway, Stuart C, 1955, Ag 2,23:2
Hemingway, Stuart C Mrs, 1956, F 6,23:4
Hemingway, W Linn, 1954, S 23,33:6
Hemingway, Walter C, 1952, Mr 22,13:3
Hemingway, Wilfrid H, 1943, Ap 22,23:2
Heminway, Buell H Jr, 1941, D 8,23:1
Heminway, Edwin H, 1951, D 6,33:1
Heminway, Harry H Mrs, 1943, N 1,17:4
Heminway, Homer, 1911, O 22,II,15:4
Heminway, John H Mrs, 1964, O 5,33:2
Heminway, Merrit, 1956, N 14,35:3
Heminway, Montine Mrs, 1941, D 10,25:3
Hemker, Arthur H, 1954, My 23,88:5
Hemle, Frank J Mrs, 1937, Ja 5,23:2
Hemley, Benjamin, 1937, D 15,25:3
Hemley, Frederick, 1946, N 12,29:4
Hemley, Jacob, 1948, N 4,29:5
Hemlock, Edward J, 1947, N 15,17:5
Hemmendinger, Max, 1959, Je 6,21:6
Hemmens, Henry J, 1951, Ja 29,19:4
Hemment, Harold J, 1939, Jl 4,13:4
Hemment, John C Mrs, 1949, Jl 7,25:2
Hemmer, J Peter, 1905, Mr 22,9:6
Hemmer, John G, 1937, Ja 24,II,8:1
Hemmerdinger, Henry, 1947, Je 17,25:2
Hemmerdinger, Monroe E, 1962, F 27,33:2
Hemmerich, Alfred, 1945, S 26,23:3
Hemmerich, Hugo, 1951, O 23,29:4
Hemmerick, George, 1954, Ap 15,29:2
Hemmershaej, Nilhelm, 1916, F 15,11:6
Hemmes, Emma L Mrs, 1942, Ap 29,21:6
Hemmeter, Henry B, 1948, Jl 20,24:3
Hemmeter, Herbert S, 1943, Mr 16,19:3
Hemmi, Aida, 1940, D 21,17:6
Hemmick, Roland J Mrs, 1919, S 23,17:3
Hemming, Amy F, 1954, Jl 13,23:2
Hemming, Emile Sr, 1964, Ag 1,21:5
Hemming, Harold A, 1947, Mr 26,25:2
Hemming, Thomas D R Brig-Gen, 1919, Ja 10,13:6
Hemming, W E G, 1953, O 18,87:1
Hemminger, Edward F, 1959, Ag 29,17:6
Hemminger, Graham L, 1949, D 21,29:5
Hemminger, Ralph W, 1968, N 9,33:3
Hemmingford, Hiram P, 1940, O 11,21:6
Hemminghaus, Roy G, 1960, Ag 27,19:6
Hemmings, Harry H, 1958, S 28,88:4
Hemmler, Charles, 1954, Ag 28,89:3
Hemond, Conrad J Mrs, 1950, Mr 1,27:4
Hempel, Fred, 1941, N 26;23:4
Hempel, Frieda, 1955, O 8,19:2
Hempel, Gustave A Mrs, 1948, Ap 29,24:2
Hempel, Herbert P, 1953, My 23,15:6
Hempel, I V Capt, 1920, Ja 16,9:5
Hempel, Meta Dr, 1903, N 11,9:6
Hemphill, Albert W, 1955, N 13,89:2
Hemphill, Boyd, 1955, Mr 2,27:1
Hemphill, Boyd Mrs, 1955, Mr 2,27:1
Hemphill, Claude L, 1961, Jl 6,29:5
Hemphill, Clifford, 1966, Ag 30,36:2
Hemphill, Clifford Mrs, 1956, F 8,33:2
Hemphill, Epolie A Mrs, 1937, Mr 12,23:3
Hemphill, Frederick A, 1949, Mr 3,25:5
Hemphill, Horace F, 1941, D 5,23:3
Hemphill, J C, 1927, N 21,23:5
Hemphill, John M Mrs, 1953, S 22,31:3
Hemphill, John W, 1957, F 3,76:1
Hemphill, Robert H, 1941, Ap 24,21:4
Hempling, Jules, 1956, Ja 27,23:1
Hempstead, Charles H, 1962, D 4,41:3
Hempstead, Charles T, 1908, Mr 5,7:6
Hempstead, Clark, 1952, Jl 1,23:2
Hempstead, David B, 1937, Je 9,25:5
Hempstead, Donald E, 1962, Ja 18,29:3
Hempstead, Emma S Mrs, 1942, Ag 24,15:5
Hempstead, Harris, 1938, F 1,21:2
Hempstead, Harry N (por),(will, Ap 12,24:3), 1938, Mr 27,II,6:3
Hempstead, Harry N Mrs, 1943, Ja 10,50:3
Hempstead, John L, 1942, Ag 24,15:5
Hempstreet, W J, 1903, O 3,9:6
Hempy, Margaret M Mrs, 1941, Ja 3,19:5
Hemrich, Louis M, 1955, Ja 6,27:2
Hemsath, Karl Rev Dr, 1953, F 27,21:3
Hemschel, Harris Mrs, 1949, Ag 7,61:3
Hemsley, Estelle (funl), 1968, N 8,47:3
Hemsley, Harry, 1951, Ap 9,25:4
Hemstreet, George P, 1943, Jl 24,13:7
Hemstreet, H Harry, 1952, O 19,88:7
Hemstreet, Ralph E, 1949, My 17,25:5
Hemstreet, Shelton C, 1962, F 4,82:1
Hemstreet, William Col, 1920, O 16,13:4
Hemus, Benjamin O, 1960, N 25,27:1
Hemus, Percy (por), 1943, D 23,19:2
Hemy, Charles Napier, 1917, O 1,13:6
Hemy, Thomas M, 1937, Ap 3,19:5
Henaghan, Patrick A, 1961, D 13,43:1
Henbry, Phil, 1939, Ap 11,23:5
Hench, La Verne Willis, 1968, Jl 4,19:2
Hench, Philip S, 1965, Ap 1,35:1
Henchie, Samuel A, 1950, N 11,15:4
Henchy, John J, 1947, Ja 3,21:3
Henck, George D, 1941, Ja 6,15:2
Hencke, Everett W, 1960, F 22,17:1
Henckel, Countess de Donnesmark, 1884, F 14,2:7
Henckel, George C, 1956, S 4,29:3
Henckel, James R, 1940, F 9,19:3
Hencken, Albert C, 1951, Mr 12,25:1
Hencken, Henry Mrs, 1965, Ja 17,88:4
Hencken, William F, 1952, S 4,27:4; 1953, My 19,29:2
Hencle, Miles S, 1939, F 14,19:3
Hendecourt, Edouard Emile Auguste Count, 1917, D 22,11:5
Hendee, Abner, 1912, My 21,13:3
Hendee, Alvin M Rev, 1925, My 3,5:1
Hendee, Ann E Mrs, 1951, Mr 24,13:5
Hendee, Ceilan C, 1941, Jl 29,15:6
Hendee, George M, 1943, Je 18,21:4
Hendee, George W, 1906, D 7,11:3
Hendee, Harold C, 1952, My 20,25:2
Hendee, Harold F, 1966, Je 28,42:3

Hendel, Christian P, 1950, Mr 2,27:1
Hendel, James M Mrs, 1956, Mr 16,31:6
Hendel, John R, 1941, Mr 13,21:2
Hendel, Pastoriza F Mrs, 1937, My 8,19:6
Hendel, Richard, 1938, Je 30,23:4
Henderosn, Herbert J, 1947, Mr 4,25:3
Hendershot, Charles D, 1946, Ag 10,13:6
Hendershot, J Blair, 1955, Jl 1,21:4
Hendershot, Theodore W, 1961, Je 22,31:2
Henderson, A, 1935, O 21,1:2
Henderson, A J, 1930, D 25,21:4
Henderson, A M Collings, 1957, F 5,23:5
Henderson, A T, 1947, N 28,27:2
Henderson, Adeline, 1915, N 26,13:6
Henderson, Albert, 1938, D 29,20:2
Henderson, Albert H, 1951, O 12,27:1
Henderson, Alex, 1947, D 19,25:1
Henderson, Alex I, 1961, Jl 24,23:2
Henderson, Alexander, 1943, D 30,17:2
Henderson, Alexander Commodore, 1901, Ja 14,7:2
Henderson, Alexander D, 1964, Jl 10,29:2
Henderson, Alfred C, 1951, N 24,11:1
Henderson, Alfred R, 1954, D 19,84:2
Henderson, Alice E, 1954, Je 25,21:2
Henderson, Anne C, 1947, F 12,25:5
Henderson, Annie R Mrs, 1938, My 13,19:2
Henderson, Archibald, 1876, Jl 17,8:3; 1963, D 7,27:1
Henderson, Archibald G (will, Mr 20,29:7), 1947, F 24,19:3
Henderson, Archibald H, 1954, F 18,31:4
Henderson, Arthur, 1937, O 24,II,8:7
Henderson, Arthur (Lord Rowley), 1968, Ag 30,30:2
Henderson, Bancroft W, 1966, Ja 2,76:1
Henderson, Bertha E Mrs, 1942, Mr 5,23:4
Henderson, Brooks Ex-Sen, 1913, Ap 13,IV,7:6
Henderson, Cam, 1956, My 4,25:5
Henderson, Charles, 1937, Ja 8,20:2; 1939, Ap 30,45:3; 1946, O 5,17:5; 1951, Jl 11,23:5
Henderson, Charles B, 1937, Mr 23,12:3; 1954, N 9, 27:1
Henderson, Charles E, 1919, Ap 11,11:3
Henderson, Charles F, 1944, Ag 2,15:3; 1944, O 19, 23:1
Henderson, Charles F Mrs, 1950, F 9,29:1
Henderson, Charles H, 1941, Ja 12,44:5
Henderson, Charles L, 1949, Mr 28,21:4
Henderson, Charles R Dr, 1915, Mr 30,11:4
Henderson, Charles W, 1947, N 5,27:5; 1949, Jl 11,17:5
Henderson, Chester B, 1939, Mr 22,23:5
Henderson, Chester Mrs, 1943, O 1,19:4
Henderson, Cicero A, 1939, D 10,69:1
Henderson, Clay S, 1948, N 17,27:5
Henderson, Daniel M, 1955, N 14,27:2
Henderson, Daniel W, 1946, D 1,79:1
Henderson, David, 1908, My 27,7:3
Henderson, David B, 1906, F 26,9:1
Henderson, David Mrs, 1944, O 31,19:4
Henderson, David Mrs (F Raymond), 1961, Je 22, 31:3
Henderson, David Sir, 1921, Ag 19,13:5
Henderson, Del, 1956, D 5,39:2
Henderson, Don C, 1908, Ja 10,7:5
Henderson, Donald G, 1941, S 16,23:2
Henderson, Donaldina F, 1951, S 16,85:1
Henderson, Douglas R, 1962, N 1,31:4
Henderson, Earl Y, 1950, Ag 23,29:2
Henderson, Edgar A, 1967, Mr 30,45:3
Henderson, Edward C Mrs, 1953, O 24,15:3
Henderson, Edward Cairns, 1923, My 12,15:4
Henderson, Edward M, 1968, Ag 23,39:3
Henderson, Edwin, 1939, Jl 4,13:5
Henderson, Eliot M Mrs, 1963, Jl 4,17:2
Henderson, Elizabeth, 1953, S 16,33:2; 1958, F 28,21:1
Henderson, Elmer J, 1953, Jl 31,19:3
Henderson, Ernest K, 1952, N 11,29:3
Henderson, Ernest Sr, 1967, S 7,53:3
Henderson, Ettie Mrs, 1909, O 8,9:4
Henderson, Fletcher H, 1952, D 31,15:5
Henderson, Francis D, 1955, My 12,29:2
Henderson, Francis E, 1943, N 9,21:5
Henderson, Francis Mrs, 1957, D 26,19:2
Henderson, Francis R (por), 1941, N 14,23:1
Henderson, Frank C, 1943, Ag 29,39:2
Henderson, Frank C Mrs, 1957, N 22,25:3
Henderson, Frank G, 1940, Ja 4,23:2
Henderson, Frank Mrs, 1944, O 30,19:2; 1950, Ap 21, 23:1
Henderson, Fred, 1957, Jl 19,19:4
Henderson, Frederick B, 1921, F 11,11:3
Henderson, Frederick K, 1945, Mr 20,19:2
Henderson, G Bert, 1942, My 19,19:2
Henderson, G C, 1927, S 1,23:6
Henderson, G Lt-Col, 1903, Mr 23,7:2
Henderson, Gail W, 1951, O 22,23:5
Henderson, George, 1939, Jl 19,19:6; 1940, F 6,22:2
Henderson, George A, 1944, Je 6,17:4
Henderson, George D, 1950, Je 16,25:2; 1957, My 30, 19:2
Henderson, George H, 1949, Je 21,25:4; 1959, Je 26, 25:4
Henderson, George I, 1937, Jl 27,21:2
Henderson, George L, 1954, Je 24,27:3
Henderson, George R, 1964, N 30,33:4
Henderson, George S, 1941, Je 20,21:2
Henderson, George T, 1963, Ap 29,31:2
Henderson, H C, 1933, N 27,17:1
Henderson, Harold H Mrs, 1944, Ap 6,23:4
Henderson, Harold R, 1942, Jl 16,19:2
Henderson, Harry V K, 1939, F 25,15:3
Henderson, Helen, 1956, My 7,27:5
Henderson, Helen M Mrs, 1939, Je 7,23:2
Henderson, Henry M, 1909, Ag 31,7:7
Henderson, Homer W Mrs, 1968, Je 22,33:5
Henderson, Horace E, 1941, Ag 4,13:2
Henderson, Howard Mrs, 1965, Je 28,29:5
Henderson, Hubert D, 1952, F 24,85:1
Henderson, Ida R, 1950, Je 19,21:4
Henderson, Ira, 1958, N 12,37:2
Henderson, Isaac, 1884, N 14,2:3
Henderson, J C, 1884, Mr 12,5:5
Henderson, J H, 1928, D 13,29:3
Henderson, J Howard, 1945, D 20,23:2
Henderson, Jacob, 1952, Ja 20,86:1
Henderson, James, 1937, Ap 13,25:3; 1945, N 23,24:2; 1949, D 12,34:3; 1951, Jl 7,13:5; 1952, O 8,31:5; 1958, Ja 21,26:6
Henderson, James A, 1956, S 5,27:6
Henderson, James D, 1940, Mr 8,22:2
Henderson, James E Mrs, 1940, Je 30,32:7
Henderson, James J Sr, 1946, Je 15,21:6
Henderson, James Mrs, 1947, Ja 9,23:3
Henderson, James R, 1943, F 15,15:4
Henderson, James Sir, 1914, My 3,13:4
Henderson, Jessie I, 1954, N 1,27:4
Henderson, John, 1901, Jl 23,7:6; 1953, Jl 22,27:3
Henderson, John A, 1947, S 17,25:2
Henderson, John Brooks, 1923, Ja 5,11:6
Henderson, John E, 1954, Ja 16,15:3
Henderson, John J, 1941, F 18,24:2; 1946, Ja 3,19:3; 1953, Ja 26,19:5; 1955, Mr 24,31:4
Henderson, John M, 1947, S 21,60:3
Henderson, John Mrs, 1907, Jl 30,7:6
Henderson, John P, 1939, Ag 6,36:8
Henderson, John R, 1957, N 11,29:5
Henderson, John S, 1939, D 24,14:5; 1940, Jl 6,15:5
Henderson, Joseph H, 1951, O 19,27:1
Henderson, Joseph M, 1941, Jl 18,19:6
Henderson, Joseph W, 1957, Jl 26,19:2
Henderson, Julia W Mrs, 1941, Ap 2,23:5
Henderson, Justin, 1942, Mr 1,44:4
Henderson, Kenneth A, 1950, Ja 2,23:5
Henderson, Laura Mrs, 1944, N 30,23:3
Henderson, Laurence E, 1966, Ag 6,23:2
Henderson, Lawrence J, 1942, F 11,21:3
Henderson, Lord of Ardwick (J Henderson), 1950, F 27,19:1
Henderson, Lucie A, 1953, S 1,24:4
Henderson, Lucien, 1967, S 23,31:5
Henderson, Lucius J, 1947, F 19,25:1
Henderson, Luis M, 1950, D 7,35:5
Henderson, Luther L Sr Mrs, 1966, O 22,31:1
Henderson, Luther Mrs, 1967, Je 7,51:6
Henderson, Martha, 1912, Je 3,9:5
Henderson, Melvin, 1954, Je 19,15:5
Henderson, Mildred K, 1952, Mr 10,21:6
Henderson, Nora, 1949, Mr 24,28:3
Henderson, Norman P, 1963, Ap 1,27:3
Henderson, Oren V, 1951, S 4,27:4
Henderson, Parker A, 1925, Jl 27,13:3
Henderson, Paul, 1951, D 20,32:2
Henderson, Paul G, 1950, Je 1,27:5
Henderson, Peter, 1944, Ja 15,13:6; 1946, Jl 6,15:6
Henderson, Peter H, 1953, Je 6,17:3
Henderson, Phil E, 1955, Ap 27,31:4
Henderson, Ralph M, 1952, D 18,29:5; 1958, Ap 6,88:3
Henderson, Ralph S, 1966, D 2,39:3
Henderson, Ralph W, 1957, Je 21,25:3
Henderson, Randell, 1955, My 10,29:2
Henderson, Randolph R, 1966, O 20,43:5
Henderson, Reed, 1964, My 23,23:3
Henderson, Reginald Sir, 1939, My 3,23:3
Henderson, Richard, 1961, My 30,17:2
Henderson, Robert, 1942, F 18,19:5; 1956, F 7,31:2; 1965, My 22,31:4; 1966, My 31,43:4
Henderson, Robert B, 1940, My 15,25:3
Henderson, Robert E, 1960, Ja 15,31:4
Henderson, Robert J, 1953, Mr 31,31:1
Henderson, Robert M Gen, 1906, Ja 30,9:6
Henderson, Robert V, 1961, N 20,31:6
Henderson, Robert W, 1955, D 29,23:1
Henderson, Russell S, 1961, Ag 27,85:2
Henderson, Samuel J, 1942, O 18,52:3
Henderson, Samuel Mrs, 1952, N 23,89:1
Henderson, Stuart A, 1945, F 18,34:3
Henderson, Thomas, 1955, F 23,27:2
Henderson, Thomas B G, 1946, Ja 1,27:2
Henderson, Thomas J Gen, 1911, F 7,9:4
Henderson, Thomas Mrs, 1950, Jl 14,21:5
Henderson, Thomas P, 1966, Mr 22,41:1
Henderson, Thomas S, 1959, Ap 19,86:4
Henderson, Thomas T, 1954, Mr 27,17:3
Henderson, Varnum S, 1953, Je 9,14:6
Henderson, Victor, 1949, My 11,29:3
Henderson, Virginia, 1952, Jl 17,23:4
Henderson, W K (por), 1945, My 30,19:3
Henderson, Walter B, 1939, Jl 11,19:6
Henderson, Walter B Mrs, 1952, N 28,26:5
Henderson, Walter C, 1947, Ja 2,27:4
Henderson, Walter G, 1938, Mr 24,23:5
Henderson, Walter Mrs, 1949, S 23,24:3
Henderson, Washington, 1903, O 3,9:6
Henderson, Will I, 1960, Ag 29,25:1
Henderson, Will I Mrs, 1946, S 26,25:1
Henderson, William, 1907, My 7,9:6; 1942, F 13,21:2
Henderson, William D, 1944, My 27,15:7
Henderson, William E Mrs, 1944, D 26,19:2
Henderson, William G, 1956, Jl 30,21:4
Henderson, William H, 1961, S 28,41:4
Henderson, William J, 1945, My 11,19:5; 1948, S 25, 17:4; 1951, Mr 27,29:2
Henderson, William Mrs, 1949, N 5,13:4
Henderson, William P Mrs, 1949, Jl 19,30:3
Henderson, William R, 1948, Mr 27,13:6
Henderson, Yandell (por), 1944, F 20,36:1
Hendery, Robert J, 1956, Je 4,29:4
Hendey, Alfred E, 1940, Mr 9,15:2
Hendler, L Manuel, 1962, Ap 13,35:4
Hendler, Michael, 1952, Je 9,23:4
Hendon, George A, 1941, O 27,17:2
Hendren, Benjamin F, 1958, Ap 6,88:3
Hendren, Paul, 1957, D 1,88:3
Hendrian, Aug W, 1940, F 22,23:3
Hendrian, Otto A, 1956, Je 24,76:8
Hendrick, Albert C, 1912, F 7,11:3
Hendrick, Arthur C, 1940, Ag 3,15:6
Hendrick, Burton J (por), 1949, Mr 25,23:1
Hendrick, Charles C Dr, 1918, Je 27,11:6
Hendrick, Charles O, 1944, S 25,17:4
Hendrick, E, 1930, O 30,25:1
Hendrick, Ellwood Mrs, 1962, O 2,39:2
Hendrick, Frank E, 1951, My 26,17:4
Hendrick, Frank J, 1919, D 21,22:4
Hendrick, George B, 1938, Ap 1,23:5
Hendrick, Harold E, 1946, Ja 27,42:3
Hendrick, Harvey, 1941, O 30,23:5
Hendrick, Hugh L, 1950, Jl 27,25:4
Hendrick, Katherine, 1911, Je 27,9:5
Hendrick, Michael J, 1922, S 10,28:3
Hendrick, Roe L, 1939, Ag 9,17:2
Hendrick, T A Bp, 1909, D 1,9:5
Hendrick, Wallace M, 1956, Ja 29,92:6
Hendrick, William A Mrs, 1964, Je 10,45:4
Hendricks, A R, 1939, F 18,15:2
Hendricks, Abraham H, 1942, S 10,27:4
Hendricks, Charles, 1949, Mr 8,25:4
Hendricks, Dudley C, 1942, F 5,21:5
Hendricks, Edmund, 1909, O 28,9:3
Hendricks, Eldo L, 1938, N 24,27:3
Hendricks, Elwood B, 1955, F 4,21:2
Hendricks, Francis, 1920, Je 10,11:5
Hendricks, H H Mrs, 1954, My 28,23:5
Hendricks, Helene E Mrs, 1939, Ag 25,15:4
Hendricks, Henry H, 1904, My 28,9:5
Hendricks, Henry S, 1959, Mr 15,88:8
Hendricks, Isabelle F C Mrs, 1940, Ja 12,17:1
Hendricks, J, 1877, Ja 8,5:5
Hendricks, Jane T Mrs, 1874, F 3,2:3
Hendricks, John B, 1949, F 27,69:2
Hendricks, John C, 1943, My 14,20:3
Hendricks, John Mrs, 1947, Jl 27,44:7
Hendricks, John T, 1949, Ag 30,27:3
Hendricks, Oliver G (por), 1948, Mr 21,60:4
Hendricks, Peter H S, 1951, Mr 1,27:2
Hendricks, Rodger, 1961, Ap 1,17:4
Hendricks, Rowena, 1939, Ja 10,19:3
Hendricks, Samuel E (por), 1939, Jl 29,15:6
Hendricks, Simon J, 1938, Ja 18,23:5
Hendricks, T A, 1933, N 20,16:1
Hendricks, T A Vice-Pres, 1885, N 26,1:1
Hendricks, Thomas A Mrs, 1903, N 4,9:6
Hendricks, Thomas G, 1946, Jl 10,23:5
Hendricks, William L, 1951, My 30,21:3
Hendricks, William R, 1953, O 14,29:3
Hendricks, William W, 1943, D 2,27:2
Hendricksen, James J, 1943, Mr 28,24:6
Hendrickson, Albert, 1952, Ja 8,27:1
Hendrickson, Albert J, 1955, Ja 10,23:4
Hendrickson, Albert W, 1951, Ap 18,31:3
Hendrickson, Arthur Ward, 1968, My 13,43:2
Hendrickson, Catherine Mrs, 1937, Jl 3,15:6
Hendrickson, Charles E, 1937, Je 24,25:5
Hendrickson, Charles E Ex-Judge, 1919, Jl 23,10:3
Hendrickson, Edmund H Mrs, 1956, Jl 17,23:4
Hendrickson, Elizabeth Mrs, 1939, F 12,44:5
Hendrickson, Finley C, 1940, N 25,17:4
Hendrickson, Frank F, 1940, S 20,23:5
Hendrickson, George E, 1963, S 1,56:5
Hendrickson, George L, 1963, D 19,33:1
Hendrickson, Glenn H, 1962, Jl 23,21:2
Hendrickson, Harold A, 1962, Ja 31,31:3
Hendrickson, Harold W, 1954, D 5,89:2
Hendrickson, Harry, 1953, Mr 19,29:4
Hendrickson, Harry M, 1942, D 17,29:4
Hendrickson, Harry W, 1943, Ag 12,19:4
Hendrickson, Herbert, 1903, Je 12,16:2
Hendrickson, Herbert E, 1939, My 9,23:2
Hendrickson, Howard, 1943, My 19,25:4
Hendrickson, Irwin S, 1946, Je 3,21:4
Hendrickson, James, 1949, Ag 7,60:5

Hendrickson, James G, 1937, N 27,17:4
Hendrickson, James Mrs (C Bruce), 1959, Ap 6,27:4
Hendrickson, John B, 1959, My 3,87:2
Hendrickson, John H, 1963, My 1,39:1
Hendrickson, Joseph A, 1945, Mr 30,15:3
Hendrickson, Judson C, 1939, S 16,17:4
Hendrickson, Nathaniel C, 1940, My 16,23:2
Hendrickson, Ralph S, 1939, O 21,15:2
Hendrickson, Reba C, 1924, D 25,17:4
Hendrickson, Robert C, 1964, D 8,45:1
Hendrickson, Roy T, 1968, N 4,47:4
Hendrickson, Skidmore Dr, 1917, S 1,7:3
Hendrickson, Susanna E Mrs, 1948, Ap 26,23:4
Hendrickson, Warren V, 1938, Ap 15,19:3
Hendrickson, William D, 1947, Ag 2,13:3
Hendrickson, William H Rev, 1920, D 25,7:6
Hendrickson, William W Rear-Adm, 1920, Je 2,11:4
Hendrie, George M, 1942, N 29,65:1
Hendrie, Gideon F, 1938, My 8,II,6:5
Hendrie, John Mrs, 1944, O 24,23:2
Hendrie, John Sir, 1923, Jl 18,15:4
Hendrie, Mabel L, 1959, Mr 25,35:1
Hendrix, Andrew B, 1907, My 11,7:2
Hendrix, Claude R, 1944, Mr 23,19:3
Hendrix, Clifford R, 1953, My 9,19:5
Hendrix, Haile, 1953, Ag 13,25:1
Hendrix, Joseph C, 1904, N 9,5:7
Hendrix, Minnie E Mrs, 1938, Je 7,23:1
Hendrix, Stafford, 1953, Ja 13,29:2
Hendrix, Stafford Mrs, 1957, Ja 24,29:2
Hendrix, Wilbur F, 1939, Je 29,23:4
Hendrixson, Charles E, 1951, N 2,23:3
Hendrixson, John E, 1949, O 9,94:4
Hendrixson, Walter S Mrs, 1950, My 8,23:3
Hendrixson, Walter Scott Prof, 1925, Jl 2,19:6
Hendron, Frank T, 1943, O 16,13:3
Hendron, James J, 1943, Je 29,19:4
Hendry, Charles, 1944, My 4,19:3
Hendry, Charles Sr, 1941, Jl 18,19:5
Hendry, Charles W Mrs, 1947, Jl 4,13:6
Hendry, David Mrs, 1944, Jl 27,17:3
Hendry, George B Capt, 1937, F 22,17:3
Hendry, Hugh Campbell Dr, 1911, Ja 30,9:4
Hendry, John W, 1957, Ap 19,21:3
Hendry, Robert S, 1957, My 3,27:2
Hendson, Nethro, 1939, Ag 4,18:7
Hendy, James C, 1961, Ja 16,27:5
Heneage, George J A, 1940, N 8,21:3
Heneage, Harry R, 1950, S 3,38:3
Heneage, Henry G Lord, 1954, Ja 27,27:3
Heneault, Maurice G, 1944, Jl 16,31:1
Heneberger, Andrew E, 1948, D 9,33:3
Henebry, John J, 1951, Je 15,23:3
Henegan, James F, 1954, S 28,29:2
Heneker, William Sir, 1939, My 25,26:4
Henel, John, 1941, Jl 15,20:3
Henel, John Mrs, 1947, Je 24,23:4
Henes, William, 1940, O 9,25:2
Henessey, Ellen T, 1944, My 24,19:6
Henessy, James, 1950, My 12,27:5
Henessy, William J Mrs, 1950, F 1,29:4
Heney, Charles F Mrs, 1945, O 2,23:5
Heney, Charles Mrs, 1908, Ja 15,9:6
Heney, Francis J (por), 1937, N 1,21:3
Heney, Francis J Mrs, 1911, Ja 27,11:5
Heney, John P, 1967, N 13,47:3
Hengel Muller von Hengervar, Ladislas Baron, 1917, Ap 27,11:4
Hengell, H C Rev, 1937, My 21,21:4
Hengerer, Julius, 1944, Mr 22,19:1
Hengerer, Julius Mrs, 1958, S 27,21:5
Hengler, May, 1952, Mr 18,27:3
Hengsbach, Curt F J, 1952, Je 17,27:4
Hengstenberg, E W Dr, 1869, Je 4,5:4
Hengstenberg, Hugh H, 1958, Mr 30,88:6
Hengstenberg, William, 1951, Jl 7,13:5
Henican, Joseph P Jr, 1963, Mr 12,7:8
Henick, Bernard Mrs, 1957, S 30,31:5
Henie, Selma Mrs, 1961, Ag 15,29:5
Henie, Wilhelm, 1937, My 11,25:3
Henig, Jacob, 1955, D 2,27:4
Henigan, James P, 1950, F 28,29:3
Henin, Benjamin L A, 1946, D 1,78:5
Hening, Crawford D, 1944, Mr 2,17:1
Hening, James C, 1955, F 19,15:5
Henion, David Mrs, 1950, Ap 10,19:4
Henion, Herbert E, 1966, F 1,31:3
Heniot, Hans L, 1960, S 21,32:3
Henius, Henry, 1962, Jl 5,3:1
Henius, Lillian M Mrs, 1925, Mr 31,19:3
Henius, M, 1935, N 16,15:3
Henjes, Gerd H, 1943, S 24,23:4
Henke, Cresense, 1951, F 6,27:4
Henke, Gustav A, 1953, Mr 18,31:2
Henke, Kenneth A, 1967, Ag 13,80:8
Henke, Robert C Mrs, 1956, Ja 4,27:4
Henke, Warren J, 1957, O 16,32:3
Henkel, August H, 1961, Mr 15,39:1
Henkel, George, 1903, N 1,7:6
Henkel, George E, 1950, Ag 24,27:5
Henkel, Myron F, 1947, N 12,27:4
Henkel, Paul, 1957, Ag 27,29:2
Henkel, Richard V, 1954, S 5,51:2
Henkel, William, 1919, Mr 29,13:4
Henken, Charles H, 1951, Ja 10,27:2
Henker, Bruno, 1948, S 10,23:4
Henkes, Frederick, 1941, S 1,15:5
Henkin, Charles L Dr, 1937, D 20,27:3
Henkin, Leo J, 1952, S 5,27:5
Henkle, Charles Z, 1949, O 4,27:3
Henkle, James R, 1940, F 8,23:4
Henkle, Manuel Mrs, 1946, N 21,31:1
Henkle, Orvis T, 1956, D 18,31:5
Henkle, Thomas H, 1948, My 22,15:4
Henle, Frederic, 1885, My 20,5:4
Henle, Frederick S, 1953, N 1,86:7
Henlein, Elmer C, 1953, Mr 9,29:3
Henlein, Paul L, 1952, F 29,23:2
Henley, Charles D, 1947, Mr 26,25:4
Henley, Frances E, 1955, My 16,23:2
Henley, Hobart, 1964, My 23,23:2
Henley, J W, 1884, D 10,5:4
Henley, John H, 1950, Mr 24,25:3
Henley, Lloyd W, 1925, N 28,15:5
Henley, Norman W, 1946, Jl 16,24:2
Henley, Reuben H, 1940, F 17,13:2
Henley, William Ernest, 1903, Jl 13,7:4
Henley, William J, 1946, Jl 9,21:4
Henley, William O, 1957, D 17,35:3
Henline, Ralph G, 1949, D 10,17:3
Henline, Roy B (por), 1949, My 24,27:3
Henline, Walter J (Butch), 1957, O 10,33:1
Henly, James Mrs, 1959, Ap 7,33:1
Henly, Neil O, 1944, Mr 16,19:2
Henn, Frederick C, 1945, Ja 12,15:5
Henn, Ida, 1950, My 25,29:5
Henn, John, 1942, Mr 5,23:3
Henn, Peter Rev, 1937, O 12,25:4
Henn, Thomas J, 1945, Ja 12,15:2
Henna, David J, 1949, O 15,15:2
Henna, J Julio Dr, 1924, F 3,23:1
Hennan, Clarence W, 1956, Mr 1,33:2
Henne, Ernest L, 1940, Ja 25,21:4
Henneberg, Otto, 1951, S 21,24:3
Henneberg, Siegfried G, 1946, Mr 28,25:2
Henneberg, Victor H, 1961, Je 15,43:4
Henneberg, Willy, 1961, S 18,29:4
Henneberger, Barbi (Barbara Marie), 1964, Ap 13, 3:2
Henneberger, Herman Col, 1924, Ap 30,19:2
Henneberry, Michael, 1950, Ag 27,89:3
Hennebert, Victor E, 1947, D 3,29:2
Hennefield, Norman, 1960, Mr 11,25:3
Hennefrund, Henry, 1963, Ag 21,33:2
Hennegan, William A, 1955, Ap 22,25:5
Hennekens, Adolfo, 1952, Ap 6,91:4
Hennell, Herman, 1957, Jl 3,23:5
Hennelly, George A, 1950, Ja 27,23:3
Henneman, Harry E, 1960, Mr 8,33:4
Henneman, John Bell Dr, 1908, N 28,9:5
Hennemann, Charles E, 1938, Je 24,19:4
Hennemann, Francis, 1951, Ja 18,27:1
Hennen, William D, 1941, F 1,17:5
Hennequin, Alfred Dr, 1914, My 2,9:6
Henner, Irving, 1962, Je 4,29:5
Hennesey, Joseph F, 1939, D 2,17:3
Hennesey, William A, 1942, Ja 16,22:4
Henness, Robert, 1948, Ag 4,22:2
Hennessey, Alphonsus R Mrs, 1945, Mr 1,21:3
Hennessey, Edward F, 1940, Ag 8,19:4
Hennessey, Eugene, 1948, Ag 4,21:2
Hennessey, Francis D, 1958, F 27,27:3
Hennessey, Frank C, 1941, N 11,14:3
Hennessey, Frank E, 1945, Ja 13,11:6
Hennessey, George B, 1940, D 29,24:7
Hennessey, J Joseph, 1956, Mr 9,23:2
Hennessey, James, 1955, N 26,19:4
Hennessey, James A Mrs, 1951, Je 15,24:2
Hennessey, John, 1938, Ap 19,21:4
Hennessey, John J, 1938, S 28,25:2; 1945, S 3,23:2
Hennessey, John P, 1953, My 3,88:7
Hennessey, John Sir, 1891, O 8,4:7
Hennessey, Joseph J Mrs, 1960, My 6,31:2
Hennessey, Joseph L, 1950, Ja 26,28:2
Hennessey, Katherine, 1953, D 12,14:6
Hennessey, Michael J, 1940, D 2,23:4
Hennessey, Philip J Jr, 1965, Ap 5,31:5
Hennessey, Raymond F, 1957, D 20,24:3
Hennessey, Raymond G Mrs, 1967, O 4,51:3
Hennessey, Richard J Judge, 1937, F 4,21:2
Hennessey, Robert J, 1940, D 12,27:4
Hennessey, Walter H, 1954, Mr 8,27:3
Hennessey, William H Jr, 1955, Ja 27,23:4
Hennessey, William J, 1946, N 10,63:6
Hennessy, A A, 1920, Mr 11,11:5
Hennessy, Daniel F, 1937, N 21,II,9:2
Hennessy, Daniel J, 1959, D 24,20:2
Hennessy, David B, 1947, Ag 26,23:4
Hennessy, David J, 1941, F 1,17:5
Hennessy, Dennis F, 1950, Ag 31,25:5
Hennessy, Edward, 1943, Jl 1,19:3
Hennessy, Forbes J, 1916, Ja 1,11:6
Hennessy, Frank, 1947, O 30,25:2
Hennessy, George R J (Lord Windlesham), 1953, O 10,17:6
Hennessy, Helen M, 1953, Jl 22,27:6
Hennessy, James J, 1961, Ja 30,23:3
Hennessy, James S, 1874, My 8,8:4
Hennessy, John, 1875, O 24,6:6
Hennessy, John A, 1951, Ap 23,25:1
Hennessy, John A Mrs, 1944, Mr 21,19:2
Hennessy, John Collins, 1903, D 16,9:4
Hennessy, John F, 1951, Ja 19,25:4
Hennessy, John F Mrs, 1961, Je 27,33:5
Hennessy, John J, 1951, Je 8,27:5
Hennessy, John L, 1955, Jl 3,33:1
Hennessy, Joseph R, 1958, Ag 3,81:2
Hennessy, Michael E, 1955, My 14,19:4
Hennessy, Raymond, 1965, S 27,3:5
Hennessy, Robert J, 1962, N 27,37:1
Hennessy, Roland B, 1939, F 3,15:5
Hennessy, Simon, 1946, Ag 20,27:3
Hennessy, Simone B, 1949, O 29,3:3
Hennessy, Sophia R Mrs, 1921, F 5,11:4
Hennessy, Thomas F, 1954, My 20,31:5
Hennessy, Wilfrid A, 1944, Ja 10,17:5
Hennessy, William Capt, 1912, N 30,13:3
Hennessy, William J, 1945, Ag 21,21:4
Hennessy, William P, 1947, My 27,26:2
Hennessy, William T, 1962, Jl 27,25:5
Hennesy, James P, 1949, My 17,25:1; 1953, My 3,88:2
Henneuse, Clarence A, 1939, Ja 6,21:6
Henney, John L W, 1950, Ap 15,15:2
Henni, J M Archbishop, 1881, S 8,5:4
Hennig, Boniface, 1945, Ja 25,19:3
Hennig, Gerhart R, 1965, Ap 5,31:5
Hennig, Otto C Mrs, 1946, My 16,21:2
Hennigan, William S, 1942, Jl 6,15:4
Hennigar, William E, 1945, F 21,19:2
Henniger, Henry Mrs, 1950, Mr 8,25:3
Hennigh, Mary E Mrs, 1941, Je 4,23:3
Hennighan, John J Mrs, 1954, D 14,33:3
Hennighausen, Louis P, 1918, F 3,15:2
Hennigson, Eugene, 1955, O 10,27:4
Hennihan, James W, 1951, D 4,33:1
Henniker, Arthur Mrs, 1923, Ap 5,19:6
Henniker, Lord, 1902, Je 28,9:6
Henning, A F, 1938, F 2,19:4
Henning, Adolph, 1940, N 24,49:2
Henning, Andrew B, 1944, Je 14,19:5
Henning, Arthur F, 1965, Ap 2,35:3
Henning, Charles A mrs, 1958, Je 5,31:3
Henning, Clarence I B, 1939, Ja 27,19:1
Henning, Cotton, 1948, D 10,26:2
Henning, E R, 1949, Je 1,31:5
Henning, Elbert H, 1946, N 4,25:4
Henning, George, 1942, F 3,19:5
Henning, Gustavus C, 1911, Ja 1,11:2
Henning, Harry W, 1955, N 19,19:6
Henning, Holcombe M, 1961, Ja 17,37:1
Henning, Hugo, 1941, Ja 27,15:2
Henning, Jay, 1940, Ja 8,15:5
Henning, John L, 1914, Ap 23,13:4
Henning, Joseph Rev, 1912, Jl 4,7:5
Henning, Mary S Mrs, 1941, D 12,25:3
Henning, Thomas I, 1949, Ja 9,73:1
Henning, Valentine, 1958, N 7,28:2
Henning, William J, 1938, O 25,23:4
Henninge, Margaret E, 1947, Mr 29,15:4
Henninger, Albert E, 1960, Ap 21,31:2
Henninger, Charles H, 1948, F 20,28:2
Henninger, Herman, 1961, My 16,43:1
Henninger, John H, 1950, Mr 27,23:5
Henninger, Otto, 1939, Ag 5,15:5
Hennings, Betty, 1939, O 27,23:4
Hennings, Ivar, 1950, N 12,92:6
Hennings, Thomas C Jr (funl, S 17,23:6; will, S 21,-18:8), 1960, S 14,1:1
Henningsen, C T Gen, 1877, Je 15,4:5
Henningsen, George E, 1943, Ag 10,19:5
Henningsen, George W, 1945, Ja 30,19:1
Hennion, Foster C, 1940, Ag 3,17:3
Hennion, John A, 1946, Ag 9,17:6
Hennion, John F, 1961, Mr 19,43:1
Hennock, Frieda (Mrs W H Simons), 1960, Je 21, 33:4
Hennrich, Kilian J, 1946, N 24,79:3
Hennson, Celestin, 1915, Mr 15,11:5
Henoch, Hanley, 1967, My 13,33:5
Henoch, Phillip Mrs, 1953, Ja 26,19:4
Henop, Louis Philip, 1918, Je 29,11:5
Henri, Duke of Parma, 1939, My 11,25:6
Henri, R, 1929, Jl 13,15:3
Henrich, Anthony G, 1962, Ap 28,25:5
Henrich, Anthony G Mrs, 1962, F 4,82:3
Henrich, John B, 1942, N 28,13:5
Henrich, John S, 1950, Jl 11,31:1
Henrich, Nicholas C, 1941, N 8,19:2
Henrich, Robert, 1966, Mr 3,33:5
Henrici, Harry H, 1938, Mr 25,19:4
Henricks, Arthur P, 1965, D 18,29:3
Henricks, George C, 1947, Ja 11,19:6
Henricks, Harold H, 1955, N 21,29:4
Henrickson, Fritz, 1941, Ap 1,23:2
Henrickson, Jacob T Mrs, 1953, My 20,29:2
Henricot, Fernand Mrs, 1945, Ja 29,13:1
Henrie, Eugene Francois Marie (Duke of Harcourt), 1908, My 18,7:5
Henrie, Harrison C, 1948, Ap 25,68:7

Henriette, Elizabeth Princess, 1917, O 20,13:4
Henriksen, Arthur L, 1962, Ag 28,31:2
Henriksen, Gustav, 1939, O 9,19:4
Henrikson, Carl Mrs, 1939, Jl 20,19:2
Henriod, Alfredo, 1942, Ja 5,20:2
Henriot, Emile, 1961, Ap 16,86:3
Henriques, Alida M, 1942, My 18,15:4
Henriques, Arthur Alberto de Campos, 1922, N 9,19:4
Henriques, Basil, 1961, D 3,88:3
Henriques, Clarence A, 1917, Je 9,11:5
Henriques, D M (funl, Se 4,5:2), 1875, S 2,4:5
Henriques, George, 1873, Ja 21,2:7
Henriques, George C, 1945, F 4,38:6
Henriques, Henry A Dr, 1921, Ag 20,7:7
Henriques, Henry Straus Quixano, 1925, N 14,15:4
Henriques, Mae A, 1951, Ap 11,29:3
Henriques, O K, 1951, Ja 26,23:2
Henriques, Vernon C, 1949, D 9,31:5
Henriques, William H, 1950, Mr 11,15:3
Henriquez, Angela Mrs, 1937, Je 22,14:4
Henriquez, Carlos, 1943, Je 10,21:3
Henriquez, Haim C, 1942, O 2,25:3
Henriquez, Philip L, 1943, Mr 18,19:3
Henriquez y Carvajal, Federico (trb lr, F 26,26:7,, 1952, F 22,21:5
Henrotin, Charles, 1914, Jl 26,5:6
Henrotin, Charles Mrs, 1922, Je 30,17:6
Henrotin, Edward, 1945, Jl 31,19:4
Henrotin, Fernand Dr, 1906, D 10,7:5
Henrotin, Frederick F, 1963, O 3,35:5
Henrotin, Mabel Mrs, 1925, Jl 17,15:5
Henrotin, Norris B, 1962, My 15,39:4
Henry, A, 1883, D 7,2:2; 1934, Je 5,23:2
Henry, Albert W, 1948, N 9,27:5
Henry, Alex E, 1941, Ja 1,23:4
Henry, Alexander Dr, 1925, Jl 16,9:3
Henry, Alexander Jr, 1946, Ja 2,19:1
Henry, Alfred, 1953, Ja 23,19:4
Henry, Alfred E, 1952, Ja 22,29:1
Henry, Alfred P, 1948, F 7,15:4
Henry, Ambrose D (por), 1939, Mr 2,21:4
Henry, Arthur J, 1955, Ap 19,31:4
Henry, Arthur J Mrs, 1945, S 25,25:1
Henry, Arthur L C, 1941, Jl 11,15:6
Henry, Arthur Mrs, 1956, S 3,13:4
Henry, Arthur W, 1947, N 4,26:2
Henry, Barklie M, 1966, S 6,47:1
Henry, Baron Thring, 1907, F 6,9:6
Henry, Beulah W Mrs, 1939, S 11,19:3
Henry, Bower, 1939, Ap 21,23:5
Henry, C Lady, 1927, My 12,27:5
Henry, Charles A, 1942, Jl 4,17:4; 1943, N 16,23:1
Henry, Charles D, 1943, Mr 25,21:4
Henry, Charles E, 1939, Ja 28,15:5
Henry, Charles F, 1955, Je 9,29:3
Henry, Charles J, 1914, Ag 31,7:6
Henry, Charles K P, 1949, S 16,28:2
Henry, Charles L, 1939, Mr 27,16:2
Henry, Charles Solomon Sir, 1919, D 28,23:3
Henry, Charles V, 1957, D 11,31:2
Henry, Charles W, 1946, Jl 29,14:6
Henry, Chester C, 1953, S 17,29:2
Henry, Clara H, 1957, Jl 16,25:2
Henry, Clare M, 1953, O 27,27:4
Henry, Clement S, 1944, My 1,15:5
Henry, Clifford West, 1921, F 10,7:4
Henry, Cowden T, 1952, Ag 20,25:4
Henry, Cyril Lt, 1916, Ap 15,13:3
Henry, Daniel W, 1939, F 26,39:3
Henry, David, 1946, D 4,31:1
Henry, David H Mrs, 1941, S 25,25:6
Henry, David W, 1949, Ap 13,29:3; 1955, O 13,31:2
Henry, Dayton M, 1962, N 28,39:5
Henry, Denis Stanislaus, 1925, O 2,23:6
Henry, Dewitt P, 1946, Jl 11,23:1
Henry, Dominick, 1942, F 1,42:1
Henry, Dominick Mrs, 1938, F 25,17:3
Henry, Dorothy D, 1958, Je 2,27:4
Henry, Duke of Mecklenburg, 1942, N 5,25:2
Henry, E R Mrs, 1875, O 3,7:2
Henry, E Schermerhorn, 1904, O 27,9:5
Henry, E Sir, 1931, F 21,17:3
Henry, Earle F, 1941, Jl 12,13:1
Henry, Edmond Winston, 1872, O 20,3:2
Henry, Edward M, 1940, D 1,62:2
Henry, Edward M Gen, 1905, Je 22,9:6
Henry, Edward W, 1942, Jl 18,13:4; 1946, F 4,25:5
Henry, Fannie E, 1937, S 29,23:3
Henry, Francis J, 1953, Ja 26,19:4
Henry, Francis M, 1937, S 26,II,8:4
Henry, Frank, 1968, Ap 15,54:3
Henry, Frank C Mrs, 1959, Ag 27,27:5
Henry, Frank F, 1961, F 24,29:2
Henry, Frank F (est tax appr), 1962, Ag 22,22:2
Henry, Frank G, 1959, Ja 22,31:4
Henry, Frank H, 1951, O 22,23:4
Henry, Frank M, 1947, F 19,25:5
Henry, Frederick A, 1949, Ja 16,68:3
Henry, Frederick E, 1950, S 6,29:3
Henry, Frederick W, 1944, Ap 12,21:5
Henry, George K G, 1941, Mr 23,45:2
Henry, George Mrs, 1952, Ag 30,13:5
Henry, George S, 1958, S 3,33:2
Henry, George W, 1964, My 24,92:6
Henry, Goodwin Mrs, 1950, F 2,27:5
Henry, Guy V, 1967, D 4,47:1
Henry, Guy V Gen, 1899, O 28,7:5
Henry, H Ashton Rev, 1920, Mr 6,11:5
Henry, Harold J, 1947, O 12,76:3
Henry, Harrison H, 1962, Ap 23,29:5
Henry, Harry S, 1909, Je 25,9:5
Henry, Heloise L Mrs, 1940, F 28,21:1
Henry, Henry C Jr, 1951, Mr 8,31:5
Henry, Herbert, 1951, S 8,17:3
Henry, Hiram P Col, 1920, Ja 31,11:4
Henry, Howard H, 1917, Ap 1,19:2
Henry, Howard H Mrs, 1924, N 15,13:5
Henry, Howard K, 1953, Jl 6,17:5
Henry, Howard R L, 1955, Je 14,29:3
Henry, Hugh C, 1945, O 15,17:6
Henry, Hugh R, 1946, Ag 10,13:3
Henry, Hugh T, 1946, Mr 13,29:2
Henry, Huntington B, 1954, Ja 28,27:4
Henry, Ira W, 1940, Ap 26,21:2
Henry, J B Mrs, 1878, D 14,8:3
Henry, J Fred, 1952, Ag 8,17:3
Henry, J Norman (por), 1938, O 5,23:1
Henry, J Norman Mrs, 1967, Ap 19,45:2
Henry, J Prof (see also My 14), 1878, My 17,5:6
Henry, J W, 1902, D 13,9:6
Henry, Jacob S, 1958, Ag 12,29:5
Henry, James, 1879, Ag 12,8:4
Henry, James (por), 1949, Mr 10,27:4
Henry, James B, 1938, S 1,23:3
Henry, James E, 1959, F 11,39:4
Henry, James M, 1958, D 29,15:4
Henry, James R, 1950, My 15,21:5
Henry, James T, 1951, Jl 8,61:2
Henry, Jay, 1951, D 25,31:4
Henry, Jennie A Mrs, 1952, S 28,77:2
Henry, John, 1874, My 21,9:1; 1902, Ag 17,1:6; 1948, S 12,72:1
Henry, John B, 1947, Je 4,27:2
Henry, John C Rev, 1909, O 6,9:3
Henry, John E, 1949, F 15,23:2
Henry, John F, 1944, My 13,19:3
Henry, John F R, 1954, Ag 3,19:3
Henry, John G, 1941, Ja 20,17:5
Henry, John J, 1939, Mr 30,23:4; 1958, Jl 22,27:4; 1962, Ja 9,16:6
Henry, John J Capt, 1918, D 29,18:8
Henry, John M, 1939, Je 12,17:3
Henry, John P, 1947, O 1,29:3
Henry, John R, 1949, O 17,23:3
Henry, John S, 1954, S 18,15:6
Henry, John T, 1941, N 25,37:5; 1943, Je 12,13:3
Henry, Jones E, 1940, S 25,27:6
Henry, Joseph C, 1954, F 10,29:3
Henry, Joseph V, 1949, Ja 13,23:5
Henry, Joseph W, 1942, Mr 3,24:3
Henry, Joshua J, 1868, S 19,4:7
Henry, Jules, 1941, Je 11,21:5
Henry, Julius, 1907, Je 3,7:5
Henry, Leigh V, 1958, Mr 12,31:4
Henry, Leland Boyd Rev Dr, 1968, S 1,53:2
Henry, Leo S, 1947, Ag 14,23:3
Henry, Lewis, 1941, Jl 24,17:6
Henry, Lewis C, 1959, My 25,29:4
Henry, Lindsay R, 1959, Je 17,35:3
Henry, Lloyd G, 1951, Ag 7,25:5
Henry, Lyman H, 1945, D 14,28:3
Henry, Margaret A, 1947, Ja 14,25:5
Henry, Margaret Mrs, 1952, Ja 24,28:2
Henry, Martin P (por), 1955, D 7,39:4
Henry, Martin P Mrs, 1955, My 1,88:7
Henry, Maxwell, 1944, Ap 8,14:6
Henry, Melinger E (por), 1946, F 1,24:2
Henry, Michael J Rev, 1922, O 4,23:5
Henry, Morton J, 1945, Ap 20,19:3
Henry, Mrs, 1879, Ap 19,2:3
Henry, Nelson Herrick Maj-Gen, 1923, Mr 16,17:4
Henry, Noah, 1960, Je 7,35:5
Henry, P J Capt, 1865, My 28,6:5
Henry, P S, 1933, Ap 12,19:1
Henry, Patrick A, 1943, D 13,23:3
Henry, Patrick Capt, 1908, N 24,9:5
Henry, Paul, 1958, Ag 25,21:4
Henry, Paul A Sr, 1950, F 26,76:6
Henry, Peter J, 1948, D 31,15:2
Henry, Peyton J, 1952, Ap 4,25:4
Henry, Phil Mrs, 1948, Ag 5,21:5
Henry, Philip, 1968, D 7,20:1
Henry, Philip W, 1947, N 9,72:5
Henry, Philip W Mrs, 1946, Ja 13,44:2
Henry, Prince Consort of Netherlands, 1934, Jl 4,15:1
Henry, Prince of Prussia, 1929, Ap 21,26:1
Henry, Prince of the Netherlands, 1879, Ja 14,2:6
Henry, Raymond B, 1955, Jl 30,17:1
Henry, Rev Bro, 1919, F 9,20:5
Henry, Richard F, 1939, N 2,23:2
Henry, Richard M, 1946, Ja 4,21:1
Henry, Robert A C, 1962, Ja 3,33:1
Henry, Robert C, 1937, S 17,25:5
Henry, Robert E, 1955, O 24,27:4; 1957, Mr 17,87:1
Henry, Robert K, 1946, N 21,31:1
Henry, Robert L, 1920, Je 2,11:2
Henry, Roy J, 1958, Jl 8,27:1
Henry, Ryder Mrs, 1965, Ap 25,88:3
Henry, S F Mrs, 1879, Ap 11,3:4
Henry, S T, 1957, Mr 31,88:8
Henry, Samuel C, 1949, Ap 24,76:2
Henry, Sarah H Mrs, 1938, Je 7,23:2
Henry, Seton, 1946, O 13,59:3
Henry, Sheldon S, 1947, Ag 21,23:5
Henry, Sidney L, 1940, F 28,21:4
Henry, Sidney M, 1959, Mr 17,33:4
Henry, Simeon A, 1906, My 29,11:7
Henry, Sterling P, 1943, Mr 19,19:4
Henry, Stuart, 1953, F 18,31:5
Henry, T P, 1901, D 15,9:5
Henry, Taylor, 1964, My 12,37:5
Henry, Theodore R, 1944, Ap 19,23:3
Henry, Thomas, 1945, S 9,46:4
Henry, Thomas J, 1956, O 28,89:2
Henry, Thomas W, 1946, N 28,27:1
Henry, Victor, 1954, Ja 2,11:4
Henry, W, 1878, My 24,5:5
Henry, W Laird Sr, 1940, Jl 6,15:2
Henry, Walter H, 1954, O 7,23:5
Henry, Wilbur, 1952, F 8,23:3
Henry, William, 1947, Ap 7,23:4; 1948, Ap 8,25:6
Henry, William A, 1954, Mr 21,88:3
Henry, William E Mrs, 1949, D 15,35:5
Henry, William F Col, 1937, N 30,23:1
Henry, William L, 1955, N 1,31:4
Henry, William M, 1937, Je 15,23:4; 1941, Mr 16,45
Henry, William T Rev Dr, 1925, Je 27,11:6
Henry of Reuss, Prince, 1913, Mr 30,IV,7:5
Henry-Ruffin, Margaret E Mrs, 1941, F 20,19:1
Henryk, Henry J, 1952, S 22,23:3
Henrympa, David W, 1949, Ap 13,29:1
Henrys, Paul P, 1943, N 12,21:5
Henschel, Albert E, 1925, Ag 25,17:5
Henschel, Charles R, 1956, O 3,33:3
Henschel, David, 1955, Ag 19,19:2
Henschel, G, 1934, S 11,21:3
Henschel, Georg Mrs, 1901, N 7,2:6
Henschel, Herbert L, 1966, O 1,32:5
Henschel, Louis K, 1945, N 29,23:5
Henschel, Morris J Mrs, 1956, Ap 8,84:4
Henschel, Otto, 1961, Ag 28,25:5
Henschel, Sid W, 1968, O 19,37:5
Henschien, H Peter, 1959, F 14,21:1
Henschot, Ernest, 1961, Jl 1,17:1
Hensel, Charles, 1946, S 11,7:2
Hensel, Clarence H, 1960, F 14,82:6
Hensel, George W Jr, 1943, F 8,19:4
Hensel, Herman D Mrs, 1958, My 19,25:2
Hensel, John C, 1954, My 5,31:4
Hensel, Robert S, 1946, Mr 14,25:2
Hensel, Walter, 1963, D 21,11:7
Hensel, William, 1949, S 19,8:5
Hensel, William H, 1941, Ja 15,23:3
Henseleit, Herman J, 1949, F 26,15:2
Henseler, Bernard J, 1963, Ap 29,31:1
Hensen, Arthur, 1939, N 13,19:3
Henserson, John S Mrs, 1952, S 22,23:5
Hensey, Margaret E, 1956, S 18,35:5
Henshall, Joseph Alexander Dr, 1925, Ap 5,5:2
Henshaw, Arthur G Sr, 1944, Ag 16,19:3
Henshaw, Edward M, 1943, S 23,21:4
Henshaw, Franklin, 1942, D 8,25:1
Henshaw, Frederick V, 1941, Mr 24,17:5
Henshaw, George, 1952, O 22,27:4
Henshaw, George F Mrs, 1956, Ja 14,19:7
Henshaw, George H, 1937, O 13,23:1
Henshaw, Glen C, 1946, Ap 7,46:5
Henshaw, Jay I, 1943, D 4,13:2
Henshaw, John E, 1939, S 6,23:5
Henshaw, John H Sr, 1952, N 21,26:3
Henshaw, Julia W Mrs, 1937, N 21,II,9:3
Henshaw, Richard Mrs, 1952, Jl 16,25:4
Henshaw, Richard T (por), 1938, Ag 31,15:3
Henshaw, Robert H, 1937, Mr 12,24:3
Henshaw, Samuel, 1907, Jl 24,7:6; 1941, F 6,22:2
Henshaw, Samuel M, 1948, O 6,29:2
Henshaw, Sidney, 1941, S 12,21:4
Henshaw, Stanley, 1950, S 26,31:5
Henshaw, W T, 1949, Ap 17,76:3
Henshel, Otto C, 1950, S 12,27:3
Henshell, Edward H, 1951, Ja 7,76:4
Henshew, Thomas, 1914, Mr 4,11:6
Hensing, William O, 1946, O 26,17:4
Hensinger, Lester P, 1947, My 30,21:2
Henske, Andrew C, 1950, Jl 11,31:4
Hensle, Charles W, 1947, N 4,25:5
Hensler, E (Countess d'Edla), 1929, My 22,27:
Hensler, James R, 1953, S 13,85:1
Hensley, Harry C, 1951, Mr 13,31:1
Hensley, J B Sr, 1958, Jl 26,15:4
Hensley, Leighton, 1945, Ja 5,15:1
Hensley, Minor, 1950, My 31,2:6
Henson, Arthur J, 1941, D 1,19:4
Henson, George W, 1952, Ag 3,61:1
Henson, Henry B, 1940, D 29,24:7
Henson, Henry B Mrs, 1938, N 5,19:6
Henson, Herbert H (por), 1947, S 29,21:3
Henson, J Rev (Uncle Tom), 1883, My 6,1:7
Henson, Leslie, 1957, D 3,35:2

Henson, Llewellyn L Rev, 1937, Ag 27,19:3
Henson, Matthew A (Matt), 1955, Mr 10,27:4
Henson, Matthew Mrs (Matt), 1968, Mr 15,39:1
Henson, Philip Truman, 1968, Ja 11,37:2
Henson, Poindexter Smith Rev Dr, 1914, Ap 25,15:7
Henson, Swaney G, 1961, O 16,29:4
Henssel, Herman H, 1949, Je 23,27:4
Henstridge, Frederick T, 1958, Jl 16,29:1
Henszey, William P, 1909, Mr 24,9:3
Henton, H Benne, 1938, Jl 11,17:3
Hentsch, Max C, 1949, O 5,29:5
Henty, G A, 1902, N 17,9:5
Hentz, Frederick J, 1941, Jl 16,17:6
Hentz, George L, 1949, S 17,17:5
Hentz, Harry Leon, 1918, N 3,2:1
Hentz, Henry (funl, O 2,23:3), 1924, S 30,23:3
Hentz, Leonard S (will, Ja 20,29:5), 1949, Ja 8,15:2
Hentz, Mary R, 1943, Mr 14,25:2
Henwood, Abraham, 1938, Ja 10,17:4
Henwood, Berryman, 1955, Mr 8,27:2
Henwood, Hervey B, 1938, S 12,17:5
Henwood, William J, 1941, Je 19,21:4
Henze, Harry J, 1943, Mr 18,19:2
Henze, I Eleanor, 1952, S 30,31:3
Henze, Louis H J, 1938, Mr 28,15:2; 1967, O 27,45:3
Henze, William Joseph, 1910, Ja 28,9:4
Henzel, Norbet J, 1955, O 18,37:3
Hepbron, George T, 1946, My 1,25:2
Hepburn, A Barton (por), 1922, Ja 26,17:3
Hepburn, A Barton Mrs, 1956, Ag 16,25:3
Hepburn, Andrew Dousa Dr, 1921, F 15,9:5
Hepburn, Andrew H, 1967, Mr 2,35:2
Hepburn, Andrew H Mrs, 1948, Je 3,25:4
Hepburn, Arthur J, 1964, Je 1,29:2
Hepburn, Barton (will), 1955, O 16,83:3
Hepburn, Charles Fisher, 1923, S 19,9:6
Hepburn, Charles J, 1942, O 13,23:1
Hepburn, Emma J Mrs, 1941, Ja 4,13:4
Hepburn, Frederick T, 1956, Je 17,92:7
Hepburn, Glen, 1968, S 13,61:3
Hepburn, Henry Charles, 1912, O 10,11:4
Hepburn, James C Dr, 1911, S 22,11:5
Hepburn, James P, 1948, My 21,23:3
Hepburn, John, 1956, Mr 31,15:6
Hepburn, John T, 1956, Mr 2,23:3
Hepburn, Mitchell F, 1953, Ja 6,29:1
Hepburn, Nan K, 1937, Jl 4,II,7:3
Hepburn, Neil J Dr, 1918, My 28,13:8
Hepburn, Neil J Dr Mrs, 1903, Je 30,7:6
Hepburn, Robert G, 1953, D 29,23:1
Hepburn, Sarah Curtis, 1925, O 16,21:4
Hepburn, Thomas N, 1962, N 21,33:4
Hepburn, Thomas N Mrs, 1951, Mr 18,90:3
Hepburn, Thomas T 2d, 1954, Jl 8,25:3
Hepburn, W B R, 1939, F 24,19:5
Hepburn, William McG, 1960, F 29,27:1
Hepburn, William P, 1916, F 8,11:5
Hepburn, William P Mrs, 1961, Je 28,35:2
Hepenstal, George W, 1942, Ag 16,45:3
Hepler, B E, 1940, My 13,17:4
Hepler, Carroll D, 1948, S 23,29:6
Hepler, J Frank, 1946, S 3,19:5
Hepler, J Raymond, 1962, Ap 10,43:4
Hepler, Oliver M, 1958, My 11,87:1
Hepner, Rufus B, 1959, Je 24,31:4
Hepp, George P Mrs, 1949, My 5,27:5
Hepp, Rudolph, 1946, Mr 7,25:1
Heppe, Florence J, 1941, S 8,15:2
Heppe, Frederick, 1954, Jl 5,11:4
Heppenheimer, Ernest J, 1955, Ja 24,23:3
Heppenheimer, F M, 1878, Ap 21,7:1
Heppenheimer, Otto Mrs, 1952, S 27,17:6
Heppenheimer, W C, 1933, S 17,36:1
Heppenheimer, William C Jr, 1968, Ja 20,29:3
Heppenstall, C W, 1945, Ja 17,21:2
Heppenstall, Robert B, 1966, F 22,23:1
Hepperle, Henry J, 1954, F 3,23:4
Heppes, George P, 1948, Je 13,68:3
Heppner, Joseph B, 1952, Ap 2,33:4
Heppner, Richard P, 1958, My 15,29:6
Heppner, William F, 1943, N 9,21:3
Heps, Henri C Mrs, 1949, Jl 3,27:2
Heptig, William L Mrs, 1958, S 14,84:2
Hepworth, Cecil, 1953, F 11,29:2
Hepworth, G H Dr, 1902, Je 9,9:5
Hepworth, John T, 1938, Jl 8,17:2
Hepworth, John T Mrs, 1952, Mr 27,29:5
Hepworth, W (Hepworth Dixon), 1879, D 28,7:5
Hequembourg, Harry C, 1938, Ja 3,21:3
Hequembourg, James T (Ted), 1917, N 30,13:4
Herald, Heinz, 1964, Jl 23,27:3
Herald, James F, 1963, O 28,27:3
Herald, William, 1938, N 2,6:2
Herald, William C, 1964, Mr 12,35:5
Heraty, Michael P, 1912, Ja 31,11:5
Herb, Isabella C, 1943, My 30,27:2
Herb, Jacob, 1939, N 11,15:6
Herb, Philp, 1967, Ag 27,89:1
Herb, Robert, 1965, D 14,43:2
Herbach, Joseph, 1943, N 1,18:2
Herbach, Joseph D, 1951, Ag 28,23:1
Herbach, Louis, 1956, N 17,21:6
Herben, Grace F Mrs, 1938, Jl 23,13:6
Herben, Stephen J, 1967, D 26,33:2
Herben, Stephen J Rev Dr, 1937, F 23,27:4
Herbener, Eugene G Mrs, 1938, Ap 16,13:4
Herbener, George H, 1952, N 6,29:4
Herber, Henry J, 1952, Ap 16,27:2
Herber, Howard T, 1966, Ag 23,39:4
Herber, John, 1951, Ag 16,27:4
Herberer, Andrew, 1954, S 22,29:4
Herberich, Bernard, 1948, Ja 31,19:4
Herbermann, Alfred A, 1964, My 6,47:4
Herbermann, Charles George Dr, 1916, Ag 25,7:3
Herbermann, Elizabeth P, 1959, Ag 13,27:2
Herbermann, Henry F, 1964, Ap 8,43:4
Herbermann, Henry Mrs (Mar 24), 1963, Ap 1,35:7
Herbert, Alex, 1941, My 9,21:3
Herbert, Alfred E, 1957, My 27,31:3
Herbert, Arthur A Sr, 1941, Ap 4,21:2
Herbert, Arthur H, 1948, Jl 20,24:3
Herbert, Arthur J Sir, 1921, S 1,15:4
Herbert, Aubrey, 1923, S 28,7:3
Herbert, Aubrey D, 1943, Ap 21,25:1
Herbert, August J, 1952, D 30,19:3
Herbert, Benjamin F, 1940, My 9,23:2
Herbert, C M Maj, 1871, D 7,8:4
Herbert, Charles F, 1949, Je 18,13:5
Herbert, Clarence Mrs, 1948, Ap 13,27:2
Herbert, Claude Mrs, 1950, Mr 16,32:2
Herbert, Clifford V, 1962, Ja 3,33:1
Herbert, Daniel, 1908, Ap 29,9:6; 1910, S 15,9:5
Herbert, E W M, 1906, N 6,9:5
Herbert, Edward, 1959, O 29,33:1
Herbert, Edward Sr, 1944, Je 27,19:4
Herbert, Emilio L, 1944, S 15,19:6
Herbert, Ewing, 1947, Mr 17,23:2
Herbert, F Hugh, 1958, My 18,86:4
Herbert, Frank M Jr, 1968, My 17,47:2
Herbert, Frank M Mrs, 1950, S 21,32:2
Herbert, Fred, 1955, Je 12,87:1
Herbert, Fred W, 1942, Ja 8,21:3
Herbert, Frederick D, 1955, Ag 5,19:1
Herbert, Frederick D Jr Mrs, 1966, S 13,47:1
Herbert, G F, 1876, Ag 22,5:4
Herbert, George H (por),(Coco), 1949, Ag 19,17:6
Herbert, George S, 1942, Ja 31,17:3
Herbert, Harry C, 1943, D 16,28:2
Herbert, Harry M, 1937, O 8,23:2
Herbert, Henry (por), 1947, F 21,19:1
Herbert, Henry, 1950, My 12,27:4
Herbert, Henry L Mrs, 1943, Ja 22,19:4
Herbert, Henry W, 1940, S 15,48:1
Herbert, Henry W Justice (por), 1937, D 25,15:1
Herbert, Hilary A, 1919, Mr 7,13:3
Herbert, Hugh, 1952, Mr 13,29:3
Herbert, J F J, 1932, D 5,17:3
Herbert, J R Gen, 1884, Ag 6,5:1
Herbert, J Stanley, 1959, Ja 31,19:4
Herbert, J W, 1934, Ag 27,15:4
Herbert, Jack (H N Songcrant), 1957, Je 12,35:5
Herbert, Jacob, 1960, Ja 29,25:3
Herbert, Jerome Mrs, 1959, F 12,27:4
Herbert, John, 1923, F 19,15:4
Herbert, John A, 1943, D 12,69:1; 1966, Ag 13,25:5
Herbert, John J (Bro Sabinus), 1955, My 14,19:4
Herbert, John W Mrs, 1945, Ag 10,15:4
Herbert, Joseph, 1940, Mr 15,23:2
Herbert, Joseph M, 1939, O 1,53:2
Herbert, Katherine W Mrs (por), 1945, Ja 31,21:4
Herbert, Le Roy B, 1951, Mr 22,31:4
Herbert, Malcolm A, 1950, S 3,38:5
Herbert, Martha B Mrs, 1940, N 21,29:2
Herbert, Matthew S, 1945, Jl 15,15:3
Herbert, Michael H Sir, 1903, O 1,9:1
Herbert, Michael Lady, 1923, N 20,19:4
Herbert, Octave B, 1941, D 26,13:2
Herbert, P O, 1880, Ag 30,5:5
Herbert, Percy J, 1951, O 11,37:1
Herbert, Preston, 1941, N 30,69:3
Herbert, Reginald Earl of Pembroke, 1960, Ja 14,33:2
Herbert, Richard A, 1960, Ap 14,31:3
Herbert, Robert B, 1954, Ja 15,19:4
Herbert, Rubin Mrs, 1960, Ap 7,84:7
Herbert, Sidney (Earl of Pembroke), 1913, Ap 2,11:5
Herbert, Sidney (will, O 27,26:2), 1939, Mr 23,23:1
Herbert, Sidney Lord, 1861, Ag 18,5:4
Herbert, T F Mrs, 1927, F 25,21:4
Herbert, Victor, 1924, My 28,23:4; 1948, Ja 29,23:3
Herbert, William, 1918, Je 8,11:5
Herbert, William C, 1952, Ap 7,25:6
Herbert, William G, 1956, Mr 15,31:3
Herbert, William H, 1944, Je 25,29:3
Herbert, William M, 1950, O 25,35:2
Herbert, William P, 1942, Mr 26,23:6
Herbert, William V, 1962, Jl 6,25:1
Herbert, Wyman D, 1940, My 12,48:5
Herbert of Lea, Elizabeth Lady, 1911, O 31,9:3
Herbertz, Charles W, 1960, Je 15,15:1
Herbes, William H, 1939, F 9,21:2
Herbhold, Richard A E, 1958, Ap 19,21:5
Herbig, Elwood H, 1940, My 6,17:5
Herbig, Frank J, 1942, O 29,23:6
Herbinson, William, 1950, N 1,35:2
Herbold, Christopher, 1951, Je 5,31:3
Herbst, Arthur, 1953, Mr 3,27:2
Herbst, Bernard H, 1950, N 21,31:4
Herbst, Charles, 1960, Jl 1,25:2
Herbst, Christian E, 1942, F 16,17:2
Herbst, Edwin J, 1954, Mr 30,27:4
Herbst, Frank R, 1943, D 17,27:1
Herbst, Frederick G, 1945, Ap 13,17:3
Herbst, Frederick L, 1948, Jl 15,23:1
Herbst, Harry, 1950, N 4,17:6
Herbst, Irving, 1949, F 15,24:2
Herbst, Louis C, 1940, Ap 14,45:1
Herbst, Mark, 1956, F 21,33:4
Herbst, Robert H, 1951, My 16,35:5
Herbst, S Charles, 1941, F 25,23:4
Herbst, Stephan, 1946, S 4,23:2
Herbst, Vernon B, 1950, Ag 30,32:2
Herbst, Wallace J, 1947, Jl 14,21:4
Herbster, Edward N, 1941, F 28,19:1
Herckenrath, Walter A, 1954, N 10,33:4
Hercock, William R, 1943, Jl 21,15:4
Hercod, Robert, 1953, Ja 31,15:3
Hercov, Max, 1949, Je 19,68:3
Herczeg, Geza, 1954, F 21,68:5
Herd, Alexander (Sandy), 1944, F 19,14:8
Herd, John W, 1951, S 28,31:2
Herd, John W Mrs, 1956, Jl 3,25:4
Herde, Joseph N Sr, 1950, Mr 24,26:2
Herdegen, Henry E, 1951, Ap 20,29:1
Herdegen, John G, 1956, S 30,86:6
Herder, Carl D, 1947, Jl 26,13:6
Herder, George, 1955, Ap 6,29:4
Herder, Ralph B, 1955, Ja 10,23:5
Herder, William, 1952, Mr 7,23:1
Herdina, John W, 1951, F 7,29:3
Herdina, William J, 1957, S 5,29:5
Herdman, John W, 1948, F 25,23:4
Herdman, Oscar, 1938, Jl 10,29:5
Herdman, William, 1940, Ja 7,48:3
Herdman, William Sir, 1924, Jl 23,15:3
Herdrick, Simon Rev, 1937, Ja 1,23:2
Herdt, William C, 1952, F 12,27:3
Heredia, Carlos M de, 1917, Je 17,19:4
Heredia, Nicolas, 1901, Jl 13,1:2
Hereford, Melvin D, 1940, O 26,15:4
Hereford, Viscount of (R C Devereux), 1952, Ap 17, 29:4
Hereford, William F, 1953, D 23,25:4
Herel, Frank J, 1967, Ag 19,25:2
Herendeen, Fred, 1962, Je 5,41:2
Herendeen, Frederick W, 1941, Je 21,17:4
Herendeen, James H, 1945, Jl 24,23:1
Herendeen, Thomas G, 1957, Ag 8,23:6
Herer, Nathan, 1954, F 6,19:3
Herer, William V, 1966, Jl 1,35:2
Hereth, Walter H, 1944, F 11,19:2
Herff, Jesse, 1943, O 7,23:6
Herford, Beatrice, 1952, Jl 20,52:1
Herford, Brooke Rev, 1903, D 22,9:4
Herford, O, 1935, Jl 6,13:3
Herfort, Philip A, 1921, Mr 26,13:5
Herfurth, Theodore, 1950, F 13,21:1
Hergenhan, Arnold E, 1948, Ag 27,19:3
Hergenhan, John C, 1953, Ap 16,29:3
Hergert, Charles, 1946, D 14,15:1
Hergert, Frederick W Mrs, 1957, Je 2,86:4
Hergert, Herman C, 1948, S 3,19:3
Hergert, John H, 1949, N 20,93:1
Hergert, Raymond, 1959, Ja 13,47:3
Hergesell, Hugo (por), 1938, Je 8,23:5
Hergesheimer, Ella, 1943, Je 25,17:5
Hergesheimer, Joseph E (funl plans, Ap 28,31:4), 1954, Ap 26,25:1
Hergesheimer, Russell U, 1940, Mr 27,21:5
Herget, Henry G, 1943, Ja 6,27:2
Herget, Louis E, 1957, N 3,89:1
Heribert, Herbert J, 1948, Ag 20,17:2
Herine, Charles Mrs (Kath), 1965, D 6,37:4
Hering, Albert S, 1943, F 24,21:5
Hering, C, 1880, Jl 27,3:4
Hering, C Dr, 1926, My 11,27:1
Hering, Daniel W (por), 1938, Mr 25,19:3
Hering, Elise Ward, 1923, Ja 14,6:2
Hering, Frank E, 1943, Jl 12,15:2
Hering, Frederick, 1942, N 19,25:3
Hering, H Brooks, 1957, N 19,33:2
Hering, Henry (por), 1949, Ja 17,19:1
Hering, Herman J, 1954, N 12,21:1
Hering, Hermann S, 1940, My 16,23:4
Hering, Hollis W, 1949, My 1,88:5
Hering, John W, 1937, My 26,25:4
Hering, Joshua Dr, 1913, S 24,9:6
Hering, Oswald C, 1941, Mr 8,19:5
Hering, Rudolph Dr, 1923, My 31,15:5
Heringman, Hyman, 1967, My 16,45:4
Heritage, Clarence, 1940, O 29,25:1
Heritage, George C, 1945, O 16,23:4
Heritage, Harry M, 1948, Jl 9,19:2
Herk, Isidor H, 1944, Jl 6,15:4
Herkimer, Bert S Mrs (cor, Mr 7,38:5), 1967, Mr 6, 28:7
Herkimer, Robert Henry Dr, 1917, Ja 17,9:3
Herkner, Anna, 1959, D 5,23:4
Herkness, Malcolm, 1940, Mr 15,23:2
Herkomer, Hubert von Sir, 1914, Ap 1,13:3

Herkowitz, Samuel A, 1941, Ap 18,21:1
Herlands, Jacob D, 1959, Jl 25,17:6
Herlehy, Patrick Mrs, 1955, S 20,31:1
Herles, Emil F, 1951, Ag 31,15:3
Herles, Emil F Mrs, 1948, N 15,25:6
Herlich, George W, 1964, Ag 5,33:1
Herlich, George W Mrs, 1959, Ap 1,37:2
Herlich, Gilbert A, 1955, Ap 14,36:3
Herlihy, Charles M, 1945, Ja 28,37:1
Herlihy, Edward L, 1948, N 2,25:2
Herlihy, Elizabeth M, 1953, O 29,31:1
Herlihy, Frank J, 1955, S 23,25:4
Herlihy, John A, 1962, F 11,86:4
Herlihy, John J, 1949, N 26,15:1
Herlihy, Thomas J, 1942, N 3,24:2
Herlihy, William, 1954, Ja 1,23:2
Herlihy, William R, 1954, Ag 1,84:6
Herlin, Emil (por), 1943, Ja 7,19:3
Herling, Felix R, 1947, O 29,28:2
Herling, Morris, 1960, Mr 2,37:3
Herlinger, Ralph D, 1948, F 4,23:2
Herlinger, Theodore, 1952, F 3,84:2
Herlithy, Walter F, 1956, O 7,86:7
Herlitz, Julius, 1953, Jl 9,25:4
Herlitzka, Amedeo, 1949, Jl 14,27:4
Herlt, Anna M, 1953, Mr 28,17:5
Herlt, Herman Mrs, 1952, Mr 25,27:4
Herly, Louis, 1952, Jl 15,21:3
Herm, Lloyd L, 1950, D 20,31:4
Herma, Frank E, 1956, Mr 1,33:2
Herma, John L, 1966, S 21,47:4
Herma, John L Mrs (P West), 1965, Jl 1,31:4
Herman, Abraham, 1947, Mr 27,27:1
Herman, Abraham M, 1956, Ja 13,23:6
Herman, Abraham Mrs, 1945, My 7,17:3
Herman, Agnes Mrs, 1944, Ag 14,24:2
Herman, Alexander, 1967, Je 30,37:3
Herman, Benjamin, 1957, D 31,17:2
Herman, Benjamin J, 1951, Jl 4,17:4
Herman, Bernard, 1952, My 4,90:4
Herman, Bernard F, 1950, Ag 31,25:5
Herman, Bro Bros of St Francis Xavier, 1956, D 26, 27:4
Herman, Carl W, 1943, S 19,48:8
Herman, Charles E, 1948, Je 21,21:5
Herman, Charles F, 1947, Je 10,27:3
Herman, Charles H, 1958, Jl 20,65:1
Herman, Charles Mrs, 1963, N 20,40:1
Herman, Charles W Mrs, 1946, Mr 27,27:4
Herman, Chris, 1942, F 25,19:2
Herman, David, 1965, Mr 7,82:1
Herman, David B, 1953, D 28,21:3
Herman, Earl L, 1949, D 31,15:4
Herman, Elizabeth H Mrs, 1941, My 22,21:2
Herman, Eugene, 1949, Ja 23,68:3
Herman, Frank H, 1938, D 2,23:2
Herman, Fred W, 1951, Mr 28,29:2
Herman, Gregory, 1957, My 9,31:3
Herman, Harry E, 1964, My 17,86:5
Herman, Henry, 1958, O 14,37:4
Herman, Henry Dr, 1921, Jl 13,9:4
Herman, Henry M, 1948, Ja 15,23:2
Herman, Henry R, 1943, Ag 22,36:4
Herman, Henry W, 1955, Jl 16,15:6
Herman, Isidor C, 1943, Ap 5,19:6
Herman, Jack, 1960, My 20,31:2
Herman, Jack Mrs, 1960, F 27,19:3
Herman, Jacob, 1947, Je 29,48:6
Herman, Jacob G, 1952, D 2,36:6
Herman, James R, 1951, Jl 10,27:3
Herman, Jan, 1946, O 2,29:4
Herman, Jane L Mrs, 1937, Ja 17,II,8:7
Herman, Jesse H, 1959, Ap 6,27:5
Herman, John M, 1955, Mr 18,28:3
Herman, Jules, 1958, O 7,35:2
Herman, Leon E, 1956, Mr 19,31:4
Herman, Louis, 1965, Ag 31,33:5
Herman, Louis L, 1938, N 23,21:2
Herman, Louis Mrs, 1947, S 8,21:4
Herman, M Robert (por), 1947, Je 20,19:1
Herman, Martin A, 1942, D 11,23:2
Herman, Michael B, 1958, S 28,88:5
Herman, Milton C, 1951, Ja 23,27:1
Herman, Moses, 1954, O 22,27:3
Herman, Nathan L, 1963, Ap 4,47:5
Herman, Oscar W, 1939, Ja 28,13:6
Herman, Raphael, 1946, Ap 9,27:3
Herman, Raymond I, 1953, D 28,21:4
Herman, Robert E, 1966, Ja 12,21:1
Herman, S James, 1942, F 22,27:1
Herman, S Mrs (will), 1939, D 6,27:5
Herman, Sam, 1953, Ag 5,23:6
Herman, Samuel, 1951, N 26,25:3
Herman, Samuel Mrs, 1946, Mr 12,25:2; 1957, Ag 17, 15:5
Herman, Sidney W Mrs, 1967, Ja 28,27:1
Herman, Sophie Mrs, 1938, Ja 15,15:2
Herman, Sydney H, 1949, N 2,27:5
Herman, W F, 1938, Ja 17,19:6
Herman, William, 1956, Ja 8,87:1
Herman, William A, 1943, F 19,19:4
Herman, William C, 1950, Mr 5,93:1
Herman, William J, 1956, F 26,89:2; 1961, N 9,35:1
Herman, William J Mrs, 1964, F 24,25:4
Herman, William P, 1965, F 9,37:2
Hermance, De Witt C, 1905, Ap 17,1:6
Hermance, Edgar Martindale Dr, 1913, D 23,9:6
Hermance, Ella R Mrs, 1938, D 6,23:2
Hermance, George W, 1960, O 29,23:4
Hermance, Harry P, 1937, Je 1,23:4
Hermance, Jacob, 1879, D 4,3:5
Hermance, John C Rev Dr, 1907, S 23,9:6
Hermance, W Oakley, 1953, Je 14,84:1
Hermance, William, 1947, N 29,13:3
Hermann, Andrew G, 1954, Ag 28,15:6
Hermann, Arthur W, 1960, Ag 20,19:5
Hermann, Bruno, 1902, Ap 30,9:4
Hermann, chas J Mrs, 1959, Ag 30,83:2
Hermann, Edwin S, 1958, Ap 3,31:3
Hermann, Ernst, 1942, S 1,19:4
Hermann, Fred W, 1941, Ag 31,23:3
Hermann, Frederick J, 1954, O 12,27:2
Hermann, George K, 1916, S 13,9:6
Hermann, Herman, 1947, F 28,23:5
Hermann, John W Mrs, 1956, Mr 11,89:1
Hermann, Joseph A, 1950, Mr 2,27:4
Hermann, Leo, 1948, Je 30,25:5
Hermann, Louise, 1946, Jl 3,25:5
Hermann, Robert F, 1966, Je 1,47:1
Hermann, Siegwart, 1956, N 28,35:1
Hermann, Solomon (por), 1949, S 8,29:3
Hermann-Leon, Charles, 1908, Ja 1,9:5
Hermannsson, Halldor, 1958, Ag 31,57:3
Hermans, Jan H, 1947, F 26,25:2
Hermans, Louis M, 1943, O 23,13:5
Hermanson, Flora, 1951, N 23,29:1
Hermanspan, John H, 1950, Je 8,31:1
Hermant, Abel, 1950, S 30,17:2
Hermant, Percy, 1959, Jl 25,17:6
Hermen, George R, 1947, N 17,21:5
Hermenze, James C, 1961, D 30,19:5
Hermes, Andreas, 1964, Ja 5,92:4
Hermes, John R, 1947, My 16,23:3
Hermes, Leonard E, 1955, Ja 21,23:1
Hermes, William B, 1949, N 11,29:4
Hermias, Rev Bro, 1937, My 27,23:3
Hermida, Jorge (F G Ortega), 1967, N 2,47:4
Hermina, Mother, 1916, Ap 26,13:7
Hermiston, George J, 1944, N 14,23:5
Hermite, Charles, 1901, Ja 15,9:5
Herms, Rudolph R, 1950, Mr 7,27:3
Hermson, Harry, 1944, Je 21,19:6
Hern, Edmund J, 1949, Ag 17,23:4
Hernandez, Albert Jr, 1953, Je 4,29:4
Hernandez, Alfredo, 1967, Mr 16,47:2
Hernandez, B Frank, 1947, Mr 17,23:3
Hernandez, Benigno C, 1954, O 21,27:2
Hernandez, Emanuel V, 1937, F 1,19:3
Hernandez, Jose Manuel Gen, 1921, Ag 26,13:5
Hernandez, Mateo, 1949, N 26,15:5
Hernandez, Placido, 1954, F 1,23:5
Hernandez, Rafael, 1965, D 13,39:3
Hernandez, Randolph J, 1951, Ja 14,85:2
Hernandez, Roberto, 1960, O 11,45:3
Hernandez, Silverio, 1947, Ja 28,24:3
Hernandez Fornos, Evenor, 1945, S 26,23:2
Hernandez Suarez, Emmanuel (funl plans, Jl 3,11:6), 1954, Jl 1,2:3
Hernbrooke, Francis D Rev, 1903, D 6,7:6
Herndon, Agnes, 1921, Ja 1,9:4
Herndon, Charles, 1966, S 15,39:4
Herndon, E Julian, 1963, Ag 27,31:3
Herndon, Hugh, 1954, Ap 21,29:2
Herndon, Hugh Jr, 1952, Ap 6,89:1
Herndon, J Laurence, 1961, N 14,36:5
Herndon, James B Jr, 1953, Ja 5,21:1
Herndon, John C, 1957, Ja 6,88:8
Herndon, John G, 1957, Jl 1,23:6
Herndon, Richard G, 1958, Jl 15,25:5
Herndon, Richard G Mrs, 1948, Ag 5,21:6
Herndon, T H Col, 1883, Mr 29,5:5
Herndon, W L Mrs, 1878, My 11,4:7
Herndon, William K, 1941, Je 18,21:2
Herne, Chrystal, 1950, S 20,31:1
Herne, Clarence H, 1942, S 22,21:1
Herne, E D C, 1941, Je 9,19:2
Herne, J A, 1901, Je 3,7:6
Herne, James A Mrs, 1943, F 9,23:5
Hernisch, Friedrich, 1925, Mr 20,19:5
Hernon, John L, 1954, O 18,25:2
Hernstadt, Sidney J, 1946, F 20,25:3
Hernstadt, William L, 1964, Ag 18,31:4
Herntrich, Volkmar, 1958, S 16,8:5
Hero, Andrew Jr, 1942, F 8,48:5
Hero, George, 1952, F 15,25:2
Hero, Simon, 1959, Ag 18,29:2
Herod, Bergen, 1955, Ag 8,21:2
Herod, Stewart R, 1942, Ag 6,19:2
Herold, Anna, 1956, My 21,25:6
Herold, Charles J, 1938, Je 6,17:5
Herold, Ernest J, 1950, Je 27,29:5
Herold, F, 1882, Je 2,5:3
Herold, George F Mrs, 1924, Ag 10,24:3
Herold, Harvey T, 1949, Je 26,60:3
Herold, Hieronimus, 1942, D 25,17:5
Herold, J Christopher, 1964, D 11,39:1
Herold, Julius E, 1941, Mr 21,21:1
Herold, Justin, 1942, F 4,19:3
Herold, Mary A R Mrs, 1921, Je 9,15:4
Herold, Matthew G, 1960, Ja 7,30:1
Herold, Otto F Mrs, 1943, Ag 9,13:6
Heron, Charles R, 1941, Ap 12,15:3
Heron, John, 1958, F 17,23:4
Heron, John M, 1920, Ag 17,13:3
Heron, Matilda (see also Mr 8), 1877, Mr 12,8:1
Heron, Raymond A, 1960, Ja 23,21:2
Heron, Robert E, 1948, D 10,26:2
Heron, Robert H Mrs, 1946, Ja 28,19:1
Heron, Sergt, 1881, Ap 16,5:4
Heron, Virginia A Mrs, 1938, My 22,II,7:4
Heroult, Paul, 1914, My 15,15:5
Herouy, Blattengeta, 1938, S 20,23:2
Heroy, Helen H Mrs, 1942, Jl 16,19:4
Heroy, James H Mrs, 1964, S 17,43:4
Heroy, James H Sr, 1950, S 5,27:3
Heroy, Newman L Rev, 1937, F 22,17:4
Heroy, William W, 1923, D 27,13:3
Herpers, Henry F, 1944, Ja 28,17:3
Herpers, Richard, 1961, O 12,29:3
Herpin, Alfred E, 1947, Ja 4,16:4
Herr, Albert M Mrs, 1948, O 17,76:1
Herr, Charles H, 1942, N 25,23:2
Herr, Crescentius A, 1964, Je 21,84:8
Herr, Dougal, 1960, Ag 27,19:6
Herr, Dougal Mrs, 1948, Je 11,23:3
Herr, E M, 1932, D 25,13:1
Herr, Eddie, 1943, Jl 20,22:3
Herr, Edward B Sgt-Maj, 1904, F 15,7:6
Herr, George S, 1961, S 16,19:6
Herr, H T, 1933, D 20,21:3
Herr, Harvey E, 1948, Mr 14,73:2
Herr, Herman A, 1966, F 26,25:4
Herr, Horace H, 1943, Mr 17,21:2
Herr, Jacob O, 1968, Mr 8,39:4
Herr, John K, 1955, Mr 13,86:1
Herr, Laurence J, 1956, Je 13,37:4
Herr, Morton R, 1968, Ja 7,84:8
Herr, Park A, 1957, Ag 15,21:5
Herr, Park A Mrs, 1959, Jl 12,73:1
Herr, Ralph M, 1945, Je 28,19:3
Herr, Rose Mrs, 1940, Ag 19,17:4
Herr, Von H, 1925, S 7,11:5
Herr, Walter J, 1949, N 29,30:2
Herr (Bro Anthony), 1964, Mr 26,35:1
Herraiz, Eduardo B, 1949, N 23,29:3
Herran, Tomas Dr, 1904, S 1,7:6
Herrel, George, 1955, Ja 12,27:5
Herrel, Louise Mrs, 1937, N 9,23:3
Herrell, William J, 1951, F 5,23:4
Herren, F Irwin, 1952, F 5,29:5
Herrera, Antonio, 1917, Jl 17,9:5
Herrera, Ariosto, 1952, Ag 8,17:2
Herrera, julio, 1951, Ap 12,33:4
Herrera, Luis A de, 1959, Ap 10,29:3
Herrera, Primitivo, 1953, Ja 27,25:2
Herrera de Hora, M, 1934, Ja 27,13:1
Herrera de la Torre, Evaristo, 1951, D 15,13:6
Herrera Guevara, Luis, 1945, Jl 4,13:8
Herrera y Franchi, Alberto, 1954, Mr 19,23:5
Herrera y Oria, Angel Cardinal, 1968, Jl 29,31:1
Herrero, y Espinosa Cardinal, 1903, D 10,9:4
Herrero de Collantes, Ignacio Marquis of Alero, D 10,89:1
Herres, Fred J, 1953, Jl 21,23:5
Herreshoff, Charles F, 1954, F 2,27:4
Herreshoff, Eugenia T Mrs, 1940, Jl 24,21:6
Herreshoff, Francis L, 1956, Ag 25,15:5
Herreshoff, Frederick, 1920, Mr 24,9:5
Herreshoff, J B Francis Mrs, 1924, O 6,19:5
Herreshoff, John B, 1915, Jl 21,11:3
Herreshoff, Nathanael G (por), 1938, Je 3,21:1
Herreshoff, Nathanael G Mrs, 1950, Jl 23,56:3
Herrett, Emery J, 1955, D 8,37:2
Herrey, Hermann, 1968, O 12,37:3
Herrick, A, 1878, Je 16,7:1
Herrick, A B, 1882, D 29,5:3
Herrick, A H, 1903, N 18,9:3
Herrick, Albert B, 1938, Ap 21,19:1
Herrick, Alfred B, 1937, N 24,23:5
Herrick, Alonzo Mrs, 1956, S 24,27:3
Herrick, Anna Mrs, 1938, Je 25,15:4
Herrick, Anson, 1868, F 7,5:6
Herrick, Arthur D, 1965, Ap 27,37:4
Herrick, Asbury H, 1965, Jl 12,27:1
Herrick, Barrett, 1954, O 31,88:5
Herrick, Catherine Mrs, 1937, Ja 10,II,10:4
Herrick, Charles C Mrs, 1943, Ja 9,13:3
Herrick, Charles J, 1960, Ja 23,21:4
Herrick, Cheesman A, 1956, F 28,31:5
Herrick, Chester A, 1955, O 15,15:5
Herrick, D-Cady, 1926, F 22,17:3
Herrick, David S, 1954, Ja 24,84:5
Herrick, David S Mrs, 1941, Ja 19,40:2
Herrick, E Hicks, 1941, N 5,23:6
Herrick, Edward C, 1862, Je 22,6:1
Herrick, Edward F, 1957, Ap 11,31:2
Herrick, Edward L, 1968, Ap 10,43:2
Herrick, Edward R, 1966, Ja 10,25:4
Herrick, Eleanor K Mrs, 1948, O 12,25:5

Ierrick, Elias J, 1915, Ja 21,9:4
Ierrick, Elinore M Mrs (mem ser set, D 25,29:3), 1964, O 12,29:3
Ierrick, Ernest A, 1950, Ag 26,13:4
Ierrick, Evelyn H Mrs, 1967, Ap 4,43:3
Ierrick, Everett C, 1957, F 14,27:6
Ierrick, Everett Dr, 1914, Ap 2,11:5
Ierrick, Francis H, 1940, S 13,23:5
Ierrick, Frank C, 1939, Mr 11,17:5
Ierrick, Frederick C, 1943, Ap 7,25:2
Ierrick, G Frank, 1956, Ag 24,19:6
Ierrick, George, 1955, My 10,20:5
Ierrick, George L, 1948, Ap 27,25:2
errick, George L Mrs, 1941, S 5,21:4
errick, George W, 1943, Jl 7,19:6
errick, Gerardus P, 1955, S 10,17:4
errick, H Terhune Mrs, 1964, Je 18,35:3
errick, Harold, 1945, Ap 26,23:4
errick, Harold Mrs, 1947, My 20,25:5
errick, Harry M, 1943, S 12,53:1
errick, Henry B, 1938, Ap 27,23:3
errick, Henry C, 1954, Ja 12,23:2
errick, Horace T, 1948, O 8,26:3
errick, Howard J, 1944, D 8,21:5
errick, Hugh H, 1916, My 1,11:4
errick, J H, 1903, Mr 12,9:2
errick, Jacob B, 1864, Ja 5,1:3
errick, James B, 1954, Mr 9,27:3
errick, James Buclin Mrs, 1919, O 10,13:3
errick, James Frederick Mrs, 1944, D 3,57:2
errick, John Jacob, 1916, Ja 31,11:4
errick, John O, 1955, D 25,48:6
errick, John P, 1961, F 5,80:7
errick, Joshua, 1874, Ag 31,1:6
errick, L R, 1877, S 5,4:7
errick, Lott R Justice, 1937, S 19,II,6:8
errick, Marcus A, 1871, N 14,2:7
errick, Mary L Mrs, 1948, D 7,31:4
errick, Myron T Mrs, 1918, S 16,11:8
errick, Newton J, 1947, Ja 4,15:6
errick, Newton J Mrs, 1944, Ja 10,17:2
errick, Osgood E Rev Dr, 1906, O 2,9:6
errick, Parmely W (por),(will, Jl 14,44:2), 1937, Jl 8,23:1
errick, Parmely W Jr, 1957, Mr 13,31:5
errick, Parmely W Mrs, 1956, D 27,25:2
errick, Robert, 1938, D 24,15:1
errick, Robert F, 1942, O 15,24:2
errick, Robert F H Jr, 1941, My 2,21:6
errick, Russell, 1937, S 22,27:4
errick, Stephen, 1947, N 13,28:2
errick, W Wilson, 1960, F 2,35:2
errick, Walter R (por), 1945, Ag 30,21:4
errick, Walter R, 1953, Jl 21,23:5
errick, William C, 1940, Ap 6,17:5
errick, William Post Dr, 1923, Mr 14,19:4
errick, William W, 1945, Je 2,15:1
errick C Judson, 1960, Ja 30,21:1
erridge, William D, 1961, S 23,19:5
erridge, William D Mrs (por), 1938, My 13,19:3
erridge, William G, 1952, Jl 15,21:1
erries, William, 1909, Jl 5,7:5
errigel, Emil A, 1950, D 12,33:2
errigel, Fred Jr Mrs, 1941, S 25,25:3
erriman, George, 1944, Ap 27,23:5
erriman, George F, 1939, Je 1,25:1
erriman, J A Gen, 1875, S 5,12:3
erriman, Jefferson D Mrs, 1950, F 25,17:2
erriman, Rudolph F, 1964, F 19,39:3
erriman, Susan, 1945, Jl 31,19:2
erriman, Wallace J, 1943, Ag 29,38:8
erriman, William H, 1918, Jl 31,9:5
errimann, Louis J Mrs, 1953, S 18,23:2
errin, Albert J, 1945, Mr 16,15:2
erring, A M, 1926, Jl 19,15:5
erring, Arthur, 1938, F 4,21:2
erring, Charles E Rev Dr, 1921, My 25,17:4
erring, Charles R, 1946, Ag 29,27:4
erring, Charles W, 1953, Mr 25,31:5
erring, Clyde L, 1945, S 16,42:3
erring, Donald G Jr, 1962, Ap 5,33:2
erring, Elbert (see also F 21), 1876, F 22,2:7
erring, Fanny, 1906, My 19,11:6
erring, Frank S, 1966, Je 16,47:2
erring, George, 1906, N 3,9:5
erring, George D, 1952, F 4,17:3
erring, Harold M, 1953, O 9,27:2
erring, Harry T, 1945, Ap 21,13:7
erring, Harry T Mrs, 1915, S 2,9:5
erring, Hubert C Rev Dr, 1920, Ag 7,5:6
erring, J Harry Mrs, 1947, N 4,25:1
erring, Jessie M, 1952, S 19,23:3
erring, Lawrence, 1943, O 24,44:4
erring, Leah B Mrs, 1941, Ja 24,17:2
erring, Menzies F, 1951, F 28,27:2
erring, Rose Mrs, 1923, Je 28,15:4
erring, S C, 1881, Je 25,8:4
errington, Arthur, 1950, Mr 30,29:1
errington, Charles Mrs, 1942, F 3,20:2
errington, Florence T Mrs, 1941, Mr 23,44:2
erriot, Edouard (funl plans, Mr 28,31:3; funl, Mr 31,88:6), 1957, Mr 27,31:1
erriot, Edouard Mrs, 1962, S 26,39:4

Herriott, David P, 1953, S 17,29:4
Herriott, Irving, 1953, N 19,31:2
Herriott, Paul, 1918, My 3,15:3
Herrity, John E, 1941, F 19,21:4
Herrle, Colin, 1952, D 17,33:5
Herrlein, Harry G, 1962, D 24,8:6
Herrlin, John S O Jr, 1960, My 3,39:2
Herrlinger, Albert P, 1937, Jl 11,II,5:2
Herrlinger, Edward, 1952, Jl 22,25:1
Herrman, Charles, 1938, Jl 12,20:1; 1945, Ag 16,19:4
Herrman, Eduard, 1937, Ap 25,II,8:4
Herrman, Ferdinand H, 1966, N 20,88:8
Herrman, Henry (will, My 12,9:6), 1955, My 6,23:5
Herrman, Henry Mrs, 1911, Jl 6,9:4
Herrman, Henry W, 1951, My 11,28:3
Herrman, M, 1927, F 15,25:3
Herrman, Max F, 1950, F 10,23:3
Herrman, Max S, 1962, Ap 10,43:1
Herrman, Seymour, 1956, Ap 2,23:2
Herrman, William G, 1965, N 8,35:4
Herrmann, A, 1896, D 18,5:1
Herrmann, A (Garry), 1931, Ap 26,1:2
Herrmann, Adolph, 1941, Ja 23,21:2
Herrmann, Albert M, 1950, Je 6,29:2
Herrmann, Alfred C, 1940, F 17,13:5
Herrmann, August M, 1966, Je 6,41:2
Herrmann, Benjamin E, 1961, Mr 24,31:2
Herrmann, Charles A Mrs, 1944, Je 6,17:5
Herrmann, Charles E Mrs, 1958, Ag 13,27:4
Herrmann, Daniel, 1947, Je 27,21:4
Herrmann, Edgar G, 1951, D 31,13:3
Herrmann, Elsa H Mrs, 1949, S 30,23:3
Herrmann, Emil, 1968, S 6,43:3
Herrmann, Erich S, 1953, Je 12,27:2
Herrmann, Frank S, 1942, Je 26,21:5
Herrmann, Fred, 1961, N 11,23:5
Herrmann, Frederick G, 1938, Jl 9,13:5
Herrmann, Gaston J, 1959, Mr 22,87:2
Herrmann, George M, 1945, F 24,11:5
Herrmann, Gustav (will), 1952, Ja 13,56:4
Herrmann, Henry F, 1964, O 14,45:4
Herrmann, Herbert, 1959, Jl 2,26:1
Herrmann, John, 1959, My 19,33:4
Herrmann, John A (cor, Mr 13,21:2), 1950, Mr 12, 92:2
Herrmann, John C, 1943, Ap 11,49:2
Herrmann, Joseph, 1908, D 12,11:2; 1967, Mr 28,39:5
Herrmann, L Edward, 1942, Ja 1,25:2
Herrmann, Lewis M, 1965, F 15,27:2
Herrmann, Lillian S Mrs, 1938, Mr 22,21:3
Herrmann, Louis J Mrs, 1948, Jl 26,17:2
Herrmann, Martin, 1952, Mr 25,27:2
Herrmann, Maurice, 1921, Je 29,15:3
Herrmann, Milton C, 1950, Mr 13,21:2
Herrmann, Nathan, 1912, Ag 24,9:7
Herrmann, Otto E Jr, 1945, S 22,17:5
Herrmann, Prestidigitateur, 1887, Je 9,1:1
Herrmann, Richard, 1941, My 1,23:4
Herrmann, Samuel L Prof, 1913, F 13,15:4
Herrmann, Theodore, 1953, Je 27,15:3
Herrmann, Theodore L, 1925, D 25,17:5
Herrmann, Urbine J, 1939, Jl 4,13:5
Herrmann, Uriah, 1910, Ag 8,7:5
Herrmann, William E, 1937, Je 4,23:2
Herrmann, William F, 1954, S 16,29:4
Herrmann, William G Mrs, 1946, O 22,25:3
Herrmann, William P, 1949, Jl 28,23:4
Herrnstein, Albert E, 1958, Ag 16,17:4
Herrold, Russell D, 1960, S 30,27:1
Herrold, Walter W, 1950, Ja 13,23:1
Herron, Albert E Mrs, 1948, Mr 11,27:2
Herron, Alden J, 1964, N 15,86:8
Herron, Alhenon, 1951, My 19,15:2
Herron, Archie, 1948, Ag 31,42:2
Herron, Ashley M, 1951, Je 19,29:4
Herron, Charles, 1942, Ap 17,17:2
Herron, Daniel A, 1942, Jl 28,17:3
Herron, F J Gen, 1902, Ja 10,7:7
Herron, France E, 1966, S 5,15:5
Herron, Frank, 1953, S 7,11:3
Herron, Frederick W, 1967, S 11,45:2
Herron, George, 1925, O 11,5:1
Herron, George D Prof, 1914, Ja 14,11:6
Herron, George F, 1956, Ag 29,29:5
Herron, Howard M, 1962, My 6,88:2
Herron, James H, 1948, Mr 31,25:4
Herron, James P, 1967, D 22,31:3
Herron, John B, 1955, My 27,23:2
Herron, John S, 1947, S 14,60:7; 1954, Jl 11,73:3
Herron, John W (funl, Ag 7,11:7), 1912, Ag 6,9:6
Herron, Joseph, 1938, N 21,19:2
Herron, Leroy W, 1948, O 14,29:5
Herron, Maria C, 1954, O 2,17:4
Herron, Patrick M, 1938, O 13,23:5
Herron, S Davidson, 1956, Ja 28,17:5
Herron, Schuyler F, 1951, Mr 7,33:3
Herron, Thomas J, 1946, F 13,23:2
Herron, W S, 1939, Jl 22,15:4
Herron, William, 1922, S 30,13:6
Herron, William A, 1959, Mr 21,21:2
Herron, William Mrs, 1948, F 24,26:3
Herrouet, Jean M, 1961, Ja 16,27:4
Hersam, John E, 1949, Je 11,17:6

Hersam, John E Mrs, 1959, O 26,29:5
Hersam, V Donald Sr, 1966, Ap 30,31:5
Hersch, Charles H, 1951, Jl 11,23:6
Hersch, Jacob H, 1959, Je 19,25:4
Hersch, William A, 1950, O 15,104:2
Herschdorfer, Manuel, 1958, Jl 8,27:4
Herschede, Edward F, 1951, S 29,17:6
Herschel, Alexander Stewart Prof, 1907, Je 19,7:5
Herschel, Alfred, 1959, Je 3,35:3
Herschel, Arthur H, 1953, Ap 29,29:5
Herschel, John Sir, 1871, My 13,4:7
Herschel, Maximilian, 1903, Jl 29,7:6
Herschel, William James Sir, 1917, O 26,15:4
Herschell, Baron, 1899, Mr 2,5:1
Herschell, John C, 1950, Je 17,15:1
Herschell, William, 1939, D 3,60:5
Herschenrader, Phillip Laurence, 1925, Ap 10,19:4
Herscher, Josephine Mrs, 1940, Ap 28,37:1
Herschkowitz, Max, 1966, D 27,32:7
Herschman, Arthur, 1944, D 4,23:3
Herschmann, Amelia C, 1953, S 7,19:3
Herschmann, Arthur J, 1950, Mr 11,15:3
Herse, Henry C, 1940, Ja 11,23:5
Herselle, David, 1967, Ag 1,33:3
Herseman, Elton C, 1922, Ja 4,13:4
Hersey, Edwin S, 1950, Jl 31,17:5
Hersey, Evelyn W, 1963, N 4,35:5
Hersey, George L, 1951, F 25,85:1
Hersey, George M, 1951, Mr 2,25:3
Hersey, George N, 1950, N 10,27:4
Hersey, Harold B, 1956, Mr 19,31:1
Hersey, Harry A, 1950, O 12,31:5
Hersey, Harry C, 1940, Ap 21,42:2
Hersey, Henry B, 1948, S 25,17:6
Hersey, Ira G, 1943, My 7,19:4
Hersey, John Corey, 1909, Mr 31,11:4
Hersey, M M Mrs, 1904, Je 1,1:6
Hersey, Mary L Mrs, 1937, N 11,25:2
Hersey, Rexford B, 1965, My 29,27:5
Hersey, Roscoe M, 1945, Mr 20,19:4
Hersey, Roscoe M Mrs, 1966, O 13,45:4
Hersey, William R, 1947, Ja 2,28:2
Hersh, Edmund S, 1968, Mr 12,43:2
Hersh, Edward S, 1945, D 27,19:4
Hersh, Edward W, 1952, Jl 11,17:4
Hersh, Grier, 1941, Ap 25,19:6
Hersh, Liebman, 1955, Je 11,15:4
Hersh, Louis F Mrs, 1947, N 24,23:3
Hersh, Nelson, 1902, N 21,9:5
Hersh, Phil Mrs, 1937, D 25,15:3
Hersh, Sydney L, 1940, Mr 10,51:4
Hershberg, Joseph, 1953, O 29,31:4
Hershberger, J Irvin, 1941, O 17,23:5
Hershdorfer, Sol, 1941, Je 31,19:4
Hershenstein, Charles, 1954, Je 28,19:6
Hershey, A S, 1933, Je 13,19:2
Hershey, Chauncey A, 1946, N 2,15:5
Hershey, Clarence H, 1950, Ja 31,23:2
Hershey, Don, 1968, N 6,47:2
Hershey, Edith P Mrs, 1942, Ag 24,15:2
Hershey, Ezra F, 1949, Ag 9,26:3
Hershey, Frank S, 1942, S 26,15:2
Hershey, Harry B, 1967, S 1,28:7
Hershey, Henry H, 1939, Mr 9,21:4
Hershey, J Willard, 1943, S 28,25:5
Hershey, John C, 1952, Ag 31,44:6
Hershey, Milton S (por), 1945, O 14,44:1
Hershey, Reuben Mrs, 1947, O 18,16:2
Hershfield, Alex S, 1963, Je 8,25:6
Hershfield, Alta Mrs, 1943, Mr 15,14:2
Hershfield, Harry Mrs, 1960, Je 13,27:2
Hershfield, Henrietta S Mrs, 1937, F 15,17:4
Hershfield, Henry G, 1937, My 15,19:6
Hershfield, Isadore (por), 1949, N 11,26:2
Hershfield, Levi, 1954, Jl 18,57:2
Hershfield, Lewis H, 1910, D 6,13:4
Hershfield, Louis, 1916, Jl 1,11:6
Hershfield, Marvin, 1966, Jl 12,43:2
Hershkowitz, Frederick E, 1951, S 1,11:6
Hershkowitz, Samuel, 1963, O 30,39:1
Hershman, Abraham M, 1959, Ap 7,33:4
Hershman, Abraham M Mrs, 1955, Je 14,29:1
Hershman, Charles L, 1965, Jl 11,68:5
Hershman, Morris, 1945, Je 10,32:2
Hersholt, Jean (funl, Je 5,35:2), 1956, Je 3,86:1
Hershon, Arthur H, 1964, Mr 29,60:6
Hersi, Daud A, 1965, Ap 20,39:3
Herske, Arthur R Mrs, 1957, O 14,27:4
Herskovits, Max, 1950, Ja 19,27:2
Herskovits, Mortimer, 1952, Ja 5,7:1
Herskovitz, Melville, 1963, F 27,16:1
Herskowitz, Harry, 1954, N 29,25:1
Herskowitz, Julius, 1947, Je 30,19:5
Herskowitz, Max, 1954, Jl 3,11:4
Hersloff, Nils B, 1956, O 27,21:5
Hersohn, William W, 1957, Jl 19,19:6
Herson, James F, 1944, Jl 11,15:5
Herson, Joseph P Rev, 1937, My 7,25:3
Herson, Michael, 1950, F 9,29:3
Herson, O Ogden, 1961, D 21,27:2
Herst, Herman Jr Mrs, 1954, S 8,32:4
Herst, Herman Mrs, 1956, Jl 30,21:5
Herstein, Bernard, 1939, Je 9,21:4

Herstein, Henry Mrs, 1956, D 26,27:3
Herstein, Karl M, 1961, Je 3,23:2
Hert, Alvin T Mrs, 1948, Je 9,29:1
Hert, Alvin Tobias, 1921, Je 8,17:6
Hert, Benedict S, 1945, D 27,19:5
Hertel, Albert Prof, 1912, F 21,11:4
Hertel, Carl W, 1940, Jl 5,13:4
Hertel, Fredrika W, 1959, Jl 7,33:4
Hertel, Hjalmar, 1966, F 18,33:3
Hertel, John A, 1938, S 4,16:5
Hertel, Joseph H, 1950, Jl 8,13:5
Hertel, Walter, 1966, D 22,33:2
Herten, Austin N, 1961, N 4,19:1
Hertenstein, Charles, 1950, Jl 22,15:6
Hertenstein, Frederick, 1943, Ja 22,19:2
Herter, Albert, 1950, F 16,23:3
Herter, Albert Mrs, 1946, O 3,27:6
Herter, Christian A, 1910, D 6,13:4
Herter, Christian A (funl, Ja 4,41:2), 1967, Ja 1,1:4
Herter, Louis A, 1937, F 11,23:5
Herter, Lydia A, 1951, S 14,25:3
Hertford, Marquess of, 1940, F 17,13:4
Hertford, Marquis of, 1884, Ja 26,5:2
Hertford, Marquis of (Hugh de Gray Seymour), 1912, Mr 24,15:3
Hertie, John C, 1923, Ap 2,17:5
Hertling, George F Von Count, 1919, Ja 6,13:1
Herts, H B, 1933, Mr 28,19:1
Herts, Harold H, 1957, Ag 13,27:1
Herts, Harry H, 1965, Ag 20,29:4
Herts, Jacques H, 1959, Ag 25,31:4
Herts, Robert J Mrs, 1942, My 20,19:5
Hertwig, Frederick A, 1960, Jl 1,25:4
Hertwig, Richard von Prof, 1937, O 5,25:1
Herty, Charles H Jr, 1953, Ja 18,92:5
Hertz, Adolph H, 1945, N 26,21:4
Hertz, Alfred (por), 1942, Ap 18,15:3
Hertz, Arthur M, 1965, Ja 6,39:4
Hertz, Douglas G, 1967, N 30,47:1
Hertz, Douglas G Mrs, 1940, Ja 11,25:1
Hertz, Emanuel (por), 1940, My 24,19:1
Hertz, Frederick, 1964, N 25,37:4
Hertz, John D (will, D 1,30:1), 1961, O 10,43:1
Hertz, John D Jr, 1968, My 13,43:2
Hertz, John D Mrs (Feb 4), 1963, Ap 1,35:7
Hertz, John J, 1962, Ja 16,33:2
Hertz, Joseph, 1958, My 14,33:4
Hertz, Joseph H (por), 1946, Ja 15,23:1
Hertz, Milton, 1941, F 5,19:1
Hertz, Morris Mrs, 1958, Jl 13,68:8
Hertz, Nils, 1964, S 19,27:4
Hertz, Otto, 1956, S 1,15:5
Hertz, Paul, 1961, O 24,37:3
Hertz, Richard, 1961, Ag 3,23:3
Hertz, Russell J, 1949, Ag 23,23:2
Hertz, Samuel, 1924, Jl 22,15:4
Hertz, Simon, 1913, Mr 20,11:4
Hertz, Sol, 1960, F 27,19:5
Hertz, Walter, 1956, F 27,23:2
Hertz, William, 1942, O 19,19:6
Hertzberg, Charles S L, 1944, Ja 13,21:3
Hertzberg, George R R, 1942, S 18,22:4
Hertzberg, Louis, 1944, D 18,19:4; 1960, S 8,35:4
Hertzberg, William, 1955, Jl 14,23:5
Hertzberg, William Mrs, 1955, N 27,88:5
Hertzig, Charles, 1968, Ap 15,43:2
Hertzig, Charles Mrs, 1940, Mr 29,21:2
Hertzig, Emanuel, 1956, My 18,25:2
Hertzler, Arthur E, 1946, S 13,7:3
Hertzler, Robert R, 1957, D 16,29:3
Hertzler, William, 1940, Je 18,23:3
Hertzman, Charles L, 1937, Ja 2,14:1
Hertzmann, Lewis Mrs, 1947, Mr 22,13:3
Hertzog, J B M (por), 1942, N 22,52:1
Hertzog, J B Prof, 1901, S 14,7:5
Hertzog, Lucy S, 1951, Ag 14,23:1
Herve, Francois, 1947, Ap 23,25:1
Herveux, Jane, 1955, Ja 16,93:1
Hervey, Abbie F Mrs, 1939, Mr 20,17:6
Hervey, Augustus Lord, 1875, My 30,7:1
Hervey, Charles S (por), 1944, Jl 23,35:3
Hervey, Charles S Mrs, 1942, D 31,15:4
Hervey, Clifford R, 1947, O 19,64:1
Hervey, Ella Mrs, 1938, D 25,14:7
Hervey, Harry, 1951, Ag 13,17:3
Hervey, Henry D, 1941, S 14,51:4
Hervey, James B, 1949, Mr 19,15:4
Hervey, John D, 1955, Je 15,31:3
Hervey, John L, 1948, Ja 2,23:1
Hervey, Mary B, 1939, N 21,23:4
Hervey, Walter L, 1952, O 15,31:1
Hervey, Walter L Mrs, 1945, F 12,19:3
Hervey, William Anderson Prof, 1918, D 26,11:5
Hervey, William E, 1944, N 8,17:4
Hervey, William Rhodes, 1953, F 3,25:1
Hervey-Bathhurst, Lady, 1957, N 22,25:2
Hervieu, Paul, 1915, O 26,11:4
Hervieux, Edward O, 1947, N 13,27:4
Herwig, Gannett, 1966, Ap 21,39:5
Herwig, H F, 1907, F 1,9:4
Herwig, J C G, 1949, F 20,61:1
Herwig, Joseph L, 1905, Je 28,9:6
Herwig, W J, 1949, Ag 31,23:2
Herwitz, Harry K, 1947, Jl 14,21:3
Herwitz, Michael W, 1952, Jl 13,61:3
Herz, Alex, 1939, Jl 23,29:4
Herz, Armin J, 1954, Ag 15,84:6
Herz, Arthur O, 1949, O 11,33:7
Herz, Arthur S, 1954, Jl 12,19:5
Herz, Carl, 1952, D 22,25:4
Herz, Cornelius Dr, 1898, Jl 7,7:1
Herz, Ernst, 1966, Ap 6,43:3
Herz, Fred W, 1938, S 9,21:3
Herz, Herman, 1955, O 12,31:1
Herz, Herman Mrs, 1958, Ja 13,29:5
Herz, Herman Sr Mrs, 1951, Jl 31,21:4
Herz, Isador, 1955, D 31,13:3
Herz, Jenny K Mrs, 1942, N 28,13:3
Herz, Max, 1951, N 9,27:2
Herz, Ralph, 1921, Jl 13,9:4
Herz, Rudolph, 1956, Ja 5,34:1
Herz, Simon, 1951, F 6,27:5
Herz, Theodore, 1966, Jl 26,35:4
Herz, Victor A, 1941, Ag 25,15:5
Herzberg, E, 1880, Mr 6,2:7
Herzberg, Harry H Mrs, 1943, N 14,56:5
Herzberg, Joseph G Mrs, 1964, Ag 30,92:8
Herzberg, Joseph Mrs, 1953, Je 28,61:1
Herzberg, Max J, 1958, Ja 22,27:3
Herzberg, Max J Mrs, 1956, Jl 9,23:6
Herzberg, Philip, 1914, D 4,11:6
Herzberg, Robert A, 1960, O 21,33:1
Herzberg, Theodore Mrs, 1951, Mr 28,29:4
Herzberger, Parker Mrs, 1949, F 3,24:2
Herzbrun, Henry, 1953, O 17,15:1
Herzel, Paul, 1956, My 12,19:5
Herzer, Jacob H, 1907, Ja 5,9:5
Herzer, Karl Pierce, 1968, F 1,37:2
Herzfeld, Ernst E, 1948, Ja 23,23:1
Herzfeld, Jacob Mrs, 1952, My 19,17:4
Herzfeld, Max, 1967, Ja 19,31:5
Herzfeld, Walter, 1968, S 12,47:4
Herzfelder, H Lionel, 1961, O 22,86:7
Herzig, Arthur J, 1954, My 8,17:7
Herzig, Benjamin H, 1956, Je 18,25:1
Herzig, C S, 1926, N 19,25:4
Herzig, George B, 1925, O 30,21:3
Herzig, Leonard S, 1957, Mr 14,29:1
Herzig, Leonard S Mrs, 1946, Ap 13,17:5
Herzig, Milton A, 1951, N 24,11:4
Herzka, Lloyd I, 1958, F 21,24:1
Herzl, Arthur, 1947, D 20,17:6
Herzl, Theodor Dr, 1904, Jl 4,5:6
Herzl, Theodore, 1925, S 5,13:6
Herzl, Theodore Mrs, 1907, N 25,9:4
Herzman, Harry I, 1947, Ja 11,19:4
Herzog, Adrien B, 1949, Mr 30,25:1
Herzog, Arthur, 1942, F 1,43:2
Herzog, Charles, 1952, Ap 24,16:6
Herzog, Charles L (Buck), 1953, S 6,50:3
Herzog, Eli H, 1957, Mr 22,23:2
Herzog, Felix B, 1912, Ap 22,11:4
Herzog, Frank E, 1941, N 6,23:5
Herzog, Frederick, 1915, Jl 15,9:4
Herzog, Harry Mrs, 1949, D 12,33:1
Herzog, Herbert H, 1962, Ag 18,19:5
Herzog, Isaac H (funl, Jl 27,25:1), 1959, Jl 26,69:1
Herzog, Jack, 1964, Ja 22,37:1
Herzog, James B, 1964, Ja 3,23:2
Herzog, Joseph L, 1953, Ap 21,27:2
Herzog, Joseph Mrs, 1947, D 25,21:3; 1951, D 8,11:6
Herzog, Joseph W, 1954, F 5,20:4
Herzog, Leo, 1952, Je 12,34:3
Herzog, Lester W, 1950, S 25,23:3
Herzog, Louis, 1917, Mr 21,11:4; 1950, Ja 17,27:2
Herzog, Max, 1881, Ap 14,8:1
Herzog, Max A, 1963, N 19,41:3
Herzog, Milton, 1953, N 4,33:1
Herzog, Paul M, 1925, N 13,19:5
Herzog, Ralph S, 1949, D 1,31:5
Herzog, Rayne M, 1968, O 2,39:1
Herzog, Rudolf, 1943, F 5,21:5
Herzog, Samuel A (por), 1946, Ja 17,23:3
Herzog, Siegmund, 1943, Ja 17,44:5
Herzog, Sol A, 1955, Mr 1,25:2
Herzog, Wilhelm, 1960, Ap 20,39:2
Herzov, Harry L, 1940, My 8,23:4
Herzwig, Olaf N, 1944, Ap 14,19:5
Hesburgh, Theodore B Mrs, 1968, F 19,39:3
Hesburgh, Theodore B V, 1960, Mr 1,33:3
Hesch, Oscar, 1966, S 20,47:4
Heschel, Abraham J, 1967, Jl 26,39:2
Hescock, Ethan A S, 1964, My 4,29:3
Heselton, William H, 1953, N 15,89:2
Heser, Herman, 1953, D 10,47:1
Hesilrige, Arthur G M, 1953, Ap 14,27:3
Hesing, Washington Mrs, 1918, Jl 5,11:5
Heskin, Cornelius J, 1952, Ja 10,29:1
Heslep, Charter, 1963, Jl 31,29:4
Hesley, Karl D Mrs, 1937, Mr 31,24:2; 1963, My 1, 39:2
Heslin, Matthew J, 1966, S 25,37:3
Heslin, Matthew J Mrs, 1959, O 8,39:4
Heslin, Thomas W, 1968, Ag 2,33:2
Hespelt, E Herman, 1961, S 9,19:7
Hess, A F, 1933, D 7,23:1
Hess, Abraham, 1938, Mr 9,23:4
Hess, Adam, 1947, O 17,22:5
Hess, Adolph, 1922, Ap 13,19:6
Hess, Albert J, 1946, Mr 21,25:3
Hess, Albert S, 1955, Mr 29,29:4
Hess, Alfred F Mrs, 1960, Ap 11,31:3
Hess, Alton, 1953, Ap 12,88:2
Hess, Amelia, 1941, N 26,23:5
Hess, Anton Prof, 1909, Ap 13,9:5
Hess, Arad F, 1951, Ag 5,73:2
Hess, Arthur, 1955, Mr 23,31:2
Hess, Arthur M, 1949, N 19,17:3
Hess, Bede, 1953, Ag 9,76:2
Hess, Benjamin M, 1958, Jl 7,27:5
Hess, Benjamin Mrs, 1948, Ag 20,17:3
Hess, Billy, 1954, Mr 26,21:1
Hess, Carl A, 1953, My 12,27:4
Hess, Charles A, 1907, O 27,9:5
Hess, Charles A Mrs, 1944, F 27,38:3
Hess, Charles F, 1938, Ap 17,II,6:4; 1946, Ag 8,2
Hess, Charles H, 1943, Ag 2,15:5
Hess, Charles M, 1952, O 4,17:7
Hess, Clara L, 1950, Ap 6,29:1
Hess, Clarence T, 1941, Ap 18,21:4
Hess, Damian C, 1941, Jl 3,19:4
Hess, Dorothea C, 1961, S 20,29:6
Hess, E B, 1941, Ja 10,19:2
Hess, Edward, 1949, N 14,27:5
Hess, Edwin A, 1963, My 21,37:3
Hess, Elizabeth G Mrs, 1955, F 2,27:1
Hess, Elmer, 1961, Mr 30,29:1
Hess, Emil C, 1966, Ja 16,82:7
Hess, Enos H, 1941, Ja 27,15:4
Hess, Everett, 1950, Ag 8,29:4
Hess, Fannie L, 1941, Mr 5,21:1
Hess, Fenne M Jr, 1967, F 19,89:1
Hess, Finley B, 1968, Ja 19,44:3
Hess, Freas L, 1959, N 8,88:3
Hess, Fred W, 1954, Ja 6,31:1
Hess, Friederich, 1941, O 9,23:1
Hess, Gabriel L, 1940, Ap 14,44:6
Hess, George C, 1957, Ag 22,27:5
Hess, George F, 1954, Ap 17,13:4
Hess, George G, 1941, Je 29,32:3
Hess, Gerald A, 1956, Ja 30,27:5
Hess, Grace K Mrs, 1942, F 24,21:2
Hess, Harold M, 1962, O 3,41:4
Hess, Harry, 1964, Mr 26,35:3
Hess, Harry B, 1960, My 1,87:2
Hess, Harry H, 1949, Ag 16,23:1
Hess, Herbert W, 1949, F 22,23:1
Hess, Herman W, 1962, N 2,31:4
Hess, Howard W, 1947, D 27,13:4
Hess, Isaac S, 1940, Je 5,25:4
Hess, Isadore, 1945, Mr 21,23:4
Hess, J Edward, 1914, S 15,11:5
Hess, Jacob, 1904, F 20,9:2
Hess, Jacob Mrs, 1946, D 12,29:2
Hess, James, 1949, D 3,15:4
Hess, John, 1939, Ap 11,16:2
Hess, John B Mrs, 1949, O 30,87:3
Hess, John E Mrs, 1914, Ag 14,11:7
Hess, John F, 1951, Mr 6,27:3
Hess, John J, 1949, Ap 26,25:3
Hess, John R Jr, 1954, Ja 8,21:3
Hess, Joseph W, 1944, D 3,57:2
Hess, Julian S, 1956, Ap 15,89:1
Hess, Julius H (por), 1955, N 3,31:3
Hess, Klara Mrs, 1951, O 7,86:8
Hess, Louise E, 1959, Jl 10,25:4
Hess, Max, 1968, S 2,19:2
Hess, Max Mrs, 1955, N 29,29:3
Hess, Milos, 1946, Jl 18,25:4
Hess, Mores, 1965, Ap 12,35:2
Hess, Morris, 1946, Ja 16,23:1
Hess, Mortimer H, 1968, Mr 7,43:3
Hess, Myra, 1965, N 27,1:3
Hess, Myron, 1950, N 7,27:5
Hess, Newman W, 1957, O 30,29:2
Hess, Otto T Mrs, 1944, Ap 1,13:6
Hess, Peter, 1967, Ap 5,47:1
Hess, Peter C, 1952, Ap 5,15:6
Hess, Philip (Bro Ignatius), 1959, Ap 8,37:4
Hess, Philip Hanson Jr Dr, 1913, F 28,13:5
Hess, R J Dr, 1901, Mr 25,7:7
Hess, Roy M, 1949, Je 26,60:5
Hess, Rudolph B Mrs, 1944, S 30,13:4
Hess, Samuel, 1956, N 25,89:1
Hess, Selmar, 1917, Mr 1,13:4
Hess, Seth G, 1958, Je 19,31:3
Hess, Sidney P, 1965, My 6,39:1
Hess, Simon B, 1949, D 8,33:3
Hess, Sol (por), 1942, Ja 1,25:4
Hess, Sol, 1953, F 1,89:2
Hess, Victor F, 1964, D 19,29:1
Hess, Walter L, 1950, D 9,15:5
Hess, Wendell F, 1954, Ap 23,27:2
Hess, William C, 1952, Ap 4,25:3
Hess, William F, 1947, Je 11,27:2
Hess, William J, 1937, N 5,23:5
Hess, Willy, 1939, F 28,20:2
Hessberg, Albert, 1920, Jl 27,13:5
Hessberg, Fredericka C Mrs, 1937, My 8,19:4

Hessberg, H M, 1931, Jl 23,19:1
Hessberg, Irving K, 1948, O 5,25:2
Hessberg, Max, 1906, My 4,9:5
Hessberg, Rufus R, 1940, Ja 7,49:2
HessburG, James P, 1953, F 21,13:6
Hesse, A J B, 1879, Ag 9,5:2
Hesse, Andre, 1940, D 24,15:2
Hesse, Charles J Sr, 1960, D 13,31:2
Hesse, Clyde R, 1940, Mr 19,25:5
Hesse, Ferdinand, 1946, My 25,15:5
Hesse, Frank M, 1952, Jl 11,17:2
Hesse, George W, 1951, O 4,33:1
Hesse, Harold G, 1950, Ja 28,13:4
Hesse, Henry, 1937, F 14,II,8:5
Hesse, Hermann, 1962, Ag 10,19:2
Hesse, John W Mrs, 1944, My 19,19:4
Hesse, Joseph Mrs, 1949, Ap 12,30:4
Hesse, Louis, 1949, Ap 5,29:5
Hesse, Louis H, 1943, Ap 9,21:4
Hesse, Nelson S, 1944, Mr 30,21:2
Hesse, Nevada Mrs, 1923, My 12,15:5
Hesse, Olga A Mrs, 1942, My 13,19:5
Hesse, Seymour D, 1967, D 3,84:6
Hesse, Victor, 1945, S 29,15:4
Hesse-Wartegg, von Baroness (Minnie Hauk), 1912, N 19,15:4
Hesselbach, Charles F Sr, 1951, Ja 4,30:2
Hesselbach, Charles V, 1959, F 14,21:4
Hesselbach, Henry J, 1939, F 2,19:2
Hesseler, Lola, 1921, D 26,13:1
Hesseler, Rene, 1921, D 26,13:1
Hesselgren, Kerstin, 1962, Ag 22,33:3
Hesselink, Henri, 1947, My 14,25:3
Hesselman, Leo W, 1959, Jl 28,27:5
Hesseltine, William B, 1963, D 9,35:2
Hessen, Joseph V, 1943, Mr 24,23:4
Hessenbruch, Hermann M, 1960, D 28,27:2
Hessenbruch, Hermann M Mrs, 1962, Ap 7,25:2
Hesser, August G, 1952, Mr 19,29:1
Hesser, Frederic W, 1954, Ap 2,27:2
Hesser, Frederick H, 1967, F 11,29:4
Hessert, Edmund C Sr, 1959, Jl 7,33:2
Hessert, Emil C Jr, 1954, Mr 30,27:1
Hessey, David C, 1968, Jl 25,33:5
Hessey, J J Evans, 1956, Mr 27,35:2
Hessey, Peter, 1947, F 24,19:3
Hessian, John J, 1939, O 13,23:3
Hessing, Jacob, 1944, Ap 21,19:2
Hession, Brian, 1961, O 9,35:4
Hession, Edward J, 1950, My 7,106:2
Hession, Jess, 1950, D 13,35:1
Hession, John G, 1939, Mr 18,17:4
Hession, John W, 1962, F 2,30:1
Hession (Sister Mary Joan), 1966, F 15,36:2
Hessler, Charles, 1953, Ja 30,21:1
Hessler, Dayton S, 1943, F 26,19:4
Hessler, DeWitt, 1946, Jl 4,19:5
Hessler, Elmer H, 1939, F 21,19:3
Hessler, Frederick C, 1967, Ag 10,37:1
Hessler, George F, 1954, F 3,23:3
Hessler, Howard H, 1962, N 28,39:1
Hessler, John C, 1944, Jl 31,13:6
Hessler, William H, 1965, Ap 16,29:5
Hesson, Horace W, 1946, O 30,27:2
Hesson, Horace W Mrs, 1945, N 15,19:5
Hesson, Hugo T, 1948, Ja 7,25:4
Hester, Ada L G Mrs, 1942, D 29,22:2
Hester, C L V Col, 1903, D 4,9:5
Hester, Charles B, 1965, N 30,41:4
Hester, Charles B Mrs, 1963, Mr 27,4:5
Hester, Charles R Mrs, 1954, Jl 7,31:6
Hester, Eugene G, 1942, Mr 10,19:3
Hester, H C Kendall, 1951, Je 1,23:4
Hester, John K, 1965, Ap 8,39:1
Hester, Lucy G, 1951, D 5,35:5
Hester, Paul V, 1953, O 10,17:6
Hester, S C B Mrs, 1901, Ap 29,7:6
Hester, St C, 1933, My 27,13:3
Hester, William Col, 1921, Je 10,13:3
Hester, William Van A, 1963, My 4,25:1
Hester, William Van Arden (por), 1924, D 15,17:4
Hesterberg, George J, 1939, Je 8,25:5
Hesterberg, Henry, 1917, S 26,13:5; 1950, Jl 1,15:3
Heston, Alfred M, 1937, N 11,25:6
Heston, E Edgar Mrs, 1948, D 17,27:4
Heston, Eliza Jones, 1925, Ap 11,13:2
Heston, Florence (Mrs H Cavanaugh), 1963, Jl 2, 26:5
Heston, Herbert Jr, 1951, O 15,25:4
Heston, Newton Rev, 1865, Jl 15,8:4
Heston, Willie (Wm M), 1963, S 11,43:3
Hetfield, A S, 1877, F 11,4:7
Hetfield, Emily L, 1940, S 17,23:4
Hetfield, Margaret T Mrs, 1940, N 14,23:2
Hetfield, Walter L Jr (por), 1940, S 18,23:1
Hetfield, Walter L Jr Mrs, 1953, Je 20,17:4
Heth, Edward H, 1963, Ap 28,87:5
Hetherington, Arthur F Mrs, 1958, Mr 2,89:2
Hetherington, Bartholomew L Mrs, 1964, Mr 26,35:4
Hetherington, Charles, 1938, S 12,17:5
Hetherington, Elizabeth N Mrs, 1941, S 23,23:6
Hetherington, Ethel, 1939, F 18,15:3
Hetherington, Ferris S, 1957, Jl 1,23:3
Hetherington, Hector, 1965, Ja 17,88:4
Hetherington, Howard H, 1952, O 22,27:1
Hetherington, James A 2d Mrs, 1960, Je 5,86:4
Hetherington, James H Com, 1917, S 18,9:6
Hetherington, Janet, 1954, Jl 27,21:2
Hetherington, John Mrs, 1939, N 23,27:4
Hetherington, Robert Rev, 1937, Ja 28,25:3
Hetherington, Seth C (por), 1955, S 13,31:4
Hetherton, Edward S Maj, 1914, O 14,11:5
Hetherton, James A, 1953, My 13,29:1
Hetherton, Jerome M, 1955, Jl 7,27:1
Hethey, Gustave, 1944, My 19,19:5
Hetrick, Clarence E F, 1941, O 14,23:1
Hetrick, Clarence Mrs, 1950, Ag 31,25:5
Hetrick, D Murray, 1941, F 3,17:1
Hetrick, George R, 1949, Ja 26,25:1
Hetrick, Llewellyn E, 1959, Ja 22,32:1
Hetrick, Wm H, 1960, S 28,39:3
Hetson, Isidore, 1963, S 20,33:2
Hett, Clarence H, 1937, Je 13,II,6:7
Hett, Edward, 1915, Ag 15,13:5
Hett, John E, 1956, S 26,33:4
Hettche, John J, 1961, Ja 21,21:2
Hettel, Arthur J, 1943, Jl 17,13:6
Hetterick, Edith S Mrs, 1952, Jl 11,17:3
Hettesheimer, Carl A, 1949, Ag 11,24:5
Hettich, Albert T, 1949, My 13,23:4
Hettinger, Mathias, 1937, Mr 9,23:1
Hettler, Oscar C (por), 1948, Je 30,25:3
Hettrick, Ames B, 1953, D 30,23:5
Hettrick, George D, 1953, N 5,31:5
Hettrick Geo Mrs, 1950, Mr 27,23:4
Hetz, Frank W, 1963, D 22,34:5
Hetz, Harold A, 1947, Ag 31,37:1
Hetzel, Carl C, 1939, Ap 11,23:4
Hetzel, Charles A Mrs, 1953, Je 13,15:5
Hetzel, Charles E, 1943, S 27,19:5
Hetzel, Foster G, 1961, O 2,31:3
Hetzel, Frederick V, 1946, F 24,44:3
Hetzel, George, 1944, O 16,19:4
Hetzel, Henry W, 1941, F 10,17:4
Hetzel, James, 1945, Mr 28,23:2
Hetzel, Ralph D, 1947, O 4,17:3
Hetzer, Lillie L, 1937, Ap 18,II,9:2
Hetzler, George A, 1940, Je 22,15:2
Hetzler, Theodore (por), 1945, Ag 14,21:2
Hetzler, Theodore Mrs, 1961, Jl 25,28:1
Hetznecker, John, 1940, My 23,23:5
Heubener, Erich K, 1951, My 8,31:4
Heublein, Arthur C Mrs, 1967, My 27,31:4
Heublein, Gilbert F, 1937, Mr 23,23:5
Heublein, Gilbert W, 1967, My 29,25:2
Heubner, Martin E, 1953, Mr 28,17:3
Heubsch, A Rev Dr, 1884, O 11,5:2
Heubsch, Frank J, 1944, Ag 29,17:3
Heudle, George L, 1922, O 1,28:4
Heuel, Emil Dr, 1920, Ag 12,9:3
Heuer, George J, 1950, D 16,17:6
Heuer, Harry H (will), 1959, My 28,31:2
Heuer, Henry F, 1941, Ag 21,17:4
Heuer, Herman F, 1945, S 24,19:1
Heugel, Aug F, 1940, Ja 6,13:1
Heughes, Walter L, 1942, Je 26,21:3
Heughlin, T Von, 1876, N 7,4:7
Heuillard, Voerges, 1952, O 12,5:1
Heuisler, Catherine A J Mrs, 1937, F 21,II,10:4
Heuisler, William F, 1949, O 19,29:1
Heulings, Lloyd, 1953, S 20,86:6
Heuman, Charles C, 1940, Jl 1,19:6
Heumann, Emil N, 1951, Ag 9,21:6
Heumann, Michael, 1937, O 31,II,10:5
Heumann, Monroe, 1939, Mr 16,23:1
Heumann, Sol (will, S 17,9:8), 1949, S 12,21:2
Heun, Arthur, 1946, Je 21,23:2
Heureaux, Gen, 1899, Jl 27,1:2
Heurich, Christian (por), 1945, Mr 9,19:3
Heus, John G, 1939, Ag 13,29:2
Heuschling, P F X T, 1883, My 26,5:5
Heuser, Christian, 1945, Ja 19,19:1
Heuser, Frank J Sr, 1951, N 6,29:6
Heuser, Frederick W J, 1961, Ja 26,29:3
Heuser, Frederick W J Mrs, 1944, O 14,13:1
Heuser, Gerhard W, 1945, D 30,14:2
Heuser, Julius R, 1941, Ag 30,13:3
Heuser, Leon V, 1953, My 10,88:2
Heusinkveld, David W sr, 1955, Je 26,77:2
Heuslein, Emma C Mrs, 1939, O 31,23:6
Heuslein, I Leonard Mrs, 1942, My 15,19:2
Heuss, John (funl, Mr 25,41:3), 1966, Mr 22,41:1
Heuss, John Mrs, 1951, Ap 15,92:4
Heuss, Theodor (funl plans; trb, D 14,27:1; funl, D 18,41:5), 1963, D 13,35:1
Heuss, Theodor Mrs, 1952, Jl 20,53:3
Heuss, William H, 1955, F 22,21:1
Heusser, Ed, 1956, Mr 2,23:4
Heusser, John F, 1962, Ja 5,29:2
Heussner, Carl E, 1951, Ja 3,27:2
Heussner, John G, 1955, N 13,89:1
Heustis, George F, 1942, Jl 4,17:5
Heustis, Harry S, 1947, Ap 16,25:6
Heustis, Lewis Mrs, 1942, Ap 11,13:6
Heuven Goedhart, G J van, 1956, Jl 10,31:4
Hevell-Thurlow-Cumming-Bruce, Thomas John (Baron Thurlow), 1916, Mr 15,11:5
Hevenor, Alfred Mrs, 1946, F 18,21:5
Hevenor, Richard S, 1957, O 10,33:2
Hever, James L, 1911, S 27,13:6; 1959, Jl 23,27:2
Heverin, Cator, 1903, Mr 19,9:5
Heverly, Lloyd, 1948, My 9,V,4:8
Heveron, William, 1946, Ja 26,13:4
Hevesh, Joseph, 1958, Je 12,31:4
Hevesi, Francis, 1952, Ap 2,33:3
Hevesi, Simon, 1943, Mr 4,20:1
Hevesy, George von, 1966, Jl 6,42:1
Hevey, John A, 1947, Ag 17,52:6
Hevia, Carlos, 1964, Ap 4,28:1
Hevia Alcalde, Aurelio, 1945, Ja 24,22:3
Heward, Charles G, 1939, Je 4,48:6
Heward, Leslie H, 1943, My 4,23:3
Hewart, Lord (por), 1943, My 6,19:1
Hewat, Richard Mrs, 1947, Mr 8,13:1
Hewat, Thomas, 1943, Ag 16,15:2
Hewatt, Fred A, 1948, Ja 14,25:1
Heweker, Charles B, 1938, Ap 27,23:5
Hewes, Alanson B, 1956, N 25,89:1
Hewes, Clarence B, 1962, Ap 23,29:3
Hewes, Earl D, 1956, Jl 13,19:5
Hewes, Frank W, 1939, Ag 19,15:2
Hewes, Frederic W, 1962, N 6,33:5
Hewes, Joel F, 1952, Mr 5,29:5
Hewes, Lawrence S, 1950, Ag 31,25:3
Hewes, M Lewin, 1940, F 17,13:4
Hewes, R Kermit, 1943, Ap 21,25:5
Hewes, Thomas, 1957, Je 17,23:4
Hewes, Virgil H, 1942, Mr 23,15:3
Hewett, Charles G, 1941, Jl 26,15:3
Hewett, E A (see also Je 3), 1877, Je 5,8:3
Hewett, Edgar L (por), 1947, Ja 1,33:3
Hewett, Frank V C, 1957, D 29,48:8
Hewett, Mary C J Mrs, 1943, Ap 13,25:5
Hewett, Merritt A, 1962, Ap 28,25:4
Hewett, Stanley, 1954, Ag 12,25:2
Hewett, Waterman Thomas, 1921, S 14,19:4
Hewett-Thayer, Harvey W, 1960, Je 17,31:2
Hewish, Edgar M, 1943, Ap 13,25:5
Hewit, Hamilton W, 1947, F 20,25:4
Hewitt, A F, 1882, Je 6,5:2
Hewitt, A S, 1903, Ja 19,1:7
Hewitt, Abram S, 1912, Ag 15,9:4
Hewitt, Alden, 1940, D 28,15:4
Hewitt, Alfred F, 1939, D 21,26:5
Hewitt, Ann C (Mrs F Nicholson), 1956, F 11,13:3
Hewitt, Arthur P Mrs, 1956, F 25,19:4
Hewitt, Bertha E, 1966, F 24,37:2
Hewitt, Brower, 1958, N 6,37:5
Hewitt, Caroline D, 1961, Je 27,33:3
Hewitt, Cecil M, 1958, Je 2,27:1
Hewitt, Charles, 1879, N 3,4:7
Hewitt, Charles G Dr, 1920, Mr 2,11:4
Hewitt, Charles J (por), 1940, Je 23,31:3
Hewitt, Charles M, 1916, Mr 17,11:7
Hewitt, Charles T, 1945, Mr 21,23:3
Hewitt, Clarence H, 1952, S 4,27:5
Hewitt, Clifford, 1942, S 2,23:3
Hewitt, Conrad, 1947, Ap 27,60:1
Hewitt, Dan S, 1956, Ja 30,27:5
Hewitt, E A, 1878, Je 8,8:6
Hewitt, E Clifford, 1953, Ap 14,27:3
Hewitt, Earl S, 1959, Je 30,31:3
Hewitt, Edward C, 1966, Ag 15,27:3
Hewitt, Edward R, 1957, F 20,33:1
Hewitt, Edward R Mrs, 1945, N 4,44:1
Hewitt, Edward S, 1962, Je 3,88:2
Hewitt, Edward S Mrs, 1960, Je 30,29:6
Hewitt, Eleanor (funl, N 29,13:3), 1924, N 28,15:4
Hewitt, Elmer, 1951, My 28,21:2
Hewitt, Elmer L, 1942, Mr 29,45:1
Hewitt, Erskine (will, Je 7,44:2), 1938, My 23,17:5
Hewitt, Frank C, 1950, N 27,25:1
Hewitt, Frederick C, 1908, Ag 31,7:6
Hewitt, Frederick R, 1952, Ja 8,27:4
Hewitt, George, 1940, Mr 16,15:3; 1944, Je 26,15:5; 1949, F 24,23:3
Hewitt, George A, 1963, My 20,31:3
Hewitt, George B, 1939, Je 25,37:1
Hewitt, George D Mrs, 1952, Ja 9,29:4
Hewitt, George E, 1948, Ap 3,15:4
Hewitt, George F, 1922, My 26,19:6
Hewitt, George W, 1954, My 28,23:5
Hewitt, Harrison, 1938, F 25,17:2
Hewitt, Harvey S, 1964, D 25,29:4
Hewitt, Henry M, 1957, My 21,35:4
Hewitt, Irenaeus Mrs, 1946, My 29,24:3
Hewitt, J Robert, 1961, Ag 1,31:4
Hewitt, James C, 1946, S 13,7:3
Hewitt, Jessie, 1944, F 29,17:4
Hewitt, Jessie L Mrs, 1942, Ja 11,44:1
Hewitt, John, 1881, Mr 10,5:5
Hewitt, John E, 1967, F 11,29:4
Hewitt, John E Mrs, 1953, Mr 30,21:3
Hewitt, John H, 1960, D 11,88:8
Hewitt, John Haskell Prof, 1920, O 7,15:2
Hewitt, John N B Dr, 1937, O 20,23:5
Hewitt, John T, 1950, My 15,21:5
Hewitt, John T Mrs, 1948, Ja 22,27:2
Hewitt, John V, 1964, N 30,33:1

Hewitt, John W, 1953, My 26,29:3
Hewitt, Joseph F, 1957, Je 10,27:2
Hewitt, Joseph T, 1968, Ja 19,39:3
Hewitt, Joseph W (por), 1938, Jl 9,13:3
Hewitt, Josiah M, 1964, F 2,89:1
Hewitt, Leo C, 1954, Ja 4,19:4
Hewitt, Louis F, 1965, N 20,35:6
Hewitt, Maryon C Mrs (Mrs M C McCarter), 1939, My 1,42:1
Hewitt, Max A Mrs, 1944, O 28,15:1
Hewitt, Mott Cannon, 1904, Ja 30,9:5
Hewitt, Ogden B, 1963, O 18,31:1
Hewitt, Orville M, 1955, O 31,25:1
Hewitt, Oscar E, 1955, F 7,21:2
Hewitt, Peter Cooper, 1921, Ag 26,13:6; 1921, S 15, 15:3
Hewitt, Robert, 1913, O 7,13:5
Hewitt, Robert A Mrs, 1945, O 18,23:5
Hewitt, Robert Mrs, 1944, D 27,19:5
Hewitt, Robert P, 1957, Ja 12,19:5
Hewitt, Ross I, 1954, My 24,27:1
Hewitt, Ross W, 1951, Ja 11,25:4
Hewitt, S, 1930, O 17,23:3
Hewitt, Sid W, 1952, O 18,19:3
Hewitt, Theodore B, 1952, N 27,31:4
Hewitt, Thomas Browning, 1921, Ja 8,11:6
Hewitt, Thomas D, 1941, F 21,19:4
Hewitt, Walter C, 1940, Ja 19,19:4
Hewitt, William D, 1924, Ap 24,19:3
Hewitt, William E, 1944, F 26,13:1; 1948, F 3,26:2
Hewitt, William F, 1955, Mr 23,31:4
Hewitt, William M, 1946, Jl 21,40:2
Hewitt, William S, 1939, Mr 9,21:2; 1955, My 17,29:4
Hewlett, Ambrose W, 1945, Ap 16,23:5
Hewlett, Arthur T, 1951, N 13,30:3
Hewlett, Arthur T 2d, 1953, Ja 25,85:1
Hewlett, C Russell, 1913, N 12,9:6
Hewlett, Carrie L, 1959, My 19,33:4
Hewlett, Charles A, 1956, F 13,27:6
Hewlett, E M, 1934, My 25,21:3
Hewlett, George, 1951, O 2,27:2
Hewlett, George T, 1912, O 12,11:6
Hewlett, Henrietta Mrs, 1937, My 24,19:5
Hewlett, Herbert E, 1947, Mr 12,25:4
Hewlett, J Monroe (por), 1941, O 19,44:5
Hewlett, John Divine, 1903, Ag 30,7:7
Hewlett, Joseph M Sr, 1954, O 20,29:3
Hewlett, Joseph S, 1966, D 21,39:3
Hewlett, Maurice, 1923, Je 16,11:5
Hewlett, Palmer A, 1945, Ap 10,19:2
Hewlett, Percy W, 1944, S 30,13:5
Hewlett, Robert, 1944, Je 4,41:1
Hewlett, Samuel L Mrs, 1954, Ag 14,15:5
Hewlett, Walter J, 1941, Ag 5,19:2
Hewlett, Walter J Mrs, 1947, My 14,25:5
Hewlett, William H, 1940, Je 15,15:4
Hewlett, William N, 1949, Jl 17,57:2
Hewson, Addinell, 1938, O 28,23:2
Hewson, Austin, 1946, Je 27,21:2
Hewson, George F, 1958, F 14,24:1
Hewson, Robert J, 1960, Je 28,31:5
Hewson, Victor, 1908, S 1,7:5
Hewston, John J, 1959, Ja 25,92:6
Hexamer, A C Mrs, 1957, O 26,21:5
Hexamer, Charles J Dr, 1921, O 16,22:3
Hexner, Ervin Paul Dr, 1968, My 17,44:1
Hexter, Irving B, 1960, My 23,29:4
Hexter, Joseph, 1954, S 27,21:3
Hexter, Max, 1952, D 25,29:4
Hexter, Roy M, 1954, Ag 16,17:2
Hey, Colby F, 1943, O 2,13:5
Hey, Frederick, 1948, F 29,60:4
Hey, James, 1940, Jl 3,17:3
Hey, Judson, 1948, Mr 8,23:3
Heybeck, Harry H, 1944, O 28,15:4
Heyboer, Linde A, 1964, N 11,43:4
Heybrock, Jan P, 1952, F 26,27:2
Heyburn, John E, 1953, F 26,25:2
Heyburn, Weldon Brinton Sen, 1912, O 18,11:3
Heyburn, William, 1939, Ap 23,III,6:8
Heycamp, Bp, 1874, O 30,1:5
Heyd, Albert, 1938, Ag 26,17:4
Heyd, Ernest, 1952, Jl 22,25:4
Heyd, Ernst, 1955, F 26,15:2
Heyd, Frank X, 1947, D 20,17:2
Heyde, Charles F Mrs, 1949, Ap 9,17:6
Heyde, Gustav von der, 1943, My 11,21:4
Heyde, Hannah Louisa Whitman, 1908, Jl 19,7:7
Heydecke, Franklyn, 1956, Jl 4,19:2
Heydecker, Edward L Mrs, 1956, Ja 2,21:5
Heydecker, William C, 1942, F 23,21:2
Heydegger, William L Jr, 1954, Jl 4,30:5
Heyden, Edward B, 1950, Ap 20,29:3
Heyden, Peter Count, 1907, Je 29,7:6
Heyden, Theodore E Mrs, 1943, Ap 10,17:5
Heydenreich, Louis Victor, 1919, S 14,22:3
Heydinger, William J, 1925, Ja 17,15:5
Heydler, John A (funl, Ap 22,86:6), 1956, Ap 19,31:5
Heydon, Charles G, 1945, My 10,23:5
Heydorn, Hugo R, 1962, F 3,21:1
Heydorn, William A, 1958, O 16,37:1
Heydrick, David M Rev, 1904, F 16,9:6
Heydrick, L C, 1959, F 22,88:4
Heydrick, William J, 1953, D 21,31:4
Heydt, Charles E, 1963, O 5,25:3
Heydt, Charles O, 1958, Ja 6,39:1
Heydt, George F, 1953, Ag 17,15:5
Heydt, George F Mrs, 1959, Jl 8,29:2
Heydt, Herman (por), 1941, Ag 5,19:5
Heydt, Louis J, 1960, Ja 30,13:2
Heye, Carl T (por), 1946, Je 23,40:1
Heye, George G (will F 7,23:2), 1957, Ja 21,25:3
Heyel, Herbert W, 1951, Ag 17,17:3
Heyen, Constant, 1947, Ag 24,58:2
Heyer, A Lester Mrs, 1952, Je 27,23:3
Heyer, Adolph, 1948, Jl 3,15:4
Heyer, Andrew L, 1950, F 9,29:2
Heyer, Arthur P, 1943, F 17,21:4
Heyer, Charles, 1961, D 28,27:1
Heyer, Charles A, 1942, Jl 13,15:4
Heyer, Edith, 1924, Ja 28,15:4
Heyer, Harriet S Mrs, 1939, Ag 5,15:5
Heyer, Herman, 1950, Je 2,23:1
Heyer, Hobert E, 1950, My 12,27:1
Heyer, Walter, 1947, Ap 21,27:5
Heyer, William D Dr, 1916, F 7,11:2
Heyes, Edwin B, 1956, Je 10,89:1
Heyes, Herbert, 1958, Je 5,31:4
Heyker, Mattias F, 1953, O 29,31:4
Heyking, Baron von, 1915, Je 17,11:7
Heyl, Ashton B Mrs, 1949, D 26,29:2
Heyl, Carl F, 1952, F 25,21:4
Heyl, Charles E Sr, 1952, Ag 15,16:7
Heyl, Ernest O, 1947, My 15,25:1
Heyl, Ernst O Mrs, 1959, My 31,76:4
Heyl, H Frau, 1934, Ja 24,17:4
Heyl, Isaac C, 1954, Ap 21,29:1
Heyl, Juliet F, 1942, F 4,20:2
Heyl, William L, 1941, Ap 13,38:2
Heylen, Thomas, 1941, N 2,52:2
Heyliger, William Mrs, 1947, Jl 5,11:6
Heylman, Henry B, 1944, F 18,17:4
Heylman Hy B Mrs, 1951, Jl 29,69:3
Heym, Gerhard M, 1959, F 26,31:4
Heym, Thomas, 1965, Jl 24,3:5
Heyman, Cecelia A Mrs, 1942, Ag 28,19:5
Heyman, Clarence H, 1952, Jl 15,21:2
Heyman, Eric S, 1957, Jl 28,60:4
Heyman, Frederick K, 1964, Jl 24,27:3
Heyman, Herbert M, 1946, Ap 16,25:3
Heyman, Herman C, 1958, F 22,17:1
Heyman, Ignatz Mrs, 1952, D 3,33:3
Heyman, Irving A, 1953, My 2,15:2
Heyman, Irving I, 1963, Je 1,21:3
Heyman, Jacob Mrs, 1964, N 24,39:1
Heyman, Katherine R, 1944, S 29,21:6
Heyman, Louis, 1958, Ja 23,27:3
Heyman, Marcus B Dr (funl, O 9,23:3), 1925, O 8, 27:5
Heyman, Marcus B Dr, 1925, D 9,27:4
Heyman, Marcus B Mrs, 1956, O 27,21:3
Heyman, Max Mrs (K Sandwina), 1952, Ja 22,29:3
Heyman, Melville, 1938, N 11,25:4
Heyman, Morris, 1965, N 6,29:5
Heyman, Nicholas, 1943, Ag 30,15:4
Heyman, Nicholas N, 1964, Mr 10,37:3
Heyman, Oscar, 1949, D 10,17:3
Heyman, Oscar Mrs, 1960, S 15,37:2
Heyman, Simon, 1941, O 15,21:1
Heyman, William, 1967, My 9,47:2
Heymann, Erick, 1949, N 25,31:4
Heymann, Ernest F, 1965, F 11,39:2
Heymann, Hans, 1949, O 2,82:5
Heymann, Joseph C, 1940, O 24,25:4
Heymann, Julius, 1965, Mr 24,43:4
Heymann, Leo A, 1947, Je 23,23:3
Heymann, Lida G (por), 1943, Ag 8,36:7
Heymann, Louis H, 1942, Jl 4,17:5
Heymann, Melvin, 1963, Jl 21,65:1
Heymann, Paul, 1944, My 23,23:3
Heymann, Roy A, 1962, Ja 2,29:2
Heymann, Seligmann Prof, 1903, S 2,14:4
Heymann, Seymour E, 1959, D 28,23:4
Heymann, Seymour E (died Dec 59, cor), 1960, Ja 5,31:1
Heymann, Sophie G Mrs, 1942, F 28,17:1
Heymann, Walter M Jr, 1961, O 11,47:4
Heymans, Corneille Jean Francois Dr, 1968, Jl 19,35:3
Heymans, Henri, 1945, S 17,19:4
Heymsfeld, Ralph T, 1962, My 20,86:1
Heyn, Daniel, 1955, F 12,15:2
Heyn, Edward T, 1950, Je 1,27:3
Heyn, Otto P, 1915, S 30,11:6
Heyn, Robert E, 1954, N 30,29:6
Heyn, Roman H, 1942, N 22,52:2
Heyn, Roman H Mrs (will, O 7,37:2), 1960, Ag 23, 29:2
Heyne, Arthur E, 1952, N 27,31:4
Heyne, Charles W Mrs, 1953, Mr 9,29:4
Heyne, Fred T Sr, 1966, My 25,47:3
Heyniger, C Lambert, 1960, O 30,86:6
Heyniger, William L, 1958, Mr 30,88:7
Heyninx, Albert, 1955, S 1,23:4
Heyrovsky, Jaroslav, 1967, Mr 28,45:3
Heyser, Carl J Sr, 1958, O 17,29:2
Heyser, Frederick L, 1951, O 26,23:3
Heyson, Harry G, 1946, O 18,23:5
Heyward, Du Bose Mrs, 1961, N 20,31:4
Heyward, DuBose (por), 1940, Je 17,15:5
Heyward, Duncan C, 1943, Ja 25,13:4
Heyward, Frank, 1879, O 8,8:3
Heyward, Jane S Mrs, 1939, Je 12,17:5
Heyward, Monroe H, 1962, S 18,39:4
Heyward, Samuel W, 1940, Ap 25,23:4
Heywood, Albert S, 1938, Je 1,23:2
Heywood, Anne (Mrs A H Reid), 1961, Ja 23,23:3
Heywood, C Fay, 1938, My 14,15:7
Heywood, Charles, 1937, Mr 20,19:6
Heywood, Charles Maj-Gen, 1915, F 27,11:6
Heywood, Charles W, 1941, N 2,53:2
Heywood, Donald, 1951, N 24,28:6
Heywood, George Dr, 1909, Jl 31,7:6
Heywood, George H, 1953, O 11,89:1
Heywood, Harry B, 1953, Ag 7,19:4
Heywood, Henry E, 1941, Je 9,19:5
Heywood, Johnson, 1950, Ap 8,13:5
Heywood, Johnson Mrs, 1950, Ap 8,13:5
Heywood, Robert R Sr, 1956, O 4,33:2
Heywood, Seth, 1938, Ja 27,21:1
Heywood, W Scott, 1950, N 30,33:1
Heyzer, Charles H, 1904, F 10,9:6
Heyzer, Charles H Mrs, 1925, Je 5,17:4
Hg, Albert, 1916, Ja 9,17:5
Hiam, T A Col, 1937, Ja 1,23:3
Hiatt, Casper W, 1924, Jl 21,11:5
Hiatt, Lucile, 1965, Mr 1,27:3
Hiatt, Walter S, 1956, Je 23,17:6
Hibbard, Addison, 1945, My 19,19:5
Hibbard, Alida V Mrs, 1938, S 13,23:4
Hibbard, Angus S, 1945, O 22,17:5
Hibbard, Charles L, 1947, N 16,76:3
Hibbard, Charles L Mrs, 1948, Jl 7,46:1
Hibbard, Edna (Mrs Lester Bryant), 1942, D 27,34:3
Hibbard, Ellery A, 1903, Je 25,12:6
Hibbard, Frank, 1957, N 5,31:4
Hibbard, Frank C, 1942, Ag 4,20:2
Hibbard, Frederick C, 1950, D 13,35:2
Hibbard, Frederick Mrs, 1950, S 5,27:2
Hibbard, Frederick P, 1943, Ag 24,19:2
Hibbard, George A, 1910, My 30,11:5
Hibbard, George Albee, 1910, Je 2,9:4
Hibbard, Halo, 1953, D 17,37:4
Hibbard, Harry W, 1950, My 28,45:2
Hibbard, Henry D, 1942, O 18,52:2
Hibbard, Henry D Mrs, 1946, Mr 29,23:3
Hibbard, Isaac L, 1924, Ap 15,21:2
Hibbard, James Dr, 1903, S 2,7:6
Hibbard, John D, 1937, N 18,23:3
Hibbard, John Van O, 1960, My 5,35:5
Hibbard, Otto M Mrs (H M Gruppe), 1958, Je 30, 19:3
Hibbard, Ralph B, 1950, O 9,25:4
Hibbard, Ralph B Mrs, 1943, N 22,19:2
Hibbard, Ralph G, 1904, Ja 27,9:7
Hibbard, Thomas, 1938, O 5,23:4
Hibbard, W G, 1903, O 12,7:7
Hibbard, Walter, 1953, N 27,27:3
Hibbard, William G Jr Mrs, 1961, D 6,47:2
Hibbard, William W, 1957, Ja 6,89:1
Hibbard, Winona A, 1947, Ag 20,21:2
Hibben, J G Mrs, 1933, Je 19,15:3
Hibben, James H, 1959, Je 17,35:1
Hibben, Sheila (Mrs P Hibben), 1964, F 21,27:1
Hibben, Thomas E, 1952, Mr 21,24:5
Hibberd, Dilworth P, 1953, My 3,89:2
Hibberd, Edward N, 1955, Mr 17,45:1
Hibberd, Ferdinand C, 1953, F 8,91:4
Hibberd, Hayward A, 1955, Ap 4,29:2
Hibbert, Harold, 1945, My 15,19:4
Hibbert, James Mrs, 1943, O 27,23:5
Hibbert, Joseph W, 1943, D 21,27:2
Hibbert, Leonard E, 1942, O 15,23:1
Hibbett, Richard, 1945, Ap 1,36:4
Hibbitt, George W, 1965, D 20,35:4
Hibbitt, Joseph J, 1945, S 18,23:3
Hibbs, Chlora E Mrs, 1941, Ja 27,15:3
Hibbs, Manton E, 1957, Ag 10,15:2
Hibbs, Raymond S, 1960, F 18,33:4
Hibbs, Russell, 1954, N 25,29:2
Hibbs, Russell A Mrs, 1968, D 17,47:2
Hibbs, William L, 1941, O 9,23:2
Hibicht, Harvey H, 1954, Je 29,27:4
Hibler, Alfred W Sr, 1951, S 15,15:4
Hibler, Orlo Mrs, 1952, O 25,17:4
Hibler, Wilfred S, 1956, Je 29,21:2
Hibner, Joseph F, 1945, Ag 15,19:2
Hibshman, Edward K, 1964, Ag 25,33:5
Hibshman, H Z, 1942, Mr 18,23:6
Hibson, James Albert, 1907, Ja 11,9:5
Hice, Arthur E, 1963, Jl 25,25:4
Hice, George S, 1951, D 30,24:2
Hichborn, Charles S, 1941, D 30,19:4
Hichborn, Franklin, 1963, D 31,19:4
Hichborn, George F, 1959, Ag 7,23:1
Hichborn, Philip Rear-Adm, 1910, My 2,9:6
Hichens, Robert S, 1950, Jl 22,15:3
Hicinbothem, Leah L Mrs, 1940, Ap 2,25:4
Hick, Charles M, 1947, F 14,21:2
Hick, Walter R, 1951, F 23,27:5

Hickcox, Charles G, 1943, N 18,23:2
Hicke, Michael P, 1948, S 11,15:5
Hickenlooper, Andrew Gen, 1904, My 13,9:6
Hickenlooper, Margaret B, 1943, My 17,15:4
Hickenlooper, Nathan O, 1961, My 31,33:4
Hickens, Edward E Mrs, 1951, Ja 7,77:2
Hickernell, Latimer F, 1963, D 17,39:2
Hickerson, J Allen, 1959, My 23,25:5
Hickerson, Robert A, 1963, My 11,25:4
Hickerson, Robert L, 1961, F 3,17:3
Hickerson, William D, 1949, D 20,31:4
Hickey, Agnes K Mrs, 1939, F 7,19:2
Hickey, Alfred J Sr, 1961, My 11,37:5
Hickey, Andrew J, 1942, Ag 21,19:5
Hickey, Andrew S Mrs, 1944, F 4,16:2
Hickey, Arthur T, 1966, Ag 2,33:2
Hickey, Austin T, 1951, O 23,29:2
Hickey, Bridget Mrs, 1922, D 27,17:5
Hickey, C A Mrs, 1873, Ap 27,5:3
Hickey, C J, 1943, D 6,23:3
Hickey, Charles, 1939, My 30,18:1
Hickey, Clarence, 1945, Je 21,19:2
Hickey, Cornelius, 1937, Ja 18,17:1
Hickey, Cornelius J, 1959, Mr 1,86:2
Hickey, Daniel F B, 1966, O 23,88:2
Hickey, Daniel J, 1940, Mr 20,27:1
Hickey, Daniel W, 1946, Mr 26,29:5
Hickey, David F, 1946, F 23,13:4
Hickey, David H, 1952, Je 5,31:5
Hickey, David J Msgr, 1937, F 3,23:1
Hickey, Dorr S, 1942, N 1,52:8
Hickey, Doyle O, 1961, O 21,21:5
Hickey, E J, 1944, Ja 14,19:1
Hickey, Edward J, 1953, S 23,31:2
Hickey, Edward L, 1937, Jl 14,21:2
Hickey, Edward V, 1949, Jl 27,24:3
Hickey, Edwin, 1947, D 13,15:3
Hickey, Ellen E Mrs, 1942, F 15,44:2
Hickey, Frank E, 1951, Jl 8,61:1
Hickey, Frank J, 1947, Mr 6,25:2; 1954, N 26,29:3
Hickey, Frederic H, 1958, S 16,27:1
Hickey, George F, 1939, S 17,49:1
Hickey, George H, 1949, Ja 26,25:3
Hickey, George 3d, 1964, O 17,29:6
Hickey, Harry A, 1952, F 29,23:4
Hickey, Harry M, 1948, S 13,21:2
Hickey, Harry R C, 1958, Ap 10,29:4
Hickey, Harry W, 1951, F 16,25:3
Hickey, Harvey J, 1959, D 1,39:3
Hickey, J Garrett, 1954, Ja 22,27:3
Hickey, James, 1948, Ag 31,26:2
Hickey, James A, 1957, O 12,19:5
Hickey, James C, 1952, Ap 4,33:5
Hickey, James F, 1940, Ag 22,20:2; 1962, Je 6,41:3
Hickey, James H, 1950, Mr 25,13:2
Hickey, James J, 1941, O 28,23:1
Hickey, James J Mrs, 1941, O 21,23:3
Hickey, James Mrs, 1949, Mr 15,27:3
Hickey, James Samuel Dr, 1912, Ja 27,11:4
Hickey, James W, 1957, Mr 11,25:4
Hickey, Jeremiah G, 1960, Mr 30,37:5
Hickey, John, 1903, N 17,3:2; 1939, D 1,23:2
Hickey, John D, 1966, Ag 14,88:3
Hickey, John F, 1938, Mr 12,17:5; 1966, N 4,39:3; 1968, O 30,47:3
Hickey, John Family of, 1903, N 17,3:2
Hickey, John H, 1952, Ap 16,28:3
Hickey, John J, 1937, Ag 17,19:4; 1938, Mr 5,17:4
Hickey, John J (por), 1943, N 23,26:2
Hickey, John J, 1948, O 15,23:1; 1951, Je 16,15:3; 1955, N 29,29:2; 1962, Ap 11,43:4
Hickey, John K, 1963, Je 26,39:4
Hickey, John M, 1915, Je 8,13:5
Hickey, Joseph A, 1955, Jl 10,72:2
Hickey, Joseph V, 1942, Ja 23,19:5
Hickey, Katherine Mrs, 1940, S 26,14:4
Hickey, Lawrence, 1937, Ap 24,19:2; 1949, D 28,32:3
Hickey, Leo A, 1954, Ja 30,17:2
Hickey, Leo J (por), 1937, D 26,II,7:1
Hickey, Marie L, 1943, F 23,21:5
Hickey, Mary A Mrs, 1954, F 16,25:5
Hickey, Mary I, 1946, N 7,31:5
Hickey, Mary J, 1955, F 3,23:3
Hickey, Matthew E, 1967, Jl 23,61:1
Hickey, Michael A, 1947, N 8,17:3
Hickey, Michael J, 1945, Ja 12,15:1; 1952, N 6,29:1
Hickey, Michael Mrs, 1949, Ja 16,68:3
Hickey, Patrick, 1942, Mr 10,19:2
Hickey, Patrick E, 1947, F 27,21:5
Hickey, Patrick J, 1942, Ap 15,21:6; 1958, Jl 13,68:8
Hickey, Patrick V, 1939, Ja 6,21:2
Hickey, Phil J, 1939, O 30,17:3
Hickey, Philip J, 1965, Mr 21,86:8
Hickey, Preston L, 1962, S 29,23:5
Hickey, Richard H Jr, 1950, N 26,90:6
Hickey, Ross A, 1943, N 4,23:5
Hickey, Rudy, 1957, Mr 31,89:1
Hickey, Sherman Jr, 1948, Ag 29,56:6
Hickey, Stephen, 1949, Jl 30,1:1
Hickey, Thomas F, 1940, D 11,27:3; 1954, O 9,17:5; 1961, Ag 28,25:5
Hickey, Thomas J, 1949, My 5,27:5; 1960, Ap 18,29:5
Hickey, Thomas J Mrs, 1938, Je 13,19:1; 1965, Jl 6, 33:1
Hickey, Thomas L, 1963, Jl 3,27:3
Hickey, Tom, 1956, S 17,27:6
Hickey, Turner P, 1962, Mr 26,31:2
Hickey, W A Rev, 1933, O 5,21:4
Hickey, W Austin, 1968, D 18,47:2
Hickey, W Gen, 1866, Ja 6,1:2
Hickey, Weyman P Sr, 1951, N 28,31:3
Hickey, William D Msgr, 1924, F 2,13:6
Hickey, William H, 1944, N 20,21:6; 1960, Ag 10,31:2
Hickey, William J, 1953, D 24,15:2
Hickey, William P, 1947, Mr 7,25:2
Hickfield, John, 1942, O 22,23:1
Hickie, William, 1950, N 4,17:4
Hickin, Eugene, 1952, O 18,19:3
Hickin, William H, 1963, My 1,39:5
Hicking, William N, 1947, Ap 20,60:2
Hickley, Leonard A Mrs, 1959, Mr 6,25:3
Hicklin, Francis M Mrs, 1945, Ja 23,19:2
Hickling, Charles W, 1942, My 18,15:3
Hickling, George, 1954, Jl 28,23:5
Hickling, Horace C B, 1948, S 15,32:2
Hickling, William, 1947, Ap 11,25:2
Hickman, Edith C Mrs, 1959, F 1,84:6
Hickman, Edward, 1939, Ag 2,19:6
Hickman, Edwin N, 1953, Mr 10,29:2
Hickman, Frederick K, 1941, Jl 3,19:3
Hickman, George J, 1957, S 2,13:4
Hickman, Herman (funl plans, Ap 29,29:4; funl, Ap 30,33:4), 1958, Ap 26,19:1
Hickman, Howard C, 1950, Ja 1,42:5
Hickman, J Parker Jr, 1952, Ag 31,45:1
Hickman, J Parker Sr, 1946, F 19,25:2
Hickman, Lucian G, 1940, D 9,19:4
Hickman, R Nelson, 1965, Jl 27,33:2
Hickman, Reginald E, 1955, D 13,39:4
Hickman, Robert L (Beau), 1873, S 3,5:5
Hickman, Sallie M Mrs, 1948, Ja 23,23:4
Hickman, William H, 1939, F 13,15:4
Hickmott, William J Jr, 1952, Ja 13,88:6
Hickock, Arthur S, 1945, Jl 2,15:6
Hickok, Allen S, 1947, Ja 6,23:1
Hickok, C R, 1901, Mr 29,9:6
Hickok, Chandler H, 1949, Ja 27,23:2
Hickok, Francis W, 1951, Jl 22,61:1
Hickok, George Starr, 1904, S 28,9:5
Hickok, Guy C, 1951, My 20,88:7
Hickok, Henry Rev Dr, 1901, My 23,9:5
Hickok, James S, 1956, Ag 10,17:1
Hickok, Lorena, 1968, My 3,54:3
Hickok, Paul R, 1945, Ja 23,19:3
Hickok, Ralph K, 1947, Ap 25,21:4
Hickok, S Rae (por), 1945, D 11,25:1
Hickok, William Hyatt Dr, 1908, Jl 12,9:7
Hickok, William O, 1946, F 17,42:4; 1957, Ap 30,29:5
Hickox, Charles G Mrs, 1952, Ja 21,15:4
Hickox, Charles R, 1959, Mr 23,31:3
Hickox, Edward P, 1942, D 8,25:2
Hickox, Ralph, 1957, D 3,35:4
Hickox, Ralph W, 1910, Mr 28,9:3
Hickox, S V R, 1872, Ag 18,1:7
Hickox, Waldo A Mrs, 1950, Mr 8,27:3
Hicks, A Boice, 1948, N 21,88:2
Hicks, A L, 1923, Ap 14,13:5
Hicks, A M, 1929, Ja 15,29:2
Hicks, Alfred Col, 1916, Mr 10,9:6
Hicks, Arthur W, 1937, Je 4,23:1
Hicks, Benson B Mrs, 1953, Je 2,29:3
Hicks, Bernard J, 1956, My 18,25:4
Hicks, Betty J, 1946, Ag 31,15:3
Hicks, C M, 1878, O 8,8:5
Hicks, C Williams, 1944, Je 15,19:4
Hicks, Charles B, 1949, My 22,88:2
Hicks, Charles B Jr, 1945, N 16,19:4
Hicks, Charles C, 1941, O 25,17:5
Hicks, Charles H N, 1958, N 25,33:2
Hicks, Charles T (Oct 9), 1965, O 11,61:2
Hicks, Charles T Mrs, 1957, Ap 20,17:2
Hicks, Clarence J (por), 1944, D 23,13:5
Hicks, Cuthbert, 1944, S 14,23:4
Hicks, De Forest, 1920, Ja 1,15:2
Hicks, Douglas M, 1964, N 9,33:5
Hicks, E John, 1939, Mr 20,17:3
Hicks, E Pierpont, 1948, S 17,25:5
Hicks, Edgar F, 1937, Ag 23,19:5
Hicks, Edgar G Mrs, 1958, S 17,37:3
Hicks, Edward E, 1940, O 19,17:5
Hicks, Edward H, 1949, Ag 12,17:5
Hicks, Edward L Jr, 1941, S 11,23:1
Hicks, Edward S, 1952, F 15,25:4
Hicks, Edward W, 1938, My 20,19:2
Hicks, Edwin, 1920, Jl 18,22:5
Hicks, Edwin J, 1951, S 18,31:4
Hicks, Elias P, 1947, S 13,11:3
Hicks, Eliza Mrs, 1925, Ag 12,21:5
Hicks, Frank, 1941, N 16,57:3
Hicks, Frank M, 1959, F 13,17:2
Hicks, Frank Mrs, 1945, F 13,23:2
Hicks, Frederick C (funl, D 20,11:1), 1925, D 18,23:4
Hicks, Frederick C, 1953, S 9,29:6; 1956, My 1,33:5
Hicks, Frederick C N (Bishop of Lincoln), 1942, F 12,23:2
Hicks, Frederick H, 1955, Ap 29,23:3
Hicks, George, 1954, Jl 20,19:1
Hicks, George B, 1873, My 3,6:7
Hicks, George C, 1937, Ja 18,17:2
Hicks, George F, 1965, Mr 18,33:4
Hicks, Gilbert L, 1951, F 16,25:2
Hicks, H Melville Mrs, 1956, Jl 26,25:5
Hicks, Hamilton, 1959, Je 6,21:4
Hicks, Harold H, 1947, Ja 4,15:3
Hicks, Harry O, 1952, F 6,29:2
Hicks, Harry W, 1960, Mr 13,87:1
Hicks, Harry Wade Mrs, 1953, F 9,27:5
Hicks, Helen G, 1964, Ja 9,31:1
Hicks, Henry, 1954, O 22,27:4
Hicks, Herbert E, 1946, Ap 29,22:3
Hicks, Hervey C, 1944, Ag 15,11:4
Hicks, Horace M, 1940, Jl 21,28:7
Hicks, Inoge Archibald Overton, 1907, My 2,11:6
Hicks, Ira E, 1941, My 13,23:6
Hicks, Isaac L, 1945, Ap 17,23:1
Hicks, J D, 1923, My 10,19:4
Hicks, James P, 1952, Ag 14,23:2
Hicks, John (Irish Pepper), 1883, F 17,2:4
Hicks, John D, 1907, D 22,9:4
Hicks, John D Mrs, 1924, O 30,19:4
Hicks, John E, 1944, Ap 24,19:4
Hicks, John M W, 1944, Mr 23,19:3
Hicks, John W, 1938, Je 20,15:5
Hicks, John W Jr (por), 1945, Je 2,15:3
Hicks, John 3d, 1952, Ja 20,85:1
Hicks, Joseph Lawrence Dr, 1915, Ag 20,11:6
Hicks, Joseph P, 1945, N 24,19:4
Hicks, Julia C, 1948, S 14,29:4
Hicks, L D, 1905, Je 18,7:6
Hicks, Leslie R, 1940, Ag 30,19:3
Hicks, Lonnie, 1953, F 21,13:3
Hicks, M Waite, 1956, Jl 29,64:7
Hicks, Malcolm B, 1962, Je 9,25:2
Hicks, Mary L Mrs, 1940, Je 29,15:6
Hicks, Morris L, 1961, Ag 22,29:5
Hicks, Percy B, 1955, Je 3,23:4
Hicks, Percy E, 1952, S 15,25:2
Hicks, Preston T, 1939, S 20,27:5
Hicks, R Randolph, 1951, Jl 2,23:5
Hicks, R Wentworth, 1937, Mr 26,21:2
Hicks, Rachel, 1878, Ag 18,12:1
Hicks, Raymond M, 1962, O 13,25:4
Hicks, Rebecca Y Mrs, 1937, Ja 11,20:2
Hicks, Reese V, 1943, O 4,17:2
Hicks, Roy C, 1942, Ap 29,21:4
Hicks, Russell, 1957, Je 2,86:3
Hicks, Seymour (por), 1949, Ap 7,29:5
Hicks, Sidney Mrs, 1912, S 4,11:4
Hicks, Sylvanus Jr, 1942, Ap 18,15:5
Hicks, T Edward, 1965, My 29,27:2
Hicks, T H Sen, 1865, F 14,1:4
Hicks, Victor S, 1952, F 2,31:2
Hicks, W M, 1943, Jl 6,21:5
Hicks, Wallace D, 1949, Jl 20,25:5
Hicks, Walter R, 1937, D 6,27:3
Hicks, William, 1907, S 17,11:6; 1951, S 20,31:3
Hicks, William C, 1944, D 16,15:7
Hicks, William C Mrs, 1938, Ap 29,21:3
Hicks, William D, 1939, My 9,23:4
Hicks, William E, 1942, My 17,47:5
Hicks, William H, 1942, F 15,45:3
Hicks, William Marlon Capt, 1908, N 30,9:4
Hicks, William V, 1939, S 19,26:2
Hicks, Xenophon, 1952, N 3,27:5
Hicks-Beach, Michael, 1952, Jl 8,27:3
Hicks-Lord, Annette W W, 1896, Ag 7,9:1
Hickson, Joseph H, 1943, D 6,23:4
Hickson, Lady, 1938, Jl 12,19:2
Hickson, Leslie M, 1968, Ja 4,34:5
Hicok, John S, 1967, Mr 2,35:2
Hidalgo, Diago, 1961, F 2,29:4
Hidalgo, Ernesto, 1955, O 16,86:1
Hidalgo, Joseph Sr, 1951, Ap 20,30:6
Hidayatullah, Ghulam H, 1948, O 5,25:2
Hidden, Thomas B, 1918, S 6,13:3
Hidden, Walter Mrs, 1950, Ap 11,31:3
Hiden, Joseph H Dr, 1937, S 12,II,7:2
Hides, J G, 1938, Je 20,15:4
Hidey, Ralph M, 1949, Ja 7,21:1
Hidinger, Leroy L Sr, 1951, N 13,29:5
Hidlebrand, Jesse R, 1951, S 20,31:5
Hidock Jno J, 1960, D 13,31:4
Hieber, Eugene A, 1950, S 27,32:3
Hieber, George M, 1946, Ag 20,27:4
Hieber, Johannes von, 1951, N 8,29:4
Hiegel, Anthony, 1950, F 20,25:4
Hielscher, Leah Z Mrs, 1954, Ag 28,15:4
Hier, Frank, 1959, Je 11,66:1
Hier, Frederick P Jr, 1956, My 3,31:2
Hierl. Konstantin, 1955, S 25,92:8
Hieronymus, Enoch, 1941, D 19,25:2
Hieronymus, William P, 1957, F 12,27:3
Hiers, Glenn S, 1954, S 8,31:3
Hiers, H Houston Mrs, 1946, O 24,27:5
Hiett, George W Mrs, 1947, S 1,19:4
Higa, Shuhei, 1956, O 25,33:2
Higashi-Kuni, Morihiro Mrs (funl, Jl 27,31:3), 1961, Jl 23,69:1
Higbee, Arthur W, 1947, Mr 16,60:2

Higbee, Charles E, 1908, Ag 13,7:4
Higbee, Clarence W, 1967, S 11,45:1
Higbee, E Y Rev Dr, 1871, D 11,1:6
Higbee, Frederick P, 1947, O 16,28:3
Higbee, Irving J, 1955, Ap 10,88:6
Higbee, Juva N, 1942, S 12,13:6
Higbee, Lenah S Mrs, 1941, Ja 12,46:1
Higbee, Myrtle R, 1949, Jl 6,30:1
Higbee, William B, 1938, O 26,23:4
Higbee, William E, 1940, Mr 23,13:3
Higbee, William S, 1939, S 14,23:4
Higbie, Anne E, 1951, Ap 4,29:4
Higbie, Calvin H, 1914, S 30,9:6
Higbie, Carlton M, 1955, Mr 2,27:5
Higbie, George H, 1938, Je 23,21:2
Higbie, Gilbert H, 1941, Ag 27,19:5
Higbie, Hamilton A, 1941, Ja 16,23:3
Higbie, Harrison S, 1950, D 29,19:1
Higbie, Henry H, 1947, Ag 5,23:4
Higbie, Howard E, 1967, O 7,29:3
Higbie, Oscar W, 1943, Je 5,15:3
Higbie, William H, 1948, S 1,48:5
Higby, Everett, 1964, Mr 6,28:3
Higby, Harlow G Mrs, 1947, S 4,25:6
Higby, James H, 1913, D 24,11:6
Higby, William F, 1949, Je 25,13:2
Higby, William F Mrs, 1948, Ja 7,25:3
Higdon, E K, 1961, Ap 21,33:3
Higger, Michael, 1952, N 24,23:5
Higginbotham, Alfred L, 1967, Je 23,39:3
Higginbotham, Henry E Mrs, 1960, Jl 8,21:2
Higginbotham, Marcus, 1953, Ja 11,91:1
Higginbotham, Roswell G, 1943, My 27,28:8
Higginbotham, W C Mrs, 1944, Mr 26,42:1
Higginbottom, Sam, 1958, Je 12,31:3
Higgins, A Foster, 1916, N 29,11:3
Higgins, Aaron L, 1942, Jl 18,13:2
Higgins, Aaron L Mrs, 1942, Ap 29,21:2
Higgins, Ada G, 1958, Ap 21,23:4
Higgins, Aldus C, 1948, S 12,72:3
Higgins, Alfred J, 1954, F 18,31:2
Higgins, Alfred K Mrs, 1965, Ja 25,37:4
Higgins, Alfred Mrs, 1949, Je 14,31:2
Higgins, Algernon Sidney, 1913, O 15,11:5
Higgins, Alice, 1923, Ja 8,17:6
Higgins, Alice B Mrs, 1953, Ag 24,23:5
Higgins, Allan H W, 1959, Jl 21,29:5
Higgins, Andrew J, 1942, Ap 25,13:1; 1952, Ag 2,15:1
Higgins, Andrew J 3d, 1959, My 12,27:3
Higgins, Annie M Mrs, 1952, F 9,13:6
Higgins, Anthony Ex-Sen, 1912, Je 27,13:5
Higgins, Arthur, 1945, My 4,19:4; 1955, My 15,86:4
Higgins, Arthur S, 1938, F 19,15:1; 1947, F 19,25:2
Higgins, Arthur T Mrs, 1948, O 14,30:2
Higgins, C L (Ox), 1953, Ja 11,91:3
Higgins, Carroll E, 1964, Ag 24,27:2
Higgins, Cecil Campbell, 1922, F 27,13:6
Higgins, Charles A Sr, 1943, D 19,48:6
Higgins, Charles A Sr Mrs, 1948, Ag 27,18:4
Higgins, Charles F, 1946, Ap 5,25:6
Higgins, Charles H, 1954, N 23,35:4; 1961, Jl 27,31:3
Higgins, Charles H Mrs, 1955, Jl 1,21:5
Higgins, Charles J, 1940, S 13,23:5
Higgins, Charles M (por),(will, Mr 31,14:5), 1937, Mr 15,23:3
Higgins, Charles M Mrs, 1955, D 1,35:2
Higgins, Charles P, 1922, Ag 20,26:4
Higgins, Charles S Sr, 1950, Je 12,27:5
Higgins, Charles W Dr, 1937, Ag 20,17:4
Higgins, Daniel P, 1950, Ja 10,29:1; 1953, D 27,60:3
Higgins, Daniel P Mrs, 1963, Jl 20,19:5
Higgins, Dean, 1945, D 19,25:3
Higgins, Edgar, 1951, Ag 26,62:4
Higgins, Edgar F, 1938, My 29,II,6:8
Higgins, Edmund S, 1943, D 19,48:7; 1952, My 14,27:2
Higgins, Edward, 1922, F 24,12:5; 1945, Ag 13,19:3
Higgins, Edward C, 1944, Je 19,19:6
Higgins, Edward F, 1963, Ap 22,27:2
Higgins, Edward J, 1947, D 15,25:1; 1954, F 11,29:4; 1963, S 6,29:2
Higgins, Edward J Mrs, 1952, Ap 22,29:5
Higgins, Edward P Mrs, 1944, F 1,19:2
Higgins, Edward R Mrs, 1967, Jl 30,64:4
Higgins, Edward T, 1948, Ag 4,21:5
Higgins, Edward W, 1947, Ag 5,23:2
Higgins, Edwin W, 1950, Jl 10,21:2; 1954, S 25,15:6
Higgins, Eliza S G Mrs, 1939, Ja 21,15:4
Higgins, Elizabeth (Sister Mary Augustine), 1914, Ap 14,11:6
Higgins, Elizabeth M, 1939, F 2,19:3
Higgins, Elvin M, 1938, Ap 7,23:3
Higgins, Eugene (will, Ag 21,1:2), 1948, Jl 30,17:3
Higgins, Eugene, 1958, F 20,25:1
Higgins, F Harrison, 1937, D 4,17:2
Higgins, Francis, 1913, N 16,IV,7:5
Higgins, Francis E, 1915, Ja 5,15:5
Higgins, Francis W Dr, 1903, D 19,9:5
Higgins, Frank J, 1937, Mr 16,23:2; 1954, S 3,17:5
Higgins, Frank W Ex-Gov (trb, F 14,9:5; funl, F 15,11:3), 1907, F 13,9:1
Higgins, Frederick A, 1957, Je 24,23:6
Higgins, Frederick R, 1941, Ja 9,21:3
Higgins, George, 1947, S 3,25:4
Higgins, George R, 1955, Ag 12,19:4
Higgins, George W, 1946, O 30,27:4
Higgins, Gerald, 1948, Ap 12,21:5
Higgins, Gordon F, 1957, O 16,35:1
Higgins, H Joseph, 1951, Je 26,29:1
Higgins, Harriet G Mrs, 1941, My 8,23:3
Higgins, Harry B, 1963, D 26,27:4
Higgins, Harry C, 1948, D 21,31:3
Higgins, Helene M, 1948, Ag 22,62:4
Higgins, Henry C, 1948, F 25,23:2
Higgins, Henry E, 1944, Mr 16,19:5
Higgins, Henry S, 1951, O 11,37:5
Higgins, Herbert J, 1949, Je 20,10:3
Higgins, Herbert N, 1964, Jl 21,33:4
Higgins, Howard C, 1924, F 8,19:4
Higgins, Howard L Capt, 1924, F 8,19:4
Higgins, Hubert H, 1952, D 3,33:5
Higgins, J J Rev, 1925, N 10,25:4
Higgins, J Wallace, 1956, Jl 14,15:5
Higgins, Jack, 1925, F 20,17:3
Higgins, James A, 1949, Ja 20,27:4; 1962, N 28,39:1
Higgins, James A Mrs, 1953, S 11,21:1
Higgins, James C, 1958, Je 13,23:2
Higgins, James F, 1939, Mr 28,23:4; 1939, Ap 11,24:3
Higgins, James H, 1938, Ag 1,13:5
Higgins, James J, 1940, Jl 1,19:5; 1940, Ag 11,31:3; 1952, F 5,29:3
Higgins, James J Rev, 1918, O 2,13:2
Higgins, James L (will), 1938, Ap 3,II,2:8
Higgins, James P, 1955, Mr 26,15:1
Higgins, James T, 1940, Mr 2,13:2
Higgins, Jeremiah J, 1940, F 20,21:4
Higgins, John, 1938, Ag 14,34:2
Higgins, John C, 1965, Mr 20,27:3
Higgins, John F, 1953, O 9,27:2
Higgins, John F A, 1948, Je 3,25:5
Higgins, John G, 1951, O 21,92:5
Higgins, John H, 1961, F 6,21:1
Higgins, John J, 1948, S 11,15:2; 1950, My 19,27:4; 1956, Ja 2,21:3
Higgins, John J Rev, 1910, Ap 18,9:6
Higgins, John P, 1955, Ag 3,23:5
Higgins, John R, 1940, Ap 23,24:2; 1950, N 21,32:2
Higgins, John W, 1946, Jl 12,17:3; 1961, O 20,33:1
Higgins, Joseph E, 1942, Je 29,15:5
Higgins, Joseph F, 1961, D 16,25:6
Higgins, Joseph I, 1947, O 8,25:2
Higgins, Joseph L, 1946, Ja 17,23:3
Higgins, Joseph L Mrs, 1947, Jl 19,13:5
Higgins, Joseph P, 1961, S 12,33:3
Higgins, Joseph R, 1939, N 29,23:3
Higgins, Joseph T Dr, 1915, Ag 23,9:5
Higgins, Josephine, 1924, Ap 7,17:5
Higgins, Josiah B, 1948, Ag 16,19:4
Higgins, Julia D Mrs, 1955, F 9,27:2
Higgins, Kessie Hoyt Mrs, 1924, F 22,15:3
Higgins, Louis Capt, 1871, S 2,8:4
Higgins, Louis S, 1944, My 15,19:3
Higgins, Margaret Mrs, 1943, Ag 5,15:4
Higgins, Marguerite (Mrs W E Hall), 1966, Ja 4,27:1
Higgins, Mark H, 1960, O 19,8:3
Higgins, Mary F, 1958, F 20,25:4
Higgins, Michael C, 1941, F 4,21:3
Higgins, Michael J, 1954, S 3,17:2
Higgins, Michael L, 1925, N 9,19:5
Higgins, Michael W, 1945, F 14,19:6
Higgins, Milton Prince Mrs, 1925, Ja 10,13:4
Higgins, Myron J, 1941, Ja 15,23:2
Higgins, Nathaniel D, 1882, Ja 12,5:1
Higgins, Norris, 1943, O 21,27:5
Higgins, Orrin T, 1912, S 15,II,15:6
Higgins, Patrick A, 1943, D 9,27:2
Higgins, Patrick J, 1937, D 18,21:3
Higgins, Patrick L, 1940, O 7,17:5
Higgins, Paul, 1952, O 25,23:5
Higgins, Peter A, 1941, Jl 5,11:4
Higgins, Peter F, 1953, Ag 9,77:2
Higgins, Peter T, 1946, Ap 25,21:4
Higgins, R Paul, 1949, Ja 14,24:2
Higgins, Raymond Dr, 1953, F 17,27:3
Higgins, Raymond L, 1959, Jl 12,72:5
Higgins, Reyburn A, 1952, Ap 16,27:2
Higgins, Richard, 1939, F 1,23:8
Higgins, Richard H (por),(will, D 1,24:2), 1937, Mr 8,19:1
Higgins, Richard H Mrs, 1953, Mr 5,27:3
Higgins, Richard Mrs, 1939, F 1,23:8
Higgins, Robert, 1941, My 27,24:3
Higgins, Robert G, 1955, My 21,17:6
Higgins, Simeon S Mrs, 1964, My 19,37:3
Higgins, Susan R Mrs, 1940, Ja 24,21:4
Higgins, Sylvester J, 1945, D 26,19:2
Higgins, Thaddeus, 1943, O 11,19:5
Higgins, Thomas, 1944, F 22,23:5; 1947, F 9,62:4
Higgins, Thomas A, 1947, Jl 8,23:4
Higgins, Thomas F, 1943, My 30,27:1; 1950, N 12, 92:6; 1956, S 23,84:5
Higgins, Thomas F Dr, 1937, Mr 25,25:4
Higgins, Thomas F Jr, 1960, D 24,15:5
Higgins, Thomas J, 1916, O 13,11:4; 1965, F 9,37:4
Higgins, Thomas K, 1939, F 2,19:4
Higgins, Thomas V, 1954, Ap 17,26:2
Higgins, Thomas W, 1957, Ap 22,25:3
Higgins, Victor, 1949, Ag 25,23:5
Higgins, Walter S, 1942, N 19,25:2
Higgins, Warner A, 1961, Ja 16,27:2
Higgins, Wesley, 1944, D 6,23:4
Higgins, William, 1938, Mr 5,17:5
Higgins, William A, 1941, N 19,23:1
Higgins, William A Jr, 1964, Mr 9,29:3
Higgins, William C, 1940, F 8,23:4
Higgins, William F, 1947, F 6,23:4; 1952, My 18,92:6; 1956, Ap 10,31:3
Higgins, William G, 1943, F 12,19:4
Higgins, William H, 1948, D 19,38:2
Higgins, William J, 1937, Ag 30,24:4; 1940, Ap 28, 36:3; 1943, O 8,19:5; 1950, Ag 31,26:2
Higgins, William L, 1951, N 20,31:4
Higgins, William M, 1938, Ag 21,32:6
Higgins, William M Dr, 1937, N 6,17:4
Higgins, William P, 1961, O 9,35:1
Higgins, William V, 1943, Ap 3,15:4
Higgins, William W, 1951, N 3,17:2
Higginson, A Henry Mrs, 1925, Ja 25,7:1
Higginson, Alex H, 1958, N 15,23:6
Higginson, Clarence H, 1959, N 5,35:2
Higginson, Emily W Mrs, 1941, D 4,25:2
Higginson, Eugene A, 1943, Ag 25,19:2
Higginson, F J, 1931, S 13,II,8:1
Higginson, Francis J Mrs, 1938, My 23,17:5
Higginson, Francis Lee, 1925, Ag 20,19:6; 1925, Ag 23,7:4
Higginson, G W A Sir, 1927, F 2,25:3
Higginson, Henry C, 1909, F 14,11:5
Higginson, Henry L Maj, 1919, N 16,22:1
Higginson, James Jackson, 1911, Ja 6,9:4
Higginson, Margaret G Mrs, 1940, S 21,19:5
Higginson, Mary P T Mrs, 1941, Ja 12,44:8
Higginson, Richard A, 1957, S 23,27:3
Higginson, Robert B, 1968, Jl 30,39:1
Higginson, Robert H, 1954, Mr 29,19:4
Higginson, Stephen Tyson, 1919, My 2,13:6
Higginson, T F, 1877, D 27,8:2
Higginson, Thomas Wentworth, 1911, My 10,11:5
Higginson, William, 1943, Ag 6,15:1
Higginson, William J, 1945, F 27,19:5
Higgiston, John E, 1951, Ap 28,15:6
Higgon, Byron E, 1961, N 17,35:4
Higgons, John A, 1951, S 4,27:4
Higgons, John A Jr, 1965, My 11,39:3
Higgons, Mae B, 1944, My 30,21:5
Higgons, Warren W, 1938, D 30,15:2
Higgs, Edgar P, 1953, S 3,21:3
Higgs, Edward, 1950, Jl 30,60:2
Higgs, Elgar I, 1951, O 29,23:5
Higgs, Horace S, 1939, My 17,23:6
Higgs, Mary Mrs, 1937, Mr 21,II,8:1
Higgs, Robert H, 1964, Ap 16,37:1
Higgs, Vivian G, 1955, Mr 12,19:2
Higgs, William H, 1947, S 27,15:3
Higgs, William J, 1943, My 23,43:3
Higgs, Z R Mrs, 1951, My 5,17:5
Higgs, Zephaniah, 1954, Jl 25,69:2
High, Douglas G, 1952, Ag 1,18:3
High, E Nelson, 1943, Ja 30,15:4
High, Elmer L, 1955, N 23,23:4
High, Frank A, 1948, Jl 2,21:5
High, Frank A Mrs, 1957, S 12,31:3
High, George H, 1945, My 22,19:4
High, Harold E, 1941, My 5,17:6
High, Henry C, 1955, My 11,31:1
High, Hermon A Mrs, 1957, Jl 5,17:1
High, John E, 1945, Jl 10,11:5
High, John J Mrs, 1949, Mr 15,27:5
High, John M, 1924, Ap 26,15:4; 1957, S 7,19:6
High, Robert K, 1967, Ag 31,33:1
High, Samuel H Sr, 1945, Je 19,19:3
High, Stanley H, 1961, F 4,19:1
Higham, Charles F (por), 1938, D 25,14:8
Higham, J Stephens, 1946, D 30,19:5
Higham, James, 1872, Jl 10,8:4; 1952, Ja 24,47:3
Higham, Jane S, 1949, My 18,27:1
Higham, Justis C Mrs, 1956, Jl 3,25:5
Highfield, Frederick P, 1959, My 8,28:3
Highfield, James B, 1955, D 29,23:3
Highfield, William J, 1943, Ag 14,11:5
Highland, Alder E, 1951, Ag 19,86:1
Highland, Cecil B, 1957, F 7,27:4
Highland, John N Sr, 1949, Ag 4,23:5
Highlands, Andrew A, 1937, S 12,II,6:8
Highlands, John Ashley, 1920, Ap 16,13:4
Highley, Edgar, 1944, O 18,21:1
Highley, John L, 1951, Je 23,15:6
Highman, H Ainsley (por), 1946, O 10,27:5
Highman, Henry, 1941, Ap 4,21:4
Highsmith, James D, 1939, O 19,24:2
Hight, Clarence A, 1945, Jl 2,15:3
Hight, Francis E, 1941, Mr 31,15:2
Hight, Frank S, 1939, F 11,15:3
Hight, Jean W, 1967, Ap 7,37:3
Hight, Pearl, 1957, Mr 6,31:2
Highton, John E, 1937, Mr 27,15:1
Hightower, E Kermit, 1963, O 8,44:1
Hightower, Emmett D, 1967, D 17,92:6
Hightower, W Harrison, 1947, F 10,29:4
Hightshoe, Ray, 1941, My 23,21:5

Higi, George S, 1953, D 13,86:5
Higier, Daniel H, 1949, Je 9,31:2
Higinbotham, Henry B, 1937, O 13,23:1
Higinson, Howard S, 1946, Mr 5,25:4
Higley, Adelbert P, 1944, F 19,13:1
Higley, Brodie G, 1946, Je 5,23:5
Higley, Charles, 1874, Ag 13,5:4; 1943, Ag 4,17:5
Higley, Charles W, 1945, Jl 24,23:5
Higley, Henry R Prof, 1918, My 2,13:8
Higley, Homer H, 1938, Jl 26,19:2
Higley, Louis A, 1955, Ap 13,29:3
Higley, Warren, 1911, Mr 24,11:3
Higman, John H, 1955, Ap 18,23:2
Higman, Martha V Mrs, 1940, Ja 14,42:4
Hignell, Millard F, 1938, N 13,44:6
Higueras Fuentes, Jacinto, 1954, N 21,87:2
Hijar, Duchess of, 1948, S 9,27:4
Hijikata, Hisaakira, 1942, Ag 26,19:5
Hikaru, Shizue, 1950, N 3,27:1
Hiken, Nat, 1968, D 9,47:1
Hikmet, Nazim, 1963, Je 4,39:4
Hilaili, Ahmed Naguib el, 1958, D 12,2:5
Hilb, Gus, 1955, My 6,23:3
Hilb, Myron R, 1946, F 26,25:5
Hilberg, John Jr, 1948, O 6,29:4
Hilberry, Clarence B, 1966, Ja 11,29:3
Hilberry, Howard K, 1955, My 26,31:4
Hilbert, Charles P, 1963, D 2,37:4
Hilbert, Constantine J, 1960, Ag 30,29:4
Hilbert, David, 1943, F 20,13:1
Hilbert, Dorothy W Mrs, 1940, Jl 7,25:4
Hilbert, Egon, 1968, Ja 20,26:4
Hilbert, William E, 1961, F 26,3:3
Hilbert, William M, 1956, S 20,33:4
Hilborn, Jacob, 1941, Ap 27,38:1
Hilborn, Jerome S Mrs, 1956, My 30,21:3
Hilborn, Lloyd T, 1946, Je 26,25:3
Hilbun, Ben, 1963, D 15,86:3
Hilburn, Allen N, 1948, Mr 7,69:1
Hild, Frank A Mrs, 1947, Ja 28,23:4
Hild, Oscar F, 1950, Ap 25,31:3
Hildburgh, Walter L, 1955, N 27,89:1
Hilde, John C, 1938, F 5,15:2
Hildebrand, Adolf von, 1921, Ja 19,11:4
Hildebrand, Adolph M, 1943, F 17,21:3
Hildebrand, Charles C, 1950, F 24,23:2
Hildebrand, Charles E Mrs, 1949, F 13,77:1
Hildebrand, Dan M, 1942, D 6,76:3
Hildebrand, E Fritjof, 1947, Je 10,27:3
Hildebrand, Emil, 1941, F 5,19:5
Hildebrand, Eugene, 1943, Ag 27,17:6
Hildebrand, H Edward, 1965, Jl 24,21:3
Hildebrand, Ira P, 1944, N 12,48:5
Hildebrand, J, 1878, S 2,8:3
Hildebrand, John C, 1961, Jl 9,77:2
Hildebrand, John S Mrs, 1945, Je 8,19:5
Hildebrand, Lewis K, 1938, D 4,60:6
Hildebrand, Roswell C, 1952, Je 7,19:2
Hildebrand, William, 1963, N 20,43:4
Hildebrand, William C, 1948, Mr 5,21:4
Hildebrandt, Charles G, 1949, O 5,29:6
Hildebrandt, Clifford W, 1941, Ja 9,21:1
Hildebrandt, Edward, 1947, Ap 29,22:4
Hildebrandt, Edward H Mrs, 1943, Mr 31,19:2
Hildebrandt, George, 1948, My 18,24:2
Hildebrandt, George B, 1939, Je 10,17:2
Hildebrandt, H Thornton, 1965, S 1,37:3
Hildebrandt, Howard L, 1958, N 12,37:3
Hildebrandt, Howard L Mrs, 1962, Mr 19,29:4
Hildebrandt, John N, 1952, N 26,23:3
Hildebrandt, Louis A, 1946, F 27,25:5
Hildebrandt, Meinhard, 1950, D 7,33:2
Hildebrandt, Walter J, 1940, S 27,23:2
Hildebrant, C Q, 1953, Ap 2,28:3
Hildebrant, Ernst Sr, 1948, N 27,17:2
Hildeburn, William L, 1947, Ag 9,13:5
Hildegard, Princess, 1948, F 12,23:2
Hildegarde, Sister, 1920, Mr 16,9:4
Hildegarde, Sister (Bernauer), 1959, N 1,86:3
Hildemann, John F, 1938, My 14,15:4
Hildemann, Louis E, 1957, N 11,29:1
Hildenberger, Martin G, 1945, My 7,17:2
Hildenbrand, Henry, 1907, F 11,9:4
Hildenbrand, Karl, 1938, Ap 5,21:3
Hildenbrand, Louis C, 1948, Ag 15,61:1
Hildenbrand, Wilhelm, 1908, F 22,7:5
Hilder, Jacob, 1937, My 8,19:3
Hilder, Moritz, 1947, Ja 28,24:2
Hilderbrand, Harry A, 1946, My 28,21:3
Hilderbrandt, Henry, 1911, F 8,9:5
Hilderbrandt, William A, 1954, Mr 3,27:4
Hildick, Walter H, 1959, F 10,33:3
Hilditch, Frank H, 1958, My 8,29:4
Hilditch, Frederick W, 1943, Mr 21,26:7
Hilditch, William R Mrs, 1963, N 23,29:2
Hildner, Jonathan A C, 1952, Ja 27,76:2
Hildreth, Albert H, 1942, Ja 24,17:4
Hildreth, Arthur G, 1941, F 22,15:4
Hildreth, E Raymond, 1946, My 29,24:3
Hildreth, Edgar P, 1941, S 25,25:1
Hildreth, Elizabeth, 1938, Jl 3,12:7
Hildreth, George W, 1959, Jl 13,27:5
Hildreth, George W Mrs, 1947, O 20,23:3
Hildreth, Harold M, 1965, N 4,47:3
Hildreth, Harry F, 1940, O 24,25:4
Hildreth, Helen R, 1921, S 23,15:6
Hildreth, J Augustus, 1952, S 21,89:3
Hildreth, James, 1903, Je 15,7:6
Hildreth, James Col, 1907, N 10,9:5
Hildreth, James H, 1944, Ag 22,17:6
Hildreth, John, 1942, Ap 29,21:4
Hildreth, John L Jr Mrs, 1964, Ag 8,19:6
Hildreth, John Lewis Dr, 1925, N 28,15:6
Hildreth, Joseph S, 1960, D 16,33:1
Hildreth, Lewis, 1945, Je 26,19:5
Hildreth, Loring T, 1915, Ap 2,11:6
Hildreth, M Frances, 1958, D 5,31:3
Hildreth, Melvin D (funl plans, D 25,21:1), 1959, D 24,19:1
Hildreth, Richard, 1865, Ag 2,5:1
Hildreth, Richard D, 1941, My 30,15:2
Hildreth, Richard Mrs, 1867, S 17,4:7
Hildreth, Richard P, 1958, Jl 22,27:4
Hildreth, Robert D, 1956, Ap 23,27:5
Hildreth, S C, 1929, S 25,31:3
Hildreth, Samuel C Mrs, 1961, Ag 30,33:4
Hildreth, Samuel P, 1950, Ag 15,29:2
Hildreth, Stanley B, 1941, Ja 13,15:4
Hildreth, Walter D, 1940, Ja 14,42:4
Hildreth, Walter Edward, 1917, S 15,11:5
Hildreth, Warren Dr, 1937, O 19,25:4
Hildreth, William O, 1954, D 11,13:2
Hildt, Howard J, 1962, S 18,39:1
Hildt, Thomas, 1952, My 13,30:3
Hildum, Clayton E, 1952, Mr 28,23:4
Hildyard, Reginald (Sept 29), 1965, O 11,61:2
Hilebrand, W F Prof, 1925, F 8,7:2
Hileman, Al, 1948, Ja 22,27:2
Hileman, Emmett A, 1952, Mr 25,27:1
Hiler, Edward, 1951, O 15,25:3
Hiler, Herbert F Sr, 1947, O 19,66:4
Hiler, Hilaire, 1966, Ja 21,47:3
Hiler, Lewis E, 1957, Ja 31,27:1
Hiles, Harrison N, 1958, Ja 20,23:5
Hiley, S Baynham, 1940, My 13,17:2
Hilfert, Edward C, 1959, S 6,73:1
Hilferty, Daniel J, 1951, D 18,31:3
Hilfinger, Fred, 1951, Jl 14,13:2
Hilfrank, Edward, 1952, F 21,27:2
Hilfrich, Antonius, 1947, F 8,17:2
Hilgard, Eugene Weidemar, 1916, Ja 9,17:5
Hilgartner, Henry L Dr, 1937, Je 10,23:5
Hilgeman, Harold E, 1952, D 26,15:3
Hilgenberg, William F, 1959, D 23,27:1
Hilgendorff, William Mrs, 1947, Ap 22,27:4
Hilger, Charles, 1949, Ag 23,23:5
Hilgerdt, Folke, 1956, Jl 17,23:2
Hilips, Thomas J, 1939, Ap 12,23:3
Hilken, Henry G, 1937, Mr 21,II,8:3
Hilker, F William, 1948, S 7,25:4
Hilker, George F, 1964, Ja 29,30:4
Hilkie, Curtis E, 1945, D 21,21:1
Hilkoff, Michael Prince, 1909, Mr 22,7:3
Hilkowich, Abe M, 1941, Je 8,49:1
Hill, A Albert, 1945, F 12,19:3
Hill, A D Dr, 1912, Mr 25,11:4
Hill, A G S, 1904, My 18,2:5
Hill, A M, 1943, O 11,19:2
Hill, Agnes N, 1945, My 22,19:4
Hill, Albert D, 1942, S 11,21:3
Hill, Albert E Mrs, 1956, O 5,25:4
Hill, Albert Mrs, 1945, Je 29,15:4
Hill, Albert P, 1949, N 15,26:3
Hill, Albert R, 1943, My 7,19:5
Hill, Alex E, 1940, Mr 18,18:2
Hill, Alfred E, 1940, Ap 23,23:2
Hill, Alfred W, 1948, O 9,19:2
Hill, Alonzo Rev, 1871, F 2,5:3
Hill, Ambrose A, 1952, Ja 30,25:4
Hill, Amelia L, 1962, O 25,39:3
Hill, Andrew W, 1945, Mr 28,23:1
Hill, Angeline W Mrs, 1951, Ag 13,17:6
Hill, Annie L W Mrs (will), 1940, Mr 31,41:7
Hill, Anthony J, 1952, Mr 23,92:1
Hill, Archibald A, 1907, N 27,7:6
Hill, Arthur, 1909, D 8,11:5
Hill, Arthur D, 1947, N 30,76:3
Hill, Arthur E (por), 1939, Mr 17,21:1
Hill, Arthur E, 1953, Ap 9,27:3
Hill, Arthur F, 1939, F 9,21:3
Hill, Arthur G, 1946, D 12,29:3
Hill, Arthur J, 1964, Ap 23,39:3
Hill, Arthur Lady, 1944, F 14,17:6
Hill, Arthur W Mrs, 1948, S 18,17:4
Hill, Ashby E, 1959, My 28,31:3
Hill, Augustus R, 1949, Ja 11,31:1
Hill, B H, 1882, Ag 17,5:3
Hill, B P, 1958, Ja 17,25:1
Hill, Beckett, 1908, D 28,7:7
Hill, Benjamin D, 1960, F 15,27:4
Hill, Benjamin H, 1951, Jl 14,13:4; 1952, My 27,27:1
Hill, Bert H, 1958, D 3,37:4
Hill, Bert H Mrs, 1954, D 19,85:2
Hill, Berton C, 1947, D 11,33:1
Hill, Bessie Mrs, 1946, N 27,25:4
Hill, Beverley S, 1953, Ag 9,77:1
Hill, Billy Mrs, 1950, Je 7,29:6
Hill, C Walter, 1938, D 19,23:5
Hill, C Walton, 1948, F 17,25:3
Hill, Calvin C, 1943, Mr 18,19:4
Hill, Caroline R Mrs (mem ser, Paris; she died Mar '65,), 1965, S 28,3:8
Hill, Carolyn C Mrs, 1942, F 25,19:4
Hill, Carrie L, 1961, Ag 3,23:4
Hill, Casper R, 1945, Ja 26,21:1
Hill, Catherine A Mrs, 1941, Ja 29,17:5
Hill, Charles, 1946, My 25,15:4
Hill, Charles A Mrs, 1960, Ag 10,31:4
Hill, Charles B, 1941, O 3,23:3; 1959, N 29,86:3
Hill, Charles C, 1952, Ja 13,89:2
Hill, Charles D, 1910, O 22,11:4; 1941, Mr 8,19:2; 1958, F 20,25:3
Hill, Charles E, 1913, O 6,7:4
Hill, Charles E Rev, 1908, O 15,9:7
Hill, Charles F, 1940, Ja 25,21:5
Hill, Charles H, 1908, Ag 29,9:4; 1944, Ja 3,22:3
Hill, Charles H Jr, 1958, Jl 18,45:1
Hill, Charles H Jr Mrs, 1958, Jl 18,45:1
Hill, Charles J, 1938, N 3,23:4
Hill, Charles L, 1956, D 10,31:4
Hill, Charles Mrs, 1951, D 20,32:2; 1953, D 29,23:3
Hill, Charles R, 1942, Ag 16,44:8
Hill, Charles S, 1948, Ja 8,25:2
Hill, Charles W, 1907, F 7,9:6; 1938, Ag 4,17:4; 1940, D 25,27:1
Hill, Chester W, 1941, Ap 9,25:6
Hill, Christopher Dudley Dr, 1925, Ap 21,21:6
Hill, Clara M, 1955, Jl 15,21:4
Hill, Clarence E, 1955, Mr 17,45:2
Hill, Clarence Edward Capt, 1953, F 2,21:3
Hill, Clarence H, 1965, S 6,15:5
Hill, Claude A, 1938, S 28,25:5
Hill, Clifford R Sr, 1940, S 17,23:6
Hill, Clyde H, 1966, Ja 2,76:1
Hill, Cora M, 1941, D 2,24:3
Hill, Crawford, 1960, Ap 4,29:5
Hill, D J, 1932, Mr 3,19:1
Hill, Dana C, 1949, Ap 30,13:5
Hill, David, 1943, Ja 15,17:4; 1950, Jl 18,29:2
Hill, David B (funl, O 23,13:4), 1910, O 21,11:1
Hill, David F Mrs, 1946, F 11,29:4
Hill, David Jayne Mrs, 1923, Ja 17,17:6
Hill, David L, 1943, N 14,56:6
Hill, David Mrs, 1916, F 24,13:6
Hill, David R, 1950, O 16,27:2
Hill, David S, 1951, N 12,25:1
Hill, David S Jr, 1958, Ja 27,27:3
Hill, Dean, 1942, Jl 16,19:5
Hill, Dudley L, 1951, Ja 1,50:7
Hill, E Eugene, 1957, Mr 29,21:1
Hill, E Munson, 1939, Mr 5,49:2
Hill, E Munson Mrs, 1947, My 21,25:5
Hill, E Rowland, 1948, Ag 26,22:3; 1949, Ja 8,15:5
Hill, E Rowland Mrs, 1950, S 8,31:4
Hill, E Scott, 1959, Jl 5,57:1
Hill, E Vernon, 1950, My 18,29:5
Hill, Earl W, 1950, Jl 6,27:3
Hill, Eben C, 1940, Je 16,39:1
Hill, Eben C Mrs (C S Bailey), 1961, D 25,23:3
Hill, Ebenezer, 1915, F 27,11:5; 1966, Ja 21,47:4
Hill, Ebenezer J, 1917, S 27,13:3
Hill, Ebenezer Mrs, 1954, My 9,88:2
Hill, Edgar G, 1955, Ja 22,11:5
Hill, Edgar P, 1938, N 27,48:4
Hill, Edgar S, 1946, Jl 22,21:5
Hill, Edith K, 1950, N 7,27:5
Hill, Edmund A Rev, 1912, Ja 3,13:4
Hill, Edmund Y, 1942, Mr 31,21:2
Hill, Edward A, 1946, Ja 9,23:2
Hill, Edward B, 1957, O 16,32:5; 1960, Jl 10,72:3
Hill, Edward B Mrs, 1942, Mr 3,23:3
Hill, Edward E, 1951, Ja 1,17:1
Hill, Edward F Mrs, 1943, S 23,21:3
Hill, Edward J, 1958, Ap 4,24:1
Hill, Edward M, 1963, Jl 7,52:6
Hill, Edward S Mrs, 1949, D 12,33:2; 1953, Jl 14,27:5
Hill, Edward T (cor, Ja 16,21:1), 1956, Ja 15,93:2
Hill, Edward Y, 1941, Ag 27,19:3
Hill, Edwin C, 1957, F 13,35:3
Hill, Eliza C T Mrs, 1941, Ja 10,19:5
Hill, Ella C, 1947, Mr 13,27:2
Hill, Ellen E, 1945, Ja 15,19:4
Hill, Elmer C, 1949, O 4,27:3
Hill, Emile N, 1961, Je 7,41:3
Hill, Emory, 1940, D 5,25:1
Hill, Enoch (por), 1942, My 14,19:3
Hill, Ernest, 1958, My 20,33:4
Hill, Ernest A L, 1942, F 4,19:3
Hill, Ernest W Mrs, 1951, F 6,27:4
Hill, Eugene S, 1948, N 30,28:2
Hill, Everett Mrs, 1947, O 20,23:2
Hill, Florence A, 1953, Mr 27,23:2
Hill, Florence E Mrs, 1941, Ap 29,19:5
Hill, Floyd M, 1919, My 19,17:6
Hill, Foster, 1952, Jl 6,1:4
Hill, Francis J, 1948, Ja 20,23:5
Hill, Francis R, 1941, Je 23,17:6
Hill, Francis X, 1953, O 15,33:3
Hill, Frank, 1939, Ap 27,25:2; 1955, D 17,23:4

Hill, Frank A, 1903, S 13,7:5; 1961, Ap 24,29:4
Hill, Frank D, 1912, My 30,11:6
Hill, Frank F, 1937, Je 29,21:2
Hill, Frank J, 1944, Ag 23,19:5; 1958, O 9,37:3
Hill, Frank M, 1939, O 16,19:6
Hill, Frank Mrs, 1953, Je 1,23:4
Hill, Frank O, 1944, My 7,46:2
Hill, Frank P, 1941, Ag 25,15:3
Hill, Frank P Mrs, 1940, F 1,21:2
Hill, Fred C, 1950, Ja 17,27:2
Hill, Fred S Sr, 1951, Ja 29,19:4
Hill, Fred W, 1950, Je 28,27:5; 1950, D 10,105:1
Hill, Frederick, 1952, Mr 6,31:2
Hill, Frederick A Col, 1907, S 1,7:6
Hill, Frederick C Mrs, 1944, N 7,27:1
Hill, Frederick Stanhope, 1913, S 27,13:6
Hill, G Albert, 1965, D 29,26:4
Hill, G Birkbeck, 1903, Je 26,3:5
Hill, G Everett, 1949, D 14,31:4
Hill, George, 1916, D 28,9:4; 1948, O 21,27:3
Hill, George A, 1951, N 13,29:4
Hill, George A Jr, 1949, N 3,29:4
Hill, George Anthony, 1916, Ag 19,9:5
Hill, George B, 1941, Je 29,33:2
Hill, George C, 1950, Ag 22,27:4
Hill, George E, 1952, Ja 20,85:1
Hill, George E Sr, 1962, S 29,23:4
Hill, George F, 1943, S 5,28:7
Hill, George H B, 1911, D 19,13:4
Hill, George J Mrs, 1947, N 17,21:5
Hill, George M, 1950, My 1,25:3
Hill, George Mrs, 1954, F 18,31:4
Hill, George P, 1942, Ap 10,17:2
Hill, George R, 1962, O 4,39:4
Hill, George T, 1948, Ja 1,23:5
Hill, George T Mrs, 1950, D 6,33:4
Hill, George W, 1914, Mr 31,11:4; 1946, S 14,7:3
Hill, George W C, 1952, Jl 30,23:2
Hill, Gordon S, 1949, My 9,25:5
Hill, Grosvenor B, 1944, Mr 21,20:2
Hill, Grover B, 1961, O 13,35:2
Hill, Gus, 1937, Ap 21,23:3
Hill, H C, 1948, Mr 28,48:5
Hill, H Clinton, 1942, Ap 28,21:1
Hill, H J, 1932, Ja 30,17:1
Hill, Hamnett P, 1942, D 16,25:3
Hill, Harley S Mrs, 1949, D 14,31:2
Hill, Harold O, 1963, F 27,16:1
Hill, Harry, 1896, Ag 28,1:3; 1953, Ja 24,15:2; 1954, Ja 14,29:2
Hill, Harry A, 1941, Mr 22,15:5
Hill, Harry G, 1951, F 16,25:4
Hill, Harry H Jr, 1965, F 13,21:4
Hill, Harry J Mrs, 1946, Jl 20,13:4
Hill, Harry W, 1953, Mr 24,31:4
Hill, Hattie L Mrs, 1941, S 22,15:6
Hill, Helen, 1951, O 18,29:4
Hill, Helen E Dr, 1920, Mr 21,22:3
Hill, Helen L Mrs, 1963, D 29,43:1
Hill, Henry A, 1959, Je 21,92:6
Hill, Henry C, 1956, D 9,87:3
Hill, Henry G, 1952, Ap 29,27:3
Hill, Henry K, 1953, S 17,29:3
Hill, Henry L, 1956, D 9,88:1
Hill, Henry M Mrs, 1944, D 11,23:5
Hill, Henry R Brig-Gen, 1921, S 4,18:4
Hill, Herbert C, 1944, Ap 12,21:5
Hill, Homer, 1968, Ap 4,47:2
Hill, Horace F, 1924, Jl 20,20:4
Hill, Horace R, 1939, D 22,19:2
Hill, Howard C, 1940, Je 26,23:5
Hill, Howard L, 1961, Ag 23,33:5
Hill, Ira J, 1955, My 25,33:3
Hill, Ira L, 1940, S 3,17:2
Hill, Ira R (por), 1947, Ja 21,24:3
Hill, Irvine S, 1944, N 9,27:5
Hill, Isaac B, 1939, D 25,23:5
Hill, J C C Dr, 1904, F 19,9:5
Hill, J D Maj, 1885, Je 19,2:6
Hill, J Foster, 1955, Ja 13,27:2
Hill, J N, 1932, Jl 5,15:1
Hill, J Parker, 1947, Mr 27,27:3
Hill, J Stevenson, 1963, Je 2,85:1
Hill, J W, 1879, O 2,5:4; 1936, O 14,26:1
Hill, J Wesley, 1873, Jl 24,1:6
Hill, Jack B, 1941, Ja 20,17:2
Hill, Jacob S, 1942, N 29,64:7
Hill, James, 1903, Je 13,9:6
Hill, James A, 1941, Jl 1,23:4; 1961, N 13,31:2
Hill, James A Mrs, 1944, Ja 11,19:2
Hill, James B, 1908, Mr 22,9:5; 1952, Ap 1,29:5
Hill, James H, 1922, D 12,19:5
Hill, James J, 1916, Je 1,11:4
Hill, James J Mrs, 1921, N 23,15:3
Hill, James Jr (funl, Ja 29,25:3), 1960, Ja 28,31:3
Hill, James M, 1912, O 4,13:4
Hill, James O, 1961, My 30,17:2
Hill, James P, 1939, S 13,25:2; 1950, Je 10,17:3
Hill, James P Mrs, 1951, Mr 5,21:4
Hill, James T, 1946, S 15,10:1
Hill, Jennie Mrs, 1921, N 21,15:1
Hill, Jeremiah J, 1942, N 10,27:5
Hill, Jerome, 1909, Ap 8,11:5; 1947, D 22,22:2
Hill, Jessica M, 1951, Ja 26,21:5
Hill, John, 1884, Jl 25,5:1; 1943, Ap 10,17:2; 1946, D 5,31:5; 1953, Ja 24,15:2
Hill, John A, 1951, Mr 11,92:4; 1956, My 29,27:3
Hill, John B, 1940, Ja 17,21:2; 1947, S 5,19:2; 1953, N 18,31:2
Hill, John B Mrs, 1950, Ap 7,25:4
Hill, John C Mrs, 1956, Jl 23,23:5
Hill, John E, 1947, Ja 1,33:2; 1947, Jl 9,23:4
Hill, John Edward Gray Sir, 1914, Je 20,9:4
Hill, John F, 1959, Ag 17,23:4
Hill, John F Ex-Gov, 1912, Mr 17,15:3
Hill, John G, 1951, D 6,34:3; 1953, Jl 22,27:2
Hill, John H, 1938, Jl 12,19:2
Hill, John J, 1940, F 10,15:4; 1943, N 20,13:6; 1947, F 22,13:3
Hill, John Lindsay, 1911, Ja 17,9:5
Hill, John M, 1944, N 16,23:6
Hill, John Mrs, 1946, Ja 28,21:3
Hill, John P, 1922, N 1,19:5; 1941, My 24,15:1; 1944, Ap 14,19:3
Hill, John Q, 1959, Jl 29,29:3
Hill, John R, 1938, Ag 19,19:1
Hill, John R Mrs, 1946, D 2,25:3
Hill, John S, 1954, O 15,23:3; 1961, Jl 30,68:1
Hill, John W, 1951, Ag 13,17:1
Hill, Joseph, 1943, Mr 6,13:4; 1947, F 28,23:5
Hill, Joseph A, 1938, D 14,25:2
Hill, Joseph F, 1953, Ag 21,17:4
Hill, Joseph H, 1955, O 17,27:5; 1958, Jl 12,15:4
Hill, Joseph H Mrs, 1946, O 10,27:4
Hill, Joseph J, 1950, Ja 10,29:3
Hill, Joseph W, 1950, Mr 4,17:4
Hill, Joseph Warren Rev, 1921, Ap 3,22:3; 1921, Ap 6, 15:5
Hill, Joshua, 1915, O 5,11:6
Hill, Julien H, 1943, D 2,27:5
Hill, Katherine M, 1939, S 26,23:3
Hill, L E (see also N 25), 1877, N 27,8:5
Hill, L L, 1946, Ap 5,25:6
Hill, L M, 1883, O 17,4:6
Hill, Lamar W, 1937, Je 25,21:5
Hill, Laurence S, 1957, Jl 26,19:1
Hill, Lavinus D, 1942, F 21,19:5
Hill, Lawrence Mrs, 1968, My 13,43:3
Hill, Leonard, 1950, D 5,31:1
Hill, Leonard E, 1952, Ap 1,29:4
Hill, Leonard L, 1940, Je 7,23:5
Hill, Leslie P, 1960, F 16,40:1
Hill, Leslie P Mrs, 1955, F 23,27:5
Hill, Lester S, 1961, Ja 10,47:3
Hill, Lewis B, 1955, Jl 20,27:4; 1958, F 6,25:1
Hill, Lewis R Mrs, 1947, N 10,29:2
Hill, Lindley H, 1952, F 29,23:2
Hill, Logan G, 1961, O 14,23:3
Hill, Louis, 1948, Ap 28,27:3
Hill, Louis C, 1938, N 7,19:5
Hill, Louis D (por), 1945, Je 26,19:5
Hill, Louise B, 1959, O 8,39:4
Hill, Lucy, 1912, D 30,7:4
Hill, Luther L Mrs, 1947, Ag 14,23:1
Hill, Luther R, 1965, Je 1,39:2
Hill, Lyall H, 1955, F 9,25:3
Hill, Marcus L, 1947, Ja 8,24:3
Hill, Martha C Mrs, 1944, Je 1,19:1
Hill, Mary A, 1966, Ag 12,31:5
Hill, Mary A Mrs, 1948, Je 11,23:5
Hill, Mary E, 1947, Ja 10,22:3
Hill, Mary G T Mrs, 1941, Ja 12,44:7
Hill, Matthew D, 1944, Ap 7,19:1
Hill, Maurice C, 1963, Je 5,41:4
Hill, Max (por), 1949, O 19,29:6
Hill, Milton E, 1956, Ag 4,15:5
Hill, Milton P, 1948, O 10,78:2
Hill, Morgan, 1913, N 26,11:6
Hill, Mortimore F, 1951, Jl 28,11:2
Hill, Muriel K, 1942, F 21,19:3
Hill, N S Jr, 1936, O 19,19:1
Hill, Nathaniel P, 1965, Ag 12,27:2
Hill, Nicholas, 1859, My 4,4:6
Hill, Nineian, 1946, Ap 16,25:5
Hill, Norman, 1944, Ja 9,42:6
Hill, Norman C, 1954, My 22,15:5
Hill, Norman N, 1950, F 18,15:3
Hill, Norman W, 1955, D 7,39:4
Hill, Octavia, 1912, Ag 15,9:3
Hill, Olin W, 1951, S 30,73:1
Hill, Orville O, 1951, Jl 11,23:3
Hill, Oscar B, 1951, Ap 9,25:6
Hill, Oscar B Mrs, 1952, Ag 22,21:5
Hill, Oscar E Mrs, 1953, N 25,23:2
Hill, Oscar S, 1942, Ja 10,18:1
Hill, Patrick, 1953, O 22,29:3
Hill, Patrick Mrs, 1955, Je 9,29:1
Hill, Patty S Mrs (por), 1946, My 26,32:1
Hill, Paul S Sr, 1947, Jl 28,15:1
Hill, Percival S, 1925, D 8,25:5
Hill, Percival S (funl, D 11,23:3), 1925, D 9,27:4
Hill, Percival S, 1941, S 26,23:2
Hill, Phil M, 1952, Ag 6,21:1
Hill, Phil S, 1954, Ja 18,23:2
Hill, Philip Adams, 1925, Ja 13,19:5
Hill, Philip E, 1944, Ag 16,19:5
Hill, R S, 1952, Je 18,27:4
Hill, Ralph, 1950, O 20,27:6
Hill, Ralph S, 1954, D 18,15:4
Hill, Ralph W S, 1954, Ag 3,19:2
Hill, Raymond A, 1966, N 6,88:5
Hill, Raymond T, 1956, Ja 7,17:5
Hill, Reuben, 1947, O 14,27:2
Hill, Rev Dr, 1882, Jl 9,8:6
Hill, Richard, 1908, N 9,7:5
Hill, Richard Mrs, 1942, Ja 7,19:3
Hill, Richard O H, 1950, Je 23,25:4
Hill, Richard W, 1941, Jl 19,13:5; 1947, Ja 12,59:7
Hill, Robert, 1937, N 20,17:4; 1938, Ap 19,21:5
Hill, Robert C (por), 1947, Mr 1,15:3
Hill, Robert C Mrs, 1955, D 28,23:3
Hill, Robert E, 1957, Jl 11,25:2
Hill, Robert E L, 1957, Ap 25,31:3
Hill, Robert E Mrs, 1958, My 12,29:2
Hill, Robert E Rev Dr, 1913, O 5,IV,17:6
Hill, Robert H, 1915, O 15,11:4
Hill, Robert Mrs, 1952, F 6,29:5
Hill, Robert P, 1937, O 30,19:6; 1961, My 31,33:2
Hill, Robert T, 1941, Jl 29,15:6; 1945, F 26,19:3
Hill, Robert W Rev, 1937, Mr 16,23:6
Hill, Roderic, 1954, O 7,23:6
Hill, Roger W, 1957, Je 29,17:5
Hill, Roland, 1956, My 29,27:4
Hill, Rolla B, 1963, Je 6,35:5
Hill, Roscoe R, 1960, O 30,86:1
Hill, Rowland, 1873, S 6,1:6
Hill, Rowland D, 1960, N 9,35:3
Hill, Rowland Sir, 1879, Ag 28,2:3
Hill, Roy L, 1946, Je 22,19:2
Hill, S, 1931, F 27,21:1
Hill, S P Mrs (Ellen Corcoran), 1879, My 17,2:6
Hill, Samuel, 1943, O 20,21:4
Hill, Samuel B, 1958, Mr 19,31:5
Hill, Samuel R Mrs, 1925, Ag 3,15:6
Hill, Samuel S Mrs, 1946, O 29,25:2; 1961, D 25,2
Hill, Sanford J, 1963, Je 5,41:5
Hill, Sara B, 1950, F 1,29:2
Hill, Sidney B, 1967, O 18,47:1
Hill, Stanley B, 1964, Ag 25,33:2
Hill, Sydney W, 1964, Ag 13,32:5
Hill, Theodore Mrs, 1956, My 25,23:1
Hill, Thomas A, 1955, D 29,23:2
Hill, Thomas A (will), 1955, D 31,16:8
Hill, Thomas C, 1950, S 6,29:4; 1951, N 17,17:5
Hill, Thomas G F Mrs (por), 1947, F 24,19:3
Hill, Thomas H, 1951, Ja 10,27:4
Hill, U C, 1875, S 4,5:2
Hill, Uriah, 1914, N 16,9:5
Hill, Van Dyke Mrs, 1960, S 9,29:2
Hill, W T Rev, 1937, O 20,23:4
Hill, W Wallace, 1949, Ag 27,13:5
Hill, Walker, 1922, O 7,15:6
Hill, Walter, 1947, Ja 3,21:1
Hill, Walter B, 1950, O 31,27:1
Hill, Walter Branard, 1905, D 29,9:6
Hill, Walter F, 1940, Jl 14,30:7
Hill, Walter H, 1948, Ap 14,27:5
Hill, Walter J, 1944, Mr 6,19:2
Hill, Walter K, 1947, N 24,23:5
Hill, Walter L Sr, 1944, Je 28,23:2
Hill, Walter N, 1955, Je 30,25:2
Hill, Walter O, 1963, Ag 29,29:5
Hill, Walton C Mrs, 1944, Ap 28,19:3
Hill, Warren E, 1962, Ap 4,43:2
Hill, Warren R, 1945, Ap 12,23:5
Hill, Wayne B, 1959, D 21,27:4
Hill, Wilhelmina E Mrs (will), 1962, O 9,29:8
Hill, Will, 1948, O 18,25:7
Hill, William, 1938, Ja 29,15:5
Hill, William (por), 1942, My 15,19:1
Hill, William, 1945, Ag 27,19:4; 1946, Ja 13,44:2
Hill, William A, 1951, Jl 23,17:6
Hill, William A Jr, 1964, My 11,31:5
Hill, William A Mrs, 1963, Jl 4,17:2
Hill, William B, 1945, Ja 24,21:2; 1953, Ap 21,2 1962, Mr 1,31:1
Hill, William B Mrs, 1946, Ja 11,22:3
Hill, William C, 1940, Ag 3,15:4; 1948, Ap 12,2
Hill, William D Mrs, 1951, S 28,31:1
Hill, William E, 1940, Ap 25,23:5; 1966, My 5,4
Hill, William F, 1941, Ap 21,19:3; 1953, N 7,17:
Hill, William F Sr, 1948, Je 22,25:4
Hill, William G, 1953, My 18,21:6
Hill, William H, 1937, Ja 30,17:6; 1941, Ja 17,1 1942, S 1,19:5; 1953, Jl 7,27:6; 1959, N 28,21:
Hill, William J (por), 1940, D 25,27:1
Hill, William J, 1941, My 25,37:2
Hill, William Jr, 1951, Ag 6,1:2
Hill, William L, 1951, Ja 6,15:4
Hill, William M, 1939, F 7,20:1; 1952, Jl 6,50:5
Hill, William Mrs, 1950, My 10,31:3
Hill, William O, 1956, Je 1,23:5
Hill, William P, 1946, S 13,7:3
Hill, William P T, 1965, D 9,47:4
Hill, William R, 1918, Je 17,13:8; 1948, S 25,17 1951, Ap 9,25:5
Hill, William R Mrs, 1950, O 27,29:4
Hill, William S, 1939, O 13,23:4
Hill, William T, 1952, Ag 12,19:4

Hill, William W, 1940, Mr 20,27:2
Hill, William Z, 1953, N 12,43:5
Hill, Willis J, 1951, D 1,13:6
Hill, Willoughby F, 1954, My 10,23:5
Hill, Winfield S, 1961, Jl 9,77:2
Hill, Winifred C Mrs, 1941, D 30,19:2
Hill-Tout, Charles, 1944, Jl 1,15:5
Hillar, Moises, 1951, S 27,31:5
Hillard, Catherine C, 1943, Je 1,23:2
Hillard, Charles, 1945, F 13,23:1
Hillard, Charles W, 1921, Mr 9,13:4
Hillard, F A, 1885, F 12,2:4
Hillard, Harry R, 1943, Jl 27,17:4
Hillard, Katherine, 1915, N 4,11:4
Hillard, Robert D Mrs, 1945, F 2,19:4
Hillard, Tuthill R, 1944, My 2,19:5
Hillary, Arthur J, 1966, Ag 28,93:2
Hillary, Edgar I, 1940, Jl 12,15:5
Hillas, Mary M Mrs, 1942, Je 25,23:2
Hillas, Robert J, 1940, My 18,15:5
Hillas, Robert M, 1956, F 10,21:4
Hillbom, Henrik, 1948, Mr 23,25:2
Hille, Frederick W, 1938, Je 9,23:4
Hille, George C, 1942, Ag 1,11:4
Hille, Herman, 1962, My 1,38:1
Hille, William G, 1960, Ag 27,19:5
Hilleary, Clarence L, 1951, Mr 16,31:4
Hilleary, Edgar D, 1942, O 11,56:8
Hilleary, Richard W, 1941, Je 29,32:3
Hilleboe, Guy L, 1957, My 8,37:4
Hilleboe, Paul B, 1960, My 16,31:2
Hillebrand, Harold N, 1953, Ja 28,27:3
Hillebrand, Joseph, 1940, Ap 23,23:5
Hillebrand, Karl, 1884, N 5,5:4
Hillebrend, Fred Mrs (V Michelena), 1961, Ag 27, 85:1
Hillegas, Eugene, 1939, O 10,23:5
Hillegas, Howard Clemens, 1918, Ja 30,9:5
Hillegas, Milo B, 1961, S 12,33:5
Hillegass, Horace R, 1945, Jl 6,11:4
Hillegeist, Willard M, 1940, Je 4,23:2
Hillegom, Jan S van, 1961, Je 1,8:3
Hillegom, Jan S van Mrs, 1961, Je 1,8:3
Hillemacher, Lucien, 1909, Je 19,7:5
Hillen, Peter J, 1945, Ap 24,19:3
Hillenbrand, E Francis, 1925, S 25,21:5
Hillenbrand, Frederick J, 1947, Ag 12,23:5
Hiller, Adelbert D, 1946, F 20,25:5
Hiller, Alma E, 1958, Je 22,76:7
Hiller, Donald F, 1941, Jl 12,13:5
Hiller, Edward F N, 1941, Mr 1,15:2
Hiller, Emily von, 1961, Ap 22,25:5
Hiller, F, 1885, My 12,5:4
Hiller, George A, 1948, Je 30,25:5
Hiller, George J Sr, 1953, Je 18,29:4
Hiller, Harvey M, 1956, D 28,21:4
Hiller, Isaac E, 1948, Mr 16,27:3
Hiller, John Jr, 1955, Jl 17,61:2
Hiller, Margaret F, 1940, F 18,41:2
Hiller, Nicolai H, 1963, S 25,43:2
Hiller, Otto P, 1944, Ag 12,11:4
Hiller, Paul W, 1947, O 7,27:1; 1964, O 25,88:7
Hiller, Paul W Mrs, 1939, Ag 31,19:4
Hiller, Robert E, 1952, Ag 18,15:1
Hiller, Robert H, 1944, Je 14,19:6
Hillerich, J A (por), 1946, N 30,15:4
Hillerich, John A Mrs, 1959, Ag 2,81:2
Hillerich, Ward A, 1949, N 28,27:4
Hillery, James P, 1956, My 30,21:5
Hillery, James P Mrs, 1952, F 22,21:3
Hillery, John D, 1956, Mr 26,29:4
Hillery, Thomas J Sr Mrs, 1958, Jl 3,25:4
Hilles, Charles D, 1949, Ag 29,17:1
Hilles, Charles Mrs, 1949, Ag 9,25:4
Hilles, Robert L, 1964, Ap 30,35:5
Hilles, William S Mrs, 1954, Je 12,15:6
Hilles, William Smedley, 1925, Mr 21,13:4
illhouse, Charles B, 1937, D 29,21:5
illhouse, Francis, 1951, Ja 27,13:2
illhouse, Hildegarde S Mrs (will, Je 5,15:3), 1942, My 31,38:5
illhouse, James, 1938, S 19,19:1
illhouse, Julia T Mrs, 1941, O 23,23:6
illhouse, Mansfield Lovell, 1908, F 8,7:5
illhouse, Percy A, 1942, S 29,24:2
illhouse, Thomas Gen Mrs, 1903, Mr 17,2:5
illhouse, William, 1943, Ap 13,25:4
illiard, Albert W, 1955, Mr 12,19:6
illiard, Arthur G, 1938, Je 20,15:6
illiard, Charles C, 1963, N 13,41:2
illiard, Charles E, 1940, N 25,17:2
illiard, G S, 1879, Ja 22,5:4
illiard, Idella Mrs, 1961, Ag 19,18:8
lliard, J Vance, 1959, F 1,84:3
illiard, John, 1939, N 2,23:3; 1945, Ag 19,39:2
illiard, John D, 1949, Je 22,31:6
illiard, Louis Henri Marie, 1918, F 26,13:4
lliard, Mack C, 1965, D 21,37:1
lliard, Marion, 1958, Jl 17,27:2
lliard, Mary C Mrs, 1940, Mr 27,21:4
lliard, Patrick R Mrs, 1957, My 8,37:2
lliard, R C, 1927, Je 8,25:3
lliard, Raymond M, 1966, Jl 5,37:1

Hilliard, Roy, 1953, Je 26,19:4
Hilliard, Thomas G, 1956, Ap 27,27:3
Hilliard, Thomas J, 1952, Mr 27,29:3
Hilliard, Thomas J Mrs, 1950, D 26,23:4
Hilliard, Thomas M, 1922, O 3,21:5
Hillias, Peg, 1960, Mr 20,86:7
Hillier, Alfred J, 1949, Ap 5,29:1
Hillier, Charles H M, 1922, D 19,19:4
Hillier, Richard V S, 1957, F 13,35:6
Hillig, Otto, 1954, S 14,27:4
Hillis, David S, 1942, N 10,27:3
Hillis, Elizabeth C Mrs, 1940, Je 29,15:5
Hillis, James G K, 1914, Ag 18,9:6
Hillis, John P, 1942, D 15,28:3
Hillis, Marg Mrs, 1902, Ap 21,9:5
Hillis, Margaret, 1949, My 31,24:3
Hillis, N D, 1929, F 26,27:1
Hillis, Thomas J, 1946, Je 26,25:3; 1948, Mr 2,23:4
Hillison, Henry I, 1960, D 9,31:1
Hillison, Morris Mrs, 1945, Jl 7,13:6
Hillkowitz, Phil (por), 1948, Ja 31,19:4
Hillman, Alex, 1946, Ag 13,27:3
Hillman, Alex L, 1968, Mr 27,47:3
Hillman, Alex Mrs, 1949, D 21,29:1
Hillman, August C, 1952, S 13,17:5
Hillman, Beriah T Judge, 1925, S 3,25:6
Hillman, Carl R, 1954, Ag 3,19:2
Hillman, Clifford Mrs, 1944, D 19,21:1
Hillman, Clifford T, 1942, S 2,23:2
Hillman, Frederick, 1940, D 13,23:3
Hillman, Frederick A, 1923, Ap 24,21:4
Hillman, George Washington, 1917, Jl 8,15:5
Hillman, Gordon M, 1968, O 6,84:8
Hillman, Guy, 1951, Jl 14,13:2
Hillman, Harry L, 1945, Ag 10,15:1
Hillman, Henry A, 1966, Ja 13,25:1
Hillman, Henry A Mrs, 1955, N 20,88:8
Hillman, Herbert V, 1957, O 30,29:2
Hillman, Hildemar M, 1957, My 12,87:2
Hillman, Hilel Mrs, 1946, S 26,25:2
Hillman, Isaac, 1962, O 12,31:2
Hillman, Joel, 1951, Ag 18,11:4
Hillman, John H Jr, 1959, S 26,23:3
Hillman, John L, 1957, Jl 15,19:5
Hillman, Leo, 1941, My 1,23:6
Hillman, Milton E, 1943, Jl 27,17:5
Hillman, Molly, 1908, D 23,9:5
Hillman, Oliver Street Dr, 1968, My 9,47:4
Hillman, Roland M, 1953, Ja 4,76:3
Hillman, Rudolph H, 1956, F 15,31:3
Hillman, Sidney, 1946, Jl 11,1:4
Hillman, Willard C, 1960, Mr 12,21:1
Hillman, William (funl, Je 5,41:5), 1962, Je 1,27:3
Hillman, Willis G Mrs, 1955, Je 3,23:3
Hillman (Sister Mary Vincent), 1962, D 4,41:4
Hillmann, Louis, 1937, D 14,25:5
Hillmuth, Edward A, 1950, Ja 27,24:3
Hillock, Edward F, 1939, Mr 30,23:6
Hillock, Robert T, 1953, My 31,72:5
Hillpot, Arthur K, 1953, Jl 24,13:6
Hillpot, Minnie, 1952, Ja 11,21:2
Hillquit, Jacob, 1939, F 26,39:4
Hillquit, M, 1933, O 9,1:7
Hillquit, Nina E, 1958, Mr 17,29:4
Hills, Alfred Kimball Dr, 1920, My 4,11:1
Hills, Anna Bulkley Mrs, 1921, S 16,17:4
Hills, Arthur T, 1915, Ag 8,13:6
Hills, Charles W, 1950, Ap 3,23:2
Hills, Charles W Jr, 1943, S 20,21:2
Hills, Chauncey H, 1903, D 12,9:6
Hills, Clarence A, 1941, Je 19,21:4
Hills, Clarence F, 1952, Jl 8,27:3
Hills, Edward E, 1959, N 21,23:7
Hills, Edward R, 1953, S 15,31:1
Hills, Edward W, 1947, Ag 9,13:6
Hills, Euegen I, 1947, My 14,25:2
Hills, Frank Waterman, 1924, D 3,11:3
Hills, Fred M, 1939, D 17,49:3
Hills, Frederic W, 1966, Mr 9,41:1
Hills, Frederick S, 1938, Jl 21,21:6
Hills, George F, 1920, F 21,13:4
Hills, George H Dr, 1937, D 4,17:5
Hills, Gladys, 1944, Je 13,19:5
Hills, Guy D, 1948, Ag 5,21:3
Hills, Harry A, 1950, Je 12,27:3
Hills, Harry C, 1950, Mr 6,21:5
Hills, Harry E, 1946, Ag 30,17:4
Hills, J Edward, 1942, Je 13,15:4
Hills, J R, 1882, S 9,8:5
Hills, James Edwin, 1915, Mr 20,13:5
Hills, James M, 1951, Mr 5,21:2
Hills, Jay C, 1949, N 23,29:3
Hills, John W, 1938, D 25,14:6
Hills, Joseph L, 1954, Jl 9,17:5
Hills, Joseph W, 1944, Ja 13,21:1
Hills, Laurence (por), 1941, Mr 29,15:3
Hills, Laurence Mrs, 1951, Ja 11,25:4
Hills, Lawrence R, 1956, Ag 27,19:5
Hills, Lee Mrs, 1961, Ag 7,23:4
Hills, Leonard Dwight, 1917, Mr 29,13:5
Hills, Reuben B, 1954, Ja 5,27:1
Hills, Rollin Dr, 1937, Mr 15,3:5
Hills, Samuels, 1943, Ag 5,15:1

Hills, Therie R Mrs, 1941, My 16,23:5
Hills, William, 1959, S 3,27:5
Hills, William E Mrs, 1944, O 17,23:5
Hills, William G, 1949, Ap 20,27:1
Hills, William I, 1939, N 10,23:2
Hills, William R, 1904, Ja 9,9:6
Hillsbeck, Charles E, 1937, Mr 10,23:3
Hillsberg, Abraham, 1967, Je 27,39:1
Hillsinger, Andrew J Mrs, 1945, Jl 28,11:6
Hillson, David P, 1951, D 18,31:3
Hillson, David R, 1947, N 4,25:3
Hillson, Joseph, 1923, Mr 14,19:4
Hillson, Max S, 1957, Ja 7,25:5
Hillton, Ned, 1967, Ag 18,33:3
Hilly, Arthur J W Mrs, 1962, My 14,29:4
Hilly, John C Mrs, 1960, S 11,82:6
Hillyard, George Mrs, 1946, Ag 8,21:3
Hillyard, George W, 1943, Mr 26,19:3
Hillyer, Clarence W, 1949, D 20,31:3
Hillyer, D B Mrs, 1932, D 9,21:6
Hillyer, E W Judge, 1882, My 11,2:4
Hillyer, Ellison, 1943, My 5,27:4
Hillyer, Ernest, 1958, Jl 8,27:4
Hillyer, Ernest Mrs, 1953, Je 7,82:5
Hillyer, Frederick L, 1950, Je 10,17:5
Hillyer, H Stanley, 1955, Ja 3,27:4
Hillyer, Homer W, 1949, Ja 4,19:2
Hillyer, James A, 1925, Mr 21,13:4
Hillyer, John Blake, 1909, Ja 29,9:5
Hillyer, Kenneth E, 1952, My 13,23:2
Hillyer, Marion, 1937, Je 6,II,8:7
Hillyer, Merton C, 1937, Mr 29,19:5
Hillyer, Rafael Mrs, 1961, O 12,35:5
Hillyer, Rana, 1954, S 6,15:4
Hillyer, Robert (funl plans, D 28,27:4), 1961, D 25, 23:1
Hillyer, V M, 1931, D 22,23:3
Hillyer, William H, 1959, O 27,37:4
Hillyer, William S, 1951, S 16,84:5
Hillyer, William S Gen, 1874, Jl 13,4:7
Hilman, William Mrs, 1948, N 15,25:5
Hilmer, Sofia, 1948, Ap 19,23:1
Hilmi, Abbas 2d (por), 1944, D 22,17:1
Hilowitz, Jacob, 1951, S 7,29:1
Hilpert, Chris O, 1948, Jl 13,27:5
Hilpert, Ernest, 1952, Jl 8,27:3
Hilprecht, Herman Vollrat, 1925, Mr 20,19:5
Hilsberg, Alex, 1961, Ag 11,23:1
Hilsberg, Alex Mrs, 1962, My 24,21:6
Hilsee, David E, 1952, Jl 13,60:4
Hilsinger, Alburtis C, 1940, Jl 15,15:2
Hilson, Cleveland, 1948, Ja 19,23:5
Hilson, Edwin I, 1952, Jl 15,21:3
Hilson, Laura Mrs (will), 1942, Ja 6,45
Hilt, Edward H, 1938, Mr 23,23:3
Hilt, Fred K, 1944, Jl 12,19:4
Hiltbrand, John R, 1940, F 14,21:2
Hiltebrant, Arthur Mrs, 1965, Ja 12,37:3
Hiltebrant, John, 1940, Ja 17,21:4
Hiltebrant, O Raymond, 1954, N 30,29:1
Hilterhaus, Fred, 1965, Mr 25,37:4
Hiltman, G P, 1881, Je 11,5:1
Hiltman, John W (por), 1941, Ap 16,23:4
Hiltner, John K, 1955, S 30,25:3
Hilton, Alfred M, 1954, My 15,15:4
Hilton, Alice B Mrs, 1962, My 31,27:4
Hilton, August H Mrs, 1947, Ag 27,23:5
Hilton, Charles A, 1937, O 11,21:6
Hilton, Charles H, 1942, Mr 23,15:5
Hilton, Charles J, 1942, Ja 10,15:1
Hilton, Edward Banker, 1908, O 8,9:4
Hilton, Elizabeth Louise d'Artois-Traver Dr, 1917, Je 17,19:3
Hilton, Esther M, 1958, O 11,23:1
Hilton, F W, 1882, Ja 20,5:6
Hilton, Fred W, 1937, Ag 14,13:6
Hilton, George P Maj, 1909, O 8,9:4
Hilton, H Stuart, 1962, Ja 7,88:7
Hilton, Harold H, 1942, My 7,19:1
Hilton, Harry L, 1946, Mr 14,25:4
Hilton, Hattie King Mrs, 1906, Ag 27,7:7
Hilton, Henry, 1899, Ag 25,1:5
Hilton, Henry G, 1905, Ag 10,7:6
Hilton, Henry H, 1948, Ap 11,73:1
Hilton, Henry Mrs, 1885, F 22,7:4
Hilton, Isaac S, 1951, My 28,21:4
Hilton, J, 1878, O 9,5:4
Hilton, J Butler, 1906, Ja 21,7:6
Hilton, James (will, D 25,13:8), 1954, D 21,27:1
Hilton, James (will), 1955, Ja 14,16:1
Hilton, James B, 1947, Ap 30,25:2
Hilton, Johanna, 1948, Ap 19,23:5
Hilton, John G M, 1955, Ap 26,29:1
Hilton, John G M Mrs, 1958, My 2,27:4
Hilton, Joseph C, 1942, Ja 31,17:2
Hilton, Joseph Mrs, 1960, Ap 2,23:4
Hilton, Norman E Mrs, 1947, Mr 4,25:1
Hilton, Prescott W, 1951, Ja 25,25:5
Hilton, Robert J, 1871, Jl 4,5:5
Hilton, Robert S, 1943, O 13,23:2
Hilton, Robert W, 1946, My 26,32:4
Hilton, Rose, 1959, O 10,21:5
Hilton, Ruben H Mrs, 1946, O 16,27:2

Hilton, Samuel J, 1941, S 21,44:1
Hilton, Stockridge C, 1960, Ap 27,37:4
Hilton, T A, 1948, S 7,25:3
Hilton, William F, 1924, Ap 26,15:4
Hilton, William L, 1952, Mr 2,92:5
Hilts, Erwin R, 1955, S 25,93:3
Hilts, Harry B, 1960, My 17,37:4
Hilts, Phil J, 1955, F 8,53:4
Hiltz, Robert A, 1955, O 13,31:4
Hilyard, Edgar G, 1954, Je 3,27:4
Hilyard, Norman, 1947, O 12,76:6
Hilyer, Abram, 1947, Je 24,23:1
Hilzinger, Charles Mrs, 1959, Ag 9,89:3
Hilzinger, May E Mrs, 1944, Jl 25,19:5
Himber, Ellis, 1946, S 6,21:3
Himber, Richard, 1966, D 12,47:1
Himelfarb, Herschel, 1964, Ja 21,29:3
Himelright, Raymond S, 1955, Ap 1,27:5
Himelson, Rudolph, 1954, My 29,15:5
Himes, Charles Francis Dr, 1918, D 8,22:3
Himes, Frank, 1942, Ap 22,24:3
Himes, John A Dr, 1923, Ag 12,26:5
Himes, Joseph H (will), 1960, S 25,5:4
Himes, Raymond, 1948, Ja 17,17:6
Himes, Walter G, 1946, My 14,21:1
Himich, John J, 1949, Ap 22,24:3
Himley, H A, 1927, F 1,27:1
Himlyn, William, 1968, O 28,47:3
Himman, Oscar, 1904, F 12,9:4
Himmel, Isaac, 1950, S 17,105:2
Himmel, J J Rev, 1924, N 4,21:1
Himmelberger, Charles M, 1947, O 3,26:2
Himmelberger, Earl G, 1954, O 12,27:5
Himmelhoch, Herman, 1943, Jl 7,19:4
Himmell, Oscar P, 1937, O 21,24:3
Himmell, Sophie (Mrs Hy Himmell), 1966, Mr 30, 45:2
Himmelman, William H, 1938, F 2,19:4
Himmelmann, Henry A, 1921, D 21,19:6
Himmelmann, Sterling, 1963, Ag 19,25:1
Himmelreich, Ferdinand, 1937, D 13,27:5
Himmelsbach, Charles J, 1925, O 28,25:5
Himmelsbach, George A, 1950, Ja 17,27:3
Himmelsbach, Jeanette P, 1949, Mr 13,76:2
Himmelstein, Aaron, 1959, D 20,60:3
Himmelstein, Samuel, 1956, Jl 30,21:4
Himmelstein, Urius, 1949, S 3,13:2
Himowitz, David Mrs, 1949, F 12,17:6
Himpler, Francis G, 1916, S 15,11:4
Himsel, William D, 1946, Jl 12,17:3
Himstead, Ralph E, 1955, Je 10,25:4
Himsworth, Hines H, 1962, Ag 7,29:4
Hin Wong, 1939, F 16,21:3
Hinan, Dale D, 1949, D 28,25:3
Hinan, Robert B, 1943, Jl 27,17:6
Hinch, Arthur E Mrs, 1942, My 22,21:5
Hinch, Edward J, 1950, O 15,105:1
Hinch, James H, 1950, Ag 29,27:4
Hinch, John A, 1941, Ag 13,17:4
Hinchcliffe, Daniel, 1944, Ja 2,38:5
Hinchcliffe, George, 1945, Ja 19,19:1
Hinchcliffe, Harry J Mrs, 1946, D 1,78:3
Hinchcliffe, J Henry, 1938, Jl 30,13:3
Hincher, Millard F, 1949, Ag 5,19:2
Hinchey, Arthur Sr, 1952, D 31,15:3
Hinchey, E Reginald, 1952, O 7,29:2
Hinchey, W John, 1939, Ap 29,17:7
Hinchliff, Theron P, 1947, Ag 15,17:4
Hinchliffe, James C, 1941, O 7,23:2
Hinchliffe, James C Mrs, 1949, Ag 13,12:2
Hinchliffe, John, 1915, Mr 19,11:6
Hinchliffe, Louis V, 1960, Je 12,86:8
Hinchliffe, Richard, 1903, D 16,9:5
Hinchman, C Russell, 1944, Ap 7,19:4
Hinchman, Frederick B, 1951, F 17,15:2
Hinchman, Harry G, 1941, Ja 9,21:5
Hinchman, Lydia S M Mrs, 1938, D 5,23:5
Hinchman, Ralph P, 1938, Ja 31,19:5
Hinchman, William B, 1954, Je 28,19:4
Hinchman, William H, 1911, S 25,9:4
Hinchman, William W, 1963, F 23,7:2
Hinck, Claus F Jr, 1961, D 31,48:5
Hinck, George W, 1962, Ap 30,27:1
Hinck, Otto H, 1954, N 25,29:5
Hincken, George A, 1940, My 24,19:3
Hinckernell, Louis M, 1962, Jl 14,21:4
Hinckle, Anton C Capt, 1903, Ag 9,7:6
Hinckley, Allen C, 1954, Ja 29,19:2
Hinckley, Benjamin S, 1940, My 8,23:2
Hinckley, Bert J, 1941, S 13,17:5
Hinckley, Dwight Mrs, 1952, Ag 2,15:2
Hinckley, Edward B, 1940, S 18,23:3
Hinckley, Frank C Jr, 1953, Jl 23,23:4
Hinckley, Frank E, 1950, O 31,27:1
Hinckley, Frank L, 1959, S 9,41:2
Hinckley, George W, 1946, Mr 22,21:3; 1950, N 6,27:2
Hinckley, Grace B, 1949, Ag 10,21:5
Hinckley, Harold D Capt, 1937, Mr 1,19:4
Hinckley, John A, 1940, F 17,13:1
Hinckley, Julian, 1955, Je 19,93:1
Hinckley, Livingston S Dr, 1920, F 26,11:4
Hinckley, Robert, 1941, Je 3,21:6
Hinckley, Thomas, 1918, N 9,13:5
Hincks, Carroll C, 1964, O 1,35:1
Hincks, Edward Y Mrs, 1944, Je 10,15:2
Hincks, Sarah, 1962, O 29,29:2
Hincks, William B Maj, 1903, N 9,7:5
Hincks, William T Mrs, 1956, O 4,33:2
Hind, A, 1933, Mr 2,17:3
Hind, Arthur M, 1957, My 23,33:3
Hind, Arthur Mrs, 1945, Je 23,13:2
Hind, C L, 1927, S 1,23:3
Hind, Cecil, 1952, Je 13,23:2
Hind, Cora, 1942, O 7,25:1
Hind, George U Sr, 1950, O 25,35:5
Hind, J Henry, 1944, Jl 22,15:5
Hinde, Thomas W, 1952, D 8,41:5
Hindemith, Paul (H C Schonberg trb, D 30,17:4), 1963, D 30,1:2
Hindenburg, Oskar von, 1960, F 13,19:3
Hindenburg, P Von, 1934, Ag 2,1:8
Hindenlang, Gustav A, 1952, O 22,27:6
Hinder, Eleanor M, 1963, Ap 14,92:7
Hindes, Edwin W, 1943, N 21,56:4
Hindes, Matitiahu, 1957, F 14,27:4
Hindle, Charles F, 1946, N 26,29:4
Hindle, F Lawton, 1960, N 5,23:4
Hindle, Frank L Dr, 1925, F 13,17:3
Hindle, Oswald J, 1952, Ag 23,13:5
Hindle, Thomas H, 1940, Ja 14,42:8
Hindle, Wilfred H, 1967, Je 1,44:1
Hindley, Charles T, 1956, N 9,31:5
Hindley, Edward B, 1952, S 7,86:5
Hindley, Howard L, 1943, My 12,25:2
Hindman, Ambrose C, 1942, My 27,23:4
Hindman, Charles A, 1955, F 12,15:4
Hindman, Geldon, 1966, Je 14,48:1
Hindman, L Bennett, 1950, Ap 20,29:1
Hindman, Robert Sr, 1968, Ja 11,33:2
Hindmarch, Pachal R, 1949, Ag 6,17:6
Hindmarsh, H C, 1956, D 21,23:2
Hinds, Arthur, 1947, S 6,17:2
Hinds, Asher C, 1919, My 3,15:6
Hinds, Asher E, 1943, Ja 22,20:2
Hinds, Benjamin H, 1908, S 9,9:5
Hinds, Bessie L, 1953, F 10,27:3
Hinds, David, 1952, Mr 19,29:3
Hinds, Ephraim Mrs, 1904, O 3,9:5
Hinds, Ernest (por), 1941, Je 18,21:3
Hinds, Fannie A, 1951, My 20,89:1
Hinds, Fred, 1905, My 6,2:4
Hinds, Fred W, 1943, Je 6,44:1
Hinds, Frederick J, 1939, O 26,48:2
Hinds, Grace E Marchioness Curzon, 1958, Jl 1,31:4
Hinds, Harold B, 1955, O 12,31:2
Hinds, Harriet C Dr, 1912, Je 6,11:4
Hinds, Henry, 1964, Ag 7,29:2
Hinds, John B L, 1940, Je 29,15:5
Hinds, John T, 1904, F 3,9:6
Hinds, Louis A, 1943, D 23,19:3
Hinds, Nellie E Mrs, 1938, Mr 25,20:4
Hinds, Peter J, 1939, Ja 18,19:4
Hinds, Ritchie K, 1957, Ag 2,19:4
Hinds, Samuel S, 1948, O 14,29:1
Hinds, William M Sr, 1955, Ap 27,31:4
Hine, Albert C, 1944, Ag 8,17:3
Hine, C De L, 1927, F 14,17:4
Hine, Caroline Mrs, 1921, F 27,22:4
Hine, Cecil C, 1952, Ja 12,13:6
Hine, Edward A Mrs, 1950, Jl 24,17:5
Hine, F L, 1927, O 10,21:4
Hine, Henry N, 1957, My 12,86:5
Hine, Lewis W, 1940, N 4,19:6
Hine, Lucius W, 1947, Ja 7,27:2
Hine, T G Macauley Dr, 1937, Ap 27,23:4
Hine, Thurber T, 1943, N 12,21:3
Hine, Walter F, 1954, F 22,19:5
Hine, Walter R, 1954, S 24,23:3
Hineline, Edson S, 1960, Jl 23,19:2
Hinemon, John H Jr, 1959, Mr 5,31:1
Hiner, Benjamin J, 1937, O 27,31:2
Hiner, Edwin M, 1948, Jl 21,23:5
Hiner, Ward B, 1948, D 8,32:3
Hiner, Zern, 1940, Je 5,25:4
Hinerfeld, Benjamin B, 1957, Ag 5,21:5
Hines, Albert B, 1953, S 27,84:4
Hines, Albert B Mrs, 1955, Jl 29,17:4
Hines, Bernam G, 1953, Ja 18,92:7
Hines, C Judge, 1901, Je 7,6:5
Hines, Charles, 1966, O 20,43:5
Hines, Christopher J, 1903, D 4,9:5
Hines, Duncan, 1959, Mr 16,31:1
Hines, Edward, 1942, Ap 11,13:3
Hines, F H, 1929, My 9,29:3
Hines, Frank A, 1915, F 6,11:6
Hines, Frank Mrs, 1948, Ja 13,25:1
Hines, Frank T, 1960, Ap 5,37:1
Hines, Frank W Mrs, 1953, Mr 22,86:1
Hines, George H, 1946, D 18,29:6
Hines, George J (will), 1942, D 15,24:6
Hines, H K Capt, 1926, N 14,28:5
Hines, J Donald, 1957, Mr 1,23:4
Hines, James F, 1943, N 1,17:5
Hines, James J (funl plans, Mr 27,32:1; funl, Mr 30,19:6), 1957, Mr 26,1:5
Hines, James J Mrs, 1957, S 1,56:6
Hines, James S, 1941, Jl 13,28:7
Hines, John A, 1944, Mr 15,19:2
Hines, John F, 1941, O 21,23:2
Hines, John L Gen, 1968, O 14,47:1
Hines, John L Mrs, 1958, Mr 9,87:1
Hines, John P, 1951, My 30,21:5
Hines, John W, 1943, O 1,19:2
Hines, Joseph D, 1941, N 26,23:1
Hines, Joseph W, 1963, My 5,86:8
Hines, Lewis G, 1960, Ja 22,27:1
Hines, Loretta Mrs, 1938, Ap 1,23:4
Hines, Michael, 1916, S 13,9:6
Hines, Nora I, 1937, Ap 29,21:4
Hines, Patrick H (Bro Lloyd), 1955, Ja 10,23:5
Hines, Phil A, 1948, F 27,22:2
Hines, Phil A Mrs, 1940, My 6,17:2
Hines, Ralph J, 1950, My 28,44:5
Hines, Ralph J Mrs, 1961, Jl 31,19:5
Hines, Roland J, 1966, Ag 28,92:4
Hines, Russell H, 1953, Jl 6,17:6
Hines, Samuel E, 1939, N 18,17:7
Hines, Sharon, 1956, Ja 6,8:2
Hines, T Elliot, 1940, Jl 16,17:4
Hines, Theodore J, 1952, My 27,56:6
Hines, Thomas F, 1940, Ag 1,21:2
Hines, Thomas G, 1945, Ja 27,11:2
Hines, Thomas J, 1950, Jl 29,13:2
Hines, W D, 1934, Ja 15,15:1
Hines, William C, 1951, N 22,31:1
Hines, William E, 1917, D 14,13:4
Hines, William F, 1950, Ja 17,27:5
Hines, William J, 1937, O 13,23:5; 1939, Jl 17,19:2
Hiney, George H, 1950, Je 26,27:4
Hing-Sing, Leo, 1946, Ap 1,27:4
Hinga, Don, 1954, Ap 25,87:1
Hingsburg, Frederick C, 1959, Mr 28,17:4
Hingslage, Henry H, 1951, Ja 10,28:2
Hingston, Donald A, 1950, N 20,25:2
Hingston, E P, 1876, Je 13,5:6
Hingston, James W, 1940, Ja 30,20:3
Hingston, Samuel A, 1944, D 2,13:1
Hingston, William Sir, 1907, F 20,11:6
Hink, George L Mrs, 1947, N 21,27:3
Hink, Norbert, 1939, F 22,21:4
Hinkamp, Clarence N, 1961, O 28,21:2
Hinke, William J, 1947, Ja 3,21:4
Hinkel, Daniel A, 1950, My 27,17:5
Hinkel, Frank W, 1946, Ap 3,25:1
Hinkel, Frederick C, 1951, My 17,31:4
Hinkel, Frederick W, 1950, D 6,33:2
Hinkel, Howard M, 1958, N 11,30:3
Hinkel, James F, 1951, Mr 27,29:4
Hinkel, Mary D Mrs, 1942, Mr 8,42:2
Hinkel, Thomas S, 1968, Je 3,45:1
Hinkelman, Alex, 1942, Jl 10,17:2
Hinkhouse, Fred J, 1956, S 8,17:5
Hinkhouse, John F Mrs, 1945, Mr 15,23:5
Hinkhouse, Paul M, 1963, N 7,34:2
Hinkhouse, Paul Mrs, 1964, Je 14,84:6
Hinkins, George S, 1958, S 24,27:3
Hinkle, Anthony Howard, 1911, My 26,13:4
Hinkle, Beatrice M, 1953, Mr 1,92:6
Hinkle, Charles G, 1964, O 31,29:4
Hinkle, Edward, 1949, S 13,29:3
Hinkle, Elmer F, 1957, N 2,21:5
Hinkle, Eugene E, 1944, Mr 8,19:5
Hinkle, Frederick W Mrs, 1952, Mr 16,90:2
Hinkle, Fritz C, 1943, My 25,23:3
Hinkle, Hannah Mrs, 1941, Ag 8,15:3
Hinkle, J R, 1949, Mr 31,25:4
Hinkle, Phil, 1949, Je 25,13:5
Hinkle, Rose O, 1950, My 30,18:2
Hinkle, William M, 1940, N 22,23:2
Hinkley, Alonzo G, 1965, S 2,31:3
Hinkley, Alonzo G Mrs, 1944, D 20,23:2
Hinkley, Frank, 1941, Mr 11,23:3
Hinkley, J William 3d, 1967, Ag 29,37:3
Hinkley, James W, 1904, Ap 12,1:4
Hinkley, James William Capt, 1911, Je 20,9:5
Hinkley, John, 1940, Jl 19,19:3
Hinkley, John L, 1948, My 13,25:5
Hinkley, Mary, 1947, D 12,27:2
Hinkley, Mary M Mrs, 1941, Mr 4,23:2
Hinkley, Nelson P, 1939, Mr 26,III,7:1
Hinkley, Royce E, 1968, D 6,47:4
Hinkley, Vern, 1951, Ja 9,29:4
Hinkley, Walter B, 1947, Ap 8,28:2
Hinks, Kennett W Mrs, 1963, My 4,25:4
Hinkson, John R Dr, 1904, F 6,9:5
Hinkston, Emily, 1947, My 18,60:2
Hinlein, Joseph H, 1950, Ag 11,19:2
Hinman, Addison H, 1938, Ag 30,17:3
Hinman, Archie S, 1939, S 15,23:1
Hinman, Benjamin P, 1920, Jl 31,7:4
Hinman, Bert A, 1947, N 7,23:5
Hinman, Eugene Dr, 1937, Ja 21,24:1
Hinman, Frank, 1961, D 19,33:2
Hinman, Frank N, 1940, Mr 19,25:2
Hinman, G W, 1927, Ap 1,23:5
Hinman, George E, 1961, Mr 20,29:2
Hinman, George W Mrs, 1951, N 1,29:1
Hinman, Harold J, 1955, F 22,21:5
Hinman, Harold P, 1964, Jl 19,65:1

Hinman, Harvey D, 1954, Jl 12,19:5
Hinman, Jennie, 1945, Jl 17,13:7
Hinman, M L, 1907, My 4,9:6
Hinman, Morton E, 1952, O 25,17:5
Hinman, Russell, 1912, Ap 30,11:5
Hinman, Samuel M, 1953, Ja 8,30:2
Hinman Elsie Mrs, 1958, Mr 11,29:1
Hinneken, Florent J, 1955, Jl 4,11:3
Hinners, Frank A, 1960, Ap 6,41:5
Hinners, Herbert F, 1960, Ag 31,29:4
Hinners, Herman C, 1941, Ja 6,15:5
Hino, Ashihei, 1960, Ja 25,27:2
Hinrichs, Alfred E, 1950, S 26,32:4
Hinrichs, Arthur J, 1949, D 3,15:2
Hinrichs, Charles A, 1958, Ja 1,25:4
Hinrichs, Edgar G, 1967, Ja 18,43:3
Hinrichs, Frederick W, 1944, F 18,17:2
Hinrichs, Gustav, 1942, Mr 27,23:2
Hinrichs, Gustav Mrs, 1939, Jl 11,19:4
Hinrichs, Hayo H, 1966, Mr 30,45:3
Hinrichs, John A E, 1945, D 27,19:3
Hinrichs, John J, 1951, S 16,85:1
Hinrichs, Louis, 1967, S 5,43:3
Hinrichs, Oscar, 1943, O 5,25:5
Hinrichsen, Max, 1965, D 21,37:4
Hinrichsen, W H, 1907, D 19,9:5
Hinsdale, Elizas B Mrs, 1912, O 23,13:6
Hinsdale, F Gilbert, 1940, O 13,49:3
Hinsdale, Guy, 1948, Ap 29,23:2
Hinsdale, Ira A, 1952, N 25,29:3
Hinsdale, Ira Mrs, 1968, F 21,47:3
Hinsdale, James Mrs, 1952, Mr 29,15:3
Hinsdale, Mary L, 1946, My 24,19:3
Hinsdale, Ray S, 1955, Jl 16,15:5
Hinsdale, Roy Seymour, 1925, Ap 29,21:4
Hinsdale, S B, 1903, D 29,9:6
Hinsdale, Wilbert B, 1944, Jl 26,19:5
Hinsdale, William G, 1940, Jl 17,21:5
Hinsdale, William Russell, 1922, F 11,13:2
Hinshaw, Carl (funl plans, Ag 7,27:2; funl, Ag 9,25:5), 1956, Ag 6,23:3
Hinshaw, David, 1953, N 7,17:1
Hinshaw, David Mrs, 1949, Jl 12,27:4
Hinshaw, Foster A, 1953, O 31,17:4
Hinshaw, Harry E, 1959, Ag 25,31:3
Hinshaw, William W, 1947, N 28,27:5
Hinshelwood, Cyril, 1967, O 12,45:1
Hinsie, Leland E Mrs, 1960, Je 3,31:1
Hinsley, Arthur, 1943, Mr 17,22:2
Hinsley, Howard E, 1925, N 23,21:4
Hinson, Eugene T, 1960, Je 10,31:2
Hinson, Joseph H, 1937, Mr 27,15:4
Hinssen, Edmund F, 1954, Jl 7,31:3
Hintelmann, William H, 1958, Ja 26,88:3
Hinteman, Walter T, 1952, S 22,23:4
Hintemeyer, Felix Msgr, 1924, Jl 2,19:5
Hinterleiter, J Fred, 1942, D 16,25:4
Hintermeister, John H, 1945, F 12,19:5
Hintermeister, John H Mrs, 1957, Ja 23,29:4
Hintlian, Deran S, 1966, F 4,31:4
Hinton, Alexander C Capt, 1909, N 14,13:4
Hinton, Alfred P, 1940, D 3,25:3
Hinton, Andrew U, 1919, N 19,13:2
Hinton, Arthur Mrs (Kath Goodson), 1958, My 13, 29:5
Hinton, Charles H, 1907, My 2,11:6
Hinton, Charles L, 1950, O 14,19:2
Hinton, Charles W, 1947, Jl 22,24:2
Hinton, Eugene H, 1958, Je 13,23:5
Hinton, Harold B (funl plans, Mr 14,88:6; funl, Mr 17,31:3), 1954, Mr 13,15:1
Hinton, Harry, 1948, Ap 18,70:2
Hinton, Henry L, 1913, O 8,11:6
Hinton, Howard, 1920, Ap 2,15:4
Hinton, Howard Mrs, 1921, D 21,19:5
Hinton, J William Mrs, 1963, My 17,33:4
Hinton, John F S, 1966, D 21,39:4
Hinton, John H Dr, 1905, Ap 27,11:6
Hinton, R J Col, 1901, D 24,3:4
Hinton, Ralph T Sr, 1952, D 20,17:4
Hinton, Robert T, 1948, Ja 25,56:5
Hinton, Sarai I Mrs, 1962, My 29,31:3
Hinton, Wilfred J, 1949, Je 23,27:6
Hinton, William A, 1959, Ag 9,88:6
Hintz, Alfred E, 1962, My 21,33:3
Hintz, Daniel T Sr, 1947, Ja 11,19:3
Hintz, Erwin E, 1954, Ap 30,23:3
Hintz, Howard W, 1964, O 20,37:3
Hintz, John R C, 1966, Ja 30,84:1
Hintz, William G Sr, 1945, Je 13,23:5
Hintze, Paul von, 1941, Ag 24,34:1
Hinz, Paul C, 1954, F 2,27:4
Hinzpeter, Dr, 1907, D 30,7:5
Hioki, Eki, 1926, O 20,25:5
Hiort, Frederick W Sr, 1963, Jl 13,17:6
Hipkins, Calvin C, 1939, Je 13,23:5
Hipkiss, Edwin J, 1955, S 2,17:4
Hipp, Carroll D, 1956, F 18,19:4
Hipp, Mary, 1942, My 22,21:3
Hipp, W Frank, 1943, Ja 4,15:1
Hippard, George R, 1939, F 9,21:4
Hippelheuser, Richard H, 1959, Je 27,23:6
Hippensteel, C L, 1937, S 21,25:3
Hipper, F, 1932, My 26,25:1
Hipple, John E, 1939, D 24,14:7
Hipple, John F, 1942, Mr 20,19:3
Hippler, William G, 1937, Jl 17,15:5
Hippold, Fred, 1943, S 22,26:7
Hippolitus, Paul D, 1949, Je 11,18:7
Hippolyte, F G, 1896, Mr 26,1:1
Hipsh, Harold M, 1957, My 25,21:5
Hipsher, Edward E, 1948, Mr 9,23:3
Hipsley, Elmer Rodies, 1968, D 14,45:2
Hipson, Harry H, 1959, S 9,41:3
Hirachand, Walchand, 1953, Ap 9,27:5
Hiraga, Yuzuru, 1943, F 18,23:3
Hirakawa, Kiyokaze, 1940, F 3,13:3
Hirano, Chie, 1939, Ap 10,17:6
Hiranuma, Kiichiro, 1952, Ag 22,2:3
Hiranuma, Ryozo, 1959, F 15,87:2
Hiraschman, Stuard (will), 1953, Ja 8,32:1
Hirata, Tosuke Count, 1925, Ap 14,23:3
Hird, George S, 1950, Je 22,27:1
Hird, Isabel H, 1947, Jl 11,15:1
Hird, John A, 1939, Mr 5,48:5
Hird, Lewis A, 1954, F 23,27:1
Hird, Lewis A Mrs, 1938, My 21,15:6
Hird, S Ainsworth, 1962, F 26,27:2
Hird, Samuel Mrs, 1957, Ap 23,31:5
Hird, Thomas F, 1953, Jl 2,23:6
Hird, William O, 1955, F 11,23:3
Hirdansky, Samuel H Rev, 1909, Je 4,7:5
Hire, Charles, 1952, S 10,29:4
Hire, Linval J Mrs, 1949, Jl 9,13:4
Hires, Charles E, 1937, Ag 1,II,7:1
Hires, Charles R Jr, 1956, Mr 24,19:1
Hires, Harrison S, 1962, Je 8,31:4
Hires, Harrison S Mrs, 1966, F 25,31:4
Hires, John E Mrs, 1955, O 9,86:3
Hires, Lillian C Mrs, 1942, N 7,15:1
Hires, Russell R, 1959, Ag 27,27:4
Hirigaray, Jean, 1953, Ja 3,15:3
Hirliman, George A, 1952, Ap 1,30:3
Hirner, Robert A, 1957, N 13,32:4
Hirning, Ludwig, 1951, N 13,29:3
Hirons, Frederic C, 1942, Ja 24,17:2
Hirons, J Gardner Dr, 1922, Ap 20,17:4
Hirose, Arthur P, 1944, D 10,54:6
Hirrschoff, Ernest A F, 1951, S 15,15:2
Hirsch, Aaron J, 1948, Ja 15,23:4
Hirsch, Albert, 1915, D 7,13:5
Hirsch, Alcan, 1938, N 25,23:3
Hirsch, Alex, 1962, O 12,32:5
Hirsch, Alex W, 1950, O 6,27:4
Hirsch, Alfred, 1947, F 8,6:2
Hirsch, Angelo, 1937, Ag 3,23:5
Hirsch, Anna Mrs, 1937, O 3,II,8:2
Hirsch, Barney B, 1959, Ap 23,31:3
Hirsch, Baroness de, 1899, Ap 2,7:1
Hirsch, Benjamin J, 1958, Mr 19,31:5
Hirsch, Caesar, 1940, My 19,42:4
Hirsch, Caroline B Mrs, 1950, Ja 16,26:3
Hirsch, Charles S (por), 1938, S 26,17:4
Hirsch, Daniel, 1940, S 16,19:5
Hirsch, David, 1901, Je 29,9:6; 1943, Jl 25,31:1
Hirsch, Dora, 1955, Jl 24,64:1
Hirsch, Edgar A, 1967, Ag 22,39:2
Hirsch, Edward, 1921, F 8,11:4
Hirsch, Emil Gustav Dr, 1923, Ja 8,17:5
Hirsch, Felix, 1940, My 26,35:2
Hirsch, Feodore C, 1924, Ap 2,19:4
Hirsch, Francis F, 1965, S 14,39:6
Hirsch, Fred M, 1948, S 14,29:4
Hirsch, Gordon B Mrs, 1947, Ap 13,60:6
Hirsch, Gustav, 1959, Ja 8,29:2
Hirsch, H R, 1936, Mr 16,17:5
Hirsch, Harold, 1939, S 26,23:4
Hirsch, Harry, 1962, Ag 24,25:1
Hirsch, Harry B, 1944, Jl 18,19:3
Hirsch, Harry Mrs, 1965, D 12,87:1
Hirsch, Helen, 1965, Je 21,29:4
Hirsch, Henry, 1922, N 16,19:5
Hirsch, Henry P, 1945, F 20,19:6
Hirsch, Herbert A, 1939, My 30,17:2
Hirsch, Herbert S, 1961, Je 23,29:1
Hirsch, Hiram H Mrs, 1949, O 6,31:2
Hirsch, I Henry (por), 1947, Ag 26,23:3
Hirsch, I Seth (por), 1942, Mr 25,21:3
Hirsch, Ira, 1953, Mr 1,53:4
Hirsch, Irving M, 1958, O 22,35:5
Hirsch, Isaac E, 1942, Mr 4,19:1
Hirsch, Isaac M, 1904, Ja 26,16:2
Hirsch, Jack D, 1957, Ja 20,92:5
Hirsch, Jacob, 1955, Jl 5,29:4
Hirsch, John, 1952, Ap 8,29:5
Hirsch, Jonas Mrs, 1962, My 5,27:5
Hirsch, Jose L Dr, 1918, Mr 18,13:5
Hirsch, Joseph, 1916, Ja 18,11:6; 1923, Je 1,19:6
Hirsch, Joseph B, 1951, D 1,13:4
Hirsch, Julius, 1961, Ag 15,29:1
Hirsch, Laurence J, 1955, Je 24,21:2
Hirsch, Leo, 1950, Ap 16,105:1
Hirsch, Leon M, 1909, F 5,7:5
Hirsch, Leon Mrs, 1967, O 20,47:1
Hirsch, Louis, 1938, F 14,17:2; 1960, Jl 22,23:4
Hirsch, Louis A, 1924, My 14,19:5; 1941, Mr 20,21:3
Hirsch, Lwarence M, 1962, Mr 11,86:6
Hirsch, Marcus, 1950, D 18,31:5
Hirsch, Martin, 1952, Mr 26,29:5
Hirsch, Marx, 1964, Ag 26,39:4
Hirsch, Maurice de Baron (por), 1896, Ap 22,5:3
Hirsch, Max (funl, Jl 27,13:5), 1925, Jl 25,11:6
Hirsch, Max, 1943, Je 27,32:3; 1968, Ap 16,47:1
Hirsch, Max A L, 1944, D 5,23:2
Hirsch, Max Mrs, 1941, Ap 9,25:3; 1956, Je 25,23:2
Hirsch, Max S, 1959, My 30,17:3
Hirsch, Melvin M, 1961, Jl 2,32:1
Hirsch, Morris, 1940, Je 5,25:3; 1946, Je 18,25:2; 1962, Mr 5,23:1
Hirsch, Morris J, 1925, N 12,25:5
Hirsch, Morse S, 1959, Ag 1,17:3
Hirsch, Nathan, 1947, My 20,25:3; 1962, Jl 18,29:5
Hirsch, Oscar, 1965, Ap 22,33:3
Hirsch, Phillip Mrs, 1960, D 27,29:3
Hirsch, Reuben, 1960, F 14,82:8
Hirsch, Robert B, 1924, S 24,19:4
Hirsch, Samuel, 1939, O 8,49:2
Hirsch, Sidney M, 1962, Ap 13,35:2
Hirsch, Sol, 1967, My 15,43:2
Hirsch, Stefan, 1964, S 30,43:3
Hirsch, Sylvan H, 1945, D 6,27:5
Hirsch, Walter A, 1938, Ag 21,33:3
Hirsch, William, 1943, N 30,27:2
Hirsch, William Dr, 1937, F 16,23:4
Hirsch, William Mrs, 1940, My 4,17:5
Hirschbaum, August, 1967, S 13,47:1
Hirschbeck, Joseph Mrs, 1961, Ag 20,86:2
Hirschberg, Adolph, 1937, Jl 18,II,7:4
Hirschberg, Arthur, 1961, F 3,25:2
Hirschberg, Benjamin, 1960, N 22,35:1
Hirschberg, Carl, 1923, My 26,15:6
Hirschberg, Henry, 1963, Je 21,29:4
Hirschberg, Isidor, 1960, Ag 15,23:4
Hirschberg, Julius Dr, 1925, F 18,19:3
Hirschberg, M H, 1929, Mr 19,31:3
Hirschberg, Max, 1964, Je 22,27:5
Hirschberg, Max B, 1957, Ap 29,25:1
Hirschberg, Ralph, 1962, Jl 13,23:1
Hirschberg, Sanford L, 1965, My 31,17:5
Hirschberg, William H, 1952, Je 17,27:3
Hirschberger, Jakob, 1966, F 26,25:5
Hirschberger, Joseph, 1954, N 10,33:3
Hirscheider, Joseph E J, 1947, F 12,25:2
Hirschenbaum, Aaron Dr, 1968, D 31,27:3
Hirschfeld, David B, 1940, Ap 9,23:4
Hirschfeld, Isador, 1965, F 6,25:4
Hirschfeld, Joseph Mrs, 1946, Ja 13,44:2
Hirschfeld, Kurt E, 1960, O 9,86:4
Hirschfeld, Max, 1942, Ag 19,19:4
Hirschfeld, Samuel, 1946, D 14,15:2
Hirschfeld, Siegfried, 1952, Je 21,15:4
Hirschfelder, Arthur D, 1942, O 12,17:2
Hirschfelder, Charles M, 1948, Mr 19,23:3
Hirschfield, Benjamin L, 1937, Ja 3,II,8:3
Hirschfield, David, 1950, Ap 8,13:3
Hirschhorn, Elmer, 1958, Je 21,19:1
Hirschhorn, Fred (will, My 21,3:7), 1946, My 1,25:5
Hirschhorn, Herman, 1955, Mr 22,31:3
Hirschhorn, Max Mrs, 1966, F 13,84:4
Hirschhorn, William A, 1966, F 20,88:6
Hirschl, Charlotte Mrs, 1940, D 10,25:2
Hirschland, G S, 1942, Mr 18,23:6
Hirschland, Kurt M, 1957, Ja 4,23:1
Hirschland, Richard S, 1961, Ja 1,49:1
Hirschler, Richard, 1947, N 21,27:2
Hirschman, Edward A, 1951, My 3,29:3
Hirschman, Henrietta Mrs (will), 1941, F 11,15:2
Hirschman, Henry, 1917, Je 30,11:4
Hirschman, Herman S, 1954, Jl 16,21:4
Hirschman, Jesse, 1939, Je 19,15:6
Hirschman, Morris, 1951, D 4,33:4
Hirschman, Simon V, 1965, Je 7,37:1
Hirschman, Stephen D (will), 1948, Ap 14,29:2
Hirschman, Stuard, 1952, D 18,29:4
Hirschmann, Adolph, 1954, N 12,21:5
Hirschmann, Adolph Mrs, 1937, Je 29,21:6
Hirschmann, Alfred, 1941, D 17,27:2
Hirschovitz, Gustav J, 1942, D 6,77:1
Hirschthal, Meyer, 1951, O 16,31:2
Hirschtritt, Moses, 1961, F 6,23:1
Hirschwald, Rudolph M, 1959, Je 20,21:6
Hirsdansky, Simon, 1956, Jl 11,29:6
Hirseman, Felix, 1915, My 1,13:6
Hirsh, A Bern, 1945, D 22,19:5
Hirsh, Alfred C, 1946, D 16,23:3
Hirsh, Allan M, 1951, D 22,15:3
Hirsh, Benjamin, 1943, Ap 8,23:2
Hirsh, Edward M, 1943, N 16,23:5
Hirsh, H, 1933, My 2,17:1
Hirsh, Harry, 1949, Ja 12,27:4
Hirsh, Harry R Mrs, 1953, D 10,47:1
Hirsh, Joseph E, 1954, Ja 24,85:1
Hirsh, Leon, 1903, My 21,9:4
Hirsh, Leon F, 1948, My 20,29:4
Hirsh, Leonard F, 1962, F 13,35:2
Hirsh, Max, 1959, Ap 10,17:3
Hirsh, Nathan, 1956, Mr 21,38:2
Hirsh, Samson, 1881, Ap 10,2:4
Hirsh, Sidney V, 1957, Jl 21,61:1

Hirshbein, Peretz, 1948, Ag 18,25:3
Hirshberg, Abraham S, 1953, F 1,88:7
Hirshberg, Bernard, 1947, Mr 16,60:3
Hirshberg, Herbert S, 1955, S 16,23:4
Hirshberg, Maximilian W, 1958, F 1,19:6
Hirshfeld, Clarence F, 1939, Ap 20,23:2
Hirshfeld, Jerome Mrs, 1947, S 30,25:2
Hirshfield, Ira W (por), 1948, D 30,22:2
Hirshman, Herbert J, 1954, Ap 12,17:5
Hirshon, Charles, 1925, O 10,15:5
Hirshon, Hugh H, 1955, My 16,23:4
Hirshon, Maurice H Mrs, 1949, Ap 5,29:2
Hirshon, Walter Mrs, 1953, Je 25,27:2
Hirshorn, Mrs, 1944, My 25,23:7
Hirshowitz, Benjamin R, 1960, Ja 9,21:4
Hirsimaki, Charles E, 1961, Mr 16,37:4
Hirst, Albert, 1945, Ag 12,40:6
Hirst, Barton C Jr, 1943, Ja 19,19:1
Hirst, Claude R, 1942, My 4,19:2
Hirst, Edward H, 1960, O 1,19:3
Hirst, Francis W (trb lr, F 27,20:7), 1953, F 23,25:1
Hirst, George E, 1949, D 10,18:3
Hirst, George H, 1954, My 11,29:1
Hirst, George S, 1968, Je 18,44:5
Hirst, Gertrude M, 1962, Ja 15,27:5
Hirst, Henry B, 1874, Ap 1,4:7
Hirst, Isadore, 1948, D 30,19:4
Hirst, Jesse W, 1952, Ap 30,27:1
Hirst, John A, 1945, Ja 12,15:2
Hirst, John Cooke Dr, 1925, O 5,21:4
Hirst, Lord (por), 1943, Ja 23,13:1
Hirst, Otto C, 1961, D 30,19:5
Hirst, Virginius B, 1952, My 10,21:6
Hirst, William E, 1948, O 6,29:2
Hirst, William H, 1940, Ja 2,19:1
Hirst, William L, 1958, Ag 19,27:2
Hirst, William L Mrs, 1954, O 17,84:4
Hirst-Gifford, Ida Mrs, 1948, Jl 28,23:2
Hirstius, Sherwood G, 1949, Ap 27,27:1
Hirt, Harry O, 1951, D 13,34:3
Hirt, Herman L, 1945, Ap 13,17:4
Hirt, Robert C, 1966, N 15,47:2
Hirt, William E, 1963, Je 26,39:3
Hirten, William J, 1938, Je 13,19:4
Hirtenstein, Aaron, 1945, F 26,19:4
Hirtenstein, Paul, 1959, Jl 17,26:6
Hirth, Emma P, 1951, My 10,31:5
Hirth, Henry K, 1951, Mr 14,33:4
Hirtz, Theodore S, 1965, Ap 14,42:1
Hirtz, William Sr, 1948, N 22,21:2
Hirtzel, Emil J, 1965, Ap 6,39:2
Hirtzel, Emil J Mrs, 1964, O 24,29:2
Hirx, Louis M, 1963, Ap 5,47:1
Hirzel, Carl H, 1945, Je 15,19:5
Hiscock, Charles, 1903, O 24,9:6
Hiscock, Frank Ex-Sen, 1914, Je 19,13:5
Hiscock, Frank H (por), 1946, Jl 3,25:3
Hiscock, Frank H Mrs, 1937, Ap 17,17:4
Hiscock, Gertrude T Mrs, 1939, Ap 21,23:2
Hiscox, Anna S Mrs, 1938, Ap 1,23:3
Hiscox, David C, 1942, My 13,19:3
Hiscox, David F, 1953, Jl 14,27:1
Hiscox, Guy D, 1938, Ap 8,19:5
Hiscox, John Mrs, 1940, Ag 31,13:2
Hiscox, Marjorie, 1960, S 9,29:3
Hiser, Philip, 1960, Ag 21,85:1
Hisgen, Thomas L, 1925, Ag 28,13:5
Hislaire, Rene, 1951, Ag 24,15:5
Hislop, Graham S, 1938, Mr 26,15:5
Hislop, Thomas W Sr, 1949, Ap 12,29:2
Hiss, Charles A Mrs (will, Ap 12,20:8), 1958, Ap 5, 15:1
Hiss, George C, 1966, Jl 10,69:1
Hiss, Margaret O Mrs, 1953, D 24,15:6
Hiss, Phil, 1940, D 16,23:6
Hiss, William J, 1941, My 4,53:3
Hissam, Benjamin V, 1951, Je 18,23:6
Hissem, Martin L, 1939, My 11,25:5
Histed, Ernest W, 1947, My 28,25:5
Histed, George W, 1937, S 4,15:5
Histo, Indian Scout, 1939, Mr 26,III,6:7
Hitch, Frederic Delano, 1911, Mr 22,11:5
Hitch, Henry F, 1913, O 12,15:3
Hitch, Joseph Delano, 1925, D 16,25:4
Hitch, Meyhew R, 1956, S 10,27:2
Hitch, Nathaniel, 1938, F 1,21:5
Hitchcock, A M (Capt Kneely), 1883, Mr 22,5:5
Hitchcock, Albert, 1959, Ja 20,35:1
Hitchcock, Alfred M, 1941, Ap 15,23:1
Hitchcock, Amos B, 1953, O 17,15:5
Hitchcock, B H, 1903, Ap 25,9:5
Hitchcock, Basil, 1938, N 24,27:6
Hitchcock, Carl H, 1954, D 3,27:3
Hitchcock, Center, 1908, D 24,7:6
Hitchcock, Charles A, 1955, My 14,19:6
Hitchcock, Charles B Mrs, 1955, N 18,25:3
Hitchcock, Charles Jr, 1916, F 18,11:7
Hitchcock, Charles Y, 1943, Ag 16,15:4
Hitchcock, Curtice (por), 1946, My 4,15:3
Hitchcock, D C, 1879, D 27,4:7
Hitchcock, De Witt Clinton Mrs, 1908, S 7,5:6
Hitchcock, Earl C, 1960, Ag 16,29:2
Hitchcock, Edward Dr, 1925, D 26,15:6
Hitchcock, Edward Prof, 1911, F 16,11:5
Hitchcock, Edward Rev, 1864, Mr 6,5:2
Hitchcock, Edwin F, 1949, Mr 1,25:4
Hitchcock, Edwin R, 1950, D 5,31:1
Hitchcock, Eldred, 1959, Ap 14,35:4
Hitchcock, Ella L C Mrs, 1942, O 11,56:5
Hitchcock, Ethan Allen, 1909, Ap 10,9:4
Hitchcock, F, 1926, Ap 20,27:3
Hitchcock, F H, 1935, Ag 6,17:3
Hitchcock, F St Clair, 1945, Je 8,19:3
Hitchcock, Frank, 1944, D 19,38:6
Hitchcock, Frank C, 1937, Mr 16,23:5
Hitchcock, Frank J, 1938, Ap 27,23:6
Hitchcock, Frank L, 1957, Je 1,17:3
Hitchcock, Frederick C (por), 1937, Je 29,21:3
Hitchcock, Frederick Mrs, 1944, My 9,19:4
Hitchcock, G M, 1934, F 3,13:1
Hitchcock, George, 1944, Ag 27,33:2
Hitchcock, George P, 1957, My 16,31:4
Hitchcock, George P Mrs, 1963, S 19,27:6
Hitchcock, Gilbert M Mrs, 1925, My 9,15:5
Hitchcock, Gladys, 1944, F 29,8:8
Hitchcock, Guy N, 1950, Ag 2,25:3
Hitchcock, Harry M, 1943, S 21,23:3
Hitchcock, Hattie H Mrs, 1941, S 27,17:3
Hitchcock, Henry, 1902, Mr 19,9:5
Hitchcock, Henry F Dr, 1912, Je 20,11:6
Hitchcock, Henry H, 1950, Mr 7,27:4
Hitchcock, Horace G, 1961, Ag 11,23:1
Hitchcock, Horace G Mrs, 1964, N 22,86:6
Hitchcock, Howard L, 1951, F 8,33:3
Hitchcock, J R Col (see also Ap 13), 1878, Ap 16,8:3
Hitchcock, James C, 1939, N 7,25:5
Hitchcock, James F, 1959, Je 25,29:1
Hitchcock, John F, 1938, Ag 14,32:8
Hitchcock, John M, 1912, F 12,11:5
Hitchcock, Josephine Lloyd Mrs (funl, Ag 22,13:5), 1915, Ag 21,7:6
Hitchcock, Lemuel Mrs, 1950, Ap 19,29:3
Hitchcock, Lucius W, 1942, Je 19,23:3
Hitchcock, Nevada D Mrs, 1937, Mr 27,15:4
Hitchcock, Ora S, 1951, Ap 27,23:4
Hitchcock, P W, 1881, Jl 11,4:7
Hitchcock, P W Mrs, 1877, My 20,6:7
Hitchcock, Paul C, 1957, Ag 30,19:2
Hitchcock, R, 1929, N 26,31:1
Hitchcock, R B Commodore, 1888, Mr 25,10:7
Hitchcock, R D Dr, 1887, Je 18,1:6
Hitchcock, Raymond Mrs (Flora Zabelle), 1968, O 8,47:2
Hitchcock, Reuben Mrs, 1956, Ap 8,84:7
Hitchcock, Ripley, 1918, My 7,13:3
Hitchcock, Ripley Mrs, 1903, S 2,7:6; 1958, D 31,38:3
Hitchcock, Samuel A, 1873, N 25,1:6
Hitchcock, Samuel M, 1939, Ja 8,43:3
Hitchcock, T Sr Mrs, 1934, Ap 2,17:4
Hitchcock, Thomas Sr (por),(will, O 12,46:2), 1941, S 30,23:1
Hitchcock, Welcome G, 1909, Jl 22,7:5
Hitchcock, Wilbur K Mrs, 1937, S 10,23:2
Hitchcock, William, 1915, F 23,13:4
Hitchcock, William C, 1937, Ag 13,17:5
Hitchcock, William F, 1940, O 20,50:1
Hitchcock, William H, 1953, Ap 20,25:5
Hitchen, James, 1937, F 28,II,8:5
Hitchens, Arthur P, 1949, D 11,92:8
Hitchens, Gideon W, 1945, My 4,19:2
Hitchings, Anna M B Mrs, 1941, Ja 19,40:8
Hitchings, Benjamin G, 1943, D 19,48:6
Hitchings, Edson F Prof, 1937, S 9,23:4
Hitchings, Grant G, 1951, Jl 5,25:5
Hitchins, Clayton S, 1958, O 15,39:4
Hitchins, Henry J, 1911, F 18,11:5
Hitchins, W E G, 1943, Jl 2,19:4
Hitchler, Theresa, 1955, O 22,19:6
Hitchman, Robert F, 1925, O 21,23:3
Hitchner, Howard C, 1947, Je 12,25:5
Hitchock, A Roy, 1946, Jl 16,23:4
Hitchock, Charles Henry Prof, 1919, N 8,13:3
Hitchock, Loranus E Judge, 1920, Mr 16,9:6
Hitchock, Thomas, 1910, Je 21,9:5
Hite, Charles J, 1914, Ag 23,13:7
Hite, Cornelius B, 1943, O 11,19:3
Hite, Earle P, 1943, Ap 23,17:5
Hite, George E Jr, 1950, N 2,31:4
Hite, George E Mrs, 1943, F 28,49:2
Hite, Howard O, 1960, Ag 23,29:5
Hite, Lewis F, 1945, Ap 28,15:4
Hite, Mabel, 1912, O 23,13:5
Hite, W C Capt, 1882, D 7,5:1
Hite, William F, 1941, My 9,21:6
Hiter, Charles T, 1954, Ja 28,27:3
Hites, C Harry Sr, 1955, Mr 2,27:1
Hitler, Adolf (death reptd), 1945, My 2,1:8
Hitlin, Alex, 1960, Mr 24,33:2
Hitner, Joseph G, 1950, N 14,31:2
Hitschmann, Edward E, 1957, Ag 2,19:4
Hitsman, John Mrs, 1938, Ap 27,23:3
Hitsman, Phil, 1938, Ag 18,19:3
Hitt, George C, 1944, Mr 11,14:8
Hitt, Robert R, 1906, S 21,9:3
Hitt, Robert R Mrs, 1949, F 2,27:2
Hitt, Robert S R, 1938, Ap 17,II,6:5
Hitt, Rodney, 1945, Jl 15,15:4
Hitt, W F Mrs, 1936, S 4,22:5
Hitt, William F R, 1961, Ap 24,29:2
Hittell, John B, 1944, Jl 5,17:3
Hittinger, Christian G, 1947, N 8,17:5
Hittinger, Norman J, 1947, F 4,25:1
Hittle, James A, 1940, F 19,17:3
Hittleman, Edward B, 1951, Ap 6,25:5
Hittleman, Yetta Mrs, 1951, F 2,23:3
Hittler, George M, 1947, Ag 6,23:4
Hittner, Isidore, 1959, My 22,27:1
Hitwell, Abraham L, 1945, D 30,14:1
Hitz, George F, 1946, Jl 2,25:2
Hitz, George F Mrs, 1952, Ja 1,25:2
Hitz, Joseph F A, 1939, F 14,2:8
Hitz, Ralph (por),(will, Mr 2,8:3), 1940, Ja 13,15:
Hitz, W, 1935, Jl 4,15:4
Hitz, William A, 1949, S 4,40:6
Hitzel, Harry, 1941, O 6,17:2
Hitzelberg, John A Mrs, 1954, O 24,88:8
Hitzelberger, Charles, 1938, F 20,II,8:6
Hives, Ernest W, 1965, Ap 25,88:1
Hix, John M, 1944, Je 7,19:5
Hix, William Preston Col, 1911, O 24,13:6
Hixon, Charles D, 1941, Ja 31,19:2
Hixon, Jessie, 1937, D 9,25:4
Hixon, Joseph H, 1937, F 17,22:2
Hixon, Warren H, 1948, Je 16,29:1
Hixon, William L, 1942, Ap 3,21:4
Hixson, Arthur G, 1938, Ap 19,21:5
Hixson, Arthur W, 1963, Ag 10,17:2
Hixson, Arthur W Mrs, 1958, Ag 16,17:2
Hixson, Edward B, 1952, Ja 20,85:2
Hixson, Elsie B Mrs, 1944, Mr 30,21:5
Hixson, Frederick D Mrs, 1952, My 23,21:5
Hixson, Frederick Whitlo, 1924, N 24,17:3
Hixson, George B Mrs, 1944, O 7,13:6
Hiznay, Joseph M, 1948, F 1,60:5
Hjertberg, Ernest W, 1951, D 17,32:6
Hjertberg, Herman, 1955, O 23,86:6
Hjjar, Grigorios, 1940, N 2,15:4
Hjoerne, Harald Prof, 1922, Ja 8,22:3
Hjort, Alfred, 1944, D 14,23:6
Hjort, Johan, 1948, O 9,19:6
Hjorth, B A, 1937, F 21,II,10:4
Hjorth, Lawrence R, 1950, Jl 10,21:3
Hlacha, Ranier F, 1943, Je 5,15:2
H'Lavac, Harvey, 1962, Mr 8,31:1
Hlavac, Sylvester, 1938, S 24,17:5
Hlavin, Vincent H, 1948, S 22,31:2
Hlebik, John A, 1938, My 15,II,7:2
Hlewicki, John, 1946, My 14,21:3
Hlinka, Andreas, 1938, Ag 17,19:3
Hlond, Aug, 1948, O 23,15:1
Hnat, Frank, 1952, Je 3,29:3
Hnatow, Alex, 1954, Ap 5,25:4
Ho, Christian P Mrs, 1950, Jl 25,27:2
Ho Cheng-Chun, 1961, My 9,39:4
Ho-Ching Yang, 1964, N 19,39:3
Ho Hon, 1951, Ag 29,25:5
Ho Jo San, Arthur, 1948, N 22,21:3
Ho Pao-hsu, 1963, My 13,29:3
Ho Tsunyue, 1948, N 21,88:1
Hoade, D Ivison, 1945, Ja 24,21:1
Hoadley, Arthur G, 1946, O 29,25:1
Hoadley, Avery M, 1937, Mr 19,23:3
Hoadley, Bert G, 1937, S 13,21:5
Hoadley, Charles W, 1942, F 17,21:2
Hoadley, Charles W Mrs, 1949, Ag 23,23:1
Hoadley, Edward M, 1942, Ja 28,19:5
Hoadley, Franklin R, 1957, S 15,84:4
Hoadley, Frederick, 1965, Ap 5,31:5
Hoadley, G A, 1936, My 19,23:4
Hoadley, George, 1955, D 17,23:2
Hoadley, Lee D, 1940, Ap 2,25:3
Hoadley, Lemuel G, 1937, Mr 31,24:1
Hoadley, Nelson T, 1952, Ag 10,60:5
Hoadley, Russell H Mrs, 1949, O 9,94:4
Hoadly, Ex-Gov, 1902, Ag 27,3:5
Hoag, Charles H, 1938, Ja 4,23:3
Hoag, Edgar L, 1958, Jl 28,23:4
Hoag, Edith F Mrs, 1940, Jl 30,19:4
Hoag, Elbert C Rev, 1937, My 15,19:2
Hoag, Francis, 1948, D 19,76:2
Hoag, Francis Mrs, 1940, Je 24,15:5
Hoag, Frank S, 1945, Ag 24,19:5
Hoag, Gilbert T, 1952, S 18,29:4
Hoag, Harry I, 1940, N 5,25:4
Hoag, Harry S, 1943, Ja 23,13:5
Hoag, Henry T Mrs, 1944, Ag 18,13:1
Hoag, Irving D, 1953, Ja 27,25:3
Hoag, J Paul (por), 1955, S 15,33:5
Hoag, Jack Sr, 1954, Ap 24,17:4
Hoag, James, 1925, O 14,25:3
Hoag, James H, 1953, S 14,27:3
Hoag, John, 1942, Jl 31,15:4
Hoag, John Jr, 1957, Ag 22,27:5
Hoag, Mary V Mrs, 1955, Ja 1,13:1
Hoag, Percy L, 1942, D 22,25:2
Hoag, R B, 1883, Ag 14,1:5
Hoag, Samuel T, 1938, My 1,II,6:4
Hoag, Walter C, 1943, F 10,25:5
Hoag, Walter P, 1938, Ap 13,25:5

Hoag, Ward B, 1947, S 17,25:4
Hoag, William, 1950, Je 6,29:1
Hoag, Wilson F, 1947, My 2,21:4
Hoagg, Kirke K, 1951, D 12,37:5
Hoagland, Anna M, 1947, D 6,15:3
Hoagland, Charles L (por), 1946, Ag 3,15:3
Hoagland, Chester F, 1947, Mr 18,27:5
Hoagland, Cornelius D, 1941, Jl 16,17:4
Hoagland, Dan P Mrs, 1947, Ag 2,13:6
Hoagland, Dennis R, 1949, S 6,27:4
Hoagland, Edgar M, 1904, Ag 5,7:6
Hoagland, George T, 1903, O 31,9:6
Hoagland, Henry V, 1966, N 9,39:4
Hoagland, Hudson, 1904, Ja 31,7:6
Hoagland, Irvin P, 1951, D 5,35:3
Hoagland, John A, 1942, Ap 18,15:6
Hoagland, John A Mrs, 1944, F 24,15:2
Hoagland, John Capt, 1912, S 3,11:4
Hoagland, John H, 1962, Ja 14,85:1
Hoagland, Joseph C, 1967, N 2,47:4
Hoagland, Mahlon L Mrs, 1957, Ag 22,27:2
Hoagland, Mary C, 1946, S 26,25:5
Hoagland, Mary E Mrs, 1941, D 23,21:2
Hoagland, Norman, 1961, O 9,35:4
Hoagland, Porter, 1958, Ag 10,94:1
Hoagland, Raymond, 1956, Mr 8,29:2
Hoagland, Russell Mrs, 1953, Ag 16,77:2
Hoagland, Thomas G Mrs, 1953, D 11,34:6
Hoagland, Victor E H, 1937, My 18,23:3
Hoagland, Walter F, 1952, Je 22,69:1
Hoagland, Warren, 1967, Je 13,47:2
Hoagland, Warren L, 1954, My 25,21:6
Hoagland, William W, 1943, O 13,23:3
Hoague, George, 1951, D 7,28:3
Hoak, Edward K, 1954, Ap 21,29:3
Hoan, Daniel W, 1961, Je 12,29:3
Hoan, Daniel W Mrs, 1941, D 29,15:4; 1952, Jl 18,19:5
Hoar, E R, 1895, F 1,9:5
Hoar, Edward P, 1965, N 17,48:1
Hoar, Fred A, 1947, Mr 15,13:3
Hoar, Friend, 1945, My 30,19:5
Hoar, George Frisbie Sen, 1904, S 30,1:1
Hoar, Henry, 1909, Jl 23,7:5
Hoar, James J, 1945, S 20,23:6
Hoar, Patrick, 1943, S 23,21:4
Hoar, Rockwood, 1906, N 2,11:6
Hoar, Roger S, 1963, O 18,31:1
Hoar, Samuel, 1952, Ag 19,23:2
Hoar, Thomas A, 1938, F 20,II,9:1
Hoard, Frank W, 1939, N 26,42:4
Hoard, Harry H, 1950, My 27,17:4
Hoard, Prescott D Mrs, 1944, O 31,19:3
Hoard, William D Ex-Gov, 1918, N 23,11:2
Hoare, Alfred, 1938, N 9,23:6
Hoare, Edward Le Mesurier Maj, 1913, S 4,9:3
Hoare, Geoffrey, 1965, My 29,27:7
Hoare, Henry, 1947, Mr 28,23:3
Hoare, Henry Mrs, 1947, Mr 28,23:3
Hoare, John J, 1950, Ap 5,31:5
Hoare, Mrs, 1872, Mr 16,8:4
Hoare, Reginald, 1954, Ag 13,15:4
Hoare, Samuel J G Viscount of Templewood, 1959, My 9,21:4
Hoare, Thomas H, 1965, N 18,47:1
Hobaica, Saleme Mrs, 1952, Jl 23,23:2
Hoban, Charles F, 1949, Ap 22,24:3
Hoban, Charles J, 1944, Ja 31,17:3
Hoban, Edward F, 1966, S 23,37:4
Hoban, George, 1943, F 3,19:5
Hoban, Harold J, 1938, Jl 15,17:5
Hoban, James D, 1943, Jl 5,15:2
Hoban, James J, 1945, O 29,19:1
Hoban, M J Rev, 1926, N 14,II,9:1
Hoban, Owen A, 1952, D 23,23:5
Hoban, Peter J, 1961, S 16,19:5
Hoban, Thomas H, 1947, F 4,25:4
Hoban, Thomas J, 1944, D 19,21:2
Hoban, Walter C, 1939, N 24,23:5
Hobart, Alice T, 1967, Mr 15,47:1
Hobart, B, 1877, Ja 31,2:3
Hobart, Citzen F A, 1903, O 15,9:7
Hobart, D S, 1905, Mr 29,9:3
Hobart, Donley, 1921, O 14,17:4
Hobart, Doty, 1958, N 17,31:3
Hobart, Emma H Mrs, 1941, My 12,17:4
Hobart, Esther J T Mrs (por), 1941, Ja 9,21:1
Hobart, Garret A, 1941, S 30,23:5
Hobart, Garret A Mrs, 1960, S 11,82:6
Hobart, Garret A Vice President, 1899, N 22,3:1
Hobart, George H, 1959, My 25,29:3
Hobart, George S, 1938, N 2,23:2
Hobart, H Bentley, 1958, My 22,29:3
Hobart, H C Gen, 1902, Ja 27,7:6
Hobart, Harold P, 1968, S 26,47:1
Hobart, Henry M (por), 1946, O 12,19:5
Hobart, Henry M, 1954, F 13,13:4
Hobart, J E, 1880, S 18,3:7
Hobart, Leonora, 1937, N 23,23:6
Hobart, Lewis P, 1954, O 20,29:5
Hobart, Lowell F Jr, 1951, S 22,17:3
Hobart, Lowell F Sr Mrs, 1958, O 26,88:7
Hobart, Marguerite Mrs, 1949, Mr 8,25:1
Hobart, Minnie W Mrs, 1939, Jl 30,29:2
Hobart, Newton B, 1938, Je 25,15:4
Hobart, Pasha (C A), 1886, Je 20,3:3
Hobart, Ralph H, 1949, D 30,19:4
Hobart, Richard T, 1954, S 19,89:2
Hobart, Samuel O Sr, 1949, Ap 10,76:4
Hobart, W T Mrs, 1928, My 12,4:3
Hobart, William H Sr, 1965, F 22,21:3
Hobbes, Halliwell, 1962, F 23,29:3
Hobbes, Halliwell Mrs, 1968, Ap 11,45:3
Hobbie, Alonzo D, 1956, Ap 12,31:4
Hobbie, J Reeve Rev, 1903, My 14,9:7
Hobbie, J Willard Mrs, 1941, My 17,15:6
Hobbie, John R Mrs, 1953, Jl 20,17:6
Hobbie, William R Mrs, 1943, Mr 8,15:2
Hobbins, James R (por), 1949, N 15,25:1
Hobble, John L, 1942, Ag 20,19:3
Hobbs, Alan, 1945, S 27,21:5
Hobbs, Alex F, 1950, Ja 1,42:6
Hobbs, Angier B, 1938, Jl 25,15:5
Hobbs, Charles A, 1953, D 22,31:5
Hobbs, Charles B, 1944, O 10,23:4
Hobbs, Charles D, 1951, Ap 15,92:7
Hobbs, Clarence W, 1944, Jl 22,15:6
Hobbs, Douglas B, 1949, O 12,29:5
Hobbs, Edward A, 1919, My 25,20:4
Hobbs, Edward H Maj, 1907, Ag 13,7:6
Hobbs, Edward L, 1948, Jl 1,23:5
Hobbs, Edwin H, 1942, D 16,25:1
Hobbs, Edwin W, 1955, O 14,27:5
Hobbs, Elon S, 1948, N 12,24:2
Hobbs, Elon S Jr, 1946, O 1,23:4
Hobbs, Frank E Lt-Col, 1911, Ap 13,13:6
Hobbs, Franklin W, 1955, Je 17,23:5
Hobbs, Franklin W Mrs, 1954, Ja 4,19:1
Hobbs, Franklyn, 1948, D 19,76:3
Hobbs, Frederick, 1942, Ap 12,45:3
Hobbs, Frederick D, 1948, Ap 27,25:3
Hobbs, G Warfield, 1957, Ap 26,25:5
Hobbs, Helen D, 1948, Ja 22,27:3
Hobbs, Helen M Mrs, 1940, N 1,25:2
Hobbs, Horace P, 1957, Ja 7,25:5
Hobbs, J F, 1928, D 9,II,8:2
Hobbs, J Howard Mrs, 1947, Ja 19,53:2
Hobbs, Jack B, 1963, D 22,34:4
Hobbs, John, 1874, Ap 9,5:3; 1958, My 10,21:2
Hobbs, John H, 1948, D 5,92:3
Hobbs, John Mrs, 1947, Ag 23,13:5
Hobbs, John S Mrs, 1944, N 24,23:3
Hobbs, Joseph W, 1963, Ag 21,33:4
Hobbs, Kenneth S, 1945, O 31,23:4
Hobbs, Leland S, 1966, Mr 7,27:1
Hobbs, Stephen B, 1951, Ag 25,11:4
Hobbs, Talbot, 1938, Ap 22,19:3
Hobbs, Thomas F, 1953, D 27,61:1
Hobbs, Wellington M, 1946, Ag 2,19:1
Hobbs, William A, 1943, Ja 14,21:5
Hobbs, William F, 1939, F 12,45:2
Hobbs, William Herbert, 1953, Ja 2,16:4
Hobby, Alfred G Mrs, 1954, D 17,31:3
Hobby, Elizabeth Beckett Morey Mrs, 1907, Jl 2,9:6
Hobby, Ferdinand F, 1937, Ap 9,21:5
Hobby, Ferdinand F Mrs, 1955, Jl 19,27:3
Hobby, G Willard, 1960, Ag 15,23:4
Hobby, Husted, 1872, Mr 15,2:6
Hobby, J O Jr, 1941, Ap 5,17:6
Hobby, J Oakley Jr Mrs, 1949, D 1,31:3
Hobby, Josephine, 1950, Ja 31,24:2
Hobby, Theodore Y, 1958, F 24,19:4
Hobby, Walter T Mrs, 1952, O 19,88:7
Hobby, William O, 1941, D 13,21:5
Hobby, William P (trb; funl, Je 9,35:4), 1964, Je 8, 29:2
Hobday, Frederick T G Sir, 1939, Je 25,37:2
Hobday, R W, 1942, N 20,23:2
Hobe, E H, 1940, Ap 20,17:5
Hobe, William W, 1961, N 2,37:2
Hobelman, David E, 1945, Ja 27,11:6
Hoben, Francis H, 1946, Ag 21,28:3
Hoben, James T, 1947, Jl 8,23:1
Hoben, Lindsay, 1967, Ja 9,39:2
Hobens, Jack, 1944, Mr 27,19:5
Hober, Rudolf O A, 1953, S 7,19:6
Hoberecht, Grace Mrs, 1956, D 14,29:3
Hoberg, Harry M, 1954, O 1,23:3
Hoberman, Dora Mrs, 1942, S 3,16:8
Hoberman, Herman Mrs, 1941, N 28,23:2
Hoberman, Jacob, 1948, Ja 22,27:2
Hobert, Leonard T, 1955, My 27,23:6
Hobhouse, Charles, 1941, Je 28,15:4
Hobhouse, Henry, 1937, Je 28,19:5
Hobin, John F, 1948, My 25,27:5
Hoble, C Miggs, 1907, Mr 9,9:6
Hoblitzell, Charles Beatty, 1904, Ja 3,9:5
Hoblitzell, Hugh, 1944, N 28,23:1
Hoblitzell, John D Jr, 1962, Ja 7,88:4
Hoblitzell, William C, 1962, O 2,39:3
Hoblitzelle, Harrison, 1949, D 6,32:5
Hoblitzelle, Karl, 1967, Mr 10,39:3
Hobrecht, Arthur H R, 1912, Jl 8,9:5
Hobson, A Augustus, 1954, Je 20,84:4
Hobson, Arthur E, 1937, N 29,23:4
Hobson, Arthur L, 1946, N 10,64:3
Hobson, Capt, 1880, O 13,5:2
Hobson, Charles M, 1949, D 6,31:4
Hobson, E H Gen, 1901, S 15,7:6
Hobson, Geoffrey D, 1949, Ja 7,22:3
Hobson, George P Mrs, 1944, My 7,46:1
Hobson, Graham B, 1937, S 22,27:4
Hobson, Henry B, 1965, Ag 8,64:4
Hobson, Henry Sir, 1968, F 9,27:2
Hobson, J R A, 1938, Jl 23,13:4
Hobson, John, 1967, D 5,50:7
Hobson, John A, 1940, Ap 2,25:3
Hobson, John J, 1950, F 1,29:4
Hobson, Joseph I, 1937, Ag 23,19:2
Hobson, Joseph Mrs, 1912, Je 12,13:5
Hobson, Oscar R, 1961, Je 19,27:2
Hobson, Ralph S, 1940, Ap 19,21:5
Hobson, Richmond P Jr, 1966, Ag 10,41:3
Hobson, Richmond P Mrs, 1966, N 16,47:2
Hobson, Richmond P Rear-Adm, 1937, Mr 17,25:1
Hobson, Robert L, 1941, Je 7,17:5
Hobson, Russell B, 1951, Mr 6,27:1
Hobson, Samuel G, 1940, Ja 5,20:3
Hobson, Stanley H, 1961, F 16,31:1
Hobson, Thayer, 1967, O 20,47:1
Hobson, Thomas, 1954, Ag 30,17:4
Hobson, Wilder, 1964, My 25,33:4
Hobson, William H, 1960, Jl 7,31:5
Hobson, William H Jr, 1961, Ag 5,17:4
Hobson, William W, 1945, Ja 5,15:4
Hoby, John C J, 1938, Mr 26,15:4
Hoch, August Dr, 1919, S 25,15:6
Hoch, Bertalan, 1944, Jl 12,19:5
Hoch, E W Ex-Gov, 1925, Je 3,23:4
Hoch, Fred, 1938, Ag 11,17:5
Hoch, George F, 1966, F 24,37:5
Hoch, Homer, 1949, Ja 31,19:5
Hoch, John A, 1944, Ap 4,21:5
Hoch, John Dr, 1937, D 23,21:6
Hoch, Paul H, 1964, D 16,46:3
Hoch, Walburga Mother, 1924, D 27,9:4
Hoch, William, 1939, Jl 9,30:5; 1953, Ja 31,15:4
Hochberg, Charles B, 1964, Mr 3,35:2
Hochberg, Hilda Mrs, 1960, N 8,29:2
Hochberg, Irving, 1966, Je 1,47:1
Hochberg, Lew A, 1966, F 4,31:1
Hochberger, Samuel, 1966, Jl 14,35:2
Hochbrunn, William F, 1948, N 2,25:4
Hochderffer, Willard J, 1951, My 22,31:2
Hocheimer, Henry Rev, 1912, Ja 26,11:5
Hochenberg, Benjamin J, 1943, Ja 10,48:3
Hochenberg, Harry M, 1964, Je 9,35:5
Hochenberg, William S, 1947, My 5,23:2
Hochendoner, Louis, 1951, Ja 3,25:2
Hochevar, John, 1952, F 10,92:2
Hochfeld, Leo, 1957, Jl 1,23:4
Hochgreve, Chris, 1939, S 13,25:4
Hochhauser, Edward, 1960, Jl 9,19:4
Hochhauser, William, 1954, Jl 19,19:4
Hochheimer, Rita, 1964, Ja 21,29:3
Hochheiser, Max I, 1955, D 4,88:7
Hochlerner, Reuben, 1952, Mr 29,15:6
Hochlerner, Tobias, 1966, S 12,45:3
Hochman, Ben S Mrs, 1961, My 18,35:1
Hochman, George, 1945, Ag 17,17:1
Hochman, Jacob, 1961, N 15,43:3
Hochman, Louis, 1965, Ap 24,29:3
Hochman, Robert, 1968, Je 6,47:2
Hochman, Sidney P, 1963, Mr 18,15:2
Hochman, Sol Mrs, 1962, Mr 7,35:2
Hochmuth, Bruno A, 1967, N 15,1:8
Hochreich, David R, 1956, Ap 1,88:7
Hochrein, Arnold, 1939, N 7,25:6
Hochschild, Mauricio, 1965, Je 15,41:4
Hochschild, Max, 1957, Je 2,86:4
Hochsprung, George W, 1957, F 4,19:5
Hochstadler, Gustave, 1953, Jl 30,23:2
Hochstadter, Albert F, 1903, Jl 5,7:5
Hochstadter, Albert F Mrs, 1945, D 7,21:3
Hochstadter, Bernard, 1960, My 25,39:1
Hochstadter, Edwin A, 1946, D 31,18:4
Hochstedler, Charles E, 1940, Je 3,15:4
Hochstein, David, 1919, Ja 28,9:4
Hochstein, Harold B, 1963, My 2,35:4
Hochstetter, Ralph, 1955, My 28,15:5
Hochstetter, Ralph (will), 1956, Je 21,15:4
Hochstetterm, Clara B Mrs, 1953, Jl 25,11:5
Hochstrasser, Thomas H, 1947, Jl 17,19:3
Hochswender, George H, 1948, D 1,29:5
Hochuli, Albert G (por), 1949, O 14,27:2
Hochuli, Henry, 1958, My 28,31:1
Hochwald, Adolph, 1958, S 2,25:1
Hochwalt, Albert F, 1938, Jl 25,15:6
Hochwalt, Frederick G (funl, S 14,43:6), 1966, S 6, 48:1
Hock, August E, 1958, Ja 16,29:1
Hock, Franck C, 1945, N 21,21:3
Hock, Fred B, 1938, Jl 30,13:5
Hock, Frederick W, 1939, O 7,17:6
Hock, Frederick W Mrs, 1947, Ap 28,23:1
Hock, Joseph, 1945, Ap 23,19:6
Hock, Julius (Hermit of the Meadows), 1912, O 12, 11:6
Hock, William G, 1967, O 29,84:4
Hockaday, Ela, 1956, Mr 28,31:4

Hockaday, J A Judge, 1903, N 21,9:6
Hockema, Frank C, 1956, F 4,19:2
Hocken, Horatio C, 1937, F 19,19:1
Hocken, Richard E, 1948, Ag 14,13:2
Hockenbeamer, A F, 1935, N 12,19:1
Hockenberger, C W, 1923, O 31,15:3
Hockenberger, George, 1965, My 25,41:4
Hockenberry, Raymond N, 1951, O 20,15:6
Hockenbury, E J, 1951, D 7,27:1
Hockenbury, Edson J, 1943, Mr 10,19:5
Hockenbury, Franklin E, 1965, Ag 16,27:5
Hockensmith, Wilbur D, 1951, Ag 21,27:4
Hocker, Alfred F (por), 1948, F 13,21:1
Hocker, Elizabeth M V, 1949, My 24,27:3
Hocker, Frank, 1910, Jl 31,7:5
Hocker, J William Sr, 1943, Jl 14,19:2
Hocker, John W Mrs, 1951, My 8,31:4
Hockett, Maurice Z, 1954, Ag 22,93:2
Hockett, Robert C Mrs, 1963, N 6,41:3
Hocking, Arthur J, 1938, Ap 12,23:4
Hocking, Arthur L, 1941, Mr 21,21:2
Hocking, James H, 1957, N 1,27:3
Hocking, Joseph, 1937, Mr 5,21:1
Hocking, William E, 1966, Je 13,39:3
Hocking, William E Mrs, 1955, My 17,29:4
Hockley, Claude C, 1941, Mr 5,21:5
Hockman, John E, 1940, My 7,25:5
Hockman, John H, 1910, O 15,11:5
Hockman, William H, 1945, Ja 9,19:4
Hockmeyer, Otto, 1939, Je 14,23:2
Hockstader, Leonard A, 1962, My 12,23:4
Hockstader, Leonard A Mrs, 1961, Ap 25,35:2
Hockstader, Thomas H, 1967, N 20,47:3
Hocomb, Bexley, 1958, S 27,21:2
Hoctor, Elizabeth K Mrs, 1952, Jl 7,21:5
Hoctor, Frank, 1960, O 2,84:3
Hoctor, John, 1942, Mr 28,17:5
Hoctor, John C, 1937, Je 23,25:4
Hoctor, William C, 1953, Je 9,27:5
Hodapp, Robert L, 1949, Ag 26,20:8
Hodas, Joseph H, 1962, Ag 17,23:5
Hodder, Alfred, 1907, Mr 4,9:6
Hodder, Alfred W H Rev, 1914, Ag 4,11:6
Hodder, C Victor, 1947, Jl 14,21:5
Hodder, J D Mrs, 1931, N 20,23:1
Hodder, James R, 1962, S 21,30:7
Hodder, Leslie, 1964, Ag 3,25:4
Hodder, Matthew H, 1911, O 19,13:5
Hodder, William C Mrs, 1963, Jl 5,19:4
Hoddick, William A, 1948, Ja 22,27:1
Hode, Hal, 1949, Ap 8,26:5
Hodecker, Edward, 1957, D 11,31:4
Hodek, Frank Sr, 1940, Mr 26,21:1
Hodell, Charles W, 1925, Mr 29,7:1
Hodell, Henry L, 1949, O 9,93:1
Hodencamp, Charles, 1944, F 3,19:3
Hodenpyl, A G, 1933, Ap 24,15:2
Hodenpyl, Anthony J G, 1907, My 11,7:2
Hodenpyl, Eugene Dr, 1910, My 7,9:5
Hodenpyl, George H, 1942, My 27,23:2
Hodes, Charles, 1964, Mr 9,29:5
Hodes, Henry I, 1962, F 15,29:2
Hodes, James, 1968, Ja 15,47:1
Hodes, Robert, 1966, Ja 30,84:4
Hodes, Robert M, 1962, N 25,86:4
Hodgart, John, 1949, D 15,35:4
Hodgdon, Anderson, 1948, Jl 13,27:4
Hodgdon, Charles, 1953, N 26,31:4
Hodgdon, Frank T Jr, 1962, O 10,51:6
Hodgdon, Frank W, 1923, Ja 27,13:3
Hodgdon, Frederick C (por), 1946, N 17,68:2
Hodgdon, Frederick C Mrs, 1952, Je 18,27:5
Hodgdon, George I, 1957, Ja 31,27:2
Hodgdon, Katherine I, 1942, Ja 31,17:6
Hodgdon, Raymond F, 1951, Ag 28,23:3
Hodgdon, Samuel K, 1922, Ap 7,17:5
Hodgdon, Warren O, 1949, Mr 29,25:4
Hodge, Albert L Col, 1920, Mr 19,13:5
Hodge, Arthur S, 1950, Ja 25,28:5
Hodge, Bachman G, 1961, Ja 6,27:2
Hodge, Carl Mrs, 1961, D 22,23:2
Hodge, Caspar W Rev Dr, 1937, F 27,17:5
Hodge, Charles H, 1949, F 16,25:3
Hodge, Charles Mrs, 1950, F 7,27:1
Hodge, Edward B, 1945, Je 20,23:2
Hodge, Edward D Mrs, 1942, Mr 6,21:2
Hodge, Frank M, 1943, Ja 24,43:2
Hodge, Frederick A, 1955, N 17,35:5
Hodge, Frederick W, 1956, S 30,86:4
Hodge, G Howard, 1966, My 16,37:1
Hodge, George, 1952, My 27,27:2
Hodge, George B, 1938, Jl 19,22:1
Hodge, George C, 1947, D 2,29:5
Hodge, Henry W, 1919, D 22,15:1
Hodge, Henry W Mrs, 1962, O 25,39:1
Hodge, Hugh B Jr Mrs, 1963, N 26,37:1
Hodge, J Aspinwall, 1916, Mr 23,4:7
Hodge, J Aspinwall Mrs, 1907, Ja 8,9:2
Hodge, John (por), 1937, Ag 11,23:3
Hodge, John R, 1963, N 13,41:2
Hodge, Malcolm, 1956, D 24,13:2
Hodge, Margaret E, 1943, N 14,57:1
Hodge, Nelson Wellington, 1905, Mr 15,9:6
Hodge, Percy, 1948, Ag 6,17:3
Hodge, Richard G, 1944, D 21,21:5
Hodge, Sarah B, 1956, F 21,33:4
Hodge, Shurly C, 1943, Ag 30,15:5
Hodge, T Barry, 1953, Ag 21,17:3
Hodge, Thomas H, 1942, S 9,23:6
Hodge, Thomas H Mrs, 1937, F 2,23:2
Hodge, W, 1932, Ja 31,7:1
Hodge, Walter, 1940, Ap 25,23:3
Hodge, Walter S, 1948, D 28,21:3
Hodge, William B, 1947, My 15,25:2; 1947, O 17,21:2
Hodge, William H, 1939, Ja 22,35:3
Hodgeboom, Nicholas, 1950, My 17,29:2
Hodgeman, Eugene Mrs, 1954, Ja 17,95:4
Hodgens, Alex M 2d, 1952, Jl 26,13:5
Hodgens, DAvid L, 1953, N 1,86:4
Hodgens, Harvey C, 1954, Ag 2,17:2
Hodges, A LeRoy, 1954, Ap 6,30:3
Hodges, Abel B W, 1942, Ap 8,19:4
Hodges, Albert B, 1944, F 5,15:4
Hodges, Alfred, 1925, My 15,19:5
Hodges, Amory G Mrs, 1943, S 27,19:2
Hodges, Andrew H, 1957, Ja 12,19:4
Hodges, Arnall P, 1945, O 10,21:2
Hodges, Arthur, 1949, S 24,13:6
Hodges, Arthur H, 1941, O 27,17:4
Hodges, Axel H, 1953, Ap 30,31:5
Hodges, Bonnie (Mrs Wm Galt Chipley), 1968, D 20,47:1
Hodges, C H, 1954, Je 17,29:2
Hodges, Campbell B (por), 1944, N 24,23:5
Hodges, Charles, 1957, N 24,87:3; 1964, O 9,40:1
Hodges, Charles D Jr, 1957, N 6,35:1
Hodges, Charles E (por), 1937, Ja 23,17:5
Hodges, Charles H Jr, 1961, Je 24,21:6
Hodges, Charles L Maj-Gen, 1911, D 27,11:4
Hodges, Claudius B, 1947, Je 25,25:2
Hodges, Courtney H, 1966, Ja 17,47:1
Hodges, Curits A, 1954, Ja 2,12:3
Hodges, Earl W, 1941, O 15,21:5
Hodges, Earl W Mrs, 1960, Je 10,31:2
Hodges, Edith C, 1902, N 22,2:1
Hodges, Edward C, 1903, D 16,9:5
Hodges, Edward Dr, 1914, N 1,17:4
Hodges, Edward P, 1954, O 15,24:1
Hodges, Frank, 1947, Je 5,26:3
Hodges, Frank A Jr, 1963, Ap 14,92:5
Hodges, Frederick, 1943, Je 13,44:6
Hodges, G M Mrs, 1949, Mr 4,21:6
Hodges, George, 1919, Mr 15,15:2
Hodges, George C, 1944, F 8,15:2
Hodges, George Dr, 1919, My 28,15:2
Hodges, George G, 1949, Jl 6,27:2
Hodges, George H, 1947, O 8,25:3
Hodges, George H Mrs, 1966, O 2,86:3
Hodges, George S, 1953, Ap 14,27:2
Hodges, George T Capt, 1905, Mr 22,9:6
Hodges, Gilbert T, 1959, Jl 5,56:1
Hodges, Gilbert T Mrs, 1958, My 26,29:3
Hodges, Harry M Capt, 1923, Mr 17,13:2
Hodges, Henry C, 1963, Jl 16,31:4
Hodges, Henry Jr Mrs, 1949, Jl 16,13:5
Hodges, Henry W, 1941, Mr 15,17:3
Hodges, J A, 1936, D 16,27:3
Hodges, James B, 1938, My 8,II,6:8
Hodges, James M, 1873, F 15,8:5
Hodges, James W, 1924, Ja 23,17:4
Hodges, Jesse R, 1960, D 24,15:1
Hodges, John C, 1967, Jl 8,25:3
Hodges, John H Mrs, 1947, N 2,72:4
Hodges, Joseph H, 1948, Ja 9,21:3
Hodges, Leigh M, 1954, Ap 5,26:3
Hodges, Leroy, 1944, D 20,23:2
Hodges, Lester O, 1967, Je 8,47:5
Hodges, Levi, 1944, N 3,21:4
Hodges, Lowell B, 1951, My 22,31:1
Hodges, Munsey S, 1962, Ag 8,32:1
Hodges, Paul, 1967, Je 2,46:3
Hodges, Ransom F, 1958, Mr 11,18:6
Hodges, Richard E, 1962, S 28,33:4
Hodges, Samuel A, 1938, My 26,25:2
Hodges, Vernon E, 1942, S 16,23:3
Hodges, Walter E, 1942, Je 17,23:6
Hodges, Wetmore, 1957, Ap 4,33:2
Hodges, William F, 1954, My 16,86:4
Hodges, William V, 1965, Ap 19,29:4
Hodges, Wyllys R, 1938, Jl 15,17:4
Hodgetts, Alfred Rev, 1920, Ag 18,9:6
Hodgetts, James C, 1953, S 26,17:3
Hodgewood, Montgomery A, 1944, O 9,23:5
Hodgins, Anthony Rev, 1922, My 25,19:4
Hodgins, Frederic B, 1943, My 12,25:3
Hodgins, Frederic B Mrs, 1948, S 8,29:3
Hodgins, George Sherwood, 1919, Ja 19,21:4
Hodgins, J Herbert, 1949, S 5,17:5
Hodgins, John, 1952, Jl 4,13:5
Hodgins, John E, 1914, O 12,9:4
Hodgins, Tottenham S Mrs, 1953, S 22,31:1
Hodgins, William H Capt, 1912, O 18,11:3
Hodgkin, D C, 1939, S 28,25:3
Hodgkin, H T, 1933, Mr 28,19:5
Hodgkin, John P Mrs, 1961, D 27,25:5
Hodgkin, William N, 1961, S 8,31:2
Hodgkins, Augustus L, 1942, Jl 13,15:5
Hodgkins, Clarence E, 1943, F 16,19:3
Hodgkins, Henry H, 1925, N 9,19:5
Hodgkins, Howard B, 1943, F 25,28:8
Hodgkins, Lemuel G, 1951, D 28,21:4
Hodgkins, Orsamus H, 1944, Ja 10,17:2
Hodgkins, Royal T, 1938, F 1,21:6
Hodgkins, Royal T Mrs, 1958, F 9,88:6
Hodgkins, Wellington, 1953, Je 27,15:3
Hodgkinson, C H, 1961, My 13,19:5
Hodgkinson, Francis (por), 1949, N 6,92:1
Hodgkinson, Harold H, 1947, O 11,17:6
Hodgkinson, M Elliott, 1950, Ja 8,76:4
Hodgkinson, Maurice E Mrs, 1956, Ja 7,17:1
Hodgkinson, Walter, 1950, D 13,35:3
Hodgkinson, William Mrs (Sara), 1968, S 6,43:2
Hodgkiss, George K, 1964, Ag 23,87:2
Hodgman, Abbott Dr, 1901, F 27,9:6
Hodgman, Burns P, 1938, N 20,39:1
Hodgman, C A, 1944, N 28,23:1
Hodgman, Frederick A, 1937, D 17,25:1
Hodgman, Frederick A Mrs, 1951, D 20,31:2
Hodgman, George B Mrs, 1946, N 16,19:4
Hodgman, John E Mrs, 1949, Je 21,25:1
Hodgman, S Theodore, 1939, N 27,17:4
Hodgman, Stephen T Jr, 1957, O 3,29:1
Hodgsdon, Daniel B Capt, 1916, S 11,9:4
Hodgskin, J B, 1879, Mr 21,4:7
Hodgskin, James B Sr, 1957, Mr 21,31:4
Hodgson, A Percival, 1954, Ja 14,29:3
Hodgson, Albert J, 1943, O 8,19:2
Hodgson, Casper W, 1938, F 18,19:2
Hodgson, Edward L, 1903, S 23,7:6
Hodgson, Elizabeth R Mrs, 1941, Ag 21,17:6
Hodgson, Ernest F, 1948, O 4,23:3
Hodgson, Hariette E Mrs (will), 1940, Ap 30,23:4
Hodgson, Harold, 1960, Ag 23,30:1
Hodgson, Henry H, 1961, N 26,88:4
Hodgson, Henry W, 1942, Je 26,21:6
Hodgson, Horace M, 1941, N 20,27:5
Hodgson, Hyland L, 1961, Jl 25,27:1
Hodgson, John H, 1951, Mr 22,31:3
Hodgson, John Helms, 1915, D 5,3:6
Hodgson, John R, 1940, Ja 17,23:6
Hodgson, Joseph C, 1937, Ag 2,19:4
Hodgson, Laurence C, 1937, Mr 25,22:3
Hodgson, Leyland, 1949, Mr 18,25:3
Hodgson, Michael A, 1954, Ja 14,29:2
Hodgson, Morton S, 1954, D 5,88:3
Hodgson, N Hull Mrs, 1912, Jl 22,7:6
Hodgson, Norman J H Mrs, 1938, D 30,16:1
Hodgson, Ralph, 1948, Ja 29,24:2; 1962, N 4,88:6
Hodgson, Richard, 1905, D 21,9:6
Hodgson, Robert J Jr, 1949, Ag 31,23:3
Hodgson, Stuart, 1950, My 11,29:3
Hodgson, W B, 1880, Ag 26,2:5
Hodgson, W R Mrs, 1946, Ag 8,21:6
Hodgson, Walter W, 1949, S 27,27:2
Hodgson, William R, 1958, Ja 25,19:2
Hodigk, John (funl plans, O 22,19:6; funl, O 23,86 1955, O 20,35:3
Hodkin, Morris Mrs, 1962, Ag 18,19:2
Hodkins, Frances, 1947, My 16,24:2
Hodkinson, Franklin C, 1953, F 24,25:3
Hodkinson, Samuel M, 1940, Ja 5,19:1
Hodler, Ferdinand, 1918, My 21,13:7
Hodnett, John F, 1965, O 21,47:4
Hodnett, John R, 1940, F 13,23:3
Hodnette, John K, 1966, Je 15,47:3
Hodnette, Mary E, 1966, Je 15,47:3
Hodous, Lewis, 1949, Ag 10,21:5
Hodsdon, Edward C, 1945, Ja 10,23:5
Hodson, Arthur W, 1944, My 28,34:1
Hodson, C, 1928, Ja 14,17:1
Hodson, Carey P, 1945, Ag 28,19:4
Hodson, Clarence Mrs, 1963, Ag 28,33:5
Hodson, Frank, 1920, D 9,13:3
Hodson, Frederick J, 1943, My 12,25:3
Hodson, George E, 1942, N 15,56:4
Hodson, George E Mrs, 1951, F 14,30:4
Hodson, George L, 1967, My 23,47:1
Hodson, Harry S, 1954, Jl 17,13:2
Hodson, Jasper D, 1948, Mr 31,25:2
Hodson, Keith L B, 1960, Jl 6,7:1
Hodson, Leslie A, 1966, N 23,39:1
Hodson, Lowell C, 1954, Ap 13,31:4
Hodson, William, 1939, O 20,23:4
Hodson, William Mrs, 1952, O 15,31:2
Hodur, Francis Prime-Bishop, 1953, F 17,34:2
Hodza, Fedor Dr, 1968, S 19,47:4
Hodza, Milan, 1944, Je 29,23:1; 1944, Jl 2,20:6
Hodza, Milan Mrs, 1961, Je 6,37:3
Hoe, Alfred G, 1948, Je 30,25:5
Hoe, Annie L D Mrs (cor, Je 15,15:6; will, Je 16 1940, Je 12,25:5
Hoe, Arthur I, 1956, Ag 31,17:4
Hoe, Charles R Jr, 1939, O 8,49:2
Hoe, Edward S, 1921, F 27,22:3
Hoe, Frederic H, 1937, Ag 13,17:5
Hoe, J C, 1880, S 14,5:4
Hoe, Laura C, 1942, N 26,27:6
Hoe, Margaret, 1916, Je 3,13:5
Hoe, R, 1884, S 14,9:4

Hoe, R M, 1886, Je 9,5:4
Hoe, Richard M, 1925, D 23,19:3
Hoe, Robert, 1960, F 9,31:1
Hoe, Robert 3d (funl, O 8,9:3), 1909, S 23,11:1
Hoeber, Arthur, 1915, Ap 30,13:4
Hoeber, Emil William Dr, 1906, O 6,6:5
Hoeber, Paul B, 1937, Ag 21,15:1
Hoechner, Ernest C, 1966, My 30,19:5
Hoedt, W Hubert, 1950, Mr 16,31:4
Hoefer, Charles Mrs, 1960, Ag 7,84:6
Hoefer, Charles W, 1953, Ag 25,21:2
Hoefer, Frederick E, 1941, Ap 22,21:2
Hoefer, George (funl, N 23,33:4), 1967, N 20,47:1
Hoefer, Karl, 1939, My 14,III,7:3
Hoefer, William F Jr, 1937, O 25,36:1
Hoeffer, Paul, 1949, S 3,13:6
Hoeffer, William Howard, 1968, Ja 21,77:2
Hoeffler, William C, 1955, My 18,31:2
Hoeffner, Frank A, 1947, S 12,21:4
Hoefle, Hugo, 1944, S 9,15:4
Hoefler, Alex G, 1940, D 12,27:3
Hoefler, Raymond L, 1966, Je 29,47:2
Hoeflich, Fritz, 1937, S 3,17:2
Hoefling, Peter Sr Mrs, 1947, D 25,21:5
Hoefner, Kate W, 1949, S 1,21:4
Hoeg, Reed E, 1948, F 19,23:2
Hoeger, August Mrs, 1949, Je 13,19:5
Hoeger, Frederick T, 1954, Jl 22,23:3
Hoegerle, Alfred, 1953, Ja 23,20:3
Hoegg, Daniel W, 1954, My 24,27:3
Hoehenlohe-Langenburg, Gottfired zu Prince, 1960, My 12,35:2
Hoehing, A C Rev, 1885, Je 11,2:2
Hoehl, Albert F, 1946, Jl 19,19:6
Hoehler, Francis C, 1944, Je 20,19:4
Hoehling, Adolph A, 1941, F 19,21:1
Hoehn, Francis V, 1943, Je 2,25:2
Hoehn, George Mrs, 1949, Ja 21,22:3
Hoehn, Henry A, 1950, O 11,33:2
Hoehn, Herbert A, 1965, D 5,89:1
Hoehn, Hugh J, 1941, N 28,23:5
Hoehn, Matthew, 1959, My 14,33:2
Hoehn, Robert G, 1960, N 25,27:5
Hoehn, Werner, 1940, Jl 3,17:5
Hoeing, Matthew J, 1948, Ag 6,17:2
Hoejer, Torvald, 1962, Ja 11,33:2
Hoekstra, Anthony, 1953, O 21,29:2
Hoekstra, Jurien, 1951, F 14,29:5
Hoekstra, Robert, 1946, N 2,15:4
Hoel, Sigurd, 1960, O 15,23:6
Hoeland, William A, 1962, Ap 4,43:4
Hoell, George S, 1957, D 17,35:4
Hoellman, Joseph B, 1954, O 5,27:3
Hoelscher, Edward H, 1947, Ap 13,60:5
Hoelscher, Paul Msgr, 1916, D 28,9:4
Hoelter, Herbert F, 1948, Ap 13,28:3
Hoelzel, John P Mrs, 1952, Ap 2,33:2
Hoelzel, Thilo C, 1952, F 4,17:5
Hoelzer, Gustav W, 1957, Ag 11,80:3
Hoelzer, John M, 1942, F 5,21:5
Hoen, A G Dr, 1911, Mr 30,11:4
Hoen, Adolph G, 1947, Jl 7,17:4
Hoen, Augustus Mrs, 1956, Ja 5,33:2
Hoen, Maude L, 1947, Jl 6,41:1
Hoener, Max E, 1951, Jl 8,61:2
Hoenig, Charles A, 1938, Mr 10,21:6
Hoenig, Edward, 1952, My 4,91:1
Hoenig, John F Mrs, 1949, F 18,23:3
Hoenig, Joseph I, 1967, Ja 2,19:4
Hoenig, Morris J, 1957, Ja 16,31:4
Hoenighausen, Anna (Mother Rose Gertrude), 1962, My 9,43:4
Hoenigsmann, Oswald, 1950, Mr 18,13:6
Hoens, Herman J, 1953, O 20,29:5
Hoenshied, Ralph J, 1950, Jl 23,57:1
Hoepfner, H L, 1877, F 4,12:3
Hoepfner, K M Oswald, 1957, Je 20,29:2
Hoepfner, William R, 1938, F 3,23:5
Hoepker-Aschoff, Hermann, 1954, Ja 16,15:5
Hoepli, M Henry Mrs, 1966, S 22,47:3
Hoerbiger, H, 1931, O 13,21:1
Hoerdt, Eugene J, 1954, S 7,25:3
Hoerger, Frederick, 1941, Ja 20,17:4
Hoerle, Edward W Mrs, 1966, F 5,29:6
Hoerle, Justus, 1955, My 20,25:4
Hoerner, Grant, 1966, S 14,47:2
Hoerner, Joseph F, 1951, N 14,31:2
Hoernle, R F Alfred, 1943, Jl 22,19:3
Hoerring, H E, 1909, F 15,7:4
Hoerrner, William H, 1956, N 29,35:1
Hoerst, George W, 1945, Jl 30,19:5
Hoert, Harry L, 1957, N 28,31:5
Hoerup (Denmark), 1902, F 16,7:6
Hoes, Ernest P Mrs, 1943, S 29,21:4
Hoes, Guy M, 1938, Ap 20,23:2
Hoes, Pirie Van Burren, 1904, F 6,9:6
Hoes, William M, 1922, N 6,15:5
Hoesch, George D, 1944, O 20,19:4
Hoesch, L G A von, 1936, Ap 11,7:1
Hoessel, Karl A, 1947, O 11,17:3
Hoest, Hugo A E, 1944, Mr 25,15:5
Hoetjes, Peter, 1937, Ag 20,17:5
Hoett, John J, 1951, Ja 23,27:5
Hoetzendorff, Francis Conrad von, 1925, Ag 27,19:6
Hoetzsch, Otto, 1946, Ag 31,15:4
Hoey, Anne M, 1941, O 6,17:4
Hoey, Christopher W, 1960, Ja 14,33:1
Hoey, Clyde R (funl, My 16,88:1), 1954, My 13,29:1
Hoey, Edward P, 1941, Ja 19,40:6
Hoey, Frank A, 1937, Mr 18,25:2
Hoey, Fred, 1949, N 18,3:7
Hoey, George, 1907, Ag 19,7:6
Hoey, Granville B, 1943, Ap 27,23:2
Hoey, James, 1943, Ja 24,42:3
Hoey, James F Mrs, 1946, Ag 16,21:4
Hoey, James J, 1941, N 11,23:1
Hoey, Jane Margueretta, 1968, O 7,47:3
Hoey, John, 1892, N 15,1:7
Hoey, Joseph L Rev, 1913, Ap 12,11:4
Hoey, Marion A, 1944, Mr 22,19:6
Hoey, Peter E, 1958, Je 12,31:5
Hoey, Robert, 1902, F 22,2:4
Hoey, Samuel, 1944, O 12,27:5
Hoey, William, 1942, Jl 3,17:2
Hoey, William J, 1951, N 11,90:8
Hoey, William Mrs, 1901, O 19,9:6
Hof, Harry J Sr, 1953, Jl 7,27:2
Hof, Henry, 1948, Ap 5,21:4
Hof, Samuel Maj-Gen, 1937, Mr 11,23:1
Hofacker, Theodore, 1947, S 28,60:7
Hofackermoser, Edouardo, 1940, F 10,15:5
Hofbauer, Isfred I, 1961, Mr 15,39:4
Hofeld, Henry, 1939, Ag 27,34:3
Hofeldt, Henry, 1961, O 16,29:2
Hofer, Karl, 1955, Ap 4,29:2
Hofer, Myron A, 1963, My 14,39:4
Hofer, Paul Jr, 1960, Jl 30,17:1
Hoff, Almeth W, 1950, S 23,17:2
Hoff, Arthur B Mrs, 1949, Mr 6,72:3
Hoff, August C, 1964, Jl 30,27:4
Hoff, Charles W, 1956, F 3,23:3
Hoff, Clifford M, 1967, Ag 20,88:1
Hoff, David G, 1949, Ja 18,24:3
Hoff, Edward T, 1947, S 14,60:5
Hoff, Frederick, 1949, Je 23,27:2
Hoff, Frederick J, 1951, F 15,31:4
Hoff, George, 1937, Ja 3,II,8:3
Hoff, Guy, 1962, S 28,25:6
Hoff, H K Rear-Adm, 1878, D 26,5:4
Hoff, Harry G, 1945, D 30,14:7
Hoff, Howard C, 1947, N 23,72:6
Hoff, Jacob H Prof, 1911, Mr 3,11:4
Hoff, Jeremiah J, 1905, Je 30,9:4
Hoff, John J, 1939, D 4,23:4
Hoff, John J Mrs, 1938, D 20,25:6
Hoff, John J Mrs (will), 1939, F 8,21:3
Hoff, John J Mrs (will), 1940, My 16,28:1
Hoff, Joseph S, 1960, Jl 26,29:5
Hoff, Louis R, 1960, Mr 22,37:2
Hoff, Max, 1941, Ap 28,17:2
Hoff, Olaf, 1924, D 25,17:4
Hoff, Sgt, 1902, My 30,9:1
Hoff, Waldemar, 1947, Jl 18,17:6
Hoffa, Harry C, 1947, S 20,15:2
Hoffacker, Albert Mrs, 1949, Ag 16,23:4
Hoffbauer, Charles, 1957, Jl 28,60:7
Hoffbeck, Nelson P, 1947, Je 6,23:2
Hoffberg, Albert, 1947, Je 21,17:1
Hoffberg, Albert Mrs, 1943, Je 25,17:4
Hoffberg, Jack Mrs, 1963, My 15,39:1
Hoffberg, Nathan M, 1956, Mr 8,29:5
Hoffberger, Samuel H, 1961, My 1,29:5
Hoffe, Monckton, 1951, N 5,31:3
Hoffecker, Charlotte J Mrs, 1937, F 3,23:2
Hoffecker, William D, 1940, Ja 3,22:3
Hoffenberg, Louis B, 1949, O 28,24:2
Hoffenberg, Marvin J Mrs, 1968, Jl 18,33:5
Hoffenstein, Edward, 1955, Ja 2,77:1
Hoffenstein, Samuel (por), 1947, O 7,27:1
Hoffer, Carl W, 1954, Jl 18,56:3
Hoffer, Daniel L, 1941, Ap 16,23:2
Hoffer, Frederic S Sr, 1950, Ap 20,29:4
Hoffer, Jay E, 1962, Ja 6,19:4
Hoffer, Jay E Mrs, 1958, D 6,23:5
Hoffer, John Mrs, 1949, Jl 25,15:5
Hoffer, Willi, 1967, O 30,45:4
Hofferberth, Carl, 1951, My 15,64:6
Hofferberth, Carl Mrs, 1951, My 15,64:6
Hofferman, Albert M, 1958, Ap 8,29:1
Hoffheimer, Herbert Sr Mrs, 1954, F 27,13:4
Hoffheimer, Jerome H, 1949, Ag 1,17:3
Hoffherr, Frederic G (mem ser, O 24,37:5), 1956, O 12,29:3
Hoffhine, John, 1949, Ag 1,17:5
Hoffhine, John Mrs, 1944, Ja 13,21:4
Hofflin, Martin, 1938, F 15,25:2
Hoffman, A K Dr, 1871, My 6,5:2
Hoffman, Aaron, 1924, My 28,23:5
Hoffman, Abraham, 1951, Je 5,31:2
Hoffman, Abram, 1958, F 25,27:1
Hoffman, Abram D, 1952, S 25,31:5
Hoffman, Al, 1960, Jl 23,19:4
Hoffman, Albert, 1960, Jl 21,27:1
Hoffman, Albert A, 1954, My 6,33:4
Hoffman, Albert B, 1940, Ag 10,13:6
Hoffman, Albert H, 1954, Jl 13,23:1
Hoffman, Albert L Mrs, 1919, Ag 27,11:3
Hoffman, Alex L, 1955, S 29,33:4
Hoffman, Alfred C, 1939, Ap 9,7:2
Hoffman, Alfred J, 1946, Ag 16,21:2; 1965, Ja 17,88:5
Hoffman, Arnold, 1962, Ag 26,82:4
Hoffman, Arthur, 1945, Ap 25,23:4; 1954, N 4,31:3; 1961, O 3,36:6; 1962, Ja 13,21:2
Hoffman, Arthur G (por), 1947, F 17,19:3
Hoffman, Arthur H, 1943, O 11,19:4
Hoffman, Arthur Mrs, 1962, F 21,45:2
Hoffman, Arthur S, 1966, Mr 15,39:3
Hoffman, Arthur W, 1946, S 15,9:8
Hoffman, Aug, 1938, F 8,21:4
Hoffman, Augustus Henry, 1874, Ja 22,5:1
Hoffman, Augustus L, 1945, D 11,25:4
Hoffman, B Franklin Mrs, 1941, Jl 2,21:4
Hoffman, B Mrs, 1938, Ap 21,19:1
Hoffman, Ben Z, 1954, O 15,23:4
Hoffman, Benjamin, 1922, My 21,30:2
Hoffman, Benjamin R, 1958, Je 20,23:2
Hoffman, Bernard, 1937, S 20,23:5
Hoffman, Bradford, 1924, N 5,19:5
Hoffman, Burrall, 1903, S 13,7:5
Hoffman, C F, 1884, Je 9,5:5
Hoffman, C Fenno, 1942, Ap 27,15:3
Hoffman, Carl, 1946, N 15,24:3
Hoffman, Carl E Mrs, 1952, Mr 8,13:4
Hoffman, Ch Fred Mrs, 1903, S 10,7:5
Hoffman, Charles, 1947, F 10,29:1
Hoffman, Charles E, 1947, Je 14,15:5
Hoffman, Charles F, 1948, Mr 25,27:2
Hoffman, Charles Frederick (funl, S 1,7:5), 1919, Ag 29,11:5
Hoffman, Charles H, 1958, Ag 24,87:1
Hoffman, Charles I, 1945, Je 8,19:4
Hoffman, Charles I Mrs (por), 1948, Ap 16,19:3
Hoffman, Charles J, 1942, My 8,23:6
Hoffman, Charles L, 1949, D 23,22:2
Hoffman, Charles M, 1949, D 29,26:3
Hoffman, Charles Mrs, 1966, O 15,29:5
Hoffman, Charles O, 1963, N 1,33:2
Hoffman, Charles S, 1947, Mr 11,27:3
Hoffman, Charles T, 1951, Ag 15,1:2
Hoffman, Charlotte Mrs, 1938, Jl 5,17:6
Hoffman, chas L, 1940, Mr 14,23:2
Hoffman, Clare, 1967, N 5,86:2
Hoffman, Clarence S Mrs, 1948, Ag 7,15:6
Hoffman, Clifford P (Biff), 1954, Ja 30,17:3
Hoffman, Conrad Jr, 1958, Ag 10,92:2
Hoffman, Corbit S, 1951, S 25,29:4
Hoffman, Coulter H, 1952, O 21,29:2
Hoffman, D B, 1943, Ag 7,11:6
Hoffman, Dallas W Mrs, 1947, S 27,15:4
Hoffman, David, 1961, Je 23,29:3
Hoffman, David J, 1951, D 19,31:2
Hoffman, David Mrs (Mercedes), 1965, F 27,25:3
Hoffman, Dean Meck, 1968, Je 8,31:4
Hoffman, Donald C, 1938, Ap 22,19:1
Hoffman, E, 1883, D 1,5:4
Hoffman, E M Gen, 1901, My 16,2:3
Hoffman, Ed, 1947, My 21,25:4
Hoffman, Edward B, 1950, D 23,15:5
Hoffman, Edward L, 1943, F 13,11:2
Hoffman, Edward R, 1953, N 26,32:3
Hoffman, Edwin W Sr, 1961, Ag 7,23:6
Hoffman, Elmer O, 1957, Ag 30,19:1
Hoffman, Elwood C (Bill), 1962, Ja 24,33:2
Hoffman, Emma Mrs, 1960, D 28,20:3
Hoffman, Enid M, 1954, O 11,27:5
Hoffman, Enoch F, 1951, My 27,69:1
Hoffman, Ethel M, 1952, Ja 29,25:1
Hoffman, Eugene F, 1963, N 23,29:5
Hoffman, F S, 1928, D 22,17:2
Hoffman, Felix E, 1953, Jl 20,11:5
Hoffman, Felix E Mrs, 1953, Jl 20,11:5
Hoffman, Forest (Nubbins), 1949, Ap 1,26:3
Hoffman, Francis B (funl, S 22,19:6), 1924, S 21,29:2
Hoffman, Francis Burrall, 1925, F 9,17:3
Hoffman, Francis R, 1939, O 3,23:5
Hoffman, Frank, 1943, Mr 15,13:3; 1948, O 28,30:3
Hoffman, Frank K Mrs (por), 1940, Mr 22,19:3
Hoffman, Frank M, 1953, Ap 4,13:6
Hoffman, Fred Mrs, 1953, Ap 3,23:3
Hoffman, Fred W, 1961, O 26,35:4
Hoffman, Frederick J, 1952, My 17,19:5; 1967, D 26, 33:3
Hoffman, Frederick L (por), 1946, F 25,26:2
Hoffman, Frederick L, 1947, Ja 19,53:6
Hoffman, Frederick L Mrs, 1949, O 13,27:1
Hoffman, Frederick S, 1954, S 27,21:4
Hoffman, G M, 1936, N 2,21:1
Hoffman, George, 1922, Ja 13,15:4
Hoffman, George A, 1955, O 13,31:4
Hoffman, George C, 1950, Mr 7,28:2
Hoffman, George F, 1951, F 6,27:6
Hoffman, George G, 1957, O 10,33:1
Hoffman, George J, 1937, Je 11,23:4
Hoffman, Gustave A, 1945, Ag 31,17:2
Hoffman, H Louis, 1946, My 20,23:4
Hoffman, Hallock E, 1951, Jl 24,26:2
Hoffman, Harold G (funl, Je 8,27:5), 1954, Je 5,17:1
Hoffman, Harold H, 1942, Je 29,15:4
Hoffman, Harold W, 1937, Ja 28,25:4
Hoffman, Harry, 1947, Ag 19,23:5; 1951, Jl 31,22:7

Hoffman, Harry B, 1942, S 9,23:3
Hoffman, Harry C, 1942, N 13,23:5
Hoffman, Harry H, 1948, Ja 21,25:4
Hoffman, Harry L, 1961, S 22,33:3
Hoffman, Harry T, 1949, My 4,29:2
Hoffman, Harry W, 1941, Je 10,23:5; 1956, Ja 26,29:2
Hoffman, Helen, 1940, Mr 4,15:3
Hoffman, Helen F, 1941, My 17,15:6
Hoffman, Herbert H, 1951, D 2,90:4
Hoffman, Herman, 1968, S 25,43:1
Hoffman, Herman M, 1939, Je 28,21:4
Hoffman, Herman S, 1912, N 24,II,17:5
Hoffman, Hermann, 1947, Je 5,35:5
Hoffman, Howard B, 1945, Je 8,19:4
Hoffman, Hugh F, 1951, Ap 22,89:2
Hoffman, Hugo W Rev, 1917, F 4,19:3
Hoffman, Ida Mrs, 1958, F 4,21:2
Hoffman, Ira O, 1943, My 6,19:2; 1948, Je 1,23:5
Hoffman, Irving, 1968, D 10,77:1
Hoffman, Irving M, 1948, Ag 6,17:3
Hoffman, Jay L, 1957, My 11,21:6
Hoffman, J B, 1877, N 19,5:3
Hoffman, J E, 1926, N 20,17:4
Hoffman, J Harry, 1941, Ja 4,13:4
Hoffman, J Paul, 1956, O 7,87:1
Hoffman, J T, 1888, Mr 25,5:3
Hoffman, Jacob, 1905, S 11,1:6
Hoffman, Jacob (will), 1906, Ja 10,9:6
Hoffman, Jacob, 1956, Je 23,17:4
Hoffman, Jacob B, 1962, Je 22,25:3
Hoffman, Jacob Mrs, 1951, O 10,23:4
Hoffman, Jacob V C, 1947, D 29,18:2
Hoffman, Jacques, 1938, Mr 19,15:3
Hoffman, James, 1884, N 13,5:5
Hoffman, James D, 1950, Jl 6,27:1
Hoffman, James J, 1954, Je 22,27:5
Hoffman, Jeane (Mrs A McIntosh), 1966, O 1,31:1
Hoffman, Jessie H Mrs, 1949, Ap 6,29:1
Hoffman, John, 1938, Ap 15,20:2; 1940, Ja 8,15:1
Hoffman, John C, 1940, Ap 24,23:2; 1950, Je 2,23:3
Hoffman, John H, 1938, F 18,19:3
Hoffman, John J, 1950, O 17,31:4; 1953, Ja 17,15:6
Hoffman, John L (por), 1938, N 24,27:3
Hoffman, John M, 1952, S 24,33:4
Hoffman, John N, 1947, Mr 12,25:3; 1951, My 25,27:2
Hoffman, John W, 1947, Ja 5,53:5; 1953, Jl 5,49:1
Hoffman, John W Jr, 1947, D 17,29:2
Hoffman, Josef, 1904, F 2,9:7
Hoffman, Joseph, 1951, F 9,25:1; 1954, Je 3,27:4; 1965, Ap 2,35:2
Hoffman, Joseph B, 1968, Mr 13,53:4
Hoffman, Joseph E, 1943, F 18,23:4
Hoffman, K Lawrence, 1947, My 22,27:2
Hoffman, Lawrence H, 1946, Ap 25,21:2
Hoffman, Lefferts Suydam, 1922, My 21,30:2
Hoffman, Leon, 1940, O 29,25:5
Hoffman, Leon J, 1955, Ap 23,19:2; 1965, Jl 17,25:5
Hoffman, Leonard D, 1954, Ja 29,19:2
Hoffman, Lew, 1952, Mr 12,27:3
Hoffman, Liebert, 1940, Ag 16,15:5
Hoffman, Louis, 1937, D 7,25:3
Hoffman, Louis A von Baron, 1909, F 5,7:6
Hoffman, M, 1927, Jl 9,13:5
Hoffman, M C, 1942, Mr 18,23:2
Hoffman, Malvina (funl, Jl 14,36:1), 1966, Jl 11,1:8
Hoffman, Max, 1944, S 17,41:1; 1954, F 21,68:3
Hoffman, Michael, 1955, Je 21,31:4
Hoffman, Michael H, 1944, Mr 8,19:2
Hoffman, Michael J, 1947, My 14,25:4
Hoffman, Morris Mrs (F Heller), 1964, Ja 13,35:1
Hoffman, Morris S, 1958, S 12,25:2
Hoffman, Mortimer B, 1937, Ap 24,19:2
Hoffman, Murray (funl, My 11,8:2), 1878, My 8,5:3
Hoffman, Nathan, 1951, S 4,27:2
Hoffman, Nicholas F, 1941, Ap 3,23:5
Hoffman, O H Jr, 1967, Ag 29,37:2
Hoffman, Oskar, 1954, Ag 1,85:1
Hoffman, Paul, 1943, S 13,19:4
Hoffman, Paul C Sr, 1960, Ag 16,29:3
Hoffman, Paul G, 1960, Je 22,18:5
Hoffman, Paul G Mrs, 1961, My 18,35:2
Hoffman, Perry A, 1958, Ag 24,87:1
Hoffman, Peter M, 1948, Ag 1,56:5
Hoffman, Phil, 1948, N 10,29:2
Hoffman, Phil F Dr, 1953, F 4,27:5
Hoffman, Phil F Mrs, 1940, O 1,23:3
Hoffman, Philip, 1915, Mr 22,9:5; 1968, D 16,47:1
Hoffman, Philip H, 1924, Ap 10,23:4
Hoffman, Philip Mrs, 1947, My 22,27:3
Hoffman, Philip W, 1946, O 8,23:4
Hoffman, R P, 1942, F 16,17:1
Hoffman, Ransom P, 1959, S 3,27:5
Hoffman, Raymond S, 1961, D 30,19:2; 1962, Ja 1,23:5
Hoffman, Renaud, 1952, N 22,23:2
Hoffman, Richard, 1909, Ag 19,7:3
Hoffman, Richard B, 1943, O 20,21:4
Hoffman, Richard Curzon Sr Mrs, 1925, My 19,21:4
Hoffman, Richard Dr, 1968, Je 13,47:4
Hoffman, Robert, 1946, Mr 4,23:4
Hoffman, Robert J, 1959, Ja 26,29:2
Hoffman, Robert V A, 1953, Ag 12,31:5
Hoffman, Rolf, 1951, Mr 31,30:8
Hoffman, Rolf Mrs, 1951, Mr 31,30:8
Hoffman, Romaine C, 1942, My 12,19:3

Hoffman, Russell J, 1943, O 25,15:5
Hoffman, S V, 1880, O 7,2:2
Hoffman, Sam Mrs, 1952, S 29,23:4
Hoffman, Samuel, 1939, S 1,17:4; 1957, Jl 6,16:1
Hoffman, Samuel A, 1955, Je 18,17:5
Hoffman, Samuel D, 1957, O 16,35:3
Hoffman, Samuel R, 1946, Ag 28,27:5
Hoffman, Samuel S, 1946, Ag 4,45:2
Hoffman, Samuel V, 1942, F 24,22:2
Hoffman, Samuel V Mrs, 1962, D 4,41:2
Hoffman, Selma, 1950, F 22,29:1
Hoffman, Seth, 1948, Ag 3,25:3
Hoffman, Silas, 1910, Jl 13,7:6
Hoffman, Sophia C, 1905, S 13,9:6
Hoffman, Stephen R, 1961, Je 13,35:2
Hoffman, Stoddard, 1941, Jl 7,15:1
Hoffman, Sylvanus D, 1905, Mr 20,7:4
Hoffman, T Kenneth, 1962, Mr 2,30:3
Hoffman, Tage E, 1950, S 1,21:4
Hoffman, Theodore H, 1952, Ag 5,19:5
Hoffman, Theodore H C, 1948, My 27,25:1
Hoffman, Theodore Q, 1951, Jl 23,17:5
Hoffman, Thomas, 1914, O 24,13:1
Hoffman, Thomas G, 1963, O 23,41:3
Hoffman, W Harold, 1958, Je 7,19:2
Hoffman, W L, 1948, O 12,25:5
Hoffman, Waldo B, 1946, F 22,25:3
Hoffman, Walter F, 1949, Je 17,23:2; 1950, F 6,25:2
Hoffman, Walter H, 1945, F 13,23:4
Hoffman, Walter H Jr, 1955, Ag 25,23:6
Hoffman, Walter J, 1967, Jl 3,17:3
Hoffman, Walter J Mrs, 1942, Ja 30,19:3
Hoffman, Wickham Mrs, 1903, S 27,7:6
Hoffman, William, 1909, Je 9,7:4; 1946, Mr 23,13:6; 1950, Jl 9,69:2; 1950, Jl 10,21:4; 1951, Ap 15,92:1; 1960, N 29,37:2
Hoffman, William A, 1958, N 15,23:6; 1966, N 10,47:2
Hoffman, William C, 1954, Jl 13,13:2
Hoffman, William D, 1940, Ap 3,23:1
Hoffman, William F, 1939, Jl 5,17:6; 1949, Jl 1,19:2; 1951, My 11,27:1; 1964, Mr 23,29:5
Hoffman, William H, 1955, Mr 15,29:1
Hoffman, William H Mrs (por), 1944, Ap 5,19:2
Hoffman, William L, 1940, N 20,21:4
Hoffman, William M V, 1947, Mr 3,21:1
Hoffman, William M V Jr, 1944, D 6,23:4
Hoffman, William M V Mrs, 1957, My 25,21:4
Hoffman, William Mrs, 1938, Ja 26,23:3; 1958, Je 28, 17:4
Hoffman, William O Mrs, 1951, F 17,15:4
Hoffman, William S, 1957, Ap 27,19:5
Hoffman, William W, 1966, Mr 9,41:4
Hoffman, William X Mrs, 1957, Je 1,17:4
Hoffman, Wilmer, 1954, My 22,15:6
Hoffman, Winton A, 1952, D 21,53:1
Hoffman, Wolfgang, 1956, Mr 26,29:1
Hoffman, Wray B, 1950, Ap 11,31:4
Hoffmann, Adolf, 1940, Je 3,15:4
Hoffmann, Adolph, 1940, Ap 6,17:4
Hoffmann, Alfred, 1959, Ap 23,31:4
Hoffmann, Anna E Mrs, 1940, Ap 6,17:3
Hoffmann, Arnold, 1966, Ag 23,39:1
Hoffmann, Aug, 1940, Ja 17,21:4
Hoffmann, Bernard, 1949, Jl 8,19:4
Hoffmann, Carl J, 1963, My 25,25:5
Hoffmann, Eberhard, 1957, Je 18,33:1
Hoffmann, Edgar F, 1965, S 6,15:5
Hoffmann, Edward M, 1962, Je 17,81:1
Hoffmann, Ernesto, 1943, Mr 31,19:3
Hoffmann, Ernst, 1956, Ja 4,12:7
Hoffmann, Ernst Mrs, 1956, Ja 4,12:7
Hoffmann, Frederick, 1952, Ag 22,21:3
Hoffmann, Gustave P, 1940, Mr 27,21:4
Hoffmann, Heinrich, 1957, D 18,35:3
Hoffmann, Henry G, 1953, Jl 29,23:5
Hoffmann, Isaac N (funl, O 30,11:5), 1918, O 28,11:3
Hoffmann, Jacob, 1947, Mr 15,13:3; 1951, Mr 18,89:1
Hoffmann, John C, 1958, S 2,25:2
Hoffmann, John P Msgr, 1922, Ag 22,17:5
Hoffmann, Josef, 1956, My 26,17:5
Hoffmann, Joseph E, 1925, S 23,25:4
Hoffmann, Joseph M, 1964, Ag 19,37:5
Hoffmann, Louis Mrs, 1943, Ap 17,17:5
Hoffmann, Margaret C, 1953, N 23,27:2
Hoffmann, Max Jr, 1945, Ap 1,38:2
Hoffmann, Otto, 1956, S 23,84:1
Hoffmann, Paul (Bro Conrad), 1956, Ja 13,23:3
Hoffmann, Rebecca, 1944, Mr 28,19:7
Hoffmann, Richard H, 1967, Je 19,35:3
Hoffmann, Theodore H Mrs, 1942, F 7,17:6
Hoffmann, Walter, 1952, Mr 25,27:1
Hoffmann, William, 1903, F 13,9:6; 1923, Ag 17,13:5
Hoffmann, William F, 1956, My 2,31:4
Hoffmann, William F Sr Mrs, 1968, Ap 2,47:3
Hoffmaster, P J, 1951, Mr 20,29:1
Hoffmeister, William, 1955, Jl 26,25:5
Hoffmeister, William F, 1951, My 29,25:2
Hoffmer, George C, 1905, Ap 16,14:2
Hoffmeyer, Anton W Mrs, 1949, Je 20,19:4
Hoffmeyer, John J, 1953, Ja 22,23:2
Hoffmeyer, Joseph, 1947, Jl 30,21:4

Hoffmire, Arthur E (por), 1943, S 1,19:5
Hoffmire, Emma, 1949, My 13,23:3
Hoffmire, Mary O, 1951, Ja 6,15:4
Hoffmire, William, 1909, Mr 9,9:6
Hoffner, George C, 1958, Ag 27,29:4
Hoffner, Henry M Jr, 1948, Je 4,23:4
Hoffner, Joseph P, 1948, O 9,19:3
Hoffner, William H Mrs, 1948, Ap 17,15:2
Hofford, Robert F, 1953, Ap 22,29:3
Hofford, Webster J, 1950, Ap 5,31:5
Hoffpauir, Curley C, 1962, Ja 1,23:6
Hoffritz, Edward Mrs, 1951, Ap 20,29:2
Hoffschmidt, Walter A, 1956, Ja 6,24:2
Hoffses, Ray W, 1942, Mr 31,21:2
Hoffspiegel, George, 1950, Jl 26,25:4
Hoffstot, Frank N, 1938, D 26,23:5
Hofft, Fred B, 1955, O 22,19:5
Hofheimer, Lester Mrs, 1963, Ag 12,21:4
Hofheimer, Solomon Mrs, 1947, D 24,21:2
Hofheinz, Roy Mrs, 1966, D 2,39:4
Hofheinz, Rudolph Mrs, 1944, N 23,31:5
Hofman, Arthur F, 1956, Mr 12,27:3
Hofman, Catherine Mrs, 1924, Mr 21,19:4
Hofman, Emil F, 1951, My 15,19:1
Hofman, Norbert, 1951, Ap 19,31:4
Hofman, William, 1944, Jl 2,19:2
Hofman, William F, 1950, Je 6,29:1
Hofmann, Alfred J, 1957, Jl 6,15:2
Hofmann, B H A, 1943, D 3,23:3
Hofmann, Charles, 1961, Ja 18,33:4
Hofmann, Charles L Mrs, 1963, Jl 25,25:4
Hofmann, Charles P, 1962, My 18,31:1
Hofmann, Charles P Mrs, 1942, Ag 22,13:4
Hofmann, Else, 1960, Ap 30,23:5
Hofmann, Emil Mrs, 1956, Mr 25,92:1
Hofmann, Emma S Mrs, 1939, Mr 26,III,7:2
Hofmann, Frederick, 1955, Ag 14,80:3
Hofmann, Fritz, 1956, N 1,39:6
Hofmann, H G Maj-Gen, 1942, F 2,5:4
Hofmann, Hans, 1966, F 18,1:8
Hofmann, Hans Mrs, 1963, Ap 21,86:4
Hofmann, Henry, 1942, O 18,52:5
Hofmann, John, 1954, Ag 31,21:3
Hofmann, John B, 1954, Ag 21,17:1
Hofmann, John M, 1955, Ap 13,29:3; 1955, O 21,27
Hofmann, Josef, 1957, F 18,1:8
Hofmann, Joseph A, 1951, Jl 30,17:4
Hofmann, Marie Mrs, 1956, Je 25,23:5
Hofmann, Tabea, 1954, Ja 4,19:5
Hofmann, Walter H, 1952, Ja 27,77:2
Hofmannsthal, Hugo von Mrs, 1959, N 11,35:1
Hofmans, Greet, 1968, N 22,47:1
Hofmeister, Henry, 1962, Ja 9,47:2
Hofmeister, Henry H, 1948, Ja 15,23:4
Hofmeister, William, 1937, Ap 23,21:1
Hofmeyr, Jan H, 1948, D 4,19:1
Hofrichter, Justine M Mrs, 1952, Jl 10,31:2
Hofsass, John A, 1958, My 24,21:6
Hofstadter, Herman, 1941, N 16,57:1
Hofstadter, Meyer, 1958, S 6,17:5
Hofstatter, Earl S, 1952, Ja 20,85:2
Hofstatter, Edwin A, 1960, Ag 9,27:3
Hofstatter, Ernest W, 1937, D 24,20:2
Hofstatter, Lulu E Mrs, 1940, F 17,13:5
Hogaboom, George B, 1954, Ja 1,23:3
Hogan, Aloysius J (por), 1943, D 18,15:1
Hogan, Anna M Mrs, 1957, F 11,29:2
Hogan, Austin Mrs, 1940, Je 29,15:3
Hogan, Barnard F, 1955, S 27,35:5
Hogan, Ben, 1916, N 3,13:6
Hogan, Bernard J, 1937, Jl 15,19:3
Hogan, C Newall, 1963, N 20,40:3
Hogan, Carl T, 1968, Jl 4,19:3
Hogan, Carl T Mrs (Marjorie), 1968, Ap 22,47:1
Hogan, Cecilia G, 1956, Jl 16,21:5
Hogan, Charles H, 1939, N 12,48:6
Hogan, Charles L (por), 1941, S 6,15:4
Hogan, Charles L Mrs, 1956, O 6,21:3
Hogan, Charles M, 1905, My 21,6:1
Hogan, Charles Washington, 1915, Mr 3,11:5
Hogan, Coleman, 1949, Mr 10,27:5
Hogan, Dana, 1945, D 15,17:1
Hogan, Daniel J, 1965, My 31,17:3
Hogan, Daniel W Jr, 1957, N 14,33:3
Hogan, David J, 1940, Ja 4,23:4
Hogan, Denis, 1938, Ap 16,13:5
Hogan, Edward A Jr, 1957, S 1,57:1
Hogan, Edward G, 1937, Ag 17,19:4
Hogan, Edward T, 1953, O 6,29:3
Hogan, Elmer F, 1954, My 6,33:3
Hogan, Francis X, 1944, O 3,23:2
Hogan, Frank, 1941, F 23,39:5
Hogan, Frank (Shanty), 1967, Ap 8,31:2
Hogan, Frank G Sr, 1962, F 26,27:2
Hogan, Frank J (por), 1944, My 17,19:5
Hogan, Frank J, 1945, F 20,19:2
Hogan, Franklin, 1945, Ap 24,19:3
Hogan, George, 1943, Mr 26,19:3
Hogan, George G Father, 1925, Je 12,19:6
Hogan, George W, 1938, Je 2,23:4
Hogan, Gerrit L Mrs, 1953, My 27,31:4
Hogan, Harry E, 1946, O 13,59:6
Hogan, Harry J, 1946, N 17,68:2

Hogan, Hector, 1960, S 3,17:3
Hogan, Henry, 1904, Ja 17,8:2
Hogan, Henry M, 1968, Je 4,44:2
Hogan, Henry M Mrs, 1952, Mr 28,23:2
Hogan, Homer S, 1952, Mr 16,91:2
Hogan, Howard, 1948, Ap 21,27:2
Hogan, J D, 1883, D 18,5:2
Hogan, James, 1954, My 4,29:2
Hogan, James A, 1939, N 21,26:4; 1944, Ag 31,17:4
Hogan, James E Justice, 1915, S 24,11:6
Hogan, James G, 1949, Ag 25,23:3
Hogan, James H (por), 1948, Ja 14,25:1
Hogan, James H, 1948, F 15,60:2
Hogan, James J, 1910, Mr 21,9:3; 1941, My 27,23:2; 1942, Jl 16,19:4
Hogan, James P, 1943, N 6,13:4; 1949, Jl 27,23:2
Hogan, Jasper, 1954, Jl 10,13:5
Hogan, Jerome Sgt, 1937, Ag 12,19:5
Hogan, John A, 1941, Jl 17,19:5
Hogan, John B, 1950, S 12,27:3
Hogan, John C, 1950, Ja 17,27:5
Hogan, John E, 1940, N 20,21:2
Hogan, John F, 1939, My 4,23:5
Hogan, John H, 1909, S 4,7:5; 1940, S 11,25:3
Hogan, John J, 1944, Je 10,15:4
Hogan, John J Dr, 1937, Mr 18,25:2
Hogan, John James Bp, 1913, F 22,11:4
Hogan, John L, 1947, Mr 28,23:2
Hogan, John M, 1951, S 23,85:2
Hogan, John P, 1961, Je 13,35:1
Hogan, John V, 1960, D 30,19:2
Hogan, John V L (funl), 1961, Ja 1,48:1
Hogan, John W Mrs, 1945, D 6,27:3
Hogan, Joseph C Mrs, 1960, D 21,31:1
Hogan, Joseph E W, 1952, N 2,88:4
Hogan, Joseph S, 1961, Mr 5,86:8
Hogan, Joseph V, 1951, Je 8,27:3
Hogan, Joseph W, 1948, D 3,25:2
Hogan, Leo L, 1948, Je 5,15:5
Hogan, Leo M, 1943, F 16,19:6
Hogan, Luke, 1954, D 22,23:2
Hogan, M Dr, 1882, D 19,5:1
Hogan, Malachi, 1911, S 4,7:6
Hogan, Martin, 1901, N 27,9:6
Hogan, Martin F, 1961, N 21,39:2
Hogan, Martin J, 1951, F 9,25:1
Hogan, Martin J Rev Dr, 1922, My 23,17:4
Hogan, Martin Rev, 1912, D 1,II,17:2
Hogan, Mary A Mrs, 1941, O 4,15:1
Hogan, May Edward, 1905, Ja 15,1:2
Hogan, Michael F, 1965, F 9,37:1
Hogan, Michael F Mrs, 1962, Je 30,19:6
Hogan, Michael J, 1940, My 8,23:2; 1950, O 3,31:5; 1954, Mr 12,21:3; 1959, Ap 15,33:1
Hogan, Michael J Mrs, 1944, My 21,44:2
Hogan, Michael J P, 1966, O 30,88:8
Hogan, Michael J P Mrs, 1962, My 9,43:5
Hogan, Mildred R F Mrs (will), 1956, D 13,26:6
Hogan, Orville J, 1952, N 6,29:4
Hogan, Parke V, 1949, Jl 22,19:2
Hogan, Patrick J, 1949, F 18,23:3
Hogan, Raymond J, 1952, Mr 11,27:5
Hogan, Reginald R Mrs, 1953, S 12,17:4
Hogan, Ridgewood Mrs, 1948, Mr 19,23:4
Hogan, Robert C Mrs, 1956, N 30,23:1
Hogan, Robert G, 1941, Jl 29,15:4; 1954, N 11,31:1
Hogan, Robert J, 1963, D 18,41:4
Hogan, Russell J, 1955, Ag 5,19:3
Hogan, Samuel J, 1949, S 1,21:5
Hogan, Scott M, 1954, Ap 24,17:5
Hogan, Society Kid (S de Lorenzo), 1962; Ap 11,43:4
Hogan, Sophie S, 1941, Ag 30,13:6
Hogan, T Franklin, 1944, Ja 13,21:3
Hogan, T J, 1940, Ag 25,35:2
Hogan, Thomas B, 1957, Ap 6,19:5
Hogan, Thomas J, 1938, Ja 20,23:4; 1948, Ap 28,27:5
Hogan, Thomas S, 1941, Ja 19,40:3
Hogan, Timothy A, 1945, D 18,27:4
Hogan, W H, 1877, My 16,8:2
Hogan, William, 1938, Je 15,23:6; 1947, O 28,26:2
Hogan, William A, 1951, Je 20,27:2; 1955, N 16,35:3; 1957, Jl 8,23:2
Hogan, William F, 1943, Ag 26,17:5
Hogan, William F Mrs, 1947, F 9,61:2
Hogan, William G, 1937, N 19,23:2; 1944, Je 28,23:6
Hogan, William J, 1946, Ap 9,27:2
Hogan, William P, 1947, Ja 14,25:4
Hogan, William R, 1940, N 7,25:3; 1953, S 11,21:2
Hogan, William S, 1938, N 7,19:2; 1947, F 23,53:3
Hogarth, A Moore, 1947, Mr 13,27:4
Hogarth, Donald M, 1950, Je 28,27:5
Hogarth, Georgina, 1917, Ap 21,13:5
Hogarth, Lionel, 1946, Ap 17,25:1
Hogarty, Edward J, 1942, S 1,19:2; 1957, O 28,28:1
Hogate, Kenneth C, 1947, F 12,25:1
Hogate, Sarah Mrs, 1937, D 7,25:3
Hogdon, Benjamin A, 1941, Ap 8,26:2
Hoge, B Lacy Mrs, 1954, Ap 20,29:3
Hoge, Charles C, 1941, N 19,23:2
Hoge, F Huber Mrs, 1964, S 16,31:5
Hoge, Gordon, 1947, Ap 2,27:5
Hoge, Huber (por), 1941, Ap 7,17:2
Hoge, J H Col, 1903, F 15,7:6
Hoge, John O, 1953, N 19,31:3
Hoge, Joseph F D, 1955, S 7,31:3
Hoge, Peyton H, 1940, O 13,34:4
Hoge, W J Rev Dr, 1864, Jl 31,6:5
Hoge, Wendell P, 1939, N 15,23:6
Hoge, William M Mrs, 1956, Ag 9,25:1; 1959, Jl 12, 73:2
Hogeboom, Francklyn, 1946, Ja 11,21:3
Hogeboom, Henry, 1872, S 13,5:4
Hogeboom, John A, 1944, N 8,17:5
Hogeland, Alexander Col, 1907, Je 18,7:5
Hogeland, Horace B, 1958, Ap 3,31:3
Hogemann, Dietrich Capt, 1917, My 19,13:5
Hogenae, Charlotte, 1947, O 23,25:4
Hogerton, Sydney, 1967, S 16,33:1
Hogerty, Elizabeth, 1949, My 25,29:2
Hogg, Charles Benner, 1911, Ja 7,9:5
Hogg, Douglas Lady, 1925, My 11,17:4
Hogg, Frank S, 1951, Ja 2,23:3
Hogg, Herbert H Rev, 1937, Ag 18,19:4
Hogg, Hope W Prof, 1912, F 17,11:4
Hogg, James R, 1941, O 30,23:3
Hogg, James Stephen, 1906, Mr 4,9:3
Hogg, John L, 1945, Jl 6,11:6
Hogg, Thomas, 1942, S 1,19:5
Hogg, Thomas E, 1949, Mr 10,27:4
Hogg, Thomas H, 1958, F 25,27:3
Hogg, Victor, 1955, O 15,15:6
Hogg, William B Rev, 1937, Ja 16,17:3
Hogg, William C, 1952, O 6,25:2
Hogg, William C Mrs, 1945, Jl 31,19:3
Hogg, William Mrs, 1960, Ag 29,25:5
Hogg, William R, 1937, Mr 16,23:1
Hoggatt, Clarissa E, 1939, Ja 1,24:8
Hoggatt, Wilford B, 1938, F 27,II,9:3
Hoggatt, Wilford B Mrs, 1962, Mr 31,25:4
Hogge, Elijah, 1939, Ap 4,25:1
Hogge, Morgan G, 1937, Je 4,23:4
Hoggson, Noble F, 1939, O 26,23:4
Hoggson, W J, 1933, My 14,30:1
Hoggson, William J Mrs, 1955, D 8,37:2
Hoghton, James de, 1938, N 5,19:2
Hogie, Minnie, 1874, D 18,5:2
Hogins, Henry H Capt, 1916, Ag 9,11:6
Hogland, Frank G, 1938, D 14,25:3
Hogle, Horace, 1943, O 28,23:5
Hogle, James A, 1955, S 16,23:2
Hogle, John Mrs, 1912, Jl 30,9:5
Hogsett, James L, 1952, Mr 30,93:2
Hogshead, F M, 1941, Ap 27,38:2
Hogshead, John W, 1949, Ap 13,29:4
Hogshead, Luther Dr, 1937, Ja 1,23:2
Hogstrom, Hazel A, 1950, N 3,27:1
Hogue, Clayton M, 1942, O 6,23:1
Hogue, J David, 1958, S 13,19:5
Hogue, John R, 1958, O 9,37:4
Hogue, Mark C, 1925, Jl 31,15:6
Hogue, Martha W Mrs, 1951, F 12,23:2
Hogue, Mary J, 1962, S 13,37:4
Hogue, Richard W Jr, 1961, Ap 1,17:6
Hogue, Robert F, 1957, Mr 11,25:3
Hogue, Roswell A, 1954, D 3,27:3
Hogue, Thomas J Sr, 1948, Ja 1,23:1
Hoguet, J Peter (por), 1946, Je 18,25:1
Hoguet, J Peter Mrs, 1955, N 23,23:1
Hoguet, Ramsay C, 1937, S 1,19:4
Hoguet, Robert L, 1961, Ja 26,29:5
Hoguet, Robert L Mrs (Louise L), 1965, Mr 27,27:3
Hoh, Paul J, 1952, Ja 21,15:2
Hoh, Philip J, 1943, S 13,19:6
Hohauser, Albert, 1941, Ag 2,15:2
Hohbein, Earl W, 1961, O 14,23:6
Hohe, John C, 1948, F 5,24:2
Hoheb, Albert S, 1940, S 15,48:2
Hohelohe-Langenburg, Prince of (Hermann Ernest Bernard), 1913, Mr 12,11:4
Hohenadel, John, 1958, Jl 15,25:3
Hohenberg, Bernard, 1944, S 7,23:3
Hohenberg, Ernst Prince, 1954, Mr 6,15:6
Hohenloe-Schillingfuerst, Ernst Prince, 1947, Je 19,21:3
Hohenlohe-Oehringen Christian zu, Prince, 1926, My 16,30:2
Hohenlohe-Schillingfurst, Egon zu Prince, 1915, D 29, 11:5
Hohenlohe-Schillingsfurst, Conrad, 1918, D 25,15:6
Hohensee, Frederick W, 1952, Jl 26,13:5
Hohenthal, E L G, 1928, D 9,31:5
Hohenthal, William D, 1949, F 9,28:2
Hohenzollern, Eitel F Prince (por), 1942, D 9,28:2
Hohenzollern, Fdk Prince, 1904, D 3,9:4
Hohl, Adolph G, 1944, N 8,17:6
Hohl, John, 1947, Ag 6,23:3
Hohl, Sebald M, 1937, My 18,23:4
Hohl, Walter C, 1950, Jl 16,69:3
Hohl, William M, 1952, Jl 8,27:3
Hohler, Thomas, 1946, Ap 24,26:3
Hohlmann, William E, 1945, D 24,15:3
Hohly, Harold Frederick, 1968, F 2,35:1
Hohman, Arthur, 1943, Ag 4,17:4
Hohman, George Dr, 1924, F 26,17:2
Hohman, Harry, 1952, Ap 30,27:4
Hohmann, Daniel A, 1966, D 3,39:4
Hohmann, Frederick W, 1938, Ja 26,23:4
Hohmann, Henry C, 1941, O 31,23:3
Hohmel, Edward, 1939, D 14,27:5
Hohmyer, Arthur K, 1947, F 13,23:5
Hohn, Charles E, 1942, Mr 9,21:7
Hohn, Charles E Mrs (Maia Bang), 1940, Ja 4,24:2
Hohneker, Fred C, 1946, N 9,17:2
Hohner, Ernst, 1965, O 18,35:1
Hohner, Matthew, 1962, Ja 24,33:4
Hohorst, Henry, 1938, D 24,15:5
Hoidale, Einar, 1952, D 7,88:5
Hoier, Thomas P, 1951, D 21,28:2
Hoile, Mary A, 1941, Ap 10,23:3
Hoiles, Arthur J, 1948, Ag 25,25:4
Hoiles, George F, 1961, S 6,37:1
Hoiriis, Holger (por), 1942, Ag 9,43:3
Hoisel, Max W, 1954, Mr 19,23:2
Hoisington, Frederick R, 1951, Mr 18,88:5
Hoisington, Frederick R Mrs, 1955, Ja 24,23:4
Hoisington, Herbert A, 1943, F 7,48:3
Hoist, John H, 1905, F 15,9:5
Hoisted, Harold L, 1955, Je 14,29:4
Hoit, Evvie V Mrs, 1942, Ja 29,19:4
Hoitsma, Harry, 1964, Je 12,35:4
Hojnacki, Leo P, 1946, Mr 11,25:2
Hoke, Archie S, 1957, Mr 6,31:1
Hoke, Edward, 1954, F 11,29:1
Hoke, Kremer J (por), 1944, F 7,15:4
Hoke, Kremer J Mrs, 1962, Jl 17,25:1
Hoke, Martha, 1939, Je 23,19:4
Hoke, Michael, 1944, S 25,17:2
Hoke, Robert Frederick Gen, 1912, Jl 4,7:5
Hoke, Robert L, 1966, F 3,32:1
Hoke, Samuel E, 1956, S 27,35:5
Hoke, W H Ex-Justice, 1925, S 14,19:4
Hoke, Walter W, 1947, Jl 19,13:4
Hoke, William E, 1944, Ja 26,19:4
Hokinson, Helen E, 1949, N 2,1:8
Holabird, John A, 1945, My 5,16:2
Holabird, Roy R, 1949, Mr 17,25:2
Holabird, Samuel Beckley, 1907, F 5,9:6
Holabird, William, 1923, Jl 20,13:6
Holadak, Emil, 1944, Je 12,19:5
Holaday, William P, 1946, Ja 30,25:3
Holahan, Edward C (Sept 30), 1965, O 11,61:2
Holahan, Edward J, 1948, Ag 10,22:3
Holahan, Frank E, 1955, O 8,19:6
Holahan, George R, 1944, D 31,26:6
Holahan, George R Jr, 1938, Je 2,23:2
Holahan, Maurice F, 1905, Ja 16,9:4
Holaman, Louis G, 1945, D 17,21:2
Holand, Hjalmar R, 1963, Ag 9,23:1
Holbein, Edgar A, 1948, Ag 13,15:5
Holbein, Montagu, 1944, Jl 12,19:4
Holben, Ralph, 1965, Jl 26,23:6
Holberg, Herbert M, 1941, Ja 13,15:4
Holbert, Harry H, 1962, S 18,39:1
Holbert, Hayward J, 1956, S 11,35:2
Holbert, Thomas C, 1943, My 4,23:4
Holborn, Frederick, 1954, F 12,25:6
Holbrook, Alfred H Mrs, 1940, My 29,23:3
Holbrook, Alva M, 1916, Ag 23,9:4
Holbrook, Arthur, 1946, D 27,20:3
Holbrook, Arthur T Mrs, 1947, Je 8,60:2
Holbrook, B Dwight, 1945, S 12,25:5
Holbrook, Benjamin P, 1937, Jl 22,19:5
Holbrook, Chalmers, 1953, S 20,86:6
Holbrook, Charles E, 1944, N 7,27:6
Holbrook, Charles S, 1950, O 28,17:3
Holbrook, Clark, 1941, Mr 14,21:4
Holbrook, Daniel, 1915, Mr 22,9:5
Holbrook, David H, 1962, Ag 29,29:5
Holbrook, Edward, 1919, My 20,17:6
Holbrook, Edward F, 1951, D 27,21:4
Holbrook, Edwin M, 1905, Mr 19,9:4
Holbrook, Elmer A, 1957, F 22,21:2
Holbrook, Emily H Mrs, 1943, My 11,21:1
Holbrook, Frank M, 1954, Je 23,25:5
Holbrook, Frank W, 1948, Ap 3,15:1
Holbrook, Frederick, 1909, Ap 29,9:4; 1920, F 7,11:3
Holbrook, Frederick H, 1957, Je 4,35:5
Holbrook, G Thomas, 1965, O 28,43:5
Holbrook, Helen, 1960, Ag 16,29:2
Holbrook, Henry F Mrs, 1953, Ja 29,27:4
Holbrook, Henry G, 1954, Je 22,27:3
Holbrook, Howard, 1918, Ap 20,13:8
Holbrook, Iowa Legislator, 1884, F 2,3:3
Holbrook, James, 1864, Ap 30,4:5; 1953, Ja 11,90:6
Holbrook, John W, 1963, D 26,28:3
Holbrook, Joseph, 1884, Je 13,5:3
Holbrook, Levi, 1922, Jl 27,17:6
Holbrook, Lucius R, 1952, O 20,23:2
Holbrook, Martin Mrs, 1939, S 13,25:3
Holbrook, Melvin, 1958, Jl 21,15:8
Holbrook, Northrop, 1958, Ap 28,23:2
Holbrook, Percy, 1941, Jl 30,17:6
Holbrook, Robert W, 1949, My 3,25:6
Holbrook, Seymour L Mrs, 1940, N 7,25:4
Holbrook, Standish Mrs, 1944, O 10,23:4
Holbrook, Stewart H, 1964, S 4,29:4
Holbrook, W A Gen, 1932, Jl 19,17:3
Holbrook, W C Justice, 1904, Mr 28,1:3
Holbrook, William Dr, 1903, Ap 28,9:5
Holbrooke, Dan, 1957, Ja 29,31:5

Holbrooke, Joseph, 1958, Ag 7,25:4
Holbrow, James W, 1912, N 18,11:5
Holby, John D, 1966, Je 16,47:5
Holcolmb, Robert, 1951, O 14,V,5:7
Holcomb, Abel Sutherland Dr, 1923, Jl 17,19:5
Holcomb, Alex M, 1939, Ja 21,15:5
Holcomb, Alfred E, 1956, S 15,17:5
Holcomb, Allan T, 1956, Mr 13,27:4
Holcomb, Allan T Mrs, 1952, O 27,27:4
Holcomb, Carlos O, 1921, N 21,15:3
Holcomb, Carlos O Mrs, 1921, N 21,15:3
Holcomb, Charles A, 1963, O 25,31:5
Holcomb, Charles F, 1958, Je 24,31:1
Holcomb, Charles T Mrs, 1950, Jl 4,17:3
Holcomb, Chauncey P, 1944, Ag 21,15:4
Holcomb, Clark W, 1950, Je 5,23:3
Holcomb, Evelyn A, 1952, Ag 29,23:3
Holcomb, Frederick B, 1946, My 31,23:2
Holcomb, Frederick W, 1949, D 10,17:5
Holcomb, Horace B, 1938, D 13,26:2
Holcomb, Horace H, 1955, O 20,36:2
Holcomb, J Rogers, 1947, Je 18,25:4
Holcomb, John P, 1949, N 12,15:1
Holcomb, Joseph Mrs, 1944, D 1,23:1
Holcomb, Lorrie R, 1951, F 12,23:1
Holcomb, Lynn, 1948, N 13,15:2
Holcomb, Richard R, 1960, Jl 3,32:3
Holcomb, Richmond C, 1945, Ap 3,19:5
Holcomb, Robert Mrs, 1947, Ag 1,17:3
Holcomb, Thomas, 1965, My 25,41:1
Holcomb, Thomas Mrs, 1962, Ag 16,27:3
Holcomb, Walter S, 1938, Ag 18,19:1
Holcomb, Winfield A Dr, 1937, D 10,25:1
Holcomb, Wynn, 1956, Ja 1,51:1
Holcombe, Albert H, 1954, O 26,27:2
Holcombe, Charles D, 1948, Jl 6,23:4
Holcombe, Charles S, 1951, Ja 27,13:4
Holcombe, Durward B, 1968, D 14,45:3
Holcombe, G Newell, 1958, S 16,28:1
Holcombe, Jesse W H, 1939, Ja 29,33:1
Holcombe, John L, 1964, F 29,21:5
Holcombe, John M Jr, 1951, My 16,35:1
Holcombe, Kenneth H, 1939, My 8,17:5
Holcombe, Oscar Fitzallen, 1968, Je 20,45:1
Holcombe, W F Dr, 1904, Mr 18,2:3
Holcombe, Walter P, 1951, Ag 2,21:2
Holcombe, Willis B, 1949, N 25,31:4
Holdaway, Thomas V, 1947, Ja 30,25:2
Holdbrook, Parker K, 1938, F 17,21:4
Holdcroft, Samuel W, 1941, F 4,22:3
Holde, Artur, 1962, Je 25,29:4
Holden, Alex, 1943, Ag 27,17:2
Holden, Alice M, 1951, D 26,25:5
Holden, Arthur, 1948, Ap 10,13:5
Holden, Arthur B, 1946, Ja 23,27:2
Holden, Arthur C, 1923, Je 11,13:4
Holden, Ben E, 1956, My 11,27:4
Holden, Benedict M, 1937, F 20,17:2
Holden, Benedict M Jr, 1966, Mr 19,29:3
Holden, Benjamin F, 1940, Je 28,19:3
Holden, Capel Gen Sir, 1937, Mr 31,24:2
Holden, Carl F, 1953, My 19,29:3
Holden, Charles, 1960, My 3,39:1
Holden, Charles A, 1940, F 6,21:2; 1960, O 14,33:1
Holden, Charles Edwards, 1924, D 28,5:2
Holden, Charles R, 1945, Mr 6,21:5
Holden, Daniel Judson, 1903, Je 22,7:5
Holden, Delos, 1943, Mr 19,20:2
Holden, Dorothy V Mrs, 1955, Ja 11,28:8
Holden, E G, 1927, D 28,23:5
Holden, Edgar Dr, 1909, Jl 20,7:6
Holden, Edmund Mrs, 1953, Ja 26,19:3
Holden, Edward, 1938, Ja 29,15:6; 1947, Je 18,25:4; 1950, Ag 29,27:5
Holden, Edward C, 1956, S 13,35:4
Holden, Edward H, 1920, Ag 10,13:5
Holden, Edward P Jr, 1967, Mr 9,39:2
Holden, Edward Singleton Dr, 1914, Mr 17,11:4
Holden, Edward Sir, 1919, Jl 24,9:3
Holden, Edwin R, 1914, F 14,11:6; 1953, F 9,27:3
Holden, Everett M, 1956, Je 30,17:5
Holden, Frank E, 1938, O 15,17:2
Holden, Frank H, 1937, My 30,18:8
Holden, Frank Howell Mrs, 1968, N 26,47:2
Holden, Fred H Mrs, 1946, Ja 16,23:1
Holden, Frederick C, 1944, Ag 29,17:2
Holden, George A, 1916, My 19,11:7; 1944, Ag 21,15:5
Holden, George A Mrs, 1952, Ap 7,25:5
Holden, George H, 1937, D 14,25:1
Holden, George J, 1951, Mr 21,33:3
Holden, George M, 1947, Mr 31,23:5
Holden, George P Mrs, 1949, Je 7,31:1
Holden, George Sir, 1937, S 27,21:3
Holden, Guerdon S, 1959, D 18,29:3
Holden, Hale (por), 1940, S 24,23:3
Holden, Hale Jr, 1954, Jl 1,25:1
Holden, Henry D, 1953, Ja 19,23:3
Holden, Herbert, 1967, Ap 19,45:2
Holden, Horace M Mrs, 1944, Ja 26,5:3
Holden, Isaac V, 1903, Je 26,9:6
Holden, J S, 1934, Ag 13,13:4
Holden, James, 1925, Je 14,5:2
Holden, James B, 1967, Ja 26,33:4
Holden, James C, 1908, Ja 14,7:6
Holden, James F, 1946, My 15,21:3
Holden, James L, 1923, Mr 14,19:4
Holden, John, 1949, Ag 16,23:5
Holden, John A, 1941, F 13,19:5
Holden, John E, 1963, Je 18,41:4
Holden, John F, 1955, D 26,19:4
Holden, John S (see also Jl 30), 1903, Jl 31,7:6
Holden, Jonas Hannibal Com, 1915, S 30,11:7
Holden, Joseph, 1919, Ap 25,15:3
Holden, Katherine B, 1915, D 8,15:5
Holden, Katherine V K Mrs, 1938, Ag 27,13:4
Holden, L Dean, 1906, F 15,7:6
Holden, L Wales, 1944, Jl 18,19:2
Holden, Lansing C, 1938, N 16,23:1
Holden, Lansing C Jr, 1924, O 4,13:3
Holden, Leo Mrs, 1956, Mr 10,17:3
Holden, Lester S, 1944, N 5,53:1
Holden, Lewis H, 1954, F 12,25:2
Holden, Liberty E, 1913, Ag 27,7:6
Holden, Lord, 1951, Jl 7,13:4
Holden, Louis E, 1942, Ap 13,16:2
Holden, Louis H, 1946, Jl 10,23:3
Holden, Mary, 1953, Mr 4,27:4
Holden, Mary C Mrs, 1937, Ja 8,19:2
Holden, Mary D Mrs, 1940, Ag 15,19:2
Holden, Max (por), 1949, Jl 6,30:1
Holden, Oliver, 1882, Mr 22,5:5
Holden, Robert F, 1944, N 18,13:4
Holden, Robert G, 1913, S 11,11:6
Holden, Robert Rev, 1901, Mr 13,9:5
Holden, Roy J, 1945, D 17,21:3
Holden, Ruth, 1917, Ap 24,11:4
Holden, Stephen, 1955, N 26,19:4
Holden, Thomas Jr, 1945, S 17,19:5
Holden, Thomas S, 1958, N 4,27:5
Holden, Timothy N Mrs, 1948, Mr 16,27:1
Holden, Walter H Jr, 1949, Ja 15,17:5
Holden, Ward A Dr, 1937, Ja 25,19:3
Holden, William, 1944, My 18,19:3
Holden, William A C, 1941, S 21,44:1
Holden, William H, 1940, N 20,21:2
Holden, William H Mrs, 1954, D 19,28:2
Holdenson, Peter, 1952, Je 1,84:4
Holder, Arthur E, 1937, Ja 7,21:5
Holder, Charles A, 1955, Ap 4,29:3
Holder, Charles F Dr, 1915, O 12,11:5
Holder, Charles L, 1961, Ap 15,21:3
Holder, Edward P, 1951, S 6,31:5
Holder, Francis T, 1912, Ag 23,9:6
Holder, Frederick C, 1944, S 17,42:1
Holder, Frederick William Sir, 1909, Jl 24,7:4
Holder, Geneva P (Mrs Oliver Holder), 1966, Ja 4, 27:3
Holder, George, 1951, Ag 17,17:2
Holder, Grover C Sr, 1948, S 10,23:2
Holder, Thornton F, 1961, Ap 20,33:2
Holderith, Frank J Mrs, 1946, O 5,17:6
Holderith, Lawrence J, 1951, Je 30,15:5
Holderith, Peter A Sr, 1951, F 20,25:3
Holderman, Bertram D, 1949, D 30,19:3
Holderman, Carl, 1959, My 21,31:3
Holderman, Nelson M, 1953, S 4,34:8
Holderness, George A, 1947, D 24,22:3
Holderness, Roy W, 1954, Ap 6,29:6
Holdert, H M C, 1944, Jl 25,19:3
Holdgman, Fred, 1871, Ag 17,3:2
Holding, Arthur F, 1949, Ag 28,72:8
Holding, Claude J, 1949, Jl 24,52:6
Holding, Elizabeth S Mrs, 1955, F 9,27:2
Holding, Herbert H, 1949, Ap 30,13:6
Holding, Hunter Mrs, 1950, Mr 15,29:1
Holding, John Jr, 1941, Ap 9,25:5
Holdman, Oro E, 1947, N 7,23:4
Holdridge, Edgar T, 1909, My 2,11:5
Holdridge, Newton C, 1939, Je 4,49:2
Holdridge, Percy A, 1957, Je 11,35:4
Holdship, Charles F, 1946, Ja 6,40:3
Holdstein, George, 1956, O 26,29:1
Holdstein, Harry, 1950, O 12,31:2
Holdstein, Walter M, 1968, N 23,47:2
Holdsworth, Adelaide K Mrs, 1953, Ag 12,31:3
Holdsworth, Fred J, 1946, N 7,31:4
Holdsworth, George J Mrs, 1948, F 15,60:2
Holdsworth, Herbert, 1949, Jl 9,13:4
Holdsworth, William, 1944, Ja 3,21:3
Holdsworth, William H, 1951, S 1,11:5
Hole, Allen D Mrs, 1939, Ap 8,15:1
Hole, Dean, 1904, Ag 28,9:6
Hole, Elmer C, 1945, Mr 1,21:5
Hole, James W, 1950, S 26,31:1
Hole, Leonard H, 1957, My 1,37:5
Hole, Leonard Hanna, 1910, Jl 9,7:5
Hole, Richard Jr, 1940, O 7,17:4
Holeman, Jan, 1963, Ap 14,28:8
Holenstein, Thomas, 1962, N 1,31:2
Holey, George, 1955, S 29,33:4
Holey, Thomas J, 1943, Ag 20,15:4
Holgan, James E, 1952, Ag 27,27:4
Holgan, Stephane, 1882, Ja 21,2:6
Holgate, Claude E, 1937, Mr 31,24:2
Holgate, Robert B, 1956, D 27,25:3
Holgate, Thomas F, 1945, Ap 12,23:3
Holick, David L, 1949, Jl 13,27:2
Holick, Jack, 1950, F 17,24:3
Holicky, Joseph, 1945, O 14,43:1
Holiday, Billie (E Fagan),(funl plans, Jl 20,25:3), 1959, Jl 18,15:5
Holiner, Mann, 1958, N 1,19:6
Holke, Walter, 1954, O 13,31:6
Holl, F, 1884, F 8,4:7
Holl, George V, 1955, Mr 14,23:4
Holl, Jerome A, 1946, Je 4,23:3
Holl, John C Mrs, 1937, My 8,19:5
Holl, John F, 1939, Ja 11,19:4
Holla, J Edward, 1939, F 21,19:2
Holladay, Charles B, 1946, Ja 28,19:3
Holladay, Edmund B Mrs, 1954, Ap 1,31:2
Holladay, Edwin W, 1951, Je 24,73:1
Holladay, Jesse, 1907, O 17,9:5
Holladay, Mary S Mrs, 1937, O 6,25:3
Holladay, Waller, 1937, F 27,17:2
Hollaender, Sidney, 1955, Ag 23,23:5
Hollaman, Rich W, 1946, Mr 24,46:5
Holland, Albert H, 1953, N 16,25:3
Holland, Albert J, 1941, Jl 3,19:1
Holland, Albert O Mrs, 1944, S 29,21:3
Holland, Alexander, 1885, Mr 13,2:2
Holland, Ambrose J, 1953, Je 10,29:4
Holland, Arthur G Dr, 1937, S 15,23:6
Holland, Arthur L, 1956, Jl 11,29:6
Holland, Charles A Dr, 1937, N 21,II,9:1
Holland, Charles H (por), 1943, Jl 13,21:4
Holland, Charles H, 1951, D 30,24:4
Holland, Charles H Mrs, 1945, F 5,15:5
Holland, Charles J, 1950, N 24,35:1; 1958, S 18,31:
Holland, Charles T, 1941, Ja 17,17:5
Holland, Clarence A, 1951, Ag 5,73:1
Holland, Clarence D, 1945, Ap 4,21:4
Holland, Clifford Milburn, 1924, O 28,23:3
Holland, Daniel A, 1952, N 13,31:1
Holland, David H, 1941, Je 27,17:5
Holland, Dewey B, 1966, Jl 27,39:3
Holland, Dorothy, 1941, Mr 28,23:4
Holland, E M (funl, N 29,13:4), 1913, N 25,11:5
Holland, E Sir, 1926, My 25,27:4
Holland, Edward J, 1946, Ap 28,42:3; 1950, Ag 11
Holland, Edward W, 1941, O 24,24:3
Holland, Edwin J, 1941, Mr 26,23:4
Holland, Elmer J, 1968, Ag 10,27:5
Holland, Ernest O, 1950, Je 1,27:1
Holland, Ezekiel U, 1939, Mr 11,17:4
Holland, Frances E, 1938, F 23,23:5
Holland, Francis E, 1941, D 14,69:1
Holland, Francis J, 1961, Jl 4,19:5
Holland, Frank, 1924, N 6,19:5
Holland, Frank D, 1947, Ap 10,25:2
Holland, Frank J, 1950, Jl 10,21:4
Holland, Frank P, 1944, Ag 27,33:3
Holland, Frank P Mrs, 1939, My 18,25:3
Holland, Frank W, 1956, O 7,87:1
Holland, George, 1870, D 29,1:7; 1910, F 18,7:4; Ag 19,23:4
Holland, George F, 1958, S 11,33:4
Holland, George J, 1945, Jl 21,11:6
Holland, George W F, 1962, Je 15,27:2
Holland, H Albert, 1958, Ag 11,21:2
Holland, Harry, 1948, Jl 6,23:2
Holland, Harry Mrs, 1965, Ja 31,88:8
Holland, Helen M, 1947, Mr 1,15:2
Holland, Helen M Mrs, 1957, F 1,25:2
Holland, Henry F, 1962, Jl 19,27:1
Holland, Henry F Jr, 1964, Jl 7,42:6
Holland, Henry S Dr, 1948, Ag 29,56:5
Holland, Henry Sir, 1873, O 29,1:5
Holland, Henry Thurston (Viscount Knutsford), 1914, Ja 30,9:5
Holland, Horace B, 1960, F 11,36:1
Holland, Isadore G, 1944, My 21,44:4
Holland, J Burnett, 1954, S 5,51:2
Holland, J G, 1881, O 13,5:5
Holland, J Monroe, 1941, N 22,19:1
Holland, James P, 1941, N 10,17:2
Holland, Jeremiah D, 1925, D 17,23:5
Holland, Jerome P, 1959, D 30,21:5
Holland, John, 1956, D 16,86:4
Holland, John A Mrs, 1943, Jl 2,19:5
Holland, John B, 1953, Je 30,23:2
Holland, John B Col, 1923, O 28,23:2
Holland, John E, 1957, Ag 28,27:4
Holland, John J, 1955, Mr 30,29:5
Holland, John P, 1914, Ag 13,9:6
Holland, John W, 1947, Je 1,60:2; 1953, F 21,13 1959, My 17,84:1
Holland, Joseph, 1945, Ja 23,19:4
Holland, Joseph F, 1942, S 28,17:4; 1955, O 14, 1967, My 20,35:4
Holland, Joseph G Mrs, 1958, Jl 4,19:1
Holland, Julian, 1961, F 27,27:3
Holland, K C, 1876, O 20,8:5
Holland, Lady, 1866, D 4,4:6
Holland, Leicester B, 1952, F 8,23:1
Holland, Leonard M, 1945, F 6,19:3
Holland, Margaret T Mrs, 1948, Ag 10,21:3
Holland, Michael P, 1914, Je 11,11:6
Holland, Mildred (por), 1944, Ja 29,13:2

Holland, Moorhead B, 1946, Ap 13,17:6
Holland, Nelson, 1961, Mr 26,93:1
Holland, Opal Mrs, 1947, Ag 16,13:5
Holland, Peter O, 1939, N 16,23:2
Holland, Richard H, 1921, Ag 1,11:6
Holland, Robert A Jr Mrs, 1954, F 9,27:4
Holland, Robert B, 1955, Ap 26,29:3
Holland, Robert C, 1942, Je 19,23:4
Holland, Robert E (por), 1946, Ag 3,15:4
Holland, Rupert S, 1952, My 5,23:3
Holland, Rush L, 1944, Ja 17,19:4
Holland, Sidney, 1951, O 1,23:5
Holland, Sidney G, 1961, Ag 5,17:2
Holland, Sidney W (por), 1937, D 3,23:4
Holland, Simon, 1950, D 25,19:5
Holland, Simon Mrs, 1956, Ja 2,21:4
Holland, T S, 1875, D 15,7:3
Holland, Thomas, 1947, Ap 23,25:4
Holland, Thomas E, 1955, Ap 6,29:2
Holland, Thomas H, 1947, My 18,60:3
Holland, Thomas Mrs, 1955, My 12,29:1
Holland, Timothy P, 1948, Je 25,23:5
Holland, Ubert C, 1957, F 27,27:4
Holland, Victor T, 1953, My 8,25:3
Holland, Vyvyan, 1967, O 11,47:1
Holland, W J, 1932, D 14,21:1
Holland, Wade D, 1938, Mr 30,21:6
Holland, William, 1942, D 29,21:3
Holland, William A, 1937, Ja 4,7:5
Holland, William F, 1950, My 14,108:2
Holland, William Mrs, 1937, Ag 7,15:5
Holland, William R Sr, 1945, O 29,19:3
Holland, William S Mrs, 1951, Mr 4,92:3
Holland, William V, 1967, Ag 10,37:4
Holland, Zay, 1941, N 8,19:3
Holland-Martin, Christopher J, 1960, Ap 6,41:3
Holland-Martin, Robert M, 1944, Ja 28,17:1
Hollander, Abraham H, 1961, S 1,17:2
Hollander, Adolph, 1950, Ja 19,28:3
Hollander, Al G, 1948, Jl 29,21:4
Hollander, Albert Mrs, 1947, S 17,25:5
Hollander, Alex, 1938, Mr 14,15:5
Hollander, B, 1934, F 7,20:1
Hollander, Benjamin W, 1957, S 12,31:4
Hollander, Charles, 1957, Ag 4,81:1
Hollander, David R, 1959, My 20,35:5
Hollander, E Rand, 1948, Ap 18,71:3
Hollander, Edward A, 1964, Je 15,29:4
Hollander, Edward Mrs, 1943, Mr 10,19:3
Hollander, Emanuel, 1961, N 26,88:3
Hollander, Emil E, 1947, S 12,21:5
Hollander, Eric, 1960, D 6,41:1
Hollander, Franklin, 1966, Mr 26,29:5
Hollander, George E, 1939, My 23,23:2
Hollander, George H, 1941, Jl 1,24:5
Hollander, H Louis, 1960, Mr 24,33:3
Hollander, Harry, 1963, S 14,25:4
Hollander, Herbert E, 1952, Mr 7,23:1
Hollander, Irving, 1952, Ja 27,76:5; 1960, O 19,45:3
Hollander, Jacob H, 1940, Jl 10,19:5
Hollander, Joseph, 1939, Ap 23,III,6:7; 1940, F 28,21:6
Hollander, Julius, 1946, Ja 14,19:3; 1954, Jl 27,21:5
Hollander, L Preston, 1953, S 28,25:4
Hollander, Leonard A, 1958, N 12,37:2
Hollander, Lewis W, 1962, Jl 12,29:2
Hollander, Louis P (est appr), 1910, Mr 26,9:4
Hollander, Max L (por), 1943, F 21,32:7
Hollander, Michael (por), 1947, O 21,24:2
Hollander, Michael Mrs, 1968, Ap 29,43:4
Hollander, Morris, 1945, Je 3,31:1
Hollander, Morton, 1965, Je 28,29:2
Hollander, Samuel, 1947, Ag 12,23:3; 1957, My 23, 33:5
Hollander, Sumner R, 1957, D 13,27:1
Hollander, Sumner R Mrs, 1937, Jl 21,21:5
Hollander, Theodore C, 1939, O 13,23:5
Hollander, Walter J, 1943, Jl 30,15:4
Hollander, William, 1954, Je 14,21:4
Hollander, William H, 1947, F 24,19:4
Hollander, William K, 1958, Mr 19,31:4
Hollands, John B, 1939, Jl 9,31:3
Hollard, Auguste, 1943, Ag 3,19:4
Hollbach, John, 1941, D 30,19:2
Hollberg, Edward W, 1962, Je 14,33:5
Holle, Nell L L Mrs, 1956, My 30,21:3
Holleb, Herbert B, 1955, Je 29,29:3
Holleman, James R Mrs, 1942, Jl 3,17:4
Hollen, Edwin S, 1961, Ja 20,26:3
Hollenbach, John G, 1942, F 4,19:1
Hollenbach, Louis J Sr, 1954, O 16,17:2
Hollenback, Anna J Mrs, 1937, S 10,24:3
Hollenback, William M, 1968, Mr 14,43:3
Hollenbaugh, George O, 1950, O 18,33:2
Hollenbeck, Edwin E, 1943, Ag 16,15:2
Hollenbeck, Everett, 1939, Ag 30,17:4
Hollenbeck, Henry S, 1942, S 20,39:2
Hollenbeck, Jacob G, 1939, My 3,23:2
Hollenbeck, Lloyd L, 1956, F 9,31:1
Hollenberg, Arthur V, 1956, My 13,86:2
Hollenberg, Benno A Dr, 1914, Ja 3,11:6
Hollenberg, Samuel, 1964, Ag 19,37:3
Hollender, Edward R, 1944, Mr 9,17:4
Hollender, Jerome S, 1967, My 27,31:4
Holler, Francis J, 1939, Je 3,15:7
Holler, George, 1937, O 13,23:2
Holler, John H, 1949, D 18,88:3
Holler, Lawrence, 1949, S 8,29:1
Holler, Marie W, 1942, Jl 7,19:4
Holleran, Leslie G, 1959, F 8,86:4
Hollesen, Harry H, 1953, Ja 28,27:3
Holley, A L, 1882, Ja 30,5:1
Holley, Alfred T, 1953, S 4,15:2
Holley, Allan J, 1944, My 1,15:1
Holley, Earl, 1958, D 7,88:3
Holley, Edward L Mrs, 1953, Ap 16,29:1
Holley, Erving, 1954, Mr 25,29:4
Holley, Eugene T, 1947, N 1,15:6
Holley, Frank H, 1949, O 10,23:1
Holley, George M, 1963, Je 28,30:3
Holley, Grace S, 1947, Jl 18,17:4
Holley, Horace H, 1964, Ja 31,27:3
Holley, Ira H, 1966, Ag 28,93:3
Holley, James A, 1947, Ap 23,25:3
Holley, John M, 1914, Je 21,15:6
Holley, Joseph W, 1958, Jl 17,27:2
Holley, Lee A, 1938, Ag 14,32:8
Holley, Lynn, 1968, Jl 23,30:2
Holley, Myle J, 1960, N 20,86:5
Holley, William, 1943, Mr 28,24:5
Holley, William L, 1945, Ag 1,19:5
Holliday, Edgar P, 1946, S 27,23:1
Holliday, Frederick T, 1951, Jl 17,27:5
Holliday, Guy H, 1937, Ag 2,19:5
Holliday, Harry J (por), 1942, F 4,19:5
Holliday, Houghton Mrs, 1945, Je 30,17:4
Holliday, James R, 1943, D 27,19:4
Holliday, John, 1938, N 22,24:5
Holliday, John H Mrs, 1950, Mr 12,93:1
Holliday, Judy (J Tuvim),(funl, Je 10,35:2; will, S 4,21:5), 1965, Je 8,1:7
Holliday, R C, 1885, Ja 19,2:5
Holliday, Ralph C, 1949, Ag 27,13:3
Holliday, Robert C, 1947, Ja 2,27:2
Holliday, Robert P, 1959, Ja 2,25:1
Holliday, Samuel N, 1953, D 9,11:4
Holliday, Wallace T, 1950, N 8,29:5
Holliday, William E, 1948, Jl 14,23:4
Hollidge, C Crawford, 1939, Mr 30,23:5
Hollie, James W, 1951, D 17,31:5
Holling, Thomas L, 1966, N 27,86:6
Hollingdale, Frederick W, 1948, Jl 26,17:2
Hollinger, D Wilson (por), 1945, Ja 30,19:6
Hollinger, Irving, 1944, Ja 19,19:3
Hollinger, John R, 1964, Ag 31,25:4
Hollinger, Joseph, 1939, D 30,15:6
Hollinger, Lena Mrs, 1951, Jl 2,13:2
Hollinger, Walter A, 1947, Ag 4,17:4
Hollings, Francis J, 1956, Mr 21,38:2
Hollings, William H Mrs, 1947, Ap 29,28:2
Hollingshead, Esther S Mrs, 1938, Ag 1,13:6
Hollingshead, George G, 1958, Mr 18,29:5
Hollingshead, George G Mrs, 1952, Je 17,27:4
Hollingshead, Gordon, 1952, Jl 10,31:3
Hollingshead, Harold H, 1956, N 21,27:5
Hollingshead, Harold H Mrs, 1953, O 24,15:2
Hollingshead, Harry T, 1942, My 31,38:5
Hollingshead, John, 1904, O 11,9:5
Hollingshead, Lowell, 1966, Je 2,43:2
Hollingshead, Richard M, 1945, My 16,19:1
Hollingshead, Richard M Sr Mrs, 1959, S 5,15:5
Hollingshead, Sylvia S Mrs, 1937, My 7,30:3
Hollingshead, Willard J Mrs, 1944, Mr 16,19:4
Hollingsworth, Amor Mrs, 1938, D 9,25:3
Hollingsworth, Ceylon E, 1949, Mr 8,26:3
Hollingsworth, Ellis, 1917, Mr 15,11:5
Hollingsworth, Frank, 1950, Ap 22,19:6
Hollingsworth, Harry L, 1956, S 18,35:2
Hollingsworth, Harry L Mrs, 1939, N 28,25:3
Hollingsworth, Henry, 1937, Ag 2,19:5
Hollingsworth, Henry S, 1905, Mr 14,9:6
Hollingsworth, Herbert B Mrs, 1949, D 20,31:4
Hollingsworth, Louisa M, 1957, Ap 19,21:4
Hollingsworth, Miller, 1958, S 10,33:1
Hollingsworth, Richard J, 1964, D 22,29:3
Hollingsworth, Richard J Mrs, 1945, Jl 6,11:5
Hollingsworth, S Dr, 1884, S 17,5:3
Hollingsworth, Thomas H, 1952, D 2,31:4
Hollingsworth, William, 1881, Ap 5,3:1
Hollingsworth, William A, 1967, D 11,47:4
Hollingsworth, William I, 1937, O 1,21:1
Hollingsworth, William T P, 1942, O 1,23:6
Hollins, Alfred, 1942, My 18,15:3
Hollins, De Ruyter M, 1925, O 24,15:7
Hollins, Edith C, 1908, D 29,9:6
Hollins, Evelina K Mrs, 1938, Mr 15,23:3
Hollins, Frank C (est, Ap 10,9:6), 1909, Mr 5,9:5
Hollins, G N, 1878, Ja 20,7:4
Hollins, George G, 1954, Ja 26,27:3
Hollins, Gerald V, 1955, N 30,33:4
Hollins, Harry B, 1938, F 25,17:3
Hollins, Harry B Jr, 1956, D 8,19:4
Hollins, Marion (por), 1944, Ag 29,17:1
Hollinshead, Redferne (por), 1937, O 7,27:2
Hollinshed, Charles, 1949, O 1,13:3
Hollis, Allen, 1955, Ap 27,31:2
Hollis, Austin W Dr, 1921, N 8,19:5
Hollis, Ella A, 1949, My 23,23:1
Hollis, Emil R, 1954, Ap 1,31:1
Hollis, Ernest V, 1965, Ja 10,92:3
Hollis, Frank, 1944, Je 2,15:4
Hollis, George Tearing, 1903, Ag 7,7:6
Hollis, Harwood L, 1947, Ap 29,27:3
Hollis, Henry F, 1949, Jl 13,27:2
Hollis, Henry P, 1939, Ag 8,17:4
Hollis, Henry S, 1942, Ag 24,15:1
Hollis, I H, 1906, D 15,11:6
Hollis, James B, 1954, S 20,23:3
Hollis, James S, 1951, My 19,15:4
Hollis, John B, 1940, D 17,25:5
Hollis, Leslie, 1963, Ag 10,17:3
Holliss, Charles F Mrs, 1949, O 26,27:3
Holliss, Roy C Mrs, 1955, D 6,37:2
Hollister, Abram H, 1947, My 26,22:2
Hollister, Buell, 1966, Ag 27,29:5
Hollister, Buell Mrs, 1963, N 14,35:3
Hollister, Charles E, 1943, N 20,13:5
Hollister, Clay H, 1940, F 19,17:5
Hollister, Clay H Mrs, 1949, My 22,88:6
Hollister, Clifford F, 1941, Ja 12,46:1
Hollister, E W Mrs, 1932, Ag 10,15:5
Hollister, Elizabeth C W Mrs (will), 1939, N 11,17:2
Hollister, Evan (por), 1943, Ja 4,15:1
Hollister, Frank, 1939, Ja 1,25:1
Hollister, Franklin C, 1947, N 24,23:5
Hollister, Franklin Mrs, 1955, Ja 20,31:6
Hollister, Frederick K Mrs, 1965, S 1,37:1
Hollister, Frederick M, 1946, O 21,31:5
Hollister, G H, 1881, Mr 25,5:3
Hollister, George B, 1952, Ja 6,93:1
Hollister, George C, 1949, My 10,26:2
Hollister, George C Mrs, 1959, S 10,35:5
Hollister, Granger A, 1924, Ja 21,17:4
Hollister, Harold E, 1955, D 20,31:3
Hollister, Harry L, 1944, S 10,45:2
Hollister, Hector, 1966, D 30,25:4
Hollister, Helen, 1942, Ap 17,17:3
Hollister, Henry M, 1940, My 12,48:4
Hollister, Horace P, 1939, Ja 19,19:3
Hollister, Howard C Judge, 1919, S 26,13:4
Hollister, John C Judge, 1903, Ag 30,7:6
Hollister, John Quincy Adams Maj, 1907, F 11,9:5
Hollister, Joseph, 1946, F 19,26:2
Hollister, Len D, 1946, D 5,32:3
Hollister, Paul Mrs (Carl I), 1962, D 12,14:7
Hollister, Ralph F, 1946, F 8,19:4
Hollister, Richard, 1949, Ja 7,21:3
Hollister, Sarah H Mrs, 1942, D 29,19:2
Hollister, Sherwood C, 1960, N 30,37:3
Hollister, William H, 1912, Ja 3,13:4
Hollizer, Harry A, 1946, Ja 16,24:2
Holljes, Edward L, 1951, F 4,76:5
Holljes, Herman R D, 1948, N 15,25:2
Holljes, Nelly, 1946, F 13,23:1
Hollman, Frank Sr Mrs, 1948, S 24,25:2
Hollman, Julius Z, 1964, Ap 25,29:5
Hollmeyer, John G, 1955, Jl 5,29:1
Hollohan, Jessie L, 1948, S 9,27:5
Hollopeter, Ralph Mrs, 1945, Ja 30,19:5
Hollos, Alex Z, 1948, S 12,72:2
Hollow, Frank H, 1946, My 12,44:3
Holloway, Charles, 1941, Ja 28,20:2
Holloway, Charles M Com, 1916, Ap 25,11:6
Holloway, Clarence Mrs, 1950, F 5,85:1
Holloway, D P, 1883, S 10,5:3
Holloway, D P Mrs, 1864, D 18,4:1
Holloway, Daniel Sr, 1956, F 7,31:2
Holloway, Edward M Mrs, 1946, Ag 15,25:4
Holloway, Edward S, 1939, N 7,28:3
Holloway, Emma F, 1964, D 9,47:4
Holloway, Frank P, 1947, D 14,76:4
Holloway, George T Maj, 1914, Ag 2,15:5
Holloway, George W, 1953, Jl 7,27:3
Holloway, H Stanley Mrs, 1950, Ja 24,31:3
Holloway, Harry A (por), 1946, O 15,25:5
Holloway, Harry D, 1939, Mr 18,17:2
Holloway, Henry F, 1940, Ap 20,17:6
Holloway, Hubert, 1961, Mr 2,27:1
Holloway, Hubert Mrs, 1947, S 21,60:6
Holloway, J Henry, 1952, Je 24,29:4
Holloway, J Morgan Mrs, 1959, F 20,26:1
Holloway, John W, 1949, Je 4,13:5
Holloway, Murray S, 1943, D 26,32:3
Holloway, Reuben R Mrs, 1940, D 1,62:3
Holloway, Sidney J, 1964, S 9,43:3
Holloway, T B, 1936, Ag 19,21:4
Holloway, Thomas T, 1940, Mr 15,23:1
Holloway, Tom, 1940, Je 2,44:5
Holloway, William G, 1959, Ja 8,29:4
Holloway, William H Mrs, 1951, Ja 14,84:3
Holloway, William R Col, 1912, Ja 1,13:3
Holloway, William Rev, 1914, F 9,7:4
Hollowell, Ada Mrs, 1954, Ap 29,31:1
Hollowell, Fred S, 1960, Ap 20,39:5
Hollowell, James S, 1951, Ja 30,25:4
Hollreiser, Raymond, 1947, N 2,73:1
Holls, George Frederick William, 1903, Jl 24,3:3
Holls, Martin, 1939, Jl 9,31:2
Hollwedel, John E Jr, 1949, Mr 12,17:3
Hollweg, Theobald von Bethmann Mrs, 1914, My 11, 11:5

Hollweg, William, 1942, N 18,26:4
Holly, Buddy, 1959, F 4,66:3
Holly, Ferdinand L, 1962, Ap 18,39:2
Holly, Flora M, 1960, N 20,86:7
Holly, Frank W, 1904, Ja 17,7:6
Holly, Graham R, 1953, Mr 26,31:2
Holly, Howard L, 1948, N 5,25:1
Holly, James, 1949, Ag 29,17:5
Holly, James T Rev Dr, 1911, Mr 21,11:5
Holly, Leland B, 1939, Jl 13,19:6
Holly, Margaret C, 1937, F 4,21:4
Holly, Robert J, 1942, My 10,43:1
Holly, Samuel E, 1939, N 25,17:2
Holly, W, 1931, Ag 5,19:3
Holly, William H, 1947, Je 4,27:1; 1958, Ja 31,21:2
Holly, William P, 1957, F 21,27:2
Hollyer, Samuel, 1919, D 30,13:3
Hollywood, Edwin L, 1958, My 17,19:5
Holm, Alfred J, 1947, Ag 1,17:2
Holm, Aug, 1941, O 15,21:7
Holm, Charles H, 1941, My 18,43:4
Holm, Clemens F, 1950, D 17,84:3
Holm, Floyd R, 1954, Ag 9,17:2
Holm, Gladstone, 1951, O 8,21:4
Holm, Gustav, 1940, Mr 14,23:5
Holm, Herbert F, 1953, Jl 5,49:1
Holm, James M, 1958, My 14,33:3
Holm, John, 1946, O 23,27:2
Holm, John C Mrs, 1959, Ja 16,27:3
Holm, Mike, 1952, Jl 7,21:2
Holm, Wilhelm, 1953, D 28,21:3
Holm-Hansen, Bjarne A, 1948, My 2,76:5
Holma, Harri, 1954, Ap 15,29:5
Holman, Alfred, 1947, Je 16,21:2
Holman, Alfred F, 1950, N 23,35:4
Holman, Arthur A, 1938, Ja 6,19:5
Holman, Bud L, 1964, Je 1,29:4
Holman, C Dudley Mrs, 1948, My 31,19:5
Holman, Charles J Mrs, 1944, Mr 15,19:5
Holman, Charles T, 1968, F 5,35:5
Holman, Chester R, 1953, Je 27,15:6
Holman, Delavan Van H, 1964, Jl 18,19:4
Holman, Eugene, 1962, Ag 14,31:1
Holman, Frank N, 1940, Ap 18,23:4
Holman, George B, 1943, Mr 20,15:3
Holman, George W Jr Mrs, 1941, Je 22,32:4
Holman, Guy, 1946, Ap 14,46:1
Holman, Harry, 1947, My 4,60:8
Holman, Herbert C, 1949, Jl 28,23:2
Holman, Howard F, 1954, My 6,33:1
Holman, Joseph W Jr, 1956, My 22,33:4
Holman, Julia, 1879, Ag 19,5:5
Holman, Justin B, 1924, Ap 19,13:5
Holman, Louis A, 1939, D 15,25:4
Holman, May, 1939, Mr 21,23:5
Holman, Nat E, 1962, N 13,37:3
Holman, Nat Mrs, 1967, D 1,47:3
Holman, Omer, 1955, My 11,31:1
Holman, Rufus C, 1959, N 28,21:1
Holman, Samuel N, 1941, O 31,23:2
Holman, W S, 1897, Ap 23,7:5
Holman, Wallace F, 1947, Ap 14,27:3
Holman, William H Jr, 1950, My 12,27:4
Holman, William L, 1953, Je 24,25:4
Holman, William M, 1947, F 24,19:2
Holman-Hunt, William, 1910, S 8,9:5
Holmberg, Allan R, 1966, O 14,40:4
Holmberg, C William, 1956, Ja 31,29:1
Holmberg, Charles G, 1950, Ja 28,13:3
Holmberg, Edgar T, 1957, Ap 28,86:6
Holmberg, Edward A, 1965, Mr 24,46:5
Holmberg, J Milton, 1947, Mr 17,17:1
Holme, Axel L, 1953, Ja 4,76:4
Holme, Brant, 1952, D 4,35:2
Holme, Edgar R, 1944, My 4,19:5
Holme, Horace, 1959, Je 2,35:4
Holme, Ida V Mrs, 1941, Je 11,21:3
Holme, John G, 1922, D 1,17:4
Holme, Jonathan L B, 1939, F 7,19:2
Holme, L R, 1926, Je 18,23:5
Holme, Pauline W Mrs, 1940, Je 15,15:2
Holme, Raymond A, 1965, My 12,47:4
Holme, Richard M, 1952, My 21,27:2
Holmershausen, E A Rev, 1873, N 11,1:2
Holmes, A Bertram, 1961, Ag 21,23:3
Holmes, Ada E Mrs, 1944, Ja 4,17:3
Holmes, Addison, 1922, Mr 28,17:4
Holmes, Albert D, 1949, O 20,29:6
Holmes, Alex, 1939, Je 3,15:5
Holmes, Alfred E Mrs, 1955, F 5,15:4
Holmes, Alfred W, 1952, O 20,23:5
Holmes, Alice, 1914, Ja 20,9:6
Holmes, Alice D Mrs, 1942, Ap 19,44:6
Holmes, Allen W, 1947, Jl 8,23:4
Holmes, Alpheus, 1948, N 24,23:5
Holmes, Amy E, 1922, F 24,12:6
Holmes, Andrew A, 1939, S 25,19:2
Holmes, Annie D Mrs, 1937, N 30,23:3
Holmes, Anthony M, 1941, N 14,23:3
Holmes, Artemas, 1944, Ap 1,13:1
Holmes, Arthur, 1948, Jl 9,19:3
Holmes, Arthur B (will), 1944, Mr 28,36:2
Holmes, Arthur D, 1956, Jl 20,17:2
Holmes, Arthur H, 1943, Mr 17,21:3
Holmes, Astley C, 1959, N 17,35:1
Holmes, Augusta, 1903, Ja 29,9:5
Holmes, Beatrice G, 1951, N 22,31:3
Holmes, Ben, 1939, S 7,25:6; 1943, D 3,23:5
Holmes, Benjamin Mrs, 1950, F 24,24:1
Holmes, Benjamin P Mrs, 1940, Ap 23,23:5
Holmes, Bertram H, 1959, D 18,29:3
Holmes, Bradford B, 1967, O 10,42:2
Holmes, Burton, 1958, Jl 23,27:1
Holmes, C J, 1936, D 8,25:5
Holmes, Carrie E, 1945, Ja 24,21:1
Holmes, Charles G Mrs, 1953, Mr 21,17:2
Holmes, Charles H, 1938, O 11,25:4; 1950, D 6,33:1
Holmes, Charles L, 1942, D 28,19:2
Holmes, Charles S, 1943, Ja 18,15:2
Holmes, Charles W, 1940, Ja 20,15:3; 1940, Ap 18,23:5
Holmes, Christian R Dr, 1920, Ja 10,11:4
Holmes, Christian R Mrs, 1941, S 30,23:4
Holmes, Christopher C, 1913, S 28,7:6
Holmes, Clarence A, 1944, Ja 28,17:4
Holmes, Clayton Wood, 1919, Jl 15,11:2
Holmes, Clinton A, 1948, Ja 2,23:1
Holmes, Crosley, 1945, Mr 3,13:4
Holmes, Daniel Henry, 1908, D 16,11:5
Holmes, David G, 1944, Mr 3,16:3
Holmes, David G Mrs, 1940, S 2,15:3
Holmes, David H Dr, 1918, Ag 25,19:1
Holmes, David S, 1904, F 7,7:6
Holmes, David V, 1940, O 5,15:7
Holmes, Dudley, 1941, Ag 16,15:2
Holmes, Duncan A, 1953, Ap 5,76:5
Holmes, E, 1946, My 4,15:6
Holmes, E J, 1884, Jl 29,5:5
Holmes, Edgar R, 1964, D 4,40:3
Holmes, Edmund R, 1950, D 5,32:4
Holmes, Edward J, 1950, My 30,17:2
Holmes, Edward W, 1940, Ag 3,15:5
Holmes, Edwin R, 1961, D 11,31:2
Holmes, Edwin Thomas, 1920, F 13,11:3
Holmes, Eliza Mrs, 1922, Ja 21,13:4
Holmes, Elizabeth B Dr, 1937, Jl 27,21:3
Holmes, Ellen W Mrs, 1938, O 15,17:5
Holmes, Elliott, 1944, Je 16,12:5
Holmes, Elmer H, 1958, Jl 9,27:3
Holmes, Ernest, 1960, Ap 9,23:2
Holmes, Ernest A, 1956, Jl 25,29:4
Holmes, Ernest R, 1959, Ja 9,27:2
Holmes, Eugene A, 1956, Je 16,19:2
Holmes, Francis R, 1943, N 20,13:4; 1965, Mr 6,25:5
Holmes, Frank, 1940, Jl 12,15:1; 1952, Ja 6,92:2
Holmes, Frank B, 1948, Ag 22,60:4
Holmes, Frank E, 1940, D 24,15:5
Holmes, Frank G, 1946, Je 10,21:4; 1954, Ap 21,29:5
Holmes, Frank H Capt, 1915, S 30,11:5
Holmes, Frank J, 1941, S 20,17:6
Holmes, Franklin B, 1949, Je 1,31:5
Holmes, Fred G Mrs, 1949, N 6,92:5
Holmes, Fred L, 1946, Jl 28,39:1
Holmes, Frederick B, 1949, Mr 12,17:3
Holmes, Frederick C, 1938, Ja 13,21:4
Holmes, Frederick F, 1943, Je 17,21:3
Holmes, Frederick M, 1948, Jl 1,23:2
Holmes, George (por), 1938, Mr 8,19:4
Holmes, George, 1953, Mr 19,29:2; 1953, Jl 22,27:2
Holmes, George A, 1962, Mr 14,39:2
Holmes, George F, 1945, Mr 10,17:3
Holmes, George I, 1966, Jl 8,35:2
Holmes, George J Dr, 1968, D 30,31:4
Holmes, George J Mrs, 1966, Jl 14,35:5
Holmes, George M R, 1944, S 14,23:7
Holmes, George R (por), 1939, F 13,15:4
Holmes, George Rev (Bp of Attrabasca), 1912, F 4, 13:4
Holmes, George S, 1955, Ag 22,21:6
Holmes, George S Mrs, 1944, F 3,19:5
Holmes, Gerald A, 1948, Ap 20,27:3
Holmes, Gertrude M Mrs, 1941, Ap 3,23:2
Holmes, Gilbert B Jr, 1967, Ja 19,69:7
Holmes, Glenn E, 1947, Ag 18,17:4
Holmes, Grace A, 1954, Ap 1,31:3
Holmes, H Clyde, 1963, Je 4,39:4
Holmes, Harold V, 1951, N 5,31:4
Holmes, Harold W Mrs, 1959, Ja 29,27:1
Holmes, Harry, 1941, Je 29,33:1
Holmes, Harry A, 1952, F 23,11:4
Holmes, Harry N, 1955, Mr 19,15:3; 1958, Jl 3,25:3
Holmes, Harvey N, 1952, Mr 28,23:2
Holmes, Harvey R, 1948, My 12,27:1
Holmes, Helen, 1938, N 26,15:4; 1950, Jl 10,21:3
Holmes, Henry, 1912, Ag 19,9:6
Holmes, Henry A, 1963, Ag 16,28:3
Holmes, Henry A Mrs, 1965, Ap 20,39:3
Holmes, Henry B, 1943, Jl 10,13:5
Holmes, Henry H, 1945, Ja 4,19:4
Holmes, Henry L, 1941, S 5,21:4
Holmes, Henry Mrs, 1949, Mr 1,25:4
Holmes, Herbert F, 1951, D 6,33:2
Holmes, Herbert W, 1945, S 22,17:3
Holmes, Howard, 1945, S 20,23:3
Holmes, Hugh G, 1907, Ag 12,7:7
Holmes, Isaac E, 1867, Mr 1,5:4

Holmes, J Alden, 1951, Jl 6,23:2
Holmes, J Edward, 1942, Ja 12,15:4
Holmes, J R, 1946, N 6,23:5
Holmes, Jabish, 1948, Je 12,15:1; 1961, O 14,23:5
Holmes, James, 1950, O 1,104:4
Holmes, James E Rev Dr (por), 1937, Mr 20,19:3
Holmes, James G, 1952, F 29,23:1
Holmes, James H Capt, 1907, N 23,9:5
Holmes, James M, 1966, Ag 29,29:4
Holmes, James M Col, 1925, Jl 20,15:6
Holmes, Jesse A, 1951, O 21,92:4
Holmes, Jesse H (por), 1942, My 29,17:4
Holmes, John, 1961, O 23,29:1; 1962, Je 23,23:5
Holmes, John A Mrs, 1939, F 20,17:5
Holmes, John A Sr, 1957, N 16,19:3
Holmes, John E, 1954, My 20,31:4
Holmes, John F Dr, 1924, Ap 28,15:4
Holmes, John F Mrs, 1944, N 2,19:5
Holmes, John Field, 1922, My 23,17:4
Holmes, John H (funl, Ap 6,31:2), 1964, Ap 4,1:
Holmes, John H Mrs, 1961, My 29,19:3
Holmes, John M, 1951, O 26,23:3
Holmes, John McClellan, 1911, Je 23,11:4
Holmes, John Milton Rev, 1871, S 21,8:3
Holmes, John Mrs, 1947, Je 21,17:4
Holmes, John P, 1960, My 30,17:5
Holmes, John R, 1920, Ja 6,15:1
Holmes, Jonathan H, 1952, D 14,90:3
Holmes, Joseph (Lord Dovercourt), 1961, Ap 25
Holmes, Joseph Austin, 1915, Jl 14,9:5
Holmes, Joseph Drexel Mrs, 1911, N 13,9:4
Holmes, Joseph E, 1952, Ja 22,29:3
Holmes, Joseph L, 1951, My 22,31:1
Holmes, Josephine P Mrs, 1943, N 28,69:2
Holmes, Julia B Mrs, 1939, Ap 25,23:5
Holmes, Julius C, 1968, Jl 16,39:1
Holmes, Lawrence, 1950, Ap 4,29:4
Holmes, Louis R, 1950, Ag 25,21:5
Holmes, Ludwig Rev Dr, 1910, N 9,9:2
Holmes, Madeleine, 1949, Je 2,28:2
Holmes, Malcolm H, 1953, Je 17,38:2
Holmes, Manfred J Mrs, 1939, Je 9,21:4
Holmes, Marcellus B, 1945, Ja 13,11:2
Holmes, Mary E Mrs, 1937, My 19,23:2
Holmes, Mary H Mrs, 1960, Mr 16,37:3
Holmes, Mary Jane Mrs, 1907, O 8,11:5
Holmes, Merrill J, 1962, My 24,35:4
Holmes, Morris B Mrs, 1949, D 6,31:5
Holmes, Morris Mrs, 1952, Ap 14,19:3
Holmes, Nicholas 2d, 1955, Ag 27,15:2
Holmes, O W, 1935, Mr 6,1:2
Holmes, Oliver W (por), 1894, O 8,1:5
Holmes, Oliver W, 1937, S 25,17:5; 1943, N 25,
Holmes, Palmer W, 1947, My 2,22:2
Holmes, Patrick, 1950, Jl 13,25:6
Holmes, Paul B, 1964, Mr 11,39:3
Holmes, Percy C, 1950, N 21,31:2
Holmes, Peter J, 1951, Mr 5,21:2
Holmes, Philip W, 1906, Ag 25,7:6
Holmes, Ralston S, 1966, Ja 6,27:1
Holmes, Richard E, 1954, O 17,86:6
Holmes, Richard L, 1957, Jl 23,27:1
Holmes, Richard S Mrs, 1948, S 30,27:3
Holmes, Richard Still Rev, 1912, S 7,11:6
Holmes, Robert, 1940, My 11,19:6
Holmes, Robert B, 1923, Ap 6,17:4; 1945, My
Holmes, Robert D, 1870, Mr 13,5:3
Holmes, Robert H, 1949, D 20,31:3
Holmes, Robert R, 1965, D 25,13:4
Holmes, Rosina Bond, 1909, N 23,9:5
Holmes, Roy H, 1949, Ja 4,19:2
Holmes, Rudolph W, 1953, Ap 26,87:1
Holmes, Russell B, 1949, S 30,23:3
Holmes, Samuel J, 1964, Mr 8,87:1
Holmes, Samuel Platner, 1907, Ag 7,7:6
Holmes, Sara F Mrs, 1937, Jl 13,19:5
Holmes, Sarah Esther Mrs, 1922, Ja 13,15:5
Holmes, Sidney, 1949, N 8,31:3
Holmes, Stanley H, 1938, Mr 28,15:4
Holmes, Sterling Mrs, 1952, O 16,29:2
Holmes, Stoney, 1947, Ap 1,27:4
Holmes, T H Gen, 1863, Ag 15,5:1
Holmes, Taylor, 1959, O 2,29:1
Holmes, Thomas, 1918, Mr 28,11:8
Holmes, Thomas B, 1918, Ja 11,15:3
Holmes, Thomas M, 1945, Jl 17,13:6
Holmes, Tommy, 1950, Ja 5,26:6
Holmes, Urban T, 1940, Ap 20,17:2
Holmes, W Arthur, 1956, N 2,27:4
Holmes, W H, 1933, Ap 21,17:3
Holmes, Walter B, 1954, O 16,17:5
Holmes, Walter F, 1959, Je 21,92:6
Holmes, Walter W, 1938, N 14,19:5
Holmes, Wesley B, 1942, F 14,15:6
Holmes, Willard N, 1956, Ag 5,77:1
Holmes, William, 1937, Jl 15,19:1; 1940, F 1 1951, F 9,15:2
Holmes, William A, 1940, N 20,21:3
Holmes, William Elliott Mrs, 1953, F 10,27:
Holmes, William H, 1940, N 3,57:2
Holmes, William H (por), 1948, Ja 7,25:3
Holmes, William H A, 1943, Mr 7,38:6
Holmes, William H Dr, 1903, D 2,9:6

Holmes, William K, 1940, Ap 14,44:8
Holmes, William L Mrs, 1958, Je 17,29:2
Holmes, William M, 1961, N 9,35:1
Holmes, William M Mrs, 1951, S 23,84:6
Holmes, William Mrs, 1947, Je 5,25:1
Holmes, William S, 1948, Ap 5,21:5
Holmes, William T, 1940, Jl 29,13:5; 1955, Mr 8,27:1
Holmes-Gore, Ellen Martyr Mrs, 1915, Je 19,9:6
Holmewood, Benedict Mrs, 1952, Jl 15,21:3
Holmgren, Charles A, 1942, O 15,24:3
Holmgren, Ernest G, 1949, Ag 28,72:7
Holmgren, Henry R, 1942, Ja 26,15:3
Holmgren, Israel F, 1961, O 4,45:3
Holmgren, John, 1963, Jl 13,17:3
Holmgren, Trygve, 1952, Ag 28,23:2
Holmok, Harry G, 1959, S 4,21:1
Holmpatrick, Hans W H Baron, 1942, S 7,19:3
Holmquist, August S, 1953, Mr 25,31:4
Holmquist, Charles H Mrs, 1937, Ja 19,23:3
Holmquist, Henry C, 1952, F 15,26:2
Holmquist, Hijalmar, 1945, F 5,15:5
Holmquist, Karline, 1943, Jl 2,19:6
Holmquist, Magnus Mrs, 1952, D 6,21:2
Holmsberg, Charles O, 1938, My 28,15:5
Holmsen, Nicholas, 1962, F 27,33:3
Holmstrand, Abel, 1949, Ja 25,23:3
Holnstein, Mildred H von Countess, 1942, F 1,43:2
Holober, George, 1948, D 15,33:4
Holober, Samuel, 1957, F 21,27:3
Holoch, Robert F, 1965, Je 6,85:2
Holohan, James B (por), 1947, F 1,15:1
Holohan, Thomas J, 1943, F 3,19:5
Holohan, William J Mrs, 1943, S 3,19:4
Holomany, Anthony J, 1952, D 4,35:5
Holosnyany, Alexis Rev, 1937, N 6,17:6
Holota, John, 1951, Mr 11,V,3:2
Holowchak, Joseph P, 1955, Ag 30,27:3
Holpp, Jacob Mrs, 1948, My 11,25:5
Holquin Lloreda, Jorge, 1951, Ag 26,80:5
Holran, Francis T, 1939, Ag 25,15:4
Holran, Herbert G, 1966, S 22,95:4
Holreth, Walter H, 1952, Jl 22,25:2
Holroyd, Fred, 1954, Mr 5,19:1
Hols, William G A, 1949, My 17,25:4
Holsaple, Roland N, 1940, N 1,25:3
Holsapple, Frank B, 1952, S 20,15:5
Holsapple, Frederick, 1950, Jl 12,29:5
Holsapple, Lloyd B, 1959, F 15,86:1
Holscher, Margaret, 1955, Ap 12,29:1
Holscher, Theodore F, 1960, Jl 11,29:2
Holschue, George J, 1943, My 11,21:3
Holsendorf, Benjamin E, 1944, O 24,23:4
Holsey, Joseph R, 1968, Jl 1,33:3
olsey, Samuel D, 1954, Jl 30,17:4
olshouser, David M, 1967, Ap 15,31:1
olske, Louis R, 1957, O 10,33:5
olske, Louis R Mrs, 1949, My 18,27:5
olslag, Claude J, 1945, Je 12,19:5
olsley, Henry E, 1956, N 21,27:6
olsman, Gerald, 1951, Ja 12,27:2
olsman, Mary M, 1961, F 28,33:4
olst, Christian A, 1949, S 5,17:3
olst, Ernie, 1947, O 11,17:6
olst, G, 1934, My 26,17:2
olst, Hermann Eduard von Prof, 1904, Ja 21,1:4
olst, John, 1950, Ja 13,23:2
olst, Louis J R, 1940, Ap 14,45:3
olst, Willem, 1938, Mr 26,15:3
olstad, Sigurd H, 1954, O 15,23:2
olste, Julia E, 1959, Je 10,37:2
olstein, Adolph M, 1938, Ag 4,17:5
olstein, Casper, 1944, Ap 9,34:6
olstein, David M, 1964, O 16,39:2
olstein, Frederick Mrs, 1947, Ap 2,13:1
olstein, Friedrich von, 1909, My 9,11:4
lstein, George M, 1943, My 30,26:2
lstein, Gustavus M Mrs (will), 1952, Ag 8,17:2
lstein, Horst, 1945, N 24,19:6
lstein, John M Mrs, 1943, Jl 24,13:2
lstein, Joseph, 1948, D 23,20:2
lstein, Mark G, 1952, O 19,88:4
lstein, O, 1934, Mr 24,16:3
lstein-Ledreborg, Count, 1912, Mr 2,13:5
lsten, Edward L (trb lr, Ag 2,28:5), 1960, Jl 23, :5
lsten, Frederick, 1949, Ja 9,72:2
lsten, Richard M, 1959, Je 30,31:4
lsti, Rudolf (por), 1945, Ag 5,37:1
lston, Edwin C, 1938, My 4,23:2
ston, Ernest H, 1960, F 1,27:6
ston, George A, 1953, Je 11,29:4
ston, William H, 1963, O 29,36:6
swade, James F, 1942, Ja 8,21:3
t, Abner D, 1940, Ja 16,23:4
t, Albert L, 1944, Mr 17,17:6
t, Alfred Mrs, 1943, My 10,19:2
t, Andrew H, 1956, N 24,19:4
t, Anna B, 1952, Ag 8,17:5
t, Arthur E, 1942, Ja 14,21:1
t, Benjamin J, 1954, Je 28,19:5
t, Calvert, 1938, Je 30,23:6
, Carlyle H, 1949, S 19,23:3
, Charles, 1953, O 16,27:1

Holt, Charles L, 1941, Ap 27,38:8
Holt, Charles O, 1952, N 29,17:4
Holt, Charles P Prof, 1910, Jl 21,7:5
Holt, Clarence E, 1920, Jl 7,11:2
Holt, Clarence E Mrs, 1953, Ja 5,21:2
Holt, Clarence R, 1940, D 25,27:3
Holt, Curtis, 1960, Ja 28,31:4
Holt, Donald W, 1967, F 17,37:1
Holt, Edward Mrs, 1947, S 10,27:4
Holt, Edwin B, 1946, Ja 27,42:5
Holt, Elijah W, 1950, N 1,35:5
Holt, Elise, 1873, D 30,4:7
Holt, Erwin A Mrs, 1942, My 29,17:1; 1950, O 28,17:3
Holt, Eugene Jr, 1946, F 3,40:1
Holt, Felix, 1954, Je 4,23:1
Holt, Frank, 1914, O 20,13:5
Holt, Frank L, 1957, D 25,31:5
Holt, Frank Mrs, 1959, Ja 30,27:2
Holt, Frank O, 1948, Ap 2,24:2
Holt, Frank W, 1939, N 13,19:5
Holt, Fred, 1942, N 12,25:3
Holt, Fred P, 1951, F 6,27:3
Holt, Frederick H Mrs, 1949, F 3,23:1
Holt, G C, 1931, Ja 27,23:2
Holt, George B, 1961, Mr 29,33:2
Holt, George C Ex-Judge, 1925, N 27,17:4
Holt, George L Mrs, 1943, D 25,13:5
Holt, George Lyttleton Capt, 1968, O 31,47:4
Holt, George Mrs, 1949, Ja 23,68:3
Holt, H, 1926, F 14,28:1
Holt, H A, 1881, Mr 5,3:7
Holt, Hamilton, 1951, Ap 27,23:1
Holt, Harold, 1939, Ag 6,18:6; 1953, S 4,34:1; 1955, My 29,44:6
Holt, Harold E, 1967, D 17,1:5
Holt, Harry S (funl, My 2,27:2), 1964, Ap 29,41:1
Holt, Hattie M (will), 1940, Ja 8,17:2
Holt, Henry, 1941, S 3,23:2; 1944, Mr 3,15:4; 1956, F 6,23:4
Holt, Henry C, 1955, F 21,21:5
Holt, Henry E, 1949, N 10,31:4
Holt, Henry Jasper, 1922, F 6,13:3
Holt, Henry Mrs, 1947, Je 20,19:1
Holt, Henry W, 1947, O 5,68:3
Holt, Herbert S (por), 1941, S 29,17:1
Holt, Isabella (Mrs H Finnie), 1962, Mr 13,32:3
Holt, Ivan L, 1967, Ja 13,23:1
Holt, Ivan L Mrs, 1958, Ag 7,25:2
Holt, Jack, 1951, Ja 19,25:1
Holt, Jacob Farnum Dr, 1908, S 1,7:5
Holt, James Smith, 1920, Mr 10,11:4
Holt, John C Jr, 1952, Jl 31,23:2
Holt, John E, 1944, Je 2,5:3
Holt, John H, 1946, D 24,17:1
Holt, John I, 1920, N 12,15:5
Holt, Joseph P, 1964, D 1,41:4
Holt, L Emmet Mrs, 1952, S 28,78:4
Holt, Lady, 1939, D 11,23:5
Holt, Lawrence S, 1937, Ja 16,17:5
Holt, Lucius H, 1953, Ja 21,31:1
Holt, Luther Emmett Dr, 1924, Ja 15,19:4
Holt, M S, 1939, Ap 1,19:2
Holt, Philetus H, 1874, Jl 18,4:6; 1915, Ap 21,13:6; 1947, My 26,21:4
Holt, Philip Herbert, 1914, N 28,13:5
Holt, R, 1931, Jl 6,17:2
Holt, Reginald V, 1957, D 11,31:4
Holt, Richard, 1952, F 9,13:5
Holt, Richard D, 1941, Mr 23,44:4
Holt, Robert P, 1950, Jl 29,13:4
Holt, Robert P Mrs, 1944, Mr 22,19:1
Holt, Rush D, 1955, F 9,27:1
Holt, Russell D Sr, 1956, Jl 28,17:6
Holt, Samuel, 1948, O 10,78:2
Holt, Samuel E, 1949, N 24,31:3
Holt, Saxon W, 1940, Ap 1,19:4
Holt, Sidney, 1944, Mr 11,13:4
Holt, Sidney T, 1953, Ja 10,17:6
Holt, Stella, 1967, Ag 29,37:1
Holt, T B, 1941, N 12,23:1
Holt, Thaddeus Goode Mrs, 1915, S 5,11:5
Holt, Thomas S, 1948, N 22,22:2
Holt, Vivian G, 1945, Jl 9,11:6
Holt, Vyvyan, 1960, Jl 30,17:3
Holt, W H, 1901, My 11,9:6
Holt, Walter B, 1964, Ag 28,29:5
Holt, Walter C, 1959, S 29,36:3
Holt, Walter H, 1957, D 9,35:4
Holt, William F, 1951, N 23,29:3
Holt, William H Judge, 1919, Mr 7,13:3
Holt, William R, 1947, S 13,11:3
Holt, William W, 1953, Mr 28,17:4
Holt-Harris, John E, 1956, O 16,34:2
Holt-Harris, William M Mrs, 1948, Jl 20,23:6
Holtam, Walter W, 1937, D 9,25:2
Holtan, Mabel, 1947, S 13,11:2
Holtaway, Walter Mrs, 1945, F 7,21:1
Holtcamp, John H, 1952, Ja 5,11:3
Holter, Edwin O, 1964, Je 8,29:3
Holter, Friedrich, 1941, O 8,23:2
Holterbosch, Hans, 1960, Jl 31,69:2
Holterhoff, Adolph Mrs, 1951, Je 27,29:3
Holterman, Edward H, 1954, Mr 30,27:5

Holtermann, C Henry, 1960, Ap 30,23:5
Holtermann, Henry J Sr, 1951, S 22,17:4
Holters, John G, 1968, N 28,37:1
Holthausen, Arend Mrs, 1955, My 26,31:2
Holthausen, Carl F Sr, 1966, O 13,45:1
Holthusen, Adolf H, 1942, D 29,21:4
Holthusen, John, 1957, O 25,27:2
Holtje, Fred Comr, 1937, Je 25,21:5
Holtkamp, Walter H, 1962, F 14,33:1
Holtman, Anna M, 1940, Ja 28,32:1
Holton, Charles R, 1949, Jl 17,57:3
Holton, Charles W, 1942, Ap 13,15:6
Holton, Curtis R, 1961, S 1,17:1
Holton, D P Dr, 1883, Je 9,2:3
Holton, Edward P Mrs, 1951, O 14,88:6
Holton, Frank, 1942, Ap 18,15:7
Holton, Frank Mrs, 1951, Ap 24,29:1
Holton, Frederick A Mrs, 1951, Ag 17,17:4
Holton, George C, 1937, N 15,23:4
Holton, Grace, 1964, Ja 29,33:1
Holton, Herbert M, 1951, My 5,17:5
Holton, Howard, 1957, D 7,21:1
Holton, Irene L Mrs, 1943, N 25,25:1
Holton, J F Prof, 1874, Ja 27,4:7
Holton, James S, 1955, Mr 27,86:8
Holton, John S, 1946, N 1,23:2
Holton, John S W Mrs, 1947, D 6,15:4
Holton, Joseph J, 1958, F 24,19:4
Holton, Joseph L, 1947, Ja 4,15:4
Holton, Susan M, 1951, O 8,21:3
Holton, Wilbur S, 1957, Ap 23,31:4
Holton, Winfred B, 1957, Jl 13,17:1
Holtorf, Henry F, 1937, My 25,27:4
Holtz, Abram I, 1945, Ag 5,37:1
Holtz, Albert, 1958, Ag 18,19:5
Holtz, Alex, 1957, Je 11,35:3
Holtz, Frederick L, 1960, D 15,43:2
Holtz, Harold B, 1964, S 21,31:4
Holtz, Harold B Mrs, 1945, N 16,19:2
Holtz, Isador, 1960, Jl 20,29:2
Holtz, Max (funl, Je 22,13:4), 1917, Je 21,13:4
Holtz, Max I, 1940, Je 25,23:2
Holtz, Theodore, 1964, My 12,37:4
Holtzapple, George E, 1946, F 23,13:2
Holtzberg, Abraham, 1951, Ja 13,15:2
Holtzclaw, Jack G, 1955, D 14,39:4
Holtzendorff, von Adm, 1919, Je 11,15:4
Holtzman, Aaron G, 1965, My 31,17:4
Holtzman, David Mrs, 1954, D 27,17:5
Holtzman, Isadore, 1961, D 19,29:5
Holtzman, Isidor Mrs, 1962, Jl 1,56:7
Holtzman, Jacob, 1940, Jl 5,13:6
Holtzman, Stephen F, 1957, N 21,30:2
Holtzmann, David M, 1965, Mr 3,41:4
Holtzmann, Henry (por), 1940, D 17,25:4
Holtzmann, Henry Mrs, 1945, My 30,19:4
Holtzmann, Howard M Mrs, 1967, Ag 4,29:2
Holtzmann, Jacob, 1925, S 25,21:6
Holtzmann, Jacob L, 1963, Jl 12,25:4
Holub, Albert, 1950, Ap 2,92:3
Holub, Emil, 1902, F 22,7:5
Holub, Joseph, 1912, Ja 31,11:5
Holub, Joseph S, 1958, Ja 30,23:1
Holub, Michael Mrs, 1952, O 29,29:6
Holveck, Joe, 1950, My 22,21:5
Holway, Amy R, 1949, Mr 11,25:4
Holway, Edward J Sr, 1954, Ap 10,15:3
Holway, Edward T, 1938, D 3,19:2
Holway, Jerome R, 1943, S 10,23:1
Holwell, Joseph J, 1946, My 28,21:4
Holwell, Joseph J Mrs, 1937, D 11,19:1
Holwill, William F, 1923, F 26,13:5
Holy, Alfred, 1948, My 24,19:3
Holy, Antonin, 1942, Je 13,15:2
Holy, James, 1924, S 4,19:6
Holyoake, George J, 1906, Ja 23,9:5
Holyoke, T, 1877, F 21,5:5
Holyoke, Thomas, 1907, N 22,9:5
Holz, Albert H, 1945, S 6,25:4
Holz, Ernest R, 1938, D 23,19:1
Holz, Henry C, 1955, My 5,33:2
Holz, Julius, 1941, Ag 14,17:6
Holz, Richard E (por), 1943, Je 23,21:1
Holz, Richard Mrs (por), 1937, Ja 7,21:4
Holz, William C, 1940, O 10,25:4
Holzapfel, Sebastian, 1940, Ap 18,23:3
Holzapfel, William H, 1957, D 18,35:4
Holzberg, Barend P, 1950, S 27,31:1
Holzberg, Julius, 1961, Ag 7,23:3
Holzderber, John Jr, 1937, Je 29,21:3
Holzer, Eric, 1968, My 7,47:2
Holzer, Jacob A (will), 1938, Mr 22,44:1
Holzer, Leo, 1950, Ja 27,23:3
Holzer, Marcell M, 1962, Ap 15,80:4
Holzer, Otto H, 1951, N 13,29:2
Holzhauer, William C, 1955, Je 8,29:2
Holzhausen, Albert H, 1954, N 8,21:1
Holzhausen, William L, 1951, Jl 27,19:4
Holzhauser, Rudolph Mrs, 1948, Mr 31,25:5
Holzinger, Karl J Jr, 1952, Ap 25,23:2
Holzinger, Karl L, 1954, Ja 16,15:1
Holzknecht, Karl J, 1956, Mr 25,74:1
Holzmacher, Henry G, 1961, Mr 10,27:1

Holzmacher, Theodore T, 1963, N 18,33:1
Holzman, Benjamin F, 1963, My 10,34:1
Holzman, Joseph Mrs, 1957, Ap 15,29:4
Holzman, Lawrence J, 1953, Ap 14,27:1
Holzman, Samuel D, 1950, O 8,104:2
Holzman, William, 1956, S 9,84:8
Holzmann, Abe, 1939, Ja 18,19:2
Holzmann, John, 1957, Mr 31,88:7
Holzrichter, Fritz Mrs, 1952, F 2,13:3
Holzwarth, Franklin J, 1948, N 19,27:2
Holzwasser, Alexander S, 1943, Ag 29,38:8
Holzwasser, Charles S, 1944, O 8,44:2
Holzworth, Sarah S Mrs, 1961, D 20,33:3
Homa, Marko Mrs, 1949, Mr 13,76:1
Homack, Alex, 1949, Ap 24,78:1
Homan, Benjamin Sr, 1946, Je 26,25:2
Homan, Dennis G, 1956, F 7,31:1
Homan, Eugene Mrs, 1954, Je 17,29:4
Homan, Frank D, 1954, Mr 30,27:2
Homan, Frank H, 1947, N 5,27:3
Homan, Franklin L, 1943, Jl 15,21:4
Homan, George L, 1942, My 30,15:5
Homan, George L Mrs, 1948, Mr 9,23:4
Homan, H Frank, 1953, Ja 12,27:5
Homan, Harold, 1941, Ap 28,15:4
Homan, Harry E, 1940, Jl 21,29:1
Homan, Helen W Mrs, 1961, Ap 8,19:2
Homan, Hermon Bell, 1914, My 25,11:6
Homan, J Albert, 1952, My 6,29:3
Homan, J Jerome, 1952, Ag 9,13:6
Homann, Carl J Mrs, 1961, Ja 19,29:1
Homans, Eugene V, 1965, O 30,35:6
Homans, Howard P, 1962, N 13,37:4
Homans, J E Rev, 1882, Ag 4,5:2
Homans, John, 1954, Je 8,27:2
Homans, John Dr, 1903, F 8,8:2
Homans, John 2d Dr, 1902, My 5,9:6
Homans, Rockland T, 1954, F 25,31:3
Homans, Sarah L Mrs, 1910, My 3,13:5
Homans, Sarah S, 1954, D 20,29:2
Homans, Sheppard, 1952, Mr 31,19:1
Homans, Sheppard Mrs, 1956, Je 6,33:4
Homberg, Octave, 1941, Jl 11,15:6
Homden, Judson B, 1953, Ja 8,27:1
Home, Dowager Countess of, 1966, S 27,47:4
Home, Earl of, 1951, Jl 13,21:2
Home, John, 1938, O 21,23:4
Home, The Spiritualist (see also Ap 6), 1876, Ap 8, 1:5
Homelius, Frank H, 1941, N 21,17:3
Homelius, Frank H Mrs, 1944, S 16,13:4
Homer, Arthur C, 1950, N 5,93:1
Homer, Arthur P, 1940, O 11,21:2
Homer, C W Rev Dr, 1905, Ap 8,11:6
Homer, Charles F, 1911, Jl 14,7:6
Homer, Charles Mrs, 1954, Ag 15,85:1
Homer, Demetre, 1952, S 29,16:7
Homer, Dudley D, 1955, My 18,31:4
Homer, Edward, 1948, Mr 5,21:4
Homer, Edward C, 1952, Ja 29,25:5
Homer, Eugene M, 1952, My 31,17:3
Homer, Francis T Mrs, 1939, S 16,17:5
Homer, George, 1871, Jl 8,1:6
Homer, H, 1883, Mr 14,2:4
Homer, Helen, 1944, My 30,21:5
Homer, John L, 1953, N 7,17:5
Homer, Joy (por), 1946, O 25,23:3
Homer, Langley S, 1950, D 13,35:4
Homer, Lorin L Mrs, 1943, S 21,23:1
Homer, Louise, 1921, N 20,22:3
Homer, R Baldwin, 1940, My 29,23:5
Homer, Sidney, 1953, Jl 11,11:3
Homer, Sidney Mrs, 1947, My 7,1:6
Homer, Warden, 1919, O 6,17:4
Homer, Winslow, 1910, O 1,13:3
Homes, Arthur D, 1958, Ag 22,21:1
Homes, Henry, 1958, N 10,29:2
Homeyer, Elizabeth Mrs, 1940, S 15,48:2
Homeyer, William F, 1948, N 19,27:4
Homlok, Alex H, 1963, Ap 7,85:6
Homma, Robert I, 1961, N 1,39:4
Homma, Robert I Sr Mrs, 1962, Ap 26,33:4
Hommedieu, John B l' Dr, 1913, F 22,11:4
Hommel, Peter A, 1948, Je 16,29:4
Hommel, Robert H, 1949, Mr 5,18:2
Hommel, Rudolf P, 1950, Mr 19,54:3
Hommon, Karol R, 1965, O 12,93:6
Homolka, Florence Mrs, 1962, N 28,39:4
Homolka, Oscar Mrs, 1938, Ap 6,23:6
Homsey, Sam Jr, 1963, Ag 20,33:5
Homsher, Fred L, 1950, My 4,27:1
Homsher, John G, 1938, S 14,23:5
Homuth, Karl, 1951, Mr 20,29:4
Honaman, Walter H, 1943, My 25,23:2
Honan, Daniel J, 1947, N 27,31:1
Honan, James H Dr, 1917, N 14,15:4
Honan, John, 1955, S 14,35:4
Honan, Michael, 1952, Ap 8,29:2
Honan, Raymond J, 1944, O 7,13:2
Honcharik, Walter, 1951, O 7,86:5
Honda, Kotaro, 1954, F 13,13:6
Hondlow, David L, 1939, Mr 18,17:2
Hondlow, Francis H, 1946, Ja 14,19:3
Hondlow, Margaret, 1953, My 10,88:1
Hondlow, S, 1878, F 22,8:2
Hone, Augustus C, 1939, S 18,19:4
Hone, Frederick de Peyster, 1925, My 4,19:5
Hone, Harold, 1939, Jl 10,19:4
Hone, Harold Mrs, 1960, Jl 10,72:3
Hone, John, 1915, Mr 22,9:3; 1923, F 24,11:5
Hone, John Mrs, 1950, Ag 30,31:4
Hone, Joseph B, 1913, Ja 1,17:4
Hone, Josephine Hoey Mrs, 1905, Je 7,9:3
Hone, Nathaniel, 1917, O 19,13:7
Hone, R G, 1927, F 27,30:3
Hone, Rosella K, 1945, Jl 10,11:5
Honeck, H C, 1934, My 2,21:3
Honeck, John G W, 1939, My 5,23:2
Honecker, Edward J, 1966, Ag 20,25:4
Honegger, Arthur (funl, D 3,17:5), 1955, N 29,29:1
Honegger, Oscar P, 1941, D 27,19:4
Honeij, James A Dr, 1924, Ja 25,17:5
Honer, William F, 1948, N 12,23:4
Honerkamp, Frederick W Sr, 1960, F 23,32:1
Hones, L William, 1945, D 25,23:3
Hones, Sidney M, 1957, Mr 16,19:5
Honess, Arthur P, 1942, D 18,27:3
Honess, George G, 1959, F 15,86:7
Honeste Celestin, Bro, 1964, S 6,56:4
Honey, Albert A, 1903, D 6,2:1
Honey, Edgar T, 1948, Je 4,23:1
Honey, G, 1880, My 30,7:5
Honey, Mary T, 1941, O 19,47:2
Honey, Robertson, 1941, Ag 31,23:2
Honey, Robertson Mrs, 1958, Ja 24,23:4
Honeycutt, Jesse V Mrs, 1958, Ap 7,21:4
Honeyford, Lyle B, 1939, Ap 3,15:4
Honeyman, David, 1947, My 20,25:4
Honeyman, George Essex Sir, 1875, S 19,1:4
Honeysett, John, 1942, F 12,23:4
Honeywell, Frank, 1940, Ap 4,23:3
Honeywell, George H, 1947, F 7,24:2
Honeywell, Harry E, 1940, F 11,48:3
Honeywell, J Frank, 1951, Ag 8,25:5
Honeywell, Mark C, 1964, S 14,33:4
Honeywill, Albert W, 1939, O 8,48:8
Honig, Edward M, 1952, Je 11,29:5
Honig, I, 1884, N 3,2:6
Honig, Jacob A, 1958, Jl 31,23:4
Honig, Joseph E, 1961, My 30,17:3
Honig, Julius, 1957, My 27,31:3
Honig, Leo Mrs, 1953, Ap 25,15:3
Honig, Milton (Arth M), 1965, Je 30,37:3
Honig, Pieter, 1965, My 16,88:3
Honig, Walter, 1952, My 7,27:5
Honig, William, 1951, Ap 4,29:3
Honigsberg, Allan, 1966, Mr 23,48:1
Honikel, George F, 1952, O 20,23:2
Honikel, Harry F, 1953, Ja 21,31:2
Honing, William A, 1948, N 3,27:2
Honkamp, Edward F, 1943, Ag 23,15:7
Honnaker, Hedley, 1960, Jl 11,29:3
Honness, John F, 1946, Ag 17,13:6
Honnold, Fred C Dr, 1937, O 16,19:4
Honnold, William L, 1950, My 7,108:2
Honold, J Frank, 1964, S 17,43:3
Honor, Hirsch W Mrs, 1954, S 10,23:2
Honor, Leo L, 1956, O 26,29:2
Honore, H H Mrs, 1902, Ja 24,1:6
Honore, Harriet D Mrs, 1938, Jl 18,3:7
Honore, Henry Hamilton, 1916, Ag 17,11:5
Honore, Henry Mrs, 1906, My 7,1:6
Honore, Lockwood, 1917, S 1,7:3
Honore, Paul, 1956, Ap 14,17:4
Honsinger, Frank, 1923, F 10,13:4
Honska, E R, 1949, Ja 30,60:8
Honssinger, Oscar, 1961, S 28,41:4
Honstrater, Ernest A, 1939, O 31,23:5
Honthumb, Benno W, 1957, Je 26,31:3
Honti, Nandor, 1961, S 20,29:5
Hoober, John A, 1950, S 26,31:1
Hoobler, B Raymond, 1943, Je 13,44:7
Hood, A G (Jos), 1880, Jl 10,3:4
Hood, Albert L Jr, 1941, Jl 13,29:1
Hood, Alex N Sir, 1937, Je 3,25:4
Hood, Archer L, 1944, Mr 23,19:5
Hood, Arthur A, 1965, D 11,33:4
Hood, Arthur B, 1962, Jl 24,27:3
Hood, Arthur N, 1950, F 1,29:4
Hood, Basil Capt, 1917, Ag 8,7:4
Hood, Bessie D, 1952, D 24,17:6
Hood, Caleb B, 1940, Mr 16,15:4
Hood, Carl, 1944, Ja 3,21:2
Hood, Charles, 1949, Mr 8,25:5
Hood, Charles C, 1939, D 10,69:2
Hood, Charles H, 1937, N 23,23:3
Hood, Charles Mrs, 1953, N 14,17:3
Hood, Charles N, 1954, Ja 31,88:1
Hood, Clarence, 1952, D 22,25:4
Hood, Clarence O, 1944, N 8,17:5
Hood, Clifford E, 1949, Ap 29,23:4
Hood, David, 1959, My 26,35:1
Hood, E P Rev, 1885, Je 13,2:6
Hood, Edward C, 1961, O 6,35:4
Hood, Edward J, 1943, Ag 12,19:5
Hood, Edward W Mrs, 1950, S 30,17:2
Hood, Edwin M, 1923, Ag 10,11:3
Hood, Edwin M Mrs, 1943, O 14,21:2
Hood, Elizabeth Y, 1946, D 7,21:3
Hood, Emily Mrs, 1945, O 31,23:2
Hood, Ernest, 1952, O 26,89:2
Hood, F James, 1949, N 11,25:3
Hood, Frazer (por), 1944, Je 20,19:5
Hood, Fred R, 1956, Ap 11,33:1
Hood, Frederic C, 1942, D 26,9:2
Hood, George C Mrs, 1958, Ap 17,31:4
Hood, George E, 1960, Mr 9,33:4
Hood, Harry, 1954, My 20,31:5
Hood, Hattie, 1937, Jl 7,23:4
Hood, Helen L, 1938, Mr 8,19:4
Hood, J B Gen, 1879, Ag 31,6:7
Hood, J B Mrs, 1879, Ag 30,3:3
Hood, J Douglas, 1966, O 23,88:8
Hood, Jeanette L, 1962, S 17,31:5
Hood, Jennings, 1951, D 27,21:3
Hood, John D, 1964, Jl 19,64:2
Hood, John H, 1949, Ag 3,23:2
Hood, John Jr, 1954, Ag 5,23:5
Hood, John M Gen, 1906, D 18,9:4
Hood, John M Jr, 1941, Je 17,21:4
Hood, John R, 1960, My 15,86:7
Hood, John Rear-Adm, 1919, F 12,13:5
Hood, John W, 1949, My 21,13:2
Hood, L Gerald, 1964, Jl 6,29:4
Hood, Lord Adm, 1901, N 18,7:4
Hood, Louis, 1946, Jl 27,17:1
Hood, Mary G, 1938, S 20,23:3
Hood, Mary M, 1937, Jl 3,15:2
Hood, Melvin L, 1943, S 15,27:5
Hood, Myer S, 1909, S 9,9:7
Hood, Phil G, 1938, N 20,39:2
Hood, R, 1934, Ag 15,17:1
Hood, Richard P, 1955, O 15,15:1
Hood, Richard W, 1953, O 4,88:4
Hood, Robert L, 1959, F 10,33:1
Hood, Solomon P, 1943, O 14,21:5
Hood, Thomas, 1874, N 21,1:2
Hood, Thomas C, 1956, Jl 20,17:4
Hood, Vance R, 1945, Ja 22,17:5
Hood, Wallace P, 1948, Je 27,52:7
Hood, Walter D, 1937, D 27,15:5
Hood, Walter S, 1955, Ap 5,29:4
Hood, Walter S Mrs, 1942, F 14,15:5
Hood, William C, 1940, Ja 22,15:2
Hoodin, Joseph H, 1959, O 3,19:6
Hoodless, William H, 1947, O 22,29:4
Hooe, James C Mrs, 1944, Ja 23,38:1
Hooey, Robert E, 1949, D 1,31:5
Hooey, William C Mrs, 1952, Ja 24,28:2
Hoofien, E Siegfried, 1957, Jl 8,23:1
Hoogland, Andrew, 1879, S 2,8:2
Hoogstraaten, Willem van, 1965, S 14,39:3
Hoogstraten, Otto S Count, 1941, Jl 22,19:3
Hoogveld, J H E J, 1942, Ag 26,19:5
Hook, Cecil, 1938, F 6,II,9:3
Hook, Charles R, 1963, N 15,35:1
Hook, Charles R Jr, 1961, D 20,33:1
Hook, Edward A, 1945, Jl 28,11:4
Hook, F Edward Mrs, 1945, Ja 13,11:3
Hook, J M, 1884, Mr 28,5:3
Hook, James Clark, 1907, Ap 16,11:5
Hook, James L, 1958, N 23,88:8
Hook, James W, 1957, O 23,33:2
Hook, John A, 1943, F 8,19:3
Hook, Melville M, 1950, O 15,104:3
Hook, Thomas F, 1952, F 6,29:2
Hook, W F Rev Dr (see also O 21), 1875, O 2
Hook, William C Judge, 1921, Ag 12,13:6
Hooke, Albert W, 1954, D 5,88:3
Hooke, F Howard, 1953, My 14,29:2
Hooke, Harvey L, 1949, Mr 10,28:2
Hooke, Henry B, 1954, My 5,31:3
Hooker, Brian, 1946, D 29,37:5
Hooker, C O, 1957, N 8,29:4
Hooker, Charles E, 1951, O 24,31:3
Hooker, Charles L, 1947, O 27,21:1
Hooker, Clarence R, 1938, Mr 10,21:2
Hooker, Donald R, 1946, Ag 3,15:6
Hooker, Duncan C, 1953, Jl 27,19:1
Hooker, Edgar F, 1951, O 10,23:3
Hooker, Edward Com, 1903, My 2,9:4
Hooker, Edward G, 1967, Mr 30,45:1
Hooker, Edward N, 1957, Ja 14,23:2
Hooker, Edward W, 1915, S 4,7:5
Hooker, Elon H (por),(died intestate, Je 9,23:2 1938, My 11,19:1
Hooker, Elon H Mrs, 1956, Je 7,31:2
Hooker, Emily M Mrs, 1937, My 23,II,11:2
Hooker, Frank A Justice, 1911, Jl 11,7:5
Hooker, Gen (Fighting Joe), 1879, N 1,5:3
Hooker, George W, 1946, Je 4,23:6
Hooker, H D, 1901, Je 12,9:6
Hooker, Harry M, 1949, Ap 10,76:2
Hooker, Henry S, 1964, My 19,37:1
Hooker, Horace W (por), 1937, Ag 31,23:5
Hooker, Horace W Mrs, 1953, Ap 23,29:5; 19 Ap 20,43:1
Hooker, J Murray, 1940, Ag 7,19:5
Hooker, Joseph D Sir, 1911, D 12,11:5

Hooker, Mary A, 1938, D 9,26:1
Hooker, Paul, 1940, Ja 13,15:2
Hooker, R S, 1932, D 25,12:1
Hooker, Ramson S, 1957, Ap 12,25:1
Hooker, Richard, 1967, N 26,84:4
Hooker, Robert J, 1961, Ap 9,86:4
Hooker, S C, 1935, O 14,17:3
Hooker, Samuel Lucius Mrs, 1918, S 30,9:6
Hooker, Sarah H, 1879, F 2,5:6
Hooker, Sherman A, 1953, F 27,21:3
Hooker, T M, 1884, Ja 25,3:4
Hooker, Thomas, 1924, O 29,21:2
Hooker, W F, 1938, D 25,14:8
Hooker, Warren B, 1920, Mr 6,11:6
Hookey, Edward M Sr, 1948, Ag 20,17:3
Hooks, C G Mrs, 1903, F 18,9:6
Hooks, David M, 1937, Jl 9,21:3
Hooks, Dominick, 1959, Mr 12,31:5
Hooks, Henry Mrs, 1952, My 30,15:2
Hooks, Matilda, 1952, Je 29,59:6
Hooks, Michael E, 1948, Ag 10,21:5
Hookway, A Thomas, 1958, S 5,27:1
Hookway, John A, 1939, N 5,49:3
Hookway, William C Sr, 1961, D 21,27:4
Hool, James A, 1940, Ap 15,17:5
Hoolahan, Frank E H, 1944, S 16,13:5
Hoolahan, Frank E Mrs, 1941, Mr 13,21:1
Hoole, Harry J, 1963, S 24,39:4
Hoole, John T, 1958, S 22,31:5
Hooley, A G, 1918, My 4,15:8
Hooley, Charles, 1944, N 28,23:4
Hooley, Ernest T, 1947, F 13,23:2
Hooley, Francis G, 1962, Ap 25,39:1
Hooley, James D, 1943, Mr 4,19:5
Hooley, John W Mrs, 1945, Mr 28,23:5
Hooley, Mark O, 1956, F 23,27:3
Hooley, Walter, 1954, O 24,88:6
Hoolihan, William F, 1946, N 17,68:3
Hoop, Harry M, 1946, Ja 23,27:4
Hoop, Josef F, 1959, O 20,39:4
Hooper, Albert A, 1964, Ap 15,39:2
Hooper, Alcaeus, 1938, Jl 2,13:6
Hooper, Alfred E, 1948, D 11,15:1
Hooper, Arthur S, 1963, Ag 7,33:5
Hooper, Ben W, 1957, Ap 19,21:2
Hooper, Byron, 1960, Ag 28,83:2
Hooper, Carl A, 1950, N 25,13:2
Hooper, Charles, 1941, My 5,17:3
Hooper, Claude E, 1954, D 16,38:2
Hooper, Clifford F T, 1954, Je 8,27:3
Hooper, Dudley R, 1963, D 18,41:4
Hooper, Edward P, 1955, O 19,33:3
Hooper, Ella G Mrs, 1942, N 3,23:2
Hooper, Florence Mrs, 1952, Ja 3,27:2
Hooper, Frank, 1943, Je 14,17:5
Hooper, Frank C, 1954, D 11,13:5
Hooper, Franklin W, 1914, Ag 2,15:5
Hooper, Fred M, 1938, Jl 17,27:4
Hooper, Frederic C, 1963, O 5,25:4
Hooper, H B, 1965, Ap 10,29:3
Hooper, H Russell, 1950, Ag 4,21:3
Hooper, Horace E Mrs, 1951, My 7,25:4
Hooper, Horace Everett, 1922, Je 14,19:5
Hooper, J Hugh, 1951, My 14,25:4
Hooper, J L, 1934, F 23,19:1
Hooper, J Leon Rev Dr, 1968, S 7,29:4
Hooper, J R, 1950, Mr 5,92:4
Hooper, James L, 1964, F 12,33:4
Hooper, John B, 1950, Jl 28,21:5
Hooper, John J, 1961, Mr 19,88:7
Hooper, John Jr, 1947, Ag 13,23:1
Hooper, John W, 1959, O 23,29:1
Hooper, John W Mrs, 1950, Mr 28,31:3
Hooper, Katrine (Mrs Jas R), 1964, Ja 31,27:5
Hooper, Lloyd P, 1950, Mr 12,94:5
Hooper, Louis L, 1945, Ap 15,14:7
Hooper, M Louise, 1948, D 15,33:2
Hooper, Martha H Mrs, 1937, My 12,23:3
Hooper, Mary, 1947, F 13,23:1
Hooper, Mary J T Mrs, 1941, S 27,17:7
Hooper, Noel J, 1953, Jl 21,23:2
Hooper, Nora, 1906, Ap 18,11:5
Hooper, Osman C, 1941, My 12,17:2
Hooper, Reginald S, 1945, S 4,23:4
Hooper, Richard B, 1945, My 25,19:4
Hooper, Richard Mrs, 1944, D 30,11:5
Hooper, Robert A, 1962, D 3,31:2
Hooper, Robert C, 1908, Ag 14,7:4
Hooper, Robert P, 1958, Jl 7,27:2
Hooper, Robert P Mrs, 1958, My 13,29:3
Hooper, Stanford C, 1955, Ap 7,27:1
Hooper, T N, 1903, N 25,9:5
Hooper, W H, 1882, D 31,2:4
Hooper, W W Rev, 1905, Ap 17,5:6
Hooper, Will P, 1938, Ja 25,21:2
Hooper, William D, 1945, F 15,19:3; 1961, Ja 9,39:5
Hooper, William F, 1946, N 8,23:3
Hooper, William Leslie Prof, 1918, O 4,13:2
Hooper, William R Mrs, 1949, Je 10,27:5
Hoopes, Edward, 1965, O 28,43:3
Hoopes, H Townsend, 1944, Je 15,19:3
Hoopes, Johannes, 1949, Ap 16,15:2
Hoopes, Josiah, 1904, Ja 17,7:5
Hoopes, Macmillan Mrs, 1963, N 28,39:4
Hoopes, Maurice, 1949, F 16,25:3
Hoopes, Maurice Mrs, 1951, O 17,31:3
Hoopes, Wilford L, 1945, Ag 2,19:6
Hoopes, William, 1924, Ja 11,17:3
Hoopes, Wilmer W, 1955, N 6,87:1
Hoopingarner, Newman L, 1958, Ja 29,27:1
Hoople, Ross E, 1946, Je 19,21:2
Hoople, Roy, 1949, O 10,23:4
Hoople, William C, 1943, S 3,19:1
Hoopman, Edward H, 1956, Je 12,35:2
Hoops, Arthur, 1916, S 17,19:3
Hoops, Frederick C, 1941, Je 18,21:1
Hoops, Herman L, 1961, Mr 30,29:1
Hoops, Paul C, 1959, N 18,41:3
Hoops, Thomas, 1946, My 27,23:1
Hoops, William T, 1940, Je 1,15:4
Hoornbeek, Frank B, 1949, N 26,15:2
Hoornbeek, Thomas C, 1940, Ja 13,15:4
Hoos, Edward, 1912, O 25,13:3
Hoos, Edward H, 1946, Jl 6,15:3
Hoos, Marguerite E, 1943, Ag 19,19:1
Hoos, Marie Mrs, 1940, D 4,27:5
Hoos, William L Jr, 1943, Mr 15,13:1
Hoose, Donald J, 1963, S 29,86:2
Hoosman, Al, 1968, O 29,47:3
Hooson, Fred Q, 1955, D 19,27:3
Hoost, John H, 1951, Mr 13,31:2
Hoot, Harold T Mrs, 1949, F 24,24:2
Hoot, J Weldon, 1950, N 11,15:6
Hooten, James C, 1911, Ja 16,11:5
Hooton, Earnest A, 1954, My 4,29:1
Hooton, Mott Gen, 1920, Je 1,15:1
Hoots, Rosa M Mrs, 1938, Ap 26,21:4
Hooven, Robert J Mrs, 1944, Je 29,23:5
Hooven, Robert L, 1949, N 18,29:5
Hooven, Samuel L, 1949, D 17,17:2
Hooven, William A, 1958, N 15,23:2
Hoover, A Pearson (trb lr, S 29,16:7), 1951, S 18,32:2
Hoover, Alden R, 1940, Ap 30,22:2
Hoover, Alden R Mrs, 1948, Mr 28,49:1
Hoover, Anna M Mrs, 1938, F 24,19:1
Hoover, Arthur L, 1947, O 14,27:2
Hoover, Arthur O J (Lord Rankeillour), 1958, My 27,31:3
Hoover, C Walter Maj, 1937, N 9,23:2
Hoover, Carl H, 1951, My 28,21:6
Hoover, Charles E, 1947, D 20,17:5
Hoover, Charles L, 1949, My 1,89:1
Hoover, Charles P, 1950, N 16,31:5
Hoover, Charles R Mrs, 1943, D 1,21:4
Hoover, Dickerson N, 1944, O 24,23:3
Hoover, Earl E, 1939, Ja 9,15:3
Hoover, Elenore L, 1954, F 10,29:4
Hoover, Eliza Mrs, 1955, F 25,21:5
Hoover, Ellison, 1955, Mr 19,15:3
Hoover, Ellison Mrs, 1954, Je 2,31:2
Hoover, Frank G, 1954, D 5,89:1
Hoover, Frank S, 1946, D 12,29:6
Hoover, George O, 1941, D 27,19:3
Hoover, George W, 1950, Jl 29,13:2
Hoover, Harry C, 1949, N 29,29:4
Hoover, Harry W, 1953, Mr 19,29:5
Hoover, Harvey D, 1958, My 14,33:5
Hoover, Henry C, 1955, O 11,39:2
Hoover, Herbert C Sr (funl ser, O 23,1:2; burial, O 26,1:4), 1964, O 21,1:8
Hoover, Herbert Mrs, 1944, Ja 8,13:1
Hoover, Herbert W, 1954, S 17,27:1
Hoover, I H, 1933, S 15,19:1
Hoover, Jeremiah F, 1964, Mr 28,19:1
Hoover, John, 1950, Ap 30,102:4
Hoover, Joseph W, 1952, S 16,29:2
Hoover, Katherine, 1951, S 19,31:2
Hoover, Loring R, 1966, Mr 20,86:8
Hoover, Mary I B Mrs, 1940, O 5,15:6
Hoover, Matthew H, 1940, F 20,21:3
Hoover, Merle M, 1961, Je 3,23:2
Hoover, Norman R, 1959, Ag 12,29:1
Hoover, Norman R Mrs, 1955, S 27,35:2
Hoover, Percy D, 1940, N 15,21:3
Hoover, Ray, 1965, Jl 10,25:4
Hoover, S C, 1951, O 6,19:1
Hoover, S Earle, 1945, Je 8,19:5
Hoover, Stuart, 1965, Jl 5,17:4
Hoover, Theodore J, 1955, F 6,89:1
Hoover, Theodore J Mrs, 1940, S 4,23:5
Hoover, William H, 1938, My 4,23:1; 1952, Je 7,19:5
Hoover, William M, 1945, N 21,21:3
Hoover, William M Mrs, 1960, D 25,43:1
Hoover, William R Mrs, 1947, Jl 27,45:1
Hopcroft, J L, 1954, Mr 29,19:1
Hope, Arthur F, 1946, Je 4,23:5
Hope, Arthur H, 1938, S 1,23:2
Hope, Charles E, 1942, F 17,21:2
Hope, Charles F Dr, 1937, Mr 9,2:7
Hope, Chester R, 1963, N 28,39:4
Hope, Danny, 1959, S 6,60:4
Hope, Duncan M, 1944, O 21,17:4
Hope, Edson, 1955, Ag 20,17:6
Hope, Edward, 1958, F 26,27:5
Hope, Eugene M Sr Mrs, 1947, S 27,15:2
Hope, Francis X Sr, 1948, D 29,21:1
Hope, Frank R, 1953, Ag 4,21:1
Hope, Frederic, 1937, Ap 22,23:1
Hope, Frederick H, 1946, Ja 12,15:5
Hope, George, 1940, F 12,17:4; 1959, Jl 13,27:5
Hope, Harry M, 1949, Jl 29,21:5
Hope, J Howard, 1945, My 23,19:5
Hope, J William, 1964, My 1,35:2
Hope, James, 1943, Jl 26,19:4
Hope, James A, 1952, Ja 19,15:4
Hope, James Mrs, 1941, Ap 6,48:8
Hope, James T, 1952, S 9,31:2
Hope, James W Mrs, 1951, My 24,35:6
Hope, Jimmy, 1905, Je 3,4:1
Hope, John A, 1955, Ja 3,27:4
Hope, John Adrian Louis (Marquess of Linlithgow), 1908, Mr 2,9:5
Hope, John E, 1957, F 14,27:1
Hope, John G, 1946, Ap 11,25:2
Hope, John S Mrs, 1947, Ag 20,21:4
Hope, M Frank, 1940, My 15,25:2
Hope, McIlroy, 1947, N 9,73:1
Hope, Norman S, 1958, Ag 16,17:2
Hope, Robert A, 1964, Ag 2,77:1
Hope, Robert D, 1951, Mr 25,72:6
Hope, Samuel, 1946, Jl 2,25:4
Hope, Sidney, 1946, Ag 26,23:1
Hope, Victor A (Lord Linlithgow), 1952, Ja 6,92:1
Hope, Vida, 1963, D 25,33:5
Hope, Walter E, 1948, Ag 17,21:1
Hope, Walter E Mrs, 1951, Ap 22,88:2; 1956, N 14, 35:2
Hope, Will, 1940, Mr 2,13:7
Hope, William C, 1937, N 8,24:1; 1965, F 3,35:4
Hope, William C Mrs, 1943, S 5,28:4
Hope, William J, 1962, Ag 7,29:3
Hope-Simpson, James Sir, 1924, O 9,23:5
Hopeman, Albert A, 1963, Ap 5,48:1
Hopeman, Bertram C, 1958, S 29,27:4
Hoper, Carl H, 1947, My 12,21:3
Hoper, Francis Mrs, 1912, Ag 31,7:3
Hopes, Robert W, 1963, S 8,86:5
Hopf, Albert C, 1947, Ag 12,23:2
Hopf, Ernest A, 1951, S 25,29:5
Hopf, George M, 1949, S 8,29:1
Hopf, Harry A (por), 1949, Je 4,13:3
Hopf, Otto, 1959, Ap 29,33:1
Hopf, Werner, 1953, N 30,1:1
Hopf, William V, 1940, F 13,23:2
Hopfe, Fred W, 1947, My 23,23:1
Hopgood, Roy C (por), 1940, N 27,23:5
Hopkins, A, 1881, Je 16,5:2
Hopkins, A Col, 1926, Je 19,15:1
Hopkins, A J Ex-Sen, 1922, Ag 24,15:5
Hopkins, A Smith, 1908, Ap 24,9:4
Hopkins, Adoniram J Mrs, 1941, Ja 21,21:2
Hopkins, Albert A, 1939, Je 11,44:6
Hopkins, Albert Mrs, 1950, S 4,17:6
Hopkins, Albert Prof, 1872, My 26,5:6
Hopkins, Alden, 1960, S 18,86:5
Hopkins, Alex, 1951, Ja 24,27:4
Hopkins, Alexis L, 1958, Jl 22,27:3
Hopkins, Alfred (por), 1941, My 6,21:4
Hopkins, Allen L, 1958, D 2,37:3
Hopkins, Allison R, 1904, Ja 14,9:6
Hopkins, Amasa A Mrs, 1947, F 19,25:4
Hopkins, Angus, 1942, Mr 2,19:5
Hopkins, Anson S, 1939, Jl 7,17:1
Hopkins, Arthur, 1939, N 11,15:4; 1950, Mr 23,29:1; 1952, My 27,27:1
Hopkins, Arthur Mrs, 1938, Ja 22,15:2
Hopkins, Arthur T, 1942, D 20,44:5
Hopkins, B Smith Sr, 1952, Ag 28,23:1
Hopkins, Ben F, 1955, D 27,24:3
Hopkins, Bishop, 1868, Ja 10,1:2
Hopkins, Carroll William Judge, 1968, S 3,43:1
Hopkins, Charles, 1953, Ja 2,15:3
Hopkins, Charles A (cor, S 13,85:1), 1953, S 12,17:3
Hopkins, Charles A, 1958, F 1,19:4
Hopkins, Charles A Col, 1916, Ja 30,17:6
Hopkins, Charles A Mrs, 1939, N 29,23:5; 1951, Je 24,72:5
Hopkins, Charles Mrs, 1945, N 20,21:4
Hopkins, Charles O, 1948, Ja 26,19:4
Hopkins, Charles R Mrs, 1960, D 28,27:2
Hopkins, Charles S, 1941, Je 25,21:2
Hopkins, Clarence F, 1956, Je 12,35:4
Hopkins, Clarence V, 1945, D 27,19:3
Hopkins, Clarence W, 1950, Mr 21,32:3
Hopkins, Clifford W, 1941, My 5,17:5
Hopkins, Crosby J, 1952, Jl 3,25:4
Hopkins, Cyril G Dr, 1919, O 9,15:4
Hopkins, David J Mrs, 1964, Jl 13,33:2
Hopkins, David M, 1938, Ap 23,15:5
Hopkins, David P, 1949, Ja 14,23:2
Hopkins, Dwight L, 1955, Ja 11,25:3
Hopkins, E J, 1901, F 5,9:6
Hopkins, Edward A, 1941, D 27,19:5
Hopkins, Edward Robey Maj, 1921, Ag 17,11:6
Hopkins, Edwin F, 1942, Ag 11,19:6
Hopkins, Edwin M, 1946, Je 14,21:4
Hopkins, Edwin M Mrs, 1944, Jl 31,13:4
Hopkins, Elias B, 1940, S 23,17:5
Hopkins, Ellen D Mrs, 1939, F 4,15:3

Hopkins, Emma B, 1952, N 3,27:6
Hopkins, Ernest M, 1964, Ag 14,27:1
Hopkins, Ernest M Mrs, 1950, My 19,27:4
Hopkins, Evan H, 1938, Je 29,19:2
Hopkins, Evan H Mrs, 1948, O 29,25:2
Hopkins, F W, 1934, Jl 13,17:6
Hopkins, Fancher M, 1943, S 15,27:3
Hopkins, Floyd D Mrs, 1944, My 4,19:5
Hopkins, Frances S Mrs, 1941, Jl 30,17:3
Hopkins, Frank, 1924, Jl 17,15:6
Hopkins, Frank A Mrs, 1948, Ag 5,21:3
Hopkins, Frank E Col, 1937, Ag 5,23:5
Hopkins, Frank L, 1957, D 29,48:5
Hopkins, Frank T, 1945, Jl 26,19:6; 1945, N 2,19:4
Hopkins, Fred M, 1954, D 16,37:3
Hopkins, Fred M Mrs, 1955, Ja 1,13:3
Hopkins, Frederick E, 1941, Jl 2,21:4
Hopkins, Frederick G (por), 1947, My 17,15:1
Hopkins, Frederick H, 1949, D 17,17:4
Hopkins, Frederick K Mrs, 1943, Ap 23,17:3
Hopkins, Frederick M, 1948, My 13,25:2
Hopkins, Frederick M Mrs, 1952, Ja 27,77:2
Hopkins, Frederick T, 1965, Mr 3,41:3
Hopkins, George (will), 1958, Ja 7,24:2
Hopkins, George A, 1957, D 10,35:5
Hopkins, George Bates, 1920, D 14,17:5
Hopkins, George H, 1906, Mr 7,9:5
Hopkins, George W Mrs, 1944, Ap 1,13:1
Hopkins, Gerald P, 1945, Ap 28,15:3
Hopkins, Gerard, 1961, Mr 21,37:2
Hopkins, Grant S, 1952, D 22,25:4
Hopkins, Guy, 1937, N 18,23:3
Hopkins, Harold B, 1958, S 13,19:4
Hopkins, Harrison, 1951, Ja 9,30:5
Hopkins, Harry Jr, 1948, Ag 7,15:1
Hopkins, Harry L, 1946, Ja 30,1:6
Hopkins, Harry L Mrs (por), 1937, O 8,23:3
Hopkins, Harvey S, 1950, Mr 1,27:5
Hopkins, Harvey S Mrs, 1946, My 24,19:3
Hopkins, Henry Dr, 1908, Ag 19,7:6
Hopkins, Henry Jr, 1949, O 16,88:4
Hopkins, Henry N, 1942, Ag 29,15:1
Hopkins, Herbert C, 1946, Mr 21,25:5
Hopkins, Herbert Mrs, 1956, My 22,33:1
Hopkins, Homer A, 1954, Ag 6,17:3
Hopkins, J A H Mrs, 1951, Mr 20,29:3
Hopkins, J C Judge, 1877, S 7,4:7
Hopkins, J Gardner, 1951, F 28,27:5
Hopkins, James, 1907, My 22,9:4; 1947, S 22,23:6
Hopkins, James A, 1954, Jl 24,13:6
Hopkins, James B, 1944, Ja 10,17:4
Hopkins, James E, 1958, My 21,33:2
Hopkins, James H, 1943, Ap 17,17:1
Hopkins, James H Capt, 1921, N 30,17:4
Hopkins, James J, 1952, N 16,89:1; 1962, My 22,38:1
Hopkins, James J Dr, 1923, Ag 18,9:6
Hopkins, James W, 1952, Ag 11,15:3
Hopkins, Jared W Mrs, 1951, Mr 2,25:3
Hopkins, Jean L, 1950, Mr 2,27:2
Hopkins, Jefferson F, 1939, Je 28,21:4
Hopkins, Jefferson F Mrs, 1961, F 3,25:2
Hopkins, Jesse, 1924, N 26,19:4
Hopkins, Jesse L, 1946, Jl 14,37:2
Hopkins, John A H, 1960, Je 16,33:1
Hopkins, John Adm, 1916, Ag 1,9:5
Hopkins, John C, 1942, My 16,13:3; 1951, Jl 18,29:2
Hopkins, John D Col, 1909, O 25,7:5
Hopkins, John D Mrs, 1909, N 6,9:4
Hopkins, John E, 1963, Ag 18,80:7; 1965, Je 10,36:1
Hopkins, John F, 1943, Ap 6,21:5
Hopkins, John H, 1939, Jl 15,15:5; 1951, S 14,25:4
Hopkins, John J, 1942, Ja 19,20:1; 1947, N 23,74:5
Hopkins, John J (funl plans, My 5,88:2; funl, My 7,35:5), 1957, My 4,21:1
Hopkins, John J, 1962, My 19,27:2
Hopkins, John Judge, 1902, My 20,9:6
Hopkins, John L, 1938, F 7,15:3
Hopkins, John M, 1946, O 16,27:4
Hopkins, John Mrs, 1939, Ag 15,19:5
Hopkins, John S, 1873, D 25,1:2
Hopkins, John T, 1945, Jl 23,19:5
Hopkins, Joseph H Mrs, 1949, Mr 12,17:4
Hopkins, Joseph M, 1951, Mr 15,29:2; 1952, S 12,21:1
Hopkins, Kenneth, 1953, F 6,15:2
Hopkins, L Wallace, 1953, Jl 31,19:2
Hopkins, Lindsey, 1937, Ag 18,19:2
Hopkins, Linton C Sr, 1943, Jl 1,19:4
Hopkins, Louis B, 1940, Ag 11,30:7
Hopkins, Louis D, 1955, Ja 31,19:3
Hopkins, Louis G, 1937, N 18,23:6
Hopkins, Lucius (see also S 29), 1876, O 1,12:1
Hopkins, Marcellus, 1907, D 8,11:5
Hopkins, Margaret, 1956, Ag 8,25:6
Hopkins, Margaret F, 1952, Jl 11,17:5
Hopkins, Marguerite S Mrs, 1939, O 16,19:5
Hopkins, Mark, 1878, Ap 8,4:7; 1887, Je 18,1:5
Hopkins, Mary A, 1960, N 10,47:2
Hopkins, Mary C Mrs, 1937, My 29,17:5
Hopkins, Mary Mrs, 1941, O 16,21:3
Hopkins, Melvin, 1948, Ja 21,25:4
Hopkins, Murat W, 1955, D 17,23:5
Hopkins, Nathaniel F, 1925, N 29,13:1
Hopkins, Nathaniel R, 1952, Jl 22,25:2
Hopkins, Nathaniel R Mrs, 1954, D 17,31:5
Hopkins, Nathaniel R 2d, 1956, Mr 21,37:4
Hopkins, Nevil M (por), 1945, Mr 27,19:4
Hopkins, Niles Mrs, 1960, Ag 31,29:5
Hopkins, Niles S, 1949, Ja 11,31:6
Hopkins, Oliver P Mrs, 1952, Mr 1,15:4
Hopkins, Orville H, 1925, S 9,25:5
Hopkins, P W Sen, 1879, F 8,8:1
Hopkins, Ralph, 1945, Mr 9,19:3
Hopkins, Ralph H, 1956, Mr 2,23:1
Hopkins, Richard, 1921, Je 7,17:5; 1955, Mr 31,27:4
Hopkins, Richard J (por), 1943, Ag 29,38:6
Hopkins, Richard M, 1962, O 13,25:3
Hopkins, Richard S, 1940, Je 22,15:5; 1958, Jl 20,65:1
Hopkins, Robert, 1916, Jl 17,11:2
Hopkins, Robert B, 1942, Mr 11,19:2
Hopkins, Robert C, 1962, Ja 31,31:4
Hopkins, Robert H, 1942, O 8,27:4; 1946, O 17,23:4
Hopkins, Robert J, 1943, N 19,19:1
Hopkins, Robert M, 1955, My 10,29:3
Hopkins, Rome, 1940, N 23,17:4
Hopkins, Rose, 1948, F 7,17:7
Hopkins, Roy S, 1947, O 26,70:6
Hopkins, Russell F, 1919, Jl 17,13:4
Hopkins, S G, 1932, Je 23,21:5
Hopkins, S M Prof, 1901, O 30,9:5
Hopkins, Samuel H, 1950, Je 21,27:3
Hopkins, Samuel S, 1905, Je 28,9:5
Hopkins, San Francisco Millionaire, 1878, N 3,10:5
Hopkins, Selden G Mrs, 1951, Ja 31,25:2
Hopkins, Sidney Wright, 1913, D 13,13:7; 1923, Ag 10,11:2
Hopkins, Squire Benjamin, 1904, My 22,2:3
Hopkins, Stephen, 1945, D 12,20:3
Hopkins, Stephen V, 1937, Je 13,II,7:2
Hopkins, Stephen W, 1942, Je 7,43:1; 1956, O 17,35:3
Hopkins, Stephens A, 1945, Ap 22,36:3
Hopkins, Susan S, 1944, Mr 23,19:4
Hopkins, Sydney B, 1939, Jl 21,19:4
Hopkins, Thomas A, 1964, Je 23,33:5
Hopkins, Thomas J, 1939, D 28,22:3
Hopkins, Thomas S, 1925, Ap 18,15:7
Hopkins, Timothy Earle, 1924, Ag 21,11:4
Hopkins, Victor J, 1947, D 22,21:1
Hopkins, Vincent C, 1964, Ap 4,28:1
Hopkins, W W, 1938, Mr 9,23:4
Hopkins, Walter, 1945, Ag 25,11:2
Hopkins, Wilber S, 1949, N 28,27:5
Hopkins, William B, 1952, Mr 17,21:4
Hopkins, William F, 1961, F 23,27:4
Hopkins, William H Mrs, 1940, Je 28,19:3
Hopkins, William M, 1942, N 1,52:4
Hopkins, William O, 1958, O 14,37:5
Hopkins, William R, 1958, Je 3,31:2; 1961, F 10,24:2; 1964, D 21,29:4
Hopkins, William T, 1945, Ag 19,40:5
Hopkins, Zoe C Mrs, 1943, Ja 3,43:1
Hopkinson, Alfred Sir, 1939, N 13,19:5
Hopkinson, Charles, 1962, O 17,39:2
Hopkinson, Charles W, 1950, My 16,31:2
Hopkinson, E, 1933, My 4,17:1
Hopkinson, Edward Jr, 1966, Ap 8,31:2
Hopkinson, Ernest Mrs, 1948, Ja 4,52:2
Hopkinson, George, 1950, Jl 5,31:4
Hopkinson, George M, 1962, S 8,19:4
Hopkinson, Henry Mrs, 1953, My 1,21:3
Hopkinson, J H, 1884, Jl 27,3:2
Hopkinson, John N, 1965, Mr 13,25:5
Hopkinson, Oliver, 1905, Mr 11,9:4; 1943, O 10,49:3
Hopkinson, Richard D, 1948, Je 15,27:2
Hopkinson, Robert A (will), 1947, N 23,43:4
Hopkinson, W Morton, 1941, O 16,21:5
Hopkinson, William, 1941, Jl 25,15:4
Hopkirk, Howard W, 1963, My 18,27:2
Hopler, Frank J, 1943, Ap 18,48:6
Hopler, Otho M Sr, 1951, Ja 4,30:2
Hopler, Wheeler, 1948, F 26,23:1
Hopley, Mary C, 1948, D 12,92:7
Hopley, Russell J, 1949, N 24,31:3
Hoplock, Frank, 1946, Je 9,40:6
Hopmann, Albert, 1942, Mr 18,23:5
Hopmans, Petrus, 1951, F 20,25:2
Hopp, Hermann, 1961, Mr 1,33:2
Hopp, Julius, 1937, S 5,II,6:5
Hopp, Leo, 1955, Je 3,23:5
Hopp, Percy R, 1950, Ja 31,24:2
Hoppaugh, William, 1942, D 19,19:3
Hoppe, Alfred B, 1965, Ag 1,76:5
Hoppe, Alice B Mrs, 1946, D 10,31:1
Hoppe, Carl F R, 1948, Jl 7,46:1
Hoppe, Frances M Mrs, 1937, Mr 12,23:4
Hoppe, Hannah Mrs, 1950, N 13,27:2
Hoppe, Herman, 1941, My 23,23:7
Hoppe, James O Dr, 1968, My 30,25:4
Hoppe, John Daniel, 1968, Ja 15,47:3
Hoppe, Otto B, 1942, Ag 5,19:5
Hoppe, Richard, 1950, D 7,33:4
Hoppe, Robert G, 1945, Mr 13,23:5
Hoppe, Willie (Wm Fredk), 1959, F 2,1:3
Hoppen, William R, 1944, D 29,15:4
Hoppenfeld, Jacob, 1964, Je 30,33:4
Hoppenfeld, Joacob Mrs, 1953, N 27,29:6
Hoppenjans, William H, 1949, D 26,29:3
Hoppens, Ernest W, 1947, Jl 31,21:4
Hopper, A Raymond, 1961, D 31,48:7
Hopper, Albert G, 1948, Jl 17,16:8
Hopper, Arthur, 1953, F 4,27:2
Hopper, Arthur J, 1937, My 25,27:3
Hopper, Charles H, 1916, Je 18,18:5
Hopper, Clara F, 1951, Jl 14,13:6
Hopper, D, 1935, S 24,23:1
Hopper, Edna W (funl plans, D 17,37:4), 1959, D 1 39:4
Hopper, Edward, 1967, My 17,1:7
Hopper, Elmer F Sr, 1940, Ag 25,36:5
Hopper, Euphemia W, 1944, Ap 29,15:2
Hopper, Francis W, 1940, S 24,23:1
Hopper, Franklin F, 1950, N 30,33:1
Hopper, Franklin F Mrs, 1937, S 16,25:1
Hopper, George B, 1961, D 7,43:4
Hopper, George H, 1937, D 18,21:5
Hopper, George Whitfield, 1919, Je 22,15:4
Hopper, H Boardman, 1962, Jl 27,25:3
Hopper, Harry C, 1956, Jl 10,31:4
Hopper, Harry W, 1952, N 23,89:2
Hopper, Harry W Mrs, 1941, Ag 13,17:5
Hopper, Hedda (ashes buried, My 4,47:3), 1966, F 32:1
Hopper, Henry, 1939, N 19,39:2
Hopper, Henry S, 1953, My 27,31:5
Hopper, Herbert A, 1937, N 27,17:3
Hopper, Hugh L, 1959, F 14,21:5
Hopper, J Blauvelt, 1943, N 25,25:4
Hopper, James H, 1937, Jl 24,15:6
Hopper, James M, 1956, Ag 30,25:3
Hopper, John A, 1951, Ag 14,23:4
Hopper, John H Col, 1911, My 8,11:5
Hopper, John H Mrs, 1951, F 3,15:3
Hopper, John J, 1923, My 17,19:6
Hopper, John T, 1864, Jl 21,2:6
Hopper, Katie H Mrs, 1964, Ja 9,31:1
Hopper, Lloyd L, 1951, F 4,76:4
Hopper, Loretta B, 1948, Ja 20,23:1
Hopper, Magnus T, 1950, My 4,27:5
Hopper, Mary J, 1955, My 18,31:1
Hopper, Nellie K Mrs, 1940, Je 9,44:3
Hopper, Orin C Sr Mrs, 1950, Ja 21,17:6
Hopper, Orion C, 1941, O 24,24:3
Hopper, Otis L, 1951, Mr 27,29:3
Hopper, Raymond E, 1953, Jl 29,23:6
Hopper, Rex DeV, 1966, Je 22,47:1
Hopper, Richard J (por), 1941, Ja 22,21:4
Hopper, Robert, 1937, Jl 23,6:8
Hopper, Samuel, 1905, Mr 7,9:6
Hopper, Vonnon S Sr, 1948, F 27,21:3
Hopper, W Earl, 1957, Ag 22,27:1
Hopper, Walter E Rev, 1937, Je 1,23:2
Hopper, Walter F, 1959, Ag 2,80:5
Hopper, William, 1943, Ja 15,17:2
Hopper, William De Mattos, 1912, Ja 23,11:4
Hoppes, James G, 1949, D 19,27:2
Hoppes, James L, 1955, N 16,35:2
Hoppin, Bayard C, 1956, N 2,27:5
Hoppin, Benjamin, 1923, Je 5,21:5
Hoppin, Curtis B, 1905, Mr 30,9:6
Hoppin, Frances S, 1940, Mr 6,23:4
Hoppin, Francis L (por), 1941, S 10,23:4
Hoppin, Frank Mrs, 1956, Mr 30,19:2
Hoppin, Frederick S, 1946, F 14,26:2
Hoppin, Gerard B, 1950, Ag 30,31:3
Hoppin, Hamilton Louis, 1921, Ap 19,17:6
Hoppin, Helen A Mrs, 1953, Jl 11,11:4
Hoppin, James Mason Rev Dr (will, N 22,10:7), 1906, N 16,9:6
Hoppin, Jessie R, 1949, Ja 21,21:4
Hoppin, John J, 1961, Ag 30,33:2
Hoppin, Joseph Clark Dr, 1925, F 1,7:2
Hoppin, Mary D Mrs, 1905, Mr 1,9:5
Hoppin, Tracy, 1958, F 17,23:1
Hoppin, William W, 1913, Ja 4,9:3
Hoppin, William W (por), 1948, My 29,15:3
Hoppin, William Warner Mrs, 1923, Mr 12,15:4
Hopping, Andrew D, 1951, Ja 12,27:3
Hopping, Clyde E, 1955, Ja 7,22:3
Hopping, Daniel M, 1939, Mr 26,III,6:8
Hopping, Daniel M Mrs, 1953, Je 10,29:1
Hopping, David S, 1961, N 22,33:2
Hopping, W Frank, 1959, Ja 18,88:4
Hopping, Walter B, 1942, Ag 1,11:6
Hoppman, Frank, 1946, F 12,28:2
Hoppock, Moses A, 1946, S 4,23:4
Hopps, L, 1876, O 26,4:7
Hopshe, Abdour, 1917, Mr 15,11:5
Hopson, George Bailey Rev Dr, 1916, Ag 31,9
Hopson, Harry M, 1942, Mr 27,23:4
Hopson, Howard C, 1949, D 23,21:1
Hopson, William A, 1922, Mr 16,17:5
Hopson, William H, 1950, Mr 10,27:3
Hoptay, Michael Sr, 1951, S 13,31:5
Hopton, Charles, 1951, Je 11,25:3
Hopwood, A, 1928, Jl 2,19:4
Hopwood, Alex I, 1949, D 29,25:3
Hopwood, Clifford M, 1943, Jl 14,19:6
Hopwood, Freeman, 1937, Ja 19,24:3
Hopwood, Herbert G, 1966, S 16,37:1
Hopwood, Irving P, 1925, S 8,21:6

Hopwood, Isaiah B Rev Dr, 1911, Ja 3,11:5
Hopwood, J Osborne, 1955, Ap 6,29:4
Hopwood, John A, 1953, N 26,31:5
Hoquet, Robert J, 1909, O 9,9:5
Hora, John C Mrs, 1949, F 12,17:5
Hora, John O, 1946, Jl 19,19:4
Horack, H Claude, 1958, My 24,21:7
Horacy, William, 1952, Mr 20,29:3
Horak, Agnes Mrs, 1941, S 14,49:2
Horak, Frank J, 1955, Jl 13,25:5
Horak, Harold C, 1949, Ap 22,23:2
Horakh, Albert G, 1950, D 14,35:5
Horan, Albert J, 1960, Jl 17,61:2
Horan, Bernard I, 1937, Ag 31,23:4
Horan, Catherine, 1955, D 21,29:2
Horan, Catherine B Mrs, 1937, Mr 19,23:1
Horan, Dennis A, 1941, Jl 10,19:5
Horan, Edward F, 1942, O 15,23:2
Horan, Frank D, 1961, F 8,31:1
Horan, Frank J, 1965, Jl 19,27:4
Horan, James A, 1938, N 12,15:4; 1938, D 30,16:1
Horan, James F, 1917, D 16,23:1
Horan, James H, 1954, Mr 16,29:5
Horan, John Daniel, 1904, D 3,9:4
Horan, John F, 1942, Je 3,23:4; 1958, My 4,88:7
Horan, John J, 1944, D 12,23:4
Horan, John M, 1938, F 5,15:5
Horan, John N Mrs, 1947, Je 25,25:3
Horan, John S (Bro Lucidius), 1911, F 4,13:4
Horan, John T, 1960, D 24,15:6
Horan, Leo Mrs, 1938, F 1,21:4
Horan, Martin P, 1941, Ap 8,25:2
Horan, Michael A, 1940, Ja 20,15:1
Horan, Michael J, 1953, Ap 5,23:3
Horan, Patrick F, 1937, N 28,II,8:5
Horan, Patrick J, 1954, Jl 16,21:3
Horan, Raymond B, 1957, Ag 23,19:5
Horan, S Gartland, 1947, S 3,25:6
Horan, Thomas J, 1945, Ja 11,23:3; 1946, F 10,42:3
Horan, Thomas P, 1956, S 10,27:4
Horan, William E, 1954, Jl 15,27:4
Horan, William F (funl plans, My 28,31:1; funl, My 30,21:2), 1958, My 27,31:1
Horan, William H, 1906, Jl 13,9:5
Horan, William J, 1952, Ap 30,27:4
Horberg, Carl L, 1955, Ag 20,17:5
Horburgh, Charles S, 1945, Ja 18,19:4
Horch, Charles M, 1944, Ja 9,42:1
Horch, Franz J, 1951, D 16,91:1
Horcheler, William, 1942, D 21,23:3
Hord, Arnold H, 1951, Ja 13,15:2
Hord, Eugene F, 1940, Mr 21,25:6
Hord, John H, 1949, Ap 16,15:6
Hord, Percy F, 1943, Ja 9,13:2
Hord, R C Judge, 1874, F 13,1:4
Hord, William Banfill, 1917, My 1,13:6
Horder, Edward Y, 1947, O 11,17:6
Horder, Thomas J Lord, 1955, Ag 14,80:3
Hordern, Agnes, 1954, D 2,31:2
Hordern, Arch, 1950, Ap 18,31:1
Hordijk, Gerard, 1958, O 17,29:5
Hordyk, Margaret M Mrs, 1953, F 25,27:2
Hore, Amy, 1948, Jl 23,19:5
Hore, William J, 1950, Je 13,27:2
Hore-Belisha, Leslie, 1957, F 17,93:1
Hore-Ruthven, Alex Earl of Gowrie, 1955, My 4,29:3
Horeis, Elizabeth C Mrs, 1941, S 24,23:1
Horeis, Louisa Mrs, 1943, N 22,19:3
Horelick, Samuel, 1962, Mr 7,35:3
Horenburger, Frederick W, 1957, My 9,31:2
Horenburger, Herman, 1941, Ap 20,44:1
Horenstein, Perry S, 1959, Jl 14,29:5
Horetz, Charles, 1953, Ja 27,25:2
Horey, Arthur M, 1937, Ap 14,26:1
Horgan, Andrew B Mrs, 1961, Je 30,25:3
Horgan, Arthur J, 1911, S 20,13:5
Horgan, Charles S (por), 1948, Ag 15,25:3
Horgan, Daniel E Rev, 1951, Jl 12,25:2
Horgan, Francis J, 1939, O 13,23:5
Horgan, Frank D, 1947, D 15,25:4
Horgan, Harry R, 1954, Mr 19,24:4
Horgan, Henry Vincent, 1918, Jl 25,11:4
Horgan, Joe, 1953, Jl 29,23:5
Horgan, John J, 1967, Jl 22,26:1
Horgan, John P, 1948, My 2,76:3
Horgan, Joseph, 1951, N 13,29:3
Horgan, Matthew W, 1940, Je 17,15:3
Horgan, Maurice M, 1946, Ag 14,26:2
Horgan, Michael J, 1952, Jl 3,25:4
Horgan, Stephen H (por), 1941, Ag 31,23:1
Horgan, Thomas P Jr, 1964, F 19,39:3
Horgan, William A, 1962, Ap 11,43:3
Horgen, Peter M, 1955, Mr 2,27:2
Horger, E L, 1943, O 23,13:5
Hori, Tomokazu, 1944, Mr 25,15:5
Horie, William J, 1952, My 26,23:4
Horikiri, Zenbei, 1946, N 27,25:2
Horine, Ernest E, 1941, D 13,21:6
Horine, George L, 1948, D 2,29:3
Horine, Merrill C, 1958, Ja 24,23:2
Horitz, Joseph F, 1961, D 6,47:6
Horkan, Michael J, 1949, D 14,31:5
Horkay, Stephen J, 1960, Ag 17,31:1
Horkheimer, Harold D, 1951, Ja 14,84:5
Horland, Aaron H, 1963, Ap 12,27:2
Horlaville, Leon B, 1952, Ja 9,29:3
Horle, George L, 1953, Ja 31,15:5
Horle, Lawrence C F, 1950, O 29,92:8
Horler, Sidney, 1954, O 28,35:2
Horler, Thomas Sr, 1949, Jl 15,19:3
Horlick, Arabella Mrs (will, Jl 15,17:1), 1938, Jl 10, 31:3
Horlick, James Sir, 1921, My 10,17:4
Horlick, W, 1936, S 26,15:3
Horlick, William Jr (will, Ap 5,26:8), 1940, Ap 2,26:2
Horlick Alex J, 1950, Je 7,29:3
Horling, Joseph A, 1946, D 3,32:2
Horman, Harold A, 1958, N 22,21:5
Horman, John F, 1940, Mr 20,27:2
Hormel, Benjamin F, 1960, Ag 10,31:4
Hormel, George A (por), 1946, Je 6,21:1
Hormel, George A Mrs, 1946, Mr 24,46:6
Hormel, Henry D, 1963, O 26,27:6
Hormel, Herman, 1937, Ja 6,23:4; 1944, My 10,19:2
Hormel, Jay C, 1954, Ag 31,21:1
Hormel, John G, 1960, O 4,43:2
Hormell, Aug, 1940, O 23,23:3
Horn, Arthur, 1956, N 4,87:1
Horn, Arthur F, 1949, F 15,23:1
Horn, Benjamin, 1947, My 4,60:4
Horn, Bertha E, 1955, Je 29,29:2
Horn, Charles A, 1953, My 30,15:5
Horn, Charles J Sr, 1945, Jl 5,13:6
Horn, Charles M, 1958, Ja 21,29:3
Horn, Charles Sr Mrs, 1953, Ja 30,21:2
Horn, Claude S, 1937, My 22,15:4
Horn, David, 1966, O 25,48:2
Horn, David W, 1962, Ag 8,31:5
Horn, E E (Eph), 1877, Ja 4,5:4
Horn, Edgar G, 1949, Ap 3,77:2
Horn, Edward J, 1937, Mr 10,23:6
Horn, Edward T Mrs, 1946, Ag 17,13:1
Horn, Elmer L, 1950, Je 30,23:4
Horn, Ferdinand R, 1939, My 10,23:4
Horn, Francis G, 1943, Ag 6,15:3
Horn, Franklin S Mrs, 1946, Ap 6,17:5
Horn, Fraser M, 1956, N 14,35:5
Horn, Fred W, 1903, Jl 15,7:6
Horn, Frederick, 1950, Ja 5,25:5
Horn, H Schuyler, 1965, Mr 29,33:4
Horn, Harold, 1921, Jl 30,9:5
Horn, Harry J, 1951, D 8,11:1
Horn, Harry S, 1948, N 30,27:4
Horn, Henry (cor, Ag 18,35:2), 1966, Ag 17,39:3
Horn, Henry J, 1940, D 30,17:4
Horn, Henry Lester, 1873, Mr 11,5:3
Horn, Herman E, 1962, N 27,37:2
Horn, John, 1938, Je 13,19:3; 1961, N 2,37:5
Horn, John F, 1938, Jl 6,23:6
Horn, John H, 1871, Ag 10,8:2
Horn, John H Mrs, 1954, Jl 6,23:5
Horn, John J, 1958, Ag 1,21:2
Horn, Joseph V (will, O 22,19:3), 1941, O 14,23:2
Horn, Leslie H, 1960, Jl 19,29:2
Horn, Lester C Mrs, 1938, D 8,28:1
Horn, Martin I, 1951, Ap 3,27:1
Horn, Martin L, 1950, O 10,31:6
Horn, Mary A, 1941, My 10,15:2
Horn, Max, 1944, N 27,23:4; 1952, Ag 5,19:3; 1959, My 22,27:3
Horn, Melchior H, 1952, N 30,87:3
Horn, Morris (por), 1945, D 27,19:4
Horn, Nellie L Mrs, 1947, O 4,17:3
Horn, Oscar J, 1952, Jl 9,27:4
Horn, Ralph C, 1950, My 29,17:4
Horn, Raymond E, 1960, Jl 18,27:4
Horn, Richard G, 1947, S 22,23:5
Horn, Robert J, 1952, S 2,23:4
Horn, Roy, 1947, N 25,29:2
Horn, Sam, 1952, Mr 8,13:3
Horn, Samuel S, 1942, Mr 13,20:3
Horn, Sydney B, 1949, Jl 7,25:1
Horn, Walter B, 1912, O 12,11:6
Horn, Walter L (por), 1938, D 30,15:1
Horn, Walter L, 1939, Ja 1,25:1
Horn, Whittier E, 1952, Ap 26,23:3
Horn, Wilbur F Dr, 1937, O 17,II,9:2
Horn, William, 1941, Je 10,23:4
Horn, William C, 1959, My 24,88:5
Horn, Winnie, 1910, N 29,11:4
Hornaday, Frank A, 1951, F 10,13:1
Hornaday, J P, 1935, D 25,27:4
Hornaday, John A, 1950, N 29,33:1
Hornaday, Josephine C Mrs, 1939, Ja 17,21:4
Hornaday, W D, 1942, D 7,27:3
Hornaday, William T Dr (por), 1937, Mr 7,II,9:1
Hornady, John R, 1948, Mr 2,23:5
Hornbeck, Arthur L, 1951, N 20,31:2
Hornbeck, Calvin D, 1953, Je 2,29:4
Hornbeck, Charles H, 1940, F 16,19:4
Hornbeck, Daniel C, 1940, Je 2,44:7
Hornbeck, Fred C, 1940, Mr 24,31:1
Hornbeck, Harvey F, 1937, N 19,23:2
Hornbeck, Joel Mrs, 1948, Je 2,29:5
Hornbeck, John W, 1951, Mr 1,28:2
Hornbeck, Stanley K, 1966, D 12,47:4
Hornbeck, Thomas B, 1963, S 15,87:1
Hornberger, Charles F, 1947, N 5,27:2
Hornberger, Gustav O, 1958, Jl 17,27:2
Hornblass, Baruch M (will), 1945, Ja 20,12:3
Hornblow, Arthur Sr, 1942, My 7,19:4
Hornblower, Chief Justice, 1864, Je 14,2:2
Hornblower, E T, 1901, D 20,9:6
Hornblower, Emily A S Mrs (will), 1938, Jl 13,18:8
Hornblower, George Sanford Mrs, 1968, Ja 22,44:2
Hornblower, Henry (por), 1941, Ap 13,39:1
Hornblower, Joseph C, 1908, Ag 26,7:6
Hornblower, Ralph, 1960, S 19,31:4
Hornblower, Ralph Jr Mrs, 1960, F 8,29:4
Hornblower, W H, 1883, Jl 17,4:7
Hornblower, W H Rev, 1883, My 22,8:3
Hornblower, William B, 1957, Ag 9,19:5
Hornblower, William Butler Judge, 1914, Je 17,11:1
Hornbostel, Charles J, 1945, Jl 24,23:2
Hornbostel, Hans G, 1957, Ap 3,31:6
Hornbostel, Henry, 1961, D 14,43:3
Hornbrook, James J, 1942, O 2,25:3
Hornbruch, Hugo Mrs, 1946, Ap 23,21:1
Hornby, Albert, 1925, D 18,23:3
Hornby, Cecil R, 1952, Je 9,23:4
Hornby, Frederick H (por), 1942, O 20,21:1
Hornby, Harry P Sr, 1948, D 5,92:4
Horne, Aaron C, 1952, N 28,25:2
Horne, Alton A, 1956, O 29,29:3
Horne, Ashley Col, 1913, O 24,11:5
Horne, Bernard C Mrs (Bessie Anthony), 1912, N 23,15:6
Horne, Berry H, 1959, Jl 2,25:2
Horne, Charles, 1950, Ap 17,23:2
Horne, Charles E Mrs, 1947, Mr 27,27:2
Horne, Charles F (por), 1942, S 16,23:5
Horne, Charles H, 1951, Ap 27,23:2
Horne, Cyril Morton Capt, 1916, F 2,11:4
Horne, Dentz, 1956, Jl 13,19:4
Horne, E H, 1953, Mr 17,29:1
Horne, Edmund C, 1948, Ap 26,23:2
Horne, Edward A, 1950, Mr 27,23:3
Horne, Elizabeth M Mrs (will), 1939, Ja 25,19:1
Horne, Frank A, 1939, Mr 23,23:5
Horne, Frank A Mrs, 1954, Ja 16,15:5
Horne, Franklin J, 1959, Jl 26,69:3
Horne, Frederick J, 1959, O 21,43:1
Horne, Frederick R, 1963, N 3,89:1
Horne, George (Sonny), 1959, S 29,39:4
Horne, George A, 1959, My 15,29:1
Horne, H Field, 1948, N 29,23:2
Horne, Hal (por), 1955, Je 9,29:2
Horne, Henry P Mrs, 1956, D 2,87:2
Horne, Herman H (por), 1946, Ag 17,13:4
Horne, Herman H Mrs, 1951, My 26,17:3
Horne, I S, 1959, S 2,29:4
Horne, Ida M Mrs, 1938, S 15,25:5
Horne, Jacob W, 1953, F 6,20:5
Horne, James A, 1944, F 5,15:4
Horne, James Q, 1946, O 7,31:6
Horne, James W, 1942, Je 30,21:2
Horne, John A, 1921, Ja 7,13:2
Horne, Joseph (will, Ap 8,28:3), 1948, Ap 3,15:5
Horne, Joseph A, 1950, O 4,31:4
Horne, Joseph A Mrs (will), 1964, Ag 25,37:7
Horne, Lord of Stirkoke, 1929, Ag 15,23:1
Horne, Marsh Mrs, 1958, N 29,21:5
Horne, Mathryn E, 1947, Ja 9,23:4
Horne, Mina, 1967, Ap 25,43:3
Horne, Ottora, 1956, N 29,35:4
Horne, R H, 1884, Mr 18,5:4
Horne, Robert L, 1954, O 1,23:2
Horne, Thomas K B, 1941, D 2,24:2
Horne, Viscount (por), 1940, S 4,23:3
Horne, William D, 1960, D 7,43:1
Horne, William D Mrs, 1938, N 17,25:2
Horne, William E, 1955, Je 30,25:3
Horne, William T, 1944, Ap 13,19:3
Horne, William W Mrs, 1947, Ap 10,25:2
Hornecker, Henry, 1951, Mr 13,31:3
Hornedo, Alfredo, 1964, Mr 17,35:3
Horneman, Paul, 1965, Mr 1,27:2
Horner, Alex M, 1959, O 29,33:4
Horner, Arthur, 1968, S 5,47:3
Horner, Benjamin L, 1924, S 3,17:1
Horner, Benjamin R, 1939, F 5,40:4
Horner, Charles F, 1967, F 8,31:1
Horner, Clarence H, 1961, N 26,87:4
Horner, Clarence H Mrs, 1958, Je 22,76:2
Horner, David A Mrs, 1953, D 15,39:5
Horner, E W Mrs, 1879, Jl 12,5:5
Horner, Frank W, 1939, F 10,23:3
Horner, G R, 1939, N 9,23:5
Horner, Henry L, 1940, O 7,1:3
Horner, Horace K, 1968, My 21,47:3
Horner, Howard O, 1952, Jl 13,60:2
Horner, J S, 1883, F 9,3:7
Horner, J V (Vic), 1955, D 24,13:3
Horner, Jake, 1951, S 23,85:5
Horner, John, 1942, Ag 2,16:4
Horner, John W, 1904, Ja 26,9:6
Horner, John W Mrs, 1968, O 26,37:5
Horner, Joseph Jr, 1960, S 20,39:2
Horner, Julia S B Mrs, 1961, D 7,43:4

Horner, Justus, 1937, Ag 27,19:5
Horner, Leonard S, 1943, Ag 2,15:3
Horner, Louis E, 1950, Ja 17,27:2
Horner, Norman G, 1954, Mr 9,27:1
Horner, Pierre J, 1949, Mr 24,27:4
Horner, Robert J, 1922, F 27,13:6
Horner, Robert L, 1945, D 17,21:4
Horner, S, 1952, Ag 19,12:2
Horner, Samuel, 1912, N 4,11:5
Horner, Seward L, 1962, Ap 25,39:4
Horner, Sidney A, 1949, D 31,15:2
Horner, Simpson W Mrs, 1947, Ja 29,25:3
Horner, William J, 1950, Mr 27,23:3
Horner, William Mrs, 1945, N 6,19:5
Horner, William S, 1944, N 17,19:1
Horney, Karen, 1952, D 5,27:2
Hornfeck, Herman G, 1956, Jl 19,27:1
Hornfeck, Maximillian R, 1968, O 27,82:8
Hornickel, Gottlieb Mrs, 1953, O 8,29:4
Hornig, Elise Mrs, 1937, F 2,23:6
Hornig, Elmer O, 1962, Ja 11,33:4
Hornig, George R, 1954, Je 3,27:2
Hornig, Herman, 1942, Je 21,36:7
Horniman, Annie, 1937, Ag 9,19:4
Horning, George Mrs, 1946, Ap 24,26:2
Horning, John O Mrs, 1952, Je 23,19:5
Horning, Louis P, 1947, D 31,15:3
Horning, V H, 1948, D 6,25:2
Horning, William A, 1959, Mr 3,33:3
Hornlake, Frank L, 1942, S 12,15:4
Hornor, Abraham, 1939, N 16,23:2
Hornor, Townsend, 1923, Ag 6,11:2
Hornor, William M, 1937, Ja 19,23:4
Hornsby, Bertram, 1943, Jl 2,19:3
Hornsby, Don, 1950, My 23,29:4
Hornsby, Hubert, 1939, Je 5,17:3
Hornsby, John A, 1939, Je 6,23:4
Hornsby, Leslie H, 1966, Jl 4,15:3
Hornsby, Marion A, 1947, F 2,57:4
Hornsby, Rogers, 1963, Ja 7,8:2
Hornsby, Rogers Jr, 1949, D 24,28:2
Hornsrud, Christopher, 1960, D 14,39:2
Hornstein, Ignus O (por), 1937, D 31,15:1
Hornstein, Joseph, 1951, Je 19,29:3
Hornstein, Samuel L, 1965, Jl 4,37:2
Hornstine, Harry H, 1962, Ap 15,80:7
Hornstrater, William H, 1947, D 2,29:3
Hornthal, De Witt L, 1905, S 22,9:7
Hornung, Charles D Mrs, 1953, S 2,25:4
Hornung, E W, 1921, Ap 8,13:4
Hornung, Edward, 1947, Mr 31,23:4
Hornung, Elizabeth Mrs, 1940, Mr 21,25:3
Hornung, Howard V, 1950, D 18,31:3
Hornung, J Thomas, 1939, N 26,43:2
Hornung, Otto, 1958, O 16,37:5
Hornung, Paul, 1942, S 29,23:5
Hornung, William H, 1943, Jl 20,19:3
Horobin, George J, 1947, Ja 31,23:3
Horobin, Joseph T, 1942, F 4,20:2
Horovitz, Bela, 1955, Mr 9,27:4
Horowitz, Abraham, 1957, D 10,35:1
Horowitz, Barnet, 1953, Je 12,27:3
Horowitz, Benjamin, 1954, My 16,86:5
Horowitz, Charles, 1940, Jl 31,17:3; 1965, My 10,33:2
Horowitz, Charles S, 1950, Ap 29,15:6
Horowitz, Edward, 1946, Ap 29,21:3
Horowitz, Harris, 1955, Je 28,27:4
Horowitz, Harry, 1962, Ja 4,33:2
Horowitz, Henry, 1955, O 2,87:2
Horowitz, Isaac, 1961, Mr 23,33:2
Horowitz, Isador, 1964, Ap 29,41:3
Horowitz, Isidore, 1956, D 15,25:4
Horowitz, Israel, 1957, O 15,33:1
Horowitz, Israel S, 1958, F 2,86:2
Horowitz, Jack, 1952, N 24,23:4
Horowitz, Jacob, 1953, S 19,15:3
Horowitz, Joseph, 1947, Ap 16,25:3; 1949, My 6,25:1; 1962, S 9,84:5
Horowitz, Joseph N, 1946, S 6,21:2
Horowitz, Julius L, 1965, Ja 18,35:4
Horowitz, L George, 1959, F 9,29:3
Horowitz, Leonard B, 1954, D 9,33:2
Horowitz, Leopold, 1950, Jl 6,27:2
Horowitz, Louis, 1922, F 15,13:2; 1941, Mr 25,26:1
Horowitz, Louis J, 1956, D 3,1:2; 1962, My 31,27:2
Horowitz, Marcus I, 1949, Ja 10,25:5
Horowitz, Mitchell A, 1960, S 4,69:1
Horowitz, Moses, 1910, Mr 7,9:5
Horowitz, Moses A, 1956, Ag 15,29:4
Horowitz, Murray A, 1960, Ag 10,31:3
Horowitz, Nathan, 1943, N 29,19:4
Horowitz, Nathan Mrs, 1965, Je 19,29:4
Horowitz, Oscar, 1962, My 7,31:2
Horowitz, Philip, 1946, Ja 18,20:2; 1959, D 22,31:4; 1965, Ja 3,85:1
Horowitz, Phineas, 1946, Mr 27,27:3
Horowitz, Samuel I, 1937, N 18,23:6
Horowitz, Samuel Mrs, 1948, N 9,27:3; 1958, D 31, 38:4
Horowitz, Solomon, 1958, My 20,33:2
Horowitz, William R, 1952, My 6,29:2
Horpy, Isaac, 1958, N 30,87:1
Horr, A R, 1958, N 6,37:1
Horr, Clarence W, 1955, Jl 8,23:3
Horr, Edward F, 1955, F 24,27:5
Horr, George E, 1961, Je 29,33:5
Horr, John V, 1948, Mr 18,27:5
Horr, L William, 1941, Ja 15,23:2
Horr, Marquis F (Bill), 1955, Jl 2,15:5
Horrabin, James F, 1962, Mr 3,21:3
Horrax, Gilbert, 1957, S 29,86:6
Horre, George W, 1939, Ap 9,III,7:1
Horre, George W H, 1961, S 2,15:5
Horre, William H, 1960, My 31,31:3
Horre, William H Mrs, 1951, S 7,29:3
Horrell, Martin, 1957, My 29,27:5
Horridge, Thomas G, 1938, Jl 26,19:5
Horrigan, Bernard E, 1948, Ja 11,56:2
Horrigan, Edward F, 1945, N 20,21:2
Horrigan, Timothy J, 1938, Ap 23,15:4
Horrmann, Curt A, 1945, D 10,14:5
Horrmann, Frances Mrs, 1940, F 13,23:5
Horrock, Erwin N, 1956, D 28,21:2
Horrocks, Edward E, 1940, My 7,25:3
Horrocks, Frederick H, 1954, N 15,27:2
Horrocks, Harry, 1944, Ja 30,37:1
Horrocks, James H, 1941, Ag 15,17:3
Horrocks, William, 1941, Ja 28,19:4
Horrworth, Charles A, 1967, Ag 1,33:3
Horry, William S Mrs, 1951, Ja 20,15:5
Horsburgh, Barbara, 1953, N 23,27:4
Horsburgh, Gordon S Capt, 1937, O 27,31:6
Horsburgh, James J, 1947, Je 14,15:1
Horsburgh, Robert H, 1949, F 13,76:6
Horsburgh, Walter N, 1941, Mr 26,23:5
Horsch, Charles E, 1949, Je 14,32:2
Horsey, Frederick B, 1937, O 7,27:4
Horsey, Henry H, 1942, Ja 7,19:3
Horsfall, Bessie, 1954, Ja 24,85:1
Horsfall, Herbert, 1955, Ag 23,23:5
Horsfall, Lloyd P, 1949, D 27,23:5
Horsfall, R Bruce, 1948, Mr 28,48:6
Horsfall, St John, 1949, Ag 21,V,3:7
Horsfall, Zaidee T, 1955, Je 11,15:3
Horsfield, Frederick H T, 1939, D 28,21:4
Horsley, C E (see also F 29), 1876, Mr 3,8:6
Horsley, Cecil D, 1953, Mr 11,29:4
Horsley, J Shelton, 1946, Ap 8,27:3
Horsley, Robert S, 1962, O 3,41:2
Horsley, Terence, 1949, Ap 25,3:2
Horsman, Edward Imeson Jr, 1918, Jl 29,11:6
Horsman, John, 1883, Ag 10,5:5
Horsnell Horace, 1949, F 12,17:6
Horst, Andrew L, 1940, My 31,19:4
Horst, E Clemens, 1940, My 25,17:3
Horst, George H, 1946, Je 1,13:2
Horst, Henry W, 1953, O 10,17:1
Horst, John, 1951, S 30,74:4
Horst, Louis, 1964, Ja 24,24:2
Horst, Miles, 1968, Ap 8,47:2
Horst, Rudolf H, 1941, N 14,23:6
Horster, Charles Mrs, 1944, F 23,19:5
Horstick, Simon M, 1958, My 23,23:3
Horstman, August George Dr, 1917, S 28,11:6
Horstman, Carl F, 1954, Jl 29,23:4
Horstman, Richard A, 1952, N 4,29:1
Horstman G M, 1927, F 17,23:5
Horstmann, Alfred, 1948, Ag 14,13:2
Horstmann, Ignatius F, 1908, My 14,9:6
Horstmann, Ignatius J, 1962, Ap 15,80:8
Horstmann, J H, 1954, F 14,92:1
Horstmann, Lali Mrs, 1954, Ag 26,27:6
Horstmann, William H Mrs, 1960, Ag 5,23:4
Horswell, Charles, 1943, D 24,13:2
Hort, Walter M, 1957, S 16,31:5
Horta, Victor, 1947, S 9,31:6
Horter, Charles M, 1938, Ap 13,25:3
Horter, Earl, 1940, Mr 30,15:1
Horter, John, 1937, D 19,II,8:8
Horthy, Eugene, 1953, N 25,23:2
Horthy, Nicholas (funl, F 21,27:4), 1957, F 10,1:6
Horthy, Nicholas Mrs, 1959, Ja 10,17:5
Horti, Michael, 1961, N 12,86:7
Horton, A Bart, 1947, S 16,23:4
Horton, Albert J, 1958, Mr 7,23:4
Horton, Alexander Mrs, 1946, Ja 19,14:2
Horton, Alfred M, 1955, Ap 29,23:3
Horton, Andrew Z, 1944, O 30,19:5
Horton, Arthur, 1944, My 15,19:5
Horton, Arthur B Mrs, 1951, S 28,31:5
Horton, Arthur E, 1948, Ag 9,19:4
Horton, Arthur W, 1949, F 5,15:6
Horton, Arthur W Jr Mrs, 1956, Ja 22,88:6
Horton, Asadata D, 1965, Mr 7,83:1
Horton, Benjamin, 1942, Je 7,42:1
Horton, Benjamin J, 1963, Je 30,56:5
Horton, Benjamin J Mrs, 1947, Ap 5,19:5
Horton, Betsey, 1880, Ja 5,5:6
Horton, Bryson D, 1945, D 15,17:2
Horton, Burrett W, 1908, Je 21,11:7
Horton, Caroline L, 1903, Ag 30,9:6
Horton, Charles A, 1955, Mr 1,25:1
Horton, Charles B, 1959, Jl 19,69:1
Horton, Charles B 2d Mrs, 1963, Je 15,23:6
Horton, Charles C, 1943, Ap 15,25:1
Horton, Charles F, 1944, Je 3,13:1
Horton, Charles M, 1952, Jl 1,23:2
Horton, Charles R, 1957, N 27,31:1
Horton, Charles S, 1944, D 16,15:4
Horton, chas B, 1944, N 5,54:3
Horton, Chase Mrs, 1967, O 1,84:3
Horton, Chauncey F Mrs, 1945, S 6,25:5
Horton, Clarence H, 1949, F 26,15:1
Horton, Clark W, 1966, D 10,38:6
Horton, Clinton T, 1953, Ja 27,25:1
Horton, Cornelius J, 1940, Je 21,21:2
Horton, Cornelius J Mrs, 1947, Ag 8,17:3
Horton, Daniel E, 1954, N 6,17:4
Horton, David, 1954, O 3,87:2
Horton, Douglas Mrs, 1944, Je 6,17:1
Horton, Douglas Rev Dr, 1968, Ag 23,39:1
Horton, Dudley R, 1952, Ag 16,15:4
Horton, Edmund P, 1949, Ag 16,23:5
Horton, Edson J, 1948, Ag 28,15:2
Horton, Edward A Jr, 1950, Je 28,27:4
Horton, Edward G Mrs, 1947, Ja 6,23:2
Horton, Edward J, 1942, Ja 28,19:1
Horton, Elliott A, 1951, N 26,25:5
Horton, Elmer G, 1949, My 31,23:1
Horton, Elsie, 1947, Ag 18,17:4
Horton, Elvin H Mrs, 1949, My 4,29:1
Horton, Ernest A Mrs, 1952, N 6,29:5
Horton, Eugene E, 1947, Ap 23,25:1
Horton, Ezra J, 1941, S 26,24:2
Horton, Frank, 1940, Je 27,23:3
Horton, Frank J, 1946, O 7,31:2
Horton, Frank L, 1942, Mr 31,21:4
Horton, Frank N, 1965, Ap 5,31:6
Horton, Frank O, 1948, Ag 18,25:2
Horton, Franklin, 1942, My 21,19:5
Horton, Fred B Mrs, 1954, Jl 21,27:4
Horton, Frederic E, 1954, F 25,31:1
Horton, Frederic J, 1962, N 25,86:4
Horton, Frederic L, 1964, F 10,27:3
Horton, Frost, 1944, Mr 25,15:4
Horton, George (por), 1942, Je 10,21:3
Horton, George A, 1945, F 5,15:5; 1960, Ap 4,2
Horton, George B, 1938, Ag 18,20:2
Horton, George Mrs, 1953, Ap 17,25:2
Horton, George S, 1940, Jl 22,17:4
Horton, George T (por), 1945, Mr 20,19:3
Horton, George W, 1913, S 17,9:3
Horton, Grace, 1943, F 2,19:4
Horton, H Albert, 1948, Jl 28,23:3
Horton, H Clark, 1938, O 1,17:4
Horton, H Frost, 1946, My 17,21:1
Horton, H H, 1934, Jl 3,19:1
Horton, Hal, 1948, N 23,29:2
Horton, Harold M, 1951, S 26,31:5
Horton, Harriette, 1948, O 1,25:2
Horton, Harry A, 1945, Ja 5,15:2
Horton, Harry C, 1941, Ja 5,44:8
Horton, Harry L, 1915, D 18,11:5; 1956, My 1
Horton, Harry M, 1948, O 29,25:2
Horton, Harry M Mrs, 1942, Jl 10,17:3
Horton, Henry, 1939, Ag 14,15:5
Horton, Henry A, 1948, Jl 3,15:3
Horton, Henry P, 1947, F 24,19:1; 1949, S 29,
Horton, Herbert L, 1957, D 30,23:1
Horton, Herman D, 1959, My 2,23:5
Horton, Hiram C, 1950, O 22,93:1
Horton, Howard L V Mrs, 1954, D 2,31:2
Horton, J Warren, 1967, My 11,47:3
Horton, James, 1905, Je 29,9:6
Horton, James B, 1945, Ag 31,17:2
Horton, James H Mrs, 1953, Ja 30,21:1
Horton, James Madison, 1914, Je 27,7:6
Horton, Jay T, 1942, N 13,23:4
Horton, Jesse P, 1953, Ja 12,27:3
Horton, Jeter R, 1939, Ja 5,23:4
Horton, John Sr Mrs, 1948, Ag 10,21:4
Horton, L, 1926, D 16,27:3
Horton, Leroy D, 1945, Jl 23,19:5
Horton, Lester (trb, N 8,II,15:7), 1953, N 3,
Horton, Lydiard, 1945, Ja 20,11:5
Horton, Max, 1951, Jl 31,22:4
Horton, McDavid, 1941, O 18,19:5
Horton, Melvin R, 1948, D 11,15:5
Horton, Myer B, 1957, Ag 26,23:4
Horton, Nathan Clarence, 1913, N 5,13:6
Horton, O R, 1939, Je 16,23:4
Horton, Ralph, 1967, Jl 16,65:1
Horton, Ralph C, 1949, N 2,12:2
Horton, Ralph E, 1943, D 31,16:8
Horton, Richard F, 1948, O 14,29:3
Horton, Robert E, 1945, Ap 23,19:3
Horton, Roderick G, 1939, Je 22,23:5
Horton, Roy A, 1953, Mr 16,19:1
Horton, S Wentworth, 1960, O 4,43:4
Horton, Salmon, 1937, Mr 21,II,9:2
Horton, Samuel B, 1942, N 4,23:1
Horton, Sarah A K Mrs, 1942, Ap 16,21:5
Horton, Sarah Mrs, 1938, S 6,21:3
Horton, Spencer T, 1948, Je 18,23:4
Horton, Theodore S, 1939, Ap 16,III,7:1
Horton, Thomas A, 1959, Ja 11,88:5
Horton, Vosburgh Mrs, 1949, N 2,27:2
Horton, W E, 1935, S 14,15:1
Horton, W H, 1902, D 13,9:5; 1928, Mr 7,2

Horton, Walter, 1952, Ap 1,29:4
Horton, Walter M, 1966, Ap 24,86:6
Horton, Walter S, 1944, Mr 14,19:4
Horton, Wilkins P, 1950, F 2,27:1
Horton, William, 1947, Jl 8,23:4
Horton, William A, 1940, O 30,23:3
Horton, William B, 1949, My 22,88:8
Horton, William E, 1938, O 25,23:3
Horton, William S S, 1959, Je 23,33:2
Horton, William T, 1956, Mr 13,27:2
Horton, William T Mrs, 1955, N 11,25:3
Horton, William W, 1950, D 12,33:5
Horton-Billard, Peter H, 1951, Je 10,92:4
Horty, Peter A, 1942, Ja 13,22:2
Horty, Thomas, 1949, My 13,24:2
Hortz, Phil H, 1948, F 21,13:4
Horvat, Casimir, 1960, Ja 5,31:4
Horvath, Dmitri Gen, 1937, My 17,19:1
Horvath, Imre, 1958, F 4,29:1
Horvath, Joseph (will, D 24,15:6), 1937, My 11,25:3
Horvath, Julius, 1945, Mr 16,15:4
Horvath, Kolman C, 1939, N 22,21:3
Horvath, Louis Mrs, 1947, O 21,23:2
Horvath, Michael H, 1945, F 17,13:3
Horvath, Rudolph J, 1940, S 29,43:3
Horvath, Stephanie, 1960, Ap 28,35:4
Horvath, Walter J, 1957, N 29,29:2
Horvitz, Aaron, 1968, S 18,47:1
Horvitz, Samuel A, 1956, Je 16,19:4
Horvitz, William A Dr, 1968, My 16,47:3
Horwedel, Francis X, 1944, N 8,17:5
Horwich, Benjamin, 1942, O 4,53:2
Horwich, Bernard, 1949, Ap 24,76:3
Horwich, Joseph (will), 1954, D 31,14:5
Horwich, Joseph (cor on Dec 31 obituary), 1955, Ja 7,15:6
Horwill, Edward T, 1924, Ag 9,11:6; 1924, Ag 10,24:4
Horwill, Emily M Mrs, 1940, S 5,23:4
Horwin, C Jerome, 1954, Ap 26,25:4
Horwin, Murray, 1956, Ag 3,19:4
Horwitz, Alfred S, 1954, F 4,25:5
Horwitz, Benjamin Mrs, 1907, Je 2,7:6
Horwitz, Charles K (por), 1949, Je 15,29:2
Horwitz, Gene Mrs, 1953, Je 22,21:4
Horwitz, James W, 1947, Jl 30,21:2
Horwitz, Julius, 1951, F 2,24:2
Horwitz, Max, 1945, Ja 23,19:2
Horwitz, Nathan, 1947, O 15,27:3
Horwitz, Orville Dr, 1913, Ja 29,11:5
Horwitz, Richard, 1950, D 15,32:4
Horwitz, Richard Mrs, 1957, Mr 6,31:4
Horwitz, Samuel, 1954, N 21,87:1
Horwitz, Samuel A, 1948, O 26,31:4
Horwood, Charles S, 1942, Jl 22,19:3
Horwood, Murray P, 1957, Je 9,88:8
Horwood, William (por), 1943, N 19,19:3
Horwood, William H, 1945, Ap 8,35:1
Hosack, Dr, 1871, Mr 7,5:2
Hosch, John H, 1956, O 29,29:5
osch, John H 3d, 1953, S 14,19:4
oschna, Carl, 1911, D 24,II,9:4
oschske, Rose, 1924, Jl 8,19:3
ose, Titus S, 1948, N 25,31:2
osek, Frank Mrs, 1954, Jl 17,13:6
oser, Frank A, 1943, D 1,21:6
osey, Charles M Rev, 1937, Ja 1,23:3
osey, John, 1954, Ja 22,27:2
osey, John J, 1947, S 25,29:5
osford, A J, 1877, Ag 9,5:6
osford, Charles F Jr, 1953, Ap 13,27:5
osford, Charles F Sr, 1941, Ap 5,17:4
osford, Harry, 1941, Ag 5,19:5
osford, Harry Jr, 1945, Ag 9,21:4
osford, Harry P, 1943, Ja 7,19:5
osford, Howard L, 1963, Ag 31,17:6
osford, Roger F, 1955, N 16,35:1
osford, Samuel C, 1875, Je 29,4:7
osford, Samuel E, 1912, Ja 12,13:6
sford, Willard D Sr, 1951, D 26,25:1
sford, William B, 1940, O 28,17:6
shour, Harvey S, 1951, O 12,27:2
sic, James F, 1959, Ja 15,33:3
sie, Alexander Sir, 1925, Mr 11,21:5
sie, Robert, 1959, Je 27,23:5
singer, George N, 1944, F 17,19:2
sken, Robert J, 1945, Ja 18,19:3
skin, Harold F, 1948, Ag 24,23:2
sking, Albert J, 1941, S 7,51:4
sking, E R C, 1945, S 3,23:4
sking, Floyd J, 1962, Jl 6,25:2
sking, Walter P, 1940, O 21,17:6
sking, William, 1943, F 5,21:2
skins, A H Sir Adm, 1901, Je 22,9:6
skins, Al, 1947, Je 22,52:6
skins, Carl S, 1947, Jl 6,40:5
skins, Doris, 1953, O 4,88:2
skins, Fred, 1966, Ap 21,39:4
skins, Halford L, 1967, S 15,47:3
skins, James D, 1960, Ap 4,29:2
skins, John C, 1961, F 19,86:2
skins, John D C Brig-Gen, 1937, Mr 3,23:5
skins, John H, 1957, F 10,86:7
skins, John M, 1944, Ag 2,15:5; 1964, Mr 31,35:1

Hoskins, John P, 1944, My 27,15:6
Hoskins, Roy G, 1964, N 8,89:1
Hoskins, Thomas L, 1940, O 3,25:6
Hoskins, Tracy M Mrs, 1957, O 5,17:4
Hoskins, William L Mrs, 1942, O 6,23:2
Hoskins, Winfield S, 1961, Jl 6,29:1
Hoskinson, Orien E, 1960, D 10,23:4
Hosler, Fred M, 1940, O 25,21:5
Hosler, Fred W, 1952, O 31,25:2
Hosler, Paul M Mrs, 1950, F 21,25:1
Hosler, William E, 1952, O 5,89:1
Hosley, H Everton, 1956, N 22,33:2
Hosley, Henry H Com, 1908, Ja 7,7:5
Hosmer, A A Col, 1902, F 2,7:6
Hosmer, Abby, 1939, S 1,17:5
Hosmer, Charles B, 1942, N 17,25:2
Hosmer, Clare C, 1940, My 7,25:2
Hosmer, Elwood B, 1946, O 26,17:5
Hosmer, Field Linn, 1914, Ja 10,9:6
Hosmer, Frank A, 1918, My 29,13:5
Hosmer, Frank H (Sept 26), 1965, O 11,61:2
Hosmer, G W, 1881, Jl 8,2:7
Hosmer, George E, 1944, Je 28,23:4
Hosmer, George W Dr, 1914, Je 4,11:6
Hosmer, Harriet, 1908, F 22,7:5
Hosmer, J B, 1878, S 26,5:6
Hosmer, James Ray Col, 1923, O 18,19:2
Hosmer, Joseph B Mrs, 1947, Jl 3,21:5
Hosmer, O E, 1879, Ja 9,5:2
Hosmer, Orick M, 1938, My 3,23:1
Hosmer, Phil B, 1942, N 4,23:4
Hosmer, Ralph S, 1963, Jl 20,19:5
Hosmer, Sidney, 1951, Ag 28,23:2
Hosmer, W H C, 1877, My 24,5:4
Hosmer, Walter A, 1948, Je 6,72:6
Hosni, Ahmed, 1961, D 28,27:2
Hosokowa, Ona Mrs, 1940, Ag 12,15:5
Hosp, Ferdinand J, 1955, Jl 17,60:7
Hospitalet, Tomas B, 1954, Mr 19,24:5
Hoss, Elijah Embree Bp, 1919, Ap 24,11:4
Hossack, Archibald B, 1964, Jl 3,21:2
Hossain, Syud, 1949, F 26,15:7
Hossenlopp, Frank S, 1942, N 26,27:2
Hossler, Melvin, 1946, O 12,19:2
Hossler, William H, 1939, Ja 15,38:4
Hoste, Julius (funl, F 6,19:6), 1954, F 2,27:3
Hoster, Herman A, 1951, My 16,35:2
Hoster, Theodore G Mrs, 1968, D 14,45:3
Hoster, William, 1942, Ap 16,21:3
Hostetler, Joseph C, 1958, D 3,37:5
Hostetter, D Herbert Jr Mrs, 1950, Je 13,28:2
Hostetter, David H Jr, 1950, Mr 14,25:2
Hostetter, Gordon L, 1962, F 25,88:4
Hostetter, Harry B, 1946, D 28,15:3
Hostetter, Harry G, 1948, D 25,17:3
Hostetter, T R, 1902, Ag 4,7:6
Hostettler, Ernest G, 1951, O 18,25:5
Hostler, Arthur C, 1940, F 9,19:4
Hostlot, L E Rev, 1884, F 2,5:4
Hostrup, Jacob W, 1955, My 26,31:2
Hotaling, Alice L, 1948, O 19,27:1
Hotaling, Arthur, 1941, My 10,15:3
Hotaling, Arthur Mrs, 1953, Ja 16,24:3
Hotaling, Charles H, 1945, S 13,23:4
Hotaling, Edward M, 1946, Ag 7,27:3
Hotaling, Elmer E, 1950, Jl 23,56:3
Hotaling, Elmer P, 1947, My 18,60:8
Hotaling, Ezra V, 1942, Ag 12,19:5
Hotaling, George P, 1938, S 28,25:3
Hotaling, Herbert C, 1938, Ap 16,13:2
Hotaling, Jane A Mrs, 1938, N 20,39:3
Hotaling, William, 1937, D 9,25:2
Hotchener, Henry Mrs, 1945, Mr 7,22:2
Hotchiss, Edgar J, 1942, D 9,27:1
Hotchkill, Willard E, 1956, S 20,29:7
Hotchkin, Walter B Col, 1916, Je 7,13:5
Hotchkin, Walter B Col (funl, Je 12,11:2), 1916, Je 10,11:6
Hotchkiss, B B, 1885, F 15,2:2
Hotchkiss, Berkeley, 1960, My 3,39:1
Hotchkiss, Bruce Mrs (D Larson), 1965, Mr 2,38:7
Hotchkiss, Charles E, 1939, Ja 18,19:4
Hotchkiss, Charles Truman Gen, 1914, Ag 29,9:6
Hotchkiss, Charles W, 1916, O 30,9:4
Hotchkiss, Charles W Jr, 1963, N 10,86:5
Hotchkiss, Chauncey Crafts, 1920, D 16,17:4
Hotchkiss, Clayton E, 1940, F 24,13:2
Hotchkiss, E Wadsworth Mrs, 1952, My 10,21:2
Hotchkiss, Edward Hopkins, 1913, D 8,11:4
Hotchkiss, Edwin G, 1947, Jl 11,15:3
Hotchkiss, Eli Hubbell, 1917, Mr 17,13:5
Hotchkiss, Elmore D, 1938, O 10,19:5
Hotchkiss, Frederick A, 1945, Ja 4,19:3
Hotchkiss, Frederick D, 1937, N 4,25:3
Hotchkiss, G W, 1878, Jl 6,5:3
Hotchkiss, George B, 1953, Mr 29,93:2
Hotchkiss, George W, 1943, Mr 27,14:8
Hotchkiss, H L, 1929, My 11,19:5
Hotchkiss, H Stuart, 1947, S 17,25:5
Hotchkiss, Henry B, 1922, Mr 21,19:6
Hotchkiss, Henry De Witt Justice, 1922, Mr 7,13:5
Hotchkiss, Henry G, 1963, Ag 31,17:1
Hotchkiss, Henry T, 1939, D 20,28:5

Hotchkiss, Hiram C Mrs, 1945, N 4,43:1
Hotchkiss, Horace L Jr, 1954, O 26,27:2
Hotchkiss, Horace L Mrs, 1941, S 1,15:4
Hotchkiss, Julius, 1878, D 24,5:3
Hotchkiss, Loyal D, 1964, Ap 17,32:5
Hotchkiss, Marie O (will, Jl 15,15:7), 1938, Jl 8,17:6
Hotchkiss, Mary L Mrs, 1938, Ap 14,23:4
Hotchkiss, Nestor M, 1961, Ja 6,27:3
Hotchkiss, Norman M, 1937, Ag 11,24:2
Hotchkiss, Ralph R, 1957, My 19,88:4
Hotchkiss, Russell, 1881, Ja 12,5:4
Hotchkiss, Thomas W, 1953, Ap 1,29:4
Hotchkiss, Velono, 1882, Ja 5,5:5
Hotchkiss, Willard E Mrs, 1951, Ja 12,26:3
Hotchkiss, William B, 1939, Je 11,44:7
Hotchkiss, William C, 1948, Ja 12,19:5
Hotchkiss, William H, 1950, Je 7,29:2
Hotchkiss, William K, 1945, Je 17,25:1
Hotchkiss, William O, 1954, Je 21,23:5
Hotchkiss, William O Mrs, 1949, Ap 6,29:4
Hotchner, Maurice, 1945, Ja 30,19:4
Hotchner, Saul, 1921, Jl 21,15:4
Hoth, Henry J, 1957, Je 6,31:4
Hothersall, John M (por), 1943, F 5,21:4
Hotine, Martin, 1968, N 15,47:2
Hotkinson, Raymond, 1966, Ag 27,29:3
Hotopp, Carl F, 1966, D 11,89:2
Hotsenpiller, Herbert O, 1953, Ag 25,21:3
Hotsford, Harry L, 1945, S 6,25:5
Hotten, John Camden, 1873, Je 15,1:5
Hotten, Ralph, 1949, My 10,25:5
Hottenroth, Gustave, 1949, O 25,27:2
Hottenstein, A (will), 1938, F 6,40:6
Hottenstein, Fred M Mrs, 1962, N 22,29:1
Hottenstein, Henry K, 1947, Ag 20,21:5
Hottenstein, Marcus S Mrs, 1955, Ja 19,27:2
Hottes, Alfred C, 1955, Mr 3,27:1
Hottmann, Frederick, 1942, N 29,60:1
Hottmann, Louisa Mrs, 1942, N 29,60:1
Hotton, B J Mrs, 1957, Jl 8,23:4
Hottum, C H, 1959, S 24,37:3
Hotung, Edward S K, 1957, Jl 3,23:4
Hotung, Robert, 1956, Ap 27,28:1
Hotvedt, Thorbjorn Mrs, 1964, My 13,47:5
Hotz, Henry, 1956, My 5,19:5
Hotz, Robert S Mrs, 1967, Ap 4,43:4
Houben, Max, 1949, F 11,29:5
Houchin, Margaret, 1955, Ja 10,23:4
Houchin, Waldo P, 1952, My 4,91:1
Houck, Courtney C Mrs, 1942, Ag 2,39:4
Houck, Frederick A, 1954, O 20,29:2
Houck, George E, 1951, O 30,29:1
Houck, John P, 1962, Ap 22,80:5
Houck, Leo, 1950, Ja 22,76:5
Houck, Lewis H, 1945, Ap 18,23:3
Houck, Mary B V Mrs, 1937, S 24,21:4
Houck, Richard Henry Mrs, 1968, Ja 11,37:2
Houck, Roy S Mrs, 1941, F 22,15:5
Houck, William G, 1942, My 6,19:3
Houck, William J, 1942, Ja 29,19:2
Houck, William L, 1960, My 6,31:2
Houde, Albert J, 1960, N 8,29:5
Houde, Camillien, 1958, S 12,25:1
Houdin, Jean E R, 1871, Jl 4,5:5
Houdini, H, 1926, N 1,1:2
Houdini, Harry Mrs, 1943, F 12,19:5
Houdry, Eugene J, 1962, Jl 19,27:3
Hougardy, John L, 1947, Ap 26,13:6
Hougate, Charles W, 1947, D 2,30:2
Hough, Alfred Lacey Brig-Gen, 1908, Ap 29,9:6
Hough, Benezet Judge, 1918, Ja 3,9:8
Hough, Bert, 1960, Ap 30,23:5
Hough, C M, 1927, Ap 23,17:5
Hough, Carlos E, 1941, D 4,25:3
Hough, Charles E, 1945, D 14,27:4
Hough, Charles M Mrs, 1938, Mr 8,19:2
Hough, David L, 1938, O 13,23:5
Hough, Donald, 1965, My 13,34:6
Hough, Edgar G, 1941, D 13,21:7
Hough, Edgar S Mrs, 1942, Ag 4,19:2
Hough, Edward B, 1950, My 15,21:5
Hough, Edward C, 1959, Ja 25,94:1
Hough, Emerson, 1923, My 1,21:3
Hough, Frank O, 1958, My 18,86:8
Hough, Frank Pennybacker White, 1918, N 7,15:4
Hough, Fred, 1918, My 18,13:4
Hough, George A, 1955, O 14,36:6
Hough, George A Mrs, 1948, Jl 20,24:2
Hough, George L, 1950, N 28,31:1
Hough, George Washington, 1909, Ja 3,11:5
Hough, Harold V, 1967, Ja 5,37:2
Hough, Harry, 1947, Ja 9,23:5
Hough, Harry Mrs, 1943, Mr 14,26:2
Hough, Harry W, 1944, My 9,19:1
Hough, Henry B Mrs, 1965, Je 22,21:2
Hough, Henry H (por), 1943, S 10,23:1
Hough, Hugh (Wm W Morrell), 1942, O 16,19:2
Hough, Ira D (por), 1939, Ja 13,19:5
Hough, John E, 1903, N 10,9:5
Hough, John K, 1951, D 30,24:5
Hough, John R, 1964, F 22,21:3
Hough, Joseph H, 1937, Ag 11,24:1
Hough, Mary H, 1941, Jl 26,15:6

Hough, Perry B, 1962, Ap 10,43:4
Hough, Richard W, 1968, Ap 1,45:4
Hough, Robert H, 1960, Ap 2,23:4
Hough, Roger, 1953, S 12,17:3
Hough, Romeyn B, 1942, D 23,19:1
Hough, Romeyn Beck, 1924, S 3,17:1
Hough, Seabury B Sr Mrs, 1960, Je 18,23:5
Hough, Waldern E, 1938, Ja 2,41:2
Hough, Walter L, 1951, Ap 26,29:4
Hough, Walter R, 1942, My 30,15:5
Hough, Warwick Ex-Justice, 1915, O 29,13:7
Houghland, Mason, 1959, Ap 26,86:6
Houghtaling, Byron F, 1939, D 20,20:4
Houghtaling, David H, 1913, F 16,II,7:4; 1968, D 25, 31:3
Houghtaling, Earle H, 1944, N 15,27:5
Houghtaling, George E, 1945, F 18,34:1
Houghtaling, James Mrs, 1950, S 27,31:1
Houghtaling, Lewis, 1947, S 14,60:7
Houghtaling, Richard, 1946, S 23,23:3
Houghtaling, Walter A, 1943, Je 10,21:6
Houghteling, James L, 1962, Ap 29,86:6
Houghten, Ferry C, 1945, Ja 26,21:1
Houghton, A A, 1928, Ap 20,23:3
Houghton, A C, 1914, Ag 12,9:1
Houghton, Alanson B (por), 1941, S 17,23:1
Houghton, Alanson B (will), 1942, O 4,11:5
Houghton, Alanson B Mrs, 1945, S 10,19:3
Houghton, Albert F (por), 1937, D 21,23:1
Houghton, Albert P, 1944, Ja 25,19:3
Houghton, Ansmore Dinsmore, 1916, Je 6,13:5
Houghton, Arthur D, 1938, Ja 25,22:3
Houghton, Augustus F, 1951, S 25,29:2
Houghton, Augustus S Sr, 1948, S 26,77:1
Houghton, Bert, 1939, Je 18,37:1
Houghton, Charles E, 1940, Jl 4,15:4
Houghton, Charles Mrs, 1964, N 1,89:2
Houghton, Charles R Col, 1914, Ap 8,13:6
Houghton, Clarence Sherill, 1917, F 19,11:4
Houghton, E Russell Mrs, 1954, S 26,87:1
Houghton, Edward F, 1951, D 6,33:3
Houghton, Edward R, 1955, My 18,31:1
Houghton, Elihu R Mrs, 1920, Ag 23,11:6
Houghton, Elmer G, 1945, F 15,19:4
Houghton, Ernest B, 1941, Jl 25,15:5
Houghton, Eugene H, 1949, Ja 20,28:2
Houghton, Frank R Mrs, 1943, Ap 29,21:5
Houghton, Frederick, 1950, Ap 30,102:6
Houghton, Frederick M, 1943, Ja 24,43:1
Houghton, Frederick P Rev Dr, 1953, Ag 17,15:3
Houghton, G H Rev, 1897, N 18,1:7
Houghton, George, 1909, S 1,9:4
Houghton, George A, 1942, O 27,25:3
Houghton, George Clarke Rev Dr, 1923, Ap 21,11:5
Houghton, George Stearns Prof, 1909, Jl 20,7:6
Houghton, H C, 1901, D 2,1:4; 1957, Je 18,33:1
Houghton, H O, 1906, Je 15,9:6
Houghton, Hadwin, 1919, Ag 27,11:4
Houghton, Harris A, 1946, S 4,23:2
Houghton, Henry C, 1956, N 18,89:2
Houghton, Henry E, 1963, S 23,29:3
Houghton, Henry L, 1948, Je 19,15:4
Houghton, Herbert P, 1964, My 13,47:4
Houghton, Herbert R, 1958, Ja 31,21:3
Houghton, James T Mrs, 1959, Je 5,27:1
Houghton, James W Mrs, 1913, Ag 12,7:6
Houghton, James Warren Justice, 1913, F 15,15:4
Houghton, John, 1913, Ag 9,7:5
Houghton, Joseph Goodhue, 1916, Ja 17,11:5
Houghton, Leonard T, 1961, Ag 30,33:1
Houghton, Lord (R M Milnes), 1885, Ag 12,5:3
Houghton, Lucy E, 1953, Ag 3,17:4
Houghton, M H, 1907, S 8,7:5
Houghton, Mabel H Mrs, 1938, F 14,17:4
Houghton, Robert F, 1959, Je 11,33:4
Houghton, Roy M, 1958, Ag 13,27:1
Houghton, Royal, 1873, Ap 1,5:5
Houghton, Stanley, 1913, D 11,11:4
Houghton, Stanley W, 1951, N 7,29:6
Houghton, Theodore L, 1872, Ja 7,8:5
Houghton, W E, 1948, Mr 6,13:3
Houghton, Walter E, 1941, Mr 23,45:2
Houghton, William M, 1960, D 28,27:1
Houghton, William M Mrs, 1955, Ag 7,73:3
Houghton, William O, 1941, My 14,21:1
Houghton, William W, 1957, Jl 20,15:5
Houghwot, John, 1940, Je 5,25:3
Houisee, Auguste, 1948, S 10,23:3
Houk, George Mrs, 1968, S 14,31:5
Houlahan, Harry C G, 1950, Ag 18,21:3
Houlahan, Harry J, 1949, Je 14,31:1
Houlahan, James M, 1965, F 11,39:2
Houlahan, Patrick H, 1939, F 12,45:1
Houlahan, Thomas F, 1945, Ap 15,14:6
Houldsworth, Hubert, 1956, F 2,25:2
Houle, George A, 1938, Ja 11,23:5
Houle, Hormisdas, 1939, D 20,35:1
Houlgate, Carroll E, 1959, Ag 1,17:3
Houlihan, Anna, 1950, Ag 20,76:3
Houlihan, Daniel, 1941, O 21,23:5
Houlihan, Daniel J Mrs, 1940, Ag 31,13:3
Houlihan, David F, 1964, Je 10,45:3
Houlihan, Frank D, 1939, Je 23,19:4
Houlihan, Henry C, 1968, D 30,31:4
Houlihan, James A, 1961, Mr 9,29:5
Houlihan, James A Mrs, 1955, O 11,39:2
Houlihan, Jeremiah A, 1949, S 13,29:3
Houlihan, John W, 1945, O 22,17:3
Houlihan, Joseph T, 1947, F 2,57:4
Houlihan, Marguerite, 1964, My 5,43:4
Houlihan, Michael J, 1925, S 22,25:4
Houlihan, Thomas F, 1950, S 14,31:4; 1961, Ag 16,31:4
Hounslow, Roper, 1919, Je 11,15:4
Houpert, Andre, 1963, Ap 7,86:1
Houpert, Henri J, 1957, Je 24,23:4
Houpt, Harry, 1925, N 14,15:4
Houpt, William P Sr, 1958, F 1,19:2
Hourigan, Andrew, 1952, Jl 28,15:2
Hourigan, John A, 1951, N 7,29:4
Hourigan, Joseph B, 1952, Ja 30,26:8
Hourigan, Mollie, 1945, Jl 1,17:3
Hourihan, Patrick J, 1951, N 24,11:4
Hourwich, Isaac A, 1925, S 4,21:6
Hourwich, Isaac A Dr, 1924, Jl 11,13:6
Hourwich, Isaac A Mrs, 1947, F 28,23:4
Hourwich, Iskander, 1968, My 29,39:3
House, Augustus P Mrs, 1951, D 25,31:5
House, Billy, 1961, S 27,41:2
House, Boyce, 1961, D 31,48:8
House, Cecil G, 1965, Ap 22,33:5
House, Charles L, 1961, O 14,23:3
House, E C, 1928, S 7,23:5
House, Edith, 1949, Jl 3,26:8
House, Edward A, 1954, F 5,20:4
House, Edward H, 1938, Mr 29,1:3
House, Erwin Rev, 1875, My 21,6:7
House, Eugene W, 1951, Ja 10,28:2
House, Florence E, 1957, N 4,27:4
House, Frederick B (por), 1925, N 24,25:5
House, Frederick B, 1925, N 25,21:3
House, Garry C, 1956, Ap 20,25:4
House, George, 1949, F 9,27:3
House, George A, 1959, Mr 2,27:2
House, George W, 1951, Ja 11,26:3
House, H Sherburne, 1945, F 25,37:1
House, Harry A, 1939, F 15,23:5
House, Helen W Mrs, 1948, Ja 24,15:4
House, Herbert C, 1957, F 14,27:5
House, Homer C, 1938, Ag 30,17:3
House, Homer D, 1949, D 22,23:4
House, Hudson H, 1961, O 24,37:5
House, J H, 1936, Ap 20,19:4
House, John A, 1941, D 7,76:2
House, John H, 1959, Ja 11,88:3
House, John H Mrs, 1947, S 23,25:2; 1961, F 27,27:2
House, Judson, 1945, Ja 7,38:2
House, Loulie H Mrs, 1940, D 27,20:3
House, R Shard S, 1903, S 26,9:4
House, Robert B Jr, 1953, O 21,29:3
House, S A, 1903, Ag 24,7:7
House, Samuel T, 1947, Ja 14,25:3
House, T W, 1923, Ag 16,15:4
House, Wallace B, 1942, Jl 21,19:3
House, William A, 1925, Ja 28,17:3
Householder, Fred W, 1950, Jl 2,24:6
Householder, M C, 1938, D 18,48:8
Houselander, Caryll, 1954, O 14,29:1
Houseman, Charles M, 1957, Ap 17,31:1
Houseman, Daniel, 1944, My 14,46:1
Houseman, Lena, 1903, S 20,20:2
Houseman, M Hampden, 1911, Mr 2,9:2
Housen, Morris, 1963, O 7,31:2
Housen, Phillip, 1952, Mr 11,27:3
Housepian, Moses M, 1952, D 12,29:3
Houser, Alfred (will), 1958, Je 25,29:1
Houser, Benjamin F, 1952, Ja 16,25:2
Houser, Edgar W, 1923, O 16,21:4
Houser, Frederick W, 1942, O 13,23:2
Houser, Gilbert, 1951, Jl 18,29:2
Houser, Gilbert L Mrs, 1951, Jl 18,29:2
Houser, John D (por), 1938, My 14,15:3
Houser, John N, 1949, N 8,31:3
Houser, John S, 1947, Je 27,21:2
Houser, Karl M, 1967, Ja 7,27:5
Houser, Lionel F, 1949, N 15,25:4
Houser, Theodore I Sr Mrs, 1954, Jl 24,13:5
Houser, Theodore V, 1963, D 18,41:3
Houser, William A, 1955, My 11,31:4
Houskeeper, William G, 1962, Mr 25,88:4
Housler, G Herman, 1961, N 8,35:5
Housley, Burton E Mrs, 1942, Ja 16,22:4
Housley, Guy J, 1953, Ja 18,93:1
Housley, William, 1953, Jl 14,27:4
Housman, A E, 1936, My 2,15:1
Housman, Arthur A (funl, Ag 24,7:4), 1907, Ag 22, 7:5
Housman, Charles, 1952, F 1,21:4
Housman, Frederick, 1945, D 30,14:6
Housman, George W, 1950, Ag 17,27:1
Housman, Harold, 1958, My 20,33:3
Housman, Jacob I Capt, 1916, Mr 22,13:4
Housman, John J, 1951, Ja 21,76:8
Housman, Laurence, 1959, F 21,21:4
Housman, Rosalie L, 1949, O 29,15:4
Housman, Stella S B Mrs (will), 1954, F 6,21:6
Housman, William, 1903, N 23,7:3
Housman, William P, 1947, My 7,27:3
Housmann, Gustav N, 1948, My 12,27:3
Houson, Charles H, 1942, F 25,19:4
Houssaye, Charles, 1942, My 16,13:3
Houssaye, Henri, 1919, S 26,13:4
Houssaye, Henry, 1911, S 25,9:4
Houst, Henry O, 1949, Ja 25,23:1
Houst, Henry R Rev, 1937, Mr 8,19:1
Houston, Alfred, 1965, Mr 6,25:2
Houston, Andrew J, 1941, Je 27,17:5
Houston, Benjamin F, 1951, N 29,33:2
Houston, Buchanan, 1945, Mr 22,23:4
Houston, Buchanan Mrs, 1956, Ja 22,88:6
Houston, Byran Mrs, 1953, Je 24,26:4
Houston, C Frederick Mrs, 1947, D 18,29:3
Houston, Charles A, 1951, O 17,31:5
Houston, Charles F, 1945, D 21,21:4
Houston, Charles H, 1950, Ap 26,29:4
Houston, Charles M Mrs, 1947, Ap 28,23:5
Houston, Charles R Mrs, 1957, Je 5,35:3
Houston, Charles W, 1945, F 8,19:1
Houston, Chester M, 1938, Je 21,19:5
Houston, Clarence P, 1965, O 12,47:1
Houston, Clyde E, 1945, Ja 10,23:5
Houston, David, 1903, Je 19,9:6; 1940, Mr 30,15:6
Houston, David F (por), 1940, S 3,17:1
Houston, David F Mrs, 1940, Ja 23,21:5
Houston, Edwin J, 1914, Mr 2,9:4
Houston, Edwin W Rear Adm, 1905, Mr 9,14:4
Houston, F L, 1936, D 30,21:1
Houston, Francis A, 1919, F 12,13:5
Houston, Frederick Mrs, 1950, My 30,18:2
Houston, G Porter, 1946, D 28,15:6
Houston, G S Sen, 1880, Ja 1,5:2
Houston, George F, 1944, N 14,23:4
Houston, George H, 1949, Jl 11,34:3
Houston, Gilbert (Cisco), 1961, Ap 30,86:5
Houston, Grafton, 1949, Ap 12,29:3
Houston, Hale, 1945, D 28,15:1
Houston, Harold W, 1947, Ja 18,15:2
Houston, Herbert S, 1955, My 16,23:3
Houston, Herbert S Mrs, 1949, Jl 28,23:2
Houston, Herbert W, 1961, Ap 16,86:7
Houston, Hough, 1952, Mr 19,29:5
Houston, Howard G, 1939, N 5,49:3
Houston, James B, 1903, My 29,9:5
Houston, James Mrs, 1944, S 26,23:3
Houston, John C, 1953, Ja 3,15:2
Houston, John J, 1957, Ap 3,31:3
Houston, John L, 1938, Ap 5,21:2
Houston, John W, 1944, F 13,41:2
Houston, John W B, 1940, D 19,25:2
Houston, L Stuart A, 1960, D 22,23:3
Houston, Lewis W, 1945, Ap 8,36:3
Houston, Livingston W Mrs, 1959, Je 26,52:1
Houston, Nelson T Com, 1913, Mr 13,11:3
Houston, Noel, 1958, S 10,33:2
Houston, Nora, 1942, F 21,19:3
Houston, Omer T, 1948, S 6,13:4
Houston, Otho S, 1917, My 9,11:2
Houston, Persis D, 1956, S 19,37:3
Houston, Philip K, 1958, D 7,88:1
Houston, R P Sir, 1926, Ap 15,27:4
Houston, Robert G, 1946, Ja 30,25:3
Houston, Robert H, 1944, F 18,17:3
Houston, Robert J, 1946, F 24,44:2
Houston, Robert L, 1968, D 22,52:7
Houston, Robert R, 1938, N 15,23:4
Houston, Sam Gen, 1863, S 20,3:6
Houston, Sam J, 1939, D 16,17:4
Houston, Samuel, 1912, Je 26,13:4
Houston, Samuel E Mrs, 1957, F 28,27:2
Houston, Samuel F, 1952, My 3,21:3
Houston, Samuel F Mrs, 1940, F 24,13:2
Houston, Samuel W, 1951, F 17,15:5
Houston, Sid, 1941, Ap 17,23:3
Houston, Thomas, 1949, Je 22,31:2
Houston, Thomas Mrs, 1960, Mr 16,37:2
Houston, William, 1947, Ja 12,59:2
Houston, William H, 1947, S 10,27:5
Houstoun, Alex J, 1961, D 18,35:2
Houtart, Maurice J, 1939, F 2,19:1
Houtchems, Ray C, 1956, D 24,13:2
Houtermans, Friedrich G, 1966, Mr 3,33:5
Houtz, Philip, 1968, Ag 5,47:1
Houvet, Etienne, 1949, Ap 27,27:6
Houx, Edwin W, 1941, O 7,23:1
Houx, John F Mrs, 1958, S 2,25:4
Houze, Harry G, 1958, Ag 23,15:5
Houze, Leon J, 1940, Ja 23,21:6
Houze, William M, 1946, F 21,21:5
Hovan, Jan, 1953, N 12,31:4
Hovanec, Frank, 1960, S 5,15:1
Hovde, Bryn J, 1954, Ag 11,25:1
Hoveka, Nikinor, 1951, N 23,29:4
Hovell, Albert A, 1953, Ja 17,15:4
Hovenden, Janet M, 1955, Mr 7,27:5
Hovenden, Martha M, 1941, F 28,19:4
Hover, Augustus, 1942, My 25,15:6
Hover, Barton L, 1942, Jl 2,21:4
Hover, Ernest G, 1951, S 16,85:2
Hover, John C, 1949, N 18,29:4
Hover, Peter A, 1951, N 18,91:2

Hoverter, William C, 1938, D 14,25:1
Hovey, Burton M, 1946, Jl 16,23:1
Hovey, Carl, 1956, Je 27,31:3
Hovey, Carl Mrs (S Levien), 1960, Mr 20,86:8
Hovey, Charles H, 1957, N 18,31:1
Hovey, Charles P, 1859, My 2,5:2
Hovey, Edmund Otis, 1924, S 27,16:2
Hovey, Frank D, 1941, F 4,21:4
Hovey, Frederick H, 1945, O 21,46:4
Hovey, George R (por), 1943, Ja 30,15:3
Hovey, Harry E, 1953, N 3,31:4
Hovey, Henry Emerson Rev, 1909, Ag 7,9:5
Hovey, Henry W Maj, 1908, N 16,9:5
Hovey, Horace Carter Rev, 1914, Jl 28,7:4
Hovey, Lewis R, 1959, O 9,29:1
Hovey, Otis E (por), 1941, Ap 16,23:1
Hovey, Otis E Mrs, 1948, Je 24,25:4
Hovey, Rex W Mrs, 1947, S 13,11:4
Hovey, Rexford W, 1957, Jl 8,23:4
Hovey, Robert, 1954, F 18,31:1
Hovey, Sarah T Mrs, 1941, S 27,17:4
Hovey, Theodore C, 1938, Ap 27,23:4
Hovey, Vernon F, 1960, Je 14,34:3
Hovey, Will W, 1941, D 11,27:6
Hovey, William A Jr, 1962, Ap 7,52:6
Hovey-King, Alvin, 1938, D 28,26:6
Hovgaard, Commodore, 1910, Mr 17,9:4
Hoviland, Carl I, 1961, Ap 18,37:1
Hoving, Mary O F Mrs, 1955, Mr 31,29:8
Hovsepiantz, Garegin, 1952, Je 23,19:4
How, Blanche B B Mrs, 1940, N 15,21:2
How, Dana G, 1964, Jl 10,30:1
How, J E, 1930, Jl 23,23:7
How, K Mrs, 1882, Mr 18,5:1
How, Louis, 1947, O 4,17:2
How, Moses, 1881, Je 27,5:4
Howard, A C Maj, 1901, F 25,1:5
Howard, A T (Bert), 1951, My 16,35:6
Howard, Ada L, 1907, Mr 7,9:6
Howard, Albert, 1947, O 21,23:3
Howard, Albert C, 1910, Jl 5,13:6
Howard, Alford E, 1950, Ap 26,29:3
Howard, Alfred P, 1948, N 13,15:6
Howard, Allen B, 1940, My 1,23:2
Howard, Almern C, 1954, N 7,87:4
Howard, Alonzo H, 1950, Ja 8,78:3
Howard, Alsa C, 1955, Mr 2,27:3
Howard, Alvin P, 1937, S 30,23:1
Howard, Andree, 1968, Ap 19,3:3
Howard, Andrew J Mrs, 1963, Je 3,29:5
Howard, Arthur L, 1937, Je 22,23:3
Howard, Arthur W, 1947, Ap 14,27:2; 1950, Jl 12,29:5
Howard, Bart B (por), 1941, F 13,19:3
Howard, Beale R Mrs, 1939, O 4,25:5
Howard, Benjamin Chew, 1872, Mr 14,5:6
Howard, Besse D, 1960, S 30,27:5
Howard, Bion H, 1942, Jl 20,13:3
Howard, Bronson, 1908, Ag 5,5:4
Howard, Bronson Mrs, 1914, Je 23,11:4
Howard, C, 1931, D 7,19:1
Howard, C Edgar Jr, 1951, S 8,17:4
Howard, C T, 1885, Je 1,5:3
Howard, Carl Mrs, 1952, D 17,33:3
Howard, Carrie L, 1951, Ag 5,72:5
Howard, Cecil de B, 1956, S 7,24:2
Howard, Celia H, 1950, My 24,29:1
Howard, Charles, 1883, N 9,5:5; 1955, Ja 28,20:2
Howard, Charles A, 1945, Je 16,13:3; 1958, Ja 6,39:2
Howard, Charles B, 1945, Ag 12,39:3
Howard, Charles B Mrs, 1953, Ja 4,76:4
Howard, Charles C, 1916, Ja 5,13:8
Howard, Charles C Mrs, 1943, D 11,15:2
Howard, Charles D, 1944, O 30,19:6
Howard, Charles M, 1940, S 11,25:4; 1942, My 20, 20:3; 1946, D 14,15:2
Howard, Charles O, 1955, D 20,31:4
Howard, Charles P, 1938, Jl 22,17:3; 1966, Jl 4,15:4
Howard, Charles S, 1951, Mr 3,13:4
Howard, Charles S Sr, 1950, Je 7,29:5
Howard, Charles T, 1939, S 7,25:1; 1949, F 22,23:2
Howard, Charles W, 1947, Jl 25,17:5; 1966, My 2,37:1
Howard, Charles Webster, 1908, Jl 19,7:7
Howard, Cilius L, 1946, Mr 8,21:4
Howard, Clara, 1951, F 28,27:2
Howard, Clara H Mrs, 1940, S 14,17:4
Howard, Clare M, 1967, Jl 21,31:4
Howard, Clarence C, 1942, Ja 15,19:5
Howard, Clarence C Dr, 1924, F 16,13:6
Howard, Clarence H Jr, 1943, O 23,13:2
Howard, Clifford, 1942, My 21,19:4
Howard, Clinton C, 1955, Jl 18,21:4
Howard, Clinton N, 1955, Ap 27,31:4
Howard, Clinton W (por), 1949, S 24,13:1
Howard, Clyde M, 1942, F 3,19:3
Howard, D L, 1936, D 15,25:4; 1951, Je 7,33:3
Howard, David, 1941, D 22,17:2
Howard, Douglas A Capt, 1925, Jl 9,19:4
Howard, Dowell J, 1957, F 24,85:2
Howard, Dudley B, 1965, D 5,89:1
Howard, E G F Baron of Glossop, 1883, D 3,5:5
Howard, E P, 1933, S 2,11:3
Howard, E Sir, 1928, My 2,25:2
Howard, Earl D, 1956, Jl 15,60:3
Howard, Ed, 1948, Ja 15,23:1
Howard, Eddy, 1963, My 24,32:1
Howard, Edgar, 1951, Jl 20,21:3
Howard, Edgar B, 1943, Mr 19,19:1
Howard, Edmund B, 1964, Jl 23,27:3
Howard, Edward, 1946, Mr 7,25:3
Howard, Edward C Mrs, 1951, Mr 11,93:1
Howard, Edward D, 1954, Je 9,31:5
Howard, Edward F, 1948, N 15,25:4
Howard, Edward P, 1943, Mr 15,13:5
Howard, Edward Tasker, 1918, Ag 9,11:8
Howard, Edward W S, 1946, Mr 17,44:4
Howard, Edwin J, 1939, Ap 27,25:1
Howard, Eleanor S Mrs, 1937, N 10,25:5
Howard, Elisha R Mrs, 1953, Ag 29,17:2
Howard, Ellis E, 1962, Ag 10,19:5
Howard, Elmer A, 1921, My 5,17:4
Howard, Emeline, 1948, N 10,29:4
Howard, Enrique Adm, 1913, D 8,11:4
Howard, Ernest, 1939, Jl 21,19:2
Howard, Ernest E, 1953, Ag 21,17:2
Howard, Ernest Mrs, 1945, Ap 3,19:4
Howard, Eugene, 1965, Ag 3,31:1
Howard, Eugene S, 1951, Je 2,19:3
Howard, Everette B, 1950, Ap 5,31:3
Howard, Floarda, 1961, Jl 15,19:3
Howard, Floyd E, 1957, Jl 28,61:2
Howard, Francis W (por), 1944, Ja 19,19:3
Howard, Frank, 1940, My 21,23:4; 1940, Je 30,32:3
Howard, Frank A, 1964, S 27,86:7
Howard, Frank B, 1945, O 16,23:6
Howard, Frank E, 1963, My 24,31:3
Howard, Frank H, 1946, S 13,7:2
Howard, Frank J, 1944, Ja 11,19:2
Howard, Frank J Mrs, 1953, F 3,25:3
Howard, Frank O, 1947, Ja 15,26:2
Howard, Frank T, 1952, N 28,25:1
Howard, Fred E, 1937, F 5,21:3
Howard, Fred R, 1939, F 20,17:6
Howard, Fred W, 1956, Ja 29,92:2
Howard, Frederick, 1911, Ag 6,II,9:6
Howard, Frederick A, 1940, F 8,23:4
Howard, Frederick C, 1947, Jl 5,11:5
Howard, Frederick H, 1948, Jl 16,19:5; 1961, Ag 17, 27:4
Howard, Frederick H C Mrs (Madeleine, Dowager Countess of Effingham), 1958, Je 20,23:1
Howard, Frederick P, 1953, Ja 5,21:2
Howard, George A, 1966, Je 24,37:2
Howard, George C, 1941, Ag 20,19:6
Howard, George C Mrs, 1908, O 17,9:4
Howard, George D, 1949, O 15,15:4
Howard, George H, 1942, S 15,23:6; 1960, Ap 19,37:4
Howard, George J L'E (Earl of Carlisle), 1963, F 19,8:6
Howard, George L, 1940, Ja 16,23:1; 1953, F 11,29:1
Howard, George Mrs, 1962, Jl 12,29:4
Howard, George W, 1939, D 19,26:3
Howard, Graeme K, 1962, D 7,39:2
Howard, Grenvill, 1939, Ap 15,19:2
Howard, Grover T, 1904, F 16,9:6
Howard, Guy M, 1955, N 23,23:2
Howard, Guy W, 1966, My 14,31:2
Howard, H, 1933, Je 30,17:3
Howard, H Waring Jr, 1940, Mr 28,24:2
Howard, Harold M, 1959, Ag 9,88:8
Howard, Harry, 1940, O 1,23:2; 1941, Mr 15,17:2; 1942, Je 27,13:5
Howard, Harry A, 1957, Jl 28,61:2
Howard, Harry C, 1942, F 11,21:4; 1946, Je 29,19:3
Howard, Harry G, 1943, Ap 7,25:4
Howard, Harry G Mrs, 1950, My 27,17:6
Howard, Harry W, 1955, Ag 27,15:2
Howard, Hartley Jr, 1921, N 7,15:4
Howard, Harvey J, 1956, N 7,31:2
Howard, Hector H, 1960, My 13,31:6
Howard, Heermance M, 1950, Jl 30,60:5
Howard, Henry, 1905, S 23,9:4; 1923, Jl 2,15:6; 1951, Ag 27,19:1
Howard, Henry D, 1942, Jl 23,19:2
Howard, Henry H Mrs, 1945, O 8,15:3
Howard, Henry Lady, 1907, D 4,9:5
Howard, Henry Sir, 1921, My 5,17:4
Howard, Henry Ward Beecher, 1906, Ap 18,11:5
Howard, Henry Waring Sr, 1925, N 3,25:5
Howard, Herbert, 1938, My 16,17:5; 1952, S 4,27:6
Howard, Herbert G, 1958, S 17,32:4
Howard, Herbert H, 1937, N 5,23:2
Howard, Howland M (por),(will, F 7,25:2), 1945, Ja 1,21:1
Howard, Hugh Melville, 1919, F 20,13:4
Howard, Ida Lydia, 1907, Mr 5,9:6
Howard, J Campbell Mrs, 1953, Ag 7,19:5
Howard, J G, 1931, Jl 19,21:5
Howard, J J, 1901, Ap 19,9:6
Howard, J M, 1871, Ap 3,1:5
Howard, J M B (Mar 8), 1963, Ap 1,35:8
Howard, J N, 1901, D 8,7:6
Howard, J R, 1903, My 26,9:6
Howard, Jack, 1957, D 24,15:2
Howard, Jack R Mrs, 1962, Je 20,32:6
Howard, Jacob Painter, 1968, Ja 25,37:3
Howard, James H, 1951, Ja 19,25:5
Howard, James Leland, 1906, My 2,9:6
Howard, James M, 1955, Ap 1,27:3
Howard, James M Jr Mrs, 1945, D 5,27:7
Howard, James Quay, 1912, N 17,17:5
Howard, James R, 1954, Ja 28,27:5
Howard, James T, 1951, N 28,31:1
Howard, Jasper V, 1939, Mr 13,17:5
Howard, Jerome, 1952, Ja 19,15:6
Howard, Jerusha Stokes Mrs, 1924, Ap 19,13:5
Howard, Joe (Jos E),(cor, Je 4,85:2), 1961, My 21, 87:1
Howard, Joe Mrs (Miriam), 1967, O 9,47:3
Howard, John, 1925, Mr 27,19:6
Howard, John A, 1938, Je 7,23:5; 1940, Jl 4,15:2
Howard, John C, 1957, Ap 16,33:3
Howard, John D, 1941, Ag 21,17:4
Howard, John E, 1949, Mr 8,25:3
Howard, John G, 1940, Jl 17,21:3
Howard, John H, 1965, F 22,21:4
Howard, John J, 1941, Ja 25,15:2
Howard, John K, 1965, Mr 3,41:3
Howard, John L, 1949, D 23,22:3
Howard, John L Mrs, 1946, My 30,21:3
Howard, John M, 1945, N 11,41:1
Howard, John Mrs, 1948, Ag 20,17:4
Howard, John R Jr, 1953, Ja 26,22:5
Howard, John T, 1941, N 6,23:5; 1964, N 21,29:3
Howard, John T Mrs, 1954, Mr 8,27:5
Howard, John W, 1944, Ja 29,13:4
Howard, Jon Hayes, 1968, Jl 30,39:1
Howard, Joseph, 1952, Ja 19,20:6
Howard, Joseph A, 1958, Ap 16,33:2
Howard, Joseph E, 1952, Jl 31,23:3
Howard, Joseph H, 1953, S 29,29:1
Howard, Joseph Jr (funl, Ap 4,9:6), 1908, Ap 1,7:5
Howard, Joseph K, 1951, Ag 27,19:6
Howard, Joseph Platt, 1909, D 14,11:4
Howard, Kathleen, 1956, Ag 17,19:5
Howard, Kenneth P, 1962, S 4,33:1
Howard, Laurent, 1901, D 18,9:4
Howard, Lawrence C, 1959, My 1,29:2
Howard, Leone E, 1945, Ap 30,19:3
Howard, Leroy T Col, 1937, O 2,21:1
Howard, Lily B Mrs, 1938, N 10,27:4
Howard, Lord of Penrith (por), 1939, Ag 2,19:3
Howard, Lou F, 1957, My 30,19:5
Howard, Lucille Bournes Mrs, 1968, Ja 21,76:4
Howard, Lucinda, 1962, D 22,8:1
Howard, Mack N, 1947, F 4,25:1
Howard, Margaret, 1919, Ag 30,7:6; 1949, Jl 18,17:6
Howard, Margaret Lady (Dowager Countess of Suffolk and Berkshire), 1968, Mr 6,47:1
Howard, Marguerite E, 1939, Jl 27,19:5
Howard, Marjorie, 1958, My 8,29:4
Howard, Martha C, 1959, Mr 20,31:2
Howard, Mary Ann Mrs, 1925, Ja 22,19:5
Howard, Michael J, 1945, My 11,19:4; 1945, D 5,25:4
Howard, Nannie M Mrs, 1939, D 27,21:2
Howard, Neil R, 1955, Ap 20,33:5
Howard, Nelson A, 1940, S 22,49:2
Howard, Nelson W, 1937, Jl 20,23:2
Howard, Oliver O Mrs, 1911, Ag 2,7:6
Howard, Oscar F, 1942, Ja 8,22:2
Howard, Oscar R, 1950, My 14,106:6
Howard, Paul B, 1958, N 2,89:1
Howard, Paul D, 1956, Ap 29,86:8
Howard, Paul G, 1958, Je 1,87:1
Howard, Perry W, 1961, F 2,29:1
Howard, Peter D (funl, Mr 5,33:3), 1965, F 26,29:2
Howard, Phil W, 1949, Je 25,13:5
Howard, Philip E, 1946, Je 24,31:4
Howard, Philip E Mrs, 1943, Ap 13,25:1
Howard, Philip L 2d, 1961, Je 22,31:3
Howard, Ralph E, 1951, S 15,15:4
Howard, Randolph L, 1967, Mr 7,41:1
Howard, Richard W, 1967, N 12,83:5
Howard, Robert B Mrs, 1957, Mr 25,13:4
Howard, Robert E, 1953, D 21,31:4
Howard, Robert E Jr, 1952, Je 6,23:3
Howard, Robert Jared Bliss Dr, 1921, Ja 11,11:4
Howard, Robert L, 1945, F 27,19:2
Howard, Robert M, 1955, O 14,27:6
Howard, Robert R, 1955, Mr 5,17:6
Howard, Roscoe, 1950, F 21,25:4
Howard, Rossiter, 1950, Ja 3,25:2
Howard, Rossiter Mrs, 1961, O 13,35:5
Howard, Roy W (cor, N 22,86:6; will, D 3,51:4), 1964, N 21,1:1
Howard, Roy W Mrs, 1965, Ja 31,88:7
Howard, Rufus, 1952, Mr 29,15:2
Howard, Sam, 1949, O 5,29:3; 1967, D 14,47:3
Howard, Samuel A Jr, 1959, S 9,41:2
Howard, Samuel O, 1947, Ap 27,60:1
Howard, Shemp, 1955, N 24,29:4
Howard, Sidney (por), 1946, Je 13,27:4
Howard, Sidney Mrs, 1964, D 2,47:1
Howard, Stanley Mrs, 1958, Ag 5,27:3
Howard, Stanley W, 1951, Je 13,29:5
Howard, Susan E Mrs, 1941, Ja 19,40:2
Howard, Tasker Jr, 1952, F 22,21:2
Howard, Thomas B Rear-Adm, 1920, N 11,13:2
Howard, Thomas H, 1904, Je 7,7:7
Howard, Thomas W Sr, 1942, Ja 8,21:5

Howard, Tom, 1955, F 28,19:4; 1961, O 9,35:3; 1965, Mr 29,33:4
Howard, Ulie J, 1947, O 18,15:4
Howard, Velma S Mrs, 1937, Mr 11,23:3
Howard, Vincent W, 1963, Ag 17,19:3
Howard, W Franck, 1955, D 1,35:4
Howard, W O, 1933, My 12,17:5
Howard, Walter E Dean, 1912, Ap 13,13:5
Howard, Walter S, 1954, Jl 29,23:2; 1954, N 14,89:3
Howard, Wilbert F, 1952, Jl 13,61:2
Howard, Wilfred Mrs, 1950, S 23,17:3
Howard, William, 1944, Ja 26,19:2
Howard, William B, 1925, Jl 7,19:5
Howard, William C, 1953, S 24,33:2; 1966, Ag 15,27:1
Howard, William Daniel, 1925, My 7,19:5
Howard, William E, 1946, My 9,21:5
Howard, William F Mrs, 1948, Mr 15,23:2
Howard, William G, 1948, O 31,88:7
Howard, William H, 1959, Ap 1,37:3
Howard, William J, 1941, My 2,21:1
Howard, William J K, 1954, F 22,19:2
Howard, William S, 1953, Ag 3,17:6
Howard, William T, 1907, Ag 1,7:6
Howard, William W, 1963, N 1,33:4
Howard, Willie, 1949, Ja 13,23:1
Howard, Willie Mrs, 1947, O 29,33:5
Howard, Wingate C, 1949, Mr 19,15:3
Howard, Winthrop R, 1951, Ag 13,17:4
Howard-Flanders, Richard L, 1939, Ag 17,21:5
Howard-Smith, Logan, 1937, S 24,21:4
Howardson, Tobias Mrs, 1946, Ap 18,27:1
Howarth, Alice H, 1939, Je 1,25:1
Howarth, Edward A, 1943, S 11,13:5
Howarth, Harry A S, 1955, Ap 23,19:2
Howarth, Henry A, 1924, Mr 13,17:5
Howarth, Joseph, 1949, Jl 18,17:6
Howarth, Mark A, 1950, Ap 22,19:5
Howarth, Mary J Mrs, 1938, D 30,15:3
Howarth, Thomas F, 1940, N 3,57:2
Howarth, W Kenneth, 1963, O 3,35:3
Howarth, Walter E, 1963, Jl 13,17:5
Howat, Alexander, 1945, D 11,25:3
Howat, Clarence W, 1946, Jl 23,25:3
Howatt, George R, 1959, D 5,23:3
Howatt, Gerald, 1909, Ag 20,7:5
Howatt, John, 1949, O 24,23:4
Howatt, Joseph P, 1942, Je 13,15:5
Howcroft, Ernest E, 1947, D 10,31:4
Howcroft, Ernest Mrs, 1951, D 30,25:1
Howcroft, Sarah M Mrs, 1938, Ap 13,25:1
Howden, Arthur W, 1939, Je 16,23:5
Howden, Frederick B, 1940, N 13,23:4
Howden, U Fred, 1962, D 28,8:5
Howe, Albert W, 1944, D 3,58:7
Howe, Alex C, 1948, D 25,17:5
Howe, Alfred F, 1924, D 13,15:3
Howe, Amasa, 1950, S 13,27:5
Howe, Andrew F, 1961, F 9,31:1
Howe, Annie E Mrs, 1916, S 19,11:4
Howe, Annie W Mrs, 1916, S 17,19:1
Howe, Anthony G, 1957, D 8,88:7
Howe, Arthur, 1955, Mr 29,30:5
Howe, Arthur B, 1956, Ap 20,25:2
Howe, Arthur L, 1942, Je 27,13:6
Howe, Arthur M (por), 1947, O 16,27:4
Howe, Arthur M Mrs, 1946, Jl 28,39:2
Howe, Arthur O, 1951, N 28,25:2
Howe, Arthur R, 1949, F 25,24:3
Howe, Arthur W, 1953, Ja 22,23:1
Howe, Arthur W Mrs, 1943, O 11,19:3
Howe, Asa V, 1943, D 29,18:2
Howe, Barbara M, 1939, Ja 19,19:4
Howe, Ben (por), 1946, D 13,23:1
Howe, Burton A, 1957, F 14,27:2
Howe, Carl, 1946, N 10,64:2
Howe, Carl E, 1966, Ag 3,37:2
Howe, Charles B, 1958, Mr 10,23:4
Howe, Charles H, 1964, Je 14,85:1
Howe, Charles M Dr, 1920, D 20,13:5
Howe, Charles P, 1949, Mr 19,15:1
Howe, Charles S, 1939, Ap 19,23:4
Howe, Charles S Mrs, 1938, D 13,26:1
Howe, Charlotte, 1949, Mr 21,23:3
Howe, Claire J, 1946, Ap 2,27:1
Howe, Clarence D (funl plans, Ja 2,25:3), 1961, Ja 1,48:1
Howe, Clifton D, 1946, F 24,43:1
Howe, Deering, 1948, N 8,21:4
Howe, E F, 1947, O 13,23:1
Howe, E J M D, 1905, Mr 15,9:6
Howe, Earl, 1929, Ja 11,23:3
Howe, Earl (F R H P Curzon), 1964, Jl 27,31:2
Howe, Edgar W (por),(will O 9,17:5), 1937, O 4,21:1
Howe, Edgar Wellington Col, 1923, Je 15,19:6
Howe, Edward F, 1937, S 20,23:1
Howe, Edward L, 1952, Ap 29,27:3
Howe, Edward S, 1949, Ag 13,11:5
Howe, Elias Jr, 1867, O 5,2:1
Howe, Elmer Parker, 1918, Je 19,11:7
Howe, Ernest J, 1943, Ja 8,19:2
Howe, F E Col, 1883, My 24,1:6
Howe, F Stanley, 1957, Mr 15,25:1
Howe, Fisher, 1940, Ag 13,19:4
Howe, Fisher Mrs, 1924, Ja 15,19:2
Howe, Flora Lady, 1925, Ap 15,19:4
Howe, Florrimon M, 1941, S 8,15:5
Howe, Frances S, 1937, S 4,15:6
Howe, Frank E, 1925, N 20,21:4; 1943, Ap 3,15:4; 1956, Jl 21,15:1
Howe, Frank H, 1940, N 16,17:2
Howe, Frank L, 1948, D 12,93:1; 1951, Mr 2,25:3
Howe, Frank M, 1949, O 22,17:3
Howe, Frank R, 1968, Jl 9,35:6
Howe, Fred B, 1941, Ag 17,39:2
Howe, Fred H, 1941, Mr 23,45:2
Howe, Fred M, 1956, Mr 19,31:2
Howe, Frederic C (por), 1940, Ag 4,33:1
Howe, Frederick L, 1921, Ag 10,13:6
Howe, Frederick P, 1911, My 20,13:6
Howe, George, 1955, Ap 17,87:1; 1967, F 26,84:6
Howe, George A Sr, 1943, N 12,21:3
Howe, George H, 1950, F 6,25:3; 1955, Ap 15,24:1
Howe, Grace R, 1956, Ap 6,25:4
Howe, H A, 1880, F 17,5:2
Howe, H A Dr, 1926, N 4,27:3
Howe, H J, 1903, My 28,9:6
Howe, Harland B, 1946, Ap 23,21:2
Howe, Harold, 1968, D 19,47:2
Howe, Harold J, 1946, Je 22,19:2
Howe, Harriet A, 1948, Je 8,25:4
Howe, Harrison E (por), 1942, D 12,15:1
Howe, Harry, 1949, D 2,29:2
Howe, Henry B, 1946, Je 14,22:3
Howe, Henry L Jr, 1944, Je 1,19:2
Howe, Henry Marion (funl, My 28,22:3), 1922, My 17,19:4
Howe, Henry W Jr, 1953, Ja 20,25:2
Howe, Herbert B, 1957, My 3,28:1
Howe, Herbert B Mrs, 1958, My 2,27:3
Howe, Herbert D, 1922, Ja 27,15:5
Howe, Herbert F, 1941, F 17,15:3
Howe, Herbert M Dr, 1916, O 2,11:5
Howe, Horace L, 1941, F 3,17:2
Howe, Hubert S, 1957, F 5,23:2
Howe, Irwin M Mrs, 1955, Je 1,33:4
Howe, J M Dr, 1885, F 7,2:5
Howe, J W S (funl), 1871, Jl 24,3:1
Howe, James A, 1953, D 18,29:2
Howe, James C, 1957, Je 30,69:3
Howe, James R Jr, 1955, Je 16,31:1
Howe, James Robinson, 1914, S 23,9:4
Howe, Jane Endicott Mrs, 1909, D 4,11:5
Howe, John, 1905, Mr 15,9:6; 1914, My 14,11:5
Howe, John A, 1955, S 11,85:1
Howe, John B, 1942, Ag 19,19:2; 1943, My 17,15:5
Howe, John Edward, 1908, S 18,7:4
Howe, John J, 1946, My 5,46:6
Howe, John K, 1917, Mr 5,11:5
Howe, John P, 1967, Jl 23,61:1
Howe, John S, 1948, My 24,20:2
Howe, Joseph, 1873, Je 2,5:6
Howe, Joseph D, 1944, Jl 30,35:4
Howe, Julia C Mrs, 1937, Ap 21,23:2
Howe, Julia Ward, 1908, My 28,7:3
Howe, Kenneth J, 1945, Ja 2,19:3
Howe, L, 1928, D 29,17:3; 1942, Mr 18,23:2
Howe, L M, 1936, Ap 19,1:1
Howe, Leon, 1949, Ap 20,27:4
Howe, LeRoy K, 1965, Mr 6,25:1
Howe, Leslie L, 1941, N 12,24:2
Howe, Lewis H Mrs, 1938, Ap 19,21:4
Howe, Lincoln H, 1964, My 23,23:4
Howe, Louis M Mrs, 1955, Je 15,31:5
Howe, Lyman J, 1949, O 18,28:3
Howe, Mark A De W Sr (will, D 23,17:5), 1960, D 7,43:3
Howe, Mark DeW, 1967, Mr 1,43:1
Howe, Marshall Mrs, 1957, S 24,35:5
Howe, Minnie E, 1939, Je 24,17:2
Howe, Murray, 1941, Je 24,19:3
Howe, N S, 1907, Mr 1,9:6
Howe, Olive W, 1947, Ja 31,23:3
Howe, Otis W, 1957, N 9,27:3
Howe, Paul C, 1948, D 9,34:3
Howe, Paul S Rev, 1937, O 8,23:2
Howe, Percival S Jr, 1965, My 16,88:5
Howe, Percy R, 1950, Mr 1,27:1
Howe, Raymond C B, 1951, My 18,27:1
Howe, Raymond R, 1953, O 13,29:3
Howe, Robert E L Mrs, 1950, O 2,23:5
Howe, Robert Martin Capt, 1914, O 2,11:6
Howe, Robert T Mrs, 1944, Je 20,19:3
Howe, S G Dr (funl, Ja 14,4:7), 1876, Ja 10,1:6
Howe, S L, 1877, F 28,5:2
Howe, Samuel B (por), 1941, F 18,23:1
Howe, Samuel G Mrs (mem, O 31,9:5), 1910, O 18, 9:1
Howe, Samuel Gridley Mrs, 1922, Ap 11,19:5
Howe, Samuel O, 1906, Mr 18,1:3
Howe, Samuel R, 1957, D 10,35:2
Howe, Solomon A, 1944, My 13,19:4
Howe, Stanley H, 1955, Mr 31,27:2
Howe, T O (funl, Mr 30,2:4), 1883, Mr 26,1:6
Howe, Thomas, 1943, N 16,23:3
Howe, W F, 1902, S 3,9:5
Howe, W H, 1929, Mr 17,II,7:1
Howe, Wallis E Mrs, 1951, S 9,89:2
Howe, Walter, 1890, Ag 23,1:5; 1945, Ja 24,22:2; 1948, D 17,27:4; 1966, Ap 10,76:4
Howe, Walter B (will, Mr 5,10:7), 1954, F 21,68:1
Howe, Walter B Mrs, 1964, S 16,31:6
Howe, Walter Gen, 1915, N 10,13:2
Howe, Walter N, 1937, Jl 1,27:5
Howe, Willard B Mrs, 1949, Jl 4,13:5
Howe, William A, 1940, S 14,17:4
Howe, William A Mrs, 1955, Mr 10,27:4
Howe, William D, 1946, D 7,21:4
Howe, William D Mrs, 1944, F 18,17:5
Howe, William Dr, 1906, N 29,9:5
Howe, William F, 1907, F 14,9:5; 1952, N 10,25:4; 1963, Ap 26,35:1
Howe, William H, 1942, F 6,19:4
Howe, William L, 1952, F 28,27:5
Howe, William P, 1911, Mr 15,13:5; 1940, N 18,19: 1957, Mr 19,37:3
Howe, William Read, 1923, N 30,15:3
Howe, William T H, 1939, Ag 20,32:3
Howe, Winifred E, 1966, Ag 16,39:5
Howe, Winthrop K Sr, 1954, Ag 21,17:6
Howe, Woodbury K, 1949, Ja 17,19:2
Howell, Albert M Mrs, 1952, Ap 3,35:1
Howell, Albert S, 1951, Ja 4,29:5
Howell, Alex, 1954, N 1,27:5
Howell, Alex R, 1941, D 15,19:5
Howell, Alfred, 1950, Mr 8,27:1
Howell, Alfred C, 1961, S 11,27:5
Howell, Alfred C Mrs, 1947, Ja 19,52:1
Howell, Alice P, 1959, Jl 10,25:2
Howell, Alice V, 1947, Ag 6,23:5
Howell, Allan C, 1954, Mr 11,31:4
Howell, Alleyne C, 1964, Ag 22,21:4
Howell, Anna B, 1953, My 22,27:1
Howell, Annie F Mrs, 1937, N 22,19:4
Howell, Arthur J, 1942, N 30,23:5
Howell, Arthur W, 1962, O 23,37:2
Howell, B Huntting, 1953, F 28,17:6
Howell, Baxter C, 1952, N 11,29:2
Howell, Beatrice (Mrs B L Rose), 1957, O 23,33:
Howell, Blair D, 1953, Ag 25,21:3
Howell, C, 1936, N 15,II,8:1
Howell, C W, 1882, Ap 6,2:5
Howell, Carl L, 1945, Ja 18,19:1
Howell, Carlyle H Mrs, 1944, D 23,13:3
Howell, Charles E, 1944, N 20,21:3
Howell, Charles F, 1940, Jl 21,29:2; 1943, Je 7,13:
Howell, Charles H, 1947, Ag 19,23:5
Howell, Charles H Mrs, 1944, Ja 18,19:1
Howell, Charles M Sr, 1941, D 15,19:3
Howell, Charlotte K, 1952, Je 23,19:3
Howell, Clarence A (funl, Je 15,31:1), 1955, Je 11
Howell, Clark Mrs, 1922, Mr 24,9:5
Howell, Claude B, 1945, N 26,21:5
Howell, Cortlandt, 1918, My 22,13:6
Howell, Corwin, 1961, Je 19,27:6
Howell, Daniel L, 1938, N 18,21:4
Howell, David A, 1944, My 25,21:6
Howell, DeWitt C, 1965, Ja 19,33:1
Howell, Donald T, 1958, Jl 6,56:8
Howell, Edmund O, 1966, S 1,35:5
Howell, Edmund W, 1953, Ja 4,76:6
Howell, Edward H, 1956, N 25,88:5
Howell, Edward Mrs, 1955, D 23,17:3
Howell, Edwin A, 1954, N 6,17:6
Howell, Edwin A Mrs, 1953, Ja 20,25:3
Howell, Edwin F, 1920, Ja 7,19:3
Howell, Edwin H, 1965, D 13,39:3
Howell, Edwin H Mrs, 1948, Mr 25,28:3
Howell, Ellen Mrs, 1959, N 27,26:6
Howell, Elmer B, 1954, F 18,31:2
Howell, Fitzherbert, 1960, Je 2,33:1
Howell, Fleming, 1941, Ja 10,19:2
Howell, Francis G Rev, 1915, Mr 5,9:6
Howell, Frank H, 1943, D 29,17:1
Howell, Frank J, 1957, Je 16,84:3
Howell, Fred S, 1943, O 17,48:4
Howell, Fred S Mrs, 1948, D 28,21:2
Howell, Frederick H, 1948, Jl 12,19:4
Howell, G E, 1937, My 9,V,8:8
Howell, George, 1874, Ag 31,1:2
Howell, George Foster, 1925, Ap 9,23:5
Howell, George N, 1963, O 22,37:4
Howell, Gideon L, 1949, Ja 14,23:4
Howell, H C, 1884, O 7,2:1
Howell, Hampton P, 1941, D 12,25:6
Howell, Harold D, 1939, F 19,39:1
Howell, Harriette, 1947, D 30,24:2
Howell, Harry B, 1947, Ap 29,27:4
Howell, Harry D, 1948, Ja 9,21:4
Howell, Harry H, 1938, F 26,15:4
Howell, Harry P, 1942, N 3,24:2
Howell, Henry W, 1938, Jl 14,21:4
Howell, Henry W Jr, 1958, O 18,21:5
Howell, Henry W Sr Mrs, 1960, Ap 13,40:1
Howell, Herbert P (por), 1944, Ag 1,15:4
Howell, Ida E, 1946, N 10,64:2
Howell, Isabel M, 1951, S 3,13:4
Howell, J B, 1880, Je 18,2:3
Howell, James, 1897, Ja 28,7:5; 1921, O 4,15:6 My 28,21:5
Howell, James C Mrs, 1951, Jl 12,25:5

Howell, James E, 1916, S 27,11:6; 1956, Mr 24,19:3
Howell, James F, 1951, S 3,13:4
Howell, James W, 1938, S 21,25:2
Howell, Jesse, 1945, Ja 9,19:2
Howell, Jesse M, 1951, My 8,31:3
Howell, John A, 1947, Mr 21,21:2; 1953, Ap 5,76:4
Howell, John A Mrs, 1947, Jl 4,13:6
Howell, John Adams Rear-Adm, 1918, Ja 12,11:4
Howell, John C, 1943, Mr 13,13:6; 1961, Je 11,86:6
Howell, John D Mrs, 1946, F 5,24:3
Howell, John E, 1948, Je 12,15:4
Howell, John F, 1960, Mr 17,19:2
Howell, John J, 1944, Mr 6,19:4
Howell, John T Dr, 1937, Jl 11,II,4:7
Howell, John W (por), 1937, Jl 29,19:3
Howell, John W, 1951, Ja 28,76:2
Howell, John W Mrs, 1953, Ag 19,29:4
Howell, Jordan, 1954, Ag 22,92:3
Howell, Joseph A, 1960, F 18,33:4
Howell, Joseph M Dr, 1937, D 28,22:2
Howell, Josephine T Mrs, 1939, F 4,15:4
Howell, Julius F, 1948, Je 21,21:3
Howell, L, 1941, Mr 11,24:2
Howell, Laurence T, 1954, Ag 22,93:1
Howell, Lawrence B, 1963, Ap 23,37:3
Howell, Leone D, 1960, My 11,39:4
Howell, Lewis J, 1956, O 16,33:3
Howell, Lewis R, 1961, Ap 28,31:1
Howell, Lillian C, 1951, F 15,31:2
Howell, Lloyd M Mrs, 1943, Mr 20,15:1
Howell, Louis Mrs, 1916, Jl 30,15:4
Howell, Lucy C, 1945, Ap 12,23:4
Howell, M Hadden, 1944, Je 19,19:3
Howell, Margaret, 1951, Jl 22,61:3
Howell, Mary I, 1948, Je 15,27:4
Howell, Max D, 1967, Ja 21,31:4
Howell, Maxwell D (will), 1941, O 8,16:4
Howell, Millard F (Dixie), 1960, Mr 19,21:5
Howell, Murray D, 1950, O 3,31:4
Howell, Perdita P Mrs, 1953, Ag 1,11:4
Howell, Phil J, 1956, Mr 8,29:3
Howell, R, 1878, N 9,8:5
Howell, R B, 1933, Mr 12,28:1
Howell, R Carson, 1954, Je 21,23:2
Howell, Rapelje Mrs, 1949, F 27,69:1
Howell, Reese M, 1967, Mr 8,45:4
Howell, Reid, 1941, My 22,21:1
Howell, Riley P, 1943, Ap 18,48:6
Howell, Robert G, 1960, D 25,42:1
Howell, Robert H, 1944, N 25,13:6
Howell, Robert M, 1957, My 18,19:4
Howell, Robert W, 1951, Ja 27,13:6
Howell, Russell B, 1951, F 1,25:4
Howell, Samuel C, 1903, Jl 13,7:5
Howell, Sidney A, 1955, F 19,15:5
Howell, Sidney K, 1951, D 31,13:3
Howell, T P, 1878, D 4,3:2
Howell, Theodore F, 1938, S 22,23:4
Howell, Thomas, 1948, Ja 25,57:1
Howell, Thomas M (por), 1945, My 12,13:4
Howell, Thomas Mrs, 1943, Ag 15,39:2
Howell, Walter C Mrs, 1954, Mr 9,27:1
Howell, Walter F, 1944, O 25,21:6
Howell, Walter R, 1949, Mr 16,27:5
Howell, Wilbur F, 1937, N 23,23:3; 1967, Ap 5,47:3
Howell, Wilbur S Mrs, 1956, Ap 6,25:3
Howell, William, 1946, Ap 26,21:1; 1953, Ag 27,25:2
Howell, William E, 1949, D 24,15:1
Howell, William F, 1956, N 13,37:2; 1964, Jl 10,29:2
Howell, William G, 1925, N 18,23:4
Howell, William H, 1944, D 25,19:5
Howell, William H (por), 1945, F 7,21:5
Howell, William Mrs, 1952, F 9,13:5
Howell, William O, 1945, Mr 24,17:4
Howell, William P, 1948, Mr 30,23:5
Howell, William W, 1942, Ap 15,21:3
Howell, Wilson S, 1943, S 19,48:3
Howells, Alvin P, 1938, Ap 14,23:5
Howells, David P, 1939, Mr 30,23:5
Howells, Effie C Mrs, 1941, Jl 31,17:4
Howells, Eldon, 1947, Mr 28,23:1
Howells, Evan, 1950, My 13,17:5
Howells, George A, 1937, Je 10,23:1
Howells, Gertrude W Mrs, 1939, Ag 23,21:3
Howells, John M, 1959, S 23,35:4
Howells, Joseph Alexander, 1912, Ag 11,II,11:5
Howells, Mildred, 1966, Ap 20,47:1
Howells, Vincent A, 1958, Mr 15,17:4
Howells, William C, 1940, Ap 4,23:5
Howells, William D Mrs, 1910, My 8,II,13:4
Howells, William D 2d, 1954, S 5,50:1
Howells, William Dean (por),(funl, My 13,11:3), 1920, My 12,11:1
Hower, Frederick, 1918, F 2,11:8
Hower, Harry S, 1941, O 11,17:4
Hower, Harry S Jr, 1958, F 23,92:8
Hower, V Allen Mrs, 1968, Ap 15,43:1
Howerton, Huey B Jr, 1953, N 25,23:1
Howerton, Philip F, 1968, My 20,47:2
Howerton, Robert D, 1943, D 6,23:4
Howes, Alfred P, 1948, Ag 22,61:1
Howes, Arthur W, 1941, Ap 12,15:5
Howes, Benjamin A, 1952, Ja 11,22:2
Howes, Benjamin Mrs, 1950, O 30,27:5
Howes, Bessie E, 1956, Mr 11,88:7
Howes, Cecil C, 1950, My 19,92:3
Howes, Daniel H Mrs, 1962, S 3,15:3
Howes, Edward T, 1964, My 11,31:4
Howes, Ernest A, 1940, F 11,49:2
Howes, Ernest G, 1951, O 8,21:5
Howes, Frank M, 1949, D 25,26:5
Howes, Franklin J Sr, 1961, My 27,23:3
Howes, H Perry, 1952, S 5,27:3
Howes, H Perry Mrs, 1945, Mr 22,23:3
Howes, Helen S Mrs, 1943, N 15,19:2
Howes, Henry S, 1954, F 1,23:2
Howes, Herbert H, 1940, N 10,57:1
Howes, Horace (est), 1871, Mr 14,1:4
Howes, I Garfton, 1952, Ag 22,21:1
Howes, James E, 1941, D 28,28:8
Howes, James E Mrs, 1954, Ag 25,27:4
Howes, Kingsley Mrs, 1942, Mr 28,17:4
Howes, Leander T Mrs, 1943, F 6,13:2
Howes, Osborn, 1907, Ap 10,7:7
Howes, Reuben W 3d, 1949, Mr 3,25:3
Howes, Reuben Wing Rev, 1919, N 26,13:1
Howes, Richard H, 1940, D 3,25:3
Howes, S B, 1901, My 19,2:4
Howes, Samuel H, 1954, D 7,33:3
Howes, Stanwood, 1954, Ag 31,21:4
Howes, Susan L, 1964, Ap 23,39:4
Howes, Walter S, 1952, F 18,19:4
Howes, William E, 1952, Ap 8,29:4
Howes, William F, 1939, Ja 6,21:4
Howes, William W, 1962, Ja 16,33:1
Howeson, John H C E, 1951, Ja 13,15:2
Howey, Walter C (funl, Mr 24,27:1), 1954, Mr 22, 27:3
Howey, Walter C Mrs, 1954, Ja 27,27:2
Howey, William J, 1938, Je 8,23:2
Howgate, George W, 1950, N 18,6:4
Howgate, H W, 1901, Je 2,2:5
Howick Tom, 1948, N 23,29:5
Howie, Brison, 1949, My 19,29:2
Howie, Henry D Mrs, 1956, F 6,23:4
Howie, John R, 1949, Je 14,31:2
Howie, Robert A Jr, 1944, N 10,19:3
Howie, Robert G, 1954, Ag 3,19:3
Howie, William M, 1951, Ap 10,27:3
Howiey, Thomas P, 1940, Ag 4,23:5
Howison, Henry Lycurgus, 1914, D 31,9:4
Howison, Robert W, 1966, O 28,31:2
Howitt, Frederick E, 1939, Ag 26,15:7
Howitt, Harold, 1939, Mr 12,III,7:1
Howitt, John N, 1958, Ja 25,19:4
Howitt, Louis R, 1953, N 22,88:1
Howitt, V A Mrs, 1960, My 28,21:6
Howitt, W, 1879, Mr 4,5:4
Howitz, Charles R, 1962, Ja 18,29:3
Howk, H J Dr, 1926, Ap 9,3:1
Howland, Alice, 1943, Ja 7,10:7
Howland, Amasa W, 1939, S 2,17:6
Howland, Arthur C, 1952, Mr 30,93:1
Howland, Arthur H, 1952, Ap 5,15:4
Howland, Arthur V, 1949, D 4,108:5
Howland, Benjamin F, 1942, Je 8,15:6
Howland, Blanche, 1943, Je 18,22:3
Howland, Charles F, 1953, S 23,31:2
Howland, Charles R, 1946, S 22,63:4
Howland, Clarence Mrs, 1955, F 7,21:2
Howland, D R, 1949, Ap 8,25:1
Howland, Edgar Orville Rev, 1922, Mr 18,13:5
Howland, Edith, 1949, S 9,25:4
Howland, Edward A, 1911, Ag 28,7:5
Howland, Edward J, 1939, Ja 26,21:5
Howland, Esther, 1942, Mr 31,21:4
Howland, Eugene Mrs, 1951, N 18,91:2
Howland, F Arthur, 1952, Ap 27,91:1
Howland, Francis A, 1951, Je 5,31:3
Howland, Frank L, 1946, F 6,23:6
Howland, Fred A, 1953, Mr 31,31:2
Howland, Fred A Mrs, 1952, Je 21,15:3
Howland, Frederick Hoppin, 1916, Je 7,13:7
Howland, G G, 1903, My 10,7:5
Howland, Gardner, 1941, Je 4,23:2
Howland, George C, 1954, Je 6,87:1
Howland, George K, 1958, My 6,35:2
Howland, George T, 1911, S 25,9:4
Howland, Goldwin W, 1950, Jl 13,25:2
Howland, Henry C Mrs, 1913, F 24,11:4
Howland, Henry E, 1913, N 9,IV,7:5
Howland, Herbert, 1939, D 27,21:3
Howland, Hewitt H (por), 1944, My 11,19:1
Howland, Horace, 1908, Ap 1,7:6
Howland, Horace Mrs, 1956, Ag 6,23:2
Howland, Irving H, 1946, Ag 2,19:5
Howland, Isabel, 1942, D 6,76:1
Howland, J Dr, 1926, Je 21,19:5
Howland, J Hoyt, 1940, Jl 21,29:3
Howland, Jesse A, 1945, N 7,23:6
Howland, Jesse A Mrs, 1944, Jl 20,19:3
Howland, Joby A, 1939, Ag 14,15:2
Howland, John D, 1951, D 27,21:3
Howland, John G, 1947, Je 19,21:5
Howland, John H, 1942, O 12,34:6
Howland, Joseph A Mrs, 1912, Ja 10,17:4
Howland, Joseph G, 1949, Jl 5,24:3
Howland, Joseph M, 1949, Ag 13,11:2
Howland, Leroy A, 1959, Ag 28,23:1
Howland, Llewellyn, 1957, Ja 7,25:4
Howland, Mary, 1943, Ja 7,10:7
Howland, Meredith, 1912, Ap 6,11:5; 1937, N 24,23:6
Howland, Nathaniel J, 1955, F 17,27:5
Howland, Paul, 1942, D 24,15:1
Howland, Reeve B, 1944, My 13,19:2
Howland, Richard G S, 1937, S 13,21:4
Howland, Richard W, 1952, My 21,28:5
Howland, Russell, 1945, Ap 17,23:6
Howland, S S Mrs, 1902, Je 1,9:3
Howland, Samuel S Mrs, 1945, Ja 24,22:2
Howland, Samuel Shaw, 1925, Ap 29,21:5
Howland, Silas W (por), 1938, S 2,17:1
Howland, Thomas E Sr, 1962, Mr 4,86:3
Howland, Thomas J, 1944, N 29,23:4
Howland, William, 1945, My 3,23:4
Howland, William Bailey (funl, Mr 1,13:4), 1917, F 28,11:5
Howland, William Capt, 1875, Je 25,6:5
Howland, William Le Grand, 1915, Jl 28,9:4
Howland, William R, 1943, Ja 15,17:3
Howland-Shearman, Charles H, 1941, D 15,19:2
Howle, Francis, 1938, D 23,19:4
Howlett, Alfred Ames, 1905, F 1,9:3
Howlett, Edwin J, 1912, Jl 19,9:6
Howlett, Edwin Sr, 1914, Je 16,9:6
Howlett, Francis E, 1943, Je 25,17:5
Howlett, James D, 1965, My 14,37:2
Howlett, James R, 1939, O 11,27:5
Howlett, John J, 1951, Mr 23,21:2
Howlett, Morris E, 1939, My 26,23:3
Howlett, Walter M Mrs, 1961, N 14,36:4
Howley, Bartholomew M, 1940, S 3,17:2
Howley, Clarence P, 1950, Ap 4,29:3
Howley, Daniel P, 1944, Mr 11,14:7
Howley, Francis H, 1952, F 15,26:2
Howley, Frank A, 1943, D 24,13:4
Howley, John F, 1947, Mr 15,13:4
Howley, Matthew J, 1949, S 20,17:3
Howley, Michael F Archbishop, 1914, O 21,11:6
Howley, Thomas P Mrs, 1943, My 29,13:4
Howley, Vincent J, 1967, Ja 25,43:3
Howley, William R, 1941, Ap 19,15:3
Howlin, Olin, 1959, S 21,31:3
Howorth, Edgar F, 1947, N 25,32:5
Howorth, James W Mrs, 1961, N 9,35:4
Howorth, John, 1945, Mr 26,19:4
Howroyd, Joshua Mrs, 1947, O 17,21:1
Howry, Charles B Mrs, 1942, Ag 1,11:5
Howry, Kenneth A Mrs, 1967, Ja 30,29:1
Hows, John A, 1874, S 29,5:2
Howse, Hilary E (por), 1938, Ja 3,21:5
Howse, J Reid, 1955, Mr 2,27:3
Howson, Albert S, 1960, Ag 3,29:5
Howson, Elmer T, 1944, S 2,11:2
Howson, F A, 1926, Je 30,25:5
Howson, Henry, 1937, Jl 7,23:1
Howson, Hubert (por), 1943, O 9,13:4
Howson, J Howard Mrs, 1946, Jl 8,29:4
Howson, Roger, 1962, Ap 23,29:2
Howze, R L Gen, 1926, S 20,23:5
Howze, S Perry Mrs, 1949, N 6,92:4
Hoxie, Albert N, 1942, Ag 21,19:6
Hoxie, Charles A, 1941, O 14,23:6
Hoxie, Edward E, 1949, Je 21,25:2
Hoxie, George H, 1959, Ap 12,87:1
Hoxie, N B Jr, 1907, Mr 26,9:4
Hoxie, R L, 1930, My 1,29:3
Hoxie, Rosa P Mrs, 1938, N 1,23:1
Hoxie, Timothy W, 1941, My 12,17:4
Hoxie, Vinnie Ream Mrs, 1914, N 21,13:4
Hoxsey, B W, 1881, D 9,5:3
Hoxsey, J M B, 1946, Ag 29,27:4
Hoxsey, Mary I, 1940, Mr 4,15:4
Hoxsey, T D Gen, 1881, My 31,5:5
Hoxter, Frieda Mrs, 1955, Mr 7,48:1
Hoxter, Jacob, 1955, My 25,33:1
Hoxter, Jacob Mrs, 1964, Ja 23,31:3
Hoxter, Oliver O, 1944, Ja 20,19:5
Hoxton, Llewellyn K, 1957, Ag 30,19:2
Hoy, Albert Charles, 1925, Ja 31,13:5
Hoy, Austin Y, 1962, Ag 16,27:5
Hoy, Austin Y Mrs, 1960, Ag 2,29:5
Hoy, D F, 1930, D 7,II,8:1
Hoy, Edmund R, 1957, F 11,29:6
Hoy, Edward F Sr, 1941, N 22,19:5
Hoy, Frank C, 1950, N 3,27:4
Hoy, H Victor, 1960, D 1,35:2
Hoy, Jane C, 1948, Jl 14,24:3
Hoy, Joseph, 1947, D 9,29:3
Hoy, Mary B Mrs, 1937, N 7,II,9:2
Hoy, Mary L, 1951, S 26,31:1
Hoy, Robert W, 1947, O 18,16:2
Hoy, Vincent R, 1953, Je 3,31:2
Hoy, William A (por), 1938, O 4,25:3
Hoy, William D, 1948, D 19,76:4
Hoy, William E (Dummy), 1961, D 16,25:2
Hoy, William J, 1949, Ag 31,23:2

Hoyal, Robert L Mrs, 1961, Je 8,35:2
Hoye, Harry W, 1962, Jl 15,60:3
Hoye, Henry J, 1942, Ap 27,15:2
Hoye, Stephen M, 1938, Ag 1,13:5
Hoye, Vincent C, 1938, F 25,17:1
Hoye, Warren F, 1954, Je 18,23:5
Hoyer, Charles E, 1941, Ja 2,23:5
Hoyer, Eric Mrs, 1955, Ja 4,21:1
Hoyer, Frans T G, 1962, Ap 19,18:4
Hoyer, Frederick F Dr, 1912, Ag 27,9:6
Hoyer, George E, 1959, Ap 9,31:2
Hoyer, Jan, 1954, D 16,37:1
Hoyer, Theodore B F, 1943, Je 2,25:2
Hoyes, John H, 1945, D 19,14:7
Hoyhurst, Hicks, 1882, D 25,8:4
Hoyland, Colin G, 1963, Ap 2,28:7
Hoyle, Emmanuel Sir, 1939, My 10,23:4
Hoyle, Harry, 1958, S 3,33:3
Hoyle, James, 1946, Je 17,21:6
Hoyle, Numa R, 1951, Jl 8,60:2
Hoyle, Pettus V, 1966, Jl 23,25:2
Hoyle, Rhonald J, 1968, Ja 28,76:3
Hoyle, William J, 1954, O 27,29:5
Hoyler, Cyril N, 1959, O 23,10:5
Hoyme, Robert, 1950, O 22,92:5
Hoyne, Maclay, 1939, O 2,17:3
Hoyne, T, 1883, Jl 30,5:1
Hoyne, Thomas M, 1941, S 30,23:6
Hoyne, Thomas T, 1946, D 19,29:2
Hoynes, Dan A, 1950, Ag 30,31:2
Hoyningen-Huene, George, 1968, S 23,35:2
Hoyns, Henry, 1945, Ja 24,21:1
Hoyns, Henry Mrs, 1961, N 24,28:6
Hoyo, Hervey H, 1948, S 21,27:6
Hoysradt, Warren J (trb, F 4,24:1), 1944, F 2,21:5
Hoystradt, Louis, 1950, S 7,31:4
Hoyt, A M, 1903, Je 19,9:5
Hoyt, Adrian H Dr, 1920, O 22,15:5
Hoyt, Albert E, 1924, Mr 6,17:4
Hoyt, Alfred Dudley Capt, 1914, Ja 9,11:5
Hoyt, Alfred W, 1911, N 21,9:5
Hoyt, Allen G (por), 1941, N 5,23:3
Hoyt, Anne S, 1951, Jl 11,23:5
Hoyt, Arthur C, 1941, Jl 14,13:5; 1957, S 4,33:2
Hoyt, Arthur C Mrs, 1937, N 10,25:3
Hoyt, Arthur Steven Prof, 1924, Mr 17,15:5
Hoyt, Beatrix, 1963, Ag 15,29:3
Hoyt, Belding A, 1940, Ap 4,23:5
Hoyt, Burnham, 1960, Ap 8,31:2
Hoyt, C A, 1903, Ap 19,7:4
Hoyt, C Sherman (funl plans, Mr 22,41:4), 1961, Mr 20,29:3
Hoyt, Carman, 1905, Je 12,1:6
Hoyt, Carol, 1941, Je 25,21:3
Hoyt, Charles, 1940, F 25,38:8
Hoyt, Charles B, 1938, Mr 12,17:5; 1949, Mr 26,17:5
Hoyt, Charles E, 1937, Jl 11,II,5:2
Hoyt, Charles H, 1900, N 21,1:5
Hoyt, Charles H Capt, 1922, Ja 20,15:4
Hoyt, Charles L, 1940, Je 29,15:7
Hoyt, Charles Sr, 1951, Ag 1,23:2
Hoyt, Charles W H, 1950, Mr 31,32:6
Hoyt, Charles W H Mrs, 1943, S 4,13:6
Hoyt, Chester J, 1938, N 19,17:2
Hoyt, Chester J Mrs, 1946, Jl 9,21:1
Hoyt, Clare J Mrs (por), 1941, Mr 11,23:3
Hoyt, Colgate (funl, F 2,17:5), 1922, Ja 31,12:5
Hoyt, Colgate, 1963, S 14,25:1
Hoyt, Colgate Mrs, 1908, S 16,9:5
Hoyt, E E, 1903, Ap 15,9:6
Hoyt, Edward C, 1925, N 29,13:1
Hoyt, Edward K, 1938, Je 27,17:2
Hoyt, Edwin, 1874, My 16,4:7; 1948, Jl 30,18:4
Hoyt, Edwin C, 1954, O 22,27:3
Hoyt, Edwin C Mrs, 1965, Ag 7,21:3
Hoyt, Eliza M W Mrs, 1942, Jl 25,13:5
Hoyt, Elizabeth W, 1939, Ag 17,21:2
Hoyt, Ella P Mrs, 1937, Ja 19,23:1
Hoyt, Elmer S, 1957, N 17,87:1
Hoyt, Elton M, 1942, D 24,15:3
Hoyt, Elton 2d, 1955, Mr 17,45:3
Hoyt, Ernest L, 1943, S 29,21:3
Hoyt, Eugene F Dr, 1913, My 27,11:5
Hoyt, F M, 1903, Ag 15,7:6
Hoyt, Fanny L, 1960, F 8,29:3
Hoyt, Ferdinand A, 1944, D 9,15:4
Hoyt, Francis Deming, 1922, Jl 22,7:5
Hoyt, Frank C, 1949, Je 30,23:4
Hoyt, Frank H, 1922, Mr 1,5:5; 1939, F 9,21:5
Hoyt, Frank W, 1945, D 29,13:2
Hoyt, Franklin C (por), 1937, N 14,II,10:4
Hoyt, Franklin G, 1940, Mr 30,15:4
Hoyt, Franklin S, 1948, S 26,76:2
Hoyt, Frederick A, 1965, O 27,47:5
Hoyt, Frederick M, 1940, Jl 8,17:2
Hoyt, George B, 1948, Je 12,15:4
Hoyt, George H, 1904, N 21,1:4; 1938, O 12,27:2; 1946, Ap 4,25:3
Hoyt, Gilbert F, 1942, My 28,17:5
Hoyt, Goold, 1911, Ap 23,11:5
Hoyt, Grace E, 1950, O 21,17:3
Hoyt, H Norman, 1949, O 24,23:3
Hoyt, Harold C, 1956, Ja 18,31:2
Hoyt, Harold W, 1953, Jl 10,19:5
Hoyt, Harriet M, 1948, Mr 13,15:4
Hoyt, Henry A, 1967, D 17,93:1
Hoyt, Henry M, 1910, N 21,9:5
Hoyt, Henry Reese (funl, Ja 8,11:6), 1921, Ja 6,11:4
Hoyt, Henry W, 1912, My 26,15:5
Hoyt, Hervey H, 1948, S 21,27:2
Hoyt, Hiram C, 1948, Ja 12,19:2
Hoyt, Homer Sr Mrs, 1947, Ag 19,23:6
Hoyt, Howard Clark, 1907, N 24,9:7
Hoyt, Ira F, 1942, My 29,17:3
Hoyt, Irene E, 1953, Ja 21,31:5
Hoyt, Irving F, 1943, D 23,20:2
Hoyt, James, 1937, S 7,21:1
Hoyt, James H, 1917, Mr 22,11:4
Hoyt, Janet Ralston Chase Mrs, 1925, N 20,21:3
Hoyt, Jerry, 1955, Jl 12,31:4
Hoyt, Jesse, 1882, Ag 15,5:1; 1902, Ja 13,7:6; 1968, O 15,47:2
Hoyt, Jesse E, 1953, My 4,23:3
Hoyt, John A, 1957, F 18,27:5
Hoyt, John C, 1946, Je 23,40:7
Hoyt, John E, 1954, S 14,27:3
Hoyt, John G, 1947, O 15,27:3
Hoyt, John S, 1954, Mr 31,27:4
Hoyt, John S Mrs, 1952, D 2,36:6
Hoyt, John T, 1962, F 8,31:2
Hoyt, John T N, 1943, Ap 17,17:4
Hoyt, John Wesley, 1912, My 24,13:5
Hoyt, John Wesley Mrs, 1912, S 24,13:6
Hoyt, Joseph B, 1942, S 17,25:4
Hoyt, Joseph B Mrs, 1913, Mr 9,IV,7:4
Hoyt, Josephine, 1938, Mr 30,21:6
Hoyt, Julia (Mrs A C Giles),(will, N 26,12:5), 1955, N 1,31:2
Hoyt, Leo T, 1954, Je 18,23:3
Hoyt, Leon G, 1964, O 9,39:1
Hoyt, Lydia, 1959, Ap 27,27:3
Hoyt, M, 1877, F 15,5:3
Hoyt, Mark D, 1941, F 14,17:2
Hoyt, Mary Cleveland Mrs, 1914, Jl 30,9:5
Hoyt, Melvin A, 1925, N 18,23:4
Hoyt, Miles A, 1944, My 14,46:2
Hoyt, Morgan H, 1953, F 24,25:1
Hoyt, Morton M, 1949, Ag 22,21:5
Hoyt, Newton H, 1959, O 24,21:5
Hoyt, Oliver, 1887, My 4,1:6
Hoyt, Oliver C, 1946, Jl 15,25:5
Hoyt, Osmon P, 1939, Ap 5,25:6
Hoyt, Phelps B Mrs, 1958, N 2,89:1
Hoyt, Phil D, 1950, Jl 5,31:1; 1950, N 24,27:1
Hoyt, R F, 1935, Mr 8,21:1
Hoyt, R M, 1903, Ja 8,1:4
Hoyt, R Rev, 1878, O 12,5:4
Hoyt, Randell Mrs, 1911, Ap 6,11:4
Hoyt, Ray, 1950, My 23,29:2
Hoyt, Ray S, 1958, Mr 17,29:4
Hoyt, Raymond, 1946, O 9,27:1
Hoyt, Richard C, 1939, O 14,19:5
Hoyt, Richard S, 1957, Jl 17,27:1
Hoyt, Robert E, 1953, D 20,76:3
Hoyt, Roy C, 1943, O 11,19:4
Hoyt, Russell P, 1951, O 27,19:2
Hoyt, Samuel E, 1939, O 13,23:3
Hoyt, Samuel O, 1954, N 2,27:3
Hoyt, Samuel W Jr, 1962, Mr 8,31:2
Hoyt, Stanley S, 1960, Ap 14,31:4
Hoyt, Stephen, 1950, Ap 1,15:2
Hoyt, Stephen B, 1961, Ap 7,23:4
Hoyt, T J Col, 1882, O 26,4:7
Hoyt, Thomas A, 1903, Je 30,7:5
Hoyt, Virginia S (will), 1939, Je 8,9:1
Hoyt, W H Rev Father, 1883, D 12,4:7
Hoyt, W M, 1925, D 18,23:2
Hoyt, Walter S, 1920, Jl 15,7:3
Hoyt, Wilhelmina G Mrs, 1940, S 6,21:6
Hoyt, Willard E, 1948, Ja 21,26:3
Hoyt, Willard E Jr, 1960, Ag 22,25:4
Hoyt, William, 1902, D 24,9:5
Hoyt, William B, 1915, Je 12,11:6
Hoyt, William E, 1916, Ap 3,13:5
Hoyt, William Elbridge, 1917, Mr 24,11:5
Hoyt, William H, 1957, S 7,19:5
Hoyt, William Mrs, 1950, Mr 26,96:1
Hoyt, William P, 1952, Mr 15,13:5
Hoyt, William Sprague, 1905, Ap 29,11:6
Hoyt, William T, 1954, My 22,15:4
Hoyt, William T Mrs (por), 1947, Jl 17,19:4
Hoyt, William W, 1954, D 2,31:1
Hoyt, Winfield S Mrs, 1945, Je 11,15:5
Hoyt, Zelotes, 1947, Ap 22,26:3
Hoyte, Clason, 1912, Mr 25,11:4
Hoyte, George F, 1918, N 18,15:5
Hozack, John, 1951, N 1,19:3
Hozar, Faik, 1954, Ja 10,86:4
Hozumi, N Baron, 1926, Ap 7,23:4
Hozumi, Shegeto, 1951, Jl 31,22:3
Hraba, Felix Mrs, 1939, My 26,23:2
Hrabeska, Alexander L, 1947, F 19,25:3
Hraman, William O Mrs, 1956, F 8,33:5
Hrawi, George, 1964, Mr 1,83:3
Hrbek, Frank, 1951, O 27,19:3
Hrbek, Sara, 1948, F 9,17:1
Hrdina, Henry Sr, 1945, Ja 9,19:4
Hrdlicka, Ales (por), 1943, S 6,17:3
Hreha, Joseph Jr, 1949, My 12,31:2
Hribar, Martin, 1945, O 19,23:5
Hritz, John, 1942, D 9,27:5
Hrouda, Joseph, 1954, F 24,25:1
Hrozny, Bedrich, 1952, D 20,17:1
Hruby, Allan J, 1939, N 19,39:1
Hrucelak, Mikolay, 1950, O 8,13:2
Hruda, Frank G, 1966, Jl 7,37:1
Hruska, Stephen L, 1945, F 7,21:4
Hrusovsky, Francis, 1956, S 12,37:2
Hrycak, Paul V, 1958, Ap 4,21:3
Hryhoriev, Nikifor Y, 1953, Ag 7,19:5
Hsia, Yun Dr, 1968, Ag 10,27:4
Hsiang, Ve-Shuen, 1961, S 16,8:1
Hsien Feng, Emperor (I Chu, Hien Fung), 1861, N 21,6:1
Hsu, Leonard S Mrs, 1958, F 19,27:2
Hsu Fu Lin, 1958, Ja 14,30:4
Hsu Kuang-ping, Mrs, 1968, Mr 4,37:4
Hsu Mo, 1956, Je 30,17:4
Hsu Pei-hung, 1953, S 28,25:5
Hsu Sze-Hao, 1961, Ag 11,24:1
Hsu Tsung-chi, 1923, Ap 10,21:4
Hsu Tsung-han, 1944, Mr 11,13:2
Hsu Wei-yang, 1952, Mr 21,2:6
Hsu Yung-chang, 1959, Jl 13,27:4
Hsun, Prince, 1951, Mr 31,15:4
Hu Cheng-Tse, 1949, Ap 16,15:3
Hu Jo-shan, 1962, S 22,3:3
Hu Shih (trb, F 27,32:2), 1962, F 25,89:1
Hu Tsung-Nan, 1962, F 15,29:4
Huang, Wen E, 1940, My 11,19:5
Huang Ching, 1958, F 13,29:4
Huang Yen-pei (funl, D 25,13:2), 1965, D 22,31:3
Huard, Serge, 1944, Mr 23,19:4
Hub, Carlton M, 1960, Ja 18,27:1
Hubach, Frederick J, 1941, Ja 19,41:1
Hubach, Louis A, 1943, S 23,21:3
Hubal, August E, 1952, Ag 30,13:7
Huband, George D, 1943, My 3,17:5
Hubar, Max A, 1962, My 16,41:5
Hubard, Archibald B, 1952, My 28,29:3
Hubard, Archibald B Mrs, 1954, Ja 7,31:3
Hubard, Lyttleton E, 1963, Je 9,87:1
Hubatka, Charles Sr Mrs, 1945, D 18,27:1
Hubay, Jeno de S, 1937, Mr 13,19:3
Hubb, Irving G, 1952, Jl 23,23:5
Hubback, John H, 1939, N 8,23:2
Hubbard, Albert W Mrs, 1943, S 7,23:3
Hubbard, Andrew C Rev Dr, 1907, Ap 20,9:6
Hubbard, Anna Eliza Mrs, 1909, Je 6,9:5
Hubbard, Arnold B, 1950, D 19,25:5
Hubbard, Benjamin H, 1940, Ja 9,23:5
Hubbard, Benny, 1964, Mr 30,29:4
Hubbard, Bernard R, 1962, My 29,31:4
Hubbard, C E, 1928, Ag 26,II,12:2
Hubbard, C Russell Mrs, 1965, Ja 5,33:1
Hubbard, Cal Mrs, 1964, Mr 1,83:2
Hubbard, Calvin J, 1952, Ja 14,19:6
Hubbard, Catherine W Mrs, 1954, Mr 15,25:5
Hubbard, Ch W Bp, 1903, D 27,14:1
Hubbard, Charles, 1875, D 29,4:5; 1915, O 23,11:
Hubbard, Charles D, 1951, S 20,31:2
Hubbard, Charles J, 1950, Ag 2,1:2
Hubbard, Charles W, 1943, My 17,15:5
Hubbard, Charles White, 1905, Ja 28,1:6
Hubbard, Chauncey K, 1962, F 25,89:2
Hubbard, Daniel B, 1908, Mr 28,9:6
Hubbard, Deane G, 1959, Mr 13,29:3
Hubbard, Demas, 1873, S 3,5:5
Hubbard, E Kent (will), 1943, My 8,8:7
Hubbard, E Kent Mrs (will, Ag 13,11:6), 1941, Ja 26,37:1
Hubbard, Edgar W, 1947, F 23,54:5
Hubbard, Edward F, 1949, My 25,29:2
Hubbard, Edwin D, 1956, S 19,37:2
Hubbard, Elijah K, 1941, Ag 8,15:6
Hubbard, Elisha D Mrs (will, Ap 3,54:8; est appr 1,25:6), 1959, Mr 19,33:2
Hubbard, Elisha D Mrs (est tax acctg), 1960, N 26:7
Hubbard, Elizabeth Dr (Mrs Benj A Hubbard), 1967, My 23,47:3
Hubbard, Emily S Mrs, 1949, D 20,31:2
Hubbard, Eugene E, 1953, Ap 6,19:4
Hubbard, F Elmore, 1943, S 22,23:5
Hubbard, F Mc K, 1930, D 27,13:1
Hubbard, F W, 1882, S 29,5:2
Hubbard, Francis (por), 1944, N 7,27:4
Hubbard, Frank B, 1954, Ap 8,27:5
Hubbard, Frank D, 1955, F 10,31:6
Hubbard, Frederick A, 1956, Jl 18,27:4
Hubbard, G Evans, 1950, Jl 25,27:3
Hubbard, G Munroe, 1953, D 31,19:3
Hubbard, George B (Amos Moore), 1958, Jl 7,
Hubbard, George D, 1958, Je 13,23:5
Hubbard, George E, 1954, F 25,31:3
Hubbard, George H, 1948, N 13,15:2
Hubbard, George L, 1881, Ja 12,5:4
Hubbard, George M, 1944, N 13,19:4
Hubbard, George W, 1955, Jl 25,19:4

Hubbard, Gorham, 1962, Ag 29,29:2
Hubbard, Guy R, 1948, D 13,23:4
Hubbard, H Warren, 1946, S 7,15:4
Hubbard, Harlan Page, 1903, D 1,9:6
Hubbard, Harriet F (will), 1948, N 6,8:6
Hubbard, Harry A, 1947, S 7,60:5
Hubbard, Harry Mrs, 1953, Jl 22,27:2
Hubbard, Harry V, 1946, F 1,23:2
Hubbard, Helen, 1946, D 27,20:2
Hubbard, Henry Capt, 1904, F 16,9:6
Hubbard, Henry D, 1943, Je 27,32:8
Hubbard, Henry E, 1957, Ap 7,88:5
Hubbard, Henry F, 1954, O 13,31:4
Hubbard, Henry M Mrs, 1945, Je 12,19:4
Hubbard, Henry V, 1947, O 8,25:2
Hubbard, Hiram Wilbur, 1922, Ap 1,15:5
Hubbard, I Lewis, 1941, Jl 9,21:6
Hubbard, Isaac M, 1937, Ag 16,19:5
Hubbard, James Capt, 1905, Je 27,9:5
Hubbard, John A, 1872, Ag 1,1:6
Hubbard, John C, 1946, Je 13,27:3; 1954, Ag 3,19:2
Hubbard, John J, 1939, F 8,23:5
Hubbard, John K Rev, 1952, D 15,25:4
Hubbard, John Mrs, 1955, Ag 8,21:5
Hubbard, John T Judge, 1937, Ja 19,23:3
Hubbard, John T L, 1954, Ap 25,87:1
Hubbard, John W (por), 1947, Je 4,27:3
Hubbard, Joseph B Mrs, 1958, Je 12,31:4
Hubbard, Joseph D, 1957, D 12,29:5
Hubbard, Joseph S, 1954, S 15,33:2
Hubbard, Leroy, 1938, S 1,23:4
Hubbard, Lester T, 1958, My 10,21:6
Hubbard, Lucius F, 1913, F 7,11:5
Hubbard, Lulu M (Mrs P McGrath), 1966, O 22,31:5
Hubbard, Mabel P Mrs, 1941, D 8,23:2
Hubbard, Moses G, 1967, Jl 30,64:6
Hubbard, Moses G Sr, 1947, D 13,15:3
Hubbard, Murray Mrs, 1943, Jl 10,13:4
Hubbard, Nathaniel T, 1875, My 9,7:3
Hubbard, Nelson E, 1942, S 7,19:5
Hubbard, Norman S, 1945, S 21,21:3
Hubbard, Oliver P M, 1948, O 6,29:3
Hubbard, Oliver W Sr, 1951, D 27,21:5
Hubbard, Oscar, 1937, Jl 14,21:6
Hubbard, Osman H, 1941, Ja 6,15:1
Hubbard, Philip P, 1945, Ap 7,15:6
Hubbard, Platt, 1946, My 8,25:3
Hubbard, Provost Mrs, 1949, Mr 25,23:4
Hubbard, R B ex-Gov, 1901, Jl 13,7:6
Hubbard, R D, 1884, F 29,5:6
Hubbard, Ralph K Mrs, 1939, D 31,18:5
Hubbard, Reuben, 1942, Mr 6,22:2
Hubbard, Richard J, 1939, Ja 9,15:4
Hubbard, Richard L Mrs, 1967, Ja 19,31:5
Hubbard, Richard P Mrs, 1941, F 24,15:5
Hubbard, Robert B, 1938, Ap 17,II,7:3
Hubbard, Robert F, 1949, My 30,13:3
Hubbard, Robert J Mrs, 1953, Ap 20,25:6
Hubbard, Rufus P, 1939, Ja 8,43:2
Hubbard, Ruth W, 1955, D 8,37:3
Hubbard, S Dana Dr, 1937, Jl 14,22:1
Hubbard, S T, 1933, Mr 23,17:1
Hubbard, Samuel, 1949, Mr 6,72:7
Hubbard, Samuel E, 1938, Ap 5,21:2
Hubbard, Samuel T, 1962, D 27,7:4
Hubbard, Samuel T Mrs, 1943, My 2,44:8
Hubbard, Samuel T Sr Mrs, 1961, D 5,39:6
Hubbard, Sanford, 1955, My 23,23:1
Hubbard, Socrates Com, 1907, Mr 13,9:6
Hubbard, Stephen A, 1963, Ag 27,31:3
Hubbard, Susan P Mrs, 1952, Ag 15,16:4
Hubbard, Therese, 1940, S 6,21:5
Hubbard, Thomas, 1943, Jl 7,19:4
Hubbard, Thomas H Mrs, 1921, My 16,15:4
Hubbard, Thomas Hamlin Gen, 1915, My 20,11:5
Hubbard, W C, 1927, N 25,21:5
Hubbard, W H Rev Dr, 1913, F 1,13:5
Hubbard, Walter E Mrs, 1953, N 1,87:2
Hubbard, Walter Jr, 1944, My 14,46:4
Hubbard, Wilbur W, 1938, S 14,23:5
Hubbard, William F, 1942, Ag 3,15:6
Hubbard, William G Mrs, 1954, Jl 25,69:2
Hubbard, William H, 1937, S 9,23:2
Hubbard, William N, 1948, Ap 22,27:5
Hubbard, William N Jr, 1953, Ja 15,27:3
Hubbard, William S, 1944, S 2,11:5
Hubbard, William T, 1913, Ag 23,7:2; 1921, F 24,13:6
Hubbard, William W, 1954, Ja 23,13:5
Hubbard, Wynant D, 1961, D 10,88:5
Hubbeell, Horatio Gen, 1875, Jl 27,4:7
Hubbel, Harold G Mrs, 1951, Ap 23,25:4
Hubbel, Ira H, 1938, Mr 11,19:2
Hubbell, Allan H, 1964, Mr 15,86:4
Hubbell, Benjamin, 1943, Mr 1,19:2
Hubbell, Benjamin S, 1953, F 23,25:4
Hubbell, Burt G, 1925, Ja 25,7:2
Hubbell, Charles B, 1939, Jl 25,19:1
Hubbell, Charles C, 1948, Jl 20,23:3
Hubbell, Charles E Mrs, 1946, Mr 26,29:5
Hubbell, Charles M, 1951, S 28,31:4
Hubbell, D D, 1957, S 8,84:4
Hubbell, De Witt, 1952, Ag 26,25:2
Hubbell, Delmer F, 1964, D 11,39:1
Hubbell, Edward W, 1941, O 30,23:4
Hubbell, F C, 1947, My 4,60:3
Hubbell, F M, 1930, N 12,23:4
Hubbell, Frederick B, 1960, O 5,41:4
Hubbell, Frederick B Mrs, 1943, Ja 26,19:1
Hubbell, Frederick W, 1959, Mr 15,88:2
Hubbell, George F, 1945, Jl 12,11:7
Hubbell, George L, 1959, Mr 15,89:1
Hubbell, George L Mrs, 1955, O 12,31:5
Hubbell, George O, 1938, D 26,24:4
Hubbell, George W Jr, 1958, Je 6,24:1
Hubbell, Grover C, 1956, D 11,39:4
Hubbell, Harold G, 1952, D 16,31:3
Hubbell, Harvey, 1968, Jl 13,27:4
Hubbell, Henry L Rev, 1908, F 29,7:6
Hubbell, Henry M Mrs, 1945, Mr 15,23:3
Hubbell, Henry S, 1949, Ja 10,25:4
Hubbell, Henry Wilson Brig-Gen, 1917, D 17,13:4
Hubbell, Henry Wilson 3d, 1968, My 1,47:4
Hubbell, Irving L, 1951, N 20,31:4
Hubbell, James F, 1948, Je 12,15:1
Hubbell, James W Mrs, 1960, D 4,88:7
Hubbell, James Wakeman (por), 1944, Jl 21,19:1
Hubbell, Jesse P, 1954, F 3,23:3
Hubbell, Jesse P Mrs, 1954, F 23,27:2
Hubbell, John, 1880, Ja 28,5:6
Hubbell, John B Capt, 1907, Jl 10,7:5
Hubbell, John E Mrs, 1954, Ap 17,13:4
Hubbell, Laura S, 1946, Ja 13,44:4
Hubbell, Leon S, 1948, O 6,29:1
Hubbell, Lyman P, 1943, My 23,42:5
Hubbell, Minor C, 1948, Ja 13,25:1
Hubbell, Nathan T Rev, 1905, Mr 5,9:3
Hubbell, Ralph G, 1956, N 20,37:2
Hubbell, Raymond, 1954, D 14,34:3
Hubbell, Richard Mrs (K Alanova), 1965, S 3,27:3
Hubbell, Stewart B, 1944, Jl 25,19:4
Hubbell, Vincent B, 1966, Ap 27,47:2
Hubbell, William, 1875, My 4,6:7
Hubbell, William Mrs, 1916, O 21,11:3
Hubbert, Edward B, 1948, D 10,26:2
Hubbert, Frances, 1967, Mr 20,31:4
Hübbert, Minnie B Mrs, 1942, Ap 24,17:2
Hubble, Edwin P, 1953, S 29,29:1
Hubbs, Edward (por), 1948, My 19,27:3
Hubbs, John B, 1938, My 28,15:5
Hubbs, John I Mrs, 1950, S 12,27:4
Hubbs, Ken, 1964, F 16,40:1
Hubbs, Robert C, 1955, My 2,21:5
Hubby, Frank W Jr, 1967, D 13,47:4
Hubby, Frank Winfield Sr, 1918, N 9,13:5
Hubby, Germain A, 1955, D 26,19:4
Hubby, Lester M, 1949, N 11,25:4
Hubel, G Andrew, 1957, Ja 7,25:3
Hubel, Otto C, 1949, Ja 20,27:5
Huben, Rudolf von, 1908, Mr 4,7:6
Huben, William J, 1943, Je 26,13:4
Hubeny, Anthony, 1957, My 25,21:4
Hubeny, Frank, 1956, S 8,17:1
Hubeny, Jeremiah, 1951, Jl 22,61:3
Hubeny, Joseph, 1953, Ag 21,17:3
Hubeny, Maximilian J, 1942, Jl 3,17:1
Huber, Abbot V, 1941, My 31,11:2
Huber, Albert, 1961, Mr 30,29:4
Huber, Anthony, 1940, F 28,21:3
Huber, Carl A, 1944, Je 2,15:2
Huber, Carl L, 1948, S 19,76:5
Huber, Carl W, 1956, My 6,87:1
Huber, Charles D, 1959, My 3,86:2
Huber, Charles E Jr, 1946, F 16,13:4
Huber, Charles F, 1966, Ag 22,33:3
Huber, Charles H Mrs, 1917, Je 8,11:5
Huber, Charles J, 1953, D 23,26:4
Huber, Charles W, 1947, My 8,25:5
Huber, David R, 1955, Mr 6,88:2
Huber, Edward C, 1954, Jl 29,23:6
Huber, Edward G, 1946, Jl 24,27:2
Huber, Elmer J, 1954, O 5,27:3
Huber, Erwing, 1951, Ag 19,85:2
Huber, Frank H, 1964, D 4,39:2
Huber, George H, 1916, Je 27,11:7
Huber, George J Sr, 1942, Mr 2,19:4
Huber, George W, 1954, Je 25,21:3
Huber, H Christian, 1937, N 5,23:6
Huber, Harold, 1959, O 1,40:2; 1962, N 13,37:2
Huber, Harold L, 1945, F 6,19:2
Huber, Harry I, 1945, D 3,21:2
Huber, Henry C, 1946, S 10,7:5
Huber, Jean P, 1962, Ap 7,25:5
Huber, John B Dr, 1924, F 18,13:1
Huber, John D, 1939, O 12,25:4
Huber, John F.Jr, 1949, My 8,77:1
Huber, John Y Jr Mrs, 1954, Je 11,23:1
Huber, Joseph, 1906, Ja 8,9:6; 1945, Ja 23,19:6; 1951, Ap 3,27:2
Huber, Joseph D, 1954, D 31,13:3
Huber, Juanita Mrs (Billie), 1965, My 24,31:4
Huber, Lester W, 1950, My 14,106:4
Huber, Marie Mrs, 1944, Mr 4,13:2
Huber, Max, 1960, Ja 2,13:5
Huber, Milton G, 1948, Je 16,29:4
Huber, Nace F, 1948, Ag 17,21:3
Huber, Paul S (por), 1946, S 27,23:2
Huber, Raphael M (Louis T), 1963, S 24,39:1
Huber, Ray A, 1958, F 4,29:5
Huber, Richard M, 1965, Mr 10,41:1
Huber, Rudolph D, 1955, S 23,25:2
Huber, Samuel H Mrs, 1968, Je 11,44:2
Huber, Thomas B, 1941, Mr 30,49:1
Huber, Wharton, 1942, Mr 14,15:5
Huber, William H, 1945, O 29,19:4
Huber, William Mrs, 1959, My 21,31:1
Huber, William R, 1942, My 18,15:6
Huberich, Charles H, 1945, Je 19,19:5
Huberland, Elias, 1958, S 11,33:2
Huberland, Elias Mrs, 1967, Mr 6,29:5
Huberman, Bronislaw, 1947, Je 17,25:1
Huberman, Leo, 1968, N 10,88:6
Huberman, Ralph, 1961, Mr 15,39:4
Hubert, Anna, 1956, O 20,21:2
Hubert, Arthur H, 1950, N 15,31:4
Hubert, Benjamin F, 1958, My 1,31:5
Hubert, C, 1928, Mr 18,I,25:1
Hubert, C Royce, 1964, Mr 1,83:3
Hubert, Edward L Mrs, 1956, S 1,15:5
Hubert, Ernest O, 1956, Ag 24,19:4
Hubert, Lucien, 1938, My 19,21:3
Hubert, Philip Gengembre, 1911, N 17,13:5; 1925, Ja 5,21:4
Hubert, R I, 1944, N 19,50:2
Hubert, Rene, 1942, S 5,13:4
Hubert, Theodore P, 1960, Ap 6,41:4
Huberth, Harry G, 1956, D 17,31:1
Huberth, Martin F, 1960, Je 3,31:1
Huberth, Martin F Jr, 1968, Ja 5,24:2
Huberti, Eugene T, 1953, S 30,31:4
Hubertus, Karl Wilhem Prince of Hohenzollern, 1950, Ap 9,87:3
Huberty, Joseph, 1941, Jl 10,19:1
Huberty, Martin R, 1960, D 15,43:3
Huberty, Oliver A, 1944, Jl 27,17:5
Huberty, Paul Sr, 1943, O 29,19:2
Hubin, Frank B, 1949, D 5,23:3
Hubinger, Frederick J, 1937, Jl 18,II,7:3
Hubka, Merle E, 1956, Jl 6,21:4
Hubka, Vernon E, 1958, O 17,30:1
Hubler, Edward L, 1965, D 29,29:5
Hubler, George W, 1948, S 12,72:4
Hubler, Harry C, 1960, Ap 15,23:1
Hubley, Richard C, 1957, O 31,28:1
Hubley, Warren F Mrs, 1968, Ja 15,47:1
Hublitz, George, 1944, Ap 3,21:3
Hublou, P, 1947, Ja 14,25:4
Hubman, Fred Mrs, 1949, My 25,29:5
Hubner, C W, 1929, Ja 4,25:2
Hubner, Edmund H, 1954, Ag 4,21:3
Hubner, George, 1941, Ap 30,19:5
Hubner, K, 1880, S 27,5:6
Hubner, William C, 1945, Ja 3,17:3
Hubner, William G C, 1945, S 20,23:5
Hubsch, Milton R, 1958, Ap 27,87:1
Hubsch, William Mrs, 1956, Ag 9,25:2
Hubschman, Albert, 1956, Ja 9,25:2
Hubschman, Herbert, 1964, S 22,39:2
Hubshman, Louis, 1950, F 2,27:2
Hubsmith, John A, 1951, F 12,23:3
Huc, Evariste Regis Rev, 1860, Ap 21,4:5
Huch, Ricarda, 1947, N 20,30:3
Huchmeister, Hermann W, 1923, F 2,15:4
Huck, Arthur Mrs, 1960, Ap 18,29:2
Huck, Benedict, 1963, O 1,39:3
Huck, Francis A, 1945, Ag 4,11:3
Huck, Francis E (por), 1939, Je 8,25:5
Huck, John G Jr, 1942, Mr 19,21:3
Huck, W M Mrs, 1936, Ag 26,21:3
Huck, William Jr, 1953, N 13,27:3
Huck, William Jr Mrs, 1943, Mr 27,14:7
Hucke, Robert W, 1960, F 17,35:4
Huckel, John F Mrs, 1943, Jl 10,13:3
Huckel, Margaret J, 1954, Ag 21,17:1
Huckel, Oliver (por), 1940, F 4,40:3
Huckel, Samuel Jr, 1917, Ap 20,13:4
Huckel, William, 1954, S 20,23:3
Huckel, William Rev, 1914, Ag 31,7:6
Huckett, Hugh C Mrs, 1964, Ap 7,35:3
Huckin, Paul G Sr, 1952, N 28,25:1
Huckin, Thomas J, 1958, My 14,33:2
Huckins, Elmer S, 1938, S 22,9:8
Huckins, John B, 1949, Ag 26,20:5
Huckins, Olga van Slyke Owens (Mrs Stuart Huckins), 1968, Jl 13,27:3
Huckle, Thomas O, 1954, S 22,29:2
Huda, Frank, 1949, S 22,31:4
Huda, Rudolph E, 1946, Jl 11,23:2
Hudacek, Mary Mrs, 1942, Jl 15,19:2
Hudaky, Edward K, 1954, O 16,36:4
Hudd, Alfred E, 1958, F 4,29:4
Hudd, Charles Sr, 1937, O 7,27:3
Hudd, Nellie C, 1940, N 19,23:5
Huddeston, John H Dr, 1915, O 31,7:4
Huddle, J Klahr, 1959, Mr 18,37:2
Huddle, John P, 1940, Ja 28,32:2
Huddleson, I Forest, 1965, My 28,33:4
Huddleston, George, 1960, Mr 1,33:4
Huddleston, Hubert, 1950, O 3,31:4
Huddleston, Myrtle Mrs, 1937, Ja 30,17:3

Huddleston, Robert B, 1948, S 18,18:2
Huddleston, Robert P, 1947, F 4,25:3
Huddleston, Sisley, 1952, Jl 18,19:3
Huddy, Joseph, 1939, Ja 5,23:4
Huden, John C, 1963, Jl 12,25:6
Hudes, Henry L, 1961, N 4,19:5
Hudgings, William F, 1937, O 18,17:1
Hudgins, Arthur Tod Capt, 1923, Mr 2,15:4
Hudgins, Edward W, 1958, Jl 30,29:5
Hudgins, Ellis B, 1949, My 31,23:2
Hudgins, Houlder, 1917, Ap 20,13:4; 1963, Jl 22,23:2
Hudgins, Morgan, 1965, My 25,41:4
Hudiburg, Will N, 1922, Mr 9,17:5
Hudlar, James D Mrs, 1945, O 30,19:3
Hudler, Dailey M, 1946, Je 5,23:2
Hudler, Harry, 1925, F 2,17:3
Hudlow, Edward W, 1955, Jl 28,23:5
Hudnall, Cecil J Mrs, 1950, My 7,106:6
Hudnall, Leonard V, 1959, Je 28,68:7
Hudnut, David A Mrs, 1908, S 20,9:5
Hudnut, E L, 1878, My 10,12:3
Hudnut, Frank, 1954, F 12,25:6
Hudnut, Joseph, 1968, Ja 17,47:1
Hudnut, Richard A Mrs, 1919, S 14,22:4
Hudnut, William H, 1963, Ag 17,19:1
Hudnutt, Arthur C, 1950, Jl 7,19:5
Hudnutt, Dean, 1943, O 12,27:4
Hudson, Albert S, 1947, Ap 22,27:2
Hudson, Alexander Barks Mrs, 1908, Mr 1,9:6
Hudson, Alfred E, 1956, My 27,89:1
Hudson, Alfred W, 1965, My 18,39:4
Hudson, Almeda Mrs, 1959, D 4,32:1
Hudson, Annie Mrs, 1955, My 6,23:2
Hudson, Arthur M, 1945, D 25,23:1
Hudson, Austin, 1956, N 30,23:4
Hudson, Brewster T Mrs, 1955, N 20,89:1
Hudson, Buell W, 1966, Mr 21,33:5
Hudson, Charles, 1881, My 7,5:3
Hudson, Charles B, 1939, Je 29,23:6; 1942, Ap 13, 15:5; 1968, D 30,31:4
Hudson, Charles B Mrs, 1946, N 26,29:1
Hudson, Charles I, 1921, N 16,19:3
Hudson, Charles R, 1941, Ja 19,40:7
Hudson, Charles Tracy Col, 1921, N 18,17:3
Hudson, Clarence W, 1943, My 12,25:1
Hudson, Claude S, 1952, D 29,19:2
Hudson, Cornelius, 1945, F 28,23:5
Hudson, Darwin S, 1959, Ag 14,21:2
Hudson, Darwin S Mrs, 1954, O 3,87:2
Hudson, David E, 1946, F 9,13:2
Hudson, Donald, 1967, Je 13,64:2
Hudson, Dora S Mrs, 1940, D 9,19:4
Hudson, E D, 1881, Ja 1,2:5
Hudson, Earl J, 1959, Ag 22,17:3
Hudson, Earl R, 1954, S 21,27:4
Hudson, Edmund A Mrs, 1943, F 22,17:5
Hudson, Edward M Capt, 1916, S 7,9:2
Hudson, Erastus M (por), 1943, S 18,17:3
Hudson, Eric Mrs, 1956, O 13,19:6
Hudson, Ernest R, 1960, O 27,37:2
Hudson, Frank, 1950, D 27,27:1
Hudson, Frank A Jr, 1952, S 16,29:3
Hudson, Fred C, 1944, O 18,21:4
Hudson, Frederick (funl, O 25,1:2), 1875, O 22,1:6
Hudson, George, 1872, Ja 2,2:7
Hudson, George C, 1943, Mr 25,21:1
Hudson, George Mrs, 1944, O 22,45:1
Hudson, George S, 1940, My 6,17:5
Hudson, H Kierstede, 1954, Je 22,27:2
Hudson, H Kierstede Mrs, 1943, F 14,48:7
Hudson, H R, 1940, Mr 10,49:2
Hudson, Harold W, 1943, Ja 16,13:6
Hudson, Harry, 1951, N 20,31:3
Hudson, Harvey B, 1951, Ap 8,93:1
Hudson, Henrietta (Mrs H H Billwiller), 1942, Ap 4, 13:2
Hudson, Henry A, 1903, N 1,7:6
Hudson, Henry E Judge, 1873, Je 5,1:2
Hudson, Hoyt H, 1944, Je 15,19:6
Hudson, Irving P, 1949, F 25,23:1
Hudson, J Cramer, 1943, Je 5,15:5
Hudson, J Jones, 1946, O 23,27:3
Hudson, J L, 1912, Jl 6,7:4
Hudson, James Fairchild, 1915, My 4,15:6
Hudson, James H, 1947, Ag 22,15:2
Hudson, James S Mrs, 1950, D 28,25:1
Hudson, John, 1918, Je 18,13:6
Hudson, John F, 1945, Je 20,23:3
Hudson, John P, 1912, N 27,13:6
Hudson, Joseph H, 1949, Mr 15,27:1
Hudson, Joseph H Rev, 1937, S 27,21:4
Hudson, Joseph K Gen, 1907, My 6,9:3
Hudson, Joshua Hillary, 1909, Jl 23,7:6
Hudson, Lon, 1957, Ag 30,19:5
Hudson, Loren R, 1954, Ja 26,27:3
Hudson, Manley O, 1960, Ap 14,31:3
Hudson, Mary E, 1963, Jl 31,29:4
Hudson, Maurice R, 1943, Ap 20,23:3
Hudson, Max B, 1959, F 22,88:4
Hudson, Paul, 1950, Ag 24,27:3
Hudson, Paul Mrs, 1939, My 9,24:3
Hudson, Percy K, 1962, Mr 15,35:3
Hudson, R F Mrs, 1951, Mr 31,15:1
Hudson, R T, 1966, D 12,47:1
Hudson, Ray L, 1937, N 8,24:1
Hudson, Raymond G Mrs, 1948, D 19,76:6
Hudson, Richard de L, 1959, O 9,29:4
Hudson, Richard F, 1950, Ja 14,15:2
Hudson, Richard F Jr, 1959, S 27,86:3
Hudson, Richard F Sr, 1965, D 17,39:1
Hudson, Richard Prof, 1915, F 23,13:4
Hudson, Robert, 1937, Ja 7,22:1
Hudson, Robert G, 1950, Ja 6,22:3
Hudson, Robert S Viscount, 1957, F 3,76:4
Hudson, Rose A, 1951, Ag 11,11:6
Hudson, Roy C, 1955, Ap 2,17:5
Hudson, Samuel E, 1941, Je 18,21:5
Hudson, Samuel E Mrs, 1956, My 7,27:5
Hudson, Susan E J Mrs, 1913, S 27,13:6
Hudson, T J Prof, 1903, My 27,9:3
Hudson, Theresa Mrs, 1949, O 12,30:6
Hudson, W H, 1908, Ag 21,7:5; 1922, Ag 30,15:6
Hudson, W S, 1881, Jl 22,5:6
Hudson, Walter E, 1937, My 5,25:4
Hudson, Walter F, 1951, Ap 4,29:4
Hudson, Walter Guy Dr, 1920, O 31,22:3
Hudson, Wilbur F, 1905, Ap 11,11:6
Hudson, William C, 1915, O 19,11:4; 1938, N 5,19:6
Hudson, William C Mrs, 1947, Ap 30,25:4
Hudson, William Capt (M H Miles), 1903, F 12,2:1
Hudson, William E, 1938, N 20,39:2
Hudson, William M, 1960, Mr 24,33:1
Hudson, Woodward, 1938, Ag 18,20:2
Hudson-Alexander, Caroline, 1948, Ja 24,15:2
Hudspeth, Claude B, 1941, Mr 20,21:3
Hudspeth, Perdita, 1955, N 21,29:4
Hudspeth, William, 1945, Jl 31,19:5
Hudtwalker, George W Sr, 1956, Mr 3,19:3
Hue, Otto, 1922, Ap 20,17:4
Huebbler, Berta, 1925, Ja 2,15:4
Huebener, Frederick, 1940, O 2,23:3
Huebener, Theodore Mrs, 1937, O 31,II,11:2
Hueber, Charles, 1950, Ja 3,25:2
Hueber, G, 1879, Ja 27,5:5
Hueber, Gustave, 1951, Ap 24,29:5
Hueber, Mary, 1948, F 29,60:4
Huebner, Albert J, 1948, Je 23,27:1
Huebner, Ambrose, 1941, F 6,21:4
Huebner, Emma D, 1938, Jl 29,17:4
Huebner, Erwin A, 1963, S 29,86:6
Huebner, Grover G, 1964, Mr 12,35:3
Huebner, Robert D, 1963, My 15,39:2
Huebner, Solomon S, 1964, Jl 18,19:2
Huebner, Walter, 1959, Mr 30,31:4
Huebsch, Arthur, 1950, My 9,29:2
Huebsch, B W, 1964, Ag 8,19:1
Huebsch, Rudolph W, 1945, Jl 10,11:4
Hueffer, Ford M Mrs, 1949, My 27,21:3
Hueffer, O M, 1931, Je 23,25:5
Huefner, Joseph A, 1946, D 9,25:4
Huehnlein, Adolf, 1942, Je 19,23:5
Huelat, John H, 1943, Jl 14,19:2
Huelgerth, Ludwig, 1939, Ag 16,23:5
Huelsdonk, John, 1946, O 26,17:5
Huelsen-Haeseler, Georg von Count, 1922, Je 22,15:6
Huelsenbeck, Ernest, 1942, Ja 29,19:5
Huelsenbeck, Harry L, 1941, N 26,23:5
Huelsenbeck, William F Sr, 1946, O 16,27:3
Huene, Catherine H Baroness, 1956, Ja 22,88:5
Huene, Ernest W, 1948, Ag 21,16:2
Huene, Frederick, 1914, Ja 16,9:5
Huenefeld, E G von, 1929, F 6,27:1
Huenerberg, Karl, 1948, Ap 9,24:2
Hueneryager, Albert E Mrs, 1943, Je 27,32:2
Huenlich, Charles M, 1966, Je 2,43:1
Hueppe, Ferdinand, 1938, S 16,21:2
Huerstel, Maurice G, 1945, Je 25,17:2
Huerta, Petro, 1952, Ag 23,19:2
Huertas, Esteban, 1943, Ag 1,38:8
Huertas, J E, 1869, Mr 29,5:5
Hueser, Harry Mrs, 1946, Ap 19,29:5
Huesmann, George Prof, 1902, N 7,9:5
Huess, Chester A, 1942, Ja 29,19:2
Huested, Percy L, 1953, Mr 24,31:2
Huester, Fred J, 1949, O 7,31:2
Huestis, C H, 1951, Ag 14,23:1
Huestis, George E, 1952, Jl 18,19:1
Hueston, Edward A, 1967, Jl 22,25:3
Hueston, Frank M, 1941, N 15,17:3
Hueston, Henry M, 1951, Jl 24,25:5
Hueston, Jeremiah, 1951, Ag 7,25:6
Huet, Stanislaw, 1961, Mr 16,37:4
Huether, George E, 1937, S 21,35:5
Huetor de Santillan, Marquis de, 1957, N 11,29:5
Huette, Walter B, 1944, F 3,19:4
Huettig, Hugo G, 1948, Jl 21,23:2
Huettner, Alfred F, 1955, S 28,35:5
Huey, Arthur B, 1939, N 17,21:2
Huey, Arthur J, 1942, S 29,23:2
Huey, Arthur S, 1924, S 17,23:3
Huey, Isaac H, 1953, Mr 26,31:2
Huey, John Sr, 1946, Mr 19,27:3
Huey, Nettie J Mrs (will), 1958, Mr 30,61:4
Hufeland, Marie A, 1941, Ja 28,19:2
Hufeland, Otto, 1940, O 16,23:4
Huff, Abraham T, 1907, Ag 8,7:6
Huff, Charles H, 1959, Jl 17,21:1; 1963, S 21,21:1
Huff, Charles S, 1966, D 13,47:5
Huff, Charlotte M, 1945, Je 1,15:2
Huff, Clarence J, 1943, Ag 19,19:6
Huff, Dale L, 1952, O 27,27:1
Huff, Edmund N Jr (Theodore), 1953, Mr 17,35:7
Huff, Edmund N Mrs, 1957, My 15,35:3
Huff, Florence A, 1943, Ap 13,25:2
Huff, Forrest, 1947, Ag 21,23:4
Huff, Frederick P, 1924, F 14,17:4
Huff, George F, 1912, Ap 18,13:5
Huff, Harry A, 1952, My 24,19:6
Huff, Harvey A, 1959, My 28,31:4
Huff, Herbert W, 1954, N 23,35:2
Huff, J Wesley, 1950, Ja 27,24:2
Huff, J Willard Mrs, 1954, F 27,13:4
Huff, John C, 1949, D 9,32:2
Huff, John S, 1959, Ap 8,37:3
Huff, Julian Burrell, 1923, D 25,17:3
Huff, Lloyd Burrell Col, 1915, My 6,13:6
Huff, Myron R, 1946, O 10,27:3
Huff, Neal J, 1958, S 16,27:2
Huff, Nicholas, 1952, Ap 9,31:5
Huff, Roy V, 1943, Mr 18,19:1
Huff, S W Mrs, 1952, Ja 13,89:1
Huff, Samuel R, 1949, Ag 30,27:3
Huff, Scott M, 1942, F 26,19:2
Huff, Sidney L, 1962, N 12,29:4
Huff, Slaughter W, 1947, O 17,22:4
Huff, Victor C Mrs, 1956, Ja 28,17:6
Huff, William K, 1964, Mr 12,35:4
Huff, Wilmer R, 1951, Jl 29,24:1
Huffaker, Edward C, 1937, Ja 4,29:1
Huffard, Cloyd H, 1956, Je 11,31:6
Huffard, Paul P, 1960, O 31,31:5
Huffcut, Ernest W (funl, My 6,9:3), 1907, My 6,9:3
Huffines, Robert L Jr Mrs, 1959, My 24,88:3
Huffington, B Walter, 1950, Jl 15,13:1
Huffman, Clive S, 1948, N 11,27:3
Huffman, Frank H, 1952, Je 7,19:7
Huffman, Harry R, 1949, Ap 10,76:3
Huffman, Harvey, 1938, D 1,23:6
Huffman, J L, 1882, D 13,5:1
Huffman, James W Mrs, 1958, Mr 13,29:4
Huffman, Marshall A, 1940, Mr 14,23:1
Huffman, Oscar C (por), 1941, My 6,21:1
Huffman, Oscar C Mrs, 1949, S 12,21:1
Huffman, Otto V Dr, 1937, Je 10,23:2
Huffman, Stanley C, 1952, Ag 8,17:6
Huffman, William F, 1949, S 10,17:2
Huffman, Wilson Mrs, 1948, Ap 16,23:3
Huffnagle, Harry W, 1958, Ja 29,27:4
Hufnagel, Bernard, 1940, D 28,15:4
Hufnagel, Bernard Mrs, 1949, Ap 30,13:6
Hufnagel, Cliff, 1949, Ja 4,40:2
Hufnagel, Frederick B, 1954, My 17,24:3
Hufnagel, George F, 1944, Mr 13,15:2
Hufnagel, J George, 1944, My 6,15:4
Hufnagle, Bernard, 1919, N 8,13:2
Hufnale, John J, 1949, Jl 17,56:1
Hufner-Harken, Helen Mrs, 1910, N 9,9:2
Hug, C, 1929, My 18,19:4
Hug, Ludwig F Mrs, 1951, Ja 19,25:6
Huganir, Elma, 1959, Mr 5,20:2
Hugard, Jean, 1959, Ag 15,17:5
Huge, Albert H, 1952, Ag 23,13:3
Hugenberg, Alfred, 1951, Mr 13,31:5
Hugentugler, E S, 1949, N 24,31:4
Huger, Alfred, 1872, My 15,1:6; 1938, My 19,21:2
Huger, Dan E, 1904, F 16,9:6
Huger, Daniel E, 1967, O 13,39:3
Huger, Margaret Mrs, 1938, Ag 27,13:6
Huget, Adolph H, 1952, F 7,27:2
Huget, J Percival, 1958, Mr 12,32:1
Hugg, Alfred Ex-Judge, 1904, Ja 22,9:6
Hugg, John L, 1953, Jl 25,11:3
Huggard, Arthur W, 1954, Mr 26,21:4
Huggard, C Willis, 1962, My 7,31:3
Huggard, Ernest D, 1954, Ap 18,88:6
Huggard, Ethel F, 1968, Jl 5,25:1
Huggard, John T, 1964, F 1,23:4
Huggard, Richard, 1948, Mr 4,25:1
Huggard, William, 1939, Jl 4,13:6
Hugger, Gustave, 1951, Ap 29,89:2
Huggett, Irving H, 1952, Ag 18,17:4
Huggett, Martin C, 1953, Mr 29,93:1
Huggins, Arthur, 1946, Jl 3,25:3
Huggins, Floyd W, 1947, S 26,23:4
Huggins, Francis X, 1949, O 23,84:2
Huggins, G Ellsworth (est tax appr), 1954, D 31,8
Huggins, George A, 1960, Ja 1,19:2
Huggins, George A Mrs, 1941, Ap 9,25:4
Huggins, George F, 1941, Je 8,49:2
Huggins, George F Mrs, 1942, Ap 7,22:3
Huggins, Gurry E, 1951, Ja 7,76:3
Huggins, J Earl Mrs, 1963, D 2,37:4
Huggins, John R, 1954, N 21,87:1
Huggins, Joseph, 1944, S 20,23:3
Huggins, R Paul, 1960, Ag 10,31:4
Huggins, Raleigh R, 1938, F 22,21:5
Huggins, Robert Mrs, 1964, N 25,37:2
Huggins, Walter L, 1940, Ap 19,21:2
Huggins, William L, 1941, My 25,36:8

Huggins, William Lady, 1915, Mr 26,13:3
Huggins, William Sir, 1910, My 13,9:6
Hugh, H P Rev, 1902, N 18,9:5
Hugh, John J, 1949, Ja 10,25:2
Hughan, Evelyn W, 1947, D 14,78:3
Hughan, Jessie W, 1955, Ap 11,23:4
Hughart, Arthur A, 1938, D 29,20:3
Hughart, J H P, 1917, Ag 17,9:7
Hughes, Aaron Konkle Rear-Adm, 1906, My 6,9:6
Hughes, Adella P Mrs, 1950, Ag 24,27:4
Hughes, Adrian G, 1941, D 9,31:1
Hughes, Albert C, 1957, Ag 5,21:2
Hughes, Albert Mrs, 1946, Ap 24,25:2
Hughes, Albert P, 1938, N 30,23:3
Hughes, Albert R, 1964, N 11,43:4
Hughes, Alfred, 1951, S 23,86:1
Hughes, Alice E Mrs, 1941, Jl 3,19:1
Hughes, Andrew J, 1907, Mr 22,11:5; 1946, Jl 12,17:2
Hughes, Andrew P, 1948, Mr 23,25:2
Hughes, Andrew P Mrs, 1946, D 13,23:3
Hughes, Annie, 1954, Ja 13,31:5
Hughes, Archbishop, 1864, Ja 4,8:1; 1882, Ja 4,8:3
Hughes, Archibald Mrs, 1943, Ja 3,43:1
Hughes, Archie E, 1942, F 7,17:3
Hughes, Arthur, 1949, Jl 14,27:5
Hughes, Arthur J, 1943, Je 6,44:6
Hughes, Arthur M, 1962, Ag 21,33:4
Hughes, Augustus S, 1942, Jl 24,20:3
Hughes, Avery E, 1951, D 4,33:3
Hughes, Bernadette B, 1955, Mr 8,27:1
Hughes, Bernard, 1871, Ap 15,8:4; 1959, Jl 26,69:2
Hughes, Brian G (funl, D 11,23:4), 1924, D 9,25:1
Hughes, C F, 1934, My 29,19:1
Hughes, Catherine A Mrs, 1940, S 28,17:7
Hughes, Charles, 1950, Jl 23,56:5
Hughes, Charles A, 1953, Ja 30,22:3
Hughes, Charles D, 1951, Mr 30,23:1
Hughes, Charles Dr, 1937, F 12,23:3
Hughes, Charles E, 1948, Ag 28,1:4
Hughes, Charles E Jr, 1950, Ja 23,23:1
Hughes, Charles E Jr Mrs, 1963, Mr 13,7:6
Hughes, Charles E Mrs (por),(will, D 14,12:2), 1945, D 7,21:1
Hughes, Charles F, 1914, F 2,7:5; 1939, Ap 11,23:6; 1951, D 25,31:3
Hughes, Charles F Mrs, 1941, My 3,15:3
Hughes, Charles H, 1956, O 30,37:3
Hughes, Charles James Jr Sen, 1911, Ja 12,13:2
Hughes, Charles M, 1947, D 3,30:3; 1967, Jl 22,25:3
Hughes, Charles M Mrs, 1949, My 3,25:4
Hughes, Charles R, 1938, Ag 12,17:5
Hughes, Charles T, 1943, Ap 23,17:2
Hughes, Charles Turner, 1909, My 6,9:6
Hughes, Chester, 1961, Je 28,35:1
Hughes, Chris J, 1941, Ap 16,23:4
Hughes, Clarence F, 1938, F 27,II,8:3
Hughes, D E Dr, 1902, O 29,1:6
Hughes, Dan, 1959, D 6,86:7
Hughes, Daniel J, 1955, Ag 9,25:4
Hughes, David, 1949, D 16,31:4
Hughes, David C Mrs, 1914, D 30,11:6
Hughes, David M, 1907, Ja 9,9:5
Hughes, David W, 1953, My 2,15:6
Hughes, Dennis A, 1948, My 4,25:4
Hughes, Donald J, 1960, Ap 13,39:3
Hughes, Donnell Dr, 1915, Ap 9,11:5
Hughes, Dorothy H (Mrs G Cobban Jr), 1960, Jl 2, 17:2
Hughes, Dudley C, 1942, My 6,19:5
Hughes, E B Maj, 1901, Mr 8,7:6
Hughes, Earl N, 1959, S 20,87:2
Hughes, Edward E (por),(will, F 8,20:2), 1940, Ja 20,15:3
Hughes, Edward J, 1939, Ap 27,25:4; 1943, S 13,19:6; 1944, Je 29,23:6
Hughes, Edward M, 1903, S 29,9:4; 1951, F 3,15:6
Hughes, Edward P, 1939, D 20,28:2; 1948, D 3,25:3; 1966, N 10,47:3
Hughes, Edward P Mrs, 1958, Ap 27,86:6
Hughes, Edward V, 1949, F 25,24:2
Hughes, Edward W, 1939, N 10,23:5
Hughes, Edwin, 1965, Jl 19,27:3
Hughes, Edwin B, 1957, My 10,27:1
Hughes, Edwin H, 1950, F 13,21:3
Hughes, Edwin H Jr, 1959, Ap 28,35:3
Hughes, Edwin H Mrs, 1938, S 19,19:2
Hughes, Eleanor, 1942, S 29,25:8
Hughes, Eleanor C, 1962, F 27,33:1
Hughes, Elizabeth Phillips, 1925, D 20,11:2
Hughes, Ellen A Mrs, 1937, S 29,23:2
Hughes, Elwood A, 1956, My 2,31:6
Hughes, Etta, 1920, Jl 29,9:3
Hughes, Eugene E, 1956, D 24,13:5
Hughes, Eugene E Mrs, 1937, Ja 31,II,9:2
Hughes, Eugene J, 1952, Ap 8,29:4
Hughes, Eugene Mrs, 1957, S 6,21:1
Hughes, Eugene V, 1942, Ag 30,42:6
Hughes, Everett S, 1957, S 8,84:6
Hughes, F Massie, 1960, D 24,15:5
Hughes, F Wade, 1944, N 30,23:3
Hughes, Felix, 1961, S 12,33:3
Hughes, Felix Mrs, 1941, My 14,21:3
Hughes, Florence, 1943, Mr 3,23:5; 1943, N 5,19:1
Hughes, Forrest R, 1951, Ja 6,15:5
Hughes, Francis W, 1953, Ja 18,93:2
Hughes, Francois L, 1940, O 16,23:3
Hughes, Frank (por), 1938, Mr 18,19:3
Hughes, Frank, 1942, Je 30,21:2; 1945, Ja 11,23:1
Hughes, Frank B, 1938, Ja 14,23:4
Hughes, Frank J, 1946, Ag 31,15:2; 1951, F 11,89:1; 1951, F 22,31:2; 1955, Jl 22,23:3
Hughes, Frank J Mrs, 1955, Mr 5,17:5
Hughes, Frank M, 1947, Ap 18,21:3
Hughes, Frank V, 1956, N 3,23:6
Hughes, Franklin R, 1947, Ja 18,4:2; 1948, F 7,15:5
Hughes, Frederick A, 1942, Ap 3,21:5
Hughes, Frederick G, 1959, O 6,39:1
Hughes, Frederick J, 1950, Je 17,15:4
Hughes, General, 1949, Jl 30,15:5
Hughes, George, 1872, My 4,1:7; 1942, Je 20,13:6; 1951, S 18,31:4
Hughes, George A, 1943, Jl 29,19:4
Hughes, George A (por), 1944, S 11,17:5
Hughes, George C, 1938, D 17,15:5
Hughes, George E, 1916, Ap 8,15:4
Hughes, George F, 1943, N 26,23:2
Hughes, George G Mrs, 1956, Je 2,19:6
Hughes, George H, 1955, Ap 26,29:2
Hughes, George I, 1937, My 21,21:4; 1950, Jl 21,19:3; 1953, N 28,15:7
Hughes, George J, 1957, O 25,27:3
Hughes, George P, 1967, Jl 1,23:4
Hughes, George Rev, 1904, O 11,9:5
Hughes, George T, 1945, O 9,21:3
Hughes, George W R, 1944, F 29,17:4
Hughes, Gethrin, 1953, Je 11,29:4
Hughes, Gilbert C, 1947, Ap 15,25:2
Hughes, Grover C, 1938, Ap 1,23:2
Hughes, Gruney O, 1948, Jl 1,23:4
Hughes, Harley C, 1948, F 26,23:1
Hughes, Harold K, 1962, Ap 15,81:2
Hughes, Harold L (por), 1955, Je 5,85:1
Hughes, Harriet E, 1949, S 25,92:4
Hughes, Harry A, 1952, Jl 29,21:2
Hughes, Harry W, 1953, Jl 28,19:4
Hughes, Hatcher, 1945, O 20,11:3
Hughes, Hector J Mrs, 1947, F 10,29:1
Hughes, Helen, 1920, Ap 19,15:1
Hughes, Helen S, 1955, My 8,88:4
Hughes, Henry, 1901, Mr 13,9:5; 1904, Ja 9,9:6
Hughes, Henry G, 1943, F 18,23:5
Hughes, Henry J, 1953, N 14,17:7
Hughes, Henry T, 1955, D 16,30:1
Hughes, Henry Weldon, 1924, Mr 16,23:2
Hughes, Herbert Col, 1917, Ja 18,11:2
Hughes, Howard R, 1951, Ag 20,19:5
Hughes, Howard W, 1945, Je 21,19:3
Hughes, Hugh, 1945, Jl 1,17:2
Hughes, Hugh J, 1944, D 24,26:4
Hughes, Isobel M Mrs, 1956, D 18,31:5
Hughes, Ivor T P, 1962, Ag 18,19:6
Hughes, J J, 1941, Mr 6,21:5
Hughes, J K Mrs, 1950, Je 17,15:1
Hughes, James, 1940, Ag 10,13:4; 1952, N 30,88:7; 1954, Mr 21,88:6; 1960, Mr 27,V,1:2
Hughes, James A, 1953, O 10,17:4; 1965, S 7,39:3
Hughes, James A Jr Mrs, 1956, O 28,89:2
Hughes, James A L, 1946, Ja 4,21:4
Hughes, James F, 1950, O 27,30:3; 1953, S 23,31:4
Hughes, James H (por), 1949, F 23,27:5
Hughes, James H, 1951, My 30,21:2; 1953, Ag 30,89:2
Hughes, James H Jr, 1938, Jl 4,4:6
Hughes, James H Mrs, 1959, S 13,84:8
Hughes, James J, 1942, Ag 31,17:6; 1946, S 27,23:5; 1953, N 26,31:5; 1955, Mr 23,31:1
Hughes, James L, 1944, Ap 10,19:3
Hughes, James M, 1951, Ja 26,23:3
Hughes, James P, 1951, My 31,27:4
Hughes, Jeremiah J, 1948, O 7,29:3
Hughes, John, 1903, D 12,9:6; 1939, Je 28,21:5; 1949, F 13,76:2; 1951, F 9,25:3
Hughes, John A, 1942, My 26,21:3
Hughes, John C, 1952, Ja 29,25:2
Hughes, John D, 1944, Ag 10,17:4; 1967, S 4,21:3
Hughes, John E, 1963, Ag 3,17:6
Hughes, John E Mrs, 1947, N 15,17:6
Hughes, John F, 1924, Je 23,19:6; 1948, Ja 15,23:3; 1953, Je 4,29:1
Hughes, John H, 1953, Ag 8,11:5
Hughes, John J, 1939, Ap 15,19:4; 1942, O 8,27:3; 1943, S 20,21:6; 1944, Ap 2,39:3; 1945, D 17,21:2; 1953, Mr 27,23:4; 1956, Je 22,23:4
Hughes, John J Father, 1919, My 6,15:5
Hughes, John J Mrs, 1949, S 8,29:3
Hughes, John J Sr, 1951, Jl 25,23:4
Hughes, John L, 1964, Ja 7,33:1
Hughes, John L Mrs, 1965, Ap 5,31:5
Hughes, John M, 1909, Mr 21,11:5
Hughes, John Mrs, 1943, D 21,27:1
Hughes, John N, 1947, D 15,25:4
Hughes, John P, 1943, N 18,23:5
Hughes, John R, 1941, O 28,23:4; 1941, N 30,68:2
Hughes, John T, 1945, S 29,15:6; 1958, N 10,29:4; 1960, O 16,88:6
Hughes, Joseph A, 1952, My 1,29:6
Hughes, Joseph B, 1944, Jl 11,15:4; 1947, O 7,27:3
Hughes, Joseph C, 1916, Ag 30,9:4
Hughes, Joseph E, 1937, Ap 13,25:5; 1947, Ja 29,25:4; 1963, S 28,19:3
Hughes, Joseph F, 1949, F 26,15:4; 1961, My 30,17:5
Hughes, Joseph H, 1941, Jl 12,13:4
Hughes, Joseph W, 1945, N 3,15:5
Hughes, Josephine, 1940, Ag 27,21:4
Hughes, Josiah N, 1939, N 10,23:3
Hughes, Katherine, 1925, Ap 28,21:4
Hughes, Katherine A, 1945, F 20,19:5
Hughes, Kenneth L, 1960, S 25,88:7
Hughes, Lady, 1939, Mr 19,III,7:3
Hughes, Laura A C Dr, 1920, Jl 31,7:6
Hughes, Lee W, 1964, Ja 27,23:4
Hughes, Leonard, 1951, Je 8,27:3
Hughes, Liana M, 1949, Je 16,29:1
Hughes, Lizbeth B, 1966, Ja 22,29:4
Hughes, Lloyd, 1958, Je 9,23:3
Hughes, Louis W, 1961, D 21,27:5
Hughes, Margaret, 1946, O 25,30:6
Hughes, Margaret P, 1941, My 5,17:4
Hughes, Martin, 1940, Ap 27,15:6
Hughes, Martin C, 1952, D 19,32:3
Hughes, Mary, 1941, Ap 4,21:4
Hughes, Mary J Mrs, 1947, N 17,23:1
Hughes, Mary Ursula Mother, 1942, S 18,22:3
Hughes, Matthew J, 1946, S 28,17:1
Hughes, Melaine Mrs, 1950, S 29,27:4
Hughes, Michael J, 1955, Je 23,29:4; 1956, Je 23,17:2
Hughes, Michael T, 1944, S 21,19:5
Hughes, Nicholas J Rev, 1909, Ap 20,9:5
Hughes, O H, 1940, Ap 28,36:3
Hughes, Oliver John Davis Dr, 1908, Mr 6,7:4
Hughes, Patrick, 1946, My 8,25:2; 1956, N 26,27:4
Hughes, Patrick J, 1947, D 28,40:6
Hughes, Paul, 1947, Je 4,27:1; 1955, My 29,45:2
Hughes, Percy, 1952, Ap 25,23:2
Hughes, Peter Dr, 1917, O 2,13:6
Hughes, Phil, 1953, Ja 26,22:6
Hughes, Presmul D, 1922, My 15,17:6
Hughes, R A Rev, 1903, Mr 11,3:2
Hughes, R Ford, 1964, Ap 26,88:4
Hughes, R H, 1903, Je 18,9:6
Hughes, Ray O, 1959, Ap 12,86:5
Hughes, Raymond G, 1939, N 26,42:5
Hughes, Raymond M, 1958, S 23,33:4
Hughes, Richard, 1950, D 10,104:4
Hughes, Richard J Mrs, 1950, N 21,31:1
Hughes, Richard M Commodore, 1937, Ag 23,19:4
Hughes, Richard Ormond Rev, 1921, My 25,17:4
Hughes, Richard P (funl plans, N 7,26:5; funl, N 10,35:1), 1961, N 6,37:4
Hughes, Robert, 1946, Mr 5,25:3; 1958, Jl 11,45:2
Hughes, Robert E, 1967, Ja 17,39:4
Hughes, Robert G, 1959, Je 26,25:4
Hughes, Robert G Mrs, 1960, My 5,35:1
Hughes, Robert J, 1939, Ap 10,17:3; 1960, Ja 4,29:2
Hughes, Robert Judge, 1901, D 11,9:4
Hughes, Robert M, 1940, Ja 16,23:4
Hughes, Robert P, 1964, Ap 15,39:5
Hughes, Robert P Maj-Gen, 1909, O 29,9:5
Hughes, Robert P Mrs, 1961, Jl 31,19:4
Hughes, Rowland R, 1957, Ap 4,33:1
Hughes, Rupert, 1956, S 10,27:3
Hughes, Rupert Mrs, 1945, Mr 24,32:6
Hughes, Rupert S, 1944, Ja 4,17:2
Hughes, Russell H Mrs, 1954, Jl 27,21:5
Hughes, Ruth, 1941, Ag 21,17:2
Hughes, Sam Sir, 1921, Ag 24,11:5
Hughes, Samuel, 1940, Mr 26,21:3
Hughes, Samuel T (por), 1948, Ap 7,25:4
Hughes, Samuel W, 1954, S 18,15:7
Hughes, Sidney W, 1963, D 21,23:4
Hughes, Stanley C, 1944, D 15,19:3
Hughes, T Rowland, 1949, O 25,27:3
Hughes, Thomas, 1896, Mr 24,5:3; 1937, Jl 14,21:4; 1946, Ag 6,25:4
Hughes, Thomas A, 1925, Jl 23,19:5; 1947, S 17,25:2; 1947, O 5,68:5
Hughes, Thomas Bayless Rev Dr, 1917, Jl 28,15:3
Hughes, Thomas C, 1872, S 17,8:5; 1957, D 18,35:4
Hughes, Thomas E, 1957, My 6,29:5
Hughes, Thomas F, 1947, Ap 4,23:4
Hughes, Thomas H, 1944, My 26,19:5
Hughes, Thomas H Mrs, 1957, F 13,35:4
Hughes, Thomas J, 1950, F 7,27:2; 1956, F 10,21:2
Hughes, Thomas J Sr, 1939, O 30,17:4
Hughes, Thomas L, 1955, N 15,29:1
Hughes, Thomas L Sr, 1941, F 21,19:3
Hughes, Thomas M, 1956, Ja 13,23:4
Hughes, Thomas P, 1912, Ag 30,9:5
Hughes, Thomas P Mrs, 1915, F 28,3:6
Hughes, Thomas Patrick Rev, 1911, Ag 9,9:4
Hughes, Thomas W, 1957, Ap 21,89:1
Hughes, Vern C, 1943, Mr 1,19:5
Hughes, Vincent L, 1957, Mr 11,25:2
Hughes, Violet L, 1955, O 28,25:2
Hughes, W A C Sr, 1940, Jl 14,31:2
Hughes, W F, 1871, Ap 6,4:2
Hughes, W J, 1878, D 7,2:4
HugheS, W Jonse, 1962, S 2,57:1
Hughes, Wallace T, 1959, Ja 13,47:1
Hughes, Walter I, 1946, Ag 3,15:2

Hughes, Walter L, 1949, N 27,104:7
Hughes, Walter T Mrs, 1964, Je 18,35:2
Hughes, Wendell L Mrs, 1953, O 20,29:2
Hughes, Willard F, 1959, Mr 17,30:4
Hughes, William, 1906, N 3,1:6; 1951, O 3,36:3; 1953, F 4,27:2
Hughes, William A, 1938, F 24,19:4; 1939, My 7,III,7:1
Hughes, William B Mrs, 1957, Je 15,17:5
Hughes, William C, 1955, Ja 5,23:5
Hughes, William D F, 1964, Ja 15,31:2
Hughes, William D Rev, 1908, F 6,7:5
Hughes, William Devereaux Rev, 1909, Ja 11,9:7
Hughes, William E, 1944, Mr 19,41:3; 1948, D 23, 20:2; 1964, Mr 11,39:4
Hughes, William H, 1951, Ag 6,21:6
Hughes, William H Rev Dr, 1925, My 19,21:4
Hughes, William Hastings, 1907, Ap 21,9:4
Hughes, William J, 1943, Ja 5,20:2; 1952, O 15,31:5
Hughes, William J Mrs, 1948, Je 30,25:5
Hughes, William K, 1956, Je 11,31:4
Hughes, William L, 1957, F 21,27:3
Hughes, William M, 1942, Ap 26,39:2; 1952, O 28,31:1
Hughes, William Mrs, 1950, My 1,25:4
Hughes, William S, 1940, Je 1,15:4
Hughes, William Sen (funl, F 3,15:2), 1918, Ja 31,9:5
Hughes-Stanton, Herbert Sir, 1937, Ag 4,19:3
Hughett, Joseph L, 1954, S 30,31:5
Hughey, George H, 1943, Jl 2,19:3
Hughey, James, 1945, Mr 30,15:2
Hughey, Mott B, 1940, N 29,21:4
Hughitt, M, 1928, Ja 7,17:5
Hughitt, Marvin Jr, 1949, F 8,26:2
Hughson, George W, 1941, S 6,15:1
Hughson, John, 1937, Ag 13,17:3
Hughson, Shirley C, 1949, N 17,29:5
Hughson, Walter Rev, 1908, S 6,9:2
Hughston, Regan, 1951, O 4,33:4
Hughston, Regan Mrs, 1958, Ag 25,21:1
Hugi, Frank W, 1957, Jl 20,15:6
Hugi, John R, 1959, F 1,85:2
Hugli, Ernest W, 1948, F 24,25:2
Hugo, Albert C, 1957, Je 26,31:5
Hugo, Charles, 1871, Mr 18,1:2
Hugo, F M, 1930, D 31,17:3
Hugo, Francois (funl), 1874, Ja 17,3:4
Hugo, Francois Victor, 1873, D 27,1:7
Hugo, Georges Victor, 1925, F 6,17:5
Hugo, John A, 1952, Mr 4,27:2
Hugo, Louis C F, 1940, Mr 31,46:3
Hugo, Valeska Mrs, 1948, Ja 5,20:3
Hugo, Victor (funl, My 31,1:3), 1885, My 23,1:7
Hugon, August, 1961, Jl 31,19:4
Hugson, Walter, 1944, S 14,23:3
Huguelet, Guy A, 1955, Jl 24,64:5
Huguenin, Charles, 1964, Ag 22,21:5
Huguenot, Harry A, 1954, Ap 28,31:1
Hugues, Clovis, 1907, Je 12,9:5
Hugues, John F, 1960, F 25,29:3
Huguet, Maxine, 1940, Ja 7,48:4
Hugus, Anna L, 1949, Mr 31,25:4
Hugus, Wright, 1958, Ap 27,86:2
Hugus, Z Zimmerman (por), 1944, D 30,11:3
Huhlein, Charles F, 1938, S 12,17:2
Huhn, Adolph, 1940, Mr 21,25:2
Huhn, Bruno, 1950, My 15,21:3
Huhn, Bruno Mrs, 1943, D 15,27:4
Huhn, George, 1903, O 31,9:6
Huhn, George A 3d, 1945, Ap 8,36:1
Huhn, Harry E, 1956, S 17,27:5
Huhn, John R Jr, 1955, Ap 9,13:6
Huhn, Samuel Parham, 1919, S 30,19:3
Huhn, Tevis, 1967, Ag 14,31:3
Huhn, William H T, 1958, Ag 26,29:2
Huhndorff, Carl, 1961, My 4,37:3
Huhner, Leon, 1957, Mr 1,23:1
Huidekoper, Frederic L, 1940, Mr 8,22:4
Huidekoper, Frederic W Mrs, 1914, My 31,5:6
Huidekoper, Frederick Wolters, 1908, Ap 30,9:5
Huidekoper, R S Dr, 1901, D 18,9:5
Huidekoper, Reginald S, 1943, S 29,21:5
Huidobro, Carolina Holman, 1909, Ap 14,11:5
Huidobro, Vincente, 1948, Ja 4,52:1
Huie, Carl W, 1950, Jl 25,27:5
Huie, Irving V A, 1957, Ag 31,15:3
Huish, George Mrs, 1954, Ap 12,29:5
Huisman, Coenraad, 1955, D 8,37:1
Huizenga, Lee S, 1945, Ag 8,23:4
Huizinga, Arnold V C P, 1953, S 2,25:4
Huizinga, Henry, 1945, D 12,27:1
Huizinga, Johan, 1945, Mr 23,19:5
Hujber, Stephen, 1951, F 28,28:5
Huke, Allen J, 1956, O 5,25:3
Huke, Angelina H Mrs, 1925, D 1,25:4
Hukill, Ralph W, 1948, Ja 12,19:3
Hula, George, 1951, S 2,48:5
Hulatt, Henry, 1956, Ja 26,29:4
Hulbert, A B, 1933, D 26,18:1
Hulbert, Arthur H Prof, 1937, My 26,25:5
Hulbert, Chauncey P Prof, 1925, Je 19,19:5
Hulbert, Edmund D, 1923, Mr 31,13:5
Hulbert, Eri Baker Dr, 1907, F 18,9:6
Hulbert, George H, 1948, My 24,19:5
Hulbert, George M Mrs, 1955, Je 22,30:2
Hulbert, Harold S, 1949, F 15,23:4
Hulbert, Henry C, 1912, Ap 25,13:5
Hulbert, Homer B (por), 1949, Ag 6,17:1
Hulbert, Louise Deming, 1912, O 25,13:2
Hulbert, Mary A Mrs, 1939, D 18,23:5
Hulbert, Mary V, 1957, N 16,19:1
Hulbert, Mary Woodward Mrs, 1921, My 4,10:5
Hulbert, Murray, 1950, Ap 27,29:1
Hulbert, Olive W, 1940, My 23,23:1
Hulbert, Prescott M, 1961, Mr 24,27:8
Hulbert, Robert S, 1925, D 21,21:5
Hulbert, Roscoe C, 1955, Je 25,15:4
Hulburd, Charles H, 1924, Ja 15,19:4
Hulburd, David W, 1940, S 3,17:1; 1960, S 22,27:4
Hulburd, Hugh E, 1955, F 16,29:2
Hulburd, Lucius S, 1938, S 9,21:1
Hulburd, Merritt, 1939, Ja 23,13:1
Hulburd, Philip E, 1966, Mr 29,41:3
Hulburt, Harry L, 1942, F 28,17:1
Hulburt, Ray G, 1947, Ap 16,25:6
Hulce, Henry C, 1937, F 27,17:5
Hulchanski, Stephan, 1950, D 4,29:2
Huldermann, Bernard, 1922, My 6,11:5
Huldschinsky, Paul O, 1947, F 3,20:2
Huldtgren, Oscar, 1942, F 22,III,7:4
Hulen, Annie S Mrs, 1942, S 15,23:3
Hulen, John A, 1957, S 15,82:3
Hulen, Rubey M, 1956, Jl 8,36:3
Hulen, William F, 1947, O 4,17:2
Hulet, Frank E, 1944, Ag 30,17:5
Hulett, Edwin L, 1942, Ag 31,17:6
Hulett, George A, 1955, S 8,31:2
Hulett, John B, 1954, F 24,25:2
Hulett, Kirk A, 1941, Ja 16,23:3
Hulett, Mason, 1943, F 9,23:4
Hulick, George, 1968, Mr 21,53:1
Hulick, George W Mrs, 1956, Ja 11,31:3
Hulick, Harry, 1946, Ag 7,27:5
Hulick, James E, 1961, Ag 9,33:4
Hulick, William H, 1948, Ja 9,21:3
Hulie, George C Mrs, 1950, N 26,89:4
Huling, Caroline A, 1941, Mr 12,21:4
Huling, Edward B Mrs, 1940, O 12,17:5
Huling, Mark, 1951, O 24,31:4
Huling, Ray G, 1949, Je 7,31:5
Huling, Robert C, 1950, Jl 27,25:2
Hulings, Willis J Gen, 1924, Ag 10,24:4
Hulitar, Michael de Mrs (Cosmy), 1961, Je 12,29:4
Huljus, Christian, 1942, F 23,21:6
Hulka, Jaroslav H, 1958, Je 20,23:5
Hull, Albert E, 1922, Ag 19,11:6
Hull, Albert W, 1966, Ja 23,89:3
Hull, Amy L (Mrs E W Scherr), 1959, F 14,21:2
Hull, Annie M, 1948, N 24,23:2
Hull, Arthur B, 1945, S 11,23:5; 1951, Ag 28,23:5
Hull, Arthur B Mrs, 1943, Mr 2,19:2
Hull, Arthur G, 1941, N 13,27:1
Hull, Aureluis B, 1907, F 16,9:6
Hull, Barney Capt, 1875, Ag 29,1:7
Hull, Brice S, 1948, Ja 4,52:1
Hull, Burton E, 1958, N 9,89:1
Hull, Charles A, 1948, Ag 31,23:2
Hull, Clark L, 1952, My 11,92:3
Hull, Cordell (funl, Jl 27,23:1; will, Ag 3,14:8), 1955, Jl 24,1:3
Hull, Cordell Mrs (funl, Mr 28,88:3), 1954, Mr 27, 17:1
Hull, Courtlandt P Jr, 1948, D 21,31:2
Hull, Daniel S, 1953, Ap 21,27:4
Hull, Deryl, 1962, My 18,31:3
Hull, Deryl Mrs, 1961, Ja 11,47:2
Hull, E, 1879, F 27,8:2
Hull, Earl L, 1960, O 10,31:3
Hull, Edward G, 1947, Ap 4,23:1
Hull, Edward M, 1950, Ap 12,28:2
Hull, Edward Mrs, 1953, Ja 12,27:5
Hull, Edward Prof, 1917, N 28,13:5
Hull, Edward T, 1938, Ag 28,32:5
Hull, Elbert O, 1955, S 7,31:1
Hull, Elinor V Mrs, 1939, F 1,21:5
Hull, Ernest H, 1937, Jl 2,21:3
Hull, Ferdinand S, 1940, N 22,23:4
Hull, Firman, 1953, Ap 9,27:6
Hull, Forest P, 1939, Je 26,15:5
Hull, Francis B, 1946, Ja 30,25:4
Hull, George A, 1941, Mr 20,21:4; 1947, Ap 7,23:4
Hull, George C, 1958, My 19,25:1
Hull, George H, 1921, Mr 15,11:3
Hull, George H Mrs, 1943, D 11,15:5; 1964, S 3,29:3
Hull, Gertrude, 1947, Mr 25,25:4
Hull, Gordon F, 1956, O 9,35:1
Hull, H H, 1876, Je 18,2:6
Hull, Harrison S, 1952, Ja 9,29:5
Hull, Harry A, 1948, F 15,60:2
Hull, Harry E, 1938, Ja 17,19:1
Hull, Harry E Mrs, 1955, Je 7,33:4
Hull, Harry R Mrs, 1917, My 22,13:3
Hull, Harwood, 1950, F 7,27:1
Hull, Henry E, 1947, S 1,19:3
Hull, Henry Mrs, 1944, D 5,23:2
Hull, Howard G Sr, 1952, Ap 29,27:5
Hull, Howard Mrs (M Anglin),(funl plans, Ja 9,33:1), 1958, Ja 8,47:1
Hull, Ida F Mrs, 1951, Ap 23,25:5
Hull, J A T, 1928, S 28,27:5
Hull, J Arthur, 1960, Mr 5,19:5
Hull, J Arthur Mrs, 1942, Je 21,36:7
Hull, J Harry, 1946, Mr 22,21:3
Hull, J Hayden, 1955, Ja 15,13:3
Hull, James F, 1923, Ag 11,9:5
Hull, James H, 1950, D 4,29:5
Hull, John A, 1941, Mr 3,15:2
Hull, John A (por), 1944, Ap 18,21:4
Hull, John B, 1947, My 8,25:2
Hull, John C, 1946, Ja 1,28:2; 1947, Ja 8,23:4
Hull, John Frank, 1907, Jl 6,7:4
Hull, Joseph, 1943, Ja 18,15:3
Hull, Joseph L, 1951, Ag 9,21:4
Hull, Josephine, 1957, Mr 13,31:2
Hull, Lawrence C Jr, 1952, F 16,13:3
Hull, Lawrence Cameron Prof, 1916, O 17,13:2
Hull, Lewis, 1945, Ja 13,11:5
Hull, Lytle, 1958, Je 27,25:4
Hull, Merlin, 1953, My 18,21:1
Hull, Morton D (por), 1937, Ag 22,II,6:4
Hull, Nathan A, 1943, O 14,21:1
Hull, Norman C, 1938, Jl 2,13:6
Hull, Orison V, 1947, Ja 12,59:5
Hull, Paul D, 1950, O 21,17:4
Hull, Richard O, 1957, D 1,88:4
Hull, Robert Bruce Dr, 1914, Ap 13,11:4
Hull, Robert E, 1951, N 13,29:3
Hull, Robert Mrs, 1953, Je 6,17:6
Hull, Roger B, 1942, Ja 24,17:5
Hull, Roger B Mrs, 1964, S 16,31:1
Hull, Royal C, 1949, Ap 18,25:1
Hull, S T, 1903, Ap 3,9:6
Hull, Sernadius S, 1940, Je 2,44:5
Hull, Shelly, 1919, Ja 15,11:2
Hull, Talcott B, 1940, Mr 8,21:4
Hull, Thomas E, 1964, Jl 18,19:5
Hull, Thomas F, 1939, Mr 6,15:4
Hull, Vera B Mrs, 1953, Ag 11,27:4
Hull, Vincent K (por), 1940, Ag 21,19:3
Hull, Vincent K Mrs, 1963, Ap 12,27:2
Hull, W H, 1877, S 19,4:6
Hull, Walter C, 1941, N 29,17:1
Hull, William C, 1948, D 22,23:1
Hull, William E (por), 1942, Je 1,13:1
Hull, William H H, 1908, S 22,9:6
Hull, William I, 1939, N 15,23:4
Hull, William I Mrs, 1958, Jl 6,57:2
Hull, William L, 1956, Mr 25,74:1
Hull, William W, 1948, N 30,27:2
Hullah, John, 1884, F 23,1:4
Hullihen, Walter, 1944, Ap 15,11:4
Hulling, Charles C Mrs, 1955, Jl 20,27:2
Hullinger, Edward B, 1956, F 16,29:5
Hullinger, Edwin Ware, 1968, O 28,47:1
Hullings, Edward P, 1942, S 14,15:5
Hullivan, Michael W, 1949, Jl 19,29:4
Hullstrung, William J, 1960, Ja 7,29:1
Hully, Ernest, 1957, O 16,35:3
Hulman, Herman, 1913, Jl 5,9:6
Hulme, Edward M, 1951, Jl 12,25:6
Hulme, Harold Mrs, 1962, Ap 21,20:7
Hulme, John W Mrs, 1946, Ja 18,20:2
Hulme, Norman, 1964, Jl 16,31:4
Hulme, Thomas, 1939, O 11,27:2
Hulme, Thomas W (por), 1939, S 24,43:1
Hulme, Thomas W Mrs, 1940, Ja 16,23:4
Hulmes, Bert, 1960, D 6,37:4
Hulnick, Michael, 1952, Jl 11,17:5
Hulquist, John, 1922, S 5,17:4
Hulsapple, Eustace, 1956, Mr 14,33:2
Hulsapple, Harry, 1952, F 17,86:5
Hulsart, C B, 1876, My 1,8:3
Hulsart, C Raymond (por), 1937, D 1,23:3
Hulsart, C Raymond Mrs, 1955, D 21,29:5
Hulsart, George W, 1938, O 28,23:2
Hulsart, J Howard, 1944, S 12,19:6
Hulsart, John, 1947, S 23,25:2
Hulsart, Pierre M Sr, 1956, S 20,33:5
Hulsberg, Albert G, 1948, S 3,19:4
Hulsbergen, H G, 1953, O 15,33:1
Hulse, Abram C, 1947, My 6,27:2
Hulse, Albert E, 1944, My 7,46:2
Hulse, Charles A, 1951, Jl 10,27:4
Hulse, Charles H, 1944, Je 21,19:4
Hulse, Curtis, 1953, Ja 16,24:3
Hulse, Frances A, 1937, D 18,21:1
Hulse, Freeman T, 1943, My 1,15:3
Hulse, Herbert L, 1939, Je 29,23:6
Hulse, Hiram R (por), 1938, Ap 11,15:1
Hulse, John B, 1871, Ap 17,8:2
Hulse, John B (por), 1941, Ag 22,15:4
Hulse, John H, 1962, My 28,29:4
Hulse, Levi S, 1938, F 18,19:5
Hulse, Wilfred C, 1962, Ja 11,33:3
Hulse, William A, 1938, Ap 9,17:5; 1944, Je 1 1953, Jl 6,17:4
Hulse, William H, 1957, F 11,25:4
Hulse, William S, 1950, Jl 16,68:8
Hulseberg, Edward H, 1943, O 6,23:1
Hulsebosch, Gerard F, 1960, Ag 26,25:1
Hulshizer, R Van Syckel Mrs, 1903, D 2,9:5

Hulsizer, Ann Mrs, 1907, D 22,9:4
Hulsizer, Judson K, 1946, My 28,21:4
Hulskamper, William H, 1944, N 1,23:3
Hulsmann, Frederick, 1937, Ag 2,19:4
Hulst, Charles W, 1938, N 10,27:5
Hulst, Charles W Mrs, 1952, Ag 1,17:2
Hulst, George D, 1944, N 12,49:2
Hulst, John, 1955, S 16,23:3
Hulst, Nelson P Dr, 1923, Ja 12,15:3
Hulsteyn, J C van, 1947, Mr 4,25:5
Hulstrom, Henry, 1940, N 27,23:4
Hulswit, Charles L Mrs, 1955, O 8,19:3
Hulswitt, Rudy, 1950, Ja 17,27:5
Hult, Adolph, 1943, Mr 7,38:5
Hult, Adolph J Mrs, 1967, D 11,47:5
Hult, Britta, 1950, My 19,27:2
Hult, Ellis G Mrs, 1947, O 8,25:4
Hult, Eugene Edward Comr (funl, My 10,44:4), 1968, My 7,47:1
Hultberg, Grant (por), 1938, N 12,15:5
Hulten, Charles M, 1967, Ja 9,36:8
Hultgreen, Odd, 1966, Jl 20,41:5
Hultgren, Emil J, 1911, F 25,11:5
Hultgren, Robert A Mrs, 1964, Ap 17,35:3
Hultman, Eugene C, 1945, Ap 23,19:6
Hulton, W A H, 1941, My 11,44:6
Hultquist, Charles O, 1949, Ap 23,13:2
Hultquist, Earle O, 1963, Ap 4,47:4
Hultquist, Victor J Sr, 1968, Ja 20,26:6
Hults, Eugene A, 1946, N 30,15:1
Hultslander, Joseph D, 1943, Jl 19,15:4
Hultz, Fred S, 1961, Ap 19,39:4
Hulvey, Charles N, 1937, My 20,21:5
Humaes, Johan, 1952, O 5,88:7
Human, Alfred E, 1962, S 30,86:1
Human, Phil Sr, 1952, Ag 21,19:5
Human, Theodore, 1955, Mr 30,29:5
Humason, Thomas A, 1957, D 12,29:4
Humason, Virgil R, 1905, My 7,1:4
Humbert, Ada E, 1939, My 29,15:4
Humbert, C, 1927, N 3,27:1
Humbert, Dolly, 1952, F 2,13:5
Humbert, George Jackson, 1907, D 13,11:3
Humbert, John H, 1942, D 30,23:2
Humbert, William A, 1943, F 16,20:2
Humbert I, King of Italy (see also Jl 30), 1900, Jl 31,1:6
Humbeutel, Charles Mrs, 1942, Ja 2,23:3
Humbird, J A, 1911, Ag 6,II,9:6
Humbird, Jacob W, 1937, Ap 3,19:6
Humble, Henry W, 1941, Ja 13,15:3
Humblet, Charles, 1942, N 12,25:5
Humboldt, Charles, 1964, Ja 25,23:4
Humboldt, F H A von Baron (funl, My 23,2:5), 1859, My 19,4:6
Hume, A Rev, 1884, N 22,5:3
Hume, Agnes H, 1961, O 17,39:4
Hume, Alfred, 1950, D 26,23:1
Hume, Arthur C, 1942, Ja 19,20:2
Hume, Barbara J, 1966, My 27,43:2
Hume, Benita, 1967, N 5,86:5
Hume, Cornelius, 1938, Jl 19,22:1
Hume, Cyril, 1966, Mr 28,33:1
Hume, Cyril Mrs, 1925, My 25,17:6
Hume, Edgar E, 1952, Ja 25,21:1
Hume, Edmund, 1960, O 15,23:5
Hume, Edmund Mrs, 1948, My 12,28:3
Hume, Edward H (mem ser set, F 11,29:5; mem ser, F 21,27:3), 1957, F 10,85:1
Hume, Edward S Rev, 1908, Ja 11,9:6
Hume, Frederic W Mrs, 1947, Je 22,52:8
Hume, H Nutcombe, 1967, D 23,23:2
Hume, Herbert C, 1948, N 20,13:2
Hume, James W, 1940, Ap 10,25:5
Hume, John T, 1949, Ag 17,23:5
Hume, Julia Cracraft Mrs, 1920, N 16,15:2
Hume, Leland, 1939, Ag 28,19:2
Hume, Nelson (por), 1948, Je 15,27:3
Hume, O F, 1959, O 31,23:6
Hume, Raphael, 1957, F 18,27:5
Hume, Rita, 1953, D 30,4:6
Hume, Robert E (por), 1948, Ja 5,19:1
Hume, Robert E Mrs, 1962, Ag 15,31:4
Hume, Thomas Rev Dr, 1912, Jl 16,9:6
Hume, Walter F, 1951, Ag 2,21:5
Hume, William J (por), 1938, F 15,25:5
Hume-Gibbons, Robert, 1937, Mr 19,23:5
Humelbaugh, Jesse C, 1922, Ja 26,17:4
Humera, Victor, 1956, Ap 21,17:4
Humes, Albert H, 1947, Jl 30,21:2
Humes, Augustine L, 1952, S 26,21:5
Humes, Augustine L Mrs, 1954, F 5,19:2
Humes, Charles L, 1950, S 24,104:4
Humes, Charles T, 1937, N 5,23:4
Humes, Chester E, 1952, Mr 3,21:4
Humes, David, 1959, S 10,35:6
Humes, J Fred, 1957, Mr 18,27:4
Humes, Larry C, 1925, F 6,17:5
Humeston, Edward J, 1948, F 21,13:5
Humiston, Charles E, 1940, N 5,34:2
Humiston, Howard B, 1940, Je 23,30:7
Humiston, Mary G W Mrs, 1948, Jl 18,52:7
Humiston, Wallace D, 1941, Ag 22,15:1
Humiston, William H (funl, D 7,21:5), 1923, D 6,19:4
Humiston, William H, 1943, Je 17,21:2
Humm, Albert, 1953, S 28,25:1
Humm, Edmund F, 1951, O 19,27:4
Humme, A A, 1943, My 22,13:2
Hummel, A F, 1951, Ap 12,33:2
Hummel, A H, 1926, Ja 24,1:7
Hummel, Alfred, 1950, D 9,15:3
Hummel, August, 1959, O 18,87:1
Hummel, Charles F, 1953, Mr 26,31:2; 1962, Ja 5,29:5
Hummel, Charles W Mrs, 1950, O 25,35:2
Hummel, Dorothy, 1948, My 27,25:1
Hummel, Francis M, 1956, Mr 5,23:5
Hummel, George F, 1952, D 22,25:3
Hummel, George H, 1946, Ag 29,27:3
Hummel, Gustave, 1943, Ap 16,21:5
Hummel, John E, 1959, My 20,35:3
Hummel, John P, 1944, N 15,27:2
Hummel, Joseph S, 1963, Jl 19,25:4
Hummel, Jules H, 1944, Mr 11,13:5
Hummel, Ragnar A, 1959, Ag 7,21:1
Hummel, Ragnar A Mrs, 1951, Ag 1,23:4
Hummel, Ralph, 1955, Jl 28,2:4
Hummel, Ralph Jr, 1955, Jl 28,2:4
Hummel, Rufus J, 1958, Je 10,33:2
Hummel, Theodore F, 1944, S 21,19:5
Hummel, William L, 1950, Mr 13,21:3
Hummell, George A, 1944, N 15,27:1
Hummler, Frank, 1941, N 25,25:4
Humpage, Frederic R, 1954, Je 21,23:5
Humperdinck, Engelbert Prof, 1921, S 29,17:5
Humpfer, Frederick G, 1943, O 30,15:1
Humpfer, George W, 1953, Je 12,27:4
Humphrey, A L (por), 1939, N 2,23:1
Humphrey, A P, 1928, Ag 21,23:1
Humphrey, Albert E, 1962, Je 30,19:3
Humphrey, Anna Mrs, 1951, Ja 4,29:5
Humphrey, Arthur L, 1946, Mr 22,22:2
Humphrey, Barry Mrs, 1947, N 28,27:3
Humphrey, Burt J (por),(will, D 20,20:5), 1940, D 12,27:1
Humphrey, Burt J Mrs, 1939, O 15,49:3
Humphrey, C F Gen, 1926, Je 5,17:5
Humphrey, C S, 1947, Ap 27,60:3
Humphrey, Carl T, 1938, F 8,21:4
Humphrey, Charles E, 1968, O 13,85:1
Humphrey, Charles E Mrs, 1952, Ja 18,27:2
Humphrey, Chauncey B, 1958, Ja 6,39:3
Humphrey, David W, 1950, Je 12,27:5
Humphrey, Doris (Mrs C F Woodford), 1958, D 30, 32:1
Humphrey, Dudley S Mrs, 1945, Ap 18,23:5
Humphrey, Edward B, 1944, O 23,19:5
Humphrey, Edward C, 1945, Ja 4,19:5
Humphrey, Edward F, 1960, F 7,85:1
Humphrey, Eugene F, 1958, F 23,93:1
Humphrey, Fletcher Mrs, 1953, Ja 21,31:5
Humphrey, Frank H, 1937, D 12,II,8:3
Humphrey, Frank J, 1953, O 26,21:3
Humphrey, G Ward, 1953, Ap 13,27:4
Humphrey, George, 1947, Je 19,21:3
Humphrey, George S, 1940, D 4,27:4
Humphrey, Gilbert E, 1951, Je 26,29:4
Humphrey, Glenn H, 1945, O 10,21:2
Humphrey, Hal, 1968, D 31,27:3
Humphrey, Harry A, 1946, D 16,23:2
Humphrey, Helen F, 1963, Ag 26,27:4
Humphrey, Henry, 1951, S 4,27:3
Humphrey, Henry B, 1948, S 20,25:2
Humphrey, Henry H, 1959, Je 10,37:4
Humphrey, Henry L, 1950, D 16,17:3
Humphrey, Howard R, 1965, F 25,31:3
Humphrey, Howard S, 1946, O 22,25:5
Humphrey, Hubert H Sr, 1949, N 26,15:1
Humphrey, Isaac, 1868, Ja 2,2:4
Humphrey, J M, 1881, N 14,5:3
Humphrey, James (funl, Je 21,2:5), 1866, Je 17,5:1
Humphrey, John, 1949, My 4,30:2
Humphrey, John P, 1944, Jl 5,17:4
Humphrey, John V Mrs, 1943, D 7,27:4
Humphrey, John W, 1951, Mr 18,89:1
Humphrey, L H Sen, 1902, Mr 18,9:7
Humphrey, Lambert Mrs, 1958, F 19,27:2
Humphrey, Lucius D, 1957, O 13,86:7
Humphrey, Lyman U Ex-Gov, 1915, S 13,9:5
Humphrey, Maria H, 1943, Jl 20,19:5
Humphrey, Marie E I Mrs, 1941, Mr 30,49:2
Humphrey, Nathan M, 1946, Mr 13,29:4
Humphrey, Norman D, 1955, N 1,31:3
Humphrey, Orville, 1940, Ag 14,19:5
Humphrey, Ralph, 1967, Ag 28,31:4
Humphrey, Raymond V, 1913, Jl 7,5:2
Humphrey, Robert G, 1956, Je 22,23:4
Humphrey, Robert W, 1943, D 19,48:4
Humphrey, Theodore F Mrs, 1955, Ag 25,23:3
Humphrey, W E, 1934, F 15,19:1
Humphrey, W Warren, 1942, O 31,15:2
Humphrey, Walter B, 1966, O 12,43:2
Humphrey, William, 1951, S 2,49:1
Humphrey, William A, 1940, Ja 3,21:5
Humphrey, William F, 1960, F 4,31:5
Humphrey, William R, 1962, My 23,45:4
Humphrey, Wirt E, 1940, Ja 29,16:2
Humphrey, Wolcott J, 1959, F 11,39:4
Humphrey, Zephine, 1956, N 16,27:4
Humphreys, A A Gen, 1883, D 29,5:5
Humphreys, A C, 1927, Ag 15,17:3
Humphreys, A S Judge, 1916, Ag 26,7:4
Humphreys, C Blake, 1949, F 11,23:4
Humphreys, Cecil (por), 1947, N 8,17:1
Humphreys, Charles E, 1940, Ap 26,21:2
Humphreys, Charles W, 1940, Ja 30,20:2
Humphreys, Charles W Mrs, 1963, N 28,39:1
Humphreys, Clifton S, 1953, D 25,17:5
Humphreys, David C, 1938, O 6,23:2
Humphreys, Desmond Mrs, 1938, Ja 4,23:1
Humphreys, Ernest G, 1949, D 29,25:5
Humphreys, Frank L Dr, 1937, Jl 19,16:1
Humphreys, Frederic E, 1941, Ja 21,21:3
Humphreys, Frederic P, 1950, Ag 20,76:1
Humphreys, Frederick H Dr, 1919, Ja 16,13:3
Humphreys, George A, 1952, My 30,15:3
Humphreys, George H, 1953, Ap 17,25:5
Humphreys, George M, 1954, Je 25,21:1
Humphreys, George W, 1947, F 6,23:3; 1949, N 8,31:1
Humphreys, H N, 1879, Jl 2,5:4
Humphreys, Harry E, 1954, O 22,27:3
Humphreys, Harry E Jr, 1967, S 4,21:1
Humphreys, Henry H, 1905, F 27,1:6
Humphreys, Howard R, 1960, Jl 30,17:6
Humphreys, Hugh, 1937, F 12,23:1
Humphreys, Hugh G, 1958, O 29,35:2
Humphreys, J (see also, No 29), 1883, N 30,1:7
Humphreys, J, 1936, Jl 11,15:1
Humphreys, James J, 1937, Ja 25,19:3
Humphreys, John P, 1944, F 4,15:3
Humphreys, John S, 1958, Jl 2,27:1
Humphreys, Joseph, 1904, My 22,7:5
Humphreys, Landon, 1965, F 12,29:2
Humphreys, Marie C, 1906, D 2,7:5
Humphreys, Martin J, 1942, Ap 26,39:1
Humphreys, Mary Gay, 1915, O 15,11:5
Humphreys, Murray, 1965, N 24,24:5
Humphreys, O F, 1944, S 14,23:6
Humphreys, Owen, 1954, O 12,27:2
Humphreys, Phebe W Mrs, 1939, Je 20,21:5
Humphreys, Richard D Mrs, 1937, S 2,21:2
Humphreys, Richard F Dr, 1968, Ag 9,35:1
Humphreys, Richard T, 1938, D 4,61:2
Humphreys, Robert E, 1962, O 30,35:1
Humphreys, Robert G, 1965, O 17,86:6
Humphreys, Russell G, 1949, N 10,31:2
Humphreys, Thomas E, 1953, N 19,31:4
Humphreys, Thomas E Mrs, 1950, Jl 1,15:3
Humphreys, Travers, 1956, F 21,33:2
Humphreys, Wilbur M, 1948, Ag 15,61:2
Humphreys, William, 1953, Mr 25,31:5
Humphreys, William Bro, 1937, Jl 4,II,7:2
Humphreys, William E, 1957, Ag 16,19:1
Humphreys, William J, 1949, N 12,15:3
Humphreys-Johnstone, John, 1941, Ap 18,21:2
Humphries, Albert, 1955, Mr 23,31:2
Humphries, Andrew K, 1957, Je 22,15:3
Humphries, Arthur G, 1953, Ja 23,20:3
Humphries, E H Bertram Mrs, 1940, F 13,23:3
Humphries, George A Mrs, 1948, S 21,27:1
Humphries, James H Dr, 1968, Mr 14,43:1
Humphries, John A, 1949, My 13,23:2
Humphries, John D, 1942, O 23,22:4; 1945, Ag 1,19:6
Humphries, John E Judge, 1915, My 30,13:6
Humphries, John H Mrs, 1955, Ja 14,21:2
Humphries, Robert E, 1957, O 23,33:3
Humphries, William A Sr, 1945, Jl 16,11:7
Humphris, F H, 1947, Je 19,21:6
Humphriss, Charles H Mrs, 1940, S 10,23:6
Humphry, Catherine M, 1924, O 10,19:5
Humphry, James, 1944, Ap 29,15:5
Humphrys, Julian Mrs, 1956, F 8,33:3
Humphrys, William J Mrs, 1958, My 17,19:5
Humpston, Millicent E, 1948, Ja 28,23:4
Humpstone, Ernest B, 1954, Ap 3,15:3
Humpstone, Harold D, 1963, Je 28,29:2
Humpstone, Mabel H Mrs, 1939, N 12,48:7
Humpstone, O Paul (por), 1946, Ja 24,22:2
Humpstone, O Paul Mrs, 1960, Jl 3,32:3
Humpton, William G, 1948, My 9,68:5
Humstone, Walter C, 1925, Mr 13,19:3
Hun, John G, 1945, S 16,44:2
Hun, John G Mrs, 1964, Jl 23,27:4
Hun, Marcus T, 1920, F 29,22:3
Hund, William H, 1943, My 10,19:3
Hundiak, John Mrs, 1958, Mr 8,17:5
Hundley, Joseph H, 1940, Ap 30,22:2
Hunefeld, John W, 1945, Je 9,13:4
Huneker, James G Mrs, 1950, O 28,17:2
Huneker, James Gibbons (por), 1921, F 10,7:1
Huneker, Minnie U, 1942, My 27,25:7
Hunerwadel, Otto K, 1952, Ag 1,17:4
Hung Shen, 1955, Ag 30,27:5
Hung Shih-lu, 1955, Ap 27,31:5
Hungate, Wilson, 1943, Ap 13,26:2
Hungelmann, Paul, 1957, Ap 9,33:1
Hunger, Frank A, 1961, O 15,88:6
Hunger, Walter L, 1951, Je 10,93:2
Hunger, William E, 1954, S 2,21:2
Hungerford, Charles S Sr, 1957, Ja 21,25:1

Hungerford, Churchill Sr, 1940, O 17,25:2
Hungerford, Clark, 1962, O 19,31:2
Hungerford, Edward (por), 1948, Jl 30,17:4
Hungerford, Frederick B, 1945, Jl 9,11:5
Hungerford, Jonathan D, 1961, Ap 28,31:1
Hungerford, L Phillips, 1947, Je 22,52:5
Hungerford, Louis S, 1948, Jl 27,25:3
Hungerford, Margaret (The Duchess), 1897, Ja 25, 2:5
Hungerford, Mona, 1942, Jl 19,30:8
Hungerford, Robert, 1949, Jl 24,52:4
Hungerford, S H, 1867, My 25,1:6
Hungerford, Samuel J, 1955, O 9,87:1
Hungerford, Theodore Albert, 1903, N 25,9:5
Hungerford, U T, 1926, Je 17,23:3
Hungerford, Victor W, 1949, Mr 5,17:3
Hungerford, William, 1873, Ja 16,5:6
Hunicke, Felix Herman Capt, 1913, S 13,11:5
Hunicke, Raymond S, 1960, Mr 10,31:1
Hunkele, Herbert J Sr, 1952, Ap 27,90:4
Hunkele, Philip, 1964, Ag 3,25:3
Hunken, George J, 1947, S 14,60:4
Hunkins, Sterling, 1967, S 21,47:3
Hunloke, Philip (por), 1947, Ap 3,25:4
Hunn, Edward B, 1956, Je 8,25:2
Hunn, Ernest F, 1963, My 14,39:3
Hunn, John T S Mrs, 1944, Ap 17,23:2
Hunneman, William C Jr, 1958, Ja 24,23:1
Hunneman, William C Jr Mrs, 1960, D 15,43:4
Hunner, Guy L, 1957, Jl 16,26:1
Hunner, Max (por), 1947, N 10,29:1
Hunnewell, Frank S Mrs, 1945, My 1,23:3
Hunnewell, H H, 1902, My 21,9:5
Hunnewell, Hillman B, 1954, F 9,27:4
Hunnewell, Hillman B Mrs, 1952, Ag 8,17:5
Hunnewell, Hollis H Mrs, 1924, My 28,23:4
Hunnewell, Hollis Horatio, 1922, Ja 25,15:6
Hunnewell, James Frothingham, 1910, N 13,11:3
Hunnewell, James M, 1954, Mr 23,27:4
Hunnewell, John A, 1937, Mr 12,24:1
Hunnicutt, J H, 1880, O 10,7:5
Hunnicutt, Julian P, 1947, N 21,27:4
Hunnikin, Arthur Mrs, 1958, Mr 1,17:3
Hunniston, David Mrs, 1908, Jl 20,9:6
Hunold, Hekla W Mrs, 1964, N 14,29:3
Hunsaker, Daniel M, 1953, My 21,31:3
Hunsaker, Jerome C Mrs, 1966, S 12,45:4
Hunsberger, Ambrose, 1949, Jl 10,56:6
Hunsberger, Byron K Mrs, 1954, Ap 18,88:6
Hunsberger, Charles A, 1949, D 17,17:5
Hunsberger, J Newton, 1947, N 3,23:6
Hunsher, Nathan, 1948, Ja 14,25:2
Hunsicker, H Alvin, 1943, D 15,27:4
Hunsicker, Horace H, 1966, Ag 9,37:1
Hunsicker, Stanley H, 1949, Mr 16,27:4
Hunsicker, William C, 1939, Ja 11,19:1
Hunsiker, Harold W, 1939, Ap 6,25:3
Hunsinger, Edward P, 1960, Ag 27,19:2
Hunt, A R, 1925, N 3,25:4
Hunt, Adelbert B, 1957, D 23,23:1
Hunt, Adlei S, 1954, My 26,29:4
Hunt, Albert F Jr, 1947, Ap 19,15:5
Hunt, Alexander Everett, 1914, S 16,11:7
Hunt, Alfred B, 1947, Je 25,25:2
Hunt, Alice M, 1956, D 2,86:2
Hunt, Alice Treat, 1908, Je 9,7:6
Hunt, Arthur Prince Rev, 1925, Jl 4,11:6
Hunt, Aylmer Byron, 1925, My 5,21:4
Hunt, Beekman, 1942, F 19,19:5
Hunt, Bethel T, 1955, My 15,86:4
Hunt, Bruce A, 1949, N 23,29:5
Hunt, C Bradley, 1945, Ag 22,23:5
Hunt, C S (see also O 16), 1876, O 18,8:1
Hunt, C W, 1932, Jl 24,22:3
Hunt, Charles C, 1940, O 17,25:4; 1948, Jl 25,48:3; 1953, Ag 8,11:3
Hunt, Charles D, 1914, S 27,15:6
Hunt, Charles Havens, 1872, Jl 15,4:6
Hunt, Charles J, 1951, Ja 2,23:2; 1963, Ag 15,29:3
Hunt, Charles J Justice, 1925, S 29,27:5
Hunt, Charles L Mrs, 1960, Ap 3,86:5
Hunt, Charles R, 1939, Je 15,23:5
Hunt, Charles S, 1940, S 11,25:1
Hunt, Charles T, 1957, S 12,31:3
Hunt, Charles W, 1911, Mr 28,13:5; 1938, Ag 18,19:2
Hunt, Charles W Mrs, 1953, D 12,19:3
Hunt, Clara W, 1958, Ja 12,86:8
Hunt, Clark C, 1954, Jl 11,73:2
Hunt, Clifford P, 1939, D 16,17:5
Hunt, Clifford P (will), 1940, F 4,44:1
Hunt, Clyde D, 1941, F 2,45:2
Hunt, Cornelia D, 1944, S 26,23:5
Hunt, Cyprian C, 1920, Ag 17,13:5
Hunt, Daniel L Mrs, 1945, Mr 19,19:4
Hunt, David H, 1911, Ja 20,11:4
Hunt, David Hopkins, 1918, Ja 4,11:8
Hunt, Dominic P, 1946, Mr 28,25:2
Hunt, Dominick, 1943, Je 26,13:2
Hunt, Douglas L, 1952, Ag 24,89:1
Hunt, Duane G, 1960, Ap 1,33:4
Hunt, E B Maj, 1863, O 2,4:5
Hunt, Earl R, 1957, Je 28,23:2
Hunt, Eden B, 1949, Mr 31,25:1
Hunt, Edgar W, 1960, Je 9,33:6
Hunt, Edmonds E Mrs, 1940, Mr 3,2:3
Hunt, Edward A, 1949, My 8,76:5
Hunt, Edward C, 1950, My 10,31:2
Hunt, Edward E, 1953, Mr 6,20:5
Hunt, Edward L, 1952, O 10,25:1; 1967, D 2,39:5
Hunt, Edward L Jr, 1963, Je 8,25:5
Hunt, Edward L Mrs, 1945, My 5,16:2; 1953, Mr 24, 42:3
Hunt, Elizabeth Mrs, 1909, Ap 15,9:4
Hunt, Ella A, 1944, Ag 16,19:5
Hunt, Ellsworth J, 1942, S 25,21:3
Hunt, Elmer F, 1957, Ap 11,31:4
Hunt, Elmer Munson, 1968, Je 30,52:8
Hunt, Emory W, 1938, My 22,II,7:1
Hunt, Ernest C Sr, 1960, Je 13,27:2
Hunt, Ernest M, 1960, D 22,26:2
Hunt, Eugene, 1953, Ag 15,15:2
Hunt, Everett L Mrs, 1953, Mr 13,25:5
Hunt, F E, 1881, F 4,4:7
Hunt, F W, 1878, O 21,5:2
Hunt, Floyd B, 1966, Jl 19,39:3
Hunt, Frank C, 1945, D 17,21:3
Hunt, Frank D, 1950, Jl 2,25:1
Hunt, Frank W, 1906, N 26,2:4
Hunt, Frazier, 1967, D 28,31:1
Hunt, Fred L, 1944, F 10,15:1
Hunt, Furman, 1885, Je 22,5:7
Hunt, G Everett, 1937, Ap 2,23:1
Hunt, G G, 1876, Ja 30,7:2
Hunt, G W (see also Jl 30), 1877, Ag 1,1:5
Hunt, G W P, 1934, D 25,23:4
Hunt, Gaillard, 1924, Mr 21,19:3
Hunt, Garnett E, 1962, F 3,21:5
Hunt, George F, 1958, O 3,29:4
Hunt, George H, 1942, N 28,13:6
Hunt, George Mrs, 1947, N 3,23:3
Hunt, George P, 1951, My 23,35:4
Hunt, George R, 1940, Ag 21,19:2; 1948, Ag 13,15:5
Hunt, George S P, 1956, Ag 13,19:5
Hunt, George T, 1947, Ap 20,60:5
Hunt, George W, 1940, Ja 12,17:4
Hunt, Glenn J Mrs, 1954, Ja 1,23:2
Hunt, Grace A C Mrs, 1937, F 6,17:6
Hunt, Graham P Sr, 1953, S 9,29:4
Hunt, Hamlin Mrs, 1966, D 3,39:4
Hunt, Harold L, 1954, Jl 17,13:6
Hunt, Harriet L, 1960, O 5,41:5
Hunt, Harry B, 1959, Ap 11,21:3
Hunt, Harry C, 1946, Ag 14,25:1
Hunt, Harry E, 1949, F 17,23:1; 1951, O 16,31:3
Hunt, Harry H, 1937, D 2,25:4
Hunt, Harry J, 1954, Ja 14,29:1
Hunt, Harry L, 1956, D 18,31:2
Hunt, Harry N, 1937, Ag 8,II,7:3
Hunt, Harry P, 1954, Ag 5,23:1
Hunt, Harry S, 1949, My 7,13:6
Hunt, Henry A, 1938, O 4,25:2
Hunt, Henry F (will), 1940, Ap 4,14:3
Hunt, Henry H H, 1952, S 20,15:5
Hunt, Henry L, 1940, Mr 27,21:4
Hunt, Henry T, 1956, Mr 2,23:2
Hunt, Herbert, 1918, F 1,9:5
Hunt, Herbert V Mrs, 1947, O 20,23:2
Hunt, Isaac L, 1939, My 13,15:5
Hunt, Israel Gen, 1875, S 11,4:7
Hunt, J D, 1877, Je 5,8:5
Hunt, J Hamilton, 1925, Ag 16,5:2
Hunt, J Jay Mrs, 1942, S 1,20:3
Hunt, J S Dr, 1875, N 24,5:2
Hunt, J Wardley, 1937, My 11,25:4
Hunt, James, 1958, S 14,85:1
Hunt, James G, 1949, D 10,17:2
Hunt, James H Jr, 1947, My 23,24:3
Hunt, James L, 1907, Je 24,7:6
Hunt, James M, 1914, Je 23,11:4
Hunt, James Mrs, 1944, N 2,19:3
Hunt, James R Dr (por), 1937, Jl 23,19:3
Hunt, Jane Mrs, 1867, O 13,4:6
Hunt, Jarvis, 1941, Je 17,21:5
Hunt, Jeremiah H, 1952, Mr 7,23:3
Hunt, Jerome Rev, 1923, D 29,13:6
Hunt, Jerry, 1960, Ag 31,58:8
Hunt, John A, 1955, S 29,33:4
Hunt, John C, 1945, S 30,46:3; 1947, N 4,25:4
Hunt, John D, 1940, Mr 17,51:2
Hunt, John E Mrs, 1960, Ag 12,19:3
Hunt, John F, 1957, My 6,29:3
Hunt, John J, 1949, F 23,27:3; 1950, Mr 11,15:4
Hunt, John L H Dr, 1918, Jl 19,13:6
Hunt, John M, 1950, N 15,31:4
Hunt, John O, 1957, F 14,27:6
Hunt, John R, 1940, Ag 5,13:5
Hunt, John Rev, 1923, D 17,17:4
Hunt, John W Mrs, 1952, Mr 17,21:2
Hunt, John Ward, 1912, Ja 1,13:3
Hunt, Joseph L Mrs, 1940, Ap 17,23:4
Hunt, Julia T Leigh, 1872, F 25,1:4
Hunt, Kathryn Mrs, 1937, Ap 27,23:2
Hunt, L, 1933, O 6,20:1
Hunt, L Clarence, 1948, Ag 20,17:2
Hunt, Leavitt J, 1960, Ag 22,25:4
Hunt, Leigh, 1859, S 13,1:3
Hunt, Leigh H Dr (por), 1937, D 17,25:1
Hunt, Leigh R, 1948, Ap 18,69:1
Hunt, Leo W, 1954, Ja 7,31:3
Hunt, LeRoy P Gen, 1968, F 10,33:3
Hunt, Livingston, 1938, S 9,8:1; 1943, Ja 19,19:1
Hunt, Livingston Jr, 1953, F 26,25:5
Hunt, Lynn B, 1960, O 13,37:2
Hunt, M Imogene, 1950, Ja 15,85:1
Hunt, Mandilla M S Mrs, 1951, O 2,27:3
Hunt, Marshall, 1956, S 9,84:2
Hunt, Martin J, 1954, Ja 10,86:1
Hunt, Mary A, 1938, N 26,15:1
Hunt, Mary Ann Ladhens, 1908, Je 7,9:6
Hunt, Mary H Mrs, 1906, Ap 25,13:6
Hunt, Mazie N Mrs, 1937, Jl 5,17:5
Hunt, Mercer, 1943, F 7,48:5
Hunt, Merle F, 1959, F 20,25:5
Hunt, Merton L, 1950, Ap 27,29:4
Hunt, Myron, 1952, My 29,27:4
Hunt, Oren G Mrs, 1948, Ap 10,13:3
Hunt, Ormond E, 1967, Ja 5,37:1
Hunt, Otto, 1968, Ja 22,47:2
Hunt, Patrick K, 1948, D 4,19:2
Hunt, Paul, 1949, Ag 22,21:2
Hunt, Peter, 1967, Ap 16,82:7
Hunt, Philip A, 1961, N 17,72:1
Hunt, Preston J Mrs, 1954, D 25,11:5
Hunt, R C, 1919, F 19,13:3
Hunt, R L, 1922, My 12,19:4
Hunt, R M, 1895, Ag 1,5:4
Hunt, Raymond E, 1945, Jl 2,15:3
Hunt, Reid, 1948, Mr 11,27:4
Hunt, Richard C, 1954, D 13,27:1
Hunt, Richard R, 1925, Ap 1,23:4
Hunt, Richard W Mrs, 1958, Ja 22,27:4
Hunt, Ridgley Lt, 1916, F 24,13:4
Hunt, Robert H, 1937, O 3,II,9:1
Hunt, Robert I, 1937, Ja 10,II,10:7
Hunt, Robert J Sr, 1941, Mr 4,23:1
Hunt, Robert W, 1951, Ap 2,25:4
Hunt, Robert W Capt, 1923, Jl 12,17:3
Hunt, Rolla E, 1941, Ag 11,13:2
Hunt, Roy A (will, N 2,42:1), 1966, O 22,31:2
Hunt, Roy A Mrs, 1963, F 23,7:5
Hunt, S B, 1880, Ap 21,5:3
Hunt, S B Dr, 1884, Ap 28,5:1
Hunt, Samuel L, 1941, Ja 31,19:2
Hunt, Sanford B, 1943, Mr 31,19:5
Hunt, Seth B (por), 1948, Je 23,27:1
Hunt, Stephen G Mrs, 1952, N 2,88:1
Hunt, Sumner P, 1938, N 21,19:5
Hunt, Susan A R Mrs, 1941, Mr 19,22:3
Hunt, Sydney A Mrs, 1946, O 28,27:3
Hunt, T, 1878, Ja 21,4:7
Hunt, T W, 1930, Ap 13,28:5
Hunt, Theodore B, 1966, Je 9,47:3
Hunt, Thomas, 1947, Ja 27,23:1
Hunt, Thomas H, 1938, S 30,21:5; 1941, Ag 13,17
Hunt, W H, 1884, F 28,5:2
Hunt, W M, 1879, S 9,2:3
Hunt, Walter A Mrs, 1951, F 20,25:5
Hunt, Walter E, 1966, O 25,48:3
Hunt, Walter L, 1952, My 24,19:5
Hunt, Walter R, 1955, N 4,29:4
Hunt, Washington Ex-Gov, 1867, F 3,8:4
Hunt, Washington Mrs, 1905, F 14,9:3
Hunt, Westley M, 1950, Je 29,29:1
Hunt, Westley M Mrs, 1952, N 4,29:1
Hunt, Willard, 1953, S 10,25:5
Hunt, William, 1864, Mr 6,6:3
Hunt, William (por), 1944, Jl 10,15:4
Hunt, William, 1957, Ag 24,15:4
Hunt, William A Sr, 1944, Je 2,15:3
Hunt, William B, 1953, D 21,31:6
Hunt, William F, 1951, Ap 14,15:1
Hunt, William H, 1949, F 5,16:2; 1957, Je 30,69
Hunt, William J, 1941, Ap 7,17:1; 1947, Mr 25,2
Hunt, William M, 1965, Jl 22,31:5
Hunt, William P, 1966, Ap 18,29:3
Hunt, William S, 1940, Ja 27,13:1
Hunt, William Talmadge, 1916, My 23,11:5
Hunt, Willis A (Bill), 1954, Ap 1,31:5
Hunter, Adolph, 1948, Mr 20,13:6
Hunter, Albert E (autopsy, Ap 8,74:4), 1959, A 66:1
Hunter, Albert R, 1954, D 3,27:3
Hunter, Althea G Mrs, 1948, Ag 4,21:2
Hunter, Amelia, 1952, Jl 30,23:1
Hunter, Andrew H, 1962, My 25,33:4
Hunter, Anna M, 1938, D 9,25:2
Hunter, Arthur, 1904, Ja 27,9:7; 1964, Ja 29,33
Hunter, Arthur Mrs, 1925, Ag 22,11:5
Hunter, Benjamin J, 1958, F 20,25:5
Hunter, Bruce T, 1941, Mr 30,49:2
Hunter, C F, 1884, Jl 21,2:6
Hunter, C Winfield, 1947, Ap 9,25:4
Hunter, Cartwright M (Pinky), 1955, Jl 24,64
Hunter, Charles Augustus, 1921, My 5,17:4
Hunter, Charles E, 1951, Ja 4,29:4; 1964, Jl 26
Hunter, Charles F, 1946, Mr 29,23:2
Hunter, Charles G, 1956, O 5,25:2
Hunter, Charles H, 1942, My 9,13:1; 1951, D
Hunter, Charles W, 1958, S 26,27:4

Hunter, Clara M, 1965, S 12,86:7
Hunter, Clifford G, 1948, My 28,23:2
Hunter, Colin, 1904, S 26,9:6
Hunter, Colin Mrs (por), 1940, Ap 30,21:2
Hunter, Dard, 1966, F 22,23:2
Hunter, David G, 1960, My 21,23:5
Hunter, Doncarolos, 1953, S 5,15:5
Hunter, Dwight Williams Dr, 1924, D 24,15:3
Hunter, E Rev, 1877, O 19,5:2
Hunter, Edgar H, 1957, Ap 18,29:4
Hunter, Edward C, 1938, N 22,24:2
Hunter, Edward J, 1938, Ag 16,19:2; 1957, Ag 31,15:5
Hunter, Ellis, 1961, S 22,33:1
Hunter, Ernest E, 1947, N 3,23:5
Hunter, Evan A, 1954, F 1,23:3
Hunter, F Heyward Mrs, 1959, Ap 27,27:5
Hunter, F K M Mrs, 1949, S 4,40:5
Hunter, F K Middleton, 1968, Ja 19,44:1
Hunter, Forest, 1946, Je 20,23:5
Hunter, Frances T, 1957, Mr 4,27:5
Hunter, Frank A Jr, 1943, Ja 24,42:3
Hunter, Frank Lt, 1923, N 13,21:4
Hunter, Frank Mrs, 1950, S 7,31:3; 1966, F 16,43:3
Hunter, Fraser Mrs, 1939, Mr 1,21:4
Hunter, Frederick L, 1943, F 24,21:5
Hunter, Frederick W, 1919, F 23,18:1
Hunter, G J, 1879, Ag 22,5:4
Hunter, George, 1920, Ja 31,11:3; 1947, Ag 31,36:7
Hunter, George B, 1965, S 12,86:7
Hunter, George B sir (por), 1937, Ja 22,21:3
Hunter, George D Mrs, 1947, Ap 26,13:6
Hunter, George F, 1949, D 10,17:4
Hunter, George F Mrs, 1946, S 21,15:5
Hunter, George H V, 1943, My 22,13:3
Hunter, George K, 1940, F 3,13:2
Hunter, George M, 1961, S 14,31:2
Hunter, George T (will, O 8,104:2), 1950, O 4,31:5
Hunter, George W 2d, 1948, F 5,23:2
Hunter, Glenn, 1945, D 31,17:1
Hunter, Graham C Mrs, 1942, Jl 9,21:5
Hunter, Graham Mrs (P Dougherty), 1959, S 3,27:2
Hunter, Guy O, 1955, F 12,15:6
Hunter, Guy O Mrs, 1954, S 8,32:4
Hunter, H C, 1881, Jl 19,8:2
Hunter, Harrison, 1923, Ja 3,13:4
Hunter, Harry, 1881, F 16,5:3
Hunter, Harry G, 1954, N 5,5:1
Hunter, Harry J, 1955, Je 4,15:5
Hunter, Henry B, 1955, Je 4,15:2
Hunter, Henry H, 1944, Mr 28,19:2
Hunter, Hester, 1938, S 9,21:2
Hunter, Hocking H, 1872, F 7,5:5
Hunter, Howard O, 1964, F 23,84:5
Hunter, Hubert S, 1940, O 21,17:5
Hunter, Ida C, 1957, D 31,17:3
Hunter, Isaiah T, 1941, Jl 19,13:1
Hunter, J Du B, 1883, Ja 13,5:3
Hunter, J E, 1956, N 17,21:6
Hunter, J K, 1873, F 17,8:3
Hunter, J Keith, 1961, O 1,87:1
Hunter, J L, 1903, Ap 10,9:5
Hunter, J Lawrence, 1955, Ja 8,13:6
Hunter, J Lawrence Mrs, 1954, F 14,92:5
Hunter, J Rufus, 1951, Mr 5,21:2
Hunter, Jackie, 1951, N 22,31:3
Hunter, James, 1940, F 16,19:3
Hunter, James B, 1941, D 1,19:2
Hunter, James B (Sept 16), 1965, O 11,61:2
Hunter, James C, 1954, O 8,23:2
Hunter, James D, 1947, Ja 8,24:2
Hunter, James F, 1961, S 10,87:1
Hunter, James S Mrs, 1960, N 23,29:2
Hunter, James T, 1952, Ja 7,19:3
Hunter, Jenny (will, S 25,30:1), 1948, S 19,78:3
Hunter, Jeremiah, 1943, Ja 23,13:1
Hunter, Jesse C, 1945, N 12,21:4
Hunter, Jim, 1949, Je 7,31:3
Hunter, John, 1942, My 18,15:2; 1945, D 14,27:2
Hunter, John C, 1947, Je 14,15:3
Hunter, John F, 1957, D 21,19:5
Hunter, John F Mrs, 1953, Ap 14,27:4
Hunter, John Irvine, 1924, D 12,21:5
Hunter, John M, 1954, O 7,23:5
Hunter, Jones R, 1948, Ja 2,23:2
Hunter, Joseph B, 1947, O 21,24:2
Hunter, Joseph F, 1940, O 13,49:1
Hunter, Joseph R, 1949, Ja 28,21:2
Hunter, Joseph W, 1950, F 16,23:3
Hunter, Junius K, 1959, D 5,23:5
Hunter, Louis V, 1961, N 6,37:5
Hunter, Lt, 1873, O 1,1:6
Hunter, Mabel R, 1948, D 10,25:1
Hunter, Malcolm D, 1953, My 31,72:3
Hunter, Marcus, 1904, D 21,9:3
Hunter, Mason, 1921, F 2,11:5
Hunter, Matthew A, 1961, Mr 25,25:5
Hunter, Maurice, 1966, Mr 4,30:1
Hunter, McGill, 1958, Ap 5,15:6
Hunter, Merlin H (por), 1948, Je 1,23:3
Hunter, Nicholas V, 1950, O 21,17:4
Hunter, Norman, 1958, My 25,86:4
Hunter, Norman W, 1955, O 15,15:5
Hunter, P Rev, 1926, D 20,21:1
Hunter, Patricia, 1949, O 19,26:2
Hunter, Paul E, 1953, Ag 11,27:2
Hunter, Paul M, 1944, Ap 30,46:3
Hunter, Percy E, 1937, My 27,23:4
Hunter, R M, 1935, Mr 21,23:4
Hunter, Ralph, 1939, N 26,43:1
Hunter, Ralph N, 1951, Ag 23,23:5
Hunter, Rex A, 1948, Ap 21,28:3
Hunter, Richard R, 1966, Je 23,39:4
Hunter, Robert, 1942, My 17,46:2; 1949, Jl 8,19:4
Hunter, Robert A, 1962, N 24,23:2
Hunter, Robert F, 1946, D 31,18:5
Hunter, Robert H, 1914, Jl 2,9:7
Hunter, Robert L, 1950, N 3,27:2
Hunter, Robert Mrs, 1964, Jl 8,35:3
Hunter, Robert W Mrs, 1909, Ag 30,7:6
Hunter, Ross, 1949, Je 16,29:3
Hunter, Rowland L, 1958, Ap 12,19:3
Hunter, Roy D, 1944, N 15,27:6
Hunter, Russell H, 1944, Ag 11,15:3
Hunter, Russell V, 1955, Mr 22,31:4
Hunter, Samuel, 1943, D 7,27:1
Hunter, Samuel L, 1937, Mr 27,15:2
Hunter, Sarah H, 1945, D 27,19:2
Hunter, Seaman, 1958, Jl 17,27:3
Hunter, Seaman Mrs, 1949, Mr 30,25:5
Hunter, Stanley A, 1960, Ja 9,21:5
Hunter, Stanley E Mrs, 1963, D 12,39:3
Hunter, T Haynes, 1944, Ap 18,21:3
Hunter, Thomas Dr (funl, O 16,11:6), 1915, O 15, 11:5
Hunter, Thomas L, 1948, Je 20,60:6
Hunter, Thomas M, 1918, Mr 5,11:4
Hunter, Thomas P, 1915, My 26,13:7
Hunter, Vincent Mrs, 1945, My 17,19:3
Hunter, Virgil H, 1938, D 25,15:3
Hunter, W H, 1918, Ap 23,13:5
Hunter, W J, 1953, My 3,88:3
Hunter, W Sutherland Mrs, 1946, S 15,9:6
Hunter, Walter S, 1954, Ag 5,23:6
Hunter, Wayne L, 1960, S 7,41:2
Hunter, William, 1882, My 11,2:4; 1949, Mr 9,25:2
Hunter, William A, 1948, Je 2,29:3; 1964, D 15,43:3
Hunter, William A Mrs, 1944, Ap 12,21:5
Hunter, William Armstrong Rev Dr, 1920, Mr 6,11:6
Hunter, William B, 1942, D 10,25:5
Hunter, William H, 1941, S 10,23:1
Hunter, William M, 1951, N 22,31:2
Hunter, William Q, 1941, Je 19,21:2
Hunter, William R, 1939, Ag 28,19:6
Hunter, William R Mrs, 1908, Ap 18,9:5; 1949, Ja 15, 17:4
Hunter, William Robinson, 1915, Ag 15,13:6
Hunter, William T, 1950, Je 12,27:4; 1951, Ap 21,17:2
Hunter, William W, 1945, My 10,23:3
Hunter, Willis O, 1968, N 9,33:2
Hunter-Blair, David Sir, 1939, S 14,23:5
Huntfield, Lady, 1943, Mr 4,19:3
Hunting, Gardner, 1958, N 23,88:2
Hunting, George C Mrs, 1946, Ja 14,19:4
Hunting, George Coolidge Bp, 1924, F 8,19:5
Hunting, Harold B, 1958, Ap 17,31:5
Hunting, Irving A, 1945, Ja 31,21:3
Hunting, Irving A Mrs, 1947, Ja 6,23:4
Hunting, John S, 1949, Ja 23,68:7
Hunting, Nathaniel S Dr, 1937, N 22,19:4
Hunting, Stanley E, 1947, D 16,33:3
Hunting, Tony E Mrs, 1960, N 13,88:3
Hunting Horse (Tsa-Toke), 1953, Jl 2,23:5
Huntington, Albert T, 1952, O 6,25:5
Huntington, Alonzo S, 1941, Ag 4,13:5
Huntington, Andrew Tyler, 1915, Ja 28,9:4
Huntington, Ann, 1903, D 14,7:4
Huntington, Annette, 1953, F 25,27:4
Huntington, Archer M (trb lr, D 20,30:7), 1955, D 12,31:5
Huntington, B N, 1882, N 11,5:1
Huntington, Benjamin H, 1912, Ja 10,17:4
Huntington, C, 1927, Jl 13,23:5
Huntington, C H, 1904, Ja 21,7:5
Huntington, C P, 1900, Ag 15,1:4
Huntington, Charles G Mrs, 1952, Ap 17,29:4
Huntington, Charles H G, 1957, D 26,19:3
Huntington, Charles Pratt, 1919, O 16,17:3
Huntington, Charles R, 1915, O 29,13:6
Huntington, Charles W, 1942, My 24,42:7
Huntington, Constant, 1962, D 7,39:1
Huntington, Daniel, 1906, Ap 20,11:5
Huntington, Daniel T, 1950, My 4,27:6
Huntington, De Witt Clonton, 1912, F 9,9:5
Huntington, Dwight W, 1938, N 27,48:5
Huntington, E, 1881, Ap 19,5:3
Huntington, E Dr, 1865, D 14,8:4
Huntington, E Irving, 1962, N 22,29:1
Huntington, Earl of, 1875, S 17,1:5
Huntington, Edith C Mrs, 1940, O 4,23:4
Huntington, Edward V, 1952, N 26,23:2
Huntington, Edward V Mrs, 1966, Jl 27,39:4
Huntington, Edwin H, 1962, S 30,86:7
Huntington, Elizabeth Q Mrs, 1937, S 1,19:4
Huntington, Elizabeth S, 1883, O 9,8:3
Huntington, Ellery C, 1945, S 20,23:1
Huntington, Ellsworth, 1947, O 18,15:3
Huntington, Emily, 1909, D 7,9:4
Huntington, Eunice Alling Mrs, 1909, Je 28,7:5
Huntington, F Bache, 1947, Mr 11,28:3
Huntington, F D Bp, 1904, Jl 12,1:3
Huntington, Ford, 1949, Ja 30,61:1
Huntington, Francis C, 1916, Mr 16,13:7
Huntington, Francis C Mrs, 1958, D 3,37:3
Huntington, Frank C, 1941, Ja 6,15:3
Huntington, Frederic D Mrs, 1948, Jl 7,46:1
Huntington, Frederick R, 1925, Je 2,23:2
Huntington, Frederick W, 1953, Jl 7,27:4
Huntington, G S, 1927, Ja 6,27:3
Huntington, George B, 1943, Mr 5,17:3
Huntington, George D Dr, 1904, Jl 12,1:3
Huntington, George H, 1953, Ag 4,21:4
Huntington, George R, 1923, N 4,23:2
Huntington, H E, 1927, My 24,25:1
Huntington, Harriet S, 1906, Je 28,7:6
Huntington, Henry B, 1965, O 15,45:3
Huntington, Henry E Mrs, 1924, S 17,23:1
Huntington, Herbert A, 1950, Mr 20,21:2
Huntington, Horace, 1903, Jl 20,7:6
Huntington, Howard W, 1958, S 17,30:6
Huntington, I L, 1903, Ag 22,9:6
Huntington, J O S, 1935, Je 30,28:3
Huntington, J W P, 1869, Je 27,5:3
Huntington, James H, 1945, Ja 7,38:1
Huntington, James Judge, 1908, My 3,11:4
Huntington, James Lincoln Dr, 1968, My 6,47:2
Huntington, L D Mrs, 1904, O 25,9:6
Huntington, Lawrence D, 1946, D 20,23:3
Huntington, Margaret W, 1958, Ap 19,21:1
Huntington, Marie V Mrs, 1940, Je 29,15:5
Huntington, Mary C, 1946, Ja 23,27:2
Huntington, Mary E, 1942, S 25,21:3; 1943, Je 22,19:5
Huntington, Oliver Whipple, 1924, Ag 26,11:3
Huntington, Philip, 1966, Ja 30,84:6
Huntington, R Graham, 1957, Ja 20,92:3
Huntington, Richard T, 1964, D 3,49:5
Huntington, Robert, 1952, My 29,27:3
Huntington, Robert P, 1949, Mr 13,76:5
Huntington, Robert P Mrs, 1919, D 25,13:3; 1942, S 28,17:6
Huntington, Robert W, 1949, Ja 23,68:6
Huntington, Robert Watkinson Col, 1917, N 6,13:4
Huntington, Roger S, 1954, My 31,13:5
Huntington, Roger W, 1943, D 15,27:3
Huntington, Samuel, 1923, Mr 10,13:4
Huntington, Samuel Mrs, 1903, Jl 19,7:6
Huntington, Samuel V V, 1939, S 21,23:5
Huntington, T P, 1884, My 30,5:1
Huntington, Theodore G Dr, 1937, Ja 27,21:5
Huntington, Thomas, 1941, Ap 11,21:1
Huntington, Tuley F, 1938, My 5,23:3
Huntington, W Chapin, 1958, O 7,35:4
Huntington, Warner D, 1938, N 26,16:2
Huntington, William R (por; funl, Jl 28,9:4), 1909, Jl 27,7:1
Huntington, William R, 1954, Ja 2,11:2
Huntington, William R Mrs, 1942, Mr 19,21:5
Huntington, Wright, 1916, S 22,7:5
Huntington Cooke, Mary Mrs (Mrs Josiah Cooke), 1911, My 22,11:4
Huntley, C R, 1926, S 18,15:5
Huntley, Charles H, 1948, D 17,28:3
Huntley, E D Rev Dr, 1909, F 13,9:4
Huntley, Fred J, 1951, S 15,15:4
Huntley, G P, 1927, S 22,29:3
Huntley, G P Mrs, 1948, Mr 17,25:3
Huntley, George, 1950, Ja 9,25:1
Huntley, Harry B, 1951, F 8,33:2
Huntley, Hubert B, 1958, N 4,27:4
Huntley, Justus R, 1960, Mr 25,27:2
Huntley, Marchioness of, 1939, My 18,25:2
Huntley, Robert, 1940, Mr 10,49:1
Huntley, Samantha Mrs, 1949, Je 21,25:5
Huntley, Walter W, 1943, O 4,17:1
Huntley, William, 1956, Je 13,37:1
Huntley, William H Sr, 1949, S 4,41:1
Huntley, Willis A, 1939, Ja 6,21:5
Huntly, Marquess of, 1937, F 21,II,11:2
Huntman, Gerard H Rev, 1924, S 22,19:5
Hunton, Eppa Gen, 1908, O 12,9:6
Hunton, George K, 1967, N 13,47:2
Huntoon, Alberto D, 1943, Ap 24,13:5
Huntoon, Benjamin Bussey, 1919, Ag 10,23:4
Huntoon, Charlotte M, 1951, Jl 24,25:4
Huntoon, Frank M, 1948, D 23,19:4
Huntoon, Franklin T, 1922, Ap 10,15:4
Huntoon, Louis D, 1947, F 23,53:4
Huntoon, Oscar C Mrs, 1941, D 10,25:5
Huntoon, Samuel W, 1955, Ap 12,29:4
Huntoon, William C Mrs, 1950, My 17,29:4
Huntress, Carroll B, 1952, N 30,86:4
Huntress, Frank G sr, 1955, Jl 31,69:2
Huntress, Frank G Sr Mrs, 1962, Ag 25,22:1
Huntsman, Edward, 1903, Jl 19,2:5
Huntsman, John F, 1943, My 4,23:6
Huntsman, Robert F R, 1945, Je 1,15:3
Huntsman Jno F Mrs, 1960, Je 25,21:4
Huntting, Henry R, 1942, S 8,23:3
Huntting, Henry T W, 1961, Ag 24,29:2
Huntting, James M, 1939, Ja 13,19:4

Huntting, Jeremiah M, 1937, O 1,21:1
Hunziker, Emil, 1901, Mr 2,9:5
Hunziker, Ernest, 1951, Mr 25,72:5
Hunziker, Gustav A, 1951, My 3,29:3
Hunziker, Otto F, 1959, N 16,31:6
Hunzinger, Emil W (will, D 9,13:1), 1937, D 1,23:4
Hunzinger, John H, 1947, Ap 22,27:2
Huot, Vincent M, 1950, N 7,27:4
Huott, Edmond J, 1950, Mr 28,31:3
Hupart, Harry, 1959, S 17,39:4
Hupel, Wally Mrs, 1944, My 20,15:6
Hupfel, Adolph G, 1917, Jl 15,15:3; 1945, O 11,23:4
Hupfel, Adolph G Mrs, 1948, D 7,31:2
Hupfel, Anton C G (will Ag 17,17:4), 1937, Ag 2,19:5
Hupfel, Christian G, 1939, D 6,25:4
Hupfel, J C G Mrs, 1905, F 5,7:6
Hupfel, Mathilde D Mrs, 1944, O 15,44:2
Hupfeld, Herman, 1951, Je 9,19:6
Hupfer, Bertha, 1953, Ag 18,17:8
Hupke, Thomas, 1959, S 9,41:3
Hupp, Don S, 1942, F 5,21:5
Hupp, Louis G, 1961, D 12,43:1
Huppe, F R, 1941, Je 3,21:4
Huppe, William, 1937, Ag 3,18:3
Huppe, William Mrs, 1937, Ag 3,18:3
Huppenbauer, Harry F, 1956, Ap 6,25:4
Huppenbauer, John Rev, 1922, Mr 11,13:5
Hupper, Roscoe H, 1967, My 10,47:1
Huppert, Alois, 1956, Ja 5,95:2
Huppert, Elmer I, 1944, Jl 1,15:2
Huppert, Erwin, 1944, Ap 3,21:4
Huppert, S Marie, 1958, O 21,33:4
Huppuch, Milton K, 1951, N 19,23:4
Huppuch, Winfield A, 1940, O 8,25:4
Hurban, Vladimir (por), 1949, O 27,27:1
Hurbaugh, Verne Mrs, 1951, Jl 18,29:3
Hurd, Barritt Newton, 1907, S 24,11:6
Hurd, Benjamin F, 1941, Je 1,40:2
Hurd, Carlos F, 1950, Je 9,23:5
Hurd, Charles E, 1910, Ap 23,11:6
Hurd, Charles G, 1956, Je 29,21:4
Hurd, Charles W B, 1968, My 18,33:4
Hurd, Clara C Mrs, 1941, Ag 20,19:3
Hurd, Don S, 1959, Ja 16,28:3
Hurd, Edward A Col, 1968, N 14,47:2
Hurd, Emily F B Mrs, 1941, O 27,17:2
Hurd, Eugene, 1941, My 21,23:2
Hurd, Ferris E, 1956, Ap 5,29:2
Hurd, Frances A, 1948, Ap 24,15:3
Hurd, Frank B, 1941, Ja 2,23:1
Hurd, Frank B Mrs, 1940, Mr 14,23:4
Hurd, Franklin B, 1946, N 20,31:5
Hurd, George F (por), 1941, D 18,27:3
Hurd, George H, 1938, F 13,II,7:1
Hurd, H Gordon, 1954, F 9,27:4
Hurd, H M, 1927, Jl 20,23:5
Hurd, Hanford B, 1963, Ap 10,39:3
Hurd, Harry B, 1943, Ag 3,19:3
Hurd, Harry E, 1958, Ag 22,21:2
Hurd, Harry H S, 1938, Ja 6,19:5
Hurd, Harvey B, 1906, Ja 21,7:6
Hurd, Imogene W Mrs, 1942, D 24,15:4
Hurd, John Mrs, 1949, D 12,33:4
Hurd, Kenneth B Mrs, 1954, Ap 9,17:2
Hurd, Lee M, 1945, My 16,19:3
Hurd, Lee M Mrs, 1944, N 26,56:4
Hurd, Loren C, 1957, S 30,31:6
Hurd, Lyman E, 1938, O 30,40:7
Hurd, Mary C, 1949, D 24,15:5
Hurd, Nathaniel S Mrs, 1946, Ja 16,23:2
Hurd, Percy A, 1950, Je 6,30:2
Hurd, Porter, 1960, O 1,19:2
Hurd, Ralph A, 1963, O 21,31:3
Hurd, Ray E, 1952, O 7,29:6
Hurd, Richard M, 1941, Je 7,17:5
Hurd, Russell R, 1949, O 8,13:1
Hurd, W Wallace, 1940, Ja 29,15:3
Hurd, William A, 1948, Ag 11,22:2
Hurd, William B Jr, 1915, Mr 23,9:6
Hurd, William F, 1956, S 16,85:1
Hurden, Martin D, 1947, S 27,15:4
Hurden, Stephen D Sr, 1945, Ag 29,23:5
Hurdis, Charles E Mrs, 1955, O 11,39:2
Hurdiston, Mary B D Mrs, 1939, Ag 29,21:4
Hurdman, Frederick H, 1951, Je 15,23:4
Hurdman, G Charles, 1948, F 20,27:2
Hurdman, George C Mrs, 1958, D 11,13:5
Hurdon, John D, 1956, Mr 28,31:3
Hurel, Gustav, 1925, O 27,23:4
Hurevitz, Abe M, 1959, My 23,25:6
Hurff, Clark J, 1943, Jl 26,19:5
Hurford, James R, 1953, Ag 12,31:1
Hurh, Alex, 1941, Ja 3,19:2
Huribut, Clarke Stanley, 1924, O 2,23:3
Huribut, Pierre Proal, 1914, Mr 26,11:6
Hurin, Silas E, 1946, Je 6,21:6
Hurja, Emil, 1953, My 31,72:1
Hurlbert, Frances C K Mrs, 1941, D 22,17:2
Hurlbert, Francis W, 1944, D 5,23:6
Hurlbert, Francis W Mrs, 1958, My 30,21:2
Hurlbert, Le Roy Mrs, 1962, O 28,88:5
Hurlbert, William Henry Mrs, 1922, My 12,19:5
Hurlbert, Willis Mrs, 1947, My 25,62:3
Hurlburt, Henry F, 1924, Ap 18,19:5
Hurlburt, Russell B, 1938, Jl 18,13:4
Hurlburt, W Merritt, 1953, Ja 8,27:2
Hurlburt, Wilbur F Sr, 1961, F 3,23:1
Hurlbut, Edward H, 1954, S 15,33:3
Hurlbut, Elisha D Mrs, 1937, Mr 9,23:5
Hurlbut, Floyd, 1948, Jl 17,15:6
Hurlbut, Frank H, 1947, Ap 23,25:3
Hurlbut, Frank M, 1912, Ja 3,13:5
Hurlbut, George H Mrs, 1959, Ap 27,27:2
Hurlbut, Gordon B, 1960, D 15,52:4
Hurlbut, Gordon B Mrs, 1960, D 15,52:4
Hurlbut, Harry J, 1958, D 9,41:2
Hurlbut, James W, 1967, Mr 27,33:3
Hurlbut, Jed W, 1950, D 10,104:4
Hurlbut, Mary C, 1944, Jl 22,15:5
Hurlbut, Olive R, 1961, D 19,33:4
Hurlbut, R C, 1942, N 18,25:4
Hurlbut, Stephen A, 1882, Ap 3,1:3; 1955, D 25,48:2
Hurlbut, W H, 1895, S 7,5:6
Hurlbut, W W, 1877, Jl 3,4:6
Hurlbut, William N, 1956, F 5,86:6
Hurlbutt, Ralph B, 1951, N 19,23:5
Hurle, Frank G, 1946, D 25,29:5
Hurler, George A, 1946, N 30,15:4
Hurley, Alec, 1913, D 7,VIII,19:4
Hurley, Ambrose D, 1949, Mr 22,25:3
Hurley, Anson, 1961, Je 25,54:8
Hurley, Anson Mrs, 1961, Je 25,54:8
Hurley, Arthur, 1941, N 3,19:2
Hurley, Catherine E, 1951, Ja 27,13:1
Hurley, Charles F, 1946, Mr 25,25:2
Hurley, Daniel, 1945, Jl 17,13:5
Hurley, Daniel H, 1946, N 25,27:4
Hurley, Daniel J, 1945, O 17,19:5; 1962, N 17,25:2
Hurley, Denis M, 1960, N 5,23:4
Hurley, Denis P, 1955, Je 11,15:2
Hurley, E N, 1933, N 15,21:1
Hurley, Edmund G, 1918, Ap 12,13:8
Hurley, Edward, 1938, Jl 5,17:5
Hurley, Edward A, 1942, S 17,25:1
Hurley, Edward F, 1941, N 24,17:3; 1943, Ap 30,21:4; 1957, Jl 10,27:4
Hurley, Edward N Jr, 1948, F 26,24:2
Hurley, Edward T, 1950, N 30,33:3
Hurley, Edward W, 1911, Ja 24,9:5
Hurley, Eleanor F, 1953, Je 18,29:2
Hurley, Elizabeth S Mrs, 1909, N 17,9:4
Hurley, Francis, 1950, My 31,29:6
Hurley, Francis B, 1965, Jl 12,27:4
Hurley, Frank, 1962, Ja 17,33:5
Hurley, Frank E Mrs, 1955, Ag 18,23:3
Hurley, Frank J, 1953, Je 29,21:5
Hurley, Frank J Sr, 1950, Ja 24,31:1
Hurley, Frederick T, 1946, Jl 2,25:5
Hurley, George, 1954, Mr 11,31:1
Hurley, Gordon L, 1945, F 10,11:3
Hurley, Harrison C, 1960, My 16,31:4
Hurley, Hugh T, 1964, F 8,23:4
Hurley, Ira, 1951, F 12,23:3
Hurley, James, 1964, Ap 7,32:3
Hurley, James B, 1951, S 15,15:5
Hurley, James E, 1910, Ag 17,7:4; 1953, Ag 14,19:4
Hurley, James E Sr, 1958, O 1,37:5
Hurley, James F, 1945, Ag 20,19:4
Hurley, James G, 1951, Je 12,29:4
Hurley, James H, 1952, Ag 11,15:6
Hurley, Jeremiah, 1943, F 14,48:6
Hurley, Jeremiah J, 1950, Mr 28,32:3; 1950, S 18,23:3; 1967, O 31,45:1
Hurley, John A, 1951, Ag 8,25:3
Hurley, John E, 1939, S 25,19:5; 1957, Mr 7,29:2
Hurley, John F, 1967, D 7,52:8
Hurley, John J, 1946, N 11,27:4; 1960, D 29,25:5
Hurley, John J Mrs, 1944, Ja 28,17:2
Hurley, John P, 1940, Mr 15,23:4; 1944, D 31,26:3; 1950, Ag 31,25:1
Hurley, John R, 1953, Je 22,21:5
Hurley, John R Jr, 1941, Jl 23,19:3
Hurley, John R Mrs, 1961, Je 25,54:8
Hurley, John S, 1943, D 6,23:2
Hurley, Joseph D, 1941, Ja 13,15:3
Hurley, Joseph L, 1956, Ap 30,23:3
Hurley, Joseph P, 1967, O 31,45:3
Hurley, L Eldon, 1942, F 10,20:3
Hurley, Lawrence F, 1953, Ja 12,27:1
Hurley, M Frank, 1947, My 17,16:3
Hurley, M Frank Mrs, 1954, Ja 23,13:2
Hurley, Malcolm F Sr, 1954, F 24,25:4
Hurley, Marcus, 1941, Mr 29,15:2
Hurley, Margaret H, 1967, N 12,87:1
Hurley, Margaret Mrs, 1939, N 8,23:3
Hurley, Martin J, 1946, O 9,27:5
Hurley, Neil C, 1948, Ag 4,22:3
Hurley, Neil C Jr, 1965, F 11,39:3
Hurley, Nellie E, 1949, Je 23,27:2
Hurley, Patrick J, 1945, My 21,19:2; 1947, Jl 28,15:4; 1948, Jl 8,23:1
Hurley, Patrick J (funl), 1957, Ap 2,31:4
Hurley, Patrick J (funl plans, Ag 1,27:1; funl, Ag 3,17:5), 1963, Jl 31,29:1
Hurley, Patrick J, 1968, My 2,47:5
Hurley, Raymond J, 1956, My 30,21:2
Hurley, Robert, 1937, O 4,21:4
Hurley, Robert A, 1955, F 3,23:3
Hurley, Robert Augustine, 1968, My 5,87:2
Hurley, Robert G, 1946, Je 25,21:2
Hurley, Robert T, 1938, Ag 15,15:5
Hurley, Sally, 1937, O 12,25:5
Hurley, Stephen E, 1955, My 11,31:5
Hurley, T D Judge, 1926, O 4,23:5
Hurley, Thomas J, 1907, D 14,9:6
Hurley, Timothy J Rev, 1920, F 6,13:3
Hurley, Vernon H Sr, 1961, Je 21,37:4
Hurley, Vincent, 1964, My 30,17:6
Hurley, W A (Bill), 1952, S 13,17:3
Hurley, W L Mrs, 1943, Ap 3,15:2
Hurley, Walter J, 1949, Je 19,68:6
Hurley, William, 1948, Je 24,25:4
Hurley, William E, 1949, Ap 6,29:3; 1957, N 26,27:3
Hurley, William F, 1942, My 25,15:6; 1956, Jl 30,21
Hurley, William H, 1953, Je 9,27:2
Hurley, William J, 1953, Mr 4,27:4
Hurley, William J Mrs, 1944, Je 17,13:1
Hurley, William James, 1908, Je 10,7:2
Hurley, William L, 1957, O 12,19:5
Hurley, William M, 1937, S 20,23:2
Hurley (Sister Anna Gabriel), 1965, Mr 18,33:4
Hurliman, Charles H, 1951, S 21,24:3
Hurlin, Marshall W, 1965, Ja 9,25:5
Hurlock, Clinton E, 1952, Ja 22,29:2
Hurlong, Herman P, 1953, S 26,17:4
Hurlstone-Piper, Vernon H, 1940, N 3,57:2
Hurn, James A Rev, 1937, My 31,16:1
Hurni, Edward J, 1941, O 8,23:5
Huron, George B, 1953, N 5,31:2
Hurowitz, Samuel W, 1967, Ag 15,39:1
Hurrell, Alfred (por), 1938, Je 24,19:3
Hurrell, Henry, 1941, Jl 16,17:5
Hurrey, Charles D, 1958, Ag 5,27:3
Hurry, Edmond Abdy, 1912, Ap 9,11:4
Hurry, Gilford Col, 1920, Ja 20,7:2
Hurry, Renwick C, 1954, Ja 25,19:2
Hurry, Renwick C Mrs, 1950, Ap 11,31:4
Hurry, Renwick W, 1961, Ap 1,17:4
Hurst, Albert E, 1938, O 24,17:6
Hurst, Albert Mrs, 1952, Jl 27,57:1
Hurst, Albert S, 1944, Ap 2,39:2
Hurst, Allan, 1960, Ja 1,19:3
Hurst, Carlton B, 1943, Ag 29,38:5
Hurst, Cecil (Mar 27), 1963, Ap 1,35:8
Hurst, Charles W, 1947, F 20,25:3
Hurst, Clarence T, 1949, Ja 19,27:2
Hurst, David H, 1953, O 6,29:3
Hurst, Don, 1952, D 8,41:3
Hurst, Edward A, 1953, Ag 21,17:4
Hurst, Elmore W, 1915, Jl 22,9:5
Hurst, Ervin Mrs, 1946, My 2,21:1
Hurst, F W J Mrs, 1873, Ag 15,8:3
Hurst, Fannie (mem ser, Mr 1,37:1; will, F 29,37: 1968, F 24,1:3
Hurst, Frederick E, 1945, Ag 21,21:4
Hurst, J A, 1882, D 19,5:1
Hurst, John, 1952, My 30,15:5
Hurst, John E, 1947, Ja 9,23:4
Hurst, John S, 1949, D 23,22:2
Hurst, Nancy J Mrs, 1938, Ja 30,II,8:5
Hurst, R F, 1941, My 4,53:1
Hurst, R Franklin Mrs, 1948, O 31,88:5
Hurst, R L, 1943, Ja 1,23:2
Hurst, Ralph W, 1956, Ag 11,13:5
Hurst, Sandy L, 1960, Je 24,27:4
Hurst, Tim C Mrs, 1944, F 4,15:1
Hurst, Vida, 1958, Ja 9,33:3
Hurst, William G, 1950, Je 14,31:4
Hurst, Z T, 1949, Ap 21,26:3
Hurston, Zora N, 1960, F 5,27:1
Hurt, Annie W Mrs, 1942, D 26,11:4
Hurt, Charles A Sr, 1949, F 25,23:3
Hurt, Edward Woods, 1918, S 27,13:7
Hurt, Everett R, 1961, F 9,31:5
Hurt, Henry H, 1945, O 5,23:2
Hurt, Henry H S Mrs, 1952, Ap 18,25:3
Hurt, Huber W, 1966, N 23,39:1
Hurt, Huber W Mrs, 1948, N 4,29:4
Hurt, J M Judge, 1903, Ap 21,9:5
Hurt, John, 1966, N 4,39:1
Hurt, John B, 1966, Ag 9,37:3
Hurt, John S, 1943, N 28,69:1
Hurt, Joseph Sr, 1947, Jl 19,13:4
Hurt, Marlin, 1946, Mr 22,21:4
Hurt, Robert, 1940, Je 27,23:2
Hurt, Rudolph J, 1947, My 19,21:3
Hurtado, Romulo Mrs, 1954, Ag 24,21:5
Hurtado de Mendoza, Luis, 1944, Ag 29,17:5
Hurteau, Clement, 1952, My 13,23:1
Hurter, Marguerite (Mrs M H Schumacher), F 10,21:2
Hurtig, Benjamin, 1909, F 14,11:6
Hurtig, J, 1928, Mr 10,17:5
Hurtig, Joseph, 1939, D 4,23:3
Hurtin, Edwin M, 1951, F 17,15:2
Hurton, Thomas J, 1948, Jl 23,19:1
Hurtt, Cecil H, 1941, Jl 14,13:2
Hurtt, Francis W Mrs, 1907, Ag 2,7:4
Hurtt, James H 3d, 1956, N 10,19:5

Hurttig, Frederick W, 1944, Je 23,19:3
Hurtubise, Joseph R, 1955, F 2,27:4
Hurty, George A, 1959, D 6,86:1
Hurtzig, Ernest H, 1949, F 24,23:4
Hurwich, Louis Mrs, 1964, Ap 29,41:4
Hurwit, Harry, 1963, S 9,27:3
Hurwitt, Elliott S, 1966, Ap 6,43:3
Hurwitz, Abraham, 1949, O 14,27:4
Hurwitz, Ben Mrs, 1948, Je 24,25:2
Hurwitz, David Mrs, 1964, D 18,33:3
Hurwitz, Henry, 1961, N 21,39:1
Hurwitz, Henry Mrs (R Sapin), 1961, Je 19,27:2
Hurwitz, Hyman, 1966, My 2,37:1
Hurwitz, Irving, 1959, Ja 6,33:3
Hurwitz, Jacob, 1937, N 28,II,8:5; 1947, F 6,23:5
Hurwitz, Louis L, 1949, S 11,96:4
Hurwitz, Max C, 1967, Ja 4,43:4
Hurwitz, Maximilian, 1963, N 15,35:3
Hurwitz, Morris J, 1957, Mr 12,33:3
Hurwitz, Nathan Rabbi, 1923, My 23,21:5
Hurwitz, Robert S, 1941, Mr 10,17:5
Hurwitz, Samuel Rabbi, 1937, D 24,17:5
Hurwitz, Saul M, 1960, Je 23,29:1
Hurwitz, Shaia, 1960, My 19,37:5
Hurwitz, Shmaryohu L, 1938, Je 12,38:8
Hurwitz, Solomon T H, 1920, Ja 13,13:3
Hurwitz, Stephen J, 1957, My 16,31:1
Hurwitz, Wallie A, 1958, Ja 7,47:4
Hurzeler, Alphons N, 1959, Ag 21,21:2
Hurzeler, Hans, 1949, Je 12,78:4
Husband, James D (por), 1943, Ap 20,23:3
Husband, Joseph, 1938, S 22,23:2
Husband, Richard W, 1924, Ap 10,23:4
Husband, Walter W, 1942, Ag 1,11:4
Husbands, Arthur C, 1964, Mr 1,83:1
Husbands, Edna P, 1956, F 11,17:1
Husbands, Florence E, 1965, Jl 11,68:6
Husbands, Sam H, 1955, N 3,31:1
Husch, Richard G (por), 1948, Jl 3,15:4
Husch, Sylvester B Mrs, 1946, Ap 29,21:5
Huse, C Burton, 1947, Ap 22,27:3
Huse, Caleb Col, 1905, Mr 13,7:6
Huse, Clair L, 1954, S 17,27:3
Huse, Emery, 1961, Jl 9,77:2
Huse, Eugene F, 1961, Jl 9,77:1
Huse, Gustav Mrs, 1940, Je 21,21:1
Huse, Harry P Mrs, 1949, O 19,29:4
Huse, John O, 1954, Je 30,27:6
Huse, Norris A, 1937, Ja 8,20:1
Huse, Raymond H, 1954, Ja 30,17:5
Huse, Robert E, 1951, Mr 29,27:3
Huse, Robert S, 1942, Ap 24,17:1
Huse, Sibyl M, 1939, Ap 6,25:6
Huse, William N, 1957, Ja 17,29:4
Husein Bey, Abdul Hak, 1919, F 23,18:3
Husek, Joseph, 1947, Mr 31,23:4
Huser, Paul, 1956, Ag 22,29:5
Huser, Thomas E, 1948, N 25,31:3
Husey, C L, 1934, D 5,23:4
Hush, Hugh J, 1960, Mr 4,25:2
Hush, Joseph, 1903, N 3,1:4
Hushebeck, Harry W, 1940, Jl 23,19:2
Husher, Frank M, 1944, D 5,23:3
Husher, John J, 1947, O 6,21:5
Hushion, Alice M Mrs, 1939, N 9,23:2
Hushion, Timothy, 1939, Mr 24,21:3
Hushion, William J, 1954, Ja 30,17:2
Husid, Harry, 1957, Mr 16,19:5
Husik, David N, 1955, N 22,35:3
Husik, Isaac, 1939, Mr 23,23:3
Husing, Edward B (Ted),(funl plans, Ag 21,81:2), 1962, Ag 11,17:2
Husing, Martin E, 1967, Ag 3,33:4
Husk, Carlos Dr, 1916, Mr 21,11:7
Husk, Harold C, 1953, N 17,31:5
Husk, Harry C, 1945, My 4,20:2
Husk, James H, 1947, F 22,13:2
Husk, Richard, 1949, Ap 11,25:5
Husk, Wilbur C, 1942, F 17,21:1
Huske, Clement W Mrs, 1946, Ag 8,21:5
Huskins, C Leonard, 1953, Jl 28,19:7
Huskinson, Patrick, 1966, N 25,37:1
Husman, John L, 1957, N 13,35:3
Huson, A Gordon, 1958, Ag 12,29:5
Huson, C J, 1928, D 16,30:6
Huson, Harry W Mrs, 1951, Mr 31,15:4
Huson, Jennie M, 1940, D 23,19:2
Huss, Frank Sr, 1962, Ja 7,88:6
Huss, George M, 1941, F 11,23:2; 1947, F 20,25:3
Huss, Henry H, 1953, S 19,15:4
Huss, Pierre J (mem ser, Mr 26,29:4), 1966, Mr 23, 47:3
Hussa, Louise, 1939, D 5,27:1
Hussa, Theodore F, 1939, D 6,25:3
Hussain, Altaf, 1968, My 26,84:3
Hussakof, Louis, 1965, My 14,37:2
Hussander, Allan B, 1961, My 12,26:5
Hussarek, M von, 1935, Mr 7,23:1
Hussein, Abd Essalam, 1949, Ag 23,24:4
Hussein, Ben Ali, 1918, Ag 23,9:7
Hussein Ibn Ali, 1931, Je 5,23:1
Hussein Zahiri, Mohammed, 1965, O 20,35:1
Hussen Said Bey, M Min, 1947, D 12,27:4
Husserl, Clara Mrs, 1952, S 23,33:2
Husserl, Edmund, 1938, Ap 29,21:2
Hussey, Abram, 1937, Ag 21,15:6
Hussey, Alfred R, 1947, Ag 12,24:3; 1964, N 8,88:3
Hussey, Carlye P, 1959, N 3,31:1
Hussey, Charles H, 1950, N 3,27:5
Hussey, Charles L Mrs, 1950, N 25,13:3
Hussey, Charles W, 1944, Jl 4,19:6
Hussey, Clarence L, 1925, D 7,21:4
Hussey, Cornelius J, 1923, F 20,17:3
Hussey, Edward E, 1939, O 29,40:4
Hussey, Erwin Albert Capt, 1917, My 7,9:5
Hussey, Francis X, 1960, N 1,39:5
Hussey, Frederic V, 1943, Je 16,21:5
Hussey, George, 1960, Je 8,39:5
Hussey, George B Mrs, 1912, Ja 9,13:6
Hussey, George F 3d, 1966, Ag 27,29:3
Hussey, George W, 1952, Ag 1,18:4
Hussey, Harry B, 1953, F 27,21:4
Hussey, Hathorne, 1953, My 2,15:4
Hussey, Henry, 1923, Ag 19,26:4
Hussey, J E, 1932, S 22,21:5
Hussey, James L, 1955, Je 23,29:1
Hussey, John B, 1960, Mr 18,26:2
Hussey, John E, 1944, Ja 29,13:3
Hussey, John Jr, 1903, S 26,9:4
Hussey, John L, 1966, Je 29,47:3
Hussey, Joseph Mrs, 1953, N 21,13:6
Hussey, Mary, 1938, My 13,19:5
Hussey, Mary I, 1952, Je 23,19:3
Hussey, Miriam, 1959, Ja 9,27:3
Hussey, Nolen, 1960, S 22,27:3
Hussey, Nolen Mrs, 1962, F 21,45:1
Hussey, Orin N, 1942, Ap 29,21:4
Hussey, Raymond, 1953, Ap 16,29:5
Hussey, Roland D, 1959, O 31,23:6
Hussey, Samuel, 1913, N 11,13:6
Hussey, Thomas J S, 1939, Ap 20,23:5
Hussey, Virginia A, 1947, Ap 14,27:2
Hussey, W J Prof, 1926, O 30,17:5
Hussey, William C, 1950, N 14,31:4
Hussey, William H, 1967, Mr 9,41:7
Hussey, William H Mrs, 1961, Jl 10,21:1
Hussey, William Howland, 1919, My 3,15:6
Hussie, J Vincent, 1942, Mr 20,19:5
Hussien, Myrtle I Princess (will), 1963, Mr 23,3:4
Husslein, Joseph C, 1952, O 21,29:2
Husson, Frederic M, 1962, S 20,33:3
Husson, Harry L, 1966, S 1,35:2
Husta, Carl, 1951, N 7,29:4
Hustace, Allerton M, 1951, D 25,31:5
Hustead, Frank H, 1952, Mr 5,29:3
Husted, Albert H Dr, 1912, O 17,11:5
Husted, Augustus Mead, 1917, F 17,11:4
Husted, Charles L, 1944, N 29,23:3
Husted, Clarissa J Mrs, 1938, D 27,17:2
Husted, Clarke E, 1948, O 11,23:1
Husted, Donald R, 1939, Ag 19,15:5
Husted, Eliphalet P, 1924, F 24,21:3
Husted, Ellery, 1967, Jl 19,39:4
Husted, Frank A, 1956, Ap 19,31:1
Husted, Harvey Mrs, 1948, N 28,92:4
Husted, James W, 1892, S 26,1:5; 1925, Ja 4,7:2
Husted, John G W Mrs, 1964, N 18,47:1
Husted, Joseph B, 1905, Ap 24,5:1
Husted, M Edison, 1958, Ag 7,25:1
Husted, Martha E, 1938, F 1,21:1
Husted, Mills H Jr Mrs, 1951, O 14,88:6
Husted, Paul H, 1951, D 16,89:2
Husted, Robert, 1948, S 3,19:2
Husten, Harvey, 1957, S 28,17:3
Husting, Berthold J, 1948, S 4,15:6
Husting, Eugene Jr, 1947, Ag 28,23:5
Hustis, Daniel, 1953, F 5,23:5
Hustis, Guy E, 1939, O 29,40:6
Hustis, James H Sr, 1942, S 19,15:1
Hustis, Samuel, 1956, My 8,33:3
Hustis, Samuel Mrs, 1940, Ap 24,23:5
Hustis, Sarah G Mrs, 1941, Mr 9,40:7
Hustis, Willis J Mrs, 1937, D 8,25:5
Hustleby, Hiram Mrs, 1944, N 7,27:4
Huston, Aubrey, 1948, S 14,29:4
Huston, Bayone W Mrs, 1937, F 21,II,10:3
Huston, Charles L, 1951, Mr 15,29:3
Huston, Charles L Mrs, 1952, F 23,11:6
Huston, Claudius H, 1952, Ag 16,15:3
Huston, David, 1939, Ja 19,19:5
Huston, Davis T, 1942, Jl 29,17:5
Huston, Frederick P, 1947, D 30,23:5
Huston, Frederick P Mrs, 1959, Mr 25,35:3
Huston, Harry D, 1939, Jl 8,15:4
Huston, Henry A, 1957, My 7,35:4
Huston, Hiram L, 1903, Jl 2,9:6
Huston, Howard H, 1949, Ap 15,23:3
Huston, Howard R, 1955, Je 10,25:3
Huston, Howard R Mrs, 1948, Ag 29,59:4
Huston, J R D, 1959, O 27,37:4
Huston, John, 1957, Jl 11,25:3
Huston, Richard, 1943, Mr 3,23:2
Huston, Robert W, 1947, S 27,15:2
Huston, Roscoe B, 1949, N 7,27:3
Huston, Samuel, 1950, Jl 21,19:4
Huston, Stewart Mrs, 1948, Ap 22,27:3
Huston, T P, 1875, D 29,4:5
Huston, Thomas W Col, 1916, D 21,11:3
Huston, Tillinghast L (por), 1938, Mr 30,21:4
Huston, Tillinghast L Mrs, 1949, N 5,14:2
Huston, W E, 1950, O 4,31:4
Huston, Walter, 1950, Ap 8,13:1
Huston, William A, 1954, F 3,23:3
Huszagh, Kenneth A, 1950, Ja 12,27:5
Hut, Rudolph W, 1958, S 15,21:4
Hutaff, John H, 1949, Ap 14,25:2
Hutchens, Floyd G, 1962, Jl 12,29:3
Hutchens, Harry, 1939, Ja 6,21:4
Hutchens, James H, 1938, D 23,19:3
Hutchens, James H Mrs, 1945, Ja 18,19:5
Hutchens, John K Mrs, 1963, N 9,25:1
Hutchens, Martin J Mrs, 1943, Mr 3,23:3
Hutchens, Raymond D (por), 1946, Ap 18,27:4
Hutcheon, Alex, 1956, Ja 21,21:2
Hutcheon, Daniel C, 1952, F 23,11:6
Hutcherson, Dudley R, 1960, S 3,17:4
Hutcheson, Ernest, 1951, F 10,13:1
Hutcheson, Ernest Mrs, 1940, N 6,23:5
Hutcheson, Grote (por), 1948, D 16,29:1
Hutcheson, William A, 1942, N 20,23:3
Hutcheson, William A Mrs, 1959, Jl 25,17:5
Hutcheson, William L, 1953, O 21,29:1
Hutcheson, William L Mrs, 1948, O 28,29:3
Hutchings, Chauncey E, 1951, My 28,21:4
Hutchings, Clifford E, 1954, Ap 6,29:4
Hutchings, Dewitt V, 1953, F 17,34:1
Hutchings, George F Mrs, 1957, Ap 24,33:1
Hutchings, George L, 1937, D 5,9:2
Hutchings, Henry E, 1942, Mr 5,24:3
Hutchings, Henry M, 1937, Ja 10,II,10:2
Hutchings, Herbert E, 1950, F 23,27:2
Hutchings, Hugh H, 1937, N 8,23:4
Hutchings, M L, 1940, Ag 19,17:6
Hutchings, Oscar G, 1950, Ap 23,95:6
Hutchings, Richard H, 1947, O 29,28:2
Hutchings, Richard H Jr, 1938, D 15,27:4
Hutchings, Samuel B, 1942, F 14,15:2
Hutchings, William, 1866, My 5,4:7
Hutchings, William H, 1911, Ag 26,9:5
Hutchings, William J, 1949, Je 18,13:4
Hutchins, Arthur W, 1958, Jl 21,21:5
Hutchins, Augustus S, 1948, F 20,28:2
Hutchins, Carroll B, 1954, O 6,25:3
Hutchins, Charles P, 1938, D 29,19:3
Hutchins, Charles T, 1920, Ag 11,9:5
Hutchins, Chaucey S, 1947, Ag 19,23:5
Hutchins, E B, 1939, D 13,27:6
Hutchins, Edith, 1917, F 1,11:4
Hutchins, Francis S, 1924, Jl 3,15:5
Hutchins, Frank E, 1942, Mr 29,45:2
Hutchins, Frank F, 1942, F 24,21:5
Hutchins, Frank R, 1937, Ap 2,23:6
Hutchins, George Y, 1942, Je 13,15:1
Hutchins, Gordon, 1952, My 25,94:4
Hutchins, Gordon L, 1945, D 1,23:3
Hutchins, Hamilton Capt, 1924, Ag 30,9:7
Hutchins, Harley D (will), 1941, Je 26,26:4
Hutchins, Harry C, 1948, S 4,15:6
Hutchins, Henry T, 1960, S 24,23:4
Hutchins, Hilda, 1947, Je 28,9:1
Hutchins, Hiram Rev, 1903, Ap 20,7:5
Hutchins, Horace A Col, 1914, O 1,11:3
Hutchins, Hurd, 1966, Je 6,41:5
Hutchins, J Warner Col, 1925, F 5,19:4
Hutchins, Jere C, 1943, F 25,21:1
Hutchins, John, 1865, Jl 26,8:4; 1945, Je 15,19:5
Hutchins, John B, 1946, N 28,27:3
Hutchins, John Mrs, 1944, Jl 15,13:1
Hutchins, Leroy W (por), 1946, Je 22,19:4
Hutchins, Margaret, 1961, Ja 5,31:3
Hutchins, Mason C, 1953, Ag 31,17:1
Hutchins, Mason C Mrs, 1945, F 9,15:4
Hutchins, Melburn W, 1911, N 5,II,15:5
Hutchins, Paul I, 1947, Mr 10,21:5
Hutchins, Robert G, 1949, My 2,25:2
Hutchins, Samuel, 1943, N 12,21:1
Hutchins, Stephen, 1883, F 23,5:4
Hutchins, Stilson, 1912, Ap 23,13:5
Hutchins, Walter S, 1946, Mr 19,28:2; 1951, Mr 2,25:1
Hutchins, William H, 1940, O 15,23:2
Hutchins, William J, 1958, F 22,17:3
Hutchins, William J Mrs, 1960, Mr 29,37:1
Hutchinson, A Alex, 1949, Mr 8,25:3
Hutchinson, Abraham, 1880, D 23,3:2
Hutchinson, Abram S Capt, 1907, Jl 6,7:4
Hutchinson, Addison O, 1937, Ap 21,23:5
Hutchinson, Albert, 1952, My 27,27:1
Hutchinson, Albert F, 1953, Je 12,27:5
Hutchinson, Annie G, 1950, Ja 22,78:1
Hutchinson, Arthur, 1937, D 13,27:5
Hutchinson, Arthur E, 1951, Ag 19,84:4
Hutchinson, Arthur J, 1951, Jl 29,69:2
Hutchinson, Asa, 1884, D 1,2:5
Hutchinson, Asa B, 1874, D 25,5:2
Hutchinson, Aubrey V, 1960, Je 8,39:3
Hutchinson, B, 1927, S 18,II,9:1
Hutchinson, B Edwin, 1961, S 29,35:3
Hutchinson, Benjamin P Mrs, 1909, Mr 25,9:5
Hutchinson, Bennett W, 1941, N 30,68:1

Hutchinson, C Hare, 1902, O 19,7:6
Hutchinson, Cary T, 1939, Ja 19,19:5
Hutchinson, Charles, 1950, Mr 10,27:4
Hutchinson, Charles H, 1942, Ap 17,17:3
Hutchinson, Charles L, 1924, O 8,19:4; 1944, Ja 12, 23:4
Hutchinson, Charles M, 1951, O 28,85:1
Hutchinson, Charles P, 1957, D 15,86:6
Hutchinson, Charles R McC Mrs, 1959, D 5,23:2
Hutchinson, Charles S, 1942, N 11,25:2
Hutchinson, Daniel L Jr, 1940, Mr 19,25:4
Hutchinson, David J, 1942, S 1,19:2
Hutchinson, David W, 1946, D 29,35:5
Hutchinson, Don W, 1949, Je 20,19:4
Hutchinson, Donald J, 1945, Je 1,15:4
Hutchinson, Dorothy, 1956, Ja 22,89:2
Hutchinson, E Lillian, 1962, N 8,39:1
Hutchinson, E Rev, 1885, Mr 4,5:6
Hutchinson, Eberly G, 1951, Mr 11,92:3
Hutchinson, Edward, 1945, S 18,24:3
Hutchinson, Edward H, 1938, F 26,15:5
Hutchinson, Elizabeth Parks Mrs, 1925, My 9,15:4
Hutchinson, Elmer T, 1954, S 15,33:2
Hutchinson, Elwood E, 1951, D 28,21:2
Hutchinson, Ely C, 1955, N 13,88:3
Hutchinson, Emilie J, 1938, Ja 13,21:1
Hutchinson, Ernest N, 1938, Ja 31,19:3
Hutchinson, Eva Mrs (will), 1939, D 20,32:3
Hutchinson, F L, 1932, F 27,17:1
Hutchinson, Frank D Mrs, 1941, Ja 24,17:2
Hutchinson, Frank J, 1958, F 25,27:1
Hutchinson, Frank L, 1937, N 19,23:4
Hutchinson, Frank S, 1946, N 12,29:3; 1955, Je 7,33:4
Hutchinson, Franklin Mrs, 1945, Ap 2,19:3
Hutchinson, Frederick C, 1964, N 13,35:3
Hutchinson, George A, 1954, Ja 16,15:2
Hutchinson, George E, 1945, O 30,19:2
Hutchinson, George W, 1945, Mr 25,38:1
Hutchinson, Guy, 1941, D 12,25:2
Hutchinson, H Earle, 1937, F 16,23:1
Hutchinson, Hamilton, 1909, O 25,7:5
Hutchinson, Harold S, 1948, Jl 2,21:3
Hutchinson, Harry F, 1943, D 19,48:4
Hutchinson, Henry E, 1914, My 10,IV,7:6
Hutchinson, Herbert S, 1942, N 27,23:4
Hutchinson, Holland H, 1968, O 8,44:2
Hutchinson, Horace F, 1920, D 31,11:4
Hutchinson, Ira, 1881, Ag 10,5:6
Hutchinson, Irving K, 1945, Ja 29,14:2
Hutchinson, Irving N, 1944, Jl 22,15:3
Hutchinson, J Judge, 1903, D 18,9:5
Hutchinson, J W, 1953, My 30,15:5
Hutchinson, James, 1937, Ap 7,25:1
Hutchinson, James F, 1941, D 26,14:2; 1964, Mr 27, 27:3
Hutchinson, James H, 1942, Ja 26,15:2
Hutchinson, James P, 1943, Ap 10,17:1
Hutchinson, James P Mrs, 1905, Ap 12,9:6; 1964, Jl 24,27:1
Hutchinson, James Sir, 1946, Je 13,27:4
Hutchinson, Jenette Mrs, 1939, Ap 7,11:2
Hutchinson, John, 1941, My 30,15:6; 1948, My 25, 27:2; 1951, Mr 20,29:2; 1951, Ap 24,29:2
Hutchinson, John M, 1940, Mr 8,22:2
Hutchinson, John S Maj, 1911, Ap 6,11:5
Hutchinson, John Stewart Lt, 1916, S 3,19:6
Hutchinson, John T, 1958, Je 7,19:2
Hutchinson, John W, 1908, O 30,9:5; 1937, F 27,17:5
Hutchinson, Jonathan Sir, 1913, Je 24,11:6
Hutchinson, Joseph B Mrs, 1960, O 20,35:5
Hutchinson, Joseph L, 1951, My 22,31:1
Hutchinson, Knox T, 1957, Jl 1,23:3
Hutchinson, Lavinia S, 1955, Jl 9,15:1
Hutchinson, LeRoy J, 1957, Ja 18,22:4
Hutchinson, Lincoln, 1940, My 23,23:5
Hutchinson, Matthew S, 1941, My 4,53:1
Hutchinson, Maxwell, 1955, N 21,29:3
Hutchinson, Maynard C Mrs, 1943, F 8,19:4
Hutchinson, Maynard Mrs, 1964, Ja 25,23:5
Hutchinson, Miller R (por), 1944, F 18,17:1
Hutchinson, Morris Mrs, 1959, Mr 11,35:5
Hutchinson, Morton C, 1959, Ja 21,31:2
Hutchinson, Myron R, 1953, N 23,27:1
Hutchinson, Nathan M Mrs, 1943, Ap 6,21:4
Hutchinson, Norman F Mrs, 1947, N 18,29:2
Hutchinson, Oliver C, 1937, Ap 8,23:3
Hutchinson, Oscar W, 1939, S 28,25:1
Hutchinson, Paul, 1956, Ap 16,27:1
Hutchinson, Pemberton S, 1903, Je 28,7:6
Hutchinson, Randall, 1942, N 15,56:5
Hutchinson, Robert, 1939, Je 13,23:5
Hutchinson, Robert G, 1945, S 24,19:4
Hutchinson, Robert H, 1946, My 14,21:2
Hutchinson, Robert L, 1957, F 20,33:5
Hutchinson, Robert P, 1956, Ja 8,86:7
Hutchinson, Samuel, 1876, Je 16,4:7
Hutchinson, Shade, 1943, D 30,18:2
Hutchinson, St John, 1942, O 25,46:2
Hutchinson, Susan A, 1945, S 29,15:2
Hutchinson, Sydney E, 1950, F 26,77:1
Hutchinson, W H Sgt, 1873, Ja 31,8:5
Hutchinson, W Spencer, 1948, My 27,25:3
Hutchinson, Walter J (por), 1942, Ap 12,45:1
Hutchinson, Walter V, 1950, My 1,25:3
Hutchinson, William, 1951, Jl 28,11:2
Hutchinson, William A, 1950, Ja 17,27:2
Hutchinson, William B, 1949, Mr 30,25:5
Hutchinson, William B (Sept 23), 1965, O 11,61:3
Hutchinson, William B Sr, 1964, Ja 9,31:4
Hutchinson, William H, 1907, Jl 9,7:6; 1945, N 1,23:5; 1961, Ja 1,48:6
Hutchinson, William H Rev, 1916, Ja 14,9:5
Hutchinson, William H Sr, 1904, Jl 7,16:2
Hutchinson, William J, 1947, D 23,24:2; 1952, Ja 8, 27:4; 1959, N 26,37:2
Hutchinson, William K (funl, My 29,27:4), 1958, My 26,29:3
Hutchinson, William S, 1945, D 24,16:4
Hutchinson, William W, 1952, F 28,27:3
Hutchison, Alex J, 1955, Je 29,29:2
Hutchison, Alex Mrs, 1949, Mr 2,25:1
Hutchison, Archibald, 1951, Jl 15,60:4
Hutchison, Archibald Mrs, 1946, D 11,31:4
Hutchison, Bruce C, 1955, My 13,25:2
Hutchison, C E, 1942, O 2,25:6
Hutchison, Charles E Mrs, 1942, N 25,23:2
Hutchison, Charles W Mrs, 1937, Ap 14,25:4
Hutchison, Elmo H, 1964, Je 26,29:4
Hutchison, Graham S (por), 1946, Ap 5,25:2
Hutchison, James E, 1944, Je 14,19:7
Hutchison, James L, 1937, Mr 21,II,8:5
Hutchison, Joseph F, 1949, F 10,27:4
Hutchison, Lord (Robt), 1950, Je 14,31:2
Hutchison, Percy Mrs, 1950, Mr 7,27:3
Hutchison, R A Dr, 1937, D 13,27:6
Hutchison, Ralph C, 1966, Mr 16,45:1
Hutchison, Robert, 1960, F 14,84:4
Hutchison, Robert M, 1952, My 6,29:4
Hutchison, Roland C, 1951, Ja 7,76:6
Hutchison, Thomas, 1937, O 23,15:7
Hutchison, William E, 1952, Ap 6,90:5
Huter, Harry Mrs, 1956, Ja 30,27:5
Huth, Anna C, 1955, Ja 25,25:2
Huth, Godfrey C, 1946, Mr 27,27:4
Huth, Harry O, 1948, Mr 24,25:4
Huth, Herman J, 1947, O 11,17:5
Hutheesing, Krishna N Mrs, 1967, N 10,51:3
Huther, Angus E, 1947, Ap 25,22:2
Huther, Warren B, 1945, Ja 21,39:1
Huthman, John, 1948, Je 17,25:1
Hutin, Marcel, 1950, O 21,17:5
Hutlin, Maurice, 1910, Mr 17,9:5
Hutman, Edward C Prof, 1937, N 19,23:4
Hutner, Nathan M, 1954, My 25,27:3
Hutschenruyter, Wouter, 1944, Ja 9,42:2
Hutschnecker, Arnold Mrs, 1966, D 15,47:3
Hutson, Clarence D, 1950, Ag 7,19:3
Hutson, Donald M Mrs, 1951, My 16,35:2
Hutson, E Archbishop, 1936, O 23,23:1
Hutson, Frank A, 1946, Ja 21,23:1
Hutson, Frederick L, 1956, Ag 29,29:5
Hutson, Frederick L Mrs, 1950, Ap 18,31:4
Hutson, John B, 1964, My 6,47:3
Hutson, John R Jr, 1959, S 4,21:4
Hutson, Norman P, 1959, Mr 21,21:6
Hutson, Phil L, 1942, Mr 15,42:6
Hutson, R B, 1943, S 24,30:5
Hutt, Anna Mrs, 1941, S 25,25:2
Hutt, Henry, 1950, Ja 20,19:2; 1952, Je 26,29:3
Hutt, Henry W, 1947, O 16,28:3
Hutt, Herman G, 1952, Je 14,15:4
Hutt, James Wesley, 1905, Je 27,9:3
Hutt, John W, 1937, S 20,23:2
Hutt, Louis C Mrs, 1942, O 3,15:5
Hutt, Orla T, 1951, F 26,23:5
Hutt, Orla T Mrs, 1953, My 13,29:3
Hutt, W Leon, 1948, Je 19,15:6
Hutt, William H, 1947, My 7,27:5
Hutten, Baroness von (B Riddle), 1957, Ja 29,31:5
Hutten, Edwin T, 1945, N 25,48:5
Huttenbach, Louis, 1950, Ja 13,24:2
Huttenbauer, Emil, 1951, Jl 21,13:3
Huttenloch, Morton W (por), 1941, Mr 19,21:4
Huttenlocher, Frederick H, 1954, N 30,29:3
Huttenlocher, Gustav, 1945, Je 22,15:4
Hutter, Francis, 1964, My 26,39:4
Hutter, George, 1879, Ag 3,8:5
Hutter, Howard J, 1966, Jl 3,34:7
Huttig, Charles H, 1913, Jl 13,II,11:4
Huttig, Charles M, 1952, Je 24,29:5
Huttle, Otto, 1949, D 7,31:5
Huttleston, Leonard C, 1964, D 10,58:1
Hutto, Jackson S, 1956, Je 26,29:5
Hutton, A J White, 1961, S 28,41:5
Hutton, Albert, 1958, N 12,37:4
Hutton, Alton E, 1951, Je 26,29:2
Hutton, Amy S Mrs, 1939, D 30,15:5
Hutton, Andrew, 1952, Ag 2,15:2
Hutton, B H, 1884, F 19,5:5
Hutton, Charles W, 1949, F 3,23:4
Hutton, Clyde D, 1964, Mr 12,35:1
Hutton, David B, 1944, D 9,15:4
Hutton, David B Mrs, 1953, D 31,19:4
Hutton, Dick, 1950, D 2,13:6
Hutton, Edward F, 1962, Jl 12,29:1
Hutton, Edward Gen, 1923, Ag 6,11:2
Hutton, Frank B, 1950, My 11,29:4
Hutton, Frank H, 1938, F 7,15:3
Hutton, Franklyn L, 1940, D 6,23:4
Hutton, Franklyn Laws Mrs, 1917, My 3,15:4
Hutton, Frederick Remsen, 1918, My 15,13:4
Hutton, Gaum M, 1916, Jl 10,11:5
Hutton, Gaun M Mrs, 1925, F 26,21:4
Hutton, George Mrs, 1957, Mr 25,25:2
Hutton, George V Mrs, 1955, Ja 14,21:1
Hutton, James A Capt, 1911, Jl 3,7:5
Hutton, James M (will, Mr 6,26:7), 1940, Mr 2,13:1
Hutton, James M Jr, 1967, D 27,34:3
Hutton, James Morgan Sr Mrs, 1968, F 10,33:2
Hutton, John, 1874, Jl 17,4:6
Hutton, John A, 1947, Ja 15,25:2
Hutton, John E, 1955, Ap 9,13:6
Hutton, John L, 1951, My 14,25:6
Hutton, John Lt, 1918, F 16,11:8
Hutton, John W (funl), 1912, My 22,13:5
Hutton, John W Mrs, 1954, Je 9,31:4
Hutton, Joseph R, 1945, Ja 25,19:2
Hutton, Laurence, 1904, Je 11,9:6
Hutton, Leon C, 1965, My 19,47:1
Hutton, Mancius S, 1880, Ap 12,5:2
Hutton, Marion C, 1940, D 9,19:5
Hutton, Martius H Rev, 1909, D 20,9:2
Hutton, Maurice, 1940, Ap 6,17:6
Hutton, May Arkwright, 1915, O 7,9:7
Hutton, R Warren, 1946, Jl 26,21:1
Hutton, Robert L, 1964, S 24,41:2
Hutton, Robert L Mrs, 1957, Mr 25,25:4
Hutton, Russell J H, 1947, Mr 23,60:3
Hutton, Thomas J, 1940, O 20,49:2
Hutton, W E, 1934, S 9,34:1
Hutton, W V, 1949, Ap 1,25:1
Hutton, Walter S, 1950, D 8,30:2
Hutton, William H Jr Mrs, 1967, Ag 21,31:3
Hutton, William Jr, 1937, Ag 15,II,7:1; 1956, F 21,33:
Hutton, William Mrs, 1950, Ag 23,29:3
Hutty, Alfred, 1954, Je 29,27:4
Hutty, Susan Mrs, 1948, Ap 13,27:4
Hutz, C Eric, 1964, F 14,33:5
Hutz, Rudolf, 1950, Mr 30,29:1
Hutzler, Charles G 2d, 1955, My 18,31:1
Hutzler, David, 1915, Ja 22,11:4
Hutzler, Ella J Mrs, 1942, Je 23,19:5
Hutzler, Elsa W, 1953, Mr 24,31:2
Hutzler, Henry, 1921, D 17,13:4
Hutzler, Morton D, 1945, Ja 24,22:3
Huunewell, Arthur, 1904, O 18,9:6
Huus, Carl M Sr, 1952, F 12,27:4
Huvelle, Rene H, 1959, Ap 24,27:3
Huver, George W, 1948, Jl 30,17:2
Huxford, Frederick W, 1946, D 22,41:8
Huxford, Walter S, 1958, F 14,24:1
Huxham, Sydney S, 1956, D 31,13:6
Huxham, Trevor S, 1964, My 23,23:3
Huxley, Aldous L, 1963, N 24,1:1
Huxley, Aldous Mrs, 1955, F 13,86:1
Huxley, Florence, 1955, My 28,15:6
Huxley, Frederic C, 1949, F 10,27:2
Huxley, Henry M, 1954, Ag 21,17:5
Huxley, T H Prof, 1895, Je 30,16:4
Huxley, Thomas Henry Mrs, 1914, Ap 6,9:5
Huxley, Walter, 1955, Ag 1,19:2
Huych, Ansel B, 1959, Ap 22,33:2
Huyck, Frank C, 1938, N 20,39:3
Huyck Francis C Mrs, 1958, Je 25,29:3
Huyler, Byron M, 1937, Jl 21,21:4
Huyler, Clyde, 1922, Je 19,15:4
Huyler, Coulter D, 1955, S 8,31:4
Huyler, Coulter D Mrs, 1957, Mr 4,27:6
Huyler, F De K, 1927, My 31,21:1
Huyler, Fred, 1968, My 27,47:3
Huyler, Harold C, 1964, Jl 12,68:4
Huyler, John S (will, O 7,11:4), 1910, O 2,II,13:4
Huyler, Kate Mrs, 1939, Ap 28,25:3
Huyler, Louis M, 1961, S 15,30:6
Huyler, Peter E, 1956, Je 26,29:1
Huyler, Robert I, 1961, Jl 18,29:2
Huynh Thuc Khang, Min, 1947, Ap 25,6:3
Huypsoon, Arnold, 1925, Jl 3,13:5
Huysmans, Camille Ex-Premier, 1968, F 26,37:2
Huysmans, Gerard, 1948, Mr 19,23:2
Huysmans, Jaris Karl, 1907, My 13,9:6
Huysmans, Louis, 1915, S 10,11:5
Huzar, Elias, 1950, D 29,20:2
Huzza, Robert Mrs, 1910, N 18,11:5
Hvass, Charles T, 1953, Ja 10,17:3
Hvolbeck, John, 1940, Ag 3,15:3
Hwang Min-chao, Mrs, 1951, N 6,33:3
Hwang Sing, Gen, 1916, N 1,11:4
Hyam, Leslie A, 1963, S 11,43:1
Hyames, Judson, 1949, Ag 20,11:2
Hyams, Chapman H 3d, 1964, S 14,33:1
Hyams, Harry, 1938, F 19,15:4
Hyams, Henry Sr, 1921, N 29,17:5
Hyams, John, 1940, D 11,28:3
Hyams, Joseph A (por), 1943, Ja 27,21:5
Hyams, Louis, 1941, O 16,21:3
Hyams, Mortimer N, 1964, D 29,27:2
Hyamson, Moses (por), 1949, Je 11,17:5
Hyatt, Abram M Mrs, 1950, My 23,29:1

Hyatt, Alpheus Prof, 1902, Ja 16,9:5
Hyatt, Annie Y, 1948, Je 28,19:2
Hyatt, Bertha E (will), 1959, D 9,25:2
Hyatt, Clarence T, 1947, N 27,31:2
Hyatt, Earl M, 1949, O 10,23:3
Hyatt, Egbert, 1937, D 3,23:3
Hyatt, Elizabeth M Mrs, 1940, O 6,48:3
Hyatt, Frank K, 1958, Jl 14,21:1
Hyatt, Frank K Mrs, 1950, O 2,23:3
Hyatt, G E L, 1880, Ap 9,8:3
Hyatt, Guy, 1950, My 1,25:2
Hyatt, Hannah N, 1950, Je 12,27:2
Hyatt, Herbert R, 1948, S 7,25:2
Hyatt, James L, 1939, N 13,19:3
Hyatt, James L Mrs, 1942, Ja 23,20:2
Hyatt, John, 1955, Jl 18,13:7
Hyatt, John B Mrs, 1946, S 5,27:3
Hyatt, John Wesley, 1920, My 11,9:4
Hyatt, Jonathan Duell, 1912, D 20,15:4
Hyatt, Lester P, 1947, S 3,25:4
Hyatt, Lewis L, 1903, Ag 29,7:5
Hyatt, Mabel E D, 1946, Ap 15,27:5
Hyatt, Nathaniel, 1903, Jl 31,7:6
Hyatt, Nathaniel I, 1959, O 21,43:3
Hyatt, Pollock F, 1904, Ja 18,7:4
Hyatt, Ralph W, 1943, S 15,27:3
Hyatt, Ramon E, 1951, Ja 3,27:2
Hyatt, Reuben H, 1939, Jl 19,19:6
Hyatt, Sam C Mrs, 1953, D 29,23:4
Hyatt, Schuyler M, 1962, Je 3,88:1
Hyatt, Stanley Portal, 1914, Jl 2,9:6
Hyatt, Stephen, 1879, Ag 26,5:4
Hyatt, Thaddeus P, 1952, D 17,33:3
Hyatt, Thomas D, 1925, Ja 26,17:4
Hyatt, W H, 1903, My 20,9:4
Hyatt, Walter E, 1961, Ap 14,30:2
Hyatt, Walter J Mrs, 1943, Jl 28,15:2
Hyatt, William E, 1944, Mr 7,17:2
Hyatt-Woolf, Charles, 1938, O 21,23:1
Hybinette, Noak V, 1937, S 11,17:3
Hydari, Lady Akbar, 1940, Je 16,39:2
Hyde, A Lewis Rev, 1937, F 4,21:3
Hyde, Albert F, 1948, N 19,28:2
Hyde, Alex C, 1956, Jl 11,29:5
Hyde, Alexander, 1881, Ja 12,5:4
Hyde, Alvan W, 1946, O 26,17:3
Hyde, Andrew P, 1941, D 19,25:4
Hyde, Anna S, 1948, F 10,23:1
Hyde, Arthur, 1950, F 4,15:5
Hyde, Arthur J W Mrs, 1954, Je 5,17:6
Hyde, Arthur M, 1947, O 18,15:4
Hyde, Arthur P S (por), 1943, D 28,18:2
Hyde, Arthur P S (mem ser planned), 1944, My 20, 15:5
Hyde, Arthur Sewall Capt, 1920, F 26,11:4
Hyde, Burdon P, 1948, F 5,24:3
Hyde, Carl C, 1965, Ja 21,31:4
Hyde, Charles, 1901, Je 13,9:6; 1942, N 27,23:2
Hyde, Charles A, 1947, Ag 30,15:5
Hyde, Charles C, 1952, F 14,27:1
Hyde, Charles F Sr, 1964, N 18,47:4
Hyde, Charles L Mrs, 1947, Jl 5,11:4
Hyde, Charles Livingston, 1925, Ja 25,7:2
Hyde, Charles S, 1947, Mr 5,25:5
Hyde, Clarence R, 1940, F 10,15:6
Hyde, Clarence R Mrs, 1943, Ja 18,15:3
Hyde, Clinton J Mrs, 1939, Jl 7,17:1
Hyde, David V, 1952, D 7,88:3
Hyde, Donald F, 1966, F 6,92:4
Hyde, Donald R Mrs, 1950, N 19,92:3
Hyde, Douglas, 1949, Jl 13,27:1
Hyde, Douglas Mrs, 1939, Ja 1,17:4
Hyde, Duncan C, 1957, F 28,27:2
Hyde, E F, 1933, Mr 19,32:3
Hyde, E Francis Mrs, 1918, Jl 31,9:5
Hyde, Edgar R, 1960, Ag 29,25:1
Hyde, Edward R, 1940, F 5,17:5
Hyde, Elise M Sister, 1956, Ag 31,17:4
Hyde, F Stillman, 1967, Ap 24,33:3
Hyde, Francis deL Mrs, 1959, Ag 29,17:3
Hyde, Francis Sir, 1937, Jl 29,19:6
Hyde, Frank D, 1957, Mr 28,31:5
Hyde, Frank D Mrs, 1942, My 11,15:5
Hyde, Frank E, 1906, D 3,9:4
Hyde, Fred, 1943, N 22,19:5
Hyde, Frederick, 1939, Ja 25,22:1
Hyde, Frederick E, 1944, O 13,19:4
Hyde, Frederick W, 1943, Ja 14,21:2; 1961, O 21,21:5
Hyde, Fritz C, 1948, S 6,13:5
Hyde, George, 1963, D 3,43:3
Hyde, George A, 1944, S 25,17:4
Hyde, George C, 1949, My 21,13:6
Hyde, George D Mrs, 1954, Je 19,15:5
Hyde, George G, 1954, Ag 4,21:2
Hyde, George P, 1945, S 4,23:5
Hyde, Gertrude S, 1964, N 14,29:6
Hyde, H B, 1899, My 3,5:1
Hyde, Harriet V Dr, 1953, Ag 17,15:6
Hyde, Henry B Mrs, 1922, Je 25,26:3
Hyde, Henry G Mrs, 1938, N 28,15:5
Hyde, Henry M, 1951, Jl 23,17:6
Hyde, Henry N Mrs, 1949, D 29,25:4
Hyde, Henry S, 1917, F 3,13:4
Hyde, Herbert E, 1954, Ag 27,21:4
Hyde, Isabella, 1948, Mr 3,23:4
Hyde, J E Hindon Mrs, 1948, Ja 27,25:1
Hyde, James B, 1925, O 9,23:4
Hyde, James F C, 1944, Ag 8,17:2
Hyde, James H, 1959, Jl 27,25:2
Hyde, James H Mrs (por), 1948, O 10,76:2
Hyde, James M, 1943, Jl 20,19:5
Hyde, James Nevins Dr, 1910, S 8,9:5
Hyde, James R, 1950, Jl 18,29:4
Hyde, James W, 1945, F 5,15:3
Hyde, Joel W Dr, 1907, S 23,9:6
Hyde, John, 1950, D 19,29:2
Hyde, John J, 1950, O 31,27:4
Hyde, John McEwen Brig-Gen, 1916, O 26,11:7
Hyde, John S, 1917, Mr 19,11:4
Hyde, Joseph H, 1952, My 7,27:3
Hyde, Leslie Mrs, 1953, Mr 1,92:8
Hyde, Liberty, 1947, F 24,19:4
Hyde, Lillia B Mrs (will), 1939, N 18,9:3
Hyde, Lloyd W, 1962, Je 14,33:2
Hyde, Louis K, 1947, S 12,21:4
Hyde, Louis K Mrs, 1943, Mr 19,19:1
Hyde, Marjorie M Mrs, 1939, N 20,19:4
Hyde, Mark P, 1952, Je 5,31:5
Hyde, Marthe L Mrs, 1944, Jl 28,13:4
Hyde, Mary M Stevens Mrs, 1905, My 3,9:5
Hyde, Mary R, 1937, D 25,15:4
Hyde, Mary T Mrs, 1937, Jl 14,22:2
Hyde, Melville, 1948, O 31,88:5
Hyde, Mildred K Mrs, 1937, F 26,21:4
Hyde, Nelson W, 1964, F 3,27:2
Hyde, Paul H, 1956, Je 23,17:6
Hyde, Phoebe, 1967, Ag 11,31:5
Hyde, R Scott, 1944, S 26,23:4
Hyde, Ralph M, 1941, Mr 28,23:2
Hyde, Reed W, 1962, F 1,31:2
Hyde, Robert J, 1964, Ja 20,43:2
Hyde, Salem, 1924, Ap 7,17:5
Hyde, Seymour J, 1915, F 15,7:4
Hyde, T Norton, 1939, Ap 20,23:4
Hyde, Theophilus R, 1962, Mr 17,25:5
Hyde, Thomas, 1940, Mr 3,45:2
Hyde, Thomas A Rev, 1937, F 9,23:4
Hyde, Thomas B, 1942, Jl 26,30:6
Hyde, Wallace W, 1966, Mr 8,30:2
Hyde, Walter B, 1950, S 8,32:5
Hyde, Wilbur H, 1947, My 26,21:2
Hyde, William De Witt Dr, 1917, Je 30,11:7
Hyde, William H, 1943, F 8,19:3
Hyde, William H Mrs, 1943, My 2,45:1
Hyde, William M M, 1943, Ja 27,21:1
Hyde, William S, 1948, O 3,67:1
Hyde, William T, 1947, F 4,26:2; 1951, N 2,23:3
Hyde, William T Mrs, 1962, Je 15,27:5
Hyde, William Waldo, 1915, O 31,17:4
Hydeman, Edwin M (por), 1940, Ap 1,19:1
Hyder, Fred M, 1937, S 3,17:3
Hyder, K Lee, 1947, Ag 13,23:1
Hyderabad, Nizam of (Nawab Mir Osman Ali Khan Bahadur), 1967, F 25,1:8
Hydock, Peter C Mrs, 1944, D 21,21:4
Hydon, William M, 1948, Ap 27,25:4
Hyer, Benjamin B, 1937, N 20,17:3
Hyer, Frederick C, 1958, O 8,35:2
Hyer, Harold, 1953, Je 2,29:5
Hyer, J K, 1882, F 13,5:5
Hyer, Lewis W, 1957, F 27,27:3
Hyer, Peter M, 1941, N 4,23:3
Hyer, Raymond T, 1967, F 14,43:1
Hyer, Tom, 1864, Je 27,2:4
Hyers, John S, 1943, Ja 28,19:2
Hyett, Francis, 1941, My 20,23:6
Hylan, Donald, 1968, Je 21,41:3
Hylan, J F, 1936, Ja 12,1:6
Hylan, Miriam L Mrs, 1942, My 9,13:6
Hylan, Thomas F, 1942, Jl 25,13:2
Hyland, Alexis, 1943, F 9,23:5
Hyland, Ambrose, 1954, O 4,50:3
Hyland, Clarence, 1952, Ag 30,13:4
Hyland, Edward J, 1954, Ag 1,85:1
Hyland, Francis E Rev, 1968, F 2,35:3
Hyland, Francis J, 1958, Jl 15,25:2
Hyland, Frederick C, 1943, Ag 25,19:5
Hyland, George J, 1951, Ag 15,27:2
Hyland, John, 1913, S 9,7:6; 1944, Ja 23,37:1
Hyland, John J, 1924, Jl 27,23:4; 1949, N 25,31:3; 1950, Ja 24,31:2
Hyland, John J (por),(will, N 20,88:2), 1955, N 13, 88:7
Hyland, John J, 1960, Ja 13,48:1
Hyland, John J Mrs, 1946, N 26,29:6
Hyland, John R, 1961, S 5,35:4
Hyland, John T Mrs, 1945, O 20,11:2
Hyland, John W, 1950, Ag 18,21:4
Hyland, Joseph V, 1960, S 23,29:1
Hyland, Lily M, 1962, Jl 20,25:3
Hyland, Matthew P, 1956, Ja 14,19:4
Hyland, Maurice J, 1939, Ap 25,23:4
Hyland, Patrick J, 1948, Ag 20,17:1
Hyland, Philip D, 1958, Mr 21,21:2
Hyland, Raymond Mrs, 1960, Ja 31,92:3
Hyland, Richard V, 1952, S 22,23:1
Hyland, Robert F, 1950, D 15,31:5
Hyland, Robert J, 1959, N 30,31:5
Hyland, Sarah Mrs, 1956, S 15,17:3
Hyland, William F, 1962, Ag 10,19:5
Hyland, William F Mrs, 1952, F 8,23:3
Hyland, William H, 1937, Ag 26,21:4
Hyland, William J, 1939, F 24,19:2
Hyland, William Mrs, 1950, Jl 19,31:4
Hylander, Clarence J, 1964, O 11,88:7
Hylas, Michael J, 1942, D 5,15:1
Hylen, Carl, 1939, Ag 6,27:2
Hylkema, George J, 1948, F 26,23:2
Hylleberg, Peter A, 1945, N 16,19:2
Hylton, Jack, 1965, Ja 30,27:1
Hylton, Lord, 1945, My 28,19:4
Hylton-Foster, Harry, 1965, S 3,27:2
Hyman, Abraham, 1952, Mr 28,24:5; 1966, D 24,19:4
Hyman, Abraham Mrs, 1968, N 25,47:1
Hyman, Benjamin H, 1956, Jl 5,25:5
Hyman, Bernard E, 1951, Ja 13,15:4
Hyman, Bernard H, 1942, S 9,23:3
Hyman, C S, 1926, O 10,29:1
Hyman, David, 1959, Je 2,35:5
Hyman, David E, 1951, Je 21,27:3
Hyman, David M, 1925, S 19,15:4
Hyman, Eli, 1902, D 31,1:6
Hyman, G M, 1936, O 30,23:5
Hyman, George, 1959, Mr 1,86:7
Hyman, Harold L, 1962, My 17,37:3
Hyman, Harry, 1968, N 22,47:4
Hyman, Henry, 1937, My 18,13:3; 1951, N 14,31:1
Hyman, Herbert R, 1939, Mr 31,21:4
Hyman, Herbert R Mrs, 1937, D 7,25:3
Hyman, Herman, 1941, Ag 7,17:2
Hyman, Irving, 1961, Mr 8,33:2; 1960, N 24,29:6
Hyman, Jacob, 1942, S 11,21:2
Hyman, John J, 1949, Ja 26,25:4
Hyman, Joseph C (por), 1949, F 9,27:1
Hyman, Julius, 1946, O 30,27:3
Hyman, Lawrence A Mrs, 1955, S 8,31:1
Hyman, Louis, 1942, Jl 1,25:2
Hyman, Mac (McKenzie H), 1963, Jl 18,27:4
Hyman, Marcus, 1939, Ja 1,24:8
Hyman, Mark (por), 1946, Je 22,19:1
Hyman, Max, 1955, N 30,33:3
Hyman, Montague E, 1942, N 17,25:6
Hyman, Morris A, 1910, Mr 30,12:2
Hyman, Mortie, 1951, Ag 17,17:3
Hyman, Moses S, 1913, S 10,9:6
Hyman, Myers, 1950, S 21,20:1
Hyman, Oscar, 1954, F 23,27:2
Hyman, Ralph, 1964, Jl 10,29:3
Hyman, Richard H, 1967, Ja 2,19:2
Hyman, Ruth, 1951, Ap 26,32:3
Hyman, Samuel I, 1917, Jl 13,9:6
Hyman, Samuel L, 1948, Jl 15,23:5
Hyman, Samuel Mrs, 1953, Jl 20,17:4
Hyman, Sol A, 1945, Jl 31,19:2
Hyman, Solomon, 1924, Ag 22,13:3
Hyman, Stanley E Mrs (S Jackson), 1965, Ag 10, 29:1
Hyman, W B, 1884, Ag 10,7:3
Hyman, Wallace M, 1942, S 1,19:4
Hyman, William A, 1966, Jl 11,29:1
Hymans, Frederick, 1959, Mr 24,39:1
Hymans, Harry C, 1965, My 15,31:3
Hymans, Max, 1961, Mr 8,33:3
Hymans, Paul M (por),(cor, Mr 10,17:4), 1941, Mr 9,40:4
Hymans, S L, 1884, My 23,5:5
Hymanson, Abraham (por), 1949, Ap 25,23:4
Hymer, John B, 1953, Je 18,32:1
Hymer, Warren (por), 1948, Mr 27,13:5
Hymers, William D, 1937, S 20,23:2
Hymes, Edward, 1938, Mr 15,II,6:8
Hymes, Edward Jr, 1962, O 18,39:4
Hymes, Maurice J, 1944, Je 29,23:2
Hymovich, Leo, 1967, O 24,47:3
Hyna, William Sr, 1943, Ap 22,23:3
Hynard, Gilbert N, 1944, My 20,15:3
Hynard, Samuel Mrs, 1951, Ag 31,15:1
Hyndmam, Rosalind Traukers Mrs, 1923, Ap 10,21:4
Hyndman, Edward Sr, 1953, D 15,39:3
Hyndman, Henry M, 1921, N 23,15:4
Hyndman, Matthew J, 1949, N 27,104:4
Hyndman, William C H Judge, 1919, S 25,15:6
Hynds, Harold D, 1966, Jl 3,34:6
Hynds, William M, 1948, Ja 30,23:1
Hyne, J Cutcliffe, 1944, Mr 11,13:5
Hynek Franciszek, 1958, S 10,8:6
Hyneman, Edwin I, 1946, Ag 4,46:1
Hyneman, Herman L, 1907, D 24,7:6
Hyneman, L, 1879, F 27,3:2
Hyneman, Ruth, 1942, Ap 25,13:4
Hynes, Charles E, 1946, F 13,23:5
Hynes, Charles Mrs, 1949, Ja 11,27:3
Hynes, Edward G Dr, 1925, Mr 16,19:5
Hynes, Edward J, 1943, Ja 21,21:5
Hynes, Eugene J Mrs, 1960, Jl 23,19:3
Hynes, Floyd J, 1965, Je 10,35:1
Hynes, Frank A, 1952, Jl 17,23:4
Hynes, George T, 1952, O 10,25:3

Hynes, J J, 1938, D 2,24:2
Hynes, John L, 1955, F 2,27:4
Hynes, John W Rev, 1953, F 6,20:4
Hynes, Maurice P, 1939, Mr 28,23:4
Hynes, Patrick, 1942, Ag 6,19:5
Hynes, Patrick W, 1950, Ag 9,29:3
Hynes, Richard B, 1945, Mr 22,23:1
Hynes, Thomas, 1903, Jl 27,7:7
Hynes, Thomas J, 1945, D 30,14:7
Hynes, Thomas V, 1941, Ap 1,23:5
Hynes, Thomas V Lt, 1922, N 28,21:6
Hynes, Walter A, 1949, Ag 23,23:2
Hynes, William A Mrs, 1956, Je 8,25:4
Hynes, William F, 1952, My 19,17:4
Hyney, Fayette A, 1948, Je 29,23:1
Hynicka, R K, 1927, F 23,23:5
Hynninen, Paavo J, 1960, My 21,23:6
Hynson, J, 1943, F 13,11:1
Hynson, James N, 1944, O 1,45:1
Hynson, Joseph, 1923, D 4,21:3
Hynson, William G, 1940, S 11,25:3
Hynson, William G Jr, 1950, Je 19,21:6
Hyre, Sarah E Mrs, 1949, O 22,17:4
Hyrne, Edward D, 1942, Mr 14,15:2
Hyser, Charles L, 1954, O 17,84:5
Hyshiver, Solomon, 1947, S 19,23:3
Hyslop, David J, 1949, N 10,31:2
Hyslop, George H, 1965, Je 29,35:1
Hyslop, James H Dr, 1920, Je 18,11:3
Hyslop, John, 1947, N 25,29:1
Hyslop, John Mrs, 1913, N 13,11:5
Hyslop, Josephine F (cor, Je 9,45:2), 1940, Je 8,15:4
Hyvernat, Henry, 1941, My 31,11:4

I

I-See-O Kiowa Indian, 1927, Mr 12,15:3
Iacombe, August L, 1950, O 26,31:3
Iacona, Chris, 1948, Mr 19,25:2
Iaconnetti, Carlo, 1924, Je 28,13:4
Iacopeta, Samuel Mrs, 1946, D 14,15:4
Iaeger, W G W Col, 1903, Jl 16,7:6
Iams, Ross L, 1952, Mr 31,19:2
Iams, Samuel H, 1941, Ja 19,40:8
Ianiri, John C, 1964, Je 18,35:4
Iannaccone, Constantino, 1952, Jl 19,15:4
Iannarone, Liberatore, 1963, D 8,86:1
Iannelli, Alfonso, 1965, Mr 26,35:1
Iannucci, Marino, 1953, N 17,31:4
I'Anson, Joseph D, 1947, Ap 5,19:4
Iarussi, Michael, 1942, N 4,24:2
Iason, Jacob M, 1946, D 22,42:1
Iavicoli, Frank, 1950, Jl 25,27:3
Iba, Zylfa Mrs, 1954, N 26,29:3
Ibanez, Vicente Blasco Mrs, 1925, Ja 22,19:5
Ibanez del Campo, Carlos, 1960, Ap 29,31:1
Ibargueren, Carlos, 1956, Ap 5,29:2
Ibarra Garcia, Oscar, 1949, Jl 27,23:5
Ibaugh, Charles M, 1951, Jl 4,17:6
Ibbotson, Edward D Mrs, 1944, D 23,13:6
Ibbotson, Joseph D, 1952, Jl 1,23:3
Iberlucea, E del Valle Sen, 1921, Ag 31,13:5
Ibert, Jacques, 1962, F 7,37:1
Ibn Abdul Rahman, Mohamet, 1943, Jl 28,15:6
Ibn Saud, Abdul Aziz King of Saudi Arabia (cor D 18,40:4), 1953, N 10,1:4
Ibrahim Halim, Prince of Egypt, 1951, S 25,29:3
Ibscher, Hugo, 1943, My 29,13:5
Ibsen, Henrik (funl plans, My 26,11:4), 1906, My 24, 9:1
Ibsen, Henrik Mrs, 1914, Ap 4,15:5
Icely, Lawrence B, 1950, Ag 9,29:5
Ichelson, Rose R, 1961, D 21,27:2
Ichikava, Sadanji, 1940, F 23,15:4
Ichikawa, Hikotaro, 1946, Ap 4,25:2
Ichimura, Kiyoshi, 1968, D 17,47:2
Ichimura, Uzaemon, 1945, My 9,23:5
Iciek, Stanislus A, 1944, Mr 18,13:3
Ickelheimer, Henry R, 1940, D 9,19:4
Ickes, H L Mrs, 1935, S 1,1:4
Ickes, Harold L, 1952, F 4,1:6
Ickes, Howard R, 1938, Ag 27,13:6
Ickes, Paul A, 1950, Mr 13,21:1
Ickes, Sydney F, 1945, D 14,27:3
Icove, Samuel J, 1953, Jl 24,13:5
Iddesleigh, Earl of (Sir Stafford Hy Northcote), 1887, Ja 13,1:1
Iddings, Carl, 1962, Mr 8,31:3
Iddings, John W, 1952, O 23,31:5
Iddings, Lewis Morris, 1921, D 28,15:6
Iddings, Paul L, 1951, F 14,29:5
Iddins, Harry, 1940, Ag 6,20:4
Ide, A Harris, 1943, O 16,13:2
Ide, Alexandra L B Mrs, 1938, Mr 6,II,8:7
Ide, Charles E, 1959, Ag 19,29:1
Ide, Charles W, 1903, N 3,7:6
Ide, Edwin D, 1938, N 3,23:4
Ide, Edwin E, 1939, Ja 4,21:2
Ide, George E Adm, 1917, F 13,11:5
Ide, George Edward (funl, Jl 13,22:5), 1919, Jl 10, 15:3
Ide, George H, 1942, Jl 27,15:4
Ide, George P Jr, 1954, Ja 19,26:3
Ide, Henry C, 1921, Je 14,15:3
Ide, Henry C Mrs, 1957, Ap 29,25:3
Ide, Henry E, 1913, S 3,9:4
Ide, Herbert S Mrs, 1950, Mr 12,92:4
Ide, James M, 1923, Mr 3,13:4
Ide, Jesse A, 1923, Mr 3,13:4
Ide, John J, 1962, Ja 13,21:1
Ide, Joseph H, 1965, D 9,47:2
Ide, Laverne M, 1914, My 18,9:6
Ide, Misao, 1943, My 30,26:1
Ide, Robert Leonard, 1916, My 11,11:6
Ideda, Torajiro, 1939, F 9,21:4
Idell, Albert E, 1958, Jl 8,27:4
Idelsohn, Abra Z, 1938, Ag 15,15:4
Idelson, Idel, 1943, Ja 16,13:6
Ides, Orestes D, 1963, Ag 5,29:5
Idleman, Finis S (por), 1941, Mr 23,45:1
Idler, Edwin, 1953, Ag 17,15:1
dler, Frank G, 1947, N 27,32:2
dler, Herman C, 1951, Je 19,29:2
dler, Percy B D, 1945, S 4,23:3
doate, Camilo, 1941, Ja 1,23:4
donas, Angelo, 1958, Jl 17,27:4
driss, Moulay Prince (Dec 21), 1963, Ap 1,35:8
enni, Phil F, 1949, N 24,31:5
erardi, Gordon S, 1966, F 18,33:4
evers, John Capt, 1925, Jl 14,21:5
ezzi, Thomas, 1945, O 22,19:4
fft, George N, 1947, Ag 16,13:4
fill, Edward P, 1950, My 26,23:4
fill, James P, 1965, Ja 23,25:3
fill, Walter P, 1951, F 25,87:2

Iftikharuddin, Mian, 1962, Je 7,35:3
Igersheimer, Joseph, 1965, N 8,35:3
Igglesden, Charles, 1949, Je 27,27:2
Iglauer, Charles S, 1954, O 1,23:1
Iglauer, Samuel Mrs, 1958, D 31,19:2
Iglehart, Charles Mrs, 1958, My 22,29:6
Iglehart, Edwin T, 1964, F 2,89:2
Iglehart, Ferdinand C Rev Dr, 1922, Jl 22,7:7
Iglehart, Francis N, 1944, F 22,24:2
Iglehart, Nannie D S Mrs, 1940, My 7,25:2
Iglesias, Antonio, 1953, O 4,88:4
Iglesias, Eudoxia C F Mrs, 1938, Je 25,15:5
Iglesias, Luis S, 1938, D 8,27:3
Iglesias, Pablo, 1919, Je 14,13:5; 1925, D 10,25:5
Iglesias, Santiago, 1939, D 6,25:1
Iglesias, Teofolio A, 1942, Ap 30,19:5
Ignagaki, Rene-Georges, 1967, Mr 3,35:3
Ignatieff, Natalie, 1944, Ag 30,17:3
Ignatieff, Nicholas, 1952, Mr 30,93:2
Ignatieff, Nicholas Pavolich Count, 1908, Jl 5,9:6
Ignatiev, Alexis A, 1954, N 21,86:7
Ignatius, Bro (P Hess), 1959, Ap 8,37:4
Ignatius, Father (Jos Leycester Lyne), 1908, O 17, 9:4
Ignatius, Johannes, 1941, Mr 4,23:3
Ignatius, Milton B, 1966, Ag 11,33:3
Ignatius, Mother (C Wallace), 1952, Ag 4,15:5
Ignatius Ephrem I, Patriarch, 1957, Je 26,31:5
Ignatoff, David, 1954, F 27,13:4
Ignatov, Alex M, 1956, Jl 21,15:4
Ignatov, Nikolai F, 1967, Ap 28,41:1
Ignatov, Nikolai G, 1966, N 15,47:3
Ignelzi, Louis G, 1958, Ja 13,29:4
Igo, James E, 1956, S 24,27:5
Igoe, Charles A, 1965, Jl 21,37:3
Igoe, Florence E Mrs, 1952, Ap 6,90:6
Igoe, Hype (por), 1945, F 12,19:2
Igoe, Margaret, 1941, O 28,23:4
Igoe, Mary S Mrs, 1925, Jl 19,7:3
Igoe, Michael J, 1943, Jl 13,10:7
Igoe, Peter J, 1962, Mr 24,25:5
Igoe, Peter Mrs, 1956, Ap 5,29:3
Igoe, William L, 1953, Ap 21,27:5
Igstaedter, Oscar, 1937, S 28,23:5
Igumnov, Konstantin N, 1948, Mr 26,22:2
Ihde, Herman, 1943, Mr 7,38:4
Ihle, Leo, 1956, S 3,13:4
Ihlefeld, Minnie, 1946, Ap 10,27:4
Ihmsen, Max F, 1921, My 5,17:5
Ihnen, William G, 1954, Jl 9,17:1
Ihrig, Adolph, 1951, F 28,27:3
Ihrig, Roscoe M, 1940, N 24,51:2
Iiams, Thomas M, 1959, Ag 23,92:5
Iida, Hisatsune, 1956, O 17,35:1
Ijams, George E, 1964, Mr 23,29:5
Ijams, J Horton, 1957, Mr 12,33:4
Ijanatti, Theresa Mrs, 1924, Ag 22,13:6
Ijuin, Goro Adm, 1921, Ja 15,13:2
Ikawa, Tadao, 1947, F 20,26:3
Ikeda, Hayato (funl plans, Ag 14,23:1; funl, Ag 18,-35:5), 1965, Ag 13,1:8
Ikeda, Seihin, 1950, O 9,25:1
Ikelheimer, Ida, 1937, Ag 24,22:1
Ikelheimer, Julius B, 1947, D 11,33:5
Ikerd, Stanley, 1952, Ag 30,13:4
Ikier, Edward E, 1957, O 31,31:4
Ikki, Kitokuro, 1944, D 18,19:2
Ikle, Charles F, 1963, O 21,31:4
Ikramullah, Mohammad, 1963, S 14,25:4
Ilberg, Frederick W K Dr, 1916, Jl 11,9:7
Ilcewicz, Wladyslaw, 1957, O 2,33:2
Ilch, Alfred D, 1954, Ap 2,27:2
Ilch, Alfred P, 1963, Je 17,25:3
Ilchester, Earl of (G S H Fox-Strangways), 1959, O 30,27:1
Ildefonse Lambing, Sister, 1937, Jl 28,19:1
Ildephonsus Damian, Bro, 1952, Jl 30,24:7
Iler, George H, 1948, Ag 12,21:2
Iler, Henry C, 1950, D 1,25:1
Iles, Alfred H, 1946, S 20,31:5
Iles, Edmisten W, 1944, Ap 5,19:2
Iles, George, 1942, O 4,53:1
Iles, John H, 1951, My 30,22:2
Iley, Harold R, 1951, N 19,23:3
Ilf, Ilya, 1937, Ap 15,23:4
Ilg, Henry P L, 1948, Je 22,25:3
Ilg, John C, 1965, Jl 10,25:5
Ilg, Joseph A, 1949, Ja 21,21:4
Ilgenfritz, Carl A, 1967, S 12,47:2
Ilgenfritz, Edwin K, 1958, My 14,33:4
Ilgenfritz, McNair (will, My 31,64:5), 1953, Ap 14, 27:6
Ilgenfritz, Wilbur F, 1942, Je 8,15:5
Iliff, David G, 1953, Ja 1,23:3
Iliff, John, 1880, F 13,4:7; 1956, O 27,21:5
Iliff, William L, 1951, F 5,23:4
Iliffe of Yattendon, Baron (Edgar M Iliffe), 1960, Jl 26,29:3
Ilinger, Albert, 1940, Ag 1,21:4

Ilinski, Janusz, 1961, Je 17,21:3
Ilkeston, Lord (B S S Foster), 1952, Ja 5,11:2
Ilkowitz, Simon Mrs, 1965, Jl 11,68:7
Ill, Bernard J, 1955, F 6,88:7
Ill, Carl H, 1943, Mr 29,15:4
Ill, Charles L, 1939, My 5,23:5
Ill, Edmund W, 1950, Ap 3,2:4
Ill, Edward J, 1942, Je 10,21:4
Ill, Edward J 2d Mrs, 1960, Ag 4,25:4
Ill, Ida, 1949, Je 15,29:1
Illanes, Gregory H, 1943, S 11,13:4
Illas, Arturo, 1947, N 24,23:3
Illava, Karl, 1954, My 17,23:4
Illch, Julius, 1946, F 28,23:3
Ille, F Wilson, 1949, Mr 23,27:3
Illein, Anton F Sr, 1950, My 9,29:5
Illera, Arthur E, 1956, D 16,86:2
Illia, Arturo U Mrs, 1966, S 6,47:3
Illiano, Emilio, 1944, My 3,19:2
Illica, Luigi, 1919, D 18,13:4
Illich, Nicholas, 1939, O 26,23:3
Illing, Meta, 1909, D 27,7:6
Illing, Theodore J, 1945, My 16,19:1
Illingsworth, Benjamin, 1914, F 24,11:5
Illington, M, 1934, Mr 12,17:1
Illingworth, George C, 1945, Ap 2,19:3
Illingworth, Gordon, 1959, Ag 9,89:2
Illingworth, Lord, 1942, Ja 25,40:3
Illingworth, Minnie D Mrs, 1938, Jl 22,17:5
Illingworth, Percy, 1915, Ja 4,11:5
Illingworth, Robert H, 1922, Ap 25,17:5
Illions, Harry A Mrs, 1950, Ja 12,28:2
Illions, Marcus C, 1949, Ag 14,68:5
Illman, G Morton, 1956, F 14,29:3
Illman, Paul E, 1952, O 9,31:1
Illman, Robert I B, 1951, Ja 4,29:2
Illmer, Louis, 1958, Jl 19,15:7
Illowizi, Henry Dr, 1911, Ap 21,11:5
Illsley, William A, 1945, Ja 3,17:1
Ilsemann, Sigurd W, 1952, Je 8,86:3
Ilsen, Elizabeth G Mrs, 1938, Ja 18,23:4
Ilsen, Martin, 1946, O 26,17:6
Ilsey, Silas A Col, 1918, Ja 10,13:3
Ilsley, Catherine Mrs, 1940, N 6,23:4
Ilsley, Francis G Rev, 1925, Jl 27,13:5
Ilsley, George E, 1951, Ap 10,27:1
Ilsley, Henry R, 1948, N 14,76:1
Ilsley, J P, 1902, Ja 16,9:5
Ilsley, James L, 1967, Ja 15,84:5
Ilsley, L C, 1945, N 24,19:6
Ilsley, William, 1945, N 27,23:5
Iltis, Charles H Jr, 1952, D 22,17:6
Iltis, H M, 1957, S 6,21:4
Iltis, Hugo, 1952, Je 23,19:5
Ilton, Alfred I, 1960, My 19,37:5
Ilton, Paul, 1958, Ja 13,29:2
Ilundain y Esteban, Eustace Cardinal (por), 1937, Ag 11,23:5
Ilychev, Alex, 1952, Mr 3,21:1
Ilyin, Peter A, 1950, Je 30,23:4
Imai, Toshimior, 1959, Je 16,35:4
Imaizumi, Teisuke, 1944, S 13,19:2
Imamura, Akitsune, 1948, Ja 3,14:3
Imatz, Charles, 1938, D 8,21:3
Imbach, Gertrude, 1951, Jl 1,50:4
Imber, Naphtall Herz (funl, O 11,9:4), 1909, O 9,9:4
Imbernon, Anacleto A, 1940, S 14,17:5
Imbert, Louis E, 1956, My 20,86:8
Imbert, Paul, 1948, My 13,2:4
Imbert-Terry, Henry, 1938, Ja 4,23:3
Imbleau, Joseph E L, 1955, Ja 15,13:3
Imboden, Daniel C, 1965, N 14,88:6
Imboden, Harry M, 1951, Je 15,23:3
Imboden, Henry M, 1963, Je 11,37:3
Imbrey, Fred E, 1937, Je 10,23:4
Imbrey, S Howard, 1948, Jl 4,27:2
Imbrie, Andrew C, 1965, Ag 22,83:1
Imbrie, Charles K, 1958, Je 27,25:1
Imbrie, William M, 1937, Mr 25,25:1; 1945, Ap 30,19:2
Imchanitzky, Michael J, 1945, O 23,19:7
Imelda Teresa, Sister (Susan Swift), 1916, Ap 24,13:5
Imelis, Oskar, 1954, Ja 10,86:1
Imes, Benjamin A Mrs, 1944, N 21,25:3
Imes, Birney, 1947, Je 19,21:1
Imes, Elmer S, 1941, S 12,22:2
Imes, G Lake Mrs, 1957, Ja 22,29:1
Imhof, Adolf E, 1956, F 25,19:6
Imhof, Lawrence W, 1968, F 28,47:4
Imhof, Roger, 1958, Ap 18,23:4
Imhoff, Berthold, 1939, D 21,26:6
Imhoff, Joseph M, 1944, F 12,13:2
Imhoff, Max Dr, 1937, Ja 21,23:3
Imig, Heinrich, 1956, F 25,19:5
Imlay, Edward, 1943, Ja 9,13:5
Imlay, Eugene L, 1952, N 10,25:2
Imlay, Joseph L, 1951, Mr 9,25:5
Imlay, Lrin E, 1941, Je 10,23:3
Immaculate, Sister (Order of St Benedict), 1960, Jl 19,29:3

Immanuel, Max, 1951, D 10,29:5
Immediato, Gerardo, 1939, O 23,19:3
Immediato, Ralph J, 1950, Ja 9,25:5
Immel, Harry D, 1958, Ap 1,31:4
Immel, John H, 1946, My 21,23:4
Immel, Ray K, 1945, Ap 14,15:5
Immen, Charles D, 1949, Ja 14,23:4
Immen, Chris Mrs, 1953, Ap 9,27:1
Immerglueck, Arthur, 1949, Ap 6,29:2
Immerman, Connie, 1967, O 25,47:1
Immerman, George Mrs, 1963, Ag 15,29:1
Immerman, Joseph, 1950, Ja 6,21:3
Immerman, Saul, 1945, D 15,17:4
Immerman, Walter R, 1950, D 4,29:2
Imms, A D, 1949, Ap 5,29:4
Imparato, Giovanni, 1957, Ag 27,29:1
Impekoven, Anton, 1947, My 22,27:2
Impellitteri, Gaetano R (Thomas), 1953, Ja 1,23:5
Impellitteri, Joseph, 1949, Mr 6,73:1
Impellitteri, Vincent Mrs (funl, My 30,21:3), 1967, My 27,31:1
Impellittiere, Ray, 1967, Ag 23,45:1
Imperato, Forest, 1961, Ja 1,48:5
Imperatore, John J, 1945, S 5,23:5
Imperatori, Charles J, 1949, Je 17,23:3
Imperiale, Cesare Marquis, 1940, Ap 24,23:3
Impey, Arthur E Mrs (L Cotton), 1962, O 10,47:4
Impey, Arthur W, 1944, Ja 16,42:4
Imray, Edith P Mrs, 1939, Ap 22,17:5
Imray, Howard H, 1943, Je 5,15:2
Imrie, Daniel F, 1955, Jl 19,27:3
Imrie, George T, 1943, Ag 30,15:5
Imrie, John H, 1953, Jl 7,27:4
Imrie, John M, 1942, Je 20,13:4
Imrie, Margaret B, 1941, Ap 25,19:6
Imwolde, Herman F, 1947, S 10,27:1
Inaguet, Alfred Joseph, 1916, N 12,23:2
Inarra, Paul, 1948, D 27,21:4
Inaudi, Jacques, 1950, N 28,31:4
Inayatullah Khan, Sirdar, 1946, Ag 15,25:4
Inbusch, Edward H, 1944, S 1,13:2
Incababian, Jacob, 1913, F 28,13:5
Ince, Alexander (mem ser set, Ja 28,47:4), 1966, Ja 29,33:2
Ince, Charles R, 1964, Ap 12,86:7
Ince, Godfrey, 1960, D 21,31:1
Ince, John, 1947, Ap 11,25:5
Ince, John E, 1909, Ja 20,9:4
Ince, John E Mrs, 1952, Jl 29,21:1
Ince, John F, 1941, O 31,23:1
Inch, George F, 1938, N 30,23:2
Inch, Richard Rear-Adm, 1911, Ap 22,13:6
Inch, Robert A, 1961, Ja 13,29:1
Inch, Sydney R, 1964, Mr 13,34:1
Inch, Thomas T, 1962, O 31,37:4
Inchape, Lord, 1932, My 24,19:3
Inchcape, Lord, 1939, Je 21,23:4
Inches, Henderson, 1947, Jl 19,13:3
Inchiquin, Baron of (Donough Edw Foster O'Brien), 1968, O 20,86:3
Inclan, Miguel, 1956, Jl 28,17:2
Inculetz, Ion, 1940, N 20,21:2
Indahl, Mauritz C, 1941, Ja 26,36:2
Inderlied, Clarence, 1944, My 28,33:1
Indian Chief, George Capt, 1873, S 26,5:4
Indick, Mandel I, 1950, Ag 12,13:5
Indiverci, Anna Mrs, 1954, Jl 4,1:1
Indjeian, Matheos, 1950, Jl 28,21:5
Indore, Maharaja of (Yeshwant Rao Holkar), 1961, D 6,47:2
Indorf, John F, 1946, N 22,23:2
Indy, V d', 1931, D 4,23:1
Infantado, Duke, 1947, Ja 5,53:7
Infante, Pedro (funl, Ap 18,11:2), 1957, Ap 16,10:5
Infeld, Leopold Dr, 1968, Ja 17,51:2
Infeld, Lydia H, 1965, Mr 5,33:1
Infield, Gerald L, 1957, Ag 2,19:4
Infosino, Carmelo J, 1961, N 20,31:5
Ing, Z T Mrs, 1947, Jl 19,13:6
Ingalabe, Maurice C, 1960, F 27,19:1
Ingall, C Milo, 1942, Mr 8,43:1
Ingallis, Arthur Mrs, 1945, D 2,46:2
Ingalls, Albert G, 1958, Ag 15,22:7
Ingalls, Albert S, 1943, Ag 9,13:6
Ingalls, Albert S Jr, 1955, My 6,23:3
Ingalls, Albert S Sr Mrs, 1962, Mr 31,25:5
Ingalls, Blair C, 1940, F 25,39:3
Ingalls, Charles A, 1949, My 10,25:2
Ingalls, Charles H, 1925, S 29,27:5
Ingalls, Claude E, 1950, Ag 9,29:1
Ingalls, Clyde, 1940, Mr 18,17:3
Ingalls, E L, 1953, Ja 13,27:4
Ingalls, Edith M, 1952, O 23,31:2
Ingalls, Ernest K Mrs, 1940, Jl 11,19:4
Ingalls, Ezra J Mrs, 1955, O 11,39:3
Ingalls, Fay, 1957, N 25,31:3
Ingalls, Fay Mrs, 1966, O 3,50:3
Ingalls, Frederick A, 1938, D 13,25:3
Ingalls, Frederick W, 1959, F 1,84:5
Ingalls, G H, 1931, Je 15,19:3
Ingalls, G Howard, 1959, Ja 19,27:4
Ingalls, George H Mrs, 1958, Ap 20,84:4
Ingalls, Henry A Brig-Gen, 1937, Mr 30,23:1
Ingalls, Herbert F, 1951, Mr 24,13:4
Ingalls, J Kibben, 1938, Ja 11,23:5
Ingalls, James Warren Dr, 1922, S 29,19:6
Ingalls, John J Sen, 1900, Ag 17,9:5
Ingalls, Louis S Mrs, 1956, F 7,31:4
Ingalls, Melville E, 1914, Jl 12,5:5
Ingalls, Melville E Jr, 1922, S 23,15:5
Ingalls, Ralph M, 1941, Mr 3,15:2
Ingalls, Robert I Sr, 1951, Jl 13,21:5
Ingalls, Sheffield, 1937, Ja 19,23:4
Ingalsbe, Harvey D Mrs, 1946, Ag 17,13:5
Ingamellis, Rex, 1955, D 31,5:6
Ingate, Salvatore J, 1965, F 28,88:4
Ingber, David A, 1961, O 28,21:3
Ingber, Isaac W, 1960, D 16,33:3
Ingber, Isaac W Mrs, 1948, N 10,29:4
Inge, Alfred, 1953, Jl 8,27:3
Inge, John C, 1946, Ap 2,27:3
Inge, W R Mrs, 1949, Ap 24,76:1
Inge, William R (funl, Mr 3,27:2), 1954, F 27,13:1
Ingeborg, Princess of Sweden (funl, Mr 20,29:1), 1958, Mr 13,29:2
Ingebrethsen, Christian Mrs, 1944, F 29,17:4
Ingebretsen, Carl, 1943, Jl 14,19:5
Ingebretsen, Hans B, 1951, Mr 6,27:5
Ingebretsen, Herman S, 1961, N 14,36:2
Ingebretsen, James A, 1940, Je 18,23:5
Ingebretsen, Jens I, 1950, Ag 3,23:3
Ingebretsen, Jens Mrs, 1948, Mr 4,25:5
Ingebritsen, Otis C, 1958, My 13,29:2
Ingelow, Jean, 1897, Jl 21,5:2
Ingels, Edward V, 1959, Je 30,31:3
Ingels, Howard P, 1951, Je 1,26:2
Ingelson, Reinhold N, 1939, My 16,23:4
Ingen, Bernard J Mrs, 1944, O 20,19:3
Ingenieros, Jose Dr, 1925, N 2,23:5
Ingenohl, F von, 1933, D 20,22:3
Ingerbretsen, Carl T, 1955, Ap 27,31:5
Ingerman, Sergius (por), 1943, F 19,19:3
Ingersley, Kay, 1945, Jl 15,15:5
Ingersoll, Adelaide M C Mrs, 1942, O 1,23:4
Ingersoll, Albert C Jr, 1965, S 1,24:7
Ingersoll, Andrew J, 1944, O 27,23:5
Ingersoll, Benjamin C, 1945, D 7,21:3
Ingersoll, C Jared Mrs, 1939, Ja 22,34:7
Ingersoll, C R Ex-Gov, 1903, Ja 26,9:6
Ingersoll, Charles A, 1941, D 25,25:1
Ingersoll, Charles A Judge, 1860, F 9,2:6
Ingersoll, Charles Dennis, 1905, Ja 9,7:4
Ingersoll, Charles E Mrs, 1944, Ap 19,23:2
Ingersoll, Colin M, 1948, Ap 8,25:2
Ingersoll, Colin McCrae, 1903, S 14,7:5
Ingersoll, E C, 1879, Je 3,1:2
Ingersoll, E Rev, 1883, F 7,5:5
Ingersoll, Edward Mrs, 1961, Mr 15,39:3
Ingersoll, Edward P Rev, 1907, F 6,9:6
Ingersoll, Ernest (por), 1946, N 14,29:1
Ingersoll, Ernest, 1949, Ap 15,23:2
Ingersoll, Ernest Mrs, 1953, Ap 24,23:4
Ingersoll, Eva A Mrs, 1923, F 3,13:4
Ingersoll, Francis G Mrs, 1943, Ap 12,23:4
Ingersoll, Frank Mrs, 1950, Jl 26,25:5
Ingersoll, Franklin D, 1954, Jl 14,27:2
Ingersoll, G, 1903, S 30,9:6
Ingersoll, G P, 1927, F 24,23:5
Ingersoll, Genevra, 1941, Ja 18,15:4
Ingersoll, George R, 1950, My 30,17:4
Ingersoll, Grace, 1947, O 17,21:1
Ingersoll, Hamilton, 1940, D 24,15:2
Ingersoll, Herbert C, 1947, Ag 2,13:5
Ingersoll, Howard L, 1943, S 14,23:2
Ingersoll, Hubert J, 1947, Ag 1,17:2
Ingersoll, J C, 1903, Je 7,4:3
Ingersoll, James W D Prof, 1921, Ap 20,13:6
Ingersoll, Jeremiah C, 1961, D 13,43:3
Ingersoll, John A, 1954, Mr 24,27:1
Ingersoll, John H W, 1967, S 23,31:4
Ingersoll, John W, 1945, S 27,21:3
Ingersoll, Mary E Mrs, 1964, D 26,17:4
Ingersoll, Oliver R, 1914, Ja 10,9:5
Ingersoll, R I, 1928, S 6,25:3
Ingersoll, R Sturgis Mrs, 1968, Ap 30,47:2
Ingersoll, Ralph J, 1872, Ag 27,1:5
Ingersoll, Ralph Mrs, 1948, Ap 3,15:4
Ingersoll, Raymond P, 1949, N 29,29:1
Ingersoll, Raymond V, 1940, F 25,1:3
Ingersoll, Robert A, 1950, S 21,31:5
Ingersoll, Robert G, 1899, Jl 22,3:1
Ingersoll, Robert S Jr, 1968, My 24,47:4
Ingersoll, Roy C, 1966, F 1,35:1
Ingersoll, Samuel Mrs, 1908, Ag 7,5:4
Ingersoll, Somers H, 1937, F 21,II,10:7
Ingersoll, Stephen L, 1956, Jl 24,25:2
Ingersoll, Stuart H Mrs, 1964, Ap 5,86:6
Ingersoll, T C, 1884, F 8,2:6
Ingersoll, William E, 1909, Ag 14,7:6
Ingersoll, William H, 1946, Ag 25,46:1
Ingersoll, William M, 1947, Jl 25,18:2
Ingerson, Walter C, 1947, D 30,24:3
Ingerson, William E, 1968, S 24,47:2
Ingerton, Phil S, 1951, Jl 9,25:5
Ingham, Charles S, 1949, Je 16,29:5
Ingham, Clara N Mrs, 1946, F 15,25:1
Ingham, Clark L, 1954, Ja 9,15:3
Ingham, Edward T, 1948, Ja 5,19:5
Ingham, Harriet, 1959, My 20,35:3
Ingham, Harry G, 1948, Ag 28,16:2
Ingham, Harry S, 1955, Ap 5,29:2
Ingham, Harvey (por), 1949, Ag 22,21:3
Ingham, Harvey Sr Mrs, 1951, O 30,29:2
Ingham, John A (por), 1944, Mr 21,19:4
Ingham, John A Mrs, 1954, Mr 21,89:2
Ingham, John H, 1954, N 12,21:1
Ingham, Lucius E, 1957, Mr 4,27:2
Ingham, Mary H, 1937, Ja 2,11:4
Ingham, Samuel, 1881, N 11,5:1
Ingham, Thomas, 1957, N 25,31:4
Ingham, William A, 1967, N 28,51:5
Ingham, William H, 1943, N 18,23:4
Inghelbrecht, Desire E, 1965, F 15,27:4
Ingle, Arthur H, 1954, Jl 2,19:4
Ingle, Edward T, 1958, Mr 22,17:3
Ingle, Henry B, 1941, Ag 13,17:5
Ingle, J Addison Bp, 1903, D 8,9:4
Ingle, John, 1937, D 3,23:4
Ingle, William O, 1943, S 3,19:3
Inglee, Abner B, 1941, F 11,23:2
Inglee, Charles T (por), 1941, Ap 4,21:3
Inglee, Charles T Mrs, 1939, Je 24,17:5
Inglee, Charles W, 1950, S 9,17:4
Inglee, Clinton, 1946, D 22,41:1
Inglee, Minnie Mrs, 1952, O 16,29:2
Inglee, William B, 1949, O 25,27:5
Inglee, Willis B, 1950, Jl 22,15:4
Inglehart, Asa Stewart Dr, 1916, Mr 21,11:6
Inglehart, George G, 1955, S 21,33:2
Ingles, Elsie Dr, 1918, F 11,9:5
Ingles, Robert T, 1950, F 2,21:4
Inglesby, John T, 1963, D 27,23:3
Inglesh, Arthur E Mrs, 1946, Ja 13,44:3
Ingling, Evangeline L, 1952, Mr 31,19:2
Inglis, Alexander James, 1924, Ap 13,27:4
Inglis, Cornelia B, 1949, D 31,15:1
Inglis, D Rev (see also D 16), 1877, D 19,8:2
Inglis, David I, 1954, S 9,32:4
Inglis, Edward S, 1946, S 22,60:5
Inglis, Edwin B, 1950, F 14,26:2
Inglis, Edwin B Mrs, 1949, Ag 21,69:1
Inglis, Elizabeth, 1948, S 12,74:2
Inglis, Franklin P, 1955, D 16,30:2
Inglis, George D, 1908, O 25,13:3
Inglis, J A, 1878, Ag 27,1:2
Inglis, Jack, 1938, Ap 28,23:5
Inglis, James, 1950, Mr 17,23:4
Inglis, James F, 1956, F 3,23:4
Inglis, James Smith, 1907, D 14,9:4
Inglis, John J, 1946, S 4,23:5
Inglis, Lindsay M, 1966, Mr 18,39:1
Inglis, Nora R M Mrs, 1937, S 10,23:4
Inglis, Robert S (por), 1949, My 22,88:4
Inglis, Warren W Sr, 1949, D 21,30:2
Inglis, William O, 1949, S 22,31:6
Inglis, William W, 1953, Ja 20,25:1
Ingman, Ralph, 1940, Ag 4,33:3
Ingold, Robert L, 1956, O 4,33:1
Ingold, William F, 1958, Ag 25,21:5
Ingraham, Andrew C, 1960, D 19,27:3
Ingraham, Arthur, 1914, D 2,13:5
Ingraham, Arthur Sr Mrs, 1957, Ja 1,23:2
Ingraham, Corinne V Mrs, 1940, N 29,21:2
Ingraham, D P, 1881, D 14,5:1
Ingraham, D Phoenix, 1915, Ap 9,11:5
Ingraham, E Morton, 1945, Ag 24,19:1
Ingraham, Edgar B, 1965, D 7,47:3
Ingraham, Edward, 1949, O 28,23:4
Ingraham, Edward Mrs, 1951, F 20,25:4
Ingraham, Edyth Newcomb, 1906, My 10,9:4
Ingraham, Elmer, 1944, O 16,19:4
Ingraham, Franc D, 1965, D 7,47:1
Ingraham, Frances T (will), 1942, Ag 22,10:2
Ingraham, G L, 1931, Ja 25,28:1
Ingraham, George, 1912, My 13,9:6; 1951, Mr 5,2
Ingraham, George L Mrs, 1937, D 24,20:2
Ingraham, George S, 1944, Jl 19,19:5
Ingraham, Harold C, 1950, F 26,76:7
Ingraham, Harry E, 1954, Ap 6,30:4
Ingraham, Henry A, 1962, S 20,34:1
Ingraham, Henry C M, 1911, F 17,9:5
Ingraham, Herbert R Rev, 1968, N 3,88:7
Ingraham, John H Maj, 1937, Ja 19,23:4
Ingraham, Lloyd, 1956, Ap 5,29:5
Ingraham, Norman R, 1944, S 22,19:5
Ingraham, Orange S, 1940, Jl 24,21:4
Ingraham, P, 1934, My 1,24:1
Ingraham, Robert G, 1957, F 26,29:1
Ingraham, Rosa L Mrs, 1941, F 5,19:3
Ingraham, Symmes H, 1947, Mr 8,13:3
Ingraham, Th H, 1904, My 28,1:6
Ingraham, Walter A, 1939, F 26,39:3
Ingraham, William A (por), 1943, Je 3,21:5
Ingraham, William M, 1908, Je 9,7:6; 1951, O 13,
Ingraham, William W Jr, 1957, Ag 27,29:4
Ingram, Alfred O, 1956, Jl 12,23:5
Ingram, Augustus E, 1937, N 11,25:2
Ingram, Bruce, 1963, Ja 9,8:3
Ingram, Carl E, 1948, Mr 3,24:2

Ingram, Clarence J, 1956, Ja 1,51:1
Ingram, E W (Billy), 1966, Mr 21,31:2
Ingram, Edward L, 1938, Jl 26,19:5
Ingram, Franklin, 1909, Jl 28,9:4
Ingram, George O, 1961, Jl 14,23:5
Ingram, Harry, 1952, Mr 18,27:4
Ingram, Harry M, 1939, N 17,21:4
Ingram, Henry H, 1942, Jl 24,20:2
Ingram, Herbert E, 1965, F 17,43:5
Ingram, Horace C, 1946, D 1,76:2
Ingram, Ira M, 1938, Ag 12,17:3
Ingram, James, 1914, Je 8,7:5
Ingram, James F, 1951, Jl 16,21:5
Ingram, John C, 1960, F 27,19:2
Ingram, John Kells, 1907, My 2,11:6
Ingram, John L, 1955, O 9,87:3
Ingram, John S, 1947, Ag 27,23:4
Ingram, Jonas H, 1952, S 11,31:1
Ingram, Marshall, 1945, F 28,23:5
Ingram, Orrin H, 1963, Ap 27,25:5
Ingram, Peter T, 1948, D 21,31:1
Ingram, Rev Dr, 1879, Mr 24,2:7
Ingram, Rex, 1950, Jl 23,57:1
Ingram, Thomas R, 1944, Ja 17,19:5
Ingram, Tolbert R, 1960, Ja 18,27:4
Ingram, Walt, 1959, O 27,44:3
Ingram, William D, 1939, N 26,43:2
Ingram, William H, 1954, Mr 5,19:2
Ingram, William T, 1939, Ja 24,19:4
Ingram, William T Mrs, 1957, F 18,27:1
Ingram, Winfield S, 1938, Ag 24,21:3
Ingrassia, Frank, 1947, D 9,29:3
Ingrish, George A, 1946, D 18,29:2
Ings, Walter, 1947, N 21,27:1
Ingwersen, Charles, 1903, N 21,9:6
Ingwersen, Harry E, 1968, Je 22,33:3
Ingwersen, Louis, 1903, Je 23,7:6
Ingwerson, Timothy H, 1963, My 25,25:5
Inhulsen, John, 1956, Je 9,17:5
Iniguez, Leonor G, 1941, O 31,23:2
Inke, Sheldon A, 1958, S 27,21:5
Inloes, Orion E, 1949, Ag 9,25:1
Inman, Albert H, 1948, Ag 23,17:3
Inman, Charles M, 1940, Ap 20,17:2
Inman, Charles S, 1946, Ag 3,15:3
Inman, Eber L, 1946, Ap 7,46:2
Inman, Edward K, 1956, S 4,29:3
Inman, Eli G Mrs, 1945, Ag 7,24:3
Inman, Frank A, 1949, D 28,32:2
Inman, Harry A, 1945, My 11,19:5
Inman, Horace J, 1953, My 24,88:2
Inman, Hugh T, 1910, N 16,11:5
Inman, J H, 1896, N 6,1:7
Inman, Melbourne, 1951, Ag 12,78:6
Inman, Ondess L, 1942, Jl 22,19:4
Inman, Robert G, 1962, Ag 30,29:4
Inman, Samuel G, 1965, F 21,77:1
Inman, Samuel M, 1915, Ja 13,9:3
Inman, W, 1881, Jl 7,5:3
Inman, Walker P, 1954, S 20,23:3
Inman, Walker P (overdose of barbituates, Mr 19,-35:5; inq set), 1955, Mr 18,4:6
Inman, William Commodore, 1874, O 24,7:3
Inman, William P, 1959, N 22,86:4
Inman, Willie L, 1951, Ja 5,21:1
Innecken, Gustave A Mrs, 1950, F 23,27:3
Innecken, Herman C, 1946, F 20,25:5
Innerarity, Lewis A R, 1947, Ag 25,17:5
Innerfield, Irving L, 1965, S 4,21:5
Innes, Charles H, 1939, My 28,III,7:4
Innes, Colin W, 1964, D 5,31:5
Innes, Edward K Mrs, 1958, O 6,31:4
Innes, Elizabeth R, 1939, F 6,13:5
Innes, Frank H (por), 1947, Ap 8,27:1
Innes, James, 1957, My 25,24:6
Innes, John, 1941, Ja 14,21:4
Innes, Otto G, 1959, Jl 10,25:3
Innes, T Christie Mrs, 1948, Mr 13,15:2
Innes, W (Scotty), 1954, Je 25,21:1
Innes, William C C, 1948, O 8,25:2
Innes, William M, 1941, Jl 24,17:7
Innes, William T Mrs, 1950, Ap 6,29:3
Innes-Brown, Charles, 1960, Mr 4,25:1
Inness, Eliza M, 1941, N 11,23:4
Inness, G Jr, 1926, Jl 29,19:5
Inness, Joseph, 1967, N 2,47:1
Inness, Julia G R Mrs, 1941, My 25,36:8
Inness-Brown, Benjamin H, 1957, F 13,35:1
Innet, Edward S, 1939, Mr 17,21:3
Innhausen, Prince, 1908, Ja 17,9:7
Innis, George, 1903, N 27,9:5
Innis, Harold A, 1952, N 9,90:1
Innis, Margaret Mrs, 1939, Je 8,25:4
Innis, Ruth D Mrs, 1939, Jl 8,15:3
Innis, William R, 1920, O 22,15:4
Innis, William R Mrs, 1923, Jl 26,15:4
Innis, William S, 1943, D 3,23:2
Innitzer, Theodor (funl O 15,15:2), 1955, O 9,86:1
Innocenti, Ferdinando, 1966, Je 22,47:2
Innocenti, Umberto, 1968, O 11,47:3
Inouye, Enryo Dr, 1919, Jl 18,11:4
Inouye, Gen, 1908, D 17,9:4
Inouye, Kaoru Marquis, 1915, S 2,9:6
Inouye, Tetsujiro, 1944, D 8,21:4
Inscho, Carson G, 1955, N 14,18:4
Inscho, Jesse, 1947, O 12,76:4
Inscho, Suzie Mrs, 1952, Je 10,27:4
Inselbuch, Samuel, 1962, Jl 30,23:5
Inselbuck, E, 1936, Jl 7,19:6
Inselman, George, 1966, My 2,37:3
Insinger, Frederic N, 1950, Ap 30,102:7
Inskip, Arthur, 1951, D 25,31:2
Inskip, Betty, 1945, Ag 7,24:2
Inskip, J S Rev, 1884, Mr 8,2:7
Inskip, James T, 1949, Ag 7,61:3
Inskip, John S, 1961, S 9,19:4
Inskip, John S Mrs, 1956, Je 20,31:3
Inslee, Clifton W, 1957, Jl 5,18:8
Inslee, Edwin W, 1942, Ja 21,17:2
Inslee, Edwin W Mrs, 1952, N 23,89:1
Inslee, Isaac, 1903, Ag 20,9:6
Inslee, Princilla Ayres, 1914, Ja 31,11:5
Inslee, William L, 1945, Ag 14,21:4
Insler, Bertha, 1956, Mr 29,27:5
Insley, Earle, 1937, O 15,23:4
Insley, Edward, 1924, S 22,19:5
Instenes, Margrette Mrs, 1948, F 11,27:2
Instone, Samuel Sir, 1937, N 10,25:3
Insull, Frederick W, 1939, Ja 15,39:1
Insull, Joseph, 1941, O 13,17:4
Insull, Martin J (por), 1947, My 5,23:3
Insull, Samuel, 1938, Jl 17,1:7
Insull, Samuel J, 1964, Ag 20,29:3
Insull, Samuel Sr Mrs, 1953, S 24,33:5
Intemann, Alfred F Mrs, 1963, S 16,35:3
Intemann, Carl F, 1952, Jl 14,17:4
Intemann, William H, 1939, S 9,17:3
Inten, Ferdinand von, 1918, Ja 17,13:2
Interland, Joseph J, 1949, F 13,76:2
Intermann, John H, 1947, Je 6,23:2
Interrante, Giuseppe, 1941, N 19,23:3
Intner, William, 1964, D 7,35:4
Intorrella, Emanuele, 1948, Jl 25,49:2
Intropidi, Ann Mrs, 1906, Mr 20,9:5
Intropidi, Josie Mrs, 1941, S 20,17:3
Intropidl, Frederick, 1908, Ja 29,7:5
Intropodi, Ethel, 1946, D 19,29:4
Inukai, Ken (cor, Ag 30,29:2), 1960, Ag 29,25:3
Inukai, Kyohei, 1954, Je 4,23:1
Invader, Lord (R Grant), 1961, O 18,43:2
Inverarity, David Sr, 1955, N 24,29:5
Inverchapel, Lord (formerly Sir A C Kerr), 1951, Jl 6,23:1
Inverclyde, Baron, 1901, F 13,7:7
Inverclyde, Lord, 1905, O 20,5:2
Inverclyde, Lord (J A Burns), 1957, Je 19,35:3
Inverforth, Lord (A K Weir), 1955, S 18,87:1
Inverness, Duchess of, 1873, Ag 4,4:6
Inverso, Ralph, 1954, My 7,23:2
Inwood, John O, 1952, Mr 9,92:4
Inwright, John C, 1943, S 19,49:1
Inzucchi, Dominick, 1943, N 13,13:2
Iocolano, Frank, 1920, O 15,13:3
Iodice, Renato P, 1963, Ap 4,47:2
Iola, B Dave, 1950, O 7,19:4
Ion, Theodore P, 1940, My 4,17:4
Ionescu, Nae, 1940, Mr 16,15:4
Ions, Robert M, 1949, Mr 11,26:3
Iorio, Michael, 1937, Ag 12,19:4
Ipatieff, Vladimir Mrs, 1952, D 10,35:4
Ipatieff, Vladimir N, 1952, N 30,87:3
Ipp, Isaac, 1941, Jl 23,19:6
Ipp, Isaac Mrs, 1938, N 5,19:6
Ippolito, Anna Mrs, 1945, F 3,11:2
Ippolito, Charles, 1953, O 26,21:4
Ippolitov, I M, 1935, Ja 29,21:3
Ipsen, Ernest L, 1951, N 4,86:3
Iqbal, Mohammed, 1938, Ap 21,19:5
Iraci, John (por), 1937, N 25,31:4
Iralson, Mose, 1949, My 2,25:2
Iredale, Thomas, 1937, S 22,23:6
Iredell, Charles J, 1949, O 24,23:3
Iredell, Frank W, 1944, F 18,17:1
Iredell, Harvey, 1944, O 14,13:5
Iredell, Samuel, 1950, N 7,27:2
Irelan, Andrew H, 1958, Mr 30,88:7
Irelan, Anna M M Mrs, 1937, Ag 5,23:3
Irelan, Charles M, 1959, O 31,23:2
Irelan, Singer B, 1956, Je 19,29:3
Irelan, Singer B Mrs, 1941, My 5,17:3
Ireland, Albert, 1947, Jl 1,25:4
Ireland, Alleyne, 1951, D 24,13:4
Ireland, Andrew L Col, 1873, Ag 8,2:2
Ireland, C Raymond Mrs, 1938, My 6,21:4
Ireland, Charles O, 1948, Mr 10,27:4
Ireland, Chester D, 1923, O 21,23:1
Ireland, Col, 1864, O 2,1:4
Ireland, Earl W, 1947, Ja 28,23:3
Ireland, Edward B, 1948, Ja 4,52:4
Ireland, F A W, 1949, Jl 19,29:4
Ireland, Frederick G, 1915, D 29,11:5
Ireland, George B, 1951, My 18,27:2
Ireland, George S, 1951, Ap 24,29:3
Ireland, George T, 1963, S 1,56:5
Ireland, James H, 1956, N 28,35:5
Ireland, James S, 1942, N 2,21:2; 1945, Ag 8,25:3
Ireland, Jere H, 1940, D 6,23:3
Ireland, John, 1880, Ap 22,4:7
Ireland, John A, 1954, S 1,27:4
Ireland, John Archbishop (por), 1918, S 26,13:1
Ireland, John J, 1953, F 12,28:3
Ireland, John M Mrs, 1954, N 30,29:1
Ireland, John T, 1947, D 28,40:2
Ireland, Loretta F, 1950, Ap 8,13:5
Ireland, Matthew B, 1950, Mr 22,27:3
Ireland, Maurice, 1951, Mr 29,27:4
Ireland, Merritte W, 1952, Jl 10,31:5
Ireland, Milton S, 1941, Mr 2,42:4
Ireland, R L, 1928, F 18,1:4
Ireland, R Livingston Mrs, 1961, O 23,30:1
Ireland, Ray W, 1968, Ja 27,29:1
Ireland, Richard H, 1952, Ag 26,25:3
Ireland, Robert B, 1939, S 23,17:2
Ireland, Rutherford, 1940, Jl 30,19:3
Ireland, Samuel, 1924, O 7,23:4
Ireland, Sophia Mrs, 1871, Ja 19,5:2
Ireland, Thomas E, 1950, Ag 8,29:5
Ireland, Thomas H Sr, 1940, O 22,23:3
Ireland, W H, 1878, Jl 16,2:3
Ireland, William A, 1941, Ja 18,15:4; 1951, D 2,91:2
Ireland, William E, 1956, My 23,31:4
Ireland, William H Dr, 1904, Ja 13,9:5
Ireland, William S Sr, 1951, F 15,31:2
Iremonger, Edward E, 1966, Jl 26,35:4
Iremonger, Edward E Mrs, 1962, Jl 1,56:8
Iremonger, Frederic A, 1952, S 16,29:3
Iremonger, Frederick B, 1958, Je 15,76:5
Iremonger, Robert S, 1942, S 9,23:6
Irene, Princess of Prussia, 1953, N 12,31:3
Ireton, Louis A, 1951, O 2,27:3
Ireton, Peter L, 1958, Ap 28,23:5
Ireton, Robert E, 1949, D 13,31:4
Irey, Elmer L, 1948, Jl 20,24:3
Irias, Julian (por), 1940, N 21,29:6
Irigoyen, Carlos, 1946, O 12,19:6
Irigoyen, H, 1933, Jl 4,13:1
Irimescu, Radu Mrs, 1943, D 1,21:1
Irinarch, Archbishop, 1952, Mr 12,27:1
Irion, Hermann, 1963, D 1,85:1
Irion, Norman C Mrs, 1950, Je 6,29:5
Iris, Esperanza, 1962, N 11,89:1
Irish, Edward F, 1944, Jl 9,36:2
Irish, Frank A, 1914, S 20,15:4
Irish, Howard, 1938, Je 6,17:3
Irish, James W, 1942, D 15,27:4
Irish, Ned Mrs, 1968, Ap 2,47:2
Irish, O H, 1883, Ja 28,7:3
Irish, Robert L Dr, 1937, Je 7,19:3
Irish, Rolland E, 1960, Ag 6,19:5
Irish, Russell C, 1954, O 12,27:3
Irish, William E, 1958, O 28,35:5
Irish, William H, 1955, D 24,13:3
Irish, William S (por), 1943, My 15,15:1
Irma, Sister, 1946, F 5,24:2
Irmisch, George W, 1937, O 4,21:5
Irmisch, Louis W, 1940, Mr 19,25:3
Ironmonger, Cornelius, 1948, My 2,77:1
Ironmonger, Frank M, 1939, D 10,68:4
Irons, Albert R, 1959, Ag 18,29:4
Irons, Courtland P, 1948, Ja 20,23:2
Irons, David Prof, 1907, Ja 24,9:3
Irons, Ernest E (death ruled manslaughter, Ja 20,-35:3), 1959, Ja 19,27:3
Irons, Harold G, 1949, Ap 10,77:1
Irons, Henry C, 1925, N 14,15:4; 1962, N 16,31:3
Irons, Herbert C, 1958, N 2,88:4
Irons, James Anderson Gen, 1921, Jl 30,9:6
Irons, Robert H, 1939, Ja 6,22:2
Irons, W J Rev, 1883, Je 20,4:6
Irons, William G, 1962, Ag 17,23:1
Ironside, Allan S, 1944, Je 2,15:5
Ironside, Fred A Jr, 1955, Jl 21,23:5
Ironside, Henry A, 1951, Ja 17,28:4
Ironside, William E Lord, 1959, S 23,39:1
Irr, Clement A, 1950, Ja 5,26:3
Irre, Emline, 1956, My 24,31:3
Irrera, Joseph, 1923, N 7,17:6
Irrera, Raymond, 1959, Ja 8,29:3
Irrgang, Charles W Sr, 1955, Ag 18,23:2
Irsch, Frank E Mrs, 1956, Ja 15,93:2
Irsch, Frank Jr Mrs, 1947, Ag 6,23:5
Irvin, A Charles, 1945, Ja 31,21:4
Irvin, Calvin J, 1952, Mr 28,23:3
Irvin, Dick, 1957, My 17,25:4
Irvin, Donald F, 1953, Jl 2,23:5
Irvin, Fannie, 1968, Ap 24,47:3
Irvin, Fay, 1951, My 26,17:3
Irvin, James H, 1954, Jl 23,17:4
Irvin, James K, 1950, Ja 24,31:1
Irvin, Jesse O, 1950, O 19,31:4
Irvin, John K, 1939, Ap 18,23:2
Irvin, John L, 1957, Je 27,25:5
Irvin, Leslie L, 1966, O 11,47:3
Irvin, Lilbourn C, 1954, S 28,29:1
Irvin, Olive, 1923, N 3,16:5
Irvin, Oscar W, 1953, Jl 23,23:5
Irvin, Richard, 1938, My 25,23:6
Irvin, Richard Mrs, 1918, Je 7,13:6
Irvin, Stanley P, 1951, Ag 2,21:5

Irvin, W Dr, 1865, N 28,1:3
Irvin, William A, 1952, Ja 2,25:1
Irvin, William A Mrs, 1956, Je 8,25:4
Irvin, William C, 1947, D 19,25:3
Irvin, William Mrs, 1910, N 5,7:5
Irvin, William Rev Dr, 1909, F 24,9:5
Irvin, Willis Sr, 1950, Ag 9,29:2
Irvine, Alex F, 1941, Mr 16,45:1
Irvine, Alex S, 1948, Jl 17,15:4
Irvine, Benjamin F, 1940, My 2,23:3
Irvine, Clara C Mrs, 1941, Mr 24,17:1
Irvine, E Eastman (por), 1948, S 24,25:1
Irvine, Edward J, 1940, Jl 20,15:6
Irvine, F, 1931, Je 24,23:5
Irvine, George T, 1938, Ag 26,17:3
Irvine, Harry, 1951, Ag 8,25:4
Irvine, Helen Lowry Mrs, 1968, Ja 18,39:1
Irvine, Horace H, 1947, F 28,24:2
Irvine, Howard T, 1948, N 27,17:5
Irvine, Ingram N W Rev Dr, 1921, Ja 25,11:5
Irvine, J J, 1930, Mr 23,31:1
Irvine, James C, 1952, Je 13,23:5
Irvine, James J Mrs, 1947, Jl 14,21:5
Irvine, James Sr, 1947, Ag 26,23:5
Irvine, Joseph M (will), 1956, Ag 14,53:2
Irvine, Lydia W Mrs, 1941, Ap 16,23:5
Irvine, Maurice H, 1960, Ag 30,29:3
Irvine, Robert, 1942, My 28,17:3
Irvine, Robert T Dr, 1921, N 5,13:5
Irvine, Robert Tate Prof, 1968, Je 25,41:2
Irvine, Theodora, 1952, Ag 17,76:6
Irvine, Thomas J, 1950, Mr 9,30:5
Irvine, W Bay, 1963, Je 19,37:4
Irvine, W Gen, 1882, N 21,2:3
Irvine, W H, 1936, Ag 29,II,7:2
Irvine, W R D, 1933, O 31,21:5
Irvine, William, 1964, O 9,39:1
Irvine, William B, 1949, Ap 22,23:1
Irvine, William G, 1937, Jl 2,21:4
Irvine, William H (por), 1943, Ag 21,11:6
Irvine, William H, 1962, Ap 15,80:5
Irving, Aemilius Sir, 1913, N 28,15:6
Irving, Alex D, 1941, F 8,15:4
Irving, Alexander Duer, 1910, Je 14,11:4
Irving, Anna D, 1957, N 14,33:3
Irving, Ben, 1968, F 8,49:4
Irving, Catherine A, 1911, O 3,13:5
Irving, Charles, 1865, Je 4,1:6
Irving, Charles E, 1955, N 22,35:1
Irving, Christopher, 1957, D 19,31:3
Irving, Clifford Mrs, 1959, My 10,70:4
Irving, Cornelia C, 1922, Jl 8,11:7
Irving, Francis R Jr, 1950, S 11,23:5
Irving, Frank, 1948, Ja 12,19:3
Irving, Frank D, 1950, F 8,27:5
Irving, Frank J (por), 1938, Mr 31,23:4
Irving, Frederick C, 1957, D 25,31:6
Irving, G G H Maj-Gen, 1937, D 13,27:5
Irving, Gardner, 1923, Ag 28,17:5
Irving, George, 1908, O 7,9:4; 1943, Jl 31,13:2; 1961, S 12,33:2
Irving, George B, 1961, Jl 27,31:5
Irving, George E, 1941, F 12,21:4
Irving, George I, 1942, D 25,17:6
Irving, George Mrs, 1943, N 11,23:3
Irving, George R, 1952, Ap 15,27:4
Irving, Guy, 1923, O 10,21:3
Irving, Harry R, 1960, My 26,33:4
Irving, Henry, 1945, Ag 27,19:5
Irving, Henry A, 1945, D 29,13:3
Irving, Henry Brodribb, 1919, O 18,13:5
Irving, Henry Sir, 1905, O 14,1:7
Irving, Herbert Mrs, 1951, Jl 4,17:5
Irving, Isabel, 1944, S 2,11:3
Irving, J S, 1881, Ap 3,7:3
Irving, James Capt, 1885, F 20,2:6
Irving, Jan, 1944, Ja 6,23:4
Irving, Jim, 1908, O 28,7:5
Irving, John, 1950, N 30,33:4
Irving, John Duer, 1907, Ap 7,9:5
Irving, John Duir Prof, 1918, Jl 29,11:8
Irving, John F, 1944, Je 3,13:5
Irving, John Treat, 1906, F 28,9:6
Irving, Kelville E, 1953, O 26,21:4
Irving, Leonard, 1957, Ja 27,84:7
Irving, Louis du P, 1961, D 12,43:2
Irving, Louise H, 1964, Mr 9,29:1
Irving, Minna, 1940, Jl 24,21:3
Irving, P M, 1876, F 27,2:6
Irving, Percival R, 1904, Ap 15,3:3
Irving, Peter (por), 1944, D 29,15:1
Irving, Richard, 1941, F 3,20:2
Irving, Robert A, 1913, Ja 26,17:2
Irving, Robert A Mrs, 1945, Mr 27,19:4
Irving, T Rev, 1880, D 21,5:1
Irving, Thomas H (cor, N 19,23:3), 1954, N 17,31:3
Irving, Walter E, 1958, My 6,35:3
Irving, Walter H, 1951, My 24,35:4
Irving, Washington (funl, D 2,4:6), 1859, N 30,1:1
Irving, William H, 1950, Je 5,23:5
Irwin, Agnes K Mrs, 1952, F 29,23:1
Irwin, Alex, 1940, S 5,23:4
Irwin, Alphonso Dr, 1937, Ja 12,23:2
Irwin, Amory T, 1947, My 12,21:4
Irwin, Andrew P, 1944, Ap 18,21:3
Irwin, Arthur B, 1958, F 20,25:5
Irwin, Arthur F, 1952, Jl 6,48:8
Irwin, Bernard John Dowling Brig-Gen, 1917, D 16, 23:1
Irwin, Blair, 1904, Ja 29,9:6
Irwin, Charles P Sr, 1951, O 23,29:3
Irwin, D, 1883, D 2,7:2
Irwin, David, 1924, F 22,15:3
Irwin, David K, 1941, N 16,56:5
Irwin, Dorothy, 1961, O 14,23:5
Irwin, Dudley M, 1945, Mr 2,20:2
Irwin, Edward, 1937, F 26,21:5
Irwin, Edward P, 1939, Jl 27,19:2
Irwin, Elisabeth, 1942, O 17,15:3
Irwin, Elmer S, 1950, N 7,27:5
Irwin, Florence, 1956, S 28,27:1
Irwin, Francis B, 1947, Mr 28,23:3
Irwin, Frank, 1948, D 27,22:2
Irwin, Frank G, 1939, D 27,21:2
Irwin, Frank J, 1942, Ag 5,19:2
Irwin, Frank N, 1940, N 12,23:6
Irwin, Frank N Mrs, 1954, S 8,32:3; 1965, Jl 16,27:3
Irwin, George C, 1943, Ag 14,11:5
Irwin, George F, 1956, F 7,31:2
Irwin, George M, 1941, N 12,23:1
Irwin, Godfrey, 1959, Ja 8,29:1
Irwin, H Franklin, 1957, Ag 17,15:1
Irwin, Harry, 1953, My 23,15:6
Irwin, Harry C, 1947, My 24,15:6
Irwin, Harry N, 1955, Ja 29,15:3
Irwin, Harry S, 1956, Ja 9,25:4
Irwin, Henry M, 1939, O 14,19:4
Irwin, Herbert J, 1959, O 22,37:4
Irwin, Hugh L, 1953, D 10,47:2
Irwin, Isabella M, 1937, Ap 3,19:5
Irwin, James B, 1965, My 5,47:1
Irwin, James C, 1940, Mr 21,25:1
Irwin, James F, 1961, Ja 19,29:4
Irwin, James J Jr, 1939, Ag 6,36:8
Irwin, John, 1949, Ap 2,15:3; 1954, S 10,23:3
Irwin, John A, 1912, Jl 4,7:5
Irwin, John Arthur Dr, 1912, Je 2,II,13:6
Irwin, John H, 1948, N 18,27:1
Irwin, John H Mrs, 1953, Ap 18,19:4
Irwin, John Rear Adm, 1901, Jl 29,7:6
Irwin, John V, 1967, Ja 31,31:1
Irwin, John W, 1960, O 14,33:1
Irwin, Joseph W, 1964, Ap 21,33:4
Irwin, Kilshaw M, 1960, O 5,41:4
Irwin, Louis S, 1943, Ag 5,15:2
Irwin, May (por),(will, N 5,17:6), 1938, O 23,41:1
Irwin, Murray, 1938, N 8,23:1
Irwin, Noble E Rear-Adm (por), 1937, Ag 12,19:5
Irwin, P, 1878, Ap 26,5:5
Irwin, Payson, 1951, D 26,25:3
Irwin, Phil J, 1948, Ag 22,60:5
Irwin, Robert, 1925, Ja 7,25:4; 1941, My 17,15:2; 1945, Ap 27,19:2; 1960, O 2,85:1
Irwin, Robert A, 1965, Jl 30,22:5
Irwin, Robert B, 1951, D 13,34:2
Irwin, Robert B Mrs, 1949, Ap 24,76:7
Irwin, Robert E, 1937, Mr 1,19:1
Irwin, Robert F, 1946, Ja 1,27:3
Irwin, Robert W, 1953, Je 29,21:4
Irwin, Roscoe, 1955, Ja 29,15:3
Irwin, Royal W, 1950, F 10,24:2
Irwin, S Leroy Mrs, 1937, Ap 21,23:1
Irwin, Samuel F, 1937, F 11,23:3
Irwin, Spencer D Mrs, 1944, My 19,19:3
Irwin, Stafford L, 1955, N 24,29:5
Irwin, Theodore, 1902, D 26,7:5
Irwin, Theodore Mrs, 1962, Mr 29,33:2
Irwin, Thomas A, 1940, D 6,27:3
Irwin, Virginia (Mrs C Tucker), 1957, Jl 3,23:3
Irwin, W Hartwell, 1956, Ap 11,33:4
Irwin, Wallace, 1959, F 15,87:1
Irwin, Wallace Mrs (Laetitia), 1965, S 7,39:2
Irwin, Walter W, 1948, Jl 15,23:6
Irwin, Will, 1948, F 25,23:1
Irwin, Will J, 1960, Ja 17,72:4
Irwin, William, 1903, Ja 1,9:5; 1942, Je 9,23:1
Irwin, William A, 1943, Ag 8,37:3; 1967, Ap 25,43:4
Irwin, William B, 1943, D 29,17:3
Irwin, William G, 1914, Ja 29,9:6; 1943, D 15,27:3
Irwin, William J, 1939, My 29,15:3
Irwin, William P M, 1942, O 24,15:3
Irwin-Martin, Jean C, 1955, F 23,27:5
Irwine, Robert L, 1957, Mr 28,31:2
Isaac, Abraham, 1947, Mr 9,60:3
Isaac, Alfred, 1958, Ag 24,86:3
Isaac, Alfred E, 1950, Je 15,31:5
Isaac, Edward J, 1954, Jl 30,17:4
Isaac, Joseph Mrs, 1951, Ag 21,27:1
Isaac, Jules, 1963, S 7,19:4
Isaac, Julius, 1952, Mr 4,27:1
Isaac, Julius Mrs, 1945, O 9,21:4
Isaac, Max (por), 1947, Ag 13,23:5
Isaac, Max Mrs, 1964, Ap 3,33:2
Isaac, Moses, 1945, D 6,27:3
Isaac, Phil J, 1939, My 23,23:2
Isaac, Sig, 1947, D 29,17:4
Isaac, Simon, 1942, Ja 28,19:2
Isaac, William, 1943, F 10,25:3
Isaac, William H, 1948, S 1,23:1
Isaacman, Adolph, 1953, Jl 23,23:1
Isaacman, Adolph Mrs, 1954, O 27,29:1
Isaacs, Abram S Dr, 1920, D 23,11:5
Isaacs, Ainslie B, 1946, Ag 27,27:4
Isaacs, Albert L, 1964, Jl 26,56:5
Isaacs, Alick, 1967, Ja 28,27:2
Isaacs, Ally G, 1956, Je 12,35:2
Isaacs, Archibald E Dr, 1913, Mr 15,13:5
Isaacs, Arthur B, 1948, Je 25,23:2
Isaacs, Bendet Mrs, 1938, Ag 31,15:2
Isaacs, Benjamin, 1948, O 29,25:2
Isaacs, Carl D, 1957, F 5,23:4
Isaacs, Charles Godfrey, 1925, Ap 18,15:5
Isaacs, Claude R, 1953, S 13,84:7
Isaacs, Clifford, 1953, Ja 10,17:5
Isaacs, Coleman E (cor; funl plans, F 23,27:2), 1956 F 22,27:2
Isaacs, Coleman E Mrs, 1958, Ag 10,92:2
Isaacs, David L Mrs, 1958, Ja 26,88:3
Isaacs, E J, 1903, Mr 3,16:3
Isaacs, George, 1952, O 2,29:4
Isaacs, Gerald R (Marquess of Reading), 1960, S 21,37:2
Isaacs, Harry, 1937, S 27,21:4; 1961, Ja 9,39:5
Isaacs, Harry E, 1954, Ag 2,17:5
Isaacs, Harry Mrs, 1924, D 30,17:5
Isaacs, Henry, 1938, My 14,15:6; 1954, D 8,35:3; 1956, Ja 9,25:4
Isaacs, I Robert, 1953, Jl 29,23:2
Isaacs, Irving, 1965, My 26,47:3
Isaacs, Irving H, 1959, Ja 25,92:4
Isaacs, Isaac (por), 1948, F 11,28:2
Isaacs, Isaac C, 1937, My 4,25:3
Isaacs, Isaac S, 1906, D 8,11:6
Isaacs, Joseph A, 1952, Ja 16,25:2
Isaacs, Joseph H, 1944, Ag 7,15:1
Isaacs, Lewis J, 1941, D 14,69:2
Isaacs, Lewis M (por), 1944, D 13,23:5
Isaacs, Lewis M Mrs, 1956, Ja 11,31:1
Isaacs, Meyer S, 1904, My 25,7:6
Isaacs, Montefiore, 1902, Je 3,9:5
Isaacs, Mortimer E, 1962, Je 27,35:2
Isaacs, Nathan, 1941, D 19,25:6
Isaacs, Rufus, 1942, F 10,19:3
Isaacs, S M Rabbi (see also My 20,21), 1878, My 23,8:1
Isaacs, Samuel, 1939, O 16,19:6
Isaacs, Samuel S, 1958, Mr 15,17:5
Isaacs, Stanley M (funl, Jl 14,21:1), 1962, Jl 13,1:4
Isaacs, Theodore M Mrs, 1952, S 19,23:2
Isaacs, William H, 1941, Je 13,19:5
Isaacs, William M, 1915, My 27,11:6; 1918, S 11,13
Isaacsen, Rosa Mrs, 1941, Ap 6,48:6
Isaacson, Alex, 1953, Mr 26,93:1
Isaacson, C D, 1936, F 16,II,10:4
Isaacson, Charles E, 1966, O 5,42:8
Isaacson, Hyman B, 1922, Ja 2,17:5
Isaacson, Isaac B, 1946, My 19,40:5
Isaacson, Jack, 1960, N 23,29:4
Isaacson, Mira, 1939, S 10,50:4
Isaacson, Rousseau M Sr, 1948, Ja 14,25:2
Isaacson, Samuel A, 1963, Ag 22,27:5
Isaacson, William J Mrs (B Kavinoky), 1965, F 5, 31:3
Isaak, Abe, 1953, Ag 31,17:2
Isabel, Alex, 1953, Ja 26,19:3
Isabel, Thomas, 1938, Je 18,15:4
Isabell, Fred, 1951, Je 21,27:3
Isabell, William D, 1950, O 24,29:5
Isabella, Archduchess, 1931, S 6,20:1
Isabella, Princess of Portugal, 1876, Ap 24,5:4
Isabelle of France, Duchess of Guise, 1961, Ap 22,
Isacksen, Frederick A, 1949, Ag 14,69:2
Isacowitz, David, 1942, Je 29,15:4
Isacs, Herman H Jr, 1964, Ja 3,23:4
Isacson, Hyman, 1962, S 28,33:1
Isakov, Ivan S, 1967, O 13,36:2
Isaly, Samuel, 1946, D 5,31:6
Isaminger, James C, 1946, Je 18,25:4
Isbell, B E, 1948, O 22,25:1
Isbell, C Harold, 1941, Je 14,17:3
Isbell, Ernest L Col, 1937, N 25,31:4
Isbell, Frank, 1941, Jl 16,17:3
Isbell, John A, 1965, Jl 26,23:4
Isbell, Orlando S, 1922, Jl 21,11:5
Isbells, Charles E, 1937, Ja 10,II,10:2
Isbill, Paul M, 1951, O 12,28:2
Isbills, William L Sr Mrs, 1950, Ag 11,19:5
Isbister, A K, 1883, My 31,5:5
Isbrandtsen, Cornelius, 1940, F 1,21:3
Isbrandtsen, Hans J (will, My 27,33:4; buried, Je 5,27:5), 1953, My 14,29:1
Isbrandtsen, Hans J Mrs, 1959, F 5,31:2
Ischie, W Vaughn, 1962, My 26,25:3
Ischudi, Hugo von, 1911, N 25,II,13:5
Iscol, Fred, 1967, Mr 26,68:6
Iscol, George, 1953, Ja 14,31:3
Isdale, Malcolm G, 1947, Mr 14,24:3
Isdebsky, Vladimir, 1965, Ag 21,21:6
Isel, Thomas G, 1968, N 9,33:3

Isele, Charles H, 1940, N 5,25:2
Iseley, Donald B, 1949, N 14,27:2
Iselin, A Mrs, 1931, Ap 5,26:3
Iselin, Adrian, 1905, Mr 29,9:3
Iselin, Adrian Mrs, 1954, My 28,23:2
Iselin, Adrian 2d, 1961, Jl 7,25:1
Iselin, Allston Mrs, 1962, O 20,25:4
Iselin, Arthur, 1952, My 7,27:5
Iselin, Arthur Mrs (will, N 11,33:1), 1953, N 6,28:4
Iselin, C O, 1932, Ja 2,11:3; 1933, N 11,15:1
Iselin, Ernest, 1954, Ja 11,25:1; 1968, F 14,47:2
Iselin, Ernest Mrs, 1946, Mr 4,23:3
Iselin, Georgine (will Jl 17,14:4), 1954, Jl 1,25:6
Iselin, Henry S Mrs, 1954, Jl 26,17:5
Iselin, Jean-Pierre, 1961, Jl 27,31:5
Iselin, Louise Caylus, 1909, D 5,13:6
Iselin, Nathan, 1963, Je 15,23:3
Iselin, O'Donnell Mrs, 1951, Ap 4,29:2
Iselin, Oliver, 1963, O 9,40:6
Iselin, Oliver Mrs (por), 1949, Ap 10,76:2
Iselin, William E (will, F 4,19:4), 1937, Ja 27,21:1
Iselin, William Goddard, 1909, S 6,7:7
Iselin, William O, 1956, Mr 8,29:5
Isely, Jeter A, 1954, O 1,23:3
Isely, Jeter A Mrs, 1957, My 20,25:4
Iseman, Garret, 1919, D 11,13:3
Iseman, George L, 1940, Ap 19,21:1
Iseman, Harold M, 1964, Jl 17,27:6
Iseman, Iseman I, 1941, Ja 12,45:2
Iseman, John E 3d, 1951, D 15,15:6
Iseman, Lawrence L, 1951, F 2,23:3
Iseman, Percy R, 1942, Je 15,19:2
Isen, Nathan D, 1945, Jl 28,11:3
Isenbarth, Frank W, 1945, N 27,23:4
Isenbera, Martens H, 1964, Mr 6,31:1
Isenberg, Alfred P, 1952, Mr 16,90:4
Isenberg, Arnold, 1965, F 27,25:5
Isenberg, David, 1937, F 1,19:5; 1952, My 23,21:3
Isenberg, Harry, 1958, F 2,86:6
Isenberg, Harry N, 1954, S 22,29:4
Isenberg, Henry R, 1939, Ap 25,23:1
Isenberg, Hiemie D, 1953, Je 30,23:2
Isenberg, Otto Mrs, 1923, Ap 3,23:4
Isenborg, Paul, 1903, Ja 17,9:1
Isenegger, Raymond, 1965, Jl 29,27:4
Iserman, Harvey Rev, 1937, D 17,32:4
Isermann, Samuel, 1949, F 4,24:3
Isgar, Charles H, 1955, N 5,19:1
Ish-Kishor, Jacob, 1948, Ag 23,17:2
Isham, Alfred F Mrs, 1950, S 11,23:3
Isham, Charles, 1919, Je 10,13:4
Isham, Charles B, 1951, N 18,91:1
Isham, Charles Mrs, 1938, N 22,24:1
Isham, Edward S Jr Mrs, 1953, Ja 30,21:1
Isham, Edwin S, 1937, O 7,27:3
Isham, Frederick S, 1922, S 9,13:5
Isham, H H, 1922, My 16,19:5
Isham, Howard E Mrs, 1966, N 28,39:2
Isham, L Scott, 1950, D 2,13:4
Isham, Mary K, 1947, S 30,25:1
Isham, Mary L Mrs (will), 1939, Mr 7,43:1
Isham, Norman, 1943, Ja 2,11:4
Isham, Phillips, 1953, Ag 30,88:5
Isham, Pierepont, 1872, My 11,10:3
Isham, Ralph H (funl, Je 18,17:2), 1955, Je 15,31:2
Isham, Samuel, 1914, Je 13,9:4
Isham, Vere, 1941, F 20,19:2
Isham, William B (est, Ap 10,9:6), 1909, Mr 24,9:3
Isham, William B Mrs, 1948, Jl 31,15:2
Isherwood, Ernest, 1952, Jl 15,21:4
Isherwood, James E, 1945, N 18,44:2
Isherwood, Joseph, 1937, O 25,19:4
Isherwood, Percy, 1952, Mr 10,21:5
Isherwood, William, 1946, My 30,21:4
Ishi, Itaro, 1954, F 9,27:5
Ishikawa, Kin-ichi, 1959, Ag 20,25:2
Ishill, Joseph, 1966, Mr 17,39:2
Ishimoto, Shiaroku Gen, 1912, Ap 3,13:5
Ishiwara, Kanji, 1949, Ag 16,23:3
Ishiwata, Sotaro, 1950, N 5,93:1
Ishkhanian, Houri, 1947, Ja 1,33:2
Isidor, Joseph S, 1941, F 15,15:4
Isiminger, Russell S, 1956, N 4,87:2
Ising, Walter K, 1950, S 25,23:4
Iskenderian, Parnag, 1956, Ja 17,33:3
Iskenderian, Yervant P, 1949, S 22,31:5
Isler, Charles, 1948, Ja 7,25:3
Isler, Charles J, 1950, My 4,27:2
Isles, Philip, 1960, O 20,35:3
Ismail, Pasha, 1895, Mr 3,5:2
Ismail, Shaikh M, 1944, F 6,42:2
Isman, Felix, 1943, S 13,19:3
Isman, Morris, 1958, D 29,15:4
Ismay, Bower Capt, 1924, My 26,17:6
Ismay, Hastings L Lord, 1965, D 18,29:4
Ismay, J Bruce Mrs, 1964, Ja 1,25:3
Ismay, Joseph B, 1937, O 19,25:2
Ismay, Joseph E, 1937, D 14,25:5
Ismay, Mary, 1947, F 13,26:6
Ismay, T H Mrs, 1907, Ap 10,7:7
Ismay, Thomas Henry, 1899, N 24,7:2
Isogaya, Rensuke, 1967, Je 9,45:2
Isola, Emile, 1945, My 18,19:5
Isola, Henry E, 1963, N 10,87:1
Isola, Vico C, 1951, D 6,33:4
Isom, Edward W, 1962, Ja 21,88:3
Isomura, Toyotaro, 1939, O 27,23:4
Isovitz, Hyman, 1949, D 5,23:2
Israel, A Cremieux, 1944, Mr 23,19:2
Israel, Achille F, 1939, Ja 21,15:4
Israel, Albert R, 1944, D 27,19:4
Israel, Alexandre, 1937, Ag 24,21:5
Israel, Arthur Jr, 1966, S 5,15:6
Israel, Arthur Sr Mrs, 1951, Ap 1,93:1
Israel, Benjamin, 1962, My 19,27:4
Israel, Bernard J, 1952, N 10,25:1
Israel, Charles C, 1961, D 16,25:3
Israel, Daniel N, 1947, F 21,19:2
Israel, David H, 1959, O 16,31:3
Israel, David H Mrs, 1963, D 31,19:4
Israel, David M, 1956, D 3,29:2
Israel, David Mrs, 1953, Ag 15,15:2
Israel, Edward L, 1941, O 20,17:5
Israel, Fred, 1958, Ag 10,93:2
Israel, Frederick K, 1952, Ap 22,29:4
Israel, George I, 1961, Mr 10,27:2
Israel, George R, 1938, Mr 15,23:4
Israel, Harold E, 1961, O 10,43:4
Israel, Harris, 1941, Je 5,23:3
Israel, Harry, 1961, S 3,61:1
Israel, Harry Mrs, 1958, Ag 16,17:6
Israel, Isaac, 1949, Ap 5,30:5
Israel, Jacob L, 1944, Je 14,19:6
Israel, Joseph S Mrs, 1964, Jl 30,27:5
Israel, Jourdan M, 1944, N 14,23:5
Israel, Leon, 1955, Ja 13,27:4
Israel, Max, 1957, N 24,87:2
Israel, Morris, 1911, O 21,13:5
Israel, Mortimer H, 1938, Ja 28,21:3
Israel, Moses, 1957, Ap 19,21:4
Israel, Nathan Mrs, 1956, Ag 24,19:5
Israel, Richard H, 1959, Je 22,25:5
Israel, Rogers, 1921, Ja 12,15:2
Israel, Samuel, 1955, Ap 22,25:4
Israel, Samuel Mrs, 1962, Mr 17,25:2
Israeli, Clara, 1953, Ja 17,15:6
Israeli, Phineas Mrs, 1959, Mr 6,25:3
Israels, Charles Henry, 1911, N 14,13:5
Israels, David, 1946, Ja 7,19:1
Israels, Josef, 1911, Ag 13,II,9:5
Israels, Josef 2d, 1954, Jl 17,13:3
Israelson, William, 1955, Ja 29,29:8
Isreal, Samuel, 1944, Je 15,19:2
Isreeli, Arnold K, 1962, Je 20,32:6
Issaacs, Joel, 1949, Mr 7,21:4
Isseks, Samuel S, 1951, Ja 21,77:1
Isserman, Morris, 1947, My 25,61:1
Issertell, A Norman, 1955, O 19,33:4
Issler, Jacob, 1950, Je 25,68:8
Issod, Abraham, 1956, S 15,17:1
Istel, Andre, 1966, S 7,47:2
Istomin, P S, 1948, Ap 14,27:1
Iswolsky, Marguerite Mrs, 1942, N 21,13:5
Iszard, Mary Mrs, 1923, D 12,21:2
Iszard, S French, 1949, O 1,13:3
Iszard, Walter R Dr, 1921, F 19,11:5
Italiano, Thomas Mrs, 1948, S 21,27:3
Iten, Charles J, 1957, Ag 22,27:4
Iten, Frank J, 1946, D 8,79:2
Iten, Louis C, 1943, Ag 14,11:4
Ito, M, 1934, F 20,21:1
Ito, Masanori, 1962, Ap 22,80:5
Ito, Michio, 1961, N 7,33:3
Ito, Nobufumi, 1960, Ap 5,37:5
Ito, Yoji, 1955, My 12,29:3
Ito, Yuji, 1963, N 4,35:3
Itogaki, Taisukei Count, 1919, Jl 27,22:5
Itter, Harry A, 1940, Jl 15,15:5
Ittleson, Henry (por), 1948, O 28,29:5
Ittman, Abraham, 1914, S 17,9:4
Ittman, Irenee H, 1964, Je 23,33:1
Ittner, Martin H (por), 1945, Ap 24,19:3
Iturbi, Maria T Mrs, 1940, Ja 3,21:1
Iungerich, Eldred E, 1947, F 9,61:2
Iungerich, Helene, 1954, Mr 14,89:1
Iunian, Grigore, 1940, D 21,17:2
Ivamy, Fred, 1937, O 26,23:1
Ivan, Rosalind, 1959, Ap 7,33:1
Ivan, Stanislaz J, 1939, Jl 5,5:8
Ivanek, Boles B Mrs, 1960, Ag 3,29:4
Ivanoff, Alex, 1942, Mr 31,19:5
Ivanoff, Alexander Gen, 1925, Ja 28,17:3
Ivanov, Ilya I, 1967, My 5,39:3
Ivanov, Lev N, 1957, S 9,25:5
Ivanov, Viacheslav, 1949, Jl 28,23:2
Ivanovic, Vladimir, 1963, My 15,40:2
Ivanowski, Sigismund, 1944, Ap 13,19:4
Ivanowski, Sigismund Mrs, 1941, Je 9,19:4
Ivans, Arthur F, 1966, Jl 11,29:1
Iveagh, Earl of, 1927, O 8,17:5
Iveagh, Earl of (R E C L Guinness), 1967, S 15,47:1
Ivella, Vittori, 1966, Je 10,45:4
Ivens, Herbert B Mrs, 1943, S 6,17:4
Ivens, William, 1957, Je 22,15:6
Ivens, William H Sr, 1947, Ag 12,24:2
Ivers, James D Sr, 1964, Je 14,84:5
Iversen, Andreas A Mrs, 1956, S 30,87:2
Iversen, Berge, 1952, Ap 10,29:5
Iversen, Iver, 1953, N 13,27:4
Iversen, John M, 1953, Jl 18,14:8
Iversen, Lorenz, 1967, Ap 14,39:1
Iversen, Olaf, 1959, Ag 28,23:3
Iversen, Oscar B Mrs, 1951, Jl 22,61:2
Iversen, Reginald J Mrs, 1968, N 5,47:2
Iverson, Alex Mrs, 1950, Jl 26,25:5
Iverson, David N, 1946, O 1,23:3
Iverson, Emil W, 1960, F 22,17:3
Iverson, Ferdinand L, 1944, Ja 2,39:1
Iverson, Gustave A, 1945, My 10,23:4
Iverson, Robert P, 1964, S 9,43:3
Iverson, Robert W, 1921, N 10,19:5
Ives, Alfred E, 1963, Ap 13,19:5
Ives, Anice, 1949, Jl 10,57:2
Ives, Archer W, 1949, O 27,27:1
Ives, Arthur S, 1944, S 16,13:3
Ives, Benoni I Rev Dr, 1912, D 10,15:4
Ives, Bertha S Mrs, 1944, D 25,19:5
Ives, Brayton Gen, 1914, O 23,11:4
Ives, Caleb A, 1937, D 30,19:4
Ives, Cameron, 1959, S 18,63:3
Ives, Charles E, 1954, My 19,31:1
Ives, Charles K Mrs, 1943, Ag 3,19:5
Ives, Charles L Mrs, 1963, N 23,29:6
Ives, Charles M, 1940, My 19,42:4
Ives, Chauncey, 1961, F 7,33:5
Ives, Edward B Capt, 1903, D 31,9:5
Ives, Edwin, 1907, S 8,7:5
Ives, Edwin I, 1941, My 22,21:4
Ives, F W Dr, 1924, Jl 6,21:3
Ives, Frank, 1947, F 19,25:2
Ives, Frank Mrs, 1954, Ap 29,31:4
Ives, Franklin Titus, 1910, Ja 31,7:7
Ives, Frederic D Mrs, 1953, Ag 9,77:2
Ives, Frederic E (por), 1937, My 28,21:1
Ives, Frederick M, 1960, F 17,35:2
Ives, Frederick M Mrs, 1946, S 11,7:2
Ives, George A, 1942, S 18,21:4
Ives, George Mrs, 1941, Jl 8,19:2
Ives, Guy E, 1955, My 20,25:2
Ives, H Douglas, 1945, Ag 15,19:5
Ives, H S, 1894, Ap 18,5:5
Ives, H W, 1928, Ap 14,19:5
Ives, Halsey Cooley Prof (funl, My 11,11:5), 1911, My 7,II,11:4
Ives, Harry D, 1938, Ja 24,23:4
Ives, Henry G, 1940, N 19,23:5
Ives, Henry S, 1950, Mr 29,29:4
Ives, Henry S Mrs, 1957, Jl 15,19:4
Ives, Herbert E, 1953, N 15,88:5
Ives, Irving M, 1962, F 25,88:1
Ives, Irving M Mrs (por), 1947, Jl 8,23:4
Ives, J Moss, 1939, Ap 9,III,6:8
Ives, James E, 1943, Ja 3,42:4
Ives, John, 1955, F 3,23:5
Ives, John G, 1944, Ja 4,17:5
Ives, John N, 1942, D 8,25:6
Ives, John W, 1958, Ja 3,23:2
Ives, Kenneth G, 1953, Mr 12,27:1
Ives, Kenneth Mrs, 1964, S 14,33:4
Ives, L S Dr, 1867, O 14,5:4
Ives, Lawson C, 1867, Jl 5,3:7
Ives, Leland D Mrs, 1953, F 2,21:3
Ives, M E Mrs, 1903, My 19,9:6
Ives, Nathaniel H, 1950, O 9,25:3
Ives, Nathaniel H Mrs, 1945, Ja 5,15:5
Ives, Neil M, 1946, S 15,10:1
Ives, Olive L, 1955, Ja 31,19:4
Ives, Otto L, 1951, F 15,31:3
Ives, Paul P, 1955, My 22,88:1
Ives, R B, 1934, Ja 3,19:3
Ives, Robert H, 1875, Jl 7,5:6
Ives, S Mary, 1947, S 13,11:5
Ives, Sherwood B, 1907, F 19,9:6
Ives, Sherwood B Dr, 1907, F 23,9:6
Ives, William, 1916, Ag 22,9:4
Ives, William H, 1937, O 28,25:2
Ives, Winifred, 1918, My 11,13:8
Ivey, Alphonso L, 1949, Ag 20,11:6
Ivey, Joseph B, 1958, Ap 5,15:3
Ivey, Leon B, 1955, Je 16,31:4
Ivey, Paul W, 1950, O 13,29:1
Ivey, T N Dr, 1923, My 16,19:4
Ivie, Alvin E, 1954, Je 2,31:4
Ivie, Alvin Mrs, 1956, Ag 19,92:1
Ivie, Joseph H, 1942, Jl 23,19:3
Ivie, William G, 1938, D 31,15:5; 1939, Ja 5,23:4
Ivimey, Muriel Dr, 1953, F 28,17:4
Ivins, Albert L, 1954, Je 24,27:3
Ivins, Augustus Mrs, 1914, Ja 5,9:6
Ivins, Benjamin F P, 1962, D 5,47:5
Ivins, Benjamin T P Mrs, 1949, Mr 24,27:4
Ivins, Charles H, 1914, F 9,7:4
Ivins, Emma L Y Mrs, 1940, Jl 25,17:2
Ivins, George C, 1959, F 11,39:3
Ivins, Haddon (por), 1941, S 6,15:1
Ivins, Haddon Mrs, 1946, Jl 18,25:4
Ivins, James S Y, 1960, My 27,31:4
Ivins, Sarah, 1958, Mr 5,31:2
Ivins, William M Jr, 1961, Je 16,33:4

Ivins, William M Jr Mrs, 1948, Ag 23,17:4
Ivins, William Mills (funl, Jl 27,9:5), 1915, Jl 24,9:5
Ivison, D B, 1903, Ap 7,9:5
Ivison, H, 1884, N 27,5:4
Ivison, William C, 1951, Je 28,25:2
Ivler, Isidore, 1955, Je 10,25:2
Ivliyev, Ivan D, 1966, F 13,7:2
Ivory, James H, 1948, Ja 6,23:2
Ivory, James T, 1964, Ap 17,35:2
Ivory, Percy M, 1962, F 7,37:3
Ivory, Percy V E, 1960, Je 27,25:3
Ivy, Charles, 1945, D 16,40:2
Ivy, Joseph W, 1950, N 4,17:6
Iwai, Tatsumi, 1908, My 25,7:6
Iwakura, Tomosada Prince, 1910, Ap 1,11:5

Iwanaga, Yukichi, 1939, S 2,17:4
Iwanicki, Henry, 1960, Ap 23,23:4
Iwasaki, Koyata, 1945, D 5,25:5
Iwasaki, Yanosuke Baron, 1908, Mr 26,7:7
Iwase, Ryo, 1944, N 2,19:4
Iwashita, Yashutaro Adm, 1937, F 19,19:2
Iwata, Chuzo, 1966, F 23,39:4
Iwinska, Estera, 1963, S 12,37:5
Ix, Alex F, 1953, Ap 30,31:4
Ix, Frank (por), 1955, D 31,13:4
Ix, Frank J Jr, 1967, F 21,47:4
Ix, Frank Mrs, 1948, F 2,19:1
Ix, William E Sr Mrs, 1957, Ap 17,31:5
Iyer, Allada K K, 1953, O 4,88:3
Izaguirre, Carlos, 1956, Jl 20,17:3

Izard, Thomas C, 1960, Jl 22,23:2
Izeki, Minoru, 1945, Je 7,19:5
Izer, George W Rev Dr, 1917, S 15,11:4
Izgur, Leon, 1939, S 30,17:3
Izinicki, Michael, 1951, O 8,21:5
Izod, Jadk, 1952, Je 1,84:5
Izotov, Nikita A, 1951, Ja 17,27:1
Izquierdo, Luiz, 1949, S 8,29:2
Izquierdo y Sanchez, Emeterio, 1951, Mr 21,33:1
Izrastoff, Constantin, 1953, Ja 8,27:2
Izsak, Ignacio, 1955, Ja 29,15:1
Izzard, William T, 1959, Je 19,25:2
Izzet Pasha, Ahmed Marshall (por), 1937, Ap 2,2
Izzo, Joseph V, 1951, Je 5,31:3
Izzo, Mary F Mrs, 1961, Ja 1,49:1

J

a'afar, Dato Onn Bin, 1962, Ja 20,21:3
aakobs, Ned, 1956, O 4,33:5
abara, Benjamin M, 1964, My 24,92:7
abara, Carolyn A (funl, N 23,43:4), 1966, N 20,39:6
abara, James (funl, N 23,43:4), 1966, N 18,6:1
abara, Richard M, 1956, Ap 13,25:4
abbara, Hassan, 1959, My 4,29:5
abelman, Otto, 1943, Ja 7,19:3
ablin, Robert, 1949, N 29,29:4
ablons, Jacob J, 1938, Mr 8,19:5
ablons, Joseph M, 1962, N 17,25:3
ablonski, Adam F, 1946, Ag 3,15:4
ablow, Abe, 1967, N 24,43:2
ablow, George, 1953, My 14,29:4
ablow, Harry L, 1953, Je 19,21:5
aborg, Christine, 1938, Ja 19,23:3
abotinsky, Vladimir, 1940, Ag 5,13:3
abotinsky, Vladimir Mrs, 1949, D 23,22:2
abr, Saleh, 1957, Je 7,4:7
abry, Saadullah el, 1947, Je 21,17:2
abson, Thomas, 1942, Ap 13,15:3
bureck, Charles C Capt, 1919, Jl 16,13:3
aburek, Otto A, 1953, My 19,29:1
burg, Henry K Sr, 1963, S 23,29:6
ccard, Jules A, 1959, My 1,29:1
ches, Leopold, 1939, Ja 24,19:3
chter, Louis, 1955, Ag 2,23:3
cini, Stefano, 1952, Je 1,85:1
ck, Alexander, 1943, My 3,17:2
ck, Emanuel J (por), 1942, Ag 22,13:6
ck, Frank E, 1939, Ag 29,21:4
ck, Frederick L, 1951, My 5,17:6
ck, George Mrs, 1957, O 13,86:6
ck, H Wesley, 1955, Je 21,31:4
ck, James B, 1963, Ag 14,33:3
ck, James R, 1944, Ap 18,21:5; 1952, Ja 7,19:3;
957, Ag 3,15:3
ck, John C, 1958, Ap 13,83:3
k, John F, 1943, Jl 16,17:6
k, John Harrison Col, 1905, Ap 23,9:6
k, John Mrs, 1925, Jl 22,19:5
k, L Foster, 1952, Je 17,27:3
k, Peter M (por), 1944, Ap 21,19:1
k, Richard, 1952, Jl 1,23:6
k, Rodney L, 1957, Ap 24,33:4
k, William,S, 1945, Ap 22,35:1; 1960, Je 5,86:1
k, William Y, 1955, O 16,86:3
kaway, William A, 1944, Ap 23,42:6
ke, K Mrs, 1941, Ja 17,36:3
kel, Max, 1954, Mr 28,88:5
ker, Edward G, 1942, F 7,17:3
kes, Hervey L, 1956, Jl 21,15:6
kh, Ernest, 1959, Ag 18,29:1
kie, William, 1954, S 20,23:2
kle, George H, 1939, O 22,40:7
kler, John J, 1958, Jl 1,31:1
kley, A M, 1950, F 21,25:4
kling, Daniel C (will, Ap 5,19:2), 1956, Mr 15,
:1
klitsch, Fred L, 1937, Jl 19,15:5
man, Charles A, 1950, Je 5,23:2
man, Edward F, 1940, Ap 29,15:5
man, Ex-Coroner (funl), 1871, Ap 7,8:4
man, Fred W, 1959, Ag 29,17:3
man, Glenn E, 1950, O 31,27:1
man, Harold, 1961, Jl 10,21:6
man, Jack J, 1954, D 8,35:1
man, Lena, 1943, Mr 4,19:5
man, Margaret M, 1954, Ja 13,31:2
man, Thomas H, 1942, S 21,15:3
man, William H, 1947, D 19,26:3
ovics, Michael, 1949, D 9,31:4
s, Arthur G, 1958, Jl 13,68:7
s, Ivan, 1950, F 15,27:4
s, Margaret (will), 1963, Ag 17,16:6
s, Morris H, 1958, O 16,37:1
s, Stanley S, 1960, Ja 7,29:4
sen, Ben, 1952, D 29,19:3
son, A M Mrs, 1958, S 13,19:6
son, A V Williams Dr (por), 1937, Ag 9,20:1
on, Abner Rev, 1874, Ap 20,1:4
on, Adolphus A, 1949, F 1,25:2
on, Alan R, 1965, Je 20,72:7
on, Albert A, 1939, Jl 31,13:6
on, Albert L Mrs, 1949, Mr 11,25:4
on, Albert M, 1948, D 8,31:2
on, Alex F, 1960, S 1,27:1
on, Alfred G, 1965, Je 26,29:5
on, Alfreda C, 1941, D 9,31:3
on, Allan H, 1941, D 8,23:1
on, Alonzo M Sr, 1944, Mr 4,13:3
on, Alta E, 1948, S 17,25:3
on, Alton C, 1941, Ja 7,23:3
on, Andrew, 1904, F 4,9:6; 1957, Ja 5,17:4
on, Andrew F, 1963, Ap 20,27:5
on, Andrew J, 1948, D 14,29:4; 1957, My 18,19:2
on, Andrew Jr, 1865, Ap 22,4:1

Jackson, Andrew Maj, 1901, Je 30,7:6
Jackson, Andrew Sr, 1952, S 1,17:4
Jackson, Andrew 4th, 1953, My 24,88:1
Jackson, Aquilla, 1940, Jl 14,31:3
Jackson, Archibald L, 1946, Je 5,23:6
Jackson, Arnold Ross, 1968, Ag 17,27:2
Jackson, Art, 1949, Mr 21,27:5
Jackson, Arthur C, 1941, Ap 8,26:2; 1943, O 27,23:4
Jackson, Arthur E, 1949, Ja 16,68:5
Jackson, Arthur H Mrs, 1946, Ap 24,25:1
Jackson, Arthur T, 1943, D 14,28:2
Jackson, Aunt Molly (Mrs M Stames), 1960, S 3,17:4
Jackson, Barbara, 1954, Je 4,20:3
Jackson, Barry, 1961, Ap 3,33:2
Jackson, Blanche H, 1949, Je 29,27:2
Jackson, Bruce, 1954, F 21,68:2
Jackson, Burris C, 1967, D 27,34:5
Jackson, Byron H, 1939, My 17,23:6
Jackson, C H Commodore, 1878, Ag 6,5:3
Jackson, C S Mrs, 1956, F 5,86:5
Jackson, C T, 1880, Ag 31,4:7
Jackson, Campbell N, 1941, Ap 14,17:5
Jackson, Carl, 1953, N 20,23:1
Jackson, Carl F, 1949, N 1,27:5
Jackson, Carl N, 1946, O 16,28:3
Jackson, Carl Z, 1943, F 19,19:4
Jackson, Catherine E, 1945, F 2,19:5
Jackson, Charles, 1949, N 15,21:5
Jackson, Charles Carroll, 1916, F 20,15:4
Jackson, Charles D, 1964, S 30,88:6
Jackson, Charles E, 1956, N 4,86:4
Jackson, Charles F, 1945, My 5,15:4
Jackson, Charles H, 1911, Je 7,9:4; 1921, Jl 7,11:4;
1942, My 7,19:6; 1955, Mr 2,27:3; 1962, Ag 8,31:4
Jackson, Charles T Jr, 1948, Je 6,72:5
Jackson, Charles W, 1966, Ja 20,35:2
Jackson, Charles W Mrs, 1960, D 29,25:4
Jackson, Chevalier, 1958, Ag 17,87:1
Jackson, Chevalier L, 1961, Ja 15,86:4
Jackson, Claiborne F, 1862, D 28,1:4
Jackson, Clarence J, 1940, N 15,21:4
Jackson, Clarence S, 1961, O 14,23:6
Jackson, Clifford B, 1951, Ja 15,17:5
Jackson, Clifford L, 1955, Ap 2,17:4
Jackson, Clyo, 1942, S 15,23:5
Jackson, Cora M, 1950, Mr 5,92:4
Jackson, Cornelius, 1955, My 7,17:5
Jackson, D C, 1877, Mr 29,5:2
Jackson, Daniel D (por), 1941, S 2,17:5
Jackson, Daniel D 2d, 1957, D 19,31:2
Jackson, Daniel H, 1925, N 11,23:4
Jackson, David J, 1924, Ag 10,24:3
Jackson, David R, 1918, Ja 26,13:8; 1940, Ja 3,21:2
Jackson, Don, 1946, Ag 28,27:5
Jackson, Donald E, 1955, N 4,29:2
Jackson, Dudley C, 1953, Ag 7,19:3
Jackson, E Conover, 1904, F 18,9:6
Jackson, E Fenwick, 1947, Mr 25,25:3
Jackson, E W Rev, 1873, Je 22,4:7
Jackson, Ed, 1954, N 19,23:3
Jackson, Edith L, 1961, Jl 25,27:1
Jackson, Edward, 1942, O 30,19:4
Jackson, Edward D, 1939, D 6,25:1
Jackson, Edward G, 1950, Ag 1,23:2
Jackson, Edward H, 1945, Ja 12,15:2
Jackson, Edward H Mrs, 1943, N 18,23:3
Jackson, Edward Q, 1950, F 5,85:1
Jackson, Edward W, 1940, Jl 7,25:4; 1941, S 6,15:6;
1944, F 2,21:4
Jackson, Edwin B, 1951, Ap 17,29:2
Jackson, Edwin E Jr, 1919, My 27,15:5
Jackson, Elihu E Ex-Gov, 1907, D 28,7:5
Jackson, Elizabeth L, 1958, Ja 21,29:2
Jackson, Elmas W, 1942, Ap 3,21:3
Jackson, Emanuel, 1946, O 19,21:2
Jackson, Emery, 1953, Ap 2,27:4
Jackson, Emma Mrs, 1954, My 20,31:4
Jackson, Erle L, 1954, Ap 10,15:5
Jackson, Ernest G, 1938, Mr 7,17:3
Jackson, Ernest L Sr, 1951, Je 5,31:2
Jackson, Ethel, 1957, N 25,31:2
Jackson, Ethel E, 1960, N 21,29:5
Jackson, Evangeline P Mrs, 1942, My 19,19:6
Jackson, F Ellis, 1950, F 10,23:5
Jackson, Felix, 1940, Mr 26,21:5
Jackson, Frank, 1947, D 31,15:4
Jackson, Frank A, 1941, F 4,22:2
Jackson, Frank D, 1938, N 17,25:6
Jackson, Frank W, 1919, Ja 9,11:2; 1955, Mr 11,25:2
Jackson, Franklin P Jr, 1941, Ap 25,19:5
Jackson, Fred W, 1904, Je 15,7:6
Jackson, Frederick, 1953, My 24,88:4
Jackson, Frederick A, 1941, Mr 27,23:3
Jackson, Frederick D, 1945, D 21,21:2
Jackson, Frederick E, 1949, Ja 30,61:1
Jackson, Frederick G, 1938, Mr 14,16:3
Jackson, Frederick H, 1915, Jl 29,9:6
Jackson, Frederick Huth, 1921, D 5,17:2
Jackson, Frederick J, 1953, O 29,31:2

Jackson, Frederick J F, 1941, D 2,23:5
Jackson, Frederick T, 1949, Je 14,31:3
Jackson, Frederick W, 1958, Ja 11,17:5; 1959, F 20,
25:3; 1965, F 17,40:1
Jackson, Gardner, 1965, Ap 18,80:4
Jackson, George A, 1940, F 8,23:1; 1941, O 5,49:2
Jackson, George F, 1948, S 21,27:3; 1957, N 16,19:1
Jackson, George G, 1941, Ja 10,19:4
Jackson, George H, 1914, Jl 9,7:4; 1954, Je 28,19:5;
1955, Mr 15,26:7
Jackson, George Mrs, 1949, O 9,92:6
Jackson, George P, 1953, Ja 23,19:2
Jackson, George Thomas Dr, 1916, Ja 4,13:7
Jackson, George W, 1951, Ag 9,21:4
Jackson, George Washington, 1922, F 6,13:3
Jackson, Gerald N, 1944, Mr 18,13:5
Jackson, Gilbert, 1959, Je 17,35:5; 1960, My 30,17:5
Jackson, Gilbert S, 1960, Jl 11,29:3
Jackson, Grace E (est acctg), 1954, F 17,25:6
Jackson, Guert G, 1938, Je 18,15:4
Jackson, H Arnold Mrs, 1961, My 3,37:4
Jackson, H C L, 1954, O 20,29:4
Jackson, H E, 1895, Ag 9,1:3
Jackson, H Kirk, 1960, Jl 19,29:4
Jackson, H Nelson, 1955, Ja 16,92:1
Jackson, Harold G, 1950, F 16,23:3; 1950, Ag 6,2:8
Jackson, Harold L, 1938, S 13,23:3
Jackson, Harrison S, 1963, N 19,41:2
Jackson, Harry, 1923, My 29,15:4; 1953, Ag 4,21:6;
1958, Jl 31,23:1; 1960, My 31,31:2; 1960, Jl 11,29:4
Jackson, Harry C, 1957, Ja 19,15:4
Jackson, Harry E, 1945, S 11,23:2; 1960, F 5,27:2
Jackson, Harry L, 1953, Mr 6,20:8
Jackson, Harry S, 1943, My 5,27:5
Jackson, Hart, 1882, Ap 14,5:3
Jackson, Harvey D, 1940, N 13,23:2
Jackson, Helen, 1946, Ap 13,17:4
Jackson, Helen B, 1925, Ap 24,19:4
Jackson, Helen H, 1885, Ag 13,5:5
Jackson, Henry, 1940, O 5,15:3; 1950, O 3,31:1
Jackson, Henry A, 1916, S 6,9:5; 1943, O 7,23:4
Jackson, Henry E, 1939, Ap 22,17:2
Jackson, Henry H, 1955, My 29,44:4
Jackson, Henry J Mrs, 1960, Je 13,27:2
Jackson, Henry Prof, 1921, S 26,15:6
Jackson, Henry S, 1939, Je 25,37:2
Jackson, Henry Sir, 1937, F 24,23:4
Jackson, Herbert, 1951, D 15,13:5
Jackson, Herbert W, 1966, Mr 28,33:4
Jackson, Holbrook, 1948, Je 18,24:2
Jackson, Horace, 1938, My 29,II,6:8
Jackson, Horace A, 1952, Ja 29,25:1
Jackson, Howard I, 1948, Ap 14,27:3
Jackson, Hugh E, 1957, Je 14,25:4
Jackson, Hugh R, 1966, Mr 9,41:1
Jackson, I Irwin, 1955, Ja 7,21:5
Jackson, Isaac, 1946, Ap 14,46:1
Jackson, J, 1927, Ja 15,15:1
Jackson, J Allen, 1938, D 2,23:3
Jackson, J C, 1882, F 8,5:6
Jackson, J Calvin, 1947, D 9,29:2
Jackson, J Chester, 1947, Ja 8,23:4
Jackson, J Hugh, 1962, Ja 23,33:1
Jackson, J P, 1880, D 18,2:5
Jackson, J Vernal, 1958, S 11,34:1
Jackson, J W Prof Dr (see also Jl 29), 1877, Jl 30,4:6
Jackson, Jacob L, 1939, D 25,23:4
Jackson, James, 1903, Mr 15,1:4
Jackson, James A, 1943, S 10,23:2; 1960, N 18,31:3;
1962, Ja 3,33:4
Jackson, James B, 1945, F 9,15:2
Jackson, James Capt, 1937, My 21,21:1
Jackson, James E, 1949, Jl 3,26:5
Jackson, James F, 1937, Ap 27,23:1
Jackson, James H, 1940, O 29,25:2
Jackson, James L, 1956, Ap 24,32:1
Jackson, James Mrs, 1949, Ja 22,13:1
Jackson, James R, 1938, Jl 29,17:3
Jackson, Jay Mrs, 1958, S 14,84:1
Jackson, Jerome A, 1942, Jl 2,21:4
Jackson, Jerome J, 1941, Jl 15,19:3
Jackson, Jess H, 1957, Ja 4,23:1
Jackson, Jesse B, 1947, D 6,15:6
Jackson, Jewel J, 1948, O 14,29:1
Jackson, Joe (por), 1942, My 15,21:6
Jackson, Joe (Shoeless), 1951, D 6,34:2
Jackson, John, 1946, Jl 14,38:5
Jackson, John A, 1939, Ja 14,17:4; 1950, Mr 2,27:4;
1951, O 2,27:3
Jackson, John Bishop, 1885, Ja 7,5:5
Jackson, John Brinckerhof, 1920, D 21,13:5
Jackson, John C, 1953, Ja 4,77:1
Jackson, John D, 1961, Mr 18,23:1
Jackson, John D (est inventory), 1962, Ap 21,17:1
Jackson, John F, 1948, Ap 28,28:2
Jackson, John G, 1959, Ap 28,35:1
Jackson, John H, 1944, D 17,37:2; 1950, O 29,92:1;
1951, Jl 31,21:3
Jackson, John H Mrs, 1953, Je 10,29:4; 1968, Ja 18,
39:3

Jackson, John J, 1948, Ap 2,23:1; 1961, O 17,39:1
Jackson, John Jay Ex-Judge, 1907, S 3,9:5
Jackson, John L (por), 1948, S 4,15:2
Jackson, John Mrs, 1949, O 12,29:2
Jackson, John O, 1950, D 13,35:4
Jackson, John P, 1948, Ap 3,15:3
Jackson, John Prof, 1883, My 18,5:4
Jackson, John R, 1949, Ja 23,68:3
Jackson, John Sir, 1919, D 16,13:4
Jackson, John W, 1952, Ja 6,93:2; 1953, Ag 8,11:6
Jackson, John W Mrs, 1948, My 6,25:4
Jackson, Joseph, 1946, Mr 6,27:3
Jackson, Joseph C Mrs, 1955, Ap 13,29:1
Jackson, Joseph Cooke, 1913, My 23,13:5
Jackson, Joseph H, 1955, Jl 16,15:4
Jackson, Joseph J, 1952, Ap 25,23:1
Jackson, Joseph L, 1953, N 6,27:3
Jackson, Joseph W Dr, 1937, N 29,23:5
Jackson, Josephine A, 1946, Ja 1,28:2
Jackson, Kathleen C, 1966, F 5,29:5
Jackson, Kenneth M, 1939, My 8,17:5
Jackson, Keziah, 1907, F 9,9:6
Jackson, L E Mrs, 1904, Ja 11,1:2
Jackson, Lambert L, 1952, Mr 30,94:1
Jackson, Lawrence A, 1954, Ag 9,17:1
Jackson, Lawrence S, 1941, S 17,23:6
Jackson, Lee, 1945, Ag 17,17:2
Jackson, Leroy Mrs, 1938, O 26,23:2
Jackson, Lewis E, 1945, O 31,23:5
Jackson, Lewis Mrs, 1944, Ag 7,15:2
Jackson, Louis, 1946, O 10,27:6
Jackson, Lyle, 1951, F 21,27:1
Jackson, M Roy, 1944, Ja 24,17:3
Jackson, Margaret, 1938, Ap 22,19:5
Jackson, Margaret A, 1952, Ja 15,27:5
Jackson, Margaret C Mrs, 1947, My 4,60:6
Jackson, Margaret H, 1939, Je 26,23:3
Jackson, Maria J Mrs, 1908, Ja 24,7:5
Jackson, Maude C D, 1956, Je 14,33:4
Jackson, Merrick T Mrs, 1953, F 25,27:4
Jackson, Milton P, 1961, O 30,29:3
Jackson, Monty J, 1944, Je 13,19:4
Jackson, Myron R, 1949, Ap 17,76:5
Jackson, N Gratz, 1944, O 16,19:4
Jackson, Nannie Nye Mrs, 1905, Mr 11,9:4
Jackson, Oliver H, 1942, Je 3,24:3
Jackson, Oliver W, 1941, S 16,23:4
Jackson, Omer S, 1940, Je 2,44:4
Jackson, Oscar E, 1947, F 28,23:1
Jackson, Paul E, 1960, S 20,39:1
Jackson, Paul F Mrs, 1944, Jl 22,15:3
Jackson, Paul R Mrs, 1951, N 3,17:3
Jackson, Pearsall B, 1939, F 14,19:2
Jackson, Pearsall B Mrs, 1963, N 9,25:1
Jackson, Percy H, 1961, Jl 7,25:4
Jackson, Percy R, 1941, D 25,25:2; 1944, N 9,27:3
Jackson, Percy Van de L (por), 1941, Ap 5,17:1
Jackson, Percy Van de L Mrs, 1964, Ap 13,29:5
Jackson, Peter H, 1908, Je 18,9:4
Jackson, Phil L Mrs, 1950, O 23,23:2
Jackson, Phil Ludwell, 1953, F 15,93:2
Jackson, Phillip Nye, 1911, Mr 4,11:6
Jackson, R B, 1929, Mr 21,31:5
Jackson, Ralph L, 1952, Ag 15,15:2
Jackson, Reginald H, 1939, S 9,17:3
Jackson, Richard, 1956, Ja 2,3:8
Jackson, Richard N Mrs, 1967, Je 22,39:4
Jackson, Richard P, 1960, Ap 22,29:1
Jackson, Richard S Mrs, 1956, F 5,87:2
Jackson, Richard W, 1952, S 12,23:3
Jackson, Robert, 1916, Ap 29,11:4
Jackson, Robert A, 1948, Ag 27,19:2
Jackson, Robert C, 1944, N 20,21:5; 1963, S 15,86:4
Jackson, Robert E Mrs, 1950, Mr 10,27:1
Jackson, Robert G Mrs, 1948, Ja 13,26:2
Jackson, Robert H (funl, O 13,31:1; will O 23,17:1), 1954, O 10,1:2
Jackson, Robert M S Dr, 1865, Ja 29,4:6
Jackson, Robert McL, 1964, S 16,31:5
Jackson, Robert Mrs, 1942, D 14,23:1
Jackson, Robert T, 1948, O 26,31:3; 1953, O 27,27:5
Jackson, Robert T Mrs, 1947, N 24,23:2
Jackson, Roland Mrs, 1939, Ja 11,19:3
Jackson, Roland P, 1959, Ag 23,93:1
Jackson, Rufus, 1949, Mr 7,21:6
Jackson, Rufus H, 1906, Je 28,7:6
Jackson, S Eugene, 1947, Ja 21,23:4
Jackson, Samuel, 1949, Mr 20,76:4
Jackson, Samuel C, 1961, N 2,37:3
Jackson, Samuel D, 1951, Mr 9,25:3
Jackson, Samuel M Gen, 1907, My 9,9:5
Jackson, Samuel Macauley Rev Dr, 1912, Ag 4,II,11:6
Jackson, Samuel Mrs, 1955, Ja 4,21:5
Jackson, Sarah V, 1945, F 17,13:2
Jackson, Saul Dr, 1872, Ap 6,1:6
Jackson, Schuyler B, 1914, Jl 30,9:4
Jackson, Shirley (Mrs S E Hyman), 1965, Ag 10,29:1
Jackson, Sidney J, 1960, F 27,19:5
Jackson, Sidney R, 1956, Ag 31,17:3
Jackson, Stanley, 1947, Mr 10,21:4
Jackson, Stewart Mrs, 1954, Jl 2,19:2
Jackson, Stonewall J, 1957, Mr 16,19:6
Jackson, Stonewall Mrs, 1915, Mr 25,11:5
Jackson, Sydney A, 1953, Ap 19,90:2
Jackson, T P, 1876, Ap 9,7:3
Jackson, Theodore, 1961, My 30,17:4
Jackson, Theodore F, 1913, Je 19,11:5
Jackson, Theodore K, 1945, S 25,26:2
Jackson, Theron S, 1944, Je 1,19:6
Jackson, Thomas B, 1941, D 10,25:2
Jackson, Thomas H Gen, 1937, Ap 9,21:5
Jackson, Thomas L, 1954, S 8,31:3
Jackson, Uriah S, 1912, Je 12,II,17:5
Jackson, Victor S, 1948, Ap 2,23:3
Jackson, W A, 1927, N 15,29:1
Jackson, W C, 1938, N 1,23:3
Jackson, W C Mrs, 1938, N 22,24:5
Jackson, W H, 1903, Jl 20,7:6
Jackson, W H Gen, 1903, Mr 31,9:6
Jackson, W Montgomery, 1960, Mr 13,86:7
Jackson, W Reginald, 1964, Je 26,29:4
Jackson, Walter, 1944, F 5,15:3; 1947, Ag 27,23:5
Jackson, Walter C, 1959, Ag 13,27:4
Jackson, Walter H, 1958, Ag 12,29:3
Jackson, Walter M, 1908, N 16,9:4
Jackson, Walter M Dr, 1908, N 17,7:4
Jackson, Walter Montgomery, 1923, Mr 14,19:4
Jackson, Warren W, 1967, N 22,47:2
Jackson, Webster S, 1958, O 11,23:2
Jackson, Wilfred J, 1959, Mr 14,23:4
Jackson, William, 1925, S 3,25:3
Jackson, William A, 1946, O 9,27:2
Jackson, William B, 1944, Je 9,15:4
Jackson, William B Col (por), 1937, Ja 21,23:4
Jackson, William C Jr (funl plans), 1955, Je 19,23:1
Jackson, William D, 1937, Ag 1,II,6:3
Jackson, William E, 1943, Ap 17,17:2
Jackson, William F, 1913, My 18,IV,7:6; 1956, F 28, 31:1
Jackson, William F Lord of Glewstone, 1954, My 4, 29:5
Jackson, William G, 1943, F 19,19:2
Jackson, William H, 1908, N 26,9:7; 1912, F 26,11:4; 1915, Ap 5,11:4; 1939, Ap 28,25:2; 1941, Ap 20,42:8; 1942, Ag 7,17:3
Jackson, William H Mrs, 1941, Ag 21,17:3
Jackson, William H Rev, 1925, O 19,21:4
Jackson, William Henry, 1942, Jl 2,21:4
Jackson, William I, 1947, S 12,22:2
Jackson, William J Mrs, 1940, Ja 8,15:2
Jackson, William K (por), 1947, N 25,32:2
Jackson, William K Jr, 1955, Ja 26,25:2
Jackson, William Lawles (Lord Allerton), 1917, Ap 5,13:6
Jackson, William M, 1950, S 8,31:3
Jackson, William P, 1939, Mr 8,21:1; 1945, Ja 15,19:4
Jackson, William R, 1938, D 27,17:3; 1940, Ag 6,20:4; 1946, N 25,27:5
Jackson, William R Mrs, 1951, Je 6,24:3
Jackson, William S, 1951, Je 2,19:2; 1955, D 1,35:2
Jackson, William S 3d, 1955, Je 23,15:2
Jackson, William W, 1953, Ja 30,21:5
Jackson, Willie (O Tobin), 1961, N 14,36:1
Jackson, Willis K, 1942, N 6,23:2
Jackstead, Conrad W, 1951, My 12,21:2
Jackvony, Louis V, 1950, D 25,19:3
Jacob, Bartholomew Mrs, 1958, My 23,23:3
Jacob, Benno, 1945, F 1,23:4
Jacob, C Albert, 1940, D 11,27:4
Jacob, Charles, 1952, Ag 13,23:7
Jacob, Charles H, 1953, Je 9,27:5
Jacob, Charles Mrs, 1950, N 27,25:3
Jacob, Charles W, 1940, Jl 9,21:2; 1945, F 20,19:1
Jacob, Charles W Mrs, 1949, Ap 7,29:4
Jacob, Claud, 1948, Je 3,25:2
Jacob, Edward H Sr, 1955, F 5,15:3
Jacob, Ernest O, 1966, Ag 3,37:1
Jacob, George H, 1957, S 30,31:4
Jacob, Hedwig J, 1943, Je 22,19:5
Jacob, Henrich E, 1967, N 10,47:3
Jacob, Howard L Sr, 1948, Ap 16,23:2
Jacob, Ike H, 1925, Mr 7,13:6
Jacob, John F, 1954, Je 16,31:3
Jacob, Lawrence Mrs, 1958, Je 2,27:1
Jacob, M, 1943, Mr 23,20:3
Jacob, Morris, 1959, Jl 5,57:1
Jacob, Myrl L, 1948, N 14,76:4
Jacob, Naomi, 1964, Ag 28,29:1
Jacob, Robert, 1944, Mr 15,19:2
Jacob, Robert Jr, 1954, My 31,13:6
Jacob, William H Mrs, 1949, F 14,19:5
Jacobaeus, Hans C Dr, 1937, O 30,19:3
Jacober, Arthur, 1962, Ap 10,43:2
Jacober, James L, 1952, Ap 20,92:3
Jacober, Milton C (por), 1947, D 27,13:6
Jacober, Milton C Mrs, 1965, Ap 23,35:3
Jacobi, Abraham Dr (por),(funl, Jl 14,11:3), 1919, Jl 12,9:3
Jacobi, Arthur J, 1955, D 29,23:3
Jacobi, Emile H Mrs, 1943, D 14,27:2
Jacobi, Felix, 1952, Ap 3,35:4
Jacobi, Freda Mrs (por), 1939, Ja 20,19:2
Jacobi, Frederick, 1952, O 25,17:3
Jacobi, George E, 1945, N 16,19:2
Jacobi, Gustave, 1905, Mr 13,12:4
Jacobi, Harold (por), 1939, Ja 1,25:1
Jacobi, Harold, 1940, Ja 5,20:2
Jacobi, Herman W Mrs, 1946, Ag 8,21:3
Jacobi, J Edward, 1968, S 10,44:5
Jacobi, Laura, 1944, Jl 31,13:4
Jacobi, Mary Putnam Dr, 1906, Je 12,9:5
Jacobi, Otto, 1938, S 11,II,11:1
Jacobi, Pablo, 1961, N 6,37:3
Jacobi, Sanford (por), 1938, N 29,23:3
Jacobi, Victor (funl, D 13,19:3), 1921, D 11,22:3
Jacobi, William F, 1964, F 14,29:1
Jacobini, L Cardinal, 1887, F 27,8:7
Jacobinoff, Sascha, 1960, F 21,93:1
Jacobius, Lawrence, 1950, S 27,31:3
Jacobovits, Morris J, 1950, Ag 15,29:5
Jacobowski, Rose Mrs, 1921, Ja 4,13:3
Jacobs, Aaron J, 1942, Jl 11,13:4; 1961, Ap 29,23:
Jacobs, Abraham, 1964, Je 1,29:2
Jacobs, Abraham L, 1921, S 15,15:5
Jacobs, Abraham Lincoln, 1923, Ja 19,17:5
Jacobs, Albert I, 1964, D 27,64:1
Jacobs, Albert P, 1950, Ag 11,19:3
Jacobs, Alexander, 1968, Je 4,47:1
Jacobs, Alexander W, 1945, Ag 9,21:5
Jacobs, Alonzo F, 1952, Ag 16,16:3
Jacobs, Andrew Mrs, 1909, My 1,9:4
Jacobs, Angela, 1951, F 11,88:4
Jacobs, Arthur E, 1947, My 5,23:2
Jacobs, Avron M, 1946, Je 16,40:3
Jacobs, Ben, 1945, Ja 30,19:3
Jacobs, Benjamin G, 1957, S 20,25:1
Jacobs, C T, 1942, O 28,23:6
Jacobs, C W, 1949, D 2,29:1
Jacobs, Charles, 1937, Mr 15,23:3; 1940, Je 30,33
Jacobs, Charles M (por), 1938, Mr 31,23:1
Jacobs, Charles Mathias, 1919, S 12,13:5
Jacobs, Charles Mrs, 1948, My 14,23:3
Jacobs, Clem V, 1948, S 16,29:6
Jacobs, Daniel, 1867, My 15,8:4
Jacobs, David, 1940, Je 14,21:5; 1955, D 3,17:5; D 16,47:6
Jacobs, Edward, 1961, D 23,23:6
Jacobs, Edwin E, 1953, N 1,86:4
Jacobs, Edwin L Mrs, 1962, Ap 30,27:2
Jacobs, Elmer R, 1937, N 18,23:5
Jacobs, Esther Mrs, 1952, Je 25,29:2
Jacobs, Etta, 1952, Mr 26,29:2
Jacobs, Eugene, 1968, S 28,33:5
Jacobs, Everett, 1942, My 21,19:5
Jacobs, Frank B (por), 1944, Jl 2,19:2
Jacobs, Frederick H Rev, 1910, N 26,9:5
Jacobs, George F, 1956, Je 10,88:3
Jacobs, George W Mrs, 1959, Ja 18,88:5
Jacobs, H B Mrs, 1936, O 22,25:4
Jacobs, H R, 1915, Ja 2,9:7
Jacobs, Hannah J, 1940, My 15,25:5
Jacobs, Harold D, 1959, Jl 22,27:3
Jacobs, Harry, 1940, Mr 2,13:2; 1953, Ja 1,23:5
Jacobs, Harry B, 1955, Jl 25,19:4
Jacobs, Harry L, 1964, Mr 17,35:4
Jacobs, Harry M, 1951, N 26,25:3
Jacobs, Harry S, 1947, Je 4,27:3
Jacobs, Harry W, 1950, Jl 24,17:2
Jacobs, Henri I, 1957, D 20,27:4
Jacobs, Henry, 1963, Ja 23,7:6
Jacobs, Henry B, 1939, D 20,28:5
Jacobs, Henry V, 1947, Ap 2,28:3
Jacobs, Henry W, 1925, Ja 6,25:5
Jacobs, Horace, 1914, Ag 5,13:4
Jacobs, Irving, 1964, My 15,36:7
Jacobs, Irving L, 1952, Ag 5,19:6
Jacobs, Isaac, 1944, O 27,23:3
Jacobs, Isaac R, 1942, O 10,15:3
Jacobs, Isidore, 1956, Ja 22,88:2
Jacobs, J, 1881, My 30,6:3
Jacobs, J Warren, 1947, F 28,23:2
Jacobs, Jack, 1940, Ag 2,15:3
Jacobs, Jacob, 1959, O 15,39:2
Jacobs, Jacob A, 1956, F 6,23:4
Jacobs, Jacob Capt, 1922, D 10,6:3
Jacobs, Jacob L, 1948, Ja 30,24:2
Jacobs, Jacob S, 1950, O 8,104:2
Jacobs, Jacques, 1957, Ja 28,23:4
Jacobs, James J, 1946, O 4,23:4
Jacobs, Jay J, 1957, Je 8,19:4
Jacobs, Jerome J, 1954, N 23,33:1
Jacobs, Jesse, 1948, O 9,19:3
Jacobs, Joe, 1940, Ap 25,24:2
Jacobs, Joel F, 1958, Je 30,19:3
Jacobs, John, 1940, D 26,19:5
Jacobs, John D, 1945, O 19,23:2
Jacobs, John F Jr, 1953, Ap 4,13:4
Jacobs, John M, 1961, F 3,25:2
Jacobs, Joseph, 1942, Mr 18,23:5; 1967, Mr 2
Jacobs, Joseph Dr, 1916, F 1,11:1
Jacobs, Joseph E, 1919, Je 5,13:2
Jacobs, Joseph J, 1956, Jl 28,17:5
Jacobs, Joseph W, 1919, F 6,11:2
Jacobs, L H Mrs, 1951, F 6,27:4
Jacobs, Leo, 1951, D 18,31:4; 1966, S 24,23:
Jacobs, Leo B, 1945, Mr 8,23:1
Jacobs, Leslie W Mrs (M Flint), 1960, F 28
Jacobs, Levi, 1905, Je 8,9:6
Jacobs, Lloyd H, 1954, Je 3,27:3
Jacobs, Louis, 1942, Jl 16,19:2; 1953, Ja 24,1

Jacobs, Louis (est tax appr), 1954, Ap 23,29:2
Jacobs, Louis M, 1959, S 12,21:4; 1968, Ag 9,35:5
Jacobs, M Rev Dr, 1871, Jl 24,1:6
Jacobs, Marion L, 1950, Mr 20,21:5
Jacobs, Mark, 1940, Ap 9,23:4
Jacobs, Marvin, 1967, Ja 12,39:2
Jacobs, Matt C, 1958, S 14,84:3
Jacobs, Maurice R Mrs, 1941, My 6,21:5
Jacobs, Max, 1958, F 28,13:3; 1960, Je 28,31:2; 1962, Ap 22,81:1
Jacobs, Meyer, 1950, Je 4,92:1
Jacobs, Meyer C, 1944, Ag 19,11:4
Jacobs, Meyer Mrs, 1956, N 25,88:3
Jacobs, Michael Jr, 1938, Mr 6,II,8:3
Jacobs, Michael S (Mike), 1953, Ja 25,84:1
Jacobs, Michel, 1958, F 6,27:5
Jacobs, Moe, 1954, Ag 2,17:4
Jacobs, Montague, 1967, Je 13,64:2
Jacobs, Morris, 1923, N 8,19:5; 1942, Ja 26,10:7; 1956, Jl 22,61:4
Jacobs, Morris B, 1965, Jl 14,37:1
Jacobs, Murray, 1964, Ag 31,25:3
Jacobs, Nathan B, 1956, F 16,29:3
Jacobs, Nathan E, 1939, O 25,23:4
Jacobs, Nellie C Mrs, 1944, F 9,19:3
Jacobs, Perry F, 1954, Ag 3,19:2
Jacobs, Phil P (por), 1940, Je 13,23:3
Jacobs, Ralph, 1956, Mr 13,27:5
Jacobs, Ralph J, 1937, Mr 26,21:2
Jacobs, Ralph K, 1950, O 2,23:1
Jacobs, Ralph K Jr, 1961, D 10,88:6
Jacobs, Ralph Mrs, 1966, Ag 19,33:3
Jacobs, Randall, 1967, Je 20,39:2
Jacobs, Raymond P, 1954, F 5,19:1
Jacobs, Rebecca Mrs, 1953, Jl 15,25:5
Jacobs, Reberta E Mrs, 1949, Mr 20,76:4
Jacobs, Robert H, 1959, D 18,30:1; 1961, Mr 12,87:1
Jacobs, Roland H, 1937, Jl 12,20:3
Jacobs, Rudolph, 1953, Mr 19,29:3
Jacobs, S M Jackson, 1952, Je 9,23:4
Jacobs, S Willard, 1960, Jl 3,32:4
Jacobs, Samuel, 1953, Jl 31,19:4
Jacobs, Samuel E, 1949, N 14,27:5
Jacobs, Samuel J Mrs, 1949, Ap 2,15:4
Jacobs, Samuel K, 1954, Ag 11,25:2
Jacobs, Samuel M, 1941, Ap 25,19:4
Jacobs, Samuel Mrs, 1937, Je 8,25:1; 1966, Ag 9,37:2
Jacobs, Samuel W, 1938, Ag 22,13:4
Jacobs, Sarah N, 1925, Mr 26,23:5
Jacobs, Saul, 1966, S 7,41:4
Jacobs, Silas F, 1949, O 19,29:2
Jacobs, Simon, 1955, My 21,17:5
Jacobs, Simon M, 1963, Ag 7,33:1
Jacobs, Sol J (will), 1959, Ag 8,15:6
Jacobs, Stephen H B, 1946, Ag 7,27:5
Jacobs, T Ralph, 1939, Ja 11,19:2
Jacobs, Terrell M, 1957, D 26,19:4
Jacobs, Thomas H B, 1938, Jl 31,33:3
Jacobs, Thomas Mrs, 1961, Ag 20,86:3
Jacobs, Thornwell Sr, 1956, Ag 5,76:7
acobs, Tillie Mrs, 1955, D 27,23:3
acobs, W W (por), 1943, S 2,19:3
acobs, Walter, 1954, Mr 2,25:3
acobs, Walter A, 1967, Jl 14,31:2
acobs, Walter B Mrs, 1948, Mr 9,23:2
acobs, Walter F, 1952, My 22,27:2
acobs, Walter H, 1945, My 22,19:4
acobs, Walter L Mrs, 1964, S 16,31:6
acobs, Whipple, 1952, Ag 20,25:3
acobs, William, 1948, F 15,60:3; 1953, O 2,21:5
acobs, William C Dr, 1915, Jl 24,9:6
acobs, William F (funl plans, My 19,88:4; funl, My 21,35:2), 1957, My 16,31:3
acobs, William H, 1938, Mr 3,21:3
acobs, William I, 1937, S 1,19:3
acobs, William Leroy, 1917, Ap 9,13:5
acobs, William P, 1948, Jl 26,17:1
acobs, William S, 1951, D 27,21:2
acobsen, Alfred, 1952, Ja 5,11:5; 1967, D 19,47:2
acobsen, Alfred Jr, 1964, Ja 14,31:3
acobsen, Anders, 1947, Jl 4,13:6
acobsen, Carlyle Mrs, 1955, N 10,35:3
cobsen, Charles C, 1948, D 19,76:3
cobsen, Charles R Lt-Comdr, 1937, My 16,II,9:1
cobsen, Charles S, 1957, Ja 15,29:1
cobsen, Clarence Mrs, 1957, D 21,19:3
cobsen, Halvor, 1946, Ja 7,20:2
cobsen, Henry I, 1949, My 26,30:2
cobsen, J Arthur, 1947, S 21,60:6
cobsen, James J, 1945, D 23,18:7
cobsen, Jean Mrs, 1944, Ap 27,23:5
cobsen, Keith, 1953, F 9,29:8
cobsen, Owen P, 1958, D 3,37:2
cobsen, Peter N, 1938, Je 28,19:5
cobsen, Pierre, 1957, Jl 2,7:8
cobsen, Sibyl V Mrs, 1964, O 21,43:8
cobsen, Walter, 1955, Ja 20,31:3
cobsen, William S, 1955, Ap 11,23:6
cobsohn, Moritz Rev, 1910, Jl 3,II,7:4
cobsohn, Sally, 1952, Jl 12,13:5
cobsohn, Sally Mrs, 1962, Ag 18,19:4
obson, Abe H Mrs, 1954, D 28,23:1
obson, Abraham Mrs, 1937, Jl 23,19:5

Jacobson, Alan A Mrs, 1962, Jl 23,21:1
Jacobson, Albert D Dr, 1920, My 4,11:3
Jacobson, Albert W, 1947, Ja 12,7:2
Jacobson, Alfred F, 1941, O 5,49:2
Jacobson, Alfred H, 1963, Mr 20,16:1
Jacobson, Archie, 1960, Je 28,31:2
Jacobson, Aron H Mrs, 1958, Je 19,31:3
Jacobson, Arthur C, 1958, O 16,37:3
Jacobson, Avram Mrs, 1945, O 15,17:5
Jacobson, B E Dr, 1918, My 17,13:8
Jacobson, Barnett, 1941, Mr 1,15:3
Jacobson, Barnett Mrs, 1949, Ap 19,25:3
Jacobson, Benjamin, 1949, Ja 19,28:2; 1950, N 6,27:3
Jacobson, Bernt A, 1966, Ap 24,86:7
Jacobson, Charles A, 1942, O 13,23:3
Jacobson, Charles A Mrs, 1959, D 26,13:5
Jacobson, Charles Mrs, 1942, Je 6,13:6
Jacobson, Conrad C, 1962, Ag 30,29:2
Jacobson, David B, 1955, Ja 3,27:5
Jacobson, Eddie, 1955, O 26,31:3
Jacobson, Edward A, 1947, Jl 25,17:6
Jacobson, Ferdinand, 1948, Mr 24,25:4
Jacobson, Frank B, 1948, S 30,27:5
Jacobson, George, 1952, Mr 20,29:4
Jacobson, Gunther, 1951, Mr 11,92:3
Jacobson, Gustave S, 1944, D 27,20:2
Jacobson, Harris A, 1941, D 23,21:2
Jacobson, Harry S, 1965, D 6,37:5
Jacobson, Harry S Mrs, 1951, O 23,29:4
Jacobson, Herman, 1961, Ag 7,23:5
Jacobson, Hymie, 1952, Ja 9,29:5
Jacobson, Isaac, 1952, F 22,21:4
Jacobson, Jacob, 1962, Ap 30,27:2
Jacobson, Jacob L, 1948, Ja 15,23:4
Jacobson, John, 1963, Jl 15,29:5
Jacobson, Joseph, 1952, My 23,21:2
Jacobson, Joseph P, 1961, O 16,29:3
Jacobson, Julius G Mrs, 1938, S 10,17:4
Jacobson, Kenneth H, 1952, Ag 31,45:2
Jacobson, Leonard L, 1946, S 28,17:3
Jacobson, Louis, 1952, D 12,29:6
Jacobson, Louis J, 1963, D 9,35:3
Jacobson, Marcus A, 1948, F 28,15:4
Jacobson, Max, 1947, D 25,21:3
Jacobson, Max L, 1957, Ag 11,81:2
Jacobson, Max Mrs, 1944, Je 17,13:1
Jacobson, Milton, 1964, O 11,88:5
Jacobson, Moritz, 1961, Jl 17,21:5
Jacobson, Morris M, 1949, O 24,23:2
Jacobson, Moses P, 1945, My 1,23:4
Jacobson, Nicholas Mrs, 1948, S 30,28:2
Jacobson, Norman, 1944, Mr 12,38:3
Jacobson, Orville K (Bud), 1960, Ap 15,24:1
Jacobson, Oscar, 1956, N 26,27:4
Jacobson, Peter N, 1948, D 12,92:2
Jacobson, Phil Mrs, 1956, D 20,29:4
Jacobson, Ralph H, 1959, S 12,21:4
Jacobson, Richard N, 1966, Ap 1,35:2
Jacobson, Robert, 1944, F 1,19:2
Jacobson, Robert Mrs, 1949, Mr 23,27:4; 1954, D 28, 23:3
Jacobson, Robert P, 1957, My 5,88:7
Jacobson, Sam, 1947, Ja 1,33:5
Jacobson, Samuel J, 1966, O 13,45:2
Jacobson, Samuel M, 1939, Jl 5,17:4
Jacobson, Selly Mrs, 1915, Jl 3,7:6
Jacobson, Shaye, 1948, Ja 15,23:4
Jacobson, Sidney, 1907, Jl 16,7:5; 1959, D 8,45:5
Jacobson, Sidney O, 1954, My 5,28:6
Jacobson, Simon Rev, 1921, O 22,13:6
Jacobson, Terrence Prof, 1912, N 4,11:5
Jacobson, Theodore, 1948, Jl 16,19:4
Jacobson, Victor H, 1959, Ag 24,21:3
Jacobson, Walter, 1947, Ja 27,25:2
Jacobson, Walter H, 1956, D 21,23:3
Jacobson, William, 1944, Mr 11,13:2
Jacobsson, Edward G, 1961, My 5,29:2
Jacobsson, Per, 1963, My 6,1:3
Jacobstein, Harry, 1955, N 8,29:4
Jacobstein, Meyer, 1963, Ap 19,43:2
Jacobstein, Meyer Dr, 1937, F 18,21:3
Jacobucci, Michael A, 1955, Ap 1,28:2
Jacobus, Bentley V N, 1941, Mr 14,21:5
Jacobus, C Russell, 1958, My 27,31:4
Jacobus, Clifford, 1942, S 16,23:4
Jacobus, David S, 1955, F 12,15:1
Jacobus, David S Mrs, 1951, N 6,29:4
Jacobus, Dewitt V, 1950, Mr 17,23:1
Jacobus, Elmer W Mrs, 1965, Ja 19,33:2
Jacobus, George R, 1965, Jl 23,29:1
Jacobus, Harold C, 1951, N 8,29:4
Jacobus, Harold S, 1937, Ap 6,23:5
Jacobus, Harold S Mrs, 1960, F 17,35:3
Jacobus, Herbert C, 1965, Jl 26,23:5
Jacobus, John W, 1948, Je 14,23:4
Jacobus, Josephine M Mrs, 1940, Mr 24,30:7
Jacobus, Leroy, 1957, S 22,86:7
Jacobus, Louis, 1912, Je 7,13:3
Jacobus, Mandeville C, 1910, F 17,9:5
Jacobus, Martha M Mrs, 1909, Ag 24,9:5
Jacobus, Martin R, 1956, Mr 24,19:4
Jacobus, Melancthon Rev Dr, 1937, N 1,21:2
Jacobus, Nelson E Sr, 1957, Ap 23,31:2

Jacobus, Nelson L, 1941, N 13,27:4
Jacobus, Roland A, 1942, Mr 28,17:2
Jacobus, Roland A Mrs, 1939, Ap 21,23:1
Jacobus, Rosabelle, 1951, N 13,29:5
Jacobus, Roy M, 1964, Jl 27,31:3
Jacobus, Theodore I, 1946, Mr 30,15:4
Jacobus, William, 1948, F 18,27:5
Jacobus, Worthington Mead, 1925, Je 17,21:5
Jacobwitz, David, 1941, O 25,17:3
Jacoby, Abraham I, 1960, D 11,88:6
Jacoby, Adolph, 1959, Ap 13,31:3
Jacoby, Clark E, 1942, Ag 25,23:3
Jacoby, Douglas P A, 1945, Ag 27,19:5
Jacoby, Elmer A, 1951, F 7,29:4
Jacoby, Emerich, 1959, O 29,33:3
Jacoby, Frank, 1952, Je 9,23:5; 1954, S 16,29:5
Jacoby, Fred Sr Mrs, 1955, Mr 13,86:1
Jacoby, Frederick, 1966, Ja 13,25:5
Jacoby, George W, 1937, F 24,24:2
Jacoby, George W (por),(will, S 24,20:1), 1940, S 12, 25:1
Jacoby, Gerhard, 1960, Ag 20,19:5
Jacoby, Gustav, 1912, Je 22,13:5
Jacoby, H Murray, 1955, Ja 28,20:1
Jacoby, Harold Mrs, 1945, Ag 2,19:4
Jacoby, Henry, 1959, Ap 4,19:5
Jacoby, Henry E, 1952, Jl 14,17:5
Jacoby, Henry S, 1955, Ag 3,23:4
Jacoby, J, 1877, Mr 8,4:6
Jacoby, Jerome J, 1954, Jl 29,23:6
Jacoby, Joseph R, 1962, Jl 10,33:2
Jacoby, Josephine, 1948, N 15,25:3
Jacoby, Kurt, 1968, S 2,19:4
Jacoby, Leo S, 1965, My 31,17:4
Jacoby, Maclear, 1965, Ag 10,29:2
Jacoby, Max, 1911, Ap 9,13:4; 1951, F 20,25:4
Jacoby, Morris Mrs, 1959, F 15,86:8
Jacoby, Nat D, 1948, Ja 27,25:4
Jacoby, Paul E, 1954, Ag 4,21:2
Jacoby, Raymond W, 1959, D 16,41:3
Jacoby, Samuel, 1938, Ap 30,15:4
Jacoby, Victor, 1960, N 8,29:2
Jacoby, Wilmer M, 1959, Mr 7,21:3
Jacobziner, Harold, 1966, F 9,39:3
Jacocks, Everett W, 1947, Ag 7,21:3
Jacocks, George T, 1944, Ja 11,19:4
Jacocks, Harold H, 1967, O 28,31:5
Jacomo, Antonio, 1951, Ja 18,27:3
Jacoponi, Armando, 1956, Ja 9,25:1
Jacopozzi, F, 1932, F 7,27:2
Jacoubs, Louis J, 1956, F 15,31:5
Jacoves, Felix N, 1961, My 8,35:1
Jacoway, Henderson M Mrs, 1957, Mr 28,31:3
Jacquart, Charles E, 1955, F 3,23:4
Jacquelin, Herbert T B Mrs, 1953, Jl 9,25:2
Jacquelin, John H, 1910, D 9,11:4
Jacquemin, William G, 1944, Mr 29,21:3
Jacques, Alfred G, 1939, F 23,23:4
Jacques, Camille, 1955, O 1,19:5
Jacques, Clara Mrs, 1924, My 20,21:4
Jacques, David R, 1905, Ja 20,1:3
Jacques, Eugene Mrs, 1915, Ag 7,7:7
Jacques, Frank D, 1951, Ag 2,21:4
Jacques, Henri C, 1954, Ap 23,27:4
Jacques, Herbert, 1916, D 22,9:3
Jacques, Jean B, 1956, F 26,89:2
Jacques, John W, 1944, D 14,23:2
Jacques, Louis Sr, 1948, S 16,29:3
Jacques, M, 1954, Jl 25,68:6
Jacques, Marvin S, 1952, N 28,25:3
Jacques, Philip, 1908, Ap 12,7:7
Jacques, Prince of Bourbon-Parma, 1964, N 6,26:5
Jacques, Richard R, 1958, My 31,15:6
Jacques, Robert A, 1956, Ja 17,33:2
Jacques, Wilfred H, 1954, Jl 6,23:3
Jacques, William, 1964, Ap 8,43:4
Jacquet, Edward A, 1948, Ja 5,19:2
Jacquet, Gustave, 1909, Jl 14,7:5
Jacquez, George W, 1909, Jl 9,7:3
Jacquier, Louis, 1946, Ag 9,17:4
Jacquier, Paul, 1961, Mr 5,86:8
Jacquin, George I, 1953, N 14,17:6
Jacquin, Max, 1954, S 28,29:5
Jacquish, Thomas, 1913, Jl 21,7:6
Jacquot, F E, 1952, Ja 11,22:2
Jacuzzi, Joseph, 1965, Ja 7,31:2
Jadassohn, Alex, 1948, D 23,20:3
Jadel, Celeste, 1948, N 1,25:4
Jadlowker, Hermann, 1953, My 15,23:4
Jadull, Frederick W, 1953, D 22,31:4
Jadwell, Sarah E Mrs, 1942, S 6,30:8
Jadwin, E, 1931, Mr 3,29:3
Jaeckel, Albert F (por), 1949, Mr 31,25:5
Jaeckel, Charlotte Mrs, 1950, Ap 28,21:2
Jaeckel, Hugo, 1939, Mr 9,22:2
Jaeckel, John P, 1941, Je 17,21:2
Jaeckel, T, 1935, D 28,15:3
Jaeckel, Theodore Mrs, 1947, S 16,23:6
Jaeckel, Walter F, 1947, D 30,24:3
Jaecker, Harry C Mrs, 1943, D 16,27:2
Jaeger, Adolph C, 1956, Ag 14,25:5
Jaeger, Alphons O, 1953, Jl 23,23:3
Jaeger, Andrew P Sr, 1940, D 17,26:2

Jaeger, Annie Mrs, 1944, F 14,17:4
Jaeger, Arthur L, 1950, S 18,23:3
Jaeger, Charles C, 1949, Ja 10,25:5
Jaeger, Charles H, 1942, S 13,53:1
Jaeger, Charles L, 1954, S 25,15:6
Jaeger, Charles T, 1942, S 29,24:2
Jaeger, David G, 1955, Ap 7,27:2
Jaeger, Ellsworth, 1962, Ag 9,25:5
Jaeger, F L, 1948, N 16,29:6
Jaeger, Ferdinand J, 1949, My 25,29:2
Jaeger, Francis M, 1904, F 14,7:6
Jaeger, Frank, 1943, Mr 21,26:3
Jaeger, Frank A Sr, 1954, Je 28,19:3
Jaeger, Fred O, 1949, N 29,29:3
Jaeger, Frederick W, 1942, Jl 20,13:2
Jaeger, George, 1949, Ag 12,17:5
Jaeger, Gustav Prof, 1917, My 18,13:7
Jaeger, Gustave L, 1922, O 21,13:4
Jaeger, Hans, 1954, Mr 2,25:5
Jaeger, Harry A, 1952, Je 17,27:4
Jaeger, Henry, 1946, O 13,62:4; 1956, S 1,15:5
Jaeger, Irwin F, 1961, F 11,23:2
Jaeger, John, 1946, My 2,21:2
Jaeger, Joseph, 1924, Jl 7,15:4; 1951, My 18,27:3
Jaeger, Julius, 1942, Ja 25,41:3
Jaeger, Louis C, 1962, Ap 17,35:3
Jaeger, Martha, 1963, D 3,43:1
Jaeger, Michael, 1948, S 9,27:2
Jaeger, Robert T, 1951, Ap 24,29:2
Jaeger, Samuel J, 1968, F 6,43:3
Jaeger, Theodore F, 1942, Mr 26,23:2
Jaeger, Walter, 1925, Jl 14,21:6
Jaeger, Werner W, 1961, O 20,33:1
Jaegerjuber, Max, 1917, Ap 10,13:6
Jaegers, Albert, 1925, Jl 23,19:6
Jaegers, Augustine, 1952, D 8,41:4
Jaeggi, William A, 1943, F 20,13:4
Jaegle, Anthony J, 1948, D 8,31:3
Jaegle, Robert F, 1950, My 24,29:4
Jaekels, Raymond, 1938, Ja 17,19:1
Jaen, Nicola V, 1950, S 17,105:2
Jaenicke, Bruno (por), 1946, D 27,19:3
Jaeobsen, Ernest O, 1917, Ja 24,9:3
Jaernefelt, Edvard A, 1958, Je 24,31:2
Jaffa, Adele S, 1953, Ja 21,31:1
Jaffares, James, 1937, My 6,25:4
Jaffcoat, Harry R, 1948, Jl 12,19:5
Jaffe, Abram S, 1963, Je 27,33:1
Jaffe, Arthur Mrs, 1968, Jl 5,25:1
Jaffe, Bernard, 1944, Ap 19,23:5
Jaffe, Boris, 1962, S 20,34:1
Jaffe, Charles, 1941, Jl 16,17:4; 1949, F 20,60:1
Jaffe, George, 1953, O 25,89:1
Jaffe, Isidor, 1956, Je 20,31:1
Jaffe, Jacob K, 1960, Ap 9,23:4
Jaffe, Jean (funl plans, D 1,29:3), 1958, N 23,88:4
Jaffe, Joseph O, 1947, My 15,25:3
Jaffe, Leo Mrs, 1946, My 7,21:2
Jaffe, Leon, 1958, Ag 18,19:5
Jaffe, Lester A, 1953, Mr 29,92:1
Jaffe, Lou, 1959, O 22,37:4
Jaffe, Louis I, 1950, Mr 13,21:2
Jaffe, Louis M, 1968, Mr 24,93:1
Jaffe, Louis N, 1944, Ag 2,15:6
Jaffe, Matthew Mrs, 1953, N 25,23:3
Jaffe, Morris, 1961, My 22,31:2
Jaffe, Nat, 1945, Ag 7,23:3
Jaffe, Phil Mrs, 1955, Mr 17,45:4
Jaffe, Ralph, 1956, O 17,35:4
Jaffe, Richard H Dr, 1937, D 19,II,8:6
Jaffe, Sam Mrs, 1941, Mr 1,15:5; 1951, Mr 22,31:3
Jaffe, Solomon E Rabbi, 1923, N 16,17:2
Jaffe, Zebulin, 1962, Ap 26,33:5
Jaffee, Charles, 1955, N 8,31:4
Jaffee, Charles D, 1937, O 13,23:6
Jaffee, Herman Mrs, 1948, O 5,25:4
Jaffee, Leo H, 1952, O 7,29:4
Jaffee, Louis J, 1953, Ja 16,23:2
Jaffee, Mortimer G, 1960, O 8,23:4
Jaffer, Louis A, 1948, Ap 21,27:2
Jaffer, Roslyn Mrs, 1939, Ap 7,21:4
Jaffin, Abraham E, 1952, N 27,31:3
Jaffin, Barney, 1950, Jl 9,69:3
Jaffin, John J, 1964, My 2,27:4
Jaffin, William, 1937, F 3,23:1
Jaffray, Clive T, 1956, N 17,21:3
Jaffray, Edward S, 1924, F 6,19:5; 1937, Je 8,25:6
Jaffray, Howard S, 1912, D 21,13:4
Jaffray, Julia K (por), 1941, My 23,21:1
Jaffray, Reginald, 1944, My 8,19:1
Jaffray, Reginald Mrs, 1945, Jl 31,19:2
Jaffray, Reginald R, 1947, Je 9,21:5
Jaffray, Richard P, 1950, Je 29,29:1
Jaffray, Robert, 1902, Ap 13,7:6
Jaffray, Robert Sen, 1914, D 19,13:5
Jaffray, William G, 1949, D 29,26:2
Jafnel, Otto B, 1946, Je 22,19:3
Jageler, John F, 1946, F 18,21:3
Jagels, Charles, 1950, Ag 8,29:3
Jagels, Charles A Mrs, 1950, Mr 20,21:4
Jagels, Claus H C, 1945, D 17,22:2
Jager, Harry, 1942, My 29,17:2
Jager, Henry, 1949, S 7,29:1
Jager, Philip Dr, 1925, N 19,25:4
Jagerhuber, Anton, 1912, Ap 10,13:5
Jaggar, Thomas A, 1953, Ja 19,23:1
Jaggar, Thomas Augustus Rev Dr, 1912, D 15,17:4
Jaggard, Robert H, 1948, N 18,27:3
Jaggard, William, 1947, Ap 30,25:6
Jagger, Albert, 1940, Ag 14,19:5
Jagger, Arthur M, 1957, N 12,37:2
Jagger, Claude N Mrs, 1940, D 14,17:3
Jagger, Ira F, 1946, S 4,23:3
Jagger, Ivan C, 1939, F 18,15:5
Jagger, Samuel B, 1948, S 3,19:1
Jagmetty, Joshua S, 1944, My 3,19:5
Jagmetty, Victor F, 1943, Jl 6,21:3
Jago, William H, 1925, O 4,5:2
Jagoe, James Harvey, 1914, Jl 15,9:6
Jagow, G Von, 1935, Ja 13,33:1
Jagow, Paul F, 1960, O 10,31:1
Jagrosseau, Msgr, 1941, Ja 21,21:4
Jagu, Fernand, 1939, D 4,23:5
Jahanbani, Mohammed Hossein, 1954, My 1,10:6
Jahenny, Marie J, 1941, Mr 13,21:5
Jahiel, Richard (por), 1955, Je 3,23:3
Jahn, Alfredo, 1940, Je 13,23:3
Jahn, Augusta A Mrs, 1938, Ja 12,21:3
Jahn, Francis P, 1941, Ag 5,19:4
Jahn, Frank J, 1948, My 14,23:4
Jahn, Gustave A Maj, 1906, Je 17,9:6
Jahn, Henry R, 1954, My 4,29:3
Jahn, William F, 1956, O 3,29:1
Jahn, William F Mrs, 1956, O 3,29:1
Jahncke, Ernest L (trb lr, N 29,36:5), 1960, N 17,37:4
Jahne, Charles E, 1963, S 30,29:4
Jahnke, Charles B, 1941, My 7,25:3
Jahoda, Hedwig E F, 1961, D 24,36:7
Jahr, George M, 1942, My 30,15:2
Jahries, Gus, 1937, Mr 31,46:7
Jahrsdorfer, O Edward, 1938, S 13,23:3
Jahss, Samuel A, 1943, Je 1,23:3
Jailer, Joseph W (mem ser plans, N 3,39:1), 1960, Ag 24,29:3
Jaime, Don, 1931, O 3,17:6
Jais, Adele Mrs, 1940, Je 27,23:4
Jais, Jacob D, 1953, Ag 27,25:5
Jaisohn, Phil, 1951, Ja 6,15:4
Jakob, Christofred, 1956, My 9,33:4
Jakob, Max, 1955, Ja 6,27:3
Jakobb, Christian A Mrs, 1960, Jl 15,23:4
Jakobowicz, Stefan S, 1946, Mr 31,46:4
Jakobsen, J Neil, 1952, Mr 25,27:1
Jakobson, August M, 1963, My 25,25:5
Jakobsson, Gustav H, 1947, O 26,70:4
Jakowski, Hilary G, 1966, Mr 13,86:7
Jakowski, Vladmir M, 1948, Ja 28,23:3
Jaksch, Abbot, 1939, Ja 5,23:2
Jaksch, Wenzel, 1966, N 28,39:4
Jaktchin, Georg, 1944, F 18,17:2
Jakubiak, Jakob, 1947, Ag 3,53:2
Jakubiak, Martin, 1947, Ag 3,53:2
Jakubik, John J, 1950, Je 16,25:3
Jakubowski, John Mrs, 1952, My 8,31:5
Jal, Auguste, 1873, Ap 28,1:4
Jalan, Dansidhar, 1943, Ja 9,13:4
Jalbert, Adelard A, 1960, My 31,31:3
Jalbert, Horace H, 1960, D 18,84:4
Jalhay, Eugenio A, 1950, D 1,25:2
Jalkut, Lee D Mrs, 1955, Ag 4,25:2
Jallade, Louis E, 1957, F 27,27:1
Jaller, Abraham A, 1957, My 27,31:4
Jaloux, Edmond (por), 1949, Ag 24,25:4
Jalowetz, Heinrich, 1946, F 4,25:5
Jaluzot, Jules, 1916, F 23,13:5
Jamais, Juan, 1950, S 25,23:4
Jamar, Armand, 1946, D 18,29:4
Jambon, Marcel, 1908, O 1,9:7
Jambor, Louis, 1954, Je 12,15:4
Jamerson, H Curby, 1966, O 26,47:3
Jamerson, H Curby Mrs, 1952, D 22,25:4
James, Aelfric Sr, 1951, Je 9,19:2
James, Albert, 1913, D 25,9:4
James, Albert E, 1952, Ap 26,23:2
James, Alex, 1953, Je 2,29:5
James, Alexander, 1946, F 27,25:5
James, Alfred P, 1946, O 12,19:5
James, Alonzo Mrs, 1947, Ja 31,23:5
James, Alvah B, 1958, S 23,33:1
James, Ambrose Sr, 1939, N 7,28:3
James, Arthur, 1946, My 24,19:3
James, Arthur C (por), 1941, Je 5,23:1
James, Arthur C, 1957, Je 5,35:5
James, Arthur C Mrs, 1941, My 16,23:5
James, Arthur L, 1964, D 14,35:3
James, Arthur Mrs, 1948, My 4,25:5
James, Austin F, 1952, Ap 15,27:3
James, Bart M, 1966, D 24,19:3
James, Benjamin, 1961, Ja 27,48:1
James, Billy, 1965, N 21,87:1
James, Bushrod Dr, 1903, Ja 7,9:6
James, C F Col, 1903, F 20,9:6
James, Carrie Mrs, 1950, Ap 19,1:2
James, Carvel Mrs (N Talmadge),(funl, D 29,48:7), 1957, D 25,31:1
James, Carver M Mrs (Norma Talmadge),(will, Ja 2,22:4; cor), 1958, Ja 6,22:2
James, Charles C, 1957, O 2,33:4
James, Charles E, 1925, O 3,15:5
James, Charles F Mrs, 1903, D 27,7:6
James, Charles H, 1957, Je 14,25:4; 1965, N 16,47:2
James, Charles I, 1925, S 10,25:4
James, Charles I Mrs, 1937, D 7,25:4
James, Clairborne M, 1940, Ag 1,21:5
James, Clarence E, 1947, D 16,33:2
James, Cyrus R Rev, 1937, Ag 25,21:5
James, D K, 1957, D 31,17:1
James, D Willis, 1907, S 14,9:5
James, Daniel, 1955, D 18,93:1
James, Darwin R, 1908, N 20,9:2
James, Darwin R (por), 1937, Ag 8,II,7:1
James, Darwin R Jr, 1955, Je 19,92:5
James, Darwin R Mrs, 1912, Ap 1,13:5
James, David, 1903, Ag 27,9:5
James, David E, 1952, S 23,33:3
James, David J, 1940, D 1,62:4
James, Edmund Janes Dr, 1925, Je 20,13:6
James, Edward, 1950, O 28,17:3
James, Edward C, 1940, My 14,23:6
James, Edward C Jr, 1940, Je 6,25:4
James, Edward H, 1954, O 7,23:1
James, Edward J Mrs, 1948, Ag 30,17:1
James, Edward P, 1943, Je 19,13:2
James, Edward P Mrs, 1944, Mr 19,41:3
James, Edward R, 1954, D 18,15:6
James, Edwin, 1882, Mr 7,10:3
James, Edwin L, 1951, D 4,1:2
James, Edwin W, 1967, D 25,21:4
James, Eldon R, 1949, Ja 3,23:5
James, Eldon R Mrs, 1958, Jl 20,64:8
James, Elias O, 1954, S 16,29:4
James, Eliza E Mrs, 1941, D 18,27:5
James, Elmer, 1959, Ap 24,27:4
James, Emerson D, 1967, Ap 13,43:3
James, Ernestine W Mrs, 1939, D 20,28:5
James, Eugene W, 1937, Mr 9,23:5
James, Everett, 1955, Mr 9,27:4
James, F J Lt, 1864, S 11,8:2
James, Fleming, 1959, S 13,84:8
James, Francis M, 1953, My 8,25:4
James, Frank, 1915, F 19,9:6
James, Frank A, 1965, D 10,47:1
James, Frank H, 1938, O 1,17:4
James, Frank L Dr, 1907, My 21,9:6
James, Frank Mrs, 1944, Jl 7,15:4
James, Frank T Mrs, 1942, S 9,23:2
James, Franklin E, 1948, Ag 6,17:5
James, Frederic W, 1948, D 30,19:3
James, Frederick K, 1940, Ja 6,13:6
James, Frederick T, 1961, My 10,45:4
James, G W, 1883, N 17,2:2
James, Gail, 1949, D 5,26:4
James, Geoffrey M, 1937, F 19,19:2
James, Geoffrey M Mrs, 1960, Ag 14,93:1
James, George Abbot Mrs, 1908, My 30,7:6
James, George E, 1950, Ja 31,23:3
James, George H, 1952, Mr 21,24:3
James, George Payne Rainsford, 1860, Je 27,4:6
James, George R (por), 1937, Mr 10,23:3
James, George R, 1965, Mr 3,41:3
James, George S, 1946, Jl 23,25:4
James, George T, 1952, N 13,31:5
James, George Wharton, 1923, N 9,17:5
James, Gladden, 1948, Ag 29,56:3
James, Guy, 1953, S 16,33:3
James, H F, 1879, Je 7,5:2
James, H Percy, 1957, F 4,19:4
James, H T, 1952, F 15,25:1
James, Harold M (will), 1964, Ag 22,15:6
James, Harold W, 1965, My 5,28:1
James, Harold W Mrs, 1963, O 26,27:1
James, Harrie A, 1939, My 3,24:2
James, Harriett Webb, 1923, Je 4,15:6
James, Harry B, 1921, Je 9,15:4
James, Harry B Mrs (A Cleveland), 1954, Ja
James, Harry L, 1944, S 19,21:2
James, Henry (por),(funl, Mr 4,11:7), 1916, F
James, Henry, 1947, D 15,25:3; 1957, Jl 15,19
James, Henry A, 1938, Ja 2,42:1; 1966, Je 24,
James, Henry Dwight, 1903, D 27,7:5
James, Henry J Mrs, 1941, F 20,19:5
James, Henry Mrs, 1946, My 4,15:4; 1960, Ag
James, Henry Sr, 1882, D 20,5:1
James, Herman G, 1959, N 27,29:3
James, Holman, 1946, F 6,23:3
James, Horace D, 1925, O 17,15:4
James, Howard Mrs, 1909, Mr 6,7:4
James, Huntington, 1947, Ap 9,25:3
James, Irene A, 1940, N 3,57:1
James, J O, 1883, Je 27,1:6
James, J W, 1915, Ag 31,9:5
James, J William, 1957, O 25,27:1
James, James A, 1962, F 13,35:5
James, James O, 1959, O 19,29:1
James, Jenkin, 1949, N 2,27:6
James, Jesse, 1946, N 20,23:3
James, John, 1941, Ag 1,15:4
James, John E Dr, 1910, F 17,9:5
James, John H, 1947, O 17,22:2

James, John J, 1951, F 8,23:5
James, John M Mrs, 1952, N 8,17:4
James, John Sylvester, 1921, Ap 10,22:3
James, John T (Fakir), 1953, F 20,19:3
James, John W, 1951, Ap 10,27:3
James, John Wells, 1915, O 22,11:5
James, Joseph H, 1948, F 13,21:1
James, Joshua, 1958, Mr 31,27:3
James, Jules, 1957, Mr 13,31:5
James, Julian Mrs, 1922, Ap 12,21:5
James, Lee R F, 1959, Mr 16,31:5
James, Lee W, 1963, Je 27,33:1
James, Lee W Mrs, 1956, My 12,19:6
James, Leon C, 1956, Jl 20,17:4
James, Leon C Mrs, 1955, O 13,32:1
James, Levin Mrs, 1944, D 10,54:3
James, Lewis L, 1959, F 22,88:5
James, Linwood C, 1942, N 11,25:4
James, Lionel, 1955, Je 1,33:5
James, Louis, 1910, Mr 6,II,11:3
James, Lucy W Mrs, 1938, Ja 21,20:3
James, M E Clifton, 1963, My 10,33:3
James, M R, 1936, Je 13,17:6
James, Macgill Mrs, 1947, Ap 15,25:5
James, Marguerite, 1955, F 19,15:5
James, Marquis (funl N 23,23:2), 1955, N 20,89:1
James, Milton C, 1962, S 18,39:3
James, Monasche, 1944, D 10,54:3
James, Murray, 1956, N 21,27:5
James, Nathaniel W, 1911, Jl 25,7:5
James, Nelson P, 1937, Mr 21,II,8:4
James, Norman Mrs, 1943, N 2,25:5
James, Norman W, 1953, Ag 3,17:5
James, Oliver B, 1955, Ap 21,29:2
James, Ollie M Mrs, 1961, S 18,29:6
James, Ollie M Sen, 1918, Ag 29,7:3
James, Percy G, 1941, Ap 25,19:2
James, Peter, 1954, Ag 24,27:2
James, Peter B, 1964, N 4,39:3
James, Philip Mrs, 1945, Jl 21,11:5
James, Proctor, 1955, Jl 28,23:4
James, Ralph E, 1941, My 12,17:2
James, Ralph H Mrs, 1944, O 28,15:6
James, Reese D Mrs, 1954, Ag 13,15:5
James, Reginald W, 1964, Jl 9,33:1
James, Rian, 1953, Ap 27,23:5
James, Richard C, 1949, Ag 24,25:4
James, Richard L, 1956, Je 3,86:8
James, Robert C Dr, 1920, N 15,15:5
James, Robert F, 1959, N 21,23:4
James, Robert Francis Lt, 1917, N 17,13:4
James, Robert K, 1950, Ap 6,29:4
James, Robert L, 1955, Ap 12,29:4
James, Rorer A, 1921, Ag 7,22:5
James, Rover A Jr (will, My 25,4:6), 1937, My 21, 21:2
James, Roy L, 1944, N 4,15:2
James, Samuel H, 1946, D 17,31:4
James, Stanley B, 1951, N 2,23:3
James, Stephen R, 1948, Mr 16,27:2
James, T L, 1944, Jl 29,13:4
James, Thomas D, 1939, N 1,23:4
James, Thomas L, 1946, D 13,23:3
James, Thomas L Mrs, 1910, N 20,II,13:4
James, Thomas Lemuel Gen, 1916, S 12,11:3
James, Thomas M, 1940, Mr 9,15:2; 1942, Jl 9,21:5
James, Thomas W, 1961, Je 8,35:1
James, Tom, 1948, Je 3,25:2
James, Ulysses S, 1944, N 26,57:1
James, Ursula Lady, 1966, Ag 27,29:4
James, W, 1885, F 24,2:3
James, W B, 1927, Ap 7,25:3
James, W Frank, 1945, N 18,44:2
James, W L, 1966, Ag 27,29:4
James, W M Sir, 1881, Je 8,2:5
James, Walter B Mrs, 1946, Ag 16,21:4
James, Walter M Mrs, 1941, F 23,15:2
James, Walter S, 1943, Jl 22,19:4
James, Ward B, 1940, My 10,24:4
James, Warner, 1947, Je 24,23:2
James, Will, 1942, S 4,23:3
James, Willard W, 1964, Mr 2,27:5
James, William (funl, Ag 28,9:5), 1910, Ag 27,7:5
James, William, 1948, N 19,27:4; 1961, S 28,41:2
James, William B, 1956, Ap 3,35:2
James, William C, 1955, O 3,27:5
James, William D, 1948, Ap 18,72:6
James, William F, 1943, D 16,27:2; 1955, O 15,15:6
James, William G, 1947, Ag 15,17:2
James, William H, 1951, Mr 15,29:5
James, William H Mrs, 1954, Jl 21,27:6
James, William J, 1941, Ja 6,15:4; 1956, N 4,87:1
James, William L, 1943, Ja 11,15:2
James, William M, 1942, Jl 11,13:1
James, William Q, 1952, F 20,29:5
James, William Rev, 1917, F 23,11:6
James, William S, 1964, Mr 1,83:1
James, William T, 1937, Ja 27,21:5
James, William Thomas, 1913, O 2,11:4
James, Willis, 1916, Ap 29,11:4
James Anthony, Sister (Murray), 1955, Jl 11,23:4
James of Hereford, Baron, 1911, Ag 19,7:6
Jameson, Albert E C, 1944, Ag 3,19:1
Jameson, Andrew, 1941, F 16,41:1
Jameson, Anna Brownell, 1860, Ap 7,1:3
Jameson, Arthur H, 1958, F 7,21:4
Jameson, Booth T, 1956, D 20,29:5
Jameson, Charles M, 1905, Mr 22,9:6
Jameson, Charles R, 1961, O 24,37:4
Jameson, Edwin C, 1945, S 4,23:5
Jameson, Edwin T, 1968, O 1,48:1
Jameson, Ephraim Hall Emery Rev, 1907, O 14,9:6
Jameson, George L, 1961, Ag 8,30:1
Jameson, Henry Dr, 1924, F 14,17:4
Jameson, House B Mrs (E Taliaferro), 1958, Mr 3, 27:3
Jameson, Howard L, 1942, Jl 3,17:3
Jameson, John B, 1960, Mr 11,25:4
Jameson, John B Mrs, 1952, D 1,23:2
Jameson, John D Mrs, 1956, S 13,35:4
Jameson, John F Dr (por), 1937, S 29,23:1
Jameson, Lean der Starr Sir, 1917, N 27,13:3
Jameson, Louis B Mrs, 1955, Ap 11,23:4
Jameson, Max A, 1960, D 7,44:8
Jameson, Max Mrs, 1953, Ja 18,93:1
Jameson, Minor S, 1955, My 22,89:2
Jameson, Nathan C, 1910, Ag 28,II,9:6
Jameson, Ovid B Mrs, 1937, My 18,23:3
Jameson, Patrick C, 1939, O 28,15:2
Jameson, Richard H, 1946, D 5,32:2
Jameson, Robert H, 1943, S 25,15:6
Jameson, Robert M, 1923, S 20,4:5
Jameson, Robert W, 1953, Ap 12,89:2
Jameson, Russell P, 1954, Je 4,23:2
Jameson, Thomas, 1943, Ap 24,13:6
Jameson, Wallace E, 1938, N 22,23:4
Jameson, William Commodore, 1873, O 8,5:4
Jameson, William G, 1939, N 17,21:7
Jameson, William R, 1940, Je 14,21:5
Jamet, Albert, 1948, Ag 25,25:3
Jamieson, Alex, 1937, My 3,19:2
Jamieson, Arthur, 1941, S 4,21:2
Jamieson, Crawford, 1967, Jl 4,19:4
Jamieson, Edward, 1962, Ag 11,17:6
Jamieson, Edward C, 1942, Je 19,23:2
Jamieson, Francis A (trb, F 1,26:2; funl, F 2,35:2), 1960, Ja 31,94:1
Jamieson, G W, 1868, O 4,5:6
Jamieson, Gus, 1920, Ag 23,11:4
Jamieson, Harriet B Mrs, 1939, O 17,25:5
Jamieson, J Paul, 1944, D 31,25:1
Jamieson, James, 1949, Ja 14,23:4
Jamieson, James C, 1957, Ag 19,19:4
Jamieson, James P, 1941, N 29,17:1
Jamieson, James S, 1950, Ja 23,23:3
Jamieson, Lawrence, 1947, N 20,30:3
Jamieson, Leland (por), 1941, Jl 10,19:6
Jamieson, Mary S Mrs, 1938, Je 14,21:4
Jamieson, Percy F, 1948, N 11,27:3
Jamieson, William D, 1949, N 20,92:8
Jamin, Charles Mrs, 1952, Ja 8,27:2
Jamison, Abbie N Mrs, 1955, Ag 11,21:4
Jamison, Alcinous B, 1938, N 16,23:3
Jamison, Ann (Mrs E Calligan), 1961, Ap 18,37:3
Jamison, Charles Arbuckle, 1915, Jl 23,9:7
Jamison, Clifton I, 1959, Ap 12,86:4
Jamison, David L, 1947, Ja 23,26:2
Jamison, Edward S, 1959, F 15,84:5
Jamison, Edward S Mrs, 1952, Mr 8,13:5
Jamison, Frank H, 1943, O 23,13:2
Jamison, George H, 1945, Jl 12,11:5
Jamison, H Stuart, 1942, N 14,15:3
Jamison, Harry N, 1949, N 16,30:5
Jamison, Harry V, 1942, D 10,30:1
Jamison, Howard E, 1958, Mr 1,17:5
Jamison, Howard L, 1951, O 13,17:4
Jamison, Hugh D, 1945, F 14,19:5
Jamison, Inez M Mrs, 1942, Mr 14,15:2
Jamison, J M, 1880, Mr 24,4:7
Jamison, James Mrs, 1953, F 17,34:3
Jamison, Jay N, 1952, N 20,31:5
Jamison, John M, 1950, D 18,31:5
Jamison, John O Sr, 1937, Jl 15,19:1
Jamison, John W, 1947, O 13,23:2
Jamison, M I Rev, 1920, Mr 5,13:3
Jamison, Margaret A, 1942, N 19,25:2
Jamison, Martha A (will, Ag 5,22:3), 1941, Jl 17,19:2
Jamison, Samuel C, 1946, Je 19,21:5
Jamison, William, 1954, O 15,23:1
Jamison, William D, 1955, D 9,27:6
Jamison, William L, 1949, D 15,35:6
Jamke, Frederick, 1921, O 22,22:2
Jamme, Anna C, 1939, Jl 5,17:1
Jamme, Bernard E, 1954, O 15,23:2
Jamme, Louise A, 1953, Je 7,82:5
Jammer, Jacob S, 1952, Mr 17,21:3
Jammes, Francis, 1938, N 2,23:4
Jamont, Edouard Fernand Gen, 1918, O 21,15:4
Jamouneau, Leslie H, 1963, N 5,28:3
Jamouneau, Osmond D, 1946, Ap 24,25:1
Jamouneau, Walter H, 1951, D 21,27:3
Jamous, Mukhamar Abu, 1941, Ag 31,22:3
Janacek, L, 1928, Ag 14,23:1
Janareli, Joseph, 1960, Ap 8,31:1
Janauschek, Mme, 1904, N 30,9:3
Jancikovic, Toma, 1952, Ja 6,9:2
Jandolo, Augusto, 1952, Ja 14,19:4
Jandorek, Aug, 1941, S 12,22:3
Jandorf, Louis C, 1952, My 3,21:2
Jandrisevits, Peter, 1967, N 2,47:4
Jane, Fred T, 1916, Mr 10,9:7
Jane, Robert S, 1958, D 3,37:4
Jane Frances, Sister (H D Leibell), 1956, S 19,37:2
Janecke, Walther, 1965, O 21,47:2
Janensch, Ernest W Jr, 1963, O 10,41:3
Janer, Ramon I, 1950, Ap 25,31:1
Janes, Arthur L, 1951, S 10,21:5; 1953, Mr 22,86:1
Janes, Charlotte, 1876, Ag 17,8:5
Janes, E S Bp (funl, S 22,8:2; mem ser, N 17,2:7), 1876, S 19,4:6
Janes, Gordon, 1956, Jl 23,23:5
Janes, Henry Dr, 1915, Je 11,15:5
Janes, Henry E, 1937, Mr 23,23:2
Janes, John M Mrs, 1944, D 14,23:1
Janes, Julian A Mrs, 1946, N 4,25:4
Janes, Lester, 1961, Jl 16,69:2
Janes, Robert W Mrs, 1950, D 9,15:6
Janes, William S, 1964, O 2,37:3
Janewax, Edmund, 1951, D 24,13:4
Janeway, Edward Gamaliel Dr, 1911, F 11,11:3
Janeway, Frank L, 1964, Je 22,27:3
Janeway, H L Jr, 1903, Mr 23,9:5
Janeway, Harry L Mrs, 1945, O 6,13:1
Janeway, Henry Harrington Dr, 1921, F 2,11:5
Janeway, Henry L, 1957, O 19,21:2
Janeway, Henry Latimer, 1909, O 19,9:5
Janeway, Hugh H, 1921, Ja 1,9:4
Janeway, J J Col, 1926, Jl 31,11:3
Janeway, Orice W Jr, 1949, Mr 2,25:3
Janeway, Theodore C, 1968, O 12,37:5
Janeway, Theodore C Mrs, 1956, My 11,27:1
Janeway, Theodore Caldwell Dr, 1917, D 28,11:3
Janeway, William R, 1945, Je 17,25:1
Janeway, William R Mrs, 1946, My 30,21:4
Janicki, Benjamin, 1937, F 13,13:2
Janicula, George T, 1938, Jl 8,17:2
Janiewicz, Dennis S, 1948, D 9,33:2
Janin, Alban, 1948, Ap 27,25:5
Janin, Albert S Mrs, 1948, My 12,27:3
Janin, Jules, 1874, Je 20,4:6
Janin, Jules (funl), 1874, Jl 6,5:3
Janis, Elsie (will, Mr 11,75:1), 1956, F 28,1:2
Janis, Frank H, 1955, S 9,23:5
Janis, Hal (Harold E), 1959, Jl 23,27:4
Janis, Lee D, 1959, Mr 27,23:1
Janis, Percy, 1907, Ap 18,11:4
Janis, Roy J Sr, 1952, Ap 25,23:2
Janis, Sidney Mrs, 1963, N 12,41:2
Janitschek, Adolph, 1964, My 16,25:3
Janitschek, John, 1945, My 21,19:5
Janitzky, Emanuel J, 1953, D 15,39:2
Janke, Frank H, 1953, Ja 3,15:4
Janke, H Alfred, 1939, O 12,25:5
Jankins, Hettie Mrs, 1911, Ja 5,9:4
Jankowski, Ralph, 1951, N 20,31:2
Jannaris, Anthony Dr, 1909, Ap 30,9:5
Janney, John B, 1960, Ag 17,17:2
Janney, Laurence A, 1955, N 16,35:5
Janney, Ralph D, 1952, My 15,31:4
Janney, Reynold Mrs, 1948, My 30,34:2
Janney, Russell, 1963, Jl 15,29:4
Janney, Stuart S, 1940, Ap 12,24:2
Janney, Walter C, 1944, O 13,19:5
Janni, Alfredo C (por), 1938, Mr 3,21:5
Jannicky, Ernest E, 1957, Mr 15,25:3
Jannings, Emil, 1950, Ja 3,25:3
Jannings, Orin, 1966, O 26,47:2
Jannings, Ralph W, 1954, Jl 21,27:4
Janoff, Barney, 1950, Ap 13,29:1
Janos, Samuel, 1949, Mr 31,25:2
Janov, Isadore, 1956, Je 13,37:4
Janover, Cyrus J, 1957, My 11,21:5
Janover, Daniel W, 1950, Ja 19,27:4
Janovsky, Felix B, 1953, D 9,11:5
Janowitz, Hans, 1954, My 26,29:3
Jansen, Abram E, 1944, F 3,19:3
Jansen, Edward O (por), 1947, Ag 14,23:3
Jansen, Ernest G, 1959, N 26,37:3
Jansen, Gerard J Mrs, 1955, Ag 6,15:5
Jansen, Harry A (Dante the Magician), 1955, Je 18, 17:6
Jansen, Henry, 1937, Ja 11,20:1; 1965, My 11,39:2
Jansen, Jacob C, 1948, D 29,21:2
Jansen, John A, 1948, Ja 16,21:2
Jansen, John H, 1944, Jl 9,36:2
Jansen, John J, 1960, D 4,88:5
Jansen, Lincoln J, 1959, Ja 5,29:3
Jansen, Marie, 1914, Mr 21,13:6
Jansen, Peter C, 1957, My 14,35:1; 1959, N 15,86:6
Jansen, William Dr, 1968, F 23,30:1
Jansen, William F, 1949, N 19,17:4
Janser, Peter T, 1959, My 7,33:4
Jansky, Karl G, 1950, F 15,27:3
Janson, Albert, 1959, Ap 22,33:3
Janson, C William, 1957, D 22,42:4
Janson, Christian W, 1950, S 18,23:4
Janson, John H L, 1945, Je 14,19:5; 1961, Mr 10,27:2
Janson, John M, 1954, D 22,23:4
Janson, Leon M, 1950, Jl 6,27:5

Janson, Paul, 1913, Ap 19,11:4
Janson, Paul E (por), 1944, Jl 5,17:4
Janson, Pierre, 1951, Je 14,8:4
Janson, Walter C, 1962, O 20,25:5
Janss, Albert F, 1952, O 4,17:6
Janss, Herman, 1940, My 12,48:1
Janssen, Alb-Edouard, 1966, Mr 30,45:4
Janssen, Aug L, 1939, N 17,21:3
Janssen, August Jr, 1945, Ja 11,23:4
Janssen, August Mrs, 1955, Ap 28,29:3
Janssen, Bernard W, 1960, Ag 10,31:3
Janssen, Charles H, 1960, Ja 21,31:4
Janssen, Charles L (por), 1941, Ja 23,21:3
Janssen, Georges, 1941, Je 18,21:5
Janssen, Henry K, 1948, Ja 30,23:1
Janssen, Herbert, 1965, Je 4,35:4
Janssen, John Bp, 1913, Jl 9,7:6
Janssen, Peter, 1908, F 21,7:6
Janssen, Pierre Jules Caesar Prof, 1907, D 24,7:5
Janssen, Webster E Mrs, 1960, Mr 18,25:2
Janssens, Enrico Msgr, 1925, Jl 25,11:5
Janssens, Jean B, 1964, O 6,1:1
Janszen, August J, 1948, My 20,29:4
Jantausch, Pavel, 1947, Jl 2,23:3
Jantz, Otto Sr, 1955, Je 5,85:1
Jantzen, William, 1942, D 6,77:1
Jantzer, Peter G Mrs, 1951, Ja 27,13:5
Jantzer, Ray H, 1959, Ag 28,23:4
January, Emory L Mrs, 1948, Ap 29,23:2
Januchowski, Vincent, 1950, Ja 18,31:3
Januk, John J, 1951, O 14,89:3
Januschau, Elard V, 1937, Ag 17,19:4
Januschowsky-Neuendorff, Georgine von, 1914, S 8, 11:6
Januszewski, Frank, 1953, Je 11,29:3
Janvier, Ernest P, 1962, My 5,27:6
Janvier, Francis D, 1940, Ag 23,15:3
Janvier, Francis D Mrs, 1940, Jl 26,17:4
Janvier, Francis Herbert, 1908, D 25,7:5
Janvier, Marie-Albert, 1939, Ap 29,17:5
Janvier, Thomas Allibone, 1913, Je 19,11:5
Janvier, Walter, 1911, Ja 30,9:4
Janvier, William O, 1951, Ja 12,27:1
Janvrin, George M, 1939, F 6,13:3
Janvrin, Joseph E Dr (funl, D 24,9:4), 1911, D 22, 13:3
Janvrin, Joseph E Mrs, 1942, Ag 14,17:3
Janz, Carl J, 1952, D 23,23:3
Jaoul, Andre, 1954, N 13,15:6
Japanese Prince Imperial, 1878, S 2,1:6
Japha, Alfred, 1952, S 4,27:4
Japha, Solomon E Lt-Col, 1922, N 26,6:3
Japour, Thomas, 1953, O 26,21:6
Jappe, James L E, 1959, Ag 17,23:4
Japy, Andre, 1960, Mr 7,29:2
Japy, Edgar, 1942, F 15,44:2
Jaqua, Frank, 1948, Ap 6,23:3
Jaquay, Samuel (Bro Antonius), 1925, Ja 27,13:2
Jaquays, Homer M, 1953, Ja 11,90:4
Jaques, Albert F, 1950, O 19,31:4
Jaques, Arthur D, 1949, Ag 5,19:3
Jaques, Edmund, 1959, O 3,19:3
Jaques, Francis, 1943, Ag 4,17:3
Jaques, George B, 1910, N 14,9:4
Jaques, Henry P Mrs, 1943, N 26,23:4
Jaques, Herbert, 1953, My 2,15:4
Jaques, James T, 1943, My 8,15:3
Jaques, Nelson, 1947, Jl 2,23:4
Jaques, Norman, 1949, F 1,25:5
Jaques, Washington, 1913, Mr 13,11:4
Jaques, Washington L, 1942, O 22,21:4
Jaques-Dalcroze, Emile, 1950, Jl 3,15:4
Jaquet, Paul F, 1951, Mr 23,21:5
Jaqueth, Charles A, 1940, Je 13,23:5
Jaquett, G P, 1882, O 7,5:4
Jaquett, Warren R, 1960, D 25,43:1
Jaquette, William A, 1945, Jl 5,13:7
Jaquillard, Henry, 1912, Ag 19,9:6
Jaquillard, Robert, 1951, Ap 18,31:1
Jaquish, Ben M, 1949, Mr 19,15:1
Jaquith, Allen F, 1960, O 2,85:1
Jaquith, Amos B, 1937, D 14,25:2
Jaquith, Charles H, 1940, F 10,15:5
Jaquith, Harold C (por), 1943, Ap 21,25:3
Jaquith, Horace J, 1961, Jl 8,19:7
Jaquith, Joseph F Mrs, 1947, O 21,23:2
Jaquitte, A B (Prof Gregg), 1883, Ap 14,1:3
Jaquot, J L, 1938, F 23,23:3
Jara, Pina S de, 1949, Mr 1,26:3
Jara, Placido, 1952, Ap 10,29:1
Jara Corona, Heriberto Maj-Gen (funl, Ap 20,34:3), 1968, Ap 19,47:1
Jaraczewski, Count, 1881, Mr 28,2:3
Jaramillo, Emilio, 1949, O 24,23:5
Jaramillo, Esteban (por), 1947, N 23,72:5
Jaramillo, Jose R, 1945, S 24,19:4
Jaramillo, Ricardo, 1949, Ag 26,20:7
Jarazever, David, 1947, S 8,21:5
Jarbeau, Vernona, 1914, O 17,11:4
Jarboe, Arthur V, 1964, Mr 20,33:2
Jarcho, Jacob, 1952, N 25,29:3
Jarcho, Julius, 1963, My 15,39:2
Jarcho, Julius Mrs, 1955, Jl 20,27:5
Jarcho, Martin D, 1967, Mr 23,35:1
Jarck, Berneice H, 1956, My 13,86:5
Jarden, Charles R, 1940, My 10,24:3
Jarden, Richards, 1946, O 19,21:3
Jardetzky, Wencelas S, 1962, O 23,37:3
Jardine, Alex, 1949, F 24,23:2
Jardine, George, 1882, F 13,5:5
Jardine, Henry H Mrs, 1948, D 16,29:4
Jardine, James T, 1954, O 25,27:3
Jardine, John E Sr, 1956, Mr 17,19:5
Jardine, John F, 1937, N 18,23:3
Jardine, R W B Sir, 1927, F 1,27:5
Jardine, Thomas V Mrs, 1962, My 29,31:6
Jardine, Walter S, 1937, O 20,23:4
Jardine, William M, 1955, Ja 18,27:3
Jardot, Arthur J Jr, 1952, Je 14,15:3
Jarecka, Tadeusz Mrs, 1954, Mr 8,27:3
Jarecka-Maurin, Benigna, 1953, S 26,17:6
Jarecki, Alex, 1941, Ap 28,15:2
Jarecki, Edmund K, 1966, O 16,89:2
Jarecki, Felix, 1948, Mr 31,25:5
Jarecky, Herman Dr, 1937, Mr 15,23:3
Jaremko, Peter, 1966, D 28,17:3
Jaret, David, 1961, My 1,29:4
Jarett, Lester, 1944, Ap 4,21:5
Jaretzki, Alfred (funl, Mr 18,21:5), 1925, Mr 15,26:5
Jaretzki, Alfred Jr Mrs, 1938, F 6,II,9:2
Jaretzki, Tillie S Mrs, 1941, Je 4,23:3
Jarka, Alexius A, 1965, Ag 18,35:4
Jarka, Clement A, 1947, S 2,21:5
Jarka, Franz, 1952, D 4,35:5
Jarlath, Bro, 1941, S 30,23:3
Jarlsberg, Fritz W, 1942, Jl 29,17:4
Jarman, Charles, 1947, Je 1,60:5
Jarman, Frank S, 1941, F 19,21:3
Jarman, George W, 1939, S 21,23:1
Jarman, George W Mrs, 1955, Mr 22,31:2
Jarman, James, 1953, Je 14,84:2
Jarman, James F, 1938, Ag 24,21:5; 1956, Ja 9,25:5
Jarman, Joseph L, 1947, N 17,21:1
Jarman, Pete, 1955, F 18,21:1
Jarmel, Benedict, 1968, Mr 28,57:6
Jarmulowsky, Harry, 1947, Ja 28,24:3
Jarmulowsky, Sender (mem, Je 21,13:5), 1912, Je 2, II,13:5
Jarnagin, J R, 1943, Ja 16,13:1
Jarnagin, Rufus, 1940, My 5,53:2
Jarooszewicz, Georgi, 1953, Ap 12,89:2
Jarorvgnskiwanski, Paul, 1915, F 24,9:5
Jaros, Alfred L, 1967, Mr 21,43:4
Jaros, Kazmiz, 1952, N 20,31:3
Jaroszewics, Vladyslaw, 1947, Je 6,23:4
Jaroszewski, Zigmond, 1950, S 3,38:4
Jarre, Cyrillus R, 1952, Mr 15,4:8
Jarrell, J Frank, 1941, O 22,23:5
Jarrell, J Frank Mrs, 1937, N 30,23:1
Jarrell, Randall (death ruled accident, N 9,19:1), 1965, O 15,20:3
Jarrell, Sanford, 1962, Ja 31,31:2
Jarres, Karl, 1951, O 21,93:1
Jarret, Victor, 1953, Jl 27,19:2
Jarrett, Arthur L, 1960, Je 14,37:3
Jarrett, Arthur R Dr, 1922, My 3,21:5
Jarrett, Dan, 1938, Mr 15,23:5
Jarrett, Delta I, 1949, F 24,23:5
Jarrett, Edwin S, 1938, D 27,17:5
Jarrett, Elizabeth, 1952, Mr 27,29:4
Jarrett, Harry, 1942, Ja 31,17:2
Jarrett, Henry, 1959, S 5,15:4
Jarrett, Henry C, 1903, O 15,9:7
Jarrett, Henry T, 1955, Je 18,17:5
Jarrett, James H, 1943, Ap 10,17:1
Jarrett, John T, 1945, Mr 20,19:4
Jarrett, Lester Mrs, 1952, Je 11,29:2
Jarrett, Lola M Mrs, 1948, Jl 20,23:3
Jarrett, Mary C, 1961, Ag 5,17:3
Jarrett, Orvis K, 1954, Mr 15,25:5
Jarrett, R Frank, 1948, S 11,15:3
Jarri, George, 1925, My 18,15:4
Jarris, Fred A, 1952, My 5,23:5
Jarrold, Ernest, 1912, Mr 21,11:4
Jarrott, John, 1938, Je 17,21:4
Jarrows, Samuel, 1950, Ag 17,28:3
Jarvais, Walter H, 1945, O 6,13:4
Jarvie, J N, 1929, Je 22,17:5
Jarvie, James N Mrs, 1912, Je 24,9:4
Jarvie, John Gibson, 1964, D 30,25:4
Jarvie, William Dr, 1921, N 18,17:6
Jarvinen, Akilles, 1943, Mr 8,15:5
Jarvis, Adeline Mrs, 1911, Ap 17,11:5
Jarvis, Aemilius, 1940, D 20,25:4
Jarvis, Alpha C, 1938, D 2,23:3
Jarvis, Anna M, 1948, N 25,31:1
Jarvis, Arthur C, 1968, Ag 18,88:6
Jarvis, Benjamin E, 1940, Ap 12,23:4
Jarvis, Bertram, 1949, Jl 1,19:6
Jarvis, Charles W, 1949, Ja 21,21:4
Jarvis, Chester D, 1948, Mr 28,48:5
Jarvis, Claude S, 1953, D 10,48:3
Jarvis, David W, 1937, Mr 31,24:1
Jarvis, DeForest C, 1966, Ag 19,33:2
Jarvis, Ebenezer T, 1938, S 9,21:2
Jarvis, Edward R, 1960, My 7,23:2
Jarvis, Ellen A, 1957, Ja 24,29:3
Jarvis, Elsinore, 1944, F 1,23:2
Jarvis, Everett S, 1951, Ag 26,80:4
Jarvis, H Gildersleeve Dr, 1968, Je 1,27:6
Jarvis, Harry W, 1941, Ap 23,21:6
Jarvis, Henry W, 1948, O 28,29:2
Jarvis, James A Mrs, 1946, Ja 22,27:2
Jarvis, James E, 1963, Mr 23,7:1
Jarvis, James M Col, 1922, Mr 11,13:5
Jarvis, John, 1950, Ja 16,26:4; 1950, O 4,31:3
Jarvis, John W, 1951, Mr 11,93:1
Jarvis, Judson, 1885, My 30,5:6
Jarvis, Nelson W, 1938, S 16,21:2
Jarvis, Pierce L, 1905, Je 25,7:2
Jarvis, Porter M Mrs, 1963, N 28,39:4
Jarvis, Robert B, 1968, D 24,20:4
Jarvis, Robert M, 1964, D 24,19:1
Jarvis, Robert Y (por), 1943, O 17,48:6
Jarvis, Rodney S, 1955, S 21,33:4
Jarvis, Rodney S Mrs, 1944, S 14,23:5
Jarvis, Samuel, 1953, Ag 1,11:4
Jarvis, Samuel M, 1913, D 27,9:6
Jarvis, Thomas W, 1955, Mr 22,31:2
Jarvis, Van Zandt, 1940, Ap 19,21:3
Jarvis, W R, 1943, Ja 28,19:5
Jarvis, Walter J, 1905, D 5,4:7
Jarvis, William, 1859, O 25,2:4
Jarvis, William O, 1944, Mr 28,19:3
Jarzebowski, Casimir, 1964, Mr 8,86:5
Jaschke, Charles, 1925, Ap 17,21:4
Jasie, William, 1955, Ja 15,13:5
Jasie, William Mrs (por), 1945, Mr 2,19:1
Jasina, Michael, 1949, F 5,15:4
Jasinski, John Z, 1951, Ap 3,27:3
Jasinsky, Alice E T, 1950, Je 25,68:2
Jasion, Frank, 1952, D 20,17:5
Jaslow, Bert Mrs (A Schein), 1967, Ja 29,76:7
Jaslow, Leonard A, 1938, Mr 6,II,8:3
Jaslowski, Adam, 1952, Je 3,29:3
Jasny, Naum, 1967, Ap 24,33:1
Jaso, James V, 1957, N 8,29:1
Jason, William C, 1943, Jl 10,13:6
Jaspar, Henri, 1939, F 16,21:5
Jasper, Edward W S, 1954, Ap 25,87:3
Jasper, Edward W S Mrs, 1949, Je 17,23:2
Jasper, Emil, 1904, F 22,5:6
Jasper, John, 1915, F 8,7:4
Jasper, Julius, 1945, Ag 13,19:4
Jasper, Louis, 1959, O 14,43:1
Jasper, William H, 1921, Ag 14,22:4
Jass, Rudolph, 1950, O 8,104:7
Jassinowsky, Pinchos, 1954, Je 26,13:4
Jasskulska, Jennie Mrs, 1938, S 26,17:3
Jasson, Theodore, 1948, Mr 1,23:5
Jastram, Edward P, 1954, Jl 24,13:1
Jastram, Raymond M, 1956, My 3,31:4
Jastremski, Leon Gen, 1907, N 30,7:4
Jastrow, Helen B Mrs, 1940, Ja 30,20:4
Jastrow, Joseph, 1944, Ja 9,43:1
Jastrow, Morris Jr Dr, 1921, Je 23,17:6
Jaszi, Oscar (mem ser, F 25,25:6; trb lr, F 26,28 1957, F 14,27:5
Jatinen, George O, 1966, N 18,43:2
Jatlow, Louis, 1965, My 31,17:4
Jaubert, Caroline, 1883, Ja 7,2:7
Jaubert, Comte, 1874, D 24,6:1
Jaubert, Ernest F, 1942, Ja 7,19:5
Jauck, Walter Mrs, 1943, Ja 14,21:4
Jaures, Louis Adm, 1937, N 1,21:2
Jaurett, Albert F, 1938, D 18,48:6
Javarone, Victor A, 1967, D 15,47:2
Javits, Morris Mrs, 1951, Ap 23,25:1
Javor, Pal, 1959, Ag 15,17:4
Jawish, Henry K, 1941, Mr 15,17:3
Jaworower, Bernard L, 1909, Je 26,7:3
Jaworowski, Aug, 1938, Je 25,15:6
Jaworski, Henry, 1937, S 25,17:6
Jaxheimer, Erwin R Mrs, 1965, Je 8,41:3
Jaxon, Honore J, 1952, Ja 12,13:5
Jay, Augustus, 1919, D 27,9:5
Jay, C W, 1884, D 11,2:5
Jay, Charles Mrs, 1945, N 22,35:3
Jay, Cornelia, 1907, O 19,9:6
Jay, De Lancey K (por), 1941, Mr 28,23:1
Jay, E K Mrs, 1932, D 15,19:1
Jay, Frank, 1966, Ag 21,92:6
Jay, Frederick, 1950, S 24,104:8
Jay, Griff, 1951, F 4,76:3
Jay, Gustave, 1949, Jl 28,24:2
Jay, John, 1894, My 6,9:5
Jay, John C, 1941, Ja 23,21:1
Jay, John Clarkson Dr, 1923, N 8,19:5
Jay, John Clarkson Mrs, 1914, My 9,11:6
Jay, John Mrs (funl, O 20,9:3), 1909, O 19,9
Jay, John Mrs, 1952, Ja 4,23:4
Jay, John W, 1939, Mr 25,15:1
Jay, Kenneth E, 1965, Ag 4,35:1
Jay, Mary R, 1953, O 5,27:3
Jay, P A, 1933, O 19,19:1
Jay, Pierre, 1949, N 25,31:1
Jay, Pierre Mrs, 1965, S 11,27:5
Jay, Webb, 1952, Je 5,31:5
Jay, William, 1858, O 16,4:4

Jay, William Col (funl, Ap 2,11:6), 1915, Mr 29,9:5
Jaycox, Calvin T, 1949, D 26,29:5
Jaycox, Mary Mrs, 1907, Ap 16,11:2
Jaycox, W H, 1927, F 4,19:3
Jaycox, Walter H Mrs, 1953, O 9,27:2
Jaye, Robert, 1950, S 17,104:6
Jayme, J Phil, 1940, O 20,49:1
Jayme, J Phil Mrs, 1952, Ja 6,93:2
Jayne, Abbie, 1946, D 25,29:5
Jayne, John K, 1957, Jl 17,27:3
Jayne, Leslie C, 1964, S 23,47:2
Jayne, W S Mrs, 1903, My 11,9:6
Jayne, Wilfred H, 1961, Ag 13,89:1
Jaynes, Charles L, 1954, N 3,29:2
Jaynes, Earl H, 1947, Je 21,17:5
Jaynes, Edward L, 1940, My 30,18:3
Jaynes, Judson, 1952, Mr 8,13:5
Jayson, Cornelius, 1966, Je 7,47:3
Jayson, Louis L, 1960, Ag 13,15:4
Jeacock, Thomas, 1957, Ja 14,23:3
Jeakens, David, 1944, Ag 18,13:3
Jeal, Edward R, 1955, S 21,33:5
Jean, Elsie, 1953, Je 11,29:5
Jean, Emile, 1957, O 13,85:5
Jean Agnes, Sister (M Mulligan), 1960, My 7,23:4
Jean Anne, Sister (Sisters of Charity), 1957, Ag 31, 15:6
Jean Marie, Mother (Greeley), 1957, S 27,19:4
Jean Marie, Sister, 1947, Je 18,25:1
Jean Marie, Sister (Baird), 1953, Mr 24,42:3
Jeandheur, Frederic, 1954, Ap 4,87:1
Jeanes, Anna T, 1907, S 25,9:5
Jeanes, Henry S Jr, 1966, N 9,39:2
Jeanes, Lucy N Mrs, 1942, Ja 25,41:1
Jeanette, Oliver C, 1957, Ap 21,89:2
Jeanmard, Jules B, 1957, F 24,84:3
Jeanmarie, William, 1949, Je 7,31:2
Jeanmene, Leo F, 1951, F 3,15:6
Jeanne, Frank, 1954, Ja 26,27:2
Jeanne d'Arc, Sister (Benedictine Sisters), 1956, N 17,21:6
Jeanneney, Jules, 1957, Ap 29,25:4
Jeanneret, Charles E (Le Corbusier),(funl plans, Ag 29,84:5), 1965, Ag 28,1:2
Jeanneret, Edward A, 1916, Je 23,11:6
Jeanneret, Rene, 1950, S 6,29:1
Jeannert, Marie, 1939, Ja 17,22:3
Jeannette, Joe, 1958, Jl 4,19:1
Jeans, James, 1946, S 17,7:1
Jeans, Philip C, 1952, O 24,23:2
Jeavons, Madelaine Mrs, 1941, My 7,25:2
Jeavons, William R Mrs, 1951, O 20,15:5
Jeayes, Allan, 1963, S 22,86:5
Jebb, Richard, 1905, D 10,7:7
Jebens, Henry H, 1950, Ap 25,31:6
Jebsen, Gustav, 1951, Ja 23,27:4
Jebsen, Marghetta, 1955, My 17,29:3
Jeck, George G, 1956, Jl 9,23:4
Jeck, Howard S, 1949, D 30,20:2
Jeck, Theodore H, 1957, Jl 17,27:2
Jeckel, Charles H, 1962, Ag 29,29:1
Jeckel, Frank Sr, 1952, My 23,21:5
Jeckell, George A Mrs, 1952, Ja 6,92:6
Jecminek, Alois, 1944, Ja 27,19:5
Ject-Key, David Wu, 1968, Ap 16,44:2
Jedd, Gerry, 1962, N 29,37:2
Jedel, Sidney S, 1958, N 25,33:4
Jedlicka, Francis W, 1950, Ja 10,29:1
Jedlicka, George J, 1959, My 29,23:2
Jedlicka, Joseph J, 1951, Je 3,92:8
edlicka, Theodore J, 1950, Ap 19,29:5
edvabnik, Abram, 1949, D 20,31:2
eenqueiro, Guerra, 1923, Jl 9,13:5
effares, James Mrs (will), 1953, F 14,30:7
effcott, Edward W, 1960, Je 21,34:1
efferds, Jerome V (J Smith), 1962, F 4,82:3
efferies, George C, 1949, F 22,23:4
efferies, Jack P Mrs, 1963, N 9,25:2
efferies, Richard M, 1964, Ap 21,37:2
efferis, Albert W, 1942, S 15,24:3
efferis, C Rodney, 1962, Mr 24,25:4
efferis, Jay H, 1952, My 13,23:1
efferis, William M Rev Dr, 1916, Mr 5,21:6
effers, Alexander, 1903, Ag 6,7:6
effers, Boley, 1942, F 28,17:1
ffers, Charles W (trb lr, Ap 24,16:6), 1954, Ap 17, 13:7
ffers, Edward A, 1952, D 8,41:3
ffers, Eliakim Tupper Dr, 1915, N 19,11:5
ffers, Gannie Gypsy Queen, 1884, Ap 16,5:2
ffers, George P, 1948, Ag 3,25:1
ffers, Henry F, 1949, N 9,27:1
ffers, Henry W Sr, 1953, Jl 19,57:1
ffers, John S, 1939, Ja 5,23:5
ffers, Katherine M, 1959, My 17,72:6
ffers, LeRoy, 1926, Jl 26,1:4
ffers, Martha Mrs, 1939, Ja 13,19:2
ffers, Robert, 1947, Ag 3,52:8
fers, Robinson, 1962, Ja 22,23:1
fers, Robinson Mrs, 1950, S 3,38:4
fers, Sara E J, 1954, F 12,25:3
fers, Thomas J, 1937, Mr 14,II,8:5
fers, W Lindley, 1945, F 12,20:3
Jeffers, W N, 1883, Jl 24,5:6
Jeffers, William, 1940, Ap 11,25:2
Jeffers, William M, 1953, Mr 7,15:5
Jefferson, Albert W, 1943, Je 13,44:6
Jefferson, Arthur S (S Laurel),(funl, F 27,25:2), 1965, F 24,41:1
Jefferson, Bernard L, 1939, Ag 10,19:1
Jefferson, Carl S, 1941, Je 3,21:6
Jefferson, Charles B, 1908, Je 24,7:4
Jefferson, Charles E Rev Dr (por), 1937, S 13,21:3
Jefferson, Charlie, 1911, Jl 14,7:4
Jefferson, Cyrus, 1883, N 23,3:5
Jefferson, Edward, 1937, O 13,23:4
Jefferson, Edward F, 1952, N 6,29:5
Jefferson, George S, 1951, F 11,89:1
Jefferson, Harley W, 1958, Mr 24,27:5
Jefferson, Henry C Mrs, 1941, Ag 26,19:3
Jefferson, Hilton W, 1968, N 20,47:2
Jefferson, Howard M, 1954, N 16,29:5
Jefferson, John H, 1941, N 22,19:5
Jefferson, John P, 1958, N 29,21:2
Jefferson, Joseph, 1905, Ap 24,1:1
Jefferson, Joseph (will), 1905, Jl 23,7:6
Jefferson, Joseph Mrs, 1924, Ag 15,13:6
Jefferson, Joseph W, 1919, My 2,13:6
Jefferson, Josephine D, 1921, Jl 19,15:6
Jefferson, Matthew, 1939, Ap 25,23:4
Jefferson, Ralf W, 1921, S 10,11:4
Jefferson, Samuel Mitchell Dr, 1914, F 21,11:3
Jefferson, Stephen P, 1951, O 10,23:5
Jefferson, William T, 1955, Jl 1,21:6
Jefferson, William T Mrs, 1956, Ag 9,25:4
Jefferson, William W, 1946, F 14,26:2
Jeffery, A B P Mrs, 1938, Mr 3,21:4
Jeffery, Arthur, 1959, Ag 5,27:3
Jeffery, David E, 1960, Ja 5,31:2
Jeffery, E P, 1943, Jl 10,13:1
Jeffery, E T, 1927, S 25,II,9:1
Jeffery, George Clinton Dr, 1913, F 12,15:4
Jeffery, John B Maj, 1925, S 22,25:4
Jeffery, Kenneth L, 1952, D 31,15:2
Jeffery, Oscar, 1925, O 19,21:4
Jeffery, Thomas B, 1910, Ap 4,9:4
Jeffery, William P, 1952, N 1,21:5
Jefferys, Charles W, 1951, O 9,29:6
Jefferys, Edward M, 1946, Ag 28,27:2
Jefferys, Robert Sr, 1944, S 1,13:5
Jefferys, Upton S, 1950, Ja 10,29:4
Jefford, Joseph L, 1948, F 24,25:3
Jeffords, Alex H, 1952, N 12,27:5
Jeffords, Clyde R, 1938, Ag 8,13:5
Jeffords, Elsa Judge, 1885, Mr 20,2:4
Jeffords, Ernest H, 1946, D 13,24:2
Jeffords, Olin M, 1964, O 13,39:3
Jeffords, Walter M (will, O 7,5:6), 1960, S 29,35:1
Jeffress, Albert G, 1925, D 30,17:5
Jeffress, E B, 1961, My 24,41:2
Jeffress, Thomas F, 1938, Ap 20,23:5
Jeffrey, Adam B, 1908, Mr 19,7:4
Jeffrey, Alexander, 1915, S 5,11:6
Jeffrey, Alexander MacLean Dr, 1918, S 3,11:3
Jeffrey, Borden A, 1945, Ja 10,23:4
Jeffrey, E Howard, 1959, Ja 3,17:1
Jeffrey, Edward A, 1964, Je 20,25:5
Jeffrey, Frank M, 1942, Ja 11,45:1
Jeffrey, Frank M Mrs, 1940, Je 29,15:6
Jeffrey, Frederick, 1908, Je 22,7:2
Jeffrey, George A, 1954, Ja 12,23:3
Jeffrey, John, 1947, Je 20,19:5
Jeffrey, John G, 1939, Je 14,23:2
Jeffrey, John M, 1956, Mr 11,89:1
Jeffrey, John P, 1951, N 15,29:3
Jeffrey, Joseph A, 1944, D 27,19:1
Jeffrey, Margaret, 1945, S 12,25:5
Jeffrey, Nicol, 1940, Jl 22,17:2
Jeffrey, Peter G, 1914, O 26,9:5
Jeffrey, Roy M, 1958, N 3,37:4
Jeffrey, Thomas B, 1943, N 28,68:4
Jeffrey, Wallace, 1955, Ap 6,29:3
Jeffrey, William, 1966, Ja 9,56:8
Jeffrey, William L, 1956, Ag 18,17:5
Jeffrey, William W Capt, 1922, Ja 29,22:1
Jeffreys, Charles, 1950, Je 4,92:4
Jeffreys, Charles Peter B, 1910, N 26,9:5
Jeffreys, Elizabeth, 1940, Mr 15,23:6
Jeffreys, Ellis (por), 1943, Ja 22,19:3
Jeffreys, George, 1962, Ja 28,76:8
Jeffreys, George D Lord, 1960, D 20,33:4
Jeffreys, Upton S Mrs, 1947, Ja 29,25:1
Jeffreys, William H, 1945, My 16,19:4
Jeffreys, William howard, 1924, My 16,9:3
Jeffries, Benjamin Jay Dr, 1915, N 24,13:6
Jeffries, Charles N (Jack), 1960, Jl 17,61:1
Jeffries, E H, 1884, Ja 22,5:3
Jeffries, Edward C, 1949, Ja 6,23:2
Jeffries, Edward J, 1939, S 12,25:5
Jeffries, Edward J Jr, 1950, Ap 3,23:1
Jeffries, Frederick L, 1949, N 21,25:3
Jeffries, Harry E, 1949, N 21,25:4
Jeffries, Henrietta Mrs, 1955, Mr 30,29:4
Jeffries, Henry C, 1945, Ja 14,40:3
Jeffries, James G, 1951, Ag 7,25:2
Jeffries, James J (Jim),(will, Mr 14,15:2), 1953, Mr 4,1:1
Jeffries, Maud, 1946, S 28,17:2
Jeffries, Thomas H Jr, 1948, Ja 28,23:2
Jeffries, Walter S Sr, 1954, O 12,27:5
Jeffries, William A, 1948, F 23,25:5
Jeffries, William H Mrs, 1960, S 14,43:4
Jeffries, William J, 1949, S 3,13:6
Jeffries, William W, 1906, F 25,9:6
Jeffries, Zay, 1965, My 22,31:1
Jeffs, Charles, 1959, O 26,29:5
Jeffs, William S, 1951, S 30,72:5
Jeger, Santo W, 1953, S 25,21:3
Jehl, Francis, 1941, F 11,24:2
Jehle, Arthur O, 1950, F 12,84:4
Jehle, August, 1945, S 14,23:3
Jehle, Charles A P, 1939, Ap 20,23:5
Jehlicka, Franz, 1939, Ja 5,23:3
Jehlinger, Charles, 1952, Jl 30,23:1
Jehu, Ivor S, 1960, O 9,86:3
Jekels, Ludwig, 1954, Ap 5,25:4
Jekely, Laszlo Mrs, 1949, D 11,92:5
Jelalian, Ira N, 1940, Je 8,15:3
Jelenek, Paul, 1949, Ag 10,21:5
Jelf, Arthur S, 1947, F 28,23:2
Jelf, Ernest, 1949, S 2,17:4
Jelf, George Edward Rev, 1908, N 21,9:2
Jelf, W E Rev, 1875, O 21,1:1
Jelin, Abraham, 1946, My 24,19:4
Jelin, Dora Mrs, 1948, O 5,25:4
Jelinek, George, 1949, N 6,92:3
Jelinek, Otto K, 1950, Ag 19,13:5
Jelis, Pierre C Mrs, 1952, Ap 29,27:4
Jelke, F Bartholomay, 1967, Jl 4,19:5
Jelke, Ferdinand F (will), 1953, S 4,13:6
Jelke, John F (will, Ja 9,38:3), 1965, Ja 2,19:3
Jellachich de Buzim, Joseph Count, 1859, Je 8,4:4
Jelle, Ralph H, 1946, Ag 22,27:3
Jelleff, Frank R, 1961, Ap 29,23:3
Jellenik, Felix, 1924, Mr 14,17:3
Jellett, Stewart A Jr, 1940, N 26,23:3
Jelley, Annie D Mrs, 1941, D 11,27:4
Jelley, Arthur L, 1942, Je 25,23:4
Jelley, William, 1961, My 6,31:6
Jellico, Benjamin W Mrs, 1950, Jl 11,31:3
Jellicoe, Dowager Countess of (Florence G), 1964, My 13,47:5
Jellicoe, J H Capt, 1914, S 9,9:2
Jellicoe, J R, 1935, N 21,1:2
Jelliffe, Smith E (por), 1945, S 26,23:1
Jelliffe, Smith Ely Dr, 1916, Mr 4,11:6
Jelliffe, Taylor, 1907, S 2,7:6; 1951, Ap 18,31:1
Jelliffe, William Leeming, 1925, Ja 23,19:4
Jelliffe, William R, 1959, D 27,60:6
Jelliffe, William R Mrs, 1960, F 5,27:1
Jellinek, Arthur, 1945, Ja 27,11:6
Jellinek, Bruno L, 1943, S 1,19:4
Jellinek, Edward L, 1943, My 21,19:6
Jellinek, Elvin M, 1963, O 23,41:4
Jellinek, Frances (F Williams),(cor, Ja 29,27:4), 1959, Ja 28,31:4
Jelling, David, 1961, S 21,35:4
Jellinghaus, C Frederic, 1946, Ap 23,21:2
Jellinghaus, Carl C, 1957, O 9,35:3
Jellinghaus, Eduard, 1944, Mr 17,17:1
Jellison, Benjamin H Capt, 1924, Ap 6,27:1
Jellison, Melvin, 1947, S 11,29:7
Jellovitz, John L, 1960, Mr 16,37:3
Jemmott, Beresford C, 1959, Mr 25,35:3
Jen-Kung Li (por), 1948, Mr 6,13:3
Jen Pi-shih, 1950, O 29,92:1
Jen Ying Yen, 1953, Ag 11,27:6
Jena, Carl J von, 1881, Mr 11,5:2
Jena, Frank, 1944, Ap 18,21:5
Jenckes, Edward N, 1941, Ap 10,24:3
Jenckes, Robert D, 1954, My 13,29:2
Jenckes, T A, 1875, N 5,4:6
Jencks, Althea M Mrs, 1950, N 29,33:3
Jencks, Francis May, 1918, S 14,11:3
Jencks, Frank E, 1957, Ja 15,29:1
Jencks, Frederick T, 1948, Je 9,29:4
Jencks, Howard W, 1951, N 17,17:4
Jencks, Millard H (por), 1945, F 15,19:1
Jenett, Henry, 1950, F 12,85:1
Jenick, Samuel, 1915, Ag 13,9:3
Jenifer, Frank M, 1950, My 27,17:2
Jenifer, Thomas M, 1946, F 20,25:5
Jenison, E Darwin, 1948, Jl 19,19:5
Jenk, Joseph H, 1953, F 10,27:4
Jenkel, Henry, 1938, Mr 17,21:4
Jenkel, Walter C, 1946, Ap 20,13:3
Jenkins, A Arthur, 1957, Je 12,35:5
Jenkins, Ab (funl, Ag 14,25:1), 1956, Ag 11,13:3
Jenkins, Alfred A Dr, 1937, N 20,17:1
Jenkins, Alfred H, 1955, Mr 3,27:1
Jenkins, Anna A Mrs, 1940, Ja 9,23:4
Jenkins, Annie E Mrs, 1941, Mr 9,41:4
Jenkins, Archibald, 1881, Ap 23,5:4
Jenkins, Arthur, 1903, N 9,7:6; 1946, Ap 26,21:1
Jenkins, Arthur W, 1944, Ap 18,21:2
Jenkins, Augustus C, 1924, F 24,21:3
Jenkins, Bertrand H, 1965, Je 6,85:2
Jenkins, Burris A (por), 1945, Mr 14,19:1
Jenkins, Burris A Jr, 1966, F 27,84:1

Jenkins, Burris Sr Mrs, 1946, F 16,13:3
Jenkins, C F, 1934, Je 7,23:4
Jenkins, C F Jr, 1947, Je 21,17:5
Jenkins, C H, 1916, Je 22,11:6
Jenkins, C J, 1883, Je 15,5:4
Jenkins, Carl B, 1965, D 3,35:6
Jenkins, Catherine Mrs, 1937, N 26,26:4
Jenkins, Charles H, 1944, Jl 26,19:5
Jenkins, Charles J, 1954, D 9,33:1
Jenkins, Charles Q, 1952, S 1,17:6
Jenkins, Charlotte Coles Mrs, 1911, D 27,11:4
Jenkins, Clarence C, 1958, S 19,27:3
Jenkins, D C, 1940, My 9,23:4
Jenkins, D J Rev, 1937, Ag 1,II,7:3
Jenkins, David, 1940, My 20,17:2
Jenkins, David J, 1946, D 17,38:3
Jenkins, David R, 1967, Je 17,31:4
Jenkins, Dick, 1956, O 22,29:5
Jenkins, Donald V Mrs, 1957, S 1,56:6
Jenkins, Donald W, 1962, D 8,27:3
Jenkins, Donelson Caffery, 1908, Je 21,11:7
Jenkins, Dudley, 1956, Mr 3,20:3
Jenkins, Dudley Mrs, 1956, Mr 3,20:3
Jenkins, E Fellows, 1923, My 17,19:4
Jenkins, E O, 1884, Ap 21,5:1
Jenkins, Edward, 1910, Je 7,9:4
Jenkins, Edward A, 1958, Ja 1,25:4
Jenkins, Edward C, 1956, F 1,31:2
Jenkins, Edward E, 1950, Je 19,21:5
Jenkins, Edward P, 1958, Jl 6,56:4
Jenkins, Edward S, 1903, N 25,3:2; 1948, My 1,15:6
Jenkins, Edwin G, 1940, Ap 16,23:3
Jenkins, Elizabeth, 1878, Je 11,5:4
Jenkins, Ellen, 1908, Ag 13,7:3
Jenkins, Elwood O Mrs, 1950, Je 4,92:3
Jenkins, Emerson E, 1967, My 24,47:4
Jenkins, Emma H Mrs, 1942, Mr 13,19:3
Jenkins, Enos, 1941, Mr 25,23:5
Jenkins, Ernest T, 1950, N 10,27:5
Jenkins, Esther M, 1956, Ap 5,29:4
Jenkins, Felix A, 1947, Mr 5,25:5
Jenkins, Forrest L, 1959, S 9,41:4
Jenkins, Frances, 1942, D 27,34:1
Jenkins, Francis, 1924, My 22,17:6
Jenkins, Francis A, 1960, Ag 7,84:8
Jenkins, Frank E, 1952, Ja 20,85:2
Jenkins, Frank Mrs, 1944, N 27,23:3
Jenkins, Frederick C, 1954, F 6,19:2
Jenkins, Frederick D Mrs, 1947, Jl 19,13:6
Jenkins, Frederick L, 1919, F 8,15:5
Jenkins, Frederick W, 1940, Ap 13,17:4
Jenkins, Frederick W Mrs, 1953, N 25,23:2
Jenkins, Gail B, 1943, D 21,27:3
Jenkins, George, 1957, Ap 4,33:4
Jenkins, George D, 1940, D 21,17:3
Jenkins, George R, 1963, Jl 6,15:4
Jenkins, Georgia, 1950, Ja 19,28:2
Jenkins, Guy H, 1957, My 6,29:6
Jenkins, H H Mrs, 1934, Ap 25,22:1
Jenkins, Hannah C Mrs, 1947, Je 14,15:2
Jenkins, Hannah Mrs, 1878, Jl 6,5:2
Jenkins, Harold E Mrs, 1961, Ap 22,25:2
Jenkins, Harry, 1941, N 18,25:5
Jenkins, Harry H, 1945, S 30,46:2
Jenkins, Harry J, 1949, N 1,28:2
Jenkins, Hayes R, 1960, Ag 7,85:1
Jenkins, Henry, 1948, F 26,23:3
Jenkins, Henry B, 1867, My 19,5:4
Jenkins, Henry P, 1954, F 2,27:4
Jenkins, Herbert W, 1940, F 15,19:5
Jenkins, Herschel V, 1960, Ap 14,31:1
Jenkins, Hester D, 1941, Ap 24,21:4
Jenkins, Hugh C Mrs, 1961, N 1,39:2
Jenkins, Hugh S, 1951, Jl 8,61:2
Jenkins, J H, 1939, O 29,41:2
Jenkins, J J, 1885, Mr 14,5:2
Jenkins, J W Col, 1903, Je 25,7:5
Jenkins, James B, 1903, Jl 31,7:6
Jenkins, James C Judge, 1922, Ap 8,15:5
Jenkins, James G Judge, 1921, Ag 7,22:5
Jenkins, James J Mrs, 1952, F 8,23:3
Jenkins, James M, 1967, F 21,47:2
Jenkins, James W, 1954, Mr 25,29:2
Jenkins, Jane E Mrs, 1954, Ap 26,25:4
Jenkins, John C, 1958, D 10,39:4
Jenkins, John E Mrs, 1947, Mr 2,60:2
Jenkins, John G, 1908, Mr 16,7:4
Jenkins, John Jones (Lord Glantowe), 1915, Jl 28,9:5
Jenkins, John L, 1953, F 25,27:4
Jenkins, John M, 1958, My 2,27:3
Jenkins, John S, 1947, S 5,19:4
Jenkins, John T, 1949, Je 10,27:3
Jenkins, John W, 1958, O 2,37:2
Jenkins, Jonathan L Rev Dr, 1913, Ag 16,9:6
Jenkins, Leon A, 1950, Mr 4,17:6
Jenkins, Lonie H Mrs, 1963, S 29,87:2
Jenkins, Louis L, 1937, Je 18,21:3; 1939, Ag 25,15:3
Jenkins, Louis W, 1950, Mr 14,25:3
Jenkins, MacGregor, 1940, Mr 7,23:3
Jenkins, Mary S, 1946, F 16,13:1
Jenkins, Merwin S, 1959, O 7,43:5
Jenkins, Micah Maj, 1912, O 20,II,15:4
Jenkins, Michael, 1915, S 8,13:6
Jenkins, Michael Mrs, 1911, Mr 6,7:6
Jenkins, Miles E Mrs, 1917, Jl 4,9:4
Jenkins, Murray G, 1937, S 27,21:5
Jenkins, Nettie Mrs, 1952, My 30,15:1
Jenkins, Newell S Dr, 1919, O 1,17:2
Jenkins, Newton, 1942, O 17,15:2
Jenkins, Osborne, 1953, Ja 3,15:1
Jenkins, Owen B, 1925, Jl 18,13:5
Jenkins, Owen B Mrs, 1955, N 20,89:2
Jenkins, Paul W, 1960, Je 25,21:6
Jenkins, Percy, 1947, Ag 21,23:6; 1951, Ja 10,27:5
Jenkins, Phillip R, 1952, Ag 28,23:5
Jenkins, R D, 1968, N 27,47:3
Jenkins, Ralph B, 1956, Jl 4,19:5
Jenkins, Ralph C (por), 1946, O 3,27:3
Jenkins, Ralph C Mrs, 1944, Ja 7,18:3
Jenkins, Ray H Mrs, 1962, F 18,92:2
Jenkins, Robert, 1962, Jl 1,56:6
Jenkins, Robert B, 1958, Ja 9,33:5
Jenkins, Robert Jr, 1942, Ag 22,13:6
Jenkins, Ruth Mrs, 1951, Ja 18,27:1
Jenkins, Sarah F Mrs, 1942, Ag 29,15:4
Jenkins, Stephen Lt, 1913, O 11,15:2
Jenkins, Stewart D, 1958, Ag 5,27:1
Jenkins, Sylvanius F Mrs, 1943, D 19,48:4
Jenkins, T A, 1935, Mr 25,15:6
Jenkins, T Courtenay, 1942, Ag 27,19:2
Jenkins, Theodore F, 1940, O 8,25:2
Jenkins, Thomas A, 1938, Je 6,17:3; 1959, D 22,31:4
Jenkins, Thomas C, 1907, O 26,11:5; 1940, N 19,23:4
Jenkins, Thomas L, 1940, Jl 30,19:2
Jenkins, Thomas Mrs, 1950, Mr 8,25:2
Jenkins, Thomas N, 1962, S 11,34:1
Jenkins, Thomas R, 1925, Je 1,15:2
Jenkins, Tom, 1957, Je 20,29:3
Jenkins, V Clement, 1964, S 22,39:2
Jenkins, Verne H, 1952, F 26,27:3
Jenkins, W Gwynn, 1954, My 29,15:3
Jenkins, Walter F (por), 1946, F 15,26:3
Jenkins, Walter F Mrs, 1941, O 23,23:6
Jenkins, William, 1944, D 9,15:6; 1949, Je 15,29:1
Jenkins, William H, 1948, F 12,23:3
Jenkins, William H Jr, 1952, Ag 29,23:5
Jenkins, William H Sr, 1945, D 7,21:2
Jenkins, William L, 1903, S 28,7:5; 1904, O 21,6:3; 1957, Jl 27,17:3
Jenkins, William M, 1941, O 20,17:5
Jenkins, William O, 1963, Je 5,41:4
Jenkins, William R Mrs, 1949, Ag 30,27:4
Jenkins, William Sr, 1941, F 18,23:6
Jenkins, William T Dr, 1921, Je 26,22:4; 1921, Je 29, 15:2
Jenkinson, C Edward, 1953, Je 7,83:1
Jenkinson, George H, 1946, S 8,46:5
Jenkinson, James, 1879, Ap 3,8:2
Jenkinson, R C, 1930, Ag 31,II,4:1
Jenkinson, Stephen L Mrs, 1949, Mr 13,76:8
Jenkofsky, William Sr, 1952, D 29,19:3
Jenks, Albert E, 1953, Je 9,27:1
Jenks, Almet, 1966, F 3,31:4
Jenks, Almet F, 1924, S 21,29:1
Jenks, Almet Francis Ex-Justice, 1924, S 19,23:3
Jenks, Alonzo, 1941, Jl 7,15:6
Jenks, Arthur B (por), 1947, D 16,33:3
Jenks, Arthur Whipple Rev Dr, 1922, Ap 20,17:4
Jenks, Clifford W, 1950, D 26,23:3
Jenks, Daniel, 1942, F 11,22:2
Jenks, Edmund B, 1953, F 12,28:4
Jenks, Edward N, 1962, Ja 23,33:3
Jenks, Edwin B, 1945, Jl 18,27:3
Jenks, Edwin B Mrs, 1952, N 14,23:4
Jenks, Eldred J, 1966, Ag 22,33:3
Jenks, Ernest E, 1965, F 1,23:3
Jenks, Frank D, 1949, My 12,31:4
Jenks, Frank Mrs, 1957, Je 12,35:4
Jenks, Frank W, 1962, My 15,39:5
Jenks, Fred C, 1944, F 16,17:5
Jenks, George A, 1908, F 11,7:6
Jenks, J W, 1929, Ag 25,27:1
Jenks, John S, 1946, Mr 15,21:2
Jenks, Jonathan, 1941, Ja 19,41:2
Jenks, Leon E, 1940, Mr 10,48:5
Jenks, Livingston, 1937, My 8,19:2
Jenks, Mary C Mrs, 1937, O 21,24:2
Jenks, Maurice (por), 1946, My 21,24:2
Jenks, Maurice L, 1950, Je 13,27:3
Jenks, N M, 1884, N 13,5:5
Jenks, Nicholas C, 1958, N 17,31:4
Jenks, Orrin R, 1951, Je 19,29:5
Jenks, Paul R, 1953, F 17,34:1
Jenks, Phoebe Mrs, 1907, Ja 22,9:6
Jenks, Pierre G, 1942, Je 15,19:5
Jenks, Ralph C, 1948, Mr 2,23:4
Jenks, Raymond, 1943, D 29,17:4
Jenks, Richard A Mrs, 1944, O 14,13:7
Jenks, Stanley, 1953, Mr 9,29:1
Jenks, Stanley Mrs, 1950, N 8,29:3
Jenks, Thomas A, 1948, F 16,21:3
Jenks, William, 1938, Mr 17,21:6
Jenks, William J, 1960, Ja 18,27:2
Jenks, William Mrs, 1946, S 20,31:2
Jenks, William O, 1945, Ja 11,23:2
Jenks, William P, 1955, Jl 31,68:4
Jenks, William P Mrs, 1957, My 6,29:4
Jenks, William Rev Dr, 1866, N 18,3:7
Jennan, John E, 1905, Je 23,7:5
Jenne, James N Dr, 1937, S 10,24:3
Jenner, George, 1946, D 17,38:3
Jenner, Harry A, 1943, N 8,19:5
Jenner, Herbert S, 1943, F 3,19:3
Jenner, Hugh B Mrs, 1948, S 4,15:4
Jenner, Lycurgus L, 1950, Mr 19,95:5
Jenner, William A Dr, 1937, Ja 22,21:4
Jenner, William Allen, 1915, Mr 15,11:5
Jenner, William Allen Mrs, 1925, N 22,9:1
Jenner-Just, Herbert, 1940, N 14,23:2
Jenness, Leslie G Dr, 1968, Jl 4,19:2
Jenness, Mary, 1947, F 21,20:3
Jenness, Richard E, 1941, Ap 19,15:2
Jennette, Charles, 1942, D 20,44:7
Jenney, Bernard A, 1939, Ap 4,25:2
Jenney, Charles Albert, 1919, N 19,13:2
Jenney, Charles F Justice, 1923, N 30,15:2
Jenney, Charles S, 1956, N 26,27:4
Jenney, Edward B, 1954, N 21,87:2
Jenney, Francis L, 1949, Jl 13,28:2
Jenney, Julie R, 1947, D 22,21:2
Jenney, Lucian W, 1943, Ag 25,19:4
Jenney, Malcolm, 1946, Mr 15,21:3
Jenney, Ralph E, 1945, Jl 14,11:6
Jenney, Shirley C Mrs, 1952, D 31,15:1
Jenney, William Le Baron, 1907, Je 16,7:5
Jenney, William S, 1946, Je 7,19:4
Jenney, William S Mrs, 1937, S 28,23:1
Jenning, George T, 1943, O 10,49:1
Jennings, A K, 1933, Ja 28,13:3
Jennings, Al, 1961, D 27,10:5
Jennings, Albert G, 1946, Jl 28,39:2
Jennings, Albert H, 1953, Je 22,21:3
Jennings, Alpheus, 1945, N 17,17:4
Jennings, Alvin H Mrs, 1967, Ag 31,33:4
Jennings, Alvin R Mrs, 1954, N 30,29:4
Jennings, Annie B, 1939, Jl 28,17:3
Jennings, Annie J Mrs, 1941, O 1,21:2
Jennings, B Brewster, 1968, O 3,47:3
Jennings, Bernard, 1948, My 9,56:5
Jennings, Charles B, 1950, My 11,30:5; 1958, Ap 2, 31:6
Jennings, Charles H, 1953, F 6,20:5
Jennings, Charles J, 1943, S 24,23:2
Jennings, Charles S, 1961, Je 21,37:6
Jennings, Clarence S Mrs, 1944, Ag 30,17:4
Jennings, David, 1955, F 17,27:2
Jennings, Dewitt C, 1937, Mr 2,21:2
Jennings, Dudley L, 1944, My 19,19:5
Jennings, Ebenezer, 1911, O 23,11:5
Jennings, Edgar S, 1956, Je 11,31:3
Jennings, Edward A, 1958, S 11,33:4
Jennings, Edward J, 1951, D 13,34:3
Jennings, Edward J Sr, 1949, N 3,29:3
Jennings, Edward Mrs, 1958, Jl 27,61:3
Jennings, Edwin L, 1941, N 24,17:4
Jennings, Elias P Mrs, 1943, Je 21,17:3
Jennings, Ella A Dr (Mrs Jas Wilson McDonald), 1908, D 3,9:5
Jennings, Ellsworth M, 1943, O 4,17:2
Jennings, Elzy D, 1938, Ap 29,21:5
Jennings, Ephraim J, 1925, N 1,9:1
Jennings, Ernest A, 1942, Je 21,36:8
Jennings, Erwin M, 1937, Mr 5,21:1
Jennings, Everett, 1949, N 8,31:4
Jennings, F X (Frank), 1950, Jl 31,17:3
Jennings, Frank, 1968, O 9,47:4
Jennings, Frank P, 1943, Mr 14,24:5
Jennings, Frank W, 1948, Ja 19,23:2
Jennings, Fred A, 1953, F 7,15:6
Jennings, Frederick Beach (funl, My 29,15:3), 19 My 27,11:4
Jennings, Frederick C, 1948, Ap 18,68:4
Jennings, Frederick E, 1953, My 25,25:1
Jennings, Frederick H, 1946, Ap 8,27:4
Jennings, George E, 1904, Ja 7,9:5
Jennings, George J Jr, 1968, Ag 20,41:3
Jennings, Gilbert P, 1941, Ap 18,21:1
Jennings, H A, 1928, F 1,1:2
Jennings, H Gordon, 1953, Ja 13,32:4
Jennings, Harry F, 1951, F 3,15:4
Jennings, Harry K, 1937, S 5,II,7:1
Jennings, Henry A, 1937, Jl 30,19:3
Jennings, Henry M Capt, 1915, O 26,11:5
Jennings, Henry S, 1943, N 21,56:3
Jennings, Herbert C, 1961, Ag 23,33:4
Jennings, Herbert Mrs, 1951, Ap 4,29:5
Jennings, Herbert S (por), 1947, Ap 15,25:1
Jennings, Hughie Mrs, 1943, O 25,15:5
Jennings, Irwin G, 1955, Ag 24,27:5
Jennings, Isaac, 1939, Mr 2,21:5
Jennings, Ivor, 1965, D 20,35:5
Jennings, J Stanton, 1958, O 5,87:2
Jennings, James A, 1937, D 25,15:2
Jennings, James B, 1943, F 27,13:4
Jennings, James J, 1957, Ag 17,15:4
Jennings, James V, 1943, Ap 14,23:5
Jennings, Jean B Mrs (will), 1949, My 30,8:3
Jennings, Jean B P Mrs, 1949, My 3,25:1
Jennings, Jim, 1957, My 14,35:5

Jennings, John E, 1945, My 26,15:4; 1948, Mr 2,23:3
Jennings, John E Mrs, 1954, My 8,17:3
Jennings, John F, 1954, Je 29,27:2
Jennings, John G, 1937, N 22,19:3
Jennings, John J, 1909, Jl 1,9:6; 1953, D 9,11:1; 1959, Je 17,35:2
Jennings, John P, 1941, Je 20,21:2
Jennings, Joseph, 1939, Ag 5,29:2
Jennings, Joseph A, 1954, Je 30,27:5
Jennings, Joseph H Mrs, 1949, F 23,27:5
Jennings, Joseph M, 1943, Je 26,13:2
Jennings, L Mrs, 1929, My 13,23:5
Jennings, Laetus Mrs, 1964, S 6,56:5
Jennings, Laura H Mrs, 1939, Jl 10,19:1
Jennings, Lynn F, 1958, Mr 30,88:3
Jennings, Mabelle, 1944, Mr 10,15:2
Jennings, Mary L, 1948, Ja 18,60:4
Jennings, Michael J, 1952, O 14,31:5
Jennings, Michael J Mrs, 1962, Ag 30,29:5
Jennings, Myra F Mrs, 1940, Ap 26,21:5
Jennings, Napoleon A, 1918, D 16,15:3
Jennings, Newell, 1965, F 18,33:3
Jennings, Oliver G Mrs, 1964, My 7,37:4
Jennings, Oliver H, 1956, Je 26,35:6
Jennings, Oscar H, 1953, F 8,88:2
Jennings, Otto E, 1964, F 1,23:4
Jennings, Patrick L, 1937, Je 5,17:5
Jennings, Percy H, 1951, O 3,36:2
Jennings, Percy H Mrs, 1963, D 18,41:1
Jennings, Phil B, 1949, Jl 31,61:1
Jennings, Philander R (funl), 1914, S 25,11:7
Jennings, Preston J, 1962, F 5,31:4
Jennings, Ralph C, 1959, Ja 8,29:2
Jennings, Richard, 1953, Ap 19,91:1
Jennings, Robert B, 1954, Ja 3,89:2
Jennings, Robert E, 1965, Mr 19,35:5
Jennings, Robert J, 1940, O 18,21:3
Jennings, Rutherford, 1957, Ag 6,27:3
Jennings, Sallie, 1940, Ag 17,15:4
Jennings, Samuel C, 1952, D 24,17:3
Jennings, Samuel S, 1962, Ja 16,33:3
Jennings, Stanley T, 1937, Ag 28,15:6
Jennings, Stephen L, 1959, Mr 10,36:1
Jennings, Theron O, 1947, F 12,25:4
Jennings, Thomas A, 1951, F 24,13:5
Jennings, Thomas E, 1967, F 1,39:2
Jennings, W, 1933, Ja 10,21:3
Jennings, W S Mrs, 1963, Ap 26,35:1
Jennings, Walter D, 1945, My 19,19:2
Jennings, Walter L, 1944, S 3,26:7
Jennings, Walter M, 1952, Ja 18,27:4
Jennings, Walter Sr, 1949, Je 28,28:3
Jennings, Warren G, 1959, D 12,23:5
Jennings, Wayne L, 1960, N 9,42:3
Jennings, William, 1912, My 18,13:6; 1952, D 17,33:3
Jennings, William H, 1944, My 16,21:6
Jennings, William J, 1950, F 28,29:3
Jennings, William N, 1946, S 11,7:5
Jennings, William Sherman, 1920, F 28,11:4
Jennison, Albert H, 1955, Ag 22,21:6
Jennison, C R Col, 1884, Je 28,3:4
Jennison, Ralph D, 1956, Jl 27,21:2
Jennrich, Aug F W, 1939, Ja 25,22:1
Jenny, Conrad G, 1944, S 20,23:6
Jenny, E, 1878, D 11,2:2
Jenny, Herbert L, 1956, Ag 20,21:2
Jenny, Murray J (M Jordan), 1962, Jl 4,21:5
Jennys, Harold W, 1967, Ag 12,25:4
Jenoves, William, 1964, S 5,19:3
Jenrick, William F, 1942, O 26,15:4
Jens, Arthur M, 1965, Mr 24,43:1
Jensen, Abbie G C Mrs, 1939, Ja 5,23:4
Jensen, Adelaide D, 1942, My 1,19:5
Jensen, Adolph Mrs, 1949, Ja 21,21:3
Jensen, Alice G Mrs, 1944, S 1,13:2
Jensen, Allan Mrs, 1963, My 4,25:5
Jensen, Anders K, 1956, N 22,33:5
Jensen, Andrew P Sr, 1949, F 20,60:3
Jensen, Axel G, 1945, My 6,38:1
Jensen, Axel K, 1955, My 19,29:6
Jensen, Carl, 1959, Ag 1,17:5
Jensen, Carl C, 1954, Ja 26,27:5
Jensen, Charles, 1948, Mr 20,13:1
Jensen, Charles H, 1925, Mr 6,19:5
Jensen, Christ, 1964, Ja 1,25:3
Jensen, Christian, 1941, Ag 23,13:2; 1943, O 31,48:7
Jensen, Daniel C, 1959, S 25,29:3
Jensen, Dorothy Mrs, 1952, D 19,32:5
Jensen, Eddy, 1949, Jl 30,15:4
Jensen, Elizabeth Mrs, 1951, Ag 3,21:1
Jensen, Elmer C, 1955, Ap 25,23:3
Jensen, Erik M, 1950, Ja 27,23:2
Jensen, Frederick, 1952, N 14,23:2
Jensen, Frederik W, 1958, Mr 31,27:2
Jensen, Gustav, 1951, Ja 10,27:5
Jensen, Gustav B, 1954, Je 28,19:6
Jensen, Gustav H, 1957, O 26,21:4
Jensen, Gustav Mrs, 1951, Ja 10,27:5
Jensen, Harold J, 1953, Jl 11,11:6
Jensen, Henry J, 1944, Mr 20,17:3
Jensen, Henry M, 1961, Ja 13,27:2
Jensen, J Harding, 1954, S 22,30:1
Jensen, J Lawrence, 1949, S 5,17:3
Jensen, Jens, 1951, O 2,27:1
Jensen, Jens C, 1954, Ag 14,15:5
Jensen, Jens K, 1955, My 15,86:4
Jensen, Jens M, 1950, Ag 1,23:3
Jensen, Johannes V, 1950, N 26,91:1
Jensen, John C, 1957, O 22,33:2
Jensen, John M Mrs, 1946, Ag 5,21:3
Jensen, Just C, 1942, My 24,42:4
Jensen, Knud E, 1960, Ag 27,13:3
Jensen, Knud V, 1939, Je 5,7:2
Jensen, Lorenz, 1943, N 13,13:6
Jensen, Martin L, 1949, N 29,30:3
Jensen, Max, 1946, Ap 26,21:4; 1952, My 17,19:4
Jensen, Niels J, 1947, D 3,29:3
Jensen, Olof, 1942, F 22,III,7:4
Jensen, Otto K, 1962, Jl 25,33:4
Jensen, Peter L, 1961, O 27,33:1
Jensen, Ralph A, 1946, Mr 14,25:4
Jensen, Robert F, 1959, D 3,37:3
Jensen, Stanley H, 1956, S 24,27:4
Jensen, Talma Mrs, 1959, F 1,85:1
Jensen, Thomas, 1963, N 17,86:5
Jensen, Thomas D, 1953, Je 30,23:4
Jensen, Thorwald, 1951, O 10,23:5
Jensen, Wilhelm Dr, 1911, N 25,II,13:5
Jensen, William E, 1955, D 28,24:6
Jensen, William F, 1962, Ap 11,43:2
Jenson, Andrew (por), 1941, N 20,27:3
Jenson, Harry P, 1949, O 18,27:4
Jenss, J Gordon, 1942, Jl 25,13:6
Jenssen, Charles K, 1941, Ag 31,22:3
Jenssen, Jacob D, 1951, Ap 18,31:4
Jente, Albert H, 1940, F 3,13:2
Jente, Richard, 1952, Ag 23,13:2
Jenter, Christina Mrs, 1914, Ag 27,11:5
Jenter, Martin T C, 1951, S 22,17:4
Jentes, Harry, 1958, Ja 22,27:2
Jenvey, William R Rev, 1924, F 7,17:5
Jephson, Arthur Jermy Mounteney Lt, 1908, O 23,9:4
Jephson, Edward, 1943, O 26,23:1
Jeppson, John R, 1958, N 3,37:4
Jepsen, Neil P, 1954, Mr 2,25:2
Jepsen, Walter, 1949, My 8,76:6
Jepson, Alfred H, 1954, O 15,23:2
Jepson, Charles A Jr Mrs, 1965, Ag 22,82:7
Jepson, Charles A Mrs, 1954, O 3,87:2
Jepson, Charles H, 1940, Ag 5,15:7
Jepson, Edgar, 1938, Ap 12,23:5
Jepson, Frank, 1951, Ap 13,23:5
Jepson, Harry B, 1952, Ag 25,17:5
Jepson, John C, 1949, My 7,13:2
Jepson, John J, 1951, Ja 12,27:2
Jepson, Paul N, 1949, O 25,27:2
Jeralds, Thomas W Mrs, 1949, Mr 8,25:1
Jerauld, Frederick N C, 1946, Jl 29,21:5
Jerauld, Frederick N C Mrs, 1937, Ja 19,23:4
Jerdan, William, 1869, Jl 27,5:4
Jerebker, Morris, 1954, Mr 31,13:2
Jeremiah, Edward J, 1967, Je 8,47:2
Jeremy, Ralph E, 1918, My 10,11:5
Jerez, Maxemo, 1881, Ag 12,5:2
Jerez, Remigio, 1943, My 29,13:2
Jergens, Andrew, 1967, F 24,35:3
Jergens, Herman, 1946, My 1,25:2
Jerger, Joseph A, 1950, Jl 6,27:5
Jerichau, J A, 1883, Jl 26,5:3
Jerie, Richard M, 1960, Ap 27,37:1
Jerkens, Thomas D, 1952, D 2,36:5
Jermain, Marie C, 1938, N 15,23:4
Jerman, Thomas P Mrs, 1961, N 22,18:5
Jerman, William B, 1941, O 3,23:5
Jermane, William W, 1942, Ag 14,17:2
Jermon, John G, 1956, Ap 28,17:6
Jermyn, Earl (Marquess of Bristol), 1960, Ap 6,41:3
Jermyn, Frank H G, 1910, Ja 4,13:4
Jernberg, George H Mrs, 1953, Je 26,19:4
Jernegan, Holmes M Dr, 1917, Je 1,9:5
Jernegan, Marcus, 1949, F 22,23:5
Jernegan, Marcus W Mrs, 1947, O 13,23:4
Jernigan, James P Brig-Gen, 1968, S 16,47:3
Jerningham, Charles Edward Wynne, 1921, F 8,11:5
Jerolamon, Harold C, 1957, D 10,35:1
Jeroliman, Henry, 1903, D 11,5:3
Jerolman, Harry W Mrs, 1937, Mr 30,24:2
Jeroloman, John, 1908, Ag 22,7:5
Jerome, Addison Gould Mrs, 1909, Jl 2,7:4
Jerome, Albeus, 1941, My 4,53:2
Jerome, Anita de S Mrs, 1941, N 20,27:6
Jerome, Ben M, 1938, Mr 29,21:2
Jerome, Bro (J B Roese), 1959, Je 10,37:1
Jerome, Charles B, 1954, Jl 29,23:5
Jerome, Edwin, 1957, F 10,86:6; 1959, S 12,21:2
Jerome, Ernest G Mrs, 1947, D 7,76:2
Jerome, Eugene D, 1960, S 20,39:2
Jerome, Frank, 1941, My 5,17:2
Jerome, Frank C, 1941, D 18,27:2
Jerome, Franklin S, 1948, Je 24,26:2
Jerome, Harry, 1938, S 13,23:5
Jerome, J K, 1927, Je 15,27:3
Jerome, James V, 1946, Ag 31,15:3
Jerome, Jerome K Mrs, 1938, O 31,15:2
Jerome, John L, 1903, N 23,7:3
Jerome, Joseph, 1937, Je 26,17:5
Jerome, L R, 1888, Ag 13,5:5
Jerome, L W, 1891, Mr 5,8:1
Jerome, Rev Bro, 1912, D 14,15:3
Jerome, Roswell H, 1872, F 11,4:6
Jerome, Sister (Kelly; Benedictine), 1958, F 25,27:4
Jerome, Victor J, 1965, Ag 8,64:4
Jerome, W T, 1934, F 14,19:1
Jerome, William F, 1943, My 2,44:5
Jerome, William K, 1942, My 9,13:1
Jerome, William Mrs (Maude Nugent), 1958, Je 4, 33:1
Jerome, William T Jr, 1952, O 3,23:3
Jerome, William Z, 1946, Ap 2,27:2
Jerpe, John M, 1949, Mr 11,25:2
Jerram, M, 1933, Mr 21,20:3
Jerrell, Everett J, 1946, Mr 28,25:3
Jerrick, Walter F, 1953, O 26,21:4
Jerrold, Douglas, 1964, Jl 24,27:4
Jerrold, Laurence, 1918, N 6,17:4
Jerrold, Mary, 1955, Mr 4,23:1
Jerrold, W B, 1884, Mr 11,2:2
Jersek, Walter J, 1943, F 16,19:5
Jersek, Walter Mrs, 1963, Je 25,33:2
Jersey, Countess of, 1945, My 23,19:4
Jersey, Earl of (Geo Hy Robt Child Villiers), 1924, Ja 1,23:2
Jersey, Lord (Victor Alb Geo Villiers), 1915, Je 1, 15:7
Jersin, Alexander, 1943, Mr 3,23:4
Jerski, Morton Mrs, 1963, Je 22,23:4
Jerue, Joseph E, 1959, S 9,41:4
Jervey, Henry, 1942, O 1,23:2
Jervey, Huger W, 1949, Jl 28,24:2
Jervey, James P, 1947, Mr 14,23:5
Jervis, J B, 1885, Ja 14,2:4
Jervis, John F, 1948, Ja 23,23:2
Jervis, William Mrs, 1904, Ap 23,9:5
Jervis-White-Jervis, Henry, 1947, S 19,23:5
Jervis-White-Jervis, John H, 1943, Ja 20,11:2
Jerwan, Shikar S, 1941, D 12,26:2
Jerzabek, Anton, 1939, Mr 27,15:4
Jerzmanowski, Ezram, 1909, F 13,9:4
Jesaitis, Joseph Mrs, 1963, Je 27,33:2
Jeschke, Rudolf P, 1948, My 1,15:6
Jeselsohn, Benjamin, 1948, Mr 26,21:1
Jeshurin, Ephim, 1967, O 27,45:4
Jeske, Carl R, 1938, Jl 14,21:5
Jeske, Fred, 1957, N 25,31:4
Jeske, John J, 1944, My 12,19:4
Jesky, Ralph, 1956, D 15,6:2
Jesmer, John J, 1954, Je 27,69:2
Jesner, Frederick, 1946, Je 9,40:3
Jespersen, Henry L Jr, 1945, Jl 7,13:3
Jespersen, Holger B, 1947, Jl 2,23:3
Jespersen, Otto, 1943, My 16,43:1
Jess, Frank B Mrs, 1946, O 14,29:2
Jesschonnek, H, 1943, Ag 21,3:4
Jesse, F Tennyson (Mrs H M Harwood), 1958, Ag 7,25:3
Jesse, George N, 1938, Ap 3,II,7:2
Jesse, Joseph P, 1959, Ag 7,23:1
Jessel, Carl, 1912, My 27,11:4
Jessel, G Sir, 1883, Mr 22,5:5
Jessel, Joseph Mrs, 1955, Jl 6,27:3
Jessel, Lord, 1950, N 2,31:5
Jessel, Patricia (Mrs Geo Feinberg), 1968, Je 11,47:1
Jesser, Frederick W, 1947, My 29,21:3
Jessett, Arthur, 1952, My 20,19:2
Jessner, Leopold, 1945, D 15,17:5
Jessop, Earl P (por), 1940, My 24,19:3
Jessop, Ford R, 1938, Je 8,23:3
Jessop, George H, 1915, Mr 23,9:5
Jessop, Gilbert L, 1955, My 12,29:4
Jessop, Joseph S, 1953, S 3,22:7
Jessop, W M, 1935, Ag 28,17:3
Jessup, A D, 1881, Jl 6,2:5
Jessup, Aaron Z, 1938, Mr 31,23:4
Jessup, Albert B, 1941, Ja 26,37:2
Jessup, Anna H, 1940, Jl 13,13:2
Jessup, Charles A, 1945, Ap 14,15:2
Jessup, David S D, 1952, F 3,85:2
Jessup, David S D Jr, 1961, Ja 8,86:2
Jessup, Edgar B, 1961, My 14,86:6
Jessup, Elon H, 1958, F 27,27:4
Jessup, Everett C Dr, 1968, Jl 3,32:2
Jessup, Everett C Mrs, 1967, D 18,47:1
Jessup, Frederick N Rev, 1919, D 9,17:4
Jessup, George P, 1942, My 19,19:5
Jessup, George P Mrs, 1904, F 6,5:2; 1955, N 27,89:1
Jessup, George S, 1937, Ap 20,25:1
Jessup, Henry H Rev, 1910, Ap 29,9:4
Jessup, Henry Harris Mrs, 1907, D 24,7:5
Jessup, James M, 1968, D 21,37:3
Jessup, John C, 1945, My 26,15:6
Jessup, Nelson O, 1924, Ap 24,19:3
Jessup, Peter M, 1948, O 7,29:2
Jessup, Samuel Rev Dr, 1912, Jl 17,9:4
Jessup, Stanbury A, 1914, Ap 10,13:5
Jessup, Stanley, 1945, O 27,15:5
Jessup, Stuart D, 1950, N 30,33:3
Jessup, Stuart D Mrs, 1953, D 30,24:3
Jessup, Theodore C, 1955, Ap 6,29:2
Jessup, Walter A (por), 1944, Jl 8,11:5

Jessup, William E, 1943, Ag 12,19:2
Jessup, William H, 1940, S 20,23:5
Jessup, William Mrs, 1950, My 26,23:2
Jessup, William Rev, 1920, D 15,15:4
Jessup, William S, 1943, D 1,21:5
Jessurum, Samuel H, 1948, S 20,25:5
Jessurun, Albert E, 1938, My 28,15:5
Jester, Alexander, 1907, Ag 20,7:5
Jester, Beauford H, 1949, Jl 12,27:1
Jester, Claude W, 1953, F 15,92:1
Jester, Edward P, 1937, Ag 29,II,7:3
Jesualda Lafranchi, Sister (Sisters of the Sacred Heart), 1953, Mr 19,29:2
Jesup, Alpheus D, 1950, Ap 30,102:4
Jesup, Edward N, 1947, N 3,23:6
Jesup, Morris K, 1908, Ja 26,9:2
Jesup, Morris K Mrs, 1914, Je 18,11:5
Jesup, Richard M, 1954, Ag 30,17:4
Jesus, Adrian of Bro, 1910, Je 14,11:5
Jesus, Angel de, 1951, My 1,29:3
Jesus e Sousa, Agostino de, 1952, F 23,11:2
Jeter, Frank, 1955, S 17,15:4
Jeter, George D, 1963, N 1,34:5
Jeter, J B, 1880, F 19,5:4
Jett, Ewell K, 1965, Ap 29,35:4
Jett, Frank Mrs, 1949, My 6,25:2
Jett, John Mrs, 1951, D 7,27:3
Jett, Millard, 1956, Je 20,31:1
Jett, Shelby M (por), 1944, Ag 11,15:6
Jette, Eric R, 1963, F 26,7:8
Jette, Louis Amable Sir, 1920, My 6,11:1
Jette, Roger G, 1951, O 2,27:1
Jetter, Anna, 1950, Jl 11,31:5
Jetter, Arthur, 1963, S 16,35:1
Jetton, Walter, 1968, Ja 30,38:1
Jetty, Alderette H Mrs, 1951, Ja 4,29:2
Jeudwine, Hugh, 1942, D 3,25:5
Jeune, Irving R, 1951, O 9,29:4
Jeunet, E Alexis, 1944, S 28,19:5
Jevenois, Pedro, 1941, My 14,21:4
Jevne, Jack A, 1941, S 7,50:1
Jevon, Victor A, 1945, Jl 19,23:4
Jevons, Alfred O, 1950, D 20,32:3
Jevons, Reginald W, 1944, D 17,37.1
Jevons, Stanley, 1955, Je 30,25:1
Jevons, W S Prof, 1882, Ag 16,5:3
Jewel, James E, 1939, N 9,23:5
Jewell, Anna, 1950, My 4,27:4
Jewell, Archibald J, 1953, O 26,21:3
Jewell, Arthur N, 1960, Je 25,21:6
Jewell, Charles A Col, 1905, Je 26,7:2
Jewell, Charles H, 1939, Je 12,17:5; 1939, Jl 25,19:5
Jewell, Charles I, 1951, O 28,84:4
Jewell, Clayton D Mrs, 1945, Jl 5,13:4
Jewell, Ditmas, 1905, Mr 5,9:3
Jewell, Edward A, 1947, O 12,76:2
Jewell, Emory L, 1949, O 22,17:2
Jewell, Enoch, 1948, O 5,25:5
Jewell, Esther, 1883, F 27,5:4
Jewell, Frank M, 1940, F 19,17:1
Jewell, Fred S Dr, 1903, D 29,9:6
Jewell, George W Mrs, 1944, My 9,19:5
Jewell, Harry S, 1945, Ag 26,44:7
Jewell, Harvey, 1881, D 9,5:3
Jewell, Herbert Stuart Maj, 1920, O 3,22:4
Jewell, John, 1953, Mr 25,31:5
Jewell, John V, 1937, O 14,25:3
Jewell, Lyman B, 1917, N 21,13:4
Jewell, Marshall, 1883, F 11,7:2
Jewell, Mary F Mrs, 1948, O 8,25:2
Jewell, Ogden Mrs, 1943, D 28,17:2
Jewell, Pliny, 1869, Ag 29,1:4
Jewell, Pliny Mrs, 1903, O 12,7:7
Jewell, Ralph, 1960, Ap 30,23:4
Jewell, Ray L, 1959, Mr 26,31:1
Jewell, Richard L, 1967, Mr 19,92:8
Jewell, Ross Dr, 1925, Ja 9,17:3
Jewell, Sargent H, 1941, O 8,23:2
Jewell, Sargent H Mrs, 1950, Je 26,27:1
Jewell, T Bronson, 1950, N 6,27:4
Jewell, Thomas A Mrs, 1938, My 23,17:4
Jewell, W H Gen, 1912, Ja 4,13:4
Jewell, Walter H, 1942, F 2,15:1
Jewell, Walter L, 1950, D 27,27:4
Jewell, William E, 1943, S 11,13:2
Jewell, William H, 1943, Ag 18,19:6; 1957, D 16,29:2
Jewett, A D Lawrence 2d, 1954, My 13,29:3
Jewett, Charles A G, 1953, F 7,15:3
Jewett, Charles C, 1868, Ja 10,1:2
Jewett, Charles Dr, 1879, Ap 4,5:5; 1910, Ag 7,II,9:4
Jewett, Charles Taylor Dr, 1918, Ja 20,17:1
Jewett, Edward H, 1944, Ap 30,45:1
Jewett, Edward H Mrs (M Sherwood), 1953, Ap 18, 19:4
Jewett, Edwin S Col, 1910, F 15,9:5
Jewett, Elizabeth R Mrs, 1940, Jl 28,27:3
Jewett, Ezekiel, 1877, My 19,1:8
Jewett, Francis A Mrs, 1950, S 23,17:4
Jewett, Frank B, 1949, N 19,17:1
Jewett, Frank B Mrs, 1948, D 19,76:1
Jewett, Franklin S Mrs, 1947, F 28,23:1
Jewett, Frederic A Dr, 1923, Ja 20,13:5
Jewett, Freeland, 1937, O 20,23:2
Jewett, G P Pollen, 1963, Ap 21,86:8
Jewett, George, 1938, Je 11,15:5
Jewett, George F, 1956, N 24,19:4
Jewett, George R Col, 1937, F 12,23:2
Jewett, Gertrude A Mrs, 1956, Ag 13,19:3
Jewett, Guernsey R, 1952, Ap 1,29:2
Jewett, Guernsey R Mrs, 1952, O 4,17:6
Jewett, H J, 1898, Mr 7,1:4; 1933, Je 16,17:6
Jewett, Harvey C Jr, 1953, F 19,23:3
Jewett, Henry E, 1940, N 9,17:4
Jewett, J B, 1876, Ja 24,1:3
Jewett, James R, 1943, Ap 1,23:4
Jewett, James W, 1944, My 3,19:2
Jewett, John H, 1939, S 21,23:2
Jewett, John Howard, 1925, S 19,15:4
Jewett, John L, 1873, Je 14,8:2
Jewett, John N, 1904, Ja 16,9:6
Jewett, Kennon, 1956, Je 12,35:1
Jewett, Levi Dr, 1908, Ja 8,9:5
Jewett, Levi Mrs, 1908, Ja 8,9:5
Jewett, Margaret W Mrs (will), 1939, Ja 19,11:2
Jewett, Marius S, 1947, S 12,21:5
Jewett, P A Dr, 1884, Ap 11,5:3
Jewett, Phelps D, 1947, O 13,23:4
Jewett, Robert J, 1954, S 10,23:2
Jewett, Sarah Orne, 1909, Je 25,9:4
Jewett, Sherman S, 1941, Ag 24,35:3
Jewett, Simeon B, 1869, Jl 29,6:1
Jewett, Stanley P, 1944, Mr 9,17:4
Jewett, T L Judge, 1875, N 5,4:6
Jewett, T S, 1940, N 18,19:2
Jewett, William S, 1944, O 26,23:3
Jewett, William W, 1941, D 16,27:2
Jewitt, Asa C, 1925, Jl 24,13:7
Jewitt, Homer M, 1952, Je 29,56:3
Jewkes, Francis R Jr, 1958, Ag 24,87:1
Jewkes, Frank R Jr Mrs, 1968, Mr 23,31:4
Jex-Blake, Sophia Dr, 1912, Ja 9,13:5
Jeze, Gaston, 1953, Ag 7,19:3
Jezek, Jaroslav, 1942, Ja 3,19:2
Jezer, Phil, 1955, My 19,29:2
Jha, Amar N, 1955, S 3,15:6
Jibbes, Frederick H, 1957, D 3,35:5
Jigger, Madge D B Mrs, 1948, Je 3,25:2
Jiggetts, John P, 1966, F 19,27:2
Jilemnicky, Peter, 1949, My 21,13:3
Jill, Joseph J, 1958, D 1,29:6
Jillings, David S, 1953, Ap 23,29:2
Jilson, Ralph A Jr Mrs (cor, Jl 2,25:2), 1946, Jl 1,31:4
Jimenez, Jeronimo, 1923, F 21,15:4
Jimenez, Juan R, 1958, My 30,21:2
Jimenez, Juan R Senora, 1956, O 29,29:4
Jimenez, Manuel F, 1952, Ap 15,27:4
Jimenez-Berroa, Jose M, 1917, Ja 20,11:3
Jimenez de la Guardia, Adolfo, 1958, Jl 20,30:2
Jimenez Oreamuno, Ricardo (por), 1945, Ja 6,11:3
Jimenis, J Oswald, 1941, S 25,25:4
Jimerson, Earl W, 1957, O 6,85:1
Jimerson, Royal W, 1958, Ag 4,21:5
Jiminez Lopez, Miguel, 1955, Ag 24,27:1
Jimmie the Bum, 1903, S 7,3:6
Jimmy the Paup, 1903, D 15,6:3
Jin Lung-po, 1957, O 15,30:2
Jinarajadasa, C, 1953, Je 20,17:6
Jindra, Charles J, 1948, Ag 24,23:2
Jingeleski, Joseph J, 1962, Mr 22,35:4
Jinishian, Asadoor J, 1959, F 11,39:1
Jinnah, Fatima (funl, Jl 11,14:6), 1967, Jl 10,31:1
Jinnah, Mohammed Ali, 1948, S 12,1:6
Jirka, Frank J Sr, 1963, N 20,40:3
Jishkariane, Nikifor, 1950, Ag 15,29:5
Jlavonoly, Maximilian von Count, 1906, N 25,9:6
Jnoes, Mary D, 1912, Mr 7,11:4
Joachim, Hans S, 1956, O 8,27:4
Joachim, Harold H, 1938, Ag 2,19:3
Joachim, Henry, 1941, Ag 19,21:6
Joachim, Joseph, 1907, Ag 16,7:6
Joachim, Max, 1939, Ja 5,23:4
Joachim, Metropolitan, 1950, Ja 27,23:2
Joachim, William, 1955, Jl 7,27:1
Joachim, William B, 1950, Ap 4,29:4
Joachimson, Martin, 1944, F 8,15:3
Joad, Cyril E M (will, Ag 18,10:6), 1953, Ap 10,21:1
Joakim, Stanley D, 1965, Ja 19,33:4
Joan Miriam, Sister, 1946, Mr 15,21:4
Joanis, Fred Mrs, 1950, Ap 3,23:3
Joanna, ex-Queen of Tahita, 1935, Mr 11,17:1
Joanna, Princess of Rumania, 1963, F 20,12:8
Joanne, A L, 1881, Mr 4,2:6
Joannes, Amba, 1942, Je 23,19:5
Joannes, Francis Y, 1952, Je 22,70:4
Joannides, Minas Sr, 1952, S 9,31:4
Joanovici, Joseph, 1965, F 7,92:4
Job, H Allen, 1947, Ap 2,27:5
Job, Robert B, 1961, S 7,35:2
Job, Thomas, 1947, Ag 2,13:4
Jobbagy, Thomas A, 1938, Je 18,15:5
Jobbins, Edward K, 1951, Ap 23,25:1
Jobbins, Hedley Mrs, 1946, Ap 22,21:4
Jobe, Howard D, 1950, Ap 30,102:5
Jober, Stanley J Mrs, 1941, O 1,21:4
Jobes, Walter, 1946, N 12,29:4
Jobes, Warren L J, 1944, Ag 19,11:3
Jobin, Francis X, 1954, F 5,20:3
Joblin, Miller Mrs, 1953, F 6,19:2
Jobling, James W, 1961, N 11,23:5
Jobson, Alex B, 1951, N 6,29:5
Jobson, F J, 1881, Ja 5,5:3
Jobson, Rachel D Mrs, 1940, Jl 20,15:6
Jobson, Wemyss Dr, 1876, My 30,8:2
Jobst, Conrad, 1957, Ag 29,27:5
Jocelyn, Louis P, 1942, F 24,21:4
Jocelyn, Mary E Mrs, 1937, O 19,26:2
Jocelyn, S Rev Father (mem ser, Se 22,8:4), 1879, Ag 19,5:5
Jocelyn, Stephen P Brig-Gen, 1920, Mr 9,11:5
Joch, Joseph, 1944, Ap 30,46:1
Jocham, Edward D, 1946, O 12,19:5
Jochelman, David, 1941, Jl 11,15:5
Jochelson, Waldemar Prof, 1937, N 2,28:2
Jochem, Hugo, 1948, Ag 10,21:5
Jocher, John C, 1946, Jl 20,13:5
Jochimsen, Edward P, 1949, F 3,24:3
Jochmus, A J Gen, 1881, S 25,5:4
Jochum, Andrew, 1960, S 17,23:6
Jochum, Henry L, 1949, F 11,23:5
Jockers, Frank E, 1951, Je 25,19:4
Jockin, Henri A, 1941, Ap 17,23:4
Jocknick, A J W, 1903, Mr 29,1:2
Jockum, J Harry Jr, 1947, Jl 22,23:3
Jockwig, John H, 1944, D 6,23:2
Jodidi, Samuel L, 1945, Ja 2,19:5
Jodkowski, Jozef, 1950, Ja 5,25:1
Jodoin, Raymond J, 1925, S 4,21:6
Joehr, Adolf, 1953, Jl 1,29:2
Joel, George W F, 1959, Ap 29,33:2
Joel, Ira D, 1952, Je 1,84:5
Joel, J B (will), 1941, Je 1,3:3
Joel, Jack B, 1940, N 14,23:1
Joel, Jack B Mrs, 1937, D 18,21:5
Joel, S B, 1931, My 23,17:1
Joel, S B Mrs, 1919, Ag 19,13:4
Joel, William V Mrs, 1950, S 6,29:4
Joelson, Harry, 1943, Ag 12,19:1
Joelson, Morris S, 1958, Ag 21,25:3
Joerg, Oswald Dr, 1920, N 6,13:2
Joerg, Wolfgang L G, 1952, Ja 9,29:1
Joergens, Arthur O, 1958, F 1,19:2
Joergensen, Hans, 1948, S 22,31:2
Joern, Charles E, 1958, My 23,23:2
Joerne, Herman, 1907, S 21,9:4
Joesting, Herb, 1963, O 3,35:4
Jofe, Isaac, 1960, D 25,42:1
Joffe, Abraham D Mrs, 1937, D 30,19:4
Joffe, Abram, 1960, O 15,23:4
Joffe, Boris M, 1960, My 29,57:1
Joffe, Isaac, 1953, Ja 26,19:4
Joffe, Joseph, 1960, Ap 5,37:1
Joffe, Judah A, 1966, S 17,29:4
Joffe, Judah A Mrs, 1963, Ag 15,29:2
Joffe, Luba A, 1960, Mr 15,39:3
Joffe, Maxwell S, 1950, My 5,21:4
Joffe, Philip M, 1962, N 24,23:5
Joffe, Reuben S, 1938, N 11,25:5
Joffe, Solomon A, 1964, N 9,33:4
Joffee, Mark S (por), 1941, Je 28,15:4
Joffre, J J C, 1931, Ja 3,1:3
Joffre, Joseph Mme, 1956, Ja 19,33:4
Joham, Josef, 1959, Ap 9,31:1
Johana, Sister (J Zhrun), 1952, Ja 3,27:3
Johaneson, Bland (Mrs L Gaynor), 1962, Jl 12,2
Johaneson, Clover B Mrs, 1963, My 31,25:1
Johanigman, Sterling E, 1953, N 21,13:4
Johanknecht, Edwin, 1960, Je 29,33:4
Johann, A, 1931, Ap 28,27:3
Johann, Jose R, 1959, Je 25,29:2
Johann-Georg, Prince of Saxony, 1938, N 25,23:2
Johannes, Albert H, 1955, Mr 6,88:1
Johannes, Francis Bp, 1937, Mr 14,II,8:7
Johannes, Prince of Liechtenstein, 1959, S 5,15:2
Johannesen, Grant Mrs, 1950, O 7,10:5
Johannesen, Ole, 1940, Mr 31,45:2
Johannesen, Svend E, 1944, D 23,13:4
Johannessen, Isaac E, 1950, Jl 6,28:5
Johannessen, Jakob A, 1954, O 5,27:1
Johannessen, Ole, 1945, O 15,17:5
Johannesson, Sigvald, 1953, F 23,25:5
Johanns, Frederick L, 1943, My 15,15:2
Johanns, Otto F, 1949, Ag 31,23:5
Johannsen, Albert, 1962, Ja 13,21:2
Johannsen, Alfred J, 1963, S 1,57:2
Johannsen, Anton, 1951, F 10,13:5
Johannsen, Claude H, 1953, Jl 18,14:7
Johannsen, Oskar A, 1961, N 8,35:3
Johannson, Asmunder P, 1953, O 24,15:3
Johannssen, Mary Mrs, 1952, N 28,25:2
Johansen, Alfred V, 1960, Ag 16,29:4
Johansen, Beppo R, 1946, Jl 24,27:3
Johansen, Charles K, 1944, Ag 2,15:6
Johansen, Dedrick, 1948, Ag 23,17:4
Johansen, George P, 1964, S 17,43:2
Johansen, Harry T Jr Mrs, 1964, Jl 7,35:1
Johansen, Henry, 1946, Je 27,21:3
Johansen, J Wilson, 1916, My 21,19:4
Johansen, John C, 1964, My 24,93:1
Johansen, John C Mrs (J MacLane), 1964, Ja

Johansing, Harry C Sr, 1954, O 7,23:5
Johanson, Carl A E, 1941, F 17,15:1
Johanson, Casimir V, 1952, O 29,29:5
Johanson, John P, 1937, D 16,27:2
Johanssen, Marco, 1965, F 23,33:4
Johansson, Carl E, 1943, O 1,19:5
Johl, Max G, 1957, Ap 3,31:1
Johl, Max G Mrs, 1957, Je 20,29:2
Johlin, Jacob M, 1954, Jl 23,17:1
John, Alice, 1956, Ag 11,13:5
John, Andrew, 1907, Jl 18,7:5
John, Augustus, 1938, Jl 18,13:5
John, Augustus (funl, N 3,35:1), 1961, N 1,1:3
John, Benjamin E, 1952, Jl 20,53:1
John, Charles O, 1955, F 2,27:2
John, David W Mrs, 1950, O 19,31:3
John, George, 1944, F 16,17:3
John, Goscombe, 1952, D 16,31:4
John, Griffith Rev Dr, 1912, Jl 26,9:6
John, J S Dr, 1937, Ag 12,19:4
John, John Price Durbin, 1916, Ag 8,9:6
John, Jonathan B, 1956, Jl 18,27:2
John, King of Abyssinia, 1889, Ap 4,1:2
John, Lisle C, 1959, Ap 9,31:5
John, Maurice D, 1954, Ja 21,31:1
John, Norman E, 1945, S 3,23:2
John, Prince, 1919, Ja 20,15:5
John, Robert, 1938, Je 5,45:3
John, Waldemar A P, 1964, O 12,29:4
John, William J, 1942, O 7,25:3
John Berchmans, Sister (Murphy), 1949, S 1,21:4
John Marie, Sister (Sisters of Charity), 1953, Ap 12, 89:1
John of Denmark, Prince, 1911, My 28,II,9:4
John William, Bro (Reul), 1966, Mr 19,29:3
John XXIII, Pope (Angelo G Roncalli), 1963, Je 4,1:8
Johncox, Bertha, 1948, D 4,19:3
Johncox, John Capt, 1920, My 27,11:3
Johncox, Lewis W, 1941, Ja 14,21:4
Johnen, Louis J, 1960, Ja 22,27:1
Johner, Peter Mrs, 1944, F 4,16:3
Johnes, Arthur, 1880, Mr 30,7:7
Johnes, Charles B, 1949, Ap 8,25:4
Johnes, E R, 1903, Mr 29,7:6
Johnes, Goldsmith Denniston, 1913, Mr 20,11:4
Johnosn, Frank E, 1958, D 7,88:5
Johns, Albert C, 1948, Je 9,29:5
Johns, Albert N, 1948, N 16,25:6
Johns, Arthur Mrs, 1903, N 30,7:6
Johns, Arthur W Sir, 1937, Ja 14,21:4
Johns, Benjamin M Jr (por), 1949, O 26,27:2
Johns, Carl O, 1942, Ap 19,44:1
Johns, Charles W, 1939, S 17,49:3
Johns, Christina Mrs, 1942, My 22,21:6
Johns, Craig, 1937, Ag 18,19:3
Johns, Craig Mrs (Sara), 1965, Ag 22,83:1
Johns, Edward B, 1946, N 14,29:2
Johns, Edward G, 1937, F 9,23:3
Johns, Elliott Mrs, 1955, N 28,31:5
Johns, George H Sr, 1947, D 17,29:3
Johns, George S (por), 1941, Jl 17,19:1
Johns, H W Mrs, 1951, N 3,17:5
Johns, Harold G, 1948, Ap 23,23:3
Johns, Harold W, 1962, Ag 25,19:4
Johns, Joshua L, 1947, Mr 17,23:5
Johns, Joshua L Mrs, 1940, Ap 4,23:3
Johns, Louis E, 1964, Je 13,23:6
Johns, Marshall E, 1914, O 3,11:6
Johns, Myles W, 1952, Je 5,31:4
Johns, Richard Rev, 1917, F 22,11:4
Johns, Roy B, 1957, Jl 26,19:2
Johns, T D Gen, 1883, Ag 2,4:7
Johns, W L, 1953, S 4,34:1
Johns, Wallace W Jr, 1952, Je 5,31:3
Johns, Walter P, 1947, My 11,62:2
Johns, Warren A, 1946, N 19,21:1
Johns, Wilbur, 1967, Jl 16,64:4
Johns, Willard T, 1956, Ap 20,25:3
Johns, William A, 1960, Ja 18,27:4
Johns, William A Mrs, 1941, Je 2,17:5
Johns, William H (por), 1944, Ap 18,21:1
Johns, William H Mrs, 1953, Je 24,25:4
Johnsen, Bjornulf, 1959, My 28,31:2
Johnsen, Carl F, 1950, O 24,29:4
Johnsen, Cilla Mrs, 1937, Ja 14,21:3
Johnsen, Martin O, 1945, My 1,23:4
Johnsen, N, 1932, D 7,21:3
Johnshoy, Howard G, 1967, Mr 25,3:4
Johnson, A B, 1935, Ja 9,20:1
Johnson, A Dexter Mrs, 1955, O 24,27:4
Johnson, A E, 1933, Mr 18,13:4
Johnson, A G, 1879, F 8,1:6
Johnson, A Herbert, 1938, F 17,21:5
Johnson, A Howard, 1943, D 10,27:2
Johnson, A J, 1884, Ap 23,5:6
Johnson, A L (funl), 1901, Jl 6,7:5
Johnson, A LeRoy, 1967, Ja 27,45:3
Johnson, A M Col, 1903, Ap 22,9:5
Johnson, A Robert, 1950, Mr 31,32:5
Johnson, A S (see also F 3), 1878, F 6,8:6
Johnson, Abram O, 1950, Ag 30,31:4
Johnson, Abram W, 1949, N 19,17:3
Johnson, Ada M, 1962, N 20,35:1
Johnson, Addison, 1939, Ap 4,25:1
Johnson, Addison F, 1944, N 7,27:4
Johnson, Adelaide Mrs, 1955, N 11,25:4
Johnson, Alba B Jr, 1938, Mr 22,21:4
Johnson, Alba B Mrs, 1944, O 25,21:4
Johnson, Albert, 1948, Jl 4,26:7; 1957, Ja 19,15:6; 1964, Je 29,27:5
Johnson, Albert A, 1963, Je 1,21:4
Johnson, Albert L, 1917, N 25,23:4; 1923, Ja 10,23:5; 1949, F 20,60:4; 1952, F 1,21:3
Johnson, Albert M, 1948, Ja 8,25:4
Johnson, Albert Mrs, 1957, Ja 22,29:3; 1959, F 20,26:1
Johnson, Albert R, 1960, Mr 17,33:2; 1967, D 22,31:1
Johnson, Albert S, 1957, F 22,21:3
Johnson, Albert S Mrs, 1945, S 15,15:5
Johnson, Albert T, 1947, Ap 27,60:2
Johnson, Albert W, 1957, Mr 23,19:3
Johnson, Albin, 1947, O 1,29:5
Johnson, Alex, 1941, My 18,43:1
Johnson, Alex C, 1938, Mr 20,II,8:4
Johnson, Alex L P Mrs, 1939, O 23,19:5
Johnson, Alexander Bryan Dr, 1917, S 6,11:3
Johnson, Alexander E, 1918, Je 12,13:5
Johnson, Alexander L P, 1947, Ap 29,28:2
Johnson, Alfonso, 1950, Mr 9,29:1
Johnson, Alfred B, 1945, O 9,21:1
Johnson, Alfred H, 1958, F 21,23:1
Johnson, Alfred J, 1937, Ap 14,25:4
Johnson, Alfred S Dr, 1925, My 25,17:5
Johnson, Alfred W, 1963, D 9,35:2
Johnson, Alfred W Mrs, 1962, S 30,86:6
Johnson, Algot K, 1946, Je 27,22:2
Johnson, Algot S, 1963, Ag 23,25:2
Johnson, Alice A E, 1920, O 23,13:6
Johnson, Alice E, 1945, Jl 19,23:5
Johnson, Allan C, 1955, Mr 3,27:1
Johnson, Alvan R, 1925, Ap 23,21:2
Johnson, Alvin H, 1950, O 1,104:3
Johnson, Alvin S Mrs, 1961, F 27,27:1
Johnson, Alvin W, 1958, D 31,38:4
Johnson, Ambrose A, 1950, Ag 20,77:2
Johnson, Amory K, 1942, O 25,46:2
Johnson, Amos Dr, 1882, D 11,5:5
Johnson, Andrew, 1875, Ag 1,1:1; 1876, Ja 12,2:4; 1879, N 12,3:3; 1944, My 9,19:7; 1957, Mr 18,27:4
Johnson, Andrew K, 1947, N 25,32:5
Johnson, Andrew L, 1949, D 28,32:2
Johnson, Andrew Mrs, 1876, Ja 17,1:6
Johnson, Andrew N Mrs, 1951, Jl 11,23:5
Johnson, Andrew R, 1966, Ag 28,93:1
Johnson, Andrew W, 1964, F 8,23:5
Johnson, Anna K Mrs, 1948, Mr 28,48:5
Johnson, Anne M, 1947, O 6,21:4
Johnson, Anton Mrs, 1949, F 2,27:3
Johnson, Arnold M (funl plans, Mr 11,25:3; will, Mr 15,33:5), 1960, Mr 10,31:4
Johnson, Arnold M (est tax appr), 1961, Je 10,13:4
Johnson, Arnold P, 1955, Ap 21,29:4
Johnson, Arthur, 1946, F 5,23:2
Johnson, Arthur C, 1937, Ja 12,24:2
Johnson, Arthur C Sr, 1950, N 12,92:3
Johnson, Arthur D, 1937, Ag 7,15:6
Johnson, Arthur E, 1949, Ap 25,23:3
Johnson, Arthur F, 1950, Je 10,17:6; 1962, D 29,4:6
Johnson, Arthur G Mrs, 1946, Mr 31,46:4
Johnson, Arthur L, 1955, My 17,29:5; 1965, N 24,39:4
Johnson, Arthur L Mrs, 1961, Mr 5,86:6
Johnson, Arthur N, 1940, Jl 12,15:4
Johnson, Arthur P, 1950, D 27,27:4
Johnson, Arthur W, 1943, O 18,15:3; 1946, O 11,23:3; 1963, Ag 22,27:4
Johnson, Ashmore C, 1960, Ag 10,31:3
Johnson, Aubrey P, 1947, Je 12,25:3
Johnson, Augustus Henry Ward, 1914, Mr 17,11:4
Johnson, Augustus J, 1962, Jl 5,25:2
Johnson, Austin G, 1948, F 12,23:4
Johnson, Axel A, 1958, Ag 4,21:4
Johnson, Axel A (will), 1959, F 19,63:1
Johnson, Axel G, 1946, Jl 17,23:1
Johnson, Aymar, 1942, Ap 7,21:5
Johnson, B B, 1931, Mr 29,1:5
Johnson, B E, 1907, F 10,7:6
Johnson, B N, 1932, F 20,15:1
Johnson, Bascom, 1954, O 21,27:1
Johnson, Benjamin, 1918, My 30,11:4; 1959, S 30,37:2
Johnson, Benjamin F, 1955, F 6,88:1
Johnson, Benjamin F 5th, 1967, F 24,35:3
Johnson, Benjamin Jr, 1952, F 27,27:2
Johnson, Bernard F, 1951, Jl 17,27:4
Johnson, Bernard L, 1947, D 24,21:2
Johnson, Bernice A Mrs, 1941, Jl 18,19:3
Johnson, Bernie, 1951, My 27,69:1
Johnson, Bert J, 1943, F 18,23:1
Johnson, Blackburn W, 1958, Jl 4,19:1
Johnson, Bradish (funl, Ag 2,11:6), 1918, Ag 1,11:5
Johnson, Bradish G, 1944, Je 10,15:7
Johnson, Bradley T Gen, 1903, O 6,9:5
Johnson, Branch, 1950, D 1,25:4
Johnson, Broadus, 1966, Jl 23,25:5
Johnson, Bror A, 1948, My 20,29:5
Johnson, Bumpy (Ellsworth R Johnson),(funl, Jl 12,13:1), 1968, Jl 10,46:5
Johnson, Burges (Feb 23), 1963, Ap 1,35:8
Johnson, Burges Mrs, 1955, Je 29,29:4
Johnson, Burgh S, 1963, Ag 1,27:5
Johnson, Burris M, 1946, O 12,19:3
Johnson, Byron R, 1942, S 7,19:5
Johnson, C Edwin, 1954, Ja 23,13:5
Johnson, C Fred, 1950, S 10,94:2
Johnson, C Haldane, 1953, Ja 19,23:1
Johnson, C Harry, 1959, Je 18,31:5
Johnson, C Hudson, 1943, Je 21,17:5
Johnson, C N, 1954, O 8,23:5
Johnson, C Oscar, 1965, N 27,31:3
Johnson, C Reid, 1959, Mr 9,29:1
Johnson, C Wadsworth Mrs, 1937, Ja 21,23:3
Johnson, C Wallace, 1947, O 3,25:4
Johnson, Cal, 1953, F 5,23:2
Johnson, Caleb E, 1924, Ag 9,11:5
Johnson, Caleb E Mrs, 1939, My 22,17:4
Johnson, Carl A (por), 1942, Mr 4,19:5
Johnson, Carl A, 1954, Mr 4,25:2
Johnson, Carl G, 1957, Ja 11,23:2; 1966, Mr 27,43:3
Johnson, Carl H, 1949, O 28,23:1; 1955, Ag 19,19:4
Johnson, Carl L, 1946, Ag 18,44:3
Johnson, Carl O, 1952, N 8,17:4; 1965, Ag 13,26:7
Johnson, Carl R, 1948, S 9,27:4; 1966, N 23,39:2
Johnson, Carl W, 1951, Je 8,27:2; 1956, Je 6,33:5
Johnson, Carroll, 1917, My 2,11:5
Johnson, Carroll D Mrs, 1967, Ja 18,43:4
Johnson, Carroll I, 1965, O 28,43:4
Johnson, Cave, 1866, N 28,1:7
Johnson, Cecil, 1946, D 28,15:4
Johnson, Charles, 1879, Ap 17,1:3; 1885, My 21,5:3; 1946, D 2,25:4; 1949, Je 27,28:3; 1950, Ag 13,77:1
Johnson, Charles A, 1937, Ap 11,II,8:1; 1950, D 8, 29:1; 1953, F 9,27:3; 1956, My 30,21:4
Johnson, Charles A C, 1957, Ja 6,89:1
Johnson, Charles C, 1939, O 11,27:1; 1942, F 21,19:2
Johnson, Charles C Jr, 1949, N 27,104:4
Johnson, Charles D, 1947, Ja 29,25:2
Johnson, Charles E, 1940, My 11,19:4; 1942, O 11, 56:1; 1943, F 15,15:3; 1950, Mr 21,29:3; 1964, N 14, 29:3
Johnson, Charles E Jr, 1958, S 29,27:4
Johnson, Charles F H, 1952, My 10,21:3
Johnson, Charles F H Mrs, 1955, O 14,27:1
Johnson, Charles F Jr, 1959, Ag 10,27:4
Johnson, Charles F Jr Mrs, 1960, My 21,23:3
Johnson, Charles G, 1948, F 8,60:5; 1957, O 15,33:1
Johnson, Charles H, 1948, O 29,26:2; 1948, N 1,23:4; 1951, F 18,78:5; 1953, O 30,23:4; 1955, Ag 23,23:3
Johnson, Charles H Mrs, 1941, S 13,17:4; 1958, Ja 3, 23:3; 1962, N 17,25:4
Johnson, Charles I, 1944, Ja 4,17:4
Johnson, Charles J, 1941, Ag 24,35:3
Johnson, Charles K, 1956, O 1,27:5
Johnson, Charles K Mrs, 1958, My 27,31:4
Johnson, Charles L, 1940, Ag 14,19:3; 1949, D 8,33:4
Johnson, Charles Mrs, 1949, D 14,31:1
Johnson, Charles N, 1938, Jl 18,13:4
Johnson, Charles S, 1956, O 28,88:4
Johnson, Charles S Mrs, 1965, F 5,31:4
Johnson, Charles W, 1912, Jl 23,9:4; 1939, F 22,21:5; 1945, Ja 30,20:3; 1954, Jl 14,27:2
Johnson, Chauncey W, 1937, D 19,II,8:8
Johnson, Chester L Mrs, 1950, D 12,33:5; 1962, O 14, 86:8
Johnson, Chic (H Ogden), 1962, F 28,33:1
Johnson, Christian, 1938, D 20,25:3; 1946, Ag 18,46:6
Johnson, Clarence, 1916, Mr 9,13:7
Johnson, Clarence C, 1959, D 5,23:2
Johnson, Clarence C Mrs, 1954, O 1,23:2
Johnson, Clarence E, 1945, Mr 17,13:5; 1961, O 31, 31:5
Johnson, Clarence S, 1950, Je 14,31:4
Johnson, Claude, 1949, Ag 12,17:2
Johnson, Claude E, 1943, Mr 5,18:2
Johnson, Cleon R, 1964, My 3,87:1
Johnson, Clifford, 1956, D 21,30:7
Johnson, Clifford L, 1952, F 27,27:2
Johnson, Clifton, 1953, Mr 24,39:4
Johnson, Clinton G, 1959, Ja 27,33:4
Johnson, Conrad A, 1960, O 2,84:1
Johnson, Content, 1949, N 13,93:1
Johnson, Cornelia T Mrs, 1938, Jl 26,19:5
Johnson, Courtney Mrs, 1967, My 6,31:4
Johnson, Crawford, 1942, D 10,25:6
Johnson, Curtis B, 1950, O 7,19:3
Johnson, Cyrus Mrs, 1907, D 23,9:7
Johnson, D B Dr, 1928, D 27,23:5
Johnson, Daniel Mrs, 1957, Mr 6,31:5
Johnson, Daniel Premier (funl mass set, S 30,10:1), 1968, S 27,1:3
Johnson, Darrell F, 1962, Je 16,19:3
Johnson, David, 1908, F 3,9:5; 1911, Je 30,9:3
Johnson, David A, 1946, S 5,27:5
Johnson, David C (por), 1942, D 21,23:1
Johnson, David C, 1965, F 12,29:2
Johnson, David C Mrs, 1946, F 22,25:2
Johnson, David E, 1952, Ag 7,21:2
Johnson, David J, 1944, O 8,44:3
Johnson, David L, 1951, O 9,29:5
Johnson, David Mrs, 1955, Ag 24,27:4
Johnson, Davis, 1921, Mr 19,11:6
Johnson, Dean F, 1957, O 16,32:6

Johnson, Dean M, 1950, N 8,29:5
Johnson, Dewey, 1941, S 19,23:2
Johnson, DeWitt C Mrs, 1952, N 28,25:3
Johnson, Don, 1951, Mr 19,32:6
Johnson, Don A Mrs, 1943, Ap 26,19:5
Johnson, Don L, 1950, S 28,31:4
Johnson, Douglas W (por), 1944, F 25,17:1
Johnson, Douglas W, 1944, Mr 12,38:2
Johnson, Douglas W Mrs, 1938, O 12,27:2
Johnson, Duncan S, 1937, F 17,21:2
Johnson, Dwight B, 1951, Mr 12,25:1
Johnson, Dwight F, 1949, Ap 25,23:3
Johnson, Dwight Mrs, 1903, D 22,9:5
Johnson, E Dana, 1937, D 11,19:1
Johnson, E Gordon, 1957, Ap 16,33:6
Johnson, E Herbert, 1968, Mr 12,43:2
Johnson, E Kendall, 1950, Ja 10,29:2
Johnson, E Lewis, 1939, Mr 18,17:3
Johnson, Earl C, 1949, Ja 11,31:1
Johnson, Earl W, 1953, F 25,27:2
Johnson, Ebenezar Platt, 1914, Ag 19,9:6
Johnson, Ebert B, 1947, Ja 23,26:3
Johnson, Edd, 1955, Mr 10,28:1
Johnson, Edgar, 1939, O 29,40:7
Johnson, Edgar D, 1950, Ja 27,24:2
Johnson, Edgar D Mrs, 1948, D 23,19:5
Johnson, Edgar H, 1944, S 13,19:3
Johnson, Edgar M, 1937, My 1,19:3; 1941, O 3,23:3
Johnson, Edgar W, 1949, N 2,27:5
Johnson, Edith C, 1954, Ag 9,17:5
Johnson, Edmund C, 1959, Ap 2,31:2
Johnson, Edna B, 1942, D 9,28:2
Johnson, Edna M, 1949, Je 10,27:4
Johnson, Edward, 1913, My 30,7:6; 1940, D 25,27:2; 1949, S 29,29:5; 1951, Je 17,84:5; 1952, D 8,41:1; 1956, My 23,31:4
Johnson, Edward (funl plans, Ap 22,33:3; mem ser set, Ap 29,33:1), 1959, Ap 21,35:1
Johnson, Edward A, 1944, Jl 25,19:6; 1949, Jl 16,13:2
Johnson, Edward D, 1943, Mr 2,19:1; 1948, D 6,25:4
Johnson, Edward E, 1953, O 14,29:3
Johnson, Edward F, 1948, Jl 7,46:2; 1956, Ja 29,92:6
Johnson, Edward F Mrs, 1951, S 27,31:1
Johnson, Edward G, 1948, Jl 17,16:2
Johnson, Edward H, 1956, Ap 9,27:3
Johnson, Edward Hine, 1924, S 24,19:4
Johnson, Edward L, 1954, Ap 13,31:4
Johnson, Edward M, 1946, F 6,23:2; 1949, Jl 27,23:2
Johnson, Edward Mrs, 1946, F 28,23:1
Johnson, Edward P, 1937, Ag 4,19:4; 1941, D 1,19:5
Johnson, Edward P Dr, 1924, Je 1,8:1
Johnson, Edward R, 1960, Ap 13,39:3
Johnson, Edward S (por), 1949, Ja 1,13:1
Johnson, Edwards, 1947, F 14,21:1
Johnson, Edwin, 1944, F 9,19:1; 1950, Ap 11,31:2; 1956, D 23,31:2
Johnson, Edwin A, 1946, F 18,21:2
Johnson, Edwin C, 1948, O 3,64:3
Johnson, Edwin F, 1872, Ap 20,2:4
Johnson, Edwin J, 1964, Ap 15,25:8
Johnson, Edwin M, 1946, N 23,15:2
Johnson, Egbert, 1906, F 1,9:5
Johnson, Eldridge R (por), 1945, N 15,19:1
Johnson, Eldridge R Mrs, 1961, Ja 6,27:3
Johnson, Eli, 1944, My 13,19:3
Johnson, Eli B, 1943, My 2,44:6
Johnson, Elias, 1951, Jl 18,29:4
Johnson, Elizabeth, 1954, S 16,29:5
Johnson, Elizabeth F, 1963, My 4,25:4
Johnson, Ellsworth E, 1948, Mr 28,48:2
Johnson, Ellsworth J Mrs, 1948, Ja 25,56:6
Johnson, Elmer C, 1958, Ja 1,25:5
Johnson, Elmer E, 1946, My 10,19:1
Johnson, Elmer E S, 1959, My 19,34:1
Johnson, Elmer H Mrs, 1965, Je 11,31:2
Johnson, Elmer J, 1940, N 5,25:6
Johnson, Elmer S, 1947, Ja 25,17:2
Johnson, Elsworth J, 1938, Jl 21,21:3
Johnson, Emil A W, 1944, Mr 17,17:4
Johnson, Emily Pauline, 1913, Mr 8,15:4
Johnson, Emma, 1943, F 24,21:3
Johnson, Emma A, 1937, Jl 10,15:4; 1954, Ja 28,27:5
Johnson, Emma B R Mrs (will), 1938, Ap 30,15:1
Johnson, Emma L H Mrs, 1942, Ja 25,41:2
Johnson, Emma R Mrs, 1937, O 8,23:3
Johnson, Emory L, 1957, Ap 25,31:5
Johnson, Emory R, 1950, Mr 8,25:3
Johnson, Emory R Mrs, 1957, N 11,29:4
Johnson, Emsley W, 1950, Ap 13,29:5
Johnson, Enoch L, 1968, D 10,47:1
Johnson, Enoch M, 1950, Jl 15,13:5
Johnson, Ephraim, 1937, D 1,23:3
Johnson, Ephraim Mrs, 1954, Ag 26,27:3
Johnson, Erland A, 1941, Ap 12,15:6
Johnson, Ernest, 1937, D 19,40:3; 1939, Ja 27,19:2
Johnson, Ernest A, 1959, Ap 14,35:2
Johnson, Ernest E, 1957, Ap 13,19:4; 1962, Mr 10,21:3
Johnson, Ernie, 1952, My 2,25:2
Johnson, Ervin D, 1942, Ag 9,42:8
Johnson, Ervin D Mrs, 1966, Ag 16,39:4
Johnson, Estelle (por), 1939, Mr 15,23:4
Johnson, Eugene A, 1924, Ja 4,13:5
Johnson, Eugene H, 1948, S 25,17:6
Johnson, Evan M Gen, 1923, O 14,6:3
Johnson, Evan M Rev, 1865, Mr 20,8:2
Johnson, Evan Malbone, 1915, Jl 9,11:5
Johnson, Everard L Mrs, 1947, Jl 14,21:4
Johnson, Everett H, 1961, F 22,25:5
Johnson, F, 1939, Ag 24,11:5
Johnson, F Coit, 1944, O 20,20:2
Johnson, F Ernest Mrs, 1962, F 17,19:2
Johnson, F Harold, 1950, S 4,17:6
Johnson, F Merle, 1950, D 3,88:5
Johnson, F Raymond, 1965, Ag 14,23:4
Johnson, Fanda B Lt, 1923, Ja 11,21:6
Johnson, Fannie Mrs, 1942, F 1,43:3
Johnson, Florence M, 1954, Mr 23,27:1
Johnson, Florence W, 1949, Ag 9,25:4
Johnson, Floyd M, 1951, S 29,17:3
Johnson, Forrest B Mrs, 1948, Ag 6,17:2
Johnson, Francis, 1944, N 27,23:5
Johnson, Francis E Sr, 1968, Je 23,73:1
Johnson, Francis K, 1963, Je 13,33:3
Johnson, Frank, 1949, O 21,25:1
Johnson, Frank A, 1953, Ag 18,23:4
Johnson, Frank A Mrs, 1960, Ap 28,35:6
Johnson, Frank E, 1955, Je 4,15:6
Johnson, Frank E Lt, 1937, N 20,3:4
Johnson, Frank E Mrs, 1943, Ag 11,19:5; 1946, Ja 5, 13:4
Johnson, Frank H Sr, 1954, Ja 24,84:5
Johnson, Frank J, 1942, My 27,23:4; 1942, Ag 20,19:1
Johnson, Frank Mrs, 1950, F 25,17:5
Johnson, Frank P, 1946, F 20,27:3
Johnson, Frank T, 1939, Ja 2,23:4
Johnson, Franklin P, 1939, D 12,27:2
Johnson, Franklin R, 1939, Jl 20,19:6
Johnson, Franklin Rev Dr, 1916, O 10,11:6
Johnson, Franklin W, 1956, F 20,23:1
Johnson, Fred, 1963, My 17,33:1
Johnson, Fred C, 1947, S 15,17:2
Johnson, Fred E, 1940, Mr 22,20:2
Johnson, Fred H, 1949, O 24,23:5
Johnson, Fred L Mrs, 1956, Je 2,20:1
Johnson, Fred W, 1955, Ag 2,23:4
Johnson, Frederic B, 1951, Je 28,25:4
Johnson, Frederic Iver, 1920, D 10,15:4
Johnson, Frederic L, 1937, F 28,II,9:3
Johnson, Frederic M, 1942, Ap 14,21:4
Johnson, Frederic M Mrs, 1961, Jl 18,29:1
Johnson, Frederick, 1958, N 19,37:4
Johnson, Frederick B, 1937, D 4,17:3
Johnson, Frederick F, 1943, My 10,19:4
Johnson, Frederick G, 1941, O 21,23:1
Johnson, Frederick H, 1949, Ap 12,29:3
Johnson, Frederick M, 1944, Ag 19,11:2
Johnson, Frederick Mrs (M MacKinnon), 1962, S 24, 29:4
Johnson, Frederick O, 1948, Ja 26,19:3
Johnson, Frederick R, 1945, Je 18,19:1
Johnson, Frederick R Sr, 1951, Ja 3,27:1
Johnson, Frederick W, 1941, F 15,15:6
Johnson, G, 1936, N 1,II,10:5
Johnson, G A, 1934, Ap 2,17:3
Johnson, G C, 1878, Mr 26,4:7
Johnson, G Frank, 1945, Je 20,23:2
Johnson, G H S, 1881, N 6,7:4
Johnson, G Leonard Jr, 1963, S 29,86:4
Johnson, Gail Borden, 1918, S 8,23:1
Johnson, George (por), 1944, Je 6,17:1
Johnson, George, 1961, Ap 18,37:2
Johnson, George A, 1942, D 27,34:2
Johnson, George Albert, 1916, Mr 6,13:5
Johnson, George B, 1939, Ja 24,19:1
Johnson, George C, 1946, Ag 14,25:5; 1965, D 8,43:1
Johnson, George E, 1938, O 24,17:4; 1943, Ag 13,17:6; 1949, S 21,31:2
Johnson, George E H, 1951, Mr 28,29:3
Johnson, George F, 1948, Je 19,15:3
Johnson, George F (por), 1948, N 29,23:1
Johnson, George F, 1957, Jl 18,25:4
Johnson, George F Mrs, 1947, O 2,27:6
Johnson, George H, 1940, Ap 21,42:3; 1952, My 22, 27:5; 1959, O 14,43:2
Johnson, George L, 1939, D 13,27:5
Johnson, George M, 1963, Ap 21,86:5
Johnson, George Mrs, 1948, Ja 3,13:2; 1952, O 3,23:4
Johnson, George P, 1938, F 3,23:4; 1940, N 19,23:5
Johnson, George P Mrs, 1948, Mr 12,23:4
Johnson, George Pryor, 1909, D 17,11:3
Johnson, George Q, 1939, Ja 26,21:4
Johnson, George S, 1948, My 22,15:2
Johnson, George S Judge, 1951, Jl 2,23:6
Johnson, George S Rev, 1951, N 27,31:4
Johnson, George V, 1951, F 23,27:3
Johnson, George W, 1944, F 26,13:4; 1948, D 9,34:3; 1953, My 25,25:2
Johnson, George W Capt, 1921, Je 28,15:5
Johnson, George W Col, 1904, F 6,5:3
Johnson, George Z, 1872, Jl 3,1:6
Johnson, Gerald C, 1961, N 24,28:6
Johnson, Grace F Mrs (will), 1963, D 18,38:1
Johnson, Grace J Mrs, 1953, N 3,32:3
Johnson, Gus A, 1942, Je 2,23:3
Johnson, Gustaf J, 1944, Ag 13,35:2
Johnson, Gustav W, 1950, D 28,25:4
Johnson, Gustave, 1949, My 3,25:4
Johnson, Gustave A, 1948, My 2,77:1
Johnson, Guy A, 1957, O 3,29:2
Johnson, Guy Black, 1923, Ap 23,15:6
Johnson, Gwendolyn E, 1956, Ag 20,21:2
Johnson, H, 1934, F 23,19:2
Johnson, H Douglas Sr, 1951, F 21,27:1
Johnson, H J, 1882, Je 8,5:4
Johnson, H Tallman, 1958, Je 16,23:3
Johnson, H V, 1880, Ag 18,2:6
Johnson, H W, 1881, S 17,5:5
Johnson, Hallett, 1968, Ag 12,35:2
Johnson, Hans, 1940, F 4,38:4
Johnson, Hardesty, 1952, Ap 24,31:1
Johnson, Harlan, 1940, F 6,21:2
Johnson, Harold A (cor, Mr 26,31:1), 1953, Mr 25, 31:4
Johnson, Harold B, 1937, D 25,15:5; 1949, My 19,30:
Johnson, Harold B Mrs, 1951, Ag 28,23:3
Johnson, Harold E, 1953, N 5,35:2
Johnson, Harold F, 1956, Ap 14,17:3
Johnson, Harold P, 1949, Ag 12,17:5
Johnson, Harriet, 1958, S 11,33:4
Johnson, Harriet A, 1959, Ja 28,31:5
Johnson, Harriet L, 1958, Ap 28,23:5
Johnson, Harris B, 1941, Ap 26,15:6
Johnson, Harrison B Mrs, 1949, S 17,17:5
Johnson, Harry B Mrs, 1946, Ap 5,25:1
Johnson, Harry F Mrs, 1960, Mr 18,25:2
Johnson, Harry H, 1952, Ja 23,27:3
Johnson, Harry L, 1921, S 7,13:4
Johnson, Harry M, 1950, Ja 27,24:2
Johnson, Harry N, 1947, O 2,27:6
Johnson, Harry S, 1943, N 30,27:2; 1951, F 22,31:1
Johnson, Harry T, 1938, D 25,15:1; 1958, S 25,33:1
Johnson, Harry T F, 1950, D 7,33:3
Johnson, Harvey F, 1959, Ap 24,27:3
Johnson, Helge S Mrs, 1949, O 3,17:5
Johnson, Henry, 1925, O 15,23:5; 1938, Je 14,21:2; 1944, F 17,19:2; 1953, Ja 26,19:2
Johnson, Henry A, 1941, Ja 2,16:1; 1942, My 16,13:
Johnson, Henry B, 1942, Ja 8,21:1
Johnson, Henry C, 1955, Ag 27,15:4
Johnson, Henry Clark Prof, 1904, My 11,2:4
Johnson, Henry E, 1941, Je 20,17:5
Johnson, Henry Gov, 1864, S 11,8:2
Johnson, Henry L, 1907, S 10,7:6; 1947, D 5,25:3
Johnson, Henry Lincoln, 1925, S 11,23:5
Johnson, Henry M, 1952, Ag 2,15:6
Johnson, Henry Prof, 1918, F 8,11:8; 1953, O 4,88:
Johnson, Henry U, 1939, Je 5,17:4
Johnson, Henry W, 1962, Ja 25,31:1; 1963, My 22,
Johnson, Herbert, 1946, D 6,23:1
Johnson, Herbert A, 1939, F 21,19:2; 1944, Jl 4,19:
Johnson, Herbert F Mrs, 1949, Jl 12,27:3
Johnson, Herbert G, 1959, F 16,29:2; 1962, Ap 11,
Johnson, Herbert M, 1937, Mr 17,25:5
Johnson, Herbert S, 1942, S 27,48:1
Johnson, Herbert S Mrs, 1959, Mr 4,31:3
Johnson, Herbert T, 1942, N 5,25:6
Johnson, Herman, 1947, Ja 27,23:4; 1947, O 30,25
Johnson, Herman L, 1954, O 15,23:3
Johnson, Herrick Rev Dr, 1913, N 21,9:6
Johnson, Herschel V, 1966, Ap 17,86:7
Johnson, Hewlett (funl, O 28,41:3), 1966, O 23,1
Johnson, Hiram W, 1945, Ag 7,1:1
Johnson, Hiram W Mrs, 1955, Ja 26,25:2
Johnson, Hobart S, 1942, My 30,15:5
Johnson, Hobart S Mrs, 1955, N 21,29:4
Johnson, Holgar J Mrs, 1966, My 3,47:1
Johnson, Horace, 1946, Ag 27,27:3
Johnson, Horatio S, 1944, Ja 17,19:5
Johnson, Hosmer Mrs, 1966, Ja 14,39:2
Johnson, Howard A, 1955, F 2,27:3
Johnson, Howard C, 1952, Je 10,27:2
Johnson, Howard E (por), 1941, My 2,21:3
Johnson, Howard E Sr, 1955, Jl 25,19:2
Johnson, Howard L, 1938, Je 1,23:4
Johnson, Howard P, 1960, F 9,31:3
Johnson, Howard W Mrs, 1968, Ap 12,35:3
Johnson, Hubert F, 1953, O 29,31:3
Johnson, Hugh S (por), 1942, Ap 16,21:1
Johnson, Hugh S Mrs, 1949, Ag 18,22:2
Johnson, Ida E Mrs, 1940, Jl 3,17:3
Johnson, Irving P (por), 1947, Mr 2,60:1
Johnson, Isaac C Mrs, 1954, Ja 30,17:4
Johnson, Isaac H, 1941, D 16,28:2
Johnson, J, 1929, Ja 24,27:1
Johnson, J A, 1941, O 3,23:4
Johnson, J A Capt, 1883, Mr 8,5:4
Johnson, J C, 1865, My 21,4:1; 1941, My 30,15:
Johnson, J E, 1951, F 15,31:1
Johnson, J Edward, 1958, D 4,39:2; 1967, Mr 24
Johnson, J Edwin, 1943, O 3,48:4
Johnson, J Edwin Jr, 1954, Mr 23,29:8
Johnson, J Ford, 1962, F 11,87:1
Johnson, J Fred Jr, 1950, My 4,27:1
Johnson, J G, 1931, S 8,25:5
Johnson, J G Rev Dr, 1905, Mr 24,2:5
Johnson, J Hegeman, 1960, Ag 25,29:6
Johnson, J Howard, 1954, Ap 28,31:4
Johnson, J Kennedy, 1946, S 21,15:6
Johnson, J Leroy, 1961, Mr 28,35:2

Johnson, J Monroe, 1964, Jl 3,21:4
Johnson, J Nunnally Mrs, 1946, Ap 9,27:4
Johnson, J Percy H, 1952, My 7,27:2
Johnson, J R, 1941, My 30,15:1
Johnson, J Roberts, 1955, Mr 5,17:3
Johnson, J Rosamond, 1954, N 12,21:1
Johnson, J T C, 1938, O 27,23:2
Johnson, J W, 1932, S 2,15:6
Johnson, J Wesley, 1915, O 4,9:5
Johnson, Jacob, 1909, Ag 18,9:6
Johnson, Jacob W, 1944, O 20,19:5
Johnson, James, 1942, Ja 19,20:1; 1942, Ap 2,22:2; 1948, D 31,15:1; 1952, Mr 12,16:4
Johnson, James A, 1938, N 24,27:2; 1939, Ap 6,25:2
Johnson, James A C, 1937, D 18,21:6
Johnson, James B Sr, 1953, Ag 29,17:5
Johnson, James C, 1940, Je 1,15:3
Johnson, James F, 1939, Ap 29,17:6; 1942, Jl 20,13:2
Johnson, James G, 1916, D 30,9:5
Johnson, James Gibson Mrs, 1905, Mr 18,11:5
Johnson, James H, 1940, Mr 10,49:2
Johnson, James J, 1943, My 9,40:6
Johnson, James Mrs, 1947, D 28,40:1
Johnson, James N, 1953, N 10,31:4
Johnson, James P, 1949, N 1,27:1; 1955, N 18,25:1
Johnson, James P Mrs, 1957, My 19,89:1
Johnson, James Riley, 1909, F 20,7:5
Johnson, James Riley Rev Dr, 1909, F 20,7:5
Johnson, James S, 1949, N 15,25:2
Johnson, James T, 1938, Ap 3,II,6:7
Johnson, James W, 1939, O 9,19:5; 1940, Jl 10,19:4
Johnson, James William, 1924, Ja 13,23:1
Johnson, Jane Mrs, 1937, Mr 3,9:3
Johnson, Jed, 1963, My 9,37:1
Johnson, Jennie D Mrs, 1938, F 20,II,9:1
Johnson, Jesse E, 1945, F 11,40:4
Johnson, Jesse Ex-Justice, 1918, N 2,15:4
Johnson, Joe Mrs, 1960, O 14,33:1
Johnson, John, 1873, S 5,2:5; 1874, F 10,8:5; 1907, Je 25,7:6; 1947, My 14,25:5
Johnson, John A, 1907, O 10,9:4; 1938, Ag 6,13:3; 1948, F 22,48:3
Johnson, John A Gov (funl; est, S 25,11:4), 1909, S 24,11:3
Johnson, John B, 1950, Ap 9,85:1
Johnson, John B Dr, 1903, O 8,9:5
Johnson, John B Mrs, 1961, F 11,23:5
Johnson, John C, 1919, D 14,22:4; 1950, D 28,25:4
Johnson, John D, 1952, Mr 21,23:4
Johnson, John E Mrs, 1943, F 20,13:1
Johnson, John F, 1941, S 21,45:2
Johnson, John F (L Bader), 1966, S 17,29:3
Johnson, John G, 1944, F 15,17:5; 1956, Jl 27,21:2
Johnson, John H Dr, 1937, N 12,21:3
Johnson, John H Mrs, 1943, F 10,25:5
Johnson, John J, 1942, Mr 19,21:4
Johnson, John L, 1945, S 13,23:3; 1946, Jl 14,36:5
Johnson, John L Ex-Judge, 1915, Mr 26,13:2
Johnson, John N, 1940, S 25,27:3
Johnson, John Q A, 1938, Ap 10,II,6:8
Johnson, John Q A Jr, 1953, D 12,19:3
Johnson, John R, 1948, Mr 7,69:1; 1953, N 6,27:3
Johnson, John R Mrs, 1942, O 5,19:2
Johnson, John Rev Dr, 1907, Ap 9,9:5
Johnson, John S, 1903, O 14,9:6
Johnson, John T, 1941, Ap 27,38:2; 1942, F 1,43:1; 1949, O 21,26:2
Johnson, John V, 1923, Ap 5,19:5
Johnson, John W, 1950, My 24,30:3; 1960, D 13,31:4
Johnson, John W F, 1938, N 29,24:1
Johnson, Joseph, 1924, Ap 14,17:3; 1937, Je 18,21:2; 1942, Mr 9,19:5
Johnson, Joseph A, 1961, O 14,23:2
Johnson, Joseph C, 1946, N 18,23:2
Johnson, Joseph F, 1939, Ag 29,21:3
Johnson, Joseph French, 1925, Ja 23,19:5; 1925, Ja 24, 13:4
Johnson, Joseph H, 1938, D 11,61:2
Johnson, Joseph J, 1946, N 20,31:2
Johnson, Joseph L, 1943, O 13,23:2; 1945, Jl 20,19:6
Johnson, Joseph P, 1937, D 21,23:4
Johnson, Joseph T Mrs, 1956, S 29,19:5
Johnson, Josephus Mrs, 1945, Mr 5,19:2
Johnson, Jotham, 1967, F 9,39:2
Johnson, Julian, 1965, N 14,89:2
Johnson, Julius F, 1950, Ja 28,13:6
Johnson, Julius M, 1946, Je 20,23:2
Johnson, Julius P, 1948, Mr 31,25:3
Johnson, Karl A, 1959, F 18,33:4
Johnson, Katherine, 1948, Ja 11,56:3; 1955, My 12, 29:2; 1959, My 23,25:4
Johnson, Katie, 1957, My 9,31:5
Johnson, Keith, 1879, Ag 22,3:1
Johnson, Kenneth, 1960, S 8,35:1
Johnson, Kenneth A, 1962, My 2,37:2
Johnson, Kenneth D, 1958, N 7,27:1
Johnson, Kenneth S, 1946, Jl 2,25:1; 1956, O 18,33:3
Johnson, Kyril A W, 1947, Ag 8,17:4
Johnson, L Byron, 1962, Je 12,37:4
Johnson, L V Mrs, 1937, Je 6,5:3
Johnson, Lambert D Sr, 1955, Jl 30,17:3
Johnson, Larry, 1949, F 13,77:1
Johnson, Laura G M Mrs, 1941, Ap 25,19:2
Johnson, Laura M, 1939, Ja 4,21:3
Johnson, Laurence, 1925, Je 16,21:5
Johnson, Laurence A, 1962, Je 28,63:4
Johnson, Lee P, 1964, Ap 6,31:1
Johnson, Leeds, 1952, O 14,31:3
Johnson, Leeds (est tax appr), 1954, My 18,34:1
Johnson, Leo A, 1960, Je 2,33:1
Johnson, Leo J, 1953, Ja 13,27:1
Johnson, Leo M, 1945, Je 21,19:3
Johnson, Leon, 1952, N 17,25:5
Johnson, Leonard H Mrs, 1952, F 18,19:3
Johnson, Leonard N, 1968, Ap 2,47:3
Johnson, Leonard T, 1946, D 4,31:2
Johnson, Leslie S, 1947, Mr 20,27:4
Johnson, Leslie S Mrs, 1950, Jl 15,13:1
Johnson, Lester B, 1948, Je 30,25:1
Johnson, Lester G, 1950, S 20,31:4
Johnson, Lewis, 1964, Je 20,25:6
Johnson, Lewis J, 1952, Ap 17,29:1
Johnson, Lewis J Mrs, 1952, Ja 19,15:5
Johnson, Lewis M, 1953, Mr 2,23:4
Johnson, Lewis R, 1967, My 17,47:1
Johnson, Lewis W, 1939, F 3,15:2
Johnson, Ligon, 1951, Mr 30,23:1
Johnson, Lillian H Mrs, 1941, N 12,24:2
Johnson, Lincoln, 1957, S 4,33:3
Johnson, Linder H, 1955, Ag 5,19:4
Johnson, Lindley, 1937, F 23,27:6
Johnson, Lloyd W, 1962, My 18,31:2
Johnson, Loomis C, 1942, O 14,25:6
Johnson, Loren B T, 1941, D 15,19:6
Johnson, Lorenzo M, 1904, N 30,9:4
Johnson, Louis, 1910, N 14,9:5
Johnson, Louis A, 1907, S 13,7:4
Johnson, Louis A (funl plans, Ap 26,46:1; will, My5,22:7), 1966, Ap 25,31:2
Johnson, Louis C, 1942, S 27,49:2
Johnson, Louis E, 1947, Ag 4,17:4; 1952, Ja 9,29:3
Johnson, Louis M, 1946, My 22,21:3
Johnson, Louise G, 1943, O 12,27:2
Johnson, Lowell F Mrs, 1964, Ja 7,33:2
Johnson, Lucius E, 1921, F 10,7:2
Johnson, Lucius W Rear-Adm, 1968, Ja 15,47:2
Johnson, Luther A, 1965, Je 7,37:3
Johnson, Luther B, 1963, Ag 9,23:6
Johnson, Luther H, 1939, My 8,17:4
Johnson, M, 1936, S 14,27:1
Johnson, M Clark, 1957, Mr 1,23:1
Johnson, M Neville Mrs, 1948, D 12,92:2
Johnson, Mabel P Mrs, 1942, S 27,49:2
Johnson, Main, 1959, D 13,86:4
Johnson, Malcolm, 1958, F 28,21:2
Johnson, Manning R (funl), 1959, Jl 26,23:3
Johnson, Marc D, 1946, My 10,19:1
Johnson, Marcellus A, 1955, Je 25,15:2
Johnson, Margaret, 1948, F 5,24:3
Johnson, Margaret L, 1959, N 22,86:5
Johnson, Margaret M Mrs, 1937, Ag 22,II,7:2
Johnson, Margaret Mrs, 1910, Ag 18,9:5
Johnson, Marguerite K Mrs, 1938, Je 17,21:4
Johnson, Marie L, 1953, Jl 22,27:3
Johnson, Marion A, 1964, N 10,47:2
Johnson, Marmaduke Col, 1871, N 22,4:7
Johnson, Martin Nelson Sen, 1909, O 22,7:4
Johnson, Martin P, 1948, Ja 18,60:8
Johnson, Martin W Mrs, 1952, F 20,29:5
Johnson, Mary C P Mrs, 1940, Ap 30,22:2
Johnson, Mary M Mrs, 1960, Ag 6,19:6
Johnson, Mary Mrs, 1937, Ap 25,4:4
Johnson, Maude Mrs, 1938, Mr 10,21:1
Johnson, Mauritz I, 1938, Ag 5,17:4
Johnson, Max S Maj-Gen, 1968, Ja 10,43:2
Johnson, Melville Mrs, 1951, F 5,40:6
Johnson, Melvin M, 1957, D 20,24:5
Johnson, Melvin M Jr, 1965, Ja 10,92:4
Johnson, Melvin M Mrs, 1947, D 11,33:4
Johnson, Melvin W, 1954, Mr 23,27:5
Johnson, Mildred C, 1963, S 17,35:1
Johnson, Mildred G, 1962, Mr 2,29:2
Johnson, Milton H, 1949, F 2,27:1
Johnson, Milton J, 1962, S 30,86:6
Johnson, Milton O, 1957, S 4,34:5
Johnson, Milton W Mrs, 1954, Mr 2,25:3
Johnson, Minnie E, 1952, D 13,21:5
Johnson, Minnie S Mrs, 1954, Ja 16,15:1
Johnson, Monroe M, 1950, Jl 20,25:4
Johnson, Montgomery H, 1952, F 8,23:5
Johnson, Mortimer L Rear-Adm, 1913, F 15,15:4
Johnson, Moulton K Mrs, 1950, Ag 2,25:5
Johnson, Murdock P, 1948, Mr 21,60:2
Johnson, Myrtle, 1953, Ap 11,17:4
Johnson, N H Judge, 1869, My 3,2:4
Johnson, Nathan C, 1951, Ag 27,19:5
Johnson, Nathaniel, 1940, Je 30,33:2
Johnson, Nelson, 1954, Mr 24,27:4
Johnson, Nelson T, 1954, D 4,17:5
Johnson, Nestor, 1949, Ap 21,26:2
Johnson, Nils, 1937, Mr 21,II,9:2
Johnson, Norman G Mrs, 1951, My 25,27:5
Johnson, Norman L, 1961, N 20,31:4
Johnson, O H Perry, 1939, My 27,15:4
Johnson, O Rudolph, 1966, O 29,29:4
Johnson, Ogden, 1962, Ja 9,48:1
Johnson, Olaf Mrs, 1950, Mr 14,25:2
Johnson, Olive Mrs, 1939, Mr 12,III,6:8
Johnson, Oliver, 1889, D 11,2:5; 1940, F 27,21:4
Johnson, Oliver C, 1951, N 27,31:5
Johnson, Orrin, 1943, N 25,25:1
Johnson, Orville C, 1939, Ag 10,19:2
Johnson, Osa H Mrs (will, Jl 8,29:7), 1953, Ja 8,30:1
Johnson, Oscar, 1949, O 23,86:4
Johnson, Oscar G, 1962, Je 3,88:8
Johnson, Oscar J, 1946, Mr 11,25:2
Johnson, Oscar Mrs, 1912, Ap 21,II,13:3
Johnson, Oscar P, 1941, O 5,49:2
Johnson, Oscar T, 1958, Jl 26,15:6
Johnson, Otis R, 1957, Jl 3,23:5
Johnson, Otto A, 1944, Mr 9,17:6
Johnson, Owen, 1952, Ja 28,17:1
Johnson, Owen Mrs, 1910, Je 18,9:6
Johnson, P H, 1933, N 30,40:3
Johnson, Palmer O, 1960, Ja 26,33:2
Johnson, Palmer W, 1946, Ja 26,13:5
Johnson, Pamela C, 1952, F 28,27:2
Johnson, Paul B, 1943, D 27,19:3
Johnson, Paul B Sr Mrs, 1968, N 9,33:3
Johnson, Paul C, 1961, Ag 8,29:3
Johnson, Paul E Mrs, 1938, N 4,23:4; 1952, N 27,31:1
Johnson, Paul J, 1950, Ja 30,17:4
Johnson, Paul S, 1942, Ja 22,17:4
Johnson, Peirce, 1956, Ap 20,25:2
Johnson, Percy J, 1950, N 3,27:5
Johnson, Percy L, 1958, O 25,21:3
Johnson, Perry E, 1950, Ap 20,29:5
Johnson, Pete, 1967, Mr 24,31:3
Johnson, Peter S, 1947, S 25,29:4
Johnson, Phelps, 1926, F 21,II,9:1
Johnson, Philip E, 1960, S 4,68:8
Johnson, Philip G (por), 1944, S 15,19:3
Johnson, R, 1929, Ag 9,7:3; 1931, O 4,II,6:1
Johnson, R Randolph, 1938, Ap 15,19:4
Johnson, R W, 1879, Jl 28,4:7
Johnson, R W W H, 1878, Ag 28,2:6
Johnson, Ralf C, 1874, N 16,5:1
Johnson, Ralph L, 1955, Mr 12,19:5
Johnson, Ralph M, 1940, My 24,19:5
Johnson, Ralph M Dr, 1937, O 17,II,9:3
Johnson, Ralph W, 1945, Ja 18,19:5
Johnson, Rankin, 1957, N 4,29:4
Johnson, Ray B, 1950, Ap 13,29:2
Johnson, Ray P Jr (funl plans, Mr 29,40:7), 1964, Mr 28,19:5
Johnson, Ray P Mrs, 1963, N 20,43:1
Johnson, Raymond A, 1957, S 8,84:5
Johnson, Raymond D, 1949, Je 30,23:4
Johnson, Raymond G Sr, 1949, Je 21,25:5
Johnson, Raymond H, 1957, N 24,86:7
Johnson, Raymond L, 1952, D 31,15:2
Johnson, Rebekah, 1958, S 13,19:4
Johnson, Redford K, 1966, Jl 13,43:4
Johnson, Reeves K, 1957, Ag 10,15:2
Johnson, Reeves K Sr Mrs, 1959, O 29,30:4
Johnson, Reginald F, 1938, Mr 8,19:2
Johnson, Remsen, 1940, F 23,15:1
Johnson, Remsen Jr, 1957, Je 3,27:5
Johnson, Reverdy (see also F 11), 1876, F 12,5:2
Johnson, Reverdy, 1907, Jl 16,7:6
Johnson, Reverdy Mrs, 1873, Mr 20,1:3
Johnson, Richard A, 1964, Jl 30,27:4
Johnson, Richard Benedict, 1924, Ap 24,19:4
Johnson, Richard G, 1945, S 22,17:5
Johnson, Richard H, 1940, D 13,23:1
Johnson, Riche H, 1951, Je 4,27:5
Johnson, Rita, 1965, N 3,39:4
Johnson, Robert, 1938, Mr 3,21:4
Johnson, Robert A, 1910, F 21,9:6; 1956, O 2,35:4
Johnson, Robert B, 1966, Ag 25,37:3
Johnson, Robert C, 1937, D 12,II,8:6; 1951, Ap 4,29:3
Johnson, Robert Col, 1869, Ap 24,3:6
Johnson, Robert E, 1921, Je 25,11:6
Johnson, Robert H, 1943, Ag 26,17:6
Johnson, Robert H (por), 1948, My 26,25:5
Johnson, Robert H, 1952, Ja 26,13:6; 1960, N 9,35:4
Johnson, Robert I, 1946, Ag 6,25:4
Johnson, Robert K, 1944, Ja 5,17:3
Johnson, Robert L, 1966, Ja 20,35:2
Johnson, Robert M, 1948, Jl 30,18:3
Johnson, Robert S Jr, 1955, O 29,19:1
Johnson, Robert Sir, 1951, Ag 29,25:3
Johnson, Robert U (por), 1937, O 15,23:1
Johnson, Robert U Mrs, 1925, Ja 1,27:3
Johnson, Robert W, 1953, D 15,39:1; 1954, Ap 30,18:8
Johnson, Robert Wood, 1968, Ja 31,41:1
Johnson, Roe S, 1939, Ap 25,23:4
Johnson, Roger A, 1954, F 10,29:3
Johnson, Roger A Mrs, 1954, D 2,31:5
Johnson, Roger B C, 1946, Jl 6,15:6
Johnson, Romulus T, 1952, My 9,23:4
Johnson, Roscoe H, 1957, N 15,27:1
Johnson, Rose L, 1946, Ag 30,17:2
Johnson, Rossiter Mrs, 1917, Ja 5,9:3
Johnson, Roswell O, 1938, Je 20,15:3
Johnson, Roy D, 1937, D 25,15:6
Johnson, Roy E, 1961, My 21,86:4
Johnson, Roy H, 1947, Ap 1,27:2
Johnson, Roy W, 1947, D 3,29:2; 1965, Jl 23,29:2

Johnson, Roy W Mrs, 1962, O 22,29:3
Johnson, Royal C (por), 1939, Ag 3,19:1
Johnson, Rudolph O H, 1954, Jl 16,21:3
Johnson, Rufus H Rev, 1915, D 28,11:3
Johnson, Russell, 1907, Mr 27,9:6
Johnson, Russell (por), 1940, Ag 19,17:4
Johnson, Russell R, 1945, S 1,11:4
Johnson, Russell S, 1939, Ap 6,25:6
Johnson, Russell W, 1961, My 9,39:4
Johnson, S, 1882, My 12,5:2
Johnson, S Fisher, 1904, Je 2,9:5
Johnson, S Orie, 1951, Ag 8,25:2
Johnson, S Taylor, 1942, My 30,16:8
Johnson, S W, 1881, D 14,5:2
Johnson, Sally M, 1957, Mr 25,25:4
Johnson, Sam (J Ray) (see also N 4), 1876, N 5,9:2
Johnson, Samuel Capt, 1872, D 31,1:3
Johnson, Samuel I, 1948, F 26,23:5
Johnson, Samuel K Dr (will, O 21,17:2), 1937, Ag 5, 23:4
Johnson, Samuel L, 1945, Ja 19,19:2
Johnson, Samuel Rev, 1882, F 21,5:5
Johnson, Samuel W Prof, 1909, Jl 22,7:5
Johnson, Sara J MRs, 1941, Ag 22,15:2
Johnson, Sarah, 1944, S 16,13:6
Johnson, Sarah P Mrs, 1941, Ap 30,19:3
Johnson, Scott, 1953, D 15,39:2
Johnson, Scclcy A, 1945, Ap 30,19:2
Johnson, Seeley Mrs, 1940, My 19,43:2
Johnson, Seth P, 1965, Je 8,41:3
Johnson, Seymour, 1946, F 7,23:3
Johnson, Seymour L, 1955, O 20,35:4
Johnson, Sherman F, 1952, Mr 10,21:4
Johnson, Sherrod C, 1961, F 26,93:1
Johnson, Sidney G, 1951, My 12,21:3
Johnson, Sidney T, 1952, Ag 13,21:2
Johnson, Silas W, 1945, Ag 3,17:3
Johnson, Simeon J, 1957, Ap 10,33:4
Johnson, Skuli, 1955, Je 4,15:4
Johnson, Solomon B, 1964, F 23,25:1
Johnson, Solomon W, 1913, Ja 21,13:5
Johnson, Stanley, 1939, Ap 4,25:6; 1948, N 16,29:4
Johnson, Stanley A, 1959, My 26,35:2
Johnson, Stanley B, 1940, S 23,17:4
Johnson, Stephen, 1950, O 10,31:2
Johnson, Stephen A, 1954, D 4,17:3
Johnson, Stephen Maj, 1903, Je 22,7:6
Johnson, Stephen S, 1938, F 1,21:5
Johnson, Stephen W, 1947, Je 21,17:1; 1964, S 3,29:4
Johnson, Stewart, 1926, S 12,12:3; 1961, F 5,81:2
Johnson, Stuart H Mrs, 1966, F 28,27:3
Johnson, Sveinbjorn, 1946, Mr 20,23:4
Johnson, T E, 1954, My 21,27:1
Johnson, T L, 1880, Jl 22,2:4
Johnson, Teodoro, 1961, Ap 4,37:3
Johnson, Theodore Benedict, 1918, O 1,13:2
Johnson, Theodore E Sr, 1962, N 11,89:1
Johnson, Theodore J, 1946, Mr 12,25:5
Johnson, Theodore M, 1940, Ag 22,19:1
Johnson, Theodore Polhemus, 1906, N 16,9:6
Johnson, Theodore R, 1939, S 21,23:2
Johnson, Theodore T Mrs, 1945, Je 26,19:4
Johnson, Theophilus, 1952, D 20,17:7
Johnson, Thomas, 1947, D 17,29:5
Johnson, Thomas A, 1960, S 25,88:4
Johnson, Thomas A Chief-Justice, 1872, D 7,8:1
Johnson, Thomas B, 1943, D 26,32:5
Johnson, Thomas C, 1951, Ja 31,25:2
Johnson, Thomas J, 1941, Ap 29,19:3
Johnson, Thomas J Mrs, 1949, F 20,60:8
Johnson, Thomas L (funl), 1911, Ap 12,13:4
Johnson, Thomas L, 1945, D 3,21:4
Johnson, Tillman B, 1939, Mr 1,21:3
Johnson, Tillman D, 1953, N 2,25:4
Johnson, Titian W, 1946, N 20,31:2
Johnson, Tom C, 1941, S 13,17:4
Johnson, Tom L, 1911, Je 12,11:4; 1950, Mr 8,25:3
Johnson, Tom W, 1952, N 26,23:4
Johnson, Tracy A, 1945, Ap 16,23:4
Johnson, Treat B, 1947, Jl 29,21:5
Johnson, U Grant, 1940, Ja 23,21:5
Johnson, Victor E, 1942, Je 11,23:3
Johnson, Victor J, 1950, S 24,104:3
Johnson, Victor M, 1941, D 31,17:2
Johnson, Victor S, 1943, Ag 30,15:7
Johnson, Vinton Mrs, 1947, Jl 18,17:6
Johnson, Virgil L, 1942, O 7,25:5
Johnson, W A Col, 1903, S 3,7:7
Johnson, W F, 1931, Mr 29,28:2
Johnson, W F Rev, 1926, Jl 7,25:5
Johnson, W Gerald, 1963, F 9,8:7
Johnson, W H, 1880, O 3,12:1; 1901, Je 29,9:6
Johnson, W H M, 1948, Ag 12,21:4
Johnson, W M, 1928, S 12,27:5
Johnson, W MacLean, 1965, N 7,88:2
Johnson, W Norman, 1942, N 18,26:3
Johnson, W Ogden, 1947, S 15,17:3
Johnson, Wait C Col, 1937, Ag 3,23:2
Johnson, Walker A, 1947, My 8,25:2
Johnson, Wallace B, 1967, Ag 30,43:2
Johnson, Walter, 1946, D 11,31:1; 1956, Jl 7,13:6
Johnson, Walter A, 1947, Ap 1,27:4; 1958, Jl 24,25:4
Johnson, Walter B (por), 1941, My 11,44:6

Johnson, Walter B Dr (funl, Ag 2,5:4), 1925, Ag 1, 11:6
Johnson, Walter C, 1963, Ap 17,41:1
Johnson, Walter C Sr, 1966, S 1,35:3
Johnson, Walter D Mrs, 1951, F 5,23:4
Johnson, Walter De Forest, 1925, My 23,15:6
Johnson, Walter De Forest Rev, 1925, My 20,23:4
Johnson, Walter F, 1948, Jl 14,23:2
Johnson, Walter G Sr, 1947, O 31,23:3
Johnson, Walter H, 1944, Mr 31,21:1; 1952, Ja 28,17:6
Johnson, Walter H Jr Mrs, 1957, Ap 14,86:4
Johnson, Walter J, 1959, Ag 25,31:6
Johnson, Walter L, 1959, Ag 8,17:4; 1966, D 21,39:2
Johnson, Walter P Jr, 1961, Mr 29,33:2
Johnson, Walter R, 1965, Ja 18,35:4
Johnson, Walter S, 1945, Mr 13,23:4
Johnson, Walter W Sr, 1951, N 10,5:6
Johnson, Warren F, 1967, Ap 10,35:1
Johnson, Warren W, 1960, F 21,92:8
Johnson, Wayne, 1947, Mr 12,25:1
Johnson, Wayne H, 1964, Jl 6,29:3
Johnson, Welton V, 1954, N 27,13:5
Johnson, Wendell, 1965, Ag 31,33:1
Johnson, Weston T Mrs, 1954, S 4,11:6
Johnson, Wilbur E, 1942, Ja 9,21:2
Johnson, Wilbur S, 1925, S 5,13:5
Johnson, Will R, 1948, N 20,13:5
Johnson, Willard H, 1957, Jl 19,19:3
Johnson, William, 1865, N 11,4:6; 1866, Ja 11,4:2; 1875, O 12,4:7; 1907, My 15,9:4; 1941, My 8,23:4; 1947, Jl 14,21:2; 1948, Je 2,29:3; 1950, N 7,27:2; 1950, D 14,35:4; 1957, Mr 7,29:3; 1968, Jl 7,53:2
Johnson, William A, 1943, My 17,15:6; 1956, My 11, 27:1
Johnson, William B, 1872, Ap 18,3:3; 1954, S 24,23:4; 1955, N 10,35:1
Johnson, William C, 1938, Je 26,27:3; 1940, Ap 19, 21:5; 1943, O 9,13:6; 1951, Jl 27,19:1; 1952, D 6,21:6
Johnson, William C Mrs, 1945, Jl 16,11:6; 1949, My 20,27:3
Johnson, William Christie, 1917, Ap 29,19:5
Johnson, William D, 1950, Je 2,24:3
Johnson, William Dr, 1963, N 5,22:8
Johnson, William E, 1911, Ap 2,II,13:4; 1944, Mr 1, 19:5
Johnson, William E (por), 1945, F 3,11:1
Johnson, William E, 1946, My 5,44:4; 1958, Je 21, 19:2; 1960, D 6,41:2
Johnson, William E Mrs, 1963, N 7,34:2
Johnson, William F, 1938, N 12,15:4; 1942, Ap 14, 21:4; 1965, O 25,37:2
Johnson, William F Rev, 1903, O 19,7:6
Johnson, William G (Bunk), 1949, Jl 9,13:6
Johnson, William H, 1941, Mr 11,23:5; 1942, N 15, 58:2; 1947, D 16,33:3; 1948, O 2,15:3; 1955, S 6,25:1; 1956, Jl 29,64:6; 1963, N 29,37:1; 1967, Ap 28,41:2
Johnson, William H A, 1947, Mr 29,15:5
Johnson, William H Mrs, 1937, N 16,23:2; 1941, My 2,21:3
Johnson, William J, 1942, F 23,21:2; 1946, Ja 17,23:2; 1964, My 19,37:4
Johnson, William L, 1903, D 14,2:4; 1952, Ja 28,17:4; 1959, Mr 10,36:1; 1961, S 18,29:4
Johnson, William M, 1942, O 2,25:5; 1956, Ap 27,27:4; 1959, S 14,29:4
Johnson, William Mrs, 1949, O 9,92:2; 1950, Ja 18, 31:1
Johnson, William N Dr, 1937, Ja 24,II,8:8
Johnson, William P, 1941, N 25,26:3; 1956, Ag 14,25:3
Johnson, William P Mrs, 1948, S 1,24:2
Johnson, William R, 1940, Ap 30,21:2; 1949, Jl 15, 19:2; 1949, S 15,27:4; 1962, Ag 27,15:2
Johnson, William S, 1937, Mr 4,23:3
Johnson, William T, 1943, S 26,48:2
Johnson, William W, 1907, Jl 21,7:7; 1924, Ap 19,13:5
Johnson, William W Mrs, 1943, Mr 5,18:3
Johnson, Willis, 1922, D 30,13:5
Johnson, Willis S Mrs, 1952, My 20,25:4
Johnson, Wilner E, 1917, Jl 30,9:7
Johnson, Wilson Sr, 1941, F 19,21:4
Johnson, Wingate M, 1963, S 13,29:1
Johnson, Wolcott Howe, 1912, Ja 16,13:3
Johnson, Woodbridge O, 1951, Jl 25,23:3
Johnson, Zoe M, 1939, Je 20,21:4
Johnsson, Wilbur S, 1925, S 4,21:4
Johnston, A F Mrs, 1931, O 6,27:5
Johnston, Albert S, 1948, D 27,22:2; 1953, Ap 13,27:2
Johnston, Albert T, 1943, F 10,25:4
Johnston, Albert W, 1952, Ag 24,88:3
Johnston, Alex, 1951, D 1,13:3
Johnston, Alex C, 1952, Ag 9,13:5
Johnston, Alex C Mrs, 1961, Mr 9,29:2
Johnston, Alex Keith Dr, 1871, Jl 13,8:2
Johnston, Alex Sr, 1959, Mr 24,89:2
Johnston, Alexander, 1945, My 1,23:4
Johnston, Alfred B, 1951, Jl 23,17:6
Johnston, Alice M, 1945, Ag 28,19:3; 1953, Ap 17,25:5
Johnston, Alva, 1950, N 24,35:1
Johnston, Alvanley, 1951, S 18,31:1
Johnston, Arch, 1948, F 2,20:2
Johnston, Arthur, 1950, Ag 16,29:4
Johnston, Arthur H, 1941, O 15,21:4

Johnston, Arthur J, 1954, My 3,25:5
Johnston, Arthur W, 1949, Je 18,13:2
Johnston, B M, 1879, O 1,5:6
Johnston, Benjamin F, 1937, Mr 11,24:1
Johnston, Benjamin F Mrs, 1953, Ap 9,27:2
Johnston, Bert, 1952, Ja 20,85:2
Johnston, Bertha, 1953, F 22,61:1
Johnston, Brady S Mrs, 1952, Mr 20,12:2
Johnston, C, 1880, My 1,5:4; 1931, O 17,17:5
Johnston, C Harmon, 1945, O 25,21:2
Johnston, C Stuart, 1939, Jl 25,3:7
Johnston, C W, 1941, Jl 5,11:2
Johnston, Campbell S, 1959, Ja 11,88:5
Johnston, Caroline B Mrs, 1939, My 28,III,7:1
Johnston, Charles, 1905, N 4,4:2; 1943, Ag 13,17:6
Johnston, Charles E, 1950, Jl 4,17:1; 1951, Jl 11,23:4
Johnston, Charles G, 1960, Je 5,86:4
Johnston, Charles R, 1943, Ap 16,21:4
Johnston, Charles T, 1937, F 19,20:1
Johnston, Charles T Jr, 1957, Jl 8,23:3
Johnston, Charles W, 1950, O 26,31:5
Johnston, Christopher Dr, 1914, Je 28,15:5
Johnston, Claudius, 1951, S 11,29:1
Johnston, Clifford C Mrs, 1965, N 14,88:8
Johnston, Cyril F, 1950, Ap 1,15:2
Johnston, D W, 1942, Jl 7,6:5
Johnston, David, 1961, Ap 19,39:3
Johnston, Donald E (Oct 10), 1965, O 11,61:3
Johnston, Douglas H, 1939, Je 29,23:1
Johnston, E Crommelin, 1964, O 5,33:3
Johnston, E D, 1952, D 10,35:4
Johnston, Earl S, 1940, Jl 6,15:3
Johnston, Earle R, 1958, Jl 25,19:4
Johnston, Edgar, 1951, F 21,27:4
Johnston, Edgar A, 1950, Ja 12,27:2
Johnston, Edward H, 1947, S 1,19:4
Johnston, Edward P, 1953, My 13,29:4
Johnston, Edytha (Mrs A E Morgan), 1958, Mr 2C 29:3
Johnston, Elizabeth Mrs, 1941, Ap 7,17:2
Johnston, Emma L, 1949, Je 4,13:4
Johnston, Eric A (funl, Ag 29,29:5; will, Ag 31,15:8 1963, Ag 23,1:4
Johnston, Ernest H, 1964, S 11,33:3
Johnston, Ernest H Mrs, 1950, O 8,104:4
Johnston, Esther M, 1968, Ja 21,77:1
Johnston, F Cliffe, 1950, N 25,13:2
Johnston, Fannie J Mrs, 1952, F 27,27:2
Johnston, Frank B, 1956, My 25,23:5
Johnston, Frank H, 1946, Je 30,38:3
Johnston, Frank Jr, 1941, My 16,23:3
Johnston, Frank S, 1938, Ja 28,21:3
Johnston, Franklin, 1945, S 20,23:5
Johnston, Franz, 1949, Jl 11,17:6
Johnston, Frederick M Mrs, 1959, S 24,37:3
Johnston, G, 1934, Mr 9,19:1
Johnston, Gail A, 1943, S 14,23:2
Johnston, George, 1950, N 7,27:6
Johnston, George B Mrs, 1960, Je 22,35:2
Johnston, George Ben Dr, 1916, D 21,11:3
Johnston, George C, 1937, Jl 6,19:6
Johnston, George C Mrs, 1960, Je 12,86:8
Johnston, George H, 1943, Mr 28,24:2
Johnston, George N, 1947, Ap 6,60:5
Johnston, George P, 1953, Je 11,29:1
Johnston, George S, 1965, O 16,27:4
Johnston, George W, 1938, Ap 4,17:5; 1944, Mr 1
Johnston, George W Sr, 1950, Ja 12,27:2
Johnston, Gerald M, 1944, N 24,23:1
Johnston, Glenn C, 1958, Ag 7,25:3
Johnston, Greenhow, 1958, Jl 28,23:4
Johnston, H E Mrs, 1903, Jl 4,1:6
Johnston, H Sir, 1927, Ag 1,19:3
Johnston, H Stuart, 1949, Ja 26,25:3
Johnston, Harold E, 1945, My 17,19:5
Johnston, Harold H, 1954, Ap 19,23:2
Johnston, Harold Whetstone, 1912, Je 18,11:5
Johnston, Harry B, 1955, F 23,27:4
Johnston, Harry L, 1948, Jl 18,53:1
Johnston, Harry M, 1967, F 5,89:1
Johnston, Helen, 1955, N 23,23:5
Johnston, Henry A, 1956, Ag 26,85:2
Johnston, Henry A Mrs, 1947, Mr 23,60:2
Johnston, Henry C Dr, 1937, O 4,21:3
Johnston, Henry J Rev, 1937, S 1,19:6
Johnston, Henry P Prof, 1923, Mr 3,13:5
Johnston, Henry S, 1965, Ja 8,29:1
Johnston, Herbert, 1942, My 2,13:6
Johnston, Homer K, 1947, N 28,27:1
Johnston, Howard E, 1964, Mr 23,29:2
Johnston, Hugh M, 1961, Mr 28,35:3
Johnston, Ida B Mrs, 1941, D 24,17:4
Johnston, Iredell Killaly, 1953, F 23,25:4
Johnston, Ivan M, 1960, Je 3,31:2
Johnston, J, 1883, D 28,2:3
Johnston, J E Gen, 1891, Mr 22,1:7
Johnston, J Edward, 1951, O 18,29:3
Johnston, J Harold, 1965, F 3,35:2
Johnston, J Harold Mrs, 1964, Ap 15,39:2
Johnston, J Shepard, 1950, Ja 15,85:1
Johnston, J T, 1893, Mr 25,2:2
Johnston, J W, 1952, Je 7,19:5
Johnston, Jack, 1951, O 31,29:5

Johnston, Jack (Mar 18), 1963, Ap 1,35:8
Johnston, James A, 1954, S 7,26:1
Johnston, James Chew Maj, 1918, My 12,21:2
Johnston, James E, 1948, Ja 6,23:4; 1954, Mr 22,27:4
Johnston, James F, 1960, F 20,23:4
Johnston, James H, 1952, F 23,11:5; 1956, F 9,32:2; 1962, My 16,41:5
Johnston, James J (por), 1946, My 8,25:1
Johnston, James M, 1967, D 29,28:1
Johnston, James N Jr, 1953, Ja 14,31:5
Johnston, James R, 1920, O 9,15:3
Johnston, James S, 1944, Ap 6,23:6
Johnston, James W, 1873, D 13,6:6
Johnston, Jasper K, 1946, N 30,15:3
Johnston, Jeanne L, 1938, D 8,27:4
Johnston, Jersey Jim, 1903, N 17,1:2
Johnston, John, 1879, D 3,2:6; 1950, N 25,13:5; 1957, F 10,87:1; 1957, Mr 23,19:6
Johnston, John A, 1940, Ja 6,13:1; 1950, Jl 25,27:4
Johnston, John B, 1947, Je 25,25:4; 1958, Ag 5,27:1; 1960, Ja 13,47:2
Johnston, John B Mrs, 1947, Je 5,25:2
Johnston, John F, 1948, My 10,21:1; 1950, Je 18,76:2
Johnston, John H, 1951, O 28,84:8
Johnston, John Henry, 1919, Mr 18,11:2
Johnston, John K, 1952, Ag 26,27:7
Johnston, John L, 1946, Ap 17,25:6; 1956, D 9,88:1; 1958, Jl 15,25:1
Johnston, John Mrs, 1949, S 7,29:2
Johnston, John T Mrs, 1953, Ap 29,21:4
Johnston, John W, 1950, Jl 26,25:4; 1953, Mr 18,31:2
Johnston, John W Mrs (Betty Blossom), 1957, S 22, 87:2
Johnston, Joseph E, 1947, Ag 30,15:6
Johnston, Joseph F Sen (funl, Ag 11,7:6), 1913, Ag 9, 7:5
Johnston, Joseph S, 1966, Ap 6,43:3
Johnston, Josephus, 1952, D 16,31:4
Johnston, Lemuel R Mrs, 1951, My 30,21:2
Johnston, Leon H, 1961, Je 12,29:5
Johnston, Leon S, 1955, F 20,88:5
Johnston, Lewis A Mrs, 1951, O 5,27:3
Johnston, Lockwood A, 1952, N 29,17:4
Johnston, Louis W (est appr, My 9,25:3), 1963, My 5,86:8
Johnston, Lucian, 1940, O 23,23:3
Johnston, M, 1936, My 10,II,9:1
Johnston, Mabel, 1943, Mr 31,19:4
Johnston, Malcolm Maj, 1917, Je 7,11:5
Johnston, Malcolm S, 1950, Ag 30,31:2
Johnston, Martha J, 1941, Ap 9,25:8
Johnston, Mary (will), 1967, Mr 2,32:3
Johnston, Mary A W Mrs, 1941, S 20,17:5
Johnston, Matthew F, 1955, Mr 25,23:4
Johnston, Morris L, 1952, Mr 10,21:5
Johnston, Ned, 1955, Ja 2,77:1
Johnston, Olin D (mem ser, Ap 20,18:4; funl, Ap 21,45:4), 1965, Ap 19,29:1
Johnston, Oscar G, 1955, O 5,36:2
Johnston, Percy H, 1957, Ja 3,33:2
Johnston, R Grant Mrs, 1948, S 14,29:2
Johnston, R Horace, 1949, O 23,84:2
Johnston, Richard A, 1939, Mr 22,23:6
Johnston, Richard E, 1943, N 3,25:5
Johnston, Richard H Mrs, 1958, Mr 10,23:5
Johnston, Richard J, 1955, D 21,32:8
Johnston, Richard L, 1961, F 21,35:2
Johnston, Richard T, 1951, O 23,29:2
Johnston, Robert, 1946, My 6,21:2
Johnston, Robert A, 1904, My 4,16:2; 1947, My 19, 21:4
Johnston, Robert B Sr, 1947, S 3,25:3
Johnston, Robert F, 1960, F 18,33:4
Johnston, Robert H, 1914, O 27,11:7; 1942, S 3,19:3
Johnston, Robert I, 1954, Ap 27,29:4
Johnston, Robert J, 1944, S 13,19:5
Johnston, Robert J Jr, 1966, N 21,45:1
Johnston, Robert M, 1940, F 3,13:2
Johnston, Robert M Mrs, 1957, Je 21,25:4
Johnston, Robert Matteson, 1920, Ja 29,9:5
Johnston, Robert Mrs, 1945, Ja 18,19:3; 1951, Ja 5, 21:2
Johnston, Robert Rev, 1916, Mr 5,21:5
Johnston, Robert S, 1944, F 20,36:4
Johnston, Robert W, 1940, D 19,25:4
Johnston, Roland E Jr, 1963, D 20,29:3
Johnston, Root, 1949, Ja 6,24:2
Johnston, Ross P, 1952, Ja 18,27:5
Johnston, Rufus Perry Rev Dr, 1924, Ag 25,13:4
Johnston, Rufus Z, 1959, Jl 5,56:1
Johnston, Rufus Z Mrs, 1951, D 26,25:4
Johnston, Russell Z, 1959, O 5,31:5
Johnston, Ruth, 1952, F 23,11:3
Johnston, Samuel, 1947, Ap 16,25:5
Johnston, Samuel J, 1950, N 23,35:5
Johnston, Sherwood, 1939, Ag 9,17:4
Johnston, Stanley, 1962, S 14,31:1
Johnston, Stephen L, 1938, S 24,17:4
Johnston, T C, 1964, Ja 25,10:7
Johnston, T N J, 1869, Mr 20,11:7
Johnston, Theodore S Mrs, 1945, O 19,23:4
Johnston, Theresa V Mrs, 1939, Jl 22,15:7
Johnston, Thomas, 1965, S 6,15:3
Johnston, Thomas A, 1957, S 11,33:4
Johnston, Thomas A Mrs, 1953, Ag 8,11:6
Johnston, Thomas D, 1952, Ja 23,27:3
Johnston, Thomas J, 1948, S 28,27:1
Johnston, Thomas R, 1967, Je 22,39:2
Johnston, Thomas S, 1942, S 26,15:5
Johnston, Tilghman, 1946, Mr 29,23:3
Johnston, Vernon T, 1959, O 18,87:1
Johnston, Victor A, 1967, Mr 16,47:2
Johnston, W A Mrs, 1950, S 7,31:5
Johnston, W H, 1933, F 21,19:6
Johnston, W W Dr, 1902, Mr 23,7:6
Johnston, W Warren, 1947, Mr 20,28:2
Johnston, Waldo C, 1938, N 12,15:5
Johnston, Walter B, 1957, Je 5,35:5
Johnston, Walter J, 1949, F 6,76:5
Johnston, Walter L, 1958, Ap 13,84:3
Johnston, Walter S, 1915, Jl 24,9:6
Johnston, Wayne A, 1967, D 6,51:3
Johnston, William, 1917, Ag 28,7:4; 1948, Mr 8,23:3
Johnston, William A (por), 1937, Ja 24,II,8:8
Johnston, William A, 1937, Ag 7,15:2; 1940, Ap 16, 23:3; 1949, Ja 6,23:3; 1950, My 12,27:4; 1962, F 6, 32:6
Johnston, William B, 1942, D 30,23:1; 1948, N 20,13:5
Johnston, William Caldwell, 1953, Ja 10,17:3
Johnston, William D, 1949, O 13,27:3
Johnston, William F, 1950, My 15,28:4
Johnston, William G, 1913, Je 2,7:4
Johnston, William H, 1937, Mr 28,II,9:1; 1945, Jl 10, 11:4; 1964, Ap 2,33:5
Johnston, William H M, 1948, Ag 13,15:3
Johnston, William J, 1907, Ap 30,9:6; 1922, N 30,19:5; 1959, N 9,31:5
Johnston, William M, 1946, My 2,21:3
Johnston, William Mrs, 1963, Jl 31,29:4
Johnston, Wilson A, 1962, S 19,39:4
Johnstone, A Sir, 1932, Ag 2,17:5
Johnstone, Alex C, 1956, Je 9,17:1
Johnstone, Andrew, 1954, Ja 7,31:3
Johnstone, Andrew B, 1955, Ja 22,11:3
Johnstone, Arthur, 1938, F 7,15:5
Johnstone, Arthur E, 1944, Ja 25,19:5
Johnstone, Bernard S, 1907, Ja 11,9:5
Johnstone, Charles T (por), 1940, O 9,25:4
Johnstone, Edward R, 1946, D 30,19:5
Johnstone, Ethel M, 1949, Ag 11,23:2
Johnstone, Florence, 1925, D 2,25:4
Johnstone, Francis U, 1937, Ap 20,25:3
Johnstone, George J, 1945, My 24,19:4
Johnstone, Hampden L, 1941, Jl 4,13:4
Johnstone, Harcourt, 1945, Mr 2,19:2
Johnstone, Harold H, 1953, Je 3,31:4
Johnstone, Herbert G, 1958, D 7,88:4
Johnstone, Hugo R Mrs, 1942, O 4,53:2
Johnstone, J Jeffrey Rev Dr, 1909, Jl 25,7:6
Johnstone, Jack, 1942, Ap 19,43:1
Johnstone, James, 1955, O 9,87:2
Johnstone, James T, 1963, Ap 11,33:2
Johnstone, Jessie St C Mrs, 1937, Ap 24,19:4
Johnstone, Jocelyn, 1903, Ag 26,7:6
Johnstone, John F, 1948, O 10,77:1
Johnstone, John James, 1909, Ag 25,9:4
Johnstone, John M, 1953, Ja 17,15:5
Johnstone, Leonard R, 1952, My 8,31:2
Johnstone, Oscar H, 1937, N 27,17:2
Johnstone, R Le G, 1926, D 5,30:5
Johnstone, R M, 1958, Je 24,31:6
Johnstone, Rae (W R), 1964, Ap 30,35:5
Johnstone, Ralph W, 1951, Ag 14,23:4
Johnstone, Robert, 1938, O 27,23:6
Johnstone, Robert B, 1963, D 17,39:3
Johnstone, Robert LeG, 1966, S 19,43:3
Johnstone, Russell R, 1944, Je 21,19:3
Johnstone, Thomas, 1950, Mr 12,92:4
Johnstone, Will B, 1944, F 7,15:6
Johnstone, William C, 1951, My 14,25:3
Johntry, Edward, 1961, Jl 25,15:6
Johore, Sultan of (Ibrahim Iboni Almarhum Abu Bakar), 1959, My 8,27:3
Joiner, Columbus H, 1947, Mr 29,15:3
Joiner, Franklin, 1960, O 30,86:6
Joiner, Webber A, 1940, O 20,49:2
Jokai, Maurus, 1904, My 6,9:5
Jolas, Eugene, 1952, My 29,27:2
Jolesch, Samuel, 1953, Mr 30,21:4
Joley, Albert, 1957, Ja 19,15:3
Joliat, Emile, 1952, Mr 21,23:1
Joline, Adrian Hoffman, 1912, O 16,13:6
Joline, Benjamin F, 1952, Ag 27,27:4
Joline, Benjamin F Mrs, 1949, Mr 10,27:3
Joline, C O, 1885, F 18,5:6
Joline, Dorothy E, 1948, S 20,25:4
Joline, G Earle Sr, 1947, F 3,19:5
Joline, George P, 1940, Ja 20,15:3
Joline, Jeanie T Mrs, 1941, O 4,15:5
Joline, William F, 1950, Ap 8,26:7
Joliot-Curie, Irene Mme (funl, Mr 22,35:4), 1956, Mr 18,89:1
Joliot-Curie, Jean Frederic (funl plans, Ag 16,17:5), 1958, Ag 15,21:1
Jolis, Jac, 1953, N 17,31:5
Jollen, Jules Rev Father, 1912, Ag 27,9:6
Jolles, Hendrik R (por), 1949, Ap 23,13:1
Jolles, Otto J M Prof, 1968, Jl 20,27:3
Jollett, Raymond F, 1949, O 4,27:1
Jolley, Alvin J, 1948, Ag 28,15:4
Jolley, David H, 1948, S 5,40:2
Jolley, John Jr, 1939, Jl 19,19:5
Jolley, Le Roy, 1918, Je 5,11:5
Jolley, Norman K, 1951, N 16,5:4
Jollie, Emma, 1947, S 10,27:3
Jollie, Walter P, 1941, N 2,53:2
Jolliffe, Albert J Mrs, 1950, Jl 19,32:3
Jolliffe, Carey C, 1957, F 25,25:5
Jolliffe, Norman H, 1961, Ag 2,29:1
Jolliffe, Norman Mrs, 1938, Je 2,23:3; 1966, My 16, 37:1
Jolliffe, R Norman (por), 1949, My 2,25:3
Jolliffe, Ruby M, 1968, Jl 14,64:7
Jollon, Alfred J, 1946, My 3,21:4
Jollos, Victor, 1941, Jl 6,27:1
Jolly, Carlos J, 1951, O 17,31:2
Jolly, Jane Mrs, 1945, Mr 22,23:5
Jolly, John W, 1950, S 2,15:4
Jolly, Louis E, 1938, S 29,25:2
Jolly, Robert, 1952, My 15,31:5
Jolowicz, Ernst, 1958, N 15,23:5
Jolowicz, Ernst Mrs, 1956, Ap 21,17:2
Jolson, Al, 1950, O 24,1:7
Jolson, Harry, 1953, Ap 28,27:2
Jolson, Harry Mrs, 1948, Mr 14,72:5
Joly, A H, 1880, D 6,5:2
Joly, Charles J, 1906, Ja 5,11:3
Jomier, Georges F A, 1950, Je 14,31:1
Jomini, Henri Baron, 1869, Ap 7,7:3
Jompulsky, Harry, 1966, Ap 12,39:1
Jonaghy, John J, 1943, Ap 12,23:6
Jonah, Albert L, 1953, My 23,15:4
Jonah, Frank G, 1945, D 9,44:4
Jonah, William E, 1938, Je 10,21:3
Jonap, Alfred M, 1951, My 10,31:1
Jonas, Alberto, 1943, N 11,23:3
Jonas, Alexander, 1912, Ja 30,9:5
Jonas, Alfred E, 1954, S 27,21:5
Jonas, Benjamin F Ex-Sen, 1911, D 22,13:5
Jonas, Daniel H Mrs, 1960, D 10,23:5
Jonas, Israel S, 1925, Ap 25,15:6
Jonas, James A, 1955, S 13,31:2
Jonas, John, 1950, Jl 7,19:3
Jonas, Joseph, 1948, Ja 22,27:2
Jonas, Julius, 1959, Ap 22,33:2
Jonas, Leon, 1958, O 1,37:4
Jonas, Maryla (Mrs E G Abraham), 1959, Jl 5,56:4
Jonas, Max Mrs, 1956, O 4,33:4
Jonas, Murray, 1956, Jl 21,15:4
Jonas, Nathan S (por), 1943, O 18,15:1
Jonas, Nathan S Mrs, 1943, Je 2,25:5
Jonas, Oscar N, 1968, Jl 22,35:4
Jonas, Paul, 1959, O 8,42:5
Jonas, Ralph, 1952, Ap 30,27:1
Jonas, Ralph Mrs, 1938, N 6,49:2
Jonas, Richard A Sr, 1960, Jl 28,27:4
Jonas, Rosalie M, 1953, Ja 11,91:2
Jonas, Salvo Mrs, 1959, Ap 21,35:3
Jonas, Samuel, 1955, N 16,35:3
Jonas, Selda Mrs, 1938, N 8,23:3
Jonas, Walter L, 1938, S 26,17:4
Jonas, Will A, 1951, Ap 9,25:4
Jonas, William, 1915, N 13,11:6
Jonassen, Tonnes O, 1953, S 18,24:4
Joncas, Leo, 1956, O 16,33:3
Jonckheer, Johan J, 1946, S 22,60:7
Jone, Richard M, 1917, Ag 2,9:4
Jones, A A, 1927, D 21,25:5
Jones, A L, 1934, Mr 3,13:1
Jones, A Merritt, 1954, Ja 24,84:4
Jones, A S, 1879, Ap 29,2:2
Jones, Aaron J Sr, 1944, My 14,46:3
Jones, Abbott H, 1939, Je 13,23:6
Jones, Abram N, 1956, Je 6,33:2
Jones, Ada C, 1946, O 23,27:1
Jones, Adam L Mrs, 1947, Mr 22,14:2
Jones, Addison H Jr, 1939, My 17,23:4
Jones, Addison P Mrs, 1961, Je 27,33:1
Jones, Adrian, 1938, Ja 25,22:3
Jones, Adrian H, 1946, Je 14,21:4
Jones, Agnes B Mrs, 1940, Ja 30,19:4
Jones, Alan M, 1941, My 17,15:3
Jones, Albert B, 1959, S 3,27:5
Jones, Albert E, 1946, Mr 25,26:2
Jones, Albert H, 1952, Je 26,29:2
Jones, Albert M, 1967, My 14,86:4
Jones, Albert N, 1924, Je 15,23:1
Jones, Albert S, 1937, Mr 21,24:1
Jones, Alexander L, 1943, Je 14,17:5; 1943, O 30,15:6
Jones, Alfred, 1943, Ja 26,19:4
Jones, Alfred B, 1965, O 16,27:3
Jones, Alfred H, 1937, F 21,II,10:7
Jones, Alfred T, 1953, Ja 17,15:6
Jones, Allen A, 1950, Je 20,27:2
Jones, Allen N, 1958, Mr 11,29:2
Jones, Allie G, 1947, Ag 19,23:4
Jones, Almer V, 1960, F 21,92:8
Jones, Andrew B, 1942, Mr 26,23:5
Jones, Aneurin, 1904, S 7,7:6
Jones, Anna, 1925, Ja 26,17:4

Jones, Anna E, 1953, Ag 21,17:5
Jones, Anna Mrs, 1909, Ap 15,9:4
Jones, Anna S Mrs, 1940, Jl 18,19:3
Jones, Archibald Sr, 1951, F 2,23:2
Jones, Arthur, 1952, Ja 22,29:3
Jones, Arthur A Mrs, 1963, My 29,33:4
Jones, Arthur B, 1943, D 14,28:2
Jones, Arthur C, 1964, O 24,29:4
Jones, Arthur E, 1939, Jl 25,19:4
Jones, Arthur F, 1940, Mr 23,13:4
Jones, Arthur F Mrs, 1942, My 28,17:1
Jones, Arthur H, 1938, O 5,23:2; 1949, Jl 10,56:6; 1961, N 15,43:5
Jones, Arthur J, 1943, Ja 3,42:4; 1962, My 3,33:1; 1963, Ag 30,21:2
Jones, Arthur Kingsley, 1914, Ap 9,11:4
Jones, Arthur L, 1941, Jl 19,13:5
Jones, Arthur M, 1960, N 26,21:4
Jones, Arthur Mason Lt, 1917, D 8,15:7
Jones, Arthur O, 1953, My 27,31:4
Jones, Arthur P, 1950, Ap 3,24:2
Jones, Arthur R (Sept 23), 1965, O 11,61:3
Jones, Arthur S, 1946, Jl 26,21:3
Jones, Arthur T, 1951, F 10,13:4
Jones, Arthur W, 1945, S 26,23:3; 1957, Mr 8,25:4
Jones, Augustine, 1925, S 11,23:6
Jones, Avonia (Mrs Brooke), 1867, O 6,8:5
Jones, B F Jr, 1928, Ja 2,31:5
Jones, B P, 1885, My 16,8:2
Jones, Barclay L, 1945, Ja 5,15:6
Jones, Barry Holme, 1919, Ap 4,11:3
Jones, Bassett, 1960, Ja 25,27:1
Jones, Ben (Benj A), 1961, Je 14,19:4
Jones, Ben Mrs, 1959, Je 11,33:4
Jones, Benjamin, 1940, My 30,18:4
Jones, Benjamin E Rev, 1904, Ja 18,1:5
Jones, Benjamin F, 1903, My 20,9:3
Jones, Benjamin H, 1950, S 23,17:4
Jones, Benjamin R, 1942, Mr 23,15:2
Jones, Benjamin R Mrs, 1953, F 23,25:3
Jones, Bernard B, 1953, My 7,32:3
Jones, Bert A Mrs, 1964, My 29,29:3
Jones, Bert L, 1942, Je 20,13:5
Jones, Billy (por), 1940, N 24,49:1
Jones, Bob Sr Dr, 1968, Ja 17,47:2
Jones, Bobby, 1938, Mr 10,21:4
Jones, Bradley, 1957, Mr 9,19:2
Jones, Breckinridge, 1965, N 7,89:2
Jones, Bruce P, 1963, My 21,37:4
Jones, Buell F, 1947, N 18,29:2
Jones, Burr F, 1952, O 1,33:5
Jones, Burtowilon, 1950, Ap 9,84:2
Jones, Byron Q, 1959, Ap 1,37:1
Jones, C Anson Mrs, 1908, Ja 1,9:3
Jones, C Drummond, 1946, Ja 3,20:3
Jones, C Edward, 1941, Ja 11,17:3
Jones, C Floyd, 1939, O 12,25:5
Jones, C H M, 1944, My 26,19:3
Jones, C N, 1913, Ja 7,11:5
Jones, C Sharpless, 1951, Je 19,29:3
Jones, C W, 1897, O 13,2:5; 1940, Je 8,15:4
Jones, C Walker, 1950, N 27,25:1
Jones, C Wesley, 1948, O 5,25:1
Jones, Cadwalader M, 1919, N 19,13:3
Jones, Carl A, 1950, Jl 24,17:4
Jones, Carl H, 1958, S 3,33:4
Jones, Carl W, 1957, Ja 6,88:1
Jones, Carleton C, 1943, Jl 9,17:4
Jones, Carleton P, 1952, My 18,92:6
Jones, Carlisle, 1952, S 24,33:4
Jones, Caroline Ogden, 1915, S 7,13:6
Jones, Carroll W, 1950, Ag 9,29:1
Jones, Carter H, 1946, My 8,25:5
Jones, Catesby L Mrs, 1943, D 28,17:4
Jones, Catesby T, 1967, S 10,83:1
Jones, Catherine P Mrs, 1947, S 19,23:3
Jones, Cecil C, 1943, Ag 20,15:5
Jones, Charles, 1938, D 9,25:5; 1940, D 13,23:2; 1950, Ja 11,23:2; 1956, Mr 20,23:3
Jones, Charles A, 1939, D 6,25:2; 1966, My 22,86:5
Jones, Charles A Mrs, 1948, Ag 14,13:1
Jones, Charles B, 1942, N 18,26:3; 1946, D 8,77:8; 1966, Ag 5,31:4; 1967, Ag 22,34:3
Jones, Charles C, 1951, O 31,29:2
Jones, Charles D, 1944, N 26,58:3
Jones, Charles E, 1939, N 2,23:5
Jones, Charles F Mrs, 1945, Ja 7,38:4
Jones, Charles G, 1938, Je 26,27:2; 1948, O 5,25:4
Jones, Charles H, 1939, Jl 16,31:2; 1941, Ap 19,15:2; 1941, N 10,17:2; 1943, Ja 14,21:2; 1949, Ag 23,23:2; 1957, Jl 15,19:5
Jones, Charles H Col, 1913, Ja 28,11:4
Jones, Charles J, 1953, Ap 18,19:4
Jones, Charles J Rev Dr, 1907, S 10,7:4
Jones, Charles K, 1952, D 21,53:1
Jones, Charles L, 1946, Je 15,21:4; 1964, Ag 12,35:5
Jones, Charles Landon, 1916, Ja 3,13:2
Jones, Charles M, 1959, Ap 13,31:4
Jones, Charles M Mrs, 1949, N 15,26:4
Jones, Charles R, 1944, Mr 27,19:6
Jones, Charles S, 1938, Ap 23,15:1
Jones, Charles T, 1911, Je 28,11:5
Jones, Charles W, 1944, Ag 17,17:6; 1964, D 6,89:1
Jones, Chauncey J, 1941, Jl 14,13:6
Jones, Cheney C, 1954, Jl 16,21:5
Jones, Chester H, 1959, Jl 25,17:3
Jones, Chester L, 1941, Ja 14,21:3
Jones, Chester N, 1940, Je 14,21:5
Jones, Clarence C, 1946, F 3,40:1; 1954, My 16,88:3
Jones, Clarence E, 1937, My 26,26:4
Jones, Clarence G, 1952, Ag 17,76:3
Jones, Clark F, 1962, Ap 13,35:2
Jones, Claude, 1962, Ja 19,31:2
Jones, Claude A, 1948, Ag 9,20:3
Jones, Claude H, 1953, Ja 22,23:4
Jones, Clement J, 1940, Mr 11,15:5
Jones, Clement R, 1939, Ag 17,21:2; 1945, S 5,23:2
Jones, Cleophas B, 1953, N 14,17:4
Jones, Clifford, 1948, D 20,25:4
Jones, Clifford L, 1956, My 27,88:3
Jones, Clyde A, 1947, My 13,25:3
Jones, Coleman B, 1959, Mr 5,31:1
Jones, Coleman D Mrs, 1947, Je 19,21:5
Jones, Creel B Mrs, 1966, Jl 5,27:2
Jones, Cyril H Mrs, 1949, F 3,24:3
Jones, Cyril J, 1964, My 1,35:2
Jones, Cyrus R Jr, 1941, Ag 31,22:6
Jones, D C, 1952, D 15,25:2
Jones, D P, 1903, F 1,7:5
Jones, Dan W, 1949, D 20,31:2
Jones, Daniel F Dr, 1937, S 12,II,7:2
Jones, Daniel H, 1950, D 22,24:2
Jones, Daniel M, 1950, Ag 22,27:5
Jones, Daniel S, 1920, Ag 20,9:4
Jones, Daniel W, 1942, Ag 5,19:4
Jones, Daniel Webster Ex-Gov, 1918, D 26,11:4
Jones, Dave R, 1965, F 4,31:5
Jones, David, 1881, Ja 18,8:2; 1948, Ag 10,22:2; 1949, My 9,25:2; 1952, F 25,21:1; 1960, Ap 30,23:5
Jones, David Benton, 1923, Ag 24,11:6
Jones, David D, 1956, Ja 25,31:5
Jones, David E, 1948, Ja 16,21:3
Jones, David H, 1955, D 1,35:1
Jones, David H E, 1919, D 16,13:3
Jones, David J (Potato Jones), 1962, Ag 8,31:2
Jones, David J, 1966, Jl 30,25:1
Jones, David L, 1958, Ja 2,29:4
Jones, David M, 1946, Mr 13,29:1
Jones, David N, 1948, Ja 5,19:2
Jones, David R Floyd, 1871, Ja 10,5:2
Jones, David S, 1911, Ap 12,13:4
Jones, David W Dr, 1937, Ja 19,23:5
Jones, Davis, 1942, F 17,21:3
Jones, De L Floyd Col, 1902, Ja 20,2:6
Jones, Delbert L, 1952, Je 16,17:4
Jones, Dewey, 1939, Ap 11,24:3
Jones, DeWitt C Jr Mrs, 1966, Mr 17,39:3
Jones, DeWitt Clinton Jr, 1968, Mr 3,88:7
Jones, Don K, 1944, Ap 4,21:4
Jones, Donald D M Mrs, 1960, Mr 4,25:2
Jones, Donald F, 1963, Je 20,33:1
Jones, Dorothea E, 1947, Je 8,60:5
Jones, Dorothy D Mrs, 1938, Ja 8,15:3
Jones, Douglas P Jr, 1964, Je 17,43:1
Jones, Duane, 1961, Je 17,21:4
Jones, Dunham C, 1954, Mr 25,29:5
Jones, Dwight A, 1913, D 9,11:5
Jones, Dwight B, 1958, F 17,23:2
Jones, E A, 1933, F 21,19:3
Jones, E D, 1954, My 8,17:1
Jones, E Douglas, 1902, D 11,16:2
Jones, E E, 1877, Je 29,5:1
Jones, E Earl, 1940, D 28,15:3; 1959, Je 14,86:2
Jones, E L, 1929, Ap 10,29:3
Jones, E Lester, 1944, Ag 3,19:2
Jones, E Milton Mrs, 1945, Je 23,13:5
Jones, Earl J, 1957, D 24,15:2
Jones, Easley S, 1947, F 20,25:3
Jones, Edgar A, 1950, F 12,84:1
Jones, Edgar D, 1956, Mr 27,35:3
Jones, Edward, 1882, N 21,5:2
Jones, Edward A, 1909, O 24,13:2; 1945, S 22,17:1
Jones, Edward A Mrs, 1946, O 29,25:5
Jones, Edward D, 1947, S 7,60:2; 1966, D 6,47:3
Jones, Edward Davis, 1920, F 17,9:3
Jones, Edward E, 1943, My 23,42:7
Jones, Edward F, 1951, My 28,21:4; 1960, Jl 16,19:2
Jones, Edward F Gen, 1913, Ag 15,7:6; 1913, Ag 16, 9:6
Jones, Edward H, 1944, Ja 6,23:1; 1956, My 29,27:4; 1960, Ja 9,21:4
Jones, Edward J, 1953, Ja 15,27:1
Jones, Edward L, 1939, F 19,39:2
Jones, Edward Mrs, 1909, Ja 10,13:4
Jones, Edward N, 1939, Mr 1,21:2
Jones, Edward N Mrs, 1957, Mr 4,27:4
Jones, Edward Priv, 1919, My 14,17:6
Jones, Edward R Prof, 1937, O 23,15:7
Jones, Edward S, 1947, Ja 17,23:4
Jones, Edward W, 1958, N 6,37:4
Jones, Edwin E, 1942, N 4,23:3
Jones, Edwin J, 1938, Mr 13,19:2
Jones, Eleazer, 1873, F 11,1:4
Jones, Eliza F Mrs, 1940, Jl 11,19:2
Jones, Elizabeth D Mrs, 1941, O 3,23:5
Jones, Elizabeth S, 1951, Jl 19,23:3
Jones, Elliot R, 1948, Je 7,19:2
Jones, Ellis, 1948, D 6,25:3
Jones, Ellis E, 1951, O 4,33:1
Jones, Ellis O, 1967, Ag 2,37:4
Jones, Elmer A, 1948, Ja 18,60:8
Jones, Elmer E, 1944, Mr 17,17:3
Jones, Elmer G, 1963, N 18,33:3
Jones, Elmer R, 1943, D 4,13:4
Jones, Elmer R (funl, Ag 20,86:4), 1961, Ag 19,1
Jones, Elwood C, 1948, D 24,18:2
Jones, Elzy L, 1952, Je 23,19:3
Jones, Emmet A, 1948, My 28,23:4
Jones, Emmett L, 1940, Ap 1,19:4
Jones, Enos L, 1941, N 2,55:4
Jones, Ernest, 1869, Ja 28,4:7; 1956, D 2,86:2; 195 F 12,29:1; 1965, Ag 1,77:3
Jones, Ernest G, 1948, D 23,19:4; 1962, Ap 8,86:3
Jones, Erwin T, 1938, Je 2,23:5
Jones, Eugene, 1946, O 2,29:4
Jones, Eugene K, 1954, Ja 12,23:5
Jones, Eugene K Jr, 1964, D 1,41:4
Jones, Eugene W, 1964, D 13,86:4
Jones, Evan, 1951, Jl 6,23:2
Jones, Evan C, 1939, N 8,23:4
Jones, Evan M, 1949, Ap 23,13:3
Jones, Evan R Maj, 1920, Ja 17,11:4
Jones, Evan S, 1949, Je 1,31:2
Jones, Evans Mrs, 1948, My 27,25:4
Jones, F A, 1934, Mr 14,19:3
Jones, F D, 1929, Ap 20,19:5
Jones, F Robertson, 1941, D 28,28:3
Jones, F Robertson Mrs, 1965, Jl 31,21:4
Jones, Florence V A, 1949, Jl 6,27:1
Jones, Frances C Mrs, 1962, S 11,34:1
Jones, Francis C, 1938, Ap 20,23:6
Jones, Francis P, 1941, Ja 7,23:2
Jones, Francis Wiley, 1914, Ap 1,13:4
Jones, Frank, 1938, Ap 13,25:3; 1945, My 13,20. 1955, Jl 6,27:1
Jones, Frank A, 1947, Ja 19,53:4
Jones, Frank B, 1951, N 21,25:3
Jones, Frank C (por), 1949, Ja 22,13:3
Jones, Frank C, 1962, Ap 14,25:2
Jones, Frank C Mrs, 1959, Ag 11,27:1
Jones, Frank D, 1951, Jl 1,50:6
Jones, Frank E, 1941, My 22,21:3; 1947, Mr 2,6
Jones, Frank H, 1954, O 22,27:5
Jones, Frank L, 1953, D 22,31:6
Jones, Frank P, 1939, F 28,19:3
Jones, Frank P Jr, 1951, D 20,31:3
Jones, Frank R, 1939, Ap 11,24:2; 1948, Mr 31,
Jones, Frank S, 1946, N 28,27:3; 1952, O 12,89
Jones, Franklin D, 1964, My 9,27:2
Jones, Franklin D Mrs (R Bradley), 1963, Ag
Jones, Franklin M, 1946, S 9,9:4
Jones, Frayser, 1956, Ap 23,27:4
Jones, Fred G, 1951, Je 6,31:1
Jones, Fred W, 1949, S 14,31:5; 1950, N 18,15:
Jones, Frederic W, 1943, D 21,27:2
Jones, Frederick G, 1951, Je 7,33:1
Jones, Frederick M, 1962, My 28,29:3
Jones, Frederick P, 1946, D 14,15:3
Jones, Frederick S, 1944, Ja 15,13:1
Jones, Frederick William, 1915, Je 30,11:6
Jones, Fuzzy Q (A St John), 1963, Ja 23,7:5
Jones, G H, 1928, N 22,25:3
Jones, G W, 1884, N 15,2:4
Jones, Gardner D, 1940, My 8,23:2
Jones, Gardner M, 1941, My 20,23:2
Jones, Gareth, 1958, D 2,37:1
Jones, Garrett E, 1949, Ja 18,23:4
Jones, George, 1891, Ag 12,4:6
Jones, George (funl, Je 1,17:4), 1921, My 29
Jones, George (por), 1946, O 1,23:3
Jones, George, 1949, Ja 1,3:5
Jones, George A, 1949, My 14,13:5
Jones, George C, 1924, Ja 1,23:2; 1940, Ag 18 1946, F 9,13:6; 1963, O 29,36:6; 1965, Mr 2
Jones, George D, 1945, D 3,21:3
Jones, George E, 1939, F 14,19:5; 1946, D 13
Jones, George F, 1913, Ag 18,9:5; 1946, Mr 2 1966, F 23,39:2
Jones, George G, 1955, S 16,23:3; 1961, Jl 4,
Jones, George H, 1941, Jl 7,15:5; 1946, Ag 2 1948, Jl 24,15:6; 1949, My 13,24:2; 1953, M
Jones, George H Mrs, 1941, Ja 10,19:2; 1944, 19:2
Jones, George Heber Rev Dr, 1919, My 13,1
Jones, George M, 1940, Ja 7,49:2; 1952, Ja 1
Jones, George P, 1944, O 15,44:6
Jones, George S, 1938, Ap 2,15:6
Jones, George T, 1943, Je 9,21:4
Jones, George T Mrs, 1943, Ja 14,21:4
Jones, George W, 1905, Mr 4,9:4; 1941, Jl 1 1948, Je 9,29:3; 1949, Ja 16,68:8; 1951, N 8 1953, O 24,15:3; 1955, Ja 29,15:2
Jones, George W Mrs, 1950, Je 3,15:5; 1957, 37:3
Jones, Gilbert, 1960, F 10,37:4
Jones, Gilbert E, 1925, O 25,9:1
Jones, Gilbert S, 1954, D 6,27:6
Jones, Glenn I, 1942, Jl 19,30:5
Jones, Golden Rule S M, 1904, Jl 13,7:7

Jones, Gomer P, 1951, Mr 31,15:2
Jones, Gordon H, 1966, S 30,47:2
Jones, Gordon H Mrs, 1951, S 25,29:3
Jones, Gordon T, 1954, D 14,33:1
Jones, Grenville R, 1957, O 9,35:2
Jones, Griffith J, 1955, Ja 30,84:3
Jones, Grinnell, 1947, Je 25,25:6
Jones, Grosvenor M, 1952, N 13,31:3
Jones, Grover, 1940, S 25,27:6
Jones, Gus T, 1963, O 1,39:3
Jones, Guy C, 1948, D 4,13:3
Jones, Guy Mrs, 1949, Jl 3,27:1
Jones, Gwendolen S, 1956, D 31,13:5
Jones, Gwethalyn, 1959, Je 21,92:7
Jones, H A (por), 1929, Ja 8,31:1
Jones, H Bp Mrs, 1903, My 10,7:5
Jones, H Ennis (por), 1946, N 23,15:4
Jones, H Farquhar, 1951, Ag 21,27:2
Jones, H Seaver, 1958, S 14,84:4
Jones, H V, 1928, My 25,25:3
Jones, H Williams Mrs, 1950, Jl 29,13:4
Jones, Harold A Mrs, 1964, S 4,29:3
Jones, Harold Colbert, 1924, Jl 19,9:5
Jones, Harold E Mrs, 1966, Ja 29,27:5
Jones, Harold F, 1962, Mr 31,25:2
Jones, Harold L, 1949, Ja 26,25:1
Jones, Harold S, 1960, N 5,23:3
Jones, Harold W, 1959, S 3,27:5
Jones, Harriet D, 1938, Ja 21,19:4
Jones, Harriet L Mead Mrs, 1923, Ap 12,19:5
Jones, Harrison, 1949, Mr 9,25:5
Jones, Harry, 1948, F 6,23:3
Jones, Harry B, 1947, D 6,15:6
Jones, Harry C, 1938, O 4,25:2
Jones, Harry F, 1963, Ap 9,31:4
Jones, Harry H, 1954, My 2,88:5
Jones, Harry I, 1958, Jl 15,25:1
Jones, Harry Mrs, 1949, D 1,31:3
Jones, Harry S V, 1942, Ja 11,45:1
Jones, Harry T, 1955, D 11,89:1
Jones, Harry W, 1946, F 25,25:5
Jones, Harry W Mrs, 1955, Je 3,23:4
Jones, Harvey C, 1945, N 17,17:5
Jones, Harvey P, 1948, S 25,17:3
Jones, Haydon, 1954, Ja 31,88:1
Jones, Helen L (Elcita), 1903, F 25,1:2
Jones, Henrietta B Mrs, 1957, Ap 30,29:4
Jones, Henry C, 1942, My 16,13:5; 1945, Mr 13,23:4
Jones, Henry C Dr, 1906, D 5,11:5
Jones, Henry L, 1944, O 13,19:5
Jones, Henry Lloyd, 1968, D 31,27:1
Jones, Henry R, 1916, O 22,23:3
Jones, Henry R Capt, 1912, Jl 21,II,11:4
Jones, Henry W, 1917, Ag 24,7:2; 1957, Ap 14,86:1
Jones, Henry W F Rev Dr, 1915, S 27,9:4
Jones, Herbert, 1951, Jl 19,23:3
Jones, Herbert A, 1950, Je 16,25:4
Jones, Herbert C Jr Mrs, 1949, F 1,25:3
Jones, Herbert G, 1958, Je 24,31:3
Jones, Herbert L, 1940, F 14,21:5
Jones, Herbert V, 1949, Ag 28,72:7
Jones, Herbert W, 1946, Je 19,21:3
Jones, Herman L, 1952, S 13,17:3
Jones, Herman W, 1948, F 1,60:3
Jones, Hillary P (por), 1938, Ja 2,40:1
Jones, Hilton I, 1955, My 4,29:5
Jones, Homer W, 1960, Mr 15,39:2
Jones, Horace C, 1940, Ag 30,19:5
Jones, Horace L, 1954, N 1,27:5
Jones, Howard, 1943, Je 29,19:1
Jones, Howard B, 1950, O 31,27:2
Jones, Howard E, 1937, Ap 18,II,9:2; 1944, Jl 8,11:6
Jones, Howard E Mrs, 1943, Ag 26,17:3
Jones, Howard G, 1939, O 21,15:3
Jones, Howard H (por), 1941, Jl 28,13:4
Jones, Howard P, 1953, Mr 28,17:4
Jones, Howard S, 1956, Ap 18,31:3
Jones, Howell A, 1966, F 3,31:2
Jones, Hubert, 1946, Ap 3,25:4
Jones, Hugh W, 1952, Ja 24,27:1
Jones, Hugh X, 1948, Je 27,52:3
Jones, Humphrey Capt, 1922, Jl 9,26:4
Jones, Hurley, 1953, Je 18,32:2
Jones, I Thomas Judge, 1907, Ja 11,9:5
Jones, Idwal, 1964, N 17,42:3
Jones, Inis W, 1938, N 27,48:4
Jones, Ira, 1960, Ag 31,29:1
Jones, Ira C, 1941, N 26,23:1
Jones, Isaac, 1937, Mr 16,23:2
Jones, Isaac H (cor, S 14,23:1), 1956, S 9,84:8
Jones, Isham, 1956, O 20,21:4
Jones, Ishmond, 1962, Ja 26,31:4
Jones, Israel C, 1906, Ja 7,7:6
Jones, Israel C Dr, 1917, D 7,13:5
Jones, Iwan E, 1945, My 26,15:1
Jones, J Addison, 1949, My 9,25:6
Jones, J B, 1881, Jl 26,2:6
Jones, J Burnett Mrs, 1951, D 23,23:1
Jones, J Clarence (por), 1942, N 16,19:1
Jones, J D Dr, 1903, Ja 6,9:4
Jones, J G, 1878, Mr 25,5:6
Jones, J Horace, 1937, Mr 23,24:1
Jones, J Jackson, 1940, Je 21,21:4
Jones, J Jefferson, 1941, N 2,53:3
Jones, J K, 1943, Jl 8,19:5
Jones, J Latta, 1946, O 1,23:3
Jones, J Levering, 1920, N 26,13:3
Jones, J M Judge, 1904, Jl 12,7:6
Jones, J Morgan, 1961, My 13,19:5
Jones, J N, 1939, O 26,23:5
Jones, J Q (see also Ja 3), 1878, Ja 5,2:2
Jones, J Rev, 1877, Ap 25,2:6
Jones, J Richter Col, 1863, My 31,3:6
Jones, J Russell, 1909, Ap 12,7:4
Jones, J Russell Mrs, 1949, F 7,19:2
Jones, J S Gen, 1903, Ap 12,7:6
Jones, J Share, 1950, D 3,88:3
Jones, J W, 1881, S 8,5:4
Jones, J Walter, 1954, Ap 1,32:3
Jones, J Wesley, 1905, D 16,6:5; 1961, F 12,86:4
Jones, J William, 1954, O 3,87:1; 1958, D 9,41:1
Jones, J William Jr Mrs, 1963, O 21,31:4
Jones, J Wyman, 1904, O 28,7:2
Jones, Jack P, 1961, Ap 8,19:2
Jones, Jacob B, 1954, F 9,27:3
Jones, Jacob R Mrs, 1957, Ap 3,31:1
Jones, James, 1912, Mr 18,11:6
Jones, James A, 1937, O 13,23:3; 1950, My 27,17:5; 1966, N 19,33:3
Jones, James B, 1938, O 13,23:5; 1947, Ag 11,23:4
Jones, James C, 1946, Jl 15,25:5
Jones, James C ex-Gov, 1859, O 31,4:5
Jones, James D, 1948, N 10,29:2
Jones, James E, 1925, Je 12,19:6; 1939, Ja 1,24:8; 1949, F 20,60:2
Jones, James E Col, 1918, Ja 4,11:5
Jones, James F, 1959, S 8,35:1
Jones, James G, 1905, Ap 24,9:6
Jones, James H, 1956, O 15,25:4
Jones, James H Mrs, 1958, D 10,40:1
Jones, James K (funl, Je 3,7:4), 1908, Je 2,7:6
Jones, James L, 1940, Jl 7,25:2
Jones, James M Jr, 1940, F 8,23:1
Jones, James S, 1940, Ag 18,37:2
Jones, James Sr, 1960, O 5,41:2
Jones, James T, 1953, My 7,31:5
Jones, Jane A, 1951, N 10,17:3
Jones, Jane L, 1946, S 13,7:2
Jones, Janet C, 1958, Ag 23,15:5
Jones, Jay S (por), 1940, Je 4,24:2
Jones, Jean S Mrs, 1939, My 13,15:3
Jones, Jefferson, 1965, D 9,47:5
Jones, Jenkins Lloyd Rev, 1918, S 13,11:1
Jones, Jennie M Mrs, 1941, D 10,20:6
Jones, Jerome, 1940, S 25,27:5
Jones, Jerry, 1938, Je 4,15:2
Jones, Jess W, 1962, Je 26,33:1
Jones, Jesse E, 1937, O 25,19:4
Jones, Jesse H (funl plans, Je 3,86:4; funl Je 5,35:5), 1956, Je 2,1:2
Jones, Jesse H Mrs, 1962, Ag 21,33:2
Jones, Jesse Jr Mrs, 1949, Je 8,30:3
Jones, Jessie B, 1944, S 14,23:3
Jones, Joe (Jos J), 1963, Ap 10,39:5
Jones, John, 1876, Ap 7,4:6; 1948, Jl 17,15:6
Jones, John A, 1939, Je 19,15:4; 1940, D 13,26:6; 1941, My 12,17:1; 1944, Ja 14,19:2; 1956, Ag 23,27:5
Jones, John A Jr, 1957, O 3,29:3
Jones, John B, 1954, D 12,89:2
Jones, John C, 1945, N 7,23:3
Jones, John D, 1942, Ap 20,21:4
Jones, John D R, 1953, Ja 31,15:5
Jones, John E, 1944, O 18,21:4
Jones, John Edward Mrs, 1913, Je 3,9:4
Jones, John F, 1939, F 6,13:5; 1950, N 12,92:6; 1958, Je 13,23:3
Jones, John F V, 1939, Je 22,23:4
Jones, John F X, 1944, Ja 9,42:2
Jones, John G, 1956, Ag 18,17:3; 1958, Ag 4,21:5
Jones, John H, 1960, Mr 8,33:4
Jones, John J, 1941, N 22,19:6; 1947, Jl 25,17:5; 1948, S 20,25:1
Jones, John L Mrs, 1958, N 22,21:2
Jones, John M, 1937, N 30,23:6
Jones, John M Sr, 1952, Je 28,19:3
Jones, John Mrs, 1954, Ag 1,84:2
Jones, John P, 1947, N 17,21:2; 1951, My 23,35:3; 1958, F 11,31:3; 1965, Ap 18,80:8
Jones, John P Capt, 1910, My 26,9:5
Jones, John P Rev Dr, 1965, Mr 4,31:3
Jones, John Paul, 1907, N 17,9:5; 1964, Je 17,43:4
Jones, John Percival Ex-Sen, 1912, N 29,15:6
Jones, John Price, 1964, D 24,19:2
Jones, John R, 1963, Ag 22,27:1
Jones, John R Mrs, 1948, Je 8,26:2
Jones, John S, 1949, Ap 22,23:2; 1955, Ja 5,23:1
Jones, John T, 1946, Ag 16,21:6; 1955, Mr 4,23:4
Jones, John W, 1918, S 30,9:4; 1937, My 26,25:5; 1946, Jl 5,30:7; 1955, Mr 2,27:4; 1957, Jl 26,19:4
Jones, John W Mrs, 1918, S 30,9:4; 1964, Jl 4,13:3
Jones, Jonathan, 1960, Je 27,25:1
Jones, Jonathan H, 1950, Ap 26,29:2
Jones, Joseph, 1942, Je 21,36:7; 1957, Ja 16,31:1; 1957, Ap 23,31:1; 1963, Mr 12,7:8
Jones, Joseph A Mrs, 1960, Ag 19,23:1
Jones, Joseph E, 1967, Mr 15,47:4
Jones, Joseph H, 1951, Ap 1,92:1
Jones, Joseph J, 1938, Je 12,39:2
Jones, Joseph Mrs, 1963, Mr 12,7:8
Jones, Joseph R, 1937, F 17,22:2
Jones, Joseph W, 1957, Je 6,31:2
Jones, Josephine K (est), 1906, Ag 8,12:4
Jones, Joshua, 1938, Jl 25,15:3
Jones, Joshua H, 1955, D 15,37:4
Jones, Karl V Sr, 1962, Ag 19,88:3
Jones, Kay C (Mrs J W Fulweiler), 1959, Je 6,21:4
Jones, Kennedy, 1921, O 21,15:5
Jones, Kenneth A N, 1964, O 12,25:2
Jones, Kenneth M, 1956, S 5,20:5
Jones, Kenneth M Mrs, 1964, O 17,29:4
Jones, Kenyon S, 1951, Ja 11,26:3
Jones, L L, 1932, D 6,21:4
Jones, Lamoyne A Mrs, 1940, F 26,15:4
Jones, Lattie G Mrs, 1942, O 24,15:1
Jones, Laura B Mrs, 1942, N 24,25:3
Jones, Laura E, 1948, S 23,29:3
Jones, Laura W Mrs, 1937, F 23,27:4
Jones, Lawrence, 1954, O 22,27:4
Jones, Lawrence L, 1941, O 22,23:4
Jones, Lawson R, 1940, Ap 27,32:4
Jones, Le Roy F, 1958, My 29,27:1
Jones, Leander P, 1907, Mr 19,9:5
Jones, Leo C, 1953, Jl 26,69:1
Jones, Leon F, 1940, Ja 6,13:5
Jones, Leonard, 1946, Jl 19,19:3
Jones, Leonard W Mrs, 1947, O 10,25:3
Jones, Leonidas S, 1937, Je 26,17:4
Jones, LeRoy G, 1967, N 25,39:4
Jones, Lester M, 1938, Mr 31,23:4; 1954, Je 18,23:2
Jones, Lester T, 1959, F 13,27:3
Jones, Lewellyn Bp, 1918, Ja 10,13:3
Jones, Lewis Jr, 1945, O 2,23:2
Jones, Lewis R, 1945, Ap 2,19:5
Jones, Lewis R Mrs, 1958, F 26,27:3
Jones, Lincoln, 1953, Ja 2,15:5
Jones, Lindley M, 1948, Je 15,28:3
Jones, Livingston E, 1941, Ag 31,22:3; 1959, F 28,19:5
Jones, Livingston E Mrs, 1958, Ag 17,85:2
Jones, Llewellyn E, 1950, My 8,23:3
Jones, Llewellyn W, 1950, O 12,31:3
Jones, Llewellyn W Jr, 1964, Ag 5,33:1
Jones, Lloyd E, 1958, Ja 4,15:2
Jones, Lloyd P, 1950, Je 6,29:4
Jones, Lloyd W, 1958, My 22,29:5
Jones, Lombard C, 1944, Ag 18,13:5
Jones, Louis C, 1945, D 30,14:5
Jones, Louis G, 1949, D 8,33:3
Jones, Louis K, 1940, S 29,44:2
Jones, Loyd A, 1954, My 18,30:4
Jones, Lydia I, 1958, F 5,27:4
Jones, Lydia W Mrs, 1942, D 15,27:3
Jones, Lynds, 1951, F 13,31:3
Jones, M, 1927, Ag 13,13:5
Jones, M (Mother), 1930, D 1,21:1
Jones, M Ashby, 1947, Ja 3,22:2
Jones, M C, 1903, Ag 17,7:5
Jones, M H, 1883, Je 2,5:1
Jones, M Paul, 1950, O 17,31:4
Jones, Madison S, 1951, Ap 10,27:2
Jones, Margaret A Mrs, 1937, O 19,26:3
Jones, Margaret G, 1943, O 12,27:5
Jones, Margaret S Mrs, 1949, Jl 31,60:2
Jones, Margo (funl plans, Jl 26,25:2; trb, Jl 31,II,1:5), 1955, Jl 25,19:3
Jones, Marguerite E, 1962, Ja 25,31:2
Jones, Marie G, 1955, S 14,35:4
Jones, Marion H Mrs, 1956, Jl 25,29:4
Jones, Mark P Jr, 1959, Ag 23,93:1
Jones, Marshall N, 1941, S 10,23:6
Jones, Martha Bradt Mrs, 1968, Mr 6,47:3
Jones, Martin B, 1950, N 24,35:2
Jones, Martin B Mrs, 1951, Jl 4,17:3
Jones, Marvin F, 1952, Mr 28,29:5
Jones, Mary Alice, 1968, Ja 3,40:2
Jones, Mary E Mrs, 1938, Ja 4,23:1
Jones, Mary F (will, Mr 3,43:3), 1937, F 18,21:4
Jones, Mary H Mrs, 1949, F 10,27:4
Jones, Mary P, 1960, N 7,35:4
Jones, Matt B (por), 1940, Jl 2,22:2
Jones, Matthew C, 1937, O 17,30:4
Jones, Mattison B, 1941, O 13,17:3
Jones, Maude A Mrs, 1940, Je 4,23:3
Jones, Melinda Mrs, 1875, D 15,7:3
Jones, Melvin, 1961, Je 2,32:1
Jones, Melvin H, 1951, Ap 21,17:1
Jones, Melvin Mrs, 1954, Je 6,87:1
Jones, Meredith L Col, 1918, D 28,11:6
Jones, Michael, 1937, Mr 29,19:3
Jones, Mildred, 1954, O 22,27:1
Jones, Millard F, 1950, Mr 26,94:3
Jones, Milo Hotchkiss Dr, 1903, Jl 28,7:6
Jones, Morgan, 1939, Ap 24,17:2; 1951, S 22,17:5
Jones, Mortimer D, 1953, S 22,31:4
Jones, N Forrest, 1954, S 28,29:6
Jones, Nathan H, 1953, Ap 20,25:5
Jones, Nathan Solomon, 1906, Mr 27,9:6
Jones, Nathaniel D, 1912, Ag 19,9:6
Jones, Nathaniel Parker, 1903, O 13,9:6
Jones, Nathaniel W, 1943, S 25,15:4

Jones, Neason, 1951, Ja 18,27:5
Jones, Neason Mrs, 1948, S 16,29:1
Jones, Needham L, 1947, S 1,19:2
Jones, Nellie F Mrs, 1942, O 2,25:2
Jones, Newton C, 1948, S 15,31:4
Jones, Nicholas A, 1946, Ag 27,27:2
Jones, Norine (will), 1966, D 10,28:8
Jones, Norman L, 1940, N 16,17:3
Jones, Norris, 1942, S 19,15:6
Jones, Norton T, 1951, D 20,31:2
Jones, O C, 1937, Ag 2,19:3
Jones, O Garfield, 1957, F 20,33:2
Jones, Obediah, 1948, Je 5,15:2
Jones, Olive M, 1953, Ag 12,31:4
Jones, Oliver Livingston Mrs, 1918, O 23,13:2
Jones, Orsino E, 1907, Ja 26,9:5
Jones, Oscar, 1946, O 9,35:2
Jones, Owen, 1874, My 4,1:7; 1878, D 27,5:2; 1884, Ap 19,5:2
Jones, Owen M, 1951, Ap 9,25:5
Jones, P M, 1883, O 3,5:1
Jones, P W, 1941, Mr 16,44:6
Jones, Parry, 1963, D 28,23:3
Jones, Patrick, 1937, S 4,15:7; 1940, Ap 5,21:4
Jones, Paul, 1941, S 5,21:5; 1948, D 27,21:3; 1965, Ag 5,29:2
Jones, Paul C, 1948, N 29,23:3
Jones, Paul D, 1959, Jl 27,25:4
Jones, Paul G, 1960, Je 10,31:6
Jones, Paul H, 1949, Jl 6,27:1
Jones, Paul L, 1942, Mr 15,42:5
Jones, Paul M, 1966, D 31,19:2
Jones, Paul Mrs, 1946, Je 28,21:4; 1950, Mr 14,25:4
Jones, Paul R (por), 1942, N 11,25:3
Jones, Paul R Mrs, 1943, Ag 6,21:4
Jones, Paul T Mrs, 1954, D 7,33:4
Jones, Paul W, 1955, Mr 9,27:1
Jones, Pauline, 1965, Mr 14,20:5
Jones, Pauline S, 1943, N 11,23:4
Jones, Pembroke, 1919, Ja 25,11:5
Jones, Percival S, 1951, Mr 27,29:2
Jones, Percy H, 1941, Mr 2,42:2
Jones, Percy L, 1941, Ag 10,36:8
Jones, Percy T, 1948, Ja 22,27:4
Jones, Percy V, 1940, F 14,21:4
Jones, Perry W, 1949, N 25,31:3
Jones, Peter H, 1950, Ja 18,31:4
Jones, Phil J, 1949, S 2,17:4
Jones, Philip Howard William, 1921, Je 18,9:5
Jones, Phineas, 1957, S 30,31:3
Jones, Pierce, 1949, Mr 20,76:3
Jones, Preston Z, 1960, O 27,37:3
Jones, Pryce, 1903, Ap 24,9:6
Jones, Quay, 1947, Ja 14,25:2
Jones, Quill, 1954, Jl 28,23:2
Jones, R D, 1925, Je 14,5:2
Jones, R E, 1929, Jl 21,22:1
Jones, R Glenn, 1964, O 10,29:4
Jones, R Hugh, 1950, Ja 25,27:3
Jones, R J, 1929, Ja 10,29:3
Jones, R Owen Mrs, 1944, Mr 9,17:2
Jones, R Sir, 1933, Ja 16,15:1
Jones, R W H, 1878, N 11,1:3
Jones, Ralph B, 1952, Jl 8,27:6
Jones, Ralph M, 1946, Ag 24,11:3
Jones, Ralph R, 1951, Jl 27,19:3
Jones, Raymond, 1953, Je 23,29:2
Jones, Raymond E, 1944, Ap 26,19:2; 1967, Ja 24,28:7
Jones, Reginald L (por), 1949, Ja 15,17:3
Jones, Richard, 1909, Jl 2,7:4
Jones, Richard A, 1950, S 3,38:4
Jones, Richard A Jr (por), 1939, Ag 23,21:4
Jones, Richard C Col, 1903, S 14,7:5
Jones, Richard F, 1945, N 25,49:1; 1965, S 15,47:2
Jones, Richard H, 1938, Ja 16,II,9:3
Jones, Richard J Mrs (will), 1946, Jl 30,21:1
Jones, Richard L Sr, 1963, D 5,45:3
Jones, Richard Seelye, 1968, O 30,47:4
Jones, Richard T Rev, 1923, My 18,19:2
Jones, Richard W, 1938, F 8,22:2; 1951, Ap 27,23:3
Jones, Richard W Sr Mrs, 1943, Jl 26,19:4
Jones, Robert, 1943, Mr 28,25:1
Jones, Robert A, 1960, Ag 14,93:1
Jones, Robert A Mrs, 1966, Mr 1,37:4
Jones, Robert B, 1948, Ag 15,61:2
Jones, Robert C, 1964, Ap 8,43:2
Jones, Robert E (trb lr, D 5,II,7:4), 1954, N 27,13:1
Jones, Robert E Mrs, 1942, Ag 2,38:7
Jones, Robert F, 1949, F 4,23:2; 1949, Ap 17,76:3; 1968, Je 24,37:4
Jones, Robert H, 1947, D 23,23:2; 1958, Ja 22,3:6
Jones, Robert L, 1950, Ag 9,29:3; 1953, My 18,21:4; 1956, Ja 18,31:5
Jones, Robert M, 1940, Ap 9,23:3
Jones, Robert M Mrs, 1951, Ja 1,17:2
Jones, Robert Mrs, 1952, Ja 10,29:1
Jones, Robert O (por), 1947, My 16,23:3
Jones, Robert P, 1956, Jl 17,21:1
Jones, Robert P Mrs, 1961, Ja 15,86:3
Jones, Robert R, 1952, D 29,19:6
Jones, Robert T, 1937, S 24,21:5; 1958, Je 12,31:5
Jones, Robert W, 1947, D 3,29:2
Jones, Robertson G (por), 1938, Ag 19,19:1
Jones, Roderick, 1962, Ja 24,33:3
Jones, Roland M, 1945, N 28,27:4
Jones, Rowland, 1939, Je 1,25:2
Jones, Roy D, 1950, Ja 9,23:3
Jones, Roy H, 1948, Ap 11,72:3
Jones, Roy J, 1939, Jl 28,17:3
Jones, Roy M, 1951, N 15,29:2
Jones, Ruel A, 1941, O 22,23:4
Jones, Rufus M (por), 1948, Je 17,25:1
Jones, Rufus M Mrs, 1952, O 28,31:2
Jones, Russell C, 1961, F 22,25:4
Jones, Russell L Mrs, 1954, D 3,28:2
Jones, Ruth E, 1940, S 18,23:1
Jones, Ruth M Mrs, 1942, Je 25,23:5
Jones, Ruth W, 1949, O 29,15:3
Jones, S Fosdick, 1946, Mr 25,25:3
Jones, S Minot, 1912, O 11,11:3
Jones, Sad Sam (Saml P), 1966, Jl 7,37:1
Jones, Salome Hanna Mrs, 1907, Ap 16,11:5
Jones, Sam P Rev, 1906, O 16,9:4
Jones, Samuel, 1957, Jl 3,23:5
Jones, Samuel B, 1955, D 31,13:5
Jones, Samuel C, 1939, Mr 2,21:1
Jones, Samuel C Mrs, 1903, Ag 10,7:7
Jones, Samuel D, 1962, Ap 17,35:3
Jones, Samuel G, 1944, S 19,21:5
Jones, Samuel H, 1941, Ag 31,23:2
Jones, Samuel R, 1949, Je 19,68:3
Jones, Samuel S, 1954, Ap 20,29:3
Jones, Samuel T, 1946, O 6,56:4
Jones, Sara P Mrs, 1938, S 26,17:1
Jones, Sarah E Mrs, 1937, O 6,25:6
Jones, Sarah R N Mrs, 1940, S 6,21:3
Jones, Seward W, 1948, Je 28,19:3
Jones, Shelby C, 1955, My 9,23:4
Jones, Sidney, 1946, Ja 30,25:6
Jones, Silas P, 1953, My 18,21:4
Jones, Simon D, 1939, Je 24,17:6
Jones, Southgate, 1949, Ja 7,21:4
Jones, Spike (Lindley A),(funl, My 5,47:4), 1965, My 2,88:1
Jones, Stanley B, 1968, Mr 2,29:4
Jones, Stanley P, 1961, S 29,35:4
Jones, Stanly W Mrs, 1959, D 21,27:3
Jones, Stephen G, 1959, Ap 11,21:6
Jones, Stewart, 1949, S 27,27:3
Jones, Sue Duff D Mrs, 1941, Jl 23,19:4
Jones, Sullivan W, 1955, Ja 27,23:4
Jones, Sullivan W Mrs, 1947, Jl 24,21:4
Jones, T C Mrs, 1967, D 26,33:1
Jones, T Carlyle, 1966, My 4,47:4
Jones, T Catesby, 1946, D 22,41:3
Jones, Theodore F Prof, 1968, N 20,47:4
Jones, Theodore J Mrs, 1957, O 31,31:4
Jones, Therese A Mrs, 1938, D 31,15:2
Jones, Thomas, 1943, O 29,19:4
Jones, Thomas A, 1943, O 17,48:6; 1956, Ja 31,29:1
Jones, Thomas A D (Tad), 1957, Je 20,29:1
Jones, Thomas B Mrs, 1951, O 11,37:3
Jones, Thomas C, 1938, N 16,23:3; 1955, D 22,23:5
Jones, Thomas D, 1954, N 23,35:1
Jones, Thomas G, 1949, Mr 8,25:2; 1963, N 5,31:2
Jones, Thomas G Judge, 1914, Ap 30,11:6
Jones, Thomas G Mrs, 1956, O 6,21:5
Jones, Thomas H, 1948, Ap 16,23:1; 1955, O 16,86:3
Jones, Thomas J, 1950, Ja 6,21:1
Jones, Thomas J Mrs, 1937, N 3,23:2
Jones, Thomas Jr, 1869, F 2,5:3
Jones, Thomas Logan, 1915, My 19,13:5
Jones, Thomas M, 1947, Jl 31,21:1
Jones, Thomas R, 1951, My 21,27:5
Jones, Thomas S, 1961, N 19,88:6; 1964, Ap 10,35:1
Jones, Thomas W, 1951, O 10,23:4; 1954, S 28,29:5
Jones, Tom E, 1944, Ja 11,20:3
Jones, Townsend, 1916, S 17,19:4
Jones, Townsend S Mrs, 1946, Ap 26,21:4
Jones, U S G Mrs, 1950, N 30,33:4
Jones, V Merle, 1941, Jl 18,19:4
Jones, Vernon H, 1947, Je 23,23:5
Jones, W Alton (funl plans, Mr 3,45:1; funl, Mr 6,-32:5), 1962, Mr 2,15:1
Jones, W Edwin, 1939, Mr 1,21:5
Jones, W G Mrs, 1907, Je 14,7:5
Jones, W H, 1880, My 1,5:4
Jones, W L, 1926, N 27,17:4; 1932, N 20,28:1
Jones, W Marvery, 1939, S 26,23:4
Jones, W P, 1944, S 30,13:6
Jones, W Paul, 1955, Ja 21,23:4
Jones, W Rand, 1968, Mr 9,29:3
Jones, W S, 1933, D 7,23:5
Jones, W Strothers, 1954, Mr 24,27:3
Jones, W W, 1957, N 1,23:2
Jones, Wallace A, 1953, O 13,29:5
Jones, Wallace S Mrs, 1964, D 30,25:1
Jones, Wallace T, 1946, My 30,21:5
Jones, Walter (funl), 1922, My 26,19:6
Jones, Walter A, 1943, S 4,13:3
Jones, Walter B (trb lr, Ag 10,16:6), 1963, Ag 2,27:5
Jones, Walter C, 1943, S 24,23:3
Jones, Walter F, 1947, S 11,27:6
Jones, Walter G, 1941, Jl 26,15:4; 1954, O 10,87:2
Jones, Walter H, 1944, Mr 12,38:2
Jones, Walter M, 1944, Ja 12,24:3
Jones, Walter P, 1950, S 16,19:4
Jones, Walter R (will, F 25,9:3), 1938, F 6,II,8:4
Jones, Walter R, 1954, Mr 9,27:5; 1964, Mr 1,83:2
Jones, Walter S, 1968, Ag 2,33:4
Jones, Walter T, 1967, O 5,39:3
Jones, Walter W, 1951, D 24,13:3
Jones, Ward E, 1953, F 22,63:3
Jones, Ward K, 1944, O 17,23:5
Jones, Warren C, 1952, Je 20,23:4
Jones, Warren D, 1953, N 27,27:1
Jones, Warren H, 1937, F 15,17:4
Jones, Webster, 1941, Mr 14,21:2
Jones, Wellington D, 1957, Jl 25,23:2
Jones, Wellington Mrs, 1944, My 29,15:5
Jones, Wellington S, 1948, F 3,25:3
Jones, Wendell, 1956, F 19,92:5
Jones, Wesley N Mrs, 1943, N 27,13:3
Jones, Wesley R Mrs, 1944, Ap 1,13:4
Jones, Whitney W, 1959, Je 2,35:3
Jones, Wilbur, 1946, Ag 23,19:2
Jones, Wilfred E, 1954, D 31,14:4
Jones, Willard, 1938, D 29,19:2
Jones, Willard C, 1962, F 24,27:2
Jones, Willard F, 1967, Ag 20,88:1
Jones, William, 1865, D 12,8:3; 1920, N 28,22:4; 1938 F 8,22:1; 1944, Jl 23,35:3; 1947, Mr 18,27:4; 1948, My 21,23:4; 1950, O 20,28:2; 1954, Jl 21,27:4; 1959, D 20,60:3
Jones, William A, 1941, Ap 11,21:5; 1941, Ag 13,17:2 1943, D 9,27:4; 1944, F 6,42:4; 1946, D 22,42:2
Jones, William A Bp, 1921, F 18,11:5
Jones, William A Brig-Gen, 1914, N 15,3:6
Jones, William Atkinson, 1918, Ap 18,13:8
Jones, William B, 1942, F 3,20:2
Jones, William B Mrs, 1949, F 5,15:3
Jones, William Carey Prof, 1923, O 4,23:3
Jones, William E, 1937, D 19,II,8:7; 1954, Je 11,23:3
Jones, William F, 1941, S 14,50:2; 1945, D 9,45:1
Jones, William G, 1944, Jl 11,15:5
Jones, William H, 1941, Ap 5,17:4; 1944, O 11,21:3; 1947, Mr 16,61:1; 1953, O 19,21:4; 1954, Ap 28,31
Jones, William L Sr, 1954, D 21,27:5
Jones, William Lloyd, 1874, Mr 14,9:2
Jones, William Mrs, 1951, Jl 31,21:4
Jones, William N Mrs, 1957, Mr 18,27:5
Jones, William O (funl, D 31,4:2), 1922, D 30,13:3
Jones, William O, 1937, Jl 31,15:5; 1938, Jl 31,33:3; 1950, Ap 18,31:5
Jones, William O Mrs, 1961, O 1,86:3
Jones, William R, 1955, Ag 20,17:7; 1967, Ap 9,92:7
Jones, William S, 1939, Ag 2,19:4; 1940, Mr 12,23:4 1949, O 13,27:2; 1951, F 8,33:4; 1954, F 18,31:4
Jones, William Strother Rev Dr, 1918, Ag 20,9:5
Jones, William T, 1942, Jl 19,30:7; 1962, Ag 10,19:2
Jones, William V, 1941, Ag 10,37:2
Jones, William W, 1950, My 30,17:4; 1959, Ap 14,3
Jones, Willie T, 1963, D 30,21:4
Jones, Willis S, 1956, N 13,37:1
Jones, Wyatt, 1951, Jl 7,13:7
Jones (Silent Becky), 1905, Mr 20,5:5
Jones-Murdoch, Celia Mrs, 1923, Jl 23,13:3
Jonescu, Take, 1922, Je 22,15:6
Jonet, Frank, 1951, Ag 19,86:1
Jonez, Hinton D, 1953, O 12,27:4
Jong, Jacques R de, 1943, Ap 9,21:5
Jong, Johannes de (funl plans, S 10,17:6; funl S 14,-35:3), 1955, S 9,23:1
Jong, Van Rijswijk de, 1946, Ag 1,23:2
Jongen, Joseph, 1953, Jl 15,25:6
Jongers, Alphonse, 1945, O 3,19:5
Jonick, Joseph L, 1967, S 19,51:3
Jonkel, Jon M, 1959, Jl 1,25:6
Jonker, Jacobus, 1944, My 18,19:1
Jonklaas, Ernest M, 1956, Ja 1,51:2
Jonkman, Sarah Mrs, 1953, O 31,17:1
Jonnard, Claude, 1959, Ag 28,23:2
Jonnart, C A C, 1927, O 1,19:4
Jonsson, Axel, 1950, Ja 12,27:5
Jonsson, Nils P, 1953, Ap 28,27:2
Jonsson, Thorsten, 1950, Ag 8,29:1
Jonston, Fred H, 1951, Mr 20,29:2
Joodha Shum Shere Jung Bahadur Rama, 1952, N 23:3
Joos, August W, 1961, Ap 12,41:1
Joos, Charles E, 1951, Ja 8,17:5
Joost, Martin, 1920, F 26,11:4
Jope, Clifford H, 1959, D 31,21:3
Joplin, J Porter, 1938, D 25,15:2
Jopling, Alfred Charles, 1923, S 18,21:6
Jopling, Reginald F, 1942, O 21,21:4
Jopson, Reginald K, 1957, My 29,27:3
Joraimon, John F Rev, 1924, N 16,7:2
Joralemon, Abram Mrs, 1903, N 25,9:5
Joralemon, Albert J, 1956, Jl 11,29:4
Joralemon, John L S Sr, 1952, Jl 18,19:3
Joralemon, L Dinwidie, 1956, My 3,31:2
Jorawarsinghji, Thakore Sahib Shri, 1940, O 1,23:
Jordahn, Gus, 1938, F 11,24:2
Jordal, Louis H, 1951, D 24,1:1
Jordan, A, 1934, S 5,21:1
Jordan, Albert C, 1964, O 17,29:4; 1966, S 19,43:
Jordan, Albert E, 1903, Jl 5,7:5
Jordan, Alfred E, 1952, Ap 26,23:6

Jordan, Alfred E Mrs, 1940, Mr 23,13:5
Jordan, Ambrose L, 1865, Jl 18,4:6
Jordan, Arthur, 1955, O 21,27:3
Jordan, Bobby, 1965, S 11,27:2
Jordan, Bridget M, 1948, Je 5,15:4
Jordan, C N, 1903, F 27,2:4
Jordan, Charles B, 1941, Ap 23,21:5
Jordan, Charles C, 1951, F 22,31:2
Jordan, Charles L, 1950, Ja 28,13:6
Jordan, Charles P, 1945, My 24,19:5
Jordan, Chester B, 1943, Mr 31,20:3
Jordan, Chester B Ex-Gov, 1914, Ag 25,9:6
Jordan, Cyrus, 1904, Ja 18,7:4
Jordan, D S, 1931, S 20,II,6:1
Jordan, Dana S, 1951, My 28,21:6
Jordan, Daniel, 1945, Mr 26,19:3
Jordan, David F, 1942, Ag 22,13:3
Jordan, David S Mrs, 1952, O 25,17:5
Jordan, E Boyd, 1959, Mr 29,80:2
Jordan, E O, 1936, S 4,19:3
Jordan, Eben D, 1916, Ag 2,9:1
Jordan, Eben D Mrs, 1920, N 5,15:6
Jordan, Edward B, 1951, Jl 20,21:4
Jordan, Edward C, 1940, O 15,23:1
Jordan, Edward F, 1967, Ap 25,43:4
Jordan, Edward S, 1941, F 6,21:3; 1958, D 31,38:1
Jordan, Edwin J, 1903, S 8,7:6
Jordan, Elijah, 1953, My 19,29:1
Jordan, Elizabeth, 1947, F 25,25:1
Jordan, Emily (Mrs Jno F Chamberlain), 1912, F 20, 11:4
Jordan, Emily G, 1947, N 13,27:4
Jordan, Emmett F, 1954, D 24,13:2
Jordan, Eugene P, 1942, My 2,13:3
Jordan, Evart L, 1958, Je 24,23:6
Jordan, Francis X, 1937, O 27,31:5
Jordan, Frank B Mrs, 1949, F 18,23:3
Jordan, Frank C, 1940, Ja 19,19:6; 1943, Je 27,32:2
Jordan, Frank R, 1941, D 28,28:8
Jordan, Frank S, 1949, S 22,31:4
Jordan, Franklin I, 1956, N 5,31:2
Jordan, Fred D, 1947, N 13,27:5
Jordan, Fred S, 1958, Ja 11,17:5; 1960, My 2,29:4
Jordan, Fred W, 1941, F 15,15:4
Jordan, Frederick, 1903, Jl 21,9:6; 1949, N 5,13:2
Jordan, Frederick F, 1938, O 11,25:4
Jordan, Frederick P, 1946, O 26,17:3
Jordan, Frederick P Mrs, 1946, O 26,17:3
Jordan, George C, 1938, D 25,15:3
Jordan, George Clifford, 1873, N 16,4:6
Jordan, George F, 1951, Ap 10,36:8
Jordan, George T, 1959, My 18,27:1
Jordan, Harry B, 1949, S 15,27:2
Jordan, Harry E, 1947, Ja 28,24:2
Jordan, Harry T, 1949, O 8,13:6
Jordan, Harvey B, 1965, Ap 9,33:1
Jordan, Heinrich E K, 1959, Ja 14,27:2
Jordan, Henry, 1955, O 6,29:2
Jordan, Howard W Mrs, 1958, N 18,37:2
Jordan, J H, 1874, Mr 27,3:1
Jordan, J Leroy, 1954, D 14,33:3
Jordan, J P, 1932, Jl 23,11:1
Jordan, J Paul, 1968, My 25,35:2
Jordan, James F, 1943, My 21,20:3
Jordan, James H, 1943, O 20,21:5
Jordan, James L Mrs, 1954, O 9,17:3
Jordan, Jim Mrs (Marian),(funl, Ap 11,37:3; will Ap 16,66:2), 1961, Ap 8,19:1
Jordan, Jimmy, 1957, D 5,35:4
Jordan, John A, 1946, Jl 25,21:5
Jordan, John A Mrs, 1950, O 12,31:3
Jordan, John J, 1944, Mr 5,36:1
Jordan, John L, 1962, Jl 9,31:5
Jordan, John Sir, 1925, S 15,25:3
Jordan, John T, 1946, D 4,31:3
Jordan, Joseph A, 1956, My 7,27:5
Jordan, Joseph S, 1944, Jl 12,19:6
Jordan, Joseph V, 1947, Je 4,27:2
Jordan, Jules, 1925, Jl 23,19:6
Jordan, Julia C, 1948, O 8,25:3
Jordan, Julian W, 1944, F 20,36:4
Jordan, Julie V, 1949, N 17,29:4
Jordan, Katherine T, 1937, Jl 27,21:2
Jordan, Kenneth L, 1959, N 12,35:5
Jordan, Lawton D, 1958, S 6,17:4
Jordan, Llewelyn D, 1944, F 20,36:4
Jordan, Louis, 1954, Jl 23,17:3
Jordan, Mahlon K, 1967, Jl 3,17:6
Jordan, Mary (Johnson), 1881, Mr 1,2:2
Jordan, Mary (Mrs C C Cresson), 1961, My 16,43:1
Jordan, Mary A, 1941, Ap 15,23:4
Jordan, Max O, 1957, S 4,34:6
Jordan, Minnie H, 1956, Ag 12,84:3
Jordan, Murray (M J Jenny), 1962, Jl 4,21:5
Jordan, Orlando S, 1968, O 5,35:4
Jordan, Orvis F Mrs, 1950, Ja 30,17:4
Jordan, Percy E, 1943, My 25,23:3
Jordan, Phil, 1965, Je 27,55:8
Jordan, Phil F, 1951, Je 7,33:1
Jordan, Philip M, 1961, Ap 2,76:2
Jordan, Philip R, 1943, N 12,21:5
Jordan, Phineas G, 1942, N 18,26:4
Jordan, Phoebe S, 1940, Ja 15,15:6
Jordan, R B, 1878, N 11,8:1
Jordan, R C, 1941, Ag 9,15:5
Jordan, Ralph B, 1953, S 23,32:3
Jordan, Raymond E, 1967, Ag 18,33:3
Jordan, Reuel M, 1962, Jl 28,19:4
Jordan, Richard, 1958, Ag 30,15:3
Jordan, Riverda H, 1950, S 13,27:4
Jordan, Robert B, 1940, Je 6,25:3
Jordan, Roy E Sr, 1951, My 14,25:4
Jordan, Samuel M, 1952, Je 25,29:3
Jordan, Samuel M Mrs, 1954, Mr 9,27:4
Jordan, Sara M (Mrs P Mower), 1959, N 22,86:6
Jordan, Sloan B Mrs, 1951, S 22,17:4
Jordan, Stanley, 1965, N 9,43:3
Jordan, Stephen Mrs, 1950, Ja 3,25:4
Jordan, Stroud, 1947, D 30,24:2
Jordan, Theodore C, 1942, F 10,19:2
Jordan, Thomas D, 1908, Jl 15,5:5
Jordan, Thomas J, 1954, O 12,27:5
Jordan, Thomas M, 1942, F 11,22:2
Jordan, Thomas W, 1956, Mr 5,23:6
Jordan, Verner C, 1963, My 23,37:4
Jordan, W Donald, 1962, Je 30,19:3
Jordan, W M, 1903, Ja 28,9:6
Jordan, Walter C, 1950, N 14,31:3
Jordan, Wesley, 1924, Mr 13,17:5
Jordan, Wilfred, 1959, O 16,31:3
Jordan, William A Mrs, 1951, O 11,37:5
Jordan, William B, 1946, Ja 10,23:3
Jordan, William Capt, 1921, D 12,15:2
Jordan, William F, 1953, O 31,17:6
Jordan, William G Mrs, 1966, Ja 21,47:1
Jordan, William J, 1955, My 9,23:4
Jordan, William M, 1966, Ja 11,29:1
Jordan, William P, 1947, My 8,25:3
Jordania, Noah, 1953, Ja 12,27:5
Jordanoff, Assen, 1967, O 19,47:4
Jorden, B, 1951, Ja 26,23:3
Jordi, Jose E, 1952, S 18,29:4
Jordon, Benjamin P, 1955, Je 9,29:2
Jordon, James W, 1942, Mr 16,15:4
Jores, Ernest F, 1950, Jl 28,21:3
Jorgensen, Andrew C, 1954, Ja 27,27:4
Jorgensen, Carl Mrs, 1950, Mr 14,25:4
Jorgensen, Frank F, 1943, N 9,21:2
Jorgensen, Johanna Mrs, 1944, My 8,19:2
Jorgensen, Johannes, 1956, My 30,21:2
Jorgensen, Jonas C, 1965, S 4,21:6
Jorgensen, Jorgen A, 1941, S 11,23:3
Jorgensen, K F, 1948, Ag 15,60:3
Jorgensen, Rolf L, 1958, Ag 6,25:5
Jorgenson, Margaret (will), 1954, N 13,9:6
Jorgulesco, Jonel, 1966, N 8,39:2
Jorio, Domenico Cardinal, 1954, O 22,27:1
Jorissen, Andre L, 1958, Mr 1,17:4
Jorjani, Reza, 1950, Ap 16,104:8
Jorlett, Stephen J, 1951, F 21,27:5
Jorn, Karl, 1947, D 20,17:2
Jorns, M J, 1909, My 18,9:5
Joroff, Dora Mrs, 1952, D 14,71:3
Joroff, Oscar, 1945, Mr 30,15:4
Jorquera, Humberto, 1963, Ap 18,35:5
Jorrin, Miguel, 1965, My 9,87:2
Jory, Edwin A, 1957, Ag 13,27:5
Jory, Grace E Mrs, 1961, Ag 18,21:5
Jose, August, 1961, N 2,37:2
Jose, Richard J, 1941, O 21,23:1
Jose, Victor R Jr, 1958, Je 18,33:3
Josef, Walter, 1954, Jl 24,31:1
Josef Franz, Archduke of Habsburg, 1957, S 27,19:1
Joseffy, Rafael, 1915, Je 26,9:5
Joseffy, Teri, 1937, Je 8,25:3
Josefovits, Teri, 1958, N 26,29:5
Joseloff, Robert, 1962, F 26,27:4
Joseloff, Robert Mrs, 1956, My 24,31:4
Joseloff, Samuel, 1957, Je 13,31:2
Josenhans, Anna, 1948, O 14,29:2
Joseph, A C Mrs, 1938, S 15,25:2
Joseph, Abram G Mrs, 1968, F 1,37:3
Joseph, Anna Mrs, 1957, D 31,18:1
Joseph, Arthur, 1906, F 21,9:4; 1947, N 23,74:4; 1956, S 24,27:4
Joseph, Barnet, 1945, My 11,19:4
Joseph, Barnett, 1967, Ag 16,41:4
Joseph, Barnett Mrs, 1962, My 12,23:4
Joseph, Barney, 1943, N 14,56:2
Joseph, Belle Mrs, 1941, O 18,19:4
Joseph, Benjamin M, 1950, Je 7,59:2
Joseph, Blanche, 1966, N 1,41:1
Joseph, Bro (Patk L Kenny), 1909, N 28,11:5
Joseph, Bro (Ira Dutton Jones), 1913, Ja 21,13:5
Joseph, Bro, 1943, My 14,20:3
Joseph, Bro Azarias, 1948, Je 13,68:7
Joseph, Charles, 1938, F 17,21:2; 1940, Ap 17,23:3
Joseph, Daniel B, 1946, S 10,7:6
Joseph, David H, 1966, Ag 27,29:1
Joseph, David J Sr, 1954, D 14,33:3
Joseph, Edward M, 1962, Je 5,41:5
Joseph, Ellis S, 1938, S 18,44:6
Joseph, Emile, 1937, S 15,23:6
Joseph, Francis, 1951, F 9,25:4; 1958, Je 18,33:3
Joseph, H Belden, 1961, Ag 24,29:5
Joseph, Henry Mrs, 1950, Jl 23,56:3
Joseph, Herman, 1967, Ja 16,41:3
Joseph, Herman Mrs, 1920, N 25,15:6
Joseph, Horace W B, 1943, N 16,23:5
Joseph, Hugo S, 1942, F 4,20:2
Joseph, Irving, 1943, Mr 27,13:5
Joseph, Irwin S, 1960, O 8,23:3
Joseph, Israel, 1919, Ja 11,13:2
Joseph, Jacob Rabbi, 1902, Jl 29,9:4
Joseph, Jacob Rev, 1922, F 13,13:5
Joseph, Jeremiah, 1954, Je 30,27:4
Joseph, Jesse S, 1943, Ag 27,17:4
Joseph, Lazarus (funl, My 25,47:5), 1966, My 24, 47:1
Joseph, Leon E, 1951, D 3,31:3
Joseph, Leopold, 1937, Ag 10,19:2
Joseph, Louis W (Joe Frisco), 1958, F 18,27:3
Joseph, M Henry, 1949, Ja 12,27:3
Joseph, Maurice, 1960, N 16,41:4
Joseph, Maurice Mrs, 1943, O 2,13:2
Joseph, Max, 1946, Jl 14,36:6
Joseph, Michael, 1958, Mr 18,29:5
Joseph, Milton E, 1957, Je 30,68:6
Joseph, Morris, 1947, Je 6,23:3
Joseph, Mother, 1938, D 23,19:4
Joseph, Nathan, 1958, F 26,27:1
Joseph, Osborne W, 1966, F 25,31:4
Joseph, Oscar L, 1938, Je 27,17:6
Joseph, Percy A, 1951, My 7,25:3
Joseph, Preston, 1960, D 12,29:2
Joseph, Samuel, 1910, Mr 16,9:4; 1959, F 10,33:1
Joseph, Samuel D, 1961, Mr 19,89:2
Joseph, Samuel G, 1944, O 6,23:2
Joseph, Samuel J, 1962, Mr 20,37:2
Joseph, Samuel L, 1938, F 11,23:4
Joseph, Sarah K Mrs, 1937, Ag 26,21:4
Joseph, Sidney, 1951, F 25,84:8
Joseph, Sidney H, 1906, Ap 14,11:4
Joseph, Solomon, 1942, N 25,23:4
Joseph, Theodore H, 1951, F 2,23:1
Joseph, Victor H M, 1961, S 1,17:3
Joseph, W Herbert, 1952, Ja 29,25:3
Joseph, William, 1968, Mr 28,47:4
Joseph, William F, 1955, F 1,29:3
Joseph Anthanasius, Bro (J Savole), 1951, Jl 30,17:4
Joseph Clare, Sister, 1941, Ja 24,17:4
Joseph Edward, Bro, 1958, Ja 7,47:4
Joseph Ferdinand, Archduke of Hapsburg, 1942, Ag 29,15:1
Joseph Marie, Sister, 1939, Ja 13,19:4
Joseph Rosarii, Sister, 1951, N 25,86:1
Joseph VII Ghanima, Patriarch, 1958, Jl 10,27:1
Josephi, Emanuel A, 1919, D 4,17:2
Josephi, Isaac A, 1954, Je 5,17:2
Josephi, Marion G, 1956, D 7,27:4
Josephi, Nettie C Mrs, 1937, S 9,23:2
Josephine, Mother (Galassi), 1958, N 9,88:8
Josephine Angela, Duchess d'Uzes, 1966, S 10,29:4
Josephine Rosaire, Sister (E E C Rea), 1960, F 11, 35:4
Josephs, Charles S, 1947, Ag 7,21:4
Josephs, Harry, 1880, S 7,5:6
Josephs, Joseph I, 1968, Ag 14,43:5
Josephs, Joseph S, 1955, O 14,27:2
Josephs, Paul, 1958, Je 24,31:2
Josephs, Ralph, 1960, Je 30,29:5
Josephson, Aksel G S, 1944, D 14,23:3
Josephson, Anne, 1956, Ag 3,19:1
Josephson, Beno, 1921, Ag 5,13:5
Josephson, C I, 1939, N 26,42:6
Josephson, Edgar, 1948, Jl 17,16:7
Josephson, Herbert O, 1962, Je 28,31:4
Josephson, Herman A, 1954, My 18,29:2
Josephson, Joseph, 1953, Ja 4,76:8
Josephson, Joseph A, 1937, Mr 26,22:1
Josephson, Julius, 1925, O 16,21:5
Josephson, Leon, 1966, F 26,25:4
Josephson, Louis, 1957, Ja 21,25:5
Josephson, Victor, 1938, S 12,17:6
Josephson, Walter S, 1940, Mr 10,48:3
Josephthal, Fritz, 1954, F 15,23:5
Josephthal, Giora, 1962, Ag 23,29:3
Josephthal, L M, 1929, My 24,27:1
Josephthal, Sydney Mrs, 1916, Mr 12,19:4
Josephy, Edward Mrs, 1940, Mr 19,25:2
Josephy, Hugo Mrs, 1945, N 23,23:3
Josey, Lenoir M, 1953, S 2,25:3
Josey, Robert A, 1954, F 1,23:5
Joshi, N M, 1955, My 31,27:3
Joshua, Seth Rev, 1925, My 23,15:6
Josiah, Hannah C Mrs, 1954, D 31,4:6
Josias, Herman, 1937, Ap 16,23:3
Josif, Metropolitan, 1957, Jl 6,16:6
Josika-Herczeg, I de, 1935, Ap 1,19:3
Joskey, Frank H, 1955, Jl 7,27:4
Joslin, Allen R, 1955, O 29,19:3
Joslin, Asher W, 1951, N 8,29:4
Joslin, B F Dr, 1885, Ap 21,4:7
Joslin, Clarence A, 1953, Je 13,15:1
Joslin, Doyle, 1953, Ag 19,29:6
Joslin, Elliott P, 1962, Ja 30,29:3
Joslin, Francis W, 1915, Ag 27,9:6
Joslin, Frank L, 1951, Ja 14,84:7
Joslin, George H, 1945, S 26,23:6

Joslin, J Oscar, 1903, N 8,7:6
Joslin, Philip C, 1961, Je 20,33:3
Joslin, Theodore G (por), 1944, Ap 13,19:1
Josling, Stanley, 1951, Ja 24,27:5
Joslyn, Charles Durant, 1925, Mr 6,19:5
Joslyn, Charles M Col, 1920, Ag 5,7:5
Joslyn, David L, 1943, Je 9,21:3
Joslyn, Frank L, 1938, D 21,23:1
Joslyn, Frederic, 1968, N 15,47:4
Joslyn, Harry P, 1941, Ap 18,21:6
Joslyn, Sarah H Mrs (por), 1940, F 29,19:1
Joslyn, William A, 1958, Ja 30,23:1
Josovsky, Imro, 1910, F 12,9:4
Joss, John H, 1955, Ap 1,27:6
Jossefowitz, Zelik, 1949, Ja 29,13:6
Josselyn, Edgar A, 1943, Ap 28,23:4
Josselyn, Elizabeth W Mrs, 1942, D 2,25:4
Josselyn, Lewis, 1944, F 17,19:4
Josslyn, George B, 1951, D 29,11:1
Jost, Chase, 1954, Mr 4,25:5
Jost, Elaine M, 1961, Ja 9,39:4
Jost, F Arthur, 1953, N 25,23:1
Jost, Frank R, 1962, N 22,29:2
Jost, Gertrude A, 1954, S 7,25:3
Jost, Theodore A, 1963, D 19,33:2
Jost, William J Jr Mrs, 1948, S 15,31:4
Josten, John A, 1942, Je 26,21:5
Jostes, Frederick A, 1952, My 20,25:4
Joswiak, Theodore J, 1957, N 14,33:3
Jouard, Farel, 1941, Ap 28,15:4
Joubert, Andrew P, 1950, Ag 31,25:2
Joubert, Eldon G, 1940, N 22,23:2
Joubert, Pietrus Jacobus Gen, 1900, Mr 29,3:4
Joubert de la Ferte, Philip, 1965, Ja 22,43:2
Jouett, J E Adm, 1902, O 2,9:5
Jouett, John H, 1968, O 22,47:3
Jouffret, Gabriel A, 1954, O 4,27:5
Joughin, James L, 1954, Ag 19,23:3
Jouhaux, Leon (funl, My 3,25:1), 1954, Ap 29,31:1
Jouine, George P F, 1957, My 9,31:2
Jourard, Paul E, 1950, D 2,13:3
Jouravleff, Alex M (will), 1957, Ag 24,3:6
Jourdain, Paul, 1954, D 29,23:2
Jourdan, James Gen, 1910, N 2,11:4
Jourdan, John (funl, O 14,2:6), 1870, O 10,5:4
Jourdan, Joseph H (por), 1938, N 26,15:1
Jourdan, William B, 1944, Mr 1,19:5
Jourdan, William G, 1947, S 1,19:3
Jourdon, Ted, 1961, S 24,86:2
Journeay, George S Mrs, 1944, Jl 14,13:4
Journeay, Helen, 1942, Ja 3,19:5
Journet, M, 1933, S 7,21:4
Journey, Martin, 1937, N 28,II,8:5
Journoud, Anatole, 1939, My 28,III,6:5
Jouvaud, Lucien, 1950, Ja 18,31:5
Jouvenel, H de, 1935, O 5,15:2
Jouvenel, Robert de, 1924, Jl 3,15:5
Jouvet, Louis (trb, Ag 18,7:2; funl Ag 22,23:2), 1951, Ag 17,17:1
Jovanovich, Dozada J, 1960, O 28,31:5
Jovanovich, Ilya M, 1956, D 23,30:3
Jovanovich, Jovan, 1939, Je 21,23:5
Jovanovitch, Branko Gen, 1921, My 1,22:3
Jovine, Francesco, 1950, My 1,25:4
Jovino, John S, 1953, S 8,31:4
Jovino, John S Jr, 1942, O 20,21:4
Jowett, Benjamin, 1893, O 2,4:6; 1963, O 15,39:3
Jowett, Genevieve E Mrs, 1939, Mr 10,23:2
Jowett, Hannah Mrs, 1911, S 16,7:5
Jowett, John Henry Dr (funl, D 21,17:5), 1923, D 20, 17:3
Jowitt, Henry, 1949, My 12,31:6
Jowitt, Samuel M, 1964, Ap 19,84:8
Jowitt, William A, 1957, Ag 17,15:1
Joy, Charles F, 1921, Ap 15,15:4
Joy, Charles T, 1956, Je 7,31:3
Joy, Clyde R, 1951, F 28,28:4
Joy, D, 1928, S 23,26:3
Joy, Edmond P, 1963, Jl 7,52:8
Joy, F W, 1928, F 3,23:5
Joy, Ferdinand J, 1953, N 3,32:7
Joy, Frederick T, 1941, Ap 15,23:4
Joy, H B, 1936, N 7,17:1
Joy, Homer T (por), 1949, O 10,23:3
Joy, James E, 1950, Ja 24,31:2
Joy, James R, 1957, Jl 2,27:3
Joy, John C, 1950, N 25,13:5
Joy, John M, 1943, O 14,21:1
Joy, John T, 1944, N 25,13:2
Joy, Joseph F, 1957, F 21,27:1
Joy, Kenneth H, 1950, Ja 26,27:3
Joy, Leonard W, 1961, N 24,31:1
Joy, Leslie W, 1953, O 22,29:4
Joy, Matthias P, 1949, Jl 31,60:6
Joy, Maurice, 1944, Ap 28,19:2
Joy, Milton R, 1954, D 3,27:4
Joy, Nicholas, 1964, Mr 17,35:3
Joy, Robert Mrs, 1946, S 23,23:3
Joy, Russell T, 1938, Je 11,15:3
Joy, Thaddeus, 1942, D 4,25:5
Joy, Wilbur R, 1960, Je 22,56:5
Joy, William L, 1937, Ap 14,25:3
Joy, William M, 1938, F 7,15:4

Joyce, Adrian D, 1954, Ag 26,27:1
Joyce, Alice, 1955, O 10,27:3
Joyce, Arthur S, 1951, F 10,13:5
Joyce, Arthur T, 1966, Mr 7,27:1
Joyce, Charles E, 1937, F 6,17:3
Joyce, Charles R, 1953, S 11,21:3
Joyce, Christopher T Sr, 1968, O 27,83:1
Joyce, Coleman J, 1941, Je 7,17:6
Joyce, Costumer, 1873, F 25,8:5
Joyce, Edgar C, 1953, Jl 29,23:6
Joyce, Edward J Sr, 1967, Ja 31,31:1
Joyce, Edward S, 1942, Je 24,19:5
Joyce, Edward T, 1944, Ja 13,21:2
Joyce, Elmer S, 1938, Mr 31,23:1
Joyce, Ernest E M, 1940, My 5,52:1
Joyce, Eugene T Col, 1903, N 24,9:5
Joyce, Francis P, 1952, Je 28,19:2
Joyce, Frank, 1944, N 3,21:2
Joyce, Gussie Mrs, 1938, D 26,24:4
Joyce, Horace, 1937, Mr 28,II,8:8
Joyce, J F, 1880, Je 25,2:5
Joyce, J St George Mrs, 1940, Mr 9,15:2
Joyce, James, 1941, Ja 13,15:1
Joyce, James J, 1953, S 12,17:5; 1958, Ag 25,21:5
Joyce, James Mrs, 1951, Ap 13,23:3
Joyce, James S, 1944, Ja 5,18:3
Joyce, John, 1946, F 20,25:4; 1948, D 28,22:2
Joyce, John A Col, 1915, Ja 19,9:6
Joyce, John C, 1950, O 21,17:3
Joyce, John E, 1946, D 10,32:3; 1959, Ap 16,33:4; 1963, N 18,33:4
Joyce, John F, 1943, Jl 3,13:6; 1956, D 11,39:2
Joyce, John H, 1948, Jl 21,23:2
Joyce, John J, 1944, Jl 4,19:3
Joyce, John J Sr, 1938, Ag 7,33:3
Joyce, John M, 1964, D 10,47:1
Joyce, John P, 1925, Jl 8,17:5
Joyce, John S, 1952, Ap 20,92:6
Joyce, John V, 1940, My 20,17:4
Joyce, John W, 1942, S 6,30:8
Joyce, Joseph E, 1938, N 27,48:6
Joyce, Joseph P, 1954, Mr 17,31:5
Joyce, Joseph R, 1958, O 30,31:5
Joyce, Kenyon A (funl, Ja 19,36:1), 1960, Ja 12,45:6
Joyce, Lawrence E, 1946, Jl 2,25:4
Joyce, Leo H, 1942, D 8,25:2
Joyce, Martin A, 1962, My 23,45:2
Joyce, Mary D Mrs, 1941, N 5,23:2
Joyce, Merton F, 1955, Ag 23,23:4
Joyce, Michael, 1940, D 10,25:1
Joyce, Michael J, 1941, N 9,52:2; 1949, Jl 19,29:2
Joyce, Michael P, 1954, F 20,17:5
Joyce, Nora, 1920, My 19,11:5
Joyce, Patrick F, 1938, O 22,17:5; 1966, F 25,84:4
Joyce, Patrick J (por), 1946, N 11,27:5
Joyce, Patrick Weston Dr, 1914, Ja 9,11:5
Joyce, Peggy H (Mrs A C Meyer),(funl plans, Je 14,25:5), 1957, Je 13,31:4
Joyce, Peggy H (Mrs A C Meyer),(est appr), 1959, Ap 21,37:1
Joyce, R D Dr, 1883, N 9,2:2
Joyce, R Edwin Jr, 1959, N 23,31:3
Joyce, Richard M, 1958, Ja 24,23:2
Joyce, Richard Mrs, 1944, Mr 25,15:6
Joyce, Robert A, 1941, O 17,23:5
Joyce, Robert F, 1946, Ap 5,25:1
Joyce, Robert Jr, 1925, N 14,15:5
Joyce, Stanislaus, 1955, Je 18,17:6
Joyce, T Frank, 1938, Jl 31,33:4
Joyce, Thomas, 1937, S 3,17:3
Joyce, Thomas A Sr, 1947, S 14,60:2
Joyce, Thomas F, 1966, S 10,29:4
Joyce, Thomas F Jr, 1965, D 19,84:7
Joyce, Thomas H, 1964, Ap 14,37:2
Joyce, Thomas W, 1937, Ap 25,II,8:8; 1945, Mr 22, 23:5
Joyce, Timothy J, 1947, F 21,20:2
Joyce, Walter Capt, 1937, N 25,31:5
Joyce, Walter F Jr, 1968, Je 19,47:1
Joyce, William, 1954, Mr 9,27:1
Joyce, William B, 1962, Ag 6,25:3
Joyce, William F, 1946, F 23,13:1
Joyce, William H, 1941, O 2,25:5
Joyce, William M, 1941, My 10,15:2
Joyce, William T, 1951, My 22,31:3
Joyner, Andrew, 1951, Mr 27,29:4
Joyner, Andrew J, 1943, S 2,19:1
Joyner, Crawley F Jr, 1958, Ag 6,25:4
Joyner, Frank, 1941, Ag 27,19:5
Joyner, Harry T, 1958, Jl 28,23:1
Joyner, Malinda Mrs, 1937, Jl 21,21:3
Joyner, Nevill, 1952, D 6,21:4
Joyner, Sterling J, 1942, Ja 30,19:2
Joynes, L S, 1881, Ja 19,5:3
Joynes, Levin, 1942, Je 20,13:4
Jozoff, Martin, 1963, Jl 23,29:4
Jozsa, Stephen, 1954, F 24,25:3
Jrodan, William A, 1945, Ag 26,44:6
Juan, Edward, 1941, Jl 4,13:3
Juan, Lloyd V, 1947, Je 15,60:5
Juarez, President, 1872, Jl 25,5:6
Jubb, John B Mrs, 1948, Je 2,29:4
Juby, Henry C, 1941, N 20,27:2

Juchhoff, Edna Z, 1938, O 8,17:5
Juchhoff, Frederick, 1953, D 16,35:2
Juckett, Edwin A, 1960, Mr 5,19:5
Juckett, Frank A, 1957, My 15,35:3
Jud, Herman H Mrs (Sept 17), 1965, O 11,61:2
Juda, Mary, 1951, Jl 10,27:4
Judah, Henry M Col, 1866, Ja 21,1:6
Judah, Mrs (Mrs Torrence), 1883, Mr 3,5:3
Judah, Noble B, 1938, F 27,II,9:1
Juday, Chauncey, 1944, Mr 30,21:3
Judd, Archibald M, 1951, Jl 17,27:2
Judd, Arthur A, 1953, F 19,23:1
Judd, Arthur N, 1949, Jl 8,19:4
Judd, Benjamin F, 1938, Ap 23,15:6
Judd, Betsey, 1876, Je 16,4:7
Judd, C C, 1877, Jl 10,4:6
Judd, Charles A, 1942, Mr 18,23:2
Judd, Charles E, 1937, F 26,21:5
Judd, Charles H, 1946, Jl 19,19:1; 1949, My 13,23:2
Judd, Clark S, 1963, O 22,37:4
Judd, Clifford K, 1941, Jl 4,13:5
Judd, E S, 1935, D 1,II,11:1
Judd, Edward S, 1949, Ja 13,23:4
Judd, Edwin U, 1922, Je 28,15:6
Judd, Francis L Mrs, 1946, Ja 23,27:4
Judd, Frank A, 1959, N 18,41:4
Judd, George E Jr, 1961, Jl 2,32:5
Judd, George W Mrs, 1952, F 15,25:2
Judd, Harold B, 1962, My 7,31:2
Judd, Henry C Sr, 1915, Ag 1,15:6
Judd, Henry E, 1956, My 25,23:2
Judd, Hugh, 1948, Ag 24,23:5
Judd, John W, 1948, Je 7,19:5
Judd, Joseph A, 1937, Ap 10,19:2
Judd, Joseph Sr, 1959, Ap 4,19:4
Judd, Joseph Sr Mrs, 1949, O 8,13:3
Judd, Lawrence McCully, 1968, O 6,85:1
Judd, Leon B, 1951, D 27,21:3
Judd, Max, 1906, My 8,9:2
Judd, Morton F, 1939, Je 29,23:5
Judd, N B, 1878, N 12,5:2
Judd, Orrin R, 1955, Mr 7,27:5
Judd, Orrin R Mrs, 1947, N 21,28:2
Judd, Stanley G, 1954, Ap 25,87:1
Judd, Stuart E Mrs, 1940, Mr 3,44:2
Judd, Susie F N Mrs, 1955, Ag 13,13:1
Judd, Thomas H, 1953, S 16,33:3
Judd, Walter S, 1938, Je 3,21:5
Judd, Wilbur W, 1939, My 30,17:3
Judd, William B Mrs, 1949, Ag 23,24:2
Judd, William C, 1946, Ja 2,19:1
Judd, William N, 1955, Ja 15,13:1
Judefind, William B, 1941, Mr 16,45:2
Judefind, William L, 1951, N 15,29:2
Judell, Arthur, 1959, Je 28,68:8
Judell, Arthur Mrs, 1959, S 28,31:5
Judels, Joseph E Mrs, 1968, Ja 3,47:1
Judes, Isaac E, 1949, Je 16,29:2
Judet, Ernest, 1943, My 27,28:7
Judge, Arthur H, 1955, Jl 21,23:3
Judge, Charles T, 1938, S 28,25:6
Judge, Cyril B Mrs, 1954, Jl 18,56:4
Judge, Denis A, 1941, Mr 23,45:2
Judge, Edward C, 1937, D 8,25:2
Judge, Edward V, 1950, S 14,31:1
Judge, Gerald A, 1948, Ap 27,25:5
Judge, Henry A, 1949, Ja 30,60:5
Judge, J Tangney, 1937, Ag 23,19:4
Judge, Jack (por), 1938, Jl 29,17:3
Judge, James A, 1942, O 27,25:5; 1953, Jl 22,27:4
Judge, James T, 1957, Mr 31,88:8
Judge, Joe (Jos I), 1963, Mr 13,7:2
Judge, John B, 1948, N 9,27:1
Judge, John C, 1938, S 17,17:6
Judge, John H, 1954, S 7,26:1
Judge, John H Mrs, 1914, D 19,13:4
Judge, John J, 1948, Mr 2,24:3; 1949, N 6,92:4
Judge, John P, 1954, Ap 10,15:1
Judge, John R, 1950, Jl 18,29:5
Judge, Joseph M, 1966, Je 28,42:2
Judge, Martin, 1946, Ap 18,27:4
Judge, Michael, 1939, S 28,25:3
Judge, Michael F, 1940, D 23,19:5
Judge, Paul J Mrs, 1960, Mr 23,37:1
Judge, Philip S, 1968, Ag 2,33:2
Judge, Thomas B, 1942, N 11,25:2
Judge, Thomas J, 1937, Mr 23,24:2; 1956, D 1,21
Judge, W Q, 1896, Mr 23,5:6
Judge, William J, 1939, Jl 1,17:5
Judge, William J (por), 1949, My 21,13:5
Judge, William J, 1953, F 15,92:4
Judge, William J Mrs, 1937, My 7,30:2
Judges, George, 1960, N 1,39:5
Judic, Anne, 1911, Ap 15,13:6
Judith, Mme, 1912, O 28,11:4
Judkins, C E H, 1878, O 9,4:6
Judkins, Charles O Mrs, 1948, D 27,22:2
Judkins, Henry E, 1937, Mr 7,II,8:3
Judkins, Joseph B Sr, 1964, Ja 1,25:4
Judkins, Leonard, 1949, D 2,29:2
Judkins, Murray L, 1950, Je 17,15:3
Judkins, Thomas C, 1963, My 16,35:3
Judkins, William D Mrs, 1953, Mr 3,27:1

Judkoff, Theodore, 1948, Je 25,23:1
Judkyn, John N, 1963, Jl 28,41:1
Judovich, Bernard D, 1956, S 15,17:3
Judson, Abbey A, 1902, D 9,9:4
Judson, Albert L, 1923, F 17,13:4
Judson, Alice, 1948, Ap 4,60:4
Judson, Annie Mrs, 1874, Mr 11,3:6
Judson, Arthur G, 1938, F 8,21:3
Judson, Benjamin F Jr Mrs, 1956, S 1,15:6
Judson, Benjamin Franklin Jr, 1953, F 13,21:2
Judson, Burton F, 1942, N 3,23:5
Judson, Charles C, 1946, N 6,23:1
Judson, Charles H, 1937, Ag 30,21:4
Judson, Charles York, 1907, F 17,9:6
Judson, Chester, 1949, Jl 27,23:3
Judson, Cornelia, 1939, S 20,27:3
Judson, Cyrus F (por), 1941, Je 24,19:6
Judson, Cyrus F Jr, 1956, S 11,35:3
Judson, E B, 1902, Ja 16,2:2
Judson, Edmund L, 1946, Mr 7,25:5; 1947, Ag 16,13:6
Judson, Edward, 1916, Jl 14,11:6
Judson, Edward Mrs, 1914, S 22,11:5
Judson, Edward Rev, 1914, O 24,13:7
Judson, Elmer, 1940, S 8,49:2
Judson, Fletcher W, 1955, N 10,35:1
Judson, Frank W, 1957, F 10,86:5
Judson, Frederic N, 1919, O 19,22:4
Judson, George D, 1937, Ap 16,23:2
Judson, H P, 1927, Mr 5,15:5
Judson, Harriet Mrs, 1922, F 13,13:5
Judson, Harry B, 1951, F 14,29:3
Judson, James McI Mrs (Clara I), 1960, My 25,39:2
Judson, John B, 1953, Mr 8,89:5
Judson, John E, 1962, N 17,25:5
Judson, Katrina I Mrs, 1955, My 30,13:6
Judson, Lemuel B, 1957, Ag 23,19:2
Judson, Oliver B, 1950, Mr 7,27:4
Judson, Philo, 1876, Mr 26,7:5
Judson, Robert O, 1948, Jl 12,19:5
Judson, Roland, 1948, Je 18,23:2
Judson, Ross W, 1946, Mr 13,29:2
Judson, Victor, 1956, Ja 28,17:5
Judson, Walter P, 1946, S 20,32:3
Judson, Wilber Mrs, 1952, S 5,27:2
Judson, Wilbur, 1951, Ag 10,15:3
Judson, William, 1903, Ag 5,7:6
Judson, William D, 1943, Ja 17,44:7
Judson, William F, 1949, Ja 22,13:2
Judson, William H, 1938, S 15,25:3
Judson, William Pierson, 1925, F 13,17:4
Judy, E W, 1938, Mr 26,15:6
Juechle, Edward, 1951, D 24,13:4
Juelsberg, Tyorkil Mrs, 1941, F 27,19:5
Juenger, Frederick, 1946, O 22,25:2
Juengerkes, Herman A, 1960, My 10,37:5
Juergenson, Hans Prof, 1912, S 6,9:6
Juffe, Isidore, 1941, D 19,27:7
Jugenheimer, Phil J, 1941, N 5,23:4
Juhasz, William P, 1967, O 2,47:4
Juhring, Henry L, 1914, Ap 19,IV,7:5
Juhring, Louis W, 1951, Jl 19,23:5
Juhring, William J, 1938, Ag 31,15:1
Juht, Ludwig, 1957, Ja 21,25:3
Juilliard, Augustus D, 1919, Ap 30,11:4
Juilliard, Frederic A, 1937, Je 30,24:1
Juin, Alphonse-Pierre (funl plans, Ja 28,27:5), 1967, Ja 27,45:1
Julay, Steven G, 1949, S 10,17:5
Jules, Caroline E Mrs, 1937, D 1,23:7
Jules-Bois, H A, 1943, Jl 3,13:5
Juley, Peter A (por), 1937, Ja 14,21:3
Julia, R Albert, 1937, Mr 14,8:4
Julia Catherine, Sister, 1945, Mr 9,19:2
Julian, Arthur N, 1951, Ag 12,77:3
Julian, Bro (P Cook), 1952, F 24,86:2
Julian, C, 1933, D 13,23:4
Julian, Clarence, 1937, F 4,21:1
Julian, Cyril J, 1954, Ap 19,23:1
Julian, Doggie (Alvin F), 1967, Jl 29,25:4
Julian, Edward W, 1939, S 30,17:6
Julian, Frank, 1937, N 29,23:6
Julian, George E, 1945, My 10,23:2
Julian, Godfrey H Mrs, 1950, S 19,31:2
Julian, John A, 1945, Ja 31,21:1
Julian, John M Dr, 1907, N 25,9:4
Julian, Joseph, 1951, S 22,17:4
Julian, Paul Mrs, 1937, Mr 14,II,8:4
Julian, Rupert, 1943, D 31,16:6
Julian, William A, 1949, My 30,1:4
Julian, William A Mrs, 1949, Mr 27,76:2
Juliana, Mother (Sisters of Bon Secours), 1951, Je 24,72:5
Juliana, Sister, 1946, Jl 6,15:5
Juliand, Henry R, 1954, Je 23,25:4
Juliand, Martha B Mrs, 1943, Je 29,40:4
Julianelle, Louis A, 1944, Ag 13,36:1
Julianelli, Charles A, 1962, Mr 13,32:3
Juliano, Carmine, 1959, N 17,35:3
Juliano, John, 1951, Ja 11,26:2
Juliano, Katherine Mrs, 1948, Ja 16,21:2
Julich, Herman, 1940, N 14,23:2
Julicher, Peter J, 1960, D 8,35:3
Julien, Gilbert, 1938, F 21,19:5
Julien, Harold M, 1961, S 24,1:7
Julien, J Ralph, 1962, My 28,29:5
Julier, Charles F, 1937, N 9,23:1
Julier, Henry V Mrs, 1952, Ja 27,76:5
Julier, Joseph, 1945, Mr 22,23:2
Julihn, Louis G, 1960, O 5,41:1
Julin, Jacob von, 1942, F 21,20:2
Julius, Churchill, 1938, S 3,13:4
Julius, George A, 1946, Je 29,19:2
Julius, Oscar H, 1965, Jl 31,21:1
Juliusberger, Otto, 1952, Je 8,85:1
Jull, Morley A, 1959, O 26,29:4
Julliard, Augustus D, 1919, Ap 26,15:5
Julliard, Augustus D Mrs, 1916, Ap 3,13:3
Julliard, Rene, 1962, Jl 2,29:5
Jullien, Andre Cardinal, 1964, Ja 11,23:1
Jullien, Cyrus S, 1962, N 14,39:2
Jullien, Louis George, 1860, Mr 31,8:2
Julliot, Henri, 1923, Mr 22,19:5
Jully, George W, 1949, F 11,23:2
Julstedt, Clas J, 1950, F 7,27:2
July, Aunt, 1905, Je 23,1:6
July, Nicholas A, 1939, Ap 21,23:4
Jumel, Eliza B Mme (widow of Aaron Burr), 1865, Jl 18,4:5
Jumelle, Clement, 1959, Ap 13,10:4
Jump, A Preston Sr, 1941, Ja 3,19:4
Jump, Eugene T, 1959, D 25,21:1
Jump, Henry D, 1949, N 19,17:6
Jump, Henry D Mrs, 1940, D 11,27:4
Junda, John, 1956, D 20,29:2
Jundt, Charles, 1945, Ap 25,23:4
June, Harold I, 1962, N 23,30:8
June, William, 1945, O 1,19:2
Juneau, William J, 1949, O 19,23:4
Jung, Adolph, 1949, Jl 27,23:4
Jung, Al, 1949, D 24,15:1
Jung, Albert, 1958, Je 13,23:4
Jung, August, 1952, Ap 18,25:3
Jung, Carl G (funl plans, Je 8,35:5), 1961, Je 7,1:2
Jung, Carl G Mrs, 1955, N 30,33:2
Jung, George H Jr, 1948, Je 24,25:4
Jung, Guido, 1949, D 28,25:1
Jung, Harold F, 1959, O 26,29:3
Jung, Jacob K, 1948, S 25,17:4
Jung, Moses, 1960, O 13,37:3
Jung, Phil, 1941, Jl 1,24:5
Jung, Philip, 1943, S 12,52:3
Jung, Salar Sir, 1883, F 10,2:3
Jung-Clemenceau, Therese, 1939, F 11,15:4
Junge, Henry, 1939, Jl 19,19:5
Jungherr, Erwin L, 1965, Ap 18,81:2
Junglas, William P, 1943, Je 8,22:2
Jungman, Bror H, 1945, N 30,23:2
Jungman, William, 1949, D 29,25:3
Jungmann, Harold L, 1958, Ja 27,27:1
Jungmann, Julius, 1943, Ja 1,23:3
Jungmeyer, Jack, 1961, Je 29,33:4
Jungnickel, Robert, 1949, D 24,15:5
Jungschlaeger, Leon N, 1956, Ap 20,1:8
Junguito, Javier Bp, 1911, O 23,11:5
Junien Victor, Bro, 1940, O 17,25:6
Junker, Alex F, 1956, My 25,23:3
Junker, Charles H, 1944, Je 24,13:2
Junker, Howard R, 1951, Ja 7,76:8
Junker, Jules X, 1943, Ag 29,39:4
Junkers, H, 1935, F 4,15:3
Junkin, Chevalier J Mrs, 1943, Ap 26,19:4
Junkin, H D, 1956, N 7,31:5
Junkin, Janet, 1961, D 13,43:2
Junkin, John E, 1940, F 17,13:7
Junkin, Malcolm P, 1958, Ag 29,23:4
Junkins, Samuel A, 1909, Ap 11,11:3
Junkins, Sydney E, 1944, O 4,19:1
Juno, Hasty P C Mrs, 1958, N 10,29:2
Junod, Charles F, 1925, D 9,27:4
Junod, L H, 1926, Ag 4,19:3
Junod, Louis H Mrs, 1960, Ap 1,33:4
Junod, Marcel, 1961, Je 17,21:5
Junod, Ray L, 1958, F 7,21:1
Junor, David Rev, 1912, S 3,11:6
Junor, Kenneth F Dr, 1915, S 28,11:3
Junta, Pearl Mrs, 1951, My 24,35:5
Jupp, Henry Sir, 1939, Ap 10,17:3
Jura, George, 1951, Je 23,15:4
Jurado, Enrique, 1965, Ap 1,35:2
Juras, Joseph B, 1944, Ap 30,45:1
Jurasz, Anthony T, 1961, S 21,35:3
Juraszek, Joseph V, 1968, My 22,47:4
Jurchak, Peter P, 1948, D 21,25:3
Jurenev, Serge B, 1960, N 13,88:1
Jurez, Norberta B de Mrs, 1938, Ap 9,7:5
Jurgatis, John P, 1958, O 21,33:5
Jurgens, Anton, 1945, Mr 14,19:5
Jurgens, Carl, 1909, N 27,9:4
Jurgens, Carl H, 1952, D 22,25:3
Jurgens, Constance, 1952, Je 5,31:4
Jurgens, Karl L Sr, 1951, N 28,31:1
Jurgensen, Hans, 1945, Je 29,15:4
Jurick, Frank W Mrs, 1952, Jl 16,25:2
Jurist, Alfred E Mrs, 1961, My 18,35:5
Jurist, Charles, 1952, S 2,23:3
Jurist, David, 1954, Mr 11,31:3
Jurist, Martin, 1948, F 7,15:5
Jurist, Simeon N, 1963, My 29,33:3
Jurji, Edward J Mrs, 1957, Ap 25,31:4
Jurkat, Frank A, 1954, Ap 7,31:4
Jurke, Louis, 1941, S 17,23:6
Jurman, Samuel Mrs, 1955, O 19,33:5
Jurney, Chesley W, 1947, Ja 29,25:1
Jurovics, Nicholas, 1944, N 16,23:6
Jury, Frank J, 1962, Je 21,31:5
Jurzykowski, Alfred, 1966, My 31,43:2
Jusserand, J J, 1932, Jl 19,17:1
Just, Aldredo (more details, Ag 9,37:1), 1966, Ag 8, 27:5
Just, Alexander, 1904, Ja 19,9:6
Just, Ernest E, 1941, O 29,23:5
Just, Frank H, 1953, My 11,27:3
Just, George A, 1964, Mr 24,33:2
Just, George Alexander, 1918, D 28,11:3
Just, Harcourt, 1951, Ja 15,17:2
Just, Paul A, 1959, N 6,29:3
Just, T Duncan, 1955, S 14,35:4
Just, Theodor K, 1960, Je 15,41:4
Juster, Emanuel M, 1946, Ag 25,45:1
Juster, Milton A, 1954, D 26,61:3
Juster, Vincent D, 1958, Ag 1,21:5
Justesen, Clifford L, 1961, S 28,41:4
Justh, E, 1883, D 18,5:2
Justh, Edward Center, 1914, Ag 9,15:5
Justh, Gustave, 1946, Jl 4,19:4
Justh, Julius, 1917, O 12,11:6
Justi, Ludwig, 1957, O 20,86:2
Justice, Emma Mrs, 1957, Jl 6,15:2
Justice, Ewan, 1922, O 18,19:4
Justice, Hilda (will), 1940, My 22,19:5
Justice, Sidney E, 1951, F 15,31:4
Justice, Theodore, 1924, My 3,15:4
Justice, Warren T, 1945, Je 3,32:2
Justin, Bro (Shannon), 1961, Je 25,76:6
Justin, Joel D, 1950, F 22,29:1
Justin, Rev Bro (Steph McMahon), 1912, F 29,11:5
Justis, Francis M, 1958, Je 2,27:3
Justis, Justa G Mrs, 1943, N 3,25:5
Justis, Lyle, 1960, S 13,37:2
Justo, A P, 1943, Ja 11,3:6
Justo, Augustin P de Mrs, 1942, D 27,34:5
Justus, Andrew, 1949, Ja 28,22:2
Justus, Bro, 1937, D 19,II,9:1
Justus, Charles, 1946, Je 14,21:4
Justus, Irving J, 1943, Ja 16,13:5
Justus, Joseph, 1942, S 1,19:6
Juszko, Jeno, 1954, Ja 6,31:1
Juta, Jan Mrs, 1966, O 18,40:4
Jutkovitz, Alexander, 1947, Mr 6,25:3
Jutkovitz, Jacob, 1937, S 27,21:1
Jutson, Robert P Mrs, 1958, F 19,27:4
Jutte, Maximillian E, 1960, Ja 15,31:4
Jutten, William J, 1937, D 15,25:1
Juul, Earl H, 1942, Ja 6,24:2
Juul, Ralph, 1955, N 8,31:4
Juve, Walter, 1944, D 14,23:2
Juvelier, Kalman, 1939, D 15,25:5
Juvenal, James B, 1942, S 4,23:4
Juzek, Thomas J, 1949, Ja 5,25:2
Juzek, William, 1942, Jl 7,19:4
Juzwik, Steve, 1964, Je 8,29:4

K

Kaa, Herman van der, 1947, Ag 3,52:1
Kaan, George W, 1943, Ap 16,21:4
Kaas, George E, 1953, Ja 1,23:6
Kaas, Louis A, 1945, F 10,11:1
Kaas, Ludwig, 1952, Ap 26,23:1
Kaase, John H, 1951, S 8,17:3
Kabakjian, Dicran H, 1945, N 15,19:4
Kabakoff, Jacob Mrs, 1947, N 26,23:5
Kabatznick, Benjamin, 1945, N 12,21:2
Kabayama, Sukehide, 1941, Mr 20,21:5
Kabayama, Sukenori Adm, 1922, F 9,17:4
Kaber, Joseph W, 1955, Jl 2,15:3
Kaberle, Joseph A, 1949, F 3,24:3
Kabinoff, Milton, 1954, N 13,10:1
Kabis, Charles L, 1957, F 14,27:6
Kable, George W, 1950, N 7,27:3
Kable, William Gibbs Col, 1920, Jl 6,15:1
Kabnick, Herbert H, 1966, Ja 12,21:2
Kaboolian, Karekin, 1959, S 13,84:5
Kabrich, William C, 1947, Ja 29,26:3
Kachaloff, Vassili, 1948, O 1,25:3
Kachurin, Philip, 1947, Ja 21,23:1
Kacmaczky, Alexander P Mrs, 1945, Ag 6,15:2
Kaczmarek, August, 1949, Je 21,25:1
Kaczynski, Zygmunt, 1953, Jl 25,3:7
Kadane, Joseph C, 1937, D 3,23:4
Kade, Lillian, 1953, Mr 22,86:5
Kadel, Donald McN, 1960, Mr 31,33:2
Kadel, Fred J, 1950, Ja 17,27:4
Kadel, George J, 1951, Ap 11,29:6
Kadel, John, 1954, D 7,33:3
Kaden, Hans, 1961, N 22,33:3
Kader, Abd-el, 1940, Ap 16,23:2
Kader, Cadi A, 1955, Ja 3,27:5
Kades, Aaron, 1944, Mr 27,19:2
Kades, Louis S, 1938, Ja 5,21:4
Kadetz, Moss M, 1954, My 14,23:4
Kadien, T C Sr, 1932, Ap 28,21:1
Kadien, Thomas C Jr, 1950, S 23,17:3
Kadin, Charles Mrs, 1960, O 7,35:2
Kadin, Musfika, 1961, Jl 20,27:1
Kadir, Abdul, 1961, Ja 22,85:1
Kadir, Abdul Prince, 1925, Jl 21,21:2
Kadis, Isador, 1958, Ja 26,89:1
Kadish, Harry, 1949, Mr 31,25:5
Kadish, Harry L, 1963, N 3,89:2
Kadish, Morris Mrs, 1963, Ag 22,27:1
Kadison, Leib, 1947, S 26,23:4
Kadlen, Marcus A Dr, 1908, D 16,11:5
Kadman, Leo, 1963, D 28,23:4
Kadomtsev, Erasmus S, 1965, Mr 11,33:2
Kadow, August, 1961, Ja 16,27:5
Kadrey, Richard H, 1956, Jl 27,21:4
Kadwit, Harry J, 1946, F 4,25:2
Kadyk, David J, 1952, My 31,17:4
Kaeding, Charles D, 1942, S 10,27:2
Kaehn, George C, 1947, Jl 6,41:6
Kaelber, Henry J Jr, 1948, Ap 21,27:3
Kaelber, J Herbert, 1947, Ja 28,23:2
Kaelber, William G, 1948, N 22,21:4
Kaelin, Charles, 1951, N 2,24:2
Kaelin, Daniel Mrs, 1939, D 31,19:1
Kaelin, Frank V, 1957, Mr 22,23:5
Kaelin, George H, 1955, Je 4,15:6
Kaemmerling, Gustav Mrs (est acctg), 1958, My 10, 15:2
Kaempf, Johannes Dr, 1918, My 27,13:6
Kaempf, John T, 1939, S 19,25:2
Kaempfer, John P, 1951, O 7,87:1
Kaempfer, Sarah C Mrs, 1938, F 10,21:5
Kaempffert, Waldemar B (funl plans, N 29,35:4), 1956, N 28,35:2
Kaesche, Max B Jr, 1948, O 3,67:4
Kaess, Israel, 1956, O 29,29:6
Kaessig, Emill, 1905, Ap 5,9:6
Kaestle, George J, 1943, Jl 29,19:4
Kaestner, Christian, 1951, Mr 27,29:5
Kaeyer, Erik, 1948, Jl 4,26:8
Kafandaris, George, 1946, Ag 29,27:2
Kafer, J Dana, 1937, Mr 23,23:3
Kafer, John C, 1906, Ap 1,11:4
Kafer, Lester S, 1948, D 23,19:2
Kaffenberg, Walter, 1948, My 25,27:6
Kaffenburgh, Albert W Mrs, 1955, Ag 18,23:2
Kafka, Benjamin H, 1944, F 14,17:5
Kafka, Otto, 1939, Mr 25,15:4
Kafka, Samuel, 1948, S 21,27:3
Kaftal, Wladyslaw, 1960, N 29,37:4
Kagami, Kenkichi, 1939, My 28,III,7:1
Kagan, Abraham S, 1963, O 28,27:4
Kagan, Benjamin, 1950, O 21,17:5
Kagan, Irving, 1958, My 19,25:1
Kagan, Leo B, 1957, Ap 23,31:1
Kagan, Michael G, 1967, N 9,61:6
Kagan, Morris, 1950, F 8,27:3
Kagan, Samuel, 1967, Jl 6,29:3
Kagan, Sergius, 1964, Mr 2,27:4
Kagan, Solomon R, 1955, Ag 1,19:3
Kagawa, Toyohiko, 1960, Ap 24,88:6
Kage, Wilhelm, 1960, N 30,37:4
Kagel, Lewis A Mrs (E Todd), 1965, D 27,25:2
Kagel, Maurice E, 1951, N 21,25:2
Kagey, Charles L, 1941, O 14,23:5
Kagey, Rudolf (por), 1946, My 14,21:3
Kahal, Irving, 1942, F 8,49:2
Kahan, Leon, 1968, Ja 30,38:3
Kahan, Mack Mrs, 1965, S 9,42:8
Kahan, Sol B, 1961, N 14,39:3
Kahan, Yaakov, 1960, N 21,29:4
Kahana, Uriel, 1965, S 11,27:3
Kahanamoku, Duke Paoa (funl, Ja 29,31:1), 1968, Ja 23,43:3
Kahane, Benjamin B, 1960, S 19,31:1
Kahane, Jack, 1939, S 8,23:4
Kahane, L I, 1950, O 15,104:4
Kahanec, John, 1952, N 29,17:2
Kahaner, Maxwell J, 1954, S 8,31:4
Kahelewai, Carl, 1938, O 10,8:6
Kahgee, Amos, 1954, N 26,29:2
Kahili, William, 1963, Ag 27,31:2
Kahl, Charles, 1941, F 6,21:5
Kahl, Fritz, 1944, D 25,19:5
Kahl, Henry L, 1949, F 1,25:2
Kahl, William E, 1954, My 25,27:1
Kahle, F J, 1942, Jl 15,19:3
Kahle, Marcell, 1909, D 19,11:5
Kahlenberg, Louis A, 1941, Mr 20,22:2
Kahler, Albert C, 1943, O 23,13:5
Kahler, Basil A, 1948, S 8,29:2
Kahler, Elmer I, 1948, O 29,26:2
Kahler, Fred T, 1950, Ap 13,29:2
Kahler, Harry A, 1959, Je 8,27:3
Kahler, Hugh M Mrs, 1962, Ap 14,25:3
Kahler, John L, 1949, F 27,69:2
Kahler, Susan E, 1949, D 24,15:5
Kahlke, Charles E, 1958, O 12,83:4
Kahlo, Frida (Mrs D Rivera), 1954, Jl 14,27:4
Kahlo, George D Dr, 1916, F 13,15:5
Kahmann, Ruth, 1943, Je 14,17:5
Kahn, Aaron, 1911, D 26,9:5
Kahn, Adolph E, 1925, Jl 8,17:4
Kahn, Albert (por), 1942, D 9,27:1
Kahn, Albert D, 1960, S 28,39:4
Kahn, Albert H, 1948, My 20,29:2
Kahn, Alex, 1962, Mr 12,31:3
Kahn, Alex L, 1940, My 28,23:2
Kahn, Alex Mrs, 1962, O 30,35:2
Kahn, Alexandre, 1943, Je 20,35:1
Kahn, Alfred H, 1955, Ag 18,23:5
Kahn, Arthur, 1959, Je 25,29:5; 1963, My 29,33:2
Kahn, Arthur H, 1961, Mr 11,21:6
Kahn, August, 1952, Jl 29,21:2
Kahn, Benjamin, 1905, Ap 28,6:1
Kahn, Benjamin M Mrs, 1968, My 6,47:2
Kahn, Bennett J, 1951, S 16,85:1
Kahn, Bernard, 1955, Ap 27,31:2
Kahn, Charles M, 1944, Ag 11,15:5
Kahn, Charles Mrs, 1962, N 10,25:4
Kahn, David, 1916, Ag 12,9:8; 1958, My 18,86:6
Kahn, David E, 1968, D 9,47:1
Kahn, David Mrs, 1957, My 22,33:1
Kahn, David W, 1966, Mr 29,41:2
Kahn, David W Mrs, 1962, S 14,31:5
Kahn, Dorothy C, 1955, Ag 27,15:6
Kahn, Edmund F, 1949, D 25,26:4
Kahn, Edward, 1959, F 23,23:1
Kahn, Edward H Mrs, 1964, S 3,29:1
Kahn, Elliott M, 1961, Je 17,21:5
Kahn, Ely J Mrs, 1962, Ag 23,29:4
Kahn, Emanuel G, 1953, F 12,27:2
Kahn, Erich I (trb lr, Mr 18,II,9:2), 1956, Mr 6,31:2
Kahn, Ernest L, 1963, O 20,88:6
Kahn, Eugene H, 1959, D 2,43:4
Kahn, Eugene W, 1943, N 2,25:4
Kahn, Felix, 1924, S 12,21:5
Kahn, Felix E, 1950, Jl 27,25:3
Kahn, George A, 1958, Ap 19,21:2
Kahn, Gordon J, 1953, O 17,15:2
Kahn, Gus, 1941, O 9,23:4
Kahn, Harry, 1957, My 26,92:4
Kahn, Harry B, 1952, Ag 19,23:1
Kahn, Harry C, 1940, N 2,15:1
Kahn, Henry, 1945, Je 8,19:3
Kahn, Henry K, 1966, My 3,47:2
Kahn, Henry L, 1955, S 10,17:5
Kahn, Henry R, 1942, Mr 3,23:2
Kahn, Henry S, 1948, Jl 4,26:7
Kahn, Herbert J, 1958, F 13,29:2
Kahn, Herman, 1937, Ag 24,21:1; 1941, S 27,17:6; 1946, Ag 24,11:6
Kahn, Herman M, 1953, Ap 25,15:3
Kahn, Howard, 1951, Mr 30,23:4
Kahn, Isadore, 1937, S 20,23:5
Kahn, Isidor N, 1955, Ag 13,13:6
Kahn, Ivan, 1951, Ap 6,25:1
Kahn, J Herman, 1954, O 3,86:8
Kahn, Jack, 1948, N 11,27:5
Kahn, Jack B, 1943, S 25,15:5
Kahn, Jack Mrs, 1948, N 4,23:4
Kahn, Jacob S, 1945, Mr 28,23:1
Kahn, James M Mrs, 1939, O 12,25:4
Kahn, Jerome J Mrs, 1946, D 19,41:2
Kahn, Jonas Mrs, 1940, Mr 6,23:4
Kahn, Joseph (por), 1940, Jl 29,13:4
Kahn, Joseph H, 1946, Mr 26,29:1
Kahn, Joss, 1951, D 29,11:3
Kahn, Julian Mrs, 1960, D 1,35:1
Kahn, Julius, 1924, D 22,17:3; 1942, N 6,23:6
Kahn, Julius Mrs (por), 1948, N 17,27:5
Kahn, Julius Mrs, 1963, My 8,36:5
Kahn, L Stanley, 1964, Ag 11,33:4
Kahn, Lazard Mrs, 1954, F 2,27:1
Kahn, Leo, 1905, My 3,11:2
Kahn, Leo A, 1939, F 20,17:2
Kahn, Leo M, 1960, Mr 30,37:2
Kahn, Leon S, 1948, S 16,29:1
Kahn, Leopold (Adm Dot), 1918, O 26,11:5
Kahn, Lester M, 1951, Je 1,23:3
Kahn, Lionel J, 1939, N 1,23:4
Kahn, Louis, 1925, F 15,7:2; 1962, Ag 21,33:4; 1967, Ja 29,76:5
Kahn, Louis E, 1958, S 28,88:3
Kahn, Louis J, 1947, Ag 21,23:4; 1958, Ap 9,36:2
Kahn, Louis L, 1965, F 17,43:3
Kahn, Louis W, 1948, Mr 25,27:3
Kahn, Lucian L, 1947, Ag 7,21:2
Kahn, M D Dr, 1926, Ap 10,17:3
Kahn, M Randolph, 1945, Ja 12,15:5
Kahn, Mack, 1960, My 1,87:1
Kahn, Manuel, 1959, O 3,19:6
Kahn, Maurice, 1950, S 14,31:3
Kahn, Maurice L, 1940, Je 27,23:5
Kahn, Max (por), 1947, D 28,40:3
Kahn, Max, 1952, Je 4,27:1
Kahn, Max Dr, 1937, S 24,21:4
Kahn, Max Mrs, 1945, My 16,19:1
Kahn, Maximillian, 1922, N 1,19:5
Kahn, Melville L, 1964, Ja 6,47:3
Kahn, Milton, 1956, S 8,17:4
Kahn, Montifiore G, 1958, F 11,31:3
Kahn, Moritz (por), 1939, Ja 17,21:5
Kahn, Morris, 1937, S 11,17:6; 1943, N 11,23:4; 195 Ag 15,29:4
Kahn, Morton C, 1959, Je 1,27:3
Kahn, Moses W, 1957, Mr 29,21:1
Kahn, Nathan, 1953, Ag 28,17:2
Kahn, Noah A, 1957, Je 21,25:4
Kahn, Norman, 1953, Ag 21,17:4
Kahn, O H, 1934, Mr 30,1:3
Kahn, Oscar I, 1952, My 31,17:1
Kahn, Otto C, 1964, O 14,45:1
Kahn, Otto C Mrs, 1965, D 8,47:4
Kahn, Otto H, 1924, S 13,13:2
Kahn, Otto H Mrs, 1949, My 16,21:1
Kahn, Robert, 1952, Mr 28,23:3
Kahn, Robert J, 1962, Ag 29,29:4
Kahn, Roger W, 1962, Jl 13,23:2
Kahn, Ruth Mrs, 1952, F 16,13:6
Kahn, Sam L, 1958, Jl 8,27:2
Kahn, Samuel, 1921, Ja 21,15:6; 1953, S 11,21:4; 19 Ag 31,32:3; 1958, Mr 15,17:6
Kahn, Seymour L, 1966, Je 24,37:2
Kahn, Sidney H, 1943, D 31,16:8
Kahn, Silas F, 1914, Mr 10,9:4
Kahn, Sol, 1947, Mr 14,23:2
Kahn, Sydney, 1916, Ag 19,9:4
Kahn, Victor, 1941, N 15,17:3
Kahn, William, 1939, F 6,13:4
Kahn, William B, 1963, D 21,23:1
Kahn, William M, 1943, D 8,23:2
Kahnt, Ferdinand C, 1958, Ag 23,15:6
Kahnweiler, Louis, 1915, My 28,13:5
Kahr, Arthur, 1963, My 5,86:5
Kahr, David Y, 1951, Ja 29,19:2
Kahrmann, Elizabeth L Mrs, 1951, N 4,86:4
Kahrs, Anna B Mrs, 1942, F 2,15:3
Kahrs, Joseph, 1948, Mr 29,21:5
Kaib, Daniel J, 1947, N 5,27:6
Kaicher, Francis A, 1954, D 5,88:3
Kaid Mahaou Said, 1924, Mr 21,19:4
Kaidanovsky, Samuel P, 1964, D 6,88:3
Kaiden, Maxwell H, 1952, Ap 10,29:4
Kaier, Richard, 1939, Ja 12,19:3
Kaighin, Alfred H, 1965, Ap 7,43:4
Kaighn, Charles B, 1949, My 15,90:4
Kail, Louis, 1956, Je 16,19:2
Kaila, Erkki, 1944, D 10,54:3
Kailes, Louis, 1959, My 1,29:1
Kaimer, Julius C, 1949, F 4,23:3
Kain, Florence M, 1962, Ag 3,23:4
Kain, Richard B, 1948, F 16,21:5
Kain, Thomas J, 1938, My 29,II,7:2
Kain, William P, 1962, N 2,31:3
Kaine, Joseph M, 1960, D 18,85:1
Kaine, Patrick F, 1946, F 9,13:2
Kains, Archibald C, 1944, D 27,19:5
Kains, Maurice G, 1946, F 26,25:5

Kains, Sherwood, 1957, D 29,49:1
Kainz, Josef, 1910, S 21,9:4
Kairer, Howard F Sr, 1948, O 5,25:5
Kairys, Stepanos, 1964, D 17,41:1
Kaiser, Albert D, 1955, N 2,35:4
Kaiser, Albert H, 1939, S 21,23:4
Kaiser, Alois Rev Dr, 1908, Ja 6,7:4
Kaiser, Arthur R, 1961, O 9,35:4
Kaiser, Ben, 1943, O 23,13:2
Kaiser, C Hillis, 1961, Ag 10,27:2
Kaiser, Charles, 1945, Mr 13,23:5; 1955, F 28,19:1
Kaiser, Charles A, 1953, Ap 10,21:2
Kaiser, Charles E, 1955, Ja 5,23:4
Kaiser, Chris, 1951, S 24,27:3
Kaiser, Dorothy E, 1943, Je 27,32:7
Kaiser, Emanuel M, 1942, Jl 3,17:6
Kaiser, Frank B, 1950, N 4,17:6
Kaiser, Fred G, 1953, N 28,15:6
Kaiser, Frederick W Sr, 1954, Jl 14,27:2
Kaiser, George, 1945, Je 6,21:3
Kaiser, H M, 1931, Mr 24,27:1
Kaiser, Harry, 1955, D 26,19:3
Kaiser, Henry B Mrs, 1958, Jl 18,21:4
Kaiser, Henry J (mem ser set; funl plans, Ag 26,27:4), 1967, Ag 25,1:3
Kaiser, Henry J Jr (est appr, Je 28,11:5), 1961, My 3,37:2
Kaiser, Henry J Mrs, 1951, Mr 16,31:5
Kaiser, J William, 1956, O 12,29:5
Kaiser, Jakob, 1961, My 8,35:1
Kaiser, Jakob Mrs, 1952, Ag 19,23:1
Kaiser, Jerome A, 1968, Ja 15,47:2
Kaiser, John B, 1961, D 14,43:1
Kaiser, John C, 1944, Je 11,45:2
Kaiser, John H, 1939, My 19,21:2
Kaiser, Joseph, 1942, N 1,52:4; 1948, O 17,76:2
Kaiser, Katherine M, 1949, F 1,25:1
Kaiser, Leon S, 1951, Ap 8,92:3
Kaiser, Lewis, 1946, Ja 15,23:5
Kaiser, Louis, 1937, Jl 16,19:2
Kaiser, Louis A Mrs, 1950, My 1,25:4
Kaiser, Louis H Mrs, 1954, O 20,29:2
Kaiser, Morris B, 1954, My 12,31:4
Kaiser, Newton, 1946, Mr 26,29:5
Kaiser, Nicholas J, 1941, Ap 5,17:3
Kaiser, Paul C, 1951, Je 5,31:2
Kaiser, Richard W, 1963, O 21,31:1
Kaiser, Robert M, 1943, Ja 20,19:1
Kaiser, William A, 1954, Je 2,31:4
Kaiser, William E, 1953, My 22,27:2
Kaiser, William F, 1950, My 5,22:2
Kaiser, William J Capt, 1913, F 4,11:5
Kaiser, William L, 1948, Mr 30,24:3
Kaiser Shumshere Jang Bahadur Rana, 1964, Je 8,29:4
Kaishian, Stepan, 1957, S 2,13:5
Kaisrova, Marie Mrs, 1954, Ja 24,84:3
Kaitz, Isidor, 1962, S 17,31:1
Kaiulani, Hawaiian Princess, 1899, Mr 18,9:1
Kaiv, Johannes, 1965, N 22,37:4
Kajanus, R, 1933, Jl 7,17:1
Kajee, Abdolla I, 1948, Ja 6,23:2
Kajiwara, Kaye, 1952, Mr 19,41:2
Kajiwara, Kaye Mrs, 1952, Mr 19,41:2
Kajiwara, Takuma, 1960, Mr 12,21:4
Kakela, Wayne, 1955, F 10,31:3
Kakeles, Seligman, 1903, N 30,7:5
Kakels, Moses S Dr, 1924, Ja 1,23:2
Kakerbeck, John, 1960, Je 11,21:6
Kakowski, Alex, 1938, D 31,15:6
Kalaidjian, Mihran T, 1955, S 19,25:4
Kalakaua, King of Hawaii Islands, 1891, Ja 21,5:3
Kalan, John M, 1950, O 18,33:5
Kalanianaole, E Princess, 1932, F 20,15:3
Kalanianaole, J Kuhio Prince, 1922, Ja 8,22:3
Kalas, Franklin T, 1964, Je 26,29:3
Kalash, Louis Sr, 1948, My 28,23:4
Kalashen, Mark J, 1939, Ag 24,19:2
Kalashnikoff, Nicholas, 1961, Ag 18,21:4
Kalatte, Michael E Mrs, 1953, Mr 26,31:4
Kalb, Frank H, 1944, F 14,17:6
Kalb, George D, 1943, My 6,19:2
Kalb, John, 1957, Mr 29,21:4
Kalb, John H, 1941, Je 23,17:4
Kalb, John J, 1937, O 2,21:5
Kalb, Mary R Sister, 1952, Ap 30,27:2
Kalb, Maxwell, 1962, O 8,23:4
Kalb, Robert M, 1968, D 17,50:5
Kalbach, Andrew E, 1920, F 3,15:2
Kalbach, Stanley W, 1955, Mr 28,27:1
Kalbacher, Paul, 1944, Mr 1,19:1
Kalbfeld, Philip, 1967, O 29,85:2
Kalbfleisch, E L, 1905, F 7,9:5
Kalbfleisch, Ella W Mrs, 1940, Ag 7,19:6
Kalbfleisch, George, 1966, N 19,33:3
Kalbfleisch, Martin, 1873, F 13,1:3
Kalbfleisch, Theodore F, 1944, O 24,23:2
Kalbflelach, Frederick W, 1906, Je 30,7:6
Kalbfus, Edward C, 1954, S 7,25:1
Kalbfus, Joseph Mrs, 1939, Mr 6,15:3
Kalbfus, Joseph P C, 1944, O 24,23:5
Kalblein, Peter, 1951, N 6,29:2
Kaldenberg, Frederick E, 1923, O 11,21:3
Kaldor, Alex, 1965, Ag 12,27:2

Kale, John (funl, Ag 26,5:4), 1960, Ag 22,5:8
Kaleb, William T, 1959, Ap 29,33:1
Kalec, Joe, 1950, My 15,21:2
Kalef, M, 1946, N 23,15:3
Kalenderian, Vahan, 1950, O 6,27:4
Kaler, James Otis, 1912, D 12,13:3
Kales, F H, 1883, N 10,5:2
Kales, John D, 1941, Mr 2,42:5
Kales, Max, 1958, My 6,35:1
Kales, William R, 1942, D 5,15:2
Kaletsky, Theodore, 1952, My 22,27:3
Kaletzsky, Julius Rev, 1915, Jl 4,11:5
Kaley, Harry W, 1954, Mr 2,25:2
Kalfayan, Puzant H, 1959, My 28,31:4
Kalff, Jan, 1944, Je 2,15:3
Kalfides, Basil, 1962, Mr 28,39:3
Kalich, Bertha Mrs, 1939, Ap 19,23:1
Kalichevsky, Anatole, 1937, Ap 4,II,11:3
Kalik, Max (will, D 31,20:6), 1939, N 30,21:6
Kalika, Phil, 1954, Ap 30,23:3
Kalikow, Joseph, 1955, F 9,27:1
Kalilima, Daniel, 1952, Ag 15,15:4
Kalin, Jerome, 1952, D 25,29:6
Kalinoski, Edward, 1965, Je 3,35:2
Kalinowski, Alex, 1951, Je 21,27:5
Kalisch, Burnham, 1942, Jl 20,13:5
Kalisch, Leonard, 1924, Ap 15,21:2
Kalisch, S, 1930, Ap 30,25:3
Kalisch, Samuel Jr, 1958, O 27,27:3
Kalischer, Alex S, 1955, Jl 15,21:5
Kalish, Abraham L, 1949, D 24,15:2
Kalish, Al (Al Kelly),(funl plans, S 8,47:3), 1966, S 7,47:3
Kalish, Ben, 1956, Ag 8,25:2
Kalish, Charles A, 1921, S 17,13:6
Kalish, Edwin L, 1921, Mr 22,17:4
Kalish, Irving, 1961, Je 12,29:3
Kalish, Jacob, 1952, D 7,89:2
Kalish, Julius Mrs, 1945, Ja 23,19:2
Kalish, Louis, 1966, Mr 5,27:6
Kalish, Max (por), 1945, Mr 19,19:3
Kalish, Richard Dr, 1921, Je 22,15:4
Kalish, Samuel, 1968, Jl 17,43:4
Kalish, Samuel I, 1957, Je 8,19:6
Kalisher, Joseph Dr, 1915, Ja 28,9:4
Kaliska, William G, 1945, O 31,23:4
Kaliski, Arthur, 1946, N 21,31:5
Kaliski, David J, 1966, Ag 22,33:3
Kalitz, William C, 1941, My 23,21:3
Kaliz, Armand, 1941, F 4,22:3
Kalk, Flora S Mrs, 1953, Jl 19,56:4
Kalker, William, 1966, Ag 20,25:5
Kalkhof, Oscar W, 1938, O 11,25:3
Kalkhoff, G Frederick, 1944, Ag 17,17:6
Kalkhurst, Eric, 1957, O 14,27:2
Kalkstein, Morris, 1968, S 5,57:6
Kall, Charles E, 1948, Je 22,25:2
Kall, Mary Mrs, 1937, D 14,25:4
Kalla, Alex Sr, 1957, Ag 31,15:5
Kallay, Benjamin, 1903, Jl 14,7:6
Kallay, Nicholas de, 1967, Ja 15,84:7
Kallberg, Hugo, 1949, F 2,27:1
Kallberg, Jennie Mrs, 1963, D 19,33:4
Kalle, Edward A, 1938, Ag 25,3:8
Kallem, Morris J, 1953, Mr 15,93:2
Kallen, Samuel, 1955, Ja 14,21:2
Kallenberg, Herman, 1941, Mr 26,23:1
Kallich, Isaac, 1962, Je 25,29:1
Kallies, Harry, 1939, Mr 26,III,6:6
Kalligan, Henry F, 1946, Ap 25,21:4
Kalligan, Thomas J Mrs, 1955, Je 1,33:4
Kallio, Kyosti, 1940, D 20,5:1
Kallish, Louis, 1968, N 1,47:3
Kallman, Alvan E, 1964, S 4,29:2
Kallman, E F, 1946, N 9,17:6
Kallman, Frances S Mrs, 1965, D 15,47:1
Kallman, Julius, 1947, D 8,25:3
Kallman, Karl, 1945, O 24,21:2
Kallman, Saul, 1943, Je 3,21:4
Kallman, William L, 1966, Je 22,47:1
Kallman Donald, 1958, Mr 8,17:6
Kallmann, Franz J, 1965, Mr 13,37:1
Kallmeyer, Leroy J, 1966, Jl 19,39:3
Kallock, Herbert F, 1951, Ap 3,27:4
Kallock, Ralph N, 1950, N 3,28:4
Kallop, Harry G, 1962, Ag 3,23:2
Kallwitz, Oscar Prof, 1913, O 2,11:4
Kalman, A L, 1925, Ja 26,17:4
Kalman, Arthur A (cor, Ap 21,88:8), 1957, Ap 17, 31:2
Kalman, Emmerich, 1953, O 31,17:1
Kalman, Nicholas L, 1944, Jl 27,17:2
Kalmanoff, Joseph, 1968, N 6,39:1
Kalmanowitz, Abraham I, 1964, F 17,31:4
Kalmanson, Alex Mrs, 1959, My 9,21:6
Kalmar, Bert, 1947, S 19,23:4
Kalmbach, Frederick W Sr, 1953, Ag 1,11:6
Kalmine, Harry M, 1964, Jl 19,65:2
Kalmuk, Paul, 1963, O 31,33:3
Kalmus, Herbert T, 1963, Jl 12,25:1
Kalmus, Herbert T Mrs, 1965, N 18,47:4
Kalmus, Nathaniel I, 1965, My 19,47:2
Kalmus, Nathaniel I Mrs, 1964, My 31,76:7

Kalmykow, Andrew D, 1941, Ja 31,19:4
Kalnitsky, Chya Mrs, 1944, Ap 4,21:4
Kalnoky, G S Count, 1898, F 14,7:2
Kalocsay, Geza, 1961, Ja 24,29:4
Kalocy, James, 1949, Je 21,25:4
Kalodner, David, 1948, F 25,23:2
Kalodner, Edwin J, 1964, Je 9,35:2
Kalogeropoulos, N, 1927, Ja 9,II,13:1
Kalomiris, Manolis, 1962, Ap 4,43:5
Kalonyme, Louis K, 1961, Je 9,33:4
Kalser, Erwin, 1958, Mr 28,25:3
Kalsom, Princess, 1964, Je 21,14:2
Kalsow, Hugo, 1942, Ja 3,19:5
Kalstrand, Leo W, 1949, Ja 7,22:2
Kalt, Hyman, 1961, S 29,35:5
Kalt, Joseph Mrs, 1946, N 19,31:2
Kalt, Pryor H, 1962, Ap 23,29:4
Kalt, William J, 1968, Ap 30,47:3
Kaltchas, Nicholas S, 1937, O 27,31:4
Kaltenbach, Ernst, 1907, F 11,9:5
Kaltenbach, Henry J, 1940, N 13,23:6
Kaltenbach, Henry J Mrs, 1944, N 24,23:1
Kaltenbacher, Joseph, 1949, Ja 7,21:1
Kaltenback, Katherine, 1951, Ap 25,29:2
Kaltenborn, Franz, 1946, Ag 28,27:2
Kaltenborn, H V (Hans von Kaltenborn),(funl, Je 19,29:5), 1965, Je 15,1:7
Kalter, Max, 1942, My 19,20:2
Kalteux, Frank M, 1959, Jl 12,72:6
Kalteyer, Frederick J, 1938, D 22,22:1
Kaltman, Louis, 1964, Ap 6,31:2
Kalvin, Henry M, 1959, O 5,31:4
Kamaiky, Leon Mrs, 1954, O 23,15:6
Kamamura, Count, 1904, Ag 16,7:6
Kamber, Morris, 1937, S 9,23:4
Kamber, Robert, 1920, Ja 18,22:4
Kambestad, Howard F, 1958, Ag 31,56:8
Kamelman, Louis Mrs (por), 1948, Mr 2,23:5
Kamen, A J, 1953, My 8,25:5
Kamen, George, 1955, D 31,13:5
Kamen, George Mrs (K Pfeffer), 1966, Ja 9,56:4
Kamen, Kate, 1949, O 29,1:8
Kamen, Kay, 1949, O 29,1:8
Kamen, Nathan, 1958, Ja 27,27:2
Kameneff, L B, 1936, Ag 25,3:5
Kamenetzky, Heiman M Rabbi, 1915, Je 2,13:6
Kamenetzky, Max, 1952, Je 4,27:2
Kamenoff, Ralph J, 1953, Jl 23,23:5
Kamens, Irvine J, 1955, D 16,29:1
Kamens, William, 1946, Ja 21,23:3
Kamensky, Joseph S, 1954, N 23,35:4
Kameny, Emil, 1958, Je 27,25:4
Kamera, Ivan P, 1952, Ja 24,27:4
Kamerdze, William E Mrs, 1951, Ag 24,15:2
Kamerick, Herbert E, 1949, O 30,84:3
Kamholz, Frederick P Mrs, 1958, S 2,25:4
Kamiat, Arnold H, 1962, My 6,88:4
Kamichoff, Stefan, 1952, Jl 8,27:4
Kamil, Sol J, 1951, Mr 14,33:5
Kamimura, HiKonojo Vice-Adm, 1916, Ag 8,9:5
Kamin, Max J, 1958, My 24,21:4
Kamin, Sally Katz (Mrs Martin Kamin), 1968, N 23, 47:4
Kamine, Benjamin R, 1958, S 19,28:1
Kaminester, Irving, 1950, N 23,35:3
Kaminow, Nathan I, 1961, Ja 8,86:5
Kaminski, John, 1963, Jl 28,65:2
Kaminski, Szymon, 1950, Jl 7,19:4
Kaminsky, Alexander H, 1937, S 27,21:3
Kaminsky, Isaac, 1946, Je 17,21:2
Kaminsky, Jacob, 1963, Je 16,84:2
Kaminsky, Max, 1960, Ja 21,31:2
Kaminsky, Paul, 1955, S 4,56:3
Kaminsky, Paul M, 1947, My 31,13:4
Kamioner, L, 1932, My 5,19:1
Kamischnikoff, Leo, 1961, D 3,88:6
Kamiyama, Sojin, 1954, Jl 30,17:6
Kamke, Charles E, 1938, S 28,25:5
Kamkov, Fyodor, 1951, Jl 20,21:1
Kamm, Emanuel L, 1962, F 28,33:3
Kamm, Isaac, 1941, My 20,23:4
Kamm, Louis, 1950, My 5,21:3
Kamm, Milton T, 1948, N 21,88:2
Kamm, Minnie W, 1954, N 8,21:2
Kamm, Rose Mrs, 1956, S 17,27:3
Kammann, Henry F, 1949, My 2,25:4
Kammari, Mikhail D, 1965, S 25,6:1
Kammer, Charles, 1954, D 13,27:3
Kammer, Herbert A, 1966, Mr 4,33:4
Kammer, Hugo, 1950, My 28,44:7
Kammer, Hugo Mrs, 1951, N 2,24:4
Kammer, Joseph, 1951, Ja 2,23:3
Kammerer, F, 1928, S 28,27:3
Kammerer, F Stanley, 1968, Jl 12,31:4
Kammerer, Frederick W, 1953, Ja 13,27:4
Kammerer, Paul T Jr, 1939, Mr 3,23:5
Kammerer, Percy G, 1946, N 15,23:2
Kammerer, Robert J, 1913, S 6,7:3
Kammerer, Titus, 1951, Je 9,19:5
Kammerer, Walter G, 1938, Je 19,29:1
Kammerer, William F Mrs, 1939, Ag 1,19:5
Kammler, Edward A Sr, 1954, O 3,86:8
Kamp, Alphonse (Ike), 1955, F 27,87:3

Kamp, George S, 1948, Ap 7,25:5
Kamp, Henry, 1963, My 1,39:3
Kamp, Henry C, 1950, Ja 14,15:6
Kamp, Joseph, 1944, Je 20,19:6
Kamper, Louis, 1953, F 25,27:5
Kampf, Frederick H, 1941, S 13,17:5
Kampf, Herbert Mrs, 1966, Ap 7,39:3
Kampf, Robert T, 1950, Ag 10,25:3
Kamplin, Reinhart J, 1942, Ag 12,19:1
Kampner, Adolph, 1939, Ja 5,23:4
Kamrass, Phil, 1951, S 9,90:1
Kamski, Katherine B Mrs, 1951, D 7,27:2
Kan, Edward B, 1959, S 13,84:2
Kan, H A M J van, 1944, Jl 13,17:5
Kan, Johannes B, 1947, My 10,13:4
Kan, Louis S, 1961, S 21,35:3
Kan, Robert (cor, D 27,37:2), 1967, D 26,33:1
Kan, Samuel R, 1962, My 31,27:2
Kan Set-hing, 1925, My 29,17:6
Kana, Jan, 1958, Mr 16,86:7
Kanaday, Johnson Mrs, 1954, Ag 10,19:5
Kanaly, Thomas J, 1953, F 16,21:2
Kananack, Wolff Mrs, 1958, Ja 15,39:3
Kanane, John T, 1951, Ag 23,23:3
Kanane, John T Mrs, 1954, S 23,33:2
Kanarek, Adam Mrs (P Moore), 1964, Je 8,59:5
Kanarek, David S, 1953, F 26,25:3
Kanayan, Dro, 1956, Mr 10,17:5
Kandel, Abraham I, 1941, N 22,19:5
Kandel, Charles, 1958, Ap 22,33:4
Kandel, Charles Mrs, 1962, N 27,37:3
Kandel, I L (Isaac L), 1965, Je 15,41:1
Kandel, Isaac L Mrs, 1949, Ag 6,17:3
Kandel, Morris J, 1957, Ja 13,84:7
Kandel, Otto A, 1956, Mr 6,31:2
Kander, Lizzie B Mrs, 1940, Jl 26,17:6
Kandinsky, Wassily (por), 1944, D 19,21:4
Kandl, Leopold, 1951, N 22,31:3
Kandler, Paul A, 1954, My 5,31:3
Kane, A C Mrs, 1926, Jl 25,II,7:1
Kane, Abraham, 1943, S 28,25:2
Kane, Albert J, 1943, D 13,23:5
Kane, Alice M, 1950, Je 10,17:2
Kane, Andrew J, 1949, D 23,21:2
Kane, Annie E, 1942, Ap 6,15:3
Kane, Arthur J, 1939, Ag 29,21:3
Kane, Arthur J Jr, 1958, Je 6,23:1
Kane, Arthur M, 1938, Je 6,17:3
Kane, Arthur R, 1940, F 23,15:2
Kane, Arthur S Jr, 1955, F 23,27:2
Kane, Benjamin N, 1965, Mr 12,33:1
Kane, Bernard Sr, 1950, Ag 19,13:5
Kane, Carl J, 1940, F 22,23:2
Kane, Charles F, 1940, F 8,23:5
Kane, Charles V, 1945, Ag 14,21:2
Kane, Clarence B, 1964, N 15,86:8
Kane, Colin A, 1939, Mr 19,III,7:2
Kane, Cornelius J, 1905, Je 10,2:5; 1947, My 18,60:8
Kane, Daniel J, 1937, Je 17,23:3
Kane, David, 1951, O 26,24:3
Kane, De Lancey Astor Col, 1915, Ap 5,11:5
Kane, DeLancey I, 1940, Ag 1,21:4
Kane, Dominic, 1949, D 26,29:5
Kane, E O, 1932, Ap 2,23:3
Kane, Edward, 1942, Ja 12,15:4
Kane, Edward A, 1964, Mr 14,23:5
Kane, Edward J, 1951, F 23,27:1; 1964, D 3,45:5
Kane, Edward J Mrs, 1947, F 23,53:4
Kane, Edward M, 1951, Jl 20,21:2
Kane, Edward Mrs, 1952, My 17,19:6
Kane, Edward Sr Mrs, 1949, Je 21,25:2
Kane, Eleanora A I Mrs, 1938, O 23,40:5
Kane, Elizabeth E Mrs, 1953, Ag 6,21:4
Kane, Florence B, 1943, My 16,43:2
Kane, Frances, 1909, Jl 19,7:4
Kane, Francis F, 1955, My 28,15:1
Kane, Frank, 1955, Jl 30,17:4; 1968, D 1,86:4
Kane, Frank G, 1943, Ap 8,23:3
Kane, Frank Sr, 1937, F 3,23:5
Kane, Frederick L (cor, Mr 15,25:4), 1954, Mr 14, 88:1
Kane, G P, 1878, Je 24,1:4
Kane, George F, 1952, F 9,13:1; 1954, S 17,27:2
Kane, George M, 1950, O 15,104:2
Kane, Grenville, 1943, Jl 18,35:3
Kane, Grenville Mrs, 1940, O 5,15:5
Kane, H V Sr, 1948, Jl 27,25:3
Kane, Harold M, 1947, S 17,25:3
Kane, Harry, 1949, N 18,29:4; 1958, Mr 13,29:2
Kane, Harry C Mrs, 1957, My 13,31:5
Kane, Harry F, 1947, S 4,25:4
Kane, Harry J, 1940, Mr 25,16:2
Kane, Harry P, 1954, My 4,29:2
Kane, Helen (Mrs D Healy), 1966, S 27,47:3
Kane, Helen A, 1955, Ag 18,23:5
Kane, Henry Coey Sir, 1917, F 1,11:4
Kane, Henry H Dr, 1906, Jl 1,9:5
Kane, Herbert W, 1947, Jl 20,44:1
Kane, Howard F, 1946, Jl 25,21:3
Kane, I Howell, 1941, O 20,17:2
Kane, J, 1926, D 9,27:1
Kane, J G, 1877, Jl 6,5:2
Kane, Jack, 1961, Mr 28,35:4
Kane, James, 1945, Ap 19,27:2
Kane, James J, 1944, Ag 11,15:4; 1945, F 23,17:2; 1947, O 3,26:3; 1956, Jl 10,31:2
Kane, James Johnson Adm, 1921, Mr 11,15:5
Kane, James M, 1949, S 28,27:5
Kane, James W, 1968, Ap 21,80:8
Kane, Jasper T, 1960, Ap 22,31:2
Kane, John, 1947, My 14,25:1; 1958, Ja 29,27:1
Kane, John A, 1950, Ap 20,29:5; 1954, Ja 7,31:1
Kane, John B, 1943, Ag 16,15:2
Kane, John F, 1939, Mr 31,21:2; 1943, Je 26,13:2; 1951, S 18,31:4; 1954, Jl 15,27:3; 1959, Ap 30,31:1; 1965, Je 15,41:2
Kane, John H, 1960, N 30,37:1
Kane, John I Mrs, 1938, Je 2,23:5
Kane, John J, 1946, N 10,63:4; 1948, Jl 16,19:5; 1948, S 15,31:2; 1959, Ap 17,25:2; 1961, Mr 6,25:3; 1966, My 29,56:8
Kane, John J Mrs, 1948, D 12,93:1
Kane, John K, 1937, N 16,23:3
Kane, John M, 1947, D 1,21:4
Kane, John N, 1951, S 11,29:1
Kane, John P, 1907, Jl 10,7:5; 1944, Je 16,19:4; 1949, Ja 15,17:6
Kane, Joseph, 1957, Mr 10,88:5
Kane, Joseph M, 1937, Je 10,23:4; 1950, N 26,90:6
Kane, Katherine T, 1947, Ap 12,17:4
Kane, L L, 1927, Je 2,25:3
Kane, L S, 1884, D 25,5:2
Kane, Leo A, 1961, Ja 20,29:2
Kane, Margaret T, 1940, Ap 14,44:8
Kane, Martin T, 1944, Jl 20,19:2
Kane, Mary (Mother Mary Benita), 1953, O 4,87:1
Kane, Maurice R, 1965, N 29,35:5
Kane, Melvin T, 1959, Ja 24,19:4
Kane, Michael, 1949, Ap 8,25:4
Kane, Michael F, 1908, Ag 4,7:5
Kane, Michael J, 1955, Ag 4,25:4
Kane, Michael James Mrs, 1947, F 27,21:2
Kane, Michael M, 1948, D 3,25:1
Kane, Nat D, 1955, S 4,56:1
Kane, Nora, 1945, Ag 11,13:6
Kane, Nora B Mrs, 1924, Jl 23,15:3
Kane, Patrick, 1960, D 15,43:3
Kane, Patrick J, 1945, Je 19,19:3
Kane, Paul V, 1959, Jl 4,15:2
Kane, Peter F Mrs, 1953, F 13,21:3
Kane, Pierce D, 1938, Jl 10,31:3
Kane, Rebecca, 1958, N 2,89:2
Kane, Robert L, 1940, N 27,23:1
Kane, Robert L Jr, 1958, Ja 1,25:2
Kane, S E, 1933, Je 1,19:3
Kane, S Nicholson (burial plans, N 20,10:4), 1906, N 16,10:3
Kane, Samuel J, 1958, Ap 16,33:4
Kane, T L Gen, 1884, Ja 2,8:2
Kane, Theodore F Rear-Adm, 1908, Mr 15,9:3
Kane, Theodore P, 1943, Ap 16,21:1
Kane, Thomas E, 1955, Ja 16,93:1
Kane, Thomas F, 1913, S 18,11:5; 1939, D 21,26:8; 1948, Mr 20,13:6; 1950, Ap 5,31:2; 1952, F 4,17:2
Kane, Thomas G, 1947, Ja 14,25:3
Kane, Thomas H, 1957, Jl 1,23:2
Kane, Thomas J, 1953, Je 28,61:1
Kane, Thomas L, 1959, Je 16,35:5
Kane, Thomas P, 1923, Mr 3,13:4; 1940, Je 1,15:5; 1949, Jl 19,29:2
Kane, Valentine B, 1961, Ap 2,76:3
Kane, Vincent J (por), 1948, Ap 17,15:1
Kane, Vincent J, 1949, Ap 27,27:3
Kane, W H Mrs, 1941, Ap 27,39:1
Kane, Walter J (Sept 30), 1965, O 11,61:3
Kane, Walter J Sr, 1961, My 1,29:5
Kane, Walter T, 1960, Ag 10,31:3
Kane, Walter W, 1941, D 16,27:4
Kane, Whitford (trb lr, D 30,II,3:4), 1956, D 18,31:3
Kane, William, 1907, S 3,9:6; 1943, Mr 29,16:2; 1949, My 4,30:2
Kane, William A, 1966, Mr 1,37:5
Kane, William B, 1949, D 15,35:3
Kane, William C Mrs, 1956, Ap 3,35:2
Kane, William Capt, 1901, D 21,9:3
Kane, William E, 1943, Je 5,15:3; 1945, O 13,15:4
Kane, William F, 1954, F 27,13:5
Kane, William H Mrs, 1912, F 4,13:4
Kane, William J, 1942, S 29,23:1; 1951, N 21,25:4; 1952, Ja 17,27:4; 1954, Mr 28,87:4
Kane, William J Mrs, 1950, O 1,104:2
Kane, William Mrs, 1939, Ag 17,21:2
Kane, William P Dr, 1906, N 29,9:5
Kane, William S, 1955, My 2,21:3
Kane, William T, 1946, D 30,19:3
Kane, Woodbury, 1905, D 6,11:5
Kaneff, Max, 1962, S 12,39:1
Kanegsberg, Alan, 1960, N 26,21:6
Kanegsberg, Henry, 1952, F 12,27:6
Kanegsberg, Jule W, 1966, Ja 18,34:2
Kaneko, Kentaro, 1942, My 17,47:5
Kaneko, Kentaro Mrs, 1916, Ja 3,13:3
Kanellos, Vassos Mrs, 1937, Jl 28,19:2
Kanelos, Alexander G, 1947, S 30,25:5
Kanelos, Andrew G (will), 1959, D 12,16:2
Kanemitsu, Tsuneo, 1955, Mr 6,88:1
Kanengieser, A Sigmund, 1940, Ap 8,19:2
Kaney, George F, 1948, Ja 24,15:3
Kaney, Patrick J, 1948, S 24,25:2
Kang Yung Chang, 1965, Ag 4,35:4
Kania, Joseph L, 1953, Ap 13,27:2
Kania, Stanley Mrs, 1949, Ag 19,17:5
Kanigsberg, J Clarence, 1938, S 21,25:2
Kanin, Charles A, 1959, Ja 30,28:1
Kanity, Hans von Count, 1913, Jl 1,9:4
Kann, Arnold, 1948, D 28,21:1
Kann, Emil A, 1961, Mr 12,86:3
Kann, George, 1944, Mr 21,19:1
Kann, Maurice, 1952, My 16,23:3
Kann, Nathan B, 1937, F 13,13:4
Kann, Ulysses S, 1947, Ap 9,25:4
Kannee, Tina Mrs, 1939, F 23,23:2
Kannellopoulus, Kanellos, 1944, Jl 14,13:5
Kannengiesser, David, 1957, Ag 28,27:4
Kanner, Joseph, 1963, N 21,39:1
Kanner, Morton H, 1943, Je 11,19:1
Kanno, Gertrude B, 1937, Ag 17,19:4
Kano, Jigoro, 1938, My 4,23:4
Kanolt, Clarence W, 1963, N 29,34:4
Kanouse, Carl W, 1944, Je 8,21:6
Kanouse, George E, 1952, N 15,17:3
Kanowitz, Alex D, 1959, Mr 10,36:1
Kanpp, Mary W Mrs, 1945, F 27,19:3
Kanrich, Albert D, 1960, Je 22,35:1
Kansas, Rocky (R Tozze), 1954, Ja 11,25:3
Kansas, Sidney, 1968, N 15,47:4
Kanski, Arthur D, 1959, Je 26,25:5
Kanst, Frederick L, 1937, O 12,25:2
Kant, Rudolph M, 1951, Jl 31,21:2
Kantack, Walter W, 1953, Ja 22,23:5
Kanter, Elias A, 1963, O 21,31:1
Kanter, Herman M, 1956, Ja 23,25:4
Kanter, Lloyd B, 1949, Ja 28,21:4
Kanter, Samuel (por), 1945, F 18,34:1
Kantner, Anton, 1952, O 11,19:3
Kantner, Rudolph J, 1957, D 1,88:4
Kantonowicz, Ernst H, 1963, S 10,39:2
Kantor, Barnet, 1946, O 22,25:4
Kantor, Harry M, 1963, Je 20,33:4; 1963, O 8,44
Kantor, Henry, 1954, F 9,17:3
Kantor, Jack, 1959, S 29,36:2
Kantor, John L, 1947, Je 27,22:2
Kantor, Joseph, 1954, Ap 24,17:4
Kantor, Michael (M Singer), 1958, N 30,87:2
Kantor, Oscar, 1966, Je 16,47:1
Kantor, Samuel, 1959, Ag 22,17:5
Kantor, Seymour, 1959, O 14,43:1
Kantor, Siegfried, 1957, D 10,35:4
Kantorowicz, Herman, 1940, F 14,21:1
Kantro, Isidore, 1942, N 22,53:1
Kantro, Samuel W, 1960, F 7,84:4
Kantrowitz, Bernard A, 1962, Ap 18,39:3
Kantrowitz, Bernard A Mrs, 1962, Jl 21,19:6
Kantrowitz, Eliezer, 1946, Jl 30,23:4
Kantrowitz, Joshua, 1938, S 17,17:2
Kantrowitz, Sidney H, 1965, Mr 15,31:3
Kantz, Yngvar A, 1967, F 5,88:7
Kantzler, George K, 1957, N 3,88:4
Kantzler, George R Mrs, 1957, F 12,27:3
Kanupp, Otis L, 1951, Je 28,25:5
Kany, Arthur S, 1963, Ag 15,29:2
Kanzer, Reuben, 1912, O 17,11:5
Kanzinger, Albt C, 1957, Jl 23,27:4
Kanzler, Ernest C, 1967, D 12,47:3
Kanzler, Hugo, 1911, Je 13,9:5
Kanzler, S, 1952, D 16,31:2
Kapell, Isadore, 1953, My 10,88:1
Kapell, William, 1953, O 30,1:2
Kapelsohn, Rebecca E (por), 1946, D 17,38:4
Kaphan, Ludwig Mrs (Gertrude), 1968, Jl 9,3
Kapilow, Harry H, 1956, Ap 9,27:1
Kapiolani, Dowager Queen in Hawaii, 1899, Jl
Kapit, Louis I, 1950, Ap 25,31:1
Kapkowski, Adolph, 1964, Jl 4,13:2
Kapkowski, Edward W, 1948, Je 23,27:1
Kaplam, Rubin, 1924, Jl 22,15:4
Kaplan, Aaron, 1937, Ag 11,24:4
Kaplan, Abraham, 1939, Jl 15,16:6; 1947, Ag
Kaplan, Abraham (cor, Je 26,33:1), 1962, Je
Kaplan, Abraham A, 1962, Ap 19,31:3
Kaplan, Abraham V, 1956, Je 23,17:4
Kaplan, Abram, 1952, Jl 3,25:4
Kaplan, Abram I, 1959, My 16,23:5
Kaplan, Albert A, 1962, Ap 2,31:5
Kaplan, Albert L, 1951, My 23,36:2
Kaplan, Allen, 1951, Mr 10,28:6; 1960, Jl 13,3
Kaplan, Benjamin, 1955, O 26,31:4
Kaplan, Benjamin G, 1952, F 27,27:4
Kaplan, Bernard M (por), 1941, N 23,52:3
Kaplan, Boris, 1945, D 27,19:2
Kaplan, Carl Mrs, 1954, O 16,17:3
Kaplan, Chaim, 1946, Je 21,23:2
Kaplan, Charles M Mrs, 1949, N 10,31:4
Kaplan, David, 1953, Ja 16,23:4; 1965, Jl 16,2
Kaplan, David M, 1952, D 1,23:5
Kaplan, David Mrs, 1958, O 13,53:5
Kaplan, Don, 1952, N 19,29:4
Kaplan, Eliezer, 1952, Jl 14,17:1
Kaplan, Fanya (Dora), 1958, Ja 9,8:4

Kaplan, Frank G, 1938, Mr 15,23:4
Kaplan, Frank R S, 1957, O 5,17:3
Kaplan, Gabriel L, 1968, S 18,47:2
Kaplan, George, 1940, F 5,17:5; 1956, N 22,66:3
Kaplan, Gershan Mrs, 1959, F 22,88:5
Kaplan, Harold C, 1958, O 8,35:3
Kaplan, Harris, 1940, N 20,21:2
Kaplan, Harry A Mrs, 1964, Ag 30,93:2
Kaplan, Harry M, 1949, D 26,12:4
Kaplan, Harry Mrs, 1954, N 9,27:3
Kaplan, Herbert I, 1949, Ap 8,26:3
Kaplan, Herman, 1959, Mr 1,86:5; 1963, N 1,33:2
Kaplan, Herman B, 1957, Ja 6,89:2; 1966, Je 16,47:1
Kaplan, Herman M, 1964, Ap 9,31:4
Kaplan, Hyman, 1951, My 3,29:3; 1954, My 8,17:6
Kaplan, Hyman A, 1947, Jl 10,21:5
Kaplan, Hyman S (cor, Ap 21,23:2), 1950, Ap 19, 29:3
Kaplan, Irving, 1957, Ag 18,83:1; 1962, O 26,31:5
Kaplan, Irving J, 1952, O 9,31:3
Kaplan, Isaac, 1937, S 4,15:6
Kaplan, Isaac H, 1956, F 13,27:5
Kaplan, Israel, 1951, S 11,29:4
Kaplan, Israel Rabbi, 1917, Ja 26,9:2
Kaplan, Izzy, 1949, Ap 5,29:1
Kaplan, Jacob, 1944, Mr 22,19:2
Kaplan, Jacob J, 1960, Ag 9,27:2
Kaplan, Joseph, 1960, N 14,31:4; 1964, Ap 26,88:6
Kaplan, Joseph Mrs, 1951, My 19,15:3
Kaplan, Julius, 1939, N 30,21:6; 1950, Mr 21,32:2
Kaplan, Julius Mrs, 1954, F 16,25:5
Kaplan, Ladislav, 1962, S 25,37:4
Kaplan, Lawrence Mrs (Sylvia), 1968, Je 27,43:3
Kaplan, Louis, 1954, F 25,31:6; 1957, D 7,21:4
Kaplan, Louis Mrs (Esther), 1966, N 2,45:3
Kaplan, Matthew H, 1966, F 23,39:2
Kaplan, Maurice S, 1951, Ag 6,21:4
Kaplan, Meyer, 1958, N 30,86:2
Kaplan, Meyer J, 1956, Je 21,31:5
Kaplan, Meyer S Mrs, 1915, Jl 3,7:4
Kaplan, Michael, 1952, Mr 30,93:3
Kaplan, Michael L, 1959, O 5,31:3
Kaplan, Moe, 1955, Mr 19,15:5
Kaplan, Mordecai, 1951, F 2,23:1
Kaplan, Mordecai Mrs, 1958, My 4,89:1
Kaplan, Morduch L, 1943, My 26,23:1
Kaplan, Morris, 1945, My 28,19:5; 1964, F 15,23:6
Kaplan, Moses, 1966, Ag 17,36:5
Kaplan, Murray Mrs, 1959, My 1,29:3
Kaplan, Nathan, 1947, N 18,29:4; 1948, F 17,25:2; 1953, Ag 12,31:2
Kaplan, Nathan H, 1956, Ja 5,33:2
Kaplan, Nathaniel Judge, 1968, S 14,28:1
Kaplan, Paul S Dr (funl), 1918, Ja 8,15:7
Kaplan, Phil, 1952, N 25,29:4; 1952, D 25,29:3
Kaplan, Robert, 1965, N 26,37:3
Kaplan, Rose, 1917, Ag 8,7:4
aplan, Rudolph, 1944, O 7,13:3
aplan, S Ray, 1967, Mr 2,35:4
aplan, Sam, 1955, N 17,35:2
aplan, Samuel, 1951, D 29,11:5
aplan, Simcha, 1952, F 22,21:2
aplan, Simon, 1961, N 4,19:2
aplan, Stanley Mrs, 1956, O 7,87:1
aplan, Theodore, 1964, S 23,47:2
aplan, William Mrs, 1950, F 8,27:4
aplander, Morris H, 1950, Ja 30,3:8
aplanoff, Irbain-Khan Prince (por), 1947, O 12,76:5
aplansky, Shlomo, 1950, D 9,15:5
aplen, Alex, 1959, Je 18,31:4
aplon, Abraham, 1939, S 29,23:2
aplon, J Jerome, 1961, D 11,31:6
aplow, Joseph, 1961, O 18,43:2
aplowitz, Morris, 1939, Mr 22,23:1
aplowitz, Yale, 1946, Ag 29,29:7
aplun, Jacob, 1965, Ja 12,37:2
aplun, Murray L, 1941, Je 25,21:4
aplus, David B, 1968, N 23,47:3
aplus, Isadore, 1958, O 24,33:2
aplus, Leo, 1949, Je 23,27:3
apmarski, Joseph A, 1956, Ap 11,33:5
apnek, Samuel, 1950, Ag 18,21:3
apner, Thomas, 1957, O 5,17:1
apner, Zodak, 1953, O 21,29:4
app, Carl G, 1962, Je 28,31:4
app, Charles, 1950, F 1,29:2
app, F, 1884, O 28,2:2
app, F Isabelle (Mrs L H Harris), 1965, Mr 23,39:4
app, George E, 1948, D 28,21:4
app, George E Mrs, 1944, S 14,23:5
app, Jack, 1949, Mr 26,17:2
app, Louis A, 1962, Ag 1,31:1
app, Morton E, 1961, F 19,86:2
app, Phillip, 1944, Ja 2,38:8
app, Roland, 1965, Jl 31,21:1
app, Vincent F, 1947, D 9,29:1
appel, Alex, 1958, S 8,29:3
appel, Alex Mrs, 1961, O 25,37:4
appel, August, 1954, O 7,23:3
appel, Fred A, 1966, D 27,35:2
appel, Jerome E, 1951, F 8,23:8
appel, Samuel, 1957, N 12,37:1
ppel, William J, 1967, Ja 21,31:3

Kappeler, Alfred, 1945, O 31,23:5
Kappelhoff, William, 1967, Ap 2,93:1
Kappelmann, Otto C W, 1960, Mr 6,86:1
Kappen, Otto H, 1947, Jl 15,23:2
Kappenberg, Aloysius G, 1957, Ag 29,27:2
Kapper, Frederick P, 1938, Ap 27,23:4
Kappers, Cornelius U A, 1946, Jl 30,23:4
Kappes, Carl H, 1938, Ap 26,21:2
Kappes, Carl H Jr, 1962, Ja 3,33:3
Kappes, Charles, 1916, N 21,11:3
Kappes, George Jr (Oct 7), 1965, O 11,61:3
Kappes, J Henry Prof, 1915, O 27,11:6
Kappes, Karl, 1943, N 18,23:4
Kappeyne, Jacobus Mrs, 1955, My 31,27:3
Kapps, Charles A, 1963, Jl 7,53:1
Kappstatter, Adam, 1960, O 22,23:5
Kappus, Adolph Jr, 1961, N 25,24:3
Kappus, Adolph Mrs, 1938, D 1,23:5
Kapreilian, Harry C, 1953, Ag 14,19:2
Kapriellian, H Kruger, 1949, D 20,31:1
Kapros, John Mrs (M Tobias),(cor, Ap 16,33:5), 1959, Ap 15,33:2
Kaprow, Abraham, 1947, Ag 18,17:2
Kaprow, Gedaliah, 1951, Ap 13,23:2
Kapsenberg, G, 1944, Ja 9,42:1
Kapurthala, Maharani of (Dowager Princess Brinda), 1962, Ag 9,25:2
Kapy, Gabriel, 1949, F 18,23:4
Kara, Meger Z, 1945, F 11,40:2
Karabatos, James J, 1961, Je 12,29:5
Karabekir, Kiazim, 1948, Ja 27,25:4
Karafin, Samuel, 1942, Ja 28,19:4
Karageorges, P Spiros, 1957, Ap 19,21:3
Karageorgevitch, Alexis Princess, 1938, Je 27,17:4
Karageorgevitch, Arsene Prince, 1938, O 20,23:3
Karagheusian, Arshag, 1963, S 25,43:1
Karagheusian, Miran, 1948, O 8,26:3
Karaivanov, Ivan, 1960, Mr 28,29:3
Karakas, Harry J, 1960, Mr 4,25:2
Karamanli, Prince Suleyman Bey, 1945, O 19,23:4
Karangasem, Anak Agung Agung Anglurah K'tut Rajah, 1967, Ja 8,3:1
Karapetoff, Vladimar (por), 1948, Ja 12,19:1
Karasek, John C, 1951, F 27,27:2
Karasik, Louis, 1959, S 13,84:4
Karasyk, Tamara Mrs, 1937, Ap 22,23:2
Karauloff, M, 1911, Ja 2,9:4
Karavaev, Peter, 1952, Je 12,33:4
Karayev, Dzhuma D, 1960, My 10,37:1
Karber, John, 1912, Ag 14,9:5
Karboski, John W, 1964, Ja 17,40:1
Karch, Arthur W, 1940, Ap 30,21:3
Karch, John G, 1962, O 28,88:7
Karch, Michael, 1947, O 1,29:5
Karcher, Leonard D Mrs, 1950, Jl 24,17:2
Karcher, Walter T, 1953, S 5,15:2
Karczewski, Stanley, 1951, Mr 19,27:2
Kardas, Joseph E, 1958, Jl 9,27:5
Kardel, Benjamin L, 1947, Jl 27,45:1
Kardon, Samuel Mrs, 1960, Ag 25,29:2
Kardorff, Wilhelm von, 1907, Jl 23,7:6
Karel, John C, 1938, D 5,23:2
Karelitz, Abraham Y (Hazon Ish), 1953, O 25,88:7
Karelitz, George B (por), 1943, Ja 20,19:3
Karelitz, Michael B, 1963, N 5,31:4
Karelsen, Frank E Mrs, 1968, O 2,39:5
Karen, Benjamin, 1958, Jl 3,25:4
Karen, J D (Jack), 1951, D 28,21:3
Kares, Edward H, 1948, S 28,27:2
Kares, Edward H Mrs, 1943, D 17,27:4
Karfiol, Bernard, 1952, Ag 17,76:3
Karfiol, Henri, 1952, Ag 27,27:3
Karfunkle, Benjamin, 1924, Je 21,13:6
Karger, Gus J, 1924, D 19,21:4
Karger, Gustav J (funl, N 18,25:4), 1924, N 17,19:5
Karger, Louis, 1947, N 12,27:2
Karger, Ralph M Mrs, 1944, O 11,21:5
Karger, Samuel I, 1950, O 17,31:2
Kargere, Minna Mrs (por), 1941, N 12,23:5
Kargl, George F (Bro Amandus Hy), 1952, F 15,25:3
Karibzhanov, Fazyl K, 1960, Ag 26,25:4
Karig, Walter, 1956, O 1,27:3
Karim, Mufid A, 1947, S 3,26:6
Karins, James J, 1951, Ag 14,23:4
Karinska, Maria, 1942, Ja 16,21:3
Karker, Maurice H, 1951, N 20,31:2
Karklinsh, Karlis, 1962, O 13,25:1
Karkunoff, Robert F, 1942, Ap 25,13:2
Karl, Aloysius S, 1962, F 17,19:4
Karl, Edward F, 1967, Mr 22,47:3
Karl, Francis J, 1938, Jl 15,17:4
Karl, John C, 1946, F 27,25:5
Karl, John Mrs, 1956, Ap 17,31:3
Karl, Marie (Sister Rose Eleanore), 1964, Ap 4,28:4
Karl, Martin J, 1964, Mr 11,39:4
Karl, Peter A, 1959, O 2,29:3
Karl, Pincus, 1953, Ag 25,21:2
Karl, Stephen E, 1957, Jl 9,27:2
Karl, Tom, 1916, Mr 20,11:3
Karl, William, 1944, Ap 16,42:2
Karl, William A, 1963, S 10,39:5
Karl, William F, 1960, Ja 18,27:4
Karl I, King of Wurtemberg, 1891, O 7,4:7

Karlberg, John S, 1942, My 3,54:2
Karle, George J Sr, 1941, D 7,76:2
Karlen, Ernest J, 1951, My 3,29:4
Karlen, Jacob J, 1955, S 2,17:4
Karletsky, Morris, 1949, Je 8,29:4
Karlfeldt, E, 1931, Ap 9,25:3
Karlin, Henry, 1951, Mr 17,15:5
Karlin, Isaac W, 1962, Ja 22,23:2
Karlin, Jack, 1944, Jl 7,15:4; 1962, S 27,37:3
Karlin, Leon J, 1955, Jl 6,27:2
Karlin, William (por), 1944, D 7,25:3
Karlsen, Arnt, 1951, Je 16,15:5
Karlson, Charles B, 1958, N 29,21:6
Karlson, Gustav V, 1963, My 11,25:4
Karlweis, Oscar, 1956, Ja 25,31:1
Karm, Earl, 1946, Jl 22,23:3
Karm, O W, 1923, Je 14,19:5
Karman, Murray, 1949, Mr 29,26:3
Karmany, Lincoln, 1943, D 27,19:3
Karmel, Alex Mrs, 1964, Mr 26,35:1
Karmel, Frank Mrs, 1950, Ag 24,27:3
Karmel, Ralph R, 1951, Ap 28,15:6
Karn, Albert E, 1958, Ag 24,87:1
Karn, Christian, 1952, Ja 1,25:2
Karn, Estella H, 1957, Mr 14,29:4
Karn, Frederick J, 1940, D 5,25:4
Karn, Frederick W, 1939, N 16,23:4
Karn, Norman K, 1966, Mr 24,39:4
Karn, Roy B Mrs, 1961, Ag 13,88:6
Karn, Willard S, 1945, Ap 29,38:1
Karnebeek, Herman A van, 1942, Ap 3,21:2
Karnell, I Max, 1946, D 28,16:2
Karnes, Clarence, 1947, S 21,V,5:1
Karnes, Faye E, 1952, Mr 19,29:4
Karnes, Morris, 1966, Ja 30,84:6
Karnes, Paul H, 1947, S 6,18:2
Karney, Rex L, 1966, N 18,43:3
Karni, Leon J, 1953, O 6,29:5
Karni, Yehuda, 1949, Ja 4,19:2
Karno, Fred, 1941, S 19,23:4
Karno, Fred Jr, 1961, F 4,19:3
Karnofsky, Harry, 1947, Ap 25,21:3
Karns, Charles W, 1941, Jl 5,11:5
Karoff, Robert B, 1966, Jl 6,42:2
Karolik, Maxim, 1963, D 21,23:1
Karolik, Maxim (will), 1964, Ja 7,40:2
Karolik, Maxim Mrs, 1948, Ap 22,27:1
Karolyi, Countess, 1937, My 19,5:2
Karolyi, Imre, 1943, Jl 25,31:2
Karolyi, Jules Countess, 1940, Je 27,23:4
Karolyi, Michael Count, 1955, Mr 21,25:3
Karonwe, 1905, Mr 3,6:1
Karow, David Mrs, 1960, Ap 3,86:6
Karp, Albert, 1965, Je 21,29:1
Karp, Albert Mrs, 1941, F 22,15:1
Karp, Archie S, 1952, Ja 18,27:3
Karp, Edmund I, 1965, O 21,47:4
Karp, Frank L, 1966, N 6,89:1
Karp, Horia, 1943, D 4,13:5
Karp, Lazarus, 1938, My 25,23:2
Karp, Leon, 1951, Ag 3,21:5
Karp, Maurice F, 1960, Je 9,33:4
Karp, Maurice F Mrs, 1958, Mr 19,31:1
Karp, Milton J, 1955, Ja 19,27:5
Karp, Morris S, 1958, Ja 18,15:6
Karp, Sophie, 1904, Ap 1,9:6
Karpe, Eugene S, 1950, F 25,4:3
Karpeles, Maurice J, 1951, Je 22,25:3
Karpen, Leo, 1955, S 4,56:1
Karpen, Michael, 1950, Jl 1,15:2
Karpf, Jacob J, 1943, Je 22,20:3
Karpf, Jerome J, 1964, Ag 18,31:2
Karpf, Nat M, 1968, Jl 28,64:7
Karpick, John J, 1960, Ja 16,21:5
Karpinski, Stanley J, 1943, N 17,25:5
Karpinsky, A P, 1936, Jl 16,17:3
Karpinsky, Vyacheslav A (cor, Mr 24,43:3), 1965, Mr 23,39:4
Karplus, Richard, 1958, N 19,37:2
Karpovich, Michael, 1959, N 8,88:6
Karr, A, 1890, O 2,4:7
Karr, Arthur J, 1939, F 7,19:4
Karr, Edward B, 1958, Je 21,19:1
Karr, Frank, 1954, Mr 30,27:1
Karr, Harry Mrs (Rebecca), 1968, F 16,37:2
Karr, Joseph, 1959, My 16,23:2
Karr, M Louise, 1949, Ja 9,72:2
Karr, Mary K, 1954, F 7,88:5
Karr, Walter G, 1946, S 19,31:4
Karraker, Cyrus H, 1966, F 7,29:3
Karreman, Anthony E, 1946, Ag 19,25:3
Karrer, Conrad, 1946, Ag 22,27:5
Karrick, David B, 1960, Ag 7,85:1
Karrick, Henrietta L B Mrs, 1939, F 9,21:5
Karrsten, Fritz, 1951, Ag 27,19:5
Karsch, B, 1932, Ja 21,21:1
Karsch, John H, 1953, S 1,23:2
Karscher, Abraham E, 1949, Jl 28,23:6
Karsh, Yousuf Mrs, 1961, Ja 26,29:4
Karshmer, Ernest E, 1965, S 10,35:2
Karslake, Henry, 1942, O 20,21:5
Karslake, J Sir, 1881, O 6,5:3
Karsner, David, 1941, F 22,15:3

Karson, Nat, 1954, S 28,29:3
Karst, Esther, 1954, F 24,25:4
Karst, Harry F, 1956, Je 16,19:2
Karst, Lulu V, 1947, N 16,76:5
Karsten, Karl G, 1968, My 26,84:1
Karstens, William, 1954, S 15,33:6
Karszo-Siedlewski, Jan, 1955, Jl 10,75:2
Kartak, Franz A, 1947, F 20,25:2
Kartashoff, George, 1960, S 16,28:5
Kartell, Barnett, 1957, Ap 13,19:5
Kartevold, Theodor, 1953, Ag 7,19:2
Kartluke, Herman F, 1943, N 22,19:3
Karutz, Henry C, 1942, Ja 8,21:2
Karvel, Charles T, 1964, Ag 21,30:5
Karzas, Andrew, 1940, Je 2,45:2
Karzas, William, 1963, S 25,43:2
Kas, Thomas, 1954, Jl 21,27:4
Kasab, Harten, 1940, Ap 3,23:4
Kasabach, Haig H, 1943, S 2,19:2
Kasanin, Joseph S, 1946, My 6,21:3
Kasch, Herman, 1950, S 24,104:4
Kasch, Herman F, 1951, Ja 5,21:3
Kaschel, Gustav A Sr, 1946, S 27,23:5
Kasdan, Alfred S Mrs, 1960, Jl 19,29:2
Kase, Ralph S, 1956, Jl 18,27:1
Kase, Shunichi, 1956, S 10,27:4
Kasel, Frank V, 1947, N 3,23:3
Kasemieresak, Piotr, 1905, My 5,9:2
Kasen, Noah, 1954, Mr 15,25:4
Kasen, William B, 1939, F 20,17:1
Kasenkina, Oksana S Mrs, 1960, Jl 27,29:2
Kaser, Harold I, 1945, Ag 24,19:2
Kaser, Louis J, 1958, Ag 18,19:5
Kasey, Arthur E S, 1954, D 26,61:1
Kash, Kelly, 1955, Ag 17,27:6
Kashani, Abolghassem, 1962, Mr 15,35:2
Kashata, Joseph, 1951, Jl 8,60:3
Kashdan, Phil, 1940, Ag 21,19:3
Kashdin, Morris, 1958, Ja 19,86:6
Kashin, Gordon C, 1964, Jl 24,27:1
Kashin, Maurice A, 1946, Ja 1,27:2
Kashins, Sol, 1963, Ap 25,33:2
Kashner, Edward A Mrs, 1946, F 12,28:1
Kashowitz, Joseph, 1961, O 17,39:2
Kashowitz, Joseph Mrs, 1948, F 17,25:5
Kashowitz, Max, 1945, O 10,21:2
Kasin, Louis, 1941, S 24,23:1
Kasinski, Michael, 1950, Ja 10,29:3
Kaske, John J, 1950, My 10,31:2
Kaskel, Alfred L, 1968, Jl 7,53:1
Kaskel, C Clarence, 1962, F 8,32:1
Kaskel, Dave J, 1940, Ap 10,25:3
Kaskel, Nat C, 1937, N 12,21:2
Kaskel, Paul, 1963, D 19,33:3
Kaskell, Ralph L, 1938, Jl 13,21:4
Kaskell, Theresa, 1951, Mr 31,15:5
Kaskey, Abel J, 1945, Jl 18,27:5
Kaskie, Sig, 1954, Mr 11,34:7
Kaslov, Steve, 1949, F 18,24:3
Kasmire, E, 1879, S 3,8:2
Kasmire, William G, 1948, Mr 4,25:2
Kasner, Edward, 1955, Ja 8,13:5
Kasner, Henry P, 1943, F 15,15:2
Kasoff, Morris A, 1966, Mr 24,39:4
Kasover, Nathan, 1954, S 29,31:5
Kasovsky, Samuel, 1948, Mr 17,25:4
Kaspar, Eugene W, 1953, Ag 24,23:5
Kaspar, Karl (por), 1941, Ap 22,21:3
Kasparek, Adam, 1939, Jl 10,19:5
Kasper, Charles, 1960, Je 15,41:1
Kasper, Frederick J Sr, 1954, O 21,27:5
Kasper, Hans, 1954, Ag 1,85:3
Kasper, John W H, 1961, Ja 6,27:4
Kasper, Leonard S, 1967, Mr 13,37:2
Kasper, Michael G, 1938, O 15,17:5
Kasper, Peter J, 1938, Ap 6,23:3
Kasper, Victor H, 1948, Mr 16,28:2
Kaspereit, Otto K, 1952, S 20,15:5
Kaspersson, Karlis, 1962, Ja 26,31:1
Kasprzak, Francis A, 1948, My 1,15:2
Kass, Abram, 1949, Jl 17,58:3
Kass, Barnet, 1957, Ja 12,19:4
Kass, Charles, 1967, N 16,47:1
Kass, David, 1955, Ap 2,17:2
Kass, David Mrs, 1966, Ap 3,85:2
Kass, Harry Mrs, 1956, Jl 10,31:5
Kass, Henry, 1942, Mr 7,17:3
Kass, Howard, 1953, F 8,89:1
Kass, Max, 1959, Ja 2,25:2
Kass, Mitchel Mrs, 1951, Ag 6,21:4
Kass, Nathan I, 1964, Ag 28,35:6
Kass, Robert, 1951, O 30,29:4
Kass, William R, 1951, Mr 15,29:4
Kass, William R Mrs, 1952, Mr 5,29:4
Kassapian, Dikran Mrs, 1952, D 17,33:3
Kassel, Art, 1965, F 5,31:5
Kassel, David, 1949, Ja 30,60:6
Kassel, Jack, 1967, Je 25,68:4
Kassel, Lewis P, 1956, D 22,19:6
Kassenbaum, John E, 1955, Ap 13,29:6
Kassern, Tadeusz, 1957, My 3,27:1
Kassewitz, Benjamin, 1949, Jl 16,13:1
Kassler, Kenneth, 1964, S 29,43:1

Kassman, Elly (Mrs B C Meyer), 1960, My 26,33:2
Kassner, Leo, 1945, Je 21,19:2
Kassner, Rudolf, 1959, Ap 2,31:3
Kasson, Burt Z, 1943, S 28,25:3
Kasson, David, 1958, Je 4,31:5
Kasson, Frank, 1952, Mr 14,20:6
Kasson, Henry C, 1924, D 8,19:4
Kasson, John A, 1910, My 19,9:4
Kasson, Lee B Mrs, 1937, My 14,23:6
Kassover, Irving, 1958, Ja 19,86:8
Kassover, Joel Mrs, 1967, N 20,47:3
Kassover, Julius, 1954, Ag 27,21:3
Kassvan, Louis, 1966, D 14,47:3
Kast, Edward R (por), 1944, Je 4,42:1
Kast, Ludwig (por), 1941, Ag 16,15:3
Kast, Ludwig Mrs, 1943, Ag 17,17:5
Kastein, Joseph, 1946, Je 14,21:5
Kasten, Alfred W (por), 1948, Ap 16,23:4
Kasten, Sam, 1953, Mr 5,27:2
Kasten, Walter, 1950, O 19,31:1
Kasten, William H, 1963, D 21,23:4
Kastendieck, Henry F, 1942, Ja 20,19:3
Kastendieck, Julian Mrs, 1944, O 5,23:1
Kaster, J P, 1938, D 14,25:6
Kastl, Alex E, 1937, S 9,23:5
Kastle, J William, 1949, S 26,25:4
Kastler, Donald M, 1947, Je 10,27:2
Kastlin, George J, 1949, Ja 1,13:5
Kastner, Alfred, 1948, My 26,25:5
Kastner, Ch Prof, 1903, My 2,9:5
Kastner, Edgar P, 1954, D 28,23:1
Kastner, Edward J, 1958, F 13,29:5
Kastner, Franklin H, 1940, O 9,25:3
Kastner, Henry P, 1947, My 29,21:3
Kastner, Hermann, 1957, S 10,33:1
Kastner, John A, 1940, Mr 16,15:4
Kastor, Alfred B, 1963, Je 5,41:3
Kastor, Louis, 1942, Ag 20,19:2
Kastor, Sigmund, 1947, O 22,29:3
Kasumov, Mir Bashir, 1949, Ap 24,76:8
Kasznar, Kurt S Mrs, 1948, Je 21,21:2
Kaszuba, Christian Mrs, 1937, Ap 21,23:3
Kaszubski, Joseph L, 1953, Jl 20,17:5
Katayama, Haruko Mrs, 1938, S 8,23:3
Katchadourian, Sarkis, 1947, Mr 9,60:5
Katcher, Arthur D, 1950, O 18,33:5
Katcher, Harry B, 1964, Jl 4,13:4
Katcher, Samuel, 1942, N 13,23:6
Katchigian, Kigore Mrs, 1946, O 24,29:7
Katchko, Adolph, 1958, S 17,37:2
Katchouny, Vahan, 1952, N 13,31:3
Kateb, Elias S, 1965, F 13,21:2
Katel, Jacques, 1965, My 9,87:1
Kateley, Pearl Mrs, 1953, My 30,15:3
Katelus, George, 1945, O 16,23:2
Kates, Edgar J Mrs, 1949, Je 28,27:2
Kates, Henry, 1924, O 18,15:6
Kates, Herbert S, 1947, F 26,25:2
Kates, Jerome, 1956, Jl 19,27:1
Kates, John B, 1947, My 1,25:5
Kates, Max L, 1958, D 30,35:1
Kath, Henry J, 1949, Ja 12,27:5
Kathigasu, Sybil Mrs, 1948, Je 17,25:5
Kathleen, Sister, 1948, F 7,15:1
Katholicos, Khoren, 1938, Ap 13,25:6
Kathrens, Joseph R, 1939, Jl 14,19:5
Katibah, Habib I, 1951, F 17,15:6
Katilungu, Lawrence, 1961, N 11,2:5
Katju, Kailash Nath Dr, 1968, F 18,80:4
Katkoff, Michael, 1887, Ag 2,2:4
Katlowitz, Dora Mrs, 1937, D 3,24:3
Kato, Kanji (por), 1939, F 9,21:3
Kato, Katsuji, 1961, S 7,35:3
Kato, Sotomatsu (por), 1942, F 13,4:6
Kato, T Viscount, 1926, Ja 28,1:7
Kato, Tomosaburo, 1923, Ag 24,11:3
Katovsky, Abraham, 1945, My 16,19:4
Katsampes, Peter A, 1939, Je 16,23:2
Katscher, Robert, 1942, F 25,20:3
Katschthaler, Johann Cardinal, 1914, F 28,9:4
Katsh, Hyman S, 1946, My 20,23:5
Katsh, Joseph I, 1963, Je 27,33:2
Katske, Floyd, 1951, Ja 16,29:2
Katske, Paul A, 1949, D 28,25:2
Katske, Paul A Mrs, 1961, Ap 3,33:2
Katsura, Taro Prince, 1913, O 11,15:3
Katte, E B, 1928, Jl 20,19:5
Katte, Walter Col, 1917, Mr 5,11:5
Kattell, Thomas B, 1947, Jl 23,23:6
Kattelman, Harry, 1950, N 21,31:4
Katten, Simon, 1937, Jl 15,19:4
Kattenhorn, Martin S, 1959, Ap 28,35:3
Katterjohn, Monte, 1949, S 11,94:5
Katterman, Emil G, 1949, O 20,29:3
Kattermann, Aug F, 1937, D 31,15:2
Kattermann, Emil D, 1959, Ap 30,31:4
Katyuskyj, Maksyn, 1949, D 26,5:1
Katz, A Ray, 1938, Mr 20,II,9:1
Katz, Aaron, 1956, Jl 7,13:4
Katz, Abner R, 1964, N 15,86:7
Katz, Abram K, 1917, N 3,15:7
Katz, Albert, 1942, O 3,15:2
Katz, Alex E, 1955, Ap 6,29:4

Katz, Alex S, 1948, Ap 18,68:6
Katz, Alex S Mrs, 1956, Je 12,35:5
Katz, Alfred Mrs, 1949, O 8,13:6
Katz, Arthur, 1947, N 10,29:2
Katz, Benjamin, 1956, Jl 11,29:5
Katz, Benne Mrs, 1955, S 23,25:3
Katz, Bernard, 1946, Ag 30,17:5
Katz, Chaim M (funl), 1964, N 19,39:4
Katz, Charles, 1950, F 19,76:4; 1968, My 7,41:3
Katz, David, 1942, D 30,23:2
Katz, David Mrs (Lenore Brundige), 1968, Mr 25, 41:4
Katz, David N, 1968, Ja 27,29:4
Katz, David W, 1968, Ag 18,89:2
Katz, Davis M, 1958, Ja 23,27:1
Katz, Elihu, 1956, Jl 21,15:6
Katz, Emil, 1953, Ap 28,27:2; 1966, D 21,32:7
Katz, Ernest, 1963, My 11,25:4
Katz, Ernest H, 1955, My 30,13:5
Katz, Esau A, 1948, Ap 6,23:4
Katz, Feldie, 1952, Je 3,29:3
Katz, Harry, 1958, F 1,19:4; 1958, Je 19,31:3
Katz, Harry D, 1965, Ja 22,43:4
Katz, Harry L, 1955, F 4,21:3; 1956, F 19,92:2
Katz, Hedi K, 1960, D 8,35:3
Katz, Herbert Mrs, 1914, Ap 17,11:6
Katz, Herman, 1948, O 26,31:4; 1957, Jl 16,26:1
Katz, Howard J, 1952, Jl 19,15:5
Katz, Isaac, 1937, Je 20,II,7:2; 1943, O 11,19:1; 195 N 10,19:6
Katz, Isaac Mrs, 1952, O 27,27:3
Katz, Jacob, 1950, Mr 26,92:5; 1952, N 21,25:3; 19 N 9,27:6
Katz, Jacob Mrs, 1938, F 14,17:3; 1960, F 13,19:3
Katz, Jacob S Mrs, 1952, S 4,27:1
Katz, Joseph, 1957, N 10,85:5
Katz, Joseph A, 1953, Ap 21,27:1
Katz, Joseph P, 1945, Jl 8,11:6
Katz, Lawrence J, 1957, Jl 23,25:2
Katz, Leon, 1941, Ap 6,49:2
Katz, Leonard S, 1937, Ja 18,17:5
Katz, Louis, 1948, F 6,23:3; 1956, S 16,84:1; 1965, My 6,39:1
Katz, Louis D Mrs, 1943, N 18,23:1
Katz, Louis Mrs, 1965, Ap 26,31:3
Katz, Manne, 1962, S 10,29:3
Katz, Marcel, 1951, Je 17,86:1
Katz, Marcel Mrs, 1950, N 22,25:1
Katz, Max, 1945, O 17,19:4; 1946, Ap 20,13:2; 196 Ap 2,35:2
Katz, Max J, 1957, O 29,31:4
Katz, Max L, 1946, Jl 12,17:4
Katz, Maxwell, 1945, Jl 29,40:6; 1950, Je 20,27:3
Katz, Maxwell C, 1951, My 10,31:3; 1958, Ag 17,8
Katz, Meyer Mrs, 1955, Je 14,29:5
Katz, Michael, 1950, Jl 6,27:5
Katz, Mike, 1952, Je 6,23:4
Katz, Moishe, 1960, Je 6,29:5
Katz, Morris, 1950, Ap 17,23:4; 1952, Ja 3,27:3; 19 Ap 18,31:1
Katz, Morris I, 1957, Jl 21,60:2
Katz, Moses, 1941, Je 15,36:7
Katz, Murray, 1950, D 20,31:2
Katz, Nahum E, 1946, Jl 24,27:4
Katz, Nathan, 1952, O 23,31:4; 1967, Je 7,51:2
Katz, Paul J, 1964, Mr 26,26:4
Katz, Paul J Mrs, 1964, Mr 26,26:4
Katz, Philip Mrs, 1944, S 16,13:4
Katz, Reuben Mrs, 1954, Ja 26,27:4
Katz, Reuven, 1963, N 4,35:3
Katz, Ruben, 1957, S 28,17:4
Katz, Rudolf, 1961, Jl 24,23:5
Katz, Sadie, 1947, Ap 14,27:4
Katz, Sam, 1942, F 20,17:2; 1961, Ja 13,29:1
Katz, Samuel, 1911, Ag 14,7:5; 1951, D 3,31:4; 19 Ag 20,27:3; 1964, D 7,35:1
Katz, Samuel H, 1960, Mr 5,19:2
Katz, Samuel M, 1941, Ja 22,21:3
Katz, Samuel Mrs, 1955, Je 23,29:1; 1961, My 31,
Katz, Samuel Mrs (E Raphael), 1964, Mr 7,23:4
Katz, Saul, 1965, D 28,25:4
Katz, Simon, 1958, Je 28,17:4
Katz, Stanley, 1964, Ag 6,29:2
Katz, Sydney M, 1965, Ap 24,29:2
Katz, Wallace, 1950, Ap 27,29:3
Katz, Walter, 1957, Ja 7,25:3
Katz, William, 1960, Mr 10,31:2
Katz, William P (por), 1941, Mr 3,15:2
Katzell, Kiva Mrs, 1947, Ap 25,21:3
Katzen, Jacob L, 1959, Ag 5,27:4
Katzenbach, F S, 1929, Mr 14,27:1
Katzenbach, George A, 1939, Jl 7,17:4
Katzenberg, A S, 1937, S 8,23:3
Katzenberg, Julius, 1907, Mr 5,9:6
Katzenberg, Max, 1912, My 25,13:6
Katzenberger, Raymond Mrs, 1948, F 14,13:1
Katzenelenbogen, Jehuda, 1920, Ap 12,15:3
Katzenellenbogen, Adolf, 1964, O 1,35:5
Katzenmeyer, George, 1941, My 27,20:2
Katzenstein, Jacob, 1943, D 4,13:2
Katzenstein, Leon E, 1919, Ag 6,9:2
Katzenstein, Martin L, 1955, Jl 23,17:4
Katzenstein, Martin L Mrs, 1943, My 25,23:1

Katzenstein, Sarah F Mrs, 1938, Ap 18,15:5
Katzenstein, Simon, 1912, Ag 27,9:2
Katzenstein, William S, 1950, My 21,106:3
Katzenstine, Zalicia, 1924, Jl 12,9:6
Katzentine, A Frank, 1960, Mr 28,29:1
Katzer, Frederick X Archbishop, 1903, Jl 21,9:5
Katzin, Eugene M, 1966, My 24,47:2
Katzka, Emil, 1966, Mr 21,33:2
Katzman, Harriet J (H Toby), 1952, Mr 4,1:6
Katzman, Louis, 1914, D 27,3:6; 1943, N 14,57:2
Katzman, Nathan, 1965, N 22,37:3
Katzman, Salo, 1956, My 19,19:4
Katzmann, Frederick G, 1953, O 17,15:4
Katznelson, Berl, 1944, Ag 14,15:6
Katznelson, Harry, 1965, F 11,39:3
Kauder, Fred S, 1948, D 20,25:2
Kauder, Sydney J, 1957, N 30,21:5
Kauderer, John G Mrs, 1947, F 10,29:3
Kauders, Otto, 1949, Ag 9,25:1
Kaudy, John C, 1953, S 3,22:8
Kaufer, Edouard E, 1937, N 30,23:5
Kauff, George H, 1958, Ap 11,25:2
Kauffer, Edward M, 1954, O 23,15:3
Kauffman, Carl, 1951, Jl 9,25:5
Kauffman, Isidore, 1947, Ja 16,25:4
Kauffman, J Harry, 1953, F 2,21:2
Kauffman, James B, 1957, Mr 18,27:5
Kauffman, James L, 1963, O 22,38:1
Kauffman, James Lee, 1968, Je 7,39:1
Kauffman, John R Jr, 1941, F 20,20:3
Kauffman, Lesser, 1939, Mr 13,17:2
Kauffman, Nathan, 1948, D 23,19:4
Kauffman, Percival C, 1914, Ap 10,13:6
Kauffman, Reginald W, 1959, Ap 26,86:5
Kauffman, Reginald W Mrs, 1952, Ag 14,23:6
Kauffman, Roland P, 1959, O 5,31:3
Kauffman, Samuel Hay, 1906, Mr 16,9:5
Kauffman, William A, 1953, Ap 14,27:5
Kauffmann, Albert W, 1948, D 30,19:2
Kauffmann, Alfred, 1959, Ag 8,17:6
Kauffmann, Felix I, 1953, N 16,25:4
Kauffmann, Florence H, 1945, Mr 28,23:4
Kauffmann, George M Mrs, 1948, Ag 12,21:5
Kauffmann, Harry H, 1959, Ja 29,27:2
Kauffmann, John J, 1948, O 31,88:6
Kauffmann, Otto Mrs, 1947, O 17,21:2
Kauffmann, Phil G, 1954, Je 11,23:3
Kauffmann, R, 1927, S 20,29:4
Kauffmann, Rudolph M, 1956, N 30,23:2
Kauffmann, Victor, 1941, My 7,25:2
Kaufherr, Daniel C Mrs, 1942, Ja 18,44:2
Kaufhold, Arthur F, 1937, Mr 12,24:2
Kaufhold, Donald L, 1956, Jl 8,64:2
Kaufman, A, 1919, D 11,13:3
Kaufman, A Spencer, 1958, Ap 1,31:1
Kaufman, Abel, 1955, Je 30,25:4
Kaufman, Abraham, 1955, Jl 19,27:4
Kaufman, Abraham Mrs (Priscilla), 1968, F 9,27:1
Kaufman, Abram, 1943, N 4,23:4
Kaufman, Agnes Boulton Mrs, 1968, N 26,53:4
Kaufman, Albert, 1963, Jl 4,17:2
Kaufman, Alex Mrs, 1961, D 25,23:5
Kaufman, Alexander, 1947, S 6,18:2
Kaufman, Alfonse, 1954, Ag 13,15:5
Kaufman, Alfred, 1941, O 3,23:1
Kaufman, Andrew, 1941, O 12,52:3
Kaufman, Anton Mrs, 1939, F 17,19:4
Kaufman, Arthur D, 1937, O 5,25:3
Kaufman, August, 1949, Ap 14,25:4
Kaufman, Benjamin, 1908, Jl 2,9:6; 1948, Je 20,62:2; 1952, Ap 11,23:4
Kaufman, Benjamin H, 1937, Je 2,23:3
Kaufman, Bruner, 1940, S 16,19:2
Kaufman, Carl, 1959, N 20,31:2
Kaufman, Charles, 1950, Jl 12,29:6
Kaufman, Charles E Dr, 1937, D 4,17:6
Kaufman, Charles J, 1942, Ja 29,19:4; 1956, Je 16,19:3
Kaufman, Charles K, 1941, S 1,15:6
Kaufman, Charles Mrs, 1943, O 31,48:6
Kaufman, Clarence W Jr, 1961, Ag 27,85:2
Kaufman, D J, 1939, N 16,23:4
Kaufman, Daniel W, 1921, S 1,15:2
Kaufman, David, 1958, S 27,21:5
Kaufman, David E (will, S 23,42:5), 1962, S 7,29:3
Kaufman, Edwin H, 1948, F 5,23:4
Kaufman, Edwin P, 1964, Ap 22,47:3
Kaufman, Elias Mrs, 1947, D 21,54:1
Kaufman, Emanuel, 1958, Je 15,76:6
Kaufman, Enit, 1961, Ja 20,26:1
Kaufman, Frank, 1942, My 30,15:3; 1943, D 21,28:2; 1956, My 4,51:5
Kaufman, Frank M (est acctg), 1958, S 20,11:8
Kaufman, Frederick, 1947, Jl 25,17:3; 1950, Ag 17,27:4
Kaufman, Gabe, 1947, N 11,27:1
Kaufman, George F, 1955, Ag 3,23:5
Kaufman, George S (funl, Je 5,31:3; will, Je 16,30:1), 1961, Je 3,1:4
Kaufman, George S Mrs (por), 1945, O 7,44:3
Kaufman, Gerald L, 1968, Ap 21,81:1
Kaufman, Harry, 1961, Ag 23,33:4
Kaufman, Harry A, 1944, N 19,50:3
Kaufman, Harry M, 1951, Ja 3,27:2
Kaufman, Harry Mrs, 1947, Je 15,60:6
Kaufman, Henry, 1951, S 20,31:1
Kaufman, Henry H, 1939, My 8,17:4
Kaufman, Herbert, 1947, S 7,63:3
Kaufman, Herman, 1958, Mr 11,29:3
Kaufman, Herman Mrs (cor, Jl 13,17:5), 1944, Jl 12, 19:3
Kaufman, Hyman, 1922, O 27,17:4
Kaufman, Irving, 1958, Ja 5,86:3
Kaufman, Isadore, 1941, Ag 12,19:6
Kaufman, Jack, 1954, Ja 14,29:5
Kaufman, Jacob, 1944, O 14,13:5
Kaufman, James A, 1957, Je 20,29:1
Kaufman, Jay, 1947, Mr 29,15:4
Kaufman, Jerome S Mrs, 1967, Ag 26,28:3
Kaufman, John B (Sept 15), 1965, O 11,61:3
Kaufman, John W, 1957, N 16,19:1
Kaufman, Joseph, 1918, F 2,11:4; 1954, Je 16,31:3; 1961, Ja 18,33:4; 1963, Je 16,84:2
Kaufman, Joseph A, 1962, Ja 14,84:6
Kaufman, Joseph S, 1940, Je 15,15:6; 1961, Jl 16,69:2
Kaufman, Julius, 1914, Ag 5,13:6; 1962, Je 6,41:3
Kaufman, Lawrence Willard Dr, 1968, D 29,53:2
Kaufman, Leo, 1955, Mr 22,31:2
Kaufman, Leon F, 1954, Mr 26,21:4
Kaufman, Lewis, 1937, Ap 3,19:2
Kaufman, Louis, 1945, D 13,29:3; 1948, S 26,76:3; 1956, F 9,32:1
Kaufman, Louis G (por), 1942, Mr 11,19:1
Kaufman, Louis J, 1903, Je 19,9:5; 1954, O 1,49:6
Kaufman, Louis K, 1925, Jl 16,9:3
Kaufman, Louis M, 1962, F 9,29:4
Kaufman, Louis R, 1964, Ag 20,29:2
Kaufman, Marcus, 1968, Ap 24,47:2
Kaufman, Marjorie, 1952, F 10,92:2
Kaufman, Max, 1950, My 10,31:5
Kaufman, Michael, 1938, Je 19,28:7
Kaufman, Michael J, 1946, Mr 25,25:4
Kaufman, Michael J Mrs, 1964, D 25,29:3
Kaufman, Milton, 1949, N 1,27:3
Kaufman, Moe H, 1954, S 15,33:3
Kaufman, Morris, 1960, Jl 8,21:3
Kaufman, Nathan Myron, 1918, N 26,15:3
Kaufman, Nettie M Mrs, 1940, N 2,15:3
Kaufman, Paul D, 1952, F 9,30:8
Kaufman, Percy S, 1960, Je 15,41:3
Kaufman, Philip Mrs, 1945, Jl 6,11:4
Kaufman, Robert E, 1960, O 11,45:1
Kaufman, S Jay, 1957, Je 21,25:3
Kaufman, Samuel, 1938, Je 21,19:6; 1944, Mr 25,15:3; 1944, D 23,13:5; 1947, Ap 16,25:3; 1950, D 6,33:1; 1960, Je 16,33:1
Kaufman, Samuel H, 1960, My 6,31:1
Kaufman, Samuel M, 1965, O 18,35:1
Kaufman, Samuel Mrs, 1951, Ja 28,76:1; 1960, F 20, 23:5; 1961, My 3,37:1
Kaufman, Sandor, 1950, Mr 31,31:3
Kaufman, Selma R, 1910, Mr 14,7:4
Kaufman, Sidney A, 1957, F 5,23:1
Kaufman, William H, 1924, Ap 4,19:6
Kaufman, William T, 1940, Ap 3,23:3
Kaufman, Yetta Mrs, 1938, S 25,41:6
Kaufmann, Albert A, 1965, Ag 5,29:4
Kaufmann, Albert A Mrs, 1948, D 24,18:3
Kaufmann, Alexander, 1946, My 10,19:4
Kaufmann, Alfred, 1951, N 15,29:5
Kaufmann, Arthur, 1937, O 31,II,11:3
Kaufmann, Arthur R, 1956, O 22,29:1
Kaufmann, Ary, 1956, N 8,39:2
Kaufmann, Augusta M Mrs, 1942, My 6,19:2
Kaufmann, Augustus Mrs, 1944, Ag 16,19:4
Kaufmann, Baruch, 1919, O 31,13:5
Kaufmann, Berthold (por), 1949, Mr 11,25:5
Kaufmann, Carl F, 1939, Ap 4,25:2
Kaufmann, Charles H, 1968, Je 11,47:3
Kaufmann, Christian, 1939, Ja 24,19:4
Kaufmann, Constantine von Gen, 1882, My 17,5:5
Kaufmann, David, 1946, Je 22,19:2
Kaufmann, Edgar J, 1955, Ap 16,19:3
Kaufmann, Edgar J Mrs, 1952, S 8,21:3
Kaufmann, Edgar Mrs, 1962, Ja 26,8:2
Kaufmann, Edmund I, 1950, Jl 18,29:3
Kaufmann, Edward, 1924, S 16,23:4; 1965, Ja 17,88:8
Kaufmann, Edward Mrs, 1946, My 10,19:4
Kaufmann, Felix, 1949, D 25,26:6
Kaufmann, Ferdinand H, 1961, S 1,17:2
Kaufmann, Frederick A, 1941, F 13,19:6
Kaufmann, Fritz, 1952, N 8,17:6
Kaufmann, George A Mrs, 1958, N 14,27:4
Kaufmann, Gordon B, 1949, Mr 2,26:2
Kaufmann, Gottlieb, 1903, D 14,7:4
Kaufmann, Gustav G, 1944, Ja 6,23:1
Kaufmann, Henry, 1952, F 3,84:3; 1955, Mr 14,23:5
Kaufmann, Henry Jr Mrs, 1952, Ap 4,25:4
Kaufmann, Herbert M, 1950, Mr 21,29:3
Kaufmann, Isaac, 1921, Jl 19,15:6
Kaufmann, Joseph M Mrs, 1961, Mr 21,37:1
Kaufmann, Josie F Mrs, 1939, N 14,23:2
Kaufmann, Jules, 1966, F 20,88:3
Kaufmann, Julius, 1937, O 26,23:5; 1963, O 16,45:5
Kaufmann, Karl M, 1951, F 11,88:2
Kaufmann, Louis W, 1964, Mr 2,27:4
Kaufmann, M J, 1967, Jl 2,35:1
Kaufmann, Maurus, 1949, Mr 2,25:4
Kaufmann, Morris Mrs, 1942, S 23,25:3
Kaufmann, Nathan, 1938, Ag 5,17:4
Kaufmann, Nathan Mrs, 1948, Mr 25,27:5
Kaufmann, Otto, 1946, Je 22,19:3
Kaufmann, Robert D, 1959, Ap 20,31:1
Kaufmann, S W, 1929, Ja 26,17:1
Kaufmann, Theodore (por), 1938, F 27,II,9:2
Kaufmann, Victor R, 1943, F 6,13:4
Kaufmann, William, 1949, Je 11,17:2
Kaul, Jacob, 1949, D 25,26:6
Kaul, Paul, 1952, Ja 3,27:1
Kaula, William J, 1953, Ja 27,25:4
Kaulbach, Hermann, 1909, D 10,11:5
Kaulback, Frank S, 1956, D 22,19:3
Kaulen, Hugo, 1954, Je 12,15:3
Kaulfers, Harry, 1947, Ja 30,25:4
Kaulfuss, Arthur E Mrs, 1946, S 18,31:4
Kaulfuss, Julius E, 1956, Mr 28,31:5
Kaull, James T, 1950, O 2,23:4
Kaulla, Otto, 1955, Jl 10,72:1
Kaumeyer, C Ellison, 1967, Je 23,31:8
Kaun, Alexander S, 1944, Je 24,13:5
Kaung, Z T, 1958, Ag 28,27:1
Kaup, Felix F Msgr, 1940, Mr 19,25:3
Kaupe, Albert G, 1939, S 23,17:5
Kaupe, William B, 1939, Mr 4,15:4
Kaupp, Carl B, 1952, O 30,31:3
Kaupp, Frederick W Mrs, 1942, N 3,23:5
Kaur, Rajkumari A Princess, 1964, F 7,31:4
Kaus, Francis J Mrs, 1958, Mr 17,29:2
Kaus, Herbert R, 1939, Mr 12,III,7:1
Kaus, J Emil, 1946, Ag 28,27:4
Kauser, Alice, 1945, S 10,19:5
Kautsky, Benedikt, 1960, Ap 3,87:1
Kautsky, Frank H, 1959, O 13,39:2
Kautsky, L, 1945, Je 18,5:6
Kautten, Emil Rev, 1912, Ja 9,13:5
Kautz, A, 1927, S 11,II,9:1
Kautz, Albert Rear-Adm, 1907, F 7,9:6
Kautz, Frank A S, 1952, My 15,31:6
Kautz, Frederick G, 1956, Ap 11,33:1
Kautz, Friedrich G, 1958, F 6,27:4
Kautz, George, 1951, Ap 16,25:2
Kautz, John A, 1938, My 19,21:4
Kautzky, Joe Sr, 1938, Ag 31,15:5
Kautzky, Karl J (por), 1938, O 18,25:1
Kautzky, Theodore, 1953, My 19,30:4
Kautzman, Charles P, 1937, D 28,21:2
Kautzmann, Gottlob, 1937, O 2,21:4
Kauzmann, Albert, 1941, Mr 8,19:4
Kavan, Anna, 1968, D 7,47:2
Kavanagh, Arthur, 1938, S 23,27:4
Kavanagh, Bertram P Sr, 1964, O 11,88:6
Kavanagh, Charles J Mrs, 1949, N 12,15:2
Kavanagh, Charles M, 1957, Mr 8,25:1
Kavanagh, Clarence, 1955, My 21,17:6
Kavanagh, Denis J, 1966, My 4,47:2
Kavanagh, Gardner C, 1944, F 28,17:4
Kavanagh, Giles, 1952, D 10,35:3
Kavanagh, Henry E (Ted), 1958, S 18,31:5
Kavanagh, Henry E Mrs, 1949, N 2,27:3
Kavanagh, James E, 1957, D 13,27:3
Kavanagh, James Orville, 1968, Jl 12,31:4
Kavanagh, John A C, 1954, My 1,15:3
Kavanagh, John J, 1951, Jl 27,19:2
Kavanagh, Joseph, 1903, Mr 28,9:6
Kavanagh, Joseph A, 1942, O 29,23:4; 1957, Ja 8,31:4
Kavanagh, Joseph D, 1946, Ag 24,11:6
Kavanagh, Joseph J, 1941, Ag 26,19:2
Kavanagh, Marcus A (por), 1938, Ja 1,19:1
Kavanagh, Matthew H, 1937, Ag 2,19:5
Kavanagh, Maurice F, 1944, Mr 23,19:5
Kavanagh, Michael D, 1943, D 10,27:2
Kavanagh, Michael P, 1952, Ap 13,77:1
Kavanagh, Patrick, 1967, D 1,47:1
Kavanagh, R Vincent, 1957, Ap 3,31:1
Kavanagh, Vincent, 1959, Jl 24,25:4
Kavanagh, William A, 1949, My 25,29:5
Kavanagh, William F Sr, 1963, O 13,87:2
Kavanagh, William L, 1941, D 29,15:4
Kavanah, Raymond E, 1955, Ap 26,29:1
Kavanaugh, Arthur G Com, 1920, F 24,13:5
Kavanaugh, Dennis, 1937, Jl 15,19:2
Kavanaugh, Edward J, 1938, Jl 20,19:2
Kavanaugh, Edward T, 1962, My 5,27:6
Kavanaugh, Emmett P, 1956, S 6,25:2
Kavanaugh, George W, 1951, S 8,17:5
Kavanaugh, George W Mrs, 1954, Ja 24,84:6
Kavanaugh, H H Bp, 1884, Mr 20,5:5
Kavanaugh, J Martin, 1946, Ja 1,27:4
Kavanaugh, James R Mrs, 1961, Je 8,32:4
Kavanaugh, James V, 1961, O 4,45:3
Kavanaugh, William F, 1937, Jl 15,19:3
Kavanaugh, William H, 1939, My 8,17:3
Kavanaugh, William J, 1946, F 13,23:1
Kavanaugh, William M, 1915, F 22,9:4
Kavasch, John, 1959, D 3,37:3
Kavasz, Mariska (Mrs D Peterson), 1960, Ag 28, 83:2
Kaveberg, Martin, 1956, Jl 17,23:4
Kaventy, Thomas, 1946, Mr 30,15:5
Kaveny, James C, 1955, Ag 28,84:3
Kaveny, Martin S, 1952, Ag 25,17:5

Kavesh, Harry, 1953, N 27,19:6
Kavey, Abraham H, 1953, Je 6,17:6
Kavezian, Omnig I, 1953, Ag 25,21:5
Kavina, Karel, 1948, Ja 23,23:4
Kavinoky, Bernice (Mrs W J Isaacson), 1965, F 5, 31:3
Kavookjian, Howard H, 1967, Ja 4,43:3
Kavovitz, Nathan, 1942, O 28,23:5
Kavy, Morris Mrs, 1964, Jl 6,29:2
Kawabe, Torashiro, 1960, Je 27,25:3
Kawai, Kanjiro, 1966, N 19,33:3
Kawai, Michi, 1953, F 14,17:1
Kawai, Misao, 1941, O 13,17:5
Kawaii, Kazuo, 1963, My 5,86:8
Kawakami, Jotaro, 1965, D 4,31:4
Kawakami, Kanichi, 1968, S 13,47:4
Kawakami, Kiyoshi K, 1949, O 13,27:5
Kawal, Al Mrs, 1951, Ag 28,23:2
Kawamata, Giichi, 1959, N 11,35:1
Kawamura, K Viscount, 1926, Ap 29,23:4
Kawamura, Karyo, 1954, S 2,21:6
Kawananakoa, Princess D, 1945, Ap 17,23:2
Kawecki, Paul, 1939, Mr 24,21:4
Kawut, Isaac, 1953, S 13,85:2
Kay, Abraham S, 1963, Jl 11,29:3
Kay, Alfred, 1949, F 15,23:4
Kay, Benny, 1960, Ja 23,21:2
Kay, Charles, 1946, O 2,29:4
Kay, Colin C, 1945, Je 8,19:3
Kay, Fred H (por), 1943, Jl 11,35:1
Kay, George F, 1943, Jl 21,15:2
Kay, George J Mrs, 1953, Ag 23,88:5
Kay, Gertrude, 1939, D 19,26:3
Kay, Helen Mrs (funl, Ap 7,20:3), 1960, Ap 1,27:4
Kay, Herbie, 1944, My 12,19:6
Kay, Jack, 1951, N 11,89:5
Kay, Jacob M Capt, 1948, F 23,25:3
Kay, James, 1944, Ap 23,42:6
Kay, John, 1884, Mr 23,5:5; 1951, S 10,21:3
Kay, John D, 1938, Jl 29,6:4
Kay, Joseph B, 1950, Ag 9,29:5
Kay, Joseph W, 1955, O 27,33:4
Kay, Leon L, 1959, N 25,29:2
Kay, Lillian S, 1939, Ag 12,13:5
Kay, Robert, 1949, S 17,17:1
Kay, Robert B, 1944, O 15,45:1
Kay, Robert J, 1955, My 1,88:8
Kay, Robert N, 1947, F 25,25:4
Kay, Wendell H, 1953, D 15,44:8
Kay, William, 1949, Je 15,29:2; 1951, Jl 8,61:2
Kay, William B, 1948, Je 26,18:2
Kay, William D, 1944, F 8,16:3
Kay, William H Mrs, 1957, Jl 8,23:6
Kay, William H Sr, 1953, S 30,31:3
Kay, William M, 1941, Je 28,15:5
Kay, William S, 1943, Ap 9,21:5
Kay, William V, 1950, Je 23,25:3
Kay-Skrzypeski, Kazimerz, 1964, Ja 23,36:5
Kaya, Yoshiko Princess, 1941, N 27,23:5
Kayaloff, Yasha, 1948, N 25,41:6
Kayar, S A, 1962, Mr 2,29:3
Kayden, Philip M, 1925, Mr 24,23:3
Kaye, Aaron M, 1958, Ja 14,30:5
Kaye, Albert P, 1946, O 9,27:6
Kaye, Alexander Mrs, 1945, My 17,19:4
Kaye, Arthur E, 1947, Ag 3,52:7
Kaye, Avedis H, 1944, N 16,23:3
Kaye, George J, 1951, D 12,37:2
Kaye, George L, 1965, My 12,47:5
Kaye, Lillian, 1944, Jl 18,19:2
Kaye, Sidney, 1967, Ag 8,39:2
Kaye, Walter, 1945, Jl 11,11:6
Kaye-Smith, Sheila, 1956, Ja 16,21:1
Kayes, George C, 1952, Mr 20,29:1
Kayfetz, Isidore, 1947, My 2,21:3
Kaylin, Edward S, 1959, S 21,31:4
Kaylor, Thomas W, 1945, S 9,45:2
Kaylor, Wallace A, 1947, Je 13,23:4
Kaylor, William G, 1951, Ap 27,23:6
Kayn, Hilde B Mrs, 1950, Ag 31,25:3
Kaynor, Warren F, 1947, F 24,19:4
Kayopolous, Peter, 1952, Ja 1,27:5
Kays, Henry T, 1958, Jl 28,23:4
Kays, R V Mrs, 1967, Jl 6,35:2
Kays, Thomas M, 1946, Mr 9,13:4
Kayser, Alex, 1952, O 6,25:3
Kayser, Charles D Dr, 1937, Ja 2,14:3
Kayser, Emile F, 1939, Ap 17,17:2
Kayser, Fred, 1950, My 15,21:5
Kayser, George B, 1956, Ja 21,21:5
Kayser, Gustave A, 1945, Mr 23,20:2
Kayser, Harry C, 1944, My 6,15:1
Kayser, John B Rev, 1903, S 13,7:5
Kayser, Julius, 1920, Mr 10,11:4
Kayser, Julius Mrs, 1943, D 14,27:4
Kayser, Louis Mrs, 1939, Mr 29,23:3
Kayser, Milton, 1956, F 18,19:2
Kayser, O William, 1968, Mr 28,57:6
Kayser, Paul B Mrs, 1947, D 9,29:2
Kayser, Reuben, 1950, Ap 15,15:2
Kayser, Rudolf, 1964, F 7,32:3
Kayton, Alvin J, 1955, Ap 6,29:4
Kaytor, Albert J, 1963, Ag 24,19:3

Kazakevich, Emmanuil G, 1962, S 23,86:3
Kazakov, Vasily (Marshal), 1968, My 27,47:3
Kazan, Abraham E Mrs, 1963, D 2,37:4
Kazan, Avraam E, 1946, N 21,32:3
Kazan, Molly (Mrs E Kazan),(funl, D 18,37:8), 1963, D 15,86:4
Kazanjian, Bedros Jr, 1957, F 23,17:6
Kazanjian, Calvin, 1948, Jl 30,17:5
Kazanjian, Harry Mrs, 1949, S 7,29:2
Kazankin, Alex F, 1955, Mr 25,21:3
Kazantzakis, Nikos, 1957, O 29,31:1
Kazaras, John, 1961, My 17,37:2
Kazier, Marion H Dr, 1917, Jl 21,11:4
Kazimir, Joseph R, 1951, Jl 25,24:2
Kazlauski, John, 1949, Jl 4,24:1
Kazunas, Michael R, 1958, O 3,18:5
Keady, Patrick, 1908, O 8,9:4
Keady, Thomas J, 1964, F 13,31:3
Keafy, John, 1947, S 20,15:5
Keagle, Donald M, 1951, F 23,27:2
Keagle, Merle Mrs, 1950, D 9,15:4
Keagy, Henry, 1938, Mr 8,19:1
Keahon, Patrick H, 1906, Jl 7,7:3
Kealey, Daniel S, 1943, D 29,18:2
Kealey, Edward, 1941, Mr 3,15:2
Kealing, J B, 1927, D 8,29:3
Kealy, Eugene P, 1959, My 24,89:2
Kealy, J Capt, 1884, Ja 5,2:6
Kealy, Michael F, 1960, N 25,27:4
Kealy, Philip J, 1944, Ag 27,33:4
Kealy, William P, 1942, O 30,19:4
Kean, Abram, 1945, My 21,19:2
Kean, Alexander Livingston, 1922, N 29,17:4
Kean, C Warren, 1944, Mr 4,13:3
Kean, Charles, 1868, Ja 24,1:2
Kean, Charles D, 1963, O 17,35:1
Kean, Charles Mrs (Helen Tree), 1880, Ag 22,7:5
Kean, Cyrus V, 1920, Mr 18,11:5
Kean, David, 1964, Ja 31,25:6
Kean, David L, 1955, Je 2,29:3
Kean, E A, 1927, D 14,29:5
Kean, Elizabeth d'Hauteville, 1922, D 12,19:4
Kean, Hamilton F, 1941, D 28,29:1
Kean, Hamilton F Mrs, 1943, Ag 25,19:3
Kean, John, 1949, O 25,27:3; 1956, D 1,21:2
Kean, John Ex-Sen, 1914, N 5,11:6
Kean, John J, 1938, D 4,60:5
Kean, John J Msgr, 1917, Ja 8,11:4
Kean, John Mrs, 1912, Mr 10,15:4
Kean, Joseph E (por), 1944, S 28,19:4
Kean, Mary Mrs, 1924, Je 18,19:4
Kean, Otho V, 1940, S 1,21:2
Kean, Otho V Mrs, 1956, Ag 2,25:5
Kean, Reginald S, 1959, Je 23,33:2
Kean, Samuel A, 1913, Jl 13,II,11:4
Kean, Susan Livingston, 1925, Jl 4,11:4
Kean, William B Mrs, 1953, Je 28,61:1
Kean, William L, 1937, D 18,21:4
Keane, Adelaide J, 1960, Jl 25,23:5
Keane, Albert W, 1939, Jl 12,19:6
Keane, Anna C Mrs, 1906, Ja 13,9:5
Keane, Arthur G, 1949, N 29,30:3; 1963, O 28,27:4
Keane, Betty (Mrs P H Bergson), 1964, Mr 4,34:6
Keane, Charles E, 1947, Jl 24,21:3
Keane, Charles P, 1950, My 29,17:3
Keane, Cornelius A, 1944, Jl 29,13:6
Keane, Daniel J, 1960, Ap 9,23:5
Keane, Doris (por), 1945, N 26,21:4
Keane, Edward J, 1942, Je 6,13:3
Keane, Fannie S Mrs, 1939, Je 19,15:5
Keane, Frances D Mrs, 1942, S 1,19:5
Keane, George A, 1942, Jl 8,23:5
Keane, George P, 1951, Ap 18,31:3
Keane, James A, 1955, S 20,31:1
Keane, James F Capt, 1937, F 3,23:4
Keane, James H, 1953, D 11,31:2
Keane, John, 1949, Ap 5,29:3
Keane, John A C, 1957, Je 8,19:4
Keane, John Daniel, 1948, F 19,23:3
Keane, John J, 1950, Je 13,27:3; 1958, N 27,29:2
Keane, John J (details, por, Ja 8,89:1), 1967, Ja 7, 27:5
Keane, John J Mrs, 1947, Jl 8,23:5
Keane, John J Sr, 1948, O 5,25:4
Keane, Lee A, 1958, F 9,88:8
Keane, Michael, 1946, My 8,25:5
Keane, Michael Sir, 1937, Ag 12,19:6
Keane, Patrick, 1952, Ja 10,30:2
Keane, Raymond R, 1948, Ap 9,23:2
Keane, Richard M, 1951, Ja 7,77:1
Keane, Richard V, 1946, Ap 27,17:3
Keane, Robert Mrs, 1947, Ag 31,36:7
Keane, Theodore J, 1952, My 16,24:3
Keane, Thomas A, 1943, N 3,25:2
Keane, Thomas E Mrs, 1949, Mr 5,17:4
Keane, Thomas F, 1948, D 17,28:2
Keane, Thomas J, 1939, Je 28,21:4; 1947, Mr 16,60:3
Keane, Thomas P, 1945, Jl 15,15:5
Keane, William E, 1955, F 16,29:1; 1967, My 7,87:1
Keane, William J, 1955, My 24,31:2
Keaney, Paul M, 1951, N 17,17:5
Kear, Edward L, 1951, Jl 16,21:5
Kear, Francis Capt, 1908, Mr 7,7:7

Kear, Francis J, 1962, N 21,33:3
Kear, Frank S, 1946, S 26,25:4
Kear, Rebecca V Mrs, 1940, D 1,61:2
Kearins, Michael F, 1949, My 28,15:2
Kearney, Aaron M, 1951, Ja 21,77:1
Kearney, Alex J, 1948, Ag 1,56:5
Kearney, Andrew F, 1959, F 7,19:2
Kearney, Andrew T, 1962, Ja 12,23:4
Kearney, Anna C, 1947, S 17,25:6
Kearney, Augustine J, 1945, D 4,30:2
Kearney, Bernard J, 1945, My 9,23:1
Kearney, Bernard L, 1940, Mr 11,15:1
Kearney, Dennis, 1907, Ap 26,9:5
Kearney, Edward B Mrs, 1943, My 17,15:5
Kearney, Edward Jr, 1916, Ap 5,13:5
Kearney, Emelie S F Mrs, 1947, N 6,27:4
Kearney, Ernest W, 1942, Je 20,13:6
Kearney, Frank A, 1958, D 4,39:3
Kearney, Frank J, 1947, F 21,20:3
Kearney, George F, 1960, Ja 27,33:4
Kearney, George L, 1952, Ap 29,27:4
Kearney, H J, 1933, My 1,15:5
Kearney, Harry A, 1948, My 24,19:5
Kearney, Henry W, 1950, Ag 5,15:6
Kearney, J Watts, 1903, D 26,2:2
Kearney, James A, 1944, Mr 12,37:2
Kearney, James H, 1947, N 22,15:2
Kearney, James J, 1945, Jl 30,19:2
Kearney, James L D, 1939, Ap 6,25:5
Kearney, John A, 1950, My 22,21:2
Kearney, John F, 1944, Jl 22,15:5; 1956, D 13,37:
Kearney, John F Msgr, 1923, Ap 12,19:5
Kearney, John J, 1957, N 10,86:8
Kearney, John L, 1945, Ag 4,11:6
Kearney, John Mrs, 1955, S 7,31:4
Kearney, John V, 1961, F 24,21:1
Kearney, Joseph J, 1939, N 20,19:5
Kearney, Joseph T, 1961, Mr 7,35:1
Kearney, Margaret J, 1951, N 20,31:3
Kearney, Matthew A Mrs, 1946, Je 14,21:4
Kearney, Maurice D, 1943, My 14,19:1
Kearney, Michael, 1937, O 24,II,8:7
Kearney, Michael E, 1956, D 2,86:1
Kearney, Monte Mrs, 1950, S 18,23:3
Kearney, P, 1933, Mr 29,13:1
Kearney, Patrick B Mrs, 1954, My 16,86:4
Kearney, Peadar, 1942, N 25,23:5
Kearney, Peter J, 1953, Mr 24,31:3
Kearney, Raymond A (funl plans, O 3,33:5; funl, 6,21:6), 1956, O 2,35:1
Kearney, Richard J, 1956, Jl 9,23:5
Kearney, Robert S, 1959, Ja 25,92:2
Kearney, Thomas, 1924, Ja 7,19:4
Kearney, Thomas A, 1941, N 8,19:5
Kearney, Thomas H, 1956, O 22,29:2
Kearney, Thomas K, 1950, O 13,29:2
Kearney, Thomas W, 1939, Ag 21,13:4
Kearney, Vincent J, 1948, Mr 16,28:2
Kearney, Warren, 1947, N 10,29:1
Kearney, William F, 1941, F 26,21:4; 1942, Ap
Kearns, Agnes S Mrs, 1959, Ag 29,17:6
Kearns, Alfred J (Soldier), 1957, S 11,33:3
Kearns, Allen B, 1956, Ap 22,85:3
Kearns, Anna C Mrs, 1938, N 23,21:4
Kearns, Carrie W, 1939, S 7,25:4
Kearns, Charles A, 1967, F 10,35:2
Kearns, Edward A, 1961, D 27,27:2
Kearns, Edward J, 1949, D 22,23:4
Kearns, Edythe A Mrs, 1966, Jl 27,39:2
Kearns, Francis J, 1957, S 19,29:2
Kearns, Frank C, 1961, Ag 28,25:3
Kearns, Frank J, 1956, S 29,19:4
Kearns, George T, 1955, S 26,23:4
Kearns, Jack (J L McKernan), 1963, Jl 8,29:2
Kearns, James A, 1945, N 11,42:6
Kearns, James J, 1950, F 16,23:5
Kearns, James J Mrs, 1953, Je 11,29:3
Kearns, John A, 1941, Ag 21,17:1
Kearns, John W, 1952, My 2,25:2; 1962, Ja 16,
Kearns, Joseph P Sr, 1961, F 9,31:4
Kearns, Joseph S, 1962, F 18,93:2
Kearns, Joseph T, 1951, O 23,29:1
Kearns, Matthew S, 1946, N 26,29:3
Kearns, Michael H Mrs, 1954, F 4,25:3
Kearns, Nick, 1949, Mr 13,76:1
Kearns, Stephen H, 1944, Ja 18,19:5
Kearns, Thomas, 1957, Mr 1,20:6
Kearns, Thomas F, 1959, Jl 21,29:1
Kearns, Thomas J, 1941, Mr 20,21:1
Kearns, Thomas L Sr, 1945, O 26,19:1
Kearns, Thomas Sen, 1918, O 19,15:2
Kearns, Thomas V, 1954, D 10,28:4
Kearns, William G, 1962, Jl 7,17:3
Kearns, William H, 1944, Ag 17,17:6
Kearns, William H Mrs, 1957, O 26,21:4
Kearny, George H Capt, 1907, F 19,9:6
Kearny, James C, 1960, D 6,41:1
Kearny, James Lawrence, 1921, D 17,13:4
Kearny, Mary, 1955, Ag 25,23:6
Kearny, Phil, 1951, D 31,13:6
Kearny, Philip J, 1958, Ag 2,17:7
Kearny, Thomas, 1942, Jl 15,19:5
Kearny, Thomas J, 1903, O 4,7:6

Kearons, William M, 1948, Ag 15,60:2
Kearsley, John R, 1954, Ja 4,19:3
Kearsley, Mary J, 1940, Jl 8,17:5
Kearton, Cherry (por), 1940, S 29,44:1
Keary, Charles F, 1917, O 28,21:1
Keary, Henry Lt-Gen Sir, 1937, Ag 14,13:6
Keasbey, Edward Q, 1925, Je 8,15:4
Keasbey, Frederick W Mrs, 1966, My 21,31:3
Keasbey, George MacCulloch, 1924, Ag 2,9:6
Keasbey, Henry M, 1939, F 28,20:2
Keasbey, Louisa E, 1941, Mr 17,17:4
Keasbey, Marguerite A, 1960, Jl 1,25:2
Keasey, Miles A, 1948, My 5,25:3
Keaster, Agnes J Mrs, 1941, Ag 26,19:1
Keaster, John, 1941, Je 23,17:4
Keat, Maude Z Mrs, 1938, O 23,41:2
Keates, George Mrs, 1953, D 15,39:1
Keathen, Marjorie, 1966, S 22,47:1
Keathley, Hampton Mrs, 1937, O 1,21:3
Keating, Andrew B, 1955, Ja 5,23:4
Keating, Anna G, 1955, My 22,89:1
Keating, Arthur, 1967, D 14,47:1
Keating, Bernard J, 1957, Je 3,27:3
Keating, Bert M, 1967, Jl 5,39:4
Keating, Charles H, 1948, S 16,29:6
Keating, Cletus, 1964, Je 21,84:5
Keating, David M, 1950, O 19,31:4
Keating, Edward, 1965, My 20,27:4
Keating, Edward C, 1958, D 30,35:3
Keating, Edward F, 1967, Mr 1,37:1
Keating, Edward L, 1952, Jl 22,25:3
Keating, Edward M, 1954, O 8,23:4
Keating, Edward P, 1945, Ap 8,36:2
Keating, Eugene M Mrs, 1953, N 3,31:4
Keating, Fred, 1961, Jl 1,17:1
Keating, Frederick L C, 1923, D 24,11:6
Keating, George E, 1954, F 17,31:2
Keating, Grace, 1944, F 29,17:4
Keating, Herbert F, 1962, N 25,86:4
Keating, Isaac H B, 1947, Ap 19,15:4
Keating, J, 1934, Jl 9,15:5
Keating, Jack T, 1951, D 19,31:1
Keating, James, 1924, Je 12,17:5; 1947, F 15,15:2
Keating, James A, 1965, Je 23,41:2
Keating, James E, 1952, My 22,27:1
Keating, James P, 1919, My 25,20:5
Keating, James V, 1944, Mr 15,19:4
Keating, Jerome B, 1939, Je 30,19:2
Keating, John B, 1940, N 6,23:3
Keating, John F, 1946, S 16,5:4; 1962, My 27,92:8; 1967, N 25,39:3
Keating, John G, 1968, Ja 30,38:4
Keating, John H Sr, 1963, Ja 22,15:6
Keating, John J, 1947, Ag 24,56:1
Keating, John J Sr, 1941, N 22,19:2
Keating, John L, 1941, F 20,19:3
Keating, John Mrs, 1945, Ap 12,23:1
Keating, John P, 1943, F 24,21:4; 1947, Jl 18,17:2; 1952, My 20,25:2
Keating, John S, 1945, Mr 21,23:2
Keating, Joseph A, 1947, F 25,25:1
Keating, Joseph T, 1950, O 4,31:1
Keating, Kenneth B Mrs, 1968, S 18,47:2
Keating, Larry, 1963, Ag 27,31:3
Keating, Laurence F, 1968, N 9,33:4
Keating, Linus, 1941, D 6,17:2
Keating, M De Chantal Mother, 1917, Je 6,11:5
Keating, M T, 1878, O 20,7:3
Keating, Margaret A Mrs, 1942, S 28,17:5
Keating, Maurice F, 1949, Mr 24,27:4
Keating, Michael F, 1959, Ja 30,27:2
Keating, Michael H, 1945, O 4,23:2
Keating, Nora T, 1951, O 6,19:5
Keating, Patrick F, 1951, Ag 2,21:1
Keating, Patrick I, 1941, Mr 12,21:5
Keating, Paul, 1954, F 20,17:6
Keating, Peter M, 1959, F 22,88:4
Keating, Peter Sr, 1947, Ap 16,25:3
Keating, Peter Sr Mrs, 1947, O 31,23:2
Keating, Ralph, 1960, Ag 16,29:2
Keating, Ralph H, 1960, Ap 15,24:1
Keating, Robert E, 1938, N 24,27:5
Keating, T Frank, 1939, Ap 18,23:1
Keating, Thomas A, 1962, O 26,31:1
Keating, Thomas E, 1943, D 31,15:2
Keating, Thomas F, 1917, Jl 14,7:4
Keating, William E Mrs, 1956, Jl 6,21:4
Keating, William J, 1960, S 29,35:4; 1963, Mr 26,9:6; 1963, My 21,37:2
Keating, William J Mrs, 1967, O 31,45:1
Keating, William R, 1962, Ap 27,35:3
Keatinge, Harriette C Dr, 1909, N 12,11:6
Keatinge, William B, 1966, My 4,47:3
Keaton, Buster (Jos F), 1966, F 2,1:3
Keaton, Clifton H, 1960, F 11,35:2
Keaton, Joseph, 1946, Ja 15,23:3
Keaton, Joseph Mrs, 1955, Jl 22,23:4
Keaton, Russell, 1945, F 15,19:1
Keator, Beverley, 1952, F 28,27:3
Keator, Eugene H, 1946, Jl 16,23:4
Keator, Frederic Rose, 1925, My 19,21:3
Keator, Frederic William Rev, 1924, F 1,17:5
Keator, Grace, 1955, Mr 11,25:2
Keator, Harry F, 1959, Je 5,27:4
Keator, Randall M Sr, 1958, D 7,88:1
Keats, Frederick J Mrs, 1958, F 27,27:3
Keats, Harry L, 1941, O 19,47:3
Keats, Mildred, 1953, My 9,19:3
Keats, Sidney, 1961, Ap 9,86:5
Keats, William H, 1961, Ja 16,27:3
Keaver, Patrick H, 1949, Jl 6,27:1
Keavney, William T, 1950, S 7,31:3
Keaw, Louis, 1908, Ap 27,9:4
Keay, Louise K Mrs, 1941, N 1,15:5
Keays, Frederick L, 1950, S 9,17:2
Keays, George J, 1952, Ja 12,13:3
Keays, Harold, 1945, D 28,15:4
Kebart, Carl, 1920, S 24,15:2
Kebart, Jules C, 1966, My 22,86:6
Kebbon, Eric, 1964, Ap 19,84:5
Kebbon, Richard A, 1949, My 9,25:5
Keble, John Rev, 1866, Ap 15,5:4
Kebler, Gustave, 1924, D 26,15:5
Kebler, John A, 1907, Ap 13,11:6
Kebler, Leonard, 1961, S 22,33:1
Kebler, Leonard Mrs, 1963, My 1,39:5
Kebler, Lyman F, 1955, Mr 5,17:6
Keblinger, Wilbur, 1953, My 16,19:4
Kebreau, Antonio, 1963, Ja 15,16:1
Kechedzhi, Nikolai, 1951, Ja 4,29:4
Kechele, D V, 1958, S 15,21:4
Keck, Alfred, 1951, Ja 13,15:6
Keck, Arthur C, 1939, F 24,19:1
Keck, Charles (trb lr, My 3,28:7), 1951, Ap 24,29:1
Keck, Charles E, 1942, S 25,21:2
Keck, Charles H, 1955, D 21,29:2
Keck, Emil C, 1948, Mr 26,22:2
Keck, Ernst M, 1942, N 6,23:1
Keck, Frank Maj, 1925, Je 26,17:5
Keck, Frederick, 1958, Ag 16,17:4
Keck, J Fred, 1943, Je 30,21:5
Keck, Joseph, 1946, Ap 16,25:2
Keck, Maxfield H, 1943, Mr 8,15:4
Keck, Russell A, 1950, Ap 3,23:3
Keck, Stanton, 1951, Ja 21,78:2
Keck, Wernpard, 1909, Mr 26,9:4
Keck, William M (will Ag 28,37:3), 1964, Ag 21,29:1
Keck, William M Sr (est acctg), 1965, Je 30,23:5
Kedah, Sultan of (Sir Badlishah), 1958, Jl 14,21:1
Keddell, James S, 1950, D 11,25:1
Keddie, David, 1907, Mr 31,9:8
Keddie, Henrietta, 1914, Ja 10,9:5
Keddie, James, 1942, O 8,27:1
Keddie, Margaret C Mrs, 1938, Mr 18,19:4
Kederich, Charles H, 1941, Jl 1,23:1
Kederich, George A, 1947, S 11,27:2
Kederick, Harry C B, 1951, Mr 2,25:2
Kedroff, Nicholas J, 1944, My 17,19:4
Kedrovich, Vladimir K, 1944, Mr 31,21:3
Kedrovsky, J S, 1934, Mr 18,35:1
Kee, George F, 1943, Ja 2,11:4
Kee, John, 1951, My 9,33:1
Keeble, Glendinning, 1947, Jl 22,24:3
Keebler, Phil Mrs, 1949, Je 23,27:2
Keebler, Walter G, 1952, Ap 8,29:2
Keech, Frank B Mrs, 1937, F 9,23:1
Keech, George T, 1937, Jl 9,21:6
Keech, George T Mrs, 1947, Ap 5,19:3
Keech, George W Mrs, 1919, O 23,13:3
Keech, John S, 1945, D 16,40:5
Keedick Lee, 1959, Ag 18,29:2
Keedy, Charles C Mrs, 1944, F 9,19:4
Keedy, Edwin R, 1958, N 27,29:3
Keeefe, Daniel E, 1941, Jl 14,13:6
Keefauver, Clarence R, 1952, Je 17,28:5
Keefe, Charles J D Mrs, 1940, D 29,24:6
Keefe, Charles S, 1946, Jl 20,13:5
Keefe, Daniel C, 1962, O 28,89:1
Keefe, David, 1940, My 11,19:6
Keefe, David A, 1943, My 19,25:3
Keefe, Edward M, 1952, Jl 23,23:4
Keefe, Edward V, 1957, F 6,25:5
Keefe, Elizabeth Mrs, 1938, S 7,36:6
Keefe, F Clyde, 1958, Ja 22,28:3
Keefe, Frank B, 1952, F 6,29:1
Keefe, Frank G, 1956, Mr 16,23:3
Keefe, Frederick H, 1943, N 27,13:6
Keefe, Gerard, 1953, Mr 4,54:7
Keefe, Grace, 1954, S 17,27:6
Keefe, James H Sr, 1951, Ap 13,23:1
Keefe, John A, 1942, N 2,21:1
Keefe, John B, 1953, My 25,25:4
Keefe, John H, 1921, O 21,15:6
Keefe, John H Sr, 1953, Ag 3,17:6
Keefe, John J, 1960, Ag 21,84:5
Keefe, John W, 1946, S 10,7:5
Keefe, Joseph F, 1951, N 24,11:5
Keefe, Lawrence J, 1957, Mr 24,86:8
Keefe, Lawrence J Mrs, 1953, My 15,23:1
Keefe, Lawrence V, 1951, Jl 28,8:8
Keefe, Patrick, 1937, Jl 19,15:4
Keefe, Paul S, 1967, N 28,51:8
Keefe, Pierce, 1940, My 11,19:6
Keefe, Rose (Mother Mary Aloysius), 1913, O 11, 15:4
Keefe, Rudyard T, 1952, Jl 13,61:1
Keefe, Tammis, 1960, Je 6,29:5
Keefe, Thomas B, 1949, Mr 17,25:3
Keefe, Thomas J, 1955, D 19,27:1
Keefe, Thomas M, 1964, S 23,47:4
Keefe, Walter L, 1950, Jl 14,21:3
Keefe, Walter R, 1957, Jl 2,27:4
Keefe, William J, 1955, S 15,33:3
Keefe, William J Mrs, 1956, N 17,21:3
Keefer, B Ray, 1947, Ag 18,17:5
Keefer, Charles D, 1942, Jl 26,30:8
Keefer, Frank R, 1954, My 17,23:3
Keefer, Henry D, 1947, My 7,27:3
Keefer, Henry H, 1948, Ja 30,23:3
Keefer, Ivan W, 1965, Ja 9,25:6
Keefer, Phil B, 1949, Ja 17,19:2
Keefer, Reuben, 1941, My 4,52:2
Keefer, William C Mrs, 1946, Ag 7,27:1
Keefer, Winifred J Mrs, 1952, F 14,27:3
Keeffe, L Richard, 1964, Ja 8,37:1
Keegan, Arthur I, 1958, O 4,21:1
Keegan, Arthur P, 1949, N 23,29:4
Keegan, Charles E, 1966, Jl 6,45:1
Keegan, Edward J, 1953, Ja 1,23:5; 1957, O 30,29:3
Keegan, Edwin A, 1906, Jl 3,9:6
Keegan, Frederick H, 1942, O 22,21:1
Keegan, George F Sr, 1947, F 28,23:2
Keegan, J Edward, 1937, F 28,II,8:7
Keegan, James T, 1950, O 20,27:3
Keegan, John, 1945, F 17,13:5
Keegan, John F, 1942, My 6,19:4
Keegan, John H, 1938, Jl 8,17:2
Keegan, John S, 1964, Ag 27,33:2
Keegan, John W, 1956, Ag 6,23:3
Keegan, Joseph E, 1960, Je 4,23:5
Keegan, Joseph J, 1955, Ja 15,13:1
Keegan, Joseph J Mrs, 1950, Ja 16,26:2
Keegan, Joseph M, 1950, O 17,31:1
Keegan, Josephine (Mrs M Smith), 1966, Ag 27,29:5
Keegan, Katherine, 1950, F 10,23:4
Keegan, Kevin, 1948, S 22,31:4
Keegan, Lawrence V Sr, 1957, O 27,87:1
Keegan, Margaret C Mrs, 1940, O 10,25:6
Keegan, Mary Mrs, 1903, D 10,1:3
Keegan, Michael, 1948, S 3,19:3; 1950, F 8,27:2
Keegan, Owen J, 1940, Jl 11,19:2
Keegan, Paul W, 1954, Ja 21,31:1
Keegan, Robert F, 1947, N 5,27:1
Keegan, Robert V, 1950, D 6,33:1
Keegan, Vincent J, 1952, S 13,17:4
Keegan, Vincent L, 1963, My 9,37:1
Keegan, William G, 1949, Ag 27,13:6
Keegan, William H, 1944, S 8,19:5
Keegan, William J, 1954, Jl 31,13:3
Keegan, William L, 1943, Jl 1,19:2
Keehn, George W, 1946, F 27,25:4
Keehn, Grant Mrs, 1961, F 2,29:2
Keehn, Roy D, 1949, F 22,24:2
Keel, Charles H, 1950, F 9,29:6
Keel, Chester, 1954, Ja 16,15:3
Keel, Elmo W Mrs, 1961, N 26,88:7
Keelan, Harry J, 1940, Ap 25,23:2
Keelan, Patrick F, 1955, F 18,22:2
Keelan, Patrick F Mrs, 1950, Ag 15,19:3
Keelan, Thomas J, 1946, Ja 3,19:1
Keeland, John A, 1946, Jl 13,15:2
Keeler, Adele C, 1961, O 7,23:2
Keeler, Alexis Capt, 1909, Ja 8,9:5
Keeler, Alton S, 1960, F 4,31:1
Keeler, Anna Mrs, 1940, My 30,17:3
Keeler, Anson W, 1943, S 30,21:2
Keeler, Arza B, 1959, Ja 12,39:4
Keeler, Benjamin A, 1965, D 22,31:1
Keeler, Benjamin C, 1962, My 13,88:8
Keeler, Charles A, 1947, S 18,25:6
Keeler, Charles E, 1940, Mr 31,44:8
Keeler, Daniel, 1948, F 27,21:3
Keeler, David B, 1915, S 7,13:5
Keeler, Edith Mrs, 1954, Ja 1,23:3
Keeler, Edward B, 1937, Ag 4,19:2
Keeler, Farnam J, 1953, Ja 6,29:1
Keeler, Floyd Y, 1954, Ap 23,27:3
Keeler, Frank H, 1960, N 8,29:2
Keeler, Frederick S, 1941, Ja 8,19:4
Keeler, Harold R, 1953, Ag 21,18:5
Keeler, Harry, 1939, D 20,25:2
Keeler, Harry F, 1954, Ja 9,15:5
Keeler, Harry Jr, 1947, Mr 1,15:5
Keeler, Horace B, 1945, N 15,19:4
Keeler, Howard E, 1950, F 28,29:5
Keeler, Howard L, 1948, N 28,92:7
Keeler, Isaac M, 1907, F 18,9:6
Keeler, Isaac P, 1942, S 27,48:4
Keeler, John, 1912, D 2,11:4
Keeler, John Henry, 1909, O 18,7:5
Keeler, Josephine, 1950, Ap 5,31:5
Keeler, Lansing Mrs, 1955, Je 2,29:5
Keeler, Leonarde (por), 1949, S 21,31:3
Keeler, Lester A, 1965, Je 5,31:5
Keeler, Louis W, 1939, N 7,25:3
Keeler, Nellie, 1903, Je 18,1:4
Keeler, O B, 1950, O 16,27:4
Keeler, Ralph W, 1956, O 19,27:3
Keeler, Ralph W Mrs, 1944, Jl 2,20:2

Keeler, Raymond M, 1959, N 18,41:4
Keeler, Robert R, 1959, My 28,31:3
Keeler, Samuel J, 1948, F 13,21:4
Keeler, Stephen E (mem ser, O 1,27:4), 1956, S 27, 35:3
Keeler, Thadeus H Mrs, 1950, F 11,15:4
Keeler, Thomas Jefferson, 1919, My 19,17:5
Keeler, Wendell P, 1951, F 19,23:4
Keeler, William B Dr, 1937, F 12,23:5
Keeler, William H, 1948, Jl 29,21:5
Keeler, William Mrs, 1957, My 8,37:2
Keeler, William R, 1941, My 26,19:6
Keeler, William S, 1937, F 25,23:3
Keeley, Charles, 1943, F 28,49:2
Keeley, Daniel, 1943, Ag 10,21:7
Keeley, Edward S, 1919, Ag 2,7:6
Keeley, Ellen J Mrs, 1941, My 4,52:3
Keeley, Frank, 1943, Ag 10,21:7
Keeley, Frank J, 1949, Ap 13,29:2
Keeley, Harry J, 1948, Ag 7,15:6
Keeley, Hugh J, 1945, Ag 2,19:5
Keeley, J, 1934, Je 8,21:4
Keeley, J Fred, 1944, My 23,23:2
Keeley, James, 1943, My 26,23:4
Keeley, John J, 1949, Jl 27,23:2
Keeley, Joseph F, 1947, Ag 22,15:3
Keeley, Michael H, 1903, N 29,7:5
Keeley, Milton R, 1940, Ap 3,23:2
Keeley, Phil D, 1941, My 13,24:2
Keeley, R Mrs, 1899, Mr 13,7:3
Keeley, Thomas J, 1950, Mr 15,29:3
Keeley, Thomas P, 1947, F 24,19:2
Keeley, William J, 1940, Ag 27,21:6
Keeling, Edward, 1954, N 24,23:5
Keeling, Hugh, 1955, F 5,15:6
Keeling, Robert J Rev Dr, 1909, D 10,11:5
Keeling, Stewart, 1943, Jl 19,15:4
Keelips, Robert W, 1963, My 14,39:5
Keelty, James, 1944, Je 16,19:3
Keely, David F, 1958, Jl 24,25:5
Keely, J E W, 1898, N 19,7:4
Keely, John A, 1955, Ap 10,89:1
Keemle, Louis F, 1952, N 20,31:3
Keen, Benjamin B, 1964, N 22,86:6
Keen, Ed L (por), 1943, O 8,19:1
Keen, Edward V W, 1947, O 20,23:5
Keen, Eliot, 1939, Mr 28,23:4
Keen, Forrest M Dr, 1968, O 26,37:3
Keen, Frank A, 1939, O 13,23:1
Keen, Frank H Mrs, 1945, Ja 12,15:3
Keen, Frederick L, 1954, Je 14,21:1
Keen, Harry R, 1945, My 22,19:2
Keen, Jules, 1906, N 1,9:5
Keen, Kennard G Jr, 1966, Je 25,31:4
Keen, Kennard J, 1943, My 11,21:2
Keen, Mary P Mrs, 1941, N 14,23:1
Keen, Oscar, 1913, Ja 10,11:4
Keen, Owen A, 1940, Mr 30,15:1
Keen, Paul E, 1958, N 21,29:2
Keen, Paul Mrs, 1956, F 26,89:1
Keen, Samuel M, 1943, S 30,21:4
Keen, Victor, 1955, Ja 31,19:3
Keen, W Ralph, 1954, Jl 16,21:6
Keen, W W, 1932, Je 8,19:6
Keen, William M, 1950, Mr 6,21:2
Keena, James T, 1924, Ja 9,21:3
Keena, Martin J, 1965, Ag 23,31:4
Keena, Michael T, 1943, My 28,21:2
Keenahan, Martin B, 1949, Ag 4,23:5
Keenan, Albert J, 1947, O 4,17:1
Keenan, Albert J Jr, 1968, Ag 15,37:2
Keenan, Alex L, 1948, Ap 2,23:2
Keenan, Bernard Rev, 1877, F 20,1:5
Keenan, Chris, 1948, Mr 27,13:4
Keenan, Chris C, 1940, Ap 3,23:4
Keenan, Christopher C Mrs, 1960, Ag 21,84:5
Keenan, Daniel S, 1953, S 10,25:4
Keenan, Edward J, 1965, Mr 26,35:3
Keenan, Eugene C, 1955, N 26,19:4
Keenan, F, 1929, F 25,23:3
Keenan, George F, 1967, Mr 23,35:4
Keenan, George F Dr, 1937, O 27,31:4
Keenan, Harold E (funl Ja 19,25:4), 1954, Ja 15,9:2
Keenan, Hilda, 1940, Ag 22,19:2
Keenan, Hugh V, 1952, N 9,91:1
Keenan, James, 1950, Ap 4,30:3
Keenan, James A, 1938, Je 5,44:7; 1958, Ag 27,29:3
Keenan, James B, 1950, Je 6,29:5
Keenan, James C Mrs, 1953, Jl 29,23:3
Keenan, James J, 1961, Ag 29,31:1
Keenan, James R, 1907, Mr 16,9:6
Keenan, John, 1904, Mr 4,9:5
Keenan, John D, 1954, Ap 13,31:5
Keenan, John F, 1942, Ja 10,15:3
Keenan, John J, 1940, Je 7,23:4; 1940, O 4,23:6; 1948, N 13,15:6
Keenan, John L, 1942, S 26,15:5; 1944, Ja 8,13:6
Keenan, Joseph, 1940, Ap 11,25:1
Keenan, Joseph B, 1954, D 9,33:1
Keenan, Joseph C, 1954, O 30,17:5
Keenan, Joseph D Mrs, 1954, F 13,13:4
Keenan, Joseph J, 1953, Ag 31,17:3
Keenan, Joseph J Mrs, 1941, Jl 18,19:5
Keenan, Joseph W, 1947, F 27,21:2
Keenan, Lawrence F, 1943, Mr 8,15:5
Keenan, Luke A, 1924, D 16,25:4
Keenan, Michael, 1940, Ja 21,34:8
Keenan, Mildred H, 1955, Jl 11,23:5
Keenan, P Frank Mrs, 1937, F 3,23:1
Keenan, P H, 1876, Mr 15,5:1
Keenan, Patrick, 1907, My 6,9:1
Keenan, Peter, 1949, Ap 8,26:4
Keenan, Peter B, 1923, Je 20,19:5
Keenan, Peter J, 1940, D 28,15:4; 1952, Ag 16,15:6
Keenan, Phil K, 1940, S 12,25:5
Keenan, Robert H, 1950, Jl 7,19:3
Keenan, Teresa, 1953, My 10,88:4
Keenan, Thomas, 1906, Ag 4,7:5; 1940, O 9,25:3
Keenan, Thomas A, 1947, My 21,25:1
Keenan, Thomas J, 1948, O 15,23:2
Keenan, Thomas J Rev (will, My 19,23:3), 1937, My 7,II,8:3
Keenan, Thomas W, 1950, Jl 7,19:4
Keenan, W Carrol, 1949, Je 18,13:4
Keenan, Walter (por), 1941, O 5,49:1
Keenan, Walter F Jr, 1940, Mr 19,25:3
Keenan, Walter M Sr, 1956, Ag 29,29:5
Keenan, Walter Mrs, 1939, Ap 19,23:5
Keenan, William D, 1949, D 7,31:4
Keenan, William F, 1949, Ja 28,22:2
Keenan, William J, 1952, Mr 29,15:1
Keene, Albert J, 1940, D 28,15:4
Keene, Alfred M, 1937, F 9,23:5
Keene, Benjamin, 1951, N 18,91:2
Keene, Charles H, 1965, My 2,89:1
Keene, Charles J, 1942, F 1,43:2
Keene, Charles W, 1957, S 15,84:5
Keene, Emory, 1951, N 19,23:4
Keene, Floyd E, 1938, N 17,25:5
Keene, Foxhall P, 1941, S 26,23:5
Keene, George E, 1948, O 15,23:4
Keene, Henry, 1906, S 10,7:5
Keene, Henry C Maj, 1940, Mr 25,15:3
Keene, Henry C Mrs, 1940, Mr 25,15:3
Keene, James R Mrs, 1916, O 10,11:7
Keene, John O, 1943, My 28,21:5
Keene, Laura, 1873, N 7,5:3
Keene, Lillian, 1948, Ja 22,27:3
Keene, Marcel S, 1954, Mr 27,17:3
Keene, Marcel S Mrs, 1956, My 28,27:6
Keene, Mary L Mrs, 1942, Ap 20,21:4
Keene, Mattie, 1944, S 3,26:5
Keene, T W, 1898, Je 2,7:6
Keene, Tom (G Duryea), 1963, Ag 7,33:2
Keene, Walter B, 1953, Je 12,27:5
Keene, Wilson B, 1960, My 4,45:3
Keenehan, John F Rev, 1925, N 13,19:4
Keenen, George E, 1942, My 15,19:4
Keener, Frank E, 1967, My 12,47:4
Keener, H James, 1954, O 22,27:5
Keener, Martha E Mrs, 1958, Je 3,31:4
Keener, Myrtle D Mrs, 1939, Mr 17,21:1
Keener, Sam, 1954, Ap 4,89:1
Keener, William A Ex-Justice, 1913, Ap 23,11:5
Keeney, A G Mrs, 1948, N 21,88:3
Keeney, Caldwell B, 1959, My 23,25:4
Keeney, Frank A, 1958, N 2,88:8
Keeney, Fred C, 1914, My 14,11:4
Keeney, Frederick T, 1952, S 25,31:4
Keeney, George A Jr, 1965, My 2,89:2
Keeney, James C, 1948, D 17,27:2
Keeney, James M, 1948, Je 8,25:4
Keeney, Myra G, 1948, Ag 23,18:2
Keeney, Perry H, 1943, Jl 28,15:2
Keeney, Ralph D Jr, 1952, S 19,23:3
Keeney, Ralph D Mrs, 1959, Ap 14,35:2
Keeney, Russell W, 1958, Ja 12,86:2
Keeney, Sarah D Dr, 1925, N 14,15:5
Keeney, Seth L, 1913, Mr 14,9:2
Keenholts, Frederick E, 1950, Je 17,15:5
Keenlyside, Robert W, 1958, S 21,86:7
Keens, Thomas, 1953, N 26,32:3
Keeny, Spurgeon M Mrs, 1959, Ap 14,35:3
Keep, Albert, 1907, My 14,11:6
Keep, Charles C Mrs, 1944, Ap 23,43:4
Keep, Charles H, 1941, Ag 31,22:4
Keep, Charles H Mrs, 1954, D 26,61:1
Keep, Frank Mrs, 1957, Ap 26,25:2
Keep, Frederic A, 1911, Je 4,II,11:5
Keep, Harry V, 1938, F 13,II,7:3
Keep, Harry V Mrs, 1950, My 20,15:4
Keep, Henry, 1869, Jl 31,5:1
Keep, J L Dr, 1882, Ag 22,8:6
Keep, J Lester Dr, 1916, O 1,23:5
Keep, John J, 1947, D 15,25:2
Keep, Oliver D, 1965, F 20,25:2
Keep, Oliver Hildreth Jr Mrs, 1908, Ap 10,9:5
Keep, Robert P, 1967, Ap 5,47:4
Keep, Robert P Dr, 1904, Je 4,9:6
Keep, Robert P Mrs, 1965, S 13,35:2
Keep, Wallace I, 1945, My 11,19:5
Keers, Walter F, 1952, My 27,27:1
Kees, Natalie E Mrs, 1950, D 28,25:1
Kees, Valere J Mrs, 1957, Mr 16,19:2
Keese, Francis Suydam Col, 1907, Ag 19,7:6
Keese, Franklin H Mrs, 1939, N 12,48:7
Keese, G Pomeroy, 1910, Ap 24,II,13:4
Keese, Marty, 1909, Je 28,7:1
Keese, William Linn, 1904, O 4,9:6
Keese, William R, 1919, Ja 15,11:2
Keeshan, Alfred G, 1962, F 3,21:2
Keesing, Felix M, 1961, Ap 23,86:6
Keesing, Isaac, 1966, Ag 27,29:5
Keesing, John Maurice, 1968, S 20,47:2
Keesing, Leonard, 1964, Ap 10,39:5
Keesling, Lloyd N, 1940, Mr 19,25:6
Keesom, Willem H, 1956, Mr 5,23:2
Keester, William J, 1967, S 19,51:6
Keeton, Forest M, 1944, Ap 5,19:6
Keeton, Robert K, 1957, Ja 23,29:3
Keeton, Thomas W Sr, 1955, D 9,27:3
Keets, Charles G, 1952, F 13,29:2
Keeveny, Thomas W, 1951, Ag 14,23:3
Keever, Edwin F, 1949, D 19,27:5
Keevers, Bernard V, 1938, Mr 13,II,9:2
Keevil, Arthur W, 1944, Mr 22,19:3
Keevil, George J, 1949, Ja 7,22:2
Keevil, Harry E, 1953, F 20,19:2
Keevil, Pauline Mrs, 1905, Je 21,14:5
Keevill, John H, 1945, S 3,23:5
Keezer, Max, 1941, F 2,44:2
Kefauver, Estes (Carey E), 1963, Ag 11,1:2
Kefauver, Estes Mrs, 1967, N 21,47:1
Kefauver, Grayson N, 1946, Ja 6,40:2
Kefauver, Robert C, 1958, F 20,25:2
Kefer, George, 1948, My 14,23:4
Kefer, Paul A, 1941, F 23,40:1
Keffer, Frank M, 1960, D 31,17:4
Keffer, Karl Jr, 1945, Jl 15,15:6
Keffer, Roscoe H, 1954, My 23,88:5
Kegel, W Percy, 1952, S 17,31:5
Kegel, W Percy Mrs, 1946, F 16,13:4
Kegel, Will C, 1942, My 3,53:2
Kegelman, Lillie A, 1945, Jl 12,11:4
Kegg, William B, 1966, Ag 15,27:3
Kegler, Tydvil E Mrs, 1941, Jl 10,40:3
Kegreiss, Frederick J, 1950, Ap 13,29:2
Kehaya, Ery, 1964, My 25,33:1
Kehir, James J, 1957, D 28,17:4
Kehl, Frederick W, 1938, Ag 18,20:2
Kehl, Karl J, 1949, My 11,29:2
Kehl, Ralph, 1951, Jl 20,23:5
Kehlbaugh, Edmond H, 1924, Ap 4,19:5
Kehlenbeck, Albert W, 1943, Mr 19,19:3
Kehler, William E, 1950, My 2,29:4
Kehm, Harry C, 1949, Jl 1,19:4
Kehnroth, Charles Henry Dr, 1906, Jl 3,9:6
Keho, John W Mrs, 1948, F 27,21:4
Kehoe, Charles D, 1953, O 14,29:4
Kehoe, Charles J, 1967, F 6,29:2
Kehoe, Chris J, 1942, Ja 22,18:4
Kehoe, Cyril C, 1942, Je 9,23:1
Kehoe, Edwin J, 1940, F 13,23:3
Kehoe, Elizabeth F, 1963, N 29,37:3
Kehoe, Frank, 1942, Jl 25,13:6
Kehoe, George, 1939, F 21,19:2
Kehoe, George R, 1938, Ag 30,17:6
Kehoe, Gerard J, 1956, Mr 16,23:5
Kehoe, J Walter, 1938, Ag 21,32:5
Kehoe, John, 1948, Je 1,46:1
Kehoe, John H, 1920, Mr 30,11:5
Kehoe, John J, 1956, Jl 20,17:2
Kehoe, John L, 1949, Je 24,23:2
Kehoe, Joseph F, 1960, D 6,37:5
Kehoe, Joseph J, 1950, My 16,31:5
Kehoe, Michael Mrs, 1937, Ag 9,19:2
Kehoe, Myles E, 1943, N 12,21:2
Kehoe, Patrick, 1904, Ja 13,9:6; 1950, D 27,28:2
Kehoe, Richard A, 1950, Je 8,32:4
Kehoe, Richard D, 1949, D 9,31:3
Kehoe, Thomas J, 1943, N 22,19:4
Kehoe, William F, 1923, D 25,17:2
Kehoe, William H, 1938, Ja 26,23:6
Kehoe, William J, 1949, My 19,29:2
Kehr, Cyrus, 1941, Jl 15,19:6
Kehr, Ferdinant, 1950, F 13,21:4
Kehr, Frank F, 1948, S 16,29:3
Kehr, Henry D, 1959, Ja 10,17:4
Kehrer, Joseph V, 1948, Je 29,23:3
Kehs, Paul, 1954, My 8,17:3
Keiber, Edward J, 1939, D 6,25:2
Keidan, Harry B, 1943, Ag 17,17:3
Keidel, Louis A, 1954, Ag 21,17:2
Keifer, Andrew C, 1940, Jl 30,19:2
Keifer, Isidore Mrs, 1967, Ap 14,39:2
Keifer, J W, 1932, Ap 23,15:3
Keiffer, Leslie E, 1962, Ap 29,86:5
Keifler, Albert J, 1957, Mr 16,19:6
Keighley, Alexander, 1947, Ag 3,52:2
Keighley, Charles P, 1938, S 16,3:6
Keightley, Fred, 1945, My 13,20:8
Keightly, Thomas, 1872, N 18,4:7
Keigwin, Albert E, 1951, S 22,17:1
Keigwin, Albert Newton Rev Dr, 1920, Mr 12,1
Keigwin, Henry W Mrs, 1958, Ja 9,33:1
Keil, Alfredo Mrs, 1939, O 9,19:5
Keil, Frank C, 1957, O 17,33:5
Keil, Gustav B, 1938, Mr 21,15:4
Keil, Harry, 1967, Je 16,43:1

Keil, Henry F, 1955, O 9,87:1
Keil, John A, 1962, Mr 7,35:1
Keil, John A Sr, 1957, Ja 15,29:1
Keil, Peter A, 1957, O 15,30:5
Keil, Sophia V, 1957, Jl 10,27:2
Keil, Vincent A, 1955, O 14,27:3
Keil, William Mrs, 1949, Ag 6,17:3
Keila, Louis, 1954, Jl 25,69:3
Keilbach, Arthur F, 1960, My 27,31:5
Keilberth, Josef, 1968, Jl 22,35:4
Keiley, Benjamin, 1943, F 18,23:2
Keiley, Benjamin J Bp, 1925, Je 18,21:6
Keiley, J D Maj, 1901, N 27,2:2
Keiley, James A Rev, 1905, Ap 4,11:1
Keiley, Jarvis, 1944, Ap 3,21:5
Keiley, John J, 1957, Ap 22,25:4
Keilhau, Wilhelm, 1954, Je 10,31:1
Keilholz, William F, 1918, Ag 12,9:4
Keiling, Karl E, 1967, Mr 21,43:3
Keiling, Karl E Mrs, 1952, D 26,15:4
Keiling, Robert F, 1967, Mr 29,45:4
Keiller, George T, 1873, Ag 21,5:4
Keillor, Colin, 1957, Ag 26,13:3
Keilson, Jacob, 1958, D 11,13:4
Keilson, Jacob F, 1963, Ag 8,27:3
Keilson, Max, 1953, N 12,31:1
Keilt, Bernard J, 1943, My 28,21:6
Keilt, James, 1939, Ap 6,25:5
Keily, Cornelius J, 1961, O 24,37:2
Keily, Denis E Mrs, 1945, N 18,44:1
Keily, Joseph, 1952, N 13,31:5
Keim, Addison, 1957, S 8,84:8
Keim, C Ralph, 1950, Mr 23,29:5
Keim, Charlotte, 1944, My 29,15:5
Keim, George de B, 1943, Jl 10,13:3
Keim, George De Bennville, 1925, Ja 12,15:3
Keim, George H, 1955, Mr 22,31:3
Keim, Julia G, 1938, O 24,17:5
Keim, Lewis M, 1940, D 6,27:2
Keim, Melville Mrs, 1949, F 9,27:4
Keim, Mildred, 1911, Mr 12,II,13:2
Keim, Raoul D, 1952, D 26,15:4
Keim, W Franklin Mrs, 1960, My 23,29:5
Keim, William J, 1941, Ap 22,21:1
Keimig, Anthony A Mrs, 1945, N 9,19:4
Keimig, Charles B, 1954, N 15,27:5
Keimig, Charles B Mrs, 1954, O 17,87:1
Keimig, John E, 1946, N 12,29:2
Keimig, Louis J, 1943, Ja 25,13:2
Keimig, Peter A, 1944, Jl 6,15:4
Keimig, Walter A Mrs, 1946, Je 21,23:4
Keinard, Benjamin F, 1947, Jl 26,13:5
Keinath, Warren G, 1963, Ag 26,27:3
Keinz, Frank M, 1951, Ag 3,21:3
Keiper, Frank W, 1950, Je 17,15:4
Keiper, Raymond, 1950, Mr 16,31:3
Keir, Ernest H, 1950, Mr 7,28:5
Keir, John L Gen Sir, 1937, My 4,25:3
Keiser, Clarence B Mrs, 1947, Jl 15,23:2
Keiser, Clarence E, 1958, Jl 23,27:2
Keiser, Elmer E, 1954, Mr 30,27:4
Keiser, George, 1942, Ja 4,49:1
Keiser, George C, 1956, Mr 24,19:2
Keiser, George E, 1939, N 19,39:2
Keiser, James R, 1938, F 9,19:3
Keiser, Paul L, 1942, Ag 6,19:3
Keish, William C, 1948, O 13,25:1
Keisker, Frank H, 1943, Ag 19,19:1
Keister, Paul M, 1959, F 11,39:2
Keitel, Erika von, 1943, My 4,23:3
Keitel, Harry J, 1954, Je 23,26:4
Keith, A Paul, 1918, O 31,13:1
Keith, Alexander Rev, 1880, F 13,2:3
Keith, Allen P, 1947, S 27,15:6
Keith, Arthur, 1944, F 10,15:4
Keith, Arthur B, 1944, O 7,13:3; 1955, Ja 8,13:1
Keith, Arthur R, 1952, O 13,21:6
Keith, B Mrs (body recovered, Ja 21,18:2), 1964, Ja 20,16:8
Keith, Benjamin F (will), 1914, Ap 25,15:4
Keith, Charles A Mrs, 1952, Ap 4,33:7
Keith, Charles F Mrs, 1950, Mr 1,27:4
Keith, Charles O, 1941, Mr 11,23:4
Keith, Charles P, 1939, Ap 24,17:4
Keith, Clara T Mrs (will), 1939, Jl 29,18:3
Keith, Darwin M Mrs, 1950, My 30,17:5
Keith, Dayton, 1939, Mr 9,21:4
Keith, Dora W Mrs, 1940, D 28,15:5
Keith, Edson, 1939, F 5,40:4
Keith, Edward H, 1938, D 11,60:6
Keith, Ella, 1953, Mr 30,21:3
Keith, Forbes, 1953, Mr 14,15:4
Keith, Frank, 1957, S 6,21:2
Keith, Frederic A Jr, 1954, Mr 2,25:4
Keith, Frederick F, 1949, My 9,25:5
Keith, Frederick S, 1951, Ap 6,25:1
Keith, George G, 1943, O 1,19:3
Keith, Hal, 1956, Ja 12,27:1
Keith, Harold C, 1961, S 9,19:5
Keith, Harry P, 1958, Ap 27,86:2
Keith, Harry P Mrs, 1945, Mr 10,17:1
Keith, Hartford D, 1955, Ap 20,33:2
Keith, Henry H, 1946, D 4,31:2
Keith, Homer, 1950, F 16,23:4
Keith, Horace A, 1938, Ja 19,23:5
Keith, Horace G, 1947, Ag 9,13:6
Keith, Ian, 1960, Mr 27,86:6
Keith, J A H, 1931, F 23,17:5
Keith, J Robert Mrs, 1956, Jl 13,19:2
Keith, James D Mrs, 1946, Je 16,40:3
Keith, James R, 1965, F 22,21:4
Keith, Jerome Jr, 1940, D 8,69:1
Keith, John S, 1955, Jl 4,11:5
Keith, Joseph, 1942, My 26,21:6
Keith, Katherine I, 1944, D 25,19:6
Keith, Lindley J, 1952, Mr 14,23:3
Keith, Louis G, 1957, Je 12,35:3
Keith, M C, 1929, Je 15,17:5
Keith, Mary L, 1948, Ap 5,21:4
Keith, Maxine (funl plans, Mr 15,39:3), 1966, Mr 12, 27:5
Keith, Minor C Mrs, 1944, Mr 16,19:6
Keith, Myron E, 1946, O 28,27:4
Keith, Nathaniel S Dr, 1925, Ja 28,17:3
Keith, Orlando S, 1940, F 15,19:5
Keith, Richard L, 1958, Ap 29,29:2
Keith, Robert, 1940, Ag 17,15:4
Keith, Robert E, 1952, S 2,23:5
Keith, Robert H, 1942, Mr 20,19:4
Keith, Royden J, 1955, Ja 6,27:2
Keith, Royden J Mrs, 1965, Mr 7,82:8
Keith, Russell, 1960, Ap 10,86:7
Keith, Sipron C, 1916, Ja 14,9:6
Keith, Thomas, 1963, Je 18,41:7
Keith, Thomas R, 1937, Mr 14,II,9:1
Keith, Virginia S, 1945, S 12,25:4
Keith, Walter W, 1925, S 3,25:5
Keith, Warren D, 1937, D 17,25:5
Keith, Wilfred D, 1966, N 10,47:2
Keith, William, 1911, Ap 14,11:4
Keith, William H, 1965, Ja 18,35:2
Keith, William J, 1940, S 17,23:5
Keithley, E Clinton, 1955, Ap 29,23:4
Keithley, Thomas W, 1938, S 13,23:5
Kekkonen, Jussi, 1962, Ap 3,39:2
Kelaghan, William L, 1951, Je 29,21:2
Kelaher, Francis J, 1951, Mr 20,29:4
Kelaher, John P, 1955, D 24,13:2
Kelaher, Peter E, 1965, Mr 3,41:4
Kelam, William Jr, 1944, Ap 22,15:4
Kelantan, Sultan of (Prince Ibrahim Bini Almarhum), 1960, Jl 10,72:3
Kelber, Jacob C, 1948, Mr 9,23:1
Kelber, Jacob C Mrs, 1948, N 7,89:1
Kelby, Charles H, 1944, Ag 2,15:1
Kelce, L Russell, 1957, Jl 1,23:4
Kelcey, Guy Mrs, 1965, My 19,47:3
Kelcey, Herbert, 1917, Jl 11,9:5
Kelcey, William E, 1952, Jl 18,19:4
Kelchner, Charles R, 1953, Ja 7,31:2
Kelchner, Charles S (cor, O 2,37:2), 1958, S 20,19:5
Kelchner, Warren, 1965, Je 11,31:1
Kelder, Abram, 1949, Ap 22,23:2
Kelder, Edward, 1943, Mr 12,17:2
Kelder, Peter Mrs, 1946, O 28,27:3
Kelder, Rufus, 1948, Mr 23,25:4
Kelder, Sanford, 1951, S 7,29:3
Keleher, Arthur C F, 1956, Mr 13,27:3
Keleher, Bernard J, 1945, N 25,49:1
Keleher, Cornelius J, 1951, N 10,17:6
Keleher, Daniel J, 1938, Mr 26,15:2; 1952, O 14,31:4
Keleher, Elizabeth L Mrs, 1946, My 27,23:1
Keleher, Michael J, 1945, N 27,23:2
Keleher, Timothy J, 1962, Jl 25,33:2
Keleher, William T, 1961, Ag 21,23:4
Kelekian, Dikran G, 1951, Ja 31,23:4
Kelemen, Chrysostom J, 1950, N 9,33:2
Kelgard, William P, 1960, N 22,35:5
Kelgman, Marvin, 1949, Ap 14,11:1
Kelham, Katherine B Mrs, 1942, N 12,25:2
Keliher, Francis T, 1960, F 3,33:4
Keliher, John A, 1938, S 22,23:2
Keliher, Tim, 1954, F 17,31:5
Keliher, William J, 1942, Ja 5,13:1
Keljikian, Sarkis B, 1955, O 5,35:2
Kelk, Charles, 1940, Ja 12,17:5
Kelker, Henry C, 1943, Jl 13,21:6
Kelker, Rudolph F Jr, 1957, Ap 20,17:6
Kell, Claude O, 1955, Jl 6,28:1
Kell, William H Col, 1916, F 10,11:4
Kellam, Floyd E, 1958, O 16,37:1
Kellam, Jesse C Mrs (funl, F 10,16:4), 1964, F 8,23:4
Kellam, Ralph N, 1946, D 12,29:1
Kellan, Eldridge T, 1949, S 6,27:5
Kelland, Clarence B, 1964, F 19,39:1
Kelland, Thomas, 1938, S 30,21:2
Kelland, Thomas Mrs, 1943, Jl 2,19:6
Kellar, Arthur J, 1940, D 4,27:2
Kellar, Arthur J Mrs (N Revell), 1958, Ag 14,29:3
Kellar, Chambers, 1950, My 20,15:2
Kellar, Harry, 1922, Mr 11,13:6
Kellar, Herbert A, 1955, O 11,39:5
Kellas, Eliza, 1943, Ap 11,49:1
Kellas, Katherine M, 1941, D 25,25:3
Kellaway, Herbert J, 1947, S 7,61:1
Kelle, Edward J, 1962, Jl 29,60:1
Kellegrew, Alexander R, 1968, Je 20,45:2
Kelleher, Cornelius A Mrs, 1940, Je 16,39:1
Kelleher, Daniel, 1948, O 14,30:2
Kelleher, Dennis E, 1951, Ja 28,76:1
Kelleher, Edgar, 1947, Je 13,23:1
Kelleher, Edward A (por), 1945, Ag 3,17:4
Kelleher, Edward J Sr, 1951, D 17,32:2
Kelleher, Elizabeth F, 1944, O 31,19:2
Kelleher, Frank J, 1966, O 24,39:3
Kelleher, Gerald A, 1943, Jl 12,15:2
Kelleher, Gerald A K Mrs, 1966, My 8,82:3
Kelleher, Goodman, 1953, Mr 2,23:3
Kelleher, Harry A, 1943, F 22,17:1
Kelleher, Hugh G M, 1961, Ag 24,29:6
Kelleher, James R, 1942, S 16,23:5
Kelleher, James W Mrs, 1940, F 27,21:2
Kelleher, John B, 1947, Ap 24,25:6
Kelleher, John P, 1960, Ag 23,29:3
Kelleher, John P (Bro Clement Eustace), 1964, N 8, 89:1
Kelleher, Louis F, 1946, N 27,26:2
Kelleher, Michael P, 1942, Je 30,21:6
Kelleher, Michael T, 1958, N 1,19:3
Kelleher, Robert J, 1956, O 2,35:2
Kelleher, Thomas F, 1952, D 4,35:2
Kelleher, Thomas J, 1945, Ap 15,14:7; 1953, F 21,13:5
Kelleher, William J, 1953, Ja 8,30:2; 1953, Ag 15,15:5
Kelleher, William P Jr, 1939, Ap 23,III,6:6
Kellems, David Mrs, 1949, D 23,22:3
Kellems, Edgar E, 1953, D 25,17:6
Kellenberg, Edward J, 1966, F 19,27:4
Kellenberger, Levi M, 1950, Ag 25,21:3
Keller, Abraham, 1954, My 20,27:4
Keller, Adam, 1915, Ja 11,9:4
Keller, Adam V, 1956, N 30,23:4
Keller, Adolph, 1951, F 21,27:4; 1963, F 12,4:6
Keller, Albert (por),(cor, O 24,23:5), 1939, O 23,19:3
Keller, Albert G, 1956, N 1,39:3
Keller, Albert T, 1940, D 23,19:3
Keller, Alex S, 1958, My 18,87:1
Keller, Alex W, 1961, Ja 21,21:5
Keller, Alexander S Mrs (Carolyn), 1968, Ag 1,31:5
Keller, Alton H, 1959, F 10,33:4
Keller, Andrew, 1903, D 29,9:6
Keller, Anton, 1945, N 16,19:2
Keller, Arnold B, 1964, Ja 17,40:1
Keller, Arthur I, 1924, D 3,11:3; 1924, D 5,21:5
Keller, August Sr, 1947, Ag 22,15:1
Keller, Ben H, 1946, D 28,15:4
Keller, Benjamin F, 1963, O 27,88:8
Keller, Charles, 1946, Jl 10,23:5; 1949, S 18,95:3
Keller, Charles C, 1951, Ja 16,29:5
Keller, Charles F, 1952, My 20,25:1
Keller, Charles K, 1937, D 20,27:3
Keller, Charles O, 1946, My 9,21:5
Keller, Charles S, 1954, My 16,86:5
Keller, Christian F, 1950, D 23,15:6
Keller, Constance M, 1948, S 6,13:3
Keller, D C, 1950, F 12,84:4
Keller, Dan H, 1967, Ag 10,37:3
Keller, Dennis K, 1962, F 27,33:2
Keller, Donald, 1959, My 15,29:2
Keller, Edward, 1952, S 11,32:3
Keller, Edward H, 1942, D 15,27:5
Keller, Edwin B, 1914, Mr 2,9:4
Keller, Eldon H, 1951, My 22,31:1
Keller, Eleanor, 1948, O 2,15:5
Keller, Elizabeth Mrs, 1941, Ap 24,21:2
Keller, Emil E, 1938, Ja 9,43:1
Keller, Ernest G, 1961, Je 5,31:4
Keller, Ernest Mrs, 1968, Ap 8,47:3
Keller, Ernst P Mrs, 1946, Jl 14,36:4
Keller, Ethel E Mrs, 1937, My 22,18:1
Keller, Ezekiel E, 1949, S 29,29:3
Keller, F Wilson, 1954, My 8,17:4
Keller, Frank J, 1949, S 27,27:4
Keller, Frank R, 1947, Ap 1,28:3
Keller, Franklin J, 1940, S 19,23:2; 1947, F 6,23:6
Keller, Franz H J, 1951, N 13,29:4
Keller, Fred J, 1955, S 13,23:4
Keller, Frederick, 1904, Mr 13,7:4; 1948, O 25,23:3; 1960, Ja 17,86:4
Keller, Frederick A Sr, 1963, O 14,29:4
Keller, Frederick C, 1937, D 16,27:6
Keller, Frederick H, 1961, Je 21,37:6
Keller, Frederick J, 1945, Ap 28,15:2
Keller, Frederick L, 1939, Ja 11,19:2
Keller, Friedrich von, 1960, My 10,37:4
Keller, G F, 1884, F 24,7:4
Keller, Garnett V, 1939, Je 9,21:3
Keller, George D, 1949, O 6,18:6
Keller, George H, 1942, Je 15,19:3
Keller, George H Mrs, 1950, N 19,93:1
Keller, George Mrs, 1946, Je 29,19:5
Keller, Gert, 1966, Je 13,39:4
Keller, Gertrude P Mrs, 1937, Ag 8,II,7:2
Keller, Harold E, 1953, N 22,89:1
Keller, Harold H, 1942, Mr 13,19:1
Keller, Harry, 1956, N 21,27:4
Keller, Harry E, 1948, Ja 24,16:2
Keller, Helen (funl plans, Je 3,45:1; funl, Je 6,48:6), 1968, Je 2,1:2
Keller, Helen R, 1967, Ja 24,37:2

Keller, Henry, 1944, N 23,31:2
Keller, Henry G, 1949, Ag 4,23:2
Keller, Henry Jr, 1954, N 23,33:1
Keller, Herbert, 1943, O 11,19:2
Keller, Herbert B, 1953, F 24,25:5
Keller, Herbert C, 1949, N 27,104:4
Keller, Hiram H, 1959, Jl 31,23:4
Keller, I Prof, 1904, S 8,7:1
Keller, Irving G, 1941, My 1,23:6
Keller, J Orvis, 1963, Jl 27,17:4
Keller, Jacob, 1907, My 8,7:6
Keller, Jacob W Maj, 1913, D 3,15:5
Keller, James E, 1953, Ag 27,25:2
Keller, James T, 1957, My 21,35:4
Keller, Jay E Mrs, 1938, Ap 9,17:3
Keller, John C, 1959, Mr 11,35:2
Keller, John F, 1937, O 28,25:1
Keller, John G, 1945, F 1,23:3; 1951, Ja 22,17:3
Keller, John J, 1944, Je 27,19:5
Keller, John J Mrs, 1938, Mr 13,II,9:3
Keller, John L Mrs, 1959, Jl 3,17:5
Keller, John W, 1919, Mr 6,11:1
Keller, Joseph F, 1961, Mr 23,33:1
Keller, Joseph M, 1941, F 25,23:2
Keller, Joseph S, 1939, My 23,23:5
Keller, Joseph W, 1960, S 16,31:3
Keller, Joseph W Mrs, 1962, Jl 2,29:4
Keller, Julia A Mrs, 1937, Ag 7,15:4
Keller, Julius, 1945, F 27,19:5
Keller, K T Mrs, 1961, My 21,86:5
Keller, Kaufman T, 1966, Ja 22,29:1
Keller, Kenneth, 1960, Mr 21,29:2
Keller, Kent E, 1954, S 5,50:1
Keller, Lewis, 1937, D 20,27:2
Keller, Louis (funl, F 19,22:4), 1922, F 17,15:5
Keller, Manfred, 1959, Je 20,21:1
Keller, Martin, 1953, Ap 21,27:1
Keller, Meyer, 1960, S 14,43:4
Keller, Murray P, 1919, Mr 18,11:2
Keller, O E, 1927, N 22,29:3
Keller, O E M, 1956, N 6,35:4
Keller, Oliver J, 1968, Ja 6,29:1
Keller, Otto Mrs, 1953, Jl 23,23:1
Keller, Paul, 1943, D 23,19:5
Keller, Paul H, 1955, F 14,19:2
Keller, R F L, 1954, Je 22,27:4
Keller, R O, 1907, My 10,7:4
Keller, Ralph J, 1959, Mr 31,30:2
Keller, Randolph M, 1950, Ja 5,26:7
Keller, Robert A, 1962, Ap 14,25:2
Keller, Robert J, 1938, Ja 15,15:3; 1946, O 8,23:4
Keller, Robert Mrs, 1956, Jl 15,60:5
Keller, Theodore, 1938, Jl 23,13:3
Keller, Thomas W, 1925, My 30,9:6
Keller, Valentine F, 1937, Ag 8,II,6:7
Keller, Vaneltine, 1951, My 4,27:2
Keller, W Benton, 1958, Jl 24,25:5
Keller, Walter, 1940, Jl 9,21:5; 1968, D 11,47:2
Keller, Walter F, 1955, S 3,15:5
Keller, William A, 1962, Ap 19,31:4
Keller, William B Jr, 1944, Mr 16,19:4
Keller, William C, 1963, Ap 15,29:4
Keller, William F, 1946, O 16,27:3
Keller, William H, 1945, Ja 17,21:4
Keller, William J, 1959, Jl 24,25:1
Keller, William L, 1959, Jl 12,72:4
Keller, William S, 1949, Mr 11,25:2
Keller, William T, 1947, N 26,23:4
Keller, Zachariah W Mrs, 1951, N 29,33:5
Kellerman, Charles, 1939, Mr 30,23:5
Kellerman, Ernest T, 1950, N 24,35:1
Kellerman, Harry W, 1940, Jl 4,15:2
Kellerman, Henry A Jr, 1939, Mr 21,24:2
Kellerman, Marcus, 1948, D 8,32:3
Kellerman, Prof, 1908, Mr 11,7:6
Kellerman, William H, 1953, S 13,85:2
Kellermann, Bernard, 1951, O 19,27:5
Kellersberger, Eugene R, 1966, Ja 31,39:1
Kellerschon, Julius, 1925, My 29,17:6
Kellett, John A, 1948, N 5,26:3
Kellett, W Wallace, 1951, Jl 23,17:4
Kellett, William F, 1947, Ja 22,23:5
Kellett, William H, 1962, Jl 18,29:5
Kelleweay, Theodore W, 1953, F 9,27:3
Kelley, Abraham F, 1946, My 26,32:6
Kelley, Albert H Rev, 1909, Jl 23,7:5
Kelley, Albert M, 1945, Ja 9,19:1
Kelley, Albert T Mrs, 1946, N 11,27:4
Kelley, Albert Tevis, 1921, Ja 4,13:3
Kelley, Aldridge D, 1941, O 22,23:3
Kelley, Alvah J, 1942, Je 5,17:5
Kelley, Anthony, 1950, Mr 25,13:4
Kelley, Arnold Mrs, 1956, Mr 23,27:4
Kelley, Augustine B (funl plans, N 24,87:2; funl, N 26,30:2), 1957, N 21,33:3
Kelley, Augustus W, 1957, Ja 27,84:4
Kelley, Austin Price, 1920, Ap 28,11:6
Kelley, Bob, 1966, S 10,29:5
Kelley, Catherine R, 1958, Jl 15,25:3
Kelley, Charles, 1946, D 5,31:1
Kelley, Charles A, 1947, Jl 31,21:2
Kelley, Charles B, 1961, Jl 27,31:5
Kelley, Charles B Capt, 1937, My 21,21:1
Kelley, Charles F, 1941, O 3,23:1
Kelley, Charles H, 1955, F 13,86:5
Kelley, Charles S, 1937, Jl 22,19:5; 1948, Ap 11,73:1
Kelley, Charles S Jr, 1959, O 29,30:5
Kelley, Clarence V, 1944, Ja 25,19:3
Kelley, Clarenton, 1938, N 23,21:1
Kelley, Cornelius F, 1957, My 13,31:2
Kelley, Cornelius J MRs, 1955, N 14,27:4
Kelley, Dana, 1966, F 9,39:4
Kelley, Daniel P, 1943, D 31,16:7
Kelley, David J Mrs, 1951, Mr 3,13:1
Kelley, David N, 1942, My 16,13:6
Kelley, E Thomas, 1943, D 4,13:3
Kelley, Ed C Mrs, 1950, D 31,42:7
Kelley, Edgar S (por), 1944, N 13,19:3
Kelley, Edgar S Mrs, 1949, Ap 4,23:4
Kelley, Edward D Mrs, 1948, My 21,23:5
Kelley, Edward J, 1960, My 14,23:2; 1962, Ja 25,31:1
Kelley, Edward L Sr, 1954, S 17,27:3
Kelley, Edward W, 1938, S 6,21:3; 1944, Ap 4,21:5
Kelley, Elmer W, 1949, Ap 4,23:4
Kelley, Eugene C, 1953, My 16,19:4
Kelley, Eugene F Mrs, 1953, D 18,29:4
Kelley, F A, 1931, O 17,17:1
Kelley, F Mrs, 1932, F 18,19:2
Kelley, Francis C, 1948, F 2,19:1
Kelley, Francis J, 1948, Je 26,18:2
Kelley, Francis R, 1939, My 19,21:6
Kelley, Frank B Mrs, 1941, D 21,41:1
Kelley, Frank H, 1953, N 21,13:2
Kelley, Frank J, 1940, Ja 12,17:2
Kelley, Frank J Mrs, 1957, Ag 6,27:5
Kelley, Frank M, 1947, Ag 26,23:5
Kelley, Frank P, 1938, S 13,23:1
Kelley, Frank S, 1942, S 29,23:4
Kelley, Frederic P Mrs, 1951, My 5,17:2
Kelley, Frederick G, 1945, F 28,23:3
Kelley, George B, 1954, Mr 6,15:3
Kelley, George E, 1944, D 19,21:3
Kelley, George L, 1938, Ag 25,19:3; 1953, Jl 29,23:3
Kelley, George P, 1950, Ja 26,27:2
Kelley, George R, 1942, F 9,15:4
Kelley, Gerald, 1939, Ja 4,21:4
Kelley, Gertrude, 1955, Mr 1,25:2
Kelley, Grace J Mrs, 1939, O 12,25:4
Kelley, Grace O, 1951, Ag 14,23:5
Kelley, Harlan W, 1957, D 2,27:6
Kelley, Harold H, 1965, N 7,88:1
Kelley, Henry A, 1945, F 23,17:3
Kelley, Hubert W, 1959, O 6,39:1
Kelley, J Herbert, 1948, Jl 18,53:2
Kelley, Jacob S, 1950, Mr 20,21:4
Kelley, James, 1938, F 15,25:5
Kelley, James A, 1938, Mr 10,21:4; 1940, O 16,23:4
Kelley, James Douglas Jerrold Com, 1922, My 1,17:1
Kelley, James E, 1943, N 12,21:2; 1952, N 10,25:4
Kelley, James F, 1950, F 2,27:2
Kelley, James J, 1951, N 14,31:4
Kelley, James M, 1960, Je 4,23:5
Kelley, James P, 1949, Mr 3,25:5; 1952, N 18,31:3
Kelley, James R Mrs, 1947, Ja 21,23:2
Kelley, James T, 1945, N 12,21:2
Kelley, Janette, 1958, My 31,15:4
Kelley, Joe, 1943, Ag 15,38:8
Kelley, John, 1943, Je 1,23:4
Kelley, John A, 1919, Je 1,22:3
Kelley, John C, 1938, Ja 8,15:1
Kelley, John D Mrs, 1914, Ag 20,11:5
Kelley, John E, 1945, F 4,38:1; 1951, S 21,23:3; 1953, F 5,23:3
Kelley, John J, 1944, Mr 5,36:1; 1946, Ag 20,27:6
Kelley, John M Jr, 1958, O 14,37:5
Kelley, John Rev, 1866, Ap 29,5:5
Kelley, John T, 1942, Ap 28,21:1
Kelley, Joseph A Mrs, 1953, Ap 9,27:2
Kelley, Joseph B, 1964, S 28,29:6
Kelley, Joseph F Mrs, 1946, F 28,23:3
Kelley, Joseph J, 1937, Ap 18,II,8:5
Kelley, Joseph W, 1959, My 27,35:3
Kelley, Katherine, 1939, Je 23,19:1
Kelley, Lawrence C, 1945, O 25,21:3
Kelley, Leo F, 1958, F 25,27:3
Kelley, Leon, 1960, Ap 7,35:3
Kelley, Leon L, 1945, F 17,13:4
Kelley, Leon M, 1947, S 25,29:6
Kelley, Lillian Mrs, 1951, Ag 23,23:1
Kelley, Louis J, 1965, My 1,31:2
Kelley, Mark, 1960, Ap 23,23:5
Kelley, Martin F, 1949, N 13,92:3
Kelley, Martin V, 1955, F 24,27:3
Kelley, Mary, 1941, Je 8,49:2
Kelley, Mary D, 1956, Jl 31,23:1
Kelley, Mary E, 1963, O 18,31:2
Kelley, Matthew, 1958, My 4,88:4
Kelley, Michael, 1909, Jl 19,7:1
Kelley, Michael J (por), 1955, Je 7,33:2
Kelley, Nicholas, 1965, O 29,43:1
Kelley, Oliver G, 1955, F 26,15:3
Kelley, Patrick H, 1925, S 12,15:5
Kelley, Paul M, 1940, Ag 11,31:2
Kelley, Peter F, 1944, Ja 21,17:4
Kelley, R W, 1928, Ag 5,25:3
Kelley, Regina C, 1944, N 17,19:4
Kelley, Richard C, 1937, F 7,II,9:1
Kelley, Robert H, 1953, D 30,23:4
Kelley, Robert M, 1953, Ag 24,23:4
Kelley, Robert W Mrs, 1949, F 19,15:2
Kelley, Robert W Mrs (will), 1949, Mr 2,23:5
Kelley, Russell G, 1940, Ap 8,20:4
Kelley, Samuel D, 1938, My 10,21:4
Kelley, Samuel F, 1965, Ja 6,39:2
Kelley, Samuel H, 1941, O 27,17:6
Kelley, Selden D, 1949, Ap 10,76:8
Kelley, Stephen D, 1947, Ja 9,24:3
Kelley, Stephen G, 1955, Ap 18,23:5
Kelley, T W, 1901, F 17,7:6
Kelley, Thomas E, 1948, Je 30,25:3
Kelley, Thomas F, 1948, F 18,27:2; 1960, D 4,88:8
Kelley, Thomas F Mrs, 1955, Ja 29,15:3
Kelley, Thomas J 3d, 1958, D 30,35:1
Kelley, Timothy J, 1943, Ap 15,25:5
Kelley, Truman L, 1961, My 3,37:5
Kelley, Vanness D, 1945, My 28,19:5
Kelley, W D, 1890, Ja 10,5:2
Kelley, William, 1916, Jl 3,9:6; 1948, Ag 31,26:2
Kelley, William A, 1938, Ap 27,23:2; 1964, Je 6,23:4
Kelley, William H, 1942, My 10,42:6; 1943, S 22,23:4
Kelley, William H Ex-Judge, 1910, Mr 15,7:4
Kelley, William S, 1925, My 2,15:6
Kellicott, William Erskine, 1919, Ja 30,13:4
Kellie, Albert G, 1941, Ag 13,17:4
Kellie, Eugene A, 1953, Ja 18,53:1
Kelligrew, Jere J, 1950, Jl 14,21:4
Kelligrew, Jeremiah J Mrs, 1962, Ap 16,29:4
Kelliher, Fred H, 1955, Jl 24,64:1
Kelliher, Leona, 1957, D 20,24:2
Kelliher, Sarah F Mrs, 1938, Mr 21,15:3
Kellin, Jacob J Mrs, 1949, Je 1,32:2
Kellin, Mike Mrs, 1963, My 13,20:7
Kelling, Rudolph, 1959, Je 16,35:3
Kellington, Howard B, 1951, Ja 29,19:3
Kellino, Roy, 1956, N 20,37:4
Kellman, Anthony, 1951, Jl 25,23:2
Kellman, Leon, 1965, N 19,39:3
Kellner, Andrew G, 1950, Jl 5,31:5
Kellner, Charles B Mrs, 1964, Ap 22,47:5
Kellner, Charles L, 1950, My 28,44:7
Kellner, Chris Mrs, 1950, Mr 2,27:2
Kellner, Franz, 1951, N 28,31:2
Kellner, Gustave, 1959, Jl 20,25:5
Kellner, Gustave Mrs, 1958, My 1,31:4
Kellner, Hans K, 1959, Ja 11,88:4
Kellner, Hans W, 1968, Ag 13,36:5
Kellner, John A Rev, 1910, Ag 24,9:5
Kellner, Samuel, 1961, F 7,33:4
Kellock, Harold, 1953, N 22,88:5
Kellock, James, 1903, My 6,9:6
Kellog, E N, 1903, D 14,1:4
Kellog, George Mrs, 1948, F 19,23:5
Kellog, Orlando, 1865, Ag 26,5:4
Kellogg, A Hinman Mrs, 1878, O 14,8:5
Kellogg, A P, 1934, Jl 22,22:4
Kellogg, Abraham L, 1946, Ag 26,23:6
Kellogg, Andrew P Mrs, 1959, S 19,23:6
Kellogg, Anne G (est), 1910, Mr 26,9:4
Kellogg, Arthur P Mrs, 1964, F 17,31:3
Kellogg, Asa B, 1950, Ap 28,21:3
Kellogg, Augustus C, 1941, N 9,53:2
Kellogg, Augustus G, 1954, S 27,21:3
Kellogg, Augustus Mrs, 1940, Mr 28,24:4
Kellogg, Benjamin A, 1940, Mr 2,13:5
Kellogg, Brainerd Prof, 1920, Ja 10,11:4
Kellogg, Charles (trb lr, S 13,28:7), 1949, S 5,17:6
Kellogg, Charles E, 1956, Jl 2,21:2
Kellogg, Charles M Dr, 1924, D 4,21:4
Kellogg, Charles P, 1957, D 29,49:1
Kellogg, Charles W, 1950, Ag 29,27:2
Kellogg, Charles W Mrs, 1952, My 8,31:3
Kellogg, Chester B, 1954, N 6,17:1
Kellogg, Clara Louise Mrs, 1916, My 17,11:6
Kellogg, Clifford W, 1938, F 2,19:2
Kellogg, Commander, 1874, O 9,4:7
Kellogg, Daniel F, 1920, O 29,15:2
Kellogg, Daniel F Mrs, 1943, N 30,27:3
Kellogg, Daniel Mrs, 1914, D 24,9:4
Kellogg, Day O, 1874, Ag 11,4:6
Kellogg, E Welles, 1948, S 12,74:2
Kellogg, Edgar R Brig-Gen, 1914, O 9,9:4
Kellogg, Edward, 1908, S 10,9:6; 1951, Je 11,25:1
Kellogg, Edward L, 1948, Ag 12,22:2
Kellogg, Edward R, 1923, Jl 5,15:4
Kellogg, Edward W, 1960, My 31,31:3
Kellogg, Edwin E, 1937, S 8,23:1
Kellogg, Elijah Rev, 1901, Mr 18,7:7
Kellogg, Elizabeth C Mrs, 1872, S 13,5:4
Kellogg, Ensign H Mrs, 1908, Ag 2,7:7
Kellogg, Evans S, 1947, Ja 17,23:2
Kellogg, F Leonard, 1941, D 21,40:7
Kellogg, Fannie H, 1939, O 11,30:3
Kellogg, Fay, 1918, Jl 12,13:6
Kellogg, Francis F, 1956, D 26,27:1
Kellogg, Frank B, 1937, D 22,1:2
Kellogg, Frank B Mrs (por), 1942, O 3,15:4
Kellogg, Frank L Mrs, 1952, F 15,25:3
Kellogg, Frank W, 1943, D 21,27:2
Kellogg, Franklin M, 1939, Ja 8,42:5

Kellogg, Fred C, 1960, S 29,35:2
Kellogg, Frederic R Mrs, 1967, Jl 10,31:2
Kellogg, Frederick H, 1944, Mr 28,19:3
Kellogg, Frederick Mrs, 1925, O 26,19:5
Kellogg, Frederick S, 1961, Jl 16,69:1
Kellogg, Frederick S Mrs, 1956, Je 27,31:5
Kellogg, Frederick W, 1940, S 6,21:1
Kellogg, Frederick W Mrs, 1958, My 1,31:4; 1958, Ag 18,19:4
Kellogg, G G, 1883, Ap 19,5:3
Kellogg, G Paul, 1951, Ap 7,15:5
Kellogg, George (see also My 21), 1878, My 24,8:4
Kellogg, George, 1903, O 1,9:5
Kellogg, George D, 1955, S 21,33:5
Kellogg, George W, 1944, D 20,23:3
Kellogg, Gertrude, 1903, Ap 21,9:5
Kellogg, Gertrude E, 1943, O 8,19:1
Kellogg, Gideon P, 1951, Ap 6,20:4
Kellogg, Gordon H, 1955, Ag 23,24:2
Kellogg, Harold F, 1964, Ja 23,31:4
Kellogg, Harry W, 1965, Jl 14,37:4
Kellogg, Henry K, 1956, D 6,37:1
Kellogg, Henry K W Mrs, 1961, S 3,60:3
Kellogg, Henry T, 1942, S 7,19:1
Kellogg, Henry T Mrs, 1958, O 6,31:5
Kellogg, Herbert S, 1937, O 15,23:4
Kellogg, Howard Jr, 1962, Jl 18,29:2
Kellogg, J A, 1929, S 9,25:3
Kellogg, James C Jr Mrs, 1954, F 13,13:7
Kellogg, James G, 1963, Ap 16,35:1
Kellogg, James L, 1938, Jl 9,13:6
Kellogg, James W Mrs, 1953, Je 14,85:1
Kellogg, John H (por), 1943, D 16,28:2
Kellogg, John H (por), 1943, D 16,28:2
Kellogg, John L, 1950, Ap 4,29:4
Kellogg, John M Ex-Justice, 1925, Ja 17,15:4
Kellogg, John Marshall Dr, 1915, O 19,11:4
Kellogg, Joseph A Mrs, 1952, S 2,23:1
Kellogg, Julia A, 1914, D 23,13:4
Kellogg, Karl H, 1955, D 23,17:4
Kellogg, Lois S, 1957, My 16,31:5
Kellogg, Louis L Mrs, 1943, Ja 22,19:4
Kellogg, Louise P, 1942, Jl 13,15:1
Kellogg, Loyal C, 1871, N 27,1:2
Kellogg, Luther Laflin, 1918, D 7,15:3
Kellogg, Luther Laflin Mrs, 1912, O 6,II,17:4
Kellogg, MacIntosh, 1950, Ap 8,13:6
Kellogg, Martin, 1903, Ag 27,7:6
Kellogg, Michael J, 1942, Mr 29,45:1
Kellogg, Minot C, 1915, Ja 9,11:4
Kellogg, Morris W, 1952, F 23,11:1
Kellogg, Morris W Mrs, 1952, S 6,18:8
Kellogg, Nelson, 1940, Ap 29,15:4
Kellogg, Nelson A, 1945, N 24,19:4
Kellogg, Paul U (trb lr, N 5,34:5), 1958, N 2,88:5
Kellogg, Paul V, 1956, S 12,37:1
Kellogg, Richards, 1938, Jl 2,13:5
Kellogg, Robert Mrs, 1937, O 7,27:4
Kellogg, Royal S, 1965, F 14,88:3
Kellogg, Spencer Jr, 1944, D 21,21:1
Kellogg, Stephen W, 1904, Ja 28,9:6; 1952, D 25,29:5
Kellogg, Sylvester A Judge, 1904, Mr 13,7:5
Kellogg, Thomas M, 1950, Ja 25,27:2
Kellogg, Thomas P, 1951, My 8,31:1
Kellogg, Vernon L Dr, 1937, Ag 9,19:2
Kellogg, W Curtiss, 1903, N 28,9:4
Kellogg, W K Mrs, 1948, F 17,25:4
Kellogg, Walter G, 1956, Je 24,76:8
Kellogg, Warren F, 1943, My 8,15:4
Kellogg, Waters, 1953, Ag 31,17:1
Kellogg, Will K, 1951, O 7,87:1
Kellogg, William C, 1917, Ag 16,11:7
Kellogg, William G, 1961, Mr 20,29:3
Kellogg, William S, 1940, D 8,71:2
Kellogg, Winthrop H, 1966, Je 4,29:5
Kellogg-Smith, Jewell, 1956, N 15,35:4
Kellor, Frances, 1952, Ja 5,11:2
Kellow, Arthur Mrs, 1951, S 12,31:4
Kellow, Martin, 1954, O 13,31:4
Kells, Clarence H, 1954, Mr 26,21:5
Kells, Edward W, 1952, Jl 2,25:3
Kells, Foster W, 1951, Jl 10,27:3
Kells, Frank E, 1941, Je 18,21:5
Kells, Herbert R, 1945, My 27,26:1
Kellum, Donald R, 1954, O 19,27:2
Kellum, Manford R, 1953, Jl 22,27:4
Kellum, Winford, 1951, Ag 12,76:7
Kellway, Cedric V, 1963, Je 16,84:4
Kelly, Addison W, 1942, Mr 24,19:5
Kelly, Agnes H Mrs, 1937, Ja 16,15:1
Kelly, Al (A Kalish),(funl plans, S 8,47:3), 1966, S 7, 47:3
elly, Albert E, 1960, S 4,68:8
elly, Albert G, 1947, Ja 21,23:4
elly, Albert G Mrs, 1954, N 28,87:2
elly, Albert J, 1964, Je 24,37:5
elly, Alfred A, 1967, D 31,44:8
elly, Alice C, 1943, S 3,19:5
elly, Allen, 1916, My 17,11:6
elly, Alvin A (Shipwreck), 1952, O 12,57:3
elly, Ambrose, 1952, F 14,27:4
elly, Andrew F, 1950, D 20,32:3
elly, Andrew J, 1948, Je 9,29:1

Kelly, Anna (Sister Demetria), 1958, My 12,29:4
Kelly, Anna L, 1946, Jl 21,39:1
Kelly, Annie, 1879, Ap 28,1:6
Kelly, Anthony, 1953, S 26,17:5
Kelly, Anthony J, 1949, Ap 19,26:4
Kelly, Aquin S, 1948, Jl 21,23:4
Kelly, Arch, 1941, O 20,17:4
Kelly, Arthur H, 1938, Ap 10,II,6:7; 1939, Jl 26,19:1; 1951, Ap 18,31:2
Kelly, Arthur H Jr, 1957, D 25,31:6
Kelly, Arthur J, 1943, Ag 2,15:3; 1947, D 29,17:3
Kelly, Arthur W, 1959, O 27,37:3
Kelly, B Joseph, 1952, My 21,27:2
Kelly, Bernard A, 1940, Ja 25,21:5; 1965, Ap 20,39:2
Kelly, Bernard D, 1937, Jl 13,19:1
Kelly, Bernard M, 1958, My 8,29:4
Kelly, Blanche M, 1966, S 13,47:3
Kelly, Brian J, 1945, D 18,27:2
Kelly, Caleb G, 1960, Ja 31,92:6
Kelly, Carlos D, 1967, N 7,39:4
Kelly, Catherine A (Mother Mary Aloysia), 1953, D 30,23:2
Kelly, Catherine E, 1957, Jl 27,17:1
Kelly, Cecilia C, 1966, My 16,37:2
Kelly, Charles, 1938, O 27,23:4; 1942, Ja 27,21:1; 1943, Je 8,21:2
Kelly, Charles E, 1938, Je 14,21:2
Kelly, Charles E (por), 1939, Ja 19,19:4
Kelly, Charles E, 1962, Je 8,31:3
Kelly, Charles E Mrs, 1951, Jl 29,68:5; 1966, Ja 28, 47:5
Kelly, Charles F, 1960, Je 7,35:1
Kelly, Charles H, 1938, Je 5,45:2
Kelly, Charles J, 1921, Je 25,11:6
Kelly, Charles J Msgr, 1911, N 17,13:5
Kelly, Charles L, 1939, Mr 29,23:6
Kelly, Charles V, 1957, Ja 13,84:3
Kelly, Christopher J, 1952, D 29,14:3; 1962, N 6,33:2
Kelly, Clare M, 1957, Ag 21,4:3
Kelly, Clark L, 1952, Je 22,70:5
Kelly, Cornelius F (por), 1938, Ap 17,II,7:1
Kelly, Cornelius F Mrs, 1956, Mr 24,19:4
Kelly, Cuthbert (por), 1948, Ap 30,23:4
Kelly, D Theodore, 1962, N 11,88:8
Kelly, D Theodore Mrs, 1963, Je 29,23:2
Kelly, Daniel, 1950, N 11,15:6
Kelly, Daniel A, 1952, My 8,31:5
Kelly, Daniel F, 1952, Ja 13,89:2
Kelly, Daniel G, 1962, Mr 11,86:3
Kelly, Daniel J, 1950, Mr 12,92:3; 1952, Jl 16,25:4; 1954, Ja 3,90:4
Kelly, Daniel W, 1937, Ja 3,II,8:7
Kelly, David F, 1952, F 18,19:2
Kelly, David J, 1965, Je 21,29:3
Kelly, David Mrs, 1964, Mr 9,29:3
Kelly, David V, 1959, Mr 28,17:5
Kelly, Denis A Sr, 1950, Je 11,92:2
Kelly, Denis J, 1950, F 16,23:5
Kelly, Dennis E, 1954, My 8,17:4
Kelly, Dennis E Mrs, 1956, Jl 12,19:1
Kelly, Dennis F, 1938, Jl 24,28:6; 1951, Jl 16,21:5
Kelly, Donald J, 1961, Ap 22,25:2
Kelly, E J Commodore, 1901, Jl 28,5:5
Kelly, Edmund P, 1937, D 1,23:6
Kelly, Edward A, 1941, Jl 14,13:5
Kelly, Edward A Msgr, 1925, Ag 25,17:6
Kelly, Edward D, 1943, Ja 11,15:6; 1947, My 5,23:5
Kelly, Edward F, 1942, S 5,13:3; 1959, Je 20,21:4
Kelly, Edward J, 1938, O 28,23:4; 1943, Ja 17,18:5; 1946, Ja 18,19:2; 1946, F 22,25:2; 1950, O 21,17:1; 1953, Jl 31,19:4; 1954, D 5,88:6; 1956, D 20,29:2; 1959, Ja 13,47:2; 1959, Je 19,25:1
Kelly, Edward J Mrs (funl, Ap 28,15:4), 1955, Ap 23,19:4
Kelly, Edward M, 1958, Jl 6,56:3
Kelly, Edward M Sr, 1957, Ag 28,27:5
Kelly, Edward Mrs, 1959, N 8,88:2
Kelly, Edward T, 1938, Mr 26,15:6
Kelly, Edwin M, 1961, Jl 5,33:3
Kelly, Elizabeth J, 1906, Je 24,9:6
Kelly, Elizabeth L, 1960, Ap 15,24:1
Kelly, Ellsworth, 1958, Jl 22,27:3
Kelly, Elsie R Mrs, 1943, Je 7,13:4
Kelly, Enos J, 1946, Jl 31,27:3
Kelly, Eric P, 1960, Ja 4,29:2
Kelly, Ernest A, 1953, Je 22,21:2
Kelly, Eugene, 1894, D 20,13:7; 1912, Ja 19,11:6; 1945, N 17,17:3
Kelly, Eugene A, 1959, D 17,37:2
Kelly, Eugene J, 1957, Ag 21,27:4
Kelly, Eva Mrs, 1924, N 19,21:3
Kelly, Evander F, 1944, O 28,15:6
Kelly, Evelione T Baroness (cause unknown, Jl 23), 1959, Ag 29,7:4
Kelly, F M, 1882, D 12,5:3
Kelly, F Sir, 1880, S 19,7:5
Kelly, Felix J, 1953, Ap 16,29:6
Kelly, Finton Sr, 1937, Mr 9,23:2
Kelly, Florence F (por), 1939, D 18,23:3
Kelly, Frances H, 1966, Ap 25,31:5
Kelly, Francis C Mrs, 1950, O 27,30:2
Kelly, Francis E, 1950, N 29,33:1
Kelly, Francis J, 1942, S 4,24:2; 1953, Ag 4,21:5

Kelly, Francis P, 1960, D 30,19:2
Kelly, Frank, 1916, Jl 17,11:2
Kelly, Frank A, 1943, D 11,15:6
Kelly, Frank J, 1950, N 10,27:1; 1953, S 26,17:2
Kelly, Frank L, 1954, Mr 26,21:5
Kelly, Frank R, 1967, Jl 7,31:1
Kelly, Frank S, 1960, Je 3,31:1
Kelly, Frank V, 1946, Jl 6,15:1; 1947, Jl 10,21:4; 1948, O 5,26:2
Kelly, Frank W, 1947, Mr 10,22:2
Kelly, Fred, 1954, Jl 1,25:5
Kelly, Fred C, 1959, My 24,89:1
Kelly, Fred F, 1944, Je 7,19:3
Kelly, Fred W Jr, 1954, N 2,51:8
Kelly, Frederick W, 1953, F 19,23:5
Kelly, G, 1927, Jl 10,23:1
Kelly, G B, 1934, F 17,15:1
Kelly, G L, 1953, Jl 28,19:4
Kelly, George, 1951, N 20,31:4; 1952, Mr 14,20:5; 1954, Jl 18,46:4
Kelly, George A, 1958, My 30,21:4
Kelly, George E, 1943, Ap 3,15:2
Kelly, George F J, 1960, O 8,23:3
Kelly, George H, 1952, Ag 18,17:4; 1956, Je 1,23:2
Kelly, George L Mrs, 1951, Je 28,25:1
Kelly, George M, 1921, Ap 6,15:5
Kelly, George Mrs, 1959, O 15,39:4
Kelly, George P, 1957, Ag 2,19:5
Kelly, George S, 1947, My 21,25:4
Kelly, George T (por), 1948, N 29,23:3
Kelly, George T Mrs, 1938, Ap 18,15:4; 1943, Jl 16, 17:3
Kelly, George V, 1949, Ap 10,78:4
Kelly, George W, 1948, Je 15,27:2
Kelly, Gerald, 1964, Ag 4,30:1
Kelly, Gerald C, 1959, Je 23,33:1
Kelly, Glenn M, 1954, Ap 11,87:2
Kelly, Grace V, 1950, Ja 12,28:3
Kelly, H J, 1953, Je 8,29:3
Kelly, Hannah, 1941, D 23,21:3
Kelly, Harold O, 1955, D 14,39:2
Kelly, Harry F, 1959, Ja 24,19:5
Kelly, Harry J, 1941, Je 16,15:4; 1952, Ja 24,47:3
Kelly, Harry J R, 1947, O 19,64:6
Kelly, Harry Mrs, 1951, Mr 27,29:3
Kelly, Harry P, 1947, D 28,40:5
Kelly, Harry T, 1953, N 19,31:1
Kelly, Harvey J, 1963, S 6,30:1
Kelly, Helen M Mrs, 1952, Ag 2,15:7
Kelly, Henry A, 1942, O 24,15:1
Kelly, Henry A Mrs, 1950, S 27,31:3
Kelly, Henry C, 1941, Je 28,15:3
Kelly, Henry Capt, 1903, My 10,7:5
Kelly, Henry E, 1942, Ag 9,42:8
Kelly, Henry S, 1960, Ja 9,21:5
Kelly, Henry T (por), 1941, S 9,23:4
Kelly, Henry T Mrs, 1952, O 5,89:1
Kelly, Herbert, 1950, Je 22,27:3
Kelly, Herbert J, 1960, Jl 5,31:4
Kelly, Herbert J Mrs, 1963, Jl 28,64:2
Kelly, Homer B, 1953, Ap 16,29:4
Kelly, Horace B, 1944, Ja 28,18:2
Kelly, Howard A (por), 1943, Ja 13,23:3
Kelly, Howard A, 1966, Mr 29,41:3
Kelly, Howard C, 1952, D 16,31:3
Kelly, Hubert (funl, Ap 7,25:3), 1962, Ap 4,43:4
Kelly, Hugh, 1908, O 31,9:5; 1944, Je 12,19:4; 1960, D 3,23:4
Kelly, Hugh C, 1944, N 14,23:4
Kelly, Hugh M, 1949, D 12,34:3
Kelly, Hugh S (por), 1955, My 20,25:2
Kelly, Hugh T, 1944, S 13,19:3
Kelly, Hugh W, 1942, Ag 5,19:4
Kelly, Ironton A, 1952, O 21,29:3
Kelly, J Bertram, 1960, Je 28,31:1
Kelly, J D, 1936, N 5,27:3
Kelly, J E, 1884, Ja 21,1:3; 1933, My 27,13:1
Kelly, J Frederick, 1947, S 3,25:3
Kelly, J R, 1958, O 31,14:5
Kelly, J Redding, 1939, D 9,15:4
Kelly, Jack, 1957, D 30,23:5
Kelly, Jack (J Schneiderman), 1965, D 5,89:1
Kelly, Jack D, 1964, O 21,47:2
Kelly, James, 1871, Ja 11,1:2; 1874, N 5,5:7; 1909, Je 14,7:4; 1947, Jl 18,17:5; 1954, My 8,17:4; 1955, F 15,27:1; 1960, Jl 17,62:3
Kelly, James A, 1944, Mr 9,17:4; 1962, Mr 4,86:6; 1965, My 9,86:4
Kelly, James E, 1939, S 4,19:5; 1953, S 29,29:3
Kelly, James E Mrs, 1952, Ja 22,29:5
Kelly, James F, 1937, Je 22,23:6; 1943, My 22,13:6; 1946, O 25,23:5; 1957, F 16,17:4
Kelly, James F Jr, 1940, D 21,17:4
Kelly, James H, 1911, O 2,11:2; 1944, F 19,13:5
Kelly, James J, 1945, O 31,23:2; 1950, N 30,33:2; 1953, Ja 16,23:4; 1954, My 6,33:5; 1962, Ag 8,31:1
Kelly, James J Judge, 1937, Jl 26,19:6
Kelly, James Kerr, 1903, S 16,9:5
Kelly, James L, 1944, O 5,23:5; 1961, S 7,35:2
Kelly, James M, 1953, Je 29,21:5; 1958, Ja 12,86:5
Kelly, James Mrs, 1944, Je 18,36:2
Kelly, James N, 1949, Jl 2,15:5
Kelly, James P, 1940, Mr 21,25:2; 1943, Je 9,21:4; 1956, Jl 13,19:1; 1962, Je 6,41:2

Kelly, James R, 1949, Mr 16,27:3
Kelly, James S, 1957, Ap 15,29:4; 1958, Ja 27,27:2
Kelly, James T, 1947, Ag 13,23:2
Kelly, James W, 1939, My 29,15:1
Kelly, James W Jr Mrs, 1951, Ap 24,29:2
Kelly, James W Mrs, 1947, F 8,17:3
Kelly, James W Sr, 1951, Ag 15,27:3
Kelly, Jeremiah J, 1940, Jl 24,21:4
Kelly, Jeremiah J Mrs, 1946, Mr 29,23:4
Kelly, Jesse M, 1954, F 7,36:5
Kelly, Jim, 1946, D 20,23:4
Kelly, Jimmy (por), 1948, Ja 10,15:3
Kelly, John, 1886, Je 2,1:5; 1918, Mr 23,13:4; 1964, Ja 3,24:3
Kelly, John A, 1937, F 12,23:5; 1937, My 18,23:2; 1946, My 2,21:2; 1946, S 7,15:2; 1956, My 4,25:4; 1959, Mr 25,35:4; 1961, F 4,19:6
Kelly, John A Bro, 1959, O 28,37:5
Kelly, John A Mrs, 1965, Ag 11,35:4
Kelly, John A Sr, 1951, Ap 10,27:2
Kelly, John B, 1950, Ap 6,29:3; 1957, Je 23,85:1
Kelly, John B Sr (funl plans, Je 23,29:1; funl, Je 25,21:5), 1960, Je 21,33:1
Kelly, John D, 1948, Ag 20,17:4
Kelly, John E, 1956, D 20,29:2; 1958, Ap 24,31:3; 1966, N 23,39:3
Kelly, John F, 1940, O 24,25:4; 1940, D 1,62:5; 1956, My 13,86:6; 1961, S 6,37:2; 1965, Jl 12,27:3
Kelly, John F Jr, 1949, Ja 27,24:2
Kelly, John F Msgr, 1961, Ag 6,85:1
Kelly, John Forrest, 1922, O 16,15:4
Kelly, John H, 1938, Mr 15,23:5; 1941, Mr 11,23:2; 1948, Je 24,25:3; 1954, D 31,13:2
Kelly, John J, 1921, Ag 20,7:6; 1941, Jl 8,19:6; 1942, Jl 22,19:5; 1946, Mr 19,27:1; 1946, D 9,25:3; 1948, Je 20,60:3; 1951, Ja 25,25:2; 1951, O 3,33:3; 1955, S 5,11:5; 1957, N 21,33:2; 1957, D 14,21:4; 1963, N 17,86:5; 1966, Mr 18,39:2; 1967, Ag 24,37:4; 1968, O 31,43:5; 1968, N 29,45:4
Kelly, John J Dr, 1951, N 10,17:3
Kelly, John J Jr, 1957, Ag 27,29:1
Kelly, John J Mrs, 1938, D 6,23:3; 1943, F 25,21:4; 1966, O 2,86:6
Kelly, John Jerome, 1918, Ap 29,13:5
Kelly, John L, 1948, Je 23,27:1
Kelly, John L Jr, 1965, Mr 19,35:3
Kelly, John M, 1943, O 24,45:1; 1956, F 2,25:4
Kelly, John M Msgr, 1968, S 19,47:2
Kelly, John P, 1939, F 8,23:5; 1948, My 17,19:6; 1956, Ag 11,13:6
Kelly, John P Mrs, 1949, Je 17,23:5
Kelly, John R, 1941, O 29,23:3; 1944, D 25,19:4
Kelly, John T, 1922, Ja 17,17:4; 1943, Ag 20,15:5
Kelly, John V, 1953, My 13,29:1
Kelly, Joseph, 1923, F 10,13:4; 1962, Je 20,35:4
Kelly, Joseph A, 1965, My 24,31:5
Kelly, Joseph B, 1949, Ja 31,19:5
Kelly, Joseph D, 1953, F 7,15:1; 1961, Je 19,27:5; 1967, Ag 30,43:3
Kelly, Joseph E, 1942, N 17,25:2; 1945, F 1,23:1; 1950, Ag 18,21:4
Kelly, Joseph F, 1949, D 20,31:2
Kelly, Joseph Henry Rev Father, 1916, My 28,17:4
Kelly, Joseph I Mrs, 1953, Ag 4,21:2
Kelly, Joseph J, 1938, Ag 17,19:1; 1939, D 15,25:1; 1950, Mr 24,25:2; 1963, Jl 8,29:4
Kelly, Joseph M, 1951, F 4,77:2; 1951, Je 15,23:4
Kelly, Joseph M Mrs, 1953, Ap 27,23:5
Kelly, Joseph P, 1965, Ag 6,27:2; 1968, S 4,47:3
Kelly, Joseph P Mrs, 1963, S 15,86:8
Kelly, Joseph S, 1956, Jl 18,27:1
Kelly, Josephine C, 1957, O 6,85:2
Kelly, Josephine H, 1955, F 12,15:6
Kelly, Kathryn, 1961, Je 15,18:5
Kelly, Kyren P, 1947, Ja 9,23:1
Kelly, L S, 1928, D 18,31:3
Kelly, L T Luke, 1966, Ap 20,25:4
Kelly, Lee E, 1959, F 4,33:1
Kelly, Lena M, 1949, Jl 14,27:5
Kelly, Leo A, 1955, N 27,89:2
Kelly, Leo C, 1944, Ag 28,11:6
Kelly, Leo E, 1937, O 24,II,8:7
Kelly, Leo J, 1963, Je 26,39:4
Kelly, Leo J Mrs, 1963, Je 3,29:4
Kelly, Leslie M Mrs, 1949, D 7,64:4
Kelly, Luke L, 1952, F 8,23:2
Kelly, M J, 1940, N 21,29:2
Kelly, Margaret (Sister Alice), 1958, Je 24,31:5
Kelly, Margaret J Mrs, 1941, Ja 3,19:3
Kelly, Mark, 1952, D 7,89:1
Kelly, Mark E, 1965, F 11,39:3
Kelly, Martin F Mrs, 1949, My 19,29:3
Kelly, Martin J, 1953, My 14,29:4
Kelly, Martin J Jr, 1968, N 7,47:3
Kelly, Martin J Sr, 1960, Ap 11,31:1
Kelly, Mary (Sister Mary Norberta), 1958, Je 27,25:2
Kelly, Mary E, 1961, My 11,37:3
Kelly, Matthew D, 1951, Mr 11,94:4
Kelly, Matthew F, 1967, Jl 14,29:3
Kelly, Matthew M, 1947, My 11,60:5
Kelly, Matthew W, 1955, Je 4,15:4
Kelly, Maurice P, 1964, D 15,44:1
Kelly, Melvin H, 1966, F 16,43:5
Kelly, Michael, 1940, Mr 9,15:5; 1958, Ja 26,88:5
Kelly, Michael E, 1912, Jl 29,9:5
Kelly, Michael F Mrs, 1951, F 5,23:1
Kelly, Michael J, 1873, Je 28,7:3; 1940, O 9,25:1; 1943, O 20,21:3; 1950, Je 29,29:2; 1952, Mr 14,23:4; 1952, Je 8,86:6; 1957, N 30,21:4
Kelly, Monroe, 1956, Ag 31,17:1
Kelly, Mortimer B, 1961, Mr 10,27:2
Kelly, Myra (Mrs Allan Macnaughtan), 1910, Ap 1, 11:5
Kelly, Nancy Mrs, 1905, Mr 10,2:3
Kelly, Nell, 1939, D 20,28:2
Kelly, Nicholas J, 1954, F 23,27:2
Kelly, O A, 1942, S 13,53:2
Kelly, Oakley G, 1966, Je 7,47:3
Kelly, Oliver, 1924, My 19,17:3
Kelly, Owen A, 1949, O 8,13:5
Kelly, Pat, 1959, O 6,39:4
Kelly, Patrick, 1938, Jl 25,15:6; 1951, My 23,35:1
Kelly, Patrick B, 1948, Je 8,26:2
Kelly, Patrick H, 1937, Ja 26,21:2; 1939, Ja 25,21:4
Kelly, Patrick J, 1949, Mr 28,21:2; 1949, O 6,31:1
Kelly, Paul, 1956, N 7,31:5
Kelly, Paul A, 1959, O 6,39:1
Kelly, Paul H, 1947, Mr 12,25:4
Kelly, Peter, 1920, My 5,11:4
Kelly, Peter J, 1958, Ja 17,25:5
Kelly, Philip C, 1967, My 22,43:1
Kelly, R, 1910, Ja 10,9:2
Kelly, R B, 1949, My 7,13:5
Kelly, Ralph, 1962, Ja 27,21:2
Kelly, Raymond, 1951, Ag 26,38:1; 1962, Mr 1,31:5
Kelly, Raymond H, 1952, Je 27,23:2
Kelly, Raymond J, 1967, Ja 9,39:3
Kelly, Raymond J Mrs, 1956, S 13,35:5
Kelly, Renee (Mrs H Allen), 1965, S 2,31:1
Kelly, Rev Father, 1873, Jl 7,1:6
Kelly, Richard (por), 1938, S 23,27:1
Kelly, Richard, 1948, My 16,71:3
Kelly, Richard A, 1946, Mr 14,25:4
Kelly, Richard B, 1922, D 4,17:4
Kelly, Richard F, 1940, D 27,20:2
Kelly, Richard F Rev, 1937, D 19,II,9:2
Kelly, Richard J, 1947, N 28,23:4
Kelly, Richard M, 1948, My 20,29:3
Kelly, Robert, 1916, Ja 7,13:4; 1949, Je 21,25:5; 1960, My 10,37:6
Kelly, Robert A, 1959, D 21,27:2; 1962, Je 25,29:2
Kelly, Robert E, 1948, Ag 28,15:3
Kelly, Robert E Mrs, 1957, Je 27,25:4
Kelly, Robert L, 1954, D 16,37:5
Kelly, Robert W, 1965, Ja 14,35:2
Kelly, S Paul, 1957, Jl 7,61:2
Kelly, Samuel H, 1925, D 19,17:5
Kelly, Samuel Sir, 1937, F 10,23:2
Kelly, Sarah A Mrs, 1942, Je 7,43:3
Kelly, Sarah C, 1939, Ag 18,19:5
Kelly, Sherman L, 1952, Ag 22,21:1
Kelly, Stephen Dr, 1922, F 12,22:3
Kelly, T H, 1933, Ja 23,13:3
Kelly, T Howard, 1967, Jl 26,36:1
Kelly, Thomas, 1939, Mr 22,23:5; 1945, D 7,21:4; 1949, Ag 20,11:5; 1951, N 22,31:5; 1953, F 6,19:4
Kelly, Thomas A, 1947, D 11,33:4; 1950, Je 10,17:4; 1950, Jl 17,21:6
Kelly, Thomas A Mrs, 1957, Ap 6,19:5
Kelly, Thomas B, 1952, Mr 31,19:4
Kelly, Thomas C, 1950, Ap 15,15:2; 1955, Je 4,15:6; 1958, Ap 24,31:1
Kelly, Thomas Dr, 1919, Ja 19,21:5
Kelly, Thomas E Mrs (Margt C), 1965, Jl 12,27:1
Kelly, Thomas F, 1944, O 22,45:2; 1946, O 18,23:4
Kelly, Thomas F Jr, 1942, Ja 4,48:2
Kelly, Thomas F Sr, 1951, F 8,33:1
Kelly, Thomas F Sr Mrs, 1948, D 5,92:4
Kelly, Thomas G, 1965, Je 16,44:1
Kelly, Thomas H, 1949, D 30,19:5
Kelly, Thomas H F, 1944, F 11,19:5
Kelly, Thomas H Mrs, 1926, Ap 22,25:3
Kelly, Thomas J, 1908, F 7,7:3; 1940, N 5,34:1; 1952, Je 14,15:6; 1955, Je 17,23:4; 1964, Je 10,45:4
Kelly, Thomas J Mrs, 1940, Je 28,19:4
Kelly, Thomas J Sr, 1948, Ap 24,15:1
Kelly, Thomas P, 1940, Je 21,21:3; 1946, D 13,23:4; 1952, Je 26,29:3; 1953, Ag 24,23:4
Kelly, Thomas R, 1941, Ja 19,40:3
Kelly, Thomas S Mrs, 1966, Je 15,47:2
Kelly, Thomas V, 1960, S 16,28:5
Kelly, Thomas W, 1966, My 24,43:7
Kelly, Timothy C, 1960, Ag 17,31:5
Kelly, Timothy J, 1938, S 2,17:3; 1963, Jl 16,21:4
Kelly, Vincent B, 1921, Ap 29,15:4
Kelly, W Boulton Mrs, 1959, Jl 16,27:3
Kelly, W E, 1929, S 21,19:1
Kelly, W Howard, 1950, O 13,29:3
Kelly, W J, 1927, O 12,27:3
Kelly, Wager S, 1944, Mr 5,35:1
Kelly, Walter A, 1942, D 19,19:5
Kelly, Walter C (por), 1939, Ja 7,15:4
Kelly, Walter C, 1943, S 27,19:4
Kelly, Walter F, 1947, Mr 3,21:3
Kelly, Walter H, 1951, F 9,25:3; 1953, Mr 26,31:5
Kelly, Walter J, 1949, F 6,76:4; 1967, My 22,43:2
Kelly, Walter Sr Mrs, 1959, F 13,27:4
Kelly, William, 1944, N 30,23:3; 1957, Je 24,4:3
Kelly, William A, 1939, Ag 4,13:4; 1959, O 23,29:1; 1963, S 30,29:2
Kelly, William A Dr, 1963, D 28,23:2
Kelly, William A Mrs, 1962, S 18,39:1
Kelly, William B, 1943, Ag 4,17:4
Kelly, William E, 1948, N 27,18:2
Kelly, William F, 1945, Mr 7,21:2; 1949, Jl 18,17:6; 1950, S 19,31:1; 1965, N 7,88:4
Kelly, William F Jr, 1947, Ja 5,53:2
Kelly, William H, 1939, Jl 4,13:7; 1943, D 20,23:5; 1948, Jl 19,19:2; 1961, O 4,45:2; 1965, F 22,21:1
Kelly, William I, 1947, Mr 8,13:4
Kelly, William J, 1924, O 20,17:6; 1937, Ap 11,II,8:7; 1940, Jl 12,15:2; 1941, Ja 1,23:6; 1946, Ja 1,28:2; 1949, Mr 1,26:3; 1949, My 18,27:6; 1954, Ap 4,88:2
Kelly, William J (por), 1955, My 31,27:4
Kelly, William J, 1963, Jl 16,21:2; 1968, S 19,47:3
Kelly, William M, 1943, Ap 2,21:2
Kelly, William M (will, Ja 28,18:4), 1949, Ja 11,27:5
Kelly, William M, 1949, Jl 24,53:1
Kelly, William Mrs, 1951, Ap 7,15:4
Kelly, William P, 1947, Ap 26,13:4; 1963, My 28,28:6
Kelly, William P Mrs, 1941, N 5,23:3
Kelly, William P Sr, 1954, F 3,23:2
Kelly, William R, 1960, N 16,41:2
Kelly, William S, 1946, Je 24,31:5
Kelly, William S Rev, 1908, Ap 20,7:4
Kelly, William T, 1944, Ja 7,17:5; 1946, Jl 1,31:4; 1955, Ap 8,29:2
Kelly, William T Mrs, 1949, N 24,32:3
Kelly (Sister Jerome), 1958, F 25,27:4
Kelly-Kenny, Thomas Gen, 1914, D 27,3:6
Kelman, J, 1929, My 4,19:3
Kelman, Phil, 1950, Je 30,23:2
Kelmenson, Nathan, 1967, Ap 18,41:1
Kelnberger, Joseph G, 1967, Je 20,39:1
Kelp, George F, 1951, O 4,33:4
Kelsall, George A, 1949, Ja 6,24:3
Kelsay, Harry T Dr, 1909, Jl 28,9:5
Kelser, Raymond A, 1952, Ap 17,29:2
Kelsey, Aaron L, 1955, N 17,35:3
Kelsey, Alan M, 1964, O 7,47:3
Kelsey, Albert, 1950, My 9,29:3
Kelsey, Arthur C, 1965, Jl 3,19:5
Kelsey, Arthur J Mrs, 1960, Ja 4,29:3
Kelsey, C H, 1930, My 1,29:1
Kelsey, Carl, 1953, O 17,15:6
Kelsey, Carlton, 1944, O 29,43:1
Kelsey, Clarence, 1943, Ap 19,19:3
Kelsey, Edwin O, 1949, Ja 28,21:2
Kelsey, Edwin R, 1946, Mr 9,14:2
Kelsey, Ernest W Dr, 1937, F 11,23:1
Kelsey, Everett N, 1968, S 18,47:3
Kelsey, F Ellis, 1966, N 17,47:4
Kelsey, F W, 1927, My 15,28:1
Kelsey, Fred A, 1961, S 5,35:3
Kelsey, Fred B, 1948, N 4,30:3
Kelsey, Frederick P Mrs, 1925, F 15,7:3
Kelsey, Frederick T Sr, 1957, O 13,86:5
Kelsey, Harold D, 1948, F 27,21:1
Kelsey, Harry S, 1957, D 1,88:8
Kelsey, Harry W, 1942, D 21,23:1
Kelsey, Henry C, 1920, My 15,15:3
Kelsey, Horace, 1944, S 22,19:3
Kelsey, Horatio N, 1952, Ap 20,94:3
Kelsey, Hugh A, 1958, N 1,19:3
Kelsey, James E, 1939, My 9,24:4
Kelsey, James T, 1962, F 12,23:4
Kelsey, John F, 1939, Ap 16,III,7:2
Kelsey, John F Mrs, 1956, Je 25,23:2
Kelsey, Joseph A, 1938, S 14,23:2
Kelsey, Joseph J Sr, 1952, N 12,27:2
Kelsey, Joseph S, 1951, Ag 8,25:6
Kelsey, Louise H, 1944, Ap 1,13:3
Kelsey, Marion S, 1954, Mr 3,27:3
Kelsey, Mary (por), 1948, Mr 24,25:5
Kelsey, Minnie C Mrs, 1947, Ag 17,54:3
Kelsey, O, 1934, Ag 21,17:3
Kelsey, Preston T, 1957, Mr 9,19:2
Kelsey, Preston T Mrs, 1949, Mr 9,25:4
Kelsey, Raymond T, 1949, Ja 16,69:1
Kelsey, Stephen T, 1965, Jl 24,21:4
Kelsey, Stephen T Mrs, 1962, My 8,39:3
Kelsey, W H, 1879, Ap 22,2:4
Kelsey, William B Mrs, 1947, D 10,31:1
Kelsh, Matthew J, 1958, D 7,88:6
Kelso, Alex, 1937, D 18,21:3
Kelso, Alex Mrs, 1937, D 18,21:3
Kelso, Edward E, 1938, Ag 27,13:6
Kelso, F M Gen, 1907, N 28,7:4
Kelso, Harold, 1950, My 25,13:5
Kelso, James A, 1951, N 5,31:1
Kelso, James E, 1948, Ag 12,22:2
Kelso, John B, 1950, My 20,15:2
Kelso, T, 1878, Jl 27,5:2
Kelso, William G Jr, 1938, S 13,23:2
Kelson, Everett S, 1949, My 17,25:5
Kelston, Leon, 1961, F 5,80:6
Kelter, William D C Rev Dr, 1925, D 5,19:4
Keltie, J S Sir, 1927, Ja 13,25:5

Kelton, Pert, 1968, O 31,43:2
Kelton, Robert, 1941, N 24,17:6
Kelton, Robert Col, 1924, Je 28,13:6
Kelty, Alfred J, 1951, Mr 15,29:5
Kelty, John D, 1948, Ja 29,23:2
Kelty, Paul R, 1944, Mr 13,15:3
Kelway, Phyllis, 1945, Ap 16,23:4
Kem, James P, 1965, F 25,32:1
Kemai, Ahmed, 1905, Ap 26,5:3
Kemal, Yahya, 1958, N 3,37:4
Kemal-ed-Din Hussein, 1932, Ag 8,15:6
Kemball, Walter F, 1953, O 13,29:5
Kemberton, H Philip Jr, 1968, S 5,47:1
Kemble, Charles Col, 1865, O 8,5:4
Kemble, Charles S, 1938, O 4,25:3
Kemble, E W, 1933, S 20,21:3
Kemble, Francis W, 1957, My 15,35:4
Kemble, Harrison H Sr, 1942, Je 12,21:4
Kemble, Henrietta H Mrs, 1948, Ag 17,21:2
Kemble, William, 1881, N 8,5:2
Kemble, William F (por), 1949, Ja 9,73:1
Kemble, William F Mrs, 1960, Ag 10,31:4
Kemble, William J, 1963, Je 25,33:4
Kemble, William P, 1957, My 15,35:2
Kemeny, Emry, 1962, Jl 7,17:2
Kemeny, George, 1952, Mr 17,21:5
Kemeny, Stefan v Baron, 1904, N 18,9:4
Kemeny, Zoltan, 1965, Je 18,35:3
Kemery, Philo, 1945, Ap 14,15:3
Kemery-Harding, Timor G, 1955, S 20,35:3
Kemether, Charles, 1950, Mr 26,92:4
Kemeys, Edward, 1907, My 12,9:5
Kemezis, Joseph, 1954, F 25,31:4
Kemler, Edgar J, 1960, D 4,88:6
Kemler, Joseph L, 1962, Jl 4,21:1
Kemm, Theodore, 1938, Ag 23,17:4
Kemmer, Frank R, 1966, F 28,27:3
Kemmer, Joseph F, 1962, My 17,37:2
Kemmerer, Benjamin T, 1960, S 25,88:3
Kemmerer, Edwin W, 1945, D 17,21:1
Kemmerer, John L (por), 1944, Mr 5,35:1
Kemmerer, John L Mrs, 1943, Ap 28,23:3
Kemmerer, Mahlon, 1925, D 30,17:4; 1963, N 18,33:3
Kemmler, Christopher Capt, 1937, My 28,21:2
Kemmy, James Mrs, 1956, O 5,25:2
Kemmy, Roy V, 1953, F 4,27:1
Kemnitz, Edward, 1955, O 2,86:6
Kemnitz, Ernest J, 1942, Jl 1,25:3
Kemp, Alan R, 1961, F 15,35:5
Kemp, Albert M, 1944, Ja 6,23:4
Kemp, Alex N, 1955, Ag 15,15:4
Kemp, Alex N Mrs, 1955, Jl 15,21:4
Kemp, Archie, 1949, S 21,43:3
Kemp, Arthur T, 1945, Ja 26,21:2
Kemp, Catherine L Mrs, 1941, Ap 11,22:3
Kemp, Charles E, 1908, My 17,9:5
Kemp, Chouteau, 1919, My 21,17:6
Kemp, David F, 1957, O 11,27:2
Kemp, Donald F, 1959, F 4,23:1
Kemp, E Sir, 1929, Ag 13,25:1
Kemp, Edwin L, 1944, D 31,26:6
Kemp, Ellwood L, 1938, S 1,23:4
Kemp, Frank L, 1947, O 9,25:2
Kemp, G Frank, 1954, Mr 7,91:2
Kemp, G Le Roy, 1956, My 16,35:5
Kemp, George E, 1938, Je 5,44:8
Kemp, George F, 1940, Ja 30,19:3
Kemp, George William, 1912, D 25,11:5
Kemp, Harold F, 1968, Jl 4,19:4
Kemp, Harry H, 1960, Ag 9,27:3
Kemp, J F, 1926, N 18,23:1
Kemp, J Howard, 1945, Ja 7,38:3
Kemp, James, 1958, Mr 6,27:5
Kemp, James W, 1967, Jl 29,25:4
Kemp, James W Mrs, 1944, Ap 21,19:6
Kemp, Jan C G, 1947, Ja 2,27:5
Kemp, John A, 1963, N 27,37:1
Kemp, John B Sr, 1957, My 24,25:4
Kemp, John J, 1938, N 1,23:4
Kemp, Joseph I, 1943, D 7,27:3
Kemp, Lady, 1957, Je 28,23:3
Kemp, Lena, 1937, Ja 17,II,8:8
Kemp, Lloyd N Mrs, 1952, My 23,21:2
Kemp, Marion M, 1963, S 20,33:2
Kemp, N C Mrs, 1937, D 8,25:4
Kemp, Peter, 1937, N 19,23:4
Kemp, Philip C, 1960, Ja 26,33:2
Kemp, R, 1880, Ap 17,8:3
Kemp, Robert, 1959, Jl 4,15:5
Kemp, Robert M, 1940, Jl 17,21:5
Kemp, Sophie, 1914, My 26,11:3
Kemp, Stanley W, 1945, My 19,19:5
Kemp, Theodore Dr, 1937, My 22,18:2
Kemp, Theodore H, 1951, Ag 24,15:5
Kemp, Thomas, 1944, F 7,15:5
Kemp, W, 1881, D 22,2:1
Kemp, W Wallace, 1948, D 25,18:3
Kemp, William, 1908, Ag 15,7:4
Kemp, William E Mrs, 1953, Je 27,15:5
Kemp, William F Sr, 1956, S 3,13:2
Kemp, William Mrs (H Shields), 1963, Ag 8,27:2
Kemp, William W, 1946, My 16,21:2
Kemp, Williard H Sr Mrs, 1949, F 12,17:2
Kemp, wm J, 1958, D 4,39:1
Kempe, Augusta, 1948, My 20,29:2
Kempen, August, 1953, Ja 31,15:6
Kemper, A A, 1948, F 28,15:4
Kemper, Charles, 1950, My 15,21:1
Kemper, Collin, 1955, N 28,31:3
Kemper, Collin Mrs (Latham Hope), 1951, Ap 11, 29:1
Kemper, Dolly, 1943, My 10,19:3
Kemper, Dolores S Mrs, 1955, Mr 9,27:3
Kemper, Edward I, 1965, Mr 17,45:5
Kemper, Graham H Mrs, 1947, O 19,66:4
Kemper, Harry T, 1943, O 19,19:3
Kemper, James A, 1949, Jl 10,57:1
Kemper, James B, 1942, O 25,44:6
Kemper, John M Mrs, 1961, S 3,60:3
Kemper, Ruth Powell Mrs (Billie), 1968, N 26,47:2
Kemper, Thomas R, 1937, S 5,II,6:6
Kemper, William T (por), 1938, Ja 20,23:1
Kempf, Joseph Mrs, 1950, D 29,20:2
Kempf, Louis A, 1962, Ap 6,36:1
Kempf, Louis W, 1947, Je 16,21:4
Kempf, Nicholas, 1942, S 4,24:3
Kempf, Paul, 1947, Ap 20,60:4
Kempf, Paul Mrs, 1966, O 10,41:2
Kempf, William C, 1965, Je 18,35:3
Kempfner, Joseph, 1951, O 3,33:2
Kempie, Hal, 1938, O 20,23:5
Kempinski, Hans, 1940, D 6,23:2
Kempinski, Leo A, 1958, My 27,29:5
Kemple, Frederick C, 1938, My 22,II,7:2
Kempner, Bernard, 1945, D 15,17:6
Kempner, Clarence, 1951, Mr 19,27:4
Kempner, Daniel W, 1956, O 17,35:4
Kempner, David W, 1958, Jl 21,21:4
Kempner, Harry, 1958, D 1,29:5
Kempner, Isaac H Jr, 1953, O 21,29:5
Kempner, Isidor H (por), 1944, Jl 21,19:5
Kempner, Isidor H Mrs, 1952, Mr 29,15:2
Kempner, M, 1927, My 12,27:6
Kempner, Otto, 1914, O 10,11:6
Kempner, Paul H, 1956, Ap 14,17:5
Kempner, Paul H Mrs, 1961, N 4,19:1
Kempner, Seymour, 1948, N 18,27:2
Kempshale, Thomas, 1865, Ja 15,1:3
Kempshall, Anna S, 1961, N 3,35:1
Kempshall, E E Rev, 1904, Ap 1,9:6
Kempson, Ewart, 1966, My 7,31:2
Kempson, Grover C, 1949, Ja 31,19:3
Kempson, John F, 1939, Ag 1,19:4
Kempson, P Tertius Mrs (Julie Hart Beers), 1913, Ag 15,7:6
Kempson, St G Mrs, 1902, Ja 12,2:7
Kempson, St George, 1907, Ag 13,7:6
Kempter, Richard, 1943, Je 21,19:5
Kempthorne, John A, 1946, F 26,25:4
Kempton, Donald E Mrs, 1949, Ap 16,15:1
Kempton, Edwin, 1916, F 28,9:2
Kempton, Elizabeth A, 1952, D 23,23:3
Kempton, Grace C Mrs, 1939, Mr 24,21:5
Kempton, Joe F, 1946, My 18,19:5
Kempton, John T, 1950, Jl 19,31:2
Kempton, Kenneth P, 1955, Je 13,23:6
Kempton, Leland H, 1947, Mr 6,25:4
Kempton, Melvin H, 1955, Ag 2,23:3
Kemsley, Viscount (Jas Gomer Berry), 1968, F 7,47:1
Kena, Nana K 2d, 1961, Ag 29,31:4
Kenah, Thomas J, 1944, D 23,13:2
Kenah, Thomas J Mrs, 1947, Ap 3,25:1
Kenamore, Charles B, 1959, F 5,31:4
Kenan, W R Capt, 1903, Ap 15,9:6
Kenan, William R Jr, 1965, Jl 29,27:2
Kenan, William R Jr Mrs, 1947, F 13,24:2
Kenarney, Henry W, 1958, O 2,37:3
Kenaston, Rolla S, 1949, Je 18,13:5
Kendal, Albert H, 1942, Jl 24,20:2
Kendal, M, 1935, S 15,39:1
Kendal, William Hunter (Wm Hunter Grimston), 1917, N 8,15:4
Kendal, Wolf Mrs, 1950, F 22,29:4
Kendall, Albert H, 1948, S 7,25:4
Kendall, Albert S, 1941, My 14,21:5
Kendall, Amos, 1869, N 13,3:7
Kendall, Burton W, 1966, Mr 31,40:1
Kendall, Calvin N Dr, 1921, S 3,9:6
Kendall, Charles H, 1949, Ag 29,17:4
Kendall, Clarence M, 1949, F 28,19:4
Kendall, Curtis P, 1949, Jl 5,23:4
Kendall, Daniel R, 1912, Ja 5,13:4
Kendall, Doric Mrs, 1959, S 20,86:7
Kendall, Edgar G, 1939, Ap 29,17:4
Kendall, Elizabeth K, 1952, My 22,27:4
Kendall, Elmer E Mrs, 1947, Ap 9,25:2
Kendall, Ezra, 1910, Ja 24,9:4
Kendall, Florence H M Mrs, 1939, Ja 21,15:4
Kendall, Francis H, 1937, O 9,19:6
Kendall, Francis R, 1952, Je 4,27:3
Kendall, Frank E, 1946, Ag 16,21:5
Kendall, Frank E Dr, 1937, My 14,23:5
Kendall, Fred H, 1951, S 15,15:3
Kendall, Frederick C, 1957, N 7,35:1; 1965, Ja 13,25:3
Kendall, Frederick H, 1942, Je 5,17:4
Kendall, Frederick Mrs, 1950, Ap 15,15:1
Kendall, Frederick O, 1942, O 20,21:4
Kendall, Frederick W, 1943, Ag 11,19:2
Kendall, George H, 1924, Ap 25,17:3
Kendall, Harry F, 1939, Je 29,23:4
Kendall, Harry H, 1950, Mr 22,27:4
Kendall, Harry T, 1952, My 4,91:1
Kendall, Harvey C, 1949, D 30,19:1
Kendall, Henry, 1946, My 10,19:4
Kendall, Henry E, 1949, S 3,13:4
Kendall, Henry G, 1965, N 29,35:4
Kendall, Henry H, 1943, Mr 1,19:5
Kendall, Henry M, 1966, Ja 14,39:3
Kendall, Henry Mrs, 1938, O 13,23:2
Kendall, Henry P, 1959, N 4,35:1
Kendall, Henry W, 1955, S 13,31:4
Kendall, Herbert P, 1944, Ja 3,21:4
Kendall, Ira H, 1950, S 28,31:3
Kendall, J F, 1931, Ag 10,15:5
Kendall, John C, 1941, Mr 17,17:5
Kendall, John F, 1945, S 13,23:4
Kendall, Joseph, 1919, F 14,13:3
Kendall, Joseph S, 1903, Ap 22,9:5
Kendall, Julian L, 1945, D 22,19:2
Kendall, Kay (Mrs R Harrison),(funl plans, S 9,41:4), 1959, S 7,15:5
Kendall, Kay (Mrs R Harrison),(est value set), 1960, Mr 9,5:6
Kendall, Messmore, 1959, My 2,23:2
Kendall, Myron A, 1962, My 24,35:2
Kendall, N E, 1936, N 5,27:5
Kendall, Oliver W, 1948, Ap 22,27:5
Kendall, Oren E, 1954, S 9,31:2
Kendall, Ralph C, 1967, Mr 13,37:4
Kendall, Ralph E, 1964, Ja 30,29:2
Kendall, Russell, 1922, Mr 16,17:5
Kendall, Sergeant, 1938, F 17,21:4
Kendall, Theodore R, 1946, F 5,24:3
Kendall, Thomas E, 1953, Ja 14,31:4
Kendall, Thomas R, 1953, D 23,26:3
Kendall, Vaughan, 1945, S 16,43:1
Kendall, Waldo S, 1957, D 23,23:5
Kendall, Walter G, 1946, Je 9,40:6
Kendall, Warren C, 1964, Mr 15,87:1
Kendall, William, 1953, F 20,19:2
Kendall, William B, 1922, Ja 28,13:4
Kendall, William B Mrs, 1942, N 1,52:5
Kendall, William C, 1939, Ja 29,32:8
Kendall, William G, 1943, D 27,20:3
Kendall, William M (will, Ag 28,21:1), 1941, Ag 9, 15:1
Kendall, Winfield Mrs, 1943, O 17,48:5
Kende, Herbert A Mrs, 1967, Je 24,29:1
Kendell, George S, 1948, S 24,25:4
Kenderdine, Jesse Mrs, 1950, Mr 21,29:3
Kendig, Calvin M, 1952, O 15,31:5
Kendig, H Evert, 1950, Ap 19,29:3
Kendig, John R, 1946, Je 11,23:2
Kendig, Kate, 1956, N 21,27:6
Kendig, Mary M Mrs, 1947, O 30,25:4
Kendig, Roscoe B, 1917, My 12,11:6
Kendig, Willard C Dr, 1937, D 28,21:3
Kendis, James, 1946, N 16,19:3
Kendler, Julius Mrs, 1948, Jl 28,23:4
Kendrick, Arthur B, 1954, Jl 1,25:5
Kendrick, Ashley W, 1939, Ja 28,13:5
Kendrick, Benjamin B, 1946, O 29,25:4
Kendrick, Benjamin B Mrs, 1950, D 3,88:6
Kendrick, D E, 1944, Jl 27,17:1
Kendrick, Eliza H, 1940, Ap 12,23:5
Kendrick, Ernest P, 1957, Ja 19,15:2
Kendrick, G W, 1946, O 30,30:2
Kendrick, George R, 1949, F 25,24:3
Kendrick, George W Jr, 1916, F 27,17:5
Kendrick, Horace, 1941, My 28,25:1
Kendrick, J, 1877, My 29,4:7
Kendrick, J B, 1933, N 4,15:1
Kendrick, J William, 1944, Jl 7,15:4
Kendrick, James E Jr, 1967, F 13,33:3
Kendrick, John Mills Bp, 1911, D 18,11:4
Kendrick, Miss, 1882, Je 13,5:2
Kendrick, Morris R, 1947, S 29,21:4
Kendrick, Raymond H Mrs, 1956, Jl 8,64:5
Kendrick, Robert R, 1945, O 11,23:4
Kendrick, Rodney, 1941, Jl 23,19:4
Kendrick, Rufus, 1908, F 21,7:7
Kendrick, S S, 1881, Je 27,5:4
Kendrick, Sarah E Mrs, 1949, N 21,25:3
Kendrick, Stanley, 1951, F 15,31:4
Kendrick, Stephen, 1944, S 29,21:4
Kendrick, T C Dr, 1884, F 13,5:2
Kendrick, T Frank, 1949, Ap 19,25:5
Kendrick, Thomas F, 1940, D 8,69:2
Kendrick, Tobias J, 1938, D 25,14:6
Kendrick, W Freeland, 1953, Mr 21,17:1
Kendrick, Ward H, 1948, Ja 31,19:2
Kendrick, William M, 1937, My 26,25:1
Kendricks, Edward J, 1956, F 19,93:2
Kendrigan, James, 1953, Jl 17,17:4
Kendrik, John F, 1951, Je 19,30:4
Kendzielawa, Steve, 1943, Jl 17,13:7
Kene, C Eugene, 1954, My 10,23:4
Kene, Emma E Mrs, 1938, Ag 25,19:5
Keneally, Joseph L, 1963, O 9,40:5

Keneally, P J, 1909, My 29,7:4
Keneally, Patrick D, 1954, Ag 5,23:3
Kenealy, Alexander, 1915, Je 27,15:4
Kenealy, Anselm E J, 1943, D 19,48:3
Kenealy, E V H, 1880, Ap 17,8:1
Kenealy, Matthew H, 1950, F 27,19:4
Kenealy, William J, 1958, Mr 5,31:4
Keneas, George, 1968, D 31,27:1
Kenedy, Louis, 1956, N 17,21:3
Kenefic, William J, 1939, F 11,15:5
Kenefick, Daniel J, 1949, D 27,23:3
Kenefick, Joseph A Dr, 1919, S 11,15:3
Kenefick, Thomas Dr, 1916, Ag 1,9:5
Kenefick, Thomas W Judge, 1923, Ag 27,11:3
Kenefick, William, 1921, Ja 26,7:4
Keneh, John F, 1954, Je 27,68:5
Kenehan, Gilbert P, 1949, Mr 17,25:4
Keneipp, George E, 1958, Mr 8,17:3
Kenely, Daniel J, 1956, My 4,25:3
Kenely, John C, 1963, Je 30,56:5
Kenely, John P Mrs, 1949, S 27,27:4
Kenely, Michael J, 1956, O 28,89:1
Kenerson, Arthur W, 1954, Mr 10,25:3
Kenfield, John Sr, 1958, Ja 21,29:2
Kengla, Leo F Jr, 1953, S 4,16:4
Kengla, Leo F Sr Mrs (por), 1949, S 15,27:6
Kenick, Charles W Mrs, 1940, S 17,23:4
Kenilworth, Lady, 1953, O 21,30:7
Kenilworth, Lord (J D Siddeley), 1953, N 4,33:2
Kenin, Mayer, 1954, S 21,27:1
Kenison, Ervin M, 1942, My 14,19:5
Keniston, Davis B, 1954, F 22,19:2
Kenjockey, Aged Seneca Indian, 1866, Ap 15,6:1
Kenlon, Andrew M, 1937, N 10,25:4
Kenlon, John (por), 1940, My 31,19:1
Kenlon, John G, 1948, Je 15,28:3
Kenlon, Walter J, 1937, Mr 5,21:2
Kenly, J R, 1928, Mr 2,25:3
Kenly, W L, 1928, Ja 12,27:3
Kenly, William L Mrs, 1943, Ja 9,13:5
Kenmare, Countess of, 1873, S 8,1:6; 1944, My 22,19:4
Kenmare, Earl of, 1941, N 15,17:6
Kenmare, Earl of (V E C B Castlerosse), 1943, S 21, 23:1
Kenmare, Earl of (G R D Browne), 1952, F 15,25:2
Kenmey, James, 1955, O 21,27:1
Kenna, Edward D Mrs, 1953, N 22,88:1
Kenna, Esther (Sister Esther Maria), 1956, Jl 4,19:4
Kenna, Frank, 1947, D 27,13:5; 1964, N 12,37:3
Kenna, James P, 1951, Ja 25,25:1
Kenna, John F, 1953, Je 4,29:3
Kenna, John J Mrs, 1945, Ag 28,19:3
Kenna, John Mrs, 1947, N 4,25:2
Kenna, Michael, 1946, O 10,27:1
Kenna, Roger, 1959, Mr 26,31:2
Kenna, William B, 1948, Jl 4,26:7
Kenna, William J, 1939, Ja 13,19:3
Kennahan, George H, 1946, Mr 21,25:4
Kennaird, Arthur Fitzgerald Lord, 1923, Ja 31,19:5
Kennally, Thomas A, 1965, My 28,33:1
Kennamer, Charles B, 1955, Je 4,15:5
Kennamer, T J, 1938, S 29,25:1
Kennan, Ben A, 1938, N 27,48:6
Kennan, Emaline Mrs, 1940, My 28,23:5
Kennan, Ernest V, 1950, F 3,23:3
Kennan, Owen, 1963, Jl 13,17:3
Kennan, Richard C, 1942, N 15,59:3
Kennard, Arthur W, 1937, Jl 6,19:4
Kennard, Clyde, 1963, Jl 5,19:2
Kennard, Frank B, 1943, S 7,23:5
Kennard, Frederic H, 1937, F 26,22:1
Kennard, Howard, 1955, N 14,27:3
Kennard, J, 1879, Mr 8,8:4
Kennard, John H, 1939, Mr 8,21:5
Kennard, Joseph S, 1944, Ag 16,19:5
Kennard, Lady, 1950, Ja 28,13:4
Kennard, Martin P, 1903, N 14,9:6
Kennard, Reginald P Mrs, 1947, Jl 18,17:5
Kennard, Victor P, 1953, Ag 16,77:2
Kennard, William M, 1952, My 8,31:1
Kennard, William P Mrs, 1953, S 29,29:5
Kennard, William W, 1938, D 18,48:8
Kennaway, Ernest, 1958, Ja 3,23:1
Kennaway, James, 1968, D 25,31:1
Kenne, Alex B Mrs, 1964, Ap 18,29:4
Kenneally, John J, 1937, O 13,23:1
Kenneally, William P (por), 1944, N 22,19:3
Kennebeck, John E, 1937, Ja 27,21:2
Kennedy, Adam G, 1949, Ag 31,23:2
Kennedy, Albert E, 1938, My 11,19:1
Kennedy, Alex, 1953, Ja 4,77:1
Kennedy, Alex M, 1939, Ja 16,15:1
Kennedy, Alexander Lord, 1912, Ap 9,11:4
Kennedy, Alfred G, 1940, My 17,19:6
Kennedy, Alfred J, 1941, D 30,19:3
Kennedy, Alfred J (por), 1944, Jl 29,13:3
Kennedy, Alfred J, 1944, Ag 1,15:3
Kennedy, Ambrose J, 1950, Ag 30,31:4
Kennedy, Amos D 3d, 1947, F 25,26:3
Kennedy, Andrew, 1957, Mr 26,33:4
Kennedy, Andrew J (por), 1939, O 3,23:2
Kennedy, Andrew J, 1958, Ap 7,21:3
Kennedy, Andrew Mrs, 1942, My 10,42:7
Kennedy, Andrew R, 1953, Ap 11,17:3
Kennedy, Ann E N Mrs, 1964, D 2,47:2
Kennedy, Anthony Jr, 1960, Je 15,41:2
Kennedy, Anthony K, 1945, Jl 2,15:5
Kennedy, Arch R S, 1938, O 26,23:4
Kennedy, Arthur, 1951, F 4,76:5
Kennedy, Arthur G, 1954, Ap 23,27:2
Kennedy, Arthur M, 1955, F 17,27:4
Kennedy, Banks, 1944, N 4,15:2
Kennedy, Bert W, 1959, Ap 18,23:4
Kennedy, C Edward, 1955, O 24,27:4
Kennedy, C W, 1901, Ag 4,5:6
Kennedy, Charles A B, 1951, S 1,11:7
Kennedy, Charles A Sr, 1946, Mr 28,25:5
Kennedy, Charles E, 1943, O 26,23:2
Kennedy, Charles Marquess of Ailsa, 1956, Je 3,86:6; 1957, Je 3,27:6
Kennedy, Charles O (trb lr, S 14,II,5:1), 1958, S 9, 35:2
Kennedy, Charles R, 1950, F 17,24:4
Kennedy, Charles W Mrs, 1946, D 20,23:4
Kennedy, Clarence H, 1941, Jl 23,19:4
Kennedy, Clarence Mrs, 1968, D 1,86:3
Kennedy, Colin, 1950, My 26,23:3
Kennedy, Colin B, 1942, Je 17,23:4
Kennedy, Cornelia L, 1957, Je 12,35:3
Kennedy, Cornelius E (por), 1939, Ja 3,17:4
Kennedy, Cornelius J, 1957, Je 13,31:3
Kennedy, Crammond, 1918, F 21,11:3
Kennedy, Daniel A, 1950, Mr 22,27:2
Kennedy, Daniel C, 1947, O 11,17:5
Kennedy, Daniel E, 1946, Je 11,23:1
Kennedy, Daniel J, 1937, N 16,23:4; 1942, My 4,19:5; 1948, D 2,29:2
Kennedy, Daniel P, 1941, N 7,23:4
Kennedy, David A, 1938, Je 9,23:6
Kennedy, David M, 1939, N 12,49:3
Kennedy, David S, 1938, Ag 29,13:4
Kennedy, Davidson, 1942, Ap 5,42:1
Kennedy, Dennis T, 1947, S 24,23:5
Kennedy, Dion W, 1946, Ja 16,23:2
Kennedy, Donald B, 1949, Jl 26,28:6
Kennedy, Donald F, 1947, N 22,15:5
Kennedy, Douglas M, 1966, O 9,86:7
Kennedy, Duncan, 1906, Ap 14,11:4
Kennedy, Duncan C, 1947, S 24,23:3
Kennedy, E Carey, 1959, Je 10,37:3
Kennedy, E R, 1926, Ap 27,25:3
Kennedy, Edgar (por), 1948, N 10,29:3
Kennedy, Edgar S, 1955, Ja 25,25:2
Kennedy, Edward (trb lr, D 4,46:6), 1963, N 30,27:2
Kennedy, Edward A, 1943, D 16,27:1; 1944, O 18, 21:1; 1945, D 3,21:2
Kennedy, Edward E, 1946, D 8,79:5
Kennedy, Edward F, 1963, Je 22,23:4
Kennedy, Edward J, 1960, D 20,33:4
Kennedy, Edward P, 1958, My 29,27:2
Kennedy, Edwin J, 1954, O 28,35:3
Kennedy, Eugene A, 1955, Ja 9,87:2
Kennedy, Ezra J Jr, 1967, N 25,39:4
Kennedy, F Laird, 1939, D 4,23:2
Kennedy, Forester L, 1949, Je 10,27:1
Kennedy, Foster, 1952, Ja 8,27:1
Kennedy, Frances, 1941, Ja 19,40:3
Kennedy, Francis J, 1950, Mr 2,27:3
Kennedy, Francis W, 1939, Jl 12,19:4
Kennedy, Frank, 1922, D 7,19:6
Kennedy, Frank G, 1952, O 28,31:1
Kennedy, Frank J, 1946, My 21,23:1
Kennedy, Frank M, 1965, Mr 22,33:4
Kennedy, Frank M Mrs, 1948, Ap 15,25:3
Kennedy, Frank Prof, 1937, Ap 15,24:3
Kennedy, Frank W, 1962, Mr 26,31:1
Kennedy, Fred, 1958, D 6,23:2; 1962, N 1,31:3
Kennedy, Fred I, 1949, My 11,29:3
Kennedy, Fred T, 1954, S 6,15:5
Kennedy, Frederick F, 1944, S 4,19:5
Kennedy, Frederick N, 1946, F 15,25:2
Kennedy, Frederick W, 1952, D 19,31:2; 1957, O 5,17:5
Kennedy, G N Judge, 1901, S 8,7:6
Kennedy, George A, 1960, Ag 17,31:3
Kennedy, George C, 1940, Jl 12,15:1
Kennedy, George E, 1953, Ag 28,17:3
Kennedy, George H, 1942, D 7,27:6
Kennedy, George H Jr Mrs, 1940, S 13,23:3
Kennedy, George J, 1941, My 23,21:3
Kennedy, George P (por), 1946, Mr 1,22:2
Kennedy, Gordon A, 1960, S 9,29:2
Kennedy, Grafton C Mrs, 1945, D 20,23:4
Kennedy, H, 1936, D 13,II,8:8
Kennedy, H D Mrs, 1953, Mr 13,27:1
Kennedy, H D Rev, 1925, O 15,23:5
Kennedy, H Van Rensselaer, 1912, Jl 14,II,11:6
Kennedy, Hamilton, 1954, Ap 4,88:6
Kennedy, Harold, 1937, O 13,23:5
Kennedy, Harold C (por), 1944, Ja 18,19:3
Kennedy, Harrison H, 1963, Ag 4,80:3
Kennedy, Harry, 1938, Ja 10,17:2
Kennedy, Harry A, 1958, Je 16,23:4
Kennedy, Harry Baldwin, 1968, O 4,47:2
Kennedy, Harry D Mrs, 1955, Ag 14,80:4
Kennedy, Harry E, 1924, Ag 18,13:4
Kennedy, Harry H Mrs, 1959, My 4,29:4
Kennedy, Harry V, 1951, S 19,31:3
Kennedy, Harvey, 1917, S 1,7:6
Kennedy, Helen F, 1958, Mr 16,86:4
Kennedy, Henry B, 1966, Ag 18,32:6
Kennedy, Henry P, 1968, Ag 2,33:1
Kennedy, Herbert W, 1951, Jl 26,21:4
Kennedy, Howard, 1948, D 11,15:5
Kennedy, Howard A, 1938, F 16,21:5
Kennedy, Howard S (por), 1938, Ja 21,20:2
Kennedy, Howard S, 1964, Ja 11,23:1
Kennedy, Howard Sr, 1905, Ap 19,11:4
Kennedy, Hugh F, 1955, Ag 17,27:4
Kennedy, Ida G Mrs, 1948, Je 3,25:5
Kennedy, Isabel P, 1954, N 26,29:2
Kennedy, J Arthur (por), 1946, S 21,15:3
Kennedy, J Carroll, 1947, Je 25,25:5
Kennedy, J J Msgr, 1906, Ap 14,11:4
Kennedy, J L, 1865, Ja 11,5:1
Kennedy, J M, 1871, O 15,5:3
Kennedy, J Russell, 1915, Ja 8,11:5
Kennedy, J Wilmer, 1939, My 6,17:5
Kennedy, Jack, 1948, Je 18,23:4
Kennedy, James, 1922, Ag 16,9:5
Kennedy, James A, 1916, Ja 12,13:4
Kennedy, James B Rev, 1908, Je 4,7:7
Kennedy, James C, 1904, Ap 21,3:2; 1951, Ap 25,2
Kennedy, James C Jr, 1957, S 20,25:4
Kennedy, James C Jr Mrs, 1963, D 1,85:1
Kennedy, James Dr, 1884, Mr 30,2:5
Kennedy, James E, 1938, Ag 23,17:2; 1961, My 17, 37:2
Kennedy, James F, 1959, Mr 24,39:4
Kennedy, James G, 1951, F 14,29:3
Kennedy, James J, 1941, D 7,76:2; 1943, O 12,27: 1946, F 21,21:2
Kennedy, James J Mrs, 1951, F 7,29:5
Kennedy, James M, 1965, Je 29,35:3
Kennedy, James M Mrs, 1940, D 15,60:4; 1954, D 13:3; 1964, O 21,47:1
Kennedy, James N, 1956, F 6,23:2; 1964, Jl 26,56:
Kennedy, James R (funl, N 23,29:5), 1963, N 19,
Kennedy, James S, 1939, F 14,19:3
Kennedy, James W, 1957, Ap 24,33:5
Kennedy, Jane Mrs, 1925, O 13,23:4
Kennedy, Jean, 1910, Jl 1,7:4
Kennedy, Jerome D, 1948, N 5,26:3
Kennedy, Jerome K, 1950, O 20,27:6
Kennedy, Joan, 1956, O 13,19:6
Kennedy, John, 1948, S 7,25:4
Kennedy, John A, 1873, Je 21,5:2; 1947, O 11,17: 1955, Jl 29,17:3
Kennedy, John B, 1961, Jl 25,27:1
Kennedy, John C, 1962, My 12,23:6
Kennedy, John D, 1940, F 6,22:2
Kennedy, John E, 1942, Ag 13,19:4
Kennedy, John F Rev, 1921, S 6,15:5
Kennedy, John J, 1940, S 27,23:5; 1941, Ag 8,15: 1942, D 21,23:2; 1943, D 27,19:3; 1945, Ap 1,3 1947, F 22,13:3; 1947, S 9,31:2; 1951, O 12,27: 1955, Ag 11,21:5; 1959, Mr 5,31:4
Kennedy, John L, 1946, S 1,36:2
Kennedy, John M, 1949, Jl 27,23:3
Kennedy, John N Judge, 1914, Je 19,13:5
Kennedy, John P, 1870, Ag 21,5:3; 1944, O 25,2 1948, Ap 15,25:5
Kennedy, John R, 1941, F 16,40:7
Kennedy, John R Mrs, 1948, Je 1,23:2
Kennedy, John S, 1950, F 14,26:2
Kennedy, John S Mrs, 1959, Ag 18,29:3
Kennedy, John Sr, 1953, My 2,15:5
Kennedy, John Stewart (funl, N 2,9:4), 1909, N
Kennedy, John Stewart, 1909, N 4,11:4
Kennedy, John T, 1944, Ja 25,19:3; 1948, My 4, 1958, Jl 18,21:4
Kennedy, John W, 1944, Jl 15,13:6; 1945, S 29, 1961, My 17,37:4
Kennedy, Joseph, 1908, Ja 10,7:5; 1938, N 19,1
Kennedy, Joseph A C, 1937, Ag 5,23:5
Kennedy, Joseph C, 1949, My 6,25:3
Kennedy, Joseph D Jr, 1951, Je 19,29:3
Kennedy, Joseph D Sr, 1957, N 4,29:2
Kennedy, Joseph E, 1959, Ja 10,17:5
Kennedy, Joseph F, 1954, S 3,17:4
Kennedy, Joseph J, 1951, Jl 31,22:5
Kennedy, Joseph P, 1944, Ap 19,23:6
Kennedy, Joseph P Mrs, 1942, Mr 5,23:5
Kennedy, Joseph S Mrs, 1946, My 3,21:3
Kennedy, Joseph T, 1966, My 17,47:3
Kennedy, Joseph W, 1957, My 6,29:1; 1966, D
Kennedy, Joyce, 1943, Mr 13,13:2
Kennedy, Katherine (will), 1956, Ja 11,33:3
Kennedy, L, 1936, D 29,21:3
Kennedy, L P, 1956, Ag 1,23:6
Kennedy, Laurence S (por), 1955, N 29,29:3
Kennedy, Leo, 1939, D 12,27:4
Kennedy, Logan L, 1962, N 5,31:5
Kennedy, Lyle H, 1958, N 2,88:6
Kennedy, Margaret (Mrs D Davies), 1967, A
Kennedy, Margaret C, 1956, N 27,30:5
Kennedy, Margaret Mrs, 1941, O 22,23:6; 194 26:3
Kennedy, Margaret R Mrs, 1942, Ja 25,34:2
Kennedy, Maria Mrs, 1913, Je 12,9:5

Kennedy, Marie R Mrs, 1954, D 31,14:6
Kennedy, Martin, 1912, S 28,13:6
Kennedy, Martin J, 1942, Ap 8,11:3; 1955, O 29,19:4
Kennedy, Martin J Mrs, 1963, Je 15,23:4
Kennedy, Martin Jr, 1944, My 20,15:5
Kennedy, Martin Mrs, 1950, Ap 9,85:1
Kennedy, Mary, 1955, Je 11,15:3
Kennedy, Mary E, 1955, Ja 9,87:2
Kennedy, Mary Mrs, 1941, Ja 5,45:2
Kennedy, Matthew (Pat), 1957, Je 17,23:1
Kennedy, Matthew F, 1925, Mr 26,23:3
Kennedy, May, 1965, Ap 14,42:1
Kennedy, Mazie E, 1941, O 29,24:2
Kennedy, Merna, 1944, D 21,21:2
Kennedy, Michael F, 1945, My 15,19:5; 1954, Jl 4,31:2
Kennedy, Michael J, 1916, Ap 15,13:5; 1949, N 2,1:8
Kennedy, Michael J (est tax appr; left no will), 1954, Je 2,29:1
Kennedy, Miles C, 1965, Mr 7,82:7
Kennedy, Miles D, 1968, S 28,33:5
Kennedy, Millard B, 1947, Jl 22,23:4
Kennedy, Minnie Mrs, 1947, N 24,23:2
Kennedy, Morgan T, 1956, O 16,33:2
Kennedy, Morgan T Mrs, 1957, Ag 15,21:2
Kennedy, Myles Burton, 1914, Je 13,9:5
Kennedy, O'Neil, 1943, Ag 25,19:5
Kennedy, Olla A, 1952, Je 10,27:4
Kennedy, Owen S, 1937, Je 7,19:3
Kennedy, Patrick, 1919, Jl 3,10:2
Kennedy, Patrick A, 1944, F 15,17:3
Kennedy, Patrick F, 1943, Ag 28,11:2; 1947, Ag 17, 54:4
Kennedy, Patrick J, 1906, Ja 5,11:3
Kennedy, Patrick Mrs, 1948, Jl 30,18:3
Kennedy, Paul B Jr, 1959, D 2,43:4
Kennedy, Paul P, 1967, F 3,31:1
Kennedy, Paul S, 1951, Je 8,27:3
Kennedy, Peter A, 1950, Ap 20,29:4
Kennedy, Peter M Sr, 1949, Ja 22,13:4
Kennedy, Philip L, 1961, Je 15,43:1
Kennedy, Phineas B, 1963, My 5,87:2
Kennedy, Phineas B Mrs, 1952, D 29,19:4
Kennedy, R G, 1881, S 18,7:1
Kennedy, R J, 1935, S 26,23:1
Kennedy, R Oakley, 1959, Ja 31,19:5
Kennedy, Ralph A, 1961, F 20,27:4
Kennedy, Raymond D, 1942, N 7,15:5
Kennedy, Raymond D Mrs, 1960, S 22,27:4
Kennedy, Rex B, 1953, Je 3,31:2
Kennedy, Rich D, 1964, My 7,20:5
Kennedy, Richard, 1913, Ag 22,9:6
Kennedy, Richard A, 1942, Ja 4,48:4
Kennedy, Richard L, 1950, S 7,31:3
Kennedy, Richard O Mrs, 1962, Je 23,23:2
Kennedy, Robert Buchanan Dr, 1917, Je 28,11:4
Kennedy, Robert Dr, 1922, My 27,13:5
Kennedy, Robert E, 1937, O 2,21:5; 1941, N 23,51:6
Kennedy, Robert J, 1956, My 16,35:2
Kennedy, Robert M (por), 1946, Je 18,25:4
Kennedy, Roderick S, 1953, My 20,29:4
Kennedy, Roger L J, 1966, Ja 15,27:4
Kennedy, Roger M, 1954, Mr 22,27:4
Kennedy, Roland A, 1960, Ag 5,23:3
Kennedy, Rose Mrs, 1942, Ja 25,41:2
Kennedy, Sam M, 1941, O 30,23:1
Kennedy, Samuel J, 1948, Ag 26,4:8
Kennedy, Samuel P, 1940, Mr 18,17:3
Kennedy, Samuel V, 1915, Je 3,11:5
Kennedy, Sherman S, 1961, N 6,37:2
Kennedy, Sidney J, 1954, D 29,23:3
Kennedy, Sinclair, 1947, Ag 6,23:5
Kennedy, Solon P, 1964, My 2,27:4
Kennedy, Stanley C, 1968, Ap 21,80:5
Kennedy, Stephen, 1948, S 18,17:4
Kennedy, T Blake, 1957, My 22,33:5
Kennedy, T J, 1879, Jl 25,5:5
Kennedy, Thomas, 1912, F 18,II,13:4; 1951, F 19,23:3; 1963, Ja 21,7:5
Kennedy, Thomas A, 1946, F 21,21:3
Kennedy, Thomas B, 1905, Je 20,9:4
Kennedy, Thomas E, 1947, Ap 12,17:3; 1956, Mr 6, 31:4
Kennedy, Thomas F, 1955, O 19,33:5; 1956, D 23,30:8
Kennedy, Thomas F Msgr (funl, S 4,11:5), 1917, Ag 30,11:7
Kennedy, Thomas H, 1950, O 29,93:1
Kennedy, Thomas J, 1950, S 9,17:3; 1951, Ag 11,11:5; 1953, F 6,19:2; 1954, Mr 14,88:2; 1955, Jl 30,17:1; 1958, Ag 5,27:5
Kennedy, Thomas Jr, 1961, O 31,31:6
Kennedy, Thomas L, 1946, Ag 7,27:6; 1947, D 21, 29:3; 1959, F 14,21:1
Kennedy, Thomas L Mrs, 1940, D 3,25:3
Kennedy, Thomas Mrs, 1953, D 13,86:2; 1959, D 1, 39:1
Kennedy, Thomas Rev, 1913, Ag 9,7:7
Kennedy, Timothy V A, 1963, O 31,34:2
Kennedy, Tom (Oct 6), 1965, O 11,61:3
Kennedy, Tom Mrs, 1950, Jl 11,31:4
Kennedy, Vincent D, 1954, Ja 8,21:2
Kennedy, W C, 1923, Ja 18,15:6
Kennedy, W E, 1958, O 19,86:5
Kennedy, W E Dr, 1883, Je 11,5:1
Kennedy, W J Dr, 1937, N 11,25:4
Kennedy, Walter B (por), 1945, D 31,17:5
Kennedy, Walter S, 1954, Ap 29,31:5
Kennedy, Warda H, 1943, Mr 19,19:3
Kennedy, Will J, 1948, Ap 9,23:4
Kennedy, Willard, 1955, O 25,33:4
Kennedy, William, 1918, Je 20,11:4; 1938, Ap 9,17:4
Kennedy, William (por), 1938, Ap 29,21:1
Kennedy, William, 1949, Mr 5,17:6; 1952, O 25,17:1
Kennedy, William C, 1956, N 21,27:3
Kennedy, William Costello, 1923, Ja 25,19:6
Kennedy, William E, 1953, Jl 14,27:5; 1961, F 27,27:3; 1962, Ja 23,33:3; 1964, O 12,29:2
Kennedy, William G, 1951, D 5,35:3
Kennedy, William H, 1914, S 26,11:7; 1939, D 22,19:3; 1940, Ja 18,23:6; 1945, O 12,23:5; 1947, O 9,25:3; 1956, Ag 8,25:2; 1958, Ap 14,25:3
Kennedy, William H J, 1948, Ag 24,23:2
Kennedy, William J, 1924, Jl 1,21:5; 1939, N 2,23:6; 1941, Je 21,17:2; 1941, Ag 12,19:2; 1945, Ap 27,19:4; 1947, Ag 18,17:2; 1948, Ap 22,27:4; 1955, O 23,86:6
Kennedy, William J Mrs, 1951, O 23,29:1; 1954, N 7, 88:5
Kennedy, William Jr, 1960, My 19,37:2
Kennedy, William L, 1942, Je 29,15:4; 1948, Ja 17,18:2
Kennedy, William M, 1954, F 18,31:4
Kennedy, William Mrs, 1951, D 12,37:5
Kennedy, William P, 1954, Jl 27,21:3
Kennedy, William Parker, 1968, My 15,47:1
Kennedy, William R, 1948, Ja 9,22:2
Kennedy, William R Sir, 1915, Ja 18,9:5
Kennedy, William Robert Adm, 1916, O 10,11:6
Kennedy, William T, 1965, Jl 11,68:8
Kennedy, William W, 1959, Ag 19,29:1
Kennedy-Purvis, Charles E, 1946, My 28,21:1
Kennel, William Lt (funl, F 21,11:6), 1921, F 18,11:5
Kennell, Edna M, 1943, S 20,21:5
Kennelly, Albert L, 1968, My 1,47:3
Kennelly, Arthur E, 1939, Je 19,15:3
Kennelly, Bryan (funl, D o1,13:5), 1923, D 29,13:4
Kennelly, Bryan L Mrs, 1950, Ja 31,23:1
Kennelly, Edward F, 1966, S 18,84:2
Kennelly, Eugene (G Morgan), 1940, Ag 16,15:5
Kennelly, Frank J, 1945, D 23,18:2
Kennelly, James A, 1951, Jl 15,61:2
Kennelly, Jeremiah J, 1940, Je 29,15:5
Kennelly, John L, 1937, Jl 17,15:6
Kennelly, Joseph P, 1940, Je 6,25:3
Kennelly, Martin H (est acctg, D 5,6:7), 1961, N 30, 37:2
Kennelly, William Mrs, 1922, Jl 6,19:5
Kenner, Albert W, 1959, N 13,29:4
Kenner, Arthur, 1953, F 28,17:5
Kenner, Carl, 1916, Jl 10,11:4
Kenner, Edward J, 1955, Ja 23,85:1
Kenner, Frank T, 1961, Mr 12,87:1
Kenner, Isidor, 1947, Jl 31,21:2
Kenner, William C Mrs, 1938, Mr 10,21:5
Kennerly, Martha M, 1956, My 24,31:4
Kennerly, William, 1944, S 9,15:4
Kenneson, Thaddeus D, 1924, My 30,15:5
Kennet, Kathleen Lady, 1947, Jl 26,13:6
Kennet, Lord (E H Young), 1960, Jl 12,35:4
Kenneth-Smith, Kenneth Mrs, 1954, Je 22,27:1
Kennett, A Crosby Mrs, 1950, Ja 22,76:4
Kennett, Charles, 1947, Ja 13,21:3
Kennett, Charles Sr, 1950, Mr 23,36:4
Kennett, Ella F Mrs, 1952, N 12,27:4
Kennett, Thomas Aiguier, 1911, Je 30,9:4
Kennett, Thomas M, 1958, S 2,25:2
Kenney, Annie, 1953, Jl 11,11:5
Kenney, Arthur Mrs, 1950, Ap 25,31:3
Kenney, Bartholomew F, 1944, D 20,23:1
Kenney, Bryant E Mrs, 1951, S 14,25:2
Kenney, Bryant F, 1958, Jl 15,25:3
Kenney, C D, 1902, D 12,9:6
Kenney, C J, 1881, S 18,7:1
Kenney, Caleb S (por), 1943, N 1,17:3
Kenney, Charles H, 1954, Ja 15,20:3
Kenney, Clara M, 1942, S 13,53:3
Kenney, Clifford, 1954, Ap 26,25:5
Kenney, Craig M (C McDonnell), 1956, N 26,27:5
Kenney, Edward C, 1948, O 22,25:3
Kenney, Edward W, 1942, Mr 10,19:3
Kenney, Elizabeth Mrs, 1909, Ja 31,11:7
Kenney, Frank B, 1945, F 26,19:3
Kenney, Frank J, 1947, S 26,23:6; 1960, My 28,21:5
Kenney, Franklyn R, 1954, N 26,29:3
Kenney, Fred C, 1951, F 2,24:2; 1952, F 12,27:2
Kenney, Frederick J, 1939, F 24,19:2
Kenney, George, 1955, F 1,29:5
Kenney, George T, 1942, Ap 7,22:4
Kenney, George W, 1946, My 29,24:2
Kenney, Henry F, 1908, Ja 11,9:6
Kenney, Henry J, 1960, O 9,86:6
Kenney, Hugh J, 1954, My 15,15:3
Kenney, Irene T, 1945, Ap 26,23:5
Kenney, J Arthur, 1954, S 2,21:6
Kenney, J Stanley, 1963, O 8,44:1
Kenney, James, 1909, S 10,9:6
Kenney, James P, 1955, Mr 13,86:7
Kenney, John A, 1946, Jl 15,25:6; 1950, Ja 30,17:1
Kenney, John B, 1873, Jl 17,4:7
Kenney, John F, 1950, Mr 22,27:1
Kenney, John J, 1912, Ag 16,9:5; 1942, O 21,21:6; 1960, Mr 31,33:2
Kenney, John J Mrs, 1944, F 8,15:1; 1950, My 1,25:4
Kenney, John L, 1955, Ap 25,23:5; 1966, Mr 27,86:7
Kenney, Joseph E, 1947, N 20,29:3
Kenney, Lewis H, 1955, Mr 28,27:3
Kenney, Martin J, 1940, O 26,15:3
Kenney, Matthew, 1947, Ag 3,52:7
Kenney, Matthew F, 1949, Ap 19,25:4
Kenney, Paul V, 1951, Jl 11,23:3
Kenney, Peter H, 1950, S 30,17:6
Kenney, R R, 1931, Ag 15,13:5
Kenney, Richard S, 1962, Mr 10,21:6
Kenney, Samuel, 1947, Mr 14,23:4
Kenney, Stephen V, 1937, O 14,25:5
Kenney, Stewart A, 1943, Ja 1,23:4
Kenney, Thomas, 1907, My 7,9:6
Kenney, Thomas A, 1953, Ja 9,21:4
Kenney, Thomas C, 1958, Mr 30,88:7
Kenney, Thomas Capt, 1937, Je 2,23:5
Kenney, Timothy A (por), 1938, Ja 20,23:4
Kenney, Vincent J, 1965, My 22,31:2
Kenney, Walter, 1950, O 22,92:4
Kenney, William E, 1941, S 7,49:1; 1946, Jl 4,19:6
Kenney, William F, 1940, Ag 11,31:2; 1941, Ag 10, 37:1; 1948, O 16,15:4
Kenney, William P (por), 1939, Ja 25,21:1
Kenney, William P, 1953, Ja 11,91:2
Kennicott, Col, 1866, O 14,5:4
Kennicott, Donald, 1965, S 14,39:5
Kennicott, Donald Mrs, 1941, Mr 7,21:2
Kennicott, Ransom E, 1939, Je 25,36:6
Kennicutt, David R, 1949, Ap 20,27:2
Kennington, Eric H, 1960, Ap 16,17:6
Kennish, William R, 1951, S 8,17:1
Kennon, Beverly R, 1938, D 28,21:5
Kennon, Jack, 1961, Ap 22,25:5
Kennon, Laura H V, 1965, Mr 30,47:4
Kennon, Mabel I Mrs, 1942, Ja 7,20:2
Kenny, Andrew J, 1941, N 3,19:5
Kenny, Arthur C, 1945, Ap 30,19:1
Kenny, Arthur J (por), 1943, Ap 22,23:2
Kenny, Bert, 1941, Ag 13,17:4
Kenny, Charles F Mrs, 1954, N 6,17:3
Kenny, Cyril Mrs, 1953, N 26,31:2
Kenny, E, 1927, Ap 20,25:5
Kenny, Edward, 1947, F 9,61:1
Kenny, Edward J A Rev, 1913, S 6,7:4
Kenny, Elizabeth Sister, 1952, N 30,1:3
Kenny, Francis P, 1956, Je 30,17:2
Kenny, Fred G, 1946, Mr 4,23:3
Kenny, Gene, 1959, Ag 3,25:4
Kenny, Harold Francis, 1925, D 11,23:3
Kenny, Henry B, 1949, Ja 29,13:3
Kenny, Henry R, 1945, S 11,23:5
Kenny, J Fred, 1960, F 16,37:2
Kenny, James, 1939, F 2,19:3
Kenny, James J, 1937, Mr 28,II,8:7
Kenny, John J, 1947, D 16,33:1; 1965, Ag 16,27:6
Kenny, John J Dr, 1920, Jl 25,20:5
Kenny, John M, 1958, F 26,27:2
Kenny, John M Mrs, 1950, Jl 2,24:5
Kenny, John P, 1916, N 21,11:3
Kenny, John R, 1943, Ap 1,23:2
Kenny, John W, 1940, Je 27,23:5
Kenny, Joseph F, 1951, Mr 29,27:2
Kenny, Joseph T, 1959, Ap 22,33:1
Kenny, Josephine Mrs, 1941, Je 5,24:4
Kenny, Laurence J, 1958, D 30,35:4
Kenny, Leo N, 1950, Mr 6,21:4
Kenny, Leon, 1948, Jl 18,54:4
Kenny, Martin J, 1955, Ja 19,27:1
Kenny, Matthew, 1918, My 27,13:5
Kenny, Michael B, 1963, O 1,39:1
Kenny, Michael J, 1946, N 23,15:6; 1952, Ja 22,29:5
Kenny, Michael Mrs, 1953, Jl 21,23:4
Kenny, Nicholas J Capt, 1924, My 10,13:4
Kenny, Norbert J, 1958, S 3,33:4
Kenny, Patrick, 1941, N 1,15:6
Kenny, Patrick F, 1941, S 19,24:2; 1967, Je 26,33:2
Kenny, Patrick F Mrs, 1951, Je 29,21:4
Kenny, Patrick L (Bro Joseph), 1909, N 28,11:5
Kenny, Robert W, 1944, N 15,27:2
Kenny, Thomas, 1950, Ja 17,27:4
Kenny, Thomas A, 1960, Ap 27,37:5; 1965, D 4,31:6; 1966, My 25,47:2
Kenny, Thomas Augustus, 1914, Jl 9,7:4
Kenny, Thomas B, 1950, Jl 25,27:2
Kenny, Thomas F, 1957, D 6,29:3
Kenny, Thomas J, 1940, Je 1,15:6; 1949, My 19,29:4
Kenny, Thomas Sr, 1939, F 28,20:3
Kenny, Timothy B, 1946, Mr 12,25:2
Kenny, Walter F, 1946, My 16,21:1
Kenny, William, 1946, F 10,42:7
Kenny, William F, 1951, Ag 14,23:1
Kenny, William F Mrs, 1946, D 29,35:5
Kenny, William J K, 1913, O 15,11:5
Keno, Edward B, 1949, Ja 6,23:1
Kenrick, George H Sir, 1939, My 30,17:5
Kenrick, John, 1942, Jl 5,29:3
Kenrick, P R Archbishop, 1896, Mr 5,1:4
Kensel, G N Lt-Col, 1881, Ap 18,5:5

Kensett, John F, 1873, Ja 9,2:4
Kensett, John Frederick, 1872, D 15,1:4
Kensing, Frederick W, 1945, Ap 12,23:5
Kenson, Harold, 1950, O 6,17:6
Kent, A Atwater Jr Mrs, 1957, N 6,35:3
Kent, Ada H, 1942, Jl 1,25:4
Kent, Albert E, 1942, Je 27,13:6
Kent, Alfred B, 1939, My 20,15:3
Kent, Anna Mrs, 1914, Je 17,11:6
Kent, Arthur A, 1949, Mr 5,17:3
Kent, Arthur A (will), 1949, Mr 31,50:4
Kent, Arthur H, 1940, My 15,25:6
Kent, Arthur L, 1945, Ja 26,21:4
Kent, Benjamin J, 1951, Ap 3,22:3
Kent, Beryl, 1959, Ag 13,27:4
Kent, Carl, 1959, D 15,40:2
Kent, Charles, 1923, My 23,21:6
Kent, Charles Foster Prof, 1925, My 4,19:5
Kent, Charles I Mrs, 1948, Ja 14,25:4
Kent, Charles M, 1954, Ag 16,17:5
Kent, Craig, 1905, My 2,11:6
Kent, Crauford, 1953, My 15,23:1
Kent, Dan E, 1943, Ap 20,23:4
Kent, Daniel, 1925, D 27,7:2
Kent, David, 1965, Jl 14,37:3
Kent, Douglas, 1953, Ja 25,85:2
Kent, E Ex-Gov, 1877, My 20,6:7
Kent, E N, 1882, D 10,7:5
Kent, Edward G, 1940, Mr 26,21:1
Kent, Edward H, 1953, Ja 24,15:5
Kent, Edward H Col, 1904, Ja 28,9:6
Kent, Edward L, 1944, Je 24,13:3
Kent, Edward R, 1961, S 26,39:4
Kent, Edwin C, 1938, Jl 12,20:1
Kent, Edwin N, 1947, Je 9,21:3
Kent, Edwin V, 1955, Ap 5,29:1
Kent, Ernest N, 1940, D 18,25:1
Kent, Frances E, 1945, D 3,21:2
Kent, Frank J, 1943, N 14,57:1
Kent, Frank L, 1947, O 4,17:4
Kent, Frank R (trb, Ap 17,30:5), 1958, Ap 15,33:1
Kent, Fred I, 1954, O 26,27:1
Kent, Fred I Mrs, 1951, My 8,31:3
Kent, G L, 1884, D 24,2:7
Kent, George A, 1948, Ja 29,24:3
Kent, George E, 1954, N 25,29:2
Kent, George E Jr, 1962, Ag 23,29:3
Kent, George E Mrs, 1954, D 24,13:1
Kent, George H, 1941, N 6,23:2
Kent, George R Mrs, 1955, O 18,37:4
Kent, Gilbert R, 1942, Ja 25,40:8
Kent, Grace E, 1944, N 21,25:2
Kent, H A, 1962, Ja 6,19:6
Kent, Halsey W, 1940, Mr 12,23:3
Kent, Harold A, 1950, D 12,33:2
Kent, Harry, 1961, S 28,41:5
Kent, Harry C, 1938, N 26,15:2
Kent, Henry F, 1946, Ap 17,25:2
Kent, Henry Oakes, 1909, Mr 22,7:5
Kent, Henry R, 1954, Ag 6,17:3
Kent, Henry T Mrs, 1946, Jl 31,27:2
Kent, Henry W (por), 1948, Ag 30,25:1
Kent, Herbert A, 1960, Jl 20,29:1
Kent, Horace M, 1954, Ja 17,92:3
Kent, Hugh, 1956, Ap 4,29:3
Kent, Ira R, 1945, N 11,42:3
Kent, J Harry, 1903, Jl 14,7:6
Kent, James, 1939, Je 24,17:4
Kent, James D, 1937, Je 27,II,7:2
Kent, James J, 1951, Je 10,93:1
Kent, James W, 1955, Mr 4,23:4
Kent, Jason S Mrs, 1943, S 5,28:8
Kent, John, 1872, S 19,9:2
Kent, Joseph C, 1937, D 15,25:5
Kent, Julia Winans, 1907, Ja 18,7:5
Kent, Larue J, 1950, Ap 27,29:2
Kent, Leonard Jr, 1953, Ag 10,23:5
Kent, LeRoy, 1967, Mr 15,47:2
Kent, Louis F, 1962, F 18,92:2
Kent, Marvin, 1908, D 12,11:2
Kent, Moss A, 1961, Ag 22,29:2
Kent, Moss A Mrs, 1942, Ja 30,20:3
Kent, Oscar A, 1940, Je 15,15:4
Kent, Pierre L, 1937, O 5,25:1
Kent, R D, 1938, N 26,16:3
Kent, Ralph S, 1949, Ap 4,23:3
Kent, Raymond A (por), 1943, F 27,13:1
Kent, Raymond R, 1948, N 2,25:3
Kent, Revere W, 1953, Ja 23,19:4
Kent, Richard, 1964, Ja 15,31:1
Kent, Richard B, 1938, F 15,25:4
Kent, Richard J, 1943, N 21,56:3
Kent, Richard T, 1964, S 15,37:1
Kent, Robert H, 1961, F 4,19:2
Kent, Robert J, 1941, Ag 13,17:4
Kent, Robert M Jr, 1921, O 19,19:4
Kent, Robert T, 1947, My 24,15:6
Kent, Rockwell Sr Mrs, 1947, O 22,29:2
Kent, Roland G, 1952, Je 28,20:7
Kent, Ronald W, 1958, Jl 21,21:2
Kent, Russell, 1940, O 31,23:6
Kent, S Miller, 1948, N 13,15:5
Kent, Sidney B Mrs, 1951, F 16,25:3
Kent, Sidney J, 1939, D 4,23:2
Kent, Sidney Mrs, 1961, D 30,19:3
Kent, Sidney R (por), 1942, Mr 20,19:1
Kent, Silas S, 1943, My 18,23:5
Kent, Stephen B, 1914, Ja 26,7:6
Kent, Stephen W Mrs, 1953, F 22,63:3
Kent, Stephenson, 1954, Mr 30,27:3
Kent, Thomas M, 1940, Je 16,38:8
Kent, W H B, 1947, D 27,13:3
Kent, Walter, 1962, Je 15,27:5
Kent, Warner W, 1958, Mr 13,29:2
Kent, William, 1910, O 28,9:6; 1918, S 19,13:3
Kent, William (por), 1945, O 6,13:2
Kent, William J, 1938, Mr 3,21:1
Kent, William J Mrs, 1959, O 16,31:2
Kent, William M, 1961, Je 15,43:2
Kent, William Mrs, 1910, Ap 22,9:5; 1947, My 18, 60:3; 1952, Ag 16,15:1
Kent, William R, 1965, Ag 15,83:3
Kent, William W, 1955, N 7,29:2
Kent, William W Mrs, 1950, Ag 8,29:5
Kent, Willys P, 1957, O 17,33:3
Kenter, William H Sr, 1952, F 5,29:1
Kenton, Edwin C, 1954, Ag 20,19:4
Kentworth, Charles M, 1959, Mr 6,25:5
Kentworthey, Charles E, 1958, Mr 27,33:4
Kentz, Frederick C Mrs, 1957, D 10,35:1
Kentz, John J, 1957, Jl 12,21:5
Kentz, Mary E, 1965, O 27,47:5
Kenward, Harold Sir, 1947, Ag 29,27:5
Kenway, Gawen P, 1943, O 15,19:4
Kenway, James L, 1924, Ja 22,17:4
Kenway, Mary M, 1966, Ag 19,33:3
Kenwell, Isaac, 1940, Je 12,25:6
Kenwick, Archbishop, 1863, Jl 9,4:6
Kenworth, Theodore H Mrs, 1958, Ja 11,17:5
Kenworthy, Claire, 1949, Jl 31,61:2
Kenworthy, Frank L, 1939, O 6,25:5
Kenworthy, George, 1959, N 11,35:4
Kenworthy, Murray S, 1951, N 6,29:4
Kenworthy, Robert W, 1960, O 1,19:5
Kenworthy, Samuel P, 1942, N 16,19:6
Kenworthy, Samuel S (por), 1940, My 19,42:3
Kenworthy, Thomas H, 1952, Ja 17,27:1
Keny, Walter R, 1944, Ap 12,21:4
Kenyon, Alan D, 1945, N 13,21:4
Kenyon, Albert J, 1937, Ja 20,21:2
Kenyon, Alden H, 1958, F 26,27:2
Kenyon, Archibald, 1953, Mr 11,29:5
Kenyon, Benn, 1944, D 8,21:3
Kenyon, Charles C, 1937, Mr 27,15:2
Kenyon, Charles H, 1955, Jl 28,23:2
Kenyon, Charles L, 1961, S 19,35:4
Kenyon, Clarence, 1956, Jl 11,29:4
Kenyon, Daniel S, 1949, D 3,15:3
Kenyon, Douglas H, 1964, F 5,35:6
Kenyon, Edmund L, 1966, D 17,33:4
Kenyon, Edward R Maj-Gen, 1937, My 20,21:3
Kenyon, Elmer, 1949, My 14,13:5
Kenyon, Frank C Jr, 1967, My 14,86:5
Kenyon, Frederic G, 1952, Ag 25,17:5
Kenyon, Frederick M, 1942, S 10,29:3
Kenyon, George, 1937, S 9,23:2
Kenyon, George H Brig-Gen, 1910, My 8,II,13:4
Kenyon, Gorlin D Mrs, 1954, Ap 15,29:2
Kenyon, Harry E, 1962, N 26,29:4
Kenyon, Harry L (por), 1949, My 8,78:2
Kenyon, Henry D, 1940, O 4,23:2
Kenyon, Howard N, 1958, Ja 2,27:2
Kenyon, J Miller, 1940, O 3,25:2
Kenyon, James B, 1924, My 12,17:6
Kenyon, James H (por), 1939, Ap 11,23:4
Kenyon, John S, 1959, S 7,13:6
Kenyon, Josephine H, 1965, Ja 11,45:4
Kenyon, L M Mrs, 1879, Ap 18,5:2
Kenyon, Leo J, 1959, Mr 16,31:4
Kenyon, Leslie, 1914, Ja 4,15:4
Kenyon, Lewis C, 1945, Ja 10,23:2
Kenyon, Lewis D, 1942, Ja 2,23:2
Kenyon, Nelson Townley, 1922, Ja 26,17:4
Kenyon, Otis A, 1949, F 4,24:3
Kenyon, Otis A Mrs, 1958, O 14,37:1
Kenyon, Ralph W, 1907, O 15,9:4
Kenyon, Ralph W Mrs, 1956, My 13,86:5
Kenyon, Richard B, 1951, D 31,15:6
Kenyon, Robert E, 1967, Je 29,43:4
Kenyon, Robert N, 1939, Mr 3,23:4
Kenyon, Sidney F, 1952, F 18,19:2
Kenyon, Thomas W, 1945, Je 23,13:2
Kenyon, Thomas W Mrs, 1941, Mr 14,21:3
Kenyon, W S, 1933, S 10,38:1
Kenyon, Wallace, 1938, D 7,19:3
Kenyon, Wallace D Mrs, 1956, Ja 12,27:2
Kenyon, William C, 1951, My 7,25:4
Kenyon, William E, 1944, D 16,15:3
Kenyon, William M, 1944, F 12,13:2
Kenzel, Francis X (por), 1943, D 24,13:3
Kenzel, Josephine G Mrs, 1939, F 10,23:5
Keoch, Thomas, 1919, Je 12,15:5
Keogan, George E, 1943, F 18,23:2
Keogan, Ramona, 1941, F 8,15:6
Keogh, Alexander, 1918, Ag 11,17:3
Keogh, Alois J, 1939, S 17,49:2
Keogh, Andrew, 1953, F 14,17:4
Keogh, Douglas S, 1959, Ap 28,36:1
Keogh, Edward A, 1965, N 18,47:3
Keogh, Edward S, 1953, S 13,85:2
Keogh, Edward S Mrs, 1938, Je 12,39:3
Keogh, Frank B Mrs, 1964, O 26,31:3
Keogh, Frank K, 1944, Mr 2,17:3
Keogh, George, 1941, Ag 23,13:4
Keogh, James P Mrs, 1958, Ap 17,31:3
Keogh, Jerome, 1953, Ja 13,27:3
Keogh, John J, 1955, F 15,27:1
Keogh, John Sr, 1960, Mr 6,86:7
Keogh, John W, 1960, O 16,88:5
Keogh, Martin J Mrs, 1947, Ja 29,25:5
Keogh, Ross F, 1941, S 19,23:2
Keogh, Thomas F, 1957, Je 23,84:4
Keogh, William, 1878, O 2,5:4; 1944, Ja 16,42:6
Keogh, William B, 1956, Ap 8,84:4
Keogh, William T, 1947, O 28,25:3
Keohg, James P, 1939, Ja 18,19:2
Keon, Joseph J, 1962, Jl 11,35:5
Keon, Miles Gerald, 1875, Je 14,5:4
Keon, Rita M, 1947, S 24,23:4
Keough, Austin C, 1955, Ap 21,29:4
Keough, Earl J, 1950, N 12,92:4
Keough, Edward, 1945, Mr 11,39:1
Keough, Edward J, 1946, O 20,60:8
Keough, Edwin J, 1951, Je 13,29:3
Keough, Francis P, 1961, D 9,27:2
Keough, George R, 1951, O 24,31:4
Keough, Hugh E, 1912, Je 10,9:6
Keough, James B, 1943, N 15,19:3
Keough, James H Mrs, 1938, F 16,21:3
Keough, M J, 1928, O 25,29:3
Keough, Matthew J, 1952, My 2,25:3
Keoughan, Sidney H, 1940, Mr 29,22:2
Keown, Eric O, 1963, F 16,8:7
Keown, Robert W, 1955, Ja 8,13:2
Kepecs, Jacob, 1947, Jl 12,13:3
Kepes, Martin A, 1954, My 28,23:1
Kephart, Quinter, 1940, D 26,3:3
Kephart, William H Rev Dr (por), 1937, Jl 29,1
Kepler, Asher R (por), 1942, Ag 12,19:3
Kepler, Asher R Mrs, 1945, Mr 31,19:3
Kepler, Roswell J, 1960, Mr 7,29:4
Kepler, Thomas S, 1963, My 3,32:2
Kepler, Walter E Sr, 1955, S 3,15:6
Kepler, William R, 1950, Mr 12,94:4
Keplinger, Warren E, 1951, Ag 19,84:4
Kepner, Arch, 1949, N 28,27:5
Kepner, Charles D, 1943, Ap 26,19:3
Kepner, Edward A, 1957, Ag 26,23:5
Kepner, William A Mrs, 1957, My 5,88:8
Keppel, Benjamin B Sr, 1953, Mr 3,27:4
Keppel, Charles J, 1953, Ja 24,15:4
Keppel, Colin, 1947, Jl 10,21:5
Keppel, David, 1956, O 15,25:2
Keppel, Derek, 1944, Ap 28,19:4
Keppel, Frances M Mrs, 1941, D 20,19:1
Keppel, Frederick D, 1950, S 15,25:2
Keppel, Frederick P (por), 1943, S 9,25:1
Keppel, Frederick P Mrs, 1961, S 15,33:1
Keppel, George Mrs, 1947, S 14,60:5
Keppel, Henry Adm Sir, 1904, Ja 18,7:3
Keppel, James S Col, 1921, Ja 31,9:4
Keppel, Mary H, 1949, Ap 30,13:4
Kepple, E P, 1936, N 21,17:1
Kepple, Ernest P Mrs, 1917, Ja 29,11:4
Kepple, Ethel P Mrs, 1938, Ap 24,II,7:1
Kepple, James P Mrs, 1958, S 3,33:1
Keppler, Adam N Mrs, 1940, Mr 24,31:2
Keppler, Carl R (por), 1939, D 28,21:3
Keppler, Emil C, 1942, My 22,21:4
Keppler, Frederick L, 1940, Ag 1,21:4
Keppler, George V Mrs, 1949, D 20,31:4
Keppler, Ignatius, 1961, N 14,36:2
Keppler, Rudolph, 1923, Je 6,21:4
Keppler, Tobias A, 1956, N 16,27:4
Keppler, Wilhelmine S Mrs, 1937, Je 5,17:2
Ker, John E Dr, 1918, O 26,11:5
Ker, Merle F, 1957, N 19,30:2
Ker, W P Prof, 1923, Jl 20,13:5
Ker, W W Capt, 1902, Ja 1,7:5
Ker, William H, 1939, F 18,15:2
Kerans, J Mark, 1952, D 11,33:1
Kerbaugh, Henry S, 1939, Mr 1,21:1
Kerbawy, Basil M Mrs, 1937, D 1,23:1
Kerbeck, Jerome L, 1957, N 21,33:3
Kerber, Cyril J, 1954, D 11,13:1
Kerber, Otto A, 1942, S 25,21:1
Kerber, William, 1945, O 3,19:1
Kerby, Clarence D, 1956, F 27,23:5
Kerby, Frederick M, 1955, F 27,86:4
Kerby, Joseph J, 1968, Jl 22,35:3
Kerby, Marion, 1956, D 20,29:2
Kerby, Robert L, 1956, D 3,22:7
Kerby, W J, 1936, Jl 28,19:4
Kerchick, Samuel, 1950, My 11,29:5
Kerchner, Edward Dr, 1916, Ag 21,11:6
Kerchove de Denterghem, Andre de, 1945, A
Kerekes, Frank, 1965, O 28,43:2
Kerens, Richard C, 1916, S 5,9:3
Kerens, Richard C Mrs, 1914, My 30,11:4

Kerensky, Alexander Mrs, 1946, Ap 11,25:4
Kerer, Keith R, 1953, Jl 16,3:5
Keresey, David H, 1937, Ja 11,20:1
Keresey, George F, 1950, O 6,27:3
Keresey, John M, 1954, Ap 19,23:5
Keresey, John W, 1942, D 5,15:6
Keresey, Mary D Mrs, 1941, Ja 27,15:1
Keresey, Raymond, 1961, My 11,37:4
Keresey, Redmond, 1903, Ap 19,7:4
Keresey, Redmond Jr, 1943, Ap 18,48:6
Keresey, Thomas M, 1957, Ap 6,19:5
Keresman, Mary Mrs, 1954, O 27,29:2
Keresman, Peter Mrs, 1948, Ag 14,13:3
Kerestedjian, Haik, 1963, Ap 1,27:3
Kereszturi, John, 1958, Jl 13,68:7
Kerewsky, Phil H, 1952, Jl 31,23:6
Kerfoot, Annie H Mrs, 1940, F 20,21:1
Kerfoot, Branch P, 1947, S 24,23:5
Kerfoot, F H Rev, 1901, Je 23,2:5
Kerfoot, J B Bp, 1881, Jl 12,5:3
Kerfut, Thomas, 1944, My 28,34:2
Kerge, Louis A, 1943, N 5,19:4
Keri, Paul, 1960, Ja 19,35:4
Kerillis, Henri de (trb lr, Ap 22,32:6), 1958, Ap 12, 19:2
Kerin, Thomas A, 1940, D 8,69:1
Kerin, William J, 1960, N 21,29:1
Kerins, John S, 1950, Mr 8,25:1
Kerjeger, Adm, 1880, My 24,4:7
Kerjegu, F de, 1882, F 14,5:4
Kerk, Charles H, 1952, D 25,29:4
Kerkam, Earl, 1965, Ja 22,43:4
Kerker, Gustave Adolph, 1923, Je 30,11:3
Kerkhoff, Johannes, 1948, F 21,13:3
Kerkhoff, Johnston D, 1958, My 3,8:1
Kerkhofs, Fernand, 1947, Ap 16,25:4
Kerlan, Irvin, 1963, D 30,21:2
Kerland, Thomas Capt, 1910, Ja 18,11:3
Kerley, Charles G (por), 1945, S 8,15:3
Kerley, Charles G Mrs, 1942, O 25,46:1
Kerley, J Hoyt, 1955, N 21,29:4
Kerley, John A, 1937, O 13,23:3
erley, Laurence B Mrs, 1950, Ap 28,21:4
erley, Mary E, 1950, F 23,27:1
erley, Thomas, 1940, Mr 14,23:5
erlin, Malcolm, 1952, Ap 4,33:6
erlin, Robert T, 1950, F 23,27:4
erlin, Ward D (por), 1948, Ag 24,23:3
erlin, Ward D Mrs, 1965, O 17,86:1
ermaingant, Louis de, 1966, Je 11,31:3
erman, Frederick R, 1956, N 5,31:6
erman, Moe, 1958, Ag 16,17:4
erman, William H, 1948, F 20,27:3
ermath, James J, 1966, F 13,84:2
ermek, Ace, 1953, Ap 30,31:5
ermet, Tillman, 1966, Ja 1,17:1
ermode, John T, 1944, D 16,15:2
ern, Abraham, 1951, Jl 15,60:3
ern, Abraham Mrs, 1964, N 25,37:3
ern, Adolph P, 1956, O 13,19:5
ern, Conrad J, 1956, D 21,23:4
ern, E Clarence, 1966, Ap 21,39:2
rn, Edward K, 1920, S 10,11:3
rn, Elizabeth Mrs, 1937, Ag 29,II,7:4; 1956, Ja 15, 2:6
rn, Ernst, 1948, F 7,15:1
rn, Frank J, 1941, D 27,19:2
rn, George, 1952, Jl 17,23:5; 1966, D 1,47:5
rn, George C, 1950, Je 9,23:5
rn, George V Mrs, 1946, O 24,27:5
rn, George W Mrs, 1948, Ag 29,60:2
rn, Herbert A, 1951, Ja 13,15:6
rn, Herbert F, 1943, Ag 29,39:2
rn, Howard L, 1947, My 13,26:2
rn, Howard L Mrs, 1946, Ap 21,47:2
rn, J E, 1941, Ja 17,17:2
rn, Jacob J, 1941, F 2,44:2
rn, Jerome, 1945, N 12,21:1
rn, John, 1956, Jl 15,61:2
rn, John D, 1948, N 25,32:2
rn, John H, 1948, Ap 8,25:1
n, John W Mrs, 1951, Mr 5,21:2
n, John Worth Ex-Sen (funl, Ag 19,15:1), 1917, g 18,7:3
n, Joseph E, 1952, Je 23,19:4
n, Julius H, 1948, My 29,15:6
n, Louis, 1946, O 30,27:3
n, Louis Mrs, 1946, S 29,62:1
n, Martin F, 1948, Ja 18,60:7
n, Maximilian, 1964, Ag 1,21:4
n, Paul B, 1953, D 17,37:5
n, Regina Mrs, 1938, Jl 12,19:4
n, Robert A, 1950, My 25,29:2
n, W, 1916, F 1,11:7
n, William A, 1964, My 11,31:2
n, William C, 1967, N 12,87:2
n, William J, 1962, Ag 27,23:5
n, William P, 1966, Je 29,47:4
naghan, William S, 1950, My 31,29:4
nahan, Coulson Mrs, 1941, Ja 18,15:4
nan, Charles H, 1947, Jl 2,23:3
nan, Edward F, 1951, D 28,21:2
nan, Elizabeth Butler, 1920, D 26,22:2

Kernan, Eugene, 1912, O 5,13:6
Kernan, Francis J (por), 1945, F 7,21:1
Kernan, Francis K, 1944, Mr 12,38:3
Kernan, Francis K Mrs, 1941, Ap 7,17:3
Kernan, George A, 1946, Ag 13,27:2
Kernan, George De S Mrs, 1962, F 13,35:3
Kernan, Hubert D, 1946, N 9,17:5
Kernan, James J Mrs, 1950, N 25,13:1
Kernan, James Lawrence, 1912, D 15,17:5
Kernan, John A Mrs, 1950, S 14,31:2
Kernan, John D, 1922, D 30,13:5; 1961, Jl 23,69:1
Kernan, Joseph A, 1917, S 23,23:1
Kernan, Joseph F, 1958, Je 8,88:5
Kernan, Michael J, 1953, D 17,37:4
Kernan, Peter J Sr, 1950, O 4,31:1
Kernan, Robert P, 1955, Ja 3,27:3
Kernan, Walter N, 1940, Ag 6,22:5
Kernan, Xenia Mrs, 1944, N 7,27:5
Kernell, John, 1903, D 20,11:3
Kerner, Ch H, 1904, Je 22,9:6
Kerner, Charles H, 1947, Je 13,23:2
Kerner, Frederick W, 1942, D 12,17:3
Kerner, Gustav, 1954, O 12,27:3
Kerner, H J, 1880, S 14,3:1
Kerner, Herman L Mrs, 1958, Ja 5,86:2
Kerner, Howard S, 1949, N 12,8:3
Kerner, John T, 1946, Ap 20,23:6
Kerner, Otto, 1952, D 14,91:1
Kerner, Richard, 1958, Ja 31,22:1
Kerner, Robert J, 1956, D 1,21:5
Kerner, Samuel, 1954, Ja 6,31:4
Kerner, William R, 1950, Je 7,29:4
Kerney, J, 1934, Ap 9,17:1
Kerney, J Edward, 1940, My 5,52:2
Kerney, James E Mrs, 1960, Je 19,88:3
Kerney, John E Mrs, 1950, Ap 23,95:5
Kerney, Joseph A, 1959, Je 30,31:2
Kerney, Thomas L, 1966, D 27,35:1
Kernkamp, Gerhard W, 1943, O 12,27:4
Kerno, Ivan S, 1961, Ap 16,86:4
Kernochan, Eliza S Mrs, 1914, D 21,9:4
Kernochan, Frederic Justice, 1937, Ja 10,II,9:1
Kernochan, H P, 1903, Ap 26,9:6
Kernochan, Henry P Mrs, 1916, S 2,7:4
Kernochan, J Frederick Mrs, 1922, Ag 12,9:6
Kernochan, James L, 1903, O 6,9:5
Kernochan, James P Mrs, 1917, F 27,11:3
Kernochan, Marshall R, 1955, Je 10,25:5
Kernochan, Marshall R Mrs, 1953, O 28,29:2
Kernochan, William Seymour, 1904, Ap 12,1:3
Kernot, Henry, 1874, O 27,4:7
Kerns, Eugene J, 1958, S 3,33:4
Kerns, F (see also S 23), 1877, S 24,8:1
Kerns, Francis J, 1951, Mr 24,13:3
Kerns, George M, 1951, Je 14,27:3
Keron, John E, 1938, Jl 31,33:3
Keron, John E Mrs, 1950, N 9,33:3
Kerpel, Esteban, 1942, O 9,21:3
Kerpel, Martin, 1949, Mr 16,29:3
Kerper, Alver H, 1950, Mr 27,23:3
Kerr, Abram T, 1938, Ag 16,19:5
Kerr, Albert B, 1945, Je 22,15:4
Kerr, Alex J, 1942, My 15,19:5
Kerr, Alex M, 1952, Mr 1,15:4
Kerr, Alfred, 1939, D 27,21:4; 1948, O 14,30:2
Kerr, Alvah Milton, 1924, S 27,16:3
Kerr, Andy Mrs, 1963, D 22,34:4
Kerr, Angus, 1961, Ja 3,27:6
Kerr, Anna W, 1938, D 1,23:2
Kerr, Arthur M, 1951, Jl 14,13:6
Kerr, C Herbert, 1925, Ag 20,19:6
Kerr, Charles, 1950, F 17,23:5
Kerr, Charles L C Mrs, 1943, Ja 30,15:4
Kerr, Charles V, 1949, N 1,27:3
Kerr, Charles W, 1951, Jl 19,23:3
Kerr, Charlotte, 1965, My 12,47:4
Kerr, Clarence D, 1957, S 21,19:1
Kerr, Daniel A, 1951, N 18,90:4
Kerr, Daniel J, 1937, My 1,19:3
Kerr, David G, 1948, O 19,27:1
Kerr, David R, 1961, D 9,27:4
Kerr, Dickie (Richd H), 1963, My 5,87:1
Kerr, Donald C, 1956, F 29,28:6
Kerr, Duncan J (por), 1940, O 9,25:1
Kerr, E Coe, 1949, Ja 28,21:4
Kerr, Edward A, 1937, Je 1,23:5
Kerr, Edward C, 1945, N 7,23:2
Kerr, Edwin J, 1917, Ag 19,15:1
Kerr, Errol, 1951, Ap 19,31:3
Kerr, F, 1933, My 3,17:3
Kerr, Frank M, 1948, N 23,29:4; 1953, S 28,25:3
Kerr, Frederick B, 1962, N 2,31:5
Kerr, Frederick W Sr, 1951, My 23,35:3
Kerr, George, 1925, Je 22,15:5; 1954, Mr 24,27:3
Kerr, George F, 1953, O 23,23:2; 1954, Ag 19,23:5
Kerr, George Francis Mrs, 1925, Ja 2,15:4
Kerr, George H, 1949, Je 25,13:5
Kerr, George H Sr Mrs, 1951, Ja 14,85:2
Kerr, George Mrs, 1913, My 30,7:6
Kerr, George R, 1937, Ag 14,13:5
Kerr, George W, 1955, Ja 8,13:7
Kerr, George W Mrs, 1943, N 7,57:1
Kerr, Gervas H, 1943, Jl 10,13:4

Kerr, Harrison D, 1939, Ja 11,19:1
Kerr, Harry D, 1957, My 22,33:2
Kerr, Harry G Lt, 1917, Jl 7,9:7
Kerr, Harry H, 1963, S 2,15:4
Kerr, Harry M, 1911, O 9,11:4
Kerr, Henry C Mrs, 1962, D 3,32:1
Kerr, Howard J, 1946, Ap 26,21:5
Kerr, Hugh, 1901, F 3,7:6
Kerr, Hugh T, 1950, Je 28,27:3
Kerr, Ida, 1938, N 13,45:2
Kerr, Isabelle D, 1959, O 13,39:2
Kerr, Ivan E, 1942, Ja 19,20:2
Kerr, J B, 1878, Ja 28,4:7; 1928, F 29,25:5
Kerr, J Dean, 1954, My 1,15:2
Kerr, J K, 1876, F 27,2:6
Kerr, J Willard, 1957, O 28,28:1
Kerr, James (funl, N 1,9:4), 1908, O 31,9:2
Kerr, James, 1941, O 31,23:2
Kerr, James A, 1947, Ja 20,25:2
Kerr, James F, 1925, Je 15,15:6; 1946, S 21,15:1
Kerr, James L, 1942, F 7,17:2
Kerr, James M Jr, 1942, F 1,43:3
Kerr, James Mrs, 1949, Je 25,13:4
Kerr, James S, 1943, O 12,27:4
Kerr, James T, 1949, Ap 15,23:1
Kerr, Jerome F, 1964, Je 3,43:4
Kerr, John, 1879, S 6,5:4; 1956, N 11,86:4
Kerr, John A, 1940, F 10,15:2
Kerr, John B, 1939, Je 26,15:4
Kerr, John C, 1962, F 6,35:3
Kerr, John G, 1957, Ap 25,31:2
Kerr, John H, 1945, D 19,25:2; 1958, Je 23,23:4
Kerr, John H Mrs, 1949, Je 6,19:2
Kerr, John J, 1949, My 9,25:3
Kerr, John T Rev Dr, 1921, D 25,20:3
Kerr, Joseph, 1944, Je 13,19:6; 1953, Ja 4,77:2
Kerr, Julia B Mrs, 1940, Mr 8,21:5
Kerr, Justine C Mrs, 1916, S 13,9:6
Kerr, Kenneth A, 1963, Jl 21,64:4
Kerr, LeGrand, 1956, Ag 12,84:5
Kerr, Lewis G Jr Mrs, 1967, Je 8,47:4
Kerr, Lewis S Jr, 1956, Jl 4,19:3
Kerr, Logan M, 1951, O 18,29:4
Kerr, Louis, 1943, Je 4,21:3
Kerr, Louis S Mrs, 1942, S 20,41:5
Kerr, M, 1877, F 28,2:5
Kerr, M C, 1876, Ag 20,6:7
Kerr, Margaret G Mrs, 1941, Ap 2,23:1
Kerr, Mark E F, 1944, Ja 21,17:3
Kerr, Mary E Mrs, 1943, Ag 1,39:1
Kerr, Medard, 1952, Je 25,29:3
Kerr, Michael J, 1940, S 10,23:4
Kerr, Muriel (Mrs N Benditzsky), 1963, S 20,33:4
Kerr, Owen B, 1947, Jl 13,44:6
Kerr, Percival M, 1949, Ap 13,29:5
Kerr, Phyllis S, 1949, Ap 13,29:5
Kerr, R Kenneth, 1953, My 11,27:4
Kerr, Robert A, 1912, Ap 29,11:5
Kerr, Robert B, 1944, My 29,15:5
Kerr, Robert B Jr, 1959, N 19,39:3
Kerr, Robert C, 1951, Jl 8,1:2; 1954, F 28,92:1
Kerr, Robert S (funl, Ja 5,8:2), 1963, Ja 2,1:4
Kerr, Ruthven S Sr, 1947, F 18,25:1
Kerr, Samuel K, 1953, Je 23,30:5
Kerr, Sophie, 1965, F 8,25:3
Kerr, Thomas, 1952, My 23,21:3
Kerr, Thomas R, 1949, My 14,13:1
Kerr, W H Mrs, 1903, My 29,9:6
Kerr, W S Mrs, 1953, Jl 31,19:4
Kerr, Walter, 1920, Ap 26,13:4
Kerr, Walter B, 1948, Ap 17,15:3
Kerr, Walter C, 1910, My 9,7:6
Kerr, Walter C Mrs, 1951, D 25,31:6
Kerr, Walter Lord, 1927, My 13,23:5
Kerr, Walter R, 1942, Ag 25,23:1
Kerr, Wilbur F Sr, 1968, D 7,47:3
Kerr, William, 1944, D 22,17:2; 1953, Mr 20,23:5; 1955, Jl 1,21:1
Kerr, William A Mrs, 1943, Ja 17,44:4
Kerr, William D, 1947, Ja 10,21:3
Kerr, William H, 1948, My 14,23:4
Kerr, William M, 1940, S 29,44:2; 1942, My 21,19:3
Kerr, William Mrs, 1952, My 23,21:3
Kerr, William T, 1953, Jl 2,23:2
Kerr, William W Mrs, 1947, N 12,27:2
Kerrick, George L, 1949, S 13,29:3
Kerrick, Harrison S, 1939, My 18,25:4
Kerridge, W H, 1940, Ap 20,17:5
Kerrigan, C F, 1934, My 23,19:3
Kerrigan, Charles J, 1940, F 26,15:3
Kerrigan, George E, 1951, Je 24,73:1
Kerrigan, J Warren, 1947, Je 10,27:2
Kerrigan, James J, 1956, S 6,25:4; 1967, Ap 2,93:1
Kerrigan, Joseph J, 1952, D 27,7:8
Kerrigan, Joseph P, 1949, Ag 5,19:3
Kerrigan, Joseph R Mrs, 1948, My 4,26:2
Kerrigan, Margaret, 1944, Ap 29,15:3
Kerrigan, Michael E, 1940, Jl 14,31:2
Kerrigan, Patrick J, 1950, Jl 25,27:5
Kerrigan, Philip Jr, 1958, N 26,29:2
Kerrigan, T A Col, 1902, S 28,7:5
Kerrigan, Thomas, 1938, Mr 13,II,8:5
Kerrigan, Tom (Thos F), 1964, My 8,33:3

Kerrigan, Walter C, 1957, Jl 17,27:4
Kerrigan, William F, 1943, N 9,21:3
Kerrigan, William J, 1938, Ag 5,17:3
Kerrigan, William Wallace, 1953, F 21,13:2
Kerrigon, George H, 1963, Ap 23,37:3
Kerrison, Charles, 1906, O 18,9:2
Kerrison, Philip D, 1944, Ja 25,19:4
Kerrl, Hanns (por), 1941, D 15,19:4
Kerry, Norman, 1956, Ja 13,23:5
Kerschner, J George Rev, 1937, F 20,17:3
Kerschner, W Sherman, 1964, O 18,89:2
Kersey, Charles A, 1945, D 24,15:4
Kersey, Hattie Mrs, 1950, S 6,58:3
Kersh, Gerald, 1968, N 8,47:1
Kershaw, Arthur R, 1944, Ag 9,17:6
Kershaw, Ernest, 1944, D 19,21:4
Kershaw, Frederick, 1943, My 20,21:2
Kershaw, Henry W, 1922, N 1,19:5
Kershaw, John A, 1946, Ja 17,23:4
Kershaw, John A Mrs, 1946, D 10,31:1
Kershaw, Sybil A, 1942, Ag 17,15:6
Kershaw, Wilette (Mrs W K Lamar), 1960, My 16, 31:4
Kershaw, William D Mrs, 1949, My 3,25:3
Kershaw, William H, 1965, F 12,29:4
Kershaw, William J, 1956, D 30,32:4
Kershman, John, 1951, Je 28,25:5
Kershner, Claude B, 1960, Je 1,39:5
Kershner, Cora L Mrs, 1949, S 14,31:5
Kershner, David T, 1949, S 10,17:1
Kershner, Edwin, 1947, S 4,25:6
Kershner, Frances M Mrs, 1941, Ag 11,13:1
Kershner, Frederick Doyle, 1953, Ag 26,27:1
Kershner, George A, 1952, O 31,25:4
Kershner, Robert C, 1944, Ja 17,19:5
Kershow, Edward V Mrs, 1940, S 20,23:5
Kerslake, John Mrs, 1948, Mr 4,25:5
Kerslake, Seabourne F, 1949, O 1,13:6
Kersta, Lawrence G Mrs, 1952, D 18,29:2
Kerstein, Isidore S, 1962, Jl 1,56:8
Kersten, Andries, 1947, Je 21,17:5
Kersten, Armand, 1949, S 1,21:5
Kersten, Felix, 1960, Ap 21,31:3
Kersten, George Mrs, 1910, S 4,9:5
Kersten, Harold J, 1955, Mr 4,23:5
Kersten, Kurt, 1962, My 22,38:1
Kerstetter, Frank L, 1949, Je 29,27:2
Kerstetter, G B Sen, 1940, Mr 9,17:5
Kerstetter, M Irene, 1964, My 17,86:5
Kersting, Vincent J, 1960, Ap 18,29:4
Kertesz, Zoltan I Dr, 1968, Ag 28,44:8
Kertzer, David Mrs, 1951, Ag 26,77:1
Kervan, Jack R, 1966, O 3,47:4
Kervick, Francis W, 1962, My 11,31:2
Kervin, William, 1939, O 22,40:7
Kerwick, Michael R, 1948, Jl 7,46:1
Kerwin, Andrew J, 1944, N 15,27:4
Kerwin, Charles M, 1955, N 3,31:1
Kerwin, Edward E, 1918, S 19,13:2
Kerwin, Edward P, 1949, My 10,25:2
Kerwin, Elizabeth L Mrs, 1938, My 17,23:4
Kerwin, Ellen Mrs, 1941, S 25,25:1
Kerwin, Eugene F, 1961, D 29,23:2
Kerwin, Hugh L, 1937, Je 11,23:5
Kerwin, James, 1953, Ja 24,15:2
Kerwin, James C Justice, 1921, Ja 30,22:3
Kerwin, James J, 1938, Je 9,23:4; 1947, S 25,29:2
Kerwin, John F, 1937, Ag 6,17:2; 1964, O 13,39:7
Kerwin, John M, 1963, O 20,88:6
Kerwin, Lawrence J Sr, 1946, Je 21,23:5
Kerwin, Mary A, 1964, Mr 16,31:2
Kerwin, Michael Gen, 1912, Je 21,13:4
Kerwin, Michael J, 1942, D 21,23:2
Kerwin, Patrick (Feb 2), 1963, Ap 1,36:1
Kerwin, Patrick J, 1943, F 1,15:4
Kerwin, Philo C Maj, 1903, D 22,9:5
Kerwin, Thomas E, 1956, N 30,23:4
Kerwin, Walter A Rev, 1937, O 1,21:4
Kerwin, William J, 1941, Ap 22,21:3
Kerzhentzeff, Platon, 1940, Je 4,23:4
Keschner, Moses, 1956, S 1,15:6
Keser, Otto A, 1950, D 31,42:6
Keshelak, Peter P, 1938, Jl 6,23:5
Keshen, Claire, 1954, Ag 27,21:5
Keshen, Herman L, 1962, Ag 26,83:1
Keshen, Meyer, 1946, F 23,13:4
Keshub, Chunder Sen, 1884, Ja 9,4:7
Kesinger, Earl V, 1946, My 14,21:2
Kesler, Carl R, 1956, Jl 3,25:6
Kesler, Robert W Mrs, 1964, My 25,33:3
Kesling, Elmer, 1961, Mr 13,29:2
Kesmir, Halit N, 1948, Mr 24,25:2
Kesner, Harry G, 1950, O 15,104:3
Kesner, Harry G Mrs, 1948, O 25,23:6
Kesner, Richard L, 1962, Ja 19,63:2
Kessanly, Rosa G Mrs, 1939, Ap 6,25:2
Kessel, Adam, 1946, S 23,23:2
Kessel, Barney, 1951, N 19,23:4
Kessel, Charles W, 1957, N 15,28:3
Kesselhaut, Louis, 1951, Ja 24,27:3
Kessell, Arthur C, 1942, Ap 17,17:3
Kessell, Herman H, 1955, Ap 14,29:4
Kesselman, Abraham H, 1941, F 17,15:5; 1963, Ag 13,31:1
Kesselman, Robert D, 1942, F 27,18:2
Kesselmeyer, William, 1953, Ag 14,19:3
Kesselring, Albert, 1960, Jl 17,60:1
Kesselring, Alexander M, 1943, S 13,19:6
Kesselring, Joseph, 1967, N 6,47:2
Kessenich, Frank J, 1940, D 8,68:2
Kessenich, Gregory J, 1958, N 20,35:6
Kessick, Martin, 1946, Ja 7,19:3
Kessinger, A C, 1928, Je 30,17:5
Kessinger, Albert R, 1941, F 25,23:1
Kessinger, Frank A Sr Mrs, 1952, O 28,31:4
Kessler, Abraham I, 1965, My 17,35:4
Kessler, Adams Jr, 1944, Je 6,17:4
Kessler, Adolph Mrs, 1910, O 10,9:5
Kessler, Alex, 1956, Ag 1,23:2
Kessler, Alfred, 1919, My 11,22:4
Kessler, Alfred A Jr, 1956, D 2,86:1
Kessler, Barnett, 1954, Je 11,23:3
Kessler, David, 1920, My 15,15:4; 1947, Jl 22,23:3
Kessler, Elizabeth, 1963, Ap 23,37:4
Kessler, Emil G, 1951, Ja 16,29:1
Kessler, Eugene G, 1940, Je 21,21:3
Kessler, Eugene G Mrs, 1962, S 4,31:6
Kessler, Frank D, 1950, Ag 1,23:4
Kessler, Frank J, 1945, D 25,23:5
Kessler, Fred W, 1963, My 3,31:3
Kessler, Frederick C Jr, 1943, My 30,26:3
Kessler, George A, 1920, S 14,11:1
Kessler, George Jr, 1952, D 10,35:4
Kessler, George W, 1918, O 24,13:2
Kessler, H J J, 1943, S 29,21:1
Kessler, Harry, 1939, D 16,17:3; 1949, My 20,27:4; 1964, F 27,31:4
Kessler, Harry Count, 1937, D 3,23:3
Kessler, Harry G Mrs, 1958, Je 3,31:1
Kessler, Henry, 1946, N 15,24:2
Kessler, Henry B, 1962, S 12,39:4
Kessler, Henry Clay Brig-Gen, 1907, S 11,9:6
Kessler, Henry Mrs (Jessie), 1968, F 24,29:5
Kessler, Ida Mrs, 1948, F 8,60:7
Kessler, Isidor F, 1949, O 8,13:1
Kessler, John H, 1943, Ja 2,11:4
Kessler, Joseph, 1954, D 2,31:2
Kessler, Julius, 1940, D 11,27:4
Kessler, Leopold, 1944, Ja 5,17:2
Kessler, Louis R, 1961, Ja 21,21:5
Kessler, Michael, 1955, N 3,31:1
Kessler, Morris, 1954, My 20,35:5; 1956, S 17,27:3
Kessler, Morris W Mrs, 1962, N 11,89:1
Kessler, Nathan, 1960, D 4,88:8
Kessler, Paul, 1966, O 6,47:3
Kessler, Phil F, 1951, Mr 23,21:3
Kessler, Richard W Mrs, 1963, Jl 16,21:1
Kessler, Samuel J, 1966, Je 11,31:1
Kessler, Sarah J Mrs, 1940, O 2,23:2
Kessler, Warren L Mrs, 1962, N 1,31:3
Kessler, William, 1904, Ja 16,9:6
Kessler, William B, 1956, F 20,23:3
Kessler, William C, 1957, Ag 31,15:6
Kessler, William J, 1943, Jl 21,15:6
Kessner, Barney, 1951, F 4,76:5
Kesten, Paul W, 1956, D 6,37:2
Kestenbaum, Alfred, 1961, Jl 18,29:3
Kestenbaum, Edward, 1963, N 6,41:3
Kestenbaum, Milton L, 1967, S 16,33:3
Kestenbaum, Phil, 1955, Ap 17,87:2
Kestenbaum, Toby, 1956, D 2,86:4
Kester, Donald, 1941, F 24,6:4
Kester, Frederick H, 1942, Ag 11,19:3
Kester, Joseph, 1952, Mr 22,13:6
Kester, P, 1933, Je 21,17:3
Kester, Reese B, 1940, S 16,19:2
Kester, Reuben P, 1945, Mr 20,19:2
Kester, Robert L, 1951, Ja 7,78:4
Kester, Robert L Jr Mrs, 1954, Ap 22,30:3
Kester, Roy B, 1965, O 23,31:6
Kester, Vaughan, 1911, Jl 6,9:4
Kestin, Joseph, 1954, Je 23,25:1
Kesting, Ted Mrs, 1967, Ja 19,35:4
Kestler, Arthur A, 1943, N 8,19:5
Kestler, C A, 1937, O 6,25:5
Kestler, George A, 1937, Mr 13,19:5
Kestler, Herman J, 1955, Ja 16,93:2
Kestnbaum, Meyer, 1960, D 15,43:4
Ketcham, Alfred L, 1950, Je 6,29:3
Ketcham, Alice B, 1953, Ja 19,23:1
Ketcham, Benjamin, 1957, Ap 23,31:1
Ketcham, Charles A, 1942, My 15,19:5
Ketcham, Charles A Mrs, 1945, Je 13,23:4
Ketcham, Charles B, 1953, Ap 3,24:4
Ketcham, Charles H, 1951, Ja 20,15:2
Ketcham, Chester O Sr, 1944, O 20,19:5
Ketcham, David W, 1941, Mr 12,22:2
Ketcham, Earl D, 1941, Mr 27,23:4
Ketcham, Edward C, 1964, My 8,33:2
Ketcham, Edward V Sr, 1953, N 3,31:2
Ketcham, Francis I, 1937, Mr 4,23:4
Ketcham, Frank A, 1950, Ja 25,27:3
Ketcham, Frank H, 1944, F 13,41:3
Ketcham, Frank H Mrs, 1945, O 24,21:3
Ketcham, Frank V, 1915, Je 5,9:4
Ketcham, Gaston, 1943, N 3,25:6
Ketcham, George E, 1962, Mr 8,31:1
Ketcham, George Franklin, 1923, F 16,13:5
Ketcham, George W, 1921, Jl 24,22:4
Ketcham, Harry J, 1943, Mr 5,17:1
Ketcham, Harry M, 1957, D 16,29:4
Ketcham, Helen R Mrs, 1938, Mr 31,23:3
Ketcham, Henry Belden, 1920, N 17,13:2
Ketcham, Herbert W, 1940, Ap 23,23:5
Ketcham, Huldah E Mrs, 1944, F 17,19:1
Ketcham, Isaac A, 1915, Mr 30,11:4
Ketcham, John C, 1941, D 5,23:3
Ketcham, John E, 1959, Je 4,31:4
Ketcham, John H, 1906, N 5,1:1
Ketcham, John L, 1942, N 3,23:3
Ketcham, Milford H, 1943, Je 2,25:1
Ketcham, Milton B, 1937, Jl 28,19:2
Ketcham, Norman, 1950, O 26,31:2
Ketcham, Orman W Mrs, 1941, D 25,25:2
Ketcham, Parley S, 1967, My 18,47:4
Ketcham, Stanley R, 1947, My 13,25:4
Ketcham, Stuart T, 1955, My 7,17:6
Ketcham, Theodore V, 1938, D 28,26:4
Ketcham, Thomas E Gen, 1916, Ja 27,11:5
Ketcham, Tuthill, 1955, Jl 15,21:5
Ketcham, Valentine O, 1957, My 16,31:1
Ketcham, Valentine T, 1940, Jl 24,21:3
Ketcham, Victor A, 1947, Jl 21,17:4
Ketcham, Walter S, 1948, D 20,25:5
Ketcham, Wilbur D, 1904, Mr 2,9:6
Ketcham, William A Capt, 1921, D 28,15:5
Ketcham, William P, 1937, S 8,23:4
Ketchel, Leon, 1942, Ap 18,15:5
Ketchem, J S, 1903, Ag 21,9:6
Ketchum, Archie, 1920, Ap 20,9:5
Ketchum, Arthur, 1963, Mr 19,7:7
Ketchum, Chambers Mrs, 1904, Ja 28,9:5
Ketchum, Charlotte H, 1948, Ja 30,23:3
Ketchum, D P, 1878, O 19,8:5
Ketchum, Edgar, 1882, Mr 4,5:2
Ketchum, Edwin P, 1962, F 13,35:3
Ketchum, Florence L, 1945, F 19,17:3
Ketchum, George A Dr, 1906, My 31,7:7
Ketchum, George F, 1943, Ja 27,21:4
Ketchum, John Buckout, 1914, D 9,13:7
Ketchum, John D, 1962, Ap 26,33:2
Ketchum, Joseph, 1884, N 25,2:6
Ketchum, Leonard C Sr, 1946, My 8,25:2
Ketchum, Mahlon E, 1946, Jl 6,15:6
Ketchum, Millimento W Mrs, 1941, D 4,25:3
Ketchum, Morris, 1880, Ja 3,5:2
Ketchum, Omar B, 1963, Jl 26,25:1
Ketchum, Silas, 1880, Ap 27,2:3
Ketchum, W W, 1879, D 8,5:2
Ketchum, William H, 1937, N 25,31:3
Ketelaar, William B, 1959, Ja 4,88:4
Ketelbey, Albert W, 1959, N 27,29:2
Ketelsen, Arthur H, 1950, F 19,76:2
Keteltas, Eugene, 1876, Ag 26,3:1
Keteltas, Mary, 1921, Mr 25,15:5
Ketenring, Elizabeth (Mme Begue), 1906, O 2
Ketler, Albert Dr, 1968, S 14,31:5
Ketron, Harold W, 1946, D 24,17:5
Kett, William R, 1916, Ap 15,13:5
Kettell, G F Rev, 1883, Mr 20,5:1
Kettell, George F, 1949, O 20,10:3
Kettell, John S, 1953, Ag 18,23:2
Kettelle, John D Mrs, 1921, S 23,15:5
Kettenburg, Grace, 1967, Ag 23,45:2
Ketter, Arthur W, 1949, D 5,23:2
Ketterer, Frank C Jr, 1950, My 23,29:3
Ketterer, Gustav, 1953, Jl 15,25:5
Kettering, Charles F (will, D 6,14:1), 1958, N
Kettering, Charles F Mrs, 1946, My 2,21:4
Kettering, Ralph T, 1958, Ap 9,33:3
Ketterson, Alex, 1952, Jl 25,17:5
Kettig, William H, 1939, Ag 4,13:6
Kettle, A Earl, 1941, Ja 4,13:5
Kettle, A J, 1916, S 24,19:3
Kettle, Ira, 1944, Je 2,15:5
Kettle, Joseph B, 1944, S 19,21:6
Kettle, Joseph F, 1941, O 3,23:6
Kettle, Marguerite, 1939, My 5,23:4
Kettle, Russell Sir, 1968, Je 21,41:1
Kettleman, J W, 1884, Ag 15,3:6
Kettles, Richard C Jr, 1966, S 6,47:2
Kettner, Frederick M, 1952, Ag 14,23:4
Kettner, Harry C, 1940, S 29,43:2
Kettner, Henry G, 1954, Jl 7,31:1
Kettner, Mangus G, 1951, Mr 7,33:3
Ketz, Henry F, 1955, Ap 16,19:5
Keucher, Werner G, 1957, S 19,29:1
Keuffel, August J, 1956, Ap 9,27:2
Keuffel, Willie L E, 1952, My 6,29:5
Keuffel, Willy G, 1942, My 18,15:4
Keune, Theodore Dr, 1916, F 27,17:4
Keuper, Vincent P Mrs, 1954, D 27,17:5
Keutgen, William O Mrs, 1943, Ag 24,19:3
Keuwet, Georges, 1947, Je 28,13:3
Kevan, John W, 1956, Mr 27,35:4
Kevan, William, 1907, S 11,9:6
Kevand, Julius H, 1949, S 30,24:2
Keve, Russell J, 1968, Mr 19,44:3
Keveney, Thomas S, 1951, Ap 18,31:5

Keveney, William D, 1958, Mr 13,29:4
Kevenhoerster, Bernard, 1949, D 10,18:2
Keveny, James W, 1937, Mr 9,23:3
Keves, Thomas A Jr, 1965, D 6,37:2
Kevill, John P, 1941, Ja 4,13:2
Keville, William J, 1960, N 16,41:2
Kevin, Bro, 1947, O 14,27:2
Kevin, J Richard, 1945, Ja 10,23:5
Kevin, J Richard Mrs, 1952, Ap 10,29:4
Kevin, Julia, 1953, S 10,25:4
Kevin, Mary Sister, 1955, F 6,88:6; 1956, Ja 14,19:2
Kevlin, James C Mrs (Ivy Larric), 1968, F 22,32:7
Kevorkian, Mihran H, 1946, D 14,15:4
Kevs, C C Rev Dr, 1876, F 3,4:7
Kew, Cyril A, 1949, Ag 25,23:3
Kew, Loring R, 1947, D 1,22:3
Key, Ben W (por), 1940, Je 6,25:1
Key, Charles W, 1964, D 10,47:2
Key, Einar, 1954, Ag 15,85:1
Key, Ellen, 1926, Ap 26,19:5
Key, Fred A, 1939, F 28,19:5
Key, Grace M Mrs, 1940, Jl 11,19:3
Key, James L (por), 1939, My 29,15:1
Key, John Francis, 1920, Ag 3,9:3
Key, Joseph S Bp, 1920, Ap 7,11:5
Key, L M, 1880, D 4,2:1
Key, Paul D Mrs (Ruth C), 1965, Ap 13,37:1
Key, Pierre V (por), 1945, N 29,23:6
Key, Sewall, 1948, My 17,19:5
Key, Stefan, 1950, Ja 11,23:4
Key, T H Prof, 1875, D 1,4:7
Key, Valdimer O Jr, 1963, O 5,25:2
Key, William S, 1959, Ja 7,33:4
Key-Oberg, Rolf, 1959, Ja 24,19:5
Key-Smith, Francis S, 1951, F 28,27:4
Keydel, Oscar F, 1954, O 27,29:1
Keyes, A, 1934, O 19,23:4
Keyes, Agnes F, 1949, O 8,13:4
Keyes, Allen L, 1951, N 17,17:3
Keyes, Allen R, 1954, O 14,29:4
Keyes, Ambrose J, 1948, Jl 18,54:4
Keyes, Baldwin L Mrs, 1947, Ag 10,53:2
Keyes, Bertha A, 1959, S 4,19:3
Keyes, Charles H Mrs, 1947, Mr 11,28:3
Keyes, Charles Henry Dr, 1925, Ja 17,15:5
Keyes, Charles R, 1942, My 20,19:2
Keyes, Chet A, 1955, O 18,37:2
Keyes, Clift B, 1938, D 8,28:1
Keyes, Clinton W, 1943, Ag 6,15:4
Keyes, Conrad S, 1962, Ja 23,33:4
Keyes, Edward A, 1943, Mr 18,19:5
Keyes, Edward L, 1949, Mr 17,26:2
Keyes, Edward Lawrence Dr, 1924, Ja 25,17:5
Keyes, Edward M Sr, 1959, N 2,31:4
Keyes, Edward W (por), 1947, D 9,29:3
Keyes, Eugene C, 1963, My 3,31:4
Keyes, Frank A, 1943, Jl 26,19:4
Keyes, Frederick A, 1938, Jl 28,19:5
Keyes, Freeman, 1871, Je 12,1:6
Keyes, Geoffrey, 1967, S 19,51:6
Keyes, George J, 1945, Ja 15,19:3
Keyes, Grace B, 1950, N 12,92:6
Keyes, Harold B, 1965, Ja 24,80:8
Keyes, Harold C, 1953, My 29,25:5
Keyes, Henry W (por), 1938, Je 20,15:3
Keyes, Homer E, 1938, O 9,45:2
Keyes, Homer E Mrs, 1938, My 24,19:4
Keyes, Howard Mrs, 1950, O 3,31:4
Keyes, Jay G, 1938, Ja 22,18:3
Keyes, Jennie C (will), 1942, F 12,24:4
Keyes, John, 1937, Ja 11,20:2; 1944, D 22,17:1; 1965, Mr 28,93:1
Keyes, John B, 1874, N 28,2:5
Keyes, John Baker, 1922, Ap 28,17:6
Keyes, John M, 1952, Ap 5,15:5
Keyes, John M Mrs, 1951, D 1,13:7
Keyes, Joseph A, 1956, Ag 2,25:2
Keyes, Katherine M, 1938, D 17,15:6
Keyes, Lawrence W, 1954, Jl 27,21:5
Keyes, Leo I (por), 1941, D 21,41:1
Keyes, Leonhard A, 1964, N 13,35:2
Keyes, Levi, 1946, Jl 17,23:3
Keyes, Margaret, 1941, Ja 7,23:4; 1957, Ap 24,33:4
Keyes, Michael J, 1959, Ag 1,17:3
Keyes, Minnie E Mrs, 1960, Ja 17,86:3
Keyes, Nelson B, 1958, Ag 17,87:2
Keyes, Patrick A, 1942, O 17,15:4
Keyes, Richard G, 1967, Mr 25,23:2
Keyes, Roger J B, 1945, D 27,19:1
Keyes, Rowena K (por), 1948, N 11,27:3
Keyes, Samuel J, 1948, N 28,92:3
Keyes, Thomas A, 1940, Mr 28,24:3
Keyes, Thomas B, 1938, O 3,15:6
Keyes, Thomas F, 1937, N 19,23:2
Keyes, William, 1903, Ag 27,2:1; 1939, D 27,21:3
Keyes, William A, 1947, F 10,29:4
Keyes, William J, 1937, D 12,II,9:2
Keyfitz, Arthur, 1953, Ap 7,29:1
Keyl, Theodore S, 1949, Jl 20,25:4
Keyl, Theodore S Mrs, 1959, Ap 27,27:4
Keynes, J N Mrs, 1958, F 14,24:1
Keynes, Lord, 1946, Ap 22,1:4
Keys, Alonzo L, 1940, D 13,23:3
Keys, Clement M, 1952, Ja 13,89:1
Keys, David R, 1939, Jl 12,19:5
Keys, E C, 1902, D 9,9:5
Keys, George F, 1946, O 16,27:5
Keys, John F, 1865, My 31,4:1
Keys, John L, 1948, S 17,25:3
Keys, Loren D (cor, O 28,45:2), 1964, O 27,39:2
Keys, Nelson, 1939, Ap 27,25:2
Keys, Pliny W, 1942, O 8,27:4
Keys, William A, 1941, F 8,15:5
Keys, William A Jr, 1948, Jl 5,15:2
Keys, William A Mrs, 1937, N 13,19:3
Keys, William E, 1940, Ja 9,23:1
Keys, William T, 1953, Mr 14,15:1
Keyser, Adelaide J, 1943, Ap 11,48:3
Keyser, Agnes, 1941, My 13,23:2
Keyser, Arthur, 1955, Jl 14,23:5
Keyser, C Naaman Mrs, 1950, S 22,31:5
Keyser, Cassius J, 1947, My 9,21:4
Keyser, Charles P, 1944, Mr 22,19:6
Keyser, E Lee, 1950, Ap 27,29:3
Keyser, E S, 1881, Mr 12,2:7
Keyser, Earle E, 1955, My 12,29:3
Keyser, Ephraim, 1937, Ja 28,25:4
Keyser, Ernest W Mrs, 1960, Jl 5,31:2
Keyser, Frank D, 1961, My 23,39:4
Keyser, Henry T, 1924, D 21,5:2
Keyser, Irving C, 1955, O 26,31:4
Keyser, Jacob S, 1949, Ja 2,60:4
Keyser, John J, 1946, N 8,23:4
Keyser, Margaret M Mrs, 1938, Ap 26,21:4
Keyser, Minna, 1959, Jl 20,25:4
Keyser, Ralph K (cor, Mr 12,23:3), 1940, Mr 11,15:3
Keyser, Ralph S, 1955, Ap 22,25:1
Keyser, Samuel S (will, Ap 1,17:2), 1939, F 4,15:4
Keyser, W Elby, 1943, Mr 11,21:1
Keyser, W Fenwick, 1968, Ag 6,37:4
Keyser, William, 1904, Je 4,1:4
Keyser, William Jr Mrs, 1956, Ap 6,26:2
Keyserling, Herman Count (por), 1946, Ap 29,22:2
Keyserling, William, 1951, O 29,17:2
Keysor, Leonard, 1951, O 13,17:6
Kezerian, Albert, 1956, D 21,23:4
Kezman, Louis, 1946, Ag 29,27:4
Khachadourian, Karekin, 1961, Je 24,21:6
Khadiga, Princess, 1951, F 23,27:4
Khai Dinh, 1925, N 7,15:4
Khaled, Tewfic, 1951, Ag 4,15:4
Khalidi, Hussein F, 1962, F 8,31:1
Khalidi, Ismail Ragib Dr, 1968, S 6,43:2
Khalifa bin Harub bin Thwain, Seyyid Sir (Sultan of Zanzibar), 1960, O 10,31:2
Khalil, Khwaja F, 1962, O 6,25:4
Khalil, Mahmoud, 1953, D 29,23:2
Khama, Tshekedi (funl, Je 18,31:5), 1959, Je 10,37:1
Khammao Vilay, Phaya, 1965, Jl 26,23:2
Khampan, Prince, 1966, Jl 27,39:3
Khan, Ali-Kuli Mrs, 1950, Je 25,68:4
Khan, Hamidullah Sir (Nawab of Bhopal), 1960, F 5,27:4
Khan, Maulvi T, 1963, Ag 20,33:2
Khan, Mohammed Akram (Maulana), 1968, Ag 19, 37:2
Khan, Prince Sardar Mohammed Hashim, 1953, O 28, 29:1
Khan, Salim, 1957, Jl 13,17:6
Khan, Shafa'at A, 1947, Jl 19,13:3
Khan, Shaikh Ul Mashaikh, 1948, Jl 4,26:7
Khan, Yephrem, 1912, My 23,13:5
Khannikov, Nikolai, 1948, My 1,15:2
Kharas, Ralph E, 1966, My 19,47:1
Kharasch, Morris S, 1957, O 11,27:4
Kharin, Ivan Gen, 1923, Je 8,19:5
Kharitonoff, Fedor M, 1943, My 31,17:6
Kharitonov, Mikhail P, 1953, O 14,29:1
Khartabil, Marwan, 1963, Mr 16,7:2
Khashaba, Ahmed, 1954, Ja 21,31:3
Khayat, Azeez, 1943, O 11,19:2
Khaykat, Khaylil Dr, 1923, My 31,15:4
Kheel, Aaron, 1942, D 14,28:2
Kheel, Samuel, 1943, F 21,32:7
Kheel, Samuel Mrs, 1952, F 12,27:4
Kheireddine, Abud an, 1941, D 9,40:4
Khenkin, Vladimir, 1953, Ap 21,27:1
Kher, Bal G, 1957, Mr 9,19:5
Khin, Selwyn, 1950, Je 16,11:1
Khitrin, Lev N, 1965, Ja 22,43:3
Khlopin, V G, 1950, Jl 14,21:1
Khmel, Vsevolod K, 1947, Ag 4,17:5
Khmeleff, Nikolai P, 1945, N 3,15:4
Khmylov, Kalin T, 1955, Ja 14,21:3
Kho Sin Kie, 1947, F 3,19:5
Khodakoff, Maxim, 1950, Ap 25,31:5
Khoshtaryia, Simon G, 1965, O 15,45:3
Khosrofian, Anterang, 1939, O 21,5:5
Khouri, Alfred, 1962, Jl 28,19:5
Khouri, Anis G, 1951, Ag 14,23:3
Khouri, Faris el-, 1962, Ja 4,33:3
Khouri, Fawwaz el, 1957, O 13,2:6
Khouri, Michael G, 1944, Jl 2,19:3
Khouri, Peter, 1946, S 10,7:1
Khoury, Bechara el-, 1964, Ja 12,93:1
Khoury, Esau el Mrs, 1957, S 28,17:2
Khrabroff, Nicholas, 1940, N 27,23:2
Khrabroff, Nicholas Mrs, 1949, D 7,31:4
Khrulev, Andrei V, 1962, Je 13,41:5
Khrunichev, Mikhail V, 1961, Je 3,23:1
Khryukin, Timon T, 1953, Jl 23,2:2
Khuang, Apaiwong Ex-Premier, 1968, Mr 16,31:4
Khuen-Hedervary, Charles Count, 1914, Ap 26,IV,7:6
Kiachif, Ali A, 1965, N 24,39:4
Kiaer, Herman S Mrs (mem ser set, O 20,47:3), 1967, Ap 24,33:2
Kiam, Omar, 1954, Mr 30,27:3
Kiamie, Jamile N, 1956, Mr 3,19:2
Kiamie, Najeeb Mrs, 1955, D 19,27:4
Kiang, Chiping H C, 1968, S 10,44:3
Kibbe, Charles, 1957, Ag 22,27:5
Kibbe, George F, 1940, Mr 24,30:8
Kibbe, Harry H, 1944, S 3,26:7
Kibbe, Harry U, 1922, N 4,13:6
Kibbe, Harry U Mrs, 1943, S 16,21:2
Kibbe, William C Gen, 1904, Ja 26,9:6
Kibbe, William J, 1967, Ag 1,33:3
Kibbe, William V, 1946, Mr 15,21:2
Kibbee, Guy B, 1956, My 25,23:1
Kibbee, William B, 1941, Je 9,19:2
Kibbey, Joseph H 2d Ens, 1953, F 1,88:3
Kibel, Joseph J, 1965, N 2,34:1
Kibler, A Franklin, 1955, Ja 25,25:5
Kibler, A Lewin, 1949, Jl 14,27:3
Kibler, Charles S, 1946, F 27,25:4
Kibler, William G, 1959, N 7,23:2
Kibler, William J, 1943, F 26,19:3
Kibling, Frank L, 1956, Ap 17,31:4
Kibling, Kay I Mrs, 1957, Ap 13,38:1
Kibrick, Herbert V, 1960, D 1,35:2
Kice, Luther H, 1952, Je 1,84:8
Kice, William W, 1951, Ap 1,93:2
Kich, Anthony, 1946, My 7,21:5
Kichler, L D, 1949, O 6,31:2
Kichline, C Preston, 1951, F 27,27:4
Kichline, Howard F, 1956, N 29,35:3
Kichline, Joseph, 1946, S 25,27:2
Kick, Theophile Jr, 1941, S 24,23:4
Kickam, C J, 1882, Ag 24,2:7
Kickham, Edward L, 1944, Ag 12,11:3
Kidd, Alexander, 1965, My 30,51:3
Kidd, Benjamin, 1916, O 3,11:3
Kidd, Beresford J, 1948, My 17,19:3
Kidd, C Dr, 1926, My 30,II,7:1
Kidd, Clifford S, 1952, F 12,27:2
Kidd, E Wilson, 1953, N 11,31:3
Kidd, Edwin S, 1968, Ag 23,39:3
Kidd, Eliza W, 1952, D 13,21:1
Kidd, Francis L, 1946, Je 10,21:5
Kidd, Francis L Jr, 1962, Je 17,81:2
Kidd, Frank W, 1950, Jl 20,25:3; 1952, S 27,17:4
Kidd, Frank W Mrs, 1959, Je 30,31:3
Kidd, Franklin J, 1942, D 11,23:1
Kidd, George F, 1952, F 1,21:3
Kidd, George H, 1937, D 25,15:2
Kidd, Glenn O (funl plans, Je 2,46:8), 1967, Je 1,43:2
Kidd, Harvey S, 1942, Ag 20,19:4
Kidd, J H Gen, 1913, Mr 20,11:4
Kidd, James H Mrs, 1944, O 16,19:4
Kidd, Jemima C Mrs, 1943, O 16,13:5
Kidd, John, 1951, D 2,89:2
Kidd, John R Sr, 1962, My 4,33:4
Kidd, John T, 1950, Je 3,15:4
Kidd, Louis W, 1941, My 30,15:2
Kidd, M G Col, 1884, F 3,7:2
Kidd, Phil C, 1954, S 20,23:3
Kidd, Robert B, 1954, F 19,34:2
Kidd, Robert J, 1943, F 5,21:4
Kidd, Robert Wilson Rev, 1915, Mr 10,13:5
Kidd, Ronald Mrs (Kathleen M), 1961, F 25,21:4
Kidd, Thomas, 1904, Je 19,7:7
Kidd, Thomas I, 1941, N 9,52:8
Kidd, Thomas Mrs, 1903, O 30,9:6
Kidd, W R, 1879, O 7,2:6
Kidd, Willett A, 1952, Jl 6,49:2
Kidd, William E, 1965, Je 14,33:3
Kidd, William Mrs, 1959, Jl 4,15:6
Kidde, Frank, 1949, O 6,31:4
Kidde, Frank Mrs, 1962, Ag 25,19:5
Kidde, Kyle B, 1950, Ag 30,31:4
Kidde, Walter (por), 1943, F 10,25:1
Kidder, A M, 1903, Ap 27,7:5
Kidder, Alfred V, 1963, Je 15,23:4
Kidder, Amos M, 1967, F 28,34:1
Kidder, Arthur E, 1940, Mr 11,15:2
Kidder, Augusta R Mrs, 1939, My 3,23:3
Kidder, Benjamin Harrison, 1909, O 28,9:4
Kidder, Camilla G, 1921, O 22,13:6
Kidder, Charles A, 1938, Ap 11,15:3
Kidder, Charles W, 1944, Ag 7,15:4
Kidder, Edward Hartwell, 1921, Jl 23,7:6
Kidder, H T, 1902, Jl 15,9:5
Kidder, Henry A, 1940, Ag 4,32:8
Kidder, Henry M, 1949, Ap 28,31:3
Kidder, Henry P Mrs, 1951, Jl 29,68:5
Kidder, Homer H, 1950, D 6,33:3
Kidder, J P, 1883, O 4,2:4
Kidder, Jerome F, 1949, Je 19,70:4
Kidder, Josephine B Mrs, 1937, My 3,19:5

Kidder, Kathryn, 1939, S 8,23:2
Kidder, Nathaniel T, 1938, Jl 14,21:6
Kidder, Walter Dr, 1872, Ja 30,8:6
Kiddoo, J B, 1880, Ag 20,5:2
Kiddy, Arthur W, 1950, F 22,29:3
Kido Koiu, 1877, Jl 3,4:6
Kidric, Boris, 1953, Ap 12,89:1
Kidson, Edward, 1939, Je 14,23:2
Kidston, Ross H, 1954, O 23,15:4
Kidwai, Rafi A, 1954, O 25,27:4
Kidwai, S R, 1953, Je 23,13:4
Kidwell, Elizabeth W, 1964, Jl 9,33:5
Kidwell, Francis Mrs, 1950, Je 7,29:1
Kieb, Aug A, 1940, Je 3,15:4
Kieb, Harriet L Mrs, 1954, O 13,31:2
Kieb, Raymond F C, 1956, Mr 13,27:1
Kieb, Raymond F C Mrs, 1956, My 11,27:1
Kieb, William A, 1948, My 26,25:3
Kieb, William A Mrs, 1946, O 27,63:5
Kiebitz, Otto, 1940, S 11,25:2
Kiechler, Christian, 1924, D 28,5:2
Kieckhefer, F A W, 1919, Mr 27,13:3
Kiefer, Adam P, 1939, My 18,25:5
Kiefer, Anthony, 1950, D 18,31:2
Kiefer, Asa E, 1937, F 4,21:3
Kiefer, C Raymond, 1954, Ja 2,11:5
Kiefer, Carl J, 1961, My 14,86:6
Kiefer, Edward J, 1952, F 5,29:4
Kiefer, Elizabeth, 1952, N 29,17:2
Kiefer, Emil, 1941, S 6,15:2
Kiefer, Frederick, 1953, Ja 9,21:1
Kiefer, George C, 1945, Ag 19,39:2; 1950, Je 13,27:2
Kiefer, Herman Dr, 1911, O 12,9:4
Kiefer, Isidor, 1961, O 17,39:2
Kiefer, J Morris, 1951, N 17,17:3
Kiefer, Jacob, 1944, D 31,25:1
Kiefer, Karl Z, 1948, Ag 12,21:4
Kiefer, Laurence, 1960, Mr 15,39:1
Kiefer, Paul W, 1968, S 3,43:2
Kiefer, Rupert Father, 1914, My 16,11:6
Kiefer, William F, 1948, N 17,27:2
Kieff, David D, 1946, O 28,27:2
Kieffer, Adah L, 1947, N 24,23:3
Kieffer, Dale W, 1959, Ag 21,21:2
Kieffer, David Mrs, 1946, S 8,44:2
Kieffer, Frank W, 1947, F 10,29:3
Kieffer, George, 1952, F 9,13:5
Kieffer, George C Mrs, 1941, Mr 10,17:4
Kieffer, George L Rev Dr (por), 1937, Ap 26,1:4
Kieffer, John B, 1948, N 3,27:5
Kieffer, Peter H, 1956, O 25,33:5
Kiefhaber, Ernest Mrs, 1958, O 31,29:2
Kiefordorf, William J, 1939, D 6,25:2
Kieft, Ray J, 1946, D 29,37:3
Kiehl, Harry Ray, 1968, Ja 19,47:1
Kiehl, John Mrs, 1962, My 23,45:1
Kiehl, Samuel J, 1960, Je 19,88:3
Kiehle, Frederick A, 1953, Mr 24,42:3
Kiehn, Arthur W, 1950, Mr 31,31:3
Kiehnel, Richard, 1944, N 4,15:5
Kiehnle, William V, 1955, Mr 23,31:5
Kiekhaefer, A C, 1950, O 10,31:1
Kiekhofer, William H, 1951, Ag 3,21:4
Kiel, Aug W Mrs, 1950, F 4,15:2
Kiel, August, 1943, D 31,16:7
Kiel, Cornelius J Dr, 1937, N 15,23:5
Kiel, Henry W, 1942, N 27,23:5
Kiel, Max R, 1956, Mr 7,28:3
Kiel, Richard, 1939, My 12,21:4
Kieldsen, James N, 1948, Ap 19,23:4
Kieley, Jarvis Mrs (M P Brewster), 1960, Mr 8,33:2
Kielgas, Milton R, 1960, Ap 24,89:1
Kielman, Frederick C, 1954, F 14,93:1
Kielty, Patrick F, 1939, S 22,23:1
Kiely, Charles E, 1948, D 31,15:4
Kiely, Charles F, 1951, Jl 21,13:5
Kiely, Daniel H, 1959, N 1,86:5
Kiely, Daniel J, 1937, Ag 24,21:2
Kiely, Edmund J Mrs, 1940, Mr 19,25:5
Kiely, Humphrey J, 1944, Mr 28,19:4
Kiely, John, 1952, N 29,17:4
Kiely, John F, 1966, Mr 5,27:1
Kiely, John J (por), 1940, Ag 24,13:3
Kiely, John M, 1941, Je 2,17:2
Kiely, Leo P, 1966, Je 15,47:3
Kiely, Patrick F Mrs, 1948, Jl 2,21:4
Kiely, Patrick S Mrs, 1951, O 7,86:5
Kiely, Tom, 1951, N 7,29:3
Kiely, William, 1939, D 1,23:5
Kiem, J Clayton, 1958, Ja 16,29:2
Kienboeck, Viktor, 1956, N 26,27:2
Kiendl, Frederick W, 1952, D 20,17:3
Kiene, William O C, 1947, N 13,27:2
Kiener, Michael J, 1949, Je 8,29:4
Kienholz, Aaron R, 1967, N 11,33:2
Kienle, Anselm, 1940, Ag 2,15:5
Kienle, Eugene, 1950, Ja 15,84:1
Kienle, Roy H, 1957, S 3,27:1
Kienzl, Wilhelm, 1941, O 4,15:5
Kienzle, George J, 1965, Mr 22,33:2
Kienzle, William A, 1950, Mr 31,32:2
Kiepura, Jan, 1966, Ag 16,39:1
Kier, Carol, 1968, My 3,47:3
Kier, George E Sr, 1952, Jl 21,19:6
Kieran, Daniel E, 1945, Ja 22,17:5
Kieran, Daniel R, 1945, Mr 26,19:6
Kieran, J M, 1936, Ap 26,II,11:1
Kieran, James M Jr, 1952, Ja 11,21:2
Kieran, John Mrs, 1944, Je 14,19:6
Kieran, Leo A, 1952, Mr 24,25:3
Kieran, Thomas, 1951, S 8,7:2
Kieran, William Msgr, 1921, D 22,15:5
Kierans, John J, 1950, Mr 22,27:1
Kierdorf, Frank, 1958, Ag 8,17:1
Kiernan, Anna A, 1951, Mr 31,15:5
Kiernan, Augustine, 1940, My 31,19:4
Kiernan, Cortland Mrs, 1940, S 19,23:5
Kiernan, Daniel F Sr, 1957, Ap 20,17:2
Kiernan, E J Mrs, 1881, Mr 27,10:4
Kiernan, Eugene F (Bro Michl), 1964, Ag 5,33:1
Kiernan, Frank (por), 1945, Mr 10,17:3
Kiernan, Frank Mrs, 1937, F 25,23:2
Kiernan, George, 1923, My 11,17:5
Kiernan, George W, 1956, Ap 21,17:4
Kiernan, Henry F, 1948, F 21,13:5
Kiernan, Henry P, 1942, N 2,21:4
Kiernan, Horatio S (por), 1941, Je 28,15:6
Kiernan, James A, 1956, O 7,86:6
Kiernan, James E, 1953, Ja 3,15:1; 1957, O 7,27:4
Kiernan, James F, 1942, Ap 10,17:4
Kiernan, James G Dr, 1923, Jl 3,13:4
Kiernan, James M, 1941, Jl 16,17:5
Kiernan, John E, 1953, O 13,29:5; 1961, Je 3,23:2
Kiernan, John J, 1939, Ag 7,15:6; 1948, Ap 22,27:5; 1951, N 28,31:3
Kiernan, John J Mrs, 1937, S 25,17:4; 1952, My 7, 27:5; 1954, N 3,29:3
Kiernan, Joseph, 1954, N 24,23:3
Kiernan, Joseph A, 1950, Jl 26,25:4
Kiernan, Joseph F, 1943, O 22,17:6; 1948, Ag 16,19:5
Kiernan, Joseph F Mrs, 1951, N 4,87:1
Kiernan, Joseph M, 1959, F 15,86:8
Kiernan, Joseph T, 1946, Ag 22,27:5
Kiernan, Michael, 1923, N 5,17:5
Kiernan, Owen M, 1940, S 15,48:8
Kiernan, P J, 1882, My 23,2:2
Kiernan, Patrick, 1925, Ja 24,13:5; 1943, Ap 9,21:5
Kiernan, Patrick J, 1947, Je 17,25:3
Kiernan, Thomas, 1939, Ap 5,25:2
Kiernan, Thomas A, 1947, D 5,25:3
Kiernan, Thomas F, 1961, Je 22,31:1
Kiernan, Thomas F Mrs, 1940, Je 15,15:2
Kiernan, Thomas J, 1945, O 28,43:1; 1966, Ap 3,84:1; 1967, D 29,27:2
Kiernan, Thomas K, 1914, Ag 1,9:5
Kiernan, Vincent J, 1951, Ja 30,25:5
Kiernan, William A, 1957, Ap 6,19:3
Kiers, Frank, 1953, Ap 20,25:3
Kierschner, Alfred, 1937, S 13,21:5
Kierschner, Gretha Mrs, 1940, Mr 26,21:5
Kierstead, Wilson G, 1906, D 18,9:5
Kiersted, Andrew W Rear-Adm, 1910, My 12,11:4
Kiersted, H T, 1882, S 14,5:6
Kiersted, Harvey B Mrs, 1964, My 11,31:3
Kies, William S, 1950, F 3,23:1
Kiesel, Frederick W, 1955, Je 11,15:2
Kieselbach, Henry A, 1953, D 9,11:1
Kieser, Charles F, 1968, Mr 26,45:2
Kieser, Henry S, 1941, Jl 13,29:3
Kiesewetter, Helmuth von M, 1963, Jl 8,29:3
Kiesewetter, Louis F, 1943, N 20,13:7
Kiesewetter, Otto B, 1950, Ap 30,102:4
Kiesewetter, Walter, 1949, Ja 22,13:5
Kiesler, Frederick J (funl, D 30,23:2), 1965, D 28,27:1
Kiesler, Frederick J Mrs, 1963, S 4,39:3
Kiesling, Walter, 1962, Mr 3,21:1
Kiess, Paul C, 1942, Ja 20,19:2
Kiessling, Calvin, 1956, Jl 2,21:5
Kiessling, Calvin Mrs, 1947, Mr 23,60:7
Kiest, Edwin J (por),(will, Ag 14,20:5), 1941, Ag 12, 19:1
Kietzman, William A, 1961, Ag 31,27:4
Kiev, I Edward Mrs, 1964, Je 30,33:5
Kievit, Cornelius W, 1938, Mr 17,21:5
Kievit, Jacob, 1954, Je 13,89:1
Kifer, Edwin H, 1949, Ap 15,23:4
Kiffin, John E, 1959, N 14,21:2
Kifner, Paul, 1964, Ag 12,35:3
Kift, Jane L, 1957, N 7,35:3
Kift, Robert Mrs, 1955, O 20,36:2
Kift, William M, 1951, D 13,33:4
Kiger, Charles J, 1960, D 17,23:4
Kiggell, Launcelot E, 1954, F 26,19:2
Kiggins, Charles B, 1949, Ja 8,15:6
Kiggins, Edward T, 1946, D 8,77:1
Kiggins, H Guyon, 1943, N 19,19:2
Kiggins, Henry, 1905, F 4,9:4
Kiggins, John Mrs, 1955, Mr 7,27:5
Kiggins, Keith, 1957, N 23,19:4
Kiggins, Murray C, 1938, Je 2,23:5
Kiggins, Symmes Mrs, 1945, Je 16,13:5
Kiggins, Willard A Sr Mrs (will, Je 1,21:5), 1951, My 19,15:5
Kightlinger, Clifford V, 1959, Mr 9,29:3
Kightlinger, Craig M, 1958, Je 11,35:3
Kihl, Viggo, 1945, Jl 12,11:4
Kihlmire, Charles W, 1946, D 6,23:5
Kihm, Frank J, 1914, O 3,11:6
Kihn, Alfred C Mrs, 1959, Ja 18,88:3
Kihn, Charles E (por), 1940, N 17,48:1
Kihn, W Langdon, 1957, D 13,27:1
Kihn, William J, 1958, F 1,19:6
Kikoler, Sigmund Mrs, 1940, Jl 14,13:6
Kikorev, Peter I, 1946, Ag 22,27:2
Kikuchi, Dairoku Baron, 1917, Ag 21,9:3
Kikuchi, Kan (por), 1948, Mr 8,23:5
Kil-So-Quah, 1915, S 5,11:4
Kilander, H Frederick Dr, 1968, D 7,47:5
Kilarjian, Albert R, 1955, S 4,56:1
Kilarjian, Nishan S, 1954, O 1,23:2
Kilbane, Johnny, 1957, Je 1,17:3
Kilbert, Louis Mrs, 1940, Ag 21,19:2
Kilbon, Roland, 1952, N 25,29:4
Kilborn, Charles H Mrs, 1958, Je 13,23:4
Kilborn, Horace M, 1923, My 30,15:4
Kilborn, Janet M, 1945, My 16,19:3
Kilborn, Melville G, 1955, Ap 3,86:5
Kilborn, Orson, 1956, Ja 9,25:3
Kilborn, William L, 1913, Ag 3,II,9:4
Kilborn, William T, 1957, Ag 15,21:3
Kilborne, Charles T, 1925, Ag 1,11:5
Kilborne, Robert S Mrs, 1968, O 25,47:4
Kilborne, Robert S 3d, 1966, Ja 1,17:6
Kilbourn, E J, 1873, Mr 15,7:4
Kilbourn, Edward B, 1938, S 7,25:4
Kilbourn, Edward E, 1912, My 26,15:5
Kilbourn, Frank B, 1949, My 22,89:1
Kilbourn, Hallett, 1903, Ap 15,9:6
Kilbourn, Horace O, 1953, Je 15,29:6
Kilbourn, Jonathan F, 1943, Ja 19,20:3
Kilbourn, Joseph B, 1964, My 12,37:5
Kilbourne, Byron A, 1951, Ap 12,33:1
Kilbourne, Byron A Mrs, 1952, Jl 1,23:1
Kilbourne, Ch E Maj, 1903, D 2,9:5
Kilbourne, Charles E, 1963, N 13,41:4
Kilbourne, Edward Mrs, 1951, F 10,13:6
Kilbourne, Edwin Ingersoll, 1968, O 14,47:4
Kilbourne, Fannie (Mrs H A Schubart), 1961, S 31:4
Kilbourne, Kenneth A, 1962, Mr 30,33:1
Kilbourne, Lincoln F Mrs, 1952, Jl 26,13:4
Kilbracken, Lord (H J Godley), 1950, O 15,10
Kilbreth, J William, 1958, Jl 24,25:5
Kilbreth, J William Mrs, 1961, S 2,15:6
Kilbreth, James T, 1912, O 28,11:4; 1954, Jl 31,
Kilbreth, John G, 1952, Ag 18,17:2
Kilbreth, John W, 1918, Jl 11,11:4
Kilbreth, Mary G, 1957, Je 28,23:5
Kilbride, Michael J, 1949, Jl 10,57:1
Kilburn, Clifford S, 1943, Ja 8,20:2
Kilburn, Colin H H, 1953, Ag 29,17:5
Kilburn, Elizabeth, 1946, D 21,19:6
Kilburn, George E Sr, 1950, Mr 21,32:4
Kilburn, Henry T, 1961, N 23,31:1
Kilburn, Homer A, 1941, Jl 23,19:3
Kilburn, Russell R, 1964, Ja 23,31:3
Kilby, Charles, 1945, My 20,32:1
Kilby, Charles B, 1942, Ap 17,17:2
Kilby, Harry, 1955, Ap 15,23:3
Kilby, Hood, 1943, My 15,15:3
Kilby, James P, 1938, Mr 28,15:4
Kilby, Thomas E, 1943, O 23,13:4
Kilcarr, Thomas, 1941, Ja 30,21:2
Kilcourse, James F, 1945, F 25,38:1
Kilcoyne, Patrick H, 1967, Ap 29,35:4
Kilcoyne, Patrick H Mrs, 1952, My 13,23:3
Kilcullen, Francis D Mrs, 1959, F 20,26:1
Kilcullen, John M Sr, 1949, Mr 14,19:6
Kilcullen, Joseph A, 1957, Ap 24,33:3
Kilcup, Ernest I, 1961, Jl 11,31:2
Kildare, Owen Mrs, 1967, Mr 23,35:2
Kilday, Frank, 1920, My 27,11:3
Kilday, Paul Joseph Judge (funl, O 16,47:3), O 13,84:4
Kildegaard, Axel C, 1947, S 29,21:4
Kilduff, Daniel J, 1943, N 22,19:5
Kilduff, William Mrs, 1950, Je 16,25:5
Kilduffe, Robert A, 1943, Ap 7,25:3
Kileen, Matthew, 1946, D 11,31:2
Kilenyi, Edward Sr, 1968, Ag 16,33:2
Kilenyi, Julio, 1959, Ja 30,28:1
Kilets, G F, 1876, Ja 8,5:2
Kiley, Aloysius B, 1949, Mr 2,26:3
Kiley, Catherine, 1948, N 15,25:1
Kiley, Edward A, 1946, Ja 30,25:4
Kiley, James A, 1938, F 3,23:3
Kiley, James S, 1950, O 1,105:1
Kiley, Jed, 1962, My 15,39:1
Kiley, Johanna, 1948, N 15,25:1
Kiley, John F, 1952, D 5,27:1
Kiley, Miles D Rev, 1937, N 26,21:6
Kiley, Moses E, 1953, Ap 16,29:3
Kiley, Patrick A, 1964, Je 16,39:4
Kiley, Stephen A, 1962, Je 16,19:5
Kiley, Thomas, 1880, S 7,2:3
Kiley, Thomas A, 1954, Je 15,29:5
Kiley, Timothy S, 1955, My 14,19:3
Kiley, Walter F Sr, 1952, Mr 5,29:4
Kiley, William A, 1947, Jl 22,23:2

Kiley, William C Mrs, 1950, N 17,27:1
Kilgallen, Dorothy (Mrs R T Kollmar),(funl plans, N 11,50:6), 1965, N 9,43:1
Kilgallen, Martin H, 1922, Ja 13,15:6
Kilgallen, Thomas E, 1957, Ap 15,29:4
Kilgannon, Marion, 1943, N 14,57:2
Kilgellon, John E, 1945, Ap 10,19:4
Kilger, Julian F, 1939, O 26,23:6
Kilgo, John C Bp, 1922, Ag 12,9:6
Kilgore, Alson R, 1959, My 23,25:5
Kilgore, Anna M Mrs, 1938, F 24,19:1
Kilgore, Ben, 1951, My 30,22:2
Kilgore, Bernard, 1967, N 15,1:7
Kilgore, Carrie Burnham Mrs, 1909, Je 30,7:2
Kilgore, Daniel, 1882, Mr 22,5:5
Kilgore, Eugene S, 1942, Ja 3,32:3
Kilgore, George E, 1944, Ag 6,37:2
Kilgore, Harley M (funl, Mr 3,19:2), 1956, F 29,31:1
Kilgore, John D, 1956, D 12,39:2
Kilgore, John E, 1959, D 14,31:1
Kilgore, Q H Mrs, 1945, Je 12,19:5
Kilgore, Tecumseh, 1959, N 24,37:2
Kilgour, Charles E, 1954, F 21,69:2
Kilgour, David E, 1946, O 12,19:3
Kilgour, John Fletcher, 1904, N 2,1:5
Kilgour, M Belle, 1938, Je 17,21:5
Kilgus, Fred, 1953, Ja 30,22:6
Kilgus, George J, 1959, Ag 16,82:1
Kilgus, Louis D, 1937, Ag 6,17:1
Kilham, Eleanor B, 1937, Ap 6,23:4
Kilham, Walter H, 1948, S 12,74:3
Kilian, Frank, 1944, N 25,13:1
Kilian, George W, 1966, S 9,45:3
Kilian, Henry C, 1958, My 13,29:4
Kilian, James A, 1958, Mr 21,21:1
Kilian, Louis, 1949, Mr 19,15:3
Kilian, Theodore P, 1954, My 15,15:4
Kilian, William A, 1938, Je 9,23:4
Kiliatscho, Mark G, 1952, Jl 24,27:2
Kiliman, Frank, 1952, Mr 13,29:4
Kilkenny, Martin, 1950, D 24,22:2
Kilkenny, Thomas R Mrs, 1949, Mr 22,25:2
Kilker, Adrian J, 1944, D 31,26:4
Kilker, John H, 1945, S 12,25:4
Killaby, H H, 1874, Mr 29,1:7
Killackey, John F, 1952, Ag 14,23:4
Killackey, William J, 1948, Ja 16,21:2
Killam, Elson T, 1968, My 28,47:2
Killam, Ida L, 1945, N 25,49:1
Killam, Isaac W (funl Ag 11,21:6), 1955, Ag 8,21:4
Killam, Izaac W Mrs (will, Ag 4,8:3), 1965, Jl 28, 35:4
Kille, Milton B, 1950, Ja 28,13:2
Killea, William J, 1963, D 1,85:1
Killearn, Lord (Miles Lampson), 1964, S 19,27:3
Killebrew, Dilla, 1909, Jl 28,9:4
Killebrew, Joseph B Col, 1906, Mr 18,11:6
Killeen, Andrew A, 1939, S 25,19:5
Killeen, Edward V, 1954, N 13,15:4
Killeen, Edward V Mrs, 1956, S 29,19:4
Killeen, Henry W, 1943, Ap 27,24:3
Killeen, John G, 1946, Jl 30,23:6
Killeen, John H, 1947, My 3,17:2
Killeen, John J, 1942, Mr 21,17:7
Killeen, Patrick A, 1956, Ag 29,29:4
Killeen, Thomas Rev, 1907, Jl 31,7:5
Killefer, Wade, 1958, S 5,27:3
Killefer, William L (Reindeer Bill), 1960, Jl 4,15:3
Killefer, William Mrs, 1954, Mr 13,15:3
Killeher, Ramond, 1922, Je 25,26:2
Killelea, John J, 1953, My 10,88:3
Killen, Arthur H, 1939, Ag 29,21:4
Killen, Clair, 1937, My 8,19:2
Killen, Frank W, 1940, F 18,43:5
Killen, Harold J, 1952, Ap 2,33:2
Killgore, Charles, 1940, F 13,23:4
Killgore, Edward W, 1956, Je 8,25:3
Killgore, J E Reese, 1941, S 25,25:5
Killgore, J Ralph, 1962, F 6,35:2
Killgore, Joseph L, 1918, Ja 16,11:4
Killgrew, John F, 1968, Ja 9,32:6
Killhoff, Dolores, 1950, O 8,71:3
Killhour, William F, 1944, Ja 17,19:3
Killiam, Paul, 1942, Ag 1,11:7
Killian, A L, 1950, S 3,39:1
Killian, Ammon A, 1945, Jl 10,11:6
Killian, Bernard, 1914, N 9,9:5
Killian, Erw J, 1951, Je 14,27:5
Killian, Frank B, 1950, My 22,21:2
Killian, John A, 1957, D 12,29:1
Killian, John C, 1957, Je 21,25:1
Killian, Julius N Maj, 1913, Ag 31,11:4
Killian, Michael, 1903, F 2,2:6
Killick, Stephen H M (por), 1938, Ap 19,21:3
Killilea, Frances L Mrs, 1938, Ap 10,II,6:7
Killilea, Frank J, 1954, F 27,13:4
Killilea, Thomas Capt, 1916, Mr 31,11:6
Killilea, Thomas R, 1947, Jl 6,41:1
Killimett, Joseph J, 1951, O 17,31:5
Killin, Edward C, 1942, Mr 17,21:5
Killinger, Donald W, 1949, O 20,29:1
Killion, Al L, 1943, My 10,19:5
Killips, Thomas, 1955, D 7,39:1
Killits, John M (por), 1938, S 14,23:1
Killmayer, Wilma J, 1946, Je 2,44:7
Killmer, David, 1948, Je 4,23:2
Killmer, E Thomas, 1953, F 15,93:1
Killmer, Miles I, 1961, O 30,29:2
Killoran, John A, 1962, Je 22,25:4
Killough, Isabel Y, 1945, Jl 31,19:1
Killough, James Henry, 1919, O 3,15:3
Killough, James Jr Mrs, 1957, Jl 6,15:6
Killoy, William J, 1946, D 6,23:4
Killpatrick, Clarence, 1911, Jl 23,9:6
Kilmartin, James L, 1950, Ag 18,21:5
Kilmartin, Michael J, 1949, D 14,31:2
Kilmarx, Louis, 1951, F 23,27:5
Kilmarx, Louis E, 1959, Ja 29,27:2
Kilmer, Aline M Mrs (por), 1941, O 2,25:3
Kilmer, Cornelia S, 1918, My 9,13:5
Kilmer, George L, 1947, Je 20,19:5
Kilmer, Hervey E, 1939, Mr 19,III,7:2
Kilmer, Hugh, 1965, Ja 25,37:4
Kilmer, Jonas M, 1912, My 14,11:4
Kilmer, Joyce Sgt, 1918, Ag 26,11:4
Kilmer, S Andral Dr, 1924, Ja 15,19:2
Kilmer, Theron W (por), 1946, Ag 1,23:3
Kilmer, Theron W Mrs, 1947, Ap 25,22:3
Kilmer, Walter H, 1945, S 13,23:1
Kilmer, Willis S (will, Jl 24,19:5), 1940, Jl 13,14:8
Kilmon, Iva L W Mrs, 1951, Je 25,19:5
Kilmorey, Earl of (Chas Francis Needham), 1915, Jl 29,9:6
Kilmuir, Earl of (D M Fyfe), 1967, Ja 28,27:1
Kilner, Ehrick B, 1945, N 6,19:1
Kilner, Frederick D, 1916, S 27,11:7
Kilner, Herbert, 1937, O 13,23:3
Kilner, Thomas P, 1964, Jl 4,13:6
Kiloh, Robert C Mrs, 1958, Ag 4,21:5
Kilpack, Bennett, 1962, Ag 21,33:1
Kilpatrick, Frederick H, 1957, Mr 28,31:3
Kilpatrick, Harry C, 1952, N 3,27:2
Kilpatrick, Howard M, 1957, Mr 19,37:3
Kilpatrick, James L, 1962, F 14,35:2
Kilpatrick, John D, 1949, F 1,25:2
Kilpatrick, John R (trb lr, My 10,36:6; funl, My 11,-39:1), 1960, My 8,1:3
Kilpatrick, Joseph Rev, 1908, Je 25,9:5
Kilpatrick, Judson Gen, 1881, D 7,5:4
Kilpatrick, Julia, 1877, Ja 2,4:6
Kilpatrick, O Arnold, 1957, Mr 25,25:5
Kilpatrick, Ringland F, 1955, N 5,19:4
Kilpatrick, Samuel, 1947, Je 5,25:4
Kilpatrick, Thomas, 1902, N 24,5:4
Kilpatrick, Van E, 1946, F 10,41:1; 1961, Ja 16,27:5
Kilpatrick, Walter F Mrs, 1947, Jl 2,23:4
Kilpatrick, Walter K (por), 1949, S 27,27:2
Kilpatrick, William D, 1949, F 21,23:6; 1950, Ap 16, 104:3
Kilpatrick, William H, 1937, Ja 13,23:3
Kilpatrick, William J, 1948, F 7,15:5
Kilpinen, Yrjoe, 1959, Mr 4,31:4
Kilrain, Jake (por), 1937, D 23,21:1
Kilroe, Edward L, 1968, Ap 30,47:2
Kilroe, Edward P, 1955, Ja 8,13:3
Kilroe, Edwin P, 1953, Jl 10,19:4
Kilroe, James M, 1945, Mr 1,21:6
Kilroy, Edward A, 1958, Je 8,88:6
Kilroy, Elmer J, 1961, N 7,33:5
Kilroy, James J, 1962, N 26,29:4
Kilroy, Matt, 1940, Mr 3,45:1
Kilroy, Rich R, 1958, My 10,21:5
Kilsby, Joseph F, 1954, O 15,23:2
Kilsheimer, James B Jr, 1950, Jl 1,15:6
Kiltgord, Marius, 1944, Jl 22,15:6
Kilty, Augustus H Rear-Adm, 1879, N 11,5:3
Kilventon, George D, 1945, S 12,25:3
Kilvert, Benjamin S C, 1946, Mr 31,46:6
Kilvert, Maxwell A Mrs, 1947, F 5,23:5
Kilworth, Thomas K Mrs, 1951, S 27,31:2
Kim, Chaik, 1951, F 2,3:5
Kim, David M, 1950, Je 16,25:2
Kim Chong Oh, 1966, Mr 31,40:1
Kim Sang Young, 1951, Je 24,72:5
Kim Sung Soo (funl F 25,21:1), 1955, F 20,89:2
Kim Yung Han, 1954, Mr 9,8:4
Kimasaki, Kyo, 1923, O 4,23:3
Kimball, Abbott, 1968, S 3,43:1
Kimball, Albert E, 1947, F 1,15:5
Kimball, Allen R, 1951, D 8,11:4
Kimball, Alonzo, 1923, Ag 28,17:5
Kimball, Amos S Brig-Gen, 1909, O 12,9:6
Kimball, Amos W Col, 1921, Je 2,13:4
Kimball, Annie M Mrs (will), 1941, F 21,12:2
Kimball, Arabel M, 1949, Ag 11,23:5
Kimball, Arthur G, 1940, D 24,15:4
Kimball, Arthur G Mrs, 1945, N 29,23:3
Kimball, Arthur L, 1943, Mr 22,19:1
Kimball, Arthur R Mrs, 1950, D 8,29:2
Kimball, Arthur S, 1948, Ja 28,23:5
Kimball, Charles E (will, Mr 16,26:8), 1938, Mr 4, 23:3
Kimball, Charles M, 1952, D 18,29:3
Kimball, Charles V, 1949, Mr 29,26:3
Kimball, Charles W, 1940, F 7,21:3
Kimball, Clarence, 1952, Ja 9,29:3
Kimball, Clinton L Mrs, 1949, Jl 26,27:3
Kimball, Comer J, 1966, Mr 31,40:1
Kimball, Cornelia Adams, 1917, My 18,13:7
Kimball, David W, 1953, Je 11,29:2
Kimball, Day, 1955, Ap 30,17:6
Kimball, Dexter S, 1952, N 2,88:6; 1957, Ap 30,29:3
Kimball, Dwight D, 1958, Ja 12,86:4
Kimball, Edward, 1901, Je 6,9:6
Kimball, Edward M, 1938, Ja 5,21:4
Kimball, Edward P, 1937, Mr 16,23:3
Kimball, Eleanor C, 1950, Ag 3,23:6
Kimball, Elwell F, 1957, Mr 29,21:1
Kimball, Elwell F Mrs, 1949, F 6,77:1
Kimball, Ephraim G, 1939, Jl 19,19:5
Kimball, Eugene, 1882, Ag 3,2:4
Kimball, Eugenia Mrs, 1942, O 2,25:5
Kimball, Eunice Marsh, 1907, Mr 12,9:6
Kimball, Everett, 1948, Jl 27,25:2
Kimball, F J, 1903, Jl 28,7:5
Kimball, Fannie H Mrs, 1942, Je 26,21:3
Kimball, Fiske, 1955, Ag 16,23:3
Kimball, Fiske Mrs, 1955, Mr 3,27:4
Kimball, Florence Mrs, 1950, S 18,23:5
Kimball, Francis, 1940, F 18,41:1
Kimball, Francis H, 1919, D 29,9:3
Kimball, Francis N, 1966, N 9,39:2
Kimball, Francis P, 1965, My 14,37:1
Kimball, Francis P Mrs, 1963, Ap 28,88:5
Kimball, Frank T, 1954, Je 16,31:4
Kimball, Frederic A, 1957, Jl 2,27:3
Kimball, Frederic C Mrs, 1951, Je 21,27:4
Kimball, Frederick B, 1955, D 20,31:3
Kimball, Frederick S, 1946, D 17,38:4
Kimball, G Cook, 1942, Ja 13,19:2
Kimball, Gardner W, 1938, Mr 14,16:4
Kimball, George, 1954, Je 10,31:5
Kimball, George E, 1967, D 7,52:6
Kimball, George S, 1951, Jl 6,23:2
Kimball, George T, 1953, Ja 3,15:4
Kimball, George W, 1941, S 21,44:2
Kimball, Grace N, 1942, N 20,23:2
Kimball, Gustavus S, 1937, Ap 23,21:4
Kimball, H Earle, 1952, N 26,23:1
Kimball, H I, 1933, O 17,21:3
Kimball, Harry G, 1945, N 24,19:2
Kimball, Harry S, 1951, D 18,31:2; 1957, Mr 12,33:5
Kimball, Henry E, 1947, Jl 23,23:4
Kimball, Henry J, 1960, Ja 20,31:5
Kimball, Herbert H, 1944, Jl 18,19:5
Kimball, Herman Porter, 1914, Je 26,13:6
Kimball, Horace Mrs, 1907, D 25,7:6
Kimball, Hunter, 1956, Je 30,17:5
Kimball, Ingalls Mrs, 1949, S 22,31:3
Kimball, J B, 1879, My 20,5:3
Kimball, J Brewster, 1965, Mr 30,47:4
Kimball, James B, 1909, N 10,9:4
Kimball, James H (por), 1943, D 22,23:1
Kimball, James N, 1943, Jl 23,17:5
Kimball, John H, 1937, N 27,17:5
Kimball, Joseph C, 1943, My 11,21:4
Kimball, Joseph Rev Dr, 1874, D 8,1:6
Kimball, Justin F, 1956, O 9,35:3
Kimball, Kate F, 1917, Ja 18,11:3
Kimball, Katherine, 1949, Mr 24,27:5
Kimball, LeRoy E, 1962, N 29,37:3
Kimball, LeRoy E Mrs, 1968, Ja 10,43:1
Kimball, Leuman W, 1905, Je 7,9:5
Kimball, Lt Col, 1863, Ap 16,8:1
Kimball, Marcus M, 1939, O 18,25:6
Kimball, Marguerite, 1954, O 23,15:2
Kimball, Maulsby Mrs, 1950, N 15,31:4
Kimball, Maynard C, 1942, D 17,37:4
Kimball, Miles W, 1949, D 10,18:3
Kimball, O, 1878, Ag 2,5:4
Kimball, Otis, 1912, F 4,13:5
Kimball, Palmer, 1943, Ja 13,23:3
Kimball, Ralph H (por), 1947, Ag 24,56:1
Kimball, Reginald G, 1960, Ag 24,29:4
Kimball, Reginald Stevens Dr, 1968, O 12,37:4
Kimball, Reuel Baker Dr, 1919, Ap 19,17:4
Kimball, Richard H, 1942, N 1,52:5
Kimball, Robert D, 1939, S 4,19:5
Kimball, Robert D Mrs, 1957, Ja 26,19:5
Kimball, Robert Jackson, 1903, O 4,7:6
Kimball, Robert S, 1945, S 24,19:4
Kimball, Ruth E, 1961, F 17,27:1
Kimball, Samuel Fisher, 1908, Ja 16,9:5
Kimball, Samuel G, 1948, D 7,31:3
Kimball, Silas, 1937, Mr 7,II,8:5
Kimball, Stockton, 1958, F 8,19:2
Kimball, Stuart E, 1950, Jl 21,19:4
Kimball, Sumner I, 1923, Je 22,17:4
Kimball, T Weller, 1944, Ag 7,15:5
Kimball, Tel Clarence, 1952, Ja 11,21:3
Kimball, Wallace D, 1950, Jl 16,69:2
Kimball, Walter, 1944, My 9,19:3
Kimball, Walter C, 1943, D 10,27:1
Kimball, Walter G, 1951, Ap 1,92:5
Kimball, Wilbur R (por), 1940, Jl 31,17:3
Kimball, Will D, 1950, Ap 25,31:1
Kimball, Winfield A, 1950, Ja 4,35:2
Kimbark, Earle G, 1960, N 3,39:2
Kimbark, Frederick, 1947, Jl 28,15:1

Kimbel, Anthony F, 1963, D 8,86:6
Kimbel, Charles E, 1949, Jl 3,26:6
Kimbel, Charles M, 1944, F 10,15:5
Kimbel, George R, 1955, My 27,23:2
Kimbell, Charles R, 1951, Je 26,29:4
Kimbell, Kay, 1964, Ap 14,34:8
Kimbell, Robert E, 1954, Mr 5,19:1
Kimber, Arthur Clifford Rev, 1909, Jl 27,7:3
Kimber, Harry G, 1966, F 5,29:4
Kimber, Joshua Rev, 1912, D 5,17:5
Kimber, Robert B, 1961, Ag 21,23:2
Kimber, Robert B Mrs, 1946, N 25,27:4
Kimberley, Anna C Mrs, 1954, O 8,23:3
Kimberley, Charlotte A Mrs, 1939, D 28,22:3
Kimberley, Countess Margaret of, 1950, Ja 6,21:1
Kimberley, George E, 1905, Ja 8,9:5
Kimberley, L A Adm, 1902, Ja 29,9:6
Kimberley, Lord, 1902, Ja 9,9:5
Kimberley, Peter L, 1905, Je 5,9:7
Kimberley, William C, 1945, O 4,23:2
Kimberlin, Amelia, 1953, My 22,27:6
Kimberling, Mark O, 1964, D 16,43:3
Kimberly, Charles H, 1959, Ag 28,23:2
Kimberly, D W, 1937, N 13,19:5
Kimberly, Floyd, 1944, F 9,19:1
Kimberly, George B Capt, 1923, Jl 31,17:5
Kimberly, George M, 1948, S 12,72:4
Kimberly, James C, 1961, O 19,35:2
Kimberly, John A, 1954, O 13,31:4
Kimberly, John P, 1948, Ap 9,23:4
Kimberly, Nelson H, 1955, Ag 23,23:4
Kimberly, Oliver A, 1965, Jl 18,68:3
Kimberly, P L, 1884, D 21,2:3
Kimberly, Robert L Gen, 1913, Je 17,11:4
Kimble, Albert L, 1953, Ag 9,77:4
Kimble, Charles B, 1939, Ap 1,19:3
Kimble, Daughton H, 1949, N 17,29:3
Kimble, Elbert M, 1946, Ag 17,13:1
Kimble, Evan E, 1956, Mr 17,19:3
Kimble, Evan E Mrs, 1956, O 27,21:4
Kimble, Leslie D, 1958, S 21,86:6
Kimbley, Frank R, 1938, D 3,20:1
Kimbley, Frederick P, 1957, D 23,23:4
Kimbough, Elizabeth Mrs, 1952, Je 2,22:3
Kimbrell, Basil S, 1944, O 7,13:2
Kimbro, Virginia M, 1961, My 4,37:3
Kimbrough, Hal C, 1955, Mr 22,31:3
Kimbrough, Robert A Jr, 1967, Jl 2,35:1
Kimbrough, Thomas C, 1946, Ja 1,28:3
Kime, Allan B, 1957, My 1,37:2
Kime, Charles R, 1958, Ja 23,21:4
Kime, Ellis E, 1941, Ag 28,10:3
Kime, Posey, 1958, Je 9,23:2
Kime, Robert R, 1956, D 2,86:1
Kime, Urban W, 1938, Ja 18,23:5
Kime, Verdon L Mrs, 1952, Jl 3,25:6
Kimer, Mary Mrs, 1940, D 14,17:1
Kimes, Ira L (por), 1949, F 5,15:5
Kimes, Russell A, 1963, Ap 12,27:1
Kimes, Stanley, 1967, N 20,47:4
Kimm, Walter E, 1950, Je 14,31:3
Kimmel, Daniel D, 1944, Je 11,46:1
Kimmel, Frank, 1964, Jl 18,19:1
Kimmel, Frank H, 1953, O 24,15:2
Kimmel, Henry, 1959, Jl 28,27:3
Kimmel, Henry W, 1949, My 28,15:4
Kimmel, Herman H, 1915, N 1,11:6
Kimmel, Herman Mrs, 1950, Ag 15,29:1
Kimmel, Husband E Rear-Adm, 1968, My 15,1:4
Kimmel, Jess, 1961, Je 1,35:4
Kimmel, Louis, 1943, O 16,13:5
Kimmel, Mordecai, 1953, My 5,29:2
Kimmel, Samuel Mrs (Beatrice), 1968, S 7,29:4
Kimmel, Saul, 1956, My 25,23:4
Kimmel, William G, 1940, D 14,17:6
Kimmelberg, Emil W (por), 1941, O 8,23:4
Kimmelman, Charles, 1966, O 20,43:2
Kimmelman, Leonard J, 1955, Je 28,27:4
Kimmelman, Ralph, 1947, Je 5,25:4
Kimmelman, Simon, 1953, S 28,25:3
Kimmerer, George C, 1952, N 26,23:2
Kimmerle, Albert, 1953, O 1,29:2
Kimmerle, August, 1949, My 11,30:8
Kimmerle, Frederick, 1937, O 1,21:5
Kimmerle, G L Mrs, 1946, Ja 11,21:3
Kimmerle, George J, 1943, Jl 28,15:4
Kimmeth, George J C, 1948, Je 2,29:6
Kimmey, Frank H, 1954, Ag 28,15:7
Kimmey, Harry A, 1956, Ja 13,23:5
Kimmey, Jennie, 1947, Jl 15,23:5
Kimmich, Frederick A, 1952, D 27,9:5
Kimmick, Charles A, 1949, My 19,29:2
Kimmins, Anthony, 1964, My 20,43:1
Kimmins, Grace, 1954, Mr 4,25:3
Kimmins, James, 1942, Mr 28,17:6
Kimmins, John Capt, 1902, F 24,9:3
Kimney, Charles W, 1949, O 11,31:4
Kimpton, Lawrence A Mrs, 1963, Mr 7,7:2
Kimter, Emma E, 1941, Ap 27,38:4
Kimzey, Paul W Mrs, 1947, Jl 23,23:6
Kin, David George (David Geo Plotkin), 1968, Ap 1,45:1
Kin, H, 1934, Ja 23,19:5
Kinahan, Patrick J, 1945, Ap 7,15:4
Kinahan, William Mrs, 1950, My 11,29:1
Kinard, James P, 1951, Je 2,19:5
Kinard, Kerwin W, 1943, Ap 3,15:1
Kinasoshvili, Robert S, 1964, Ap 30,35:5
Kinast, Robert L, 1947, O 22,29:1
Kinber, Adella S, 1939, Ja 29,11:2
Kincade, Gerard M, 1949, S 21,31:4
Kincaid, Charles E, 1906, N 3,9:3
Kincaid, Daniel W Mrs, 1950, N 30,33:3
Kincaid, Earle H, 1961, D 15,37:5
Kincaid, Elbert A, 1958, Ja 17,30:1
Kincaid, Elmer L, 1956, N 24,19:4
Kincaid, Julia M, 1946, O 10,27:5
Kincaid, Robert L, 1960, My 23,29:4
Kincaid, Stella M, 1940, Ap 23,23:4
Kincaid, Thomas F, 1950, Mr 26,93:1
Kincaid, Thomas W Rear-Adm, 1920, Ag 13,9:4
Kincaid, William, 1967, Mr 28,45:1
Kincaid, William W, 1946, My 22,21:2
Kincaid-Smith, Thomas M H, 1939, Ja 2,24:3
Kincannon, Linda (por), 1946, O 24,27:5
Kincel, Peyton, 1945, Jl 6,11:1
Kincey, Floyd S, 1944, Mr 11,13:3
Kinch, Frederick A, 1939, O 26,23:5
Kinch, Frederick A Mrs, 1944, Ag 3,19:3
Kincheloe, Charles F, 1950, Jl 13,25:4
Kincheloe, David H, 1950, Ap 17,24:2
Kincheloe, Iven C Jr (funl, Ag 2,17:2), 1958, Jl 27, 39:1
Kind, Constantine, 1960, My 20,29:4
Kind, Oscar, 1950, D 22,23:2
Kind, Oscar Mrs, 1947, D 25,21:3
Kind, Phil, 1953, Ja 25,85:2
Kindall, Lloyd E, 1950, N 17,28:3
Kindelan Duany, Alfredo, 1962, D 15,14:6
Kindelberger, E Crosby, 1950, Ag 7,19:3
Kindelberger, James H (funl plans, Jl 29,60:7), 1962, Jl 18,19:1
Kindell, Katie, 1940, Ja 2,19:3
Kinder, Ellis, 1968, O 18,47:1
Kinder, John J, 1956, Jl 26,25:2
Kinder, Ralph, 1952, N 16,87:1
Kinder, Ralph P, 1968, Mr 20,47:3
Kinder, William, 1955, Ja 26,25:2
Kinder, William R, 1949, Ja 16,68:4
Kinderman, John Mrs, 1956, Jl 11,29:3
Kindermann, George, 1947, My 28,25:5
Kindersley, Richard Torin Sir, 1879, O 25,2:3
Kindersley, Robert M Lord, 1954, Jl 22,23:6
Kindervater, Rudolph, 1948, My 28,23:5
Kindig, Albert, 1941, My 12,17:4
Kindig, Theodore P, 1941, Mr 12,21:4
Kindig, Waldo J, 1967, Jl 31,27:3
Kindle, Edward M, 1940, Ag 30,19:1
Kindleberger, Charles P Mrs, 1939, Ag 27,34:6
Kindleberger, David Rear-Adm, 1921, Mr 26,13:6
Kindleberger, E Crosby Mrs, 1959, N 14,21:2
Kindleberger, Jacob, 1947, Ja 2,27:5
Kindler, Hans (will, S 27,32:4), 1949, Ag 31,23:4
Kindler, Henry N, 1959, F 21,21:2
Kindler, Oscar L, 1949, My 29,36:4
Kindler, Oscar L Mrs, 1943, D 25,13:6
Kindley, Anna E Mrs, 1958, N 7,28:1
Kindley, Bradley W Rev, 1937, Ap 22,23:3
Kindley, Field E Capt, 1920, F 2,13:1
Kindlund, Martin G, 1968, Ag 26,39:3
Kindlund, Martin G Mrs, 1948, Ja 5,20:2
Kindre, Thomas A, 1950, Ag 12,13:1
Kindred, John C, 1953, O 26,21:4
Kindred, John J Dr, 1937, O 25,19:4
Kindred, John J Mrs, 1947, Ap 29,27:1
Kindy, William H, 1946, O 4,23:1
Kineon, G G, 1943, Ag 23,15:6
Kineon, James P, 1956, Ja 17,33:4
Kineon, James P Mrs, 1965, D 4,31:5
Kiner, William, 1961, My 20,23:3
Kiney, William A, 1953, Je 24,25:5
King, A H, 1901, S 22,7:6
King, A Paul, 1964, Jl 21,33:3
King, A Rowden, 1968, Ja 9,43:1
King, Abel, 1948, F 3,25:1
King, Ada P, 1954, Mr 23,27:1
King, Adam C, 1945, D 27,20:2
King, Agnes Mrs, 1941, O 15,21:5
King, Albert, 1944, Ag 31,17:3
King, Albert B, 1948, S 10,23:1
King, Albert J, 1948, Ja 17,18:3
King, Alex, 1959, Ag 30,82:8
King, Alexander, 1945, Jl 22,38:2; 1965, N 17,47:1
King, Alfred B, 1949, N 21,25:5
King, Alfred C, 1941, Ap 22,21:1
King, Alfred E, 1947, Mr 31,23:1
King, Alfred F, 1948, Ap 18,68:4
King, Alfred W V, 1957, Jl 4,19:4
King, Algernon Sidney, 1914, D 16,15:5
King, Allen, 1951, S 17,21:6
King, Alonzo H, 1959, O 8,39:1
King, Alpha K, 1938, My 10,21:4
King, Alvin O, 1958, F 23,92:2
King, Amy B Mrs, 1937, F 25,23:3
King, Andres, 1951, Ag 23,23:5
King, Anita (Mrs T McKenna),(will, Je 15,21:6), 1963, Je 11,37:2
King, Anson D, 1949, F 19,15:3
King, Archie W, 1951, F 27,27:2
King, Arklay, 1941, Ja 29,17:6
King, Arthur, 1953, Ag 10,23:5
King, Arthur A Rev, 1912, My 29,11:5
King, Arthur B, 1962, Ap 14,25:1
King, Arthur C, 1958, Ja 24,23:1
King, Arthur D, 1952, My 12,25:3
King, Arthur E, 1946, N 11,27:1
King, Arthur L, 1962, Mr 19,29:2
King, Arthur M, 1938, F 18,19:2; 1954, Ag 29,89:2
King, Arthur S, 1957, Ap 26,25:4
King, Augustus Fleming, 1920, Mr 6,11:5
King, Barney F, 1943, F 16,19:3
King, Barrington, 1866, F 4,3:4
King, Basil, 1928, Je 23,15:5
King, Basil Mrs, 1947, N 16,76:7
King, Beatrice P, 1937, Jl 13,20:2
King, Benjamin, 1945, D 17,21:3
King, Benjamin J, 1961, Mr 31,27:4
King, Benjamin P, 1942, My 25,15:5
King, Bertell W, 1968, My 25,35:1
King, Bonner Mrs, 1952, Je 16,17:2
King, C, 1933, Mr 18,13:4
King, C G Y, 1937, F 22,17:5
King, C H, 1882, S 3,2:6
King, C LeRoy Sr, 1953, F 27,21:2
King, Cameron H, 1954, D 13,27:2
King, Campbell, 1953, O 17,15:2
King, Carol Mrs, 1952, Ja 23,27:1
King, Caroline B Mrs (por), 1947, D 4,31:4
King, Carolyn P Mrs, 1938, Je 30,23:2
King, Catherine C, 1951, Ja 2,23:1
King, Charles, 1867, S 30,5:1; 1938, D 7,23:2
King, Charles (por), 1944, Ja 12,24:2
King, Charles A, 1917, Jl 25,11:5; 1941, My 8,23:5 1950, Mr 3,27:8
King, Charles A Mrs, 1954, Ja 8,21:2
King, Charles B, 1862, Mr 21,1:3; 1957, Je 24,23:3
King, Charles B Mrs, 1941, N 12,23:4
King, Charles C, 1938, Mr 22,21:4
King, Charles D B (funl, S 11,27:4), 1961, S 5,35
King, Charles D B Mrs, 1950, D 11,25:4
King, Charles E, 1950, F 28,29:1
King, Charles F, 1940, Ja 23,21:1
King, Charles G, 1945, S 15,15:5; 1951, O 14,89:2
King, Charles H, 1948, Ag 5,21:6; 1950, My 11,2
King, Charles J, 1939, Jl 4,13:1
King, Charles K, 1952, Je 1,84:8
King, Charles L, 1950, Ag 6,72:7
King, Charles Mrs, 1954, Jl 7,31:4
King, Charles S, 1951, Mr 25,73:1
King, Charles W, 1920, S 5,19:4; 1940, My 1,23:1 1956, Ag 8,25:4; 1966, S 14,47:1
King, Charles Webster, 1920, S 2,9:3
King, Chester A, 1946, Ag 21,27:5
King, Chris C, 1939, Jl 5,17:4
King, Chris E, 1948, My 14,23:2
King, Christopher J A, 1955, O 10,27:3
King, Clara E, 1954, Ap 6,30:3
King, Clarence, 1901, D 25,7:5
King, Clarence D, 1957, Mr 26,33:3
King, Clarence L, 1941, Ap 19,15:5
King, Clark W, 1962, Ag 15,31:2
King, Claude B, 1945, F 14,19:5
King, Clifford H, 1950, Ja 10,29:4
King, Clifton, 1951, N 6,29:1
King, Clyde Lyndon Dr (por), 1937, Je 22,23:1
King, Cora S, 1939, N 22,21:2
King, Cyrus S Mrs, 1958, My 26,29:4
King, D H MacDougal Dr, 1922, Mr 19,28:3
King, Dana C, 1957, D 8,88:8
King, Dana M, 1952, Ap 22,29:1
King, Daniel W Mrs, 1967, N 1,47:2
King, David, 1882, Mr 9,5:2
King, David B, 1943, Jl 21,15:6
King, David H Jr, 1916, Ap 21,11:4
King, Delcevare, 1964, Mr 22,77:1
King, Dennis Mrs, 1963, S 28,19:2
King, Donald D, 1967, N 20,47:2
King, Donald S, 1963, S 1,56:4
King, Donald S Mrs, 1968, Je 20,45:3
King, Dorothy W, 1953, My 6,31:4
King, Douglas H, 1968, F 11,92:3
King, E J, 1929, F 18,23:5
King, E L, 1933, D 28,19:1
King, E L Sr, 1949, D 13,31:1
King, Earl S, 1911, S 5,7:6
King, Edward, 1875, S 3,4:6; 1908, Ja 17,9:3; 1 N 20,9:3; 1922, Jl 9,26:4; 1941, Ap 20,43:2
King, Edward (Ned), 1962, N 15,37:1
King, Edward B, 1937, Mr 30,23:6
King, Edward B Mrs, 1947, Ap 18,21:1; 1947, 13:3
King, Edward C, 1961, D 8,37:2
King, Edward E, 1950, F 16,23:4
King, Edward J Mrs, 1925, N 7,15:5
King, Edward L, 1915, N 20,13:6
King, Edward M, 1945, Mr 16,15:3
King, Edward P, 1952, Ja 31,27:2
King, Edward P Jr, 1958, S 2,25:1
King, Edward S, 1958, My 26,29:3

King, Edward T Mrs, 1958, F 6,27:1
King, Edward V, 1943, O 3,48:4
King, Edwin B, 1950, D 26,23:2
King, Edwin D, 1954, O 17,86:7
King, Edwin J, 1940, S 18,23:6
King, Edwin S, 1961, My 5,29:3
King, Elbridge G, 1948, Ag 10,21:3
King, Eldon P, 1962, N 13,37:3
King, Eleanor A, 1949, Jl 8,19:6
King, Elias P, 1947, Jl 26,13:5
King, Elizabeth F Mrs, 1937, My 10,19:6
King, Ellen A Mrs, 1949, Mr 5,17:5
King, Ellsworth L Mrs, 1953, Jl 12,65:4
King, Elmer, 1945, O 11,23:3
King, Elmer Mrs, 1938, D 29,19:3
King, Emma, 1966, Jl 2,23:4
King, Emmett C, 1953, Ap 23,29:5
King, Emmett R, 1939, Ja 9,15:4
King, Ernest J (funl, Je 30,17:1), 1956, Je 26,1:3
King, Ernest J Mrs, 1950, F 9,29:3
King, Ernest L, 1954, Jl 10,13:4
King, Ernest M, 1955, O 11,39:4
King, F P Mrs, 1942, Mr 18,23:4
King, Ferman, 1955, D 2,33:4
King, Forest S, 1947, Jl 15,23:5
King, Francis G, 1950, F 10,24:2
King, Francis J, 1963, Jl 8,20:1
King, Francis Mrs, 1948, Ja 18,60:3
King, Francis P, 1952, S 13,17:6
King, Frank, 1951, Ja 23,27:5
King, Frank H, 1919, Ap 4,11:3
King, Frank M, 1953, N 9,35:2
King, Frank M S, 1940, Jl 27,13:5
King, Frank O Mrs, 1959, F 8,86:2
King, Frank T, 1940, Je 14,21:3
King, Franklin G, 1946, S 7,15:2
King, Fred C, 1924, D 3,11:2; 1924, D 6,15:6
King, Fred E, 1940, D 11,28:2
King, Fred W, 1966, Jl 13,43:4
King, Frederick A, 1939, N 1,23:3
King, Frederick DeLancy, 1919, Ag 6,9:1
King, Frederick E Dr, 1937, Ap 6,23:4
King, Frederick G, 1937, N 2,25:1
King, Frederick J, 1948, Jl 28,23:5
King, Frederick L, 1947, N 9,72:4
King, Frederick P, 1958, Mr 4,29:4
King, Frederick W, 1938, My 13,19:4
King, G Stewart, 1959, Ja 9,27:1
King, Gelston T, 1961, O 26,35:5
King, George A, 1947, D 28,43:3
King, George C, 1942, Ja 7,19:4; 1947, D 22,21:2
King, George C Mrs, 1944, F 24,15:5
King, George G Mrs, 1939, Ag 4,13:3
King, George Gordon, 1922, Ap 1,15:4
King, George H, 1947, Jl 29,21:4
King, George P, 1962, My 6,88:4
King, George S, 1903, D 9,9:5; 1943, Ap 3,15:5; 1966, Je 14,47:4
King, George T, 1944, N 3,21:1
King, George W, 1941, S 27,17:2; 1956, My 26,17:7
King, George W Mrs, 1939, Ap 5,25:4; 1956, Je 28,29:2
King, Georgiana G, 1939, My 5,23:4
King, Gerald, 1955, D 4,88:3
King, Gerald E, 1955, Ag 3,23:5
King, Gilbert L, 1964, Mr 1,83:2
King, Gilbert Snowdon, 1908, N 26,9:6
King, Gurnos, 1939, Ja 31,21:5
King, Gustave A, 1949, Ap 16,15:5
King, Guy, 1956, My 25,23:2
King, Guy B Mrs, 1953, Ja 8,27:1
King, H C, 1934, F 28,19:1
King, H Capt, 1884, F 16,4:7
King, H Clay Gen, 1903, D 11,2:7
King, Hamilton, 1912, S 3,11:6; 1952, Ja 8,27:3
King, Hamilton G, 1941, Ap 25,19:2
King, Hamilton G Mrs, 1947, N 29,13:4
King, Harold, 1966, Ja 20,35:1
King, Harold R, 1952, Ja 30,25:4; 1956, D 11,36:1; 1957, Ap 24,33:4
King, Harriet G Mrs, 1950, Mr 29,29:4
King, Harry E, 1963, Jl 2,26:7
King, Harry L, 1942, Mr 14,15:4
King, Harry N, 1946, Ag 20,28:2
King, Harry O Mrs (I S Greenway), 1953, D 19,15:1
King, Harry R, 1945, Ap 19,27:4; 1945, Ag 9,21:5
King, Harvey G, 1947, Ap 7,23:2
King, Helen, 1955, Mr 10,27:3
King, Henrietta M Mrs, 1925, Ap 1,23:3
King, Henry L P, 1952, O 30,31:2
King, Henry S, 1943, S 7,23:2; 1947, O 25,19:1
King, Henry V, 1956, Mr 31,15:6
King, Henry W, 1938, My 18,21:5
King, Herbert H, 1949, Mr 12,17:6
King, Herbert Maxon Dr, 1917, Je 25,11:6
King, Herbert P, 1951, Ja 18,27:1
King, Herbert T, 1944, D 16,15:6
King, Herman, 1942, D 26,11:4
King, Hezekiah, 1905, Je 7,9:5
King, Homer D, 1961, F 22,25:1
King, Homer S, 1919, D 20,11:4
King, Horace Mrs, 1924, S 13,13:5
King, Horace W, 1951, Ap 25,29:4
King, Horatio, 1897, My 21,3:2
King, Horatio Collins Gen, 1918, N 16,13:5
King, Horatio Gen, 1917, Ag 11,7:5
King, Horatio Mrs, 1925, Mr 30,17:5
King, Howard I, 1947, My 22,27:5
King, Howard L, 1958, S 22,31:6
King, Hoyt, 1946, D 29,37:4
King, Hubert C, 1953, O 18,87:1
King, Hugh A, 1948, Ap 22,27:3
King, Hugh P, 1966, Ja 14,39:5
King, Hugh P Mrs, 1946, Mr 28,25:1
King, Hugo Mrs, 1943, Jl 24,13:3
King, Hyman, 1949, Je 23,27:5
King, Irvin, 1939, Ag 31,19:6
King, Irving C, 1945, D 19,25:1
King, Isabella C, 1943, Mr 12,17:2
King, Ivan D, 1956, Ja 2,21:6
King, J Edward, 1960, Jl 24,65:1
King, J Elmer, 1952, My 30,15:5
King, J Scott, 1946, Ja 7,19:4
King, J Scott (por), 1955, Jl 13,25:2
King, J T, 1878, Ag 26,8:2; 1926, My 14,23:1
King, J Travis, 1943, Ja 31,45:1
King, James, 1939, Jl 13,19:4; 1957, Ja 30,29:5
King, James A, 1938, My 24,19:3; 1952, Ag 1,18:3
King, James C (Bro Azarias), 1965, S 3,27:4
King, James C Mrs, 1955, My 13,25:1
King, James E (will, My 29,17:5), 1947, Mr 11,27:2
King, James F, 1966, My 20,44:3
King, James G Mrs, 1955, N 8,31:4
King, James H, 1953, N 15,89:1; 1955, Jl 15,21:5
King, James H Mrs, 1949, Ja 29,13:5
King, James Kossuth Dr, 1914, S 22,11:6
King, James L, 1945, O 5,23:3
King, James L Mrs, 1949, S 30,23:1
King, James M Dr, 1907, O 4,11:6
King, James M Mrs, 1947, S 30,25:3
King, James P, 1951, N 7,29:5
King, James R Jr, 1951, F 27,27:1
King, James S, 1925, Ap 11,13:4; 1949, Ap 21,26:5
King, James T, 1944, F 28,17:3
King, James W, 1953, D 15,39:2
King, James W Capt, 1905, Je 7,9:5
King, Jessie Caldwell Mrs, 1925, Jl 25,11:6
King, Joaquin S, 1952, O 21,29:1
King, John, 1917, Ja 4,11:4; 1954, Mr 23,27:3
King, John A Ex-Gov, 1867, Jl 8,5:4
King, John A Jr, 1957, F 23,17:4
King, John B, 1944, Jl 18,19:3
King, John B Mrs, 1967, My 20,35:4
King, John C Mrs, 1954, O 15,23:1
King, John D, 1965, Je 21,29:5
King, John E, 1937, O 25,22:1; 1938, N 27,49:2; 1941, Jl 29,15:4; 1951, Je 27,29:4
King, John E Sr, 1960, Ag 20,19:1
King, John F, 1944, Ag 30,17:4
King, John G, 1952, Je 8,85:1
King, John Garfield, 1952, O 25,17:4
King, John H, 1943, O 29,19:4; 1951, Je 7,33:5
King, John J, 1941, S 13,17:4; 1948, My 4,25:3
King, John L, 1949, S 6,27:4; 1966, S 18,84:3
King, John M, 1937, N 29,23:5; 1949, Ja 12,27:3
King, John Mrs, 1959, Mr 3,33:3
King, John R, 1951, F 15,19:7
King, John R Maj, 1918, Jl 19,13:6
King, John Rev, 1875, My 11,7:4
King, John S, 1904, Mr 6,7:6
King, John W Mrs, 1941, Ap 16,23:3
King, Jonas Rev, 1869, Je 15,5:3
King, Joseph, 1957, Ja 10,29:4
King, Joseph E, 1964, My 7,37:3
King, Joseph G, 1947, Ap 22,27:2
King, Joseph H, 1909, N 21,13:4
King, Joseph J Mrs, 1950, S 21,31:5
King, Joseph L, 1944, Ag 12,11:4
King, Joseph Mrs, 1966, S 2,31:4
King, Joseph R, 1959, Je 29,29:2
King, Joseph R Mrs, 1948, O 22,25:2
King, Joseph W, 1940, Mr 26,21:4
King, Josias R Col, 1916, F 12,11:6
King, Judson, 1958, Jl 5,17:5
King, Julia C Mrs, 1939, Ja 23,13:5
King, Karl, 1943, Je 28,21:1
King, Kathryn, 1954, Ja 12,23:2
King, Kenneth T, 1957, Ag 9,19:2
King, Landreth H, 1944, D 17,38:5
King, Lawrence A, 1943, O 15,19:2
King, Leon, 1951, F 18,76:4
King, LeRoy, 1962, Jl 10,33:2
King, LeRoy A, 1942, Je 6,13:2
King, Leslie, 1947, O 12,79:3
King, Lewis C, 1951, S 21,24:2
King, Lloyd S, 1955, Ja 10,23:5
King, Lorenzo H, 1946, D 18,29:5
King, Loretta, 1909, Ag 8,9:5
King, Louis F Mrs, 1953, F 8,88:5
King, Louis R, 1938, Ag 5,17:3
King, Lucian L, 1951, Mr 28,29:4
King, Lucy A Mrs, 1944, Je 17,13:6
King, Luther, 1944, O 9,23:3
King, Luther R, 1945, O 23,17:4
King, Lyman M Jr, 1953, O 15,33:2
King, Margaret, 1906, Jl 3,9:7
King, Margaret J, 1950, F 18,15:6
King, Mark J, 1949, N 12,15:4
King, Mark J Mrs, 1948, Jl 1,23:3
King, Martin E, 1965, Ja 22,44:1
King, Martin E Mrs, 1965, O 16,27:4
King, Martin H, 1967, N 22,47:1
King, Martin L Mrs, 1944, Ag 25,13:6
King, Mary A Mrs, 1941, Mr 15,17:4
King, Mary B Mrs, 1937, O 29,22:3
King, Mary L, 1940, N 16,17:5
King, Mary Leroy, 1904, Ja 9,9:2
King, Mary Rhinelander, 1909, Ag 14,7:5
King, Mason H, 1960, Ja 13,48:3
King, Melville S, 1950, Ag 2,25:4
King, Melvin L, 1946, Ag 12,21:6
King, Mervin A, 1941, Je 26,23:4
King, Michael, 1937, O 1,21:2
King, Michael J, 1941, Jl 22,19:6
King, Michael Mrs, 1966, N 26,35:3
King, Milton J, 1948, Ja 24,15:4
King, Milton W Mrs, 1967, Ap 26,47:3
King, Moreland B Mrs, 1958, O 21,33:4
King, Morland, 1958, Mr 19,31:5
King, Morris L Mrs, 1939, My 22,17:4
King, Moses, 1909, Je 13,9:5
King, Moses (Mosey), 1956, D 12,46:4
King, Moses (Mosey),(est acctg), 1957, Mr 8,23:6
King, Nathaniel, 1937, Ap 25,II,8:4
King, Nelson, 1949, O 29,15:2
King, Noble C, 1949, N 2,27:5
King, Nora A, 1950, Je 3,15:6
King, Norbert T, 1957, F 2,19:5
King, Nosmo, 1949, Ja 14,24:2
King, Oliver K, 1960, Jl 6,33:3
King, Orville T Mrs, 1955, Je 28,27:5
King, Oscar A Dr, 1921, S 14,19:5
King, Oswin K, 1942, Ap 16,21:3
King, Otis B, 1951, Jl 4,17:4
King, Otto S, 1942, F 2,15:2
King, Padraic D, 1945, Ap 14,15:2
King, Patrick F, 1950, O 28,17:5
King, Patrick H Maj, 1872, O 17,1:6
King, Patrick Mrs, 1952, D 27,9:2
King, Paul B, 1947, N 26,23:5
King, Paul C, 1942, My 18,15:1
King, Paul H, 1942, My 19,20:3
King, Percy J, 1939, Je 24,17:6
King, Peter, 1961, My 15,31:4
King, Phil, 1938, Ja 8,15:4; 1948, Ja 28,23:3
King, Philip C, 1960, D 16,38:5
King, Philip M, 1966, Jl 11,29:2
King, Philip W R, 1923, Ja 3,13:4
King, Phoeby Mrs, 1951, Ap 9,25:3
King, Preston, 1865, N 5,4:6
King, Preston E, 1942, F 28,17:6
King, Preston L, 1940, Ap 3,23:1
King, R H, 1903, My 27,9:3
King, Rachel L, 1949, Ap 12,29:5
King, Ralph M, 1950, D 6,33:1
King, Ralph S, 1925, My 16,17:7
King, Rayburn S, 1966, Jl 14,35:3
King, Raymond W, 1961, F 5,80:5
King, Richard, 1914, Ja 6,13:6
King, Richard M, 1954, N 16,29:1
King, Robert, 1865, Je 20,5:3; 1881, My 11,8:2
King, Robert B, 1952, Ap 28,19:4
King, Robert C, 1943, Jl 18,34:7
King, Robert C Mrs, 1955, F 25,21:2
King, Robert C Sr, 1949, Je 18,13:6
King, Robert D, 1955, My 29,44:4
King, Robert E, 1950, Jl 11,31:1; 1955, Je 11,15:5
King, Robert J, 1946, Je 2,44:5
King, Robert M, 1941, D 29,15:5
King, Robert N, 1951, My 13,88:5; 1962, Ja 4,33:2
King, Robert P, 1949, N 16,30:4
King, Robert R Sr, 1946, N 27,25:4
King, Robert V Mrs, 1951, F 8,34:2
King, Robert W, 1938, Mr 20,II,8:4; 1964, My 27,39:1
King, Robert W Mrs, 1955, D 8,37:1; 1962, My 23,45:4
King, Ross L Mrs, 1956, Je 9,17:5
King, Rudolph F, 1961, S 10,86:1
King, Rufus, 1953, O 5,27:4
King, Rufus D, 1952, F 9,13:3
King, Rufus E Rev, 1921, N 8,19:5
King, Rufus H, 1867, Jl 10,4:6
King, Russell H, 1947, Ap 27,60:7
King, Russell S, 1956, S 20,33:4
King, S, 1933, Je 15,17:1
King, S G, 1882, Ag 16,5:4
King, S LeRoy, 1957, Je 1,17:6
King, S Quay, 1952, O 25,17:2
King, S Stanley, 1945, Ja 6,11:1
King, S T, 1878, Ag 6,5:2
King, S W, 1878, Je 29,5:3
King, S W Rev, 1878, Jl 1,8:2
King, Samuel A, 1937, Je 1,23:3
King, Samuel Archer Prof, 1914, N 4,7:7
King, Samuel B, 1961, My 14,86:3
King, Samuel E, 1947, Ag 31,36:8
King, Samuel J, 1945, F 9,16:3; 1952, N 13,31:5
King, Samuel T, 1940, N 24,49:2
King, Samuel W, 1959, Mr 26,31:1
King, Simeon Woodrow, 1921, My 5,17:4
King, Sion J Jr, 1944, F 6,42:1

King, Spencer C, 1945, Ja 10,23:2
King, Stanley, 1951, Ap 29,89:1
King, Stanley M, 1943, Jl 28,15:2
King, Stanley Mrs, 1967, F 18,29:3
King, Stanton H, 1939, N 11,15:5
King, Stephen T, 1922, Ap 4,17:5
King, Sylvan N, 1966, Mr 1,37:5
King, Tarant P, 1941, N 24,17:2
King, Thomas B, 1924, Jl 24,13:4
King, Thomas J (por), 1939, S 14,23:6
King, Thomas J Mrs, 1952, Ja 23,27:4
King, Thomas M, 1911, S 15,9:5
King, Thomas Starr Rev, 1864, Mr 5,3:2
King, Thomas W, 1940, Mr 21,25:3; 1943, D 5,64:4
King, Truby, 1938, F 10,21:5
King, Victor, 1957, Je 14,25:5
King, Victor L, 1958, O 13,29:3
King, Victor Mrs, 1946, Mr 23,13:4
King, Vincent M, 1942, N 24,25:4
King, Virginia P Mrs, 1959, N 4,41:6
King, W D, 1948, Ag 11,22:3
King, W F, 1883, Mr 13,5:4
King, W G, 1882, Je 10,5:1
King, W Irving, 1956, Je 6,33:2
King, W J Leslie, 1949, S 15,27:2
King, W L, 1936, D 12,19:3
King, W Marshall, 1957, Je 26,31:4
King, W Mills, 1956, Je 8,25:5
King, W Mills Mrs, 1954, Ag 28,15:6
King, W S, 1882, Je 30,2:2
King, W W, 1905, Mr 9,7:6
King, Wallace S, 1939, Ap 16,III,7:3
King, Walter G, 1953, Ja 15,27:4
King, Walter N, 1952, Jl 7,21:4
King, Walter W Mrs, 1950, O 11,33:6; 1950, O 31,27:4
King, Warner, 1941, Ag 14,17:2
King, Warner Mrs, 1957, O 1,33:2
King, Warren W, 1961, Je 12,29:6
King, Watson Mrs, 1948, F 15,60:5
King, Welty S, 1948, Ag 20,17:3
King, Wilfred, 1943, F 23,21:1
King, Willard V, 1955, My 3,31:1
King, Willford I, 1962, O 19,20:6
King, William, 1915, S 14,11:5; 1925, Je 17,21:4; 1965, Mr 24,43:1
King, William A, 1907, F 4,9:5; 1968, O 5,35:4
King, William A E, 1945, D 15,17:4
King, William B, 1945, Jl 3,13:2
King, William C, 1941, Ag 18,13:5
King, William E, 1943, S 5,28:6
King, William F, 1943, Je 24,21:1
King, William F (por), 1944, Jl 16,32:1
King, William F, 1953, Je 7,83:1
King, William F Dr, 1916, Ap 24,13:4
King, William Fletcher Dr, 1921, O 25,17:5
King, William H, 1942, Jl 25,13:6; 1944, Jl 25,19:4; 1949, N 28,27:1; 1951, Mr 21,33:1
King, William H Mrs, 1942, Mr 15,42:5
King, William J Jr, 1956, Mr 14,33:5
King, William J Mrs, 1942, O 22,21:5
King, William L, 1956, Ag 25,15:4
King, William L M, 1950, Jl 23,1:2
King, William Mrs, 1944, Mr 22,19:5
King, William N, 1943, D 31,15:4
King, William P, 1949, Mr 4,21:4; 1957, Je 21,28:7
King, William R, 1951, N 22,32:3
King, William Ryerson, 1919, D 31,7:4
King, William Vinton, 1923, D 3,17:3
King, William W Jr, 1947, Jl 16,23:3
King, Woods, 1947, Ja 16,25:2
King, Wunsz, 1968, Ap 22,47:3
King, Wyllys S, 1939, Mr 30,23:4
King, York Adam Rev, 1968, Je 1,27:4
King Charles XV of Sweden, 1872, S 20,4:7
King-Farlow, Sydney C, 1957, N 28,31:5
King-Hall, George, 1939, S 12,25:6
King-Hall, Stephen Lord, 1966, Je 2,43:4
King-Harman, Charles A Sir, 1939, Ap 19,23:4
King Lunalilo, of the Sandwich Islands, 1874, F 18,5:6
King-Smith, LeRoy, 1955, Ja 3,27:4
Kingdon, Frank, 1937, Ap 10,19:5
Kingdon, H Tully Bp, 1907, O 12,9:1
Kingdon, Mary Carter Mrs (funl, Je 13,9:5), 1911, Je 10,13:5
Kingdon, William, 1944, S 20,23:3
Kingdon-Ward, Frank, 1958, Ap 11,25:4
Kingery, Lisle B, 1940, Jl 12,15:3
Kingery, Robert, 1951, N 14,31:4
Kingham, Samuel B, 1957, F 11,29:3
Kinghorn, Henry B, 1907, S 6,9:6
Kinglake, W C, 1881, O 29,5:1
Kinglsey, Philip, 1903, Je 16,7:6
Kingma, John G, 1957, N 1,27:3
Kingman, Arthur G, 1953, Ap 2,27:2
Kingman, C Amey, 1950, Ja 25,28:4
Kingman, Daniel C Brig-Gen, 1916, N 16,11:4
Kingman, Dong Mrs, 1954, Je 15,29:2
Kingman, Eugene A, 1961, D 25,23:5
Kingman, Henry, 1937, S 22,27:2
Kingman, Henry S, 1968, D 13,47:2
Kingman, J W Judge, 1903, D 19,9:5
Kingman, John A, 1939, Ag 22,19:6
Kingman, John J, 1948, Jl 23,19:5
Kingman, Ralph W, 1950, F 5,85:1
Kingman, Robert, 1940, Ag 9,15:6
Kingman, Russell B, 1959, Mr 13,29:3
Kingman, Samuel E, 1952, Ap 13,77:2
Kingman, Thomas S, 1903, O 11,7:6
Kingman, William C, 1954, Mr 26,21:2
Kingman, William Livermore, 1924, My 9,19:5
Kingon, J, 1880, O 23,2:7
Kingore, Grant, 1964, Ap 14,37:4
Kingsbury, A N, 1880, D 12,10:4
Kingsbury, Agnes A, 1959, D 26,13:3
Kingsbury, Albert (por), 1943, Jl 29,19:3
Kingsbury, Albert Mrs, 1945, N 19,21:4
Kingsbury, Alice, 1937, Ap 5,20:1
Kingsbury, Amy K Mrs, 1938, Mr 10,21:4
Kingsbury, Arthur W, 1942, O 18,52:2
Kingsbury, Benjamin F, 1946, Jl 9,21:4
Kingsbury, Byron H, 1942, Ag 16,45:2
Kingsbury, C P, 1879, D 25,5:2
Kingsbury, Charles A, 1946, Ja 23,27:2
Kingsbury, Chester G, 1950, Je 30,23:3
Kingsbury, Chester G Mrs, 1949, O 28,24:3
Kingsbury, Dana W, 1942, F 10,19:3
Kingsbury, Edward H, 1951, Mr 17,28:4
Kingsbury, Edward M, 1946, Ja 24,21:1
Kingsbury, Edward M Mrs, 1957, Ap 9,33:2
Kingsbury, Edward R, 1940, My 2,24:3
Kingsbury, Edwin F, 1954, Mr 6,15:5
Kingsbury, Francis H, 1903, O 15,9:7
Kingsbury, Frank D, 1954, Ap 17,13:5
Kingsbury, Fred B, 1949, D 22,23:4
Kingsbury, Frederick H, 1942, Ap 28,21:3
Kingsbury, Frederick H Mrs, 1949, Je 2,28:3
Kingsbury, George O 2d, 1949, D 28,25:3
Kingsbury, Harry D, 1949, Ja 16,68:2
Kingsbury, Harry D Mrs, 1956, My 25,23:3
Kingsbury, Hazel, 1964, My 27,39:3
Kingsbury, Herbert D Mrs, 1914, S 19,11:3
Kingsbury, Howard T Col (por), 1937, Je 5,17:1
Kingsbury, Jerome, 1944, Jl 16,32:3
Kingsbury, Kenneth R, 1937, N 23,23:4
Kingsbury, Nathan Corning, 1920, Ja 25,22:2
Kingsbury, Paul, 1949, Ja 16,68:3
Kingsbury, Ralph, 1925, D 21,21:4
Kingsbury, Seldon H, 1950, Ja 2,23:3
Kingsbury, Susan M, 1949, N 29,30:2
Kingsbury, William H Rev, 1907, O 12,9:6
Kingsbury, William M, 1953, Ap 13,27:2
Kingsford, Howard N, 1950, F 10,24:2
Kingsford, Irving B, 1967, S 24,84:7
Kingsford, Walter, 1958, F 8,19:3
Kingsland, A C, 1878, O 15,5:4
Kingsland, Blanche V Mrs, 1941, Ag 18,13:4
Kingsland, Cornelius F, 1912, Je 29,11:5
Kingsland, Cornelius V V, 1945, D 17,21:4
Kingsland, Daniel, 1881, O 2,5:4
Kingsland, Edmund W, 1912, D 19,15:3
Kingsland, Elbert Hall, 1923, Ja 11,21:6
Kingsland, Ella, 1905, Ap 30,1:5
Kingsland, Emma V Mrs, 1940, Ap 3,23:4
Kingsland, George L, 1952, Ap 24,31:4
Kingsland, J Edward, 1950, Ja 26,27:2
Kingsland, John A, 1946, N 13,27:4
Kingsland, Stephen W Mrs, 1948, My 27,25:3
Kingsland, William D, 1941, S 23,23:2
Kingsland, William M (will, Je 21,2:5), 1906, Je 1,9:5
Kingsland, William M Mrs, 1919, Ag 11,11:4
Kingsley, Arthur L, 1954, D 9,33:4
Kingsley, Bruce G, 1962, Mr 31,25:4
Kingsley, Calvin Bishop, 1870, Ap 10,1:7
Kingsley, Caroline P, 1939, D 9,15:3
Kingsley, Charles, 1944, D 3,58:6
Kingsley, Charles F, 1939, D 2,17:5
Kingsley, Charles R, 1941, Je 26,23:5
Kingsley, Charles R Mrs, 1937, O 28,23:3
Kingsley, Charles W, 1955, My 26,31:1
Kingsley, Charles W Mrs, 1942, Ap 7,21:4
Kingsley, Chester W, 1904, Ja 2,9:3
Kingsley, Cornelius L, 1945, Je 1,15:3
Kingsley, Darwin P Mrs, 1962, Ap 11,43:4
Kingsley, E E, 1952, Jl 30,24:6
Kingsley, Edward D (por), 1945, Ja 3,17:3
Kingsley, Edward L, 1962, F 1,31:4
Kingsley, Elizabeth S Mrs, 1957, Je 8,19:2
Kingsley, Emeline M Mrs, 1942, N 22,53:1
Kingsley, Florida, 1937, Mr 20,19:2
Kingsley, Frances H, 1953, Jl 9,25:4
Kingsley, George C, 1957, Mr 21,31:3
Kingsley, Henry R, 1942, S 29,24:2
Kingsley, Howard L, 1948, Ap 9,23:4
Kingsley, James A, 1918, Ja 25,11:8
Kingsley, John, 1959, Mr 13,26:5
Kingsley, John H Mrs, 1943, Ja 29,19:5
Kingsley, John J, 1939, Mr 16,23:5
Kingsley, Joseph T Mrs, 1947, Jl 17,19:5
Kingsley, Levi G Gen, 1915, Je 28,9:6
Kingsley, Lewis, 1872, F 8,5:6
Kingsley, Lewis W (will, My 7,24:3), 1939, Ap 18, 23:5
Kingsley, Maurice, 1910, N 14,9:6
Kingsley, Maurice Mrs, 1920, Je 3,11:4
Kingsley, Neil Mrs, 1941, D 18,27:4
Kingsley, Omar (Ella Zoyara), 1879, My 28,5:4
Kingsley, Ralph H, 1952, Ja 5,11:1
Kingsley, Richard J, 1951, Ag 31,15:4
Kingsley, Robert J, 1968, Je 21,41:3
Kingsley, Rose Georgina, 1925, Ag 19,19:6
Kingsley, Sherman C, 1946, Mr 1,22:3
Kingsley, Theodore, 1964, My 14,35:5
Kingsley, W C, 1885, F 21,1:7
Kingsley, W J, 1929, F 15,23:3
Kingsley, Walton P, 1958, F 13,29:3
Kingsley, Willey J P Dr, 1912, Ja 27,11:4
Kingsley, William H (por), 1945, N 2,19:5
Kingsley, William M (por), 1942, S 8,23:1
Kingsmill, Harold, 1945, Mr 27,19:6
Kingsmill, Hugh, 1949, My 17,25:2
Kingsome, John, 1950, Jl 18,29:3
Kingson, Milton S, 1959, Ag 5,27:5
Kingston, Arthur C, 1949, F 9,27:4
Kingston, George F, 1950, N 21,31:5
Kingston, Gertrude, 1937, N 9,24:3
Kingston, Harry, 1951, Jl 6,23:1
Kingston, Herbert C, 1945, Ja 13,11:4
Kingston, Richard J, 1950, F 28,30:2
Kingston, Swan, 1947, O 31,23:5
Kingston, William H, 1948, Ap 18,72:4
Kingston, Winifred (Mrs C R Runyon), 1967, F 5, 88:5
Kington, Randall K, 1959, O 13,39:4
Kiniry, Francis A, 1949, D 3,15:4
Kinkade, William, 1945, F 9,15:3
Kinkade, William Mrs, 1941, O 24,24:2
Kinkaid, Herbert R, 1946, Ja 8,24:3
Kinkaid, Mary H Mrs, 1948, O 21,27:3
Kinkaid, Moses Pierce, 1922, Jl 7,17:6
Kinkead, Beatrice Mrs, 1947, N 12,27:5
Kinkead, Cornelia D, 1949, Ap 15,23:2
Kinkead, Ellis Guy Mrs, 1922, Ap 22,9:5
Kinkead, Eugene F, 1960, S 7,42:1
Kinkead, Geoffrey R, 1952, N 22,23:3
Kinkead, George B, 1940, F 27,21:2
Kinkead, George H, 1946, Ap 27,17:5
Kinkead, Herbert E, 1941, S 17,23:3
Kinkead, John H, 1904, Ag 17,7:6
Kinkead, John Mrs, 1944, F 26,13:2
Kinkead, Robert E Mrs, 1953, F 5,23:2
Kinkead, Thomas H, 1941, S 27,17:4
Kinkead, W Kenneth, 1957, Je 19,35:2
Kinkead, William L, 1948, F 10,23:3
Kinkead, William L Mrs, 1951, Ja 14,84:3
Kinkel, Albert, 1939, S 6,23:4
Kinkel, Albert Mrs, 1939, Ap 18,23:4
Kinkel, Henry, 1944, S 7,23:5
Kinkel, J G, 1882, N 16,5:5
Kinkel, John Mrs, 1959, Ap 8,37:2
Kinkeldey, Carl W, 1949, Jl 13,28:2
Kinkeldey, Otto, 1966, S 21,47:1
Kinkhead, Cleves, 1955, O 18,37:2
Kinkley, Melvin F, 1949, Jl 13,27:3
Kinksley, D P, 1932, O 7,21:1
Kinley, David (por), 1944, D 4,23:3
Kinley, John W, 1959, Ap 14,35:6
Kinley, Richard C, 1950, Ag 12,13:3
Kinloch, Lucy, 1951, S 21,23:2
Kinloch, Robert E, 1960, Jl 13,35:4
Kinloch-Cooke, Clement (por), 1944, S 5,19:4
Kinman, Leo M, 1960, O 14,33:3
Kinmond, R D, 1948, Ap 19,23:1
Kinmonth, J Lyle, 1945, N 19,21:5
Kinmonth, J Lyle Mrs, 1965, Jl 21,37:5
Kinmonth, Robert, 1872, Ag 14,8:4
Kinmouth, Hugh S Dr, 1920, Jl 23,15:4
Kinnaird, Emily C, 1947, S 12,21:3
Kinnally, James H, 1957, F 10,86:5
Kinnaly, Eugene T Mrs, 1948, Mr 4,25:5
Kinnan, Alexander P W Mrs, 1944, N 5,54:6
Kinnan, Alexander Phoenix Waldron, 1924, Ja 24,1
Kinnan, Morris E, 1968, Ap 15,43:3
Kinnane, Charles H, 1954, Ap 29,31:2
Kinnane, Jack, 1943, Mr 30,26:3
Kinnard, Leonard H, 1957, D 29,49:2
Kinnard, Leonard H Mrs, 1941, Mr 23,45:1
Kinne, Benjamin B, 1944, O 7,13:3
Kinne, Brayton E, 1939, Ja 24,19:5
Kinne, Burdette I, 1947, O 22,29:3
Kinne, Charles E Mrs, 1944, Ja 16,41:6
Kinne, Clarence E, 1950, S 14,32:2
Kinne, George L, 1951, Ap 6,25:2
Kinne, Helen Prof, 1917, D 31,7:7
Kinne, Henry G Mrs, 1937, Ag 29,II,7:1
Kinne, Judge, 1869, S 29,4:5
Kinne, Lewis O, 1949, Ap 13,29:1
Kinne, Linn, 1950, Mr 14,25:1
Kinne, Marion E, 1955, Ja 25,25:4
Kinne, William H, 1943, Mr 19,19:2
Kinnear, David J, 1967, My 1,37:3
Kinnear, Guy, 1942, Ap 19,44:4
Kinnear, Ronald, 1954, D 12,88:3
Kinnear, Thomas J, 1944, O 30,19:4
Kinnear, William R, 1944, Ag 18,13:4
Kinnear, Wilson S, 1941, Ag 9,15:5
Kinnell, Murray, 1954, Ag 14,15:3
Kinnelly, Thomas Sr, 1957, Jl 17,27:3
Kinnen, Mathias, 1943, Mr 10,19:3
Kinner, Albert V Mrs, 1966, Mr 31,39:5

Kinner, Winfield B, 1957, Jl 7,61:1
Kinnere, Raymond J Mrs, 1956, N 16,28:1
Kinney, Arthur S, 1955, Ag 4,25:1
Kinney, Asa Mrs, 1952, Ja 25,21:1
Kinney, Asa S, 1961, Mr 4,23:6
Kinney, Belle (Mrs L Scholz), 1959, Ag 28,23:5
Kinney, Benjamin A, 1937, Je 26,17:6
Kinney, Benjamin I, 1937, S 2,21:2
Kinney, Carl W, 1950, F 27,19:1
Kinney, Charles J, 1956, O 16,33:2
Kinney, Charles Spencer Dr, 1920, O 28,15:5
Kinney, Edward B, 1950, D 15,31:5
Kinney, Francis S, 1908, Ap 5,11:4
Kinney, Frank P, 1941, Ag 6,17:3
Kinney, Franklin S, 1871, Jl 14,2:5
Kinney, George A, 1963, N 22,31:5
Kinney, Gilbert, 1952, Mr 13,29:1
Kinney, Gilbert Mrs, 1956, Ja 31,29:4
Kinney, Harold V, 1938, N 6,48:8
Kinney, Herbert R, 1948, D 7,32:2
Kinney, Ira L, 1952, S 28,78:8
Kinney, J Ernest, 1943, Ap 20,23:1
Kinney, J Sterling, 1958, F 1,19:1
Kinney, Jacob M, 1955, Ja 20,31:2
Kinney, Jennette, 1954, Ap 30,23:2
Kinney, John A, 1967, S 25,45:3
Kinney, John F, 1938, Ja 9,42:1
Kinney, John J, 1940, Je 28,19:2
Kinney, John J Mrs, 1949, D 16,31:5
Kinney, Joseph I, 1949, F 10,27:5
Kinney, Joseph R Jr, 1960, Jl 24,65:2
Kinney, Kenneth K, 1957, N 29,29:4
Kinney, Michael E, 1957, Mr 6,31:3
Kinney, Morris, 1945, O 9,21:2
Kinney, Oscar F, 1949, Mr 24,28:3
Kinney, Patrick R, 1953, Je 2,29:3
Kinney, Ralph D, 1962, Ap 7,51:3
Kinney, Robert L, 1940, Je 2,44:8
Kinney, Samuel M, 1964, Je 29,27:5
Kinney, Sydney C, 1955, N 25,28:1
Kinney, T Wylie, 1966, My 25,47:4
Kinney, Thomas C, 1908, Jl 19,7:7
Kinney, Thomas I Mrs, 1950, D 19,29:1
Kinney, Thomas P Mrs, 1907, D 27,7:6
Kinney, Troy, 1938, Ja 30,II,8:8
Kinney, Troy Mrs, 1952, Ja 13,88:4
Kinney, Volney P, 1937, Ag 20,17:3
Kinney, W B, 1880, O 22,5:3; 1925, Ja 7,25:4
Kinney, William, 1947, N 15,17:4
Kinney, William C Mrs, 1947, Ja 24,21:4
Kinnicutt, Francis H, 1939, Jl 4,13:4
Kinnicutt, Francis P Mrs, 1910, O 27,11:6
Kinnicutt, Francis Parker Dr, 1913, My 2,11:3
Kinnicutt, G Herman, 1943, D 7,27:2
Kinnicutt, G Hermann Mrs, 1947, Je 4,27:4
Kinnicutt, Leonard P, 1911, F 7,9:4
Kinnicutt, William H Mrs, 1948, My 18,23:2
Kinnie, Margaret E, 1939, F 17,20:2
Kinnier, James C, 1942, My 5,21:4
Kinnoch, Peter A, 1951, Ja 26,23:4
Kinnosuke, Adachi, 1952, Ja 31,27:3
Kinnoull, Countess of, 1938, D 16,25:4
Kinnoull, Earl of (Archibald Fitzroy Geo Hay), 1916, F 8,11:2
Kinnoull, Lord, 1938, Mr 20,II,8:5
Kinnucan, Henry L Mrs, 1941, S 16,23:3
Kinoshita, Tomosaburo, 1944, N 23,31:4
Kinross, Cecil J, 1957, Je 22,15:5
Kinross, Lord, 1939, Jl 29,15:3
Kinsella, Arthur, 1938, My 29,II,6:5
Kinsella, Edward A, 1944, Jl 7,15:6
Kinsella, Edward W, 1948, D 17,28:3
Kinsella, George F, 1952, Ja 11,21:4
Kinsella, Kathleen F, 1951, F 4,77:1
Kinsella, Michael B, 1949, Ap 21,25:2
Kinsella, Patrick B, 1957, Ja 21,25:4
Kinsella, Patrick J, 1942, My 28,17:5
Kinsella, Richard F, 1939, O 15,49:1
Kinsella, Richard J, 1925, Ag 13,19:5
Kinsella, T, 1884, F 12,5:3
Kinsella, Thomas F, 1952, S 29,23:5
Kinsella, Thomas J, 1937, Ja 25,19:3
Kinsella, Thomas P, 1946, Jl 23,25:3
Kinsella, William, 1949, O 31,25:3
Kinsella, William F, 1942, Ag 16,45:2
Kinsey, Alfred C (funl plans, Ag 27,19:6; funl, Ag 28,27:1), 1956, Ag 26,1:3
Kinsey, Alfred S, 1943, Ap 8,23:4
Kinsey, Alonzo W, 1904, F 14,7:6
Kinsey, Carroll B, 1945, Jl 19,23:5
Kinsey, Charles S, 1952, Je 8,86:5
Kinsey, E Lee, 1961, My 27,23:5
Kinsey, E Marshall, 1955, O 29,19:4
Kinsey, Eugene A, 1939, Ja 2,24:4
Kinsey, Frank H Mrs, 1943, Ap 28,23:3
Kinsey, Fred, 1943, F 20,13:5
Kinsey, Harold C, 1949, Je 26,60:4
Kinsey, Henry R, 1942, O 14,25:3
Kinsey, Howard F, 1947, O 5,68:4
Kinsey, Howard O, 1966, Jl 28,33:4
Kinsey, Margaret J H Mrs, 1937, Ja 15,21:2
Kinsey, Robert G, 1964, S 20,89:2
Kinsey, Wendell H, 1951, S 18,31:3
Kinsey, William A, 1951, O 31,29:4
Kinsgland, Ambrose, 1924, N 14,19:5
Kinsie, Paul M Mrs, 1961, Ag 30,33:1
Kinskey, Walter C, 1941, My 30,15:3
Kinsky, Ulrich, 1938, D 20,26:2
Kinsley, Charles L, 1944, Ap 8,13:5
Kinsley, Clayton J, 1942, O 28,23:6
Kinsley, Earle S, 1949, Ja 13,23:4
Kinsley, Edward W, 1944, Ap 15,11:2
Kinsley, George S, 1945, Je 23,13:3
Kinsley, Joseph E, 1952, Mr 30,93:1
Kinsley, Mart T, 1947, O 7,27:3
Kinsley, Philip, 1960, My 22,86:8
Kinsley, William J, 1916, Mr 26,21:4
Kinsloe, Charles L, 1953, O 16,27:4
Kinsloe, Charles Mrs, 1937, Mr 13,19:4
Kinsman, Arthur J, 1964, Je 13,23:2
Kinsman, Arthur M, 1939, N 29,23:4
Kinsman, Charles W, 1954, F 16,25:5
Kinsman, Ezbon G, 1965, Je 14,33:2
Kinsman, Frederick J, 1944, Jl 18,19:2
Kinsman, J Warren, 1965, F 16,35:4
Kinsman, James M, 1942, S 6,31:2
Kinsman, William A, 1943, F 15,15:3; 1964, F 9,88:4
Kinsner, William, 1949, Ap 6,29:3
Kinsolving, Arthur B, 1951, Ag 16,27:5; 1964, Je 16, 39:4
Kinsolving, Arthur B Mrs, 1962, Ap 28,25:3
Kinsolving, George Herbert Mrs, 1925, S 27,7:4
Kinsolving, Grady, 1939, Jl 19,19:4
Kinsolving, L L, 1929, D 19,27:3
Kinsolving, Walter O, 1965, Ag 8,64:7
Kinsolving, Walter O Mrs, 1956, F 28,31:2
Kinstadter, William, 1947, My 30,21:2
Kinter, John F, 1951, Ja 30,25:2
Kinter, W A, 1946, Jl 16,23:6
Kintner, Adrian C, 1946, O 22,25:2
Kintner, George, 1941, S 11,23:3
Kinton, Ambrose J, 1942, N 22,52:2
Kintsler, Joseph N, 1954, F 27,13:6
Kintzing, Frank T, 1944, Jl 24,15:6
Kintzing, W F, 1884, O 14,5:3
Kinum, Andrew, 1937, O 7,27:2
Kinzer, J Roland, 1955, Jl 26,25:3
Kinzer, R J, 1952, Ag 31,45:2
Kinzie, Andrew L, 1949, Jl 28,23:6
Kinzie, Charles, 1946, Ja 25,24:3
Kinzler, Frederick W, 1961, O 28,21:2
Kinzler, Jacob, 1966, D 23,25:5
Kinzley, G Walter, 1938, D 14,25:5
Kinzley, Joseph C, 1947, Je 8,60:4
Kinzley, Joseph Mrs, 1947, Ag 5,23:6
Kiobassa, Peter, 1905, Je 24,9:5
Kip, Charles A, 1940, Ap 14,44:8
Kip, Charles H, 1942, Ap 1,21:6
Kip, Edward, 1964, O 18,89:2
Kip, Garrett Mrs, 1950, Jl 31,17:4
Kip, Henry, 1883, Ja 18,5:5
Kip, I Jr, 1885, My 16,2:5
Kip, Isaac L Dr, 1911, O 7,13:6
Kip, Kermit F, 1957, Je 22,15:6
Kip, Lor Col, 1903, F 24,9:6
Kip, Percy N, 1940, Je 11,25:5
Kip, Ruloff F, 1953, Ap 9,27:4
Kip, Thomas H, 1938, Je 20,15:4
Kip, Walter S, 1940, Je 13,23:4
Kip, William V B (will, Ja 27,19:2), 1937, Ja 15,22:2
Kip, William V P Mrs, 1957, F 12,27:3
Kipa, Wadym, 1968, S 3,43:1
Kipe, Horace S, 1966, Mr 1,37:2
Kipfer, Albert Mrs, 1942, Ap 1,21:4
Kiphuth, Robert J H, 1967, Ja 9,39:1
Kiphuth, Robert J H Mrs, 1941, Je 8,49:2
Kipley, Joseph, 1904, F 7,7:6
Kipling, Arthur W, 1947, S 18,25:6
Kipling, Arthur W Mrs, 1963, Jl 31,29:3
Kipling, Caroline B Mrs (por), 1939, D 20,25:1
Kipling, John L, 1911, Ja 31,9:4
Kipling, R, 1936, Ja 18,1:4
Kiplinger, Cora M Mrs, 1947, Ag 12,23:1
Kiplinger, Herman M, 1957, Mr 8,25:3
Kiplinger, Willard M, 1967, Ag 7,29:2
Kipnis, Leon, 1966, Je 9,47:2
Kipnis, Leonid L, 1968, S 13,47:3
Kipp, Benjamin A, 1942, Ag 26,19:3
Kipp, Burdett, 1937, Ja 24,II,8:4
Kipp, Calvin P, 1958, D 29,15:1
Kipp, Carlton G, 1945, My 14,17:3
Kipp, Charles E, 1950, O 27,29:3
Kipp, Charles J, 1965, My 2,88:1
Kipp, Charles J Dr, 1911, Ja 14,11:6
Kipp, Daniel P Mrs, 1938, F 15,25:2
Kipp, David, 1954, Mr 15,25:4
Kipp, David C, 1938, Ag 15,15:5
Kipp, Edward H Mrs, 1940, S 23,17:5
Kipp, George Washington, 1911, Jl 26,9:6
Kipp, John A, 1954, S 23,33:4
Kipp, Karl, 1954, My 11,29:3
Kipp, Leonard, 1922, D 22,15:5
Kipp, S Arthur, 1954, S 3,17:3
Kipp, S Arthur Mrs, 1940, Je 8,15:6
Kipp, Stanley C, 1940, Jl 19,19:4
Kipp, Theodore, 1941, My 30,15:6
Kipp, V K, 1958, Jl 30,29:4
Kipp, Walter A, 1941, D 4,25:2
Kipp, Warren A, 1951, D 22,15:4
Kipp, Warren A Mrs, 1952, Ja 23,27:3
Kipp, William Halstead Col, 1918, Ag 21,9:4
Kipping, Frederic S, 1949, My 1,88:6
Kipsey, Grover F, 1961, O 1,87:1
Kir, Felix Canon, 1968, Ap 26,43:2
Kira, Princess of Prussia, 1967, S 9,31:2
Kirafly, Verona A, 1946, S 5,27:2
Kiralfy, Imre, 1919, Ap 29,15:3
Kiraly, Nicholas, 1950, D 26,23:3
Kiraly, Victor, 1955, Jl 8,23:2
Kirby, Alfred L, 1964, Jl 5,43:2
Kirby, Andrew S Mrs, 1945, O 28,44:4
Kirby, Annie M, 1937, Ja 12,23:1
Kirby, Austin E, 1938, D 1,23:3
Kirby, Austin E Mrs, 1943, Ap 18,48:4
Kirby, Burnett T, 1939, Mr 7,21:2
Kirby, C Valentine, 1947, S 28,60:6
Kirby, Charles A, 1950, Ap 25,31:5
Kirby, Charles L, 1954, Ap 8,27:4
Kirby, Charles W Mrs, 1941, My 8,23:5
Kirby, Daniel B, 1953, D 28,21:3
Kirby, David Barclay, 1920, Mr 4,11:5
Kirby, David N, 1952, Ap 9,31:3
Kirby, Dunne W, 1959, S 10,35:6
Kirby, Edmund, 1942, Mr 25,21:1
Kirby, Edmund H, 1950, O 29,92:6
Kirby, Edmund W, 1946, F 16,13:5
Kirby, Edward B, 1968, Jl 8,39:3
Kirby, Francis G, 1951, Ja 14,84:6
Kirby, Frank B, 1941, Ag 21,17:2
Kirby, Frank G, 1950, O 23,23:4
Kirby, Frank M, 1939, Ag 29,21:4
Kirby, Fred M (will, O 26,9:1), 1940, O 17,25:3
Kirby, George A, 1955, My 8,88:5
Kirby, Grover C, 1949, Mr 7,16:4
Kirby, Gustavus T (funl, Mr 2,23:2), 1956, F 29,31:3
Kirby, Gustavus T Mrs, 1941, D 24,17:2
Kirby, Harris C, 1959, O 18,87:1
Kirby, Homer C, 1961, O 6,35:1
Kirby, Hugh L, 1937, N 20,17:3
Kirby, James F, 1966, F 10,34:1
Kirby, James Mrs, 1946, Je 26,25:4
Kirby, James N, 1949, Ja 1,11:8
Kirby, James P, 1948, O 14,29:4
Kirby, John, 1957, Ap 14,86:2
Kirby, John B, 1942, Ag 11,19:4
Kirby, John D, 1913, F 6,11:5; 1949, O 18,27:2
Kirby, John H, 1940, N 11,19:5; 1952, F 19,29:4
Kirby, John Jr, 1925, D 31,15:4
Kirby, John N, 1952, F 4,17:4
Kirby, John P, 1943, Ag 18,19:4
Kirby, John P Mrs, 1956, Ag 7,27:2
Kirby, John T, 1968, Ap 3,52:1
Kirby, John V, 1948, D 21,31:2
Kirby, John W Jr, 1947, My 27,25:1
Kirby, Josiah M, 1964, F 6,29:2
Kirby, Kate M, 1938, Ap 22,19:5
Kirby, Leonard (see also Mr 5), 1878, Mr 7,5:4
Kirby, Merretta F Mrs, 1938, Ap 26,21:3
Kirby, Norman A, 1957, Je 19,35:3
Kirby, Phil H, 1948, Ap 17,19:5
Kirby, Robert J (por), 1944, Ja 16,43:1
Kirby, Robert J Mrs, 1944, D 8,21:1
Kirby, Rollin, 1952, My 10,21:1
Kirby, Rollin (est appr), 1954, F 6,21:1
Kirby, Rollin Mrs, 1943, Ag 10,19:2
Kirby, Russell T, 1941, Je 7,17:3
Kirby, S R, 1876, Mr 8,8:1
Kirby, Stanley J, 1959, Ag 2,81:2
Kirby, Thomas, 1937, Je 11,23:4
Kirby, Thomas Ellis (funl, Ja 19,13:4), 1924, Ja 18, 17:1
Kirby, W F Justice, 1934, Jl 27,17:2
Kirby, Wallace M, 1949, Je 28,27:2
Kirby, Wilfred S, 1948, F 10,23:2
Kirby, William F Mrs, 1949, Jl 5,23:2
Kirby, William J, 1944, O 15,44:2; 1957, F 25,25:4
Kirby, William P, 1915, N 7,21:5
Kirby-Smith, Joseph L, 1939, N 6,23:5
Kirbye, J Edward, 1939, N 14,23:2
Kirch, Edwin A, 1940, D 30,17:5
Kirchenbaum, Abraham I, 1949, N 14,27:3
Kirchenstein, August M, 1963, N 7,37:1
Kircher, Charles E, 1948, Ap 18,68:5
Kircher, Conrad, 1938, Ap 5,21:2
Kircher, Edward A, 1958, Ja 27,27:3
Kircher, George Sr, 1948, N 9,27:3
Kircher, John H, 1937, O 3,II,9:1
Kircher, Julius, 1940, My 27,19:5
Kircher, Robert C, 1953, Jl 6,17:6
Kirchgasner, George L, 1964, My 30,17:3
Kirchgessner, Charles A, 1943, Ap 21,26:2
Kirchheimer, Otto, 1965, N 23,45:1
Kirchheimer, Sigmund, 1920, Ap 28,11:6
Kirchhof, Grover C, 1958, O 1,37:4
Kirchhofer, Hugo, 1955, Je 19,92:4
Kirchhoff, Bernard C, 1940, Ap 14,45:2
Kirchhoff, Charles William Henry, 1916, Jl 24,9:5
Kirchhoff, William C, 1938, N 18,21:2
Kirchmayer, Jerzy, 1959, Ap 13,31:4

Kirchmyer, Joseph G, 1944, Mr 9,17:3
Kirchner, Felix, 1954, Jl 21,27:4
Kirchner, George H, 1938, Ag 23,17:2
Kirchner, Henry J, 1943, Ja 29,19:3
Kirchner, Henry P, 1957, Je 16,84:4
Kirchner, John, 1944, O 15,44:5
Kirchner, Karl A, 1949, Ja 12,27:2
Kirchner, Karl F, 1964, F 11,40:1
Kirchner, Philipp, 1955, N 20,89:2
Kirchner, Ralph J, 1952, Ja 8,27:2
Kirchner, Stanley J, 1950, My 27,17:5
Kirchoff, Frederick C, 1947, D 14,80:4
Kirchoff, William C Mrs, 1945, F 7,21:3
Kirchwey, George W (por), 1942, Mr 5,23:1
Kirchwey, Karl W, 1943, O 30,15:3
Kirchwey, Mary F, 1942, Mr 26,23:5
Kirdar, Lutfi (funl, F 20,8:3), 1961, F 18,17:3
Kirdorf, Emil, 1938, Jl 14,21:1
Kireker, C Frank Mrs, 1949, O 29,15:6
Kirgan, John M, 1953, Je 25,27:6
Kirk, A Raymond, 1949, N 4,27:4
Kirk, Abby, 1951, Ja 2,23:2
Kirk, Alan G, 1963, O 16,45:1
Kirk, Althea A Mrs, 1942, O 11,56:7
Kirk, Annie, 1951, S 7,29:2
Kirk, Arthur G, 1959, Ap 18,23:5
Kirk, Bernard F, 1953, Ja 18,92:8
Kirk, Charles A (por), 1947, Je 18,25:4
Kirk, Charles D, 1945, Ap 10,19:2
Kirk, Charles E, 1949, D 24,15:1
Kirk, Charles S, 1947, N 30,76:6
Kirk, Daniel P, 1943, Jl 1,19:5
Kirk, Donald, 1943, Ag 13,19:3
Kirk, E N Brig-Gen, 1863, Jl 25,2:5
Kirk, Ed N Rev, 1874, Mr 28,7:5
Kirk, Edward J, 1950, Ap 7,25:2; 1961, Je 13,35:3
Kirk, Edwin, 1955, N 18,25:3
Kirk, Ernest, 1921, N 3,19:3
Kirk, Eugene E Mrs, 1952, S 24,33:5
Kirk, Frank C, 1963, O 30,39:1
Kirk, George A, 1951, My 11,27:1
Kirk, George V, 1947, Je 22,52:4
Kirk, George W, 1962, Mr 23,33:3
Kirk, George 3d, 1950, D 25,32:8
Kirk, Hannah M, 1951, My 19,15:3
Kirk, Harris C, 1960, Mr 15,39:1
Kirk, Harris E, 1953, N 8,89:1
Kirk, Harry A, 1955, Je 16,31:2
Kirk, Harry D Sr, 1945, N 16,19:2
Kirk, Harry I, 1967, Je 5,43:2
Kirk, Helena (Mrs M Ames), 1908, Je 25,9:5
Kirk, Henrietta L Mrs, 1944, S 10,46:1
Kirk, Hiram Merritt, 1918, Mr 13,11:8
Kirk, Howard, 1941, N 30,68:4
Kirk, Howard K, 1939, Ap 7,22:3
Kirk, J W, 1943, D 14,27:3
Kirk, Jack Mrs, 1952, Je 26,29:3
Kirk, James F, 1939, D 14,27:5; 1942, My 8,21:5
Kirk, James P, 1951, S 1,11:2
Kirk, John, 1948, My 24,19:6
Kirk, John B, 1904, N 2,9:4
Kirk, John L, 1947, F 28,23:4
Kirk, John Mrs (F Baker), 1954, N 15,27:4
Kirk, John R Dr, 1937, N 8,23:4
Kirk, John Sir, 1922, Ja 16,13:4; 1922, Ap 5,17:5
Kirk, John T, 1956, Mr 12,27:3
Kirk, John W, 1963, My 4,25:5
Kirk, Joseph A, 1944, S 21,19:5
Kirk, Kenneth E, 1954, Je 9,31:2
Kirk, Leander R, 1955, S 20,31:5
Kirk, Marie R Sister, 1945, O 25,21:1
Kirk, Maurice H, 1954, Ja 31,88:4
Kirk, Max, 1956, S 27,35:1
Kirk, Montgomery, 1878, My 22,1:5
Kirk, Myron R Mrs, 1959, F 28,19:6
Kirk, Norman T, 1960, Ag 14,93:1
Kirk, Raymond E, 1957, F 7,27:3
Kirk, Raymond V (por), 1947, My 29,21:6
Kirk, Rev Dr, 1874, Ap 1,1:7
Kirk, Robert Horner, 1925, N 25,21:5
Kirk, Robert J, 1937, F 15,17:4
Kirk, Robert L, 1960, Ag 13,15:3
Kirk, Sophia, 1950, Ag 18,21:1
Kirk, Stuart L, 1951, S 19,31:4
Kirk, T Allen, 1961, My 21,87:3
Kirk, Theodore H, 1960, S 19,31:1
Kirk, Thomas, 1939, Mr 18,20:4
Kirk, Thomas F, 1960, Je 3,31:4
Kirk, Traine C Mrs, 1959, Ag 14,21:3
Kirk, Walter F, 1955, Jl 29,17:4
Kirk, Walter J, 1946, My 14,21:1
Kirk, Walter R, 1964, Je 18,35:4
Kirk, William, 1919, D 23,9:2
Kirk, William A, 1957, S 28,17:5
Kirk, William B G, 1967, Ja 10,40:2
Kirk, William E J, 1941, F 20,19:4
Kirk, William F, 1960, N 13,88:4
Kirk, William H, 1922, N 25,13:5; 1950, Ag 7,19:5
Kirk, William Mrs, 1946, Jl 9,21:5
Kirk, William P, 1964, Ja 8,37:3
Kirk, William T, 1938, Je 29,19:3; 1958, S 23,33:5
Kirk, Zachary T, 1939, F 18,15:2
Kirkaldy, Margaret, 1959, Mr 21,21:5

Kirkbride, Charles K, 1944, Je 21,19:5
Kirkbride, Elizabeth A Mrs, 1941, My 8,23:2
Kirkbride, Franklin B (trb lr, O 5,34:7), 1955, S 29, 33:1
Kirkbride, Fred G, 1938, N 1,23:5
Kirkbride, Joseph A, 1962, Ag 12,80:1
Kirkbride, T S, 1883, D 18,5:2
Kirkbride, Thomas H, 1939, N 18,17:4
Kirkbride, Walter G, 1956, D 9,89:1
Kirkbride, Walter H, 1944, D 21,21:6
Kirkbridge, Mary B, 1967, Mr 29,45:3
Kirkby, Cyril S, 1949, S 17,17:4
Kirkby, W, 1880, Jl 8,3:2
Kirkby, William West Rev Dr, 1907, S 6,9:6
Kirkeby, Marius, 1938, S 19,19:4
Kirkegaard, Theodore A, 1953, S 4,34:1
Kirkendall, Frederic C, 1925, D 21,21:5
Kirkendall, Frederick G 2d, 1945, Ag 8,23:6
Kirkendall, George T, 1945, Je 28,19:3
Kirker, James B Maj, 1868, Mr 1,6:5
Kirkey, James J, 1952, Mr 22,13:2
Kirkham, Augustus, 1912, Mr 10,15:4
Kirkham, Frederick C, 1956, Je 12,35:2
Kirkham, George C, 1954, S 23,33:3
Kirkham, George D, 1939, Ap 24,17:3
Kirkham, H L D (por), 1949, Mr 19,15:5
Kirkham, J C, 1876, Ag 6,6:6
Kirkham, Stanton D, 1944, Ja 8,13:6
Kirklady, A, 1934, Ap 17,21:5
Kirkland, Alfred T, 1951, Mr 27,29:1
Kirkland, C P, 1883, Ag 8,5:3
Kirkland, Charles B, 1937, Mr 17,25:4
Kirkland, Charles P Capt, 1911, O 4,13:5
Kirkland, Francis J, 1940, S 24,23:4
Kirkland, Frank W, 1949, S 29,29:4
Kirkland, Frederic R, 1961, Ag 17,27:3
Kirkland, Frederic R Mrs, 1958, My 24,21:4
Kirkland, Gordon A, 1953, Je 24,25:3
Kirkland, Henry B Mrs, 1956, N 13,37:1
Kirkland, Henry W, 1950, Je 20,27:4
Kirkland, James A, 1940, Jl 29,13:5
Kirkland, James H, 1939, Ag 6,37:3
Kirkland, John F, 1950, My 6,15:6
Kirkland, John Thaw, 1909, D 25,7:4
Kirkland, Lawrence A (por), 1943, Jl 14,19:3
Kirkland, Leigh G (por), 1942, D 27,34:1
Kirkland, Margaret K Mrs, 1940, D 27,19:2
Kirkland, Owen A, 1963, D 29,42:6
Kirkland, Patrick W, 1948, N 6,13:6
Kirkland, R Mason, 1947, Jl 9,23:1
Kirkland, Robert D, 1943, O 14,22:2
Kirkland, W A Adm, 1898, Ag 13,7:5
Kirkland, Weymouth, 1965, F 4,31:2
Kirkland, William, 1952, S 13,17:4
Kirkland, William A Mrs, 1909, F 17,9:4
Kirkland, William C, 1943, O 30,15:5
Kirkland, William R, 1955, Je 6,27:3
Kirkland, William R Mrs (Barbara), 1968, Ag 13, 36:4
Kirkland, William R 3d, 1967, Mr 20,31:2
Kirkland, Winifred M, 1943, My 15,15:3
Kirklin, Byrl R, 1957, Mr 4,27:2
Kirkman, Christian W, 1937, Ap 9,21:1
Kirkman, Frederick, 1947, Ag 9,13:5
Kirkman, John D, 1952, Je 6,23:4
Kirkman, Marshall M, 1921, Ap 19,17:6
Kirkman, Robert P Mrs, 1953, Jl 21,23:2
Kirkman, Robert W, 1956, Je 10,88:6
Kirkman, Sidney A, 1953, My 12,27:4
Kirkman, Sidney A Mrs, 1954, Mr 11,34:8
Kirkman, Thomas B, 1960, Jl 8,21:1
Kirkman, Thomas Mrs, 1960, S 28,39:1
Kirkman, Van Leer, 1951, Mr 6,27:2
Kirkmyer, James A, 1944, Ap 27,23:2
Kirkner, Jacob, 1909, D 15,11:3
Kirkover, Harry D Mrs, 1938, Ja 28,21:2
Kirkpatrick, Alice S Mrs, 1941, Ag 29,17:3
Kirkpatrick, Andrew Judge, 1904, My 4,9:5
Kirkpatrick, Andrew M, 1955, Je 15,31:5
Kirkpatrick, Arthur, 1941, Ag 12,19:3
Kirkpatrick, Arthur J E, 1955, O 27,33:2
Kirkpatrick, Charles, 1951, D 23,14:4
Kirkpatrick, Charles Sir, 1937, Ja 5,23:5
Kirkpatrick, David E, 1950, S 21,31:1
Kirkpatrick, Edwin A, 1937, Ja 5,23:4
Kirkpatrick, Frank F, 1946, Ap 16,25:1
Kirkpatrick, Frank O, 1947, N 10,29:3
Kirkpatrick, George, 1950, F 8,27:4
Kirkpatrick, George R, 1937, Mr 20,19:3
Kirkpatrick, George U, 1940, Ap 21,43:2
Kirkpatrick, Harlow B, 1948, D 2,29:5
Kirkpatrick, Harold H, 1951, Jl 31,21:4
Kirkpatrick, Ivone, 1964, My 26,39:4
Kirkpatrick, James Mrs, 1945, Je 11,15:3
Kirkpatrick, John B, 1949, Ja 13,23:2
Kirkpatrick, John P, 1946, D 18,30:3
Kirkpatrick, John P Mrs, 1947, D 22,21:2
Kirkpatrick, Laura B, 1945, D 1,23:5
Kirkpatrick, Malcolm, 1955, My 25,33:3
Kirkpatrick, Mary S Mrs, 1944, Ja 20,19:2
Kirkpatrick, Maude Mrs, 1950, Mr 2,27:4
Kirkpatrick, N Willard, 1951, Jl 7,13:4
Kirkpatrick, Ralph, 1949, Ap 8,26:5

Kirkpatrick, Snyder S, 1909, Ap 7,11:5
Kirkpatrick, T Bruce, 1965, F 11,39:2
Kirkpatrick, W Howard, 1944, Je 2,15:4
Kirkpatrick, William D, 1961, Jl 21,23:2
Kirkpatrick, William E, 1940, O 3,25:3
Kirksey, Guy, 1961, Ja 7,19:3
Kirkup, J Milford Jr, 1962, Mr 29,33:3
Kirkus, Alfred R, 1939, Ap 12,23:3
Kirkus, Frederick M, 1939, F 17,19:2
Kirkus, William Rev, 1907, Jl 11,7:6
Kirkwood, Allan S, 1951, Jl 29,69:2
Kirkwood, Arthur P, 1957, Je 11,35:1
Kirkwood, David Lord, 1955, Ap 17,86:3
Kirkwood, Elwood, 1944, D 11,23:5
Kirkwood, Jack, 1964, Ag 4,30:2
Kirkwood, James, 1963, Ag 25,82:7
Kirkwood, John G, 1959, Ag 11,27:5
Kirkwood, John L, 1959, My 24,88:4
Kirkwood, Maclean, 1963, O 25,31:1
Kirkwood, Robert G, 1950, O 5,32:2
Kirkwood, Robert O, 1942, Mr 5,23:5
Kirkwood, Thomas, 1906, N 10,9:4
Kirkwood, Thone S, 1947, Mr 14,23:4
Kirkwood, W Chester, 1949, F 7,19:2
Kirkwood, William A, 1942, S 24,27:5
Kirkwood, William P Mrs, 1954, My 9,88:2
Kirley, Patrick J, 1965, Ja 30,27:2
Kirlin, J P, 1927, D 23,19:3
Kirlin, Louis F Sr, 1947, Ja 29,25:1
Kirlin, Louis F Sr Mrs, 1950, Mr 23,36:2
Kirmayer, Frank H, 1953, Ag 12,31:2
Kirmayer, Paul J, 1964, S 6,56:3
Kirmse, Marguerite (Mrs G W Cole), 1954, D 13, 27:2
Kirn, George J, 1947, Jl 7,17:4
Kirn, William H, 1937, My 2,II,9:1
Kirnan, William, 1948, Ja 31,19:3
Kirner, Lee J, 1959, F 2,25:2
Kiroack, Howard, 1951, My 15,31:4
Kiroff, S, 1934, D 2,1:4
Kirpal, Frederick J Mrs, 1948, D 24,18:4
Kirpatrick O'Farril, Guillermo, 1952, Ja 9,29:4
Kirsch, Bernard, 1944, D 10,54:3
Kirsch, Bernard M, 1953, Ag 25,21:2
Kirsch, Carl G, 1937, Ap 1,23:2
Kirsch, David, 1947, N 6,27:4
Kirsch, Felix M, 1945, Mr 23,20:3
Kirsch, Guy W, 1950, S 29,27:5
Kirsch, Jacob Mrs, 1959, My 24,88:3
Kirsch, John P, 1941, F 6,21:5
Kirsch, Karl M Mrs, 1962, D 5,47:5
Kirsch, Ralph, 1963, My 28,37:1
Kirsch, Ralph Mrs, 1960, Ja 27,33:3
Kirsch, Rose, 1941, S 29,17:6
Kirsch, Rudolph G, 1959, S 24,37:4
Kirsch, Samuel, 1956, Jl 4,19:5; 1958, Ap 10,29:4
Kirschbaum, Arthur, 1958, My 30,22:1
Kirschbaum, Harry M, 1959, D 3,37:3
Kirschbaum, Richard W, 1948, N 21,88:5
Kirschbaum, William G, 1941, Ja 12,45:2
Kirschber, Bradley H, 1941, My 29,19:2
Kirschberg, Joseph, 1947, Mr 19,26:2
Kirschen, Rolman, 1925, Je 4,19:4
Kirschen, Sidney, 1959, Mr 22,87:1
Kirschenbaum, Benjamin F, 1946, Ja 5,13:1
Kirschenbaum, Charles, 1949, F 20,60:2
Kirschenbaum, Charles W, 1949, Ag 9,26:3
Kirschenbaum, Jacob, 1946, O 26,17:4
Kirschenbaum, Morris, 1955, Ja 4,21:1
Kirschgessner, George, 1939, Mr 26,III,7:1
Kirschke, Paul T, 1962, S 19,39:4
Kirschmer, Charles L, 1949, D 16,31:2
Kirschner, Albert, 1952, Jl 22,25:2
Kirschner, B W Mrs, 1915, F 26,9:4
Kirschner, Charles L Mrs, 1941, O 18,19:3
Kirschner, Efraim, 1942, N 19,25:5
Kirschner, Isaac, 1942, O 9,21:5
Kirschner, Jacob M, 1953, Ap 25,15:3
Kirschner, K A Martin Dr, 1912, S 15,II,15:6
Kirschner, Theodore Mrs, 1953, My 12,27:3
Kirschstein, Benjamin, 1958, Ap 6,88:4
Kirschstein, Henry J, 1950, Mr 11,15:2
Kirshbaum, Helen, 1939, Ja 23,13:4
Kirshner, James M, 1952, S 18,29:3
Kirsner, Raymond B, 1953, Je 8,29:5
Kirsopp, Edgar C B, 1960, My 29,56:3
Kirstein, Albert F Sr, 1942, Jl 30,21:3
Kirstein, Henry E, 1940, D 8,71:3
Kirstein, Jane (Mrs Geo G Kirstein), 1968, Jl 2
Kirstein, Louis E (por), 1942, D 11,23:1
Kirstein, Louis E Mrs, 1952, Jl 31,23:2
Kirsten, Albert Jr Mrs, 1947, S 28,61:1
Kirsten, Arthur Jr, 1959, D 7,31:2
Kirsten, Frank R, 1948, Ap 12,21:6
Kirsten, Frederick K, 1952, N 22,23:5
Kirsten, George W Mrs, 1951, O 13,17:6
Kirsten, Warren F, 1952, Ap 29,27:3
Kirtland, George D, 1954, S 6,15:3
Kirtland, Jacob H, 1962, N 7,39:3
Kirtland, Kenneth C, 1946, F 11,29:3
Kirtland, Lucian S, 1965, O 12,48:1
Kirtland, Milton P, 1944, My 19,19:5
Kirton, Charles F A, 1949, My 25,29:5

Kirton, Cooper N, 1939, O 21,15:5
Kirtz, Harry M, 1949, F 26,15:4
Kirtzman, Nicholas, 1963, Ap 1,27:5
Kirvay, Julius P, 1950, N 15,32:2
Kirwan, Arthur J, 1945, My 8,34:2
Kirwan, E J (see also N 26), 1876, N 28,8:3
Kirwan, Francis W, 1943, Je 21,17:4
Kirwan, John Capt, 1907, F 12,9:6
Kirwan, John J, 1954, F 22,19:2
Kirwan, Martin W Mrs, 1944, Ja 5,17:2
Kirwan, Richard H, 1965, My 8,31:4
Kirwan, William F, 1948, My 12,28:3
Kirwin, Aloysius, 1966, N 20,67:1
Kirwin, Daniel, 1938, F 14,17:5
Kirwin, Lawrence E, 1938, Jl 16,13:7
Kirwin, Richard J, 1937, N 30,23:1
Kirwin, Thomas J, 1959, Ag 19,30:1
Kiryuhkin, Nikolai I, 1953, D 19,15:4
Kisch, Bruno Z, 1966, Ag 13,25:4
Kischke, John L, 1949, O 11,34:4
Kisco, Frank J, 1952, O 14,34:2
Kiselev, Anisim F, 1952, Je 18,27:6
Kiselev, Yevgeny D (trb, Ap 19,43:1), 1963, Ap 18, 35:3
Kiselewski, Joseph Mrs, 1954, Je 7,23:5
Kiser, Donald J, 1945, Ja 6,11:2
Kiser, John W, 1959, My 26,35:4
Kiser, John W Jr Mrs, 1953, Ap 29,30:4
Kiser, John W Mrs, 1948, D 3,25:5
Kiser, Louise K, 1954, Ap 2,27:4
Kiser, May P Mrs, 1942, F 28,17:6
Kiser, Owen E, 1958, Ja 15,29:3
Kiser, Samuel E, 1942, Ja 31,17:2
Kiser, William H, 1943, D 19,48:5
Kisevalter, George, 1941, Mr 12,21:5
Kish, Felicia, 1960, S 17,23:6
Kishorr, Gideon, 1951, Jl 14,13:2
Kishpaugh, Joseph, 1945, N 14,19:1
Kishpaugh, Ralph J J, 1941, Ap 28,15:4
Kisilewsky, Julian Mrs, 1956, Mr 30,19:3
KisKadden, Adams Mrs, 1916, Mr 19,19:6
Kiskadden, John M, 1937, Jl 7,23:4
Kisling, Moise, 1953, Ap 30,31:1
Kisner, Ambrose P, 1946, O 12,19:1
Kiss, Max, 1967, Je 23,39:1
Kiss, Rodolphe, 1953, F 5,23:4
Kiss de Ittebe, Maria J von Mrs (K Schratt),(por), 1940, Ap 19,21:5
Kissam, Albert W, 1943, My 17,15:5
Kissam, Albert W Mrs, 1945, F 18,34:1
Kissam, Benjamin J, 1907, Jl 12,7:6
Kissam, Daniel Embury Dr, 1903, D 25,7:6
Kissam, George P Mrs, 1904, N 15,1:4
Kissam, Harold H, 1963, Jl 28,65:2
Kissam, Harriet, 1908, Ap 9,9:4
Kissam, J B, 1885, Ap 28,5:5
Kissam, Samuel H, 1915, Ap 19,9:5
Kissam, W V, 1903, N 22,7:5
Kissam, William A, 1950, Ja 30,17:5
Kissam, William A Mrs, 1949, D 17,17:5
Kissane, Cyril, 1938, Ap 25,15:2
Kissane, James J, 1938, Mr 8,3:6
Kissane, John W, 1953, Ap 4,13:1
Kissane, William J, 1954, S 19,89:1
Kissel, Caroline T Mrs (will), 1953, Jl 28,19:2
Kissel, Charles M, 1947, My 2,21:1
Kissel, George, 1942, O 16,19:4
Kissel, John, 1938, O 4,25:2
Kissel, Peter F F Mrs, 1948, N 27,17:4
Kissel, Rudolph H (por), 1942, Ap 1,21:2
Kissel, Rudolph H Jr, 1937, Ap 10,19:3
Kissel, Rudolph H Mrs, 1950, Ja 21,17:3
Kissel, Stanislaus, 1952, Je 6,23:3
Kissel, W Thorn, 1960, My 27,31:2
Kissel, W Thorn Mrs, 1960, My 26,33:2
Kissel, Wilhelm, 1942, Jl 20,13:3
Kisseleff, Count, 1872, D 14,5:6
Kissell, Eleonora M, 1966, Ag 3,37:2
Kissen, Murray, 1958, F 18,27:4
Kissenberth, George, 1946, O 3,27:3
Kissick, Joseph, 1959, Mr 14,23:2
Kissin, Yekuthiel, 1950, Je 26,27:5
Kissinger, Clifford W, 1938, Ja 29,15:2
Kissinger, John R, 1946, Jl 16,23:2
Kisslan, Joseph J, 1946, Ap 11,25:5
Kissling, Beryl C Mrs, 1954, D 28,23:3
Kissling, Ernest G, 1939, Jl 3,13:5
Kissling, John, 1938, Jl 26,19:5
Kissling, Louis A (por), 1946, Je 14,21:3
Kissman, Joseph, 1968, Ja 2,37:2
Kissman, Joseph Mrs, 1964, O 10,29:2
Kist, Alfred, 1954, Ag 5,23:2
Kistakovsky, Vladimir, 1952, O 24,23:2
Kistemeckers, Henry, 1938, Ja 22,18:2
Kister, Frank F, 1937, Ap 6,23:1
Kister, Frank F Mrs, 1959, Ja 4,87:2
Kister, Fred W, 1938, S 26,17:3
Kister, George F, 1964, O 30,26:3
Kister, Ida K Mrs, 1938, N 20,38:8
Kister, Marion, 1958, Ja 7,47:3
Kister, William C, 1946, D 10,31:4
Kistler, Douglas S, 1942, Je 28,33:2
Kistler, Frank E, 1960, N 16,41:2
Kistler, Frederick Mrs (C Carlstedt), 1953, My 31, 72:1
Kistler, George, 1942, Ja 19,17:4
Kistler, Oliver F, 1945, N 28,27:4
Kistler, Raymon M, 1965, Mr 18,30:4
Kistler, Raymon M Mrs, 1959, D 20,60:8
Kistler, S, 1880, Mr 20,8:3
Kistler, Sedgwick, 1952, Ap 30,27:5
Kistler, Sedgwick Mrs, 1952, S 13,17:4
Kistler, Seth W, 1946, Ag 10,13:4
Kistler, William C Capt, 1968, O 26,37:5
Kistler, William E, 1951, Ap 26,29:5
Kistner, Merrill M, 1963, My 25,25:5
Kitain, Boris, 1959, Ap 21,38:1
Kitain, Marie Mrs, 1964, S 4,29:1
Kitchel, Alice L Mrs, 1938, Mr 17,21:3
Kitchel, Allan F, 1963, Ap 26,35:3
Kitchel, Anna T, 1959, My 30,17:4
Kitchel, Cornelius P, 1947, Ja 15,25:4
Kitchel, Farrand de Forest, 1908, My 25,7:2
Kitchel, Lloyd, 1950, Jl 3,15:5
Kitchel, W Lloyd (por), 1947, Je 3,25:1
Kitchel, W Lloyd Mrs, 1945, Mr 5,19:3
Kitchell, Charles Mrs, 1948, Ag 10,21:1
Kitchell, Charles W, 1956, Ap 21,17:4
Kitchell, Harry B Mrs, 1954, D 7,33:4
Kitchell, William Parkhurst, 1908, Ap 5,11:4
Kitchen, Conway N, 1963, My 31,25:3
Kitchen, Dorothy Follis, 1923, Ag 16,15:4
Kitchen, H W Dr, 1907, O 1,11:6
Kitchen, James, 1906, My 26,11:6
Kitchen, John B Jr, 1952, D 5,27:2
Kitchen, John H Mrs, 1948, D 4,19:2
Kitchen, John R, 1950, Ag 19,13:6
Kitchen, John S Surgeon, 1872, My 9,1:2
Kitchen, Karl K, 1949, Ap 12,29:1
Kitchen, Millard F, 1944, Mr 30,21:4
Kitchen, Myra Mrs, 1938, D 16,25:5
Kitchen, Theodore, 1906, O 4,9:4
Kitchen, W M, 1876, S 22,5:1
Kitchen, William G, 1939, Ja 28,15:2
Kitchen, William K, 1939, S 3,19:3
Kitchener, Earl, 1937, Mr 30,23:2
Kitchener, Frederick Walter Gov, 1912, Mr 8,13:5
Kitchens, T Neal (por), 1949, Ap 26,25:1
Kitchens, Wade H, 1966, Ag 23,39:4
Kitchin, Anthony W, 1951, Mr 21,33:3
Kitchin, Charles H, 1952, Ag 8,29:3
Kitchin, Claude, 1923, Je 1,19:5
Kitchin, Thurman D, 1955, Ag 29,19:6
Kitchin, William Walton Ex-Gov, 1924, N 10,17:2
Kitching, Edward J, 1945, Ja 8,17:5
Kitching, Frank Wilberforce, 1917, N 17,13:4
Kitching, George E, 1905, F 25,9:3
Kitching, Robert N 3d, 1953, Ap 23,29:3
Kitching, Theodore E, 1941, Ja 6,15:2
Kitchlew, Saifuddin, 1963, O 10,41:1
Kite, Earle L, 1954, Ap 8,27:3
Kite, Mary L Mrs, 1945, Ag 22,23:5
Kite, Owen W, 1946, Ja 10,23:2
Kite, Sam, 1962, Ap 8,86:2
Kite, Thomas, 1938, Mr 19,15:2
Kite, William H, 1948, N 17,27:2
Kite, William H Mrs, 1952, Jl 23,23:5
Kithcart, Lawrence, 1948, Ja 18,60:4
Kithcart, Robert B, 1941, S 11,23:4
Kitiyakara, Nakkhatra Mangala Prince, 1953, F 12, 27:3
Kitselman, Alva S, 1940, Mr 7,23:5
Kitson, Albert Sir, 1937, Mr 9,23:5
Kitson, Anne M Mrs (por), 1937, Mr 26,22:2
Kitson, Arthur, 1937, O 2,21:4
Kitson, H H Mrs, 1932, O 30,37:6
Kitson, Harry D, 1959, S 26,23:1
Kitson, Henry H, 1947, Je 27,21:5
Kitson, Lady, 1947, My 29,21:5
Kitson, Nellie Mrs, 1940, Ap 28,37:1
Kitson, Roland D (Lord Airedale), 1958, Mr 21,21:1
Kitson, Samuel J, 1906, N 10,9:4
Kitson, Sydney W, 1951, Ag 31,15:2
Kitt, Charles H, 1949, Mr 15,27:3
Kitt, Edward, 1951, O 16,31:2
Kitt, S A, 1948, D 6,25:5
Kittay, Abraham I Mrs, 1954, Je 25,21:2
Kittay, Phil, 1957, D 20,24:3
Kittel, Joseph John, 1904, Mr 17,1:3
Kittel, Walter E, 1922, Ag 4,15:7
Kittell, Clyde S, 1955, Mr 24,31:5
Kittell, Donald D, 1947, Ap 18,21:2
Kittell, James S Rev Dr, 1937, Ap 18,II,8:6
Kittell, William F, 1968, Mr 27,47:1
Kittelle, Sumner E W, 1950, D 30,13:5
Kittenplan, Reuben, 1960, My 29,37:1
Kittermaster, Harold B, 1939, Ja 15,39:3
Kittilsen, Edward, 1939, Mr 23,23:4
Kittinger, Harold D (will, N 22,13:5), 1947, O 6,21:4
Kittinger, Irvine J, 1941, Jl 15,20:2
Kittinger, Irvine J Sr Mrs, 1957, D 29,48:2
Kittinger, Theodore A, 1939, O 6,25:4
Kittle, Abraham, 1920, D 13,15:6
Kittle, Frank C, 1951, Mr 20,29:3
Kittle, Hugh D Sr, 1967, My 26,47:2
Kittleman, William H, 1960, Ja 13,47:2
Kittler, Alfred, 1943, Ap 24,13:6
Kittner, Violet, 1940, Jl 23,19:6
Kitto, Charles W, 1960, D 28,27:1
Kittredge, A O, 1903, Mr 29,7:5
Kittredge, Abbott Eliot Rev Dr, 1912, D 18,15:4
Kittredge, Arthur Beard Ex-Sen (funl, My 9,11:5), 1911, My 5,11:4
Kittredge, Arthur E, 1962, Jl 16,32:2
Kittredge, Benjamin R, 1951, Je 2,19:3
Kittredge, Charles A, 1944, My 27,15:3
Kittredge, Charles J, 1944, D 14,23:5
Kittredge, Edward H, 1944, Ja 1,13:5
Kittredge, Elsie M, 1954, Mr 25,29:5
Kittredge, Frank A, 1954, D 12,88:3
Kittredge, Frank E, 1941, Jl 9,21:2
Kittredge, George L (por), 1941, Jl 24,17:1
Kittredge, George L Mrs, 1951, Mr 12,25:3
Kittredge, George W, 1914, Ja 3,11:5
Kittredge, George W (por), 1947, Ag 24,58:1
Kittredge, Harry C, 1947, S 18,25:4
Kittredge, Henry C, 1967, F 20,37:3
Kittredge, Joseph Mrs, 1956, Je 8,25:5
Kittredge, Josiah E Rev Dr, 1913, D 23,9:5
Kittredge, Linus E, 1959, N 25,29:4
Kittredge, Mabel, 1955, My 9,23:2
Kittredge, Rufus J, 1947, Ag 18,17:4
Kittredge, Samuel D, 1939, N 7,25:4
Kittredge, Sarah F Mrs, 1903, F 28,3:5
Kittredge, Tracy B, 1957, D 24,15:1
Kittredge, William A, 1945, Jl 27,15:6
Kittredge, William R, 1949, Ja 20,27:4
Kittredge, Winifred R Mrs, 1947, My 27,25:5
Kittrell, James W, 1939, O 4,25:2
Kittrell, William H, 1966, Ap 26,45:4
Kittridge, Michael J Jr, 1939, O 10,23:4
Kitts, Clarence A, 1950, Ja 1,42:4
Kitts, Jimmie, 1952, D 14,90:4
Kitts, Willard A 3d, 1964, N 23,37:1
Kitz, Alfred F, 1950, F 11,15:4
Kitzinger, Frederick, 1947, My 25,60:6
Kitzler, Frederick C, 1948, N 30,27:3
Kitzler, Sidney H, 1960, D 30,20:1
Kitzmeyer, U F W Rev, 1923, Jl 3,13:4
Kivel, George (por), 1945, Mr 3,13:1
Kivel, John Justice, 1924, Ap 2,19:5
Kivelson, Harvey E, 1960, D 1,35:5
Kiven, Nathan J, 1960, O 18,39:1
Kivett, Tunis, 1962, F 18,92:3
Kivlen, Thomas Judge, 1873, D 2,5:3
Kivlihen, Francis P, 1951, Jl 18,33:2
Kivy, Julius, 1967, F 17,37:2
Kiwanuka, Joseph, 1966, F 24,37:4
KixMiller, William, 1945, Ap 15,14:8
Kiyosawa, Kiyoshi, 1945, My 23,19:1
Kiyose, Ichiros, 1967, Je 28,45:2
Kiyoura, Keigo, 1942, N 7,15:4
Kizer, Benjamin F Sr, 1949, Ap 13,29:5
Kizer, Elmer E Mrs, 1954, N 9,27:4
Kizer, Noble (por), 1940, Je 14,21:5
Kjaer, Ejnar, 1947, Je 19,21:2
Kjellgren, Bengt R F, 1968, N 12,43:3
Kjellman, Franz, 1907, Ap 23,9:4
Kjellstrom, Erik T H, 1956, N 8,39:4
Kjelsberg, Betzy A K Mrs, 1950, N 3,28:3
Kjems, Christian P, 1957, Je 25,29:4
Klaas, Ferdinand, 1948, Jl 5,15:5
Klaber, William, 1943, F 21,32:5
Klabin, Wolf, 1957, Mr 17,86:8
Klaboe, Nicholas, 1944, Je 9,15:4
Klabouch, Frank J, 1945, Ag 24,19:4
Klackner, Christian, 1916, Jl 5,11:6
Klackner, John, 1916, N 21,11:2
Klaeger, Robert H, 1965, My 28,33:3
Klaer, Harvey, 1952, Ag 25,17:4
Klaer, Jacob Mrs, 1917, Ag 24,7:2
Klaesius, Paul K, 1948, Jl 22,23:3
Klaess, Francis J, 1958, O 14,37:1
Klaess, John J, 1951, Ap 15,92:4
Klaessig, Emil, 1940, N 12,23:4
Klaestad, Helge, 1965, My 26,47:3
Klafter, Simeon H, 1965, O 19,43:3
Klag, Henry Sr, 1912, Ag 14,9:4
Klages, John L, 1959, O 31,23:2
Klages, Raymond, 1947, Mr 22,13:6
Klahold, William C, 1940, Jl 3,17:2
Klahr, Evelyn G, 1941, Ja 17,17:4
Klahre, Hugo Sr, 1967, Mr 4,27:5
Klaif, Morris, 1967, S 16,33:3
Klain, Zora, 1952, N 7,23:2
Klairborn, Alfred N, 1951, Mr 26,23:5
Klami, Unno, 1961, My 30,17:3
Klamroth, Wilfried, 1944, Ja 17,19:2
Klaner, Fred, 1955, Ap 22,25:5
Klansky, Jacob J, 1968, F 22,32:7
Klapp, Eugene (por), 1938, My 13,19:1
Klappenberger, Ernest, 1946, Ja 28,19:4
Klapper, Isaac, 1956, Ag 6,23:3
Klapper, Morris, 1966, N 6,89:2
Klapper, Paul, 1952, Mr 26,29:1
Klaptoz, Adalbert, 1955, Ag 11,23:8
Klar, John A, 1952, Ag 23,13:4
Klar, Samuel Mrs, 1959, My 22,27:3
Klar, Zoltan, 1966, Ja 5,31:1

Klaristenfeld, Sam, 1968, D 1,86:6
Klarman, Jack, 1960, Ap 30,23:5
Klarmann, Emil G, 1963, S 1,57:1
Klarsfeld, Jerome R, 1955, N 19,19:2
Klas, Norman J, 1949, My 30,13:4
Klase, Howard A, 1947, N 6,27:3
Klase, James L Mrs, 1959, My 10,86:8
Klase, John T, 1946, S 14,7:6
Klase, Thomas J, 1951, D 22,15:3
Klasek, Charles J, 1949, Ja 18,23:5
Klasen, Franz, 1943, Ap 23,17:3
Klass, Bertrand, 1962, S 19,39:4
Klass, Gustav J, 1947, Ag 18,17:1
Klass, Raymond N, 1954, N 20,17:3
Klass, Richard J, 1947, Je 24,23:5
Klassen, August, 1956, Jl 31,23:2
Klatcik, Michael, 1957, Ja 8,31:4
Klath, Thormod O, 1943, O 2,13:3
Klatsky, Harry, 1952, D 15,25:3
Klatte, Henry A, 1944, Jl 2,20:1
Klatte, John A, 1953, Ap 4,13:5
Klatz, Boruch Mrs, 1949, N 16,29:2
Klatzkin, Jacob, 1948, Mr 28,49:1
Klatzko, Anna Mrs, 1951, Ag 18,17:3
Klau, David W, 1961, Mr 13,29:1
Klau, Nathan, 1938, F 17,21:4
Klauber, Adolph, 1933, D 8,23:5
Klauber, Alfred S, 1947, S 8,21:4
Klauber, Bernard S, 1964, Ap 26,89:2
Klauber, Chester D, 1953, Mr 30,21:2
Klauber, Edward, 1954, S 24,23:1; 1959, N 6,29:1
Klauber, Edward A, 1954, My 2,89:2
Klauber, Edward Mrs, 1943, O 10,49:1
Klauber, Harry I, 1948, S 30,27:2
Klauber, Henry, 1943, N 26,23:1
Klauber, Joseph C Mrs, 1949, Jl 12,27:2
Klauber, Julia Mrs, 1947, Mr 8,13:6
Klauber, Rosina Mrs (cor, My 15,30:2), 1940, My 12,48:3
Klauberg, August H, 1956, Ja 8,86:7
Klauberg, August H Mrs, 1956, Ja 8,86:7
Klauberg, Charles J, 1964, F 29,21:3
Klauberg, Minnie Mrs, 1942, Mr 30,17:4
Klauberg, William, 1946, Mr 3,46:4
Klauberg, William J, 1920, D 3,15:4
Klauck, William, 1944, Mr 31,13:6
Klauder, Charles Z, 1938, O 31,15:3
Klauder, Charles Z (will), 1939, Ja 22,18:1
Klauder, Francis E Rev, 1912, Jl 30,9:6
Klauder, Joseph V, 1962, Ap 5,33:2
Klauer, Kilian, 1942, F 8,50:1
Klauer, William H, 1952, D 5,27:4
Klaus, Anna M, 1956, Mr 21,37:5
Klaus, F J (Fee), 1951, F 15,31:4
Klaus, Frank A, 1948, F 9,17:1
Klaus, Fred R, 1949, N 26,15:4
Klaus, Henry, 1957, Je 6,31:3
Klaus, Henry Jr, 1954, N 16,29:5
Klaus, Leon L, 1956, S 25,33:2
Klaus, Samuel, 1963, Ag 3,17:5
Klausmann, Harry, 1967, S 9,31:4
Klausmann, Joseph B, 1963, S 14,25:3
Klausner, Hubert, 1939, F 13,15:2
Klausner, Joseph, 1958, O 28,35:4
Klausner, Julius, 1964, Mr 8,86:7
Klausner, Siegfried, 1947, Jl 12,13:7
Klausner-Cronheim, Irma, 1959, Ap 26,86:6
Klaussmann, Eric K, 1954, D 31,13:6
Klavan, Joshua, 1953, Jl 29,23:2
Klaw, Alonzo, 1944, Ja 13,21:4
Klaw, M, 1936, Je 15,21:1
Klawans, Bernard, 1958, Ja 22,27:4
Klayer, Chester C, 1945, Je 8,19:5
Kleagle, Jersey, 1924, Ag 6,13:3
Kleban, Louis E, 1942, Ja 9,21:4
Kleban, Milton, 1957, F 10,86:6
Kleban, Myron J, 1966, D 8,47:1
Klebanow, Joseph H, 1956, Jl 18,27:1
Klebaur, Louis D, 1941, D 19,25:3
Klebe, Otto P M Mrs, 1947, My 5,23:3
Klebe, Werner G Mrs, 1945, Je 18,19:4
Kleber, Chester C, 1960, N 29,37:2
Kleber, Clement O Dr (por), 1937, Jl 16,19:4
Kleber, Jackson O, 1958, O 31,29:3
Kleberg, Caesar, 1946, Ap 16,25:6
Kleberg, R J, 1932, O 11,21:5
Kleberg, Richard M Sr, 1955, My 9,23:4
Kleberg, Robert J Jr Mrs, 1963, Je 13,33:1
Kleberg, Robert Sr Mrs, 1944, Jl 31,13:4
Klebes, Albert H Mrs, 1953, F 15,92:1
Klebes, Ralph D, 1952, Je 7,19:3
Klebes, Roy W, 1955, Ag 16,49:2
Klebicki, Nicholas, 1949, N 22,29:5
Klebs, Arnold C, 1943, Mr 9,23:4
Kleckler, Henry, 1963, Ap 10,39:4
Kleckner, David, 1963, O 15,39:1
Kleckner, Leonard Mrs (Lois Andrews), 1968, Ap 6, 40:2
Kleckner, Martin S, 1958, My 2,27:3
Kleckner, Ralph Mrs, 1959, Ag 6,27:5
Kleckner, W A, 1956, Ja 3,31:4
Klee, Emil, 1940, My 1,23:4
Klee, Hans, 1959, My 26,35:2
Klee, Kathryn, 1954, Jl 11,72:2
Klee, Lawrence M, 1957, Ja 2,27:2
Klee, Leon, 1940, F 16,19:3
Klee, Paul, 1940, Jl 3,17:2
Klee, Sigmund, 1952, D 23,23:3
Klee, Simon J, 1947, Je 5,25:4
Klee, Walter H, 1953, S 4,15:2
Kleeberg, Gordon S P, 1946, Je 23,40:4
Kleeberger, Frank L, 1942, S 15,23:2
Kleefeld, Fred H, 1952, Mr 8,13:1
Kleeman, Arthur O, 1946, S 3,19:1
Kleeman, Arthur S, 1965, My 3,33:3
Kleeman, Emil H, 1949, Mr 8,25:1
Kleeman, Erich E, 1966, Jl 18,27:2
Kleeman, F Julian, 1940, S 5,23:4
Kleeman, James, 1949, F 2,27:1
Kleeman, Louis, 1947, Je 11,27:6
Kleemola, Kauno, 1965, Mr 13,25:5
Klees, Ludwig, 1909, Ap 19,9:5
Klees, William E Mrs, 1949, Je 6,19:5
Kleffmann, Theckla Mrs, 1941, Mr 2,42:8
Klehm, Louise, 1941, F 24,15:5
Klehr, William, 1944, My 11,19:6
Kleiber, Erich, 1956, Ja 28,17:3
Kleig, James F, 1939, Ap 3,15:2
Kleihauer, Cleveland, 1960, S 17,23:4
Kleiman, I Ernest, 1955, N 26,19:4
Kleiman, Jack, 1964, Je 3,43:4
Kleiman, Jacob, 1951, N 30,23:1
Kleiman, Samuel J, 1952, Ja 3,27:4
Klein, Aaron, 1948, F 9,17:3; 1951, Je 5,31:4
Klein, Abraham, 1952, F 5,29:5
Klein, Adolf, 1946, S 16,5:5; 1950, Ja 24,31:2; 1950, S 28,31:3
Klein, Adolf Mrs, 1949, O 22,17:3
Klein, Adolph, 1950, S 9,17:6
Klein, Adolph I, 1968, Ag 11,73:1
Klein, Adolph Mrs, 1962, N 9,35:2
Klein, Adolph P Mrs, 1948, Ag 23,19:1
Klein, Agnes Mrs, 1963, S 26,36:1
Klein, Albert, 1943, S 2,19:6; 1958, O 5,87:1
Klein, Albert M, 1955, O 18,37:2
Klein, Albert W, 1945, Ap 4,21:3
Klein, Alex, 1958, Ag 2,17:5
Klein, Alexander, 1946, My 25,15:5
Klein, Alfred, 1904, F 23,7:6
Klein, Alfred J, 1944, My 21,43:1
Klein, Alfred M, 1963, N 6,41:4
Klein, Allen, 1963, Jl 17,31:4
Klein, Andrew, 1967, Jl 10,28:4
Klein, Andrew C, 1947, F 4,27:7
Klein, Anthony W, 1944, Ja 26,19:2
Klein, Aron, 1943, My 4,23:1
Klein, Arthur, 1964, N 3,31:1
Klein, Arthur F, 1942, Ja 11,46:1
Klein, Arthur G Justice (will, Mr 7,60:2), 1968, F 22, 31:1
Klein, Arthur H, 1955, Je 7,33:1
Klein, Arthur W, 1960, Jl 14,27:5
Klein, Aug C (por), 1948, F 6,26:6
Klein, August B, 1945, D 9,44:3
Klein, August P, 1943, My 19,25:2
Klein, Bernard, 1938, N 26,15:3; 1953, Je 9,27:3
Klein, Bert M, 1947, My 2,21:3
Klein, Bruno Oscar, 1911, Je 25,11:4
Klein, Charles, 1937, O 27,31:1; 1950, O 17,31:5
Klein, Charles D, 1949, D 21,29:1
Klein, Charles F A Mrs, 1954, N 4,31:4
Klein, Charles H (Chuck), 1958, Mr 29,17:1
Klein, Charles H, 1959, My 28,31:4
Klein, Charles L, 1949, Je 14,32:4
Klein, Chester, 1962, Jl 2,29:2
Klein, D Emil, 1956, Ja 17,33:2
Klein, David, 1944, My 6,19:5; 1952, Ja 17,27:3; 1959, Jl 7,33:5
Klein, David J, 1940, O 3,25:6
Klein, David Mrs, 1967, N 30,47:3
Klein, E Allen, 1939, Ap 25,23:2
Klein, Edward E Dr, 1925, F 12,19:4
Klein, Edward F, 1962, My 30,19:4
Klein, Edward H, 1955, My 19,29:6
Klein, Edward J, 1949, My 12,31:5
Klein, Edward J Mrs, 1947, N 11,27:1
Klein, Edward L, 1945, Ja 15,19:3
Klein, Edward Mrs (R Taylor), 1961, Ja 22,85:1
Klein, Elias, 1945, Ja 20,11:4; 1949, Mr 24,28:2
Klein, Emanuel, 1949, Jl 6,27:2; 1959, D 20,60:6
Klein, Emil, 1937, Mr 13,19:5; 1963, Ag 8,27:5
Klein, Emil F, 1954, D 10,27:5
Klein, Emma S Mrs, 1941, Ag 20,19:5
Klein, Eugene, 1944, My 1,15:4
Klein, Eugene Mrs, 1954, Ja 7,31:2
Klein, Frank W, 1948, Ag 21,15:3
Klein, Fred, 1943, Mr 17,21:1
Klein, Frederick, 1953, Jl 28,19:4
Klein, Frederick B, 1950, Jl 30,61:1
Klein, Frederick B Mrs, 1958, O 16,37:4
Klein, George W, 1943, F 17,21:2
Klein, George W Mrs, 1949, Mr 22,25:3
Klein, Harry, 1963, N 21,39:3
Klein, Harry M, 1953, Ja 6,29:2
Klein, Harry M J, 1965, Ag 29,84:6
Klein, Harry T, 1965, Ja 26,37:1
Klein, Harry W, 1965, Ag 26,33:2
Klein, Henri F, 1944, D 1,23:2
Klein, Henry, 1952, Mr 20,29:5; 1960, D 11,88:8
Klein, Henry C, 1940, Jl 29,13:4; 1950, Mr 9,29:5
Klein, Henry Dr, 1952, My 31,17:5
Klein, Henry H, 1955, Jl 18,21:3
Klein, Henry J, 1937, O 11,21:5
Klein, Henry Mrs, 1944, S 28,19:5
Klein, Henry R, 1965, Ja 23,25:5
Klein, Herman, 1903, N 14,9:6
Klein, Howard F, 1967, Ja 18,43:2
Klein, Hyman (cor, N 29,25:5), 1954, N 28,87:2
Klein, I A, 1944, Ja 25,19:4
Klein, Irvin E, 1947, N 19,28:3
Klein, Irving, 1958, Je 8,88:8; 1966, Ap 18,29:2
Klein, Irving N, 1954, O 6,25:3; 1964, Ap 5,87:1; 1 D 21,37:1
Klein, Isaac H, 1919, Jl 6,20:4
Klein, Isaac Mrs, 1949, Je 7,31:3
Klein, Isadore, 1966, My 22,86:8
Klein, J Warren, 1957, Je 30,68:5
Klein, Jack, 1960, Mr 11,26:1
Klein, Jacob, 1943, O 7,23:4; 1948, Ap 15,25:5; 19 O 16,17:4
Klein, Jacob H Sr, 1937, Ap 17,17:5
Klein, Jacob M, 1946, F 8,19:3
Klein, Jacob Mrs, 1964, Ja 5,92:5
Klein, Johan Adam, 1875, My 30,7:1
Klein, John, 1940, Ap 27,15:2
Klein, John C, 1938, Ap 27,23:4
Klein, John F, 1945, D 5,25:5
Klein, John J, 1942, N 15,58:1
Klein, John M, 1956, Jl 19,27:4
Klein, John Mrs, 1943, Ja 6,25:2
Klein, Joseph, 1939, Mr 2,21:6; 1943, Ja 8,19:5; 1 Ag 28,23:2; 1949, Ag 17,23:6; 1949, D 14,31:1; F 4,31:4
Klein, Joseph C, 1949, Ag 26,20:4
Klein, Joseph Frederic, 1918, F 12,11:2
Klein, Joseph J Mrs, 1968, Mr 22,47:3
Klein, Joseph M, 1961, O 29,88:7
Klein, Joseph M Mrs, 1959, D 6,86:8
Klein, Julius, 1958, N 15,23:2; 1961, Je 16,33:2
Klein, Julius J, 1951, Ja 30,25:5
Klein, Kalman Mrs, 1952, Ag 17,77:1
Klein, Lazarus, 1954, O 5,27:2
Klein, Leo H, 1953, S 20,87:1
Klein, Leo L, 1962, Jl 25,33:5
Klein, Leo M, 1960, F 12,27:3
Klein, Leon, 1962, Ja 14,84:5
Klein, Leroy, 1963, Jl 8,29:4
Klein, Lester C (por), 1945, Mr 10,17:5
Klein, Lewis, 1943, O 9,13:5
Klein, Louis, 1938, Ja 11,23:4; 1939, Ja 20,19:3; O 25,17:3; 1942, Je 6,13:6
Klein, Louis A, 1953, Je 24,25:5
Klein, Louis J, 1945, Ap 17,23:2
Klein, Louis P, 1949, Mr 26,17:3
Klein, Ludwig, 1959, My 3,86:3
Klein, Manuel, 1919, Je 2,15:6
Klein, Martin A, 1955, Je 8,29:6
Klein, Martin Mrs, 1950, N 26,90:3
Klein, Mary E Mrs, 1940, Ag 6,19:5
Klein, Maurice, 1947, O 28,25:4
Klein, Maurice I, 1945, N 23,23:2
Klein, Maurice M, 1963, Ap 17,41:4
Klein, Max, 1945, Ja 11,23:4; 1957, Ap 2,31:1
Klein, Max M, 1955, Je 14,29:5
Klein, Max Mrs, 1956, Jl 5,25:3
Klein, Melanie, 1960, S 23,29:2
Klein, Michael, 1966, Jl 17,68:3
Klein, Mildred, 1939, N 14,23:2
Klein, Milton M (por), 1948, F 27,21:3
Klein, Murray, 1950, Je 8,31:5
Klein, Nat, 1955, Ja 19,27:4
Klein, Nicholas, 1951, O 23,29:5
Klein, Norman, 1948, O 31,88:5
Klein, Paul, 1964, My 13,47:5
Klein, Paul R, 1953, O 22,29:4
Klein, Peter, 1941, Je 29,32:7; 1942, Jl 20,13:4
Klein, Peter F, 1948, Jl 17,15:2
Klein, Randolph S, 1954, S 4,11:3
Klein, Regina, 1965, N 21,86:8
Klein, Richard A, 1962, My 14,29:4
Klein, Robert, 1941, Ag 29,17:4; 1958, Ap 10,2
Klein, Roelof, 1960, F 14,84:1
Klein, Roger H (ed), 1968, Jl 11,37:3
Klein, Rudolph M, 1937, Ap 15,17:2
Klein, Samuel, 1942, O 21,21:5; 1942, N 16,19: Ja 29,68:4; 1956, Ap 3,35:1; 1956, Jl 28,17:5
Klein, Samuel Dr, 1937, Ap 18,II,9:2
Klein, Samuel J, 1951, F 17,15:5
Klein, Samuel Mrs, 1955, N 21,29:5
Klein, Sarah Mrs, 1940, My 19,42:3
Klein, Sidney, 1958, Jl 30,29:1
Klein, Sigmund, 1950, O 23,23:1
Klein, Simon, 1938, Ja 9,43:2
Klein, Simon Mrs, 1944, O 26,23:5; 1948, Ap 1
Klein, Simon R, 1939, Ag 20,32:5
Klein, Sophie Mrs, 1951, My 27,68:1
Klein, W Royden Mrs, 1937, Ap 13,25:3
Klein, Walter A, 1947, Jl 15,23:3
Klein, William, 1942, D 4,25:6; 1954, O 11,27: Ja 18,37:2

Klein, William C Mrs, 1955, D 9,27:5
Klein, William G, 1943, O 23,13:4
Klein, William H, 1949, Ja 30,60:3
Klein, William I, 1949, D 2,29:3
Klein, William J, 1942, My 5,21:4
Klein, William L, 1957, Ja 4,23:2
Klein, William Mrs, 1942, Je 17,23:4
Kleinbardt, Ernest, 1962, Ja 8,39:5
Kleinbaum, Elihu N, 1967, Mr 16,47:4
Kleinberg, Chester E, 1961, Jl 24,23:3
Kleinberg, Samuel, 1957, S 7,19:2
Kleinberg, Samuel Mrs, 1941, F 10,17:3
Kleinberg, William, 1918, Ap 9,13:4
Kleinberger, Harry, 1947, Je 7,13:5
Kleindienst, Francis J, 1956, Jl 19,27:4
Kleindinst, Edgar L, 1939, N 30,21:3
Kleindinst, George G, 1960, Mr 23,37:2
Kleine, Anton G, 1957, S 25,29:4
Kleine, Frederick, 1953, Jl 22,27:2
Kleine, Gustave Mrs, 1947, Ap 28,23:3
Kleine, Henry E, 1941, Je 19,21:5
Kleine, Katherine E, 1944, Ja 5,17:4
Kleine, Walter F, 1944, Ja 5,17:1
Kleinelp, William Sr, 1950, D 24,34:1
Kleiner, Charles, 1943, N 13,13:5
Kleiner, George, 1960, Jl 18,27:5
Kleiner, Hugo P, 1963, D 16,33:4
Kleiner, Isaac L, 1947, Jl 6,41:2
Kleiner, Israel S, 1966, Je 12,86:6
Kleiner, Israel S Mrs, 1956, My 16,35:5
Kleiner, Rheinhart, 1949, My 13,23:4
Kleiner, Simon B, 1962, Jl 13,23:3
Kleinert, Emil J Sr, 1960, O 23,89:1
Kleinert, Harry I, 1953, D 19,15:2
Kleinert, Herminie E, 1943, Jl 28,15:3
Kleinfeld, Alfred, 1964, Mr 18,41:5
Kleinfeld, Edward I, 1960, O 20,35:4
Kleinfeld, Max, 1939, O 6,25:5; 1949, Jl 5,23:3
Kleinhans, Florence A, 1956, S 30,87:1
Kleinhans, Paul O, 1945, Ag 4,11:1
Kleinhans, Phil L Sr, 1949, D 25,26:7
Kleinhaus, Herman I, 1953, My 19,29:4
Kleinhaus, Samuel, 1940, Ag 6,19:4
Kleinholz, Frank Mrs, 1945, O 20,11:3
Kleinkauf, Henry, 1942, Ag 5,19:5
Kleinke, Norbert G, 1950, Mr 17,24:5
Kleinklaus, Louis J Mrs, 1967, Ap 25,43:2
Kleinle, Leroy J, 1957, Mr 11,25:1
Kleinman, Herman J, 1947, Ap 22,27:4
Kleinman, Jacob, 1946, Ag 11,45:1
Kleinman, Maurice, 1953, S 2,25:2
Kleinman, Moshe, 1948, N 30,27:2
Kleinman, Samuel, 1952, Ap 8,29:2
Kleinmann, Laura, 1960, D 3,23:6
Kleinoschegg, Willi, 1955, S 4,56:2
Kleinschmidt, Frank H, 1939, My 27,15:5
Kleinschmidt, Harry E, 1960, Jl 26,29:2
Kleinstub, Louis Mrs, 1949, My 14,13:6
Kleinwaks, Adolph, 1957, Je 15,17:6
Kleis, Phil Mrs, 1952, Jl 28,15:2
Kleiser, Clare, 1956, Je 18,25:1
Kleiser, George W, 1952, D 1,23:3
Kleiser, Grenville, 1953, S 1,23:3
Kleiser, Hugh N, 1946, O 17,23:1
Kleiser, Lorentz, 1963, My 30,17:2
Kleissler, Edward E Sr, 1950, D 20,31:1
Kleist, Daniel K, 1947, Ag 5,23:5
Kleist, Ewald von, 1954, N 6,17:3
Kleitsch, Joseph Mrs, 1950, Ag 6,73:2
Kleitz, George, 1941, Jl 26,15:2
Kleitz, William L, 1957, N 20,35:1
Klem, Bill Mrs, 1955, D 22,23:5
Klem, John W, 1949, F 10,27:1
Klem, William J (Bill), 1951, S 17,21:1
Klem, Xavier Mrs, 1950, Je 24,13:4
Klemann, George F, 1959, N 14,21:6
Klemann, John A, 1955, Jl 17,61:2
Klemann, Leonard R Rev, 1968, F 14,47:3
Klemanski, Leon, 1951, Ag 8,25:3
Klemas, Morris, 1959, Je 20,21:1
Klementis, William Mrs, 1945, Jl 16,11:7
Klemfuss, Harry C, 1961, F 17,24:5
Klemin, Alex, 1950, Mr 15,29:1
Klemke, John Mrs, 1939, Ja 19,19:2
Klemko, Henry F, 1950, N 1,35:3
Klemm, Frederick M, 1955, S 30,25:4
Klemm, Gustav, 1947, S 6,17:6
Klemm, Leroy A P, 1938, N 22,24:2
Klemm, Russell, 1948, Je 14,23:2
Klemm, Russell Mrs, 1963, Ap 18,35:3
Klemme, Ronald M, 1957, N 23,19:3
Klemmer, Conrad, 1956, Jl 25,29:2
Klemmer, Lee C, 1960, D 8,35:4
Klemmt, Maynard O, 1959, Mr 27,23:1
Klemperer, Charles, 1962, Mr 19,29:4
Klemperer, George, 1946, D 26,25:4
Klemperer, Paul, 1960, Jl 31,69:2; 1964, Mr 4,37:1
Klemperer, Ralph J, 1947, Ap 8,27:1
Klemperer, Wolfgang B, 1965, Mr 27,27:4
Klempin, August G, 1958, My 25,87:1
Klemyer, John De Witt Maj, 1914, Ja 30,9:5
Klenatic, Elizabeth, 1922, Jl 15,9:6

Klendon, Jack, 1952, Ap 13,77:2
Klenert, Abram, 1943, Mr 9,23:5
Klenert, Isadore V, 1963, S 20,33:4
Klenett, Louis B, 1946, S 28,17:5
Klenk, Louis P, 1946, My 13,21:3
Klenk, William R, 1954, D 30,17:1
Klenke, William, 1945, My 7,17:2
Klenke, William W, 1961, S 16,19:1
Klenner-Dombrowski, Rudolph Ferdinand von (Marquis of Patteri), 1914, Je 2,11:6
Klenze, Camillo von, 1943, Mr 19,19:1
Klepac, Joseph, 1959, My 26,35:5
Klepfer, Edward L, 1950, Ag 10,25:4
Klepp, Aug, 1941, My 13,23:2
Kleppe, Otto W, 1952, Ap 24,31:3
Kleppel, Isadore Mrs, 1968, O 22,47:2
Klepper, Arthur A, 1950, Ja 10,29:4
Klepper, Julius I, 1955, Je 16,31:5
Klepper, Julius I Mrs, 1960, Ja 17,86:5
Klepper, Max, 1947, N 19,27:3
Klepper, Max Francis, 1907, My 6,9:2
Klepper, Paul, 1946, Je 12,27:5
Klepper, William H, 1959, Je 27,23:4
Kleppner, Samuel, 1940, Ja 18,23:1
Kleppner, Samuel Mrs, 1955, Ap 19,31:2
Kleps, Albert F, 1947, O 11,17:2
Kleps, Albert F Mrs, 1948, Ag 16,19:5
Klerekoper, Jacgues, 1950, D 16,17:5
Klerr, Edward D, 1961, Ag 12,17:2
Kless, Michael J, 1944, Mr 14,19:1
Klett, Gottlieb Jr, 1952, S 3,29:2
Klett, Robert E, 1941, Ap 3,23:4
Klett, William H, 1948, Jl 29,21:5
Kletter, Louis, 1965, N 12,48:1
Klettke, William G, 1939, Ja 23,13:1
Kletzing, Elmer L, 1947, Ag 24,57:1
Kletzsch, Herman C, 1938, N 7,19:4
Kleufer, Harry B, 1951, Mr 16,31:1
Kleutgen, Francis K, 1953, D 10,47:4
Klevan, Oscar J, 1963, Jl 4,15:8
Kley, Alfred Mrs, 1945, F 13,23:5
Kliban, Louis Mrs, 1961, F 9,31:4
Klibscheidl, Uti I, 1955, N 23,23:3
Kliche, Curt, 1955, S 13,31:1
Klickmann, F Henri, 1966, Je 27,35:4
Kliefken, John W, 1944, F 3,19:2
Klieforth, Ralph G, 1966, Mr 22,41:3
Kliegl, A, 1927, My 21,19:6
Kliegl, Alfred H, 1967, My 11,47:2
Kliegl, Herbert A, 1968, O 6,84:7
Kliegl, John H, 1959, O 1,35:5
Kliegman, David, 1937, O 3,II,9:2
Kliegman, Joseph H, 1953, Ag 17,15:1
Kliene, Robert J H, 1945, Je 2,15:4
Klier, Roman, 1950, F 1,29:3
Kliesrath, Victor W (por), 1939, D 22,19:3
Kliger, Israel K, 1944, S 25,17:4
Kligman, David, 1966, D 8,47:4
Klikoff, Waldemar A, 1960, Ap 4,29:3
Klima, Frank E, 1949, N 8,31:2
Klimback, J Charles, 1957, Ag 3,15:6
Kliment, Gustav, 1953, O 23,23:4
Klimke, Alois, 1954, O 28,35:4
Klimm, Lester E, 1960, D 18,84:6
Klimoff, Wladimis A, 1941, S 26,23:5
Klimov, Vladimir Y, 1962, S 11,33:4
Klimper, Charles H, 1939, O 19,23:5
Klin, Alex G, 1951, Ap 22,88:4
Klinck, Arthur W, 1959, Ag 11,27:5
Klinck, Chris, 1903, Je 4,9:7
Klinck, Clarence, 1938, O 18,25:6
Klinck, Edwin G, 1950, Ag 8,29:3
Klinck, George, 1884, F 24,3:6
Klinck, Jacob C (por), 1944, O 18,21:1
Klinck, William, 1942, F 1,43:2
Kline, A L, 1930, O 14,25:3
Kline, Abbie L Mrs, 1939, My 9,24:3
Kline, Alan L, 1949, Je 30,23:5
Kline, Alice B, 1955, Je 12,87:1
Kline, Allan B, 1968, Je 16,68:6
Kline, Benjamin J, 1953, F 25,27:3
Kline, Bert F Sr, 1956, S 27,35:6
Kline, C Mahlon, 1967, Ap 4,43:5
Kline, Charles A Jr, 1961, D 16,25:3
Kline, Charles D Dr, 1937, N 4,25:5
Kline, Charles H, 1967, Mr 29,45:4
Kline, Charles Mrs, 1958, D 7,88:3
Kline, Charles T, 1956, Mr 29,27:3
Kline, Chester M, 1955, Je 12,87:1
Kline, E Hall, 1951, Ap 19,31:4
Kline, Edward J, 1958, Ap 2,31:3
Kline, Edwin, 1956, O 4,33:1
Kline, Eugene B, 1945, F 28,23:4
Kline, Francis A, 1947, D 8,25:4
Kline, Frank J, 1944, S 10,45:1
Kline, Franz, 1962, My 15,39:1
Kline, George, 1937, Ag 10,19:5; 1952, D 26,15:3
Kline, George W Rear-Adm, 1922, Je 29,15:5
Kline, H Eugene, 1945, S 27,21:5
Kline, Harry, 1964, Ap 18,29:5
Kline, Harry D, 1959, Jl 4,15:2
Kline, Henry B, 1951, N 3,17:5
Kline, Henry Mrs, 1948, Je 10,25:4

Kline, Homer J, 1940, Jl 23,19:2
Kline, Ira M, 1964, Ap 21,37:2
Kline, J Alex, 1951, My 18,27:3
Kline, J W, 1937, N 9,23:2
Kline, Jacob, 1957, D 18,35:1
Kline, Jacob Brig-Gen, 1908, Mr 24,7:5
Kline, James A, 1944, Ja 5,17:2
Kline, Jay C Mrs, 1956, Ja 6,23:3
Kline, John H, 1937, F 3,24:1
Kline, John M, 1950, F 4,15:6
Kline, John W, 1951, D 27,21:4
Kline, John W E, 1951, S 30,73:1
Kline, Joseph, 1908, F 5,7:5; 1951, Mr 23,21:2
Kline, Judson S, 1942, S 24,27:3
Kline, Juel W Mrs, 1953, Ag 6,21:5
Kline, Lester M Mrs, 1953, N 13,27:2
Kline, Lillian A, 1947, F 19,25:5
Kline, Mahlon N, 1909, N 28,11:5
Kline, Mahlon R, 1947, Ap 4,23:4
Kline, Mark A, 1940, Ap 26,21:3
Kline, Nathaniel Mrs, 1964, Mr 2,27:2
Kline, Nick, 1958, Jl 10,27:4
Kline, Percy E, 1951, Mr 10,13:4
Kline, Ray W, 1967, Ag 3,33:2
Kline, Raymond A, 1948, S 8,29:3
Kline, Rena Mrs, 1939, Mr 20,19:5
Kline, Richard Mrs, 1952, My 22,27:5
Kline, Robert F Mrs, 1948, Ap 4,60:3
Kline, Robert R, 1943, F 8,19:2
Kline, Russell, 1957, F 15,23:5
Kline, Samuel L, 1951, O 17,31:4
Kline, Samuel Mrs, 1960, Mr 31,33:4
Kline, Selden E, 1956, Mr 17,19:5
Kline, Sol, 1945, Ja 4,19:1
Kline, T D, 1904, Ja 11,7:6
Kline, Virgil C, 1966, My 27,43:4
Kline, Virgil P, 1917, Ja 19,7:3
Kline, Virginia, 1951, Mr 17,15:4
Kline, Webster H, 1951, N 21,25:2
Kline, Whorten A, 1946, N 21,31:3
Kline, William E Mrs, 1953, Je 19,21:4
Klinedinst, David P, 1940, S 25,27:3
Klinedinst, Louis M, 1953, Ag 11,27:3
Klinedinst, Milford S, 1960, F 8,29:2
Klinefelter, Harvey E, 1947, O 7,27:3
Klineman, David, 1959, Mr 17,33:2
Kling, Caroline Beatty Mrs, 1925, My 6,23:5
Kling, Charles, 1959, D 13,86:4
Kling, Edward Jr, 1954, Je 20,85:2
Kling, George, 1957, Ja 19,15:4
Kling, Gerald Clarke, 1915, S 20,9:5
Kling, Herman, 1941, Mr 29,15:6
Kling, Jehiel, 1960, Ag 23,29:2
Kling, John, 1947, F 1,15:5
Kling, John B, 1949, S 15,27:3
Kling, John J, 1954, O 6,25:3
Kling, Julius, 1959, Ag 24,21:3
Kling, Pearla S, 1950, My 18,29:3
Kling, Saxon, 1940, Jl 30,19:1
Kling, Vetalis H, 1938, Jl 2,13:5
Klingaman, Jacob L, 1966, Jl 6,42:1
Klingaman, Orie E, 1941, Ja 27,15:1
Klingbeil, Tobias, 1953, Je 6,17:5
Klingberg, John E, 1946, Je 8,21:6
Klinge, Gustave, 1940, Ap 28,36:4
Klinge, Johanna M, 1958, S 21,87:3
Klinge, John H, 1964, N 26,33:4
Klingelfuss, Paul F, 1968, Ap 16,47:2
Klingenberg, Alfred, 1944, S 12,19:5
Klingenberg, August, 1952, Ag 13,2:2
Klingenberger, Jerome J, 1954, Ja 27,27:1
Klingensmith, Frank L, 1949, Ag 29,17:3
Klingenstein, Conrad F, 1956, Ag 22,29:1
Klingenstein, Jacob Mrs, 1949, D 13,38:3
Klingenstein, William, 1961, N 4,19:5
Klinger, A A (Atwood A Klinger), 1967, F 24,35:1
Klinger, Harry, 1942, Ag 15,11:5
Klinger, Karle Mrs, 1949, Ap 26,26:3
Klinger, Louis, 1955, Ja 29,15:2
Klinger, Oliver C, 1954, Ap 24,17:4
Klinger, Paul T, 1944, S 17,42:2
Klinger, Philip Mrs, 1960, D 12,29:3
Klinger, William J Mrs, 1941, Ja 30,21:5
Klinghoffer, Isaac Mrs, 1951, F 24,13:2
Klinghoffer, Lawrence, 1954, My 16,86:4
Klinginsmith, John G, 1947, D 6,15:5
Klingle, Christine Mrs, 1949, Ag 25,23:5
Klingler, Albert, 1958, Mr 10,23:2
Klingler, Jay W, 1954, Jl 31,28:7
Klingman, William W, 1959, D 29,25:4
Klingsberg, Louis M, 1949, F 27,68:5
Klingsmith, Frank A, 1959, S 23,35:2
Klingstedt, Paul T, 1954, D 18,15:4
Klink, Agnes K Mrs, 1943, Ap 21,25:5
Klink, Emory J H, 1941, Ja 31,19:4
Klink, Joseph J Jr, 1946, D 3,32:3
Klinkerfues, E F W Prof, 1884, Ja 29,5:4
Klinkert, Jan R, 1965, D 23,28:7
Klinkhamer, Herman, 1939, N 25,19:7
Klinkhart, John W, 1943, Jl 9,17:3
Klinksick, Theodore, 1957, Mr 27,31:4
Klintworth, John P L, 1941, S 9,23:4
Klion, Samuel M, 1962, O 24,39:1

Kliot, Nathan, 1965, O 23,31:4
Klipfel, George J Rev, 1914, My 22,13:6
Klipp, Fred, 1939, Ja 16,15:4
Klippel, Lester B, 1940, S 30,17:3
Klipper, Harry, 1956, Ap 6,26:2
Klipstein, Ernest C, 1923, Ap 30,15:5
Klitgaard, Kaj E, 1954, Ja 1,23:2
Klitgord, Otto, 1960, Ap 21,31:1
Klithermes, William H, 1945, F 6,19:5
Klitsman, Meyer, 1958, D 9,41:4
Klitz, Robert H, 1948, Ap 27,25:2
Klitzner, Samuel L, 1960, S 6,35:3
Kloberg, Clara, 1949, D 15,35:4
Klobusicky, Andrew, 1957, O 22,33:4
Klock, John N, 1938, My 9,17:6
Klock, Joseph E, 1945, N 10,15:4
Klock, Paul R, 1950, Jl 17,21:4
Klocke, Eugene L, 1948, My 31,19:5
Klocke, John H, 1961, My 29,19:4
Klockson, George W, 1940, Ap 3,23:3
Kloeb, Charles A, 1909, O 26,9:5
Kloeble, Harry A, 1946, Jl 30,23:3
Kloeckner, Peter, 1940, O 7,18:2
Kloeppel, Robert, 1961, Jl 13,29:2
Klohr, Arthur P Mrs, 1957, Je 24,23:4
Kloizner, Jack Mrs, 1957, Jl 17,27:2
Kloman, Francis R, 1951, Je 21,27:2
Kloman, Henry F, 1942, Ag 30,42:6
Kloman, Young, 1909, F 5,7:5
Klonarakis, Emanuel, 1940, Ja 29,15:5
Klonis, Bernard, 1957, Je 22,15:4
Klooz, L Fred, 1939, F 5,40:5
Klopfer, Bertram, 1946, Ap 20,21:2
Klopfer, Hans M, 1961, Je 9,33:4
Klopp, Francis J, 1940, Je 26,23:3
Klopp, Henry I, 1945, Mr 9,19:4
Klopp, Onno, 1903, Ag 10,7:6
Klopsch, Louis Dr (mem, Ap 13,11:4), 1910, Mr 10, 9:4
Klopsch, Louis Mrs, 1943, My 23,42:3
Klopstock, Paul, 1946, My 5,44:4
Klorer, John D, 1951, Jl 17,27:1
Klorfein, Julius, 1958, N 29,21:1
Klose, Otto R W, 1943, My 9,40:7
Klosk, Herbert, 1963, S 23,29:5
Klosowiski, Laura Mrs, 1944, Ag 14,24:2
Kloss, Julius, 1956, Je 28,29:5
Kloss, William T, 1952, Jl 5,15:2
Klosterman, Julius A, 1963, O 5,25:2
Klosty, Lee, 1960, Jl 6,33:3
Klothe, Crawford S, 1948, F 25,23:5
Klothe, Edward C, 1949, D 10,17:6
Klots, Allen T, 1965, Ja 2,19:1
Klots, Henry D, 1914, Mr 20,11:5
Klotz, Anna S, 1959, Jl 29,29:1
Klotz, Clarence F Mrs, 1944, S 24,46:3
Klotz, Gustav F (G Sun), 1959, O 2,29:3
Klotz, Jack, 1957, Ap 14,86:8
Klotz, John R MacPherson, 1968, Ja 11,33:2
Klotz, Joseph, 1954, F 17,31:3
Klotz, L L, 1930, Je 16,21:3
Klotz, Louis, 1949, N 13,92:4
Klotz, Nathan, 1949, D 23,21:4
Klotz, Otto Dr, 1923, D 29,13:4
Klotz, Robert L, 1950, Ja 31,23:2
Klotz, Ruth, 1965, My 5,47:4
Klotz, Solon T, 1948, N 27,17:4
Klotz, Theodore, 1947, S 17,25:5
Klotz, Walter C, 1941, Jl 1,23:1
Klotzberger, Edward L, 1958, O 17,29:4
Klov, Emil N, 1946, Jl 30,23:5
Klovekorn, Joseph, 1948, D 18,19:4
Klubertanz, Ferdinand, 1940, S 5,23:4
Klubock, Abraham H, 1944, N 24,23:3
Klubock, Abraham H Mrs, 1944, S 21,19:3
Kluchitsky, Nicholas Prof, 1925, F 3,13:4
Kluck, A von, 1934, O 20,15:1
Kluckhohn, Carl F, 1952, Mr 18,27:5
Kluckholn, Clyde K M, 1960, Jl 30,17:1
Klue, Harold E Mrs, 1959, Je 6,21:5
Kluehs, Alfred, 1968, D 25,31:2
Kluepfel, Cornelius, 1960, F 13,19:4
Kluepfel, Karl, 1909, Je 27,7:5
Klug, Edward A, 1957, D 6,29:2
Klug, John J, 1944, Ja 4,17:5; 1948, Ap 6,23:5
Klug, Norman R, 1966, O 26,47:3
Klug, Otto, 1948, D 12,92:7
Kluge, Albert C, 1956, Je 29,21:2
Kluge, E H Mrs, 1953, O 17,15:5
Kluge, Edgar M, 1962, Ap 30,27:3
Kluge, Edward Theodore Rev, 1912, S 22,II,17:5
Kluge, Emile H, 1947, Ag 13,23:3
Kluge, Ernest J J, 1953, My 5,29:1
Kluge, Frederick, 1958, S 7,87:3
Kluge, Harry H, 1958, Jl 29,23:1
Kluge, Walter, 1954, F 18,31:4
Kluge, William Mrs, 1949, Mr 23,27:3
Kluger, Ernest Mrs, 1964, Ap 16,37:2
Kluger, Harry, 1937, F 14,II,9:1
Kluger, Harry Mrs, 1949, Ag 4,23:4
Klugescheid, Richard C, 1968, N 1,47:3
Klugh, Paul B, 1941, Jl 16,17:4
Klugherz, John A, 1953, Ag 30,60:4
Klugherz, Leo H, 1941, O 19,47:3
Klugman, Bornatt Mrs, 1955, S 4,56:6
Klugman, Jerome, 1948, Ja 30,23:4
Klugman, Samuel, 1943, Je 23,21:3
Klugmann, Joe, 1951, Jl 19,23:3
Kluin, Chris, 1949, Ap 28,31:2
Kluin, Herman Sr, 1951, Ja 14,84:3
Klukofsky, Eli (E Kaye), 1952, Ag 22,4:6
Klumback, Joseph J, 1945, Jl 24,23:4
Klump, Henry G, 1948, Je 27,52:5
Klumph, Arch C, 1951, Je 5,31:2
Klumpp, Carl S, 1947, D 19,25:1
Klumpp, Charles Mrs, 1962, S 16,86:5
Klumpp, Christian, 1937, Mr 9,23:1
Klumpp, Fred C, 1959, N 2,31:4
Klumpp, John B, 1955, Mr 31,27:3
Klumpp, Margaret M, 1965, My 3,33:1
Klunder, John S, 1947, My 18,60:3
Klune, Frederick C, 1938, O 26,23:4
Klurfeld, Arthur M, 1961, Ag 4,21:5
Klusmeier, William H, 1948, N 29,23:2
Klusmeyer, George H, 1949, D 13,31:2
Klusmeyer, William (por), 1941, S 19,23:3
Kluss, Charles L, 1967, Ag 8,39:3
Kluth, Charles R Jr, 1966, Ap 26,45:1
Kluth, Robert, 1921, S 24,11:4
Kluttz, Adam A Mrs, 1947, Je 1,62:6
Klyman, Julius, 1963, Je 2,84:5
Klyver, Henry P, 1940, Je 23,31:1
Kmetz, John, 1950, N 19,93:2
Kmetz, John T, 1968, Jl 31,27:1
Knab, Max, 1954, Mr 27,17:4
Knabb, Howard M, 1950, Je 25,68:3
Knabbe, Frederick, 1945, My 25,19:2
Knabe, Henry A, 1951, Ja 26,23:2
Knabe, Martin C Jr, 1941, Ag 8,26:3
Knabe, Richard D, 1903, Je 21,7:6
Knabe, William, 1939, Mr 1,21:5
Knabenshue, Frederick G, 1953, Je 27,15:2
Knabenshue, Paul (por), 1942, F 2,15:3
Knabenshue, Roy, 1960, Mr 7,29:3
Knack, Frank P, 1954, D 22,23:2
Knack, Frederick J, 1965, Ap 25,88:7
Knacke, Mathilda R Mrs, 1942, Je 10,21:3
Knaebel, Ernest, 1947, F 20,25:5
Knaggs, Donald W, 1958, D 29,15:4
Knaizik, Michael, 1951, N 23,29:2
Knakal, Anton, 1953, My 27,31:3
Knall, David E, 1939, Je 13,23:3
Knandel, Clyde Mrs, 1960, Je 25,21:5
Knap, Joseph D, 1962, Ja 20,21:3
Knaplund, Paul A, 1964, Ap 11,25:3
Knapp, A L, 1881, My 25,4:7
Knapp, Ada M Mrs, 1948, O 26,31:2
Knapp, Alfred H, 1949, Ja 3,23:4
Knapp, Alfred M, 1951, Mr 13,31:3
Knapp, Alice S Mrs (will), 1962, Ja 17,8 4
Knapp, Allen A, 1946, D 5,31:1
Knapp, Andrew S, 1961, Mr 10,27:5
Knapp, Anna, 1938, F 13,II,7:2
Knapp, Arnold H, 1956, Mr 1,34:1
Knapp, Arthur Blair Dr, 1968, My 15,47:3
Knapp, Arthur E, 1965, My 16,88:3
Knapp, Arthur Mrs, 1954, S 4,11:5
Knapp, Arthur Sr, 1946, Je 23,40:2
Knapp, Augustus, 1917, Jl 30,9:6
Knapp, Benjamin G, 1960, Ja 5,31:2
Knapp, Bradford, 1938, Je 12,38:8
Knapp, C Stanley, 1960, Jl 7,31:3
Knapp, Charles H, 1925, Ja 30,17:4
Knapp, Charles J, 1916, Je 2,11:5; 1946, Ag 2,19:4
Knapp, Charles N, 1965, Ag 20,29:2
Knapp, Charles O, 1956, N 29,35:4
Knapp, Charles S, 1943, Ag 9,13:6; 1950, Ap 21,23:2
Knapp, Charles W, 1953, S 16,33:4
Knapp, Charles W Mrs, 1916, D 8,9:2
Knapp, Charles Welbourne (por),(funl, Ja 8,9:5), 1916, Ja 7,13:1
Knapp, Christine B Mrs, 1937, Jl 20,23:6
Knapp, Clarence Mrs, 1944, Ap 28,19:3
Knapp, Clarence V, 1950, Ap 10,19:1
Knapp, Clifford S, 1950, Ja 31,23:3
Knapp, Clyde W, 1940, F 2,17:3
Knapp, Cyrus Dr, 1871, S 26,8:2
Knapp, David, 1958, Ap 26,19:6
Knapp, David V, 1943, O 18,15:4
Knapp, David V Mrs, 1944, Je 2,15:4
Knapp, David W, 1951, N 25,86:2
Knapp, Deloss, 1952, D 16,31:4
Knapp, Dorothy H, 1945, Ag 21,11:5
Knapp, Dorothy M, 1950, Je 23,25:1
Knapp, Edgar A, 1945, Jl 31,19:4
Knapp, Edward, 1939, Jl 19,19:5
Knapp, Edward A, 1951, My 22,31:1
Knapp, Edward J, 1925, N 20,21:1; 1944, Ja 12,23:4
Knapp, Edward Mrs, 1949, Je 15,29:3
Knapp, Edward S, 1940, Ap 6,17:7
Knapp, Edward S Mrs, 1938, D 1,23:4
Knapp, Edwin L, 1938, D 30,15:1
Knapp, Edwin N, 1955, Je 15,31:5
Knapp, Edwin R, 1952, Mr 27,29:4
Knapp, Elder Jacob, 1874, Mr 5,5:3
Knapp, Enos Mrs, 1949, Jl 16,13:5
Knapp, F H, 1883, Je 24,7:4
Knapp, Florence Mrs (por), 1949, O 27,27:5
Knapp, Frances L, 1941, Ag 1,15:3
Knapp, Frank, 1947, F 11,27:1
Knapp, Frank A, 1937, O 26,23:4
Knapp, Frank S, 1949, N 5,13:4
Knapp, Fred, 1939, Jl 2,15:3
Knapp, Fred A, 1960, My 22,86:4
Knapp, Fred D, 1941, Ap 29,19:4
Knapp, Frederick C, 1946, Ag 13,27:4
Knapp, Frederick H, 1955, Mr 16,33:1
Knapp, G, 1883, S 27,1:7
Knapp, George E, 1944, Mr 24,19:5
Knapp, George H, 1925, Ap 10,19:4; 1944, S 20,23:2; 1952, Ja 10,29:1
Knapp, George O, 1945, Jl 24,23:3
Knapp, George O Mrs, 1924, N 11,23:2
Knapp, George Perkins Rev, 1915, O 2,11:2
Knapp, George S, 1940, Jl 9,21:4; 1947, Ja 5,53:5
Knapp, Georgia, 1946, O 30,27:3
Knapp, Gilbert H, 1958, Mr 8,17:5
Knapp, Gilbert H Mrs, 1957, Jl 24,25:3
Knapp, Gunther, 1953, Ag 3,5:6
Knapp, H G, 1881, O 19,5:5
Knapp, Harold A, 1938, Mr 25,19:1
Knapp, Harold D, 1946, Je 3,21:3
Knapp, Harold J, 1955, Ja 26,25:3
Knapp, Harold L, 1949, O 26,27:5
Knapp, Harry J, 1944, D 19,21:2
Knapp, Harry K, 1943, D 19,49:2
Knapp, Harry S Rear-Adm (funl, Ap 10,12:5), 192 Ap 7,13:6
Knapp, Herman Dr, 1911, My 2,11:4
Knapp, Hiram M, 1942, Mr 25,21:2
Knapp, Homer, 1941, D 9,31:2
Knapp, Horace J, 1914, F 7,11:5
Knapp, Howard A, 1955, My 27,23:1
Knapp, Howard W, 1945, O 19,23:5
Knapp, J F, 1884, D 17,2:3
Knapp, J M, 1926, D 17,23:4
Knapp, J Maxwell, 1953, S 16,33:2
Knapp, James B, 1943, Je 11,19:3
Knapp, James G, 1912, F 11,II,13:3
Knapp, James H, 1939, Jl 1,17:6
Knapp, James L, 1943, Ja 15,17:2
Knapp, John A, 1939, F 4,15:3
Knapp, John B, 1958, Mr 13,29:3
Knapp, John C, 1944, My 15,19:6
Knapp, John D, 1941, O 5,49:2
Knapp, John H, 1938, D 4,61:2
Knapp, John Joseph Capt, 1915, S 28,13:5
Knapp, John L, 1940, My 24,19:3
Knapp, John W, 1941, F 25,23:5
Knapp, Joseph F, 1952, O 24,23:1
Knapp, Joseph P, 1951, Ja 31,25:1
Knapp, Joseph P Mrs, 1960, Ja 6,35:1
Knapp, Joseph W, 1954, D 22,23:2
Knapp, Karl W, 1958, Ap 28,23:3
Knapp, Kemper K, 1944, F 24,15:3
Knapp, Kemper K (will), 1944, Mr 4,6:7
Knapp, Kemper K (will), 1944, My 17,21:8
Knapp, Lawrence C Mrs, 1950, Ap 7,25:2
Knapp, Leo A Mrs, 1966, N 27,87:1
Knapp, Leslie M, 1959, S 29,36:2
Knapp, Lewis H, 1938, Ag 26,17:5
Knapp, Lorenzo H, 1955, S 21,33:2
Knapp, Malcolm H, 1951, Ap 7,15:6
Knapp, Margaret E Mrs, 1939, My 24,23:4
Knapp, Martin A Judge, 1923, F 11,6:2
Knapp, Mary A Mrs, 1938, N 27,49:1
Knapp, Matthew G, 1946, Mr 30,15:1
Knapp, Maurice, 1966, Mr 15,39:1
Knapp, McKinstry Amos Dr, 1917, N 2,15:4
Knapp, Morgan C, 1959, O 7,43:1
Knapp, Nathaniel, 1941, F 7,19:5
Knapp, Otto, 1918, Mr 18,13:5
Knapp, Richard E, 1960, Mr 10,31:1
Knapp, Robert D Mrs, 1950, Mr 19,95:3
Knapp, Robert P, 1954, Mr 16,29:5
Knapp, Robert T, 1957, N 8,29:2
Knapp, S F Jr, 1882, O 28,2:6
Knapp, Sanford Reynolds, 1922, Ap 18,17:4
Knapp, Sarah E Mrs, 1942, My 9,13:2
Knapp, Seaman Asahel Dr, 1911, Ap 3,9:5
Knapp, Shepherd, 1946, Ja 13,43:1
Knapp, Sheppard, 1906, O 27,9:6
Knapp, Sidney M, 1948, Ja 5,19:5
Knapp, Susan T, 1941, N 25,25:2
Knapp, Thomas P Mrs, 1950, D 26,23:3
Knapp, Vernon W, 1945, My 15,19:3
Knapp, Virgil T J, 1944, F 4,15:2
Knapp, W Gray, 1948, Ap 22,27:2
Knapp, Walter H, 1944, D 15,19:4; 1951, Ja 26,
Knapp, Walter R, 1952, Je 29,59:6
Knapp, William, 1875, S 14,4:7
Knapp, William H, 1945, My 25,19:2
Knapp, William Ireland Prof, 1908, D 7,9:5
Knapp, William J, 1947, Jl 21,17:2
Knapp, William R, 1874, Ap 11,1:4
Knapp, Woodford H, 1944, Ap 11,19:3
Knapp, Zachariah, 1939, Jl 6,23:1
Knapp-Fisher, Edward, 1940, D 1,62:6
Knapp Phil N Mrs, 1955, S 13,31:1

Knappe, Adolph H, 1964, Ag 13,32:5
Knappe, Leo J, 1948, F 2,20:2
Knappek, Paul G, 1964, My 6,47:1
Knappen, Frank J, 1943, Mr 1,19:3
Knappen, Theodore T, 1951, Mr 22,31:1
Knapper, Joseph S, 1954, My 6,33:4
Knapperberger, William Mrs, 1952, Ja 6,93:1
Knappert, Laurentius, 1943, Jl 14,19:2
Knappertsbusch, Hans, 1965, O 27,47:2
Knappmann, George W, 1937, N 27,17:3
Knaub, William L, 1947, S 30,25:2
Knauer, Anna M Mrs, 1941, F 27,19:3
Knauer, Arthur F, 1963, Ap 29,31:2
Knauer, Carroll, 1951, F 21,27:1
Knauer, Charles H, 1950, Mr 24,25:1
Knauer, George Sr, 1957, N 17,86:6
Knauf, George M Dr, 1968, Je 21,41:2
Knauf, Henry, 1950, Ap 17,24:3
Knauff, Carl G B, 1944, N 2,19:1
Knauff, William A, 1948, Mr 28,48:5
Knaufft, Ernest, 1942, Ap 23,23:3
Knauft, Edwin R, 1952, Ap 3,36:3
Knaupp, John F, 1948, Jl 7,46:4
Knaur, Richard I Mrs, 1948, My 10,21:3
Knaus, G Norman, 1956, Mr 30,19:4
Knaus, William A Mrs, 1948, N 1,23:4
Knauss, Edward G, 1954, Ag 24,21:3
Knauss, Frederic E, 1958, Je 11,35:2
Knauss, Harrison E, 1938, Ja 3,21:4
Knauss, Samuel M, 1944, Ap 4,21:5
Knauss, William F, 1951, S 30,73:1
Knauss, William H, 1953, Je 17,27:3
Knauth, Arnold W, 1960, O 15,23:3
Knauth, Oswald W, 1962, Jl 14,21:2
Knauth, Oswald W Mrs, 1965, Ap 12,35:2
Knauth, Percival Mrs, 1946, Ag 31,15:6
Knauth, Theodore W, 1962, N 15,37:5
Knawa, William A, 1949, Je 19,68:2
Kneass, Edward D, 1954, O 29,21:3
Kneath, Watkin W, 1948, Ja 5,19:2
Knebel, A G (por), 1938, Ap 23,15:4
Knebel, Charles T, 1950, Ag 18,21:2
Knebel, Mark P, 1943, F 5,21:4
Knebelkamp, C H, 1939, Je 4,48:6
Knecht, Albert A, 1954, D 7,33:4
Knecht, Bessie, 1903, N 10,5:6
Knecht, Edwin K, 1959, Ag 6,27:4
Knecht, Eugene (will), 1945, Ja 25,21:1
Knecht, George G, 1952, O 10,25:1
Knecht, Harry, 1940, Jl 31,17:2
Knecht, Harry I, 1966, Je 20,30:4
Knecht, Louis, 1941, O 20,18:2
Knecht, Peter J, 1941, Ap 20,44:1
Knecht, Sigmund, 1952, Ja 5,11:4
Knecht, William F, 1949, F 26,15:4
Kneedler, Benjamin L, 1954, O 8,23:1
Kneedler, Henry M, 1939, Ap 16,III,7:2
Kneeland, Adele, 1937, S 17,25:3
Kneeland, Elbert W (por), 1941, My 21,23:2
Kneeland, Frederick R, 1943, N 10,23:5
Kneeland, Herbert A, 1951, O 17,31:4
Kneeland, James K, 1958, Mr 19,31:1
Kneeland, S F Gen, 1926, Ag 31,17:3
Kneeland, Yale Mrs, 1955, F 24,27:1
Kneely, Capt (A M Hitchcock), 1883, Mr 22,5:5
Kneip, Herbert J, 1955, Ap 30,17:1
Kneip, William, 1945, F 3,11:5
Kneipp, S Father, 1897, My 22,7:3
Kneisel, Carl, 1946, Ag 6,25:4
Kneissl, Robert L, 1944, D 28,19:5
Kneitel, Frances S, 1960, S 13,37:3
Kneitel, Seymour H (cor, Ag 1,21:4), 1964, Jl 31,24:1
Knell, Frank J, 1968, N 8,47:2
Knell, G Robert Mrs, 1957, O 6,84:7
Knell, John, 1962, Jl 18,29:5
Knell, William V, 1945, My 25,19:2
Kneloff, Max, 1922, My 8,17:4
Kneloff, Max Mrs, 1922, My 8,17:4
Knepp, James W, 1953, Je 13,15:5
Kneppenberg, Henry C Jr, 1948, N 5,25:2
Knepper, George E, 1940, Ja 8,15:4
Knepper, Harry H, 1941, S 10,23:6
Knepper, Henry, 1958, Je 25,29:3
Knepper, Herman (por), 1946, Ap 21,45:1
Knerr, Calvin B, 1940, S 30,17:6
Knerr, George H, 1953, Mr 18,31:6
Knerr, Harold H (por), 1949, Jl 9,13:4
Kneser, William W, 1951, F 23,27:3
Knetsch, Nancy (funl, Ap 14,24:2), 1966, Ap 12,32:5
Knetzer, John E, 1959, Jl 11,19:4
Kneuer, Anne E, 1960, Ja 29,25:4
Knevals, Emily (est tax appr), 1954, S 17,12:6
Knevals, Sherman W, 1908, D 5,9:2
Knevels, Gertrude, 1962, Ap 8,86:5
Knevels, John W, 1952, F 20,29:3
Knevels, Mary E, 1957, Ja 22,29:2
Knewitz, John J (funl, Mr 14,29:2), 1957, Mr 11,25:4
Knibbs, James, 1901, Ap 17,9:5
Knibbs, John W Jr, 1953, Jl 7,27:2
Knickerbacher, J F, 1882, N 17,5:2
Knickerbacker, John, 1947, Je 17,25:4
Knickerbocker, A B, 1951, O 8,41:1
Knickerbocker, A B Mrs, 1951, O 8,41:1
Knickerbocker, Charles K, 1940, Ja 8,15:5
Knickerbocker, Cholly (M H B Paul), 1942, Jl 18, 13:5
Knickerbocker, Clair B, 1943, O 21,27:2
Knickerbocker, Curtis E, 1942, F 16,17:5
Knickerbocker, Edwin Van Berghen, 1968, S 11,47:2
Knickerbocker, Frank D, 1967, Je 22,39:2
Knickerbocker, Frederick H, 1955, My 27,23:3
Knickerbocker, H R Mrs, 1949, Ja 6,23:5
Knickerbocker, Harry H, 1948, My 11,25:2
Knickerbocker, Henry J Mrs, 1943, Ja 3,42:3
Knickerbocker, Herman, 1908, D 15,9:5
Knickerbocker, Hubert Renfro, 1949, Jl 13,1:8
Knickerbocker, McClellan, 1948, N 6,13:4
Knickerbocker, Patrick J Mrs, 1959, O 20,39:3
Knickerbocker, Reginald C, 1942, Je 23,19:5
Knickerbocker, Stephen H, 1943, Jl 23,17:3
Knickerbocker, Thomas A, 1922, N 9,19:3
Knickerbocker, William E, 1960, D 22,23:4
Knickerbocker, William H, 1937, D 4,17:3
Knickerbocker, William L Mrs, 1968, Ap 18,47:4
Kniepen, Ernest J, 1946, D 30,19:4
Knieriem, John Capt, 1903, Jl 30,7:6
Knieriemen, Norma H, 1959, Mr 20,32:1
Knierim, Harry M Mrs, 1947, Ag 26,23:4
Knies, Arthur C, 1948, F 28,15:4
Knies, George J, 1949, Ja 19,27:4
Kniffen, Harry, 1939, Jl 13,19:5
Kniffen, Richard Mrs, 1957, Ag 14,25:4
Kniffin, Charles, 1938, D 21,23:4; 1946, My 8,25:6
Kniffin, Charles D, 1951, Jl 4,17:4
Kniffin, Edgar A Mrs, 1957, Ap 5,27:3
Kniffin, Edward W, 1952, Jl 22,25:4
Kniffin, George H, 1948, Je 15,27:4
Kniffin, Howard S Mrs, 1957, N 12,37:1
Kniffin, Paul P, 1961, Ag 22,29:1
Kniffin, William H, 1951, Mr 1,28:2
Knight, A L, 1906, Mr 7,9:5
Knight, A Russell, 1962, O 21,89:2
Knight, Alex, 1937, Ag 1,II,7:2
Knight, Alfred, 1958, N 1,19:4
Knight, Alice Gilman, 1919, F 26,11:4
Knight, Alonzo B, 1923, Ag 4,13:4
Knight, Alson, 1903, Ap 19,7:4
Knight, Althea B, 1921, N 1,19:4
Knight, Arch S, 1938, Ag 29,13:6; 1939, Je 30,19:1
Knight, Arthur A, 1948, S 7,25:1
Knight, Arthur H, 1937, Je 9,25:3
Knight, Arthur R, 1958, F 2,86:4
Knight, Arthur S Mrs, 1951, N 21,25:4
Knight, B Jay Mrs, 1963, Jl 6,15:3
Knight, C Carroll, 1957, My 21,35:5
Knight, Carl D, 1940, F 29,19:4
Knight, Casper, 1948, Jl 1,23:1
Knight, Charles A, 1950, O 23,23:1
Knight, Charles A Mrs, 1938, Mr 5,17:3
Knight, Charles C, 1950, S 26,31:2
Knight, Charles H, 1958, Ap 16,33:2
Knight, Charles L Mrs, 1965, N 13,29:1
Knight, Charles P, 1961, My 26,33:4
Knight, Charles R, 1953, Ap 17,25:3
Knight, Charles R Mrs, 1957, Jl 13,17:5
Knight, Charles Wesley, 1925, Ag 19,19:7
Knight, Charles Y, 1940, My 10,23:3
Knight, Clara C, 1946, Ja 3,20:2
Knight, Clarence D, 1945, Je 15,19:4
Knight, Clarence S, 1944, O 31,19:5
Knight, Claud B Mrs, 1955, D 11,88:5
Knight, Clifford, 1957, D 26,19:4
Knight, Daniel J, 1940, O 24,25:4
Knight, Daniel Ridgway, 1924, Mr 10,15:4
Knight, Daniel Ridgway Mrs, 1909, Ag 16,7:5
Knight, David G Jr, 1948, N 18,28:2
Knight, E R Dr, 1883, Ja 24,5:5
Knight, Earl W, 1948, Ag 1,57:2
Knight, Edgar W, 1953, Ag 8,11:1
Knight, Edward A, 1937, Ap 11,II,8:7
Knight, Edward F (por), 1949, F 26,15:3
Knight, Edward H, 1948, F 29,60:3
Knight, Edward J Bp, 1908, N 18,9:2
Knight, Edward J Rev, 1908, N 16,9:6
Knight, Edwin B, 1949, Jl 26,27:1
Knight, Erastus C, 1923, S 4,17:3
Knight, F E, 1903, My 5,9:6
Knight, F H, 1903, Je 2,9:7
Knight, Floyd A, 1948, N 10,29:3
Knight, Frank A, 1956, Jl 7,13:5
Knight, Frank H Dr, 1918, N 23,11:2
Knight, Frank M, 1958, Ag 4,21:2
Knight, Frank McL, 1958, Mr 10,23:2
Knight, Frank R, 1945, Ja 16,19:5
Knight, Fred M, 1960, My 24,37:1
Knight, Fred W, 1946, Ap 10,27:1
Knight, Frederic B, 1948, Je 21,21:4
Knight, Frederick H Maj, 1922, S 18,13:5
Knight, Frederick J Mrs, 1943, My 9,40:4
Knight, Frederick Mrs, 1963, Je 27,33:4
Knight, Frederick S, 1950, D 6,33:3
Knight, Frederick T, 1948, Mr 11,27:1
Knight, G Laurence Mrs, 1941, My 11,44:5
Knight, G W, 1932, F 11,22:1
Knight, Galen V, 1950, Ag 1,23:4
Knight, Gardner F, 1962, Ap 19,31:1
Knight, George, 1951, S 25,29:3
Knight, George A, 1916, Je 28,11:4
Knight, George A Sr, 1946, F 19,25:5
Knight, George L (por), 1948, Mr 29,21:4
Knight, George T Rev, 1911, S 11,9:4
Knight, George W, 1937, F 12,23:6; 1952, My 16,23:4; 1959, F 5,31:3
Knight, Gerald W (por), 1937, Ap 12,17:3
Knight, Goodwin J Mrs, 1952, O 30,31:2
Knight, Gordon F, 1961, F 4,19:5
Knight, H Stanley, 1947, Je 9,21:1
Knight, Harold, 1961, O 5,37:4
Knight, Harold A, 1954, N 3,29:3
Knight, Harry C, 1949, Jl 21,26:2
Knight, Harry E, 1951, Mr 14,33:5; 1953, Mr 23,23:3
Knight, Harry H, 1948, Je 30,26:3
Knight, Harry S Mrs, 1945, Je 4,19:5
Knight, Henry, 1949, Ag 16,23:4
Knight, Henry B, 1960, F 11,36:1
Knight, Henry G, 1942, Jl 14,20:5
Knight, Henry H, 1959, Mr 8,86:5
Knight, Henry L, 1944, Ja 28,17:3
Knight, Henry W, 1917, Jl 4,9:7
Knight, Herbert M, 1948, Ag 20,17:2
Knight, Herbert W, 1953, Ja 15,27:4
Knight, Horace D, 1951, F 11,88:4
Knight, Howard R (por), 1947, O 8,25:1
Knight, I W, 1939, Ap 11,24:4
Knight, Ira W, 1959, F 18,33:3
Knight, J K Col, 1903, Ag 23,7:5
Knight, J P, 1881, Mr 29,4:7
Knight, J Stephen, 1961, Ja 6,27:2
Knight, Jack, 1945, F 26,19:4
Knight, James, 1939, Ap 19,23:4
Knight, James M, 1950, F 14,25:4
Knight, Jesse A, 1947, D 15,22:7
Knight, Jesse Judge, 1905, Ap 10,9:5
Knight, John, 1955, Je 16,31:1; 1956, Jl 10,31:5; 1964, Je 12,35:2
Knight, John A, 1966, Ap 9,25:3
Knight, John C, 1952, Ja 12,13:3
Knight, John E, 1946, F 21,21:4
Knight, John E Mrs, 1950, Mr 24,25:1
Knight, John George David Brig-Gen, 1919, Je 10,13:4
Knight, John Lindmark Capt, 1912, Mr 6,11:4
Knight, John O Mrs, 1940, Ag 2,15:5
Knight, Jonathan Dr, 1864, Ag 28,4:6
Knight, Joseph D, 1951, Jl 10,27:4
Knight, Joseph H, 1942, N 4,24:2
Knight, Joseph S, 1946, N 11,27:1
Knight, Josephine, 1937, F 17,22:2
Knight, L Aston (por), 1948, My 9,68:3
Knight, Lillian Mrs, 1950, O 17,31:2
Knight, Lora J, 1945, Je 28,19:2
Knight, Mary M, 1949, N 11,25:2
Knight, Melvin C, 1955, Ap 28,29:3
Knight, Milton, 1905, Mr 28,9:4
Knight, Montgomery, 1943, Jl 26,19:5
Knight, Newell C, 1946, Mr 14,25:1
Knight, Norbert E, 1949, Ag 1,19:3
Knight, Ora W Dr, 1913, N 12,9:7
Knight, Paul K, 1957, Ag 25,86:7
Knight, Percival, 1923, N 29,21:4
Knight, Peter A, 1941, F 4,21:1
Knight, Peter O (por), 1946, N 27,25:4
Knight, Raymond, 1953, F 13,22:5
Knight, Richard, 1947, D 6,15:3
Knight, Richard A, 1943, Mr 8,15:4
Knight, Richard V, 1949, O 31,25:5
Knight, Robert, 1912, N 27,13:6; 1950, Mr 10,27:3
Knight, Robert A, 1958, Ap 14,27:4
Knight, Robert A Mrs, 1942, Jl 9,21:5
Knight, Robert P, 1966, My 1,88:6
Knight, Rufus S, 1949, F 13,76:3
Knight, Samuel, 1943, Ja 29,19:4
Knight, Sarah A (est), 1914, Je 12,13:4
Knight, Seymour H, 1954, O 21,27:1
Knight, Silas Partridge, 1919, Je 14,13:6
Knight, Sophie A C Mrs, 1939, Ja 18,19:2
Knight, T R, 1956, Mr 16,23:2
Knight, Theodore, 1954, N 24,23:5
Knight, Thomas D, 1938, Ap 29,21:2
Knight, Thomas E Jr Lt-Gov, 1937, My 18,23:1
Knight, Thomas W, 1911, Ja 20,11:4
Knight, Walker C, 1952, Je 6,23:4
Knight, Walter D, 1959, Ja 28,31:2
Knight, Walter H, 1946, Jl 17,23:4
Knight, Walter J Mrs, 1950, D 1,25:6
Knight, Webster 2d Mrs, 1965, O 30,35:2
Knight, Wilbur Clinton Dr, 1903, Jl 30,7:6
Knight, Willard C, 1915, N 27,15:5
Knight, William, 1944, D 29,15:3
Knight, William A, 1957, F 12,27:4
Knight, William Angus Prof, 1916, Mr 5,21:6
Knight, William B, 1945, Jl 2,15:4
Knight, William D, 1959, Ap 30,31:4
Knight, William Henry, 1925, My 14,19:2
Knight, William R, 1943, Mr 9,23:4
Knighten, Lauana, 1956, S 24,27:2
Knighton, Bert M, 1961, O 8,87:2
Knighton, John A, 1954, Ag 20,19:4
Knighton, John A Mrs, 1956, D 17,31:1
Knighton, Samuel, 1939, Jl 28,17:6

Knighton, Willis S, 1964, Ap 9,31:3
Knights, Charles C, 1963, My 13,29:2
Knights, Ernest G, 1956, O 10,39:4
Knightsmith, W, 1932, F 14,29:1
Kniley, John Mrs, 1941, Mr 24,17:5
Kniola, Michael P, 1944, S 19,21:4
Knipe, Alden A, 1950, Mr 24,30:2
Knipe, Alden A Mrs, 1958, O 26,88:5
Knipe, David, 1953, Mr 4,27:4
Knipe, George Dr, 1921, Ja 6,11:3
Knipe, Isobel, 1967, Ap 20,44:1
Knipe, J F Gen, 1901, Ag 19,7:6
Knipe, James Nelson Rev, 1924, F 3,23:1
Knipe, John R, 1939, Ag 1,19:3
Knipe, Joseph B, 1946, S 5,27:4; 1951, O 5,27:4
Knipe, Norman L, 1961, Jl 25,28:2
Knipe, William H, 1959, My 29,23:3
Knipp, Charles T, 1948, Jl 9,20:2
Knippenberg, John G, 1944, My 2,19:6
Knisell, Sidney L, 1941, Ag 8,15:4
Knisely, J Herman, 1937, Jl 1,27:5
Knisely, Oscar E, 1940, Ja 10,21:3
Kniskern, Frank, 1938, N 21,19:6
Kniskern, Leslie A, 1961, Mr 21,37:3
Kniskern, Philip W, 1961, My 21,86:6
Knispel, Christian J, 1951, D 20,31:3
Knitel, Maximilian R, 1954, Mr 15,25:4
Knittle, Earl J Mrs, 1955, N 18,25:3
Knittle, John F, 1949, My 31,23:3
Knittle, Verdie J, 1940, S 6,21:4
Knittle, Walter A (por), 1948, Je 19,15:3
Kniveton, James, 1956, N 14,35:4
Knize, Frederick, 1949, O 29,15:6
Knob, Fred J, 1952, N 13,31:2
Knobel, Frederick J, 1949, Ag 24,26:5
Knobel, John R, 1951, S 7,29:5
Knobel, Morris, 1964, S 19,27:4
Knoblauch, C E, 1934, O 12,25:4
Knoblauch, Charles E Mrs, 1950, N 29,33:3
Knoblauch, David C, 1955, F 20,88:8
Knoblauch, Frederick F, 1955, Jl 14,23:5
Knoblauch, Frederick F Jr, 1949, D 25,26:6
Knoble, Charles E, 1941, F 4,21:1
Knobloch, David C, 1967, Mr 2,35:2
Knobloch, Edward G Mrs, 1942, Je 17,23:3
Knobloch, Harry F X, 1960, Ag 17,31:3
Knobloch, Valentine, 1948, F 3,25:3
Knoblock, Edward (por), 1945, Jl 20,19:4
Knoblock, Morris, 1945, D 29,13:3
Knoch, Ernst, 1959, Mr 22,87:1
Knoch, Leland, 1942, My 3,53:1
Knoch, Ulrich, 1945, D 5,25:2
Knoche, G Alfred Mrs, 1941, My 24,15:1
Knochenhauer, Karl, 1939, Jl 3,3:3
Knochenhauer, Wilhelm, 1939, Je 29,23:6
Knode, Oliver M, 1962, Ap 9,29:2
Knodle, Charles A, 1941, N 27,23:5
Knoedler, Charles L (por), 1944, Mr 7,17:1
Knoedler, Edmund L Mrs, 1910, Ap 21,11:5
Knoedler, Elmer L, 1947, D 12,27:3
Knoedler, M, 1878, Ap 15,5:5
Knoedler, R F, 1932, O 5,21:1
Knoedler, Roland F Mrs, 1922, Ja 22,22:1
Knoefel, Aug F, 1941, Ag 29,17:5
Knoell, John, 1942, My 11,15:3
Knoell, John Jr, 1952, S 3,30:4
Knoepfle, August A, 1962, Ap 18,39:1
Knoepfle, Herman, 1948, Mr 16,28:3
Knoepfler, Albert, 1958, My 15,29:2
Knoeppel, Alfred W, 1937, S 9,23:4
Knoeppel, Harold C, 1946, Mr 20,23:2
Knoeppel, John H, 1916, Jl 28,11:6
Knoeppel, John Mrs, 1943, O 6,23:2
Knoeppel, Raymond J, 1951, Je 22,25:3
Knoerle, Harold M, 1954, O 21,27:4
Knoerzer, Arthur T, 1943, Mr 28,24:1
Knoizen, Arthur S, 1950, Ap 30,102:6
Knoke, Edward J Mrs, 1952, Je 6,23:3
Knoke, Herman W, 1958, Ap 12,19:2
Knoles, Tully C, 1959, N 30,31:3
Knolhoff, Arthur C, 1968, Mr 8,39:3
Knoll, Gustave F, 1946, O 25,24:2
Knoll, Hans G, 1955, O 10,30:3
Knoll, Jacon, 1946, S 11,7:2
Knoll, Max, 1957, Je 1,17:2
Knoll, Maximilian, 1947, My 18,60:6
Knollys, Edward G W T Viscount, 1966, D 4,89:1
Knollys, Francis Viscount, 1924, Ag 16,11:7
Knollys, W Sir, 1883, Jl 12,3:1
Knoop, Harry A, 1955, D 21,29:2
Knoop, William A, 1967, S 12,47:4
Knopack, Arthur, 1954, Je 11,23:2
Knopf, Alfred A Mre (Blanche), 1966, Je 5,86:1
Knopf, Almira F Mrs, 1941, D 9,31:3
Knopf, Carl S, 1942, Je 24,19:3
Knopf, Hans, 1967, N 4,33:5
Knopf, J Raymond, 1954, N 9,27:5
Knopf, Otto Mrs, 1954, Ag 18,29:5
Knopf, S Adolphus, 1940, Jl 16,17:1
Knopf, Samuel, 1944, O 10,23:1
Knopf, Samuel Mrs, 1945, Ag 4,11:4
Knopke, Alfred F, 1947, Ja 20,25:3
Knopp, Oscar, 1952, N 6,29:5
Knopp, Robert F, 1948, Ag 14,13:3
Knorpp, Gustav, 1903, Jl 19,7:6
Knorr, Arthur, 1966, My 26,47:2
Knorr, Charles A, 1937, S 24,21:4
Knorr, Fred, 1960, D 27,29:1
Knorr, Harry, 1962, Ap 17,35:4
Knorr, John K Jr, 1956, S 19,37:4
Knorr, John Mrs, 1951, O 13,17:6
Knorr, Martin G, 1959, Ja 31,19:4
Knorr, Thomas, 1911, D 14,13:4
Knortz, Karl, 1918, Jl 28,19:3
Knote, Heinrich, 1953, Ja 16,24:3
Knote, Heinrich Mrs, 1907, Ap 23,9:4
Knote, John M, 1948, O 10,76:7
Knothe, Adolph C, 1950, O 16,27:4
Knothe, C Frederick, 1904, F 17,9:7
Knothe, Charles J, 1940, N 20,21:4
Knothe, Frank F, 1944, My 7,45:1
Knott, A Leo Gen, 1918, Ap 19,13:6
Knott, Agnes R, 1948, Ja 29,24:3
Knott, Annie M Mrs, 1941, D 21,40:6
Knott, David H, 1954, My 5,31:1
Knott, David H Mrs, 1951, N 2,24:2
Knott, Ernest W, 1942, S 3,19:2
Knott, Gene, 1937, Je 7,19:2
Knott, George C, 1959, N 15,86:7
Knott, George H, 1966, Je 26,72:7
Knott, Harry Mrs, 1949, Ja 27,23:3
Knott, J O, 1952, Je 12,33:4
Knott, James, 1906, S 6,9:6
Knott, James E, 1963, O 3,35:1
Knott, James Mrs, 1913, O 29,11:6
Knott, John F, 1963, F 18,17:8
Knott, Joseph Proctor, 1911, Je 19,9:5
Knott, Middleton O, 1954, Ja 6,31:3
Knott, Ralph B, 1954, My 3,25:3
Knott, Richard W Mrs, 1951, S 20,31:4
Knott, Richard Wilson, 1917, D 28,11:5
Knott, Thomas A, 1945, Ag 17,17:3
Knott, Thomas W, 1954, My 9,89:1
Knott, William H, 1943, Ja 11,15:5
Knott, William J, 1951, O 26,23:5
Knott, William J Mrs, 1943, S 4,13:2
Knotts, A F, 1937, O 4,21:3
Knotts, Benjamin, 1965, Je 2,45:3
Knotts, G Lloyd, 1950, N 29,33:4
Knotts, Howard C (por), 1942, N 24,25:3
Knotts, J Owen, 1949, Ja 29,13:5
Knotts, Thomas E, 1921, Mr 27,22:3
Knotts, Thomas E Mrs, 1954, Ap 8,27:3
Knoud, Michael J Mrs, 1967, F 11,29:5
Knous, William L, 1959, D 12,23:5
Knower, H M, 1940, Ja 13,15:5
Knower, Henry D, 1939, N 27,17:5
Knower, Henry M Mrs, 1954, Ag 17,21:4
Knower, Leonard G, 1952, Ja 8,27:5
Knowitch, Benjamin, 1949, D 29,25:3
Knowiten, Ebenezer, 1874, S 17,4:7
Knowland, Daniel P Mrs, 1943, Ap 28,23:1; 1953, Je 5,27:5
Knowland, Joseph R, 1966, F 2,35:4
Knowland, Joseph R Jr, 1961, O 7,23:1
Knowland, Joseph R Jr Mrs, 1962, Ja 11,33:1
Knowles, A Stanley, 1951, D 19,31:3
Knowles, Albert W, 1937, Jl 7,23:3
Knowles, Allen Leroy, 1944, O 20,19:4
Knowles, Archibald C, 1951, O 2,28:3
Knowles, Archibald C Mrs, 1947, Mr 20,27:3
Knowles, Arthur F, 1951, S 4,27:2
Knowles, Augusta O Mrs, 1937, F 12,23:1
Knowles, C O Mrs, 1952, My 8,31:5
Knowles, Charles A, 1950, F 2,27:3
Knowles, Charles E, 1965, Je 17,33:2
Knowles, Charles E Mrs, 1965, Ap 14,41:3
Knowles, Charles G, 1938, S 6,37:8
Knowles, Charles George Frederick Vice-Adm, 1918, Mr 5,11:8
Knowles, Charles O, 1956, D 4,39:4
Knowles, Charles W, 1954, My 15,15:1
Knowles, Daniel, 1905, Ap 6,11:6
Knowles, Edward F, 1964, F 5,35:6
Knowles, Edwin, 1902, Ap 15,9:7
Knowles, Edwin B, 1967, My 19,39:2
Knowles, Edwin M, 1943, F 11,19:1
Knowles, F Wendell Mrs, 1944, Ja 28,17:1
Knowles, Frank C, 1957, Ja 11,24:1
Knowles, Frederic Lawrence, 1905, S 21,9:5
Knowles, Frederick E, 1946, My 8,25:3
Knowles, Frederick M, 1959, F 15,86:5
Knowles, Harry Sr, 1945, Mr 20,19:3
Knowles, Harry W Jr, 1966, S 6,47:2
Knowles, Hartley R, 1953, O 8,29:2
Knowles, Harvey C, 1964, Mr 6,28:5
Knowles, Henry S, 1951, Mr 20,29:4
Knowles, Herbert M Capt, 1937, F 13,13:6
Knowles, Horace E, 1952, Ap 23,29:4
Knowles, Horace G, 1937, N 3,23:4
Knowles, James, 1916, D 24,15:1
Knowles, James A, 1941, S 3,23:4
Knowles, James B, 1944, D 21,21:2
Knowles, James Sheridan, 1862, D 20,4:6
Knowles, James Sir, 1908, F 14,7:5
Knowles, Joe, 1942, O 23,22:3
Knowles, John Fletcher, 1903, O 27,9:5
Knowles, John L, 1954, F 22,19:4
Knowles, John W, 1937, Ja 10,II,10:8
Knowles, Joseph F, 1909, N 11,9:4
Knowles, L C A Mrs, 1926, Ap 27,25:2
Knowles, Lawrence C, 1965, My 3,33:1
Knowles, Lucius J, 1920, N 27,13:4; 1961, Ja 16,27:3
Knowles, Lucy C, 1943, D 29,18:2
Knowles, Mabel W, 1949, D 1,31:3
Knowles, Mary Mrs, 1915, Ag 1,15:2
Knowles, Percival G, 1959, Ap 26,86:8
Knowles, Percival G Mrs, 1951, Ja 23,27:2
Knowles, Philip E, 1920, Je 11,13:3
Knowles, R B, 1882, F 14,5:2
Knowles, Raymond A, 1953, F 4,27:3
Knowles, Raymond H, 1961, D 7,43:5
Knowles, Richard George, 1919, Ja 2,9:2
Knowles, Robert B, 1958, D 5,31:4
Knowles, Robert E, 1946, N 16,19:4
Knowles, Ryland S, 1940, Ag 28,19:4
Knowles, Thomas C, 1949, F 20,60:2
Knowles, Thomas H, 1939, Ag 5,15:4
Knowles, Vernon, 1951, D 29,11:5
Knowles, Watts R Mrs, 1960, Ap 16,17:4
Knowles, Wilbur Mrs, 1944, Ag 15,17:5
Knowles, Wilbur S, 1944, My 13,19:5
Knowles, Wilhelmina C, 1952, Ap 17,29:4
Knowles, William F, 1946, Mr 17,44:6
Knowles, William G, 1946, S 28,17:5
Knowles, William H, 1939, Ap 26,23:4; 1959, My 11, 27:1
Knowles, William J, 1938, N 22,23:4
Knowles, William K Mrs, 1954, Je 8,27:2
Knowles, William W, 1944, Ja 20,19:5
Knowlington, Thomas Dr, 1937, Jl 30,19:5
Knowlson, James S, 1959, Mr 7,21:3
Knowlson, Lee K Sr Mrs, 1952, My 18,92:4
Knowlson, Walter S, 1939, N 22,21:1
Knowlton, Austin Mrs, 1924, My 19,17:3
Knowlton, Bill, 1944, F 27,38:3
Knowlton, Chase H, 1958, Mr 26,34:5
Knowlton, Daniel C, 1966, Mr 7,27:2
Knowlton, Daniel C Mrs, 1955, My 6,23:1
Knowlton, Dexter A, 1903, N 20,9:5
Knowlton, Don R, 1949, Mr 11,26:3
Knowlton, Eben J, 1938, Ja 11,23:3
Knowlton, Edward J, 1943, D 14,28:2
Knowlton, Elizabeth Mrs, 1953, Ap 3,23:1
Knowlton, Ernest S, 1947, F 3,19:5
Knowlton, Frank W, 1938, D 11,60:5
Knowlton, Grace E, 1941, Mr 2,43:2
Knowlton, H J, 1903, Ap 27,7:5
Knowlton, H M, 1902, D 19,9:5
Knowlton, Harry D, 1947, Mr 20,27:2
Knowlton, I S C, 1871, Je 12,1:6
Knowlton, John, 1937, N 2,28:2
Knowlton, John A, 1960, N 23,29:3
Knowlton, Lewis D, 1956, My 29,27:5
Knowlton, Marcus P Ex-Justice, 1918, My 8,11:5
Knowlton, Mark, 1904, F 13,9:5
Knowlton, Robert A, 1968, My 28,47:2
Knowlton, Sylvia B Mrs, 1937, Ap 3,19:1
Knowlton, Theodore E, 1953, Jl 21,23:2
Knowlton, Theodore E Mrs, 1955, My 8,89:2
Knowlton, Thomas A, 1940, F 16,3:5
Knox, Alex D, 1960, D 3,23:5
Knox, Alfred Curtis, 1925, D 11,23:3
Knox, Andrew, 1949, Je 12,79:4
Knox, Andrew J, 1940, S 16,19:4
Knox, Andrew J Sr, 1952, Jl 14,17:4
Knox, Arthur S, 1952, My 11,93:2
Knox, Benjamin C, 1960, Ja 29,25:1
Knox, Betty, 1963, Ja 26,7:3
Knox, Charles A, 1951, Mr 11,92:6
Knox, Charles E, 1938, N 2,23:1
Knox, Charles Edwin, 1919, Je 3,13:5
Knox, Charles H, 1906, My 30,7:6
Knox, Charlotte D, 1945, D 12,27:3
Knox, Douglas, 1940, My 4,17:6
Knox, Dudley W, 1960, Je 12,86:5
Knox, Earle S, 1953, My 21,31:6
Knox, Edmund A Rev Dr, 1937, Ja 17,II,8:5
Knox, Edward M (funl, Mr 30,13:6), 1916, Mr 29, 11:3
Knox, Edward M Mrs, 1914, F 9,7:5
Knox, Ernie, 1963, O 17,46:1
Knox, Errol, 1949, O 18,27:2
Knox, Frank Mrs, 1958, S 23,33:2
Knox, Franklin, 1944, Ap 29,1:4
Knox, George C, 1941, Ja 8,19:1
Knox, George L, 1944, Ap 19,23:3
Knox, George P, 1950, O 31,27:3
Knox, George W Rev, 1912, Ap 27,13:4
Knox, Grannell E, 1948, Ja 20,23:2
Knox, Harry, 1953, N 12,43:7; 1963, S 26,35:2
Knox, Harry A, 1957, Je 5,35:5
Knox, Harry G Rear-Adm, 1923, Ag 31,15:6
Knox, Harry S (por), 1947, Ja 22,23:3
Knox, Harvey A, 1948, My 14,23:3
Knox, Helen, 1959, Ap 8,37:1
Knox, Helena L (will), 1939, O 31,9:3
Knox, Henry C, 1923, Ap 12,19:4
Knox, Herbert A, 1939, Ap 12,23:3

Knox, Herbert G Mrs, 1960, Je 14,37:1
Knox, Herbert H, 1944, Ag 18,13:2
Knox, Howard A, 1949, Jl 28,23:5
Knox, Irving S, 1949, N 24,31:1
Knox, J Emmet, 1961, Mr 29,33:5
Knox, J H Rev, 1903, Ja 23,9:6
Knox, J J, 1892, F 10,8:4
Knox, J J Gen, 1876, F 2,4:6
Knox, J P, 1882, Je 4,7:1
Knox, James E, 1958, My 8,29:3
Knox, James L, 1944, D 12,23:2
Knox, James M, 1960, My 11,39:1
Knox, James P, 1947, F 6,23:3
Knox, James W, 1952, Ag 21,19:4
Knox, James W T, 1941, D 1,19:5
Knox, John, 1948, Mr 25,27:1; 1958, N 16,88:8
Knox, John A, 1953, My 11,27:3
Knox, John A Mrs, 1938, S 30,21:3
Knox, John Armoy, 1906, D 20,7:3
Knox, John Bradfute, 1924, Ag 7,15:5
Knox, John C, 1966, Ag 24,51:1
Knox, John Jay, 1913, Ja 7,11:6
Knox, John Jay Mrs, 1922, Ag 16,9:5
Knox, John Mason, 1919, O 23,13:3
Knox, John P Mrs (K M Flannigan), 1954, Ag 10, 19:6
Knox, John W, 1961, O 21,21:3
Knox, Joseph N, 1937, Jl 17,15:6
Knox, Kenneth, 1951, N 21,28:8
Knox, Lena B, 1955, D 14,39:1
Knox, Leonard K Mrs, 1953, Mr 10,29:2
Knox, Louise C Mrs (por), 1942, Ja 12,15:3
Knox, Louise C Mrs, 1942, F 16,25:7
Knox, Maryal, 1955, N 6,87:1
Knox, Neville Y, 1951, O 7,87:2
Knox, Paul W, 1965, Je 22,21:2
Knox, Philander C (funl, O 16,22:3), 1921, O 15,13:6
Knox, Raymond C, 1952, Ja 27,77:1
Knox, Renwick M, 1954, Ja 7,31:3
Knox, Reuben Mrs, 1944, D 27,19:2
Knox, Robert C, 1942, Ap 10,17:2; 1946, Jl 18,25:2
Knox, Robert V, 1950, N 26,90:3
Knox, Roger, 1951, S 6,31:4
Knox, Ronald A (funl, Ag 30,19:2), 1957, Ag 26,23:1
Knox, S B P Dr, 1922, Jl 1,13:5
Knox, S R, 1883, N 23,2:2
Knox, Samuel L G, 1947, My 9,22:3
Knox, Samuel M, 1924, Ap 10,23:5
Knox, Seymour H, 1915, My 17,9:4; 1948, S 12,74:3
Knox, Stuart K, 1941, Je 29,33:2
Knox, Susan R, 1959, Je 13,21:6
Knox, Taber, 1949, My 8,77:1
Knox, W Curtis, 1944, Je 27,19:4
Knox, W E, 1927, F 5,1:6
Knox, W E Rev, 1883, S 22,1:6
Knox, W J Dr Senator, 1867, N 14,1:4
Knox, Walter Mrs, 1940, Ap 2,25:3
Knox, Walter R, 1951, Mr 4,92:4
Knox, Warren C, 1950, Je 25,68:2
Knox, William B, 1940, Ap 2,26:4; 1945, Ag 15,19:1
Knox, William E Mrs, 1956, O 31,33:6
Knox, William G, 1953, N 21,13:2
Knox, William H, 1953, O 7,29:3
Knox, William J, 1944, My 17,19:3
Knox, William K, 1938, Ap 15,19:4
Knox, William S Mrs, 1947, N 12,27:4
Knubel, Frederick H (por), 1945, O 17,19:1
Knubel, Frederick H Mrs, 1950, Mr 19,92:4
Knubel, Frederick R, 1957, O 24,33:2
Knubel, John A, 1959, Ja 11,88:4
Knucken, George D, 1940, S 21,19:3
Knucksen, Edgar, 1940, Ap 20,17:3
Knudsen, Alfred, 1954, My 9,89:2
Knudsen, Alfred M, 1947, Ap 23,25:3
Knudsen, Anna K Mrs, 1951, S 5,31:4
Knudsen, Christian L, 1967, F 23,35:2
Knudsen, Enger A, 1961, Mr 18,23:3
Knudsen, G D, 1928, D 2,31:5
Knudsen, Hans R, 1962, N 5,31:5
Knudsen, Hugo, 1955, N 28,31:3
Knudsen, Ivan, 1920, Mr 28,22:2
Knudsen, Jack, 1947, F 3,19:1
Knudsen, Karl Sir, 1937, N 27,17:2
Knudsen, Martin, 1943, Jl 27,17:2
Knudsen, Morris H, 1943, N 18,23:3
Knudsen, Sigurd, 1955, Ap 13,29:2
Knudsen, William S, 1948, Ap 28,27:1
Knudsen, William S Mrs, 1950, Ap 18,31:1
Knudson, Albert C, 1953, Ag 30,90:1
Knudson, Bennett O, 1964, Jl 1,35:5
Knudson, Charles P, 1956, O 14,86:7
Knudson, James K, 1963, O 15,39:1
Knudson, John I, 1959, Ag 26,29:5
Knudson, Karl E, 1953, Jl 26,69:1
Knuelle, Charles, 1950, S 16,19:2
Knuhl, Adolf, 1937, D 31,15:4
Knup, Jacob, 1937, Ja 9,17:4
Knupfer, Charles, 1949, Ja 14,23:5
Knupfer, Walter, 1954, S 8,31:2
Knupp, Richard, 1940, Ja 7,48:5
Knushevitsky, Svyatoslav, 1963, F 20,12:8
Knust, John J G, 1954, Ja 28,27:3
Knust, Leo F, 1946, Ag 10,13:4
Knust, William, 1962, Ag 14,31:2
Knuth, Christian B, 1948, Jl 5,15:3
Knuth, Maria A, 1955, My 25,33:5
Knutsford, Lord, 1931, Jl 28,21:3
Knutson, Harold, 1953, Ag 22,15:1
Knutson, Henry C, 1963, Ag 6,31:5
Knuzsen, Knuz A, 1941, Je 21,17:4
Knyveth, R Hugh Capt (funl, Ap 18,13:5), 1918, Ap 16,13:4
Ko Ching-Shih, 1965, Ap 10,30:1
Ko Kun Kua, Prof at Harvard, 1882, F 15,1:6
Koar, William H, 1952, Mr 23,92:1
Kob, Robert L, 1961, Ja 18,30:4
Koback, Samuel A, 1939, Ag 5,15:4
Kobak, Disraeli W, 1956, F 18,19:5
Kobak, Edgar, 1962, Je 5,41:3
Kobak, Morris, 1962, Ag 24,37:3
Kobayachi, Seizo, 1962, Jl 6,25:4
Kobayashi, Icizo, 1957, Ja 26,19:2
Kobb, George, 1964, Je 10,45:3
Kobbe, Frederick W, 1946, S 6,21:5
Kobbe, George C, 1923, Mr 12,15:4
Kobbe, George L, 1954, My 3,25:6
Kobbe, Herman, 1966, Jl 23,25:2
Kobbe, Philip F, 1906, S 22,7:6
Kobbe, Walter, 1947, Ag 14,23:4
Kobe, Samuel J, 1958, Ag 28,27:2
Kobeleff, Konstantin, 1966, Ag 9,37:2
Kobelt, Arnold A, 1962, Ap 7,25:2
Kobelt, Karl, 1968, Ja 7,85:1
Kober, Adolf, 1958, D 31,19:1
Kober, Albert G, 1943, O 7,23:3
Kober, Alice, 1950, My 17,29:4
Kober, Arthur Mrs, 1951, My 19,15:2
Kober, Charles W, 1951, Mr 9,25:3
Kober, G M, 1931, Ap 25,19:3
Kober, Georgia L, 1942, S 17,25:4
Kober, Joseph E, 1940, Jl 20,15:6
Kobernuss, Louis F, 1955, Ap 14,29:3
Koberski, Walter, 1942, Je 12,22:3
Kobes, Herbert R, 1959, Ja 11,88:3
Kobesky, Eddie, 1952, F 16,13:3
Kobets, Sergei S, 1953, Ap 24,24:6
Kobik, William J, 1967, O 28,31:5
Kobitzsch, Adolph Mrs, 1945, N 14,19:5
Koblenz, William, 1961, F 3,23:1
Koblenzer, Hugo, 1939, D 4,23:1
Koblenzer, S James, 1951, S 5,31:3
Kobler, Albert J (will, My 19,23:3), 1937, Ja 4,29:2
Kobler, E W, 1933, Ag 11,15:3
Koblet, Hugo, 1964, N 6,37:4
Kobrin, Leon (por), 1946, Ap 1,28:2
Kobrin, Leon Mrs, 1961, Ag 30,33:1
Kobrin, Nathan, 1965, Ap 14,41:1
Kobs, John, 1968, Ja 27,29:5
Koburger, Charles W, 1965, Mr 21,86:5
Kobus, B Paul, 1956, Ag 2,25:2
Kobus, Mary W Mrs, 1954, D 15,31:5
Kocan, George Mrs, 1964, Ap 4,28:5
Koch, Alfred J, 1951, N 8,29:4
Koch, August, 1946, S 24,30:3
Koch, Bernard A, 1943, Mr 8,15:3
Koch, Bernard A Mrs, 1951, O 4,33:2
Koch, Carl, 1937, Je 19,15:6
Koch, Carl B, 1948, S 1,24:3
Koch, Carl E, 1967, O 30,45:3
Koch, Charles, 1945, N 25,50:3
Koch, Charles G, 1949, Je 30,23:3
Koch, Charles J, 1953, N 23,27:2
Koch, Charles Rudolph Edward, 1916, Jl 22,9:7
Koch, Edward E, 1947, Jl 3,21:6
Koch, Edward J, 1954, D 5,89:1
Koch, Edward R, 1947, Ag 29,17:2
Koch, Edward W, 1946, F 10,42:5
Koch, Ernest, 1944, Ap 23,41:2
Koch, Ernest H Jr, 1958, Ja 29,27:4
Koch, Ernest W, 1961, F 26,92:2
Koch, Frank, 1922, D 6,19:4; 1937, Jl 5,17:6
Koch, Frank A, 1951, Je 23,15:3
Koch, Frank C, 1944, Ag 25,13:6
Koch, Fred C (por), 1948, Ja 27,26:2
Koch, Frederick, 1952, My 9,23:5
Koch, Frederick A, 1967, Ja 16,41:4
Koch, Frederick C, 1949, O 18,27:2
Koch, Frederick C Sr, 1950, Ap 7,25:1
Koch, Frederick G Jr, 1952, F 26,28:3
Koch, Frederick H (por), 1944, Ag 18,13:3
Koch, George D, 1949, S 9,26:3
Koch, George W H, 1937, Ja 17,II,2:4
Koch, Gustave, 1949, F 26,15:3
Koch, Gustave Mrs, 1945, D 4,29:5
Koch, Harry C, 1955, F 18,21:3
Koch, Henry, 1939, S 8,23:3
Koch, Henry E, 1960, Ap 21,31:4
Koch, Herman, 1924, My 23,19:5; 1940, Je 8,15:4
Koch, Hiram, 1937, N 29,23:4
Koch, Irving, 1959, Ja 20,35:5
Koch, Jean L Mrs, 1940, Ap 18,23:2
Koch, John D, 1953, D 18,29:3
Koch, John H, 1961, N 5,89:1
Koch, Joseph C, 1943, D 9,27:3
Koch, Joseph J, 1956, F 14,29:4
Koch, Joseph Judge, 1902, Ag 29,9:5
Koch, Julius A, 1956, F 12,88:7
Koch, Lauge, 1964, Je 7,86:5
Koch, Lewis A, 1963, Ap 6,19:1
Koch, Louis, 1958, Je 29,68:7
Koch, Markus, 1962, Mr 1,31:4
Koch, Mathilde L, 1948, Je 20,60:8
Koch, Max C P, 1953, N 9,35:3
Koch, Millard F, 1948, Mr 31,25:3
Koch, Oscar F, 1951, Ap 26,29:5
Koch, Otto F Sr, 1948, O 14,29:5
Koch, Paul, 1956, F 18,19:6
Koch, Ralph A, 1953, Mr 16,22:5
Koch, Reinhard, 1939, Je 28,21:6
Koch, Richard Dr, 1910, O 16,II,13:4
Koch, Robert N Mrs, 1957, S 25,29:1; 1964, O 31,29:1
Koch, Robert Prof, 1910, My 28,9:3
Koch, Roscoe H Mrs, 1946, S 24,29:1
Koch, Rudolf, 1957, Je 9,89:1
Koch, Rudolph C, 1937, S 29,23:4
Koch, Rudolph J, 1955, Ap 5,26:6
Koch, Samuel, 1905, My 7,7:3
Koch, Samuel P, 1939, S 15,23:2
Koch, Spencer B, 1939, F 5,40:2
Koch, Theodor (por), 1940, O 30,23:4
Koch, Theodore, 1957, Mr 27,31:5
Koch, Theodore W, 1941, Mr 24,17:6
Koch, Vivienne (Mrs J F Day), 1961, N 30,37:4
Koch, W Walter, 1962, Mr 23,33:3
Koch, Walter, 1944, N 26,56:6
Koch, William, 1937, F 11,23:5; 1945, F 13,23:2
Koch, William A, 1953, D 24,15:1
Koch, William J, 1908, Mr 1,9:4
Koch Krefft, Osvaldo, 1963, Ap 18,35:3
Koch-Weser, Erich, 1944, N 4,15:6
Kochanski, P, 1934, Ja 13,13:4
Kochen, Max, 1965, F 10,42:1
Kochenderfer, Gerald, 1952, Ag 28,23:3
Kochendorfer, John, 1954, S 4,11:5
Kocher, Albert, 1941, My 10,15:5
Kocher, John H, 1937, Ag 15,II,7:4
Kocher, Joseph Mrs, 1943, Je 16,21:4
Kocher, Lawrence E, 1960, S 3,17:6
Kocher, Theodore Dr, 1917, Ag 5,17:3
Kochersperger, Earl, 1964, Ag 7,29:6
Kochersperger, Edmund S, 1952, S 9,31:5
Kochersperger, Hiram M, 1945, D 29,13:6
Kochmeister, Samuel, 1963, My 4,25:3
Kochs, August (will), 1960, D 7,51:5
Kochubei, Anton D, 1966, D 17,33:4
Kochurov, Yuri, 1952, Je 1,84:5
Kocialkowski, Leo, 1958, S 29,27:3
Kocian, Jaroslav, 1950, Mr 9,29:1
Kocinsky, Ruth, 1955, N 28,31:2
Kocon, Ferdinand, 1940, N 23,17:6
Kocova, Mila, 1951, F 11,88:3
Kocsis, Paul, 1958, Mr 3,16:3
Kocur, Joseph H, 1951, Jl 20,21:3
Koczalski, Raoul, 1948, N 26,23:4
Koczinski, Joseph P, 1954, N 2,27:3
Koda, George, 1952, O 15,31:3
Kodaly, Zoltan, 1967, Mr 7,38:3
Kodaly, Zoltan Mrs, 1958, N 24,29:4
Kodama, Gentaro Gen, 1906, Jl 23,7:6
Kodama, Hideo, 1947, Ap 8,27:3
Koder, Frank J, 1943, Ap 8,23:4
Koe, Lancelot C, 1941, F 20,19:3
Koe, Samson H, 1964, S 15,37:1
Koeb, Emil, 1948, Je 8,25:6
Koebel, John L, 1941, N 18,25:2
Koebele, Frank J, 1940, Jl 27,13:3
Koech, Edward, 1952, O 16,29:1
Koecher, George W, 1946, S 12,7:4
Koechlin, Charles, 1951, Ja 3,27:5
Koechlin, Maurice, 1946, Je 12,27:4
Koechling, Ethel, 1944, Ap 15,11:3
Koechling, Phil J, 1948, O 5,25:3
Koeck, Joseph A, 1948, Jl 11,50:8
Koecker, Leonora L, 1940, My 5,52:2
Koeckert, Frederick W, 1962, F 10,23:2
Koegel, Peter F, 1945, Ag 5,37:2
Koegel, William F Mrs (Barbara), 1968, O 18,53:4
Koegl, Richard A, 1959, Ag 1,17:6
Koegler, Emil, 1947, Mr 8,13:1
Koegler, George, 1956, S 15,17:6
Koegler, George H, 1941, Ja 15,23:4
Koegler, Richard A, 1943, Ag 24,19:4
Koehl, Albt M, 1956, Ja 29,92:6
Koehl, Hermann (por),(comment, O 16,X,6:6), 1938, O 9,45:1
Koehler, Arthur, 1967, Jl 18,37:1
Koehler, Charles A, 1941, Ap 25,19:1
Koehler, Charles G Jr, 1956, Jl 24,25:4
Koehler, David M, 1903, D 4,9:4
Koehler, Edward W, 1950, My 8,23:4
Koehler, Ernest F, 1943, My 12,25:4
Koehler, Ferdinand C, 1940, D 19,25:4
Koehler, Fred, 1959, Mr 31,30:3
Koehler, Frederick C, 1942, O 31,15:5
Koehler, Frederick R, 1947, Ap 27,60:2
Koehler, George M, 1943, My 17,15:2
Koehler, George R, 1949, O 25,27:4
Koehler, H J Col, 1927, Jl 2,17:5
Koehler, Hans C, 1949, O 7,31:3

Koehler, Harry A, 1957, O 19,21:2
Koehler, Heinrich, 1949, F 7,19:3
Koehler, Herbert A Sr, 1967, Ja 26,33:1
Koehler, Hoffmann Mrs, 1948, Mr 28,48:3
Koehler, Hugo W, 1941, Je 19,21:1
Koehler, Joseph, 1948, D 21,28:5
Koehler, Joseph M Mrs, 1964, D 28,29:4
Koehler, Karl F, 1952, Ja 29,25:1
Koehler, L M Col, 1924, Jl 18,13:5
Koehler, Louis C, 1941, Jl 24,17:3
Koehler, Philip H, 1946, Ag 8,21:6
Koehler, Robert, 1955, My 26,31:5
Koehler, Robert H, 1962, Ag 23,29:4
Koehler, Wilhelm, 1959, N 5,35:4
Koehler, William C, 1953, N 28,15:2
Koehler, William C Mrs, 1941, F 23,40:8
Koehn, Walter H, 1941, N 4,23:3
Koehne, Louise S Mrs, 1942, F 2,15:4
Koehnle, Bert A, 1955, Ap 20,33:6
Koelble, Alphonse G, 1946, D 19,29:4
Koeleman, Dirk J, 1964, Je 27,25:2
Koelle, Wilhelm G, 1943, My 3,12:1
Koeller, David Jr, 1955, Ja 14,21:1
Koellhoffer, Conrad H, 1939, Je 20,21:4
Koellhoffer, John F, 1958, Ja 25,19:5
Koellhoffer, William, 1938, Ag 12,17:5
Koelling, Louis C, 1939, Ag 30,17:6
Koellmer, John J, 1939, Ja 13,19:3
Koelmel, George, 1952, Ag 5,19:1
Koelsch, August, 1918, O 28,11:3
Koelsch, Carl A, 1943, Je 4,21:4
Koelsch, Carl J, 1957, O 2,33:3
Koelsch, Henry A Jr, 1938, Ja 19,14:3
Koelsch, Henry A Mrs, 1963, Jl 24,31:5
Koelsch, Peter, 1903, Ap 12,7:5
Koelsch, William F H, 1942, O 31,15:1
Koemmenick, Louis Mrs, 1944, Mr 1,19:4
Koempel, Edward C, 1962, N 12,29:3
Koempel, J Alex, 1941, N 13,27:1
Koenan, Josephine Agnes, 1917, S 2,13:2
Koeneke, Henry W (por), 1944, N 18,13:5
Koenig, A George, 1957, Ja 27,85:2
Koenig, Adrianu, 1944, F 10,15:4
Koenig, Barbara E, 1952, Mr 13,29:4
Koenig, Carl, 1942, Ag 24,15:4
Koenig, Carl F, 1955, Ja 28,19:1
Koenig, Charles C, 1944, Ag 9,17:2
Koenig, Charles F, 1938, My 21,15:5
Koenig, Edwin C, 1960, Jl 6,33:3
Koenig, Emil L, 1957, Je 28,23:4
Koenig, Frederick, 1947, Mr 19,26:3
Koenig, Frederick A G, 1956, Jl 1,57:1
Koenig, Frederick Mrs, 1910, Ag 28,II,9:5
Koenig, George A, 1959, D 21,27:3; 1967, Ap 4,43:1
Koenig, George A Prof, 1913, Ja 16,17:5
Koenig, George C, 1950, N 25,13:4
Koenig, George L, 1962, Je 30,19:6
Koenig, Henry, 1949, Jl 21,25:3
Koenig, Herman, 1949, Je 24,23:2
Koenig, Herman E, 1940, Ag 24,13:5
Koenig, Jacob, 1937, O 12,25:1
Koenig, Jennie Mrs, 1943, Je 8,22:2
Koenig, John, 1938, Ja 4,23:3
Koenig, John Jr, 1951, Ag 28,23:5
Koenig, Len, 1949, Je 13,25:2
Koenig, Leo, 1960, N 29,37:5
Koenig, Leo Rev, 1919, O 14,17:3
Koenig, Marcus, 1958, F 8,19:1
Koenig, Mary F F Mrs, 1957, Je 5,35:2
Koenig, Morris (por),(will, D 7,25:5), 1939, D 2,17:4
Koenig, Nicholas, 1956, Je 17,92:5
Koenig, Otto, 1918, S 24,13:5
Koenig, Otto Mrs, 1950, F 14,25:2
Koenig, P, 1933, S 10,39:1
Koenig, Samuel S (funl, Mr 21,25:2), 1955, Mr 18, 27:1
Koenig, Samuel S Mrs, 1939, Je 19,15:2
Koenig, Walter, 1949, S 4,40:4
Koenig, William, 1943, My 30,26:6
Koenig, William H, 1943, My 7,19:2
Koeniger, Karl W, 1961, Ap 17,29:2
Koeniger, Walter, 1943, D 17,27:5
Koenigsberg, Max, 1947, S 29,21:6
Koenigsberg, Moses (por), 1945, S 22,17:4
Koenigsberg, Nicolas de Sr, 1952, Ag 2,15:2
Koenigsberg, Samuel S, 1962, Ap 12,35:4
Koenigsberger, Lawrence, 1951, D 4,33:4
Koenigsreuther, Rene W Mrs, 1958, D 11,13:3
Koenneke, Clifford N, 1959, F 8,86:3
Koepchen, Caroline M N Mrs, 1941, S 11,23:1
Koepchen, Henry, 1957, N 28,31:2
Koepchen, W, 1936, S 9,27:4
Koepel, Norbert F, 1967, Je 27,39:3
Koepfler, Andrew J, 1957, Ja 9,31:1
Koepfli, Joseph O, 1942, O 2,25:3
Koeppe, Robert J, 1952, F 14,27:2
Koeppel, Arthur E, 1956, N 27,37:3
Koeppel, George, 1947, Ag 2,13:4
Koeppel, Martin, 1960, Ja 2,13:3
Koeppel, Nathan Mrs, 1946, D 22,41:4
Koeppel, Samuel, 1941, Mr 18,23:5
Koerbel, Samuel J, 1947, Je 4,27:1
Koerber, Kenneth A, 1956, Jl 27,21:2
Koerber, Ruth, 1954, O 18,25:5
Koerner, Albert E, 1953, Jl 26,69:1
Koerner, Anthony, 1946, D 4,31:3
Koerner, Anthony C T, 1941, Ap 23,21:6
Koerner, Arthur A, 1947, F 12,25:3
Koerner, Bernhard Gen, 1920, Mr 27,13:3
Koerner, C Byron, 1957, Ag 13,27:1
Koerner, Charles, 1937, D 22,25:5
Koerner, Charles W (por), 1946, F 4,25:4
Koerner, Frederick W, 1961, Je 24,21:5
Koerner, Herman W, 1940, O 29,25:6
Koerner, John, 1938, D 17,15:4
Koerner, Leon J Mrs, 1959, Jl 28,27:3
Koerner, Rulley, 1967, N 4,33:4
Koerner, Theodor, 1951, N 12,25:2
Koerner, Theodor (funl plans, Ja 6,88:6; funl, Ja 11,23:4), 1957, Ja 5,17:1
Koerner, Theodore, 1957, My 5,88:6
Koerner, William, 1940, Jl 2,21:4
Koerner, William H D, 1938, Ag 13,13:7
Koerper, Karl, 1957, Ap 10,33:5
Koert, Jan, 1911, F 4,13:5
Koerzer, Otto, 1952, Je 20,23:6
Koessler, John A, 1951, My 26,17:6
Koester, Alfred A, 1968, Mr 15,39:3
Koester, Ernest, 1909, Ag 3,7:4
Koester, Frederick E, 1943, Jl 22,19:1
Koester, Frederick W, 1940, My 2,23:3
Koester, George R, 1939, Ja 2,24:2
Koester, Herman, 1964, Je 10,45:4
Koester, Oscar W, 1952, D 5,27:3
Koester, Phil E, 1954, Jl 1,25:2
Koestle, George, 1941, Mr 5,21:3
Koestler, Mamaine Mrs, 1954, Je 4,23:2
Koestler, Samuel, 1960, Ap 5,37:2
Koestler, Samuel Mrs, 1960, Jl 21,27:1
Koestner, John, 1949, S 7,29:4
Koestring, Ernst, 1953, N 22,88:4
Koether, Bernard G, 1941, Jl 10,19:2
Koettiltz, Reginald Dr, 1916, Ja 17,11:3
Koetzle, Frederick G, 1955, O 22,19:3
Koewing, Jessie S Mrs, 1937, S 28,23:4
Koff, Sidney C, 1950, My 28,44:6
Koffka, Kurt, 1941, N 23,52:1
Koffler, Camilla (Ylla),(funl, Ap 1,2:6), 1955, Mr 31, 2:3
Koffler, Emil, 1946, F 15,25:2
Koffler, Irving, 1950, Ag 16,29:3
Koffler, John J, 1963, Ag 26,27:4
Koffler, Joseph, 1946, N 3,64:3
Koffsky, Samuel, 1953, Ja 17,15:2
Koftoff, Reuben Mrs, 1943, Mr 30,21:4
Kogan, Claude Mme, 1959, O 18,1:7
Kogan, David H, 1938, N 25,23:4
Kogan, Zinovy, 1954, My 29,15:6
Kogel, Christopher F, 1959, Jl 30,27:4
Kogen, I B, 1938, N 14,19:4
Kogler, Albert, 1959, My 8,54:1
Kohan, Joseph H, 1959, N 12,35:4
Kohan, Morris I, 1950, Ja 21,17:4
Kohansky, Mendel Mrs, 1955, O 31,25:1
Kohen, Edward H, 1951, Jl 31,21:1
Kohl, Benjamin H, 1953, O 27,27:4
Kohl, Carl C Jr, 1955, Mr 19,15:1
Kohl, Charles E, 1910, N 13,11:3
Kohl, Edmund F, 1960, Je 1,39:4
Kohl, Edwin Phillips, 1968, Ja 12,27:1
Kohl, Frank E Mrs, 1948, D 5,92:3
Kohl, Henry (por), 1937, Mr 11,23:3
Kohl, J G, 1871, Je 8,1:2
Kohl, J J, 1957, S 20,25:1
Kohl, Maurice P, 1965, D 16,50:8
Kohl, Ralph B, 1952, Jl 29,21:4
Kohl, Raymond, 1950, Jl 9,69:3
Kohl, Valentine, 1942, Mr 20,19:3
Kohl, Walter W, 1949, Mr 16,27:3
Kohl, Walter W Mrs, 1942, My 20,19:2
Kohl, William J, 1942, Je 7,43:3
Kohlbeck, Valentine Rt Rev, 1937, F 19,20:1
Kohlbecker, Frank, 1950, Ag 7,19:4
Kohlberg, Alfred, 1960, Ap 8,31:2
Kohlberg, Alfred Mrs, 1951, N 3,17:3; 1968, F 12,53:7
Kohlberger, Joseph Mrs, 1949, My 7,13:5
Kohlbrugge, Jacob, 1941, S 19,23:3
Kohleberg, Eugene L, 1940, Ja 15,15:5
Kohlemetz, William C, 1950, F 9,29:5
Kohlenberger, Frederick, 1962, Jl 18,29:3
Kohler, Adolph J, 1942, D 31,15:2
Kohler, Alfred C, 1963, Jl 15,9:2
Kohler, Arthur S Mrs, 1963, O 20,88:6
Kohler, Carl, 1954, Jl 15,27:4
Kohler, Carl J Sr, 1960, N 18,10:4
Kohler, Charles (funl, Je 17,11:4), 1913, Je 5,11:4
Kohler, Charles, 1957, S 25,12:6
Kohler, Charles F, 1962, Jl 18,29:3
Kohler, Charles H Capt, 1925, D 11,23:3
Kohler, Charles H Mrs, 1947, Ja 23,23:1
Kohler, Charles J, 1942, Jl 4,17:4
Kohler, Charles L (por), 1945, F 27,19:3
Kohler, Charles L Mrs, 1940, Jl 4,15:6
Kohler, David A, 1951, F 5,23:3
Kohler, Edgar J (por), 1941, O 11,17:4
Kohler, Elmer P, 1938, My 25,23:5
Kohler, Evangeline, 1954, Ag 28,15:3
Kohler, F, 1934, F 1,19:4
Kohler, Ferdinand N, 1957, D 28,17:2
Kohler, Frank R Sr, 1955, O 24,27:3
Kohler, Fred, 1938, O 29,19:3
Kohler, Fred Mrs, 1948, Ja 27,25:3
Kohler, Fred S, 1961, Ag 24,29:4
Kohler, Fred W, 1940, Mr 5,24:3
Kohler, G A E, 1932, Ap 30,15:3
Kohler, Harry W, 1961, N 28,32:8
Kohler, Henrietta, 1943, D 9,27:3
Kohler, Henry, 1943, My 18,23:5
Kohler, Herbert C, 1953, D 29,23:3
Kohler, Herbert V Mrs, 1953, Mr 9,29:6
Kohler, Isidor F, 1948, Jl 11,53:2
Kohler, Jacob Mrs, 1947, Ap 21,27:5
Kohler, James P, 1941, Ag 5,20:3
Kohler, John F, 1957, Ag 10,15:6
Kohler, John H, 1959, O 13,39:4
Kohler, L David, 1964, Ja 25,23:4
Kohler, L Frank, 1946, Ja 15,23:3
Kohler, Laura A Mrs, 1953, D 14,31:4
Kohler, Louis H, 1950, S 26,31:3; 1955, Je 14,29:4
Kohler, M J, 1934, Jl 25,17:1
Kohler, Marie C, 1943, O 12,27:3
Kohler, Max J, 1922, D 23,13:6
Kohler, Milton W, 1942, My 25,15:6
Kohler, Myron H, 1947, F 11,27:5
Kohler, Nathan, 1964, Je 23,33:4
Kohler, Richard F, 1940, D 3,25:1
Kohler, Robert F, 1938, Ap 5,21:5
Kohler, Rose (por), 1947, O 6,21:1
Kohler, Steoh H, 1939, F 7,19:1
Kohler, Veronica M Mrs, 1937, Jl 3,15:2
Kohler, Walter J, 1940, Ap 22,17:1
Kohler, Walter J Mrs, 1947, F 3,19:2
Kohler, William, 1961, F 26,92:3
Kohler, William A, 1953, Ja 30,21:5
Kohler, William G, 1937, N 25,31:5
Kohler, William P, 1938, Ap 14,23:4; 1951, F 9,25:4
Kohler, Wolfgang, 1967, Je 12,45:3
Kohlhaas, Paul F, 1964, Ap 19,85:2
Kohlhaas, Reynold, 1915, O 4,9:5
Kohlhass, Herman T, 1951, Ap 26,18:4
Kohlhepp, Frederick B, 1948, N 1,23:5
Kohlhepp, Frederick B Mrs, 1943, Ag 20,15:3
Kohlman, Marion B Mrs (will), 1950, Ag 17,25:6
Kohlmann, Henry J, 1943, D 20,23:4
Kohlmann, Hugo, 1965, O 27,47:5
Kohlmann, Hugo Mrs, 1965, Ag 11,35:2
Kohlmar, Lee, 1946, My 16,21:4
Kohlmar, Lee Mrs, 1944, N 23,31:2
Kohlmeier, William, 1903, D 27,7:6
Kohloff, Paul, 1955, F 25,21:4
Kohlrausch, Eduard, 1948, Ja 26,19:4
Kohlreiter, Nathan, 1961, Ja 18,30:3
Kohlrieser, John C, 1957, Je 21,25:4
Kohlrieser, Melvin, 1950, Je 4,V,2:1
Kohlsaat, Amelia, 1950, D 24,34:1
Kohlsaat, C C Judge, 1918, My 13,13:6
Kohlsaat, Ernest W, 1919, Mr 14,13:3
Kohlsaat, Herman Henry (por),(funl, O 19,7:2), 1924, O 18,15:1
Kohlsat, J C, 1876, Mr 8,8:1
Kohlstedt, Edward D Mrs, 1942, D 23,19:4
Kohman, Henry A, 1952, Ag 17,76:7
Kohman, Minnie Mrs, 1942, Ap 7,21:5
Kohn, Achilles H, 1965, Ap 28,45:5
Kohn, Adolph T, 1948, S 8,29:3
Kohn, Albert M, 1944, Je 6,17:3
Kohn, Alex, 1962, Ap 5,33:5
Kohn, Alfred A, 1939, S 17,49:2
Kohn, Alois, 1925, S 30,23:4
Kohn, Armin, 1940, O 9,25:2
Kohn, Arnold, 1922, Je 19,15:6
Kohn, Benjamin, 1943, D 15,28:3
Kohn, Bernard, 1941, My 24,15:2
Kohn, Boris B, 1953, Ap 26,86:2
Kohn, Daniel, 1942, O 31,15:3
Kohn, David A, 1903, N 13,7:5
Kohn, Edward, 1909, Ag 13,7:6; 1939, S 25,19:3
Kohn, Emanuel, 1954, Ap 27,29:1
Kohn, Emil, 1914, Ap 3,11:5
Kohn, Emil W, 1944, N 4,15:6
Kohn, Erwin, 1962, Ag 9,25:4
Kohn, George E, 1952, Ag 5,19:5
Kohn, Harry I Mrs, 1947, F 14,21:2
Kohn, Harry R, 1939, Mr 21,23:6; 1964, Jl 21,33:4
Kohn, Henry H, 1938, D 24,15:3; 1944, D 27,20:2
Kohn, Henry H Mrs, 1942, D 12,17:2
Kohn, Herman S, 1937, N 21,II,9:1
Kohn, Hezekiah (funl, Mr 27,13:4), 1912, Mr 25,
Kohn, Irving, 1941, S 5,21:6
Kohn, Irving H, 1945, N 12,21:3
Kohn, Isidor, 1938, O 11,27:4
Kohn, Isidore E, 1964, Jl 24,27:4
Kohn, Jacob Mrs, 1955, S 3,15:5
Kohn, Jacob Rabbi, 1968, S 11,51:1
Kohn, Jerome, 1948, Jl 13,6:5
Kohn, Jerome A, 1958, Jl 12,15:2
Kohn, Jerome L, 1964, Ja 19,76:5
Kohn, Joseph S, 1950, D 22,23:3
Kohn, L Winfield, 1956, Ag 17,19:4

Kohn, Leon A, 1956, Ag 19,92:8
Kohn, Louis, 1950, N 26,90:4
Kohn, Martin I, 1949, D 10,17:5
Kohn, Martin J, 1925, O 14,25:3
Kohn, Max Mrs, 1943, Ag 30,15:6
Kohn, Michael, 1962, Ap 22,81:1
Kohn, Murry, 1942, S 12,13:4
Kohn, Nathan S, 1966, My 9,39:1
Kohn, Otto, 1965, Jl 11,69:3
Kohn, Paul A, 1945, S 9,45:1
Kohn, Ralph A, 1945, Mr 5,19:5
Kohn, Richard, 1963, O 14,29:5
Kohn, Richard Mrs, 1966, Jl 8,35:1
Kohn, Robert D, 1953, Je 17,27:3
Kohn, Robert D Mrs, 1955, N 7,29:4
Kohn, Sallie Mrs, 1938, F 14,4:7
Kohn, Samuel Dr, 1909, N 27,9:4
Kohn, Samuel T, 1955, F 6,88:6
Kohn, Sol H, 1920, N 18,15:4
Kohn, W C, 1943, Mr 15,13:2
Kohn, Walter T, 1964, Ap 16,37:2
Kohn, William L, 1954, O 10,84:2
Kohn, Yetta Mrs, 1950, D 23,16:2
Kohner, Arthur W, 1950, Ag 17,27:3
Kohnfelder, Abraham L, 1952, F 16,13:4
Kohnfelder, Abraham L Mrs, 1961, F 9,31:2
Kohnle, Robert C, 1952, D 30,19:4
Kohns, Hermine S Mrs, 1922, O 19,21:5
Kohns, L, 1927, Ja 19,23:3
Kohns, Lazarus (funl, D 6,13:4), 1910, D 4,13:4
Kohns, Lee Mrs, 1952, Je 21,15:3
Kohnstamm, Edward G (por), 1939, N 21,23:4
Kohnstamm, Frank R, 1959, Ag 11,27:4
Kohnstamm, Lorenzo J Dr, 1904, Ap 20,2:5
Kohnstamm, Lothair S, 1950, Ja 31,23:4
Kohon, Benjamin Mrs, 1946, N 24,76:6
Kohon, Isidore, 1945, Ja 20,11:5
Kohout, Jerome, 1951, Ag 11,11:4
Kohout, John J, 1948, Ag 23,19:6
Kohout, Joseph G, 1955, N 12,19:3
Kohr, Hugo J, 1958, Ja 22,27:2
Kohr, Hugo J Mrs, 1963, My 18,27:5
Kohrhardt, Frederick H, 1940, My 15,25:5
Kohs, Samuel C Mrs, 1943, S 9,25:4
Koht, Halvdan, 1965, D 13,39:4
Kohut, Alex Mrs, 1951, Ag 12,79:3
Kohut, G A, 1934, Ja 1,23:1
Koike, Jitsutaro, 1938, Ap 25,15:2
Koine, John F, 1940, My 24,19:2
Koiner, C W, 1947, S 30,25:5
Koiner, George W, 1939, Ag 11,15:4
Kojan, Arthur E, 1958, My 30,21:4
Kok, Arie, 1951, Ja 11,25:5
Kok, Johannes de (por), 1940, O 29,25:3
Kokatnur, Vaman R, 1950, Ag 15,15:1
Kokeritz, Carl von Mrs, 1948, F 14,13:1
Kokeritz, Helge, 1964, Mr 28,19:1
Kokinchak, George Mrs, 1951, F 12,23:5
Koklova, Olga, 1955, F 14,20:5
Kokolski, John, 1968, My 1,47:3
Kokoskie, James M, 1968, Je 4,44:3
Kolachov, Paul J, 1956, Mr 8,29:4
Kolanke, Stephen F, 1946, N 28,27:1
Kolar, Steve, 1941, Mr 26,23:5
Kolar, Victor, 1957, Je 17,23:5
Kolarov, Vassil P Premier, 1950, Ja 23,13:3
Kolars, Charles C, 1937, Mr 27,15:4
Kolas, Yakub, 1956, Ag 15,29:3
Kolb, Andrew G Sr Mrs, 1949, Mr 13,76:4
Kolb, Annette, 1967, D 5,51:5
Kolb, Charles A, 1961, O 6,35:4
Kolb, Clarence, 1964, N 27,35:1
Kolb, Donald F Mrs, 1950, O 5,31:2
Kolb, E Worth, 1939, O 20,23:1
Kolb, Edmund Dr, 1925, Mr 21,13:4
Kolb, Edward O, 1950, Ap 13,29:1
Kolb, Edwin P, 1953, Je 16,27:5
Kolb, Emanuel G, 1945, Mr 6,21:4
Kolb, Emma V, 1955, S 7,31:4
Kolb, Fred, 1960, O 27,37:1
Kolb, Frederick J, 1958, N 18,37:5
Kolb, Frederick Mrs, 1949, S 1,21:6
Kolb, George A, 1903, Jl 8,16:2
Kolb, Gustave F, 1945, Ag 30,21:3
Kolb, Henry D, 1950, N 28,31:2
Kolb, Henry G, 1939, Jl 14,19:5
Kolb, Henry G Mrs, 1946, Je 5,23:2
Kolb, Isador, 1943, F 20,13:2
Kolb, Jacob C, 1966, Ja 13,25:2
Kolb, John F Mrs, 1959, O 6,39:2
Kolb, John N, 1952, Jl 2,25:2
Kolb, John W, 1943, F 18,23:4
Kolb, Joseph O, 1955, Mr 30,29:5
Kolb, Louis J, 1941, Jl 4,13:3
Kolb, Louis J Mrs, 1943, D 27,20:2
Kolb, P Val (por), 1955, D 7,39:2
Kolb, Philip, 1960, Ja 2,13:5
Kolb, R, 1928, Mr 5,23:5
Kolb, Walter, 1956, S 21,25:1
Kolb, William J, 1952, Ag 4,15:5
Kolb, William R, 1956, Mr 24,19:4
Kolb-Danvin, Charles L Mrs, 1941, My 13,23:4
Kolbe, Arno, 1942, F 20,17:3
Kolbe, Arno Mrs, 1954, S 23,33:1
Kolbe, Ferdinand C, 1959, Je 29,29:2
Kolbe, Georg, 1947, N 22,15:5
Kolbe, Harry M Mrs, 1948, Ag 2,21:1
Kolbe, James L, 1957, Mr 7,29:3
Kolbe, Joseph, 1949, Jl 1,19:3
Kolbe, Joseph T Mrs, 1947, Ja 2,27:3
Kolbe, Parke R, 1942, Mr 1,44:7
Kolbe, Theodore W, 1941, Ag 28,19:3
Kolbenheyer, Guido, 1962, Ap 14,25:2
Kolber, Charlotte Mrs, 1950, N 24,35:2
Kolber, Samuel, 1968, Ag 13,39:3
Kolberg, Herbert, 1942, F 2,15:3
Kolbert, Oswald, 1961, S 22,33:2
Kolbert, Stanley, 1960, Ja 12,45:5
Kolbmann, John I, 1955, S 28,35:4
Kolbrener, Martin M, 1967, Je 9,45:1
Kolbride, Percy, 1964, D 12,31:1
Kolby, Uriah S, 1954, Ap 27,29:3
Kolchin, Morris, 1955, Mr 7,27:5
Koldin, Harry, 1967, Ag 2,37:3
Koldofsky, Adolph, 1951, Ap 10,27:1
Koldorf, Max, 1957, Je 26,31:5
Kolehmainen, Hannes, 1966, Ja 12,21:3
Koler, Harry, 1962, S 20,33:3
Kolesnikoff, Vladimir, 1959, Jl 13,27:2
Kolev, Svetoslav, 1950, Je 1,7:4
Kolff, Cornelius G, 1950, F 28,29:1; 1950, Mr 3,25:1
Kolff, Cornelius G Jr, 1941, N 17,19:2
Kolhapur, Maharajah of, 1940, N 27,23:5; 1946, S 30, 25:6
Kolin, Mise, 1958, N 1,19:2
Kolisch, Paul, 1955, O 3,27:5
Kolischer, Gustav, 1942, Ag 12,19:2
Kolk, George B, 1945, Ag 20,19:5
Kolk, Roelof van der, 1959, Mr 11,35:4
Kolker, Edward, 1959, F 19,31:3
Kolker, Henry, 1947, Jl 18,17:3
Kolker, Lee Mrs (M Picker), 1958, N 7,27:1
Kolker, Louis, 1924, N 22,15:4
Kolkman, R, 1947, S 11,27:1
Kolkmann, John H, 1939, Jl 25,19:4
Kolkmeyer, Emeran J, 1958, Ag 20,27:4
Kolle, F Strange Mrs, 1958, Je 25,29:1
Kolle, William D, 1959, My 28,31:3
Kolleeny, Julius Mrs (R Roye), 1960, Je 13,27:5
Kollen, Daniel M, 1963, S 24,29:1
Kollen, G J Dr, 1915, S 6,9:6
Koller, Andrew, 1947, Je 29,48:3
Koller, Antal, 1952, Jl 7,21:3
Koller, Carl (por), 1944, Mr 22,19:1
Koller, Charles W, 1955, Ag 12,19:6
Koller, Edmund L, 1953, Jl 2,23:6
Koller, George J Mrs, 1942, N 30,23:1
Koller, John P, 1953, D 23,25:2
Koller, Larry, 1967, Ag 19,25:1
Koller, Paul W Rev Dr, 1937, N 12,21:3
Kolli, Nikolai, 1966, D 7,47:4
Kolliner, Sim A, 1950, Jl 19,31:2
Kolliner, Sim A Jr, 1966, F 19,27:3
Kollman, Jack, 1959, My 30,17:2
Kollmar, Herman E, 1954, My 10,23:3
Kollmar, John Mrs, 1951, Mr 14,33:4
Kollmar, Richard T Mrs (D Kilgallen),(funl plans, N 11,50:6), 1965, N 9,43:1
Kollmar, Walter H, 1950, Ag 13,76:2
Kollmorgen, Frederick L G, 1961, Ja 20,29:1
Kollmyer, William Mrs, 1950, F 24,24:1
Kollner, Max Mrs, 1942, S 16,23:1
Kollock, John H, 1942, O 26,15:4
Kollontay, Alexandra M, 1952, Mr 12,27:5
Kollsman, Paul Mrs, 1951, Jl 9,25:5
Kolman, Burton A, 1967, F 25,28:1
Kolman, Edward M, 1954, Mr 24,27:3
Kolmer, John A, 1962, D 13,4:5
Kolmer, William, 1967, Ag 9,39:2
Kolmess, Jakob, 1953, Ja 15,4:3
Kolmorgen, Erhard J (cor, N 24,35:2), 1966, N 23, 39:1
Kolod, Ruby, 1967, Ag 12,25:3
Kolodie, Irene Mrs, 1922, N 1,19:6
Kolodney, Louis, 1966, N 15,41:1
Kolodny, Anatole (por), 1948, Jl 9,19:3
Kolodziejewski, Henryk, 1953, Ap 20,25:2
Kolodziejski, Frank J, 1942, S 28,17:4
Kolotilschikov, Nikolai M, 1955, S 7,31:1
Kolowich, George J, 1955, D 10,21:4
Kolpakchi, Vladimir Y, 1961, My 19,1:3
Kolseth, Henry F, 1908, Ap 5,11:4
Kolsky, Edward, 1964, Ja 14,31:2
Kolstedt, Clarence P, 1963, Je 17,25:4
Kolster, Frederick A, 1950, Ag 1,23:2
Kolthoff, Howard C, 1950, Ap 2,93:2
Kolts, Harry J, 1948, Jl 24,15:6
Koltz, Maury J M, 1956, Je 22,23:4
Kolyer, Abram B, 1942, D 28,19:4
Kolyer, John, 1955, Jl 26,25:3
Komack, Max, 1956, Mr 11,89:1
Komar, George M, 1958, Mr 11,29:4
Komar, John J, 1946, F 25,25:2
Komara, Joseph J, 1946, Je 9,40:4
Komarewsky, Vasili I, 1957, Je 22,15:2
Komarnicki, Waclaw, 1954, Mr 23,27:1
Komaroff, George, 1957, Mr 13,31:5
Komaroff, Vladimir, 1945, D 7,22:3
Komaroff, von Marshall, 1928, My 19,4:6
Komarov, Simon A, 1964, Mr 31,35:3
Komarovsky, Mendel, 1952, Ap 3,35:4
Komatsu, Prince, 1903, F 19,9:7
Komatsu, Takashi, 1965, Mr 15,31:3
Komatsu-no-Miya, Yoriko Princess, 1914, Je 27,7:6
Kometer, Baroness (M K Feldman), 1957, N 22,25:2
Komfort, Valentine, 1943, D 6,23:5
Komie, Isaac, 1947, D 14,78:4
Komins, Benjamin, 1956, S 1,15:5
Komisarjevsky, Theodore, 1954, Ap 18,88:5
Komisarzhevsky, Vera F Mrs (Countess Muravieff), 1910, F 24,9:3
Komiss, David S, 1947, Je 11,27:5
Komlos, Emory H, 1949, O 29,3:2
Kommel, Aaron, 1920, O 22,15:6
Kommel, Louis M, 1946, N 15,23:4
Kommer, John T, 1950, O 3,31:2
Kommer, Rudolf K, 1943, Mr 29,16:2
Kommodov, N V, 1947, Je 18,25:5
Komnenos, Notis, 1950, D 5,32:2
Komora, Paul O, 1950, Jl 19,31:3
Komora, Paul O Mrs, 1950, S 4,17:5
Komoroski, Stephen F, 1952, D 11,33:2
Komorowski, Tadeusz (Gen Bor), 1966, Ag 26,33:1
Komow, Maximilian, 1965, Je 30,37:5
Komroff, Elinor M B Mrs, 1942, F 17,22:2
Kon, Alex V, 1941, Ap 30,19:5
Konald, George Frank, 1924, Mr 4,19:3
Konchalovsky, Pyotr, 1956, F 4,19:6
Konchell, Joseph, 1948, F 18,27:3
Kondakov, Alex, 1954, D 23,19:1
Kondell, Leon, 1958, My 11,86:5
Konder, Alex M, 1953, S 15,31:2
Kondo, Ichitaro, 1961, Ja 7,19:6
Kondo, Nobitake, 1953, F 21,13:3
Kondo, Rempei Baron, 1921, F 11,11:3
Kondolf, Frank N, 1944, Ag 31,17:5
Kondolf, George V Mrs, 1947, Mr 11,27:3
Kondor, Arno, 1942, F 17,21:2
Kondrup, Johann C, 1874, D 11,8:3
Konduriotis, P, 1935, Ag 23,15:1
Kone, Samuel C, 1951, F 3,15:4
Konecky, Albert M, 1955, Mr 13,86:1
Konematter, Albert, 1949, N 10,31:2
Konen, Henrich M, 1949, Ja 5,25:1
Koner, Samuel, 1966, D 18,84:8
Konetchy, Edward J, 1947, My 28,25:3
Konheim, Jerome F, 1960, D 10,23:6
Konheim, Louis, 1955, My 2,21:4
Konheim, Solomon Mrs, 1948, S 15,31:2
Konheim, Sydney, 1951, Jl 15,60:5
Konieczny, Stanislaus, 1940, O 4,23:5
Konig, George, 1913, Je 1,IV,7:6
Koniger, Maximilian J, 1940, Ap 20,17:4
Konight, Samuel Jr, 1950, Ja 28,9:2
Konijnenburg, Willem van, 1943, Mr 6,13:4
Koning, Johan F L, 1946, O 31,25:4
Koning, Paul Mrs, 1946, S 20,31:2
Konishi, Katsuishi, 1940, Ap 9,23:3
Konitza, Faik, 1942, D 16,25:2
Konizak, Carl, 1905, Ap 24,5:1
Konkle, Burton, 1944, O 25,21:2
Konkle, Creighton M, 1939, S 25,19:3
Konkle, Oscar E, 1954, N 25,29:4
Konkle, Oscar Mrs, 1941, Je 19,21:6
Konner, Jacob, 1964, Ja 30,29:3
Konnov, Ivan, 1951, Jl 16,21:4
Kono, Ichiro, 1965, Jl 9,29:1
Konopka, Alexandria Mrs, 1940, D 28,15:3
Konovitz, Israel, 1958, Jl 2,29:3
Konovitz, Israel Mrs, 1957, N 26,33:4
Konow, Henri, 1939, Ja 20,19:4
Konowitz, Isidore M, 1967, Ja 21,31:5
Konoye, Fumitaka Prince, 1956, D 11,8:3
Konrad, John C, 1923, Je 12,19:3
Konrad, John S, 1941, Mr 23,45:1
Konrad, Michael Mrs, 1947, D 3,29:4
Konrad, William, 1942, Jl 7,19:6
Konrath, George, 1945, D 22,12:8
Konselman, Charles B Jr, 1967, F 4,27:4
Konta, A, 1933, Ap 29,13:3
Konta, Geoffrey (por), 1942, N 25,23:1
Konti, Isadore (por), 1938, Ja 12,21:1
Kontos, Thomas, 1961, F 13,27:5
Konvitz, Ben Z, 1946, Je 29,19:1
Konvitz, Joseph, 1944, Je 7,19:6
Konwin, Robert S, 1965, Jl 22,31:3
Konwitschny, Franz, 1962, Jl 29,61:1
Konyot, Arthur, 1966, D 16,47:3
Konzet, John J, 1946, Ja 24,21:4
Koo, Wellington Mrs, 1918, O 11,11:3
Koob, Albert P, 1953, N 11,31:3
Koob, Ernie, 1941, N 13,27:3
Kook, Dov, 1950, Mr 9,29:1
Kook, Irving, 1955, D 30,19:2
Kook, Moses, 1954, Ag 10,19:4
Kooken, Don L, 1959, My 30,17:5
Koolhoven, Fritz, 1946, Jl 2,25:6
Koolick, Abe, 1950, Ja 24,31:3
Koon, James C, 1959, Jl 5,57:1

Koon, Ray M, 1954, Jl 5,11:5
Koon, Sidney G, 1950, S 26,31:2
Koon, Thomas W (por), 1946, D 6,24:2
Koones, J Alexander, 1906, My 29,11:7
Koons, Benjamin Franklin Prof, 1903, D 19,9:5
Koons, Charles Alfred, 1968, F 27,39:1
Koons, Charles E, 1952, O 28,31:5
Koons, Chauncey B Mrs, 1955, Ap 29,23:2
Koons, Dana R, 1965, Ja 22,43:3
Koons, Earle R, 1960, Je 21,34:1
Koons, Earle R Mrs, 1964, My 18,26:4
Koons, Edward L, 1946, F 25,25:1
Koons, Edwin W, 1947, D 1,21:5
Koons, John C (por), 1937, Ap 13,25:5
Koons, Lucius T, 1942, D 29,21:5
Koons, Tilghman B, 1946, Ja 20,43:1
Koonsen, William F, 1947, Ag 14,23:3
Koonts, Harvey H, 1940, O 18,21:3
Koontz, Alexander F Dr, 1917, Mr 6,11:5
Koontz, Amos R, 1965, F 5,31:5
Koontz, Chester B, 1954, Ja 22,27:4
Koontz, Frank L, 1943, F 1,15:3
Koontz, Fred B, 1953, O 30,23:3
Koontz, Louis K, 1951, Ag 8,25:2
Koontz, Paul, 1954, N 30,29:5
Koontz, Richard G, 1938, Je 17,21:4
Koonz, Harold A, 1955, O 9,86:1
Koonz, Marie C, 1956, Jl 23,23:4
Koop, Eugene J, 1952, Je 21,15:6
Koop, Eugene Jackson Mrs, 1968, N 20,47:2
Koop, John F, 1945, F 23,17:3
Koop, Laura H Mrs, 1948, Ag 26,21:3
Koop, William H, 1952, Ag 26,25:5
Koopman, Harry S, 1945, Mr 6,21:3
Koopman, Henry, 1919, O 27,11:5
Koopman, Henry Mrs, 1948, My 20,29:3
Koopman, John R, 1949, S 20,29:1
Koopman, Thomas O, 1952, Mr 19,29:4
Koopmann, John H W, 1945, Ja 20,11:2
Koops, Harry G, 1942, Mr 22,48:7
Kooreman, Byak, 1912, Ja 14,II,16:2
Kooreman, Fred, 1940, Jl 20,15:1
Koos, Charles Sr, 1951, O 6,19:4
Koos, E Emile, 1947, Mr 15,13:4
Koos, Edward Jr Mrs, 1953, Ja 4,77:1
Kooser, James E, 1939, Mr 6,15:3
Kooyman, Beulah L Mrs, 1965, Ag 25,48:1
Kopald, Herman G, 1957, N 1,27:1
Kopald, S L, 1953, D 27,60:8
Kopald, Sigmund, 1956, Ap 6,25:3
Kopec, Joseph, 1947, Ja 26,53:2
Kopec, William Sr, 1950, My 23,29:3
Kopecky, Joseph, 1952, Ag 24,89:1
Kopecky, Vaclav, 1961, Ag 7,23:1
Kopel, Holger A Mrs, 1940, S 14,17:2
Kopel, Oscar, 1940, My 26,34:4
Kopelman, Barnett E, 1955, Mr 24,31:5
Kopeloff, Nicholas, 1959, S 6,72:6
Koperski, Richard T, 1952, O 2,29:5
Kopetschny, Edward F, 1941, Mr 25,26:1
Kopetschny, Otto E Dr, 1937, Mr 25,25:2
Kopetsky, Joseph, 1907, S 23,9:4
Kopetzky, Samuel J, 1950, N 14,31:1
Kopf, Carroll B, 1944, F 21,15:4
Kopf, Emil A, 1944, My 24,19:6
Kopf, Harry C, 1954, Mr 28,88:5
Kopf, Harry W, 1958, Mr 20,29:4
Kopf, Hinrich, 1961, D 22,23:1
Kopf, John G, 1954, N 9,27:2
Kopf, John G Mrs, 1950, O 12,31:2
Kopf, Joseph B, 1960, Jl 17,61:1
Kopf, Joseph L, 1957, O 23,33:3
Kopf, Leo, 1953, Mr 2,23:4
Kopf, Marie Mrs, 1947, Je 7,13:6
Kopf, Maxim, 1958, Jl 8,27:1
Kopf, Morris, 1952, Ja 9,29:5
Kopf, William G, 1950, D 19,29:1
Kopfer, George, 1914, Ag 17,7:3
Kopff, Emilie Mrs (will), 1938, Je 21,17:2
Kopff, Frederick L Jr, 1966, My 18,47:1
Kopfstein, William V, 1949, S 20,29:4
Kopins, Louis J, 1950, Je 23,25:2
Koplik, Abner, 1957, O 19,21:1
Koplik, Daniel M, 1957, Ap 28,86:8
Koplik, H, 1927, My 1,II,9:1
Koplik, Irving Mrs, 1950, F 24,23:1
Koplik, Lewis H, 1945, Jl 23,19:4
Koplin, Arabham H, 1944, Ja 24,17:3
Koplin, Louis, 1949, Mr 31,25:3
Kopliner, Michael C, 1960, Jl 22,23:2
Koplovitz, Ely S, 1957, Ja 31,27:1
Koplovitz, Jacob, 1956, Je 9,17:4
Koplowitz, Abraham, 1953, F 12,27:3
Koplowitz, Abraham J, 1958, Ag 27,29:1
Kopman, Benjamin, 1965, D 5,89:2
Kopman, Benjamin Mrs (Y Blumberg), 1964, N 14, 29:6
Kopnicki, Anton, 1949, Jl 8,19:3
Kopoken, Arthur A Dr, 1968, Je 18,47:4
Kopotkov, Victor, 1952, Jl 9,27:3
Kopozynski, Leon, 1938, Ja 12,21:5
Kopp, Alexander, 1945, Ag 4,11:2
Kopp, Cornelius J, 1940, Ap 20,17:4
Kopp, Frederick U, 1950, My 14,106:8
Kopp, George, 1947, D 27,14:2
Kopp, George Cardinal, 1914, Mr 4,11:5
Kopp, Harry, 1943, O 28,23:3
Kopp, Harry F, 1946, Ag 21,27:5
Kopp, John, 1955, My 21,17:5
Kopp, Marie E, 1943, D 16,27:2
Kopp, Nicholas, 1937, Ap 17,17:4
Kopp, O H, 1881, D 13,2:4
Kopp, Sidney S, 1945, Ap 22,35:1
Kopp, William F, 1938, Ag 26,17:4
Koppang, Sigurd E, 1955, D 9,27:3
Koppel, Arthur, 1908, My 14,9:6
Koppel, Holger A, 1941, Ap 12,15:4
Koppel, Jacob, 1954, F 9,27:3
Koppel, Peggy (Mrs Edw), 1958, D 4,39:4
Koppel, Thomas A, 1963, D 17,39:4
Koppell, Alfred B, 1963, Je 1,21:6
Koppell, Henry G, 1964, D 6,88:7
Koppell, L C, 1878, Jl 29,8:2
Koppelman, Edwin L, 1937, O 16,19:5
Koppelmann, Eugene, 1942, Mr 17,22:3
Koppen, Charles A, 1945, F 15,19:3
Koppens, Madge W von, 1944, Ag 5,11:5
Kopper, David, 1956, Ap 13,25:1
Kopper, John M, 1945, Je 16,13:2
Kopper, Joseph Mrs, 1945, Mr 6,21:1
Kopper, Samuel K C, 1957, Je 5,35:1
Kopperl, Joseph I, 1951, Mr 2,25:4
Kopperl, Moritz O, 1952, S 3,30:3
Kopperl, Wladine Z Mrs, 1949, Jl 29,21:3
Kopperud, Harry L, 1939, S 20,27:5
Koppin, Henry S, 1941, Ja 29,17:5
Koppisch, Walter F, 1953, N 6,27:1
Koppleman, Jessie Mrs, 1942, F 3,20:2
Kopplemann, Herman P, 1957, Ag 13,27:2
Koprulu, Fuad, 1966, Je 29,47:5
Kops, Daniel, 1923, O 2,7:3
Kops, Max Mrs, 1955, Ag 10,25:2
Kops, Samuel, 1912, Ag 14,9:5
Kops, Waldemar (por), 1945, Ja 14,40:3
Kopsch, John, 1943, Je 6,44:6
Kopstein, Isaac, 1959, D 12,23:2
Koptman, Theodore, 1948, S 13,21:3
Kopycinski, Stephen J, 1968, O 1,47:2
Kopytov, Anatolii, 1950, Mr 11,15:1
Korab, Henri de, 1954, D 26,61:2
Koran, William M, 1957, Ap 23,31:5
Korb, Anton W, 1956, S 8,17:5
Korb, Phillip M, 1964, Ap 15,39:5
Korbel, Edward F, 1961, Ag 6,85:1
Korbel, Mario, 1954, Ap 1,31:4
Korbly, Charles A, 1937, Jl 27,21:3
Korch, Frank, 1958, S 7,87:2
Korchagin, O P, 1951, Jl 27,19:2
Korcheck, Michael, 1954, D 25,11:6
Korchinsky, Joseph E, 1942, My 16,13:1
Korda, Alex, 1956, Ja 24,31:1
Korda, Harold L, 1967, My 3,45:1
Korda, Zoltan, 1961, O 15,89:1
Kordff, Arnold, 1944, Je 4,41:2
Kordula, Edward J, 1960, F 20,23:1
Korell, Christian W, 1966, Ap 15,39:2
Korell, George W, 1945, Ap 2,19:3
Korell, George W Mrs, 1941, N 28,24:3
Koren, Ludo, 1958, Je 20,23:5
Koren, William, 1937, Ja 26,21:4
Koren, William Jr, 1956, F 8,33:1
Korenman, Hyman, 1942, N 23,23:6
Koretzky, Israel, 1946, Ja 10,23:3
Korey, A J, 1947, S 3,25:4
Korey, Harold R, 1960, N 14,31:4
Korey, Saul R, 1963, S 28,19:2
Korfanity, Adalbert, 1939, Ag 17,21:1
Korff, Howard C, 1956, Ag 16,25:6
Korff, Jacob I, 1952, S 28,78:7
Korff, Kurt, 1938, Ja 31,19:3
Korff, Nikolas Mrs, 1948, Ap 26,23:5
Korff, Oscar, 1958, Ag 13,27:4
Korff, Serge A Baron, 1924, Mr 14,17:3
Korgis, Hercules, 1961, Ag 4,21:3
Korhammer, Maximilian W, 1937, S 9,25:2
Korhammer, William M, 1951, Ag 7,25:3
Korin, Pavel D, 1967, N 24,46:1
Korinda, Peter, 1957, Mr 14,1:4
Korinek, Adolph J, 1950, N 3,27:1
Korjus, Voldemar L, 1961, Je 24,21:4
Korkes, Seymour, 1955, D 12,16:2
Korlesky, Paul F, 1960, F 10,38:1
Korman, Murray, 1961, Ag 10,27:3
Korman, Samuel H, 1948, S 18,17:3
Korman, Sigmund, 1957, Je 19,35:3
Kormann, William H, 1959, N 18,41:3
Kormendi, Eugene, 1959, Ag 16,82:8
Kormos, Hugo, 1951, D 4,33:3
Korn, Albert R, 1956, N 21,27:2
Korn, Arthur (por), 1945, D 23,18:4
Korn, Carl G F, 1951, Jl 20,21:4
Korn, Chester B, 1955, Ag 2,23:4
Korn, Chester F, 1954, N 21,87:1
Korn, Daniel L, 1957, Mr 24,87:2
Korn, Ernst A, 1939, Je 23,19:4
Korn, Eva C, 1946, Ap 12,27:3
Korn, Francis E, 1957, Ap 28,86:6
Korn, Frank W, 1943, Jl 31,13:4
Korn, Frederick A, 1948, N 11,27:1
Korn, Heinrich von, 1907, Mr 24,9:5
Korn, J M, 1956, Jl 24,25:5
Korn, Lewis W, 1938, Ag 28,32:5
Korn, Max, 1942, S 5,13:6; 1949, Ag 9,25:1
Korn, Meyer H, 1966, Ja 30,84:7
Korn, Nathan, 1941, N 23,53:1
Korn, Otto K, 1958, D 29,15:1
Korn, Samuel W Mrs, 1946, O 2,29:4
Kornacki, Joseph S, 1959, Mr 29,80:1
Kornas, Joseph, 1952, Ja 17,28:3
Kornberg, Leonard, 1963, S 24,29:1
Kornberg, Maurice Dr, 1968, Jl 18,33:5
Kornblau, Jerry, 1951, N 14,31:3
Kornblith, Abraham L, 1965, Je 29,35:2
Kornblith, Rachmil, 1959, N 25,29:2
Kornblum, Karl, 1944, My 17,19:2
Kornblum, Moses J C, 1964, S 2,37:3
Kornbluth, Cyril M, 1958, Mr 22,17:4
Kornbrath, Rudolph J, 1946, F 26,25:4
Kornder, Phil J, 1939, Mr 23,23:4
Korndorfer, Alfred, 1950, Ja 6,21:2
Korndorff, Lynn H, 1959, Ag 12,29:2
Korndorff, Lynn H Mrs, 1949, My 10,25:5
Kornelussen, Horken, 1953, My 31,32:1
Korner, Otto, 1946, S 5,27:2
Kornfeder, Joseph Z, 1963, My 4,25:2
Kornfeld, Albert, 1962, Ag 18,19:2
Kornfeld, Alfred E, 1944, Ap 9,34:2
Kornfeld, Harold, 1952, Je 1,85:1
Kornfeld, Harold B, 1946, N 25,27:4
Kornfeld, Herman, 1968, Ag 20,41:1
Kornfeld, Joseph S, 1943, Je 24,21:2
Kornfeld, Joseph S Mrs, 1958, Je 18,33:2
Kornfeld, Kurt, 1967, F 20,37:3
Kornfeld, Werner, 1961, Ap 7,31:1
Kornfelt, Joseph, 1938, F 28,6:3
Kornfield, Louis D, 1941, Ap 2,23:4
Korngold, Erich W, 1957, N 30,21:2
Korngold, Julius, 1945, S 27,21:5
Korngold, Ralph, 1964, O 30,37:5
Kornhauser, Samuel J, 1956, Ag 30,25:1
Kornicke, Joseph Sr, 1950, Ag 15,29:4
Korniechuk, Aleksandr Y Mrs (W Wasilewska), 1964, Jl 30,27:4
Kornish, Max, 1948, My 25,27:1
Kornitzer, Bela, 1964, N 25,37:3
Kornsand, Edmond S, 1966, My 14,31:1
Kornstein, Phil, 1954, D 22,23:3
Korntheuer, Joseph, 1944, Jl 18,19:3
Korobov, Anatoly V, 1967, O 5,39:2
Korobov, Ivan G, 1952, Ja 30,26:3
Korobov, Pavel I, 1965, Ag 19,31:4
Korody, Alex, 1950, Ap 13,29:2
Koroki Te Rata Mahuta Te Wherowhero, King, 1966 My 20,44:1
Korol, Alexander G, 1967, O 14,27:2
Korol, Stanley, 1952, Ja 29,25:3
Korol, Walter, 1966, O 9,86:2
Korolenko, Vladimir, 1921, D 29,15:4
Korolev, Sergei P (funl, Ja 19,10:3), 1966, Ja 16,82:
Koronefsky, Jacob, 1939, Ja 19,19:3
Koroshetz, Anton, 1940, D 15,61:1
Korotev, Constantine A, 1953, Ja 7,31:1
Korovin, Yevgeny A, 1964, N 25,37:1
Korowicz, Marek S, 1964, O 9,40:2
Koroyev, Georgi P, 1957, Je 9,88:3
Korphage, Joseph A (Bro Adelmar George), 1953, Je 22,21:1
Korsa, Arku, 1967, Ja 26,33:4
Korsak, Wladyslaw, 1950, Ja 4,46:2
Korschen, John A, 1953, Ag 11,27:2
Korseymer, Frederick W Mrs, 1953, Mr 4,27:1
Korshalla, Joseph D, 1959, Je 30,31:2
Korsmeyer, Frederick A, 1961, O 30,29:2
Korson, George K, 1967, My 25,47:1
Korsoski, John Mrs, 1914, My 14,11:5
Korsten, Bernard S, 1951, Ap 11,29:5
Korstian, Clarence Ferdinand Dr, 1968, F 23,33:3
Kort, Arthur H, 1944, Mr 12,38:5
Kortenhaus, William A, 1968, Ja 3,40:8
Kortjohn, Martin (por), 1949, O 12,29:4
Kortlander, Henry W, 1953, Mr 30,21:5
Kortlander, Max J, 1961, O 12,29:5
Kortright, James M, 1954, N 27,14:2
Kortright, Robert R, 1945, O 30,19:2
Kortright, Therese White Mrs, 1922, O 24,17:4
Kortschak, Hugh, 1957, S 20,25:4
Kortz, Ida S Mrs, 1938, Ag 25,19:5
Korves, Albert M, 1939, O 9,19:6
Korwin, Joseph M de, 1944, O 19,23:3
Kory, Jacob M, 1954, S 29,31:4
Kory, Max Mrs, 1945, Mr 25,37:2
Korylak, William, 1964, Ap 2,33:4
Korzybska, Alfred Mrs, 1954, Jl 14,27:5
Korzybski, Alfred H, 1950, Mr 2,28:2
Kosa, Emile Sr, 1955, My 12,29:1
Kosaki, Hiromichi, 1938, F 27,II,9:2
Kosanovic, Sava, 1956, N 15,35:4
Kosar, Jaromir, 1967, Ja 5,37:2
Kosberg, Benjamin, 1951, Mr 3,13:2

Kosberg, Milton, 1964, My 12,37:5
Kosberg, Semyon A, 1965, Ja 5,33:2
Kosby, Samuel, 1955, My 29,45:1
Kosch, Rudolph A J, 1946, Mr 24,44:5
Koscherak, Otto L, 1946, Ap 12,27:1
Kosches, Norris R, 1950, Mr 29,29:1
Koschwitz, William B, 1946, N 24,79:3
Koscinski, Arthur A, 1957, N 23,19:3
Kosco, John, 1950, My 29,17:4
Kosco. Jno Mrs, 1945, O 28,28:8
Kosek, Frank J, 1942, F 12,23:2
Kosek, Osvald, 1960, Ap 11,31:2
Kosh, Israel R, 1948, Ja 4,52:4
Koshalko, Charles, 1951, Ja 20,15:5
Koshetz, Abraham, 1945, N 11,42:2
Koshetz, Alexander (por), 1944, S 23,13:2
Koshetz, Nina, 1965, My 16,88:4
Koshits, Alex P, 1949, Ap 19,25:4
Koshkin, Victor I Mrs (Vera H), 1962, Jl 20,25:2
Koshland, Daniel E Mrs, 1959, Mr 8,87:1
Koshland, Edward O, 1949, Je 8,29:1
Koshland, Joseph, 1940, Je 13,23:3
Koshland, Marcus S Mrs, 1953, O 15,33:6
Koshtoyants, Khachatur, 1961, Ap 4,37:1
Kosik, C Austin, 1953, Ja 28,27:4
Kosik, Gustave, 1956, O 30,37:2
Koske, William, 1950, Mr 21,32:3
Koskenniemi, Veikko A, 1962, Ag 5,81:2
Kosko, Maria, 1965, Ap 2,35:3
Koskoff, Yale D Mrs, 1954, Jl 14,27:3
Kosky, Sophie B, 1962, N 8,39:5
Koslen, Manuel, 1950, Ap 15,15:4
Kosloff, Meyer L, 1954, Ap 23,27:2
Kosloff, P, 1935, S 28,15:5
Kosloff, Samuel, 1959, Ja 24,19:4
Koslofsky, Irving, 1940, O 19,17:3
Koslovsky, Morris, 1949, Ap 19,25:4
Koslow, Nat, 1958, Mr 24,27:3
Koslow, Oscar E, 1959, Ja 27,33:3
Koslowsky, Aaron J, 1964, My 30,17:3
Kosmack, Ruth G Mrs, 1952, Ja 14,19:4
Kosmak, George W, 1954, Jl 11,73:1
Kosmerl, Francis S (will), 1949, Ap 23,14:3
Kosmopoulos, Alice L W, 1954, Je 29,27:2
Kosmutza, Charles A Sr, 1953, O 6,29:3
Kosnoski, Anton, 1941, S 11,23:5
Kosok, Paul, 1959, O 7,43:1
Koss, C G, 1933, O 7,15:4
Koss, David, 1956, F 22,48:3; 1960, Mr 11,25:2
Koss, Fred, 1939, Jl 18,19:3
Koss, John F, 1955, Ap 13,29:4
Koss, Joseph, 1953, My 1,21:1
Kossak, Zofia, 1968, Ap 10,43:1
Kossatkino-Rostoffsky, Olga Princess, 1952, Ap 24, 31:3
Kossler, William J, 1945, N 17,17:2
Kossman, Hans R, 1956, F 14,29:2
Kossman, Samuel, 1958, Mr 25,27:1
Kossove, Boris Mrs, 1944, Ja 23,38:3
Kossovsky, Wolf, 1958, S 12,25:1
Kossuth, Egon J, 1949, Ja 12,28:2
Kossuth, Francis, 1914, My 26,11:5
Kossuth, Louis, 1884, D 18,2:1; 1894, Mr 21,5:3
Kost, Anna, 1951, D 15,13:5
Kost, Frederick W, 1923, F 24,11:6
Kost, Henry, 1945, Ap 23,19:3
Kost, John Dr, 1904, Ja 11,7:5
Kost, William, 1952, N 24,23:2
Kost, William L Mrs, 1958, Mr 27,33:5
Kostal, Emil, 1965, My 10,33:1
Kostelanetz, Nachman, 1954, My 26,29:2
Kostellow, Alex J, 1954, S 1,27:3
Koster, Elmer T, 1943, Jl 14,19:4
Koster, Florentine Mrs, 1950, Je 6,29:4
Koster, Fred H, 1958, Ja 17,25:2
Koster, Frederick J, 1958, N 20,35:5
Koster, George F, 1954, D 6,27:4
Koster, Henry H, 1961, Ag 9,33:4
Koster, Henry W, 1953, Ja 17,15:5
Koster, John, 1945, Ag 16,19:5
Koster, John J, 1967, Jl 20,37:4
Koster, John P Mrs, 1945, Ja 16,19:1
Koster, Peter M, 1944, F 26,13:6
Koster, W O A, 1947, Jl 17,19:3
Koster, Walter, 1966, D 20,43:1
Kosterin, Aleksei Y, 1968, N 13,4:5
Kosters, Paul J, 1949, My 28,15:3
Kostial, Michael, 1942, D 23,19:4
Kostik, Joseph, 1947, Ap 16,25:2
Kostikov, Andrei G, 1950, D 9,15:2
Kostiloff, Nicholas Paulovitch, 1924, Mr 3,17:5
Kostlin, Julius Prof, 1902, My 14,9:4
Kostner, J O, 1925, F 26,21:4
Kostomaroff, Historian, 1885, My 30,3:2
Kostov, Donche, 1949, Ag 11,23:4
Kostroff, Maurice, 1958, Ag 15,21:2
Kostrubala, John, 1958, O 1,37:1
Kosturkov, Stoyan, 1949, D 19,27:1
Kostyal, John A, 1956, S 9,84:4
Kosygin, Aleksei N Mrs (funl, My 4,39:2), 1967, My 2,47:2
Kosynkin, Piotr E Maj-Gen, 1953, F 18,31:4
Koszegi, Alex, 1937, D 16,27:4

Kotcher, Irwin, 1953, D 9,11:1
Kotchetovsky, Alex, 1952, Mr 4,27:2
Kotchoubey, Sergio, 1960, D 26,23:4
Koterba, Ed (trb), 1961, Je 29,12:1
Kotershall, Joseph J, 1945, D 12,27:2
Koth, Charles, 1952, Ap 1,29:4
Koth, Herbert B, 1951, F 1,25:2
Kothe, Raymond F, 1957, Ja 8,31:3
Kotila, John E, 1951, Mr 28,29:4
Kotimas, Joseph, 1913, S 11,11:6
Kotkov, Wilfred Phineas Dr, 1921, F 28,11:4
Kotlarsky, Max, 1958, Jl 26,15:2
Kotler, Aaron (funl NYC, D 3,31:1; funl Jerusalem, D 5,47:5), 1962, N 30,33:1
Kotler, Leo, 1960, Ag 22,25:4
Kotler, Max, 1943, Je 23,21:5
Kotrich, Edward J, 1957, Je 20,29:5
Kott, George Mrs, 1951, Ag 13,17:4
Kott, Otto W, 1937, D 23,21:3
Kotta, Nuci, 1965, Jl 23,29:2
Kottgen, Hector, 1962, Je 26,33:4
Kottle, Harriet, 1951, My 10,33:7
Kottler, Aaron, 1961, Jl 28,21:2
Kottler, Erwin, 1947, O 21,23:1
Kottman, Anna T, 1946, Mr 19,27:5
Kottman, William A (por), 1945, F 21,19:3
Kottmiller, Alfred, 1940, D 27,14:6
Kottner, Charles A, 1950, Ja 27,24:3
Kotulka, Merion J, 1937, My 20,21:3
Kotz, Adam L, 1940, Mr 18,17:2
Kotz, Daniel Mrs, 1947, Ap 27,60:3
Kotze, George, 1947, Ap 20,60:7
Kotze, John G, 1940, Ap 2,25:1
Kotze, Robert, 1953, Mr 16,19:5
Kotze, Stefan von, 1909, Ap 13,9:5
Kotzebue, Paul de Countess (will, My 26,32:5), 1955, My 3,31:4
Kotzen, Isidore, 1954, Jl 11,72:4
Kotzen, Max M, 1957, Mr 19,37:2
Kotzian, Henry, 1952, S 6,17:4
Kotzias, Constantine, 1951, D 9,90:5
Kotzschmar, Hermann Mrs, 1947, N 8,17:4
Kouba, Frank C, 1962, Je 16,19:4
Koudacheff, Vladimir, 1957, F 24,85:2
Koudelka, Joseph Maria Bp, 1921, Je 25,11:6
Koudrey, Vladimir, 1938, D 21,23:1
Koukol, Alois B, 1953, Ja 17,15:4
Koult, Oscar, 1959, O 3,19:5
Kountz, Palmer D, 1963, Jl 4,17:1
Kountz, Richard, 1950, O 17,31:4
Kountz, William B, 1962, D 15,14:6
Kountze, A F, 1927, Mr 16,25:4
Kountze, B W, 1901, Ag 30,7:6
Kountze, Charles B, 1911, N 19,II,15:5
Kountze, Charles T, 1938, F 1,21:2
Kountze, De Lancey (por), 1946, O 3,27:5
Kountze, Herman, 1906, N 22,9:6
Kountze, Herman D, 1947, N 20,30:3
Kountze, Herman D Mrs, 1951, Ap 28,17:7
Kountze, Luther, 1918, Ap 18,13:4
Kour, Joseph, 1954, Jl 8,23:2
Kourcik, Leon, 1967, Je 20,39:3
Kouri, Habib M, 1963, O 10,41:1
Kouri, Habid, 1946, O 10,27:5
Kourkoulis, Methodios (por), 1941, Ap 11,21:4
Kous, Nicholas, 1952, Mr 9,93:2
Koussevitzky, Moshe, 1966, Ag 24,45:1
Koussevitzky, Serge, 1951, Je 5,1:2
Koussevitzky, Serge Mrs, 1942, Ja 13,22:5
Koutroulis, Constantine, 1944, D 10,56:1
Koutzen, Boris, 1966, D 11,88:8
Koutzen, Leo, 1941, Ap 12,15:2
Kouwenhoven, Annie B Mrs, 1941, D 19,25:5
Kouwenhoven, Charles W Mrs, 1954, Jl 5,11:5
Kouwenhoven, Cornelius B, 1952, D 11,33:4
Kouwenhoven, Grace, 1960, D 18,84:5
Kouwenhoven, Holmes W, 1940, Ja 9,23:5
Kouwenhoven, Luke, 1914, D 18,13:6
Kouwenhoven, Tunis G B Mrs, 1955, Je 14,29:1
Kouwenhoven, William H, 1937, D 22,25:5
Kouwenhoven, William W, 1961, F 7,33:1
Kouyoumdjisky, Angel Mrs, 1944, Ap 29,15:2
Kovacevic, Vasily, 1961, D 16,25:2
Kovach, Edward M, 1965, F 28,88:6
Kovach, George S, 1960, N 14,31:5
Kovacic, Donald G, 1958, My 24,21:5
Kovacs, Bela (trb lr, Je 25,28:6), 1959, Je 23,33:1
Kovacs, Daniel, 1946, Ap 7,44:2
Kovacs, Ernie (funl, Ja 16,33:5; est acctg, Ja 26,16:2), 1962, Ja 14,1:3
Kovacs, Ernie (est acctg), 1966, D 20,36:5
Kovacs, Eugene, 1943, O 17,48:4
Kovacs, John, 1957, Ag 16,19:1
Kovacs, Joseph Mrs, 1949, My 28,15:5
Kovacs, Julius G, 1963, Je 6,35:3
Kovacs, Lily, 1960, O 29,23:5
Kovacs, Nicholas, 1965, S 28,3:5
Kovacs, Paul A, 1965, D 8,47:2
Kovacs, Richard, 1950, D 30,13:3
Kovacs, Stephen, 1884, Ap 17,4:7
Kovacs, Stephen J (wrong listing as Kovacs, Paul; cor, Jl 24,27:5), 1964, Jl 23,27:3
Kovalenko, Michael S, 1954, Ap 3,16:5

Kovalik, John, 1961, O 16,29:1
Kovar, Abraham J, 1965, Ag 8,64:5
Kovar, Harry L, 1954, My 23,88:5
Kovarick, John, 1945, F 20,19:2
Kovarik, Alois, 1965, N 19,39:3
Kovarik, James F, 1947, Jl 30,21:6
Kovarik, Joseph J, 1951, F 20,25:5
Kovarsky, Ilia, 1962, Jl 11,35:5
Koveleski, Emanuel, 1950, N 5,92:5
Koven, Benjamin Mrs, 1962, Ag 22,33:2
Koven, Charles W, 1941, N 11,23:1
Koverman, Ida Mrs, 1954, N 25,29:4
Kovesi, Geza, 1949, N 22,29:1
Kovner, Harold Mrs, 1939, Je 28,21:3
Kovner, Harry, 1947, Jl 28,15:6
Kovner, Milton, 1967, Ja 3,34:1
Kovner, Sidney J, 1963, Jl 17,31:3
Kowal, Chester C, 1966, S 29,47:3
Kowal, John, 1946, Jl 12,17:2
Kowalczyk, Andrew S, 1952, Ja 17,28:2
Kowalczyk, Francis P Msgr, 1968, Mr 11,41:4
Kowalczyk, Leon, 1952, Ap 6,88:2
Kowaleski, Michael, 1951, Je 3,92:3
Kowalinski, Anna C Mrs, 1942, Ja 17,17:4
Kowalke, Robert A, 1943, D 2,27:2
Kowalski, Gustav A, 1940, O 20,49:2
Kowalski, John L (J Cole), 1961, Jl 29,19:6
Kowalski, Joseph A, 1957, Mr 8,25:3
Kowalski, Leon, 1950, O 17,31:4
Kowalski, Max, 1956, Je 5,35:4
Kowalski, Shanley, 1948, D 21,28:5
Kowalski, Stanley E, 1941, N 23,51:4
Kowalski, Vincent J, 1962, O 11,39:2
Kowalsky, Morris Mrs, 1949, Mr 17,25:4
Kowalsky, Morton D, 1959, O 4,86:3
Kowarsky, Morris, 1949, F 19,15:5
Kowarsky, Saul L, 1941, Je 30,17:1
Kowat, Max, 1951, S 18,32:3
Kowsky, Julius Dr, 1924, Ag 2,9:6
Koyer, John B, 1947, Ag 30,15:2
Kozak, Andrew V, 1948, S 16,29:2
Kozak, John, 1945, D 4,29:2
Kozak, John J, 1952, D 31,15:2
Kozak, Joseph A, 1958, Mr 22,17:5
Kozak, Julius D, 1946, Je 20,23:3
Kozak, Semyon A, 1953, D 30,23:3
Kozakevich, Stefan, 1957, Ap 18,29:2
Kozar, Joseph Mrs, 1957, D 27,19:4
Kozary, Myron T, 1966, O 23,88:3
Kozelsky, Alois, 1942, Je 23,19:3
Kozera, Edward S, 1965, Ag 17,33:3
Kozicke, Bernard A, 1963, D 5,45:3
Kozin, Jacob, 1954, Ag 27,21:3
Kozinn, Joseph J, 1968, D 26,37:5
Kozinsky, Joseph, 1950, Ja 29,68:5
Koziol, Martin, 1952, O 17,27:3
Koziol, Matthew J, 1950, Mr 15,29:1
Kozlay, Charles Meeker, 1924, Ag 9,11:6
Kozlay, Percival M, 1945, O 21,46:3
Kozlek, John, 1951, Je 3,93:1
Kozlin, Leonel, 1941, Ag 23,13:5
Kozlov, Alex, 1952, Mr 22,13:4
Kozlov, Frol R (funl F 3,3:2), 1965, Ja 31,2:3
Kozlov, Peter, 1944, Ap 21,19:5
Kozlovsky, David E, 1949, Ag 15,17:3
Kozlowski, Edward S, 1959, S 18,31:2
Kozlowski, John B, 1967, O 5,39:1
Kozlowski, John J, 1947, Ja 29,25:1
Kozlowski, Leon, 1944, My 17,19:5
Kozma, Arpad, 1951, S 27,31:4
Kozmor, Edward P, 1965, Ap 27,37:1
Kozusko, John A, 1954, Ap 18,88:6
Kraak, Henrietta (Sister Mary Victoria), 1960, Ja 23,21:5
Kraak, Kornelius, 1953, Ap 12,88:5
Kraayenbrink, Antoon, 1951, Ag 17,17:3
Krabbe, Hans C, 1953, Je 30,23:4
Kracauer, Siegfried, 1966, N 28,39:1
Krack, Ferdinand, 1947, My 7,56:6
Krack, Herman, 1951, Mr 19,27:4
Kracke, Edward A, 1960, Mr 3,29:2
Kracke, Frederick J H (funl, D 5,88:2), 1954, D 3, 27:1
Kracke, Frederick T, 1953, Ja 5,21:3
Kracke, Henry Mrs, 1944, My 19,19:3
Kracke, Louis, 1956, D 24,13:2
Krackowizer, Ernst Dr, 1875, S 25,4:5
Kraeger, Edward, 1960, Jl 7,31:5
Kraeler, Joseph, 1965, N 29,35:2
Kraeling, Carl H, 1966, N 15,41:3
Kraeling, Emil C J, 1956, Jl 2,21:4
Kraemer, Casper J, 1958, N 7,27:3
Kraemer, Casper Sr, 1946, Jl 22,21:4
Kraemer, Charles F, 1952, Jl 10,31:3
Kraemer, Elmer O, 1943, S 9,25:4
Kraemer, Herman, 1939, My 13,15:5
Kraemer, Manfred, 1948, N 14,76:6
Kraemer, Oscar T, 1944, Jl 10,15:4
Kraemer, Richard M, 1925, Ag 27,19:6
Kraemer, Sam P Jr, 1956, D 17,31:4
Kraemer, Walter Mrs, 1947, Je 10,27:4
Kraemer, William H, 1962, Mr 22,35:5
Kraemer, William S Mrs, 1945, S 15,15:6

Kraenzler, William, 1945, Mr 21,23:1
Kraeth, C P, 1883, Ja 3,5:4
Kraeuter, Aug L, 1940, Je 2,44:8
Kraeuter, Phyllis M, 1964, N 11,43:2
Kraeuter, Robert, 1957, Ag 15,21:5
Krafchik, Charles W, 1950, Ap 27,33:1
Kraff, Sonia, 1955, Ja 1,13:3
Krafft, F William, 1925, S 1,21:6
Krafft, Fred A, 1953, Ag 3,17:5
Krafft, J C, 1944, Mr 29,21:3
Krafft, Paul Mrs, 1946, Jl 28,39:1
Krafft-Ebing, Prof, 1902, D 23,9:6
Kraft, Charles F, 1963, My 11,25:6
Kraft, Charles H, 1952, Mr 26,29:4
Kraft, Charles J, 1949, Ja 6,23:4
Kraft, Charles P, 1952, Ap 25,23:4
Kraft, Clarence, 1958, Mr 27,33:1
Kraft, David H, 1962, F 19,31:3
Kraft, Dorothea, 1903, Mr 13,16:2
Kraft, Edwin A, 1962, Jl 16,23:3
Kraft, Erich, 1961, Mr 13,29:1
Kraft, Frederick, 1967, Jl 9,60:6
Kraft, Frederick L, 1956, N 6,35:2
Kraft, George J, 1967, Ag 2,37:3
Kraft, Herman T, 1960, Mr 22,37:3
Kraft, J W, 1961, N 11,23:6
Kraft, J W Mrs, 1951, O 16,31:3
Kraft, James Lewis, 1953, F 17,34:1
Kraft, John N, 1952, N 15,17:4
Kraft, John W, 1965, N 27,31:4
Kraft, Julius, 1960, D 31,17:2
Kraft, Leonard J, 1958, Ja 1,25:4
Kraft, Mark A, 1962, O 18,39:2
Kraft, Max, 1963, Jl 30,29:1
Kraft, Norman, 1967, Ja 3,34:1
Kraft, Otto E, 1963, My 12,86:4
Kraft, Philip, 1968, D 4,47:2
Kraft, R Wayne, 1956, F 15,31:4
Kraft, Robert H, 1954, F 19,27:3
Kraft, Samuel Mrs, 1945, F 14,19:5
Kraft, Theodore J, 1942, D 4,25:4
Kraft, William, 1946, O 12,19:1
Kraft, William F, 1949, F 2,27:1
Kraft, William F Mrs, 1949, Mr 17,25:2
Kraft, William R, 1956, Jl 3,25:5
Krafte, Henry Mrs, 1955, Ag 31,25:4
Krag, Ole Herman Johannes, 1916, D 13,15:5
Kragh-Hansen, Ernst, 1949, Jl 20,25:4
Kraham, John C, 1958, Jl 26,15:4
Krahe, Richard, 1959, F 26,31:2
Krahmer, Charles E, 1955, S 9,23:2
Krahmer, William R, 1949, Jl 13,27:3
Kraicer, Menachem, 1964, N 12,37:3
Kraiss, William A Mrs, 1956, Ap 12,31:4
Kraissel, Frederick, 1944, Ag 5,11:7
Kraissl, Frederick Mrs, 1946, Jl 18,25:5
Krajewski, Henry, 1966, N 9,39:3
Krajger, Boris, 1967, Ja 5,34:3
Krajger, Janez, 1967, Ja 5,34:3
Krajnik, Mary Mrs, 1948, D 7,32:3
Krakauer, Jay F, 1961, My 12,29:3
Krakauer, Julius, 1912, Jl 2,11:5
Krakaur, David C (por), 1948, D 2,29:2
Krakaur, Henry G, 1952, D 15,25:3
Krakaur, Maurice J Mrs, 1956, O 4,33:1
Krake, Stanton G, 1948, D 22,23:2
Kraker, Adele G, 1946, Mr 2,13:5
Kraker, David A, 1954, Ap 25,87:1
Kraker, Florence E, 1950, Ja 5,25:3
Krako, Joseph, 1948, Je 24,25:3
Krakoff, Henry, 1953, Ap 25,15:3
Krakow, Moses H, 1960, S 3,17:6
Krakow, Richard H, 1949, N 13,93:1
Krakower, John, 1949, Ja 7,22:7
Kral, Eustach, 1940, D 27,10:5
Kraland, John, 1938, Ja 27,21:1
Kralce, William, 1937, S 22,27:2
Kralovich, Emilienne, 1960, S 20,39:3
Kralstein, David, 1949, O 5,29:5
Kraly, Hans, 1950, N 13,27:4
Kram, Abraham B, 1965, Jl 17,25:5
Kram, William, 1955, O 13,31:4
Kramar, Cyril J Rev, 1968, Mr 31,81:2
Kramar, Karl Dr (por), 1937, My 27,23:5
Kramarich, Irene (Mrs R Abruzzese), 1967, Ag 13, 80:8
Kramarsky, Felix, 1959, Je 13,21:5
Kramarsky, Siegfried, 1961, D 26,25:4
Kramer, A Sigmund, 1955, N 13,89:2
Kramer, A Walter Mrs, 1951, S 8,17:2
Kramer, Abraham F Dr, 1968, Mr 2,29:4
Kramer, Abraham Mrs, 1961, Jl 4,19:3
Kramer, Adam Maj, 1901, N 12,9:7
Kramer, Adolf F, 1944, O 16,19:6
Kramer, Albert L, 1948, Ag 9,19:6
Kramer, Albert S, 1941, Ap 24,21:2
Kramer, Alex M, 1955, Ag 26,19:3
Kramer, Arthur, 1950, F 18,15:1
Kramer, Arthur Mrs, 1959, Ag 16,82:2
Kramer, Austin L (cor, Jl 6,28:2), 1950, Jl 5,31:4
Kramer, Benjamin B, 1965, Jl 29,27:1
Kramer, Bernard, 1967, Ap 21,39:4
Kramer, Bertram S, 1964, Mr 10,37:1
Kramer, Bessie, 1915, Jl 26,9:5
Kramer, C Frank Jr, 1964, Ap 9,32:1
Kramer, Charles, 1924, Jl 25,13:5; 1943, Ja 21,21:3; 1948, Ja 10,15:2; 1950, Je 26,27:3
Kramer, Charles P, 1961, Ag 8,30:1
Kramer, Cornelius, 1949, Ja 3,23:3
Kramer, Dale, 1966, D 2,39:3
Kramer, Edward, 1946, Ap 12,27:5
Kramer, Edward A, 1941, D 29,15:3
Kramer, Edward C, 1962, F 12,23:5
Kramer, Edward I, 1956, Je 19,29:3
Kramer, Ella W Mrs, 1938, D 15,27:6
Kramer, Ernest, 1954, Je 6,87:1
Kramer, Eugene J, 1950, F 7,28:3; 1964, Ja 15,31:1
Kramer, Felix, 1965, O 19,43:1
Kramer, Floyd, 1957, Je 17,23:3
Kramer, Francis W, 1946, Jl 8,29:4
Kramer, Frank H, 1963, My 23,37:1
Kramer, Frank L, 1958, O 9,37:1
Kramer, George, 1955, Je 11,15:2
Kramer, George A, 1957, D 14,21:6
Kramer, George C, 1948, D 10,25:4
Kramer, George H, 1943, Jl 30,15:4
Kramer, George L, 1967, O 16,45:2
Kramer, George Mrs, 1958, Ap 7,21:2
Kramer, George W, 1938, O 21,23:3
Kramer, Harold, 1949, Ap 30,13:4
Kramer, Henry F, 1955, S 14,35:5
Kramer, Herman, 1942, Je 24,19:5
Kramer, Howard A, 1952, My 9,23:4
Kramer, Hyman Mrs, 1956, N 14,35:3
Kramer, Hyman S, 1963, D 26,27:1
Kramer, Irving, 1961, D 7,43:1
Kramer, Israel Mrs, 1951, N 11,90:6
Kramer, Jacob, 1948, Ja 1,23:4
Kramer, Jacob F, 1959, O 4,86:3
Kramer, Jacob J, 1954, S 16,29:2
Kramer, Jacob L, 1963, S 9,27:3
Kramer, Jacob Mrs, 1968, My 25,35:1
Kramer, Jacob R, 1966, O 8,31:4
Kramer, Jacob R Mrs, 1954, Ag 25,27:5
Kramer, Jacob W, 1961, N 17,35:1
Kramer, Jerome A, 1956, Ja 2,21:4
Kramer, John A, 1946, D 4,31:4
Kramer, John G, 1944, F 9,19:5
Kramer, Jorge Z, 1956, S 21,25:4
Kramer, Joseph, 1949, O 19,29:5; 1951, Ap 24,29:1
Kramer, Julius, 1944, D 2,13:2
Kramer, K Adolf, 1963, Jl 24,31:3
Kramer, Ledru R, 1951, Jl 18,29:1
Kramer, Leon R, 1950, My 22,21:2
Kramer, Leroy, 1945, Ag 17,17:3; 1954, Ap 12,29:5
Kramer, Lester J, 1957, N 19,33:4
Kramer, Louis, 1939, O 31,23:5; 1941, N 26,23:6; 1952, Ag 20,25:6; 1960, Ag 25,29:5
Kramer, Louis I, 1964, N 6,37:5
Kramer, Matthew J, 1953, O 31,17:6
Kramer, Max, 1920, Ap 4,22:3; 1959, Je 8,27:3
Kramer, Max J (new will filed, O 10,27:2), 1946, Je 18,25:2
Kramer, Milton A, 1955, Jl 5,29:3
Kramer, Milton L, 1965, Mr 10,41:2
Kramer, Morris, 1967, Ap 8,31:4
Kramer, N St Clair, 1958, N 27,29:6
Kramer, Nathan, 1943, Jl 29,19:2; 1953, Ap 14,27:3; 1959, D 5,23:2
Kramer, Nathan Mrs, 1947, Jl 5,11:6
Kramer, Peter R, 1951, D 24,13:5
Kramer, Philipp C, 1950, Je 25,68:2
Kramer, Rachel E Mrs, 1940, My 31,19:2
Kramer, Raymond C, 1957, Ja 25,21:1
Kramer, Richard L, 1938, Ag 22,13:3
Kramer, Robert, 1951, N 21,25:4
Kramer, Rudolph, 1964, Ja 22,37:4
Kramer, Russell R, 1966, Ap 24,86:8
Kramer, S David, 1955, Je 27,21:6
Kramer, Sam, 1964, Je 10,45:2
Kramer, Samuel E, 1963, Je 4,39:3
Kramer, Sidney, 1961, Ap 26,39:2
Kramer, Simon, 1937, Mr 7,II,8:7
Kramer, Simon P, 1940, Ap 13,17:6
Kramer, Sydney S, 1962, O 11,39:1
Kramer, Vera D Mrs, 1956, D 28,41:1
Kramer, William, 1915, Mr 25,11:6
Kramer, William A, 1944, N 13,19:4
Kramer, William C, 1937, S 23,27:2
Kramer, William F, 1948, Je 11,23:4
Kramer, Zachary, 1948, Mr 27,13:5
Kramers, H A, 1952, Ap 26,23:2
Kramm, Joseph Mrs (I Bonner),(funl plans, Jl 6,28:1), 1955, Jl 2,12:8
Kramorov, Mikhail, 1952, Ja 12,13:2
Kramp, George Mrs, 1952, Je 5,31:5
Kramp, Louis J, 1965, Jl 6,33:3
Krampner, William, 1941, N 17,19:3
Kramrath, Henry M, 1939, N 2,23:3
Kranch, Helmuth F, 1956, O 26,29:4
Krangel, Samuel J, 1952, Ag 25,17:5
Krangle, William J, 1953, O 23,23:3
Kranich, Alvin, 1944, O 29,43:1
Kranich, Hellmuth, 1902, Ja 26,7:5
Kranjnik, Eddie, 1957, Ap 21,88:8
Krans, Horatio S, 1952, Jl 30,23:2
Krans, Horatio S Mrs, 1960, N 5,23:3
Kransz, Henry P, 1947, Ap 22,27:4
Krantz, Frederick, 1938, N 1,10:6
Krantz, Hubert F, 1942, N 24,25:3
Krantz, John, 1938, Ap 19,21:4
Krantz, Jules Francois Emile Vice-Adm, 1914, F 27, 11:5
Krantz, Karl T, 1942, Mr 5,23:4
Krantz, Philip (funl, D 1,17:4), 1922, N 29,17:5
Kranz, Alfred L, 1948, Mr 22,23:4
Kranz, Frederick H, 1965, My 23,84:6
Kranz, Leon G, 1956, S 30,86:6
Kranz, Max C, 1938, D 1,23:1
Kranz, Maxim, 1961, O 17,39:2
Kranz, Otto G, 1952, S 13,17:5
Kranz, William G, 1944, Mr 7,17:2
Kranze, Bernard G, 1968, Ja 19,44:1
Kranzer, Herbert C, 1964, S 25,41:1
Kranzer, William J, 1961, Ag 17,27:1
Kranztohr, Carl Mrs, 1955, Ja 14,21:1
Krapf, Frederick C, 1960, Jl 15,23:5
Krapf, George W, 1953, N 17,31:1
Krapf, J L, 1881, D 22,2:1
Krapff, Eugene Mrs, 1944, Je 29,23:3
Krapish, Alex, 1951, Mr 28,29:3
Krapiven, Alexander N, 1947, Ja 11,19:2
Kraschel, Nelson G, 1957, Mr 17,86:6
Krash, Fred, 1956, O 5,25:5
Krashkevich, John J, 1960, O 19,45:3
Krasik, Sidney, 1965, O 18,35:5
Krasilovsky, Mike, 1961, D 18,35:1
Krasilovsky, Nathan Mrs, 1957, Jl 17,27:2
Krasinski, Zygmunt Count, 1859, Ap 14,4:1
Krasko, John, 1960, Jl 1,25:3
Krasne, Wolfe, 1952, F 29,23:2
Krasner, Ichel, 1951, O 31,29:2
Krasner, Jack, 1952, My 12,25:2
Krasnogar, Jerry, 1951, My 30,38:7
Krasnomowitz, Alex, 1958, Mr 5,31:3
Krasnor, David H, 1957, D 22,40:8
Krasnow, David, 1965, Mr 25,37:3
Krasnow, Israel Mrs, 1952, O 21,29:4
Krasny, William, 1951, N 23,29:3
Krasnykh, Arkady A, 1950, D 3,88:5
Krasowich, Joseph B, 1967, O 21,31:4
Krass, Nathan, 1949, N 23,29:1
Krass, Nathan Mrs, 1948, O 27,27:5
Krassin, L, 1926, N 25,10:1
Krasuski, Alex, 1948, N 23,29:4
Kratina, Joseph M, 1953, Mr 29,95:3
Kratoville, Charles P, 1944, S 28,19:3
Krattenmaker, J George, 1961, Ja 10,47:2
Kratz, Charles C, 1950, Ap 11,31:1
Kratz, Maxwell H, 1939, N 20,19:2
Kratz, Raymond C, 1963, O 15,39:4
Kratzel, Edward A, 1964, Mr 1,83:2
Krauch, Oscar, 1954, Ap 27,29:3
Kraus, A, 1928, O 23,29:5
Kraus, A F, 1901, N 9,9:6
Kraus, A Walter Sr, 1944, Ap 9,33:1
Kraus, Abraham F, 1943, Ja 6,25:2
Kraus, Albert F, 1954, Ag 14,15:5
Kraus, Albert F Mrs, 1965, Ap 28,45:1
Kraus, Albert W, 1948, N 3,27:5
Kraus, Alfred, 1961, My 7,87:1
Kraus, Alois, 1953, Ap 2,27:4
Kraus, Bernard C, 1949, My 15,90:3
Kraus, Bertram L, 1942, O 28,23:5
Kraus, Bessie Mrs, 1940, D 3,25:3
Kraus, Charles A, 1967, Je 28,45:1
Kraus, Charles C, 1948, N 11,27:4
Kraus, Charles M Mrs, 1948, D 21,25:4
Kraus, Charles M Sr, 1951, N 29,33:4
Kraus, Eugene R, 1952, O 6,25:4
Kraus, Ezra J, 1960, Mr 1,33:1
Kraus, Frank, 1964, S 5,19:4
Kraus, Frank Mrs, 1961, Jl 15,19:4
Kraus, Frederick, 1903, O 27,9:5
Kraus, Gabriel, 1938, Ap 6,23:5
Kraus, George J (will), 1914, Je 16,9:7
Kraus, Harry (will, S 25,17:1), 1938, S 15,25:5
Kraus, Hertha Dr, 1968, My 19,86:3
Kraus, Jack L 2d, 1954, Mr 5,39:1
Kraus, Jacob M, 1960, F 6,19:6
Kraus, James E, 1965, Jl 8,28:2
Kraus, John J, 1937, Je 5,17:4; 1950, S 26,31:3
Kraus, John P, 1954, Mr 1,25:4
Kraus, John Prof, 1918, N 3,2:1
Kraus, Louis J, 1945, Jl 24,23:1
Kraus, Maurice A Mrs, 1947, Ja 14,25:2
Kraus, Max, 1946, O 19,21:6
Kraus, Oscar, 1946, N 28,27:4
Kraus, Othmar, 1950, Jl 18,30:2
Kraus, Otto, 1952, O 31,25:4
Kraus, Paul S, 1956, N 13,37:2
Kraus, Paul T, 1955, Mr 26,15:5
Kraus, Philip, 1945, O 23,17:6
Kraus, Rene (por), 1947, Jl 17,19:1
Kraus, Romualdo, 1954, D 20,29:1
Kraus, Rudolf, 1955, Ag 3,23:5
Kraus, Rudolph W Jr, 1954, S 27,21:5
Kraus, Walter M, 1944, Ag 23,19:6
Kraus, William A, 1958, My 1,31:5

Kraus, William A Mrs, 1944, N 7,27:3
Krause, Albert H Mrs, 1952, F 18,19:5
Krause, Allen K, 1941, My 13,23:3
Krause, Arthur, 1954, S 16,29:1
Krause, Carl H, 1966, N 16,47:3
Krause, Charles H, 1949, S 20,29:3
Krause, Ernest G, 1907, F 2,9:3
Krause, Frederick, 1959, Ag 24,21:2
Krause, George, 1958, My 14,33:2
Krause, George J, 1914, Je 3,13:6
Krause, Gustav Mrs, 1944, Ap 10,19:4
Krause, H Edward, 1954, D 12,88:4
Krause, Harry A, 1948, Ap 25,70:3
Krause, Jacob B, 1948, Ag 25,25:2
Krause, Jacob Mrs, 1919, Je 29,22:4
Krause, John, 1937, N 30,23:2
Krause, John A, 1948, S 8,29:2
Krause, John F Jr, 1958, Jl 6,57:2
Krause, Joseph, 1945, Je 10,32:4; 1964, Ja 29,30:1
Krause, Louis A, 1949, Ja 26,25:5
Krause, Lucy B, 1951, N 6,29:2
Krause, Lyda F, 1939, N 1,23:5
Krause, Oliver J, 1940, D 24,15:3
Krause, Oscar O, 1958, Ja 19,86:1
Krause, Otto, 1939, Ja 23,13:3
Krause, Otto G, 1940, Ja 31,19:3
Krause, Paul C, 1952, S 18,29:1
Krause, Robert L, 1957, O 25,27:4
Krause, Thaddeus S, 1952, My 16,23:1
Krause, Verne G, 1944, N 28,23:3
Krause, William, 1961, Ag 12,17:4
Krause, William H Dr, 1911, Ja 8,13:5
Krause, William J, 1948, Ja 18,60:2
Krauser, Charles F, 1960, Ap 15,23:2
Kraushaar, John F, 1946, D 13,23:5
Kraushaar, Katherine K Mrs, 1940, F 17,13:4
Kraushaar, Meyer, 1961, Ap 4,37:2
Kraushar, Henry L Mrs, 1947, My 29,21:3
Kraushar, Leon, 1967, S 13,47:2
Krauskopf, Daniel M, 1957, Jl 28,60:6
Krauskopf, Henry, 1959, Je 20,21:4
Krauskopf, Joseph Dr, 1923, Je 13,19:5
Krauskopf, Joseph Mrs, 1954, N 24,23:6
Krausmann, Matthew A, 1942, O 8,27:5
Krauss, Alfred, 1938, S 30,21:4
Krauss, Andrew G, 1943, Ag 1,38:8
Krauss, Arnold, 1941, N 26,23:2
Krauss, Arthur H, 1954, D 18,15:5
Krauss, Arthur J, 1967, S 19,51:3
Krauss, Charles F, 1967, S 26,47:2
Krauss, Charles Sr, 1940, Ap 28,37:1
Krauss, Clemens, 1954, My 17,23:6
Krauss, David, 1950, Ag 6,72:7
Krauss, Elmer F, 1946, My 24,19:4
Krauss, Fred J Mrs, 1954, N 5,21:3
Krauss, Frederick, 1944, O 11,21:4; 1948, My 8,15:3
Krauss, George, 1953, Jl 25,11:3
Krauss, Harry K, 1955, Ap 13,29:3
Krauss, Herman D, 1966, D 11,89:2
Krauss, J F Prof, 1883, D 15,4:7
Krauss, Jacob, 1962, Mr 13,35:3
Krauss, Lawrence, 1966, My 14,31:2
Krauss, Lee, 1955, Ja 30,84:6
Krauss, Marcel S, 1955, F 3,23:4
Krauss, Sidney L, 1953, S 27,87:2
Krauss, Victor P, 1960, Ap 4,29:6
Krauss, Werner, 1959, O 21,44:1
Krausse, Joseph, 1953, O 13,29:2
Krausser, Herman F, 1956, O 12,29:5
Krausz, Wilhelm V, 1959, My 5,33:4
Kraut, Hans B, 1947, D 27,13:5
Kraut, Julius, 1939, Jl 3,13:5
Kraut, Paul, 1946, Je 12,27:5
Krauter, Harold S, 1939, N 3,21:4; 1954, Je 11,23:4
Krautheimer, Melvin, 1964, N 15,86:5
Krautter, Walter W Mrs, 1959, Mr 4,31:4
Kravchick, Hyman, 1961, D 22,23:2
Kraver, Henry, 1938, Ja 22,15:2
Kravette, N Leland, 1962, Ag 29,29:4
Kravetz, Boruch, 1956, S 3,13:6
Kravitz, Ben, 1956, D 14,29:5
Krawetz, Meyer, 1962, Jl 26,27:2
Kray, Charles B, 1957, Jl 4,19:4
Kraybill, Amos, 1953, F 7,15:4
Kraybill, Ira B, 1964, Ja 22,37:2
Krayer, Anthony, 1941, Jl 17,19:5
Krayer, Eva A, 1953, O 20,29:5
Krayer, Stephen S, 1942, N 29,65:2
Krayer, Valentine J Mrs, 1950, D 14,35:5
Kraynak, Andrew, 1945, F 16,24:3
Kraynick, Joseph F, 1947, Ag 22,15:6
Krazanskas, Mary Mrs, 1923, S 8,13:5
Kreamer, Edward, 1937, Mr 25,25:4
Kreamer, Frank H, 1952, Je 28,19:3
Kreamer, George, 1939, Ag 4,13:2
Kreamer, William, 1950, Ag 17,27:3
Kreamer, William Capt, 1916, Ag 10,9:5
Krebaum, Frederick, 1912, D 14,15:3
Krebaum, William T, 1952, D 12,29:1
Krebs, Bernard L, 1965, Jl 4,37:3
Krebs, Francis W, 1953, Jl 6,17:5
Krebs, Frank S, 1948, Ja 25,56:8
Krebs, Fred R, 1938, Je 18,15:3
Krebs, Fred W, 1942, Ap 11,13:3
Krebs, J M Rev, 1867, O 1,8:4
Krebs, Michael F, 1948, My 8,15:4
Krebs, Peter, 1945, Ja 25,19:5
Krebs, William, 1905, Ap 29,11:6
Krebs, William F, 1940, N 27,23:2
Krech, A W, 1928, My 4,25:1
Krech, Aug M, 1950, Ja 29,68:3
Krech, Frederick H, 1959, O 10,21:5
Krech, shepard Dr, 1968, D 16,50:3
Krech, Shepard Mrs (cor, S 26,47:4), 1967, S 25,45:3
Krech, Warren W Mrs, 1949, Ja 1,13:6
Krechniak, Joseph M, 1964, F 24,25:5
Krecker, Frederick Mrs, 1903, N 17,9:6
Krecker, Frederick S, 1952, N 24,23:2
Krecker, Preston S, 1958, S 5,27:1
Krecker, Preston S Mrs, 1921, Ap 27,17:4
Kreder, Karl H Mrs, 1962, S 15,25:2
Kredlow, John P, 1950, Ag 26,13:2
Kreeger, Meyer, 1961, Ap 12,41:5
Kreeger, William R, 1949, D 14,31:4
Kreenberg, Samuel K, 1947, D 1,21:5
Kreer, George W, 1941, D 13,21:4
Krefeld, William J, 1965, Ag 5,29:4
Krefting, Albert, 1949, My 30,1:8
Kregarman, S L Mrs, 1944, Ap 23,43:4
Kregelium, Herman, 1952, Ja 30,26:5
Kreger, Clarence W, 1960, N 20,87:2
Kreger, Edward A, 1955, My 26,31:1
Kreh, Henry J Sr, 1943, Jl 14,19:3
Krehbiel, Albert H, 1945, Je 30,17:6
Krehbiel, Edward, 1950, Je 17,15:6
Krehbiel, Henry E (por),(funl, Mr 22,19:4), 1923, Mr 21,17:3
Krehbiel, Henry E Mrs, 1944, N 24,23:4
Krehbiel, John J, 1950, F 12,84:3
Kreher, Max O, 1955, Ja 29,15:3
Krehl, Ludolf von Dr, 1937, My 27,23:3
Kreibohm, Paul H, 1939, Ja 15,39:2
Kreicher, George F, 1910, Ja 10,9:2
Kreidel, George A, 1956, S 8,17:5
Kreider, David A, 1959, Ap 10,29:1
Kreider, Eugene C, 1959, Mr 24,39:4
Kreider, Harold B Mrs, 1942, Ag 29,15:4
Kreider, Harry J, 1961, Ag 8,29:4
Kreider, Paul V, 1964, Je 12,35:3
Kreider, William H, 1938, N 18,21:4
Kreidler, Chester K, 1950, Ap 30,102:5
Kreidler, Minerva F Mrs, 1942, Ag 16,44:8
Kreie, Harry F Sr, 1949, N 11,25:3
Kreielsheimer, Jacob, 1945, D 5,25:5
Kreielsheimer, Lester A, 1968, Jl 10,39:2
Kreielsheimer, William, 1944, Ja 22,13:5
Kreier, George J, 1958, Ag 27,29:1
Kreier, Robert A, 1955, D 17,23:5
Kreig, George W, 1959, Ag 6,27:2
Kreig, Valentine G Mrs, 1942, D 3,27:4
Kreig, William G, 1944, Ap 15,11:6
Kreiger, Joseph P Mrs, 1949, F 23,27:5
Kreiger, Mary G, 1941, N 23,51:5
Kreiger, William H, 1946, Ag 10,13:5
Kreighbaum, Charles, 1950, Ja 24,31:1
Kreimendahl, Frank Y, 1962, O 9,41:4
Kreimer, Ralph A, 1955, Ja 25,25:3
Krein, Alex A, 1951, Ap 23,25:5
Kreiner, Frederick M, 1959, Jl 18,15:7
Kreiner, Harry P, 1941, Je 5,24:3
Kreinheder, Jerome C, 1951, F 8,33:4
Kreinheder, Oscar C, 1946, Mr 27,27:2
Kreinick, William Mrs, 1956, My 8,33:3
Kreis, Conrad, 1950, F 15,21:3
Kreis, Henry G (Jan 21), 1963, Ap 1,36:1
Kreis, Louis, 1955, My 27,23:1
Kreis, Maurice M, 1957, O 29,31:3
Kreis, Oscar C, 1956, Jl 7,13:3
Kreis, Philip J, 1945, S 15,15:4
Kreis, Rudolph, 1946, Ap 21,45:1
Kreisberg, Louis Mrs, 1945, My 30,19:4
Kreisberg, Ralph I, 1960, O 22,23:6
Kreisel, Alex, 1953, Je 4,29:6
Kreisel, Ralph Mrs, 1955, F 27,87:1
Kreiselman, Joseph Dr, 1968, O 23,47:2
Kreisinger, Henry (por), 1946, My 9,21:5
Kreisler, B Bernard, 1965, Ja 25,37:4
Kreisler, Fritz (funl plans, F 1,31:2; funl, F 2,29:4), 1962, Ja 30,1:4
Kreismann, Herman, 1911, S 23,7:4
Kreisner, Louis M, 1943, Jl 8,19:4
Kreiswirth, Chester, 1952, Mr 7,23:2
Kreitler, Carl R, 1964, Ap 26,89:2
Kreitler, John J, 1967, Je 4,86:4
Kreitman, Gertrude Mrs, 1957, Mr 31,17:2
Kreitz, Ralph W, 1941, Jl 21,15:5
Kreitzberg, Frank, 1960, O 19,45:4
Krejci, Joseph, 1950, Ag 9,29:1
Krejci, Lad E, 1953, F 27,21:4
Krekel, Charles L, 1940, Ag 4,32:8
Krekel, Henry W, 1963, Ap 18,35:5
Krekeler, Thomas, 1922, O 26,17:3
Kreldt, Anastasius J, 1921, S 18,22:3
Kreling, Charles (Tiv), 1951, Je 19,29:4
Krell, Artur, 1967, O 4,51:1
Krell, Edward H, 1966, Jl 12,43:3
Krell, Solomon C, 1955, S 6,25:3
Krellberg, Alfred S, 1939, Mr 6,15:2
Krellner, Justine, 1949, Jl 3,26:5
Krembs, Ottmar M, 1950, N 19,93:2
Krementz, Frank J, 1940, Jl 24,21:6
Krementz, Richard, 1966, D 23,25:1
Krementz, Walter M, 1959, Jl 29,29:2
Kremer, Alex, 1961, F 21,35:2
Kremer, Aloys, 1947, S 8,21:4
Kremer, Carl P, 1960, Mr 16,37:3
Kremer, Edward J, 1958, Ag 19,28:5
Kremer, Ernest W, 1961, O 20,30:4
Kremer, Geza, 1963, Je 9,86:8
Kremer, Herman, 1947, Ap 11,25:3
Kremer, Isa, 1956, Jl 9,23:4
Kremer, J Bruce (por), 1940, Jl 24,21:1
Kremer, James B, 1963, N 4,35:5
Kremer, Julius G, 1940, Ap 11,25:4
Kremer, Leonard E, 1964, O 1,35:3
Kremer, Louis, 1967, Ag 18,30:5
Kremer, Paul O, 1961, Mr 24,27:6
Kremer, Ray (Remy), 1965, F 11,39:2
Kremer, Rudolf J Dr, 1937, Ag 16,19:2
Kremer, Theodore, 1923, F 6,19:4
Kremer, Theodore H (por), 1949, N 5,13:3
Kremer, William, 1943, S 1,19:6
Kremers, Edward, 1941, Jl 11,15:2
Kremers, Ernest W, 1942, Ap 7,21:5
Kremm, Georgianna W, 1949, My 21,13:2
Kremp, Edward S, 1940, D 2,23:5
Kremsdorf, Irving, 1965, D 19,84:7
Kren, Joseph G, 1953, S 19,15:1
Krencker, Daniel, 1941, N 14,23:5
Krenek, Joseph (por), 1949, Je 16,29:3
Krener, John G, 1938, D 27,17:3
Krening, Benjamin Mrs, 1949, O 25,28:4
Krenkel, Frank J, 1951, F 25,84:6
Krenkel, K, 1881, Jl 4,8:4
Krentzlin, John N, 1968, Mr 31,48:1
Krentzlin, John N Mrs, 1968, Mr 31,48:1
Krenz, Gustav, 1914, Ag 3,11:6
Krenz, Joseph M Mrs, 1950, F 2,27:3
Krenzer, Edward Mrs, 1942, D 3,27:4
Krepela, Aldrich J, 1965, D 17,39:2
Kreplak, Jacob, 1945, S 22,17:6
Krepps, John F, 1959, N 7,23:3
Krepps, William J, 1966, Jl 22,31:4
Kreps, C David, 1949, F 19,15:3
Kreps, Max, 1944, O 23,19:6
Kresch, Maxwell, 1960, N 10,47:3
Kresch, Philip, 1964, O 19,33:5
Kresch, Samuel E, 1958, Ap 23,33:4
Kresel, Solomon, 1938, D 6,23:2
Kresevich, Joseph, 1965, Jl 6,33:1
Kresge, Albert S, 1941, Ja 22,21:5
Kresge, Anna Mrs (will), 1947, Je 6,16:4
Kresge, Catherine E Mrs, 1940, F 10,15:4
Kresge, Elijah E, 1963, S 24,39:2
Kresge, Floyd L, 1957, Ja 23,29:1
Kresge, Sebastian S, 1966, O 19,1:1
Kreshover, Max, 1967, S 15,47:2
Kresner, Lewis, 1946, D 5,31:4
Kress, Andrew G, 1956, N 25,89:1
Kress, C Adam, 1955, Ag 4,25:5
Kress, Carl, 1965, Je 15,38:1
Kress, Charles W, 1964, F 28,29:3
Kress, Claude W (por),(will, D 10,22:4), 1940, N 19, 23:1
Kress, Clyde W Mrs, 1964, D 9,50:5
Kress, Frederick J, 1939, O 7,17:5
Kress, George A, 1954, D 26,61:1
Kress, George H, 1954, Ja 20,27:3
Kress, John Dr, 1916, Ja 27,11:2
Kress, Joseph G, 1954, Jl 24,13:5
Kress, Joseph H, 1942, N 15,57:1
Kress, Louis C, 1952, Mr 14,20:6
Kress, Ralph (Red), 1962, N 30,34:1
Kress, Raymond, 1950, Jl 30,46:4
Kress, Raymond J, 1945, Ja 28,37:2
Kress, Rush H, 1963, Mr 25,7:8
Kress, Samuel H (will, O 4,70:3), 1955, S 23,25:1
Kressel, Samuel, 1968, O 23,47:1
Kresser, William J, 1939, Je 15,23:4
Kressler, Harold C, 1944, S 21,19:5
Kressler, Kenneth W, 1963, S 7,19:5
Kressley, George S, 1941, Mr 4,23:3
Kressman, F W, 1954, O 3,87:1
Kreszl, Ferdinand, 1956, Je 30,17:2
Kretchmar, Herman, 1938, Je 6,17:4
Kretchmar, Robert T, 1961, D 18,35:4
Kretcho, Edward J, 1948, My 28,23:2
Kreter, Charles F, 1968, Ag 16,33:1
Kretsch, Harry A, 1947, O 6,21:4
Kretschmar, Frederick, 1865, My 8,8:4
Kretschmar, Hermann A, 1941, N 12,23:3
Kretschmer, Ernst, 1964, F 10,27:3
Kretschmer, Herman L (will, S 29,19:2), 1951, S 24, 27:3
Kretschmer, Herman L Mrs, 1942, Ap 27,15:1
Kretser, Raymond, 1956, Jl 1,56:7
Kretz, Adolph H, 1950, D 14,35:2
Kretzchmar, George W, 1955, Ag 9,26:6
Kretzer, Frederick W Mrs, 1954, Ja 6,31:2

Kretzman, Maurice C, 1943, Ja 4,15:2
Kretzmann, Karl, 1949, Ap 4,23:3
Kretzmer, Eugene, 1955, Jl 21,23:1
Kretzner, John L Mrs, 1965, Jl 21,37:4
Kretzschmar, Charles E, 1944, Ap 13,19:4
Kretzschmar, George, 1949, Je 25,13:5
Kretzschmar, Gustave R, 1943, Ja 15,17:4
Kretzschmar, Norman R, 1943, My 6,19:3
Kreuder, Henry, 1951, Ap 30,21:5
Kreuger, I, 1932, Mr 13,1:8
Kreuger, William C, 1959, Ap 15,33:1
Kreuscher, Philip H, 1943, Je 2,25:4
Kreuter, Henry, 1938, My 21,15:3; 1954, D 1,31:2
Kreuttner, Joseph W Mrs, 1958, Jl 3,26:1
Kreutz, Alfred M, 1943, D 14,27:2
Kreutz, Theresa, 1950, O 17,31:3
Kreutzberg, Edgar C, 1955, N 16,35:4
Kreutzberg, Harald, 1968, Ap 26,47:1
Kreutzer, Erwin, 1953, Ag 25,21:1
Kreutzer, Fred A Mrs, 1944, My 28,33:2
Kreutzer, Frederick C, 1949, Ag 22,21:3
Kreutzer, Gabriel, 1921, My 24,15:4
Kreutzer, Leonid, 1953, N 1,87:1
Kreutzer, Michael, 1957, O 19,21:1
Kreutzinger, Edmund P, 1942, O 5,19:4
Kreuzer, John L, 1948, Ja 29,23:4
Kreve-Mickevicius, Vincas, 1954, Jl 8,23:4
Krever, Benjamin S, 1965, Ja 7,31:4
Krevet, Joseph J, 1967, N 16,47:3
Krevsky, Louis J, 1967, Ag 3,33:3
Krevsky, Solomon, 1954, Ap 11,87:1
Krewson, Irving C, 1962, Je 6,41:4
Krewson, Robert, 1962, Mr 24,25:4
Krewson, William Egbert 3d, 1968, My 4,39:3
Krey, A C, 1961, Jl 31,19:4
Kreyer, Albertine M Mrs, 1942, N 22,52:4
Kreymborg, Alfred, 1966, Ag 15,27:2
Kreymborg, Charles O, 1941, Ap 1,23:3
Kreyns, Stephen, 1945, F 9,16:2
Kreys, Robert, 1953, Ja 14,31:4
Kribben, Earl, 1959, Je 1,27:1
Kribbs, Benton A, 1968, Ja 13,31:3
Kribbs, George F, 1938, S 8,24:4
Krich, Harry, 1953, O 14,29:2
Krichbaum, William F, 1939, N 2,23:5
Krichell, Paul B, 1957, Je 6,31:1
Krichesky, Boris, 1949, Ag 30,27:4
Krick, Charles S, 1943, Jl 30,15:3
Krick, Francis E, 1955, Mr 15,29:3
Krick, Frederick H, 1943, My 22,13:2
Krick, Howard V, 1958, Jl 8,27:1
Kricker, Augustus Rev Dr, 1920, Mr 12,13:4
Krickl, Charles A, 1939, Ja 3,18:1
Krickl, Maurice, 1953, O 7,29:3
Kridel, Abraham M, 1908, F 10,9:4
Kridel, Alex H, 1950, Ag 6,72:6
Kridel, Frank W (funl, Jl 8,19:7), 1961, Jl 6,29:1
Kridel, Moe, 1949, S 2,17:2
Kridel, Myron M, 1967, Ja 13,23:1
Kridel, Samuel, 1952, Ag 15,16:5
Krider, Walter W, 1959, Jl 31,23:4
Kridl, Manfred, 1957, F 5,23:1
Kriebel, Hermann, 1941, F 18,24:2
Kriebel, William F Sr, 1956, S 30,86:5
Kriebie, Vernon, 1964, Ja 24,24:5
Krieg, Charles P, 1943, Jl 27,17:3
Krieg, Charles W, 1968, My 27,47:2
Krieg, Frank W, 1942, N 29,64:8
Kriegbaum, Hiller Mrs, 1959, Mr 29,80:1
Kriegel, Harry G, 1968, S 27,47:3
Kriegel, Joseph J, 1959, N 16,31:3
Krieger, Allan Mrs, 1951, Ja 18,27:3
Krieger, Anselm A, 1956, F 24,25:1
Krieger, Arthur A, 1958, S 8,29:3
Krieger, E C, 1960, N 11,31:1
Krieger, Frederick W, 1963, O 21,31:1
Krieger, George Sr, 1944, Mr 2,17:1
Krieger, Helen, 1958, Ja 30,23:3
Krieger, Jacob, 1956, Je 28,29:4
Krieger, James, 1956, Jl 10,31:1
Krieger, Joseph A Dr, 1907, Jl 21,7:7
Krieger, Louis, 1953, N 4,33:1
Krieger, Phil, 1940, Ag 21,19:4
Krieger, Samuel, 1951, D 27,21:1
Krieger, William, 1956, Ag 28,28:2
Krieger, William A, 1944, My 21,43:1; 1951, Jl 29,69:4
Krieger, William A Mrs, 1950, N 19,93:2
Krieger, William Mrs, 1956, Ag 28,28:2
Kriegshaber, Irving M, 1964, Ap 18,29:1
Kriegsheim, Heinrich, 1957, Ap 24,33:5
Kriegsman, Leo Mrs, 1949, N 18,29:2
Kriegsman, Louis G, 1967, D 25,21:4
Kriegsman, Sig, 1957, Ap 29,25:4
Krielsheimer, Max L, 1948, Je 12,15:3
Kriendler, John C (por), 1947, Ag 15,17:1
Kriendler, John C (est tax appr), 1955, My 11,29:6
Kriens, Christiaan, 1925, Je 11,19:4
Krier, Moore, 1949, Ja 30,60:6
Krier, Pierre, 1947, Ja 21,23:3
Kriessel, Christopher A, 1937, N 9,23:3
Kriete, Frank L, 1945, N 3,15:3
Kriete, Frederic M, 1959, Jl 27,25:3
Kriete, George H, 1939, Mr 25,15:1
Kriete, George O Jr, 1949, My 22,88:2
Kriete, George O Sr, 1941, Jl 8,19:6
Krigbaum, Clarence R, 1967, Ap 7,37:1
Kriger, Eli, 1946, My 19,42:4
Krikorian, Gregory, 1961, Jl 18,29:3
Krikorian, H K, 1942, D 16,25:4
Krim, Charles F, 1962, My 17,37:3
Krim, Frank A, 1946, Jl 17,23:4
Krim, George J Rev (funl, Ap 3,13:5), 1920, Ap 2, 15:1
Krim, Morris, 1954, Ja 14,29:3
Krim, Sydney, 1951, Mr 24,13:6
Krimmel, Edmund G, 1953, Mr 12,27:5
Krimmel, Paul M, 1943, F 9,23:1
Krimpen, Wilbur Mrs, 1956, Ap 4,20:6
Krimsky, Jacob, 1967, Mr 10,36:2
Krimsky, Jerrold, 1948, N 25,31:4
Kriner, Joseph F, 1944, Ap 16,42:1
Kriney, Francis W, 1964, F 12,33:4
Kriney, John A Sr, 1939, Ja 22,34:6
Kriney, Samuel L, 1964, Jl 6,29:3
Kringel, Ira C, 1945, My 19,19:4
Krinkin, David Z, 1959, O 28,37:5
Krinn, Samuel J, 1956, O 8,27:3
Krinski, Irving E, 1966, F 11,33:1
Krinsky, Alex, 1964, N 22,86:1
Krinsky, Sonia Mrs, 1941, Ap 10,23:3
Krinzman, Abraham H, 1949, Je 22,31:5
Krinzman, Ida, 1952, Ag 28,23:6
Krinzman, Nathan J, 1947, Ja 28,24:3
Krinzman, Nathan J Mrs, 1949, D 18,88:4
Kripp, William F, 1946, Ag 16,21:3
Krippendorf, Charles J, 1950, Ag 9,29:5
Krippendorf, Paul F C, 1948, F 22,48:2
Kris, Ernst, 1957, F 28,27:3
Krisanda, Andrew, 1951, D 12,37:3
Krisch, Fred F, 1952, My 10,21:1
Krisch, Henry, 1945, Ag 10,15:3
Krischer, Morris, 1950, Ag 21,19:4
Krischhoch, Patricia, 1967, Je 12,30:5
Krischker, Joseph Mrs, 1939, Mr 1,21:1
Krisher, Lalen C, 1954, S 14,27:3
Krishna, Marayan, 1949, O 31,25:5
Krishnan, Kariamanikkam S, 1961, Je 15,43:6
Krishnayya, Pasupuleti G, 1966, Ap 29,47:1
Kriss, Max, 1941, N 17,19:3
Krissel, Walter D, 1964, Mr 10,37:4
Kristal, Frank A, 1963, O 19,25:5
Kristan, Julius, 1950, My 22,21:3
Kristeller, F Vaughan, 1955, My 15,86:5
Kristeller, Frederick W, 1957, O 27,86:5
Kristeller, Lionel P, 1956, Je 28,29:3
Kristeller, Robert S Mrs, 1958, O 25,21:6
Kristeller, Walter, 1947, S 9,32:2
Kristen, Charles A, 1949, My 4,29:5
Kristensen, Knud, 1962, S 30,86:5
Kristiansen, Rolf O Mrs, 1950, S 26,31:4
Kristof, Mary J Mrs, 1942, D 4,25:6
Kristoff, Barbara Mrs, 1955, F 23,27:4
Kristoff, George Mrs, 1952, Ap 11,23:1
Kristoffersen, Magnus K, 1960, Ap 23,23:5
Kristoph, Stephen A, 1947, Ja 23,23:5
Kritler, George W, 1946, Ap 20,13:2
Kritser, Shelby, 1966, Ag 14,49:6
Kritter, William A, 1945, My 28,19:4
Kritzler, Gottfried, 1944, F 20,36:4
Krival, Israel Mrs, 1964, Je 21,84:5
Krive, Jacob, 1946, Ag 13,27:2
Kriveloff, Jacob V, 1951, Ag 19,85:1
Krivit, Ralph B, 1967, O 25,47:2
Krivobok, Vsevolod N, 1958, My 19,25:1
Krivor, Matthew G, 1949, N 30,4:2
Krivsky, Frank, 1948, F 18,28:2
Kriz, Joseph R, 1950, My 23,29:2
Krizek, Joseph F, 1940, N 21,30:2
Krnjevitch, Biserka K, 1950, Ap 28,5:8
Krock, Arthur Mrs, 1938, S 15,25:3
Krock, Joseph, 1938, F 20,II,9:2
Kroczek, Stanislaus, 1950, Ag 15,30:2
Krodel, William L, 1943, Je 4,21:2
Kroeber, Alfred, 1960, O 6,41:1
Kroeber, Richard E, 1938, F 25,17:2
Kroeck, Frederick W, 1946, S 29,62:2
Kroeger, Bernard, 1910, Ja 9,9:4
Kroeger, Frederick C, 1944, Ag 11,15:5
Kroeger, Frederick W, 1945, Ap 13,17:2
Kroeger, Peter M, 1948, My 31,19:4
Kroeger, Richard C, 1948, My 26,25:2
Kroeger, William J, 1966, Jl 26,32:1
Kroegler, Louis J, 1967, N 1,47:1
Kroeh, C F, 1928, F 4,15:6
Kroehl, George F, 1908, F 18,7:6
Kroehler, Edward W, 1951, My 14,25:4
Kroehler, Peter E, 1950, Ag 16,29:4
Kroekel, C Rudolph, 1960, My 25,39:1
Kroell, Adrienne, 1949, O 3,17:6
Kroell, Theodore Mrs, 1967, Ja 7,27:4
Kroemer, William Sr, 1947, Ap 2,27:4
Kroemmelbein, Robert J (Irish Bobby Brady), 1967, My 2,47:2
Kroemmelbein, Walter, 1951, N 28,31:4
Kroener, George E, 1948, Ja 6,23:4
Kroener, Richard, 1942, My 13,21:4
Kroesen, Frederick J, 1940, My 16,23:4
Kroether, wm A, 1958, Mr 16,86:8
Kroft, Ella L, 1947, D 9,29:2
Krofta, Kamil (por), 1945, Ag 19,39:1
Kroger, Bernard H (will, Jl 27,6:6), 1938, Jl 22,1
Kroger, Chester F, 1949, F 23,27:1
Kroger, Henry C, 1939, Mr 12,III,6:6
Kroger, Josephine B, 1937, S 9,23:1
Krogerus, Marianna, 1961, Ja 28,9:1
Krogh, Aug, 1949, S 16,27:5
Krogh, Christian, 1925, O 17,15:5
Krogh, Detlef M F, 1939, D 5,27:1
Krogh, Thor, 1968, Jl 5,25:2
Kroglund, Ludvig R, 1950, F 11,15:2
Krogman, Florence A, 1943, D 12,71:1
Krogmann, Carrie W Mrs, 1943, My 17,15:4
Kroh, George W, 1923, Ag 19,26:5
Kroh, Harry H, 1963, S 21,21:5
Kroha, George F, 1949, S 2,17:1
Kroha, Joseph F, 1940, Ap 13,17:1
Krohn, Abraham L, 1958, N 24,29:4
Krohn, Bertram, 1944, F 12,13:5
Krohn, Evelyn Mrs, 1962, Ja 31,31:1
Krohn, Irwin M, 1948, D 13,23:4
Krohn, Irwin M Sr Mrs, 1953, Ag 29,17:3
Krohn, Israel, 1952, Je 14,15:4
Krohn, Max, 1951, S 12,31:2
Krohn, Phil L, 1950, D 29,19:4
Krohn, Sidney A, 1944, F 12,13:5
Krohner, Maurice N Mrs, 1959, Je 10,37:4
Krokyn, J Frederick, 1960, D 5,31:5
Krol, Stephen, 1954, My 10,23:1
Krolik, Joseph N, 1943, O 19,19:3
Kroll, Abraham, 1964, O 15,39:1
Kroll, Adolph Jr, 1943, Jl 8,19:4
Kroll, Charles, 1960, N 12,21:2
Kroll, Charlotte, 1958, N 15,23:2
Kroll, Daniel, 1963, Ag 20,33:1
Kroll, Hans, 1967, Ag 9,39:3
Kroll, Leopold, 1946, Mr 6,27:5
Kroll, Leopold Mrs, 1942, Jl 1,14:3
Kroll, Max, 1961, F 14,37:3
Krollpfeiffer, Henry Mrs, 1952, Je 9,23:5
Kroloff, Max N, 1959, Jl 5,57:1
Krom, Asbury, 1949, Ag 4,23:5
Krom, Charles S, 1962, O 13,25:3
Krom, Edward F, 1957, N 22,26:1
Krom, Edwin H (por), 1945, Je 23,13:3
Krom, Edwin H, 1964, D 16,43:2
Krom, Edwin H Mrs, 1964, O 22,35:2
Krom, James, 1940, S 7,15:4
Krom, Jetta J Mrs, 1939, O 17,25:3
Krom, Meyer, 1958, Ap 22,33:4
Krom, Richard O, 1945, Ap 19,27:4
Kroman, Morris, 1942, F 12,23:4
Krombach, Harry L (por), 1939, Jl 27,19:6
Kromer, Leon B, 1966, S 14,47:3
Kromer, Louis, 1958, Ja 6,39:4
Kromer, Richard, 1949, O 18,27:3
Kromer, Richard Mrs, 1948, Ja 8,25:4
Kromer, Wilson H, 1954, N 19,23:4
Kromm, Edward A, 1944, N 10,19:1
Kron, Phil, 1937, D 17,25:4
Kron, William H, 1965, My 21,35:3
Kronald, Edward Mrs (S Haas), 1957, D 9,35
Kronberg, Julius, 1921, O 19,19:5
Kroncke, George, 1941, Je 19,21:2
Krone, Joel, 1944, Ap 14,19:1
Krone, Karl, 1943, Je 5,15:4
Kronenberg, Aaron, 1945, F 16,23:3
Kronenberg, Albert S, 1956, N 14,35:1
Kronenberg, Bernard Mrs, 1966, Ag 11,33:5
Kronenberg, Edward S, 1946, Jl 13,15:5
Kronenberg, Frank, 1966, S 28,47:3
Kronenberg, Franklin, 1942, Ja 28,19:2
Kronenberg, Morris, 1940, My 4,17:6
Kronenberg, Rebecca Mrs, 1950, Ag 8,29:2
Kronenwetter, Ralph E, 1950, My 8,25:7
Kroner, Robert E, 1966, Ja 1,17:1
Krones, Louis, 1955, Ag 26,19:5
Kronethal, Sylvan, 1944, F 13,42:1
Kronfeld, Morris, 1968, My 24,65:3
Kronfeld, Philip Mrs, 1955, Ag 31,25:4
Kronfeld, Rudolph, 1940, F 14,21:6
Kronfeld, Sidney M, 1964, S 8,29:1
Kronheim, Sylvan, 1943, O 5,25:4
Kronish, Ben, 1957, S 13,23:4
Kronish, Fred, 1963, S 6,30:1
Kronish, Fred Mrs, 1966, Mr 6,39:1
Kronkhite, William H, 1944, F 28,17:1
Kronmann, Edwin C, 1952, Ap 25,23:2
Kronmeyer, William C, 1951, F 8,33:4
Kronold, Hans, 1922, Ja 11,21:6
Kronold, Selma, 1920, O 19,11:4
Kronowitz, William, 1944, Ja 26,19:3
Kronsky, Samuel, 1966, Mr 8,39:3
Kronstadt, John of Father, 1909, Je 7,7:4
Kronstadt, Max, 1940, Mr 27,21:2
Kronstein, Albert, 1948, Je 15,27:4
Kronthal, Aaron N (Jimmy), 1955, D 10,21:
Kronthal, Henry, 1916, O 21,11:4
Kronthal, James S, 1953, Ap 1,30:6
Kronyak, Nicholas S, 1952, My 14,27:1

Kroon, Albert T, 1948, Jl 21,23:5
Kroos, O A (Tom), 1957, S 5,29:4
Kroosz, Charles H, 1951, My 12,21:1
Kroovand, Carl, 1960, S 3,17:3
Krop, Elmer M, 1946, N 18,23:2
Kropa, Edward L, 1965, Ag 26,33:2
Kropf, Adam, 1925, Je 6,15:6
Kropf, John, 1940, D 10,25:5
Kropf, Joseph, 1955, S 28,35:4
Kropf, Oscar A, 1938, Ag 30,17:5
Kropff, William F, 1949, D 30,19:4
Kropotkin, Peter Alexeivich Prince, 1921, Ja 30,22:4
Kropp, Charles F, 1953, My 9,19:6
Kropp, Frederic, 1941, Mr 25,23:2
Kropp, Heinrich A, 1956, Jl 31,23:1
Kropp, Robert, 1952, Mr 4,27:2
Kroppy, Joseph F, 1954, Ap 4,88:6
Krotel, George F Rev, 1907, My 18,7:3
Krotel, Paul, 1918, Mr 16,13:8
Krotinger, Myron N Mrs, 1952, Ag 28,23:3
Krotoschniner, Joachim, 1946, Mr 7,25:4
Krotoshinsky, Abraham, 1953, N 5,31:4
Krotosky, Isidore, 1947, S 21,60:3
Krotz, Alvaro, 1954, D 11,13:2
Krouner, Jacob G, 1947, Ap 8,27:1
Krouse, Elizabeth C, 1960, Ja 24,88:4
Krouse, F Michael, 1955, S 2,17:3
Krouse, Harry, 1959, O 15,39:4
Krouse, Harry E, 1942, N 16,19:4
Krouse, Henry S, 1940, Mr 6,23:3
Krouse, John, 1944, N 29,23:2
Krouse, Louis, 1949, Je 21,25:3
Krouse, Louise H Mrs, 1942, Mr 26,23:3
Krouse, Paul, 1960, Ag 30,29:1
Krout, C A, 1964, N 30,33:2
Krout, John A Mrs, 1959, D 13,86:4
Krout, Palled B, 1951, Ap 14,15:3
Krowicki, Anthony, 1948, D 9,34:3
Krows, Arthur E, 1958, My 26,29:4
Krows, Arthur E Mrs, 1939, Ag 18,19:4
Krows, Elizabeth, 1943, O 19,19:2
Kroyer, Carl W, 1950, N 11,15:5
Kroyer, Henry F Sr, 1963, S 5,31:3
Kruckeberg, Edward, 1957, F 21,27:3
Kruckman, Arnold, 1959, Jl 2,25:4
Kruczek, Stanislaus J, 1941, N 25,25:5
Kruczkowski, Leo, 1962, Ag 2,25:1
Krudener, August W, 1955, N 24,29:5
Krueger, Anthony, 1943, O 26,23:4
Krueger, Bennie, 1967, My 1,37:2
Krueger, C George, 1962, Mr 19,29:4
Krueger, Edward, 1937, Jl 19,15:6
Krueger, Ernest T, 1945, Je 20,23:3
rueger, Frederick W, 1955, Mr 10,27:1
rueger, Jess, 1967, S 16,33:4
rueger, Joseph, 1956, Mr 11,89:1
rueger, Joseph W, 1941, Ap 24,21:2
rueger, Karl Mrs, 1953, Mr 5,14:5
rueger, Morris G, 1959, F 21,21:6
rueger, Nathan, 1961, O 31,31:4
rueger, Nathan L, 1954, D 25,11:3
rueger, Nathum B, 1950, My 1,25:4
rueger, Oscar O, 1960, Ap 7,35:4
rueger, Paul W, 1946, S 7,10:3
rueger, Theodore, 1961, Ja 5,31:3
rueger, Theodore H, 1966, N 10,47:3
rueger, Walter, 1967, Ag 21,31:1
rueger, Walter Mrs, 1956, My 14,25:6
rueger, William, 1957, F 21,27:5
rueger, William C, 1943, My 10,19:2
ruell, Gustav, 1907, Ja 4,7:5
ruesi, Frank E, 1949, Ap 10,76:3
ruesi, Olga A, 1943, My 29,13:4
ruesi, Paul J, 1965, D 2,41:2
ruesi, Walter E, 1961, N 25,24:4
ruetgen, Ernest J, 1948, Jl 11,53:1
ruetgen, Ernest Mrs, 1945, O 17,19:3
rug, Adolph N, 1942, My 28,17:4
rug, Adolph N Mrs, 1951, Ja 17,27:1
rug, Alfred M, 1937, F 11,23:2
rug, Alfred M Mrs, 1948, Je 27,52:3
rug, Amelia J, 1945, N 16,19:4
rug, Andrew J, 1942, O 26,15:3
rug, Boniface Father, 1909, Jl 6,7:7
rug, Charles F, 1940, N 22,23:1
rug, Charles F Mrs, 1948, D 29,21:5
rug, Edward J, 1950, Ag 3,23:4
rug, Emil W, 1938, O 11,25:2
rug, Ernest F (por), 1948, Mr 1,23:1
rug, Florian Dr, 1924, Ag 23,9:4
rug, Frank S Sr, 1940, D 10,26:3
rug, George A, 1961, F 1,35:4
rug, George A Mrs, 1962, Jl 29,61:2
rug, George W, 1947, Je 17,28:5
ug, J Adolph, 1941, F 1,17:2
ug, John A, 1952, Ag 27,27:4
ug, Julius J Mrs, 1949, Mr 30,25:2
ug, Karl, 1952, Ap 27,91:1
ug, Solomon, 1958, Ag 30,15:5
ug, Stephen P, 1956, Ag 18,17:2
ug, Theodore F, 1938, Ja 3,21:4
uge, George, 1959, Je 24,31:5
uger, Abraham, 1959, S 14,29:6

Kruger, Albert, 1925, Ag 13,19:6
Kruger, Alma, 1960, Ap 8,31:4
Kruger, Charles, 1923, S 11,15:3; 1952, Jl 3,25:5
Kruger, Harry B, 1940, Mr 14,23:3
Kruger, Henry, 1947, Ja 19,12:4
Kruger, J W, 1941, Ap 23,21:2
Kruger, John L, 1955, Je 6,27:4
Kruger, Minnie Mrs, 1949, D 28,25:2
Kruger, Solomon Rabbi, 1919, N 9,22:3
Kruger, Stefan, 1961, O 19,35:1
Kruger-Gray, George, 1943, My 5,27:3
Krugler, Joseph A, 1950, Je 20,27:5
Krugler, Wallace, 1963, Je 6,35:5
Krugman, Bertram, 1956, Mr 20,23:4
Kruhm, Adolph, 1940, Je 7,23:5
Krulewitch, Betsy Mrs, 1924, Ap 14,17:4
Krulewitch, Harry, 1945, F 23,17:3
Krulewitch, Melvin L Mrs, 1957, Jl 18,25:2
Krulewitch, Samuel, 1937, Mr 13,19:4
Krulewitz, George L, 1961, Ap 12,41:2
Krull, Frederick H, 1943, Je 14,17:3
Krum, Charles B, 1939, F 4,15:6
Krum, Charles L, 1937, S 26,II,8:7
Krum, Chester H, 1923, O 20,15:4
Krum, Francis M, 1944, My 20,15:5
Krum, H Nelson, 1961, Jl 21,23:4
Krum, Hiram, 1903, Jl 30,7:6
Krum, Hobart, 1914, My 5,11:6
Krum, Howard L, 1961, N 15,43:4
Krum, Russell William, 1968, Ap 18,47:2
Krum, Tyrell H, 1951, Ja 25,25:2
Kruman, Abraham, 1968, S 21,33:1
Krumb, Henry (funl plans, D 30,35:1; funl, D 31,19:1), 1958, D 28,2:7
Krumb, Henry (will), 1959, Ja 6,31:1
Krumb, Henry Mrs (will), 1962, Jl 31,29:6
Krumbein, Charles, 1947, Ja 22,23:4
Krumbhaar, Edward B, 1966, Mr 18,39:3
Krumbhaar, Hugh, 1950, Mr 17,23:4
Krumbhaar, Louis, 1942, N 8,50:6
Krumbhaar, William, 1957, Ag 28,27:2
Krumboldt, Louis, 1939, O 24,23:3
Krumholz, Sigmund, 1945, Ja 27,11:3
Kruming, Paul R, 1956, Mr 24,41:5
Krumm, Fred, 1952, Ja 12,13:5
Krumm, Herbert C Lt, 1905, Ap 22,5:2
Krummen, Leo F, 1937, Je 20,II,5:4
Krumnov, Ernest, 1905, Ap 1,5:1
Krumschmidt, Eberhard A, 1956, Je 5,35:4
Krumwiede, Howard C, 1954, Ja 27,27:3
Kruna, Richard B, 1947, Jl 6,41:1
Krunchwitz, Elizabeth Mrs, 1937, Mr 22,4:3
Krundieck, Frederick C, 1938, N 12,15:6
Krunsberg, Henry H, 1937, O 4,21:4
Krupa, Frank A, 1954, N 15,27:3
Krupa, Gene Mrs, 1955, D 10,21:1
Krupa, George M, 1961, F 21,35:3
Krupa, Robert, 1961, Jl 10,17:7
Krupa, Roman, 1955, O 20,36:1
Krupensky, Anatole, 1923, D 7,21:5
Krupnick, Sidney R, 1950, O 28,17:3
Krupp, Alfred, 1887, Jl 15,4:5
Krupp, Alfried (funl, Ag 4,29:2; will, Ag 5,7:6), 1967, Ag 1,1:5
Krupp, Arthur, 1938, Ap 23,15:5
Krupp, Frank X, 1966, N 9,40:1
Krupp, Harry Z, 1944, Jl 4,19:4
Krupp, Vera Mrs, 1967, O 17,47:2
Krupp, William A, 1961, Je 22,31:5
Krupp von Bohlen und Halbach, Gustav, 1950, Ja 17, 27:1
Kruppenbacher, Frank F, 1952, Mr 27,29:5
Krupskaya, Nadezhda K Mrs (Mrs N Lenin), 1939, F 28,14:4
Krus, Frederick S, 1948, D 8,32:2
Kruse, Arthur K, 1949, Jl 27,23:1
Kruse, Claus H, 1951, S 13,31:2
Kruse, Emil T, 1947, O 3,25:2
Kruse, Frederick, 1937, O 29,21:3
Kruse, Frederick W, 1938, Mr 20,II,9:3
Kruse, George W, 1937, Jl 30,19:2
Kruse, Gustave E, 1937, D 14,25:5
Kruse, Harry C Mrs, 1953, N 27,27:5
Kruse, Harry M, 1953, N 22,88:2
Kruse, Henry S, 1960, Je 9,33:4
Kruse, Otto V, 1941, Jl 3,19:4
Kruse, Peter, 1951, Jl 18,29:3
Kruse, Simon, 1946, O 9,27:5
Kruse, Theodore A, 1937, N 4,25:6
Kruse, William F, 1952, D 28,49:1
Krusen, Henry A, 1947, Ap 28,23:2
Kruskal, Eugene, 1944, Jl 12,19:5
Kruspak, Edward J, 1967, O 31,49:4
Krussman, Leo F, 1952, N 27,31:4
Krussman, Leo F Mrs, 1949, D 28,32:2
Kruszas, Michael L, 1950, F 1,29:3
Kruszewski, Charles, 1954, Ag 31,21:2
Kruszewski, Wladyslaw, 1953, F 23,25:4
Krutak, John, 1947, S 12,21:2
Krutckoff, Charles, 1948, O 12,25:4
Krutilek, George, 1962, Ap 6,72:1
Krutovskikh, Pavel M, 1954, Mr 3,27:4
Kruttschnitt, Herbert, 1959, Jl 15,29:4

Kruttschnitt, Julius (por), 1925, Je 16,21:4
Kruttschnitt, Julius Mrs, 1941, D 20,19:1
Kruttschnitt, Theodore H, 1962, N 9,26:3
Krutzky, Paul G, 1941, Ja 5,44:7
Krych, F J, 1945, Je 27,19:5
Kryger, Brunon, 1951, N 18,91:3
Kryger, John, 1950, F 15,21:3
Kryger, Joseph A, 1944, Jl 12,19:3
Kryl, Bohimir (est tax appr), 1962, N 16,24:1
Kryl, Bohumir, 1961, Ag 10,27:6
Krylenko, Eliena (Mrs M Eastman), 1956, O 11,39:1
Kryloff, Alexei N, 1945, O 28,44:3
Krymer, Elias M, 1945, S 9,45:2
Krynine, Paul D, 1964, S 15,37:5
Kryske, Nat E, 1957, S 16,31:3
Krysostomos, Archbishop (funl, Je 13,47:3), 1968, Je 10,45:1
Krystyn, John, 1943, Ja 11,15:5
Kryszak, Anthony Mrs, 1945, Jl 17,13:4
Krzhizhanovsky, Gleb, 1959, Ap 1,37:2
Krzystoforski, Michael, 1950, O 5,31:4
Krzyzak, Leopold L, 1965, Ap 28,45:2
Krzyzanowski, Adam, 1963, F 2,8:7
Ku Chung-Chen, 1945, Ag 2,19:5
Kubal, Lawrence, 1922, Mr 24,9:3
Kubalak, Henry F, 1956, O 2,35:1
Kubasek, John J, 1950, Je 17,15:5
Kubec, August, 1946, Jl 22,21:2
Kubelik, Jan (por), 1940, D 6,23:1
Kubelle, Jordan J, 1944, Jl 25,19:4
Kubelsky, Mayer, 1946, O 15,25:3
Kuberski, Edward N, 1941, O 9,23:2
Kubicek, John, 1953, Mr 30,21:3
Kubie, Albert D, 1947, N 22,15:2
Kubie, David S, 1953, My 10,88:4
Kubie, Donald A, 1968, N 8,47:4
Kubie, Isaac Mrs (por), 1944, F 19,13:4
Kubik, Henry H Sr Mrs, 1960, F 25,29:5
Kubina, Teodor, 1951, F 16,25:2
Kubler, George A, 1944, Ja 11,20:2
Kubler, Louis E, 1957, Mr 3,84:7
Kubley, William R, 1954, F 8,23:5
Kubovy, Arieh, 1966, My 18,47:2
Kuboyama, Aikichi, 1954, S 24,10:3
Kubuski, Clarence E, 1963, My 11,25:5
Kuc, William Sr, 1950, F 24,23:4
Kucera, Louis B, 1957, My 11,21:4
Kuch, A H Mrs, 1944, O 9,23:5
Kuch, Charles F, 1942, My 6,19:5
Kuch, Herman F, 1946, F 20,25:3
Kucharzewski, Jan, 1952, Jl 5,15:4
Kuchera, Charles Sr, 1949, F 11,23:3
Kucherenko, Vladimir A, 1963, N 28,39:1
Kuchler, Henry C Mrs, 1941, D 3,25:1
Kuck, Henry D, 1947, F 14,22:2
Kuck, Julius A, 1943, Ap 12,23:5
Kuck, Julius A Mrs, 1954, S 25,15:4
Kucker, Abraham, 1952, F 17,85:1
Kuckro, William E, 1951, Ap 16,25:2
Kuckuck, Harry J, 1945, Ja 26,21:1
Kuczynski, Robert R, 1947, N 28,27:4
Kuczynski, Vincent A J, 1952, Ja 1,25:6
Kuder, Joseph, 1913, Jl 26,7:6
Kuder, Kate R Mrs, 1944, My 4,19:4
Kuder, Louis F, 1947, Ja 28,23:1
Kuder, William J, 1949, Jl 7,26:2
Kudisch, Alexis, 1947, F 24,19:5
Kudisch, Clarence P, 1965, Ag 7,21:3
Kudlich, Hans E, 1947, F 23,53:5
Kudlich, Herman G, 1946, Ja 8,24:3
Kudner, Arthur H (por), 1944, F 19,13:3
Kudner, Charles W, 1959, My 4,29:4
Kudner, Henry C Mrs, 1956, Ap 2,23:4
Kuebel, Matthew, 1951, N 3,17:4
Kuebler, Charles R, 1953, Mr 14,15:3
Kuebler, Kaethe, 1951, Je 24,72:6
Kuebler, William P, 1951, Mr 31,15:2
Kuechenmeister, Frederick W Jr, 1937, N 14,II,11:3
Kuechler, Gustave H, 1957, Ja 10,29:4
Kuegle, Albert S, 1951, My 23,35:5
Kuehl, Henry, 1955, Ja 22,11:2
Kuehl, John G W, 1950, Ag 21,19:3
Kuehn, Charles R, 1953, Mr 18,31:3
Kuehn, Ferdinand A, 1952, Ap 29,27:3
Kuehn, Louis, 1948, N 28,92:3
Kuehn, R, 1942, Mr 17,17:5
Kuehn, Theodore O, 1938, Mr 23,23:5
Kuehn, Victor A, 1960, Jl 13,35:4
Kuehn, William G Sr Mrs, 1952, D 12,29:3
Kuehne, Frederick W, 1947, Ag 23,13:4
Kuehne, Frederick W Mrs, 1948, O 12,25:6
Kuehne, Gerhard, 1959, O 5,31:4
Kuehne, Joseph C, 1952, F 9,13:6
Kuehne, Max, 1968, Mr 16,31:3
Kuehne, Percival Mrs, 1909, O 1,9:5
Kuehner, Hanns E, 1967, N 30,47:3
Kuehnert, Paul A, 1953, My 15,23:4
Kuehnle, Frederick C, 1952, My 25,92:5
Kuehnling, William, 1949, Mr 29,25:4
Kuehnreich, Zigmund, 1961, Mr 10,27:3
Kuehns, Carl, 1947, My 18,60:6
Kuelling, Albert, 1937, N 3,23:5
Kuelz, Wilhelm, 1948, Ap 11,72:7

Kuemmel, Otto, 1952, F 14,27:3
Kuemmerle, Gustave C (will, Ap 4,19:4), 1957, Mr 25,25:1
Kuempel Wm O, 1951, My 27,69:1
Kuen, Samuel E, 1937, Je 30,24:2
Kuenhold, Otto J, 1943, Jl 4,20:5
Kuenn, Harvey Sr, 1962, My 12,23:2
Kuenneke, Edward, 1953, O 28,29:1
Kuenstler, H Dr, 1882, N 28,2:2
Kuenzel, Waldemar R, 1957, O 5,17:5
Kuenzlen, Albert, 1938, S 22,23:4
Kues, Charles H, 1953, Jl 10,19:4
Kuesel, Arthur T, 1957, S 22,87:2
Kuester, Lillian J, 1955, O 31,25:5
Kuetgen, Charles G, 1948, Ja 4,52:5
Kuett, Mary B Mrs, 1941, My 12,17:3
Kufahl, Gertrude M, 1963, S 19,27:4
Kufferle, Peter, 1942, Ag 22,13:5
Kuffler, Harry A Mrs, 1965, Ap 30,36:8
Kuffler, Julius L Mrs, 1964, S 9,43:1
Kuflewski, Wladyslaw A, 1945, O 25,21:1
Kufs, Otto B, 1950, O 23,23:4
Kufta, John G Dr, 1937, O 9,19:1
Kugel, David Mrs, 1968, D 20,47:3
Kugel, Frederick A, 1960, S 8,35:1
Kugel, Harry J, 1968, My 15,47:1
Kugel, Isadore H, 1942, D 24,15:2
Kugel, Lee, 1950, Ja 19,28:3
Kugel, Maurice A, 1946, Mr 11,25:4
Kugel, Samuel, 1939, Ja 27,19:2
Kugel, Simon H, 1947, Ja 9,23:5
Kugelman, Jack, 1942, Ap 21,23:2
Kugelman, Solomon, 1937, F 24,23:5
Kugelmann, Bernhard, 1938, D 25,14:4
Kugeman, William E, 1950, N 30,33:1
Kugler, Albert J, 1945, D 6,28:2
Kugler, Charles, 1958, Ja 19,86:6
Kugler, Fred W, 1944, F 22,23:2
Kugler, Heinz W Mrs, 1947, Jl 25,17:1
Kugler, Joseph C, 1941, N 24,17:4
Kugler, Joseph W, 1956, Mr 28,31:3
Kuh, Anton, 1941, Ja 19,40:1
Kuh, Edwin J, 1941, Ja 1,23:2
Kuh, Emanuel S, 1917, Je 14,11:4
Kuhar, Aloysius, 1958, O 30,31:4
Kuhara, Fusanosuke, 1965, Ja 30,27:3
Kuhbach, Charles J, 1945, F 23,17:4
Kuhl, C Walter, 1954, Mr 27,17:2
Kuhl, Carl W Mrs, 1950, Je 22,27:2
Kuhl, Christopher H, 1950, Jl 29,13:6
Kuhl, Frank J, 1954, Mr 16,29:3
Kuhl, Herman G, 1966, Je 25,31:3
Kuhl, Louise, 1967, Ag 10,37:3
Kuhl, Philip E, 1939, Ja 4,21:3
Kuhl, Richard, 1951, F 7,29:3
Kuhl, Richard Mrs, 1948, Ja 23,27:5
Kuhlenschmidt, Richard M Sr, 1949, D 31,15:5
Kuhlman, Carl J, 1960, N 15,42:4
Kuhlman, Charles L, 1952, O 11,19:5
Kuhlman, Ernest H, 1957, F 18,27:1
Kuhlman, Gus J, 1951, Mr 10,13:5
Kuhlman, Harry E, 1960, O 10,31:1
Kuhlman, Henry T, 1950, N 19,93:2
Kuhlmann, Alvin E, 1951, S 14,26:2
Kuhlmann, Fred, 1941, Ap 20,42:4
Kuhlmann, Frederick F, 1944, N 30,23:2
Kuhlmann, Rhoda C (will), 1952, My 1,15:6
Kuhlmeier, Henry, 1951, Mr 8,29:4
Kuhn, Adam Mrs, 1959, Ja 9,25:3
Kuhn, Alvin B, 1963, S 15,86:7
Kuhn, Andrew B, 1940, Ja 15,15:5
Kuhn, Archie, 1948, S 10,23:2
Kuhn, Arthur K, 1954, Jl 9,17:5
Kuhn, Byron W, 1925, S 23,25:3
Kuhn, C Hartman, 1948, Mr 11,27:2
Kuhn, C Hartman Mrs, 1940, D 15,61:2
Kuhn, C John, 1960, Jl 27,29:5
Kuhn, Carrie T, 1954, Ja 30,17:6
Kuhn, Claire L, 1949, F 21,23:4
Kuhn, Clarence W, 1912, F 2,9:5
Kuhn, Edward J, 1959, O 20,40:1
Kuhn, Ernest H, 1961, My 23,39:1
Kuhn, Ferdinand, 1949, Je 15,29:5
Kuhn, Ferdinand J, 1953, O 14,29:4
Kuhn, Ferdinand Sr Mrs, 1967, N 25,39:2
Kuhn, Frank J, 1941, Ag 14,17:3
Kuhn, Fred, 1949, Je 27,16:6
Kuhn, Frederick J, 1942, Mr 25,21:3
Kuhn, Fritz, 1953, F 2,11:1
Kuhn, George, 1939, F 16,21:2; 1945, My 9,23:2
Kuhn, George J M, 1968, O 12,37:2
Kuhn, George J Mrs, 1944, F 18,17:4
Kuhn, George M, 1953, Je 5,27:4
Kuhn, George Richard Dr, 1915, N 7,21:6
Kuhn, George W, 1961, Mr 27,31:3
Kuhn, Harold P, 1940, Ap 16,23:1
Kuhn, Harry A, 1962, Ja 28,76:6
Kuhn, Hubert G, 1943, O 9,13:4
Kuhn, Hugh A, 1958, Ap 20,84:6
Kuhn, I Russel, 1961, Je 17,21:5
Kuhn, Isaac B Mrs, 1945, Mr 15,23:2
Kuhn, J E, 1935, N 13,21:3
Kuhn, J R, 1926, N 4,27:5
Kuhn, John J, 1947, O 19,66:6; 1958, Ja 14,33:3; 1966, O 18,45:2
Kuhn, John Mrs, 1954, Ap 24,17:4
Kuhn, Joseph G, 1943, S 1,19:6
Kuhn, Joseph J, 1965, D 27,25:2
Kuhn, Julius, 1944, Mr 24,19:4
Kuhn, Lee, 1955, D 3,17:6
Kuhn, Leo Mrs, 1948, S 9,27:4
Kuhn, Louis A, 1950, S 2,15:5
Kuhn, Louis C, 1938, Ag 8,13:2
Kuhn, Max Mrs, 1943, O 14,21:1
Kuhn, Oliver O, 1937, Jl 19,15:5
Kuhn, Paul H, 1951, F 27,27:3; 1965, Ja 27,35:1
Kuhn, Peter R, 1961, S 13,45:5
Kuhn, Philalethes, 1937, Ag 6,17:4
Kuhn, R Parker, 1963, My 29,33:5
Kuhn, Richard, 1967, Ag 2,37:2
Kuhn, Samuel F, 1955, Mr 24,31:2
Kuhn, Simon, 1919, D 11,13:3
Kuhn, Simon Mrs, 1952, Ap 23,29:6
Kuhn, Walt (por), 1949, Jl 14,27:1
Kuhn, Walt Mrs, 1961, O 23,29:2
Kuhn, Walter R, 1965, Ja 9,25:5
Kuhn, Wendel S, 1964, N 18,47:4
Kuhn, William F Dr, 1924, S 3,17:2
Kuhn, William H, 1950, O 12,31:1
Kuhnast, Frank H Mrs, 1949, Ja 27,24:2
Kuhne, Aug, 1941, Jl 30,17:5
Kuhne, Frederick Mrs, 1947, S 19,23:4
Kuhne, James S, 1951, O 22,23:3
Kuhner, Anne E, 1954, Ja 4,19:5
Kuhner, George A, 1946, Ja 26,13:4
Kuhner, George A Mrs, 1959, Jl 25,17:1
Kuhner, M Rev, 1917, S 13,13:2
Kuhnhold, William H, 1961, N 15,43:4
Kuhnle, Edmund L, 1953, My 3,89:2
Kuhnle, William, 1960, Ap 9,23:6
Kuhnlein, Robert L, 1968, My 3,54:3
Kuhnmuench, Charles J, 1944, Jl 9,35:3
Kuhnmuench, Otto J, 1943, D 20,23:5
Kuhns, Austin, 1962, Ap 22,80:7
Kuhns, Charles W, 1965, F 22,21:3
Kuhns, Harold S, 1965, Jl 5,17:5
Kuhns, Maurice S, 1949, O 11,31:2
Kuhr, Ernestus O, 1959, My 8,27:2
Kuhr, William Frederick, 1920, Mr 20,11:6
Kuichling, Emil, 1914, N 11,13:5
Kuiken, Henry A, 1956, Mr 3,23:1
Kuiken, Nicholas A, 1944, Ja 4,17:4
Kuist, Howard T, 1964, My 16,25:6
Kujur, Niclas, 1960, Jl 25,23:2
Kuker, Siegmund, 1954, O 18,25:3
Kulagin, Mikhail V, 1956, Ag 8,6:4
Kulakowski, B A Dr, 1924, N 27,19:3
Kulas, E J (will), 1952, D 9,28:5
Kulas, Elroy J, 1952, My 14,27:3
Kuleman, Frederick E, 1964, D 9,50:7
Kulenovich, Dzafer, 1944, My 26,19:4
Kulesa, Bernard, 1950, Ja 13,23:1
Kulesza, Chester W, 1963, S 2,15:5
Kulfson, August, 1943, D 10,12:6
Kuli Mirza, Riza Prince (R K Mirza), 1941, My 6,9:3
Kulikowski, Robert L, 1964, Jl 19,65:1
Kulischer, Eugene M, 1956, Ap 4,29:1
Kulka, William, 1950, Jl 20,25:4
Kulkin, Joseph S, 1957, D 30,23:4
Kulky, Henry, 1965, F 14,88:3
Kull, Albert L, 1938, Ap 5,21:6
Kull, Arthur F, 1962, Jl 12,29:3
Kull, Frederick Mrs, 1954, D 16,37:6
Kull, Irving S, 1961, Jl 26,31:5
Kull, Mary Mrs, 1905, Ag 22,7:5
Kullak, Theodore, 1882, Mr 2,5:1
Kullitis, Jekabs, 1957, O 15,33:3
Kullman, Charles J, 1914, Ap 26,IV,7:6
Kullman, Charles Sr, 1942, S 25,21:5
Kullman, Fannie Mrs, 1940, D 28,15:3
Kullman, John N, 1951, Ap 5,29:4
Kullman, Morris, 1962, S 21,29:2
Kullman, Morris Mrs, 1963, Ap 6,19:3
Kullman, Phil C Jr, 1951, N 24,11:1
Kullmann, Martin, 1939, My 14,III,7:2
Kullmer, Charles J, 1942, F 5,21:5
Kullujian, Thomas H, 1941, N 8,19:3
Kulmayer, Joseph, 1958, Ap 5,15:6
Kulnick, Charles, 1938, Ja 24,23:3
Kulow, Claudius S, 1961, Jl 2,33:2
Kulp, Abram M, 1954, D 28,23:4
Kulp, Burr R, 1946, F 28,23:3
Kulp, C Arthur, 1957, Ag 21,27:3
Kulp, Floyd B, 1962, Ap 27,35:2
Kulpa, Stanley T, 1953, F 27,21:2
Kulsen, Hans, 1948, S 30,27:3
Kultee, Gustavus, 1876, Je 23,6:6
Kumarappa, Bharatan, 1957, Je 26,31:2
Kumarappa, Jagadisan M, 1957, O 27,86:8
Kumler, F A Z, 1942, Jl 23,19:3
Kumm, Einar, 1952, Mr 5,29:5
Kummel, Henry B (por), 1945, O 24,21:3
Kummel, Max, 1953, S 1,23:2
Kummer, Frederick A, 1943, N 23,25:6
Kummer, Otto Mrs, 1948, Ag 24,23:1
Kummerow, Albert, 1948, D 24,17:4
Kump, Edith Mrs, 1941, Ap 25,19:3
Kump, Elizabeth, 1937, Ja 10,II,9:2
Kump, Herman G, 1962, F 15,29:2
Kumpf, Willard O, 1961, Je 10,23:4
Kun, Irene, 1958, F 25,27:3
Kun, Joseph L, 1961, Je 17,21:3
Kun, Ladislas (por), 1939, My 6,17:3
Kun, Magda, 1945, N 8,19:4
Kunath, Edward F, 1947, Ja 29,25:2
Kunc, Bozidar, 1964, Ap 2,33:3
Kunc, Frank J, 1963, O 27,88:3
Kunderd, Amos E, 1965, Ap 3,29:3
Kundig, Martin Rev, 1879, Mr 7,1:4
Kundt, Hans (por), 1939, Ag 31,19:3
Kung, Duke, 1919, N 17,15:3
Kung, H H (Kung Hsiang-hsi),(mem ser, Ag 23,51:1), 1967, Ag 16,41:1
Kung Ping Wang, Mrs, 1964, Ja 25,23:4
Kunhardt, H Rudolph, 1963, O 18,28:3
Kunhardt, Kingsley, 1959, N 2,31:2
Kunhardt, W B, 1933, N 24,22:3
Kuni, Asaakira, 1959, D 8,45:5
Kuni, Taka Prince, 1937, O 2,21:4
Kuni, Tomoko Princess, 1947, Je 30,19:5
Kuniansky, Max, 1953, Jl 23,23:3
Kunin, Maxwell (est appr), 1962, Ja 4,22:2
Kunin, Stanley, 1950, O 3,21:1
Kunitz, Charles, 1955, Ap 16,19:3
Kuniyoshi, Yasuo, 1953, My 15,23:1
Kunkel, Beverly W Mrs, 1956, Jl 20,17:3
Kunkel, Florence M, 1964, N 14,29:4
Kunkel, Fritz, 1956, Ap 2,23:5
Kunkel, George, 1885, Ja 26,2:4; 1937, N 9,24:3
Kunkel, Henry J, 1953, Ag 20,27:4
Kunkel, Louis E, 1950, Mr 15,29:4
Kunkel, Louis O, 1960, Mr 22,37:1
Kunkel, Otto A, 1944, Ag 17,17:3
Kunkel, P, 1880, Je 21,5:5
Kunkel, Robert S Mrs, 1950, O 5,31:3
Kunkel, William A Jr, 1948, O 8,25:3
Kunkelman, William H, 1956, Mr 30,19:3
Kunkle, Bayard D, 1953, S 15,31:1
Kunkle, Cornelius K, 1947, O 30,25:3
Kunkle, Edward C, 1941, O 16,21:2
Kunkle, John S, 1961, S 4,15:2
Kunkler, Vincent, 1951, Mr 6,27:2
Kunos, Eugene, 1961, Ja 21,21:4
Kunschak, Leopold (funl, Mr 18,31:5), 1953, Mr 92:1
Kunsman, Charles J Jr Mrs, 1956, My 5,19:5
Kunsman, Harry P, 1951, Jl 15,60:5
Kunst, George J, 1953, Ja 12,27:4
Kunst, John, 1943, F 4,23:1
Kunst, Paul H, 1951, Ap 5,29:4
Kunstadter, Albert, 1965, N 25,35:6
Kunstler, Harold L, 1960, My 6,31:3
Kuntz, Abraham, 1945, Ap 1,36:7
Kuntz, Albert, 1957, Ja 22,29:2
Kuntz, Cyrus, 1903, Jl 8,9:7
Kuntz, Daniel, 1959, Ap 11,21:1
Kuntz, Edward, 1957, Ap 11,31:2
Kuntz, Frank E, 1942, Ja 1,25:5
Kuntz, John H J, 1940, S 14,17:3
Kuntz, John J, 1960, Ja 9,21:5
Kuntz, Joseph, 1953, Ap 8,29:2
Kuntz, Nicholas G, 1958, F 9,88:5
Kuntz, William A, 1948, N 6,13:6
Kuntz, William E, 1941, S 27,17:2
Kunz, Charlie, 1958, Mr 17,29:2
Kunz, Conrad, 1946, Je 2,44:3
Kunz, Eric C, 1964, Ja 26,80:8
Kunz, Eric C Mrs, 1964, N 1,88:6
Kunz, Frederick W, 1945, F 20,19:1
Kunz, G F, 1932, Je 30,23:3
Kunz, Gustave, 1941, Je 5,23:3
Kunz, Harold G, 1960, F 6,19:6
Kunz, Herman Mrs, 1948, Jl 8,23:3
Kunz, Jakob, 1938, Jl 19,21:5
Kunz, John F, 1947, Jl 13,44:2
Kunz, Joseph W, 1962, Jl 26,27:3
Kunz, Peter J, 1940, Ag 13,19:4
Kunz, Stanley H, 1946, Ap 25,21:3
Kunz, William C, 1952, O 19,88:3
Kunze, Arthur D, 1944, F 3,19:4
Kunze, Charles H, 1948, N 3,27:4
Kunze, Donald, 1954, Jl 4,22:4
Kunze, Henry A, 1943, Mr 29,16:3
Kunze, Louis, 1947, F 7,24:2
Kunze, Max O, 1939, My 15,17:4
Kunze, Walter, 1960, Ag 13,15:7
Kunzelman, Edward, 1950, F 24,23:2
Kunzig, Phil H, 1948, S 29,29:2
Kunzig, Philip H Mrs, 1966, Jl 18,27:3
Kunzinger, Arthur, 1957, D 18,35:4
Kunzinger, Philip Jr, 1945, Ap 4,21:5
Kunzmann, Charles P, 1960, Jl 2,17:6
Kunzmann, Ferdinand L, 1948, Je 1,23:3
Kunzmann, Louis F Mrs, 1957, D 2,27:4
Kuo, Bonaventure, 1962, F 5,31:5
Kuoch, Robert H, 1949, F 2,27:1
Kuokew, F W, 1882, Ap 7,5:2
Kupala, Yanka (Ivan Lutsevich), 1942, Jl 1,23
Kupchynski, Vladimir T, 1958, Ja 9,33:2

Kupcinet, Karyn, 1963, D 1,55:1
Kuperman, Nathan, 1960, Ja 1,19:1
Kuperstein, David, 1954, O 20,29:2
Kupfer, Felix A, 1963, My 6,29:4
Kupfer, Louis, 1956, Je 25,23:5
Kupfer, Milton P, 1958, Jl 25,9:4
Kupfersmith, Meyer, 1951, Je 7,33:5
Kuplic, James Leslie, 1968, Jl 23,39:1
Kuppenheimer, B, 1903, O 28,9:6
Kuppenheimer, Jonas, 1921, My 5,17:3
Kupper, John C, 1957, Ap 16,33:5
Kupperman, Moses, 1960, Mr 11,25:1
Kupriyanov, Pyotr, 1963, Mr 15,7:4
Kupsick, Jack R, 1961, Jl 19,29:4
Kupsick, Robert H, 1960, D 31,17:3
Kurashov, Sergei V, 1965, Ag 28,21:5
Kurchatov, Igor V (funl plans, F 9,31:5; funl, F 10,-37:4), 1960, F 8,1:6
Kurdle, Albert, 1965, Ag 27,29:3
Kureck, Edward, 1947, Jl 5,11:4
Kurekhin, Ivan, 1951, Ap 13,23:2
Kurfees, James F Sr, 1956, Ja 30,27:5
Kurgans, Louis Mrs, 1966, Ja 2,22:1
Kurh, Victor, 1948, D 17,27:1
Kurig, Wasyl, 1950, O 5,26:5
Kurilenkov, Vasili, 1952, My 14,28:3
Kurimoto, George T Mrs, 1960, N 29,37:1
Kurino, Shinichiro Viscount (por), 1937, N 16,23:4
Kuriskin, Sergi, 1951, F 16,25:2
Kuritzky, Isadore Dr, 1968, Ja 31,41:3
Kurka, Robert F, 1957, D 13,27:2
Kurke, George (por), 1946, D 8,77:1
Kurkjian, Vahan M, 1961, N 1,39:1
Kurkus, Edward, 1953, O 1,29:3
Kurland, Simon Mrs, 1953, Ag 1,27:2
Kurlander, John H, 1949, Je 27,27:4
Kurman, Nathan A, 1962, N 8,39:4
Kurmes, Ernest Mrs, 1958, Jl 20,65:1
Kurn, James M, 1945, Ja 14,40:2
Kurnakov-Kozelski, Sergei N, 1949, Ag 11,23:2
Kurnitz, Harry (funl plans, Mr 20,47:1), 1968, Mr 19,44:1
Kuroki, Tamemoto Gen, 1923, F 5,15:5
Kuropatkin, Gen, 1925, Ja 24,13:5
Kurowski, John, 1951, Ag 14,23:1
Kurpiel, John, 1948, My 19,27:1
Kurr, Fred L, 1961, Jl 26,31:2
Kurras, J Fred, 1947, Ap 17,27:4
Kurrie, Harry R, 1938, D 26,23:4
Kurrus, Albert B Mrs, 1950, D 4,29:3
Kurrus, Harry J, 1949, Jl 18,17:5
Kursh, George F Mrs, 1942, Mr 20,19:5
Kurshals, Fred C, 1947, My 6,28:2
Kurshals, Jacob A, 1950, Mr 20,21:3
Kursheedt, A, 1884, Ap 20,2:6
Kursheedt, Moses M, 1942, Ap 19,43:2
Kurt, Franklin T, 1947, S 1,19:5
Kurt, Frederick Mrs, 1952, Mr 6,32:5
Kurt-Deri, Melanie, 1941, Mr 12,21:2
Kurth, Aug, 1903, Ap 12,7:6
Kurth, Chris Jr, 1953, Ag 3,17:4
Kurth, Ernest L, 1960, O 27,37:5
Kurth, Harold R, 1956, F 9,31:1
Kurth, Henry A, 1940, D 10,25:2
Kurth, John W, 1954, Ag 11,25:4
Kurth, Wilfred, 1959, Je 2,35:3
Kurthy, Zoltan, 1954, Mr 23,27:3
Kurtin, Abner (por), 1955, My 12,29:1
Kurtsniger, Charles E (por), 1946, S 25,27:1
Kurtz, Aaron, 1964, My 31,76:5
Kurtz, Adam, 1945, Ag 3,17:6
Kurtz, Adolf R C, 1939, My 6,17:4
Kurtz, Allan K, 1965, Je 2,45:4
Kurtz, Aron, 1945, Je 4,19:5
Kurtz, Aron Mrs, 1949, N 23,29:5
Kurtz, Arthur D, 1939, Ja 23,13:3
Kurtz, Arthur F Rev, 1925, F 28,13:5
Kurtz, Benjamin T, 1960, Mr 30,37:2
Kurtz, Charles, 1948, Jl 1,23:2
Kurtz, Charles M, 1909, Mr 22,7:5
Kurtz, Cyrus, 1943, Jl 24,13:2
Kurtz, Daniel H, 1950, Je 26,27:5
Kurtz, Ford, 1956, Ag 10,17:1
Kurtz, Ford Mrs, 1956, Jl 16,21:4
Kurtz, Frank B, 1962, Ja 4,33:4
Kurtz, Frederick W, 1952, Je 20,23:5
Kurtz, Henry F, 1958, Ja 9,33:4
Kurtz, Henry J, 1942, D 18,27:4
Kurtz, Henry L, 1951, N 19,23:3
Kurtz, Henry L Mrs, 1962, S 27,37:1
Kurtz, Irwin, 1965, S 1,37:5
Kurtz, Isadore J, 1953, My 9,19:4
Kurtz, James H, 1951, O 16,31:4
Kurtz, John C, 1952, D 29,19:6
Kurtz, Joseph, 1941, Jl 10,19:6
Kurtz, Kenneth S, 1953, Ap 12,89:1
Kurtz, LeRoy H, 1967, Jl 29,25:3
Kurtz, Louis C, 1950, O 2,23:5
Kurtz, Max, 1955, Mr 17,45:5
Kurtz, Max L, 1939, N 29,23:4
Kurtz, Meyer H Mrs, 1952, Ap 14,19:6
Kurtz, Morris Mrs, 1961, Ja 4,33:1
Kurtz, Nathan Mrs, 1947, My 21,25:2

Kurtz, Robert B, 1946, F 22,25:3
Kurtz, Robert M, 1941, Je 1,41:3
Kurtz, Robert R, 1952, Mr 29,15:5
Kurtz, Rubin, 1944, O 17,23:6
Kurtz, Samuel, 1957, Ja 13,84:1
Kurtz, Thomas R, 1956, Mr 8,29:2
Kurtz, Thomas R Mrs, 1962, Ja 14,84:5
Kurtz, Walter O, 1946, D 3,31:1
Kurtz, William, 1904, D 7,9:3
Kurtz, William F, 1940, D 18,25:3; 1943, Ap 5,19:5
Kurtz, William M, 1965, F 13,21:3
Kurtz, William S, 1941, Ja 20,17:5
Kurtzman, Charles, 1961, Ja 8,86:3
Kurtzman, Leon, 1962, F 24,27:3
Kurtzner, Harry M, 1953, S 5,15:5
Kurtzon, Morris, 1958, Jl 26,15:7
Kurucz, John, 1940, Jl 24,21:4
Kurusu, Saburo, 1954, Ap 8,27:1
Kurz, Frances Mrs, 1903, N 24,9:5
Kurz, G Victor, 1940, D 1,62:2
Kurz, George F, 1937, Jl 22,19:6
Kurz, Jacob, 1958, Ag 24,86:2
Kurz, Louis A Mrs, 1948, Ap 3,15:1
Kurz, Meyer, 1957, N 11,29:2
Kurz, Michael, 1958, Mr 5,31:1
Kurz, Paul H, 1956, Ja 3,31:2
Kurz, Peter, 1966, F 24,37:2
Kurz, Robert E, 1957, My 22,33:6
Kurz, Schulem, 1950, Mr 14,25:3
Kurz, William F, 1945, S 24,19:2
Kurz, William G, 1949, My 26,29:1
Kurzbauer, Elsa Mrs (cor, Je 24,27:2), 1954, Je 23, 26:6
Kurzhals, Edward, 1950, S 12,27:2
Kurzinski, Frank, 1952, S 14,36:1
Kurzman, Charles, 1940, Ag 1,21:3
Kurzman, Ferdinand, 1917, D 25,15:3
Kurzman, Julius C, 1922, F 21,17:3
Kurzman, Samuel, 1938, Mr 30,21:2
Kurzon, Charles, 1964, Mr 5,30:4
Kurzrock, Abraham H, 1965, Mr 28,93:1
Kurzrock, Julius, 1954, O 15,23:2
Kurzrok, Raphael, 1961, N 26,88:7
Kurzweg, Frank, 1946, D 2,25:2
Kurzweil, Peritz M, 1965, Jl 26,23:1
Kurzweil, Phil Mrs, 1958, Ag 27,29:4
Kurzweil, Robert, 1966, Ap 21,39:1
Kusanke, Richard, 1946, O 10,27:5
Kusanobu, Takeji, 1942, D 7,27:5
Kusch, Ernest H, 1958, Mr 24,27:5
Kusch, Harry B, 1961, Jl 22,21:5
Kusche, Julius, 1937, S 10,23:4
Kusell, James, 1909, O 22,7:2
Kusell, Jules, 1909, N 9,9:5
Kuser, A R, 1929, F 9,17:3
Kuser, Dryden, 1964, Mr 6,28:5
Kuser, Fred, 1937, Ag 6,17:4
Kuser, John L, 1937, Ag 12,19:6
Kuser, Walter, 1967, F 7,39:2
Kusevitsky, Mihal Mrs, 1950, S 7,31:3
Kush, Gustav, 1946, My 11,27:4
Kushakian, Thorgom, 1939, F 11,15:5
Kushel, Francisak Gen, 1968, My 27,47:1
Kushel, Harold, 1962, Ag 10,19:1
Kushelevitch, Joseph, 1954, D 23,19:5
Kushell, Maria D, 1953, Jl 18,13:4
Kushida, Manzo (por), 1939, S 7,25:5
Kushins, Doris, 1959, Je 21,93:2
Kushner, Bernard M, 1955, F 16,29:2
Kushner, J Irving, 1960, Ag 11,27:4
Kushner, Jefferson E Prof, 1922, Jl 1,13:6
Kushner, Nat, 1959, N 21,23:5
Kushner, Nicholas C, 1963, Ag 7,33:3
Kushwara, John M, 1950, D 19,30:3
Kusielewicz, Agnes B Mrs, 1964, Ja 26,81:2
Kusiw, Basil, 1958, Jl 26,15:4
Kuskin, Louis, 1941, Ag 20,19:6
Kuskin, Wolf, 1943, My 1,15:2
Kuskova-Prokopovich, Sergei N Mrs, 1959, Ja 17,19:4
Kusnetz, David, 1959, Je 29,29:1
Kuss, Frederick W, 1956, Jl 15,61:2
Kuss, George J, 1959, S 10,35:3
Kuss, Harry F, 1939, N 7,25:5
Kuss, Henry A, 1948, Mr 12,23:5
Kuss, Henry J Sr Mrs, 1964, Je 20,25:5
Kuss, Mayor (funl), 1871, Mr 20,1:4
Kuss, Phil H, 1942, Ag 18,22:2
Kussat, Rudolf O, 1958, Mr 25,33:4
Kussel, Alfred, 1967, Jl 2,35:2
Kussell, William, 1954, Ag 30,17:4
Kussmaul, Adolf Prof, 1902, My 29,9:6
Kussy, Herman, 1949, Ap 1,25:2
Kussy, Meyer Mrs, 1955, Ja 7,21:5
Kussy, Nathan, 1956, D 15,25:2
Kussy, Sarah, 1956, O 3,33:3
Kustner, Carl G, 1954, Je 3,27:2
Kutak, Frank J, 1949, D 4,108:6
Kutak, John A, 1938, Ja 16,II,9:2
Kutas, Michael J, 1949, O 14,27:3
Kutay, Maurice, 1959, Mr 15,88:7
Kutcher, Edward, 1947, Ja 12,21:3
Kutchin, Victor, 1939, N 23,27:3
Kutinsky, Morris Mrs, 1940, F 1,21:4

Kutisker, Meyer J, 1964, Mr 2,27:2
Kutner, Abraham A, 1957, Ap 7,88:5
Kutner, Arthur, 1903, S 11,7:6
Kutner, Morris M, 1951, Ja 9,30:5
Kutner, Nanette, 1962, O 10,47:2
Kutner, Paul, 1961, Mr 17,31:2
Kutrzeba, Stanislaw, 1946, Ja 12,15:5
Kutschbock, Robert A, 1918, Mr 3,23:1
Kutscher, Albert, 1951, Jl 20,23:3
Kutscher, Cardinal, 1881, Ja 28,5:4
Kutscher, Harry, 1941, My 2,21:2
Kutscher, Martin (por), 1947, N 1,15:3
Kutschman, Andrew Mrs, 1950, D 23,15:2
Kutsky, John, 1944, O 10,23:4
Kutsukian, John Mrs, 1945, Je 7,19:5
Kuttler, Charles A, 1959, D 27,60:5
Kuttner, Ann G Dr, 1968, My 21,47:1
Kuttner, Elsie, 1960, S 12,29:1
Kuttner, Henry, 1958, F 7,21:2
Kuttner, Julia E, 1967, N 2,47:2
Kuttner, Theodore, 1947, Jl 8,23:2
Kuttner, Theodore Mrs, 1959, Mr 29,80:2
Kuttruff, Charles, 1942, D 4,25:4
Kutz, Abraham, 1937, S 23,27:5
Kutz, Charles, 1954, O 12,27:4
Kutz, Charles W, 1951, Ja 26,23:2
Kutz, Gabriel S, 1939, Ap 17,17:6
Kutz, George Fink Rear-Adm, 1921, Ag 11,13:5
Kutz, Grace, 1950, Mr 9,30:2
Kutz, Kenneth K, 1949, Mr 28,21:5
Kutz, Milton, 1953, Je 19,21:3
Kutz, Milton Mrs (Hattie), 1965, Mr 4,31:3
Kutzleb, August, 1920, D 11,13:3
Kutzleb, August Mrs, 1920, D 11,13:3
Kutzner, Charles E, 1953, N 10,31:1
Kutzner, Pauline I, 1939, D 31,18:5
Kutzschenbach, Eugen von, 1938, Je 3,21:2
Kuusinen, Esa O, 1949, Ap 13,29:5
Kuusinen, Otto V (funl, My 20,3:2), 1964, My 18,2:4
Kuver, Fred H, 1967, Ap 15,31:4
Kuverie, Mark, 1949, Ap 14,1:1
Kuvshinoff, Vasily, 1953, O 16,27:2
Kuwait, Sultan of, 1950, Ja 31,24:2
Kuwatly, Shukri al-, 1967, Jl 1,23:1
Kuwnick, Frank A, 1950, Ap 6,29:1
Kuyawaski, Walter A, 1954, Jl 15,20:4
Kuykendall, C Porter, 1957, My 8,37:2
Kuykendall, Charles F, 1939, Mr 24,21:3
Kuykendall, Dave, 1957, Ag 10,15:5
Kuykendall, E V, 1958, F 27,27:1
Kuykendall, George, 1958, Ja 4,15:2
Kuykendall, Mitchell, 1940, N 5,25:2
Kuykendall, Nathaniel W, 1947, Ja 27,23:2
Kuykendall, Otho, 1940, N 5,25:2
Kuyper, Abraham Dr, 1920, N 9,15:3
Kuypers, John A, 1940, Mr 21,25:3
Kuzela, Joseph F Sr, 1950, N 5,92:4
Kuzma, William, 1950, O 26,31:3
Kuzmeier, Robert X, 1962, N 4,49:3
Kuzmier, Joan, 1950, F 20,41:8
Kuzmin, Anatoli N, 1954, O 30,17:5
Kuznetsov, Vassily D, 1954, Ja 29,19:2
Kuznetzoff, Adai, 1954, Ag 12,25:1
Kuznir, William, 1954, Jl 21,27:2
Kuznitzky, Erich, 1960, Mr 3,29:2
Kuzu, Hoshihisa, 1958, F 5,28:1
Kvande, Nicolai, 1943, Mr 10,19:5
Kvapil, Jaroslav, 1950, Ja 11,23:1
Kviesis, Albert, 1944, Ag 13,35:2
Kwaak, Jacobus, 1944, My 18,19:6
Kwaak, Peter G, 1942, Ja 19,17:4
Kwacho, Hiratada Prince, 1924, Mr 20,19:5
Kwalick, Harry, 1949, Je 3,25:2
Kwalick, Julius Judge, 1968, S 2,19:1
Kwan, S S, 1960, N 29,37:3
Kwan Yau Tang, 1960, Jl 6,33:4
Kwartin, Savel, 1952, S 23,33:2
Kwasigroch, Stanley J, 1947, S 29,21:1
Kwasniewski, Wanda Mrs, 1937, Ag 24,21:3
Kweetin, John, 1950, N 24,36:3
Kwei Yung-ching, 1954, Ag 13,15:6
Kwiatonski, Andrew, 1939, S 7,25:5
Kwiecien, Roman, 1953, Mr 19,29:2
Kwiek, Matthias, 1937, Mr 31,4:3
Kwis, Arthur F, 1952, Jl 10,31:5
Kyasht, Lydia, 1959, Ja 17,19:3
Kyba, Gabriel A, 1951, Jl 18,29:4
Kybal, Vlastimil, 1958, Ja 3,23:1
Kydd, Burness (por), 1955, Jl 11,23:2
Kydd, Charles, 1917, F 25,19:2
Kydd, Samuel L Mrs, 1937, Ap 5,19:5
Kyer, Charles, 1938, O 21,23:2
Kyes, L M, 1954, N 18,33:3
Kyes, L M Mrs, 1957, Je 30,68:8
Kyes, Preston, 1949, D 28,32:3
Kyff, Leonard Mrs, 1952, O 13,21:4
Kyff, Neil Mrs, 1951, Je 17,84:3
Kyjovsky, Jan, 1963, O 5,25:1
Kylar, Anton Sr, 1948, Mr 10,28:3
Kylberg, Carl, 1952, Ja 7,19:4
Kyle, Arthur C, 1960, N 5,23:5
Kyle, Billy, 1966, F 24,38:1
Kyle, Charles T, 1949, N 1,27:1

Kyle, Christopher, 1916, Ja 22,9:6
Kyle, Edwin De Wees, 1968, Ja 6,29:1
Kyle, Francis K, 1938, Ja 6,19:4
Kyle, Gordon R Mrs, 1953, Ag 10,23:4
Kyle, Howard, 1950, D 2,13:3
Kyle, J A, 1871, Mr 14,1:7
Kyle, J H Sen, 1901, Jl 2,7:5
Kyle, James J, 1941, Ap 10,23:5
Kyle, John T Mrs, 1955, N 9,33:2
Kyle, Joseph B Sr, 1961, Jl 30,69:2
Kyle, Joseph E, 1964, S 5,19:2
Kyle, M G, 1933, My 26,19:5
Kyle, Marion, 1941, O 9,23:5
Kyle, Mary Mrs, 1910, My 30,11:5
Kyle, Thomas E, 1939, My 18,25:5
Kyle, W Ray, 1965, D 4,31:4
Kyle, William D, 1953, Ap 23,29:2
Kyle, William G, 1941, My 25,37:1
Kyle, William J, 1939, Ja 8,43:2; 1944, Jl 30,35:4
Kyle, William J Sr Mrs, 1957, Ja 31,27:4
Kyler, James F, 1953, Je 1,23:5
Kylsant, Baroness, 1952, D 15,25:3
Kylsant, Lord, 1937, Je 6,II,8:6
Kynaston, Percy L, 1964, Ap 9,32:1
Kynberg, Jacob R, 1950, Jl 4,17:1
Kyndberg, Elmer, 1956, S 2,57:2
Kyne, Peter B, 1957, N 26,30:3
Kyne, Peter B Mrs, 1955, Ag 27,15:6
Kyne, William P, 1957, F 17,92:8
Kyner, William A, 1955, S 14,35:4
Kynett, Alpha G, 1939, D 27,21:2
Kynett, Harold H Mrs, 1954, Ja 27,27:1; 1965, Mr 1 31:4
Kynett, Martin W, 1950, My 6,15:2
Kynoch, Alfred E, 1948, O 24,78:5
Kynoch, William E G, 1966, Jl 18,27:5
Kyrillovna, Marie Grand Duchess, 1951, O 28,84:5
Kyrk, Hazel, 1957, Ag 8,23:5
Kyser, Emily R H Mrs, 1950, My 8,23:4
Kyser, Jacob A, 1952, Ja 31,27:3
Kysor, Leon M, 1945, O 18,23:5
Kyster, Olaf H Jr, 1959, S 16,39:4
Kyte, Arthur H, 1946, Mr 22,21:2
Kyu Chun Cho, 1965, Ap 11,92:3

L

Laage, Herbert A, 1957, F 19,31:1
Laak, Alex, 1960, S 8,14:5
Laase, Christian F J Dr, 1920, Ag 22,20:5
Laass, Gustave Rev, 1937, My 3,19:3
La Badie, Florence, 1917, O 14,23:3
Labagh, Isaac, 1876, Je 19,2:7
Labagh, Robert B, 1947, O 22,29:4
La Baie, Arthur J, 1952, N 11,29:2
Labalme, George Mrs, 1941, Je 22,32:2; 1956, Mr 27, 35:5
Laban, Rudolf, 1958, Jl 3,25:1
Laband, Paul Prof, 1918, Mr 25,11:4
Labar, Daniel E, 1939, Jl 23,29:2
Labar, James L, 1953, Ap 15,31:5
Labar, John S, 1950, Jl 10,21:4
La Bar, S Kenneth Mrs, 1950, Ap 9,85:1
Labar, Samuel P, 1941, Mr 28,23:4
Labar, Vincent, 1961, Jl 17,21:4
Labarca Hubertson, Guillermo, 1954, N 9,27:4
Labaree, B Rev, 1883, N 17,2:2
Labaree, Benjamin Rev Dr, 1906, My 19,11:6
Labaree, Mary S, 1960, Ja 9,21:1
Labaree, Robert M, 1952, Je 23,19:6
Labarge, Ernest H, 1955, Je 17,23:4
la Barraque, Christine B, 1961, F 12,87:1
la Barre, Anne de Countess, 1960, Jl 15,23:3
La Barre, Eugene, 1956, O 20,21:3
La Barre, George B, 1943, F 19,19:6
La Barre, Richard E, 1942, Je 11,23:5
Labarthe, Andre, 1967, N 13,47:1
Labat, J J, 1930, Jl 1,29:3
Labat, John B, 1954, N 4,31:4
Labate, Bruno, 1968, N 25,47:3
Labatt, Hugh F, 1956, Ap 1,88:2
Labatt, John S, 1952, Jl 9,27:3
Labatt-Simon, Harre M G, 1942, Ja 11,45:1
La Bau, Alicia, 1902, Ag 17,7:5
La Bau, James P, 1947, S 19,23:3
Labaugh, William I, 1950, Mr 29,29:3
Labaw, John P, 1949, Ap 28,31:2
Labaw, William, 1953, Ap 24,23:1
Labbe, Leon Dr, 1916, Mr 22,13:7
Labbe, Paul A, 1946, S 23,23:1
Labberton, John M, 1953, O 7,29:5
Labecki, John, 1949, F 19,15:5
La Bella, Philip T, 1960, My 10,37:5
La Bella, Vincenzo, 1954, D 28,23:1
LaBelle, Charles W, 1963, N 9,25:6
La Belle, Claude A, 1947, S 16,23:5
La Belle, Edward C, 1942, S 13,53:4
La Belle, Joseph E, 1941, Ag 21,17:5
La Belle, Orme W, 1956, D 25,25:2
Labensky, Boris P, 1950, O 26,31:2
Laber, Leo, 1947, Je 4,27:4
LaBerge, Bernard R, 1951, D 29,11:3
Laberge, Charles Joseph, 1874, Ag 9,8:3
Labetti, Nicholas J, 1955, Ag 24,27:5
Labey, James P, 1946, O 27,62:5
Labiche, E M, 1888, Ja 24,5:4
Laboissiere, Edward J, 1952, Jl 5,17:2
La Boiteaux, Mary M H Mrs, 1946, Mr 20,24:2
LaBombard, Leon F, 1965, Jl 5,17:5
LaBonne, Raymond B, 1967, Jl 12,43:2
LaBonte, Joseph F, 1940, Je 24,15:6
La Borde, Corina Mrs, 1937, N 12,22:1
Laborde, Herman, 1955, My 3,31:3
Labori, Fernand, 1917, Mr 15,11:4
La Boschin, Florence L (Mrs C Wolff), 1962, N 11, 88:5
La Bossier, Inez J, 1953, D 21,31:6
Labost, Henry, 1948, My 21,23:3
Labouchere, Albert E, 1941, S 25,25:5
abouchere, Albert E Mrs, 1943, Ap 14,23:2
abouchere, H (Lord Taunton), 1869, Jl 15,5:6
abouchere, Henry, 1912, Ja 17,13:5
abouisse, H R Mrs, 1945, S 20,23:5
aboulaye, Andre LeF de, 1966, Ag 18,32:6
aboulaye, E R L, 1883, My 26,5:5
aboulle, Alfred, 1947, S 17,25:2
abourdette, Charles P Mrs, 1943, Mr 31,19:2
aboure, Theodore, 1944, Mr 7,17:4
a Boux, Boris M, 1962, Ja 18,29:5
abovitz, Jerome, 1957, My 1,37:1
abow, Joseph J, 1967, Ag 12,25:5
abows, E, 1920, Jl 12,9:3
aBoyteaux, William H (por), 1947, Ja 5,53:1
a Branche, Ada Seagrist Mrs, 1925, Ap 11,13:4
a Branche, George M, 1961, N 20,31:5
a Brauch, V, 1882, S 7,4:7
abreche, Alma, 1940, F 3,30:7
abrinos, Peter, 1952, O 18,19:5
abriole, Pierre de, 1941, Ja 16,21:1
abrot, Sylvester Mrs, 1939, Mr 18,17:5
abrot, Sylvester W Jr, 1958, O 22,35:4
abrot, William H (por), 1949, Ap 2,15:3
aBrum, Joseph T, 1964, D 13,86:3
a Buy, Joseph S, 1942, My 29,17:3
aBuy, Walter J, 1967, S 30,33:1
aby, Thomas H, 1946, Je 23,40:5

La Caise, Noah, 1951, My 18,27:2
Lacalle, Joseph M, 1937, Je 12,15:5
Lacapria, Vincent Mrs, 1957, D 20,24:3
La Carrubba, Carmen, 1964, O 7,47:4
La Cava, Gregory, 1952, Mr 2,92:1
Lacayo, Constantino, 1954, F 20,17:4
Lacayo, Eduardo, 1945, Ja 25,19:6
Lacayo-Sacasa, Angelica, 1946, D 31,17:3
Lacayo Sacasa, Benjamin, 1959, My 5,33:4
Lacaze, Lucien, 1955, Mr 24,31:4
La Cecilia, N, 1878, D 29,10:5
Lacerda, Jacques C de, 1961, F 24,21:1
Lacerda Lago, Renota de, 1952, Mr 3,21:2
Lacerna, Francisco, 1952, F 23,11:4
Lacey, Charles, 1953, N 3,31:4
Lacey, Charles W, 1954, Ap 4,89:1
Lacey, Edward S, 1916, O 5,11:4
Lacey, Florence J, 1945, Ja 16,19:4
Lacey, Hugh J, 1954, Ja 12,23:2
Lacey, Jack, 1965, My 27,37:3
Lacey, James J, 1939, F 3,15:4; 1942, Ja 16,21:5
Lacey, James R, 1951, Jl 7,13:3
Lacey, John W, 1938, Mr 23,23:1
Lacey, Julia W Mrs, 1938, Jl 26,19:5
Lacey, Lionel, 1962, O 12,32:6
Lacey, Louise E, 1947, My 24,15:5
Lacey, Margaret E (por), 1948, D 17,27:2
Lacey, Martin T (funl, N 19,30:1), 1957, N 14,33:1
Lacey, Martin T Mrs, 1951, S 11,29:5
Lacey, Maud (will), 1949, Mr 23,19:4
Lacey, Michael V, 1952, Je 19,27:5
Lacey, Oliver L, 1961, F 2,19:3
Lacey, Robert C, 1943, D 19,48:5
Lacey, Rogers, 1947, D 10,31:3
Lacey, Thomas J (por), 1944, F 6,42:3
Lacey, Thomas Mrs, 1950, Jl 10,21:2
Lacey, Walter H, 1965, Ja 2,19:2
Lacey, Wilhelmina, 1907, Ja 29,9:4
Lacey, William H, 1950, Ap 2,92:6
Lach, Alexander, 1946, N 22,23:3
Lach, Frank, 1951, Mr 24,13:5
Lach, William A, 1953, F 25,27:4
Lachaise, G, 1935, O 19,17:1
Lachaise, Marie B Mrs, 1940, Ag 15,19:5
Lachance, Norbert, 1944, Mr 19,41:1
La Chapell, Arthur, 1945, Je 26,19:2
Lachappelle, Frederick N, 1944, Ja 13,21:3
la Chassaigne, Henri de Mrs, 1958, My 3,19:5
Lachau, Ada G de Countess, 1956, Je 16,19:6
Lachaud, C A, 1882, D 11,5:4
Lachelier, Barthelemy G, 1962, O 9,42:1
Lachenal, Adrian, 1918, Jl 1,11:6
Lachenal, Louis, 1955, N 27,11:1
Lachenauer, William G, 1964, S 12,10:8
Lachenbruch, Irving Mrs, 1965, Je 21,29:1
Lacher, Hugo E, 1951, Ja 26,24:2
Lacher, Samuel, 1952, Mr 5,29:2
Lachevre, Marcel, 1938, Jl 29,19:8
Lachlan, B S, 1930, O 22,25:1
Lachlan, Bruce S Mrs, 1952, Ag 3,60:5
Lachlan, Gertrude E, 1943, N 2,25:4
Lachlan, Happie B Mrs, 1958, Je 2,27:4
Lachlan, Robert I, 1940, N 17,50:6
Lachler, Kate S Mrs, 1945, N 21,21:1
Lachman, Arthur (cor, D 2,27:6), 1957, D 1,88:7
Lachman, Joseph Mrs, 1961, S 13,45:4
Lachman, Laurence S, 1968, Ag 7,43:1
Lachman, Maurice, 1943, Je 11,19:2
Lachman, S, 1931, D 29,21:3
Lachmann, Arthur, 1940, Mr 16,15:5
Lachmann, E J, 1944, Je 3,13:4
Lachmann, Karl Edward, 1968, Ag 31,23:2
Lachmann, Marc, 1941, Ap 23,21:3
Lachmann-Mosse, John H, 1944, Ap 19,23:3
Lachmansingh, J P, 1960, Ja 4,29:4
Lachmund, Anita (T Zanou), 1956, Ag 8,25:6
Lachmund, Herman H, 1943, S 19,III,5:7
Lachmuth, Max, 1952, My 11,92:5
Lachner, Harold, 1965, D 28,27:3
Lachoff, Harold, 1963, My 9,37:1
Laciar, Samuel L, 1943, Ja 16,13:3
Laciar, Samuel L Mrs, 1940, Ap 19,21:3
La Cierva y Penafiel, Isidoro de, 1939, Ap 19,23:4
Lack, Allan A, 1958, S 17,37:2
Lack, Frederick, 1942, Ap 8,19:2
Lack, Frederick Mrs, 1950, Jl 29,13:5
Lack, Harry C, 1942, Mr 3,24:3
Lack, J Hunter, 1949, F 14,19:4
Lack, Thomas, 1957, My 14,35:3
Lackard, Ernest W Sr, 1958, Jl 10,27:4
Lackas, Edmund Mrs, 1968, O 31,43:4
Lackas, John W, 1950, N 18,15:5
Lackaye, Helen, 1940, O 21,17:6
Lackaye, James M, 1919, Je 10,13:4
Lackaye, W, 1932, Ag 22,15:1
Lackaye, William, 1946, F 1,24:2
Lackaye, Wilton Mrs, 1919, Ag 6,9:1; 1945, Mr 11, 40:1
Lacker, Julius, 1939, Jl 16,30:7

Lackey, Frank R (por), 1944, S 15,19:4
Lackey, Franklin, 1939, Je 22,25:7
Lackey, George E, 1957, Ap 1,25:4
Lackey, Harley, 1941, N 13,27:5
Lackey, Harry A, 1937, F 4,21:4
Lackey, J Frank, 1943, Ag 12,19:3
Lackey, James B, 1950, Jl 5,31:5
Lackey, James B Mrs, 1945, Ag 26,44:7
Lackey, John, 1942, S 22,21:4
Lackey, Louis A, 1952, My 26,23:3
Lackey, Mason C, 1949, D 2,29:4
Lackey, O H, 1883, My 22,5:5
Lackey, Robert A, 1939, O 2,17:4
Lackey, William J, 1941, D 18,27:3
Lackland, Edgar C, 1944, N 23,31:2
Lackland, Frances F B Mrs, 1960, S 29,35:2
Lackland, Frank D, 1943, Ap 29,21:4
Lackland, Nannie J, 1952, S 7,83:2
Lackland, Rufus J, 1910, Mr 1,9:5
Lackman, William, 1871, Je 30,5:5
Lackritz, Joseph S, 1963, N 9,25:1
Lacks, Felix A, 1944, O 30,19:3
Lacks, George W, 1966, S 6,48:1
Lacomb, George F, 1941, Ag 27,19:2
Lacombe, Emil Henry Ex-Judge, 1924, N 29,13:5
Lacombe, Pierre L, 1944, Jl 7,15:4
Lacombe, Rufus Tryon, 1925, F 15,7:2
Lacomble, Antoine E, 1952, N 6,29:4
Lacorte, James B, 1950, Ag 29,20:6
LaCorte, Nicholas, 1966, D 5,45:3
La Corte, Salvatore F, 1945, N 29,23:2
La Coss, Louis, 1966, F 19,27:3
La Coss, Louis J, 1948, Ag 3,25:2
La Cossitt, Henry, 1962, D 3,31:3
Lacoste, Alexandre Sir, 1923, Ag 18,9:6
Lacoste, Anna, 1868, Jl 8,4:6
Lacour, Leopold, 1939, Ap 30,45:3
Lacour-Gayet, Jacques, 1953, Ag 9,77:2
Lacourse, George J, 1941, Ap 16,23:5
Lacouture, John H, 1951, My 12,21:5
La Couture, Michael A Sr, 1959, Mr 13,29:3
La Cov, Stanley I, 1956, O 1,27:1
La Croix, Francis C, 1949, O 19,29:3
Lacroix, Millies, 1941, O 13,17:5
LaCroix, Morris F, 1955, Jl 29,17:1
Lacroix, P (Bibliophile Jacob), 1884, O 18,5:1
Lacroix, William P, 1950, Mr 21,29:3
LaCrosse, Edwin L Mrs, 1956, Ja 12,27:5
Lacy, Ben R Jr Mrs, 1947, O 7,27:4
Lacy, Charles A Sr, 1940, My 15,23:5
Lacy, Charles R, 1924, Ag 15,13:7; 1951, F 5,23:3
Lacy, Daniel G, 1950, My 7,106:4
Lacy, Ed (Leonard Zinberg), 1968, Ja 8,35:1
Lacy, Edward M, 1940, Mr 27,21:3
Lacy, Ernest Prof, 1916, Je 18,18:4
Lacy, G Carleton, 1951, D 20,31:3
Lacy, Howard J, 1952, Je 28,20:6
Lacy, John, 1962, Jl 30,23:2
Lacy, L Douglas, 1951, D 27,21:2
Lacy, Lucius G, 1947, Ag 11,23:5
Lacy, Mabel V Mrs, 1943, My 12,25:5
Lacy, Mark, 1941, O 3,23:1
Lacy, Pierre T, 1956, D 26,27:3
Lacy, Richard H, 1945, Jl 4,13:5
Lacy, Richard Mrs, 1940, Ja 18,23:5
Lacy, Richmond T Jr, 1938, O 20,23:6
Lacy, Sterling B, 1955, Mr 9,27:3
Lacy, Sterling B Mrs, 1958, Ja 4,15:2
Lacy, Thomas H, 1873, Ag 21,4:6
Lacy, Thomas N, 1954, Ap 1,31:2
Lacy, Volney E, 1938, Ag 27,13:7
Lacy, Wilfred G, 1955, O 27,33:3
Ladd, Alan (funl plans, F 1,13:2; funl, F 2,88:3), 1964, Ja 30,29:1
Ladd, Anna C Mrs, 1939, Je 4,48:8
Ladd, Arthur C, 1964, D 2,47:1
Ladd, Carl E, 1943, Jl 24,13:6
Ladd, Carroll W, 1938, Ja 26,23:5
Ladd, Charles C, 1949, My 8,76:4
Ladd, Charles Rensselaer, 1903, O 28,9:5
Ladd, Delano W, 1962, Mr 4,86:6
Ladd, Edward H Jr, 1942, My 1,19:4
Ladd, Edward H Jr Mrs, 1953, S 2,25:4
Ladd, Edward W, 1949, Je 24,23:1
Ladd, Edwin Fremont, 1925, Je 26,17:6
Ladd, Fletcher Judge, 1903, D 14,7:3
Ladd, Forrest, 1959, Ag 7,6:1
Ladd, Frank, 1937, Ag 12,19:2
Ladd, Fred G, 1968, Je 17,39:4
Ladd, Fred H, 1945, Ap 15,14:6
Ladd, Fred W, 1951, Ap 29,89:2
Ladd, Frederick P, 1947, Ap 2,27:2
Ladd, George C, 1941, Jl 3,19:1
Ladd, George H, 1961, Ja 1,49:1
Ladd, George T (por), 1943, O 4,17:1
Ladd, George Trumbull Prof, 1921, Ag 9,9:5
Ladd, George U Mrs, 1937, Ap 30,22:2
Ladd, Harland A, 1952, Jl 21,19:2
Ladd, Harry W, 1955, D 16,29:4

Ladd, Henry A, 1941, Je 28,15:5
Ladd, Henry M, 1939, Ag 5,15:4
Ladd, Herbert Warren Ex-Gov, 1913, N 30,IV,7:6
Ladd, Hope, 1952, D 29,19:4
Ladd, Jesse A, 1957, D 17,35:2
Ladd, John W, 1944, Jl 22,15:5; 1951, O 31,29:1
Ladd, Laura D S Mrs, 1943, My 22,13:2
Ladd, Margaret S Mrs, 1938, Ap 13,25:5
Ladd, Maynard, 1942, Mr 11,19:4
Ladd, Niel M, 1940, My 21,23:5
Ladd, Samuel T, 1948, Mr 28,48:3
Ladd, T W, 1882, D 14,5:2
Ladd, Tallman Mrs, 1962, O 13,25:5
Ladd, W W, 1927, S 13,31:4
Ladd, Walter G Mrs (will, S 14,18:2), 1945, Ag 28, 19:3
Ladd, William B, 1937, Ag 11,24:2
Ladd, William F, 1943, S 11,13:1
Ladd, William John, 1914, Ag 3,11:6
Ladd, William P, 1941, Jl 2,21:1
Ladd, William P Mrs, 1961, Jl 23,69:3
Ladd, William S, 1949, S 18,92:1
Ladd, William S Mrs, 1964, Ap 13,29:2
Ladd-Franklin, C Mrs, 1930, Mr 6,23:3
Ladden, John J, 1956, Jl 24,6:6
Ladds, John A, 1957, N 5,31:2
Lademan, Oscar E, 1953, D 16,35:5
Lademann, Erich W, 1954, Jl 9,17:1
Laden, H W, 1946, Ag 10,13:6
Laden, Thomas J, 1952, Ja 22,29:4
Ladenburg, Emil, 1902, Ja 5,4:3
Ladenburg, Emily S Mrs, 1937, Ag 10,19:1
Ladenburg, Rudolf W, 1952, Ap 5,15:5
Ladendorf, Bernard C, 1940, My 24,19:1
Ladendorf, Frank H, 1943, Ap 27,23:2
Laderburg, Julius, 1966, Ja 20,35:1
Laderchi, Paolo R, 1940, Jl 8,17:4
Laderer, Henry, 1958, O 6,31:5
Laderman, Isidor, 1952, D 7,88:6
Ladeuze, Paulin (por), 1940, F 11,48:4
Ladew, Edward Mrs, 1910, Ap 23,11:6
Ladew, J Harvey, 1940, F 18,41:1
Ladew, Rebecca K Mrs, 1905, Ap 27,11:6
Ladin, Louis J, 1951, S 16,85:1
Ladin, Melvin E, 1966, My 10,25:1
Ladin, Paul, 1940, Mr 9,15:3
Ladin, Phil, 1955, Ap 29,23:3
Ladislaw, Peter Mrs, 1944, S 28,19:3
Ladlee, Donald, 1942, S 9,25:1
Ladner, Albert H Jr, 1955, My 21,38:8
Ladner, Grover C, 1954, My 28,23:2
Ladner, Grover C Mrs, 1942, F 25,19:1
Ladner, Henry, 1952, S 11,32:3
La Dow, Augustus M, 1952, N 21,25:2
La Dow, Charles, 1904, D 18,7:7
La Dow, George A, 1875, My 11,2:7
La Dow, Stanley V, 1945, D 9,45:1
Ladrach, Aaron G, 1947, Ap 9,25:1
Ladreda, Jose M F, 1954, S 21,27:4
Ladreyt, Casimir, 1877, Jl 6,4:6
Ladrigan, Frank C (Pop), 1954, Ap 16,21:2
Ladu, Arthur I, 1960, Jl 15,23:3
Ladu, Dwight B, 1954, Ag 18,29:4
Ladue, C C Dr, 1903, Ap 19,7:4
Ladue, Charles R, 1951, Mr 19,28:4
Ladue, George Mrs, 1948, O 28,29:5
Ladue, Joseph, 1901, Je 28,7:6
Ladue, William B, 1954, O 22,28:1
Ladue, William H, 1903, Ag 25,7:6
LaDue, William O, 1942, F 11,21:4
La Duke, Nora Mrs, 1942, F 2,15:3
Lady, William F, 1949, S 7,30:5
Laedlein, John Frederick, 1920, F 28,11:4
Laeger, Otto W, 1964, Ap 19,84:4
Laemar, Robert, 1943, O 16,13:4
Laemmle, Carl Sr (por),(will, S 27,28:6), 1939, S 25, 19:1
Laemmle, Edward (will, My 2,II,10:6), 1937, Ap 4, II,11:1
Laesch, Otto, 1938, O 19,23:5
Laessle, Albert, 1954, S 8,32:3
Laessle, Henry A, 1952, My 15,31:3
Lafabregue, J Edgar, 1947, Je 19,21:4
La Farge, Bancel, 1938, Ag 15,15:1
LaFarge, Bancel Mrs, 1944, S 29,21:3
La Farge, C Grant Mrs, 1944, S 19,21:2
LaFarge, Charles R Mrs, 1967, Ag 24,37:2
La Farge, Christopher, 1956, Ja 6,23:1
La Farge, Christopher G, 1938, O 12,27:3
La Farge, Christopher R Mrs, 1945, Jl 28,11:4
La Farge, Frederick Mrs, 1949, F 22,23:5
La Farge, John (funl), 1910, N 18,11:5
LaFarge, John (funl, N 28,39:5), 1963, N 25,19:1
La Farge, Margaret, 1956, My 26,17:3
La Farge, Oliver H P, 1963, Ag 3,1:4
La Farge, Peter, 1965, O 29,52:1
La Fauci, Ida Mrs, 1952, Ag 12,17:8
La Fave, Arthur J, 1962, Jl 21,19:6
Lafave, Frank E, 1944, Jl 19,19:2
Lafave, Roy G, 1943, Ap 19,19:1
Lafay, William, 1946, My 14,21:4
Lafayette, Gregory (funl, Jl 10,27:4), 1957, Jl 5,35:1
Lafayette, Gregory T Mrs (J Tyler),(funl Jl 10,27:4), 1957, Jl 5,35:1
Lafayette, O de, 1881, Mr 28,5:6
La Fayette, Paul (Comte de), 1926, Je 18,23:4
La Femina, Richard Mrs, 1959, Je 20,21:2
Lafer, Horacio, 1965, Je 30,37:4
Laferriere, French Actor, 1877, Jl 29,7:1
Laferte, Elias, 1961, F 19,86:4
Laferty, John M, 1958, F 11,31:4
LaFetra, Edward B (por), 1943, F 10,25:5
La Fetra, Gladys A, 1944, Ja 13,21:3
La Fetra, Linnaeus E, 1965, D 29,29:4
La Fetria, Lear Christian Prof, 1916, Mr 11,11:5
La Fevre, Gertrude M, 1953, Ja 6,29:5
Laff, Samuel B, 1950, Ja 25,28:5
Laffan, Michael Fitz Gibbon, 1915, Ag 20,11:3
Laffan, R M Sir, 1882, Ap 3,5:2
Laffan, William M (por),(funl, N 22,9:7), 1909, N 20,11:1
Laffen, Georgianna R Mrs, 1924, Ja 25,17:5
Lafferandre, Robert Mrs, 1939, N 25,17:5
Lafferty, Charles I, 1961, Ja 13,27:2
Lafferty, Clarence J Mrs, 1959, My 1,29:1
Lafferty, Edmund J, 1955, Mr 15,26:8
Lafferty, Edwin J, 1943, D 21,28:3
Lafferty, Elton B, 1965, D 1,47:2
Lafferty, Francis, 1941, O 24,23:5
Lafferty, John P, 1952, F 18,19:3
Lafferty, John R, 1954, Ag 28,15:6
Lafferty, Manuel M, 1953, My 24,89:1
Lafferty, Roger T, 1953, My 11,27:3
Lafferty, Roger T Mrs, 1952, S 25,31:5
Lafferty, Stanley B, 1942, N 14,15:2
Laffey, Edwin S, 1954, F 19,27:5
Laffey, Edwin S Mrs, 1955, Je 30,25:1
Laffey, John P (por), 1937, F 9,23:1
Laffey, Thomas J, 1943, Je 22,20:2
Laffin, John J, 1949, My 4,29:4
Laffin, Leo R, 1967, Ja 26,33:2
Laffitte, Pierre, 1944, D 7,25:1
Laffon, Emile, 1957, Ag 24,15:2
Laffoon, Polk, 1945, Ap 21,13:3
Laffoon, Ruby (por), 1941, Mr 2,43:1
Lafin, A H, 1878, S 29,2:5
Lafitte, Fermin E (funl plans, Ag 11,5:5; funl, Ag 12,9:6), 1959, Ag 9,89:2
Lafitte, Pierre, 1938, D 14,25:3
Lafkin, Warren E Mrs, 1957, Jl 21,61:1
LaFlame, Oliver, 1956, Mr 11,88:4
Laflamme, Herbert F, 1950, Ja 19,28:2
LaFleche, Leo R, 1956, Mr 8,29:4
Lafler, Herbert A, 1957, Mr 18,27:5
Lafleur, Henri A, 1939, Je 5,17:2
LaFleur, Joy, 1957, N 8,29:4
Lafleur, Paul, 1937, Jl 19,2:5
Lafleur, Paul Theodore Prof, 1924, F 11,15:3
Laflin, Arthur King, 1908, Ap 7,9:4
Laflin, H Dwight Col, 1914, Ag 8,9:7
Laflin, Herbert N, 1948, Je 5,15:5
Laflin, J Philbrick, 1903, F 25,9:7
Laflin, James A Mrs, 1954, My 28,23:5
Laflin, Willis, 1871, S 19,5:6
La Folette, William T, 1913, My 1,11:4
La Follette, Chester Mrs, 1964, N 8,88:5
La Follette, Philip F (funl plans, Ag 21,21:6; funl, Ag 22,83:1), 1965, Ag 19,31:2
La Follette, R M Sr Mrs, 1931, Ag 19,21:1
La Follette, Robert M Jr Mrs, 1961, D 28,27:3
La Follette, Robert Marion Sen, 1925, Je 23,19:3
La Follette, Robert R, 1967, Mr 25,3:4
Lafon, Alphonse F, 1958, N 17,31:3
Lafon, Alphonse Mrs, 1954, F 1,23:2
Lafon de Lageneste, Henri J J B, 1964, Mr 23,29:4
La Fond, William E, 1956, Ap 8,84:3
Lafont, Pierre Chere, 1873, My 3,6:7
LaFontaine, Charles Mrs, 1947, Ag 28,23:5
La Fontaine, Henri, 1943, My 27,25:5
La Fontaine, James A (will), 1950, My 3,32:6
LaFontaine (Bro Adrian Lewis), 1966, F 1,35:2
La Fontane, Samuel H, 1945, O 7,44:3
La Force, Harry C, 1946, Jl 12,17:2
Lafore, John A, 1951, S 14,25:2
La Forest, Byron J, 1947, My 6,28:2
La Forge, A T, 1878, F 13,4:7
La Forge, Charles A, 1965, D 4,31:1
LaForge, D Edson, 1948, Jl 30,17:3
LaForge, D Edson Mrs, 1957, Mr 9,19:4
La Forge, Frank, 1953, My 6,31:5
La Forge, Laurence, 1954, My 31,13:6
La Forge, Richard, 1946, Jl 10,23:5
LaForge, Richard J, 1952, Ap 18,25:2
La Forge, Sarah Mrs, 1950, Je 6,29:2
Laform, Levia A, 1940, N 8,21:4
Lafortune, Bellarmine, 1947, O 24,23:4
Lafortune, D A, 1922, O 20,17:5
LaFount, Harold A, 1952, O 22,27:5
Lafount, Harold A Mrs, 1943, Je 15,21:3
La Fountain, Alfred A, 1961, Je 3,23:3
LaFountain, Moses H, 1946, My 2,21:5
Laframboise, Arthur M, 1941, Ap 1,23:2
Laframboise, J R, 1956, Je 12,35:5
La France, Ernest, 1964, O 30,37:3
La France, Menetee, 1954, Mr 20,15:4
LaFrance, William, 1953, Jl 29,23:6
LaFrano, Tony, 1961, S 13,45:4
LaFreniere, Oliver B Mrs, 1961, S 13,45:3
Lafrentz, Arthur F Mrs, 1957, Ja 21,25:5
Lafrentz, Ferdinand W, 1954, Jl 16,21:1
L'Africain, Edward N, 1921, My 17,17:5
Lagace, Alphonse, 1940, Jl 28,27:2
Lagace, Joseph P, 1951, D 1,13:5
LaGagh, Alphonse L, 1945, O 11,23:4
Lagakos, Milton G, 1947, Ap 7,23:2
La Gamma, Frank, 1962, Ap 12,36:1
Lagarde, Ernest Dr, 1914, O 26,9:5
Lagarde, Jacqueline V de Countess, 1960, S 10,21:3
La Garde, Louis A Col, 1920, Mr 8,9:5
Lagarenne, John L, 1949, Je 19,68:6
Lagattuta, Sam, 1964, S 12,51:1
Lagay, Frank L, 1966, D 4,89:1
Lagay, R William, 1963, Jl 28,65:1
Lage, Louis de, 1947, D 16,33:3
Lagelouze, Gaston Prof, 1903, N 9,7:6
Lagemann, Eric, 1968, N 16,37:3
Lager, Carl, 1939, Jl 19,19:5
Lager, Carl H, 1949, D 13,38:1
Lager, John Boyd, 1968, S 28,33:3
Lager, John E, 1937, O 31,II,11:1
Lagercrantz, Herman, 1945, S 29,15:6
Lagergren, Carl G, 1941, O 28,23:2
Lagergren, Gustav, 1949, Ja 9,73:1
Lagerloef, Benjamin H, 1952, My 13,23:3
Lagerlof, Selma, 1940, Mr 17,49:1
Lagerman, Joseph F, 1947, O 10,25:5
Lagerquist, Walter E, 1944, F 23,19:6
Lagerwall, Charles J, 1949, O 23,86:3
Lages, William J, 1946, Ag 20,28:2
Lages, William Mrs, 1950, F 28,29:1
Laggenbauer, Victor, 1947, Je 4,27:4
Laggren, Isaac V, 1949, Ja 25,23:1
Laghi, Aldo, 1942, Ja 3,19:6
Lagonegro, Harry J, 1952, S 7,86:5
LaGorce, Gilbert G, 1959, F 21,21:5
La Gorce, John O (funl plans, D 25,21:2), 1959, D 24,19:2
La Gorce, John O (will), 1960, Ja 8,16:6
Lagorio, Antonio, 1944, N 25,13:5
Lagorio, Frank A, 1943, Jl 19,15:1
Lagoudakis, Socrates, 1944, Je 5,19:2
Lagowitz, Isador, 1960, Ag 28,83:2
Lagoyda, John, 1955, S 27,35:1
Lagrange, Benjamin, 1925, Mr 28,15:6
Lagrange, Comte de, 1883, D 9,4:4
La Grange, Frank C, 1964, Je 14,84:5
la Grange, Louis de Baron, 1919, Ag 19,13:4
LaGrone, John K, 1953, Ap 14,27:5
Laguardia, Attilio, 1959, Ja 7,33:1
la Guardia, Ernesto J de, 1961, Ap 19,39:3
LaGuardia, Fiorello H, 1947, S 21,1:1
La Guardia, Fiorello Mrs, 1921, N 30,17:4
LaGuardia, John B, 1938, N 25,23:5
LaGuardia, Richard D Mrs, 1950, D 20,31:2
la Guardia, Santiago de Gen, 1925, O 26,19:4
La Guardia, Wenceslao de, 1947, My 9,21:2
Laguex, Arthur, 1957, O 18,23:2
Lagupepa, Malietoa Samoan King, 1898, Ag 30,1:
Lahahan, Henry, 1963, Ap 10,39:2
Laharry, Nitish C, 1964, Jl 23,27:2
La Harte, Rose, 1958, Ja 23,27:4
La Haye, E de, 1944, D 13,8:1
Lahens, Charles E B, 1958, Je 15,76:6
Laherty, John J, 1957, Ap 1,25:4
Lahey, Daniel J Mrs, 1954, N 12,21:1
Lahey, Edward V, 1964, Ag 9,76:8
Lahey, Frank H, 1953, Je 28,60:3
Lahey, George F, 1947, Ja 30,25:3
Lahey, George W, 1942, Ap 14,21:2
Lahey, Harold W (cor, My 17,25:3), 1949, My 1 21:1
Lahey, Harry, 1947, Mr 10,21:3
Lahey, Henry J, 1956, My 12,19:2
Lahey, James J, 1939, Ja 7,15:5
Lahey, Joseph Mrs, 1947, Jl 1,25:1
Lahey, Marguerite D, 1958, O 22,35:2
Lahey, Robert F, 1944, Ja 2,38:4
Lahey, Thomas J Mrs, 1949, O 6,31:4
Lahey, Thomas R, 1957, D 31,17:1
Lahey, W J, 1933, Ap 3,15:1
Lahiff, Thomas, 1943, O 9,13:3
La Hines, Arthur D (por), 1942, D 12,17:4
La Hines, Arthur D Mrs, 1951, Ag 21,27:3
Lahiri, Sarat, 1941, My 6,21:3
Lahm, David E, 1958, Ag 1,21:2
Lahm, F S, 1931, D 31,19:3
Lahm, Frank P, 1963, Jl 9,31:1
Lahm, Jacob P, 1948, D 7,31:4
Lahm, Mortimer, 1967, Mr 29,45:1
Lahm, Renee D Mrs, 1945, My 9,23:6
Lahmann, Rudolf, 1905, O 28,5:2
Lahn, Louis, 1958, N 1,19:5
Laholm, Eyvind, 1958, Jl 20,65:3
Lahon, Clara B Mrs, 1953, N 28,15:4
Lahr, Bert (funl, D 7,52:1), 1967, D 5,1:5
Lahr, Frederic W, 1960, Jl 30,17:6
Lahr, John M, 1968, F 5,35:1
Lahrbusch, I, 1877, Ap 6,8:3
Lahrheim, Jacob, 1947, S 29,21:1

Lai Chuan-chu, 1965, D 26,69:2
Lai Jo-ju, 1958, My 21,33:1
Laidlaw, Alexander H, 1946, Ag 19,25:3
Laidlaw, Alexander Hamilton Dr, 1908, Jl 31,5:4
Laidlaw, Benjamin P, 1940, My 8,23:4
Laidlaw, Charles E, 1909, F 5,7:4
Laidlaw, Daniel, 1950, Je 3,15:3
Laidlaw, Elliot C R, 1960, My 26,33:2
Laidlaw, Henry B Mrs, 1917, O 16,19:5
Laidlaw, James L Mrs (por), 1949, Ja 26,26:2
Laidlaw, Joseph, 1913, Ja 6,9:5
Laidlaw, Loper B, 1941, Ap 5,17:4
Laidlaw, Mary J, 1954, N 11,31:1
Laidlaw, Patrick P Mrs, 1940, Mr 23,26:6
Laidlaw, Robert E, 1938, D 22,21:6
Laidlaw, Robert R Mrs, 1955, Ja 1,13:6
Laidlaw, Robert Sir, 1915, N 6,11:6
Laidlaw, W, 1936, My 21,23:3
Laidlaw, Walter L, 1937, My 15,19:6
Laidlaw, William R, 1911, Ag 9,9:5; 1940, Ag 1,21:5
Laidlein, Paul, 1925, F 8,7:2
Laidler, Francis, 1955, Ja 7,21:3
Laidlow, Richard E, 1953, Je 16,27:4
Laidman, James S, 1964, Jl 4,13:3
Laifer, Fred, 1958, My 27,29:1
Laifer, Max D, 1956, N 27,38:1
Laighton, Florence M, 1943, Ja 17,44:5
Laighton, Oscar, 1939, Ap 5,25:5
Laighton, Thomas B, 1866, My 29,2:2
Laihanen, Onni, 1956, Ap 26,33:4
Laimbeer, Francis E, 1941, O 25,17:6
Laimbeer, George M, 1962, Ja 27,21:4
Laimbeer, John Jr, 1949, Ag 18,21:6
Laimbeer, John Jr Mrs, 1952, O 15,31:1
Laimbeer, N S Mrs, 1929, O 26,17:4
Laimbeer, R H Jr, 1934, F 20,24:4
Laine, Damaso T, 1938, N 9,23:4
Laine, David Mrs, 1955, My 22,88:1
Laine, Jean, 1940, Ag 10,13:3
Laing, Alex Mrs, 1960, F 15,27:2
Laing, Allen B, 1961, Ap 3,33:3
Laing, Andrew L Mrs, 1960, D 2,29:2
Laing, Chester W, 1967, F 14,43:2
Laing, Chester W Mrs, 1967, Mr 1,43:3
Laing, Edward A, 1951, Ag 10,15:5
Laing, Francis, 1947, D 22,21:3
Laing, Frederick W, 1959, Jl 15,29:2
Laing, George, 1956, Ap 3,35:2
Laing, George H, 1955, Ja 12,27:4
Laing, George H Mrs, 1952, Jl 2,25:5
Laing, George S, 1948, Mr 7,68:6
Laing, George T Mrs, 1945, O 1,19:1
Laing, Gordon J (por), 1945, S 3,23:5
Laing, H V D, 1958, S 2,25:1
Laing, Harry A, 1950, Ja 9,25:5
Laing, James, 1957, Ap 30,29:1
Laing, James A, 1961, O 26,35:2
Laing, James Sir, 1901, D 16,9:6
Laing, Minnie E Mrs, 1943, Mr 31,20:3
Laing, Neff, 1953, N 2,25:5
Laing, Phil A, 1948, S 5,40:4
Laing, Robert, 1967, Ap 30,86:7
Laing, Sallie Reber, 1885, Mr 19,2:5
Laing, Samuel M, 1944, Ja 11,20:2
Laing, Sarah S, 1948, Ja 2,23:1
Laing, William A, 1954, Jl 21,27:3
Lair, Howell P Mrs, 1959, Je 2,35:3
Lair, Jane Seymour Mrs (Jane Seymour), 1956, Ja 31,29:2
Laird, A Wilson, 1966, Mr 18,39:4
Laird, Allyn V, 1945, S 5,23:4
Laird, Annie L, 1939, Je 1,25:4
Laird, Charles A, 1937, N 10,25:2
Laird, Charles H Jr, 1940, Je 21,21:6
Laird, Clinton N Mrs, 1942, N 4,23:5
Laird, D Clarkson, 1941, Ag 20,19:4
Laird, David, 1914, Ja 13,9:6
Laird, Donald A Mrs, 1938, Ja 31,19:3
Laird, E Cody, 1961, Ap 10,31:2
Laird, Emily, 1937, S 30,23:3
Laird, Eugene Mrs, 1948, Jl 18,52:6
Laird, Frederick A, 1940, Je 14,21:5
Laird, George A, 1953, N 19,31:1
Laird, George S, 1942, D 2,25:4
Laird, George Thomas, 1907, Mr 26,9:4
Laird, Gilbert, 1944, O 4,20:2
Laird, Grace M, 1952, Mr 26,29:4
Laird, Harry A, 1938, My 4,23:5
Laird, James A, 1942, N 4,23:4
Laird, James R, 1937, S 1,19:5
Laird, John A, 1955, Ja 12,27:3
Laird, John B, 1953, Ag 30,88:4
Laird, John E, 1952, D 2,31:4; 1955, Je 20,21:5
Laird, John M, 1942, Je 22,15:1
Laird, Joseph R Rev, 1937, F 17,22:2
Laird, Joseph T 3d, 1950, Je 1,27:4
Laird, Mary A B du P Mrs, 1938, Ag 28,33:4
Laird, Nathaniel, 1952, Ja 17,27:4
Laird, Philip D, 1947, D 27,13:5
Laird, Reginald M Mrs, 1968, D 1,86:5
Laird, Richard, 1967, N 9,50:8
Laird, Robert, 1940, O 26,15:5
Laird, Robert H, 1950, D 29,20:2
Laird, Samuel Rev Dr, 1913, D 18,9:6
Laird, Samuel W, 1945, Ag 11,13:3
Laird, Walter J, 1957, Je 5,35:2
Laird, Walter S, 1950, My 17,29:3
Laird, Warren P, 1948, F 19,23:1
Laird, Warren P Mrs, 1947, Ap 4,23:2
Laird, William, 1942, Jl 1,25:4
Laird, William J, 1953, O 27,27:3
Laird, William Sir, 1901, Ag 15,7:5
Lais, Father, 1921, D 27,13:5
Laise, Clemens A Mrs, 1944, Ja 11,19:2
Laiser, George H, 1945, Ag 10,15:4
Laisi, Lauri T (por), 1947, Je 19,21:4
Laist, Frederick, 1963, Je 17,25:2
Laistner, Max L W, 1959, D 12,23:5
Lait, George, 1958, Ja 13,29:4
Lait, Jack Jr, 1961, Ag 19,17:2
Lait, Jacquin L (Jack),(will, Ap 8,29:8), 1954, Ap 2, 27:1
Laite, Charles, 1937, F 18,21:5
Laitin, Yale J, 1967, N 14,47:1
Laity, Harold S, 1964, O 8,43:1
Laity, John C, 1941, S 9,23:2
Laizure, Elmer L, 1947, D 19,25:4
Lajeunesse, Deliante Mrs, 1947, Ap 1,27:1
La Joie, Hubert J, 1959, Je 19,25:3
Lajoie, Napoleon (funl, F 10,33:1), 1959, F 8,86:2
Lakasky, Adolph, 1954, Jl 27,21:3
Lakatos, Vitez G, 1967, My 25,47:4
Lake, Amzi, 1959, Ap 9,31:3
Lake, Arthur G Mrs, 1944, D 19,21:5
Lake, Austen R, 1964, Je 13,23:1
Lake, Carrie M, 1946, F 6,23:3
Lake, Chester H Mrs, 1937, F 15,17:5
Lake, Christopher J, 1938, D 15,27:5
Lake, Clinton E, 1956, D 25,25:5
Lake, Delos, 1882, Ag 9,1:6
Lake, Denton D, 1941, Ja 6,18:2
Lake, Dorothy A, 1950, D 2,13:5
Lake, Edward C, 1957, F 10,87:1
Lake, Elvin, 1946, Je 22,19:4
Lake, Everett J, 1948, S 17,25:1
Lake, Ezra, 1937, Ag 20,17:4
Lake, Frankie, 1947, Ja 21,7:3
Lake, Fred Mrs, 1944, S 27,21:3
Lake, Frederick W, 1943, O 7,23:1
Lake, George B, 1954, N 7,88:8
Lake, George C, 1947, Ja 3,22:2
Lake, George G, 1951, F 14,30:3
Lake, Harley W Sr, 1964, O 26,31:5
Lake, Harold S, 1967, Ap 8,31:3
Lake, Harrison M, 1940, Ap 22,17:2
Lake, Harry E, 1959, S 4,19:3
Lake, Harry Y, 1945, Ap 19,27:4
Lake, Henry E, 1938, Je 26,27:1
Lake, Henry G, 1942, Jl 19,30:7
Lake, Howard C, 1943, N 17,25:3
Lake, Ira, 1954, Jl 27,21:4
Lake, James Col, 1873, F 14,6:7
Lake, Jess V, 1939, Ja 26,21:2
Lake, Jesse D, 1950, Ja 29,68:5
Lake, Jimmy, 1967, S 17,85:1
Lake, John, 1960, Je 29,33:5
Lake, John R, 1939, Jl 13,19:4
Lake, John W, 1965, S 12,86:3
Lake, Joseph F Mrs, 1959, My 28,31:2
Lake, Kirsopp, 1946, N 12,29:5
Lake, Lehman Blew Capt, 1913, N 19,9:6
Lake, Lew, 1939, N 6,23:1
Lake, Mack C, 1954, N 11,31:2
Lake, Martin S, 1952, Ag 29,23:4
Lake, Mayhew L, 1955, Mr 17,45:2
Lake, Percy, 1940, N 18,19:4
Lake, Peter (Grand Central Pete), 1913, Jl 18,9:6
Lake, R Verne, 1943, F 19,19:2
Lake, Richard C, 1953, Je 23,29:3
Lake, Robert A, 1945, D 19,25:3
Lake, Sarah M, 1947, Ja 31,23:4
Lake, Sidney, 1962, N 30,33:1
Lake, Simon, 1914, O 29,11:4; 1945, Je 24,22:1
Lake, Simon Mrs, 1956, Mr 6,31:5
Lake, Stuart N, 1964, Ja 28,31:2
Lake, Theodore Mrs, 1937, Ag 20,17:2
Lake, Thomas T, 1950, D 5,31:4
Lake, Victor E, 1944, O 7,13:5
Lake, Walter H, 1937, O 2,21:2
Lake, William C, 1950, F 19,76:2
Lake, William D Mrs, 1953, F 11,29:2
Lake, Willis S, 1947, D 6,15:2
Lake, Zera W, 1949, N 21,25:2
Lake-Hickok, Agnes Mrs, 1907, Ag 23,7:5
Lakeman, Earl L, 1955, Ap 5,29:4
Lakeman, Ernest W, 1948, O 27,27:3
Laken, Isidore, 1966, O 18,45:3
Lakestream, Frank D, 1955, F 21,21:5
Lakestream, Henry Mrs, 1947, Ap 4,23:3
Lakey, George H, 1938, Mr 2,19:3
Lakhovsky, Arnold, 1937, Ja 9,17:5
Lakhovsky, Georges, 1942, S 1,20:3
Lakhtionov, Oleg, 1953, F 18,31:3
Lakin, Allan R, 1951, Je 30,15:4
Lakin, Ella F, 1964, Mr 11,39:2
Lakin, Harry P, 1958, Mr 19,31:2
Lakin, Herbert C, 1952, D 30,19:5
Lakin, Oliver, 1938, Ap 9,17:5
Laking, Francis Henry Sir, 1914, My 22,13:7
Laking, Guy Francis Sir, 1919, N 24,15:2
Lakota, Gregory, 1950, O 8,13:2
Lakowka, Anthony F, 1941, O 3,23:6
Laks, Sol, 1966, D 7,47:1
Lalak, Frank, 1961, My 12,29:2
Lalak, Frank Mrs (D McCann), 1961, My 10,45:3
Lalande, Alice, 1961, S 19,14:2
Lalanne, Charles E, 1945, Je 23,13:5
Laliberte, Alfred, 1952, My 8,31:5
Laliberte, J Adelard, 1956, Jl 15,61:1
Laliberts, J A, 1955, Jl 19,27:3
Lalique, Rene (por), 1945, My 10,23:5
Lalk, E A, 1943, F 3,19:2
Lalle, Henry de, 1949, F 16,25:5
Lallemand, Louis, 1938, S 4,16:5
Lalley, Francis A, 1963, Ag 12,21:3
Lalley, Frank E, 1939, Mr 4,15:4
Lalley, Harry W, 1948, S 15,31:4
Lalli, Nicola, 1958, F 27,27:4
Lally, Edward A, 1905, My 7,7:3
Lally, Jane K Mrs, 1937, S 21,25:6
Lally, John F, 1941, D 13,21:6
Lally, John P, 1942, Ag 12,19:4
Lally, Martin, 1943, Je 1,23:3
Lally, Michael, 1903, N 6,7:4
Lally, Michael F, 1944, My 16,21:4
Lally, Thomas, 1920, O 15,13:4
Lally, Thomas J, 1953, O 16,27:4
Lally, Thomas V, 1963, Je 19,37:1
Lally, Virginia, 1951, My 7,25:5
Lally, William J, 1937, N 24,23:2
Lally-Tollendal, Count, 1877, N 30,2:2
La Londe, Bernard E Mrs, 1960, Mr 23,37:4
Lalor, Bernard E, 1959, Je 13,21:3
Lalor, John, 1884, F 23,8:4
Lalor, R J, 1884, Je 30,5:4
Lalor, Robert E Mrs, 1951, My 19,15:6
Laloux, Victor, 1937, Jl 14,21:5
Lamac, Carl, 1952, Ag 3,61:2
Lamade, Charles D, 1949, Jl 12,27:3
Lamade, Dietrick (por), 1938, O 10,19:3
Lamade, George Mrs, 1948, My 10,21:4
Lamadrid, Joaquin M Mrs, 1908, Ag 11,5:6
Lamana, Peter, 1907, S 7,9:7
Lamanna, Leonard, 1956, Ja 16,21:1
Lamanna, Theodore J, 1963, S 12,37:5
Lamantia, Benjamin, 1953, My 9,19:3
Lamar, Adolph Dr, 1916, Jl 26,11:6
La Mar, Alfred Col, 1924, Je 12,17:5
Lamar, D, 1934, Ja 14,1:2
Lamar, Ernest E, 1949, Ag 16,23:1
Lamar, Gazaway B, 1874, O 8,4:7
Lamar, Joseph R Mrs, 1943, Ap 28,23:1
Lamar, Joseph Rucker Justice (por),(funl, Ja 6,13:4), 1916, Ja 3,13:1
Lamar, L Q C, 1893, Ja 24,1:1
Lamar, L Q Judge Mrs, 1903, O 28,9:5
Lamar, Napoleon, 1939, S 5,23:5
Lamar, Wilette K Mrs (W Kershaw), 1960, My 6, 31:4
Lamarche, Charles A, 1940, Ja 30,19:2
Lamarche, John V, 1943, Jl 24,13:2
Lamarine, Wilford E, 1950, Je 29,29:5
La Marmora, A T, 1878, Ja 6,7:2
Lamaro, Richard, 1948, N 2,25:2
Lamarre, Victor de, 1955, Mr 15,29:4
Lamartine, Alphonse de, 1869, Mr 2,7:3
Lamason, Howard O Mrs, 1953, Ap 7,29:4
Lamasse, Henry, 1952, Jl 22,25:4
Lamater, Walter A Mrs, 1940, Ap 3,23:4
Lamatsch, Frederick, 1953, O 12,27:5
Lamay, Joseph C, 1953, Ja 31,15:1
Lamaze, George, 1940, My 28,23:1
Lamb, Albert E Mrs (will), 1943, Jl 1,21:7
Lamb, Albert R, 1959, N 24,37:2
Lamb, Andrew J Dr, 1953, F 11,29:1
Lamb, Arthur B, 1952, My 16,23:2
Lamb, Arthur S, 1958, S 6,17:5
Lamb, Bernard, 1942, Ap 26,40:1
Lamb, Bert E, 1941, Jl 29,15:3
Lamb, Blanche H Mrs, 1937, Je 12,15:5
Lamb, Charles, 1961, O 3,39:4
Lamb, Charles A, 1945, Ja 23,19:5
Lamb, Charles R (por), 1942, F 23,21:1
Lamb, Cora H, 1940, Je 26,23:5
Lamb, David C, 1951, Jl 8,60:4
Lamb, Dean (death ruled suicide, N 18,51:1), 1955, N 3,24:3
Lamb, Donald W Mrs (R Findlay),(por), 1949, Jl 14, 27:4
Lamb, E R, 1906, Ja 12,9:6
Lamb, Edward, 1942, Mr 20,19:2
Lamb, Edwin E, 1943, Mr 4,19:5
Lamb, Edwin T, 1919, N 11,13:3
Lamb, Elbert N, 1951, Ap 25,29:6
Lamb, Ernest H (Lord Rochester), 1955, Ja 14,21:4
Lamb, Eugene Mrs, 1945, Ja 16,20:2
Lamb, Ford R, 1941, O 28,23:1
Lamb, Frank A Mrs, 1952, N 14,23:1
Lamb, Frank I, 1953, Ag 10,23:6

Lamb, Frank J, 1949, Ja 5,26:2
Lamb, Fred E Mrs, 1937, Mr 30,23:2
Lamb, Frederic W Mrs, 1951, Ap 5,29:2
Lamb, Frederick D Mrs, 1944, Ap 6,23:3
Lamb, Frederick S Mrs, 1954, D 7,33:2
Lamb, Gene, 1948, Ag 21,15:2
Lamb, George, 1964, Jl 29,33:3
Lamb, George B, 1956, S 22,17:4
Lamb, George E, 1950, S 29,27:5
Lamb, George R Mrs, 1947, Jl 27,44:6
Lamb, George W, 1939, O 31,23:4; 1948, Ag 2,21:5
Lamb, Gilbert D, 1940, Je 3,15:5
Lamb, Ginger (Mrs Dana Lamb), 1967, F 28,37:2
Lamb, Hal S, 1950, S 10,92:3
Lamb, Harold A, 1962, Ap 10,43:1
Lamb, Harry H, 1953, My 6,31:5
Lamb, Henry C (por), 1941, Mr 7,21:5
Lamb, Hugh, 1903, Ap 4,9:6; 1959, D 9,45:5
Lamb, J H Rev, 1924, F 2,13:6
Lamb, James A, 1961, N 17,35:2
Lamb, James D, 1960, D 12,29:3
Lamb, James H, 1940, Jl 26,17:5
Lamb, John Cameron Sir, 1915, Ap 1,15:6
Lamb, John E, 1914, Ag 24,9:5
Lamb, John E S, 1954, Ap 14,29:3
Lamb, John J, 1940, Je 8,15:4
Lamb, Joseph F, 1964, F 3,27:3
Lamb, Joseph F Mrs, 1958, Ja 13,29:4
Lamb, Joseph P, 1946, My 21,23:3
Lamb, Peter J, 1947, Jl 9,23:2
Lamb, Raymond S, 1957, Mr 2,21:3
Lamb, Richard, 1909, Mr 26,9:4; 1962, Jl 29,61:2
Lamb, Richard H, 1959, D 5,23:2
Lamb, Robert E, 1959, My 31,76:4
Lamb, Robert K, 1952, Ag 27,27:3
Lamb, Rolond O, 1921, N 15,19:4
Lamb, Stella W Mrs, 1942, Je 2,23:2
Lamb, Stephen A, 1952, N 29,17:4
Lamb, Thomas, 1938, Ja 26,23:5
Lamb, Thomas W, 1942, F 27,17:4
Lamb, Torrance K, 1953, My 13,29:2
Lamb, Wallace E, 1961, N 28,37:4
Lamb, William, 1903, O 24,7:5; 1947, Ap 18,21:2
Lamb, William A, 1949, O 15,15:1
Lamb, William Col, 1909, Mr 24,9:3
Lamb, William F, 1952, S 9,31:1
Lamb, William P, 1958, N 7,27:2
Lambach, Walter, 1943, F 6,13:1
Lambacher, Edward, 1952, F 18,19:2
Lamback, Aime B, 1947, S 17,25:4
Lambain, Alfred Cochran Dr (funl, N 10,11:5), 1911, N 8,13:3
Lambart, Ernest C O, 1945, Je 28,19:5
Lambden, Howard R, 1943, Jl 17,13:4
Lambdin, John O, 1923, Ap 27,17:5
Lambe, Ben H, 1959, Jl 5,56:1
Lambe, Charles, 1960, Ag 31,29:2
Lambe, Reginald R, 1966, O 2,87:1
Lambeau, Curly (Earl), 1965, Je 2,45:1
Lambelet, Carl H, 1952, Je 23,19:2
Lambermont, Baron, 1905, Mr 7,9:6
Lamberson, Frank, 1938, F 10,21:5
Lamberson, George E Sr, 1950, Je 1,27:4
Lamberson, Owen B, 1954, My 28,23:3
Lambert, A, 1930, Ja 1,19:3
Lambert, A V, 1930, My 30,19:1
Lambert, Adrian V S, 1952, O 17,27:3
Lambert, Adrian V S Mrs, 1947, S 25,29:6
Lambert, Albert B, 1946, N 13,27:3
Lambert, Albert D, 1948, Jl 29,21:3
Lambert, Alex (por), 1939, My 10,23:1
Lambert, Alex Mrs, 1938, Ja 14,23:4
Lambert, Arlof E, 1947, F 19,25:2
Lambert, Arthur J, 1949, Ag 8,15:4
Lambert, Arthur J Mrs, 1950, My 23,29:3
Lambert, August V Mrs, 1954, My 8,17:5
Lambert, Basil G (Prof Lamberti), 1950, Mr 15,29:1
Lambert, Benjamin F, 1949, S 24,13:5
Lambert, Byron J, 1952, O 30,31:4
Lambert, C E, 1907, D 11,11:3
Lambert, Charles E, 1955, S 8,31:1
Lambert, Charles I, 1954, Ap 24,17:3
Lambert, Charles L, 1949, D 30,19:1
Lambert, Charles Mrs, 1958, Ja 28,27:4
Lambert, Charles P, 1956, Ag 16,25:3
Lambert, Charles W, 1949, S 20,29:4
Lambert, Chris, 1968, Jl 29,38:5
Lambert, Constant, 1951, Ag 22,23:3
Lambert, Dave, 1966, O 4,47:1
Lambert, David, 1948, Ja 8,25:3; 1952, Ja 20,84:2
Lambert, Donald, 1962, My 9,43:6
Lambert, Donaldson L, 1968, D 15,21:1
Lambert, Donaldson L Mrs, 1968, D 15,21:1
Lambert, Edward H, 1937, Ja 14,22:1
Lambert, Edward W Dr, 1904, Jl 19,7:6
Lambert, Elizabeth W Mrs, 1942, Ag 21,19:2
Lambert, Emma M Mrs, 1949, Ag 23,23:5
Lambert, Ernest W, 1952, N 7,23:3
Lambert, Frederick C, 1944, O 22,46:5; 1958, S 4,29:3
Lambert, Frederick C Mrs, 1964, Jl 1,35:5
Lambert, Frederick D, 1948, Ap 22,27:1
Lambert, George, 1915, Ag 4,11:5; 1948, Je 9,29:5; 1958, F 18,27:1
Lambert, George S, 1942, Ap 4,13:6
Lambert, George T Mrs, 1960, O 26,39:2
Lambert, Gerard B, 1967, F 26,84:3
Lambert, H Bertram, 1963, Jl 16,21:3
Lambert, Harold M, 1963, Ag 29,29:5
Lambert, Harry, 1947, Mr 8,13:4
Lambert, Harry B, 1942, F 4,19:2
Lambert, Harry C, 1958, Mr 2,89:2
Lambert, Henry W Mrs, 1964, Ja 11,23:5
Lambert, James, 1951, D 3,31:5; 1957, Mr 29,21:4
Lambert, James C, 1940, N 30,17:4
Lambert, James C Mrs, 1942, My 19,19:5
Lambert, John A, 1937, D 13,27:3
Lambert, John B T, 1953, O 15,33:4
Lambert, John Col, 1922, Mr 7,13:5
Lambert, John H Sr, 1960, My 22,86:7
Lambert, John J, 1940, F 29,19:5
Lambert, John L, 1967, My 26,39:7
Lambert, John M, 1937, Ja 10,II,10:7
Lambert, John T, 1939, S 15,23:3
Lambert, John W, 1952, My 21,27:5
Lambert, Joseph E, 1957, Je 29,17:6
Lambert, Julius J, 1921, N 12,13:5
Lambert, Katherine, 1949, F 11,23:5
Lambert, Lavina D, 1941, Je 24,20:2
Lambert, Lawrence Mrs (R Crawford), 1966, Ja 8, 26:1
Lambert, Louis F, 1954, N 17,31:4
Lambert, Louis Rev, 1910, S 26,13:5
Lambert, Louis V C, 1958, Ja 27,27:2
Lambert, Nicholas H, 1945, F 13,23:4
Lambert, Noah D Mrs, 1953, Ag 12,31:5
Lambert, Norman P, 1965, N 6,29:6
Lambert, Otis, 1954, Je 13,88:2
Lambert, Percy M Mrs, 1949, My 10,25:3
Lambert, Richard E (est acctg), 1956, Ag 30,21:2
Lambert, Richard J, 1946, Mr 7,25:2
Lambert, Richard M Capt, 1937, Ap 29,21:5
Lambert, Robert A, 1960, N 21,29:4
Lambert, Robert K (por), 1946, O 4,23:3
Lambert, Samuel W, 1942, F 10,19:1
Lambert, Stanley Sr, 1967, Ap 30,86:8
Lambert, Sylvester M (por), 1947, Ja 11,19:1
Lambert, Theodore W, 1946, F 23,13:1
Lambert, Thomas, 1925, Mr 26,23:3
Lambert, Thomas A, 1946, My 2,21:5
Lambert, Thomas R, 1948, F 10,23:4
Lambert, Walter Davis, 1968, O 29,47:2
Lambert, Walter E Mrs, 1959, Jl 28,27:2
Lambert, Walter Merton, 1968, O 25,47:5
Lambert, Walter R, 1943, Ap 2,21:1
Lambert, Ward L, 1958, Ja 21,29:3
Lambert, William, 1909, Ja 2,9:6
Lambert, William H Maj, 1912, Je 2,II,13:6
Lambert, William Mrs, 1949, My 11,29:5
Lambert, Wilton J Mrs, 1959, Ja 9,25:3
Lambert, Woolf W, 1964, O 29,35:4
Lamberti, Fiore Mrs, 1951, My 30,21:4
Lamberto, James, 1943, Ag 27,17:3
Lamberton, Albert M, 1960, S 26,33:5
Lamberton, Anne, 1960, Jl 21,27:1
Lamberton, Benjamin P Mrs, 1911, Je 30,9:4
Lamberton, Benjamin Peffer Rear-Adm, 1912, Je 10, 9:5
Lamberton, Chess, 1953, My 19,29:1
Lamberton, George D, 1949, S 6,27:2
Lamberton, James M, 1915, Mr 29,9:4
Lamberton, John Porter, 1917, Jl 28,7:7
Lamberton, Robert, 1952, Jl 21,19:5
Lamberton, Robert E, 1941, Ag 23,13:3
Lambertson, Bertram S, 1963, O 19,25:5
Lambertson, Charles H, 1950, Je 8,32:2
Lambertson, Charles Lytle, 1906, N 27,9:5
Lambertson, William C, 1962, Jl 13,20:4
Lambeth, Charles F, 1947, Ap 26,13:4
Lambeth, William A, 1944, Je 25,29:1
Lambiase, Charles P Justice, 1968, Je 26,47:4
Lambiase, Emil R, 1952, Je 22,68:4
Lambie, John E Jr, 1958, Je 21,19:3
Lambie, Thomas, 1954, Ap 17,13:4
Lambirth, William H, 1950, Ag 4,21:4
Lambley, John, 1904, F 25,9:5
Lambooy, J M J H, 1942, Je 21,36:7
Lambord, Benjamin, 1915, Je 9,13:5
Lamborn, Arthur H Mrs, 1946, Mr 6,27:3
Lamborn, Bayard T, 1942, Ja 9,21:4
Lamborn, Elizabeth F, 1953, Ja 13,27:2
Lamborn, Samuel W, 1946, Ag 26,23:5
Lamborn, William J, 1946, Je 17,21:3
Lambrakis, Dimitri, 1957, Ag 13,27:4
Lambrakis, Gregory (funl, My 29,8:1), 1963, My 27, 8:6
Lambrecht, Ferdinand H, 1948, My 20,29:4
Lambrecht, William A Jr, 1940, Je 30,32:6
Lambrechts, Ragnar F, 1945, Je 16,13:5
Lambrianides, Lambros, 1953, D 14,31:4
Lambros, Peter A, 1961, Je 3,23:4
Lambros, Peter S, 1947, Ap 6,60:8
Lambruschini, Raphael Sen, 1873, Ap 5,3:7
Lambsdorff, Gustav von Lt-Gen Count, 1937, D 24, 19:2
Lambson, Anna H Mrs, 1942, O 5,19:4
Lambton, Catherine Duchess of Leeds, 1952, D 7,88:4
Lambton, Ernest B, 1954, S 13,23:3
Lambton, George, 1945, Jl 24,18:7
Lambury, Lord (L P Lord), 1967, S 14,47:4
Lambusta, Nicholas, 1952, D 17,33:1
Lambuth, David, 1948, Ag 24,24:2
Lambuth, Walter R Bp, 1921, S 28,19:6
Lamdeth, Aubrey C, 1944, Jl 28,13:2
Lamdin, A Gist, 1960, Ag 2,29:2
Lamdin, Philip, 1947, D 18,29:2
Lamdin, William D, 1945, Je 1,15:3
Lame, Herman F, 1954, Mr 2,25:3
Lame, William Dr, 1907, Mr 15,9:4
Lamendola, Frank J, 1964, Jl 19,64:2
Lament, Harold H, 1963, S 19,27:4
Lamenty, Walter J, 1945, O 12,23:3
Lamer, Joseph S Mrs, 1954, O 27,29:3
La Mer, Victor K, 1966, S 28,47:3
Lamerdin, John P, 1937, D 19,8:5
Lamere, George, 1956, D 24,13:4
Lamesta, Michael, 1957, My 25,21:5
la Meurthe, Henry D de Mrs, 1942, Ja 1,25:4
Lamey, Arthur F, 1963, Je 6,35:5
Lamey, Hiram T, 1947, D 28,40:5
Lamiell, John E, 1942, O 29,23:5
Lamington, Lord, 1940, S 18,23:4
Lamiroy, Hendrik, 1952, My 11,92:5
Lamkay, Jacob, 1924, D 27,9:5
Lamkay, Louis, 1967, F 20,37:5
Lamke, William, 1950, My 31,29:1
Lamkin, Harry, 1903, Ag 7,7:7
Lamkoff, Paul, 1953, Mr 12,25:1
Lamley, John REv Dr, 1911, Ja 30,9:4
Lamm, Gustav H, 1959, S 10,35:3
Lamm, Lucian, 1955, Ja 10,23:6
Lamm, Martin, 1950, My 7,41:2
Lammasch, Heinrich Prof, 1920, Ja 9,17:1
Lamme, Benjamin G, 1924, Jl 9,19:5; 1924, Jl 11,1
Lamme, Charles W, 1955, D 15,37:2
Lammel, Anthony Msgr, 1911, Ag 28,7:5
Lammerding, Frank A, 1948, O 2,15:1
Lammerding, Frank J, 1957, Je 2,86:4
Lammerding, John C V, 1958, My 3,19:3
Lammerding, John C W Mrs, 1954, O 29,21:3
Lammerding, Ruth Mrs, 1961, F 25,21:1
Lammering, Henry R, 1963, Jl 18,27:5
Lammers, Charles J, 1958, N 25,33:3
Lammers, Charles N, 1950, Ap 8,13:5
Lammers, Howard M Jr, 1946, Je 22,19:3
Lammert, Peter, 1944, Ap 21,19:5
Lamneck, Elmer J, 1955, D 15,37:3
Lamon, Francis H, 1948, Mr 7,68:5
Lamon, Francis H Mrs, 1947, Ap 19,15:2
Lamon, Harry M, 1942, Ag 7,17:6
Lamon, Hartog J, 1954, S 17,27:1
LaMonaca, Joseph Sr, 1955, F 19,15:5
Lamond, David T Mrs, 1950, Mr 26,92:4
Lamond, Felix, 1940, Mr 17,51:4
Lamond, Felix Mrs, 1951, N 13,29:2
Lamond, Frederick, 1948, F 22,48:5
Lamond, John K, 1959, D 11,34:8
Lamond, M David, 1946, Jl 20,15:2
Lamond, Walter E, 1940, F 4,40:7
Lamons, Thomas P, 1946, Mr 4,23:2
La Mont, Charles, 1904, F 24,9:4
Lamont, Charles A, 1873, S 7,8:3
Lamont, Clarence F, 1949, Ag 10,22:6
Lamont, Clifford, 1904, Ag 14,9:6
Lamont, Clifford F, 1943, Ag 9,13:5
Lamont, Daniel, 1950, My 6,15:6
Lamont, Daniel Scott (funl plans, Jl 25,7:6; funl, 27,1:3), 1905, Jl 24,1:7
Lamont, Elizabeth K, 1958, Je 27,25:4
Lamont, Forrest, 1937, D 18,21:4
Lamont, G D, 1876, Ja 16,2:7
Lamont, Hammond, 1909, My 7,9:4
Lamont, Hammond Mrs, 1953, My 24,89:2
LaMont, Harry, 1957, My 10,27:5
Lamont, Harry K, 1941, Ja 19,40:5
La Mont, John M, 1947, F 25,25:4
Lamont, Moses, 1944, F 28,17:3
Lamont, Owen (F P Clark), 1952, Ja 18,28:8
Lamont, Robert, 1967, Ag 17,37:3
Lamont, Robert P, 1948, F 20,27:1
Lamont, Robert P Mrs, 1950, Mr 15,29:3
Lamont, Samuel C Mrs, 1945, Ja 7,38:4
Lamont, Thomas L, 1950, S 17,104:5
Lamont, Thomas L Mrs, 1949, Mr 27,76:4
Lamont, Thomas Mrs, 1915, D 29,11:5
Lamont, Thomas Mrs (est tax appr), 1957, Ag
Lamont, Thomas Rev, 1916, Ap 8,15:7
Lamont, Thomas S (funl, Ap 13,43:2; will, Ap 34:1), 1967, Ap 11,1:1
Lamont, Thomas W, 1948, F 3,1:4
Lamont, Thomas W Mrs, 1952, D 30,19:1; 195 23:3
La Mont, Walter D (por), 1942, Ja 20,19:4
Lamont, Walter M, 1945, O 7,45:2
La Montagne, Edward Mrs, 1948, N 25,31:5
La Montagne, Harry, 1959, Je 15,27:2
La Montagne, Harry Mrs, 1948, D 23,19:2
La Montagne, Maurice, 1918, O 3,13:2
La Montagne, Montaigu, 1938, Ja 30,II,9:2
La Montagne, Morgan, 1958, Ap 21,23:5

La Montagne, Rene, 1910, O 15,11:5; 1948, Ap 23,23:4
La Montagne, Robert W, 1959, Mr 17,33:1
Lamonte, A C, 1916, Ja 17,11:4
Lamonte, Carloine B, 1946, D 13,23:1
La Monte, G M, 1927, D 25,II,5:1
La Monte, George, 1913, O 20,7:4
Lamonte, George M Mrs, 1956, F 10,21:4
Lamonte, George V, 1961, S 28,41:6
LaMonte, John L, 1949, O 3,17:6
La Monte, Theodore (mass planned), 1968, N 26, 53:6
Lamonte, Wellington, 1952, Mr 4,27:4
LaMoore, Parker, 1954, N 13,15:3
Lamore, Edward C, 1958, Ag 12,29:1
L'Amoreaux, P C, 1933, S 3,16:4
Lamoreaux, Wilbur, 1963, My 12,86:2
Lamorelle, Joseph F, 1937, F 19,19:5
Lamorelle, Paul, 1937, Ag 22,II,7:3
Lamoriciere, Gen, 1865, S 26,5:3
La Moriniere, Francois, 1911, Ja 5,9:4
Lamoroux, Wendell Prof, 1907, Ap 2,11:5
Lamorte, J P H, 1884, My 3,2:3
LaMorte, Michael, 1953, Mr 7,15:4
Lamos, Thomas, 1951, Jl 2,10:2
Lamote de Grignon, Ricard, 1962, F 7,37:4
Lamothe, Gustave Justice, 1922, N 25,13:5
Lamotte, Arthur, 1947, Jl 19,13:6
La Motte, Ellen N, 1961, Mr 4,23:5
Lamotte, Walter, 1951, N 27,31:5
La Mountain, A A, 1941, F 22,15:6
La Mountain, George W, 1948, Ap 24,15:4
La Mountain, Prof, 1873, Jl 8,3:2
Lamoure, Charles T, 1950, F 17,23:4
La Moure, William T, 1937, N 25,31:3
Lamoureux, Arthur R (Bro Clement Peter), 1962, O 29,29:4
Lamoureux, Eugene E, 1948, N 23,29:2
Lamoutte, Alex C, 1948, O 18,23:4
Lamoutte, Louis A, 1943, Ag 14,11:5
Lamoy, Kenneth W, 1954, Je 19,15:3
Lampadius, John, 1954, F 5,20:3
Lampard, Charles A, 1941, O 26,43:1
Lampe, Christian, 1960, Ap 10,85:3
Lampe, Ernest W, 1966, O 22,31:4
Lampe, J Dell, 1949, Ap 3,76:2
Lampe, William E, 1950, Ag 17,27:2
Lampe-Lengyel, Josef S Mrs, 1951, F 18,77:1
Lampert, Henry, 1941, Ag 29,17:2
Lampert, Hyman, 1956, Je 29,21:1
Lampert, Morris, 1946, Jl 26,21:5
Lampert, William B, 1950, Mr 9,54:4
Lampert, Wilson W, 1964, Je 16,39:4
Lamperti, Giovanni, 1910, Mr 19,9:4
Lamphear, Amos S, 1957, O 28,27:5
Lamphear, Clarence P, 1955, Je 21,31:4
Lamphear, Henry L, 1948, Mr 20,13:2
Lamphear, Henry L Mrs, 1946, Jl 16,23:2
Lamphear, Roy H, 1959, Ja 26,29:4
Lampher, Cornelius Capt, 1873, My 8,5:4
Lamphier, Eugene H, 1959, N 14,21:5
Lamping, Thomas J Mrs, 1948, Mr 19,23:2
Lampis, Giuseppe, 1956, My 31,27:4
Lampke, Louis J, 1956, Ag 9,25:4
Lampkin, William Mrs (Daisy E), 1965, Mr 12,33:3
Lampl, Carl G, 1962, S 14,31:1
Lampl, Joseph G, 1957, Ag 3,15:5
Lampl, Walter, 1945, D 25,14:4
Lampland, Carl O, 1951, D 15,13:3
Lampland, Oscar, 1937, Je 22,23:4
Lampland, Oscar Mrs, 1960, D 9,31:3
Lampman, Arch O, 1939, My 15,17:3
Lampman, Ben Hur, 1954, Ja 25,19:5
Lampman, Charles, 1939, Ag 22,19:4
Lampman, Edward G, 1941, Ja 29,17:1
Lampman, Emma, 1943, Mr 3,23:4
Lampman, H Frank, 1941, O 12,53:2
Lampman, Leonard B, 1939, My 23,23:4
Lampman, Lewis Dr Mrs, 1904, Ja 9,9:6
Lamport, Alex, 1961, S 11,27:5
Lamport, Arthur M (por),(will, N 19,21:2), 1940, N 9,17:1
Lamport, Arthur M Mrs, 1939, Je 25,37:3
Lamport, Hiram K, 1907, Ja 24,9:5
Lamport, Mary E, 1952, Ja 11,22:2
Lamport, Mary P, 1944, D 18,19:5
Lamport, Samuel C, 1941, S 14,49:1
Lamport, Samuel C Mrs, 1951, O 5,27:2
Lamport, Solomon Mrs, 1957, O 13,85:4
Lamport, William K, 1948, D 31,16:3
Lamprecht, Karl Prof, 1915, My 12,13:5
Lamprecht, William H, 1917, Jl 12,11:8
Lamprey, Louise, 1951, Ja 16,29:6
Lamprey, Sarah, 1944, Ap 14,19:5
Lampson, C M Sir, 1885, Mr 14,5:2
Lampson, Miles (Lord Killearn), 1964, S 19,27:3
Lampson, Ray D, 1947, Ap 2,27:2
Lampton, Elizabeth W, 1903, Ap 22,9:5
Lampton, William James (por), 1917, My 31,11:5
Lampus, George J, 1941, Je 1,41:2
Lampworth, William, 1937, My 17,19:4
Lams, J Herbert, 1952, O 19,87:3
Lamsdorff, Count, 1907, Ap 2,11:5
Lamsdorff, Vladimir Nicolaievitch Count, 1907, Mr 20,9:6
Lamson, C, 1880, Ap 23,2:7
Lamson, Carl, 1966, Mr 7,27:3
Lamson, Daniel R, 1963, Jl 6,15:5
Lamson, Elliott W, 1948, D 7,31:2
Lamson, Fred M, 1940, Je 16,38:7
Lamson, Gardner, 1940, My 8,23:5
Lamson, Guy C Mrs, 1943, F 2,19:2
Lamson, Hoswell H Capt, 1903, Ag 16,7:6
Lamson, John L, 1941, Jl 6,27:1
Lamson, Julius G Mrs, 1951, F 26,23:3
Lamson, Kenneth W Mrs, 1967, O 28,31:4
Lamson, Lindsay J, 1951, D 29,11:3
Lamson, Margaret J Mrs, 1925, N 13,19:4
Lamson, Moses W, 1942, Ap 16,21:5
Lamson, Otis F, 1956, D 13,37:5
Lamson, Robert L Mrs, 1952, Ag 23,13:4
Lamson, Warren A, 1940, S 4,23:5
Lamson, William A, 1914, Mr 23,11:3
Lamson, William M, 1962, Je 2,19:2
Lamson-Scribner, Frank, 1938, F 23,23:2
LaMura, Frederick P, 1944, Mr 30,21:5
Lamy, Anthony, 1943, Mr 19,25:2
Lamy, Edgar D Mrs, 1937, N 24,23:4
Lamy, Edmund, 1962, S 8,19:5
Lamy, Etienne Victor, 1919, Ja 10,13:4
Lamy, George Mrs, 1912, N 27,13:5
Lamy, Henry B Jr, 1957, F 18,27:3
Lan, Samuel, 1962, N 27,37:3
Lanagan, Frank R, 1955, D 17,23:3
Lanagan, James F, 1937, Ag 8,II,6:7
Lanahan, Francis H Mrs, 1948, Ap 19,23:5
Lanahan, Frank H 3d, 1953, Jl 14,27:1
Lanahan, John Rev Dr, 1903, D 9,9:5
Lanahan, Joseph A, 1938, Je 3,21:2
Lanahan, William R, 1941, Ag 28,19:4
Lanahan, William W, 1948, Ag 31,24:3
Lanahan, William Wallace Mrs, 1921, Mr 28,11:3
Lanard, Thomas S, 1951, Je 1,23:4
Lanard, William M, 1958, Ag 5,27:1
Lanauze, C D, 1952, Je 17,27:4
Lanbord, Howard F, 1942, O 8,27:4
Lancashire, Frederick W Mrs, 1943, N 19,19:2
Lancaster, Ada E Mrs, 1940, N 29,21:5
Lancaster, Arthur, 1941, Je 17,21:4
Lancaster, Bruce, 1963, Je 21,29:1
Lancaster, C C Randall Mrs, 1903, Ag 10,7:6
Lancaster, Charles Dr, 1903, Jl 7,7:6
Lancaster, Charles L, 1937, O 10,II,8:8
Lancaster, D Rev, 1880, My 29,2:4
Lancaster, Edward S, 1965, Je 3,35:3
Lancaster, Florence E, 1947, My 8,25:2
Lancaster, Frank E, 1903, N 28,9:5
Lancaster, Frederick Mrs, 1948, F 4,23:2
Lancaster, George P, 1954, Jl 21,27:3
Lancaster, Harold, 1948, F 8,60:7
Lancaster, Helen N, 1967, F 28,34:3
Lancaster, Henry C, 1954, Ja 31,88:5
Lancaster, Henry P Mrs, 1959, Je 27,23:2
Lancaster, Isabelle Mrs, 1922, Mr 26,27:2
Lancaster, J Eugene, 1939, Mr 28,23:2
Lancaster, James H, 1961, S 13,45:1
Lancaster, Jim, 1961, Ja 28,19:5
Lancaster, John E Mrs, 1951, S 3,13:6
Lancaster, Joseph, 1924, D 14,7:2
Lancaster, Joseph A, 1949, N 26,15:6
Lancaster, L Lt, 1919, D 26,11:5
Lancaster, Mary E Mrs, 1944, Ap 22,15:5
Lancaster, Nathaniel D, 1937, Ap 7,25:3
Lancaster, Robert, 1945, D 5,25:3
Lancaster, Robert A, 1957, My 8,37:3
Lancaster, Robert A Jr, 1940, Ag 28,19:4
Lancaster, Tom, 1947, Ag 5,23:6
Lancaster, Walter B, 1951, D 11,33:3
Lancaster, William C, 1965, N 8,35:4
Lancaster, William W, 1957, Jl 16,25:5
Lance, Andrew H, 1943, Mr 14,24:7
Lance, H Kiefer, 1939, N 10,23:3
Lance, H Kiefer Mrs, 1938, S 16,21:3
Lance, Harold B, 1949, D 26,29:3
Lance, Hobart, 1949, O 27,27:5
Lance, John H Mrs, 1944, N 30,23:5
Lance, Richard O, 1954, O 19,27:6
Lance, Saul J, 1965, Jl 18,68:5
Lance, Wayne M Sr, 1953, Ja 14,31:2
Lance, Wesley L Mrs, 1965, Ap 5,31:5
Lancelot, Pierre, 1957, O 8,6:4
Lancet, M Mortimer, 1956, My 26,17:4
Lanchantin, Eugene Fabian, 1968, Ja 4,37:1
Lanchester, Henry V, 1953, Ja 18,93:1
Lanchner, Abraham J, 1957, O 19,21:3
Lanchner, Samuel H, 1958, F 5,27:1
Lancia, Vincenzo, 1937, F 16,23:4
Lancis, Ricardo R, 1950, My 26,23:4
Lancraft, William M, 1903, S 20,7:6
Lancton, Walter H, 1957, O 10,33:2
Land, Arthur Mrs, 1948, Ag 1,56:2
Land, Charles Henry Dr, 1922, Ag 4,15:7
Land, Emory S Mrs, 1956, Mr 14,33:4
Land, Frank S, 1959, N 10,47:1
Land, George A, 1953, Ja 21,31:1
Land, John, 1874, O 30,1:6
Land, John H, 1938, Ja 29,15:2
Land, Joseph Foster Dr, 1912, O 31,13:5
Land, Mary A, 1958, Jl 15,25:2
Land, Morris, 1950, N 14,31:3
Land, Morris Mrs, 1945, O 28,43:1
Land, Murray, 1956, Ap 28,17:5
Land, Paul H, 1951, S 21,23:4
Land, Rome R, 1948, S 3,19:1
Land, S E Mrs, 1941, F 20,20:3
Land, Walter W, 1955, Jl 24,64:3
Landa, Harry, 1951, D 13,33:5
Landaburu, Laureano, 1950, N 22,26:2
Landale, Cecil D, 1938, S 1,23:3
Landan, John R Mrs, 1955, S 29,38:3
Landard, Philippe, 1905, S 2,6:7
Landau, Abraham, 1960, F 11,35:3
Landau, Annie, 1945, Ja 25,19:3
Landau, Benjamin, 1944, My 1,15:5
Landau, Bruno, 1965, Je 6,85:1
Landau, David Mrs, 1946, My 26,32:4
Landau, David S, 1951, Ap 17,29:3
Landau, Edmund Mrs, 1963, My 14,39:2
Landau, Ezekiel, 1965, Ag 20,29:3
Landau, Frank E, 1951, Ag 1,23:6
Landau, George M, 1956, Ap 12,31:4
Landau, H Sidney, 1965, N 19,39:1
Landau, Henrietta (found alive by Dr, Mr 5,54:7; died), 1966, Mr 7,53:2
Landau, Hyman, 1958, F 17,23:1
Landau, Isaac, 1959, My 11,27:5
Landau, Jacob, 1952, F 1,21:3
Landau, Lev Davidovich Dr, 1968, Ap 3,1:2
Landau, Lilly, 1965, Mr 30,47:1
Landau, Louis, 1942, Ap 21,23:1
Landau, Maurice C, 1960, S 16,28:5; 1962, O 18,39:3
Landau, Morris M, 1949, N 7,27:4
Landau, Sidney Mrs (P Rowland), 1963, Je 17,25:4
Landau, Toni, 1942, Ap 10,17:2
Landau, Zisha, 1937, Ja 18,17:3
Landau de Maroth, Willy, 1958, O 20,29:4
Landauer, Georg, 1954, F 6,19:5
Landauer, I Nathan Mrs, 1960, Ap 25,29:1
Landauer, Jacob, 1946, O 27,62:4
Landay, Arch W, 1948, D 23,19:3
Landay, James B, 1965, Ap 8,39:5
Landay, Max, 1959, Ja 26,29:5
Landby, John P Mrs, 1948, Je 19,15:6
Lande, David S Mrs, 1955, Jl 11,23:4
Lande, Isaac, 1941, N 8,19:4
Landeck, Frederick H, 1944, Ja 11,20:3
Landeker, Alfonse F, 1947, O 26,68:4
Landeker, Alfonse F Mrs (E E Borg), 1961, O 9,35:4
Landenberger, Frederick, 1943, D 18,15:5
Landenberger, Leopold, 1967, My 5,39:1
Lander, Anthony J, 1950, F 5,85:1
Lander, Cecil H, 1949, Mr 19,15:6
Lander, Edward Judge, 1907, F 3,7:6
Lander, Everett J Sr, 1955, Ap 23,19:6
Lander, Frank, 1941, F 11,23:2
Lander, George J, 1946, F 19,25:4
Lander, George W, 1955, Ag 15,15:2
Lander, John B, 1921, Jl 22,11:6
Lander, John M, 1905, O 9,9:4
Lander, Norman W, 1959, O 30,27:3
Lander, Stephen C, 1949, O 29,15:3
Lander, W W, 1876, O 15,5:1
Landera, Pedro P, 1944, S 30,13:3
Landeron, John W Capt, 1912, F 19,9:6
Landers, Charles E, 1956, D 18,31:2
Landers, Charles S, 1946, Jl 28,39:1
Landers, Charles S Mrs, 1961, O 5,37:3
Landers, Douglas J, 1925, D 16,25:4
Landers, Frank E, 1953, Mr 17,29:3
Landers, George B, 1949, Mr 25,23:4
Landers, George F, 1939, Ja 24,19:2
Landers, Harvey E, 1959, My 24,88:3
Landers, Howe S (por), 1943, Mr 16,19:1
Landers, James L, 1957, My 4,21:5
Landers, Joseph O, 1940, Je 19,23:6
Landers, Leland L, 1956, Ja 18,31:1
Landers, Maurice F, 1948, Mr 8,23:4
Landers, Patrick, 1944, Mr 12,37:2
Landers, Patrick H, 1941, D 24,17:3
Landers, Wilbur N, 1965, Mr 26,35:5
Landers, Ziba A, 1939, Je 20,21:4
Landes, Bertha K (por), 1943, N 30,27:3
Landes, Elmer S, 1949, Ap 19,25:2
Landes, Fred Mrs, 1956, Jl 4,19:1
Landes, Gene B, 1956, N 10,19:6
Landes, George A, 1939, Je 8,43:2
Landes, Ira D, 1947, D 21,52:5
Landes, Joseph C, 1937, Ap 1,23:2
Landes, Joseph W, 1962, Ag 1,31:4
Landes, W Stuart, 1968, O 30,47:5
Landes, William G, 1956, D 16,86:3
Landesberg, Charles K, 1957, O 20,86:5
Landesberg, Edward, 1941, F 21,19:3
Landesco, Alex, 1963, S 5,31:4
Landesman, Henry, 1955, Ap 6,29:5
Landesman, Henry M, 1946, My 23,21:1
Landesmann, Ernest W, 1947, Ja 4,14:4
Landeta, Felipe, 1945, O 3,19:3
Landfear, Harry W, 1949, O 23,86:4
Landfear, Lucius R, 1948, F 15,60:4

Landfield, Jerome B, 1954, N 23,35:1
Landgon, Neilner M Dr, 1948, Ag 29,56:3
Landgraf, Howard M, 1946, Ja 17,23:2
Landgraf, William, 1964, D 23,27:2
Landgrebe, Karl, 1955, My 14,19:2
Landgren, Elizabeth, 1942, N 11,25:6
Landi, Almo, 1948, N 24,23:3
Landi, Anthony, 1943, Je 24,21:4
Landi, Elissa, 1948, O 22,25:3
Landi, Fidardo, 1918, Ja 3,9:8
Landi, Frank J, 1953, Mr 26,31:5
Landi, Orlando, 1945, Mr 1,21:4
Landi, Oscar, 1958, N 12,37:1
Landi, Rocco, 1940, D 16,13:2
Landin, Colin, 1954, O 22,27:5
Landin, Paul, 1942, Ja 16,21:5
Landing, James A, 1948, My 9,68:4
Landini, Mauro, 1956, O 2,35:1
Landino, Bernard, 1953, My 14,29:4
Landis, Albert L, 1950, N 10,27:1
Landis, Arthur, 1951, F 3,15:5
Landis, Benson Y, 1966, N 11,43:1
Landis, Carney, 1962, Mr 6,35:1
Landis, Cary D, 1938, My 11,19:2
Landis, Charles Beary, 1922, Ap 25,17:5
Landis, Charles K Jr, 1949, S 19,23:5
Landis, Charles W, 1944, Mr 23,19:6
Landis, David, 1925, Jl 16,19:5
Landis, Edgar B, 1950, Je 24,13:2
Landis, Ely, 1960, Jl 15,23:4
Landis, F, 1934, N 16,23:1
Landis, George E, 1950, D 10,68:5
Landis, Harry R, 1950, My 1,25:3
Landis, Henry R M Dr, 1937, S 15,23:4
Landis, Irwin F, 1955, My 24,31:4
Landis, J F Reynolds, 1939, O 20,23:4
Landis, James D, 1914, Ja 19,9:5
Landis, James M (funl, Ag 3,25:4), 1964, Jl 31,1:4
Landis, John D, 1951, Ja 12,27:3
Landis, Katherine, 1921, N 24,19:6
Landis, Kenesaw M, 1944, N 26,56:2
Landis, Kenesaw M Mrs, 1947, Ag 28,23:1
Landis, Kenesaw M 2d, 1949, Jl 13,27:4
Landis, Merkel, 1960, O 1,19:1
Landis, Norman, 1956, My 24,31:3
Landis, Ruth M, 1958, O 8,35:3
Landis, Stanley W, 1953, Je 18,29:2
Landis, Stella M Mrs, 1967, Je 16,43:4
Landis, Thomas J S, 1939, D 27,21:2
Landis, Walter S, 1944, S 16,13:3
Landis, William A Dr, 1937, Ja 1,23:4
Landis, William W, 1942, Ap 9,19:5
Landman, D M Mrs, 1948, F 29,60:5
Landman, Gustave Mrs, 1949, Ag 9,25:3
Landman, Isaac, 1946, S 5,27:1
Landman, J Henry, 1961, Ja 19,29:2
Landman, Louis, 1944, F 9,19:6
Landman, Louis Dr, 1922, Ja 26,17:4
Landman, Louis W, 1952, Ag 16,15:6
Landman, Solomon, 1951, My 21,27:4
Landmesser, Charles E, 1947, Jl 3,21:3
Landmesser, Frank H, 1954, F 21,68:2
Landmesser, Fred, 1948, F 13,21:2
Landolf, Bluch, 1952, O 24,23:3
Landolfe, Lorenzo, 1959, Mr 3,33:1
Landolfi, Joseph, 1951, Ag 22,16:2
Landolt, Frederick H, 1944, Ap 17,23:3
Landon, Benson, 1942, D 28,19:2
Landon, Clarence G, 1954, Mr 14,89:1
Landon, Dwight K, 1939, My 3,23:3
Landon, Edith G Mrs, 1953, Ap 22,29:2
Landon, Edward H Mrs, 1918, Ap 12,13:8
Landon, Edwin, 1951, Ap 25,29:4
Landon, Francis G, 1947, D 3,29:5
Landon, Frederick W B Sir, 1937, O 28,25:1
Landon, Freeman, 1947, Jl 7,17:4
Landon, George I, 1914, Je 23,11:6
Landon, H H Maj, 1926, N 10,27:2
Landon, Harry, 1954, N 8,21:5
Landon, Herman, 1960, Mr 24,33:2
Landon, Howard F, 1950, F 18,15:2
Landon, Hugh M, 1947, Ap 3,25:3
Landon, John M, 1938, Ap 28,23:4
Landon, Judson Stuart, 1905, S 7,7:6
Landon, Kirk, 1953, F 23,25:3
Landon, Mary, 1951, Je 19,29:5
Landon, P, 1927, Ja 24,17:4
Landon, Sealand W Mrs, 1945, My 30,19:2
Landon, Sealand Whitney, 1919, S 30,19:3
Landon, Sidney W, 1953, Mr 10,29:2
Landon, T H, 1882, D 5,7:4
Landon, T J Mrs, 1872, S 23,5:5
Landon, Thomas H Rev, 1917, Jl 31,9:4
Landor, Henry Savage, 1924, D 29,15:4
Landor, Walter Savage, 1864, O 12,4:5
Landore, Brown, 1945, O 11,23:3
Landouzy, Louis Dr, 1917, My 12,11:7
Landow, Max, 1960, N 19,21:2
Landowne, Joseph, 1965, D 28,27:3
Landowska, Eva, 1925, Ja 1,27:3
Landowska, Wanda, 1959, Ag 17,23:2
Landowski, Paul M, 1961, Ap 3,33:4
Landreth, Burnet Jr, 1941, O 5,48:5
Landreth, James V, 1960, S 21,32:3
Landreth, L Scott Jr, 1949, Je 8,30:4
Landreth, Symington P, 1942, Jl 18,13:2
Landreth, William B, 1941, D 10,25:1
Landreville, Louis J, 1940, My 21,23:3
Landrick Jerome, Bro, 1944, F 23,19:4
Landrine, Lawrence B, 1961, D 17,82:6
Landrine, Mary, 1953, My 8,25:3
Landriot, J F A T Archbishop, 1874, Je 10,1:7
Landrith, Ira, 1941, O 12,52:2
Landroth, Oliver E, 1950, N 21,31:5
Landrum, Ernestine L, 1946, S 28,17:1
Landrum, Grace, 1951, Ap 22,88:1
Landrum, Margaret, 1953, O 23,23:4
Landrum, Robert B, 1962, Jl 26,27:4
Landry, Auguste C P R Sen, 1919, D 21,22:4
Landry, George A, 1961, F 1,35:6
Landry, J A, 1881, Mr 22,2:2
Landry, John H, 1967, Je 16,43:3
Landry, Narcisse A, 1941, Ap 19,15:1
Landry, Pierre A Sir, 1916, Jl 29,9:6
Landry, Robert, 1960, Ag 31,29:2
Landry, William A, 1962, Jl 19,27:5
Landsberg, Frank J, 1951, Jl 6,23:1
Landsberg, Henry Mrs, 1951, Ja 30,25:2
Landsberg, Kate Mrs, 1942, Mr 7,17:4
Landsberg, Klaus, 1956, S 18,35:4
Landsberg, M, 1927, D 10,17:5
Landsberg, Paul M, 1964, N 7,27:5
Landsberger, Hans, 1964, Mr 18,41:3
Landsberger, Siegfried W, 1955, D 14,39:4
Landsbury, George, 1945, Je 16,13:2
Landsbury, John J, 1958, Ag 20,27:3
Landsdowne, David Powell, 1953, F 28,17:5
Landseadel Wm, 1948, O 15,23:4
Landseer, Charles, 1879, Jl 23,5:6
Landseer, Edwin Sir, 1873, O 3,4:7
Landseer, T, 1880, Ja 21,2:7
Landseidel, Walter W, 1949, N 4,23:2
Landsheft, Charles, 1959, S 5,15:6
Landsiedel, Harry, 1965, D 27,25:1
Landsman, Arthur A, 1959, Ag 1,17:6
Landsman, Isidore J, 1963, D 13,36:3
Landsman, Lawrence, 1964, Jl 26,57:1
Landsman, Ned, 1960, My 4,45:4
Landsman, Ralph, 1960, Mr 27,87:1
Landstad, Hans, 1957, D 10,35:4
Landsteiner, Karl (por), 1943, Je 27,32:1
Landt, Daniel, 1961, F 26,92:8
Landt, Jack, 1959, Ag 22,17:2
Landt, Mathias, 1948, S 9,27:4
Landt, Matthias Mrs, 1959, F 17,31:2
Landucci, Alfred, 1962, Ja 28,76:8
Landwehr, August H, 1937, Jl 16,19:5
Landwehr, Dorothea M, 1937, My 28,21:4
Landwehr, Edgar G, 1959, Ja 7,33:3
Landwehr, Harry C, 1968, N 8,47:2
Landwehr, Henry, 1957, S 29,87:1
Landy, Abraham, 1951, Ag 28,23:2
Landy, Alvin, 1967, S 24,84:6
Landy, Edwin F, 1947, N 23,76:2
Landy, F Emmet, 1943, Mr 13,13:5
Landy, George, 1955, Ag 11,21:2
Landy, Grace G Mrs, 1938, Ja 12,21:2
Landy, Harold, 1938, Je 20,15:5
Landy, James, 1875, Jl 28,4:6
Landy, James J, 1948, Ag 3,26:3
Landy, James Mrs, 1953, D 21,31:5
Landy, Joseph A Mrs, 1940, D 26,19:4
Landy, Ludwig, 1953, Ap 16,29:6
Landy, Michael M, 1938, Ag 10,19:5
Landy, Rae D, 1952, Mr 7,23:4
Lane, Abigail, 1962, Ag 25,19:5
Lane, Abraham B, 1903, S 1,7:6
Lane, Abram B Mrs, 1903, F 15,2:5
Lane, Ada Mrs, 1914, Ap 12,15:4
Lane, Adolphus, 1876, F 16,4:7
Lane, Aidan W, 1949, Ja 13,23:5
Lane, Albert, 1955, Ap 26,16:6
Lane, Albert A, 1967, My 26,47:1
Lane, Albert S, 1940, My 3,21:3
Lane, Alfred, 1940, Ja 13,15:1
Lane, Alfred C, 1948, Ap 17,15:5
Lane, Alfred J, 1941, S 19,23:1
Lane, Anthony, 1882, Ag 11,5:2
Lane, Arthur, 1952, My 16,23:3
Lane, Arthur B (will, O 9,28:7), 1956, Ag 14,25:1
Lane, Arthur E, 1951, Jl 13,21:3
Lane, Arthur E Mrs, 1946, My 25,15:3
Lane, Arthur Mrs, 1941, Jl 21,15:4
Lane, Arthur S, 1938, Jl 18,13:4
Lane, Benjamin C, 1940, N 29,21:3
Lane, Benjamin L Mrs, 1945, My 24,19:5
Lane, C C, 1967, D 28,31:1
Lane, Carlos D (Carl), 1960, S 1,27:1
Lane, Charles A Mrs, 1948, D 30,19:2
Lane, Charles E, 1939, Ap 16,III,6:7; 1947, D 28,43:2; 1948, Ja 1,23:2
Lane, Charles E Mrs, 1941, O 12,53:1
Lane, Charles J, 1953, Ag 30,89:2
Lane, Charles M, 1909, Ap 24,7:3
Lane, Charles P, 1938, Ap 30,15:5
Lane, Charles S, 1938, F 3,23:2
Lane, Charles W Jr Mrs, 1952, D 25,29:6
Lane, Chester T (trb lr, Mr 19,32:5), 1959, Mr 13, 29:1
Lane, Clarence H, 1942, Ja 28,19:4
Lane, Clem, 1958, O 28,35:5
Lane, Clifford M, 1947, N 28,27:2
Lane, Cora B Mrs, 1952, Ja 6,93:1
Lane, David, 1885, Ja 28,5:3
Lane, David H, 1925, Ja 25,7:2
Lane, David W, 1941, Ja 14,21:2
Lane, Dennis, 1942, Ag 11,19:4
Lane, Derick, 1938, N 1,23:2
Lane, Dick Mrs (D Washington),(funl, D 19,28:6), 1963, D 15,79:1
Lane, E W, 1876, Ag 27,6:7
Lane, E William, 1955, O 18,37:5
Lane, Eastwood, 1951, Ja 23,27:4
Lane, Edgar C, 1956, O 5,25:2
Lane, Edward, 1959, Je 7,86:4
Lane, Edward B, 1941, S 18,25:2
Lane, Edward C, 1959, D 5,23:6
Lane, Edward W, 1942, Mr 24,19:3
Lane, Effel, 1942, F 18,19:2
Lane, Elbert H Mrs, 1949, Ag 7,60:4
Lane, Elinor Macartney Mrs, 1909, Mr 17,9:3
Lane, Elmer S, 1961, Ap 29,46:3
Lane, Eugene, 1958, Jl 22,28:1
Lane, F P L, 1945, Ag 29,23:3
Lane, F Thatcher Mrs, 1967, Ap 2,93:2
Lane, Francis J Msgr, 1968, Ap 1,45:3
Lane, Francis R Dr, 1937, Mr 29,19:3
Lane, Francis T Luquer, 1916, F 4,9:7
Lane, Frank B, 1943, Ap 10,17:4
Lane, Frank E, 1948, Ja 11,58:6
Lane, Franklin F, 1947, Ja 31,23:3
Lane, Frederick C, 1945, S 2,32:2
Lane, Frederick H, 1952, Jl 15,21:1
Lane, Frederick H Mrs, 1942, F 9,15:2
Lane, French, 1938, O 29,19:5
Lane, G W, 1883, D 31,5:3
Lane, G W (see also, Ja 1), 1884, Ja 3,8:3
Lane, Gardiner M, 1914, O 4,15:5
Lane, Gardiner M Mrs, 1954, S 13,23:2
Lane, Genevieve, 1938, O 14,23:2
Lane, George, 1925, S 25,21:6
Lane, George D, 1917, My 30,9:4
Lane, George E, 1937, F 24,23:5
Lane, George P, 1953, D 29,23:4; 1968, Mr 28,57:[illegible]
Lane, George T, 1940, Ja 14,42:6; 1960, Jl 27,29:1
Lane, Gerould T, 1961, Ja 14,23:2
Lane, Gertrude, 1953, N 23,27:4
Lane, Gertrude B (por), 1941, S 26,23:1
Lane, H Richardson, 1963, O 21,31:5
Lane, Harold F Mrs, 1955, Ag 28,84:4
Lane, Harold M Mrs, 1943, Ag 25,19:4
Lane, Harry C, 1946, O 18,24:2
Lane, Harry J, 1943, O 28,23:2
Lane, Harry N, 1941, My 7,25:4
Lane, Harry Sen, 1917, My 24,13:2
Lane, Hazel, 1950, Ap 19,29:1
Lane, Henry M, 1960, Mr 8,33:2
Lane, Herbert J, 1938, O 26,23:4
Lane, Howard A, 1961, O 27,33:4
Lane, Howard V, 1950, Mr 6,22:3
Lane, Irving J, 1953, O 29,31:1
Lane, Isaac Rev, 1937, D 6,27:3
Lane, J O'Gorman, 1950, Mr 28,32:2
Lane, J W, 1927, My 23,21:3
Lane, Jack (J Teitelbaum), 1964, Ja 21,29:2
Lane, James H, 1866, Jl 3,5:3; 1939, N 18,17:5
Lane, James Mrs, 1948, O 4,23:5
Lane, James R, 1944, D 8,21:4
Lane, James W, 1959, S 24,37:1
Lane, Jennie R Mrs, 1938, Je 14,21:2
Lane, Jeremy, 1963, S 20,33:1
Lane, John, 1925, F 4,21:4
Lane, John A, 1947, Jl 8,23:3
Lane, John C, 1958, F 9,88:6
Lane, John F, 1949, D 21,29:3
Lane, John Gen, 1914, D 26,7:4
Lane, John H, 1942, Jl 19,30:8
Lane, John I, 1949, O 2,82:6
Lane, John J, 1937, Ap 8,23:1; 1945, My 16,19:3 1954, Ap 3,15:3; 1958, O 11,23:3
Lane, John L Dr, 1937, D 3,23:2
Lane, John M, 1942, Jl 6,15:3
Lane, John Mrs, 1952, Je 12,34:6
Lane, John Q Gen, 1903, Jl 14,7:6
Lane, John W, 1938, Ag 11,17:4
Lane, Joseph, 1881, Ap 21,5:2; 1966, N 10,47:2
Lane, Joseph A, 1965, N 15,37:4
Lane, Joseph E, 1946, O 6,59:4; 1950, O 29,93:1
Lane, K B, 1878, Mr 16,3:4
Lane, Katherine F Mrs, 1952, Ja 21,15:4
Lane, Kenneth A, 1959, D 16,41:2
Lane, Laurence W Sr, 1967, F 22,29:3
Lane, Leota (Mrs J Day), 1963, Jl 27,17:3
Lane, Leslie C, 1954, Mr 16,29:1
Lane, Loring, 1909, Mr 21,11:6
Lane, Louis, 1940, S 19,23:2
Lane, Lupino, 1959, N 11,35:3
Lane, Marcus D L, 1872, S 16,1:3
Lane, Martin B, 1955, Mr 14,23:3

Lane, Mary Mrs, 1951, D 18,31:4
Lane, Maude Mrs, 1925, My 16,17:5
Lane, Merritt, 1939, Je 24,17:3
Lane, Merritt Mrs, 1955, F 4,19:8
Lane, Mervin L, 1953, N 9,35:4
Lane, Michael Mrs, 1948, Ja 13,25:4
Lane, Mills B (por), 1945, Ag 7,24:2
Lane, Morton P, 1948, N 7,88:4
Lane, Moses R, 1955, Ag 6,15:2
Lane, N, 1876, O 26,4:7
Lane, Nathan, 1962, My 30,19:4
Lane, Nathaniel Plumm, 1912, N 7,13:5
Lane, Norman E, 1966, My 17,47:3
Lane, Oren C Mrs, 1940, S 29,43:1
Lane, Orren C Rev, 1917, My 13,21:1
Lane, Patrick H Mrs, 1945, D 20,23:3
Lane, Peter C, 1949, Ag 29,17:3
Lane, Ralph, 1965, F 9,37:2
Lane, Ralph J, 1955, Ap 23,19:4
Lane, Rembrandt P, 1964, D 20,69:1
Lane, Richmond D, 1960, Jl 28,27:4
Lane, Robert P, 1953, Mr 31,32:3
Lane, Robert R, 1959, N 1,85:8
Lane, Rollin S Mrs, 1945, D 11,25:2
Lane, Ronald Gen Sir, 1937, Mr 8,19:2
Lane, Rose Wilder Mrs, 1968, N 1,47:4
Lane, Rufus H, 1948, Ap 21,27:5
Lane, Samuel A Mrs, 1942, My 21,19:4
Lane, Samuel M (mem ser set), 1967, O 2,48:1
Lane, Sanford H, 1944, Jl 12,19:6
Lane, Sarah P Mrs, 1903, Jl 28,7:6
Lane, Sig, 1965, Ja 2,19:3
Lane, Smith E, 1909, F 2,9:5
Lane, Thomas, 1942, Ag 18,21:2
Lane, Thomas A, 1963, Jl 21,64:7
Lane, Thomas M, 1947, Jl 13,44:6
Lane, Victor, 1946, Je 24,31:3
Lane, Wallace R, 1946, My 25,15:1
Lane, Walter A, 1940, Ja 22,15:4
Lane, Warren C, 1943, Ap 26,19:4
Lane, Warren D, 1938, Ja 11,23:4
Lane, William A (por), 1943, Ja 18,15:1
Lane, William Channing, 1923, F 10,13:5
Lane, William E Jr, 1962, Jl 10,33:5
Lane, William F, 1940, My 14,23:5
Lane, William H, 1946, Je 9,40:6
Lane, William J, 1941, Ja 4,13:4
Lane, William P, 1938, N 6,49:3
Lane, William P Jr, 1967, F 8,31:2
Lane, William T, 1937, O 27,31:3
Lane, Wolcott G, 1956, N 12,29:5
Lane-Jackson, Nicholas, 1937, O 27,31:3
Lanehart, James P, 1947, Ja 9,23:2
Lanehart, James P Mrs, 1941, Jl 5,11:5
Lanehart, Louis N Dr, 1920, Ap 26,13:4
Lanel, E, 1916, Ja 12,13:4
Lanergan, Ann Mother, 1951, S 24,27:2
Laneri, Eugene, 1965, Mr 15,31:3
Lanesborough, Earl of (H C Butler), 1950, Ag 24, 27:2
Laney, Calvin C, 1941, Ag 24,34:3
Laney, Francis B, 1938, Ap 26,21:1
Laney, John E, 1955, My 8,89:2
Laney, Joseph C, 1948, Ag 18,25:1
Lanfair, Charles H, 1943, S 15,27:5
Lanfair, Lawrence C, 1948, Ap 23,23:2
Lanfear, James H, 1937, Ag 1,II,7:3
Lanford, John A, 1940, Jl 3,17:4
Lanfranconi, Luigi, 1938, Ja 26,23:1
Lanfrey, Pierre, 1877, N 17,5:1
Lang, Albert F (Al), 1960, F 28,82:4
Lang, Albert G, 1960, Ag 10,31:5
Lang, Albert Rev, 1937, N 3,23:3
Lang, Alfred C, 1955, My 15,86:5
Lang, Alfred E, 1950, Jl 7,19:2
Lang, Alfred L, 1949, O 6,31:6
Lang, Alois, 1954, Mr 12,21:6
Lang, Andrew, 1912, Jl 22,7:5
Lang, Anton (por), 1938, My 19,21:1
Lang, Benjamin Johnson, 1909, Ap 5,7:4
Lang, Bernard D, 1956, S 6,25:2
Lang, Bill, 1948, Ap 2,23:4
Lang, Carl, 1945, S 6,25:2
Lang, Cecilia, 1960, Ag 3,29:5
Lang, Charles, 1941, Ja 3,19:5; 1947, Je 15,60:6
Lang, Charles A, 1959, Je 2,35:2
Lang, Charles A Mrs, 1952, My 16,23:3
Lang, Chester H, 1961, Je 16,33:1
Lang, Christopher D, 1956, Je 17,92:3
Lang, Clara, 1952, Jl 15,21:1
Lang, Currier, 1964, Mr 20,33:3
Lang, Currier Mrs, 1961, Mr 19,88:8
Lang, David S, 1940, Ap 5,21:2
Lang, Dora S Mrs, 1937, Jl 17,15:6
Lang, Edmund (por), 1940, N 2,15:1
Lang, Edward A, 1939, D 29,15:2
Lang, Edward C, 1947, D 15,25:5
Lang, Elizabeth H, 1957, Ja 16,31:4
Lang, Elmer J Mrs, 1957, N 19,33:3
Lang, F, 1878, Jl 3,5:4
Lang, Frank, 1942, My 23,15:4; 1947, Ap 5,19:3
Lang, Frank C, 1921, My 21,13:1
Lang, George, 1948, My 28,23:2
Lang, George F, 1946, N 13,27:2
Lang, George Mrs, 1949, Je 3,25:4
Lang, George W, 1937, Ag 26,21:3
Lang, Georgi, 1948, Jl 27,25:2
Lang, Gustav, 1950, Mr 31,32:6
Lang, H Becket, 1965, Ap 23,35:2
Lang, H R, 1934, Jl 26,19:3
Lang, Harry, 1953, Ag 4,21:1; 1956, Ap 2,23:3
Lang, Harry J, 1949, Je 5,92:6
Lang, Harry Mrs, 1962, Ja 26,31:2
Lang, Harry W, 1966, D 20,43:2
Lang, Henry Mrs, 1941, Ap 5,17:5; 1943, F 6,13:3
Lang, Herbert B, 1959, Jl 26,68:3
Lang, Herman E, 1943, Jl 20,19:5
Lang, Herman R Mrs, 1938, Je 19,29:2
Lang, J Harvey Mrs, 1953, Jl 9,25:3
Lang, Jack, 1959, D 22,31:3
Lang, James C, 1937, S 26,II,8:2
Lang, James H, 1949, Je 12,76:1; 1961, Mr 14,35:4
Lang, James R, 1946, Jl 25,21:6
Lang, Jennings Mrs (will), 1952, D 17,28:6
Lang, John, 1950, O 11,33:5; 1958, Jl 9,27:4; 1959, My 24,88:4
Lang, John J, 1948, My 12,27:3
Lang, John L Mrs, 1960, D 1,35:4
Lang, John M, 1952, N 15,17:2
Lang, John Marshall Rev, 1909, My 3,7:7
Lang, John Mrs, 1960, Ja 27,33:2
Lang, Joseph, 1940, O 13,49:2; 1954, Ja 24,85:1
Lang, Joseph C, 1937, Je 24,25:3
Lang, Karl F, 1952, S 24,33:4
Lang, Kaufman, 1903, N 10,5:6
Lang, Kaufman Mrs, 1903, N 10,5:6
Lang, Leo Mrs, 1957, S 21,19:3
Lang, Leon S, 1956, Ap 27,27:2
Lang, Lewis F, 1956, D 28,21:4
Lang, Lord, 1945, D 6,27:1
Lang, Louis, 1962, Je 12,37:4
Lang, Malcolm, 1941, F 26,21:4
Lang, Martin R, 1965, My 11,39:4
Lang, Matheson (por), 1948, Ap 13,27:3
Lang, Morris, 1964, Ag 23,87:1
Lang, Nick, 1939, Ap 20,23:3
Lang, Ossian, 1945, S 13,23:6
Lang, Otto U, 1940, Jl 25,17:5
Lang, Patrick J, 1944, N 15,27:2
Lang, Phil H, 1954, N 24,23:3
Lang, Philo S, 1948, D 5,92:4
Lang, Richard R, 1942, S 6,31:1
Lang, Robert H, 1948, F 8,60:5
Lang, Robert W, 1954, Ag 30,17:6
Lang, Rudolph C, 1949, Je 25,13:3
Lang, Rudolph Mrs, 1958, Mr 7,23:2
Lang, Sebastian F, 1947, D 8,25:3
Lang, Theodore Sr, 1942, S 30,23:5
Lang, Theresa J, 1947, Ja 20,25:3
Lang, Thomas B Mrs, 1946, O 29,25:5
Lang, Ulrich, 1946, Ap 20,23:5
Lang, Walter C (por), 1940, Je 11,25:6
Lang, Will, 1968, Ja 23,43:3
Lang, William A, 1951, Ja 22,17:4; 1967, Ap 26,47:2
Lang, William F, 1947, Mr 25,25:2
Lang, William J, 1943, S 26,48:2; 1944, Ag 16,19:4
Lang, William P, 1955, Jl 27,23:2
Langan, Ambrose, 1942, My 4,19:3
Langan, George J, 1954, N 9,27:1
Langan, John J, 1956, Jl 15,60:5; 1959, Mr 5,31:3
Langan, John P Rev, 1913, S 30,13:6
Langan, John T (por), 1946, S 3,19:5
Langan, Joseph G, 1952, Ja 15,27:3
Langan, Thaddeus A, 1945, D 3,21:2
Langan, Thomas A Mrs, 1947, Je 21,17:4
Langan, Thomas L, 1951, Ap 8,92:5
Langan, William T, 1953, Ja 3,15:3
Langaskens, Maurice, 1946, D 27,20:2
Langbank, Joseph L, 1943, Jl 30,15:5
Langbaum, Theodore, 1968, S 16,47:2
Langbein, Charles Mrs, 1950, Ja 7,18:3
Langbein, Louis, 1946, Ag 6,25:1
Langdale, A Barnett, 1965, F 6,25:1
Langdale, John W (por), 1940, D 11,27:5
Langdan, Nathan S, 1944, Mr 28,19:6
Langden, Joseph, 1953, Mr 19,29:6
Langdon, Arthur N, 1963, N 1,33:1
Langdon, Chauncy T, 1961, O 1,86:3
Langdon, Courtney Prof, 1924, N 20,23:5
Langdon, Dudley, 1919, Je 26,9:3
Langdon, Elizabeth W, 1923, Je 1,19:6
Langdon, Emma F Mrs, 1937, D 2,25:6
Langdon, Francis E, 1944, Ag 30,17:3
Langdon, Frank M, 1941, Ap 29,19:2
Langdon, Frederic Mrs, 1954, Jl 15,27:4
Langdon, Frederick M, 1937, D 3,24:3
Langdon, G W, 1903, Ag 2,7:5
Langdon, H H Dr, 1937, My 7,25:1
Langdon, Harry, 1944, D 23,13:3
Langdon, Howard A, 1939, Ja 29,33:3
Langdon, Ida, 1964, O 10,29:4
Langdon, Jervis, 1952, D 17,33:4
Langdon, Loomis L Brig-Gen (cor, Ja 9,9:4), 1910, Ja 8,9:4
Langdon, Mary B Mrs, 1943, Ap 23,17:4
Langdon, Ned F, 1955, Ap 28,29:1
Langdon, Roy L, 1956, D 23,30:4
Langdon, Russell C, 1963, N 8,31:1
Langdon, Sophia E Mrs, 1941, Ag 4,13:4
Langdon, Stephen H Dr, 1937, My 20,21:1
Langdon, Thomas (will), 1960, Ja 14,2:4
Langdon, Thomas P, 1903, N 24,9:5
Langdon, Walter Galbraith, 1923, Mr 27,19:5
Langdon, Walter T, 1958, My 9,23:1
Langdon, Warren H Lt, 1921, Ja 21,15:6
Langdon, William C, 1947, Ap 12,17:4
Langdon, William H (por), 1939, Ag 11,15:6
Langdon, William R, 1963, Jl 20,19:4
Langdon, Woodbury, 1921, O 25,17:5
Langdon, Woodbury Gusdorf, 1919, Ap 21,15:3
Langdon-Brown, Walter, 1946, O 4,23:3
Lange, A H Mrs, 1950, S 25,23:1
Lange, Albert C, 1947, F 5,23:3
Lange, Alex H, 1956, Mr 13,27:5
Lange, Alexis F, 1924, Ag 30,9:7
Lange, Arthur, 1956, D 8,19:5
Lange, Augusta H, 1941, Mr 12,21:3
Lange, Carl F Prof, 1937, My 28,21:3
Lange, Charles, 1953, Mr 14,15:2
Lange, Charles W, 1964, Ag 11,33:4
Lange, Christian L, 1938, D 12,19:1
Lange, Dorothea (Mrs P S Taylor), 1965, O 14,47:2
Lange, Emma E, 1938, My 24,19:3
Lange, Frank, 1909, F 23,9:2
Lange, Frederick W, 1947, Ap 9,25:5
Lange, George H, 1953, Je 23,29:3
Lange, Gustav Mrs, 1953, My 20,29:5
Lange, Gustave A, 1953, My 20,29:2
Lange, H Julius Mrs, 1924, N 3,17:4
Lange, Hans, 1960, Ag 15,23:5
Lange, Harry W, 1942, S 10,27:5
Lange, Henry A, 1960, Ja 21,31:4
Lange, Henry C, 1949, Mr 25,23:1
Lange, Henry H, 1943, N 3,25:3
Lange, Herman T, 1938, Je 4,15:6
Lange, Hugo Dr, 1937, Ag 29,II,7:3
Lange, Hugo V, 1923, Mr 26,13:4
Lange, John D, 1916, Ap 20,13:6
Lange, John R, 1949, My 3,25:2
Lange, Joseph de, 1948, Ja 31,19:4
Lange, Julius O Mrs, 1941, Ag 6,17:1
Lange, Leo B, 1957, D 16,29:3
Lange, Linda B, 1947, Ap 25,21:5
Lange, Oscar, 1965, O 4,4:1
Lange, Otto A, 1954, Ja 10,86:2
Lange, Otto F, 1965, My 8,31:5
Lange, Robert E Mrs, 1946, N 28,27:3
Lange, Theodore S, 1950, Mr 16,31:2
Lange, William A, 1943, Ag 7,11:6; 1950, Jl 25,27:1; 1957, F 4,19:5
Lange, William P, 1946, N 11,27:4
Langel, Henry, 1947, Jl 5,11:6
Langeli, Luigi, 1951, S 25,29:4
Langelier, Francis Sir, 1915, F 9,9:6
Langell, Alex H, 1953, Ap 7,29:2
Langeloth, Jacob, 1914, Ag 15,9:6
Langenbach, Raymond T, 1943, O 20,21:5
Langenbacher, Dominic, 1939, Je 10,17:2
Langenbahn, Theodore W, 1967, N 27,47:2
Langenberg, Frederick C Dr, 1937, Ap 5,19:2
Langenberg, Joseph V, 1944, Ja 10,17:3
Langenburg, Gustave C, 1915, N 29,11:5
Langenieux, Jean M, 1953, Ap 7,29:4
Langenus, Alan G Mrs, 1966, N 17,47:3
Langenus, Gustave L, 1957, F 1,25:4
Langenus, Gustave L Mrs, 1957, F 22,21:4
Langer, Aaron Mrs, 1942, Mr 1,45:1
Langer, Adolph A (por), 1948, Ap 29,24:2
Langer, Charles, 1938, F 21,12:5
Langer, Frank E, 1952, N 28,25:2
Langer, Frederick, 1963, Je 5,41:1
Langer, Frieda, 1968, D 23,39:1
Langer, Herbert L, 1966, F 26,25:4
Langer, Hyman D, 1951, D 10,29:4
Langer, Joseph, 1944, Ja 29,13:1
Langer, Lena, 1956, Je 18,25:1
Langer, Louis E, 1957, Ag 24,15:3
Langer, Matthew A, 1967, Je 25,68:8
Langer, Norbert J Sr, 1966, Ag 20,25:3
Langer, Ralph Dr, 1968, Jl 31,41:3
Langer, Robert, 1967, Ja 8,88:7
Langer, Robert A, 1966, Mr 17,43:6
Langer, Rudolph A, 1958, D 26,2:6
Langer, Rudolph E, 1968, Mr 13,53:3
Langer, Solomon, 1963, Ap 23,37:2
Langer, Tevia, 1950, Mr 21,32:3
Langer, William (funl plans, N 10,47:5; trb, N 11,-35:1), 1959, N 9,1:7
Langer, William Mrs (funl, Ag 8,17:5), 1959, Ag 5, 27:3
Langer von Langendorff, Diana Baroness (Miss Evyan), 1968, Ag 21,42:1
Langerfeld, Paul Mrs (Mina), 1968, N 3,89:1
Langerman, Frederick, 1941, S 11,23:5
Langerman, Joseph, 1951, Mr 24,13:5
Langerman, Nathaniel S, 1963, D 25,33:1
Langermann, Aug, 1942, Ag 30,39:3
Langevin, Eldon K, 1949, Mr 15,27:4
Langevin, Hector Sir, 1906, Je 12,4:3

Langevin, Louis Philip Adelard Archbishop, 1915, Je 16,11:5
Langevin, Medause, 1944, Mr 4,13:3
Langevin, Paul, 1946, D 20,23:1
Langfeld, Herbert S, 1958, F 26,27:3
Langfeld, Louis F, 1937, Je 19,15:4
Langfeld, William R, 1941, D 25,25:5
Langfelder, Frederick, 1960, Ag 31,29:4
Langfitt, W C, 1934, Ap 21,15:4
Langfitt, William C Mrs, 1954, D 14,33:4
Langfitt, William S, 1945, Ap 18,23:5
Langford, Arch M, 1942, F 9,15:4
Langford, Daniel B (will), 1954, D 21,4:4
Langford, E L Col, 1902, Jl 26,9:4
Langford, Edward J, 1945, D 20,23:3
Langford, George, 1964, Je 18,35:4
Langford, Harry, 1952, N 14,23:1
Langford, Herbert E, 1941, Ag 3,35:3
Langford, Lee E, 1956, My 26,17:6
Langford, Lillian J Mrs (will, Mr 7,2:2), 1937, Mr 4, 8:2
Langford, Malcolm S, 1962, N 20,36:1
Langford, Menalcus, 1937, D 29,21:2
Langford, Sam, 1956, Ja 13,23:1
Langford, Thomas P Mrs, 1942, N 21,13:2
Langford, Thomas R, 1945, Mr 23,20:2
Langford, William, 1955, Jl 22,23:2
Langford, William S, 1942, Mr 3,23:3
Langford-Baker, Clifford, 1945, Ja 28,38:5
Langfus, Anna Mrs, 1966, My 14,31:3
Langhaar, Henry L Mrs, 1945, Ja 29,13:6
Langham, Cornelius K Sr, 1939, D 21,23:4
Langham, Peter, 1958, O 7,29:3
Langhammer, Paul W, 1938, My 29,II,6:5
Langhanke, Helen Mrs, 1947, Ja 20,25:1
Langhanke, Otto, 1943, F 5,21:1
Langheinz, Henry Mrs, 1945, Jl 3,13:2
Langheinz, Louis E G, 1966, S 2,31:3
Langhoff, Wolfgang, 1966, Ag 26,33:1
Langhorne, Agnes S, 1950, Jl 14,21:5
Langhorne, C P Mrs, 1903, O 8,5:6
Langhorne, Chriswell Babney, 1919, F 15,11:4
Langhorne, Edmund G Mrs, 1951, F 13,31:2
Langhorne, George T, 1962, Ja 26,31:1
Langhorne, J C, 1912, Jl 26,9:6
Langhorne, James A D, 1950, My 14,106:6
Langhorne, John Devall, 1915, N 26,13:6
Langhorne, Mable J Mrs (will), 1955, Mr 6,35:2
Langhorne, Marshall, 1942, D 22,26:2
Langhorne, William H, 1938, Je 10,21:4
Langhorst, Frederick, 1947, Je 7,13:1
Langhorst, George, 1948, D 29,21:4
Langhorst, Harry J, 1952, Ja 22,29:4
Langhorst, Paul H, 1945, F 23,17:4
Langie, Mary B Mrs, 1950, My 28,44:6
Langkjaer, Svend, 1948, My 5,25:4
Langland, Howard F (Bro Gerard), 1960, Mr 6,84:5
Langlard, Abbe H, 1944, Ag 29,17:5
Langle, Richard R Jr, 1965, Jl 27,33:4
Langler, Lawrence P, 1948, N 7,89:1
Langley, Allan L, 1949, N 18,35:1
Langley, Cortlandt J, 1959, S 3,27:2
Langley, Elizabeth E, 1949, F 9,27:3
Langley, Ernest F, 1954, S 23,33:4
Langley, Frank E, 1938, Ap 26,21:4
Langley, Frederick O, 1947, Ja 24,22:3
Langley, George J, 1941, Ja 27,15:1
Langley, Hurbert, 1947, Ja 2,27:1
Langley, J N Prof, 1925, N 7,15:4
Langley, James M, 1968, Je 24,37:2
Langley, John W, 1950, Je 30,23:3
Langley, John W Mrs, 1948, Ag 16,19:5
Langley, Leonard D, 1940, F 8,23:3
Langley, S P, 1906, Mr 3,9:5
Langley, Samuel P, 1946, F 10,40:5
Langley, Samuel Pierpont Prof, 1906, F 28,9:3
Langley, T C Archbishop, 1868, O 29,4:7
Langley, William C, 1962, F 9,29:3
Langley, William C Mrs, 1949, Je 30,23:4
Langlie, Arthur B, 1966, Jl 25,27:1
Langlois, Cyril O, 1957, Je 20,29:4
Langlois, Ernest F, 1954, F 6,19:4
Langlois, Ferdinand H, 1954, Mr 4,25:2
Langlois, Hippolyte, 1912, F 13,11:4
Langlois, J Albert, 1964, Ja 30,30:2
Langlotz, Arthur S, 1966, Jl 21,33:2
Langlotz, Carl A Prof, 1915, N 26,13:6
Langmack, Carl J, 1956, Mr 15,31:4
Langman, Harry, 1963, D 19,33:4
Langmann, Gustav Adolph Dr, 1916, Mr 28,13:6
Langmore, William, 1956, Je 22,23:6
Langmuir, Arthur C (por), 1941, My 15,23:1
Langmuir, Arthur C Mrs, 1943, Je 29,21:7
Langmuir, Charles H, 1944, O 8,43:1
Langmuir, Dean, 1950, Ja 9,25:5
Langmuir, Irving, 1957, Ag 17,1:4
Langmuir, John D, 1959, Ap 5,86:8
Langmuir, Peter B, 1967, Ap 20,43:4
Langner, Herbert B, 1965, Ag 4,35:5
Langner, Herbert Mrs, 1959, Ap 4,19:4
Langner, Lawrence, 1962, D 28,8:5
Langner, Lawrence (will), 1963, F 6,5:7
Langr, Frank J, 1966, Ag 6,23:4
Langrall, Leander, 1937, Ag 5,23:2
Langredge, W B, 1883, Ag 6,5:1
Langren, Frances (Mrs Hy Helprin), 1968, Ag 9,35:2
Langreth, George L, 1962, F 26,27:5
Langreuter, H Capt, 1911, My 5,11:4
Langridge, William H R, 1958, N 6,37:5
Langrish, J Mrs, 1948, Ja 3,13:5
Langrock, Edwin G, 1967, Ja 7,27:5
Langsam, William L, 1964, Mr 29,61:3
Langsenkamp, Frank H, 1953, Mr 17,29:1
Langshaw, Edward E, 1949, Ja 9,72:5
Langshaw, Walter H, 1947, Mr 20,28:2
Langslet, Bjarne I, 1959, Jl 26,68:4
Langslow, Harry R, 1942, Ap 9,19:1
Langspecht, Otto, 1945, O 27,15:6
Langstadt, Albert C, 1938, S 1,23:4
Langstaff, John E, 1948, Ja 17,17:2
Langstaff, Richard T, 1942, Mr 29,45:1
Langstaff, Will, 1953, Jl 3,19:5
Langstaff, William Sr Mrs, 1945, Ag 10,15:2
Langston, Eugen M, 1947, Mr 10,21:4
Langstroth, Clifford B, 1961, My 26,33:1
Langstroth, Francis Ward, 1925, O 28,25:5
Langstroth, Frederick E, 1940, N 12,23:1
Langstroth, Thomas W, 1940, Ap 23,23:2
Langthorn, Jacob S, 1955, O 25,33:5
Langthorne, Jane M, 1957, O 23,33:2
Langton, Daniel W Mrs (Berenice), 1960, Mr 25,27:1
Langton, George Jr, 1952, Je 2,42:6
Langton, Gore, 1873, D 29,2:2
Langton, James A, 1943, F 13,11:5
Langton, John A, 1946, Ag 12,21:6
Langton, John H, 1941, Je 23,17:4
Langton, Mabel F, 1959, D 19,27:5
Langtry, Albert P, 1939, Ag 28,19:5
Langue, Frederick R, 1965, Mr 21,86:6
Languedoc, Georges Francois E, 1924, S 30,23:3
Langworthy, Arthur M, 1945, O 17,19:3
Langworthy, Edward Phelps, 1953, F 24,25:5
Langworthy, Harry W Sr, 1951, Je 3,95:3
Langworthy, Henry J, 1944, Mr 12,38:2
Langworthy, Herman M, 1956, Ag 24,19:5
Langworthy, Mary P Mrs, 1941, Mr 5,21:1
Langworthy, W G, 1941, Jl 7,15:1
Langworthy, William F, 1947, Jl 25,17:3
Langworthy, William N, 1943, D 27,20:3
Langworthy, William P, 1962, S 25,37:3
Lanham, Charles F, 1939, Ag 5,15:6
Lanham, Edward, 1939, S 26,23:5
Lanham, Fritz D, 1965, Ag 3,31:2
Lanham, Henderson L, 1957, N 11,19:3
Lanham, John W, 1939, Je 23,19:4
Lanham, McCall, 1959, Ap 1,37:3
Lanham, S W T Ex-Gov, 1908, Jl 31,5:4
Lanheady, Thomas J, 1957, Ap 11,31:3
Lani, Maria (Mrs M Ilyin), 1954, Mr 13,15:6
Lania, Leo, 1961, N 10,36:1
Laniel, Rene, 1964, Jl 4,13:1
Lanier, Albert G Mrs, 1964, Ja 12,92:6
Lanier, Berwick B, 1957, F 14,27:2
Lanier, C, 1926, Mr 8,19:3
Lanier, Charles, 1918, D 6,15:4
Lanier, Charles D, 1945, N 19,21:3
Lanier, Charles D Mrs, 1962, Ag 11,17:5
Lanier, Edmund Capt, 1872, F 27,5:2
Lanier, George H, 1948, S 18,18:2
Lanier, H B Mrs, 1931, O 28,23:3
Lanier, Haskell D, 1950, Ap 28,10:2
Lanier, Henry Mrs, 1967, O 9,47:3
Lanier, Henry W, 1958, Mr 11,29:5
Lanier, Henry W Mrs, 1958, D 31,19:2
Lanier, J F D, 1881, Ag 28,7:2
Lanier, J F D Mrs, 1903, Je 22,7:6
Lanier, John J, 1942, S 18,21:3
Lanier, P W, 1958, O 14,37:3
Lanier, Raphael O, 1962, D 20,8:1
Lanier, Raymond R, 1958, N 25,66:6
Lanier, Robert, 1912, Mr 27,13:4
Lanier, S Mrs, 1931, D 30,19:3
Lanier, Sidney, 1881, S 9,5:1
Lanier, Sidney M Jr Mrs, 1961, S 17,86:7
Lanier, Will S, 1948, Mr 13,15:1
Lanigan, Charles L, 1949, D 17,17:5
Lanigan, James A rev Dr, 1912, Ag 21,9:6
Lanigan, John R, 1953, S 18,23:2
Lanigan, Mary (Sister M Concepta), 1959, My 20, 35:4
Lanigan, William U, 1953, S 14,27:5
Lanigon, Joe, 1944, N 29,23:3
Lanin, Joseph L, 1961, O 4,45:3
Laning, A P, 1880, S 5,7:3
Laning, Eugene L R, 1952, N 29,17:5
Laning, Harris, 1941, F 3,20:1
Laning, Victor P, 1957, Ag 18,82:1
Lanini, Alfred, 1956, Ja 23,25:2
Lank, Frank A, 1921, N 17,17:4
Lank, Grace, 1956, Ja 15,92:8
Lank, Henry C, 1946, Ap 20,13:4
Lank, James T, 1952, N 7,23:4
Lankau, Metislaus C, 1962, D 8,27:1
Lankenau, Elizabeth, 1955, F 10,31:5
Lankenau, F D, 1901, Ag 31,7:6
Lankenau, F J, 1939, Jl 17,19:6
Lankenau, Henry, 1953, My 16,19:5
Lankering, Adolph, 1937, F 4,21:4
Lankering, George, 1940, Mr 5,23:5
Lankes, Julius J, 1960, Ap 24,88:5
Lankester, R Sir, 1929, Ag 16,21:5
Lankewich, Joseph, 1937, Ja 4,15:4
Lankford, Grace W Mrs, 1967, N 1,47:1
Lankler, Ralph C Mrs, 1961, Ja 29,84:8
Lankow, Edward, 1940, Ja 30,20:2
Lanman, Charles F, 1950, Je 8,32:2
Lanman, Charles R, 1941, F 21,19:1
Lanman, David H, 1940, Ag 4,33:3
Lanman, Jonathan T, 1952, My 24,19:5
Lanman, Joseph A, 1945, Mr 21,23:5
Lanman, Joseph Rear-Adm, 1874, Mr 14,7:2
Lanman, Maurice H Sr, 1951, Mr 24,13:3
Lanman, Thomas H, 1961, Mr 29,33:5
Lann, Jack, 1958, My 9,23:1
Lann, Max E, 1949, Mr 21,23:4
Lannan, Louis E, 1943, O 12,27:5
Lannefeld, Walter E, 1949, D 6,31:3
Lannelongue, Odilon Prof, 1911, D 23,9:5
Lannen, John J, 1952, D 30,19:5
Lanner, Katti, 1908, N 16,9:6
Lannig, George A, 1950, S 8,31:1
Lannin, J J, 1928, My 16,16:1
Lanning, Carl G, 1966, D 5,45:3
Lanning, Charles E, 1949, S 3,13:6
Lanning, Don, 1960, F 15,27:3
Lanning, Edward V, 1948, Ja 27,25:1
Lanning, Floyd M, 1940, My 18,15:3
Lanning, Frank R, 1952, Jl 22,25:1
Lanning, Frederic J, 1961, D 9,27:6
Lanning, Henry M, 1946, N 8,23:2
Lanning, J Melville, 1947, Je 3,25:1
Lanning, Leo J, 1963, Ag 27,31:4
Lanning, Percy L, 1937, Ja 11,20:3
Lanning, Samuel A, 1940, Mr 11,15:2
Lanning, William Mershon Judge, 1912, F 17,11:5
Lannon, Arthur M, 1951, S 28,31:3
Lannon, James, 1948, N 23,30:2
Lannon, James A, 1954, My 29,15:5
Lannon, James P, 1957, Ja 1,23:3
Lannon, John D Mrs, 1956, My 20,86:8
Lannon, Martin F, 1950, N 28,31:4
Lannon, Mary, 1938, F 8,21:5
Lannon, Michael J, 1961, N 9,35:4
Lannuier, Shirley A, 1964, My 13,47:3
La Noce, Howard Mrs, 1950, My 2,29:2
Lanouette, Adolphus Mrs, 1952, Je 10,27:5
Lanouette, Daniel W, 1947, Jl 25,17:5
Lanphear, Mary E Mrs, 1945, O 23,17:5
Lanpher, Louis A Rev Dr, 1909, Ag 27,7:6
Lanphere, Charles N, 1940, My 24,19:2
Lanphere, Fremont C Mrs, 1951, D 29,11:6
Lanphere, Gladys (cor, O 8,22:7), 1948, O 7,33:1
Lanphier, Robert C, 1939, Ja 30,13:5
Lanrezac, Charles Gen, 1925, Ja 19,17:4
Lansburgh, James, 1917, O 30,15:4
Lansburgh, Percy W, 1940, My 22,23:3
Lansburgh, Richard H, 1942, Je 5,17:4
Lansburgh, Robert S, 1960, Ja 27,33:4
Lansbury, George, 1940, My 8,23:1
Lansdale, Elizabeth C B Mrs, 1937, O 26,23:4
Lansdale, Henry, 1959, Ja 30,27:4
Lansdale, Henry N, 1964, N 6,37:2
Lansdale, Herbert P Jr Mrs, 1950, Mr 21,32:4
Lansdale, Herbert P Mrs, 1953, Mr 4,27:5
Lansdell, Elizabeth Mrs, 1945, Ja 19,19:4
Lansdell, Julien B, 1961, S 25,33:2
Lansdell, Robert H, 1958, Je 21,19:2
Lansden, Dick Latta, 1924, Ag 10,24:4
Lansden, Ollie P Mrs, 1952, S 16,29:3
Lansdowne, Lady, 1965, F 18,25:2
Lansdowne, Marquis of, 1863, F 17,5:3
Lansdowne, R Marquess of, 1927, Je 5,25:3
Lansing, A B Capt, 1880, F 12,2:5
Lansing, A Ten Eyck, 1937, F 14,II,8:7
Lansing, Ambrose, 1959, My 29,23:5
Lansing, Anna M, 1948, D 10,25:2
Lansing, Arthur B Mrs, 1904, O 14,7:5
Lansing, Barbara L Mrs, 1941, S 27,17:6
Lansing, Bradford R, 1912, F 5,9:4
Lansing, Charles E, 1946, Mr 14,25:2
Lansing, Clarence T, 1949, Ag 26,19:1
Lansing, Cleveland C, 1943, Ap 19,19:4
Lansing, Cleveland Mrs, 1944, My 2,19:5
Lansing, E F Mrs, 1934, Ag 20,13:1
Lansing, Edwin Y Maj, 1937, Ap 28,23:5
Lansing, Emma L Mrs, 1939, Ag 21,13:4
Lansing, Emma S, 1956, D 12,39:3
Lansing, Gerrit Y, 1940, My 18,15:6
Lansing, Gulian, 1952, Ja 10,29:4
Lansing, Harry, 1958, Je 24,31:4
Lansing, Hugh H, 1950, Ja 7,17:5
Lansing, Isaac C F, 1874, N 21,9:7
Lansing, J A Rev, 1884, Jl 23,5:1
Lansing, John E, 1958, S 29,27:5
Lansing, John Ernest Mrs, 1968, Jl 12,31:4
Lansing, Louis S, 1950, N 10,27:2
Lansing, R, 1878, O 5,1:6; 1928, O 31,1:6
Lansing, Raymond P Mrs, 1964, Ja 23,31:4
Lansing, Roscue U, 1941, My 17,15:5

Lansing, Samuel B, 1950, Je 18,76:1
Lansing, Susan Y, 1911, Ja 16,11:5
Lansing, W E, 1883, Jl 30,5:5
Lansing, W Yates, 1938, S 5,15:6
Lansing, William, 1939, Mr 22,23:2
Lansingh, Van R, 1956, N 17,21:5
Lansky, Gabriel, 1959, Mr 29,80:2
Lansner, Herbert, 1952, Ag 19,23:4
Lanston, Aubrey G, 1960, Ag 26,25:4
Lant, Edwin B, 1947, Ja 10,21:1
Lantelme, French Actress, 1911, Jl 26,9:5
Lanter, Fred M, 1960, Jl 1,25:3
Lanterman, Claude E, 1951, Je 3,92:5
Lanterman, E Tracy (por), 1941, F 9,48:1
Lanterman, George C Mrs, 1949, Jl 6,27:3
Lanterman, W Stanley, 1946, Jl 13,15:4
Lanthear, Harry A, 1950, N 19,93:2
Lanthier, John H, 1916, Ja 7,13:5
Lantry, F J Mrs, 1901, D 23,7:1
Lantry, Francis J, 1922, O 8,30:4
Lantry, J J Police Capt, 1926, O 10,II,9:1
Lantry, Joseph P, 1959, My 31,77:2
Lantry, Joseph W, 1921, Jl 31,22:4
Lantry, Thomas B, 1949, O 11,34:1
Lantry, Thomas H, 1938, N 25,23:3
Lantsberry, Frederick C A H (por), 1939, Je 30,19:4
Lantz, Christian, 1955, O 17,27:4
Lantz, Harvey L, 1958, Ap 5,15:2
Lantz, Henry L, 1953, My 12,27:4
Lantz, Jesse H, 1912, Mr 21,11:4
Lantz, Simon E, 1952, D 28,48:6
Lantzis, Saul, 1956, N 12,29:4
Lanux, Pierre de, 1955, Mr 13,87:2
Lanvin, Jeanne, 1946, Jl 7,36:5
Lanyi, Dezso, 1951, Ap 25,29:3
Lanyon, Peter, 1964, S 3,29:4
Lanyon, Searle H, 1952, Ag 12,19:3
Lanz, Henry, 1945, N 3,15:4
Lanz, R Stanley Jr, 1960, Ja 31,59:7
Lanz Duret, Miguel, 1940, N 22,23:6; 1959, Mr 25,35:3
Lanza, Anthony J, 1964, Mr 24,35:4
Lanza, Clara Marquise, 1939, Jl 15,15:6
Lanza, Frank, 1960, Mr 3,29:1
Lanza, Giovanni, 1882, Mr 10,5:1
Lanza, Joseph, 1961, Ja 29,84:8
Lanza, Lucy R, 1950, My 2,29:1
Lanza, Manuel G, 1943, D 25,13:3
Lanza, Mario (A A Cocozza),(funl plans, O 9,29:3), 1959, O 8,39:1
Lanza, Mario Mrs, 1960, Mr 12,15:5
Lanza, Salvatore Mrs, 1957, Ap 15,29:2
Lanza, Silvio A, 1968, Ag 1,31:4
Lanza, Socks (Jos Lanza), 1968, O 11,47:2
Lanza di Scalea, Pietro, 1938, My 30,11:5
Lanzer, Charles, 1903, F 20,6:5
Lanzetta, James J, 1956, O 29,29:3
Lanzetta, Mary C Mrs, 1947, Je 9,21:4
Lanzillotti, Nicholas, 1949, O 21,25:1
Lanzit, Mortimer, 1960, My 8,88:5
Lanzner, Joseph, 1952, F 18,19:3
Lao, Julian, 1952, Ag 30,13:5
La Ossa, Ernesto de, 1961, S 6,31:1
L'Aoureaux, George H, 1948, F 17,25:5
Lapadula, Anthony C, 1961, F 2,29:2
Lapaire, Hughes, 1967, Ja 3,37:3
La Palme, A Napoleon, 1950, N 2,31:4
Lapan, Henry, 1960, N 12,21:5
La Parcerie, Cora, 1951, Ag 29,25:2
Lapaugh, Arthur S, 1946, N 15,23:3
Lapaugh, William H, 1944, F 9,19:2
LaPaugh, William H Mrs, 1948, F 20,27:1
Lapauze, Jeanne, 1921, Ja 4,13:3
La Paz, Emilio de, 1951, Ag 31,15:1
Lape, Bertha, 1942, Ja 20,19:1
Lape, George F, 1952, Ja 14,19:3
La Pearl, Harry, 1946, Ja 15,23:2
Lapeire, Franklyn J, 1962, My 6,88:3
La Pella, Anthony, 1940, O 20,14:7
La Pena, Marino de, 1921, Je 11,13:5
La Penna, Joseph, 1950, Je 22,27:2
Lapensohn, Harry, 1952, Mr 5,29:4
Laperruque, Savarin's chef, 1904, S 20,9:6
Lapetina, Frank M Sr, 1943, Ja 27,21:3
Lapey, Percy G, 1944, F 6,42:1
Lapeyrouse, Maury, 1965, D 20,35:5
Lapham, Anna R, 1953, Ap 2,27:3
Lapham, Arthur J, 1954, Mr 11,31:2
Lapham, Claude, 1957, My 12,87:2
Lapham, Claude E, 1956, S 25,33:5
Lapham, Dudley H, 1960, My 31,31:4
Lapham, E Gerry, 1921, S 17,13:6
Lapham, Edward M Mrs, 1956, Ag 21,29:4
Lapham, George D Mrs, 1951, Mr 27,29:5
Lapham, Henry G, 1939, D 17,49:1
Lapham, Jesse John, 1911, F 12,12:3
Lapham, Lewis H Mrs (cor, My 18,25:1), 1956, My 17,31:5
Lapham, Nathan D, 1958, My 6,35:1
Lapham, Roger D, 1966, Ap 18,29:2
Lapham, Ruth H Mrs, 1942, N 14,16:3
Lapham, W Z, 1873, O 27,1:5
Lapiana, Fred G, 1956, S 23,84:7
La Pice, John, 1950, D 17,85:2
La Pico, Peter M, 1884, F 19,5:5
Lapidas, Benjamin, 1942, F 9,23:8
Lapienski, John J, 1951, Ja 20,15:4
Lapierre, Arthur W, 1952, Ag 5,19:1
La Pierre, Guy M, 1952, D 13,21:4
Lapierre, Louis A, 1952, D 3,33:6
La Pierre, Louis Mrs, 1944, F 14,17:6
La Pierre, Margaret G Mrs, 1940, D 12,27:5
Lapierre, Ramon Sr, 1950, D 21,29:5
Lapigio, O Serena di Baron, 1941, D 6,17:1
Lapin, Adam, 1961, Ag 25,25:5
Lapin, Sidney, 1959, N 2,31:1
Lapiner, Moses Mrs, 1940, Je 13,23:4
La Pish, Benjamin, 1952, Je 11,29:2
La Plac, St James, 1951, Je 13,29:3
Laplace, Ernest Dr, 1924, My 16,9:3
La Place, John, 1904, Ja 25,5:1
Laplace, Louis B, 1953, D 28,21:3
Laplace, Louis B Mrs, 1953, D 22,31:6
La Place, Louis J, 1960, Ap 20,39:3
LaPlante, Joseph D, 1946, Ag 27,27:3
LaPlante, Wilfred J, 1950, N 29,36:6
La Plaza, Victorino de Dr, 1919, O 3,15:3
Lapman, Maurice, 1951, N 11,90:8
Lapoint, William H, 1948, Ja 1,23:4
La Pointe, Albert A, 1951, D 25,31:5
LaPointe, Ernest, 1941, N 27,23:1
Lapointe, Francis J, 1953, D 1,2:7
Lapointe, George W Jr, 1951, Jl 26,21:5
La Pointe, Harriet Mrs, 1939, F 22,21:4
Lapointe, Ralph, 1967, S 14,47:3
Lapolla, Garibaldi M, 1954, Ja 14,29:3
Lapolla, Michael, 1962, Ap 22,80:8
LaPolt, Harold S, 1946, Ja 25,24:2
Laporte, Alphonse A, 1962, O 30,35:3
LaPorte, Anna M, 1956, S 27,35:3
Laporte, Frank B, 1939, S 26,23:3
La Porte, George, 1954, S 18,15:5
Laporte, George L, 1947, Je 17,25:2
Laporte, William F Sr, 1958, My 18,86:4
La Porte, William R, 1955, Ja 15,13:5
Lapp, Albert W, 1951, Je 14,27:4
Lapp, Charles A, 1944, Mr 21,19:3
Lapp, Charles E Sr, 1951, S 10,21:5
Lapp, Charles W, 1938, N 19,17:2
Lapp, Harvey E, 1953, My 14,29:3
Lapp, John A, 1960, D 31,17:6
Lapp, John A Mrs, 1938, D 2,23:4
Lapp, John S, 1953, My 3,88:8
Lapp, Robinson G, 1960, Ja 23,21:1
Lappano, Ernest, 1962, Mr 2,30:1
Lappe, Charles F Sr, 1952, F 7,27:3
Lappe, Charlotte N S, 1950, F 13,35:4
Lappe, Edward Jr, 1950, F 8,27:5
Lappe, Edward Mrs, 1948, D 25,17:2
Lappen, Morris L, 1947, Je 24,23:2
Lappin, Elizabeth G, 1949, F 15,23:4
Lappin, Harry A, 1945, Ag 17,17:6
Lappin, John B, 1950, F 31,43:2
Lapponi, Giuseppe Dr, 1906, D 8,11:5
Laprade, Lloyd, 1953, N 7,17:4
Laprade, P R De, 1883, D 15,4:7
Lapsley, Gaillard T, 1949, Ag 18,22:2
Lapsley, John W Mrs, 1953, Ap 2,27:2
Lapsley, John Willard, 1921, S 10,11:4
Lapsley, Joseph B, 1955, D 18,93:1
Lapworth, Charles A, 1955, Jl 19,27:6
Laque, John B, 1938, My 3,23:1
Laquer, Fritz O, 1954, My 31,13:2
Laqueur, Ernest (por), 1947, Ag 24,56:4
Lara, Edward M, 1948, S 14,30:2
Lara, Leonidas, 1951, Je 26,29:2
Lara, Raul, 1957, Je 19,35:4
Laraba, Bob, 1962, F 17,20:8
Larabee, Joseph C, 1940, Ag 22,20:3
Laragh, Grace Mrs, 1941, O 8,23:3
Laragh, Harry J, 1938, Je 20,15:5
Laramee, Georges, 1947, Jl 15,23:2
Laramee, Harry J, 1956, Ja 7,17:2
Larard, J, 1879, Ja 31,3:2
Larbaud, Valery, 1957, F 5,23:4
Larbig, William P, 1943, Ap 17,17:2
Larcade, Edouard, 1945, F 6,19:6
Larchar, L Embury Mrs, 1937, Ap 5,19:2
Larchar, Lucy, 1949, Jl 10,56:6
Larchar, Sumner F, 1966, Jl 9,27:4
Larco Herrera, Rafael, 1956, Mr 16,23:3
Larcom, Lucy, 1893, Ap 19,11:1
Larcombe, Dudley T R, 1944, D 6,23:2
Larcombe, Samuel, 1937, O 21,24:2
Lardennois, Georges L, 1940, Ja 7,48:1
Lardin, Paul, 1942, Ja 15,19:2
Lardner, Dionysius Dr, 1859, My 20,4:5
Lardner, Henry, 1954, Mr 6,15:4
Lardner, Henry A, 1952, D 28,48:7
Lardner, J L Rear-Adm, 1881, Ap 13,5:3
Lardner, John A, 1960, Mr 25,28:1
Lardner, John J, 1948, O 7,29:4
Lardner, John Mrs, 1962, Ap 5,33:4
Lardner, R W, 1933, S 26,21:1
Lardner, Rex (por), 1941, Je 24,19:3
Lardner, Ring Mrs, 1960, F 16,37:2
Lardner, William P, 1950, Ag 8,29:3
Lare, William S, 1952, S 18,29:1
Lareau, Earl P, 1948, Jl 15,23:3
Laredo Bru, Federico, 1946, Jl 8,29:1
Laree, Daniel H, 1968, Mr 20,47:3
Lares, James, 1961, F 9,31:3
Lares, Roberto P, 1950, Mr 29,29:2
Larey, Lorraine M, 1944, Jl 30,35:3
Larg, Frederico, 1947, Ap 3,25:1
Largay, Arthur O, 1957, Ag 4,81:2
Largay, James W, 1955, Ja 29,15:4
Large, Alvin L, 1943, Jl 20,19:5
Large, Donald C, 1956, My 23,31:4
Large, George H (cor, Ag 18,19:5), 1939, Ag 16,23:3
Large, George H Mrs, 1937, Ja 6,23:2
Large, George K, 1958, D 25,2:5
Large, George K (will), 1959, Ja 7,18:1
Large, John B, 1947, Ag 30,15:7
Large, John Howard, 1924, Ap 8,19:2
Large, Rex, 1944, Jl 18,19:3
Large, Rex Mrs, 1967, F 15,41:2
Largeman, Morris, 1956, D 4,39:4
Largey, James W, 1943, Ja 27,21:2
Largo Caballero, Francisco, 1946, Mr 23,13:1
Larguier, Leo, 1950, N 1,35:5
Largy, Arthur J, 1939, N 1,23:5
Largy, Charles B, 1939, D 8,25:2
Laria, Anthony A, 1951, D 5,35:5
Larice, Albina M Mrs, 1946, N 19,7:2
Laridon, G A, 1903, My 31,7:6
La Riew, Frederick J, 1942, Ja 7,19:5
Larimer, Robert S, 1941, Ag 25,15:3
Larimore, Dudley T Mrs, 1943, Jl 11,35:2
Larimore, Earle (por), 1947, O 24,23:1
Larimore, H H, 1946, Jl 7,36:2
Larimore, Joseph H, 1944, Ap 20,19:4
Larionov, Aleksei, 1960, S 25,88:7
Larionov, Michael, 1964, My 12,37:2
Larisch, Demeter, 1959, O 9,29:4
Larison, William K Mrs, 1951, N 8,29:2
Lariviere, Amanda Mrs, 1943, Jl 10,13:2
Lark, Charles T, 1946, O 5,17:5
Lark-Horovitz, Karl, 1958, Ap 16,33:3
Larke, Alfred G, 1964, Jl 5,43:3
Larke, George H Mrs, 1951, Jl 19,23:6
Larke, George Harriss, 1921, My 16,15:4
Larke, George T, 1946, F 15,26:2
Larkey, Aaron, 1956, F 2,25:5
Larkey, Benjamin, 1956, Je 24,77:1
Larkey, Charles J, 1946, F 19,25:5
Larkey, Joseph, 1958, N 21,29:5
Larkin, Adrian H, 1942, F 24,21:1
Larkin, Adrian H Mrs, 1960, D 16,38:5
Larkin, Arthur F, 1959, Ag 21,21:4
Larkin, Arthur G, 1966, Mr 9,41:4
Larkin, Arthur Mrs, 1967, Ap 2,93:1
Larkin, Austin J, 1946, Je 18,25:2
Larkin, Barbara W Mrs (B Webb), 1964, S 12,25:6
Larkin, Bessie B, 1942, Jl 31,15:6
Larkin, David H, 1938, Je 19,29:2
Larkin, Denis Mrs, 1952, My 25,92:5
Larkin, Donald R, 1958, Je 18,33:4
Larkin, Edgar Lucien, 1924, O 13,17:6
Larkin, Edmund J Mrs, 1947, Ja 19,53:1
Larkin, Edward, 1951, Ag 2,21:4
Larkin, Edward J, 1941, Je 1,40:3
Larkin, Edward L, 1959, Je 6,21:6
Larkin, Eugene L, 1959, Mr 27,24:7
Larkin, Frank J, 1952, Jl 22,25:2
Larkin, Fred V, 1954, My 25,27:3
Larkin, George A, 1955, Jl 3,32:4
Larkin, George A Mrs, 1943, Ap 13,25:3
Larkin, Henry, 1942, F 2,15:2
Larkin, Hugh P, 1955, O 5,35:4
Larkin, Irvin E, 1951, My 22,31:3
Larkin, J Leslie, 1953, O 29,31:1
Larkin, James, 1903, My 2,9:5
Larkin, James F, 1942, Je 21,36:7
Larkin, John, 1956, Jl 12,23:3; 1965, Ja 31,89:2
Larkin, John A (por), 1948, N 27,17:1
Larkin, John A, 1955, N 27,89:2
Larkin, John D Jr (por), 1945, Ap 4,21:3
Larkin, John F, 1950, Ap 27,29:4
Larkin, John H Dr (funl, Ja 20,13:5), 1923, Ja 19,17:6
Larkin, John J, 1946, O 27,63:3; 1953, Ap 6,19:5
Larkin, John J Mrs, 1943, F 4,23:4
Larkin, John Mrs, 1918, Ap 5,15:5
Larkin, John W, 1953, Ag 4,21:3
Larkin, Joseph A, 1938, O 7,23:5
Larkin, Joseph J, 1959, O 25,86:4
Larkin, Joseph Jr, 1958, Ja 21,29:3
Larkin, Josita Sister, 1903, Ag 23,7:5
Larkin, Julia R, 1944, Ap 16,41:2
Larkin, Lawrence P, 1961, Mr 22,41:2
Larkin, Leo J, 1964, Jl 30,27:5
Larkin, Lewis H, 1951, Mr 16,31:3
Larkin, Margaret, 1967, My 11,47:1
Larkin, Mark, 1963, Je 15,23:6
Larkin, Martin W, 1920, Je 11,13:3
Larkin, Mary E Mrs, 1937, N 1,21:4; 1940, Ag 24,13:6
Larkin, Michael J, 1948, D 14,29:5; 1950, Ag 2,25:5; 1954, Ag 12,25:4
Larkin, P O'Neill, 1912, Je 2,II,13:5
Larkin, Patrick F, 1956, Je 12,35:1

Larkin, Peter Mrs, 1952, O 7,29:5
Larkin, Regis M, 1949, D 1,31:4
Larkin, Ridgley, 1946, My 27,23:3
Larkin, Robert E, 1941, Ja 4,13:1; 1963, Ap 13,19:6
Larkin, Robert E Mrs, 1967, Jl 15,25:5
Larkin, Sarah M, 1939, Je 9,21:2
Larkin, Sylvester P, 1966, F 14,29:3
Larkin, T F, 1928, Jl 26,21:3
Larkin, T M Mrs, 1943, F 28,47:5
Larkin, Thomas A, 1940, D 18,25:5
Larkin, Thomas B, 1941, Mr 20,22:2; 1959, Mr 12,31:4
Larkin, Thomas E, 1967, Je 10,33:2
Larkin, Thomas F, 1940, Jl 23,19:2
Larkin, Thomas F Jr, 1954, O 22,28:1
Larkin, Thomas J, 1937, Je 10,23:3
Larkin, Thomas P, 1950, Jl 19,31:3
Larkin, Thomas W, 1943, F 8,19:6
Larkin, Wayne, 1968, S 14,25:2
Larkin, William F Mrs, 1951, Ja 31,25:4
Larkin, William J, 1938, Ja 25,22:2
Larkin, William P (por), 1945, Ap 1,36:1
Larkin, William T, 1956, Je 8,25:4
Larkins, Carl J, 1958, Mr 8,17:3
Larkins, Charles Darius, 1917, Ja 16,9:3
Larkins, Frederic M, 1954, Mr 14,88:1
Larkins, Reginald H, 1957, Ag 2,19:2
Larkowski, Helena Mrs, 1947, S 2,21:5
Larmon, Park J, 1957, Je 7,24:2
Larmon, Sigurd Mrs, 1964, O 23,39:2
Larmonth, Laura K Mrs, 1938, My 13,19:4
Larnach-Nevill, Guy T M (Lord Abergavenny), 1954, Mr 31,27:1
Larned, Albert C, 1956, Je 2,19:2
Larned, Charles W Col, 1911, Je 20,9:5
Larned, Charles W Mrs, 1949, Je 4,13:4
Larned, E C, 1884, S 19,5:4
Larned, Edwin Channing, 1915, Ag 27,9:6
Larned, Frank H, 1937, Je 23,25:4
Larned, Insley B, 1955, D 4,88:1
Larned, J I Blair Mrs, 1953, Ag 15,15:6
Larned, Linda H Mrs, 1939, Je 25,36:6
Larned, Richard M, 1938, Ap 28,23:1
Larned, W L Mrs, 1905, Ap 4,7:2
Larned, W Livingston, 1960, N 23,29:2
Larned, Walter Cranston, 1914, Je 20,9:5
Larned, William E, 1965, Je 12,31:2
Larned, William Z, 1911, Mr 31,11:4
Larner, Chester W, 1942, Je 14,46:5
Larner, Henry, 1944, F 1,20:2
Larner, Jacques, 1944, S 18,19:3
Larner, Victor, 1954, D 2,31:4
Larner, William A, 1955, Ap 28,29:3
Larney, William A, 1938, F 6,II,8:3
La Rocca, Anthony C, 1949, Je 28,27:3
La Rocca, Dominick J (Nick), 1961, F 23,27:5
La Rocca, James, 1949, Mr 5,18:2
la Roche, Baroness de, 1919, Jl 19,9:6
LaRoche, Clara R Mrs, 1963, O 5,25:2
La Roche, Cloridan, 1915, Mr 25,11:5
La Roche, F A, 1905, Mr 5,9:3
La Roche, Joan H S, 1960, Je 30,29:5
La Roche, Louis F, 1943, Jl 3,13:5
La Roche, Philip V, 1919, O 15,17:2
La Roche, William J Sen, 1908, Ap 5,11:4
La Roche, William T Dr, 1916, My 4,11:5
La Rochefoucauld, Xavier de Count, 1942, F 15,44:3
La Rochelle, J Eugene, 1950, Ap 5,31:4
La Rochelle, Lee R, 1947, Ap 30,25:3
La Rochelle Arth H, 1962, F 13,35:4
Larocque, Joseph, 1955, F 9,27:5
Larocque, Joseph Mrs, 1953, My 8,25:4
La Roe, James P, 1903, N 22,7:5
Laroe, Mark K, 1953, My 29,25:3
Laroe, Robert S, 1947, Ap 15,25:3
LaRoe, Wilbur Jr, 1957, Ap 16,33:2
Larom, Frank W Mrs, 1952, My 12,25:4
Laronne, Alfred, 1961, My 15,31:1
Laroquette, M, 1874, Ag 17,1:7
Laros, Charles F, 1953, Ap 13,27:4
Laros, Russell K, 1955, N 14,27:6
LaRosa, Charles, 1963, Ag 6,31:1
La Rosa, Frank, 1946, Je 12,27:2
La Rosa, Pasquale, 1953, O 30,23:4
La Rosa, Peter, 1968, O 7,47:5
Larose, Anthine W, 1943, D 7,27:3
La Rose, Edmund S, 1959, S 24,37:3
Larose, George, 1953, Ap 21,27:2
Larose, Lloyd J, 1960, Mr 15,39:3
La Rose, Pierre de C, 1941, F 22,15:1
La Rowe, John S, 1940, My 6,17:4
Laroza, Enrique, 1948, Mr 12,23:2
Larquey, Pierre, 1962, Ap 19,31:3
Larrabee, A K, 1880, S 14,5:4
Larrabee, Florence (Mrs F Burnham MacLeary), 1968, D 30,31:1
Larrabee, Harold A Mrs, 1965, Mr 27,27:5
Larrabee, Leon E, 1947, My 26,21:5
Larrabee, Leon Mrs, 1943, N 19,19:1
Larrabee, Stephen H, 1967, F 28,34:2
Larrabee, Walter J, 1940, F 3,13:3
Larrabee, Wilbur P, 1963, Mr 27,4:5
Larrabee, William Ex-Gov, 1912, N 17,17:5
Larranaga, Pedro, 1944, N 24,24:2
Larre, John, 1947, Jl 2,23:5
Larregla, Joaquin, 1945, Je 25,17:3
Larremore, P P, 1884, N 16,2:6
Larremore, Wilbur, 1918, Ag 12,9:7
Larric, Ivy (Mrs Jas C Kevlin), 1968, F 22,32:7
Larric, Jack, 1941, Ag 19,21:4
Larrick, George P, 1968, Ag 13,39:1
Larrimore, George K, 1942, N 12,25:5
Larrimore, Stella (Mrs R Warwick), 1960, D 2,29:1
Larrisey, Fenton P, 1950, Ja 25,27:5
Larrowe, Dwight Morgan, 1914, Ap 12,15:4
Larrowe, James E, 1943, D 14,27:2
Larsen, Alex, 1949, Jl 10,56:7
Larsen, Alfred, 1949, Jl 5,23:2
Larsen, Andrew, 1952, F 6,29:3
Larsen, Andrew P, 1948, Ag 3,26:3
Larsen, Arnold, 1940, Mr 11,15:4
Larsen, Aug, 1950, F 6,25:5
Larsen, Augusta Mrs, 1961, D 3,88:1
Larsen, Charles S, 1939, F 7,19:1
Larsen, Clarence H, 1937, Mr 27,15:5
Larsen, Darrell D, 1965, Jl 26,23:1
Larsen, Edward M, 1945, Ja 25,19:1
Larsen, Emil S, 1952, Je 1,84:4
Larsen, Erik, 1952, Ap 11,6:5
Larsen, Esper S Jr, 1961, Mr 9,30:1
Larsen, F A Duke of Mongolia, 1957, D 21,19:6
Larsen, Frederick, 1950, Ja 9,12:3
Larsen, Gabriel Mrs, 1967, My 16,45:2
Larsen, George P, 1949, F 2,27:4
Larsen, Hanna A, 1945, D 5,25:3
Larsen, Hans M Capt, 1937, S 5,II,6:5
Larsen, Harold Mrs, 1962, S 11,33:5
Larsen, Henry A, 1964, O 30,37:2
Larsen, Henry L, 1962, O 3,41:2
Larsen, Hjalmar R, 1950, Ap 2,93:2
Larsen, Joseph L, 1963, D 3,43:4
Larsen, Julius W, 1952, Ja 16,25:4
Larsen, Karl J Capt, 1944, My 28,6:1
Larsen, Karl Mrs, 1950, F 22,30:2
Larsen, Lars, 1907, My 22,9:4
Larsen, Lauritz Rev (funl, F 2,15:4), 1923, Ja 30,17:4
Larsen, Lawrence G, 1967, Ja 30,29:2
Larsen, Lewis A, 1954, Ag 26,27:4
Larsen, Lewis J, 1917, D 20,11:3
Larsen, Lisa (Mrs N Rasmussen), 1959, Mr 11,35:3
Larsen, Louis, 1953, D 19,15:5
Larsen, Louis J, 1959, Ag 19,30:1
Larsen, Magnus, 1939, D 15,25:4
Larsen, Martin, 1952, N 5,27:3
Larsen, Niels, 1944, Ja 23,38:2
Larsen, Orla A, 1963, Je 30,56:3
Larsen, Payne P Mrs, 1948, Ja 18,61:1
Larsen, Peter, 1951, My 30,21:4
Larsen, Richard L, 1949, F 23,27:2
Larsen, Robert J, 1965, Ag 26,33:4
Larsen, Torkel, 1946, S 8,44:8
Larsen, W W, 1938, Ja 6,19:3
Larson, Alfred, 1963, D 5,45:4
Larson, Andrew, 1945, S 1,11:4
Larson, Arthur H, 1957, F 4,19:3; 1960, D 9,31:2
Larson, Arthur J, 1942, Jl 1,25:6
Larson, Bror O, 1944, Jl 6,15:6
Larson, Carl W, 1954, Je 15,29:2
Larson, Charles, 1949, Mr 18,25:2
Larson, Charles H, 1950, Ap 23,92:7; 1951, D 23,22:4
Larson, Clinton, 1952, Ja 24,28:2
Larson, Dorothy (Mrs B Hotchkiss), 1965, Mr 2,38:7
Larson, Edward G, 1944, Ja 13,21:2
Larson, Emery E, 1945, N 8,19:5
Larson, F Oscar, 1940, F 9,19:5
Larson, Francis D, 1955, D 21,29:2
Larson, G Siegfried, 1950, My 27,17:6
Larson, George V, 1952, Ap 11,23:1
Larson, Gerald, 1965, Ja 7,31:2
Larson, H V, 1948, S 17,25:3
Larson, Harry A, 1939, Je 17,15:2
Larson, Harry E, 1965, Ap 26,31:4
Larson, Henry M, 1958, Je 7,19:4
Larson, Henry P, 1951, D 29,11:1
Larson, Henry P Mrs, 1942, N 2,21:2
Larson, James H, 1954, N 5,21:3
Larson, Jeanette E, 1950, Ap 25,31:2
Larson, John, 1908, O 7,9:7
Larson, John A, 1965, S 24,6:4
Larson, Laurence M, 1938, Mr 10,21:5
Larson, Lewis E, 1953, F 12,28:4
Larson, Mannie, 1939, Ja 17,22:3
Larson, Martin J, 1938, Ag 12,17:1
Larson, Morgan F, 1961, Mr 23,33:1
Larson, Per G, 1940, Jl 10,19:5
Larson, Peter R, 1943, Ag 30,15:6
Larson, Theodore E, 1965, Jl 4,37:1
Larson, Vern E, 1958, Je 23,23:2
Larson, Victor A, 1965, D 10,42:7
Larson, William J, 1952, D 20,17:6
Larson, Winford P, 1947, Ja 2,27:5
Larssen, Thorvald A, 1950, O 30,27:2
Larsson, Ernest G, 1946, Je 3,21:2
Larsson, Gustaf A R, 1940, F 6,21:3
Larsson, Hans, 1944, F 18,17:2
Larsson, Karl, 1952, My 18,92:5
Larsson, Uno, 1941, D 7,79:2
Larter, H Monroe, 1948, Mr 21,60:3
Larter, Roland, 1946, N 21,31:2
Larter, Warren R, 1938, Ja 9,42:6
Lartz, Claude B, 1956, D 10,31:5
Lartz, J Servis, 1956, Ag 22,29:3
Larue, B F, 1878, O 19,2:7
La Rue, Belmont M, 1940, Ap 19,21:5
La Rue, Benn V, 1955, N 14,27:2
La Rue, Carl D, 1955, Ag 21,93:2
Larue, Eugene C, 1947, Mr 23,60:3
Larue, Ira L, 1940, Mr 20,27:4
La Rue, John, 1954, O 16,17:1
La Rue, Jonathan, 1907, D 11,11:4
La Rue, Roy B, 1953, Jl 13,25:4
La Rue, Theodore Rev, 1917, Ag 2,9:4
La Rue, Walter M, 1941, Ja 19,40:2
Larus, Jacob, 1951, N 26,25:5
Larus, Jacob Mrs, 1968, Ag 2,33:3
La Rush, Florence M, 1937, Ja 26,21:5
Lary, J Frank, 1952, My 27,27:4
Larzelere, Walter D, 1951, F 27,27:2
Lasa, Jose Maria, 1953, F 17,27:4
Lasagni, Pietro Cardinal, 1885, Ap 22,5:5
Lasak, John (por), 1949, S 27,29:7
Lasala, Casper P, 1925, Jl 28,13:5
La Sala, Francesco, 1952, O 30,31:2
La Sala, George, 1957, N 30,21:6
LaSalle, Clint W, 1947, O 10,25:4
La Salle, Edmond O, 1950, F 17,24:3
La Salle, George W, 1924, Ap 5,15:5
Lasance, Francis X, 1946, D 13,23:2
Lasar, Jesse, 1954, Ap 17,13:7
Lasbury, Ralph C Sr, 1944, F 13,41:1
Lasby, C C Rev, 1902, N 18,9:5
Lascar Sal, 1874, N 29,10:4
Lascari, Salvatore, 1967, Mr 15,47:2
Lascelle, George T, 1951, S 17,21:4
Lascelle, Ward, 1941, Ja 20,12:1
Lascelles, Alfred G, 1952, F 11,25:6
Lascelles, F, 1934, My 26,17:6
Lascelles, Frank Cavendish Sir, 1920, Ja 3,11:2
Lascelles, John H, 1925, Jl 7,19:5
Lascelles, Mabel C Mrs, 1951, N 25,86:3
Lascelles, Robert J, 1952, N 26,24:7
Lasch, Charles F W Mrs, 1968, Mr 12,43:1
Lasch, Henry, 1908, Ja 19,11:5
Lasch, John A Sr, 1947, S 27,15:5
Lasch, William, 1944, D 21,22:2
Lasche, Alfred J M (por), 1938, N 8,23:4
Lasche, P G, 1954, F 21,68:3
Lasco, Boris, 1947, My 30,21:1
Lascoe, Henry, 1964, S 2,37:2
Lascoff, J Leon (por), 1943, My 6,19:3
Lascurain, Pedro, 1952, Jl 22,25:3
Lasell, Chester W Mrs, 1950, Ap 27,29:3
Lasell, Josiah M, 1939, S 8,23:3
Lasell, Sidney L, 1944, Ja 22,13:5
La Sere, Emile, 1882, Ag 15,5:2
Laserson, Max M, 1951, D 1,13:6
Laserte, Charles J, 1944, Ap 16,42:2
Lasette, Frank B, 1950, D 21,29:5
Lash, James H, 1949, D 19,27:1
Lash, Maria L Mrs, 1903, Ag 13,1:4
Lash, Miller, 1941, O 9,23:2
Lash, Norwood M, 1945, Jl 27,15:4
Lash, William, 1958, Mr 23,88:5
Lashar, Edith H Mrs, 1942, My 8,21:3
Lashar, J Oscar, 1948, My 29,15:4
Lashar, Walter B, 1955, N 7,29:5
La Shelle, Kirke, 1905, My 17,9:6
Lasher, Alfred W, 1958, N 18,37:3
Lasher, Charles, 1951, S 13,31:1
Lasher, Claude K, 1942, N 18,25:2
Lasher, David Mrs, 1956, F 21,33:1
Lasher, Duncan M, 1952, Jl 27,57:1
Lasher, Earl P, 1950, O 30,27:4
Lasher, Edward, 1948, F 11,28:2
Lasher, Frank B, 1939, N 22,24:8
Lasher, George A, 1938, Mr 20,II,8:7
Lasher, George S, 1964, Mr 20,33:1
Lasher, Grant R, 1959, Jl 2,25:3
Lasher, Jack, 1960, Ag 24,29:4
Lasher, Lena M Mrs, 1938, Ja 2,39:8
Lasher, William R, 1946, D 31,17:5
Lasher-Schlitt, Carl D Mrs (Dorothy), 1966, N 36:3
Lashier, Harriet Mrs, 1925, Mr 22,7:3
Lashin, Jacob, 1953, My 12,27:4
Lashin, Nathan A, 1957, O 19,21:4
Lashley, Karl S, 1958, Ag 17,86:2
Lashly, Jacob M (I Dilliard lr on rept, O 28,30: 1967, O 3,47:1
Lashman, William M, 1951, Jl 23,17:4
Lashus, George W, 1938, F 23,23:2
Lashwood, George, 1942, Ja 21,18:3
Lask, Bertha Mrs, 1951, Ap 22,88:1
Laska, Edward, 1959, Ap 29,33:3
Lasker, Albert D, 1952, My 31,1:2
Lasker, Albert D (est tax appr), 1955, Mr 11,
Lasker, Bruno, 1965, S 10,32:4
Lasker, Edouard, 1884, Ja 6,7:1
Lasker, Emanuel (por), 1941, Ja 12,45:1
Lasker, Florina, 1949, S 2,17:3

Lasker, George L, 1949, Ap 12,30:2
Lasker, Henry, 1953, D 12,19:2
Lasker, Jacob, 1941, Ja 18,15:3
Lasker, Lewis, 1957, Ap 28,86:1
Lasker, Loula D (will, Mr 14,27:5), 1961, Ja 30,23:3
Lasker, Morris, 1916, F 29,11:6
Lasker, Myles F, 1940, D 8,71:4
Lasker, Phil, 1949, O 16,88:1
Lasker, Raphael Rabbi, 1904, S 13,9:7
Laskey, Ellis A, 1968, F 6,43:3
Laskey, Henry J, 1943, Jl 21,15:6
Laskey, Joseph B, 1959, Ap 3,27:1
Laskey, Phil B, 1940, N 28,23:3
Laski, Harold J, 1950, Mr 25,13:1
Laski, Leon, 1923, Jl 29,6:5
Laski, Nathan, 1941, O 21,23:5
Laski, Nathan Mrs, 1945, Mr 2,19:3
Laskier, Frank, 1949, Jl 9,28:8
Laskin, Herbert N, 1958, N 23,88:6
Laskin, Jacob, 1958, Ag 22,21:3
Lasky, Jacob S Mrs, 1959, N 6,29:3
Lasky, Jesse L, 1958, Ja 14,33:1
Lasky, Joseph, 1968, Mr 6,47:2
Lasky, Max, 1915, F 2,7:6
Lasky, Sarah Mrs, 1946, Ja 31,21:2
Lasler, Emery L, 1940, Jl 28,26:7
Lasley, Theodore H, 1954, Ap 8,27:5
Lasner, Edwin Mrs, 1963, N 25,20:3
Lasner, Jacob, 1960, S 3,17:4
LaSor, Allan, 1953, D 22,31:5
La Spada, Salvatore, 1957, S 19,29:2
Lass, Ernest C, 1952, Jl 21,19:3
Lass, Jacob, 1950, Je 25,68:6
Lass, Louis, 1953, S 16,33:3
Lassalle, Jan, 1909, S 8,9:4
Lassans, J Pierre, 1962, Jl 6,25:3
Lasscell, William B, 1914, N 7,11:6
Lassen, Abraham L, 1957, Mr 21,31:5
Lassen, Ben, 1968, O 7,47:2
Lassen, Carl J, 1950, O 21,17:5
Lassen, Edward W Mrs, 1951, D 23,22:4
Lassen, Emil Mrs, 1953, D 16,35:5
Lassen, Emil V S Mrs, 1964, Ag 1,21:3
Lassen, Helene S Dr, 1920, Mr 27,13:3
Lassen, Larsine, 1951, Jl 24,32:8
Lassen, Louis Mrs, 1946, O 15,25:5
Lassen, May G, 1925, O 15,23:4
Lassen, Oscar (por), 1949, My 18,27:4
Lassen, Oscar Mrs, 1942, Ap 10,17:3
Lassen, Rowland W, 1958, Je 4,33:2
Lassen, Valdemar Mrs, 1961, Ap 5,37:5
Lassen, Wilhelm, 1908, Ap 7,9:4
Lasser, Donald J, 1962, F 9,29:5
Lasser, Jac A, 1948, My 8,15:4
Lasser, Jacob K, 1954, My 12,31:1
Lasser, Sarah Mrs, 1941, F 14,17:4
Lasser, Sydney, 1950, N 12,93:2
Lassere, Edward, 1947, O 8,25:1
Lasserre, Frederic, 1961, Ap 9,29:1
Lassiat, Raymond C, 1960, N 15,39:4
Lassiter, C K Mrs, 1944, D 21,21:5
Lassiter, Francis R, 1909, N 1,11:4
Lassiter, Herbert C, 1950, Jl 1,15:6
Lassiter, wm, 1959, Mr 30,31:5
Lassoe, John Van P, 1962, Je 3,88:2
Lassoe, Valdemar F, 1912, My 23,13:5
Lassoff, Theodore, 1955, Jl 9,15:4
Last, Edwin J, 1951, Mr 23,21:3
Last, Erwin, 1948, F 14,13:3
Last, Matias, 1941, Jl 21,15:4
Last, Murray A, 1953, Je 26,19:6
Last, Samuel E, 1942, S 27,48:1
Lastavica, Stefan, 1966, My 11,47:2
La Stayo, Paul H, 1942, S 6,30:6
Laster, Alan, 1965, Jl 5,17:3
Laster, Matilda C, 1964, D 25,29:4
Lasteyrie, C, 1936, Je 29,15:4
Lasteyrie, Count de, 1879, My 15,2:6
Lastic, Charles R, 1942, N 12,25:2
Lastowsky, Alex, 1950, Mr 2,27:5
Lastra Charriez, Alfonso, 1946, D 6,23:4
Lastreto, Emilio, 1946, F 24,43:1
La Sueuer, Anna B Mrs, 1958, Ag 16,17:2
Laszlo, Aladar, 1958, S 19,27:2
Laszlo, Alex F, 1963, Ap 20,27:4
Laszlo, Andras E, 1960, O 18,39:2
Laszlo, Daniel, 1958, Je 2,27:2
Laszlo, George, 1965, N 16,47:3
Laszlo, Nicholas J, 1955, N 19,19:1
Laszlo, Phil de (por), 1937, N 23,23:1
Laszowski, Gerard de Mme, 1905, Ja 12,7:2
Latane, J A Bp, 1902, F 25,9:5
Latane, J H, 1932, Ja 2,11:5
Latane, James A, 1955, N 11,25:3
Latasa, Vincente T, 1944, F 20,36:3
Latch, Edward Biddle, 1911, Ap 4,11:5
Latchaw, Austin, 1948, Ja 25,56:3
Latcher, Buel, 1948, My 23,68:5
Latcher, Buel Mrs, 1940, Ap 26,21:2
Latchford, F R, 1938, Ag 14,32:7
Latchford, Stephen F, 1960, Je 16,33:5
Latendorf, E Walter, 1957, N 19,30:2
Laterman, Edward Mrs, 1943, Mr 31,19:2
Laterre, Harvey W, 1955, O 16,87:1
La Terza, Ermenegildo, 1939, N 7,25:5
Latey, Harry N, 1948, Jl 13,27:6
Latham, Carl R Mrs, 1942, N 9,23:1
Latham, Charles A, 1944, N 28,23:4
Latham, Charles A Mrs, 1945, Je 19,19:5
Latham, Charles L, 1960, Mr 11,25:2
Latham, Clarence F, 1950, F 18,27:3
Latham, Daniel (funl), 1957, S 14,17:5
Latham, Edward W, 1939, Ap 27,25:2
Latham, Ernest B, 1945, S 4,23:4
Latham, Ernest R Mrs, 1950, My 12,27:3
Latham, Everett B Mrs, 1943, S 16,21:4
Latham, Fred G (por), 1943, F 1,15:1
Latham, Frederick P, 1961, Je 20,33:2
Latham, George W, 1947, F 26,25:5
Latham, Harry O Mrs, 1951, D 23,22:3
Latham, Hope, 1951, Ap 11,29:1
Latham, J Scott, 1942, My 25,15:4
Latham, James R, 1951, Ag 1,23:3
Latham, John C, 1909, Ag 19,7:5
Latham, John G, 1964, Jl 25,19:3
Latham, Joseph C Sr, 1948, Ja 10,15:1
Latham, Leon D Sr, 1947, N 25,32:3
Latham, LeRoy, 1938, Jl 26,19:4
Latham, M S, 1882, Mr 5,7:3
Latham, Minor W, 1968, Ja 30,38:1
Latham, Orval R, 1940, Jl 10,19:3
Latham, Peter, 1953, N 23,27:4
Latham, Pierre W, 1944, Ja 12,23:3
Latham, Vida, 1958, Ja 18,15:4
Latham, Walter A (Arlie), 1952, N 30,88:4
Latham, William G, 1953, N 10,31:5
Latham, William H Jr, 1967, Ap 18,41:1
Latham, William R, 1942, S 23,26:2
Lathan, George, 1942, Je 15,19:2
Lathan, Robert, 1937, S 27,21:4
Lathbury, Albert A Rev, 1937, Mr 2,21:2
Lathbury, Clarence, 1939, N 12,48:7
Lathero, Charles, 1960, Mr 17,33:1
Latherow, George C, 1944, D 12,23:5
Lathers, Ida, 1945, My 11,19:4
Lathers, Richard Col, 1903, S 18,7:3
Lathers, Richard Mrs, 1904, F 4,9:5
Lathrop, Alanson P, 1950, Ap 16,106:1
Lathrop, Alfred L, 1949, My 12,31:4
Lathrop, Alice L, 1940, Ap 10,25:2
Lathrop, Austin, 1921, S 21,15:6
Lathrop, Austin E, 1950, Jl 27,26:3
Lathrop, Benjamin G Mrs, 1964, O 28,45:1
Lathrop, C Huntington, 1953, F 1,88:2
Lathrop, C N, 1931, Ja 31,17:1
Lathrop, Charles H, 1941, Ja 5,44:8
Lathrop, Clarence E, 1944, Ap 7,20:3
Lathrop, Cornelia P, 1938, Ja 16,II,8:8
Lathrop, Edward P, 1940, My 6,17:2
Lathrop, Edward P Mrs, 1952, Je 1,84:5
Lathrop, Edward Rev Dr, 1906, Ap 6,11:5
Lathrop, F E, 1876, Jl 18,5:6
Lathrop, Florence M, 1947, D 17,30:2
Lathrop, Francis, 1909, O 19,9:4; 1909, O 21,9:4
Lathrop, Francis S, 1882, Mr 5,7:3
Lathrop, Francis S Mrs, 1907, Ap 2,11:5
Lathrop, Frank C Mrs, 1953, Jl 6,17:5
Lathrop, Frank W, 1960, Ag 21,84:5
Lathrop, G P, 1877, O 13,8:5; 1898, Ap 20,7:1
Lathrop, Gardiner, 1938, Ja 22,18:2
Lathrop, Gayle J (Sept 29), 1965, O 11,61:3
Lathrop, H Clinton, 1947, Mr 17,23:3
Lathrop, H O, 1951, My 13,89:1
Lathrop, Helen, 1941, Jl 17,19:1
Lathrop, Henry R, 1953, Ap 4,13:5
Lathrop, Henry R Mrs, 1953, Mr 14,15:4
Lathrop, Ida P Mrs, 1937, S 8,23:1
Lathrop, J, 1932, Ap 16,18:1
Lathrop, James Gray, 1923, S 23,7:5
Lathrop, James Roosevelt, 1907, Mr 13,9:5
Lathrop, John H, 1866, Ag 10,2:5; 1967, Ag 23,51:2
Lathrop, John Judge, 1910, Ag 25,7:5
Lathrop, John K, 1948, Ap 3,15:4
Lathrop, Joseph B, 1950, D 28,25:4
Lathrop, L H, 1883, Mr 20,2:3
Lathrop, Levi Chapman, 1909, F 3,9:6
Lathrop, Louis A Mrs, 1911, My 19,11:4
Lathrop, Mary G, 1949, Ap 5,29:2
Lathrop, Patrick I M Lt-Com, 1919, N 22,13:2
Lathrop, Ruth W, 1940, Ag 1,21:5
Lathrop, Spencer Mrs, 1958, Ap 17,31:3
Lathrop, Stephen Hubbard, 1904, F 3,9:6
Lathrop, Thomas S Mrs, 1948, Mr 27,13:5
Lathrop, Walter B, 1903, Ag 13,14:6
Lathrop, William, 1907, N 20,9:6
Lathrop, William A, 1912, Ap 13,13:5
Lathrop, William G, 1948, Ja 14,25:2
Lathrop, William M, 1950, Ja 6,21:2
Lathrope, Howard R, 1965, Ag 19,31:5
Latilla, Herbert G, 1949, Ag 20,11:4
Latimer, A E Lt-Col, 1905, Mr 21,11:4
Latimer, Arsa, 1922, Mr 22,13:3
Latimer, Asbury C (funl, F 22,7:2), 1908, F 21,7:5
Latimer, Benton R Mrs, 1948, S 15,31:1
Latimer, Brainard G, 1917, Je 1,9:4
Latimer, Charles H, 1943, N 16,23:4
Latimer, Clyde B, 1952, S 29,23:4
Latimer, Courtenay, 1944, Je 16,19:4
Latimer, Dana E, 1950, Je 3,15:6
Latimer, Elizabeth, 1912, My 16,11:3
Latimer, Empie, 1948, Ja 5,19:4
Latimer, Faith (Mrs M O Miller), 1903, My 12,9:5
Latimer, Frederick P, 1940, O 9,25:3
Latimer, George, 1945, D 14,28:3
Latimer, Herbert G, 1954, Mr 1,25:4
Latimer, J Carter, 1953, F 8,88:3
Latimer, J L, 1968, Mr 25,41:4
Latimer, Julian L (por), 1939, Je 5,17:1
Latimer, Lewis S Mrs, 1955, S 6,25:2
Latimer, Marvin L, 1953, Ap 18,19:4
Latimer, Mary E W Mrs, 1904, Ja 5,1:4
Latimer, Maxcy G, 1942, O 14,25:4
Latimer, Robert C, 1950, Je 13,27:3
Latimer, Thomas E, 1937, N 7,34:8
Latimer, W K Commodore, 1873, Mr 16,5:5
Latimer, Wendell M, 1955, Jl 7,27:1
Latimer, William N, 1922, Mr 22,13:3
Latino, Francisco, 1945, O 18,23:3
Latino, Manuel, 1957, Mr 24,86:1
Latner, Martin H Mrs, 1942, O 23,22:2
La Tona, Alexander, 1907, Jl 23,7:4
La Torella, Charles A, 1967, My 4,39:2
Latorraca, Nicolo M, 1940, Je 18,23:5
la Torre, Carlos Maria de Cardinal, 1968, Ag 1,31:3
Latorre, Fernando C, 1953, My 22,27:3
la Touche, Gaston de Pellerin de, 1920, N 4,13:4
Latouche, John T (funl, Ag 10,17:2; trb lr, S 2,II,3:8), 1956, Ag 8,25:3
Latouche, John T Mrs, 1956, Ja 30,27:3
La Tour, Charles, 1939, My 24,23:3
Latour, F S (Don), 1927, N 9,25:1
Latour, James A, 1945, F 5,15:3
la Tour, Pierre Imbart de, 1925, D 19,17:4
La Tourette, Herman R, 1943, My 6,19:2
Latourette, James Mrs, 1949, My 10,25:4
Latourette, La Forde, 1953, F 22,60:6
Latrobe, Ferdinand C Gen, 1911, Ja 14,11:5
Latrobe, Ferdinand C 2d, 1944, My 6,15:6
Latrobe, Gamble, 1922, Je 22,15:6
Latrobe, Osmun (por), 1939, D 8,25:2
Latrobe, Osmun Col, 1915, O 9,9:4
Latshaw, Benjamin I, 1942, Jl 7,20:2
Latshaw, David G, 1950, S 23,17:2
Latson, Almet R (por), 1943, F 2,19:1
Latta, A B, 1865, My 2,2:1
Latta, Cecil, 1937, D 29,5:4
Latta, Cuthbert H, 1949, F 18,24:2
Latta, J P, 1911, S 12,11:5
Latta, John (por), 1949, Je 20,19:2
Latta, John E, 1950, O 21,17:5
Latta, Matthew M, 1953, O 9,27:4
Latta, Maurice C (por), 1948, Ap 4,60:4
Latta, Robert, 1940, N 7,25:2
Latta, Thomas L, 1961, Ja 10,47:2
Latta, William J, 1938, O 1,17:3
Latta, William J Sr, 1958, Ja 8,47:1
Lattanner, Victor, 1949, Ja 18,23:3
Latter, Harry, 1961, O 5,37:2
Latter, Herbert E, 1945, Ja 16,19:5
Latter, Rose H, 1948, Jl 16,19:3
Lattes, Elijah Prof, 1925, Je 23,19:5
Lattes, Ernesto Dr, 1937, Ap 4,II,11:2
Lattey, Henry, 1937, My 26,25:5
Lattimer, David W, 1953, Ap 24,23:4
Lattimer, George M Sr Mrs, 1968, Ap 27,39:5
Lattimer, Samuel, 1946, Ag 28,27:6
Lattimer, William, 1876, O 8,6:7
Lattimore, David Mrs, 1952, N 9,91:1
Lattimore, O E Mrs, 1955, S 28,35:1
Lattimore, S A Prof, 1913, F 18,13:5
Lattin, C Irving Mrs, 1940, O 13,49:2
Lattin, Clarence L, 1939, N 23,27:4
Lattin, Frank H Dr, 1937, My 25,27:1
Lattin, Henry W, 1943, D 25,13:4
Latting, Charles P, 1943, Jl 26,19:3
Latting, Emerson Mrs, 1955, Ag 5,11:6
Latting, Walter S, 1925, Ja 24,13:4
Lattman, Jacob, 1945, D 19,25:3
Lattman, Morris, 1962, Ja 24,33:3
Lattomus, James W, 1947, Ag 5,23:3
Lattre de Tassigny, Bernard de, 1951, My 31,3:7
Lattre de Tassigny, Jean de, 1952, Ja 12,3:5
Lattre de Tassigny, Roger de, 1956, Ap 11,33:2
LaTulip, Harold J, 1962, Jl 22,64:2
Latus, George W, 1941, Mr 12,21:4
Latz, Ana D de (will), 1937, Jl 3,4:6
Latz, Augustus, 1915, Je 16,11:4
Latz, Benno E, 1953, O 3,17:2
Latz, C Irving, 1947, F 14,21:1
Latz, Milton, 1948, Ap 21,27:2
Latzer, John A, 1952, Je 30,19:4
Latzis, Jan, 1937, Mr 12,23:2
Latzko, William, 1945, F 13,23:3
Latzo, Pete, 1968, Jl 9,39:1
Lau, Ferdinand C, 1938, Ag 12,17:4
Lau, Luther C Sr, 1958, Mr 9,86:6
Lau, Max, 1943, My 31,17:2
Lau, Robert F, 1943, O 7,23:4
Lau, Robert J Rev Dr, 1925, D 8,25:4

Laub, Alex, 1951, My 15,31:5
Laub, David (Danny Murphy), 1967, Ja 1,52:1
Laub, Elias, 1949, O 7,27:4
Laub, Herbert F, 1959, My 25,29:4
Laub, Leon C, 1958, Ap 24,31:2
Laub, Moriz, 1944, Ag 13,35:1
Laub, Roswell C, 1955, N 12,19:2
Laubach, Charles M, 1941, Ja 23,21:3
Laubach, George A Mrs, 1951, N 4,86:4
Laubach, William H, 1952, Jl 20,53:2
Laubach, William H Mrs, 1951, My 31,27:3
Laube, Alfred J (por), 1949, S 28,27:5
Laube, Alfred R Mrs, 1959, S 22,39:3
Laube, Benjamin J, 1944, Ap 6,23:5
Laube, Charles A, 1951, S 6,31:2
Laube, Henri, 1884, Ag 2,4:6
Laube, Otto T, 1956, Mr 16,23:2
Lauben, John J, 1938, Mr 10,21:3
Laubenheimer, Mary M Mrs, 1939, N 24,23:5
Laubenheimer, Roy C Mrs, 1958, Ap 11,25:1
Laubenstein, Arthur E, 1966, Jl 21,33:2
Lauber, Calvin G, 1950, Ja 5,25:4
Lauber, Hubert C, 1949, D 30,19:4
Lauber, Joseph, 1948, O 19,27:4
Lauber, Urban S, 1953, F 2,21:4
Lauber, William F, 1948, Ag 25,25:1
Lauber, William Mrs, 1952, Mr 13,30:4
Laubersheimer, Daniel H, 1941, Ja 4,13:3
Laubeuf, Max, 1939, D 24,14:8
Laubscher, Ernest T, 1959, O 26,29:2
Laubshire, George M, 1948, Ja 20,23:2
Laucella, Nicholas, 1952, S 5,27:3
Lauchheimer, Charles H Brig-Gen, 1920, Ja 16,9:5
Lauchheimer, Jacob, 1925, N 13,19:6
Lauchheimer, Robert M, 1938, F 19,15:1
Laucius, Frank C, 1949, Ja 4,40:2
Lauck, Joseph E, 1957, Jl 30,23:5
Lauck, W Jett, 1949, Je 18,13:6
Lauckhardt, Ernst, 1942, Jl 11,13:3
Lauckhardt, Otto W Mrs, 1944, N 16,23:5
Lauckner, Alan K, 1966, Mr 17,43:6
Laucks, S Forry, 1942, Ap 12,44:5
Laud, Sam, 1963, Ag 2,27:4
Laudenbach, Henry B, 1943, D 30,17:1
Laudenschlager, Thurmond H, 1948, S 27,23:1
Laudenslager, Clarence, 1951, Ja 30,25:5
Laudenslager, Claude M T, 1957, N 10,86:7
Lauder, Edwin G Jr, 1955, Mr 2,27:4
Lauder, George, 1924, Ag 25,13:4
Lauder, George Jr, 1916, Ja 5,13:8
Lauder, George Jr Mrs, 1957, Mr 19,37:3
Lauder, George Mrs, 1913, N 20,11:4
Lauder, Harry, 1950, F 27,1:2
Lauder, Jack, 1950, Mr 10,27:2
Lauder, Lady, 1927, Ag 1,19:4
Lauder, Robert L, 1945, Ag 3,17:2
Lauder, William H Mrs, 1949, Je 23,27:2
Lauderback, H C, 1951, Ap 5,29:4
Lauderback, H C Mrs, 1948, S 6,13:5
Lauderburn, Frederic C, 1940, Ja 20,15:5
Lauderdale, Earl of (Rev Alf Sydney Fredk Maitland), 1968, N 29,89:4
Lauderdale, Lord of (Maitland), 1953, F 19,23:4
Laudig, Oscar O, 1945, Ja 24,21:5
Laue, Arthur E, 1966, Jl 3,34:7
Laue, Max von, 1960, Ap 25,29:3
Lauenroth, Lillian, 1915, Ag 22,13:2
Lauer, Carl F, 1957, Je 12,35:3
Lauer, Conrad N (por), 1943, Ag 3,19:3
Lauer, Conrad N Mrs, 1940, Ja 16,23:4
Lauer, Edgar J (por), 1948, N 10,29:1
Lauer, F, 1883, S 7,4:7
Lauer, George E Mrs, 1959, Ja 8,29:1
Lauer, George W, 1951, Jl 9,25:6
Lauer, Helen M, 1945, O 3,19:2
Lauer, Isidore, 1940, S 9,15:5
Lauer, John, 1959, F 11,39:3
Lauer, John B, 1941, N 28,24:2
Lauer, John H, 1962, Ap 15,80:6
Lauer, John R, 1956, N 30,23:4
Lauer, Joseph A Rev, 1905, Mr 1,9:5
Lauer, Matthew J, 1954, S 6,15:4
Lauer, Nicholas, 1953, Jl 20,17:2
Lauer, Nicholas Prof, 1937, O 9,19:3
Lauer, Stewart E, 1962, My 4,33:2
Lauer, Theodore W, 1963, Ap 27,25:6
Lauer, Vernon Mrs, 1955, S 18,87:1
Lauer, Walter, 1940, My 2,23:3
Lauer, Walter E, 1966, O 16,89:3
Lauerman, William D, 1952, S 29,23:6
Laufenberg, Walter P, 1949, F 6,76:6
Laufer, Calvin W, 1938, S 21,25:4
Laufer, Edward B Mrs, 1967, My 10,47:4
Laufer, Jacob, 1957, Je 26,31:2
Laufer, Leon D, 1954, My 5,31:5
Laufer, Louis, 1941, D 10,25:4
Lauferty, Lilian (Mrs J Wolfe), 1958, F 20,25:4
Lauffer, Joseph, 1943, Je 16,21:3
Lauffer, Vada K Mrs, 1948, My 11,25:2
Lauffer, William M, 1942, F 25,19:5
Laughlin, Alexander, 1943, Ag 31,17:1
Laughlin, Alice D, 1952, Ag 1,18:3
Laughlin, Anne I, 1947, F 28,23:1
Laughlin, Charles E, 1940, Mr 31,44:1
Laughlin, Clara E, 1941, Mr 4,23:4
Laughlin, Donald S, 1959, Jl 9,27:4
Laughlin, E V, 1938, N 19,17:2
Laughlin, Edwin B, 1939, Jl 13,19:2
Laughlin, Frank C (por), 1943, Ja 20,19:1
Laughlin, Frank S, 1942, D 16,25:2
Laughlin, Gail, 1952, Mr 14,23:4
Laughlin, George M, 1948, Ag 17,21:4
Laughlin, George M Jr (por), 1946, Mr 10,46:3
Laughlin, George M Mrs, 1949, F 15,23:5
Laughlin, George McCully Maj, 1908, D 12,11:2
Laughlin, H Hughart, 1938, Ja 3,21:1
Laughlin, Harriet M Mrs, 1940, N 1,25:5
Laughlin, Harry H, 1943, Ja 28,20:2
Laughlin, Henry A, 1922, Mr 23,13:4
Laughlin, Hice R, 1943, Jl 31,13:2
Laughlin, Hugh C, 1944, F 13,41:3
Laughlin, Irwin, 1941, Ap 19,15:3
Laughlin, Irwin Mrs, 1958, F 21,23:3
Laughlin, J B, 1928, Ag 13,17:5
Laughlin, J L, 1933, N 29,19:1
Laughlin, J Lee, 1937, N 5,23:5
Laughlin, James E Mrs, 1955, Jl 26,25:1
Laughlin, James Mrs, 1925, F 7,15:5
Laughlin, John E, 1939, S 24,44:4
Laughlin, John Jr, 1953, Ja 20,8:5
Laughlin, John Mrs, 1916, F 25,11:6
Laughlin, John S, 1945, Mr 15,23:5; 1962, Jl 11,36:1
Laughlin, John Sr, 1953, Ja 19,14:5
Laughlin, Mike (M J Loughran Sr), 1950, Je 28,27:3
Laughlin, Richard C, 1940, Ap 9,23:2
Laughlin, Robert V, 1948, Ag 24,23:4
Laughlin, Sara, 1955, S 3,15:4
Laughlin, Thomas I, 1965, Jl 22,31:3
Laughlin, Thomas K (funl, Mr 14,7:5), 1910, Mr 12, 9:3
Laughon, Absalom B, 1944, Je 20,19:3
Laughton, Charles (ed, D 18,6:2; funl, D 20,8:1), 1962, D 17,15:6
Laughton, Eliza Mrs, 1953, Mr 15,92:6
Laughton, Eliza Mrs (will), 1954, Je 3,32:6
Laughton, James F, 1962, Je 10,86:7
Laughton, Norris H, 1943, Ag 10,19:4
Laugier-Villars, Diane de, 1946, O 30,27:3
Lauinger, Frederick Sr, 1946, Mr 16,13:2
Laul, John Dr, 1924, My 14,19:6
Lauman, Arthur A, 1951, Ap 8,93:1
Lauman, George N, 1944, N 2,19:5
Lauman, Henry J Mrs, 1941, Mr 26,23:3
Laun, Albert C, 1944, Ja 13,21:5
Laundree, William, 1946, N 20,31:4
Laundrie, Eli J Jr Mrs, 1951, Jl 24,25:5
Laune, Virginia V M de, 1943, Je 15,21:3
Laune, William, 1919, S 22,11:3
Launer, Louis, 1953, Mr 12,27:4
Launitz, Robert E (funl), 1874, F 15,8:3
Laupman, Pavel P, 1957, Ap 20,17:6
Laura, M, 1936, Ap 14,22:3
Laureano, Napoleao, 1951, Je 1,26:1
Laureate, Frankie, 1949, Jl 15,19:5
Laurel, Jose P, 1959, N 6,29:1
Laurel, Stan (A S Jefferson),(funl, F 27,25:2), 1965, F 24,41:1
Laurell, George D, 1956, My 15,32:8
Laurell, Klas E, 1950, My 23,29:2
Lauren, Bertus C, 1953, Ag 20,27:1
Laurence, Abram Burtt Col, 1912, Ap 3,13:5
Laurence, Alexander J Jr, 1943, S 21,23:1
Laurence, Archer C, 1947, My 8,25:4
Laurence, Charles Edward, 1907, Ap 7,9:5
Laurence, Daniel, 1961, Ja 4,33:5
Laurence, Daniel Mrs, 1951, O 25,29:1
Laurence, E Z, 1882, Ja 15,5:5
Laurence, George Sir, 1916, F 25,11:4
Laurence, Georgia, 1923, Ja 14,6:2
Laurence, J C, 1908, F 8,7:5
Laurence, Lionel E, 1914, Ja 31,11:5
Laurence, Sydney, 1940, S 13,23:2
Laurence, William, 1921, Mr 18,15:6
Laurence, William T, 1909, Ap 9,9:4
Laurencelle, J Eugene, 1962, N 16,31:2
Laurencena, Eduardo, 1959, Jl 20,25:3
Laurencin, Marie, 1956, Je 9,17:6
Laurendeau, Francis X, 1942, O 20,21:3
Laurens, Jean Paul, 1921, Mr 24,17:4
Laurent, Charles, 1939, F 20,17:2
Laurent, Emilio, 1946, Mr 2,13:3
Laurent, Georges, 1964, S 26,23:5
Laurent, T Clifford Mrs, 1960, Jl 20,29:4
Laurenti, Camillo Cardinal (por), 1938, S 7,25:3
Laurenti, Mario, 1922, Mr 8,15:6
Laurentie, Pierre Sebastian, 1876, F 10,1:3
Laurey, Albert (Kid Ash), 1955, D 18,92:8
Laureyns, Gerard H, 1942, D 4,25:4
Laureys, Henry, 1958, Ap 27,86:2
Lauri, Lorenzo, 1941, O 8,9:6
Lauria, Larri, 1965, D 27,23:7
Lauriat, Charles E, 1937, D 29,22:2
Laurice, Carmine, 1948, N 26,23:3
Lauricella, Bartholomew Mrs, 1949, Ag 13,11:3
Lauricella, Louis F, 1961, Ja 8,86:7
Laurie, Frank A, 1959, My 24,89:1
Laurie, Henry J, 1962, Ja 16,33:4
Laurie, James A, 1954, Ag 3,19:3
Laurie, Joe Jr (will, My 7,24:7), 1954, Ap 30,23:1
Laurie, Joe Jr Mrs, 1956, Ag 22,29:2
Laurie, Joe 3d, 1955, My 11,31:5
Laurie, John D Sir, 1954, Jl 21,27:3
Laurie, Percy, 1962, F 18,93:1
Laurie, Robert D, 1953, Ap 9,27:3
Laurie, Thomas, 1952, Je 13,23:3
Laurier, Israel Dr, 1923, F 6,19:4
Laurier, Wilfrid Lady, 1921, N 2,17:5
Laurier, Wilfrid Sir, 1919, F 23,18:1
Laurillard, E, 1936, My 8,23:5
Laurin, Arne, 1945, F 19,17:5
Laurino, Alfred Mrs, 1967, S 25,45:1
Laurita, Sister (C Dwyer), 1950, Je 27,29:5
Lauritsen, Charles C Dr, 1968, Ap 14,76:8
Lauritsen, Louis, 1942, My 21,19:5
Lauritzen, Lauritz, 1964, Jl 20,25:1
Lauritzen, Lauritz Mrs, 1959, Je 21,92:8
Lauro, Peter, 1945, O 26,19:3
Laursen, Svend, 1960, F 12,27:2
Laurvik, John N, 1953, My 5,29:4
Laury, Preston A, 1942, Je 10,21:1
Laury, Theodore N A, 1946, Ja 28,19:4
Lauryssen, Gaston, 1962, O 16,39:3
Laus, Abdon F, 1945, Jl 30,19:5
Lausmann, Bohumil, 1958, Je 30,19:3
Lausten, Caltoft F, 1966, Je 16,47:6
Lautebach, Emanuel Mrs, 1946, Ag 4,45:1
Lauten, Henry G F, 1951, My 28,21:3
Lautenberg, Saul, 1952, My 20,25:5
Lautenschlager, Edward A, 1955, Ja 3,27:5
Lautenschlager, Stanton, 1950, Je 9,23:2
Lauter, Frederick Sr, 1950, Mr 21,29:3
Lauter, Herman, 1959, N 2,31:2
Lauter, Kurt C, 1959, N 21,23:2
Lauter, Philip, 1945, My 29,15:5
Lauterbach, Edward (por),(funl, Mr 7,15:4), 1923, Mr 5,15:1
Lauterbach, Edward, 1958, Jl 7,27:2
Lauterbach, Jacob S Mrs, 1942, Je 20,13:3
Lauterbach, Jacob Z, 1942, Ap 15,21:2
Lauterbach, John, 1946, N 3,64:4
Lauterbach, Richard E, 1950, S 21,31:5
Lauterborn, George, 1941, Jl 10,19:3
Lauterer, Arch, 1957, Je 11,35:1
Lauterjung, Fritz, 1949, N 22,29:2
Lauterpacht, Hersch, 1960, My 10,37:1
Lauterstein, Leon (cor, S 2,25:4), 1967, S 1,31:1
Lautier, Louis R, 1962, My 8,39:3
Lautman, David, 1956, Jl 4,19:6
Lautman, Louis, 1952, Jl 23,24:5
Lautman, Maurice, 1938, S 27,21:3
Lautner, John E, 1943, Je 29,19:3
Lautrec, Gabriel de, 1938, Jl 26,19:3
Lautrup, George W, 1956, Je 10,88:4
Lautz, Frank, 1948, Ja 15,23:2
Lautz, Frank Mrs, 1944, My 12,19:2
Lautz, John, 1944, S 19,21:4
Laux, August, 1921, Jl 24,22:4
Laux, Frank C, 1941, N 11,23:1
Laux, Howard E, 1962, Je 5,41:4
Laux, John J, 1939, F 9,21:4
Laux, Leo J, 1950, O 25,35:3
Lav, A M, 1879, D 9,5:3
Lava, Vincente, 1947, S 17,25:4
Lavachelli, Harry, 1944, S 6,19:6
Laval, Charles J, 1946, Mr 13,30:2
Laval, Jean M Bp, 1937, Je 5,17:5
Laval, Pierre Mrs, 1959, D 12,23:2
Laval, W L (Billy), 1957, Ja 22,29:5
Lavalle, Dominick, 1952, Je 5,31:4
Lavalle, Leander, 1947, F 20,26:2
Lavallee, George A, 1953, Jl 30,23:5
Lavallee, James L, 1948, F 13,21:4
Lavan, John L, 1952, Je 1,84:4
Lavanburg, F L, 1927, N 6,29:1
LaVance, Joseph E Sr, 1962, S 5,39:4
La Vanco, Frank P, 1951, Jl 17,27:2
Lavarack, John D, 1957, D 5,35:3
Lavarnway, William B, 1940, Je 11,25:2
Lave, Daniel W, 1949, Jl 28,23:3
Laveau, Marie, 1881, Je 23,2:3
La Vecchia, Louis Mrs, 1949, Je 22,31:2
La Vecchia, Nicholas, 1940, Ag 20,19:5
Lavedan, Henri L, 1940, S 21,19:6
Laveleye, Victor de, 1945, D 16,40:6
Lavell, James, 1939, Je 10,17:4
Lavell, Thomas E Mrs, 1967, N 22,47:2
Lavelle, Elizabeth G Mrs, 1937, F 23,27:5
Lavelle, Francis E, 1953, Jl 15,25:4
Lavelle, George Aloysius, 1922, My 8,17:4
Lavelle, George F, 1945, N 13,22:3
Lavelle, George J, 1952, Ja 10,29:1
Lavelle, Helen M, 1955, O 23,86:7
Lavelle, Jack, 1958, D 5,31:3
Lavelle, John M, 1951, Ag 21,27:4
Lavelle, Margaret C, 1942, Jl 16,19:5
Lavelle, Martin A, 1947, N 1,15:3
Lavelle, Michael J Mrs, 1939, O 18,1:2
La Velle, Paul B, 1942, My 6,19:5
Lavelle, Peter J, 1923, Ap 3,23:5

Lavelle, Sarsfield P, 1941, S 14,50:4
Lavelle, Tracy F, 1953, F 8,89:2
Lavelle, Walter J, 1951, My 6,93:1
Laven, Paul, 1950, My 2,30:2
Lavenberg, Leonard, 1965, My 1,31:4
Lavender, Harriet E, 1948, S 2,23:2
Lavender, James S, 1960, Ja 15,31:2
Lavender, John G, 1941, O 31,23:5
Lavender, William E, 1945, F 17,13:2
Lavene, Jacob C, 1942, Ag 17,15:6
Lavenson, Jay, 1968, Ap 15,43:3
Lavenstein, Harry H Mrs, 1957, Je 7,23:4
Lavenstein, Meyer H, 1957, Mr 26,33:2
Laventall, Louis J, 1941, D 21,41:2
Laver, William E, 1939, Ag 22,19:5
Laveran, A Dr, 1922, My 19,17:6
La Verde, Sabato, 1946, Ag 8,21:5
Laverick, William J Mrs, 1961, N 13,29:6
Laverie, James R (por), 1947, Mr 1,15:6
Laverie, Robert H, 1951, Ap 23,25:4
Laverie, Robert H Mrs, 1952, S 18,29:2
La Verne, Lucille (por), 1945, Mr 7,21:3
La Verne, Norris, 1942, D 14,23:2
Lavers, Percy L, 1960, Ag 28,30:5
Laverty, Caroline M, 1945, D 8,17:5
Laverty, Edgar R, 1955, Mr 23,31:4
Laverty, James F, 1940, Jl 11,19:2
Laverty, James P, 1939, Ap 25,23:6
Laverty, Jesse W, 1951, S 18,25:8
Laverty, Robert G, 1956, Jl 23,23:4
Laverty, Seamus Mrs, 1966, Jl 29,31:1
Lavery, Albert E, 1944, D 29,15:2
Lavery, Charles A, 1938, Ap 16,13:2
Lavery, Charles V, 1944, Je 28,23:4
Lavery, Daniel J, 1943, F 16,19:5
Lavery, Francis X, 1961, Mr 27,31:5
Lavery, Fred L, 1947, Mr 24,25:3
Lavery, Hugh A, 1961, My 2,37:1
Lavery, Hugh A Mrs, 1952, O 11,19:3
Lavery, James, 1959, N 5,35:4
Lavery, John (por), 1941, Ja 11,17:1
Lavery, John C Mrs, 1949, N 27,104:5
Lavery, Thomas C, 1944, My 17,19:6
Lavery, Urban A, 1959, Ag 21,21:4
Lavery, William G, 1961, Ag 21,23:5
Laves, Kurt, 1944, Mr 28,19:5
Lavey, Arthur D, 1956, Je 27,31:2
Lavezzo, James, 1947, O 22,30:3
Lavezzorio, John, 1962, Mr 23,33:5
Lavia, John T, 1964, Mr 18,41:4
La Vier, Alfred, 1939, F 18,15:1
Lavigerie, C M A Cardinal, 1892, N 27,16:7
Lavigne, Arthur D, 1950, Jl 19,31:3
Lavigne, G H, 1928, Mr 10,12:8
Lavigne, Jerome R, 1942, Mr 3,24:2
Lavigne, Louis A M, 1946, Jl 16,23:1
Lavin, Bernard F, 1951, D 6,33:2
Lavin, Charles M Mrs, 1943, Ag 22,36:7
Lavin, Clement J, 1952, Je 18,27:2
Lavin, Edward J, 1943, O 22,17:3
Lavin, Frank P, 1952, S 18,29:4
Lavin, Henry St C, 1965, Mr 23,39:4
Lavin, J M Dr, 1925, D 8,25:4
Lavin, John, 1963, N 10,86:4
Lavin, John J Mrs, 1955, Ja 9,87:1
Lavin, Michael, 1940, My 4,17:5
Lavin, Michael J, 1952, O 15,31:2
Lavin, Patrick A, 1951, F 12,23:5
Lavin, Patrick J, 1945, Mr 1,21:3
Lavin, Robert, 1946, Ag 19,29:3
Lavine, Harry, 1937, Jl 10,15:4
Lavine, Joseph, 1963, N 16,27:1
Lavine, Louis L, 1943, Je 5,15:1
La Vine, Mary H Mrs, 1951, O 27,19:5
Lavine, Mollie Mrs, 1947, Je 17,22:6
Lavine, Phil S, 1957, F 3,77:2
Lavine, Sidney A, 1950, Ja 18,31:2
Lavinsky, Hyman, 1952, O 8,31:3
Laviolette, Jack, 1960, Ja 11,45:3
Laviolette, Leo E, 1948, N 8,21:1
Lavis, Charles J, 1939, Ag 13,29:2
Lavis, Fred, 1950, N 26,90:3
Lavis, Maurice G, 1937, Mr 5,21:5
Lavisse, Ernest, 1922, Ag 19,11:6
La Vista, Frank W, 1963, Jl 6,15:5
Lavitrano, Luigi, 1950, Ag 3,23:1
Lavner, Harry S, 1965, Ja 23,25:6
LaVochkin, Semyon (funl, Je 12,19:8), 1960, Je 10, 31:4
Lavoie, Alphonse J, 1940, Ap 26,21:2
Lavoie, Aurel G, 1952, O 28,31:4
Lavorante, Alejandro, 1964, Ap 2,38:4
Lavoriotes, Chrysogonos, 1963, Ap 25,33:5
Lavoy, Merl, 1953, D 9,11:6
Lavrangas, Dionig, 1941, Ag 1,15:6
Lavrenev, Boris, 1959, Ja 8,29:2
Lavrenov, Ivan, 1966, D 7,47:3
Lavrovsky, Leonid, 1967, N 28,47:2
Law, Alfred L, 1959, Ap 21,35:5
Law, Andrew Bonar (funl), 1923, N 3,13:6
Law, Benedict W, 1924, F 21,17:6
Law, Bernard A, 1955, S 1,23:2
Law, Charles, 1953, Jl 23,23:3
Law, Charles B Jr, 1942, Mr 23,15:1
Law, Charles Mrs, 1937, Je 24,25:3
Law, Charles S Jr, 1955, O 25,33:4
Law, Clarence L, 1952, D 26,15:3
Law, Clarence L Mrs, 1944, S 9,15:4
Law, David H, 1945, F 22,28:2
Law, Donald E, 1967, Ja 9,39:1
Law, E, 1881, O 6,5:5
Law, E M Maj-Gen, 1920, N 1,15:6
Law, Edward M, 1943, O 11,19:5
Law, Fannie Mrs, 1941, Ap 18,23:2
Law, Francis, 1953, S 3,23:4
Law, Francis M, 1907, Ja 6,II,9:6
Law, Frank, 1941, Mr 4,23:1
Law, Frank F, 1950, Je 6,29:1
Law, Fred H, 1942, Mr 31,21:2
Law, Frederick H, 1957, S 9,25:3
Law, Frederick M, 1947, F 15,15:1
Law, George, 1881, N 19,8:1
Law, Glen C, 1950, My 1,25:2
Law, Gordon E, 1938, D 28,26:5
Law, Hayward R, 1954, Jl 8,23:2
Law, Henry I, 1955, Ja 1,13:2
Law, Herbert E, 1952, Ja 20,84:6
Law, Howard G, 1944, N 15,27:2
Law, Howard G Mrs, 1938, O 10,19:4
Law, Hugh, 1883, S 11,5:2
Law, Ilma B Mrs, 1940, N 18,19:3
Law, Isabella, 1950, Jl 28,21:3
Law, James Dr, 1921, My 11,17:5
Law, James M, 1954, D 8,35:4
Law, Jenny L, 1961, Ja 2,25:2
Law, John, 1919, Ag 31,22:2
Law, John A, 1949, D 20,31:4
Law, John B, 1962, O 16,39:1
Law, John Mrs, 1951, Je 19,29:2
Law, Leonard Mrs, 1950, O 29,95:1
Law, Louis S, 1964, Ap 2,33:4
Law, Lyman T, 1943, Ja 6,25:6
Law, Mary L, 1940, O 13,48:7
Law, Michael S, 1946, O 6,58:8
Law, Owen B, 1923, Mr 3,13:3
Law, Pierce, 1948, Ag 2,21:2
Law, R L Com, 1869, Ja 14,5:5
Law, Robert H Jr Mrs, 1948, N 19,28:2
Law, Rodman, 1919, O 15,17:3
Law, Russell (por), 1942, D 23,19:3
Law, Russell Mrs, 1956, My 21,25:5
Law, Sarah A, 1883, Mr 9,5:6
Law, Thomas A, 1967, Ap 16,83:1
Law, W H, 1881, Ap 3,7:3
Law, Wallace J, 1955, D 19,27:5
Law, Walter, 1940, Ag 10,13:6
Law, Walter F, 1956, Mr 24,19:4
Law, Walter W (funl, Ja 20,23:3), 1924, Ja 19,13:4
Law, Walter W, 1958, Ag 28,27:5
Law, Walter W Mrs, 1949, Ag 19,17:4
Law, William A Mrs, 1947, Mr 7,25:4
Law, William F, 1959, Je 11,33:4
Law, William I, 1958, My 28,31:2
Law, Willie, 1940, Je 26,23:5
LaWall, Charles H Dr, 1937, D 8,25:5
Lawall, Elmer H, 1939, D 9,15:4
Lawall, Harold J, 1948, Mr 11,27:1
La Wall, Millicent R Mrs, 1939, Je 27,23:3
Lawall, Paul, 1965, D 1,47:4
Lawand, Shaker, 1942, Je 4,19:2
Lawby, William E (por), 1944, Ja 20,19:2
Lawch, Louis, 1962, Mr 17,25:3
Lawder, Donald, 1959, Ja 17,19:4
Lawder, Edward A, 1947, Ap 14,27:2
Lawder, H Miller, 1966, Ap 5,39:2
Lawder, J L, 1965, F 27,25:2
Lawder, Robert H, 1951, My 14,25:5
Lawder, Sam R, 1950, Jl 13,25:6
Lawes, Albert L, 1966, S 23,37:1
Lawes, Charles C, 1955, Ja 22,11:6
Lawes, Ernest F Sr Mrs, 1947, Ap 22,27:2
Lawes, George, 1952, Ap 28,19:5
Lawes, Herbert J, 1964, N 4,39:2
Lawes, Lewis E, 1947, Ap 24,25:1
Lawes, Sarah Mrs, 1938, Ja 7,20:1
Lawford, Betty (Mrs B Buchanan), 1960, N 21,29:5
Lawford, Ernest E (por), 1940, D 28,15:1
Lawford, Hugh R, 1946, S 25,27:3
Lawford, Sidney, 1953, F 16,21:1
Lawford, William, 1955, S 16,23:3
Lawhead, A Louis, 1951, D 20,31:3
Lawhead, Leo A Jr, 1949, O 20,29:3
Lawhead, William D, 1968, Jl 17,43:3
Lawhon, Zim E, 1943, N 8,19:6
Lawler, Alfred J, 1952, Mr 16,90:6
Lawler, Andrew M Mrs, 1967, Jl 28,31:1
Lawler, Austin J, 1950, Je 27,29:2
Lawler, Edmond V Sr Mrs, 1953, S 22,31:4
Lawler, Edward W Sr, 1956, D 29,15:5
Lawler, Fenton J, 1951, D 30,24:2
Lawler, Francis J, 1958, O 22,35:1
Lawler, George A, 1943, Ap 30,21:5
Lawler, George S, 1941, N 2,52:8
Lawler, George W, 1939, Ag 24,19:3
Lawler, J C, 1903, S 30,9:6
Lawler, James W, 1951, N 3,17:6
Lawler, John, 1943, F 17,21:3
Lawler, John A, 1949, Ap 15,23:5
Lawler, John J, 1948, Mr 12,23:3
Lawler, Joseph, 1955, N 26,19:4
Lawler, Joseph G Mrs, 1946, My 14,21:1
Lawler, Joseph H, 1956, Jl 17,23:3
Lawler, Kathleen Mrs, 1952, Ja 14,19:3
Lawler, Michel F, 1962, S 30,86:4
Lawler, Percy E, 1949, Ja 14,23:2
Lawler, Robert J, 1942, O 2,25:2
Lawler, T G Col, 1908, F 4,7:5
Lawler, Thomas B Mrs, 1943, Jl 11,35:2
Lawler, William V, 1945, S 8,15:3
Lawles, Thomas D, 1939, Mr 28,23:1
Lawless, Albert S, 1949, Ap 20,27:3
Lawless, Emily, 1913, O 24,11:5
Lawless, Francis T, 1956, Mr 7,33:5
Lawless, John, 1951, D 24,13:4
Lawless, John L F, 1950, N 9,33:3
Lawless, John T, 1960, Ap 25,29:2
Lawless, Martin Judge, 1903, N 20,9:6
Lawless, Richard A, 1945, S 24,19:2
Lawless, Thomas F, 1953, Ap 2,27:1
Lawless, Thomas P, 1942, D 14,28:3; 1947, Je 14,15:3
Lawless, William J, 1943, D 25,13:2
Lawless, William T, 1947, N 11,27:3
Lawley, Henry S, 1957, Ag 22,27:2
Lawley, John, 1922, S 11,17:7
Lawley, John T, 1947, S 23,25:2
Lawley, William G, 1963, Ag 28,26:8
Lawlin, Richard A, 1954, Jl 21,27:5
Lawlor, Agnes (Sister Mary Leona), 1963, Ap 19, 43:2
Lawlor, Charles B, 1925, Je 1,15:2
Lawlor, Daniel J, 1950, D 27,27:2
Lawlor, David S, 1943, Ja 17,44:4
Lawlor, Ethel, 1949, S 7,30:5
Lawlor, Frank J, 1940, Ja 9,24:3
Lawlor, Jerome N, 1956, My 8,33:2
Lawlor, John F, 1957, O 30,29:2
Lawlor, Joseph J, 1939, N 23,27:3
Lawlor, Joseph M, 1955, Ag 8,21:4
Lawlor, Lily (will), 1938, D 1,21:2
Lawlor, Martin, 1959, S 4,21:3
Lawlor, Matthew J, 1946, D 26,25:4
Lawlor, Michael J Mrs, 1948, Ja 14,25:3
Lawlor, Patrick H, 1909, Mr 11,9:4
Lawlor, Roy W Sr, 1957, N 17,87:1
Lawlor, Theodore P, 1942, My 11,15:6
Lawlor, Thomas F, 1941, Ap 20,42:2
Lawlor, William F, 1959, Je 22,25:3
Lawlor, William J, 1949, Je 14,31:3
Lawman, Jasper, 1906, Ap 2,6:3
Lawney, Josephine C, 1962, Mr 1,31:2
Lawrance, Charles L, 1950, Je 25,68:1
Lawrance, Francis C Mrs, 1908, My 11,7:5
Lawrance, Howard B, 1958, D 11,13:4
Lawrence, A M, 1882, Je 12,5:4
Lawrence, Abraham R Mrs, 1915, Jl 1,11:5
Lawrence, Abraham Riker Ex-Justice, 1917, F 15,11:5
Lawrence, Adelaide C Mrs, 1937, Mr 8,19:3
Lawrence, Albert A, 1950, My 19,27:4
Lawrence, Alex Sir (cor, S 8,23:1), 1939, S 4,19:6
Lawrence, Allan, 1968, Je 17,39:3
Lawrence, Alva A, 1942, F 21,19:3
Lawrence, Amory A, 1912, Jl 7,II,11:5
Lawrence, Amos A, 1948, N 16,29:5
Lawrence, Andrew, 1942, D 2,25:4
Lawrence, Andrew W Sr Dr, 1937, O 22,24:3
Lawrence, Anna C V Mrs, 1955, S 21,33:3
Lawrence, Annie Mrs, 1940, Mr 16,15:6
Lawrence, Annie T, 1942, D 22,25:5
Lawrence, Arnette R, 1942, D 3,25:4
Lawrence, Arthur Mrs, 1951, Ap 6,25:3
Lawrence, Arthur P D, 1955, Mr 23,31:3
Lawrence, Arthur Rev, 1909, S 21,9:5
Lawrence, Arthur W (por), 1937, O 22,24:1
Lawrence, Asa, 1941, D 29,17:3
Lawrence, Ashton C, 1937, Je 21,19:2
Lawrence, Augustine Nicholas, 1919, D 3,15:2
Lawrence, Bayard C, 1959, F 14,21:4
Lawrence, Benjamin B, 1921, Ja 22,11:4
Lawrence, Benjamin F, 1965, My 11,39:3
Lawrence, Benjamin L, 1951, D 20,32:2
Lawrence, Bertha L, 1952, S 18,29:3
Lawrence, Bertram H, 1953, Mr 27,23:3
Lawrence, Bro, 1908, Je 8,7:6
Lawrence, Byron T, 1952, S 30,31:2
Lawrence, C B Judge, 1883, Ap 10,5:5
Lawrence, C E, 1940, Mr 16,15:4
Lawrence, Caleb W, 1939, My 23,23:5
Lawrence, Carl G, 1954, Ag 27,21:5
Lawrence, Carl G Mrs, 1959, My 19,33:1
Lawrence, Caroline H Mrs (will), 1939, Ap 23,III,8:3
Lawrence, Catharine, 1941, My 18,43:3
Lawrence, Catherine Mrs, 1939, My 2,23:1
Lawrence, Catherine R Mrs, 1955, Jl 28,23:6
Lawrence, Cecil V, 1949, Ja 20,27:6
Lawrence, Charles A, 1942, F 7,17:3
Lawrence, Charles Capt, 1909, Je 21,7:4
Lawrence, Charles D Mrs, 1957, Ap 21,89:2
Lawrence, Charles H, 1910, O 29,11:6; 1945, Mr 14, 19:5; 1951, Ap 1,93:1

Lawrence, Charles T Mrs, 1947, Ag 19,23:2
Lawrence, Charlotte S Mrs, 1939, Jl 27,19:5
Lawrence, Chester B Mrs, 1947, F 2,50:2; 1966, Jl 23, 25:1
Lawrence, Chester H Mrs, 1949, Ag 10,21:4
Lawrence, Christopher, 1954, Ap 22,24:2
Lawrence, Clark J, 1966, N 11,43:4
Lawrence, Clinton C, 1952, Ag 19,23:3
Lawrence, Clinton E, 1949, Jl 19,29:4
Lawrence, Clyde H, 1940, Ag 19,17:6
Lawrence, Cornelius Van Wyck, 1861, F 21,5:3
Lawrence, Cyrus J, 1908, Ja 10,7:5; 1908, Ja 13,7:4
Lawrence, D H, 1930, Mr 4,27:1
Lawrence, Daniel, 1942, F 21,19:2
Lawrence, Daniel W, 1921, My 11,17:5
Lawrence, David L (funl, N 26,35:5), 1966, N 22,1:4
Lawrence, DAvid L (est acctg filed), 1967, My 22, 84:2
Lawrence, Dora C Mrs, 1941, Ap 18,21:2
Lawrence, Dowager Lady, 1918, Ja 22,11:5
Lawrence, Dwight Alden, 1903, Jl 26,7:6
Lawrence, E A, 1883, Je 5,2:6; 1883, Jl 25,2:5
Lawrence, E F, 1946, Mr 1,22:2
Lawrence, E S, 1924, Ja 16,19:5
Lawrence, E Wallace, 1946, My 8,25:4
Lawrence, Edgar A, 1964, O 25,88:6
Lawrence, Edgar V (will), 1906, Ap 24,11:4
Lawrence, Edmund, 1944, Ag 2,15:2
Lawrence, Edson R, 1964, D 25,29:3
Lawrence, Edward, 1947, Ap 14,27:4; 1960, F 4,31:1
Lawrence, Edward F, 1945, S 8,15:6
Lawrence, Edwin R, 1938, S 28,25:5
Lawrence, Edwin R Mrs, 1952, S 10,29:3
Lawrence, Effingham, 1956, S 10,27:2
Lawrence, Effingham N, 1963, N 2,25:4
Lawrence, Elizabeth J Mrs, 1948, Mr 9,23:4
Lawrence, Ellsworth C, 1954, O 18,25:1
Lawrence, Emlen Newbold, 1925, Ag 11,21:5
Lawrence, Enoch P Dr, 1918, Jl 27,9:6
Lawrence, Ernest M, 1943, My 27,25:2
Lawrence, Ernest O (trb, Ag 29,23:3; funl Ag 31,-56:3), 1958, Ag 28,1:6
Lawrence, Eunice C Mrs, 1903, O 30,1:1
Lawrence, F E (mem ser), 1879, N 3,8:6
Lawrence, F E Rev Dr, 1879, Je 14,3:5
Lawrence, F Vinton Jr, 1955, Ja 19,27:1
Lawrence, F Vinton Mrs, 1944, D 11,23:5
Lawrence, Frances Mrs, 1941, Ja 21,22:3
Lawrence, Francis Cooper, 1911, Ag 20,II,9:6
Lawrence, Frank J, 1923, Je 18,13:6
Lawrence, Frank M, 1948, Mr 29,21:5
Lawrence, Frank P, 1957, My 28,33:4
Lawrence, Frank R (funl, O 30,11:4), 1918, O 28,11:3
Lawrence, Franklin, 1953, Ap 27,23:3
Lawrence, Franklin W, 1939, Mr 30,23:4
Lawrence, Fred T, 1940, Ja 18,23:2
Lawrence, Frederic Newbold, 1916, D 25,9:4
Lawrence, Frederick B, 1948, Mr 15,23:5
Lawrence, Frederick T Mrs, 1955, D 23,17:4
Lawrence, G Philip, 1961, Ag 10,27:3
Lawrence, G St P Sir, 1884, N 19,2:4
Lawrence, George F, 1947, O 25,19:2
Lawrence, George H Jr, 1940, Ag 2,15:5
Lawrence, George J (por), 1949, N 10,32:4
Lawrence, George Mrs, 1945, Ap 30,19:4; 1948, F 9, 17:4
Lawrence, George N, 1907, F 11,9:5
Lawrence, George P, 1917, N 22,13:5
Lawrence, George R, 1938, D 16,25:5
Lawrence, George V, 1865, O 19,4:1
Lawrence, George W, 1939, My 30,17:4; 1954, F 12, 25:3
Lawrence, George W Mrs, 1941, O 17,23:5; 1948, Ap 9,23:3
Lawrence, Gertrude, 1952, S 7,1:2
Lawrence, Gertrude E, 1941, My 2,21:4
Lawrence, Gustavus G, 1952, My 4,91:1
Lawrence, Harry C, 1939, D 21,23:5
Lawrence, Harry V, 1953, D 23,25:1
Lawrence, Helen (will), 1948, N 25,41:6
Lawrence, Henry, 1904, Mr 8,9:7
Lawrence, Henry C, 1919, S 14,22:3
Lawrence, Henry E, 1954, D 20,29:6
Lawrence, Henry W, 1924, Ap 6,27:1; 1942, Ja 25,40:5
Lawrence, Herbert, 1882, Mr 1,5:2; 1943, Ja 19,19:5; 1949, Jl 15,19:4
Lawrence, Herbert F, 1956, Ja 22,89:1
Lawrence, Herbert M, 1953, D 25,17:5
Lawrence, Herbert R, 1960, Jl 9,19:3
Lawrence, Herbert R Mrs, 1943, Je 19,13:5
Lawrence, Horace M, 1954, Ap 7,31:6
Lawrence, Howard C, 1946, Je 11,23:4
Lawrence, Isaac, 1919, Ap 18,13:3
Lawrence, Isaac A, 1903, S 2,7:6
Lawrence, Isadore M, 1950, F 8,27:1
Lawrence, J Campbell, 1954, S 26,87:2
Lawrence, J Duncan Mrs, 1945, D 18,27:4
Lawrence, J E, 1878, Jl 16,2:3
Lawrence, J G K, 1895, Je 23,1:4
Lawrence, J Joseph, 1944, Ja 27,19:4
Lawrence, J S, 1880, Je 6,7:5; 1903, Ap 2,9:5
Lawrence, James, 1904, Ag 5,7:6; 1939, Je 9,21:3; 1939, Ag 9,17:4
Lawrence, James B, 1941, D 30,19:4
Lawrence, James E, 1941, My 21,23:2; 1957, S 18,33:1
Lawrence, James Judge, 1914, Jl 5,5:6
Lawrence, James Van Horn, 1915, Jl 18,15:5
Lawrence, Janet M Mrs, 1939, N 20,19:4
Lawrence, Jeannette R Mrs, 1937, Mr 21,II,8:4
Lawrence, Jesse E Mrs, 1949, Mr 26,17:2
Lawrence, Jesse J, 1949, My 5,27:4
Lawrence, John, 1912, S 23,13:6; 1950, S 20,31:2
Lawrence, John C, 1944, Ag 27,33:2
Lawrence, John F, 1944, Ja 18,19:4
Lawrence, John H, 1959, N 23,31:3
Lawrence, John H Mrs, 1959, Ja 14,27:1
Lawrence, John J, 1942, O 16,19:2
Lawrence, John Lord, 1879, Je 28,2:5
Lawrence, John S Mrs, 1937, O 24,II,8:6
Lawrence, John W, 1945, Ja 28,37:2
Lawrence, Joseph S, 1950, Ag 26,13:4
Lawrence, Joseph Sir, 1919, O 26,22:3
Lawrence, Joseph W, 1947, My 29,22:3
Lawrence, Justus B Mrs, 1963, Ap 8,47:3
Lawrence, Katherine C, 1945, N 14,19:6
Lawrence, Lawrence S Sr, 1965, Ap 16,29:4
Lawrence, Leonard A, 1947, Ag 12,24:3
Lawrence, Leslie, 1941, F 27,19:3
Lawrence, Lewis H, 1905, Je 18,7:6
Lawrence, Lina, 1949, Ja 25,23:2
Lawrence, Louis, 1949, Mr 29,25:4
Lawrence, Lucien Jr, 1953, F 22,60:6
Lawrence, Lulu A, 1953, Ja 30,22:3
Lawrence, M J, 1922, D 1,17:5
Lawrence, Malcolm R, 1925, N 18,23:4
Lawrence, Margaret G N Mrs, 1943, Je 14,17:5
Lawrence, Maria J M (will), 1938, S 16,23:7
Lawrence, Marion, 1924, My 4,23:2
Lawrence, Mary M, 1943, Ag 25,19:2
Lawrence, Merrill L, 1925, O 24,15:6; 1953, Ap 25, 15:6
Lawrence, Mildred R, 1942, Mr 5,23:3
Lawrence, Morris, 1939, O 22,41:2
Lawrence, Mortimer W, 1967, F 27,29:1
Lawrence, Neville Mrs (por), 1947, F 22,13:1
Lawrence, Newbold T, 1968, N 20,47:1
Lawrence, Oscar, 1966, O 6,47:1
Lawrence, Parker Vesie, 1919, Je 21,15:6
Lawrence, Paul S, 1947, O 22,29:2
Lawrence, Paul W, 1951, Ja 22,17:4
Lawrence, Philip, 1882, Ag 3,8:3
Lawrence, Philip L, 1961, Ja 23,23:5
Lawrence, Prescott, 1921, N 14,15:1
Lawrence, Prescott Mrs, 1948, Ap 1,25:3
Lawrence, R B (Larry), 1951, Ja 12,27:3
Lawrence, R Burchard, 1944, N 13,19:6
Lawrence, Ralph W, 1961, Ag 9,33:5
Lawrence, Ralph W Sr Mrs, 1956, Ag 14,25:4
Lawrence, Refine L Mrs, 1946, Ja 20,42:5
Lawrence, Reginald, 1967, N 22,47:4
Lawrence, Reina A, 1948, Ja 4,23:4
Lawrence, Richard A, 1940, S 29,43:1
Lawrence, Richard F, 1966, Ap 7,36:1
Lawrence, Richard Mrs, 1961, Mr 8,33:3
Lawrence, Richard W (por), 1948, O 8,25:1
Lawrence, Richard W Mrs, 1945, Mr 1,21:1
Lawrence, Robert, 1938, Ag 18,19:2
Lawrence, Robert B, 1942, S 4,24:4
Lawrence, Robert C, 1944, F 22,23:4
Lawrence, Robert J, 1952, D 2,36:5
Lawrence, Robert S, 1957, My 31,19:4
Lawrence, Robert Sr Mrs, 1954, D 14,33:3
Lawrence, Robert V, 1950, My 25,29:4
Lawrence, Robert W, 1947, F 5,23:1
Lawrence, Roscoe, 1947, Je 13,23:5
Lawrence, Roscoe C, 1938, Ja 21,20:3
Lawrence, Rulif V, 1938, S 18,44:4
Lawrence, Ruth W, 1956, Je 16,19:6
Lawrence, Sam, 1959, O 27,37:3
Lawrence, Samuel B, 1939, Jl 27,19:4
Lawrence, Samuel B Col, 1908, Mr 20,7:6
Lawrence, Samuel C Gen, 1911, S 25,9:4
Lawrence, Samuel Gen, 1914, Mr 23,11:4
Lawrence, Seabury, 1922, O 23,15:4; 1946, Je 28,21:4
Lawrence, Stillson F, 1957, N 16,19:4
Lawrence, Susan (por), 1947, O 25,19:5
Lawrence, T B Col, 1869, Mr 22,1:1
Lawrence, T E, 1935, My 19,1:2
Lawrence, Theodore, 1941, Mr 18,23:2; 1964, Ja 13, 35:3
Lawrence, Theodore F, 1947, Je 27,21:5
Lawrence, Theron R Mrs, 1944, Ap 25,23:6
Lawrence, Thomas F, 1949, Jl 5,23:3
Lawrence, Thomas H, 1945, S 18,23:3; 1954, F 20,17:4
Lawrence, Thomas L, 1953, Ja 19,23:2; 1959, Ag 1, 17:2
Lawrence, Townsend, 1951, O 31,29:3
Lawrence, Townsend Mrs, 1913, My 17,11:5
Lawrence, Victor D, 1948, Ja 11,56:5
Lawrence, Victor H, 1958, D 5,31:1
Lawrence, Vincent, 1946, N 26,29:6
Lawrence, Vivian S Jr, 1952, F 21,27:4
Lawrence, W B, 1881, Mr 26,5:5
Lawrence, W E, 1882, F 8,5:5
Lawrence, W H Mrs, 1903, S 8,7:6
Lawrence, W Van D, 1927, My 17,29:3
Lawrence, Walter A, 1961, Mr 11,21:5
Lawrence, Walter B, 1912, Ja 13,13:4; 1955, Ag 17, 27:4
Lawrence, Walter J, 1951, D 3,31:4
Lawrence, Walter N, 1920, F 29,22:3
Lawrence, Walter R, 1940, My 30,17:4
Lawrence, Walter R Sir (cor, S 8,23:1), 1939, S 4,19
Lawrence, Walter S, 1947, F 3,19:2
Lawrence, Wardington G Mrs, 1956, Ap 19,31:2
Lawrence, Warrington G, 1938, Ag 2,19:3
Lawrence, Watson A, 1951, N 6,29:4
Lawrence, Willard C, 1952, Ja 3,46:4
Lawrence, William, 1874, Mr 7,7:4
Lawrence, William (por),(will, N 19,25:6), 1941, N 7,23:1
Lawrence, William A, 1938, Ag 4,17:5; 1941, Ap 16, 23:3
Lawrence, William C, 1944, My 23,23:3; 1950, N 21, 31:1
Lawrence, William C Mrs, 1945, Mr 23,19:2
Lawrence, William F, 1921, Ja 30,22:4
Lawrence, William G, 1950, N 30,33:3
Lawrence, William H, 1938, Mr 4,23:4; 1940, Ja 2, 19:3; 1949, Ag 10,21:2; 1960, Ja 13,48:1
Lawrence, William H Gen, 1874, N 30,5:2
Lawrence, William H Mrs, 1957, O 9,35:1
Lawrence, William H Rev Dr, 1914, D 15,13:6
Lawrence, William M Mrs, 1956, Mr 24,19:5
Lawrence, William Mrs, 1949, Ap 29,23:4
Lawrence, William P, 1958, F 8,19:4
Lawrence, William S, 1955, Jl 16,15:6
Lawrence, William S Dr, 1923, Mr 8,17:3
Lawrence, William W, 1958, Jl 26,15:4
Lawrence, William Watson, 1916, Ag 30,9:3
Lawrence, Willis, 1937, Ja 10,II,10:2
Lawrence Sixtus, Bro (Jos Dalton), 1953, Mr 10,2
Lawrenson, Jack, 1957, N 2,21:4
Lawres, John J, 1953, Ap 27,23:4
Lawrie, Alvah K (will), 1938, S 17,34:1
Lawrie, James T, 1950, Je 4,92:5
Lawrie, James W, 1947, Ja 16,25:2
Lawrie, Lee, 1963, Ja 25,11:5
Lawrie, Lee Mrs, 1937, N 29,23:6
Lawry, Raymond G, 1949, D 27,23:3
Laws, Anhony W, 1943, D 16,27:5
Laws, Archer L, 1940, F 13,23:1
Laws, Bolitha J, 1958, N 15,23:3
Laws, Carl H, 1956, Mr 2,23:3
Laws, Curtis L, 1946, Jl 8,29:4
Laws, Curtis L Mrs, 1956, D 29,15:4
Laws, Florence B Mrs, 1937, Ja 16,17:3
Laws, George W, 1945, Je 8,19:2
Laws, H Langdon, 1955, Mr 26,15:5
Laws, Henry M, 1960, O 29,23:5
Laws, J Robert, 1942, Ja 19,20:2
Laws, James W, 1938, D 10,17:4
Laws, Oscar B, 1960, F 5,27:1
Laws, R Don, 1951, N 12,25:2
Laws, Samuel Spahr Rev, 1921, Ja 10,11:5
Lawser, Charles W, 1947, D 19,25:3
Lawson, A Emil, 1951, My 31,27:2
Lawson, A Werner, 1968, Ja 15,47:4
Lawson, Al, 1951, Ag 26,38:1
Lawson, Alfred W, 1946, D 6,23:2; 1954, D 14,33
Lawson, Andrew C, 1952, Je 18,27:1
Lawson, Anna J Mrs, 1948, Ag 4,22:2
Lawson, Arnold, 1947, Ja 22,23:3
Lawson, Arthur Mrs, 1945, Jl 5,13:6
Lawson, Arthur W, 1952, My 1,29:4
Lawson, Calude S, 1964, S 11,33:2
Lawson, Charles B, 1924, Ap 8,19:2
Lawson, Charles O, 1953, N 14,17:3
Lawson, Charles W, 1941, Ag 5,19:3
Lawson, Chester B, 1961, Ag 27,84:5
Lawson, Clarence J, 1954, O 6,25:1
Lawson, Clarence J Jr, 1964, Mr 11,39:2
Lawson, Clarence J Mrs, 1960, Ap 2,23:4
Lawson, Edgar P (por), 1938, Ap 20,23:2
Lawson, Edward B, 1962, N 20,35:2
Lawson, Edward C, 1945, Jl 14,11:2
Lawson, Edward F (Lord Burnham), 1963, Jl 5,
Lawson, Ernest W, 1960, Ja 31,92:7
Lawson, Evald B (Sept 22), 1965, O 11,61:3
Lawson, Fenton, 1937, My 28,21:4
Lawson, Floyd K, 1947, S 20,15:5
Lawson, Franklin D, 1949, O 27,27:3
Lawson, George, 1945, Mr 25,38:1
Lawson, George B, 1952, F 15,25:4
Lawson, George M, 1951, S 22,17:3
Lawson, George W, 1959, S 24,37:4
Lawson, H Edward, 1943, O 1,19:4
Lawson, Harold E, 1948, S 8,29:2
Lawson, Harry, 1952, Je 13,23:4; 1968, Je 25,41:
Lawson, Helen R, 1959, N 11,35:2
Lawson, Henry M, 1951, Ja 14,84:5
Lawson, Howard H, 1953, S 4,34:2
Lawson, Iver N, 1937, Ap 2,23:4
Lawson, J Capt, 1881, F 1,5:2
Lawson, J Earl, 1950, My 14,108:1
Lawson, James, 1912, S 12,11:5; 1938, Ag 11,17
Lawson, James A Sr, 1949, Ap 23,13:2
Lawson, James H, 1945, Ap 26,23:1
Lawson, James J, 1962, Jl 24,41:4

Lawson, James S (por), 1938, D 22,21:3
Lawson, James T, 1951, Ap 12,33:5; 1957, D 14,21:5
Lawson, John, 1947, F 23,53:4
Lawson, John A, 1938, Ja 14,23:4
Lawson, John Capt, 1901, N 22,9:6
Lawson, John E, 1948, Jl 24,15:4
Lawson, John F, 1965, O 26,45:3
Lawson, John Jr, 1960, D 18,84:1
Lawson, John M Sr Mrs, 1943, Je 20,35:2
Lawson, John R, 1945, My 13,20:7
Lawson, Joseph H, 1953, O 11,89:2
Lawson, Laurin L, 1938, Ja 29,15:4
Lawson, Leonidas M Col, 1909, Mr 29,7:4
Lawson, Lionel, 1879, O 6,2:5
Lawson, Lowell A Mrs, 1954, Ag 28,15:5
Lawson, Marie A, 1956, Je 14,33:1
Lawson, Owen (Inky), 1953, Ap 5,76:4
Lawson, P F, 1949, S 11,94:3
Lawson, Reed B Mrs, 1937, F 6,17:4
Lawson, Robert, 1904, D 16,9:6; 1957, My 28,33:1
Lawson, Robert C, 1961, Jl 4,19:3
Lawson, Robert H, 1965, D 19,84:8
Lawson, Robert M, 1962, Ja 4,33:4
Lawson, Robert N, 1945, Ag 13,19:4
Lawson, Robert S O, 1954, Ap 29,31:2
Lawson, Robert W, 1952, D 3,33:5
Lawson, Roberta C Mrs (por), 1941, Ja 1,23:3
Lawson, Strang, 1960, N 6,88:3
Lawson, Thomas Goodwin Judge, 1912, Ap 17,13:6
Lawson, Thomas R, 1954, Mr 16,29:4
Lawson, Thomas W Mrs, 1906, Ag 6,1:6
Lawson, Victor E, 1960, Mr 21,29:5
Lawson, Victor F (por),(funl, Ag 25,17:3), 1925, Ag 22,11:4
Lawson, Victor F Mrs, 1914, O 3,11:4
Lawson, W C, 1953, Ja 23,19:3
Lawson, Walter B, 1955, F 12,15:2
Lawson, Walter W, 1938, Jl 19,22:6
Lawson, Wilfrid (trb lr, O 23,II,7:4), 1966, O 12,43:4
Lawson, Wilfrid Sir, 1937, Ag 30,21:5
Lawson, William, 1939, D 27,21:1; 1940, Mr 6,23:5
Lawson, William D, 1944, My 1,15:3
Lawson, William E, 1943, N 28,68:2
Lawson, William J (Uncle Bill), 1954, My 27,27:4
Lawson, William M, 1948, S 30,27:2
Lawson, William V, 1963, Ap 11,33:2
Lawson-Johnston, Percy, 1955, Je 20,21:3
Lawson-Johnston, Percy Mrs, 1957, D 17,35:1
Lawson of Beamish, Lord (Jno J Lawson), 1965, Ag 4,35:2
Lawther, Boyd M, 1950, D 20,31:1
Lawton, Abbie E, 1905, Je 12,1:6
Lawton, Alice O, 1941, Ag 22,15:5
Lawton, Carl S, 1951, My 26,17:6
Lawton, Charles F, 1942, Ja 23,19:2
Lawton, Charles T, 1959, Mr 14,33:4
Lawton, Dorothy, 1960, F 21,92:8
Lawton, Dwight L, 1961, Ag 2,29:5
Lawton, Francis, 1922, Ap 18,17:4; 1957, Ja 19,15:5
Lawton, Fred, 1939, Je 5,17:3
Lawton, George, 1957, O 9,35:3
Lawton, George A, 1940, N 22,23:2
Lawton, George Field Judge, 1925, Jl 19,7:4
Lawton, Grace E, 1941, S 11,23:6
Lawton, H W Gen, 1899, D 20,1:2
Lawton, Harriet N, 1942, F 22,26:4
Lawton, Henry J, 1951, My 5,17:2
Lawton, J Warren, 1911, Mr 29,13:5
Lawton, James M Mrs, 1920, F 9,9:4
Lawton, Joseph S, 1946, Mr 26,29:2
Lawton, Leo P, 1954, My 22,15:3
Lawton, Louis B, 1949, Jl 10,57:1
Lawton, Louis C, 1942, Jl 22,19:4
Lawton, Mary, 1945, Ja 23,19:3
Lawton, Michael W, 1952, Ja 13,89:2
Lawton, Mollie E, 1941, Je 21,17:5
Lawton, Nelson J (will), 1938, F 2,21:2
Lawton, Platt R, 1939, D 4,23:5
Lawton, Ralph W, 1943, Ag 22,36:5
Lawton, Richard E, 1950, Ja 5,25:4
Lawton, Samuel T, 1961, Ja 23,23:5
Lawton, Samuel T Mrs, 1959, My 31,76:3
Lawton, Shailer U, 1966, Ap 12,39:1
Lawton, Thais, 1956, D 19,31:2
Lawton, Walter Y Mrs, 1952, Jl 8,27:6
Lawton, William, 1943, N 23,25:4
Lawton, William C, 1941, Ap 20,43:1; 1951, Jl 9,25:4
Lawton, William F, 1964, Mr 24,35:3
Lawton, William H, 1940, D 18,25:3
Lawton, William R, 1944, Ja 3,21:2
Lawyer, Charles C, 1938, O 15,17:5
Lawyer, Charles Jr, 1949, My 20,28:3
Lawyer, Frederick C, 1937, Ap 18,II,8:7
Lawyer, Frederick Mrs, 1950, Ag 28,17:5
Lawyer, G Gould, 1949, Ja 31,19:2
Lawyer, George, 1938, Mr 30,21:3
Lawyer, George A, 1944, D 24,26:5
Lawyer, James E, 1957, Je 7,23:3
Lawyer, Louis R Mrs, 1955, Je 11,15:5
Lax, Charles C, 1959, D 10,39:4
Lax, Harry, 1955, Jl 17,60:6
Lax, Samuel, 1956, O 18,33:5
Lax, William, 1937, Je 26,17:5
Lax, William H Rev, 1937, F 8,17:3
Lay, Beirne, 1954, Mr 17,31:2
Lay, Beirne Mrs, 1945, Ap 9,19:1
Lay, Charles, 1940, My 8,23:5
Lay, Charles D, 1956, F 16,29:2
Lay, Dirk, 1944, D 9,15:3
Lay, Frank H, 1940, Jl 21,28:7
Lay, Frank M Mrs, 1948, Ap 29,23:3
Lay, G C, 1881, Ap 18,5:5
Lay, H R, 1932, Jl 28,17:5
Lay, Julius G, 1939, Ag 29,21:2
Lay, L Oscar, 1947, O 27,21:3
Lay, Merwin W, 1947, Je 9,21:3
Lay, Olive W Mrs, 1941, N 20,27:3
Lay, Robert D, 1940, Ja 3,21:4
Lay, Theodore M, 1960, Ja 6,35:2
Lay, W P, 1940, N 22,23:2
Lay, Wilfrid, 1955, Jl 3,32:4
Laycock, Charles W, 1940, N 26,23:1
Laycock, Craven, 1940, Ap 5,21:1
Laycock, John R, 1961, Je 3,23:6
Laycock, John R Mrs, 1952, Ja 16,25:3
Laycock, Joseph F, 1952, Ja 12,13:4
Laycock, Oswald L, 1951, N 7,29:3
Laycock, Robert Edward Maj-Gen Sir, 1968, Mr 11, 41:1
Layden, Leon M, 1955, F 10,31:1
Layden, Michael J, 1963, Ag 29,29:5
Layden, Thomas F, 1939, Ap 14,23:3
Layfield, Clarence J, 1948, Jl 20,23:3
Layley, Edward J, 1938, S 30,21:2
Layman, David Jr, 1952, Ja 30,26:4
Layman, David T Jr Mrs, 1947, F 23,54:3
Layman, Joseph, 1938, N 22,24:8
Layman, Peter P, 1946, Ja 14,19:4
Layman, Ray, 1923, Jl 5,15:4
Layman, Theodore D Mrs, 1951, S 17,21:5
Layman, Walter G, 1944, S 28,19:3
Laymance, Millard J, 1943, Je 25,17:1
Layne, Carney M, 1941, Mr 9,41:3
Layne, Charles W, 1956, S 22,17:6
Layne, Eric, 1966, Je 23,39:3
Layne, J Gregg, 1952, Ag 18,17:1
Layne, Maximilian Mrs, 1944, Ag 18,13:4
Layng, Grant B, 1952, S 7,20:1
Layng, James D, 1908, F 15,7:4
Laytham, Allison W, 1956, N 14,35:3
Laytham, William P, 1944, Je 3,13:6
Layton, C B, 1930, N 12,23:6
Layton, Daniel J Jr, 1963, Ag 6,31:3
Layton, David, 1948, Ag 8,56:5
Layton, Eleanor Lady, 1959, Mr 19,33:4
Layton, Francis N Mrs, 1952, Mr 9,92:4
Layton, Frank D, 1956, O 26,29:2
Layton, George R, 1949, N 7,27:4
Layton, Gloria (Mrs H Gewiss),(funl), 1965, S 7,39:3
Layton, Jacob, 1941, Jl 22,20:2
Layton, Johnny, 1956, Ja 19,33:3
Layton, Lewis W, 1964, Ap 5,71:6
Layton, Phil E Mrs, 1954, O 29,21:1
Layton, Robert T, 1941, N 5,23:2
Layton, Roy E, 1952, N 28,26:4
Layton, Sarah R, 1948, D 30,22:2
Layton, Solomon W, 1946, My 4,15:5
Layton, Walter Lord, 1966, F 15,39:1
Layton, William A, 1939, F 8,23:4; 1951, N 2,23:2
Layton, William Mrs, 1948, S 11,15:5
Layton-Bennett, Kenneth A, 1947, Ap 4,23:1
Laz, Joseph, 1951, Jl 30,17:5
Lazan, Benjamin J, 1966, Jl 5,27:2
Lazansky, Edward, 1955, S 13,31:1
Lazansky, Edward Mrs, 1956, Jl 5,25:4
Lazar, Isadore, 1948, Je 8,26:2
Lazar, J, 1877, S 7,4:7
Lazar, Joseph F, 1963, My 13,29:2
Lazar, Leo E, 1960, Je 2,33:4
Lazar, Louis A Mrs, 1949, Ag 15,17:3
Lazar, Martin, 1966, F 2,35:2
Lazar, Robert, 1952, O 2,29:5
Lazard, Desiree (Mrs H Harris), 1960, Jl 16,19:5
Lazareff, Luba Z Mrs, 1966, N 9,40:1
Lazarin, Louis, 1954, Je 21,23:5
Lazaroff, Leon, 1954, My 29,15:4
Lazarovich-Hrebelianovich, Eleanor C Princess, 1957, Ja 12,19:2
Lazarovich-Hrebeljanovich, Eugene, 1941, Ag 21,17:6
Lazarow, Jacob, 1957, Ap 21,88:8
Lazarowitz, Alfred M, 1955, My 8,89:1
Lazarowitz, Idel N, 1951, N 24,11:2
Lazarowitz, Leopold C, 1965, F 28,88:3
Lazarson, Solomon, 1944, My 20,15:6
Lazarus, Adolph Prof, 1925, Jl 24,13:6
Lazarus, Alfred A, 1953, S 4,34:2
Lazarus, Amelia B (will), 1906, Ag 2,7:2
Lazarus, Bertha Mrs, 1919, O 31,13:5
Lazarus, David, 1940, Ag 3,15:5; 1956, F 7,31:4
Lazarus, David H Mrs, 1958, My 4,88:7
Lazarus, Eldon S, 1955, Je 15,31:5
Lazarus, Emma, 1887, N 20,16:2
Lazarus, Fanny Mrs, 1939, D 28,21:3
Lazarus, Harris M, 1962, F 27,33:4
Lazarus, Herman Mrs, 1966, Ap 22,41:4
Lazarus, Hyman Judge (funl, N 17,19:5), 1924, N 15,13:5
Lazarus, Irving, 1958, Mr 29,17:1
Lazarus, Isidor, 1958, S 1,13:4
Lazarus, Izzy, 1867, S 28,8:2
Lazarus, John D Mrs, 1952, Je 11,29:1
Lazarus, Joseph A, 1965, F 6,25:4
Lazarus, Leon, 1961, O 19,35:2
Lazarus, Lester, 1961, Je 29,33:4
Lazarus, Levi, 1953, Mr 6,20:5
Lazarus, Louis J, 1949, My 17,25:3
Lazarus, Max A, 1937, Ag 8,II,7:2
Lazarus, Milton, 1955, Mr 1,25:3
Lazarus, Morris A, 1956, Ag 12,85:1
Lazarus, Mortimer C, 1953, N 25,23:1
Lazarus, Moses, 1885, Mr 10,2:3
Lazarus, Norman, 1966, O 28,41:2
Lazarus, Paul N Mrs, 1945, Mr 17,13:2
Lazarus, Paul N Sr, 1965, F 20,25:4
Lazarus, Ralph, 1903, Jl 28,7:6
Lazarus, Ray H, 1952, Mr 26,29:3
Lazarus, S, 1926, Mr 6,15:3
Lazarus, Simon, 1947, D 22,21:2
Lazarus, Sylvan D Dr, 1937, O 24,II,9:1
Lazarus, William W Dr, 1937, Ap 2,23:4
Lazcano, Fernando, 1920, S 1,13:3
Lazear, Cornelius S, 1943, Ap 14,23:5
Lazear, George C, 1954, Je 3,27:2
Lazear, Jesse W Mrs, 1946, F 27,25:4
Lazear, Robert, 1957, Ja 27,84:5
Lazell, Frederick J, 1940, S 25,27:4
Lazell, L T, 1902, Mr 1,9:6
Lazenby, Elizabeth A, 1938, Ja 2,41:1
Lazenby, Marguerita B, 1955, F 9,27:3
Lazenby, Robert S, 1941, Ap 19,15:4
Lazerow, Louis, 1939, Jl 23,29:2
Lazic, Zivojin, 1958, N 24,29:4
Lazier, Lawrence W, 1957, S 15,84:8
La Zink, William, 1944, Je 13,19:6
Lazo, Antonio, 1956, N 14,35:3
Lazo-Arriaga, Antonio, 1938, N 14,19:3
Lazor, George J, 1949, Ag 16,23:5
Lazott, Joseph, 1939, My 20,15:4
Lazrus, S Ralph, 1959, S 6,73:1
Lazure, Wilfrid, 1962, My 31,27:1
Lazurick, Robert, 1968, Ap 18,47:2
Lazzara, Cosimo D, 1968, Ap 4,47:2
Lazzari, Carolina, 1946, O 18,24:2
Lazzari, Joseph, 1937, Ag 4,19:5
Lazzari, Sylvio, 1944, Je 20,19:3
Lazzari, Virgilio, 1953, O 7,29:3
Lazzarini, Hubert P, 1952, O 2,29:2
Lazzeri, Tony (por), 1946, Ag 8,21:1
Lea, Albert G, 1938, Ap 17,II,7:1
Lea, Alice Van Antwerp Mrs, 1921, O 24,15:4
Lea, Arden O, 1946, O 26,17:2
Lea, Arthur, 1958, Ja 21,26:7
Lea, Arthur H (will, Ja 14,24:1), 1938, Ja 7,19:1
Lea, C Russell, 1955, Ja 30,84:7
Lea, Charles M Mrs, 1945, Ag 20,19:4
Lea, Clarence F, 1964, Je 22,27:4
Lea, Edward Lt, 1863, F 8,3:2
Lea, Edward P, 1959, Jl 19,69:2
Lea, Fanny H, 1955, Ja 14,21:2
Lea, Francis C, 1961, D 13,43:3
Lea, George, 1953, Ja 6,96:5
Lea, Gladys, 1965, S 11,27:2
Lea, Helen, 1953, Ap 30,33:5
Lea, Henry Charles, 1909, O 25,7:5
Lea, Homer Gen, 1912, N 2,13:5
Lea, J Tatnall, 1916, My 13,9:4
Lea, John M Judge, 1903, S 21,7:6
Lea, John W, 1964, Ja 10,43:1
Lea, Langdon, 1937, O 6,25:3
Lea, Luke (por), 1945, N 19,21:2
Lea, Overton, 1912, Je 11,9:6
Lea, Robert B, 1968, S 13,47:2
Lea, Robert C, 1946, My 23,21:2
Lea, Robert W, 1956, N 14,35:1
Lea, Russell Mrs, 1949, F 27,68:7
Lea, Sydney L W, 1966, F 1,35:3
Lea, Victor L, 1959, N 24,37:4
Lea, William H, 1939, My 13,15:5
Leach, Abby, 1918, D 30,9:4
Leach, Addison C, 1948, Ag 19,21:3
Leach, Andrew K, 1950, O 11,33:4
Leach, Ann, 1952, Ap 12,11:4
Leach, Arthur B, 1939, Ja 15,39:1
Leach, Arthur J, 1943, D 9,27:4
Leach, Benjamin, 1951, O 28,84:5
Leach, Benjamin Mrs, 1952, F 25,21:3
Leach, Charles E, 1944, S 6,19:6
Leach, Charles J, 1950, Ap 26,29:4
Leach, Cora Mrs (will), 1940, S 20,25:6
Leach, Donald W Mrs, 1948, F 3,25:3
Leach, Edward, 1924, My 6,21:5; 1940, My 5,52:1
Leach, Edward A, 1948, O 22,25:2
Leach, Elizabeth S Mrs, 1937, Jl 25,II,7:4
Leach, Ferry W, 1937, O 19,26:2
Leach, Floyd S, 1965, Ap 18,81:2
Leach, Francis J, 1954, O 16,17:6
Leach, Frank A Prof, 1905, Ja 21,9:3
Leach, Frank K, 1956, Je 8,25:3
Leach, Frank W, 1943, F 17,21:3

Leach, Frederick R, 1945, O 23,17:1
Leach, G Harvey, 1951, D 23,22:4
Leach, George, 1942, N 11,25:6
Leach, George A, 1944, D 15,19:2
Leach, George E, 1955, Jl 18,21:2
Leach, George O, 1942, My 24,42:8
Leach, George T, 1951, Ag 13,17:5
Leach, Glen C, 1942, Je 4,19:6
Leach, Harry A, 1967, F 3,31:4
Leach, J G Col, 1903, Je 10,9:6
Leach, J Sayles, 1964, Mr 17,35:4
Leach, James, 1906, N 16,9:5
Leach, James E Mrs, 1943, Ap 4,40:8
Leach, John A, 1919, Je 28,9:3; 1946, Mr 25,25:4
Leach, Lawrence R, 1956, Ja 31,29:1
Leach, MacEdward, 1967, Jl 13,37:4
Leach, May A, 1945, O 8,15:4
Leach, Murray, 1958, N 11,29:4
Leach, Raymond H, 1942, My 24,42:2
Leach, Samuel, 1909, Jl 17,7:3
Leach, Samuel B, 1965, N 14,89:2
Leach, Thomas A, 1946, Ja 31,21:4
Leach, Walter, 1939, S 21,23:4
Leach, William, 1945, Ap 25,23:5; 1949, N 23,30:5
Leach, William Mrs, 1944, Jl 28,13:2
Leach, William Mrs (Ethel), 1960, Ja 1,19:1
Leacock, Arthur G, 1947, N 29,13:2
Leacock, James J, 1948, Mr 6,13:2
Leacock, Stephen B, 1944, Mr 29,21:1
Leacock, W T, 1884, D 30,5:5
Leadbeater, Edward H, 1941, Ap 27,38:8
Leadbetter, Frederick W, 1948, D 23,19:4
Leadbetter, Guy W, 1945, N 13,21:3
Leadbitter, George P, 1955, D 22,23:4
Leaden, Michael H, 1951, Ag 7,25:1
Leaden, Thomas E, 1949, Mr 12,17:5
Leadenham, George B, 1948, S 11,15:2
Leadenham, George H, 1949, S 29,29:4
Leadenham, Harry N, 1948, Ja 6,23:3
Leader, Benjamin W, 1923, Mr 23,19:5
Leader, Colledge, 1938, D 10,17:2
Leader, Edwin O, 1958, O 7,35:1
Leader, Harry, 1946, My 11,27:5
Leader, Helen J, 1952, F 28,27:5
Leader, Jack, 1941, Je 29,32:3
Leader, Tom, 1945, Je 25,17:2
Leadie, James L, 1938, Ap 2,15:3
Leadingham, Christine S, 1943, Ap 28,23:4
Leadlay, Edward, 1951, F 8,33:5
Leaf, Elizabeth T Mrs, 1941, N 16,56:5
Leaf, Frank G, 1942, O 30,19:1
Leaf, Noel W, 1939, My 14,III,6:8
Leaf, W, 1927, Mr 9,25:3
Leaf, William B, 1938, D 15,27:4
Leaf, William N, 1948, Je 2,29:6
League, Harry M, 1937, O 19,26:1
League, Judson, 1955, O 19,33:4
Leahey, George A, 1948, N 23,29:3
Leahon, Patrick J, 1942, My 28,17:4
Leahy, Agnes B, 1960, Mr 2,37:3
Leahy, Andrew A, 1949, My 17,26:3
Leahy, Charles H, 1957, Jl 19,19:5
Leahy, Charles M, 1957, F 18,27:4
Leahy, Charles S, 1956, S 8,17:1
Leahy, Daniel J, 1944, Ap 4,21:1
Leahy, Daniel M, 1941, D 16,27:2
Leahy, David T (will, Ap 14,16:7), 1951, Mr 30,23:2
Leahy, Dennis B, 1941, D 19,25:5
Leahy, Edward L, 1953, Jl 23,23:1
Leahy, Edwin J, 1951, My 2,31:4
Leahy, Emmett J, 1964, Je 25,33:4
Leahy, Francis T, 1954, D 13,27:1
Leahy, Frank M, 1959, F 17,31:2
Leahy, Frank W, 1947, Ag 5,23:3
Leahy, Fred W, 1952, Ag 1,17:5
Leahy, George V, 1959, D 21,27:4
Leahy, J F, 1903, S 1,7:6
Leahy, Jack J, 1953, Ap 24,24:4
Leahy, James B, 1940, Ag 24,13:5
Leahy, Jeremiah J (Bro Chrysostom Austin), 1964, Ag 23,87:2
Leahy, John H, 1952, Jl 29,21:2
Leahy, John J, 1948, Ap 9,24:2
Leahy, Joseph, 1951, Mr 26,30:3
Leahy, Joseph D, 1947, Ja 3,21:2
Leahy, Lamar R, 1958, O 11,23:4
Leahy, Michael J, 1958, My 20,34:7
Leahy, Morris R, 1938, Jl 3,13:3
Leahy, Patrick Mrs, 1946, Jl 11,23:2
Leahy, Paul, 1966, Jl 5,37:3
Leahy, Raymond A Mrs, 1959, Je 15,27:4
Leahy, Stephen F, 1944, Mr 28,19:6
Leahy, Thomas, 1961, F 26,92:4
Leahy, Thomas A, 1947, D 12,27:2
Leahy, Thomas E, 1949, Jl 1,19:1
Leahy, Thomas J, 1944, Je 30,21:5; 1946, My 14,21:1; 1951, Je 13,29:4
Leahy, Thomas L W, 1960, S 4,68:5
Leahy, Timothy F, 1951, F 10,13:3
Leahy, Walter R, 1938, Je 5,45:1
Leahy, William D (funl, Jl 24,25:4), 1959, Jl 21,1:6
Leahy, William D Mrs (por), 1942, Ap 22,23:1
Leahy, William I, 1958, N 9,89:2
Leahy, William J, 1942, Jl 12,35:1
Leahy, William P, 1965, Jl 28,35:3
Leak, William H, 1958, N 22,21:6
Leake, Alice M, 1949, Mr 6,72:2
Leake, Benjamin, 1942, Ag 14,17:3
Leake, Eugene W, 1959, Ag 24,21:2
Leake, Francis M, 1921, N 10,19:5
Leake, H, 1933, Mr 29,15:6
Leake, Hunter C, 1946, Ja 25,23:4
Leake, Walter J, 1944, Ap 6,23:3
Leake, William Josiah Judge, 1908, N 24,9:5
Leake, William W, 1952, Ag 27,27:3
Leakin, George Armistead Rev, 1912, Jl 11,9:5
Leal, J R Dr, 1882, Ag 29,5:6
Leal, John Laing Dr, 1914, Mr 14,11:5
Leal, Laura E, 1909, Jl 19,7:6
Leale, C A, 1932, Je 14,21:3
Leale, Lilian, 1963, Ap 19,43:4
Leale, Loyal, 1952, S 15,25:3
Leale, M, 1934, Jl 1,24:3
Leaman, Clair S, 1955, D 15,37:4
Leaman, Claude F, 1968, N 9,33:6
Leaman, Walter E, 1958, My 29,27:5
Leaman, Walter E Mrs, 1962, S 6,31:2
Leamer, Angus B, 1943, Ag 3,19:4
Leamey, Harold G, 1951, N 7,29:4
Leaming, Anna, 1908, F 1,9:5
Leaming, Edward Dr, 1916, My 12,11:6
Leaming, George, 1940, O 27,44:3
Leaming, Jeremiah, 1908, F 1,9:5
Leaming, Jonathan F Dr, 1907, Ap 26,9:6
Leaming, Joseph R Mrs, 1950, O 20,28:3
Leaming, Thomas H, 1925, Mr 29,7:1
Leamon, Edward L, 1944, N 7,27:3
Leamy, Daniel, 1882, N 10,8:2
Leamy, Edmund, 1962, Ag 7,29:3
Leamy, Frank A, 1966, Je 26,73:1
Leamy, Frederick W, 1951, D 2,91:1
Leamy, Frederick W Mrs, 1938, S 19,19:5
Leamy, James P, 1949, Jl 24,52:7
Leamy, La Barre J Dr, 1953, F 8,88:2
Leamy, Margaret M Mrs, 1939, Ap 26,23:2
Leamy, Robert H, 1963, Jl 23,29:5
Leander, Axel J, 1940, My 24,19:3
Leander, George, 1904, Ag 24,3:5
Leap, Thomas V, 1947, Ap 15,25:1
Leapley, Forest R, 1963, Ja 16,16:1
Lear, Ben, 1966, N 2,45:1
Lear, Frederick A, 1959, N 21,23:1
Lear, Frederick R, 1950, Je 22,27:3
Lear, George, 1884, My 24,4:7
Lear, George F, 1945, N 8,19:5
Lear, Jane N Mrs, 1937, D 11,19:4
Lear, John B, 1944, Jl 26,19:2
Lear, John E, 1948, Ag 18,25:3
Lear, John Mrs, 1965, My 10,33:4
Lear, Joseph M, 1950, Ag 31,25:3
Lear, Roy A, 1944, D 5,23:3
Lear, Samuel A, 1962, S 20,33:1
Lear, William, 1940, My 5,52:1
Lear, Wilson H, 1938, S 11,II,11:2
Learch, William D, 1960, D 9,31:2
Leard, Norman W Sr, 1948, F 9,17:4
Learmonth, Frederick, 1941, Je 5,24:4
Learmonth, James, 1967, S 29,47:2
Learnard, Henry G Gen, 1937, Mr 9,23:1
Learnard, Samuel S, 1903, D 3,9:4
Learne, Jane S Mrs, 1955, Mr 5,17:5
Learned, Arthur G, 1959, D 28,23:4
Learned, Edward Jr, 1945, Jl 4,13:6
Learned, Edwin J, 1938, Jl 22,17:5
Learned, Ellin C Mrs, 1940, Ja 9,23:6
Learned, Elry H, 1948, Je 2,29:3
Learned, Frank E, 1937, O 24,II,8:5
Learned, Gearfield, 1883, Ja 30,5:3
Learned, Harry H, 1937, My 25,27:4
Learned, Henry B Mrs, 1952, Ja 28,17:1
Learned, J E, 1902, Je 16,9:6
Learned, John G, 1943, O 24,44:6
Learned, Walter Mrs, 1960, O 31,31:4
Learned, William L Judge, 1904, S 21,9:7
Learned, William S, 1950, Ja 5,26:2
Learner, Ernest R, 1948, My 16,71:2
Learney, William T, 1944, My 3,19:5
Learoyd, Arthur, 1950, Ag 30,31:5
Learoyd, Harold J, 1957, Mr 7,29:1
Learoyd, Harold J Mrs, 1945, D 4,29:4
Learsch, Louis Mrs, 1946, N 7,31:3
Learsi, Rufus (I Goldburg), 1964, Ag 4,29:2
Leary, Annie Papal Countess, 1919, Ap 27,22:3
Leary, Anson T, 1962, Ag 25,19:2
Leary, Catherine T Mrs, 1937, S 21,25:1
Leary, Charles J, 1959, Jl 11,19:2
Leary, Charles J Jr, 1953, O 22,29:3
Leary, Cornelius, 1916, D 13,15:5
Leary, Cornelius J, 1940, Ap 22,17:4
Leary, Daniel A, 1962, Mr 1,31:2
Leary, Daniel B, 1946, My 2,22:3
Leary, Daniel F, 1944, Mr 23,19:3; 1968, My 22,47:3
Leary, Daniel J, 1965, N 4,47:3
Leary, Edward B, 1942, Mr 1,44:2
Leary, Edward J, 1945, Je 6,21:5; 1948, D 3,25:4
Leary, Frances M C Mrs, 1942, Jl 10,17:6
Leary, Francis T, 1968, S 12,47:3
Leary, Frank J, 1951, Jl 4,17:2
Leary, Frederick J, 1953, N 25,23:4
Leary, George, 1942, My 9,13:1
Leary, George A, 1953, Je 23,29:3
Leary, George F, 1954, Je 13,89:1
Leary, George G, 1967, My 24,47:1
Leary, George Jr, 1955, S 19,25:2
Leary, George P, 1925, N 9,19:5
Leary, Gertrude, 1947, Ag 22,15:3
Leary, Harry B Sr, 1938, My 15,II,6:5
Leary, Henry V, 1944, Ap 6,23:4
Leary, Herbert F, 1957, D 4,39:3
Leary, J D, 1902, Ap 12,9:5
Leary, James A, 1963, O 20,88:4
Leary, James F, 1925, S 6,13:2
Leary, James H, 1942, Ag 11,19:4
Leary, James J, 1945, D 28,15:3
Leary, Jeremiah C, 1952, Ja 12,13:3
Leary, John J Jr (por), 1944, Ja 5,17:1
Leary, John J Mrs, 1942, O 25,46:1
Leary, John L, 1961, Ag 20,86:3
Leary, Lewis G, 1951, My 28,21:5
Leary, Lewis G Mrs, 1959, D 1,39:2
Leary, Mary E Mrs, 1937, Jl 17,15:5
Leary, Matthew G Sr, 1944, My 2,19:2
Leary, Michael, 1917, N 17,13:4
Leary, Montgomery E, 1954, Ja 5,27:5
Leary, Owen P, 1958, Mr 17,29:1
Leary, Peter Brig-Gen, 1911, F 14,11:5
Leary, Richard J, 1953, Ag 15,15:4
Leary, Sylvester L, 1965, Ap 29,35:1
Leary, Ted, 1945, S 28,21:4
Leary, Theodore M, 1912, F 16,9:4
Leary, Timothy, 1954, N 17,31:3
Leary, Timothy A (por), 1946, Ap 20,13:4
Leary, William (por), 1939, Ja 19,19:1
Leary, William, 1954, Jl 16,21:5
Leary, William C, 1939, O 14,19:3
Leary, William H, 1952, N 4,29:3
Leary, William H Sr, 1946, D 22,42:1
Leary, William Mrs, 1967, F 23,35:2
Leary, William P, 1943, Mr 27,14:8
Leas, Leroy P, 1954, Jl 6,23:3
Lease, Benjamin M, 1944, Mr 8,19:4
Lease, Mary E, 1964, Ag 19,37:3
Lease, Raymond E, 1958, O 2,37:4
Leask, Arthur, 1941, Ap 20,43:2
Leask, Edwin M, 1939, Ag 14,15:2
Leask, G, 1933, Ap 3,15:5
Leason, John, 1938, S 1,23:5
Leason, Percy, 1959, S 14,29:2
Leath, James E, 1955, Ja 20,31:5
Leatham, Ralph, 1954, Mr 11,34:7
Leather, Robert S, 1954, Ja 19,26:5
Leather, Walter J, 1940, My 19,42:4
Leatherbee, Frederick K, 1941, Ag 31,23:2
Leathers, Blanche D Mrs, 1940, Ja 27,13:4
Leathers, Frederick J Viscount, 1965, Mr 20,27:4
Leathers, Waller S, 1946, Ja 27,41:1
Leathers, Willard G, 1957, Ag 24,15:3
Leathes, Stanley, 1938, Jl 27,17:6
Leattor, William L, 1943, Mr 4,19:5
Leavell, David C Mrs, 1957, Ag 27,29:2
Leavell, Frank, 1949, D 8,33:1
Leavell, Ullin W, 1960, S 23,29:2
Leavelle, Charles, 1948, My 11,25:2
Leavens, B F, 1881, Ag 6,5:4
Leavens, Eric, 1959, N 18,41:4
Leavens, Frank A, 1938, Mr 24,23:1
Leavens, George D, 1915, D 23,13:4
Leavens, Jane Mrs, 1937, Jl 22,19:5
Leavens, William B, 1941, O 13,17:3
Leavenworth, Charles S, 1949, O 4,27:4
Leavenworth, E W Mrs, 1911, N 8,13:5
Leavenworth, Ellis W, 1959, Jl 28,27:2
Leavenworth, John C, 1961, Mr 2,27:3
Leavenworth, William S, 1943, Jl 3,13:3
Leaver, Raymond J, 1958, My 30,21:2
Leaver, Warren M, 1953, Jl 7,27:4
Leaverton, Alfred C, 1963, O 3,35:3
Leavitt, Adele, 1958, O 17,29:3
Leavitt, Alvin B, 1939, Je 6,23:5
Leavitt, Annie N, 1947, Je 7,13:2
Leavitt, Arthur H Mrs, 1962, S 11,33:2
Leavitt, C W, 1928, Ap 24,25:5
Leavitt, Charles, 1904, F 18,9:6
Leavitt, Charles S Mrs, 1947, Ag 4,17:5
Leavitt, Charles W Mrs, 1956, Ja 3,31:3
Leavitt, Cornelius V Mrs, 1953, Je 9,27:4
Leavitt, David, 1872, Ja 11,1:6; 1879, D 31,5:6
Leavitt, Dudley W, 1958, Mr 14,25:4
Leavitt, Edward, 1908, S 13,9:5
Leavitt, Edward R, 1923, Mr 22,19:4
Leavitt, Emanuel J Dr, 1918, O 26,11:5
Leavitt, F M, 1928, Ag 7,21:3
Leavitt, Frank M, 1953, My 2,15:6
Leavitt, Frank S (Man Mountain Dean), 1953, My 30,15:4
Leavitt, G Howland, 1923, Ap 8,6:3
Leavitt, George B Mrs, 1951, O 23,29:2
Leavitt, George O, 1919, Ap 21,15:2
Leavitt, George W, 1919, Ag 4,11:3

Leavitt, Harold W, 1957, Ag 10,15:2
Leavitt, Harry, 1949, Ja 14,23:4
Leavitt, Harry R, 1948, Ja 6,23:2
Leavitt, Henry S, 1904, F 24,9:6
Leavitt, Henry S Mrs, 1924, D 25,17:5
Leavitt, Horace H, 1966, S 8,47:3
Leavitt, Jack, 1953, F 9,27:2
Leavitt, James E C, 1957, N 4,29:5
Leavitt, Joshua Rev, 1873, Ja 17,4:7
Leavitt, Judge, 1873, My 16,5:5
Leavitt, Julian, 1939, D 11,23:2
Leavitt, Louis, 1940, Je 23,30:5
Leavitt, Maria V (por), 1947, Mr 31,23:3
Leavitt, Moses A (funl, Je 26,29:4), 1965, Je 22,35:1
Leavitt, Moses A Mrs, 1956, F 17,23:3
Leavitt, Nathan, 1966, N 15,47:2
Leavitt, Nathan R Mrs, 1955, N 7,29:4
Leavitt, Peter M, 1960, Jl 28,27:4
Leavitt, Philip B Mrs, 1965, Jl 24,21:3
Leavitt, Ralph W H, 1950, Mr 21,32:3
Leavitt, Robert G, 1942, O 4,52:7
Leavitt, Robert W, 1946, Jl 8,29:3
Leavitt, Royden, 1939, Je 5,17:6
Leavitt, Rufus, 1950, Je 6,29:2
Leavitt, Scott, 1966, O 22,31:5
Leavitt, Sheldon Mrs, 1951, Je 13,29:3
Leavitt, William Homer Mrs, 1914, Ap 16,9:4
Leavitt, William S Mrs, 1914, S 24,11:6
Leavy, Charles H, 1952, S 27,17:2
Leavy, John F, 1946, My 24,19:1
Leavy, John F Mrs, 1951, Ja 9,30:4
Leavy, Joseph T, 1952, My 9,23:3
Leavy, Leonard S, 1937, Je 13,II,7:2
Leavy, Michael J, 1968, D 19,47:2
Leaycraft, Charles M, 1940, Ja 28,32:6
Leaycraft, Charles Mrs, 1950, Je 11,92:1
Leaycraft, Edgar C, 1957, O 8,35:3
Leaycraft, Egbert R, 1943, Ag 1,39:3
Leaycraft, Frank E, 1952, O 21,29:2
Leaycraft, J Edgar, 1916, Jl 4,11:6
Leaycraft, Jeremiah, 1884, Mr 18,5:4
Leaycraft, Julia S Mrs, 1960, D 23,19:4
Leaycraft, Reginald R, 1944, Je 1,19:4
Leaycraft, William S, 1946, Mr 4,23:3
Lebair, Harold A, 1967, Jl 19,39:1
Le Barbier, Henry, 1905, Je 7,9:5
Lebarbier, Henry A, 1907, Ja 22,9:6
Lebarge, Oza J, 1948, Ag 1,58:1
Le Baron, Francis Rev Dr, 1911, F 17,9:5
LeBaron, Walter A, 1967, Jl 20,37:2
LeBaron, William, 1958, F 10,23:2
Le Barron, Lydia Bartlett Mrs, 1920, Ag 19,9:4
Lebasque, Henri, 1937, Ag 8,II,7:4
Lebeau, George J, 1938, Jl 30,13:3
Le Beau, Marie A A, 1949, My 18,27:2
Lebedeff, Aaron, 1960, N 9,35:2
Lebedeff, Ivan, 1953, Ap 2,27:4
Lebedeff, Vladimir I, 1956, Ap 1,88:3
Lebedeff, Vladimir I Mrs, 1958, Mr 3,27:3
Lebedenko, Vladimir, 1946, O 18,23:4
Lebedev-Kumach, Vasili, 1949, F 22,23:3
Lebedev-Poliansky, Pavel I, 1948, Ap 7,25:1
Lebedieff, Sergei A, 1940, N 4,19:4
Lebedinsky, Aleksandr I, 1967, S 14,47:4
Lebegott, Edward, 1956, D 25,25:3
Lebeis, Edward H, 1944, D 16,15:2
LeBel, Clarence J, 1965, Ap 15,33:2
Lebel, Jerry G Mrs, 1951, Jl 8,60:5
Le Bel, Louis J B, 1952, My 22,27:2
Lebel, Omer M, 1950, Ag 15,29:2
Lebengood, John L, 1942, F 4,19:2
Lebenson, Robert J, 1944, O 15,45:2
Lebenthal, Louis S, 1951, D 17,31:2
Leber, Charles H, 1907, O 29,11:6
Leber, Charles T (mem ser set, S 27,86:2), 1959, Jl 31,24:1
Leber, Otto H, 1965, My 29,27:5
Leber, Robert E, 1955, Ja 18,27:4
Leber, Robert E Mrs, 1948, Ap 14,27:4
Leber, Samuel F, 1939, N 2,23:6
Leber, Theodore A Mrs, 1947, Jl 26,13:6
Leber, Ulrich, 1946, Ap 27,17:3
Le Bermuth, Arthur Mrs, 1944, Ja 21,17:2
Lebert, William H, 1949, F 1,25:4
Lebesgue, Henri, 1941, Ag 7,17:5
Lebett, Charles A, 1944, F 1,19:2
Lebhar, Bertram, 1959, F 18,33:2
Lebhar, Bertram Jr Mrs, 1948, Je 18,3:4
Lebhar, Godfrey M, 1963, D 10,50:6
Lebhar, Neil F Mrs, 1948, Ap 14,27:3
Lebhar, Norman J, 1948, Jl 27,25:1
Le Blanc, Albert Mrs, 1945, Ap 22,36:1
Leblanc, Albini, 1957, My 18,3:5
Leblanc, Aug, 1948, F 17,25:4
LeBlanc, George L, 1954, Ap 7,31:3
Leblanc, George L Mrs, 1953, Jl 9,25:2
Leblanc, Georgette, 1941, O 29,23:3
Le Blanc, Joseph, 1959, My 8,86:8
Leblanc, Maurice, 1941, N 8,19:1
Leblanc, Pierre E Sir, 1918, O 19,15:2
Le Blanc, Thomas J, 1948, S 10,23:5
Le Blang, Isaac, 1950, Ja 4,35:3
Leblang, Jacob, 1943, Ja 22,19:1
Leblond, Foreman M, 1953, N 13,28:3
Le Blond, Fred Mrs, 1942, S 16,23:4
LeBlond, Hubert, 1959, Ja 1,31:3
Leblond, Richard K, 1953, Mr 18,31:5
Leblond-Zola, Denise, 1942, D 15,27:4
Lebo, Ellerslie A, 1954, O 28,35:5
LeBoeuf, Albert A, 1939, D 7,27:2
Le Boeuf, Randall L Mrs, 1943, N 23,25:2
Lebohner, Edward K, 1968, D 25,31:3
Le Bois, Alfred, 1944, Jl 1,15:3
Lebolt, J M H, 1944, F 29,17:5
Lebolt, Sidney L, 1944, S 30,13:2
Lebon, Andre, 1938, F 18,19:4
Le Bon, G, 1931, D 15,27:3
Le Bonn, Napoleon, 1901, Jl 10,7:6
Le Bosquet, Charles H, 1954, Ap 4,88:7
LeBouef, George, 1950, S 1,21:2
Le Bourgeois, Adolph Mrs, 1940, Mr 20,34:7
Le Bourveau, Harry V, 1946, Jl 10,23:3
Le Bourveau, Harry V Mrs, 1949, Ja 25,23:1
Le Boutiller, John Mrs, 1925, S 13,5:1
Le Boutiller, William G Dr, 1923, D 24,11:6
Le Boutillier, Benjamin H, 1957, S 1,57:2
Leboutillier, Charles, 1939, Ag 30,17:5
Le Boutillier, Clement, 1944, D 9,15:5
Le Boutillier, Edward H, 1940, F 12,17:5
Le Boutillier, Ella N Mrs, 1938, F 23,23:3
Le Boutillier, F, 1880, S 16,5:2
Le Boutillier, G, 1936, F 21,17:5
LeBoutillier, George, 1952, O 6,25:5
Le Boutillier, James, 1906, S 22,7:5
Le Boutillier, John H, 1924, Ap 18,19:4
Le Boutillier, Mary, 1945, Ja 1,21:2
Le Boutillier, T, 1929, S 19,1:2
Le Boutillier, Thomas Mrs, 1945, S 13,23:4
Le Boutillier, William A G, 1952, O 26,88:4
Le Boutilliere, Paul, 1938, Ap 7,23:5
Leboutte, Norbert, 1953, Ag 25,21:4
Lebovitz, Bernard, 1955, S 13,31:4
Lebovitz, Leo, 1955, Je 10,25:1
Lebovitz, Victor, 1945, Mr 10,17:5
LeBow, Alexander, 1966, Ja 15,27:6
Lebow, Herman, 1950, Ap 22,19:5
Lebow, Howard, 1968, Ja 15,47:3
Lebow, Joseph, 1964, Ja 6,47:3
Lebowitz, Benjamin J, 1945, D 12,27:2
Lebowitz, David Mrs, 1941, Ag 19,21:2
Lebowitz, Jacob, 1947, My 3,17:6
Lebowitz, Lawrence, 1948, Mr 12,23:4
Lebowitz, Louis Mrs, 1957, My 5,88:2
Lebowitz, Sidney, 1968, N 13,26:3
Leboy, J Lewis Mrs, 1959, Ag 27,27:3
Le Branchu, Jean-Yves, 1944, F 8,15:1
LeBrandt, Joseph, 1940, Je 6,25:3
Lebret, R Charles, 1952, N 27,31:2
LeBreton, David, 1953, Ag 30,35:4
Le Breton, Tomas A, 1959, F 19,31:3
Le Breton, Tomas Mrs, 1938, Je 27,17:2
Lebreux, Dorothy L, 1952, F 28,27:3
Lebreux, Napoleon E Mrs, 1947, Ja 1,34:3
Le Brocq, William J, 1940, Ag 11,30:8
Lebroke, Mary E Mrs, 1939, N 11,15:1
Le Brou, Richard K, 1949, Ap 7,29:3
Le Brun, Adele, 1915, D 24,9:4
Lebrun, Albert, 1950, Mr 7,27:1
Lebrun, Albert Mrs, 1947, O 29,27:5
LeBrun, Antoinette, 1956, N 18,89:1
Lebrun, Gabriel, 1939, N 23,27:2
LeBrun, George P, 1966, N 14,41:6
Lebrun, Hilaire O, 1941, My 11,44:4
Lebrun, J Mrs, 1928, My 11,27:6
Le Brun, Michael M, 1913, S 28,7:5
Lebrun, Rico, 1964, My 11,31:4
Le Brune, Alexandrine P, 1949, Jl 29,21:2
Lebson, Samuel, 1946, Jl 8,29:2
Lebuffe, Francis P, 1954, My 28,23:1
Lebzeltern-Collenbach, Victor Baron, 1925, N 24,25:3
Lecain, John, 1939, F 16,21:4
Le Caron, Maj, 1894, Ap 2,5:1
Lecasse, Aurelius, 1948, O 29,26:3
Lecchio, Francisco, 1943, Ja 14,21:1
Leccione, William T Mrs, 1946, Ag 1,23:3
Lecerf, Auguste, 1943, S 29,21:2
Leche, Eric D, 1953, Ag 25,21:5
Leche, Richard W, 1965, F 23,33:2
Lecher, Clara O Mrs, 1950, O 29,92:5
Lechler, George P, 1949, N 9,27:4
Lechmere-Oertel, Frederick, 1942, F 24,21:2
Lechner, Anthony F, 1955, Ag 19,19:3
Lechner, Carl, 1953, Ap 1,29:4
Lechner, Harvey, 1954, S 15,33:2
Lechner, Ludwig, 1960, Mr 17,33:4
Lechner, Mabel Mrs, 1950, Ap 19,13:3
Lechner, Sidney, 1956, O 24,37:1
Lechner, William Mrs, 1948, D 30,19:1
Lechter, Henry J Mrs, 1959, F 5,31:5
Lechthaler, Roy M, 1938, Jl 14,21:5
Lechtman, Benjamin Mrs, 1952, Ap 9,31:3
Leck, William H Mrs, 1951, Ag 24,15:3
Leckach, Joseph, 1952, Ja 20,84:8
Leckey, Robert C, 1952, Ap 11,24:3
Leckie, Arch S, 1938, Ag 25,19:5
Leckie, Frederick L, 1950, D 1,25:1
Leckie, William C, 1944, Je 5,19:5
Leckie, William J, 1943, Ja 17,45:2
Leckner, John G, 1941, Ag 31,22:8
Leckner, Myron C, 1952, S 3,29:5
Lecky, Prescott, 1941, My 31,11:2
Lecky, Robert Jr, 1939, Je 27,23:6
Lecky, W E L, 1903, O 24,9:5
Leclair, Paul L, 1967, Jl 29,9:2
Le Clear, Harry W, 1939, N 23,27:5
Le Clear, T, 1882, N 28,2:2
Leclear, Thomas, 1939, Jl 26,19:1
Le Clerc, Joseph A, 1956, N 18,88:5
Leclerc, Louise Henrietta, 1907, F 25,9:4
Le Clerc, Raoul C, 1940, D 25,27:2
Le Clerco, Remy, 1940, N 30,17:2
Le Clercq, Henri, 1945, Mr 26,19:4
Le Clere, Frank W, 1946, Mr 28,25:4
Le Cluse, Egbert E, 1948, Ja 14,25:3
L'Ecluse, Ernest A, 1945, N 15,20:2
L'Ecluse, Mary Y Mrs, 1952, N 13,31:1
L'Ecluse, Milton L, 1938, D 20,26:2
Lecocg, Alexander Charles, 1911, Mr 4,11:6
Lecocq, Alexandre Charles, 1918, O 26,11:5
Lecointe, Sadie, 1944, Jl 18,19:4
Le Compte, Edward Mrs, 1914, D 27,3:5
Lecompte, Edwin L, 1947, Mr 17,23:4
Lecompte, Irville C, 1957, Ap 8,23:2
Lecompte, John B, 1952, Jl 10,31:2
Le Compte, Joseph, 1951, Ag 27,19:3
Le Compte, William C, 1948, S 18,17:4
Le Compte, William G, 1956, Ja 15,93:1
Le Comte, Francis D, 1907, D 20,11:6
Lecomte, Georges, 1958, Ag 28,27:3
LeConey, J Alfred, 1959, N 13,29:3
Leconfield, Lord of (C H Wyndham), 1952, Ap 18, 25:2
Le Conte, Joseph N 2d, 1950, F 3,23:1
Le Conte, Joseph Prof, 1901, Jl 7,5:4
Le Corbusier (C E Jeanneret),(funl plans, Ag 29,84:5), 1965, Ag 28,1:2
Lecot, Victor Lucian Sulpice Cardinal, 1908, D 21,9:6
Le Count, Frederick D, 1943, Je 29,19:2
LeCount, John R, 1958, N 7,27:1
Le Count, Joseph F, 1953, D 12,19:4
Le Count, Josiah M, 1948, Ag 28,15:1
LeCount, Wallace E, 1956, O 21,86:5
Lecour, Edward V, 1940, Mr 14,23:6
Lecour, Joseph H, 1954, Mr 24,27:2
Lecraw, David R, 1952, N 29,17:3
Lecraw, Loring R, 1963, N 29,34:4
Lecraw, William F, 1965, Mr 21,86:7
Lecrenier, Frank S, 1941, Ag 30,13:6
LeCroix, Aurore (Mrs Hy H Hay), 1967, Je 22,39:4
Le Cron, George F, 1948, My 6,25:5
Le Cron, James D, 1961, Ja 28,19:3
Lecson, Arsenio H, 1962, Ap 16,29:1
Lecuna, Vicente, 1954, F 22,19:1
Lecuona, Ernesto (funl plans, D 4,47:2), 1963, D 1, 84:2
L'Ecuyer, Josephine Mrs, 1947, My 27,25:1
Ledasma, Delores D Mrs, 1940, O 2,23:4
Ledbetter, Homer C, 1946, O 24,27:3
Ledbetter, Huddie, 1949, D 7,36:2
Ledbetter, Huddie Mrs, 1968, Je 4,44:2
Ledbetter, J F, 1937, Jl 10,16:1
Ledbetter, John N Jr, 1967, D 27,37:1
Ledbetter, Samuel L, 1946, Mr 12,25:4
Ledbetter, William H Lt, 1937, Ag 20,17:4
Ledden, Joseph E, 1949, My 20,28:5
Ledden, William J, 1951, D 25,31:2
Leddy, C A, 1940, Ja 15,15:4
Leddy, Harry, 1937, Mr 27,15:5
Leddy, James H Mrs, 1942, F 25,19:3
Leddy, John A, 1948, O 24,76:3
Leddy, Joseph A Rev, 1937, O 27,31:5
Leddy, Leo P, 1963, Jl 18,27:2
Leddy, Margaret, 1960, Mr 19,21:6
Leddy, Martin T, 1941, Ag 19,21:5
Leddy, Peter, 1873, My 2,5:3
Leddy, Philip J Jr, 1960, Jl 6,33:2
Ledebur, Wilbur T Jr, 1960, S 4,68:7
Leden, William G, 1951, O 7,55:1
Leder, Frank E, 1962, N 9,35:2
Leder, Nathan Mrs, 1948, O 8,26:2
Leder, Seymour Mrs, 1955, D 22,23:2
Lederer, Charles, 1925, D 14,21:4; 1954, My 1,15:6
Lederer, Charlotte B Mrs, 1955, Ag 24,27:6
Lederer, Emanuel, 1917, Ag 22,7:2
Lederer, Emil, 1939, My 30,17:1; 1941, O 25,17:5
Lederer, Frederic, 1952, O 23,31:1
Lederer, George F, 1938, My 22,II,7:1
Lederer, George W, 1938, O 9,44:8
Lederer, Grace N Mrs, 1942, Ja 8,21:4
Lederer, Irving R, 1950, Ja 10,29:4
Lederer, John G Mrs, 1953, N 17,31:2
Lederer, John H Mrs, 1940, Je 22,15:3
Lederer, Ludwig G, 1960, Mr 18,25:2
Lederer, Max, 1950, Ja 26,28:2; 1952, S 14,87:1
Lederer, Miles W, 1953, D 27,60:6
Lederer, Morris W, 1963, Ag 1,27:2
Lederer, Norbert L, 1955, N 26,19:3
Lederer, Richard M Sr, 1952, Jl 26,13:3
Lederer, Richard Mrs, 1957, Je 8,19:4

Lederer, Sam, 1950, D 31,43:2
Lederer, Samuel, 1925, S 1,21:4
Lederle, Ernst Dr, 1921, Mr 15,11:3
Lederle, Francis A Col, 1909, Ag 6,7:4
Lederman, Abraham, 1963, O 4,35:2
Lederman, Anthony A, 1953, D 27,60:5
Lederman, Charles, 1965, F 26,29:4
Lederman, Jerome A, 1967, Jl 7,33:2
Lederman, M D Mrs, 1942, Jl 3,17:4
Lederman, Max (cor, Mr 13,86:6), 1960, Mr 12,21:1
Lederman, Moses D, 1952, S 8,21:2
Lederman, Neal, 1960, Mr 11,25:1
Ledlie, J H Gen, 1882, Ag 16,5:3
Lednicki, Waclaw Dr, 1967, O 31,45:2
Ledochowski, Card, 1902, Jl 23,9:2
Ledochowski, Cardinal, 1894, Jl 30,5:1
Ledochowski, Vladimir, 1942, D 14,23:3
Ledoux, Albert R Mrs, 1918, N 24,11:1
Ledoux, Albert Reid, 1923, O 25,19:5
Ledoux, Alice Benet, 1925, S 29,27:4
Ledoux, Athanasius, 1953, O 15,33:5
Ledoux, J W, 1932, N 8,21:3
Ledoux, Louis V, 1948, F 26,23:2
Ledoux, Urbain J (por), 1941, Ap 10,25:8
Ledoux, Urbain J Mrs, 1960, D 11,88:8
Ledseman, Thomas, 1955, Ja 3,29:1
Ledterman, Robert L, 1960, Ja 11,33:8
Leduc, Alma D L, 1956, Jl 19,27:5
Leduc, Henri Mrs, 1956, Je 28,29:3
Leduc, Joseph A, 1955, D 22,23:2
Leduc, Medard, 1954, Je 17,29:5
Leduc, Paul A, 1964, Ap 2,33:2
Le Due, Janvier Mrs, 1912, F 27,9:2
Ledwick, Claude, 1951, F 14,29:3
Ledwinka, Joseph, 1949, N 27,105:1
Ledwith, Frank M, 1955, N 19,19:6
Ledyard, Henry B, 1921, My 26,13:3
Ledyard, L C, 1932, Ja 8,21:1
Ledyard, L Cass Mrs, 1905, Ja 18,6:3
Ledyard, Lewis C Mrs, 1955, F 4,19:4
Lee, A H, 1869, Jl 26,5:2
Lee, A N, 1879, N 1,2:4
Lee, A W Mrs, 1938, D 21,23:5
Lee, Abram M, 1951, My 15,31:3
Lee, Addison W Jr, 1949, My 2,25:2
Lee, Adele C Mrs (will), 1941, Ag 21,17:1
Lee, Alan P, 1951, Ag 10,15:5
Lee, Albert, 1943, Mr 27,13:3; 1945, N 9,19:1
Lee, Albert E, 1942, Mr 19,21:4
Lee, Albert Lindley Gen, 1908, Ja 1,9:3
Lee, Albert R, 1959, D 5,23:6
Lee, Alfred E Mrs (D Masters), 1964, D 23,27:2
Lee, Alfred O, 1938, D 26,24:4
Lee, Alfred P, 1940, Ap 10,25:4
Lee, Algernon, 1954, Ja 6,31:1
Lee, Algernon Mrs, 1953, Ja 24,15:5
Lee, Alice, 1943, F 20,13:3
Lee, Alice L, 1952, Ap 4,25:4
Lee, Allen, 1951, F 7,29:2
Lee, Amasa C, 1962, Ap 16,29:5
Lee, Amy, 1925, D 26,15:7
Lee, Anson L, 1949, Ja 12,27:5
Lee, Anthony Mrs, 1946, Ag 13,27:4
Lee, Archie L, 1950, D 23,16:2
Lee, Arthur, 1961, My 16,43:1
Lee, Arthur C, 1937, N 18,23:5
Lee, Arthur D, 1949, F 1,25:5
Lee, Arthur E, 1964, Ja 28,31:3
Lee, Arthur J, 1947, Ap 13,60:2
Lee, Arthur L, 1956, Jl 22,61:2
Lee, Arthur L Jr, 1937, Ag 8,II,6:6
Lee, Arthur M, 1964, Je 11,33:4
Lee, Arthur M Mrs, 1950, O 27,29:4
Lee, Arthur O, 1938, Mr 13,II,8:3
Lee, Arthur T, 1953, Ja 8,27:3
Lee, Arthur V Jr, 1943, S 21,23:2
Lee, Ashton, 1941, Mr 20,21:1
Lee, B J, 1933, N 13,14:7
Lee, Baker P, 1942, D 16,25:3
Lee, Baxter, 1939, F 8,23:3
Lee, Belinda, 1961, Mr 14,30:2
Lee, Benjamin F, 1909, Ap 26,7:5; 1961, Je 7,41:1
Lee, Benjamin Franklin, 1907, Mr 4,9:5
Lee, Benjamin T, 1937, O 27,31:4
Lee, Benjamin W, 1958, Ag 1,21:1
Lee, Benno, 1961, F 6,23:3
Lee, Benno Mrs, 1946, O 24,27:4
Lee, Bert, 1946, Ja 25,23:3
Lee, Blair, 1944, D 27,19:1
Lee, Blewett, 1951, Ap 21,17:6
Lee, Bp, 1874, S 27,5:3
Lee, Bryan A, 1955, Je 21,31:1
Lee, Burton E, 1954, Jl 2,19:3
Lee, Burton J Jr, 1962, Jl 24,28:1
Lee, C Stewart, 1949, O 6,31:5
Lee, C Tennant, 1945, N 26,21:4
Lee, C W, 1926, N 26,19:4
Lee, C W Mrs, 1953, Je 11,29:3
Lee, Canada (L L C Canegata), 1952, My 10,21:5
Lee, Carlton G, 1949, Mr 28,21:4
Lee, Charles, 1953, Je 18,32:2; 1962, Ja 29,25:3
Lee, Charles A, 1947, Jl 14,21:4
Lee, Charles A Prof, 1872, F 15,8:4
Lee, Charles C Mrs, 1962, Ag 19,89:1
Lee, Charles E, 1956, Je 26,29:1; 1959, S 13,84:4
Lee, Charles F, 1942, My 25,15:6; 1948, Jl 20,23:5
Lee, Charles H, 1940, Ja 20,15:5; 1949, S 29,29:2
Lee, Charles H Jr, 1955, My 8,88:3
Lee, Charles H Mrs, 1944, My 25,21:6
Lee, Charles Northam (funl, S 2,23:5), 1925, Ag 31, 15:6
Lee, Charles R Mrs, 1946, Jl 23,25:4
Lee, Charles Rev, 1873, Jl 11,2:4
Lee, Charlotte E, 1959, D 6,86:7
Lee, Charlotte R Mrs, 1957, O 16,32:3
Lee, Chong Yung, 1954, F 2,17:5
Lee, Chris J, 1950, Ja 7,17:3
Lee, Christian A, 1944, D 15,19:5
Lee, Christopher M Judge, 1912, My 21,13:3
Lee, Chuck (Chas), 1967, Jl 6,35:2
Lee, Clara Mrs, 1947, S 2,21:4
Lee, Clarence L, 1941, Ag 16,15:1
Lee, Clarence W, 1942, N 11,25:3
Lee, Clark, 1953, F 16,21:3
Lee, Clifford S, 1940, F 9,19:5
Lee, Columbus O Jr, 1939, O 5,23:2
Lee, Cornelius S Jr, 1954, S 14,27:4
Lee, Dai-Ming, 1961, Mr 20,29:3
Lee, Daniel Mortimer Maj, 1914, Jl 29,9:6
Lee, David, 1952, Ja 18,27:4
Lee, David Bradley, 1903, Ag 26,3:2
Lee, David Russell, 1867, Ja 18,8:4
Lee, David William, 1909, Mr 24,9:3
Lee, Delia C Mrs, 1947, Ap 27,60:7
Lee, Dick (funl plans, Jl 3,17:3), 1967, Jl 2,35:1
Lee, Donald E, 1942, S 19,15:1
Lee, Donald S, 1940, Je 24,15:4
Lee, Dorothy, 1958, O 24,33:1
Lee, Dwight B, 1942, Mr 7,17:3
Lee, E, 1933, Ag 7,1:4
Lee, E W, 1927, S 10,17:5
Lee, Edith F Mrs, 1955, Ja 28,19:2
Lee, Edmund J, 1962, My 26,25:3
Lee, Edmund W, 1942, Ja 13,19:4
Lee, Edmund W Mrs, 1943, N 24,21:2
Lee, Edna (Mrs Harry J), 1963, S 27,29:2
Lee, Edward B (por), 1939, Ja 25,21:3
Lee, Edward B-H, 1956, Ja 27,23:3
Lee, Edward B Mrs, 1946, F 24,44:2
Lee, Edward E, 1942, F 10,20:3
Lee, Edward H, 1937, Ja 13,24:2
Lee, Edward Merwin Gen, 1913, Ja 3,9:5
Lee, Edward R, 1956, F 7,31:4
Lee, Edward T, 1943, D 15,27:5
Lee, Edward W, 1941, O 28,23:5
Lee, Edwin A (por), 1942, F 16,17:1
Lee, Edwin A, 1942, D 11,23:4; 1966, My 15,88:5
Lee, Edwin F (por), 1948, S 16,29:5
Lee, Eleanor, 1967, Je 1,43:3
Lee, Elizabeth F Mrs, 1942, Ap 23,24:2
Lee, Elizabeth L, 1938, Ja 29,15:2
Lee, Elmo P, 1949, Jl 27,23:2
Lee, Elwood Mrs, 1943, Ja 17,44:6
Lee, Emmitt T, 1938, Ja 30,II,9:1
Lee, Emory J, 1951, Je 4,27:3
Lee, Enoch J, 1940, Mr 14,23:3
Lee, Ernest K Mrs, 1948, My 27,25:2
Lee, Ernest R, 1965, My 24,19:1
Lee, Esther H Mrs, 1939, Ag 6,37:1
Lee, Etta G Mrs (por), 1942, Ag 24,15:4
Lee, Everett A, 1949, N 2,27:4
Lee, F R, 1879, Jl 10,2:4
Lee, Felix H, 1949, Je 14,31:3
Lee, Fitzhugh, 1954, N 14,89:3
Lee, Fitzhugh Gen, 1905, Ap 29,1:5
Lee, Florence M, 1945, S 6,25:4
Lee, Floyd J, 1942, Ja 6,24:2
Lee, Frances G Mrs, 1962, Ja 28,76:6
Lee, Francis A, 1954, D 4,17:6
Lee, Francis Bazley, 1914, My 3,13:5
Lee, Francis W Mrs, 1948, O 7,29:3
Lee, Francis X Sr, 1967, Ag 17,37:4
Lee, Francis X Sr Mrs, 1959, S 6,72:2
Lee, Frank, 1941, D 22,17:1; 1943, D 27,20:2
Lee, Frank H, 1937, Ap 14,25:3; 1952, N 22,23:5
Lee, Frank H Jr, 1958, S 21,86:8
Lee, Frank H Mrs, 1942, Mr 8,42:3
Lee, Frederic P, 1968, O 5,35:3
Lee, Frederic S (por), 1939, D 16,17:1
Lee, Frederic S Mrs, 1938, N 8,23:3
Lee, Frederick Girard, 1924, My 18,7:1
Lee, Frederick Mrs, 1943, Ja 4,15:2
Lee, Frederick W, 1937, Mr 19,23:5
Lee, G Harold, 1950, Ap 20,29:3
Lee, George B, 1943, Mr 14,26:1; 1948, Jl 14,23:5
Lee, George Bolling Mrs (cor, Jl 13,27:4), 1968, Jl 10,39:1
Lee, George C, 1950, O 30,27:3; 1955, Ag 27,15:5
Lee, George C Mrs, 1914, Ja 15,9:5
Lee, George F, 1946, F 24,44:3
Lee, George L, 1966, Ag 10,41:2
Lee, George L Sr Mrs, 1961, Jl 17,43:3
Lee, George S (por), 1949, Ja 20,27:4
Lee, George W, 1937, Ap 9,21:1; 1941, N 29,17:3; 1945, D 25,23:2
Lee, George Washington Custis Gen, 1913, F 19,11:5
Lee, Georgie M Mrs, 1938, Je 7,23:5
Lee, Gerald S (por), 1944, Ap 4,21:3
Lee, Gerald S Mrs, 1951, O 18,29:6
Lee, Gerrard S, 1957, Ag 17,15:1
Lee, Gertrude A Mrs, 1959, S 3,27:1
Lee, Gilbert C, 1941, F 8,15:2
Lee, Godwin, 1921, Mr 4,13:4
Lee, Grace E, 1961, My 11,37:3
Lee, H Frank, 1937, N 19,23:3
Lee, H Vernon, 1962, F 10,23:6
Lee, H W, 1941, Ap 18,21:3
Lee, Hal F, 1959, D 11,34:1
Lee, Halfdan Mrs, 1953, S 10,25:4
Lee, Halfdan Mrs (Kath J), 1961, O 25,37:4
Lee, Hamlin F, 1907, Mr 29,9:6
Lee, Hannah F Mrs, 1866, Ja 1,4:2
Lee, Harold G, 1951, O 15,25:3
Lee, Harold R, 1957, N 9,27:5
Lee, Harry, 1925, My 20,23:4; 1941, D 14,69:1; 194 D 20,44:8
Lee, Harry C Mrs, 1951, Ja 26,23:2
Lee, Harry D, 1940, D 18,25:3
Lee, Harry G, 1917, N 25,23:4
Lee, Harry M Mrs, 1955, Ap 19,31:2
Lee, Harry P, 1952, S 19,23:1
Lee, Harry R (por), 1938, Mr 24,23:4
Lee, Harry W Mrs, 1943, N 6,13:1
Lee, Helen, 1921, Mr 24,17:4
Lee, Helen H (funl planned, Je 26,29:1; postponed, 27,25:6), 1964, Je 22,6:4
Lee, Henry Dr, 1904, Ap 25,1:4
Lee, Henry F, 1939, My 1,23:5
Lee, Henry Flavel Rev, 1912, My 26,15:5
Lee, Henry H (por), 1941, Ag 1,15:4
Lee, Henry S Mrs, 1949, Ap 13,29:2
Lee, Herbert B, 1946, Jl 6,15:3
Lee, Herman H, 1956, Mr 8,29:1
Lee, Homer, 1923, Ja 26,17:3
Lee, Howard C, 1946, Jl 12,17:3
Lee, Howard W, 1956, My 17,31:5
Lee, Hugh J, 1944, O 1,45:3
Lee, I, 1934, N 10,15:1
Lee, Irving J, 1955, My 24,31:1
Lee, Isaac L, 1942, O 24,15:5
Lee, Isaac V, 1948, Ap 17,15:4
Lee, Isadora H, 1945, Mr 7,21:6
Lee, Ivan, 1952, N 27,31:5
Lee, J Elwood (est), 1914, Ap 11,11:5
Lee, J Gordon, 1959, My 12,35:3
Lee, J H, 1877, Ag 17,2:4
Lee, J M, 1929, N 17,31:5
Lee, J M Dr, 1926, Ja 12,31:3
Lee, J M Maj Gen, 1926, Mr 27,17:5
Lee, J R Dr, 1884, Ja 25,3:4
Lee, J Richard, 1944, N 13,21:7
Lee, James, 1941, F 7,19:3
Lee, James A Mrs, 1948, S 16,29:5
Lee, James B, 1964, Mr 28,19:3
Lee, James C L Gen, 1916, Jl 28,11:7
Lee, James C Mrs (cor, Jl 25,33:6), 1962, Jl 24,2
Lee, James Col, 1874, Je 18,5:4
Lee, James D, 1947, Mr 22,13:6
Lee, James E, 1961, F 24,21:1; 1962, Ja 15,27:4
Lee, James E Sr, 1959, Ap 25,21:5
Lee, James F, 1937, F 12,23:3
Lee, James J, 1962, Ja 10,47:2
Lee, James M, 1952, Ag 23,13:6
Lee, James P, 1941, S 15,17:1; 1950, N 18,15:5; 1 Ag 15,16:4; 1955, O 19,33:5
Lee, James S, 1937, Je 9,25:5
Lee, James S Mrs, 1951, Ja 22,17:1
Lee, James T, 1968, Ja 4,37:1
Lee, James T Mrs, 1943, F 27,13:1
Lee, James W Jr (por), 1948, S 18,17:4
Lee, James Wideman Rev, 1919, O 5,22:4
Lee, Jane (Mrs J L St John), 1957, Mr 20,37:4
Lee, Jay A J, 1954, S 13,23:2
Lee, Jenny, 1925, Ag 7,15:7
Lee, Joe, 1937, Jl 29,19:1
Lee, John, 1915, My 3,11:3
Lee, John A Dr (funl, Ap 8,11:4), 1920, Ap 6,1
Lee, John Bowers, 1914, Ap 28,13:6
Lee, John C, 1940, S 17,23:6
Lee, John C H (funl, S 5,27:1), 1958, Ag 31,57:
Lee, John D, 1937, S 8,23:5
Lee, John E, 1955, Ap 1,28:2; 1966, O 12,43:2
Lee, John F, 1946, My 15,21:2
Lee, John F Sr, 1948, O 17,76:5
Lee, John H, 1946, Je 1,13:6; 1947, Ag 6,23:5; 1 O 28,28:7
Lee, John H Col, 1873, S 14,1:6
Lee, John H Mrs, 1949, N 21,25:5; 1961, S 21,1
Lee, John H S, 1949, Jl 13,28:2
Lee, John J, 1945, Jl 15,15:6; 1954, Ja 30,17:4
Lee, John K, 1952, Mr 1,15:2
Lee, John Lloyd Rev Dr, 1906, D 2,7:6
Lee, John M Jr, 1966, Je 2,18:8
Lee, John Mason Maj, 1924, Mr 13,17:3
Lee, John P, 1939, D 8,25:3
Lee, John P Mrs, 1955, F 9,27:1
Lee, John R, 1915, Jl 23,9:7; 1967, Ap 12,42:8
Lee, John W, 1949, My 28,15:7; 1951, O 23,27: 1952, Je 7,19:5

Lee, John Y, 1939, Ap 21,23:5
Lee, Joseph A, 1954, Jl 2,19:5
Lee, Joseph D, 1941, Jl 11,15:2
Lee, Joseph Mrs, 1949, Ja 23,68:4
Lee, Joseph T, 1952, N 30,88:5; 1956, O 19,27:2
Lee, Josh B, 1967, Ag 11,31:3
Lee, Joshua M, 1951, D 1,13:6
Lee, Judy, 1958, Ag 4,21:5
Lee, Julia, 1958, D 9,41:4
Lee, Kenneth, 1967, O 20,47:3
Lee, Kui, 1966, D 5,45:5
Lee, L, 1877, Ja 22,5:6
Lee, L M, 1882, Ap 22,5:3
Lee, L Mason Mrs, 1965, D 11,33:4
Lee, Laurence F, 1961, Jl 21,23:5
Lee, Lawrence, 1963, N 24,22:8
Lee, Lawrence R Mrs, 1952, D 7,88:5
Lee, Leander R, 1955, D 8,37:4
Lee, Leonard, 1956, Ag 7,27:1
Lee, Leslie A Prof, 1908, My 21,7:6
Lee, Lester, 1956, Je 21,31:4
Lee, Lewis A, 1951, Jl 16,21:5
Lee, Lewis H, 1950, D 1,25:2
Lee, Lewis H Mrs, 1950, Je 5,23:2
Lee, Lewis Mrs, 1959, O 5,31:1
Lee, Linford H, 1956, Ap 13,25:4
Lee, Lothrop, 1946, O 16,27:2
Lee, Louis F, 1957, Mr 25,25:3
Lee, Louise F, 1962, S 23,86:6
Lee, Lowell M, 1953, Ag 28,17:3
Lee, Lucas S, 1954, O 2,17:6
Lee, M B Mrs, 1948, S 30,27:1
Lee, Margaret, 1907, Mr 14,7:6; 1914, D 27,3:5
Lee, Mary, 1951, Ja 14,86:2
Lee, Mary Custis, 1918, N 23,11:2
Lee, Mary E Mrs, 1937, O 10,II,8:5
Lee, Mary F, 1946, My 3,21:2
Lee, Mary G Mrs, 1945, F 24,11:3
Lee, Mary J, 1881, My 18,5:5
Lee, Mary M, 1957, Ag 6,27:3
Lee, Mary Tabb Bolling Mrs, 1924, My 6,21:6
Lee, Matthew T Sr, 1956, Jl 9,23:2
Lee, Milo Mortimer, 1953, F 21,13:4
Lee, Montague, 1966, N 19,33:2
Lee, Morris M, 1956, Jl 18,27:4
Lee, Muna, 1965, Ap 4,87:3
Lee, Murray G, 1965, Jl 4,37:1
Lee, Nelson, 1872, Ja 18,2:3
Lee, Nixon, 1962, F 27,33:3
Lee, Oliver G, 1942, Je 1,13:3
Lee, Oliver J, 1964, Ja 16,26:1
Lee, Oscar, 1938, Ap 15,19:2
Lee, Otis H, 1948, S 19,76:4
Lee, Pa Parish, 1904, F 25,9:4
Lee, Paul M, 1950, Ja 28,13:5
Lee, Percy H Y, 1951, S 29,17:4
Lee, Porter R, 1939, Mr 9,21:5
Lee, Porter R Jr, 1946, Ja 31,21:3
Lee, R Q, 1930, Ap 19,17:5
Lee, Raleigh W, 1959, Jl 27,25:5
Lee, Ralph A Sr Mrs, 1960, S 11,82:1
Lee, Ralph E, 1959, D 5,23:5
Lee, Raymond E, 1958, Ap 8,29:3
Lee, Richard (funl, Ag 6,19:5), 1925, Ag 5,17:6
Lee, Richard, 1953, N 25,23:3
Lee, Richard B, 1943, D 28,17:1
Lee, Richard Bland Col, 1875, Ag 7,4:6
Lee, Richard H, 1937, Ag 7,15:4
Lee, Richard H Mrs, 1957, O 26,21:2
Lee, Richard Mrs, 1966, Jl 16,25:2
Lee, Richard S M, 1961, Jl 20,27:3
Lee, Robert, 1940, F 24,13:1; 1966, N 3,39:4
Lee, Robert E, 1942, Je 14,46:2; 1963, Ja 4,4:4; 1966, Ja 15,27:3; 1966, D 17,33:4
Lee, Robert E Capt, 1914, O 21,11:5
Lee, Robert E Col, 1922, S 8,13:4
Lee, Robert E Gen (mem, O 25,8:1), 1870, O 13,4:7
Lee, Robert E Gen Mrs, 1873, N 9,5:2
Lee, Robert E Mrs, 1965, N 23,38:2; 1967, N 3,48:5
Lee, Robert E Sr Mrs, 1941, My 31,11:4
Lee, Robert E 3d Mrs, 1959, My 20,35:2
Lee, Robert Emmons, 1925, N 29,13:1
Lee, Robert H, 1956, Ap 4,29:2
Lee, Robert L, 1964, Jl 19,65:1
Lee, Robert Lincoln, 1915, F 17,11:6
Lee, Robert M, 1939, Ja 8,42:5
Lee, Robert P, 1865, Ja 29,4:6
Lee, Robert V, 1949, Ap 11,25:5
Lee, Robert W Mrs, 1954, O 5,27:5; 1959, Ja 1,31:2
Lee, Roger I, 1965, O 30,35:3
Lee, Ronald C, 1955, My 5,33:5
Lee, Rose H (Mrs G Ginn), 1964, Mr 27,27:4
Lee, Rudolph, 1955, Jl 6,27:1
Lee, S G, 1882, Ja 10,8:6
Lee, Samuel, 1924, My 5,15:3
Lee, Samuel T, 1958, My 14,33:3
Lee, Selena A Mrs, 1946, Ap 19,29:2
Lee, Shavey (L J Waye),(funl plans, Mr 17,45:4), 1955, Mr 16,33:3
Lee, Sidney Sir, 1926, Mr 4,21:1
Lee, Stephen D Gen (funl, My 30,7:5), 1908, My 29, 7:3
Lee, Stephen G, 1941, S 11,23:5; 1957, My 10,27:2
Lee, T I L, 1903, Ag 1,7:6
Lee, T P, 1939, F 5,40:5
Lee, T W, 1954, S 4,11:6
Lee, Theodore S Rev, 1911, Ag 25,7:5
Lee, Thomas, 1950, Ja 14,6:7
Lee, Thomas (Bro Adonas Thomas), 1963, S 17,35:2
Lee, Thomas A, 1953, Ja 17,15:3
Lee, Thomas B, 1950, O 19,31:1
Lee, Thomas H, 1954, Mr 18,31:1
Lee, Thomas L (est tax appr), 1965, D 23,30:7
Lee, Thurman, 1960, D 26,23:5
Lee, Timothy J, 1942, S 14,15:4
Lee, Tom, 1952, Ap 2,33:2
Lee, Umphrey, 1958, Je 24,31:3
Lee, Vernon H, 1924, Mr 18,21:5
Lee, Viscount, 1947, Jl 22,23:3
Lee, W Arthur, 1958, O 26,88:6
Lee, W C, 1929, N 3,29:1
Lee, W S, 1934, Mr 25,29:5
Lee, Walter E, 1951, Ap 7,15:6
Lee, Walter G, 1945, Ag 3,17:2
Lee, Walter H, 1952, N 11,29:2
Lee, Walter J, 1945, Ja 10,23:2
Lee, Walter J Sr Mrs, 1949, N 13,92:7
Lee, Walter N, 1956, Ja 29,92:2
Lee, Walter T, 1954, Ap 21,29:4
Lee, Walter Wright, 1911, Jl 5,11:6
Lee, Warren I, 1955, D 26,19:2
Lee, Watson Mrs, 1961, My 1,29:5
Lee, Wellington B, 1943, My 5,27:5
Lee, Whitford J, 1959, My 9,21:5
Lee, Wilbur O, 1956, Mr 14,33:4
Lee, Wilfred Mrs, 1964, Mr 1,35:2
Lee, Willard J, 1959, My 13,37:5
Lee, William, 1883, My 12,5:2; 1906, D 4,9:5
Lee, William B, 1938, Jl 31,33:5; 1946, F 18,21:4; 1946, Mr 30,15:3
Lee, William C, 1948, Je 26,17:5; 1952, Jl 23,23:3
Lee, William C Mrs, 1955, N 18,25:2
Lee, William E, 1941, Ap 29,19:2; 1955, D 7,39:1
Lee, William H, 1954, Ap 30,23:3; 1960, S 5,15:5; 1962, O 28,88:8; 1964, My 20,43:1
Lee, William H Mrs, 1945, S 29,15:6
Lee, William Henry Lawrence, 1918, N 13,13:5
Lee, William J, 1938, D 20,25:2
Lee, William J Sr, 1957, Ag 16,19:4
Lee, William Mrs, 1952, Jl 18,19:5
Lee, William P, 1937, N 12,21:2; 1941, Je 2,23:5; 1949, Jl 8,19:3
Lee, William Pray Mrs, 1918, Ja 11,15:3
Lee, William R, 1943, F 11,20:3
Lee, William S, 1949, Mr 21,23:5
Lee, William T, 1939, Jl 1,17:3
Lee, William W, 1947, N 1,15:6
Lee, William Y, 1965, Ap 13,37:3
Lee, Willis A Jr, 1945, Ag 26,43:1
Lee, Willis A Jr Mrs, 1949, Mr 24,27:2
Lee, Wilson H, 1948, My 10,22:2
Lee, Z Collins Judge, 1859, N 29,4:4
Lee-Hankey, William, 1952, F 12,27:4
Lee-Martin, Peter J Mrs, 1958, Ap 12,19:1
Lee-Martin, Richard H, 1950, Mr 8,27:3
Lee-Warner, Philip Henry, 1925, Ja 30,17:5
Leeb, Brian P Mrs, 1947, My 16,23:4
Leeb, Wilhelm R von, 1956, My 1,33:3
Leeberg, Edward, 1958, S 14,84:1
Leece, Bennett M, 1948, D 7,31:3
Leech, A Y Jr, 1953, Je 28,60:5
Leech, Al, 1912, Jl 6,7:4
Leech, Edgar L, 1949, Jl 1,19:5
Leech, Edward T, 1949, D 12,33:3
Leech, George T, 1941, Ag 6,17:4
Leech, H H, 1879, F 11,2:1
Leech, Haliburton H, 1939, My 8,17:3
Leech, Harper, 1951, My 23,35:4
Leech, Harper Mrs, 1946, D 5,31:5
Leech, Hedding B, 1966, N 2,45:4
Leech, Hedding B Mrs, 1956, S 8,17:4
Leech, Herbert C, 1967, Ap 25,43:1
Leech, Isaac E, 1956, Je 8,25:6
Leech, J Russell, 1952, F 7,27:4
Leech, James C, 1951, Ag 19,85:2
Leech, James M, 1956, Mr 4,78:4
Leech, John (funl, N 20,2:1), 1864, N 14,1:4
Leech, John, 1954, F 16,25:3
Leech, John S, 1948, Ja 30,23:2
Leech, Joseph, 1940, My 31,19:5
Leech, Mary A, 1953, O 28,29:4
Leech, Paul N, 1941, Ja 15,23:5
Leech, Ralph O (por), 1948, F 5,23:3
Leech, Stephen Sir, 1925, My 13,21:3
Leech, William J, 1949, D 14,31:6
Leedham, Cajus, 1941, O 30,23:2
Leedom, James S, 1952, Mr 25,18:2
Leedom, Marion J, 1954, S 9,32:4
Leeds, Abram L, 1938, Jl 20,19:1
Leeds, Abram L (will), 1939, Je 28,22:3
Leeds, Albert, 1938, Je 9,23:4
Leeds, Annie S Mrs, 1937, O 25,22:2
Leeds, Arthur N, 1939, Ja 27,19:3
Leeds, C C, 1949, Jl 20,25:5
Leeds, Carl S, 1957, Mr 1,23:3
Leeds, Charles S, 1939, Je 5,17:3
Leeds, Charles T, 1960, Mr 21,29:2
Leeds, Donald D, 1951, Ag 1,23:4
Leeds, Duchess of, 1874, Ap 26,10:4
Leeds, Duchess of (C Lambton), 1952, D 7,88:4
Leeds, Duke of, 1927, My 11,25:5
Leeds, Duke of (J F G Osborne), 1963, Jl 28,64:7
Leeds, Duke of (F D'A G Osborne), 1964, Mr 21, 25:1
Leeds, Edmund I, 1958, Je 2,27:5
Leeds, Edward Fowler, 1908, Ag 13,7:4
Leeds, George T, 1952, F 27,27:4
Leeds, Harry D, 1952, Mr 21,24:4
Leeds, Henry, 1946, Ag 18,46:5; 1966, Je 7,47:1
Leeds, Henry H, 1870, Mr 13,4:3
Leeds, Henry W, 1946, O 3,27:5
Leeds, Horace W, 1953, Ag 15,15:4
Leeds, J C, 1941, Mr 26,23:2
Leeds, Jeannette G Mrs, 1946, S 26,25:4
Leeds, Joseph L, 1872, My 9,1:2
Leeds, Josephine F, 1966, Je 8,43:4
Leeds, Jules C, 1952, N 10,25:3
Leeds, Laurence C Sr, 1968, Ja 2,37:1
Leeds, Mary B Dr, 1937, O 15,23:5
Leeds, Morris E, 1952, F 10,93:3
Leeds, Myron P, 1962, Ja 29,25:3
Leeds, Norman Jr, 1961, Mr 14,35:3
Leeds, Robert L, 1955, O 26,31:1
Leeds, Rudolph G, 1964, N 23,37:3
Leeds, Samuel P (por), 1946, Ja 22,27:3
Leeds, Samuel P Mrs, 1957, Mr 19,37:5
Leeds, Sarah West Mrs, 1924, Mr 27,19:5
Leeds, Shepherd E, 1946, N 5,25:4
Leeds, Stanton B, 1964, D 31,17:1
Leeds, Theodore E, 1921, Ag 7,22:5
Leeds, Warner Mifflin, 1925, Mr 26,23:5
Leeds, William B, 1908, Je 24,7:5
Leeds, William B (funl, Je 9,7:5), 1908, Jl 8,7:5
Leeds, William J, 1921, Je 7,17:4
Leedy, C Denoe, 1964, O 24,29:3
Leedy, Charles Mrs, 1947, N 13,27:4
Leedy, J W, 1935, Mr 25,15:3
Leef, David, 1957, Je 23,84:5
Leefe, A C V Mrs, 1937, O 9,19:5
Leefe, J G Lt-Col, 1903, Je 12,9:6
Leehane, Timothy J, 1960, Mr 9,33:2
Leek, William T, 1938, Ag 21,32:6
Leeker, Albert H, 1956, F 15,31:4
Leeking, Frank D, 1947, Ag 9,13:6
Leeman, George Mrs, 1961, Mr 4,23:2
Leeman, J M, 1945, Je 1,15:3
Leeman, Walter, 1951, Ap 20,30:3
Leeming, John, 1944, N 5,54:3
Leeming, Joseph, 1906, Je 23,7:4; 1968, S 29,80:1
Leeming, Thomas L, 1949, Ja 5,26:2
Leeming, Woodruff Lt-Col, 1919, N 22,13:3
Leen, Clarence W, 1937, Jl 5,17:4
Leenhouts, Edward J, 1965, S 7,39:3
Leeper, Alpharetta, 1960, Jl 8,21:1
Leeper, Clyde, 1950, My 17,29:1
Leeper, Harry D, 1954, S 28,5:6
Leeper, James C, 1958, N 9,89:1
Leeper, James L Mrs, 1965, Jl 23,26:8
Leeper, James M Rev Dr, 1922, Ap 9,28:4
Leeper, Reginald Sir, 1968, F 4,80:3
Leeper, William, 1940, Ap 18,23:3
Leer, Henry, 1915, My 21,13:6
Leer, John, 1947, My 22,27:1
Leerburger, Hannah Mrs, 1937, O 30,19:4
Leers, Gustave, 1941, Jl 1,23:1
Lees, Annie E, 1945, Jl 6,11:4
Lees, C Robert, 1947, N 9,72:4
Lees, George C, 1954, Ap 13,31:5
Lees, H C, 1929, Ja 11,23:3
Lees, Henry T, 1946, Ja 25,24:2
Lees, James, 1938, N 2,24:2
Lees, James W, 1946, Mr 29,23:2; 1951, Ja 30,25:2
Lees, John A Sr, 1949, Je 7,31:1
Lees, Leon S, 1961, Ap 28,31:1
Lees, Peter W, 1923, My 14,15:5
Lees, Timothy, 1939, Ap 30,45:3
Lees, William C, 1951, My 27,68:6
Lees, William T, 1962, Ag 29,29:4
Lees-Smith, H B, 1941, D 19,25:4
Leese, Arnold S, 1956, Ja 20,4:4
Leeser, Solomon H Mrs, 1954, N 28,87:2
Leeson, A Whitney C, 1946, O 6,56:5
Leeson, Alfred Bradford Father, 1911, N 26,15:4
Leeson, Arthur A, 1958, N 18,37:2
Leeson, Harold G, 1943, S 30,21:5
Leeson, James A, 1947, S 26,23:5
Leeson, Robert A, 1953, N 24,29:1
Leeson, Spencer, 1956, Ja 28,17:7
Leet, Frank R, 1949, D 8,33:1
Leet, G A, 1881, Mr 27,1:6
Leet, G Edwin Mrs, 1944, O 28,15:6
Leet, George K, 1947, Ja 9,23:5
Leet, Horace W, 1966, S 4,65:1
Leet, John B, 1874, D 16,8:2
Leet, Leslie N, 1949, D 12,33:4
Leete, C Sidney, 1950, O 10,31:5
Leete, Ellsworth N, 1941, Je 6,21:4
Leete, Frederick D, 1958, F 16,86:6
Leete, William H, 1956, Ag 10,17:4

Leete, William R, 1952, Jl 20,53:2
Leete, William W, 1946, My 3,22:2
Leeuw, Harry A, 1945, O 19,23:4
Leever, Sam W, 1953, My 20,29:4
Leewitz, Allen A, 1939, Mr 20,17:3
Le Faivre, Alphonse Mrs, 1945, Jl 30,19:6
Lefaivre, Eva P Mrs, 1942, Ja 13,19:4
Lefaivre, F Hayes, 1953, Jl 8,27:5
Lefaivre, Georgiana, 1951, Mr 6,27:4
Le Fanu, Henry F, 1946, S 10,7:6
Le Faucheur, Albert R Mrs, 1945, D 4,30:2
Le Faucheur, J Joseph, 1948, Mr 27,13:3
Lefaucheux, Marie-Helene, 1964, F 26,21:1
Lefaucheux, Pierre-Andre, 1955, F 12,4:5
Lefaur, Andre, 1952, D 5,27:1
Le Favour, Adjutant-Gen, 1878, Mr 2,5:3
Lefavour, Henry, 1946, Je 17,21:4
Lefavour, William B Mrs, 1945, Ja 31,21:3
Lefco, Arthur J, 1959, Jl 24,25:5
Lefcort, Louis J, 1954, N 4,31:4
Lefcort, Martin, 1966, Ap 14,39:3
Lefcourt, A E, 1932, N 14,17:1
Lefcourt, Abraham A Mrs, 1949, Ag 17,23:5
Lefeber, John F, 1943, O 19,19:1
Lefebre, Walter S, 1956, Ja 20,23:2
Lefebvre, A Henry, 1938, Je 13,19:5
Lefebvre, Channing, 1967, Ap 22,31:5
Lefebvre, Charles, 1882, My 22,5:3
Lefebvre, Hector W, 1952, Ja 21,15:1
Le Febvre, Jules (cor, Je 16,9:6), 1911, Je 15,9:3
Lefebvre, Jules J, 1912, F 25,II,11:3
Lefebvre, Marie (Mrs Chas Herman Steinway), 1924, Je 25,23:5
Lefebvre, Pierre, 1941, O 14,23:3; 1955, F 23,27:2
Lefee, Charles A, 1947, Je 26,23:5
Le Feuvre, Guy, 1950, F 17,23:1
Lefever, Florence E, 1951, My 27,68:5
Le Fever, Frank, 1950, Jl 8,13:6
Le Fever, Matthew D Mrs, 1946, Ja 16,23:4
Lefever, Ralph H, 1937, O 8,23:5
Lefever, Silas F Mrs, 1949, O 3,17:6
Lefevre, Albert A, 1951, O 14,89:1
Lefevre, Benjamin Gen, 1922, Mr 9,17:3
Lefevre, Bishop, 1869, Mr 8,2:6
Lefevre, Caroline H, 1951, F 17,15:6
Le Fevre, Edward Y, 1941, F 23,40:2
Lefevre, Edwin, 1943, F 24,21:5
Le Fevre, Egbert Dr, 1914, Mr 31,11:5
Le Fevre, Elizabeth, 1948, My 29,15:5
Lefevre, Ernesto T, 1922, D 26,13:3
Le Fevre, Eugene Mrs, 1946, Ag 7,27:2
LeFevre, Frank J, 1941, My 1,23:3
Lefevre, Frederic, 1949, S 12,21:4
Le Fevre, George H Mrs, 1948, S 12,72:2
LeFevre, Gertrude Mrs, 1942, Jl 4,17:5
Lefevre, Gustave M, 1951, D 12,37:5
Lefevre, Henry F, 1951, O 7,87:2
LeFevre, Herbert, 1941, S 16,23:6
Le Fevre, Ira D (por), 1944, Je 5,19:5
Le Fevre, James Mrs, 1916, F 13,15:5
Lefevre, James O, 1956, D 13,37:3
Le Fevre, James Rev Dr, 1914, My 7,11:6
Le Fevre, James W, 1948, Je 4,23:5
Le Fevre, Jeannette G, 1947, Ja 15,25:4
Le Fevre, Lewis, 1943, Mr 15,13:1
LeFevre, Nathan Mrs, 1942, Mr 5,23:2
Lefevre, Philip F, 1965, My 31,17:3
Lefevre, Solomon, 1945, Je 10,32:5
Le Fevre, Theodore C Mrs, 1947, O 18,15:3
LeFevre, W LeRoy, 1967, Jl 22,25:3
Le Fevre, Wallace R, 1940, S 6,21:4
Leff, Abraham, 1957, Mr 25,25:1
Leff, Benjamin, 1953, Ap 14,27:6
Leff, Frank, 1963, N 30,27:2
Leff, Harry Mrs, 1951, Jl 28,11:3
Leff, Isadore, 1968, Je 29,29:2
Leff, Samuel, 1940, Mr 15,23:5
Leff, Solomon S, 1951, O 10,23:4
Leffert, Charles N, 1953, Mr 8,90:1
Leffert, Harry J, 1952, N 3,27:3
Leffert, Herman, 1951, Mr 3,13:1
Lefferts, A Mrs, 1878, D 31,5:1
Lefferts, Allen, 1957, My 5,88:6
Lefferts, Barent, 1955, F 18,21:1
Lefferts, Barent Mrs, 1964, N 3,31:4
Lefferts, David, 1960, Je 17,31:3
Lefferts, Elizabeth, 1879, My 21,2:6
Lefferts, Frederic R, 1918, Jl 26,11:5
Lefferts, George Morewood Dr, 1920, S 23,13:5
Lefferts, Gillet, 1952, Ag 18,17:4
Lefferts, Jacob R, 1941, D 20,19:4
Lefferts, James, 1915, N 6,11:7
Lefferts, Lefferts, 1908, Ja 10,7:5
Lefferts, Louis Eugene, 1911, Ag 1,9:6
Lefferts, M C, 1928, My 1,29:5
Lefferts, Marshall (see also Jl 4), 1876, Jl 7,8:3
Lefferts, Sigourney Fay, 1907, D 13,11:6
Lefferts, Walter, 1948, N 8,21:2
Lefferts, William, 1948, Je 10,25:2
Lefferts, William H, 1919, D 20,11:4
Lefferts, William R, 1956, D 2,87:1
Leffingwell, Albert F, 1946, Ag 15,25:3
Leffingwell, Elizabeth F, 1938, D 23,19:2
Leffingwell, Elmore C, 1942, N 30,23:3; 1942, D 2,25:6
Leffingwell, M W, 1879, Je 11,5:4
Leffingwell, Maurice A, 1944, Je 3,13:1
Leffingwell, Myron C Mrs, 1915, Ap 1,15:4
Leffingwell, Russell C (funl, O 5,41:4), 1960, O 3, 31:4
Leffingwell, Russell C Mrs, 1959, F 10,33:4
Leffinwell, Lucia D, 1944, O 13,19:5
Leffler, Charles D, 1961, Ja 3,27:6
Leffler, George, 1951, Ag 6,21:3
Leffler, George L, 1958, F 16,86:6
Leffler, Jack, 1962, Jl 12,29:2
Leffler, John, 1944, F 24,15:3
Leffler, John E, 1947, Ag 27,23:6
Leffler, Ray V, 1941, Ap 11,21:4
Leffler, William S, 1964, Ag 1,21:3
Leffman, L, 1885, My 25,1:7
Lefkow, Alfred, 1946, My 18,19:5
Lefkowitch, Henry, 1959, F 1,85:1
Lefkowitz, Arnold L Mrs, 1953, Jl 16,21:5
Lefkowitz, Benjamin V, 1962, Jl 11,35:2
Lefkowitz, David, 1958, O 4,21:2
Lefkowitz, Irving J, 1949, Je 2,27:1
Lefkowitz, Joseph, 1950, O 20,28:3; 1957, Mr 10,88:5
Lefkowitz, Louis L, 1943, Mr 7,38:7
Lefkowitz, Max, 1921, S 25,22:2
Lefkowitz, Samuel Mrs (Sept 26), 1965, O 11,61:3
Lefkowitz, Samuel S, 1957, S 24,35:5
Le Fleming, Kaye, 1946, Jl 18,25:4
Lefler, Edward L, 1946, Jl 14,36:5
Lefler, Mark R, 1956, N 26,27:2
Lefler, Theodore W, 1951, D 27,21:2
Le Fonte, J L Dr, 1883, N 17,2:2
Le Fort, August, 1912, Mr 4,11:6
Le Fort, Bernard R, 1938, N 19,17:3
Le Fort, Capt, 1864, My 26,4:5
Le Fort, Edward D, 1948, Mr 5,21:3
Lefort, Marie L, 1951, Ag 8,25:6
Lefrak, Harry (funl plans; trb, Jl 3,25:3; funl, Jl 4,-17:3), 1963, Jl 2,29:2
Lefrak, Harry Mrs, 1962, N 20,35:1
Lefranc, Abel, 1952, N 27,31:6
Lefranc, E V E, 1883, S 15,5:2
Lefranc, Fernand, 1949, Mr 24,28:2
Le Frank, Felipe, 1945, S 13,23:3
Le Frank, John D, 1945, My 28,21:2
Lefroy, Sallie M Mrs, 1942, Mr 20,19:4
Lefschitz, Harris, 1921, Ag 4,15:7
Left Hand, 1911, Je 29,11:4
Leftoff, Michael, 1962, O 24,39:1
Lefton, Abe, 1958, F 26,27:5
Lefton, Al P, 1964, S 20,88:5
Leftwich, Alex Mrs, 1957, D 26,19:1
Leftwich, Alexander, 1947, Ja 14,26:3
Leftwich, Fleming C, 1940, My 25,17:4
Leftwich, George F, 1943, D 24,13:2
Leftwich, R Frank, 1962, O 8,23:4
Lefuel, H M, 1881, Ja 4,5:2
Le Fur, Louis, 1943, F 24,21:3
Lefurgy, Albert Mrs, 1945, O 16,23:4
Lefurgy, Harry E Mrs, 1947, My 17,15:5
Lefurgy, Harry P, 1949, O 20,29:5
Le Furgy, William G, 1944, Mr 30,21:4
Lega, M, 1935, D 17,17:1
Legal, Ernst, 1955, Jl 1,21:3
Le Gal, Eugene Col, 1872, Mr 23,2:7
LeGall, Marcena J, 1955, Jl 31,69:1
Le Gallais, Hughes, 1964, D 26,17:3
Le Gallienne, Richard, 1947, S 16,23:1
Le Gallienne, Richard Mrs, 1955, Mr 18,27:2
Legan, John E, 1967, S 24,84:5
Legare, Alexander B, 1943, O 24,44:3
Legarth, Jens C, 1967, Jl 31,34:8
Legat, Nicholas, 1937, Ja 25,19:4
Legate, Burton J, 1937, Ag 31,23:1
Le Gay, Charles, 1909, Ja 10,13:4
Lege, Fred M Jr, 1939, Ag 31,19:3
Legendre, Eidney, 1948, Mr 9,23:5
Legendre, Leonce, 1951, My 16,35:3
Legenhausen, Albert H, 1952, S 26,21:4
Leger, Antoine J, 1950, Ap 9,84:4
Leger, Ernest J, 1952, O 8,31:2
Leger, Fernand, 1955, Ag 18,23:1
Legere, Frederick J, 1945, N 5,19:2
Legere, George, 1953, D 24,15:2
Legett, Theodore A Rev Dr, 1906, N 26,9:5
Legeyt, Charles H, 1949, O 10,2:2
Legg, Andrew J (will), 1952, Ap 20,55:1
Legg, Arthur T, 1939, Jl 10,19:4
Legg, George A Mrs, 1937, Ag 7,15:2
Legg, Helen Merryman, 1968, O 13,84:4
Legg, J W, 1929, Ja 4,25:2
Legg, John, 1938, Mr 21,15:5
Legg, John C Jr Mrs, 1947, Ag 21,23:6
Legg, John H, 1952, O 9,31:4
Legg, Lucille A Mrs (will), 1939, Ap 27,29:1
Legg, Raymond H, 1940, Ap 8,20:4
Legg, Washington, 1920, Ag 15,20:4
Legg, William B, 1946, Ag 28,27:3
Legg, William H, 1947, Jl 18,17:5; 1951, F 20,25:4
Leggat, Andrew R, 1914, Mr 9,9:4
Leggat, Harry F, 1949, F 2,27:4; 1955, Je 21,31:2
Legge, A, 1933, D 4,19:1
Legge, Alex S, 1950, F 2,27:4
Legge, Barnwell R, 1949, Je 9,31:4
Legge, Edgar P, 1954, N 7,86:1
Legge, Edward, 1950, Ag 14,17:5
Legge, Llewellyn, 1938, Ja 16,II,8:8
Legge, Peter, 1951, Mr 10,13:4
Legge, Russell H, 1941, S 10,23:1
Leggett, Albert C, 1950, Ja 14,15:3
Leggett, Albert G (R Sterling), 1959, Ap 16,33:2
Leggett, Alfred J, 1938, Mr 8,19:3
Leggett, Charles B, 1953, Ja 26,19:2
Leggett, Charles H, 1946, O 17,23:3
Leggett, Clarence P, 1943, S 10,23:4
Leggett, Eleanore, 1944, N 19,50:2
Leggett, Eugene S (por), 1939, F 20,17:3
Leggett, F A, 1876, D 21,4:6
Leggett, Francis H, 1909, Ag 30,7:5
Leggett, Francis H (funl, S 2,9:5), 1909, S 1,9:7
Leggett, Fred B, 1956, O 23,33:5
Leggett, Frederick, 1949, D 5,23:3
Leggett, Frederick W, 1955, My 24,31:3
Leggett, Frederick W Mrs, 1954, Je 12,15:3
Leggett, George H, 1938, S 13,24:2
Leggett, Henry T, 1947, Mr 25,26:3
Leggett, J Dwight, 1946, Jl 27,17:2
Leggett, James B, 1962, Ja 17,33:1
Leggett, John H, 1938, Ag 4,17:3
Leggett, John W, 1939, Mr 17,21:1
Leggett, Lindley H Jr, 1959, Jl 25,17:6
Leggett, Louise, 1949, Ja 30,60:4
Leggett, Mortimer M, 1873, O 14,1:4
Leggett, Oliver E, 1946, Mr 19,27:1
Leggett, Samuel, 1873, My 19,5:6
Leggett, Theodore, 1883, Jl 31,4:6
Leggett, Warren F, 1948, N 21,88:1
Leggett, William F, 1955, Ja 2,77:1
Leggett, William J Rev Dr, 1925, O 29,25:6
Leggiadro, Vincent E, 1967, N 24,46:7
Leggiere, Carmen E, 1962, Ap 25,39:5
Leggiero, Marcellino, 1959, N 10,47:4
Legh, Piers, 1955, O 17,27:4
Legh, Piers Mrs, 1955, O 18,37:4
Leght, G W, 1881, Je 10,2:7
Legien, Carl Rudolph, 1920, D 27,13:5
Legier, Edward W, 1964, Ja 11,23:1
Le Gierse, William H, 1947, Ja 11,19:4
Legner, John J, 1940, O 5,15:4
Legoll, Joseph C, 1959, S 21,31:3
Legon, Ernie, 1948, Jl 29,28:2
Legore, Harry W, 1956, Je 10,88:5
Legorreta, Augustin, 1937, N 9,24:7
Le Gost, Adolph F, 1961, N 26,88:8
Le Gost, Adolphe F Mrs, 1956, Ap 17,31:1
Le Goube, Rene L, 1954, Je 15,29:4
Legouve, E W, 1903, Mr 15,7:5
Legoux, C F M, 1947, S 11,27:6
Legrain, Leon, 1963, N 2,25:1
Le Gras, Gustave Prof, 1912, Jl 24,9:4
Legros, Moise, 1949, Ag 6,17:2
Legters, Leonard L, 1940, My 21,23:4
Leguere, George, 1947, N 23,72:6
Legueu, Felix, 1939, O 5,23:3
Leguia, A B, 1932, F 7,II,7:1
Leguia, Roberto, 1945, Mr 20,19:3
Leguizamon, Guillermo, 1946, N 1,23:2
Leguizamon, Hector D, 1938, Je 27,17:4
Legvazion, Charles, 1921, Ag 17,11:5
Leh, John Mrs, 1944, S 30,13:4
Leh, William H, 1957, Ap 10,33:5
Lehahan, John J, 1952, Ap 18,25:3
Le Hand, Marguerite A, 1944, Ag 1,15:1
Lehane, Daniel J (funl, O 1,31:3), 1966, S 28,47:4
Lehane, Timothy D Mrs, 1960, My 4,45:3
Lehar, Franz, 1948, O 25,23:1
Lehardy, Eugene Col, 1874, D 29,5:1
Le Harte, Ada Mrs, 1940, My 9,23:3
Lehback, F A Rev, 1875, S 11,4:7
Leheney, Raymond F, 1956, Mr 21,37:4
Lehigh, Ernest A, 1948, Ap 11,72:4
Lehigh, Stanley G, 1948, Ap 30,23:3
Lehlbach, Edward, 1944, Ag 7,15:2
Lehlbach, Frederick A, 1946, Ap 23,21:2
Lehlbach, Frederick R (por), 1937, Ag 5,23:3
Lehlbach, Herman, 1904, Ja 11,7:6
Lehlbach, Herman B, 1949, F 12,18:2
Lehmaier, James S, 1920, O 30,11:5
Lehmaier, Louis A Mrs, 1953, Jl 28,19:5
Lehman, A, 1932, D 19,15:3; 1936, My 16,15:3
Lehman, Abraham, 1964, S 22,39:3
Lehman, Adolph, 1945, Ag 2,19:4
Lehman, Allan S (will, N 27,63:3), 1952, N 10,2
Lehman, Allan S Mrs, 1962, Ja 9,47:2
Lehman, Ambrose E Mrs, 1949, Ja 30,60:4
Lehman, Arnold M, 1964, Ag 5,33:5
Lehman, Aron H Mrs, 1949, F 8,25:1
Lehman, Arthur, 1954, My 18,29:5
Lehman, Arthur Mrs (will filed, Ag 27,31:8), 19 Ag 12,27:1
Lehman, Charles, 1967, Je 9,45:1
Lehman, Charles A, 1951, N 7,29:4
Lehman, Charles C, 1967, Jl 23,60:6
Lehman, Charles F Mrs, 1953, O 20,29:2
Lehman, Charles H, 1957, S 1,56:7; 1964, Ja 2,27

Lehman, Chester H, 1959, O 23,17:5
Lehman, Clarence O, 1945, O 23,17:4
Lehman, David S, 1915, Ap 23,13:4
Lehman, Edwin P, 1954, My 29,15:4
Lehman, Elizabeth (Sister Cordelia), 1958, Jl 29,23:2
Lehman, Emanuel, 1907, Ja 11,9:5
Lehman, Frank, 1951, Ag 28,23:4
Lehman, Frank A, 1950, My 30,17:3
Lehman, George M, 1946, Ja 21,23:1
Lehman, Harry J Sr, 1959, O 31,23:2
Lehman, Harry J Sr (est tax appr filed), 1960, D 29, 41:5
Lehman, Herbert H (trbs, D 6,15:1; funl, D 9,1:5), 1963, D 6,1:6
Lehman, Howard L, 1965, Mr 23,39:3
Lehman, Howard Mrs, 1953, N 17,31:5
Lehman, I Howard Mrs, 1958, Je 10,33:4
Lehman, Irving, 1945, S 23,1:2
Lehman, Irving Mrs, 1950, F 18,15:1
Lehman, Isadore D, 1950, My 30,17:4
Lehman, J Arthur, 1937, Ja 16,17:4
Lehman, Jack H, 1963, Ag 18,80:6
Lehman, Jeannette U Mrs, 1957, Ag 23,19:3
Lehman, Jerome, 1961, Mr 15,39:5
Lehman, John, 1937, Jl 26,19:5
Lehman, John L, 1962, Mr 21,39:1
Lehman, Joseph D, 1948, F 23,25:3
Lehman, Leo, 1948, S 24,25:2
Lehman, Leser, 1911, Ja 1,11:2
Lehman, Lester I, 1941, Mr 19,21:5
Lehman, Lester L, 1955, Mr 15,29:2
Lehman, Margaret Z M Mrs (will), 1942, Ag 14,14:3
Lehman, Marguerite Z M Mrs, 1942, Jl 22,19:4
Lehman, Max J, 1948, O 17,76:7
Lehman, Meyer H, 1918, Je 28,11:6
Lehman, Milton, 1966, O 14,40:3
Lehman, Myron G, 1963, Jl 16,31:2
Lehman, Myron G Mrs, 1964, Ap 17,35:2
Lehman, Paul, 1952, O 20,23:5
Lehman, Phil Mrs (will, N 16,25:7), 1937, N 11,25:3
Lehman, Philip, 1947, Mr 22,13:1
Lehman, R C, 1929, Ja 23,23:5
Lehman, Robert J, 1952, Ag 8,17:5
Lehman, Robert S, 1944, Ja 16,42:7
Lehman, Rowland R, 1952, F 20,29:2
Lehman, Samuel, 1920, S 1,13:3; 1947, Jl 14,21:5
Lehman, Sigmund M Mrs (will, Jl 21,9:4), 1945, Jl 14,11:4
Lehman, Walter, 1964, F 1,23:5
Lehman, William E, 1951, Jl 31,22:5
Lehman, William V, 1954, N 3,29:1
Lehman, Wilmer S Mrs, 1960, F 9,31:1
Lehmann, Alexander H, 1946, O 29,25:1
Lehmann, Anthony T, 1952, D 9,33:2
Lehmann, Augusta, 1942, Ja 6,24:2
Lehmann, Carl B, 1949, Je 20,19:5
Lehmann, Charles H, 1948, D 12,92:4
Lehmann, Charles L, 1951, My 3,29:5
Lehmann, Edward H, 1949, N 26,15:1
Lehmann, Edward J, 1954, O 14,29:5
Lehmann, Frederick T, 1943, Mr 26,19:1
Lehmann, Frederick W, 1931, S 13,28:1
Lehmann, Fritz, 1956, Ap 1,88:2; 1963, Ap 29,31:4
Lehmann, George, 1941, O 15,21:4
Lehmann, George C, 1944, N 3,21:3
Lehmann, Hans, 1949, Je 14,31:3
Lehmann, Harold Mrs, 1950, F 24,23:3
Lehmann, Harold R, 1962, Mr 14,39:4
Lehmann, Isaac, 1947, My 9,21:5
Lehmann, John J, 1942, D 26,11:2
Lehmann, Julius (will), 1954, S 9,33:2
Lehmann, Julius (will), 1955, My 17,5:2
Lehmann, Karl, 1960, D 19,27:1
Lehmann, L, 1929, My 18,19:1
Lehmann, Leo H, 1950, Je 21,27:4
Lehmann, Liza, 1918, O 18,13:2
Lehmann, Louis C Sr, 1952, Jl 11,17:5
Lehmann, Louis C Sr Mrs, 1949, D 16,31:2
Lehmann, Otto R, 1953, Ap 12,89:2
Lehmann, Otto W, 1952, Ap 27,90:5
Lehmann, Theodore A, 1955, O 26,31:2
Lehmann, William A, 1950, Ap 27,29:4
Lehmer, Derrick N, 1938, S 9,21:4
Lehmer, J D, 1903, Ap 24,9:6
Lehmiller, Harry, 1944, Jl 21,19:2
Lehmkuhl, C Edward, 1950, Ja 14,15:6
Lehmkuhl, Charles, 1952, F 16,13:1
Lehmkuhl, Harold W, 1957, N 6,35:1
Lehmony, Henri, 1882, Ap 24,4:7
Lehmuth, Charles, 1950, D 6,33:3
Lehn, Charles J, 1954, S 12,84:4
Lehn, Henry, 1940, S 15,48:2
Lehn, Herman, 1940, Ap 21,42:3
Lehn, Herman Mrs, 1956, D 4,39:1
Lehnartz, Frederick H, 1960, D 21,31:1
Lehne, Richard W, 1944, O 6,23:5
Lehnert, Richard Mrs, 1964, Jl 9,33:1
Lehnerts, Edward M, 1953, D 22,31:1
Lehnhard, Carl W Mrs, 1948, My 24,19:5
Lehon, Countess, 1880, Mr 21,1:7
Lehoven, Frank, 1948, O 19,27:4
Lehr, Abraham Mrs, 1951, N 10,17:5
Lehr, Arthur, 1960, O 31,31:1
Lehr, Charles, 1938, Ag 31,14:1
Lehr, Charles J, 1949, N 24,31:4
Lehr, Clarence E, 1948, F 1,60:5
Lehr, Conrad, 1949, My 13,23:4
Lehr, Frances A, 1941, S 4,21:3
Lehr, Frank E Sr, 1948, Mr 30,23:1
Lehr, Franklin H, 1939, D 10,68:4
Lehr, Frederick William, 1909, Ag 28,7:6
Lehr, George W, 1949, O 10,23:4
Lehr, H S, 1929, Ja 4,25:3
Lehr, Henry S Rev, 1923, Ja 30,17:4
Lehr, Herman L, 1947, S 7,60:1
Lehr, Horace, 1956, D 28,21:2
Lehr, Hyman, 1947, Je 24,23:5
Lehr, John C, 1958, F 18,27:4
Lehr, Karl, 1948, D 15,33:3
Lehr, Lew, 1950, Mr 7,28:2
Lehr, Robert, 1956, O 14,86:6
Lehr, Robert Oliver, 1923, Jl 20,13:6
Lehr, Robert Oliver Mrs, 1922, S 19,19:4
Lehr, Saul, 1948, Jl 15,23:2
Lehr, Sidney, 1950, Jl 3,15:4
Lehrbach, Phil, 1952, Ja 28,17:3
Lehrbas, Lloyd A, 1964, O 31,29:1
Lehren, James S, 1961, N 7,33:3
Lehren, James S Mrs, 1949, F 17,23:4
Lehrenkrauss, Julius, 1943, D 4,15:6
Lehrfeld, Hugo R, 1966, Ap 27,47:2
Lehrfeld, Louis, 1952, F 7,27:5
Lehrich, Henry, 1967, Jl 16,65:2
Lehrich, M Zachary, 1959, S 26,23:5
Lehrkaupt, Samuel, 1964, Ag 19,37:5
Lehrman, Hal Mrs, 1962, O 11,39:4
Lehrman, Henry, 1946, N 9,17:4
Lehrman, Jacob, 1956, Mr 30,19:4
Lehrman, Phil R, 1958, F 5,27:3
Lehrs, Henry F, 1943, Je 9,21:2
Lehtinen, Artturi, 1966, O 11,47:2
Lehto, Reino R, 1966, Jl 16,25:3
Lehtonen, Aleksi E, 1951, Mr 28,29:5
Lehtonen, Richard, 1946, Je 19,21:4
Lehy, Geoffrey B, 1917, N 9,13:5
Lehy, John Francis Rev, 1918, N 27,13:2
Lehy, Thomas A, 1963, Mr 18,15:2
Lei, Simon, 1961, Ag 27,6:2
Leib, Charles W, 1952, O 11,19:6
Leib, David D, 1941, Je 16,15:5
Leib, Julius, 1957, Jl 20,15:5
Leib, Julius Mrs, 1965, My 29,27:3
Leibel, Benjamin, 1953, S 19,15:2
Leibel, Emanuel S, 1965, F 26,29:4
Leibell, Vincent L Judge, 1968, S 23,35:1
Leibell Helen D (Sister Jane Frances), 1956, S 19, 37:2
Leibenzon, Leonid, 1951, Mr 18,88:4
Leiber, Fritz (por), 1949, O 15,15:1
Leiber, Joseph, 1939, Ag 1,10:4
Leiber, Paul E, 1955, D 5,31:1
Leiber, Richard, 1944, Ap 16,42:1
Leibersberger, Peter, 1945, O 7,44:2
Leibert, Morris W Mrs, 1956, Je 17,92:4
Leibert, Morris William Bp, 1919, Ja 12,22:4
Leibert, Owen, 1911, Mr 27,11:4
Leibfred, John J (cor, S 29,35:3), 1960, S 1,27:3
Leibfred, Sarah E Mrs, 1940, Ja 23,21:6
Leible, Arthur B, 1955, N 11,25:5
Leibman, David, 1955, Ja 3,27:3
Leibman, Nathan, 1942, Mr 10,19:1
Leibow, Leon, 1945, My 22,19:3
Leibowitz, David, 1941, D 6,17:4
Leibowitz, Max, 1950, My 28,44:6
Leibowitz, Morris Mrs, 1948, Ja 21,25:4
Leibowitz, Phil, 1940, Ag 31,13:5
Leibowitz, William, 1950, O 20,27:2
Leibson, Victor J, 1947, My 7,27:4
Leiburg, William, 1951, Ag 6,21:5
Leiby, Agnes Minerva Mrs, 1903, D 26,1:1
Leiby, E O, 1949, F 24,23:3
Leiby, Elias B, 1952, D 12,29:3
Leicester, Dowager Countess of, 1937, F 27,17:4
Leicester, Earl of, 1941, N 20,27:1
Leicester, Earl of (T W Coke), 1949, Ag 22,21:2
Leicester, Hubert Sir, 1939, Je 15,23:2
Leicester, Lady, 1940, N 7,25:5
Leicester, Robert W, 1953, Jl 3,19:1
Leicester, William F Mrs, 1968, D 20,47:1
Leicester Earl of (Thos Wm Coke), 1909, Ja 25,9:5
Leich, A H, 1932, F 13,13:5
Leich, Herbert R, 1943, Ja 31,46:3
Leicher, F A, 1960, Ja 11,45:5
Leicher, John C, 1952, N 20,31:5
Leichner, William, 1943, Ag 11,19:2
Leichtentritt, Hugo (trb, D 2,II,7:5), 1951, N 18,91:1
Leichter, Jess, 1959, Ap 30,31:3
Leichtman, Clavin Mrs, 1951, N 22,31:5
Leick, John S, 1957, S 13,23:1
Leide, Enrico Mrs, 1962, S 7,29:5
Leidenger, Joseph (will, Ag 20,35:8), 1939, Ag 12, 13:4
Leider, William, 1944, Ag 2,15:6
Leiderman, Hyman, 1938, Ja 22,18:2
Leiderman, Louis, 1950, Ap 1,15:3
Leidersdorff, John von Mrs, 1952, Ap 7,25:5
Leidesdorf, Samuel D (will, S 28,33:3), 1968, S 22, 89:1
Leidhold, William C, 1954, Mr 23,27:1
Leidich, Sylvester W, 1954, Ap 25,87:2
Leiding, Henry H, 1950, S 21,31:1
Leidy, Carter R, 1954, Ja 22,28:5
Leidy, Channing A, 1937, Ap 23,21:2
Leidy, Gertrude H, 1946, My 19,42:3
Leidy, H R Mrs, 1933, F 10,17:3
Leidy, Samuel N, 1945, S 14,23:1
Leidy, Thomas K, 1953, Ja 16,23:3
Leifer, Isador Mrs, 1953, Mr 26,31:4
Leifer, Isidor, 1947, O 13,23:2
Leifflen, Harry B, 1951, F 13,31:4
Leigh, Albert S, 1922, Mr 15,19:6
Leigh, Benjamin W, 1941, Ap 2,23:4
Leigh, Billie (Mrs H Wehrman), 1963, Ag 24,19:3
Leigh, Charles A, 1942, Ag 9,43:4
Leigh, Douglas Mrs, 1941, N 27,23:3
Leigh, Edward James, 1921, O 20,17:6
Leigh, Ernest A, 1942, Ag 16,44:7
Leigh, Frances B Mrs (will, F 2,21:3), 1939, Ja 27, 20:3
Leigh, Frances J Mrs, 1939, Ap 27,25:2
Leigh, Francis Dudley Lady, 1909, Ap 29,9:3
Leigh, Frank F Mrs, 1950, D 29,19:1
Leigh, Frederick Tollington Lt-Col, 1914, N 11,13:3
Leigh, Gene, 1937, D 10,25:2
Leigh, H S, 1883, Jl 6,3:3
Leigh, Henry C, 1949, D 31,15:3
Leigh, Henry M, 1966, O 26,47:4
Leigh, Horace, 1958, Jl 10,27:4
Leigh, James G, 1939, Mr 30,23:4
Leigh, John R, 1958, Ap 15,33:4
Leigh, John Sir, 1959, Jl 30,27:6
Leigh, Lord, 1938, My 17,23:4
Leigh, N John Mrs, 1965, N 22,37:5
Leigh, Octa C Jr, 1951, D 27,21:4
Leigh, Richard H (por), 1946, F 5,24:2
Leigh, Robert D, 1961, F 1,35:2
Leigh, Robert D Mrs, 1959, My 20,35:4
Leigh, Robert E, 1960, N 10,47:3
Leigh, Rowland C, 1943, Ja 28,19:2
Leigh, Shepard W, 1968, S 23,35:3
Leigh, Vivien (funl, Jl 13,37:4; mem ser, Ag 16,41:2), 1967, Jl 9,1:3
Leigh, William E, 1958, O 25,21:5
Leigh, William R, 1955, Mr 13,87:1
Leigh, William R Mrs (Ethel T), 1963, Ap 30,35:2
Leigh-Bennett, H C, 1903, Mr 8,5:2
Leigh-Jones, George, 1960, My 1,87:1
Leight, John Sr, 1950, D 29,20:2
Leighton, Albert, 1950, Je 22,27:5
Leighton, Anthony, 1960, My 21,23:6
Leighton, Archibald O, 1964, Ag 19,37:4
Leighton, Bert, 1964, F 12,33:2
Leighton, Carl A, 1958, F 2,86:2
Leighton, Charles, 1959, Ap 27,27:5
Leighton, Charles H, 1950, Mr 4,17:4
Leighton, Clarence T Mrs, 1952, D 8,41:3
Leighton, David R, 1951, D 1,13:1
Leighton, Delmar, 1966, My 14,31:3
Leighton, Edward E Mrs, 1952, Jl 3,25:2
Leighton, Elmer S, 1949, Je 1,31:4
Leighton, Eugene E, 1951, D 5,35:1
Leighton, Francis M Mrs, 1912, Ja 22,9:5
Leighton, Frank T, 1943, N 24,21:2
Leighton, Frederick, 1942, Je 3,23:5; 1948, Je 7,19:2
Leighton, Frederick Lord, 1896, Ja 26,3:1
Leighton, G B, 1929, D 21,19:3
Leighton, George, 1920, S 14,11:2
Leighton, George Mrs, 1954, My 28,23:5
Leighton, George R, 1966, Mr 25,41:3
Leighton, George Rev, 1903, Ag 27,1:4
Leighton, George W, 1945, Ap 27,19:3
Leighton, Harry G, 1949, Ja 20,27:4
Leighton, Hugh C, 1942, Ja 7,20:4
Leighton, J Kenric, 1965, My 4,43:5
Leighton, Jason C, 1954, D 6,27:5
Leighton, Leon E, 1947, Ag 26,23:3
Leighton, Lillianne, 1956, Mr 23,27:2
Leighton, Lord (G L Seager), 1963, O 18,31:2
Leighton, Marshall O, 1958, Ag 30,15:6
Leighton, Perry, 1967, Ja 20,43:1
Leighton, Robert E, 1953, Ja 16,23:4
Leighton, Robert L, 1943, Jl 6,21:6
Leighton, Walter M, 1945, My 24,19:3
Leighton, William E, 1952, N 11,29:1
Leiken, Robert S, 1968, O 16,47:4
Leikensohn, Abraham, 1959, Ap 15,33:4
Leimback, Joseph, 1945, D 5,25:2
Leimer, Joseph B, 1953, Ag 22,15:4
Leimer, William F, 1950, D 5,31:3
Leimkuhler, Frederick J, 1950, S 19,31:1
Lein, Irving, 1959, Ja 16,28:1
Lein, Karl R, 1947, D 9,29:5
Leinbach, A Ellsworth, 1939, F 25,15:5
Leinbach, Joseph V, 1938, Jl 6,23:1
Leinbach, Paul S, 1941, D 8,23:2
Leinbach, Roy E Sr, 1943, Jl 27,17:5
Leinbach, Thomas H, 1949, D 12,33:3
Leinbach, Thomas M Mrs, 1952, F 23,11:4
Leinen, Raymond F, 1951, Mr 30,23:2

Leiner, Gerson, 1957, Je 13,31:4
Leiner, Jacob, 1950, Ja 6,21:3
Leinhart, Rudolph H, 1937, My 22,15:5
Leiningen, Emich von Prince, 1939, Jl 25,7:6
Leininger, Albert G Mrs, 1944, N 17,19:3
Leininger, Leonard F, 1952, O 26,88:6
Leininger, Mary Angela Mother, 1940, O 7,17:1
Leininger, Philipp, 1951, O 4,33:4
Leinkram, Maurice M, 1945, S 20,23:3
Leinoff, Harry D, 1958, Jl 22,27:2
Leins, Arlene, 1938, F 25,17:3
Leins, William G, 1953, Ja 6,29:5
Leinsler, R L Brig-Gen, 1912, Ag 15,9:2
Leinster, Duchess of (Denise Orme), 1960, O 22,23:4
Leinster, Duke of, 1874, O 12,4:7
Leinster, Duke of (Maurice Fitzgerald), 1922, F 5, 22:3
Leinwand, Irving Dr, 1956, Jl 14,15:3
Leinwand, Louis, 1965, S 13,35:3
Leinwand, Solomon L, 1954, Ap 21,29:5
Leinwoll, Hyman, 1950, Ag 16,29:4
Leiper, Callender I, 1960, Ap 26,37:3
Leiper, Edwards F, 1938, D 3,19:4
Leiper, Henry M, 1960, Mr 6,86:6
Leiper, Joseph M, 1947, Mr 18,27:3
Leipheimer, Louis, 1950, My 5,22:3
Leipprand, Eric, 1949, Ja 9,72:6
Leipzig, Nate, 1939, O 14,19:3
Leipziger, Harriet Mrs, 1908, N 26,9:5
Leipziger, Henry M Dr (funl, D 4,13:1), 1917, D 2, 5:3
Leipziger, Jacob, 1944, Mr 3,15:3
Leipziger, Leo E, 1955, Mr 25,21:3
Leis, Earl F, 1939, Ap 21,23:6
Leisegang, Hans, 1951, Ap 6,25:4
Leisenring, Edward B, 1952, Je 18,27:6
Leisentritt, Frederick C Sr, 1951, Je 25,19:4
Leiser, Edward J, 1942, S 4,23:5
Leiser, Louis M, 1957, N 8,29:2
Leiser, Oscar M Capt (funl, D 10,15:5), 1917, D 9, 23:1
Leiser, William, 1965, Ja 17,88:6
Leiserowitz, Max Mrs, 1955, Ag 6,15:1
Leiserson, William M, 1957, F 13,35:5
Leishman, Chester M, 1955, My 25,33:2
Leishman, Douglass M, 1956, S 30,86:5
Leishman, John G, 1924, Mr 28,17:4
Leishman, W B Lt Gen Sir, 1926, Je 3,25:5
Leishman, William, 1958, Jl 17,27:1
Leisinger, Albert H, 1937, S 14,23:2
Leisk, Herbert N, 1964, Ja 18,23:3
Leisner, Emmi, 1958, Ja 13,29:5
Leiss, Edgar, 1958, N 12,37:4
Leiss, Frederic J, 1954, S 24,23:3
Leisser, Martin B, 1940, My 18,15:2
Leist, Christopher, 1925, D 28,15:3
Leister, Claude W, 1940, F 6,21:2
Leister, John, 1951, N 17,17:5
Leister, Maximilian H, 1954, S 21,27:4
Leister, Teresa, 1940, F 20,21:1
Leistikow, Walter Prof, 1908, Jl 26,7:7
Leistner, Charles J, 1948, F 22,48:2
Leitch, Gordon C, 1954, Je 3,27:4
Leitch, Howard W, 1953, N 3,31:1
Leitch, Joseph, 1939, Ja 4,21:3
Leitch, Joseph D, 1938, O 28,23:2
Leitch, Samuel, 1945, Jl 24,23:1
Leitch, Thomas, 1947, O 29,27:3
Leite, Duarte, 1950, S 30,17:2
Leite Ribeiro, Orlando, 1962, Je 13,41:2
Leiter, H Evans, 1958, S 13,19:6
Leiter, J, 1932, Ap 12,21:3
Leiter, Joseph Mrs, 1942, O 31,15:4
Leiter, Levi Z Mrs, 1913, Mr 7,11:5
Leiter, Thomas, 1958, Ap 27,86:5
Leiterman, Morris, 1953, N 11,31:2
Leiterman, Samuel N, 1957, O 30,29:3
Leith, Alex Jr, 1952, Ap 3,35:3
Leith, Catherine, 1958, Ja 3,23:1
Leith, Charles K, 1956, S 15,17:5
Leith, George D F, 1944, D 16,15:4
Leith, Gordon, 1941, Ap 3,23:6
Leith, John Forbes Lord, 1925, N 15,13:1
Leith, Samuel E, 1939, D 15,25:2
Leithead, John L, 1941, Ag 18,13:3
Leitman, Max, 1960, Je 28,31:4
Leitner, Arthur W, 1953, Ja 2,15:1
Leitner, Emil (por), 1941, D 13,21:3
Leitner, Frank G Sr, 1949, F 24,23:3
Leitner, Frederick L, 1957, Je 5,35:4
Leitner, George A Dr, 1937, My 19,23:3
Leitner, Jack, 1967, N 23,33:3
Leitner, Julia, 1950, S 19,31:1
Leitner, Karl, 1954, O 17,87:2
Leitner, Maud C Mrs, 1938, N 29,23:5
Leitner, R, 1945, Ja 31,3:7
Leitner, William Mrs, 1951, F 6,27:4
Leitz, Ernst, 1956, Je 16,19:5
Leitzell, Charles W, 1950, Ap 25,31:5
Leiva, Tobias, 1946, Je 7,19:2
Leja, Allen J, 1954, N 23,44:4
Lejay, Pierre, 1958, O 12,87:1
Le Jeune, George F C, 1904, Ap 13,9:2
Lejeune, Hubert, 1945, D 13,29:5
Lejeune, John A (por), 1942, N 21,13:1
Lejeune, John A Mrs, 1953, N 11,31:2
Lejeune, Jules, 1911, F 20,7:5
Le Jeune, Norman F, 1956, Ap 17,31:2
Lekach, Joseph, 1952, Ja 20,84:8
Lekberg, Carl H, 1943, F 15,15:3
Le Kites, Delbert L, 1950, N 4,6:4
LeKites-Wallace, Lillian R, 1954, Ja 17,92:2
Leland, A P, 1878, Ag 15,2:6
Leland, Abby P, 1950, N 25,13:3
Leland, Amelia V Mrs, 1948, Mr 16,27:1
Leland, Arthur S, 1950, D 23,15:3
Leland, Arthur S Mrs, 1944, Mr 14,19:2
Leland, Benjamin T, 1937, Mr 30,23:6
Leland, C A, 1949, My 26,29:3
Leland, C G, 1903, Mr 21,9:5
Leland, Charles, 1885, O 22,8:1
Leland, Charles E, 1906, Mr 1,9:6
Leland, Charles E Mrs, 1909, Ja 1,11:6
Leland, Charles H, 1925, S 15,25:5
Leland, Charles H Mrs, 1916, S 9,11:6
Leland, Claude G, 1950, Ja 23,23:4
Leland, Everard, 1946, Jl 9,22:2
Leland, Fanny A, 1902, F 9,7:5
Leland, Francis, 1885, My 17,9:2
Leland, Francis L, 1916, Mr 29,11:1
Leland, G S, 1882, Ag 3,8:1
Leland, George A Jr, 1943, S 25,15:4
Leland, H M, 1932, Mr 27,II,5:1
Leland, Harry J, 1938, N 30,24:1
Leland, Henry Perry, 1868, S 27,3:7
Leland, Henry W, 1957, Je 14,25:4
Leland, Hervey D, 1941, O 7,23:2
Leland, Hugh, 1958, My 16,25:3
Leland, J, 1883, Mr 30,5:4
Leland, Joseph D, 1968, Ap 16,47:4
Leland, Lee H, 1944, O 26,23:4
Leland, Morgan B, 1939, My 6,17:2
Leland, Oliver S, 1870, Ap 21,5:1
Leland, Richard D Sr Mrs, 1948, Ag 17,21:3
Leland, Roscoe G, 1949, O 19,29:5
Leland, Samuel, 1939, O 27,23:2
Leland, Sanford D Jr, 1938, S 16,21:5
Leland, Simeon, 1872, Ag 6,8:4
Leland, Stanley W, 1950, Je 7,29:5
Leland, T C, 1885, Je 6,2:5
Leland, W F, 1899, Ap 5,7:1
Leland, W W, 1879, Ag 10,12:2
Leland, Waldo G, 1966, O 20,43:4
Leland, Wilfred C, 1958, Ja 18,15:3
Leland, William E, 1945, Ja 13,11:5
Leland, William G, 1925, Ja 21,21:3
Leland, William H, 1948, F 25,24:2
Leland, Worth W, 1924, N 29,13:4
Leland, Z A, 1872, S 7,4:6
Le Lay, Herve, 1951, Ja 7,76:3
Lelievre, Leo, 1956, Ap 2,23:2
Lelivelt, John F, 1941, Ja 22,26:2
Lelle, Frederick W, 1962, Mr 6,35:1
Lellek, Mark, 1959, My 15,30:1
Lelli, Renata, 1962, Ag 17,23:4
Lellos, Theodore, 1947, Ja 16,25:2
Leloir, Louis, 1884, F 21,2:1
Lelong, Leone, 1905, Je 15,9:6
Lelong, Louis, 1945, D 20,23:3
Lelong, Lucien, 1958, My 12,29:3
Lely, Antiope T Mrs, 1942, My 26,21:4
Lely, Durwood, 1944, Mr 2,17:5
Lely, Nicholas G, 1958, Ag 29,23:5
Lelyveld, Edward J, 1955, Ap 2,17:3
Lem, Charlie, 1912, Ag 19,9:4
Lem, Monnen, 1956, O 2,35:1
Lema, Tony (funl plans, Jl 27,39:1; funl, Jl 29,31:1), 1966, Jl 25,1:8
Lema, Tony Mrs (funl plans, Jl 27,39:1; funl, Jl 29,-31:1), 1966, Jl 25,1:8
Lemaire, Charles J, 1944, D 20,23:4
Lemaire, Leo G, 1961, Jl 22,21:6
LeMaire, Rufus, 1950, D 4,29:4
Le Maistre, Frederic J, 1944, Ag 26,11:2
Lemaitre, Frederick (funl, F 14,5:6),(see also Ja 28,29), 1876, Ja 30,4:6
Lemaitre, Jules, 1914, Ag 7,11:5
Lemal, Richard F Mrs, 1948, Ag 18,25:5
Leman, F, 1933, F 1,18:1
Le Man, Frank, 1958, N 17,31:1
Leman, Grant W, 1945, My 29,15:3
Leman, J W F, 1953, O 18,86:5
Leman, John J, 1950, O 25,35:3
Leman, Moses H, 1913, S 8,7:4
Lemann, Monte M (died, Sept 13), 1959, S 23,39:2
Le Mar, Harold D, 1959, My 12,35:3
Le Massena, Andrew, 1955, Je 22,30:1
Lemaster, Charles A, 1923, Ag 19,26:4
Lemaux, Irving, 1952, Ap 8,29:5
LeMay, Arizona D Mrs, 1967, S 26,47:3
LeMay, Irving, 1966, Jl 19,39:2
Lemay, Joseph Mrs, 1945, Je 19,19:5
Lemay, Tracy D, 1954, Jl 29,23:5
Lembcke, Ricardo E, 1937, Ag 22,II,7:1
Lembeck, Henry, 1904, Jl 26,7:7
Lembeck, John M, 1952, S 8,21:4
Lemberg, Abraham I, 1967, Ap 28,41:2
Lembertson, William P, 1957, O 28,27:3
Lembo, Anthony, 1951, Je 26,29:5
Lembo, Joseph J, 1950, S 20,31:5
Leme da Silveira Cintra, Sebastian, 1942, O 18,55:3
Le Mee, Jacques M, 1954, Mr 27,17:2
Lemen, Gen, 1920, O 18,15:3
Lemenmeier, Paul, 1941, Ag 13,17:7
LeMesurier, Cecil, 1951, S 8,17:5
Lemieux, Donald Z, 1941, Ap 6,48:8
Lemieux, Gustave, 1956, Jl 21,15:5
Lemieux, Pierre, 1941, O 2,25:2
Lemieux, Rodolphe Sen, 1937, S 29,23:5
Leming, Joseph L, 1941, F 22,15:4
Lemkau, J H Walter, 1946, Ap 18,27:5
Lemke, Charles E, 1947, My 6,27:2
Lemke, James, 1940, Mr 18,17:4
Lemken, Charles E, 1955, F 8,27:4
Lemkin, Raphael, 1959, Ag 30,82:3
Lemkin, Samuel, 1949, O 6,31:2
Lemkuhl, Bertha H, 1957, My 17,26:2
Lemlein, Matilda, 1939, D 4,23:4
Lemler, Martin D, 1956, S 8,17:5
Lemler, Sam, 1954, My 13,29:3
Lemley, Harry J, 1965, Mr 7,81:4
Lemlich, Marcus, 1939, Ja 19,19:2
Lemly, Rowan P, 1938, Mr 6,II,8:5
Lemly, Samuel Conrad Capt, 1909, S 5,9:4
Lemm, Ellen Mrs, 1938, N 13,44:8
Lemmel, William H, 1953, Ja 30,22:4
Lemmer, George E Mrs, 1948, D 25,18:2
Lemmer, George J, 1950, D 17,84:6
Lemmerman, Fred C, 1947, O 22,29:2
Lemmerman, Fred C Mrs (will), 1951, N 17,19:6
Lemmerz, Theodore H, 1941, N 10,17:6
Lemmon, Arthur K Mrs, 1962, S 21,30:8
Lemmon, Bruce H, 1955, F 23,27:4
Lemmon, Charles M, 1944, Ag 22,17:3
Lemmon, George T, 1943, My 10,19:4
Lemmon, Guy, 1959, O 10,21:5
Lemmon, John U, 1962, Mr 31,25:3
Lemmon, Mildred N Mrs, 1967, S 4,21:1
Lemmon, Robert J, 1946, Mr 14,25:5
Lemmon, Robert S, 1964, Mr 5,30:4
Lemmon, Robert T Col, 1937, Mr 8,19:4
Lemmon, Samuel L, 1954, Ja 22,27:4
Lemmon, Samuel L Mrs, 1950, O 29,92:4
Lemmon, Thomas W, 1945, Ap 24,19:5
Lemmon, Walter S, 1967, Mr 21,46:1
Lemnitzer, Hannah B Mrs, 1952, D 14,91:2
Lemoine, James Sir, 1912, F 6,11:5
Lemon, Arthur L, 1944, Jl 21,19:5
Lemon, Charles T, 1948, Ap 7,25:4
Lemon, Grace W Mrs, 1940, D 28,15:2
Lemon, Harvey B, 1965, Jl 6,33:4
Lemon, John F, 1963, My 23,37:1
Lemon, John S, 1924, O 16,25:4
Lemon, Lee, 1939, F 12,45:1
Lemon, Luther O, 1957, Mr 1,23:4
Lemon, Peyton W, 1951, Je 1,23:4
Le Mone, Francois, 1919, O 13,13:4
Lemonnier, Andre G, 1963, Je 1,21:2
Lemore, Raymond, 1944, Jl 29,13:6
Le Moult, Adolph, 1951, Je 9,19:7
Le Moyne, Edward, 1914, F 11,11:6
Le Moyne, F J Dr, 1879, O 15,5:2
Le Moyne, Sarah Cowell, 1915, Jl 18,15:4
Le Moyne, William J, 1905, N 7,9:6
Lempe, George Gustave Dr, 1915, My 18,13:5
Lempereur, Glenn N, 1965, Je 13,84:6
Lemperly, Paul L, 1939, My 6,17:5
Lempert, Julius Dr, 1968, D 18,47:1
Lempert, Sol, 1944, D 14,23:5
Lemunyon, Walter J, 1959, S 24,37:3
Lemus, Joseph L, 1962, My 17,37:2
Lemus, Milo, 1962, O 25,39:5
Lena, Frederick T, 1964, Ap 2,33:4
Lenahan, Charles B, 1942, Je 16,23:4; 1967, Jl 26,
Lenahan, Francis J (por), 1946, Jl 8,29:4
Lenahan, Frank P, 1945, F 9,15:3; 1953, S 24,33:4
Lenahan, James L, 1962, O 11,39:4
Lenahan, John Tower, 1920, Ap 29,13:4
Lenahan, Mary (Sister Rosalie), 1923, Ja 13,13:6
Lenahan, Michael A, 1941, Ja 18,15:3
Lenahan, Richard F, 1951, S 20,21:1
Lenahan, William J, 1955, Mr 5,17:4
Lenane, Edward B, 1948, My 31,19:4
Lenane, Frank E, 1938, S 2,17:4
Lenane, Gerald M, 1948, Je 19,15:2
Lenane, John A, 1958, Ap 12,19:5
Lenartowicz, Stefan, 1961, Ag 5,17:5
Lenau, Henri B, 1952, Ap 1,29:5
Lenbach, Franz von, 1904, My 6,9:6
Lenck, Walter, 1952, S 8,21:5
Lencke, John K, 1946, S 28,17:4
Lencke, John K Mrs, 1947, Ag 14,23:1
Lendemann, William F, 1949, F 22,23:2
Lendrim, Hugh C, 1942, F 10,19:2
Lendrum, William H, 1925, Ap 14,23:5
Lenehan, Daniel J, 1945, My 18,19:4
Lenehan, Francis J, 1957, Je 21,25:4
Lenehan, George G, 1960, Jl 31,69:1
Lenehan, John J, 1937, Jl 4,II,6:8

Lenell, John J, 1875, Je 15,6:6
Lener, Jeno (por), 1948, N 5,25:3
Lenfert, John Rev, 1903, My 14,9:7
Lenfest, Bertram A, 1953, Ag 6,21:2
Lenfest, Harold C, 1967, O 29,85:1
Lenfestey, Nathan C, 1954, Ag 9,17:4
Leng, Charles W, 1941, Ja 25,15:4
Leng, John Sir, 1906, D 14,11:6
Leng, Theodore C, 1955, Mr 7,27:4
Lengel, Albert L, 1942, Ag 12,19:6
Lengel, Seranus A, 1941, Ja 9,21:2
Lengel, William C, 1965, O 12,47:1
Lengemann, John W, 1967, F 25,27:2
L'Engle, William J, 1957, N 24,87:3
Lenglen, Suzanne, 1938, Jl 4,13:3
Lenglet, Andre, 1945, D 29,16:4
Lengs, Harold J, 1946, My 7,21:5
Lengyel, Martin, 1956, O 13,19:3
Lengyel, Tibor, 1958, Mr 19,31:4
Lenhard, Joseph, 1950, Je 5,23:2
Lenhardt, Frank, 1937, S 4,15:4
Lenhardt, Paul F, 1952, Jl 19,15:5
Lenhart, Carl H, 1955, Ap 9,13:6
Lenhart, George S, 1925, Ag 14,13:6
Lenhart, Phil M, 1941, Jl 27,30:2
Lenhart, Sara, 1944, Jl 7,15:6
Lenhoff, Benjamin K, 1959, My 16,23:5
Lenichek, Frank J, 1938, Je 5,44:7
Lenihan, Bridget S Mrs, 1966, Ag 2,33:4
Lenihan, Daniel A, 1941, S 7,49:1
Lenihan, F J Rev, 1867, Ag 10,6:2
Lenihan, George J, 1952, Ja 5,11:4
Lenihan, John P, 1958, S 15,21:5
Lenihan, Mathias C, 1943, Ag 20,15:5
Lenihan, Michael J, 1958, Ag 15,21:2
Lenihan, Michael P (Rev Bro Binen Michl), 1962, Mr 26,31:2
Lenihan, Thomas E, 1962, Ap 21,20:5
Lenihan, Thomas J, 1957, D 4,39:4
Lenihan, Thomas P, 1945, O 30,19:5
Lenihan, William J, 1940, My 7,26:2
Lenihan, Winifred (Mrs F W Wheeler), 1964, Jl 30, 27:1
Lenin, Nicolai Mrs (Mrs N K Krupskaya), 1939, F 28,14:4
Lenington, R F, 1939, O 22,40:6
Lenington, Robert F Mrs, 1938, S 25,38:8
Lenke, Mark A, 1957, Je 24,23:3
Lenker, Charles E Mrs, 1940, Mr 26,21:4
Lenker, Hiram, 1950, S 24,105:1
Lenker, J N, 1929, My 18,19:5
Lenker, John L, 1964, Ag 16,93:2
Lenko, George, 1948, O 29,25:3
Lenko, Rudolf, 1958, Je 2,27:3
Lenkowsky, Samuel, 1947, Ap 18,21:1
Lenley, Jay E, 1967, O 11,47:3
Lenna, Oscar A, 1951, Ja 26,23:1
Lennan, Anna, 1942, Mr 22,49:1
Lennan, Thomas J, 1942, Ja 10,15:6
Lennard, Oswald D, 1958, Jl 2,27:1
Lennard-Jones, John, 1954, N 2,27:5
Lennartson, Andrew L, 1952, N 16,85:2
Lennen, Phil W, 1955, D 25,49:1
Lennen, Philip W Mrs, 1945, Ja 18,19:2
Lennep, Eric N van, 1961, Mr 27,31:5
Lenney, Teresa M, 1942, Mr 19,21:5
Lennig, Lucretia C, 1939, Ja 10,19:3
Lennihan, Charles Jr, 1945, My 22,19:3
Lennihan, Richard G, 1961, Je 24,21:2
Lennon, Alice Mrs, 1951, My 22,31:1
Lennon, Edmund L, 1958, F 28,13:4
Lennon, Edward C, 1962, N 10,25:5
Lennon, Edward G, 1944, D 2,13:4
Lennon, George W, 1944, N 30,23:2
Lennon, Grace B, 1949, Ja 1,13:3
Lennon, Harry D, 1961, My 13,19:5
Lennon, James H, 1967, Ag 21,31:3
Lennon, James S, 1958, Jl 3,25:1
Lennon, Johanna (Sister Aline de l'Immaculee), 1954, Jl 15,27:3
Lennon, John A, 1948, N 6,13:3
Lennon, John A Jr, 1949, N 23,29:2
Lennon, John B, 1923, Ja 19,17:6
Lennon, John J, 1940, Je 17,15:4; 1962, O 28,88:7
Lennon, Katherine H Mrs, 1953, My 20,29:3
Lennon, Mary K Mrs, 1958, Mr 10,23:4
Lennon, Michael Jr, 1950, Ja 24,53:1
Lennon, Nestor, 1913, O 16,11:4
Lennon, Patrick, 1953, Mr 11,29:2
Lennon, Patrick H, 1938, Ja 29,15:6
Lennon, Patrick J, 1961, Mr 23,33:4
Lennon, Patrick Mrs, 1944, F 17,19:2
Lennon, Ralph, 1947, Jl 31,21:1
Lennon, Robert A, 1942, D 27,34:2
Lennon, Roscoe T, 1949, My 24,27:3
Lennon, Rose Mrs, 1948, Je 26,17:2
Lennon, Thomas F (cor, Ap 6,39:4), 1967, Ap 5,47:1
Lennon, Thomas P, 1964, O 2,37:5
Lennon, William H Prof, 1913, Mr 12,11:4
Lennon, William J, 1938, Mr 27,II,7:3
Lennon, William J Sr, 1950, Ja 4,35:2
Lennon, Winfred T Mrs, 1942, F 15,45:1
Lennox, Arthur Lord, 1864, F 6,8:2
Lennox, Augustus Charles (Duke of Grafton), 1918, D 6,15:4
Lennox, Christopher J, 1951, Ja 5,21:1
Lennox, David F, 1947, F 16,57:4
Lennox, Edward L, 1950, Ag 22,27:6
Lennox, George A Sr, 1963, My 8,39:4
Lennox, Gordon Lord, 1873, N 16,4:7
Lennox, James E, 1939, O 27,23:4
Lennox, James G, 1943, Je 10,21:2
Lennox, Jane, 1941, S 4,21:3
Lennox, Lottie, 1947, Mr 10,21:5
Lennox, Marian, 1942, Mr 7,19:3
Lennox, Robert A, 1955, Ap 16,19:2
Lennox, Robert I, 1953, Je 8,29:4
Lennox, Thomas, 1951, Jl 8,61:2
Lennox, W P Lord, 1881, F 19,5:3
Lennox, Walter S, 1905, Mr 21,11:4
Lennox, William G, 1960, Jl 23,19:1
Lennox-Boyd, Donald, 1939, Ap 13,16:4
Leno, Dan, 1904, N 1,9:6
LeNoir, Lawrence A Mrs, 1948, Ag 2,21:3
Lenoir-Jousserau, Mme, 1874, Ap 12,9:6
Lenormand, Henri-Rene, 1951, F 18,76:3
Lenotre, G, 1935, F 8,21:3
Lenox, J P, 1926, F 12,19:4
Lenox, James L, 1957, Mr 18,27:1
Lenox, Joseph A, 1955, Ja 15,13:1
Lenox, P, 1880, F 19,5:5
Lenox, William J Mrs, 1946, Mr 5,25:2
Lenroot, Irvine L, 1949, Ja 27,23:1
Lenroot, Irvine L Mrs, 1942, Ap 5,41:2
Lenrow, Bernard, 1963, O 10,41:5
Lenski, Mordecai, 1964, Ja 19,76:8
Lenssen, Nicholas F, 1950, My 24,29:3
Lent, A Mrs, 1881, My 13,5:2
Lent, Abraham, 1882, N 24,5:6
Lent, Abram D, 1944, Je 23,19:3
Lent, Alexander K Rev, 1920, D 8,17:3
Lent, Andrew Mrs, 1945, Mr 16,15:2
Lent, Arthur R, 1943, D 23,19:1
Lent, B Frank, 1946, S 22,63:1
Lent, Charles A, 1937, N 7,II,9:4
Lent, Charles F, 1941, My 16,23:5
Lent, Clarence J, 1937, Mr 14,II,8:6
Lent, Davis C, 1945, D 19,25:4
Lent, Ernest Mrs, 1947, N 19,27:3
Lent, Francis W, 1962, S 6,31:2
Lent, Frank A, 1940, D 22,30:6
Lent, Frank B, 1967, D 10,87:1
Lent, Frank S Mrs, 1948, N 7,88:6
Lent, Frederick (por), 1942, D 31,15:5
Lent, Frederick J, 1950, My 16,31:4
Lent, George, 1938, Je 13,19:5
Lent, George H, 1947, Mr 3,17:5
Lent, Hattie G W Mrs, 1940, Jl 24,21:3
Lent, Herbert, 1949, Jl 9,13:4
Lent, Herbert D, 1939, O 12,25:5
Lent, Herbert D Mrs, 1944, Jl 25,19:3
Lent, Howard E Mrs, 1940, Jl 12,15:2
Lent, J Page, 1946, Ap 30,21:4
Lent, James P, 1943, Ap 21,25:3
Lent, John H, 1949, O 2,81:1
Lent, John W, 1955, Ap 2,17:3
Lent, Lewis E, 1952, F 10,92:2
Lent, Lewis E Mrs, 1952, Ja 30,25:2
Lent, Malcolm F, 1961, O 22,86:4
Lent, Max, 1938, Ag 14,32:5
Lent, Murray M, 1963, Ap 8,47:6
Lent, Norman F, 1956, Je 5,35:3
Lent, Perley A, 1949, N 26,15:5
Lent, Stanley F, 1946, N 26,29:1
Lent, Stephen H, 1954, S 4,11:4
Lent, Walter S Mrs, 1941, O 14,23:6
Lent, Willis A, 1959, Ag 29,17:2
Lentaigne, Walter D E, 1955, Je 26,76:1
Lentelli, Leo, 1962, Ja 2,30:4
Lenth, Charles W, 1947, N 12,27:4
Lenthall, J, 1882, Ap 12,4:7
Lentilhon, E, 1879, My 17,5:2
Lentilhon, Edward D, 1951, N 21,25:1
Lentilhon, Pauline de Tewes, 1922, My 31,15:1
Lentino, Amil, 1913, Je 3,9:5
Lento, Salvatore, 1952, Ag 13,21:5
Lentz, Bernard, 1961, D 15,37:2
Lentz, Carl Maj, 1923, D 22,13:3
Lentz, Charles H, 1946, Mr 21,25:4
Lentz, Edwin W, 1940, Je 27,23:2
Lentz, Edwin Warner Rev, 1925, O 23,23:5
Lentz, Frank E, 1959, Jl 10,25:5
Lentz, Herman, 1955, My 15,86:6
Lentz, William L Mrs, 1949, Mr 25,23:5
Lenygon, Francis Henry (por), 1943, Je 14,17:3
Lenz, Albert, 1946, F 22,25:4
Lenz, Arnold W, 1952, Jl 14,36:5
Lenz, Charles, 1914, Ap 8,13:6
Lenz, Charles O, 1955, Ap 10,88:3
Lenz, Charles T, 1943, Jl 22,19:5
Lenz, David M, 1938, D 15,27:5
Lenz, Edward, 1938, Mr 20,II,9:2
Lenz, Frank B Mrs, 1947, Jl 16,23:4
Lenz, G Franklin, 1947, F 3,19:4
Lenz, George, 1948, O 19,28:3
Lenz, George H, 1950, S 29,27:3
Lenz, George J Mrs, 1966, O 14,43:3
Lenz, Harold A Mrs, 1960, Jl 12,35:2
Lenz, Herbert S, 1959, D 4,31:2
Lenz, J Mayo, 1959, Ja 19,27:2
Lenz, Oscar, 1912, Je 26,13:6
Lenz, Otto, 1957, My 3,27:2
Lenz, Robert, 1962, Ap 13,35:3
Lenz, Sidney S, 1960, Ap 13,39:1
Lenzo, Bro Charisius (por), 1947, My 25,60:5
Lenzo, Thomas F, 1955, Ag 18,23:4
Lenzo, Tobia, 1947, My 6,27:4
Leo, Albert J, 1937, Mr 27,15:2
Leo, Aleander H, 1943, D 31,15:3
Leo, Arnold, 1910, O 3,9:2
Leo, Arnold C, 1916, Ja 1,11:6
Leo, Bro, 1939, Jl 6,23:5
Leo, Carl M, 1960, Ag 17,31:2
Leo, Donald C, 1954, My 23,89:2
Leo, Jack G, 1968, F 20,47:3
Leo, John P, 1923, Jl 24,21:5
Leo, John P (por), 1946, S 24,29:3
Leo, Joseph, 1945, Je 29,15:4
Leo, Joseph N, 1948, Je 19,15:3
Leo, Michael J, 1942, S 21,15:5
Leo, Michael J Mrs, 1948, Ag 10,21:4
Leo, Simeon Newton Dr, 1923, Mr 10,13:4
Leo, Stephen F Mrs, 1947, D 25,21:4
Leo XIII, Pope, 1924, O 23,21:3
Leon, Albert, 1952, Ja 27,76:5
Leon, Alexis M Dr, 1913, N 3,9:6
Leon, Anita D Mrs, 1960, Ja 19,35:2
Leon, Arthur T, 1943, D 17,28:3
Leon, Arthur T Mrs, 1948, F 11,27:4
Leon, Bro, 1947, S 27,15:2
Leon, Goodrich, 1937, N 15,23:5
Leon, Henry H, 1948, Mr 3,23:2
Leon, Irene B Mrs, 1937, Jl 17,15:6
Leon, Isaac, 1943, Jl 19,15:3
Leon, Marie A B Mrs, 1953, O 30,23:2
Leon, Maurice, 1952, O 11,19:3
Leon, Mischa, 1926, Ap 9,19:4
Leon, Regina Mrs, 1950, O 12,31:6
Leon, Samuel I, 1949, Ap 15,23:1
Leon, Simon I, 1959, Mr 31,30:3
Leon, Vitor, 1940, Ap 25,23:3
Leon y Castillo, Fernando (Marquis del Muni), 1918, Mr 13,11:4
Leonard, A S Rev, 1878, My 21,2:7
Leonard, A W, 1941, Ja 9,21:3
Leonard, Abraham J, 1963, Ap 6,19:3
Leonard, Abriel Bp, 1903, D 4,9:5
Leonard, Adna Bradway Rev Dr, 1916, Ap 22,11:5
Leonard, Albert, 1963, Jl 25,25:5
Leonard, Alistes, 1948, D 23,19:2
Leonard, Americus J, 1955, Je 16,31:4
Leonard, Amzi Mrs, 1949, N 30,27:3
Leonard, Andrew T, 1944, S 20,23:4
Leonard, Arthur G, 1949, F 5,16:2
Leonard, Arthur J, 1939, F 9,21:2; 1959, O 23,29:4
Leonard, Arthur J Mrs, 1947, Je 3,25:2
Leonard, Arthur L, 1949, O 20,29:3
Leonard, Arthur N, 1950, Mr 10,27:2
Leonard, Arthur W, 1941, D 27,19:5
Leonard, Baird (Mrs B L Zogbaum), 1941, Ja 24,17:4
Leonard, Benjamin F, 1941, F 28,19:5
Leonard, Benny, 1947, Ap 19,15:1
Leonard, Bro, 1948, Mr 27,13:4
Leonard, Burt H, 1957, Ag 7,27:3
Leonard, Charles, 1922, D 18,17:5
Leonard, Charles A, 1960, N 2,39:3
Leonard, Charles A Mrs, 1948, F 5,23:3
Leonard, Charles F, 1959, D 27,61:1
Leonard, Charles F Mrs, 1952, Ap 25,23:4
Leonard, Charles H, 1938, Mr 20,II,9:2; 1948, Ap 15, 25:5
Leonard, Charles Hall Rev, 1918, Ag 28,7:2
Leonard, Charles Lester Dr, 1913, S 24,9:6
Leonard, Charles R, 1956, Mr 10,17:1
Leonard, Charles T, 1939, Ap 18,23:5
Leonard, Charles W (por), 1941, N 3,19:3
Leonard, Chauncey M, 1874, D 4,1:6
Leonard, Chris, 1957, My 13,31:3
Leonard, Clifford C, 1957, F 17,92:1
Leonard, Clifford M, 1956, S 11,35:1
Leonard, Col (funl), 1873, S 22,1:7
Leonard, Craigh, 1964, Ag 4,29:2
Leonard, Daniel, 1905, My 2,11:6
Leonard, Daniel J, 1937, My 8,19:4; 1941, Jl 26,16:5; 1958, Ag 3,80:5
Leonard, Daniel J Sr Mrs, 1956, Ag 27,19:6
Leonard, Daniel W, 1958, Je 17,29:4
Leonard, Donald F, 1962, Mr 30,33:1
Leonard, Eddie, 1941, Jl 30,19:6
Leonard, Edgar, 1944, S 28,19:1
Leonard, Edgar C, 1938, Mr 18,19:3
Leonard, Edgar W, 1948, O 8,25:2
Leonard, Edmund M, 1954, D 17,31:1
Leonard, Edward, 1944, D 8,21:2
Leonard, Edward C Mrs, 1925, Jl 8,17:5
Leonard, Edward F (por), 1940, N 28,23:1
Leonard, Edward F, 1941, Ja 29,17:4
Leonard, Edward M, 1954, Mr 31,27:1
Leonard, Edward W, 1945, F 2,19:2

Leonard, Ella S, 1947, Ap 9,25:2
Leonard, Elof Mrs, 1941, F 24,15:3
Leonard, Elof R, 1944, Ja 28,17:2
Leonard, Elvira Mrs, 1948, Mr 25,28:3
Leonard, Emerie E, 1943, Jl 15,21:6
Leonard, Emily L Mrs, 1952, Ag 29,23:2
Leonard, Ernest J, 1950, Jl 5,32:5
Leonard, Estelle, 1955, Mr 5,17:5
Leonard, F A, 1903, Je 24,9:6
Leonard, Florence, 1955, N 23,23:2
Leonard, Frances W Mrs, 1938, Ja 8,15:3
Leonard, Francis Mrs, 1950, O 28,17:5
Leonard, Frank J, 1941, Jl 17,19:5
Leonard, Frank L, 1953, O 20,29:3
Leonard, Fred C, 1921, D 7,17:6
Leonard, Frederick C, 1960, Je 24,27:1
Leonard, George, 1952, Je 1,85:1
Leonard, George B, 1956, N 18,89:2
Leonard, George E Mrs, 1959, Ap 16,33:3
Leonard, George F, 1956, Mr 22,35:1
Leonard, George Henry, 1909, F 12,13:6
Leonard, George R, 1950, My 6,15:6
Leonard, Gerome, 1966, Ap 2,29:3
Leonard, Gus, 1939, Mr 28,24:3
Leonard, H B (Dutch),(will), 1953, S 9,20:5
Leonard, H D, 1907, Ap 9,9:6
Leonard, H Steward, 1952, My 14,28:3
Leonard, H V, 1956, Jl 10,31:3
Leonard, H V Mrs, 1944, My 17,19:4
Leonard, H Ward, 1915, F 19,9:6
Leonard, Harry, 1908, Jl 2,9:7
Leonard, Harry E, 1954, My 18,29:3
Leonard, Harry R, 1938, D 29,19:1
Leonard, Henry (por), 1945, Ap 10,19:1
Leonard, Henry G, 1946, Ap 13,17:2
Leonard, Henry Mrs, 1959, Mr 29,80:8
Leonard, Henry R, 1939, Ja 12,19:3
Leonard, Henry S, 1967, Jl 13,37:4
Leonard, Henry T Sr, 1949, D 29,25:3
Leonard, Hiram J, 1948, My 19,27:3
Leonard, Howard, 1945, O 22,17:3; 1955, Ap 14,29:3
Leonard, Hubert B (Dutch), 1952, Jl 12,13:3
Leonard, Hubert B (Dutch),(est acctg), 1954, Jl 10, 6:4
Leonard, I Roy, 1961, Mr 15,39:4
Leonard, Isaac E Sr, 1952, Ap 2,33:3
Leonard, J, 1884, Mr 7,5:2
Leonard, J B, 1864, Ja 30,8:1
Leonard, J E, 1878, My 16,1:1
Leonard, J Hampton, 1937, Ja 31,II,8:6
Leonard, Jack E Mrs, 1967, D 3,84:4
Leonard, Jackie (L Rabasco), 1955, My 12,29:1
Leonard, Jacob C, 1943, Mr 16,19:4
Leonard, Jacob N Mrs, 1948, S 1,23:2
Leonard, James, 1869, Ja 16,4:7; 1960, Je 12,86:6
Leonard, James B, 1948, D 30,19:4
Leonard, James F, 1959, O 6,39:4
Leonard, James H, 1937, D 16,27:2; 1962, Mr 14,39:2
Leonard, James J, 1945, Ap 24,19:4
Leonard, James M, 1964, Ag 19,37:5
Leonard, James T Mrs, 1950, Mr 3,26:3
Leonard, Jean, 1955, Ag 6,15:4
Leonard, Jo (Josephine M), 1963, Ag 8,27:5
Leonard, John A, 1917, O 31,13:5
Leonard, John D, 1958, S 20,19:4
Leonard, John F, 1920, Ag 7,5:5; 1937, S 25,17:4
Leonard, John J, 1938, N 18,21:4; 1946, O 26,17:3
Leonard, John J Mrs (Hazel Bowman), 1956, D 3, 29:5
Leonard, John M, 1968, O 9,47:5
Leonard, John M Mrs, 1951, Ja 18,27:5
Leonard, John N, 1948, Jl 30,18:5
Leonard, John P, 1964, Ag 12,35:3
Leonard, John W, 1938, Ja 26,23:5
Leonard, Joseph, 1960, My 2,29:1
Leonard, Joseph S, 1953, Jl 24,13:5
Leonard, Joseph V, 1959, F 14,21:5
Leonard, Julia Mrs, 1942, D 20,45:2
Leonard, Kenneth A, 1952, Mr 27,29:3
Leonard, L L, 1951, My 18,27:2
Leonard, Leon Mrs, 1952, O 14,31:3
Leonard, Leonard M, 1964, O 14,45:3
Leonard, Martia, 1963, Jl 1,29:2
Leonard, Mary L, 1940, O 8,26:2
Leonard, Mason E, 1941, Ap 20,44:1
Leonard, Maurice, 1947, Jl 28,15:5
Leonard, Maurice J, 1938, My 1,II,6:5
Leonard, Melvin, 1957, O 3,29:4
Leonard, Michael J, 1939, Ja 21,15:3
Leonard, Minnie Mrs, 1940, Ja 3,21:4
Leonard, Mortimer H Mrs, 1949, Ja 1,13:2
Leonard, Neil, 1968, S 16,47:2
Leonard, Nicholas J, 1948, Je 2,29:1
Leonard, Paul, 1948, D 31,15:3
Leonard, Peter J, 1946, S 12,7:2
Leonard, Philip Mrs, 1945, Je 20,23:3
Leonard, Ralph B, 1967, F 15,41:7
Leonard, Raymond, 1948, Ag 11,21:3; 1952, Je 2,22:6
Leonard, Rev Brother, 1938, Ag 3,19:6
Leonard, Richard D, 1943, F 3,19:2
Leonard, Robert, 1948, Ja 6,23:3
Leonard, Robert J, 1954, Ag 21,17:4
Leonard, Robert L, 1945, Je 7,19:4
Leonard, Robert Z, 1968, Ag 29,35:2
Leonard, Royal, 1962, Je 23,23:2
Leonard, Russell, 1903, Jl 20,7:6
Leonard, Russell G, 1949, N 7,27:5
Leonard, Sam, 1940, Je 10,17:5
Leonard, Stephen J, 1949, Jl 26,27:5
Leonard, Thomas, 1918, F 13,13:8
Leonard, Thomas C, 1943, Jl 5,15:4
Leonard, Thomas D, 1957, D 5,35:4
Leonard, Thomas D Mrs, 1942, S 21,15:4
Leonard, Thomas F, 1944, Ap 21,19:3; 1949, My 15, 91:1
Leonard, Thomas J, 1942, My 11,15:4; 1943, N 12,21:4
Leonard, Thomas J Sr, 1939, My 19,21:3
Leonard, Veador, 1947, S 12,22:3
Leonard, Viola A, 1952, S 6,17:1
Leonard, W A, 1930, S 22,19:1; 1932, My 21,15:5
Leonard, W A Hazard, 1952, Ap 15,27:5
Leonard, Warren A, 1949, Ja 16,68:2
Leonard, William A Mrs, 1942, Ap 24,17:2
Leonard, William Bradford, 1924, Ap 2,19:4
Leonard, William Day, 1916, N 24,13:4
Leonard, William E (por), 1944, My 3,19:4
Leonard, William F, 1950, Je 27,29:2
Leonard, William H, 1951, Ag 27,19:4
Leonard, William J, 1957, D 6,29:1
Leonard, Wirt S, 1939, S 21,23:5
Leonarda, Sister (Benedictine Order), 1956, Je 2,20:1
Leonardi, Fernando Mrs, 1959, My 21,31:5
Leonardi, Sydney B, 1942, Ap 6,15:4
Leonardi, Sydney B Mrs, 1956, My 22,33:2
Leonardo, Pasquale, 1965, Ja 11,45:4
Leonardo, Richard A, 1959, D 7,31:1
Leoncavallo, Ruggiero, 1919, Ag 10,23:4
Leone, Charles B, 1949, Ja 14,23:2
Leone, Gerome Mrs, 1944, My 5,19:3
Leone, Henry, 1922, Je 10,11:5
Leone, Joseph, 1946, Je 14,21:5
Leone, Philip, 1945, My 30,19:2
Leone, Raymond E, 1955, O 23,86:7
Leone, William, 1961, F 6,21:1
Leonett, James V, 1958, S 6,17:4
Leonetti, Michael, 1949, Ap 7,30:2
Leonhard, Edgar G, 1944, Je 30,21:2
Leonhard, Margaret V, 1949, Ag 2,19:2
Leonhard, Rudolf Dr, 1921, Ja 5,13:5
Leonhard, Theodore Rev, 1910, Ap 7,11:4
Leonhardt, A F, 1915, Ag 24,11:5
Leonhardt, Frederick H, 1956, Ap 12,31:3
Leonhardt, Harry G, 1952, Je 27,23:3
Leonhardt, Kurt A, 1951, Ja 7,77:3
Leonhardt, Phillip C, 1952, Jl 17,23:4
Leonhardt, Robert, 1923, F 3,13:4
Leoni, Arturo, 1943, Ag 6,15:6
Leoni, Leone, 1964, O 5,33:2
Leoni, Paul G, 1943, Je 24,22:2
Leonian, Leon M, 1945, Je 8,19:6
Leonidian, Bro, 1944, Ag 14,15:5
Leonidoff, Leonid, 1921, F 11,11:4
Leonori, Frank R, 1943, D 6,23:4
Leonori, William H Jr, 1943, D 26,32:3
Leontine, Bro, 1904, Ap 3,2:5
Leontios I, Archbishop, 1947, Jl 28,15:3
Leonty, Metropolitan (L Turkevich),(funl, My 21,- 35:1), 1965, My 15,31:1
Leopold, Alfred M, 1941, O 8,23:4
Leopold, August F, 1949, Mr 15,27:1
Leopold, Charles S, 1960, N 26,21:5
Leopold, David J, 1942, Ap 8,19:6
Leopold, Duke of Albany, 1884, Mr 29,5:1
Leopold, Grand Duke of Tuscany, 1870, Ja 31,1:7
Leopold, Herbert P, 1939, S 23,17:2
Leopold, Isaac Dr, 1915, Ja 21,9:4
Leopold, Isaiah E (E Wynn),(funl plans, Je 21,43:2), 1966, Je 20,1:2
Leopold, Israel, 1950, S 7,31:1
Leopold, James M, 1917, O 10,11:6
Leopold, Jerome S Dr, 1968, Ap 5,47:1
Leopold, John, 1958, My 4,88:8
Leopold, Joseph, 1938, F 8,21:6
Leopold, Joseph Mrs, 1944, Ja 21,17:3
Leopold, King of Belgium, 1865, D 19,4:6
Leopold, Leon, 1948, Jl 3,15:1
Leopold, Louis Mrs, 1960, My 7,23:5
Leopold, Ludwig, 1922, Je 12,15:2
Leopold, Raymond S, 1957, Jl 2,27:2
Leopold, Samuel, 1938, D 23,19:3; 1948, D 21,31:1
Leopold, Simon L Mrs, 1959, Jl 9,27:2
Leopold, Simon S, 1957, Jl 16,25:4
Leopold of Anhalt, Duke, 1918, S 14,11:3
Leopold of Lippe-Bresterfeld, Count, 1908, Ja 29,7:5
Leopold Salvator, Archduke, 1931, S 5,13:3
Leopoldi, Hermann, 1959, Je 29,29:3
Leopoldt, Christian F L, 1947, Ap 14,27:6
Leoser, Thomas S, 1909, My 20,9:4
Leovy, Frank A (por), 1949, Je 3,25:1
Leovy, Frank A Mrs, 1942, D 16,25:6
Le Page, Clifford B, 1948, Ja 17,17:4
Le Page, Nellie Mrs, 1910, O 24,9:6
Le Page, Sophie de V Mrs, 1938, D 13,25:4
Lepart, Anthony, 1946, My 11,27:6
Lepaul, Paul (P Braden), 1958, Je 10,33:1
Le Peer, Albert R Mrs, 1953, F 10,27:1
Lepeley, Joaquin, 1957, Mr 17,86:2
Le Pelletier, Olivier Mrs, 1945, Je 21,19:3
Lepere, John G, 1949, My 12,31:2
Lepeshinskaya, Olga B, 1963, O 4,35:2
Lepesqueur, Raymond A, 1950, D 31,14:1
Lepeta, Harry, 1949, Ap 24,76:1
Lepetrie, W C, 1948, Je 15,28:3
Lepidi, Alberto Rev, 1925, Ag 2,5:5
Lepine, Alfred (por), 1955, Ag 4,25:2
Lepine, Louis J, 1949, D 5,23:1
Lepine, Valmore J, 1951, O 16,31:1
Lepine, William J, 1903, O 9,7:4
L'Episcopo, Joseph B, 1947, S 6,17:5
Le Play, Albert Dr, 1937, Mr 11,23:4
LePlay, Pierre G F, 1882, Ap 7,5:2
Lepler, Samuel E, 1968, Jl 9,39:1
Lepley, Martin O, 1943, Ap 7,25:3
Lepley, Raymond D, 1953, S 25,21:1
Le Plongeon, Augustus Dr, 1908, D 14,9:5
Lepore, Donato A, 1952, O 17,27:3
Lepore, Frank, 1953, Je 29,21:1
Lepore, Pasquale, 1946, My 28,21:3
Le Porin, Frederic W, 1943, Mr 22,19:3
Leporsky, Nikolai, 1952, Je 18,27:6
Leport, Ernest M (por),(Bro Donation), 1943, S 2- 23:4
Lepoutre, Jacques, 1956, Mr 20,23:5
Leppart, John C, 1968, My 24,47:3
Leppelman, John, 1955, D 8,37:4
Lepper, Henry, 1945, S 1,11:5
Lepper, Howard J, 1949, D 31,15:5
Lepper, Lewis E W, 1950, F 16,24:2
Lepper, Philip, 1968, Jl 3,32:1
Lepper, William C, 1951, D 13,33:4
Leppert, Alice Mrs, 1959, D 3,37:5
Leppert, Emma C, 1947, Ap 8,27:3
Leppert, Rudolph E, 1949, O 5,29:3
Leppert, Rudolph E Mrs, 1944, O 10,21:3
Leppert, William, 1947, O 14,27:3
Leppig, John, 1937, Jl 13,20:1
Leppo, Shirley, 1956, F 28,20:6
Lepree, Michael, 1951, Ap 12,33:2
Le Pree, Peter Sr Mrs, 1948, My 15,15:2
Leprestre, Rene, 1941, Ja 19,41:1
Le Prince, Gabriella M, 1953, Mr 3,27:5
Le Prince, Joseph, 1956, F 11,17:4
Leprohon, Ernest P, 1947, D 11,34:2
Leps, Wassili, 1942, D 23,19:5
Lepsius, J Dr, 1926, Mr 31,23:3
Lequerica y Erquiza, Jose F de, 1963, Je 10,31:4
Le Quesne, Charles T, 1954, N 23,35:3
Lequien, Paul, 1941, Ja 7,23:2
Le Rallec, Blanche Mrs, 1940, Mr 20,27:3
Le Ray, James, 1878, Ja 11,2:5
Lercaro, Aurelia Mrs, 1953, My 10,88:4
Lerch, Archer L, 1947, S 11,15:4
Lerch, George R, 1949, F 25,24:3
Lerch, John G, 1966, N 17,47:3
Lerch, Louise (Mrs D G Brien), 1967, Ja 6,35:4
Lerch, Milton J Mrs, 1946, Ap 18,27:3
Lerch, Oscar E Mrs, 1964, O 7,47:1
Lerch, Walter, 1964, Ap 1,39:3
Lerche, Charles O Jr, 1966, Ag 30,36:2
Lerchenfeld-Koefering, Hugo von, 1944, Ap 20,19
Lerf, Frederick W, 1947, F 22,13:4
Leriche, Maurice, 1948, S 17,25:4
Leriche, Rene, 1955, D 30,20:1
Lerius, Joseph Van, 1876, Mr 23,2:4
Lerman, Edward, 1962, Jl 6,25:2
Lerman, Hyman, 1955, Mr 5,17:2
Lerman, Irving M, 1960, Mr 12,21:4
Lerman, Leonard S, 1963, Je 17,25:4
Lerman, Peter Mrs, 1955, N 30,33:1
Lerman, Theodore M, 1954, O 23,15:6
Lermen, John J, 1960, Mr 27,86:8
Lermer, Eugene, 1944, S 23,13:5
Lermond, Normond W, 1944, Ap 9,34:3
Lerner, A B, 1939, Ap 12,24:3
Lerner, Allen Dr, 1953, F 12,28:3
Lerner, Benjamin H, 1959, Ja 11,88:1
Lerner, Charles, 1939, N 27,17:5
Lerner, Frank Mrs, 1957, O 8,35:2
Lerner, Harry, 1949, My 2,25:4
Lerner, Hyman, 1943, Mr 4,19:2
Lerner, Israel M, 1963, Jl 2,26:8
Lerner, Jacob, 1965, Ja 13,25:4
Lerner, Joseph J (will, Jl 27,9:2), 1954, Jl 19,19
Lerner, Leo A, 1965, Mr 8,29:3
Lerner, Louis, 1938, D 1,24:2
Lerner, Ralph, 1946, Ap 26,21:4
Lerner, Samuel A, 1956, D 6,37:4
Lerner, Solomon Mrs, 1951, S 21,23:3
Lerner, William, 1961, Je 30,25:3
Lerose, Harry E, 1950, N 29,33:2
Le Rouge, Gustave, 1938, F 28,15:4
Leroux, G, 1927, Ap 17,24:2
Leroux, Jules, 1952, S 25,31:5
Leroux, P, 1880, Je 3,5:2
Leroux, Xavier, 1919, F 4,11:1
LeRoy, Albert E, 1960, Ap 7,35:4
Leroy, Alice F, 1947, N 12,27:4
Leroy, Charles Joseph, 1919, N 12,13:1
Le Roy, Cornelia, 1964, Ap 5,87:1

Le Roy, Edouard, 1954, N 12,21:5
LeRoy, Edward A, 1913, D 12,11:6
Le Roy, Frank A, 1951, N 27,31:3
Le Roy, Fred, 1948, O 8,25:4
Leroy, H M, 1947, S 8,21:5
Le Roy, Herman Mrs, 1903, Ap 24,9:4
LeRoy, Ida C, 1947, Mr 18,27:3
Leroy, James A, 1956, Mr 27,35:3
LeRoy, Joseph D, 1944, F 1,19:3
Leroy, Louis, 1944, My 11,19:4
Leroy, Marvin D, 1949, Je 27,27:3
Le Roy, Newbold Mrs, 1903, Jl 16,7:6
Leroy, Paul E, 1963, N 14,35:2
Leroy, Phyllis Mrs, 1953, N 3,8:4
LeRoy, Ralph D, 1939, Je 9,21:6
LeRoy, Robert, 1946, S 9,9:4
Le Roy, Sherman Hoyt, 1916, My 25,13:4
Leroy, Virginia Mrs, 1949, F 15,23:4
Leroy-Beaulieu, Anatole Henri, 1912, Je 17,9:7
Leroy-Beaulieu, Paul, 1916, D 11,9:5
Lerrigo, Charles H, 1955, D 6,37:4
Lerroux, Alejandro, 1949, Je 28,27:1
Lersner, Clarence L, 1948, Ap 14,27:4
Lersner, Hortense Mrs, 1940, Je 5,25:3
Lersner, Victor A, 1949, Mr 26,17:1
Lersner, Victor A Mrs, 1951, Ja 29,19:2
Lersundi, Gen, 1874, N 19,1:5
Lert, Ernest J M, 1955, F 1,29:5
Lert, Richard Mrs (V Baum), 1960, Ag 30,29:1
Lerz, Edward B, 1962, My 21,33:4
Lesage, Albert, 1954, N 15,27:2
Le Sage, George L, 1949, N 8,31:3
Le Sage, J Sir, 1926, Ja 2,13:5
Le Sage, Wilford Mrs, 1950, Ag 25,21:5
Le Saint, Edward J, 1940, S 12,25:4
LeSauvage, George R, 1961, O 22,86:1
Lescarboura, Austin, 1962, Ja 9,47:1
Lescault, Frank, 1949, Ja 30,60:5
Lesch, Carl F, 1964, Ag 15,21:4
Lesch, Frank J, 1957, Ap 16,33:1
Lesch, Rudolf (por), 1946, Mr 12,25:6
Leschen, Maurice B, 1959, S 20,87:1
Lescher, Royal W, 1957, Ja 30,29:5
Lescher, Thomas E, 1938, Ap 25,15:3
Leschetizky, Theodor, 1915, N 18,9:6
Lescohier, A William, 1951, N 18,90:7
Lescot, Gen, 1940, D 5,25:5
Lescouve, Theodore, 1940, Ap 23,23:2
Lescure, Marie Therese de Rev Mother, 1958, Ja 2, 29:2
Lese, Frederick, 1959, Je 6,21:4
Lese, Louis, 1941, Ja 10,20:2
Leselidze, K N, 1944, F 22,4:4
Lesemann, John H, 1945, Ja 11,23:5
Lesemann, Louis F W, 1941, Ap 23,21:3
Lesenger, Morris, 1957, Ag 3,15:4
Lesense, Richard H, 1946, D 20,23:1
Leser, C C Fulton, 1949, Ag 18,21:6
Leser, Frederick, 1954, Jl 17,13:2
Leser, Jacob G, 1939, O 2,17:2
Leserman, Philip 3d, 1968, D 15,86:2
Lesesne, Thomas P, 1942, Mr 5,23:2
Le Seur, Edward F, 1947, S 13,11:5
Leseur, James A, 1943, Ap 24,13:2
Le Seur, William H, 1946, S 13,7:3
Lesh, Henry F, 1949, Jl 7,26:2
Lesh, John A, 1939, Ag 8,17:2
Lesh, Paul E, 1944, O 31,19:2
Lesh, William S, 1954, Jl 16,21:3
Leshan, Edward J, 1961, N 15,43:5
Leshefsky, Johann, 1961, N 30,37:4
Lesher, A U Mrs, 1951, D 11,33:1
Lesher, Curtis C, 1941, Jl 7,15:6
Lesher, J E, 1943, Ag 7,24:3
Lesher, Raymond, 1923, Je 18,13:7
Lesher, Stephen H, 1950, Mr 25,13:3
Leshin, Joseph, 1968, S 2,19:5
Leshure, Willard R, 1944, D 17,37:1
Lesieur, J B, 1876, My 20,2:1
Lesinski, John, 1950, My 28,1:2
Lesinsky, Henry, 1924, Ap 25,17:4
Leska, Maria Y Mrs, 1952, Ja 14,19:5
Leskar, John W, 1874, S 22,5:4
Leskela, Ernest A, 1951, D 9,66:1
Leskes, Theodore, 1964, F 21,27:2
Leskom, Edwin S Mrs, 1952, My 3,21:4
Lesley, Eulalia W Mrs, 1940, Mr 21,25:5
Lesley, Everett P, 1945, Ja 18,19:2
Lesley, J P Prof, 1903, Je 3,9:5
Lesley, Neva O, 1953, Je 12,27:1
Lesley, Olive, 1950, Ap 18,31:4
Leslie, Alex, 1955, F 24,27:1
Leslie, Alexander F W, 1914, Ja 12,9:6
Leslie, Alfred A, 1941, Ja 26,37:1
Leslie, Alice U Mrs, 1938, Ap 6,23:1
Leslie, Amy, 1939, Jl 4,13:3
Leslie, Charles Robert, 1859, My 23,4:5
Leslie, Edward H, 1945, F 27,19:4
Leslie, Edwin A, 1905, Je 6,9:5
Leslie, Elizabeth M Mrs, 1952, S 29,23:6
Leslie, Frank, 1880, Ja 11,12:2
Leslie, Frank Mrs (funl, S 21,7:4), 1914, S 19,11:2
Leslie, Frederick A, 1937, F 20,17:3
Leslie, George N Rev, 1937, Ag 10,19:3
Leslie, George R, 1922, Je 16,17:7; 1942, My 29,17:4
Leslie, George W (funl, Ag 18,7:6), 1911, Ag 16,7:6
Leslie, Harry G (por), 1937, D 11,19:3
Leslie, Harry M, 1945, Ja 20,11:2
Leslie, Helen V, 1952, O 7,29:2
Leslie, James C, 1923, Jl 24,21:5
Leslie, James E Mrs, 1948, O 8,25:4
Leslie, James G, 1949, My 17,25:2
Leslie, James I, 1959, Mr 28,17:6
Leslie, Jane S Mrs, 1967, Ap 28,41:2
Leslie, John, 1944, Ja 26,19:4; 1949, D 9,31:2
Leslie, John E, 1940, Ja 28,33:2
Leslie, John M, 1945, Ap 26,23:1
Leslie, John Mrs, 1943, Ag 22,36:8
Leslie, John R Col, 1913, F 16,II,7:4
Leslie, John S, 1939, Ja 11,19:2
Leslie, Julius J, 1944, Je 29,19:7
Leslie, Lady, 1946, N 2,15:6
Leslie, Lew, 1963, Mr 12,7:6
Leslie, Maud M, 1949, My 25,29:4
Leslie, May (Mrs M W Thompson), 1965, Jl 23,26:6
Leslie, Norman B, 1942, N 29,64:8
Leslie, Norman H, 1953, Mr 16,19:4
Leslie, Preston Hopkins, 1907, F 8,9:6
Leslie, Robert J, 1952, Jl 23,23:3
Leslie, Robert Peel, 1924, N 2,7:1
Leslie, S Inglis, 1967, Je 21,47:3
Leslie, Shane Mrs, 1951, F 10,13:2
Leslie, T E Cliffe, 1882, F 14,5:2
Leslie, Thomas J, 1874, N 26,5:3
Leslie, Thomas L, 1953, S 6,52:4
Leslie, Warren, 1952, Mr 2,92:5
Leslie, Warren Jr, 1955, O 15,15:4
Leslie, William, 1939, Mr 8,21:5
Leslie, William G, 1943, Mr 1,19:2
Leslie, William H, 1940, Ja 7,48:6
Leslie, William Mrs, 1947, Ja 21,23:3
Lesnevich, Gus, 1964, F 29,21:2
Lesniak, Helen E, 1950, F 10,24:2
Lesnick, Matthew J, 1941, D 31,17:3
Lesnick, Matthew J Mrs, 1951, Ap 10,27:3
Lesnicki, Ludwig, 1956, F 26,89:1
Lesniewsky, Francis, 1945, My 18,19:4
Lesnik, Stanley Mrs, 1967, N 16,47:2
Lesoff, Morris J, 1938, Jl 3,12:7
Lesourd, Andre, 1920, My 5,11:5
Lesourd, Frank N, 1945, N 10,15:5
LeSourd, Gilbert Q, 1962, Je 23,23:4
Le Sourd, Gilbert Q Mrs, 1960, N 13,88:1
Le Sourd, Homer W, 1948, Mr 18,27:2
Lesperance, Adrian H, 1953, Je 10,32:4
L'Esperance, David A, 1942, S 19,15:4
L'Esperance, David O, 1941, S 1,15:5
L'Esperance, Elise S, 1959, Ja 22,31:1
Lespes, Leo, 1875, My 14,2:2
Lespinasse, Victor D, 1946, D 16,23:2
Less, William L 2d, 1964, Ag 13,29:5
Lessar, Paul, 1905, Ap 22,11:5
Lessard, Father, 1910, N 24,11:2
Lessard, Henry J, 1941, S 16,23:4
Lessard, Joseph W, 1950, Je 18,76:6
Lessart, Charles de, 1944, D 21,21:5
Lessenger, Mark D, 1951, Ag 3,21:3
Lessenger, Waldo E, 1955, My 16,23:5
Lesseps, Charles de Count, 1923, O 3,15:3
Lesseps, Ferdinand de, 1894, D 8,8:1
Lesseps, Paul de, 1955, Jl 13,25:4
Lesser, A J G Rabbi, 1924, O 9,23:5
Lesser, Adolph, 1945, Ap 21,13:3
Lesser, Benjamin, 1967, Mr 26,68:3
Lesser, David, 1949, N 15,26:3
Lesser, Elizabeth, 1947, F 5,23:6
Lesser, Emil C, 1945, Mr 8,23:4
Lesser, Harman, 1957, Jl 18,25:4
Lesser, Harry, 1963, Je 3,29:1
Lesser, Harry J, 1940, N 4,19:5
Lesser, Howard, 1937, S 8,23:3
Lesser, Irving M, 1964, Ag 28,29:2
Lesser, Jacob J (por), 1948, F 27,22:3
Lesser, Joseph, 1943, N 10,23:3
Lesser, Joseph Mrs, 1957, D 9,35:5
Lesser, Max, 1947, Mr 2,60:1
Lesser, Meyer, 1954, Ja 30,17:2
Lesser, Milton A, 1955, F 1,29:5
Lesser, Morris G, 1946, F 21,21:3
Lesser, Myer Mrs, 1956, N 30,23:1
Lesser, Philip P, 1964, Mr 28,19:6
Lesser, Robert, 1922, Je 22,15:7
Lesser, Rose N (funl, N 14,9:6), 1908, N 13,9:3
Lesser, Samuel, 1965, Jl 29,27:5
Lesser, Samuel C, 1948, F 6,26:6
Lesser, Simon, 1939, Ja 9,15:2
Lesser, Solomon, 1906, Ja 8,9:6
Lesser, Walter A, 1915, Je 17,11:7
Lesser, William, 1939, Jl 20,19:3
Lessey, George, 1947, Je 4,27:4
Lessey, George Mrs, 1952, Ag 21,15:2
Lessey, James A, 1906, N 19,9:4
Lessing, Arthur P, 1912, Jl 15,9:3
Lessing, Bruno (por), 1940, Ap 30,21:3
Lessing, Gunther R (Sept 28), 1965, O 11,61:3
Lessing, Lawrence A, 1941, Jl 25,15:5
Lessing, Maxwell, 1938, N 1,23:6
Lessler, Montague, 1939, F 18,15:6
Lessner, Erwin, 1959, D 26,13:2
Lessy, Alex E, 1955, F 5,15:5
Lessy, Michael, 1948, D 9,33:3
Lester, Adelaide, 1937, My 12,23:5
Lester, Andrew J Mrs, 1954, O 24,88:7
Lester, Anthony S, 1940, O 1,23:5
Lester, Arthur, 1944, My 9,19:2
Lester, Barnett B Mrs, 1960, D 1,35:4
Lester, Benjamin A, 1941, Mr 28,23:4
Lester, Bernard, 1964, N 29,86:4
Lester, C Clay, 1946, My 22,21:2
Lester, Carl H, 1966, S 20,47:2
Lester, Charles E, 1938, Ja 15,15:6
Lester, Charles F, 1938, O 17,15:5
Lester, Charles L, 1947, My 20,25:4
Lester, Charles S Judge, 1904, N 18,9:4
Lester, Claude F Prof, 1924, Ag 12,11:3
Lester, Claude W, 1963, Ag 1,27:6
Lester, Daniel K, 1924, D 27,9:4
Lester, Dudley G Mrs, 1950, Ap 11,31:3
Lester, Elliott, 1951, F 25,84:5
Lester, Fanny A, 1940, My 17,19:2
Lester, Frank S, 1946, D 7,21:2
Lester, Fred E, 1938, Ag 9,19:3
Lester, Frederick W, 1925, S 16,25:4
Lester, George B, 1949, F 9,27:2
Lester, Harold G, 1954, Ja 12,23:2
Lester, Harry, 1956, Jl 16,21:5
Lester, Henry M, 1916, Jl 4,11:6
Lester, Henry V, 1903, Ap 23,9:5
Lester, Jacob, 1947, Je 29,48:4
Lester, James, 1947, Je 7,13:3
Lester, James A, 1958, Mr 12,31:2
Lester, James U, 1945, Je 10,31:1
Lester, John C Dr, 1937, S 26,II,8:6
Lester, John J, 1942, D 10,30:2
Lester, Joseph G, 1938, Ag 25,15:2
Lester, Marcus T, 1939, Ap 23,III,7:1
Lester, Mary E, 1951, Ag 11,11:3
Lester, Maurice C, 1955, D 14,39:3
Lester, Maxwell, 1920, Ag 22,20:5
Lester, Maxwell Jr Mrs, 1957, D 3,35:4
Lester, Nathan, 1950, Je 11,92:3
Lester, Orrin C, 1958, F 27,27:3
Lester, Ralph W, 1958, N 15,23:5
Lester, Reuben L, 1941, Mr 24,17:3
Lester, Reuben L Mrs, 1960, O 19,45:2
Lester, Robert Mrs (M Vokes), 1957, S 14,19:6
Lester, Roy C, 1954, N 19,23:5
Lester, Rufus E, 1906, Je 17,9:6
Lester, S F, 1937, Ja 17,II,8:5
Lestoca, William, 1920, O 19,11:3
Lestrade, Harold J, 1958, N 13,33:1
Lestrade, James W, 1937, Ap 25,II,8:8
Lestrade, Louis G, 1952, D 17,33:2
Lestrange, Austin B Sr, 1961, My 12,29:3
LeStrange, Joseph A, 1957, Ap 23,31:4
L'Estrange, Julian (funl, O 24,13:2), 1918, O 23,13:2
l'Estrange, Richard, 1963, N 21,39:4
Le Sueur, Charles B, 1960, N 24,29:5
Lesueur, Hal H, 1963, My 10,33:1
Le Sueur, J B C, 1883, D 28,2:3
Le Sueur, Richard V, 1945, S 7,23:4
Le Sueur, Robert, 1957, Je 28,23:4
Le Sueur, Thomas E, 1938, Ja 2,42:1
LeSure, Harvey K, 1959, S 9,41:4
Lesznai, Anna (Mrs T Gergely), 1966, O 5,42:8
Leszynski, Ruth, 1966, S 15,43:5
Leszynski, Werner, 1962, Ag 8,31:2
Leszynsky, Julius, 1919, Ap 26,15:4
Le Tac, Yvonne Mme, 1957, D 27,20:3
LeTarte, Joseph A Mrs, 1959, Jl 29,29:2
Letcher, Charlotte, 1879, N 9,5:6
Letcher, H J Owen, 1967, Ap 2,93:1
Letcher, Henry W, 1948, Ap 30,23:2
Letcher, J, 1884, Ja 27,7:3
Letcher, Marion, 1948, Je 25,23:4
Letchford, Sarah W P Mrs, 1941, O 23,23:4
Letchworth, Edward J, 1958, O 23,31:3
Letchworth, Edward Sir, 1917, O 9,11:6
Letchworth, Ogden E, 1939, Mr 12,III,7:3
Letchworth, William Pryor, 1910, D 3,11:5
Letellier, Arthur Father, 1921, Ag 25,13:5
Le Tellier, Pol, 1941, Ag 4,13:3
Lethbridge, Arthur E, 1962, S 10,29:4
Lethbridge, Edgar E, 1924, Mr 21,19:2
Lethbridge, George, 1914, Jl 8,9:5
Lethbridge, George W, 1938, Je 19,29:3
Letheley, Henry, 1876, Mr 30,2:1
Lethridge, George W Mrs, 1959, Ag 5,27:4
Le Thuy, Ngo Dinh (funl, Ap 16,79:2), 1967, Ap 14, 6:4
Letondal, Henri, 1955, F 17,27:3
Letort, Robert (Sept 27), 1965, O 11,61:3
Le Tourneau, H A, 1952, Ap 30,27:3
Letourneau, Louis A, 1938, N 14,19:5
LeTourneau, Nora, 1961, Ja 12,29:4
Letourneau, Severin, 1949, D 18,88:4
Letowsky, Samuel, 1959, S 4,19:4
Le Troguer, Andre, 1963, N 12,41:2
Letsch, Frederick G, 1947, N 23,74:6

Letson, Frederick M, 1957, Mr 25,25:3
Lett, Sherwood, 1964, Jl 26,56:6
Lettan, Richard, 1939, Jl 14,19:2
Lettau, John, 1943, Ap 10,17:3
Letteau, George H, 1949, O 21,25:2
Letterhouse, George, 1958, Ap 7,21:3
Lettieri, Felice, 1954, O 3,86:6
Lettieri, Felice Mrs, 1950, Jl 8,13:5
Lettieri, Rocco, 1952, O 12,89:1
Letton, Harold W, 1948, Jl 4,27:2
Lettow-Vorbeck, Paul von, 1964, Mr 10,37:3
Letts, Arthur, 1923, My 19,13:6
Letts, Clarence W, 1953, Mr 8,88:3
Letts, F Dickinson, 1965, Ja 20,39:3
Letts, Henry T, 1946, D 21,19:5
Letts, Ira L (por), 1947, N 25,29:5
Letts, William M, 1957, F 27,27:1
Letzeisen, Helen J, 1940, Jl 28,27:2
Letzer, Albert A Mrs, 1937, Mr 3,23:2
Letzing, John J, 1937, N 14,II,10:5
Leuba, James H, 1946, D 10,31:2
Leubuscher, Frederic C, 1940, Ag 19,17:5
Leucht, Joseph Rabbi, 1920, Mr 8,9:6
Leuchtenberg, Georges Grand Duke de, 1912, My 4, 13:6
Leuchtenberg, Lizzie H Mrs, 1947, D 22,21:5
Leuchter, Max, 1949, My 16,21:2
Leudesdorff, Irving, 1961, Mr 26,93:2
Leuin, Samuel, 1941, F 11,24:3
Leullier, Robert, 1922, Jl 6,19:5
Leupp, Ada M Mrs, 1940, O 18,21:5
Leupp, Francis Ellington, 1918, N 20,15:4
Leupp, Harold L, 1952, F 13,29:1
Leupp, Julia Beach, 1904, S 25,12:3
Leupp, William H, 1925, F 24,19:2
Leur, Olga D Van der Mrs, 1940, Ag 18,37:3
Leuret, Francois, 1954, My 15,15:3
Leusch, Henry A, 1943, D 12,68:6
Leuschner, Armin O, 1953, Ap 24,23:3
Leuschner, Bruno, 1965, F 12,30:1
Leuschner, Walter R, 1949, Ja 29,13:2
Leuser, Ernst, 1903, My 24,7:3
Leute, F D, 1883, O 12,4:7
Leute, Karl M, 1954, Mr 27,17:5
Leuthauser, Theodore C, 1958, S 20,19:4
Leutner, Winfred G, 1961, D 27,27:2
Leutze, Emanuel, 1868, Jl 21,2:6
Leutze, Trevor W, 1966, Ap 26,45:3
Lev, Ray (funl plans, My 22,47:4), 1968, My 21,47:1
LeVaca, Peter Mrs, 1944, D 30,11:6
Leval, Fernand, 1963, Jl 7,52:1
Levalley, Frank A, 1942, N 3,23:1
Le Valley, Lloyd D, 1946, O 5,17:4
Levalley, Orlando, 1948, Ap 20,27:4
Levame, Albert, 1958, D 6,23:3
Levan, George K, 1954, D 12,88:7
LeVan, Harry (Carny C Carny), 1958, N 12,37:2
Levan, James M, 1947, My 29,21:4
LeVan, John N, 1954, Ag 26,27:6
Levan, Louisa, 1953, Ap 21,20:6
Levan, Paul W, 1949, O 6,31:1
Levan, Samuel Mrs, 1949, Mr 11,25:4
Levan and Melville, Earl of, 1947, Ja 16,25:5
Levand, Louis, 1953, Jl 25,11:6
Levand, Max M, 1960, Mr 22,37:1
Levandowsky, Vladimir A, 1946, Jl 14,37:1
Levane, Anthony, 1954, D 9,33:4
Levanger, Rutland, 1953, Mr 15,93:2
Levangie, George W, 1953, Ja 9,22:4
Levanowitz, Michael (Old Mike), 1953, Je 16,23:7
Levant, Benjamin, 1958, Jl 29,23:3
Levant, H Harvey, 1948, D 3,25:4
Levant, Harry L, 1945, My 13,20:3
Levant, Howard, 1960, Ap 4,29:6
Levant, Mark, 1950, My 10,31:4
Le Van Ty, 1964, O 22,32:4
Levay, Abraham Mrs, 1953, S 24,33:3
Le Vay, S Sawyer, 1967, Je 15,47:5
Leve, A Aaron, 1956, F 21,17:7
Leve, Harold R, 1942, Jl 25,13:3
Leve, J Frank, 1959, My 28,31:5
Leve, J Frank Mrs, 1941, N 17,19:3
Levee, David, 1963, O 6,88:5
LeVee, Joseph R, 1954, S 3,17:2
Leveen, Henry, 1912, Ap 3,13:5
Le Veen, Ira H, 1916, Ap 25,11:7
LeVeen, William W, 1967, Ap 2,93:2
Levegh, Pierre, 1955, Je 12,1:3
Leveille, Georges, 1956, Je 14,33:1
Level, Andrew D Sr, 1954, Je 26,13:5
Leven, Isaac, 1940, Ap 19,21:5
Leven, Joseph, 1952, Ap 7,25:4
Leven, Richard R, 1949, Ap 1,26:2
Leven and Melville, Countess of, 1941, Mr 4,23:5
Levenberg, Anna Mrs, 1944, Mr 27,19:2
Levenberg, Judah H, 1938, Ja 17,19:5
Levenberg, Julius, 1959, Ja 11,88:4
Levendovsky, John, 1946, D 12,29:4
Levene, Alexander, 1967, F 2,35:2
Levene, Anna E Mrs, 1947, Ap 1,27:1
Levene, Benjamin F, 1957, Ja 16,31:1
Levene, Louis, 1950, D 30,13:6
Levene, P A Mrs, 1947, Mr 31,23:3
Levene, Phoebus A, 1940, S 7,15:6
Levenfish, Grigory, 1961, F 10,27:4
Levenhagen, Henry A, 1940, D 29,24:5
Levenick, L B, 1947, O 28,25:3
Levens, David C Mrs, 1945, F 9,15:4
Levens, James F, 1960, N 15,39:1
Levenson, Ben, 1951, Ag 13,17:5
Levenson, Bernard, 1944, Jl 22,15:6
Levenson, Boris, 1947, Mr 12,25:4
Levenson, Charles, 1939, Je 1,25:4
Levenson, Charles Mrs, 1966, Jl 5,37:3
Levenson, Cyrus O, 1965, Ag 17,33:3
Levenson, David J, 1953, Ap 4,13:2
Levenson, Harris, 1948, O 8,25:2
Levenson, Jacob Mrs, 1956, My 3,31:4
Levenson, Jacob N, 1962, Jl 23,21:3
Levenson, Jay M, 1957, Mr 9,19:2
Levenson, Joseph A, 1946, N 30,16:2
Levenson, Max, 1942, My 12,19:4
Levenson, Max L Mrs (por), 1944, Ap 23,41:2
Levenson, Milton T, 1949, D 9,31:4
Levenson, Robert, 1952, Ag 16,15:3; 1961, Ap 29,23:3
Levenson, Walter, 1941, Ag 8,15:5
Levenstein, Aaron Mrs, 1957, My 15,35:2
Levenstein, Meyer, 1964, My 26,39:2
Leventhal, Adolph, 1941, N 3,19:3
Leventhal, Alvin A, 1965, N 24,39:3
Leventhal, Hyman Mrs, 1944, Ap 10,19:2
Leventhal, Isadore H, 1959, O 31,23:5
Leventhal, Jacob F, 1953, Jl 20,17:3
Leventhal, Joseph J (por), 1949, Ap 14,25:1
Leventhal, Joseph J, 1949, Ap 18,25:2
Leventhal, Joseph Mrs, 1950, F 23,27:5
Leventhal, Jules (lr), 1949, My 1,II,3:7
Leventhal, Louis, 1955, S 17,15:2
Leventhal, Murray J, 1954, Je 30,27:5
Leventhal, Philip Mrs, 1961, Je 23,29:3
Leventhal, Reuben, 1968, O 8,44:1
Leventon, Alex, 1950, O 14,19:4
Leventritt, D Justice, 1926, Ja 9,17:3
Leventritt, David Mrs, 1909, Jl 5,7:5
Leventritt, Edgar M, 1939, Je 2,23:3
Leventritt, George M, 1910, Je 14,11:4
Leventritt, Victor, 1968, Ag 12,35:2
L'Eveque, Francis L, 1954, Jl 26,17:4
Lever, Asbury F, 1940, Ap 29,15:4
Lever, Charles, 1872, Je 28,5:3
Lever, Charles C, 1951, S 25,29:1
Lever, G Frank, 1939, Ap 1,19:4
Lever, Haley Mrs, 1949, My 3,25:3
Lever, Hardman, 1947, Jl 2,23:2
Lever, Haseltine S, 1941, Ag 11,13:2
Lever, Hayley, 1958, D 8,31:3
Lever, J Howard Dr, 1913, Je 26,9:5
Lever, Roy, 1951, Ag 1,23:3
Lever, Thomas S Jr, 1957, F 7,27:1
Lever, William Hasketh (Lord Leverhulme), 1925, My 7,19:4
Lever, William L, 1942, F 15,45:2
Lever, William Mrs, 1913, Jl 25,7:6
Levere, J Leonard, 1953, D 31,19:3
Levere, Rose Wice Mrs, 1923, D 29,13:6
Leverence, Charles A, 1954, Ag 13,15:6
Leverenz, Robert J, 1941, Je 3,21:3
Leverett, Jules G, 1957, N 11,29:4
Leverett, Thomas F Mrs, 1944, Ap 23,41:1
Leverhulme, Lord (W H Lever), 1949, My 27,21:1
Leverich, C P (see also J 11), 1876, Ja 13,8:2
Leverich, C S, 1936, O 29,25:4
Leverich, Charles Duncan, 1925, F 19,19:3
Leverich, Henry, 1939, Ap 20,23:2
Leverich, Henry P, 1959, Ag 13,27:1
Leverich, Louis G, 1955, D 9,27:1
Leverich, Stephen D, 1916, O 13,11:3
Leveridge, Lavinia, 1951, Je 26,29:1
Levering, Frank D, 1943, My 30,26:8
Levering, Griffith G, 1955, Ag 20,17:3
Levering, Richard, 1920, Ja 30,15:4
Levering, William W, 1943, S 21,23:4
Levermann, Wilhelm, 1954, Ap 20,7:2
Levermore, C H, 1927, O 22,17:5
Leverone, Louis E, 1957, Mr 16,19:6
Leveroni, Elvira, 1924, D 27,9:4
Leverrier, M J J, 1877, S 24,5:4
Levers, David L, 1949, Mr 23,27:3
Levers, Frederick Mrs, 1945, Ag 21,21:3
Levers, Robert, 1945, D 19,26:2
Leverton, Garrett H, 1949, N 12,15:6
Leverty, John A, 1937, Ap 4,II,10:7
Leveson-Gower, George G S (Duke of Sutherland),(Feb 1), 1963, Ap 1,36:6
Leveson-Gower, William S 4th Earl of Granville, 1953, Je 26,19:1
Levetown, Harris, 1952, S 13,17:1
Levetown, Morris, 1960, S 5,15:6
Levett, Benjamin A, 1962, My 18,31:1
Levett, David M, 1914, S 29,11:6
Levett, George Mrs, 1953, Ja 27,25:2
Levetzow, Herr von, 1903, Ag 13,9:7
Levetzow, Magnus von (por), 1939, Mr 15,23:1
Levey, A L Mrs, 1954, My 14,23:4
Levey, David E, 1944, Ja 19,19:4
Levey, Edgar J (mem), 1912, Ap 30,11:4
Levey, Ethel, 1955, F 28,19:3
Levey, George P, 1951, S 19,31:4
Levey, Harold A, 1967, Je 16,43:4
Levey, Henry, 1943, N 7,56:6
Levey, Jacob J, 1955, Ag 11,21:4
Levey, James, 1955, My 13,25:2
Levey, Jules Mrs, 1959, Jl 14,29:1
Levey, Sam, 1948, Je 22,25:5
Levey, William, 1963, O 13,86:8
Levi, Albert L, 1945, Ap 22,35:1
Levi, Alfred W, 1943, Ja 12,23:5
Levi, Anthony, 1944, My 1,15:3
Levi, Carl, 1937, My 14,23:2
Levi, Emanuel (Jan 15), 1963, Ap 1,36:1
Levi, Emilio Mrs, 1961, Ap 22,25:2
Levi, Eric, 1966, Ap 26,45:3
Levi, Ernest, 1950, Ap 23,92:6
Levi, Gaston I, 1957, D 22,40:8
Levi, Gerson B, 1939, F 16,21:2
Levi, Harry, 1944, Je 14,19:4
Levi, Irving B, 1964, F 10,27:5
Levi, James R, 1948, Ja 13,25:4
Levi, John H, 1948, Ja 28,23:3
Levi, Joseph C (funl, Ja 21,21:5), 1925, Ja 19,17:1
Levi, Leo N, 1904, Ja 14,9:5
Levi, Lew, 1945, O 18,23:5
Levi, Max, 1953, Jl 2,23:6; 1956, O 10,39:5
Levi, Melvin L, 1952, Je 5,31:2
Levi, Nathaniel H (por), 1942, Mr 22,48:7
Levi, Paul, 1943, Ag 28,11:4
Levi, Rachel H Mrs, 1938, Ap 26,21:3
Levi, S George, 1951, My 30,21:5
Levi, Siegfried, 1941, Ja 4,13:3
Levi-Civita, Tullio, 1942, Ja 2,23:5
Levi della Vida, Giorgio, 1967, N 27,47:4
Levic, Emanuel, 1937, F 14,II,9:1
Levick, Gustavus, 1909, Jl 11,7:7
Levick, Hugh G Sir, 1937, Je 20,II,7:2
Levick, Louis E, 1968, N 11,47:4
Levick, Maurice E, 1945, F 21,19:5
Levick Saml, 1958, Mr 16,86:8
Levidis, Dimitrios, 1964, F 10,27:2
Le Vien, Chris, 1948, Mr 13,15:4
Levien, Louis, 1940, Ja 18,23:4
Levien, Max Mrs, 1952, Je 30,19:3
Levien, Sonya (Mrs C Hovey), 1960, Mr 20,86:8
Leviero, Anthony (funl plans, S 5,27:2; funl, S 7,23: 1956, S 4,29:1
Leviero, Augustine Mrs, 1958, O 20,29:5
Levin, Abraham, 1947, Mr 16,60:1; 1957, D 1,88:5
Levin, Abraham L, 1940, S 16,19:4
Levin, Abraham W, 1963, Ag 31,17:3
Levin, Albert A, 1949, Ag 21,68:7
Levin, Anna, 1953, Je 8,29:1
Levin, Antonio, 1947, N 18,29:3
Levin, Antonio Mrs, 1947, N 18,29:3
Levin, Axel, 1954, Jl 9,17:1
Levin, Barney, 1947, N 23,72:3
Levin, Ben Mrs, 1959, N 11,35:4
Levin, Charles E Dr, 1937, Je 26,5:4
Levin, Clarence F, 1923, Je 8,19:5
Levin, David, 1953, Jl 1,29:5
Levin, David L, 1962, S 3,15:4
Levin, Eli M, 1961, N 28,37:1
Levin, Emil N, 1964, Ja 30,29:1
Levin, Frances, 1941, My 27,23:4
Levin, Goldie B Mrs, 1937, F 20,17:4
Levin, Harry, 1945, D 12,27:2; 1950, Ap 21,23:1; 1956, S 26,33:1
Levin, Harry Mrs, 1953, Mr 20,23:3
Levin, Herman Mrs, 1963, Jl 9,31:3
Levin, Hoke, 1960, Mr 30,37:2
Levin, Hudythe M (Mrs I Nachamie), 1965, Ja 2 35:3
Levin, Isaac, 1945, Je 21,19:2
Levin, Israel, 1955, N 23,23:1
Levin, Jacob, 1952, D 19,31:3; 1958, D 8,31:5
Levin, Jacob S, 1950, Jl 1,15:2
Levin, Jasper J, 1959, F 21,21:4
Levin, Joseph B, 1946, D 14,15:5
Levin, Joseph B Mrs, 1966, O 29,29:4
Levin, Joseph D Dr, 1968, O 14,47:3
Levin, Joseph M Mrs, 1958, F 27,27:4
Levin, Julius, 1947, Mr 15,13:6; 1957, My 6,29:5
Levin, Justin Mrs, 1950, N 23,35:2
Levin, Lawrence M, 1968, Ag 6,37:2
Levin, Leonard S, 1952, Mr 28,23:3
Levin, Louis, 1963, Ap 17,41:4
Levin, Louis H, 1923, Ap 24,21:5; 1954, N 4,31:2
Levin, Lucy, 1939, S 5,23:6
Levin, Maurice, 1968, Ja 23,43:5
Levin, Maurice C, 1948, D 24,17:3
Levin, Michael, 1952, Mr 7,23:3
Levin, Milton B, 1960, Ja 9,21:2
Levin, Milton H, 1967, Ag 28,31:4
Levin, Morris, 1947, Je 29,48:5
Levin, Morris R H, 1942, N 24,26:2
Levin, Oscar, 1953, Ag 18,23:3
Levin, Philip, 1958, Ja 19,86:4
Levin, Samuel, 1939, N 26,42:4; 1948, O 20,29:5; 1949, Ap 5,30:6
Levin, Samuel A, 1960, D 1,35:4
Levin, Samuel L, 1944, Ag 10,17:4

Levin, Sarah L Mrs, 1939, Je 7,23:6
Levin, Saretta, 1880, My 7,8:3
Levin, Saul R, 1960, My 4,45:2
Levin, Sidney O, 1939, D 15,25:5
Levin, Stanley, 1958, F 3,23:2
Levin, Yehuda Leib, 1925, D 7,21:4
Levin-Shatzkes, Icchok (cor, D 17,39:4), 1963, D 16, 33:4
Levin-Shatzkes, Icchok Mrs, 1962, S 9,84:7
Levine, Abraham, 1952, Jl 20,52:1; 1953, My 9,19:5; 1966, Mr 30,45:1
Levine, Abraham I, 1967, S 23,31:5
Levine, Al, 1965, Jl 21,37:5
Levine, Alex Z, 1952, Je 17,27:2
Levine, Archie, 1961, F 15,35:4
Levine, Arnold S, 1960, Ag 27,19:6
Levine, Arthur B, 1965, Mr 29,36:2
Levine, Arthur E, 1961, D 17,82:6
Levine, Arthur I (mem ser), 1951, S 17,21:2
LeVine, Arthur I, 1958, Ja 15,29:3
Levine, Benjamin, 1942, N 7,15:1; 1955, F 19,15:5
Levine, Bernard S, 1962, N 15,37:4
Levine, Charles A, 1965, F 15,27:2
Levine, D Rev, 1926, Je 28,17:4
Levine, David, 1944, S 18,19:5
Levine, David B, 1950, Ag 8,30:2
Levine, Edmund J, 1946, Ag 1,23:5
Levine, Edmund J Mrs, 1945, Mr 13,23:2
Levine, Edward H, 1965, S 10,35:2
Levine, Edward Mrs, 1950, Ja 19,27:2
Levine, Emanuel, 1952, My 9,15:6
Levine, Esther, 1958, S 5,27:3
Levine, Eugene B, 1952, F 28,27:3
Levine, Fannie, 1943, S 28,25:2; 1966, O 7,43:5
Levine, Frank, 1948, Ag 19,21:1
Levine, Frank R, 1955, N 23,23:5
Levine, Froim, 1941, Ja 5,44:7
Levine, G Irving, 1956, D 3,29:2
Levine, George N, 1961, Jl 3,15:1
Levine, H Robert, 1964, Mr 19,33:1
Levine, Harold, 1961, Ja 19,29:5
Levine, Henry, 1951, S 24,27:3
Levine, Herman B, 1962, Jl 3,23:4
Levine, Herman B Mrs, 1966, S 1,35:4
Levine, Hyman Mrs, 1945, O 17,19:3
Levine, Irving Mrs, 1948, Ja 9,21:4
Levine, Isaac, 1961, O 28,21:5
Levine, Isadore, 1962, My 17,37:5
Levine, Israel, 1949, Mr 29,25:4
Levine, J Sidney, 1955, D 23,17:4
Levine, Jack, 1953, Ja 19,23:2; 1958, Ag 23,15:6
Levine, Jack D, 1966, D 10,37:4
Levine, Jacob, 1966, Ap 16,33:2
Levine, Jacob J, 1967, My 1,37:3
Levine, Joseph, 1943, S 22,24:2; 1947, O 9,25:3; 1950, Jl 2,24:7; 1959, My 11,27:3; 1964, Je 9,35:4
Levine, Joseph M, 1963, Ag 17,19:4
Levine, Joseph Mrs, 1941, Je 17,21:4
Levine, Joseph S, 1958, My 27,29:5
Levine, Jules C, 1941, N 28,23:2
Levine, Julius, 1949, F 1,26:3
Levine, Lena (Mrs L Ferber), 1965, Ja 11,45:3
Levine, Leon I, 1961, Ap 19,39:2
Levine, Leon Mrs, 1951, O 9,29:6
Levine, Leonard, 1968, N 4,47:5
Levine, Leopold E, 1966, My 18,47:2
Levine, Libby Mrs, 1937, Ag 12,19:1
Levine, Lillian (Mrs H Ward), 1966, My 5,47:2
Levine, Lipman, 1967, F 14,43:1
Levine, Louis, 1942, Ag 15,11:5; 1958, F 16,86:2; 1960, Ag 11,27:5; 1961, Je 23,29:5
Levine, Louis B, 1960, My 31,31:3
Levine, Louis M, 1950, My 7,106:1
Levine, Louis Mrs, 1953, Ja 27,25:3
Levine, M Carl, 1963, My 31,23:5
Levine, M S, 1933, Ag 28,13:3
Levine, Mac, 1964, Jl 15,35:4
Levine, Manuel, 1939, My 7,III,6:6
Levine, Marvin Mrs, 1966, Ag 16,39:5
Levine, Maurice I, 1952, Ja 16,25:1
Le Vine, Maurice M Mrs, 1940, D 19,25:5
Levine, Max, 1915, My 8,15:5; 1946, F 17,42:4; 1946, Jl 19,19:3; 1953, My 15,23:3; 1955, Ja 6,27:4; 1960, Jl 16,19:3
Levine, Max D, 1956, Mr 4,88:3
Levine, Mendel L, 1957, Mr 8,25:3
Levine, Mervin S Mrs, 1962, My 11,31:2
Le Vine, Merwin F, 1962, O 11,39:2
Levine, Meyer, 1937, Je 13,II,6:7
Levine, Meyer H, 1947, Ap 17,27:2
Levine, Michael, 1951, O 5,28:3; 1952, Ag 27,27:1
Levine, Milton G, 1953, Jl 30,23:6
Levine, Morris, 1962, F 11,86:4
Levine, morris J, 1964, D 30,25:4
Levine, Morris Mrs, 1945, Je 27,19:5
Levine, Moses, 1953, S 9,29:2
LeVine, Murray, 1953, N 23,27:3
Levine, Murray, 1962, S 25,37:1; 1964, N 21,29:1
Levine, Murray Mrs (L Everts), 1960, Je 3,31:4
Levine, Murry H, 1943, N 20,13:4
Levine, Nahum, 1959, D 18,30:1
Levine, Nathan J, 1953, S 22,31:5
Levine, Nathan L Dr, 1968, S 10,47:3
Levine, Nathan Mrs, 1955, S 1,23:3
Levine, Philip, 1963, D 24,17:5
Levine, Robert H, 1966, S 12,45:2
LeVine, Robert P, 1967, Ag 20,89:1
Levine, Samuel, 1947, O 16,27:4; 1948, N 2,25:4; 1949, Mr 21,23:3; 1951, N 29,33:5
Levine, Samuel A, 1966, Ap 1,35:4
Levine, Samuel M, 1964, Je 13,23:4
Levine, Samuel Mrs, 1948, Ag 17,21:4; 1951, F 8,34:2
Levine, Seth, 1968, Je 8,31:2
Levine, Seymour Mrs, 1954, D 12,88:5
Levine, Sidney H, 1957, Ag 3,15:4
Levine, Sidney J, 1949, D 28,25:4
Levine, Sidney S, 1962, S 15,25:4
Levine, Sol, 1952, Ap 16,27:4; 1952, N 1,21:4
Levine, Stanley R, 1967, Jl 3,17:4
Levine, Victor E, 1963, S 30,29:2
Levine, Zindel, 1949, Ag 17,23:3
Leviness, Arthur A, 1948, O 15,23:2
Le Viness, Clarence K, 1943, Ap 3,15:2
Le Viness, Clarence K Mrs, 1953, Jl 29,23:4
Le Viness, Osmund, 1953, Ja 24,15:2
LeViness, Ossie, 1966, Jl 7,37:2
Levinger, Alfred, 1957, F 22,21:3
Levinger, Lee J, 1966, Jl 3,35:2
Levinger, Lee J Mrs, 1958, Ja 31,21:1
Levings, Frederick R, 1955, Je 19,92:6
Levings, George E 2d, 1966, F 18,33:4
Levings, John A Mrs, 1958, F 28,21:2
Levings, N C, 1883, Je 12,4:7
Levingston, Aron, 1949, Je 16,29:4
Le Vino, Alex, 1958, Ap 2,31:1
Levino, Herman D, 1956, Jl 3,25:4
Le Vino, Selma (will), 1946, F 21,23:7
Levins, Elizabeth, 1938, N 28,15:5
Levins, James, 1922, Ag 4,15:5
Levins, James J, 1945, F 21,19:4
Levins, Peter, 1950, F 26,76:8
Levinsky, Battling (B Lebrowitz), 1949, F 13,76:3
Levinsohn, Bernard, 1958, Ja 19,87:1
Levinsohn, Charles, 1938, Je 23,21:2
Levinsohn, Herman, 1960, Jl 25,23:5
Levinsohn, James, 1921, Je 29,15:2
Levinsohn, Morris, 1948, Je 25,23:1
Levinson, Abraham, 1955, S 19,25:3
Levinson, Abraham C Rabbi, 1912, Je 9,II,15:6
Levinson, Abraham F, 1946, Jl 22,21:3
Levinson, Bernard, 1950, My 5,22:2
Levinson, Charles, 1944, Ja 14,19:3
Levinson, Charles Mrs (M Slott), 1967, Ja 25,43:2
Levinson, David, 1953, Jl 10,19:4; 1964, D 6,88:6
Levinson, David J, 1958, O 1,37:1
Levinson, David J Mrs, 1962, Ag 3,23:5
Levinson, Edward, 1945, Ag 9,21:4
Levinson, Edwin D, 1954, Ap 10,15:4
Levinson, Emanuel, 1945, O 16,23:3
Levinson, George Mrs, 1945, S 30,46:4
Levinson, Harry, 1945, Ag 5,38:3; 1949, Ap 23,13:1; 1954, N 30,29:4
Levinson, Irving L, 1950, Ag 10,25:3
Levinson, Jacob, 1955, Je 16,31:2
Levinson, Joseph, 1944, Ag 20,33:1
Levinson, Julian D, 1950, Je 3,15:3
Levinson, Max, 1943, Jl 20,19:2
Levinson, Meyer A, 1940, Ap 1,19:5
Levinson, Michael J Mrs, 1955, S 8,31:5
Levinson, Morris, 1953, Ap 26,85:3; 1967, N 15,47:1
Levinson, Nathan, 1952, O 19,87:4
Levinson, Paul, 1957, O 13,86:4
Levinson, Salmon O (por), 1941, F 3,17:1
Levinson, Salmon O Mrs, 1963, Je 12,43:2
Levinson, Samuel J (por), 1947, S 20,15:3
Levinson, Samuel J, 1956, Je 1,23:5
Levinson, Sidney O, 1954, Je 21,23:6
Levinson-Lovi, Moses W, 1955, Je 24,21:2
Levinthal, Bernard L, 1952, S 24,33:6
Levinthal, Bernard L Mrs, 1968, Jl 25,33:4
Levinthal, Fred, 1961, D 1,33:1
Levinthal, Hyman, 1962, Mr 7,35:2
Levinthall, Mitchell Mrs, 1967, Jl 9,60:8
Levinton, George, 1967, My 24,47:4
Levis, Arthur B, 1948, F 20,27:2
Levis, Ben F, 1956, O 26,29:1
Levis, Carl, 1939, O 4,25:4
Levis, Carl (will), 1940, Jl 10,17:5
Levis, Charles, 1948, D 2,29:4
Levis, David H, 1943, Ap 30,21:1
Levis, Franklin B, 1913, Ap 10,11:5
Levis, Harold J Dr, 1925, S 13,5:1
Levis, Henry, 1954, Je 8,27:4
Levis, Irving A, 1960, My 30,17:1
Levis, John M, 1942, Jl 3,17:4
Levis, Julius J, 1952, Je 4,27:3
Levis, Nelson, 1950, O 27,29:5
Levis, Norman Van Pelt, 1955, Ag 17,27:2
Levis, Robert H, 1950, O 16,27:5
Levis, Robert P, 1943, D 3,23:1
Levis, Robert P Mrs, 1955, N 26,19:4
Levis, William E, 1962, N 8,39:3
Leviseur, Frederick J Dr, 1920, Mr 20,11:6
Levison, D Marrenner, 1943, Mr 20,15:5
Levison, Ira N, 1946, D 11,32:3
Levison, Jacob B, 1947, N 24,23:5
Levison, Jacob J, 1961, Ja 3,27:5
Levison, John R, 1940, N 18,19:3
Levison, Wallace Goold, 1924, Mr 11,19:3
Levison, Wilhelm, 1947, Ja 19,53:4
Levison, William, 1961, Ap 5,37:2
Leviss, Boris, 1961, Ap 21,33:1
Levister, Benjamin F, 1950, O 26,31:2
Levitan, Benjamin W (por), 1941, Jl 24,17:4
Levitan, Solomon, 1940, F 28,22:2
Levitas, Gerson, 1940, F 26,15:5
Levitas, Irving Mrs, 1953, Ag 28,17:4
Levitas, Joseph I, 1965, Ap 23,35:2
Levitas, Matthew S, 1956, F 22,27:1
Levitas, Samuel M (trb lr, Ja 14,22:6), 1961, Ja 4, 33:1
Levitch, Bruce, 1946, Je 23,40:5
Levitch, Isaiah B, 1951, Je 1,23:3
Levitch, Oscar, 1952, Ap 8,29:4
Levitin, Benjamin, 1943, Ag 4,17:5
Levitin, Jacob, 1950, Ja 28,13:4; 1951, D 25,31:1
Leviton, Isidor, 1965, Je 10,35:3
Leviton, Isodor Mrs, 1964, O 20,37:3
Levitow, Bernhard, 1950, Jl 21,19:4
Levitt, Abraham (cor, S 5,39:2), 1962, Ag 21,33:4
Levitt, Abraham Mrs, 1965, N 21,87:1
Levitt, Adolph, 1953, O 30,23:5
Levitt, Albert (cor, Je 20,45:2), 1968, Je 19,47:3
Levitt, Alfred S, 1966, F 11,33:1
Levitt, Benjamin, 1945, Mr 16,15:4
Levitt, Benjamin Z, 1962, Ag 17,23:6
Levitt, Charles H, 1966, O 26,47:4
Levitt, George, 1966, Jl 16,25:3
Levitt, Israel A, 1941, S 13,17:6
Levitt, Israel A Mrs, 1949, Ag 3,23:2
Levitt, Jacob, 1950, Ag 23,29:3; 1963, D 4,47:1
Levitt, Joel J, 1937, Mr 29,19:5
Levitt, Lou, 1949, F 14,19:2
Levitt, Mayer Mrs, 1949, My 22,88:4
Levitt, Morris, 1948, Ag 7,15:4
Levitt, Thomas I, 1953, F 2,21:2
Levitt, Victor, 1956, S 29,19:4
Levitte, George, 1951, Ap 17,29:4
Levitus, George, 1965, Je 19,29:2
Levitz, Charles D, 1947, Ja 27,23:3
Levitz, David Dr, 1953, F 19,23:1
Levitz, Meyer, 1956, Ag 30,25:1
Levitzki, Mischa, 1941, Ja 3,19:1
Levitzky, Boris, 1958, Mr 27,33:4
Levor, Arthur S, 1959, F 7,19:1
Levorsen, Arville I, 1965, Jl 18,68:6
Levowitz, Aaron D, 1942, F 25,19:1
Levowitz, David, 1967, D 23,23:3
Levy, A J J, 1948, D 1,29:5
Levy, A Morris, 1965, D 12,86:4
Levy, Aaron, 1952, O 1,33:3
Levy, Aaron G, 1950, F 22,29:1
Levy, Aaron J (funl, N 26,19:1), 1955, N 22,35:5
Levy, Aaron Mrs, 1953, Mr 16,19:2
Levy, Aaron W, 1954, Jl 11,72:5
Levy, Abraham, 1920, D 18,13:5; 1954, Ja 1,23:4; 1954, Je 30,27:4; 1961, Ap 4,37:3
Levy, Abraham A, 1946, Ja 18,19:3
Levy, Abraham D Mrs, 1965, Ja 16,27:1
Levy, Abraham L Dr, 1968, D 1,86:5
Levy, Abraham M, 1942, Jl 22,19:2
Levy, Abraham N Mrs, 1957, S 1,56:5
Levy, Abram Col, 1937, Mr 16,23:4
Levy, Al, 1941, Mr 25,23:6
Levy, Albert L, 1958, Ap 14,25:1
Levy, Albert Sir, 1937, S 6,17:6
Levy, Alex O Mrs, 1940, Jl 19,19:6
Levy, Alfred L, 1962, Je 20,35:3
Levy, Alfred Rabbi, 1919, Jl 24,9:1
Levy, Alton, 1965, Ja 9,25:3
Levy, Amanuel, 1939, S 6,23:3
Levy, Andrew L, 1963, Ag 31,17:3
Levy, Anna J Mrs, 1942, My 12,19:5
Levy, Annie R Mrs, 1937, Ja 26,21:2
Levy, Arch, 1949, S 20,29:1
Levy, Arthur, 1938, N 21,19:2
Levy, Arthur J, 1955, My 14,19:5
Levy, Arthur Mrs, 1951, S 15,15:6
Levy, Arthur W, 1957, Ap 11,31:4
Levy, Arthur Z, 1944, Je 15,19:6
Levy, Austin T (will, D 12,31:6), 1951, N 25,86:3
Levy, Baruch, 1944, My 30,21:2
Levy, Benjamin, 1966, Ap 15,39:3
Levy, Benjamin C, 1944, Ap 9,34:1
Levy, Benjamin E, 1952, Mr 7,23:3
Levy, Benjamin E Mrs, 1951, O 8,21:3
Levy, Benjamin M, 1942, Ag 18,22:3
Levy, Benjamin Mrs, 1961, N 16,39:1
Levy, Benno B, 1960, Ap 26,37:4
Levy, Bernard, 1948, O 19,27:1
Levy, Bernard Mrs, 1943, D 27,19:2
Levy, Bert (Yank), 1965, S 5,56:7
Levy, Bert Jr, 1918, Ap 29,13:5
Levy, Berthold Mrs, 1950, N 23,38:4
Levy, C Arthur, 1940, Ap 19,21:5
Levy, C Harold, 1945, S 12,25:3
Levy, C Sedgwick, 1951, D 5,35:5
Levy, Carrie Mrs, 1952, N 24,23:2
Levy, Charles, 1945, Ap 28,15:3; 1947, S 5,20:2; 1953, F 23,25:5

Levy, Charles F Sr, 1954, My 22,15:5
Levy, Charles H, 1950, S 24,105:1
Levy, Charles M, 1940, Ap 17,23:5
Levy, Charles S, 1921, Jl 6,15:6
Levy, Charles S Mrs, 1943, O 20,21:2
Levy, Clara, 1961, O 26,35:3
Levy, Clara Mrs, 1954, N 29,25:5
Levy, Clarence B, 1942, Mr 6,21:3
Levy, Clifton H, 1962, Mr 19,29:3
Levy, Daniel, 1937, My 22,15:1
Levy, Daniel K, 1955, My 15,86:4
Levy, David, 1939, Mr 23,23:1; 1948, Ap 3,15:1
Levy, David Heine Dr, 1923, My 23,21:6
Levy, David M Mrs (funl plans, Mr 14,29:1), 1960, Mr 13,86:3
Levy, David R, 1955, F 15,27:4
Levy, David S, 1952, Je 30,19:1
Levy, David W, 1940, F 13,23:4
Levy, Diana F Mrs, 1941, D 23,21:5
Levy, Edgar A, 1958, Ja 31,22:1
Levy, Edgar E, 1960, Jl 8,21:5
Levy, Edward, 1945, O 8,15:1; 1947, O 11,17:3
Levy, Edward A, 1955, N 8,31:4
Levy, Edward D, 1960, Ag 21,85:1
Levy, Edward H, 1941, S 28,49:3
Levy, Eli H, 1953, F 20,20:3
Levy, Elliot, 1954, Ja 29,19:4
Levy, Ellis W, 1951, S 16,84:5
Levy, Emile Mrs, 1955, Ja 27,23:4
Levy, Erich, 1953, S 11,21:6
Levy, Ernest C, 1938, S 30,21:2
Levy, Ernest J Mrs, 1945, Je 11,15:3
Levy, Fabian S M, 1952, N 28,25:2
Levy, Fanny, 1949, My 20,27:3
Levy, Felix A, 1963, Je 20,33:3
Levy, Felix H, 1953, Mr 25,31:5
Levy, Felix U, 1944, N 29,23:5
Levy, Ferdinand, 1923, Jl 2,15:6
Levy, Flora Mrs, 1941, My 7,25:3
Levy, Florence N (por), 1947, N 17,22:2
Levy, Fred Sr (will, Ap 6,23:4), 1955, Mr 26,15:3
Levy, Fred Sr Mrs, 1955, Ja 30,84:8
Levy, Frederick Mrs, 1961, F 26,92:6
Levy, Garfield W, 1963, Jl 6,15:5
Levy, George A, 1951, Jl 11,23:3
Levy, George M Mrs, 1967, S 19,51:3
Levy, George Mrs, 1963, O 1,39:2
Levy, Gershen, 1947, F 23,54:4
Levy, Gerson J Mrs, 1964, Je 18,35:1
Levy, Gilbert M, 1949, Mr 18,25:2
Levy, Gustav, 1946, Ja 23,27:5
Levy, H Ralph, 1948, N 29,23:5
Levy, Harriet L, 1950, S 17,104:3
Levy, Harry C Mrs, 1948, S 18,17:2
Levy, Harry W, 1962, Mr 17,25:1
Levy, Hemiot, 1946, Je 17,21:3
Levy, Henrietta Mrs, 1941, O 11,17:1
Levy, Henry, 1937, Ap 9,21:2; 1948, D 21,31:3; 1952, My 23,21:1; 1954, Jl 18,56:6
Levy, Henry C, 1951, F 21,27:4
Levy, Herbert, 1966, Mr 13,86:3
Levy, Herman, 1920, Ap 17,15:4; 1920, N 23,13:3; 1943, O 5,25:4; 1948, D 22,24:3; 1951, O 15,25:1
Levy, Hermann, 1949, Ja 18,23:5
Levy, Howard S, 1962, O 9,41:1
Levy, Hugo, 1940, Ja 21,34:5
Levy, Hyman, 1940, F 8,23:5
Levy, I Harris, 1946, Jl 5,19:6
Levy, I Jesse, 1964, Je 16,39:3
Levy, I Joseph, 1957, My 23,33:3
Levy, I Montefiore, 1960, N 3,39:1
Levy, Isaac H, 1945, F 13,23:1
Levy, Isaac H (por), 1948, F 11,27:1
Levy, Isaac H, 1954, D 17,31:1
Levy, Isaac M, 1945, My 15,19:2
Levy, Isidore, 1947, S 29,21:3
Levy, Isidore A, 1939, D 6,25:1
Levy, Israel K, 1955, Ag 28,85:2
Levy, J Harold, 1961, F 24,29:3
Levy, J J, 1942, F 23,21:5
Levy, J Langley, 1945, My 13,20:6
Levy, J Leonard Rev Dr, 1907, Ap 21,9:5
Levy, J P Capt, 1883, S 15,5:2
Levy, Jacob, 1939, N 25,17:5; 1951, S 11,29:4; 1958, Jl 4,19:4
Levy, Jacob J, 1941, S 21,45:1
Levy, Jacob L, 1925, D 21,21:5
Levy, Jacob Mrs, 1945, S 8,15:5; 1952, Ag 13,21:3
Levy, Jacoby, 1946, D 8,79:1
Levy, James, 1924, Mr 22,15:6
Levy, Jefferson M, 1924, Mr 7,15:3
Levy, Jeremiah, 1958, O 27,27:5
Levy, John (por), 1938, Jl 14,21:3
Levy, John, 1957, Ap 17,31:1
Levy, John D Mrs (Della Fox), 1913, Je 17,11:4
Levy, John H, 1948, Mr 24,25:2; 1966, Mr 21,33:4
Levy, Joseph, 1907, N 11,7:2; 1944, S 13,19:4; 1945, O 17,19:2; 1946, Ag 20,46:4; 1950, F 3,23:4; 1952, Ap 12,11:3; 1959, Mr 7,21:1
Levy, Joseph Dr, 1952, Mr 1,15:6
Levy, Joseph L (cor, Jl 22,27:1), 1959, Jl 20,25:3
Levy, Joseph Leonard Rabbi, 1917, Ap 27,11:5
Levy, Joseph M, 1965, Ap 20,39:1
Levy, Joseph Mrs, 1954, My 22,15:2; 1958, Mr 7,24:1
Levy, Jules, 1903, N 29,9:1
Levy, Julian H, 1964, O 24,29:2
Levy, Julius, 1916, Ja 21,9:6; 1940, Mr 26,21:5
Levy, Julius H, 1959, Ja 3,17:2
Levy, Julius H Mrs, 1960, N 3,39:4
Levy, Lazarus, 1967, Ap 16,83:2
Levy, Lena Mrs, 1954, Je 10,31:5
Levy, Leo, 1953, Ja 6,29:6
Levy, Leo H, 1944, Ag 29,19:6
Levy, Leo J Mrs, 1957, D 26,19:4
Levy, Leo S, 1961, Ap 24,29:4
Levy, Leo T, 1939, Ja 12,19:5
Levy, Leon, 1942, Ag 30,42:7
Levy, Leopold, 1957, My 11,43:5
Levy, Lionel K Mrs, 1938, N 20,39:3
Levy, Lloyd J, 1941, N 28,23:1
Levy, Louis, 1904, F 13,9:5; 1937, Jl 10,15:5; 1950, S 9,17:2; 1950, D 27,28:2; 1951, Ap 6,26:2; 1951, Je 4,27:2; 1952, F 18,19:3; 1957, Ag 19,19:2; 1963, Ap 7,74:8
Levy, Louis Edward, 1919, F 18,11:6
Levy, Louis H (L H Baker), 1960, My 28,21:2
Levy, Louis Napoleon, 1921, Ap 11,11:3
Levy, Louis S, 1952, Ag 5,19:1
Levy, Louis T Mrs, 1950, F 4,15:3
Levy, Louis W, 1942, N 18,25:2
Levy, M, 1926, Ag 1,30:1
Levy, Mack H, 1958, Ja 4,15:6
Levy, Mark, 1956, Ap 15,88:7
Levy, Martin D, 1920, Mr 17,11:3
Levy, Mary B Mrs, 1953, Ap 18,19:1
Levy, Maurice, 1957, Ag 31,15:7
Levy, Maurice A, 1939, D 2,17:3
Levy, Maurice D, 1960, Ja 6,35:4
Levy, Max, 1946, My 19,40:5; 1966, Ja 4,27:3
Levy, Max J, 1952, Je 20,23:4
Levy, Meyer, 1964, F 14,29:2; 1967, Ja 27,45:1
Levy, Michael, 1875, My 6,1:6
Levy, Michael (por), 1939, N 18,17:4
Levy, Milford M, 1939, O 12,25:6
Levy, Millie A Mrs, 1940, F 1,21:2
Levy, Milton F, 1946, Je 30,38:5
Levy, Mimi C, 1965, O 18,35:4
Levy, Miriam E Mrs, 1939, S 21,23:6
Levy, Moe, 1956, My 25,23:3
Levy, Morey L, 1964, F 8,23:4
Levy, Morris, 1923, Jl 25,11:5; 1943, N 10,23:1
Levy, Morris A, 1952, Ja 9,29:4
Levy, Morris Mrs, 1913, Jl 13,II,11:4; 1956, F 29,31:2
Levy, Mose, 1948, O 27,27:1
Levy, Moses (por),(will, Ag 29,12:6), 1939, Ag 19, 15:4
Levy, Murray H, 1957, D 24,15:3
Levy, Myron B, 1956, S 23,84:8
Levy, Nat, 1963, N 23,29:5
Levy, Nathan, 1923, Ja 13,13:5; 1963, Jl 7,53:1
Levy, Nathan A, 1957, Je 11,35:2
Levy, Newman, 1966, Mr 23,47:1
Levy, Pincus Mrs, 1952, D 30,19:4
Levy, Ralph, 1939, Ag 10,19:4
Levy, Ralph J Dr, 1937, D 13,4:7
Levy, Ralph R, 1948, S 18,17:4
Levy, Raoul, 1967, Ja 1,19:1
Levy, Rene, 1954, O 6,25:3
Levy, Robert, 1944, N 24,23:4
Levy, Robert L Mrs, 1967, S 1,31:3
Levy, S Alfred, 1953, Je 2,29:5
Levy, S Oliver, 1956, S 6,25:2
Levy, Sam, 1955, Ag 7,72:5
Levy, Samuel, 1953, Mr 16,19:1; 1953, Mr 28,17:5
Levy, Samuel (est tax appr filed), 1958, N 14,8:7
Levy, Samuel D, 1940, D 26,19:3
Levy, Samuel D Mrs, 1954, Je 28,19:5
Levy, Samuel H Mrs, 1961, Mr 26,92:8
Levy, Samuel Henry, 1953, F 22,60:6
Levy, Samuel J, 1959, D 4,32:1; 1965, Jl 14,37:3
Levy, Samuel M, 1947, D 17,29:3
Levy, Samuel Mrs, 1957, Ja 17,29:1
Levy, Samuel N Mrs, 1962, Je 19,35:2
Levy, Saul, 1964, F 25,32:1
Levy, Seymour A, 1950, Je 24,13:2
Levy, Sidney, 1960, Mr 1,33:2
Levy, Simon, 1960, Mr 24,33:3
Levy, Sol J, 1959, N 24,37:2
Levy, Stuart, 1966, Je 4,29:3
Levy, Sylvia N (Mrs Milton J), 1964, N 21,29:4
Levy, T Aaron, 1955, Ja 8,13:4
Levy, Theodora G Mrs, 1925, S 28,19:5
Levy, Victor, 1961, Ag 28,25:3
Levy, W M, 1882, Ag 11,5:2
Levy, Walter C, 1965, My 16,88:8
Levy, Warren A, 1958, Ag 12,29:3
Levy, Will I, 1959, Ja 31,19:3
Levy, Wolf, 1940, D 18,25:2
Levy, Zachary, 1945, Ja 17,21:1
Levy-Despas, Andre Mrs, 1968, F 2,35:2
Lew, Abraham G, 1958, O 3,30:5
Lew, Timothy T, 1947, Ag 5,23:4
Lew, William E, 1949, F 2,28:3
Lewal, Jules Louis Gen, 1908, Ja 24,7:5
Lewald, Ernest A, 1947, D 2,29:4
Lewald, Leon T, 1962, Je 18,25:3
Lewald, Theodor, 1947, Ap 19,15:4
Lewallen, Samuel M, 1938, Ja 26,23:2
Lewando, Charles L, 1903, Ag 12,9:6
Lewandowski, H Paul Dr, 1909, D 5,13:4
Lewandowski, Joseph W, 1941, F 22,15:5
Lewandowski, Stephen M, 1966, My 27,43:1
Lewanika, Mwanawina III Sir, 1968, N 15,47:2
Lewars, Elsie S Mrs (Elsie Singmaster), 1958, O 1 37:2
Lewcock, World W, 1949, Ag 29,17:3
Lewellen, John, 1956, Jl 28,17:3
Lewellyn, John Mrs, 1940, Ap 12,24:2
Lewengood, Louis, 1913, Ja 30,11:5
Lewenhaupt, Eric, 1953, Ja 15,27:1
Lewenhaupt, Lily K E Countess, 1951, Ja 11,26:2
Lewenthal, Rebecca, 1937, Ja 4,29:5
Lewer, Peter F, 1944, Ag 22,17:2
Lewery, Leonard J, 1954, O 13,31:4
Lewes, Earl of (Hy J M Nevill), 1965, Ap 3,29:4
Lewes, G H, 1878, D 2,1:6
Lewes, George H Mrs, 1902, D 24,9:6
Lewey, Frank, 1948, Jl 8,23:3
Lewey, Frederic H, 1950, O 7,19:2
Lewey, Frederic H Mrs, 1961, F 1,35:6
Lewi, Emily, 1946, Mr 2,13:4
Lewi, Franklin L, 1946, Ag 6,25:4
Lewi, Isidor (por), 1939, Ja 3,17:1
Lewin, A C, 1952, S 18,29:2
Lewin, Albert, 1968, My 10,44:1
Lewin, Albert Mrs, 1965, F 4,31:5
Lewin, Alfred B, 1949, Je 17,23:2
Lewin, Bill, 1963, Jl 29,19:4
Lewin, Charles J, 1965, D 30,23:1
Lewin, Daniel M, 1967, Ja 23,43:2
Lewin, Edgar R, 1943, Ag 14,11:4
Lewin, Edward Mrs, 1956, Je 27,31:4
Lewin, Emmanuel, 1965, F 20,25:1
Lewin, Harry J, 1955, F 13,86:2
Lewin, Harry Mrs, 1950, O 12,31:4
Lewin, Herbert S, 1957, Ja 24,29:3
Lewin, John Mrs, 1940, Jl 13,14:8
Lewin, Julia S Mrs, 1941, N 3,19:4
Lewin, Kurt, 1947, F 13,23:5
Lewin, Lewis P, 1949, D 11,91:5
Lewin, Milton, 1967, Ja 19,35:2
Lewin, Milton H Mrs, 1958, N 8,21:4
Lewin, Morris, 1952, Je 25,29:4
Lewin, Morris G, 1958, Jl 5,17:5
Lewin, Morris I, 1950, F 16,23:1
Lewin, Murray, 1943, Jl 24,13:5
Lewin, Paul L, 1947, My 7,27:4
Lewin, Philip, 1960, My 14,23:6
Lewin, Ralph, 1955, Je 25,15:3
Lewin, Robert, 1951, Ap 24,29:3
Lewin, Samuel, 1959, Je 5,27:5
Lewin, Samuel A, 1953, Ja 15,27:2
Lewin, Samuel Mrs, 1947, D 9,29:5
Lewin, Vincent B, 1965, Ja 16,27:3
Lewin, William, 1960, Ag 25,29:4
Lewin, William O, 1944, Ag 5,11:6
Lewin-Epstein, Eliezer, 1968, F 20,47:2
Lewin-Epstein, Rechaviah, 1942, N 25,23:4
Lewine, Archibald E, 1959, O 7,43:3
Lewine, Hiram S, 1967, My 28,61:2
Lewine, Irving I, 1965, F 16,35:3
Lewine, Jerome, 1962, D 31,4:5
Lewine, Julius, 1941, My 27,23:3
Lewine, Samuel, 1913, Ag 15,7:7
Lewine, Sol, 1953, D 11,31:1
Lewinsky, Josef, 1907, F 28,9:6
Lewinsohn, Henry P, 1963, Je 18,41:5
Lewinson, Benno Mrs, 1955, Ja 23,85:1
Lewinson, Phineas, 1961, Mr 22,41:1
Lewinthal, Isidore Dr, 1922, My 18,19:6
Lewis, A, 1930, Je 14,17:5
Lewis, A Alexander Rev Dr, 1968, My 4,39:5
Lewis, A Jarratt, 1940, Ja 24,21:2
Lewis, A Jeb, 1960, Ap 10,86:6
Lewis, A L, 1947, Mr 11,27:1
Lewis, A Nelson Mrs, 1923, O 22,19:3
Lewis, A S Dr, 1926, Mr 28,II,9:1
Lewis, Abe, 1948, Mr 11,27:1
Lewis, Abraham W, 1881, F 4,8:3
Lewis, Ada (funl, S 26,17:6), 1925, S 25,21:5
Lewis, Albert J, 1953, My 5,29:5
Lewis, Albro, 1951, Ag 21,27:3
Lewis, Alex J, 1949, Ag 9,25:1
Lewis, Alex M, 1949, Je 9,31:5
Lewis, Alexander R, 1911, Ap 10,13:4
Lewis, Alfred E, 1940, F 22,23:4; 1968, Mr 29,4
Lewis, Alfred G, 1942, My 17,46:2
Lewis, Alfred H Mrs (funl, Ag 28,17:7), 1924, Ag 26,11:4
Lewis, Alfred Henry, 1914, D 24,9:5
Lewis, Alfred Walter, 1918, S 19,13:2
Lewis, Allen, 1957, Mr 21,31:5
Lewis, Alma D, 1962, Ja 25,31:1
Lewis, Alonzo V, 1946, N 9,17:4
Lewis, Amy H, 1944, F 16,17:3
Lewis, Andrew, 1952, F 3,85:2
Lewis, Andrew Jr, 1942, Ap 22,24:5
Lewis, Anne H R B Mrs, 1937, N 8,23:5

Lewis, Annie A, 1944, Je 14,19:6
Lewis, Arley C, 1952, My 27,27:2
Lewis, Art, 1962, Je 14,33:3
Lewis, Arthur C, 1952, Jl 8,27:5
Lewis, Arthur G, 1948, N 6,13:5
Lewis, Arthur M, 1959, My 3,86:3
Lewis, Arthur M Mrs, 1948, Mr 5,21:3; 1950, D 31, 42:8
Lewis, Arthur R, 1946, Mr 14,25:2
Lewis, Arthur R Jr, 1954, Mr 17,31:5
Lewis, Arthur W, 1941, S 16,23:3; 1941, D 18,27:5
Lewis, August, 1913, Mr 4,13:4
Lewis, B Palmer, 1949, Je 28,27:1
Lewis, Bedford (will), 1966, My 4,35:1
Lewis, Ben, 1944, N 14,25:2; 1959, N 15,86:4
Lewis, Benjamin, 1955, Mr 3,27:4; 1956, D 8,19:1
Lewis, Benjamin M, 1940, S 21,19:5
Lewis, Benjamin Mrs, 1947, Ja 21,23:3
Lewis, Benn, 1956, Mr 1,34:4
Lewis, Bernard, 1962, S 15,25:2
Lewis, Bert (B L Schlesinger), 1960, Ap 27,37:5
Lewis, Bert F, 1950, Ap 18,31:1
Lewis, Beulah R, 1950, N 8,29:3
Lewis, Bill (Jas A Whitfield), 1961, Ap 2,76:1
Lewis, Bill, 1961, D 24,36:2
Lewis, Bransford, 1941, My 20,23:6
Lewis, Burdette G, 1966, Ap 16,33:3
Lewis, Burton P Mrs, 1962, Je 5,41:4
Lewis, Byron L, 1950, F 8,28:2
Lewis, C B, 1957, Ap 22,25:5
Lewis, C Carlton, 1968, Mr 19,44:3
Lewis, C S (Clive S),(trb lr, D 21,22:5), 1963, N 25, 19:3
Lewis, C T, 1941, Mr 2,42:7
Lewis, Caleb A, 1964, Jl 15,32:8
Lewis, Cary B, 1946, D 10,31:4
Lewis, Cathy, 1968, N 23,47:1
Lewis, Ceylon H, 1939, Ja 18,19:4
Lewis, Charles, 1961, Mr 28,35:4
Lewis, Charles A, 1942, S 8,24:3; 1946, N 26,29:5; 1947, N 12,28:3; 1963, Ag 18,80:6
Lewis, Charles B Mrs, 1950, Ag 3,23:2
Lewis, Charles C, 1941, Je 26,23:2
Lewis, Charles Dudley, 1905, My 5,9:4
Lewis, Charles E, 1947, D 2,29:1; 1953, O 24,15:5
Lewis, Charles Edwin, 1925, Je 6,15:5
Lewis, Charles F, 1905, Mr 7,9:6; 1954, D 18,15:3
Lewis, Charles H, 1938, My 24,19:1
Lewis, Charles H B, 1940, Je 23,31:2
Lewis, Charles L, 1957, Ap 4,33:4; 1963, D 14,27:1
Lewis, Charles S, 1942, Ap 3,21:3
Lewis, Charles S Mrs, 1952, Ja 23,27:4
Lewis, Charlotte, 1948, S 4,15:1
Lewis, Charlotte Mrs, 1942, S 29,23:1
Lewis, Charlton Miner Prof, 1923, Mr 13,22:5
Lewis, Charlton T Dr, 1904, My 27,9:6
Lewis, Charlton T Mrs, 1946, D 23,23:4
Lewis, Chester F, 1949, Mr 19,15:4
Lewis, Christine M, 1958, Mr 2,89:2
Lewis, Christopher S, 1952, Ap 17,29:2
Lewis, Clarence, 1950, Ja 24,32:3
Lewis, Clarence I, 1947, F 19,25:5; 1964, F 4,33:1
Lewis, Clarence M, 1959, Ja 5,29:5
Lewis, Claude D Mrs, 1955, N 29,29:3
Lewis, Clifford H, 1946, D 27,19:2
Lewis, Clifford Jr, 1956, My 10,31:2
Lewis, Cora G Mrs, 1940, Ja 21,34:5
Lewis, Cora V, 1945, My 31,15:5
Lewis, Cornelius, 1943, Mr 28,24:3
Lewis, Cyrus E, 1941, Je 10,23:4
Lewis, D, 1928, My 14,23:7
Lewis, Dai H (por), 1943, S 9,25:5
Lewis, Daniel G, 1948, N 5,26:3
Lewis, David, 1951, Je 8,27:4
Lewis, David F, 1941, N 22,19:5
Lewis, David J, 1952, Ag 13,21:1
Lewis, David L, 1940, O 16,23:3
Lewis, David M, 1924, O 1,19:2
Lewis, David Mrs, 1953, Jl 10,19:2
Lewis, David N, 1949, N 30,1:8
Lewis, David R, 1939, Ap 9,III,6:6
Lewis, Davis B, 1939, My 27,15:3
Lewis, De Verne A, 1944, My 27,15:6
Lewis, Dean D, 1941, O 10,23:3
Lewis, Donald Mrs, 1953, Ag 9,77:3
Lewis, Dorothy R, 1954, My 18,30:3
Lewis, Dudley P, 1952, Ap 14,19:5
Lewis, Dwight M, 1948, S 2,23:5
Lewis, Dwight N, 1938, My 2,17:3
Lewis, E de M, 1880, N 25,5:6
Lewis, E Harry, 1945, Ag 23,23:4
Lewis, E Z, 1883, Mr 31,2:1
Lewis, Earle R, 1959, N 9,31:4
Lewis, Ed, 1941, Ap 30,19:2
Lewis, Ed Mrs, 1951, My 30,21:2
Lewis, Edison, 1942, Ag 14,17:2
Lewis, Edmund V, 1951, Ag 21,27:5
Lewis, Edward C, 1946, Jl 24,27:5
Lewis, Edward M, 1949, Jl 28,24:2
Lewis, Edward P C Mrs, 1903, S 23,7:6
Lewis, Edward S, 1937, D 27,15:4; 1943, N 19,19:5
Lewis, Edwin, 1959, N 30,31:3
Lewis, Edwin A Dr, 1911, Jl 18,9:6
Lewis, Edwin B, 1940, Je 4,24:2
Lewis, Edwin H, 1938, Je 8,23:3
Lewis, Edwin J, 1954, O 3,86:1
Lewis, Edwin L, 1925, Ja 1,27:3
Lewis, Effingham J, 1941, D 4,25:1
Lewis, Elizabeth F (Mrs Jno A), 1958, Ag 8,19:4
Lewis, Elizabeth O Mrs, 1940, My 16,23:2
Lewis, Elizabeth W, 1943, Ja 22,19:1
Lewis, Ella E Mrs, 1938, S 16,22:3
Lewis, Elmer J, 1945, Ja 9,19:3
Lewis, Elmore H, 1954, F 26,20:7
Lewis, Elodie H Mrs, 1953, Je 14,85:1
Lewis, Emanuel, 1964, My 27,39:1
Lewis, Emma B, 1944, Ag 29,17:2
Lewis, Emma L Mrs, 1939, My 10,23:3
Lewis, Ernest F, 1941, S 13,17:5; 1950, Ja 19,27:2
Lewis, Ernest I (por), 1947, Jl 2,23:4
Lewis, Essington, 1961, O 3,36:6
Lewis, Estelle A, 1880, N 30,1:6
Lewis, Ethel, 1944, My 3,19:3
Lewis, Ethel N Mrs, 1948, Ap 12,21:4
Lewis, Eugene A, 1951, Ap 26,29:4
Lewis, Eugene Howard, 1907, Mr 3,7:6
Lewis, Eugene R, 1953, Mr 21,17:3
Lewis, Everett L, 1937, F 8,17:4
Lewis, F Park, 1940, S 11,25:5
Lewis, F Wood, 1950, Ja 13,23:5
Lewis, Francis A Sr, 1945, Je 8,19:4
Lewis, Frank A, 1963, Ap 22,27:3
Lewis, Frank D, 1947, F 13,23:4
Lewis, Frank E, 1947, Jl 18,17:2; 1961, Je 3,23:1
Lewis, Frank G, 1945, N 20,21:3; 1947, My 17,15:5
Lewis, Frank H, 1944, S 23,13:5
Lewis, Frank J, 1960, D 22,23:1
Lewis, Frank N Dr, 1910, N 14,9:4
Lewis, Frank S, 1947, My 29,21:5
Lewis, Frank T, 1947, D 8,25:3
Lewis, Frank W (will), 1958, F 14,45:8
Lewis, Franklin, 1958, Mr 13,29:4
Lewis, Fred A, 1955, F 19,15:4
Lewis, Fred E, 1949, Je 28,28:2
Lewis, Fred I, 1960, Jl 29,25:4
Lewis, Fred M, 1938, Je 5,45:2
Lewis, Fred M Mrs, 1943, My 3,17:1
Lewis, Frederic T, 1951, Je 4,27:5
Lewis, Frederick, 1947, F 12,25:5
Lewis, Frederick G, 1946, Mr 21,25:4
Lewis, Frederick H, 1940, S 2,15:5
Lewis, Frederick L, 1923, Mr 22,19:5
Lewis, Frederick P, 1941, N 12,23:4
Lewis, Frederick W, 1948, My 1,15:5
Lewis, Frederick W Mrs, 1946, N 8,23:3
Lewis, Frederick W Rev Dr, 1968, Ag 6,37:4
Lewis, Frederick Z, 1943, Ap 7,25:4
Lewis, Fulton Jr, 1966, Ag 22,33:1
Lewis, Fulton Sr, 1944, Mr 2,17:2
Lewis, Fulton Sr Mrs, 1948, Mr 26,21:2
Lewis, G Wendell, 1962, N 25,87:1
Lewis, G William, 1938, Jl 24,28:7
Lewis, Gabriel I, 1938, S 20,23:4
Lewis, George, 1939, F 7,19:2; 1962, S 13,37:3
Lewis, George A, 1951, Ag 5,73:3; 1954, N 19,32:2; 1966, My 10,39:3
Lewis, George C, 1938, D 21,23:4; 1943, Ja 31,46:3; 1943, Ag 22,36:5
Lewis, George Chase Mrs, 1968, D 4,47:2
Lewis, George D, 1948, N 19,28:2
Lewis, George E, 1940, Ja 22,15:2; 1946, Jl 16,23:4
Lewis, George F, 1940, Ja 15,15:4; 1953, N 19,31:3; 1961, Mr 23,33:1
Lewis, George F Jr, 1960, S 28,39:1
Lewis, George H, 1947, F 22,13:2
Lewis, George H Mrs, 1962, S 15,25:1
Lewis, George Jr, 1952, N 3,29:8
Lewis, George L, 1939, Ag 21,13:4
Lewis, George M, 1938, N 8,23:2; 1966, F 28,27:4
Lewis, George S, 1938, D 30,15:4; 1946, S 13,7:2
Lewis, George S Mrs, 1939, F 5,40:7
Lewis, George T, 1962, F 27,33:4
Lewis, George W (por), 1948, Jl 13,27:1
Lewis, George W, 1951, My 19,15:5
Lewis, Georgiana King Mrs, 1924, D 9,25:3
Lewis, Gibson, 1954, N 26,29:3
Lewis, Gilbert L, 1942, O 2,25:5
Lewis, Gilbert N (por), 1946, Mr 25,25:3
Lewis, Golden F, 1947, Ja 19,52:1
Lewis, Grace Anna, 1912, F 26,11:4
Lewis, Grace Mrs, 1938, Mr 17,21:2
Lewis, Grady, 1953, Ja 5,21:1
Lewis, Griffith W, 1915, Ag 29,15:6
Lewis, Guy F, 1950, Je 1,27:5
Lewis, H A, 1937, Jl 26,19:5
Lewis, H C, 1884, Ag 19,1:4
Lewis, H E, 1927, Ag 8,17:5
Lewis, H Myron, 1966, My 1,87:2
Lewis, H O'B, 1878, My 21,1:6
Lewis, H Spencer, 1939, Ag 3,19:4
Lewis, Hal T Ex-Justice, 1903, D 11,9:5
Lewis, Harlow, 1953, O 17,15:1
Lewis, Harmon, 1963, S 23,29:2
Lewis, Harold A, 1954, O 13,31:5
Lewis, Harold C, 1942, Ag 13,19:2
Lewis, Harold L, 1954, Ap 12,29:3
Lewis, Harry, 1951, D 9,90:8; 1956, F 23,27:2
Lewis, Harry E, 1948, Ag 24,23:1
Lewis, Harry E Mrs, 1944, Jl 30,35:1
Lewis, Harry L Mrs (De S Mooers), 1960, Ja 13,47:3
Lewis, Harry M, 1957, S 6,21:3
Lewis, Harry P, 1959, Ag 29,17:3
Lewis, Harry S, 1950, O 21,17:4; 1965, Ag 10,29:1
Lewis, Hattie M (Jan 18), 1963, Ap 1,36:1
Lewis, Henry, 1903, Ag 9,7:6; 1943, O 23,13:4
Lewis, Henry C, 1958, N 30,87:1
Lewis, Henry C Mrs, 1954, D 23,19:2
Lewis, Henry G, 1912, Ag 25,II,11:5
Lewis, Henry L, 1952, Ag 12,19:5
Lewis, Henry L D, 1938, Ja 10,17:3
Lewis, Henry S, 1954, O 25,27:5
Lewis, Henry T, 1938, Ja 9,43:2
Lewis, Henry W, 1939, Mr 8,21:2
Lewis, Herbert C, 1950, O 19,31:4
Lewis, Herbert F, 1949, Je 30,23:6
Lewis, Herbert P, 1922, Mr 28,17:4
Lewis, Herbert R, 1940, My 15,25:2
Lewis, Horace E (por), 1948, D 6,25:1
Lewis, Horatio W, 1951, O 10,23:5
Lewis, Howard A, 1963, O 17,35:3
Lewis, Howard B, 1946, Ja 26,13:5; 1954, Mr 9,27:1
Lewis, Howard C, 1952, O 3,23:3
Lewis, Howard L, 1947, Mr 9,60:8
Lewis, Howard P, 1945, Je 17,26:3
Lewis, Howard T, 1949, Ag 25,23:2
Lewis, Howard W, 1940, N 9,17:2
Lewis, Howard W Mrs, 1949, Ja 18,23:2
Lewis, Howell E, 1953, D 11,31:4
Lewis, Hugh, 1937, Mr 9,24:1
Lewis, Hugh A, 1964, Ag 18,31:1
Lewis, Hugh A Mrs, 1941, My 17,15:2
Lewis, I J, 1927, Ja 7,19:4
Lewis, I N, 1931, N 10,25:1
Lewis, Ida (funl), 1911, O 26,11:6
Lewis, Ida M, 1938, Ag 23,17:1
Lewis, Ira F, 1948, Ag 29,59:3
Lewis, Ira L, 1940, Ag 30,19:3
Lewis, Irving R, 1937, N 13,19:6
Lewis, Irving S, 1964, Ag 2,77:2
Lewis, Isaac N, 1938, Ja 28,21:4
Lewis, Isaac N Mrs, 1945, S 2,32:2
Lewis, Israel, 1939, Mr 10,23:3; 1951, D 31,13:3
Lewis, Ivey F, 1964, Mr 17,35:4
Lewis, J, 1926, Ap 29,23:3
Lewis, J C, 1956, Je 15,25:4
Lewis, J F, 1876, Ag 19,8:2
Lewis, J Hamilton, 1939, Ap 10,1:2
Lewis, J Howard, 1907, Ap 25,9:5
Lewis, J M, 1881, Ap 14,5:6
Lewis, J T Mrs, 1938, S 7,21:4
Lewis, J Wilbur, 1959, My 21,31:1
Lewis, Jacob D, 1948, Jl 9,20:2
Lewis, Jacques A, 1968, Ag 6,37:3
Lewis, Jacques M, 1951, Ja 31,25:3
Lewis, James, 1896, S 11,5:3; 1947, Je 8,60:1
Lewis, James C Mrs, 1963, N 5,31:4
Lewis, James Col, 1914, Jl 12,5:5
Lewis, James E, 1939, My 26,23:5
Lewis, James F, 1952, Ag 9,13:3; 1962, S 6,31:4
Lewis, James H, 1944, Ag 27,33:3; 1952, N 14,23:2
Lewis, James M, 1938, N 22,23:5; 1954, Ap 21,29:4
Lewis, James O, 1954, Je 17,29:4
Lewis, James P Sr, 1961, O 26,35:1
Lewis, James V Msgr, 1916, Mr 26,21:5
Lewis, James W, 1938, O 29,19:3; 1964, O 28,2:5; 1968, Je 14,47:3
Lewis, Jane C K Mrs, 1938, D 2,24:1
Lewis, Jay R, 1952, Je 28,19:4
Lewis, Jerome A, 1937, Jl 27,21:1
Lewis, Jesse W, 1957, F 28,27:5
Lewis, Jessica, 1947, Je 15,60:4
Lewis, John, 1940, Ja 22,15:3
Lewis, John A, 1904, Ja 14,9:7; 1920, Jl 8,11:4; 1954, N 17,31:4
Lewis, John B, 1937, F 5,21:2
Lewis, John Beavens, 1923, N 16,17:2
Lewis, John Bowers, 1874, Ja 25,1:7
Lewis, John C, 1872, F 29,1:6; 1960, Je 3,31:3
Lewis, John Clivin Mrs, 1920, Ap 29,13:4
Lewis, John E, 1958, Ja 18,15:6
Lewis, John F, 1947, Ja 20,25:3; 1958, Ap 24,31:4
Lewis, John F Jr, 1965, S 6,15:4
Lewis, John H, 1908, F 8,7:5; 1938, N 17,25:6; 1958, O 5,87:1
Lewis, John H Mrs, 1946, Ja 31,21:5; 1953, D 25,17:2
Lewis, John I Mrs, 1947, D 17,29:3
Lewis, John L Mrs (por), 1942, S 10,27:3
Lewis, John M Mrs, 1945, D 8,17:3
Lewis, John Mrs, 1937, Jl 24,15:3
Lewis, John N, 1940, Ap 11,25:6
Lewis, John Neher, 1914, Je 16,9:6
Lewis, John P, 1961, Jl 18,29:1
Lewis, John R, 1945, F 15,19:4; 1957, Jl 19,19:2
Lewis, John S, 1963, F 23,7:1
Lewis, John W, 1963, N 7,37:3
Lewis, John W Rev Dr, 1918, Ap 11,13:3
Lewis, Jose G, 1939, F 13,15:4
Lewis, Joseph, 1961, Ag 27,84:5; 1968, N 5,47:2
Lewis, Joseph C, 1941, F 23,40:2

Lewis, Joseph J, 1954, Ag 10,19:2
Lewis, Joseph M, 1955, Ja 10,23:6
Lewis, Joseph Mrs (por), 1946, Ag 2,19:3
Lewis, Joseph P, 1942, Je 25,23:1
Lewis, Joseph S, 1942, Ja 23,19:5
Lewis, Joseph W, 1937, My 30,19:1; 1938, Ag 1,13:4; 1943, F 13,11:4; 1953, Jl 14,27:1
Lewis, Josephine D Mrs, 1939, My 2,23:2
Lewis, Josephine M, 1959, My 12,35:4
Lewis, Judd M, 1945, Jl 27,15:3
Lewis, Julius A, 1954, F 5,20:4
Lewis, Kathryn, 1962, Ja 8,39:5
Lewis, Kenneth B, 1952, N 26,23:4
Lewis, Kenneth M Jr, 1967, Jl 12,43:5
Lewis, L A (Faye), 1966, O 17,37:4
Lewis, L H, 1937, N 10,25:4
Lewis, L Logan, 1965, Mr 10,41:2
Lewis, Lawrence, 1943, D 10,28:2
Lewis, Leicester C (por), 1949, Mr 20,77:1
Lewis, Leicester S, 1956, D 10,31:4
Lewis, Leo R (por), 1945, S 9,46:2
Lewis, Leon, 1960, O 6,41:3
Lewis, Leon L, 1954, My 22,15:3
Lewis, Leonard T, 1959, Mr 14,23:5
Lewis, Liston L, 1940, F 11,49:2
Lewis, Livingstone L Dr, 1937, N 10,25:3
Lewis, Lloyd D, 1949, Ap 22,23:1
Lewis, Lloyd P, 1954, O 14,29:1
Lewis, Lloyd R, 1948, D 31,15:5
Lewis, Loran L Ex-Justice, 1916, Mr 9,13:5
Lewis, Louis Dr, 1902, F 21,9:6
Lewis, Louis J (cor, O 19,27:1), 1956, O 11,39:3
Lewis, Louis Mrs, 1953, Ag 13,25:5
Lewis, Louis S, 1949, My 26,29:3
Lewis, Louis Sostman, 1921, N 18,17:6
Lewis, Louise T, 1912, Ja 21,II,13:2
Lewis, Lucy B Mrs, 1941, Ja 15,23:5
Lewis, Luther H (Sept 20), 1965, O 11,61:3
Lewis, Lynn G, 1949, N 9,27:2
Lewis, Lynn R, 1940, Mr 26,21:2
Lewis, M Haller, 1962, N 5,31:5
Lewis, M Lee, 1959, Jl 7,37:2
Lewis, M M Dr, 1884, Ja 21,5:6
Lewis, M T, 1931, Jl 9,23:4
Lewis, Mahalas Mrs, 1966, Ag 7,80:2
Lewis, Manuel F, 1964, D 11,39:3
Lewis, Margaret C, 1953, Jl 14,27:4
Lewis, Marion L, 1951, Ja 3,27:2
Lewis, Mark C, 1951, S 29,17:1
Lewis, Martin, 1962, F 21,45:3
Lewis, Martin B, 1955, Mr 30,29:5
Lewis, Martin J, 1955, N 14,27:5
Lewis, Martin W, 1954, Ja 23,13:4
Lewis, Mary (por), 1942, Ja 1,25:1
Lewis, Mary A, 1937, F 7,II,8:6
Lewis, Mary A Mrs, 1941, Je 10,23:6
Lewis, Mary E, 1948, Ap 9,23:4
Lewis, Mary E Mrs, 1938, Mr 12,17:5
Lewis, Mary H, 1950, S 8,31:3
Lewis, Mary L Mrs, 1949, D 14,31:1
Lewis, Maurice B, 1945, Je 25,17:2
Lewis, Maurice Winfred Rev, 1925, Ag 8,11:6
Lewis, Maxwell, 1957, F 20,33:6
Lewis, Mead A, 1962, O 27,25:5
Lewis, Meade L, 1964, Je 8,18:4
Lewis, Merton E (por),(cor lr, My 5,24:7), 1937, My 3,19:1
Lewis, Milton, 1959, S 15,39:4
Lewis, Mitchell J, 1956, Ag 26,85:1
Lewis, Montgomery S, 1954, Ja 5,27:1
Lewis, Morgan (Buddy), 1968, D 9,55:4
Lewis, Morley B, 1955, D 4,88:4
Lewis, Morris, 1939, D 6,10:5
Lewis, Mortimer H, 1950, Ja 12,27:1
Lewis, Moses, 1956, D 13,37:1; 1963, D 1,84:6
Lewis, Moses Mrs, 1956, Ja 14,19:5
Lewis, Murney E, 1956, Ap 29,86:1
Lewis, Murray, 1967, O 19,47:4
Lewis, Murray Mrs, 1945, Ja 9,19:1
Lewis, N Lawson, 1950, My 3,29:2
Lewis, Nancy D, 1961, Ag 1,31:2
Lewis, Nat, 1956, Ja 27,23:3
Lewis, Nate, 1952, N 19,29:4
Lewis, Nathan, 1903, My 22,8:4
Lewis, Nathan C, 1937, Jl 27,21:2
Lewis, Neil D, 1950, My 2,30:4
Lewis, Nelson P, 1924, Mr 31,17:2
Lewis, Nelson P Mrs, 1945, N 27,23:2
Lewis, Norman D, 1953, O 17,2:7
Lewis, Norman S Mrs, 1944, Je 27,19:6
Lewis, Orlando, 1907, Jl 15,7:6
Lewis, Orlando Faulkland Dr, 1922, F 25,13:5
Lewis, Orville N, 1943, Ja 10,50:4
Lewis, Osborn G, 1948, My 8,15:3
Lewis, Oscar A, 1959, Mr 30,31:5
Lewis, Owen B, 1954, Ap 18,89:1
Lewis, P Newell, 1955, Je 1,33:4
Lewis, Palmer H Mrs, 1950, Ag 29,27:3
Lewis, Paton Mrs, 1946, D 24,17:5
Lewis, Paul C, 1953, Ja 7,31:2
Lewis, Paul V, 1955, Mr 9,27:2
Lewis, Percival C, 1943, Ja 30,15:1
Lewis, Percy Pyne, 1914, Ag 6,11:6
Lewis, Phil G Sr, 1957, N 7,35:5
Lewis, Ralph F, 1959, Ja 15,33:2
Lewis, Ralph L, 1964, O 31,29:6
Lewis, Raymond R, 1949, S 5,17:3
Lewis, Reginald M, 1960, Jl 4,15:2
Lewis, Reuben, 1946, Mr 13,29:5; 1948, My 5,25:4
Lewis, Richard, 1947, S 12,21:4
Lewis, Richard H, 1951, N 15,29:3
Lewis, Richard J, 1942, N 8,53:1
Lewis, Richard Vaughan, 1922, Jl 23,21:2
Lewis, Richard W, 1959, Ja 27,33:3
Lewis, Robert B, 1947, O 27,21:4
Lewis, Robert B Mrs, 1955, S 22,31:4
Lewis, Robert E, 1938, S 11,II,11:2
Lewis, Robert E Jr (mem ser, F 11,23:5), 1961, F 7, 36:5
Lewis, Robert E L, 1946, O 21,31:4
Lewis, Robert J, 1953, Je 27,15:3
Lewis, Robert L, 1939, D 21,26:4; 1963, N 3,88:5
Lewis, Robert M, 1958, Je 22,76:3
Lewis, Robert M Dr, 1968, N 8,47:1
Lewis, Roberto, 1949, S 23,23:4
Lewis, Roderick S, 1958, O 27,27:4
Lewis, Rosa, 1952, N 30,88:6
Lewis, Roy A, 1955, N 18,25:5
Lewis, Rufus, 1909, Mr 22,7:5
Lewis, Rupert R, 1958, My 13,29:5
Lewis, Rush F, 1949, Ap 30,13:6
Lewis, Ruth (Mrs J E Cohen), 1963, Ap 24,35:4
Lewis, Ruth E, 1954, Ja 8,21:3
Lewis, Rutherford B, 1942, Jl 5,29:1
Lewis, Sam (Horseshoe), 1954, N 11,31:3
Lewis, Samuel, 1939, Ap 19,23:4; 1945, Ja 4,19:2; 1950, O 30,27:5
Lewis, Samuel A, 1913, Je 1,IV,7:6
Lewis, Samuel A Mrs, 1903, Jl 9,7:6
Lewis, Samuel B, 1958, Ap 21,23:6
Lewis, Samuel C, 1946, O 11,23:1
Lewis, Samuel Jr, 1953, N 14,17:3
Lewis, Samuel Jr Mrs, 1962, Je 12,37:1
Lewis, Samuel M, 1959, N 23,31:2; 1960, Mr 16,37:2
Lewis, Samuel S, 1959, Ja 16,27:4
Lewis, Samuel Sir, 1903, Jl 19,4:7
Lewis, Samuel W, 1940, F 10,15:2
Lewis, Sarah R, 1954, D 23,19:5
Lewis, Saunders Jr, 1937, D 18,21:2
Lewis, Sharon (Feb 8 death laid to alcohol and drugs), 1966, F 24,75:1
Lewis, Sherman M, 1946, D 24,17:1
Lewis, Shippen, 1952, My 18,92:5
Lewis, Sidney, 1958, My 8,26:5
Lewis, Sinclair, 1951, Ja 11,1:2
Lewis, Sol P, 1959, Mr 22,87:1
Lewis, Spearman, 1954, F 5,19:2
Lewis, Spencer, 1939, F 18,15:5
Lewis, Stan, 1959, My 14,33:1
Lewis, Strangler (Ed; R H Friedrich), 1966, Ag 8,27:1
Lewis, T, 1927, O 20,29:5
Lewis, T Prof (mem ser, Je 25,5:4), 1877, My 13,6:7
Lewis, Talbot T, 1945, Ap 13,17:2
Lewis, Theodore B, 1962, Ja 13,21:1
Lewis, Theodore B Mrs, 1960, F 18,33:4
Lewis, Theodore J, 1937, Ap 16,23:3
Lewis, Thoe J Mrs, 1946, Jl 17,23:5
Lewis, Thomas (est), 1910, My 21,9:6
Lewis, Thomas, 1945, Mr 21,23:4; 1955, Ja 30,84:4
Lewis, Thomas J, 1938, Je 4,15:5
Lewis, Thomas L, 1939, My 2,24:4; 1945, D 8,17:2
Lewis, Thomas Mrs, 1943, Jl 18,34:5
Lewis, Thomas T, 1956, N 15,35:4
Lewis, Thornton, 1945, Jl 5,13:7
Lewis, Thornton Mrs, 1946, My 7,21:2
Lewis, Tracy, 1939, Ag 29,21:2
Lewis, Tracy H, 1951, N 8,29:5
Lewis, Victor C, 1942, My 6,19:2
Lewis, Victor G, 1956, N 2,27:2
Lewis, Vincent, 1946, S 18,31:2
Lewis, Virgil, 1952, Je 21,8:3
Lewis, Vivian M, 1950, Mr 15,29:2
Lewis, W B, 1884, O 16,8:4
Lewis, W D Gen, 1872, Ja 21,5:5
Lewis, W Leslie, 1955, F 4,21:2
Lewis, W Vaughn, 1961, Je 9,67:2
Lewis, Walford W, 1963, My 28,37:2
Lewis, Walker L, 1943, Ja 26,19:5
Lewis, Walter, 1947, Ja 8,24:2
Lewis, Walter E, 1946, O 30,27:4
Lewis, Walter L, 1957, Je 4,35:5
Lewis, Ward, 1955, O 7,25:3
Lewis, Warren H, 1964, Jl 4,13:6
Lewis, Warrington G, 1951, Ja 6,15:2
Lewis, Welborne, 1942, O 8,27:4
Lewis, Willard Mrs, 1940, Ja 29,15:2
Lewis, Willard P, 1953, Ag 23,88:2
Lewis, William, 1902, My 31,9:6; 1938, Jl 8,17:4; 1954, S 15,33:2; 1964, Mr 26,35:4; 1967, Ap 27,45:2
Lewis, William A, 1949, D 21,29:3
Lewis, William B Maj, 1866, N 17,1:5
Lewis, William C, 1946, N 24,79:3
Lewis, William D, 1938, N 24,27:2; 1949, S 3,13:1
Lewis, William D Mrs, 1953, Ja 5,21:4
Lewis, William Eugene, 1924, O 29,21:4
Lewis, William F, 1944, S 12,19:5
Lewis, William G W Rev, 1914, Ag 4,11:6
Lewis, William H, 1937, My 18,23:4; 1947, Jl 4,13:4; 1949, Ja 2,60:5; 1953, Mr 15,92:6
Lewis, William H G, 1943, Jl 15,21:2
Lewis, William H Mrs, 1961, Je 4,86:1
Lewis, William I, 1948, F 21,13:1
Lewis, William J, 1906, Ja 4,11:4; 1944, O 26,23:2; 1951, Je 21,13:3
Lewis, William L, 1942, D 26,9:3; 1952, Je 29,56:4
Lewis, William L Mrs, 1941, Ap 28,15:4
Lewis, William M, 1939, Ja 31,21:1
Lewis, William M (por), 1945, N 12,21:3
Lewis, William M Mrs, 1953, My 29,25:4
Lewis, William R, 1961, Ag 18,21:4
Lewis, William Rev, 1913, Ag 3,II,9:5
Lewis, William S, 1911, S 29,9:4
Lewis, William Thomas (Baron Merthyr), 1914, Ag 28,9:5
Lewis, William W, 1956, My 24,31:3
Lewis, Willie, 1949, My 19,30:3
Lewis, Willmott H, 1950, Ja 5,25:3
Lewis, Wilmarth S Mrs, 1959, My 10,86:7
Lewis, Wilson S Bp, 1921, Ag 26,13:4
Lewis, Winslow Dr, 1875, Ag 5,4:7
Lewis, Wolf, 1942, Ap 4,13:6
Lewis, Wyndham, 1957, Mr 9,19:3
Lewis, Z M Rev, 1903, Ap 30,9:6
Lewis-Hill, Samuel Mrs, 1906, O 14,6:5
Lewisohn, Adolph, 1919, My 28,15:4; 1938, Ag 18,
Lewisohn, Adolph Mrs, 1916, Jl 29,9:6
Lewisohn, Albert, 1911, Mr 15,13:5
Lewisohn, Frederick (funl plans, Jl 10,25:4), 1959, Jl 5,56:2
Lewisohn, Irene (will, Ap 22,13:1), 1944, Ap 5,19:
Lewisohn, Leonard, 1902, Mr 6,9:5
Lewisohn, Ludwig, 1956, Ja 1,50:6
Lewisohn, Mary A C Mrs, 1946, Ap 9,27:2
Lewisohn, Oscar (funl, D 6,13:4), 1917, D 4,13:4
Lewisohn, Phil Mrs, 1954, Mr 12,21:3
Lewisohn, Philip, 1917, N 21,13:4
Lewisohn, Randolph S, 1967, My 28,60:7
Lewisohn, Raphael, 1923, My 4,17:3
Lewisohn, Richard, 1961, Ag 13,89:2
Lewisohn, Richard L Sr Mrs, 1960, F 6,19:2
Lewisohn, Sam A, 1951, Mr 15,29:1
Lewisohn, Sam A (est tax appr), 1955, Ap 28,19:
Lewisohn, Samuel A Mrs, 1954, Je 15,1:7
Lewisohn, Samuel A Mrs (est tax appr), 1959, F 24:6
Lewisohn, Walter (will), 1938, Ag 24,19:2
Lewison, B, 1935, F 17,29:1
Lewison, Harold J, 1964, My 22,35:1
Lewison, Maurice, 1942, Je 18,21:1
Lewit, Charles L, 1944, Je 27,19:5
Lewit, Harry, 1939, O 24,23:4
Lewit, Richard R, 1956, Ap 2,23:4
Lewith, Edward L, 1951, F 9,25:4
Lewitin, Landes, 1966, Ja 21,48:1
LeWitt, George, 1960, Ag 21,84:7
Lewitt, Jesse E, 1948, O 13,25:1
Lewitt, Max, 1963, Jl 9,31:1
Lewitt, Samuel S, 1968, Ag 17,27:5
Lewitt, Samuel S Mrs, 1960, Ja 14,33:1
Lewitt, William, 1949, D 7,31:6
Le Witter, Arnold, 1952, Mr 28,23:1
Lewittes, Judith M, 1957, Ja 8,31:1
Lewittes, Morris, 1968, N 23,47:2
Lewittess, Meyer Mrs, 1965, My 18,39:3
Lewitus, Victor, 1960, Ja 8,23:1
Lewman, Frank J, 1964, Jl 10,30:1
Lewsen, Nicolaus, 1949, Ja 8,15:4
Lewson, Arthur C, 1964, Ag 6,29:5
Lewton, Nina Mrs, 1967, Mr 1,43:4
Lewton, Val, 1951, Mr 15,29:3
Lewy, Fred, 1950, Je 21,27:5
Lewy, Frederick J Mrs, 1954, My 28,30:1
Lewy, George S, 1939, O 12,25:3
Lewy, Hildegard, 1967, O 10,42:1
Lewy, John H, 1968, N 29,45:3
Lewy, Julius, 1963, Je 21,29:2
Lewy, Louis, 1943, Ap 11,49:2
Lewy, Raphael, 1957, D 14,21:2
Lewys, Abbie Carrington Mrs, 1925, Ap 10,19:3
Lex, E L, 1903, O 10,9:6
Lexer, Erich Dr, 1937, D 6,27:1
Lexow, C K, 1928, Jl 14,13:3
Lexow, Caroline F, 1961, Jl 14,23:3
Lexow, Clarence Ex-Sen, 1910, D 31,9:3
Lexow, Clarence Sen, 1920, S 4,9:4
Lexow, Fred, 1872, D 5,8:3
Lexow, Frederic R, 1967, N 4,33:1
Lexow, Rudolph, 1909, Jl 17,7:4
Lexow, Theodore J, 1904, Ja 26,9:6
Ley, Elizabeth C, 1950, Ap 22,19:3
Ley, Frederick T, 1958, Jl 14,21:3
Ley, Frederick T Mrs, 1965, Ag 7,21:1
Ley, Harold A, 1956, My 12,19:3
Ley, Lawrence, 1947, Ja 25,17:2
Ley, Thomas J, 1947, Jl 26,3:1
Ley, William B, 1945, Jl 26,19:3
Ley, William B Mrs, 1960, Jl 5,31:3
Leyair, George Mrs, 1916, Jl 30,15:4
Leyburn, Alfred P, 1959, My 10,87:1

Leyburn, G W Rev, 1875, S 24,4:6
Leyda, Frederick E, 1949, F 3,23:1
Leydecker, William, 1946, Je 26,25:3
Leyden, Ernst von Prof, 1910, O 6,11:4
Leyden, Francis X, 1950, O 14,19:3
Leyden, James A Mrs, 1952, Ap 1,29:4
Leyden, Thomas F H, 1959, Ap 22,33:2
Leyden, William H, 1940, Je 21,21:5
Leydenfrost, Alex, 1961, Je 16,33:1
Leyendechers, Constantine, 1945, F 10,11:1
Leyendecker, Frank J Mrs, 1962, F 11,87:2
Leyendecker, Frank X, 1924, Ap 20,22:2
Leyendecker, Hilary M, 1953, Mr 6,23:2
Leyendecker, Joseph C (will, Ag 14,25:2), 1951, Jl 26,21:4
Leyendecker, Theodore Mrs, 1957, Mr 26,33:3
Leyerle, Frank J, 1963, D 21,23:3
Leyerle, George A, 1940, Mr 20,27:1
Leyes, Charles, 1956, Mr 1,34:6
Leygues, G, 1933, S 3,16:1
Leykauf, Herbert, 1949, Ag 16,23:3
Leyko, Julius J Dr, 1937, Je 9,25:2
Leyland, James Capt, 1918, Ja 17,13:3
Leyland, John, 1924, Ja 6,23:1
Leyland, Lady, 1932, Mr 12,15:1
Leyman, Harry S, 1954, My 25,27:4
Leypoldt, F, 1884, Ap 1,5:2
Leypoldt, John B, 1947, D 17,29:4
Leypoldt, John C, 1951, O 30,29:3
Leyrer, Elmer J, 1955, Mr 12,19:6
Leys, Cecil, 1950, Je 24,13:5
Leys, Charles, 1949, My 26,29:3
Leys, James F, 1938, Ja 14,23:3
Leys, Katharine, 1951, Ap 27,23:2
Leysen, Jane A Mrs, 1939, O 6,25:2
Leysen, Ralph J, 1951, My 29,25:1
Leyser, Ada L, 1949, O 11,31:5
Leyser, George, 1947, My 14,25:3
Leyshon, Annie H, 1950, F 20,25:2
Leyshon, Hal I, 1967, Jl 10,31:3
Leysmith, Walter F (cor, Ja 14,21:4), 1955, Ja 13, 27:4
Leyssac, Paul, 1946, Ag 21,28:3
Leyton, Henry K, 1950, Je 18,76:8
Leyton, Otto, 1938, Ja 24,23:2
Lezcano, Jose A, 1952, Ja 7,19:3
Lherisson, Camille (trb lr, Ja 9,IV,13:4), 1966, Ja 2, 72:4
L'Herminier, Jean, 1953, Je 8,29:3
Lhermitte, Leon A, 1925, Jl 28,13:5
Lherner, M Andre, 1868, My 28,5:1
L'Heureux, Alfred J, 1961, Mr 2,27:4
L'Heureux, Camille, 1964, D 26,17:4
L'Heureux, Carrie M Mrs, 1945, S 12,25:3
L'Heureux, Herve J, 1957, Jl 10,27:2
Lhevinne, Josef, 1944, D 3,57:1
L'Hommedieu, Abby B Mrs, 1942, Ja 4,48:3
L'Hommedieu, Douglas C, 1958, Ag 20,27:4
L'Hommedieu, Harold C, 1951, N 19,23:4
L'Hommedieu, Harry, 1945, S 19,25:4
'Hommedieu, Henry B, 1943, My 4,23:5
'Hommedieu, Irving Mrs, 1951, O 2,28:2
'Hommedieu, James H Sr, 1950, N 11,15:2
'Hommedieu, M Cecelia H, 1941, D 16,27:2
'Hommedieu, Marie, 1968, Mr 25,41:4
'Hommedieu, Mark C, 1953, My 6,31:1
'Hommedieu, Paige B, 1950, Jl 6,27:4
'Hommedieu, Richard W, 1906, F 8,9:5
'Hommedieu, Sylvester Y, 1962, Mr 13,35:3
'Hommedieu, Sylvester Y Mrs, 1961, Mr 17,31:2
'Hommedieu, William A, 1942, O 22,21:4
hotak, Ferdinand R, 1947, Ag 3,52:5
hote, Andre, 1962, Ja 25,31:3
hotka, Fran, 1962, F 15,29:3
hotta, Charles L, 1950, Ja 15,84:5
howe, Harold R, 1945, D 30,14:5
hoyd, Fred W, 1946, O 30,27:4
i, Kuo-ching, 1961, Mr 8,33:1
i Chi-sen, 1959, O 10,21:3
i Ching-Mai, 1938, Je 29,19:5
i Chorchi, 1940, Mr 20,34:8
i Ke-nung, 1962, F 10,23:5
i Lieh-Chun, 1946, F 23,13:6
i Ming, 1966, O 22,31:6
i Shu-fan, 1966, N 25,37:1
i Tchuin, 1948, My 24,19:3
i Tsung-jen, Mrs, 1966, Mr 24,39:3
i Yuan-Hung, 1928, Je 4,3:5
iable, Annie N Mrs, 1954, F 12,25:1
achowsky, Waldemar, 1958, Ap 16,33:5
acono, Francesco, 1952, Mr 20,29:4
amadis, Germanos, 1965, Mr 15,31:4
an, Abraham A, 1961, Jl 4,19:6
an, Ragi A, 1938, S 14,23:2
an, Sahid A, 1965, My 3,33:2
ang, Lone, 1967, Je 15,47:4
ang, M T, 1941, O 15,21:4
ang Chi-chao, 1929, Ja 22,6:1
aptcheff, A, 1933, N 7,23:1
ard, Louis, 1917, S 22,11:6
ardet, Arthur Evelyn, 1923, S 5,15:4
autard, Alexander Francis Dr, 1918, Ap 23,13:5
autaud, Andre, 1951, Jl 27,19:4

Liazza, Francesco, 1942, Jl 4,17:5
Libaire, Adolph, 1920, S 7,15:1
Libaire, George, 1960, Jl 7,31:4
Libaire, Henry A, 1968, F 3,29:5
Libbet, Hervey W Sr, 1953, Je 25,27:5
Libbey, Donald S, 1959, S 28,31:5
Libbey, Edward D, 1925, N 14,15:5
Libbey, Florence S Mrs, 1938, Mr 14,16:4
Libbey, Laura Jean, 1924, O 26,7:1
Libbey, Octavus B, 1907, Ag 30,7:6
Libbey, Octavus B Mrs, 1944, N 13,19:2
Libbey, Ogden F Mrs, 1949, Mr 11,26:2
Libbey, Walter M, 1941, D 20,19:2
Libbey, Warren G, 1953, N 27,27:2
Libbey, Welding D, 1964, D 13,31:3
Libby, Arthur F, 1950, Mr 11,15:2
Libby, Charles Freeman, 1915, Je 4,11:4
Libby, Charles T, 1948, My 24,20:2
Libby, Clarence E, 1964, My 28,37:2
Libby, D T Mrs, 1949, Jl 6,30:5
Libby, Deane A, 1959, Ja 18,88:1
Libby, Deane A Mrs, 1964, Mr 24,35:1
Libby, Demorin Capt, 1909, Ag 27,7:6
Libby, Edward C, 1940, Je 18,23:2
Libby, Edward H, 1944, D 26,19:2
Libby, Eugene S, 1948, S 2,23:2
Libby, Frederick, 1945, N 26,22:3
Libby, Gracia D Mrs, 1951, Ja 15,17:5
Libby, Hattie E Mrs, 1940, Mr 20,34:8
Libby, Joseph R, 1955, Ja 22,11:4
Libby, Josephine Mrs, 1944, Mr 4,13:2
Libby, Luther, 1944, Ap 3,21:5
Libby, Norman H, 1949, Ag 18,21:1
Libby, Richardson A, 1941, N 10,17:4
Libby, Roscoe F, 1954, F 5,20:3
Libby, Samuel H, 1959, D 29,25:3
Libby, Sarah Bradbury Mrs, 1920, Mr 10,11:5
Libby, Walter, 1955, D 2,27:3
Libby, Walter G, 1939, Ap 6,25:2
Libby, Willard T, 1944, Ap 4,21:3
Libby, William H, 1948, Jl 7,46:7
Liben, Joseph, 1965, Ja 27,35:4
Liber, Benzion, 1958, Je 9,23:6
Liberace, Ettore V, 1956, Mr 9,23:3
Liberati, A, 1927, N 7,23:5
Liberati, Armond, 1951, N 22,31:5
Liberman, David M Mrs, 1922, My 18,19:6
Liberman, Etta F Mrs, 1940, O 25,21:3
Liberman, Harry, 1957, Ap 6,19:3
Liberman, Joel B, 1955, Ag 3,23:2
Liberman, Lawrence A, 1955, My 5,33:5
Liberman, Leonard, 1967, F 21,47:4
Liberman, Myron S, 1946, S 10,7:1
Liberman, Phil, 1937, Je 16,23:4
Liberman, Samuel Z, 1954, Mr 22,27:4
Liberman, Simon, 1946, Ja 6,40:6
Libermas, Baruch Pincus, 1914, F 19,9:4
Liberson, Frank, 1947, Ap 17,27:6
Libert, Louis, 1957, D 2,27:6
Liberte, Jean, 1965, Ag 25,39:3
Liberti, Frank, 1965, D 12,87:2
Libertini, Pasquale Sen (Baron of San Marco), 1940, Je 5,25:2
Liberts, Ludolfs, 1959, Mr 16,31:4
Liberty, Arthur Lasenby Sir, 1917, My 12,11:7
Liberty, Emery, 1914, S 12,9:5
Liberty, Richard W, 1953, O 18,86:4
Libglid, Jacob, 1950, Mr 31,32:6
Libich, Jean, 1968, N 13,47:3
Libidins, David, 1958, D 29,15:4
Libin, Solomon, 1955, Ap 15,23:3
Libinger, Kaye R Mrs, 1944, Jl 7,15:5
Libman, Emanuel (por), 1946, Je 29,19:1
Libman, Emanuel, 1946, Jl 2,25:2
Libow, Robert, 1960, N 30,37:4
Libowitz, Isidor, 1962, Jl 2,29:1
Libretti, Joseph, 1948, N 8,21:5
Libschutz, Morris, 1948, N 11,27:2
Libson, Robert J, 1951, S 23,86:2
Liburt, Joseph, 1959, Mr 28,17:1
Libutti, Salvatore, 1941, Ag 7,17:2
Licari, Jerome J, 1951, D 4,33:4
Licastro, Philip, 1944, F 14,17:3
Liccione, Joseph Mrs, 1945, Ja 5,15:3
License, Edward P, 1943, D 8,23:5
Lichenstein, Julius, 1945, O 27,15:4
Lichentag, Alex, 1938, Ja 15,15:3
Lichfield, Earl of (Thos Francis Anson), 1918, Jl 31, 9:5
Lichnowsky, K M von Prince, 1928, F 28,25:5
Lichstern, A J, 1928, Jl 7,13:6
Licht, Alvin A Mrs, 1948, O 24,76:5
Licht, Emanuel H Mrs, 1956, Jl 6,21:1
Licht, George A, 1960, Ag 2,29:4
Licht, Herman, 1967, Ap 11,41:2
Licht, James H, 1966, Ap 21,39:2
Licht, Louis F, 1957, Ag 17,15:2
Licht, Philip S, 1967, D 23,23:3
Licht, Sallie W, 1943, My 4,23:3
Lichten, Frances, 1961, Mr 29,33:1
Lichtenauer, Joseph M, 1912, My 20,9:5
Lichtenberg, August, 1944, F 14,17:6
Lichtenberg, Bernard, 1944, O 4,20:2

Lichtenberg, Etta Mrs, 1916, O 8,23:3
Lichtenberg, Harry F, 1954, Ap 27,29:2
Lichtenberg, Jerome M, 1959, Ag 31,21:5
Lichtenberg, Joseph, 1961, N 19,89:2
Lichtenberg, Noah, 1965, F 6,25:6
Lichtenberg, Samuel, 1956, O 2,35:3
Lichtenberg, Samuel H, 1944, O 6,23:4
Lichtenberger, Andre, 1940, Mr 26,21:3
Lichtenberger, Anthony J, 1952, F 18,19:5
Lichtenberger, Arthur Bp, 1968, S 4,47:1
Lichtenberger, Charles F, 1950, D 22,23:5
Lichtenberger, James B, 1949, Jl 9,13:1
Lichtenberger, James P, 1953, Mr 18,31:6
Lichtendorf, Max, 1962, Je 16,19:4
Lichtenfels, Russel C, 1940, Mr 10,51:3
Lichtenstadter, Sylvester H Mrs, 1952, O 21,29:3
Lichtenstein, Adolph B, 1959, D 15,39:4
Lichtenstein, Alfred, 1915, N 1,11:6
Lichtenstein, Alfred F, 1947, F 25,25:5
Lichtenstein, Charles, 1966, Ap 1,35:3
Lichtenstein, Clara K Mrs, 1937, Mr 11,24:1
Lichtenstein, Emille J, 1915, Je 11,15:5
Lichtenstein, Gaston, 1954, Ja 18,23:5
Lichtenstein, George P, 1952, Ap 27,91:1
Lichtenstein, George P Mrs, 1940, F 28,21:1
Lichtenstein, Harmon G, 1954, F 2,27:3
Lichtenstein, Isaac, 1944, Ja 24,17:4
Lichtenstein, Julius, 1953, Ja 24,15:5
Lichtenstein, Julius Mrs, 1937, My 7,25:2
Lichtenstein, Mayer, 1955, Mr 20,88:6
Lichtenstein, Morris (por), 1938, N 7,19:3
Lichtenstein, Morris, 1954, Je 5,17:4; 1962, Jl 27,25:2
Lichtenstein, Perry M, 1954, Je 15,29:3
Lichtenstein, Rae Mrs, 1952, My 17,19:3
Lichtenstein, Richard C, 1937, My 22,18:1
Lichtenstein, Robert, 1923, Je 4,15:6
Lichtenstein, Seaman, 1902, D 25,7:5
Lichtenstein, Solomon B, 1908, Je 14,11:5
Lichtenstein, Walter, 1964, Mr 15,86:2
Lichtenwalner, Norton L, 1960, My 4,45:2
Lichter, Anna (Mrs A L Mehrbach), 1942, D 10,30:1
Lichter, Ira J, 1944, Ja 9,42:2
Lichter, Jacob, 1968, F 9,27:2
Lichter, Julius, 1966, My 10,45:1
Lichter, Malvin, 1955, My 21,17:5
Lichterman, Abraham, 1942, Je 28,33:3
Lichtin, James J, 1964, Ja 29,30:4
Lichtle, William W, 1953, D 16,35:4
Lichtman, Abner, 1956, Ja 1,50:3
Lichtman, Al, 1958, D 21,24:1
Lichtman, Bertha Mrs, 1942, S 20,41:4
Lichtman, Harold B R, 1955, Ag 5,19:2
Lichtman, Robert B, 1953, F 22,28:2
Lichtman, Sol S, 1961, Je 17,21:1
Lichtwitz, Leopold (por), 1943, Mr 19,19:3
Lichty, Brucc, 1941, Mr 11,23:5
Lichty, David M, 1942, D 26,11:3
Lichty, Edson P, 1950, Jl 28,21:5
Lichty, J A, 1932, My 3,21:6
Lick, James (see also O 2), 1876, O 9,10:2
Lick, John H, 1951, O 2,27:2
Licking, Bernard P, 1952, Jl 18,19:5
Lickle, H Roland, 1939, S 15,23:5
Licklider, Albert H, 1959, Ag 4,27:4
Lickmann, William, 1940, Jl 12,15:4
Licks, Frederick C, 1957, O 13,86:5
Liddell, Charles C, 1947, Je 16,21:4
Liddell, Charles E, 1953, Mr 13,25:4
Liddell, Clive G, 1956, S 11,35:1
Liddell, Donald M, 1958, Ag 17,86:1
Liddell, Donald M Mrs, 1963, N 10,86:5
Liddell, Eric H, 1945, My 8,19:2
Liddell, George T, 1954, D 18,15:5
Liddell, Howard S, 1962, N 1,31:2
Liddell, John S Lt-Col, 1922, Jl 11,15:3
Liddell, Katherine F, 1960, Ag 26,26:2
Liddell, M H, 1936, Jl 29,19:1
Liddell, William, 1960, O 21,33:3
Liddle, Charles A, 1961, Ja 5,31:5
Liddle, Fred S Sr, 1952, D 3,33:6
Liddon, Benjamin S Judge, 1909, D 23,9:3
Liddon, H P, 1890, S 10,4:7
Liddy, Edward F, 1959, Ag 8,17:6
Liddy, Sarah, 1951, O 14,89:1
Liddy, Thomas A Sr, 1962, Jl 11,36:1
Liddy, Timothy M, 1945, N 28,27:6
Liddy, W L Rev, 1924, F 17,23:1
Liddy, William A, 1959, Jl 19,69:1
Lide, Jesse H, 1967, S 26,47:1
Lidell, J A, 1883, Jl 10,5:2
Lidgerwood, Florence V, 1947, Ap 5,19:2
Lidgerwood, Harriet, 1950, Jl 26,25:5
Lidgerwood, John H, 1910, Ja 2,II,13:5; 1955, Mr 10, 27:2
Lidgett, John S, 1953, Je 18,29:5
Lidi-Mahamed, Sultan of Monaco, 1873, S 22,5:4
Lidstone, Harold W, 1951, Ag 19,85:2
Lidzy, George B, 1941, D 21,41:1
Lie, Jonas, 1940, Ja 11,23:1
Lie, Jonas Lauritz Edemil, 1908, Jl 6,7:5
Lie, Trygve, 1968, D 31,1:5
Lie, Trygve Mme, 1960, Mr 20,87:1
Lieb, Charles C, 1956, Ap 7,19:6

Lieb, Charles C Mrs, 1954, F 23,27:3
Lieb, Clarence H, 1944, D 31,26:7
Lieb, Frank, 1946, Ja 1,28:3; 1947, My 21,25:4
Lieb, George F Mrs, 1949, Ag 19,17:2
Lieb, Herman, 1961, Jl 8,19:5
Lieb, J W, 1929, N 2,17:3
Lieb, John C Jr, 1951, Ja 13,15:3
Lieb, John J, 1966, Ap 15,39:4
Lieb, Joseph, 1946, F 3,40:1; 1948, S 5,40:6
Lieb, Joseph S Mrs, 1950, Ag 30,31:3
Lieb, Sam, 1945, O 24,21:3
Lieb, Solomon (est appr), 1905, Ag 30,16:2
Lieb, Thomas J, 1962, My 1,38:1
Lieb, William, 1951, S 6,31:2
Lieb, William A Mrs, 1947, N 4,25:2
Liebeck, Robert Mrs, 1948, Ag 5,21:5
Liebel, Willard K, 1961, Ag 3,23:3
Liebenau, Albert H, 1961, Mr 3,27:4
Liebenau, J H Gen, 1878, D 14,2:3
Liebenguth, John L, 1953, Ag 15,15:2
Liebenguth, Louis J, 1959, S 15,39:4
Liebenguth, Louis Mrs, 1957, Ap 26,25:2
Liebenow, Anna Mrs, 1947, Jl 31,21:2
Liebensu, Andrew J, 1910, My 8,II,13:4
Lieber, Albert C, 1954, N 10,33:2
Lieber, B Franklin, 1915, N 12,11:6
Lieber, Ernst Dr, 1902, Ap 1,9:6
Lieber, Francis Prof, 1872, O 3,10:5
Lieber, G Norman Brig-Gen, 1923, Ap 27,17:5
Lieber, George C, 1949, Mr 8,25:4
Lieber, Harry B, 1947, Mr 13,27:3
Lieber, Hugh G, 1961, Ag 8,29:3
Lieber, Hyman Mrs, 1951, Ja 8,17:3
Lieber, Joseph, 1960, Je 20,31:5
Lieber, Samuel, 1956, My 10,31:2
Lieber, Saul, 1939, D 4,23:4
Lieberknecht, Adam Mrs, 1943, Ap 15,25:4
Lieberman, Aaron Mrs, 1956, Mr 30,19:4
Lieberman, Abraham, 1941, Jl 4,16:5
Lieberman, Albert H, 1967, Ag 5,23:2
Lieberman, Alex, 1941, O 30,23:4
Lieberman, Chaim (Herman), 1963, My 17,33:2
Lieberman, David, 1959, Ja 22,31:1; 1967, Jl 17,29:5
Lieberman, David H Mrs, 1956, My 13,86:6
Lieberman, David P, 1960, My 17,37:2
Lieberman, Edward, 1939, D 12,27:3
Lieberman, Herman, 1941, O 22,23:3
Lieberman, Hyman, 1963, Je 7,31:3
Lieberman, Isadore, 1952, F 19,29:4
Lieberman, Jacob, 1912, Ja 7,II,15:3
Lieberman, John, 1942, F 22,26:3
Lieberman, Joseph, 1953, F 7,15:2
Lieberman, Joseph A, 1956, Ag 25,15:4; 1959, Je 5, 27:1
Lieberman, Joseph M, 1958, O 5,87:2
Lieberman, Julius, 1945, F 24,11:6
Lieberman, Lawrence J, 1960, N 14,31:5
Lieberman, M, 1935, F 9,16:1
Lieberman, Marcus, 1951, My 22,31:4
Lieberman, Max, 1948, My 30,34:4
Lieberman, Michael E, 1945, N 30,23:2
Lieberman, Nathan, 1955, Ja 21,23:4; 1962, N 6,33:2
Lieberman, Nathan Mrs, 1912, Je 6,11:4
Lieberman, Samuel H, 1964, Je 29,27:4
Lieberman, Saul, 1940, F 3,13:5
Lieberman, Simon, 1954, S 11,17:6
Lieberman, Sol J Mrs, 1956, Je 12,35:3
Lieberman, Stanley, 1968, Jl 4,19:1
Lieberman, Sylvia Mrs, 1952, N 18,15:3
Lieberman, Victor, 1937, Je 8,25:5
Liebermann, Abraham, 1963, Ag 21,33:1
Liebermann, William, 1954, Ag 10,19:6
Liebers, Albert S Mrs, 1962, Je 27,32:6
Liebers, Meyer, 1947, N 27,32:3
Liebert, A H, 1947, Je 6,23:1
Liebert, Arthur, 1946, N 11,27:4
Liebert, Frederick, 1943, Mr 27,13:4
Liebert, Gerald, 1965, O 28,43:1
Liebert, Sam, 1945, O 25,21:4
Liebert, Walter N, 1950, Je 8,31:2
Lieberthal, David, 1953, Je 12,27:2
Liebes, Leon, 1951, N 24,11:3
Liebeskind, Solon J, 1955, My 3,31:1
Liebeskind, Solon J Mrs, 1948, S 17,25:2
Liebgold, Samuel, 1943, My 30,26:4
Liebhober, Isidore Mrs, 1957, N 10,86:5
Liebig, Baron, 1873, Ap 19,7:3
Liebknecht, Otto, 1949, Je 23,27:4
Liebknecht, Wilhelm Dr, 1900, Ag 8,6:7
Liebl, Michael, 1964, Ap 12,87:2
Lieblang, Henry, 1949, D 20,31:4
Liebler, Adam, 1956, Mr 11,88:1
Liebler, Jacob F, 1950, F 5,85:1
Liebler, M Walter Mrs, 1949, S 30,23:3
Liebler, M Walther, 1942, S 22,21:2
Liebler, Theodore A, 1941, Ap 24,21:4
Liebler, Theodore A Mrs, 1944, N 19,50:6
Lieblich, Morris Mrs, 1947, N 23,72:4
Lieblich, Neil M, 1965, Jl 7,37:3
Liebling, A J (Abbott J), 1963, D 29,42:2
Liebling, Ann B, 1964, My 16,51:1
Liebling, Emil, 1914, Ja 21,9:4
Liebling, Joseph Mrs, 1956, Ag 21,29:5
Liebling, Leonard (por), 1945, O 29,19:3
Liebling, Max Mrs, 1907, O 12,9:6
Liebling, Philip, 1966, O 6,47:4
Liebling, Sally, 1909, S 17,9:5
Lieblong, Nelson, 1951, Ag 29,25:6
Liebman, Charles J, 1957, S 17,35:3
Liebman, Charles J Mrs, 1966, Ag 24,45:3
Liebman, David, 1956, S 3,13:4
Liebman, Joseph B, 1962, Je 3,88:2
Liebman, Joshua L, 1948, Je 10,25:1
Liebman, Julius, 1937, F 1,19:4
Liebman, Phil L, 1950, F 16,23:3
Liebman, Philip, 1945, D 19,25:4
Liebman, Rafael, 1942, O 19,21:5
Liebman, Walter H, 1963, N 7,37:2
Liebman, Walter H Mrs, 1962, S 21,29:1
Liebmann, Alfred, 1957, N 26,33:5
Liebmann, Alfred J, 1957, O 12,19:4
Liebmann, Alfred Mrs, 1938, Jl 16,13:5
Liebmann, Arthur E, 1960, Ap 11,31:3
Liebmann, Frederick J, 1958, My 28,31:2
Liebmann, Harry, 1937, O 4,21:3
Liebmann, Henry L, 1950, N 6,27:5
Liebmann, Herman, 1912, Mr 12,13:4
Liebmann, Hugo K, 1958, My 14,33:2
Liebmann, Joseph, 1913, Mr 27,11:5
Liebmann, Julius, 1957, O 10,33:1
Liebmann, Samuel, 1955, My 19,29:2
Liebner, Otto, 1946, N 29,25:4
Liebold, Ernest G, 1956, Mr 5,23:3
Liebovitz, Abraham L, 1964, Ag 8,19:3
Liebovitz, Abraham Mrs, 1953, N 25,23:2
Liebovitz, David, 1968, F 5,35:4
Liebovitz, Simon Mrs (por), 1944, Ap 28,19:5
Liebow, William, 1957, Ja 10,29:3
Liebowitz, Ephraim J, 1964, S 24,41:4
Liebowitz, Jack S Mrs, 1956, D 26,27:4
Liebowitz, Louis Mrs, 1954, N 30,29:2
Liebowitz, Nathan, 1951, Ja 18,27:1
Liebrecht, E Frank, 1967, Ja 31,31:5
Liebscher, Gustave, 1953, My 12,27:3
Lieburg, Max, 1962, Je 14,33:5
Lied, Susanne, 1942, N 26,27:2
Lieder, Frederick W, 1953, Jl 31,19:5
Lieder, Kurt M, 1956, Ap 6,26:2
Lieder, Paul R, 1956, My 15,31:3
Lieder, William J A, 1916, My 25,13:4
Liederbach, J C, 1962, N 3,25:1
Liedy, William J, 1950, My 26,23:3
Lief, Jacob F, 1951, O 15,25:3
Lief, Joseph Mrs, 1960, Ap 7,35:5
Lief, Nathaniel (por), 1944, D 23,13:6
Liefeld, Walter L, 1947, N 1,15:3
Liefke, Henry, 1940, F 22,23:3
Liegnitz, Augusta De Princess, 1873, Je 7,5:4
Liekefet, Harry W, 1955, Ag 10,25:1
Liem, Roland H D, 1962, F 8,31:1
Lien, Jonas, 1959, Jl 18,15:5
Lien, Joseph M, 1942, D 1,25:4
Lienau, A Williams, 1961, Jl 25,27:4
Lienau, J Henry, 1957, N 22,25:2
Lienemann, Harold J Mrs, 1943, O 26,23:5
Liengme, Adrian Mrs, 1959, Je 27,23:2
Lienhard, Rudolph, 1951, Ap 29,88:8
Lienhardt, Adolph, 1950, F 9,29:5
Lier, Paul L, 1947, F 9,61:5
Lies, B Eugenia, 1945, Ja 29,14:2
Lies, William, 1960, O 4,43:3
Liese, Harry G Mrs, 1956, My 11,28:2
Liese, W H, 1902, Mr 16,7:5
Lieske, Robert E, 1953, Ag 13,41:2
Lietz, Amos C, 1945, Jl 31,19:5
Lietz, M Christine, 1959, F 8,86:2
Lieu, Dakuin K (D K), 1962, My 8,39:4
Lieutheny-Thomsen, Hermann von der, 1942, Ag 9, 43:4
Lievegoed, A J, 1946, Je 29,19:5
Lievense, Cornelis, 1949, S 24,13:6
Liff, Henry, 1916, Je 14,13:5
Liff, Henry W, 1953, Ag 8,11:4
Liffiton, Arthur E, 1954, My 11,29:2
Lifford, Lord (E J Hewitt), 1954, Ap 8,27:5
Lifschey, Elias I, 1959, Je 27,23:6
Lifschey, Samuel, 1961, S 17,86:7
Lifschitz, Joseph, 1964, O 18,89:1
Lifschitz, Morris Mrs, 1944, Ja 31,17:3
Lifschitz, Siegmund, 1949, N 9,27:4
Lifschutz, Leopold A, 1940, O 13,49:1
Lifshey, Lawrence L, 1967, D 17,92:6
Lifshey, Oscar, 1953, My 10,88:3
Lifshey, Samuel H, 1954, N 5,46:1
Lifshitz, William, 1953, Je 23,29:4
Lifson, Harry, 1955, D 16,29:3
Lifson, William, 1916, Ja 15,9:4
Lifter, Louis M, 1957, Jl 2,27:3
Lifter, Morris, 1948, Ag 18,25:2
Liftig, Maurice D Mrs, 1952, Ag 31,44:4
Lifton, Eli, 1967, D 19,47:1
Lifton, Harold A, 1966, Ag 16,39:3
Lifton, Harold Mrs, 1962, F 5,31:4
Lifton, Louis S, 1951, Mr 12,25:2
Lifton, Oscar M, 1949, Ag 8,15:3
Ligety, Aaron Mrs, 1949, My 24,28:3
Liggan, Roland B, 1941, My 24,15:4
Ligget, J Thomas, 1949, Ap 7,30:5
Liggett, Florence, 1945, My 23,19:3
Liggett, George A, 1948, Je 29,24:3
Liggett, H, 1935, D 31,15:1
Liggett, Harold, 1964, Mr 3,35:3
Liggett, Jeannette M, 1948, Ja 14,26:2
Liggett, John E, 1939, Je 2,23:5
Liggett, John L, 1937, F 16,23:2
Liggett, Joseph, 1942, My 4,19:2
Liggett, Leigh B, 1937, D 2,25:6
Liggett, Louis K (por), 1946, Je 7,19:1
Liggett, Melvin R, 1957, Jl 21,60:7
Liggett, Richard H, 1940, D 25,27:5
Liggett, Sidney B, 1915, Ja 9,11:4
Liggett, Sidney S, 1942, My 28,17:1
Liggett, Thomas, 1942, Ag 6,19:3
Liggett, Winfield Jr Com (por), 1937, Jl 20,23:4
Liggitt, J Walter, 1955, My 29,44:2
Ligh, Charles G, 1952, N 4,29:2
Ligham, Saul T, 1958, F 10,23:1
Light, Albert A, 1948, O 8,25:3
Light, Alfred D, 1941, Ag 22,15:3
Light, Arthur B, 1958, Mr 22,17:3
Light, Arthur B Mrs, 1958, Mr 11,29:2
Light, Ben, 1965, Ja 9,25:3
Light, David H, 1941, Ag 12,19:6
Light, Everett D, 1961, O 12,2:5
Light, Frederick D, 1942, Ja 12,15:4
Light, Freeman, 1959, Ap 9,31:2
Light, Gilson D, 1941, F 27,19:2
Light, Herbert C, 1946, N 17,68:3
Light, Herman H, 1958, Ap 14,25:2
Light, Hunter U, 1954, Ap 7,31:2
Light, James (trb lr, Mr 22,II,9:2), 1964, F 12,33:1
Light, James E, 1964, F 2,88:6
Light, John C, 1952, Jl 21,19:3
Light, John H, 1945, Jl 24,23:4; 1961, Ja 22,85:2
Light, John J, 1947, Jl 1,25:3
Light, Michel, 1953, Je 12,27:1
Light, Nestor, 1951, Ja 7,77:2
Light, Norbert D, 1940, O 11,21:3
Light, Ralph A, 1937, Mr 4,23:4
Light, Roderick H, 1955, Ag 8,21:2
Light, S Rudolph, 1961, Ja 29,85:1
Light, Stephen B, 1949, Ag 23,23:3
Light, Theodore H Sr, 1958, Je 28,17:5
Light, Tole, 1956, Ag 5,77:1
Light, Wayne W, 1962, Ja 25,31:3
Light, Wesley W, 1953, Ag 29,17:4
Light, William C, 1942, S 12,13:5
Lightbody, Frank, 1945, Ja 28,38:5
Lightbourn, Robert C, 1937, My 12,23:4
Lightcap, Edward R, 1915, Je 1,15:6
Lighte, F C, 1872, F 5,8:5
Lightfoot, Arthur, 1957, S 2,13:3
Lightfoot, C E Todd, 1966, D 22,33:1
Lightfoot, James A, 1941, Mr 30,49:1
Lightfoot, Theodore A Mrs, 1924, N 13,21:4
Lightfoot, Thomas M, 1950, N 27,25:2
Lightfoot, Warren R, 1952, F 20,29:2
Lightfoot, William C, 1924, Je 5,21:5
Lightfoot, William H, 1943, S 19,48:6
Lightfoot-Boston, Lady, 1965, S 6,15:2
Lighthall, George P R, 1956, Jl 4,19:3
Lighthipe, Charles A, 1905, F 15,9:5
Lighthipe, Herbert, 1937, Ap 16,23:4
Lighthipe, Kenneth D, 1952, Mr 11,27:5
Lightipe, James A, 1925, Ap 11,13:3
Lightley, John W, 1948, Je 15,28:3
Lightman, Malcolm Sr, 1958, D 6,23:5
Lightner, Clarence A, 1938, D 8,27:2
Lightner, Lowrie H Mrs, 1944, Ag 26,11:5
Lightner, Milton Clarkson, 1968, Mr 26,45:1
Lightner, Walter L, 1951, Ap 19,31:4
Lightoller, Charles H, 1952, D 9,33:5
Lighton, Louis D, 1963, F 4,8:8
Lightstone, Abraham (por), 1955, Ag 8,21:2
Lightstone, Joseph, 1940, O 16,23:5
Lightstone, Sidney Mrs, 1956, Ag 14,25:4
Lighty, William H, 1959, My 21,31:4
Ligman, Thaddeus S, 1950, Mr 30,29:4
Lignante, William H, 1963, Ag 4,80:4
Ligne, Albert de Prince, 1963, Ap 28,45:5
Ligne, Eugene de Prince, 1960, Je 27,25:2
Ligne, Prince de, 1880, My 22,5:3
Lignier, Frederick, 1917, Ag 7,9:2
Ligon, David S, 1965, My 28,33:3
Ligotino, Charles, 1947, Mr 19,25:5
Ligouri, Francis C, 1938, O 18,25:6
Ligourie, Alfred, 1947, N 3,23:5
Ligouvi, Carmine, 1922, Jl 4,13:5
Ligtermoet, Harry, 1945, O 3,19:5
Liguori, A James, 1967, F 28,34:1
Liguori, Mother (Katherine Leigh), 1905, Je 28
Lihme, C Bai (por), 1946, O 16,27:1
Lihme, C Bai Mrs, 1956, N 10,19:5
Lihme, Harold H, 1964, D 7,35:4
Lihou, John, 1946, My 7,21:4
Likas, Frank C (will), 1955, Ap 26,31:5
Likely, David S, 1952, S 12,21:4
Likhachev, Ivan (funl Je 27,5:6), 1956, Je 26,3
Likly, William Mrs, 1944, Ja 25,19:3

Lilenthal, Pauline Mrs, 1944, Ag 12,11:6
Lilford, Baron, 1945, D 18,27:2
Lilford, Lady, 1940, Ap 10,25:5
Lilien, Ernest L, 1952, Je 18,27:2
Lilien, Jack M, 1968, O 30,47:4
Lilienfeld, Karl, 1966, S 21,47:3
Lilienstern, Solon B, 1937, My 20,21:4
Lilienthal, C H, 1883, Je 3,2:3
Lilienthal, David, 1953, D 19,15:5
Lilienthal, F W Dr, 1910, Jl 29,9:6
Lilienthal, Felix F, 1955, Mr 22,31:5
Lilienthal, Howard, 1946, My 1,25:1
Lilienthal, Jesse W Jr, 1952, Jl 1,23:3
Lilienthal, Joseph L Dr, 1955, N 20,88:8
Lilienthal, Joseph L Mrs (Edna A), 1955, Ja 25,25:2
Lilienthal, Leo, 1951, Ap 11,29:6
Lilienthal, Max, 1882, Ap 6,2:5
Lilienthal, Max P, 1949, S 15,27:5
Lilienthal, Meta L Mrs, 1948, Mr 26,21:2
Lilienthal, Richard S, 1968, Ja 31,41:1
Lilies, Frank P, 1951, My 28,21:2
Lilina, Maria P, 1943, Ag 27,17:2
Liliuokalani, Queen, 1917, N 12,13:5
Liljefors, Bruno, 1939, D 19,26:2
Liljestroems, Waldemar, 1960, N 14,31:4
Lill, Alfred J, 1956, Mr 19,31:2
Lill, Peter D, 1946, Mr 18,21:5
Lillagore, T Nelson, 1949, Ja 29,13:3
Lillard, Benjamin, 1910, Mr 7,9:4
Lillard, Caroline M H Mrs, 1941, My 11,45:2
Lillard, Charlotte, 1946, Mr 8,21:1
Lillard, George W, 1940, O 25,21:2
Lillard, Walter H, 1967, Jl 3,17:3
Lillback, Elna T, 1950, Ja 17,27:2
Lillback, John E, 1940, F 1,21:2
Lillers, Marquis, 1941, Mr 19,21:5
Lilley, Alex P Sr, 1948, F 2,19:5
Lilley, Anna E H Mrs, 1940, S 19,23:3
Lilley, Charles J, 1946, N 19,31:3
Lilley, Frank W, 1938, D 30,15:4
Lilley, George Leavens, 1909, Ap 22,9:5
Lilley, Jeanne, 1944, Je 9,15:5
Lilley, John J, 1944, O 20,20:2
Lilley, Theodore, 1967, Je 13,64:2
Lilley, Thomas H, 1954, S 19,88:7
Lilley, Walter F, 1965, Ag 5,29:3
Lilley, William Jr, 1955, Mr 21,25:4
Lilley, William Sr (por), 1939, O 18,26:3
Lillibridge, Emery L, 1939, S 16,17:3
Lillibridge, Emory L Mrs, 1943, Jl 4,21:2
Lillibridge, Harrison, 1967, D 11,47:5
Lillie, Abraham B H, 1905, D 12,9:3
Lillie, Alice C Mrs, 1937, D 29,22:4
Lillie, Amy Morris, 1967, N 23,33:5
Lillie, Andrew, 1922, N 17,17:5
Lillie, Charles A, 1964, D 1,41:1
Lillie, Egbert H, 1961, Ja 17,37:2
Lillie, Frank R, 1947, N 6,27:5
Lillie, Frank R Mrs, 1958, F 5,27:5
Lillie, Gordon W (por),(will, F 10,17:1), 1942, F 4, 19:1
Lillie, Lucie S Mrs, 1957, N 8,29:2
Lillie, Nathaniel W, 1948, Mr 1,23:1
Lillie, O R, 1946, F 23,13:3
Lillie, Ralph S, 1952, Mr 20,29:2
Lillie, Walter I, 1947, F 22,13:2
Lillien, Alex Mrs, 1949, N 17,29:2
Lilliencron, Detlev von, 1909, Jl 23,7:6
Lillienfeld, Julius E, 1963, Ag 30,21:2
Lillienfeld, Max, 1968, Mr 3,89:2
Lillienthal, Katherine, 1907, Je 13,7:5
Lilling, Charles, 1951, S 9,88:4
Lillis, Charles E, 1944, Je 1,19:5
Lillis, De Forest, 1951, S 26,31:5
Lillis, Donald C, 1968, Jl 24,41:1
Lillis, Edward J, 1948, Ag 17,22:2
Lillis, James F, 1963, Jl 8,29:5
Lillis, James J, 1941, N 19,23:4
Lillis, Martin, 1943, O 25,15:3
Lillis, Richard R, 1958, Ap 2,31:1
Lillis, Thomas E, 1939, O 9,19:6
Lillis, Thomas F (por), 1938, D 30,15:3
Lillis, Thomas J, 1865, D 17,5:5
Lillo, Samuel A, 1958, O 20,29:1
Lilly, Coral A, 1940, My 5,53:1
Lilly, D Clay, 1939, My 29,15:5
Lilly, George L, 1949, Mr 29,26:3
Lilly, George W, 1957, N 12,37:3
Lilly, George W Mrs, 1955, D 24,13:3
Lilly, Harry Mrs, 1955, O 8,19:6
Lilly, Henry, 1942, N 8,51:4
Lilly, Henry W, 1946, Jl 18,25:5
Lilly, Hugh Francis Rev, 1914, D 4,11:6
Lilly, J Joseph, 1955, O 13,31:3
Lilly, Jonathan, 1946, S 10,7:3
Lilly, Joseph, 1965, F 24,41:3
Lilly, Joseph T, 1939, N 10,23:6
Lilly, Josiah K, 1948, F 9,17:2; 1966, My 6,47:3
Lilly, Lewis, 1954, S 28,29:6
Lilly, Mary D Mrs, 1954, Ag 24,21:3
Lilly, Paul A, 1959, O 20,39:2
Lilly, Richard C, 1959, O 24,21:6
Lilly, Roy F, 1954, Ap 22,30:3
Lilly, S, 1880, Ap 4,2:6
Lilly, Scott B, 1948, Ag 20,17:1
Lilly, Thomas A, 1949, Je 23,27:3
Lilly, Thomas R, 1952, D 10,35:3
Lillybridge, Thomas, 1962, N 1,31:1
Lily Duchess of Marlborough, 1909, Ja 12,9:4
Lima, Bertram L Sir, 1919, F 25,11:2
Lima, J M, 1928, D 9,II,8:1
Lima, Joao Evangelista de, 1958, Ja 6,39:1
Lima, Joseph J T, 1952, Ja 3,27:4
Lima, M de O, 1928, Mr 25,III,31:5
Lima, Waldomiro de C, 1938, F 13,II,7:1
Lima, Wenceslau de Dr, 1920, Ja 30,15:5
Liman, Elliott I, 1961, N 5,89:1
Liman, Louis, 1958, Jl 31,23:1
Limantour, J Y, 1935, Ag 27,19:1
Limb, Claudius, 1949, Ap 6,29:4
Limbach, Henry A, 1954, Jl 21,27:5
Limbaugh, Conrad, 1960, Mr 28,3:1
Limberg, Frank B, 1952, Ap 20,92:6
Limbert, Lee M, 1966, S 13,47:3
Limbert, Roy, 1954, N 30,29:5
Limburg, H R, 1932, Ag 16,17:3
Limburg, Richard, 1916, F 6,15:4
Limburg, Richard P Mrs, 1958, S 25,33:5
Limerick, Bp of (Edw Thos O'Dwyer), 1917, Ag 20, 9:4
Limerick, Countess of, 1943, Mr 13,13:6
Limerick, Samuel R, 1938, Ja 17,19:5
Limerick, William J, 1911, O 8,II,13:5
Limmer, John M, 1874, Jl 15,5:5
Limner, Frank, 1957, My 7,35:2
Limoli, Ernest, 1965, Ap 4,87:4
Limoli, Louis, 1949, N 6,92:5
Limont, Frank T, 1956, Ag 11,13:2
Limonta, Hechevarria, 1943, Ap 13,25:1
Limouze, Percy, 1953, Ag 3,17:6
Limpery, William J, 1958, Ja 12,86:5
Limpus, Lowell M, 1957, D 20,24:3
Limpus, Robert, 1955, D 23,18:2
Limroth, Frederick J, 1953, S 7,19:2
Lin, Francis, 1952, Ja 16,25:5
Lin, Joe, 1947, D 15,25:3
Lin, John Mrs, 1948, My 25,27:3
Lin Dai (funl, Jl 20,8:6), 1964, Jl 18,11:2
Lin Pin, 1958, Jl 25,19:1
Lin Po-chu, 1960, My 30,17:6
Lin Sen, 1943, Ag 2,15:1
Lin Wei, 1955, Ag 4,25:4
Linares, Gonzales de, 1955, Mr 4,23:1
Linares, J M, 1942, F 7,7:2
Linaweaver, Luther W, 1956, Ja 6,23:3
Linbarger, Harvey R, 1959, O 2,29:2
Linbarger, Norman L, 1937, O 7,27:3
Linbarger, Sadie M, 1947, My 9,21:3
Linburn, Ernest A, 1946, My 27,23:5
Linburn, Richard E, 1967, Ag 9,39:2
Lincer, Isidor, 1949, Mr 12,17:3
Lincewicz, Anthony, 1951, F 16,25:3
Linch, Carlo A, 1957, Jl 11,25:3
Linch, Edward P, 1942, D 27,34:3
Linch, George W, 1915, D 18,11:5
Linck, Charles G, 1941, Ja 14,21:3
Linck, Jus Volney, 1925, Ap 2,21:5
Linck, Walter H, 1944, Ap 11,19:5
Lincke, Paul, 1946, S 7,15:6
Lincks, George H, 1951, Ja 13,15:4
Lincoln, Abraham Mrs, 1882, Jl 17,1:4
Lincoln, Agnes H Mrs, 1954, Ag 31,21:3
Lincoln, Alan M, 1937, D 8,25:4
Lincoln, Albert N, 1943, D 24,13:2
Lincoln, Alfred G, 1922, My 16,19:5
Lincoln, Allan B, 1950, Mr 10,28:3
Lincoln, Allen B, 1941, S 3,23:3
Lincoln, Annie F Mrs, 1941, Ap 13,38:2
Lincoln, Bishop of (F C N Hicks), 1942, F 12,23:2
Lincoln, Blanche H B Mrs, 1906, D 21,9:4
Lincoln, C G, 1884, D 18,2:2
Lincoln, Calvin, 1881, S 12,1:6
Lincoln, Charles, 1884, D 3,2:3
Lincoln, Charles M, 1950, D 23,15:1
Lincoln, Charles M Mrs, 1941, Ap 11,21:3
Lincoln, Charles S, 1941, My 21,23:5
Lincoln, Charles S F, 1965, Jl 6,34:1
Lincoln, Charles Z (funl, Jl 29,21:6), 1925, Jl 27,13:4
Lincoln, Clarence C, 1953, Mr 15,92:4
Lincoln, Clyde R, 1952, S 11,31:6
Lincoln, David F Dr, 1916, O 19,9:2
Lincoln, Donald, 1952, D 30,19:2
Lincoln, Edith W Mrs, 1963, S 10,39:4
Lincoln, Edmond E, 1958, My 16,23:6
Lincoln, Eleanor S Mrs, 1954, Ja 3,88:1
Lincoln, Elmo, 1952, Je 28,20:5
Lincoln, Ex-Gov (funl, Je 3,8:1), 1868, Je 1,1:7
Lincoln, Ezra P, 1951, My 10,31:2
Lincoln, Frank O, 1950, F 13,21:3
Lincoln, Frederic Walker, 1968, Ap 8,47:2
Lincoln, Frederick B Mrs, 1962, O 6,25:5
Lincoln, George, 1905, My 23,9:6
Lincoln, George C Mrs, 1961, F 15,35:3
Lincoln, George L Mrs, 1944, Je 21,19:4
Lincoln, Harold C, 1946, N 30,15:3
Lincoln, Harrison T, 1949, D 3,15:2
Lincoln, Harry J, 1937, Ap 21,23:3
Lincoln, Henry P, 1939, F 9,21:4; 1955, My 11,31:4
Lincoln, Isaac W, 1954, Mr 11,31:1
Lincoln, J E, 1931, Mr 16,21:3
Lincoln, J Freeman, 1962, F 13,35:2
Lincoln, Jackson S, 1941, My 5,17:2
Lincoln, James C Sr, 1923, N 29,21:4
Lincoln, James F, 1965, Je 24,35:3
Lincoln, James F Mrs, 1954, S 18,15:1
Lincoln, James G, 1948, N 18,27:2
Lincoln, Jennings S, 1952, Ja 23,27:3
Lincoln, Joel H, 1952, F 9,13:2
Lincoln, John C (will, Jl 10,15:1), 1959, My 26,35:1
Lincoln, John J, 1948, Ja 25,56:5
Lincoln, Jonathan T, 1942, F 12,23:5
Lincoln, Joseph C (por), 1944, Mr 11,13:1
Lincoln, Joseph C (will), 1944, Ap 14,13:8
Lincoln, Joseph C Mrs, 1954, Ja 20,27:4
Lincoln, Josephine V Mrs, 1942, My 29,17:5
Lincoln, Julius, 1954, Jl 22,23:4
Lincoln, Lawrence J, 1959, F 24,29:2
Lincoln, Lee R, 1943, F 23,21:4
Lincoln, Leroy A (funl, My 12,86:2), 1957, My 10, 27:1
Lincoln, Louis B, 1964, Ap 11,25:5
Lincoln, Louis B Mrs, 1958, Ja 1,25:4
Lincoln, Louis H, 1962, N 1,31:2
Lincoln, Martha Mrs, 1964, S 27,87:1
Lincoln, Murray D, 1966, N 8,39:3
Lincoln, N S, 1935, S 1,18:3
Lincoln, Nancy, 1956, D 31,13:5
Lincoln, Paul M, 1944, D 21,21:3
Lincoln, Philena P Mrs, 1940, Ap 13,17:2
Lincoln, Robert E, 1954, Ja 31,89:2; 1954, Je 20,85:2
Lincoln, Robert G, 1952, N 21,25:2
Lincoln, Robert T Mrs, 1937, Ap 1,24:2
Lincoln, Russell F, 1951, Ap 7,15:5
Lincoln, Samuel B, 1954, D 26,60:8
Lincoln, Solomon, 1907, O 17,9:6
Lincoln, Thomas Mrs, 1960, S 11,82:5
Lincoln, Walter O, 1966, My 5,48:1
Lincoln, Walter P, 1939, F 2,19:6
Lincoln, William E, 1944, F 18,17:2
Lincoln, William H, 1925, D 3,25:3
Lincoln, William L Mrs, 1937, D 3,23:1
Lincoln, Willis C, 1958, S 12,25:2
Lind, Adam, 1939, F 2,19:1
Lind, Carl H, 1956, N 11,87:1
Lind, Herbert H, 1951, Mr 3,13:3
Lind, J, 1930, S 19,23:2
Lind, Jenny (Mrs Otto Goldschmidt), 1887, N 3,5:5
Lind, John, 1951, Je 4,29:2
Lind, John A, 1954, Je 5,17:3
Lind, John E, 1954, Ja 22,27:2
Lind, John H Jr, 1958, Ja 3,21:4
Lind, Karl G, 1957, S 9,25:3
Lind, Letty, 1923, Ag 28,17:4
Lind, Lloyd L, 1961, Mr 20,29:6
Lind, Norman, 1947, Jl 20,44:1
Lind, Norman V, 1962, O 17,39:5
Lind, Olander, 1952, Mr 22,13:3
Lind, Ralph A, 1955, O 28,26:2
Lind, Rosa (Mrs Frank Wright), 1921, S 4,18:3
Lind, Samuel C, 1965, F 14,63:2
Lind, Wallace L, 1940, Ap 13,17:5
Lind, William, 1953, N 27,27:2
Lindaberry, Arthur S, 1962, F 1,31:1
Lindabury, Harrison P Sr, 1953, D 9,11:7
Lindabury, Richard V Mrs, 1925, O 10,15:6
Lindabury, Richard Vliet (por),(funl, Jl 17,15:6), 1925, Jl 16,19:4
Lindahl, Oscar N, 1952, My 7,27:2
Lindam, J C, 1882, F 12,6:7
Lindback, Christian R, 1950, Mr 21,29:4
Lindback, Christian R Mrs, 1955, Je 14,29:4
Lindbarger, Edward, 1940, Ja 18,23:2
Lindbarger, Silas C, 1921, S 11,21:2
Lindbeck, John M H Mrs, 1954, Je 7,23:1; 1965, Jl 6, 33:3
Lindberg, Carl O, 1960, S 3,17:6
Lindberg, Fritz A, 1943, Jl 21,15:2
Lindberg, Irving A, 1957, Ap 9,33:3
Lindberg, Irving A Mrs, 1942, S 18,21:2
Lindberg, John A, 1960, Ag 19,23:4
Lindberg, John C, 1954, Ag 11,25:3
Lindberg, Kay E, 1943, Jl 16,17:2
Lindberg, M Hugo Mrs, 1951, N 4,87:1
Lindberg, Otto G, 1968, Mr 14,43:1
Lindberg, Rudolph, 1950, S 11,23:5
Lindberg, Sally Mrs, 1948, Ag 18,25:2
Lindbergh, A V, 1939, N 13,19:5
Lindbergh, Charles A Sr Mrs (funl, S 17,27:2), 1954, S 8,32:5
Lindbergh, Gustaf A, 1941, Mr 11,23:3
Lindblad, Carl A, 1953, D 10,47:2
Lindblom, Ivan, 1958, Ag 29,23:3
Lindblom, John A, 1940, Ap 25,23:4
Lindbloom, Carl G Sr, 1947, D 17,29:4
Linde, Alphonze E, 1957, Jl 20,15:4
Linde, Bertram E, 1945, Mr 9,19:3
Linde, Frederick, 1912, Jl 4,7:6
Linde, Herman A Mrs, 1949, Ja 11,31:1
Linde, John F, 1967, D 9,47:2

Linde, Joseph I, 1951, S 16,83:3
Linde, Ossip L, 1940, My 1,23:2
Linde, Rudolph B von, 1942, Ag 27,19:2
Lindebaum, Daniel Mrs, 1953, D 22,31:5
Lindeberg, Harris T, 1959, Ja 11,88:4
Lindeborg, Jennie C, 1950, F 15,27:1
Lindeheim, Norvin R, 1939, Ap 8,15:4
Lindelman, H R (see also Jan 28), 1879, F 1,5:4
Lindelof, Lawrence P, 1952, O 20,23:4
Lindeman, Charles A, 1940, Ap 29,15:5
Lindeman, Eduard C, 1953, Ap 14,27:1
Lindeman, Edward Dr, 1919, Je 13,15:3
Lindeman, Frank Jr, 1963, N 28,39:4
Lindeman, Hannah, 1962, Ja 15,27:2
Lindeman, Harry H, 1963, Jl 4,17:2
Lindeman, Henry, 1920, Ap 14,9:4
Lindeman, Herman, 1871, N 29,1:6
Lindeman, Howard E, 1952, S 12,21:4
Lindeman, Louis H, 1963, O 18,31:1
Lindeman, Nathan, 1942, Ja 21,17:2
Lindeman, Phil, 1952, Ag 27,27:2
Lindeman, Phil Mrs, 1948, My 24,19:5
Lindeman, Walter Mrs, 1966, My 7,31:2
Lindemann, Adolf D, 1952, Jl 15,21:1
Lindemann, Emil, 1948, Ja 9,21:2
Lindemann, Ernest T, 1941, F 20,19:2
Lindemann, Eugene E, 1951, F 21,27:5
Lindemann, Ferdinand von, 1939, Mr 8,21:6
Lindemann, Fred H, 1958, D 4,39:4
Lindemann, Leo, 1957, S 25,29:3
Lindemann, Leo Mrs, 1959, My 17,83:2
Lindemann, Oscar, 1940, F 16,19:5
Lindemann, Paul G (por), 1938, D 14,25:3
Lindemann, Theodore C, 1940, Je 5,25:5
Lindemuth, Louis A Mrs, 1944, D 20,23:2
Lindemuth, William H, 1939, Mr 17,22:2
Linden, Anthony, 1957, Je 21,25:4
Linden, Arthur V, 1962, F 17,19:2
Linden, Carl E, 1942, N 8,51:6
Linden, Emma, 1916, Ja 8,9:5
Linden, Eugene P, 1954, Ap 13,31:3
Linden, Harold R, 1954, Ag 28,15:5
Linden, Henry A, 1874, D 19,5:1
Linden, John, 1949, D 3,15:3
Linden, John F, 1917, F 26,9:4
Linden, John Mrs, 1945, Je 16,13:3
Linden, Michael M, 1959, Jl 7,33:2
Linden, Mortimer H, 1954, N 14,89:2
Linden, Nels W, 1957, Je 11,35:4
Linden, Robert A, 1954, Mr 25,29:3
Lindenbaum, Daniel, 1954, D 25,11:5
Lindenbaum, Isidore, 1956, Ag 2,25:1
Lindenbaum, Seymour, 1954, My 23,89:2
Lindenberg, Alfred A, 1942, Ag 13,19:5
Lindenberg, John T, 1940, Ag 27,21:3
Lindenberg, Tobias, 1919, F 21,13:7
Lindenblit, Michael Mrs, 1962, Ja 31,31:3
Lindenburn, Henry, 1952, Mr 30,93:1
Lindenmeyr, Gustave, 1923, D 28,15:6
Lindenmeyr, Henry, 1957, Mr 19,37:5
Lindenthal, G, 1935, Ag 1,23:1
Linder, Albert, 1939, N 9,23:5
Linder, Albert A, 1965, Jl 25,69:1
Linder, Arthur I, 1946, F 16,13:5
Linder, Carl E, 1957, N 21,33:3
Linder, Carl P, 1943, Ap 26,19:4
Linder, Cuno, 1948, Ja 3,13:3
Linder, Frank, 1952, My 2,25:2
Linder, Fred, 1950, Ap 7,25:2
Linder, Fred E, 1949, S 7,30:4
Linder, Frederick M, 1956, O 30,37:2
Linder, George A, 1943, My 15,15:6
Linder, George H Mrs, 1940, N 8,21:4
Linder, John, 1947, Ja 13,21:2
Linder, John A, 1954, N 8,21:4
Linder, Leo J, 1962, N 29,37:5
Linder, Louis, 1913, O 20,7:4
Linder, M F, 1876, Je 8,5:2
Linder, Mark, 1950, N 11,15:5
Linder, Mary F Mrs, 1953, Ap 7,29:2
Linder, Morris, 1946, My 19,42:4
Linder, Raymond J, 1941, N 16,57:2
Linder, Solo, 1960, D 25,42:2
Linder, William (por), 1945, Ag 13,19:3
Linder, William H, 1955, D 9,27:4
Linderholm, Ernest A, 1955, Mr 22,31:4
Linderman, Bert A, 1938, O 11,25:2
Linderman, Bud, 1961, Mr 14,35:2
Linderman, Frank B, 1938, My 13,19:4
Linderman, Garrett B, 1950, Jl 28,21:1
Linderman, Max, 1944, N 6,19:4
Linderman, William H, 1954, Ag 31,21:4
Linderman, William S, 1944, D 20,23:4
Linderoth, Gustave W, 1947, My 4,60:3
Linderoth, Martin, 1951, Ja 6,15:6
Lindewall, Carl A, 1941, Je 10,23:5
Lindewall, Karlo H, 1948, My 23,69:1
Lindewurth, Chester A, 1943, Ap 24,13:1
Lindey, Henry H Mrs, 1966, O 1,31:2
Lindfeldt, William, 1947, Ja 15,25:3
Lindgren, Alex C, 1941, Ja 12,46:2
Lindgren, C Walter, 1965, Ag 9,25:1
Lindgren, E Martin, 1940, N 9,17:5
Lindgren, Elin, 1955, My 21,17:3
Lindgren, Gustave S, 1943, O 14,21:2
Lindgren, Homer D, 1942, Ap 5,41:2
Lindgren, Justa M, 1951, My 30,22:2
Lindgren, Reuben, 1943, N 18,23:5
Lindgren, Waldemar, 1939, N 4,15:5
Lindh, Eric I, 1944, Jl 5,11:2
Lindh, F Philip Mrs (Alice), 1968, O 11,47:1
Lindhagen, Carl, 1946, Mr 13,29:4
Lindhard, Povl T, 1952, F 22,21:2
Lindhe, Eric G, 1956, Ag 28,27:1
Lindheim, Benjamin F, 1960, Je 7,35:2
Lindheim, Herman Mrs, 1956, S 5,27:4
Lindheim, N R, 1928, F 9,25:5
Lindheim, Reuben, 1909, Jl 9,7:4
Lindheimer, Benjamin F (est tax acctg), 1961, D 28, 54:1
Lindheimer, Elizabeth P, 1965, F 8,25:5
Lindheimer, Horace G, 1954, D 12,88:6
Lindholm, Clifford F, 1967, Je 18,76:6
Lindholm, George W Mrs, 1941, N 11,23:5
Lindholm, Jens S, 1959, Jl 20,25:4
Lindholm, John, 1953, Mr 3,27:3
Lindholm, Oscar W, 1961, Ja 9,39:5
Lindhorst, Will L, 1954, Mr 8,27:5
Lindi, Aroldo, 1944, Mr 10,15:4
Linding, Hesser C C, 1956, Ap 12,31:5
Lindley, Allen L (por), 1941, Mr 1,15:1
Lindley, Charles Newton Col, 1920, D 1,15:5
Lindley, Curtis N Ex-Judge, 1920, N 22,15:4
Lindley, Daniel Allen, 1915, D 18,11:5
Lindley, Erasmus C, 1957, Jl 15,19:6
Lindley, Erasmus C Mrs, 1947, Ja 2,27:3
Lindley, Ernest, 1955, Je 8,29:1
Lindley, Ernest H (por), 1940, Ag 22,19:2
Lindley, Etta M, 1938, Mr 2,19:5
Lindley, Forrest P, 1945, Ja 18,19:2
Lindley, Francis, 1950, Ag 18,21:3
Lindley, Frederick A, 1942, Mr 24,19:2
Lindley, Gail E, 1956, S 26,33:1
Lindley, Granville P, 1956, D 19,31:2
Lindley, Harlow, 1959, Ag 23,92:6
Lindley, J Bryant Mrs, 1944, N 29,23:3
Lindley, John J, 1923, Ag 21,17:2
Lindley, John W Prof, 1907, D 18,9:5
Lindley, Mary L D Mrs, 1942, F 27,17:3
Lindley, Theodore J, 1922, Ap 22,9:5
Lindley, Walter C, 1958, Ja 4,15:1
Lindley, Werner L, 1948, F 2,19:5
Lindlof, Oscar K Mrs, 1954, Je 12,15:2
Lindman, Ina S, 1963, S 3,33:1
Lindmueller, Charles, 1953, My 5,29:4
Lindner, Amanda, 1951, Ap 21,17:5
Lindner, Charles R Mrs, 1945, Ap 26,23:5
Lindner, Clarence, 1952, Ja 8,27:3
Lindner, Clarence B, 1952, D 28,48:3
Lindner, Edward T, 1951, Je 11,25:6
Lindner, Esther Mrs, 1924, F 9,13:6
Lindner, Frederick A, 1947, N 9,72:6
Lindner, Georg F, 1943, Ag 25,19:1
Lindner, John, 1942, Ap 15,21:5
Lindner, Karl A, 1945, Mr 4,36:3
Lindner, Matilda, 1950, My 21,104:4
Lindner, Max, 1950, Ap 18,31:3
Lindner, Max J, 1945, S 9,45:1
Lindner, Newell D, 1961, Ag 9,33:2
Lindner, Oscar, 1941, Mr 2,42:8
Lindner, Robert, 1944, N 1,23:1
Lindner, Robert M, 1956, F 28,31:3; 1959, D 24,19:5
Lindo, Albert, 1968, My 31,29:4
Lindo, Oswald J, 1948, Mr 22,23:5
Lindon, J D, 1879, D 6,8:1
Lindop, John C Sr, 1947, O 8,25:1
Lindop, Norman L, 1952, S 9,31:5
Lindorff, Elizabeth A Mrs, 1944, N 29,23:4
Lindorff, William F, 1945, Ap 8,36:1
Lindow, Carl A, 1949, My 28,15:5
Lindquist, Albert E, 1943, D 7,27:6
Lindquist, Charles E, 1954, Mr 17,31:2
Lindquist, David L, 1944, N 12,48:4
Lindquist, Eric G, 1966, D 4,88:4
Lindquist, Ernest (Ole), 1955, F 12,15:4
Lindquist, Harry Mrs, 1967, Mr 27,33:1
Lindquist, Henry E, 1952, Ap 3,35:2
Lindquist, John A, 1961, Ag 28,25:4
Lindquist, Joseph E, 1942, Mr 21,17:4
Lindquist, Otto, 1946, D 10,31:1
Lindquist, Rupert J, 1951, My 6,92:4
Lindrath, Hermann, 1960, F 28,82:1
Lindridge, Charles D Mrs, 1964, Je 30,33:5
Lindridge, Edwin F Dr, 1925, Ja 13,19:5
Lindroth, Elmer G, 1942, S 11,21:5
Lindroth, Helen, 1956, O 12,29:3
Lindroun, Leon, 1953, D 22,31:3
Lindrum, Walter A, 1960, Jl 31,69:1
Lindrup, John A, 1958, Je 16,23:3
Lindsay, A D Lord, 1952, Mr 19,29:3
Lindsay, Albert M, 1940, F 23,15:4
Lindsay, Alex Jr, 1949, My 30,13:3
Lindsay, Alexander M, 1920, Jl 15,7:3
Lindsay, Alfred, 1908, Ap 2,7:3
Lindsay, Allan, 1914, Jl 10,9:6
Lindsay, Andrew, 1946, N 9,17:5
Lindsay, Arch L Lady, 1942, Je 1,13:3
Lindsay, Archibald L, 1943, O 16,13:6
Lindsay, Arthur, 1949, N 26,15:2
Lindsay, Arthur O, 1956, N 18,88:6
Lindsay, Arthur P, 1955, Ja 14,21:3
Lindsay, Bruce, 1945, Ag 22,23:6
Lindsay, Carolyn P Mrs, 1941, My 1,23:4
Lindsay, Charles B, 1965, Je 9,47:4
Lindsay, Charles W Sir, 1939, N 8,23:1
Lindsay, Daniel C, 1962, My 2,37:1
Lindsay, Daniel E, 1957, Ap 18,29:3
Lindsay, David, 1922, D 19,19:4
Lindsay, David (por), 1941, My 10,15:4
Lindsay, David B, 1968, My 5,86:8
Lindsay, Donald R, 1955, Je 26,77:2
Lindsay, Earl of, 1939, Ja 15,38:1
Lindsay, Edward Delano, 1915, My 2,20:5
Lindsay, Edward W, 1945, D 14,27:4; 1949, S 4,41:1
Lindsay, Elizabeth B Mrs, 1952, Ag 12,19:6
Lindsay, Elizabeth Lady, 1954, S 4,11:6
Lindsay, George, 1952, My 28,29:1
Lindsay, George A, 1937, F 9,23:3; 1957, F 20,33:3
Lindsay, George D, 1946, F 11,29:3
Lindsay, George H, 1916, My 26,11:4
Lindsay, George L, 1943, Ag 26,17:6; 1952, Ap 26,2
Lindsay, George N, 1961, D 21,27:1
Lindsay, George W, 1938, Mr 17,21:5
Lindsay, Godfrey Mrs, 1949, Ja 1,13:5
Lindsay, Guy W, 1952, S 24,33:4
Lindsay, Harris, 1905, Ag 15,1:3
Lindsay, Homer J Col, 1907, Mr 6,9:5
Lindsay, Howard (mem ser, F 16,37:1; will, F 24,-26:8), 1968, F 12,1:5
Lindsay, J S Rev, 1903, D 1,2:1
Lindsay, James, 1879, S 3,2:5
Lindsay, James L, 1943, Ag 13,17:3
Lindsay, James R, 1940, Ap 27,15:3
Lindsay, Jesse W Mrs, 1941, Ja 12,46:2
Lindsay, John, 1953, My 20,29:3
Lindsay, John D, 1951, F 8,33:3
Lindsay, John L, 1946, Ap 3,25:1
Lindsay, John R, 1956, Mr 4,88:2
Lindsay, John Wesley, 1912, Mr 7,11:5
Lindsay, Kate H Mrs, 1942, Ap 17,17:2
Lindsay, Lionel A, 1961, My 23,39:2
Lindsay, Melish M Jr, 1947, D 19,25:2
Lindsay, Merrill K, 1960, My 25,39:2
Lindsay, Philip, 1958, Ja 5,87:1
Lindsay, R B ex-Gov, 1902, F 14,9:6
Lindsay, R Bruce, 1947, F 17,19:5
Lindsay, R S Mrs, 1949, F 28,19:3
Lindsay, Ralph L, 1954, Ap 10,15:4
Lindsay, Robert G Mrs, 1965, My 18,39:3
Lindsay, Robert H, 1938, Mr 21,15:2; 1962, Ja 23,
Lindsay, Roland Mrs, 1918, My 3,15:5
Lindsay, Ronald, 1945, Ag 23,23:1
Lindsay, Samuel M, 1959, N 13,26:2
Lindsay, Samuel M Mrs (por), 1948, Mr 1,23:4
Lindsay, Samuel T, 1938, O 11,25:5
Lindsay, Thomas B Mrs, 1954, S 11,17:6
Lindsay, V, 1931, D 6,31:3
Lindsay, Vachel Mrs, 1954, Ag 9,17:6
Lindsay, W, 1878, My 27,5:3
Lindsay, Wallace M Prof, 1937, F 22,17:2
Lindsay, William B, 1921, S 18,22:3
Lindsay, William Ex-Sen, 1909, O 16,9:4
Lindsay, William J, 1958, Ap 29,29:1
Lindsell, Gerald, 1953, Je 29,21:2
Lindsell, Harry J MRs, 1953, My 31,73:2
Lindsets, Peter A, 1943, F 27,13:4
Lindsey, Ben B (por), 1943, Mr 27,13:1
Lindsey, Charles T Sr, 1953, Ja 6,29:2
Lindsey, Earl of, 1938, Ja 4,23:1
Lindsey, Emily, 1944, Mr 5,36:2
Lindsey, Frederick B, 1937, Ap 25,II,9:1
Lindsey, Frederick V (por), 1942, N 18,25:5
Lindsey, G Walter, 1941, D 4,25:6
Lindsey, Jim, 1961, Ja 25,24:3
Lindsey, Joseph B, 1939, O 28,15:5
Lindsey, Julian (por), 1948, Je 28,20:2
Lindsey, Mort, 1959, My 17,83:3
Lindsey, S D, 1884, My 1,2:4
Lindsey, T S L S Ry, 1903, Jl 21,9:6
Lindsey, William, 1922, N 26,6:3
Lindsey, William H, 1940, Jl 28,27:3
Lindskoog, John D, 1958, N 5,35:4
Lindsley, A Van S, 1885, Je 25,7:5
Lindsley, Charles, 1906, Mr 10,11:5
Lindsley, Charles A, 1948, Mr 13,15:7
Lindsley, Charles B Dr, 1937, N 18,23:3
Lindsley, Charles P Dr (will, Ap 2,3:5), 1937, 23:5
Lindsley, Clarence E, 1961, Je 6,37:2
Lindsley, Clarence E Mrs (H I Williams), 196 My 8,35:4
Lindsley, Emily E, 1944, O 19,23:1
Lindsley, Halsted, 1945, Mr 24,17:4
Lindsley, Henry D (por), 1938, N 19,17:3
Lindsley, James, 1948, S 4,15:4
Lindsley, John Nichol, 1918, Je 12,13:5
Lindsley, Lorna (Margt A S), 1956, Jl 14,15:1
Lindsley, Reginald Mrs, 1950, My 31,29:4
Lindsley, Stuart, 1942, Ja 21,17:4

Lindsley, Thomas D, 1949, Ag 6,17:6
Lindsley, Van S, 1951, Ag 6,21:4
Lindsley, Van S Mrs, 1961, F 8,31:3
Lindstedt, William E Mrs, 1944, F 27,38:4
Lindstone, Carl E, 1951, D 10,29:4
Lindstroem, Adolf, 1939, S 23,17:5
Lindstrom, Austin J, 1940, Jl 11,19:1
Lindstrom, C O, 1947, N 5,27:2
Lindstrom, Claude B, 1957, D 31,17:4
Lindstrom, Ellen, 1923, S 17,15:1
Lindstrom, Frank L, 1952, F 7,27:5
Lindstrom, Peter J, 1959, Ap 2,31:5
Lindstrom, Stanley E, 1961, My 26,33:5
Lindstrom, W J, 1940, My 25,17:5
Lindvall, Robert W, 1963, Je 7,31:1
Lindy, Jacob D, 1945, Jl 24,23:3
Line, Edgar P, 1940, N 22,23:6
Line, Francis M, 1947, O 23,25:4
Line, Harry H, 1948, Jl 30,17:1
Line, Mervin L, 1943, N 28,68:6
Line, Thomas B, 1951, Jl 14,13:4
Line, William, 1964, F 15,23:3
Lineaweaver, Thomas H, 1955, O 20,36:2
Lineback, Paul E, 1939, Mr 1,21:6
Linebarger, Paul M A, 1966, Ag 7,80:6
Linebarger, Paul M W (por), 1939, F 21,19:1
Linebaugh, Jessie J, 1948, Ag 3,25:4
Lineberger, Abel C, 1947, D 30,23:3
Lineberger, John D, 1946, D 27,19:4
Lineberger, Walter F, 1943, O 12,27:4
Linecum, Dr, 1874, D 26,2:7
Linehan, Cornelius C, 1948, Mr 11,27:3
Linehan, Daniel M, 1948, Ag 9,19:4
Linehan, Frank J, 1957, Ja 11,23:3
Linehan, Frederick J, 1966, Ja 30,84:6
Linehan, Jerome F, 1962, Mr 14,39:2
Linehan, Joseph P, 1958, Je 5,31:5
Linehan, Leo L, 1962, Jl 26,27:4
Linehan, Nicholas Sr, 1950, F 14,25:3
Linehan, Paul H, 1967, S 21,47:3
Linehan, Paul H Mrs, 1957, Jl 13,17:2
Linehan, Richard E, 1957, O 22,33:1
Linehan, William F, 1959, Mr 16,31:2
Linen, James A Jr, 1957, D 7,21:1
Linen, Robert W, 1956, Mr 7,33:4
Linenthal, Harry Mrs, 1955, F 13,87:2
Liner, Frank H, 1939, O 1,53:3
Liner, Irving L, 1944, N 28,23:2
Lines, Amelia Dr, 1909, S 13,9:6
Lines, Arthur D, 1947, Mr 15,13:5
Lines, E S Bishop, 1927, O 26,29:3
Lines, Edwin S Mrs, 1945, My 20,32:4; 1953, Ap 10, 21:4
Lines, H K, 1928, Ag 10,19:3
Lines, Ira L, 1943, Ja 22,20:2
Lines, Lester F, 1953, O 8,29:5
Lines, Mary L, 1942, O 6,23:4
Lines, Samuel D, 1903, D 13,7:6
Lines, Stephen, 1942, Jl 7,19:3
Lines, Sterling C, 1940, Ag 21,19:5
Lines, Theodore Truesdale, 1914, Ap 17,11:6
Lines, Thomas D, 1910, D 12,9:5
Lines, William S Jr, 1941, S 12,22:2
Linett, Louis Mrs, 1957, Jl 19,19:2
Linevitch, Lt-Gen, 1908, Ap 24,9:4
Liney, John J, 1961, Ja 25,33:4
Ling, Armin F, 1943, My 25,23:5
Ling, Joseph B, 1949, Ja 7,21:2
Ling, Percy, 1947, Je 17,25:1
Ling, Ping Mrs, 1959, D 2,43:2
Ling, Richie, 1937, Mr 6,17:2
Lingafelt, Georgia, 1957, Jl 25,23:4
Lingard, Catherine, 1921, Ap 21,13:5
Lingard, George, 1876, O 30,1:4
Lingborg, Oscar O, 1941, Ag 22,15:1
Linge, F John Mrs, 1949, Ap 29,23:1
Linge, Herbert M, 1946, N 25,27:3
Lingelbach, Anna Lane (Mrs Wm E), 1954, Jl 16, 21:6
Lingelbach, William E, 1962, N 25,86:4
Lingeman, Katherine, 1948, N 29,23:5
Lingenfelter, Horace D, 1948, N 18,28:3
Lingenfelter, Marcy C, 1952, Mr 18,27:3
Lingerman, George F, 1956, Ap 3,35:3
Lingham, Fred J, 1954, O 12,27:5
Lingham, M V, 1882, Mr 7,2:3
Lingle, Harvey D, 1950, Ap 18,31:4
Lingle, Henry F, 1951, N 1,29:3
Lingle, James M, 1939, Je 28,21:2
Lingle, Thomas W Mrs, 1962, Mr 8,31:4
Lingle, William H, 1941, N 5,23:3
Lingley, C R, 1934, Ja 31,17:3
Lingo, John A Jr, 1949, Jl 17,58:3
Lingo, Kelsey F, 1951, Ag 20,19:4
Lingren, John O A, 1950, Jl 7,19:4
Lings, Albert Msgr, 1915, Jl 3,7:7
Lingwood, Adrian, 1937, Ag 9,8:7
Lingwood, David, 1937, Ag 9,8:7
Linhares, Jose, 1957, Ja 27,84:2
Linherr, Caroline C, 1950, Je 7,29:3
Linhos, Conrad M, 1943, N 22,19:4
Liniger, George W, 1907, Je 9,9:5
Lininger, William G, 1943, Je 25,17:5

Linitis, Jack S, 1939, Ag 30,10:2
Link, Albert, 1965, F 15,27:2
Link, Alfred J, 1949, O 9,92:6
Link, Arthur, 1962, My 24,35:5
Link, Charles, 1941, D 18,27:3; 1946, Jl 8,29:3
Link, Charles E, 1956, S 16,84:6
Link, Conrad B Mrs, 1948, My 21,23:2
Link, Edgar B, 1959, Ap 25,21:5
Link, Edward G Mrs, 1944, S 11,17:5
Link, Francis Mrs, 1952, Jl 11,17:4
Link, Frank S, 1961, Ag 2,29:2
Link, George A, 1938, Mr 15,23:5
Link, George A Mrs, 1948, Ag 31,23:1
Link, George J Jr, 1953, My 6,31:3
Link, George K K Mrs, 1943, N 22,19:5
Link, George K Mrs, 1962, S 11,33:3
Link, George M, 1942, Mr 28,17:2
Link, Harry, 1956, Jl 6,21:2
Link, Henry A, 1950, Ap 19,29:5
Link, Henry C, 1952, Ja 10,29:1
Link, J Louis Mrs, 1945, Jl 22,37:2
Link, John H, 1955, Je 11,15:2
Link, Michael S, 1911, Ap 11,11:5
Link, Raphael, 1963, Je 22,23:4
Link, Raphael Mrs, 1944, Je 21,19:5
Link, Robert E, 1939, S 3,19:4
Link, Robert H, 1957, Ag 15,21:4
Link, Samuel B, 1961, Ap 1,17:6
Link, Stanley J, 1957, D 25,31:3
Link, Walter E, 1951, S 29,17:3
Link, William W, 1950, S 25,23:4
Linke, Charles I, 1948, F 8,60:4
Linke, Frank, 1924, Ap 17,19:4
Linke, Victor Mrs, 1958, Ag 9,13:2
Linkenbach, Charles L, 1942, Ap 13,15:2
Linker, Charles G, 1942, D 1,25:2
Linker, Henry, 1968, F 25,41:4
Linker, Phil Y, 1949, F 4,23:1
Linker, Regina Mrs, 1916, O 24,12:7
Linkman, Louis B, 1957, Ja 14,23:3
Linkomies, Edwin, 1963, S 9,27:3
Linkroum, Rachel J Mrs, 1939, Mr 24,21:5
Linley, Betty, 1951, My 11,28:3
Linlithgow, Dowager Lady, 1937, Ap 5,19:2
Linlithgow, Dowager Marchioness of (Doreen Maud), 1965, Ag 4,35:4
Linlithgow, Lord (V A J Hope), 1952, Ja 6,92:1
Linlithgow, Marquess of (Jno Adrian Louis Hope), 1908, Mr 2,9:5
Linn, Alex P (Bro Alphonsus Fidelis), 1960, F 4,31:4
Linn, Allen Mrs, 1953, S 21,25:4
Linn, Bettina, 1962, Ap 8,87:3
Linn, Charles A, 1950, S 13,27:1
Linn, Clarence F, 1950, O 31,27:1
Linn, Conn, 1953, Ja 28,27:5
Linn, Frederick Sr, 1947, My 21,25:5
Linn, Gary Mrs, 1957, Ag 2,19:1
Linn, George S Mrs (P Soberances), 1941, F 24,15:3
Linn, George W, 1966, Mr 28,33:4
Linn, Henry H, 1963, D 9,35:2
Linn, Hugh H, 1948, S 21,27:4
Linn, James P, 1937, D 17,25:3
Linn, James W (por), 1939, Jl 17,19:3
Linn, James W Mrs, 1952, My 24,19:4
Linn, Julia C, 1919, Mr 10,11:4
Linn, Ludwig C, 1950, Ap 20,29:3
Linn, Oscar H, 1945, Ja 6,11:5
Linn, Scott Mrs, 1965, Mr 4,31:1
Linn, Walter, 1961, D 8,37:3
Linn, William A, 1917, F 24,9:4
Linn, William B, 1950, Je 14,31:1
Linn, William H, 1941, O 22,23:4
Linn, Winfield Scott, 1953, F 19,23:1
Linnane, William A, 1960, My 23,29:6
Linnard, Daniel M, 1949, S 3,13:3
Linne, Hans S, 1939, N 23,27:1
Linneborn, Edward C, 1942, Mr 27,23:2
Linnehan, James M, 1945, O 14,44:3
Linnehan, Jeremiah M, 1942, Ag 10,19:6
Linnekin, Thomas J Capt, 1904, N 1,9:6
Linnekin, William S, 1938, Ap 24,II,7:3
Linnell, Clarence I, 1942, Ap 6,15:5
Linnell, Edward H Dr, 1925, Jl 28,13:5
Linnell, John, 1882, Ja 21,2:6
Linnell, William S, 1968, F 15,43:4
Linneman, Henry, 1912, Ja 8,13:5
Linney, Joseph R, 1952, F 20,29:2
Linney, William J, 1956, S 24,27:3
Linquist, Maurice F, 1947, Je 27,21:5
Linquist, Maurice F Mrs, 1937, Jl 25,II,7:3
Lins, Adolph J, 1940, N 7,25:3
Lins, John, 1957, Ap 27,19:4
Lins, William G, 1946, O 15,25:3
Lins de Barros, Joao A, 1955, Ja 27,23:1
Lins Do Rego, Jose, 1957, S 13,23:2
Linscott, Charles E, 1947, O 7,27:3
Linscott, Charles H, 1943, Ag 4,17:6
Linscott, Robert N, 1964, S 27,86:1
Linse, Walter, 1960, Je 9,8:4
Linser, Louis P, 1950, Mr 7,28:3
Linsey, William, 1905, Ap 17,9:6
Linsingen, A von, 1935, Je 6,22:2
Linsky, Harold, 1959, D 29,25:2

Linsky, Samuel A, 1950, Ja 20,25:5
Linsler, Mary Mrs, 1948, Mr 10,27:2
Linsley, Daniel E, 1937, N 30,23:4
Linsley, George T Rev, 1937, Ag 7,15:3
Linsley, J Chauncey, 1960, Mr 30,37:4
Linsly, Jared, 1878, Ja 28,3:5
Linsmann, Henry F, 1947, Jl 11,15:2
Linson, Corwin K, 1959, Je 11,33:1
Linson, John J Ex-Sen, 1915, Ag 3,9:6
Linson, Washington F, 1944, Ag 20,33:2
Linson, William H, 1938, F 12,15:5
Linstedt, William E Dr, 1914, Je 19,13:5
Lint, Perry A, 1944, Jl 27,17:6
Lint, Theodore, 1952, F 29,23:4
Linthicum, Charles Clarence, 1916, D 13,15:5
Linthicum, Daniel A, 1952, Jl 8,27:2
Linthicum, J C, 1932, O 6,23:1
Linthicum, J Charles Mrs, 1944, F 5,15:1
Linthicum, Jesse A, 1959, My 13,37:2
Linthicum, Josiah G, 1940, N 16,17:2
Linthicum, R, 1934, Ja 21,29:1
Lintilhac, Francis E, 1957, O 17,33:4
Lintner, Robert C, 1960, Jl 27,29:4
Linton, Charles, 1966, F 22,23:5
Linton, David A, 1954, Jl 20,19:4
Linton, Edward F, 1921, Mr 28,11:6
Linton, Edwin, 1939, Je 5,17:4
Linton, Frank B A, 1943, N 16,23:1
Linton, Harry J, 1954, D 19,84:6
Linton, J Marshall, 1952, Ag 2,15:3
Linton, James Dromgole Sir, 1916, O 4,11:7
Linton, Jesse, 1958, S 21,87:2
Linton, Jesse Mrs, 1955, N 2,35:2
Linton, M Albert, 1966, My 3,47:4
Linton, Ralph, 1953, D 25,17:1
Linton, Richard W, 1954, Mr 30,27:6
Linton, Robert, 1942, N 14,15:5
Linton, Robert Mrs, 1947, N 9,74:5
Linton, William, 1953, Je 5,27:4
Lintott, E Bernard Mrs, 1953, Jl 2,23:6
Lintott, Edward B, 1951, Mr 13,31:2
Lintott, Kate E J Mrs, 1968, S 13,47:4
Lintott, Mary J, 1950, F 27,19:5
Lints, Francis Mrs, 1950, O 10,31:5
Lintz, Adam H Mrs, 1956, My 2,31:3
Linus, Bro (W N Quirk), 1950, Ag 2,25:3
Linville, Charles H, 1941, O 23,23:2
Linville, Clarence, 1938, My 26,25:5
Linville, Henry R Mrs, 1943, S 11,13:6
Linwood, Earle L, 1957, Ap 30,29:1
Linxweiler, Jacob H, 1951, O 11,37:2
Linxweiler, Theresa Mrs, 1960, S 28,39:3
Linz, E W (Eddie), 1954, Jl 31,13:5
Linz, Simon, 1952, N 5,27:4
Linzel, Frank A, 1952, Ag 9,13:6
Linzel, Frank A Mrs, 1953, Je 4,29:5
Linzmayer, Joseph J, 1951, Jl 24,25:1
Liomin, Frederick, 1950, O 18,33:2
Lion, Albert F, 1956, Je 25,23:1
Lion, Hugo J, 1954, F 12,25:4
Lion, Leon M, 1947, Mr 29,15:6
Lion, Max, 1951, D 4,33:4
Lione, Michael F, 1954, Je 8,27:2
Lionetti, Domenick Mrs, 1960, F 27,19:6
Lionville, Joseph, 1882, S 11,5:3
Liota, Gasper J, 1958, F 8,19:4
Liotta, Frank V, 1965, Jl 3,19:6
Liotta, Mae C Mrs, 1943, D 20,23:4
Liotta, Orazio Mrs, 1960, Jl 29,25:2
Lipack, Louis, 1942, Mr 11,19:2
Lipari, Angelo, 1947, N 4,25:3
Lipari, Anthony I, 1953, Je 21,84:3
Lipari, Attilio F, 1938, F 15,25:6
Lipatti, Dinu, 1950, D 3,88:4
Lipchitz, Louis, 1962, Jl 31,30:2
Lipe, Walter H Mrs, 1960, Mr 21,29:3
Lipe, Willard C, 1924, S 6,11:6
Lipetz, Alphonse, 1950, Ap 12,27:4
Lipetz, Basilla B, 1955, My 27,23:3
Lipford, Walter F, 1951, My 25,27:3
Lipin, Herman, 1955, S 3,15:5
Lipkin, William, 1962, Ag 14,31:3
Lipkins, Ronald, 1966, Ap 10,76:7
Lipkint, Arthur M, 1947, O 30,26:3
Lipkint, Arthur M Jr, 1954, O 25,27:3
Lipman, Abraham, 1938, Ap 14,23:3
Lipman, Adolph, 1941, Ag 28,19:6
Lipman, Albert I Mrs, 1957, Ag 9,19:4
Lipman, Alvah S, 1911, Ap 6,11:5
Lipman, Charles B (por), 1944, O 23,19:4
Lipman, Charles K, 1919, Jl 3,13:5
Lipman, Edward C, 1959, O 3,19:3
Lipman, Frederick L, 1950, My 12,27:3
Lipman, Harry, 1958, Ag 31,57:2
Lipman, Jacob, 1958, O 24,33:1
Lipman, Jacob G (por), 1939, Ap 20,23:1
Lipman, Jerry, 1943, D 3,23:2
Lipman, Martin, 1950, Ap 9,85:1
Lipman, Nathan, 1962, Ja 26,31:2
Lipman, Philip Rabbi, 1924, Ja 15,19:4
Lipman, Rubin Mrs, 1944, My 5,19:3
Lipman, Samuel, 1938, O 8,17:4; 1962, D 2,88:8
Lipman, Samuel Mrs, 1946, D 20,24:3

Lipman, Walter L, 1952, O 28,31:2
Lipman, William T, 1950, O 25,35:4
Lipner, Abraham, 1945, F 9,15:4
Lipon, John Sr, 1950, F 21,25:1
Lipp, Albert I, 1943, F 18,23:4
Lipp, Clinton C, 1950, Ap 22,19:4
Lipp, Harvey E, 1924, Jl 31,13:6
Lipp, J J, 1958, Je 17,29:4
Lipparini, Giuseppe, 1951, Mr 7,33:3
Lippe, Constantine, 1885, Je 3,5:6
Lippe, Herman F, 1960, Je 4,23:2
Lippe, Samuel, 1941, Je 23,17:2
Lippe, Vincent S, 1946, Jl 26,21:4
Lippe, Vincent S Mrs, 1950, Jl 7,20:3
Lippe, Waldemar Prince, 1904, S 27,9:6
Lippencott, George W Mrs, 1943, O 5,25:4
Lippens, Maurice Count, 1956, Jl 15,61:1
Lipper, Aaron, 1939, N 23,27:4
Lipper, Arthur, 1956, D 11,39:1
Lippert, Harold B, 1952, Ja 15,27:3
Lippert, Leon, 1947, Je 29,48:3
Lippert, Robert H E, 1941, O 23,23:1
Lippert, Robert T, 1944, O 20,20:2
Lippert, William L, 1943, Ap 10,17:3
Lippi, Andrew F, 1951, D 15,13:6
Lippincott, Alice D, 1940, F 20,21:2
Lippincott, Arthur H, 1940, D 16,23:5
Lippincott, Arthur H Mrs (will), 1948, N 10,60:3
Lippincott, B C Rev, 1925, Ag 14,13:6
Lippincott, Benjamin C Rev Dr, 1912, Ja 21,II,13:2
Lippincott, Benjamin Mrs, 1943, D 31,16:6
Lippincott, Carter H, 1954, O 2,17:1
Lippincott, Charles S, 1956, Mr 26,29:4
Lippincott, Clifford S, 1949, Ap 9,17:2
Lippincott, De Witt G Dr, 1905, Je 9,2:1
Lippincott, Donald F, 1962, Ja 11,33:4
Lippincott, Edward N, 1948, Ag 15,60:5
Lippincott, Franklyn M, 1941, N 23,53:3
Lippincott, George C, 1951, N 22,31:2
Lippincott, Harold E, 1947, N 6,27:6
Lippincott, Harry P, 1942, Ja 23,20:2
Lippincott, Henry C, 1938, F 8,21:4
Lippincott, Henry Col, 1908, Ja 26,9:4
Lippincott, J Aubrey, 1938, O 7,23:2
Lippincott, J Bertram (por), 1940, Ja 20,15:1
Lippincott, J Bertram Mrs, 1938, My 17,23:5
Lippincott, J Dundas, 1905, Mr 7,9:6
Lippincott, Jesse T, 1938, Je 12,38:7
Lippincott, Joahua Allen Rev Dr, 1907, Ja 1,9:5
Lippincott, Job H, 1951, N 27,31:6
Lippincott, John H, 1947, N 24,23:3
Lippincott, Joseph Mrs, 1948, My 26,25:5
Lippincott, Joseph W Mrs, 1943, D 1,21:3
Lippincott, May T, 1937, Je 3,28:3
Lippincott, Norman, 1949, Ja 22,13:3
Lippincott, Ralph R, 1948, Je 16,29:1
Lippincott, Richard H, 1957, F 19,31:1
Lippincott, Robert R, 1947, O 25,19:1
Lippincott, Samuel R Jr, 1948, O 23,15:5
Lippincott, Theodore, 1909, My 13,7:6
Lippincott, Walter M, 1957, My 17,25:1
Lippincott, William A Jr, 1953, Ag 28,17:3
Lippincott, William D, 1944, F 14,17:4
Lippincott, William Henry, 1920, Mr 18,11:5
Lippincott, William J (por), 1946, Mr 11,26:2
Lippitt, Charles W Mrs, 1940, Ja 3,21:3
Lippitt, Charles Warren Ex-Gov, 1924, Ap 5,15:4
Lippitt, Costello, 1924, Ag 22,13:6
Lippitt, H F, 1933, D 29,21:1
Lippitt, Henry F Mrs, 1961, Jl 28,21:3
Lippitt, Pomeroy Mrs, 1948, Je 13,68:5
Lippitt, Robert Lincoln, 1910, Je 27,7:4
Lippman, Abraham, 1910, Mr 22,11:2
Lippman, David H, 1940, Mr 29,22:2
Lippman, Frances, 1958, Ap 19,21:6
Lippman, Francis L, 1940, F 21,3:4
Lippman, Harry, 1960, Mr 25,27:3
Lippman, Irving O, 1958, S 16,28:1
Lippman, Isaac, 1955, Je 24,19:1
Lippman, Isaac Mrs, 1943, Je 10,21:4
Lippman, Jacob Mrs, 1962, F 23,29:3
Lippman, Julie M, 1952, Ap 13,76:4
Lippman, Martin, 1954, Ja 14,29:1
Lippman, Meyer, 1944, Mr 11,13:4
Lippman, Phil, 1941, O 18,19:4
Lippmann, Dan C, 1955, D 2,27:3
Lippmann, David, 1944, N 4,15:5
Lippmann, Gabriel, 1921, Jl 14,15:4
Lippmann, George (est tax appr), 1956, My 2,22:8
Lippmann, Henry (por), 1941, Je 21,17:3
Lippmann, Henry Mrs, 1949, Jl 13,27:4
Lippmann, Lionel, 1962, Je 4,29:3
Lippmann, Mortimer Mrs, 1948, N 24,23:2
Lippold, Henry F, 1958, Ja 1,25:5
Lippold, John, 1937, Mr 3,23:1
Lipponcott, Charles P, 1957, D 21,19:5
Lippoth, Robert S, 1953, Jl 31,19:1
Lippoth, William R, 1947, N 25,32:4
Lipps, Elmer G, 1948, D 21,31:2
Lips, Julius, 1950, Ja 25,27:2
Lipscher, Milton A, 1940, O 27,45:2
Lipschitz, Ezekiel, 1940, D 12,27:6
Lipschitz, Henry Mrs, 1939, Ja 23,4:3
Lipschitz, Hyman, 1956, Ja 27,23:1
Lipschitz, Israel, 1953, S 4,34:8
Lipschitz, Jacob A, 1958, O 13,29:4
Lipschitz, Joachim, 1961, D 12,43:4
Lipschitz, Meier Mrs, 1961, Ja 4,33:2
Lipschitz, Samuel, 1959, N 24,37:1
Lipschitz-Lindley, Werner, 1948, F 3,25:2
Lipschultz, Irving, 1957, Je 18,33:3
Lipschutz, Benjamin, 1944, My 27,15:4; 1961, Je 25, 76:6
Lipschutz, Ephraim, 1949, My 12,31:4
Lipschutz, Jacob M Dr, 1912, My 10,11:4
Lipschutz, Leo, 1958, My 17,19:6
Lipschutz, Marty N Mrs, 1950, Ja 28,13:4
Lipschutz, Samuel, 1954, My 13,29:2
Lipscomb, Alex B, 1940, O 5,15:6
Lipscomb, Charles E (por), 1937, Jl 7,23:3
Lipscomb, Charles T, 1964, N 4,39:1
Lipscomb, Gaston J, 1968, Je 14,47:2
Lipscomb, Gene (Big Daddy),(funl, My 16,17:4), 1963, My 11,20:4
Lipscomb, George D, 1957, Ja 22,29:5
Lipscomb, James E, 1951, My 17,31:5
Lipscomb, M M Capt, 1903, Je 9,9:6
Lipscomb, William H, 1957, Jl 30,23:1
Lipscomb, William P, 1945, N 24,19:2; 1958, Jl 26,15:5
Lipscott, Alan, 1961, N 22,33:4
Lipset, Alfred, 1959, My 14,33:2
Lipset, Joseph, 1955, F 13,87:1
Lipset, Meyer, 1951, D 6,33:4
Lipsett, James J, 1937, N 30,23:1
Lipsett, Robert W, 1939, O 1,53:2
Lipsey, David H, 1956, Mr 29,27:5
Lipsey, Donald B, 1954, Mr 14,88:5
Lipsey, P I, 1947, Jl 17,19:3
Lipsey, William N, 1940, N 23,17:3
Lipshie, Joseph, 1968, S 29,80:2
Lipshitz, David, 1947, Ag 21,23:3
Lipshutz, Samuel Mrs, 1952, My 2,25:5
Lipsig, Irving A, 1967, O 30,45:4
Lipsit, Moise, 1958, Ag 7,25:1
Lipsitz, Herbert J, 1964, Ap 28,37:1
Lipsius, J George, 1951, F 8,33:4
Lipskar, Abraham, 1952, Ja 21,15:3
Lipski, Herman, 1967, O 8,86:1
Lipski, Jozef, 1958, N 3,37:1
Lipski, Samuel, 1956, D 5,39:3
Lipsky, Abraham, 1966, Je 6,41:2
Lipsky, Abram, 1946, My 4,15:6
Lipsky, Abram Mrs (cor on Jan 1 rept on death), 1968, Ja 7,85:1
Lipsky, Dinah R Mrs, 1941, N 14,23:5
Lipsky, Joseph, 1947, F 18,25:1
Lipsky, Louis (funl plans, My 29,33:2), 1963, My 28,37:1
Lipsky, Louis Mrs, 1959, Mr 17,33:3
Lipson, Lawrence, 1959, Mr 4,31:3
Lipson, Samuel, 1949, Jl 26,27:3
Lipstein, Philip, 1966, Ag 20,25:5
Lipstone, Louis R, 1954, Mr 20,15:5
Liptak, John Sr, 1951, Je 21,27:6
Lipton, Edgar L Mrs, 1964, My 16,25:7
Lipton, George, 1962, Mr 10,21:4
Lipton, Louis, 1966, N 28,39:3
Lipton, Louis M, 1967, Ap 10,35:3
Lipton, Maurice F, 1964, Jl 26,56:7
Lipton, T Sir, 1931, O 3,1:2
Lirio, Antonio, 1950, Ap 18,31:2
Lirot, Charles J, 1945, F 8,19:5
Lisboa, Miguel Dr, 1916, Ja 20,9:5
Lisburne, Regina, 1944, Ja 26,19:2
Lischer, Benno E, 1959, O 10,21:6
Lischer, Henry, 1903, D 9,9:5
Lischesky, Charles, 1947, O 15,27:2
Lischke, John A, 1939, D 5,27:1
Lisee, Joseph, 1946, Ag 30,17:3
Lishawa, Allen W, 1952, F 7,27:1
Lisitsyn, Peter I, 1948, F 22,48:4
Lisitzky, Ephraim E, 1962, Je 27,35:4
Lisk, Fred C, 1950, Mr 26,92:6
Liske, Victor B Mrs, 1957, Je 28,23:3
Liskin, Joseph, 1957, O 26,21:2
Liskin, Max, 1957, Ap 19,21:2
Liskin, Morris, 1953, Ja 22,23:4
Liskun, E F, 1958, Ap 21,23:5
Lisle, Arthur B, 1949, Ap 1,25:3
Lisle, Clifton, 1966, Ag 6,23:3
Lisle, Elizabeth, 1925, My 30,9:6
Lisman, Anthony A, 1910, N 16,11:5
Lisman, Frederick J, 1940, F 15,19:4
Lisman, Ralph J, 1965, Ag 3,31:3
Lisner, Sidney Mrs, 1947, O 22,29:2
Liss, Abe, 1963, D 2,37:5
Liss, Edward, 1967, F 1,39:3
Liss, Eleanor, 1944, Jl 29,13:6
Liss, Selman, 1958, S 21,87:2
Lissauer, Bernard, 1950, Mr 12,92:6
Lissauer, Bernard Mrs, 1949, My 12,31:3
Lissauer, Ernst, 1937, D 11,19:5
Lissauer, Harry, 1949, Mr 1,25:2
Lissauer, Meno, 1958, My 28,31:3
Lissberger, Benjamin (por),(will, N 23,21:6), 1937, N 20,17:2
Lissberger, L Walter, 1951, N 15,29:5
Lissel, E J K, 1880, F 29,7:5
Lissenden, David D Mrs, 1948, S 1,23:2
Lissenden, Walter A, 1947, N 18,29:5
Lissey, Bernard, 1942, Jl 11,13:5
Lissfelt, Harry L, 1945, Ja 31,21:5
Lissfelt, J Fred, 1965, Ap 17,19:6
Lissignolo, Augusta Mrs, 1939, Mr 1,21:5
Lissitzyn, James J, 1949, Ap 2,15:2
Lissman, Edward, 1962, Jl 30,23:3
Lissman, Edward Mrs, 1938, F 12,15:5
Lissman, Edward Rev Dr, 1914, Ja 29,9:6
Lissner, Arthur, 1942, O 24,15:5
Lissner, Earle deWitt, 1968, Mr 29,45:4
Lissner, Emil, 1939, Mr 31,21:6
Lissner, Ignatius, 1948, Ag 8,57:2
Lissner, Leo N, 1952, Je 18,27:2
Lissner, Morris Mrs, 1954, Mr 7,46:6
List, Emanuel, 1967, Je 24,29:5
List, Jacob S, 1967, Ag 17,37:3
List, Leonardo J Mrs, 1943, S 17,21:6
List, William H Jr, 1958, F 6,27:4
Listemann, Paul, 1950, S 21,32:2
Listemann, Sophia Mrs, 1938, N 25,23:3
Lister, Alfred H Mrs, 1950, Je 11,92:1
Lister, Alice, 1952, Je 2,10:5
Lister, Arthur S, 1948, Mr 2,23:3
Lister, Charles B, 1951, My 16,35:3
Lister, Daniel I, 1948, Ja 30,23:3
Lister, Edward J, 1967, My 12,47:3
Lister, Ernest, 1919, Je 15,22:4
Lister, Ernest Mrs, 1923, My 28,15:4
Lister, Francis, 1951, O 30,29:4
Lister, Frederick A, 1960, Jl 20,29:2
Lister, John W, 1948, N 16,29:1
Lister, Reginald Sir, 1912, N 11,11:4
Lister, Spencer Sir, 1939, S 8,23:2
Lister, Thomas, 1905, Ap 13,11:5
Lister, Thomas (Lord Ribblesdale), 1925, O 22,25:
Lister, Thomas W, 1950, O 7,19:3
Lister, Walter B, 1967, My 4,39:1
Lister, Walter B Mrs, 1967, Mr 16,47:1
Lister, Walter S, 1951, D 6,33:4
Lister, Walter S Mrs, 1952, Je 2,10:5
Lister, William, 1953, Je 14,85:1
Lister, William P, 1954, Mr 20,15:3
Lister, William T, 1944, Jl 10,15:5
Lister-Kay, Lady (por),(will, F 27,16:3), 1943, F 48:6
Lister-Kaye, Jon Sir, 1924, My 28,23:4
Listhardt, George D, 1944, My 25,21:3
Listman, Charles, 1939, My 9,24:4
Listman, George L, 1950, F 3,23:4
Liston, Cary (Mrs J H Gaiser), 1964, N 10,47:3
Liston, Emil S, 1949, O 27,27:4
Liston, Hardy Sr, 1956, O 22,29:4
Liston, Millie, 1920, F 21,13:4
Liston, Thomas E, 1951, F 11,89:1
Listowel, Earl of, 1931, N 17,25:1
Liswood, Jacques, 1963, O 12,23:4
Liszniewski, Karol Mrs, 1947, S 27,15:3
Liszt, Abbe Franz, 1886, Ag 1,7:1
Lit, David J, 1944, F 24,15:2
Lit, Jacob D (will, Ja 29,39:1), 1950, Ja 21,17:1
Lit, Jacob Mrs, 1953, O 25,88:3
Lit, S D, 1929, Mr 1,25:1
Litch, Robert L, 1962, My 1,37:3
Litchfeild, Norman, 1967, F 8,31:2
Litchfield, Arthur V, 1961, Ap 28,31:3
Litchfield, Bayard S, 1960, S 19,31:1
Litchfield, Bayard S Mrs, 1957, Ap 16,33:4
Litchfield, Charles M Mrs, 1943, D 6,23:3
Litchfield, Edmund C, 1951, Jl 6,23:4
Litchfield, Edward H, 1949, N 26,8:1
Litchfield, Edward H Dr, 1968, Mr 10,29:1
Litchfield, Edward H Mrs, 1923, Ag 11,9:6
Litchfield, Edward Mrs, 1956, Ja 8,87:1
Litchfield, Electus D, 1952, N 28,25:1
Litchfield, Everett S, 1951, D 30,24:5
Litchfield, Frank W, 1939, Mr 15,23:2
Litchfield, G A, 1937, Ap 29,21:4
Litchfield, Grace, 1944, D 5,23:5
Litchfield, H G Col, 1902, Ja 29,9:5
Litchfield, Harry R Mrs, 1965, D 28,27:4
Litchfield, Henry E, 1940, S 1,21:2
Litchfield, Lawrence Jr, 1967, O 29,85:1
Litchfield, Marion, 1961, Ja 21,21:5
Litchfield, Paul W (est acctg, S 2,29:2), 1959, N 33:1
Litchfield, Percy, 1940, Jl 3,17:4
Litchfield, Robert B, 1962, S 30,87:1
Litchfield, Wilbur L, 1939, Ap 13,23:6
Litel, John Mrs, 1955, Ap 28,29:2
Lithgow, Charles D, 1947, Mr 14,23:5
Lithgow, James, 1952, F 24,84:8
Lithgow, Leslie G, 1957, My 24,25:3
Lithgow, Robert M, 1954, O 22,27:3
Lithgow, Walter D, 1951, O 5,27:2
Lithgow, William Mrs, 1964, Ag 8,19:7
Litio, Philip E, 1955, Ag 25,23:6
Litke, Nathan, 1954, O 29,23:2
Litle, Thomas J Jr, 1941, O 7,23:3
Litoshko, Yevgeny V, 1963, F 16,8:6

Litschert, Frank P, 1951, F 16,25:2
Litt, Edward, 1963, My 2,35:4
Litt, Henry, 1953, Jl 14,27:3
Litt, Jacob, 1905, S 28,9:6
Litt, Jonas, 1956, My 14,25:4
Litt, Ruth C V Mrs, 1937, Mr 31,23:5
Litt, Walter H, 1963, My 29,33:4
Litta, B Count, 1880, Mr 4,5:6
Litta, Eugenia di Duchess, 1914, Ap 8,13:4
Litta, Mlle, 1883, Jl 8,7:5
Littauer, Kenneth P, 1968, Jl 16,39:4
Littauer, Lucius N, 1944, Mr 3,15:1
Littauer, Milton H, 1951, Jl 13,21:6
Littauer, Nathan J, 1968, Jl 7,53:1
Littauer, William (will, O 30,25:6), 1953, O 13,29:2
Littauer, William Mrs, 1948, My 16,68:4
Littaver, E Victor Dr, 1968, O 22,47:4
Littel, Clair F, 1966, My 16,37:2
Littel, Emlen T Mrs, 1964, F 8,23:6
Littell, Anna, 1941, N 7,24:2
Littell, Anne B, 1961, Mr 6,25:2
Littell, Charles S, 1942, S 19,15:5
Littell, E W, 1881, Jl 27,8:2
Littell, Elton G, 1962, F 4,82:4
Littell, Emlen T, 1937, Jl 10,15:2
Littell, F Joseph, 1956, O 3,33:3
Littell, George R Sr, 1949, N 22,29:3
Littell, Herbert L, 1951, Ag 15,27:3
Littell, Howard H, 1943, Ja 3,42:2
Littell, Isaac W Brig-Gen, 1924, My 2,19:5
Littell, Isaac W 3d, 1963, S 6,29:2
Littell, James R W, 1946, Ja 23,27:3
Littell, John W, 1903, Jl 8,9:7
Littell, Joseph R, 1950, Mr 3,25:3
Littell, Margaret, 1966, Ja 7,27:3
Littell, Philip, 1943, N 2,25:1
Littell, Robert, 1963, D 7,28:5
Littell, Robert B, 1959, My 26,35:5
Littell, Robert R, 1962, D 7,39:4
Littell, S Harrington, 1967, N 16,47:1
Littell, Theodore F, 1912, D 23,9:4
Littell, Walter R, 1955, N 16,35:3
Littell, William B, 1965, Ja 23,25:1
Litten, Arthur S, 1954, N 21,87:2
Litten, Charles P, 1967, D 12,47:1
Litten, Frederick N, 1951, Jl 27,19:1
Littenberg, Michael A, 1958, O 11,23:5
Litter, Louis, 1951, Ap 11,29:3
Litterbrant, William C Col, 1919, Jl 3,13:3
Litterer, John B, 1957, Ag 27,29:1
Litterer, John B Mrs, 1948, My 27,25:2
Litterer, William C, 1938, Ja 4,24:3
Litterick, William S Jr, 1962, F 13,12:4
Litterst, Alex C, 1953, F 13,21:4
Littick, Orville B, 1953, S 3,22:3
Littick, William O, 1941, N 30,69:3
Littig, Francis J, 1941, O 26,43:1
Littig, Harriet B, 1954, Jl 12,19:4
Littig, John V, 1938, F 3,23:3
Little, A B S, 1932, My 13,19:5
Little, A D, 1935, Ag 3,13:4
Little, Albert K, 1960, F 4,31:4
Little, Alice C, 1958, D 26,2:6
Little, Alonzo, 1954, N 16,29:5
Little, Amos R, 1906, D 17,11:5
Little, Andrew G, 1945, O 23,17:2
Little, Arthur W (por), 1943, Jl 19,15:1
Little, Arthur W Mrs, 1939, Ap 19,23:2
Little, Bascom, 1940, My 28,23:1
Little, C C, 1869, Ag 10,1:3
Little, C S, 1881, O 8,5:3; 1936, Je 7,II,8:5
Little, Carl V, 1959, Je 9,37:2
Little, Charles, 1950, Ja 10,29:4
Little, Charles Dr, 1921, D 29,15:4
Little, Charles E, 1945, Ag 3,17:3
Little, Charles H, 1947, D 21,52:4
Little, Charles Joseph Rev, 1911, Mr 12,II,13:3
Little, Chauncey, 1952, O 1,33:5
Little, Clarence A, 1946, Jl 4,19:6
Little, Clarence D, 1949, D 19,27:3
Little, Clarence J, 1963, Ap 13,19:5
Little, Clarence W, 1940, Ap 19,21:2
Little, David M, 1954, Ap 26,25:2
Little, David M Mrs, 1948, F 8,60:6
Little, Dillon A, 1950, O 27,29:5
Little, Duncan M, 1966, D 19,37:5
Little, Dwight R, 1961, Mr 29,33:4
Little, Edgar S, 1943, D 23,19:2
Little, Edith B, 1950, Ag 5,15:5
Little, Edward C, 1924, Je 28,13:5
Little, Edward H, 1964, O 19,33:5
Little, Edward P, 1940, F 18,41:3
Little, Edward S, 1940, F 8,23:5
Little, Elliotte, 1940, D 8,69:3
Little, Elmer, 1947, Jl 12,13:3
Little, Elsie, 1912, F 5,9:3
Little, Ernest L, 1957, Jl 25,29:1
Little, Eunice R Mrs, 1903, Ja 27,9:6
Little, Everett W, 1955, O 18,37:1
Little, Frank, 1944, F 6,42:5
Little, Franklin Mrs, 1963, Jl 22,23:5
Little, Fred A, 1945, D 13,29:5
Little, Frederick B, 1942, N 2,21:4
Little, Frederick S, 1950, Mr 23,36:5
Little, G Martin, 1959, N 11,35:1
Little, Gabriel C Mrs, 1944, N 19,50:1
Little, George, 1903, Jl 9,7:6
Little, George A, 1958, Ja 23,27:2
Little, George E, 1948, S 30,27:2; 1957, F 24,84:6
Little, George F, 1957, Ag 10,15:4
Little, George F Dr, 1925, D 6,13:1
Little, George J, 1937, Mr 18,25:4
Little, George T Dr, 1915, Ag 7,7:4
Little, George W, 1964, D 21,29:4
Little, George W Mrs, 1951, S 13,31:5
Little, Harry B, 1944, Ap 5,19:4
Little, Harry E, 1945, My 7,17:3
Little, Helen H B Mrs, 1937, S 21,25:1
Little, Henry, 1959, D 5,23:5
Little, Henry A, 1947, F 22,13:1
Little, Henry Mrs, 1940, D 5,25:3
Little, Henry Stafford Sen, 1904, Ap 25,9:6
Little, J, 1946, Ap 1,27:5
Little, J L Dr, 1885, Ap 5,9:3
Little, Jacob, 1865, Mr 29,4:4
Little, James F, 1938, Ag 12,17:2
Little, James H, 1947, S 7,60:6
Little, James S Sr, 1960, Ag 15,23:6
Little, John, 1937, My 17,19:3
Little, John D, 1957, Jl 31,23:5
Little, John M, 1964, Je 30,33:6
Little, John Mrs, 1920, Ja 26,7:1
Little, John T, 1951, O 12,28:2
Little, John W, 1947, Ap 4,23:3
Little, Joseph D, 1951, S 8,17:4
Little, Joseph J, 1952, Mr 20,29:3
Little, Joseph J Mrs, 1924, O 29,21:1
Little, Joseph James, 1913, F 12,15:4
Little, Joseph Sir, 1902, Jl 15,9:5
Little, Joseph V, 1938, S 28,25:1
Little, Kenneth, 1963, O 12,23:4
Little, Laura R, 1947, Mr 5,25:4
Little, Lawson, 1968, F 2,35:1
Little, Leroy L, 1925, My 1,19:4
Little, Louis M, 1960, Jl 18,27:4
Little, Louis M Mrs, 1949, N 22,29:4
Little, Louis R, 1948, N 14,76:4
Little, Luther, 1941, Ap 28,15:2
Little, Michael V, 1937, S 17,25:3
Little, Minnie L Mrs, 1942, D 4,25:5
Little, Paul N, 1954, S 18,15:5
Little, Phil, 1942, Ap 1,21:3
Little, Ralph B, 1965, Jl 29,27:5
Little, Ralph V, 1956, D 22,19:5
Little, Raymond, 1954, S 14,27:1
Little, Richard H, 1946, Ap 28,42:4
Little, Richard H Mrs, 1960, Jl 11,29:3
Little, Richard W, 1915, Jl 7,11:6
Little, Riley M, 1939, Ap 28,25:6
Little, Robbins, 1912, Ap 14,II,17:3
Little, Robert Forsyth, 1923, Jl 24,21:6
Little, Robert H, 1952, Ag 27,27:2
Little, Robert M, 1945, N 6,19:4
Little, Robert R, 1968, F 16,37:1
Little, Samuel, 1959, Ag 23,92:5
Little, Seelye W Dr, 1937, F 28,II,9:1
Little, Silas C, 1947, O 3,25:3
Little, Stephen, 1917, O 30,15:4
Little, Stephen C, 1938, F 16,21:2
Little, Stuart, 1968, My 29,39:4
Little, Susan E Mrs, 1938, O 30,41:4
Little, Teresa Mrs, 1938, Ag 12,17:5
Little, Thomas E, 1957, Ap 8,23:5
Little, Thomas F, 1942, Ja 24,17:5
Little, Thomas J, 1955, S 8,31:2
Little, W Paxton (por), 1940, Ja 9,23:4
Little, Walter J, 1960, O 14,33:2
Little, Wilbur, 1944, Ap 2,40:2
Little, Willard P Mrs, 1937, O 17,II,8:3
Little, William, 1948, O 20,29:4
Little, William A, 1940, O 2,23:1
Little, William A Mrs, 1955, Ap 7,27:5
Little, William F, 1939, Ap 21,23:2; 1946, S 20,31:2
Little, William F Sr Mrs, 1961, D 20,33:2
Little, William G, 1950, D 30,13:3
Little, William H, 1916, N 10,13:4
Little, William McCarthy (funl, Mr 15,11:6), 1915, Mr 13,13:6
Little, William N Mrs, 1959, Ap 26,87:1
Little, William Nelson Rear-Adm, 1925, Ja 5,21:4
Little, William T Mrs, 1955, Ja 9,87:2
Little, Winslow Mrs, 1965, Ap 9,33:2
Littledale, Clara S Mrs, 1956, Ja 10,31:3
Littledale, Harold A (trb lr, Ag 16,18:7), 1957, Ag 12,19:1
Littlefield, Amazon Mrs, 1948, Ja 3,13:4
Littlefield, Anna, 1952, Ja 5,11:4
Littlefield, Augustine F, 1946, My 23,21:3
Littlefield, Benjamin H (will), 1953, Jl 10,16:4
Littlefield, Catherine, 1951, N 20,31:1
Littlefield, Charles, 1902, S 1,7:6
Littlefield, Charles Edgar, 1915, My 3,11:1
Littlefield, Charles R Col, 1922, Ap 11,19:4
Littlefield, Charles W, 1939, Ag 8,17:1
Littlefield, Charles W (por), 1943, Ja 4,15:4
Littlefield, Charles W, 1961, Ag 12,17:2
Littlefield, Charles W Mrs, 1921, Ja 6,11:3
Littlefield, Edgar, 1949, S 21,31:4
Littlefield, F A Maj, 1911, Je 5,11:6
Littlefield, Frank H, 1945, Jl 26,19:4
Littlefield, Frank Mrs, 1944, My 16,21:5
Littlefield, Fred, 1946, O 16,27:3
Littlefield, Gilbert B, 1925, Ag 16,5:3
Littlefield, H C Maj, 1926, O 22,21:5
Littlefield, Harriet S, 1939, F 23,23:3
Littlefield, Henrietta, 1952, Mr 28,23:3
Littlefield, Henry K, 1952, Ap 4,25:3
Littlefield, I Allen, 1958, Je 24,31:4
Littlefield, Ivory, 1955, Mr 9,27:5
Littlefield, James B, 1947, D 4,31:5
Littlefield, James H Jr, 1946, Jl 22,21:4
Littlefield, James H Maj, 1901, Je 8,9:5
Littlefield, James H Mrs, 1957, My 10,27:4
Littlefield, Lelana H, 1924, Ap 10,23:5
Littlefield, Lloyd M, 1953, Mr 16,19:2
Littlefield, Lucien, 1960, Je 7,35:3
Littlefield, M S, 1934, Je 13,23:3
Littlefield, Minnie, 1951, O 21,92:4
Littlefield, Morton D, 1957, Ja 19,15:4
Littlefield, Nathaniel, 1882, Ag 16,5:4
Littlefield, Ralph Mrs, 1940, S 28,17:6
Littlefield, Raymond B, 1951, My 26,17:4
Littlefield, Walter, 1948, Mr 26,21:3
Littlefield, Walter Mrs, 1945, My 25,19:3
Littlefinger, Anna H Mrs, 1937, Ag 23,19:2
Littleford, Roger S Sr, 1959, My 8,27:1
Littlegreen, Sam J, 1953, Ag 14,19:3
Littlehale, Paul B Mrs, 1960, Ap 28,35:3
Littlehales, Lillian, 1949, Ag 9,25:4
Littlehales, Richard C, 1945, Je 21,19:4
Littlehales, Thomas, 1941, Jl 28,13:3
Littlejohn, A N Bishop (funl, Ag 8,7:5), 1901, Ag 4, 5:5
Littlejohn, Harry F, 1956, Ja 10,31:3
Littlejohn, James B, 1947, My 23,23:4
Littlejohn, Robert M, 1940, Ag 7,19:5
Littlejohn, Robert M Mrs, 1961, Jl 25,27:2
Littler, Edwin E, 1952, D 16,31:5
Littler, Edwin E Mrs, 1965, S 10,35:1
Littler, Ellsworth R, 1967, Mr 14,47:2
Littler, H G, 1956, Ag 4,15:6
Littles, Annabell D Mrs, 1943, N 22,19:4
Littleton, Benjamin H, 1966, Jl 8,36:1
Littleton, Douglas Marshall, 1919, Ja 5,22:4
Littleton, Jesse M, 1923, Ap 23,15:6
Littleton, Jesse T, 1966, F 26,25:2
Littleton, M W Sr, 1934, D 20,1:4
Littleton, Martin W, 1966, Ag 31,40:1
Littleton, Martin W Mrs, 1953, F 15,92:3
Littleton, Sanford, 1903, D 25,7:6
Littleton, William G, 1937, Jl 12,17:2
Littleton, William G Mrs, 1954, Ja 2,11:5
Littlewood, Frank B, 1960, S 7,37:6
Littlewood, Frank B Mrs, 1955, Ap 8,21:4
Littlewood, J Thompson, 1946, N 6,23:5
Littlewood, William, 1967, D 5,50:3
Littman, Albert, 1964, Mr 30,29:4
Littman, Carl, 1958, Ag 20,27:1
Littman, Joseph, 1953, Ag 22,15:2
Littman, Paul, 1950, N 3,27:2
Littner, Nathan, 1962, Ag 6,25:4
Litton, Abraham C, 1955, Jl 10,73:2
Littre, M P E, 1881, Je 3,5:4
Littridge, S S, 1903, S 30,9:6
Littwin, Charles, 1961, My 14,87:1
Litvin, Phil, 1951, Ag 22,25:6
Litvinov, Maxim M, 1952, Ja 2,1:6
Litwack, Abraham, 1959, Mr 6,25:5
Litwin, Harry, 1962, F 5,31:4
Litwin, Samuel, 1947, My 12,21:4
Litz, Andrew, 1949, O 9,92:2
Litz, Samuel J, 1939, S 11,19:3
Litzak, Abraham M (por), 1949, Ja 29,13:3
Litzenberg, Homer L, 1963, Je 29,23:5
Litzinger, Dorothy, 1925, Ja 6,25:5
Litzinger, Marie, 1952, Ap 8,29:3
Litzkuhn, Erwin B, 1948, S 2,24:3
Litzky, David, 1943, Mr 29,16:3
Liu, J Heng, 1961, Ag 27,84:2
Liu Hsiang, Gen, 1938, Ja 21,10:4
Liu Wen-hui, 1950, Mr 6,5:3
Liu Wen-tao, 1967, Je 13,47:2
Liu Ya-Lou, 1965, My 8,31:3
Liucci, Virgil, 1961, F 19,86:8
Liuzzi, Fernando, 1940, O 12,17:4
Liuzzi, Frank P, 1954, Ap 9,23:4
Liva, Henry, 1960, F 24,37:4
Livaccari, Philip J, 1966, Ja 11,27:4
Livanos, George M, 1964, Ap 29,41:1
Livanos, Stavros G, 1963, My 29,33:3
Liveing, George D Dr, 1924, D 27,9:4
Lively, Chauncy C, 1949, F 3,24:2
Lively, D O'C, 1933, D 2,30:3
Lively, Francis P, 1954, Mr 18,31:2
Lively, Robert D, 1943, Mr 9,23:2
Lively, Roger T, 1950, S 1,21:5
Lively, W S, 1944, O 27,23:3
Livengood, Chester R, 1942, Je 23,19:2
Livengood, Horace Mrs, 1949, Ag 24,25:5

Livengood, Horace R, 1951, Ja 1,17:4
Livengood, John E Mrs, 1941, Ap 27,38:3
Livengood, William W, 1962, Mr 15,35:3
Livergood, Ira D, 1953, Mr 6,20:7
Liveright, Ada F, 1962, D 7,39:3
Liveright, H, 1933, S 25,15:1
Liveright, Horace Mrs, 1947, F 11,27:4
Liveright, Howard, 1951, Ap 6,25:1
Liveright, I Albert Mrs, 1958, F 19,27:4
Liverman, Harry, 1961, Je 24,21:3
Liverman, Harry Mrs, 1960, Ag 9,27:5
Liverman, William Mrs, 1949, O 6,31:5
Livermore, A L Mrs, 1933, O 16,17:4
Livermore, Alvie R Jr, 1949, Ja 28,21:2
Livermore, Eliot P, 1941, F 27,19:2
Livermore, Frank D, 1951, Ag 17,17:3
Livermore, George G, 1951, Jl 4,17:5
Livermore, George Kirchway, 1968, My 20,47:3
Livermore, Harry A, 1966, Ap 18,29:3
Livermore, John R, 1906, My 4,9:3
Livermore, John Robert McDowell, 1925, My 9,15:4
Livermore, L E Rev, 1916, Ja 27,11:2
Livermore, Mary A, 1905, My 24,9:5
Livermore, Norman B, 1953, D 29,23:2
Livermore, Paul S, 1952, N 25,29:2
Livermore, Robert Sr, 1959, S 28,31:6
Livermore, Russell B, 1958, My 23,23:1
Livermore, Scott P, 1949, Mr 1,25:6
Livermore, Watson S, 1950, Mr 8,27:2
Livermore, Wendell B, 1940, Ap 4,23:5
Livermore, William R Col, 1919, S 29,13:2
Livernois, Frank, 1941, S 5,21:5
Liverpool, Earl of (Cecil Geo Savile Foljambe), 1907, Mr 25,7:5
Liverpool, Earl of, 1941, My 17,15:4
Livers, Arthur L, 1961, Ap 16,86:8
Liversay, John F B (por), 1944, Je 16,19:1
Liversedge, Harry B, 1951, N 26,25:1
Liversidge, Horace P, 1955, D 9,27:3
Liversidge, Robert M, 1947, My 21,25:4
Livesay, Everett Mrs, 1947, Ag 28,23:3
Livesay, J F B Mrs, 1953, Jl 29,23:5
Livesey, Frederick, 1961, Je 6,37:5
Liveseys, Francis B, 1925, Jl 3,13:5
Livezey, John R, 1938, N 21,19:6
Livingood, Charles J, 1952, F 27,27:4
Livingston, Alan Cameron, 1912, Ag 4,II,11:6
Livingston, Alex C, 1949, Ap 1,25:4
Livingston, Alida S, 1940, Ag 26,15:2
Livingston, Anson, 1873, Ag 6,5:7
Livingston, Archibald E, 1965, D 4,31:2
Livingston, Arnold, 1957, S 26,25:3
Livingston, Arthur, 1944, F 13,41:1
Livingston, Bancroft, 1945, My 2,23:5
Livingston, Benedict, 1967, N 13,47:2
Livingston, Burton E, 1948, F 9,17:2
Livingston, C, 1933, Ap 19,17:5
Livingston, Cambridge, 1879, S 19,5:6
Livingston, Carroll, 1904, Ap 27,9:7
Livingston, Charles A, 1946, Jl 16,23:6
Livingston, Charles P, 1938, N 22,23:4
Livingston, Chris H, 1949, Mr 30,25:3
Livingston, Crawford, 1925, N 17,25:4
Livingston, David, 1947, F 11,27:2
Livingston, David Mrs, 1944, Mr 13,15:5
Livingston, David 2d, 1949, F 16,25:1
Livingston, Donald C, 1957, Ja 19,15:3
Livingston, E Louis, 1908, Jl 16,7:7
Livingston, Eda F Mrs, 1955, O 22,19:3
Livingston, Edward, 1953, Mr 16,22:5
Livingston, Elbert C, 1946, Ja 25,23:4
Livingston, Frank B, 1948, Ja 3,13:4
Livingston, Fred H, 1945, F 13,23:1
Livingston, Frederick M, 1948, O 9,17:3
Livingston, Frederick M Mrs, 1962, S 28,33:4
Livingston, George A, 1949, Ja 5,25:1
Livingston, George E, 1941, N 14,23:1
Livingston, George L, 1961, F 12,86:2
Livingston, George W, 1937, O 19,25:2
Livingston, Gerald M, 1950, N 13,28:4
Livingston, Gilbert Robert, 1915, D 24,9:5
Livingston, Goodhue, 1951, Je 4,27:1
Livingston, Goodhue Mrs, 1960, Ja 17,86:4
Livingston, Guy H, 1948, Ja 11,56:3
Livingston, H S, 1939, D 3,60:8
Livingston, Harry A, 1963, Ag 5,16:1
Livingston, Harry A Mrs, 1951, Je 30,15:4
Livingston, Harry B, 1949, Ag 16,23:2
Livingston, Henrietta Ulrica, 1916, O 25,11:5
Livingston, Henry, 1948, S 11,15:2
Livingston, Henry S Mrs, 1949, Ag 5,19:4
Livingston, Henry W Mrs, 1923, Mr 27,19:5
Livingston, Henry 5th, 1956, Ap 2,23:4
Livingston, Herman, 1937, Ja 1,23:4
Livingston, Hermann, 1872, My 10,1:3
Livingston, Howard, 1950, Ap 25,31:3
Livingston, Hugh, 1884, Mr 12,5:5
Livingston, Idas F, 1949, Jl 5,23:3
Livingston, Ira B, 1953, Ja 8,27:1
Livingston, Irving O, 1957, My 28,34:2
Livingston, J A, 1884, S 2,4:6
Livingston, J H, 1927, Ja 28,17:4
Livingston, J Stevens, 1958, F 9,88:7
Livingston, Jacob A, 1959, Ag 18,30:1
Livingston, Jacob H, 1950, O 22,92:2
Livingston, James D Jr, 1956, Mr 30,19:2
Livingston, James D Mrs (Mar 12), 1963, Ap 1,36:1
Livingston, John G, 1961, Ja 10,47:4
Livingston, John G Mrs, 1955, Jl 4,11:6
Livingston, John H, 1916, My 15,9:6
Livingston, John H Jr, 1964, Mr 21,25:6
Livingston, John J, 1950, S 6,29:2
Livingston, John R, 1947, Jl 10,21:6
Livingston, John S Mrs, 1945, Je 1,15:4
Livingston, John Swift, 1867, My 31,2:2
Livingston, Johnston, 1911, My 8,11:5; 1939, O 11,27:4
Livingston, Julia, 1920, Mr 15,15:6
Livingston, Julian M, 1960, Mr 21,29:1
Livingston, Juliette B Mrs, 1940, My 29,23:2
Livingston, Julius I, 1910, Mr 2,9:4
Livingston, L L, 1882, F 28,7:2
Livingston, L P M, 1881, Ap 11,5:2
Livingston, La R Lt-Col, 1903, Mr 31,9:6
Livingston, Leon J, 1958, Ap 16,33:4
Livingston, Louis, 1959, Ag 20,26:2
Livingston, Louis D, 1947, Ap 20,60:7
Livingston, Lucian O Mrs, 1943, Ag 18,19:1
Livingston, Luther, 1914, D 25,11:6
Livingston, M Jr, 1879, S 13,8:2
Livingston, Manning Lt, 1863, Jl 24,4:6
Livingston, Margaret J S Mrs, 1942, Jl 25,13:3
Livingston, Margaret M Mrs, 1941, N 27,23:5
Livingston, Maturin Mrs, 1918, N 21,15:2
Livingston, Maurice Mrs, 1956, Ag 19,92:4
Livingston, Melvin J, 1956, My 25,23:2
Livingston, Meyer W (funl, My 29,11:5), 1916, My 26,11:3
Livingston, Myran J, 1968, N 14,47:2
Livingston, Noel B, 1954, Ja 18,23:4
Livingston, Park Mrs, 1957, N 19,33:4
Livingston, Paul Y, 1963, Ag 21,33:2
Livingston, Phil, 1938, Je 25,15:3; 1948, N 25,31:4
Livingston, Philip Mrs, 1908, S 17,7:6
Livingston, R E, 1933, Ja 30,13:1
Livingston, Ralph S, 1954, Je 1,27:2
Livingston, Richard M C (will), 1945, My 26,13:8
Livingston, Richard M Mrs, 1951, Ag 17,17:6
Livingston, Robert, 1948, F 20,28:2; 1951, Mr 17,15:4
Livingston, Robert E Mrs, 1910, F 11,11:6; 1944, Ag 25,13:3
Livingston, Robert F, 1950, Mr 27,23:3; 1955, Ja 16, 92:1
Livingston, Robert I, 1967, Ag 3,33:4
Livingston, Robert L, 1925, Ap 13,19:4
Livingston, Robert L Mrs, 1958, Ag 14,29:4
Livingston, Robert R, 1962, N 8,39:3
Livingston, Robert R Mrs (por), 1944, O 19,23:5
Livingston, Robert T, 1949, Je 30,23:5
Livingston, Robert Teviot, 1968, Ja 8,35:1
Livingston, Rosa (will), 1941, O 8,16:4
Livingston, S Otis, 1903, S 22,5:2
Livingston, Sanford J, 1964, N 4,39:4
Livingston, Saul A Mrs, 1960, Jl 27,29:2
Livingston, Sidney, 1946, Ja 17,23:3
Livingston, Sigmund, 1946, Je 15,21:4
Livingston, Sol Mrs, 1953, Ja 27,25:4
Livingston, Stephen M, 1955, Jl 27,23:6
Livingston, Syd, 1958, My 30,22:1
Livingston, Walter Chapman, 1909, Ja 1,11:7
Livingston, William, 1952, F 13,29:1
Livingston, William B, 1920, Je 18,11:3
Livingston, William H, 1943, Ap 9,21:4; 1951, F 7, 29:2; 1965, D 24,17:3
Livingston, William T, 1962, O 31,37:2
Livingstone, Austine E, 1944, Ja 24,17:5
Livingstone, Belle (funl, F 10,86:8), 1957, F 8,23:4
Livingstone, Charles, 1873, N 22,7:4
Livingstone, Colin H (por), 1943, F 2,19:5
Livingstone, David Rev Dr (funl, Ap 19,1:7), 1874, Ja 27,4:6
Livingstone, Dr, 1867, Mr 8,1:1
Livingstone, Helen, 1959, Ja 28,31:3
Livingstone, Henrico Mrs, 1910, Ja 14,9:3
Livingstone, Jeffrey D, 1958, F 26,27:3
Livingstone, John, 1940, Ja 24,21:1; 1945, Je 21,19:4
Livingstone, John Mrs, 1954, Ja 16,15:3
Livingstone, Richard W, 1960, D 28,27:1
Livingstone, Rob L Mrs, 1904, F 7,7:6
Livingstone, Robert Swift, 1867, Mr 1,4:6
Livingstone, Van Brugh, 1904, Mr 15,9:6
Livschutz, Mischa, 1943, Jl 15,21:2
Liwschitz-Garik, Michael M, 1959, F 9,26:2
Lizee, Albert J Mrs, 1951, My 11,28:3
Ljungberg, Frederick, 1944, Mr 13,15:5
Ljunggren, Aug, 1948, F 24,25:1
Ljunglund, Leonard, 1946, Jl 30,23:5
Llaca Argudin, Francisco, 1949, Ap 24,76:3
Lladoc, Casimiro, 1951, S 25,29:2
Llandaff, Viscount (Hy Matthews), 1913, Ap 5,15:4
Llaneras, Miguel, 1949, Mr 25,23:2
Llano, E, 1927, Ja 13,25:4
Llano, Rodrigo de (Jan 31), 1963, Ap 1,36:1
Llauger, Carlos, 1940, Ja 27,13:2
Llaverias, Federico Mrs, 1958, Mr 25,33:1
Llewellin, John J (funl, Ja 28,23:3), 1957, Ja 24,29:3
Llewellyn, Arthur, 1948, Jl 29,21:2
Llewellyn, David, 1937, Ap 4,II,10:8
Llewellyn, David R, 1940, D 16,23:5
Llewellyn, Henry J, 1940, Mr 21,26:4
Llewellyn, James R, 1962, O 18,39:3
Llewellyn, Joseph, 1940, Mr 9,15:1
Llewellyn, Karl N, 1962, F 15,29:1
Llewellyn, Mary E Mrs, 1941, D 25,23:4
Llewellyn, Maurice, 1951, O 24,32:3
Llewellyn, S J, 1925, S 5,13:6
Llewellyn, Thomas, 1947, Ap 9,25:4
Llewellyn, William (por), 1941, Ja 30,21:5
Llona, Numa Pompilio, 1907, Ap 6,7:7
Llona, Victor M, 1953, Je 7,84:3
Llopis, Carlos R, 1950, S 3,38:5
Llori, Homicide, 1953, Jl 2,31:2
Lloyd, A H, 1927, My 12,27:3
Lloyd, A S, 1936, Jl 23,21:1
Lloyd, Alice, 1949, N 18,29:4
Lloyd, Barbara E, 1954, Mr 21,89:1
Lloyd, Betty S Mrs, 1938, My 31,19:5
Lloyd, Bro (P H Hines), 1955, Ja 10,23:5
Lloyd, Carl T Mrs, 1955, Je 15,31:3
Lloyd, Charles A, 1940, N 12,23:1
Lloyd, Charles Dr, 1925, Mr 22,7:2
Lloyd, Charles E Sr, 1960, Mr 30,37:1
Lloyd, Charles M, 1948, D 7,31:5
Lloyd, Charles Mrs, 1940, S 7,15:4
Lloyd, Claude T, 1968, F 10,33:2
Lloyd, Cyrus T, 1949, D 5,23:4
Lloyd, Daniel B, 1943, D 9,27:4
Lloyd, David, 1959, Ja 20,35:4
Lloyd, David Frank, 1911, Je 7,9:4
Lloyd, De Courcy, 1944, O 18,21:3
Lloyd, Demarest (will, Jl 3,13:4), 1937, Je 25,21:3
Lloyd, E, 1927, Ap 1,23:4
Lloyd, E G Rawson, 1966, N 10,47:2
Lloyd, E Morris, 1961, F 13,27:5
Lloyd, E Morris Mrs, 1958, Jl 9,27:4
Lloyd, Edward, 1943, Mr 26,19:4; 1948, F 6,23:2
Lloyd, Edward L, 1959, Ap 1,37:5
Lloyd, Edward Mrs, 1944, O 17,23:1
Lloyd, Edward W, 1940, Je 27,23:4
Lloyd, Elizabeth E, 1957, Je 15,17:6
Lloyd, Elizabeth F Mrs, 1941, Ag 18,13:4
Lloyd, Everett T, 1947, N 16,77:1
Lloyd, Francis E, 1947, O 18,15:2
Lloyd, Francis Gen Sir, 1926, F 27,15:5
Lloyd, Francis Guerin, 1920, O 7,15:2
Lloyd, Francis W, 1950, Ap 29,15:2
Lloyd, Frank, 1960, Ag 11,18:1
Lloyd, Frank E, 1945, Mr 31,19:5
Lloyd, Frank Mrs, 1952, Mr 17,21:3
Lloyd, Frank S, 1954, Ap 2,28:3; 1957, Ja 7,25:5
Lloyd, Frank T Jr, 1962, My 9,43:3
Lloyd, Frank T Sr, 1951, N 23,29:1
Lloyd, Frederick E Mrs, 1945, My 25,9:6
Lloyd, Frederick W, 1949, N 26,15:4
Lloyd, Freeman, 1953, Ap 7,29:2
Lloyd, Freeman Mrs, 1949, S 12,21:5
Lloyd, Gaylord E, 1943, S 2,19:4
Lloyd, George, 1953, Je 15,24:8
Lloyd, George A Lord, 1941, F 6,21:1
Lloyd, George E, 1940, D 10,26:3
Lloyd, George L, 1955, Jl 16,15:5
Lloyd, George L Mrs (M Boswell), 1958, Jl 3,25
Lloyd, George W Capt, 1909, Jl 10,7:4
Lloyd, Gibbons O, 1941, Ap 21,19:5
Lloyd, Godfrey I H, 1939, F 14,19:3
Lloyd, H Rev, 1881, Ja 18,5:4
Lloyd, Harlan P Maj, 1913, O 4,13:4
Lloyd, Harold C, 1954, F 7,88:3
Lloyd, Harold H, 1949, Ap 5,30:3
Lloyd, Harold L Mrs, 1965, Mr 21,86:5
Lloyd, Henry A, 1917, Jl 27,9:6
Lloyd, Henry D, 1952, N 4,29:1
Lloyd, Henry D Mrs, 1957, D 5,35:5
Lloyd, Henry Demarest, 1903, S 29,9:5
Lloyd, Henry H, 1948, Ag 17,21:4
Lloyd, Henry W, 1950, N 16,31:2; 1961, O 8,87:3
Lloyd, Henry W Mrs, 1946, Je 29,19:2
Lloyd, Herbert G, 1939, S 24,44:8
Lloyd, Horatio G (por),(will, My 7,22:7), 1937, Ja 22,21:1
Lloyd, Howard E, 1945, Ap 15,14:5
Lloyd, Howard J, 1968, Jl 1,33:2
Lloyd, J Darsie, 1947, D 18,29:3
Lloyd, J F, 1903, Ap 26,2:3
Lloyd, J Paul, 1965, S 16,47:2
Lloyd, J R, 1952, Ag 14,23:4
Lloyd, J U, 1936, Ap 10,23:1
Lloyd, J W Mrs, 1959, Je 23,33:6
Lloyd, James H Brig-Gen, 1911, My 22,11:4
Lloyd, James T, 1944, Ap 5,19:6
Lloyd, John, 1940, Ja 29,15:2; 1946, S 19,31:3; 1 F 12,15:4
Lloyd, John A, 1947, Je 21,17:6; 1949, My 6,25:
Lloyd, John C, 1939, Ja 4,21:4
Lloyd, John E, 1947, Je 21,17:3
Lloyd, John F, 1948, Ap 23,23:3
Lloyd, John J, 1944, S 23,13:6
Lloyd, John Rev, 1924, Je 12,17:5
Lloyd, John S, 1949, F 12,17:6
Lloyd, Joseph D, 1948, Mr 31,26:2

Lloyd, Joseph P, 1964, F 8,23:3
Lloyd, Kate H, 1938, Ja 20,24:2
Lloyd, Laurence M Mrs, 1952, Mr 13,29:4
Lloyd, Lewis G Mrs, 1943, Mr 17,21:3
Lloyd, Llewellyn, 1945, S 1,11:3
Lloyd, Llewellyn Mrs, 1945, N 2,19:4
Lloyd, Llewelyn, 1949, O 3,17:5
Lloyd, Lola M Mrs, 1944, Jl 26,19:4
Lloyd, Malcolm Jr, 1949, Jl 28,23:3
Lloyd, Margaret (Mrs L A Sloper), 1960, Mr 2,37:2
Lloyd, Marie (funl, O 13,17:6), 1922, O 8,30:4
Lloyd, Milton S, 1954, My 18,30:5
Lloyd, Morton G, 1941, Ap 27,38:2
Lloyd, Nelson Ashley, 1925, Ja 28,17:4
Lloyd, Owen, 1941, Jl 10,19:5
Lloyd, Paul A, 1952, S 4,27:4
Lloyd, R McA, 1927, D 16,25:3
Lloyd, Ralph B, 1953, S 10,25:5
Lloyd, Ralph B Mrs, 1953, O 1,29:4
Lloyd, Ralph I Mrs, 1937, O 21,24:3
Lloyd, Raymond E, 1951, N 15,29:5
Lloyd, Richard L, 1937, Je 20,II,5:5
Lloyd, Robert, 1960, S 23,29:3
Lloyd, Robert E, 1951, Ap 13,23:5
Lloyd, Robert E Mrs, 1959, N 4,35:2
Lloyd, Robert M Mrs, 1959, Ag 4,27:4
Lloyd, Rodney Maclaine, 1911, My 18,11:6
Lloyd, Rollo D, 1938, Jl 26,19:2
Lloyd, Samuel, 1959, My 10,87:1
Lloyd, Stacy B, 1941, Jl 31,17:5
Lloyd, T Mortimer Mrs, 1948, O 12,25:4
Lloyd, Tex B, 1952, Jl 17,23:5
Lloyd, Thomas A, 1944, D 12,23:4
Lloyd, Thomas E, 1958, N 8,21:1
Lloyd, Thomas Francis, 1914, My 23,11:6
Lloyd, W, 1936, Ja 11,15:1
Lloyd, W Kenyon, 1954, Ag 10,19:5
Lloyd, Walter, 1947, Ja 15,26:3
Lloyd, Willard D Mrs, 1951, Ap 28,15:6
Lloyd, William, 1947, F 15,15:4
Lloyd, William (por), 1949, Ag 9,26:2
Lloyd, William B, 1946, Jl 11,23:2
Lloyd, William C, 1958, Ag 28,27:1
Lloyd, William E, 1948, S 4,15:2
Lloyd, William E Jr, 1942, O 7,25:5
Lloyd, William F, 1938, My 15,II,6:6
Lloyd, William F Sir, 1937, Je 14,23:4
Lloyd, William H, 1937, Ja 1,23:4; 1946, F 15,25:3
Lloyd, William Supplee, 1920, My 6,11:3
Lloyd-Butler, John Mrs, 1940, Ag 5,13:4
Lloyd George, David, 1945, Mr 27,1:2
Lloyd George, David Mrs (por), 1941, Ja 21,21:1
Lloyd George, Gwilym (Viscount Tenby), 1967, F 15,45:1
Lloyd George, Megan Lady (will, S 21,4:6), 1966, My 15,88:4
Lloyd George, William, 1967, Ja 26,33:4
Lloyd-Jones, Silas, 1966, Ap 25,31:5
Lloyd-Smith, Walton Lt, 1917, Ag 26,19:4
Lloyd-Smith, Wilson (will), 1940, Mr 28,25:7
Lloyds, Lloyd S Mrs, 1967, D 26,33:3
Lluberas, Arturo, 1938, Jl 21,21:5
Llufrio, Charles E, 1964, O 16,39:2
Llyn, May, 1903, F 25,16:2
Lo Cascio, Charles, 1952, N 10,25:2
Lo Conte, Gabriele, 1958, My 10,21:4
Lo Jung-huan, 1963, D 17,39:3
Lo Medico, Joseph M, 1940, Ja 27,13:3
Lo Nano, Ernest Mrs, 1953, My 13,29:5
Lo Parco, Pasquale, 1946, S 27,23:1
Lo Prete, Vincent, 1958, Mr 8,17:4
Lo Savio, Nino, 1957, My 2,31:3
Lo Surdo, Antonino, 1949, Je 9,31:2
Lo Vecchio, Salvatore J, 1943, O 14,21:3
Lo Wen-Kan (por), 1941, O 18,19:7
Loach, Minnie, 1946, My 18,19:3
Loacz, Effie L, 1950, Ag 10,25:1
Loacz, Michael, 1950, Jl 4,17:4
Loader, John W Mrs, 1911, Ja 26,11:5
Loan, B F, 1881, Ap 2,5:3
Loan, John C, 1954, S 3,17:2
Loan, Walter B, 1940, My 24,19:4
Loane, William B, 1949, D 20,31:4
Loasby, A W, 1936, N 25,23:1
Loasby, Arthur W Mrs, 1952, My 31,17:3
Loasby, Richard P, 1943, Mr 28,24:2
Loase, Frederic A, 1940, Mr 21,25:1
Loase, Herbert G, 1938, O 15,17:1
Loayza, Rojas Sen, 1922, Mr 31,17:5
Lobanoff-Rostovsky, Prince, 1896, Ag 3,5:3
Lobb, George A (por), 1939, Ap 2,III,7:3
Lobb, Mabel A, 1939, Mr 30,23:6
Lobdell, A Whitney, 1953, Ap 15,31:4
Lobdell, A Whitney Mrs, 1951, F 18,77:1
Lobdell, Alex F, 1940, F 14,21:5
Lobdell, Alex Mrs, 1953, Jl 20,17:3
Lobdell, Avis, 1942, Jl 24,19:2
Lobdell, Charles E, 1949, Ja 30,60:3
Lobdell, Charles W, 1940, O 11,21:3
Lobdell, Edwin L Mrs, 1947, Ag 24,56:4
Lobdell, Harold E, 1963, Ja 3,15:7
Lobdell, Harry H, 1946, F 5,23:4
Lobdell, Harry L, 1957, Jl 18,25:1
Lobdell, Isaac W, 1948, Ja 13,26:2
Lobdell, J E, 1875, Jl 10,4:7
Lobdell, John, 1873, Ag 14,8:3
Lobdell, Leighton, 1956, Mr 8,29:4
Lobdell, Martin E Mrs, 1944, Jl 13,17:4
Lobe, Paul, 1967, Ag 4,29:3
Lobeck, Charles C, 1950, O 9,25:3
Lobeck, Charles O, 1920, Ja 31,11:4
Lobeck, Henry, 1951, Mr 26,23:2
Lobeck Armin K, 1958, Ap 27,86:1
Lobedanz, Reinhold, 1955, Mr 6,89:2
Lobel, Jacob, 1959, S 29,39:2
Lobel, John, 1923, Jl 17,19:5
Lobel, Milton Mrs, 1965, Ap 7,43:3
Lobenstein, George J, 1942, My 2,13:5
Lobenstine, Belle W Mrs, 1940, O 22,23:4
Lobenstine, Edwin C, 1958, Jl 5,17:4
Lobenstine, Edwin C Mrs, 1964, O 31,29:3
Lobentzen, Frederic L C, 1960, Mr 17,33:4
Lober, Elmer W, 1946, N 7,31:4
Lober, George J, 1961, D 15,37:1
Lober, Louis, 1963, S 10,39:3
Lober, Max, 1946, O 8,23:5
Lober, Morris, 1942, D 15,27:6
Lobert, Hans (Jno B Lobert), 1968, S 18,44:1
Lobingier, Andrew S, 1939, Ag 1,19:4
Lobkowicz, Edward J Prince, 1959, Ja 3,17:5
Lobkowicz, George C, 1950, Ag 26,13:5
Lobkowicz, Irma Princess, 1950, Jl 18,29:4
Loblein, Eldon L, 1943, Je 14,17:4
Lobligeois, Felix, 1941, O 21,23:2
Lobo, Arthur, 1960, Mr 21,29:5
Lobo, Fernando, 1966, Ag 9,37:4
Lobo, Gustavo, 1951, O 18,29:3
Lobo, Leocadio, 1959, Jl 13,27:6
Lobo y Senior, Heriberto, 1950, D 21,29:2
LoBosco, Angelo, 1960, Jl 13,35:3
Lobosco, Joseph, 1956, Jl 16,21:5
Lobrano, Gustave S, 1956, Mr 2,23:1
Lobsenz, Jacob M, 1963, S 20,33:4
Lobsenz, Johanna, 1966, N 7,47:3
Lobsenz, Moses, 1959, Mr 30,31:2
Lobus, George A, 1965, Jl 17,9:1
Locanthi, Bartholomew, 1946, D 11,31:5
Locard, Edmond, 1966, My 5,47:2
Locas, J Albert, 1951, Jl 4,17:6
Locatelli, A, 1935, Ap 6,15:4
Locatelli, Carlo Mrs, 1949, Mr 1,25:5
Locatelli, Ercole H (por), 1949, Je 7,31:3
Locatelli, Mario, 1956, F 12,89:2
Locatelli, Umberto, 1958, O 5,87:2
Loch, Dowager Lady, 1938, Mr 14,16:3
Loch, Hans, 1960, Jl 14,27:4
Loch, Lord, 1942, Ag 16,45:3
Loch, Robert, 1947, Ja 30,25:2
Lochee, Baron (Edmund Robertson), 1911, S 14,9:6
Locher, C, 1929, Ag 18,II,5:3
Locher, Charles H (por), 1948, Ja 17,17:3
Locher, Fred, 1943, F 27,14:8
Locher, Freda Mrs, 1945, O 22,17:5
Locher, Robert E, 1956, Je 21,31:5
Lochman, Frederic I, 1945, Ag 1,19:2
Lochman, Veronica M, 1947, My 10,13:4
Lochmuller, Henry G, 1945, D 21,21:2
Lochner, Albert J, 1949, Ag 2,20:2
Lochner, George M, 1942, N 18,25:3
Lochner, Hendrik W, 1948, Ag 29,39:3
Lochner, Jacob L, 1942, N 29,65:1
Lochner, Joseph F Sr, 1939, D 15,25:2
Lochner, Martin, 1945, F 7,21:3
Lochner, William F, 1942, My 26,21:5
Lochren, William Judge, 1912, Ja 29,11:6
Lochridge, Lloyd P, 1946, Ja 11,22:3
Lochridge, Lloyd P Mrs, 1956, Ap 1,88:2
Lochrie, Howard F, 1961, S 25,33:2
Lock, George H, 1957, Ap 24,33:4
Lock, James G, 1938, Jl 27,17:2
Lock, John A, 1954, Mr 29,19:4
Lock, Leonard L, 1960, F 1,27:3
Lock, W, 1933, Ag 14,13:4
Lockard, Charles Mrs, 1956, F 27,45:2
Lockard, Elmer E, 1939, Ja 24,19:5
Lockard, James F, 1955, S 28,35:5
Lockard, Rae E Mrs, 1937, Mr 31,23:1
Lockard, Sandra, 1957, N 26,36:1
Lockart, Herbert, 1949, S 29,29:5
Locke, Alain, 1954, Je 10,31:4
Locke, Allan S, 1944, S 3,26:5
Locke, Alonzo, 1947, Ag 4,17:2
Locke, Arthur P, 1961, Ap 5,37:3
Locke, Benjamin, 1938, S 10,17:3
Locke, Benjamin H, 1959, My 26,35:2
Locke, Bessie, 1952, Ap 11,23:3
Locke, Bradford B (por), 1946, Ja 7,19:3
Locke, Bradford H, 1914, F 23,9:5
Locke, Campbell E, 1950, D 1,26:3
Locke, Charles E, 1940, Mr 5,23:6; 1948, S 25,17:2
Locke, Charles T, 1949, O 3,17:5
Locke, Clinton Rev, 1904, F 14,7:5
Locke, D R, 1888, F 16,5:3
Locke, Edward, 1945, Ap 2,19:3
Locke, F A, 1903, Je 21,7:6
Locke, F D, 1927, My 25,23:5
Locke, Florence, 1903, D 25,7:5
Locke, Frank J, 1963, Je 10,31:4
Locke, Frederick, 1925, O 3,15:6
Locke, Frederick Mrs, 1944, Ja 15,13:1
Locke, G E (Yankee), 1880, Ja 6,5:2
Locke, George D, 1942, Jl 2,21:3
Locke, George H Dr, 1937, Ja 29,19:6
Locke, Helen V Mrs, 1937, F 16,23:6
Locke, Herbert G, 1918, S 21,9:8
Locke, J D, 1883, N 29,5:4
Locke, J N (Nat), 1954, Ap 11,87:2
Locke, James S Mrs, 1964, Ja 10,43:4
Locke, James W Judge, 1922, S 7,17:5
Locke, John H, 1945, N 13,22:2
Locke, John M Mrs, 1925, Mr 7,13:6
Locke, John P, 1948, D 11,15:3
Locke, John W, 1950, N 21,31:5
Locke, L Ward, 1951, Ja 12,27:1
Locke, Leslie L (por), 1943, Ag 30,15:4
Locke, Lucien P (por), 1937, D 3,24:3
Locke, Mahlon W, 1942, F 8,49:1
Locke, Morris E, 1942, Jl 4,17:4
Locke, Morris E Mrs, 1944, Ap 16,41:2
Locke, Norman J, 1937, S 8,23:2
Locke, Richard Earl Rev, 1925, Je 27,11:6
Locke, Robert D, 1943, F 11,20:3
Locke, Robinson, 1920, Ap 21,9:4
Locke, Robinson Mrs, 1968, F 12,53:6
Locke, Roland A, 1952, D 23,23:4
Locke, Sidney E Mrs (will), 1961, My 30,6:7
Locke, Sylvanus D, 1959, S 29,39:2
Locke, Thomas F, 1951, Je 27,29:5
Locke, Thomas L, 1948, F 17,25:3
Locke, W J, 1930, My 16,23:3
Locke, Walter, 1957, O 25,27:1
Locke, Will H, 1950, O 9,25:2
Locke, William F, 1952, Ja 3,27:3
Locke, William H, 1913, Ag 15,7:4
Locke, William H Rev Dr, 1905, Je 15,9:6
Locke, William Henry, 1917, My 9,11:4
Locke, William Henry Rev, 1905, Je 16,9:6
Locke, William Mrs (will), 1946, D 17,27:3
Locker, Edward, 1967, S 8,39:1
Locker, Frederic J, 1957, O 6,85:1
Locker, Frederick, 1940, Jl 26,17:4
Locker, Jesse D (funl, Ap 21,29:4), 1955, Ap 11,23:3
Locker, John A Jr, 1962, Jl 5,23:5
Locker, Melville E, 1960, Je 10,31:3
Locker, Peyton B, 1955, Jl 5,29:4
Locker, Samuel, 1938, My 24,19:3
Locker, Tice, 1951, S 21,23:5
Locker, W Clyde, 1961, My 22,31:5
Locker-Lampson, Oliver S, 1954, O 9,17:4
Lockett, Andrew M, 1945, O 12,23:2
Lockett, Arthur H, 1957, Ja 10,29:1
Lockett, Arthur H Mrs, 1959, S 16,39:3
Lockett, Charles E S, 1966, Ag 27,29:4
Lockett, Henry W, 1949, Mr 8,25:5
Lockett, Louis, 1964, Ag 5,33:2
Lockett, S Hobart, 1960, D 16,33:4
Lockett, Samuel S, 1963, Ap 26,35:4
Lockewood, Mary Smith Mrs, 1922, N 11,13:5
Lockewood, Stephen O, 1924, My 11,7:2
Lockhart, Andrew E, 1955, Jl 18,21:2
Lockhart, Arthur M, 1942, N 10,28:4
Lockhart, Catharine Sister, 1938, S 25,39:1
Lockhart, Charles, 1905, Ja 27,7:3; 1954, Jl 15,27:6
Lockhart, Charles A, 1942, My 19,19:3
Lockhart, Charles E, 1944, D 26,19:5
Lockhart, Clinton, 1951, Je 12,29:2
Lockhart, Cyrus L, 1950, D 5,31:2
Lockhart, Edwin H, 1954, Jl 27,21:4
Lockhart, Frank P, 1949, Ag 26,19:1
Lockhart, Frederick C, 1920, Jl 1,13:3
Lockhart, Frederick C Mrs, 1948, F 26,23:2
Lockhart, Gene, 1957, Ap 1,25:3
Lockhart, Harry J, 1965, Je 27,64:8
Lockhart, Henry, 1943, Ap 15,25:1
Lockhart, James C, 1945, Je 17,26:8
Lockhart, James H, 1938, My 17,23:3
Lockhart, James H Sir, 1937, Mr 1,19:4
Lockhart, James J, 1948, Jl 18,52:5
Lockhart, Jesse P Mrs, 1948, Ap 14,27:1
Lockhart, John C, 1938, Je 14,21:1; 1953, Mr 12,27:1
Lockhart, John F, 1937, Mr 4,23:3
Lockhart, John M, 1939, Ja 24,19:2
Lockhart, L W M, 1882, Ap 11,5:1
Lockhart, Margaret, 1925, Ap 6,19:5
Lockhart, Oliver W, 1944, N 7,29:1
Lockhart, Robert, 1904, Jl 22,7:2
Lockhart, Sydney W, 1952, S 26,21:4
Lockhart, W S Dr, 1937, Je 23,25:5
Lockhart, Walter S Mrs, 1961, Jl 30,69:3
Lockhart, William A, 1942, F 24,21:5
Lockheed, Malcolm, 1958, Ag 14,29:3
Lockington, Robert, 1968, Jl 8,31:1
Lockitt, Clement, 1920, F 3,15:2
Lockitt, J, 1878, Jl 30,5:3
Lockland, Martha A Mrs, 1942, Je 24,19:1
Locklear, Omer, 1920, Ag 10,13:5
Lockley, Albert H Sr, 1951, Mr 3,13:1
Lockley, George J, 1940, Mr 18,17:4
Lockley, Harry C, 1947, Ja 17,24:2

Lockman, DeWitt M, 1957, Jl 2,27:1
Lockman, John Mrs, 1959, Mr 3,33:2
Lockman, John T Gen, 1912, S 29,13:5
Lockman, Myron A, 1943, F 7,48:5
Lockman, Myron A Mrs, 1944, F 28,17:3
Lockner, George T, 1951, Ag 18,11:5
Lockrane, O A Judge, 1887, Je 18,1:5
Lockridge, Richard Mrs, 1963, F 19,8:7
Lockridge, Ross F Sr, 1952, Ja 14,19:5
Lockridge, Willard, 1950, Jl 18,29:3
Lockrow, Winifred E, 1924, D 17,21:3
Lockroy, Edouardo, 1913, N 23,IV,7:6
Lockton, Edward, 1940, My 17,19:4
Lockton, John D Mrs, 1949, O 16,88:4
Lockward, Anna N C Mrs, 1937, Ap 15,23:4
Lockwood, Adolphus Newman, 1968, My 13,43:3
Lockwood, Alfred, 1874, Je 7,2:6
Lockwood, Alfred W, 1952, Ja 26,13:2
Lockwood, Arthur J, 1938, Mr 15,23:2
Lockwood, Belva, 1917, My 20,23:1
Lockwood, Benoni, 1952, Ag 5,19:2
Lockwood, C C Mrs, 1957, Je 26,31:1
Lockwood, C H, 1933, Ap 18,16:3
Lockwood, Charles A (funl, Je 10,33:4), 1967, Je 7, 51:1
Lockwood, Charles C (funl plans, S 23,33:4), 1958, S 22,31:2
Lockwood, Charles D, 1949, D 13,31:3
Lockwood, Charles S, 1937, Je 12,15:3
Lockwood, Clifford A, 1942, D 23,19:3
Lockwood, Clifford C, 1940, My 22,23:5
Lockwood, Clifford L, 1950, My 16,31:1
Lockwood, Cornelius W, 1946, Je 23,40:3
Lockwood, Daniel N, 1906, Je 2,9:4
Lockwood, Dean P, 1965, F 9,37:3
Lockwood, Dewitt C Mrs, 1944, S 30,13:5
Lockwood, Donald S, 1949, F 26,15:4
Lockwood, Douglas A, 1950, Je 23,25:5
Lockwood, E B, 1880, Je 13,5:3
Lockwood, Edgar, 1906, D 4,9:5; 1953, F 3,25:2
Lockwood, Edward H, 1957, Ap 6,19:3
Lockwood, Edward T, 1963, Je 9,87:2
Lockwood, Edwin J, 1967, O 21,31:1
Lockwood, Edwin M, 1949, D 14,31:2
Lockwood, Edwin M Mrs, 1949, Mr 24,27:4
Lockwood, Elijah J Mrs, 1948, Je 2,29:6
Lockwood, Elizabeth C W Mrs (will), 1939, My 4, 48:2
Lockwood, Enos Beal, 1903, D 5,9:4
Lockwood, Erville A, 1947, Mr 20,27:5
Lockwood, Estelle, 1874, O 13,12:3
Lockwood, F L, 1876, F 27,2:6
Lockwood, Florence C, 1953, S 4,34:3
Lockwood, Frances K Mrs, 1941, F 19,21:5
Lockwood, Frank M, 1954, Mr 27,17:4
Lockwood, Frank S, 1938, My 28,15:4
Lockwood, Fred R, 1940, Ja 27,13:5
Lockwood, Frederick D, 1954, My 8,17:4
Lockwood, Frederick F Mrs, 1940, Ja 6,13:1
Lockwood, Frederick R, 1953, S 4,34:3
Lockwood, Frederick R Mrs, 1954, N 21,87:1
Lockwood, Frederick S, 1952, Ja 15,27:3
Lockwood, Frederick St John Col, 1907, O 14,9:6
Lockwood, Frederick W, 1942, O 19,19:2
Lockwood, G B, 1932, F 13,13:1
Lockwood, G F, 1875, Ag 17,3:2
Lockwood, George H Mrs, 1962, Ag 30,29:3
Lockwood, George R, 1959, Ap 17,25:1
Lockwood, Guy H, 1947, O 1,29:4
Lockwood, H C Col, 1902, D 25,7:6
Lockwood, Hanford N, 1955, Je 1,33:5
Lockwood, Harold J, 1960, Ap 16,17:5
Lockwood, Harriette L, 1952, F 7,27:4
Lockwood, Harry C Mrs, 1955, Ag 8,21:4
Lockwood, Harry Thompson, 1919, S 7,23:5
Lockwood, Henrietta, 1922, Ja 13,15:5
Lockwood, Henry, 1924, Jl 11,13:6; 1925, D 7,21:3
Lockwood, Henry B, 1915, N 13,11:6; 1944, O 3,23:5; 1953, Ja 5,21:3
Lockwood, Henry B Mrs, 1950, Mr 1,27:4
Lockwood, Henry C, 1950, S 5,27:4
Lockwood, Henry C Mrs, 1952, Ag 30,13:5
Lockwood, Howard A, 1959, My 24,88:6
Lockwood, Howard Jr Mrs, 1952, N 1,21:4
Lockwood, Hubbard C, 1958, Ja 22,27:4
Lockwood, I Ferris Mrs, 1944, O 25,21:5
Lockwood, Ingersoll (funl, O 23,13:1), 1918, O 3,13:2
Lockwood, James Frederic Mrs, 1912, Ag 28,9:5
Lockwood, James K, 1922, Ja 7,13:6
Lockwood, Janet I D Mrs, 1938, O 11,25:4
Lockwood, Jeremiah, 1945, Je 8,19:1
Lockwood, Jesse H, 1925, O 28,25:5
Lockwood, John L, 1940, F 12,17:3
Lockwood, John S, 1950, Je 17,15:3
Lockwood, Joseph E, 1942, O 5,19:3
Lockwood, Joseph J, 1954, D 10,27:3
Lockwood, Joseph T Jr, 1949, O 14,27:4
Lockwood, Kate H B Mrs, 1937, Mr 27,15:2
Lockwood, Kenneth F, 1948, Ap 3,15:4
Lockwood, L A, 1883, Ja 24,5:4
Lockwood, Laura E, 1956, D 1,21:2
Lockwood, Le Grand, 1872, F 25,3:4
Lockwood, Leroy, 1955, S 4,56:8
Lockwood, Luke V, 1951, Ja 24,27:4
Lockwood, Luke V Mrs (est acctg, Mr 18,33:8), 1954, Mr 6,15:3
Lockwood, Lukea, 1905, N 21,10:4
Lockwood, Lyman B, 1961, Ap 3,33:3
Lockwood, Manice D, 1946, Ag 15,25:3
Lockwood, Marquis H, 1938, D 6,23:2
Lockwood, Mary C, 1945, N 22,35:5
Lockwood, Mary E, 1939, My 23,23:5
Lockwood, Merritt C, 1955, Ja 9,87:3
Lockwood, Nelson Capt, 1920, Ag 18,9:5
Lockwood, Phil V D, 1950, Je 30,23:4
Lockwood, Phil V D Mrs, 1939, Mr 12,III,7:2
Lockwood, Radcliffe B, 1913, D 24,11:6
Lockwood, Raymond L, 1954, Jl 27,21:5
Lockwood, Robert H, 1939, Ag 10,19:3
Lockwood, Robert M, 1938, O 4,25:4
Lockwood, Roscoe C, 1960, N 26,21:5
Lockwood, Ryland L, 1941, O 3,23:1
Lockwood, Sally Weed, 1907, Mr 5,9:6
Lockwood, Samuel, 1948, S 30,27:5
Lockwood, T Preston, 1951, Ap 1,92:2
Lockwood, T Preston Mrs, 1964, Jl 12,69:1
Lockwood, Thomas B, 1947, Ag 20,21:2
Lockwood, Thomas C, 1962, Je 2,19:4
Lockwood, Timothy S Mrs, 1944, Ag 11,15:3
Lockwood, Traviss D Mrs, 1949, Je 9,31:4
Lockwood, Vernette Le R Rev, 1903, Jl 11,7:6
Lockwood, W L, 1928, My 30,19:5
Lockwood, Walter A, 1948, S 14,29:5
Lockwood, Walter S, 1955, Mr 13,87:2
Lockwood, Ward, 1963, Jl 8,29:5
Lockwood, Warren J, 1961, F 26,92:1
Lockwood, Warren S Mrs, 1957, Mr 24,86:8
Lockwood, William A, 1966, D 17,33:4
Lockwood, William A Mrs, 1943, Jl 3,13:5; 1960, D 23,19:5
Lockwood, William H Mrs, 1945, N 13,21:3
Lockwood, William Jr, 1959, My 2,23:2
Lockwood, William R, 1954, My 4,29:2
Lockwood, William W Mrs, 1947, D 20,17:4
Lockwood, Wilton M, 1948, S 8,29:2
Lockyer, Norman Sir, 1920, Ag 17,13:4
Loco, Chief of Apache Indian Tribe, 1882, Je 21,5:6
Locock, Charles Sir, 1875, Ag 7,4:6
Locock, Guy H, 1958, Ag 26,29:3
Locognito, John, 1947, Ja 12,59:3
Lodeesen-Grevinck, John D, 1946, Jl 25,21:1
Loder, Benjamin, 1876, O 12,4:7
Loder, Benjamin C, 1946, D 20,23:4
Loder, Bertha, 1943, O 16,13:6
Loder, Eustace Maj, 1914, Jl 28,7:6
Loder, George E Mrs, 1937, Ap 18,II,9:1
Loder, George S, 1918, Ja 28,13:5
Loder, Orrin, 1945, O 24,21:5
Loder, Pamela K, 1941, My 24,15:5
Loder, Paul, 1947, Ag 16,13:3
Loder, Paul W, 1940, N 16,17:4
Loder, Roya A, 1956, D 16,86:5
Lodes, John, 1952, N 2,89:1
Lodewick, Charles Casper Col, 1907, Ag 13,7:6
Lodewick, Eugene K, 1912, Ap 1,13:6
Lodewick, Mildred, 1968, D 13,47:1
Lodge, Clarence V, 1937, D 2,25:5
Lodge, Edgar A, 1945, Ap 10,19:5
Lodge, Edward A, 1943, Ap 6,21:2
Lodge, George, 1943, Ja 12,23:4
Lodge, George C Mrs (will, Jl 23,38:6), 1960, Jl 2, 17:4
Lodge, George Cabot, 1909, Ag 23,7:5
Lodge, George E, 1954, F 9,27:5
Lodge, Harriett C, 1943, Ja 18,15:5
Lodge, Henry, 1939, Mr 10,23:3
Lodge, Henry Cabot Mrs, 1915, S 29,13:5
Lodge, Henry Cabot Sen (funl), 1924, N 13,21:3
Lodge, J Alex, 1939, D 10,68:8
Lodge, J Norman, 1964, D 19,29:2
Lodge, James T, 1950, Jl 12,29:3
Lodge, James T Mrs, 1964, N 6,37:4
Lodge, John C, 1950, F 7,27:4
Lodge, John E, 1942, D 31,15:2
Lodge, O Lady, 1929, F 21,27:5
Lodge, Oliver, 1940, Ag 23,15:1
Lodge, Oralie B D Mrs, 1939, N 16,23:2
Lodge, Robert O Mrs, 1948, Jl 24,15:3
Lodge, Rupert C, 1961, Mr 3,27:5
Lodge, Thomas H, 1948, Ap 27,25:4
Lodge, Walter, 1941, Ag 7,17:3
Lodge, William P, 1950, Je 6,29:4
Lodge, William T, 1944, Je 24,13:5
Lodijenski, Theodore A, 1947, Mr 7,25:5
LoDolce, Agostino, 1956, Ap 15,36:4
Lodolce, Antonio, 1956, Ap 28,17:2
Lodor, Richard Brig-Gen, 1917, My 10,13:4
Lods, Philip C, 1966, D 31,19:5
Lodter, Charles F, 1953, Ja 12,27:2
Lodwick, Albert I, 1961, O 23,29:1
Lodwick, David Sr, 1944, S 4,19:3
Lodwick, John, 1942, O 17,15:3; 1959, Mr 19,34:1
Lodwick, William G, 1968, Mr 8,39:4
Lodygensky, A P Col, 1905, Je 23,1:3
Lodyjensky, Ivan I, 1957, Ag 28,27:5
Loeb, Aaron M, 1939, Mr 22,23:3
Loeb, Adele, 1956, D 26,27:4
Loeb, Albert, 1902, O 13,9:4
Loeb, Albert H Mrs, 1950, Ja 25,27:2
Loeb, Arthur, 1939, D 22,19:3; 1940, Ap 10,25:3
Loeb, Arthur J, 1968, D 6,47:2
Loeb, Bena G Mrs, 1937, Mr 31,23:4
Loeb, Benjamin, 1955, S 2,17:6
Loeb, Bernard, 1953, Jl 19,32:8
Loeb, Carl A, 1966, Ap 7,39:4
Loeb, Carl M (will, Ja 11,27:8), 1955, Ja 4,21:1
Loeb, Carl M Mrs, 1953, N 30,2:8
Loeb, Clarence H, 1951, Ag 27,19:3
Loeb, Clifford W, 1940, Jl 15,15:3
Loeb, Edward, 1949, Je 2,27:2
Loeb, Emil, 1941, Je 20,21:2
Loeb, Emil Mrs, 1951, D 6,33:4
Loeb, Gustavus A, 1945, Ap 9,19:4
Loeb, Gustavus A Mrs, 1958, O 19,87:1
Loeb, Harold Mrs, 1961, Jl 15,19:1
Loeb, Harry, 1959, Je 7,86:4
Loeb, Herman A Mrs, 1962, D 3,31:3
Loeb, Howard A, 1955, N 4,29:3
Loeb, J, 1933, My 29,13:1
Loeb, Jack W Mrs, 1954, My 31,13:6
Loeb, Jacob, 1942, Ja 12,15:2
Loeb, Jacob F, 1937, Ap 1,23:1
Loeb, Jacob F Mrs, 1957, Ap 22,25:6
Loeb, Jacob W, 1957, Je 28,23:4
Loeb, Jacques Dr, 1924, F 13,19:3
Loeb, Jacques Mrs, 1951, Ag 21,27:4
Loeb, James I, 1950, D 8,29:3
Loeb, James J, 1948, Mr 28,48:5
Loeb, Joseph, 1953, My 18,21:2
Loeb, Julius, 1946, Ja 5,14:2
Loeb, Julius Mrs, 1946, N 22,23:1
Loeb, Leo, 1959, D 30,21:3
Loeb, Louis, 1909, Jl 14,7:6
Loeb, Louis Mrs, 1907, N 12,9:5
Loeb, Ludwig, 1957, My 7,35:5
Loeb, Ludwig M, 1944, N 7,27:2
Loeb, Ludwig Mrs, 1955, S 30,25:5
Loeb, Martin J, 1961, D 17,82:1
Loeb, Max B, 1907, Ag 5,7:6
Loeb, Meyer, 1959, D 20,60:5
Loeb, Michael A Mrs, 1955, O 30,88:4
Loeb, Milton A, 1954, F 13,13:2
Loeb, Milton B Mrs, 1942, My 24,43:2
Loeb, Mitchell, 1968, N 21,47:4
Loeb, Morris Dr (funl, O 10,11:4), 1912, O 9,13:5
Loeb, Morris Dr, 1912, N 17,17:5
Loeb, Morris Mrs (will), 1951, N 29,24:7
Loeb, Mortimer, 1960, Je 1,39:2
Loeb, Nathaniel J, 1961, Jl 8,19:5
Loeb, Phil, 1955, S 2,38:3
Loeb, Robert H, 1953, O 13,29:5
Loeb, Robert S, 1954, Je 21,23:2
Loeb, S I, 1929, Ja 19,17:1
Loeb, Samuel Mrs, 1946, Ja 6,40:3
Loeb, Simon J, 1945, My 4,19:3
Loeb, Solomon, 1903, D 14,7:3
Loeb, Victor A, 1953, N 14,17:4
Loeb, Virgil, 1956, Je 27,31:5
Loeb, Walter, 1948, Mr 31,25:4
Loeb, Willard E, 1958, N 28,30:5
Loeb, William (por), 1937, S 20,23:3
Loeb, William, 1941, Jl 26,30:4
Loeb, William Mrs, 1966, N 25,37:2
Loebel, Leopold, 1950, S 8,31:2
Loebel, Robert G, 1960, F 18,33:4
Loebell, Henry O, 1945, My 5,15:4
Loebenberg, Alfred L, 1951, Ja 29,19:2
Loebinger, Hugo L Mrs, 1943, Mr 9,23:4
Loebker, Joseph, 1948, D 26,52:4
Loebl, Andrew W, 1967, Jl 20,37:4
Loebl, Louis, 1950, Ag 9,29:1
Loebl, Solomon, 1925, F 5,19:4
Loeble, Carleton C, 1946, Je 30,38:3
Loeble, Charles I, 1943, Mr 17,21:4
Loebner, James, 1951, My 27,68:4
Loecher, Albert, 1954, D 8,35:1
Loeder, William J, 1907, D 7,9:6
Loefflad, Paul A, 1952, My 20,25:1
Loeffler, Andrew, 1914, Jl 3,9:3
Loeffler, C M, 1935, My 21,19:1
Loeffler, Edward H, 1945, Jl 25,23:5; 1962, Ja 19
Loeffler, Edward H Mrs (N Vernon), 1959, O 2
Loeffler, Frederick A, 1956, O 22,29:1
Loeffler, Henry, 1941, Ag 16,15:4
Loeffler, Henry D W, 1947, Jl 31,21:4
Loeffler, John A, 1947, N 21,28:3
Loeffler, John G, 1964, O 8,43:3
Loeffler, Joseph H, 1965, Ap 10,29:1
Loeffler, Joseph N, 1945, N 6,19:3
Loeffler, Milton G, 1954, Jl 27,21:4
Loeffler, Richard A, 1950, O 21,17:3
Loeffler, Rudolf, 1942, Ja 29,19:6
Loefgren, Elie, 1940, Ap 9,23:5
Loefler, Franz, 1937, Mr 7,IV,9:6
Loeher, Stephen F Mrs, 1954, F 1,23:5
Loehmann, Charles H Mrs, 1962, S 24,29:4
Loehr, Carl T, 1948, D 3,25:6
Loehr, Edward A, 1959, N 9,31:5
Loehr, Edward B Mrs, 1960, Ja 5,31:5

Loehr, Frank J, 1947, N 25,29:1
Loehr, George F, 1949, S 20,29:2
Loehr, Joseph F, 1959, Je 1,27:5
Loehr, Otto T, 1942, N 26,27:4
Loehrs, Fred H, 1955, F 6,88:2
Loeloff, Henry A, 1951, Ap 12,35:5
Loemker, Elmer, 1960, N 22,35:4
Loenard, L F, 1875, D 26,10:6
Loennrot, E Prof, 1884, Mr 30,13:2
Loeppert, Adam L, 1950, My 25,29:4
Loer, Maurice C, 1947, D 24,22:3
Loerch, George, 1952, O 2,29:2
Loery, William B, 1950, Jl 10,21:2
Loerzer, Bruno, 1960, Ag 27,19:5
Loes, Franz E, 1962, O 3,41:4
Loes, James, 1961, My 31,33:1
Loesch, Charles F, 1947, Mr 28,23:1
Loesch, Frank J, 1944, Ag 1,15:6
Loesch, George (por), 1948, D 24,17:3
Loesch, Otto E, 1941, S 3,23:4
Loesche, Alvin, 1939, Ap 18,23:4
Loesche, John A, 1940, Ag 23,15:4
Loesche, William H Sr, 1962, Je 16,19:5
Loescher, Henry A, 1941, Ap 5,17:5
Loeser, Albert D, 1956, My 24,31:3
Loeser, Charles E, 1956, Ja 26,29:4
Loeser, Christian L, 1963, My 19,86:6
Loeser, Edwin A Mrs, 1948, Mr 21,61:1
Loeser, Frederick, 1911, Ag 1,9:5
Loeser, Frederick L, 1948, Ja 24,16:3
Loeser, George, 1955, Ja 25,25:1
Loeser, Hannah, 1944, Ja 27,19:4
Loeser, Nathan, 1953, Jl 1,29:6
Loeser, Paul, 1943, D 17,27:3
Loeser, Vincent, 1918, Ap 2,13:5
Loetscher, Frederick W, 1966, Ag 2,33:1
Loetting, Diedrich, 1937, Jl 13,19:1
Loevenguth, Jay E, 1948, Jl 26,17:1
Loevin, Leopold, 1938, N 19,17:6
Loevland, J G, 1922, Ag 22,17:6
Loew, E Victor, 1950, D 27,27:1
Loew, E Victor Mrs, 1958, Ja 21,29:4
Loew, Edward Victor, 1907, N 11,7:5
Loew, Elmer J, 1965, Ag 16,27:5
Loew, Frederick W, 1909, N 8,7:7
Loew, Henry, 1943, Je 15,21:6
Loew, Herman G, 1938, Jl 19,21:5
Loew, John T Mrs, 1951, My 18,28:4
Loew, M, 1927, S 6,1:5
Loew, S Robert, 1949, Je 10,27:3
Loew, Tobias, 1880, Je 23,5:2
Loew, W G Mrs, 1936, My 25,19:5
Loew, William G, 1955, My 24,31:1
Loewe, Arthur V, 1922, Jl 27,17:6
Loewe, Ferdinand, 1925, Ja 7,25:4
Loewe, Isidor, 1910, Ag 29,7:5
Loewe, Leo, 1967, Je 1,43:1
Loewenberg, Kurt, 1966, Mr 21,33:4
Loewenberg, Sigmund, 1957, My 7,35:4
Loewengart, Sol, 1968, F 4,81:1
Loewenguth, Edgar H, 1947, S 11,27:5
Loewenheim, Arthur, 1956, N 22,33:5
Loewenstein, Ben M, 1941, O 22,23:6
Loewenstein, Emanuel, 1941, Ap 27,38:1
Loewenstein, Erich, 1945, Ag 28,19:5
Loewenstein, Herman, 1944, Jl 17,15:6
Loewenstein, Johannes, 1956, My 19,19:3
Loewenstein, Louis, 1908, F 14,7:4
Loewenstein, Maurice F, 1921, Jl 31,22:4
Loewenstein, Max, 1966, Je 9,47:3
Loewenstein, Max Mrs, 1966, Je 9,47:3
Loewenstein, William (will, Ap 14,1:3), 1938, Ja 8, 15:5
Loewenstein-Wertheim-Rosenberg, Alois zu Prince, 1952, Ja 27,77:1
Loewenstine, Frank M, 1948, S 24,26:2
Loewenthal, Bernard, 1946, D 14,15:5
Loewenthal, Daniel Rabbi, 1914, O 3,11:4
Loewenthal, Fred S, 1958, Ap 22,33:5
Loewenthal, H, 1927, N 6,30:1
Loewenthal, Julius, 1922, S 28,21:4; 1941, O 23,23:5
Loewenthal, Julius S, 1966, O 26,47:2
Loewenthal, Lucien D Mrs, 1953, Ag 15,15:6
Loewenthal, Siegfried, 1946, D 5,31:3
Loewenwarter, Paul L, 1940, O 17,25:5
Loewer, Jacob, 1940, N 20,21:4
Loewi, Joseph F, 1949, Je 6,19:4
Loewi, Mortimer W, 1967, Ja 17,39:3
Loewi, Otto, 1961, D 27,27:1
Loewinthan, Albert, 1968, Ap 6,39:4
Loewith, Walter Mrs, 1956, Ja 27,23:3
Loewl, Joseph, 1913, Ap 9,9:4
Loewstein, Clarence, 1952, Je 20,23:4
Loewy, Arnold H, 1951, S 26,31:6
Loewy, Benno (funl), 1919, Ag 22,11:6
Loewy, Bernard R, 1961, Ap 29,23:5
Loewy, Bernard R Mrs, 1953, Ja 30,21:3
Loewy, Edwin J, 1957, Ja 2,27:5
Loewy, Erwin, 1959, Jl 15,29:3
Loewy, George J, 1942, Mr 14,15:6
Loewy, Julius, 1944, N 26,57:1
Loewy, Leo H, 1956, S 17,14:5
Loewy, Maurice, 1907, O 17,9:5
Loewy, Paul, 1955, D 10,21:5
Lof, Eric A, 1957, Mr 7,29:3
Loffer, O W Dr, 1953, F 20,19:4
Lofgren, Edna, 1951, N 3,17:1
Lofgren, Knute E, 1947, D 3,30:2
Lofgren, Lewis Mrs, 1950, O 23,23:3
Lofink, Conrad A, 1954, O 30,17:4
Lofland, William C Mrs, 1950, Je 1,27:2
Lofquist, Emanuel A, 1950, Jl 23,56:4
LoFranco, Niccolo, 1951, N 13,29:3
Lofruscio, Luigi, 1940, Mr 26,21:5
Lofstedt, Andrew Mrs, 1946, Ap 8,27:1
Loft, George W (por), 1943, N 7,57:1
Loft, George W Mrs (will, Jl 21,44:5), 1962, My 17, 37:3
Loft, Louis, 1965, Ag 15,83:2
Loft, William Mrs, 1947, D 28,40:4
Lofthouse, Charles Mrs, 1947, Je 7,13:3
Loftin, Scott M, 1953, S 23,31:5
Lofting, Hugh J, 1947, S 28,60:4
Loftis, James J, 1938, O 29,19:6
Lofton, George V, 1952, S 17,31:5
Loftus, Clarence A, 1946, Je 21,23:1
Loftus, Edna, 1916, Je 17,11:5
Loftus, Frank G, 1950, F 7,27:3
Loftus, Fred H, 1951, F 12,23:4
Loftus, George H, 1959, My 29,23:2
Loftus, George J Mrs, 1947, D 27,14:3
Loftus, James, 1944, My 29,15:5
Loftus, John J, 1951, Ap 20,29:1
Loftus, Margaret E, 1951, Ap 26,29:5
Loftus, Marie C (por), 1943, Jl 13,21:1
Loftus, Marie Mrs, 1940, D 8,69:3
Loftus, Patrick, 1941, Mr 22,15:5
Loftus, Peter, 1951, Ap 6,27:1; 1964, D 29,27:1
Loftus, Raymond I, 1957, Ap 14,86:6
Loftus, Richard P, 1966, My 22,87:1
Loftus, Thomas P Mrs, 1963, N 6,41:3
Loftus, William B, 1938, Ja 22,15:2
Loftus, William B Mrs, 1954, Je 12,15:7
Loftus, William H, 1941, F 6,21:4
Logan, A D, 1869, Ag 24,4:6
Logan, Albert E, 1941, Ap 18,21:2
Logan, Albert H, 1945, Mr 21,23:2
Logan, Alberta Mrs, 1938, O 19,23:2
Logan, Arthur G, 1964, Ja 6,47:2
Logan, Arthur H, 1952, N 16,88:4
Logan, C F, 1903, S 28,7:5
Logan, Charles A, 1948, Ag 9,19:5
Logan, Charles C, 1940, Jl 4,15:4
Logan, Charles P, 1946, F 1,24:2
Logan, Dale F, 1952, O 15,31:2
Logan, Edward B (Sept 25), 1965, O 11,61:3
Logan, Edward L, 1939, Jl 7,17:5
Logan, Edward L Mrs (funl), 1957, Ja 25,21:3
Logan, Elizabeth C Mrs, 1924, Ap 26,15:4
Logan, Ella B Mrs, 1938, S 15,25:2
Logan, Ellen, 1955, Ap 5,29:1
Logan, F Chandler, 1964, F 2,89:1
Logan, Francis V, 1952, Ag 6,21:3
Logan, Frank A, 1946, Ja 28,19:2
Logan, Frank G, 1937, Jl 19,16:1
Logan, Frank G Mrs, 1943, N 2,25:3
Logan, Fred, 1937, Jl 18,II,7:2
Logan, Frederick A, 1942, F 9,15:1
Logan, Frederick W (por), 1947, F 9,62:3
Logan, George A, 1937, Ja 5,23:4; 1942, S 19,15:4
Logan, George H, 1960, Ja 9,21:2
Logan, George R, 1940, F 17,13:2
Logan, George W Capt, 1915, Ap 23,13:4
Logan, Hance J, 1944, D 27,19:5
Logan, Harold E, 1955, Ja 14,19:5
Logan, Harry A, 1957, Mr 16,19:4
Logan, Henry G, 1950, O 22,92:1
Logan, Henry J, 1940, My 1,23:2
Logan, Hugh J, 1937, Jl 5,17:4
Logan, J A, 1930, O 28,25:1
Logan, J A Sen, 1886, D 27,1:5
Logan, James P (por), 1938, O 29,19:4
Logan, James R, 1962, Jl 16,23:5
Logan, John, 1949, Ag 4,23:6
Logan, John A, 1960, Je 6,29:5
Logan, John A Mrs, 1923, F 23,13:5
Logan, John G, 1950, F 25,17:4
Logan, John P, 1951, Mr 6,27:4
Logan, John R, 1957, My 8,37:4
Logan, John T, 1945, Ja 29,14:3
Logan, John W, 1947, Ja 30,25:4
Logan, Joseph, 1961, D 12,43:4
Logan, Joseph M, 1951, N 28,31:4
Logan, Julia B Mrs, 1941, Ag 27,19:3
Logan, Lawrence J Brig-Gen, 1921, S 14,19:4
Logan, Leavitt C Rear-Adm, 1921, N 24,19:6
Logan. Leo J. 1951, F 23.27:2
Logan, Leo R, 1961, S 20,29:4
Logan, Leon M, 1939, Ja 9,15:1
Logan, Lloyd, 1938, D 30,15:5
Logan, Louis J, 1951, D 9,91:1
Logan, Malcolm R, 1961, N 12,86:2
Logan, Margaret, 1937, Ag 29,32:5; 1946, Mr 20,24:2
Logan, Margaret Mrs, 1945, Ja 12,15:3
Logan, Maria D, 1939, F 14,19:2
Logan, Marvel M, 1939, O 3,23:1
Logan, Nannie E Mrs (will), 1956, N 11,137:3
Logan, Olive (funl, Ap 30,9:5), 1909, Ap 29,9:3
Logan, Patrick, 1948, Ap 4,7:1
Logan, Patrick H, 1944, O 15,44:4
Logan, Ralph K, 1953, My 31,73:1
Logan, Robert, 1925, D 8,25:4; 1961, Ap 18,39:8
Logan, Robert F, 1959, D 12,23:1
Logan, Robert G, 1942, O 26,15:3
Logan, Robert H, 1942, Ja 11,46:1
Logan, Robert R, 1956, Je 19,29:4
Logan, Robert R Mrs, 1938, D 3,19:4
Logan, Robert S, 1947, Ap 24,25:2
Logan, Russell A, 1948, N 12,23:2
Logan, Spencer H, 1956, S 16,84:7
Logan, Stanley, 1953, F 1,88:3
Logan, Stuart, 1952, O 29,29:4
Logan, Sydney H, 1953, Ja 11,90:3
Logan, T F, 1928, Ag 10,17:5
Logan, Thomas M Mrs, 1950, Jl 3,15:5
Logan, Thomas Muldrup Logan, 1914, Ag 12,9:4
Logan, Virginia K Mrs, 1940, N 28,23:4
Logan, W N, 1941, Ag 29,17:3
Logan, Walter, 1940, Mr 12,23:2
Logan, Walter Seth, 1906, Jl 20,7:5
Logan, Warren, 1942, Ap 28,21:1
Logan, Welden A, 1941, Je 9,19:5
Logan, William B, 1951, Je 27,29:6
Logan, William Edward Sir, 1875, Je 29,4:7
Logan, William H G, 1943, Ap 7,25:2
Logan, William J, 1920, D 16,17:4; 1921, S 28,19:5; 1938, O 20,23:3
Logan, William M, 1937, Ap 3,19:6
Logan, William T, 1941, S 16,23:3
Logerot, Richard de (Marquis de Croisic), 1907, Mr 14,7:5
Logerot, Richard De Mrs (Marquise De Crossic), 1913, Mr 14,9:1
Loggins, Vernon Dr, 1968, O 4,47:3
Logie, Alfred E, 1946, D 24,17:3
Logie, Jessie, 1955, Mr 3,27:4
Logie, Margaret B, 1959, Je 19,25:2
Logie, William, 1918, O 28,11:2
Logie, William Mrs, 1945, S 9,46:3
Login, S Martin, 1940, D 5,25:4
Login, Samuel E, 1957, My 20,25:6
Loginov, Fedor, 1958, Ag 3,80:5
Loginov, Leonid, 1952, S 28,78:8
Logothetidis, Basil, 1960, F 21,92:5
Logsdon, Ralph E, 1942, Je 29,15:5
Logue, A Emmet, 1949, My 8,76:5
Logue, Cardinal, 1924, N 20,23:4
Logue, Charles A, 1938, Ag 4,17:4
Logue, Charles A Rev, 1913, S 26,11:4
Logue, Daniel C Dr, 1914, F 4,9:6
Logue, Howard H, 1948, Jl 5,15:4
Logue, Hugh A Sr, 1947, Ja 23,23:4
Logue, J Washington, 1925, Ag 28,13:5
Logue, James S, 1943, S 18,17:3
Logue, Lionel, 1953, Ap 13,27:4
Logue, Thomas A (por), 1940, Je 21,21:3
Logue, William A, 1939, Je 17,15:3
Logue, William G, 1942, D 17,29:3
Logue, Wylie G, 1937, N 28,II,9:2
Loh, Lester J, 1962, D 8,27:2
Lohbauer, Fred, 1904, F 4,7:5
Loheed, Kenneth B, 1960, S 6,35:2
Lohia, Ram M, 1967, O 12,50:1
Lohman, Ernest, 1958, S 1,13:3
Lohman, George, 1901, D 2,7:4
Lohman, Harry C, 1953, Mr 26,31:4
Lohman, Henry J, 1948, Ap 10,13:2
Lohman, J Frederick, 1940, N 17,49:2; 1964, D 9,47:3
Lohman, Jack C Mrs, 1948, My 22,15:5
Lohman, James T B, 1946, N 11,27:2
Lohman, Joseph D, 1968, Ap 27,39:3
Lohman, Zeke, 1938, Ja 20,23:5
Lohmann, Carl A, 1957, My 20,25:3
Lohmann, Herbert G, 1942, D 28,19:3
Lohmann, Herman, 1948, Ja 21,25:3
Lohmann, John H Sr, 1955, D 18,92:6
Lohmann, Leroy H, 1940, S 27,23:4
Lohmann, Oscar F, 1965, Jl 13,33:5
Lohmann, Walter, 1955, Ap 16,19:5
Lohmeyer, Frederick H, 1947, My 31,13:4
Lohmeyer, Henry F, 1963, S 1,56:4
Lohn, George L, 1947, Ag 23,13:6
Lohnaas, Harold, 1966, Ja 3,27:3
Lohnes, Carl W, 1951, D 4,33:2
Lohnes, Horace L, 1954, D 25,11:5
Lohr, Bruno A, 1948, F 14,13:3
Lohr, Floyd D, 1950, Mr 18,13:3
Lohr, Freeman D, 1946, Ja 18,19:4
Lohr, George Rev, 1937, Jl 28,14:4
Lohr, Hans, 1964, My 21,35:3
Lohr, Herman, 1943, D 7,27:3
Lohr, J Martin Mrs, 1940, S 24,23:1
Lohr, Lenox R, 1968, My 30,25:1
Lohr, Vergil C, 1951, N 18,90:4
Lohrberg, Howland O, 1953, Jl 23,23:1
Lohrke, Eugene W, 1953, My 18,21:4
Lohrke, James L, 1949, Jl 29,21:6
Lohrman, Christ, 1957, Ap 24,33:5
Lohrman, William E Sr, 1966, S 16,37:3

Lohrmann, Theodora I, 1943, Ap 24,13:3
Lohse, August, 1943, Mr 9,23:3
Lohse, George J, 1946, Ag 25,46:3
Lohsen, Clinton B, 1959, Ag 9,88:2
Loia, James, 1958, Ag 24,86:6
Loia, Michael J, 1948, F 26,23:3
Loillieux, Arthur L, 1956, O 2,35:1
Loines, Russell H Mrs, 1957, D 6,29:2
Loines, Russell Hillard, 1922, D 29,13:4
Loines, Stephen, 1919, Ja 16,13:2
Loines, Stephen Mrs, 1944, Ap 3,21:3
Loinger, Morris M, 1966, D 29,31:2
Loins, Richard A, 1907, Je 24,7:6
Loiseau, J P, 1870, Mr 6,1:3
Loisseaux, Louis A, 1947, Ja 28,24:3
Loizeaux, Charles E, 1947, My 8,25:4
Loizeaux, Elie T, 1956, Ag 7,27:3
Loizeaux, John G, 1955, O 15,15:5
Loizeaux, Joshua D Mrs, 1956, My 22,42:6
Loizeaux, P Daniel, 1952, F 9,13:6
Loizeaux, P Daniel Mrs, 1942, D 8,25:3
Lok, Lee B, 1942, N 1,53:1
Lokey, Eugene M, 1956, F 1,31:5
Lokis, Basil D, 1953, N 3,32:5
Lokitz, Daniel, 1947, F 8,17:2
Lokke, Carl L, 1960, Ap 5,37:3
Lole, Arthur F Mrs, 1964, My 12,37:4
Lolley, William H, 1957, N 7,35:2
Lollo, Vincenzo, 1946, N 20,31:4
Lomakin, Jacob M, 1958, Ag 18,19:3
Lomanto, Enzo D, 1952, Mr 17,21:4
Lomas, Alfred J, 1954, S 12,84:6
Lomas, Harold Lt, 1916, Jl 31,9:6
Lomas, Herbert, 1961, Ap 13,35:4
Lomas, Norman A, 1957, F 21,27:1
Lomas, Sidney C, 1953, Jl 29,23:3
Lomas, W B, 1880, Jl 16,5:5
Lomas, William B, 1942, S 4,23:2
Lomasney, David A, 1962, N 21,30:6
Lomasney, M, 1933, Ag 13,26:1
Lomasney, Michael J, 1945, O 13,15:2
Lomax, Clarence S, 1944, S 3,28:8
Lomax, Flippen C, 1940, Je 11,25:3
Lomax, John A, 1948, Ja 27,26:3
Lomax, John J, 1939, Ap 1,19:3
Lomax, Lansford L Gen, 1913, My 29,11:6
Lomax, Lucie V Mrs, 1945, D 26,19:4
Lomax, Thomas Henry Bp, 1908, Ap 1,7:2
Lomb, Carl F, 1939, Ja 27,19:3
Lomb, Emilie Mrs, 1940, F 9,19:2
Lomb, Henry Capt, 1908, Je 14,11:5
Lomba, Edward F Mrs, 1939, Ja 5,23:3
Lombaert, H J, 1885, Mr 11,5:6
Lombard, Alice M A Mrs, 1940, Ap 17,23:2
Lombard, Alvin O, 1937, F 22,17:4
Lombard, E H Gen, 1903, My 6,9:6
Lombard, Gulf Davenport Dr, 1907, My 24,9:7
Lombard, Jay P, 1963, S 8,86:7
Lombard, Joseph J, 1955, O 26,31:3
Lombard, Manuel H, 1938, Ja 4,23:3
Lombard, Mary G, 1942, Je 24,19:3
Lombard, Robert H, 1944, Ag 7,15:2
Lombard, Walter E, 1942, D 23,19:2
Lombard, Warren P, 1939, Jl 14,19:3
Lombardi, Alfonso A, 1966, F 12,27:4
Lombardi, Anthony, 1948, F 19,23:4
Lombardi, Carlo Mrs, 1967, Ag 12,25:5
Lombardi, Carmen A, 1959, Jl 2,25:4
Lombardi, Cynthia, 1942, Ja 11,44:2
Lombardi, David, 1966, N 21,54:1
Lombardi, Generoso, 1957, Ap 27,19:5
Lombardi, Gioacchino, 1961, Ag 2,29:3
Lombardi, Joseph J, 1964, Ap 14,37:2
Lombardi, Julius C, 1960, Ag 9,27:4
Lombardi, Louis G, 1965, Ag 6,24:6
Lombardi, Louis G Mrs, 1965, Ag 6,24:6
Lombardi, Louis T, 1955, D 11,88:8
Lombardi, Mario, 1915, Ap 23,13:4
Lombardi, Vincent J, 1968, Ag 29,35:4
Lombardo, Carlo, 1959, D 22,31:3
Lombardo, Francis, 1937, S 17,25:5
Lombardo, Gaetano, 1954, O 7,23:5
Lombardo, Gaetano Mrs, 1957, My 28,34:3
Lombardo, Joseph J Mrs, 1965, Ja 8,29:4
Lombardo, Melchiore, 1952, F 12,27:3
Lombardo, Theodore R, 1955, Jl 22,23:5
Lombardo, Toledano Vincente, 1968, N 19,40:2
Lombardo, Tom, 1950, O 28,3:1
Lombart, V, 1942, Mr 17,21:3
Lombino, Onofrio Mrs, 1951, F 24,13:2
Lombroso, Cesare, 1909, O 20,9:4
Lombroso, Ugo, 1952, Ap 11,23:3
Lome, Dupuy de, 1904, Jl 8,5:5
Lome, S C H L D de, 1885, F 2,5:6
Lomen, Alfred J, 1950, My 19,27:5
Lomen, Carl J, 1965, Ag 18,35:2
Lomis, Luigi Col, 1918, My 10,11:5
Lomonossoff, George V, 1952, N 21,25:4
Lomp, Raymond N, 1968, Ag 28,44:5
LoNano, Ernest S, 1958, O 11,23:3
Lonardi, Eduardo A (funl plans, Mr 24,19:5; funl, Mr 25,92:5), 1956, Mr 23,1:6
Lonberg, Fritz, 1959, O 10,21:4
Lonborg, Carl, 1948, Ja 28,23:3
Loncao, Ignazio B, 1947, N 22,15:5
Loncarevich, Andrew, 1950, S 21,48:2
Loncin, Msgr, 1947, Ap 24,25:6
Londergan, Harold, 1961, Je 1,35:1
Londergan, John Mrs, 1943, Ja 3,42:2
Londesborough, Earl of (Wm Francis Hy Denison), 1917, N 17,13:4
Londesborough, Earl of (Geo Francis Wm Hy Denison), 1920, S 14,11:2
Londesborough, Earl of, 1937, Ap 18,II,8:8
Londino, Joseph, 1954, Ja 17,93:2
Londino, Joseph Mrs, 1952, F 7,27:3
London, Abraham, 1925, D 13,13:1
London, Bessie M Mrs, 1947, S 9,31:2
London, Carl, 1956, Jl 2,21:3
London, Emma Mrs, 1962, Mr 11,87:1
London, Frank M (por), 1945, Mr 11,39:1
London, Frederick G, 1947, F 8,17:4
London, Frederick G Mrs, 1964, S 20,88:5
London, Fritz, 1954, Mr 31,27:5
London, Georges, 1951, S 16,84:5
London, Irving, 1967, Ap 4,43:2
London, Israel, 1968, S 24,47:1
London, Jack (funl, N 24,13:5), 1916, N 23,13:3
London, Jack, 1955, Mr 2,27:2
London, Jack (J G Harper), 1963, D 20,26:7
London, Jack Mrs, 1955, Ja 15,13:2
London, Jacob, 1965, My 16,88:3
London, John M, 1956, Ja 24,31:4
London, Jules R, 1949, Je 17,23:5
London, Louis B, 1946, Je 10,21:2
London, Louis L, 1953, Ap 3,24:3
London, M, 1926, Je 7,1:8
London, Matilda H, 1942, Ja 24,15:7
London, Meyer Mrs, 1947, Jl 19,13:2
London, Samuel, 1958, Jl 21,21:4
London, Sascha, 1950, Mr 5,94:6
London, Stephen, 1953, Ag 24,23:2
Londonderry, Dowager Marchioness of (E H Chaplin), 1959, Ap 24,27:2
Londonderry, Lady, 1951, D 20,31:4
Londonderry, Lord, 1915, F 9,9:6
Londonderry, Marquess of (por), 1949, F 12,17:5
Londonderry, Marquess of (E C S R Vane-Tempest-Stewart), 1955, O 19,33:2
Londonderry, Marquis of (G H R C W Vane-Tempest), 1884, N 7,5:6
Londos, Thomas, 1949, S 26,25:1
Londrigan, Joseph F, 1953, O 19,21:4
Lone, E Miriam, 1953, S 7,19:2
Lone, Edward Rev, 1909, F 18,7:5
Lonergan, Alice F, 1942, S 2,23:3
Lonergan, Amy R Mrs, 1937, Ag 18,19:5
Lonergan, Aneta C, 1962, Jl 12,29:2
Lonergan, Augustine (por), 1947, O 19,64:1
Lonergan, Edward, 1948, F 7,15:1
Lonergan, Edward F, 1966, Ag 23,39:3
Lonergan, J Rev, 1867, Ag 19,1:7
Lonergan, John A, 1951, Ja 7,76:5
Lonergan, John A Mrs, 1943, D 19,48:1
Lonergan, Lester Jr, 1959, D 28,23:3
Lonergan, Michael, 1953, Je 19,21:4
Lonergan, Michael P, 1946, Mr 9,13:3
Lonergan, Patrick J, 1949, O 23,84:4
Lonergan, Phil, 1940, Mr 10,48:7
Lonergan, T E Maj, 1901, N 8,9:5
Lonergan, Walter J, 1960, S 16,31:2
Lonergan, William R, 1956, Jl 18,27:2
Loney, Edward D, 1949, Jl 3,26:7
Long, Albert J, 1944, Je 15,19:5
Long, Andrew T (por), 1946, My 23,21:5
Long, Annie Mrs, 1940, Ag 19,17:6
Long, Anthony, 1955, Mr 8,27:2
Long, Arita S Mrs, 1937, S 27,21:4
Long, Arthur B, 1949, Je 28,27:4
Long, Arthur L Mrs, 1952, D 27,9:5
Long, Arthur M Mrs, 1944, Ap 1,13:4
Long, Augustus C Mrs, 1963, O 15,39:1
Long, B B, 1927, Mr 2,25:5
Long, Baron H, 1962, F 19,31:2
Long, Basil S, 1937, Ja 10,II,10:3
Long, Benjamin G, 1943, Mr 10,19:5
Long, Bert H Mrs, 1951, My 11,27:3
Long, Boaz W, 1962, Jl 31,27:3
Long, Breckinridge, 1958, S 27,21:2
Long, Breckinridge Mrs, 1959, Ja 25,92:7
Long, Brice H, 1948, F 22,48:4
Long, Byron A Mrs, 1938, D 8,27:6
Long, C I, 1934, Jl 2,19:1
Long, C O, 1904, My 13,9:7
Long, C Sterry, 1964, O 27,39:2
Long, Catherine, 1940, Ag 26,15:3
Long, Charles A Jr, 1949, Jl 8,19:2
Long, Charles Dr, 1937, Ap 8,23:2
Long, Charles E, 1940, Jl 5,13:5
Long, Charles E (por), 1942, Mr 19,21:2
Long, Charles G, 1943, Mr 6,13:2
Long, Charles G Mrs, 1951, Ap 11,29:3
Long, Charles I, 1942, N 17,26:2
Long, Charles J, 1949, O 22,17:1
Long, Charles R (por), 1946, Ja 29,25:3
Long, Chas-Francis, 1952, F 29,23:1
Long, Clarence D, 1956, N 8,39:4
Long, Clarence S, 1957, Ap 25,31:3
Long, Curtis W, 1953, D 22,31:2
Long, D Edward, 1952, D 4,35:3
Long, D Ritchie Mrs, 1958, Mr 23,89:1
Long, Daniel E, 1942, Ja 14,21:3
Long, David D, 1939, Ja 16,15:5
Long, David F, 1940, O 28,17:3
Long, Dewey E, 1968, Ap 21,80:1
Long, Doris, 1937, Ap 26,19:5
Long, E Edward, 1956, Je 25,23:6
Long, E Hugh, 1948, Ap 21,27:3
Long, E Leslie, 1941, F 28,19:1
Long, Earl K (funl, S 8,35:3), 1960, S 6,1:2
Long, Eddie, 1942, F 12,23:6
Long, Edward, 1865, O 22,4:1
Long, Edward E, 1949, Jl 8,19:5
Long, Edward J, 1949, F 20,60:6
Long, Eli, 1948, Ag 4,21:2
Long, Eli Gen, 1903, Ja 6,9:4
Long, Eli H, 1949, Je 2,28:4
Long, Elmer E, 1942, Mr 14,15:1
Long, Emile B Mrs, 1957, O 29,31:3
Long, Emilie O, 1951, Mr 31,15:6
Long, Ernest M, 1937, S 29,23:2
Long, Ferdinand G, 1948, Ja 13,25:1
Long, Florence Mrs, 1955, O 25,33:4
Long, Francis, 1916, Je 9,13:7
Long, Frank A, 1946, O 19,21:3
Long, Frank B, 1939, S 30,17:5
Long, Frank E Mrs, 1951, Ja 11,26:3
Long, Frank M, 1956, D 13,37:1; 1962, O 19,31:2
Long, Frank W, 1941, N 29,17:5
Long, Fred A, 1945, Ap 15,14:5
Long, Frederick L, 1945, D 5,25:2
Long, George A, 1958, N 21,29:5
Long, George C Jr, 1958, Jl 16,29:1
Long, George D, 1951, O 3,36:2
Long, George H, 1937, My 4,25:3
Long, George L, 1940, Jl 9,21:1
Long, George L Mrs, 1957, O 18,23:3
Long, George S, 1958, Mr 23,88:1
Long, George T, 1948, Ag 3,25:3
Long, H P, 1935, S 10,1:8
Long, Harold M, 1956, F 19,92:2; 1956, F 22,27:5
Long, Harry, 1945, D 9,V,2:5
Long, Harry B, 1957, S 17,35:1
Long, Harry V, 1949, F 11,23:3
Long, Helen M, 1951, My 5,17:4
Long, Henry, 1880, Ap 28,2:3; 1907, F 9,9:6
Long, Henry F, 1956, Mr 31,15:5
Long, Henry J, 1955, My 20,25:5
Long, Henry K, 1963, Je 22,23:6
Long, Henry S, 1954, O 14,29:2
Long, Herbert M, 1948, Je 17,25:4
Long, Homer G, 1952, My 22,27:4
Long, Howard H, 1957, F 24,84:4
Long, Howard M, 1952, D 4,35:3
Long, Howard V Mrs, 1956, Jl 19,27:1
Long, Huey P Sr, 1937, F 5,21:3
Long, Hugh W, 1964, D 14,35:3
Long, Irving G, 1942, Je 20,13:3
Long, Isaac S, 1916, My 9,11:5
Long, J C Commodore, 1865, S 7,8:2
Long, J D, 1948, D 7,31:4
Long, J H, 1882, Mr 3,2:6
Long, J L, 1927, N 1,27:3; 1933, Jl 29,11:4
Long, J Raymond, 1967, Ag 20,88:2
Long, James, 1868, Ja 17,8:5
Long, James E, 1946, D 3,31:2
Long, James J, 1944, S 20,23:2; 1955, Ap 9,13:4
Long, James M, 1950, Ag 1,23:1
Long, James Mrs, 1881, Ja 9,5:7
Long, James W, 1903, Ap 21,9:5; 1952, F 18,19:3
Long, Jesse C, 1951, Ja 3,27:4
Long, John, 1939, Ja 16,15:2
Long, John B, 1962, Mr 17,25:3
Long, John C, 1903, Jl 29,7:6
Long, John D, 1915, S 1,9:6
Long, John D (por), 1949, S 20,29:1
Long, John Davis, 1915, Ag 29,15:5
Long, John E, 1940, Mr 4,15:2; 1950, F 6,25:3; 1 O 12,29:2
Long, John F, 1948, Jl 8,23:4
Long, John J, 1947, Jl 14,21:5; 1964, Jl 19,64:3
Long, John L, 1951, Ag 6,21:5
Long, John Mrs, 1949, O 9,92:4
Long, Joseph B Mrs (will, Jl 18,14:8), 1942, Jl
Long, Joseph B Mrs (will), 1943, My 14,21:6
Long, Joseph H, 1958, D 30,35:1
Long, Joseph V Sr, 1943, Jl 19,15:2
Long, Julius T, 1965, N 12,48:1
Long, Kathleen, 1968, Mr 22,47:3
Long, Kenneth B, 1955, Je 1,33:3
Long, Kenneth M, 1949, Ag 10,21:4
Long, Kitty H Mrs, 1941, F 23,41:3
Long, Lee, 1960, D 24,15:3
Long, Leroy Y Mrs, 1950, D 30,13:3
Long, Lewis M, 1957, S 12,31:5
Long, Lily A Mrs, 1939, Jl 11,19:5
Long, Louis Dr, 1968, My 14,47:3
Long, Lucy V Mrs, 1942, Je 19,23:5
Long, Marcus Dr, 1968, My 14,47:3

Long, Marguerite, 1966, F 14,29:1
Long, Martin S, 1945, Jl 29,40:3
Long, Maurice A, 1938, Mr 1,22:2
Long, Maurice D, 1957, Mr 17,86:2
Long, Michael F, 1949, Je 3,25:2
Long, Mitchell, 1953, Ap 4,14:3
Long, Monroe Budd Dr, 1910, F 21,9:5
Long, Omera F, 1945, N 28,27:6
Long, Oren E, 1965, My 7,41:1
Long, Orie W, 1955, S 15,33:2
Long, Orville S, 1944, Mr 25,15:6
Long, Oscar L, 1945, Mr 10,17:5
Long, Paul, 1950, D 18,31:4
Long, Paul W Sr, 1961, Ap 11,37:4
Long, Percy W, 1952, O 3,23:4
Long, Perrin H, 1965, D 18,29:3
Long, Philip J, 1944, O 9,23:4
Long, R A, 1934, Mr 16,21:3
Long, Ralph H, 1948, F 20,27:3
Long, Ralph N, 1956, N 15,35:1
Long, Ralph W, 1961, N 4,19:3
Long, Raymond F, 1954, Je 20,86:1
Long, Raymond V, 1960, F 23,31:2
Long, Richard C, 1957, Mr 15,26:1
Long, Richard H, 1957, Ap 18,29:2
Long, Richard H Mrs, 1947, My 16,23:3
Long, Richard W, 1953, N 14,17:4
Long, Robert C Sr, 1948, Ag 29,56:4
Long, Robert E C, 1938, O 19,23:1
Long, Roland W, 1960, D 10,23:4
Long, Roy H, 1964, O 25,89:1
Long, Samuel, 1915, Jl 29,9:6
Long, Samuel C, 1958, Ag 5,27:2
Long, Samuel Mrs, 1947, Ap 2,27:5
Long, Sana, 1941, Mr 3,15:1
Long, Seth W, 1937, My 23,II,11:2
Long, Sheila P, 1956, Mr 1,19:4
Long, Stanley D, 1956, O 10,39:5
Long, Stanley L, 1955, Mr 24,32:2
Long, Stephen Merritt, 1905, Ap 11,11:6
Long, Sven A, 1951, N 28,31:5
Long, T Richard, 1948, Jl 12,19:5
Long, Thomas M, 1941, F 4,21:2
Long, Thomas S, 1952, N 10,25:2
Long, Walter D, 1964, Mr 3,35:4
Long, Walter E, 1961, O 26,35:5
Long, Walter H, 1952, Jl 6,48:7
Long, Walter Hume, 1924, S 27,16:2
Long, Walter L, 1943, Ag 9,13:5
Long, Walter P Mrs, 1947, D 8,25:4
Long, William A, 1948, Ag 17,21:4
Long, William C, 1963, O 17,32:6
Long, William F, 1961, Mr 4,23:3
Long, William F Mrs, 1948, N 3,27:5
Long, William H, 1954, My 29,15:5; 1957, Ap 18,29:4
Long, William H Sr Mrs, 1947, F 10,29:5
Long, William J, 1948, D 29,21:2; 1952, N 11,29:1
Long, William P, 1952, Ap 21,21:4
Long, William S, 1938, My 12,23:2
Long, William W, 1941, F 18,23:3
Longabaugh, Charles O, 1944, Je 17,13:5
Longacre, Andrew Rev Dr, 1906, F 19,9:4
Longacre, Frederick, 1950, Jl 21,19:6
Longacre, Herbert R, 1948, S 10,23:2
Longacre, J Howard, 1941, Jl 13,29:3
Longacre, James B, 1947, My 16,24:2
Longacre, John A, 1944, Ap 27,23:1
Longacre, John M, 1939, Ap 24,17:5
Longacre, Lindsay B, 1952, S 18,29:5
Longacre, Lydia, 1951, Je 22,25:2
Longaker, Edgar L, 1957, Ag 30,19:1
Longaker, L C, 1938, Ap 4,17:5
Longaker, Louis B, 1963, S 10,39:4
Longan, George B (por), 1942, O 17,15:1
Longan, Lou E W Mrs, 1938, O 20,23:4
Longboat, Tom, 1949, Ja 11,31:1
Longbottom, Albert S, 1942, Ap 17,17:3
Longbottom, Charles R Lt-Com, 1937, O 8,24:2
Longbrake, Art, 1953, N 6,27:4
Longchamp, Ben, 1942, Ag 4,20:2
Longcope, Thomas M Jr, 1946, Jl 18,25:3
Longcope, Thomas R, 1939, Ja 12,19:3
Longcope, Warfield T, 1953, Ap 26,86:1
Longden, Aladine C, 1941, Jl 13,29:3
Longden, Frederick, 1952, O 6,25:2
Longden, Henry B (por), 1948, N 9,27:3
Longden, Wilfred, 1943, F 28,47:5
Longell, Clyde Mrs, 1955, Mr 8,27:1
Longendyke, Dwight, 1937, Mr 24,25:5
Longenecker, Phil, 1954, F 2,14:7
Longergan, Lester Jr Mrs, 1942, Je 12,22:2
Longernecker, H, 1955, Ja 16,70:4
Longest, Joseph Y (will), 1956, O 20,16:6
Longfelder, William, 1939, Ja 7,15:1
Longfellow, A M, 1928, D 8,19:4
Longfellow, Ernest Wadsworth, 1921, N 25,15:4
Longfellow, Frederick W (por), 1938, O 31,15:1
Longfellow, Frederick W Mrs, 1963, S 11,43:3
Longfellow, H W, 1882, Mr 25,1:7
Longfellow, Livingston, 1963, N 14,35:4
Longfellow, Mary K, 1945, S 17,19:5
Longfellow, Raymond C, 1944, Ap 28,19:4
Longfellow, Wilbert E (por), 1947, Mr 19,25:3
Longfellow, William Pitt Preble, 1913, Ag 5,7:3
Longfield, Charles H, 1949, Mr 8,25:1
Longfield, Melvin R, 1940, Ja 26,17:4
Longfield, Reynolds, 1948, Ag 21,15:6
Longford, Earl of (E A H Pakenham), 1961, F 5,80:4
Longhi, Lorenzo G, 1950, Je 28,27:5
Longhi, Louis, 1950, Ag 4,21:3
Longhi, Silvio Sen, 1937, Jl 1,27:5
Longhorn, Chula King, 1910, O 24,9:5
Longhurst, Maurice F, 1960, Ap 26,37:5
Longini, Arthur, 1965, Je 5,31:6
Longino, Andrew H, 1942, F 25,19:5
Longino, Olin N, 1955, S 9,23:3
Longley, Edmund W, 1941, My 16,23:6
Longley, F Alan, 1946, Ja 4,21:3
Longley, George Cashel, 1917, D 22,11:5
Longley, Harry S, 1944, Ap 6,23:4
Longley, Harry S Mrs, 1964, N 6,37:2
Longley, James F Mrs, 1943, Je 10,21:3
Longley, James Wilburforce, 1922, Mr 17,17:6
Longley, Lewis E, 1954, My 4,29:3
Longley, Walter L, 1942, Ja 26,15:3
Longley, William H Dr, 1937, Mr 11,23:2
Longlin, J N, 1904, Mr 29,2:3
Longman, Evelyn B, 1954, Mr 11,34:6
Longman, George H, 1938, Ag 20,15:4
Longman, Hubert Sir, 1940, Mr 18,17:1
Longman, W, 1877, Ag 16,4:6
Longmire, Rowena, 1938, Jl 21,21:5
Longmore, Robert J, 1946, S 18,31:3
Longmore, Samuel H, 1949, O 22,17:1
Longo, Maurice M, 1958, My 15,29:4
Longo, Michael, 1943, Je 4,21:6
Longo, Thomas J, 1950, Ag 17,28:4
Longobardi, Nicholas Mrs, 1946, Ap 6,17:4
Longone, Paul (cor, Ag 10,17:1), 1939, Ag 4,13:5
Longperier, H A, 1882, Ja 15,5:5
Longsdorf, Harold E, 1955, Ag 25,23:5
Longsdorf, Harold H, 1944, Ap 30,45:1
Longsdorf, Jacob Mrs, 1956, F 28,31:2
Longshore, Clinton H, 1948, Jl 14,24:3
Longshore, Francis H, 1941, O 20,17:2
Longshore, J S, 1879, D 27,2:4
Longshore, John P, 1960, N 4,33:3
Longshore, Walter E Jr, 1957, Ag 28,27:2
Longsjo, Arthur J Jr, 1958, S 17,8:6
Longstaff, John, 1941, O 2,25:2
Longstaff, John Bailey Jr, 1968, Ap 10,43:1
Longstaff, Tom (details, Je 30,33:3), 1964, Je 29,27:3
Longstreet, Archibald Craig, 1911, My 1,11:5
Longstreet, Arthur H, 1944, Ap 6,23:6
Longstreet, Chalmer J, 1952, Mr 7,23:4
Longstreet, Elias S, 1945, Jl 10,11:7
Longstreet, George A, 1937, My 24,19:4
Longstreet, James Col, 1922, Jl 16,26:4
Longstreet, James Gen, 1904, Ja 3,9:4
Longstreet, James Mrs, 1962, Mr 4,33:1
Longstreth, Bevis, 1944, Mr 2,17:2
Longstreth, Charles, 1948, Mr 2,23:5
Longstreth, Edward T, 1946, F 11,29:2
Longstreth, Frank M, 1942, Je 29,15:5
Longstreth, Frank M Jr, 1942, Ap 24,17:2
Longstreth, Howard, 1946, D 24,17:3
Longstreth, Rebecca C, 1937, Jl 23,19:4
Longstreth, William C, 1958, Jl 26,15:6
Longua, Paul J, 1958, O 7,35:4
Longueil, Harry R, 1941, O 19,45:2
Longuet, Edgar, 1950, D 14,35:4
Longuet, Jean (por), 1938, S 13,23:3
Longuet, Marcel, 1949, D 21,30:4
Longwell, Daniel, 1968, N 22,47:4
Longwell, Eugene V, 1949, O 12,30:5
Longworth, J, 1883, D 31,5:2
Longworth, N, 1931, Ap 10,1:1
Longworth, N Murray, 1963, N 9,25:5
Longworth, Nicholas, 1863, F 15,3:4
Longworth, Nicholas Mrs, 1865, O 8,5:5; 1922, Je 28, 15:6
Longworthy, G I, 1882, Jl 29,2:7
Longyear, Edmund J, 1954, D 7,33:4
Longyear, John Munro, 1922, My 29,11:4
Longyear, Ralph V, 1950, Je 26,27:4
Longyear, Robert L, 1953, Mr 24,31:4
Longyear, Robert L Sr Mrs, 1956, Ap 5,29:4
Longyear, William A, 1937, N 26,21:2
Longyear, Willis D, 1941, Mr 18,23:3
Lonis, Ernest J, 1954, My 24,27:2
Lonn, Merton J, 1967, My 24,47:3
Lonnen, Emily M Mrs, 1939, D 30,15:2
Lono, Gen, 1907, Jl 1,7:6
Lons, Cynthia, 1939, Ap 2,III,6:7
Lonsberry, Marcus D, 1948, N 24,23:4
Lonsdale, D, 1876, Ag 19,8:2
Lonsdale, Earl of, 1872, Mr 6,5:3; 1944, Ap 14,19:3
Lonsdale, Earl of (E L Lowthar), 1953, Mr 12,27:4
Lonsdale, Edwin, 1915, S 7,13:6
Lonsdale, F Murton, 1947, Mr 29,15:2
Lonsdale, Frederick, 1954, Ap 6,29:5
Lonsdale, Herman L, 1940, Ag 17,15:3
Lonsdale, James E, 1948, Jl 29,21:4
Lonsdale, James Ralston, 1921, My 25,17:4
Lonsdale, John Brownlee (Lord Armaghdale), 1924, Je 9,17:6
Lonsdale, John G (por), 1943, Je 17,22:2
Lonsdale, Lady (por), 1941, My 13,23:2
Lonsdale, Lord, 1882, F 25,3:2
Lonsdale, William Sr, 1960, F 28,82:3
Lonsdorf, William M, 1957, Ja 26,19:4
Lonyay, Carl, 1963, My 1,39:2
Lonys, Pierre, 1925, Je 5,17:4
Loo, C T, 1957, Ag 18,82:3
Loo, F A van der, 1943, Ag 7,11:4
Loo, Ping Y, 1958, O 16,37:5
Loo, W L Sluyterman van, 1946, My 28,21:5
Looby, John C, 1953, O 14,29:2
Looby, Mary, 1960, D 28,27:5
Loofbourow, Dorothea G, 1951, F 2,23:3
Loofbourow, John R, 1951, Ja 23,27:1
Loofbourrow, John G, 1964, F 25,32:1
Loofbourrow, John Mrs (L Groody), 1961, S 17,86:4
Loog, Mary E, 1946, My 6,21:5
Look, David M, 1945, Je 22,15:5
Look, M Jerome, 1944, Jl 12,19:5
Look, Mariana, 1944, O 21,17:6
Look, Samuel L, 1942, Ap 17,17:1
Look, Samuel M, 1963, N 22,37:3
Lookaround, Angus F, 1946, Ap 17,25:2
Looker, Edward C, 1947, Ag 25,17:2
Looker, John C, 1938, S 1,23:5
Lookout, Fred, 1949, Ag 29,17:5
Lookstein, Jacob S, 1943, Jl 19,15:3
Lookup, T (Dr Evans), 1879, Ag 29,2:7
Loomes, Harry E, 1946, Mr 20,23:4
Loomis, A L Dr, 1895, Ja 24,9:7
Loomis, Alfred Fullerton, 1968, Mr 27,47:1
Loomis, Alfred L Mrs, 1904, Mr 25,9:5
Loomis, Allen, 1948, Ja 11,56:6
Loomis, Archie H, 1947, N 13,28:2
Loomis, Charles B, 1911, S 24,II,13:5
Loomis, Chester, 1924, N 14,19:6
Loomis, Corinne V, 1956, S 1,15:2
Loomis, D F, 1909, Je 8,7:5
Loomis, Eben J Prof, 1912, D 3,15:4
Loomis, Edward E (por), 1937, Jl 12,17:1
Loomis, Edward E Mrs, 1948, Jl 16,19:1
Loomis, Edward F, 1959, Jl 15,29:5
Loomis, Edwin F, 1952, N 30,88:8
Loomis, Edwin J Col, 1918, Je 24,11:5
Loomis, Elias Prof, 1889, Ag 16,4:6
Loomis, Elisha S, 1940, D 13,23:2
Loomis, Elmer H Mrs, 1951, N 9,27:3
Loomis, Emma H Mrs, 1948, F 29,60:7
Loomis, Francis B, 1948, Ag 7,15:3
Loomis, Frank, 1904, F 12,9:6; 1950, Mr 14,25:2
Loomis, Frank D, 1952, F 29,23:3
Loomis, Frank Mrs, 1939, Ag 5,15:4
Loomis, Frank N, 1941, F 4,21:6
Loomis, Fred P Mrs, 1950, Ap 24,25:2
Loomis, Frederic M, 1949, F 10,27:3
Loomis, Frederick B Prof, 1937, Jl 31,15:3
Loomis, Frederick H, 1948, Jl 3,15:5
Loomis, Frederick K, 1959, My 2,23:2
Loomis, Frederick Mrs, 1939, Mr 16,23:6
Loomis, Frederick O Gen Sir, 1937, F 16,23:2
Loomis, G A Col, 1872, Mr 6,1:6
Loomis, George F, 1940, Ja 7,48:7
Loomis, Gilbert J, 1961, O 27,33:4
Loomis, Guy, 1946, N 15,24:2
Loomis, H N, 1881, Mr 23,5:3
Loomis, Hannah S Mrs, 1939, O 22,41:2
Loomis, Harlow Mrs, 1943, N 5,19:3
Loomis, Harold V, 1956, My 30,21:5
Loomis, Harvey Noxon, 1916, S 14,7:5
Loomis, Henry B, 1939, D 3,60:2
Loomis, Henry B Mrs, 1949, Ap 30,13:4
Loomis, Henry F, 1952, Jl 9,27:6
Loomis, Henry Mrs, 1947, D 18,30:3
Loomis, Henry Patterson Dr, 1907, D 23,9:5
Loomis, Henry Rev, 1920, Ag 30,9:6
Loomis, Herbert F, 1939, Mr 18,17:4
Loomis, Homer L Mrs, 1941, D 5,24:2
Loomis, Horace, 1925, Mr 9,17:4
Loomis, J S Mrs, 1933, D 26,15:1
Loomis, James Hervey, 1914, N 4,7:7
Loomis, Jennie, 1944, Mr 9,17:4
Loomis, John Mason Mrs, 1910, O 8,11:5
Loomis, John R, 1922, D 8,17:4; 1951, Ag 16,27:5
Loomis, Karl Mrs, 1963, Ap 2,47:3
Loomis, Katherine, 1965, F 23,33:2
Loomis, Lady, 1954, S 11,17:4
Loomis, Laurus, 1922, N 25,13:5
Loomis, Lee C, 1950, Ap 9,84:4
Loomis, Lee P, 1964, F 11,40:1
Loomis, Louise R, 1958, Ja 4,15:4
Loomis, Lynn A, 1952, F 10,93:2
Loomis, M Gen, 1874, Ja 13,1:6
Loomis, Madeleine S, 1950, Ag 18,21:5
Loomis, Marion L Mrs, 1938, Mr 4,23:3
Loomis, N Edward Mrs, 1964, F 9,89:2
Loomis, Nathaniel E, 1965, N 12,48:1
Loomis, Newell C, 1960, D 14,39:1
Loomis, Orland S, 1942, D 8,25:1
Loomis, Roger Mrs, 1960, Ag 26,25:2
Loomis, Roger S, 1966, O 12,43:3
Loomis, Samuel L, 1938, Ja 12,21:5
Loomis, William A, 1952, O 18,19:7

Loomis, William F, 1964, D 24,19:5
Loomis, William H, 1913, Je 8,IV,5:6; 1917, D 1,13:5
Loomis, William W, 1947, D 10,31:3
Loonam, Bernard J, 1940, F 26,15:3
Loonam, Joseph P, 1958, Mr 5,31:5
Looney, Charles, 1937, Mr 26,22:3
Looney, Edmund D Jr, 1956, My 10,31:3
Looney, James Francis Msgr, 1968, Ap 5,47:2
Looney, James T, 1954, Mr 25,29:5
Looney, John T, 1944, F 21,15:5
Looney, Michael J, 1948, Mr 30,23:5
Looney, Thomas, 1940, My 27,19:4
Looney, Thomas F, 1948, Jl 25,48:7
Looney, William A, 1966, Ap 15,39:1
Loonie, William P, 1963, O 28,27:5
Loop, Charles L, 1915, N 18,9:6
Loop, J P, 1882, Jl 26,5:6
Loop, Jennette Shepperd Mrs, 1909, Ap 18,11:4
Loop, Martin, 1946, S 19,31:2
Loope, Warren L Mrs, 1940, Ap 21,43:1
Looper, Edward A, 1953, Ja 16,23:3
Looram, James F X, 1964, Ap 29,41:2
Loori, Joseph J, 1955, Mr 10,27:4
Loos, Carl, 1948, My 27,25:2
Loos, Charles Louis Prof, 1912, F 28,11:5
Loos, Charles W (por), 1945, Ag 2,19:3
Loos, Edward W N, 1950, Jl 10,21:1
Loos, Ernie, 1945, N 10,15:2
Loos, H Clifford, 1960, S 1,27:5
Loos, John H, 1955, Jl 2,15:5
Loos, R Beers, 1944, Mr 8,16:5
Loos, Ralph B Mrs, 1938, O 10,19:2
Loos, Richard C, 1942, D 27,34:3
Loos, Wallace M, 1944, O 8,43:1
Loose, Alfred C, 1943, O 16,13:4
Loose, Franz, 1965, Mr 30,39:6
Loose, Jacob L, 1923, S 19,4:7
Loose, Jacob L Mrs, 1945, S 27,21:6
Loose, Joseph S, 1922, Je 13,19:6
Loose, Kenneth D Mrs, 1951, My 12,21:6
Loose, Maxwell A, 1941, Ja 21,22:2
Looser, Gustave A, 1939, O 29,40:8
Loosley, Daniel R Capt, 1922, N 21,19:4
Lootens, J Ghislain, 1946, Ag 21,27:2
Lopata, Agnes Mrs, 1953, Jl 19,57:3
Lopatin, Edward, 1953, D 20,77:2
Lopatnikov, Philip P, 1947, Ag 19,23:5
Lopatto, John S, 1956, Ap 3,35:4
Loper, Arthur G, 1943, My 16,43:1
Loper, Frank Marion, 1925, F 12,19:4
Loper, Gilbert H Mrs, 1948, S 20,25:3
Loper, Harry S, 1945, My 28,19:5
Loper, R F, 1880, N 9,3:5
Loper, Walter, 1949, F 27,68:6
Lopetz, Harry, 1947, S 20,15:6
Lopez, Adriano L, 1944, Ap 22,15:5
Lopez, Albert F, 1948, Jl 18,53:1
Lopez, Alejandro, 1940, Mr 14,23:3
Lopez, Alfonso, 1959, N 21,23:3
Lopez, Alfonso Mrs, 1949, Ja 24,19:3
Lopez, Amy M Mrs, 1956, S 11,35:3
Lopez, Ana, 1955, O 11,27:5
Lopez, Angel, 1968, Jl 13,27:5
Lopez, Ansonia Mrs, 1955, D 20,27:2
Lopez, Antonio, 1912, Mr 30,13:5
Lopez, Bernardo, 1958, Ja 15,26:1
Lopez, Carlos, 1953, Ja 8,27:4
Lopez, Carlos Antonio Pres, 1862, N 15,2:1
Lopez, Carlos L, 1944, N 22,19:5
Lopez, Charles Albert, 1906, My 19,11:2
Lopez, Clement, 1947, Ja 4,15:3
Lopez, Eugenio G, 1954, S 1,27:2
Lopez, Faustina Mrs, 1962, Ap 16,29:3
Lopez, Frank G Mrs, 1956, N 22,33:4
Lopez, Giuseppe, 1966, O 5,47:3
Lopez, Giuseppe Mrs, 1966, O 5,47:3
Lopez, Ildefonso S, 1943, D 6,23:4
Lopez, J Antonio Dr, 1922, N 2,19:5
Lopez, John A, 1959, Ja 16,27:3
Lopez, John S, 1952, Ag 5,19:2
Lopez, Jose A, 1938, N 20,39:3
Lopez, Joseph E (will), 1955, Je 18,3:4
Lopez, Joseph E Mrs (cor, My 8,23:6), 1941, My 7, 25:5
Lopez, Juan H, 1944, My 19,19:5
Lopez, Louis L, 1945, Mr 13,23:6
Lopez, Luis C, 1950, N 1,35:5
Lopez, Martin, 1919, Mr 22,15:1
Lopez, Michael D, 1943, Mr 26,21:2
Lopez, P M, 1877, Ap 15,7:5
Lopez, President of Paraguay, 1870, Ap 14,5:4
Lopez, Ralph A, 1952, Ja 4,23:4
Lopez, Sabatino, 1951, O 28,85:2
Lopez, Virgil J, 1940, Ja 20,15:5
Lopez de Victoria, Cassius, 1965, Je 12,31:5
Lopez-Guillen, Jose M, 1939, Ap 15,19:5
Lopez Leyva, Francisco, 1940, D 5,25:3
Lopez Llovet, Jorge, 1965, Ap 3,29:6
Lopez Mezquita, Jose M, 1954, D 8,35:2
Lopez Mollinedo, Emilio de la C, 1941, Jl 22,19:5
Lopez Perez, Arturo, 1949, N 1,27:5
Lopez-Rey, Lucio, 1957, Ja 12,19:2
Lopez y Fuentes, Gregorio, 1966, D 13,47:5

Lopiano, Rocco Dr, 1925, N 20,21:4
LoPiccolo, James E, 1966, N 5,31:5
Lopker, Joseph L, 1955, Ja 3,27:5
Lopp, George W, 1955, Je 25,15:6
Lopp, William T, 1939, Ap 12,23:4
Loppin, Alexander J, 1945, D 11,25:1
Lopresti, A Baron, 1881, N 28,5:1
LoPrestri, Charles, 1954, D 10,27:1
Loprete, Frank, 1941, Ap 13,38:2
Loprete, Michael, 1945, N 15,19:4
Lopukhin-Demidoff, Natalie Princess, 1957, O 13,86:8
Lora, Alfredo, 1943, D 4,13:4
Lora, Antonio, 1965, O 21,47:4
Lorah, George H, 1945, Ag 31,17:4
Lorain, Lorenzo, 1882, Mr 7,2:3
Loraine, C de, 1903, F 20,16:3
Loraine, C de Son of, 1903, F 20,16:3
Loraine, Edward Col, 1872, D 31,1:3
Loraine, Percy, 1961, My 24,41:2
Loraine, Violet, 1956, Jl 20,17:4
Loram, Charles T, 1940, Jl 10,19:3
Lorance, John, 1953, N 25,23:2
Lorand, Edith, 1960, N 24,29:3
Lorand, Georges, 1918, S 3,11:3
Lorand, Sandor Mrs, 1942, Mr 27,23:5
Lorang, Nicholas, 1952, Jl 22,25:1
Loranger, Albert J, 1955, N 26,19:5
Loranger, Eli J, 1958, F 4,26:4
Loranger, Peter J, 1952, Ag 2,15:4
Loranger, Theodore, 1950, Ag 13,76:3
Lorber, Aaron N, 1959, Ap 8,37:2
Lorber, Adolf, 1953, Ap 18,19:5
Lorber, Adolf Mrs, 1956, Ap 30,23:5
Lorber, Bendit Mrs, 1942, Ap 8,19:3
Lorber, Herbert J, 1964, Ag 15,21:5
Lorber, Herman, 1958, Ja 31,21:1
Lorber, Jacob, 1954, Mr 26,21:2
Lorber, Jacob N Mrs, 1958, Je 10,33:4
Lorber, Samuel Z, 1951, Mr 8,29:4
Lorch, Adolph, 1959, Je 27,23:5
Lorch, Alex, 1951, Ag 24,15:6
Lorch, Frederick W, 1957, F 4,19:5
Lorch, Paul, 1961, Ja 9,39:3
Lorch, Raymond F, 1950, N 2,31:1
Lorch, Richard C, 1907, Je 26,7:5
Lorch, Theodore A, 1947, N 12,28:2
Lord, Albert J, 1951, Mr 2,25:3
Lord, Alex H, 1942, Mr 13,19:4
Lord, Arthur, 1925, Ap 11,13:3
Lord, Arthur C, 1952, Ag 10,61:1
Lord, Arthur D, 1944, Je 16,19:4
Lord, Arthur E, 1947, S 15,17:5
Lord, Aug M, 1941, S 15,17:4
Lord, Austin Willard, 1922, Ja 20,15:4
Lord, B G Capt, 1870, Ag 26,6:3
Lord, Bert (por),(will, Je 14,25:2), 1939, My 25,25:3
Lord, Bert Mrs, 1937, My 26,25:3
Lord, Bertram, 1948, Je 18,24:2
Lord, C Clifford, 1959, N 23,31:1
Lord, C S, 1933, Ag 2,15:1
Lord, Carl J, 1960, Mr 8,33:1
Lord, Caroline E, 1949, Mr 30,25:2
Lord, Charles B, 1967, Mr 25,23:5
Lord, Charles C, 1944, D 21,21:2
Lord, Charles E, 1942, D 11,23:5
Lord, Charles Emerson, 1953, F 26,25:1
Lord, Charles K, 1908, S 11,9:7
Lord, Chester B, 1958, O 4,21:2
Lord, Chester S Mrs, 1910, Ag 8,7:5
Lord, Chester Waiter, 1912, Ja 11,13:4
Lord, Clarkson E, 1944, O 16,19:6
Lord, Clarkson E Mrs, 1942, Ag 29,15:3
Lord, D M, 1880, Jl 15,2:7; 1930, My 28,25:4
Lord, Daisy, 1941, Ja 28,19:2
Lord, Daniel (trb, Mr 10,7:2), 1868, Mr 6,2:4
Lord, Daniel A (cor, Ja 27,23:3), 1955, Ja 16,95:4
Lord, Daniel M, 1958, Jl 30,29:2
Lord, Devereux, 1960, O 13,37:1
Lord, Edward Rev, 1921, Mr 28,11:6
Lord, Edward T S, 1957, Mr 20,37:4
Lord, Edward T S Mrs, 1966, Je 22,47:4
Lord, Edwin B, 1940, O 10,25:6
Lord, Elizabeth C, 1916, Ag 16,7:4
Lord, Ellis, 1944, Mr 1,19:2
Lord, Everett W, 1965, Ja 16,27:4
Lord, Everett W Mrs, 1947, My 23,23:3
Lord, F Townley, 1962, F 10,23:3
Lord, Frank (por), 1946, Ag 7,27:3
Lord, Frank A, 1945, Ja 20,11:5
Lord, Franklin B, 1958, D 6,23:1
Lord, Franklin B Mrs, 1958, S 9,35:2
Lord, Franklin Butler, 1908, Ja 28,9:5
Lord, Franklin W, 1938, Ag 30,17:4
Lord, Fred R, 1947, Jl 30,21:4
Lord, Frederic W, 1952, Ja 1,25:4
Lord, Frederic W Mrs, 1959, Jl 23,27:4
Lord, Frederica, 1948, D 26,52:5
Lord, Frederick, 1941, Ap 10,23:5
Lord, Frederick T, 1941, N 5,23:1
Lord, Frederick T Mrs, 1941, Jl 12,13:6
Lord, G Marston Mrs, 1945, Mr 28,23:5
Lord, George, 1951, N 26,25:4
Lord, George D, 1945, Je 30,17:6

Lord, George D Sr, 1950, F 4,15:5
Lord, George de F Mrs, 1965, Je 29,35:2
Lord, George de Forest Mrs, 1917, Ja 25,9:3
Lord, George O, 1945, Ag 11,13:2
Lord, George W, 1951, D 25,31:6
Lord, H M, 1930, Je 3,31:1
Lord, Harold W Mrs, 1942, Ja 5,17:3
Lord, Harriet, 1958, Jl 26,15:5
Lord, Harry D, 1948, Ag 11,21:3
Lord, Hartley L, 1938, N 5,19:3
Lord, Haynes, 1880, Ap 25,2:5
Lord, Heinz, 1961, F 5,80:6
Lord, Helen, 1911, Ja 4,9:3
Lord, Herbert G, 1966, N 6,89:1
Lord, Herbert M Mrs, 1944, Ag 3,19:6
Lord, Howard W, 1946, Jl 23,25:2
Lord, Howell G Mrs, 1965, Mr 31,39:4
Lord, Isabel E, 1959, F 9,29:3
Lord, J B, 1902, Je 2,9:5
Lord, J C, 1869, F 12,11:5
Lord, J Couper, 1939, Je 5,17:3
Lord, J H Cap, 1902, Jl 26,1:6
Lord, J Kenworthy, 1952, Je 5,31:5
Lord, J T, 1903, Ja 5,9:5
Lord, James F, 1945, D 15,17:3
Lord, James Jr, 1965, My 8,23:5
Lord, John (The Voice), 1968, Ja 22,47:1
Lord, John A, 1945, S 10,19:4
Lord, John B Mrs, 1947, D 21,54:2
Lord, John C, 1946, My 19,40:6
Lord, John M, 1946, Jl 30,23:1
Lord, John N, 1962, Je 20,35:5
Lord, John P, 1940, Mr 4,15:4
Lord, Joseph Edward Potter Col, 1907, My 2,11:6
Lord, Kenneth, 1941, Jl 16,17:3; 1956, Ag 25,15:4
Lord, Kenneth Mrs, 1948, O 5,26:2
Lord, Kenneth P, 1957, Ap 29,25:2
Lord, Leonard E, 1962, F 3,21:5
Lord, Leonard P (Lord Lambury), 1967, S 14,47:4
Lord, Louis E, 1957, Ja 25,21:5
Lord, Lyman L, 1948, Jl 6,23:5
Lord, Mary E, 1953, Ag 9,77:3
Lord, Mary L Mrs, 1938, N 21,19:6
Lord, Mason F, 1965, N 18,47:3
Lord, Merrill M, 1954, F 21,69:2
Lord, N H, 1929, Mr 10,28:6
Lord, N Merchant, 1944, S 17,42:1
Lord, Nathan Dr, 1870, S 10,5:3
Lord, Nellie M, 1939, Ap 20,23:5
Lord, Pauline, 1925, S 3,25:6; 1950, O 12,31:1
Lord, Pauline (est tax appr), 1954, S 28,27:1
Lord, Rivington D (por), 1938, Jl 19,22:1
Lord, Robert A, 1965, F 10,41:3
Lord, Robert H (trb lr, My 27,26:7), 1954, My 23, 90:1
Lord, Roger, 1958, F 27,27:4
Lord, Royal B, 1963, O 23,42:1
Lord, Rufus, 1869, Je 10,5:3
Lord, Russell C, 1964, Mr 19,34:1
Lord, Scott, 1937, O 7,27:3
Lord, Thomas Sr, 1879, F 8,1:5
Lord, W B, 1884, D 24,2:7
Lord, Walter R, 1952, N 16,87:2
Lord, Wheeler, 1953, Ag 6,21:5
Lord, William, 1940, Jl 24,21:6; 1953, Je 5,27:3; 19[illegible] Je 11,21:6
Lord, William A, 1909, F 1,9:6
Lord, William A (por), 1942, D 3,25:3
Lord, William Mrs, 1956, My 25,23:3
Lord, William T, 1968, N 2,37:4
Lord, William Wilberforce Rev, 1907, Ap 23,9:4
Lord, Wilmot P, 1941, F 13,19:3
Lord Jno Manners, 1874, S 10,6:7
Lordan, Dennis T, 1952, Mr 8,13:1
Lordan, Ferdinand P (por), 1948, F 2,20:3
Lordan, John J Mrs, 1918, Je 12,13:5
Lordan, Mary T Mrs, 1918, Je 14,11:4
Lordeer, Lloyd L Mrs, 1951, D 4,33:4
Lorden, George L, 1951, Mr 18,88:3
Lorden, George Mrs, 1945, Ag 4,11:3
Lordi, Alfonso A, 1942, Mr 22,49:2
Lore, Belford A, 1952, Ap 18,25:1
Lore, Charles B Justice, 1911, Mr 7,11:4
Lore, John M, 1950, Ja 23,23:5
Lore, Ludwig, 1942, Jl 9,21:6
Loreburn, Lord (Jas Jno Reid), 1923, D 1,13:4
Lored, Frank E, 1941, S 15,17:4
Loree, Hattie, 1922, Ja 2,17:5
Loree, Jessie T Mrs, 1941, O 15,21:6
Loree, Leonor F (por),(will, S 19,21:3), 1940, S 7
Loree, Robert F Mrs, 1920, F 13,11:3
Lorek, Joseph M, 1949, Ja 23,68:8
Lorella, Colie, 1943, Jl 19,15:2
Loren, Gustaf, 1939, Ap 19,23:2
Lorenc, Aleck, 1954, Ap 25,87:2
Lorence, Charles H Dr, 1921, S 20,17:6
Lorence, Johanna Mrs, 1941, S 11,23:5
Lorence, Louis, 1966, S 7,41:2
Lorensen, George, 1955, S 22,31:2
Lorentz, Hendricus A, 1944, S 6,19:4
Lorentz, John Sr, 1947, Mr 12,25:1
Lorentz, Moses L Mrs, 1953, Je 15,29:4
Lorentzen, Peter, 1952, My 23,21:2

Lorenz, Adolf, 1946, F 18,21:1
Lorenz, Albert D, 1949, N 17,29:3
Lorenz, Alfred, 1943, Jl 18,34:5
Lorenz, Alice Mrs, 1903, S 20,1:4
Lorenz, Anton, 1964, Je 25,33:1
Lorenz, Berthold H, 1952, Mr 26,27:4
Lorenz, Charles F, 1939, Je 1,25:5
Lorenz, Charles H, 1951, Ja 4,29:4
Lorenz, Daniel E, 1941, F 28,19:5
Lorenz, Edward B, 1942, N 7,15:4
Lorenz, Edward S, 1942, Jl 11,13:6
Lorenz, Egon K, 1954, F 13,13:6
Lorenz, Frederick A, 1938, Jl 24,28:5
Lorenz, Heinrich, 1966, Jl 15,31:2
Lorenz, Ira S, 1949, Ja 29,13:2
Lorenz, Joseph, 1958, Jl 21,21:5
Lorenz, Joseph S Sr, 1955, O 28,25:2
Lorenz, Karl, 1955, Je 9,29:4
Lorenz, Keith, 1952, Jl 26,13:2
Lorenz, Martin J, 1943, Ag 9,13:5
Lorenz, Otto C, 1960, Ja 26,33:2
Lorenz, Richard, 1915, Ag 4,11:6
Lorenz, Stephen J, 1961, N 30,34:4
Lorenz, William, 1884, D 30,5:5
Lorenz, William F, 1958, F 20,25:3
Lorenze, Edward J, 1939, F 5,40:6
Lorenzelli, Benedetto Cardinal, 1915, S 17,7:6
Lorenzen, Anton F, 1958, Ag 17,86:1
Lorenzen, Chris, 1949, Ap 5,29:3
Lorenzen, Elmer C, 1953, Ap 20,25:2
Lorenzen, Ernest G, 1951, F 13,31:5
Lorenzen, Peter B, 1939, Ja 14,17:5
Lorenzen, Ralph, 1942, F 20,17:4
Lorenzo, Frank A, 1952, My 31,17:6
Loretan, Joseph O, 1966, Ag 2,31:4
Loretto Francis, Sister (Thompson), 1960, Jl 24,64:6
Lorey, Gustav, 1937, Ja 26,21:2
Lorge, Irving, 1961, Ja 24,29:3
Lorge, Irving Mrs, 1968, Ja 2,41:3
Loria, Gaetano, 1946, My 1,25:2
Loria, Gino, 1954, F 1,23:2
Loridan, Walter Mrs, 1960, S 5,5:4
Lorie, Benjamin J, 1953, O 5,27:3
Lorillard, Beeckman, 1923, F 22,15:4
Lorillard, Beeckman Mrs, 1912, Mr 19,11:3
Lorillard, Griswold, 1942, S 7,19:2
Lorillard, Jacob, 1916, Ap 29,11:6; 1949, Ja 6,23:1
Lorillard, Katherine B Mrs, 1941, Jl 21,15:5
Lorillard, Louis L (will, N 18,11:6), 1910, O 23,II, 13:4
Lorillard, Louis L, 1938, My 1,II,6:8
Lorillard, Pierre (por), 1940, Ag 7,19:2
Lorillard, Pierre (por), 1943, Ap 19,19:1
Lorillard, Pierre Mrs, 1925, S 12,15:6
Lorimer, Addison B, 1951, O 14,89:2
Lorimer, Frank Mrs (F M Williams), 1958, S 22,31:3
Lorimer, George B, 1952, D 20,31:2
Lorimer, George C Rev, 1904, S 9,7:6
Lorimer, George H, 1937, O 23,1:4
Lorimer, George H Mrs, 1941, Ja 20,17:3
Lorimer, George H Mrs (will), 1942, Ja 30,10:5
Lorimer, John Mrs, 1960, Ag 17,31:2
Lorimer, John W, 1947, O 29,27:4
Lorimer, Lou (L Benjamin), 1959, D 8,45:2
Lorimer, W, 1934, S 14,27:1
Lorimer, William Jr, 1945, Ja 18,19:5
Lorimer, William S, 1941, N 3,19:5
Lorimer, Wright, 1911, D 28,9:5
Lorin, Germaine M B, 1959, Jl 24,25:1
Loring, Aaron K, 1911, S 28,9:5
Loring, Augustus Jr Mrs, 1950, S 19,31:2
Loring, Augustus P, 1938, Mr 18,19:2
Loring, Augustus P Jr, 1951, O 2,27:1
Loring, Brown, 1942, N 8,50:5
Loring, Caleb, 1954, F 24,25:4
Loring, Charles, 1961, Mr 8,33:3
Loring, Charles A, 1949, D 3,15:5
Loring, Charles G, 1867, O 10,1:7
Loring, Charles G Mrs, 1914, Ap 11,11:5; 1956, Mr 11,88:3
Loring, Charles Harding Rear-Adm, 1907, F 7,9:6
Loring, David R (por), 1949, Ag 28,72:3
Loring, Eugene, 1940, F 22,23:1
Loring, Fred P, 1950, Ag 6,72:4
Loring, Fred W, 1871, N 15,5:5
Loring, Gabriel, 1950, Mr 4,17:5
Loring, Harrison, 1907, D 27,7:6
Loring, Homer, 1939, Je 21,23:2
Loring, John A, 1947, My 9,21:3
Loring, Lee, 1962, Ag 23,29:1
Loring, Ralph A, 1953, Ja 2,15:3
Loring, Ray, 1953, D 10,47:2
Loring, Richard T, 1948, Ap 17,15:3
Loring, Robert B, 1943, N 11,23:4
Loring, Victor J, 1947, F 10,29:2
Loring, Victor J Mrs, 1951, Mr 15,29:6
Loring, W W Gen (Fereck Pasha), 1886, D 31,5:3
Loring, William C, 1959, Je 15,27:5
Loringstein, Hyman, 1951, S 7,29:4
Lorini, M Campbell, 1960, N 24,29:6
Lorini, Mario, 1943, D 14,27:3
Lorini, Prof, 1919, N 16,22:4
Lorins, Carl L Mrs, 1943, My 19,25:2

Lorio, Vincent, 1953, Ap 16,29:2
Lorne, Marion, 1968, My 10,47:3
Lorraine, Emily, 1944, Ag 6,37:3
Lorraine, Frederick, 1943, Ja 26,19:2
Lorraine, Leopold H, 1958, Mr 15,17:4
Lorraine, Lillian (Mrs J O'Brien), 1955, Ap 21,29:2
Lorraine, Theodore, 1951, D 3,31:6
Lorraine, Wellford B, 1938, N 13,45:1
Lorre, Peter (funl, Mr 27,27:4), 1964, Mr 24,35:2
Lorsch, Charles N, 1903, Jl 20,2:3
Lorson, Frank E, 1938, Mr 16,23:6
Lorson, Robert G, 1939, Ja 20,19:3
Lorsy, Ernest, 1960, Ag 14,93:2
Lorton, Eugene, 1949, O 18,28:2
Lorton, Otis, 1945, Ag 17,17:3
Lorton, Robert E, 1938, D 1,23:5
Lorut, Louis, 1881, O 2,5:4
Losada, Jose P, 1937, S 25,17:7
Losaw, Arthur F, 1952, S 25,31:5
Losch, Edward G, 1949, Ap 18,25:5
Losch, Harry, 1949, Je 28,27:1
Losch, Josephine von, 1945, N 7,23:4
Losee, Charles, 1951, N 28,31:1
Losee, Charles G, 1953, My 22,27:4
Losee, Edward F, 1951, Ap 4,29:4
Losee, Franke, 1937, N 15,23:4
Losee, Gordon P, 1948, Ja 3,13:3
Losee, Henry S, 1940, O 14,19:3
Losee, Herbert I, 1957, O 21,25:1
Losee, John P, 1962, S 5,39:3
Losee, Joseph Mrs (Paynie D), 1965, Ap 10,29:6
Losee, Lewis H (por), 1941, Ag 28,19:2
Losee, Peter, 1945, Ja 30,19:2
Losee, Walter F, 1942, D 25,17:2
Losee, William, 1951, My 8,63:3
Losee, William F, 1951, O 30,29:2
Losel, Albert B Mrs, 1955, S 10,17:5
Loser, Sophia Mrs, 1952, D 9,33:2
Losey, John C, 1948, My 12,27:5
Losey, Marie H Mrs, 1940, O 27,44:2
Losey, Raymond, 1966, Ag 6,23:5
Losey, Robert M, 1940, My 30,17:4
Losh, Rosamond, 1945, Je 2,15:4
Loshe, Lillie D, 1958, Ap 24,31:2
Losie, Thomas M, 1945, Mr 12,19:5
Losinsky, Jacob, 1941, S 20,17:4
Losner, Samuel, 1957, Ja 15,30:3
Loso, Foster W, 1952, My 6,29:1
Loss, Henrik V, 1938, Jl 9,13:5
Loss, Warren H (funl, O 31,15:5), 1921, O 30,22:3
Loss, William, 1958, Jl 17,27:2
Lossberg, F K von, 1942, My 17,22:1
Lossberg, Otto von, 1914, Jl 23,9:4
Lossberg, Victor F, 1942, Ag 28,19:6
Lossing, B J, 1891, Je 4,4:7
Lossow, Otto von, 1938, N 30,23:1
Lostalot-Bachoue, Philippe de, 1952, D 14,90:5
Lostar, Basri, 1946, N 3,63:1
Losy, Frederick A K, 1948, O 28,30:2
Lot, Ferdinand, 1952, Jl 22,25:2
Lotbiniere, Alain C J de, 1944, Ap 18,21:5
Lotbiniere-Harwood, Reginald de, 1955, Ja 21,23:5
Lotee, Herbert A, 1954, Mr 24,27:1
Loth, Edward W, 1938, Ag 9,19:3
Loth, Henry A, 1941, D 9,31:4
Loth, Leopold C, 1951, Ap 23,25:4
Loth, Mathilde, 1940, Ag 30,19:4
Loth, Moritz, 1913, F 19,11:5
Lothar, Ernest, 1961, Ap 2,76:2
Lothar, J H, 1944, Ja 12,23:3
Lothar, Nicholas, 1964, Je 5,31:4
Lothian, Jane K, 1938, F 12,15:6
Lothian, Napier Jr, 1903, Ja 4,15:1
Lothrop, Arthur E, 1957, Ag 27,29:1
Lothrop, Carl D, 1922, S 28,21:4
Lothrop, Eleanor B Mrs, 1963, Ag 7,33:3
Lothrop, Ernest E, 1952, Mr 11,27:4
Lothrop, G E, 1924, F 5,23:3
Lothrop, George E Dr, 1922, Ag 4,15:5
Lothrop, H A, 1928, Je 5,14:2
Lothrop, Samuel K, 1965, Ja 13,25:3
Lothrop, Stanley B, 1944, Mr 18,13:2
Lothrop, Theodore A, 1949, D 11,91:6
Lothrop, Thomas M, 1955, My 9,23:5
Loti, Pierre, 1923, Je 11,13:3
Lotito, Christo, 1950, My 25,29:2
Lotito, Luigi P, 1942, Ja 29,19:1
Lotka, Alfred J, 1949, D 7,31:1
Lotker, Archibald A, 1965, Ja 7,31:3
Lotowycz, Anthony (por), 1949, D 15,35:4
Lotowycz, Wladimir, 1955, Ap 30,17:4
Lotsch, Joseph J, 1961, O 29,88:4
Lotshaw, Andrew D (A Daly trb, F 25,32:2), 1953, F 24,25:3
Lotspeich, Roy N, 1951, S 10,21:3
Lotspeich, William D Dr, 1968, N 30,39:3
Lott, Arthur E, 1952, D 4,35:1
Lott, Blanche R Mrs, 1940, Ag 21,19:2
Lott, Charles H, 1925, My 2,15:5
Lott, Charles O, 1944, D 4,23:5
Lott, Edson, 1945, N 2,19:1
Lott, Ella K, 1942, Jl 11,13:6
Lott, H Stokes Jr, 1937, My 21,21:3

Lott, Harry H, 1949, F 9,27:4
Lott, Henry D, 1943, F 19,19:4
Lott, Hershel, 1945, S 18,20:4
Lott, J A Judge, 1878, Jl 21,12:1
Lott, James H, 1961, Ag 25,25:2
Lott, John Z, 1914, O 25,3:4
Lott, Leonard W, 1944, Jl 20,19:6
Lott, Martin B, 1945, Ap 18,23:5
Lott, Martin B Mrs, 1953, Je 19,22:3
Lott, Mervin, 1952, F 29,23:4
Lott, Peter, 1940, Jl 17,21:4
Lott, Rulef V, 1924, S 30,23:1
Lott, Sidney, 1958, My 17,40:2
Lott, Stephen I, 1942, Mr 4,20:3
Lott, T B, 1907, Jl 8,7:6
Lott, Theodore E, 1945, Ag 22,23:5
Lott, Van W Sr, 1946, Ap 25,21:4
Lott, Van Wyck Sr Mrs, 1948, Jl 25,48:7
Lotte, C Walter, 1942, Mr 21,17:3
Lotte, Charles E, 1954, Jl 18,57:3
Lotte, Charles E Mrs, 1963, Je 15,23:2
Lottman, George D, 1942, S 26,15:4
Lotto, Fred, 1937, D 11,19:5
Lottridge, Arthur C, 1951, N 1,29:2
Lottridge, Silas A, 1940, F 13,23:4
Lotts, William H, 1954, D 30,17:1
Lotz, Christian, 1915, O 21,11:5
Lotz, Henry J, 1942, Ag 27,19:6
Lotz, Jacob, 1940, Ap 18,23:5
Lotz, John R, 1965, D 15,47:1
Lotz, Paul P, 1945, F 21,19:4
Lotz, Peter, 1948, Ja 8,25:4
Lotze, Karl G, 1967, Ag 18,33:3
Lotze, Philip, 1925, Ja 15,21:6
Lou Tseng, Tsiang, 1949, Ja 16,69:1
Loubat, Duke de, 1927, Mr 2,25:3
Loubat, M Alphonse, 1866, O 14,5:5
Loubet, E, 1929, D 21,19:1
Loubet, Mme, 1905, Ja 16,5:3
Loucheim, James (por), 1938, D 27,17:3
Loucher, L, 1931, N 23,19:1
Louchheim, Harry F, 1941, Jl 6,28:2
Louchheim, Henry, 1903, Ag 8,7:7
Louchheim, Jerome H (por), 1945, Ap 5,23:3
Louchheim, Joseph, 1905, My 2,2:2
Louchheim, Joseph Mrs, 1954, Ap 4,88:1
Loucks, Glenn D (funl, Ag 30,29:4), 1962, Ag 28,31:3
Loucks, H L, 1928, D 30,20:3
Loucks, Irving A, 1967, Jl 18,37:3
Loucks, Otis F, 1947, O 9,25:4
Loucks, W Barner, 1963, My 4,25:4
Loucks, William D, 1957, S 12,31:4
Loucks, William Dewey Mrs, 1968, N 28,37:4
Loud, Albert L, 1940, O 8,25:7
Loud, Alexander C H, 1946, Ag 16,21:6
Loud, Edward F, 1952, Ja 20,84:2
Loud, Edward P, 1955, Ja 26,25:2
Loud, Eugene, 1908, D 21,9:7
Loud, Frederick E, 1955, S 12,25:4
Loud, Grover Cleveland, 1968, Ag 30,33:3
Loud, John W, 1937, Ja 4,29:1
Loud, William H, 1941, Ap 6,48:7
Louden, Samuel R, 1903, D 24,9:5
Louden, Thomas, 1948, Mr 17,25:5
Louden, Waldo W, 1954, Ag 22,92:5
Loudenslager, Henry C, 1911, Ag 13,II,9:5
Loudenslager, Paul E, 1948, D 9,33:4
Louderback, Arthur E Mrs, 1945, My 9,23:4
Louderback, Delancey H, 1914, Ap 10,13:5
Louderback, George D, 1957, Ja 29,31:4
Louderback, George H, 1955, Mr 12,19:4
Louderback, Harold, 1941, D 12,25:3
Louderback, Walt S, 1941, O 16,21:6
Louderbough, Harry, 1910, Ja 7,9:7
Louderbough, Harry C, 1939, D 28,21:3
Louderman, James H, 1903, N 3,7:6
Louderman, William M, 1951, D 27,21:2
Loudermilk, William W, 1952, S 20,15:6
Loudin, Milton G, 1919, D 3,15:2
Loudon, Alex Dr, 1953, F 5,23:3
Loudon, Edward, 1957, Ja 29,31:6
Loudon, Frederic, 1948, O 4,23:2
Loudon, John, 1955, N 13,88:3
Loudon, Jonkheer H, 1941, S 14,48:1
Loudon, Julian D, 1959, O 18,86:2
Loudon, Paul W, 1953, D 9,11:1
Loudon, Winfield D, 1951, Mr 13,31:4
Loudon, Winfield D Mrs, 1940, Ja 21,34:5
Loudoun, Wood D, 1937, Je 3,28:3
Loudy, Ebenezer, 1882, Ja 5,2:7
Loudy, Flavius E, 1953, Mr 21,17:6
Louer, Albert S Mrs, 1937, Je 17,24:2
Loues, Spyro, 1940, Mr 27,21:2
Loufek, George H, 1956, My 19,19:5
Lougee, Arthur L, 1952, Ja 6,92:3
Lougee, Richard J, 1960, My 17,37:3
Lougee, William R, 1955, Je 19,93:1
Lougee, William W, 1954, Ja 13,31:1
Lough, Ernest L, 1967, N 2,47:3
Lough, Ernest S G Mrs, 1943, N 16,23:2
Lough, James E, 1952, Je 4,27:6
Lough, Walter E, 1948, Jl 27,25:3
Lough, William P, 1959, Ap 13,31:5

Loughborough, John N, 1924, Ap 10,23:4
Loughborough, Robert H Mrs, 1956, Ag 21,29:2
Loughborough, Robert H R Mrs, 1952, Je 2,21:2
Loughead, Charles F Mrs (Emma Roberts), 1968, S 19,47:1
Lougheed, James Alexander Sir, 1925, N 3,25:6
Lougheed, Robert H Mrs, 1947, S 25,29:3
Lougheed, Victor, 1943, Ag 31,19:2
Lougher, E H Dr, 1926, O 13,23:3
Loughery, John T Mrs, 1947, O 9,25:2
Loughhead, Charles F, 1944, D 26,19:5
Loughin, Charles A, 1963, My 20,31:2
Loughlin, August H, 1952, Ja 6,93:2
Loughlin, James V, 1945, S 15,15:2; 1951, F 23,27:4
Loughlin, John, 1940, Ap 27,15:5
Loughlin, John Bishop, 1891, D 30,8:1
Loughlin, John F, 1950, Ag 9,29:1
Loughlin, John J, 1951, My 27,68:5; 1967, O 14,27:2
Loughlin, Joseph J, 1965, Ja 14,35:2
Loughlin, Joseph M, 1957, Jl 7,60:8
Loughlin, Mary E, 1962, O 26,31:3
Loughlin, Phil H, 1938, Jl 3,13:3
Loughlin, Raymond E A, 1953, Je 14,84:1
Loughlin, Thomas B, 1948, F 27,21:2
Loughlin, Thomas C, 1953, Je 16,27:4
Loughlin, Thomas P, 1956, S 29,19:5
Loughlin, William D, 1950, N 13,27:4
Loughlin, William J, 1943, Jl 27,17:3; 1947, D 24,22:2
Loughlin, William L, 1948, Ag 4,22:3
Loughman, Edward D, 1957, D 7,21:2
Loughman, Edward J, 1941, O 7,23:4
Loughman, Elizabeth S Mrs, 1940, Ag 14,19:4
Loughman, Henry, 1959, Ja 17,19:1
Loughman, Michael F Capt, 1937, My 24,19:1
Loughman, William J, 1952, Jl 21,19:4
Loughnane, Francis J, 1948, Ap 1,25:5
Loughnane, John J, 1955, Ag 8,23:8
Loughney, John F, 1964, Ap 3,33:4
Loughney, John V, 1942, Je 28,32:2
Loughney, John V Mrs, 1950, Ap 20,29:4
Loughran, Arthur P, 1960, Ag 23,29:1
Loughran, Charles P, 1944, F 13,41:2
Loughran, Charles P Mrs, 1949, Mr 26,17:4
Loughran, Edward, 1938, My 11,19:5
Loughran, Edward P, 1959, S 19,23:5
Loughran, Frank, 1951, My 29,25:2
Loughran, Fred J (death laid to natural causes, Ag 2,27:1), 1961, Je 29,33:4
Loughran, Frederick W Dr, 1922, Ag 8,11:5
Loughran, George A, 1959, N 4,41:5
Loughran, George A Mrs, 1959, D 4,32:2
Loughran, Harold S, 1941, N 5,23:5
Loughran, Helen, 1940, Je 22,15:4
Loughran, James F, 1954, My 11,29:4
Loughran, John, 1903, O 7,9:5
Loughran, John T, 1953, Ap 1,29:1
Loughran, Joseph Lt, 1911, S 8,7:4
Loughran, Peter J, 1968, O 14,47:5
Loughran, Robert L, 1942, Ja 28,19:5
Loughran, William H, 1963, Ap 27,25:4
Loughran, William J, 1951, Mr 27,29:3
Loughran-Olcott, Susan B Mrs, 1923, Ag 9,13:5
Loughrane, Basil, 1949, My 30,13:2
Loughrey, John J, 1941, O 6,17:3
Loughrey, May, 1952, My 4,91:1
Loughrey, Michael J, 1960, Jl 1,25:4
Loughridge, Matthew M, 1942, My 19,19:5
Loughry, James C, 1946, Ap 28,42:6
Lougovoy, Boris N, 1951, O 21,92:6
Louis, Adolph Mrs, 1922, Mr 13,15:6
Louis, Arthur O, 1966, N 11,43:3
Louis, Bernard, 1925, Jl 21,21:5
Louis, Charles Austrian Archduke, 1896, My 20,5:2
Louis, Henry, 1939, F 23,23:6
Louis, Joseph W, 1951, Mr 22,31:5
Louis, M, 1950, Jl 7,19:5
Louis, Samuel, 1907, Mr 15,9:6
Louis, Spencer S, 1952, Je 28,19:3
Louis, William F, 1966, Jl 26,35:2
Louis Bertrand, Sister (O'Connor), 1950, Ag 9,29:3
Louis-Dreyfus, Francois, 1958, Jl 4,19:2
Louis Euthyme, Bro (Desmarais), 1959, My 14,33:4
Louis of Bourbon-Parma, Prince, 1967, D 6,51:4
Louis Philippe de Boishebert Gaste de Tilly, 1908, Mr 5,7:6
Louis Roy, Bro (Alexian Bros), 1961, S 13,45:4
Louis Veronica, Sister (McHugh), 1950, N 14,31:3
Louise, Princess of Saxony (former Archduchess), 1947, Ap 1,27:5
Louise, Princess Royal, 1931, Ja 5,23:1
Louise, Queen of Denmark, 1898, S 30,6:7
Louise, Queen of Swenden (funl plans, Mr 9,35:1), 1965, Mr 8,29:1
Louise, Sister (L G Hall), 1883, Mr 29,8:2
Louise, Sister, 1937, Ap 9,21:3; 1942, F 27,17:4; 1948, Ja 18,60:5
Louise Caroline Alberta, Princess (Dowager Duchess of Argyll), 1940, F 10,2:4
Louison, Leo Mrs (A R Parisi), 1961, Mr 21,37:1
Loukomsky, Alex, 1939, F 27,15:5
Loulakakis, Emanuel, 1966, Jl 2,23:5
Louman, Harry, 1938, My 29,II,6:5
Lounsberry, Alice, 1949, N 22,29:4
Lounsberry, Frank B, 1963, Je 7,31:2
Lounsberry, Isaac R, 1959, F 26,31:5
Lounsbery, Alfred Bp, 1916, Ja 22,9:3
Lounsbery, Elliott L, 1953, Ap 19,90:2
Lounsbery, George, 1939, O 15,49:2
Lounsbery, Henry H F Mrs, 1940, Mr 13,23:5
Lounsbery, Louis M, 1957, My 12,86:2
Lounsbery, Richard, 1967, N 10,47:1
Lounsbery, Richard P, 1911, O 24,13:6
Lounsbery, William S, 1951, My 25,27:4
Lounsbury, Charles E, 1943, Ja 28,19:1; 1952, N 3,27:2
Lounsbury, Charles E Mrs, 1952, Ap 17,29:5
Lounsbury, Charles S, 1949, Mr 3,25:4
Lounsbury, Edwin D, 1941, Mr 19,21:4
Lounsbury, Edwin W Rev Dr, 1923, S 17,15:3
Lounsbury, Elmer H, 1955, Ja 3,27:1
Lounsbury, George E, 1904, Ag 17,7:6
Lounsbury, George F, 1958, Ap 13,84:4
Lounsbury, Herbert D, 1951, O 23,29:4
Lounsbury, Herbert Mrs, 1947, Jl 2,23:5
Lounsbury, Jesse P Mrs, 1945, D 15,17:3
Lounsbury, John W, 1904, Mr 19,1:2
Lounsbury, Lewis M, 1949, Mr 27,76:4
Lounsbury, Phineas C Ex-Gov, 1925, Je 23,19:4
Lounsbury, Ralph G Mrs, 1939, Ja 17,22:2
Lounsbury, Thomas R Prof, 1915, Ap 10,11:5
Lounsbury, William, 1947, Mr 25,25:1
Lourenco, Agostinho, 1964, Ag 3,25:3
Loures, George A Mrs, 1952, F 2,13:4
Louria, Alex L (por), 1949, My 23,23:3
Lourie, Adolph, 1940, D 20,25:2
Lourie, Emmanuel M, 1956, Ag 14,25:6
Lourie, Leo Mrs, 1954, Jl 29,23:6
Lourie, Samuel A, 1957, Mr 15,26:1
Lourie, Saul V Mrs, 1945, My 20,32:4
Lourin, Leon Dr, 1923, O 20,15:4
Loury, Robert J, 1919, Ja 9,11:3
Loustaunau-Lacau, Georges, 1955, F 12,15:6
Loutfi, Omar (mem ser; trb, My 19,86:8), 1963, My 18,1:3
Loutit, James F R, 1963, My 26,92:1
Loutrel, Cyrus F Mrs, 1943, D 4,13:6
Loutrel, Cyrus H, 1957, Ja 14,23:3
Loutrel, William L, 1959, Mr 31,29:2
Louttit, Tom, 1951, Mr 26,23:4
Louw, Eric H, 1968, Je 24,37:1
Louwes, Stephanus L, 1953, Ja 27,25:1
Loux, Arthur Mrs, 1951, S 28,31:2
Loux, Carl H, 1949, My 14,13:4
Loux, Edward A, 1952, Je 21,15:5
Lovallo, Joseph Mrs, 1955, F 13,86:4
Lovatt, Arthur B, 1951, O 14,88:4
Lovatt, Frederick J, 1944, D 6,23:2
Lovatt, Frederick Sr, 1943, D 27,20:2
Lovay, Edith, 1922, Je 26,13:6
Lovblad, Walter E, 1923, Jl 21,9:6
Love, Alfred H, 1913, Je 30,7:4
Love, Allen M, 1958, N 22,21:4
Love, Andrew L (Oct 7), 1965, O 11,61:3
Love, Charles E, 1955, S 28,35:2
Love, Charles J, 1953, Ag 16,76:7
Love, Cornelius R, 1961, Ja 5,31:3
Love, David E, 1937, Jl 7,23:4
Love, Dumont, 1944, Ja 3,21:3
Love, Edward Gurley Dr, 1919, S 14,22:4
Love, Edward K, 1953, Mr 23,23:4
Love, Edward L Mrs, 1962, O 23,37:1
Love, Edward T Mrs, 1950, Ag 30,32:3
Love, Edward W, 1951, Ap 2,25:5
Love, Elizabeth, 1953, My 10,88:5
Love, Elmer A, 1946, O 11,23:5
Love, Ernest C, 1947, S 30,25:2
Love, Francis H, 1958, Mr 6,27:4
Love, Frank W, 1944, Ag 5,11:3
Love, Harry H, 1966, Ag 22,41:3
Love, Hattie H Mrs, 1941, My 24,15:2
Love, I N Dr, 1903, Je 19,9:4
Love, Irving G, 1946, Ja 6,40:3
Love, J Spencer, 1962, Ja 21,89:1
Love, Jack P, 1958, Jl 18,16:8
Love, James, 1874, Ag 16,5:2
Love, James H, 1905, Ap 7,9:6
Love, James L, 1950, My 7,108:3
Love, James S, 1937, D 25,15:7
Love, John, 1881, Ja 31,5:6
Love, John E, 1949, O 10,23:4
Love, John H (por), 1942, O 12,17:5
Love, John H, 1948, D 9,33:2
Love, John K, 1952, N 2,89:2
Love, John S, 1954, D 16,37:5
Love, John W, 1948, My 7,23:2; 1958, S 22,21:1
Love, Julius D, 1945, Jl 6,11:6
Love, L Stewart, 1940, S 7,15:4
Love, Lawrence P, 1940, Ag 27,21:4
Love, Leslie C, 1949, Ap 4,23:3
Love, Mabel, 1953, My 16,19:6
Love, Mark S, 1954, S 12,84:6
Love, Montague, 1943, My 18,23:3
Love, Ray D, 1947, N 19,27:3
Love, Raymond L, 1964, Mr 24,35:2
Love, Robert C, 1950, My 31,29:5
Love, Robert J, 1951, S 20,33:8
Love, Robert Mrs, 1943, Ja 26,19:2
Love, Samuel D, 1937, Ja 31,II,8:5
Love, Stephen, 1965, Je 19,29:1
Love, Stephen C M, 1948, Mr 1,23:3
Love, Thomas (por), 1948, S 19,78:1
Love, Thomas J, 1955, Ja 3,27:3
Love, Thomas M, 1937, N 12,21:4
Love, Van Buren, 1950, Jl 14,21:4
Love, W H, 1874, Ag 5,6:6
Love, Walter J, 1968, Ap 21,80:4
Love, William F, 1959, F 19,31:3
Love, William G, 1959, N 16,31:4
Love, William J, 1947, Mr 15,13:2
Love, William Mrs, 1937, O 10,II,9:2
Love, William S, 1940, My 14,23:4
Loveday, Alex, 1962, Ja 21,88:2
Loveday, William C, 1955, Je 22,29:2
Lovegren, Carl N, 1950, N 3,28:2
Lovegrove, Norman C, 1953, Ag 16,77:3
Lovejoy, Abbie, 1948, Je 25,23:4
Lovejoy, Albert W, 1951, Jl 16,21:6
Lovejoy, Frank, 1962, O 3,41:1
Lovejoy, Frank W (por), 1945, S 17,19:3
Lovejoy, Frank W Mrs, 1961, Ag 2,29:4
Lovejoy, George, 1924, Jl 20,20:4
Lovejoy, George A Mrs, 1967, Ag 18,33:1
Lovejoy, George E Rev, 1916, D 26,11:5
Lovejoy, Irving P Mrs, 1960, F 17,35:3
Lovejoy, Jesse R (por),(will, N 11,30:6), 1945, N 2, 20:2
Lovejoy, Jesse R Mrs, 1941, Jl 25,15:4
Lovejoy, John E, 1952, Jl 14,17:5
Lovejoy, John F, 1950, Ja 11,23:4
Lovejoy, John Meston, 1968, N 11,47:4
Lovejoy, Kenneth, 1947, F 14,21:5
Lovejoy, L K A, 1877, F 5,2:6
Lovejoy, Owen, 1864, Mr 28,5:2
Lovejoy, Owen R, 1961, Je 30,27:1
Lovejoy, Parish S, 1942, Ja 22,18:4
Lovejoy, Philip, 1966, Jl 2,23:3
Lovejoy, Ralph M, 1954, D 4,17:3
Lovejoy, Thomas E (por), 1939, D 13,27:6
Lovekin, Luther D, 1937, N 21,II,9:1
Lovel, C S Gen, 1871, Ja 7,1:4
Lovelace, Daniel D, 1952, N 29,13:4
Lovelace, Delos W, 1967, Ja 19,35:3
Lovelace, Frederick L, 1943, Ap 13,25:5
Lovelace, Griffin M, 1968, Ap 2,47:3
Lovelace, Mary Caroline Countess, 1941, Ap 21,19:
Lovelace, W Randolph, 1965, D 16,42:1
Lovelace, W Randolph Mrs, 1965, D 16,42:1
Lovelace, Walter S, 1961, S 19,35:5
Lovelace, William Randolph Dr, 1968, D 5,47:3
Loveland, Charles A, 1951, D 18,31:4
Loveland, Charles D, 1960, Mr 14,29:2
Loveland, Edward R, 1960, O 26,39:4
Loveland, Ernest K Mrs, 1948, Ja 30,23:2
Loveland, Frank C Col, 1916, Je 25,18:5
Loveland, George A, 1940, Mr 31,44:3
Loveland, Henry M, 1948, My 28,23:3
Loveland, Hollis I, 1956, Ap 7,19:5
Loveland, John E Dr, 1937, S 13,21:2
Loveland, Lena B Mrs, 1940, Mr 15,23:5
Loveland, Murray Mrs, 1948, F 9,17:2
Loveland, Prescott R, 1944, Ja 22,13:4
Loveland, Roland W, 1950, F 16,23:2
Loveland, William W Mrs, 1952, Je 21,15:3
Loveless, George Mrs, 1951, S 6,31:2
Loveley, Albert L, 1943, Ap 20,23:4
Lovell, Aaron, 1902, Ap 17,9:6
Lovell, Alfred H, 1960, O 28,31:3
Lovell, Arthur C, 1948, My 23,68:4
Lovell, Caroline Mrs, 1906, O 18,9:1
Lovell, Charles E, 1959, Je 11,33:5
Lovell, Charles F, 1948, N 9,27:3
Lovell, Charles F Mrs, 1947, Jl 6,41:2
Lovell, Charles N, 1952, My 13,23:5
Lovell, Clarence R, 1947, Ag 19,23:6
Lovell, Don G Maj, 1907, O 27,9:6
Lovell, Earl B, 1948, Ag 24,23:5
Lovell, F Hallett, 1962, My 20,86:6
Lovell, Francis Henry Sir, 1916, Ja 29,9:4
Lovell, Frank F Mrs, 1950, Jl 10,21:2
Lovell, Frederick A, 1941, D 15,19:5
Lovell, Frederick H, 1948, Jl 7,46:2
Lovell, George R, 1941, My 20,23:5
Lovell, George R Mrs, 1954, Mr 6,15:5
Lovell, Harry B, 1942, Ap 26,40:1
Lovell, Harry S, 1955, N 22,35:1
Lovell, Isaac J, 1954, Mr 15,25:3
Lovell, J W, 1932, Ap 22,17:2
Lovell, Jefferson Mrs, 1948, My 5,25:4
Lovell, John F, 1951, D 31,13:5
Lovell, John H, 1939, Ap 3,19:6
Lovell, K Allen, 1923, Ag 30,13:5
Lovell, Leander D, 1947, Ja 1,33:5
Lovell, Lorenzo Mrs, 1945, Ap 26,23:2
Lovell, Louise J Mrs, 1947, My 26,21:4
Lovell, M Gen, 1884, Je 2,5:3
Lovell, Martha E, 1940, Ap 25,23:3
Lovell, Moses R (por), 1944, S 24,46:1
Lovell, Percy B, 1957, Jl 31,23:1
Lovell, Philip G, 1959, Je 21,92:3
Lovell, Ralph L, 1945, Je 5,19:2

Lovell, Raymond, 1953, O 3,17:4
Lovell, Robert W, 1948, Jl 5,15:4
Lovell, Sophia Mrs, 1922, Jl 22,7:5
Lovell, Walter (por), 1937, S 10,23:1
Lovelock, Frank A, 1947, S 19,23:4
Lovelock, John E, 1949, D 29,1:6
Lovely, Collis, 1940, Jl 4,15:3
Loveman, Amy, 1955, D 12,31:3
Loveman, Charles S, 1955, O 22,19:4
Loveman, D B, 1926, My 19,25:3
Loveman, D B Mrs, 1937, Je 9,25:2
Loveman, Ernest B, 1953, D 23,25:4
Loveman, Herbert S, 1964, Je 2,37:4
Loveman, Robert, 1923, Jl 11,19:6
Loveman, Samuel A, 1963, Ap 4,47:5
Loveman, Wesley J, 1957, Ja 10,29:2
Loven, Carl K, 1965, My 12,47:3
Loventhal, Charles D, 1952, Je 15,84:6
Lover, Samuel, 1868, Jl 9,5:3
Loveridge, Irving, 1909, Je 5,9:5
Loveridge, Stuart A, 1957, Ap 12,51:2
Loverin, Frank J, 1950, S 9,17:5
Lovering, Charles T, 1961, N 19,88:8
Lovering, Cora, 1942, Je 17,23:5
Lovering, Edward, 1941, Ap 24,21:3
Lovering, Gilman W, 1952, My 13,23:4
Lovering, Gilpin, 1953, D 17,37:2
Lovering, Henry B, 1911, Ap 6,11:4
Lovering, Joseph S, 1953, Je 12,27:1
Lovering, Leonard A Col, 1914, My 31,5:6
Lovering, N P, 1903, Ap 24,9:6
Lovering, Richard S, 1962, Jl 19,27:4
Lovering, Richard S Mrs, 1958, F 9,88:4
Lovering, W, 1876, Ag 27,8:3
Lovering, William C, 1910, F 5,7:4
Loverro, Joseph, 1952, O 8,31:1
Lovesy, Arthur H, 1942, N 2,21:3
Lovett, A B, 1945, D 29,13:5
Lovett, Charles H, 1956, Ag 15,29:3
Lovett, Edgar O, 1957, Ag 14,25:5
Lovett, Edward C, 1951, O 14,89:2
Lovett, Ernest N, 1951, S 9,88:3
Lovett, Florence Mrs, 1942, Ap 11,13:4
Lovett, Fremont L, 1953, Je 14,78:1
Lovett, Gordon B, 1949, S 5,17:5
Lovett, Henry M, 1948, F 23,25:3
Lovett, John (Jno the Orangeman), 1906, Ag 13,7:6
Lovett, John L, 1952, Mr 16,90:1
Lovett, Joseph C, 1949, Je 1,32:3
Lovett, Lewis J, 1942, Ap 29,21:5
Lovett, Louis de B, 1941, My 6,21:2
Lovett, Norman F, 1953, Ag 24,23:6
Lovett, Paul, 1959, Je 25,29:6
Lovett, Paul Mrs (Anne), 1968, O 7,47:2
Lovett, R H Judge, 1926, Ag 24,21:6
Lovett, R S, 1932, Je 20,15:3
Lovett, Raymond E, 1956, Ja 7,17:5
Lovett, Robert M, 1956, F 9,31:5
Lovett, Robert W Dr, 1924, Jl 3,15:5
Lovett, William C, 1940, Jl 2,22:2
Lovett, William P, 1947, Jl 8,24:3
Lovette, Frank H, 1968, Ag 24,29:5
Lovette, Leland P, 1967, Jl 12,43:1
Lovey, George R, 1946, Ap 18,27:2
Lovier, Arthur M, 1952, Mr 19,29:2
Loving, E Pierre, 1950, Je 27,29:4
Loving, Robert C Mrs, 1956, D 3,29:4
Lovinger, Walter, 1966, F 8,36:4
Lovingham, John S, 1960, Mr 29,37:1
Lovink, G J, 1947, D 17,29:5
Lovins, Maxwell V, 1961, F 28,33:3
Lovis, Henry C, 1943, Ap 6,21:4
Lovitz, Phil Mrs, 1950, My 26,23:4
Lovre, G A, 1949, Ag 13,11:4
Lovuola, Angela Mrs, 1943, My 15,15:2
Low, A Augustus, 1963, N 25,20:2
Low, A Richie, 1948, D 25,17:6
Low, Abbot Augustus (funl, S 28,13:5), 1912, S 26, 11:4
Low, Abraham A, 1954, N 19,23:4
Low, Adele T, 1944, S 9,15:2
Low, Archibald M, 1956, S 14,23:3
Low, Bela, 1943, F 26,19:4
Low, Benjamin R C, 1941, Je 23,18:2
Low, Bertha (will), 1940, Ag 23,12:5
Low, C Adolphe, 1907, O 16,9:5
Low, Charles H, 1949, Jl 10,56:4
Low, Clarence H, 1960, D 10,23:3
Low, Daniel, 1876, Ap 7,4:6
Low, David, 1938, O 3,15:5; 1963, S 21;1:1
Low, E M, 1881, Jl 31,6:7
Low, Edward F, 1949, Je 8,29:2
Low, Edward P (will), 1949, Je 19,68:1
Low, Ethelbert I, 1946, O 20,60:6
Low, F G, 1878, D 13,2:2
Low, Francis S, 1964, Ja 25,23:3
Low, Fred, 1954, Mr 23,27:4
Low, George, 1950, Ap 18,31:5
Low, George A, 1948, S 14,29:2
Low, George C, 1952, Ag 2,15:2
Low, George E, 1948, O 24,76:2
Low, George E Mrs, 1950, D 10,104:6
Low, Grace B, 1944, Mr 16,19:5
Low, Harry C, 1943, S 14,23:2
Low, Harry R, 1957, Jl 21,60:3
Low, Harry W, 1947, S 11,27:6
Low, Harry W Mrs, 1941, N 30,69:2
Low, Harvey L, 1951, Jl 5,25:3
Low, Henry J, 1953, Mr 20,23:2
Low, Howard G, 1944, Ja 18,19:2
Low, J Herbert, 1959, D 21,27:5
Low, J Mrs, 1927, Ja 18,25:3
Low, J Sir, 1880, Ja 30,2:7
Low, James T, 1939, F 22,21:5
Low, John A Mrs, 1951, Je 5,31:4
Low, John G Mrs, 1951, D 21,27:3
Low, John H, 1958, N 11,29:1
Low, John H Mrs, 1958, N 5,35:2
Low, John M, 1956, Ag 23,27:6
Low, Joseph T, 1942, N 17,26:4
Low, Josiah O, 1956, My 1,33:5
Low, Leo, 1960, O 7,35:2
Low, Leopold Dr, 1875, N 7,7:1
Low, Leslie, 1939, Ap 16,III,6:7
Low, Mary Mrs (Grandma; por), 1955, My 4,29:4
Low, Milton H, 1942, Jl 25,13:4
Low, Minnie, 1922, My 29,11:4
Low, Nathan S, 1956, My 3,31:4
Low, Paul R, 1944, Ap 15,11:2
Low, Philip Burrill, 1912, Ag 24,9:4
Low, Rollie B Mrs (will), 1938, Ag 20,18:8
Low, Rudolph A, 1924, Mr 20,19:5
Low, Russell C, 1957, N 4,29:5
Low, Sanford, 1964, O 7,47:2
Low, Seth (por),(funl, S 19,11:4), 1916, S 18,13:2
Low, Seth H, 1962, Ap 1,87:1
Low, Seth Mrs, 1929, Ap 2,31:4
Low, Thomas P, 1938, D 13,25:3
Low, W G, 1936, Je 29,15:1
Low, W H, 1932, N 28,15:1
Low, Werner E, 1961, Ap 29,23:5
Low, William F, 1941, F 12,21:2
Low, William G, 1945, O 10,21:3
Low, William H, 1964, O 8,43:2
Low, William H Mrs, 1909, Ap 8,11:5
Low, Willy H Mrs, 1946, My 24,19:4
Low-Beer, Bertram V A, 1955, S 28,35:1
Lowack, Charles W, 1949, D 10,17:2
Lowan, Arnold N, 1962, My 28,29:4
Lowden, B Frank, 1938, Ap 8,19:4
Lowden, Davidina M Mrs, 1938, Mr 23,23:2
Lowden, Eleanor, 1956, Je 27,31:6
Lowden, Francis V, 1961, O 26,35:6
Lowden, Francis V Mrs, 1967, Ag 25,35:3
Lowden, Frank O (por), 1943, Mr 21,26:1
Lowden, Frank O Mrs (por),(will, Jl 25,II,6:8), 1937, Jl 6,19:3
Lowden, Isabel, 1957, N 6,35:1
Lowden, John G, 1940, Ja 29,15:4
Lowden, Joseph D Mrs, 1943, D 27,19:1
Lowden, Joseph J, 1958, Je 21,19:1
Lowden, Robert Johnson, 1909, Ja 1,11:6
Lowden, Theodore G, 1951, Ja 5,22:2
Lowe, Aubrey L, 1953, S 12,17:4
Lowe, Bauma Mrs, 1948, Ag 13,15:5
Lowe, Caroline, 1946, D 30,22:5
Lowe, Charles, 1941, Jl 28,13:3
Lowe, Clifton D, 1955, D 25,48:2
Lowe, Corinne, 1952, Ap 15,27:2
Lowe, D P, 1882, Ap 13,5:3
Lowe, David, 1965, S 25,6:1
Lowe, David Sr, 1951, S 26,31:3
Lowe, Donald B, 1946, Mr 4,23:2
Lowe, Edmund P Dr, 1937, Je 25,21:5
Lowe, Edward Mrs, 1951, Ja 18,27:3
Lowe, Edward Ricketson, 1908, Ap 18,9:5
Lowe, Edwin A, 1940, Ap 15,17:5
Lowe, Elias A Mrs (H T Lowe-Porter), 1963, Ap 27, 25:1
Lowe, Ella H, 1939, My 23,23:5
Lowe, Ernest A Mrs, 1947, F 27,21:3
Lowe, Ernest R, 1943, N 14,57:2
Lowe, Francisco, 1947, F 21,20:3
Lowe, Frank, 1955, Ja 26,25:4
Lowe, Frank D, 1948, Ap 19,23:2
Lowe, Frank E Maj, 1903, D 17,9:4
Lowe, Frank E Maj-Gen, 1968, D 28,27:1
Lowe, Fred M, 1938, Mr 1,21:1
Lowe, Fred Mrs, 1953, F 11,29:3
Lowe, Fred N, 1966, Ja 9,56:6
Lowe, Garrison, 1958, D 1,29:6
Lowe, George, 1953, Ja 16,23:4
Lowe, George Mrs, 1945, Ap 3,19:5
Lowe, H Burton Mrs, 1958, N 19,37:2
Lowe, Harry W, 1940, Ag 24,13:3
Lowe, Henry W, 1954, Ja 9,15:5
Lowe, Herbert G Mrs, 1948, O 26,31:4
Lowe, Herbert Rev, 1922, Je 6,17:3
Lowe, Herman A, 1961, Mr 13,29:2
Lowe, Horatio Mrs, 1949, Je 5,92:3
Lowe, Isaac C, 1944, O 2,19:5
Lowe, Isadore J, 1964, My 15,35:3
Lowe, Jacob, 1950, Ag 23,29:5
Lowe, James E, 1943, Ja 18,15:5
Lowe, Joe Mrs, 1966, D 20,43:2
Lowe, John, 1946, S 18,31:1
Lowe, John B Sr, 1960, Je 10,31:1
Lowe, John G (will), 1939, S 30,18:8
Lowe, John H, 1953, N 17,31:1
Lowe, John J, 1951, N 2,18:4
Lowe, John M, 1948, Ag 24,23:3
Lowe, John P, 1945, S 26,23:4
Lowe, John S, 1954, Mr 24,27:4
Lowe, John T C, 1963, Jl 12,25:4
Lowe, John W, 1937, N 8,23:3
Lowe, John W Mrs, 1950, Mr 8,27:2
Lowe, John Z, 1950, N 15,31:3
Lowe, Joseph, 1954, Ag 13,15:1
Lowe, Joshua, 1945, Mr 23,19:2
Lowe, Leo H, 1950, Jl 29,13:4
Lowe, Lillian (Mrs A Tarble), 1957, Je 25,29:3
Lowe, Louisa S, 1910, F 15,9:6
Lowe, Maynard W, 1939, Jl 1,17:2
Lowe, Michael C, 1966, Ap 6,43:2
Lowe, Nathan J, 1945, Ja 10,23:5
Lowe, Perly, 1924, Jl 31,13:7
Lowe, R Girard, 1951, F 7,29:4
Lowe, R P, 1883, D 23,2:5
Lowe, Richard R, 1962, Mr 31,25:3
Lowe, Robert (Lord Sherbrooke), 1892, Jl 28,4:7
Lowe, Robert L, 1951, D 10,29:3
Lowe, Russell B, 1965, Ag 5,29:4
Lowe, Russell W, 1944, Ja 4,17:3
Lowe, Siegmund, 1962, My 17,37:4
Lowe, Stephen E, 1945, Je 15,19:5
Lowe, Susan L Mrs, 1947, O 28,25:3
Lowe, Thaddeus S C Dr, 1913, Ja 17,13:5
Lowe, Thomas, 1960, Ap 1,33:4
Lowe, Thomas C, 1943, Ja 24,43:1
Lowe, Thomas Owen Rev, 1922, S 4,13:6
Lowe, Titus, 1959, N 28,21:3
Lowe, Vincent J, 1949, Ap 20,27:1
Lowe, W M, 1882, O 13,5:2
Lowe, Walter A, 1959, Je 16,35:3
Lowe, Walter Mrs, 1941, N 15,17:5
Lowe, William A, 1944, Je 9,15:6
Lowe, William B, 1946, Ag 4,45:1
Lowe, William Ebbets, 1924, Ap 9,21:3
Lowe, William S, 1956, Mr 13,27:4
Lowe, William W, 1953, Ja 12,27:3; 1961, D 20,33:3
Lowe-Porter, Helen T (Mrs E A Lowe), 1963, Ap 27,25:1
Lowell, A L M D, 1882, O 14,2:2
Lowell, A Lawrence (will, Ja 14,18:7), 1943, Ja 7, 19:1
Lowell, Albert F, 1939, My 15,17:5
Lowell, Alfred P, 1954, Je 29,27:5
Lowell, Amy, 1925, My 13,21:2
Lowell, B F, 1879, Ag 1,5:2
Lowell, Charles R Col, 1864, O 30,6:2
Lowell, Cuthbert H, 1948, S 14,29:3
Lowell, D O S, 1928, Mr 13,29:5
Lowell, Dorothy, 1944, Jl 3,11:5
Lowell, E J Mrs, 1904, S 27,9:6
Lowell, Eugene B, 1951, Ag 17,17:4
Lowell, Francis Cabot Judge, 1911, Mr 7,11:4
Lowell, G, 1927, F 5,15:5
Lowell, Guy Mrs, 1953, Ap 17,25:2
Lowell, Helen, 1937, Je 30,24:1
Lowell, J A, 1933, D 1,20:1
Lowell, J Albert, 1950, Jl 16,68:7
Lowell, J R, 1891, Ag 13,1:7
Lowell, J R Mrs, 1885, F 18,1:4
Lowell, James B (por), 1947, O 26,70:3
Lowell, James B Mrs, 1943, D 14,27:4
Lowell, James H Mrs, 1945, Jl 13,11:7
Lowell, James R, 1960, Ja 28,31:4
Lowell, Joan, 1967, N 15,47:2
Lowell, Josephine Shaw, 1905, O 13,9:6
Lowell, Mary C, 1949, Je 28,27:2
Lowell, Mary E H Mrs, 1940, F 23,15:1
Lowell, Milton H Mrs, 1943, O 21,27:3
Lowell, Nat, 1956, N 4,87:2
Lowell, Orson B, 1956, F 11,17:5
Lowell, Otis E, 1963, Je 7,31:3
Lowell, Percival Dr, 1916, N 14,11:3
Lowell, Percival Mrs, 1954, S 27,21:2
Lowell, Ralph E, 1950, Ja 26,27:5
Lowell, Robert I Mrs, 1964, N 3,31:3
Lowell, Sherman J (por), 1940, F 4,40:7
Lowell, W Holbrook, 1943, Ap 2,21:5
Lowell, William, 1954, Je 25,21:3
Lowen, Charles J Jr, 1956, S 6,25:1
Lowen, Harold A, 1968, Ja 24,42:1
Lowen, Herbert C, 1955, Jl 27,23:6
Lowen, Irwin S, 1949, Ap 25,23:6
Lowen, Walter A, 1965, Ag 16,27:5
Lowenbraun, Isidore, 1952, Mr 31,19:3
Lowenbraun, Isidore Mrs, 1963, O 6,88:2
Lowendon, Alfred J, 1953, F 3,25:4
Lowenfeld, Viktor, 1960, My 26,33:2
Lowengard, Armand, 1944, My 23,23:3
Lowengard, Joseph, 1961, Ja 13,29:3
Lowengard, Santiago, 1954, Jl 9,17:5
Lowengrund, Ernest, 1949, F 9,27:3
Lowengrund, Margaret Mrs, 1957, N 21,33:2
Lowenhaupt, Warren H, 1967, O 5,39:4
Lowenstein, Arthur J, 1962, Ag 1,31:2

Lowenstein, Benjamin, 1941, Ag 17,38:2
Lowenstein, Casper, 1951, Mr 13,31:2
Lowenstein, David, 1938, My 14,15:5
Lowenstein, Ernst, 1950, Ag 30,32:3
Lowenstein, Gabriel, 1966, Ap 1,35:1
Lowenstein, Gabriel A, 1965, Mr 10,41:2
Lowenstein, Harry M, 1949, Ag 6,17:6
Lowenstein, Leo, 1961, N 2,37:4
Lowenstein, Leon B, 1946, O 5,17:1
Lowenstein, Louis, 1918, Jl 17,11:6; 1925, Mr 19,21:3
Lowenstein, Louis Dr, 1968, Mr 25,41:3
Lowenstein, M Louis Mrs, 1967, Ja 14,31:2
Lowenstein, Max, 1909, Je 3,9:4
Lowenstein, Otto, 1965, Mr 27,27:1
Lowenstein, Philip C, 1964, Jl 22,33:4
Lowenstein, Samuel L, 1953, Mr 13,25:4
Lowenstein, Sol, 1942, Mr 11,15:1
Lowenstein, Sol Mrs, 1941, S 20,17:6
Lowenstein, Solomon (por), 1942, Ja 21,17:1
Lowenstein, William, 1956, O 30,34:2
Lowenthal, Abraham, 1951, O 13,17:1; 1951, N 28, 31:3
Lowenthal, Albert A Dr, 1937, Mr 21,II,8:5
Lowenthal, Benjamin W, 1948, Je 11,23:3
Lowenthal, David, 1937, F 1,19:4
Lowenthal, Eugene M, 1938, Ag 22,13:5
Lowenthal, Fred G, 1958, Ag 13,27:3
Lowenthal, Isadore R, 1940, Je 6,25:6
Lowenthal, Karl, 1944, Ja 18,19:4
Lowenthal, Leo, 1944, Je 12,19:4
Lowenthal, Nathan, 1948, Mr 17,25:2
Lowenthal, Oscar, 1946, Ag 5,21:3
Lowenthal, Perry, 1923, Ag 2,15:5
Lowenthal, Sidney (por), 1944, Ja 28,17:4
Lower, Charles A, 1948, N 20,13:3
Lower, Elton, 1947, My 5,23:4
Lower, Henry, 1961, Ag 29,24:1
Lower, John H, 1951, Jl 17,27:4
Lower, M William, 1954, Ag 27,21:4
Lower, Martin L, 1948, F 23,25:2
Lower, Mary J, 1947, N 29,13:3
Lower, William B, 1960, Ap 2,23:6
Lower, William E, 1948, Je 18,23:2
Lower, William Savery, 1925, F 28,13:5
Lowerre, George H Mrs, 1939, Ag 6,37:2
Lowerre, T H, 1884, Jl 13,7:1
Lowerre, Thomas B, 1951, Je 30,15:6
Lowerre, Thomas B Mrs, 1957, Mr 5,31:2
Lowery, Arthur K, 1944, Jl 14,13:4
Lowery, Elizabeth R Mrs, 1937, N 26,21:2
Lowery, Harry E, 1941, Ap 2,23:4
Lowery, James L, 1954, O 28,35:2
Lowery, John E, 1952, Jl 9,27:6
Lowery, John F Rev, 1914, D 23,13:4
Lowery, Joseph D, 1964, Mr 19,33:1
Lowery, Marklove Mrs, 1938, Jl 28,19:2
Lowery, Thomas A, 1949, Ap 13,29:4
Lowery, Worth, 1944, D 12,23:2
Lowes, C Leslie, 1944, Je 13,19:5
Lowes, C Leslie (por), 1947, Ag 27,23:2
Lowes, Clarence M, 1937, Ap 19,21:4
Lowes, Marvin M, 1960, Jl 1,25:4
Lowie, Risa, 1960, D 12,29:4
Lowinson, Emanuel, 1937, Ag 13,11:3
Lowinson, Louis, 1952, My 9,23:4
Lowinson, Oscar, 1946, S 28,17:2
Lowitz, Elick, 1956, N 4,87:1
Lowitz, John J, 1968, N 3,89:1
Lowitz, Robert M, 1941, F 18,23:4
Lowitz, Robert M Mrs, 1955, F 12,15:2
Lowitz, Samuel Mrs, 1948, Je 27,52:6
Lowkrantz, Gunnel, 1964, N 28,21:1
Lowman, Arthur A, 1960, N 15,39:4
Lowman, E J, 1947, N 29,13:2
Lowman, Guy S, 1943, S 15,27:4
Lowman, John H, 1919, Ja 24,11:4
Lowman, John R, 1947, Je 7,13:2
Lowman, Seymour, 1940, Mr 14,23:1
Lown, Alex A, 1942, N 12,25:5
Lown, Bert, 1962, N 21,33:5
Lown, Cora E, 1941, Ag 14,17:4
Lown, George, 1955, Jl 16,15:4
Lown, George E Mrs, 1953, Jl 30,23:2
Lown, Jessie, 1940, Ag 30,19:2
Lown, Marcus M Mrs, 1943, Jl 24,13:3
Lown, Maxwell, 1950, Ap 11,31:3
Lown, Percy M, 1950, Ag 7,19:6
Lown, William, 1948, My 10,21:6
Lowndes, Arthur Rev Dr, 1917, Ja 3,11:4
Lowndes, Belloc Mrs (por), 1947, N 15,17:1
Lowndes, Charles L B, 1967, Jl 30,64:3
Lowndes, Lloyd, 1968, D 16,47:1
Lowndes, Lloyd ex-Gov, 1905, Ja 9,7:5
Lowndes, Mary E, 1947, Mr 20,27:2
Lowndes, Richard, 1905, Jl 2,7:6
Lowndes, Richard T Jr, 1905, Je 30,9:4
Lowndes, Richard T Mrs, 1944, Ja 21,17:4
Lowndes, Tasker G, 1952, Jl 11,17:1
Lowndes, W Bladen Sr, 1941, My 31,11:6
Lowndes, William Henry, 1919, Je 28,9:4
Lownes, Allan A Mrs, 1959, Ja 24,19:3
Lownestein, Ludwig, 1968, Jl 31,41:3
Lowney, Timothy E, 1950, Ag 13,76:4
Lowney, Walter M, 1921, Ap 5,19:5
Lowrey, Alva Mrs, 1949, My 16,21:1
Lowrey, B G, 1947, S 3,25:4
Lowrey, Betty, 1961, Jl 17,21:2
Lowrey, C, 1877, F 18,12:5
Lowrey, Girard C Mrs, 1945, Jl 1,17:2
Lowrey, Girard C W, 1908, Ja 19,11:4
Lowrey, Ida, 1957, Je 24,23:1
Lowrey, James H, 1960, Jl 12,35:3
Lowrey, Jeanette, 1955, Ja 13,27:4
Lowrey, John D, 1945, O 25,21:1
Lowrey, Perrin, 1965, Je 26,29:4
Lowrey, William T, 1944, My 30,21:3
Lowria, Leon Dr, 1923, Ag 28,17:4
Lowrie, Charles N (por), 1939, S 19,26:2
Lowrie, Donald, 1925, Je 26,17:5
Lowrie, Donald J, 1951, S 17,21:6
Lowrie, Howard H, 1953, Mr 26,31:4
Lowrie, Jeanette, 1937, F 23,27:2
Lowrie, John M, 1954, Mr 4,25:1
Lowrie, Rachel, 1957, N 7,35:4
Lowrie, Robert H, 1957, S 24,35:5
Lowrie, Robert J, 1961, O 11,47:3
Lowrie, Sarah D, 1957, Je 24,23:2
Lowrie, Thomas R, 1964, F 15,23:5
Lowrie, Walter, 1959, Ag 14,21:3
Lowrie, Wesley M, 1924, Jl 31,13:7
Lowrie, Will L, 1944, Ap 3,21:4
Lowrie, William L, 1945, My 25,19:4
Lowry, Alfred Jr Mrs (Grace B), 1964, N 26,33:3
Lowry, Carolyn Clay, 1925, S 20,7:2
Lowry, Charles D, 1953, D 16,35:4
Lowry, Donald R, 1955, Ag 10,25:3
Lowry, Edith B, 1945, Mr 9,19:2
Lowry, Edward G, 1943, Jl 23,17:1
Lowry, Erwin F, 1957, Ja 3,33:4
Lowry, Francis B, 1952, Ag 3,60:4
Lowry, Frank Clifford, 1968, N 28,37:5
Lowry, Frank J, 1955, Mr 29,30:2
Lowry, Helen Bullitt (Mrs Harry Irvine), 1968, Ja 18,39:1
Lowry, Hiter H, 1966, Ap 1,35:3
Lowry, Howard F, 1967, Jl 5,41:3
Lowry, Ira M, 1951, Ag 4,15:3
Lowry, James Johnson, 1916, Ag 26,7:5
Lowry, James W, 1950, D 30,31:1
Lowry, John, 1920, O 6,15:5; 1962, N 4,89:1
Lowry, John Mrs, 1947, Ap 10,25:1; 1968, F 25,76:4
Lowry, John T, 1950, Mr 12,92:4
Lowry, Judith, 1941, Mr 22,15:5
Lowry, Kieran J, 1943, D 2,27:4
Lowry, Margaret H Mrs, 1938, O 4,25:5
Lowry, Mary R Mrs, 1941, My 11,45:2
Lowry, Milton, 1954, Ap 7,31:3
Lowry, Paul H, 1944, N 6,19:2
Lowry, R B Capt, 1880, N 26,5:4
Lowry, Ralph M, 1943, Je 9,21:5
Lowry, Robert B, 1952, Mr 12,27:4
Lowry, Robert Dr (mem), 1911, Ap 17,11:4
Lowry, Robert Ex-Gov, 1910, Ja 20,11:3
Lowry, Robert Judge, 1904, Ja 28,9:6
Lowry, Robert P, 1953, Ag 31,17:1
Lowry, Rudd, 1965, D 16,48:1
Lowry, Thomas, 1909, F 5,7:5
Lowry, Thomas P Jr, 1949, Ap 27,27:6
Lowry, Walter L, 1961, S 15,33:2
Lowry, Wheaton S, 1943, My 1,15:3
Lowry, Zetta M Mrs, 1938, Jl 30,13:2
Lowsley, Augustus S, 1939, Jl 19,19:5
Lowsley, Oswald S, 1955, Je 6,27:3
Lowson, David Lindsay, 1911, Jl 5,11:5
Lowther, Albert, 1937, Jl 20,23:4
Lowther, Alice Lady, 1939, N 21,23:2
Lowther, C, 1877, Je 8,8:5
Lowther, Cecil, 1940, D 11,27:6
Lowther, Charles, 1949, Ja 24,19:3
Lowther, Christopher M, 1945, Ap 13,17:5
Lowther, Clifford, 1960, O 11,45:5
Lowther, Gerard Augustus Sir, 1916, Ap 6,13:7
Lowther, James M P, 1904, S 13,9:7
Lowther, John B Mrs, 1946, Mr 21,25:3
Lowther, John E, 1964, Je 23,33:4
Lowther, Leonard W, 1960, F 7,84:7
Lowther, Lloyd, 1941, Ap 9,25:3
Lowther, Samuel H, 1963, Ap 21,86:6
Lowther, Viscount (Anthony Edw), 1949, O 8,13:4
Lowther, William E, 1953, Jl 23,23:5
Lowy, Alex, 1941, D 26,14:2
Lowy, Arthur, 1962, Ja 18,29:3
Lowy, Felix, 1937, O 6,25:1
Lowy, Harry P, 1948, Ag 10,21:6
Lowy, Harry P Mrs, 1962, N 10,25:2
Lowy, Mannie, 1944, Mr 31,21:1
Lowy, Moriz, 1959, Mr 20,31:2
Lowy, Nicholas Mrs, 1968, Je 27,43:3
Lowy, Robert, 1956, Ja 24,32:8
Lowy, Victor, 1955, Je 6,27:5
Lowy, Wolff, 1945, Ap 5,23:2
Loy, Lawrence V, 1955, Mr 12,19:5
Loy, Thomas H, 1961, My 7,86:6
Loyak, Andrew, 1919, Jl 28,11:4
Loyal, Alfred, 1945, O 28,44:2
Loyall, George R, 1941, Ja 21,21:2
Loyd, John, 1915, O 6,11:4
Loyd, Phil H, 1952, Ja 13,89:1
Loyd, S, 1934, F 25,31:1
Loyd, Sam, 1911, Ap 12,13:4
Loyd, W, 1882, D 6,5:3
Loynes, Charles N, 1946, D 8,77:6
Loyola, Sister, 1914, Mr 23,11:4
Loysen, Milton O, 1964, Je 17,43:3
Loyson, Charles, 1909, D 5,13:4
Loyson, Paul Hyacinthe, 1921, Ap 20,13:6
Loza, Celestino Msgr, 1921, Ja 24,11:4
Lozada, Jesus E, 1948, Je 30,25:4
Lozado, Manuel, 1871, Jl 29,1:6
Lozano, Agapita S, 1945, Ap 11,23:3
Lozano, Ignacio E, 1953, S 22,31:4
Lozano, Torijos (por), 1947, Ja 6,23:3
Lozano Diaz, Julio, 1957, Ag 21,27:1
Lozano y Lozano, Carlos, 1952, F 14,5:1
Lozaw, Frank A, 1947, Ja 31,23:4
Lozier, Abraham Witton Dr, 1915, Ag 7,7:4
Lozier, Arnold T, 1948, Je 25,23:3
Lozier, Charles, 1954, Mr 29,19:4
Lozier, Charles E, 1938, My 8,II,7:3
Lozier, Charlotte Dr, 1870, Ja 4,5:2
Lozier, H A, 1903, My 26,9:5
Lozier, Matthew Z, 1959, Ap 16,33:1
Lozier, Merritt W, 1942, O 10,15:1
Lozier, Robert Ten Eyck, 1921, Ag 23,15:6
Lozo, John Peter Dr, 1968, O 3,47:1
Lozowick, Herman Mrs, 1955, Ja 20,31:4
Lozowick, Philip A, 1959, F 22,89:2
Lozuk, Nicholas, 1952, O 26,89:1
Luang Vichit Vadakan, 1962, Ap 1,86:6
Lubaitowski, F, 1954, D 8,35:3
Lubarsky, Abraham E (funl, S 3,22:1), 1920, O 2,1
Lubarsky, David A Dr, 1968, Ja 14,84:5
Lubarsky, Simon, 1957, Mr 16,19:2
Lubarsky, Wladimir, 1953, My 9,19:5
Lubart, Abraham, 1946, Ag 8,21:5
Lubash, Samuel, 1950, D 9,15:2
Lubben, Herman C, 1951, S 2,48:5
Lubben, John F, 1938, Ja 31,19:3
Lubbers, Adriaan, 1954, My 18,29:3
Lubbers, Edward S, 1962, F 25,88:5
Lubbock, F R ex-Gov, 1905, Mr 19,9:4
Lubbock, John (Lord Avebury), 1913, My 29,11:5
Lubeck, George F Sr, 1962, My 19,27:5
Lubeck, H, 1933, S 5,17:3
Lubell, Aaron D, 1940, D 8,69:1
Lubell, Abe Mrs, 1954, N 4,31:3
Lubell, Jacob J, 1954, F 28,92:4; 1957, O 16,35:4
Lubell, Mack, 1960, D 6,37:1
Lubell, Morris, 1954, D 7,33:4
Lubell, Samuel L, 1966, Jl 10,69:1
Lubell, Samuel L Mrs, 1952, D 27,9:3
Lubelsky, Joseph, 1961, O 6,35:3
Luber, Harry I, 1963, Jl 28,64:8
Luberda, Frederick S, 1968, D 24,20:7
Luberger, Charles M, 1944, My 19,19:6
Lubetkin, Louis, 1964, Jl 27,31:5
Lubetkin, Sanford W Mrs, 1967, Ap 26,47:1
Lubic, Ben, 1948, F 16,22:3
Lubin, Albert J, 1964, Mr 23,29:4
Lubin, Annie Mrs, 1941, My 24,15:1
Lubin, Arthur, 1940, Mr 30,15:3
Lubin, Charles, 1954, Mr 17,31:6
Lubin, David (funl, Ja 4,11:4), 1919, Ja 3,9:2
Lubin, Herbert, 1953, Ja 30,22:6
Lubin, Horace A, 1953, Je 7,83:1
Lubin, Jacob H, 1953, N 10,31:3
Lubin, Jacob H Mrs, 1946, My 6,21:4
Lubin, Max D, 1955, Jl 31,68:6
Lubin, Milan Mrs, 1950, Jl 8,13:4
Lubin, Milton, 1948, D 10,25:1
Lubin, Phil, 1952, Jl 28,15:5
Lubin, Samuel, 1954, Ap 4,88:1
Lubin, Sigmund (funl, S 15,15:6), 1923, S 11,15:3
Lubin, Solomon S, 1958, Ap 16,33:5
Lubinski, Kurt, 1955, Ag 20,17:3
Lubinsky, Benjamin B, 1957, Mr 28,31:2
Lubinsky, Henry, 1948, My 26,25:3
Lubis, James, 1947, D 19,26:3
Lubischer, Frank J, 1951, My 20,88:4
Lubisco, Anthony, 1949, Ja 20,27:3
Lubitsch, Ernst, 1947, D 1,21:1
Lubitz, Samuel, 1946, D 16,23:3
Lublin, Nathan A, 1961, Jl 13,29:3
Lubliner, Philip, 1968, Jl 19,35:4
Lubliner, Solomon, 1939, O 11,30:2
Luboshutz, Katherine Mrs, 1940, Je 28,19:4
Luboshutz, Lea, 1965, Mr 19,35:4
Lubow, Nathan E, 1947, Jl 22,23:2
Lubowitt, Jules J, 1954, N 10,33:2
Lubowsky, Barry, 1954, Jl 4,1:1
Lubowsky, Eli, 1954, Jl 4,1:1
Lubowsky, Eli Mrs, 1954, Jl 4,1:1
Lubrecht, Charles A, 1963, Ap 14,93:1
Lubrecht, L G, 1948, Je 16,29:4
Lubrew, G Stephen, 1953, Ja 30,21:2
Lubschez, Ben, 1963, Ag 21,33:3
Lubschez, Rose, 1955, Ja 21,23:1
Luby, David Mrs, 1947, Ja 11,19:5
Luby, John F Com, 1911, Ja 11,13:6

Luby, T C, 1901, D 1,7:6
Luby, Th Clarke Mrs, 1903, Jl 12,7:6
Luby, Walter F, 1954, O 16,17:4
Luca, Giuseppe de, 1960, My 14,23:7
Luca, Giuseppe de Signora, 1960, Ja 23,21:5
Luca, Ramon Barros, 1919, S 21,22:3
Lucacher, Harry, 1938, Mr 24,23:1
Lucacik, Stephen, 1954, O 5,27:5
Lucal, Ira D, 1951, N 6,29:3
Lucan, Earl of, 1914, Je 6,9:5
Lucan, Earl of (G C Bingham), 1949, Ap 22,24:8
Lucan, Earl of (G C P Bingham), 1964, Ja 22,37:2
Lucanese, Carmela Mrs, 1940, O 6,48:1
Lucano, Ralph V, 1963, N 21,39:3
Lucanus, Fredrick K Dr, 1908, Ag 4,7:6
Lucas, Albert, 1923, Je 16,11:6; 1946, Je 26,25:4
Lucas, Albert Durer, 1919, My 27,15:6
Lucas, Albert P, 1945, My 3,23:2
Lucas, Alfred, 1945, D 10,21:5
Lucas, Anthony, 1954, Mr 12,22:4
Lucas, Anthony R, 1941, My 14,21:2
Lucas, Armistead S, 1950, My 14,106:7
Lucas, Arthur, 1940, D 16,61:1; 1943, Jl 19,15:3; 1944, D 7,25:6
Lucas, Arthur F, 1953, Jl 9,25:6
Lucas, Arthur G, 1952, Ja 11,21:3
Lucas, Arthur V, 1937, S 9,23:3
Lucas, Carl, 1942, My 4,19:6
Lucas, Carroll F, 1947, F 22,3:3
Lucas, Charles, 1874, My 7,4:7; 1955, Ja 12,27:5
Lucas, Charles J P, 1951, My 14,25:4
Lucas, Clarence D Mrs, 1959, F 18,33:4
Lucas, Clyde G, 1941, Ja 14,21:2
Lucas, David L, 1960, Jl 5,43:1
Lucas, E N, 1948, Ag 30,25:2
Lucas, Edward J, 1945, D 5,25:4
Lucas, Edward V (por), 1938, Je 27,17:5
Lucas, Edwin E, 1940, Je 7,23:3
Lucas, Edwin J, 1946, Ag 29,27:4
Lucas, Eugene (cor, Ja 30,27:1), 1959, Ja 29,27:3
Lucas, Eugene W Van C Mrs, 1916, Ja 30,17:6
Lucas, F A, 1929, F 16,29:4
Lucas, Francis F, 1961, Je 21,37:4
Lucas, Frank, 1949, O 21,25:2
Lucas, Frank L, 1967, Je 26,33:3
Lucas, Frederick, 1946, N 5,25:5
Lucas, George C, 1964, F 4,30:8
Lucas, George W, 1942, My 30,15:3
Lucas, Gilbert, 1947, N 12,27:2
Lucas, Harry, 1939, Mr 14,21:4
Lucas, Harry H, 1944, S 9,15:5
Lucas, Harry J, 1950, S 3,38:3
Lucas, Henry C, 1937, S 22,27:5
Lucas, Henry G, 1960, S 9,30:1
Lucas, Henry H Dr, 1937, D 11,19:2
Lucas, Herbert, 1953, N 15,89:1
Lucas, Herbert J, 1957, Ap 14,86:2
Lucas, Howard J, 1963, Je 25,33:3
Lucas, J C M, 1943, O 22,17:4
Lucas, J Carrell, 1937, Mr 14,II,9:2
Lucas, J Harold, 1956, My 14,25:4
Lucas, J Harold Mrs, 1946, D 21,19:5
Lucas, James, 1874, My 4,5:6
Lucas, James A, 1952, O 5,88:6
Lucas, James A Mrs, 1950, D 30,13:3
Lucas, James J, 1939, Ja 11,19:5; 1949, F 22,23:4
Lucas, Jocelyn Lady, 1956, Ja 22,88:7
Lucas, John D, 1959, Mr 4,31:5
Lucas, John D Mrs, 1949, Ag 28,75:1
Lucas, John J, 1921, Ja 18,11:3; 1958, Jl 10,27:4
Lucas, John Mrs, 1947, O 9,25:3
Lucas, John P, 1949, D 25,26:4
Lucas, John S, 1968, N 21,47:4
Lucas, Joseph D, 1907, N 2,9:2
Lucas, Joseph L, 1949, N 20,92:3
Lucas, Joseph W, 1956, N 6,35:1
Lucas, Julian, 1944, Mr 10,15:5
Lucas, Ken (Chas K), 1965, Jl 6,33:4
Lucas, Leigh, 1963, My 26,92:8
Lucas, Louis J, 1940, Ag 15,19:2
Lucas, Mary M Mrs, 1951, My 15,31:4
Lucas, Myrtle I, 1949, D 4,108:4
Lucas, Oliver, 1948, Mr 23,25:5
Lucas, Phil H, 1942, Je 2,23:4
Lucas, R J Bp, 1938, O 9,44:7
Lucas, Robert H (por), 1947, O 14,27:3
Lucas, Rupert, 1953, Ja 15,27:5
Lucas, Sallie S Mrs, 1940, My 15,25:5
Lucas, Sam, 1948, Mr 22,23:2
Lucas, Samuel, 1865, My 6,4:6; 1948, Je 1,23:4
Lucas, Samuel Mildmay, 1916, Ja 11,11:5
Lucas, Scott W Ex-Sen, 1968, F 23,33:1
Lucas, Scott W Mrs, 1967, N 9,61:8
Lucas, Sidney Z, 1966, Jl 4,15:2
Lucas, Stephen, 1951, O 17,32:6
Lucas, T M, 1946, Ja 25,23:4
Lucas, Thomas D, 1947, F 19,25:5
Lucas, Timothy C, 1940, D 31,15:3
Lucas, Walter S, 1942, F 14,15:1
Lucas, Wilfred, 1940, D 14,17:6
Lucas, Willa B Mrs, 1961, Ja 22,84:8
Lucas, William A, 1956, My 26,17:6
Lucas, William H, 1952, S 22,23:4
Lucas, William J, 1946, Ag 15,25:4
Lucas, William P, 1960, D 17,23:6
Lucas, William V, 1945, Jl 17,13:6
Lucas, William W, 1953, Jl 19,56:5
Lucas, Y Rev, 1868, My 22,5:6
Lucas-Championniere, Just Dr, 1913, O 23,11:5
Lucas of Trudwell, Baron, 1916, D 5,11:3
Lucashick, Jacob Mrs, 1910, Jl 15,7:6
Lucca, Luciano Mrs, 1948, S 22,31:3
Lucca, Pauline, 1908, F 29,7:6
Lucca, William, 1953, F 20,19:1
Lucchesi, Adamo, 1940, Ja 10,21:5
Lucchetti, Antonio, 1952, D 20,17:5
Lucchetti, Peter J, 1944, Ja 13,21:2
Lucci, Boniface, 1957, Jl 10,27:2
Luccock, George N, 1943, F 24,21:2
Luccock, Halford E, 1960, N 6,88:2
Luce, Alice H, 1940, O 4,23:5
Luce, Almerino, 1967, Je 30,37:4
Luce, Barnard C, 1956, Je 1,23:1
Luce, Clarence, 1924, Mr 23,X,8:2
Luce, Clarence Jr, 1947, Je 8,60:6
Luce, Cyrus G ex-Gov, 1905, Je 23,7:5
Luce, David E, 1939, F 7,19:4
Luce, Deans S, 1953, Ap 10,21:3
Luce, Edna, 1941, S 23,23:5
Luce, Edward B W, 1950, Ja 21,17:3
Luce, Elizabeth S (Betsy), 1961, S 18,14:7
Luce, Francis C, 1943, Mr 28,24:5
Luce, Francis H, 1942, D 12,17:2
Luce, Fred I, 1958, Ap 13,84:7
Luce, Fred L, 1940, D 31,15:3
Luce, Frederick B, 1951, D 16,89:2
Luce, Hallock, 1940, Ja 2,19:1
Luce, Harvey G, 1955, N 26,19:2
Luce, Henry A, 1955, O 30,89:1
Luce, Henry R (funl plans, Mr 2,35:4; funl ser, Mr 4,27:2), 1967, Mr 1,1:2
Luce, Henry W (por), 1941, D 9,31:1
Luce, Henry W Mrs, 1948, N 7,88:6
Luce, Herbert P, 1958, F 24,19:2
Luce, Horatio E, 1950, Jl 31,17:5
Luce, J C, 1879, Jl 11,8:3
Luce, John D H, 1921, Ja 12,15:4
Luce, John W (por), 1942, N 26,27:4
Luce, John W, 1944, F 28,17:5
Luce, Joseph P Mrs, 1955, O 25,33:4
Luce, L A Judge, 1903, Ja 6,9:5
Luce, Leonard E, 1952, Ap 28,19:4
Luce, Leroy A, 1939, S 28,25:3
Luce, Linn, 1903, D 27,7:6
Luce, Matthew Mrs, 1962, Ja 28,76:7
Luce, Maximilien, 1941, F 27,19:3
Luce, Orvis H Mrs, 1943, O 7,23:4
Luce, R L, 1933, Mr 12,29:1
Luce, Richard W, 1955, Je 25,15:2
Luce, Robert (will, Ap 17,52:3), 1946, Ap 8,27:2
Luce, Robert E, 1958, Ja 25,19:1
Luce, Stephen B Mrs, 1921, D 25,20:3
Luce, Steph Bleecker Rear-Adm (funl, Ag 1,9:7), 1917, Jl 28,15:3
Luce, Stephen C, 1942, Ja 1,25:3
Luce, Theodore, 1949, Ag 14,68:4
Luce, Thomas C, 1944, Jl 10,15:4
Luce, Thomas J, 1941, D 3,25:3
Luce, William G, 1948, S 25,17:3
Luce, William L, 1956, Ja 25,31:5
Lucero, Felix A, 1951, Ja 24,27:1
Lucey, J, 1936, Ap 9,23:1
Lucey, John D, 1942, O 20,21:4
Lucey, John F, 1947, O 9,26:2; 1958, O 8,35:4
Lucey, John K, 1964, My 14,35:2
Lucey, Mary E, 1944, Je 6,17:3
Lucey, Michael H, 1957, D 20,27:3
Lucey, Robert E, 1961, D 3,88:5
Lucey, William J, 1952, F 5,29:4
Lucey, William S, 1957, Mr 2,21:5
Luchaire, Achille, 1908, N 15,9:5
Luchaire, Corinne, 1950, Ja 24,31:3
Luchese, Thomas G (Three Finger Brown),(funl, Jl 16,64:6), 1967, Jl 14,31:1
Luchi, Lewis, 1944, My 10,19:3
Luchow, August G, 1923, Ag 22,15:4
Luchs, Alvin S, 1949, F 4,23:2
Luchtenberg, William Mrs, 1949, Mr 30,25:4
Lucia, Alfred, 1950, Je 28,27:3
Lucia, Dominick, 1948, My 11,25:4
Luciani, Sebastiano A, 1950, D 9,15:1
Luciani, Vito, 1951, Ag 18,11:5
Luciano, Charles (Lucky),(funl plans, Ja 29,2:6; funl, Ja 30,59:3), 1962, Ja 27,1:6
Luciano, Dominick, 1958, Mr 25,33:3
Luciano, Josephine Mrs, 1953, My 7,31:1
Luciano, Tony, 1957, F 11,29:4
Lucibello, Emil Mrs, 1966, O 18,35:8
Lucid, Michael M Mrs, 1945, F 23,18:2
Lucidius, Bro (Jno S Horan), 1911, F 4,13:4
Lucido, Angelo J, 1949, Ja 24,19:4
Lucientes, Francisco, 1961, N 17,35:1
Lucier, Alvin A, 1953, Ja 27,25:4
Lucier, Gilbert, 1944, S 23,13:5
Lucifero, Alfonso, 1925, Je 19,19:7
Lucino, Marie Superior, 1904, Ja 1,7:5
Lucitt, John J, 1944, O 24,23:1
Lucitt, Maurice V, 1945, Jl 20,19:6
Lucius, Albert E, 1950, Ja 23,23:4
Lucius, Albin A, 1955, S 24,19:6
Lucius, George H, 1941, N 17,19:4
Luck, Andrew, 1937, Je 1,23:2
Luck, Bertha Mrs, 1942, F 8,48:4
Luck, Elizabeth, 1938, Mr 9,23:4
Luck, John J, 1938, S 17,17:4
Lucke, Balduin, 1954, Ap 27,29:4
Lucke, Charles E, 1951, Mr 27,29:1
Lucke, Charles E Mrs, 1958, N 4,27:4
Lucke, Edward J, 1938, N 10,27:4
Lucke, Henry J, 1948, F 26,23:4
Lucke, Jerome Bonaparte, 1923, Mr 13,22:5
Luckemeyer, Leona S Mrs (will), 1938, Ag 3,17:3
Luckenbach, Andrea Mrs, 1962, Ap 3,39:2
Luckenbach, Edgar F (por),(will, My 1,10:3), 1943, Ap 27,23:1
Luckenbach, Edgar F (est tax appr), 1958, Mr 8,34:4
Luckenbach, Edgar Mrs, 1937, Ja 12,24:2
Luckenbach, Edward, 1904, Ag 19,7:6
Luckenbach, J Lewis, 1951, Jl 5,25:3
Luckenbach, Lewis, 1906, Ag 9,9:6
Luckenbach, Lewis V, 1954, Mr 16,29:4
Luckenbill, Thomas D Mrs, 1965, N 2,33:1
Lucker, Albert E, 1954, N 11,31:3
Lucker, Eugene, 1943, Je 9,21:2
Lucker, John T, 1951, D 29,11:6
Luckett, Llewellyn F, 1940, Ja 1,24:2
Luckey, Ann, 1966, Je 21,43:4
Luckey, Charles M, 1944, S 5,19:5
Luckey, Charles P, 1966, N 20,88:4
Luckey, Charles P Mrs, 1959, D 30,22:1
Luckey, Frank M R, 1940, O 10,25:3
Luckey, George W A Mrs, 1952, Ag 18,17:1
Luckey, Henry C, 1957, Ja 1,23:4
Luckey, Hugh M, 1946, D 30,19:5
Luckey, James S Dr, 1937, Ap 8,23:5
Luckey, Leonard W A, 1942, Ja 29,19:4
Luckey, William W, 1944, F 1,20:2
Luckey, William W Mrs, 1951, Je 21,27:3
Luckhardt, Arno B, 1957, N 7,35:2
Luckhurst, Charlotte T Mrs, 1941, Ja 17,17:2
Luckie, S Blair Mrs, 1964, Ja 17,43:3
Luckie, Samuel B, 1944, D 22,17:2
Luckiesh, Matthew, 1967, N 3,48:1
Lucking, Joseph H, 1944, Ja 3,22:2
Luckman, Albert J Mrs, 1967, Ag 24,37:2
Luckman, David, 1955, S 18,87:1
Luckman, Meyer, 1944, Ja 25,21:7
Luckman, Sol, 1966, Je 4,29:4
Luckner, Felix von Count, 1966, Ap 14,39:1
Lucks, Charles B, 1938, Je 7,23:3
Lucks, Karl, 1951, D 5,35:5
Luckstone, Isidore, 1941, Mr 13,21:5
Luco, Ramon B, 1949, Ag 18,22:2
Lucon, Gino L, 1949, Ja 29,14:2
Lucon, L H, 1930, My 29,23:1
Lucy, Anna C, 1951, Ja 23,27:2
Lucy, Henry Sir (Toby M P), 1924, F 22,15:5
Lucy, James J, 1958, Je 25,29:5; 1960, My 26,33:4
Lucy, John C, 1961, Ap 26,39:1
Lucy, John H, 1948, S 29,30:3
Lucy, Mark E, 1947, My 8,25:1
Lucy, Roscoe W, 1941, Je 16,15:4
Luczak, Edward P, 1953, D 20,77:2
Luddecke, Ralph R, 1961, S 26,39:4
Ludden, Anthony P, 1964, Je 7,86:7
Ludden, Harold J, 1952, Ja 29,25:3
Ludden, John, 1951, Ja 10,27:4
Ludden, P A Bp, 1912, Ag 4,II,11:6
Ludden, Patrick A Bp, 1912, Ag 7,11:6
Ludden, William A Col, 1920, F 21,13:5
Ludden, William E, 1943, F 12,19:1
Ludder, Carsten H, 1962, Ap 8,86:6
Luddy, Llewellyn V, 1952, N 10,25:2
Ludeke, Francis X (por), 1944, S 25,17:3
Ludeking, George F Mrs, 1951, Ap 21,17:4
Ludeman, Henry F, 1956, My 8,33:1
Ludeman, Louis H, 1945, Ag 7,23:6
Luden, Georgine M, 1943, N 23,25:2
Luden, Henry, 1924, Jl 23,15:3
Luden, William H Mrs, 1950, N 28,31:3
Ludendorff, E F W Gen, 1937, D 20,1:3
Ludendorff, Erich Mrs, 1966, My 15,88:1
Luders, Alfred E, 1964, Ap 8,43:2
Luders, Arthur A G, 1964, O 8,43:5
Luders, Gustave Carl, 1913, Ja 25,15:5
Luders, Oscar F, 1937, Ag 17,19:5
Luderus, Fred, 1961, Ja 7,19:3
Ludes, George E, 1957, Ja 18,21:3
Ludewig, Edwin W C, 1966, Jl 23,25:5
Ludewig, Harold F A, 1957, N 19,33:2
Ludewig, Joseph G, 1953, F 10,27:4
Ludewig, Joseph W, 1958, Mr 18,29:3
Ludewig, William R, 1937, O 9,19:5
Ludford, Edward H Mrs, 1949, D 30,19:3
Ludgard, Mary Sister, 1952, Mr 7,23:1
Ludgate, Charles, 1918, S 23,9:2
Ludin, Carl Axel Robert, 1915, N 29,11:4
Ludin, Eugene C, 1965, My 2,89:2
Ludin, Marion B A Mrs, 1938, F 20,II,8:5

Ludin, Mohammad K, 1966, Ja 15,27:6
Ludington, Arthur C, 1914, N 12,13:4
Ludington, Benjamin L Mrs, 1912, Ag 20,9:6
Ludington, Burt D, 1957, Mr 26,33:3
Ludington, C Townsend, 1968, Ja 20,29:2
Ludington, Charles Henry, 1910, Ja 2,II,13:5
Ludington, Elliott K, 1958, O 9,37:4
Ludington, G Franklin, 1949, D 19,27:1
Ludington, Howard J, 1961, S 12,33:1
Ludington, Katherine (trb lr, Mr 21,16:6), 1953, Mr 9,29:2
Ludington, Luzerne Maj, 1922, Je 10,11:6
Ludington, Nelson A, 1940, Je 27,23:2
Ludington, Nelson J Mrs, 1953, F 18,31:5
Ludington, Nicholas S, 1966, Ja 25,41:4
Ludington, William H, 1945, Je 4,19:4
Ludins, Ryah, 1957 Ag 31,15:2
Ludka, John J, 1945, S 5,23:2
Ludlam, C S, 1934, Ap 6,28:1
Ludlam, Frank, 1939, D 9,15:4
Ludlam, Frank A, 1951, Jl 2,23:3
Ludlam, Frank Mrs, 1938, Jl 14,21:5
Ludlam, George P, 1924, Ap 15,21:3
Ludlam, Harry A, 1959, S 8,32:7
Ludlam, Harry W, 1942, Ap 24,17:4
Ludlam, Henry, 1919, D 23,9:2
Ludlam, J T, 1880, D 28,8:4
Ludlam, John Henry, 1915, F 19,9:5
Ludlam, Josephine C Mrs (will), 1938, Ag 17,20:3
Ludlam, Julia Parish, 1917, Ag 7,9:4
Ludlam, Thomas J, 1941, D 20,19:5
Ludlam, Thomas R, 1941, Ap 22,21:6
Ludlon, Thomas, 1941, Ap 21,19:2
Ludlow, Albert S, 1919, O 6,17:4
Ludlow, Alden R, 1946, N 3,61:1
Ludlow, Ann Mrs, 1939, N 7,28:5
Ludlow, Benjamin H, 1957, Mr 16,19:3
Ludlow, Charles B, 1941, F 14,17:2
Ludlow, Charles W, 1942, Mr 14,15:1
Ludlow, Clara S, 1924, S 30,23:4
Ludlow, Clifford W, 1952, O 10,25:2
Ludlow, E H, 1884, N 28,2:5
Ludlow, Edwin, 1924, F 12,17:3
Ludlow, F Milton, 1959, Ja 20,35:4
Ludlow, G Richard, 1945, S 15,15:4
Ludlow, Godfrey, 1956, D 23,30:7
Ludlow, Henry S, 1938, F 9,19:5
Ludlow, James Bettner, 1921, Je 17,13:6
Ludlow, John D, 1911, Ag 2,7:5
Ludlow, John D Mrs, 1960, F 25,29:5
Ludlow, Lady, 1945, D 1,23:5
Ludlow, Louis L, 1950, N 29,36:3
Ludlow, Louis L Mrs, 1955, O 21,27:1
Ludlow, Nicoll Mrs, 1915, N 23,13:2
Ludlow, Oliver Perry, 1903, D 10,9:5
Ludlow, Onslow Capt, 1909, S 1,9:6
Ludlow, R Archer, 1959, N 27,29:1
Ludlow, Randall H, 1908, My 4,7:4
Ludlow, Raymond W Sr, 1957, Mr 3,85:2
Ludlow, Samuel Jr, 1957, D 21,19:3
Ludlow, T W, 1878, Jl 18,5:5
Ludlow, Theodore Mrs, 1949, D 16,31:1
Ludlow, Theodore R, 1961, N 14,39:4
Ludlow, Walter, 1941, O 16,21:2
Ludlow, William Gen, 1901, Ag 31,7:6
Ludlow, William H, 1937, Mr 19,24:1
Ludlow, William H Mrs, 1954, F 24,25:3
Ludlow, William I, 1957, N 7,35:1
Ludlow, William O, 1954, Ja 22,27:3
Ludlum, Clarence A, 1948, Mr 1,23:2
Ludlum, David F, 1942, D 26,11:4
Ludlum, Herbert B, 1949, Ag 18,21:1
Ludlum, Isaac C, 1908, Ag 16,7:4
Ludlum, Seymour D, 1956, D 3,29:3
Ludlum, Seymour D Mrs, 1954, Ap 27,29:2
Ludlum, W, 1885, Ja 21,5:5
Ludlum, William, 1949, Mr 1,25:2
Ludlum, William H, 1944, My 28,33:3
Ludmerer, Oscar, 1953, Ja 1,23:5
Ludolph, William F, 1952, Ap 10,29:4
Ludt, Arthur, 1950, Jl 16,68:2
Ludt, Arthur R, 1950, Jl 14,21:4
Ludvigh, Elek, 1903, Je 25,7:6
Ludvigh, Elek J (por), 1937, F 18,21:6
Ludvigsen, Ludvig L Mrs, 1939, D 22,19:2
Ludwick, Clarence E, 1950, My 18,29:5
Ludwick, N Volney Mrs, 1961, S 29,35:2
Ludwig, Arnold E, 1956, Mr 12,27:5
Ludwig, August H, 1948, Jl 16,19:2
Ludwig, Augustus, 1943, My 11,21:5; 1964, Jl 15,35:3
Ludwig, Berthold A, 1950, O 10,31:4
Ludwig, Cathrine Mrs, 1943, Ja 6,25:5
Ludwig, Charles, 1940, Mr 30,15:5
Ludwig, Charles Benson, 1923, Jl 31,17:5
Ludwig, Clarence, 1961, F 13,27:6
Ludwig, Daniel, 1906, N 15,9:6
Ludwig, Duke of Bavaria, 1920, N 11,13:3
Ludwig, Edward J Sr, 1951, Ja 28,76:5
Ludwig, Elizabeth G, 1952, Mr 22,13:6
Ludwig, Emil, 1948, S 19,76:3
Ludwig, Emil J, 1940, Je 14,21:3
Ludwig, Francis J, 1951, F 18,77:2
Ludwig, Fred W, 1960, Mr 22,38:1
Ludwig, Frederick W, 1950, N 8,29:3
Ludwig, George G, 1951, S 22,17:6
Ludwig, Harry O Mrs, 1937, Ag 4,19:4
Ludwig, Henry C, 1948, F 1,60:2
Ludwig, Henry Jr, 1960, Jl 11,29:1
Ludwig, Herman, 1961, S 3,60:3
Ludwig, Jesse J Mrs, 1965, Ap 19,29:3
Ludwig, Leon R, 1951, N 16,25:5
Ludwig, Louis, 1945, N 25,49:1
Ludwig, Louis E, 1953, Ap 15,45:1
Ludwig, Louis Mrs, 1947, Jl 4,13:5
Ludwig, Norbert, 1960, O 31,31:5
Ludwig, Robert P, 1955, Jl 20,27:5
Ludwig, Theodore H, 1946, D 3,32:2
Ludwig, William, 1953, Jl 31,19:6
Ludwig, William W, 1945, Ag 24,19:2
Ludwig, William W Mrs, 1944, Jl 10,15:5
Ludwig III, Ex-King of Bavaria, 1921, O 19,19:4
Ludwig III, Grand Duke of Hesse, 1877, Je 14,4:6
Ludwig III, King, 1916, Ag 30,9:4
Ludwig of Hesse, Prince, 1968, Je 1,27:6
Ludwigsen, Arthur Mrs, 1953, Ja 19,23:4
Ludwigsen, Jacob, 1949, F 5,15:4
Ludwigsen, Louis A, 1949, O 26,27:3
Ludwigson, Joseph R, 1951, D 17,31:6
Ludy, Albert K, 1950, Je 12,27:3
Ludy, Albert K Mrs, 1951, Jl 5,25:4
Ludy, Charles C, 1948, Jl 9,20:2
Ludy, John B, 1944, S 13,19:6
Luebbe, Carl, 1938, Ap 24,II,7:2
Luebbers, Ernest H, 1943, S 11,13:6
Luebbers, Ernest Henry, 1918, F 27,11:5
Luebke, Friedrich W, 1954, O 17,87:2
Luechinger, Bruno, 1961, Jl 21,23:4
Luecht, Henry W, 1951, D 29,11:1
Luecke, John, 1952, Mr 23,92:1
Luecke, Wilbur H, 1965, O 14,47:5
Luedde, William H, 1952, Mr 20,29:5
Luedecker, Charles Jr, 1948, Ap 3,15:2
Luedeke, Henry, 1962, My 31,27:1
Luedeking, Robert Dr, 1908, Mr 1,9:6
Lueder, Arthur C, 1957, My 8,37:1
Lueder, Eberhard L, 1939, Mr 21,23:5
Lueder, Eberhard Mrs (F Wickham), 1962, O 21,89:1
Lueder, John C, 1940, S 18,23:1
Lueders, Annie E, 1942, Mr 12,19:1
Lueders, William H, 1939, Je 12,17:6
Luedi, Rudolf, 1943, Ja 1,23:4
Luedtke, Max, 1948, Ag 20,17:5
Luegel, Heinrich von, 1941, F 2,46:4
Lueger, Karl Dr, 1910, Mr 11,9:5
Luehrs, Leslie E, 1953, Ja 28,27:3
Luellen, Gerald H, 1961, O 21,21:3
Luello, James, 1921, Ag 17,11:5
Luening, Augustus A, 1951, F 13,31:4
Luening, Eugene, 1944, O 21,17:4
Luer, Albert O, 1945, Ap 3,19:2
Luer, Aug (por), 1942, S 23,25:4
Luer, Henry S, 1912, D 9,11:4
Luerich, Harry L, 1950, Je 9,23:3
Luerich, M M Mrs, 1939, F 14,19:1
Luers, Herbert F, 1953, Ja 26,19:4
Luerssen, Charles H, 1941, Ap 2,23:2
Luery, Michael Mrs, 1956, O 25,33:6
Luescher, M A, 1936, S 21,23:1
Luetke, Oscar, 1937, My 22,18:2
Luetscher, George D, 1941, Je 21,17:4
Luettwitz, Walther von, 1942, S 23,25:4
Luetz, Alfred, 1945, O 2,23:3
Luey, William A, 1954, D 18,15:5
Luez, Maria de la, 1951, N 1,1:2
Lufburrow, Charles B, 1956, Je 29,21:1
Lufburrow, Elizabeth S, 1938, Ja 19,23:2
Luff, John N, 1938, Ag 24,21:4
Luff, Leroy W, 1950, Mr 26,94:3
Lufkin, Chauncey F, 1956, Ja 11,31:3
Lufkin, Chauncey S, 1918, F 23,13:5
Lufkin, Elgood C Mrs, 1942, Ja 2,34:2
Lufkin, Frank W, 1943, F 8,19:1
Lufkin, George B, 1950, Ap 24,25:5
Lufkin, Hoyt D, 1949, D 27,23:2
Lufkin, John L, 1965, My 8,31:4
Lufkin, Willfred W Jr, 1957, Ap 13,19:5
Lufriu y Alonso, Rene, 1943, Mr 7,38:7
Luft, George Jr Mrs, 1955, Mr 8,27:3
Luft, George W, 1939, O 15,49:1
Luft, George W Mrs, 1946, N 29,25:3
Luft, Norbert, 1953, D 18,29:4
Luftig, Vivian C, 1963, D 31,19:1
Lugara, Joseph, 1948, S 14,29:4
Lugard, Lord, 1945, Ap 12,23:6
Lugari, Cardinal, 1914, Ag 1,9:6
Lugeon, Maurice, 1953, O 24,15:3
Luger, Carl, 1953, Ja 27,25:5
Luger, Peter, 1941, Ja 23,21:3
Lugert, Francis E, 1967, Ag 1,25:1
Lugg, Harry H, 1965, Mr 24,46:4
Lugne-Poe, A, 1940, Jl 16,17:2
Lugo, Americo, 1952, Ag 8,17:6
Lugo-Romero, Americo, 1958, My 29,27:2
Lugosi, Bela, 1956, Ag 17,19:3
Lugrin, Cecil M, 1937, N 24,23:4
Lugrin, Walter, 1940, Ja 26,17:5
Lugscheider, Frances, 1944, Ag 26,11:5
Lugue, Adolfo, 1957, Jl 4,19:3
Lugue y Rohde, Guillermo de Mrs, 1962, Ap 21,20:8
Luguer, Lea M Mrs, 1948, Je 9,29:3
Luguet, Charles (por), 1945, D 16,40:5
Luhan, Antonio Mrs (Mabel D), 1962, Ag 14,31:4
Luhan, Frank, 1959, Ja 12,39:1
Luhe, Augustus von der Dr, 1923, O 23,21:4
Luhman, George B, 1955, My 12,29:1
Luhman, William, 1937, Mr 18,25:1
Luhmann, William, 1949, N 2,27:5
Luhn, Hans P, 1964, Ag 20,29:3
Luhn, John A, 1952, Jl 2,25:5
Luhnow, C A, 1933, Jl 21,17:4
Luhring, Marie E, 1939, D 30,15:3
Luhring, Oscar R, 1944, Ag 19,11:1
Luhrs, George H, 1941, Jl 22,19:3
Luhrs, Herbert N, 1944, O 14,13:2
Luhrs, Louis C, 1948, F 2,20:2
Luhrsen, Ernest Frederick Dr, 1918, F 5,13:8
Luhy, James (funl, Je 3,23:3), 1925, My 31,5:1
Lui, Jean M del, 1946, Je 10,21:4
Luigard, Charles F, 1960, D 31,17:4
Luigi, Ramon B, 1944, Ag 16,19:3
Luiro, Tauno, 1955, N 1,31:4
Luis Phillippe, King of Portugal, 1889, O 20,5:2
Luisa de Orleans y Bourbon, Infanta of Spain, 1958, Ap 19,21:5
Luisi, Gerard, 1962, Ag 13,25:6
Luitpold, Prince (Maximillian Louis Chas), 1914, Ag 28,9:6
Luitwieler, Clarence S, 1948, Ja 5,19:3
Luiz, Jose, 1942, Je 27,13:7
Luiz Felipe, Pedro A (Dom), 1940, Ja 30,19:6
Luizet, Charles, 1947, S 22,23:5
Lukacs, Joseph J, 1953, Jl 16,21:5
Lukaszkiewicz, Chester Z, 1946, Ja 9,24:2
Lukavsky, Karel, 1954, Ja 9,15:5
Luke, Adam K, 1956, Ag 9,25:3
Luke, Arthur F, 1917, O 1,13:6
Luke, Charles W, 1939, Jl 25,13:4
Luke, Donald K Mrs, 1961, O 16,29:2
Luke, Edmon G, 1968, N 24,87:1
Luke, Frank Sr, 1939, Je 19,15:4
Luke, G G, 1884, D 22,5:2
Luke, George C, 1954, F 9,27:5
Luke, James L, 1945, My 21,19:6
Luke, John G, 1921, O 16,22:4
Luke, Joshua C, 1949, Je 3,31:1
Luke, Lord, 1943, F 24,21:5
Luke, Louis, 1959, Ap 22,33:3
Luke, Mary Sr, 1953, Ag 26,27:2
Luke, Otto Mrs, 1945, Je 13,25:7
Luke, Priscilla W S Mrs, 1962, N 3,25:3
Luke, Roman W Mrs, 1956, My 9,33:1
Luke, Thomas (por), 1948, My 13,25:1
Luke, Thomas Mrs, 1947, S 12,21:3
Luke, William, 1912, N 25,13:4
Lukeman, A, 1935, Ap 4,23:1
Lukenbach, Ralph R, 1940, F 7,21:5
Lukens, Alan Mrs, 1961, My 11,1:6
Lukens, Alan N, 1937, O 21,23:2
Lukens, Alfred B, 1946, Ap 29,19:4
Lukens, Anna Dr (will, Jl 7,9:6), 1917, Je 17,19:
Lukens, Arthur T, 1961, S 17,87:1
Lukens, Charles K, 1941, Ja 15,23:5
Lukens, Edmund T, 1940, S 18,23:5
Lukens, Edmund T Mrs, 1925, S 24,25:3
Lukens, Edward C, 1948, My 18,23:5
Lukens, Edward F, 1939, Mr 31,21:3
Lukens, George N, 1946, O 13,59:5
Lukens, Herman T, 1949, Ja 19,28:2
Lukens, Hiram S, 1959, N 26,37:5
Lukens, Howard A, 1945, Ja 25,19:4
Lukens, Irwin G, 1956, Ja 24,31:5
Lukens, James C, 1941, Je 16,15:3
Lukens, John M, 1940, D 3,25:2
Lukens, Margaret M, 1941, N 2,53:3
Lukens, Matthias Mrs, 1960, Ap 6,41:4
Lukens, Phil J, 1953, Je 8,29:4
Lukens, Ralph H Mrs, 1953, Je 8,29:4
Lukens, Rinaldo A, 1961, Je 11,86:5
Lukens, Victor H, 1952, Ag 12,19:5
Lukens, William D, 1949, My 27,21:2
Luker, David R, 1952, O 8,31:4
Lukert, Louis A, 1963, N 26,37:3
Lukert, William J Mrs, 1940, My 29,23:3
Lukey, John E, 1949, Je 18,13:1
Lukin, Phil Mrs, 1953, S 3,21:3
Lukin, Sergie G, 1948, S 3,20:3
Lukirsky, Peter I, 1954, N 19,32:2
Lukk, Gertrude J (Mrs Geo Lukk), 1966, F 22,
Lukov, Leonid, 1963, Ap 26,35:5
Luks, G B, 1933, O 30,17:1
Luks, William D, 1952, D 17,33:4
Lukyanov, Vladimir V, 1958, O 29,35:5
Luland, John C, 1940, D 25,27:4
Lull, Clifford B, 1951, Jl 7,13:5
Lull, Dorothy S Mrs, 1953, S 28,25:4
Lull, George F Mrs, 1949, F 8,25:2
Lull, H M, 1949, Mr 24,27:3
Lull, Louis J Capt, 1874, My 8,1:6
Lull, Richard S, 1957, Ap 23,31:4

Lulley, Julius, 1951, N 13,29:3
Lulling, Anthony, 1963, Jl 20,19:2
Luloff, Samuel, 1960, S 11,82:4
Lulow, Charles, 1951, Ap 11,29:5
Lum, Charles H, 1946, My 29,23:6
Lum, Charles M, 1939, F 25,15:5
Lum, Edward H, 1951, S 10,21:4
Lum, Ernest C, 1951, N 23,29:4
Lum, Frank P, 1963, N 1,34:6
Lum, Frederick H Jr, 1954, Ag 24,21:6
Lum, Frederick H Jr Mrs, 1954, Je 8,27:1
Lum, Frederick P, 1942, N 8,51:5
Lum, Hermann A, 1950, O 8,104:5
Lum, Howard E, 1938, O 1,17:4
Lum, Maryette H, 1944, F 20,36:2
Lum, Percy B, 1954, Jl 25,69:3
Lum, Ralph E Sr, 1952, My 22,13:1
Lum, Reginald P, 1949, Ja 6,23:3
Lum, S Clark, 1964, Ag 15,21:2
Luman, John A, 1957, O 31,31:4
Luman, William W, 1963, O 1,40:1
Luman, William W Mrs, 1953, N 3,31:2
Lumb, Elting, 1950, Ag 5,15:4
Lumb, George H, 1946, My 20,23:2
Lumb, Henry T, 1952, Mr 5,29:4
Lumbard, John W, 1960, Ap 10,85:4
Lumbard, Joseph E (por), 1942, O 29,23:3
Lumbard, Victor G, 1945, Ap 17,23:1
Lumberg, Neuta, 1948, D 5,92:5
Lumby, Christopher, 1946, N 4,25:4
Lumby, John R, 1941, Jl 7,15:2
Lumiere, Auguste, 1954, Ap 11,87:1
Lumiere, Louis (por), 1948, Je 7,19:3
Lumley, Alexander Mrs, 1923, My 17,19:6
Lumley, Arthur, 1912, S 28,13:7
Lumley, Arthur C, 1949, S 30,23:1
Lumley, Arthur T, 1938, Je 9,23:3
Lumley, Charles G, 1961, Je 30,25:3
Lumley, Frederick E, 1954, Jl 27,21:6
Lumley, Harry, 1938, My 23,17:4
Lumley, Margaret, 1938, Mr 7,17:3
Lummas, H Dr, 1905, Ap 15,11:5
Lummis, Benjamin R, 1937, Je 12,15:4
Lummis, C F, 1928, N 26,25:5
Lummis, George O, 1941, Je 6,21:5
Lummis, J Milton, 1953, Ap 28,27:2
Lummis, Katherine, 1947, Mr 7,25:4
Lummis, M F, 1939, F 26,38:7
Lummis, William, 1914, Mr 16,9:4
Lummis, William Maxwell Mrs, 1904, Mr 7,7:6
Lummus, J E, 1955, Jl 2,15:5
Lummus, John N, 1961, F 28,33:5
Lumpkin, Alva M, 1941, Ag 2,15:5
Lumpkin, Edwin K, 1938, F 5,15:5
Lumpkin, Harry, 1937, Ja 16,17:1
Lumpkin, Joseph H Justice, 1916, S 8,7:4
Lumpkin, Sam, 1964, Jl 11,25:5
Lumpkin, Samuel Justice, 1903, Jl 19,7:6
Lumpkin, W Ex-Gov, 1871, Ja 5,5:5
Lumpkins, J H Chief-Justice, 1867, Je 14,4:7
Lumsden, David, 1945, Ja 23,19:4
Lumsden, Leslie L, 1946, N 9,17:2
Lumsden, Simon H, 1949, Je 9,31:1
Lumsden, Tommy, 1955, Je 25,15:5
Lumsdon, Christine M V Mrs, 1937, Ap 9,21:4
Lumsdon, John, 1919, N 27,15:3
Lunacharsky, A, 1933, D 28,19:3
Lunalilo, King of the Sandwich Islands, 1874, F 18,5:6
Lunardi, Federico, 1954, N 11,31:4
Lunberg, Frank, 1920, F 9,9:4
Lunceford, Jimmie (por), 1947, Jl 14,21:5
Lund, Adolph, 1957, Ja 2,27:3
Lund, Anthon H, 1966, Ap 5,39:2
Lund, Carl A, 1945, S 20,23:4
Lund, Charlotte, 1951, Jl 17,27:4
Lund, Conrad A Mrs, 1953, D 23,26:4
Lund, Cyrus B, 1958, D 3,37:1
Lund, Emil G, 1942, My 2,13:4
Lund, Emily B, 1954, O 31,89:2
Lund, Frank W, 1941, Ag 10,37:1
Lund, Frederick, 1965, D 23,27:4
Lund, George, 1925, O 20,25:4
Lund, George E Mrs, 1944, Je 17,13:6
Lund, Gunnar, 1940, N 28,23:1
Lund, Harold M, 1946, Je 6,21:3
Lund, Harry T, 1959, D 25,21:6
Lund, Helen W, 1962, Ap 7,25:5
Lund, John, 1925, F 2,17:3
Lund, John B, 1957, Ap 10,20:4
Lund, John L, 1948, F 23,25:4
Lund, Jorgen H, 1948, Ja 6,24:3
Lund, Joseph W, 1922, My 7,28:1
Lund, Lawrence H (por), 1949, Mr 15,27:1
Lund, Marquard H Sr, 1955, F 27,87:1
Lund, Nils W, 1954, Ja 4,19:1
Lund, Oria Christian Engelsted, 1918, Je 17,13:8
Lund, Palagio B, 1919, Je 26,9:3
Lund, Reidar, 1961, F 13,27:4
Lund, Robert L, 1957, Mr 10,89:1
Lund, Rudolph O, 1954, My 23,90:1
Lund, Troels, 1921, F 14,9:6
Lund-Quist, Carl E, 1965, Ag 28,21:4
Lundbeck, Charles J Mrs, 1958, N 17,31:5
Lundbeck, G Hilmer (por), 1949, Je 19,70:2
Lundberg, Arthur H, 1947, O 16,28:3
Lundberg, Arthur H Mrs, 1949, Ag 3,23:4
Lundberg, Emma O, 1954, N 18,33:5
Lundberg, Mary E, 1945, Ag 6,15:5
Lundblad, Walter E, 1967, Ja 7,27:6
Lundborg, Florence, 1949, Ja 19,27:2
Lunde, Johann, 1938, F 13,II,7:2
Lundean, J Louis, 1961, O 26,35:5
Lundeberg, Harry, 1957, Ja 29,31:2
Lundeen, Ernest F, 1962, Jl 16,23:1
Lundell, Otto H, 1940, F 24,13:3
Lundergam, John, 1949, Jl 8,21:6
Lundergan, John, 1950, F 21,25:1
Lundgaard, Ivar, 1946, Je 9,40:6
Lundgren, Albert T, 1949, Ja 24,19:4
Lundgren, Charles J, 1937, S 24,21:5
Lundgren, Eric Mrs, 1943, N 24,21:3
Lundgren, George W, 1947, N 5,27:4
Lundgren, Nels Mrs, 1958, Jl 15,25:4
Lundgren, Oscar A, 1949, N 26,15:3
Lundgren, Oscar Mrs, 1947, S 27,15:4
Lundgren, William, 1949, F 25,23:2
Lundgren, William E, 1955, F 1,29:2
Lundie, J, 1931, F 10,21:3
Lundin, Edward Mrs, 1946, O 31,25:4
Lundin, Frederick, 1947, Ag 30,15:4
Lundin, Harold, 1954, Ja 21,31:3
Lundin, Harold F Mrs, 1949, Ag 31,23:2
Lundin, Hjaalmar, 1941, Ap 9,25:3
Lundin, Jack, 1943, S 27,19:5
Lundin, Laura M, 1944, D 31,25:2
Lundmark, Leon, 1942, My 5,21:3
Lundquist, Franklin C E, 1947, Ap 5,19:4
Lundquist, Wilton G, 1968, O 14,47:5
Lundry, C Marlin, 1945, Mr 20,19:3
Lundstedt, August, 1949, F 24,23:2
Lundstrom, Walter H, 1956, Ja 18,31:4
Lundt, Karl C, 1961, D 31,48:8
Lundt, Otto J, 1945, D 16,39:1
Lundy, A Wilson Rev Dr, 1937, Ja 5,23:4
Lundy, Ayres D, 1949, Jl 13,27:4
Lundy, Barry R Sr, 1956, Ag 18,17:3
Lundy, Elmer A, 1949, Ap 2,15:4
Lundy, F L, 1879, F 23,7:5
Lundy, Frederick, 1918, N 9,13:5
Lundy, Henry, 1903, Ap 30,9:6
Lundy, Howard W, 1955, D 22,23:1
Lundy, Joseph R, 1942, F 14,15:3
Lundy, Rev Dr, 1868, Ap 8,4:1
Lundy, William A, 1957, S 3,27:2
Lundy, William J, 1950, N 21,31:1
Lundy, Wilson T, 1963, O 3,35:2
Luneborg, Julius, 1951, My 6,93:1
Luneburg, Rudolph, 1949, Ag 20,11:3
Lunenfeld, Bernard, 1938, My 10,21:5
Lung, George A Capt, 1921, Jl 27,15:5
Lung, George Augustus Mrs, 1923, Ap 12,19:4
Lung Yun, 1962, Je 29,27:1
Lungarello, Donato, 1908, Je 22,7:3
Lunger, John B (funl, My 15,22:4), 1919, Je 14,13:6
Lungren, C M, 1927, S 6,27:4
Lungwitz, Emil E, 1950, D 12,33:2
Lunham, Clayton W, 1949, My 4,29:3
Luniewski, Joseph, 1951, Je 7,33:1
Lunjack, Charles A, 1939, F 13,15:5
Lunn, Arthur W, 1965, S 4,21:6
Lunn, Charles W, 1941, My 20,23:6
Lunn, George R (por), 1948, N 28,92:2
Lunn, Henry S Sir, 1939, Mr 19,III,6:6
Lunn, Herbert W, 1960, S 20,39:3
Lunn, James A, 1956, Je 14,33:4
Lunn, Leo J, 1940, Je 7,23:5
Lunn, Morris A, 1952, Jl 15,21:1
Lunn, Richard D, 1962, Ag 25,19:2
Lunn, William, 1942, My 18,15:4
Lunney, Dorothy O (Mrs Hank Lunney), 1963, Ap 27,25:5
Lunney, John S Mrs, 1946, O 2,29:4
Lunney, Mary, 1880, Ja 6,8:6
Lunning, Frederik, 1952, S 1,17:5
Lunning, Just (trb lr, Ag 18,34:6), 1965, Ag 12,27:3
Lunny, J J, 1929, Jl 22,19:3
Lunny, James, 1960, Ag 10,31:2
Lunny, John J, 1949, O 15,15:6
Lunsford, Charles S, 1964, Ja 31,27:1
Lunsford, Guy, 1950, Mr 16,31:4
Lunsford, Lew C, 1952, O 10,25:3
Lunsford, William B, 1949, Mr 8,25:4
Lunt, Alfred E, 1937, Ag 14,13:2
Lunt, Alfred J, 1938, D 3,19:2
Lunt, Edward C, 1941, Ja 14,21:6
Lunt, Edward C Mrs, 1953, D 27,60:8
Lunt, George C, 1952, Ja 26,13:5
Lunt, Mildred, 1940, My 11,19:6
Lunt, Samuel M, 1922, Ag 2,17:6
Lunt, Wilbur Fisk, 1908, My 29,7:3
Lunt, William E, 1956, N 12,29:3
Luntz, Darwin S, 1951, D 18,31:3
Luongo, Federico, 1957, N 6,35:3
Luongo, John O, 1962, O 17,39:3
Luongo, Vincent J, 1957, My 19,88:5
Luongo, Vito Mrs, 1957, Je 10,27:3
Lupia, Bruno, 1953, Ap 21,27:3
Lupiano, Domenick Mrs, 1958, Ja 10,23:1
Lupiano, Dominick, 1960, F 7,85:1
Lupino, Barry, 1962, S 27,37:4
Lupino, Connie Mrs, 1959, D 27,60:4
Lupino, Stanley (por), 1942, Je 10,21:5
Lupino, Wallace, 1961, O 13,35:3
Lupka, Harry, 1962, My 19,27:3
Lupo, Harry, 1953, Ja 31,15:2
Lupo, Jack, 1960, S 6,33:6
Lupo, S Quentin, 1954, O 11,27:5
Luppens, Herman C, 1941, Ja 29,17:6
Lupprian, Charles, 1949, Ja 17,19:2
Lupton, Charles M Mrs, 1944, Ap 17,23:5
Lupton, David D, 1946, D 3,31:4
Lupton, Edmund H Mrs, 1956, Ap 10,31:2
Lupton, Edmund R, 1959, F 25,31:3
Lupton, Elizabeth P Mrs, 1941, Ja 5,44:4
Lupton, J T, 1933, Ag 1,17:1
Lupton, John W, 1951, Je 4,27:5
Lupton, John W Rev, 1909, O 4,9:6
Lupton, Robert B, 1942, My 15,19:5
Lupton, William A, 1952, F 11,25:5
Lupton, William G Jr, 1960, N 8,29:4
Lupton, William R, 1955, Mr 3,27:4
Lupu, Nicolae, 1946, D 5,32:3
Luque, Crisanto, 1959, My 8,28:3
Luqueer, F T Jr Capt, 1903, Ap 1,2:3
Luqueer, Robert S, 1916, F 22,11:5
Luquer, Eloise P, 1947, D 29,17:2
Luquer, John H, 1944, O 19,23:2
Luquer, Lea Rev Dr, 1919, Je 19,13:4
Luquer, Thatcher T P, 1958, Ag 17,86:1
Luquiens, Frederick B, 1940, Ap 18,23:1
Luram, Thomas M, 1941, D 18,27:2
Lurcat, Jean, 1966, Je 7,27:4
Lurcott, Charles, 1956, My 15,32:8
Lurcott, George, 1940, Jl 31,17:6
Lurcott, George Mrs (por), 1938, My 18,21:3
Lurcy, Georgres, 1953, O 1,29:5
Lurgan, Baron, 1937, F 10,23:5
Luria, Alex L, 1951, S 9,91:1
Luria, Daniel, 1945, O 10,21:2
Luria, Frank, 1956, Jl 18,27:3
Luria, Herbert B, 1958, Mr 12,31:1
Luria, Leon, 1954, F 13,9:7
Luria, Max A, 1939, S 10,49:2; 1966, Mr 12,27:1
Luria, Richard M, 1966, Mr 13,86:5
Lurich, Charles C Jr, 1960, Ap 10,86:2
Lurie, Alex, 1951, S 25,29:3
Lurie, Annie N Mrs (will), 1938, O 25,24:3
Lurie, Charles N Mrs, 1942, S 23,25:5
Lurie, Ira A, 1958, S 29,27:4
Lurie, Irene Mrs, 1954, Mr 27,12:8
Lurie, Irving H, 1968, Ja 3,40:1
Lurie, Leib, 1948, Ag 20,17:2
Lurie, Leib Mrs, 1954, N 30,29:4
Lurie, Louis R Mrs, 1956, Mr 4,88:4
Lurie, Lucienne F Mrs, 1944, D 25,19:4
Lurie, Nathan W, 1959, N 24,37:2
Lurie, Sasha S Mrs, 1967, O 6,39:3
Lurienne, Louis A, 1911, Mr 29,13:4
Lurio, Adaline, 1949, Je 9,31:5
Lurio, Joseph, 1945, Jl 7,22:4
Lurio, Samuel R, 1966, D 2,39:4
Lurje, Elja, 1964, Je 11,33:5
Lurton, Douglas E, 1956, Ag 28,27:2
Lurton, Justice, 1914, Jl 14,9:5
Lurton, Nelson E, 1956, D 23,30:7
Lurz, Frank, 1942, Ap 11,13:6
Lusardi, Alex B, 1951, Je 19,29:1
Lusardi, Francis R, 1949, Jl 7,25:5
Lusardi, Giuseppe, 1925, Mr 5,19:5
Lusardi, John, 1948, My 8,15:5
Lusby, J W Prof, 1937, Je 28,19:4
Luschear, John W, 1947, My 23,24:3
Luscombe, Alfred, 1942, Jl 21,20:3
Luscombe, Carl, 1953, O 17,15:5
Luscombe, Don A, 1965, Ja 12,37:1
Luscombe, John H Sir, 1937, Ap 5,19:5
Luscombe, Walter G, 1939, S 14,23:2
Luscombe, Walter O, 1939, Jl 18,19:5
Luse, Andrew O, 1954, N 18,33:4
Luse, Charles W, 1953, Je 26,19:1
Luse, D Claude Mrs, 1952, Ag 19,23:5
Lush, Ernest B, 1937, F 27,17:4
Lush, Herman, 1953, F 26,25:3
Lush, Joseph (will, Ag 7,28:1; cor, Ag 8,18:1), 1959, Jl 16,27:4
Lush, Robert, 1881, D 28,5:2
Lush, William E L, 1961, My 3,37:4
Lush, William L, 1951, Ag 29,25:4
Lushbaugh, Edward B, 1942, My 26,21:3
Lusher, Joseph Mrs, 1953, S 2,25:3
Lushington, Godfrey Sir, 1907, F 6,9:6
Lusk, Clayton R, 1959, F 15,85:4
Lusk, Clayton R Mrs, 1948, S 14,29:2
Lusk, Daniel D Mrs, 1952, F 20,30:3
Lusk, Edward J, 1961, Jl 20,27:1
Lusk, Frank C, 1941, Ap 18,21:5
Lusk, Peter Mrs, 1953, N 12,31:2
Lusk, Ralph D, 1959, My 28,31:5
Lusk, Sherman W, 1956, O 13,19:5

Lusk, W C, 1940, Jl 8,17:3
Lusk, William B, 1953, Ja 14,31:5
Lusk, William C, 1913, Je 15,IV,5:5
Lusk, William C (por), 1944, F 27,38:3
Luskind, Abraham B, 1954, S 12,84:7
Lusse, Joseph C, 1944, N 2,19:4
Lussen, Frederick H, 1951, N 9,27:1
Lussier, John J, 1937, N 30,23:2
Lussier, Marc, 1951, O 1,3:5
Lust, Benedict, 1945, S 6,25:2
Lustbader, Henry, 1954, S 17,27:2
Lustbader, Maurice, 1960, Ag 12,19:4
Lustbader, Paul, 1960, D 16,38:3
Lustbader, Samuel, 1966, Jl 24,60:4
Lustbaum, Edward H, 1942, Jl 3,17:3
Lustberg, B Herbert, 1966, Ag 30,36:1
Lustberg, Morris, 1955, F 12,15:5
Lustberg, Morris Mrs, 1939, Ap 25,23:4
Luster, Charles F, 1945, Mr 10,17:4
Luster, Clifton H, 1963, My 25,25:4
Luster, Emile J, 1963, D 21,23:5
Luster, Eric W, 1955, Ap 4,29:3
Luster, George, 1946, N 19,21:1
Luster, Raymond W, 1945, Ag 27,19:4
Luster, William H Mrs, 1953, F 15,93:1
Lusterman, Isidor, 1949, D 29,26:2
Lustgarten, Emil J, 1948, S 17,25:5
Lustgarten, Henry, 1946, Je 28,21:4
Lustgarten, Maximilian J, 1959, Jl 8,29:4
Lustgarten, Meta Mrs, 1942, O 3,15:5
Lustgarten, Nathan, 1954, Jl 14,27:4
Lustgarten, S Mrs, 1940, D 23,19:3
Lustgarten, Sigmund Dr, 1911, Ja 23,7:4
Lustig, Albert A, 1953, Jl 12,65:3
Lustig, Alvin, 1955, D 5,31:1
Lustig, Bessie Mrs, 1914, S 9,9:6
Lustig, Elias, 1958, F 25,27:2
Lustig, Harry, 1956, My 11,27:1; 1957, S 28,17:4
Lustig, Henry, 1958, S 18,31:3
Lustig, Herman Rev, 1903, N 29,8:2
Lustig, Louis, 1940, My 15,25:2; 1940, Jl 19,19:2
Lustig, Maxwell, 1955, Jl 10,73:1
Lustig, Phil H (por), 1937, Ja 13,24:3
Lustig, Phil H Mrs, 1941, Je 11,21:5
Lusty, John, 1947, Je 13,23:3
Lute, E R, 1945, Ag 26,43:2
Lute, Joseph H Jr, 1946, Ag 17,13:6
Luter, John Mrs, 1966, Ja 27,33:3
Lutes, Della Mrs, 1942, Jl 14,19:2
Lutes, Henry R, 1955, Ag 12,19:1
Lutes, Joseph H, 1947, Jl 17,19:3
Lutes, Mabel M, 1953, Jl 25,11:4
Lutes, Olin S, 1967, O 18,47:1
Lutfy, George J Mrs, 1966, My 31,43:1
Lutge, Norma K Mrs, 1939, Ap 1,19:6
Luth, Frank G, 1945, D 16,40:4
Luthe, Julius K, 1951, Ap 25,20:5
Luther, Albert Sr, 1952, Jl 11,17:3
Luther, C F Mrs, 1949, Ag 14,68:1
Luther, E S, 1928, N 19,19:5
Luther, Eliot H, 1943, My 4,23:4
Luther, F S, 1928, Ja 5,29:3
Luther, Frank M, 1957, F 28,27:3
Luther, Frank W, 1967, Jl 29,25:4
Luther, Frederick M, 1938, My 29,II,6:6
Luther, George Martin, 1913, D 27,9:6
Luther, Guy S, 1945, Ja 5,15:5
Luther, Hans, 1962, My 12,23:3
Luther, Henry, 1925, Ja 23,19:4
Luther, Kendrick A, 1952, S 27,17:6
Luther, L M, 1881, Jl 22,5:6
Luther, Lawrence L, 1953, My 5,29:2
Luther, Martin, 1943, F 24,21:4
Luther, Martin F, 1949, My 19,30:3
Luther, Martin P Mrs, 1955, Mr 24,31:1
Luther, Robert Morris Rev, 1903, S 29,9:4
Luther, Roland C, 1905, Mr 7,9:6
Luther, Thomas C, 1937, D 30,19:6
Luthin, Hugo A, 1949, Mr 7,21:5
Luthin, Reinhard H, 1962, N 26,29:2
Luthin, Roswell, 1945, S 27,21:4
Luthringer, George F, 1955, Mr 12,19:4
Luthuli, Albert J (funl, Jl 31,27:4), 1967, Jl 22,1:3
Luthy, Max, 1967, F 4,27:3
Lutjen, Harry C, 1947, Ag 14,23:1
Lutjens, William E, 1939, N 26,42:7
Lutkin, Frederick Mrs, 1947, Ag 6,23:4
Lutkins, Clifford L, 1938, Ja 22,18:3
Lutkins, Frank, 1948, My 16,68:3
Lutkoff, Samuel, 1948, Ja 9,22:3
Lutomski, John C, 1941, My 4,53:1
Luton, Robert, 1950, N 22,25:3
Lutoslawski, Wincenty, 1955, Ja 5,23:3
Lutringer, Emil V, 1958, O 20,29:1
Lutringer, Leonie, 1921, O 13,15:4
Lutsevich, Ivan (Y Kupula), 1942, Jl 1,25:6
Lutsi el Sayed, Ahmed, 1963, Mr 6,4:5
Lutsky, C Israel Mrs, 1957, N 18,31:1
Lutter, Frederick, 1943, N 1,17:3
Luttfrig, Casimir Rev (Capuchin Fathers), 1912, F 14,11:4
Luttgen, Roderick G, 1960, Ja 18,27:3
Luttgen, Walter, 1922, F 28,19:1
Luttgens, Arthur A, 1967, Ja 5,37:1
Luttgens, Henry Sr, 1950, Mr 31,32:2
Luttmann, Henry D, 1945, O 4,23:6
Lutton, Albert, 1955, Ja 15,13:4
Lutton, Charles A Gen, 1913, O 21,9:7
Lutton, William B, 1949, D 13,38:1
Luttrell, John L, 1948, D 10,26:3
Luty, B E V, 1938, N 30,23:4
Lutyens, Edwin L (por), 1944, Ja 2,38:4
Lutyens, Lionel Galway Maj, 1918, Ja 27,17:3
Lutz, A George, 1959, Jl 15,29:3
Lutz, Arleight H, 1953, Ja 27,25:1
Lutz, Arthur T, 1953, S 14,27:3
Lutz, Charles H, 1945, Je 14,19:2
Lutz, Charles J, 1952, My 21,27:3
Lutz, Conrad B, 1953, Ap 26,85:2
Lutz, Daniel, 1961, Mr 15,39:5
Lutz, Elmer H, 1950, Je 26,27:1
Lutz, Francis E, 1958, D 2,37:5
Lutz, Frank E (por), 1943, N 28,69:1
Lutz, Frank J Dr, 1916, Mr 25,13:7
Lutz, Frederick C, 1942, F 1,42:8; 1944, D 23,13:6
Lutz, Frederick L Mrs, 1942, F 10,19:1
Lutz, George Mrs, 1946, Jl 30,23:5
Lutz, Harry A, 1954, Ap 20,29:3
Lutz, Harry G, 1948, N 21,88:2
Lutz, Harry N, 1947, O 5,68:3
Lutz, Hendrik V, 1951, Ag 9,21:4
Lutz, Henry F, 1938, Ja 21,20:4
Lutz, Herman A, 1949, Ap 1,25:2
Lutz, J Milton, 1945, Ag 4,11:2
Lutz, J Norbert, 1961, N 11,23:5
Lutz, Jacob, 1944, Ap 13,19:3
Lutz, John, 1947, N 19,23:1
Lutz, John A, 1953, Je 1,23:3; 1959, My 15,29:3
Lutz, John C, 1954, O 8,23:1
Lutz, John F, 1946, N 27,25:3
Lutz, John George Rev, 1922, Ap 26,19:5
Lutz, John J, 1943, My 31,17:5; 1952, S 4,27:2
Lutz, Kilian, 1942, O 21,21:6
Lutz, L Walter, 1947, S 9,31:1
Lutz, Michael P, 1946, Ja 17,23:4
Lutz, Oswald, 1944, Mr 2,17:3
Lutz, Philip, 1946, F 22,25:2
Lutz, Philip T, 1945, Ja 4,19:1
Lutz, Ralph H Prof, 1968, Ap 9,48:1
Lutz, Raymond P, 1958, Ag 31,56:1
Lutz, Richard, 1960, Mr 27,87:1
Lutz, Roland B, 1950, Ap 19,29:2
Lutz, Stephen H Dr, 1919, O 19,22:3
Lutz, Thomas, 1954, O 5,27:2
Lutz, W M, 1903, F 2,8:6
Lutz, Wilbur P, 1963, Jl 31,29:3
Lutz, Wilhelm Otto, 1915, My 14,13:5
Lutz, William M, 1955, Jl 9,15:5
Lutzke, Walter, 1938, Mr 7,17:5
Lutzow-Holm, Finn, 1950, Je 5,23:3
Luvadis, Jerry, 1938, S 7,25:1
Lux, Albert C Mrs, 1944, My 31,19:3
Lux, Arpad, 1960, S 3,17:7
Lux, Charles F, 1951, F 24,13:5
Lux, Frederick, 1958, Mr 28,25:4
Lux, H Col, 1882, Je 29,2:4
Lux, Joseph R, 1953, Ag 19,29:4
Lux, Leo A, 1949, Jl 22,19:4
Lux, Paul, 1947, Ja 26,53:4
Lux, Thomas W, 1940, Jl 27,13:5
Luxburg, Karl L von Count, 1956, Ap 6,25:2
Luxemburg, Duke of (Wm Alexander), 1912, F 27,9:2
Luxenberg, Morry, 1968, Ja 18,39:4
Luxenberger, Eugene A, 1965, Mr 18,33:4
Luxford, Donald L, 1945, Ja 21,40:3
Luxner, George Mrs, 1954, Je 29,27:4; 1959, Je 5,27:4
Luxton, George, 1962, N 2,31:2
Luyster, Cornelius H, 1964, Ja 15,31:3
Luyster, John, 1959, D 13,86:7
Luyster, John S, 1939, My 21,III,7:3
Luyties, Henry E G, 1905, Mr 22,9:6
Luz, Carlos, 1961, F 10,27:2
Luzenberg, Charles A, 1957, S 30,31:3
Luzenberg, Harry S, 1938, F 16,21:4
Luzier, Thomas J, 1947, Ap 16,25:5
Luzin, Nikolai, 1950, Mr 4,17:6
Luzzatti, L, 1927, Mr 30,25:3
Luzzatto, Ettore, 1949, S 30,24:2
Luzzatto, Joseph Mrs, 1950, Ag 30,31:1
Luzzatto, Mark Dr, 1922, S 20,21:4
Luzzi, Joseph, 1944, Jl 5,17:4
L'Verso, Frank, 1944, F 14,19:2
Lvovitch, David, 1950, Ag 19,13:2
Lyall, Beatrix M, 1948, My 10,21:2
Lyall, David, 1937, S 20,12:4
Lyall, Edna, 1903, F 10,9:7
Lyall, F W, 1901, Ag 24,7:6
Lyall, George H H, 1938, Je 1,23:5
Lyall, Harold W, 1953, Ja 5,21:2
Lyall, Herbert J, 1941, N 25,25:6
Lyall, James C M, 1949, D 23,21:2
Lyall, William (funl, Ja 15,9:6), 1916, Ja 14,9:6
Lyall, William L, 1937, Ap 17,17:3
Lyatoshinsky, Boris, 1968, Ap 16,47:2
Lyautey, I H, 1934, Jl 28,13:1
Lyautey, Louis Mme, 1953, F 10,27:2
Lybeden, Baron, 1873, N 15,2:6
Lybolt, Emeline M Mrs, 1941, My 25,37:2
Lybolt, Frank, 1925, Ja 30,17:4
Lybrand, William M, 1960, N 21,29:2
Lybyer, Albert H, 1949, Mr 29,25:2
Lycan, Donald W, 1952, O 15,31:4
Lycett, William, 1938, Ap 15,19:3
Lycett, William Mrs, 1939, F 5,41:3
Lychenheim, Morris, 1947, Je 28,13:5
Lychtenstein, Aaron A Rev, 1923, Jl 8,27:5
Lycurgos, Archbishop of Syra, 1875, N 2,4:7
Lyddy, John L, 1945, Ap 23,19:4
Lydecker, Charles E, 1920, My 7,11:3
Lydecker, Cornelius J, 1944, Ap 1,13:2
Lydecker, Frederick A, 1961, My 15,31:6
Lydecker, Garrett J Gen, 1914, Jl 10,9:4
Lydecker, Homer B Mrs, 1949, S 15,27:2
Lydecker, Irving B, 1964, S 20,89:1
Lydecker, Kenneth, 1954, Je 1,27:1
Lydecker, Rachel C, 1941, Je 19,21:2
Lydecker, Thomas W, 1949, Ja 22,13:6
Lydekker, Richard, 1915, Ap 19,9:4
Lyden, Andrew V (por), 1940, S 27,23:2
Lyden, Daniel J, 1948, O 25,23:5
Lyden, Frederick F, 1940, D 19,25:6
Lyden, J Kenneth, 1965, D 9,47:3
Lyden, John J, 1964, S 29,43:2
Lydenberg, Harry M, 1960, Ap 17,92:4
Lyder, George P, 1958, Mr 7,23:1
Lydia, Sister, 1949, Mr 8,25:3
Lydiard, Keith B, 1943, My 11,21:4
Lydig, David, 1917, O 25,15:5
Lydig, P Col, 1929, F 17,28:4
Lydig, Philip M, 1872, F 24,5:4
Lydig, R de A Mrs, 1929, O 20,1:2
Lydon, Cornelia B Mrs (will), 1966, N 21,34:6
Lydon, Eugene K, 1963, N 24,22:8
Lydon, Henry C, 1903, N 25,9:5
Lydon, Richard P (por), 1946, Mr 9,13:1
Lydon, William A, 1918, O 28,11:3
Lydston, G Frank Dr, 1923, Mr 15,19:5
Lyerly, Carl, 1957, My 14,35:5
Lyerly, Charles A Capt, 1925, Ag 10,13:6
Lyeth, John M R, 1957, D 24,15:2
Lyett, J H, 1881, Ja 11,2:2
Lyford, Frederic E Mrs, 1957, F 24,85:2
Lyford, Oliver Mrs, 1953, N 27,27:2
Lyford, Oliver S, 1952, Mr 7,23:2
Lyford, Phil, 1950, Mr 25,13:2
Lyford, S C, 1885, My 11,5:6
Lyke, Frederick S, 1939, Ap 29,17:7
Lyke, Joseph F, 1951, My 18,27:3
Lykes, Coke S, 1942, F 22,26:2
Lykes, Frederick E, 1951, N 11,91:4
Lykes, Howell T, 1942, Jl 10,17:6
Lykes, James M, 1943, N 28,68:5
Lykes, John W, 1957, My 20,25:2
Lykes, Joseph T Sr, 1967, Mr 10,36:1
Lykes, Tom M, 1941, N 11,23:3
Lykke, Chris, 1950, F 17,23:3
Lykken, Henry G, 1958, Ap 7,33:3
Lylburn, Henry C Mrs, 1959, Jl 31,23:3
Lyle, Alex G, 1955, Jl 16,15:2
Lyle, Alexander Dr, 1919, My 24,13:2
Lyle, Alfred F Rev, 1910, N 9,9:2
Lyle, Annie G, 1948, O 10,76:5
Lyle, Archibald, 1946, D 6,23:3
Lyle, David A Col, 1937, O 12,25:5
Lyle, David A Mrs (will, Jl 7,36:6), 1957, Je 24,2
Lyle, Duncan C, 1938, Mr 1,21:2
Lyle, Ethel H Mrs, 1950, D 1,26:2
Lyle, Floyd, 1962, Je 29,27:4
Lyle, Henry H, 1947, Mr 12,25:2
Lyle, Herman V, 1938, F 3,23:5
Lyle, J Irvine, 1942, Je 8,15:2
Lyle, Jack, 1944, Je 13,19:3
Lyle, Jerome K, 1966, N 8,39:2
Lyle, John H, 1964, N 25,37:4
Lyle, John S, 1912, Jl 28,II,11:5
Lyle, Julia G Mrs, 1939, D 12,31:6
Lyle, Lord, 1954, Mr 7,90:3
Lyle, Maude E, 1944, S 25,17:2
Lyle, Mervin E, 1903, S 19,7:6
Lyle, Otis D, 1941, Ja 19,40:3
Lyle, Peter, 1879, Jl 18,4:7
Lyle, Quentin E, 1964, Ap 9,32:1
Lyle, William, 1959, Je 29,29:3
Lyle, William G, 1955, N 26,19:5
Lyles, Lee, 1950, Jl 22,15:5
Lyles, Mary L, 1924, F 8,19:4
Lyles, Ruluf Mrs, 1903, My 18,7:6
Lyman, A S, 1930, Mr 8,17:1
Lyman, Abe (will, O 26,18:2), 1957, O 24,33:1
Lyman, Albert J Mrs, 1947, S 25,29:5
Lyman, Albert J Rev, 1915, Ag 24,11:6
Lyman, Albert K, 1942, Ag 14,17:5
Lyman, Alex S Mrs, 1955, D 4,89:2
Lyman, Alex V, 1959, Mr 1,86:2
Lyman, Alfred, 1940, Ja 8,15:2
Lyman, Alfred G, 1949, D 21,29:4
Lyman, Anna M Mrs, 1959, N 3,31:2
Lyman, Arthur A, 1949, Ag 25,23:1
Lyman, Arthur T, 1915, O 25,9:4

Lyman, Benjamin Smith, 1920, Ag 31,9:1
Lyman, Charles Col, 1913, Mr 26,11:3
Lyman, Charles E, 1948, F 29,60:5
Lyman, Charles H (por), 1945, Jl 25,23:4
Lyman, Charlton E, 1964, F 20,29:2
Lyman, Clifford H, 1941, S 21,42:6
Lyman, Daniel W, 1954, My 23,90:1
Lyman, David B, 1914, Ap 9,11:5
Lyman, David R, 1956, O 16,33:1
Lyman, Donald S, 1948, F 3,25:3
Lyman, Edson R, 1953, Ja 3,15:1
Lyman, Edward A, 1946, Ap 23,21:3
Lyman, Edward A Mrs, 1960, Ap 7,35:5
Lyman, Edward B, 1943, Ja 13,23:4
Lyman, Elias Jr, 1952, Ap 4,25:4
Lyman, Elias Mrs, 1915, My 21,13:6
Lyman, Elihu R, 1937, O 30,19:3
Lyman, Elizabeth Mrs, 1937, S 23,27:5
Lyman, Ellen S, 1938, Mr 6,II,9:2
Lyman, Eva S Mrs, 1952, N 11,29:2
Lyman, Francis M, 1916, N 19,21:3
Lyman, Frank E, 1938, D 13,25:5
Lyman, Frank J, 1963, D 19,33:1
Lyman, George, 1943, Ap 15,25:4
Lyman, George H Sr, 1945, My 18,19:5
Lyman, Harold C, 1947, My 22,27:5
Lyman, Harriet M Mrs, 1941, F 11,23:4
Lyman, Harrison F, 1944, My 23,23:4
Lyman, Helen, 1939, Mr 28,24:3
Lyman, Helen Mrs, 1938, Jl 30,13:6
Lyman, Henry D, 1921, F 28,11:4
Lyman, Herbert, 1941, Je 16,15:4
Lyman, J W, 1882, Mr 28,5:5
Lyman, John G, 1954, Jl 29,23:5
Lyman, John G Dr, 1937, Jl 13,19:2
Lyman, John Pickering, 1914, N 2,9:5
Lyman, Joseph B, 1872, Ja 29,1:6
Lyman, Joseph M, 1937, Jl 28,20:1
Lyman, Kenneth J, 1966, Jl 29,31:3
Lyman, Lauren D Mrs, 1947, D 11,33:4; 1957, N 2, 21:2
Lyman, Lewis B, 1946, My 10,19:2
Lyman, Martha I, 1944, Mr 18,13:5
Lyman, Michael J, 1945, D 2,45:2
Lyman, Mike, 1952, D 1,23:3
Lyman, Morris, 1968, Je 14,47:1
Lyman, Payson Williston Rev, 1924, Ap 19,13:5
Lyman, R Yale, 1941, D 24,17:3
Lyman, Ralph H, 1954, Mr 16,29:2
Lyman, Richard E, 1954, F 27,13:6
Lyman, Robert H, 1937, S 4,15:3
Lyman, Robert J, 1944, F 23,19:5
Lyman, Rollo L Prof, 1937, D 24,17:5
Lyman, Ronald T, 1962, Jl 7,17:6
Lyman, Ronald T Mrs, 1953, S 3,22:6
Lyman, Samuel Hinckley, 1910, Ag 12,7:5
Lyman, Sidney M, 1967, Jl 27,35:2
Lyman, Stuart, 1943, D 9,27:5
Lyman, Stuart Mrs, 1954, Ap 21,29:1
Lyman, Theodore, 1954, O 13,31:3
Lyman, Theodore C, 1966, Jl 22,31:2
Lyman, Theodore C Mrs, 1947, Ja 19,53:3
Lyman, Theodore P, 1941, O 14,23:4
Lyman, Theron U, 1939, S 22,23:3
Lyman, William E, 1948, Mr 16,28:3; 1952, Je 18,27:2
Lyman, William H, 1946, N 14,29:2
Lyman, William T, 1960, Ap 13,39:5
Lyman (Uncle Gad), 1885, Je 21,2:5
Lyman-Wheaton, Alfred E, 1951, O 16,31:4
Lymon, Frankie, 1968, F 28,50:3
Lynah, Henry L Dr, 1922, Ap 9,28:3
Lynah, James, 1956, F 25,19:5
Lynam, Edward, 1950, F 1,29:2
Lynam, Frank, 1950, O 10,31:5
Lynam, Fred C, 1942, Ap 12,44:8
Lynam, Malachy, 1956, Je 6,33:5
Lynam, Robert Mrs, 1961, Ja 16,27:2
Lynas, John R Com, 1937, N 17,23:5
Lynch, A, 1934, Mr 26,17:5
Lynch, A Oliver, 1950, S 3,39:2
Lynch, Abbie D Mrs, 1939, Ja 4,21:5
Lynch, Ambrose M, 1950, O 10,31:5
Lynch, Andrew G, 1966, Ja 28,47:5
Lynch, Andrew J, 1944, Mr 29,21:2
Lynch, Andrew R, 1948, Jl 4,26:7
Lynch, Anne B, 1948, O 21,27:4
Lynch, Anthony J, 1939, Je 16,23:3
Lynch, Anthony V Jr, 1964, Mr 12,35:4
Lynch, Arch S, 1948, D 21,31:2
Lynch, Arthur F, 1965, O 14,47:5
Lynch, Arthur J, 1947, Ag 7,21:6; 1950, Ap 5,31:3
Lynch, Arthur L, 1948, N 10,29:2
Lynch, Augustus M, 1955, N 27,89:2
Lynch, Austin, 1946, Ja 29,25:1
Lynch, Bartholomew A, 1956, F 5,86:4
Lynch, Benito, 1951, D 24,13:3
Lynch, Benny, 1946, Ag 7,27:4
Lynch, Bernard F Mrs, 1953, S 1,24:4
Lynch, Bernard J, 1952, Mr 29,15:3
Lynch, Carl, 1956, S 14,23:1
Lynch, Catherine, 1945, Ag 9,21:6
Lynch, Charles (por), 1938, Ja 25,22:2
Lynch, Charles D, 1950, Mr 3,25:4
Lynch, Charles F, 1942, Je 18,21:5
Lynch, Charles McK Mrs, 1957, S 3,28:1
Lynch, Charles T, 1906, Mr 8,9:4
Lynch, Clarence, 1948, S 6,13:4
Lynch, Clyde A, 1950, Ag 7,19:4
Lynch, Commodore, 1865, O 19,1:4
Lynch, Cornelius, 1940, N 13,23:2
Lynch, Cornelius F, 1938, Ap 15,19:4
Lynch, D Capt, 1884, O 11,5:2
Lynch, Daniel D Mrs, 1951, Ap 16,25:5
Lynch, Daniel F, 1942, Ja 31,17:5
Lynch, Daniel F Mrs, 1953, Jl 7,27:4
Lynch, Daniel J, 1950, D 24,34:1; 1952, N 14,23:3
Lynch, Daniel W, 1943, D 15,27:4
Lynch, David J, 1962, Ja 3,33:3
Lynch, David S, 1942, D 7,27:2
Lynch, David W, 1913, Ag 11,7:6
Lynch, Denis T, 1966, Ja 15,27:3
Lynch, E L Mrs, 1904, Ja 28,9:7
Lynch, Edmund C (por),(will, My 26,25:1), 1938, My 14,15:1
Lynch, Edward B, 1953, Ap 14,27:4
Lynch, Edward G Mrs, 1966, D 5,45:3
Lynch, Edward H, 1948, D 6,25:4
Lynch, Edward J Dr, 1968, F 19,39:1
Lynch, Edward Rev, 1865, My 7,5:5
Lynch, Elizabeth C, 1946, O 5,17:5; 1950, Ag 4,21:4
Lynch, Elizabeth M (will), 1938, Je 21,17:2
Lynch, Ella, 1943, D 6,15:2
Lynch, Ella F, 1945, S 1,11:1
Lynch, Etta M, 1943, D 11,15:3
Lynch, Eugene A, 1954, O 2,17:2
Lynch, Eugene R, 1950, S 28,31:3
Lynch, Fannie E, 1940, Ap 9,24:3
Lynch, Florence C Mrs, 1939, S 21,23:1
Lynch, Florence M Mrs, 1953, Ap 30,31:3
Lynch, Frances, 1942, My 20,14:5
Lynch, Francis, 1945, Mr 30,15:1
Lynch, Francis L Jr, 1962, Mr 14,39:3
Lynch, Frank, 1938, Ja 14,23:4
Lynch, Frank B Rev Dr, 1925, D 3,25:3
Lynch, Frank J, 1947, D 30,23:4
Lynch, Frank M, 1940, Ag 11,31:4; 1949, O 14,27:3; 1964, S 14,33:5
Lynch, Frank T Mrs, 1948, Je 8,25:2
Lynch, Frank W, 1945, Ja 13,11:5
Lynch, Franklin P, 1948, N 23,29:5
Lynch, Fred, 1968, Ja 11,33:5
Lynch, Frederick J, 1957, Jl 11,25:5
Lynch, Garry P, 1951, Mr 27,29:2
Lynch, George (funl), 1872, Ja 26,8:5
Lynch, George A, 1962, Ag 11,17:4
Lynch, George E Mrs, 1957, N 30,21:4
Lynch, George F, 1965, D 10,47:2
Lynch, George F Sr, 1955, Jl 14,23:6
Lynch, Gerald M, 1960, S 16,31:1
Lynch, Gerald R, 1945, S 2,32:1
Lynch, Gertrude C Mrs, 1940, My 30,17:3
Lynch, Hada, 1952, Ja 28,17:2
Lynch, Hannah A, 1942, F 28,17:4
Lynch, Harold J, 1953, S 12,17:2
Lynch, Harry Howard, 1940, Ap 7,45:3
Lynch, Henry C, 1961, O 8,87:2
Lynch, Henry J Rev, 1905, Ap 19,5:1
Lynch, Henry W, 1925, N 24,25:2
Lynch, Homer W, 1968, S 15,84:8
Lynch, Howard J, 1949, O 7,31:2
Lynch, Hugh J, 1939, N 26,42:5
Lynch, Humphrey J (por), 1938, Ja 25,21:1
Lynch, Isabella M, 1937, N 12,22:2
Lynch, J M, 1930, Jl 17,21:1
Lynch, J Paul Mrs, 1938, F 26,15:5
Lynch, J Rev, 1878, O 13,1:6
Lynch, Jack, 1957, F 20,66:4
Lynch, James, 1872, D 19,1:2; 1946, D 22,41:5
Lynch, James (Piggy), 1958, Ap 23,28:3
Lynch, James A, 1938, My 20,19:4; 1940, N 17,48:4; 1966, F 20,88:8
Lynch, James D, 1917, My 12,11:6; 1937, O 13,23:5
Lynch, James E, 1946, My 22,21:1; 1951, S 1,11:6
Lynch, James F, 1939, Ja 8,42:4
Lynch, James H, 1941, S 8,15:2
Lynch, James H J Mrs, 1961, Mr 31,27:3
Lynch, James J, 1925, N 5,23:6; 1939, Je 21,23:6; 1942, My 20,19:5; 1947, My 1,25:5; 1955, F 2,27:2
Lynch, James J Jr, 1950, Je 8,31:4
Lynch, James J Mrs, 1948, Ag 30,25:2
Lynch, James K, 1919, Ap 29,15:4
Lynch, James L, 1947, S 6,17:3
Lynch, James Sylvester M Msgr, 1925, D 11,23:2
Lynch, James T Mrs, 1941, O 28,23:4
Lynch, James V, 1945, D 17,22:2
Lynch, Jasper, 1942, Ap 17,17:3
Lynch, Jeremiah D, 1940, Ja 3,21:4
Lynch, Jerome M, 1951, Ap 24,29:3
Lynch, Jerome M Mrs, 1943, S 19,48:1
Lynch, Joe, 1965, S 2,31:1
Lynch, John, 1937, Mr 3,23:3; 1942, My 12,19:5; 1947, Mr 24,27:6; 1957, Jl 21,60:7; 1958, Je 17,29:3
Lynch, John A, 1938, O 3,15:2; 1940, Ap 12,23:1; 1950, D 4,29:4; 1954, Mr 10,25:3
Lynch, John B, 1939, D 5,27:5; 1954, N 23,35:3
Lynch, John C, 1937, Je 30,23:3; 1956, Mr 25,92:3
Lynch, John D, 1946, Je 24,31:3
Lynch, John E, 1903, Jl 21,9:6; 1951, Ag 3,21:6; 1954, Ja 5,27:4
Lynch, John F, 1940, S 28,17:6; 1944, Jl 7,15:5
Lynch, John F Rev, 1905, Mr 7,9:5
Lynch, John H, 1943, Jl 7,19:3; 1948, O 21,27:2; 1964, S 10,35:1
Lynch, John H Jr, 1947, Je 10,27:2
Lynch, John H Mrs, 1960, N 13,88:8
Lynch, John J, 1938, Je 29,19:5; 1939, Ag 24,19:3; 1945, Mr 17,13:2; 1945, D 30,14:3; 1957, Jl 16,25:3
Lynch, John J (Bro Andrew), 1960, My 7,23:5
Lynch, John M Mrs, 1962, My 28,29:2
Lynch, John Mrs, 1942, Jl 4,17:6
Lynch, John P, 1948, O 31,88:4; 1965, Ap 1,35:3
Lynch, John R, 1947, Ja 22,23:2; 1962, Je 13,41:3
Lynch, John R Maj, 1939, N 3,21:5
Lynch, John S, 1949, Ja 11,27:2
Lynch, John T, 1960, F 1,27:2
Lynch, John W, 1953, Jl 14,27:1; 1968, O 22,47:3
Lynch, Joseph, 1939, Ja 18,20:4; 1947, Ja 31,23:1; 1948, Ja 13,25:2
Lynch, Joseph A, 1956, Ja 14,19:2
Lynch, Joseph A Mrs, 1955, F 1,29:2
Lynch, Joseph B, 1957, F 19,31:3
Lynch, Joseph B Mrs, 1958, F 1,19:6
Lynch, Joseph J, 1946, Jl 19,19:5
Lynch, Joseph M.Mrs, 1967, Je 10,33:4
Lynch, Joseph P, 1966, Je 27,35:5
Lynch, Josiah H Mrs, 1940, D 22,31:1
Lynch, Lawrence J, 1955, Ag 17,27:2
Lynch, Leigh B, 1945, Mr 27,19:3
Lynch, Leo A, 1960, My 28,21:6
Lynch, Leo F, 1943, Jl 13,21:5
Lynch, Leo J, 1957, F 21,27:2
Lynch, Levi, 1942, D 16,25:4
Lynch, Lewis L, 1949, O 3,17:4
Lynch, Lewis M, 1947, D 14,76:6
Lynch, Luke G, 1941, Ja 24,17:4
Lynch, Mae V, 1945, S 12,25:1
Lynch, Margaret Mrs, 1945, Ag 10,15:1
Lynch, Margaret T, 1961, D 25,23:6
Lynch, Martha V J Mrs, 1948, F 5,23:3
Lynch, Martin, 1954, F 24,25:1; 1954, Mr 28,88:6
Lynch, Martin B, 1951, S 30,72:4
Lynch, Mary E, 1950, Mr 19,94:6
Lynch, Mary E Mrs, 1940, S 27,23:3
Lynch, Mary Regina Sister, 1943, O 28,23:5
Lynch, May A, 1947, Mr 9,60:2
Lynch, Michael, 1940, D 2,23:6
Lynch, Michael E, 1952, Ag 21,19:5
Lynch, Michael J, 1946, My 15,21:3
Lynch, Michael J Mrs, 1958, O 22,35:2
Lynch, Michael Mrs, 1940, D 2,23:6
Lynch, Morris T, 1941, Mr 29,15:2
Lynch, P J, 1928, S 14,27:5
Lynch, P N Bp, 1882, F 27,1:6
Lynch, Patrick, 1951, My 10,31:3
Lynch, Patrick B, 1955, Ag 10,25:3
Lynch, Patrick J Dr, 1905, Ap 23,9:7
Lynch, Patrick Mrs, 1947, D 31,15:3
Lynch, Peter, 1874, Jl 9,4:7
Lynch, Peter F, 1954, Je 20,84:6; 1968, S 23,35:3
Lynch, Phil C Mrs, 1950, Ag 8,29:4
Lynch, Phil F, 1950, Ag 23,29:5
Lynch, Phil S, 1938, O 23,41:2
Lynch, Philip J, 1945, Ja 5,15:3
Lynch, R B, 1884, Ja 15,5:3
Lynch, Rachel A C Mrs, 1938, N 3,23:5
Lynch, Raymond F, 1965, Ap 13,37:4
Lynch, Raymond J, 1955, Ap 27,31:2
Lynch, Richard B Rear-Adm, 1968, Ja 21,76:3
Lynch, Richard Mrs, 1949, Ap 9,17:4
Lynch, Robert E, 1954, D 16,37:1
Lynch, Robert J, 1954, F 25,31:2; 1955, Jl 9,15:5
Lynch, Rose Mrs, 1911, Jl 21,9:6
Lynch, Rose V, 1949, My 20,27:2
Lynch, S Walter, 1947, O 30,26:2
Lynch, Selma, 1960, Ap 20,39:1
Lynch, Theodore F, 1965, F 19,35:3
Lynch, Theodore K, 1960, S 6,42:2
Lynch, Theresa Mrs, 1903, Ja 30,9:5
Lynch, Thomas, 1903, Ag 31,1:6; 1914, D 30,11:5; 1939, Mr 2,21:2
Lynch, Thomas A, 1944, O 29,44:3; 1950, S 19,31:1
Lynch, Thomas J, 1940, Mr 20,34:7; 1941, Ja 21,22:3; 1946, O 15,25:5; 1950, Jl 11,31:2
Lynch, Thomas J Rev (funl, Ap 2,17:5), 1923, Mr 29,19:5
Lynch, Thomas M (por), 1939, F 27,15:4
Lynch, Thomas M, 1950, Ap 27,29:4
Lynch, Thomas M Sr, 1959, F 27,25:3
Lynch, Thomas P, 1950, Mr 14,25:3; 1959, Ag 7,23:2
Lynch, Thomas S, 1954, Jl 30,17:3; 1967, Ag 12,7:2
Lynch, Thomas W Mrs, 1948, Je 1,23:5
Lynch, Timothy, 1941, Je 24,19:3
Lynch, Tom, 1938, My 7,15:6
Lynch, W A Col, 1874, Ag 6,4:6
Lynch, Walter A (funl, S 14,19:5), 1957, S 11,33:1
Lynch, Walter F, 1951, Jl 27,19:3
Lynch, Walter R, 1949, F 26,30:2
Lynch, Walton D, 1962, Mr 7,35:2
Lynch, Warren J (por), 1949, Ag 5,19:1

Lynch, Wilbur H, 1948, Jl 13,28:3
Lynch, Wilbur W, 1944, Ap 27,23:5
Lynch, Will A, 1948, O 16,15:4
Lynch, Willard A, 1955, Mr 11,25:4
Lynch, Willard N, 1951, Ja 26,24:2
Lynch, William A, 1946, Ap 3,25:5; 1953, Mr 10,29:2; 1955, S 27,35:1
Lynch, William B, 1938, S 16,1:3
Lynch, William C, 1957, N 12,34:1
Lynch, William F, 1948, Ja 23,24:3; 1952, My 4,90:6; 1960, D 7,43:3
Lynch, William H, 1949, Jl 22,19:3; 1950, Je 14,31:5
Lynch, William J, 1939, Je 24,17:2; 1939, S 10,49:2; 1941, Je 25,21:5; 1944, N 21,25:5; 1948, S 15,31:3
Lynch, William R, 1962, Jl 19,27:4
Lynch, William S Mrs, 1946, Ja 15,23:2
Lynch, William W, 1950, N 14,31:1
Lynch, Willis D, 1944, Ja 27,19:3
Lynch (Bro Cornelius Peter), 1961, D 3,88:3
Lynch-Staunton, George, 1940, Mr 20,34:6
Lyncker, Baroness von, 1907, Ag 23,7:5
Lynd, J Norman, 1942, N 9,23:5
Lynd, James, 1876, Jl 1,5:5
Lynd, Margaret L, 1944, Ag 29,17:3
Lynd, Robert, 1949, O 7,31:3
Lynd, Robert Mrs, 1952, F 22,21:1
Lynd, Samuel E, 1939, F 18,15:2
Lynd, Stoughton B, 1948, Ag 27,18:3
Lyndall, Ervin, 1952, Ja 10,29:3
Lynde, Carleton J Mrs, 1940, F 13,23:5
Lynde, Charles R, 1940, Ap 16,23:2
Lynde, Charles Westley, 1906, S 4,1:5
Lynde, George Stanley Dr, 1914, N 6,11:5
Lynde, John H, 1874, Mr 13,4:7
Lynde, Rollin H, 1907, Ap 9,9:5
Lynde, Samuel A, 1940, F 23,15:3
Lynde, Sandra, 1941, My 11,44:5
Lynde, William R, 1943, F 22,17:4
Lynden, George H, 1966, My 23,41:2
Lynden, Jan C van Baron, 1946, My 20,24:3
Lyndon, Charles, 1967, My 15,43:3
Lyndon, Edward, 1940, N 7,25:5
Lynds, Henry I, 1950, Je 24,13:2
Lyne, James G, 1966, Ja 17,47:4
Lyne, Joseph Leycester (Father Ignatius), 1908, O 17,9:4
Lyne, Lewis F Jr, 1960, N 26,21:6
Lyne, Lucien A, 1954, F 26,20:3
Lyne, William Sir, 1913, Ag 4,7:4
Lyner, Maurice M, 1948, Ag 1,46:5
Lynes, Alex, 1949, My 13,23:3
Lynes, Emily A, 1943, F 2,19:2
Lynes, George B, 1938, D 23,19:2
Lynes, George P, 1955, D 7,39:4
Lynes, J C, 1936, F 28,21:3
Lynes, James P, 1948, N 9,27:2
Lynes, Twining, 1942, F 2,15:4
Lyness, Anna W Mrs, 1948, F 28,15:5
Lyness, Frederick W J, 1956, O 15,25:2
Lyness, John W, 1962, S 24,29:2
Lyness, John W Jr, 1966, Ag 20,25:5
Lynett, Edward J (will, Ap 1,25:5), 1943, Ja 2,11:3
Lynett, Edward J, 1966, F 7,29:3
Lynett, Elizabeth R, 1959, Ap 3,27:4
Lynett, James D, 1962, Mr 23,33:5
Lynett, William R, 1946, F 15,26:2
Lyng, Eugene J, 1947, Ag 22,15:5
Lyngholm, Thorvald, 1943, Jl 2,19:2
Lyngklip, Einar, 1942, Ja 13,19:4
Lynip, Franklin Mrs (Ryllis G), 1963, O 8,43:3
Lynk, George H, 1951, O 24,32:3
Lynke, Harry E, 1947, N 1,15:2
Lynn, A M, 1927, Ap 9,19:5
Lynn, Alan G, 1947, Jl 16,23:3
Lynn, Arthur L, 1948, D 8,32:3
Lynn, C Gordon, 1960, N 5,23:2
Lynn, Charles J, 1958, S 24,27:4
Lynn, Charles W, 1947, Je 4,27:4
Lynn, David, 1961, My 26,33:1
Lynn, David E, 1950, O 3,31:5
Lynn, Frank, 1964, O 25,88:3
Lynn, Frank G, 1961, Jl 23,69:2
Lynn, Frank W, 1954, S 5,1:8
Lynn, Harry G, 1957, Ag 19,19:5
Lynn, Harry G Mrs, 1948, My 16,70:2
Lynn, Harry H, 1956, F 22,27:3
Lynn, Henry, 1952, Ag 19,23:5
Lynn, J, 1933, N 22,19:6
Lynn, John, 1946, Ja 15,23:1
Lynn, John Capt, 1946, Ja 20,42:5
Lynn, John E, 1938, My 3,23:6
Lynn, John H, 1957, Je 12,35:4
Lynn, John Mrs, 1948, O 26,31:1
Lynn, Josiah E, 1903, Ap 28,5:6
Lynn, Martin T, 1954, S 28,29:6
Lynn, Norman M, 1938, N 8,23:1
Lynn, P P, 1926, My 29,15:6
Lynn, Ralph, 1962, Ag 10,19:5
Lynn, Richard H, 1958, Jl 11,13:6
Lynn, Robert, 1944, My 1,15:5; 1945, Ag 6,15:3
Lynn, Sharon, 1963, My 28,37:2
Lynn, Vincent de C, 1966, S 11,86:6
Lynn, Walter L, 1950, N 13,27:5
Lynn, Walter W, 1954, D 16,37:5
Lynn, Wauhope (funl, Ag 20,9:4), 1920, Ag 19,9:4
Lynn, William F, 1940, Jl 31,17:5
Lynn, William F Mrs, 1943, Mr 11,21:3
Lynn, William H, 1952, Ja 6,95:4
Lynn, William H Mrs, 1960, Ag 25,29:1
Lynn-Thomas, John Sir, 1939, S 22,23:6
Lynott, Matt J, 1943, Ag 31,17:4
Lynskey, Elizabeth M, 1954, D 1,31:5
Lynskey, George J, 1957, D 22,41:2
Lynt, B, 1878, Ag 1,8:2
Lyon, A Maynard, 1916, O 17,13:6
Lyon, Abraham, 1942, Je 28,33:2
Lyon, Adrian, 1950, Mr 12,94:4
Lyon, Adrian Mrs, 1959, N 5,35:3
Lyon, Alfred E, 1967, My 9,47:1
Lyon, Alfred H, 1938, D 26,24:4
Lyon, Alfred J, 1942, D 2,25:4
Lyon, Alfred L, 1957, Jl 26,19:2
Lyon, Alfred L Mrs, 1959, Mr 22,87:2
Lyon, Alice, 1937, Ap 19,21:2
Lyon, Almira, 1924, D 16,25:3
Lyon, Amos M Mrs, 1947, N 23,72:7
Lyon, Andrew H, 1961, O 26,35:6
Lyon, Arthur G, 1947, D 2,29:1
Lyon, Arthur S C, 1952, Je 17,27:2
Lyon, B B Vincent, 1953, My 22,27:2
Lyon, Benjamin B Sr, 1938, Jl 3,13:1
Lyon, Bert R, 1959, Je 9,37:3
Lyon, Caleb, 1875, S 9,4:7
Lyon, Calvin C, 1955, N 27,88:6
Lyon, Cecil A Gen, 1916, Ap 5,13:6
Lyon, Charles B Mrs, 1947, F 5,23:4
Lyon, Charles C, 1947, F 2,57:4
Lyon, Charles H, 1947, Ja 2,27:4
Lyon, Charles H Mrs (E Messler), 1953, Ja 14,31:3
Lyon, Charles Leroy, 1908, Mr 6,7:5
Lyon, Charles M, 1949, Ja 30,60:5; 1959, F 5,31:4
Lyon, Charles Mrs (J Wilson), 1953, Jl 6,17:6
Lyon, Charles W, 1945, D 22,19:2
Lyon, Chester B, 1944, Ja 12,23:4
Lyon, Clifford S Mrs, 1950, My 18,29:1
Lyon, Conant S, 1945, Ag 10,15:4
Lyon, D Everett, 1946, N 4,25:5
Lyon, D G, 1935, D 5,25:5
Lyon, D Willard, 1949, Mr 18,26:2
Lyon, Daisy E Mrs, 1941, My 30,15:3
Lyon, Damon, 1918, Jl 6,9:6
Lyon, Darwin O Dr, 1937, Ap 16,23:3
Lyon, David, 1945, Ap 21,13:5; 1957, Ag 18,44:4
Lyon, David Mrs, 1951, Ap 24,29:2
Lyon, Dolly, 1960, Je 18,23:5
Lyon, Dore Mrs, 1937, My 2,II,8:6
Lyon, E, 1880, My 8,2:2
Lyon, E Burton, 1937, Jl 10,15:1
Lyon, E Wilton, 1955, My 19,29:4
Lyon, Edmund, 1920, Ap 25,22:4
Lyon, Edward, 1883, O 14,9:3
Lyon, Edward A, 1942, Je 13,15:4; 1947, Mr 6,25:4
Lyon, Edward F, 1954, Je 25,5:6
Lyon, Edwin P, 1945, F 22,27:4
Lyon, Elias P Dr, 1937, My 6,25:5
Lyon, Elizabeth Mrs, 1942, Ja 1,36:7
Lyon, Emily F Mrs, 1940, Ja 26,17:2
Lyon, Emma, 1958, Mr 19,31:1
Lyon, Emory F, 1943, Ap 3,15:4
Lyon, Emory S, 1944, Ap 13,19:2
Lyon, Ernest, 1938, Jl 18,13:5
Lyon, Eugene L, 1954, My 21,27:3
Lyon, Eugene L Mrs, 1940, N 8,21:5
Lyon, Frank, 1961, Ja 7,19:5
Lyon, Frank M, 1953, F 6,19:2
Lyon, Frank R, 1947, Ap 17,27:5
Lyon, Frank S, 1962, My 20,86:7
Lyon, Franz F, 1945, F 17,13:5
Lyon, Fred G, 1953, Ap 22,29:5
Lyon, Fred M, 1952, Ap 2,33:5
Lyon, Fred W, 1937, Ap 14,26:2; 1943, O 18,15:4
Lyon, Frederick (will), 1938, D 13,8:3
Lyon, Frederick D Jr, 1952, Ja 27,77:2
Lyon, Frederick D Mrs (Mme DeMoss), 1960, Ag 24,29:3
Lyon, Frederick G C, 1946, Mr 18,21:4
Lyon, Frederick J, 1944, F 28,17:1
Lyon, Frederick K Mrs, 1938, Ap 10,II,7:1
Lyon, George A Rear-Adm, 1914, Mr 8,15:5
Lyon, George C, 1907, N 27,7:6
Lyon, George F (cor, My 23,23:1), 1940, My 22,23:5
Lyon, George F, 1941, My 9,21:5
Lyon, George G, 1950, Ap 26,29:1
Lyon, George J, 1939, D 20,25:2
Lyon, George Jr, 1956, Ag 17,19:5
Lyon, George R Mrs, 1949, Ja 7,22:2
Lyon, George S, 1938, My 12,23:2
Lyon, George T, 1946, D 14,15:4
Lyon, George W, 1948, S 27,23:2
Lyon, Gideon A, 1951, Ja 10,27:5
Lyon, Gilbert R, 1948, Je 28,19:2
Lyon, Harold A Mrs, 1939, Ag 2,19:5
Lyon, Harold S, 1967, O 2,48:1
Lyon, Harriet M Mrs, 1937, F 13,13:4
Lyon, Harris Merton, 1916, Je 4,21:5
Lyon, Harry, 1950, O 24,29:2
Lyon, Harry Jr, 1963, Je 1,21:6
Lyon, Harvey L, 1964, Ag 7,29:4
Lyon, Hastings, 1953, Ap 28,27:3
Lyon, Henry H Mrs, 1924, Ag 8,13:4
Lyon, Herb, 1968, Ag 7,43:1
Lyon, Herbert E, 1966, O 23,88:8
Lyon, Herbert M, 1951, My 26,17:5
Lyon, Howard S, 1951, My 22,32:4
Lyon, Irving P, 1944, N 14,23:3
Lyon, Irving W, 1961, Ja 3,29:3
Lyon, Israel Whitney Dr, 1907, F 23,9:6
Lyon, J Denniston, 1939, Ag 15,19:6
Lyon, James A, 1955, Ag 5,19:4
Lyon, James B, 1959, Ap 15,33:1
Lyon, James B Jr, 1939, Mr 5,48:6
Lyon, Jean, 1960, Ag 31,29:4
Lyon, Jesse, 1951, Mr 31,15:4
Lyon, John, 1920, Jl 13,11:4
Lyon, John Capt, 1923, F 27,19:1
Lyon, John H, 1914, O 31,11:6; 1946, O 22,25:2
Lyon, John H H, 1961, D 19,33:3
Lyon, John H H (will), 1962, N 16,18:2
Lyon, John J, 1956, Je 19,29:4
Lyon, John R, 1925, Ap 5,5:1
Lyon, John V, 1963, Je 13,33:1
Lyon, Joseph H, 1959, F 3,31:2
Lyon, Leland, 1967, S 27,47:1
Lyon, Leland H, 1957, Ja 1,23:4
Lyon, Leverett S, 1959, S 8,35:2
Lyon, Lewis, 1959, Ja 18,88:1
Lyon, Lorenzo G, 1940, O 24,25:6
Lyon, Louisa C Mrs, 1942, Ag 8,11:4
Lyon, Louisa Mrs, 1943, N 15,19:4
Lyon, Moses H, 1945, Ap 25,23:2
Lyon, Newell, 1941, Je 8,49:1
Lyon, Olen J, 1923, Ap 9,17:4
Lyon, Oliver D, 1947, O 30,25:2
Lyon, Paul, 1951, Jl 26,21:5
Lyon, Preston E, 1954, Ap 30,23:5
Lyon, Robert D, 1956, Je 14,33:5
Lyon, Robert G, 1940, Ap 12,24:2
Lyon, Samuel B Dr, 1924, My 13,21:3
Lyon, Samuel J, 1941, Ap 21,19:2
Lyon, Simon, 1946, Ja 29,25:5
Lyon, Theodore E (por), 1938, Je 24,19:4
Lyon, Thomas L, 1938, O 8,17:4
Lyon, Thomas P, 1949, Jl 30,15:2
Lyon, Thomas S, 1946, Je 2,44:4
Lyon, Thompson H, 1954, Je 11,23:5
Lyon, W C, 1932, Mr 27,II,5:7
Lyon, W J, 1903, Je 17,9:6
Lyon, W Wallace, 1942, O 12,17:4
Lyon, Walter J, 1962, F 6,32:5
Lyon, William E Jr, 1949, Je 1,32:4
Lyon, William H, 1944, Jl 26,19:3
Lyon, William I, 1938, Je 14,21:5
Lyon, William J, 1950, D 28,25:1
Lyon, William L Mrs, 1956, Je 3,85:1
Lyon, William P, 1949, D 16,31:1
Lyon, William R, 1951, Ap 23,25:4
Lyon, William S, 1916, Ag 25,7:6
Lyon, William W, 1908, O 8,9:4
Lyon, Willis H, 1950, F 28,29:1
Lyons, Adolph, 1907, F 28,9:7
Lyons, Albert L, 1947, Je 12,25:4
Lyons, Alex (por), 1939, Je 7,23:3
Lyons, Arthur J, 1939, D 29,15:3
Lyons, Barrow, 1959, Ap 7,33:2
Lyons, Bernard, 1957, S 21,19:6
Lyons, Bernard A, 1959, Ag 15,17:4
Lyons, C Raymond, 1939, Ap 15,19:5
Lyons, Champ, 1965, O 25,37:4
Lyons, Charles, 1943, N 6,13:2
Lyons, Charles H, 1942, Je 25,23:4
Lyons, Charles M, 1951, Jl 6,23:2
Lyons, Charles S, 1937, Mr 23,24:1
Lyons, Charles W, 1939, F 1,21:3
Lyons, Clarence B, 1952, Jl 21,19:4
Lyons, Clifton Mrs, 1945, Jl 10,11:3
Lyons, Daniel A, 1949, S 1,21:2
Lyons, Daniel L, 1962, My 22,37:4
Lyons, Dennis A, 1947, S 5,19:3
Lyons, Earl W, 1952, My 19,17:5
Lyons, Edgar W, 1956, Ja 25,31:3
Lyons, Edmund, 1906, Je 17,9:6
Lyons, Edmund Baron, 1858, D 14,4:5
Lyons, Edward (por), 1938, Jl 21,21:3
Lyons, Edward, 1957, N 8,29:5
Lyons, Edward J, 1945, Mr 9,19:4
Lyons, Edward M L, 1950, My 5,21:1
Lyons, Edward Mrs, 1937, N 19,23:4
Lyons, Edward P, 1950, Jl 25,27:3
Lyons, Edwin J, 1965, Mr 8,29:1
Lyons, Elizabeth M, 1950, Jl 5,1:6
Lyons, Ernest C, 1950, O 11,33:2
Lyons, Ethel H, 1946, Ag 2,19:3
Lyons, Francis P, 1943, Ap 24,13:2
Lyons, Frank J, 1968, F 14,47:4
Lyons, Garrett E, 1960, F 7,84:5
Lyons, George, 1958, F 2,87:1
Lyons, George C, 1951, My 10,31:4
Lyons, Grace, 1953, Ag 3,17:6
Lyons, Grace M, 1953, Ja 9,21:3

Lyons, Harry, 1944, Ja 31,17:4
Lyons, Harry C, 1946, F 27,25:6
Lyons, Harry V, 1945, O 30,19:3
Lyons, Harry V Mrs, 1950, Ap 26,29:4
Lyons, Hattie M Mrs, 1953, Je 21,85:2
Lyons, Henry G, 1944, Ag 11,15:4
Lyons, Henry J Rev, 1919, Ap 3,11:4
Lyons, Hugh J, 1942, Jl 18,13:2
Lyons, J A, 1882, Je 10,8:5
Lyons, J Austin, 1945, O 11,23:1
Lyons, J Curtis, 1964, Ag 24,27:6
Lyons, J J Rev (see also Ag 14), 1877, Ag 16,8:3
Lyons, J Roger, 1950, F 6,25:6
Lyons, J Sprole, 1942, Jl 13,15:5
Lyons, J Sprole Jr, 1940, D 22,31:1
Lyons, James, 1962, Je 8,31:3
Lyons, James H, 1954, My 23,89:2
Lyons, James J, 1949, O 14,28:3; 1966, Ja 8,25:1
Lyons, James L, 1956, Ag 23,27:4
Lyons, James P, 1950, Je 3,15:6
Lyons, James R, 1940, My 7,25:1
Lyons, James W, 1948, D 1,29:5
Lyons, Jeremiah P, 1963, Jl 19,25:4
Lyons, Jimmy, 1957, Je 13,31:2
Lyons, John, 1957, Ag 15,21:4
Lyons, John A, 1951, Jl 13,21:1; 1955, N 26,19:2
Lyons, John C, 1962, My 5,27:4
Lyons, John D, 1947, Mr 22,13:1
Lyons, John D Sr Mrs, 1949, My 15,90:8
Lyons, John E, 1942, D 19,19:5
Lyons, John F, 1951, Ag 19,86:4
Lyons, John H, 1961, O 27,30:7
Lyons, John J, 1940, N 25,17:4
Lyons, John J (por), 1945, Mr 1,21:1
Lyons, John J Mrs, 1951, N 18,91:2
Lyons, John M, 1939, Ap 23,III,6:6; 1957, Ag 7,27:4; 1958, My 25,87:1
Lyons, John S, 1958, Ja 8,45:1
Lyons, John Sr, 1948, F 29,60:4
Lyons, John W, 1905, Je 6,16:3
Lyons, Joseph A, 1939, Ap 10,5:5
Lyons, Joseph B, 1950, F 15,27:1
Lyons, Joseph Sir, 1917, Je 22,13:4
Lyons, Julius J, 1920, Je 3,11:4
Lyons, Justin J, 1956, My 27,88:6
Lyons, Karl M, 1955, N 16,35:2
Lyons, Kenneth, 1947, F 11,27:2
Lyons, Kermit (Ken), 1949, Ag 24,25:4
Lyons, L K, 1903, O 10,9:6
Lyons, Lawrence E, 1939, D 3,60:4
Lyons, Lawrence W, 1953, O 19,21:5
Lyons, Leo J, 1943, Jl 15,21:5
Lyons, Leo T, 1960, Jl 6,33:3
Lyons, Leopold, 1914, Ag 3,11:4
Lyons, Margaret V, 1960, S 22,27:4
Lyons, Martha S Mrs, 1942, Je 4,19:6
Lyons, Martin, 1922, O 9,15:6
Lyons, Martin J Capt, 1920, Jl 23,15:4
Lyons, Martin J Sr, 1944, F 26,13:1
Lyons, Mary L C Mrs, 1940, S 6,21:4
Lyons, Michael A, 1950, N 8,29:3
Lyons, Michael J, 1937, Ag 17,19:2; 1943, F 22,17:3; 1955, Je 7,25:6
Lyons, Michael T, 1966, S 17,29:4
Lyons, Nathan, 1946, Mr 27,27:1
Lyons, Nathaniel H, 1946, Je 18,25:4
Lyons, Nathaniel P, 1954, Ap 19,23:1
Lyons, Patrick, 1937, S 30,23:3; 1949, Ap 28,31:1
Lyons, Phil A, 1953, Je 9,27:3
Lyons, Phillip D, 1957, My 5,88:7
Lyons, R B P Lord, 1887, D 6,5:4
Lyons, Ralph J, 1945, Mr 3,13:5
Lyons, Richard J, 1959, Mr 15,89:1
Lyons, Robert E, 1946, N 26,29:4
Lyons, Robert G, 1955, F 11,23:5
Lyons, Robert J, 1950, Mr 19,92:3; 1965, Ja 2,19:1
Lyons, Robert W, 1949, F 4,24:2
Lyons, Ruth Mrs, 1951, Mr 8,29:4
Lyons, Samuel T, 1941, D 8,23:4
Lyons, Sen, 1871, Mr 13,5:1
Lyons, Stephen M, 1967, Jl 19,39:4
Lyons, Thomas A, 1940, S 30,17:4
Lyons, Thomas C, 1962, N 29,38:1
Lyons, Thomas D, 1950, S 23,17:2
Lyons, Thomas F, 1947, My 25,60:3
Lyons, Thomas H, 1946, My 22,21:5
Lyons, Thomas J, 1939, Ja 1,24:6
Lyons, Thomas J (por), 1943, My 8,15:1
Lyons, Thomas J, 1951, My 31,27:2
Lyons, Vincent, 1955, N 16,35:4
Lyons, Virginia, 1952, O 23,26:8
Lyons, W F Capt, 1871, Ag 11,8:4
Lyons, Wallace F H, 1938, O 20,23:2
Lyons, William, 1944, F 17,19:5
Lyons, William C, 1945, Je 14,19:4
Lyons, William E, 1921, Jl 3,18:2; 1948, Ag 29,56:5
Lyons, William F, 1941, Jl 4,13:2
Lyons, William H, 1904, N 12,2:1; 1943, Ap 30,21:1
Lyons, William Heath, 1908, My 3,11:4
Lyons, William J, 1945, N 22,35:4
Lyons, William T, 1952, Mr 3,21:2
Lyons, William T Mrs, 1948, S 14,29:3
Lyot, Bernard, 1952, Ap 3,35:3
Lyra, Charles, 1941, Ja 13,15:3
Lyra, Charles Mrs, 1947, S 16,23:3
Lys, Francis J, 1947, O 2,27:4
Lysaght, John J, 1951, Ja 6,15:3
Lysaght, Patrick (see also Jl 25), 1876, Jl 28,8:4
Lysaght, William R, 1945, Ap 28,15:3
Lysen, Arnoldus, 1946, Jl 12,17:3
Lyses, Charlotte, 1956, Ap 8,84:1
Lyska, Naardyn Mrs, 1946, Jl 9,21:3
Lysle, Edmond, 1953, S 2,25:4
Lysle, George H, 1947, S 25,29:2
Lysons, J Will, 1941, Jl 5,11:4
Lystad, Isak, 1945, My 30,19:4
Lyster, Arthur L S, 1957, Ag 6,27:4
Lyster, Morton J, 1944, D 1,23:2
Lyster, William J, 1947, My 22,27:3
Lytell, Bert, 1954, S 29,31:1
Lytell, Wilfred (cor, S 12,84:6), 1954, S 11,17:5
Lyter, J Wn, 1925, F 10,23:3
Lythgoe, A M, 1934, Ja 30,19:1
Lytle, George B, 1947, Jl 28,15:1
Lytle, Herbert C Jr, 1950, S 2,15:2
Lytle, Herbert J, 1951, Ja 5,21:3
Lytle, Isaac W, 1942, O 22,21:6
Lytle, James B, 1940, Ag 14,19:5
Lytle, Lafayette D, 1949, Ap 28,31:4
Lytle, Robert P, 1963, Ag 8,27:6
Lytle, Wallace B Mrs, 1941, Ap 17,23:3
Lyttelton, George William Spencer, 1913, D 6,11:6
Lyttle, J L, 1930, Ap 3,31:3
Lyttle, John D, 1948, N 27,17:6
Lyttle, Joseph Jr, 1959, F 4,33:4
Lyttle, Samuel L Mrs, 1953, Jl 9,25:5
Lyttleton, Donald V Mrs, 1947, Ag 24,56:2
Lyttleton, Edith, 1948, S 3,19:5
Lyttleton, Edward, 1942, Ja 27,21:4
Lyttleton, G W, 1876, Ap 21,4:7
Lytton, Constance Lady, 1923, My 23,21:4
Lytton, Countess, 1882, Mr 27,2:7
Lytton, Earl (E R Bulwer), 1891, N 25,1:5
Lytton, H, 1936, Ag 16,II,7:1
Lytton, Lord, 1873, Ja 19,1:3
Lytton, Nevile S Earl, 1951, F 10,13:3
Lytwnenko, Serhiy, 1964, Je 24,37:4
Lyveden, Lady (J Emory), 1949, Mr 26,7:8
Lyveden, Lord, 1926, D 30,19:3

Mac, Mc

MacAaron, Walter S, 1941, N 13,27:2
McAbee, James L, 1938, O 7,23:5
McAbee, Joseph J, 1951, S 19,31:3
McAdam, Charles V Mrs, 1965, Ja 19,33:3
MacAdam, David H, 1962, Jl 21,19:3
McAdam, Dunlap J Dr, 1925, F 16,19:4
MacAdam, E Wallace, 1953, N 18,31:3
McAdam, George Harrison, 1925, N 5,23:6
McAdam, George Mrs (Ann Fletcher), 1958, Jl 1, 31:1
McAdam, Henry Mrs, 1905, Ap 24,9:6
McAdam, Kyrie F, 1968, Jl 30,39:2
MacAdam, Thomas, 1907, Ap 20,9:6
McAdam, William A, 1949, D 9,31:1
McAdams, Edgar M, 1948, D 29,21:3
McAdams, Harold, 1960, Ap 3,86:8
McAdams, Henry W, 1905, Ap 28,2:3
McAdams, James, 1948, N 25,31:5
McAdams, James V Ex-Judge, 1924, Ja 29,19:3
McAdams, Raymond N, 1949, Ap 11,25:5
McAdams, Sherry T Jr, 1952, D 15,25:3
McAdams, Thomas B, 1958, Ja 2,29:2
McAdams, William, 1948, D 28,21:3
McAdams, William D, 1954, Ag 16,17:3
McAdie, Alexander G, 1943, N 3,25:4
MacAdie, Donald (funl, Ag 4,81:1), 1963, Ag 2,27:2
McAdie, Jack B, 1950, S 13,27:2
McAdie, William, 1943, S 30,21:1
McAdoo, Eva T, 1942, My 15,19:2
McAdoo, Henry M, 1951, Je 6,31:4
McAdoo, Joseph H, 1947, Ja 1,33:1
McAdoo, Malcolm Rose Mrs, 1922, Je 15,19:6
McAdoo, Robert H, 1937, Ja 11,19:4
McAdoo, Rowland H, 1958, Mr 8,17:6
McAdoo, William, 1930, Je 8,1:5
McAdoo, William G (will, F 23,36:5), 1941, F 2,1:5
McAdoo, William G Jr, 1960, N 29,25:6
McAdoo, William G Mrs, 1912, F 22,9:4
McAdow, Finley H, 1941, Ag 22,15:4
McAdow, Richard C Mrs, 1946, Ag 21,27:5
McAfee, Claude M, 1958, Je 24,31:1
McAfee, Cleland B (por), 1944, F 5,15:5
McAfee, Cleland B, 1944, Mr 20,17:2
McAfee, Daniel S, 1954, O 30,17:2
McAfee, Ernie, 1956, Ap 23,31:6
McAfee, Guy, 1960, F 21,92:7
McAfee, Helen, 1956, Mr 13,27:4
McAfee, Howard B, 1949, Jl 21,25:1
McAfee, James, 1884, O 2,5:5
McAfee, James B, 1954, Je 28,19:5
McAfee, James M, 1952, Ag 14,23:4
McAfee, Joseph E, 1947, Mr 15,13:3
McAfee, Knox Jr, 1953, Je 1,23:6
McAfee, Knox Lt-Col, 1925, F 27,17:6
McAfee, Lloyd T, 1942, Ja 3,19:1
McAfee, T C Col, 1903, N 26,1:4
McAfee, Thomas H Rev Dr, 1923, Jl 21,9:7
McAfee, W, 1883, O 7,2:2
McAfee, William F, 1941, O 18,19:6; 1958, Jl 9,54:1
McAffee, Jane R, 1943, Jl 13,21:5
Macaffee, John Blair, 1921, Ja 12,15:5
MacAffer, Kenneth S, 1964, Ja 11,23:2
McAghon, Cecilia W Mrs, 1940, Je 18,23:5
McAghon, Helen R, 1961, Jl 11,31:4
McAghon, Justin, 1956, N 2,27:2
McAghon, Margaret A, 1960, O 13,37:5
MacAlarney, Emma Lenore, 1925, S 15,25:4
McAlarney, John H, 1938, N 4,23:3
MacAlarney, Robert E, 1945, N 16,19:1
McAlaster, Miles D Gen, 1869, Ap 26,5:1
McAleenan, Arthur, 1947, Mr 24,25:4
McAleenan, Henry, 1913, N 25,11:6; 1948, D 7,31:3
McAleenan, Henry A (por), 1941, Je 4,23:5
McAleenan, J Austin Jr, 1957, Je 19,35:1
McAleenan, Joseph A Mrs, 1957, N 10,86:6
McAleer, George T, 1949, My 1,88:2
McAleer, Gerald A, 1941, F 1,18:3
McAleer, Hugh K, 1941, My 14,21:5
McAleer, J R, 1931, Ap 30,17:8
McAleer, John J Sr, 1959, S 1,29:2
McAleer, Joseph J, 1948, F 4,23:3
McAleer, Mary F, 1910, D 13,13:5
McAleer, Owen, 1944, Mr 10,15:5
McAleer, Ralph E, 1964, Jl 8,35:1
McAleer, Raymond V, 1962, F 28,25:5
McAleer, Thomas J, 1954, S 29,31:6
McAleer, William, 1912, Ap 20,15:5; 1952, Je 12,33:1
McAleer, William S, 1938, My 7,15:5
MacAleese, William J, 1946, Jl 22,21:2
McAlexander, U G, 1936, S 19,17:1
McAliley, R George Mrs, 1943, O 19,19:5
McAlinn, Edward J, 1950, Jl 25,27:3
MacAlister, Alex, 1938, N 23,21:1
Macalister, George R, 1960, Je 29,33:4
McAlister, Hill, 1959, N 1,86:5
McAlister, John A, 1940, Jl 12,15:4
McAlister, John B, 1948, Jl 26,17:2
McAlister, Mary T, 1938, O 13,23:2
McAlister, Percy A, 1938, My 11,19:4
Macalister, Robert, 1950, Ap 28,21:5
McAlister, Robert A, 1945, Ja 6,11:4
McAlister, William H, 1925, D 26,15:6
Macalister, William Jr, 1940, O 28,17:6
McAlister, William K Ex-Justice, 1923, My 18,19:3
MacAlister, William W, 1946, Je 24,31:3
McAll, Percy L Dr, 1937, Mr 11,24:1
McAll, Reginald L, 1954, Jl 12,19:3
McAllen, Robert G Mrs, 1967, S 15,47:1
Macallister, A K, 1942, Mr 17,21:5
McAllister, A R, 1944, O 1,46:1
McAllister, Addams S, 1946, N 27,25:3
McAllister, Albert R, 1948, F 25,23:4
McAllister, Alec Graham, 1916, S 17,19:4
McAllister, Alex J, 1937, Mr 18,25:3
McAllister, Alice Mrs, 1907, Mr 25,7:6
McAllister, Andrew, 1938, Ag 26,17:3
MacAllister, Archibald T, 1966, D 14,47:3
McAllister, Arthur D, 1957, My 5,88:8
McAllister, C A, 1932, Ja 7,23:5
McAllister, Charles L, 1947, Ag 6,23:3
McAllister, Clifford Taber Mrs, 1922, S 26,17:5
McAllister, Dan F, 1943, Jl 15,21:3
McAllister, Daniel Capt, 1920, O 26,17:4
McAllister, Daniel F, 1939, F 13,15:3
McAllister, Earl C, 1955, O 26,31:1
McAllister, Edward, 1948, S 25,17:5
McAllister, Elmer A, 1951, Ap 15,93:1
McAllister, Frank E, 1948, O 31,88:7
McAllister, Frederick D, 1942, N 18,25:2
McAllister, G Stanley Mrs, 1949, Mr 19,15:3
McAllister, George F Col, 1937, O 19,25:1
McAllister, George Mrs, 1950, N 14,31:4
MacAllister, Gordon R, 1945, Ag 17,17:5
McAllister, Gordon Rutherford, 1924, Ja 8,23:3
McAllister, Grace, 1950, F 15,27:1
McAllister, Herbert T, 1951, D 7,27:2
McAllister, Heyward Hall, 1925, D 2,25:4
McAllister, Hugh N, 1873, My 6,4:7
McAllister, J D, 1939, My 11,25:3
McAllister, J Edgar (will), 1959, Jl 22,8:6
McAllister, Jack, 1946, O 19,21:1
McAllister, James, 1946, Ja 15,23:4
McAllister, James A, 1955, N 1,31:4
McAllister, James Capt, 1916, N 7,11:4
MacAllister, James Dr, 1913, D 13,13:6
McAllister, James E, 1952, Ag 29,23:3
McAllister, James J, 1947, O 4,17:5
McAllister, Jeanne Mrs, 1939, S 15,23:1
McAllister, John, 1942, F 8,48:7; 1947, Mr 22,13:3
McAllister, John E, 1940, S 26,23:5
McAllister, M H, 1865, D 23,8:3
McAllister, Ottawa, 1947, Mr 8,13:4
McAllister, Peter F, 1946, S 6,22:2
McAllister, Ralph J, 1947, My 16,23:4
McAllister, Robert E, 1960, O 14,33:2
McAllister, Robert F, 1962, O 25,39:2
McAllister, Robert S Mrs, 1941, Je 5,23:3
McAllister, Rose A, 1950, Ag 31,25:4
McAllister, Sam A, 1903, S 16,9:6
McAllister, Sydney G, 1946, D 26,25:2
McAllister, Ward, 1895, F 1,1:3
McAllister, Ward Judge, 1908, Ap 1,7:5
McAllister, Ward Mrs, 1909, O 14,9:6
McAllister, William, 1880, Ja 6,8:3; 1912, Mr 25,11:4
McAllister, William A, 1945, Ja 12,15:5
McAllister, William B, 1956, My 9,33:4
McAllister, William F, 1950, Ag 16,29:4
MacAlman, John H, 1944, Ja 7,17:4
McAloon, Charles A, 1949, N 20,92:3
McAloon, Charles P, 1948, S 9,27:5
McAloon, Maurice G A, 1954, Ja 14,29:1
McAloon, Raymond F, 1950, Mr 6,21:4
McAloon, Vincent J, 1954, Ap 1,32:3
McAlphin, Kenneth R, 1964, F 10,27:4
McAlpin, Allan H, 1946, D 25,29:3
McAlpin, Allan H Mrs, 1956, Je 7,31:5
McAlpin, Benjamin B, 1960, Mr 15,39:2
McAlpin, Charles W, 1942, F 3,19:1
McAlpin, Charles W Mrs, 1949, My 16,21:2
McAlpin, David H 2d Mrs, 1945, Ja 10,23:2
McAlpin, Donald M, 1949, Ja 15,17:4
McAlpin, E A Mrs, 1908, Mr 11,7:5
McAlpin, Edwin A Gen, 1917, Ap 13,13:5
McAlpin, George L, 1922, N 28,21:4
McAlpin, John V, 1955, O 5,35:5
McAlpin, M Louise Mrs (will, My 5,21:2), 1938, My 2,17:4
McAlpin, William Letham, 1917, Ag 30,11:6
McAlpine, Arch D, 1949, F 28,19:4
McAlpine, C A, 1903, Ap 28,9:6
McAlpine, C Le G, 1884, Ja 12,5:3
McAlpine, Charles A, 1945, Ag 7,23:1
MacAlpine, Charles S, 1938, O 25,23:3
Macalpine, J Kenneth, 1956, N 9,29:3
MacAlpine, J Wallace, 1945, Jl 20,19:5
McAlpine, James E, 1946, Mr 28,25:1
McAlpine, Malcolm, 1967, Ap 14,39:1
MacAlpine, William, 1940, Ap 4,23:4
McAlster, William J, 1937, D 2,25:5
Macaluso, Vincent, 1946, Je 6,21:1
McAlvanah, Charles A, 1950, Je 6,29:3
McAmis, Hugh J, 1942, Ag 21,19:3
Macan, Robert J Mrs, 1945, Ja 11,23:4
McAnally, Bertha Mrs, 1944, O 14,13:4
McAnaney, Edward G, 1955, My 13,25:1
McAnaney, Edward G Mrs, 1956, Ja 1,51:1
McAnaney, George D, 1956, O 17,35:5
McAnany, Hugh, 1944, Je 3,13:2
McAnarney, Jeremiah J, 1942, F 5,21:2
McAnarney, John W, 1948, My 31,19:5
McAndless, Alva J, 1954, Ja 27,27:1
McAndrew, Dorothy, 1950, D 16,17:3
McAndrew, E B, 1943, Mr 16,19:3
McAndrew, Frank A, 1951, S 26,31:3
McAndrew, George, 1967, D 24,49:1
McAndrew, George J Mrs, 1948, N 17,27:5
McAndrew, John J, 1954, N 6,17:2
McAndrew, Joseph A, 1956, D 28,21:1
McAndrew, Patrick H, 1946, Mr 2,13:6
McAndrew, Thomas R, 1946, S 4,24:2
McAndrew, William (por), 1937, Je 29,21:1
McAndrew, William, 1949, Jl 10,57:1
McAndrews, Charles A, 1945, Je 6,21:3
McAndrews, David W, 1942, N 6,23:2
McAndrews, J R, 1928, Mr 11,II,7:1
McAndrews, James A, 1942, S 2,23:4
McAndrews, James W Maj-Gen (funl, My 3,21:5), 1922, My 1,17:2
McAndrews, Joseph J, 1943, My 19,25:2
McAndrews, Martin Mrs, 1948, S 22,32:2
MacAndrews, Richard H, 1964, S 10,35:1
McAndrews, Thomas F, 1966, My 28,27:1
McAndrews, William Robert, 1968, My 31,29:1
McAneny, George, 1953, Jl 30,23:1
McAneny, George F Mrs, 1925, Ag 11,21:3
McAneny, George Mrs, 1966, N 22,45:6
McAneny, Harold D, 1937, S 21,35:5
McAneny, Leonard G, 1953, Ja 28,27:3
McAnerney, J, 1928, Mr 23,21:3
McAnerney, Joseph A, 1954, My 24,27:6
McAnge, William N Jr, 1940, Ag 31,13:6
Macann, Theodore H, 1942, Jl 14,20:3
McAnney, Burnett O, 1962, Ag 30,29:4
McAnney, Ells T Mrs, 1941, Ap 23,21:1
McAnulty, John B, 1967, My 29,25:4
Macara, C Sir, 1929, Ja 3,27:5
McAra, Thomas, 1942, D 12,17:5
MacAran, Charles, 1955, Je 9,29:4
Macardell, Abram, 1958, Ja 11,17:4
McArdell, Abram B Mrs, 1953, Ap 25,15:5
McArdle, Andrew P, 1950, Je 2,23:3
McArdle, Arthur B, 1937, D 26,II,7:1
McArdle, Edward A, 1950, My 5,22:3
McArdle, Edward F, 1924, Ja 3,17:3
McArdle, Florence E, 1950, Je 10,17:2
McArdle, Francis H, 1951, S 2,49:1
McArdle, Frank P, 1941, S 18,25:4
McArdle, J, 1880, Jl 12,8:6
McArdle, J H, 1928, Mr 26,21:3
McArdle, James N, 1960, F 10,37:3
McArdle, John J, 1943, O 24,44:5
McArdle, Joseph D (funl, Jl 8,11:2), 1919, Jl 7,13
McArdle, Joseph H, 1938, O 24,17:6
McArdle, Joseph J (por), 1947, Jl 16,23:3
McArdle, Joseph Mrs, 1948, D 11,15:2
McArdle, Mary, 1942, Je 7,43:3
McArdle, Patrick J, 1941, O 17,23:4
McArdle, Peter J, 1940, Ja 2,20:1
McArdle, Phil J, 1950, Ap 3,23:5
McArdle, Thomas J, 1950, My 21,104:6
McArdle, Tom, 1949, D 19,27:5
McAree, John V, 1958, Mr 23,88:3
McAree, Joseph F, 1946, N 21,31:4
McArevey, John A, 1941, Jl 24,17:5
Macarius, Metropolitan, 1950, Je 29,29:3
MacArness, Charles, 1922, My 6,11:5
Macarow, Daniel, 1950, Ja 8,76:4
McArron, Edward T, 1954, My 2,89:1
MacArt, James A, 1962, O 13,25:5
McArthur, A F, 1926, D 2,27:3
McArthur, Alan G (will), 1940, Mr 30,9:1
McArthur, Alex S, 1949, Ap 7,29:5
MacArthur, Angus, 1943, My 10,19:3
McArthur, Anna P Mrs, 1948, Ja 14,25:1
MacArthur, Arthur Capt, 1923, D 3,17:3
MacArthur, Arthur Col, 1914, D 28,9:5
MacArthur, Arthur F Mrs, 1954, Mr 26,21:1
MacArthur, Arthur Lt-Gen, 1912, S 8,II,13:4
MacArthur, Arthur Mrs, 1907, O 20,9:6; 1959, O 27:4
McArthur, Charles, 1910, Jl 4,7:6
MacArthur, Charles (funl, Ap 24,31:3), 1956, Ap 86:4
MacArthur, Charles J, 1964, Je 29,27:4
MacArthur, Chester W, 1956, My 4,25:3
MacArthur, Donald P, 1955, N 19,19:3
MacArthur, Douglas (burial, Ap 12,1:4; est appr, 11,49:7), 1964, Ap 6,1:8

McArthur, Douglas H, 1942, Je 4,19:5
McArthur, Duncan, 1943, Jl 21,15:5
MacArthur, Edward G Mrs, 1959, Ap 12,86:7
MacArthur, Frederick, 1958, N 4,25:5
MacArthur, Frederick Jr, 1958, N 4,25:5
MacArthur, Harry H, 1950, Mr 1,27:1
MacArthur, Henry E, 1949, Ap 20,27:3
MacArthur, James, 1909, F 12,13:5
MacArthur, John A, 1941, Ja 5,44:5
McArthur, John C, 1873, Mr 26,8:4
MacArthur, John Gen, 1906, My 17,9:3
McArthur, John P, 1942, F 20,17:1
McArthur, John R, 1940, F 7,21:4
MacArthur, John R, 1940, D 1,62:4
MacArthur, Kathleen W, 1955, N 15,33:4
McArthur, L L, 1934, N 6,32:3
McArthur, Lawrence H, 1944, Ag 26,11:3
MacArthur, Marian Elizabeth, 1907, Je 16,7:6
MacArthur, Mary (por), 1949, S 23,23:3
MacArthur, Pauline A Mrs, 1941, My 23,21:2
MacArthur, Peter, 1948, S 28,27:4
MacArthur, Richard N, 1956, S 16,85:1
MacArthur, Robert, 1952, Je 12,33:1
McArthur, Robert A, 1947, D 30,23:3
MacArthur, Robert Stuart Dr, 1923, F 26,13:5
McArthur, Silas C H, 1903, Je 25,7:5
MacArthur, Telfer, 1960, Ja 31,92:7
McArthur, Warren, 1961, D 18,35:1
McArthur, William, 1963, O 24,33:4
McArthur, William C, 1950, Jl 11,31:1
McArthur, William G W, 1943, O 6,23:4
McArthur, William T, 1949, N 14,27:4
McArthur, Wood, 1966, My 17,47:4
MacArthur-Onslow, James W, 1946, N 18,23:5
MaCarthy, David R, 1947, N 21,28:2
Macartney, Clarence E, 1957, F 21,27:1
Macartney, Lewis F, 1957, N 2,21:4
Macartney, William N (por), 1940, Je 16,38:6
Macaskie, Francis G, 1952, Ja 21,15:4
McAskill, Joanne, 1949, Ag 2,40:8
McAskill, Norman, 1942, Jl 26,30:7
McAtee, Clyde, 1947, F 22,13:3
McAtee, Frank C, 1953, D 24,15:5
McAtee, Waldo L, 1962, Ja 18,29:4
Macatee, William L, 1950, Je 17,15:1
McAteer, Daniel A, 1960, N 27,86:4
McAteer, Howard W (por), 1946, O 23,27:4
McAteer, James J Rev, 1921, D 4,22:3
McAteer, John L, 1960, My 7,23:4
Macaulay, Alex, 1957, D 2,27:5
Macaulay, Fannie C Mrs, 1941, Ja 8,19:5
Macaulay, Frank A, 1949, N 19,17:6
Macaulay, Genevieve Mrs, 1938, N 25,23:1
Macaulay, Harry A, 1946, Jl 27,17:6
Macaulay, James, 1902, Je 20,9:3
Macaulay, John C Sr, 1951, S 14,25:3
Macaulay, Lillian M, 1942, My 23,13:2
McAulay, Lizzie J, 1937, Ag 10,19:5
Macaulay, Mary J, 1944, Jl 21,19:4
Macaulay, Robert W, 1951, Ag 3,21:3
Macaulay, Rose, 1958, O 31,29:1
Macaulay, Samuel B, 1959, D 3,37:4
Macaulay, Theodore C, 1965, Ap 23,35:6
Macaulay, Thomas Babington Lord (funl, Ja 30,1:5; will, F 10,2:5), 1860, Ja 17,1:2
Macaulay, William J B, 1964, Ja 10,43:2
Macauley, Alvan, 1952, Ja 17,27:1
Macauley, Arthur J, 1953, Ag 19,29:3
McAuley, Arthur P, 1966, Je 14,47:4
Macauley, C R, 1934, N 25,30:1
Macauley, Edward, 1964, My 19,37:4
McAuley, Edward J, 1961, O 26,35:3
Macauley, Ellen M, 1938, Ap 13,25:6
MacAuley, Ernest A, 1952, O 13,21:4
Macauley, George C Rev, 1968, Je 5,47:3
Macauley, Herbert E, 1958, Ap 20,85:1
Macauley, Irving P, 1966, Ap 5,39:1
Macauley, James, 1944, Ja 7,17:2
Macauley, James E, 1946, Je 19,21:1
McAuley, James J, 1961, F 18,19:4
Macauley, John, 1938, S 13,9:1
McAuley, John E, 1946, Ag 23,19:5
Macauley, John Mrs, 1938, S 13,9:1
McAuley, Madeline L, 1953, Ap 3,23:1
MacAuley, Mary Ann Mrs, 1922, Ja 6,17:5
Macauley, Thomas B (por), 1942, Ap 4,13:3
Macauley, Timothy A, 1953, Ap 15,31:3
McAuley, William, 1955, My 20,25:5
McAuliff, Cornelius, 1911, Ap 11,11:5
McAuliffe, Charles H, 1957, N 24,86:5
McAuliffe, Charles H C, 1965, S 5,57:2
McAuliffe, Cornelius G, 1954, N 5,21:4
McAuliffe, Daniel J, 1957, Mr 21,31:1; 1961, Ap 28, 31:4
McAuliffe, David J, 1950, My 12,27:3
McAuliffe, Dennis, 1951, O 15,10:5
McAuliffe, Eugene, 1959, Je 4,31:3
McAuliffe, Eugene P, 1948, Ag 7,15:4
McAuliffe, Everett E, 1946, S 20,31:4
McAuliffe, George B, 1954, O 2,17:6
McAuliffe, Gervais W, 1960, O 18,39:3
McAuliffe, Jack (por), 1937, N 5,23:3
McAuliffe, John, 1947, Ap 30,26:3
McAuliffe, John A, 1952, O 3,23:3
McAuliffe, John E, 1961, Mr 12,86:1
McAuliffe, John J (Bro Alfred Patrick), 1953, Ap 3, 23:2
McAuliffe, Joseph J (por), 1942, Jl 10,17:1
McAuliffe, Joseph J Mrs, 1939, Jl 16,31:4
McAuliffe, Mary G Mrs, 1954, S 24,24:3
McAuliffe, Maurice F (por), 1944, D 16,15:3
McAuliffe, Patrick Mrs, 1962, Ap 2,31:3
McAuliffe, Pierce J, 1964, Je 17,43:3
McAuliffe, Raymond J, 1952, O 12,89:1
McAuliffe, Richard J, 1959, Je 21,92:7
McAuliffe, Thomas, 1961, Ja 30,23:5
McAuliffe, Thomas F, 1922, My 20,15:6
McAuliffe, Vincent J, 1941, S 9,23:1
McAuliffe, William A, 1937, Ag 8,II,6:6
McAuliffe, William B, 1938, Ap 15,19:5
McAuliffe, William H, 1937, D 18,21:5
McAuliffe, William J, 1938, N 3,23:6; 1942, Ja 21,17:2
McAuslan, George R, 1948, Mr 26,21:4
McAveney, William J, 1946, Ag 31,15:6
McAvey, Frank Mrs, 1945, Ja 6,11:3
McAvity, Malcolm, 1944, My 1,15:3
McAvoy, Arthur T, 1953, My 14,29:3
McAvoy, Charles D, 1937, Mr 1,20:1
McAvoy, Clifford T, 1957, Ag 11,80:4
McAvoy, Daniel E, 1922, Jl 5,19:5; 1968, Mr 3,88:8
McAvoy, David H, 1948, My 2,76:5
McAvoy, Earl, 1959, F 28,19:3
Macavoy, Edmund W, 1943, S 30,21:4
McAvoy, Eugene D, 1941, F 28,19:4
McAvoy, F S, 1926, Ag 7,11:5
McAvoy, J J, 1885, My 5,8:2
McAvoy, James E Mrs, 1951, O 28,85:2
McAvoy, James J, 1954, Je 22,27:3
McAvoy, John M Mrs, 1950, N 28,31:1
McAvoy, John V, 1957, Ja 8,31:3
McAvoy, John V Justice, 1937, Ap 13,25:1
McAvoy, Michael J Rev, 1903, O 14,9:6
McAvoy, Minnie B, 1940, N 12,25:2
McAvoy, Oscar J, 1949, Jl 19,29:5
McAvoy, Raymond T, 1962, Ja 31,31:2
McAvoy, T F, 1933, Ag 4,15:1
McAvoy, Thomas D, 1966, F 13,84:3
McAvoy, Thomas J Mrs, 1947, Mr 5,25:3
McAvoy, Thomas P, 1939, F 4,15:1
McAvoy, William (Happy), 1912, Ag 26,9:6
Macavoy, William C Mrs, 1961, My 14,86:3
McAward, Patrick, 1949, Ja 7,21:4
McAweeney, Thomas P, 1955, O 5,35:2
McBain, Donald R, 1951, My 22,31:2
McBain, H L, 1936, My 8,23:1
McBain, Howard L Mrs, 1944, S 29,21:2
McBain, James W, 1953, Mr 13,27:1
McBain, John, 1952, Ja 12,13:3
MacBain, William, 1952, F 9,13:6
McBarron, James F, 1951, F 25,85:1
McBarron, James William, 1907, S 7,9:6
McBarron, John D, 1940, Ag 26,15:3
McBarron, Joseph P Sr, 1944, Mr 1,19:3
McBean, Archie L, 1950, N 23,35:1
McBean, Donald Duncan, 1918, Mr 1,11:5
MacBean, William M, 1924, F 14,17:4
McBee, Augustine E, 1925, O 6,27:4
McBee, Crosswell, 1951, Ag 30,3:6
McBee, Silas, 1951, Je 16,15:4
McBee, Silas Dr, 1924, S 4,19:4
McBerty, Frank R, 1950, F 19,79:2
MacBeth, Alexander B, 1945, Mr 21,23:1
Macbeth, Dare A, 1910, Ap 6,11:5
MacBeth, George A, 1916, F 12,11:5
MacBeth, George Duff, 1968, My 3,47:3
Macbeth, George K, 1953, Ap 22,29:4
Macbeth, George T, 1952, S 6,17:1
Macbeth, Henry Rev, 1937, Je 17,24:1
Macbeth, Madge (Sept 20), 1965, O 11,61:3
Macbeth, Orietta W C Mrs, 1952, Ap 2,33:5
Macbeth, Robert W, 1940, Ag 2,15:4
Macbeth, Wallace D, 1968, Ap 9,47:1
Macbeth, William, 1917, Ag 15,9:4
Macbeth, William J (por), 1937, Ag 6,17:3
MacBeth-Raeburn, Henry, 1947, D 7,76:4
McBey, James, 1959, D 2,43:3
McBoyle, Errol, 1949, N 7,27:3
McBratney, John, 1938, Ap 18,15:4
McBratney, Robert, 1946, S 3,19:4
McBratney, Robert Mrs, 1938, Jl 22,17:3
McBratney, William E, 1951, Ag 5,72:4
McBrayer, Ruben A, 1948, F 23,25:4
MacBrayne, Lewis E, 1954, D 31,13:4
McBrearty, Laurence E, 1961, N 8,35:3
McBrearty, Thomas A, 1940, Jl 7,25:3
McBreath, Ewing C, 1956, N 14,35:4
McBreen, Charles W, 1948, Jl 1,23:4
McBriar, Henry C, 1951, D 30,24:3
McBriarity, Patrick, 1915, O 21,11:4
McBride, Albert E, 1961, My 3,37:4
McBride, Allan C, 1945, Ja 14,5:8
McBride, Andrew F, 1946, Ja 4,21:1
McBride, Andrew J, 1956, Mr 3,19:4
McBride, Andrew S, 1953, Ja 24,15:5
McBride, Anna, 1952, F 4,17:3
McBride, Archie, 1955, Ja 22,11:4
McBride, Arthur F, 1949, D 14,31:3
MacBride, Charles A, 1947, Jl 21,17:5
McBride, Charles B, 1958, S 12,25:2
MacBride, Charles E, 1939, Jl 30,29:1
McBride, Charles J, 1942, D 27,34:7
McBride, Charles L Mrs, 1950, N 24,35:2
McBride, Charles S Mrs, 1944, Ja 12,23:3
McBride, Charles W, 1948, D 23,19:2
McBride, Clifford A, 1960, Jl 12,35:3
McBride, Clyde E Sr, 1967, Ag 22,34:4
McBride, D M, 1957, N 2,21:5
McBride, D Rankin, 1944, S 7,23:6
McBride, Daniel, 1950, Ap 13,29:4
McBride, Daniel J, 1943, Je 20,34:5
McBride, David A, 1955, Jl 3,32:5
McBride, David J, 1956, Ap 17,31:4
McBride, David L, 1941, Ap 21,19:5
MacBride, Donald H, 1957, Je 23,84:3
MacBride, Donald S, 1959, Mr 10,35:2
McBride, Earl, 1951, Ap 7,15:4
McBride, Edward, 1964, Ag 25,33:3
McBride, Elinor, 1940, N 29,21:5
MacBride, Ernest W, 1940, N 20,21:1
McBride, Euclid W, 1954, N 14,89:2
McBride, F Scott, 1955, Ap 24,86:7
McBride, Francis J, 1952, Ag 26,25:3
McBride, Frank A, 1959, Mr 15,88:3
McBride, George H, 1952, Je 30,19:4
McBride, George W Ex-Sen, 1911, Je 20,9:5
McBride, George Washington, 1925, S 4,21:3
McBride, Grace, 1918, D 30,9:4
McBride, Harry A, 1961, Ap 13,35:5
McBride, Henry, 1937, O 8,24:1; 1962, Ap 1,86:4
McBride, Herbert R Mrs, 1967, Ag 19,25:1
McBride, Hesser G, 1949, S 30,23:1
McBride, Howard E, 1942, Mr 21,17:3
McBride, Isaac, 1941, Ag 4,13:5
McBride, J, 1879, My 8,3:3
McBride, J Boyd, 1960, Ja 4,29:4
McBride, J Wilson, 1953, Je 22,21:3
McBride, James E, 1919, Ag 15,11:6
McBride, James E Mrs, 1948, Ja 8,25:2
McBride, James F, 1937, Jl 28,19:4
McBride, James Joseph, 1919, S 16,15:6
McBride, James S, 1947, S 7,60:5
McBride, James T, 1954, Ag 6,17:3
McBride, John, 1917, O 10,11:7; 1942, O 31,15:2
McBride, John B, 1952, Ja 9,29:2
McBride, John C, 1946, Je 2,44:6
McBride, John D, 1943, O 21,27:5
McBride, John F, 1947, Ap 14,27:4
McBride, John J (Exile), 1911, F 10,9:6
McBride, John J, 1950, S 10,92:5; 1957, D 2,27:4
McBride, John L, 1939, D 2,17:4
McBride, John S, 1961, N 29,41:3
McBride, John T, 1943, D 4,13:6
McBride, Joseph M, 1960, My 31,31:1
McBride, Karl R Sr, 1957, Ag 21,27:1
McBride, Margaret Lady, 1937, D 12,II,8:5
McBride, Mary F, 1959, Je 10,37:4
MacBride, Maud G Mrs, 1953, Ap 28,27:4
McBride, Maurice D, 1964, S 13,86:5
McBride, Maurice D Mrs, 1955, Jl 9,15:5
MacBride, Morrison M, 1938, Je 6,17:6
McBride, Paul H, 1942, Ja 1,25:3
McBride, Peter W, 1944, Jl 4,19:1
McBride, R B A Mrs, 1952, Ja 28,17:4
McBride, Ralph C, 1943, N 3,25:4
McBride, Richard Sir, 1917, Ag 7,9:4
MacBride, Robert I, 1940, Ja 7,48:7
McBride, Robert I Mrs, 1947, Ja 14,25:5
McBride, Robert J, 1950, S 12,27:4
McBride, Samuel, 1941, Je 3,21:1
McBride, Samuel Rev Dr, 1916, Je 22,11:6
McBride, Sylvester J, 1938, N 3,23:4
McBride, Thomas C, 1955, N 24,29:4
McBride, Thomas D, 1965, Ap 5,31:2
McBride, Thomas F, 1944, N 6,19:4; 1952, Ag 13,21:4
McBride, William A, 1941, Mr 6,21:6
McBride, William E, 1949, S 30,19:4
MacBride, William J, 1938, S 23,27:3
McBride, William L, 1959, Mr 15,88:5
McBride, William M, 1950, Ag 16,29:3; 1960, Ap 8, 31:3
McBride, William M Mrs, 1957, D 21,19:5
McBridge, Margaret L Mrs, 1950, Ag 13,76:1
McBrien, Frederick G, 1938, Jl 3,12:8
MacBrien, James (por), 1938, Mr 6,II,8:1
McBrien, Robert L, 1946, O 23,27:4
McBrien, William C, 1954, Je 19,15:4
McBrier, Charles E, 1944, F 13,42:1
McBrier, Edwin M, 1956, S 20,33:5
McBrier, Edwin M Mrs, 1938, Ag 11,17:6
McBroom, Claude V, 1958, F 9,88:2
McBroom, Victor, 1959, F 22,88:5
McBryde, John M, 1956, N 23,27:2
McBurney, Charles Dr, 1913, N 8,13:3
McBurney, Charles Mrs, 1913, Je 2,7:4
McBurney, Edgar P (will, Ja 10,15:3), 1940, Ja 7, 49:3
McBurney, Henry, 1956, Jl 3,25:1
McBurney, James Carroll, 1905, Ap 2,9:6

McBurney, James E, 1955, Mr 5,17:5
McBurnie, Thomas, 1938, Ap 22,19:6
McCaa, David G, 1954, Je 24,27:3
McCaa, George S, 1960, N 29,37:4
McCabe, Alex, 1959, Ja 19,27:3
McCabe, Alexander J, 1946, Ja 11,22:2
McCabe, Arthur E, 1945, F 10,11:1
McCabe, Caroline Mrs, 1957, Jl 20,15:6
MacCabe, Charles B, 1940, O 19,17:5
McCabe, Charles B Sr, 1946, My 1,25:3
McCabe, Charles Caldwell Bp, 1906, D 20,3:4
McCabe, Clarence J, 1948, Ag 2,21:5
McCabe, E R Warner, 1960, F 17,35:1
McCabe, Edward, 1922, O 27,17:4
McCabe, Edward J, 1952, Ag 5,19:3
McCabe, Edward J Mrs, 1954, O 30,17:3
McCabe, Elizabeth Mrs, 1940, Jl 22,17:3
McCabe, Ellin B, 1952, Ja 7,19:4
McCabe, Emmett Mrs, 1956, F 17,21:1
McCabe, Eugene, 1944, Mr 29,21:6; 1945, S 20,23:5
McCabe, Eugene F, 1964, Ag 24,27:1
McCabe, Felix F, 1965, Ap 5,31:5
McCabe, Felix R, 1953, My 22,27:5
McCabe, Francis D, 1942, D 19,19:2
McCabe, Francis X, 1948, Jl 3,15:3
McCabe, Frank, 1937, My 13,25:1; 1959, O 3,19:5
McCabe, Frank J, 1947, Jl 9,23:4
McCabe, Frank L, 1946, D 28,15:2
McCabe, Frank M, 1957, Ag 12,19:4
McCabe, Frank Mrs, 1947, Mr 17,23:4
McCabe, Frank V Mrs, 1946, Ag 30,18:2
McCabe, George T, 1955, Ja 1,13:5
McCabe, Guy S, 1949, My 5,28:2
McCabe, Harriet Calista C Mrs, 1919, S 26,13:4
McCabe, Henry J, 1959, Mr 31,29:1
McCabe, Hugh, 1869, Je 10,8:3
McCabe, Hugh P, 1955, Ap 29,23:2
McCabe, Ira E (will), 1957, Jl 2,11:1
McCabe, J J, 1930, Jl 18,19:5
McCabe, J Kenneth (Feb 15), 1963, Ap 1,36:2
McCabe, James A, 1959, Ap 22,33:4
McCabe, James F, 1951, D 14,31:2
McCabe, James P, 1949, Ja 26,25:4
McCabe, James T Sr, 1957, F 3,76:3
McCabe, James W, 1954, Je 10,31:3
McCabe, John J, 1943, Ap 26,19:6; 1945, O 14,44:5
McCabe, John J Rev, 1937, N 14,II,10:5
McCabe, John M Mrs, 1959, S 21,31:3
McCabe, John M Sr, 1949, My 10,25:2
McCabe, John P, 1911, Ja 20,11:4
McCabe, John R, 1943, D 23,19:4
McCabe, John W, 1939, Jl 8,15:1; 1943, S 29,21:2
McCabe, Joseph A, 1955, Ja 30,84:8
McCabe, Joseph V, 1962, Mr 22,35:4
McCabe, Katherine, 1941, Ap 3,23:3
McCabe, Leonard M, 1966, Ap 27,47:2
McCabe, Lida R, 1938, D 10,17:3
McCabe, Louis F, 1964, Ap 7,35:1
McCabe, M Ambrose, 1965, My 29,27:5
McCabe, Margaret F Mrs, 1940, Ap 1,19:4
McCabe, Margaret M Mrs, 1939, My 20,15:4
McCabe, Mary, 1923, Ja 5,11:6; 1941, D 3,25:5; 1949, Ap 26,23:4
McCabe, May N, 1949, Je 24,23:6
McCabe, Michael, 1940, Jl 9,21:6
McCabe, Michael J Rev, 1924, Ja 27,23:2
McCabe, Owen, 1952, Ja 15,27:5
McCabe, Patrick, 1909, O 4,9:3
McCabe, Patrick J, 1946, Ap 28,42:4
McCabe, Peter, 1940, Je 26,23:2
McCabe, Peter F, 1954, O 30,17:5
McCabe, Peter J, 1941, N 29,17:3
McCabe, Richard C, 1950, Ap 13,29:3
McCabe, Robert, 1937, Ja 19,23:4
McCabe, Robert C, 1958, F 28,13:6
McCabe, Robert C Mrs, 1967, Ja 31,31:4
McCabe, Robert J, 1950, Ag 20,77:2
McCabe, Roger D, 1942, Je 18,21:2
McCabe, Rose, 1947, S 9,31:2
McCabe, Sarah C Mrs, 1941, My 30,15:4
McCAbe, Stewart E, 1951, Jl 1,29:1
McCabe, T J Judge, 1903, Ap 18,9:5
McCabe, Thomas, 1909, N 23,9:5
McCabe, Thomas F Mrs, 1952, S 26,21:7
McCabe, Thomas J (por), 1943, Ap 6,21:3
McCabe, Thomas Mrs, 1952, Ap 4,25:3
McCabe, Thomas S, 1938, F 28,15:5
McCabe, Walter L, 1946, O 23,27:3
McCabe, Wilfred E Mrs, 1956, D 7,27:4
McCabe, William, 1924, S 30,23:3
McCabe, William A, 1949, My 28,15:6
McCabe, William F, 1939, F 11,15:6
McCabe, William F Mrs, 1955, My 28,15:6
McCabe, William Gordon Col, 1920, Je 2,11:2
McCAbe, William H, 1951, Ja 14,86:2
McCabe, William J, 1943, O 26,23:3
McCabe, William R, 1958, Ag 14,29:4
McCabe, William W, 1949, Ap 14,25:4
Maccabee, Samuel K, 1951, Ja 4,29:4
Maccabee, William J, 1947, Ja 23,23:3
McCadam, Norvin G, 1950, My 22,21:3
McCadden, David, 1943, S 4,13:3
McCadden, Edmund A, 1951, Je 27,29:5
McCadden, James, 1920, N 12,15:5
McCadden, John F, 1959, S 13,84:7
McCaddin, Howard Mrs, 1962, Ja 5,29:1
McCaddon, Joseph T, 1938, Ja 23,II,9:2
McCafferty, Frank I, 1951, S 3,13:5
McCafferty, Grattan H, 1954, D 1,31:5
McCafferty, James, 1911, Ja 28,11:5
McCafferty, James A, 1946, S 7,15:4
McCafferty, James P Father, 1904, Ja 18,7:4
McCafferty, Joseph P, 1945, Ag 3,17:4
McCafferty, Leroy, 1951, F 22,31:1
McCafferty, Thomas B, 1954, Ap 1,31:2
McCafferty, William J, 1948, Je 2,29:4; 1949, Jl 26, 27:4
McCaffery, Francis, 1962, My 20,87:1
McCaffery, Hugh Mrs, 1943, N 13,28:3
McCaffery, Michael J A, 1912, N 23,15:6
McCaffery, Paul, 1957, Ap 18,29:3
McCaffery, Richard S, 1945, Je 13,23:2
McCaffery, Richard S Mrs, 1961, Je 28,35:3
McCaffery, William T, 1939, Mr 14,21:4
McCaffray, Alys M Mrs (will), 1940, Ag 1,23:2
McCaffray, Arthur J, 1959, F 16,29:1
McCaffrey, Andrew J K M, 1965, Ap 15,33:4
McCaffrey, Carlton J, 1964, Ap 25,29:2
McCaffrey, Cornelius, 1903, D 9,4:5
McCaffrey, Eugene S, 1947, Je 15,60:5
McCaffrey, Floyd E, 1963, Je 3,29:5
McCaffrey, Francis J, 1939, My 12,21:3; 1963, Jl 14, 61:2
McCaffrey, Francis S, 1952, D 27,9:4
McCaffrey, Frank, 1939, Ag 7,15:5
McCaffrey, Frank Mrs, 1948, F 10,23:4
McCaffrey, George H, 1954, Ja 26,27:3
McCaffrey, John, 1939, Ja 3,6:7; 1951, Ag 10,15:4
McCaffrey, John B, 1960, F 5,27:3
McCaffrey, John J, 1956, S 16,84:6
McCaffrey, John P, 1967, Ag 6,76:5
McCaffrey, Joseph A, 1948, Mr 13,15:5; 1953, O 27, 27:3
McCaffrey, Joseph J, 1947, D 3,30:3
McCaffrey, Joseph T, 1957, S 1,56:8
McCaffrey, Joseph V, 1953, F 13,22:4
McCaffrey, Martin J, 1948, Ag 31,26:1
McCaffrey, Mary U Sister, 1955, F 8,27:2
McCaffrey, Michael F, 1956, N 7,31:3
McCaffrey, Michael J, 1945, Ap 12,23:3
McCaffrey, Michael J Mrs, 1949, O 27,27:5
McCaffrey, Patrick J (Bro Dominic Augustine), 1963, D 6,36:2
McCaffrey, Ralph A, 1964, S 18,32:6
McCaffrey, Thomas E, 1950, My 19,27:1
McCaffrey, William J, 1940, My 5,52:2; 1961, Ag 8, 30:1
McCaffry, Frank X, 1922, Mr 29,17:5
McCagg, Edith E K Mrs, 1942, Je 5,17:4
McCagg, George W, 1953, N 18,31:1
McCagg, Louis B, 1964, D 21,29:1
McCagg, Louis B Mrs, 1942, Je 7,42:3
McCague, David J, 1948, F 23,25:4
McCahan, David, 1954, Je 30,27:2
McCahan, Florence P Mrs, 1941, Jl 25,15:2
McCahan, Sarah C, 1947, Ap 25,22:3
McCahery, Patrick, 1955, F 2,27:5
McCahill, Charles F Mrs, 1955, Ag 23,24:2
McCahill, Frank E, 1953, Ap 5,76:3
McCahill, Frank E Mrs, 1937, S 28,23:2
McCahill, James L, 1947, Mr 29,15:4
McCahill, John J, 1955, Jl 30,17:6
McCahill, Thomas J, 1952, N 1,21:6
McCahill, William A, 1952, D 26,15:4
McCahill, William J, 1925, Je 30,19:4; 1925, Jl 2,19:6; 1925, Ag 20,19:6
McCail, G A Gen, 1868, F 27,4:7
McCain, C Curtice, 1942, Jl 15,19:4
McCain, Charles S, 1957, D 14,21:1
McCain, Donald R Mrs, 1955, O 12,31:4
McCain, Donald Rockefeller, 1968, O 28,96:1
McCain, Florence A Mrs, 1937, Ag 20,17:3
McCain, George L, 1945, S 15,15:6
McCain, George N Mrs, 1942, O 12,34:5
McCain, Henry P, 1941, Jl 28,13:2
McCain, John S, 1945, S 7,1:2
McCain, John S Mrs, 1959, My 30,17:2
McCain, Samuel A, 1964, Ap 18,29:4
McCain, William A Mrs, 1942, Jl 3,17:5
McCain, William S, 1964, Ap 14,37:4
McCaleb, Charles A, 1949, O 19,29:2
McCalip, Medford A, 1952, D 21,53:1
McCall, Ambrose V, 1968, Ap 24,47:1
McCall, Ambrose V Sr Mrs, 1957, D 18,35:4
McCall, Arthur G, 1954, O 21,27:3
McCall, Bernard F, 1954, Ag 21,17:5
McCall, Cadmus C, 1953, Mr 14,15:3
McCall, Clifford H Jr, 1965, My 26,47:4
McCall, Edward E (funl, Mr 14,17:3), 1924, Mr 13, 17:4
McCall, Edward E Mrs, 1954, Ap 24,17:4
McCall, Edwin W, 1959, Je 10,37:4
McCall, Emil J, 1955, Mr 3,27:1
McCall, Ernest J, 1950, F 14,25:3
McCall, Francis J, 1963, Jl 21,64:6
McCall, George, 1938, S 24,17:4
McCall, George A, 1956, Ap 17,31:2
McCall, George H, 1944, Je 4,42:3
McCall, Harold, 1960, D 5,31:4
McCall, Henry Sr, 1947, F 3,19:5
McCall, Howard W, 1951, Ap 30,21:2
McCall, James, 1864, Ag 13,4:6; 1923, Ja 1,15:4; 1943, N 17,25:1
McCall, James M, 1954, O 19,27:4
McCall, John, 1954, N 7,87:4
McCall, John A, 1951, Ap 12,33:5
McCall, John C, 1953, S 5,15:3
McCall, John C Mrs, 1946, O 11,23:2
McCall, John T, 1950, F 14,26:5
McCall, Joseph B Jr, 1954, Mr 27,17:4
McCall, Leo H, 1963, Je 23,84:8
McCall, Lizzie, 1942, Ap 19,43:3
McCall, Lois L, 1949, My 5,27:4
McCall, M N, 1947, Mr 10,22:3
McCall, Mary W H Mrs, 1944, O 2,19:5
McCall, Oswald W S, 1959, Je 14,86:6
McCall, Richard C, 1952, S 13,17:6
McCall, Robert S, 1949, D 5,23:5
McCall, Samuel W, 1923, N 5,17:3
McCall, Sidney (Mrs M Fenollosa), 1954, Ja 13,3
McCall, Sydney C, 1949, F 19,15:4
McCall, Thomas, 1965, S 22,6:3
McCall, U L, 1951, Jl 9,25:3
McCall, W Webb, 1953, Ag 15,15:3
McCall, William A, 1903, Ag 30,1:6
McCalla, Bowman H Rear-Adm, 1910, My 7,9:5
McCalla, John Gen, 1873, Mr 2,1:6
McCallen, Edward F, 1952, Je 20,23:6
McCallen, James A Rev, 1912, S 4,11:4
McCallen, Thomas J, 1965, S 15,47:3
McCallie, Edward L, 1960, Jl 21,27:4
McCallie, Joseph M, 1942, Ja 16,21:2
McCallie, Spencer J, 1949, O 19,29:4
McCallin, Edward H, 1938, S 23,27:2
McCallion, Edward Mrs, 1948, Ag 28,15:3
McCallion, Francis J, 1955, Ap 29,23:4
McCallion, James, 1947, O 30,25:4
McCallion, John A, 1950, My 2,29:4
McCallister, William F, 1966, Je 10,45:3
McCallon, Frank A, 1946, Je 15,21:6
MacCallum, Alexander D, 1947, N 16,76:6
McCallum, Archibald J, 1946, Je 15,21:1
McCallum, Archibald R, 1945, My 4,19:3
McCallum, Archie H, 1949, S 9,26:7
McCallum, Arthur, 1953, Ja 15,27:3
MacCallum, B Lawrence, 1952, S 28,77:1
MacCallum, Burnside, 1940, O 14,19:5
McCallum, Chester, 1939, Jl 16,31:2
McCallum, D C Gen, 1878, D 24,2:7
McCallum, Dougall, 1952, My 14,27:4
McCallum, Duncan, 1958, My 11,86:7; 1962, Ag 2 23:4
MacCallum, F M Mrs, 1959, N 7,23:4
McCallum, Frank, 1946, S 26,25:5
MacCallum, Frederick W, 1945, N 30,23:5
McCallum, George B, 1942, S 23,25:6; 1958, Ag 2 15:4
MacCallum, Harry Jr, 1954, My 20,31:3
MacCallum, J D, 1937, Je 26,17:3
McCallum, J S Capt, 1903, S 14,7:5
McCallum, James, 1937, Ag 17,19:3
McCallum, James A, 1938, N 8,23:1
McCallum, James D, 1950, F 5,85:1
McCallum, James I, 1940, F 25,39:2
MacCallum, John A (por), 1946, Ja 1,27:1
McCallum, John Sherman, 1924, My 24,15:4
McCallum, Joseph, 1953, N 13,28:3
McCallum, Lee, 1917, Jl 19,11:5
McCallum, Newton W, 1957, Ap 9,33:3
MacCallum, Norman E, 1946, S 4,24:2
MacCallum, Oda Mrs, 1955, S 14,35:4
McCallum, Russel P, 1960, Je 25,21:7
MacCallum, William B, 1938, N 3,23:6
McCallum, William B, 1946, Jl 23,25:5
McCallum, William G, 1944, F 4,15:1
MacCalman, Douglas R, 1957, F 6,25:5
MacCalman, Duncan, 1938, Mr 16,23:3
McCalmont, Alfred B Gen, 1874, My 10,7:5
McCalmont, David B, 1947, Ag 14,23:2
McCalmont, Harry, 1902, D 9,9:5
McCambley, Bernard, 1938, Ja 29,15:6
McCambley, Felix J, 1963, My 2,35:4
McCambridge, Charles J, 1940, Ja 11,23:4
McCambridge, Leonard A, 1954, N 20,17:1
McCambridge, Leonard A Mrs, 1952, Ag 15,15:2
MacCameron, Robert Lee, 1912, D 30,7:5
McCamic, Mary, 1911, Ag 3,7:5
McCammon, Arthur Mrs, 1964, Mr 5,30:4
McCammon, Bert C, 1956, O 12,29:4
McCammon, Edward E, 1938, My 17,24:4
McCammon, Eva R Mrs, 1954, O 29,21:2
McCammon, Milo F, 1967, Mr 11,29:1
McCammond, William A, 1942, O 1,23:5
McCampbell, Eugene F Dr, 1937, My 9,II,11:1
McCampbell, Leavelle (por), 1946, F 15,25:1
McCampbell, Paul R, 1955, F 3,23:4
McCampbell, Theron, 1941, Ag 5,20:2
McCampell, Coleman W Mrs, 1961, Ja 1,49:2
McCamy, Robert G, 1964, Ag 8,19:5

McCance, Andrew, 1939, Ag 31,19:5
McCance, Edward G, 1951, S 19,31:1
McCance, Robert T, 1948, Je 29,23:2
McCance, William J, 1947, D 28,40:6
McCandless, Alex U, 1954, Ap 1,32:3
McCandless, Bruce Rear-Adm, 1968, Ja 26,47:1
McCandless, Charles W, 1960, Ag 12,19:3
McCandless, Henry W, 1957, D 25,31:3
McCandless, Howard A, 1955, D 1,35:1
McCandless, James S, 1943, My 26,23:6
McCandless, Joseph H, 1951, Ap 3,27:4
McCandless, Lincoln L, 1940, O 7,17:5
McCandless, Margaret Mrs, 1916, Ap 16,21:4
McCandless, Robert, 1945, Je 5,19:3
McCandless, Robert Mrs, 1942, Je 3,24:3
McCandless, Roy A, 1945, Ja 20,11:6
McCandless, Russell, 1952, S 6,17:5
McCandless, Stanley, 1967, Ag 5,21:7
McCandless, Thomas, 1959, Jl 8,29:1
McCandless, Thomas C, 1953, N 28,15:4
McCandless, Thomas Mrs, 1949, Je 18,13:5
McCandless, W Col, 1884, Je 18,4:7
McCandless, Wilson, 1882, Jl 1,2:7
McCandless, Wilson B, 1964, D 12,31:2
McCandlish, Edward G, 1946, D 8,77:5
McCandlish, Howard S, 1955, Ag 28,85:3
McCandliss, Edgar S, 1945, F 9,15:1
McCandliss, Lester C, 1945, N 2,20:3
McCandliss, William K, 1946, O 15,25:4
McCanlass, William A, 1948, My 24,19:4
McCanless, Joseph A, 1949, O 15,15:5
McCanliss, Lee, 1968, Ag 24,29:1
McCann, Alex, 1938, Ap 15,20:2
McCann, Alexander, 1873, O 21,4:7
McCann, Alfred W Sr Mrs, 1945, F 22,27:4
McCann, Andrew Mrs, 1966, Mr 3,33:5
McCann, Bert H, 1940, F 17,13:3
McCann, Charles, 1951, Je 7,33:5
McCann, Charles E F, 1941, F 1,17:1
McCann, Charles E F Mrs (por), 1938, Mr 16,23:3
McCann, Charles H, 1940, Mr 12,23:4
McCann, Charles M, 1959, Mr 7,22:1
McCann, Charles M Mrs (Judith S), 1965, Ag 31, 33:6
McCann, Charles Sr, 1947, Mr 27,27:2
McCann, Chris B, 1949, D 9,31:5
McCann, Don, 1952, F 4,17:3
McCann, Dorothy (Mrs F Lalak), 1961, My 10,45:3
McCann, Dwight G, 1956, Mr 30,19:7
McCann, Edmund G, 1957, Ag 2,19:3
McCann, Edward S, 1966, Ag 27,29:3
McCann, Frank G Mrs, 1946, F 10,42:6
McCann, Frank J, 1942, S 18,22:4; 1956, Ja 29,93:2
McCann, Harrison K, 1962, D 22,8:2
McCann, Harrison K Mrs, 1962, D 22,8:2
McCann, Helen R, 1954, O 9,17:2
McCann, Henry E, 1943, Ap 27,24:2
McCann, Henry F, 1937, S 14,23:4
McCann, Hiram C, 1967, Je 11,87:3
McCann, Hugh, 1950, S 13,27:3
McCann, Isabelle A, 1944, F 26,13:5
McCann, Jack, 1939, Jl 30,29:2
McCann, James, 1904, F 17,9:7; 1925, Mr 22,7:3; 1955, F 17,27:2
McCann, James A, 1952, F 6,29:2
McCann, James B, 1941, O 31,23:1
McCann, James Ferdinand, 1925, S 1,21:5
McCann, James J, 1939, D 29,15:4; 1942, Ag 29,15:4
McCann, James T, 1945, F 19,17:4
McCann, John, 1939, O 10,23:3
McCann, John E, 1943, S 12,53:1
McCann, John H, 1903, S 4,7:7
McCann, John J, 1939, My 12,21:3; 1944, My 16,23:1; 1950, Je 4,92:4; 1959, D 12,23:5
McCann, John P, 1951, Je 13,29:5
McCann, John R, 1952, D 13,21:6
McCann, Joseph A, 1937, Ja 18,17:4
McCann, Joseph J, 1937, Mr 7,II,8:7; 1945, D 24,15:1
McCann, Joseph L, 1942, D 2,25:5
McCann, Joseph P, 1945, Je 26,19:5
McCann, K A, 1926, D 20,21:4
McCann, Kenneth M, 1968, D 12,47:1
McCann, Lillian, 1950, N 12,93:2
McCann, Mary, 1945, O 22,17:4
McCann, Michael J, 1906, Ja 24,9:6
McCann, Patrick J (por), 1942, Je 24,19:5
McCann, Patrick J, 1962, O 27,25:5
McCann, Phil, 1950, Mr 20,21:4
McCann, Phoebe E Mrs, 1954, Jl 25,68:8
McCann, Richard M Mrs, 1956, Je 18,25:5
McCann, Richard Mrs, 1949, F 6,77:1
McCann, Richard P, 1967, N 6,47:3
McCann, Robert E (mem ser set, My 6,32:2), 1961, My 5,9:5
McCann, Rupert, 1958, Je 19,31:6
McCann, Russell B, 1952, Mr 18,27:2
McCann, Sylvester C, 1943, Jl 3,13:5
McCann, Thomas H, 1922, O 26,17:3
McCann, Thomas J Sr, 1942, Mr 2,19:4
McCann, Walter I, 1945, My 10,23:4
McCann, Walter J, 1953, Ja 29,27:2
McCann, Walter L, 1960, N 17,37:3
McCann, Wilhilmina S Mrs, 1954, D 25,11:4
McCann, William B, 1952, O 3,23:2
McCann, William J, 1948, Mr 8,23:6
McCann, William Mrs, 1951, Je 5,31:4
McCann, William Penn, 1906, Ja 16,11:5
McCann, William R, 1949, Ag 7,60:6
McCanna, Benjamin T, 1937, My 8,19:4
McCanna, Pat, 1903, D 11,9:6
McCannel, James, 1939, Je 30,19:2
McCard, Stewart H, 1952, Ag 29,23:3
McCardell, A Leroy, 1945, D 11,25:3
McCardell, Claire (Mrs I D Harris),(funl, Mr 27,-33:5), 1958, Mr 23,1:8
McCardell, Richard P, 1948, Jl 9,19:1
McCardell, Thomas F Capt, 1914, Mr 19,9:5
McCardell, William R, 1941, Ap 20,43:2
McCardle, John, 1949, S 11,V,7:2
MacCardle, Ross C, 1964, Je 25,33:3
McCardy, R H, 1880, Ap 6,5:4
McCargar, Alfred T, 1938, F 13,II,7:1
McCarius, Bro, 1948, F 21,13:4
McCarl, James A, 1953, Ap 22,29:3
McCarl, John R (por), 1940, Ag 3,15:1
McCarley, Henry H, 1961, D 16,25:3
McCarlo, G B, 1903, Je 10,9:5
McCarnes, Mabel F, 1937, My 13,25:4
McCarney, Hugh R Sr, 1952, Jl 3,25:1
McCarney, James F, 1939, Ja 16,15:3
McCarney, John G, 1955, Jl 13,25:4
McCarney, John R, 1948, Mr 4,25:2
McCarney, William L (Billy),(por), 1948, S 25,17:5
MacCarone, Ralph Mrs, 1948, My 12,28:3
McCarran, Mary L, 1966, Mr 26,29:1
McCarran, Pat (funl O 3,87:1), 1954, S 29,1:2
McCarran, Pat Mrs, 1963, Jl 17,31:3
McCarren, Daniel G, 1963, N 8,31:3
McCarren, Frank, 1925, O 14,25:2
McCarren, Frank A, 1938, O 26,23:3
McCarren, Hugh T, 1950, D 25,19:4
McCarren, James J Mrs, 1949, Je 4,13:4
McCarren, Mary Mrs, 1911, Jl 3,7:4
McCarren, Patrick Henry Sen (est), 1915, Jl 3,7:5
McCarren, William J, 1941, Ap 6,48:6; 1952, Ag 5,19:4
McCarriagher, Daniel H (por), 1945, Ap 12,23:4
McCarrick, Francis, 1924, Je 16,15:3; 1951, F 7,26:7
McCarrick, Joseph, 1940, Ap 7,45:2
McCarroll, Betty, 1941, Ja 5,45:1
McCarroll, David R, 1965, D 4,31:2
McCarroll, Henry G, 1950, O 2,23:5
McCarroll, James R T, 1939, F 14,20:2
McCarroll, John J, 1955, Jl 4,11:3
McCarroll, John J Jr, 1950, Jl 29,13:2
McCarroll, Robert A, 1945, My 13,20:6
McCarroll, T Clyde Mrs, 1957, Jl 25,23:2
McCarron, Charles, 1937, Ag 6,17:4
McCarron, Charles R Mrs, 1952, O 22,27:5
McCarron, Francis A, 1960, Ja 4,29:3
McCarron, Hugh M, 1952, Mr 2,92:3
McCarron, James, 1952, F 22,21:1
McCarron, James A, 1952, S 15,25:2; 1960, Ag 1,23:5
McCarron, John J Rev, 1923, Ja 12,15:5
McCarron, Michael L, 1950, Ja 4,35:3
McCarron, Peter A, 1946, F 10,41:1
McCarron, Sarah A, 1964, Ja 10,43:3
McCartan, Edward, 1947, S 22,23:4
McCartan, Frederick S, 1944, My 18,19:2
McCarten, Frederich T, 1950, S 5,27:2
McCarten, George F, 1966, F 16,43:3
McCarter, George Mrs, 1943, Je 24,21:4
McCarter, George W C, 1951, F 7,24:8
McCarter, Henry, 1942, N 21,13:5
McCarter, Leo D, 1947, Ag 22,15:3
McCarter, Louis N, 1945, Ja 30,19:4
McCarter, Margaret H Mrs, 1938, S 1,23:3
McCarter, Maryon C H Mrs (Mrs Hewitt), 1939, My 1,42:1
McCarter, Richard H, 1948, Mr 22,23:5
McCarter, Robert D, 1951, Mr 12,25:4
McCarter, Robert H (por), 1941, My 31,11:1
McCarter, Robert H Mrs, 1938, Ja 9,43:2
McCarter, Thomas N, 1959, N 3,31:1
McCarter, Thomas N Mrs, 1957, D 20,27:2
McCarter, Thomas N Sr, 1955, O 24,27:5
McCarter, U H, 1931, Ag 16,II,6:1
McCarter, Uzal H, 1956, O 26,29:4
McCarter, William H, 1959, Jl 7,33:2
McCarter, William J, 1951, Ja 19,25:2
McCarthy, A J Mrs, 1949, Ja 11,27:1
McCarthy, Agnes M, 1955, Jl 22,23:4
McCarthy, Alan J, 1967, Ag 24,37:4
McCarthy, Albert G Mrs, 1959, Ap 5,86:6
McCarthy, Albert J, 1941, Ap 6,48:7
McCarthy, Albert W, 1948, Ap 14,27:5
McCarthy, Alice R Sister, 1955, N 26,19:4
McCarthy, Arthur C, 1953, Ja 19,23:4
McCarthy, Arthur P, 1946, Je 29,19:2
McCarthy, Benjamin V, 1952, S 6,17:4
McCarthy, C A, 1903, Ag 25,7:6
McCarthy, Cal, 1941, D 19,25:3
McCarthy, Cal J, 1963, Je 17,25:3
McCarthy, Callaghan, 1941, D 22,17:5
McCarthy, Callahan J, 1950, Mr 6,36:3
McCarthy, Catherine J, 1943, F 22,17:1
McCarthy, Catherine M, 1952, Je 9,23:2
McCarthy, Charles A, 1937, Je 16,23:4; 1950, My 24, 29:4
McCarthy, Charles A Dr, 1968, O 7,47:1
McCarthy, Charles D Mrs, 1968, Ja 30,38:3
McCarthy, Charles E, 1944, Jl 4,19:3
McCarthy, Charles E A, 1954, Ap 26,25:5
McCarthy, Charles F, 1942, My 9,13:6; 1944, Ag 8, 17:5; 1964, Je 16,39:3; 1968, Ja 14,84:4
McCarthy, Charles F Mrs, 1947, Mr 13,27:5
McCarthy, Charles H, 1958, S 16,27:3
McCarthy, Charles J, 1905, Je 21,7:7; 1948, F 13,21:1; 1950, Mr 11,15:1; 1952, My 27,27:4; 1957, Mr 20, 37:4
McCarthy, Charles Jr, 1939, Je 8,25:6
McCarthy, Charles L (Clem),(funl plans, Je 6,41:4; funl, Je 8,31:4), 1962, Je 5,41:1
McCarthy, Charles P, 1950, F 6,25:5
McCarthy, Charles S, 1952, O 24,23:3
McCarthy, Charles T, 1938, Ap 27,23:3
McCarthy, Clem Mrs, 1949, Mr 23,27:5
McCarthy, Corbett, 1948, O 16,15:3
McCarthy, Cornelius, 1948, My 7,23:2
McCarthy, Cornelius J, 1947, Je 14,15:2
McCarthy, D F, 1882, Ap 10,5:5
McCarthy, D J, 1954, N 10,33:1
McCarthy, Dan, 1905, F 17,5:6
McCarthy, Daniel F, 1948, Ag 9,19:3; 1950, Mr 22, 27:5; 1950, Jl 13,25:3
McCarthy, Daniel G Rev, 1968, D 18,47:2
McCarthy, Daniel J, 1938, S 15,25:2; 1943, F 22,17:4; 1947, Ap 18,21:2; 1947, Ag 20,21:1; 1958, O 11,23:4; 1967, Ap 15,31:2
McCarthy, Daniel L, 1943, Je 30,21:4
McCarthy, Daniel P, 1943, Ja 26,19:1
McCarthy, Daniel W, 1946, Ja 4,22:3
McCarthy, David M, 1968, O 27,82:2
McCarthy, Delia A Mrs, 1950, Je 25,70:1
McCarthy, Dennis, 1919, O 27,11:5
McCarthy, Dennis J, 1944, N 1,23:2; 1953, Ja 14,31:4
McCarthy, Dennis P, 1946, N 14,29:4
McCarthy, Dennis S, 1945, S 24,19:4
McCarthy, Dennis T, 1939, D 15,25:5
MacCarthy, Desmond, 1952, Je 9,23:3
McCarthy, Edmond F, 1951, O 20,15:5
McCarthy, Edna M, 1956, Ag 9,25:2
McCarthy, Edward E, 1949, O 24,23:3
McCarthy, Edward F, 1955, Je 7,33:4
McCarthy, Edward J, 1941, N 9,52:7; 1956, Ap 15, 89:1; 1957, S 16,31:5
McCarthy, Edward T, 1952, Ja 15,27:3; 1962, Ja 23, 33:1
McCarthy, Edwin H, 1950, D 10,4:3
McCarthy, Elbert T, 1948, Ag 30,17:3
McCarthy, Elizabeth, 1952, D 9,33:1
McCarthy, Ellen Mrs, 1940, D 26,19:3
McCarthy, Ernest C, 1963, N 18,33:4
McCarthy, Eugene, 1903, Ap 27,7:5; 1956, N 2,27:4
McCarthy, Eugene A, 1949, D 2,29:1; 1958, Ap 18, 23:4
McCarthy, Eugene C, 1941, Je 6,21:5
McCarthy, Eugene J, 1944, Ag 10,17:5; 1965, Ap 19, 29:4
McCarthy, Eugene T, 1954, O 11,27:5
McCarthy, F J, 1942, Ja 21,17:4
McCarthy, F J A, 1963, Jl 16,31:5
McCarthy, F Joseph, 1964, Mr 6,28:3
McCarthy, Florence, 1865, Ag 22,3:2
McCarthy, Florence (Sister Miriam Francis), 1968, Ja 25,37:2
McCarthy, Francis, 1954, Mr 29,19:4
McCarthy, Francis C, 1942, Jl 14,19:2
McCarthy, Francis J, 1947, Ag 15,17:1
McCarthy, Francis M, 1937, F 15,17:2
McCarthy, Francis P, 1941, F 20,19:1
McCarthy, Francis X, 1951, My 25,27:4
McCarthy, Frank A, 1945, My 27,25:1
McCarthy, Frank A Mrs, 1948, S 17,25:1
McCarthy, Frank B, 1943, O 10,48:7
McCarthy, Frank B Mrs, 1949, D 14,31:5
McCarthy, Frank C, 1938, D 28,21:5
McCarthy, Frank G, 1956, O 5,25:3
McCarthy, Frank J, 1957, O 2,33:4
McCarthy, Frank Mrs, 1949, Mr 16,27:5
McCarthy, Frank P, 1951, Mr 29,27:4
McCarthy, Frank W, 1963, Je 16,84:4
McCarthy, Fred, 1944, Ja 20,19:5
McCarthy, Frederick A, 1943, D 9,27:1
McCarthy, Frederick J, 1950, My 1,25:3
McCarthy, George E, 1950, F 14,25:2
McCarthy, George H, 1939, My 31,23:2; 1951, Mr 27, 29:4
McCarthy, George J, 1950, Ja 21,17:4
McCarthy, George L, 1918, Je 14,11:4; 1954, Jl 11, 72:1; 1963, Jl 10,35:2
McCarthy, George T, 1942, Ag 26,19:6
McCarthy, George T Jr, 1950, D 16,17:5
McCarthy, Gordon T, 1941, Ja 19,40:5
McCarthy, Hamilton T C P, 1939, O 25,23:6
McCarthy, Harriet F Mrs, 1954, D 14,33:1
McCarthy, Harry J, 1945, D 29,14:2
McCarthy, Henry F, 1961, Ja 27,48:1
McCarthy, Henry J, 1939, Ap 26,23:2; 1959, My 20, 35:4

McCarthy, Henry J Judge, 1903, Jl 22,7:6
McCarthy, Howard F, 1960, Je 5,86:2
McCarthy, J, 1936, Mr 22,10:3
McCarthy, J E Mrs, 1952, Mr 13,29:1
McCarthy, J M Mrs, 1944, Ja 30,37:1
McCarthy, James, 1905, Mr 23,9:6; 1925, Jl 12,7:4; 1939, Ag 10,19:2; 1944, Je 23,19:3
McCarthy, James A, 1939, Jl 18,19:6; 1961, D 29, 23:1; 1964, N 7,27:3
McCarthy, James E, 1942, Ja 18,42:2; 1958, Jl 12,15:5
McCarthy, James E Jr, 1950, Jl 8,13:5
McCarthy, James F, 1940, Mr 7,23:6; 1943, Ap 19, 19:5; 1954, My 20,31:2
McCarthy, James J, 1947, F 1,15:3
McCarthy, James L, 1944, F 7,15:6
McCarthy, James P, 1920, D 28,11:4
McCarthy, James R, 1955, Ag 4,25:3
McCarthy, James W (por), 1939, Je 29,23:3
McCarthy, Jane, 1944, Je 15,19:3
McCarthy, Jeremiah J, 1951, Mr 19,27:3
McCarthy, Jerome F, 1952, Mr 21,23:1
McCarthy, Jerry, 1953, F 7,15:2
McCarthy, Jerry Mrs, 1949, O 17,23:5
McCarthy, John, 1903, My 14,9:6; 1943, Ap 13,26:2; 1949, D 21,30:4
McCarthy, John A (por), 1939, Ap 5,25:4
McCarthy, John A (Fishhooks),(will, F 4,27:5), 1955, Ja 25,25:7
McCarthy, John A Mrs, 1951, Ja 16,29:3
McCarthy, John C, 1937, Ja 19,23:5; 1941, My 23,21:5
McCarthy, John D, 1945, Ap 8,35:1; 1955, D 24,13:5
McCarthy, John E (funl plans, Je 17,31:1; funl Je 19,88:2), 1960, Je 16,33:2
McCarthy, John F, 1939, D 10,69:1; 1949, N 14,27:1; 1950, Ja 1,43:1; 1952, Ja 28,17:4; 1958, Jl 8,27:2; 1968, F 11,92:3
McCarthy, John F Msgr, 1968, Je 28,38:1
McCarthy, John Henry, 1908, F 6,7:6
McCarthy, John J, 1941, F 13,19:4; 1942, My 22,21:6; 1943, Mr 11,21:5; 1943, Mr 20,15:1; 1943, Ag 4,17:2; 1946, S 26,25:5; 1950, O 4,31:2; 1951, S 23,86:1; 1952, Ja 17,27:2; 1952, Je 18,27:5; 1953, S 27,86:3; 1957, F 1,25:2; 1958, F 21,23:3
McCarthy, John J Mrs, 1939, N 4,15:5
McCarthy, John L, 1954, Mr 7,90:1; 1954, Jl 11,73:3
McCarthy, John M, 1905, O 21,4:4; 1940, My 21,23:4; 1951, Jl 30,17:3
McCarthy, John Mrs, 1966, My 16,37:3
McCarthy, John T, 1961, F 12,87:2
McCarthy, John V, 1944, My 28,33:2
McCarthy, John W, 1941, S 5,21:5
McCarthy, Joseph, 1943, D 19,49:1; 1960, Ja 1,19:1
MacCarthy, Joseph, 1960, S 20,39:1
McCarthy, Joseph E (funl, S 14,35:2), 1955, S 9,23:2
McCarthy, Joseph F, 1938, S 16,21:3; 1947, Ap 11, 25:5; 1960, Ja 17,86:2; 1965, Ja 22,43:1
McCarthy, Joseph J (por), 1937, F 26,21:3
McCarthy, Joseph P, 1924, My 2,19:5; 1939, D 31,18:5
McCarthy, Joseph R (funl plans, My 4,1:1; funl, My 7,35:1), 1957, My 3,1:8
McCarthy, Joseph T, 1966, Jl 18,27:3
McCarthy, Joseph W, 1965, Jl 26,23:2
McCarthy, Josephine F, 1948, N 2,25:5
McCarthy, Justin, 1912, Ap 25,13:5; 1915, Mr 9,9:4
MacCarthy, Justin, 1960, O 29,8:4
McCarthy, Justin B, 1941, O 15,21:3; 1954, D 31,13:3
McCarthy, Justin F, 1949, Jl 17,56:1
McCarthy, Justin G Sr, 1948, Ag 5,21:6
McCarthy, Justin J (funl plans, D 28,23:1), 1959, D 27,60:4
McCarthy, Katherine F, 1953, Je 9,27:5
McCarthy, Kathryn O Mrs, 1952, Ja 17,28:3
McCarthy, Lawrence, 1941, Jl 7,15:5
McCarthy, Lawrence J, 1950, Ja 27,24:2
McCarthy, Lawrence W, 1954, F 7,89:1
McCarthy, Leigh M, 1959, Mr 27,23:3
McCarthy, Leighton G, 1952, O 6,25:3
McCarthy, Leighton Mrs, 1949, N 7,27:2
McCarthy, Leo D, 1957, Ja 1,23:2
McCarthy, Leo I, 1951, O 10,23:4
McCarthy, Lillah, 1960, Ap 16,17:4
McCarthy, Lorenzo C, 1941, Je 29,32:6
McCarthy, Louis C, 1949, F 24,23:4
McCarthy, Louise, 1946, D 10,31:4
McCarthy, Marie A Mrs, 1940, D 28,15:4
McCarthy, Mary A, 1947, Mr 29,15:3; 1967, Mr 22, 47:3
McCarthy, Mary Mrs, 1922, Mr 31,17:4
McCarthy, Mary R, 1952, S 16,29:5
McCarthy, Matilda L, 1955, Mr 2,27:1
McCarthy, Matthew M, 1954, S 8,31:2
McCarthy, Maurice J (por), 1938, My 9,17:3
McCarthy, Maurice J Sr Mrs, 1945, D 30,14:8; 1959, S 8,35:1
McCarthy, Maurice Jr, 1957, My 26,92:2
McCarthy, Michael F, 1943, Ag 29,39:3; 1964, Je 27, 25:4
McCarthy, Michael J, 1944, Ja 13,21:1; 1945, D 16, 40:1
McCarthy, Michael W, 1963, D 5,45:1
McCarthy, Owen J, 1947, S 11,27:2
McCarthy, P Rev, 1877, Ag 10,3:5
McCarthy, Patrick, 1940, Ap 30,21:5
McCarthy, Patrick (por), 1941, D 12,25:5
McCarthy, Patrick, 1950, Mr 23,29:2; 1951, N 20,31:2
McCarthy, Patrick A, 1959, O 25,86:4
McCarthy, Patrick D Rev Bro, 1968, F 11,92:1
McCarthy, Patrick F, 1940, Ag 25,35:1
McCarthy, Patrick J, 1947, Jl 16,23:2; 1951, My 1, 29:3; 1952, Ap 23,29:3
McCarthy, Peter, 1919, My 30,9:6
McCarthy, Randal J, 1937, O 16,19:2
McCarthy, Ray B, 1950, Ap 17,23:1
McCarthy, Ray Mrs, 1955, Ap 30,17:2
McCarthy, Raymond G, 1964, Je 26,29:1
McCarthy, Robert F Lt, 1937, Jl 2,21:3
McCarthy, Robert H Jr, 1954, N 8,21:4
McCarthy, Robert J, 1952, D 22,25:3
McCarthy, Robert S, 1945, Ja 1,21:4
McCarthy, Roger L, 1949, Jl 1,19:4
McCarthy, Ronald J, 1964, Jl 18,19:6
McCarthy, Sadie J, 1951, Ap 14,15:5
McCarthy, Theodore K, 1963, S 24,39:4
McCarthy, Thomas, 1949, D 9,32:2
McCarthy, Thomas D, 1939, Je 25,37:1
McCarthy, Thomas F, 1921, Ag 10,13:5
McCarthy, Thomas F Mrs, 1968, My 20,47:1
McCarthy, Thomas F X Mrs, 1955, Ap 26,29:2
McCarthy, Thomas J, 1943, D 22,23:3; 1944, Je 4,34:3
McCarthy, Thomas L Mrs, 1954, Ag 24,21:6
McCarthy, Thomas M, 1925, D 23,19:4
McCarthy, Thomas S, 1947, My 10,13:5
McCarthy, Thomas T, 1952, Ag 13,21:1
McCarthy, Timothy F, 1938, F 2,19:5
MacCarthy, Timothy Mrs, 1955, Ag 21,93:2
McCarthy, Vincent J, 1950, S 8,31:1
McCarthy, Vincent P, 1948, N 10,29:1
McCarthy, Walter, 1942, Ag 30,42:4
McCarthy, Walter J, 1954, Ja 23,13:4
McCarthy, William, 1944, Jl 9,35:2; 1950, S 20,31:5
McCarthy, William E, 1949, F 25,24:2; 1962, Jl 15,60:2
McCarthy, William F, 1956, Jl 2,21:4
McCarthy, William G, 1957, Je 30,69:2; 1964, F 26, 35:1
McCarthy, William H, 1958, F 5,27:3
McCarthy, William J, 1918, Mr 1,11:4; 1940, Mr 6, 23:1; 1951, O 29,23:2; 1957, Ja 19,15:3; 1961, D 17, 83:1; 1962, Ja 28,77:2
McCarthy, William M, 1949, N 8,31:3
McCarthy, William M Mrs, 1953, Ag 2,73:3
McCarthy, William P, 1940, O 20,49:1; 1948, Mr 17, 25:3
McCarthy, William T, 1952, Ap 20,93:1
McCarthy, William V, 1954, Ja 12,23:3
McCarthy, William V Mrs, 1945, Ap 20,19:2
McCarthy, Wilson, 1956, F 14,29:1
McCartie, Charles J Mrs, 1909, Jl 3,7:4
McCartin, Henry C, 1904, F 18,9:6
McCartin, M Joseph, 1944, Ag 13,35:1
McCartin, Patrick J Jr, 1949, N 29,29:2
McCartney, Albert J, 1965, Ag 21,21:3
McCartney, Bernard J, 1955, O 1,19:2
McCartney, C Elwood, 1964, Ag 18,31:3
McCartney, David L, 1940, N 14,23:5
McCartney, Elmer Mrs, 1966, Mr 29,41:2
McCartney, Ernest L, 1942, Jl 10,17:4
McCartney, F A, 1871, Jl 20,1:6
MacCartney, F O, 1903, My 26,9:5
McCartney, Frank L, 1961, S 13,45:1
McCartney, Harold S, 1950, N 10,27:3
McCartney, Henry R, 1950, O 14,19:6
McCartney, Hoge, 1938, O 8,23:1
McCartney, Howard J, 1962, Jl 28,19:2
McCartney, James, 1940, Ja 26,17:5
McCartney, James H Mrs, 1944, Je 27,19:5
McCartney, John P, 1947, F 3,19:3
McCartney, Joseph C, 1940, Jl 6,15:7
McCartney, Mary T, 1960, Ja 5,31:2
McCartney, Richard, 1949, O 6,31:1
McCartney, Richard Mrs, 1949, Je 28,27:3
McCartney, Robert A, 1953, Ap 9,27:1
McCartney, Robert H, 1937, Ag 17,19:3
McCartney, William A Rev, 1937, Ap 20,25:3
McCarton, Peter E, 1943, Jl 7,19:3
McCarty, Allen, 1964, S 12,25:6
McCarty, Andrew J, 1953, Ap 30,31:4
McCarty, Barclay V, 1944, Jl 25,19:3
McCarty, C Walter, 1965, Je 24,35:2
McCarty, Charles F, 1965, Ja 31,88:6
McCarty, Charles H, 1965, Ap 8,39:2
McCarty, Dan, 1953, O 1,29:3
McCarty, Earl H (por), 1942, N 3,23:6
McCarty, Edward C Dr, 1937, Ja 2,14:3
McCarty, Edward T, 1946, Je 1,13:3
McCarty, Edward W, 1925, Je 11,19:3; 1939, Ja 8,43:2
McCarty, Ellen, 1942, My 8,23:5
McCarty, Elmer L, 1950, My 31,29:2
McCarty, Frederick E, 1942, Ja 12,15:2
McCarty, George S, 1945, Mr 20,19:4
McCarty, Harold J, 1958, Jl 16,29:5
McCarty, James E Jr, 1962, My 26,25:5
McCarty, John B, 1966, My 15,88:1
McCarty, John H, 1920, O 18,15:1
McCarty, Leroy J, 1950, Ja 20,25:2
McCarty, Louis J, 1940, N 14,23:4
McCarty, Lyman, 1909, O 23,11:2
McCarty, Mary Mrs, 1911, S 24,II,13:5
McCarty, Michael F, 1959, S 3,27:4
McCarty, Milburn, 1959, Je 17,35:4; 1963, Ap 27,8:5
McCarty, Norman, 1937, O 3,II,8:7
McCarty, Rebekah T, 1951, Jl 30,17:3
McCarty, S Williamson Mrs, 1947, Ap 29,27:4
McCarty, T B, 1875, S 27,1:2
McCarty, Thelma Mrs, 1950, My 27,17:1
McCarty, Thomas, 1950, My 8,23:3
McCarty, Thomas J, 1943, Ap 26,19:3
McCarty, Thomas S, 1941, Mr 29,15:2
McCarty, Timothy F Mrs, 1946, Je 1,13:2
McCarty, W Ross Dr, 1968, F 19,39:4
MacCarty, William C, 1964, My 19,37:2
McCarty, William H, 1940, S 11,26:2
McCarty, William M, 1958, S 21,86:1
McCarty, William M Mrs, 1952, D 18,29:4
McCary, Robert L, 1961, Ja 14,23:1
McCash, James Mrs (funl, N 16,9:5), 1909, N 13, 11:6
McCaskey, William S Maj-Gen, 1914, Ag 13,9:5
McCaskie, John, 1946, My 17,21:3
McCaskill, Oliver L, 1953, Ja 15,27:4
McCastline, Robert, 1963, S 14,25:3
McCastline, William H, 1953, Jl 15,25:2
McCathie, David M, 1948, N 19,28:3
McCathran, Wallach A, 1942, O 20,21:3
McCaughan, Russell C, 1957, Mr 22,23:4
McCaughan, W J Rev, 1910, Ag 1,7:2
McCaughey, Anna E, 1950, Ag 31,26:2
McCaughey, Russell J, 1939, My 1,23:5
McCaughey, William J, 1942, N 27,23:3
McCaughlin, Hector, 1903, O 22,7:6
McCaughn, Blakely D, 1942, O 17,15:6
McCaul, Joseph F, 1949, Je 20,19:4
McCaul, Verne James Lt-Gen, 1968, Mr 4,37:3
MacCaulay, James B, 1949, Ja 18,24:2
MacCaulay, Joseph, 1967, O 12,45:3
Maccaulay, William P, 1945, F 18,33:1
McCauley, Charles, 1944, Ap 9,33:2
McCauley, Charles J, 1957, Ap 26,25:4
McCauley, Charles S Commodore, 1869, My 23,1:5
McCauley, Clarice V Mrs, 1938, Je 27,17:5
McCauley, David V, 1950, Mr 4,17:5
McCauley, Dennis, 1912, My 23,13:5
McCauley, E S H Mrs, 1951, N 10,17:6
McCauley, Francis H, 1950, S 6,30:4
McCauley, Francis L, 1958, Ap 10,29:3
McCauley, Harry, 1959, My 30,17:3
McCauley, James J, 1948, Mr 28,49:1
McCauley, James W, 1958, Mr 10,23:3
McCauley, John H, 1964, F 27,31:5
McCauley, John W Dr, 1937, Mr 12,24:2
McCauley, Katharine Gordon, 1947, F 20,26:3
McCauley, Lolita, 1947, Ag 5,25:7
McCauley, Paul J (por), 1941, Jl 3,19:3
McCauley, Paul J Mrs, 1946, D 24,17:1
McCauley, Richard V, 1953, Mr 8,91:1
McCauley, Robert A, 1945, D 15,17:2
McCauley, Thomas H, 1955, O 10,27:5
McCauley, William H, 1943, Jl 4,20:4
McCauley, William J, 1952, Jl 23,23:3
McCaulley, Samuel W, 1946, O 23,27:2
McCaulley, Sybilla, 1903, Ag 1,7:6
McCausland, Benjamin, 1940, O 9,25:5
McCausland, Donald N, 1952, O 8,31:3
McCausland, Elizabeth, 1965, My 17,35:2
McCausland, Frank, 1962, Jl 15,61:1
McCausland, Fred L, 1942, O 5,19:5
McCausland, Irvin, 1952, Ap 13,77:1
McCausland, J, 1927, Ja 24,17:3
McCausland, Maurice M, 1938, Ja 15,15:5
McCausland, William J, 1945, N 6,19:4
McCaustland, Elmer J, 1941, My 17,15:2
McCaw, Henry, 1952, S 16,29:2
McCaw, Hugh C Mrs, 1950, Jl 23,57:1
McCaw, Raymond H (funl plans, Mr 24,39:1; funl 26,31:3), 1959, Mr 23,31:1
McCaw, Samuel J, 1950, Ja 8,78:2
McCaw, Walter D, 1939, Jl 8,15:4
McCaw, William G, 1942, Ap 20,21:5
McCaw, William T, 1941, Ap 5,17:5
McCawley, Edmund S, 1966, Mr 13,86:7
McCawley, Harrison B, 1947, F 17,19:4
McCawley, Sarah H Mrs, 1939, F 20,17:2
McCawley, William M Mrs, 1949, N 5,13:3
McCay, Edward A, 1945, Mr 1,21:4
McCay, Leroy W Dr (por), 1937, Ap 15,23:3
McCay, Michael J, 1958, Je 14,21:6
McCay, Robert W, 1962, Ap 23,29:3
McCay, Winsor Mrs, 1949, Mr 1,25:3
McCernan, Frank E, 1950, Ap 21,23:1
McCernan, John A, 1951, Je 19,29:2
McChain, George G, 1937, Ja 10,II,10:3
McChain, Sidney N, 1955, Ag 14,81:2
MacChesney, C T, 1928, Ag 19,27:3
McChesney, Charles E, 1947, D 5,25:1
McChesney, Charles E Mrs, 1952, Ag 24,89:2
MacChesney, Chester M, 1967, Je 25,69:1
McChesney, Dora G, 1912, Jl 6,7:4
McChesney, Ernest, 1953, N 5,31:5
McChesney, Grant G, 1944, Jl 4,19:4
McChesney, Harvey, 1951, N 14,31:1

McChesney, Herman F, 1949, D 27,24:2
McChesney, J Edward, 1947, Ja 30,25:1
McChesney, J M Col, 1865, Ag 28,5:1
McChesney, John, 1967, O 4,47:2
McChesney, John M Mrs, 1966, Je 5,86:3
McChesney, John P Jr, 1962, S 9,84:7
McChesney, Leonard W Sr, 1951, My 27,69:1
MacChesney, Nathan W, 1954, S 26,86:3
McChesney, Peter Mrs, 1954, Ja 5,27:4
McChesney, Rosalie, 1966, Ja 25,41:1
McChesney, Thomas Dewar, 1918, My 28,13:8
McChesney, William, 1938, Je 19,29:1
McChesney, William F, 1952, S 26,21:3; 1960, Ag 27, 19:5
McChristie, Alice M Mrs, 1948, Mr 16,27:3
McChristie, John C, 1946, Ap 23,21:5
McClafferty, John Mrs, 1951, Je 10,92:3
McClain, Charles W, 1952, Ap 15,27:1
McClain, Emlin, 1915, My 26,13:5
McClain, Frank B, 1925, O 12,21:4
McClain, John (funl plans, My 05,39:3), 1967, My 4, 39:3
McClain, Lynn B, 1965, F 28,88:6
McClain, Norman A, 1949, My 24,27:3
McClain, William M, 1955, Je 29,29:3
McClamroch, James Mrs, 1960, Jl 19,29:3
McClamrock, Abraham A, 1937, N 11,25:1
McClanahan, Allen B, 1967, Je 24,29:5
McClanahan, Louis Mrs, 1953, D 10,47:5
McClanahan, Walter L, 1949, D 26,29:2
McClancy, Benjamin F, 1961, Jl 29,19:6
McClancy, Joseph V S (cor, D 12,88:4), 1954, D 11, 13:2
McClane, Lenus, 1939, O 16,19:5
McClane, Walter D, 1953, My 5,29:2
MacClaren, Archibald C, 1944, N 18,13:5
MacClaren, Malcolm Mrs, 1946, Jl 24,27:4
McClarin, Hugh W, 1954, Ja 19,25:2
McClarity, Harry C Mrs, 1953, Jl 30,23:4
McClarity, John T, 1939, S 18,19:6
McClary, Ernest S, 1950, S 25,23:4
McClary, Eula Mrs, 1946, S 14,7:5
McClary, John C, 1952, F 16,13:2
McClary, Joseph A Mrs, 1949, Jl 2,15:6
McClary, Thomas A, 1948, S 23,29:5
McClaskey, Harry (H Burr), 1941, Ap 7,17:6
McClaskey Robt W, 1950, D 12,33:4
McClatchey, George R Mrs, 1948, D 11,15:2
McClatchey, Samuel H, 1941, F 26,21:4
McClatchey, Walter E, 1956, My 12,19:2
McClatchy, C K, 1936, Ap 28,21:1
McClatchy, Ella K Mrs, 1939, S 24,44:6
McClatchy, J W, 1883, O 26,4:7
McClatchy, John H, 1960, Mr 13,86:8
McClatchy, Leo A, 1945, O 3,19:2
McClatchy, V S (por), 1938, My 16,17:4
McClaughry, Robert Wilson Maj, 1920, N 10,13:6
McClave, Albert, 1924, S 21,29:2
McClave, Albert Mrs, 1949, D 12,33:2
McClave, B Duncan, 1939, My 9,23:2
McClave, Charles, 1947, Ap 3,25:5
McClave, James J Mrs, 1940, O 20,49:1
McClave, Ormande W, 1939, Mr 18,17:5
McClave, Richard, 1957, D 1,88:5
McClave, Robert B, 1953, Ja 29,27:2
McClave, Roscoe P, 1961, Je 8,35:3
McClave, S Wood Maj, 1924, My 7,21:3
McClave, Stephen W Jr, 1953, N 25,23:3
McClay, S Amour, 1958, O 5,87:2
McClay, William J, 1953, Ja 27,25:4
McClean, Francis, 1955, Ag 13,13:2
McClean, Garfield T, 1949, Jl 28,23:1
McClean, John J, 1950, Mr 23,36:2
McClean, Percy W, 1941, N 21,17:4
McClean, Stuart, 1960, Je 28,31:5
McClean, Wesley, 1941, Ag 31,22:8
McClean, William A, 1937, Ja 31,II,8:7
McClear, Louis W, 1940, Mr 26,21:2
McClearn, Hugh J, 1937, Ag 26,21:3
McCleary, E T, 1930, Ap 23,27:3
McCleary, George F, 1962, Ja 4,34:1
McCleary, John Maj, 1868, Mr 5,5:2
McCleary, William, 1920, Ja 6,15:1
McCleary, William A, 1942, S 28,17:6
McCleary, William S, 1953, N 22,88:1
McCleerey, John, 1949, S 20,29:2
McCleery, John C Mrs, 1953, My 17,88:4
McCleery, Robert W, 1959, Je 30,31:4
McCleery, William, 1957, O 31,31:3
McClees, Earle J, 1959, Ja 4,88:4
McClees, Edgar J, 1941, D 26,13:4
McClees, Kathleen, 1944, F 12,13:3
McClellan, A L, 1938, F 8,21:3
McClellan, Albert, 1962, Ag 25,19:3
MacClellan, Albert (Jan 21), 1963, Ap 1,36:1
McClellan, Arno S, 1950, O 7,19:2
McClellan, Arthur J, 1944, F 1,19:4
McClellan, Arthur Maj, 1904, F 23,7:4
McClellan, Charles H, 1966, Ja 11,27:2
McClellan, Charles Mrs (E H Dunbar), 1964, Je 21, 84:6
McClellan, Clarence S, 1953, My 31,72:8
McClellan, Clarence S Mrs, 1943, S 16,21:1
McClellan, Edwin, 1924, F 1,17:5
McClellan, Edwin Mrs, 1949, Mr 18,25:5
McClellan, G A, 1924, N 9,7:1
McClellan, G B Gen, 1885, O 30,5:1
McClellan, George B (por), 1940, D 1,61:1
McClellan, George B Mrs, 1952, D 4,35:5
McClellan, George Brinton Mrs (funl, F 18,11:6), 1915, F 14,3:5
McClellan, George E, 1956, Ap 16,27:5; 1960, Jl 18, 27:5
McClellan, George F, 1948, D 21,31:1
McClellan, George R, 1955, Jl 19,27:2
McClellan, John, 1949, S 4,40:7
McClellan, Joseph G, 1964, Ap 25,29:2
McClellan, Lewis, 1941, F 13,19:4
McClellan, Maurice S, 1950, S 21,31:4
McClellan, Otey, 1965, D 27,25:3
McClellan, Robert Mrs, 1967, S 9,31:3
McClellan, Robert W, 1947, F 12,25:2
McClellan, Samuel P, 1940, F 16,19:4
McClellan, Thomas, 1916, Ag 7,9:4
McClellan, Thomas Capt, 1882, S 25,5:6
McClellan, Vernon F, 1963, Je 3,29:3
McClellan, Walter, 1946, My 12,45:3
McClellan, William, 1950, N 16,31:4
McClellan, William A Mrs, 1952, Ap 7,25:4
McClellan, William H, 1951, My 9,33:5
McClellan, William J Jr, 1953, Je 30,23:5
McClellan, 1871, My 10,8:3
McClelland, A Russell, 1952, Ag 2,15:2
McClelland, Adam Rev Dr, 1916, S 7,9:4
McClelland, Alvin B Sr, 1948, F 10,23:2
McClelland, Annie D Mrs, 1942, S 13,53:3
McClelland, C K, 1941, Je 10,23:2
McClelland, Carl C, 1942, Jl 31,15:4
McClelland, Charles, 1942, F 6,19:5
McClelland, Charles P (por), 1944, Je 7,19:4
McClelland, Charles P Mrs, 1939, Ap 17,17:2
McClelland, Chester W, 1940, D 31,15:3
McClelland, Dalton F, 1967, N 17,47:1
McClelland, David A, 1951, F 3,15:6
McClelland, David M, 1948, S 18,17:2
McClelland, Donald, 1955, N 17,35:3
McClelland, Edmund, 1953, Je 29,21:4
McClelland, Edward B, 1941, Ag 30,13:2
McClelland, Elizabeth, 1908, Ag 11,5:6
McClelland, Elmer B, 1947, Jl 11,15:5
McClelland, George W, 1955, Ag 22,21:3
McClelland, Harold M, 1965, Jl 19,27:2
McClelland, Harold M Maj-Gen, 1965, N 21,86:7
McClelland, J Dr, 1877, Ag 5,6:7
McClelland, Jack, 1954, N 20,17:1
McClelland, James D Ex-Sen, 1919, Ja 14,11:2
McClelland, James F, 1955, My 7,17:3
McClelland, James F Mrs, 1967, Mr 5,86:8
McClelland, John A, 1943, Mr 25,21:2
McClelland, Joseph C, 1941, Jl 3,19:5
McClelland, Milton G, 1940, N 14,24:2
McClelland, Nancy V (mem ser set, O 19,29:4), 1959, O 2,29:4
McClelland, Noah H, 1954, D 16,37:2
McClelland, Ralph A Mrs, 1941, Ag 15,17:4
McClelland, Robert, 1880, Ag 31,2:6; 1949, D 17,17:2
McClelland, Rogers, 1963, D 8,86:3
McClelland, T Calvin, 1917, O 26,15:4
McClelland, V S, 1938, Mr 24,23:3
McClelland, William, 1945, Jl 12,11:4
McClelland, William (por), 1949, Ap 17,78:3
McClelland, William A, 1942, S 21,15:6
McClelland, William Mrs, 1951, F 17,15:3
McClement, John Hall, 1924, My 17,15:5
McClenaghan, George P, 1961, O 14,23:5
McClenahan, Howard Mrs, 1946, Jl 17,23:2
McClenahan, Hugh K, 1943, Jl 9,17:4
McClenahan, J Stanley, 1949, Jl 14,27:4
McClenahan, John M, 1938, Jl 7,19:3
McClenahan, Marjorie B Mrs, 1964, Jl 17,27:2
McClenahan, Robert S, 1949, N 9,28:4
McClenahan, Walter J, 1960, O 21,33:1
McClenahan, William, 1941, N 28,24:3
McClenathan, C V, 1939, Ja 3,17:3
McClendon, Caesar P, 1944, S 2,11:3
McClendon, Lloyd H, 1950, Je 2,23:5
McClennen, Edward F, 1948, Jl 3,15:2
McClenthen, William A, 1948, F 1,60:5
McCleod, Andrew, 1944, N 28,23:3
McClernand, E J Brig Gen, 1926, F 10,23:4
McClernand, George B Jr, 1951, Jl 28,11:4
McClinachan, William B Mrs, 1937, D 20,27:3
McClinchie, Kenneth A, 1961, Jl 17,21:3
McClintic, Earl C, 1964, D 21,29:4
McClintic, Frederic M, 1946, S 5,27:3
McClintic, George W, 1942, S 26,15:6
McClintic, Guthrie, 1961, O 30,29:4
McClintic, Howard H, 1938, Ag 6,13:5
McClintic, James V (por), 1948, Ap 23,23:1
McClintock, Andrew T Mrs, 1953, D 19,15:3
McClintock, Charles A, 1968, Ag 16,33:3
McClintock, Earl I, 1963, Ag 26,27:2
McClintock, Emery, 1916, Jl 11,9:5
McClintock, Euphemia, 1953, Mr 1,92:2
McClintock, Gilbert S, 1959, Je 20,21:3
McClintock, H W, 1950, O 15,104:2
McClintock, Harry K, 1957, Ap 25,31:2
McClintock, Harry T, 1953, My 28,23:3
McClintock, Harvey C, 1943, Ja 20,20:2
McClintock, Herbert D, 1956, Ag 27,19:5
McClintock, James D, 1956, Jl 4,19:5
McClintock, John Rev, 1870, Mr 5,5:2
McClintock, John T, 1939, F 5,40:3
McClintock, Lindley W, 1953, Ja 25,85:1
McClintock, Marshall, 1967, F 11,29:2
McClintock, Maxwell Mrs, 1946, Ja 3,19:4
McClintock, Miller, 1960, Ja 11,45:4
McClintock, Norman, 1938, F 27,II,9:1
McClintock, Thomas H, 1960, Je 26,72:4
McClintock, Thomas L, 1948, My 26,25:1
McClintock, Walter, 1949, Mr 27,76:7
McClintock, Wilder F, 1904, F 7,7:6
McClintock, William H Mrs, 1953, Jl 1,29:4
McClintock, William L, 1946, Ap 10,27:1
McClintock, William Mrs, 1950, Ag 10,25:2
MacClinton, Seth B Lt-Col, 1937, Mr 22,23:5
McClory, Robert B Mrs, 1967, S 5,43:3
McClosby, Felix, 1909, S 2,9:3
McCloskey, C Graham, 1954, My 11,29:4
McCloskey, Cardinal, 1885, O 10,1:1
McCloskey, Charles J, 1955, Ag 12,19:5
McCloskey, Dorothy M, 1954, O 28,35:4
McCloskey, Edwin H, 1924, Ap 26,15:4
McCloskey, Eugene T, 1952, Jl 11,17:4
McCloskey, F A, 1927, N 8,27:3
McCloskey, Frank, 1954, Jl 1,25:4
McCloskey, George Mrs, 1955, N 16,35:2
McCloskey, George W, 1925, O 14,25:2
McCloskey, Henry, 1869, Ap 28,7:2
McCloskey, Herbert, 1954, My 21,27:3
McCloskey, J Frank, 1944, D 31,26:1
McCloskey, James, 1941, D 28,28:7
McCloskey, James J, 1913, Jl 30,7:3
McCloskey, James P, 1945, Ap 15,14:6
McCloskey, John, 1940, N 18,19:2
McCloskey, John A, 1939, O 23,19:2; 1941, Ap 20, 44:1; 1947, Ag 18,17:3
McCloskey, John B, 1945, My 9,23:4; 1967, Jl 18,38:1
McCloskey, John F, 1951, N 23,29:3
McCloskey, John J, 1946, Ap 20,23:6
McCloskey, John J Jr, 1952, O 28,31:5
McCloskey, John Mrs, 1943, O 10,48:6
McCloskey, Joseph, 1939, Ap 11,23:6
McCloskey, Joseph M, 1946, N 15,23:3
McCloskey, Joseph O, 1903, Jl 8,9:7
McCloskey, Margaret, 1943, My 21,20:3
McCloskey, Matthew H, 1946, Ap 30,21:5
McCloskey, Norbert, 1944, Mr 12,37:3
McCloskey, P J, 1877, D 6,8:4
McCloskey, Robert J, 1942, F 17,21:4
McCloskey, William F Sr, 1955, Ag 23,23:4
McCloskey, William George Bp (funl, S 22,9:5), 1909, S 18,9:5
McClosky, Harry B, 1949, F 20,60:4
McClosky, John Mrs, 1937, D 10,26:3
McClosky, Louis M, 1948, F 8,60:7
McClosky, Mary L, 1942, N 1,52:4
McCloud, Bentley G, 1956, My 11,28:1
McCloud, Charles A, 1937, Mr 22,23:3
McCloud, George L, 1953, Je 17,38:2
McCloud, Harriet D, 1951, N 8,29:5
McCloud, Louis, 1948, Ap 22,27:3
McCloud, Louis Mrs, 1941, Ag 15,17:3
McCloud, Patrick, 1943, Ap 29,22:3
McCloud, Robert C, 1938, D 13,25:3
McCloud, William J, 1939, Ap 11,24:2
McCloud, William J Mrs, 1948, Je 24,25:1
McCloy, Anna S Mrs, 1959, N 15,86:8
McCloy, C H, 1959, S 20,87:1
McCloy, Henry L, 1951, Je 22,25:5
McCloy, John, 1945, My 26,15:3
McCloy, John M, 1943, My 28,21:5
McCloy, John Mrs, 1942, O 29,23:5
McCloy, Joseph F, 1965, Jl 7,37:1
McCloy, William C, 1940, Je 22,15:7
McCloy, William C Mrs, 1950, Jl 13,25:6
McCloy, William J, 1952, N 20,31:4
MacCluer, Frederick A, 1938, O 17,15:4
McCluer, Margaret Mrs, 1945, Ap 4,21:1
McClugage, David H, 1945, Ja 1,21:4
McClughan, William G, 1952, D 13,21:3
McCluney, Commodore, 1864, F 13,1:5
McClung, Benjamin G, 1940, N 10,56:1
McClung, Carl H, 1944, D 20,23:3
McClung, Clarence E, 1946, Ja 19,13:1
McClung, George H, 1952, O 11,19:2
McClung, Lee, 1914, D 20,15:5
McClung, R W Mrs, 1951, S 3,13:2
McClung, Reid L, 1961, Ag 20,86:2
McClung, Samuel A, 1945, F 9,15:2
McClung, Stanley F, 1955, Mr 17,45:5
McClung, William N, 1953, Ja 15,27:5
McClunn, David F (por), 1945, My 10,23:2
McClunn, John F, 1941, Ja 7,23:4
McClure, A K Mrs, 1877, N 28,4:7
McClure, A S, 1903, Ap 18,9:5
McClure, Alexander Kelley Col, 1909, Je 7,7:3
McClure, Arthur H, 1963, D 7,27:1
McClure, Bruce H, 1959, D 30,22:1

McClure, Charles A, 1956, F 18,19:5
McClure, Charles A Mrs, 1946, Mr 30,15:2
McClure, Charles F W, 1955, Jl 24,64:1
McClure, Charles F W Mrs, 1959, Jl 13,27:5
McClure, Charles J, 1944, D 2,13:5
McClure, David, 1872, Mr 14,8:5; 1912, My 1,13:3
McClure, Donald F, 1968, Je 30,52:4
McClure, Edward S, 1952, Mr 27,29:2
McClure, F L Mrs, 1948, N 16,29:3
McClure, Frank, 1960, Ja 25,27:5
McClure, Frank H, 1942, O 22,21:2
McClure, Frank N, 1943, Ap 27,23:5
McClure, Frank N Mrs, 1959, S 4,21:2
McClure, George C, 1952, Ap 27,90:3
McClure, George S, 1940, My 26,34:1
McClure, Halley, 1961, Ag 30,33:5
McClure, Harold M, 1951, Mr 10,13:3
McClure, Harry E Mrs, 1937, Je 2,23:2
McClure, Henry H, 1938, N 25,23:5
McClure, Hugh S, 1942, Jl 9,21:2
McClure, James C, 1962, Ag 3,23:1
McClure, James G K, 1956, Je 18,25:5
McClure, James G K Mrs, 1948, My 3,21:4
McClure, James N, 1948, N 24,23:4
McClure, James R, 1960, My 16,31:5
McClure, James Russell, 1907, F 25,9:7
McClure, Jay C, 1937, S 23,27:3
McClure, Joanna M, 1943, D 17,28:2
McClure, John F, 1940, Ap 13,17:5; 1941, Jl 16,17:4
McClure, John G Jr, 1967, My 21,86:8
McClure, John J, 1965, Mr 29,36:1
McClure, John P, 1956, F 9,31:5
McClure, Kenneth G, 1943, O 20,21:6
McClure, Lambert, 1958, My 17,19:4
McClure, Laura E, 1945, O 19,23:3
McClure, Mabel, 1943, N 30,27:2
McClure, Mary L, 1944, Je 24,13:5
McClure, Matthew T, 1964, Jl 30,27:5
McClure, Nathan D (por), 1949, F 7,38:4
McClure, Nathan R, 1950, Je 6,29:4
McClure, Nathaniel F, 1942, Je 27,13:7
McClure, Oscar, 1944, N 7,22:4
McClure, Robert A, 1957, Ja 5,17:3
McClure, Robert J Adm Sir, 1873, N 5,2:3
McClure, Robert L S, 1949, O 4,27:4
McClure, Robert O, 1952, Je 4,27:5
McClure, Roy D, 1951, Ap 1,92:3
McClure, Samuel G, 1948, D 26,52:6
McClure, Samuel S (por), 1949, Mr 23,27:1
McClure, Scott H, 1955, Je 7,33:1
McClure, Silas (will), 1949, Mr 22,27:3
McClure, Stuart L, 1960, My 9,12:5
McClure, Thomas O, 1949, Ag 30,27:1
McClure, Vashta Mrs, 1940, Ap 19,21:2
McClure, Virgil Mrs, 1947, D 7,76:2
McClure, W G, 1927, Mr 27,26:4
McClure, Walter H, 1940, My 1,23:3
McClure, William, 1916, Ag 29,9:5
McClure, William C, 1946, Mr 23,13:6
McClure, William F, 1951, Ja 4,29:3
McClure, William H, 1960, F 3,33:3
McClure, William J, 1951, Mr 28,29:3
McClure, William M, 1956, D 19,31:5
McClure, William Sir, 1939, Ap 24,17:5
McClure Smith, Hugh A, 1961, O 10,43:5
McClurg, Gilbert, 1938, D 9,26:1
McClurg, Lowrie, 1914, Je 25,9:5
McClurg, O T, 1926, Ap 21,25:5
McClurkin, John Knox Rev Dr, 1923, N 10,13:5
McClurkin, Robert, 1956, My 9,33:4
McCluskey, James, 1967, Jl 4,19:5
McCluskey, James E, 1951, Je 22,25:2
McCluskey, James J, 1910, Ag 1,7:6
McCluskey, James T, 1945, F 14,19:5
McCluskey, Leroy, 1955, O 25,33:1
McCluskey, Mary J Mrs, 1904, Ja 6,9:5
McCluskey, Thomas J Rev, 1937, Jl 15,19:1
McClusky, Charles, 1953, F 10,27:1
McClusky, George N, 1950, Je 13,27:4
McClusky, George W, 1912, D 21,13:4
McClusky, William E, 1967, Ap 21,39:3
McClymonds, Lewis K, 1903, N 8,7:7
McClymont, James, 1944, Ap 19,23:3
MacClymont, William S, 1948, S 7,25:5
McCoach, David, 1947, Mr 24,25:5
McCoach, David Jr, 1951, D 17,31:4
McCoach, Nathan F, 1944, N 10,19:5
McCoart, Richard F, 1951, F 26,23:2
McCobb, Thomas C, 1954, O 23,15:5
McCoey, Bernard, 1944, O 6,23:4
McCole, Camille J, 1939, Ja 15,38:6
McCole, Charles, 1948, Ap 28,27:3
McCole, Thomas A, 1950, S 10,92:5
MacColl, Alex, 1953, My 31,73:2
McColl, Alex L, 1962, Ag 17,23:5
McColl, David K, 1952, Ja 24,27:2
MacColl, Donald, 1947, S 30,25:4
McColl, Dugald S, 1948, D 22,23:2
McColl, Florence L Mrs, 1937, Ag 21,15:5
MacColl, Hugh F, 1953, O 18,86:6
MacColl, J R, 1931, N 24,25:3
MacColl, James A, 1956, Ap 20,25:3
McColl, John A, 1950, Ja 24,31:1
McColl, Joseph W Jr, 1959, Mr 17,33:2
MacColl, LeRoy A, 1967, Ja 22,76:4
MacColl, Mary, 1941, F 15,15:5
Maccoll, Norman, 1904, D 16,9:5
MacColl, Robert J, 1966, F 20,88:3
MacColl, William B, 1941, N 9,55:5
McCollam, John J, 1944, Je 14,19:4
McCollerm, Samuel, 1925, Mr 3,23:4
McCollester, Lee S (por), 1943, D 27,20:2
McCollester, Parker, 1954, Ja 13,31:3
McCollester, Parker Mrs, 1967, Ag 1,33:3
MacCollin, Andrew W F, 1923, Ap 26,19:5
McCollin, Fannie H, 1937, D 14,25:4
McCollin, Frances, 1960, F 27,19:3
McCollom, Harold C, 1966, Ap 13,40:2
McCollom, J C, 1883, N 18,8:7
McCollom, John H Dr, 1915, Je 15,13:5
McCollom, Kate, 1937, Ap 30,22:3
McCollom, Lucian R Dr, 1937, My 24,19:5
McCollom, Vivian C, 1959, Ag 13,27:4
McCollom, William C, 1958, D 19,2:6
McCollom, William C Mrs, 1944, N 19,50:4
McCollom, William Dr, 1909, F 24,9:5
McCollom, William E, 1943, O 14,21:6
McCollough, Albert W, 1941, My 15,23:5
McCollough, Austin E, 1944, Mr 29,21:4
McCollough, J Huston, 1942, O 2,25:4
McCollough, William B, 1954, O 19,27:5
McCollum, Earl (por), 1947, F 5,26:1
McCollum, Elmer V, 1967, N 16,47:3
McCollum, Frank V, 1949, Ap 21,25:1
McCollum, H H, 1938, D 21,23:5
McCollum, J Brewster Judge, 1903, O 5,7:6
McCollum, James B, 1960, Ap 4,29:4
McCollum, James Mrs, 1956, N 8,39:4
McCollum, John A, 1967, F 21,47:4
McCollum, John C, 1941, N 21,17:2
McCollum, John J, 1947, Ag 22,15:5
McCollum, William Sr Mrs, 1957, Mr 2,21:5
McComas, Alice Moore Mrs, 1919, D 3,15:2
McComas, Carroll, 1962, N 10,25:4
McComas, Francis, 1938, D 29,19:4
McComas, Henry W, 1939, Ap 11,24:2
McComas, Joseph P (por), 1943, O 6,23:1
McComas, Joseph P Mrs, 1941, O 30,23:5
McComas, Louis Emory Justice, 1907, N 11,7:5
McComas, O Parker, 1957, N 26,30:1
McComas, Richard T, 1941, Ag 19,21:2
McComas, Robert G, 1947, Jl 5,11:4
McComb, Arthur J, 1958, Ag 29,23:4
McComb, Arthur J Mrs, 1952, D 1,23:3
McComb, Frank E, 1950, My 13,17:4
McComb, H S, 1881, D 31,5:3
McComb, Herkimer, 1907, Mr 12,9:6
McComb, John H Mrs, 1943, My 5,27:3
McComb, John Mrs (Kate), 1959, Ap 17,25:3
McComb, Judith, 1952, Mr 21,23:4
McComb, Kemper G, 1951, Ag 30,23:2
McComb, Laura H Mrs, 1942, Mr 9,19:3
McComb, Lawrence M, 1954, Mr 30,27:2
McComb, Leonard H, 1955, F 1,29:3
McComb, Malcolm S, 1957, Mr 21,33:1
McComb, Samuel, 1938, S 12,17:5
McComb, Samuel D (por), 1944, Mr 19,41:1
McComb, William R, 1957, D 22,40:1
McCombe, Christopher J, 1954, Ap 11,86:5
McCombe, John A, 1949, Ag 4,23:3
McComber, S A Dr, 1919, N 8,13:2
McCombs, Carl E, 1949, My 7,13:4
McCombs, Charles F, 1947, My 20,25:4
McCombs, Nelson W Mrs, 1963, O 7,31:4
McCombs, Robert, 1946, F 12,25:4
McCombs, Virgil J, 1952, Ja 4,40:4
McCombs, William F, 1921, F 23,13:4
McCombs, William H, 1953, S 4,34:3
McCommon, Frank, 1914, My 24,IV,7:5
McCommons, James V, 1941, Ag 2,15:5
McConachie, G W Grant, 1965, Jl 1,31:2
McConahay, Edward O, 1952, N 7,23:3
McConathy, Osbourne (por), 1947, Ap 3,25:1
McConaty, Barton S, 1967, My 12,47:2
McConaughey, John L, 1954, D 23,19:3
McConaughy, Donald Mrs, 1947, Mr 29,15:4
McConaughy, Francis B, 1950, F 21,25:1
McConaughy, Francis E, 1946, Ja 15,23:2
McConaughy, James L, 1948, Mr 8,1:4
McConaughy, James L Mrs, 1966, Je 15,47:5
McConaughy, Samuel G Sr, 1945, D 8,17:1
McConchie, Thomas L, 1945, D 1,23:3
McCone, Alicia J, 1965, Mr 4,31:2
McCone, John A Mrs, 1961, D 7,43:2
McConihe, A Douglas Col, 1915, O 14,11:5
McConihe, Isaac, 1903, Ja 12,9:6
McConihe, John Col, 1864, Je 9,2:3
McConihe, Malcolm S, 1961, Jl 4,19:2
McConkey, Frank W Mrs, 1943, Je 12,13:5
MacConkey, Helen A, 1957, Jl 12,21:4
McConkey, James G, 1942, F 5,21:5
McConkey, John, 1917, Je 18,9:6
McConkey, M W, 1943, Jl 19,15:1
McConn, Charles M, 1953, Ap 16,30:3
McConn, William Sidney, 1873, Jl 16,5:3
McConnachie, Morton J, 1967, O 25,47:2
McConnaughey, George C, 1966, Mr 17,39:1
McConnaughey, George C Mrs, 1961, My 9,39:1
McConnaughey, Robert K, 1966, Mr 1,37:3
McConnaughy, David, 1946, Ag 21,27:3
McConnel, Murray, 1961, Ap 10,31:2
McConnel, Patrick J, 1939, N 12,49:2
McConnel, Wilfred G, 1953, N 23,27:4
McConnell, Albe W, 1946, S 3,19:3
McConnell, Alexander Daniel Judge, 1921, S 7,13:4
McConnell, Alfred, 1944, N 13,19:5
McConnell, Ambrose M, 1942, My 21,19:6
McConnell, Andrew B, 1949, Jl 4,13:6
McConnell, Arthur, 1945, Ja 16,19:4
McConnell, Brendan, 1951, D 30,24:4
McConnell, Burt M, 1960, S 25,89:1
McConnell, Charles D, 1953, Ag 17,15:5
McConnell, Charles H, 1948, O 7,29:3
McConnell, Clinton D, 1955, Ap 18,23:4
McConnell, D H, 1937, Ja 21,23:2
McConnell, David, 1940, O 16,23:5
McConnell, David H (por), 1944, Ag 6,38:3
McConnell, Donald W, 1941, F 5,19:5
McConnell, E H Mrs, 1905, Mr 28,9:4
MacConnell, Eugene P, 1943, Ap 2,21:2
McConnell, Fowler B, 1961, D 29,23:2
McConnell, Francis J, 1953, Ag 19,29:1
McConnell, Frank H, 1966, Ag 18,35:3
McConnell, Fred B, 1947, Ja 11,19:4
McConnell, Frederic, 1968, Ag 11,72:6
McConnell, George, 1948, O 12,25:1; 1954, O 21,27
1965, Ap 10,30:1
McConnell, George Jr Mrs, 1957, N 6,35:2
McConnell, George N, 1962, N 24,23:4
McConnell, Guy W, 1948, F 7,15:4
McConnell, H F, 1934, My 26,17:4
McConnell, H Hugh, 1960, Jl 12,33:2
McConnell, Harry N, 1966, S 20,47:4
McConnell, Harry W, 1963, Ap 7,86:4
McConnell, Helen Mrs, 1957, My 9,7:2
McConnell, Hugh, 1942, S 23,25:2
McConnell, Isaac Mrs, 1963, Je 24,27:2
McConnell, J Herbert, 1951, My 6,92:2
McConnell, J Miller, 1959, S 17,39:4
McConnell, J Park, 1940, F 11,49:1
McConnell, J S T Rev, 1903, S 1,7:6
McConnell, James C, 1958, My 30,21:1
McConnell, James E, 1938, Jl 8,17:3; 1954, Jl 27,21
McConnell, James Joseph Rev, 1925, D 9,27:4
McConnell, John, 1940, N 8,21:4; 1964, N 8,88:7
McConnell, John A, 1951, Je 6,31:4
McConnell, John F, 1938, Ap 1,23:5
McConnell, John H, 1958, O 19,86:2
McConnell, John Joseph (Bro Eliphus Victor), 19
Jl 28,7:6
McConnell, John W, 1950, F 11,15:1; 1963, N 7,37
McConnell, Joseph H, 1949, N 27,104:8
McConnell, Joseph Jr (funl, Ag 29,89:4), 1954, Ag 26,1:2
McConnell, Lillian, 1957, Mr 28,31:4
McConnell, Lucy, 1944, Ag 7,15:1
McConnell, Lulu, 1962, O 11,39:1
McConnell, Luther G, 1961, F 17,28:1
McConnell, Margaret Mrs, 1944, Ap 16,25:5
McConnell, Marshall, 1950, O 21,17:4
McConnell, Matthew, 1948, O 3,67:1
McConnell, Noble, 1959, S 3,27:4
McConnell, Noble Mrs, 1942, Je 13,15:1
McConnell, Oviatt, 1953, O 10,17:6
McConnell, Philip S, 1958, Ap 15,33:3
McConnell, Rebecca J Mrs, 1946, D 2,25:1
McConnell, Rex Q, 1947, Je 11,27:5
McConnell, Riley F, 1940, Jl 13,13:2
McConnell, Robert H, 1952, D 22,25:5
McConnell, Robert K, 1938, Je 14,21:5
McConnell, Roy P Mrs, 1947, Mr 21,22:3
McConnell, Samuel D, 1939, Ja 12,19:2
McConnell, Samuel K, 1950, Je 18,76:4
McConnell, Samuel P, 1955, Je 7,33:2
McConnell, Thomas, 1938, My 25,23:6
McConnell, Veronica, 1964, O 3,1:7
McConnell, W A, 1905, O 4,9:6
McConnell, William, 1942, Je 23,19:6; 1944, Ap 2
19:3
McConnell, William J, 1925, F 13,17:3; 1950, N 2
31:6; 1963, Ap 27,25:4
McConnell, William J Sen, 1925, Ap 2,21:4
McConnell, Wilson G, 1966, Ja 14,39:3
McConnico, K T, 1939, O 16,19:4
McConnochie, James F, 1947, F 17,19:5
McConnon, Thomas J, 1964, Jl 25,19:4
McConnon, William J, 1951, S 8,17:3
McConoughy, John Mrs, 1955, Ja 3,27:4
McConville, Bernard, 1917, S 23,23:1
McConville, Curran C, 1937, Ag 11,24:2
McConville, Edward A, 1948, Ap 13,27:2
McConville, George T, 1957, Ap 7,88:8
McConville, James S, 1961, Mr 17,31:2
McConville, John, 1873, S 9,5:5
McConville, Joseph A, 1967, N 28,51:5
McConville, Mathew A, 1944, Je 23,19:4
McConville (Bro Vincent), 1958, F 6,25:1
McCooey, Catherine I Mrs, 1938, Ag 22,13:6
McCooey, Francis W, 1951, Ap 6,25:3

McCooey, Frank J, 1954, Ag 3,19:1
McCooey, Frank J Mrs, 1943, Ap 14,23:2
McCooey, J H, 1934, Ja 22,1:8
McCooey, James E, 1953, Jl 12,65:2
McCooey, John H, 1950, My 13,34:4
McCooey, John H Jr, 1948, Je 24,25:4
McCooey, Margaret J, 1965, N 18,47:2
McCook, A M Gen, 1903, Je 13,9:5
McCook, Anson G Gen, 1917, D 31,7:7
McCook, Anson T, 1966, D 14,47:5
McCook, Edward M Gen, 1909, S 10,9:5
McCook, G, 1878, Ja 4,2:2
McCook, G W, 1877, D 29,5:2
McCook, H Kennedy, 1953, O 8,29:5
McCook, Henry Christopher, 1911, N 1,11:5
McCook, Hettie B Mrs, 1942, Ja 9,21:1
McCook, John B, 1946, Je 21,23:2
McCook, John J Col, 1911, S 18,11:3
McCook, Nelson, 1960, Ap 17,92:6
McCook, Phil J Mrs, 1941, N 3,19:4
McCook, Philip J, 1963, S 26,35:4
McCool, Charles E, 1944, D 12,23:1
McCool, James H, 1950, N 23,35:2
McCool, John, 1949, My 3,25:2
McCool, Patrick, 1906, F 5,2:2
McCool, Richard M, 1956, Mr 8,29:4
McCool, William P, 1963, Je 6,35:2
McCord, Alvin C, 1956, Ag 9,25:6
McCord, Bernard, 1962, D 5,47:2
McCord, Byron Mrs, 1951, F 15,31:2
McCord, Charles L, 1942, Mr 13,19:2
MacCord, Charles William, 1915, Ap 14,13:4
McCord, Clinton F, 1950, My 4,27:1
McCord, Clinton P, 1953, My 11,27:3
McCord, David W (por), 1945, O 20,11:5
McCord, David W Mrs, 1940, Ag 30,19:5
McCord, Don C, 1957, Mr 4,27:3
McCord, Frank B, 1925, N 3,25:6
McCord, Frederick A, 1953, Ap 17,25:5
McCord, George F, 1942, Mr 18,23:2
McCord, George G, 1942, Mr 21,17:5
McCord, George Henry, 1909, Ap 7,11:5
McCord, H D, 1903, Ap 27,7:5
McCord, Henry Y, 1943, Ag 19,19:5
McCord, J Stanley, 1965, O 16,27:4
McCord, Jack, 1953, N 13,27:3
McCord, James, 1903, S 25,7:5
McCord, James R, 1960, Mr 29,38:1
McCord, Jim Nance, 1968, S 3,43:2
McCord, John E, 1947, Jl 2,23:4
McCord, Joseph, 1943, Ja 30,15:2; 1943, D 31,15:2
McCord, Leon C, 1952, F 12,27:3
McCord, Mary, 1959, N 12,35:4
McCord, Miles S, 1950, F 15,27:1
McCord, Peter B, 1908, N 11,9:6
McCord, Robert, 1946, Ja 24,21:4
McCord, Robert F, 1958, Ja 5,86:7
McCord, Vera, 1949, Mr 4,21:1
McCord, William H, 1941, F 11,23:2
McCord, William P, 1918, O 24,13:2
McCordock, Howard A, 1938, N 15,23:1
MacCorison, John H, 1940, F 22,23:5
McCorkie, John Alva Dr, 1916, Ag 16,7:4
MacCorkindale, Andrew D, 1954, D 10,27:4
McCorkindale, William P, 1940, Ag 3,15:6
McCorkle, Graham, 1964, N 10,47:3
McCorkle, Roy J, 1966, My 14,31:4
McCormac, Eugene I, 1943, Ja 12,23:3
MacCormac, John (funl, Jl 26,15:6), 1958, Jl 7,27:1
McCormac, Michael C, 1945, Mr 13,23:2
MacCormac, William Sir, 1901, D 5,7:5
McCormack, Alfred, 1956, Jl 12,23:4
McCormack, Andrew, 1941, Ja 8,19:1
McCormack, Anna M, 1953, Mr 24,31:4
McCormack, Arthur T, 1943, Ag 8,36:8
McCormack, Benjamin B Mrs, 1948, Jl 19,19:2
McCormack, Charles, 1953, N 9,35:5
McCormack, Charles J (funl, Jl 13,11:6), 1915, Jl 12, 7:5
McCormack, Daniel, 1937, Mr 7,II,8:4
MacCormack, Daniel Mrs, 1939, Ja 19,19:3
MacCormack, Daniel W, 1937, Ja 1,23:1
McCormack, Denis A Mrs, 1961, Jl 17,21:1
McCormack, Donald J, 1966, Ja 9,56:5
McCormack, Edward F, 1968, Ap 21,81:1
McCormack, Edward J (funl, N 21,39:2), 1963, N 18,33:3
McCormack, Edward L, 1941, Ag 7,17:4
McCormack, Edward P, 1940, Mr 30,15:4
McCormack, Edward T, 1943, Ja 15,17:4
McCormack, Emmet J, 1965, F 25,31:1
McCormack, Frank, 1938, N 4,23:1
McCormack, Frank C, 1961, Je 4,86:2
McCormack, George H, 1954, Jl 23,17:5
McCormack, George J, 1942, S 25,21:3
McCormack, Hannah Mrs, 1938, Je 4,15:1
McCormack, Harry, 1953, Je 11,29:5
McCormack, J L, 1927, F 11,21:5
McCormack, James B Mrs, 1948, O 28,29:3
McCormack, James E, 1946, S 4,23:3; 1951, O 2,27:4
McCormack, James F, 1940, Je 3,15:4; 1966, Ja 29, 27:1
McCormack, James G, 1965, Ap 16,29:1
McCormack, James H, 1948, O 7,30:3
McCormack, James J, 1950, Ja 14,15:5
McCormack, John, 1943, Ja 9,13:5
McCormack, John (por), 1945, S 17,21:8
McCormack, John A, 1950, Ag 17,27:3
McCormack, John F, 1945, D 24,15:5; 1968, N 8,47:3
McCormack, John H, 1950, Ag 30,32:3
McCormack, John J, 1950, Mr 17,24:5; 1966, My 31, 43:1
McCormack, Joseph A, 1944, Mr 19,41:1
McCormack, Joseph H, 1951, Ap 21,17:4
McCormack, Lawrence J, 1953, Ag 16,76:8
McCormack, Lawrence P, 1968, Ap 26,43:4
McCormack, Margaret I, 1957, S 2,13:5
McCormack, Marshall, 1918, My 16,13:3
MacCormack, Mary H Mrs, 1941, Ja 10,20:2
McCormack, Owen J, 1944, S 2,11:7
McCormack, Richard Ronald Cormac Dr, 1968, D 30, 31:4
McCormack, Robert A, 1950, Ap 28,4:3
MacCormack, Robert S, 1938, S 8,24:1
McCormack, Stephen N, 1949, O 15,15:6
McCormack, Thomas, 1949, Ag 18,21:2
McCormack, Thomas B, 1952, O 9,64:4
McCormack, Thomas E, 1944, N 3,21:3
McCormack, Thomas I, 1946, Jl 9,22:2
McCormack, Thomas J, 1922, Ja 24,15:4; 1964, O 26, 31:2
McCormack, Thomas J Mrs, 1953, Jl 11,11:5
McCormack, Vincent J, 1941, D 18,27:3
McCormack, W F, 1928, Ag 26,27:5
McCormack, Walter A, 1952, F 13,29:1
McCormack, William, 1953, Ag 30,89:1
McCormack, William J, 1939, Mr 28,24:3; 1945, Ja 5, 15:1; 1965, Jl 13,33:4
McCormack, William L, 1940, My 23,23:2
McCormack, William R, 1950, Jl 21,19:3
McCormic, Robert H, 1942, Ag 14,17:5
McCormich, George, 1946, D 24,17:3
McCormick, A P Judge, 1916, N 3,13:5
McCormick, Albert E, 1961, Ja 31,29:2
McCormick, Alexander A, 1925, N 27,17:4
McCormick, Alexander Hugh Rear-Adm, 1915, Ag 23,9:5
McCormick, Alexander Mrs, 1943, O 14,21:2
McCormick, Alice, 1947, Ja 18,15:3
McCormick, Allen G, 1947, Jl 10,21:2
McCormick, Alphonse L, 1938, Ag 18,19:2
McCormick, Andrew A, 1907, F 12,9:6
McCormick, Andrew L Mrs, 1949, S 10,17:2
McCormick, Andrew Mrs, 1950, Mr 28,31:4
McCormick, Andrew P, 1944, Je 23,19:5
McCormick, Anne O Mrs, 1954, My 30,1:3
McCormick, Arthur B, 1954, N 24,23:4
McCormick, Arthur L, 1954, Je 27,69:2
McCormick, Burton D, 1940, O 31,23:2
McCormick, C H, 1884, My 14,1:6; 1936, Je 3,21:1
McCormick, Charles K, 1945, Ag 29,23:3
McCormick, Charles R, 1945, My 26,15:5; 1955, F 25, 21:1
McCormick, Charles T, 1952, Mr 23,92:1; 1963, D 24, 17:3
McCormick, Charles Wesley Rev Dr, 1920, O 21,13:5
McCormick, Chauncey, 1954, S 9,31:4
McCormick, Chauncey Mrs, 1965, Ja 14,35:3
McCormick, Clara J Mrs, 1942, My 24,42:2
McCormick, Clarence, 1945, Je 9,13:4
McCormick, Constance P Mrs, 1938, Je 27,17:6
McCormick, Cyrus H Mrs, 1923, Jl 6,13:6
McCormick, Cyrus Hall Mrs, 1921, Ja 18,11:4
McCormick, Denis Father, 1913, Mr 17,11:4
McCormick, Douglas N, 1965, Jl 31,21:5
McCormick, E O, 1923, N 2,17:3
McCormick, E R Mrs, 1932, Ag 26,17:1
McCormick, Edith, 1956, O 25,33:5
McCormick, Edith Mrs, 1943, D 22,23:2
McCormick, Edmund J (por), 1946, F 6,23:3
McCormick, Edward C Mrs, 1963, Jl 14,61:3
McCormick, Edward J, 1954, F 26,19:3
McCormick, Edward R, 1954, N 9,27:5
McCormick, Edward W, 1947, S 6,17:5
McCormick, Elizabeth, 1905, Ja 27,7:4
McCormick, Elsie (Mrs M Dunn), 1962, Je 18,25:3
McCormick, Evelyn, 1948, My 8,15:6
McCormick, F J, 1947, Ap 25,21:5
McCormick, Flora A Mrs, 1940, O 29,25:4
McCormick, Francis D, 1963, Jl 29,19:4
McCormick, Francis J, 1949, Jl 2,15:4; 1954, O 30,17:3
McCormick, Francis V, 1946, Ap 21,46:1
McCormick, Frank E, 1938, Mr 22,21:2
McCormick, Frank R, 1962, Jl 29,61:2
McCormick, Frank T, 1952, Mr 21,23:1
McCormick, Frederick L, 1960, O 3,31:5
McCormick, Garrett, 1945, Je 20,23:3
McCormick, George, 1911, Jl 23,9:6; 1953, Ja 23,20:3
McCormick, George B, 1949, Ag 23,23:4
McCormick, George Mrs, 1950, Mr 3,25:3
McCormick, Gregory A, 1953, O 7,29:4
McCormick, H G, 1902, My 27,9:5
McCormick, Hamlin F, 1937, F 7,II,8:8
McCormick, Harold F (por),(will, O 30,24:2), 1941, O 17,23:1
McCormick, Harold V, 1960, My 5,35:4
McCormick, Harry E (Moose), 1962, Jl 10,33:1
McCormick, Helen P, 1937, F 22,17:1
McCormick, Henry, 1940, F 21,19:4
McCormick, Henry B, 1941, D 28,28:5
McCormick, Herbert V, 1946, Mr 21,25:4
McCormick, Howard, 1943, O 14,22:2
McCormick, Howard Mrs, 1948, My 30,34:3
McCormick, Hugh J, 1910, Ag 29,7:5
McCormick, Islay F, 1956, Ja 11,31:1
McCormick, James, 1903, Ag 1,7:6; 1948, S 6,13:2
McCormick, James C, 1942, Ja 1,25:2; 1942, D 14,28:5
McCormick, James F, 1937, Ja 6,23:6; 1949, S 30,24:2; 1956, Jl 1,57:2
McCormick, James Father, 1903, My 31,7:6
McCormick, James H, 1912, Ap 10,13:4; 1945, Ap 30, 19:4
McCormick, James J, 1939, Ja 23,5:1
McCormick, James P, 1952, Ja 15,27:3
McCormick, James T, 1950, Mr 20,21:4
McCormick, James W, 1965, Ja 14,35:4
McCormick, John, 1944, My 27,15:6
McCormick, John A, 1939, Ap 21,23:3
McCormick, John E, 1963, Jl 31,29:2
McCormick, John F, 1943, Jl 16,17:6; 1964, S 5,19:1
McCormick, John F Jr, 1949, O 23,86:4
McCormick, John Father, 1903, Ja 24,9:5
McCormick, John G Msgr, 1925, Jl 29,21:7
McCormick, John J, 1958, Ap 27,86:6
McCormick, John J D, 1968, Ap 25,47:4
McCormick, John Jr, 1956, Ja 2,21:4
McCormick, John N (por), 1939, N 27,17:2
McCormick, John S, 1948, Ap 23,23:3
McCormick, John T, 1945, N 18,44:1; 1956, My 16, 35:3
McCormick, Julia R Mrs, 1942, Ap 22,23:4
McCormick, Katherine H, 1960, Mr 25,27:3
McCormick, Kyle C, 1965, My 24,31:1
McCormick, Lawrence, 1912, S 8,II,13:4
McCormick, Lawrence J, 1957, My 5,89:2
McCormick, Leander J, 1964, Ja 31,27:1
McCormick, Leslie T, 1942, Ap 17,17:1
McCormick, Lillian M, 1940, Mr 20,27:5
McCormick, Lynde D (funl plans, Ag 19,92:4; funl Ag 21,29:4), 1956, Ag 17,19:1
McCormick, Malcolm, 1958, Ja 30,24:1
McCormick, Margaret, 1952, My 23,21:3
McCormick, Mary J Mrs, 1938, O 11,25:4
McCormick, Mary M Mrs, 1947, My 3,17:1
McCormick, Mary V, 1941, My 26,19:6
McCormick, Matthias, 1938, F 6,II,8:3
McCormick, Maud Miller Mrs, 1901, D 25,7:6
McCormick, Medill Sen, 1925, F 27,17:3
McCormick, Michael, 1953, N 20,23:2
McCormick, Myron (funl, Ag 2,25:1), 1962, Jl 31,27:1
McCormick, Olin F, 1949, Ja 27,23:2
McCormick, Patrick J, 1953, My 19,30:3
McCormick, Peter J, 1954, Mr 15,25:4
McCormick, Peter V, 1951, N 13,29:3
McCormick, Phil S, 1954, S 30,31:5
McCormick, Phillip S Mrs, 1956, Ap 28,17:5
McCormick, R C, 1901, Je 3,7:5
McCormick, Roberdeau A, 1940, N 19,23:5
McCormick, Roberdeau A Mrs, 1938, Mr 6,II,8:8
McCormick, Robert E, 1960, N 19,21:4
McCormick, Robert E Mrs, 1942, My 16,13:1
McCormick, Robert H, 1963, D 28,23:4
McCormick, Robert Hall, 1917, Mr 15,11:2
McCormick, Robert Hall Mrs, 1922, Mr 17,17:6
McCormick, Robert R (funl plans, Ap 2,13:1; funl, Ap 5,26:6), 1955, Ap 1,1:1
McCormick, Robert R Mrs, 1939, Ag 15,19:4
McCormick, Robert Sanderson, 1919, Ap 17,11:5
McCormick, Roger S, 1968, N 14,47:1
McCormick, Ruth S Mrs, 1959, D 6,86:7
McCormick, Samuel, 1951, Ja 14,85:1
McCormick, Samuel S, 1961, D 9,27:4
McCormick, Scott Lt, 1918, Ja 20,17:1
McCormick, Stanley F, 1947, Ja 20,25:4
McCormick, Stanley Mrs (will), 1968, Ja 13,14:5
McCormick, Susan, 1947, D 14,80:5
McCormick, Thomas J, 1956, N 1,39:4; 1962, Ag 1, 31:1
McCormick, Timothy C, 1959, S 14,29:6
McCormick, Vance C (por),(will, Je 25,23:7), 1946, Je 17,21:1
McCormick, Vance C Mrs, 1953, Ja 25,85:1
McCormick, Vincent A, 1963, My 7,43:2
McCormick, Walter B, 1957, Je 17,23:5
McCormick, William, 1923, F 12,13:4; 1954, Ja 5,27:1
McCormick, William A, 1949, F 23,27:5
McCormick, William B, 1948, Ja 29,23:5
McCormick, William G, 1941, N 30,68:3
McCormick, William H, 1950, N 5,93:1; 1956, Ja 9, 25:3; 1961, Jl 7,25:5
McCormick, William Henry Rev, 1908, F 22,7:5
McCormick, William J (Barry), 1956, Ja 31,29:2
McCormick, William L, 1946, Mr 27,27:4
McCormick, William P G (por), 1940, O 17,25:6
McCormick-Goodhart, Frederick H, 1924, S 28,27:2; 1938, D 13,25:1
McCormick-Goodhart, Leander, 1965, D 18,30:4
McCormick-Goodheart, Janet P Mrs, 1956, N 23,27:4
McCornac, J Wesley, 1940, Ja 17,21:2

McCornack, Condon C, 1944, N 10,19:4
MacCornack, Eugene A, 1957, D 10,35:1
McCornack, Richard B, 1959, My 15,29:2
McCornack, Walter E, 1939, Jl 1,17:5
McCornack, Walter R, 1961, N 8,35:2
McCorristin, Joseph V, 1954, Je 1,27:4
McCorry, Julia A P Mrs, 1949, Ja 12,27:2
MacCorry, P J Rev, 1920, Ag 17,13:3
McCory, John G Mrs, 1950, Ag 9,29:2
McCosh, A G, 1881, N 1,5:3
McCosh, James, 1894, N 17,5:3
McCosh, William C, 1962, Jl 27,25:1
McCosker, Alfred J, 1959, Jl 2,25:1
McCosker, Anna E, 1951, My 25,27:4
McCosker, James, 1922, N 24,17:4
McCosker, John S, 1947, F 15,15:5
McCosker, Redmond A, 1959, Je 22,25:4
McCotter, Kenneth H, 1958, S 5,27:2
McCoull, Neil Mrs, 1951, O 10,23:5
MacCoun, Alfred A, 1962, My 7,31:1
McCoun, Frederic H, 1957, Ja 15,29:1
McCoun, W T, 1878, Jl 21,12:1
MacCount, William E, 1958, D 4,39:1
McCourt, Edward J, 1940, D 11,27:2
McCourt, George T, 1949, S 29,29:2
McCourt, James J Jr, 1962, Je 6,41:4
McCourt, John D, 1948, D 30,19:4
McCourt, John J, 1948, Ag 29,56:6
McCourt, John M, 1952, S 16,29:4
McCourt, Mark, 1941, F 28,19:5
McCourt, William, 1903, S 1,7:6; 1945, Ap 19,27:2
McCowan, David Sir, 1937, My 17,19:3
McCowan, Frank H, 1957, Ap 25,31:4
McCowan, Joseph M, 1952, Mr 30,92:6
McCowan, William L, 1953, Ja 11,90:2
MacCowatt, Horace H, 1953, D 13,86:5
McCowen, Oliver, 1942, Ag 13,19:4
McCown, Allison E, 1948, Ap 28,27:4
McCown, Andrew R, 1950, D 29,19:1
McCown, Edward C, 1946, N 15,23:2
McCown, J R, 1879, Ja 23,5:2
McCown, W Jerome, 1948, D 8,31:4
McCoy, Albert B, 1951, S 7,29:1
McCoy, Alex, 1939, Je 16,23:5
McCoy, Alex C, 1940, S 22,49:2
McCoy, Alexander W, 1944, Jl 2,19:4
McCoy, Ambrose P, 1954, F 18,31:4
McCoy, Anne, 1923, My 29,15:4
McCoy, Babe (H E Rudolph), 1962, Ap 23,29:4
McCoy, Bernard J, 1958, Ap 4,21:3
McCoy, Berryman H, 1954, Je 5,17:5
McCoy, Bessie C, 1940, Mr 23,13:3
McCoy, Bill, 1948, D 31,15:1
McCoy, Caroline S Mrs, 1940, Mr 27,21:4
McCoy, Charles G, 1947, O 24,23:1
McCoy, Clarence M, 1946, Je 18,25:1
McCoy, Clem D Mrs, 1948, Jl 16,19:5
McCoy, Conrad I (por), 1949, Jl 2,15:5
McCoy, Earl H, 1951, N 11,91:2
McCoy, Edward T Mrs, 1944, Ja 8,13:2
McCoy, Emily, 1953, My 30,15:5
McCoy, Emma A, 1945, F 15,19:1
McCoy, Ernest C, 1951, Ja 23,27:2
McCoy, Frank, 1923, Jl 19,15:4; 1940, Ap 2,26:3; 1947, Ja 17,23:2; 1954, F 10,29:5
McCoy, Frank B Col, 1917, S 28,11:6
McCoy, Frank L, 1905, Je 28,5:2
McCoy, Frank R, 1954, Je 5,17:3
McCoy, Frederic M, 1954, Mr 14,89:1
McCoy, George W, 1938, Mr 25,19:1; 1959, O 10, 21:7; 1962, F 12,23:4
McCoy, Guy, 1962, N 17,25:1
McCoy, Harold G, 1950, Jl 15,13:5
McCoy, Harry, 1937, S 2,21:4
McCoy, Henry Bayard Col, 1923, O 2,7:2
McCoy, Herbert N, 1945, My 8,19:4
McCoy, Herbert W Mrs, 1954, N 7,89:1
McCoy, Horace, 1955, D 17,23:3
McCoy, Hugh W, 1964, O 23,36:5
McCoy, Irving P Mrs, 1946, Ap 3,25:5
McCoy, Jackson, 1952, Je 28,19:1
McCoy, James Col, 1875, My 30,7:1
McCoy, James F, 1942, N 3,23:4
McCoy, James Henry Bp, 1919, Mr 23,20:4
McCoy, James P, 1951, Mr 24,13:5
McCoy, James W, 1937, S 16,25:4; 1947, F 4,25:5
McCoy, Jasper, 1951, Ag 18,11:4
McCoy, John A, 1959, Ja 18,88:5
McCoy, John C (por), 1941, Ap 18,21:3
McCoy, John J Mrs, 1957, S 29,86:2
McCoy, John P, 1938, S 20,23:1
McCoy, John W, 1961, Mr 22,41:4
McCoy, Joseph C, 1955, Ag 17,27:3
McCoy, Joseph F, 1938, S 2,17:5
McCoy, Joseph F Mrs, 1951, S 18,31:2
McCoy, Joseph J, 1963, Ag 22,27:4
McCoy, Mary Mrs, 1943, My 22,13:6
McCoy, Mary V, 1937, Ja 24,II,8:4
McCoy, Mildred Mrs, 1955, F 3,23:1
McCoy, Paul, 1966, N 3,39:3
McCoy, Percy L, 1948, My 9,68:4
McCoy, Peter J, 1958, Jl 19,15:6
McCoy, R Allen, 1947, D 5,25:4
M'Coy, R B Maj Gen, 1926, Ja 6,21:4
McCoy, Richard F, 1949, S 30,23:2
McCoy, Richard T, 1954, Mr 28,88:5
McCoy, Robert, 1951, My 16,49:3
McCoy, Robert B Mrs, 1954, N 3,29:2
McCoy, Robert E, 1950, O 25,35:2
McCoy, Samuel D, 1964, Ap 11,25:1
McCoy, Samuel D Mrs, 1960, D 10,23:5
McCoy, Stanley E, 1948, N 30,27:5
McCoy, Thomas A, 1962, F 22,25:3
McCoy, Thomas F Sr, 1950, O 10,31:2
McCoy, Thomas O, 1942, N 25,23:5
McCoy, Thomas P, 1945, Ag 17,17:4
MacCoy, W Logan, 1948, Ja 13,26:2
McCoy, Walter R, 1952, Je 21,15:3
McCoy, Wayne G, 1945, Mr 31,19:6
McCoy, Willard A, 1946, Je 15,21:5
McCoy, William H, 1941, N 17,19:4
McCoy, William J, 1953, Mr 14,15:5
McCoy, William S, 1940, Ap 21,43:1
McCrackan, William Dennison, 1923, Je 14,19:4
McCracken, Andrew V, 1963, Ja 17,8:7
MacCracken, Booth, 1948, D 5,92:2
McCracken, Charles C, 1957, Ag 4,80:6
McCracken, Charles D, 1951, Ja 29,19:2
McCracken, David H, 1953, Mr 12,27:2
McCracken, Franklin T, 1937, Ag 29,II,7:2
McCracken, Fred C, 1940, Je 23,31:2
McCracken, Fred W, 1968, Ap 23,44:4
McCracken, Frederick B, 1959, Mr 7,22:1
MacCracken, Henry Mitchell Dr (funl, De 28,11:3), 1918, D 25,15:5
McCracken, Jack D, 1958, Ja 7,47:4
MacCracken, James A, 1941, Je 22,32:6
McCracken, James S, 1944, N 30,23:6
McCracken, Joan, 1961, N 2,37:2
MacCracken, John H (por), 1948, F 2,19:1
McCracken, Josiah C, 1962, F 16,27:1
McCracken, Josiah Mrs, 1944, Ag 22,17:3
McCracken, Lawrence M, 1958, Mr 12,31:4
McCracken, Leonard J, 1942, Ag 19,19:4
McCracken, Lorenzo F, 1940, Mr 17,48:8
McCracken, Robert, 1938, Je 18,15:5
McCracken, Robert (J McTurk), 1961, Jl 23,68:5
McCracken, Robert B, 1954, O 2,17:2
McCracken, Robert J, 1947, Ja 21,23:3
McCracken, Robert S, 1949, O 5,29:4
McCracken, Robert T, 1960, D 26,23:3
McCracken, Rollo B, 1952, Je 25,29:5
McCracken, Samuel, 1951, D 29,11:6
McCracken, Samuel J, 1965, My 28,33:3
McCracken, Tracy S, 1960, D 27,29:3
MacCracken, Walter, 1940, Mr 5,24:4
McCracken, Wilfred H, 1955, S 20,31:4
McCracken, William, 1906, Ap 29,11:5; 1940, Je 14, 21:4
MacCracken, William B, 1943, Ap 2,21:1
McCracken, William J, 1948, N 29,23:4; 1949, D 4, 108:5
MacCracken, William Mrs, 1952, F 11,25:5
MacCracken, William P Sr Dr, 1937, F 2,23:3
McCrackens, Arthur J, 1959, F 2,25:3
McCrackin, Alexander Commodore, 1911, Ja 5,9:4
McCrady, John, 1968, D 25,31:2
McCrae, John D Lt-Col, 1918, Ja 30,9:5
McCrae, T, 1935, Jl 1,19:3
McCraith, Charles E, 1942, O 21,21:5; 1948, O 28,29:5
McCraith, Douglas, 1952, S 17,31:4
McCran, Thomas F (por),(funl, S 21,19:5), 1925, S 20,7:1
McCrann, James J Mrs, 1948, O 26,31:2; 1966, F 24, 37:3
McCrann, Raymond A, 1959, Ag 1,17:4
McCrary, D B, 1946, O 29,25:2
McCrary, Douglas A Mrs, 1968, Ja 15,47:3
McCrary, Frank R, 1952, Je 14,15:4
McCrary, J Reagan, 1948, Ap 10,13:1
McCrary, Pierce R, 1949, Ja 28,22:2
MacCrate, John Mrs, 1963, N 19,41:2
McCraven, James M P, 1952, D 31,15:1
McCraw, Richard, 1951, O 25,39:6
McCraw, William, 1955, N 10,35:1
McCray, Benjamin M, 1948, Mr 16,27:5
McCray, Lee H, 1961, Ap 3,33:4
McCray, Lionel G, 1948, My 28,23:2
McCray, Randolph Y, 1951, D 5,35:1
McCray, Warren T (por), 1938, D 20,26:1
McCray, Warren T Mrs, 1947, D 20,17:5
McCrea, A Wallace, 1954, Ap 8,27:3
McCrea, Abraham L, 1946, S 14,7:6
McCrea, Albert J, 1939, Ap 29,17:5
McCrea, Anna L Mrs, 1942, Jl 16,19:4
McCrea, Arch M, 1937, D 20,27:2
McCrea, Archibald Mrs, 1960, O 20,35:3
McCrea, Archie E, 1950, My 2,29:3
McCrea, Carrol, 1942, Ap 26,40:4
McCrea, Charles, 1952, O 31,25:3
McCrea, Charles H, 1946, Ag 25,46:3
McCrea, E P Commander, 1881, O 15,2:2
McCrea, Edwin L, 1939, Ap 2,III,6:7
McCrea, Florence, 1948, Jl 13,28:3
McCrea, Frederic L, 1949, N 13,93:1
McCrea, Harry O, 1942, Ja 22,18:3
McCrea, Henry Capt, 1908, Jl 20,9:6
McCrea, James (funl, Mr 31,IV,7:5), 1913, Mr 29, 15:5
McCrea, James A Col, 1923, O 18,19:2
McCrea, James A Jr, 1948, Je 20,62:3
McCrea, James A Jr Mrs, 1966, D 21,39:3
McCrea, James A Mrs, 1957, Ap 29,25:1
McCrea, James G, 1953, S 14,27:2
McCrea, John E, 1911, My 8,11:5
McCrea, Louis, 1944, N 5,53:1
McCrea, Nelson G (por), 1944, Je 1,19:1
McCrea, Roswell C, 1951, Jl 4,17:5
McCrea, Samuel H Jr, 1941, Mr 29,15:3
McCrea, Tully Gen, 1918, S 7,7:6
McCrea, Walter A, 1946, N 5,25:5
McCrea, William J, 1964, O 1,35:5
McCready, Charles Msgr, 1915, Ap 10,11:3
McCready, Donald M, 1938, My 12,23:3
McCready, Edward L, 1952, Mr 22,13:5
McCready, Ernest W, 1950, O 27,29:5
McCready, Harold, 1945, Ag 3,17:5
McCready, Leroy, 1948, S 23,29:4
McCready, Nathaniel L'Hommedieu, 1915, Mr 2,9:4
McCready, Robert H, 1952, Mr 16,90:7
McCready, Robert L (por), 1947, D 16,33:5
McCreary, George D, 1915, Jl 27,9:4
McCreary, J B, 1879, Jl 11,2:2
McCreary, J Bruce, 1938, S 14,23:2
McCreary, James B, 1918, O 9,11:3
McCreary, James T, 1925, My 20,23:5
McCreary, John J Rev, 1937, F 13,13:3
McCreary, M Louise, 1938, Mr 30,21:5
McCreary, Peter H, 1968, Je 5,47:1
McCreary, Robert E, 1950, Ja 12,27:1
McCreary, Walter H, 1946, F 19,25:5
McCreary, William C, 1954, Mr 11,31:5
McCreath, Lesley, 1957, Ag 19,19:4
McCredie, Donald, 1944, Ja 11,19:1
McCredie, Jennie C Mrs, 1937, Ja 27,21:4
McCredy, Warren H, 1966, S 5,15:4
McCree, Junie, 1918, Ja 14,11:4
McCree, Marian, 1962, D 1,25:4
McCree, Reno, 1916, My 18,11:6
McCree, Robert D, 1955, F 22,21:1
McCree, Vivian Mrs, 1948, D 22,28:3
McCreery, Andrew B, 1916, N 26,21:2
McCreery, Arthur, 1953, N 20,24:3
McCreery, C A, 1879, N 11,5:3
McCreery, Chester M, 1960, S 11,82:4
McCreery, Clifford B, 1952, O 17,27:4
McCreery, Earl W Mrs, 1955, Jl 2,15:5
McCreery, Edgar S, 1952, Je 15,84:5
McCreery, Fenton R, 1940, O 7,17:5
McCreery, Forbes R Dr, 1937, Jl 1,27:3
McCreery, Hector P, 1963, S 12,37:3
McCreery, Henry F, 1937, D 19,II,8:6
McCreery, J, 1881, S 25,5:4
McCreery, James, 1903, F 28,9:5
McCreery, James H, 1922, O 17,19:3; 1957, Jl 13,
McCreery, John A, 1948, F 1,60:2
McCreery, Lydia F P Mrs, 1939, Ja 19,19:2
McCreery, Mary McK, 1964, D 24,19:5
McCreery, Maud Mrs, 1938, Ap 12,24:2
McCreery, Richard L, 1967, O 19,42:2
McCreery, Richard S, 1938, O 20,23:4
McCreery, Samuel, 1909, Jl 4,7:7
McCreery, Samuel W, 1937, Ag 8,II,6:2
McCreery, Thomas H, 1954, O 27,29:1
McCreery, William John, 1909, Mr 24,9:3
McCreesh, John J, 1959, S 10,35:5
McCreight, Harry A, 1946, Ag 18,47:7
McCreight, Robert, 1940, My 19,42:4
McCrelis, Cornelius B, 1964, My 13,47:5
MacCrellish, William H, 1961, Je 2,32:1
MacCrisken, Edward W, 1962, O 9,42:1
McCroddan, Matthew, 1954, F 10,29:1
McCroden, Hugh J, 1958, F 18,28:5
McCrorey, Henry, 1951, Jl 14,13:4
McCrorken, Thomas F, 1956, S 21,25:2
McCrory, Daniel, 1951, F 25,87:2
McCrory, Henry, 1906, D 21,9:3
McCrory, John G, 1943, N 21,57:2
McCroskery, J Harry, 1962, Ja 24,33:4
McCroskey, Donald W, 1944, N 15,27:1
McCroskry, Brig-Gen, 1921, Mr 4,13:4
McCrosky, Carl R, 1946, O 18,24:2
McCrosky, James W Mrs, 1961, N 8,35:4
McCrosky, Theodore Tremaine, 1968, Jl 25,33:2
McCrossen, James W, 1939, Je 26,15:6
McCrudden, Edward, 1943, Mr 1,19:3
McCrudden, Francis L, 1958, Ja 19,86:1
McCrudden, George J, 1946, Je 18,25:1
McCrudden, John F, 1949, Jl 7,26:2
McCrudden, Joseph F, 1944, Je 2,15:5
McCrudden, Samuel, 1950, D 5,31:1
McCruden, Donald R, 1961, O 28,21:3
McCrum, E Howard, 1950, Je 8,31:2
MacCrum, John J, 1938, Mr 11,19:3
McCrum, Lloyd D, 1968, Ja 25,37:1
McCrystal, Edward T Maj, 1913, F 8,13:4
McCrystal, Jane (Sister Theresa Vincent), 191 My 24,13:6
McCrystal, Joseph, 1939, Je 21,23:4
McCrystle, Jerome, 1952, Je 18,27:5

McCuaig, George E, 1958, Mr 22,17:2
McCubbin, John D S, 1962, S 15,25:3
McCue, Aloysius D, 1950, N 9,33:6
McCue, Catherine B Mrs, 1942, Mr 29,45:1
McCue, Charles A, 1942, Ja 14,21:4
McCue, Edward, 1903, Jl 31,12:3
McCue, Edward J, 1945, Ag 9,21:4
McCue, Edward J Father, 1916, S 22,7:5
McCue, Eugene P, 1952, Ap 6,88:1
McCue, Eugene V, 1943, Mr 27,13:4
McCue, Francis X, 1967, O 27,45:4
McCue, Frank J, 1948, N 18,27:3
McCue, James Mrs, 1940, F 4,41:2
McCue, Jeremiah, 1938, F 21,19:4
McCue, John J, 1957, O 31,31:1; 1958, Je 22,76:2; 1960, D 25,42:2
McCue, John J Mrs, 1957, D 27,19:2
McCue, M, 1932, S 19,17:1
McCue, Martin, 1946, O 27,63:5
McCue, Martin A, 1956, Ag 11,13:2
McCue, Michael A, 1947, O 1,29:3
McCue, Patrick J Mrs, 1945, Ag 14,21:3
McCue, Richard A, 1942, D 1,25:1
McCue, Rose, 1967, Ag 26,28:2
McCue, Thomas, 1941, Mr 6,21:5
McCue, Thomas J, 1913, Ag 10,II,11:5
McCue, Thomas P, 1938, Ag 23,17:4
McCuen, Leslie E, 1942, Ag 22,13:4
McCuen, Robert W, 1945, Ag 8,23:5
McCuen, William A, 1951, Mr 17,15:4
McCuin, Carlisle, 1939, Mr 26,III,8:2
McCuin, Carlisle Mrs, 1939, Mr 26,III,8:2
McCullagh, Archibald Rev Dr, 1922, D 14,21:2
McCullagh, Clement G, 1952, Ag 6,21:1
McCullagh, Crawford, 1948, Ap 14,27:4
McCullagh, Florence C Mrs, 1939, Ag 15,19:5
McCullagh, Francis, 1956, N 26,27:2
McCullagh, George H, 1943, S 25,15:4
McCullagh, George Mrs, 1939, My 26,23:3
McCullagh, J B, 1897, Ja 1,1:5
McCullagh, John, 1917, Ja 4,11:3
McCullagh, Samuel, 1948, Jl 22,23:2
McCullagh, William Lt, 1910, Je 11,11:5
McCullars, Clayton J, 1959, My 5,33:1
McCullen, Michael F, 1941, F 17,15:2
McCullers, Carson (funl, O 4,51:1), 1967, S 30,1:6
McCullers, J Reeves Jr, 1953, N 27,27:6
McCulley, Albert C, 1950, My 4,27:5
McCulley, Arthur J, 1958, N 25,33:1
McCulley, John A, 1954, Mr 17,31:5
McCulloch, Allan R, 1925, O 11,5:1
McCulloch, Carleton B, 1949, Ap 7,30:3
McCulloch, Charles A (por), 1946, Ja 25,23:1
MacCulloch, Charles H, 1947, Je 25,25:6
McCulloch, David, 1958, Mr 6,27:2
McCulloch, David H, 1955, S 22,31:1
McCulloch, E A, 1933, Ja 24,14:1
McCulloch, Frank H Mrs, 1945, Ag 21,13:3
McCulloch, Frank J, 1946, Mr 30,15:1
McCulloch, George, 1907, D 13,11:3
McCulloch, George D, 1942, Jl 18,13:3
McCulloch, George Foulke, 1915, Mr 29,9:4
McCulloch, H J, 1903, Je 29,7:6
McCulloch, Hugh, 1895, My 25,13:5
McCulloch, James W, 1938, Mr 23,23:5
McCulloch, John, 1939, Ag 4,13:5
McCulloch, Joseph H, 1960, D 17,23:5
McCulloch, Kenneth L, 1945, Jl 22,38:1
McCulloch, May C, 1948, O 3,64:4
McCulloch, Patrick J, 1943, F 18,23:4
McCulloch, Richard, 1940, Ag 30,19:4
McCulloch, Richard Mrs, 1956, N 29,35:2
MacCulloch, Robert P, 1961, F 27,27:4
McCulloch, Robert W, 1946, F 6,23:4
McCulloch, Robert W Mrs, 1941, Ap 2,23:3
McCulloch, Roscoe C, 1958, Mr 19,31:3
McCulloch, Samuel W, 1940, O 9,25:4
McCulloch, William A, 1959, D 3,37:4
McCulloch, William P, 1957, O 4,23:3
McCulloch, William R, 1959, O 15,39:5
McCulloch, William T, 1922, Mr 25,11:3
McCulloh, Charles S, 1940, D 27,19:2
McCulloh, Gordon, 1968, Ap 2,47:1
McCulloh, James S, 1957, Jl 6,15:6
McCulloh, James S Mrs, 1956, Je 18,25:4
McCullom, John U, 1948, Ap 9,23:4
McCullouch, Charles H Jr, 1920, Ap 4,22:2
McCullough, Ashley M, 1945, Mr 20,19:5
McCullough, Austin E Mrs, 1940, N 1,25:4
McCullough, Bruce, 1950, S 26,31:2
McCullough, C B, 1946, My 7,21:4
McCullough, Charles E, 1958, N 7,28:3
McCullough, Clem B, 1948, Ag 15,61:1
McCullough, Daniel, 1905, Ap 11,11:6
McCullough, E, 1931, O 2,25:5
McCullough, Edmund R, 1962, O 14,86:8
McCullough, Edward A, 1946, N 25,27:5
McCullough, Edwin C, 1955, O 14,27:3
McCullough, Esther M, 1957, Je 15,17:4
McCullough, Frances C, 1917, Ap 13,13:5
McCullough, Frank, 1953, My 24,89:1
McCullough, Frank W, 1948, O 7,29:3
McCullough, G R, 1948, N 24,23:5
McCullough, Hall P, 1966, Ag 6,23:4
McCullough, Hall P Mrs, 1967, Je 28,45:4
McCullough, Harold A, 1964, Jl 2,31:3
McCullough, Harry E, 1963, Ap 9,31:4
McCullough, Herman L, 1946, O 8,23:5
McCullough, J Augustus, 1949, F 23,27:4
McCullough, James J, 1942, N 29,64:8
McCullough, James M, 1950, S 23,17:6
McCullough, James S Mrs (Myrtle Reed McCullough), 1911, Ag 20,II,9:6
McCullough, John, 1885, N 9,5:1; 1940, Mr 24,31:3
McCullough, John E, 1941, Mr 8,19:7
McCullough, John F Rev, 1937, Mr 23,23:5
McCullough, John G, 1915, My 30,13:4
McCullough, John G Mrs, 1955, D 15,37:2
McCullough, John Henry, 1921, D 15,19:4
McCullough, John M, 1961, S 7,35:3
McCullough, John R, 1957, S 19,29:4
McCullough, Leon, 1952, D 7,88:3
McCullough, Leon J, 1968, Je 29,29:5
McCullough, Myrtle Reed (Mrs Jas S McCullough), 1911, Ag 20,II,9:6
McCullough, Richard H, 1939, O 15,49:3
McCullough, Richard P, 1966, Mr 24,39:2
McCullough, Robert H, 1951, Ag 9,21:4; 1967, Ja 6, 35:2
McCullough, Robert L, 1963, Ap 8,47:2
McCullough, Rosa A, 1946, Ap 17,25:3
McCullough, Samuel H Mrs, 1946, My 8,25:4
McCullough, Theodore W Col, 1937, D 9,25:2
McCullough, Thomas L, 1952, N 19,22:3
McCullough, Walter A, 1951, S 30,31:5
McCullough, Walter J, 1951, Ap 26,29:4
McCullough, William C, 1940, Jl 23,19:4
McCullough, William J, 1954, Ag 8,85:3
McCullough, Willis G, 1948, D 18,19:4
McCullum, Fenelan, 1925, D 13,13:1
MacCullum, Norman, 1937, Ja 12,23:4
McCullum, Raymond, 1960, N 1,39:1
McCully, C Harold, 1965, O 14,47:2
McCully, Charles H, 1941, My 23,21:2
McCully, Edwin H, 1968, N 7,50:6
McCully, Harry M, 1947, D 2,29:4
McCully, Harry O, 1966, F 20,88:7
McCully, John E, 1938, Jl 14,21:2
McCully, Joseph, 1948, Jl 20,23:3
McCully, Newton A, 1951, Je 15,24:2
McCumber, Clifton H, 1943, Je 25,17:5
McCumber, P J, 1933, My 19,17:1
McCumber, William, 1949, Ap 6,29:5
McCune, Abbie L Mrs, 1938, O 2,49:2
McCune, Arthur C, 1952, F 20,30:2
McCune, C W, 1885, Mr 15,2:3
McCune, Charles A, 1940, O 14,19:5
McCune, Edmund C, 1950, S 5,27:3
McCune, Frederick G, 1953, O 28,29:1
McCune, Frederick G Mrs, 1960, Jl 25,23:4
McCune, George M, 1948, N 7,88:6
McCune, George S, 1941, D 6,17:3
McCune, George S Mrs, 1952, Mr 7,23:2
McCune, Janet Mrs (est acctg), 1959, D 24,31:8
McCune, John Robinson, 1923, My 15,19:4
McCune, Theodore, 1909, N 5,9:4
McCune, Thomas G, 1956, N 29,35:5
McCunn, J N Mrs, 1912, S 28,13:5
McCunn, James M, 1955, Ag 14,80:6
McCunn, John H Judge, 1872, Jl 7,1:2
McCunn, John N, 1937, Ja 14,21:2
McCurdy, Anne A Mrs, 1951, Ag 12,78:8
McCurdy, Charles A, 1941, N 11,24:2
McCurdy, Charles P Jr Mrs, 1956, Ag 31,17:2
McCurdy, D George, 1954, N 5,21:2
McCurdy, Delos, 1921, O 8,13:4
McCurdy, Fleming B, 1952, Ag 30,13:6
McCurdy, Frank, 1941, Jl 18,20:4
McCurdy, Frank M, 1950, O 22,94:5
McCurdy, Frank M Mrs, 1964, Je 26,29:4
MacCurdy, Frederick, 1965, Je 4,35:2
McCurdy, George B, 1950, Ap 20,29:2
MacCurdy, H Leigh, 1961, F 1,35:2
MacCurdy, Hansford M Mrs, 1937, My 25,27:2
MacCurdy, Harriet R, 1961, My 6,31:6
McCurdy, Harry A R, 1940, Ag 15,19:6
McCurdy, Hugh, 1908, Jl 17,7:5
McCurdy, James H, 1940, S 5,23:6
McCurdy, John A D, 1961, Je 26,31:1
McCurdy, John Mrs, 1943, My 14,19:3
MacCurdy, John T, 1947, Jl 3,21:6
McCurdy, Joseph, 1903, S 16,9:6
McCurdy, Laurence T, 1956, Ag 18,17:1
McCurdy, Mary Mrs, 1951, D 7,27:3
McCurdy, Matthew S, 1921, F 17,11:5
McCurdy, Merle M, 1968, My 7,41:3
McCurdy, Ralph G (por), 1948, Ja 11,56:1
McCurdy, Richard A, 1916, Mr 7,11:3
McCurdy, Richard A Mrs, 1910, My 2,9:4; 1910, My 5,11:5
McCurdy, Robert A, 1958, Jl 4,19:4
McCurdy, Robert H, 1951, Ja 11,26:2
McCurdy, Robert H Mrs, 1925, My 25,17:5
McCurdy, Sidney M, 1944, S 27,21:5
McCurdy, Wesley, 1961, S 16,19:4
McCurdy, William A, 1941, D 9,31:5
McCurdy, William C, 1940, Ap 20,17:3
McCurdy, William D, 1953, Ja 1,23:3
McCurdy, William E, 1967, Jl 6,29:6
McCurdy, William G, 1939, D 16,17:3
McCurdy, William J, 1968, F 15,43:2
McCurley, Lansing C, 1958, O 17,29:4
McCurley, William S, 1941, S 12,21:4
McCurrach, George, 1938, S 23,27:4
McCurrach, James C, 1966, O 24,39:4
McCurrach, Mabel C Mrs, 1940, F 19,17:2
McCurren, John T, 1943, My 5,27:3
McCusker, Barnum C, 1956, S 24,27:4
McCusker, Edward, 1965, Ja 12,37:2
McCusker, Edward Mrs (Paula), 1964, Jl 26,56:8
McCusker, F Stanley, 1957, D 3,35:2
McCusker, Francis S Mrs, 1949, Jl 8,19:5
McCusker, Harold R, 1967, O 11,47:2
McCusker, Henry, 1943, Ap 12,23:3
McCusker, Hubert J, 1967, Ja 14,31:1
McCusker, J J Rev, 1903, Ja 9,9:5
McCusker, James, 1952, My 11,92:3
McCusker, John R, 1953, Ja 26,22:6
McCusker, Mary A, 1918, O 14,11:7
McCusker, Thomas A, 1950, Ag 8,29:1
McCusker, Thomas A Mrs, 1963, Ap 28,88:4
McCusker, Thomas B Jr, 1961, Ja 28,19:3
McCusker, Thomas B Sr, 1960, Ja 27,33:4
McCutchen, Charles W Mrs, 1948, N 13,15:3
McCutchen, Joseph Dr, 1882, My 16,5:3
McCutchen, Leighton M Mrs, 1959, Ap 8,37:4
McCutchen, Lucy, 1953, O 10,17:3
McCutchen, Samuel P, 1966, Mr 8,30:1
McCutchen, Tyler Mrs, 1944, S 14,23:3
McCutchen, William M, 1954, Je 13,88:2
McCutcheon, Allen O, 1953, Ag 10,23:6
McCutcheon, Arthur S, 1951, Ap 10,27:4
McCutcheon, David C, 1925, D 21,21:5
McCutcheon, E Louise, 1950, My 12,27:3
McCutcheon, Frank M, 1949, D 3,15:2
McCutcheon, Frederick L Mrs, 1947, Jl 29,21:3
McCutcheon, Frederick M, 1950, Jl 16,69:2
McCutcheon, G B, 1928, O 24,1:2
MacCutcheon, George W, 1917, Ap 27,11:5
McCutcheon, George W Mrs, 1947, Mr 2,6:4
McCutcheon, Henry D Maj, 1920, Je 15,11:3
McCutcheon, Hugh, 1920, Ap 17,15:3
McCutcheon, James (funl;will, Jl 26,5:4), 1914, Jl 24, 9:5
McCutcheon, John, 1959, D 2,43:5
McCutcheon, John J, 1954, O 27,29:2
McCutcheon, John P, 1949, N 13,92:6
McCutcheon, John T (por), 1949, Je 11,17:3
McCutcheon, Joseph M, 1951, Je 5,31:2
McCutcheon, Lorne, 1953, D 17,37:3
McCutcheon, Louise M Mrs, 1937, Je 18,21:1
McCutcheon, Norman Lockwood, 1913, O 1,9:6
McCutcheon, Paris S, 1949, O 31,25:5
McCutcheon, Patrick F, 1944, Ap 15,11:5
McCutcheon, S G, 1884, Jl 12,5:6
McCutcheon, Thomas P, 1907, N 29,9:7
McCutcheon, Victor H, 1949, Ja 6,23:3
McCutcheon, W, 1928, Ja 28,8:8
McCutcheon, W M Dr, 1937, O 2,21:3
McCutcheon, William C (por), 1939, F 17,19:3
MacDade, Albert D Mrs, 1937, D 2,25:5
McDade, George, 1942, Ja 17,17:5
McDade, John T, 1949, Jl 20,25:4
McDaniel, Arthur B, 1943, D 27,20:3
McDaniel, Arthur S, 1941, Mr 27,23:2
McDaniel, Charles T, 1938, D 7,23:4
McDaniel, D R, 1948, D 23,19:3
McDaniel, Earl, 1945, D 8,17:2
McDaniel, Ellen, 1923, Jl 7,11:5
McDaniel, Floyd C, 1952, Ja 1,25:6
McDaniel, George M, 1944, Ag 21,15:6
McDaniel, Hattie (funl, N 2,88:1; will, N 5,17:3), 1952, O 27,27:4
McDaniel, Henry (por), 1948, Ja 25,56:7
McDaniel, J A, 1945, N 30,23:1
McDaniel, J Erskine, 1962, N 29,38:6
McDaniel, John S, 1964, N 15,86:6
Macdaniel, Leonard, 1924, O 21,23:4
MacDaniel, Margaret Mrs, 1937, Jl 22,9:4
McDaniel, Marion, 1923, Jl 7,11:5
McDaniel, Marion R, 1939, N 1,23:2
MacDaniels, Clarence J, 1958, S 15,21:4
McDaniels, D Col, 1885, Ja 31,5:3
McDaniels, William H, 1945, My 20,32:1
McDaniels, William M, 1944, Ag 17,17:4
McDannald, Alex H, 1957, D 19,31:2
McDannald, Clyde E (por), 1949, Ag 14,68:1
McDannel, Thomas H, 1942, S 4,23:6
McDarby, Robert J, 1957, Ja 9,31:5
McDavid, Adolphus J, 1957, O 22,33:5
McDavid, James L, 1939, Mr 20,17:5
MacDavitt, Madaliene, 1953, Ap 27,23:4
McDavitt, Marcellus B Mrs, 1963, O 19,25:6
McDearby, Katherine Mrs, 1948, Ap 21,27:4
McDede, Anson, 1952, S 10,29:2
McDede, Ernest H (por), 1940, N 4,19:4
McDede, Frank F, 1943, Jl 11,35:3
McDede, Joseph S, 1941, Ja 29,17:5
MacDermid, James G Mrs, 1940, N 5,25:2

McDermid, William A, 1962, My 16,41:3
McDermit, Frank M, 1922, O 5,23:3
McDermith, Janet L, 1954, Ja 31,32:6
McDermitt, Francis F Sr, 1958, Ag 29,23:5
McDermitt, Matthew P A, 1939, Je 27,23:3
McDermitt, William P A, 1961, F 19,86:6
McDermond, J Frank Jr, 1946, O 9,27:5
MacDermot, Patric R, 1946, N 29,25:4
McDermott, Ada L Mrs, 1939, F 26,38:8
McDermott, Alex P, 1958, Jl 20,65:2
McDermott, Aline L, 1951, F 17,15:4
McDermott, Allan Langdon, 1908, O 27,9:6
McDermott, Anna (Mother Mary Edw), 1953, F 7, 17:5
McDermott, Anne E, 1957, My 28,34:6
McDermott, Arthur V, 1949, D 20,31:1
McDermott, Bernard A, 1959, Je 16,35:4
McDermott, Bernard J, 1946, F 23,13:4
McDermott, Bridget Mrs, 1940, Jl 5,13:4
McDermott, Charles, 1948, Je 6,72:2
McDermott, Charles J, 1941, D 20,19:6
McDermott, Charles L, 1958, S 16,27:3
McDermott, Cleveland J, 1946, Ja 24,22:2
McDermott, Cyril L Mrs, 1952, Mr 8,13:4
McDermott, Eddie, 1947, Ap 9,25:1
McDermott, Edward J, 1947, O 15,27:4
MacDermott, Edward M, 1968, Mr 29,41:2
McDermott, Edward T, 1949, N 28,27:4
McDermott, Elizabeth, 1946, N 12,29:5
McDermott, Eugene G, 1945, S 26,23:2
McDermott, Francis, 1907, O 21,7:5
McDermott, Francis J, 1942, Je 10,21:2
McDermott, Frank P, 1921, Ja 4,13:3; 1949, N 3,29:3
McDermott, George R Prof, 1937, My 27,23:1
McDermott, George T Judge, 1937, Ja 20,22:2
McDermott, Gerald R, 1951, My 30,21:6
McDermott, H, 1884, Ja 22,5:2
McDermott, Harold, 1947, S 28,61:2
McDermott, Harold M, 1958, Jl 19,15:5
McDermott, Henry C, 1956, Mr 29,27:4
McDermott, Ida, 1950, Ja 8,77:1
MacDermott, J Edward, 1940, Jl 28,27:2
McDermott, J Francis, 1953, Ag 14,19:5
McDermott, Jack C, 1966, Mr 1,37:4
McDermott, James, 1916, Ap 8,15:7; 1941, Mr 19, 23:7; 1950, O 1,104:6
McDermott, James A, 1941, My 12,17:4
McDermott, James F, 1950, My 9,30:2
McDermott, James J, 1947, D 3,29:3; 1964, Mr 11, 39:2; 1965, Ag 20,29:4
McDermott, James O Mrs, 1966, Mr 6,93:2
McDermott, James W, 1947, Je 27,21:5
McDermott, John, 1880, Ap 20,8:3
McDermott, John A, 1965, O 18,35:2
McDermott, John B, 1954, S 20,23:5
McDermott, John C, 1955, Je 24,21:2; 1965, N 1,41:2
McDermott, John F, 1907, O 21,7:5
McDermott, John J, 1944, F 16,17:6; 1947, Mr 21,22:3
MacDermott, John L, 1938, O 12,27:6
McDermott, John M, 1943, Ap 1,23:2
McDermott, John P, 1949, F 9,28:2
McDermott, John S, 1963, Je 30,56:5
McDermott, Joseph (por), 1938, Je 11,15:5
McDermott, Joseph E, 1944, My 2,19:6
McDermott, Joseph J, 1950, N 28,31:4
McDermott, Joseph P, 1955, O 11,39:3
McDermott, Katherine, 1944, Ja 8,13:5
McDermott, Lawrence M, 1945, F 16,23:4
McDermott, Leo J, 1956, Mr 14,33:5
McDermott, Margaret E, 1949, F 22,23:2
McDermott, Martin A, 1968, S 24,44:6
McDermott, Martin P Mrs, 1942, Jl 12,35:3
McDermott, Mary E, 1948, N 16,29:3
McDermott, Mary S, 1965, F 28,88:6
McDermott, Michael F, 1952, Ja 4,23:1
McDermott, Michael J (funl plans, Ag 7,73:2; funl Ag 10,25:5), 1955, Ag 6,15:5
McDermott, Owen, 1945, O 22,17:4
McDermott, Owen Mrs, 1952, Ja 4,23:3
McDermott, Paul F, 1945, D 20,23:4
McDermott, Peter, 1964, D 10,47:1
McDermott, Ray, 1937, Ja 3,II,8:3
McDermott, Raymond M, 1938, D 20,25:5
McDermott, Richard, 1873, N 18,3:7
McDermott, Richard M, 1957, N 29,27:3
McDermott, Robert, 1953, O 8,29:2; 1963, O 5,25:3
McDermott, Robert J, 1951, Ja 6,15:5
McDermott, S Earl, 1950, Ja 31,23:2
MacDermott, Seamus, 1960, O 18,40:1
McDermott, Stephen H, 1959, Ja 28,31:4
McDermott, Terence S, 1963, Ap 6,19:4
McDermott, Theresa Mrs, 1942, Je 24,19:3
MacDermott, Thomas J, 1954, Je 18,23:3
McDermott, Thomas W, 1947, Mr 17,23:5
McDermott, Walter L, 1945, Mr 27,19:1
McDermott, William, 1941, N 5,23:5
McDermott, William C, 1938, F 4,21:3; 1960, Ag 17, 31:6
McDermott, William E, 1965, S 14,39:5
McDermott, William F, 1953, O 7,29:1
McDermott, William F (trb lr, N 23,II,3:3), 1958, N 17,31:4
McDermott, William F, 1964, O 26,31:4
McDermott, William F Sr, 1951, Ap 27,23:3
MacDermott, William H Mrs, 1948, Ag 28,15:3
McDermott, William J, 1948, N 23,29:1
McDermott, William J Dr, 1904, Mr 14,9:6
McDermott, William R, 1960, Ja 22,27:2
McDermott, William S, 1943, F 14,48:5
MacDermut, Charles K, 1948, Ap 17,15:1
McDevett, C W, 1941, D 22,17:2
McDevit, William V, 1943, N 29,19:6
McDevitt, Charles J, 1950, My 30,17:2
McDevitt, Frederick H Mrs, 1948, O 24,76:3
McDevitt, George A, 1952, O 20,23:4
McDevitt, Harry S, 1950, Ap 23,94:5
McDevitt, Herbert, 1957, O 21,25:2
McDevitt, Hugh, 1961, My 12,26:4
McDevitt, J F, 1868, Jl 15,5:2
McDevitt, J Harry, 1942, N 28,13:1
McDevitt, James, 1947, Mr 2,60:5
McDevitt, James A, 1940, F 9,19:3
McDevitt, James J Dr, 1937, My 30,19:1
McDevitt, James L, 1963, Mr 20,16:1
McDevitt, James Mrs, 1948, My 8,15:6
McDevitt, James W, 1956, N 10,19:4
McDevitt, John J, 1951, F 4,76:6
McDevitt, John J Jr, 1945, N 16,19:5
McDevitt, Joseph D Sr, 1953, Mr 22,86:8
McDevitt, Joseph T, 1949, O 6,31:4
McDevitt, Mary E, 1954, O 30,17:4
McDevitt, Michael M, 1947, D 28,43:3
McDevitt, P R, 1935, N 12,19:3
McDevitt, Thomas F, 1967, Je 14,47:3
McDevitt, William A Mrs, 1965, Ag 3,31:1
MacDiarmid, Allan, 1945, Ag 15,19:2
McDiarmid, Campbell J, 1942, My 14,19:2
McDiarmid, Errett W Prof, 1937, S 6,17:5
McDill, A S Dr, 1875, N 16,4:7
MacDill, David Dr, 1903, Ap 20,7:5
McDill, John M Mrs, 1944, Ap 18,21:4
McDivit, John A, 1938, Mr 30,21:3
McDivitt, Dewey K, 1944, F 13,41:1
McDoel, William Henry, 1916, Ap 26,13:6
Macdona, Charles, 1946, N 17,68:2
Macdona, Henry D, 1909, Ap 26,7:5
McDonach, Harry, 1955, F 1,29:4
McDonagh, Andrew J, 1942, F 11,21:5
MacDonagh, Donagh, 1968, Ja 2,37:1
McDonagh, Joseph, 1944, My 6,15:5
McDonagh, Joseph P, 1946, O 4,23:4
McDonagh, Leo A, 1945, O 29,19:3
McDonagh, Patrick J, 1939, Je 9,21:3
MacDonald, A, 1936, Ja 18,15:3
McDonald, A B, 1879, Ja 30,3:2; 1942, Ap 10,17:4
McDonald, Agnes S (Sister M Agnes Alma), 1959, Ap 9,31:4
McDonald, Alan A, 1950, Jl 7,19:6
MacDonald, Albert, 1956, N 12,29:5
MacDonald, Albert James, 1924, Ag 20,13:3
MacDonald, Alex, 1942, D 19,19:1
McDonald, Alex B, 1955, Mr 3,27:2
MacDonald, Alex E Dr, 1906, D 8,11:5
McDonald, Alex F, 1957, S 28,17:1
McDonald, Alex Mrs, 1903, D 29,9:6
MacDonald, Alex Mrs, 1955, Ap 19,31:1
Macdonald, Alexander, 1881, N 1,5:3
McDonald, Alexander, 1903, D 14,7:2; 1910, Mr 20,II, 11:3; 1947, N 26,23:2
McDonald, Alexander J Mrs, 1966, O 27,47:2
McDonald, Alice, 1943, Jl 18,35:2
MacDonald, Allan A, 1939, My 26,23:4
MacDonald, Allan H, 1951, N 9,27:5
McDonald, Allan J, 1951, N 6,29:6
McDonald, Andrew, 1923, Ap 20,17:4; 1939, My 30, 17:3; 1941, N 25,25:5; 1943, D 26,32:1
McDonald, Andrew J, 1950, My 23,29:3
McDonald, Andrew R, 1946, Jl 13,15:4
McDonald, Andrew V Mrs, 1923, Ja 21,6:3
MacDonald, Angus, 1961, F 22,25:4
McDonald, Angus B, 1952, S 14,86:1
McDonald, Angus D (por), 1941, N 16,57:1
Macdonald, Angus J Mrs, 1951, Je 16,15:5
Macdonald, Angus L, 1954, Ap 14,29:1
MacDonald, Angus Mrs, 1961, D 23,23:1
MacDonald, Anna E W Mrs, 1940, D 27,19:4
MacDonald, Anna Mrs, 1947, My 18,60:7
McDonald, Arch, 1960, O 17,29:2
Macdonald, Arch A, 1963, Ap 25,33:3
Macdonald, Archibald A, 1960, F 1,27:6
McDonald, Arthur B, 1937, F 22,17:5
Macdonald, Arthur N, 1940, F 7,21:6
MacDonald, Arthur N Mrs, 1947, S 5,19:3
MacDonald, Augustin S Mrs, 1948, Jl 16,19:2
MacDonald, Benjamin, 1950, Ag 31,26:2
McDonald, Benjamin A, 1949, Mr 3,25:5
McDonald, Bill Capt, 1918, Ja 16,11:4
McDonald, Bruce, 1946, F 4,25:2
MacDonald, Bruce W, 1943, S 18,17:5
MacDonald, Bryce J, 1968, S 29,55:1
McDonald, Burt A, 1965, My 5,47:4
MacDonald, Byrnes, 1959, O 11,86:6
McDonald, C Eric, 1939, My 18,25:6
MacDonald, C F Dr, 1926, Je 2,25:1
McDonald, C P, 1937, Mr 12,23:5
MacDonald, C P, 1942, Mr 18,23:4
MacDonald, Calvina, 1944, N 23,31:3
MacDonald, Carolyn, 1942, F 21,19:4
McDonald, Charles, 1949, Ja 8,15:3
MacDonald, Charles, 1960, D 12,29:4
McDonald, Charles A, 1951, Mr 6,27:5
MacDonald, Charles A (Bro A Paul), 1959, Je 26, 25:3
McDonald, Charles A, 1961, F 8,28:1
McDonald, Charles A Mrs, 1951, F 23,27:2
Macdonald, Charles B (por), 1939, Ap 22,17:1
McDonald, Charles C, 1950, Je 27,29:2
McDonald, Charles F, 1925, S 20,7:3
MacDonald, Charles H, 1945, S 13,23:3
McDonald, Charles R, 1948, D 31,15:1
McDonald, Charles S, 1948, N 26,23:5
Macdonald, Charles S, 1953, S 11,21:1
Macdonald, Charles Snead, 1918, Ap 27,15:8
MacDonald, Charles T Mrs, 1950, N 25,13:5
Macdonald, Chisholm N, 1952, Ap 2,33:6
MacDonald, Christie (Mrs H L Gilespie), 1962, Jl 27,25:4
Macdonald, Claude, 1960, O 14,33:2
MacDonald, Claude Sir, 1915, S 11,9:6
MacDonald, Colin C Sr, 1951, D 14,31:1
MacDonald, Cordelia H Mrs, 1941, Ag 11,13:5
McDonald, D G, 1947, My 18,60:6
McDonald, D W Ross, 1945, Je 23,13:6
Macdonald, Daniel A, 1937, O 29,21:2
McDonald, Daniel J, 1937, Je 29,21:5
McDonald, Daniel T, 1939, Ap 1,19:4
MacDonald, Dave, 1964, My 31,V,1:3
MacDonald, David, 1939, Mr 8,21:3
McDonald, David E, 1956, Ja 16,21:1
Macdonald, David I, 1953, Mr 21,17:5
MacDonald, David J, 1959, Mr 21,21:2
McDonald, Dennis J, 1939, O 9,19:5
McDonald, Don W, 1952, My 26,23:2
McDonald, Donald (por), 1937, O 9,19:1
Macdonald, Donald, 1959, D 10,39:3
MacDonald, Donald C Mrs (Betty), 1958, F 8,19:1
McDonald, Donald F, 1942, My 30,15:5
MacDonald, Donald 2d, 1952, N 4,30:3
Macdonald, Dudley S, 1959, Jl 27,25:5
McDonald, Duncan, 1947, Ap 3,25:3
MacDonald, Duncan B, 1943, S 7,23:2
McDonald, Duncan Mrs, 1952, D 10,35:3
MacDonald, E A, 1950, D 6,33:3
Macdonald, Edgar F, 1958, Mr 28,25:3
MacDonald, Edith, 1937, Ap 1,24:1
McDonald, Edmund E S, 1954, Ag 26,27:4
MacDonald, Edmund J, 1958, Jl 11,23:2
McDonald, Edward, 1954, D 11,13:2
MacDonald, Edward C, 1946, Mr 13,30:2
McDonald, Edward C, 1956, Ag 23,27:5; 1960, D 2 33:1
McDonald, Edward D, 1950, F 11,15:2
McDonald, Edward J, 1947, My 29,22:2; 1963, Je 37:4
McDonald, Edward J Mrs, 1950, Ag 21,19:4
McDonald, Edward L, 1954, O 11,27:4
Macdonald, Edward M, 1940, My 27,19:5
McDonald, Edward T, 1943, S 2,19:5; 1955, Ap 5,
McDonald, Edward W, 1949, Ag 25,23:5; 1954, Ap 12,29:3
McDonald, Edwin C Mrs, 1968, O 24,47:2
McDonald, Edwin J, 1959, Ag 13,27:4
MacDonald, Eliza, 1937, F 4,21:4
McDonald, Ellen, 1951, F 27,27:1
McDonald, Ellice, 1955, Ja 31,19:4
MacDonald, Ernest S Mrs, 1945, Mr 10,17:5
MacDonald, Estella, 1954, N 27,13:5
McDonald, Eugene E, 1954, O 1,23:3
McDonald, Eugene F Jr (will, My 21,66:4), 1958 My 16,25:2
McDonald, F, 1878, N 9,8:3
McDonald, F R, 1941, Ap 4,21:1
MacDonald, Finlay G, 1951, Mr 31,15:3
Macdonald, Forrester Mrs, 1966, D 3,39:5
McDonald, Francis, 1949, Ap 13,29:4
MacDonald, Francis C (Mr Mac), 1952, Mr 27,
MacDonald, Francis E, 1963, O 22,37:1
McDonald, Francis J, 1943, Mr 23,19:4; 1956, Je 25:5
McDonald, Frank, 1943, F 24,21:3
MacDonald, Frank, 1944, D 7,25:5
McDonald, Frank C, 1948, S 3,19:3
McDonald, Frank D, 1940, Mr 20,34:8
McDonald, Frank E, 1953, Jl 11,11:4
MacDonald, Frank J Mrs, 1954, Ag 15,84:5
McDonald, Frederic W, 1948, O 28,29:3
McDonald, Frederick, 1958, N 26,29:3
McDonald, Frederick L, 1944, My 25,21:4
McDonald, G G Mrs, 1954, D 24,13:1
MacDonald, George, 1905, S 19,9:6
McDonald, George, 1913, Jl 19,7:6
MacDonald, George, 1940, Ag 12,15:5; 1950, M 29:2
Macdonald, George, 1951, Ja 19,25:2; 1955, Ja 7
MacDonald, George, 1955, F 6,88:1; 1961, N 12
McDonald, George, 1962, Mr 17,25:4; 1968, S 1
MacDonald, George A, 1939, Mr 12,III,6:8
McDonald, George A, 1947, Mr 5,25:4
Macdonald, George E (cor, Jl 16,31:3), 1944, 13:5

MacDonald, George H, 1952, Ja 14,19:3
McDonald, George J, 1945, Mr 23,19:2
McDonald, George Mrs, 1952, Je 7,19:2
McDonald, George N, 1942, Jl 9,22:5
MacDonald, George P (por), 1944, My 28,34:1
MacDonald, George S, 1945, Mr 19,19:4
McDonald, Gerald E F, 1925, S 24,25:4
MacDonald, Gertrude L, 1950, S 5,27:4
MacDonald, Glenn, 1959, Jl 18,15:1
Macdonald, Godfrey, 1967, Ag 19,25:1
MacDonald, Gordon, 1908, Ag 15,7:6
McDonald, Grant M, 1941, D 26,13:4
McDonald, Grant M Mrs, 1951, Ja 21,76:6
McDonald, H Bower, 1907, Mr 3,7:6
McDonald, H F, 1943, S 3,19:5
Macdonald, H J, 1929, Mr 30,15:3
MacDonald, H Reid, 1956, S 1,15:6
MacDonald, H Ruthben, 1949, O 23,84:1
McDonald, Harl, 1955, Mr 31,27:1
McDonald, Harold J, 1943, Ap 26,19:1
McDonald, Harold P, 1947, S 18,25:5
McDonald, Harry, 1945, Mr 29,23:5
McDonald, Harry A, 1964, Jl 4,13:1
MacDonald, Harry B, 1963, S 11,43:1
MacDonald, Helen E, 1963, Ap 15,29:2
McDonald, Henry, 1950, Ap 5,31:5
MacDonald, Henry, 1956, Ap 25,35:1
Macdonald, Henry G Sr, 1961, O 15,88:4
McDonald, Henry M, 1941, Je 14,17:3
McDonald, Henry T, 1951, D 1,13:4
MacDonald, Herman A, 1961, Ja 6,27:1
Macdonald, Herschel H, 1960, Je 15,41:4
McDonald, Homer, 1946, Jl 14,38:4
MacDonald, Howard B, 1965, My 20,43:4
MacDonald, Howard F, 1955, O 21,27:3
McDonald, Hugh, 1949, Ap 12,30:2
MacDonald, Hugh N, 1940, My 13,17:6
McDonald, Hunter, 1937, Ag 26,21:5
MacDonald, Irving, 1958, S 12,26:1
Macdonald, J A, 1929, Ap 16,29:2
MacDonald, J Alex, 1948, N 16,29:5
McDonald, J Benjamin, 1948, F 13,21:2
McDonald, J C, 1928, Ag 13,17:3
MacDonald, J Clifford, 1963, Ag 17,19:4
McDonald, J E, 1891, Je 22,1:5; 1952, Je 14,15:1
McDonald, J Graves, 1953, Ja 1,23:6
McDonald, J K, 1953, Ja 28,27:4
McDonald, J M, 1876, Ap 21,4:7
McDonald, J P, 1922, My 11,17:4
MacDonald, J Ramsay, 1937, N 10,1:4
MacDonald, J Wiseman, 1942, N 23,23:1
MacDonald, Jack, 1961, D 16,25:5
McDonald, James, 1915, Ja 14,11:4; 1925, My 22,19:6
MacDonald, James, 1940, S 4,23:1; 1951, Ap 10,27:2
McDonald, James, 1951, Je 22,25:2
Macdonald, James, 1953, Ap 22,29:1
McDonald, James, 1953, Je 1,23:3
MacDonald, James, 1954, D 5,88:5; 1962, Je 20,35:2
MacDonald, James A, 1942, Ag 21,19:6
McDonald, James A, 1942, D 29,21:4; 1945, D 6,27:5; 1957, D 31,17:2
Macdonald, James A (Col J R Stingo), 1964, N 6, 37:1
MacDonald, James A Rev Dr, 1923, My 15,19:4
McDonald, James C, 1940, S 26,23:2
McDonald, James C Bp, 1912, D 6,15:4
McDonald, James Carnahan, 1914, Je 10,11:5
McDonald, James E, 1951, D 6,33:1
McDonald, James E Mrs, 1910, N 20,II,13:4
McDonald, James F, 1952, Ag 16,15:2
McDonald, James F Rev, 1937, Ap 20,26:1
Macdonald, James F S, 1961, Mr 13,29:1
McDonald, James G, 1940, Mr 28,23:5; 1951, N 8,29:3
Macdonald, James G, 1964, Ag 12,35:3
MacDonald, James G, 1964, S 27,86:2
MacDonald, James H, 1938, Mr 25,19:2; 1938, S 24, 17:4
McDonald, James H, 1946, D 23,23:3
McDonald, James Henry Maj, 1916, O 19,9:3
McDonald, James J, 1938, My 3,23:6; 1949, Ja 7,21:2
McDonald, James M, 1954, D 18,15:2
McDonald, James M (will, O 5,12:5), 1956, S 23,84:5
Macdonald, James M, 1959, Jl 24,25:4
MacDonald, James O, 1947, Ja 15,25:4
MacDonald, James R, 1966, Mr 7,27:3
MacDonald, James S, 1941, F 24,15:2
MacDonald, James S Mrs, 1952, N 1,21:4
McDonald, James Sr Mrs, 1945, F 2,19:2
MacDonald, James W, 1962, S 2,57:1
Macdonald, James W G, 1960, D 5,31:3
McDonald, James W Judge, 1937, Ap 2,23:1
MacDonald, James Wilson Alexander, 1908, Ag 16,7:6
McDonald, James Wilson Mrs (Dr Ella A Jennings), 1908, D 3,9:5
McDonald, Jane F, 1943, O 4,17:3
McDonald, Jay J, 1956, Ja 26,29:5
MacDonald, Jeanette A (Mrs G Raymond),(funl plans, Ja 16,27:1), 1965, Ja 15,1:2
McDonald, Jeffrey J, 1945, Ja 3,17:3
MacDonald, Jeremiah J, 1937, S 5,II,7:2
McDonald, Jesse F (por), 1942, F 26,19:5
McDonald, Joanne K, 1957, Ag 14,14:4
McDonald, John, 1939, Ja 9,15:1
MacDonald, John, 1953, Je 8,29:4
MacDonald, John A, 1939, Mr 25,2:2
Macdonald, John A, 1939, Ap 19,23:4
McDonald, John A, 1947, Ap 1,27:2
MacDonald, John A, 1958, Je 18,33:5
Macdonald, John A Sir, 1891, Je 7,1:7
MacDonald, John Alexander Mrs, 1920, S 8,11:2
McDonald, John B (funl), 1911, Mr 18,13:6
McDonald, John B Brig Gen, 1926, Mr 16,25:1
McDonald, John D, 1952, S 3,30:5
McDonald, John F, 1941, F 19,21:5; 1943, Je 7,13:2
McDonald, John H, 1938, D 23,19:4
MacDonald, John H, 1958, O 8,35:1
MacDonald, John H S, 1961, My 21,86:4
McDonald, John I, 1958, Ap 2,31:5
MacDonald, John J, 1942, My 10,43:3
McDonald, John J, 1945, N 9,19:3
MacDonald, John J, 1953, Ap 18,19:2
McDonald, John J, 1964, F 17,31:2
McDonald, John J Gen, 1912, Ja 22,9:4
McDonald, John J Mrs, 1955, Mr 9,27:2
MacDonald, John L, 1940, Ja 9,23:4
MacDonald, John M, 1961, N 22,33:3
MacDonald, John Mrs, 1939, Ja 9,17:3
McDonald, John Mrs, 1953, Mr 8,89:6
MacDonald, John P, 1937, Ag 6,17:4
Macdonald, John R, 1925, D 17,23:4
McDonald, John R Mrs, 1948, Jl 31,15:3
McDonald, John S, 1941, Jl 7,15:2
Macdonald, John S, 1954, Ja 2,11:4
Macdonald, John Sarsfield, 1872, Je 2,1:6
Macdonald, John T, 1951, Ap 4,29:4
MacDonald, John W, 1946, Ag 10,13:3; 1950, Ap 21, 23:4
MacDonald, John W Mrs, 1939, Jl 17,19:4
McDonald, Joseph, 1940, D 3,25:4; 1953, F 28,17:3; 1962, F 10,23:2
MacDonald, Joseph Brewster Mrs, 1916, Jl 11,9:7
McDonald, Joseph D, 1952, F 1,14:2
MacDonald, Joseph Dr, 1925, D 6,13:2
McDonald, Joseph F, 1951, Ap 9,25:5
MacDonald, Joseph F, 1961, O 3,36:6
McDonald, Joseph F, 1965, Ag 4,35:4
MacDonald, Joseph J, 1946, S 6,21:2
McDonald, Joseph J A, 1955, N 8,31:3
McDonald, Joseph M Lt-Col, 1925, Jl 15,17:6
McDonald, Joseph N, 1967, Ap 13,43:1
McDonald, Joseph S, 1961, Jl 12,31:1
MacDonald, Joseph T, 1960, Jl 25,23:4
McDonald, Joseph W, 1955, Ap 28,29:1
McDonald, Juett N Rev, 1937, S 7,21:4
MacDonald, K C, 1945, N 20,21:3
MacDonald, Katherine, 1956, Je 5,35:3
Macdonald, Kenneth J, 1956, My 1,33:4
MacDonald, Kenneth Mrs, 1949, Ja 12,27:2
MacDonald, Laura H Mrs, 1941, Ap 26,15:6
McDonald, Leo A, 1940, My 8,23:4
McDonald, Leon E Mrs, 1963, Je 29,23:2
McDonald, Leslie B, 1948, Jl 7,23:4
McDonald, Lillie L, 1953, Ap 24,23:3
McDonald, Lloyd D, 1954, My 17,23:4
McDonald, Louis L, 1953, Ag 14,19:5
McDonald, Louis Mrs, 1951, Ja 27,13:3
McDonald, Louis N, 1946, Ja 16,23:3
McDonald, Lyle, 1966, Ap 10,76:6
Macdonald, M A, 1941, O 14,23:2
MacDonald, M Irwin Mrs, 1918, Mr 2,13:2
McDonald, M J, 1938, Jl 12,20:2
MacDonald, Malcolm, 1953, Ap 9,27:5
McDonald, Margaret T, 1947, D 2,29:1
MacDonald, Marie, 1958, Jl 6,56:5
McDonald, Marie (Mrs D F Taylor), 1965, O 22, 44:1
McDonald, Mary, 1953, Ag 3,19:5
MacDonald, Mary G, 1960, My 28,21:6
McDonald, Mary Mrs, 1907, S 18,9:6
McDonald, Matthias J Rev, 1914, S 9,9:7
McDonald, Michael A, 1942, D 11,24:2
McDonald, Michael C, 1907, Ag 10,7:5
McDonald, Milo F, 1959, F 16,30:1
MacDonald, Milton T, 1967, O 17,47:3
McDonald, Morris, 1938, My 21,15:6
MacDonald, Moses, 1869, O 19,5:4
McDonald, Moses, 1955, Mr 18,27:2
MacDonald, Murdoch, 1957, Ap 25,31:2
McDonald, Neil, 1918, My 11,13:4
McDonald, Neil A, 1947, Ap 5,19:6
MacDonald, Norman, 1959, Je 5,27:3
McDonald, Norman C, 1958, N 30,86:1
McDonald, Patrick, 1942, Mr 29,45:3; 1948, O 16,15:6
McDonald, Patrick J (Babe),(Daley on Career, My 18,41:2), 1954, My 17,23:3
McDonald, Patrick Joseph, 1923, Ap 22,8:2
McDonald, Peter, 1944, Je 20,19:4
MacDonald, Peter F, 1954, My 17,23:4
McDonald, Philip B, 1959, O 25,86:8
MacDonald, Philip G, 1963, Jl 15,29:1
McDonald, Pirie (por), 1942, Ap 23,23:1
MacDonald, Pirie Mrs, 1950, D 20,32:2
MacDonald, Ralph Mrs, 1949, N 29,29:5
Macdonald, Ranald H Mrs, 1959, Mr 17,30:5
McDonald, Ray, 1959, F 21,25:5
Macdonald, Reuben, 1942, Jl 11,13:1
MacDonald, Richard A, 1941, Ag 8,15:3
McDonald, Richard A, 1947, Je 15,62:4
McDonald, Richard J, 1953, S 20,87:2; 1953, O 19, 21:5; 1958, Mr 14,25:4
MacDonald, Robert, 1917, Je 22,13:4
MacDonald, Robert (por), 1942, D 18,27:3
MacDonald, Robert A, 1956, O 4,33:2
McDonald, Robert F, 1958, N 22,21:4
McDonald, Robert J, 1947, My 20,25:4; 1958, Ag 20, 27:3
MacDonald, Robert Jr, 1942, Mr 10,19:1; 1957, Jl 25, 23:5
MacDonald, Roderic A, 1957, Ja 27,85:1
MacDonald, Roderick A, 1951, N 19,23:3
MacDonald, Roland A, 1947, Ja 22,23:5
MacDonald, Ronald J, 1947, S 6,17:3
Macdonald, Russell F, 1957, Je 14,25:3
McDonald, S W, 1877, Ag 24,3:3
McDonald, Samuel J, 1949, Mr 29,25:1
McDonald, Seth C, 1948, Mr 23,25:3
McDonald, Stephen A, 1964, Ap 27,31:4
McDonald, Stephen J, 1956, Ag 13,19:6; 1963, O 9, 40:5
McDonald, Stewart, 1957, Ja 4,23:2
McDonald, Thomas B, 1954, Mr 30,27:4
McDonald, Thomas F, 1937, S 14,23:6
MacDonald, Thomas H, 1911, D 4,13:5; 1957, Ap 8, 23:2
McDonald, Thomas J, 1939, Je 28,21:1
Macdonald, Thomas J Mrs, 1958, S 7,87:1
McDonald, Thomas N, 1951, Je 1,26:3
McDonald, Thomas V, 1957, Je 9,88:5
McDonald, Thomas W, 1939, F 17,19:4
McDonald, W, 1936, Ag 2,II,7:4
McDonald, W J (see also Je 3), 1878, Je 6,5:5
MacDonald, W J, 1933, Ja 8,31:4
McDonald, W K, 1871, Ap 15,2:5
McDonald, W Stewart, 1967, Mr 11,29:3
McDonald, Wallace R, 1946, My 3,21:4
Macdonald, Walter R, 1940, D 21,17:5
MacDonald, Wentworth S, 1949, O 5,29:1
McDonald, Will R, 1941, Je 7,17:2
MacDonald, William, 1938, D 16,25:3
McDonald, William, 1943, Ja 10,49:1
Macdonald, William, 1952, F 9,13:6
MacDonald, William, 1966, Ag 28,93:3
McDonald, William A, 1939, Ja 10,19:3; 1944, Je 16, 19:5
MacDonald, William A, 1946, N 10,64:1
Macdonald, William A, 1951, Mr 16,31:1
MacDonald, William A, 1961, Ag 13,88:3
Macdonald, William A Mrs, 1962, N 20,35:4
McDonald, William A Rev, 1917, Je 20,11:5
McDonald, William B Jr, 1966, N 21,35:5
McDonald, William C, 1943, Ag 28,11:3
MacDonald, William C, 1946, N 20,31:3
McDonald, William C, 1949, D 13,38:4
MacDonald, William C, 1954, O 5,27:3
McDonald, William Christopher Sir, 1917, Je 13,13:6
MacDonald, William D, 1955, S 25,92:8
Macdonald, William E, 1956, S 25,33:3
McDonald, William F, 1924, Ag 22,13:7; 1940, Ja 9, 23:2
McDonald, William H, 1906, Mr 28,9:2; 1937, Je 6,II, 8:6; 1938, D 22,21:5; 1952, F 15,26:2
Macdonald, William H Mrs, 1952, Jl 6,49:2
MacDonald, William J, 1943, Mr 26,19:3; 1946, Mr 31,46:6
McDonald, William J, 1948, Ag 3,26:2; 1959, Mr 9, 29:1; 1967, Mr 7,41:4
McDonald, William J Mrs, 1967, Ja 21,31:3
McDonald, William L, 1951, O 27,19:4
MacDonald, William M P, 1950, Mr 10,27:2
McDonald, William Ogden Dr, 1918, Mr 27,13:7
McDonald, William P, 1951, N 21,25:4; 1959, Ap 7, 33:3; 1964, O 30,38:1
MacDonald, William S, 1937, F 6,17:1
McDonald, William S, 1944, D 22,17:2
MacDonald, William T, 1938, D 2,23:1
MacDonald, William W, 1952, Ag 22,21:6
MacDonald, Willis G Dr, 1910, D 31,9:4
McDonald, Willis Jr, 1953, Je 21,84:4
McDonald, Wilson J, 1955, Ag 12,19:1
McDonald (Mother Christina Marie), 1964, Jl 9,33:2
Macdonald of Gwaenysgor, Lord (Gordon Macdonald), 1966, Ja 21,47:1
MacDonall, A P, 1927, D 20,29:5
McDonaugh, Wilfred E, 1954, D 30,17:5
McDonell, Alex A Mrs, 1959, Je 28,69:2
Macdonell, Arch C, 1941, D 24,17:1
MacDonell, Frank, 1941, F 11,23:3
MacDonell, Genevieve G E Mrs, 1938, Je 27,17:5
MacDonell, Joseph W, 1961, Ag 14,25:3
MacDonell, Stanley A, 1949, Ap 22,23:2
McDonell, William E, 1948, O 29,25:2
McDonnell, Alex J, 1951, F 8,34:2
Macdonnell, Anthony Patrick, 1925, Je 10,23:5
Macdonnell, Arch G, 1941, Ja 18,15:2
Macdonnell, Arch H, 1939, N 13,19:6
McDonnell, Austin, 1965, Mr 22,33:1
McDonnell, Bernard, 1952, Jl 2,25:3
McDonnell, Bernard C, 1959, Ag 2,80:6

McDonnell, Charles Edward Bp, 1921, Ag 9,9:3
McDonnell, Clara, 1960, N 19,21:6
McDonnell, Craig (C M Kenney), 1956, N 26,27:5
MacDonnell, Dan, 1964, S 8,29:1
McDonnell, Edward A, 1957, Je 18,33:2; 1959, Je 24, 31:5
McDonnell, Edward J, 1946, N 5,25:5
McDonnell, Edward O, 1960, Ja 7,16:2
McDonnell, Francis A Mrs, 1952, Ja 9,29:2
McDonnell, Frank, 1952, Mr 3,21:3
McDonnell, George J, 1962, D 5,47:4
MacDonnell, George N, 1953, D 11,34:5
MacDonnell, Henrietta M, 1921, F 23,13:6
McDonnell, Hubert, 1956, My 17,31:3
McDonnell, Hunter, 1944, D 28,19:1
McDonnell, James A, 1952, S 19,23:3
McDonnell, James F Sr (funl plans, Jl 14,21:3), 1958, Jl 11,23:3
McDonnell, James Mrs, 1942, S 7,21:7
McDonnell, John A, 1947, Jl 29,21:1
McDonnell, John B, 1950, Mr 9,29:4
McDonnell, John C, 1950, Ag 11,19:1
McDonnell, John F, 1948, F 29,60:3
McDonnell, John J, 1947, O 27,21:4
MacDonnell, John L, 1963, Ag 10,17:1
McDonnell, Joseph F, 1955, Mr 7,27:5
McDonnell, Joseph W Mrs, 1944, Ap 6,23:6
McDonnell, Mae F, 1956, Ap 28,17:4
MacDonnell, Mark R, 1942, D 7,27:3
McDonnell, Myles F, 1963, My 19,86:3
Macdonnell, Norman S, 1938, Ap 8,19:5
McDonnell, Patrick B, 1939, N 14,23:4
McDonnell, Patrick F, 1950, Ja 2,23:5; 1951, Ap 18, 31:4
McDonnell, Percy G, 1953, Mr 17,29:4
McDonnell, Peter, 1907, Ag 21,7:6; 1942, Ja 26,15:4
McDonnell, Peter J Mrs, 1958, Jl 14,21:5
McDonnell, R G Sir, 1881, F 7,5:6
McDonnell, Ralph A, 1939, My 27,15:5
McDonnell, Ralph E, 1947, N 26,23:2
McDonnell, Richard A Dr, 1937, S 18,19:4
McDonnell, Robert E, 1925, Jl 11,11:6
McDonnell, Robert E Jr, 1967, Mr 23,35:1
McDonnell, Sean, 1968, Je 5,47:2
McDonnell, Shomberg K Capt, 1915, N 27,15:4
McDonnell, T E, 1940, Mr 3,45:1
McDonnell, Thomas, 1964, Ap 22,47:2
McDonnell, Thomas J (funl plans, F 27,27:4; funl, Mr 3,27:2), 1961, F 26,92:7
McDonnell, William, 1943, D 18,15:1
McDonnell, William J, 1954, N 19,23:3
MacDonogh, George M W, 1942, Jl 14,20:3
McDonogh, James J Capt, 1912, Ja 28,II,13:3
McDonogh, Robert M, 1945, D 11,25:6
McDonough, Aloysius, 1967, Jl 24,27:2
McDonough, Andrew L, 1950, Mr 5,92:4
McDonough, Andrew V, 1952, F 23,11:2
Macdonough, Augustus R, 1907, Jl 22,7:5
McDonough, Bernice Mother, 1951, N 30,23:4
MacDonough, Charles Q, 1950, D 29,20:4
McDonough, Clarence, 1956, S 20,33:3
McDonough, Dennis M, 1938, S 19,19:4
McDonough, Edmund J, 1952, F 24,84:3
McDonough, Edward F, 1942, Ja 28,19:1
McDonough, Edward J, 1941, F 13,19:2
McDonough, Eugene P, 1943, D 16,27:4
McDonough, Francis A, 1968, S 11,47:2
McDonough, Francis J (por), 1943, Je 2,25:1
McDonough, Frank, 1950, Mr 4,17:3
McDonough, Frank J, 1944, Ja 26,13:2; 1949, Jl 14, 27:3; 1953, My 15,23:3
McDonough, Frankie, 1942, My 24,42:5
McDonough, George, 1949, Jl 26,27:2
McDonough, George V, 1964, D 30,25:2
MacDonough, Glen, 1924, Mr 31,17:3
McDonough, J E, 1882, F 13,2:4
Macdonough, James, 1962, Ja 28,77:1
McDonough, James A (por), 1941, Je 18,21:6
McDonough, James F, 1944, D 16,15:2
McDonough, James M, 1954, Je 9,31:4
McDonough, James V, 1959, O 9,21:3
McDonough, John A, 1950, Mr 24,25:3
McDonough, John Col, 1911, Je 22,11:6
McDonough, John F, 1948, S 6,13:6
McDonough, John H Mrs, 1957, F 11,29:6
McDonough, John J, 1953, Je 14,84:5; 1961, O 3,39:3
McDonough, John T Ex-Justice, 1917, Mr 30,11:7
McDonough, Joseph A, 1952, Je 7,19:2
McDonough, Joseph A Mrs, 1940, Ja 19,19:3
McDonough, Joseph D, 1951, O 15,25:5
McDonough, Joseph F Mrs, 1956, S 12,37:3
MacDonough, Joseph M Mrs, 1953, My 10,89:1
McDonough, Joseph W, 1958, S 8,29:4
McDonough, Margaret A, 1948, Ap 22,27:4
McDonough, Margaret M (will), 1952, O 2,27:7
McDonough, Marianne G Mrs, 1957, Ja 22,29:4
McDonough, Martin A, 1957, N 18,31:3
McDonough, Michael J, 1950, O 31,27:3
McDonough, Patrick, 1944, Ag 19,11:2
MacDonough, Patrick, 1960, Jl 16,19:4
McDonough, Patrick H, 1949, N 23,29:4
McDonough, Patrick J, 1952, Ja 2,25:4
McDonough, Patrick W, 1951, Ag 26,77:3
McDonough, Peter J Mrs, 1951, Ap 1,92:2; 1965, F 21,76:7
McDonough, Richard A, 1952, Ap 25,23:3
McDonough, Richard T, 1938, My 27,17:4
McDonough, Stephen, 1946, Jl 1,31:2
McDonough, Stephen J Mrs, 1946, Jl 18,25:5
McDonough, Susan Mrs, 1953, S 11,21:4
McDonough, Terence P, 1947, Mr 26,25:4
McDonough, Terrence J, 1937, Ap 24,19:5
McDonough, Thomas A, 1955, Jl 3,32:7
McDonough, Thomas H, 1938, O 25,23:4
Macdonough, Thomas W, 1952, N 19,29:5
McDonough, Vincent S, 1939, S 4,19:4
McDonough, Viola M, 1962, O 10,51:5
McDonough, W John, 1954, Je 20,84:4
McDonough, Walter I, 1963, N 30,27:3
McDonough, William H, 1911, My 21,II,11:4
McDonough, William Mrs, 1908, O 7,9:5
Macdonough, William O'Brien, 1913, N 18,11:6
McDonough (Mother Mary Rosa), 1961, Ja 2,25:4
McDouall, James D, 1950, Mr 22,27:2
McDouall, John S, 1949, D 9,31:4
MacDougal, Alex M, 1953, Ja 27,25:4
McDougal, C J Commander, 1881, Mr 30,5:3
McDougal, Charles B, 1939, O 29,40:7
McDougal, Clyde C, 1958, O 11,23:3
MacDougal, Donald Rev, 1920, Ap 3,13:5
McDougal, Douglas C, 1964, Ja 22,37:2
McDougal, Elliott C, 1943, S 8,23:4
MacDougal, Harry M, 1956, O 23,33:2
McDougal, James A, 1867, S 4,4:6
McDougal, James B, 1948, Ag 24,24:3
McDougal, Jerome R, 1962, My 27,92:7
McDougal, John, 1866, My 6,3:5
McDougal, Neal, 1945, Ag 15,14:7
MacDougal, Richard, 1957, F 16,17:2
McDougal, Robert, 1949, Ap 8,26:2
MacDougal, Russell K, 1956, My 4,25:4
McDougald, Daniel Mrs, 1957, Jl 31,23:4
McDougald, Frank A, 1952, Ap 24,31:4
McDougald, Robert B, 1942, My 18,15:2
MacDougald, Roman M, 1960, Je 5,86:8
McDougall, A P, 1950, Ap 26,29:2
MacDougall, Albert E, 1957, Jl 14,40:3
McDougall, Alex, 1941, Mr 1,15:4; 1948, N 4,29:3
MacDougall, Alex, 1953, Mr 14,15:6
McDougall, Alexander Capt, 1923, My 24,19:6
McDougall, Alice F Mrs (por), 1945, F 11,40:1
Macdougall, Allan R, 1956, Jl 26,25:4
McDougall, Anna P Mrs, 1937, N 9,24:2
McDougall, Arthur, 1942, My 30,15:6
MacDougall, Arthur W Mrs, 1947, F 19,25:1
McDougall, Avery, 1941, D 2,23:3
McDougall, Charles Mrs, 1955, Jl 1,21:1
MacDougall, Clinton Dugald Gen, 1914, My 25,11:6
McDougall, Colin Dr, 1915, S 20,9:5
MacDougall, David C, 1949, Jl 21,25:2
McDougall, David Rear-Adm, 1882, Ag 8,4:7
McDougall, Edward A, 1944, S 3,26:8
McDougall, Edward G, 1944, Mr 10,15:3
McDougall, Frank L, 1958, F 16,86:7
McDougall, George F, 1959, F 15,86:4
McDougall, George G, 1950, N 25,13:2
McDougall, George Rev, 1876, Mr 18,5:4
MacDougall, Hamilton C, 1945, Mr 17,13:5
McDougall, Harold, 1943, Ag 27,17:4
McDougall, Hartland B, 1947, Ap 29,28:3
McDougall, Herbert N, 1955, Je 15,31:4
MacDougall, Ida D Mrs, 1937, Je 4,23:5
MacDougall, J C Mrs, 1937, N 19,23:1
McDougall, J L, 1941, Mr 1,15:4
McDougall, James, 1922, S 19,19:4
MacDougall, James, 1949, Ja 17,19:1
McDougall, James C, 1963, D 31,19:3
McDougall, John, 1866, Ap 1,1:7
MacDougall, John L, 1956, Je 7,4:4
McDougall, John W Capt, 1908, D 6,13:4
McDougall, Kenneth, 1944, Ag 16,19:6
McDougall, Morris, 1956, D 9,87:3
McDougall, R P, 1928, Ag 30,21:3
MacDougall, Ralph G, 1954, Ag 28,15:4
McDougall, Richard, 1948, D 17,27:3
McDougall, Robert, 1938, D 16,25:1
MacDougall, Robert, 1939, N 2,23:6
MacDougall, Robert C, 1963, S 9,27:1
McDougall, Stuart E, 1957, F 16,17:6
MacDougall, Susette O Mrs, 1941, F 2,46:3
McDougall, Walter Mrs, 1951, Ja 17,27:1
McDougall, William (por), 1938, N 29,23:1
McDougall, William D (por), 1943, Mr 7,38:8
McDougle, Ivan E, 1955, O 26,31:4
McDow, George W, 1945, D 11,25:5
McDowall, Elizabeth Mrs, 1940, N 21,30:2
McDowall, James, 1944, N 15,27:4
McDowall, Jimmy, 1951, N 12,28:3
MacDowall, John L, 1942, Jl 22,19:1
McDowall, William, 1951, Mr 21,33:4
McDowell, Alexander, 1946, N 8,23:2
McDowell, Alexander Maj, 1913, O 1,9:6
McDowell, Alexander Mrs, 1925, Ap 6,19:5
McDowell, Alfred H, 1967, Mr 26,69:1
McDowell, Andrew M, 1950, Ag 12,13:1
McDowell, Arch A, 1948, Je 8,25:2
McDowell, Arthur F, 1950, O 18,33:2
McDowell, Arthur G, 1966, O 8,31:2
McDowell, Arthur R, 1938, My 16,17:3
McDowell, B Wilbur, 1964, Ap 1,39:5
MacDowell, B Wilbur Mrs, 1942, Ap 7,21:4
McDowell, C S, 1957, Jl 21,60:4
McDowell, Charles, 1942, D 21,19:6; 1945, S 1,11:
McDowell, Charles E, 1937, Ag 31,23:6; 1950, O 3 27:2
McDowell, Charles H, 1954, Mr 6,15:5
McDowell, Clarence, 1909, N 10,9:4
MacDowell, E Carleton Mrs, 1940, O 25,21:5
McDowell, Edmund W, 1939, Ap 10,17:3
MacDowell, Edward Mrs (funl plans, Ag 27,19:5; Ag 30,25:3), 1956, Ag 25,15:3
McDowell, Edward N, 1940, D 20,25:1
McDowell, Edward P, 1943, Ap 14,23:3
MacDowell, Edward Prof (funl, Ja 25,9:5), 1908, Ja 24,7:5
McDowell, Fay B, 1955, My 6,23:2
MacDowell, Francis M, 1940, Mr 9,15:4
McDowell, Frank H, 1966, Ap 18,29:4
MacDowell, Frank N, 1951, Ag 31,15:3
McDowell, George C, 1940, Ag 9,15:6
McDowell, George S, 1944, Ap 2,39:2
McDowell, Harry B, 1947, Ap 15,25:3
McDowell, Henry B Mrs, 1953, Ja 16,23:3
McDowell, Hugh, 1912, Je 18,11:5
McDowell, Hugh C, 1951, My 21,27:4
McDowell, I Gen, 1885, My 6,5:3
McDowell, J J, 1877, Ja 21,7:3
McDowell, James D Mrs, 1955, Ag 13,13:2
McDowell, John, 1911, N 13,9:5; 1947, O 26,70:6
McDowell, John G, 1948, My 8,15:4
McDowell, John M, 1961, Mr 30,29:3
McDowell, John Mrs, 1944, Mr 20,17:3
McDowell, John R, 1946, Jl 16,23:4; 1947, Mr 12 1957, D 22,40:5
McDowell, John Rev, 1863, F 22,3:6
McDowell, John Rev Dr, 1937, N 14,II,10:3
McDowell, Joseph M, 1948, N 20,13:4
McDowell, Joseph Rev Dr, 1913, Ja 5,17:2
McDowell, Lewis J, 1944, Ap 23,43:3
McDowell, Louise S, 1966, Jl 8,35:2
McDowell, Lycurgus, 1950, D 19,29:1
McDowell, M, 1936, O 15,27:3
McDowell, M Mrs (Fanny V Davenport), 1898, S 27,1:5
McDowell, Malcolm M Mrs, 1943, My 28,21:3
McDowell, Malcolm Maj, 1903, D 27,7:6
McDowell, Malcolm Marsh, 1920, Ag 18,9:5
MacDowell, Margaret I Mrs, 1942, N 28,13:4
McDowell, Mary H Mrs, 1941, My 7,25:1
McDowell, Mary S, 1955, D 7,39:5
McDowell, Maxwell E, 1954, D 17,31:5
MacDowell, Melbourne Mrs (Virginia Drew Trescott), 1912, Ja 2,11:6
McDowell, Neville L, 1939, S 13,25:5
MacDowell, Noah, 1940, N 26,23:2
McDowell, Norris S, 1940, F 11,48:5
McDowell, P, 1871, Ja 1,1:2
McDowell, Rachel K, 1949, Ag 31,23:1
McDowell, Robert, 1948, N 5,25:3
McDowell, Robert D, 1967, Ap 17,37:1
McDowell, Robert Mrs, 1943, Mr 9,23:3
McDowell, Sam Sr, 1947, Ap 18,21:2
McDowell, Samuel, 1941, Mr 24,17:4
McDowell, Samuel J Rev, 1937, Ja 12,24:2
McDowell, Samuel L, 1956, Jl 11,29:3
McDowell, Stewart H, 1947, D 21,52:6
McDowell, Ted G, 1949, D 28,25:4
McDowell, W W, 1934, Ap 10,1:5
McDowell, Walter M, 1955, S 14,35:2
McDowell, William F Bp (por), 1937, Ap 27,2
McDowell, William F Dr, 1917, S 12,11:5
McDowell, William G, 1938, Mr 21,16:1
McDowell, William George Bp, 1922, O 21,13:
McDowell, William H, 1950, Ag 4,21:5
MacDowell, William M, 1941, F 20,20:2
McDowell, William O Mrs, 1921, Mr 9,13:4
McDuff, James, 1937, Ap 1,23:3
MacDuff, James R, 1967, N 27,47:4
MacDuffee, Cyrus C, 1961, Ag 25,25:4
McDuffee, Edward A, 1957, N 28,31:2
McDuffee, George F, 1950, F 13,21:1
McDuffee, Joseph H, 1943, My 14,19:4
MacDuffie, Abby P Mrs, 1937, My 27,23:2
McDuffie, Duncan, 1951, Ap 22,89:1
McDuffie, Frederic, 1942, Ap 30,19:4
McDuffie, Irvin H (por), 1946, Ja 31,21:5
MacDuffie, John, 1941, S 22,15:4
McDuffie, John, 1950, N 3,27:1
MacDuffie, Marshall, 1967, Jl 9,60:2
McDuffie, Marshall W (por), 1945, Jl 24,23:
MacDuffie, Marshall W Mrs, 1945, O 6,13:2
McDuffie, William C, 1963, Ap 11,33:4
MacDwyer, Patrick S, 1958, Ag 4,21:6
MacDwyer, Patrick S Mrs, 1957, D 31,17:4
Mace, Charles A, 1949, Ja 5,25:4
Mace, Charles H, 1950, D 11,25:4
Mace, William H, 1938, Ag 11,17:3
MacEachen, Roderick, 1965, Jl 2,29:1
McEacher, Donald S, 1951, N 2,23:1
McEachern, Alex, 1939, O 14,19:5

MacEachern, Archibald, 1962, N 4,88:8
McEachern, John N Sr Mrs, 1949, Ap 25,23:5
McEachern, Malcolm, 1945, Ja 18,19:5
MacEachern, Malcolm T, 1956, F 4,19:5
McEachron, Karl B, 1954, Ja 25,19:3
McEldowney, Allen W, 1946, Ap 7,44:5
McEldowney, H C, 1935, Mr 10,34:1
McEldowney, J H, 1911, My 9,11:5
McEldowney, Ralph E (will, S 16,17:2), 1937, My 15,19:5
McElduff, Edward G, 1949, Ja 31,19:4
McElduff, John V, 1959, Ja 23,25:1
McElduff, Mich H, 1953, S 30,31:3
McEleney, Bridget Mrs, 1947, O 21,23:2
McElfatrick, George C, 1940, Mr 21,25:5
MacElfatrick, John Bailey, 1906, Je 7,7:5
McElfatrick, William H, 1922, S 30,13:6
McElfresh, John S, 1943, Ag 28,11:2
McElgin, James, 1955, D 9,27:2
McElhaney, Clarence W, 1943, N 26,23:4
McElhaney, Edward D, 1956, Mr 21,21:8
McElhany, Charles B, 1948, Ja 5,19:4
McElhany, J L, 1959, Je 26,25:4
McElhany, Thomas J, 1966, Jl 24,61:1
McElheran, R B, 1939, Ag 13,29:2
McElhiney, John A, 1942, D 29,21:4
McElhinney, Andrew, 1903, Jl 4,7:6
McElhinney, Andrew J, 1956, Je 29,21:4
McElhinney, Francis E, 1956, Ja 11,24:3
McElhinney, James F, 1938, Je 11,15:2
MacElhinny, John F, 1955, N 3,31:4
MacElhinny, Murray, 1968, Mr 7,43:4
McElhinny, William D, 1921, F 16,9:6
McElhone, Francis J, 1945, Ap 24,19:5
McElhone, Helen K, 1943, D 7,27:5
McElhone, James F, 1938, Ja 15,15:5
McElhone, William, 1945, My 10,23:4
McEligot, Timothy F, 1957, F 26,29:4
McElkenny, John J, 1960, N 13,88:7
McEllen, Charles R Jr, 1944, Je 15,19:6
McElligott, John J, 1946, S 7,15:1
McElligott, Joseph Mrs, 1952, Ap 18,25:2
McElligott, Mildred, 1956, Ap 17,31:4
McElligott, William J, 1956, Jl 18,27:4
McElliot, John J, 1965, N 14,89:1
McElliott, Joseph M, 1961, Mr 15,39:1
MacEllven, Charles E Mrs, 1954, D 31,13:2
McEllwee, Bridgid, 1949, Jl 3,25:4
McElmeel, Edward J, 1920, Ja 17,11:4
McElmell, Jackson Rear-Adm, 1908, Je 1,7:4
McElmoyle, John, 1938, N 26,15:1
McElnea, William H, 1960, O 9,86:7
McElory, S H, 1903, My 23,9:2
MacElree, George A, 1957, My 9,31:3
McElroth, Thomas, 1949, D 24,16:2
McElroy, Arthur E Mrs, 1953, My 14,29:2
McElroy, Benjamin L, 1948, F 2,19:4
McElroy, Bernard, 1903, D 11,9:5
McElroy, Bernard A, 1937, Ag 24,22:3
McElroy, Bernard W, 1942, My 11,15:3
McElroy, Bernard W Mrs, 1950, Ja 26,27:2
McElroy, Burgess L, 1903, Je 29,7:6
McElroy, Charles E, 1947, F 24,19:3
McElroy, Charles F, 1948, D 26,52:3
McElroy, Clayton Sr, 1946, N 28,27:5
McElroy, Daniel S, 1914, My 28,13:5
McElroy, David E, 1938, F 4,21:4
McElroy, David W, 1945, D 14,27:4
McElroy, Dennis T, 1944, Ap 29,15:5
McElroy, Francis L, 1958, S 27,21:4
McElroy, George, 1951, Ap 26,29:5
McElroy, George L Mrs, 1937, Jl 28,19:4
McElroy, Harry F, 1950, S 16,19:6
McElroy, Henry F, 1939, S 16,17:6
McElroy, Hugh, 1947, Ag 26,23:3
McElroy, Hugh Jr, 1945, Mr 3,13:5
McElroy, Irving Rev Dr, 1914, Ja 2,9:6
McElroy, James F, 1915, F 11,9:5
McElroy, James L, 1960, Ap 22,29:1
McElroy, James L Mrs, 1948, F 5,23:4
McElroy, James M, 1946, Ag 20,27:3
McElroy, James Mrs, 1962, Jl 24,28:1
McElroy, James T, 1937, Jl 2,21:4
McElroy, John A, 1955, O 8,19:2
McElroy, John E, 1915, S 17,7:6
MacElroy, John R, 1954, Ag 4,21:3
McElroy, Joseph C, 1907, Ag 22,7:5
McElroy, Joseph M, 1947, Jl 22,23:6
McElroy, Leon E, 1958, S 30,31:2
McElroy, Leon E Mrs, 1949, D 30,20:2
McElroy, Marcellus J, 1951, Mr 6,27:1
McElroy, Mary, 1951, Ag 24,15:5
McElroy, Peter J, 1961, Jl 24,23:5
McElroy, Philip F, 1963, Jl 16,31:5
McElroy, R J, 1965, F 17,43:3
McElroy, Robert (mem ser plans, Ja 24,19:3), 1959, Ja 17,19:1
McElroy, Robert H, 1937, Ag 23,19:2; 1938, Je 27,17:2
McElroy, Robert Mrs, 1942, F 9,15:3
McElroy, Thomas, 1881, O 24,2:2
McElroy, Thomas E, 1944, O 9,23:5
McElroy, Thomas J, 1948, F 25,23:2
McElroy, Thomas N, 1937, Ja 24,II,8:1
McElroy, William B, 1945, Ag 9,21:5
McElroy, William H, 1938, Ja 17,19:2
McElroy, William H Dr, 1918, N 8,15:3
McElroy, William J, 1943, Ag 1,38:7
Maceltchie, Robert, 1941, F 26,21:4
McElvein, George F, 1954, Je 9,31:4
McElveney, Daniel J Jr, 1962, Mr 19,29:1
McElvenny, Robert T, 1965, Mr 29,33:1
MacElveny, Andrew W (por), 1938, Jl 8,17:4
McElvey, Mary A Mrs, 1942, My 2,13:2
McElwain, Andrew A Jr, 1939, D 1,23:4
McElwain, Clifford E, 1946, Jl 21,40:1
McElwain, Edwin, 1960, Mr 17,33:3
McElwain, Frank A, 1957, S 20,23:5
McElwain, Harriet A, 1942, S 20,41:2
McElwain, J Franklin, 1958, Jl 4,19:4
McElwain, John S, 1925, N 26,23:5
McElwain, Mary B, 1964, F 25,31:1
McElwain, Patrick, 1946, Ja 23,27:3
McElwain, R Franklin, 1949, N 8,31:5
McElwaine, Eugene, 1941, F 14,17:4
Macelwane, Francis J, 1940, D 6,27:2
Macelwane, James B, 1956, F 16,29:1
McElwee, Anna B Mrs, 1939, D 25,23:2
McElwee, John F, 1942, Ag 23,13:5
McElwee, Joseph F, 1942, N 24,25:2
MacElwee, Roy S, 1944, F 8,15:5
McElynn, Philip J, 1960, O 21,33:3
McElynn, Thomas J, 1954, Ja 22,27:3
McElynn, Thomas J Mrs, 1954, Mr 2,25:5
McEnany, Benjamin, 1946, Mr 6,28:2
McEnany, Elwood P, 1946, F 2,13:4
McEnany, Robert N, 1921, Mr 8,11:5
McEncroe, Edward, 1909, My 22,7:5
McEneaney, Bernard (Bro Bernardine Lewis), 1963, My 1,39:5
McEneany, Annie Mrs, 1949, Mr 25,45:2
McEneany, Joseph A, 1939, Jl 11,20:3
McEnergy, Eugene, 1962, Jl 4,21:5
McEnerney, Garret W, 1942, Ag 4,19:4
McEnerney, Mary, 1946, Ap 15,27:2
McEnery, Augustin A, 1925, Jl 14,21:6
McEnery, Eugene F, 1954, S 5,51:2
McEnery, Michael J, 1952, F 3,85:1
McEnery, Samuel Douglas Sen, 1910, Je 29,7:5
McEniry, Frank, 1948, Ag 28,16:2
McEniry, Marion Mrs, 1958, Ap 23,33:2
McEnroe, James Msgr, 1925, Ja 13,19:5
McEnroe, John, 1954, My 4,29:4
McEnroe, John C, 1925, Je 4,19:5
McEnroe, Mary, 1951, Ja 27,13:4
McEnroe, P Joseph, 1966, F 2,35:5
McEnroe, William O H, 1945, Ag 19,39:2
McEntee, Bernard J, 1945, F 25,38:1
McEntee, Dwight T, 1952, My 6,29:5
McEntee, Elmer A, 1948, N 12,24:2
McEntee, Girard L, 1957, Ja 25,21:2
McEntee, James J, 1957, O 16,35:1
McEntee, John Col, 1903, D 21,7:5
McEntee, John E, 1948, S 4,15:5
McEntee, John T, 1950, S 12,27:6
McEntee, Joseph L, 1919, Ja 27,13:4
McEntee, Peter, 1922, My 3,21:6
McEntee, Peter J, 1949, Je 10,27:2
McEntee, Thomas, 1943, Je 1,24:2
McEntee, Thomas F, 1967, My 10,47:2
McEntee, Thomas L, 1946, Mr 12,25:5
McEntee, Valentine L Lord, 1953, F 12,27:4
McEntee, William J, 1946, D 4,31:3
McEntegart, Bryan J Archbishop (funl plans, O 2,39:2), 1968, O 1,47:1
McEntegart, Patrick J R, 1966, Ag 25,37:1
McEntegart, Patrick Mrs, 1952, Jl 18,19:2
McEntire, Barnie B Jr, 1961, My 26,4:5
McEntire, Frank S, 1953, My 21,31:5
McEntire, Joseph A, 1960, Ap 19,37:5
McEntire, Richard B, 1958, F 19,27:2
Maceo y Gonzalez, Jose, 1951, Ja 16,29:3
McErlane, F, 1932, O 9,3:4
McEvay, Fergus Patrick Archbp, 1911, My 10,11:4
McEvilly, Jere J, 1954, D 22,23:3
McEvily, Patrick J, 1947, Ap 21,27:5
McEvily, William J, 1956, Ap 5,77:2
MacEvitt, John C, 1942, Jl 2,21:2
McEvitt, Joseph L, 1944, Ag 17,17:5
McEvoy, A, 1927, Ja 5,21:3
McEvoy, Alex, 1953, Mr 23,23:4
McEvoy, Capt, 1905, Ap 17,5:2
McEvoy, Charles D, 1955, Jl 26,25:2
McEvoy, Charles F, 1960, Ja 10,86:6
McEvoy, Charles J, 1948, Ja 7,26:2
MacEvoy, Clifford F, 1960, S 13,37:4
MacEvoy, Clifford F Mrs, 1960, Ja 5,31:5
McEvoy, Douglas N, 1948, D 18,19:1
McEvoy, Edward D, 1957, D 2,27:2
McEvoy, Edward Q, 1952, Ag 12,10:4
McEvoy, Francis A, 1966, O 9,86:3
McEvoy, Frank E, 1954, Jl 16,21:3
McEvoy, George, 1925, Ag 9,5:4
McEvoy, George F, 1964, Jl 21,33:5
McEvoy, J A Justice, 1937, D 25,15:2
MacEvoy, J Louis, 1940, N 17,50:1
McEvoy, James E, 1941, F 14,17:2
McEvoy, James L, 1949, Ap 19,26:3
McEvoy, James P Dr, 1913, Je 10,11:4
McEvoy, John F Mrs, 1950, Mr 21,32:3
McEvoy, John J, 1962, Mr 15,32:4
McEvoy, John J Mrs, 1937, Ja 29,19:4
McEvoy, John J Rev, 1937, D 29,21:2
McEvoy, John P, 1940, N 5,34:2
McEvoy, Joseph P (funl, Ag 10,92:2; mem ser set, S 9,35:5), 1958, Ag 9,13:3
McEvoy, Katherine, 1947, O 9,25:1
McEvoy, Lawrence D Dr, 1937, Ja 31,II,8:8
McEvoy, Leo C, 1957, My 19,88:2
McEvoy, Louis A, 1953, D 18,29:4
McEvoy, Patrick, 1941, D 21,41:2
McEvoy, Patrick H, 1904, Ja 12,7:5
McEvoy, Peter P, 1948, D 4,19:1
McEvoy, Richard E Mrs, 1959, Je 25,29:5
McEvoy, Thaddeus F, 1955, F 2,27:3
McEvoy, Thomas J, 1942, N 10,27:5
McEvoy, Warren Mrs, 1958, Ag 22,21:3
McEwan, Arch W, 1941, My 13,23:2
McEwan, Arthur, 1943, Ap 21,25:4
McEwan, Calvin W, 1950, Ja 15,85:1
McEwan, David, 1943, D 2,27:2
McEwan, David Mrs, 1944, Je 19,19:3
McEwan, Edward K, 1939, Ja 25,21:3
MacEwan, Eldridge J, 1941, Mr 23,45:2
McEwan, G William, 1961, My 21,87:2
McEwan, George, 1958, Mr 28,25:1
McEwan, James Briggs, 1915, D 28,11:4
McEwan, John, 1959, S 22,35:4
McEwan, John H, 1925, D 24,13:6
McEwan, John S, 1943, Ja 1,23:5
McEwan, John Stevans Col, 1915, F 19,9:5
McEwan, Peter V Mrs, 1948, S 7,25:4
McEwan, Richard W Mrs, 1944, O 27,23:5
McEwan, Robert B, 1937, F 21,II,10:4
MacEwan, Robert S, 1968, O 25,47:3
McEwan, W L Dr, 1937, N 5,23:5
McEwan, Walter S, 1953, Ag 2,73:3
MacEwen, Alex M, 1941, Je 30,17:2
McEwen, Alfred F, 1945, N 25,49:1
McEwen, Alfred F Mrs, 1943, S 11,13:2
McEwen, Arthur, 1907, My 2,11:6
McEwen, Clifford M, 1967, Ag 7,29:5
McEwen, Daniel Church, 1909, N 2,9:3
MacEwen, David J Mrs, 1947, N 14,23:4
McEwen, Edward Mrs (May Deveraux), 1925, O 19,21:3
MacEwen, Ewen M, 1947, S 3,25:4
McEwen, Fred, 1950, N 16,31:4
McEwen, Gerald F Mrs, 1956, N 20,37:2
McEwen, Henry T Rev Dr, 1921, F 19,11:5
McEwen, Herbert N, 1944, D 26,19:5
McEwen, James H, 1946, O 9,27:4
McEwen, James L, 1913, D 31,9:5
McEwen, James R, 1952, D 28,48:6
McEwen, James R Mrs, 1941, Jl 2,21:5
McEwen, John, 1948, Je 17,25:4; 1951, My 12,21:2
McEwen, John F, 1948, Ag 21,15:3
McEwen, John M, 1952, My 18,93:1
McEwen, Kenneth M, 1952, My 2,25:5
McEwen, Leland C, 1955, Mr 18,27:3
McEwen, Malcolm H, 1948, N 6,13:5
McEwen, Merrill C, 1957, N 3,89:1
McEwen, Peter Mrs, 1962, S 7,30:1
McEwen, Robert Col, 1937, Je 4,23:2
McEwen, Robert W, 1967, Je 1,43:1
MacEwen, Walter (por), 1943, Mr 21,26:3
MacEwen, Wellington C, 1939, O 4,25:4
McEwen, William E, 1944, My 29,15:4
McEwen, William Jr Mrs, 1949, S 17,17:3
Macewen, William Sir, 1924, Mr 24,15:4
McEwing, Thomas, 1941, Ja 13,15:4
McEwing, William G, 1962, Jl 4,21:2
Macey, Phil O, 1950, My 18,29:4
McFadden, Annie J, 1955, Je 10,25:1
McFadden, Benjamin B, 1939, N 23,27:2
McFadden, Benjamin L, 1937, S 10,24:1
Macfadden, Bernarr (funl plans, O 14,27:5; funl, O 16,86:1), 1955, O 13,31:1
Macfadden, Beulah, 1961, D 3,88:3
McFadden, Charles P, 1963, Ap 10,39:4
McFadden, Clifford R, 1948, Mr 16,27:5
McFadden, Cornelius Mrs, 1950, Ja 13,23:2
McFadden, Dennis P, 1951, S 12,31:4
MacFadden, Don, 1951, Ja 7,77:1
McFadden, Edward Jr, 1954, N 30,29:2
McFadden, Elizabeth A, 1961, Jl 18,29:4
McFadden, Everett R, 1945, My 5,15:1
McFadden, F L, 1949, N 18,29:3
McFadden, Francis B, 1954, Ja 25,19:5
McFadden, Frank D, 1958, Ja 17,25:4
McFadden, G H, 1926, O 17,II,9:1
McFadden, George, 1951, My 8,31:3
McFadden, George Howard Dr, 1925, D 31,15:5
McFadden, Harvey P, 1949, Ag 14,68:1
McFadden, Haynes, 1964, Mr 11,39:4
McFadden, James A, 1952, N 17,25:4
McFadden, James B, 1954, Je 25,21:1
McFadden, John F, 1944, Ja 28,17:2; 1957, My 9,31:5
McFadden, John H, 1921, F 17,11:6
McFadden, John H Jr, 1955, Ag 18,23:4

McFadden, John H Jr (est tax appr), 1961, F 28,43:1
McFadden, John J, 1943, F 19,20:3
McFadden, Katherine (Sister Helen Grace), 1955, Ja 15,13:1
McFadden, L T, 1936, O 2,25:1
McFadden, Manus, 1955, F 18,22:2
McFadden, Mary A (Sister Mary Claudia), 1952, D 27,9:2
McFadden, Mary D, 1944, My 31,19:3
McFadden, Parmalee J, 1911, F 10,9:5
McFadden, Thomas W, 1946, Je 17,21:2
McFadden, W E Col, 1903, Je 2,6:1
McFadden, W H, 1956, N 3,23:5
MacFadden, Walter J Sr, 1960, My 25,39:2
McFadden, Walter N, 1957, Ag 25,86:2
McFadden, William, 1952, N 18,32:5
McFadden, William J Sr, 1950, Mr 29,29:5
McFaddin, Dorman, 1967, S 20,44:2
McFaddin, Harrison D, 1965, Mr 21,86:7
McFaden, Frank, 1959, O 27,37:2
MacFaden, John, 1941, Mr 23,44:2
McFadgen, Henry M, 1945, F 9,15:3
McFadyen, Bernice M, 1954, Jl 24,13:1
McFail, Wellington P, 1965, F 9,37:1
McFall, Charles, 1950, Je 15,31:3
McFall, Henry T, 1957, O 29,31:2
McFall, Jay Vaughn, 1912, D 6,15:5
McFall, John B, 1950, D 5,32:5
McFall, Robert J, 1963, Jl 20,19:1
McFall, Susan V, 1940, D 16,61:1
McFalls, Robert B, 1941, Mr 18,23:5
MacFarlan, Allan, 1943, F 11,19:2
McFarlan, Edward, 1959, O 15,39:5
Macfarlan, Frederick M, 1956, D 20,29:5
Macfarlan, Frederick T, 1937, Ag 15,II,7:2
Macfarlan, Helen R, 1940, Jl 4,15:6
Macfarlan, Robert A, 1947, F 13,23:5
MacFarlan, S Merrill, 1958, Jl 10,27:6
McFarlan, William K, 1943, D 7,27:2
McFarland, A J, 1950, N 29,33:4
MacFarland, Albert E, 1941, Je 7,17:4
McFarland, Asa, 1879, D 15,5:2
MacFarland, Benjamin S Mrs, 1959, Ap 4,19:5
McFarland, Beulah (Mrs B M Braun), 1964, Ag 11, 33:2
McFarland, Bp (funl), 1874, O 16,1:6
MacFarland, Charles S, 1956, O 27,21:1
McFarland, Chauncey L, 1949, Jl 20,25:5
McFarland, David F, 1955, F 8,27:4
MacFarland, David H, 1948, O 7,29:3
McFarland, Ellis D, 1948, O 27,27:2
McFarland, Ellis Mrs, 1947, Ja 20,25:2
MacFarland, Franklin S, 1955, N 2,35:5
McFarland, G F Mrs, 1948, Ap 17,15:5
MacFarland, George, 1942, My 17,47:1
MacFarland, George A, 1965, Ap 13,37:3
McFarland, George B Mrs, 1952, Ja 10,29:4
Mac Farland, George E, 1925, Jl 18,13:5
MacFarland, George F, 1937, N 16,23:5
McFarland, George K, 1949, D 9,32:3
McFarland, George W, 1942, F 23,21:2
MacFarland, Grenville S, 1924, F 29,17:6
McFarland, Harold B, 1940, Jl 17,21:3
McFarland, Harry A, 1937, D 2,25:6
McFarland, Harry T, 1953, Je 27,15:3
McFarland, Helena, 1963, D 23,25:4
MacFarland, Henry J, 1951, F 3,15:4
MacFarland, J Horace, 1948, O 3,67:2
McFarland, James E, 1956, Mr 1,33:4
McFarland, Janet, 1949, N 2,27:2
McFarland, Jean H, 1966, Ag 27,29:4
McFarland, John A, 1952, Jl 30,23:3
MacFarland, John C Mrs, 1940, Jl 28,26:6
McFarland, John E, 1968, D 11,41:1
McFarland, John I, 1943, F 7,48:4
MacFarland, John S, 1923, Ja 6,13:4
McFarland, John Thomas Rev Dr, 1913, D 23,9:5
McFarland, Joseph, 1945, S 23,44:5
McFarland, Joseph W, 1947, D 9,29:3
MacFarland, Laurens W, 1959, Ap 25,21:6
McFarland, Lloyd, 1948, N 24,23:4
McFarland, Margaret L Mrs, 1925, My 25,17:5
McFarland, P F, 1936, S 24,25:1
McFarland, Paul J, 1959, Ag 27,27:5
MacFarland, Robert J, 1923, O 20,15:3
McFarland, Stephen J, 1964, N 24,39:3
MacFarland, Stewart, 1939, Ag 29,21:2
McFarland, Thomas C, 1954, S 18,15:4
Macfarland, Thomas T, 1954, Ag 22,92:2
MacFarland, Thomas W, 1940, Ja 18,23:2
McFarland, Tommy (C C Bevilacqua), 1954, O 26, 27:5
McFarland, W W, 1954, Ja 30,17:5
McFarland, Warren C, 1950, O 19,31:1
MacFarland, William A, 1942, N 6,23:3
McFarland, William C Capt, 1916, S 6,9:5
McFarland, William G Mrs, 1941, Jl 28,13:5
MacFarland, William H, 1958, Je 10,33:5
McFarland, William H Jr, 1956, Ja 7,17:1
McFarland, William L Mrs, 1967, Ja 18,43:4
McFarland, William W, 1905, O 31,7:3
MacFarlane, A Cooper, 1951, S 5,31:2
Macfarlane, Alex, 1955, N 25,27:4
MacFarlane, Alex S, 1955, Mr 6,89:2
McFarlane, Arch W, 1960, Jl 25,23:5
McFarlane, Arthur E, 1945, Ap 12,23:4
MacFarlane, Charles C, 1954, O 5,27:1
Macfarlane, Charles M, 1953, Ag 17,15:1
McFarlane, Charles T, 1949, F 27,69:1
McFarlane, Clement, 1952, N 26,23:5
MacFarlane, David L, 1953, Ja 4,76:4
Macfarlane, Elna F, 1944, N 1,23:5
McFarlane, Frederick C, 1948, N 19,76:2
Macfarlane, George W Col, 1921, F 21,11:5
Macfarlane, Henry J, 1949, Mr 11,25:2
MacFarlane, Irving, 1946, Je 25,22:3
Macfarlane, J H, 1948, O 26,31:5
Macfarlane, James R Mrs, 1944, N 23,31:4
McFarlane, John, 1938, S 1,23:3
MacFarlane, John D, 1943, Ap 5,19:3
MacFarlane, John J Mrs, 1957, Mr 30,19:4
MacFarlane, John L, 1967, Ag 12,25:3
MacFarlane, John M, 1943, S 18,17:5
McFarlane, Lewis B, 1943, Je 10,21:1
McFarlane, Robert, 1951, O 23,29:3
McFarlane, Robert B, 1938, My 21,15:4
McFarlane, Vernon B, 1943, Ja 4,15:5
Macfarlane, W, 1928, Ja 20,21:3
Macfarlane, W E, 1944, O 10,23:5
MacFarlane, William C, 1945, My 15,19:5
McFarlane, William J, 1944, D 29,15:2
MacFarlane, William J, 1957, Je 27,25:4
Macfarlane, William M, 1946, Ag 9,17:4
MacFarleane, James, 1950, Mr 6,21:5
McFarrel, Joseph, 1917, N 5,15:6
McFarren, George E, 1946, Jl 4,19:2
McFate, Earl C, 1952, F 24,85:2
McFatrich, George W, 1946, N 12,29:4
McFatrich, James Burton Dr, 1914, Ap 27,11:6
McFaul, James A Rev (funl, Je 21,13:4), 1917, Je 17,19:3
MacFaul, Mabel, 1944, Ag 22,17:2
McFayden, Bertrand, 1947, N 23,72:4
McFayden, Donald, 1951, N 17,17:6
MacFayden, Harry, 1940, N 15,21:3
McFayden, Temple, 1964, My 5,43:2
McFeaters, Charlie P, 1947, F 18,25:1
McFee, Harold C, 1959, N 18,41:4
McFee, Henry L, 1953, Mr 21,17:3
McFee, Thomas W Sr, 1953, S 20,87:2
McFee, William, 1966, Jl 4,15:1
McFee, William D, 1949, S 9,25:3
McFee, William Mrs, 1952, D 26,15:3
McFeeley, Willis, 1937, N 25,31:5
McFeely, Bernard J, 1946, Mr 17,43:1
McFeely, Bernard N (por), 1949, Ag 10,21:3
McFeely, Edward, 1949, O 5,29:4
McFeely, Edward J, 1956, N 24,19:5
McFeely, Mary, 1942, Je 5,17:4
McFeely, Richard H, 1966, O 6,47:5
McFerran, J C Gen, 1872, Ap 26,1:3
McFetridge, J B, 1903, Je 7,3:6
McFetridge, Laura, 1941, D 8,23:4
Macfie, Elizabeth R Mrs, 1941, O 16,21:3
McGaath, James G, 1963, D 8,87:1
McGaffey, Elizabeth Mrs, 1944, Mr 14,19:3
McGaffigan, James H, 1960, Ja 27,30:5
McGaffin, Charles G, 1941, Mr 27,23:5
Macgahan, J, 1878, Je 11,1:3
McGahan, J A (funl), 1884, Ag 26,2:5
McGahan, John D, 1949, N 11,26:3
MacGahan, Paul, 1959, O 17,23:3
McGahey, John E, 1943, My 15,15:2
McGahuey, Dwayne L, 1950, F 21,25:5
McGall, Albert H, 1941, S 10,23:5
McGall, Quinton, 1907, Mr 16,9:6
McGalloway, M Angelo, 1940, N 1,25:3
McGann, Andrew J, 1964, Ag 14,27:4
McGann, Bernard, 1907, S 18,9:6
McGann, Francis L, 1965, Jl 26,23:5
McGann, James D, 1946, Mr 8,21:3
McGann, John J, 1953, Je 11,29:4
McGann, Mary A, 1947, Jl 16,23:3
McGann, Michael F, 1948, Ja 9,22:3
McGann, Robert G Mrs, 1949, Mr 30,25:5
McGann, Thomas J, 1937, D 28,22:1
McGannon, Robert E Mrs, 1968, D 24,20:5
McGarey, Francis D, 1950, Je 24,13:3
McGarigal, John, 1943, Je 17,21:2
McGarr, James M (Bro Boniface of Mary), 1960, F 22,17:5
McGarr, John A, 1955, N 15,29:3
McGarr, Timothy E, 1942, D 7,27:2
McGarrah, Ella, 1951, F 11,88:3
McGarrah, Gates W (por), 1940, N 6,23:1
McGarrah, Gates W Mrs, 1951, O 8,21:3
McGarrahan, William, 1894, Ap 25,2:6
McGarrett, George F, 1960, My 7,23:6
McGarrigle, Regina, 1944, Ja 10,17:3
McGarrigle, Stephen J, 1951, Ap 25,29:1
McGarrity, Daniel, 1948, Mr 16,28:2
McGarrity, Joseph, 1940, Ag 6,20:3
McGarry, Anthony H, 1949, Ag 10,21:3
McGarry, Bernard P, 1953, S 18,24:4
McGarry, David A, 1953, Ag 17,15:2
McGarry, Frank J, 1943, F 17,21:4; 1963, Jl 20,19:5
McGarry, J J, 1902, F 23,7:6
McGarry, James A, 1959, O 12,19:4
McGarry, James J, 1953, Ja 24,15:3
McGarry, James Mrs, 1909, My 3,7:7
McGarry, John A, 1941, O 2,25:6
McGarry, John B, 1953, Mr 14,15:6
McGarry, John E, 1962, S 25,37:4
McGarry, John J, 1938, Ag 13,13:5
McGarry, John L, 1949, Je 7,31:4
McGarry, John V, 1958, S 9,35:4
McGarry, Joseph B, 1948, F 20,27:1
McGarry, Joseph J, 1947, Jl 2,23:6
McGarry, Maurice Mrs, 1955, N 25,28:1
McGarry, Peter J (por), 1940, D 31,15:4
McGarry, Peter J, 1941, Ja 2,23:4
McGarry, Susie, 1948, S 1,48:7
McGarry, Thomas B, 1959, Mr 16,31:5
McGarry, Thomas H, 1963, Ap 6,19:1
McGarry, Thomas I, 1953, Mr 13,27:3
McGarry, Thomas N Mrs, 1949, Mr 1,25:2
McGarry, William A Sr, 1950, D 13,35:3
McGarry, William H, 1944, Jl 2,19:2
McGarry, William J (por), 1941, S 24,23:1
McGarry, William R, 1942, My 15,20:3
McGarty, John Mrs, 1913, Je 9,9:4
McGarvey, Charles M, 1946, Jl 2,25:5
McGarvey, Cyprian, 1953, Ap 22,29:5
McGarvey, Edward, 1967, F 13,33:3
McGarvey, Henry A, 1952, My 27,27:5
McGarvey, Henry E, 1959, N 8,88:8
McGarvey, Hugh J, 1960, F 16,37:4
McGarvey, John J, 1943, Mr 16,19:2
McGarvey, John N, 1939, Ag 15,19:3
McGarvey, John W, 1938, D 28,26:2
McGarvey, Johnny, 1937, S 19,II,6:7
McGarvey, Robert, 1952, N 1,21:6
McGarvey, Robert N, 1952, Je 29,58:3
MacGarvey, William H, 1914, D 15,13:6
McGarvey, William Msgr, 1924, F 29,17:6
MacGarvie, Robert S, 1937, N 28,II,9:2
McGary, James Walter, 1968, S 9,47:4
McGary, Paul H, 1946, Mr 6,28:2
McGaughan, Frank, 1968, D 25,31:2
McGaughey, W R, 1955, Ap 12,29:1
McGaughlin, Matilda J, 1952, Jl 25,17:3
McGaughy, James R, 1954, Je 24,27:1
McGauley, William R, 1941, Ja 23,21:1
McGaulley, John H, 1951, N 1,29:1
McGavern, John H, 1951, Jl 9,25:4
McGavern, John W, 1951, Ag 5,73:1
McGavick, Alex J, 1948, Ag 26,21:3
McGavick, John Mrs, 1947, D 23,23:4
McGavick Jno, 1958, Ap 27,86:3
McGaw, Albert C Rev, 1938, Ja 20,24:3
McGaw, Albert G Mrs, 1943, Jl 14,19:5
McGaw, Alexander, 1905, Ja 31,2:7
McGaw, Francis A, 1944, Ap 30,45:1
McGaw, Frederick M, 1950, F 7,27:3
McGay, Arthur, 1950, Ap 5,31:5
McGay, Culbert, 1957, Je 22,15:6
McGay, Frank B, 1947, My 3,17:2
McGay, John C, 1957, F 1,25:1
McGeachie, William T, 1950, O 3,31:3
McGeachin, George, 1949, Mr 4,29:2
McGeachin, George Mrs, 1958, D 31,19:3
McGeachy, Donald Mrs, 1944, F 1,19:4
McGeachy, J Burns, 1966, Ag 29,29:4
McGean, John P, 1949, N 9,28:2
McGean, Vincent de Paul Father, 1922, Ag 31,15:
McGean, Walton H, 1940, Mr 20,27:5
McGear, J Brodie, 1953, Ap 24,23:1
McGeary, James L, 1945, Ap 20,19:2
McGeary, Jon A, 1938, Mr 19,15:2
McGee, A B H Col, 1903, O 8,9:5
McGee, Albert A F, 1963, N 26,37:4
McGee, Burton J, 1941, Je 13,19:6
McGee, Charles A, 1942, Mr 6,21:5
McGee, Charles A A, 1955, Ja 12,27:5
McGee, Clarence Mrs, 1953, Ja 27,25:2
McGee, Clifford W, 1958, Ag 13,27:3
McGee, Cushman, 1962, Ag 14,32:1
McGee, Cyril, 1916, F 22,11:5
McGee, Donald W, 1937, O 27,31:5
McGee, Elizabeth A, 1946, Ja 26,13:2
McGee, Eugene D, 1967, F 19,88:7
McGee, Eugene F, 1952, Ag 7,21:3
McGee, Francis B, 1939, Jl 20,19:2
McGee, Francis G, 1952, Ag 22,21:5
McGee, George Kenny, 1968, Ja 13,31:1
McGee, Hall T, 1963, S 11,43:5
McGee, Harold J, 1955, F 24,27:2
McGee, Harry L, 1960, N 27,86:2
McGee, Henry A, 1914, O 18,3:6
McGee, Homer E, 1963, F 14,14:8
McGee, Hugh H (por), 1947, Je 3,25:5
McGee, Hugh Mrs, 1948, N 27,17:3
McGee, James, 1925, Je 23,19:5
McGee, James (M F Gray), 1961, N 21,39:5
McGee, James F, 1920, Mr 19,13:5
McGee, James P, 1941, Ja 2,23:1
McGee, James S, 1949, Jl 14,27:4
McGee, James W, 1965, Je 8,41:3
McGee, Jerry, 1945, Je 5,19:2

McGee, John B, 1951, D 18,31:2
McGee, John D, 1946, O 25,23:4
McGee, John M, 1953, Ja 31,15:2
McGee, John R, 1954, N 21,87:1
McGee, Joseph A Mrs, 1952, D 9,33:1
McGee, Lewis R, 1937, Ag 29,II,6:6
McGee, Matthew, 1949, O 30,84:5
McGee, Patrick E, 1948, N 28,96:5
McGee, Patrick J, 1953, F 6,19:2
McGee, Raymond R, 1949, Ja 28,22:3
McGee, Sam, 1940, S 10,23:2
McGee, Stanislaus, 1940, Ap 12,24:2
McGee, Thomas J, 1943, F 22,17:3
McGee, W J Dr, 1912, S 5,9:3
McGee, W Vaughan, 1912, Ag 7,11:6
McGee, Walter, 1949, Je 23,20:4
McGee, Walter M, 1952, Je 1,84:1
McGee, Walter M Mrs, 1949, Je 13,19:4
McGee, Walter V, 1945, F 18,34:2
McGee, William E, 1946, My 18,19:4
McGee, William H, 1941, Je 23,18:3
McGee, William J, 1940, Je 11,25:1
McGeechan, Edward J Sr, 1952, O 3,23:3
McGeehan, Edward A, 1937, N 9,23:1
McGeehan, Edward Mrs, 1949, N 4,27:1
McGeehan, Hugh V, 1948, Ag 19,21:3
McGeehan, John E Ex-Judge, 1968, My 18,33:3
McGeehan, John E Mrs, 1964, Ja 29,30:3
McGeehan, John W Sr, 1944, Ag 24,19:3
McGeehan, Stanley, 1950, My 15,21:2
McGeehan, W O, 1933, N 30,33:1
McGeen, D M, 1942, F 10,19:3
McGeer, Gerald G, 1947, Ag 12,23:2
McGeever, Joseph A, 1955, Mr 11,25:2
McGehee, Dan R, 1962, F 10,23:2
McGehee, Harvey, 1965, N 3,39:3
McGehee, Schaumburg Maj, 1937, N 23,23:5
McGenty, Denis C, 1959, Mr 2,27:5
McGeoch, John A, 1942, Mr 5,23:2
MacGeorge, Katherine E, 1949, S 6,27:3
McGeorge, Percy, 1937, Ap 10,19:3
McGeory, Edwin J, 1942, Ja 12,15:5
McGeory, Gertrude C Mrs, 1945, Ap 30,19:4
McGeory, John J, 1949, Ag 16,23:5
McGeory, Patrick J, 1950, Je 27,29:3
McGeory, William J, 1946, N 1,23:5
McGeough, Ralph L, 1944, S 5,19:4
McGerald, Arthur, 1903, D 21,7:4
McGettigan, Daniel I, 1947, Jl 26,13:4
McGettihan, John, 1958, Ja 17,25:4
Macgeveran, Mary E, 1941, N 8,19:5
McGevna, Philip J, 1963, Ag 4,80:2
McGhee, Charles B, 1951, Mr 25,72:5
McGhee, Charles McClung Col, 1907, My 6,9:2
McGhee, Frank G, 1955, Jl 16,15:5
McGhee, Guy W, 1947, Ja 23,23:2
McGhee, James E, 1965, Ja 27,35:4
McGhee, Joseph, 1950, Mr 1,27:5
McGhee, Paul A, 1964, Ag 7,29:3
McGhie, Isabella S, 1938, S 17,17:4
McGhie, James, 1948, My 18,23:3
McGhie, James Mrs, 1950, Ap 24,25:3
McGhie, John, 1921, Ap 30,11:4; 1951, Je 10,93:2
McGhie, John Mrs, 1937, S 30,23:1
McGhill, John Bishop, 1872, Ja 15,1:6
McGibbon, Cornelia A D Mrs, 1942, Ap 23,23:4
McGibbon, William A, 1942, Ja 20,20:2
McGibbons, John H, 1939, My 31,23:5
McGibeny, Carson G, 1947, D 29,17:3
McGiehan, Patrick H, 1946, F 22,25:1
McGiehan, Patrick H Mrs, 1943, N 21,56:6
McGiffert, A C, 1933, F 26,26:3
McGiffert, Arthur C Mrs, 1962, Je 12,37:2
McGiffert, James, 1943, Je 19,13:6
McGiffert, John R, 1949, My 11,29:2
McGiffert, Julian E, 1947, D 25,21:4
McGill, Alex, 1953, Ag 19,29:5
McGill, Alexander D, 1925, F 13,17:3
McGill, C Dr, 1881, My 6,2:6
McGill, C Harry, 1966, Mr 1,37:3
McGill, Charles A, 1949, Jl 22,19:3; 1954, N 6,17:2
McGill, Charles A Mrs, 1947, S 5,19:1
McGill, Charles J Mrs, 1966, O 11,47:1
McGill, Charles N, 1950, O 9,25:4
McGill, Clarence McCutcheon Lt-Com, 1918, O 11, 11:3
McGill, Daniel, 1955, Je 12,87:1
McGill, Earle L, 1949, N 5,13:1
McGill, Edward A, 1959, D 30,21:3
McGill, Edward T, 1941, Mr 10,17:1
McGill, Eliza A, 1949, F 18,23:1
McGill, Francis G, 1940, My 24,19:4
McGill, Fred C Mrs, 1949, D 29,25:2
McGill, G W, 1879, N 12,8:1
McGill, George, 1963, My 15,40:1
McGill, Harold A, 1952, D 3,33:4
McGill, Hugh T, 1968, O 27,82:3
McGill, Isabelle (Sister Mary Loretta), 1954, My 3, 25:2
MacGill, J H Mrs, 1947, F 28,23:3
McGill, J Tyson, 1949, Je 29,27:5
McGill, James D, 1942, Mr 6,21:2
McGill, James Rev, 1911, My 19,11:4
McGill, John D Dr, 1912, N 29,15:6
McGill, John T, 1946, Ap 12,27:4
McGill, Joseph F, 1910, F 10,7:5
McGill, Mary C, 1951, Ag 27,19:1
McGill, Nathan K Sr, 1946, My 9,21:2
McGill, Ralph Mrs, 1962, Mr 22,35:3
McGill, Ray, 1963, S 22,86:7
McGill, Richard, 1907, F 7,9:6
McGill, Rita Mrs, 1955, D 27,21:8
McGill, Theodore A, 1966, O 7,43:2
McGill, Thomas H A, 1913, N 22,15:4
McGill, Thoms O, 1947, D 3,29:1
McGill, William, 1944, Ag 31,17:4
McGill, William B, 1953, S 8,31:2
McGillan, G E, 1952, Ap 7,25:5
McGillen, J Gerald, 1952, Ag 7,21:5
McGillian, Eugene F, 1952, Ja 11,21:2
McGillicuddy, Anna Mrs, 1941, Mr 30,48:5
McGillicuddy, Brendan (Bro Brendan), 1960, Mr 9, 33:1
McGillicuddy, Daniel F, 1940, Je 1,15:5
McGillicuddy, Denis F Mrs, 1948, D 2,29:2
McGillicuddy, Eugene, 1950, Mr 23,36:4
McGillicuddy, Eugene (G Mack), 1953, Jl 9,25:5
McGillicuddy, Helen I, 1954, S 4,11:3
McGillicuddy, Michael, 1946, S 23,23:3
McGillicuddy, Michael J, 1960, N 29,37:3
McGillicuddy, Nora A, 1954, Jl 13,23:3
McGillin, Catherine Mrs, 1937, Ap 5,19:3
McGillivray, A A, 1940, D 13,23:5
MacGillivray, A J Rev, 1938, Ja 3,21:2
MacGillivray, Alex, 1958, My 25,87:2
MacGillivray, Angus, 1947, O 16,27:3
Macgillivray, Dougald, 1937, Ag 10,19:2
McGillivray, Edward W, 1947, Ja 10,21:2
McGillivray, Edwin P, 1947, Ap 30,25:4
McGillivray, James H, 1966, Mr 8,16:8
Macgillivray, John C, 1947, F 18,25:3
McGillivray, Neil B, 1949, Je 28,27:4
McGillivray, Perry, 1944, Ag 1,15:6
MacGillvary, Stanley Howard Dr, 1914, F 18,9:5
McGillvray, E K, 1908, Ja 6,7:4
McGillvray, Fred, 1967, Ap 13,43:2
McGillvray, George, 1959, Mr 3,33:4
McGillycuddy, Denis Donough, 1921, Mr 22,17:4
McGillycuddy, Ross K, 1950, Ap 29,15:6
McGilton, Anna L Mrs, 1937, Jl 11,II,4:6
McGilton, Thomas H, 1946, N 3,63:2
McGilton, William A Mrs, 1950, Ap 2,92:7
McGilvery, Neil L, 1960, Mr 29,37:2
McGilvray, David, 1967, My 16,45:3
McGilvray, Donald A Sr, 1950, N 22,25:3
McGilvray, John, 1905, F 25,9:3
McGilvray, William A, 1952, My 27,27:3
McGilvrey, John E, 1945, O 5,23:5
McGinigle, John R, 1955, Ag 14,36:5
McGinity, Frank, 1945, Jl 11,11:6
McGinity, Patrick F Mrs, 1948, S 29,29:2
McGinity, Thomas J, 1948, S 17,25:4
McGinley, Alfred E, 1940, My 8,23:2
McGinley, Anthony F, 1944, D 31,26:8
McGinley, Bernard L, 1953, D 23,25:4
McGinley, Dom M G, 1955, S 21,33:4
McGinley, Edward C, 1946, S 11,7:5
McGinley, Edward V, 1948, D 22,23:3
McGinley, John R Mrs, 1947, Ag 25,17:3
McGinley, John S, 1964, Ag 22,21:6
McGinley, Joseph E, 1947, My 3,17:2
McGinley, Joseph J, 1946, Ja 3,19:2
McGinley, Thomas A (por), 1940, Ap 14,45:1
McGinley, Thomas R, 1925, My 16,17:6
McGinley, Thomas R Mrs, 1948, Ja 16,21:2
McGinley, William, 1952, Ja 12,13:6
McGinley, William J, 1947, Ap 20,60:3
McGinn, Bernard J, 1937, Je 19,17:1
McGinn, Francis J, 1966, Mr 7,27:4
McGinn, John C, 1948, S 19,76:5
McGinn, John R Jr, 1940, Ap 6,17:6
McGinn, Joseph, 1922, O 7,15:7; 1942, S 3,19:2
McGinn, Margaret Mrs, 1952, N 25,29:2
McGinn, Marjory, 1941, N 19,25:4
McGinn, William E, 1955, My 11,31:2
McGinn, William J, 1966, Mr 15,39:2
McGinn, William P, 1939, Jl 6,23:1
McGinnes, Clyde R, 1944, F 22,23:2
McGinness, Alfred J, 1966, O 28,31:1
McGinney, Patrick J Rev, 1911, Mr 31,11:4
McGinnies, Joseph A (por),(will N 29,18:5), 1945, N 2,19:3
McGinnis, Alan R, 1960, O 22,23:4
McGinnis, Angelo, 1914, O 16,11:6
McGinnis, Charles A, 1949, Ag 12,17:5
McGinnis, Charles R, 1948, Jl 31,15:7
McGinnis, Charles T, 1955, F 25,21:5
McGinnis, Claude S, 1964, O 16,39:1
McGinnis, Edward L'Hommedieu Dr, 1925, Ap 30,21:3
McGinnis, Estelle G Mrs, 1955, Jl 19,27:5
McGinnis, Felix S, 1945, Mr 19,19:4
McGinnis, Frank Sr, 1948, My 3,21:5
McGinnis, George, 1915, Ag 22,13:4
McGinnis, James J, 1961, Mr 28,35:2
McGinnis, James S, 1949, My 5,27:2
McGinnis, John J, 1945, S 27,21:2
McGinnis, Josephine C, 1954, F 5,19:4
McGinnis, Patrick H, 1959, Je 16,35:4
McGinnis, Paul V, 1937, Ap 6,23:4
McGinnis, Pearl Mrs, 1948, Mr 1,23:5
McGinnis, Peter J, 1951, Ja 6,15:3
McGinnis, Phil, 1937, N 26,21:3
McGinnis, Robert, 1918, F 23,13:5
McGinnis, Robert B Sr, 1940, N 30,17:4
McGinnis, Stanley P, 1955, S 7,31:1
McGinnis, W F, 1932, My 17,21:3
McGinnis, William, 1938, Jl 30,13:4
McGinnis, William C, 1961, O 7,23:2
McGinniss, James A, 1937, S 29,23:2
McGinnity, J, 1929, N 15,24:3
McGinnity, William F, 1965, N 2,33:3
McGinty, Allen, 1951, Ag 27,19:1
McGinty, Bernard, 1921, Ag 11,13:5
McGinty, Cornelius V, 1958, F 14,23:4
McGinty, Edward B, 1945, Mr 2,19:2
McGinty, Francis P, 1949, Je 7,31:4
McGinty, George B, 1937, F 17,21:3
McGinty, George F, 1962, F 17,19:4
McGinty, John F, 1953, F 23,25:5
McGinty, John J, 1948, N 25,31:4
McGinty, Joseph M F Rev, 1915, Je 26,9:5
McGinty, Richard, 1939, Ap 6,25:4
McGirr, Charles J, 1949, Mr 5,18:3
McGirr, Eugene F, 1943, Ag 13,17:3
McGirr, James, 1939, D 24,14:7
McGirr, Marie F W Mrs, 1941, N 13,27:2
McGirr, Newman F, 1952, N 20,31:1
McGirr, Wilbur, 1959, My 9,21:5
MacGiure, Constance J Mrs, 1939, Ja 19,19:1
McGiverin, Michael, 1944, D 4,23:3
McGivern, Bernard L, 1949, Ja 18,24:2
McGivern, Daniel, 1915, Ag 13,9:3
McGivern, Owen Mrs, 1953, D 28,22:5
McGivney, Alter J, 1946, Ap 28,42:6
McGivney, John J, 1939, Mr 17,21:2
McGivney, P J, 1928, My 8,27:2
McGlachlin, Edward F Jr, 1946, N 10,64:2
McGlade, Agnes T (U O'Connor), 1959, F 6,25:3
McGlade, George B, 1948, Jl 9,19:3
McGlashan, R R, 1953, Mr 2,23:4
McGlasson, Grady C, 1950, Jl 2,25:1
McGlasson, Harold I, 1949, D 7,31:5
McGlasson, Oscar B, 1939, O 16,19:6
McGlaughlin, Louis E, 1947, D 18,30:2
McGlaughlin, John P, 1947, Je 4,27:4
McGlennon, Thomas P, 1957, F 12,27:5
McGlincey, John D, 1908, Ap 19,9:6
McGlinchee, Andrew J Mrs, 1953, Ag 6,21:2
McGlinchey, James M, 1961, My 6,31:6
McGlinchey, Michael J, 1952, Mr 2,92:1
McGlinchy, Pat J Father, 1903, O 20,9:7
McGlinn, Frank J, 1944, My 6,15:5
McGlinn, John A, 1946, D 1,79:4
McGloin, James F, 1953, D 24,15:3
McGloin, William J, 1907, Mr 14,7:6
McGlon, Jesse C, 1963, D 11,47:4
McGlone, Charles T Mrs, 1941, S 9,23:3
McGlone, Frank P, 1948, Jl 7,46:6
McGlone, James, 1938, D 28,26:3
McGloone, Marguerite B Mrs, 1955, O 27,33:4
McGlothlin, W J, 1933, My 29,13:4
McGlue, Michael Rev, 1937, S 10,23:1
McGlynn, Edward R, 1964, O 26,31:4
McGlynn, Edward Rev Dr, 1900, Ja 8,1:5
McGlynn, Francis H, 1965, Ap 25,88:8
McGlynn, Frank, 1951, My 19,15:3
McGlynn, Fred T, 1942, D 18,27:2
McGlynn, G W, 1881, Mr 8,8:6
McGlynn, James A, 1941, D 2,23:5
McGlynn, Joseph L, 1962, Mr 2,30:1
McGlynn, Michael T, 1959, Ap 16,33:2
McGlynn, Peter J, 1943, Mr 4,20:1
McGlynn, U S Grant, 1941, Ag 27,19:4
McGoey, Bernard, 1948, F 21,13:3
McGoey, Elizabeth Mrs, 1942, My 1,19:4
McGoey, Frank A, 1941, Ag 15,17:4
McGoey, John J, 1954, Je 19,15:5
McGoey, Matthew B, 1944, Ja 11,19:4
McGoey, Matthew B Sr, 1938, My 19,21:5
McGoey, Thomas, 1915, S 7,13:6
McGoldrick, Anna, 1938, D 10,17:4
McGoldrick, Bernard F, 1949, My 30,13:2
McGoldrick, Charles F, 1952, Ap 29,27:3
McGoldrick, Daniel J, 1950, D 20,32:3
McGoldrick, Edward J, 1938, Ag 24,21:1; 1951, Ja 10, 27:1; 1967, N 22,50:1
McGoldrick, Francis M, 1960, Ag 22,25:2
McGoldrick, James E, 1949, Ap 8,25:4
McGoldrick, James F, 1937, Ag 30,21:4
McGoldrick, James P, 1939, Ag 18,19:4
McGoldrick, John B (funl), 1911, Ag 6,II,9:6
McGoldrick, John J, 1943, N 13,13:2; 1962, Ap 4,43:1
McGoldrick, Joseph A, 1959, My 26,35:5
McGoldrick, Joseph L, 1964, D 23,30:3
McGoldrick, Loretta R, 1961, Ag 24,29:5
McGoldrick, Mary J, 1946, S 15,9:8
McGoldrick, Thomas, 1963, S 13,30:1
McGoldrick, Thomas A, 1956, Mr 10,17:5
McGoldrick, Warren P, 1964, My 20,43:3

McGoldrick (Sister Mary Alphonsus), 1961, F 15, 35:4
McGoldrick Thos A Mrs (por), 1949, My 13,23:3
McGolrick, James Bp, 1918, Ja 24,9:4
McGonagle, Bridget Mrs, 1953, Mr 2,9:7
McGonagle, William, 1940, N 6,56:8
McGonegal, John R, 1952, D 19,31:4
McGonegal, Michael F, 1940, D 8,69:1
McGonegal, Phil H Mrs, 1951, D 6,33:3
McGonigal, Celestine, 1963, S 30,29:3
McGonigal, Ethel M, 1917, F 4,19:3
McGonigal, Harry F, 1958, N 18,37:3
McGonigal, Sean, 1965, Je 2,45:4
McGonigal, William, 1940, Ap 2,25:4
McGonigle, Cornelius P, 1948, Ap 6,24:2
McGonigle, Edward J, 1947, O 24,23:5
McGonigle, James A, 1954, Ag 28,89:3
McGonigle, Robert D, 1905, Jl 6,1:2
McGonigle, William J Mrs, 1955, Ja 6,27:2
McGoodwin, Preston B, 1945, S 27,21:2
McGoodwin, Thomas Q, 1938, S 28,25:2
McGoorty, John P Mrs, 1944, S 4,19:5
McGorrill, Virgil C, 1957, N 17,86:8
McGorrisk, Daniel H, 1950, Ja 11,23:4
McGorrisk, David H Mrs, 1946, F 28,23:4
McGorry, Hugh A Jr, 1943, Ap 2,21:6
McGorry, Michael T, 1942, Ap 12,45:1
McGorry, Thomas, 1940, Ja 28,32:4
McGorty, Peter J, 1944, Je 20,19:5
McGough, Frank, 1953, O 20,29:3
McGough, John H, 1949, F 24,23:2
McGough, John J, 1940, Je 27,23:5
McGough, Lawrence, 1949, Jl 15,19:5
McGough, Louise C, 1955, Je 17,23:4
McGough, Patrick, 1940, Ag 22,19:2
McGourty, Gerald S, 1951, O 3,33:2
McGourty, James P, 1953, Mr 23,23:3
McGovern, Arthur A (por), 1942, N 2,21:3
McGovern, Bernard, 1947, Ja 16,25:3
McGovern, Catherine Mrs, 1939, N 17,21:1
McGovern, Charles C, 1950, Mr 10,27:4
McGovern, Charles F, 1942, Mr 30,17:2
McGovern, Charles F J, 1956, D 20,29:6
McGovern, Charles T, 1956, Mr 23,28:2
McGovern, Charles W, 1939, F 15,23:5
McGovern, Daniel P Mrs, 1964, Mr 22,76:7
McGovern, Edward F, 1943, Mr 4,19:2; 1946, S 5,27:5
McGovern, Elizabeth, 1949, Ag 21,68:3
McGovern, Elizabeth L, 1946, D 25,29:6
McGovern, Emmett G Mrs, 1953, F 1,88:6
McGovern, Eugene, 1968, N 4,47:2
McGovern, Felix B, 1944, D 6,23:3
McGovern, Felix Mrs, 1967, Jl 12,43:1
McGovern, Francis E, 1946, My 18,19:3
McGovern, Francis X, 1951, Jl 29,68:3
McGovern, Frank J, 1955, My 12,29:1
MacGovern, George, 1967, S 27,47:1
McGovern, George B, 1944, Mr 31,21:5
McGovern, George T, 1964, Je 17,43:2
McGovern, Harry B, 1953, D 12,19:4
McGovern, J Winslow, 1966, My 9,39:1
McGovern, James, 1909, N 7,13:5; 1945, O 11,23:1
McGovern, James B Jr, 1954, My 8,2:6
McGovern, James L, 1952, F 4,17:4; 1958, Ja 15,39:2
McGovern, James L Mrs, 1937, O 12,25:2
McGovern, James T, 1942, Ag 17,15:3
McGovern, John, 1968, F 15,43:1
McGovern, John F, 1963, D 17,39:1
McGovern, John J, 1955, Ag 3,23:3
McGovern, John Mrs (P Allenby), 1966, Mr 25,41:2
McGovern, John T, 1925, O 15,23:6
McGovern, John T (funl plans, My 28,21:7), 1960, My 27,31:1
McGovern, Joseph, 1944, Jl 25,19:5
McGovern, Joseph A, 1966, My 22,87:1
McGovern, Joseph T, 1964, Mr 26,35:4
McGovern, Lawrence J, 1948, Ap 13,27:3
McGovern, Louis V, 1946, Ap 30,21:3
McGovern, Marian, 1952, Ap 26,23:4
McGovern, Mary T, 1946, S 12,7:4
McGovern, Michael D, 1947, D 24,21:4
McGovern, Nellie M, 1937, Jl 19,15:2
McGovern, P, 1933, F 23,17:3
McGovern, Patrick, 1941, F 6,21:2
McGovern, Patrick A, 1951, N 9,27:1
McGovern, Patrick J, 1940, Je 9,45:2
McGovern, Peter P, 1952, S 21,88:2
McGovern, Phil J Jr, 1948, N 14,76:2
McGovern, Roger, 1940, O 11,21:5
McGovern, Rudolph A, 1951, Je 14,27:5
McGovern, Thomas, 1947, F 10,29:5
McGovern, Thomas A Rev, 1937, Ap 29,21:4
McGovern, Thomas F, 1961, D 1,33:4; 1966, My 27, 43:1
McGovern, Thomas J, 1956, Je 6,33:4; 1960, D 13,31:3
McGovern, Walter, 1937, Ap 21,23:4
McGovern, William J, 1951, F 26,23:3
McGovern, William M, 1964, D 14,36:1
McGovern, William Mrs, 1963, Ag 4,80:3
McGovern, William P Mrs (por), 1944, Ja 21,17:4
McGovney, Dudley O, 1947, O 17,22:3
McGowan, Alex, 1958, N 3,37:4
McGowan, Alexander D, 1943, My 12,25:2

McGowan, Allen J R, 1950, Mr 2,27:3
McGowan, Andrew J, 1955, Ja 4,21:4
McGowan, Anna M, 1941, D 30,19:3
McGowan, Arch W, 1940, Ja 21,34:5
McGowan, Arthur C, 1958, N 23,88:1
McGowan, Bernard, 1938, Je 6,17:4
McGowan, Ceceilia F, 1947, Je 8,60:4
McGowan, Charles, 1943, O 1,19:1
McGowan, Charles E, 1947, O 15,27:2
McGowan, Daniel F, 1947, N 15,17:4
MacGowan, David B Mrs, 1938, Ja 9,43:2
McGowan, Donald A, 1963, Ag 13,31:2
McGowan, Edward J, 1943, Ja 10,50:3
McGowan, Elizabeth B Mrs, 1923, Mr 22,19:5
McGowan, Francis J, 1918, O 14,11:8
McGowan, Frank A, 1915, Je 28,9:2
McGowan, Frank P, 1968, N 14,47:2
McGowan, George E, 1946, O 11,23:5
McGowan, Harry D, 1961, Jl 15,19:1
McGowan, Henry, 1948, S 10,23:4
McGowan, Hugh, 1937, Ag 19,20:1
MacGowan, J E Col, 1903, Ap 13,9:5
McGowan, James, 1966, Ja 16,83:1
McGowan, James F, 1944, Je 21,19:1
McGowan, James J, 1937, Mr 11,23:5; 1958, Ja 13, 29:4
McGowan, James Jr, 1961, Mr 16,37:3
McGowan, John, 1950, My 10,31:5
McGowan, John A, 1952, O 7,29:2; 1965, N 2,33:2
McGowan, John B Mrs, 1963, My 19,86:8
McGowan, John F, 1942, S 14,15:5; 1947, F 4,26:3
McGowan, John J (por), 1948, Mr 9,23:3
McGowan, John J, 1948, N 20,13:3; 1952, N 15,17:4; 1954, N 8,21:2; 1955, F 17,27:2; 1962, Je 8,31:3
McGowan, John J Mrs, 1962, S 18,39:3
MacGowan, John K, 1942, N 24,26:3
McGowan, John M J, 1952, Mr 9,37:1
MacGowan, John N, 1959, O 7,43:2
McGowan, John P, 1952, Mr 27,30:3
McGowan, John P Dr, 1915, Mr 1,9:4
McGowan, John Rear-Adm, 1915, Ag 14,7:6
McGowan, John S, 1941, N 14,24:2
McGowan, Joseph E, 1946, Ag 28,27:5
McGowan, Joseph J, 1964, Je 16,39:3
McGowan, Katherine, 1957, Ap 17,31:5
Macgowan, Kenneth, 1963, Ap 29,31:4
McGowan, Leo H, 1949, Jl 30,15:5
McGowan, Louis O, 1937, F 2,23:3
McGowan, Mary, 1954, Je 24,27:5
McGowan, Mary C Mrs, 1946, N 30,15:5
MacGowan, Mary F Mrs, 1938, Jl 13,21:6
McGowan, Michael, 1947, Ja 23,23:4
McGowan, Michael J, 1938, N 6,49:4
McGowan, Nettie Mrs, 1947, My 2,21:4
McGowan, Patrick, 1958, S 11,33:5
McGowan, Patrick Francis (funl, Ap 10,11:6), 1913, Ap 7,9:5
McGowan, Pattilo H, 1939, N 17,21:4
McGowan, Peter J, 1945, My 25,19:4; 1951, N 30,23:1
McGowan, Raymond A, 1962, N 15,37:3
McGowan, Raymond L Sr, 1964, Mr 13,33:5
McGowan, Roscoe E, 1966, N 6,88:3
McGowan, Thomas, 1907, Jl 16,7:6; 1948, Ag 5,21:4
McGowan, Thomas H Jr, 1949, Ja 11,27:4
McGowan, Thomas J, 1940, F 5,17:3; 1951, D 9,91:2
McGowan, Walter A, 1968, N 23,47:3
McGowan, William A (Bill),(funl, D 14,33:4), 1954, D 10,27:3
McGowan, William F, 1947, Jl 25,17:5
McGowan, William J, 1944, My 9,19:6
MacGowen, Charles J, 1960, O 27,37:5
McGowen, James Sinclair T, 1922, Ap 9,28:4
McGowen, Roscoe E Mrs, 1963, N 13,41:1
McGowin, Everette L, 1955, Ap 23,19:3
McGowin, Joseph A, 1950, Jl 23,57:2
McGown, Chester S, 1948, Ag 30,25:1
McGown, Chester S Mrs, 1954, O 20,29:3
McGown, Dana P, 1956, S 17,27:5
McGown, Harry B, 1945, Jl 3,13:3
McGown, Helen H, 1937, D 10,26:6
McGown, Henry P judge, 1904, Je 14,7:3
McGown, William F, 1943, D 13,23:3
McGown Chester C, 1958, Ja 13,29:5
McGrade, William H, 1951, D 24,13:5
McGrady, Edward, 1903, N 2,9:3
McGrady, Edward F, 1960, Jl 18,27:3
McGrail, Arthur J, 1954, Ap 14,29:3
McGrail, Frank J, 1940, Je 15,15:5
McGrail, George B, 1954, Ag 27,21:2
McGrail, George M, 1949, O 28,23:1
McGrail, John A, 1945, My 2,23:4
McGrail, Margaret T, 1947, D 22,22:2
McGrail, Patrick J, 1940, S 22,49:2
McGrail, Theresa C, 1940, D 28,15:2
McGrail, William P, 1951, Ja 22,17:2
McGrail, William P Mrs, 1967, Jl 9,60:8
McGrain, Preston, 1943, F 8,19:2
McGranahan, Floyd, 1942, Ag 29,15:4
McGranahan, James, 1907, Jl 10,7:5
McGranary, Daniel F, 1945, D 24,15:3
McGrane, Bernard G, 1957, N 24,87:2
McGrane, John F, 1945, Ap 13,17:5
McGrane, Joseph M, 1941, N 28,23:1

McGranery, James P (Dec 23), 1963, Ap 1,36:2
McGrann, Aloysius P, 1950, Ag 9,29:3; 1950, D 9,1
McGrann, Helen, 1957, O 22,33:4
McGrann, Richard P Mrs, 1947, Ap 29,28:2
McGrann, William H (por), 1945, My 3,23:5
McGrath, Alfred F, 1967, Ja 16,41:4
McGrath, Archibald F, 1967, Jl 2,35:2
MacGrath, Blain, 1939, D 10,68:7
McGrath, Charles H, 1942, S 14,15:5
McGrath, Clara L, 1956, Ja 15,92:2
McGrath, D Harold Mrs, 1955, O 30,88:5
McGrath, Daniel, 1964, Ja 9,31:1
McGrath, David F (por),(Bro Paul Edward), 1943 S 25,15:4
McGrath, David J, 1943, S 13,19:5
McGrath, Douglas G Mrs, 1968, S 7,29:2
McGrath, Edmund J, 1941, Ag 31,23:2
McGrath, Edmund P Mrs, 1957, My 11,21:3
McGrath, Edward A Mrs, 1954, My 4,29:1
McGrath, Edward F, 1948, My 28,23:3; 1960, S 7,
McGrath, Edward J, 1947, D 4,31:4; 1956, Ja 21,2 1958, Mr 27,33:1; 1964, O 27,39:2
McGrath, Edwin C, 1938, D 19,23:2
McGrath, F Sims, 1959, S 15,39:2
McGrath, F Sims Mrs, 1963, Ag 24,19:5
McGrath, Francis P (por), 1949, N 17,29:3
McGrath, Frank, 1967, My 15,43:2
McGrath, Frank E, 1961, Je 18,88:7; 1964, O 30,3
McGrath, Frank I, 1948, Ja 4,52:1
McGrath, Frank J, 1944, Ja 25,19:5; 1961, O 29,8
McGrath, Frederick T, 1952, Ag 12,19:3
MacGrath, H, 1932, O 30,37:1
McGrath, H P, 1881, Jl 6,2:5
McGrath, Harry T, 1951, N 2,23:2
McGrath, Henrietta F Mrs, 1941, Ja 20,17:4
McGrath, Henry B, 1948, Ag 31,26:2
McGrath, Henry C, 1945, Je 18,19:4
McGrath, Howard O, 1955, O 29,19:4
McGrath, Hugh C, 1941, S 8,15:6
McGrath, J Howard (est appr, N 12,16:4), 1966 23:2
McGrath, J Wade, 1960, Jl 13,35:4
McGrath, Jack, 1955, N 7,37:5
McGrath, James, 1944, Jl 21,19:5
McGrath, James E, 1967, My 12,47:3
McGrath, James F, 1942, N 16,19:5
McGrath, James G, 1947, Jl 24,21:6
McGrath, James J, 1960, Ja 1,19:1
McGrath, James J Mrs, 1945, N 4,44:2
McGrath, James Sr, 1959, Ag 23,92:6
McGrath, Jane L, 1954, Je 29,27:2
McGrath, Jefferson, 1937, Ag 23,19:2
McGrath, John, 1870, D 5,3:2; 1941, D 5,23:4; 1 N 22,88:3
McGrath, John B, 1941, Ap 24,21:2
McGrath, John B Rev, 1924, Ap 9,21:2
McGrath, John C, 1941, My 18,44:2
McGrath, John E, 1952, Ja 9,29:4
McGrath, John F, 1949, O 16,88:6; 1957, Ap 28, 1960, My 22,86:4
McGrath, John H, 1944, F 14,17:2; 1950, D 19,2
McGrath, John J, 1947, D 20,17:1; 1950, Ap 10, 1951, Mr 14,33:3; 1953, My 19,30:5; 1957, Ja 1962, Ag 31,21:3
McGrath, John J Mrs, 1944, Mr 4,13:3; 1948, N 88:1; 1953, Mr 19,29:4
McGrath, John J Rev, 1937, My 12,23:3
McGrath, John T, 1944, My 14,46:2
McGrath, John T Rev, 1924, Ap 12,15:3
McGrath, John W, 1924, F 19,15:2
McGrath, Joseph, 1905, F 21,7:5; 1943, Ap 26, 1966, Mr 27,86:7
McGrath, Joseph F, 1950, Ap 13,29:3
McGrath, Joseph L, 1948, Jl 23,19:2
McGrath, Joseph M, 1952, Ap 3,35:3
McGrath, Joseph W, 1942, Ap 14,21:2
McGrath, Larry, 1960, Jl 8,21:2
McGrath, Lawrence, 1949, F 27,68:6
McGrath, Leslie, 1953, S 22,31:4
McGrath, Margaret L, 1942, My 12,19:5
McGrath, Martin W, 1956, F 19,92:5
McGrath, Mary Mrs, 1873, Mr 16,8:3
McGrath, Mary T Mrs, 1946, Ap 11,25:5
McGrath, Matilda E, 1961, Ag 26,17:4
McGrath, Matthew E, 1956, Jl 7,13:4
McGrath, Matthew F, 1957, S 14,19:2
McGrath, Matthew J, 1941, Ja 29,1:3
McGrath, Matthew Mrs, 1944, Mr 27,19:6
McGrath, Michael, 1905, Mr 9,2:6; 1950, My
McGrath, Michael C, 1913, F 24,11:3
McGrath, Michael F Dr, 1903, Ag 12,9:6
McGrath, Michael J, 1941, My 5,17:4; 1961,
McGrath, Michael T, 1952, N 9,91:1
McGrath, P, 1929, Je 15,17:4
McGrath, Pat J Dr, 1905, Ja 29,18:1
McGrath, Patrick, 1944, My 11,19:6; 1951, Ja 1956, Je 21,31:4
McGrath, Patrick J, 1947, O 9,25:5; 1956, O
McGrath, Patrick J Mrs, 1938, Ap 6,23:5
McGrath, Patrick Mrs, 1954, Jl 18,57:2
McGrath, Paul Mrs (L M Hubbard), 1966, C
McGrath, Reuben L, 1949, S 7,29:3
McGrath, Robert P F D Capt (por), 1937, A

McGrath, Stephen J, 1962, F 5,31:5
McGrath, Stephen W, 1948, My 24,19:5; 1950, Ja 7, 17:4
McGrath, T M, 1951, S 1,11:4
McGrath, Thomas, 1937, Ap 23,21:2; 1938, Mr 20,II, 8:7
McGrath, Thomas A, 1952, My 27,27:5
McGrath, Thomas F, 1948, O 17,76:2; 1956, D 22,19:6
McGrath, Thomas J, 1945, O 25,21:3; 1949, D 14, 31:5; 1966, Ag 4,33:5
McGrath, Thomas J Mrs, 1954, My 20,31:4
McGrath, Thomas M, 1945, Ap 21,13:3
McGrath, Timothy J, 1948, O 27,28:2
McGrath, William F, 1938, Ja 25,22:2; 1956, Jl 22, 61:3; 1967, N 29,40:4
McGrath, William F Mrs, 1952, Ja 3,46:4
McGrath, William G, 1946, F 18,21:5
McGrath, William H, 1949, F 7,19:2
McGrath, William J, 1944, D 1,23:4; 1946, Ja 5,13:4
McGrattan, Andrew, 1957, D 2,27:5
McGrattan, Andrew Mrs, 1948, Jl 11,52:7
McGratty, Agnes G (will), 1938, My 10,17:6
McGratty, Charles L, 1940, D 10,25:4
McGratty, E J Mrs, 1944, Ja 13,21:3
McGratty, Edward J Sr, 1959, Mr 30,31:3
McGraw, Anthony F, 1950, Ag 5,15:5
McGraw, Curtis W, 1953, S 11,21:1
McGraw, Edward, 1954, F 10,29:2
McGraw, Harrison B, 1944, F 16,17:4
McGraw, Harry J Mrs, 1957, N 30,21:4
McGraw, Hugh E, 1956, O 19,27:4
McGraw, J, 1877, My 5,2:5
McGraw, J J, 1928, Mr 4,II,7:1; 1934, F 26,1:4
McGraw, James H Mrs, 1959, N 2,31:4
McGraw, James H Sr, 1948, F 22,48:1
McGraw, John, 1871, Jl 15,1:6
McGraw, John F, 1942, Ja 26,15:4
McGraw, John J Mrs, 1962, N 5,31:1
McGraw, John M, 1964, S 12,25:2
McGraw, Joseph A Mrs, 1954, Ap 17,13:3
McGraw, Joseph J, 1950, Ag 19,13:2
McGraw, Max (will, N 10,76:7), 1964, O 28,45:4
McGraw, Patrick, 1944, F 3,19:4
McGraw, Robert B, 1960, O 24,29:3
McGraw, Robert F, 1954, F 3,31:3
McGraw, Stanley D, 1957, Jl 11,25:2
McGraw, Theodore A Dr, 1921, S 7,13:4
McGraw, Thomas A, 1966, Ag 27,29:4
McGraw, Thomas J, 1946, D 14,15:5
McGraw, William T, 1937, My 1,19:5; 1944, Jl 30,35:3
McGray, Arthur N Mrs, 1949, My 24,27:5
McGrayne, James C, 1938, Ag 4,17:3
McGreal, Francis J, 1945, Ag 25,11:5
McGreal, Michael B, 1950, Jl 14,21:1
McGreer, John, 1908, Je 13,7:3
McGreery, Clifford, 1952, O 17,27:4
McGreevy, John P, 1941, S 16,23:6
McGreevy, Robert F, 1947, O 2,27:4
McGreevy, William S, 1950, Jl 31,17:4
McGreger, Arthur E, 1937, D 20,27:4
McGregor, A J, 1945, Ja 24,21:3
McGregor, Archie, 1945, O 4,23:4
McGregor, Arthur A, 1945, Jl 31,19:4
McGregor, Arthur J, 1945, F 12,19:4
McGregor, Atholl, 1945, N 18,43:1
McGregor, B B, 1902, S 9,2:5
McGregor, Charles D, 1954, N 11,31:2
McGregor, Charles S, 1937, Ag 9,19:6
MacGregor, Clarence, 1952, F 19,29:2
McGregor, Daniel A, 1955, F 21,21:2
Macgregor, Daniel D, 1950, Mr 17,23:5
McGregor, David, 1944, F 14,17:3; 1947, Mr 6,25:5
MacGregor, Dollie Mrs, 1954, Ja 27,27:4
McGregor, Donald F, 1944, F 18,17:2
McGregor, Donald P, 1949, Ag 17,24:2
McGregor, Douglas, 1964, O 14,45:1
McGregor, Douglas U, 1953, Je 11,29:1
MacGregor, Duncan, 1939, Je 10,17:3; 1948, Je 12, 15:5
MacGregor, Edgar J, 1957, S 3,27:4
McGregor, Ernest F, 1946, Je 2,44:4
MacGregor, George P Mrs, 1955, Je 24,19:1
McGregor, Gordon M, 1922, Mr 12,30:3
McGregor, Gregor W, 1948, D 19,76:5
MacGregor, H Patricia, 1944, Ag 27,33:3
McGregor, Harmon B, 1948, D 6,25:3
MacGregor, Harold R, 1944, F 20,11:4
McGregor, Henry F Mrs, 1949, My 25,29:2
McGregor, Hessie M, 1950, Je 19,21:3
McGregor, Ian Lt, 1920, Mr 6,11:5
McGregor, J D Gov, 1878, Ap 26,8:5
McGregor, J Harry, 1958, O 8,35:1
McGregor, James B, 1910, Mr 24,9:5
MacGregor, James C Mrs (will), 1952, N 26,15:6
MacGregor, James H, 1948, F 11,27:4
McGregor, James K, 1946, Ja 23,27:3
MacGregor, James V Mrs, 1957, S 17,35:2
McGregor, John, 1952, Je 12,33:4
McGregor, John A, 1937, S 15,23:5
MacGregor, John A, 1939, S 21,23:2
McGregor, John A, 1942, Ap 25,13:1
McGregor, John D, 1950, D 2,13:2
McGregor, Kenneth, 1947, F 23,53:7
MacGregor, Kenneth W, 1968, Ap 27,39:5
McGregor, Mabel Mrs, 1953, Ag 28,17:4
MacGregor, Mary E C, 1955, O 24,27:4
McGregor, O E, 1967, F 3,28:6
McGregor, Peter G, 1949, My 12,31:4
MacGregor, Ralph W G, 1945, Je 6,21:2
McGregor, Robert A, 1947, D 10,31:2
McGregor, Robert A Mrs, 1943, F 9,23:2
McGregor, Robert C, 1942, Je 12,21:5
McGregor, Robert G, 1944, O 31,19:6
McGregor, Robert G Mrs, 1962, My 24,35:4
McGregor, Sarah E, 1946, Ja 6,8:3
MacGregor, Theodore D Mrs, 1948, Mr 7,68:6
McGregor, Tho Gen, 1921, F 5,11:4
McGregor, W Eugene, 1939, Ap 11,23:5
MacGregor, Wallace F, 1939, Je 19,15:3
McGregor, William T, 1940, D 17,25:2
MacGregor-Morris, John T, 1959, Mr 21,21:4
Macgregor of Macgregor, Malcolm, 1958, D 6,23:4
McGrew, Clinton F, 1940, S 29,44:1
McGrew, Edward W, 1954, My 19,31:2
McGrew, Edward W Mrs, 1943, O 7,23:2
McGrew, Eva Mrs, 1951, Jl 22,61:2
McGrew, Fitzhugh (por), 1947, Ap 19,15:4
McGrew, George Harrison Rev Dr, 1917, Ag 17,9:5
McGrew, George S Col, 1912, My 16,11:4
McGrew, Irving A, 1942, Ag 21,19:1
McGrew, Irving A Mrs, 1948, Ap 29,23:1
McGrew, James Clark, 1910, S 19,7:6
McGrew, John A, 1952, My 9,23:4
McGrew, John T, 1955, Mr 8,27:1
McGrigor, Rhoderick, 1959, D 5,23:4
McGroarty, Dennis, 1909, Jl 20,7:5
McGroarty, John C Jr, 1965, Jl 13,33:2
McGroarty, John S (por), 1944, Ag 8,17:4
McGroarty, John S Mrs, 1940, My 15,25:1
McGronen, Thomas F Rev, 1914, O 6,11:6
McGrory, John T, 1946, Mr 3,45:2
McGrory, Patrick A, 1943, Ag 31,17:7
McGuane, James J, 1952, Mr 22,13:3
McGucken, William J, 1943, N 6,13:3
McGuckin, Eugene, 1937, My 10,19:5
McGuckin, Joseph I, 1943, D 7,27:4
McGuerty, John L, 1952, O 17,27:4
MacGuffie, John A, 1941, My 3,15:6
McGuffin, W L, 1950, Je 26,27:4
McGuigan, Frank, 1937, Jl 11,II,4:8
McGuigan, J Barry, 1955, Ja 11,25:1
McGuigan, J I Mrs (Clara H), 1964, F 5,35:4
McGuigan, John, 1943, O 6,23:2; 1952, Mr 30,94:2
McGuigan, Patrick, 1938, S 14,23:5
McGuigan, Patrick J, 1941, My 15,23:5
McGuill, Lawrence, 1941, Jl 25,15:4
McGuiness, Clifford, 1955, O 4,35:3
McGuiness, Cornelius P, 1957, Ap 17,31:4
McGuiness, Dennis J, 1953, Mr 30,21:3
McGuiness, James J, 1966, D 29,28:7
McGuiness, Jask, 1950, D 5,31:5
McGuiness, John, 1950, O 5,31:2
McGuiness, John J, 1949, Je 6,19:4
McGuiness, Mary Mrs, 1955, O 18,37:5
McGuiness, Peter J, 1948, Je 11,23:1
McGuiness, Thomas, 1948, Ap 13,27:3
McGuiness, Walter F, 1958, Jl 4,19:4
McGuinn, James J (por), 1947, N 11,28:3
McGuinn, Walter, 1944, Ap 2,40:2
McGuinn, Warner T, 1937, Jl 11,II,4:7
McGuinn, William B, 1959, O 30,27:2
McGuinness, Edward F, 1953, N 22,88:1
McGuinness, Edward J, 1956, Je 28,29:5
McGuinness, Eugene J, 1957, D 28,17:5
McGuinness, Hamilton, 1958, Ja 10,23:2
McGuinness, James, 1951, O 25,29:2
McGuinness, John J, 1952, O 10,25:2; 1965, Mr 13, 25:2
McGuinness, John Mrs, 1952, D 3,33:4
McGuinness, Joseph, 1922, Je 1,19:6
McGuinness, Madge C L, 1959, D 11,34:3
McGuinness, Michael F, 1945, Jl 24,23:4
McGuinness, Patrick, 1950, F 23,27:2
MacGuinness, Robert B Mrs, 1943, Mr 9,24:3
McGuire, Adrian E, 1951, F 27,27:4
McGuire, Alice Mrs, 1951, S 27,63:8
McGuire, Andrew W, 1955, Ap 8,21:2
McGuire, Arthur G, 1952, D 30,19:4
McGuire, Augustine C, 1938, Ja 28,21:5
MacGuire, C J, 1930, My 7,27:3
McGuire, Charles M, 1945, D 30,14:2
McGuire, Clarence K, 1949, O 12,30:2
McGuire, Constantine J, 1965, Ag 12,27:1
McGuire, Cyril L, 1948, S 16,29:4
McGuire, Daniel P, 1955, Jl 2,15:6
McGuire, Daniel W, 1919, Jl 17,13:4
McGuire, David, 1922, D 25,13:2
McGuire, Donald A, 1962, O 29,29:3
McGuire, E J, 1934, Ag 5,26:3
McGuire, Edward A, 1950, My 25,29:3
McGuire, Edward S, 1960, F 4,31:4
McGuire, Edwin B, 1938, Je 30,23:6
McGuire, Edwin W, 1947, N 4,25:1
McGuire, Esther M Mrs, 1953, Jl 17,17:4
McGuire, Eugene J, 1956, Ag 23,27:5
McGuire, Father, 1903, Ag 27,7:6
McGuire, Floyd E, 1964, D 11,39:2
McGuire, Francis A Dr, 1921, Mr 1,13:4
McGuire, Frank J, 1953, Je 6,17:2
McGuire, Frank J Mrs, 1948, O 19,27:4
McGuire, Fred, 1955, D 19,27:3
McGuire, Frederick T Jr, 1966, S 20,47:2
McGuire, George, 1913, N 23,IV,7:6
McGuire, George A, 1958, F 27,27:2
McGuire, George F, 1940, D 29,24:6
McGuire, Harry, 1939, F 15,23:5
McGuire, Hunter H, 1949, Ja 23,68:3
McGuire, J P, 1945, D 23,18:6
McGuire, Jack W, 1946, Ja 1,27:2
McGuire, James, 1944, Ag 9,17:3
McGuire, James A, 1949, Ja 4,40:3
McGuire, James E, 1953, Ag 13,25:2
McGuire, James J, 1938, O 12,27:4; 1946, O 7,31:1
McGuire, James K, 1923, Je 30,11:4
McGuire, James P, 1950, My 14,108:1; 1954, Ja 14, 29:3; 1955, Mr 4,23:5
McGuire, John, 1942, O 25,44:8
McGuire, John A, 1956, D 7,27:3
McGuire, John C, 1923, Ja 5,11:6; 1958, F 9,88:8
McGuire, John F Mrs, 1950, F 13,21:5
McGuire, John G, 1949, Jl 8,19:3
McGuire, John P, 1948, N 14,76:6; 1955, Ag 26,19:5; 1957, Je 1,17:4; 1963, O 15,40:1
McGuire, John Rev (funl, My 7,11:6), 1912, My 3, 11:5
McGuire, John T, 1948, Jl 27,25:2; 1950, O 28,17:6
McGuire, John W, 1958, Ja 17,25:2
McGuire, Joseph D, 1950, Ap 22,19:6
McGuire, Joseph F, 1952, Jl 30,24:8
McGuire, Joseph H, 1947, Ap 29,27:6
McGuire, Joseph J, 1951, Mr 3,13:2
McGuire, Joseph P, 1938, Jl 19,23:7
McGuire, Karl, 1949, Ja 30,61:1
McGuire, Laurence, 1949, F 15,23:6
McGuire, Lee W, 1959, O 4,86:4
McGuire, Marguerite E, 1959, Ag 20,25:2
McGuire, Mary, 1939, My 7,III,7:1
McGuire, Mary C, 1946, Mr 21,25:2
McGuire, Michael A, 1954, D 28,23:2
McGuire, Nancy, 1939, My 7,III,7:1
McGuire, Paddy (por), 1940, Jl 28,29:4
McGuire, Patrick Mrs, 1958, My 30,21:4
McGuire, Paul C, 1962, S 13,37:2
McGuire, Phil E, 1940, S 12,25:3
McGuire, Robert A, 1962, Ja 5,29:4
McGuire, Robert J, 1939, Jl 25,19:4
McGuire, Samuel A, 1949, D 13,38:4
McGuire, Stan, 1950, Ja 5,4:4
McGuire, Stuart C, 1946, O 11,23:2
McGuire, Thomas, 1942, Ja 24,8:5
McGuire, Thomas B, 1916, Jl 1,11:6
McGuire, Thomas J, 1950, O 27,29:3
McGuire, Thomas Jefferson, 1912, D 27,9:4
McGuire, Thomas L, 1944, D 30,11:5
McGuire, Vincent G, 1949, Mr 25,23:2
McGuire, W B Dr, 1883, N 29,8:4
McGuire, W D Jr, 1923, Ap 19,19:5
McGuire, Walter, 1963, S 26,35:2
McGuire, Walter P, 1951, Jl 1,50:3
McGuire, William A (por), 1940, S 17,23:1
McGuire, William A, 1947, Je 12,25:5
McGuire, William H, 1957, N 1,23:1
MacGuire, William J, 1939, Je 13,23:3
McGuire, William M, 1965, My 4,43:2
McGuirk, Alex, 1952, F 15,25:2
McGuirk, Alexander Prof, 1914, Jl 18,7:6
McGuirk, Charles J, 1943, D 5,64:5
McGuirk, Edward A, 1939, Jl 2,15:2; 1959, Ja 22,31:4
McGuirk, Edward J, 1955, F 9,25:2
McGuirk, James J Jr, 1957, Ja 13,85:1
McGuirk, John J, 1942, Mr 19,21:5
McGuirk, Joseph J, 1939, F 4,15:6
McGuirk, Laurence A, 1945, Je 20,23:4
McGuirk, Madeline, 1957, Ag 7,27:6
McGuirk, Peter, 1950, D 28,26:3
McGuirl, W T, 1933, N 14,19:1
McGunnegle, George K, 1938, Ja 19,23:2
McGunnell, Robert P, 1955, Je 26,77:2
McGuone, James J, 1938, S 30,21:6
McGurgan, James, 1937, My 2,II,9:2
McGurgan, William E, 1948, Mr 3,23:4
McGurin, Patrick J, 1944, Ag 9,17:5
McGurk, Francis A, 1956, Ag 17,19:5
McGurk, James, 1954, D 4,17:7
McGurk, James E, 1965, S 14,39:1
McGurk, Jonce I, 1947, Ja 11,1:6
McGurk, Joseph F, 1962, Je 13,41:3
McGurk, Joseph Rev, 1924, Jl 23,15:3
McGurk, Joseph W, 1939, Ja 10,19:3
McGurk, Michael, 1948, Je 24,25:6
McGurk, Robert M, 1938, D 4,60:4
McGurley, James B Mrs, 1948, Jl 5,15:3
McGurn, Barrett Mrs, 1960, F 21,92:4
McGurran, Nellie, 1955, Ag 5,19:4
McGurren, Mary, 1953, Mr 22,86:5
McGurrin, Andrew F, 1939, My 12,21:2
McGurrin, James Mrs, 1966, Jl 21,33:1
McGurrin, William, 1919, D 25,13:3
McGusty, Mary, 1939, N 26,42:5

McGusty, Robert T, 1946, Ja 29,25:3
Machado, Bernadino (por), 1944, Ap 30,46:1
Machado, Guillermo J, 1938, F 23,23:4
Machado, John Z, 1942, Ap 20,21:5
Machado, Manuel, 1947, Ja 20,25:3
Machado Hernandez, Alfredo, 1946, Ag 5,21:4
Machado y Morales, Gerardo, 1939, Mr 30,23:1
Machaels, August J, 1949, Ag 20,11:4
McHaffey, David Mrs, 1950, Ja 28,13:5
McHaffie, Alex C, 1954, Je 17,29:4
McHale, Archbishop, 1881, N 8,5:2
McHale, Frank, 1937, Ja 13,24:2
McHale, James H Mrs, 1957, My 27,31:2
McHale, Joseph A, 1950, Mr 26,96:1
McHale, Kathryn, 1956, O 9,35:3
McHale, Martin (por), 1942, Ap 3,21:5
McHale, Martin Mrs, 1951, Mr 3,13:4
McHale, Mary E, 1943, Ja 11,15:4
McHale, Patrick Rev, 1937, Mr 14,II,9:1
McHale, Richard L, 1948, My 11,26:3
McHale, Thomas A, 1944, O 26,23:2
McHale, Thomas M, 1944, Jl 13,17:4
McHale, William, 1962, O 28,16:2
McHale, William J, 1951, O 21,92:3
McHale (Mother Mary Liguori), 1963, O 17,35:4
McHarg, Arthur V, 1950, F 7,27:4
McHarg, C K Rev Dr, 1903, Ag 1,7:6
McHarg, Henry K, 1941, Ja 29,18:2
McHarg, Henry K Jr, 1943, Jl 30,15:3
MacHarg, John B, 1954, N 1,27:4
MacHarg, Malcolm (por), 1943, My 9,40:5
MacHarg, William, 1951, F 22,31:1
McHarg, William C, 1905, Je 7,9:4
McHarg, William E, 1949, Ja 7,22:3
MacHarrie, Lindsay, 1960, My 23,29:5
McHarrie, Stuart A, 1952, Ap 5,15:6
Machauer, William F Sr, 1949, Ja 29,13:1
Machen, Arthur, 1947, D 16,34:2
Machen, Arthur W, 1950, My 29,17:6
Machen, Harry L, 1948, Je 8,26:3
Machen, J Gresham Rev Dr, 1937, Ja 2,11:1
Machen, William H, 1947, Mr 9,60:7
McHenry, David J, 1953, D 20,76:3
McHenry, E W, 1961, D 22,23:4
McHenry, Elizabeth, 1956, Mr 16,23:4
McHenry, Frank A, 1937, F 5,21:3
McHenry, G, 1880, N 9,2:2
McHenry, H Cresson, 1947, D 7,78:4
McHenry, J H, 1941, Ap 11,21:4
McHenry, Joann M, 1951, Je 13,29:5
McHenry, John, 1939, D 19,26:4; 1948, O 17,78:3
McHenry, Junius H, 1953, D 5,2:7
McHenry, Luke, 1911, S 18,11:4
McHenry, Myra Mrs, 1939, Je 19,15:2
McHenry, Sylvan W, 1964, Ja 31,27:1
McHenry, Thomas, 1940, Ap 7,45:2
McHenry, W Lee, 1942, D 2,25:4
McHenry, William D, 1939, Mr 10,23:5
McHenry, William F, 1946, My 17,21:3
McHenry, William R, 1953, Ja 4,77:2
Machette, George M, 1948, Mr 10,27:1
Machette, James H, 1947, Ap 7,24:2
Machey, Charles Rev, 1919, Jl 13,22:4
Machida, Chuji, 1946, N 14,29:2
McHie, Sidmon, 1944, Ag 31,17:1
Machin, Charles Henry, 1917, Ag 18,7:4
Machin, Sara E, 1942, My 10,42:7
Machler, F Patrick, 1950, Je 11,92:2
Machlet, George F, 1937, Ag 29,II,6:8
Machold, Arthur G Sr, 1962, O 15,29:2
Machold, H Edmund, 1967, F 8,28:5
Macholdt, Wallace S, 1947, Je 2,25:2
Machos, Henry J, 1947, Je 29,48:2
McHose, Isaac, 1912, Jl 25,9:5
McHowie, John, 1948, Mr 12,23:4
Machray, Robert, 1946, Ja 27,42:4
Machris, Alfred P, 1938, Ag 26,17:6
Machson, Orris Mrs, 1947, O 5,68:4
Macht, Ephraim, 1944, D 20,23:6
McHugh, Anna R (Sister Anna), 1959, O 11,86:8
McHugh, Arthur E, 1959, Ap 28,35:3
McHugh, Bonaventure, 1944, Ja 30,38:5
McHugh, Earle H, 1949, D 29,25:5
McHugh, Edward, 1938, Mr 1,21:1; 1948, Ap 1,25:2
MacHugh, Edward, 1957, F 5,23:2
McHugh, Ellen L Mrs, 1937, Jl 19,15:5
McHugh, Eugene J, 1962, Mr 27,37:2
McHugh, Francis J, 1940, Mr 3,45:1; 1945, D 15,17:3
McHugh, Francis Patrick Rev, 1924, S 30,23:4
McHugh, Francis X, 1966, F 4,31:1
McHugh, Frank A, 1946, D 3,31:3
McHugh, Frank E Mrs, 1965, My 1,31:2
McHugh, Frank J, 1944, My 4,19:4
McHugh, George E, 1955, N 28,31:5
McHugh, George W Rev, 1950, Jl 20,25:5
MacHugh, Harold F Mrs, 1955, O 19,33:3
McHugh, J Paul, 1941, F 4,21:3
McHugh, James A, 1955, Ja 27,23:5
McHugh, James F, 1944, Je 1,19:1
McHugh, James S, 1941, My 9,21:4
McHugh, John, 1939, My 7,III,6:6; 1947, Ja 5,53:5
McHugh, John (por), 1948, Ag 2,21:3
McHugh, John A, 1950, Ap 10,19:2; 1964, S 20,88:8
McHugh, John F, 1950, O 25,35:5
McHugh, John J, 1942, Ja 27,21:3; 1942, D 30,23:1; 1951, N 2,23:1; 1954, O 28,35:2
McHugh, John Mrs, 1956, O 23,33:5
McHugh, John T, 1966, S 30,47:2
McHugh, Joseph A, 1942, Mr 16,15:2; 1967, Jl 12,43:3
McHugh, Joseph P, 1916, Je 21,11:4
McHugh, Julia A Mrs, 1947, Je 19,21:4
McHugh, Keith S Mrs, 1956, Je 15,25:4
McHugh, Lawrence F, 1941, My 17,15:3
McHugh, Lawrence P, 1966, Jl 19,39:3
McHugh, Margaret C, 1950, My 17,29:2
McHugh, Martin J, 1961, Ap 14,29:4
McHugh, Michael B, 1949, Je 26,60:5
McHugh, Michael J, 1955, F 23,27:4
McHugh, Nellie Mrs, 1949, Jl 4,24:1
McHugh, Patrick J, 1951, Jl 17,27:2
McHugh, Robert E, 1961, S 14,31:3
McHugh, Rose J, 1952, D 13,21:3
McHugh, Thomas E, 1951, O 25,29:1
McHugh, Thomas J, 1960, D 8,35:1
McHugh, Thomas J Mrs, 1943, My 22,13:4
McHugh, Vincent A, 1951, S 23,70:1
McHugh, William J Jr, 1960, O 26,39:4
McHutchison, James (por), 1940, F 4,41:1
Maciejewski, Anton F, 1949, S 26,25:1
McIlhaney, Asa K, 1946, My 27,23:1
McIlhargy, John A, 1938, Mr 3,21:5
McIlhenney, Frank C, 1939, Ag 4,13:1
McIlhenney, Horace R, 1964, O 31,29:5
McIlhenny, Edward A, 1949, Ag 9,25:2
McIlhenny, Edward A Mrs, 1958, Jl 13,69:2
McIlhenny, John D, 1925, N 24,25:3
McIlhenny, John D Mrs, 1943, Mr 11,21:4
McIlhenny, Selina B, 1950, F 11,15:5
McIlhiney, Parker Cairns, 1923, Je 22,17:4
McIllvaine, C A (por), 1948, F 29,61:1
McIllveny, Harry J, 1914, Jl 14,9:6
McIllwain, Herbert A, 1948, N 18,27:4
McIlravey, Samuel, 1957, S 28,17:2
McIlravy, William N, 1943, Ap 22,23:4
MacIlreith, R T, 1943, Jl 14,19:2
McIlroy, Samuel H, 1942, F 10,19:5
McIlroy, Walter H, 1946, Mr 23,13:5
McIlvain, Charles J Jr, 1938, Ag 31,15:5
McIlvain, Edward M, 1961, Ag 30,33:2
McIlvain, Edward M Mrs, 1950, My 24,29:1
McIlvain, Ernest C, 1938, D 5,23:3
McIlvain, Robert W, 1959, F 18,33:5
McIlvaine, Anne, 1946, Ja 22,27:4
McIlvaine, Charles P Bishop, 1873, Mr 15,7:4
McIlvaine, Clarence, 1912, D 10,15:4
McIlvaine, Donald, 1950, D 9,15:2
McIlvaine, Edwin L, 1962, Ja 17,33:3
McIlvaine, Gilbert, 1939, Ag 7,15:6
McIlvaine, James M, 1953, Je 20,17:6
McIlvaine, Tompkins, 1953, N 14,17:4
McIlvaine, William Joseph, 1946, Ja 30,3:4
McIlvan, Edwin H, 1948, Ja 17,17:5
McIlvan, William G, 1943, S 8,23:1
McIlvane, Charles A, 1947, My 4,60:4
MacIlvane, Robert, 1940, Ap 13,17:4
McIlvane, William J, 1958, Ja 27,27:4
Macilvar, Hugh, 1940, F 8,23:4
McIlveen, Joseph, 1942, Jl 6,15:4
McIlveen, Samuel J, 1940, N 1,25:4
McIlwain, Charles H Mrs, 1948, S 28,27:1
McIlwain, John F, 1961, F 20,27:2
McIlwain, Knox, 1961, Mr 31,17:2
McIlwaine, Alex Mrs, 1957, D 8,88:2
McIlwraith, Thomas F, 1964, Ap 1,39:3
McIlwraith, William, 1944, F 9,19:2
McIlyar, James O, 1954, F 22,19:1
McIndoe, Archibald H, 1960, Ap 13,39:4
McIndoe, Garnet W, 1966, O 11,43:8
McIndoe, George, 1951, D 16,91:1
MacIndoe, J Franklin, 1958, F 4,29:1
McIndoe, James Francis Brig-Gen, 1919, F 21,13:7
McIndoe, Walter J Mrs, 1946, Ap 3,25:3
McInenly, Charles W, 1939, F 1,21:4; 1949, Ja 11,31:4
McInenly, William P, 1952, D 14,91:1
McInerney, Ben, 1944, D 28,19:5
McInerney, Cornelius, 1946, S 15,9:8
McInerney, Douglas J, 1951, D 30,24:2
McInerney, Edward J, 1952, Je 12,33:4
McInerney, Francis X, 1956, Je 25,23:4
McInerney, Frank A, 1947, My 7,27:4
McInerney, George J, 1937, Jl 22,19:5
McInerney, Henry F, 1958, S 19,27:1
McInerney, J P, 1946, S 15,9:7
McInerney, James H, 1948, Jl 19,19:3
McInerney, James J, 1941, Ag 7,17:1
McInerney, James M, 1963, O 9,55:8
McInerney, John A, 1959, D 30,21:4
McInerney, John E, 1951, N 15,29:3
McInerney, John J, 1947, Ap 18,22:2
McInerney, John L, 1945, N 22,35:2
McInerney, John P, 1945, Ag 27,19:3
McInerney, Joseph A, 1939, Jl 11,19:6
McInerney, Joseph D, 1954, My 31,13:6
McInerney, Joseph J Mrs, 1945, F 16,19:3
McInerney, Mary Mrs, 1950, Ja 28,13:2
McInerney, Thomas J, 1945, S 12,23:4
McInerney, Timothy A, 1965, S 11,27:4
McInerny, T F, 1926, Ag 1,II,5:1
McInerny, William Owen, 1917, O 9,11:5
McInnerney, Thomas H, 1952, O 1,33:5
McInnerney, Thomas H Mrs, 1940, Ja 26,17:6
MacInnes, Albert G, 1965, Ja 28,30:7
MacInnes, Angus A, 1961, F 17,27:3
Macinnes, C R, 1929, S 30,25:3
MacInnes, Duncan (por), 1946, Ja 22,27:1
MacInnes, Duncan A (Sept 23), 1965, O 11,61:3
McInnes, Hamilton, 1953, S 11,21:2
McInnes, Hector, 1937, Je 20,II,6:8
McInnes, J Campbell, 1945, F 10,11:4
MacInnes, John C, 1915, F 25,9:4
McInnes, Russell, 1967, Ag 8,39:2
MacInnes, William, 1963, Je 30,56:3
McInnes, William Dr, 1925, Mr 12,19:4
MacInnis, Early C, 1948, Ag 13,15:4
McInnis, Emmett E, 1953, Ap 21,27:5
McInnis, Frank, 1959, Ja 29,27:3
McInnis, Hugh, 1941, N 6,23:2
McInnis, John F, 1949, S 8,29:2
McInnis, John P (Stuffy), 1960, F 17,35:3
McInnis, Norman K, 1952, Je 25,29:4
MacInnis, Phil H, 1941, F 22,15:3
McInnis, Raymond J, 1952, F 19,29:3
McInnis, Robert A, 1941, Ag 16,15:4
MacInnis, Robert Mrs, 1959, Jl 19,69:2
McIntee, E Teresa, 1951, S 10,21:3
McIntire, A C, 1948, D 25,17:3
McIntire, B Meredith, 1945, My 28,19:2
McIntire, Bradford O, 1938, Mr 7,17:3
McIntire, Charles, 1941, Ja 1,23:4
McIntire, Charles V, 1941, Je 11,21:6
McIntire, Clarence J, 1955, F 25,21:5
McIntire, Edward, 1941, My 9,21:4
McIntire, Edward H, 1945, S 5,23:2
McIntire, Frank, 1954, Ag 20,19:4
Macintire, Horace J, 1948, Jl 17,15:2
McIntire, Lani, 1951, Je 18,23:4
McIntire, Malcolm Mrs, 1951, Jl 4,17:6
McIntire, Reed, 1947, O 14,27:4
McIntire, Ross T, 1959, D 9,45:1
McIntire, W H, 1943, Mr 5,17:3
McIntire, William H, 1943, F 27,13:2
McIntire, William T, 1950, N 29,33:5
McIntire, William Watson, 1912, Ap 1,13:5
McIntosh, A A, 1950, Jl 4,17:2
McIntosh, A C, 1939, Ja 28,15:1
McIntosh, Albert J, 1964, Ag 12,35:5
McIntosh, Alex, 1953, My 1,21:4
McIntosh, Alex E, 1962, Ap 12,35:1
McIntosh, Allan Mrs (J Hoffman), 1966, O 1,3
McIntosh, Arthur T, 1955, N 9,33:3
McIntosh, Burr (por), 1942, Ap 29,21:3
McIntosh, Calvin F, 1941, S 5,22:3
McIntosh, Charles J, 1937, Jl 23,19:5
McIntosh, Charles K, 1950, D 23,15:3
McIntosh, Daniel F, 1945, O 27,15:4
McIntosh, David G Jr, 1940, My 10,23:5
Macintosh, Douglas C, 1948, Jl 7,46:5
McIntosh, Edward F, 1946, Jl 16,24:2
McIntosh, Edwin S (por), 1944, Ja 13,21:1
McIntosh, Elmore R, 1943, Ag 24,19:1
Macintosh, Enrique C, 1912, S 18,11:4
McIntosh, Frank, 1942, O 5,19:3
McIntosh, Franklin G, 1940, Je 13,23:5
McIntosh, George H D, 1955, Mr 15,26:8
McIntosh, Gregory K, 1952, Ag 21,19:4
McIntosh, H M, 1925, O 4,5:1
McIntosh, Hugh D, 1942, F 5,22:2
McIntosh, India (Mrs P J Dower), 1963, My 1
McIntosh, J H, 1908, N 22,11:6
McIntosh, James (por), 1948, Ja 8,25:6
McIntosh, James G, 1953, Ag 21,17:2
McIntosh, James G Mrs, 1957, Ja 22,29:3
McIntosh, James H, 1941, F 26,21:5
McIntosh, James R, 1952, My 9,23:2; 1959, D
MacIntosh, James W, 1944, N 29,23:5
McIntosh, John, 1903, My 12,9:5
McIntosh, John A, 1946, My 9,21:4
McIntosh, John D Mrs (R Wakefield), 1955, I 48:1
McIntosh, John M, 1950, O 19,31:1
McIntosh, John Mrs, 1951, My 2,31:5
McIntosh, John S, 1945, Ag 28,19:4
McIntosh, Joseph W, 1952, Ag 28,23:3
McIntosh, Montgomery E, 1946, Ag 24,11:5
McIntosh, Percival J, 1944, F 12,13:2
McIntosh, Peter, 1958, F 18,27:3
MacIntosh, Russell L, 1957, S 6,21:5
McIntosh, Samuel, 1946, O 8,23:3
McIntosh, Stanley W, 1963, O 1,39:3
McIntosh, Walter K, 1949, Mr 9,25:4
McIntosh, Wendell, 1961, O 14,17:8
MacIntosh, Willard B, 1948, Ag 7,15:5
Mcintosh, William, 1910, D 13,13:4
McIntosh, William A, 1951, Ag 9,21:5
McIntosh, William M, 1946, Jl 30,23:1
McIntosh, William Mrs, 1951, Je 11,25:3
McIntyre, Alec C, 1949, D 22,22:3
McIntyre, Alexander, 1943, Jl 8,19:4
McIntyre, Alfred R, 1948, N 29,23:2

MacIntyre, Angus J Rev, 1937, N 22,19:5
McIntyre, Arch, 1938, S 15,25:5
McIntyre, Augustine, 1954, S 7,25:3
McIntyre, Bede, 1944, Ap 12,21:6
McIntyre, Bonaventure, 1967, Ja 26,33:3
McIntyre, Brouwer D, 1966, Ja 14,39:4
MacIntyre, Carlyle F, 1967, Jl 3,17:4
McIntyre, Charles E, 1952, Ag 28,23:2
McIntyre, Charles J, 1951, Je 23,15:3
McIntyre, Daniel R, 1947, Mr 13,27:4
McIntyre, Donald R, 1957, Ja 31,27:4
McIntyre, Dugald, 1950, Jl 20,25:4
McIntyre, Edward C, 1947, Je 16,21:2
McIntyre, Edward J, 1949, S 28,27:4
McIntyre, Edward Maj, 1912, Ag 10,7:6
Mcintyre, Ewen, 1913, Ja 10,11:3
MacIntyre, Ezra Mrs, 1966, Je 20,30:3
McIntyre, Flora, 1946, Ag 7,27:1
McIntyre, Francis J, 1965, My 13,37:3
McIntyre, Frank (por), 1944, F 17,19:3
McIntyre, Frank (por), 1949, Je 9,31:1
McIntyre, Frederic M, 1948, Ag 10,22:2
McIntyre, Frederick M, 1944, Ja 22,13:3
MacIntyre, Freeman A, 1940, Je 14,21:4
McIntyre, G Donald, 1940, D 10,25:5
McIntyre, George, 1949, Ap 3,76:2; 1952, S 16,29:1
McIntyre, George D, 1950, Ag 15,30:2
McIntyre, George V, 1968, D 1,87:1
Macintyre, Gerald R, 1938, Je 1,23:5
MacIntyre, Gordon, 1952, Jl 2,25:4
McIntyre, H D, 1903, Je 19,9:5
McIntyre, Hal, 1959, My 6,39:3
McIntyre, Hector, 1945, Mr 17,13:3
McIntyre, Henry T, 1937, D 10,26:4
McIntyre, Herbert J, 1950, N 5,92:4
McIntyre, Hugh C, 1953, My 11,27:1
McIntyre, Irwin A, 1941, My 23,21:4
McIntyre, J, 1879, N 9,12:1
McIntyre, J D, 1950, F 7,27:3
McIntyre, J F, 1927, Ja 10,1:6
McIntyre, James, 1916, Ja 31,11:4; 1937, Ag 19,19:1; 1950, F 1,29:2
McIntyre, James F, 1951, Je 21,27:3
McIntyre, James P, 1957, Ap 10,33:3
McIntyre, Jane, 1943, Ap 20,23:4
McIntyre, John, 1949, Ja 18,23:3
Macintyre, John, 1953, O 30,23:4
McIntyre, John A, 1946, D 22,41:4
MacIntyre, John J, 1942, F 9,15:4
McIntyre, John J, 1960, Jl 4,15:5
McIntyre, John T, 1951, My 22,32:2
McIntyre, Joseph D, 1948, Ja 27,25:4
McIntyre, Joseph W, 1966, D 13,47:4
McIntyre, Leo A, 1944, Ap 16,41:2
McIntyre, Leona A, 1944, Ja 14,19:3
McIntyre, Louis F, 1958, O 4,21:6
McIntyre, Marvin H, 1943, D 14,27:1
MacIntyre, Mary B, 1955, Mr 29,30:3
McIntyre, Mathew, 1947, N 30,76:3
McIntyre, Molly, 1952, F 5,29:3
McIntyre, Neil, 1944, O 17,23:5; 1948, O 5,25:1
McIntyre, O E, 1967, Je 13,47:2
McIntyre, Oscar O (por),(will, D 14,28:6), 1938, F 15,25:1
McIntyre, Peter J, 1949, My 28,15:6
McIntyre, R A Mrs, 1940, Je 13,23:4
McIntyre, Richard H, 1958, Jl 11,23:5
McIntyre, Robert B, 1944, Ja 3,21:1; 1963, S 6,29:1
McIntyre, Robert Bp, 1914, Ag 31,7:5
McIntyre, Robert L, 1952, Mr 4,27:4
McIntyre, Ronald S, 1957, Ja 13,84:1
McIntyre, Rufus, 1866, My 6,3:5
MacIntyre, Thomas, 1939, Ap 5,25:4
McIntyre, Thomas, 1951, Ag 16,27:3
McIntyre, Thomas A, 1908, Jl 30,5:5
McIntyre, Thomas A Mrs, 1945, Je 5,19:5
McIntyre, Thomas J, 1945, Ja 3,17:3
McIntyre, Thomas P, 1948, O 30,15:2
McIntyre, Thomas Sr, 1937, Ap 22,23:5
MacIntyre, Willetta W, 1954, O 25,27:4
McIntyre, William A, 1950, N 11,15:1; 1957, Jl 17,27:4
McIntyre, William H, 1947, S 7,60:2; 1951, F 24,13:5; 1953, D 23,25:4
MacIntyre, William H Mrs, 1948, F 16,22:3
McIntyre, William J, 1953, N 10,31:1
McIntyre, William P, 1942, S 4,23:4
McIntyre, William R, 1946, N 20,31:1
McIntyre, William R Mrs, 1952, Mr 18,27:5
McIon, James, 1875, Jl 28,5:2
MacIravy, George W, 1964, Jl 30,27:3
MacIsaac, A Campbell, 1948, Ag 16,19:5
McIsaac, Archibald M, 1960, Ja 14,33:1
McIsaac, Charles F, 1951, Mr 3,13:3
MacIsaac, John L, 1941, Mr 26,23:4
MacIsaac, Lloyd J, 1954, Mr 30,27:3
McIver, Alex R, 1951, Je 16,15:3
McIver, Allan Mrs, 1948, S 22,31:4
McIver, Charles Duncan, 1906, S 18,9:6
MacIver, David, 1907, S 2,7:7
McIver, DeWitt T, 1955, N 5,19:1
Maciver, Enrique, 1922, Ag 22,17:6
McIver, Evander J, 1944, Ja 4,17:4
McIver, George W, 1950, Jl 25,27:2
McIver, George W 3d, 1957, F 7,49:3
McIver, Henry Judge, 1903, Ja 13,1:3
McIver, John, 1875, Jl 27,1:1
MacIver, John L, 1943, Jl 24,13:7
McIver, John W, 1940, S 25,27:2
McIver, Joseph, 1959, Ap 22,33:4
McIver, Joseph A, 1940, S 8,49:1
McIver, Leo H, 1947, O 14,27:1
McIvor, Dan, 1965, S 4,21:6
MacIvor, J Smith, 1957, Je 13,31:2
McIvor, James, 1943, Ap 8,23:4
MacIvor, James P Gen, 1904, N 4,9:5
McIvor, Nicholas Williams, 1915, F 10,11:5
McIvor-Tyndall, Alex J, 1940, D 13,23:2
McJames, Frederick J, 1959, Je 12,27:4
McJimsey, Elmer E E, 1943, F 9,23:1
McJimsey, R, 1883, D 21,2:6
McJohnston, Robert P, 1942, O 28,23:5
McJunkin, William D, 1941, Je 16,15:5
Mack, see also page 660
Mack, A F, 1947, O 19,64:5
Mack, Alfred, 1950, Ap 24,25:3
Mack, Annie T, 1943, Ag 30,15:6
Mack, Anthony J, 1944, My 31,19:2
Mack, Arthur G, 1947, Jl 20,44:3
Mack, Aug F, 1940, D 3,25:4
Mack, Bessie, 1948, F 24,25:2
Mack, D Leo, 1945, O 6,13:4
Mack, Eddie, 1944, Ag 2,15:6
Mack, Edgar M, 1946, F 13,23:2
Mack, Edwin S, 1942, Ap 11,13:5
Mack, Elizabeth, 1948, S 28,27:3
Mack, Ernest (E McLaughlin), 1942, N 14,15:3
Mack, Eugene P, 1938, O 25,23:3
Mack, Everett Mrs, 1948, Je 17,25:3
Mack, Frances C, 1950, S 20,31:3
Mack, Fred, 1950, N 5,92:5
Mack, Fred A, 1942, Je 9,24:2
Mack, Fred A Mrs, 1949, F 19,15:3
Mack, George A Sr Mrs, 1950, O 12,31:2
Mack, George E, 1948, My 24,19:2
Mack, Harry W, 1938, Ap 25,15:4
Mack, Helen W Mrs, 1938, Mr 15,23:1
Mack, Henry, 1945, Ap 9,19:3
Mack, Henry B, 1949, Ap 29,23:4
Mack, Hugo S, 1943, Ja 15,18:2
Mack, J Herbert, 1947, Mr 23,60:8
Mack, J N, 1938, F 9,19:3
Mack, J S, 1940, S 28,17:6
Mack, J S Mrs, 1944, D 7,25:3
Mack, Jacob W (por), 1948, Ja 16,21:3
Mack, Jesse Mrs, 1945, Mr 31,19:4
Mack, John A Mrs, 1943, Je 20,34:6
Mack, John D, 1941, My 16,23:3
Mack, John I, 1945, My 2,23:3
Mack, Joseph A Mrs, 1945, F 28,23:4
Mack, Julian W (por), 1943, S 6,17:1
Mack, Julian W Mrs, 1938, D 1,23:4
Mack, Merrill J, 1942, F 11,21:4
Mack, Mike, 1949, Ag 14,69:2
Mack, Millard W, 1942, Ag 7,17:4
Mack, Patrick H, 1947, Ag 17,54:4
Mack, Petie, 1949, Je 9,31:1
Mack, R Walter, 1949, D 30,19:1
Mack, Sterling C, 1949, Je 28,27:4
Mack, William (por), 1941, D 11,27:3
Mack, William H, 1941, S 24,23:4
McKaig, Archie, 1946, O 16,28:3
McKaig, Edgar S, 1954, D 25,11:4
McKaig, Harry N, 1925, O 25,9:1
McKaig, T J, 1882, My 6,2:6
McKaig, William, 1940, S 11,25:3
McKaig, William McMahon Gen, 1907, Je 8,9:4
McKaig, William W Mrs, 1940, Ap 15,17:2
Mackaill, Florence P Mrs, 1954, Ag 31,21:5
McKale, J F, 1967, Je 3,31:5
MacKall, Douglass S, 1943, F 20,13:5
Mackall, Lawton, 1968, Mr 27,47:1
Mackall, Leonard, 1937, My 20,21:5
McKall, Louis A Mrs, 1925, Ag 27,19:5
Mackall, Paul, 1954, S 17,27:3
Mackall, Samuel T Col, 1937, Ap 30,21:4
McKallagat, Peter L, 1939, Ja 22,35:1
McKallip, Charles C, 1949, F 24,24:3
McKallip, Robert L, 1956, F 27,23:3
McKammon, Joseph W, 1964, N 9,33:4
McKan, Caroline Mrs, 1871, Jl 11,5:3
McKandy, William H, 1943, F 28,49:2
McKane, J Y Mrs, 1902, O 30,9:4
McKane, James, 1913, O 19,IV,15:5
McKane, John Y, 1899, S 6,1:5
McKaney, William, 1953, O 16,27:2
McKanna, Edwin A, 1942, O 11,56:2
Mackarness, G R, 1883, Ap 21,2:6
Mackasek, Louis, 1952, S 30,31:4
McKaughan, L D, 1948, Ja 24,15:2
Mackay, A, 1879, My 1,2:4
Mackay, A D, 1951, S 19,31:2
McKay, Addison H, 1949, Jl 12,27:5
MacKay, Aeneas A (Lord Reay), 1963, Mr 12,7:5
McKay, Alex, 1953, S 5,15:3
McKay, Alex B, 1942, Ja 19,17:4
McKay, Alexander Capt, 1912, Ja 10,17:4
Mackay, Alexander G, 1920, Ap 26,13:4
Mackay, Alfred B Mrs, 1951, D 21,27:1
McKay, Ambrose N, 1924, N 19,21:3
Mackay, Angus, 1941, Mr 8,19:6
Mackay, Archibald K K, 1941, F 22,15:6
Mackay, Archibald K K Mrs, 1961, My 19,31:3
Mackay, Archie B, 1953, Ap 30,31:4
McKay, Barkuloo Mrs, 1953, Ja 26,19:5
McKay, C E Com Mrs, 1903, F 21,9:5
McKay, Charles, 1949, F 23,27:4
Mackay, Charles H, 1952, F 14,27:4
McKay, Charles H, 1953, N 8,89:1
McKay, Chester (por), 1941, S 10,23:6
Mackay, Clarence, 1938, N 13,1:3
McKay, Claude (por), 1948, My 24,19:4
McKay, David, 1956, My 17,31:3
McKay, Donald, 1880, S 22,5:5
Mackay, Donald, 1912, Mr 1,11:3; 1939, Ag 24,19:2
MacKay, Donald, 1958, Ja 6,39:5
Mackay, Donald B, 1938, S 28,25:5
McKay, Donald C, 1959, Ap 3,27:3
Mackay, Donald D, 1963, Je 23,85:2
Mackay, Donald James (Lord Reay), 1921, Ag 2,9:4
Mackay, Donald S, 1951, S 15,15:5
Mackay, Donald Sage Rev (por), 1908, Ag 28,7:1
McKay, Donald W, 1952, Ja 28,17:4
McKay, Douglas (funl, Jl 26,68:1), 1959, Jl 23,27:1
McKay, Douglas I, 1962, S 28,33:1
McKay, Douglas J, 1948, N 11,27:1
McKay, Dwight, 1940, Mr 11,15:2
McKay, E B Mrs, 1939, S 14,23:5
McKay, E Ross, 1945, Ag 17,17:1
McKay, Edward F, 1943, Jl 5,15:3
Mackay, Edward J, 1948, D 27,22:2
Mackay, Edward Mrs, 1955, N 9,33:3
McKay, Edwin J Jr, 1951, Ag 5,73:2
Mackay, Ernest J H, 1943, O 6,23:5
Mackay, Evelyn Bryant (Princess Colonna), 1919, Mr 31,13:4
Mackay, Francis A, 1949, My 11,30:3
Mackay, Frank B, 1921, F 2,11:5
McKay, Frank D, 1965, Ja 13,25:1
Mackay, Frank Finley, 1923, My 7,15:6
McKay, Frederick, 1944, Mr 2,17:6
McKay, Frederick S, 1959, Ag 23,93:3
Mackay, G M Johnstone, 1938, Jl 30,13:4
Mackay, George D, 1954, Je 30,27:4
McKay, George M Sir, 1937, Jl 20,23:4
McKay, George W, 1945, D 4,29:6
Mackay, Georgie C Mrs, 1941, Ap 13,38:2
McKay, Gordon, 1903, O 20,9:5
Mackay, Gordon, 1941, F 16,40:1
McKay, Harry J, 1952, Je 12,33:4
Mackay, Henry, 1939, Mr 6,15:4
MacKay, Henry Jr, 1939, My 17,23:4
Mackay, Henry S Jr, 1954, Jl 6,23:4
McKay, Horatio Capt, 1912, Ja 9,13:5; 1923, My 17, 19:4
Mackay, Howard, 1939, D 29,15:4
Mackay, Hugh, 1957, D 8,88:4
McKay, Hugh D, 1951, D 2,90:1
McKay, Hugh M Mrs, 1959, D 19,27:6
Mackay, Ian, 1952, O 4,17:3
Mackay, Iven G, 1966, O 1,32:3
MacKay, J Harold, 1947, Mr 19,26:2
Mackay, J W Mrs, 1928, S 6,25:5
Mackay, James, 1940, Ap 4,23:5
Mackay, James B, 1940, F 27,21:2
McKay, James M, 1937, S 8,23:2
McKay, James R, 1953, F 3,25:2
Mackay, Jennie M, 1947, F 27,21:3
McKay, Jessie, 1943, Mr 6,13:1
Mackay, John, 1905, Ap 18,11:5
McKay, John, 1909, Ap 13,9:4
MacKay, John, 1938, My 17,23:2
Mackay, John C, 1952, Jl 17,23:2
McKay, John E, 1910, My 15,II,11:4
MacKay, John F, 1954, Ja 20,27:2
McKay, John F, 1958, O 18,21:6
McKay, John G Sr, 1951, Ja 25,25:1
Mackay, John M, 1949, Mr 24,27:3
McKay, John S Dr, 1917, Mr 8,11:4
McKay, John V, 1952, D 24,17:4
McKay, John W (cor, D 5,25:1), 1940, D 3,25:4
Mackay, Joseph, 1881, Je 4,5:1
McKay, Joseph, 1941, F 15,15:5; 1950, F 3,23:4
McKay, Joseph P, 1938, O 28,23:5
Mackay, Julia Mrs, 1940, D 14,17:1
McKay, Louis E, 1948, Mr 2,23:3
McKay, Mary Mrs, 1954, D 30,17:1
McKay, Maurice P, 1962, N 17,25:1
McKay, Murdock, 1938, Jl 3,13:2
McKay, N Bruce, 1963, D 22,34:3
McKay, Nath, 1902, Jl 11,9:5
McKay, Neal H, 1951, Je 13,29:5
McKay, Neil A, 1941, Mr 5,22:3
McKay, Peter C, 1953, Jl 9,25:6
Mackay, Peter C (Prince R Monolulu), 1965, F 16, 28:4
McKay, R Frank, 1937, Je 13,II,7:1
MacKay, R H, 1941, F 18,21:4
Mackay, Robert, 1925, My 25,17:6
McKay, Robert, 1945, Je 6,21:4
Mackay, Robert F B, 1940, F 23,11:7

McKay, Robert G, 1958, N 28,30:4
McKay, Robert G Mrs, 1955, D 21,29:4
McKay, Robert J, 1941, Mr 1,15:3
Mackay, Ronald W G, 1960, Ja 16,21:3
McKay, Scott Mrs (A Sheridan),(funl, Ja 23,43:4), 1967, Ja 22,77:1
McKay, Stanley, 1951, Ja 5,24:7
Mackay, Stanley, 1956, F 3,23:3
McKay, Thomas, 1951, Mr 6,27:3
McKay, W Johnston, 1939, F 1,21:4
McKay, W Johnston Mrs, 1954, S 28,29:3
McKay, Willard S, 1959, O 18,86:6
McKay, William A, 1938, My 5,23:4
Mackay, William A (por), 1939, Jl 28,17:4
McKay, William C, 1943, N 2,25:6
McKay, William E, 1948, D 4,19:3
McKay, William G, 1943, Jl 17,13:6
Mackay, William H G, 1942, Ja 7,20:2
Mackay, William H Mrs, 1952, O 25,17:4
McKay, William K, 1944, S 24,46:3
Mackay, William Murray Mrs, 1904, My 18,9:6
McKay, William O, 1956, S 15,17:4
Mackay, William Phin Rev, 1922, O 8,30:4
McKay, William W, 1947, Jl 7,17:5
McKay, Zachary S, 1952, N 9,91:3
Mackay-Smith, Alexander Bp (trb, N 18,13:5), 1911, N 17,13:5
Mackaye, G H Mrs, 1949, Je 22,31:5
MacKaye, Hazel, 1944, Ag 12,11:5
Mackaye, Henry Goodwin Dr, 1913, F 3,11:4
MacKaye, J M, 1935, Ja 23,17:1
Mackaye, Jessie Hardy Mrs, 1921, Ap 21,13:4
MacKaye, Percy, 1956, S 1,15:3
Mackaye, Steele, 1894, F 26,1:7
Mackaye, Steele Mrs, 1924, My 16,19:2
McKeachie, William S, 1967, O 31,45:3
McKeag, Anna J, 1947, N 24,23:2
McKeag, Edwin C, 1949, D 1,31:4
McKeagan, Norman, 1950, Ja 6,22:3
McKeage, John A, 1953, Mr 1,92:4
McKeague, John M, 1951, F 20,42:1
McKean, Andrew P, 1954, Jl 7,31:4
McKean, Bernard Mrs, 1950, Ap 27,29:3
McKean, Charles W, 1941, Je 14,17:5
McKean, Clarence D, 1944, Ap 11,19:2
McKean, Commodore, 1865, Ap 23,4:6
McKean, Egbert Lt, 1918, F 12,11:2
McKean, Elizabeth, 1925, N 11,23:4
McKean, Frederick G, 1953, Je 3,31:4
MacKean, Helen V, 1939, Ap 7,21:2
McKean, Horace G Mrs, 1944, Ja 3,21:1
McKean, J S, 1951, Ap 30,23:4
McKean, James H, 1942, My 20,19:2
McKean, James W, 1949, F 11,24:2
McKean, John Bell, 1908, Je 14,11:5
McKean, John O, 1939, F 28,20:2
McKean, Katherine L P Mrs, 1940, Ja 14,43:2
McKean, Robert C, 1948, D 17,27:5
McKean, Thomas, 1942, F 9,23:8
McKean, Thomas Mrs, 1912, Ap 8,11:6
McKean, W V, 1903, Mr 30,9:7
McKean, William I, 1952, Ag 29,23:3
McKean, William S, 1939, Ap 17,17:4
McKeand, George, 1954, N 23,35:4
McKeand, James Mrs, 1944, My 24,19:3
McKeary, Thomas, 1948, My 11,25:2
McKechnie, Alexander Sr Mrs, 1947, D 11,33:2
Mackechnie, Arch, 1940, Jl 6,15:4
McKechnie, Bill, 1965, O 30,35:4
McKechnie, Frank B, 1949, F 16,25:4
MacKechnie, Harry W, 1953, F 19,23:3
McKechnie, James, 1949, Jl 12,27:2
McKechnie, John T, 1919, Mr 9,20:5
McKechnie, Peter, 1964, F 19,39:1
McKechnie, William A Mrs, 1950, N 14,32:2
McKee, Andrew K, 1946, S 3,19:4
McKee, Arthur G, 1956, F 21,33:4
McKee, Arthur G Mrs, 1948, Je 6,72:3
McKee, Benjamin H, 1958, Ap 3,31:1
McKee, Bert, 1950, S 3,38:3
McKee, Charlotte Mrs, 1910, Mr 28,9:3
McKee, Clifford, 1939, Ap 23,III,6:7
McKee, David G, 1945, O 5,23:2
McKee, David R, 1940, F 20,21:2
McKee, David Ritchie, 1924, Je 14,11:6
McKee, Donald E Mrs, 1959, Ap 11,21:3
McKee, Donald Mitchell, 1968, Je 28,38:2
McKee, Douglas, 1958, Ap 12,19:4
MacKee, Edward M, 1946, Je 4,23:2
McKee, Forest E, 1951, O 11,37:4
McKee, Frank, 1922, N 14,19:4; 1947, D 29,17:3
MacKee, Frank O, 1948, Ag 15,60:4
McKee, Frank W, 1944, Ja 31,17:4
McKee, Frederick C, 1961, Mr 6,25:2
McKee, G Ross, 1948, S 8,29:4
McKee, George M, 1946, Je 13,28:2
MacKee, George M, 1955, My 9,23:3
McKee, Gussie, 1903, Jl 8,5:2
McKee, Henry S, 1956, N 20,37:5
McKee, Henry Sellers, 1924, Je 12,17:6
McKee, Howard T, 1964, Ap 4,27:5
McKee, Howard T Jr, 1955, N 6,86:4
McKee, J, 1931, D 26,11:2
McKee, James, 1905, Ap 11,11:6; 1954, Jl 26,17:3
McKee, James H, 1945, Mr 27,19:1; 1949, Mr 25,23:1
McKee, James L Mrs, 1955, Je 18,17:3
McKee, John, 1915, Ap 16,13:4; 1917, Ag 3,9:3; 1953, D 29,23:4
McKee, John A, 1956, F 9,32:2
McKee, John B, 1948, Ap 15,25:3
McKee, John D, 1948, F 7,15:6; 1956, Je 26,29:1
McKee, John J, 1949, F 13,76:2
McKee, John L, 1965, Ap 13,37:2
McKee, Joseph A, 1962, Je 25,29:5
McKee, Joseph J, 1940, D 12,27:2
McKee, Joseph V (funl, F 1,31:6), 1956, Ja 29,93:1
McKee, Lanier, 1943, Ja 6,27:1
McKee, Lewis A, 1949, Ag 2,19:1
McKee, Lt (funl, Ag 28,4:7), 1871, Ag 12,3:2
McKee, Lydie S Mrs, 1954, My 21,27:6
McKee, Mary, 1947, O 14,27:5
McKee, Moses H (funl, Ja 26,20:4), 1919, Ja 23,13:3
McKee, Neal T, 1962, S 26,39:1
McKee, Oliver, 1928, S 1,13:5
McKee, Oliver Jr, 1948, Je 4,23:3
McKee, Paul B Mrs, 1957, N 28,31:5
McKee, Paul W, 1964, Jl 1,35:5
McKee, R D, 1943, O 19,19:5
McKee, R R, 1935, O 27,II,9:1
McKee, Ralph E, 1939, Ja 25,21:1
McKee, Ralph H, 1967, F 27,29:3
McKee, Ralph L, 1944, N 16,23:3
Mackee, Robert, 1880, Ap 14,4:7
McKee, Robert R, 1968, Ja 3,40:3
McKee, Roy B, 1952, My 27,27:2
McKee, Russell W, 1903, D 9,9:5
McKee, Samuel H, 1948, O 9,19:5
McKee, Samuel Jr, 1967, Jl 2,35:2
McKee, Stewart, 1950, My 11,29:3
McKee, Terence T, 1950, Ap 22,19:5
McKee, Thomas P, 1947, Je 17,25:2
McKee, Walter V, 1954, D 25,11:6
McKee, William A, 1942, Ja 5,17:2
McKee, William E, 1875, Jl 27,4:7
McKee, William J, 1957, F 28,27:4
McKee, William L, 1937, O 29,21:3
McKeeby, B H, 1950, Ja 9,25:4
MacKeeby, Clarence Mrs, 1953, Mr 20,23:3
McKeefe, Edward P, 1941, Ja 3,20:2
McKeefrey, J, 1927, Mr 24,25:5
McKeefrey, James F, 1941, S 19,23:1
McKeefrey, William, 1940, N 28,23:4
McKeehan, Homer H, 1938, N 24,6:8
McKeehan, Joseph P, 1950, Je 29,29:1
McKeel, Benjamin S, 1948, N 28,92:4
McKeel, Grover H, 1945, D 16,40:4
McKeel, James C, 1956, Ap 5,29:2
McKeen, Benjamin, 1947, D 17,29:2
McKeen, David, 1916, N 14,11:2
McKeen, Ernest W, 1953, My 28,23:3
McKeen, Helen J, 1943, F 13,11:3
McKeen, James, 1911, F 23,9:6
McKeen, John Savage, 1917, F 6,9:2
McKeen, William M, 1938, Jl 12,20:1
McKeen, William Riley, 1913, F 19,11:5
McKeene, James Dr, 1873, N 29,1:7
McKeever, A E Maj, 1919, D 27,9:4
McKeever, Arthur G (por), 1949, Ag 12,17:1
McKeever, Bernard F, 1941, O 30,23:1
McKeever, Buell, 1938, My 21,23:2
McKeever, Charles Gen, 1901, S 6,7:6
McKeever, Chauncey, 1939, O 22,41:2
McKeever, Edward J, 1925, My 2,15:6
McKeever, Emmet G (por), 1947, Jl 10,21:1
McKeever, George, 1938, D 17,15:4
McKeever, Gerald D, 1957, Jl 21,61:2
McKeever, Hugh, 1948, N 11,27:2
McKeever, James, 1913, Jl 3,9:4
McKeever, James J, 1944, Je 8,21:6
McKeever, James J Rev, 1921, My 17,17:6
McKeever, James Lawrence, 1919, Ag 15,11:4
McKeever, Jennie V Mrs (will, S 26,12:8), 1942, S 17,25:1
McKeever, John F, 1941, F 18,23:4
McKeever, Joseph R, 1954, Ja 13,31:1
McKeever, Mike, 1967, Ag 26,28:1
McKeever, Norman W, 1952, Je 28,19:2
McKeever, R F, 1933, Ja 1,14:1
McKeever, R T, 1927, Ap 21,27:5
McKeever, Roy S, 1950, S 24,105:1
McKeever, Stephen W (por), 1938, Mr 7,17:1
McKeever, William A, 1940, Jl 10,19:2
McKeever, William B, 1937, S 21,26:1
McKeever (Ricardo), 1883, N 2,8:2
Mackel, Charles H, 1945, Jl 29,40:3
MacKelcan, H Gordon, 1941, N 16,56:8
McKell, William E, 1964, F 23,84:6
MacKellar, Andrew, 1959, Ag 4,27:3
McKellar, Andrew, 1960, My 8,88:2
McKellar, Annie Mrs, 1944, N 23,31:5
McKellar, Don, 1945, D 22,19:3
McKellar, Donald, 1941, O 3,23:6
MacKellar, George M, 1922, Ap 6,17:5
McKellar, James S, 1952, Ag 29,23:4
McKellar, John A, 1957, Ja 18,21:2
MacKellar, John A Mrs, 1946, Jl 24,27:4
McKellar, Kenneth D (funl, O 28,27:2), 1957, O 26, 21:1
McKellar, Robert E, 1944, N 13,19:2
MacKeller, William H H, 1942, Ja 28,19:5
McKelvey, Bernard J, 1952, D 27,9:6
McKelvey, Charles W, 1957, Ja 10,29:4
McKelvey, Daniel T Sr, 1946, Ag 28,27:5
McKelvey, David, 1918, My 12,21:2
McKelvey, Edwin L, 1947, Jl 13,44:8
McKelvey, James E, 1948, Mr 6,13:6
McKelvey, James P, 1967, O 28,31:5
McKelvey, John F, 1937, N 30,23:5
McKelvey, John J, 1947, O 20,23:3
McKelvey, John S Mrs, 1958, Je 17,29:5
McKelvey, John W, 1944, Je 1,19:4
McKelvey, Mary M Mrs, 1954, D 11,13:3
McKelvey, Nellie, 1937, N 9,24:4
McKelvey, Ralph H (funl), 1957, Ap 9,33:4
McKelvey, Ralph H Mrs, 1964, Mr 17,35:3
McKelvey, William T, 1952, O 15,31:4
McKelvie, Bruce A, 1960, Ap 18,29:4
McKelvie, Julius C, 1961, O 28,21:4
McKelvie, Sam R, 1956, Ja 7,17:2
McKelvy, Francis G, 1952, My 8,31:6
McKelvy, Jeremiah D, 1963, Ja 5,8:3
McKelvy, John E, 1963, Ag 8,27:5
McKelvy, Robert, 1937, D 10,25:4
McKelvy, William Cully, 1909, Mr 1,9:2
McKelway, A J, 1953, My 1,21:1
McKelway, A J Mrs, 1950, O 31,27:4
McKelway, Alexander Jeffrey Dr, 1918, Ap 18,13:8
McKelway, Lee, 1914, Ja 7,11:5
McKelway, St Clair (por; funl, Jl 18,15:4), 1915, Jl 17,7:1
McKelway, St Clair Jr, 1954, Je 5,17:4
McKelway, Virginia B T Mrs, 1938, S 6,21:2
Macken, Luke J, 1946, My 13,21:5
Macken, May B, 1946, Je 26,25:2
Macken, Walter, 1967, Ap 23,93:1
McKendree, Charles A, 1954, S 12,84:3
McKendrew, Edward L, 1953, My 22,27:5
McKendrick, Alex, 1953, N 5,31:2
McKendrick, James, 1938, Jl 5,17:5
McKendrick, William, 1944, Ap 18,21:2
McKendry, Andrew, 1947, Je 4,27:5
McKendry, Charles, 1940, Ap 11,25:5
McKenley, Jacob A, 1866, Ja 4,1:6
McKenna, Alex A, 1962, N 22,29:5
McKenna, Alice C, 1942, N 17,25:2
McKenna, Arthur J, 1922, Ap 8,15:3; 1945, Ag 5,37:2; 1951, N 19,23:5
McKenna, Arthur L, 1941, Ap 15,23:3
McKenna, Bartholow M, 1945, Ja 24,22:3
McKenna, Bernard A, 1960, Jl 22,23:4
McKenna, Bernard J, 1947, S 16,23:3
McKenna, Bernard Rev Father, 1912, Jl 28,II,11:5
McKenna, Bridget Mrs, 1922, O 27,17:4
McKenna, Charles A J, 1948, N 25,31:4
McKenna, Charles H, 1947, N 14,23:1
McKenna, Charles H Rev (funl, F 27,11:3), 1917, F 23,11:6
McKenna, Dennis, 1943, Ap 18,48:5
McKenna, E, 1931, D 15,27:1
McKenna, Eddie, 1951, Je 1,26:1
McKenna, Edmund B, 1939, N 26,42:7
McKenna, Edward A, 1951, Mr 27,29:3
McKenna, Edward J, 1945, Jl 8,11:5
McKenna, Edward J Sr Mrs, 1951, N 6,29:4
McKenna, Edward L, 1953, Je 3,31:5
McKenna, Edward P, 1943, D 13,23:3
McKenna, Eleanor L, 1940, Mr 23,13:6
McKenna, Eugene Father, 1925, Mr 25,21:5
McKenna, Eugene J, 1942, Mr 17,22:3
McKenna, Frank, 1951, Ap 3,9:3
McKenna, Frank S, 1947, Ja 12,59:7
McKenna, Frederick J, 1952, My 30,15:3
McKenna, George L, 1959, O 1,36:1
McKenna, Harold, 1946, D 20,23:2; 1960, S 28,39:4
McKenna, Harry T, 1958, Je 19,31:4
McKenna, Hugh, 1957, My 14,35:4
McKenna, Irene E, 1966, N 26,35:4
McKenna, J, 1926, N 21,2:4
McKenna, J E, 1957, Ja 3,33:1
McKenna, J Lindsay, 1937, N 13,19:6
McKenna, James, 1955, S 6,25:1; 1957, My 5,89:1
McKenna, James A, 1941, My 23,21:5
McKenna, James A Maj, 1918, Ag 10,7:5; 1921, Jl 1 9:4
McKenna, James C, 1947, S 25,29:2
McKenna, James D, 1949, Mr 17,25:2
McKenna, James J, 1943, Je 25,17:2; 1954, D 23,19:
McKenna, James J Jr, 1948, Ag 21,15:3
McKenna, James J Sr, 1958, Mr 31,27:3
McKenna, James S, 1941, D 19,25:6
McKenna, James T, 1939, Ap 18,23:6
McKenna, John A, 1925, Je 19,19:5; 1943, My 11, 21:5; 1956, Jl 23,23:5; 1963, O 14,29:4
McKenna, John Aloysius Rev, 1913, S 18,11:5
McKenna, John F, 1967, Ap 13,43:5
McKenna, John J, 1941, F 14,17:5; 1949, Ag 29,17:5
McKenna, John P, 1948, Jl 1,23:2
McKenna, Joseph, 1938, Ap 4,17:5; 1941, D 7,79:2
McKenna, Joseph F Rev, 1937, Mr 17,25:4

McKenna, Joseph M, 1957, D 27,19:4
McKenna, Kenneth, 1948, D 18,19:2; 1962, Ja 17,33:4
McKenna, Lawrence F, 1952, Ap 25,23:1
McKenna, Loretta M, 1939, F 23,23:2
McKenna, Lou, 1943, My 22,13:4
McKenna, Mary, 1949, O 23,84:1
McKenna, Norbert A, 1964, Ap 17,35:1
McKenna, P J Rev, 1873, Jl 12,5:6
McKenna, Patrick, 1942, F 8,48:6
McKenna, Patrick E (por),(will, Ag 1,11:2), 1940, Jl 2,21:3
McKenna, Patrick H, 1961, My 9,39:1
McKenna, Patrick J, 1939, Ap 4,25:2; 1956, Mr 4,88:1
McKenna, Patrick Rev Father, 1916, Je 13,11:4
McKenna, Peter F, 1940, Mr 30,15:1
McKenna, Reginald (por), 1943, S 7,23:1
McKenna, Richard, 1964, N 2,39:1
McKenna, Roy C, 1958, Jl 13,68:8
McKenna, T J, 1903, F 24,1:2
McKenna, Thomas, 1951, S 28,31:3
McKenna, Thomas M, 1942, F 24,21:5
McKenna, Thomas P (por), 1941, Ja 21,22:2
McKenna, Timothy Mrs (A King),(will, Je 15,21:6), 1963, Je 11,37:2
McKenna, Walter H, 1949, S 25,92:4
McKenna, Walter J, 1950, Ag 16,29:4
McKenna, William F, 1947, S 15,17:4
McKenna, William H, 1946, F 17,42:4
McKenna, William J, 1950, Mr 5,92:3
Mackennan, Archibald R Mrs, 1943, Mr 4,19:3
MacKennan, Luella M Mrs, 1941, S 3,23:5
McKennee, Oscar W, 1949, Ag 12,17:4
McKennee, Thorndyke C, 1924, Ap 24,19:5
McKennell, Thomas A (por), 1942, Mr 16,15:4
McKennett, Frank Mrs, 1964, N 1,88:6
McKenney, Clara J P Mrs, 1942, Ja 17,19:1
McKenney, Descum C, 1947, S 14,60:8
McKenney, Frederic D, 1949, Je 28,27:5
McKenney, Henry P, 1940, F 26,15:5
McKenney, Herbert E, 1952, Jl 25,18:3
McKenney, James H, 1913, O 14,13:5
MacKenney, John R Mrs, 1948, F 3,25:5
McKenney, Luther F Rev, 1922, Ag 1,19:4
McKenney, Maurice R, 1967, S 18,47:2
McKenney, Patrick J, 1952, Ja 1,25:1
McKenney, Randolph E B, 1941, Mr 20,22:2
McKenney, Thomas E, 1945, My 28,19:4
McKenney, William A, 1940, Ja 12,17:3
McKenney, William E, 1950, Mr 27,23:3
McKenney, William F, 1940, Ap 18,23:3
McKenney, William V, 1938, Mr 20,II,8:2
McKennis, Herbert, 1945, D 8,17:5
McKennon, C R, 1952, O 8,31:3
McKennon, Thomas W, 1954, S 2,21:4
McKenny, Arthur F, 1945, D 14,28:3
McKenny, Hugh C, 1945, Mr 11,39:1
McKenny, Louis C, 1954, My 20,31:5
McKenny, Luke M, 1957, Mr 22,23:2
McKenny, Luke Mrs, 1939, S 9,17:4
McKenny, Thomas (Bro Alban Aloysius), 1966, Mr 19,29:4
Mackensen, August von, 1945, N 10,15:1
Mackensen, Han-Georg V von, 1947, O 21,16:3
Mackenson, Clarence T Jr, 1940, Mr 3,44:2
Mackentepe, Frederick E, 1942, Ag 12,19:2
MacKenty, John E Mrs, 1938, N 30,23:5
McKenty, Samuel H, 1959, N 13,29:4
McKenty, Thomas W, 1942, S 12,13:2
McKenzie, A, 1926, O 11,21:3
McKenzie, Aeneas J, 1948, D 13,23:3
Mackenzie, Alan S, 1939, Ja 26,21:4
Mackenzie, Alex, 1939, F 28,19:4; 1948, Ap 20,27:3; 1957, Ap 22,25:6
Mackenzie, Alexander, 1892, Ap 18,2:4
MacKenzie, Alexander, 1943, Jl 13,22:2; 1965, F 25, 31:4
MacKenzie, Alexander Cameron Dr, 1915, Mr 24,11:4
Mackenzie, Alexander M, 1943, Ja 6,25:5
McKenzie, Alexander Rev, 1914, Ag 7,11:6
McKenzie, Alfred C, 1954, D 21,27:5
McKenzie, Allen, 1949, D 31,15:3
McKenzie, Andrew D, 1953, Ja 17,15:3
McKenzie, Angus, 1952, My 21,27:4
McKenzie, Angus H, 1950, S 2,15:2
McKenzie, Angus Mrs, 1953, Jl 17,17:3
MacKenzie, Arthur Ford, 1905, Je 24,9:5
McKenzie, Arthur Mrs, 1967, Mr 2,35:2
Mackenzie, Arthur S, 1938, O 3,15:3
Mackenzie, Augustus Jr, 1942, O 29,23:1
Mackenzie, Cameron (funl, Mr 20,22:2), 1921, Mr 18,15:6
MacKenzie, Carrie A Mrs, 1942, N 11,25:4
McKenzie, Cary A, 1956, N 17,15:1
Mackenzie, Catherine, 1949, O 25,27:4
Mackenzie, Charles F, 1955, S 21,33:4
Mackenzie, Charles K, 1938, Ap 3,II,7:2
McKenzie, Charles L, 1942, N 3,23:4
MacKenzie, Charles S, 1943, My 15,15:4
Mackenzie, Charles S Mrs, 1966, S 28,47:4
McKenzie, Charles T, 1944, Jl 17,15:5
Mackenzie, Christine Lady (Mrs Compton Mackenzie), 1963, N 11,31:5
Mackenzie, Clinton (por), 1940, Mr 11,15:1
Mackenzie, Clinton Mrs, 1945, Mr 20,19:4
Mackenzie, Colin A, 1938, S 22,23:2
Mackenzie, Collin, 1939, Ap 4,25:6
MacKenzie, D D Mrs, 1938, N 3,23:5
MacKenzie, D R (see also O 18), 1877, O 19,8:5
Mackenzie, David, 1958, F 21,23:2
Mackenzie, David Mrs, 1945, F 17,13:3
MacKenzie, David W, 1952, D 24,17:6
Mackenzie, Dewitt, 1962, Ag 17,23:1
Mackenzie, DeWitt Mrs, 1962, Mr 12,19:6
Mackenzie, Donald, 1941, O 21,23:5; 1942, O 22,21:2; 1957, Ag 22,27:1
MacKenzie, Donald A, 1945, My 6,38:2
McKenzie, Donald A, 1953, Ja 30,21:3
Mackenzie, Donald B, 1943, Je 1,23:5
McKenzie, Donald K, 1949, Ap 19,25:2
Mackenzie, Donald M, 1956, Ag 13,19:6
Mackenzie, Donald Mrs, 1946, Je 28,21:4
Mackenzie, Duncan, 1945, D 18,27:3
MacKenzie, Duncan R, 1954, My 10,23:4
Mackenzie, Edward B, 1952, S 26,21:2
McKenzie, Edward E, 1952, My 16,24:3
Mackenzie, Edward Easton, 1925, S 27,7:3
Mackenzie, Edward H, 1960, D 9,31:3
Mackenzie, Ella S Mrs, 1940, Ag 21,19:3
Mackenzie, Ernest S, 1956, My 17,31:5
McKenzie, Ernie, 1961, Ja 17,37:2
MacKenzie, Fannie C, 1952, N 1,21:3
Mackenzie, Francis A, 1941, O 17,23:6
Mackenzie, Frank J, 1939, D 12,27:5
Mackenzie, G, 1882, Mr 16,5:2
Mackenzie, G H Capt, 1891, Ap 15,2:1
McKenzie, G W, 1934, Ag 25,13:1
MacKenzie, George C, 1945, Jl 16,11:7
Mackenzie, George M, 1952, Mr 27,29:1
Mackenzie, George W, 1945, Ag 7,24:2
McKenzie, George W Mrs, 1953, N 21,13:4
McKenzie, Gordon, 1938, D 27,17:4
McKenzie, H Lincoln Mrs, 1957, D 21,19:2
McKenzie, Harry C, 1963, Je 9,63:2
Mackenzie, Herbert C, 1942, S 9,23:4
Mackenzie, Howard, 1937, Ag 31,23:5
Mackenzie, Hugh, 1946, F 28,23:2
MacKenzie, Hugh S, 1959, Jl 27,25:5
Mackenzie, Ian (por), 1949, S 3,13:7
McKenzie, Isabel, 1965, Je 9,47:4
Mackenzie, J C, 1931, My 11,19:3
Mackenzie, J J Prof, 1922, Ag 2,17:5
Mackenzie, J K, 1936, S 3,21:1
McKenzie, J Robert, 1949, Mr 18,25:1
MacKenzie, J T, 1877, O 21,2:7
Mackenzie, James, 1943, S 22,23:3
McKenzie, James (Bro Adelphus Patk), 1953, Mr 28,17:5
Mackenzie, James B, 1945, D 13,29:5
Mackenzie, James C (Feb 10), 1963, Ap 1,36:1
McKenzie, James D Sr, 1962, Ja 30,29:1
McKenzie, James F, 1944, Je 28,23:6
Mackenzie, James Sir, 1925, Ja 27,13:3
Mackenzie, James W, 1947, O 2,27:4
Mackenzie, Jane G Mrs, 1942, Je 30,24:6
Mackenzie, Jeannette K, 1947, D 4,31:5
Mackenzie, Jim, 1967, Ap 29,35:4
MacKenzie, John, 1941, S 5,21:4
McKenzie, John, 1952, O 20,23:5
Mackenzie, John, 1953, O 21,29:3
Mackenzie, John, 1955, Ag 27,15:5
Mackenzie, John A, 1947, O 1,29:6
MacKenzie, John B, 1942, Ag 28,19:3
McKenzie, John C, 1941, S 18,25:2
McKenzie, John F, 1961, D 1,33:1
Mackenzie, John Jr Mrs, 1966, Mr 31,39:1
Mackenzie, John W, 1945, O 9,21:3
Mackenzie, Kenneth, 1909, D 25,7:4; 1943, Jl 13,21:6; 1945, Ap 21,13:6
McKenzie, Kenneth, 1949, N 5,13:3
Mackenzie, Kenneth Alexander J Dr, 1920, Mr 17,11:4
Mackenzie, Kenneth G, 1967, D 20,45:3
McKenzie, Leonard, 1874, Je 23,1:3
McKenzie, Lewis J, 1949, Ja 22,13:6
McKenzie, Lewis J Brig-Gen, 1925, F 9,17:3
Mackenzie, Lewis R, 1950, F 3,23:4
MacKenzie, Luther R Mrs, 1961, D 8,37:1
McKenzie, Malcolm, 1938, Ag 27,27:8; 1940, D 28, 15:5
Mackenzie, Malcolm, 1967, F 22,29:2
MacKenzie, Margaret Mrs, 1938, Ag 26,17:5
Mackenzie, Marion, 1940, F 6,21:2
MacKenzie, Mary, 1953, S 18,29:1
McKenzie, Maurice, 1944, O 27,23:5
McKenzie, Maurice Mrs, 1937, Ja 11,19:4
Mackenzie, Morell Sir, 1892, F 4,5:4
Mackenzie, Morris Robinson Slidell, 1915, Ja 17,3:5
Mackenzie, Morris S, 1910, Mr 8,9:5
Mackenzie, Murdo, 1939, My 31,23:5; 1949, D 1,31:2
Mackenzie, Percy D, 1951, My 25,27:4
McKenzie, Peter J, 1948, My 27,25:1
McKenzie, Philip, 1924, D 9,25:4
McKenzie, R E, 1952, Ja 15,27:4
McKenzie, R Monroe, 1947, Ja 23,23:3
Mackenzie, R S, 1881, N 22,5:2
McKenzie, R Tait (por), 1938, Ap 29,21:3
McKenzie, R Tait Mrs, 1952, N 23,89:2
Mackenzie, Richard, 1957, S 9,25:2
McKenzie, Robert A, 1967, Ag 29,15:1
McKenzie, Robert C, 1945, My 31,15:4
Mackenzie, Robert Mrs, 1938, Ag 2,19:5
Mackenzie, Robert R, 1953, S 8,31:2
MacKenzie, Robert Rev Dr, 1925, S 16,25:4
McKenzie, Roderick D, 1940, My 7,25:3
MacKenzie, Roderick F, 1966, Jl 21,33:3
Mackenzie, Roderick J, 1923, Mr 3,13:5
McKenzie, Roy E, 1965, Ja 16,27:4
MacKenzie, S G, 1914, N 2,9:5
McKenzie, Stewart G, 1959, N 30,31:1
MacKenzie, Stuart R, 1950, Jl 16,68:6
MacKenzie, Stuart R Mrs, 1949, Ja 4,19:1
Mackenzie, Thomas A, 1962, Ag 17,23:4
Mackenzie, Thomas H (por), 1942, Je 7,41:1
Mackenzie, W A, 1942, N 20,24:4
McKenzie, W L, 1946, F 4,25:3
McKenzie, Wallace B, 1965, D 26,68:5
Mackenzie, Wentworth P, 1951, Ja 17,27:4
McKenzie, William, 1914, Ap 13,11:5; 1947, Jl 27, 44:7; 1948, F 8,61:1; 1948, My 13,25:2
Mackenzie, William A, 1943, Ag 30,15:7
McKenzie, William C Mrs, 1904, Ja 22,9:6
McKenzie, William D, 1952, Ag 25,17:4
McKenzie, William F, 1955, O 29,19:3
McKenzie, William H Dr, 1916, My 4,11:7
MacKenzie, William H Mrs, 1952, Mr 8,13:5
McKenzie, William Lady, 1917, N 30,13:7
Mackenzie, William M, 1941, Ja 31,19:4
McKenzie, William P, 1942, S 10,27:5
Mackenzie, William P, 1944, O 1,45:1
Mackenzie, William Sir, 1923, D 6,19:3
Mackenzie, Willie, 1959, Jl 26,68:3
McKeogh, Arthur Maj (por), 1937, Je 16,23:3
McKeogh, Arthur Mrs, 1955, O 30,89:2
McKeon, Alexander, 1945, N 2,19:2
McKeon, Andrew J, 1966, Je 30,39:4
McKeon, Cornelius A, 1950, Ag 13,76:1
McKeon, Edward F, 1961, Jl 10,21:4
McKeon, Frank Mrs, 1950, Ja 27,24:2
McKeon, Frederick T, 1948, N 20,13:4
McKeon, John, 1883, N 23,8:1; 1924, Jl 22,15:5
McKeon, John A, 1941, F 15,15:1; 1959, Ja 26,29:4
McKeon, John C, 1916, Je 17,11:5
McKeon, John E, 1943, Ap 4,40:6
McKeon, John J (por), 1947, N 11,27:1
McKeon, John J, 1949, Jl 13,27:2; 1950, Je 3,15:3
McKeon, John P, 1951, Ap 30,21:3
McKeon, John W, 1955, Jl 31,68:6
McKeon, Marcelia, 1939, Ap 13,23:4
McKeon, Matthew, 1947, Ja 18,15:4
McKeon, Newton F, 1959, N 19,39:3
McKeon, Peter F, 1948, Ja 28,23:5
McKeon, Peter J, 1946, D 16,23:2
McKeon, Robert L, 1946, Ap 26,22:3
McKeon, Robert M, 1948, My 15,15:4
McKeon, Sara M, 1958, Je 21,19:5
McKeon, Thomas, 1941, F 15,15:2
McKeon, Thomas F Capt, 1925, N 21,17:4
McKeon, William P, 1953, D 28,22:4; 1959, Ap 18,23:2
McKeough, Michael J, 1960, Je 6,29:3
McKeown, Alex, 1961, Jl 12,31:4
McKeown, Austin P Mrs, 1952, D 12,29:4
McKeown, Edward J, 1950, Mr 25,11:7
McKeown, Edward V, 1951, D 21,27:3
McKeown, Francis M, 1956, N 5,31:3
McKeown, Frank E, 1967, Ag 15,36:3
McKeown, Henry F, 1949, Ja 14,23:1
McKeown, Hugh S, 1944, S 15,19:6
McKeown, Ian H, 1965, D 25,13:3
McKeown, J F, 1938, S 28,25:6
McKeown, James, 1940, Ja 19,19:3
McKeown, James F, 1942, N 30,23:5
McKeown, John, 1940, Ja 16,23:5; 1946, S 29,60:5
McKeown, John A, 1955, Ja 19,27:2
McKeown, John C, 1949, D 24,15:3
McKeown, John J, 1941, N 29,17:3
McKeown, John Mrs, 1946, Ag 12,21:5
Mackeown, Joseph J, 1943, N 6,13:2
McKeown, Maurice J, 1967, D 20,45:2
McKeown, Mitchell, 1954, Mr 16,29:4
McKeown, Robert, 1925, Ap 10,19:4
McKeown, Samuel C, 1940, Je 26,23:5
Mackeown, Samuel S, 1952, Je 2,22:3
McKeown, Stuart E, 1959, My 19,33:2
McKeown, Thomas D, 1951, O 23,29:1
McKeown, Walter W, 1957, Jl 9,29:3
McKeown, William, 1948, D 5,92:5
McKeown, William B (Bro Mac), 1953, D 10,47:4
McKeowne, Hugh J Sr, 1941, N 5,23:4
McKercher, George J, 1948, Mr 19,23:2
McKernam, Charles A, 1940, F 26,15:6
McKernan, Edward F, 1950, F 22,29:3
McKernan, Edward J, 1956, D 5,39:2
McKernan, Eugene, 1938, D 7,23:3
McKernan, Francis A, 1948, Mr 10,28:3
McKernan, Garrett Mrs, 1945, D 22,19:3
McKernan, Gerald J, 1962, N 10,25:5
McKernan, James, 1955, Mr 30,29:5
McKernan, John F, 1959, Ja 5,29:3
McKernan, John H, 1953, Mr 22,86:1
McKernan, John L (Jack Kearns), 1963, Jl 8,29:2

McKernan, Nelson M, 1961, Jl 12,32:1
McKernan, Reginald A Rev, 1957, S 11,33:2
McKernon, Edward, 1943, Mr 23,19:2
McKernon, James F, 1949, Ja 23,69:2
McKerrell, Augustus de Segur Gen, 1916, Ap 25,11:8
MacKerrow, Clarence D, 1959, O 22,37:4
McKerrow, George, 1946, F 10,42:4
Mackerson, Harry R, 1964, Ja 27,23:3
McKesson, Irving, 1958, N 11,29:4
McKesson, John Jr, 1924, S 8,15:2
McKesson, Robert I, 1958, Jl 9,27:6
Mackessy, Elizabeth, 1937, F 28,II,8:6
Mackessy, John N Sr, 1966, My 27,43:1
Mackessy, Richard P, 1946, F 24,44:2
Mackessy, Thomas F Mrs, 1950, F 27,19:4
McKetrick, Daniel H (por), 1948, My 23,68:6
McKettrick, William K Mrs, 1953, Ja 8,27:4
McKevitt, Hugh K, 1951, O 25,29:5
McKevlin, Anthony J, 1946, D 24,18:2
McKewan, Patrick J, 1943, S 15,27:2
McKewan, William D, 1953, N 11,31:2
Mackey, Angus S, 1953, O 4,87:1
Mackey, Argyle R Sr, 1968, Jl 2,41:1
Mackey, Bertha C, 1938, Je 7,23:5
Mackey, C Stanley, 1915, S 27,9:4
Mackey, Charles L Rev, 1937, Jl 14,21:5
Mackey, Cyrus F, 1940, Mr 22,19:2
Mackey, D Clinton Mrs, 1960, Jl 15,23:1
Mackey, E W M, 1884, Ja 29,5:4
Mackey, Edward W, 1940, Mr 29,21:3
Mackey, Edwin A, 1941, F 13,19:3
Mackey, Fern J, 1961, Mr 19,89:1
Mackey, Frances T, 1937, Ap 22,23:5
Mackey, Francis, 1962, Ja 1,23:5
Mackey, Frank J, 1959, Ap 3,27:4
Mackey, Fredericka B Mrs, 1945, My 13,20:3
Mackey, George Devereaux, 1922, Mr 3,13:5
Mackey, George I Mrs, 1948, Ap 25,72:2
Mackey, George W, 1903, O 7,9:6
Mackey, Goff J W, 1948, N 15,25:6
Mackey, Grover H, 1943, Ap 3,15:2
Mackey, Harry A (por), 1938, O 18,25:5
Mackey, Harry A Mrs (por), 1949, Je 23,27:3
Mackey, James B Mrs, 1959, Mr 5,31:2
Mackey, James H, 1943, N 17,25:5
Mackey, Joe Jr, 1951, F 23,27:5
Mackey, Joseph, 1961, O 31,31:2
Mackey, Joseph T, 1961, Ag 6,84:1
Mackey, Lorenzo, 1947, Mr 8,13:1
Mackey, M, 1878, Mr 21,1:6
Mackey, Maud A, 1957, Ja 31,27:4
Mackey, R W, 1879, Ja 2,5:1
Mackey, Richard, 1951, Ja 22,17:1
MacKey, Richard J, 1957, Jl 7,60:5
Mackey, Robert V Mrs, 1919, Je 13,15:5
Mackey, T D, 1903, My 15,2:4
Mackey, Thomas D Sr Mrs, 1957, F 15,23:4
Mackey, Wallace B, 1948, D 22,23:1
Mackey, William, 1951, Jl 30,21:2
Mackey, William A, 1939, F 7,19:5
Mackey, William B, 1952, Je 7,19:3
Mackey, William D, 1954, F 7,89:1
Mackey, William Fleming Ex-Sen, 1912, Jl 11,9:6
Mackey, William J, 1938, My 26,25:4; 1946, O 1,23:3
Mackey, William L, 1942, S 1,19:6
McKibben, Charles H, 1960, O 29,23:6
McKibben, John S, 1945, F 20,19:1
McKibben, Paul S, 1941, N 12,24:2
McKibben, William T, 1938, Ag 19,19:3
McKibbin, Bernice C, 1961, My 2,37:1
McKibbin, Chambers Brig-Gen, 1918, D 31,11:3
McKibbin, George, 1967, D 30,23:4
McKibbin, George B, 1960, S 15,37:2
McKibbin, George S, 1959, D 29,25:2
McKibbin, James S, 1944, Ja 23,38:2
McKibbin, Mildred (will), 1942, O 1,48:3
Mackie, Alex, 1949, D 1,31:5
Mackie, Arthur D, 1938, Jl 20,19:5
MacKie, C P, 1932, F 8,17:1
Mackie, Catherine R, 1948, Ja 9,22:3
McKie, Charles, 1952, N 8,19:5
Mackie, Daniel S, 1961, S 20,29:4
Mackie, Edwin L, 1947, Ag 19,23:3
Mackie, George F, 1948, Je 17,25:3
McKie, George M, 1941, Je 16,15:5
Mackie, Isaac S, 1963, Je 24,27:2
Mackie, James B, 1959, Mr 13,26:2
Mackie, James S, 1949, Ja 22,13:4
MacKie, James Steuart, 1922, Mr 14,15:4
McKie, John W Maj, 1917, D 18,15:5
Mackie, Joseph B C, 1942, F 24,21:2
Mackie, Mae, 1951, Jl 21,13:6
Mackie, Rufus L, 1949, D 20,31:2
Mackie, Thomas J, 1942, Je 17,23:5
Mackie, Thomas Mrs, 1959, N 26,37:2
Mackie, William L, 1941, Ap 19,15:5
McKiegan, William M, 1954, Mr 22,27:4
MacKieran, Douglas, 1950, Jl 30,1:2
McKiernan, Charles Patrick, 1917, Ag 25,7:5
McKiernan, James, 1882, D 27,5:2
McKiernan, John F, 1954, Ag 6,17:5
McKiernan, John F Mrs, 1963, Ap 7,85:8
McKiernan, Joseph L, 1949, F 16,25:2

McKiernan, Katherine G, 1939, Ag 22,19:5
McKiernan, William, 1939, My 28,III,6:8
McKiernan, William F, 1939, Mr 4,15:2
McKiernan, William J Jr, 1943, Ja 26,19:3
McKillip, Burlin G, 1950, My 17,29:3
McKillips, Budd L, 1939, Ap 7,21:2
McKillop, I Thomas, 1951, Jl 1,29:2
McKillop, J, 1880, Mr 25,2:7
McKillop, James H, 1938, Jl 12,19:5
McKillop, John A, 1947, Je 21,17:6
McKillop, William, 1937, D 22,25:2
McKillop, William M, 1952, Ap 27,91:2
McKim, Albert Vanderburgh, 1909, Jl 30,7:5
McKim, Charles D, 1950, S 28,31:1
McKim, Charles F, 1909, S 17,9:5
McKim, Clarence, 1916, F 11,11:4
McKim, J, 1936, Ap 5,II,11:1
McKim, James Rev, 1874, Je 15,4:7
McKim, Janet W, 1948, Je 7,19:5
McKim, John C, 1952, Ag 27,27:1
McKim, Joseph, 1912, Jl 10,9:2
McKim, Judson J, 1948, Mr 13,15:5
McKim, Kenneth W, 1958, N 13,33:6
McKim, Phil, 1938, D 31,15:5
McKim, Randolph H Rev Dr, 1920, Jl 16,11:4
McKim, Robert Vanderburgen Mrs, 1907, My 28,9:5
McKim, Robert Vanderburgh Dr, 1915, O 21,11:5
McKim, Samuel J, 1961, My 7,86:6
McKim, W Duncan Mrs, 1914, Jl 14,9:6
McKim, William H, 1954, Ap 11,42:2
McKim, William R, 1941, My 7,25:4
Mackin, Alex J, 1942, Jl 28,17:4
Mackin, Charles L, 1945, D 2,46:3
Mackin, James A, 1938, N 15,23:3
Mackin, James F Msgr (funl, Ap 24,19:4), 1925, Ap 21,21:5
Mackin, John E, 1950, Ja 22,76:3
Mackin, John J, 1967, N 11,33:4
Mackin, Joseph C, 1914, Mr 12,9:4
Mackin, Margaret Mrs, 1938, Ja 12,21:5
Mackin, Patrick H, 1939, F 4,15:5
Mackin, Robert N, 1959, Ag 1,17:4
Mackinder, H J Sir, 1947, Mr 8,13:3
McKiniry, Mary E, 1937, N 19,23:5
McKiniry, Richard F, 1950, Je 1,27:5
McKiniry, Thomas E, 1947, N 23,72:8
Mackinlay, Andrew, 1938, My 14,15:6
McKinlay, David A, 1948, D 21,25:3
McKinlay, Harry D, 1956, Mr 8,33:1
McKinlay, Harry G, 1941, Ag 9,15:7
McKinlay, James B, 1951, Jl 13,21:2
McKinlay, John, 1953, Mr 10,29:5
McKinlay, Wilbert L, 1944, Ag 6,37:3
McKinlay, William B, 1950, N 21,31:4
MacKinlay, William C, 1942, Ja 1,25:3
MacKinlay, 1937, Jl 22,19:5
McKinley, Abner, 1904, Je 12,9:6
McKinley, Ada S Mrs, 1952, Ag 29,23:3
McKinley, Benjamin L, 1950, N 20,25:2
McKinley, Carl Mrs, 1939, Mr 21,23:1
McKinley, Charles F, 1955, My 8,89:1
McKinley, Charles R, 1950, O 18,33:5
McKinley, Clare H, 1948, N 21,88:1
McKinley, Clarence A Mrs, 1952, Ag 20,25:5
McKinley, Edward E, 1941, O 15,21:2
McKinley, Edward G, 1947, O 31,23:3
McKinley, Eugene F, 1938, N 26,15:5
McKinley, Eugene F Mrs, 1950, O 29,92:5
McKinley, George E, 1941, Jl 26,15:2
McKinley, James A, 1940, Ja 6,13:3
McKinley, James F (por), 1941, Ja 18,15:4
McKinley, John L, 1958, Ap 21,23:6
McKinley, John M Mrs, 1951, S 4,27:4
McKinley, Louis G, 1952, N 13,31:3
McKinley, Louis H, 1949, D 21,30:4
McKinley, Michael L, 1951, My 9,33:6
McKinley, Paul B, 1937, Ja 3,II,8:6
McKinley, Richard S, 1956, Je 8,25:4
McKinley, Richard S Mrs, 1939, F 10,23:1
McKinley, W B Sen, 1926, D 8,27:1
McKinley, William, 1964, Ag 13,29:5
McKinley, William G, 1967, My 1,37:4
McKinley, William Mrs (funl), 1907, My 28,9:5
McKinnell, George E S, 1908, My 19,7:4
McKinney, A, 1882, N 3,5:5
McKinney, Alex H, 1941, Ap 23,21:7
McKinney, Alexander Mrs, 1944, Mr 9,17:2
McKinney, Arthur W, 1963, Ag 4,80:2
McKinney, B B, 1952, S 11,31:1
McKinney, Bernard, 1954, Ja 13,31:3
McKinney, Buckner A, 1939, Ap 3,15:5
Mackinney, Charles B Mrs, 1950, F 4,15:3
McKinney, Edward N, 1942, Jl 13,15:2
McKinney, Edward N Mrs, 1938, N 16,23:5
McKinney, Ernest M, 1956, Je 1,23:4
McKinney, Frank C, 1950, Ap 16,104:5
McKinney, Frederick H, 1938, Je 8,23:4
McKinney, Frederick W Mrs, 1951, N 22,31:2
McKinney, Georgia L, 1957, Je 30,69:2
McKinney, Grace, 1944, D 21,21:3
McKinney, Harry W, 1946, Ja 21,23:1
McKinney, Henry N, 1918, Ap 30,13:4
McKinney, Howard C, 1955, O 28,26:2

McKinney, Ida E (will), 1965, Ja 9,27:3
McKinney, J C, 1924, D 8,19:4
McKinney, J F, 1903, Je 14,7:6
McKinney, J Ray, 1949, F 13,76:3
McKinney, James, 1951, O 19,27:6
McKinney, James F, 1957, O 21,25:1
McKinney, James P, 1941, Ag 18,13:1
McKinney, James P Mrs, 1957, S 16,31:3
McKinney, John C, 1951, D 29,11:2
McKinney, John F, 1904, Ja 19,9:6
McKinney, John H, 1955, Ap 7,27:3; 1956, D 4,39:1
McKinney, John I (por), 1937, My 22,15:1
MacKinney, John R, 1955, Mr 9,27:1
McKinney, Kate Mrs, 1939, O 11,27:3
McKinney, Laurence, 1968, Ap 22,47:1
McKinney, Madge M, 1956, Jl 31,23:3
McKinney, Preston, 1945, O 13,15:4
McKinney, Ralph, 1944, N 25,13:5
McKinney, Ralph B, 1946, S 22,63:6
McKinney, Raymond H, 1953, Mr 29,93:1
McKinney, Raymond H Mrs, 1951, O 29,23:5
McKinney, Robert C Col, 1916, O 4,11:6
McKinney, Roessle Mrs, 1949, S 9,25:3
McKinney, Roscoe Mrs, 1948, N 13,15:3
McKinney, Samuel A, 1948, Mr 13,15:6
McKinney, Samuel P, 1952, Mr 21,23:2
McKinney, Stephen B, 1953, O 12,28:7
McKinney, Theophilus E, 1962, Jl 6,25:3
McKinney, Thompson W, 1943, F 15,15:5
McKinney, W Arthur, 1968, O 29,47:4
McKinney, William, 1949, Jl 7,25:1
McKinney, William Allison, 1923, Ja 29,15:6
McKinney, William H, 1939, N 24,23:3
Mackinney, William H, 1943, Je 11,19:1
McKinney, William K, 1952, F 28,27:5
McKinney, William M, 1955, N 10,35:2
McKinney, William N, 1945, Jl 7,13:3
McKinney, William S, 1947, F 21,20:3
McKinney, Worth E, 1947, Ja 24,21:2
McKinnie, Charles T, 1962, O 20,25:6
McKinnley, Eugene F, 1938, N 26,15:5
MacKinnon, Albert E, 1954, My 1,15:2
McKinnon, Alex B, 1955, Ap 2,17:4
Mackinnon, Allan, 1939, Ag 8,17:1
MacKinnon, Angus, 1958, Je 30,19:4
Mackinnon, Arch L, 1938, S 12,17:2
MacKinnon, Archibald, 1952, N 28,26:4
Mackinnon, Bergan A, 1951, Mr 13,31:3
MacKinnon, Clarence Rev Dr, 1937, O 9,19:2
Mackinnon, Clinton N, 1957, N 15,28:3
MacKinnon, Ellen Mrs, 1953, D 10,47:5
MacKinnon, Eugene, 1951, Ag 10,15:6
MacKinnon, Francis A, 1947, F 28,23:5
McKinnon, Frank D, 1946, Ja 24,22:2
MacKinnon, Frederick B, 1937, Ja 11,19:4
MacKinnon, George E, 1948, Ag 20,17:3
MacKinnon, George V, 1939, Je 18,37:3
MacKinnon, Hector E Sr, 1957, Ap 10,33:4
Mackinnon, James, 1945, Jl 21,11:3
MacKinnon, James A, 1958, Ap 19,21:5
McKinnon, John (mem, Jl 14,11:6), 1916, Jl 10,11
McKinnon, John H, 1952, F 29,23:1
McKinnon, John W, 1941, Jl 19,13:7
McKinnon, Judge, 1948, Ap 21,27:1
McKinnon, Kenneth, 1953, Ag 5,23:5
MacKinnon, Kenneth R, 1955, Ap 28,29:1
Mackinnon, Lauchian Sir, 1925, D 5,19:5
MacKinnon, Mary (Mrs F Johnson), 1962, S 24,2
McKinnon, Neil Norbert Rev, 1907, O 10,9:4
McKinnon, Norman Rev, 1919, D 9,17:4
McKinnon, Robert A, 1961, S 9,19:4
Mackinnon, Robert D, 1948, Je 12,15:7
McKinnon, Russell A Mrs, 1965, Je 12,31:5
McKinnon, Sarah E Mrs, 1941, Jl 23,19:5
McKinnon, Tristram Allan, 1903, Jl 13,7:4
McKinnon, William S, 1908, N 18,9:2
McKinny, Alexander, 1920, Ap 1,11:5
McKinsey, James O (will, D 31,16:4), 1937, D 1,
McKinstrie, William G, 1952, S 5,27:4
McKinstry, Addis E (por), 1941, Mr 23,44:1
McKinstry, Arthur Packer, 1921, Jl 22,11:6
McKinstry, Charles C, 1946, Jl 22,21:4
McKinstry, Charles H Mrs, 1920, Ja 12,9:1
McKinstry, De Witt E, 1944, Ja 13,19:6
McKinstry, Earle C, 1945, Ja 11,23:5
McKinstry, Edwin L, 1951, Mr 30,23:3
MacKinstry, Elizabeth C, 1956, My 14,25:3
McKinstry, Guy H, 1957, D 23,23:1
McKinstry, Helen M, 1949, Je 12,76:6
McKinstry, J C, 1942, F 10,20:3
McKinstry, Jacob H, 1941, Ap 6,48:8
McKinstry, Mark S, 1940, Jl 21,29:2
McKinstry, Willard D, 1919, My 25,20:5
McKinstry, William B, 1954, Jl 27,21:4
Mackintosh, A F, 1884, F 1,5:6
Mackintosh, Alex, 1948, Ap 16,23:3
Mackintosh, Alexander D, 1945, Ag 3,17:5
Mackintosh, Alexander Mrs, 1945, Je 11,15:4
Mackintosh, Archie E, 1956, Je 3,85:1
Mackintosh, Donald, 1943, D 9,27:3
Mackintosh, Elizabeth (G Daviot), 1952, F 14,27
Mackintosh, Frank H Mrs, 1943, N 17,25:1
Mackintosh, Frederick L, 1937, Jl 1,27:4

Mackintosh, Harriet F A M Mrs, 1941, F 19,21:2
Mackintosh, Lachlan D, 1957, Mr 22,23:4
Mackintosh, Stuart J, 1952, O 15,31:1
Mackintosh, William G, 1940, F 18,43:6
Mackintosh of Halifax, Harold V Viscount, 1964, D 29,27:3
Mackintosh of Mackintosh (will, N 21,21:6), 1938, N 15,23:6
Mackirdy, James, 1937, S 23,27:4
MacKirdy, John, 1925, My 29,17:6
McKirgan, Elmer L Mrs, 1955, Je 14,29:1
McKirgan, Elmere L, 1954, O 24,88:6
McKisack, Caroline Z Mrs, 1941, Je 3,21:5
McKisick, Lewis, 1942, Ja 7,19:5
McKissick, J Rion, 1944, S 4,19:6
McKisson, Robert E, 1915, O 15,11:4
McKitchen, Thomas J, 1957, Je 28,23:4
McKittrick, Edward, 1903, O 1,9:5
McKittrick, Fred C, 1954, O 16,17:6
McKittrick, H V Mrs, 1944, Jl 13,17:3
McKittrick, Harold V, 1958, O 6,31:5
McKittrick, James W, 1941, S 30,23:5
McKittrick, Louis A, 1950, D 19,29:1
McKittrick, Robert A, 1949, My 17,26:2
McKittrick, Roy, 1961, Ja 24,29:5
McKlaw, John Belker, 1924, Ag 26,11:3
Mackle, Clifford W, 1950, Ag 4,21:6
Mackler, Fred C, 1947, Ag 1,17:1
Mackler, Meinrod Mrs, 1947, Ap 3,25:2
Mackley, Harry A, 1949, D 27,23:4
Mackley, Walter E, 1951, O 20,15:4
Macklin, C B, 1944, Ja 24,17:5
Macklin, Charles F, 1945, Ap 17,23:1
Macklin, E H, 1946, My 1,25:5
Macklin, Francis H, 1903, My 6,9:6
Macklin, Gordon S, 1949, Jl 15,19:5
Macklin, John, 1943, F 13,11:5
Macklin, John F, 1949, O 11,34:4; 1952, S 4,27:2
Macklin, John N, 1948, My 4,25:5
Macklin, Patrick H, 1946, F 2,13:4
Macklin, William E Mrs, 1946, S 27,23:2
McKlissick, Anthony F, 1938, Ap 9,17:2
McKloskey, Howard W, 1945, N 24,20:2
McKneally, George F Sr, 1944, S 9,15:3
McKnight, Earle B Mrs, 1949, Jl 12,27:3
McKnight, Everett J Dr, 1917, D 26,9:3
McKnight, George M, 1941, Ap 12,15:5
McKnight, George W, 1951, Mr 21,33:5
McKnight, Harvey S, 1949, Jl 19,29:5
McKnight, Harvey W Rev Dr, 1914, My 30,11:7
McKnight, Irene B Mrs, 1937, Ap 12,17:3
McKnight, J Donald, 1956, O 13,19:4
McKnight, J Lee, 1941, My 16,23:3
McKnight, James H, 1938, Jl 26,19:2
McKnight, John, 1914, Je 27,7:6
McKnight, John F Mrs, 1959, Ap 30,31:3
McKnight, John W, 1939, O 1,53:2
McKnight, Joseph F, 1964, N 12,37:1
McKnight, Robert B, 1950, S 11,23:3
McKnight, Thomas, 1951, F 17,15:1
McKnight, William A P, 1951, D 1,13:7
McKnight, William G, 1940, Mr 19,42:4
McKnight, William H, 1966, Ja 1,17:5
McKnight, William Mrs, 1947, Je 20,19:2
McKnight, William S, 1949, N 18,29:3
McKowen, Robert, 1949, Ap 1,25:1
McKown, Charles P, 1948, Ag 12,22:3
McKown, Francis J, 1941, O 10,23:4
McKown, Harry C, 1963, S 6,29:1
MacKown, Leon A, 1950, Je 7,29:4
McKown, Wendell P, 1957, Ap 18,29:2
McKown, Wendell P Mrs, 1956, Jl 10,31:1
McKowne, Frank A (por), 1948, My 8,15:3
McKoy, Charles F, 1965, Mr 20,27:3
Mackrille, Alfred, 1948, Jl 12,19:4
Mackubin, George, 1964, Mr 15,86:2
McKune, Clarence Mrs, 1947, Je 17,13:5
McKusick, Leon R, 1962, Ap 16,29:3
McKusick, Marshall, 1950, D 25,19:3
McLachlan, Adam, 1954, Ja 4,19:2
MacLachlan, Alex (por), 1940, S 9,15:3
Maclachlan, Angus, 1938, S 16,21:5
McLachlan, Archibald A, 1947, D 3,29:2
McLachlan, Archibald C, 1943, Jl 17,13:2
McLachlan, Argyle, 1949, D 25,26:3
McLachlan, George A, 1956, Ag 26,85:2; 1963, Ag 31,17:4
McLachlan, Harry, 1968, D 18,47:3
McLachlan, Harry Mrs, 1954, Jl 20,19:1
McLachlan, J B, 1937, N 4,25:6
McLachlan, James, 1940, N 22,23:5
MacLachlan, James A, 1967, Ap 18,41:1
McLachlan, James D Maj-Gen, 1937, N 9,24:5
McLachlan, James Mrs, 1944, O 1,45:1; 1945, My 11, 19:4
Maclachlan, John, 1942, S 23,25:3
McLachlan, John B, 1949, Ap 14,25:5
McLachlan, John F, 1945, Ja 5,15:4
McLachlan, John K, 1945, Mr 18,42:6
Maclachlan, Murdock, 1940, F 19,17:4
McLachlan, Thomas J, 1954, Mr 10,25:5
McLachlan, William, 1941, My 31,11:1
McLachlen, Archibald, 1922, S 19,19:4
McLachlin, Ewen, 1914, My 22,13:2
McLachlin, Louis E, 1943, D 19,48:4
McLae, Henry, 1944, O 3,23:4
MacLaeon, Angus S, 1953, O 16,27:3
MacLafferty, James H, 1937, Je 11,23:3
McLagan, Angus, 1956, S 5,27:5
McLagan, Donald, 1949, D 29,25:2
Maclagan, William D Rev, 1910, S 20,11:4
McLagen, Victor Mrs, 1942, Ap 3,21:3
MacLagger, Mary M Mrs, 1951, My 17,31:2
McLaglen, Victor (funl, N 11,35:3), 1959, N 8,88:1
McLain, Chester A (trb lr, S 30,30:7), 1953, S 26,17:1
McLain, David, 1945, O 20,11:4
McLain, Dick R, 1962, Ja 6,19:5
McLain, Forrest J, 1963, Je 16,84:4
McLain, George H, 1965, Jl 13,33:3
McLain, Michael, 1943, Jl 7,19:3
McLain, Raymond S, 1954, D 15,32:1
McLain, Robert B, 1949, F 23,27:4
McLain, Robert G, 1957, S 26,25:4
McLain, William R, 1949, Mr 29,25:3
McLain, William T, 1961, F 20,27:1
McLaine, Leonard S, 1943, Jl 22,19:5
McLaine, Warren G, 1958, O 2,37:3
McLallen, Walter F, 1942, Ag 28,19:1
McLanahan, Alexander H, 1967, D 18,47:3
McLanahan, Austin, 1946, Ap 4,25:4
McLanahan, Duer Sr, 1962, Ja 11,33:1
McLanahan, George W, 1908, N 4,11:7
McLanahan, J Craig, 1946, Mr 20,23:2
McLanahan, M Hawley Mrs, 1951, Mr 19,27:4
McLanahan, Samuel Rev, 1912, N 5,13:5
McLanahan, Scott, 1946, My 21,24:2
McLanahan, William, 1950, Ja 17,27:4
McLane, Allan, 1940, S 17,23:4; 1948, Ag 7,15:6
McLane, Charles E, 1941, Je 2,17:5
MacLane, Cleveland C, 1947, Mr 18,27:1
McLane, Guy Richards, 1921, Ap 11,11:3
McLane, Guy Richards Mrs, 1912, F 25,II,11:3
McLane, James W Dr, 1912, N 26,15:4
MacLane, Jean (Mrs J C Johansen), 1964, Ja 24,24:3
McLane, John B, 1948, F 10,23:4
McLane, John Ex-Gov, 1911, Ap 14,11:4
McLane, John J, 1949, F 7,19:2
McLane, John T, 1950, D 12,33:2
Maclane, M, 1929, Ag 8,25:5
McLane, Patrick, 1946, N 14,29:3
McLane, Patrick F, 1953, N 14,17:1
McLane, Ralph, 1951, F 20,25:3
McLane, Thomas J, 1939, S 4,19:6
McLane, Thomas S (por), 1947, N 19,27:1
McLane, Thomas S Mrs, 1955, D 27,23:1
McLane, W L, 1903, My 17,7:7
McLane, W Lawrence, 1964, My 8,33:1
MacLaren, Albert, 1940, Ap 23,24:2
MacLaren, Alex, 1939, Jl 10,19:2
McLaren, Alex, 1940, O 9,25:5; 1954, Ja 13,20:5
McLaren, Alexander Rev, 1910, My 6,9:4
McLaren, Andrew R, 1943, N 3,25:5
MacLaren, Arch W, 1950, My 7,108:2
MacLaren, Archibald Dr, 1924, O 13,17:4
McLaren, Charles, 1955, Je 9,29:3
McLaren, D C Mrs, 1953, Ja 8,30:3
MacLaren, D Laurence, 1960, S 8,35:2
Maclaren, Donald, 1966, Je 11,31:2
McLaren, Donald Mrs, 1955, D 19,27:5
McLaren, Donald Rev, 1920, My 29,15:5
Maclaren, Edwin J, 1949, Jl 23,11:6
McLaren, Francis J, 1943, Mr 23,19:4
McLaren, Henry D (Lord Aberconway), 1953, My 24,89:3
McLaren, Hugh, 1952, Je 26,29:6
Maclaren, Ian (Rev Dr Jno Watson), 1907, My 7,9:5
MacLaren, Ivor, 1962, N 1,31:2
McLaren, James J, 1954, S 2,21:4
McLaren, James J Mrs, 1953, Ja 10,17:2
McLaren, James R, 1948, Ap 24,15:2
McLaren, John, 1943, Ja 13,23:2
MacLaren, John A, 1955, Je 12,86:7
McLaren, John D, 1956, S 22,17:4
McLaren, John J Lt, 1920, Ap 8,11:5
McLaren, John Jr, 1949, Ap 16,15:4
McLaren, Kenneth K, 1953, O 29,31:4
McLaren, Kenneth K Mrs, 1941, N 15,17:4
McLaren, Malcolm, 1945, S 25,25:4
MacLaren, Murray, 1942, D 25,18:3
McLaren, Olive B Mrs, 1940, F 24,13:1
McLaren, Peter, 1941, D 8,23:3
McLaren, Peter L, 1955, Ja 27,24:1
McLaren, Robert L, 1943, Ja 26,20:2
McLaren, Thomas, 1956, Je 23,17:4
McLaren, Walter W Mrs, 1949, Je 3,26:3
McLaren, William, 1953, Ja 3,15:1
McLaren, William A, 1944, F 20,36:3
McLaren, William E Bp, 1905, F 20,7:4
McLarin, Howard M, 1942, Mr 29,44:4
McLarn, Ernest S, 1965, F 2,33:2
McLarn, William D, 1967, F 23,35:4
McLarnan, Robert L, 1945, Ag 24,19:4
McLarney, Thomas J, 1955, F 12,27:6
McLarnin, Samuel Mrs, 1940, F 9,19:4
McLarnon, Harry, 1960, Ja 22,25:2
McLarty, Alex McL, 1941, Ap 24,21:2
McLarty, Norman, 1945, S 17,19:4
McLarty, Ray C, 1953, Ja 24,15:4
McLashan, Leonard, 1907, Ja 8,9:2
MacLauchlan, John, 1943, Mr 7,38:6
McLauchlan, John, 1946, O 26,17:2
McLaughan, George W, 1944, Mr 22,19:3
McLaughin, Thomas J, 1948, Ja 21,26:2
MacLaughlan, Donald S, 1938, My 7,15:5
McLaughlin, Alex G, 1951, Je 21,27:5
McLaughlin, Allan J, 1961, O 26,35:2
McLaughlin, Alonzo G (por), 1939, F 25,15:1
McLaughlin, Alonzo G Mrs, 1959, D 24,19:5
McLaughlin, Andrew C (por), 1947, S 25,29:3
McLaughlin, Andrew C Mrs, 1941, My 7,25:4
McLaughlin, Beverly, 1955, Ag 5,19:2
McLaughlin, Carroll W, 1951, N 14,31:1
McLaughlin, Charles, 1937, N 8,23:5
McLaughlin, Charles B, 1947, D 9,29:1
McLaughlin, Charles G, 1947, Ag 14,23:2
McLaughlin, Charles I, 1940, S 26,23:3
McLaughlin, Charles J, 1947, Mr 7,25:2
McLaughlin, Charles R, 1939, Jl 5,17:6
McLaughlin, Chester B, 1952, Ja 23,27:2
MacLaughlin, Claude M Mrs, 1968, S 23,35:4
McLaughlin, Clayton R, 1943, Ja 16,13:5
McLaughlin, Clifford, 1947, Ja 9,23:2
MacLaughlin, Creswell, 1946, Ja 9,23:2
McLaughlin, Daniel, 1906, S 29,7:6
McLaughlin, Daniel J, 1949, S 14,31:2
McLaughlin, Dean B, 1965, D 10,47:3
McLaughlin, Dennis, 1912, Je 7,13:4
McLaughlin, Donald F, 1945, D 17,21:4
McLaughlin, Edmund K, 1949, O 26,27:5
McLaughlin, Edward, 1947, Jl 29,21:3
McLaughlin, Edward A, 1950, Ap 2,93:1
McLaughlin, Edward B, 1955, My 18,31:4
McLaughlin, Edward F, 1954, Je 2,31:3
McLaughlin, Edward H, 1939, N 23,27:3
McLaughlin, Edward J, 1939, Ja 30,13:2; 1942, My 29,17:5; 1961, O 29,88:8
McLaughlin, Edward M, 1909, Ap 14,11:5
McLaughlin, Edward T, 1938, D 14,25:5
McLaughlin, Edwin W, 1960, D 3,23:6
McLaughlin, Ernest (E Mack), 1942, N 14,15:3
MacLaughlin, Floyd T Mrs (Ruth), 1968, Jl 26,33:2
McLaughlin, Francis L, 1939, O 2,17:4; 1961, Je 22, 31:3
McLaughlin, Frank, 1919, Jl 14,11:2
McLaughlin, Frank A, 1939, O 24,23:5; 1948, Ag 29, 60:1; 1949, Mr 24,28:2
McLaughlin, Frank B, 1950, My 13,17:7
McLaughlin, Frederic (por), 1944, D 18,19:1
McLaughlin, Frederick C, 1959, D 15,39:2
MacLaughlin, George, 1947, Mr 13,28:3
McLaughlin, George B, 1964, Ap 15,25:8
McLaughlin, George F, 1962, Ja 22,23:2
McLaughlin, George P, 1940, Je 16,39:1
McLaughlin, George S, 1944, Ag 6,37:4
McLaughlin, George V, 1967, D 8,42:1
McLaughlin, George W, 1942, O 12,17:4; 1955, N 12, 19:5
McLaughlin, Glenn D Mrs, 1943, Je 8,21:5
McLaughlin, Grace, 1916, Ap 14,9:1
McLaughlin, Grant B, 1945, S 2,32:1
McLaughlin, Henry L, 1938, Ja 10,17:2
McLaughlin, Henry W, 1950, Ag 29,27:2
McLaughlin, Hugh, 1904, D 8,1:3; 1946, F 15,25:2; 1948, Ja 21,26:2
McLaughlin, Hugh J, 1957, Ag 5,21:6
McLaughlin, Hugh Mrs, 1915, Ap 3,9:4
McLaughlin, J Fairfax, 1903, N 18,1:2
McLaughlin, J Frank, 1962, O 27,25:4
McLaughlin, James, 1943, D 12,68:3
McLaughlin, James B, 1955, N 23,23:1
MacLaughlin, James C, 1945, My 17,19:3
McLaughlin, James H, 1923, Jl 29,6:3
McLaughlin, James J, 1964, Ja 6,47:3
McLaughlin, James Prof, 1925, My 29,17:5
McLaughlin, James R, 1949, N 6,92:2
McLaughlin, James W, 1953, My 16,19:2
McLaughlin, Jane Mrs, 1942, Ap 27,15:3
McLaughlin, John, 1872, S 13,8:5; 1907, S 17,11:6; 1942, D 3,25:4; 1943, D 3,23:2; 1950, Ap 23,92:6
McLaughlin, John C, 1948, Jl 2,21:5; 1967, Ap 29,35:4
McLaughlin, John F, 1943, Mr 28,24:7; 1949, D 22, 23:3; 1955, O 30,89:1
McLaughlin, John G, 1944, Ag 30,17:2
McLaughlin, John J, 1911, Ja 20,11:5; 1949, Ap 15, 23:2; 1952, O 14,31:2; 1956, My 15,32:3
McLaughlin, John J Mrs, 1960, S 22,27:4
McLaughlin, John L, 1953, Jl 3,19:4
McLaughlin, John M, 1966, Mr 24,39:3; 1968, Je 17, 39:2
McLaughlin, John Mrs, 1960, S 1,27:4
McLaughlin, John P, 1950, Jl 3,15:2
McLaughlin, John S, 1960, Ap 28,35:5
McLaughlin, John T, 1951, My 9,33:5
McLaughlin, Joseph, 1940, D 12,34:2; 1948, N 15, 25:6; 1951, Mr 14,33:3
McLaughlin, Joseph A, 1944, Ja 10,17:3; 1949, O 22, 17:3; 1962, Ag 18,19:4
McLaughlin, Joseph C, 1945, Mr 27,19:1
McLaughlin, Joseph I, 1939, Mr 27,15:3

McLaughlin, Joseph L, 1949, Ja 18,23:5
McLaughlin, Joseph P, 1944, F 11,19:1
McLaughlin, Joseph R, 1960, My 2,29:2
McLaughlin, Joseph W, 1953, Mr 21,17:1
McLaughlin, Lalor R, 1958, N 7,28:4
McLaughlin, Lawrence A, 1956, S 25,33:1
McLaughlin, Leo A, 1940, Je 6,25:3
McLaughlin, Leo M, 1950, S 30,17:4
McLaughlin, Leon E, 1955, Ap 15,24:2
McLaughlin, Lucy A, 1944, D 3,57:2
McLaughlin, M Louise, 1939, Ja 18,19:5
McLaughlin, Manus P, 1944, Je 18,36:2
McLaughlin, Martin J, 1946, O 21,31:6
McLaughlin, Mary A, 1954, My 29,15:6
McLaughlin, Mary A Mrs, 1942, S 24,27:3
McLaughlin, Mary E, 1950, S 9,17:6
McLaughlin, Michael, 1907, F 4,9:6
McLaughlin, Michael J, 1951, N 27,31:5
McLaughlin, Nelson, 1955, Mr 4,23:3
McLaughlin, Patrick H, 1909, O 26,9:3
McLaughlin, Patrick J, 1941, Mr 2,18:1; 1957, Ag 8, 23:5
McLaughlin, Paul R, 1960, Ap 28,35:2
McLaughlin, Phil J Dr, 1937, Je 19,17:3
McLaughlin, R S Mrs, 1958, Ja 11,17:5
McLaughlin, Raymond J, 1966, N 29,39:3
McLaughlin, Rich W, 1950, N 30,26:5
McLaughlin, Richard, 1959, O 24,21:4
McLaughlin, Robert, 1945, D 10,21:2
McLaughlin, Robert G, 1959, Je 19,25:1
McLaughlin, Robert H, 1939, Ja 17,22:4
McLaughlin, Seldon B, 1937, Mr 30,24:2
McLaughlin, Stuart W, 1967, Ap 23,93:1
McLaughlin, Theodore J, 1954, O 21,27:4
McLaughlin, Thomas, 1940, Mr 29,22:2
McLaughlin, Thomas F, 1938, N 11,25:2
McLaughlin, Thomas H, 1947, Mr 18,27:1
McLaughlin, Thomas J, 1907, Ja 31,9:6; 1941, D 29, 15:2; 1942, O 1,23:4; 1945, S 2,32:2
McLaughlin, Thomas J Mrs, 1937, Mr 31,24:2
McLaughlin, Thomas P, 1948, N 28,65:3; 1953, Mr 19,29:2
McLaughlin, Vincent J, 1960, S 18,86:8
McLaughlin, W T Rev, 1924, My 1,19:4
McLaughlin, W W, 1933, O 14,15:1
McLaughlin, Warner, 1950, D 9,15:1
McLaughlin, William, 1938, D 9,25:4; 1948, F 1,60:5; 1949, Ap 23,13:2
McLaughlin, William F, 1942, Ag 6,19:6
McLaughlin, William H, 1912, My 1,13:3
McLaughlin, William J, 1962, Ag 12,80:2
McLaughlin, William J Mrs, 1947, Je 16,21:5
McLaughlin, William S, 1938, Jl 10,29:1; 1959, F 9, 29:4
McLaughlin, William T, 1960, Jl 4,15:2
McLaughlin, William V, 1965, Jl 10,25:6
McLaughlin, Zachary, 1947, N 8,17:5
McLaughry, James A, 1942, N 22,53:1
McLaughry, May G Mrs, 1952, Jl 22,25:1
McLauren, J L, 1934, Jl 30,13:3
McLaurie, Dorr W, 1954, F 12,25:1
McLaurin, George W Prof, 1968, S 6,43:3
MacLaurin, J Donald, 1957, Ja 17,29:4
Maclaurin, Richard C Dr, 1920, Ja 16,9:3
MacLaurin, Richard Mrs, 1951, Je 2,19:6
MacLaury, Bruce K, 1953, Mr 9,29:3
McLaury, Charles H, 1952, Ja 29,25:5
McLaury, D Herbert Mrs, 1952, Ag 1,17:1
McLaury, Frank Dr (por), 1937, D 9,25:3
Maclay, Alex L, 1951, My 17,31:6
Maclay, Alfred B (por), 1944, My 28,33:1
Maclay, Alfred B, 1952, My 24,19:3
McLay, Angus D, 1949, Jl 22,19:4
Maclay, Archibald M, 1923, D 15,13:3
Maclay, Edgar S, 1919, N 4,15:1
Maclay, Isaac Walter Maj, 1908, D 31,9:5
Maclay, James Prof, 1919, N 29,11:4
Maclay, Lord, 1951, Ap 25,29:2
Maclay, Mark W, 1957, F 8,23:1
Maclay, Mary E Mrs (will), 1940, Je 28,23:6
Maclay, Robert, 1920, N 27,13:5
McLay, Robert E, 1952, F 17,84:4; 1954, Ag 1,85:1
Maclay, W B, 1882, F 20,5:4
Maclay, William H, 1941, F 5,19:4
McLay, William Mrs, 1948, Je 23,27:1
Maclay, William P, 1943, Ag 3,19:4
MacLea, Robert K, 1961, Ja 9,39:5
McLeaish, Robert B Sr, 1962, Ja 9,48:1
MacLean, A E, 1939, O 29,40:4
Maclean, A K, 1942, Ag 1,11:5
McLean, Alan D Mrs, 1942, O 12,17:2
McLean, Albert W, 1871, Je 10,8:3
MacLean, Alex, 1938, S 28,25:3
McLean, Alex B, 1963, Je 20,33:5
MacLean, Alex C, 1948, F 14,13:4
Maclean, Alex T, 1950, My 16,31:3
McLean, Alexander, 1916, Ja 6,13:4
McLean, Alexander N, 1967, Mr 14,47:2
McLean, Alexander Rev, 1910, D 18,13:4
McLean, Alice Throckmorton, 1968, O 27,82:4
MacLean, Allen D, 1959, My 29,23:4
McLean, Andrew, 1903, D 21,7:5
McLean, Andrew (funl, D 7,19:5), 1922, D 6,19:4
McLean, Andrew, 1956, F 13,27:4
McLean, Angus, 1939, Ap 12,23:2
MacLean, Angus D (por), 1937, S 2,21:5
McLean, Arthur, 1918, D 30,9:4
McLean, Arthur A, 1918, Je 6,13:8
McLean, Arthur S, 1943, Mr 1,19:5
MacLean, Basil C, 1963, F 16,8:6
McLean, Benjamin, 1950, Ap 29,15:4
Maclean, Bernice L (por), 1946, Mr 9,13:5
McLean, Bob, 1966, Mr 26,V,1:8
McLean, Bridget Mrs, 1915, D 28,11:4
McLean, C Herbert, 1940, N 23,17:5
McLean, Charles, 1948, Je 12,15:3
McLean, Charles A Mrs, 1948, S 22,31:2
McLean, Charles Batchelor, 1921, Je 14,15:3
McLean, Charles C, 1948, S 23,29:3
McLean, Charles D, 1905, S 24,9:4
MacLean, Charles F, 1924, Mr 21,19:3
MacLean, Charles F Mrs (will, Jl 20,11:3), 1946, Jl 13,15:7
McLean, Charles I, 1954, Je 29,27:4
McLean, Charles M, 1950, Ap 30,103:1
McLean, Charles V, 1943, F 4,23:2
MacLean, Charles W, 1915, Jl 24,9:6
McLean, Colin M, 1941, F 3,17:5
McLean, Cornelius Col, 1908, F 20,7:6
McLean, David J, 1950, Ap 22,19:2
MacLean, Don C, 1940, N 24,49:1
Maclean, Donald A, 1963, My 3,32:2
MacLean, Donald C, 1938, Ag 3,19:4
MacLean, Donald Dr, 1903, Jl 25,7:6
MacLean, Donald F, 1956, Ag 9,25:6
McLean, Donald Mrs, 1916, My 20,11:4
MacLean, Douglas, 1967, Jl 11,37:4
McLean, Douglas, 1968, Ja 30,38:4
McLean, Douglas A, 1965, Jl 29,27:4
McLean, E B, 1902, D 28,7:5
Maclean, E K, 1951, Ja 26,24:2
McLean, E P Cons, 1903, Ja 8,9:5
McLean, Earl M, 1947, Ag 5,23:2
McLean, Edmund Jr, 1953, N 13,27:3
McLean, Edward, 1957, Je 5,35:5
McLean, Edward B (por),(will, Jl 29,17:7), 1941, Jl 28,13:1
McLean, Edward J, 1949, Mr 29,26:3
McLean, Edward Mrs, 1943, Mr 15,13:1
McLean, Elizabeth, 1954, Ja 25,19:1
McLean, Eugene E, 1906, Ja 6,9:4
McLean, Eugene L, 1957, My 29,27:2
McLean, Evalyn W, 1967, D 14,47:3
McLean, Evalyn W Mrs, 1947, Ap 27,1:2
MacLean, Ewen J, 1953, O 14,29:3
MacLean, F D, 1936, N 23,21:3
MacLean, Findlay Barnes, 1968, Jl 18,33:5
McLean, Floyd D, 1946, Mr 11,25:5
McLean, Forman M, 1956, S 9,84:1
McLean, Francis H, 1945, Je 11,15:4
McLean, Frank E, 1964, F 14,33:7
McLean, Frank Mrs, 1962, Je 16,19:3
McLean, Franklin Chambers, 1968, S 11,47:3
McLean, G P, 1932, Je 7,19:5
McLean, George, 1951, Mr 27,31:6
McLean, George E, 1938, My 5,23:5
MacLean, George E Mrs, 1922, F 25,13:4
MacLean, George H, 1939, O 21,15:6
McLean, George Hammond, 1913, F 19,11:5
McLean, George J, 1937, My 27,23:4
McLean, George J Mrs, 1959, Jl 14,29:5
McLean, George P Mrs, 1950, O 23,23:3
McLean, George W, 1962, Ag 12,81:2
MacLean, Gordon, 1948, Jl 21,23:5
McLean, Harry F, 1961, My 2,37:2
McLean, Harry I, 1957, My 29,27:1
MacLean, Harry Sir, 1920, F 6,13:4
McLean, Harvey B, 1944, D 27,19:5
Maclean, Helen G Mrs, 1958, O 26,88:5
McLean, Henry C, 1955, D 29,23:4
McLean, Henry C Dr, 1904, D 25,7:7
MacLean, Henry C Mrs, 1967, S 27,47:3
MacLean, Henry Coit, 1968, Ja 15,47:2
McLean, Henry G, 1958, O 2,37:5
McLean, Henry G Mrs, 1968, My 6,47:1
McLean, Henry R, 1942, O 13,24:2
McLean, Herbert E, 1945, Ja 11,23:1
MacLean, Howard L Mrs, 1938, F 24,19:4
McLean, Hugh, 1944, Je 2,15:3
MacLean, Hugh B, 1959, D 24,19:1
McLean, Hugh C, 1949, Ag 11,23:3
McLean, Hugh H (por), 1938, N 23,21:3
McLean, J Albert, 1949, S 9,25:3
McLean, J Allen Mrs, 1961, Je 30,27:4
McLean, Jack, 1961, Ag 30,33:4
McLean, James, 1920, Ja 8,17:1; 1952, Mr 26,29:4
MacLean, James A, 1945, Ja 20,11:6; 1953, Jl 29,23:3
Maclean, James D, 1950, D 9,15:4
McLean, James F, 1937, N 30,23:2
McLean, James H, 1956, Ap 2,23:4; 1960, N 24,29:3
McLean, James H Mrs, 1962, O 28,88:4
MacLean, James M, 1956, F 3,23:1
McLean, James S (will, O 17,26:4), 1954, S 2,21:5
McLean, Jay, 1957, N 16,19:4
McLean, John, 1872, F 10,12:2; 1951, D 15,13:6
McLean, John B, 1948, Ja 27,25:3
MacLean, John B, 1950, S 26,32:2
McLean, John D, 1948, Mr 30,23:2
McLean, John D Mrs, 1962, O 14,86:8
McLean, John Justice, 1861, Ap 5,8:2
McLean, John Milton Dr, 1968, My 3,47:2
McLean, John N, 1944, Ag 11,15:3
Maclean, John Pearse Adm, 1907, Jl 18,7:5
McLean, John R (funl, Je 11,21:5), 1916, Je 10,11:
McLean, John R Mrs (funl, S 11,11:6), 1912, S 10,
McLean, John S, 1911, Mr 27,11:4
McLean, John W, 1938, Mr 1,22:2
McLean, John Y, 1945, Mr 18,42:1
McLean, Joseph F, 1947, Jl 19,13:5
McLean, Joseph H, 1938, Ja 19,23:2
McLean, Kathryn F (K Forbes), 1966, My 17,47:1
Maclean, Lady (will, O 11,4:6), 1962, Jl 26,27:5
MacLean, M Haddon (sons to share bulk of est, O 6,27:3), 1954, S 25,15:4
MacLean, Magnus Prof, 1937, S 3,17:4
McLean, Malcolm Dr, 1924, Ja 17,15:3
MacLean, Mansell L, 1968, Jl 6,21:3
McLean, Margaret Sumner Mrs, 1905, Je 12,9:5
McLean, Marrs, 1953, My 20,29:2
McLean, Marshall, 1952, Ap 7,25:4
McLean, Marshall Mrs, 1949, Mr 30,25:6
MacLean, Mary A Mrs, 1943, Ja 18,15:3
McLean, Mary C Mrs, 1940, Mr 29,21:3
Maclean, Mary Dunlop Mrs, 1912, Jl 13,9:5
McLean, Mary S, 1914, N 19,11:6
MacLean, Matthew, 1953, Ap 8,29:5
McLean, Milton H, 1951, Mr 2,18:3
McLean, Milton H Brig-Gen, 1951, Ap 18,31:4
McLean, N C Gen, 1905, Ja 6,9:2
McLean, N H Col, 1884, Jl 8,3:2
MacLean, N Peter, 1959, My 21,31:4
McLean, Nathaniel Maj, 1871, Ap 17,5:4
Maclean, Norman, 1952, Ja 16,25:3
McLean, Norman B, 1939, Ag 21,13:5
McLean, Odber R, 1941, D 24,36:4
McLean, Peter D, 1941, My 8,23:4
McLean, Phil J, 1941, D 14,69:3
McLean, Ralph, 1948, N 30,27:4
McLean, Ray, 1964, Mr 5,33:2
McLean, Ridley Mrs, 1941, F 6,22:2
McLean, Robert, 1964, Ap 11,25:4
McLean, Robert Hamilton Col, 1915, O 29,13:5
McLean, Robert L, 1944, D 22,17:5
McLean, Robert L Mrs, 1941, S 17,23:3
McLean, Robert N Mrs, 1939, My 16,23:6
MacLean, Robinson F, 1960, N 17,37:1
MacLean, Rod, 1958, Jl 6,56:4
MacLean, Roderick Mrs, 1961, O 2,31:2
MacLean, Roy M, 1945, Mr 20,19:1
McLean, S B W, 1874, N 21,1:2
Maclean, S W, 1878, Ja 14,5:4
McLean, Simon J, 1946, N 6,23:4
MacLean, Thomas C Rear-Adm, 1919, S 9,17:6
McLean, Thomas Chalmers Rear-Adm, 1919, Ag 7:6
McLean, Thomas F, 1954, Je 7,23:3
McLean, W L, 1930, Mr 21,27:5; 1931, Jl 31,17:1
MacLean, Wallace, 1943, My 30,26:2
McLean, Wallace D, 1966, D 28,37:2
McLean, Wallace D Mrs, 1949, Ja 2,63:5
MacLean, Walter J, 1951, Jl 17,27:5
McLean, Warden Lt, 1917, Je 30,11:6
McLean, William A, 1942, Jl 26,31:1; 1949, My 25:6
MacLean, William D Mrs, 1946, N 21,32:3
McLean, William H, 1943, Ja 11,15:1
McLean, William L Jr (will, Mr 23,29:2), 1954, Mr 11,31:5
McLean, William L Mrs, 1921, My 5,17:4
MacLean, William M, 1954, O 30,17:5
McLean, William M Sr, 1944, N 30,23:4
McLean, William Mrs, 1955, N 26,19:4
McLean, William R, 1964, D 22,29:3
McLean, William S, 1938, Ja 18,23:1; 1938, N 1
McLean, William T, 1938, Ag 18,19:3
McLean, William T Mrs, 1945, S 16,42:3
MacLear, Anne B, 1938, Ap 28,23:5
McLear, Herbert G, 1950, D 23,15:5
Maclear, John F, 1942, N 19,25:4
McLear, Robert E, 1938, D 7,23:1
MacLeary, F Burnham Mrs (Florence Larrabee), 1968, D 30,31:1
McLeary, James A, 1940, Jl 20,15:2
McLeary, James Harvey, 1914, Ja 6,13:3
McLeavy, Michael P, 1953, D 31,19:5
MacLeay, Alfred A, 1939, Je 3,15:5
MacLeay, Francis R, 1949, Jl 22,19:3
McLeay, George, 1955, S 14,35:5
MacLeay, James W R, 1943, Mr 7,38:3
Macleay, Lachlan, 1952, N 2,88:4
McLeer, Edward Jr, 1944, Ja 28,17:3
McLeer, James, 1922, Ja 16,13:4
McLeer, James Mrs, 1909, F 25,7:4
McLees, William H (cor, F 12,27:1), 1953, F
MacLehose, Maitland, 1955, O 25,33:5
MacLeish, Andrew Mrs, 1947, D 20,17:6
MacLeish, Bruce Mrs, 1961, Ja 24,29:5
McLeish, James A, 1940, My 9,23:4
McLeish, Robert, 1941, My 30,15:6

McLellan, Archibald, 1917, Jl 19,11:6
McLellan, Asahel W, 1943, Ap 27,23:4
McLellan, G B, 1932, F 2,32:1
McLellan, George H, 1939, Jl 17,19:4
McLellan, Howard H, 1958, My 13,29:2
McLellan, Howard H Mrs, 1966, My 2,37:2
McLellan, Hugh D, 1953, Je 21,84:5
Maclellan, J Joseph Mrs, 1951, F 6,27:2
McLellan, James D, 1962, Ap 6,36:1
McLellan, John D, 1938, Je 4,15:3
McLellan, Norman, 1946, F 3,40:1
McLellan, William, 1954, O 24,88:6
McLellan, William J, 1942, Jl 3,17:2; 1948, Mr 30,23:1
McLellan, William W, 1960, Ap 12,33:4
McLelland, Edward S, 1943, Je 27,32:3
McLelland, Thomas, 1941, Mr 2,42:4
McLemore, Albert S Col, 1921, Jl 15,11:6
McLemore, Baskerville Y, 1941, Ag 23,13:6
McLemore, Henry, 1968, Je 24,37:4
McLemore, J H, 1953, Ag 21,17:3
McLenaghen, J O, 1950, Je 25,70:1
McLenan, John, 1865, Mr 23,2:6
McLendon, Charles C, 1940, N 2,15:4
McLendon, Charles R, 1955, Jl 13,25:4
McLendon, Jeff D, 1954, Jl 10,13:4
McLendon, Lennox P, 1968, Ag 8,33:1
McLenithan, Franklin S, 1953, F 6,19:1
McLennan, A Murray, 1943, Ja 17,45:2
MacLennan, Alex M, 1959, Ja 20,35:5
MacLennan, Alfred L, 1959, Je 7,86:8
McLennan, Colin W, 1941, Ja 8,19:5
MacLennan, Donald, 1953, O 20,29:4
McLennan, Donald D, 1966, Ap 8,31:2
McLennan, Donald R, 1944, O 15,44:4
MacLennan, Dorothy D, 1957, Ap 23,31:3
MacLennan, F P, 1933, N 20,15:4
MacLennan, Francis W, 1947, Ja 30,25:3
MacLennan, Frank P Mrs, 1955, N 17,35:2
McLennan, Fred M, 1944, Ap 30,46:4
MacLennan, Helen M, 1943, Jl 26,19:5
McLennan, Hugh Lt, 1915, My 8,15:5
McLennan, J, 1933, D 22,22:2
McLennan, Jessie, 1962, Jl 29,60:2
MacLennan, John A, 1952, F 6,29:3
McLennan, John S, 1939, S 16,17:5
McLennan, Peter B Justice, 1913, My 9,11:5
MacLennan, Roderick, 1939, Ap 17,17:4
Maclennan, Simon F, 1938, My 18,21:2
McLennan, Stewart P, 1954, Jl 27,21:6
McLennan, Thomas J, 1960, N 24,29:4
MacLennan, William F, 1909, Ag 15,7:3
McLeod, A A, 1902, Ap 20,7:5
McLeod, Alex M, 1962, S 26,39:1
McLeod, Arthur B, 1941, Ag 26,19:2
McLeod, Aubrey S, 1960, Ap 11,31:4
McLeod, Charles M, 1951, O 23,29:5
McLeod, Clarence J, 1959, My 16,23:5
MacLeod, D W, 1901, D 11,9:4
McLeod, Daniel, 1875, Ag 10,5:5
MacLeod, David A, 1937, Jl 13,19:3
MacLeod, Donald C, 1942, O 29,23:4
McLeod, Earl H, 1953, Je 23,29:2
McLeod, Edward H, 1938, Ja 4,23:4
McLeod, Edward J, 1943, O 12,27:4
MacLeod, Elizabeth S, 1939, Ja 16,15:1
MacLeod, Ernest, 1939, D 4,23:3
McLeod, Ezekiel Sir, 1920, Je 13,22:2
McLeod, F J Dr, 1911, Ag 21,9:7
McLeod, Frank H, 1944, O 26,23:5
McLeod, George B, 1958, F 5,27:4
MacLeod, George I, 1968, Ag 26,39:3
MacLeod, George R Mrs, 1950, N 14,32:3
McLeod, Grace, 1962, N 18,85:6
McLeod, Harry F Mrs, 1953, Ag 23,89:1
McLeod, Harry T (Hy), 1964, Ag 18,31:5
McLeod, Harvey Smith, 1923, F 17,13:4
McLeod, Herman L, 1955, Mr 24,32:2
MacLeod, J J R, 1935, Mr 18,17:3
McLeod, James, 1943, Je 13,44:6
McLeod, James W, 1957, F 19,31:1
MacLeod, John L K, 1946, O 30,27:6
MacLeod, John Mrs, 1945, S 15,15:5
McLeod, John Neil Dr, 1874, My 12,12:3
Macleod, John R, 1956, Je 29,21:4
MacLeod, Johnston, 1960, My 25,39:4
McLeod, Keith (will), 1952, Mr 21,21:1
MacLeod, Lewis N, 1948, My 10,21:2
MacLeod, Lincoln W Capt, 1913, Je 23,7:6
MacLeod, Louis H D, 1961, Je 21,37:2
MacLeod, Malcolm J, 1940, O 6,48:3
MacLeod, Murdoch, 1939, Mr 6,15:4
MacLeod, Murdoch C, 1941, Ja 3,19:4
MacLeod, N Mrs, 1927, F 12,15:5
McLeod, Neil, 1938, S 14,23:4
McLeod, Neil Mrs, 1954, My 2,89:2
McLeod, Norman A, 1948, Ja 26,19:3
MacLeod, Norman D, 1963, My 30,17:1
McLeod, Norman H F, 1948, Ja 15,23:3
MacLeod, Norman M, 1956, Je 16,19:6
MacLeod, Norman M Mrs, 1949, F 15,23:2
Macleod, Norman Rev Dr, 1872, Je 18,4:7
McLeod, Norman Z, 1964, Ja 28,31:5
McLeod, Robert H, 1961, My 6,31:5
McLeod, Robert M, 1949, F 7,19:5
McLeod, Samuel D, 1951, My 12,21:2
McLeod, Scott, 1961, N 8,35:1
McLeod, Stewart B, 1947, Ag 8,17:2
McLeod, Stuart C (por), 1944, Ap 17,23:3
MacLeod, Talmadge J, 1941, Ag 11,13:2
McLeod, Thomas, 1960, D 18,84:2
McLeod, Thomas B, 1939, S 15,23:3
McLeod, Thomas C, 1952, D 25,29:3
McLeod, William, 1960, Jl 3,32:5
McLeod, William A, 1937, S 9,23:1; 1945, Ag 7,24:2
MacLeod, William A, 1954, My 31,13:1
McLeod, William E, 1955, Ag 16,49:2
McLeod, William H, 1946, F 8,19:2
MacLeod, William J, 1954, Ap 6,30:3
Macleod, William R, 1957, D 16,29:4
McLernon, Charles, 1942, My 1,19:1
McLester, George W, 1965, Je 5,31:6
McLester, James S, 1954, F 9,27:5
McLester, Judson C Jr, 1965, O 24,87:1
McLester, Judson C Jr Mrs, 1958, Ag 26,29:5
MacLetchie, John G Jr, 1967, S 20,44:1
McLevy, Jasper (will, D 6,45:1), 1962, N 20,35:2
McLevy, Maximilian Mrs, 1949, My 4,29:3
McLewee, Frederick C Gen, 1913, Mr 13,11:5
Maclin, Charles C Mrs, 1962, Mr 16,31:2
McLinn, George (Stoney), 1953, Mr 9,29:3
McLintock, William, 1947, My 9,22:3; 1957, Je 19,35:3
Maclise, Deming G, 1942, O 31,15:5
McLochlin, R E, 1957, N 9,27:5
Macloskie, George Dr, 1920, Ja 6,15:1
McLoud, Anson, 1958, Jl 25,19:2
McLough, L A, 1927, F 25,21:5
McLoughlin, Allan V, 1962, Ja 15,27:5
McLoughlin, Bridget G Mrs, 1940, Ap 12,24:2
McLoughlin, D Maujer, 1915, Ja 4,11:5
McLoughlin, F Eugene, 1966, N 21,45:2
McLoughlin, F O X, 1936, Je 30,19:3
McLoughlin, F T Rev, 1865, Ag 5,4:6
McLoughlin, Fergus M, 1957, O 23,33:3
McLoughlin, Francis J, 1961, Ja 22,84:4
McLoughlin, Gerald, 1937, Ja 28,25:4
McLoughlin, Henry W Rev, 1937, My 21,21:5
McLoughlin, James, 1947, D 5,25:2
McLoughlin, James (Diamond Jim), 1955, F 8,27:2
McLoughlin, James J, 1961, S 7,35:2
McLoughlin, James W, 1950, F 20,25:2
McLoughlin, John, 1905, Ap 29,11:6; 1922, Je 28,15:5; 1945, Jl 1,18:1
McLoughlin, John J, 1953, Jl 11,11:5
McLoughlin, John P Mrs, 1960, My 8,88:7
McLoughlin, Joseph F, 1946, My 31,23:2; 1956, Ap 2, 23:5
McLoughlin, Joseph P, 1950, Je 20,27:2
McLoughlin, Lamont, 1939, Je 18,38:2
McLoughlin, Martha Mrs, 1940, D 22,31:1
McLoughlin, Maurice E, 1957, D 12,29:2
McLoughlin, Richard J, 1949, Ap 29,23:5
McLoughlin, Robert E Jr, 1964, Je 11,33:5
McLoughlin, Stephen E, 1950, N 14,31:1
McLoughlin, Thomas P, 1939, My 24,23:2
McLoughlin, Thomas P Rev, 1913, F 18,13:5
McLoughlin, William, 1951, Ap 28,32:2
McLoughlin, William A Rev, 1910, S 7,9:6
McLoughlin, William J, 1946, O 29,25:2
McLoughlin, William P, 1923, Ag 5,26:3
McLoughry, Thomas J, 1953, S 11,21:1
McLouglin, Erwin R, 1968, D 18,47:1
McLouth, Donald B (will, Jl 23,17:1), 1954, Jl 11, 72:5
McLucas, Walter S Mrs, 1952, My 9,23:2
McLucas, Walter Scott, 1953, F 6,19:3
McLuckie, William, 1946, Mr 28,25:5
McLuke, Luke (Jas S Hastings), 1921, Je 4,13:6
McLure, James N Mrs, 1947, Ap 25,21:2
Maclure, John, 1938, N 18,22:3
McLure, Norman R, 1941, Ja 23,21:5
McLurin, George W Mrs, 1966, Ag 23,39:2
McLuskey, Peter Mrs, 1951, D 16,90:1
Macluskie, John, 1937, D 27,15:2
McMackin, James J, 1942, Ap 7,21:4
McMacklin, Daniel J Msgr, 1922, Jl 13,13:2
McMahan, James I, 1951, Ap 5,29:5
McMahan, John L, 1950, D 4,29:4
McMahan, John V, 1944, Mr 28,19:1
McMahon, A Philip (por), 1947, Je 22,52:4
McMahon, Albert J, 1948, Ag 11,22:2
McMahon, Aloysius, 1941, Ap 15,23:5
McMahon, Anna Mrs, 1938, F 24,19:1
McMahon, Arlina D, 1939, O 18,26:3
McMahon, Arnold J, 1955, Je 5,85:1
McMahon, Arthur J, 1950, Ag 20,76:3
McMahon, Austin J, 1947, O 2,27:3
McMahon, Austin J Mrs, 1940, Je 8,15:5
McMahon, Bernard C, 1961, Ap 22,25:2
McMahon, Brien, 1952, Jl 29,1:6
McMahon, Catherine H Mrs, 1940, Mr 29,21:5
MacMahon, Cecil H, 1953, Ag 20,27:2
McMahon, Charles A, 1942, N 9,23:4
McMahon, Charles B, 1968, My 3,47:3
McMahon, Charles E, 1953, F 3,20:3
MacMahon, Cornelius G, 1957, O 31,28:1
McMahon, D F, 1927, S 21,29:5
McMahon, Daniel F, 1907, N 7,9:6; 1947, Ap 5,19:2
McMahon, Daniel Mrs, 1949, F 7,19:3
McMahon, Dennis, 1902, N 21,9:5
McMahon, E W, 1936, D 7,23:1
McMahon, Eaver, 1947, N 10,29:3
McMahon, Edmond, 1949, F 17,23:3
McMahon, Edmund J, 1945, Jl 15,15:5
McMahon, Edward J, 1950, Ap 17,24:2; 1957, Jl 1,23:4
MacMahon, Farren, 1946, Ag 2,19:4
McMahon, Francis C, 1955, My 11,31:1
McMahon, Francis J, 1945, Mr 15,23:2; 1953, S 26, 17:2
McMahon, Frank, 1939, D 1,23:3; 1956, Jl 26,25:2
McMahon, Frank J Mrs, 1952, O 2,29:4
McMahon, Frank Mrs, 1911, Je 29,11:4
McMahon, Frederick J, 1954, Je 3,27:2
McMahon, Harry T, 1959, S 9,41:3
McMahon, Henry, 1949, D 30,20:2
McMahon, Hugh B, 1939, Je 17,15:4
MacMahon, Hugh F E, 1939, F 20,17:1
McMahon, J Francis, 1944, Ap 9,33:2
McMahon, J Fred, 1956, My 30,21:5
MacMahon, J Gratton Judge, 1923, S 5,15:3
McMahon, J J, 1933, Ja 1,15:1
McMahon, J Raymond, 1946, S 4,23:5
McMahon, James, 1913, D 11,11:4; 1939, N 30,21:5; 1941, Je 15,36:7
McMahon, James A, 1950, My 9,29:4
McMahon, James A Sr, 1944, Mr 23,19:1
McMahon, James B, 1910, Mr 4,9:5
McMahon, James H, 1937, S 5,II,6:5; 1940, Je 21,22:2
McMahon, James J, 1925, My 19,21:3
McMahon, James M, 1940, Mr 15,23:2
McMahon, James W, 1943, F 8,20:3
McMahon, James W Sr Mrs, 1958, Je 6,23:3
McMahon, John, 1941, S 16,23:4
MacMahon, John, 1953, Jl 22,27:5
McMahon, John A, 1942, Ap 13,15:5
McMahon, John D, 1955, Ap 8,21:3
McMahon, John E Jr Mrs, 1944, My 31,19:1
McMahon, John E Maj-Gen, 1920, Ja 31,11:5
McMahon, John F, 1947, Ja 17,31:4
McMahon, John G, 1955, Jl 25,19:5
McMahon, John H, 1947, F 23,53:3
McMahon, John J, 1949, Ap 14,25:2
McMahon, John J (Sadie), 1954, F 22,19:5
McMahon, John J, 1954, O 20,29:5; 1959, Jl 7,33:5; 1961, N 26,88:4
McMahon, John J Jr Mrs, 1950, Ag 28,17:5
McMahon, John J Sr, 1946, Ja 3,19:2
McMahon, John M, 1957, Mr 8,25:3
McMahon, John P, 1949, Mr 5,18:2
McMahon, John R Mrs, 1942, Jl 20,13:4
McMahon, John Rev, 1937, Jl 2,21:4
McMahon, John S, 1950, S 16,19:4
McMahon, John T, 1950, N 29,33:2
McMahon, John W, 1959, Ag 3,25:5
McMahon, Joseph C, 1951, O 27,19:7
McMahon, Joseph F, 1944, Ja 12,23:4; 1966, Ag 31, 40:3
McMahon, Joseph H (por), 1939, Ja 7,15:1
McMahon, Joseph J, 1938, S 16,22:3
McMahon, Joseph Mrs, 1939, O 19,23:5
McMahon, Katherine E, 1924, N 11,23:2
McMahon, Lawrence S, 1960, Ag 13,15:3
McMahon, Leon J, 1948, Ap 23,23:3
McMahon, Leonard, 1955, S 5,11:5
McMahon, Lillian J, 1948, Ja 28,23:6
McMahon, Lillian Mrs, 1937, O 20,23:6
McMahon, Louis C, 1944, F 4,15:5
MacMahon, M E P M de, 1893, O 18,9:5
McMahon, Margaret M, 1953, Ja 5,21:3
McMahon, Margaret Mrs, 1907, Jl 15,7:7
McMahon, Mark L, 1962, Ag 23,29:4
McMahon, Marshal, 1870, S 9,5:5
McMahon, Marshall A, 1962, N 23,30:2
McMahon, Martin J, 1949, D 30,19:3
McMahon, Martin Mrs, 1950, My 6,15:5
McMahon, Martin T Judge, 1906, Ap 22,9:1
MacMahon, Mary Mrs, 1968, D 1,60:3
McMahon, Maurice, 1960, S 24,46:7
McMahon, Michael J, 1948, Mr 16,27:2
McMahon, Nellie G, 1948, O 25,23:5
McMahon, Pat J, 1954, O 10,1:2
McMahon, Patrick H, 1953, Mr 14,15:4
McMahon, Patrick S, 1923, Ja 22,15:6
MacMahon, Paul W A, 1957, F 22,21:1
McMahon, Raymond, 1964, F 1,23:4
McMahon, Regina A, 1954, D 22,23:4
McMahon, Richard D, 1945, Ap 7,15:3
McMahon, Richard G, 1950, Mr 28,31:4
McMahon, Roderick (Jess), 1954, N 22,23:3
McMahon, Roderick L, 1937, Mr 23,23:4
McMahon, Roger F P, 1956, Jl 6,21:4
McMahon, Stephen (Rev Bro Justin), 1912, F 29,11:5
McMahon, Sylvester L, 1944, Ap 26,19:1
McMahon, T J, 1939, My 25,25:4
McMahon, Thomas A, 1949, Ap 2,15:5
McMahon, Thomas A Mrs, 1947, Mr 20,27:4
McMahon, Thomas F, 1944, Ap 24,19:6
McMahon, Thomas J, 1941, F 8,15:2; 1947, Ja 2,27:4; 1948, F 21,13:2; 1949, F 10,27:3; 1951, Je 18,23:5; 1956, D 7,27:5

McMahon, Thomas R, 1946, O 29,26:2
McMahon, Thomas W, 1941, O 8,23:4
McMahon, Tim, 1915, D 18,11:5
McMahon, Tom, 1943, Ja 26,19:4; 1952, O 5,88:7
McMahon, W H, 1882, N 22,5:4
McMahon, William F, 1948, S 22,31:3
McMahon, William H, 1940, N 6,23:3; 1941, N 7,24:2
McMahon, William H Jr Dr, 1968, S 2,19:2
McMahon, William H Sr Mrs, 1964, Ap 29,41:1
McMahon, William J, 1941, My 21,23:4
McMahon, William S, 1955, S 5,11:2
McMahon, Willie, 1910, O 24,9:5
McMahon (Sister Maria Elena), 1968, O 19,37:4
McMaken, J G Ex-Sen, 1907, Jl 6,7:4
McMakin, Lewis, 1962, Ag 16,27:1
McMakin, Ralph B, 1949, My 21,13:5
McManaman, Edward P, 1964, Jl 19,64:2
McManamon, J Emmett, 1954, Ag 7,13:4
McManamy, Frank (por), 1944, O 5,23:1
McManamy, Robert Jr, 1950, D 23,15:5
MacManaway, Godfrey, 1951, N 4,86:4
McMane, Frederick, 1953, Mr 29,93:1
McMane, Frederick Mrs, 1953, F 24,25:1
McMane, William I, 1952, Jl 18,19:4
McMane, William J Mrs, 1959, F 28,19:5
McManis, Rumana K, 1942, O 11,56:6
McMann, Joseph P, 1941, D 20,19:2
MacMann, Peter, 1952, Mr 30,93:2
McMannis, William T, 1940, Jl 15,15:5
McMannus, John H, 1940, Ja 30,19:3
McMannus, John P, 1940, F 8,23:3
McManus, Agnes Mrs, 1959, N 17,35:4
McManus, Ambrose, 1941, Je 14,17:4
McManus, C E, 1940, Ja 17,21:4
McManus, Catherine, 1944, Je 27,19:7
McManus, Charles A Mrs, 1947, Ja 1,34:3
McManus, Charles E (por), 1946, Je 4,23:4
McManus, Charles Everett, 1924, F 21,17:6
McManus, Charles M, 1951, Ag 3,21:6
McManus, Charles T, 1953, Mr 15,93:2
McManus, Charles W, 1941, S 1,15:3
McManus, Christopher R, 1951, N 3,17:2
McManus, Edward, 1937, N 15,23:3
McManus, Edward C, 1951, My 9,33:2
McManus, Edward F, 1940, Mr 30,15:2
McManus, Edward Joseph, 1953, F 14,17:4
McManus, Edward Mrs, 1946, Je 10,21:5
McManus, Edward P, 1944, Jl 29,13:6
McManus, Emma G, 1953, Ag 19,29:4
McManus, Francis B, 1964, Ag 27,33:4
McManus, Frank E, 1960, Jl 28,27:5
McManus, George, 1954, O 23,15:2
McManus, George A, 1940, Ag 30,38:1
McManus, Harry E, 1947, F 8,17:4
McManus, Helen M, 1953, My 14,29:2
McManus, Helen T, 1942, S 21,15:6
McManus, Helen V, 1950, O 17,31:3
McManus, Hugh J Rev, 1937, Je 18,21:2
McManus, Hugh P, 1955, Jl 7,27:1
McManus, James A, 1948, O 22,25:1
McManus, James E Mrs, 1944, Ja 26,19:5
McManus, James G, 1958, S 7,87:2
McManus, James P, 1961, D 24,37:1; 1962, Je 12,37:3
McManus, James W, 1953, S 25,21:5
McManus, John A, 1960, O 9,86:6
McManus, John H, 1941, S 7,51:4; 1961, My 15,31:5
McManus, John J, 1938, D 23,19:5; 1939, Ag 30,17:3; 1944, S 9,15:5; 1944, O 12,27:2; 1946, D 24,17:5; 1955, S 9,23:5
McManus, John J Capt, 1937, My 24,19:2
McManus, John J Jr, 1966, Ja 31,39:4
McManus, John L, 1940, My 27,19:3
McManus, John P C, 1938, Je 23,21:3
McManus, John T, 1948, N 30,28:2; 1961, N 23,31:3; 1966, S 18,84:6
McManus, John T Mrs, 1950, F 23,27:4
McManus, Joseph K, 1967, S 4,21:5
McManus, Joseph V, 1956, D 14,29:5
McManus, Julia Mrs, 1945, D 24,15:2
McManus, Lawrence J, 1967, My 18,47:4
McManus, Margaret Mrs, 1942, Ap 9,19:2
McManus, Maria Mrs (funl, D 17,9:5), 1907, D 14, 9:4
McManus, Mary C Mrs, 1942, Jl 24,19:4
McManus, Mary G, 1958, Ap 30,33:4
McManus, Matthew P, 1950, Ap 21,23:4
McManus, Michael Augustine Rev Dr, 1909, N 17,9:5
McManus, Michael T, 1942, Ag 9,43:2
McManus, Myles, 1950, Ap 18,31:3
McManus, Myles J, 1943, Jl 19,15:3
McManus, Nathaniel J, 1964, Jl 23,27:3
McManus, Neil J, 1944, D 2,13:6
McManus, Nicholas A, 1962, Mr 26,31:1
McManus, Owen, 1919, Jl 26,9:6
McManus, Peter, 1938, S 5,15:3
McManus, Ralph D, 1950, Ap 19,29:5
McManus, Richard Capt, 1875, S 13,4:7
McManus, Richard G, 1965, D 27,23:7
McManus, Robert C, 1946, S 24,29:3
McManus, Sallie, 1945, N 25,49:1
MacManus, Seumas, 1960, O 24,53:8
MacManus, Seumas Mrs, 1962, S 26,39:3
McManus, T F Father, 1904, F 21,7:2
McManus, T J, 1926, Jl 31,11:5
McManus, Terence, 1903, My 16,9:6
MacManus, Terence Bellow (funl, N 21,2:5), 1861, O 19,5:2
McManus, Terence J, 1950, My 20,15:1
MacManus, Theodore F, 1940, S 13,23:4
McManus, Thomas F, 1938, N 15,23:4
McManus, Thomas J, 1937, Ag 3,23:5
McManus, Thomas W, 1942, F 3,19:3; 1945, Ja 3,17:3
MacManus, Tomas, 1945, S 21,21:5
McManus, Valentine J, 1941, Ap 12,15:1
McManus, Venerano P, 1940, S 25,27:4
McManus, Walter D, 1939, Ag 18,19:3
McManus, William F, 1939, Je 14,23:5
MacMartin, Archibald, 1881, My 8,7:1
McMartin, Charles, 1954, S 16,29:5
McMartin, Duncan, 1914, My 15,15:5
MacMartin, James M, 1955, Je 4,15:4
MacMartin, Malcolm, 1920, Je 3,11:5
McMartin, Willis F, 1967, Ag 26,27:4
MacMaster, Amelia K, 1956, Jl 12,23:3
McMaster, Andrew L, 1937, Ap 28,23:6
McMaster, Arthur C, 1963, Ap 4,47:3
MacMaster, Donald Lady, 1923, Je 8,19:5
Macmaster, Donald Sir, 1922, Mr 4,15:4
McMaster, Edward A, 1939, Jl 3,13:6
McMaster, Frederick D, 1954, N 29,25:3
McMaster, J A, 1886, D 30,5:3
McMaster, John D Mrs, 1950, Ap 5,31:2
McMaster, Juliet, 1941, N 23,53:3
MacMaster, Maxwell, 1945, S 13,23:5
McMaster, Robert, 1948, Ag 18,25:5
MacMaster, Ronald K, 1968, S 19,47:1
McMaster, Ross H, 1962, Ja 4,33:2
McMaster, S Y Rev Dr, 1875, N 6,1:6
McMaster, Samuel, 1952, D 11,33:4
McMaster, William H, 1962, N 15,37:2
McMaster, William H Mrs, 1964, Ap 17,32:5
McMasters, William H, 1968, Mr 2,29:2
McMath, Francis C, 1938, F 14,17:3
McMath, Robert E, 1968, Mr 23,31:5
McMath, Robert R, 1962, Ja 4,33:1
McMaugh, Stephen J, 1924, My 14,19:5
McMaurtrie, William J, 1946, Mr 23,13:6
McMechan, Frank H, 1939, Je 30,19:4
McMechen, Edgar C, 1953, Jl 19,56:7
McMeehan, Andrew, 1904, O 8,9:5
McMeekan, Walter, 1964, D 16,43:3
McMeekin, Lewis S, 1944, D 13,23:4
McMeekin, Robert A, 1940, Ag 4,33:2
McMein, Neysa (por), 1949, My 13,23:1
McMenamin, Bernard V, 1948, Ag 8,56:7
McMenamin, Cornelia V, 1947, Ja 30,25:5
McMenamin, George F, 1957, S 7,19:3
McMenamin, Hugh L, 1947, Jl 28,15:2
McMenamin, Hugh R Sr Mrs, 1956, My 5,19:3
McMenamin, James A, 1956, Je 14,33:3
McMenamin, James Jr, 1942, Jl 14,20:5
McMenamin, John J, 1944, Jl 9,35:3
McMenamin, S J, 1945, O 3,19:4
McMenamy, Francis X, 1949, Ja 22,13:4
McMenamy, James L Jr, 1954, Ja 5,27:3
McMeniman, Patrick T, 1954, Je 8,27:1
McMenimen, Robert A (por), 1947, Jl 31,21:1
McMenimen, Walter L, 1941, F 18,24:2
McMenimen, William V, 1965, D 26,69:1
McMenimen, William V Mrs, 1966, My 30,19:3
McMenimon, John A, 1947, D 24,21:1
McMenomy, Thomas A, 1949, Mr 3,25:2
McMichael, Charles P Lt, 1918, Ja 24,9:4
McMichael, Clayton, 1906, Ap 18,11:6; 1958, Ja 4,15:3
McMichael, Clayton Fotteral, 1907, S 29,9:7
McMichael, Emory, 1940, D 9,19:5
McMichael, Guy H Jr, 1942, Ap 2,21:4
McMichael, Joe W, 1944, F 13,18:4
McMichael, Maxwell, 1946, D 2,25:4
McMichael, Morton, 1879, Ja 7,5:4; 1904, Mr 29,9:6
McMichael, Orville W Dr, 1924, O 3,21:4
McMichael, Richard, 1903, Je 9,9:6
McMichael, Robert C, 1957, F 7,27:6
McMichael, Stanley L, 1950, Jl 30,60:1
McMichael, Thomas H, 1938, Je 24,19:2
McMichael, William P Col, 1909, My 2,11:5
McMichall, Isaac, 1911, F 23,9:4
McMicken, Edgar G, 1950, O 22,94:6
McMickle, Ernest, 1961, Jl 6,29:3
Macmillan, A, 1896, Ja 26,3:3
MacMillan, A Stirling, 1955, Ag 8,21:2
McMillan, Albert C, 1924, F 8,19:5
Macmillan, Alexander H, 1966, Ag 28,92:5
McMillan, Alvin N (Bo), 1952, Ap 1,29:1
McMillan, Andrew Mrs, 1953, Je 3,31:1
McMillan, Arch, 1948, Ja 18,61:1
McMillan, Archie B, 1947, My 5,23:5
McMillan, Arthur C, 1947, Ap 6,60:2
McMillan, Arthur C Mrs, 1953, F 22,61:2
MacMillan, Arthur D, 1938, Ja 18,23:4
Macmillan, Arthur Tarleton, 1968, Ag 14,39:2
MacMillan, Cargill, 1968, O 17,47:5
McMillan, Charles, 1943, My 22,13:2
McMillan, Charles L, 1949, Ag 10,22:2
MacMillan, Chrystal, 1937, S 22,27:3
McMillan, Claude L, 1961, F 13,27:4
McMillan, D H, 1933, Ap 15,13:6
McMillan, D W, 1936, Ag 4,19:1
Macmillan, Daniel, 1965, D 7,47:2
McMillan, Daniel A, 1946, Je 29,19:3
Macmillan, Daniel D Mrs, 1957, My 14,29:5
McMillan, Daniel H, 1908, Je 5,7:4
McMillan, Daniel Lady, 1923, F 3,13:4
McMillan, David K, 1951, Jl 28,11:6
McMillan, Dayton, 1958, My 16,5:6
McMillan, Donald, 1938, Ap 20,23:3
MacMillan, Dorothy J, 1949, F 9,27:2
McMillan, Duncan J (por), 1939, Je 28,21:5
MacMillan, Ebenezer, 1944, N 2,19:4
McMillan, Edward J, 1964, D 11,39:3
MacMillan, Edward M, 1952, D 4,35:5
McMillan, Emma, 1942, Ap 12,44:6
McMillan, Ernest H, 1951, My 22,31:3
MacMillan, Estelle, 1942, O 22,21:3
Macmillan, F O, 1936, Je 2,27:3
Macmillan, Flavius Mrs, 1948, Ag 18,25:4
McMillan, Florence, 1965, S 13,35:2
McMillan, Francis W, 1947, Ap 14,27:1
McMillan, Frank, 1953, Ja 23,19:2
McMillan, Frank A (por), 1947, D 13,15:2
MacMillan, Frederick Mrs, 1943, Ap 14,23:4
Macmillan, G A, 1936, Mr 4,21:3
McMillan, George Scholefield, 1968, O 27,82:8
McMillan, H George Mrs, 1958, My 1,31:3
McMillan, Harold G, 1950, F 28,29:5
Macmillan, Harold Mrs, 1966, My 22,86:2
McMillan, Harry D, 1956, F 24,25:3
McMillan, Herbert R, 1945, Ja 15,19:4
McMillan, Howard I, 1960, N 24,29:4
MacMillan, Hugh P, 1952, S 6,17:1
MacMillan, Hugh R Jr, 1957, O 7,27:1
McMillan, J W Gen, 1903, Mr 10,9:6
MacMillan, James H, 1958, Ag 14,29:2
McMillan, James T, 1946, S 5,27:4
McMillan, John (por), 1939, S 23,17:5
McMillan, John, 1942, Ap 27,15:6
MacMillan, John, 1951, Je 6,31:3
McMillan, John A, 1949, Ja 7,21:3
MacMillan, John A, 1952, Je 9,23:6
McMillan, John B Mrs, 1963, N 26,37:5
McMillan, John F Mrs, 1962, Ap 16,29:3
McMillan, John H, 1944, O 22,46:3
MacMillan, John H, 1947, Ja 22,23:3; 1960, D 24,
McMillan, John L, 1946, S 20,31:4
McMillan, John M, 1957, O 8,35:4; 1962, Ag 17,2
McMillan, John Mrs, 1962, Jl 21,19:2
MacMillan, John W Mrs, 1940, S 2,15:4
Macmillan, Joshua, 1965, Ap 27,75:4
Macmillan, Kerr D (por), 1938, Mr 15,23:1
MacMillan, Lida Mrs, 1940, Mr 31,44:7
MacMillan, Lincoln, 1950, S 13,27:4
McMillan, Margaret S Mrs, 1962, O 16,39:3
McMillan, Mark, 1967, O 4,47:2
McMillan, Mary, 1956, N 29,35:2
MacMillan, Newton, 1920, D 10,15:4
McMillan, Norman, 1942, O 30,19:1
MacMillan, Norman, 1950, Ag 22,27:3
MacMillan, Peter, 1943, Mr 21,27:1
McMillan, Peter, 1954, Ag 5,23:3
McMillan, Philip Hamilton, 1919, O 5,22:4
McMillan, Robert, 1945, Mr 10,17:6; 1948, Ja 1, 1948, N 15,25:1
McMillan, Robert J, 1941, O 28,23:3
McMillan, Samuel, 1924, My 8,19:5
McMillan, T F, 1930, Jl 7,19:3
McMillan, Thomas A, 1959, S 3,27:5
McMillan, Thomas S, 1939, S 30,17:6
MacMillan, Violet (Mrs J H Folger), 1953, D
McMillan, W Northrup Sir, 1925, Mr 24,23:4
MacMillan, Wade Mrs, 1949, S 22,31:3
McMillan, Walter C, 1959, Ap 25,21:4
McMillan, Walter K, 1962, D 8,27:4
McMillan, Webster C, 1951, N 25,86:5
McMillan, William D, 1948, Ag 29,56:5
MacMillan, William D, 1948, N 16,29:5
McMillan, William D Mrs, 1948, N 21,88:2
MacMillan, William J P, 1957, D 8,88:5
MacMillan, Wm Mrs, 1960, Jl 24,64:3
McMillan, William P, 1907, F 22,9:6
McMillan, William R, 1942, Je 27,13:3
McMillen, Charles R, 1953, F 3,25:5
McMillen, Charles R Mrs, 1950, Ag 16,29:4
McMillen, Clara B, 1957, My 3,27:3
McMillen, Clifford L, 1951, Ap 13,23:3
McMillen, David, 1941, My 29,19:5
MacMillen, Frank H, 1948, N 18,27:3
McMillen, Fred E, 1959, S 18,31:1
McMillen, Harlow, 1939, Je 9,21:5
McMillen, Henry C, 1937, Ag 7,6:6
McMillen, James Mrs, 1964, My 4,29:4
McMillen, Rolla C, 1961, My 7,86:2
McMillin, B, 1933, Ja 9,19:1
McMillin, Benton Mrs (por), 1949, F 26,15:4
McMillin, Emerson, 1904, N 17,1:1; 1922, Je 2
McMillin, John M, 1951, D 28,21:3
McMillin, Marion M, 1924, Ja 26,13:2
McMillin, Mina M, 1947, O 21,23:2
MacMinn, Clarence A, 1946, D 12,29:2
McMinn, William H, 1952, Je 5,31:2

McMonagle, Dewitt, 1942, Ja 1,25:5
McMonagle, Harvey D, 1941, My 11,44:5
McMonigal, Richard S, 1957, Mr 9,19:4
McMonigle, Earl E, 1946, Je 12,27:1
McMonigle, Timothy F, 1946, Jl 29,21:3
MacMonigle, William D, 1947, D 2,29:3
MacMonnies, Frederick W (por), 1937, Mr 23,23:1
MacMonnies, Juliana E Mrs, 1910, Je 6,7:4
McMorran, David W, 1945, Ja 10,23:5
MacMorran, Joe, 1955, Mr 30,29:4
McMorris, Charles H, 1954, F 13,13:1
MacMorris, Earnest, 1955, Ap 28,29:3
McMorris, Joseph, 1942, Ag 4,19:3
McMorrough, John, 1957, F 16,17:4
McMorrow, Charles P, 1943, Ja 5,19:5
McMorrow, F J, 1963, Ag 25,83:1
McMorrow, J Walter, 1954, D 27,17:4
McMorrow, John T, 1948, O 9,19:4
McMorrow, Patrick, 1915, F 24,9:6
McMorrow, Phil J, 1948, D 27,21:3
McMorrow, Thomas, 1957, N 19,30:1
MacMullan, Edward J Mrs, 1966, Je 13,39:4
McMullan, Harry, 1955, Je 25,15:2
McMullan, James, 1956, My 12,19:2
McMullen, Albert R (por), 1947, N 26,23:3
McMullen, Anthony J Rev, 1968, Ag 7,43:3
McMullen, Charles S, 1956, Mr 13,27:3
McMullen, Charles S Mrs, 1959, Ap 20,31:1
McMullen, Chester B, 1953, N 4,33:3
McMullen, Clarence, 1944, My 27,15:3
McMullen, Clements, 1959, Ja 10,17:5
MacMullen, David Rev, 1914, My 23,11:5
MacMullen, David W, 1942, O 1,23:3
McMullen, Donald B, 1967, My 29,25:1
Macmullen, Edward A, 1939, Jl 28,17:5
McMullen, Evelyn, 1952, Mr 11,27:6
McMullen, Fayette, 1880, N 10,5:3
McMullen, Francis, 1946, Ag 8,21:4
McMullen, Francis J, 1940, F 16,19:2
McMullen, Hugh A, 1937, N 7,II,9:2
McMullen, J Bp, 1883, Jl 5,5:5
McMullen, J Robert (petition for est adm filed, O 20,53:1), 1946, O 9,27:5
McMullen, James F, 1952, Jl 29,21:4
McMullen, John, 1921, Ag 31,13:3; 1939, S 8,23:4
McMullen, John C, 1947, D 7,76:3
McMullen, John J, 1944, Mr 13,15:3
McMullen, Joseph E, 1959, S 18,31:3
McMullen, Joseph H, 1968, My 3,54:3
McMullen, Kenneth W, 1951, Jl 8,61:2
McMullen, Lavelette J Mrs, 1941, Ap 28,15:4
MacMullen, Lois, 1944, F 13,42:1
McMullen, R S, 1942, Jl 3,17:5
McMullen, Richard C, 1944, F 19,13:6
McMullen, Richard F, 1938, Je 30,23:4
McMullen, Robert M, 1940, Je 15,15:2
McMullen, Vincent J, 1951, D 20,31:3
MacMullen, Wallace, 1943, Ag 11,19:1
McMullen, William, 1955, D 22,23:1
MacMullen, William Mrs, 1953, Je 19,22:3
McMullin, Jessica L Mrs, 1937, Jl 15,19:2
McMullin, John, 1944, S 15,19:4
McMullin, Joseph J, 1961, Ag 26,17:5
McMullin, Melvin, 1951, D 15,13:3
McMullin, Russell A, 1959, O 31,23:6
McMullin, Stewart N, 1924, Ag 15,13:6
McMullin, W Norman, 1949, F 22,23:4
McMullin, Walter G, 1937, Ja 9,17:5
McMullin (Sister Mary Beatrice), 1964, Je 5,31:2
McMultrie, Richard, 1947, Ag 12,23:3
MacMunn, George F, 1952, Ag 25,17:4
McMurdo, James, 1948, F 25,23:2
McMurdy, John H, 1944, My 8,19:2
McMurdy, Robert, 1941, D 4,25:5
MacMurphy, Dempster, 1939, F 23,23:5
McMurphy, Nelson M, 1940, Ja 3,21:3
McMurray, Bartholomew A, 1952, N 1,21:6
McMurray, Charles B, 1940, Ja 26,17:3
MacMurray, Charles F, 1948, Ag 25,25:1
McMurray, Dewitt, 1940, D 17,25:4
MacMurray, Donald, 1938, D 4,60:7; 1939, S 29,23:3
McMurray, Donald D, 1954, S 1,27:2
McMurray, Ebenezer, 1948, Je 22,25:5
McMurray, Eugene A, 1949, Ag 12,17:6
McMurray, Francis M, 1938, My 9,17:5
MacMurray, Fred Mrs, 1953, Je 23,29:4
MacMurray, Fred Mrs (est acctg), 1954, N 2,25:2
McMurray, Frederick S, 1958, S 27,21:4
McMurray, George J, 1961, Ja 10,47:3
McMurray, Gerald R, 1968, F 28,47:4
McMurray, H Albert, 1946, Je 11,23:4
McMurray, Henry Rutgers, 1904, Ap 20,9:5
McMurray, Howard J, 1961, Ag 16,31:2
MacMurray, Hugh H, 1941, N 12,23:2
McMurray, James E, 1943, Jl 2,19:4
MacMurray, James H, 1940, Ag 17,15:6
McMurray, James T, 1938, Ag 19,19:1
McMurray, John G, 1942, S 10,28:3
McMurray, John H Mrs, 1953, S 25,21:2
MacMurray, John R, 1939, Ap 19,23:2
MacMurray, John Van A, 1960, S 26,33:4
McMurray, Joseph P Mrs, 1960, F 18,33:3
MacMurray, Maleta A Mrs, 1965, Ag 5,29:1
McMurray, Orrin, 1945, F 2,19:4
McMurray, Robert K, 1910, Mr 10,9:4
McMurray, T P, 1949, N 18,29:4
McMurray, W F, 1934, Ja 18,21:3
McMurray, Walter J, 1951, O 20,15:3
McMurray, William, 1868, Je 1,5:6
MacMurray, William H, 1941, F 21,19:4
McMurray, William R, 1942, Mr 7,17:2; 1952, Jl 1,23:5
McMurrich, J Playfair, 1939, F 10,23:2
MacMurrough, Francis K, 1938, S 7,25:2
McMurry, Fred R, 1943, Je 29,19:2
McMurry, James A, 1938, F 20,II,9:1
McMurtie, Alfred P, 1944, Ag 31,17:4
McMurtrie, Adnah, 1946, Ag 10,13:6
McMurtrie, Douglas C, 1944, S 30,13:3
McMurtrie, Edith, 1947, Je 1,62:3
McMurtrie, Francis E, 1949, F 24,24:3
McMurtrie, Henry Dr, 1865, My 28,1:1
McMurtrie, William Dr, 1913, My 25,IV,7:7
McMurtry, Alden L, 1924, Jl 27,23:4
McMurtry, Alden L Mrs, 1954, O 27,29:4
McMurtry, Calvin D, 1937, N 15,23:6
McMurtry, Charles Wood Dr, 1914, N 26,13:4
McMurtry, George G, 1915, Ag 7,7:7; 1958, N 24,29:3
McMurtry, Lewis S Dr, 1924, F 2,13:6
McMyler, Howard T, 1953, S 9,29:2
McNab, Alex (por),(cor, Mr 9,40:7), 1941, Mr 8,19:6
McNab, Alex D, 1955, Ap 3,87:2
Macnab, Alex J, 1955, N 6,86:3
McNab, Alex J, 1956, Jl 6,21:2
McNab, Archibald P, 1945, Ap 30,19:5
McNab, Caroline H, 1952, Jl 23,23:2
McNab, G, 1927, D 29,23:5
Macnab, George T, 1941, Ag 2,15:4
McNab, John A, 1915, S 1,9:4
McNab, John L, 1950, Mr 19,92:7
Macnab, William, 1941, S 3,23:3
MacNabb, A L, 1952, F 17,84:3
McNabb, Alvin Ira, 1920, O 13,15:4
McNabb, Charles E, 1949, Ag 6,17:2
McNabb, Daniel Sir, 1937, D 28,22:2
McNabb, Duane T, 1947, O 14,27:2
McNabb, Hilliard, 1960, Ja 30,21:5
McNabb, Joseph H, 1949, Ja 6,23:4
McNabb, Robert C, 1965, Ja 21,31:2
McNabb, Samuel W, 1940, D 5,25:5
McNabb, Stanley Lt, 1915, D 16,15:4
McNabb, Vincent, 1943, Je 18,21:2
McNabb, William A, 1949, Ap 12,29:4
McNaboe, James F, 1941, Ap 11,21:1
McNaboe, John J, 1954, Je 21,23:3
MacNaghten, Frederic F, 1955, N 20,88:4
McNair, Albert D, 1947, My 9,22:3
McNair, Alexander, 1944, Ag 21,15:4
McNair, Andrew, 1905, Mr 19,9:4
McNair, Charles H, 1949, S 19,23:3
McNair, Edward E, 1943, Ja 1,23:3
McNair, Eric, 1949, Mr 13,76:4
McNair, Fred D Rear Adm, 1900, N 29,7:2
McNair, Frederick M, 1940, Je 20,23:5
McNair, Frederick V Jr, 1962, S 3,15:2
MacNair, Harley F, 1947, Je 24,24:2
MacNair, Harley F Mrs, 1942, Ap 25,13:5
McNair, Harry, 1941, O 7,23:6
McNair, Henrietta K Mrs, 1940, My 28,23:2
McNair, Hugh, 1950, F 21,25:4
MacNair, James D, 1946, My 7,21:5
MacNair, Janet, 1954, Jl 13,23:3
MacNair, Jeremiah A, 1952, Je 21,15:4
McNair, John B, 1968, Je 15,35:4
MacNair, John V, 1953, S 9,29:2
McNair, John W, 1968, N 20,47:4
McNair, Joseph V, 1950, S 1,21:2
McNair, Robert J, 1949, Ap 8,26:3; 1959, Ap 6,27:4
McNair, Stephen Y, 1938, Ap 8,19:5
McNair, Walter J, 1914, N 14,11:5
McNair, William J, 1949, Ja 25,24:3
McNair, William N, 1948, S 10,23:4
MacNair, Wilmer Mrs, 1952, Ag 21,19:6
McNairn, James C, 1954, S 11,17:6
McNall, Eugene W, 1949, Jl 24,52:6
McNall, Freeman H, 1940, D 17,25:3
McNall, Marvin L, 1947, Ag 28,23:6
McNall, Robert H Mrs, 1940, F 9,19:5
McNally, Andrew, 1904, My 8,1:6; 1954, My 21,27:3
McNally, Augustin Mrs, 1960, Je 29,33:4
McNally, Charles, 1943, Ap 20,24:2
McNally, Charles F, 1949, Ag 17,23:3
MacNally, Charles J, 1954, Ja 31,88:1
McNally, Daniel A, 1951, Ag 29,25:2
McNally, Edward J, 1937, Ag 6,17:4; 1947, Jl 13,44:2; 1967, N 4,33:1
McNally, Frank M, 1942, Jl 23,19:3
McNally, Frank Sr, 1950, D 28,25:3
McNally, Frederick George, 1907, S 17,11:6
McNally, Frederick L, 1950, Mr 25,13:5
McNally, George W, 1947, N 27,32:2
McNally, Harry, 1946, Jl 5,5:6
McNally, Hugh J, 1948, Ap 4,60:3
McNally, J Harry, 1956, F 24,25:2
McNally, James, 1924, Mr 25,21:4
McNally, James C, 1920, Ag 6,9:6
McNally, James J, 1950, Je 8,31:2
McNally, James J Jr, 1946, Ap 23,21:1
McNally, James Martin Rev Bro, 1953, F 7,15:3
McNally, Jim, 1944, Je 6,17:5
McNally, John Capt, 1937, D 4,17:7
McNally, John J, 1941, S 23,23:5; 1953, My 12,27:4
McNally, John T, 1952, N 19,29:5; 1953, Mr 8,88:3
McNally, Joseph J, 1937, F 4,21:5
McNally, Louis J, 1941, My 16,23:5
McNally, Martin J, 1958, F 4,29:3
McNally, Mary F, 1953, Jl 14,27:2
McNally, Maxwell F, 1949, My 28,15:5
McNally, Patrick Mrs, 1943, My 14,19:4
McNally, Paul A, 1955, Mr 5,17:3
McNally, Raymond A, 1942, N 13,23:5
McNally, Richard J, 1957, Ja 27,84:1
McNally, Robert C, 1941, Mr 21,21:4
McNally, Robert J, 1940, Je 20,23:6
McNally, Theodore S, 1943, My 20,21:3
McNally, Thomas J, 1944, D 8,21:1
McNally, Walter, 1945, Ag 27,19:5
McNally, William D, 1961, Jl 1,17:3
McNally, William P, 1944, D 8,21:2
McNally, William Rev, 1938, Ja 28,21:4
McNally, William T, 1945, Je 26,19:6
McNamara, Adelaide L, 1940, O 19,17:4
McNamara, Agnes, 1951, N 29,33:2
McNamara, Ambrose, 1961, Jl 28,21:3
McNamara, Andrew A, 1958, Jl 7,27:3
McNamara, Carl T, 1955, N 23,23:5
McNamara, Clara N S Mrs, 1964, D 28,29:2
McNamara, Cyrille F, 1963, O 30,39:1
McNamara, Daniel I, 1962, F 21,45:1
McNamara, Daniel L Mrs, 1959, My 31,76:6
McNamara, Edward, 1944, N 10,21:4
McNamara, Edward J, 1948, Ja 18,61:1; 1948, Ap 24, 15:3
McNamara, Francis P, 1944, Jl 4,19:5
McNamara, Francis W, 1938, S 17,17:2
McNamara, Frank H, 1948, My 24,25:3
McNamara, Frank J, 1951, Ag 11,11:5
McNamara, Frank L, 1942, N 28,13:2
McNamara, Frank X, 1957, N 11,29:2
McNamara, George, 1952, Mr 11,27:2
McNamara, George A, 1938, Je 12,39:2
McNamara, George F, 1937, D 5,II,8:7
McNamara, Harley V, 1966, D 24,19:3
MacNamara, Harry, 1958, My 19,25:3
McNamara, Howard, 1940, S 25,27:2
McNamara, James A, 1947, F 11,27:2
McNamara, James B, 1941, Mr 9,38:3
McNamara, James C, 1941, My 18,44:1
McNamara, James E, 1968, Ja 23,43:8
McNamara, James F, 1942, Ag 15,11:6; 1942, D 14, 28:2
McNamara, James G, 1968, O 12,37:1
McNamara, James P, 1942, Ja 9,21:5; 1954, Ap 6,29:4
McNamara, John, 1956, S 10,27:1
McNamara, John A, 1950, Ja 7,18:2
McNamara, John F, 1938, My 27,17:3; 1947, Jl 24, 21:4; 1959, D 6,87:1
McNamara, John G, 1958, D 5,32:1
McNamara, John H, 1937, O 9,19:3
McNamara, John J, 1941, My 8,46:2; 1944, My 28, 34:2; 1944, Je 6,17:2; 1944, S 23,13:3; 1948, Mr 14, 72:2
MacNamara, John J T, 1952, N 20,31:4
McNamara, John M, 1960, N 27,86:3
McNamara, John Mrs, 1951, My 4,27:3
McNamara, John P, 1966, S 10,29:5
McNamara, John S, 1966, F 25,31:3
McNamara, Joseph A, 1959, F 22,89:1
McNamara, Joseph A Mrs, 1965, Mr 31,39:3
McNamara, Joseph H, 1937, Ag 31,23:4
McNamara, Joseph P Mrs, 1957, O 12,19:4
McNamara, Julia R, 1948, Jl 22,23:5
McNamara, Kathleen (Mother Mary Gabriel), 1956, D 27,25:4
McNamara, Lawrence J, 1943, Ap 2,21:4
McNamara, Leo C, 1959, Ap 5,86:7
MacNamara, Lewis P, 1938, My 12,23:2
McNamara, Mary, 1939, My 13,15:4
McNamara, Mary E, 1950, S 19,31:3; 1956, Je 29,21:1
McNamara, Matthew J, 1946, O 25,23:3
McNamara, Matthew J Mrs, 1943, D 17,27:3
MacNamara, Matthew J Mrs, 1950, Mr 31,32:2
McNamara, Michael F Mrs, 1959, Ag 25,31:5
McNamara, Michael J, 1938, Jl 27,17:4; 1949, N 21, 25:4
McNamara, Patrick H, 1954, Je 23,25:1
McNamara, Patrick J, 1942, O 6,23:3
McNamara, Patrick J Msgr, 1912, Ap 16,13:5
McNamara, Patrick V (funl plans, My 4,47:2; funl, My 5,47:1), 1966, My 1,88:1
McNamara, R Reid, 1964, Ap 1,39:3
McNamara, Ray, 1942, O 16,19:2
McNamara, Robert A, 1945, S 18,23:5
McNamara, Robert Rev, 1917, O 7,23:3
Macnamara, Saunderson (F Harcourt), 1955, Ag 4, 25:5
McNamara, Stuart, 1946, O 26,17:3
McNamara, Sylvester J, 1943, F 2,20:3
MacNamara, Thomas, 1923, Ap 27,17:4
McNamara, Thomas F, 1940, D 26,19:3

McNamara, Thomas J, 1946, N 7,31:4; 1952, Ja 9,29:3
McNamara, Thomas L, 1939, Jl 22,15:6
McNamara, Thomas L Jr, 1948, Ja 28,23:4
McNamara, Thomas L Mrs, 1946, Ja 12,15:2
McNamara, Thomas P, 1937, S 19,II,7:3
McNamara, W Brendan, 1951, D 2,91:2
McNamara, William P, 1963, Je 5,41:3
McNamee, Albert P, 1957, Ja 25,21:4
McNamee, Bartlett L, 1955, S 2,17:4
McNamee, Bernard F Mrs, 1954, O 8,23:2
McNamee, Charles F, 1962, Je 12,37:4
McNamee, Charles J, 1964, My 4,29:1
McNamee, Charles R, 1967, Je 6,47:3
McNamee, Daniel F, 1958, Je 16,23:2
McNamee, Daniel V, 1939, My 31,23:4
McNamee, Edgar P, 1951, Jl 10,27:4
McNamee, Frank A Mrs, 1945, My 27,26:2
McNamee, Frank A Sr, 1954, Ag 12,25:3
McNamee, Graham, 1942, My 10,43:1
McNamee, Harold R, 1945, S 25,25:1
McNamee, Henry, 1952, Jl 2,25:3
McNamee, J Msgr, 1927, Ap 15,21:5
McNamee, James B, 1909, My 16,9:5
McNamee, James J, 1941, Ap 14,17:5; 1952, Ap 4,25:4
McNamee, James Vanderbilt Mrs, 1903, Jl 10,7:6
McNamee, John, 1914, Ap 9,11:4
McNamee, John E, 1950, Ja 4,35:4
McNamee, John L, 1938, N 5,19:5
McNamee, Luke, 1952, D 31,15:1
McNamee, Luke B Mrs, 1965, N 22,37:4
McNamee, Peter J Father, 1921, Jl 9,9:6
McNamee, Roger D, 1943, O 4,17:3
McNamee, Ronald J, 1941, Je 18,21:3
McNamee, Susan D Mrs, 1953, N 7,17:1
Macnamee, W Bruce, 1958, Je 6,23:1
McNamee, William H Mrs, 1949, O 10,23:3
McNamee, William J, 1949, My 6,25:4
McNamee, Xavier, 1952, N 23,88:1
McNanamy, Robert J, 1937, F 6,21:4
McNary, Charles L, 1944, F 26,1:2
McNary, Clarence W, 1941, O 22,23:5
MacNary, Harry C, 1968, My 17,44:2
McNary, James E, 1950, My 12,27:4
McNary, James G, 1962, Je 11,31:3
McNary, Thomas C, 1943, Jl 21,15:2
McNaugher, David, 1943, N 26,23:2
McNaugher, John, 1947, D 12,27:1
McNaught, Andrew J, 1943, Je 8,21:5
McNaught, John, 1938, Mr 14,15:6
McNaught, Robert, 1937, N 29,23:5
McNaught, Robert Morgan, 1908, Ap 18,9:6
McNaught, Roy H, 1951, Ja 20,15:3
McNaught, Samuel P, 1958, My 20,33:4
Macnaughtan, Allan Mrs (Myra Kelly), 1910, Ap 1, 11:5
McNaughten, E, 1933, Jl 12,17:6
McNaughton, Andrew G L, 1966, Jl 12,1:6
McNaughton, Arch G, 1949, O 7,27:3
McNaughton, Clarence L, 1943, Jl 8,19:5
McNaughton, Donald S, 1942, Ap 25,13:2
McNaughton, Edward T Sr, 1941, F 9,47:6
McNaughton, George D, 1949, O 10,23:3
Macnaughton, George F, 1938, Ag 10,19:4
McNaughton, Harry, 1967, F 28,34:1
McNaughton, Helen B Mrs, 1952, F 10,93:1
MacNaughton, Herbert J, 1946, Ja 22,28:2
McNaughton, Howard J, 1949, S 22,31:4
McNaughton, J A, 1952, Ap 26,23:1
MacNaughton, James, 1905, D 30,9:6
McNaughton, James, 1949, My 27,21:5
McNaughton, James J, 1956, F 9,32:1
McNaughton, James Mrs, 1944, D 26,19:6
McNaughton, John, 1925, Ja 6,25:5
McNaughton, John A, 1944, Je 2,15:3
McNaughton, John T (funl, Jl 26,39:1), 1967, Jl 20, 1:1
McNaughton, John T Mrs (funl, Jl 26,39:1), 1967, Jl 20,1:1
MacNaughton, Kenneth P, 1960, S 22,27:3
McNaughton, Lynn, 1950, F 9,29:3
MacNaughton, Margaret L, 1957, Jl 9,29:1
McNaughton, Murray W A, 1952, My 17,19:6
McNaughton, Patrick J, 1957, Ja 11,23:3
Macnaughton, Percy M Mrs, 1953, Ag 24,23:6
McNaughton, Stewart, 1943, D 16,27:4
MacNaughton, Stuart, 1940, Jl 23,19:3
McNaughton, Theodore (funl, Jl 26,39:1), 1967, Jl 20,1:1
McNaughton, Walter T, 1942, Jl 8,23:2
McNaughton, William G (por), 1949, F 6,76:5
McNay, Marion K Mrs (will, Ap 26,31:4), 1950, Ap 15,15:5
McNeal, Austin, 1948, S 29,29:3
McNeal, David Mrs, 1947, F 14,21:1
MacNeal, J Barry, 1953, Je 25,27:5
McNeal, J Hector, 1949, N 19,17:6
McNeal, J Hector Mrs, 1952, Ap 5,15:5
McNeal, Kate, 1953, Ja 11,91:3
MacNeal, Lady (por), 1937, S 12,II,7:3
MacNeal, Robert E, 1967, N 3,45:1
McNeal, Sylvester E, 1908, F 11,7:5
McNeal, Thomas A, 1942, Ag 8,11:5
McNeal, William H, 1945, Ap 8,36:1
MacNeal, William J Mrs, 1953, Je 25,27:5
McNealus, William C, 1957, O 20,86:8
McNealy, Raymond W, 1958, Jl 30,29:4
McNear, Alex S, 1940, Jl 21,29:3
McNear, Clinton, 1954, D 21,16:5
McNear, E Denman Mrs, 1955, My 16,23:5
McNear, Egerton B, 1954, D 13,27:5
McNear, Fred W, 1958, Ap 1,31:5
McNear, George P, 1947, Ag 13,23:4
McNear, Jesse, 1938, S 28,25:2
McNear, William F, 1950, F 23,27:4
McNee, John, 1939, Mr 22,23:3
McNee, Robert S, 1947, S 28,60:3
McNeedy, John T, 1948, Ja 13,26:2
McNeeley, Charles M, 1961, My 2,37:3
McNeeley, Frances, 1962, My 12,23:4
McNeely, Anna L Mrs, 1956, Ja 8,87:2
McNeely, Frank A Capt, 1912, S 20,11:6
McNeely, George H, 1945, Ja 3,17:1
McNeely, John, 1948, Ap 8,25:3
McNeely, Richard P, 1950, D 31,42:6
McNeely, William R Mrs, 1959, O 23,29:3
McNeer, Gordon P, 1967, Ja 19,35:3
MacNeice, Louis, 1963, S 4,40:1
McNeice, Peter J, 1958, Je 20,23:3
McNeil, Arch (por), 1941, O 15,21:5
McNeil, Charles A, 1951, S 19,31:2
MacNeil, Charles S J, 1944, N 19,51:5
MacNeil, Daniel B Mrs, 1951, Ja 17,28:3
MacNeil, Douglas H, 1963, My 6,29:5
McNeil, Edwin, 1875, S 14,4:7
McNeil, Esther Mrs, 1907, Ap 21,9:4
McNeil, H Laurence, 1953, Jl 3,19:2
MacNeil, Hamilton Douglas Bentley, 1924, O 10,19:5
MacNeil, Harry Mrs, 1937, My 14,23:1
McNeil, Hector (funl plans, O 13,31:4; funl, O 15,-15:3), 1955, O 12,31:1
MacNeil, Hermon A, 1947, O 4,17:1
McNeil, Hermon A Mrs, 1944, Je 23,19:6
McNeil, Hiram C Dr, 1937, Je 11,23:3
McNeil, James, 1941, O 26,43:1
McNeil, James A, 1939, N 23,27:3
MacNeil, James J, 1944, Ag 29,17:5
MacNeil, James Mrs, 1958, Ap 27,86:1
McNeil, John, 1940, Mr 4,15:3; 1953, My 16,19:4
McNeil, John A, 1964, O 19,33:5
McNeil, John V, 1938, Jl 3,13:3
McNeil, Malcolm, 1923, Je 30,11:4
Macneil, Marie S Mrs, 1952, My 2,25:4
McNeil, Mary E, 1967, N 8,40:2
McNeil, N, 1934, My 26,17:3
McNeil, Norman, 1942, Ap 12,45:1
MacNeil, Norman A, 1940, My 31,19:5
McNeil, Peter G Mrs, 1951, D 31,13:5
McNeil, Robert L, 1967, S 22,47:4
McNeil, S G S, 1936, My 9,15:3
Macneil, Sayre, 1961, D 17,83:2
MacNeil, Stephen, 1943, N 17,25:3
MacNeil, Ward J, 1946, Ag 16,21:3
McNeile, Cyril, 1937, Ag 15,II,7:3
McNeile, Evelyn A Mrs, 1950, Ap 8,13:6
McNeile, H, 1879, Ja 29,5:4
McNeill, Alex, 1954, Ap 19,23:3
McNeill, Angus, 1939, Jl 16,31:4
McNeill, Archibald H, 1951, D 4,33:2
McNeill, Arthur Y, 1959, Jl 24,25:3
MacNeill, Ben D, 1960, My 28,21:5
MacNeill, Charles M, 1923, Mr 19,17:6
McNeill, David R, 1953, Jl 14,27:2
McNeill, Donald J Jr, 1968, Ag 12,35:1
MacNeill, Eoin, 1945, O 16,23:5
McNeill, Ernest, 1938, S 7,3:2
McNeill, Frank, 1960, S 26,33:4
McNeill, George E, 1906, My 20,9:6
McNeill, Herbert H, 1949, Ja 30,60:4
McNeill, J, 1933, Ap 20,17:3
MacNeill, J G S, 1926, Ag 25,21:2
McNeill, James (por), 1938, D 13,25:1
McNeill, James, 1964, Jl 25,19:6
McNeill, James P, 1940, D 16,23:3
McNeill, John, 1952, Ag 6,21:5
McNeill, John C Gen Sir, 1904, My 27,9:6
McNeill, John F, 1962, Mr 10,21:4
McNeill, John F Mrs, 1948, S 13,21:5
MacNeill, John Rev Dr, 1937, F 12,23:6
McNeill, John Sir, 1883, My 18,5:4
McNeill, Joseph, 1950, Ap 18,31:2
McNeill, Lemuel J, 1948, O 19,27:3
McNeill, Malcolm M, 1941, Ag 16,15:6
MacNeill, Neale, 1953, Je 28,61:1
MacNeill, Neale Jr, 1957, D 11,32:1
Macneill, Norman M, 1965, Je 18,35:4
MacNeill, Samuel L, 1942, Ap 10,17:1
McNeill, Thomas W, 1958, Mr 5,31:2
McNeill, W D, 1925, Ja 18,7:1
McNeill, Walter, 1947, S 28,60:4
McNeill, Walter G, 1939, Ja 20,19:3
McNeill, Walter H, 1946, Ja 4,22:2
McNeill, Walter H Jr, 1942, Mr 23,15:2
MacNeille, Clarence T, 1946, D 6,23:1
MacNeille, Raymond, 1961, Ap 8,19:3
McNeillie, J K, 1940, Ap 25,23:3
McNeilly, J H Rev, 1922, S 29,19:6
McNeilly, John C, 1941, Je 17,21:2
McNeir, Forest W, 1957, My 11,21:3
McNeir, George (por), 1941, Je 16,15:1
McNeir, George Mrs, 1944, Mr 10,15:5
MacNeish, Harris F, 1953, S 4,34:1
Macneish, N S, 1964, Ag 25,33:2
McNelis, John F, 1954, Ja 23,13:2
McNelis, John P Mrs, 1951, Jl 23,17:5
McNell, Thomas R, 1917, O 13,13:6
McNellis, Frank, 1950, Ja 18,32:2; 1958, My 9,16:4
McNellis, John E, 1949, My 25,29:4
MacNelly, A C, 1957, N 17,86:2
McNelly, Lindsey S, 1960, O 23,88:7
McNenney, Claudio E, 1949, S 13,29:2
McNerney, James J, 1951, Mr 23,35:4
McNerney, Jerry, 1965, Ja 1,17:2
McNerney, Lawrence M, 1942, Je 3,23:2
McNerney, Neil, 1946, D 24,17:3
McNerney, Patrick J, 1946, Mr 19,27:4
McNerney, William J, 1948, N 18,27:3
McNerny, Evelyn F, 1950, O 14,19:3
McNevin, John C, 1944, Je 16,19:2
McNew, James T L, 1946, D 22,42:4
MacNichol, Archibald F, 1963, My 18,27:3
McNichol, Edward J, 1955, Ap 18,23:4
McNichol, Francis P, 1944, F 2,21:2
McNichol, Harry A, 1937, Mr 16,23:5
McNichol, Harry E, 1906, Jl 21,7:4
McNichol, James P Jr, 1961, Je 20,33:1
McNichol, James P Sen, 1917, N 15,13:4
McNichol, John, 1956, S 3,13:5
McNichol, Michael, 1937, Je 8,25:2
McNicholas, John G, 1951, Mr 14,33:4
McNicholas, John J, 1944, F 8,15:5
McNicholas, John T, 1950, Ap 23,92:3
McNicholas, John W, 1967, Je 15,47:4
McNicholas, Michael T, 1947, My 2,21:4
MacNicholl, Robert Turner Rev, 1908, F 23,7:6
McNichols, Walter, 1949, Mr 27,76:2
MacNicol, Alex M, 1961, Ja 19,29:4
McNicol, Donald M, 1953, S 19,15:6
McNicol, Edward L, 1950, Je 17,15:4
MacNicol, John R, 1950, Je 20,27:1
MacNicol, Kenneth R, 1955, Je 20,21:3
MacNicol, Roy V Mrs, 1941, F 15,15:5
McNicol, T A, 1945, F 8,19:5
McNicol, Thomas J Rev, 1937, Mr 23,23:4
McNicoll, David, 1916, N 28,13:4
McNicoll, Douglas, 1949, O 27,28:2
McNicoll, John G, 1941, Mr 1,15:5
McNicoll, Walter R, 1947, D 26,15:4
McNider, C H Mrs, 1954, Ag 26,27:3
MacNider, Hanford Lt-Gen, 1968, F 18,80:5
MacNider, William D, 1951, Je 2,19:3
McNiece, Duncan A, 1937, D 14,25:1
McNierney, Thomas J, 1938, F 15,25:4
McNiff, Francis J, 1944, Ap 29,15:4
McNiff, John, 1942, Jl 23,19:6
McNiff, Miles F Sr, 1952, Jl 23,23:5
McNiff, William J, 1945, S 2,32:1
McNiff, William T, 1952, D 8,41:4
McNinch, Frank R, 1950, Ap 21,23:3
McNish, James H, 1948, Jl 29,21:2
McNitt, Charles C, 1943, My 15,15:5
McNitt, Esther U, 1941, O 2,25:2
McNitt, Thomas, 1949, S 1,21:2
McNitt, Virgil V, 1964, Je 16,39:1
McNiven, Howard H, 1941, Ap 8,25:2
McNiven, Stuart K, 1952, Ap 24,31:4
McNomee, Harry G, 1959, Ag 1,17:6
McNomee, Harry G Mrs, 1955, Ag 30,27:1
McNulty, Anna L Mrs, 1940, Ap 10,25:1
McNulty, Arthur P, 1961, Je 14,19:3
McNulty, Casimir, 1941, Jl 4,13:5
McNulty, Charles, 1946, S 25,28:2
McNulty, Charles J, 1952, D 9,33:3
McNulty, Daniel A, 1952, My 2,25:5
McNulty, Donald S, 1962, Ja 26,31:2
McNulty, Edward C, 1953, O 16,27:5
McNulty, Eleanor S, 1958, S 14,84:5
McNulty, Frank J, 1962, N 7,39:1
McNulty, Frank P, 1948, Jl 1,23:6
McNulty, G Kneeland, 1944, N 28,23:3
McNulty, George A Sr, 1964, N 23,37:3
McNulty, George W, 1924, Ap 21,17:6
McNulty, Henry A, 1950, Jl 11,31:1
McNulty, Henry A Mrs, 1948, My 19,27:2
McNulty, Hugh J, 1947, Ja 20,25:5
McNulty, James, 1940, My 25,17:2
McNulty, James A, 1947, Ja 29,26:2
McNulty, James D, 1924, N 4,21:1
McNulty, James F, 1938, D 3,19:2
McNulty, James H Mrs, 1956, My 12,19:2
McNulty, James J, 1949, My 31,23:4
McNulty, James J Mrs, 1950, Je 8,32:2
McNulty, James L, 1948, D 19,76:4
McNulty, James W, 1937, F 1,19:2
McNulty, John, 1948, Ag 12,21:2
McNulty, John (funl Ag 2,25:4), 1956, Jl 30,21:1
McNulty, John F, 1943, Je 9,22:2
McNulty, John J, 1963, S 3,33:2
McNulty, John L (funl, Je 2,35:4), 1959, My 28,3
McNulty, John R Maj, 1912, Ja 14,II,16:1

McNulty, Martin J, 1949, Mr 18,25:3
McNulty, Matthew F, 1950, Ag 12,13:3
McNulty, Patrick J, 1943, S 4,13:2
McNulty, Patrick J Mrs, 1951, F 16,25:4
McNulty, Paul S, 1958, S 7,83:6
McNulty, Peter J, 1907, D 13,11:3; 1960, Ag 11,27:1
McNulty, Peter T, 1952, S 17,31:4
McNulty, Raymond P, 1946, My 1,25:5
McNulty, Terence Rev, 1937, O 11,21:5
McNulty, Thomas, 1960, O 13,37:2
McNulty, Thomas A, 1955, Mr 28,27:3
McNulty, Thomas F, 1954, S 19,89:2
McNulty, Thomas J, 1947, S 7,60:3
McNulty, William, 1922, Je 19,15:6
McNulty, William C, 1963, S 27,29:1
McNulty, William J, 1939, S 3,19:3; 1956, Je 1,23:2; 1957, Mr 24,87:1
McNulty, William Mrs, 1962, N 26,29:3
McNulty, William P, 1960, S 22,27:5
McNurney, William F, 1962, Ap 25,39:1
MacNutt, Barry Mrs, 1956, O 1,27:3
McNutt, Cornelius J, 1960, Ag 25,29:3
McNutt, Earl C, 1946, N 9,17:4
Macnutt, Ernest A, 1955, My 11,31:4
McNutt, J Lt-Col, 1881, Ap 17,9:4
McNutt, John C, 1949, D 11,91:4
McNutt, John C Mrs, 1947, Ja 4,15:1
McNutt, Joseph D, 1954, Ag 3,19:4
McNutt, Loran C, 1949, Ja 25,23:1
McNutt, Maxwell, 1946, Ja 4,21:4
McNutt, Patterson, 1948, O 24,78:3
McNutt, Paul V (funl plans, Mr 26,15:4; funl, Mr 29,29:3), 1955, Mr 25,23:1
McNutt, Robert B, 1945, My 16,19:4
McNutt, Willard C, 1938, O 12,27:2
McNutt, William S, 1938, Ja 27,21:4
McNylty, John F, 1953, Mr 29,92:1
MacOdrum, Donald, 1938, Je 21,19:5
MacOdrum, Maxwell, 1955, Ag 3,23:5
McOlwaine, Theodore R, 1908, F 7,7:6
Macomb, A S, 1876, My 9,3:3
Macomb, Christina L, 1945, N 7,23:5
Macomb, David Benton Rear-Adm, 1911, Ja 28,11:5
Macomb, Montgomery Meigs Brig-Gen, 1924, Ja 20, 13:1
Macomb, Thomas J, 1942, Ap 5,41:2
Macomb, W H, 1872, Ag 13,5:5
Macomber, Charles A Mrs, 1961, N 28,37:1
Macomber, Charles F, 1947, S 2,21:3
Macomber, Frank G, 1941, D 19,25:4; 1944, My 23, 23:4
Macomber, Henry W, 1941, Ja 22,21:3
Macomber, Joseph H Jr, 1940, Ja 14,42:7
Macomber, Lewis A, 1946, F 14,25:4
Macomber, M, 1933, Ja 16,15:3
Macomber, Paul Y, 1959, Ja 24,38:6
Macon, Clinton, 1947, Mr 5,25:6
Macondray, Atherton Jr, 1950, Mr 23,29:4
Macormac, Alfred R, 1959, Je 14,86:2
McOwen, Anthony, 1920, O 30,11:4
McOwen, John, 1953, F 6,20:6
McOwen, Joseph A, 1945, Ja 1,22:2; 1947, Je 24,24:2
McOwen, William H, 1948, Mr 10,27:2
Macoy, Earl H, 1940, F 15,19:4
McPadden, William H, 1953, Ja 12,27:1
McParian, Edward C, 1924, My 14,19:5
McParlan, James Mrs, 1958, Ja 30,23:3
McParland, James, 1919, My 20,17:6
McParland, John, 1923, Je 17,11:1
McParland, Patrick V, 1949, Ag 4,23:4
McPartland, Eugene J Sr, 1964, Ja 27,23:4
McPartland, Francis, 1964, D 2,50:8
McPartland, John, 1958, S 16,28:1
McPartland, Patrick F, 1945, Ja 30,19:4
McPartland, Richard, 1941, My 4,53:1
McPartland, Stephen, 1912, Ja 5,13:3
McPartland, William L (Kid), 1953, F 22,60:5
McPartlin, Raymond F, 1951, N 27,31:6
McPartlin, Stephen E, 1949, Je 13,19:3
McPeake, John R, 1948, Je 14,23:3
Macphail, Agnes C, 1954, F 14,92:3
McPhail, Alex, 1956, Mr 27,35:5
Macphail, Andrew, 1938, S 24,17:6
McPhail, Charles E, 1938, My 29,II,6:7
MacPhail, Curtis W, 1939, My 11,25:2
MacPhail, Donald T, 1941, S 18,27:2
MacPhail, Inez T Mrs, 1965, Je 20,72:6
MacPhail, James A G, 1952, S 12,21:2
MacPhail, John D, 1959, My 21,31:1
McPhail, Leonard W, 1957, F 26,29:4
Macphail, Malcolm L, 1940, Ja 6,13:2
MacPhail, Neil (por), 1949, Ap 2,15:6
McPhail, Percy R, 1938, S 18,45:2
MacPhail, Robert B, 1941, F 15,15:1; 1952, S 22,23:3
MacPhail, Simpson, 1952, D 10,35:6
MacPhail, Thomas S, 1954, Ja 14,29:1
McPhail, William R, 1944, N 14,19:5
MacPhail, Winburn L, 1949, D 1,31:3
McPharlin, Paul, 1948, O 1,26:2
McPhartlon, Peter, 1940, N 21,29:2
McPhaul, Wilbur A, 1939, Ag 2,19:4
MacPhedran, Alex, 1954, Ap 23,27:3
McPhedran, John H, 1963, Ag 22,27:3
McPhee, Colin, 1964, Ja 8,37:4
MacPhee, Donald Capt (por), 1937, Jl 9,21:5
McPhee, Howie, 1940, D 1,60:3
McPhee, John A, 1943, Ja 6,25:3; 1948, O 9,19:3
MacPhee, John J, 1941, F 19,21:2
McPhee, Polly Mrs, 1903, Ja 1,5:2
MacPherran, Ival L, 1941, F 2,43:6
MacPherran, Ralph S, 1939, N 14,23:4
McPherson, Aimee S, 1944, S 28,19:1
McPherson, Alex, 1942, F 12,23:5
MacPherson, Allan D, 1961, Je 26,51:1
MacPherson, Andrew Mrs, 1940, D 5,25:5
McPherson, Bradley, 1937, D 3,23:6
MacPherson, Burton N, 1943, Mr 17,21:1
McPherson, Charles, 1874, Je 10,1:7
Macpherson, Cluny, 1966, N 18,43:4
McPherson, Donald F, 1944, Mr 18,13:2; 1964, Mr 24, 35:4
Macpherson, Douglas V, 1949, S 5,17:2
MacPherson, E A Mrs, 1919, Ap 24,11:5
Macpherson, Ewan, 1915, D 30,13:4
McPherson, Ewen A, 1954, N 19,23:3
MacPherson, Frank, 1912, Ag 24,9:7
McPherson, Gen (funl, Jl 31,4:6;trb, Ag 2,8:3), 1864, Jl 25,4:3
McPherson, George E, 1945, Je 17,26:4
McPherson, George W, 1956, S 28,27:4
MacPherson, H P, 1949, D 28,25:1
McPherson, Harry W, 1957, O 26,21:6
McPherson, Hobart M, 1955, O 2,86:5
MacPherson, Irving P Sr, 1942, Jl 11,13:4
McPherson, J R, 1897, O 9,1:5
MacPherson, James, 1938, Mr 28,15:3
McPherson, James, 1940, D 14,17:3; 1941, Jl 18,19:4
McPherson, James D Capt, 1953, F 19,23:1
Macpherson, James E, 1939, Mr 8,21:2
McPherson, James J W, 1948, Ja 6,23:5
MacPherson, James Mrs, 1950, Je 16,25:4
MacPherson, Jeanie, 1946, Ag 27,27:2
MacPherson, John, 1962, Ap 25,39:1
McPherson, John D, 1913, N 6,11:7
McPherson, John D Dr, 1937, My 4,25:4
McPherson, John F, 1959, Ja 2,25:1
MacPherson, John R, 1955, F 17,27:3
McPherson, Logan G, 1925, Mr 25,21:5
McPherson, Lowell C, 1949, Jl 17,56:5
MacPherson, Malcolm, 1907, F 26,11:6
McPherson, Mary G, 1956, Ap 9,27:2
McPherson, Melville B, 1945, Je 26,19:4
MacPherson, Murdoch A, 1966, Je 14,47:4
McPherson, Norman C, 1939, O 17,25:4
McPherson, Oscar H, 1948, F 20,27:4
McPherson, Richard C, 1944, Ag 2,15:2
MacPherson, Robert, 1941, Mr 10,17:3
McPherson, Robert, 1950, Ja 6,22:3
MacPherson, Roy Mrs, 1953, My 3,88:1
McPherson, Roy P, 1951, F 10,13:5
McPherson, Rufus, 1901, My 29,1:2
McPherson, Samuel W Col, 1911, N 16,9:5
McPherson, Sherman J, 1920, O 15,13:4
McPherson, Smith Judge, 1915, Ja 18,9:5
Macpherson, Thomas, 1903, Ja 2,3:6
McPherson, Virginia Mrs, 1937, S 4,15:4
MacPherson, Walter H, 1955, Ap 13,29:1
McPherson, William, 1951, O 3,33:2
McPherson, William C, 1958, N 23,88:7
MacPherson, William J, 1947, Je 24,23:2
MacPhie, Elmore I, 1955, Mr 23,31:4
McPhillips, A E, 1938, Ja 25,22:3
McPhillips, Bernard, 1953, N 19,31:4
McPhillips, Bernard J, 1937, Ap 17,17:3
McPhillips, James F, 1949, Je 1,31:4
McPhillips, James Mrs, 1948, Jl 18,54:4
McPhillips, John, 1903, D 13,1:6
McPhillips, Joseph Mrs, 1947, Ja 20,25:3
McPhillips, Matthew F, 1960, D 20,33:1
McPhillips, Michael S, 1967, O 11,47:1
McPhillips, Thomas F, 1949, Je 4,13:4
McPike, Edward J, 1947, D 20,17:3
McPike, Mary, 1951, Jl 27,19:3
McPike, Sarah (por), 1943, F 27,13:3
McPoland, Charles E Mrs, 1946, My 7,21:5
McQuade, B F, 1932, O 20,29:7
McQuade, Edward A Mrs, 1967, S 6,47:1
McQuade, Edward V, 1949, Ap 25,23:3
McQuade, Edwin Mrs, 1953, Ja 7,31:1
McQuade, Emma T B Mrs, 1938, My 19,21:5
McQuade, Eugene T, 1965, O 20,47:3
McQuade, Francis A, 1967, Mr 17,41:4
McQuade, Francis P, 1938, N 3,23:4
McQuade, Francis X (will, My 13,33:5), 1955, Ap 7, 27:3
McQuade, George T, 1941, F 8,15:2
McQuade, George W, 1940, N 28,23:5
McQuade, J A, 1935, My 6,19:3
McQuade, J Gen, 1885, Mr 26,5:2
McQuade, James B, 1942, Mr 11,19:3
McQuade, John, 1903, Ap 3,9:5
McQuade, John B, 1904, F 3,16:5
McQuade, John H, 1947, Ag 25,17:4
McQuade, John J, 1955, S 24,19:3; 1956, S 20,33:5
McQuade, John S, 1947, Mr 10,21:4
McQuade, John S Jr, 1955, Ag 13,13:2
McQuade, Malcolm B, 1954, D 18,15:6
McQuade, Owen F, 1964, D 17,41:5
McQuade, Owen F Mrs, 1962, N 11,88:6
McQuade, Patrick H, 1937, Mr 1,19:3
McQuade, T B, 1902, N 17,9:5
McQuade, Thomas F, 1938, Ap 6,23:3
McQuade, Thomas J, 1955, Ja 15,13:4
McQuade, Timothy J, 1945, Je 26,19:4
McQuade, Victor J, 1961, S 10,86:1
McQuade, W O, 1874, Je 13,8:2
McQuade, Walter P, 1957, D 25,31:4
McQuaid, Bernard J Rev, 1909, Ja 19,9:5
McQuaid, Paul A, 1950, Ja 3,25:2
McQuaid, William A, 1951, Je 17,84:3
MacQuaide, James P, 1915, Jl 13,11:6
McQuaig, James B, 1944, S 18,19:3
McQuald, William P Msgr, 1913, S 20,11:5
MacQuarrie, Gordon, 1956, N 12,29:4
McQuarrie, Haven, 1953, Ag 6,21:4
McQuarrie, Irvine, 1961, S 11,27:5
McQuarrie, James L, 1939, Mr 2,21:6
McQuarrie, Joseph F, 1947, My 7,31:2
McQuary, Odell, 1948, S 2,23:4
McQuay, Homer, 1952, Ag 3,61:1
McQuay, John H, 1951, S 23,87:1
McQuay, Louis E, 1953, Ag 11,27:2
McQueen, Donald B, 1960, My 11,39:2
McQueen, Edwin M, 1944, Mr 13,15:5
McQueen, James W, 1925, Ap 21,21:5
MacQueen, James W, 1954, S 10,23:1
McQueen, John, 1867, S 6,2:3; 1945, O 18,23:3
McQueen, John S, 1941, O 24,23:2
MacQueen, Peter Dr, 1924, Ja 12,13:3
McQueen, Robert F Mrs, 1945, My 31,15:5
McQueen, Walter, 1923, Je 30,11:4
Macqueen-Pope, Walter J, 1960, Je 28,31:3
McQueeney, Andrew M, 1959, S 22,39:1
McQueeney, John J, 1939, Ag 8,17:5
McQuern, James N, 1948, Ja 1,23:4
McQuestion, Samuel, 1948, Ag 26,21:4
McQuestion, William O, 1947, N 5,27:4
McQuhae, Allen, 1960, Jl 4,15:3
McQuibban, George A Dr, 1937, Ja 31,II,8:5
MacQuigg, Charles E, 1952, Ap 25,23:4
McQuigg, Donald I, 1950, Je 9,23:4
McQuigg, Frederick W, 1941, Mr 13,21:5
McQuilkin, Elisabeth R, 1939, Ag 9,17:3
McQuilkin, Robert C, 1952, Jl 16,25:2
McQuillan, Arthur S, 1965, Mr 17,45:2
McQuillan, Daniel J, 1951, Mr 24,13:5
McQuillan, Edward, 1950, F 22,29:5
McQuillan, George, 1940, Mr 31,44:6
McQuillan, Hugh, 1947, Ag 27,23:3; 1955, O 4,35:2
McQuillan, Philip J, 1946, O 1,23:4
McQuillan, Philip J Mrs, 1944, N 21,25:6
McQuillan, Walter J, 1960, D 17,23:5
McQuillan, William J, 1949, Ap 3,76:6
McQuillan, William L, 1939, O 20,23:2
McQuillan, William P, 1942, Ja 29,19:4
McQuillen, Hugh R, 1944, S 12,19:2
McQuillen, Paul W, 1968, O 3,47:4
McQuillen, Roy H, 1941, My 20,23:7
McQuillen, Thomas A Mrs, 1943, Mr 9,23:2
McQuillen, Walter B Mrs, 1948, My 30,34:2
McQuillin, Eugene, 1937, D 12,II,9:2
McQuillin, Frank T, 1950, N 20,25:5
McQuilling, Thomas A, 1953, S 19,15:6
McQuinn, Michael J, 1914, Jl 19,5:5
McQuirk, John Msgr, 1924, N 22,15:6
Macquisten, Frederick A, 1940, Mr 2,13:6
McQuistion, R Hunter, 1959, O 4,86:4
McQuiston, Edward I, 1966, My 14,31:5
McQuiston, James M, 1952, Ag 16,16:3
McQuivy, Edwin W, 1942, Ap 6,15:5
McQuown, James B, 1953, O 23,23:2
McRae, B, 1927, My 8,29:4
McRae, Bruce, 1941, F 20,19:4
McRae, Calvin A, 1940, D 21,17:4
McRae, Cameron F Mrs, 1937, Ja 10,II,9:4
MacRae, Charles F, 1949, Mr 15,27:5
MacRae, David B, 1939, O 21,15:4
MacRae, Donald A, 1955, O 21,27:4
MacRae, Donald Mrs, 1945, F 10,11:3
McRae, Duncan, 1946, Je 27,22:2
Macrae, Duncan, 1967, Mr 24,31:4
Macrae, Elliott Beach, 1968, F 14,47:1
MacRae, Farquhar J, 1947, Mr 6,25:4
McRae, Frances E, 1956, Je 12,35:5
MacRae, Fred T, 1943, Mr 4,19:5
McRae, George W, 1950, Jl 17,21:5
MacRae, Gertrude C Mrs, 1940, Ap 18,23:1
McRae, J J Ex-Gov, 1868, Je 12,5:4
Macrae, James, 1952, Mr 19,29:2
Macrae, James E, 1951, Ja 17,27:2
McRae, James H (por), 1940, My 2,23:1
McRae, James W, 1960, F 3,33:1
Macrae, John (por), 1944, F 20,35:1
MacRae, Lester F, 1958, F 1,19:5
McRae, M A, 1930, O 12,II,6:1
Macrae, Martha B, 1950, S 1,21:3
MacRae, Murdock N, 1955, Jl 26,25:4
Macrae, Richard M, 1957, N 6,35:4
McRae, Roderick, 1960, My 7,23:5

Macrae, Roderick E, 1944, O 15,44:2
Macrae, William, 1882, F 13,5:5; 1968, D 10,47:3
McRaye, Walter J, 1946, Ag 9,17:6
Macready, Gordon N, 1956, O 19,27:5
Macready, Harry A, 1940, S 23,17:3
Macready, Nevil, 1946, Ja 10,23:4
Macready, William Charles, 1873, Ap 30,7:4
McRedmond, Edward L Mrs, 1938, Ag 9,19:2
Macree, Daniel Sir, 1882, Ja 19,5:3
McRell, James A, 1949, Mr 3,25:3
McReynolds, Douglas, 1958, My 24,21:5
MacReynolds, George, 1950, O 29,92:4
McReynolds, George E, 1954, Mr 29,19:6
McReynolds, George S, 1940, S 9,15:3
McReynolds, James C, 1946, Ag 26,1:2
McReynolds, John O, 1942, Jl 8,23:6
McReynolds, Robert P, 1952, D 21,53:2
McReynolds, Sam D, 1939, Jl 12,19:1
McReynolds, Thomas J, 1939, F 15,23:3
McReynolds, William H, 1951, Ja 18,27:5
Macri, Charles G, 1937, Ap 6,23:1
Macri, John, 1945, My 22,19:6
Macri, Ralph A, 1947, N 25,60:2
McRickard, Samuel E, 1946, Mr 19,27:2
Macrina, Mother, 1949, My 9,25:2
Macritchie, Allan, 1950, N 2,31:4
McRitchie, Donald, 1948, N 30,28:3
MacRobbie, Leslie H, 1955, Je 5,84:7
MacRobert, Rachel W Lady, 1954, S 2,21:6
MacRobert, Russell G, 1967, Jl 10,31:1
McRoberts, Arthur K Jr, 1949, Je 28,28:2
McRoberts, Edward, 1909, Mr 31,11:5
McRoberts, John H, 1949, D 30,19:2
McRoberts, Robert A, 1955, Jl 28,23:5
McRoberts, Samuel (por), 1947, S 9,31:3
McRoberts, Samuel J (por), 1946, Je 7,19:4
McRoberts, Samuel Mrs, 1946, Ja 23,27:1
McRoberts, Thomas, 1904, F 1,7:3
MacRorie, Janet, 1950, F 6,25:3
McRory, James G, 1953, F 15,51:3
MacRory, Joseph (por), 1945, O 14,42:2
MacRossie, Allan, 1940, Mr 3,44:3
McRossie, T Donald, 1943, S 3,19:6
Macrum, Edward A, 1914, My 10,IV,7:4
MacRury, J Allison, 1962, Ag 25,19:3
McShain, Joseph M, 1949, D 2,29:3
McShane, Edward A, 1968, O 8,47:2
McShane, Edward C J, 1955, O 6,29:5
McShane, Felix, 1937, F 6,17:1
McShane, Felix J Jr, 1953, Ja 2,15:4
McShane, Felix J Mrs, 1944, F 5,15:2
McShane, Frank L, 1950, N 12,93:2
McShane, Frank R, 1951, Mr 22,31:2
McShane, Henry J, 1956, F 12,89:1
McShane, James J P, 1968, D 24,20:1
McShane, John H, 1962, Ja 13,21:3
McShane, John H Mrs, 1964, S 2,37:1
McShane, Lewis L, 1955, O 21,27:1
McShane, Mary, 1938, O 16,44:4
McShane, Thomas F, 1950, D 19,29:1
McShannic, Peter R, 1946, D 1,79:5
McShea, Roger A, 1954, Jl 23,17:3
McShea, Stewart Ross, 1922, D 21,15:3
McShea, William J, 1955, Jl 23,17:6
McSherry, Annie D Mrs, 1941, Ap 9,25:3
McSherry, Felix J, 1943, F 24,21:2
McSherry, James Judge, 1907, O 24,11:5
Macsherry, S Hillen, 1939, F 24,19:3
McSorley, Edward, 1966, D 23,25:2
McSorley, Edward F, 1955, Ap 4,29:3
MacSorley, Edward J, 1948, F 11,27:5
McSorley, J T, 1879, Ag 28,2:3
McSorley, Joseph, 1963, Jl 5,19:3
McSorley, Richard T Mrs, 1952, N 17,25:5
McSorley, William J, 1943, Mr 24,23:5; 1961, D 17, 82:6
McSpadden, J Walker, 1960, F 10,37:3
McSpadden, J Walker Mrs, 1948, Jl 7,23:1
McSpadden, Sallie R Mrs (por), 1943, Ag 26,17:5
McSpadden, Warren W, 1959, Mr 14,23:1
McSparran, John A, 1944, Ja 18,20:2
McSpedon, Frank, 1939, Ja 2,23:2
McSpedon, Frank Mrs, 1948, F 21,13:4
McSpedon, Howard (funl, O 11,27:2), 1957, O 8,35:3
McSpedon, Richard W, 1964, D 13,86:5
McSpedon, William J, 1958, S 6,17:6
MacSporran, John A, 1954, F 21,68:2
MacSporran, John S, 1961, Ja 1,48:2
McStay, Arnold, 1924, Jl 30,13:5
McSurely, Alex, 1953, S 16,33:2
McSurley, William H, 1943, My 28,21:2
McSwain, J J, 1936, Ag 7,19:3
McSween, A B, 1912, S 14,13:6
McSweeney, Bernard J, 1968, Ag 23,39:2
McSweeney, Dennis, 1940, Mr 1,21:3
McSweeney, Edward E Mrs, 1944, D 1,23:2
McSweeney, Edward S, 1944, S 18,19:2
McSweeney, Eugene M, 1946, Ja 22,27:3
McSweeney, Henry, 1946, Mr 6,28:2
McSweeney, Henry Mrs (Theresa), 1968, O 7,47:1
McSweeney, James H, 1941, O 19,44:4
McSweeney, James L, 1949, Ap 26,26:2
MacSweeney, John P, 1937, O 16,19:4
McSweeney, John T, 1966, My 23,41:2
McSweeney, Lizzie J, 1947, Ap 6,60:8
McSweeney, Miles E Ex-Gov, 1909, S 30,9:6
McSweeney, Patrick Francis Msgr, 1907, F 26,11:6
McSweeney, Rebekah Mrs, 1964, Ja 1,25:4
McSwigan, Marie, 1962, Jl 18,29:4
MacSwiney, Mary M (por), 1942, Mr 9,19:3
McSwiney, Myles J, 1958, F 24,19:1
MacSwiney, Peter, 1949, N 21,25:4
MacSwiney, Sean, 1942, Ja 24,17:5
McTaggart, Edward, 1952, Ja 27,76:4
McTaggart, George A, 1956, Ag 30,25:4
Mactaggart, John A, 1960, Ap 11,31:4
McTaggart, John Dr, 1925, Ja 20,21:4
MacTaggart, John S, 1945, O 13,15:2
McTaggart, Johnny, 1946, Ap 19,29:4
MacTaggart, P Arch Mrs, 1941, O 22,23:4
McTaggart, Peter E, 1951, Ag 28,23:6
McTaggart, Walter W, 1956, Ja 28,17:6
McTague, Bernard, 1953, S 19,15:5
McTague, Charles F, 1949, Ap 29,23:1
McTague, Charles F Mrs, 1963, O 19,25:3
McTague, Hugh F, 1938, Mr 30,21:3
McTague, James A, 1963, D 27,10:5
McTague, James A Mrs (funl, Jl 19,27:4), 1956, Jl 17,13:2
McTague, John S, 1937, O 18,17:4
McTague, Joseph F, 1950, Jl 28,21:6
McTague, Lawrence J, 1965, Ap 13,37:3
McTague, William F, 1958, Jl 9,27:4
McTarnahan, John T, 1943, Ap 30,21:4
McTarnahan, William C, 1951, O 19,27:3
McTavey, Harry E, 1939, N 2,23:2
MacTavish, Charles Carroll Mrs, 1909, F 19,9:5
MacTavish, Duncan K, 1963, N 17,80:8
McTavish, Stuart, 1953, Ap 19,91:1
McTavish, Wilfred L, 1951, Mr 20,29:3
MacTavish, William C, 1968, S 17,94:3
MacTear, Margaret A Mrs, 1955, S 9,50:1
McTeer, J T Maj, 1904, Ja 8,7:4
McTeigue, Walter J Sr, 1968, D 20,47:2
McTeigue, Walter P, 1952, F 20,30:4
McTernan, Charles C, 1967, My 27,31:4
McTernan, Felix J, 1954, Je 7,23:1
McTernan, Felix J Mrs, 1953, Ap 14,27:5
McTernan, Frank J, 1955, Mr 17,45:2
McTernan, James A, 1954, Ap 25,87:1
McTernan, James E, 1958, F 20,25:1
McTernan, John, 1945, S 2,32:2
MacTier, Anthony D, 1940, D 7,17:5
McTiernan, William, 1946, Ap 18,27:4
McTighe, Edward F, 1949, N 11,26:2
McTighe, James T, 1964, O 16,39:3
McTighe, Patrick B, 1951, Jl 15,61:3
McTigue, Andrew, 1939, O 19,24:2
McTigue, Charles H, 1944, Je 28,23:6
McTigue, J G, 1928, F 15,23:1
McTigue, James J Mrs, 1956, Ja 22,89:2
McTigue, Mark, 1938, N 16,23:1
McTigue, Mike (Michl F), 1966, Ag 13,25:1
McTurk, Joe (R McCracken), 1961, Jl 23,68:5
McTurnan, Clair, 1958, O 26,88:4
Mactye, Sylvester P, 1955, Ja 11,25:2
Mactye, Sylvester P Mrs, 1955, Ja 11,25:2
Macumber, J L, 1928, D 23,17:3
Macurdy, Grace H, 1946, O 24,27:4
McVail, David Caldwell Sir, 1917, N 6,13:4
McVane, Ernest F Dr, 1937, S 10,23:2
McVann, Donald E, 1949, F 9,27:1
MacVannel, John Angus, 1915, N 11,13:6
McVarish, Charles E, 1963, S 16,35:2
McVarish, Robert H, 1949, Mr 2,25:1
McVarnish, Francis X, 1948, Jl 13,27:1
McVay, Anna P, 1962, Jl 2,29:5
McVay, Charles B, 1949, O 29,15:6
McVay, Charles B Rear-Adm, 1968, N 8,47:3
McVay, Christopher C, 1949, O 20,29:5
McVay, George, 1951, N 17,17:2
McVay, George E, 1943, N 27,13:1
McVay, George P H, 1915, S 28,11:5
McVay, Ira O, 1951, Jl 7,13:6
MacVeagh, Charles Mrs, 1948, O 17,76:3
MacVeagh, Charlton, 1963, Mr 21,16:1
MacVeagh, F, 1934, Jl 7,13:1
MacVeagh, Francis W, 1959, F 26,31:2
MacVeagh, George D Mrs, 1946, Ag 30,17:5
MacVeagh, Lincoln Mrs (por), 1947, S 10,27:5
MacVeagh, Rogers, 1943, S 21,24:2
MacVeagh, Wayne, 1917, Ja 12,13:3
McVean, David B, 1959, D 21,27:4
MacVeany, Arthur P, 1953, S 24,33:3
McVeigh, Charles S, 1962, Ag 21,33:1
McVeigh, Francis P, 1950, F 2,28:2
McVeigh, Gregory D, 1953, S 8,31:4
McVeigh, John N, 1959, Ja 16,27:3
McVeigh, John N Mrs, 1955, Ap 26,29:1
McVeigh, Margaret E, 1960, Je 17,31:1
McVeigh, Owen, 1941, Mr 12,21:5
McVeigh, Patrick J, 1943, Ag 4,17:3; 1947, O 3,25:2
McVeigh, Patrick J Mrs, 1941, N 24,17:5
McVeigh, Raymond J, 1952, Ap 7,25:6
McVeigh, Sherman, 1951, Mr 1,27:4
McVeigh, Sylvester P, 1965, O 26,45:3
McVeigh, Thomas B, 1961, O 23,29:4
McVeigh, Thomas J V, 1956, My 7,27:3
McVeigh, Thomas Mrs, 1963, D 19,33:3
McVety, Margaret A, 1949, Je 6,19:6
McVey, Adolphus G, 1912, Jl 15,9:6
MacVey, Charles T Mrs, 1944, My 12,19:4
McVey, Clarence E, 1947, N 8,17:4
McVey, Frank L, 1953, Ja 6,29:4
McVey, Frank L Mrs, 1945, Je 14,19:2
McVey, George H, 1914, Jl 26,5:7
McVey, George V, 1964, Je 11,33:4
McVey, J D, 1879, O 10,5:2
McVey, John R, 1945, My 9,23:5
McVey, Lawrence A, 1945, N 14,19:5
McVey, Lee R, 1939, Ap 20,23:2
McVey, Thomas C, 1949, S 24,13:5
McVey, William E, 1958, Ag 11,21:4
McVicar, Charlotte S Mrs, 1941, Jl 18,19:6
MacVicar, Donald G, 1956, Jl 24,28:6
MacVicar, John, 1950, Je 27,29:5
MacVicar, John G, 1945, My 5,15:4
MacVicar, John G Mrs, 1950, Ap 3,23:2
McVicar, John Rev, 1868, O 31,5:4
McVicar, Malcolm Rev, 1904, My 19,9:5
McVicar, Nelson, 1960, D 22,26:3
McVicar, Thomas, 1942, D 6,77:1
McVicar, Thomas Mrs, 1946, N 6,23:3
MacVicar, William, 1943, Ag 19,19:2
McVicar, William B Mrs, 1943, N 1,17:4
MacVichie, Duncan, 1941, Ja 19,40:7
McVickar, Dorothea C Mrs, 1938, D 12,19:2
McVickar, Edward S, 1950, F 3,24:3
McVickar, Elizabeth D Mrs, 1942, F 7,17:4
McVickar, Henry Goelet, 1919, S 15,11:6
McVickar, Henry L, 1960, S 19,31:3
McVickar, James, 1967, Mr 23,35:2
McVickar, Noel, 1962, Mr 12,31:1
McVickar, Robert, 1937, O 5,25:3
McVickar, W A Rev Dr, 1877, S 25,5:3
McVickar, William N Mrs, 1955, D 2,27:2
McVickar, William Nelson Bp, 1910, Je 29,7:5
McVicker, Horace Mrs (A Weaver), 1940, N 19,24
McVicker, Horatia (will), 1948, Ag 12,19:3
McVicker, J H, 1896, Mr 8,5:4
McVicker, Julius, 1940, Mr 13,23:4
McVicker, Walter, 1948, F 5,23:1
McVickers, Alex C Mrs, 1952, D 13,21:5
McVinney, Raymond J, 1958, S 4,31:2
McVittie, James, 1960, O 3,31:1
McVitty, Albert E, 1948, Mr 18,27:4
McVitty, Edward Q, 1954, Ap 26,25:4
McVoy, Arthur, 1944, S 17,42:2
McVoy, Arthur D, 1957, D 7,21:5
McVoy, Charles F, 1949, O 21,25:1
McVoy, Herbert C, 1951, Ag 21,27:3
McVoy, Martin Jr, 1949, Ja 9,73:1
McVoy, Raymond L, 1950, S 8,32:2
McVoy, Raymond Mrs, 1950, F 9,29:4
McVoy, William E, 1950, Mr 8,27:3
McWade, E S, 1951, Ag 14,23:3
McWade, Frank L, 1937, N 3,23:5
McWade, Frederick J, 1942, F 3,19:1
McWade, Robert, 1938, Ja 20,19:3
McWade, Robert Sr, 1913, Mr 6,11:6
McWain, Andrew J (por), 1949, Mr 6,72:7
McWain, Andrew J Mrs, 1950, D 22,24:3
McWain, Donald M, 1948, F 6,26:5
McWane, Fred, 1959, Mr 4,31:3
MacWatt, Charles, 1945, Ap 15,14:7
McWatters, Arthur Mrs, 1942, O 22,21:2
McWatters, Bernard J, 1946, Mr 23,13:1
McWeeney, George H, 1965, My 14,37:3
McWeeney, John G, 1965, Ag 6,27:2
McWeeney, Laurence R, 1956, S 28,27:4
McWeeny, Douglas L (Buzz), 1953, Ja 3,15:5
McWethy, Wilson H, 1961, F 11,23:4
Macwherter, John, 1959, N 9,31:4
McWhiney, Edgar E, 1950, Mr 12,92:3
McWhinney, Alex Mrs, 1956, Ap 9,27:1
McWhinney, Curtis A, 1947, My 28,25:4
MacWhinney, Everett S, 1961, Je 8,35:4
MacWhinney, George B, 1943, Jl 21,15:5
McWhinney, T A, 1933, N 26,32:1
MacWhinnie, J W Dr, 1885, My 6,5:3
McWhirter, Felix T Mrs, 1952, D 12,29:2
MacWhirter, John, 1911, Ja 29,11:2
McWhirter, William A, 1955, My 18,31:1
MacWhite, Michael, 1958, N 14,27:4
McWhood, Leonard B, 1939, D 5,27:4
McWhorter, Emerson H, 1937, D 10,26:2
McWhorter, Ernest D, 1950, F 1,29:5
McWhorter, Robert L, 1960, Je 30,29:2
MacWilliam, James D, 1954, Je 12,15:4
MacWilliam, Janet, 1949, Mr 14,19:6
McWilliam, John R, 1966, My 17,47:2
McWilliam, Robert, 1945, My 6,38:1
McWilliam, Townsend T, 1940, Mr 21,25:2
McWilliams, Afton, 1963, Ap 6,19:2
McWilliams, Andrea, 1941, D 4,25:1
McWilliams, Andrew, 1903, Ja 10,1:7
McWilliams, Andrew F, 1939, Ja 7,15:6
McWilliams, Charles H, 1959, Mr 31,29:2
McWilliams, Charles M, 1940, Ap 19,21:5
McWilliams, Daniel Wilkin, 1919, Ja 9,11:2

McWilliams, Daniel Wilkin Mrs, 1920, S 9,11:2
MacWilliams, Edward N (Jim), 1955, O 15,15:5
McWilliams, Eugene J, 1940, N 1,25:2
McWilliams, F A, 1938, Jl 21,21:5
McWilliams, Francis J, 1960, O 18,39:2
McWilliams, Henry, 1940, Ag 18,37:4
McWilliams, Howard, 1942, O 10,15:2
McWilliams, J A, 1945, N 13,21:5
McWilliams, James E, 1948, N 27,17:1
McWilliams, James P, 1955, Je 22,30:1
McWilliams, Kate E, 1912, O 9,13:6
McWilliams, Kimber C, 1953, D 30,23:4
McWilliams, LeRoy Msgr, 1968, Ja 27,29:4
McWilliams, Mary A Mrs, 1940, S 16,19:2
McWilliams, Phillip A, 1961, Mr 25,25:4
McWilliams, R F Mrs, 1952, Ap 14,19:5
McWilliams, Raymond J, 1946, F 13,23:4
McWilliams, Robert L, 1955, O 25,33:3
McWilliams, Samuel, 1947, S 22,23:4
McWilliams, Thomas, 1943, Je 23,21:2
McWilliams, William E, 1949, Jl 15,19:5
McWilliams, William J, 1957, My 17,25:3; 1967, Je 29,43:2
McWilliams, William R, 1954, Ap 24,17:2
McWilson, Logan W, 1964, Ag 9,76:5
Macwithey, Edward L, 1957, O 7,27:4
McWood, John E, 1943, Ap 22,23:4

M

Ma Chan-shan, 1950, D 6,33:5
Ma Hsiang-pai, 1939, N 5,49:4
Maag, Albert, 1948, My 31,19:5
Maag, Albert A, 1946, Jl 23,25:1
Maag, Edward, 1954, Ja 29,19:4
Maak, Carl, 1943, D 3,23:2
Maalouf, Georges, 1948, S 17,25:4
Maar, Edward, 1952, Ag 5,19:1
Maar, Henry J, 1944, Je 7,19:5
Maarschalk, Nicholas H, 1958, Jl 26,15:6
Maarseveen, Johannes H van, 1951, N 20,31:3
Maartens, Maarten, 1915, Ag 5,11:7
Maas, Albert van L, 1968, Ag 22,37:1
Maas, Alfred, 1942, Ja 10,18:2
Maas, Charles Oscar Lt-Com, 1919, Jl 3,10:2
Maas, Charles Sr, 1939, Je 17,15:4
Maas, Frank, 1941, My 16,23:1
Maas, John W, 1941, D 29,15:4
Maas, Joseph, 1958, My 7,35:4
Maas, Louis W, 1944, Ja 11,19:3
Maas, Maurice, 1908, Mr 1,9:4
Maas, Max A, 1966, D 4,88:4
Maas, Melvin J (trb, Ap 15,39:3; trb lr, Ap 28,36:6), 1964, Ap 14,37:1
Maas, Milton A, 1948, Mr 31,26:3
Maas, Milton A Mrs, 1953, Ap 25,15:5
Maas, Mortimer, 1952, S 22,23:1
Maas, Mortimer Mrs, 1958, Mr 8,17:3
Maas, Pauline, 1914, Ag 28,9:7
Maas, Pieter C, 1937, O 27,31:5
Maas, Robert, 1948, Jl 9,19:2
Maas, Walter S, 1955, Mr 5,17:5
Maas, William H, 1939, Mr 16,23:4
Maasen, Henry B, 1944, O 16,19:5
Maaske, Roben J, 1955, F 21,21:3
Maass, Edgar, 1964, Ja 8,37:4
Maass, Frank Mrs, 1949, Ap 8,26:5
Maass, Harold J, 1965, Ja 7,31:3
Maass, Herbert H, 1957, Ap 13,19:2
Maass, Louis, 1946, My 7,21:2
Mabbett, Fred A, 1940, Je 25,23:3
Mabbott, John M Mrs, 1948, N 28,96:5
Mabbott, Thomas Ollive Dr, 1968, My 16,48:1
Mabbs, Francis G, 1960, Ag 10,31:2
Mabbs, John W, 1946, Ag 6,25:3
Mabe, James C, 1959, My 24,89:1
Mabee, D Walter Mrs, 1949, F 1,25:4
Mabee, Fred A, 1952, N 19,29:4
Mabee, George S, 1938, My 21,15:5
Mabee, George W, 1948, My 12,27:4
Mabee, George W Mrs, 1950, My 9,29:3
Mabee, Henry N, 1913, D 12,11:6
Mabee, J P Judge, 1912, My 7,11:5
Mabee, Peter A, 1945, F 25,38:1
Mabel, Arthur M, 1942, Ap 9,19:4
Mabel, Robert C, 1940, Ja 17,21:3
Maben, Buel W, 1950, S 17,105:2
Maben, Herbert C, 1943, Ag 27,17:2
Maben, John C Jr, 1941, Jl 21,15:3
Mabey, Charles R, 1959, Ap 27,27:4
Mabey, J Corwin, 1950, D 18,31:2
Mabey, Lionel C, 1957, Ag 6,27:4
Mabie, C W, 1884, D 1,2:6
Mabie, Carroll S, 1944, Ap 6,23:5
Mabie, E C, 1956, F 11,17:5
Mabie, Edmund G, 1940, My 15,25:3
Mabie, Edward P, 1948, Ag 8,56:4
Mabie, Hamilton Wright Dr (funl, Ja 4,11:4), 1917, Ja 1,9:2
Mabie, Harold S, 1947, Ap 17,27:3
Mabie, Helen R (will, Ag 31,44:1), 1952, Ag 15,15:2
Mabie, Janet (Mrs J M Clapp), 1961, D 8,37:2
Mabie, Josephine, 1940, Ap 23,24:2
Mabie, Louise K Mrs, 1957, N 13,35:1
Mabie, Reuben A, 1942, My 13,19:3
Mabie, Sarah Colwell, 1905, F 23,9:6
Mabie, Sophia Mrs, 1942, Ap 9,20:2
Mabilleau, Leopold, 1941, F 17,15:4
Mable, Henry Clay Rev Dr, 1918, My 1,13:5
Mable, Marion C, 1914, Je 19,13:6
Mabon, Arthur F, 1960, Jl 31,68:7
Mabon, James B (por), 1941, Mr 11,23:1
Mabon, James B Sr Mrs, 1961, My 13,19:3
Mabon, S Cliffton, 1957, My 25,21:3
Mabon, S Clifton Mrs, 1942, Ag 24,15:4
Mabon, William Dr, 1917, F 10,9:4
Mabott, John M, 1938, Jl 3,13:1
Mabry, Helen M, 1960, O 8,23:1
Mabry, Sadie Mrs, 1941, Mr 22,15:5
Mabus, Charles F Mrs, 1945, O 28,44:4
Macabee, William, 1910, O 6,11:4
Macan, Helen A Mrs, 1957, Mr 26,33:4
Macatee, Mary L, 1953, N 26,31:2
Maccaferri, Signor, 1874, S 20,5:3
Maccanico, Camelo, 1921, Ag 5,13:4
Macchi, Luigi Cardinal, 1907, Mr 30,9:7
Macchi, Mauro, 1881, Ja 2,7:1
Maccoby, Max, 1956, D 28,21:2
Maccoll, Christina L, 1939, Ag 15,19:5
Mace, A Wilbur, 1961, S 23,19:1
Mace, Amos J, 1963, Je 5,41:4
Mace, Benjamin, 1878, N 21,5:2
Mace, Dan, 1885, Ap 20,5:4
Mace, Edward, 1939, D 17,49:1
Mace, Frank W, 1962, N 13,37:2
Mace, Fred, 1917, F 22,11:5
Mace, George E, 1952, Ag 16,15:5
Mace, Harry F, 1963, D 31,19:3
Mace, John W, 1958, S 27,21:1
Mace, Lloyd R, 1953, Ja 26,19:4
Mace, Margaret, 1951, D 17,31:5
Mace, Thomas D, 1952, Je 18,27:3
Macedo, Miguel S, 1959, S 28,31:3
Macedo Soares, Jose R de, 1953, O 3,17:3
Macedonio, Camela M, 1952, D 20,17:6
Macek, Vladko, 1964, My 16,25:4
Macelhone, Harry, 1958, Je 5,31:5
Mach, E von, 1927, Jl 17,II,9:1
Machacek, Gerald F, 1959, N 10,47:3
Machado, Antonio, 1939, F 24,19:3
Machado, Argemiro, 1957, N 12,37:2
Machado, Augusto, 1924, Mr 29,15:4
Machado, Christiano M, 1953, D 27,61:1
Machado, Decio de Paula, 1955, Jl 29,17:6
Machado, J T, 1935, F 2,13:6
Machado, Jose A, 1953, Ja 21,31:3
Machado, Jose A Jr, 1965, D 15,47:3
Machalske, Florentine J, 1916, Ja 17,11:4
Machamer, Jefferson, 1960, Ag 17,31:4
Machat, Hyman, 1960, Je 26,72:6
Machaty, Gustav, 1963, D 17,39:1
Machella, Thomas E, 1962, Ap 12,35:4
Machen, Henry B, 1959, O 24,21:5
Machenberg, Leo A, 1959, Ja 21,31:2
Machens, Joseph G, 1956, Ag 15,29:5
Machiavelli, Nicolo, 1961, Ja 26,29:3
Machin, Jose, 1913, S 14,II,15:5
Machin, Stanley Sir, 1939, Ag 13,29:3
Machlet, Adolph W, 1955, S 28,35:1
Machlet, Fritz W, 1952, Ja 8,27:2
Machlett, Raymond R, 1955, Ja 8,13:7
Machlis, Moses, 1957, Ap 27,19:1
Machmer, William L, 1953, My 25,25:4
Machol, Morris R Mrs (Claudia), 1968, S 15,84:6
Machold, Walter J, 1951, D 5,35:3
Machray, Robert, 1904, Mr 10,2:4
Machris, George L, 1952, O 18,19:2
Macht, David I, 1961, O 16,29:1
Macht, Harry R, 1962, F 4,82:3
Macht, Jerome I, 1952, F 5,29:2
Macia, F, 1933, D 26,1:5
Macias, Josefa E Mrs, 1939, N 18,17:2
Maciszewski, Felix, 1957, S 20,25:2
Mack, see also page 647
Mack, A W Dr, 1871, Ja 7,1:4
Mack, Alfred, 1958, Ap 1,31:4
Mack, Arthur K Mrs, 1956, D 3,29:4
Mack, Charles, 1923, F 21,15:4; 1952, Ag 2,15:7
Mack, Charles A, 1963, Jl 20,19:5
Mack, Connie (funl plans, F 10,21:5; funl F 12,89:1), 1956, F 9,1:4
Mack, E B, 1881, D 13,5:1
Mack, Earl J, 1953, Mr 3,27:2
Mack, Earle Mrs, 1955, My 5,33:5
Mack, Edward L, 1952, N 8,17:2
Mack, Francis X, 1951, Jl 24,25:3
Mack, Frank W, 1906, O 29,9:6
Mack, Gene (E McGillicuddy), 1953, Jl 9,25:5
Mack, George J, 1952, N 30,88:6
Mack, Harold A Mrs, 1965, O 26,45:1
Mack, Harry, 1957, My 3,27:4
Mack, Harry H, 1954, Jl 18,57:1
Mack, Harvey F, 1956, My 30,21:3
Mack, Helen Mrs, 1954, S 28,29:4
Mack, Henry A, 1953, My 30,15:5
Mack, Henry B Mrs, 1955, Ag 15,15:5
Mack, Howard, 1967, Jl 8,25:3
Mack, Irving J, 1960, S 6,35:2
Mack, Isaac F Col, 1912, Ap 19,15:5
Mack, James F, 1916, Ag 23,9:6
Mack, James H, 1951, N 3,17:3
Mack, James J, 1951, Ag 13,17:4
Mack, James Stephen, 1968, My 23,47:2
Mack, John, 1912, Ag 21,9:2; 1916, Ja 12,13:4
Mack, John E, 1958, F 24,19:1
Mack, John M, 1915, Ja 27,9:6; 1924, Mr 15,13:4
Mack, Joseph A, 1956, S 8,17:2
Mack, Joseph P 2d, 1955, Je 13,23:6
Mack, Joseph S, 1953, Jl 28,19:3
Mack, Julian, 1966, Ap 16,33:4
Mack, Julian W Mrs, 1968, D 23,39:2
Mack, L Alex Mrs, 1952, O 18,19:3
Mack, Laurence A, 1958, My 16,23:8
Mack, Lewis S, 1915, Ap 26,9:6
Mack, Margaret, 1956, Ag 2,25:2
Mack, Michael J, 1916, Ja 24,11:2
Mack, N E, 1932, D 26,1:7
Mack, Nila, 1953, Ja 21,31:2
Mack, Norman E Mrs, 1954, Ag 4,21:3
Mack, Pierce W, 1954, Ja 2,11:3
Mack, Ralph W Mrs, 1964, O 27,39:3
Mack, Richard, 1967, O 1,84:4
Mack, Richard A, 1963, N 27,37:2
Mack, Robert D, 1958, Mr 2,89:3
Mack, Roy (est acctg), 1961, Ap 4,27:8
Mack, Roy F, 1960, F 11,35:3
Mack, Russell V, 1960, Mr 29,37:4
Mack, Sam, 1957, O 1,33:1
Mack, Thomas Mrs, 1954, D 22,23:2; 1959, O 28,37:4
Mack, W, 1934, N 20,21:1
Mack, Walter C, 1960, S 1,27:3
Mack, Walter S Sr Mrs, 1952, Jl 7,21:3
Mack, Warren B, 1952, Jl 8,27:5
Mack, William B, 1955, S 15,33:5
Mack, William C, 1953, F 15,92:3
Mackall, William W, 1939, Ag 24,19:6
Mackau, Baron de, 1918, My 7,13:3
Macken, Michael J (will), 1960, D 30,41:3
Mackenzie, Finlay, 1955, Jl 23,17:6
Mackie, David I, 1966, F 14,29:3
Mackie, Donald W Sr, 1955, F 27,86:2
Mackie, George, 1955, Je 27,21:5
Mackie, Howard, 1952, Mr 11,27:5
Mackie, John B, 1953, Ja 12,27:2
Mackie, Joseph W, 1955, Ja 17,23:5
Mackie, Paul T, 1960, Ap 9,23:5
Mackie, Thomas J, 1955, O 8,19:5
Mackie, Thomas T, 1955, O 6,29:3
Mackiewicz, Stanislaw, 1966, F 19,27:3
Mackin, Billy, 1912, O 26,11:6
Mackin, James H, 1953, Jl 10,19:3
Mackin, John J, 1919, Ap 7,13:3
Mackland, Ray Mrs, 1961, Je 16,33:5
Mackle, Frank E, 1956, Mr 13,27:2
Mackle, Joseph A, 1953, Ap 19,90:4
Mackler, Harry, 1967, O 31,45:1
Mackler, Harry S, 1965, N 19,39:1
Mackler, John, 1952, F 17,85:2
Macklin, George E, 1905, Je 27,9:5
Macklin, John F, 1957, Ag 27,29:1
Macklin, Martin T, 1966, Ap 25,31:4
Macknet, C S, 1872, Ja 26,5:4
Macko, George, 1954, Jl 8,23:2
Macksey, Kenneth W, 1958, D 8,31:4
Mackubin, Florence, 1918, F 3,15:2
Maclin, Edward S, 1955, F 1,29:5
Macom, J Morgan, 1955, Mr 22,31:4
Macom, William J, 1958, Jl 9,27:3
Macomber, A K, 1955, O 7,25:2
Macomber, A Kingsley (will), 1958, O 25,13:6
Macomber, Alex, 1956, Mr 15,31:3
Macomber, Charles F, 1947, S 2,21:3
Macomber, De Witt B Mrs, 1951, F 28,27:3
Macomber, Ernest A Mrs, 1953, S 30,31:5
Macomber, John R, 1955, My 12,29:2
Macomber, W Sturgis, 1957, Ag 2,19:5
Macon, Clifton, 1947, Mr 5,25:6
Macon, Clifton Mrs, 1958, Jl 17,27:3
Macon, Dave (Uncle), 1952, Mr 23,92:2
Macon, Robert Bruce, 1925, O 13,23:5
Macoy, Harry B, 1952, Je 11,29:4
Macri, Vincent, 1959, D 13,86:8
Macrides, John C, 1967, D 15,94:3
Macrum, Edward K, 1953, Ja 18,92:3
Macson, Walter L, 1953, Ja 10,17:3
Macsoud, Adele S, 1953, My 22,27:5
Macy, A S Mrs, 1936, O 21,27:1
Macy, Bernard, 1955, N 17,35:4
Macy, Carleton, 1946, O 18,23:5
Macy, Carlton, 1949, Ja 6,23:1
Macy, Carlton Mrs, 1938, My 3,23:3
Macy, Charles H, 1875, Jl 23,4:7
Macy, Cromwell Gardner, 1917, O 31,13:5
Macy, Edward W, 1958, O 31,26:1
Macy, Edward W Mrs (funl plans, Jl 8,25:1), 1967, Jl 7,31:4
Macy, F H, 1903, Ap 2,9:6
Macy, Frank H, 1947, My 21,25:2
Macy, Frederick B, 1945, Ja 14,40:7
Macy, George, 1956, My 21,25:3
Macy, George I, 1937, Ag 18,19:5
Macy, Gertrude I Mrs, 1940, My 29,23:4
Macy, J A, 1932, Ag 27,15:6
Macy, J Mrs (funl), 1871, D 29,2:2
Macy, Janet P Mrs, 1942, O 13,23:5
Macy, Jared, 1882, Ja 16,8:2
Macy, Joseph, 1966, Je 24,37:1
Macy, Josiah Mrs, 1948, Mr 22,23:2
Macy, Mary S, 1950, O 17,31:1
Macy, Nelson, 1957, Ap 9,33:1
Macy, Nelson C, 1922, F 3,15:4
Macy, Norman L, 1967, Mr 7,38:5
Macy, Oliver C, 1947, Ap 20,60:3
Macy, Paul G, 1960, O 12,39:3
Macy, Paul Mrs, 1957, S 7,19:4
Macy, R B Gen, 1887, N 23,5:2
Macy, R H, 1877, Mr 31,8:6
Macy, Silvanus J, 1903, My 18,7:6

Macy, V E, 1930, Mr 22,19:1
Macy, V Everit Mrs, 1925, F 2,17:3
Macy, W Kingsland (funl plans, Jl 18,29:1; funl, Jl 19,29:2), 1961, Jl 16,1:2
Macy, William Austin Dr, 1918, My 22,13:6
Macy, William Henry, 1913, O 18,13:2
Macy, William S, 1945, Jl 31,19:3
Madacey, Joseph E, 1957, N 27,31:4
Madans, Alex, 1963, Ag 6,31:1
Madar, Rudolf, 1949, Ag 26,19:2
Madaras, John Mrs, 1944, F 7,15:6
Madariaga, Manuel R, 1959, F 1,84:8
Maday, Stefan von, 1959, Je 25,29:4
Maday, William T, 1964, Ag 10,31:5
Maddaus, Oscar Jr, 1951, S 5,31:5
Madden, Alfred L, 1947, O 19,64:1
Madden, Ann T Mrs, 1939, Ja 15,38:6
Madden, Bentley, 1957, Ag 28,27:4
Madden, C E, 1935, Je 6,21:1
Madden, Charles A, 1945, D 17,21:4
Madden, Charles G, 1945, Ag 2,19:5
Madden, Clare K, 1953, S 18,23:3
Madden, Clarence L, 1941, Ap 29,19:2
Madden, David D, 1939, S 19,25:3
Madden, E D, 1947, Mr 22,13:5
Madden, Edmund W, 1963, O 15,39:2
Madden, Edward, 1952, Mr 12,27:1
Madden, Edward J, 1966, Mr 17,39:3
Madden, Elizabeth, 1967, N 29,40:8
Madden, Elizabeth Mrs, 1947, O 2,27:2
Madden, Ellen Mrs, 1941, O 30,23:1
Madden, Eva A, 1958, Ja 25,19:1
Madden, Francis A, 1952, N 3,27:4
Madden, Frank J Sr, 1947, Ag 18,17:5
Madden, Frank Mrs, 1949, F 1,26:3
Madden, Frank X, 1940, S 22,49:1
Madden, George, 1955, S 20,31:2
Madden, George J Sr, 1955, F 25,21:2
Madden, H F, 1877, Je 12,5:2
Madden, Henry D, 1941, S 2,17:3
Madden, Howard C, 1954, F 9,27:3
Madden, J E, 1929, N 4,25:3
Madden, James, 1937, Ja 30,17:3
Madden, James H, 1953, F 17,34:3
Madden, James T, 1950, Jl 15,13:4
Madden, John F (por), 1946, My 21,23:3
Madden, John H (funl, Ja 25,7:1), 1925, Ja 23,19:5
Madden, John H, 1945, Jl 19,23:5; 1956, N 1,39:4
Madden, John J, 1943, N 25,25:5; 1963, Jl 30,29:2
Madden, John P, 1940, Mr 7,23:4; 1948, N 29,23:4
Madden, John T (por), 1948, Jl 3,15:1
Madden, John T, 1949, Ap 29,23:5
Madden, John T Jr (cor, Mr 25,41:5), 1966, Mr 24, 39:2
Madden, Joseph P, 1968, O 12,37:3
Madden, M B, 1928, Ap 28,1:2
Madden, Mary A M Mrs, 1940, F 14,21:1
Madden, Michael Capt, 1903, My 3,9:6
Madden, Michael J, 1947, O 24,23:3
Madden, Michael L, 1961, Ja 17,37:3
Madden, Owney (Owen V), 1965, Ap 24,1:4
Madden, Patrick J, 1943, D 21,27:4
Madden, Patrick V, 1939, Jl 11,19:5
Madden, Paul J, 1958, Je 2,27:5
Madden, Ralph C, 1958, O 29,35:6
Madden, Richard J, 1951, My 10,31:1
Madden, Robert, 1952, Ja 14,19:5
Madden, Sarah L Mrs, 1940, Mr 26,21:4
Madden, Theodore A, 1917, D 21,11:5
Madden, Thomas, 1948, D 28,22:3
Madden, Thomas A, 1947, Jl 30,21:6
Madden, Thomas F, 1954, Ja 22,27:1
Maddеn, Thomas J, 1942, Je 14,46:4
Madden, W Charles, 1945, N 21,21:1
Madden, Walter A, 1950, F 23,27:2
Madden, Walter D, 1945, F 6,19:5
Madden, William E, 1945, Je 14,19:5
Madden, William J, 1938, Jl 23,13:5
Madden, William L, 1943, My 11,21:4
Maddern, Mary, 1912, Ap 20,15:6
Maddern, Richard H, 1917, D 25,15:4
Maddever, Noah F, 1946, O 27,62:5
Maddigan, Arthur G, 1944, O 26,23:4
Maddigan, John P, 1950, F 26,78:1
Maddigan, Mary, 1960, Ja 4,29:4
Maddii, Pietro, 1954, F 4,25:6
Maddison, Isabel, 1950, O 24,29:3
Maddock, Archibald M, 1961, Je 4,86:6
Maddock, Aubrey L, 1949, My 19,29:3
Maddock, Charles S Jr Mrs, 1958, N 6,37:2
Maddock, Frederick R, 1962, Ag 4,19:6
Maddock, Harold S, 1938, Ap 2,15:4
Maddock, Harry Smith, 1914, Ja 25,IV,5:5
Maddock, Henry A, 1947, O 5,71:3
Maddock, John N, 1956, Mr 11,89:1
Maddock, Raymond C, 1948, D 11,15:3
Maddock, Sylvester J, 1955, Mr 1,25:5
Maddock, Walter J, 1951, Ja 26,24:2
Maddocks, John A, 1966, Ja 21,47:3
Maddox, Aaron W, 1952, Mr 13,29:4
Maddox, Claude (J E Moore), 1958, Je 23,31:6
Maddox, Flavius C, 1949, Ag 15,17:4
Maddox, Floyd, 1954, D 19,84:5
Maddox, J T (see also N 17), 1876, N 20,8:1
Maddox, Louis W, 1956, Jl 3,25:4
Maddox, Samuel T Justice (trb, Mr 14,11:2; funl, Mr 16,13:7), 1916, Mr 13,9:3
Maddox, William T, 1945, O 15,17:5
Maddox, William T Mrs, 1950, My 20,15:2
Maddren, William Dr, 1909, Ja 10,13:6
Maddry, Charles E, 1962, S 19,39:4
Maddux, David R, 1939, Je 11,45:3
Maddux, Lafayette J, 1941, O 31,23:4
Maddux, Lewis, 1907, My 15,9:6
Maddux, Parker S, 1953, N 2,25:6
Madduz, John L (por), 1937, Jl 27,21:1
Maddy, Joseph E, 1966, Ap 19,41:4
Madeira, Albert P, 1925, N 5,23:5; 1964, Ja 15,31:1
Madeira, Edward W, 1956, Je 9,17:3
Madeira, Louis C 3d, 1943, Mr 21,26:8
Madeira, Lucy (Mrs D L Wing), 1960, Je 30,29:4
Madeira, Percy C, 1942, F 23,21:6
Madeira, Percy C Jr Mrs, 1951, My 5,17:3
Madeleine, Dowager Countess of Effingham (Mrs F H C Howard), 1958, Je 20,23:1
Madeleine, Mother, 1948, My 17,19:3
Madeleine Morris, Sister, 1945, Ag 5,38:4
Madeley, Walter B, 1947, My 13,25:5
Madelin, Louis, 1956, Ag 20,21:3
Maden, Harold, 1949, O 20,29:2
Maden, Sarah, 1959, N 26,2:7
Madeo, Joseph F, 1951, Mr 23,21:5
Madeo, Lucius D, 1966, Ag 31,40:5
Mader, A Ivan Jr Dr, 1968, Je 21,41:3
Mader, Otto, 1944, S 16,13:6
Mader, Solomon D, 1946, Jl 31,27:3
Mader, William Mrs, 1948, Ap 27,25:3
Madera, Carl R, 1947, Jl 8,23:3
Maderna, Osmar, 1951, Ap 29,27:4
Madero, Francisco, 1916, S 4,7:5
Madey, Elia D, 1957, N 24,86:4
Madgets, Casmir, 1937, O 24,33:2
Madiera, Marion C Mrs, 1938, D 14,25:4
Madigan, Cecil T, 1947, Ja 15,26:3
Madigan, Edgar W Mrs, 1950, D 12,33:1
Madigan, Edith H Mrs, 1942, Je 4,19:3
Madigan, Edward, 1941, My 21,23:1
Madigan, Elinor A Mrs, 1942, D 9,27:4
Madigan, Francis A, 1968, Je 9,84:5
Madigan, James C, 1943, Ag 29,38:4
Madigan, James G Mrs, 1943, Je 11,13:5
Madigan, John B, 1918, Ja 20,17:1
Madigan, John J, 1951, F 22,31:4; 1951, My 3,29:1
Madigan, John P Mrs, 1961, D 30,19:4
Madigan, John T, 1907, My 20,9:6
Madigan, John W, 1967, Jl 26,36:2
Madigan, Joseph V, 1948, Ag 29,56:7
Madigan, LaVerne (Mrs H Bordewich), 1962, Ag 23,59:1
Madigan, Michael J, 1939, N 16,23:4
Madigan, Patrick F Mrs, 1943, Jl 12,15:5
Madigan, Slip (Edw P), 1966, O 11,43:4
Madigan, Stephen J, 1953, Je 13,15:6
Madigan, T F, 1936, Ap 20,19:1
Madigan, Thomas H, 1938, Ja 31,19:5
Madigan, William M, 1950, Je 5,23:1
Madigan (Sister Mary Servatia), 1963, Jl 13,17:4
Madill, Grant C, 1943, Mr 27,13:4
Madill, Grant C Mrs, 1941, S 6,15:3
Madison, Edmond H (funl, S 23,7:4), 1911, S 19,13:5
Madison, Hans C A, 1958, My 8,29:4
Madison, Harold L, 1950, O 5,32:2
Madison, James, 1943, Mr 30,26:5
Madison, James J Com, 1922, D 28,17:6
Madison, James V, 1943, S 14,23:6
Madison, L F, 1932, Mr 17,24:6
Madison, Mary B Mrs, 1937, Jl 25,II,7:4
Madison, Maud, 1953, O 9,27:4
Madison, Robert L, 1954, O 2,17:6
Madison, Vincent S, 1960, My 12,35:3
Madison, Zachariah H, 1938, Jl 2,13:2
Madjaroff, Rashkin, 1943, O 14,21:4
Madjeski, Edward Mrs, 1945, Je 30,17:5
Madocks, Llewellyn, 1954, Je 27,69:1
Madole, Richard, 1945, Ja 23,19:5
Madon, August L, 1946, Je 9,40:6
Madon, Jim, 1916, S 2,7:3
Madore, George, 1957, O 26,42:2
Madory, Eugene V, 1953, My 26,29:5
Madou, J B, 1877, Ap 4,4:7
Madrazo, Don R de, 1898, Ag 22,7:5
Madrazo, Mariano F, 1949, My 4,29:2
Madrazo, Raimundo de, 1920, S 18,9:2
Madre, Jeane de Countess, 1915, Mr 15,11:4
Madrid, Francisco S, 1942, My 23,13:5
Madriz, Jose Dr, 1911, My 16,13:5
Madry, Robert W, 1955, Ap 9,13:4
Madsen, Alfred W, 1954, Ja 17,93:1
Madsen, Christian, 1957, Ja 22,29:2
Madsen, Jens J, 1949, N 25,31:5
Madsen, John K, 1942, My 12,19:1
Madsen, Mads Mrs, 1949, F 10,27:4
Madsen, Martin C, 1948, Mr 8,23:4; 1954, S 5,50:1
Madsen, Robert E, 1963, O 31,33:2
Madsen, Thorbjorn, 1962, Jl 20,25:5
Madsen, Thorvald, 1957, Ap 16,33:4
Madsen, Vincent, 1961, Jl 24,23:3
Madson, Walter E, 1948, N 26,23:4
Maduro, Charles, 1947, O 6,21:3
Maduro, Denis, 1967, Ag 25,35:3
Maduro, Monti L, 1956, Ja 3,31:3
Maduro, S E L, 1951, Mr 11,92:3
Maduro, Sarah J H Mrs, 1938, Ja 5,21:5
Maeda, Michiko, 1966, Ja 29,5:1
Maeda, Toshisada, 1944, O 4,20:2
Maeder, Abbott S, 1941, S 22,15:4
Maeder, C F, 1898, N 13,8:1
Maeder, Edmund L, 1945, Ja 24,21:3
Maedler, Johan Heinrich, 1874, Mr 19,5:3
Maeger, Martin A, 1960, Jl 23,19:3
Maenan, Lord (W F K Taylor), 1951, S 23,86:2
Maenin, Joseph, 1953, Ap 30,31:2
Maenner, T H (Ted), 1958, Ja 19,87:1
Maer, S William, 1962, Ap 8,86:5
Maerlender, Adolph, 1903, D 11,9:6
Maerlender, William A, 1944, D 28,19:4
Maertins, Gustave Sr, 1941, Mr 30,49:1
Maes, Alfred, 1941, Ag 21,17:1
Maes, Camillus P Bp, 1915, My 12,13:4
Maes, Julian P, 1946, Ag 13,27:3
Maes, Urban, 1954, Mr 17,31:4
Maeser, Edward, 1942, Ag 28,19:3
Maestri, Catullo, 1952, Je 21,15:4
Maeterlinck, Maurice, 1949, My 7,13:1
Maetzel, Richard, 1958, O 17,29:1
Mafee, Frank J, 1966, Ja 30,84:7
Mafera, Joseph F, 1967, F 13,33:2
Maffi, P, 1931, Mr 17,14:2
Maffitt, Robert S Mrs, 1949, O 24,23:5
Maflin, Alfred H, 1915, Ja 12,9:4
Magafan, Jenne, 1952, O 21,29:5
Magagna, Albert, 1946, D 15,77:3
Magalhaes, Agamenon, 1952, Ag 25,17:1
Magalhaes, Frank V, 1963, Ap 3,47:2
Magan, John T, 1961, Jl 24,23:4
Magan, John W, 1958, My 30,21:5
Magan, Percy T, 1947, D 18,29:2
Magana, Gildardo, 1939, D 14,27:2
Magann, John B, 1937, My 16,II,8:6
Magarvey, John R, 1944, N 1,23:3
Magary, Alvin E, 1964, Je 15,29:3
Magaz, Antonio de, 1953, O 14,29:5
Magazine, Samuel Mrs, 1959, Ap 15,33:1
Magaziner, Louis, 1956, My 21,25:4
Magdalen, Sister, 1947, Ja 31,23:4
Magdalen, Sister St, 1938, N 16,23:3
Magdalene von Bracht, Sister, 1941, D 29,15:5
Magdich, Frank, 1952, Mr 6,31:4
Mage, Myron, 1965, Jl 26,23:1
Maged, Alan J, 1960, Je 2,33:4
Maged, Howard E, 1961, F 23,27:3
Maged, Jacob, 1939, Ap 1,19:2
Magee, A S, 1903, Ag 17,7:5
Magee, A Vedder, 1949, F 8,25:3
Magee, Alonzo H, 1948, Je 23,27:6
Magee, Anna F, 1955, My 18,31:4
Magee, Anna M, 1954, N 13,15:5
Magee, Bill, 1951, Ap 12,33:2
Magee, Carl, 1946, F 2,13:3
Magee, Charles M, 1950, Ja 21,17:1
Magee, Cuthbert G, 1963, Ag 31,17:4
Magee, Daniel, 1953, S 3,21:1
Magee, E C Mrs, 1909, My 12,7:5
Magee, Edward F, 1949, D 25,26:7
Magee, Emmett M, 1951, F 13,31:3
Magee, Forrest N, 1941, Ja 9,21:3
Magee, Fran, 1959, O 12,19:5
Magee, Fred, 1953, My 6,31:1
Magee, Genevieve Mrs, 1937, Jl 12,38:4
Magee, George W (will), 1939, F 28,20:3
Magee, Graham, 1963, D 5,41:4
Magee, Guy, 1919, Je 6,13:4
Magee, Henry I, 1942, My 2,13:5
Magee, Hubert C, 1955, My 9,23:4
Magee, J Henry Mrs, 1950, Ap 25,31:4
Magee, J Ralph Mrs, 1943, N 4,23:4
Magee, J Rodney, 1941, Ag 12,19:4
Magee, J Rodney Mrs, 1949, Ap 17,76:5
Magee, J S Mrs, 1938, Ap 21,19:3
Magee, James C, 1938, D 1,23:4
Magee, James D (por), 1948, Ap 7,25:1
Magee, James D Sr, 1946, Jl 26,21:6
Magee, James F Jr, 1955, Ap 16,19:5
Magee, James K, 1941, Jl 14,13:3
Magee, James M, 1949, Ap 18,25:6
Magee, John, 1942, Jl 16,19:2
Magee, John B, 1943, Ap 8,23:1
Magee, John F, 1960, Ag 4,25:3
Magee, John G, 1953, S 10,25:5
Magee, John L C, 1939, D 3,60:7
Magee, John Mrs, 1952, N 15,17:3
Magee, John R, 1903, N 19,9:7
Magee, John S, 1951, Ag 13,17:3
Magee, John W, 1960, D 15,43:2
Magee, Joseph B, 1957, Ag 14,25:4
Magee, Joseph T, 1945, S 10,19:4
Magee, Loretta, 1903, Ap 28,16:2
Magee, Margaret, 1952, Jl 22,25:3
Magee, Margaret M, 1961, Ag 25,25:3

Magee, Raymond L, 1944, Ag 28,11:5
Magee, Richard J, 1953, Jl 30,23:4
Magee, Robert B, 1939, My 10,23:4
Magee, Robert P, 1940, My 12,48:3
Magee, Robert P Mrs, 1941, Ja 23,22:2
Magee, Samuel B Mrs, 1952, Jl 15,21:2
Magee, W David Mrs, 1952, Jl 10,31:4
Magee, William A, 1938, Mr 26,15:4; 1953, Ja 24,15:3
Magee, William E, 1946, Ja 27,42:5
Magee, William J, 1940, Jl 3,17:3
Magee, William M, 1965, Je 15,41:2
Magel, Frank L, 1952, D 24,17:1
Magen, Harry, 1952, Ja 3,27:1
Magennis, Byron C, 1942, F 19,19:4
Magennis, Peter E Rev, 1937, Ag 31,23:6
Magennis, Thomas Msgr, 1912, F 24,11:5
Magens, E Coit Mrs, 1947, D 11,34:3
Mager, Alois, 1946, D 31,17:2
Mager, Charles A (Gus), 1956, Jl 18,27:5
Mager, F Robert, 1952, Jl 5,15:5
Mager, George, 1950, S 21,31:5
Mager, George T, 1949, Mr 4,21:3
Mager, Henry, 1947, S 26,23:2
Mager, Martin, 1937, N 9,23:4
Magera, Roman Mrs (C Stewart), 1966, Je 17,45:3
Magerkurth, George, 1966, O 8,31:2
Magerum, Mahlon R, 1942, Ap 10,17:3
Mages, Kenneth P Mrs, 1956, Ja 14,19:5
Maggia, Clement, 1967, D 7,2:6
Maggio, Stephen J, 1958, N 18,37:4
Maggiolo, Harry, 1953, Mr 24,31:4
Maggiolo, Henry L, 1962, Jl 16,23:4
Maggiorotti, Leone A, 1940, F 7,21:2
Maggrett, Ralph J Mrs, 1954, Mr 19,24:4
Maggs, Douglas B, 1962, S 15,25:2
Maggs, Ernest U, 1955, Je 6,27:3
Maggs, Gilbert E, 1955, Mr 26,15:2
Maghee, James M Mrs, 1958, F 12,29:4
Magher, Arthur E, 1954, Je 12,15:4
Magi, Lloyd O, 1953, My 14,29:5
Magid, Bernard, 1967, Jl 6,35:2
Magid, Isadore, 1952, D 17,33:1
Magid, Jacob M, 1951, D 9,90:3
Magid, Maurice O (por), 1940, Ag 1,21:1
Magida, Nathan, 1961, Je 1,35:2
Magidoff, Jacob, 1943, Ag 27,17:4
Magie, Abbie F, 1938, N 15,23:6
Magie, Barnes P, 1944, Ja 11,19:1
Magie, David, 1960, Ap 24,88:3
Magie, David Rev Dr, 1865, My 11,5:4
Magie, George W, 1948, Mr 2,23:2
Magie, Henrietta O, 1944, Jl 8,11:6
Magie, Lucy Belden, 1909, Ap 4,13:4
Magie, William F, 1943, Je 7,13:3
Magie, William Jay, 1917, Ja 16,9:2
Magil, Joseph, 1945, F 12,19:3
Magil, Max Mrs, 1940, O 11,21:5
Magil, William K, 1944, My 12,19:3
Magill, Andrew, 1959, N 4,35:4
Magill, Ann Elizabeth Mrs, 1916, Mr 1,11:6
Magill, Charles E, 1943, S 10,23:2
Magill, Charles J Capt, 1905, Ap 5,9:6
Magill, Charles N Mrs, 1943, Ag 29,38:7
Magill, Daniel H Sr, 1951, O 12,28:2
Magill, David, 1941, Mr 17,17:3
Magill, Edward Hicks, 1907, D 11,11:4
Magill, Frank S, 1952, N 15,17:1
Magill, George C Mrs, 1953, S 5,16:4
Magill, George P, 1954, O 5,27:3
Magill, George T, 1953, O 7,29:2
Magill, H M, 1904, S 23,1:2
Magill, Henry P, 1941, Ag 21,17:4
Magill, Joseph, 1904, F 6,9:6
Magill, Louis J Mrs, 1941, Mr 25,26:1
Magill, Pat Jr, 1949, D 26,11:1
Magill, Robert D, 1966, Je 30,39:3
Magill, Robert E, 1939, My 5,23:5
Magill, Roscoe C, 1950, Ja 5,25:3
Magill, Roswell, 1963, D 18,41:1
Magill, Urwin J Mrs, 1951, N 16,12:4
Magill, Walter H, 1958, Ap 23,33:4
Magilligan, Lawrence P A Mrs, 1957, D 12,29:4
Magilton, A L Col, 1875, D 30,4:7
Magin, Francis W, 1965, Ja 23,25:5
Magin, Henry, 1941, Ag 23,13:5
Magin, Jake, 1937, F 27,20:6
Magin, John R, 1910, Je 17,7:5
Maginn, Agnes J, 1945, Jl 12,11:7
Maginn, Edward, 1956, Jl 16,21:2
Maginn, Ivan E, 1959, S 20,86:4
Maginn, Jack F, 1967, Je 17,31:4
Maginn, James, 1910, Mr 9,9:1
Maginn, Thomas A, 1943, S 5,28:5
Maginnes, Albert H, 1966, Ja 31,39:1
Maginnis, Charles D, 1955, F 16,29:1
Maginnis, Charles D Jr, 1954, F 27,13:5
Maginnis, George W, 1947, Je 30,19:3
Maginnis, John, 1863, Mr 17,1:2
Maginnis, Robert E, 1948, S 10,23:3
Maginnis, S Abbot, 1941, S 27,17:2
Maginnis, Thomas A, 1957, S 4,33:3
Maginnis, William H, 1954, S 30,31:2
Maginot, A, 1932, Ja 7,23:3
Maginot, Francoise, 1950, Je 19,6:6
Maginot, Mme, 1941, Ag 10,37:2
Magistrati, Maria C Countess, 1939, O 22,40:4
Maglaghlin, Webb C, 1938, S 23,27:4
Maglathlin, Frank W, 1943, Ja 23,13:1
Maglathlin, Leon E, 1956, My 10,31:2
Magliaro, Dominick J, 1962, Ap 30,27:3
Maglie, Joseph L, 1956, My 19,19:3
Maglin, William H, 1958, Ja 12,86:7
Maglio, Ercole, 1949, Je 1,31:4
Magliocco, Joseph (funl), 1964, Ja 1,41:1
Maglione, Luigi, 1944, Ag 23,19:3
Maglioni, Raphael, 1953, My 29,25:5
Magloire, Clement, 1945, N 16,19:2
Magloire, Jacques, 1961, D 18,35:2
Magly, G William (por), 1938, My 18,21:4
Magna, Herman W Mrs, 1953, Ap 15,31:5
Magna, Russell W Mrs, 1960, O 19,45:4
Magnasci, Osvaldo, 1920, My 6,11:1
Magnat, Louis A, 1961, Je 3,23:1
Magne, Pierre, 1878, Je 9,7:4
Magnel, Gustave, 1955, Jl 7,27:2
Magnell, Alfred E, 1959, Mr 27,23:2
Magnelsson, William C, 1919, O 23,13:4
Magner, Edward J, 1947, N 7,23:4; 1964, Je 27,25:6
Magner, Edward J Mrs, 1946, Ap 18,27:2
Magner, Francis J, 1947, Je 14,15:4
Magner, George H, 1950, Ap 30,102:6
Magner, James J, 1944, Mr 9,17:3
Magner, James P, 1944, Je 28,23:2
Magner, James P Mrs, 1954, F 2,27:4
Magner, James R, 1960, My 18,41:3
Magner, John, 1907, Je 7,9:6
Magner, John F, 1907, Ja 28,7:4
Magner, John J, 1945, Ja 8,17:3; 1951, Je 3,93:1
Magner, John M, 1943, My 7,19:3
Magner, Joseph F, 1940, D 5,25:2
Magner, Thomas F, 1945, D 23,18:5
Magnes, David, 1922, Ap 9,28:3
Magnes, Judah L, 1948, O 28,29:1
Magnes, Judah L Mrs, 1968, D 3,47:3
Magness, Sallie Mrs, 1963, Ag 8,27:2
Magni, Alessio, 1944, Ap 14,19:6
Magni, Harry Mrs, 1946, Mr 14,25:3
Magni, Robert A Jr, 1946, Ap 18,27:5
Magnier, Anthony A, 1959, F 7,19:2
Magnier, Edward F, 1940, N 19,23:2
Magnin, Ami J Dr, 1917, N 27,13:3
Magnin, Cyril Mrs, 1948, Jl 14,23:5
Magnin, E John, 1944, N 26,57:2
Magnin, Edgar J, 1942, Jl 12,36:6
Magnin, Felix, 1941, O 12,52:1
Magnin, Jacques Mrs (K Adams), 1959, F 19,31:1
Magnolia, Joseph F, 1953, Ja 8,30:2
Magnon-Pujo, Charles Lt, 1921, F 4,11:3
Magnoni, Salvatore, 1959, O 15,39:4
Magnus, Baron, 1881, Jl 7,5:3
Magnus, Edward, 1950, Ag 19,13:1
Magnus, Elizabeth G, 1947, N 17,21:3
Magnus, Gusta V Mrs, 1940, Mr 26,21:4
Magnus, Julius, 1905, S 17,9:6
Magnus, Walter, 1952, D 31,15:5
Magnus-Levy, Adolph, 1955, F 7,21:2
Magnuson, Alfred G, 1953, Ap 13,27:5
Magnuson, E Herman, 1955, Jl 17,61:2
Magnuson, Edward, 1955, O 18,37:2
Magnuson, Fritts, 1951, Jl 19,23:1
Magnuson, Mildred, 1960, Jl 13,35:2
Magnuson, Oscar W, 1956, My 12,19:1
Magnuson, Paul B, 1968, N 6,39:1
Magnussen, J, 1926, Je 25,21:4
Magnusson, Aug, 1949, Jl 17,57:2
Magnusson, Carl E, 1941, Jl 12,13:4
Magny, Pere, 1879, F 19,5:6
Magoffin, Edward T, 1941, Ja 20,12:1
Magoffin, Ralph V D (por), 1942, My 17,47:3
Magoffin, William H, 1942, F 3,19:2
Magone, Daniel, 1904, S 5,5:6
Magonet, Mandel, 1948, Ap 30,23:5
Magonigle, Gertrude, 1939, Ap 19,23:1
Magonigle, H Van Buren Mrs, 1949, Ag 10,22:3
Magonigle, John Henry, 1919, D 23,9:2
Magoon, Charles E, 1920, Ja 15,11:3
Magoon, George H, 1943, D 7,27:5
Magoon, Mabel Mrs, 1947, D 8,25:3
Magor, B, 1933, Ja 15,24:1
Magor, Leslie D, 1961, D 24,36:8
Magor, Robert J (por), 1942, Jl 5,29:1
Magoun, G B, 1902, D 17,9:6
Magoun, Roy W, 1956, Ap 14,17:4
Magovern, James P, 1948, O 13,25:2
Magovern, John J, 1944, My 19,19:3
Magowan, David, 1952, Ap 17,29:5
Magowan, Elmer T, 1958, Ap 25,27:4
Magowan, George, 1944, Ag 14,15:4
Magowan, George H, 1948, Ag 5,21:3
Magowan, J H, 1883, N 27,5:4
Magowan, James M, 1952, F 23,11:4
Magowan, John H, 1951, Ap 8,93:1
Magowan, Zacharia, 1947, Ap 3,25:4
Magown, David E, 1872, Je 8,1:6
Magrane, Joseph J, 1941, Ag 18,13:1
Magrane, Robert, 1916, Jl 20,11:5
Magrane, Thais, 1957, Ja 29,31:5
Magrath, A Jocelyn, 1956, Ja 12,27:3
Magrath, Charles A, 1949, O 31,25:4
Magrath, Christopher Col, 1923, Ag 7,17:3
Magrath, George B, 1938, D 12,19:3
Magrath, James W, 1963, O 23,41:3
Magrath, P J, 1936, Ag 22,13:1
Magrath, William G, 1949, Ag 7,61:1
Magrattan, William A, 1952, My 26,23:4
Magrauth, Joseph W, 1949, S 30,24:2
Magrauth, Joseph W Mrs, 1949, S 30,24:2
Magraw, Lester A, 1949, Mr 27,76:5
Magri, Primo Count, 1920, N 1,15:6
Magri, Rocco, 1963, Jl 10,35:4
Magrill, George, 1952, Je 3,29:4
Magrin-Vernery, Raoul C (R Monclar), 1964, Je 4, 37:4
Magritte, Rene, 1967, Ag 16,38:4
Magruder, Belle B Mrs, 1941, O 7,23:2
Magruder, Bernard F, 1968, O 29,47:3
Magruder, Bruce, 1953, Jl 25,11:1
Magruder, Calvert Judge, 1968, My 24,47:3
Magruder, Charles, 1963, Je 5,41:2
Magruder, Charles Mrs, 1947, My 29,21:4
Magruder, David Lynn Brig-Gen, 1910, N 23,9:5
Magruder, Ernest Pendleton Dr, 1920, Jl 28,13:5
Magruder, G Lloyd Dr, 1914, Ja 30,9:5
Magruder, J B Gen, 1871, F 20,4:7
Magruder, James Dr, 1918, Ap 17,13:4
Magruder, John, 1958, My 1,31:1
Magruder, John H Jr, 1963, Ag 22,27:2
Magruder, John H Mrs, 1964, Je 6,23:5
Magruder, Julia, 1907, Je 10,7:6
Magruder, Lewis W, 1957, My 14,2:5
Magruder, Lloyd B, 1964, Mr 22,77:2
Magruder, Peter H, 1947, Ja 7,27:2
Magruder, Thomas P (por), 1938, My 27,17:1
Magruder, Thomas P Mrs, 1951, Ag 20,19:5
Magruder, W Lauson, 1952, Ap 1,29:3
Magruder, Warren K, 1944, Ap 16,41:3
Magsaysay, Exequiel, 1968, Ja 26,47:1
Magsaysay, Paterno, 1957, Mr 18,8:2
Magsaysay, Ramon, 1957, Mr 18,1:8
Maguill, Harry R, 1949, Jl 16,13:4
Maguire, Alexander H, 1947, Ja 22,23:1
Maguire, Alfred, 1949, O 15,15:4
Maguire, Arnold G, 1949, D 6,31:4
Maguire, Charles A, 1954, Mr 25,29:3
Maguire, Charles F, 1946, N 24,79:4
Maguire, Charles J, 1960, Ja 14,33:3; 1966, Je 6,41:2
Maguire, Edward B, 1949, Mr 20,76:6
Maguire, Edward J, 1937, N 4,25:6; 1951, Jl 29,69:3
Maguire, Eugene L Dr, 1937, F 28,II,8:6
Maguire, Francis J Msgr, 1917, Ja 3,11:5
Maguire, Frank, 1947, Jl 31,21:2
Maguire, Frank G Sr, 1956, N 9,29:3
Maguire, Frederick, 1961, N 5,89:1
Maguire, Gabriel R Mrs, 1953, F 20,19:4
Maguire, Hamilton E Jr, 1950, S 6,31:8
MaGuire, Helene (Sister Regina Cecilia), 1953, My 12,27:3
Maguire, Hugh Rev, 1914, Ja 23,11:5
Maguire, J Russell, 1966, N 11,43:2
Maguire, J W R, 1940, F 12,17:5
Maguire, James, 1914, O 3,11:4
Maguire, James E, 1945, My 4,20:2
Maguire, James I, 1948, Jl 30,17:2
Maguire, James J, 1940, Mr 6,23:6; 1943, F 6,13:2; 1952, Je 7,19:4
Maguire, Jeremiah De S, 1959, Ag 19,29:1
Maguire, Jeremiah Mrs, 1948, Mr 30,23:4
Maguire, John, 1908, Mr 17,7:5; 1942, Jl 23,19:4
Maguire, John F Mrs, 1962, Ag 12,81:1
Maguire, John Francis, 1872, N 3,1:7
Maguire, John J, 1940, F 22,23:1; 1941, Ap 5,17:6
Maguire, John S Mrs, 1951, D 6,33:1
Maguire, Joseph A, 1959, Mr 14,23:2
Maguire, Joseph F, 1959, S 11,27:3
Maguire, Joseph J, 1950, Ap 27,29:1
Maguire, Joseph L, 1965, Je 30,37:2
Maguire, Laurence Mrs, 1954, F 20,17:6
Maguire, Leon, 1951, D 16,90:5
Maguire, Louis W, 1959, O 20,39:4
Maguire, Margaret, 1945, Ag 31,17:4
Maguire, Mary F, 1937, D 9,25:4
Maguire, Michael Mrs, 1968, S 7,29:1
Maguire, Mickey, 1950, Je 7,29:3
Maguire, Neil, 1963, S 17,35:4
Maguire, Patricia, 1937, S 29,14:5
Maguire, Peter F, 1947, Ap 1,27:1
Maguire, Peter Rev, 1937, S 14,23:6
Maguire, Philip, 1947, My 10,13:4
Maguire, Philip B, 1959, S 7,15:4
Maguire, Richard C, 1942, Jl 11,13:5
Maguire, Ruth S Mrs, 1945, Mr 27,19:3
Maguire, Samuel W, 1938, Je 23,21:4
Maguire, Stephen A, 1950, S 22,31:4
Maguire, Thomas E, 1909, S 7,9:6
Maguire, Thomas G, 1948, Ag 16,19:4
Maguire, Thomas H M, 1964, D 13,86:4
Maguire, Thomas J, 1914, Mr 23,11:2
Maguire, Vic, 1912, Jl 10,9:6
Maguire, Walter J, 1955, Je 28,27:1

Maguire, Walter N, 1967, Ja 2,19:3
Maguire, Walter P, 1940, Ap 28,36:4
Maguire, Walter R, 1962, Ja 12,23:4
Maguire, William A, 1953, S 16,33:1
Maguire, William C, 1952, Ja 6,92:2
Maguire, William F, 1942, O 30,19:2
Maguire, William G (Sept 28), 1965, O 11,61:3
Maguire, William J Msgr, 1923, Jl 12,17:4
Maguire, William L Mrs, 1953, F 23,25:4
Maguire, Willie, 1951, N 9,27:2
Magunson, Edward, 1874, Ja 7,8:3
Magwood, William, 1951, F 18,76:4
Magyar, Bertalan Mrs, 1965, F 27,25:3
Magyar, Eugene Bp, 1968, O 21,47:4
Magyari, Imre, 1940, Ap 30,21:2
Magzen, Nathan Mrs, 1952, Ap 29,27:5
Mahady, Phil C, 1953, D 20,76:3
Mahady, Stephen A, 1951, Je 20,27:6
Mahaffey, Annie L Mrs, 1940, Mr 30,15:4
Mahaffey, J Lynn, 1948, N 3,27:3
Mahaffey, John F, 1944, Jl 22,15:5
Mahaffey, John J, 1943, My 3,17:2
Mahaffy, James R, 1943, O 8,19:2
Mahaffy, John P Sir, 1919, My 1,17:7
Mahaffy, Wilson B, 1948, O 23,15:2
Maham, John P, 1938, Ja 10,17:4
Mahan, Adm, 1914, D 2,13:3
Mahan, Bryan F, 1923, N 17,13:4
Mahan, Charles J, 1951, My 25,27:4
Mahan, Charles R, 1951, S 15,15:4
Mahan, Dennis Hart, 1925, My 30,9:4
Mahan, Edgar C, 1948, O 29,25:2
Mahan, Edna (funl plans, Ap 17,32:7), 1968, Ap 14, 76:6
Mahan, Frederick Maj, 1918, N 30,11:4
Mahan, Harold W, 1946, Jl 25,21:6
Mahan, Jack, 1955, S 3,31:5
Mahan, Jane L, 1945, Ag 28,19:5
Mahan, John R, 1949, Jl 20,25:2
Mahan, Lawrence E (por), 1946, N 20,31:3
Mahan, Lyle E, 1966, My 19,47:2
Mahan, Mary A Mrs, 1937, Ag 31,23:2
Mahan, Priscilla, 1949, S 8,29:3
Mahan, Sidney D, 1953, My 23,15:5
Mahan, Sylvester A Sr, 1947, N 4,26:3
Mahan, William, 1950, My 1,25:2
Mahan, William H Sr, 1951, F 18,78:4
Mahan, William J, 1945, D 6,27:3; 1948, Jl 27,25:4
Mahana, George S, 1957, Ag 15,21:5
Mahaney, John Mrs, 1945, Ag 30,21:5
Mahaney, William J, 1954, My 13,29:3
Mahannah, Fred L, 1941, O 13,17:5
Mahany, Martin M N Mrs, 1937, F 14,II,9:4
Mahany, Rowland B, 1937, My 4,25:4
Mahany, Thomas H, 1943, Mr 27,14:8
Mahar, Catherine Mrs, 1952, N 28,26:4
Mahar, Dennis H Prof, 1871, S 17,5:3
Mahar, Ella T, 1948, S 18,17:3
Mahar, George V Mrs, 1951, Je 7,33:5
Mahar, James A (Bro Azades Gabriel), 1966, Ja 4, 31:4
Mahar, James W, 1923, Ag 5,26:2
Mahar, John A, 1956, Ja 12,27:4
Mahar, John J, 1938, My 21,15:6; 1947, Jl 27,44:4
Mahar, Joseph G, 1965, Ag 23,31:4
Mahar, Mary E Mrs, 1958, Ag 9,13:3
Mahar, Raymond L, 1953, My 22,27:4
Mahar, Thomas, 1954, N 10,33:2
Mahar, William J, 1940, Mr 25,15:2
Maharam, Louis, 1941, Ap 6,49:2
Maharishi, Ramana, 1950, Ap 16,105:1
Maharshi, Ramana, 1950, Ap 15,15:4
Mahedy, Charles S Sr, 1952, Ap 1,29:3
Mahedy, Edward J, 1952, Ap 14,19:5
Mahedy, John S, 1938, O 8,17:6
Maher, Agnes (Sister Mary Francis), 1940, My 23, 23:4
Maher, Arthur P, 1942, Jl 26,31:3
Maher, Arthur P Mrs, 1948, S 17,25:4
Maher, Clarence J, 1950, Ag 8,29:4
Maher, Dale W, 1948, Je 9,29:2
Maher, Daniel L, 1939, Jl 12,19:6
Maher, Edward A, 1920, S 15,9:2
Maher, Edward F Mrs, 1950, Je 1,27:5
Maher, Edward J, 1940, O 7,17:1; 1942, Je 23,19:2
Maher, Ellen T, 1951, Ja 28,76:4
Maher, Frances, 1958, N 24,29:4
Maher, Frances L, 1940, Ap 23,23:1
Maher, Francis X, 1957, Je 6,31:2
Maher, Gibson, 1958, N 23,89:1
Maher, Helen, 1948, D 12,92:3
Maher, Hugh F, 1951, N 10,17:7
Maher, James, 1922, Je 27,15:4
Maher, James B, 1963, Ag 10,17:1
Maher, James Capt, 1917, Je 11,11:4
Maher, James D, 1921, Je 4,13:6
Maher, James E, 1955, F 27,86:2
Maher, James F J, 1966, D 9,47:5
Maher, James F J Mrs, 1966, O 18,45:3
Maher, James P, 1942, Jl 6,15:5; 1952, Mr 23,94:3
Maher, James S, 1940, Je 9,45:2; 1943, S 23,21:4
Maher, James T, 1941, D 6,17:4; 1963, My 9,37:3
Maher, Jeremiah J, 1942, Ap 16,21:6
Maher, John, 1940, My 15,25:6
Maher, John A, 1950, D 15,31:4
Maher, John C Mrs, 1961, D 21,27:3
Maher, John F, 1956, Ja 23,25:4
Maher, John G, 1939, Je 11,44:7
Maher, John J, 1944, My 2,19:5; 1957, Mr 31,88:4; 1960, Jl 24,64:6
Maher, John L, 1942, Ja 28,19:3
Maher, John W, 1959, Ag 27,27:5
Maher, John W Mrs, 1941, F 9,48:1
Maher, Joseph, 1949, Je 17,23:3
Maher, Joseph F, 1952, S 29,23:4
Maher, Martin, 1961, Ja 18,33:3
Maher, Martin J, 1949, Ja 9,72:2
Maher, Mary (Sister Agnes Dolores), 1962, S 15,25:2
Maher, Michael A, 1944, Ag 5,11:4
Maher, Michael J, 1945, Mr 18,42:2; 1964, O 31,29:2
Maher, P, 1931, O 13,21:5
Maher, Patrick, 1942, Ja 13,19:3
Maher, Patrick A, 1948, D 22,24:2; 1952, Ja 7,19:5
Maher, Peter, 1940, Jl 23,19:6
Maher, Robert E, 1966, Je 17,45:2
Maher, Stephen J (por), 1939, Je 7,23:2
Maher, Thomas E, 1947, O 4,17:5
Maher, Thomas F, 1938, Je 20,15:6; 1940, D 19,25:6; 1953, D 14,31:5; 1961, S 1,17:2
Maher, Thomas J, 1945, D 22,19:5; 1949, D 11,92:4
Maher, Vincent J, 1955, Jl 28,23:5
Maher, Vincent P, 1948, O 19,27:1
Maher, Walter, 1951, D 28,21:3
Maher, William, 1940, Jl 12,15:1; 1949, Ja 25,24:3
Maher, William E, 1948, D 28,21:5
Maher, William H, 1948, Mr 16,27:3
Maher, William J, 1939, F 28,20:3; 1944, S 14,23:6; 1951, O 2,27:1
Maher, William T, 1951, O 31,29:1
Maher-Howell, Margaret Mrs, 1937, F 16,23:5
Maher Pasher, Aly, 1960, Ag 25,29:2
Mahl, Herbert H, 1956, Ag 31,17:2
Mahl, William, 1918, My 14,13:6
Mahla, Walter T, 1943, Mr 10,19:3
Mahlan, John C, 1944, F 28,17:4
Mahldau, Carl J, 1963, Ag 2,27:4
Mahler, Anna, 1941, D 24,17:5
Mahler, Curt Mrs, 1952, S 27,17:3
Mahler, Donald B, 1968, N 1,47:3
Mahler, Ernst W, 1967, Ag 1,33:1
Mahler, Godfrey J, 1945, F 27,19:5
Mahler, Gustav (funl, My 23,11:6), 1911, My 19,11:1
Mahler, Gustave, 1959, Mr 31,30:3
Mahler, H H, 1953, Mr 8,90:1
Mahler, Henry Mrs, 1947, Ag 13,23:5
Mahler, Herbert, 1961, Ag 18,21:2
Mahler, Julius, 1956, Ja 8,86:8
Mahler, Max Mrs, 1959, Ap 3,27:1
Mahler, Myron A, 1960, Mr 30,37:3
Mahler, Richard F, 1952, Je 19,27:4
Mahlke, Edward A, 1939, Ja 17,21:2
Mahlon, Philip B, 1961, D 30,19:5
Mahlstad, William G, 1943, Ja 29,38:4
Mahlstedt, G H, 1927, D 17,2:6
Mahlstedt, George, 1938, O 20,23:2
Mahlstedt, George W, 1939, Ja 20,19:4
Mahlstedt, John F, 1957, Jl 8,23:5
Mahmoud, Ali, 1949, N 18,29:1
Mahmoud Bey, Prince, 1939, F 27,15:5
Mahmoud Khan Ghazi, Sardar Shah, 1959, D 26,13:3
Mahmoud Nedim Pasha, 1883, My 15,5:6
Mahmoud Pasha, Mohammed (por), 1941, F 1,17:4
Mahnken, Arthur J, 1960, Mr 20,87:2
Mahnken, Edward A Mrs, 1951, Jl 19,23:3
Mahnken, John H, 1921, O 13,15:5
Mahnken, William F, 1949, F 24,23:2
Mahon, Annie Mrs, 1954, D 22,23:4
Mahon, Arthur L, 1963, O 8,43:1
Mahon, B M, 1937, Jl 8,23:5
Mahon, Bart J, 1943, Ja 5,19:2
Mahon, Bernard H, 1955, F 26,15:5
Mahon, Charles J, 1938, Ag 3,19:5
Mahon, Charles J Mrs, 1944, Ap 12,21:5
Mahon, Dennis J, 1965, Je 14,33:4
Mahon, Edward F, 1944, N 29,23:5
Mahon, Francis H, 1967, O 14,27:2
Mahon, Harold J, 1937, F 28,II,8:7
Mahon, Hugh W, 1946, D 22,41:8
Mahon, James J, 1941, Ap 20,43:2
Mahon, John C, 1939, Ja 29,33:3
Mahon, John H Mrs, 1958, Ja 12,86:1
Mahon, John J, 1959, Je 13,21:5; 1962, F 2,29:1
Mahon, John M, 1945, Mr 29,23:3
Mahon, John P, 1957, Mr 28,31:5
Mahon, Lillias H Mrs (will), 1940, Jl 10,17:5
Mahon, Lucy, 1949, N 18,29:1
Mahon, Phil F, 1948, Je 2,29:2
Mahon, Robert (Oct 1), 1965, O 11,61:3
Mahon, Robert V, 1965, F 15,27:1
Mahon, Stephen K, 1963, Ag 26,27:3
Mahon, Walter C, 1949, Je 22,31:3
Mahon, William, 1955, Ap 24,86:5
Mahon, William D (por), 1949, N 2,27:1
Mahon, William F, 1949, F 22,23:4
Mahon, William J, 1960, Jl 10,72:4
Mahone, W Gen, 1895, O 9,13:4
Mahoney, Anna M, 1947, O 13,23:2
Mahoney, Bartholomew J, 1941, Ap 19,15:1
Mahoney, Benjamin F, 1951, Ag 1,23:4
Mahoney, Bernard J, 1939, Mr 21,23:2
Mahoney, C J Mrs, 1948, O 23,15:6
Mahoney, Charles, 1923, N 7,17:6
Mahoney, Charles H, 1966, F 1,31:4
Mahoney, Cornelius J, 1951, Ap 21,17:6
Mahoney, Daniel, 1950, Jl 22,15:3
Mahoney, Daniel J, 1949, Mr 24,28:2; 1960, S 29,35:4
Mahoney, Daniel J (ansethetic explosion blamed, Ap 3,20:6), 1963, Ap 2,47:3
Mahoney, Daniel J, 1966, Je 26,73:2
Mahoney, David Mrs, 1942, D 3,25:1
Mahoney, Dennis, 1948, N 5,26:2
Mahoney, Dennis J, 1948, Jl 26,17:5
Mahoney, Dennis W, 1913, D 1,9:4
Mahoney, Edmund J, 1961, Ap 21,33:3
Mahoney, Edmund P, 1960, Ja 21,31:4
Mahoney, Edward, 1946, Jl 26,21:4
Mahoney, Edward J, 1954, Ja 9,16:3
Mahoney, Edward J Mrs, 1937, My 15,19:3
Mahoney, Edward Mrs, 1948, My 31,19:6
Mahoney, Edward S, 1958, F 19,27:2
Mahoney, Edward W, 1955, Je 6,27:4
Mahoney, F Rev (Father Prout), 1866, Je 10,2:5
Mahoney, Florence, 1951, My 14,25:4
Mahoney, Florence C, 1961, Ag 31,27:2
Mahoney, Francis J (funl, D 28,21:1), 1956, D 24, 13:3
Mahoney, Francis W, 1948, Ag 23,17:3
Mahoney, Frank D, 1944, Ag 18,13:2
Mahoney, Frank D Mrs, 1943, Ap 13,26:2
Mahoney, George A, 1944, N 6,19:5
Mahoney, George W Col, 1910, Jl 23,7:6
Mahoney, Harry L, 1953, Mr 17,29:3
Mahoney, Helen Cox Ex-Gov, 1921, My 17,17:6
Mahoney, Henry J Rev, 1937, Jl 7,23:5
Mahoney, Ivan L Jr, 1966, O 13,45:2
Mahoney, James, 1941, My 7,25:6
Mahoney, James (Jake), 1956, D 11,36:2
Mahoney, James H Mrs, 1949, F 1,25:3
Mahoney, James J, 1908, My 10,9:4; 1956, Je 17,92:5; 1957, O 1,33:1
Mahoney, James P, 1954, F 5,19:3
Mahoney, James T, 1950, S 3,38:4
Mahoney, James Vincent, 1909, O 14,9:6
Mahoney, Jeremiah C, 1954, Ap 24,17:5
Mahoney, Jeremiah F, 1950, F 27,19:3
Mahoney, Jeremiah P, 1948, F 23,25:2
Mahoney, Jerome A, 1952, S 24,33:5
Mahoney, John, 1941, D 24,17:2; 1943, N 22,19:6
Mahoney, John A, 1948, My 19,15:5
Mahoney, John C, 1946, Jl 13,15:6
Mahoney, John F, 1957, F 24,84:1
Mahoney, John H, 1941, Ag 10,37:1; 1955, Jl 23,17:6
Mahoney, John J, 1937, Je 17,24:1; 1947, D 14,76:4; 1949, Ja 15,17:1; 1954, Ap 19,23:2; 1958, Jl 28,23:5
Mahoney, John R, 1951, F 4,77:2
Mahoney, John S, 1940, Ap 26,21:4
Mahoney, John W, 1941, My 20,23:2; 1950, F 11,15:2
Mahoney, Joseph A, 1968, S 19,47:4
Mahoney, Joseph E, 1943, Jl 14,19:3
Mahoney, Joseph F, 1949, O 21,25:2; 1955, Mr 8,27:2
Mahoney, Joseph N, 1946, Ja 3,19:4
Mahoney, Joseph P Mrs, 1949, O 6,31:1
Mahoney, Julia G Mrs, 1939, Ja 19,19:4
Mahoney, Justin T, 1965, Ag 13,29:3
Mahoney, Kate, 1946, Mr 7,25:4
Mahoney, Kevin, 1952, S 6,17:2
Mahoney, L C, 1944, O 19,23:4
Mahoney, M Bertrand, 1950, O 19,31:2
Mahoney, Margaret, 1942, F 26,19:4
Mahoney, Merchant (por), 1946, My 5,46:1
Mahoney, Michael (Klondike Mike), 1951, Ap 10, 27:5
Mahoney, Patrick J, 1952, D 16,31:4
Mahoney, Raymond J, 1943, Mr 22,19:3
Mahoney, Richard B, 1952, N 8,17:6
Mahoney, Richard J, 1948, Jl 14,23:2
Mahoney, Robert H Mrs, 1959, Jl 22,27:2
Mahoney, Thomas D, 1946, O 20,60:2
Mahoney, Thomas H, 1942, S 8,23:3
Mahoney, Thomas H Mrs, 1948, Ja 28,23:5
Mahoney, Thomas J, 1949, D 9,32:2
Mahoney, Thomas P, 1965, Je 24,35:5
Mahoney, Timothy, 1946, F 6,23:5
Mahoney, Timothy J, 1954, D 31,13:5
Mahoney, Walter, 1937, My 5,25:2
Mahoney, Walter B Mrs, 1945, N 3,15:3
Mahoney, Walter J Mrs, 1951, N 25,87:1
Mahoney, Will, 1967, F 10,35:1
Mahoney, William, 1948, Je 28,19:1; 1952, Ag 18,17:4
Mahoney, William E, 1949, Ja 1,13:5
Mahoney, William H, 1952, F 28,27:6
Mahoney, William J, 1940, F 9,19:4; 1940, S 9,15:4; 1942, Jl 9,21:3; 1944, Jl 16,31:2; 1947, Ap 29,27:1
Mahoney, William J Mrs, 1947, Mr 14,23:2
Mahoney, William J Sr, 1956, F 8,33:3
Mahoney, William M, 1939, Ja 5,23:3
Mahoney, William P, 1948, Ag 14,13:3
Mahoney, William W, 1952, N 30,86:3
Mahony, Catherine A, 1956, S 27,35:4

Mahony, Daniel J, 1937, N 18,23:1
Mahony, Frederick, 1951, D 10,29:3
Mahony, James E, 1954, Je 23,25:2
Mahony, John A, 1946, My 1,25:2
Mahony, John J Sr, 1947, Jl 1,25:5
Mahony, Lewis H, 1942, F 10,19:2
Mahony, Michael T A, 1952, D 2,31:4
Mahony, Mortimer M (por), 1949, Ja 30,60:4
Mahony, Patrick A, 1941, O 25,17:2
Mahony, Paul R, 1938, Ja 8,15:5
Mahony, Thomas F, 1951, Jl 10,27:4
Mahony, Thomas L, 1941, Ap 18,21:2
Mahony, Walter B, 1954, Ja 10,86:3
Mahony, William D, 1951, O 20,15:5
Mahood, David, 1959, F 20,25:3
Mahood, Joseph H Sr, 1964, Ja 20,43:1
Mahood, Joseph M, 1944, D 14,23:3
Mahool, J Barry, 1966, Jl 31,72:4
Mahool, James S (por), 1940, O 3,25:3
Mahorner, Matthias, 1960, F 7,84:1
Mahr, Ernest F, 1942, My 30,15:3
Mahr, George J Mrs, 1949, D 13,38:1
Mahr, Irving O, 1947, Ja 14,26:3
Mahr, Julius D, 1925, F 12,19:5
Mahu, Abel, 1958, Ap 5,15:3
Mahuran, Stuart A Dr, 1953, F 10,27:2
Mahy, George G, 1946, D 5,31:2
Maibaum, Jerome, 1964, S 24,41:3
Maibaum, Jerome Mrs, 1958, F 28,13:4
Maidat, Harold, 1941, N 28,23:3
Maiden, James C, 1958, Ja 15,29:1
Maiden, Robert K, 1939, N 25,17:2
Maiden, Stewart, 1948, N 5,25:4
Maiden, William H, 1944, Ag 26,11:4
Maider, Wesley H, 1955, Mr 5,17:3
Maidhof, William J Capt, 1937, Ap 8,23:4
Maidment, Fred H Mrs, 1949, O 31,25:5
Maidment, Frederick H, 1952, F 22,21:3
Maidment, William, 1925, O 5,21:5
Maiello, Matthew, 1954, Ap 18,50:1
Maier, Alfred D, 1964, O 20,37:3
Maier, C Fred, 1950, Ap 16,105:1
Maier, Curtis E, 1964, O 1,35:4
Maier, Edward J, 1946, D 12,29:3
Maier, Emil Mrs, 1943, D 1,21:5
Maier, Eric, 1963, Ap 23,37:2
Maier, Ernest G, 1948, Mr 8,23:4
Maier, F Hurst, 1946, N 3,64:2
Maier, George, 1943, O 22,17:3
Maier, Gustave A, 1943, Ag 13,17:6
Maier, Guy, 1956, S 25,33:4
Maier, Henry W, 1946, Ag 31,15:4
Maier, Herbert C Mrs (J S Baldwin), 1958, S 19,28:1
Maier, Herman R, 1958, O 7,35:1
Maier, Ira F, 1942, D 3,25:3
Maier, Jerome I, 1948, Ag 10,21:1
Maier, John I, 1943, N 9,21:5
Maier, Louis A Sr, 1949, Ap 12,29:5
Maier, Max, 1966, My 13,38:3
Maier, Merwin D, 1942, F 16,17:6
Maier, Otto, 1950, Mr 10,27:4
Maier, Philip J, 1945, D 16,40:2
Maier, Roland L Dr, 1968, Jl 23,39:1
Maier, Siegfried, 1965, My 22,31:3
Maier, Walter A, 1950, Ja 12,27:1; 1950, Ja 16,26:4
Maier, William, 1937, O 20,23:2
Maier, William F, 1952, Mr 20,29:4
Maier, William J (por), 1941, D 16,27:3
Maiers, Frederick E, 1949, O 16,89:1
Maigren, Harry E, 1957, D 10,35:2
Maigs, Arthur I, 1956, Je 11,31:2
Maihl, John U, 1954, Ja 5,27:3
Maihofer, Walter B, 1950, My 13,17:6
Maijgren, Thorvald, 1948, Ap 23,23:1
Maikoffske, William E, 1950, F 9,29:3
Mailer, John, 1942, Mr 14,15:2
Mailey, Henry U, 1950, N 21,31:1
Mailhiot, Adhemar, 1938, Ap 22,19:5
Mailhouse, Max, 1941, O 20,18:2
Maillart, Aime, 1871, Je 8,5:5
Maille, Roland de, 1953, Ap 8,29:5
Maillefert, B S H Prof, 1884, Ag 12,2:2
Mailler, Elizabeth C Mrs, 1937, D 1,23:3
Mailler, George, 1937, Je 15,23:3
Mailler, Harold W, 1950, Ag 9,29:3
Mailler, Janet, 1950, Ap 12,27:4
Mailler, Lee B, 1967, S 23,31:3
Mailler, Royal F Sr, 1950, D 22,23:3
Mailler, Sophia J Mrs, 1941, Ja 12,44:5
Mailler, William Henry, 1903, O 14,9:6
Mailley, Edward L, 1948, Ag 30,17:2
Mailloux, Hormisdas, 1951, Ap 15,92:2
Mailly, Joseph, 1967, Ag 1,33:2
Mailly, William, 1912, S 5,9:4
Mailly, William Mrs, 1960, Ag 16,29:5
Mailman, Samuel, 1938, Ag 4,17:4
Maimin, Mayer, 1956, Ag 31,17:1
Maimon, Jacob, 1951, Ap 17,29:5
Maimon, Judah L, 1962, Jl 11,36:1
Main, Archibald M, 1961, Ja 20,26:2
Main, Archibald M Mrs, 1955, O 31,25:5
Main, Charles T (por), 1943, Mr 7,38:4
Main, David J, 1955, Ja 18,27:4
Main, E W, 1876, Mr 16,2:2
Main, Frank W, 1954, N 19,23:4
Main, Fred L, 1950, N 10,27:2
Main, Frederic W, 1948, Je 1,23:2
Main, Frederick H, 1962, Ag 8,31:4
Main, H W Mrs, 1957, My 19,88:5
Main, Hanford, 1959, N 16,31:2
Main, Herschel, 1909, Mr 19,9:5
Main, Hershel L, 1946, Mr 15,22:2
Main, Hubert Platt, 1925, O 8,27:4
Main, J Fulton, 1968, O 10,47:3
Main, J H T, 1931, Ap 2,27:1
Main, John B, 1941, Ag 20,19:6
Main, John F, 1942, O 14,25:2
Main, John H, 1940, N 15,21:2
Main, Lafayette, 1947, Je 6,23:4
Main, Lucius C Mrs, 1954, Mr 4,25:4
Main, Walter H, 1949, Ja 18,23:2
Main, Walter H Mrs, 1944, Ja 18,20:3
Main, William B, 1954, My 23,88:6
Main, William R, 1947, Ag 28,23:3
Maina, Pauline M Mrs, 1943, D 15,27:4
Mainardy, George E Jr, 1944, F 10,15:4
Maincy, Baron de, 1880, Mr 15,5:4
Maine, Alva P, 1938, N 8,23:3
Maine, Bruno, 1962, Jl 31,27:3
Maine, Clarence A, 1962, O 21,88:7
Maine, Mary T, 1942, F 19,19:2
Maines, Charles T, 1938, O 11,25:5
Mainey, Baron De (Haase C, Dr Carlos), 1880, Mr 15,5:4
Mains, George P Mrs, 1907, Je 17,7:7
Mains, Mary A C, 1907, Je 18,7:6
Mains, Robert, 1950, D 24,35:1
Mains, Walter L, 1950, D 1,25:5
Mainus, J H, 1946, O 16,28:3
Mainzer, Anthony H, 1950, Mr 29,29:4
Mainzer, Herbert R, 1925, D 14,21:4
Mainzer, R H, 1936, Ag 7,19:5
Maione, James E, 1918, O 25,13:5
Maioran, Jeraldo, 1944, Ap 7,20:3
Maioud, Henri, 1952, N 7,4:2
Mair, Alexander, 1916, Ap 19,13:4
Mair, Edmand F, 1953, Ap 10,21:2
Mair, George, 1942, F 9,15:1; 1962, Ja 16,33:1
Mair, Hugh, 1952, Mr 24,25:5
Mair, Janet Mrs (Lady Beveridge), 1959, Ap 27,27:4
Mair, Kenneth T, 1964, D 9,50:3
Mair, Robert, 1944, Ja 5,17:3
Mair, Sarah E, 1941, F 18,23:5
Mair, William J, 1965, Ag 13,29:3
Maireder, Rona, 1938, F 20,XI,8:2
Mairena, Leopoldo R, 1944, Jl 19,19:4
Maires, Thomas W, 1941, O 13,17:3
Mairs, J D, 1881, O 4,5:3
Mairs, James H, 1947, S 1,19:4
Mairs, Katherine E Mrs, 1939, O 6,25:4
Mairs, Olney B, 1943, Ap 28,23:4; 1959, S 13,83:5
Mairs, Olney B Sr Mrs, 1949, My 8,78:1
Maisack, Paul S, 1950, My 2,29:3
Maisano, Donato, 1960, Je 11,21:6
Maisch, Charles F, 1949, Ap 1,25:3
Maisel, Bernard, 1963, Ap 23,74:3
Maisel, Carl, 1963, N 20,40:2
Maisel, Frederick C (Fritz), 1967, Ap 23,92:7
Maisel, Irving, 1957, My 29,27:2
Maisel, Jule L, 1961, S 29,35:6
Maisel, Max, 1943, Je 23,21:4
Maisel, Max N, 1959, O 18,86:7
Maisel, Robert, 1945, S 21,21:4
Maisin, Albert, 1923, F 6,19:4
Maisner, Emil, 1944, My 17,19:3
Maison, Edna, 1946, Ja 14,19:4
Maison, Rene, 1962, Jl 17,25:1
Maisonville, Barnabe, 1939, Mr 3,23:2
Maissel, Aida (Mrs J F Grahame), 1962, F 6,35:3
Maister, William T, 1907, Mr 3,7:6
Maistre, P A M Gen, 1922, Jl 26,13:4
Maitland, Adam, 1949, O 7,28:5
Maitland, Albert G C, 1958, O 10,31:3
Maitland, Alex, 1965, S 28,3:5
Maitland, Alexander, 1907, O 27,9:6
Maitland, Alfred Sydney Frederick Rev (Earl of Lauderdale), 1968, N 29,89:4
Maitland, Arthur, 1959, My 25,29:4
Maitland, David L, 1944, O 27,23:3
Maitland, Gertrude, 1938, D 29,19:4
Maitland, J A F, 1936, Mr 31,21:3
Maitland, James W, 1968, Jl 4,19:1
Maitland, James W Mrs, 1957, My 10,27:3
Maitland, Joseph, 1939, O 1,53:3
Maitland, Robert L, 1870, D 23,4:5
Maitland, Robert L Mrs, 1945, F 17,13:5
Maitland, Rollo F, 1953, Ap 9,27:2
Maitland, S S Rev, 1884, Ap 10,2:3
Maitre, Victor, 1945, S 12,25:5
Maiuri, Amedeo, 1963, Ap 8,47:3
Maixner, Henry A, 1947, Ja 24,21:1
Maixner, Henry A Mrs, 1950, N 1,35:2
Maize, Richard, 1953, O 12,27:3
Maizlish, I Paul, 1945, S 5,23:4
Maiztegui, Juan J, 1943, S 30,21:1
Majali, Atef, 1967, Jl 31,27:2
Majane, John A, 1946, F 2,13:4
Majane, John Jr, 1953, Mr 9,29:2
Majarian, Diran M, 1961, Ag 28,25:4
Majcher, Matthew Mrs, 1949, S 4,41:1
Majczek, Tillie Mrs, 1964, Jl 25,19:4
Majdrakoff, Boris (M I Boris), 1962, Jl 17,25:5
Majer, Carl T, 1949, D 11,92:6
Majer, Charles F, 1947, My 25,60:4
Majer, Emily, 1951, My 13,88:7
Majer, Ernest E, 1960, Je 11,21:6
Majer, Lester W, 1961, Jl 16,68:4
Majerone, Giorgio, 1924, Ag 9,11:6
Majeska, Yna (Mrs E Adir), 1959, O 30,27:1
Majesky, Richard A, 1952, S 23,33:5
Majewski, Boleslaw, 1943, My 15,15:1
Majewski, Bruno Capt, 1939, D 15,51:5
Majewski, Frederick H, 1956, O 29,29:5
Majkowski, Walter, 1951, Jl 25,23:2
Majo, Victor J, 1958, Mr 29,17:3
Major, Alfred J, 1940, Ap 24,23:6
Major, Cedric A, 1961, Ap 29,23:2
Major, Charles, 1913, F 14,15:3; 1938, Jl 15,17:5
Major, Charles Mrs, 1925, Je 11,19:3
Major, Charles T, 1962, Jl 3,23:2
Major, Clare T Mrs, 1954, O 10,84:1
Major, Duncan K Jr, 1947, My 28,25:4
Major, Edward K Mrs, 1938, O 1,17:4
Major, Elliott W, 1949, Jl 10,56:4
Major, Emily Moore, 1904, F 18,9:6
Major, Henry, 1923, Mr 6,21:4; 1948, S 19,76:5
Major, Henry D A, 1961, Ja 28,19:2
Major, John, 1965, O 28,43:4
Major, Joseph K, 1941, Je 12,23:2
Major, Kenneth, 1948, D 1,29:4
Major, Lillie H Mrs, 1941, Jl 1,23:5
Major, Samuel G, 1942, O 15,24:2
Major, Thomas E, 1939, Jl 3,13:6
Major, William W, 1940, Ja 15,15:5
Majur, Fred S Mrs, 1955, My 29,45:1
Makara, Steven Father, 1915, Ja 3,IX,3:2
Makarchek, S John, 1966, F 10,37:2
Makaroff, Vadim S (will, Ja 15,28:5), 1964, Ja 3,
Makaroff, Vadim S Mrs, 1961, Mr 28,35:5
Makarov, Alex G, 1957, Mr 26,33:2
Makary (Met), 1953, N 13,27:1
Makay, Alex F, 1951, S 25,29:2
Makedensky, Brayne Mrs, 1909, D 19,11:5
Makeham, Eliot, 1956, F 9,31:1
Makely, George N, 1948, Ap 15,25:4
Maken, Morris, 1960, Mr 16,37:4
Makepeace, Alex, 1937, F 12,23:4
Makepeace, Charles D, 1960, Ap 27,37:5
Makepeace, Frank B, 1942, S 25,21:4
Makepeace, Grace, 1951, F 11,89:1
Makepeace, Mary E, 1949, Ag 12,17:1
Makepeace, Walter D, 1942, Ag 28,19:4
Makepeace, William D, 1946, F 18,21:4
Maker, Lewis A, 1954, N 25,29:3
Maker, Lloyd D, 1961, Je 3,23:5
Makewen, Isabella, 1940, F 6,21:6
Makin, Joseph H, 1960, D 20,33:3
Makinen, Eero, 1953, O 29,31:4
Making, Thomas, 1946, Mr 27,27:2
Makino, Nobuaki, 1949, Ja 26,25:4
Makins, G H Sir, 1933, N 3,19:3
Makins, James C, 1946, F 23,13:1
Makiver, Harry J, 1942, S 30,23:3
Makkai, Francis A, 1949, Mr 17,25:3
Maklakiewicz, Jan, 1954, F 10,29:4
Makonnen, Ras, 1906, Mr 24,9:6
Makovsky, Constantine, 1915, O 25,9:4
Makowski, Alex J, 1963, Ag 31,17:3
Makowski, Dean, 1957, D 24,15:5
Makowski, Stanley J, 1958, Ap 5,15:5
Makowski, Waclaw, 1943, F 17,21:5
Makowsky, Barney, 1949, S 2,17:2
Makoyed, Lavrenti, 1950, Jl 5,31:2
Makransky, Harry, 1961, S 21,35:1
Makray, Eugene R, 1942, Mr 17,23:1
Makrionitis, Marios, 1959, Ap 9,31:5
Makser, William A, 1954, Mr 18,31:1
Maksimov, Matvei, 1949, My 30,13:5
Maksimov, Nickolai, 1952, My 11,93:3
Maksutov, Dmitri D, 1964, Ag 15,21:6
Makuen, G Hudson Dr, 1917, F 23,11:6
Makuen, Hattie Mrs, 1948, Jl 2,21:6
Makuszynski, Kornel, 1953, Ag 2,73:2
Malabre, Alfred L, 1964, My 25,33:5
Malach, Charles O Dr, 1915, Ag 22,13:5
Malach, Robert R, 1954, Ja 18,23:5
Malady, Owen A, 1966, D 13,47:3
Malahide, T de Lord, 1883, Ap 17,5:1
Malakis, Emile, 1954, Je 22,27:2
Malakoff, Arthur, 1960, N 25,27:3
Malakoff, Duke of, 1864, Je 7,2:3
Malament, Edward J, 1961, My 22,31:1
Malamut, Celia Mrs, 1949, Ja 29,31:1
Malamuth, Charles, 1965, Jl 15,29:2
Malan, Daniel F (funl plans, F 8,86:6; funl, F 12 1959, F 7,20:1
Malan, Francois S, 1942, Ja 1,25:2
Malan, J P, 1942, Ap 20,21:6
Malan, Sailor (Adolph G), 1963, S 18,39:2

Malan, William E, 1938, Ap 19,21:5
Maland, Joseph O, 1947, Ag 17,54:2
Malandin, Gherman, 1961, O 30,29:1
Malane, Jeffrey J, 1949, N 27,104:4
Malaney, Robert J Mrs, 1950, Ag 13,77:2
Malaney, W J, 1950, My 7,106:2
Malanga, Nicholas Mrs, 1952, O 4,17:4
Malaniuk, Eugene F, 1968, F 19,39:3
Malaparte, Curzio (C Suckert), 1957, Jl 20,15:3
Malark, Daniel, 1955, Jl 13,25:3
Malarkey, John, 1949, N 30,84:4
Malarky, Martin F, 1954, Ap 20,29:3
Malatesta, Antonio Mrs, 1961, Ap 25,35:3
Malatesta, E, 1932, Jl 26,15:1
Malatesta, Mark, 1903, Ag 29,7:5
Malatesta, Numa P (Pompilio), 1960, F 28,83:1
Malatesta, Pompolio Mrs, 1963, Ag 20,33:4
Malato, Charles, 1938, N 10,29:1
Malavazos, Antonios E, 1945, Ap 24,19:4
Malavey, Thomas, 1945, Mr 2,19:4
Malayko, George, 1945, My 3,23:5
Malbin, Mayer Mrs, 1952, My 12,25:5
Malboysson, Enrique, 1945, My 8,34:5
Malbran, Manuel E, 1942, N 14,15:2
Malburn, William P, 1945, Ap 11,23:3
Malby, George R, 1912, Jl 7,II,11:3
Malby, George R Mrs, 1943, F 7,48:2
Malby, Seth G, 1964, F 1,23:5
Malby, Walter Rives Mrs, 1921, Jl 21,15:4
Malcarney, Arthur L, 1968, My 29,36:3
Malcher, Frederick Mrs, 1948, Ja 27,26:3
Malcolm, Alex, 1961, Ja 20,29:1
Malcolm, Alex G, 1953, Ja 23,19:4
Malcolm, Alex Sr Mrs, 1949, F 1,25:5
Malcolm, Arthur B, 1951, Ag 29,25:4
Malcolm, Frederic, 1944, Ap 8,13:6
Malcolm, George A, 1955, F 19,15:5; 1961, My 18,35:3
Malcolm, Gilbert, 1965, Jl 3,19:2
Malcolm, James, 1912, S 18,11:6
Malcolm, James L, 1937, Ap 9,21:2
Malcolm, John, 1964, O 28,45:3
Malcolm, Lord, 1902, Mr 8,9:5
Malcolm, Mart M, 1961, Ja 9,39:6
Malcolm, Neill, 1953, D 22,31:1
Malcolm, Ormond Drimmie Sir, 1912, Mr 5,11:4
Malcolm, Percy E, 1945, Ag 14,21:4
Malcolm, Robert B, 1946, Je 23,40:3
Malcolm, Robert J Sr, 1952, Jl 6,49:2
Malcolm, Ronald, 1949, N 5,13:6
Malcolm, Roy, 1959, Ag 13,27:2
Malcolm, Schuyler, 1908, Mr 25,9:4
Malcolm, Thomas D, 1941, Ag 31,23:1
Malcolm, William, 1946, F 21,21:2
Malcolm, William L, 1948, Ja 19,23:1
Malcolmson, Alex Y, 1923, Ag 2,15:5
Malcolmson, Charles T, 1946, Je 1,13:3
Malcolmson, Harold T, 1950, My 7,108:2
Malcomson, George W, 1955, Je 1,33:1
Malcomson, John A Mrs, 1944, O 19,23:3
Maldarelli, Louis, 1939, F 3,15:4
Maldonado, Angel, 1955, F 1,29:3
Male, Albert, 1947, D 9,29:4
Male, Arthur F, 1967, N 30,47:2
Male, Emile, 1954, O 7,23:3
Male, Isaac, 1943, My 10,19:2
Male, James, 1947, Ja 17,23:4
Male, James Mrs, 1958, O 18,21:5
Male, Roy M, 1953, Ag 22,15:5
Male, William H Capt, 1906, N 25,9:6
Maleady, Richard G, 1965, Ag 12,27:1
Maleeney, John W, 1941, N 13,28:2
Maleeny, Robert V, 1945, O 2,23:1
Malees, John H, 1910, N 14,9:5
Malehorn, Ralph, 1954, My 1,15:3
Malek, Guindi Abdel, 1956, Ja 31,29:4
Maleska, Frank D, 1949, Ap 19,25:2
Malessa, Charles L, 1945, My 6,38:2
Malester, Isaac, 1961, Mr 6,25:2
Malet, Achilles W, 1951, Jl 23,17:3
Malet, Edward Baldwin Sir, 1908, Je 30,7:6
Malevinsky, Moses L Mrs, 1952, O 14,31:3
Malex, Stephen, 1950, Ag 30,31:5
Maley, Charles J, 1949, My 31,23:4
Maley, Dennis J, 1956, D 1,21:2
Maley, Eugenio, 1907, O 27,9:4
Maley, Frank A, 1948, N 9,27:1
Maley, James J, 1948, Ja 8,25:5
Maley, John J, 1948, Ja 13,25:3
Maley, Stephen, 1950, Mr 10,27:3
Maley, Stephen Mrs, 1962, Ja 4,33:4
Maley, Thomas J, 1948, My 22,15:5
Maley, Thomas W, 1956, F 25,19:4
Maley, Thomas W Mrs, 1961, My 17,37:2
Malgeri, John, 1959, Mr 25,35:4
Malherbe, William, 1951, O 30,29:3
Mali, John T J, 1950, N 15,31:2
Mali, Pierre, 1923, O 5,19:2
Malia, William H Mrs, 1939, Je 24,17:2
Malicheff, Michael G, 1950, N 9,33:3
Malick, Frederick E, 1952, Ja 6,95:4
Malik, Eugen, 1958, Jl 12,15:3
Malik, Josef, 1946, D 10,31:5
Malin, Henry, 1966, Ja 8,26:6
Malin, Joseph E Dr, 1937, S 29,23:5
Malin, Patrick M, 1964, D 14,35:2
Malin, W C, 1950, Jl 11,32:3
Malina, Louis, 1963, D 20,29:1
Maling, Walter B, 1947, D 27,13:3
Malinin, Mikhail S, 1960, Ja 25,27:3
Malinka, William E Sr, 1949, F 3,23:2
Malinka, William E Sr Mrs, 1949, F 3,23:2
Malinoff, Alex, 1938, Mr 21,6:3
Malinofsky, Max, 1963, My 11,25:6
Malinovsky, Rodion Y (funl plans, Ap 2,93:2), 1967, Ap 1,31:1
Malinowski, Bronislaw K (por), 1942, My 17,46:1
Malinowski, Dyonizy, 1950, Jl 29,13:5
Malinowski, Harriot R Mrs, 1946, Ap 1,27:2
Malins, R Sir, 1882, Ja 16,5:5
Malinverni, Aristide, 1952, Ja 5,31:3
Malion, Bernie, 1959, Ap 4,6:2
Malisheff, Alex, 1939, Ja 28,2:7
Malisoff, Samuel, 1961, F 5,80:8
Malisoff, William M (por), 1947, N 17,21:4
Maliszewski, Anton J, 1947, N 6,27:4
Malitz, Chaim Mrs, 1956, O 31,33:4
Malitz, Lester M, 1965, Jl 26,23:5
Malitz, Lewis (Lew Raymond), 1953, Ap 19,90:4
Maljan, Abdul, 1944, S 9,15:6
Malkan, Henry, 1946, My 1,25:4
Malkenson, Arthur L, 1956, Mr 26,29:3
Malkiel, Leon A Mrs, 1949, N 18,29:3
Malkin, Elias, 1953, Jl 19,56:5
Malkin, Henry, 1954, O 9,17:2
Malkin, Herman, 1959, Ag 25,31:4
Malkin, Isadore, 1946, Ja 27,42:2
Malkin, Manfred, 1966, Ja 10,25:6
Malkin, Morris, 1951, O 24,31:2
Malkin, William H, 1959, O 15,39:3
Malko, Nicolai, 1961, Je 24,21:2
Mall, Arthur W, 1959, O 4,86:5
Mallaby, Francis B Mrs, 1951, O 9,29:4
Mallaby-Deeley, Harry Sir, 1937, F 5,21:6
Mallalieu, Frank W, 1944, Ap 13,19:3
Mallalieu, Joshua C, 1937, Jl 31,15:4
Mallalieu, Wilbur E, 1957, Jl 28,61:1
Mallalieu, Wilbur V, 1943, N 17,25:3
Mallalieu, Willard Francis Bp, 1911, Ag 2,7:6
Mallam, Ben H, 1956, Jl 13,19:4
Mallan, Bernard K, 1956, O 3,33:5
Mallard, Dallas W, 1953, N 12,31:1
Mallard, Frederick W, 1946, S 3,19:3
Mallard, Stephen F, 1954, Je 27,68:3
Mallary, Harold T Mrs, 1944, O 10,23:2
Mallary, R Dewitt Rev, 1911, Ja 30,9:3
Mallay, Ralph J, 1949, S 16,27:4
Malle, Clyde E, 1952, My 30,15:4
Malleck, Alfred, 1953, S 1,12:5
Mallen, Frank, 1960, D 22,23:2
Mallen, James J MRs, 1954, Je 24,27:5
Maller, Annie Mrs, 1948, My 10,21:1
Maller, Julius B, 1959, My 9,21:1
Maller, Melvin, 1953, Ja 25,85:1
Malleret-Joinville, Alfred, 1960, F 22,17:3
Mallery, Charles G Mrs, 1945, Mr 8,23:4
Mallery, Charles Payson Rev Dr, 1917, S 28,11:6
Mallery, Cortlandt H, 1961, S 17,86:6
Mallery, Earl D, 1952, Jl 29,21:3
Mallery, Fred A, 1941, Ap 23,21:4
Mallery, Otto T, 1956, D 18,27:5
Mallery, Richard P, 1962, Je 12,37:2
Mallery, Richard P Mrs, 1955, Ja 10,23:3
Mallery, William S, 1952, Ag 29,24:5
Mallet, Edmond Maj, 1907, Ap 13,11:6
Mallet-Prevost, Severo (por), 1948, D 11,15:3
Mallet-Stevens, Robert, 1945, F 11,38:3
Malleterre, J G M Gen, 1923, N 28,17:2
Mallett, Charles E Mrs, 1951, Ja 6,15:3
Mallett, Charles J, 1956, D 18,31:4
Mallett, Frank J, 1944, My 28,33:2
Mallett, Frank J Mrs, 1938, My 16,17:5
Mallett, George T Mrs, 1949, Je 24,23:3
Mallett, John P, 1945, Jl 13,11:5
Mallett, John W Prof, 1912, N 8,13:4
Mallett, Montville H, 1950, Jl 31,17:5
Mallett, Norman J, 1965, N 8,35:6
Mallett, Wilbur G, 1942, Ja 13,19:2
Mallette, Frank R, 1957, Ag 9,19:4
Mallette, Frederick S, 1959, S 11,27:1
Mallette, J Vital, 1939, Ap 18,23:3
Mallette, James E, 1941, N 5,23:5
Malley, Arthur W, 1938, Jl 15,17:1
Malley, Charles E Sr, 1953, F 25,27:2
Malley, Edward, 1909, Jl 27,7:2; 1948, Ap 17,15:1
Malley, Edward J, 1943, S 23,21:2
Malley, Henry, 1948, Jl 17,15:2
Malley, James E, 1937, F 8,17:5
Malley, James F, 1961, Ja 28,19:5
Malley, John, 1942, Ap 16,21:4
Malley, John F, 1966, My 17,47:2
Malley, John L, 1953, F 4,27:3
Malley, Thomas A, 1964, D 14,35:4
Malley, Wallace W Sr, 1959, Ja 11,88:2
Malley, Walter E, 1948, F 24,25:2
Malley, Walter E Mrs, 1944, F 12,13:5
Malli, James M, 1947, Ja 29,26:3
Mallin, Fletcher D, 1937, Mr 21,II,8:1
Mallin, Isidore H, 1964, Ja 2,27:2
Mallin, Morris C, 1953, Ag 14,19:4
Mallinckrodt, Edward Jr (will, F 3,14:5), 1967, Ja 20,43:3
Mallinckrodt, George, 1968, Jl 12,31:1
Mallinson, Euphame C, 1944, Mr 25,30:2
Mallinson, George E, 1954, My 26,29:4
Mallinson, George E Mrs, 1938, My 10,21:3
Mallinson, H R, 1931, My 13,25:3
Mallinson, Herbert, 1941, O 11,17:5
Mallinson, Hiram R, 1961, D 7,43:4
Mallinson, Horton W, 1945, Jl 24,23:2
Mallinson, Joha S, 1941, D 30,19:2
Mallison, Elizabeth, 1942, O 20,21:5
Mallison, F A (see also Je 23), 1877, Je 24,7:4
Mallison, Fred, 1951, Jl 14,13:5
Mallison, Goe, 1940, Ap 17,23:6
Malloch, Archibald, 1953, S 20,87:3
Malloch, Douglas, 1938, Jl 3,13:4
Malloch, Thomas T, 1962, Mr 29,33:1
Mallock, William Hurrell, 1923, Ap 5,19:5
Mallon, Alfred E, 1947, D 2,29:1
Mallon, Carrie L M Mrs, 1940, Jl 22,17:5
Mallon, Charles A, 1951, Je 14,27:3
Mallon, Charles E, 1946, N 8,23:2
Mallon, Dwight S, 1956, Ap 8,84:1
Mallon, Frank E, 1956, Je 26,29:4
Mallon, G B, 1928, Ja 14,17:3
Mallon, George Barry Mrs, 1923, Jl 6,13:6
Mallon, Guy M Mrs, 1951, O 15,25:5
Mallon, Harry C, 1955, Ap 28,29:3
Mallon, James, 1907, Ja 20,7:6; 1945, O 20,11:5
Mallon, James E Brig-Gen, 1863, O 21,8:2
Mallon, James J, 1961, Ap 13,35:4
Mallon, John J, 1948, Ja 31,19:4
Mallon, John J Rev, 1907, Ap 17,9:6
Mallon, Joseph, 1946, F 5,23:3
Mallon, Mary, 1938, N 12,17:7
Mallon, Mary T, 1945, Mr 6,21:3
Mallon, Michael A, 1948, Mr 4,25:3
Mallon, Paul R, 1950, Jl 31,17:4
Mallon, Peter, 1879, Ja 12,12:4
Mallon, Peter F, 1959, Ag 18,29:3
Mallon, Thomas H Mrs, 1946, S 21,15:6
Mallon, Vincent M, 1955, Jl 15,21:4
Mallon, William H, 1951, F 14,30:5
Mallon, William L, 1965, Jl 16,27:3
Mallon, Winifred, 1954, Ap 5,25:3
Malloney, Merritt J, 1955, O 2,86:8
Mallory, Anna E Mrs, 1953, Ja 31,15:4
Mallory, B, 1878, D 16,1:6
Mallory, Barton L, 1938, Ap 4,17:6
Mallory, C H, 1882, Ag 27,2:3
Mallory, Cassius C, 1959, Ja 3,17:1
Mallory, Charles, 1918, Jl 9,13:6
Mallory, Charles H, 1953, Mr 16,19:4
Mallory, Chester B, 1957, S 19,29:6
Mallory, Clifford D (por), 1941, Ap 8,25:1
Mallory, Cora P Mrs, 1938, Ja 22,18:3
Mallory, Elsie W Mrs, 1942, Ja 20,19:2
Mallory, Eugene L Mrs, 1960, Ap 8,31:1
Mallory, Fannie R Mrs, 1941, Ag 21,17:5
Mallory, Francis B, 1958, My 23,23:2
Mallory, Frank B, 1941, S 29,17:2
Mallory, Frank L Mrs, 1918, N 12,13:6
Mallory, G S Rev, 1897, Mr 3,12:1
Mallory, Grant T, 1938, F 6,II,8:8
Mallory, Harry B, 1964, Jl 14,33:3
Mallory, Harry R, 1947, Jl 27,45:2
Mallory, Harry R Mrs, 1950, S 28,31:4
Mallory, Henry Lee, 1920, Ja 24,11:4
Mallory, Henry R, 1919, Mr 5,11:3
Mallory, Henry Rogers, 1919, Mr 9,20:4
Mallory, Hervey F, 1943, Jl 23,17:6
Mallory, Holmes, 1918, Mr 20,13:4
Mallory, J C Maj, 1922, N 26,6:3
Mallory, Jeremiah D, 1905, Mr 17,9:4
Mallory, John A, 1937, N 3,18:2
Mallory, John S Mrs, 1945, D 9,44:4
Mallory, Joseph S, 1952, S 14,86:1
Mallory, Lewis B, 1946, Ja 1,28:2
Mallory, Louis A Mrs, 1952, S 16,29:4
Mallory, Molla B Mrs (will, D 16,48:6), 1959, N 23, 31:4
Mallory, Patricia (Boots; Mrs H Marshall), 1958, D 2,37:4
Mallory, Philip R Mrs, 1961, Mr 21,37:5
Mallory, Robert Mrs, 1946, S 28,17:5
Mallory, Robert Sr, 1921, D 16,17:5
Mallory, Roland H, 1954, Je 19,15:5
Mallory, Stephen R, 1873, N 13,6:6
Mallory, Stephen R Sen, 1907, D 24,7:6
Mallory, Tracy B, 1951, N 13,29:6
Mallory, Virgil S, 1959, O 1,35:3
Mallory, W H, 1882, N 11,5:1
Mallory, Walter S (por), 1944, F 15,17:4
Mallory, William E, 1938, Mr 13,II,9:3
Mallory, William W, 1940, N 5,34:2
Mallouk, Elias N, 1944, Ja 13,21:2
Mallowan, Emory A, 1947, F 3,19:5
Malloy, Arthur H, 1950, D 2,13:6
Malloy, Charles A, 1953, My 28,23:1

Malloy, Dann, 1945, N 30,23:2
Malloy, Francis A Msgr, 1937, Ag 3,23:4
Malloy, J Malloy, 1945, Ja 16,19:1
Malloy, John A (por), 1943, Mr 20,15:3
Malloy, John F, 1942, D 10,30:1; 1958, F 7,21:4
Malloy, John J, 1938, D 28,21:5; 1961, N 2,37:3
Malloy, John M, 1952, Jl 9,27:4
Malloy, John W, 1940, F 14,21:4
Malloy, Joseph I, 1959, My 18,27:2
Malloy, Louise, 1947, F 27,21:4
Malloy (Bro Christian of Mary), 1961, D 7,43:2
Malluh, Antonio, 1920, Je 23,11:4
Mally, James W, 1945, Ag 16,19:2
Mally, Manuel J, 1957, Jl 26,19:5
Malm, Axel C V, 1946, Mr 15,21:2
Malm, Frank S, 1967, My 12,47:1
Malman, Christina (Mrs D Masters), 1959, Ja 15, 33:3
Malman, David A, 1941, D 4,25:6
Malmar, Edward S, 1939, Mr 6,15:2
Malmar, Girard G, 1949, Ja 13,23:3
Malmar, Mary I Mrs, 1938, O 5,23:3
Malmed, Edwin S Mrs, 1959, Jl 11,19:5
Malmed, Lawrence, 1955, N 26,19:2
Malmesbury, Lord (J E Harris), 1950, Je 13,27:2
Malmquist, Axel F, 1939, Mr 15,24:2
Malmros, Oscar, 1909, Ag 20,7:5
Malmsha, C L, 1882, O 21,4:7
Malmus, Nathan, 1921, Jl 13,9:4
Malnati, John N (por), 1938, O 6,23:3
Malnick, Max, 1950, F 26,76:4
Malo, Gina (Mrs G Brent), 1963, D 3,43:4
Malo, M, 1884, O 18,3:5
Malon, Leon, 1952, Jl 29,21:1
Malona, Walter, 1942, Ap 30,19:2
Malone, A W, 1948, S 7,25:3
Malone, Aloysius S, 1940, Je 4,23:3
Malone, Austin M, 1925, S 5,13:5
Malone, B J, 1878, F 15,8:4
Malone, Barney, 1949, N 14,27:2
Malone, Christopher E, 1967, Mr 20,31:5
Malone, Dana, 1917, Ag 14,9:5
Malone, Dennis E, 1951, F 4,76:5
Malone, Dudley F, 1950, O 6,27:1
Malone, Dudley F Mrs, 1961, O 5,37:5
Malone, E Halsey, 1938, D 31,15:5
Malone, Edward C, 1937, Jl 10,15:4
Malone, Edward J, 1944, N 10,19:2
Malone, Florence R (Sister Mary Angela), 1965, My 5,47:4
Malone, Francis A, 1951, Ag 4,15:6
Malone, Francis P, 1960, Jl 22,23:4
Malone, Frank J, 1963, Jl 29,19:1
Malone, Frederick C, 1960, N 20,87:1
Malone, George H, 1950, O 8,104:2
Malone, George T, 1962, F 3,21:1
Malone, George V, 1947, O 20,23:1
Malone, George W, 1961, My 20,23:1
Malone, Gilbert, 1962, S 17,31:2
Malone, Harry A, 1962, Ja 16,33:3
Malone, Harvey E, 1951, Ag 5,73:2
Malone, Henry Mark, 1925, Ja 6,25:5
Malone, James F, 1949, Je 22,31:3
Malone, James H, 1942, S 6,30:8
Malone, James H (Shooey), 1955, Ja 13,27:2
Malone, James M, 1957, O 16,35:2
Malone, James P, 1960, Ag 19,23:4
Malone, James T, 1959, Ap 5,86:8
Malone, James T Judge (funl, D 5,23:2), 1920, D 2, 11:3
Malone, Jock, 1964, Jl 6,29:1
Malone, John, 1906, Ja 16,2:5
Malone, John F (funl, Je 1,17:5), 1957, My 28,33:2
Malone, John J Mrs, 1949, Jl 10,56:7
Malone, John L Jr, 1947, N 16,76:6
Malone, John N, 1940, S 17,23:1
Malone, Joseph, 1937, D 14,25:1; 1949, Ja 14,23:3; 1956, Ap 25,35:4
Malone, Katherine Mrs, 1944, Je 30,21:3
Malone, L William, 1953, Mr 4,27:5
Malone, Louis T, 1951, O 27,19:4
Malone, Margaret F (Sister Stella Margt), 1942, Ja 30,20:3
Malone, Mary H Mrs, 1960, Ja 22,27:3
Malone, Michael C, 1944, S 15,19:6
Malone, Murtagh J, 1922, N 21,19:4
Malone, Nelson D, 1958, Ja 19,86:7
Malone, Owen B, 1938, Ag 27,13:6
Malone, Paul B, 1960, O 18,39:4
Malone, Perce (Pat), 1943, My 14,20:3
Malone, Phil Mrs, 1949, Jl 26,27:5
Malone, Pick (A P Maloney), 1962, Ja 24,33:3
Malone, Raymond, 1959, Mr 12,31:4
Malone, Richard A, 1939, My 26,23:5
Malone, Richard B, 1956, Ap 1,88:5
Malone, Robert J, 1966, Ag 10,41:3
Malone, Sylvester Father, 1899, D 30,7:1
Malone, Thomas F, 1949, D 28,32:3
Malone, Thomas R, 1939, N 2,23:5
Malone, Walter Judge, 1915, My 19,13:4
Malone, William J, 1961, F 10,17:4
Maloney, Andrew P (P Malone), 1962, Ja 24,33:3
Maloney, Anne, 1959, Ja 18,88:5
Maloney, Arthur M, 1962, Je 12,37:4
Maloney, Charles E, 1956, N 18,88:2
Maloney, Charles J, 1949, Mr 29,26:3
Maloney, Clifton, 1958, O 4,21:1
Maloney, Cornelius L, 1961, F 19,86:7
Maloney, Cornelius M, 1942, Ag 16,45:3
Maloney, David Mrs, 1949, Jl 22,19:2
Maloney, Denis A Rev (por), 1937, My 22,15:6
Maloney, E Coyne, 1952, D 17,33:3
Maloney, Edward, 1942, N 17,25:1
Maloney, Edward C, 1940, Ag 9,15:4
Maloney, Edward F Mrs, 1958, Je 24,31:4
Maloney, Edward P, 1940, Jl 6,15:6
Maloney, Edward R (por), 1942, O 6,23:1
Maloney, Edward W, 1944, Je 17,13:3
Maloney, Francis H, 1955, Ja 5,23:3
Maloney, Francis R, 1942, S 1,19:3
Maloney, Francis T Mrs, 1956, O 16,33:4
Maloney, George W, 1951, N 16,25:3
Maloney, Gregory, 1950, Ap 24,25:2
Maloney, Harry, 1938, D 24,15:4
Maloney, Harry L, 1949, Ap 12,29:2
Maloney, J Fred, 1955, S 24,19:6
Maloney, J Loy Mrs, 1956, Mr 11,88:2
Maloney, James, 1960, F 2,35:3
Maloney, James E, 1946, N 29,25:4; 1955, Ap 13,29:4
Maloney, James F, 1950, N 30,33:2; 1960, D 7,43:1
Maloney, James J, 1959, Je 8,27:1
Maloney, James P, 1950, My 2,29:1
Maloney, James P Father, 1903, Je 16,7:6
Maloney, Jeremiah J, 1947, Jl 2,23:2
Maloney, John A, 1958, My 4,89:2
Maloney, John C, 1955, Ag 23,23:3
Maloney, John J, 1939, Ag 28,19:5; 1945, N 23,23:5; 1949, My 21,13:4; 1952, F 18,19:6
Maloney, John J Mrs, 1943, N 27,13:1
Maloney, John J Sr, 1965, N 24,39:4
Maloney, John L, 1951, Ag 18,11:5
Maloney, John T, 1942, Ag 24,15:1
Maloney, John V, 1946, Je 11,23:1
Maloney, John W, 1958, Jl 21,21:4
Maloney, Joseph A, 1946, Ja 15,23:3
Maloney, L D, 1929, N 3,26:3
Maloney, Leonard J, 1943, N 1,17:4
Maloney, Levi L, 1937, Je 13,II,6:8
Maloney, M, 1929, My 9,29:1
Maloney, Maie S, 1955, Jl 8,23:1
Maloney, Margaret L Mrs, 1946, S 2,17:5
Maloney, Martha L Mrs, 1942, N 15,58:2
Maloney, Martin, 1939, F 12,45:2
Maloney, Martin E, 1961, Ag 18,21:4
Maloney, Martin Mrs, 1923, Ja 24,13:5
Maloney, Michael E, 1954, F 15,23:5
Maloney, Michael J, 1940, N 27,23:1; 1956, Je 10,88:6
Maloney, Michael T, 1938, Mr 2,19:3
Maloney, Monica, 1924, Ag 8,13:4
Maloney, Pat, 1904, N 15,1:6
Maloney, Patrick J, 1943, Ag 20,15:5
Maloney, Patrick J Sr, 1947, Mr 6,25:2
Maloney, Patrick T, 1942, D 23,19:5
Maloney, Peter J, 1938, D 4,60:8
Maloney, Phil J, 1952, Je 8,87:1
Maloney, Richard J (will, Ap 16,14:4), 1940, Ap 12, 23:4
Maloney, Richard L, 1962, O 6,25:3
Maloney, Robert E, 1952, F 21,27:4
Maloney, Russell (por), 1948, S 5,40:3
Maloney, Susan N Mrs, 1937, Ag 7,15:1
Maloney, T J, 1933, Ja 19,15:3
Maloney, Teresa A, 1957, N 2,21:4
Maloney, Thomas, 1938, Je 26,27:2
Maloney, Thomas A, 1962, Jl 26,27:2
Maloney, Thomas F, 1949, My 22,88:6; 1965, Ap 13, 37:2
Maloney, Thomas H Sr Mrs, 1955, F 3,23:2
Maloney, Thomas J Mrs, 1950, My 16,31:1
Maloney, Vincent T, 1953, S 13,85:1
Maloney, Walter A, 1950, O 14,19:6
Maloney, William, 1944, Ap 6,23:5
Maloney, William A, 1964, Je 10,45:1
Maloney, William E, 1964, Ja 8,37:2
Maloney, William J, 1953, S 11,21:5; 1954, F 25,31:4
Maloney, William J M A, 1952, S 5,27:1
Maloney, William P, 1940, Ja 4,24:4
Maloney, William R, 1945, D 16,39:1
Malony, William R P, 1944, My 21,44:3
Maloof, Alex, 1956, Mr 1,33:2
Maloof, Naceep S, 1964, My 8,33:3
Malool, Thomas, 1925, My 12,23:5
Malot, Hector Henri, 1907, Jl 19,7:6
Malott, M H, 1952, F 19,29:4
Malott, William E, 1945, D 30,14:1
Malotte, Albert H, 1964, N 18,47:2
Malouf, Azeez H, 1946, Ag 21,28:2
Malow, William F, 1942, My 4,19:3
Malowan, Walter, 1966, My 3,44:6
Maloy, Charles J, 1944, S 26,23:5
Maloy, Donald D, 1943, S 3,19:4
Maloy, Edward J, 1962, Jl 19,27:4
Maloy, Frank, 1961, Ja 26,29:1
Maloy, Frank J, 1951, Mr 30,23:3
Maloy, Joseph H, 1942, Jl 3,17:5
Maloy, Joseph H Justice, 1924, S 7,31:1
Maloy, Thomas P, 1942, O 14,25:3
Maloy, William J, 1952, Mr 22,13:5
Malozemoff, Alexander P, 1944, Jl 15,13:6
Malpass, Frank P, 1957, Je 5,35:4
Malpass, Joseph, 1940, O 9,25:1
Malpere, Joseph Mrs, 1958, My 2,28:3
Malraux, Pierre-Gauthier, 1961, My 24,18:6
Malraux, Vincent, 1961, My 24,18:6
Malsberger, William F, 1958, S 16,27:3
Malsch, William G, 1949, S 3,13:2
Malsin, Lane B Mrs (will, O 4,37:5), 1951, S 27,31:
Malsin, Lane B Mrs (est tax appr), 1954, Je 19,19:4
Malsin, Theodore R, 1964, Ag 2,77:1
Malsky, Maurice, 1953, Ap 15,31:4
Malsom, Frank Mrs, 1951, S 11,29:1
Malstrom, Martin, 1941, F 5,19:5
Maltbie, Armstrong, 1937, Jl 17,15:4
Maltbie, James M, 1966, O 29,29:4
Maltbie, Milo R Mrs, 1957, Ap 16,33:5
Maltbie, Robert G Sr, 1951, N 6,29:5
Maltbie, William M, 1961, D 16,25:6
Maltby, Charles S, 1948, D 4,19:3
Maltby, F Lee, 1957, N 23,19:3
Maltby, George E, 1909, Ag 2,7:6
Maltby, George Mrs, 1950, F 4,15:3
Maltby, Harry E, 1907, F 25,9:5
Maltby, Margaret E, 1944, My 5,19:6
Maltby, Ralph B, 1952, O 11,19:6
Maltby, Rufus C, 1922, Je 14,19:5
Maltby, William G, 1949, Ja 7,21:4
Maltby, William Mrs, 1950, Ap 3,24:2
Malter, Henry Dr, 1925, Ap 6,19:6
Maltese, Torie, 1942, O 9,21:3
Maltin, Bernard, 1952, Ap 11,24:3
Maltsev, Anatoly I, 1967, Jl 8,25:5
Maltsev, Ilya K, 1955, S 16,23:4
Maltz, Bob, 1966, F 22,23:2
Maltz, Harry R, 1946, F 9,13:3
Maltz, Leo, 1955, Ja 25,25:2
Maltzan, A von Baron, 1927, S 24,1:3
Maltzeff, Alexis G, 1961, Mr 16,37:5
Malusecki, Adalbert Rev, 1937, My 12,23:5
Malven, Henry H, 1938, Ja 7,19:3
Malvern, Corinne, 1956, N 10,19:3
Malvestiti, Piero, 1964, N 6,37:3
Malvin, Benjamin, 1938, Je 21,19:4
Malvina, Carola, 1915, Ja 19,9:5
Malvy, Louis-Jean, 1949, Je 10,27:5
Maly, Frank J Sr, 1939, Ja 20,19:1
Malypetr, Jan, 1947, S 30,25:3
Malyshev, Ivan S, 1966, D 1,47:4
Malyshev, Vyacheslav A, 1957, F 21,27:4
Mamaux, Al, 1963, Ja 3,15:8
Mamaux, John J, 1942, Ja 28,19:6
Mamber, Harry C, 1945, F 17,13:4
Mamelok, Emil, 1954, My 26,29:3
Mamerow, Siegfried A, 1959, Ap 12,87:1
Mamhead, Lord, 1945, N 4,43:2
Mamiani, Ferenzio Count, 1885, My 22,2:1
Mamini, Robert, 1953, D 20,77:1
Mamlet, Alfred M, 1955, S 8,31:2
Mamlet, Samuel Mrs (F Slaff), 1964, N 4,39:5
Mamlok, Hans J (por), 1940, N 12,23:4
Mamlok, Hans J Mrs, 1953, D 10,47:3
Mamlok, Hermine I, 1949, Mr 10,27:2
Mamlok, Karl H, 1962, F 5,31:4
Mamlok, Richard R, 1948, O 20,29:1
Mammen, George, 1943, D 4,13:5
Mammon, Constantine, 1951, Mr 27,29:4
Man, Ellery A, 1922, S 26,17:6
Man, Horace L, 1942, F 11,21:6
Man, William, 1906, Ja 23,9:5
Man, William F, 1948, Jl 27,25:6
Manach, Consuelo R Mrs, 1941, Ag 5,20:2
Manach, Jorge, 1961, Je 27,33:2
Managan, Timothy, 1950, Ap 29,15:4
Manahan, Edwin F, 1947, Ag 22,15:4
Manahan, Elmer G, 1947, Ja 1,33:4
Manahan, Mary G, 1940, Je 28,19:4
Manahan, Peter L, 1945, My 1,23:2
Manahan, Thomas, 1913, O 12,15:2
Manahan, Thomas J, 1959, Je 21,92:5
Manahan, Vincent D, 1944, O 26,23:5
Manak, Roberta Mrs, 1950, Je 18,76:2
Manalo, Armando D Mrs, 1961, Ag 25,25:1
Manasco, Nemesio J, 1960, N 30,37:4
Manasse, Edward, 1937, S 8,23:5
Manasse, Gerard, 1952, N 25,29:1
Manasses, Jacob, 1940, Ap 7,45:2
Manaster, Harry, 1959, Ja 23,33:1
Manbeck, Aaron E, 1937, O 14,25:3
Manby, Alan Reeve Sir, 1925, O 1,27:5
Manchee, Arthur L Mrs, 1953, O 10,17:7
Manchee, Percy D Mrs, 1947, My 25,62:2
Manchee, Wilfrid A Mrs, 1951, My 5,17:2
Mancher, Morris, 1939, S 21,23:3
Manchester, Alice G, 1958, D 29,15:4
Manchester, Annie J Mrs, 1951, Mr 9,25:4
Manchester, Charles, 1945, D 2,45:2
Manchester, Edward A, 1951, Mr 22,31:3
Manchester, Frederick F, 1951, D 23,22:5
Manchester, Harry R, 1953, Jl 26,69:2
Manchester, Harry S, 1938, Jl 16,13:2

Manchester, Henry C, 1953, Ja 16,23:2
Manchester, Horace H, 1942, Ag 13,19:6
Manchester, Horace L, 1948, F 10,23:2
Manchester, Howard R, 1942, S 11,21:1
Manchester, Irving E, 1938, Mr 7,17:4
Manchester, James G, 1948, Je 29,23:1
Manchester, Leander C Rev Dr, 1925, S 19,15:4
Manchester, Paul, 1941, Ja 28,19:5; 1957, My 26,92:4
Manchester, Paul R Mrs, 1952, D 11,33:5
Manchester, Philip S, 1962, Je 20,32:5
Manchester, Rex, 1966, Je 20,45:1
Manchester, Wilbur, 1947, D 26,15:1
Manchester, William C, 1943, My 19,25:1
Manchester, William L Mrs, 1955, S 24,19:6
Manchon, Charles F, 1964, Mr 7,23:4
Mancinelli, Luigi, 1921, F 8,7:4
Mancini, Michael Mrs (E Mussolini), 1952, My 21, 27:3
Mancini, Theodore, 1944, F 4,15:5
Manco, Frank J, 1951, Ag 18,11:4
Mancroft, Lord, 1942, Ag 18,22:4
Mancusi, Joseph J, 1948, O 11,23:4
Mancusi-Ungaro, Elvire, 1949, Mr 11,26:3
Mancusi-Ungaro, Eugenia Mrs, 1939, Ja 9,15:2
Mancusi-Ungaro, Themistocles, 1940, D 27,20:3
Mancuso, August R Mrs, 1962, O 29,24:7
Mand, George F (funl, My 6,39:4), 1965, My 2,85:2
Mand, Harvey M, 1958, Jl 30,29:3
Manda, Joseph A, 1939, S 24,44:4
Manda, Walter Sr, 1945, My 9,23:4
Mandal, Sant R, 1962, My 3,33:3
Mandel, Abraham, 1947, Ag 20,13:5
Mandel, Arthur R Dr, 1937, Mr 8,19:2
Mandel, Austin B, 1962, My 13,88:5
Mandel, Charles, 1963, S 1,56:8
Mandel, Charles I, 1950, O 5,31:3
Mandel, Edmond de Rothchild, 1920, F 14,11:4
Mandel, Edward (por), 1942, My 26,21:1
Mandel, Edward A, 1967, O 6,39:4
Mandel, Edward A Mrs, 1937, O 17,II,8:8
Mandel, Edwin F (will, Ag 9,3:7), 1963, Jl 18,27:2
Mandel, Emanuel, 1908, S 5,7:4
Mandel, Emmanuel, 1908, S 6,9:4
Mandel, Estelle, 1968, Ja 12,34:7
Mandel, Frank, 1958, Ap 22,33:3
Mandel, Frank Mrs, 1941, My 3,15:6
Mandel, Frank S, 1937, Mr 29,19:4
Mandel, G, 1943, Je 5,8:5
Mandel, Gerald, 1964, Ag 26,39:2
Mandel, Harry T, 1952, S 10,29:6
Mandel, Harvey, 1965, Mr 20,27:5
Mandel, Henry (por), 1942, O 11,57:1
Mandel, Herman, 1960, Je 22,35:1
Mandel, Herman Isaac, 1903, Jl 9,7:6
Mandel, Howard, 1968, D 17,47:1
Mandel, Irving Mrs, 1959, D 12,23:5
Mandel, Jacob, 1965, Mr 19,35:1
Mandel, Joseph, 1954, Mr 20,15:4
Mandel, Joseph D, 1953, My 15,23:4
Mandel, Julius, 1949, D 1,31:4
Mandel, Julius I Mrs, 1961, F 5,81:1
Mandel, Max (por), 1941, My 11,44:4
Mandel, Max, 1968, D 25,31:3
Mandel, Morris, 1952, Ag 17,76:3
Mandel, Nathan, 1953, Je 7,84:4
Mandel, Paul, 1965, D 20,35:3
Mandel, Simon, 1912, Ag 20,9:6
Mandelbaum, Abraham Dr, 1921, My 25,17:4
Mandelbaum, Charles Mrs, 1956, D 18,31:2
Mandelbaum, Daisy, 1916, Jl 24,9:3
Mandelbaum, Harry, 1955, My 28,15:4
Mandelbaum, Herman A (cor, Mr 4,27:1), 1952, F 27,27:1
Mandelbaum, M Joseph, 1956, My 10,31:5
Mandelbaum, Marcus, 1944, S 1,13:3
Mandelbaum, Maurice, 1949, Ja 27,24:2
Mandelbaum, Samuel, 1946, N 21,31:3
Mandelbaum, Sarah S Mrs (will, Ag 12,17:3), 1937, Ag 5,23:3
Mandelberg, Abraham, 1964, S 25,41:1
Mandelberg, David Mrs, 1964, F 5,35:3
Mandelberg, Theresa Mrs, 1925, Je 13,15:6
Mandelick, Charles E, 1952, Jl 20,52:5
Mandelick, Elizabeth Mrs, 1921, Je 23,17:5
Mandelkern, Joseph, 1940, Ja 14,42:6
Mandell, Benjamin E, 1949, O 27,27:2
Mandell, Clifford B, 1967, Ap 7,34:4
Mandell, G S, 1934, Ag 12,24:1
Mandell, Harold C, 1959, My 19,33:1
Mandell, Henry R, 1907, O 7,9:6
Mandell, Israel, 1962, S 17,31:2
Mandell, Jacob, 1943, Ap 13,25:3
Mandell, Sam, 1968, D 15,86:2
Mandell, Sammy, 1967, N 9,61:2
Mandell, Samuel P, 1920, F 15,22:3
Mandell, Serguis I, 1953, Ap 21,27:4
Mandell, William D, 1914, S 14,9:6
Mandell, Winthrop A, 1950, Mr 19,92:5
Mandella, Arthur A, 1968, Ap 30,47:3
Mandellaub, Max Mrs, 1953, My 1,21:1
Mandelstamm, Max Prof, 1912, Mr 21,11:4
Mander, Miles, 1946, F 9,13:2
Mandernach, Howard J, 1949, Ja 26,25:3

Manders, Helen E Mrs, 1941, Ja 2,14:5
Manderson, Charles Frederick Sen, 1911, S 29,9:4
Manderson, Harold A, 1950, Ag 19,13:4
Manderstroem, Count, 1873, Ag 29,4:7
Manderville, William, 1947, Ja 19,12:4
Mandes, Joseph, 1952, Ag 6,21:1
Mandeville, Charles H W, 1947, S 14,60:6
Mandeville, Christopher, 1937, S 26,II,8:6
Mandeville, Edwin, 1915, Je 11,15:4
Mandeville, Estelle Mrs, 1942, My 26,21:5
Mandeville, Frederick A, 1955, Ag 2,23:1
Mandeville, Frederick B Dr, 1909, Ap 27,11:5
Mandeville, H A Dr, 1903, F 1,7:5
Mandeville, Harry W, 1944, F 11,19:2
Mandeville, Hubert C, 1943, Mr 28,24:6
Mandeville, Hubert Mrs, 1951, N 2,24:2
Mandeville, James A, 1947, Mr 10,22:3
Mandeville, James M, 1938, My 18,21:4
Mandeville, James N, 1938, F 6,II,8:2
Mandeville, Philip J, 1944, My 2,19:5
Mandeville, Thomas P Mrs, 1943, My 12,25:5
Mandeville, William H, 1954, Mr 23,27:3
Mandic, Ante, 1959, N 16,31:5
Mandigo, Albert Mrs, 1944, Mr 11,13:6
Mandigo, Elmer J, 1951, O 27,19:6
Mandigo, John H, 1908, Ap 16,9:4
Mandigo, Joseph, 1941, F 7,19:5
Mandigo, Pauline E, 1956, Jl 18,27:3
Mandigo, Peter Mrs, 1945, Jl 25,23:4
Mandillo, Vincent F, 1938, My 21,15:4
Manditch, Lucas, 1960, Mr 13,86:6
Mandl, Felix, 1957, O 16,35:1
Mandl, Joseph G, 1942, Mr 1,45:3
Mandly, Henry Jr, 1954, O 7,23:4
Mandola, John, 1954, Jl 13,23:3
Mandot, Joe, 1956, Ag 1,8:4
Mandour, Joseph A, 1939, S 9,17:5
Mandra, Raymond, 1967, O 11,47:3
Mandre, Phil, 1947, D 3,29:2
Mandrey, William W, 1945, N 20,21:2
Mandrey, William W Mrs, 1948, Mr 17,25:2
Mandry, Walt, 1965, Ap 1,35:2
Mandukich, Svetozar, 1966, Ja 9,57:1
Mandushich, Jake A (J Allex), 1959, Ag 29,17:4
Maneck, Eugene E Mrs, 1957, F 26,29:2
Manecke, Philipp, 1943, Je 9,21:3
Manee, Basil H, 1954, O 2,17:5
Manee, Harry E, 1946, Ja 23,27:3
Maneely, Edward F, 1958, F 9,88:4
Manegold, Frank W, 1950, N 29,36:6
Maneille, M, 1869, Ag 29,2:7
Manello, Carl, 1951, S 18,32:3
Manely, Robert E, 1941, D 30,4:7
Manenionello, Giuseppe, 1939, D 31,18:5
Maner, Pitt T, 1963, Je 14,29:1
Manero, Pasquale Mrs, 1952, Jl 9,27:4
Manes, Alex H, 1940, Ag 25,36:5
Manes, Antonio, 1950, O 31,27:2
Manes, Charles S, 1944, Jl 26,19:3
Manes, Elias T, 1907, D 26,7:5
Manes, Peter, 1966, Je 3,13:5
Manet, E, 1883, My 2,5:5
Manetzakes, Stantes, 1937, My 6,36:7
Manewal, William H, 1942, S 4,23:5
Maney, C Joseph, 1954, Ja 8,21:4
Maney, Denis J Jr, 1956, Ag 20,21:4
Maney, George A, 1947, My 11,60:4
Maney, John J, 1925, F 1,7:2
Maney, Joseph J, 1956, Ap 19,31:4
Maney, Mansfield G, 1949, Mr 11,26:2
Maney, Patrick Mrs, 1956, Mr 22,35:2
Maney, Richard, 1968, Jl 2,27:1
Manfra, Frank, 1954, My 5,31:3
Manfra, Raffelinia Mrs, 1952, Ap 14,20:3
Manfred, Charles N, 1938, O 18,25:4
Manfred, Maud E, 1956, D 9,88:2
Manfredini, James M, 1953, F 21,13:4
Mangabeira, Otavio, 1960, D 1,35:4
Mangada Rosernon, Julio, 1946, Ap 16,25:5
Mangam, Daniel D Mrs, 1957, D 30,23:4
Mangam, Edgar Bedell, 1916, Ja 13,11:3
Mangan, Agnes C Mrs, 1950, D 7,33:5
Mangan, Charles, 1962, Mr 27,37:4
Mangan, Daniel C Dr, 1925, Ja 7,25:5
Mangan, Daniel J, 1944, My 7,45:1
Mangan, Edward F, 1951, S 28,31:5
Mangan, Edward M, 1956, Ap 2,16:8
Mangan, Ellen T Mrs, 1937, Ag 31,23:6
Mangan, Francis X, 1943, S 9,26:3
Mangan, Frank, 1915, O 10,17:6
Mangan, James M, 1938, Ap 2,15:6
Mangan, John, 1950, S 4,17:6
Mangan, John C Mrs, 1944, Ja 7,18:3
Mangan, John J, 1952, D 16,31:1
Mangan, Patrick J, 1944, O 3,23:2
Mangan, Patrick Mrs, 1961, Mr 4,23:2
Mangan, Paul J, 1967, S 27,47:2
Mangan, Thomas J (por), 1947, My 20,25:1
Mangan, Thomas J Mrs, 1952, S 15,25:2
Mangan, William H, 1952, F 15,25:3
Manganaro, Vincent, 1938, Ap 24,II,7:2
Mangano, Antonio, 1951, My 11,27:1
Mangano, Antonio Mrs, 1959, Mr 3,33:4

Mangano, Gaetano V, 1961, F 7,33:4
Mangano, James L, 1952, F 4,17:2
Mangasarian, Mangasar M, 1943, Je 28,21:1
Mangassarian, Roupen, 1944, My 23,23:1
Mange, Ch de Father, 1903, N 3,7:7
Mange, John I, 1951, Ja 25,25:4
Mangel, Benjamin, 1954, Je 23,25:1
Mangel, Sol Mrs, 1947, F 21,19:1
Mangels, William F, 1958, F 13,29:3
Mangelsdorf, Albert Mrs, 1948, Jl 16,19:5
Manger, Julius, 1937, Mr 29,19:1
Manger, Julius (will), 1940, Mr 16,15:1
Manger, Julius Sr Mrs, 1962, O 5,33:3
Manger, W, 1928, Jl 9,19:4
Manges, Harry L, 1948, N 14,76:2
Manges, Morris, 1944, Ja 28,18:2
Manghetti, Louis, 1913, S 18,11:3
Mangiagalli, Riccardo P, 1949, Jl 9,13:6
Mangin, Charles Gen (por), 1925, My 13,21:4
Mangin, Joseph Mrs, 1950, F 24,23:1
Mangini, Humbert E, 1956, F 20,23:5
Mangini, Joseph, 1947, Ap 9,25:1
Mangini, Peter (P Morgan), 1961, Ag 25,25:2
Mangino, Humbert C, 1955, My 11,31:4
Mangkoe Negoro VII, Sultan of Solo, 1944, Jl 26,19:5
Mangles, Edward H Mrs, 1905, Je 20,2:1
Mangnell, Oliver P, 1940, D 21,17:6
Mangogna, Phil, 1957, Ja 1,23:5
Mangold, Aurel E, 1962, F 12,23:4
Mangold, Charles F, 1948, My 10,21:1
Mangold, John H, 1944, Mr 11,13:2
Mangold, Julius J, 1962, Mr 12,31:4
Mangold, William A Jr, 1959, My 19,33:1
Mangone, George F, 1948, N 22,21:4
Mangone, Phil, 1957, D 8,89:1
Manguenzo, Ilis, 1947, S 19,23:3
Mangum, Charles S, 1939, O 2,17:4
Mangum, Minnie, 1967, S 25,45:2
Mangum, W P, 1881, Ap 1,5:4
Mangum, William P, 1861, S 28,5:1
Manhardt, John, 1952, Jl 25,17:4
Manhardt, John Mrs, 1949, Je 7,31:3
Manhardt, Leo W, 1947, Ag 15,17:5
Manheim, Ferdinand, 1948, Mr 30,23:4
Manheim, Isidore, 1967, Ja 4,43:1
Manheim, Jacob, 1944, N 21,25:3
Manheim, Nathaniel L, 1952, Ag 12,19:2
Manheim, Samuel, 1961, F 5,80:5
Manheimer, Arthur E, 1957, D 14,21:3
Manheimer, Edwin J, 1962, Ja 14,84:3
Manheimer, Eugene, 1952, S 10,29:5
Manheimer, Irving S Mrs, 1959, Je 18,31:5
Manheimer, Jacob, 1964, Mr 14,23:5
Manheimer, Jacob S, 1956, Ap 25,35:2
Manheimer, Wallace A, 1949, Je 2,27:4
Manice, Arthur R, 1950, Je 10,17:4
Manice, Edward A, 1925, Jl 28,13:6
Manice, William, 1914, Ja 20,9:6
Manice, William D, 1961, O 28,21:3
Manier, Will R Jr, 1953, F 1,88:2
Maniere, Phil M, 1950, S 6,29:4
Manierre, Benjamin F, 1910, Je 14,11:4
Manierre, Charles E (por), 1940, Ja 31,19:3
Manierre, Charles E Mrs, 1968, S 19,47:3
Manierre, George, 1924, Ja 30,19:4
Manievich, Abraham, 1942, Jl 1,25:3
Manigault, Robert S, 1945, My 13,20:5
Manigian, Matteos, 1959, Je 25,29:2
Manin, Auguste, 1949, Je 17,25:4
Manini Rios, Pedro, 1958, Jl 5,17:3
Manion, Anna (Mother Mary Regis), 1962, Je 8,31:5
Manion, Edward J, 1958, My 21,33:1
Manion, F Raymond Mrs, 1953, O 3,17:6
Manion, John, 1940, Je 5,25:5
Manion, M Celeste, 1953, N 9,35:5
Manion, Margaret Mrs, 1944, Je 19,19:5
Manion, Robert J (por), 1943, Jl 3,13:3
Manis, John J, 1942, Je 18,21:3
Maniscalco, Antonio Mrs, 1965, My 30,51:2
Manischewitz, Hirsch (por), 1943, O 10,49:2
Manischewitz, Jacob U, 1942, Mr 27,23:5
Manischewitz, Joseph (por), 1949, Mr 29,25:3
Manischewitz, Max (por), 1947, Ag 30,15:6
Manischewitz, Max Mrs, 1949, Ag 11,23:5
Manishen, James, 1948, N 21,88:1
Manissero, Romolo, 1951, My 21,27:5
Maniton, Joseph, 1912, O 26,11:6
Manitz, Emil G, 1944, O 13,19:4
Manitz, Walter B, 1951, Ag 28,23:5
Maniu, Juliu, 1951, Jl 18,2:3
Manizer, Matvei, 1966, D 22,33:5
Manke, Fred Mrs, 1938, Jl 17,26:5
Manker, Edward B, 1949, F 21,23:5
Manker, Henry M, 1943, S 18,17:1
Manker, J Lucille, 1949, O 16,88:3
Manker, Philip, 1967, Mr 25,23:1
Manker, W W, 1939, Ap 4,25:1
Mankiewicz, Frank (por), 1941, D 3,25:4
Mankiewicz, Frank Mrs, 1943, O 16,13:2
Mankiewicz, Herman J, 1953, Mr 6,23:3
Mankiewicz, Joseph L Mrs (death ruled suicide, N 26,26:1), 1958, S 28,87:3
Mankin, Harry A, 1954, Je 24,27:3

Manko, Louis H, 1950, Ag 7,19:5
Mankowski, Casimir Count, 1917, Ap 25,11:7
Manley, Addis B, 1950, Ag 23,29:5
Manley, Albert E, 1944, Ap 9,34:2
Manley, Alfred S, 1946, O 24,27:5
Manley, Andrew W, 1916, Je 19,11:5
Manley, Carleton W, 1952, Jl 20,53:3
Manley, D V R, 1937, My 28,21:5
Manley, Edgar, 1953, Je 6,17:3
Manley, Edward B Mrs, 1947, O 4,17:4
Manley, Edwin J, 1962, Jl 15,60:2
Manley, Frank C, 1937, F 18,21:5
Manley, Frank H Sr, 1946, O 7,31:1
Manley, Frank J, 1960, Ap 27,37:4
Manley, Franklin G, 1949, O 29,15:3
Manley, Frederic T, 1941, F 27,20:2
Manley, George W, 1948, N 9,27:5
Manley, H Ervin, 1950, Mr 11,15:1
Manley, Harold S, 1951, S 28,28:2
Manley, Harry L, 1959, My 15,29:2
Manley, Henry, 1921, S 26,15:2; 1949, O 28,23:4
Manley, Henry S, 1967, S 15,44:5
Manley, James, 1953, D 2,2:7
Manley, John A, 1957, D 8,88:5
Manley, John B, 1939, Jl 11,19:6
Manley, John E, 1954, My 7,23:3
Manley, John E Mrs, 1966, F 24,38:1
Manley, John W, 1942, S 29,24:2
Manley, Joseph H, 1905, F 8,9:4
Manley, Joseph L Sr, 1960, N 23,29:1
Manley, Lloyd, 1938, Ag 12,17:6
Manley, Louis E, 1960, S 8,35:2
Manley, Lucius N, 1924, Ap 2,19:5
Manley, Mark, 1940, N 9,17:4
Manley, Mart, 1956, Mr 29,27:4
Manley, Michael E, 1940, Ja 30,19:4
Manley, Minnie C F Mrs, 1941, F 17,15:3
Manley, Robert E, 1958, Ja 21,26:7
Manley, Thomas J, 1947, Mr 23,60:2
Manley, Thomas R, 1938, My 14,15:4
Manley, Thomas W, 1958, N 3,37:5
Manley, Walter F, 1947, Ja 25,17:1
Manley, Warren E, 1951, Ap 10,27:4
Manley, William B, 1962, F 5,31:4
Manley, William F, 1954, Jl 12,19:2
Manley, William J, 1952, N 3,27:4
Manley, Williston P, 1947, N 11,27:3
Manlove, Charles J, 1952, F 13,29:1
Manlove, Francis A, 1946, My 17,22:3
Manlove, George H, 1946, N 11,27:3
Manlove, Harry, 1949, Ja 1,13:2
Manly, Augustus W, 1951, S 22,17:2
Manly, Basil, 1950, My 12,27:5
Manly, C M, 1927, O 18,29:3
Manly, Charles A, 1916, Ja 23,17:3
Manly, Clarence J Col, 1937, Je 29,21:4
Manly, Ellen Mrs, 1937, Jl 14,21:1
Manly, Grace E, 1943, My 22,13:2
Manly, John M, 1940, Ap 3,23:2
Manly, L S, 1938, Je 12,38:7
Manly, Mary P Mrs, 1953, Ap 3,23:2
Manly, Matthias E Mrs, 1952, O 22,27:4
Manly, Thomas E, 1954, Jl 15,27:6
Manly, William H, 1938, N 29,23:5
Mann, A R, 1947, F 22,11:8
Mann, Abraham, 1955, Mr 26,15:2
Mann, Abraham Mrs, 1956, Jl 6,21:2
Mann, Adelia S Mrs, 1941, D 2,23:5
Mann, Albert, 1962, Mr 28,39:2
Mann, Albert C, 1948, F 2,20:3
Mann, Alden T Jr, 1966, F 28,27:4
Mann, Alex (por), 1948, N 16,29:1
Mann, Aloysius J, 1941, N 23,51:4
Mann, Amelia R Mrs, 1937, My 21,21:5
Mann, Anthony, 1967, Ap 30,86:5
Mann, Archibald I, 1961, F 9,31:4
Mann, Arthur, 1963, Ja 5,8:3
Mann. Arthur I, 1962, Ag 18,19:4
Mann, Arthur G Mrs, 1941, Mr 24,17:1
Mann, Baldwin Mrs, 1957, O 22,33:5
Mann, Barney Mrs, 1946, N 22,23:1
Mann, Benjamin, 1961, F 22,25:5
Mann, Benjamin H, 1944, N 24,24:3
Mann, Benson, 1940, Mr 21,25:2
Mann, Bernard, 1964, Ag 5,33:3
Mann, Bernard O, 1951, My 19,15:4
Mann, Carolyn Mrs, 1907, N 10,9:7
Mann, Charles F, 1941, Je 11,21:2; 1944, Ja 16,43:2; 1945, Mr 28,23:3
Mann, Charles H Rev, 1918, Ap 11,13:3
Mann, Charles Mrs, 1951, Mr 22,31:3
Mann, Charles W, 1943, D 4,13:4
Mann, chas A, 1953, Ap 5,76:8
Mann, Claire (Mrs S Nordlicht), 1960, Ja 2,13:6
Mann, Clara L, 1952, Je 23,19:5
Mann, Clarence L Jr, 1952, N 6,29:5
Mann, Conklin, 1966, Ja 18,37:4
Mann, Conklin Jr, 1956, Jl 9,23:4
Mann, Conrad H, 1943, D 28,17:3
Mann, D, 1934, N 12,19:3
Mann, Daniel, 1902, S 9,9:6
Mann, Daniel H, 1961, Ag 10,27:3
Mann, Daulton, 1941, My 16,23:2
Mann, David M, 1950, Mr 23,36:3
Mann, Delbert M Mrs, 1961, My 14,86:4
Mann, E D, 1902, Mr 31,9:6
Mann, Eben H, 1944, N 28,23:4
Mann, Edith T Mrs (will), 1942, Ag 18,34:1
Mann, Edith W Mrs, 1951, My 23,35:1
Mann, Edward C Dr, 1937, Ag 7,15:5
Mann, Elizabeth, 1954, O 29,23:2
Mann, Elizabeth S Mrs (E Softer), 1963, F 12,4:6
Mann, Ellen K Mrs, 1952, Jl 29,21:6
Mann, Ellery W, 1956, Ja 16,21:3
Mann, F N Sr, 1880, F 9,4:7
Mann, Fanny, 1942, D 28,19:4
Mann, Ferdinand Mrs, 1953, Ap 24,23:2
Mann, Floyd, 1946, D 26,30:1
Mann, Francis N Jr Col, 1912, N 29,15:6
Mann, Francis N Mrs, 1946, Ja 13,43:1
Mann, Frank, 1943, Ag 30,15:2
Mann, Frank C, 1962, O 2,39:2
Mann, Frank H, 1954, O 12,27:4
Mann, Frank Mrs, 1940, Je 23,30:7
Mann, Frederick A, 1943, Ag 17,17:5; 1957, D 27,20:2
Mann, Frederick J, 1939, Je 25,37:3
Mann, Frederick J Mrs, 1938, N 18,21:5
Mann, Frederick L, 1960, Jl 12,35:3; 1962, N 27,37:2
Mann, George E Mrs, 1960, Ag 11,27:4
Mann, George H, 1955, Jl 22,23:2
Mann, George H Mrs, 1965, Je 8,41:3
Mann, George J, 1941, N 14,23:3
Mann, Gerson, 1943, Ja 28,19:2
Mann, H A, 1934, Mr 16,22:3
Mann, Harrington (por), 1937, Mr 1,19:1
Mann, Heinrich L, 1950, Mr 13,21:4
Mann, Henry, 1915, O 17,15:4; 1937, Ap 8,7:2; 1968, Ag 26,39:4
Mann, Herbert S, 1938, Ag 25,19:1
Mann, Horace, 1859, Ag 3,8:2
Mann, Horace B, 1937, Jl 16,19:2
Mann, Horace M, 1951, Je 23,15:2
Mann, Horace T, 1940, F 10,15:4
Mann, Howard C, 1943, Ap 20,23:3
Mann, Hunter, 1966, My 7,31:2
Mann, J Frank, 1939, Mr 8,21:2
Mann, Jacob, 1968, Ag 13,39:1
Mann, Jacob J, 1960, S 15,37:3
Mann, James, 1941, S 8,15:5
Mann, James F Sr, 1959, N 16,31:4
Mann, John W, 1951, O 2,27:3
Mann, Joseph B Mrs, 1947, Je 10,27:4
Mann, Joseph F, 1951, N 6,29:1
Mann, Josiah, 1948, N 1,23:3
Mann, Klaus (por), 1949, My 23,23:1
Mann, Kristine, 1945, N 13,21:5
Mann, L, 1931, F 16,19:1
Mann, Lawrence B Mrs, 1963, D 20,29:2
Mann, Lee B, 1957, Ja 7,19:5
Mann, Leon, 1951, F 18,78:3
Mann, Lloyd O V Mrs, 1967, D 6,51:3
Mann, Louis D, 1944, My 7,45:2
Mann, Louis L, 1966, F 2,35:4
Mann, M Burr, 1942, D 15,27:5
Mann, Martha Mrs, 1952, F 15,25:3
Mann, Marvin, 1966, Ag 21,93:2
Mann, Mary E Mrs, 1940, Ja 24,21:3
Mann, Mary M Mrs, 1939, Je 27,23:2
Mann, Mathilde, 1925, F 16,19:4
Mann, Matt 2d, 1962, Ag 8,31:2
Mann, Matthew D Dr, 1921, Mr 4,13:4
Mann, Matthew D Jr, 1953, D 22,31:6
Mann, Maude F, 1955, O 16,86:6
Mann, Maurice H, 1951, My 27,69:1
Mann, Milton, 1951, My 29,25:4
Mann, Morris H, 1946, Ja 31,21:4
Mann, Morris J, 1953, D 18,29:2
Mann, N, 1926, Jl 26,15:4
Mann, Newton Mrs, 1958, Mr 5,31:3
Mann, Ormond H, 1948, D 15,33:1
Mann, Parker, 1918, D 16,15:2
Mann, Paul B (por), 1943, O 24,45:1
Mann, Peter C, 1940, Ap 24,23:2
Mann, Philip, 1959, Je 20,21:5
Mann, R R Com, 1925, Ja 4,7:2
Mann, Rachel Mrs, 1909, My 21,9:6
Mann, Ralph G, 1952, S 18,29:2
Mann, Ralph H, 1948, Ap 3,15:4
Mann, Ransford V, 1950, S 27,32:2
Mann, Richard B Com, 1925, Ja 7,25:4
Mann, Robert N, 1959, Mr 28,17:4
Mann, Robert S, 1938, My 2,17:4
Mann, Roland W, 1945, D 30,14:6
Mann, Rose Mrs, 1948, Je 2,29:1
Mann, Ruth Z S, 1959, Mr 28,17:5
Mann, S Vernon, 1950, Ja 14,15:3; 1952, Mr 1,15:2
Mann, Samuel, 1938, Je 15,23:6; 1958, S 8,29:4
Mann, Samuel Mrs, 1959, Ap 10,29:3; 1964, Ja 4,23:1
Mann, Sanford B, 1922, Ag 25,13:7
Mann, St John E, 1949, Ap 12,29:5
Mann, Stanley, 1958, Ag 21,25:2
Mann, Theodore, 1921, S 6,15:5
Mann, Thomas (funl plans, Ag 14,81:1; funl, Ag 17,27:6), 1955, Ag 13,1:2
Mann, Thomas E, 1946, My 15,21:4
Mann, Tom, 1941, Mr 14,21:3
Mann, Viktor, 1949, Ap 23,13:1
Mann, W W, 1885, F 22,3:6
Mann, Walter B, 1947, Je 26,23:2
Mann, Walter C, 1948, D 29,21:4
Mann, Walter R, 1940, Ap 5,21:2
Mann, William, 1939, My 13,15:7; 1953, Ap 7,29:5
Mann, William B, 1946, O 23,28:2
Mann, William D'Alton Col (funl, My 20,13:5), 1920, My 18,11:3
Mann, William H Mrs, 1958, Ja 13,29:4
Mann, William L Jr, 1953, Je 14,85:1
Mann. William M, 1960, O 11,45:3
Manna, Nicola, 1938, Ag 11,17:2
Mannain, John K, 1943, Jl 23,17:4
Mannel, Anton F, 1948, Je 23,27:5
Mannella, Mike, 1940, D 8,71:2
Mannen, Frank A (por), 1937, O 1,21:2
Mannen, Frank A Mrs, 1947, Jl 20,44:2
Manner, Jane, 1943, My 28,21:4
Manner, Percy H, 1938, Ap 21,19:2
Mannerheim, Carl G E, 1951, Ja 28,77:1
Mannering, Mary, 1953, Ja 22,23:3
Manners, F Rennison, 1944, D 28,19:5
Manners, John James Robert Duke of Rutland, 1906, Ag 5,9:6
Manners, John Lord, 1874, S 10,6:7
Manners, Maynard, 1938, Ja 5,21:2
Mannes, David (trb lr, My 2,22:5), 1959, Ap 25,21:
Mannes, David Mrs (por), 1948, Mr 18,27:1
Mannes, Leopold, 1964, Ag 12,35:1
Mannes, William I, 1948, D 27,21:3
Mannesmann, Reinhard, 1922, F 23,15:5
Manness, S Ervin, 1925, S 26,17:7
Manney, Charles F, 1951, N 1,29:5
Manney, Henry Newman Adm, 1915, O 26,11:6
Mannheim, Elsa K Mrs, 1940, N 5,34:2
Mannheim, Herbert W, 1958, N 16,88:4
Mannheim, Karl, 1947, Ja 10,22:3
Mannheim, Max, 1950, D 10,107:3
Mannheimer, Albert, 1957, Jl 23,27:5
Mannheimer, Fritz, 1939, Ag 11,15:1
Mannheimer, George, 1945, D 11,25:2
Mannheimer, Isaac, 1944, N 12,48:4
Mannierre, Alfred Lee, 1911, O 2,11:5
Manning, A J, 1954, F 19,34:2
Manning, A R, 1880, S 19,2:5
Manning, Abraham, 1922, D 5,19:3
Manning, Albert, 1924, F 20,19:4
Manning, Albert J Mrs, 1951, N 25,86:5
Manning, Alice L, 1944, Ag 2,15:3
Manning, Ambrose, 1940, Mr 25,16:2
Manning, Anna, 1945, F 9,16:3
Manning, Anthony B, 1957, S 28,17:5
Manning, Arthur G, 1939, My 20,15:7
Manning, Arthur J, 1956, Ag 21,29:5
Manning, Arthur L, 1967, Jl 19,39:2
Manning, Bruce, 1965, Ag 7,21:2
Manning, Cardinal, 1892, Ja 15,9:1
Manning, Catherine L Mrs, 1957, Ap 17,31:3
Manning, Charles E, 1958, My 13,29:2
Manning, Charles R, 1937, D 22,25:5
Manning, Charles W, 1961, N 30,37:3
Manning, D, 1887, D 25,5:1
Manning, Daniel, 1942, O 8,27:2
Manning, Dennis J, 1954, Ap 26,25:3
Manning, E E Mrs, 1951, Mr 24,13:6
Manning, Edmund C, 1951, Ap 16,25:5
Manning, Edward, 1919, D 25,13:3
Manning, Edward B, 1940, Ap 3,23:5; 1948, Mr 9,
Manning, Edward J, 1938, Mr 11,19:2; 1958, F 27,
Manning, Edward M Sr, 1956, S 30,86:5
Manning, Edward V, 1946, S 24,29:3
Manning, Eliza Mrs, 1924, My 30,15:5
Manning, Ella A Mrs, 1941, N 11,23:4
Manning, Emily S Mrs, 1940, O 31,23:2
Manning, Eugene A, 1945, O 6,13:4
Manning, Eugene J, 1963, My 23,37:4
Manning, Florence, 1949, D 18,88:5
Manning, Fowler, 1948, Je 16,29:2
Manning, Francis X, 1959, Ap 4,19:4
Manning, Frank A, 1939, S 26,23:1; 1949, Mr 6,72
Manning, Frank E, 1944, Ja 27,19:3
Manning, Frank O Mrs, 1947, Ap 19,15:3
Manning, Franklin H, 1944, O 23,19:3
Manning, Fred C, 1959, Jl 10,25:5
Manning, Frederick Col, 1913, Ag 5,7:3
Manning, Frederick J, 1966, D 16,47:3
Manning, Frederick R Mrs, 1957, Ag 9,19:5
Manning, G Randolph, 1953, D 2,2:7
Manning, G Rudolph Mrs, 1965, Ap 28,45:2
Manning, George L Dr, 1914, N 22,3:6
Manning, George T, 1956, D 2,87:1
Manning, Guy, 1956, S 2,57:3
Manning, Harry J, 1946, Ja 26,13:3
Manning, Henry P, 1956, Ja 13,23:4
Manning, Henry S, 1921, Jl 10,22:4
Manning, Herbert A, 1959, Ag 3,25:1
Manning, Irving H, 1944, F 3,19:3
Manning, Isaac H, 1946, F 13,23:5
Manning, J J, 1926, D 19,II,11:1
Manning, J M Rev, 1882, N 30,2:7
Manning, Jack (por), 1940, F 20,21:5
Manning, James, 1961, Je 18,88:5

Manning, James C Mrs, 1945, Ag 7,23:3
Manning, James F, 1938, My 24,19:2
Manning, James F Jr, 1949, Mr 17,25:3
Manning, James H, 1967, Je 13,47:1
Manning, James Hilton, 1925, Jl 5,3:4
Manning, James J, 1921, F 15,9:5
Manning, James S, 1938, Jl 30,13:7
Manning, John A, 1938, Mr 16,23:5
Manning, John A Mrs, 1946, Ag 11,45:1
Manning, John B, 1918, Ap 24,13:5
Manning, John E, 1954, Je 17,29:6
Manning, John F, 1937, N 17,23:5; 1939, S 21,23:4; 1945, D 30,14:3
Manning, John H, 1951, Ap 24,29:4
Manning, John J, 1947, O 21,23:4; 1953, N 8,88:4; 1962, S 6,31:2
Manning, John J Msgr, 1953, Je 23,30:4
Manning, John L, 1953, Ag 19,29:3
Manning, John L Mrs, 1955, Jl 26,25:3
Manning, John Mrs, 1922, Je 13,19:6
Manning, John T, 1949, D 28,32:3
Manning, John W, 1952, O 11,19:4
Manning, Joseph, 1946, Ag 1,23:4
Manning, Joseph J Mrs (will, N 19,15:3), 1943, N 14,56:5
Manning, Joseph P, 1944, Ja 24,17:5
Manning, Leslie B, 1940, Je 7,23:1
Manning, Lester J, 1960, Jl 2,17:4
Manning, Manny, 1948, Je 20,60:3
Manning, Mary (Sister Maria Patrick), 1958, Mr 22, 17:1
Manning, Merrill M Mrs, 1955, N 24,29:4
Manning, Michael J, 1950, Ap 10,19:6
Manning, Michael X, 1953, Ap 25,15:4
Manning, Michaele, 1964, Jl 20,25:4
Manning, Millard, 1942, Je 4,19:2
Manning, Newton S, 1947, Ag 23,13:2
Manning, Peter J, 1948, Ja 25,57:1
Manning, Phil V Sr, 1941, Ag 23,13:6
Manning, R I, 1931, S 12,17:3
Manning, Riccardo, 1954, Jl 9,17:2
Manning, Richard I Mrs, 1947, Ja 23,23:5
Manning, Robert, 1955, Ap 30,17:2
Manning, Robert D, 1947, Ag 18,17:5
Manning, Robert L, 1915, Mr 10,13:6
Manning, Roger I C, 1956, D 11,39:3
Manning, Rosalie, 1968, S 17,47:2
Manning, T C, 1887, O 12,2:4
Manning, Thomas, 1925, S 7,11:5; 1946, Ap 23,21:1
Manning, Thomas A, 1939, S 6,23:5
Manning, Thomas A Jr, 1944, My 23,23:2
Manning, Thomas A Mrs, 1944, O 31,19:2
Manning, Thomas E, 1938, My 12,23:4
Manning, Thomas J, 1950, Mr 18,13:5
Manning, Valentine R, 1941, Ja 10,19:4
Manning, Van H Jr, 1940, S 10,23:5
Manning, Vera C Mrs (V Connolly), 1964, O 14,45:2
Manning, W S, 1906, N 3,9:3
Manning, W S Maj, 1918, N 30,11:5
Manning, Wallace W, 1950, My 26,23:2
Manning, Walter H, 1938, Ja 20,23:5
Manning, Warren H, 1938, F 6,II,9:1
Manning, William F, 1954, Ja 25,19:5
Manning, William H, 1951, Ag 25,11:6
Manning, William J, 1954, Ap 22,29:3; 1962, S 29,23:5
Manning, William Lt, 1924, Ag 28,17:6
Manning, William R, 1942, O 29,23:5
Manning, William Sinkler Maj, 1921, S 8,13:4
Manning, William T, 1908, Mr 9,7:4; 1949, N 19,1:2
Manning, William T Mrs, 1954, F 13,13:2
Manning, William T Rev, 1921, Mr 16,9:4
Mannings, Hal, 1958, Ja 15,39:4
Mannino, Joseph, 1951, O 28,85:2
Mannion, Frank D, 1960, Mr 23,37:1
Mannion, James C, 1940, F 18,41:3
Mannion, James J, 1947, Ap 19,15:2
Mannion, Thomas F, 1952, Jl 8,27:3
Mannion, Thomas H, 1907, Ap 18,11:6
Mannion, Thomas H Sr, 1954, My 1,15:6
Mannisaw, Margaret, 1871, Ag 8,2:2
Mannix, Arthur J, 1952, S 19,23:4
Mannix, Daniel, 1963, N 6,41:1
Mannix, Daniel P, 1957, S 18,33:6
Mannix, Edgar J, 1963, Ag 31,17:1
Mannix, Edward F, 1959, Je 16,35:4
Mannix, Elizabeth Mrs, 1938, Mr 9,23:2
Mannix, J Walter, 1949, Ag 13,11:6
Mannix, John H, 1938, Ja 14,23:3
Mannix, John J Jr, 1952, Ag 30,13:6
Mannix, Joseph A, 1957, Ja 2,27:4
Mannix, Joseph F, 1961, My 20,23:4
Mannix, Michael F, 1950, S 19,31:2
Mannix, Timothy C, 1952, F 8,23:1
Mannlein, Benjamin Mrs, 1944, Mr 20,17:1
Mannlicher, Baron von, 1904, Ja 21,9:6
Manns, Adam, 1946, Ap 7,46:4
Manns, August, 1907, Mr 2,9:6
Manns, Frederick C, 1948, Jl 3,15:6
Mannsbarth, Franz, 1950, O 4,31:4
Mannucci, Livio, 1961, D 23,23:2
Mannuzza, Frank Mrs, 1951, D 20,31:3
Mannville, James H Capt, 1908, Ap 9,9:4
Manny, Egbert L, 1951, F 16,25:4
Manny, Frank A, 1954, N 6,17:1
Manny, J Harvey, 1954, Ap 3,19:2
Manny, Theodore, 1938, S 27,21:6
Manoff, Arnold, 1965, F 12,30:1
Manogue, John B W, 1955, Ja 6,27:2
Manoilescu, Gregorio, 1963, My 1,39:4
Manola, Marion, 1914, O 8,11:6
Manor, Anthony, 1952, My 21,27:2
Manotas, Luis E de Mrs, 1956, Jl 29,65:2
Manoukian, Kerekin, 1937, Ja 6,23:2
Manovill, Edwin G, 1958, My 5,29:4
Manowitch, Benjamin, 1942, Jl 9,22:5
Manowitz, Alex, 1951, S 4,27:1
Manro, Fred J, 1942, Je 6,13:2
Manrodt, Henry Mrs, 1954, D 3,27:2
Manross, Martha W Mrs, 1937, S 21,25:4
Manrot, Joseph, 1916, Jl 20,11:6
Mansbach, Louis H, 1940, N 10,57:1
Mansback, Irving E, 1950, N 26,91:1
Mansbridge, Albert, 1952, Ag 23,13:3
Mansell, David, 1948, Mr 27,13:2
Mansell, David A, 1953, N 13,27:1
Mansell, Harry M Mrs, 1953, O 10,17:3
Mansell, N R, 1952, S 24,33:4
Mansell-Moullin, Charles W, 1940, N 11,19:5
Manser, Harold Mrs, 1951, N 5,31:2
Mansergh, James, 1905, Je 16,9:6
Mansfield, A R, 1934, F 12,15:1
Mansfield, Albert M (funl, Mr 6,21:4), 1923, Mr 2, 15:2
Mansfield, Alfred W, 1951, Ja 1,17:2
Mansfield, Arch R, 1938, Ja 3,29:1
Mansfield, Arthur D, 1940, S 27,23:5
Mansfield, Arthur N, 1948, Jl 12,19:4
Mansfield, B, 1932, O 5,30:4
Mansfield, C Mrs, 1936, F 18,24:1
Mansfield, Clifford J, 1940, Ja 8,15:6
Mansfield, E D, 1880, O 28,2:5
Mansfield, Edward, 1947, F 7,23:4
Mansfield, Edward C, 1945, Ag 12,40:6
Mansfield, Frederick A, 1949, Ja 13,23:5
Mansfield, Frederick J, 1946, D 24,17:2
Mansfield, Frederick W, 1958, N 7,28:1
Mansfield, Frederick W Mrs, 1957, Ap 27,19:4
Mansfield, George A, 1940, D 25,27:4
Mansfield, George W, 1945, Ja 22,17:1
Mansfield, H Stanley, 1953, D 29,24:6
Mansfield, Helen C, 1957, Ag 16,19:2
Mansfield, Henry Buckingham Rear-Adm, 1918, Jl 18, 9:6
Mansfield, Horace J, 1951, My 20,88:3
Mansfield, Howard, 1938, Ag 15,15:6
Mansfield, Hubbard B, 1939, Ag 14,15:5
Mansfield, James E, 1944, S 25,17:6
Mansfield, James H, 1948, Ap 25,69:1
Mansfield, Jayne (funl plans, Jl 1,23:5; funl, Jl 4,19:4), 1967, Je 30,34:3
Mansfield, John C, 1955, Jl 18,21:5
Mansfield, John D, 1942, D 27,34:5
Mansfield, John M, 1949, F 5,15:2
Mansfield, Joseph, 1944, Jl 29,13:6
Mansfield, Joseph F, 1946, S 27,23:5
Mansfield, Joseph J, 1947, Jl 12,13:5
Mansfield, King W, 1953, Jl 28,19:5
Mansfield, King W Mrs, 1944, Ja 25,19:2
Mansfield, Patrick J, 1966, D 4,88:6
Mansfield, Patrick J Mrs, 1967, Ap 1,31:4
Mansfield, Phil C, 1942, S 2,23:4
Mansfield, Raymond A, 1949, Ja 25,24:2
Mansfield, Richard (funl, S 2,7:2), 1907, Ag 31,7:1
Mansfield, Richard (funl, Ap 6,15:4), 1918, Ap 5,15:3
Mansfield, Richard, 1944, S 15,19:5
Mansfield, Richard Mrs, 1940, Jl 13,14:7
Mansfield, Robert E, 1925, S 19,15:5
Mansfield, Roland M, 1942, F 28,17:5
Mansfield, Romaine S Rev, 1916, My 30,9:5
Mansfield, Thomas F, 1943, My 23,42:8
Mansfield, W R, 1876, Je 24,2:4
Mansfield, William (Viscount Sandhurst), 1921, N 3, 19:6
Mansfield, William D (will, O 15,13:6), 1952, O 8, 31:4
Mansfield, William K, 1944, D 8,21:5
Manshel, Charles, 1960, Mr 6,86:5
Manshel, Milton Mrs, 1949, Jl 25,15:2
Manship, Charles P, 1947, Ja 28,24:2
Manship, Charles P Sr Mrs, 1950, O 1,105:1
Manship, Harry G, 1954, Mr 30,27:5
Manship, Paul, 1966, F 1,31:3
Manship, Phil, 1942, S 20,40:1
Manship, W S, 1943, Jl 13,21:2
Mansill, Rich, 1903, Ja 6,9:5
Mansini, Fred, 1947, S 30,25:3
Manske, Albert E, 1943, O 10,48:5
Manske, Leo P, 1963, Jl 16,31:4
Manson, Alan, 1955, My 7,17:3
Manson, Alan Mrs, 1961, Ag 11,23:1
Manson, Andrew H, 1938, O 10,19:5
Manson, Charles E, 1942, Je 24,19:1
Manson, Donald, 1962, F 5,31:3
Manson, Donald Alexander, 1921, Mr 5,13:6
Manson, Donald G, 1947, S 6,18:2
Manson, Eddy Mrs, 1958, O 21,33:5
Manson, Elizabeth Mrs, 1940, F 4,41:1
Manson, F X, 1904, Mr 30,1:6
Manson, Fessenden D, 1956, Jl 5,25:3
Manson, Frank W, 1943, Mr 13,13:5
Manson, Frederick A, 1952, Jl 17,23:3
Manson, Howell T, 1944, Ja 19,19:6
Manson, Isabel M Mrs, 1952, My 21,27:2
Manson, James B, 1945, Jl 4,13:6
Manson, John T (por), 1944, F 22,23:1
Manson, John T Mrs, 1941, Je 28,15:2
Manson, John W, 1941, My 7,25:1
Manson, Louisa E Mrs, 1954, My 12,31:3
Manson, Patrick, 1922, Ap 10,15:2
Manson, Phil, 1941, O 7,23:5
Manson, Ray H, 1961, D 24,37:1
Manson, Richard, 1954, Ag 29,89:3
Manson, Willis H Mrs, 1948, My 19,28:2
Mansperger, William H, 1954, D 13,27:5
Manss, Harvey M, 1959, My 23,25:2
Manss, William H, 1941, O 8,24:3
Mansur, Frank, 1943, N 18,23:1
Mant, Reginald, 1942, Ap 1,21:1
Mantanari, Alberto, 1953, F 16,21:3
Mantani, Walter, 1963, Ap 28,88:6
Mante, Theodore, 1941, Mr 30,49:3
Mantegazza, Paul, 1910, Ag 29,7:5
Mantel, Eugene W, 1957, D 12,30:1
Mantell, Frank, 1951, O 10,23:6
Mantell, James E, 1961, Mr 4,23:2
Mantell, Joseph, 1921, F 2,11:5
Mantell, R B, 1928, Je 28,25:3
Mantell, Robert B Mrs, 1939, Ap 12,24:4
Mantell, Robert Mrs, 1911, N 1,11:5
Mantell, Sam, 1951, Ja 26,24:2
Manter, Harry, 1945, My 7,17:3
Manteufel, A Von, 1879, Jl 18,5:2
Manteuffel, E H C von, 1885, Je 18,5:6
Mantha, William L, 1951, D 16,90:6
Manthei, Richard, 1946, My 6,23:6
Manthey, Adolph A, 1956, Ag 1,23:4
Manthey-Zorn, Otto, 1963, D 8,86:4
Manthorne, Donald L, 1944, Ap 9,34:2
Manthorp, John C W, 1942, F 11,21:4
Manthorp, Richard W, 1940, F 11,48:6
Mantia, Harry J, 1948, Ag 27,19:3
Mantia, Simone, 1951, Je 30,15:6
Mantis, Constantine, 1954, N 8,21:1
Mantis, Max (cor, Ja 29,27:1), 1953, Ja 28,27:2
Mantle, Burns, 1948, F 10,23:1
Mantle, Elven C, 1952, My 7,27:2
Mantler, Heinrich, 1937, N 30,23:3
Mantler, Rudolph Mrs, 1958, N 18,37:5
Manton, Benjamin D Capt, 1911, Ag 5,7:6; 1912, Je 24,9:4
Manton, Henry B, 1941, D 21,40:7
Manton, John Mrs, 1945, Ag 6,15:3
Manton, Martin T, 1946, N 18,23:3
Manton, Michael F, 1940, My 29,23:2
Manton, Patrick J, 1948, Mr 3,23:3
Manton, Paul, 1941, D 6,17:5
Mantoux, Paul, 1956, D 23,30:8
Mantz, B Stafford, 1939, Mr 20,17:6
Mantz, B Stafford Mrs, 1937, Mr 24,25:3
Mantz, Harold E Mrs, 1961, Jl 5,33:4
Mantz, Harry W, 1947, D 27,13:3
Mantz, Paul, 1965, Jl 9,14:1
Mantz, Theodore, 1945, Ag 14,21:2
Mantzius, Carl Dr, 1921, My 18,17:4
Manuel, Anna Mrs, 1947, Je 24,23:4
Manuel, Earl V (est tax appr), 1963, Ag 30,10:2
Manuel, Former King of Portugal, 1932, Jl 3,14:1
Manuel, Henri, 1947, S 27,15:5
Manuel, William S, 1941, Ja 31,19:5
Manuela Vincente, Mother, 1946, Ja 25,23:4
Manuila, Sabin, 1964, S 22,39:1
Manuilsky, Dmitri Z, 1959, F 23,23:1
Manulis, Abraham G, 1948, F 6,23:4
Manus, Jesse L, 1965, Mr 7,82:6
Manus, R, 1942, Je 28,5:1
Manus, R S, 1942, Ag 12,3:7
Manus, Samuel, 1958, Ag 24,86:5
Manush, Catherine Mrs, 1938, Jl 3,12:7
Manush, Henry E Mrs, 1949, Je 25,13:5
Manuti, Alfred J, 1965, S 12,86:6
Manuti, John, 1964, Ap 20,29:2
Manvel, Harold E, 1960, Ja 23,21:4
Manvel, Harriet R Mrs, 1938, F 21,19:3
Manvel, Herbert F, 1950, N 10,27:6
Manvel, William C, 1940, Jl 26,17:3
Manvel, William C Mrs, 1948, F 8,60:2
Manvers, Earl of (E R Pierrepont), 1940, Ap 8,19:1
Manvers, Gervas E P Earl, 1955, F 15,27:1
Manville, A Earl, 1968, Mr 9,29:4
Manville, C B, 1927, N 28,21:3
Manville, Calerie C Mrs (por), 1941, Ag 25,15:3
Manville, Clare L, 1959, Mr 9,15:6
Manville, George P, 1945, O 13,15:6
Manville, H Edward (por), 1944, Je 28,23:3
Manville, H Edward Mrs (por), 1947, O 17,21:1
Manville, Jennie E Mrs, 1939, Je 24,17:2
Manville, Lois Mrs, 1960, O 16,88:7
Manville, Thomas F, 1925, O 20,25:3
Manville, Thomas Mrs (G Campbell), 1952, Ap 27, 56:3

Manville, Tommy (Thos F Manville Jr),(will, O 24,49:1), 1967, O 9,47:4
Manville, Tracy F (por), 1945, S 14,23:4
Manwaring, C T, 1956, N 17,21:5
Manwaring, Edward B, 1954, Ag 28,15:5
Manwaring, Elizabeth W (por), 1949, F 14,19:3
Manwaring, Robert E, 1943, Ag 24,19:4
Manwaring, Selden B, 1921, S 6,15:5
Manwell, John P, 1952, O 11,19:2
Many, Benjamin Smith, 1907, Ja 16,7:4
Many, Edmund A, 1948, Mr 23,25:1
Many, Phil H Mrs, 1949, D 13,31:3
Manypenny, William P, 1943, My 31,17:5
Manyurane, Bernard, 1961, My 9,39:1
Manz, Andrew C, 1952, N 3,29:8
Manz, Caspar O, 1954, My 19,31:3
Manz, Edwin J, 1954, F 22,19:1
Manz, Fred Mrs, 1949, N 10,31:5
Manzanares, Gustavo, 1955, Mr 12,19:2
Manzano, Senor Capt-Gen of Cuba, 1867, S 25,1:7
Manzelmann, George F, 1952, Ag 2,15:4
Manzer, Bert S, 1949, S 4,40:4
Manzer, Diane (Sister Mary Joy), 1965, My 5,47:5
Manzer, Sarah C Mrs, 1941, Ap 18,21:1
Manzetti, Leo P, 1942, F 7,17:5
Manzi, Alfred, 1937, Je 19,34:4
Manzi, Amedo, 1937, Je 19,34:4
Manzian, James, 1914, Ag 5,13:4
Manziel, Bobby, 1956, N 10,19:6
Manziolli, Vincenzo, 1909, Ja 7,9:4
Manzo, Carlo, 1955, Je 23,29:1
Manzo, Francisco, 1940, F 3,13:2
Manzoni, Alessandro Count, 1873, My 24,7:3
Manzoni, Correspondent, 1873, Je 5,1:5
Mao Hsiao-chun, 1959, F 25,5:6
Mao Tse-tung, 1940, My 24,3:4
Mapelli, James, 1951, N 3,17:1
Mapelsden, Elizabeth, 1941, Jl 26,15:5
Mapelson, Lionel S (por), 1937, D 23,21:3
Mapes, Bertha Mrs, 1941, Mr 9,40:6
Mapes, Bruce A Sr, 1961, F 20,27:4
Mapes, C H, 1935, O 11,25:4
Mapes, Carl, 1939, D 13,27:1
Mapes, Charles M, 1944, F 6,42:6
Mapes, Charles V, 1916, Ja 24,11:2
Mapes, Demarest H, 1954, My 6,33:3
Mapes, Edgar M, 1955, My 30,13:6
Mapes, Edgar M Mrs, 1951, N 28,31:3
Mapes, Edward F, 1953, S 15,31:4
Mapes, Eugene E (por), 1947, Ap 12,17:5
Mapes, Francis W Mrs, 1961, N 10,35:3
Mapes, Herbert L, 1960, F 28,82:7
Mapes, James, 1954, Mr 20,15:3
Mapes, James J, 1925, Ag 10,13:6
Mapes, John A, 1907, F 4,9:5
Mapes, Lambert G, 1951, D 19,31:3
Mapes, Laura, 1878, My 17,8:6
Mapes, Leslie B, 1955, D 23,17:3
Mapes, Minta B Mrs, 1940, Ap 15,17:1
Mapes, Raymond W Mrs, 1948, O 29,26:2
Mapes, Victor, 1943, D 12,69:1
Mapes, W D, 1901, Jl 31,7:6
Mapes, William M, 1967, Ja 21,31:2
Mapes, William S, 1946, Ja 23,27:5
Maphis, Charles G, 1938, My 16,17:3
Maple, John Blundell Sir, 1903, N 25,9:6
Maple, John D, 1949, Mr 30,25:4
Maples, Edward C, 1924, Mr 17,15:5
Maples, Harold E, 1950, Mr 6,21:4
Maples, Joseph Mrs, 1949, S 15,27:1
Maples, Mary Mrs, 1938, My 15,II,7:2
Maples, Norman D, 1949, D 16,31:3
Maples, William K, 1949, F 21,23:2
Maplesden, Anna K Mrs, 1938, Ja 20,23:4
Maplesden, Raymond J, 1959, Mr 18,37:1
Mapleson, Alfred John, 1917, Mr 27,11:5
Mapleson, Arthur, 1939, Jl 25,19:3
Mapleson, H, 1927, S 28,25:5
Mapleson, J H Col (funl, N 19,9:7), 1901, N 15,9:1
Mapleson, Lionel S Mrs, 1961, D 6,47:2
Mapother, Edward, 1940, Mr 21,25:1
Mapp, John Jr, 1953, My 26,40:4
Mapps, Charles R, 1953, Ag 28,17:1
Maps, Howard L, 1947, Ja 19,53:5
Maps, John L, 1948, F 1,60:8
Maps, Lester C, 1948, Ja 1,23:3
Mar and Kellie, Countess of, 1938, D 17,15:6
Mar Elia, Alex, 1960, D 13,31:5
Mar Ivanios, 1953, Jl 18,14:7
Mara, Frank J, 1951, N 13,29:4
Mara, Jack (Jno V),(funl, Jl 3,19:3), 1965, Je 30,37:1
Mara, Joseph A, 1958, Ja 14,33:3
Mara, Joseph A Mrs, 1966, Ap 8,31:1
Mara, Katherine H Mrs, 1939, Ap 15,19:3
Mara, Sara R, 1939, N 15,23:5
Mara, Timothy J (Tim),(funl plans, F 18,33:4), 1959, F 17,31:1
Mara, Timothy J Mrs, 1963, Jl 23,29:2
Marabini, Anselmo, 1948, O 11,23:5
Marable, Fate, 1947, Ja 19,53:2
Marabout Sidi Ahmed Saidi, 1941, N 5,23:4
Marache, Eliza A Mrs, 1937, Jl 16,19:3
Marache, Harold, 1952, N 12,27:4
Marafioti, P Mario, 1951, Je 5,31:4
Maragliano, Edward, 1940, Mr 11,15:5
Maragliotti, Vincent Mrs, 1947, D 20,17:2
Maraini, Antonio, 1963, My 25,25:6
Marakle, William A, 1941, Jl 1,23:4
Maraldo, Charles G, 1947, Je 20,19:4
Marander, Arthur, 1939, Ap 14,47:2
Marane, Joseph C, 1953, Jl 22,27:5
Marangoni, Andrea, 1965, F 15,27:4
Marano, Alfonso V, 1961, Mr 11,37:2
Marano, Ralph Jr, 1957, Jl 16,25:3
Maranon, Gregorio, 1960, Mr 28,29:1
Marans, Isadore, 1946, Ap 1,27:5
Marans, Max, 1959, S 8,35:1
Marantz, Charles B, 1961, Jl 8,19:6
Maranville, C Robert, 1962, Ap 1,86:6
Maranville, Walter J (Rabbit),(funl, Ja 10,87:1), 1954, Ja 6,46:3
Maranville, Walter J Mrs, 1954, N 27,14:3
Maras, Peter E, 1942, Ap 7,21:6
Marasco, Carmine J (mem ser, Jl 20,31:4), 1960, Jl 3,32:5
Marasco, Charles J, 1952, Ap 13,76:5
Marasco, Rocco, 1913, Ja 16,17:4
Marasin, Theodore L, 1958, S 24,27:5
Maravel, George Mrs, 1956, Mr 5,23:5
Maraventano, Salvator G, 1953, Mr 10,29:3
Maravigna, Pietro, 1964, My 27,39:2
Maraziti, Albert, 1943, S 29,21:2
Marbach, John, 1966, N 17,47:4
Marbaker, Ellsworth, 1954, Je 3,27:1
Marbeau, Emmanuel Jules Msgr, 1921, Je 1,17:4
Marbel, James E, 1961, My 9,39:1
Marberry, M Marion, 1968, Ag 17,27:3
Marble, Albert P Prescott Dr, 1906, Mr 26,11:6
Marble, Arthur H, 1945, F 17,13:2
Marble, Charles F, 1947, F 8,17:1
Marble, Delia W, 1951, Je 20,27:5
Marble, Edgar M Gen, 1908, D 25,7:5
Marble, Edwin H, 1941, Ap 17,23:4
Marble, Edwin T 2d, 1951, Mr 2,25:2
Marble, Ellen Bloom, 1918, Ja 15,13:3
Marble, Florence M, 1957, Ap 1,25:4
Marble, Frank Com, 1911, F 15,9:4
Marble, Fred E Rev Dr, 1937, Mr 27,15:1
Marble, John H (funl), 1913, N 24,11:5
Marble, John P, 1955, Je 7,33:2
Marble, John S, 1919, Je 24,13:4
Marble, Manton, 1917, Jl 25,11:5
Marble, Mary (Mrs J W Dunne), 1965, F 7,92:4
Marble, Mary T, 1943, D 23,19:1
Marble, Stephen B, 1956, Jl 22,61:3
Marble, Stuart J, 1941, N 25,25:5
Marble, Thomas L, 1952, O 25,17:2
Marble, W A, 1930, S 13,15:3
Marble, William E, 1940, My 20,17:2
Marble, William H Sr, 1954, Ag 29,88:5
Marboe, Ernst, 1957, S 29,86:8
Marburg, Amelia, 1937, S 11,17:5
Marburg, Edgar Mrs, 1958, Je 10,33:5
Marburg, Emma, 1948, Ja 11,56:6
Marburg, Louis C, 1943, Je 28,21:2
Marburg, Otto (por), 1948, Je 14,23:4
Marburg, Theodore, 1946, Mr 5,25:1
Marburg, Theodore H, 1944, Je 24,13:3
Marburg, Theodore Jr Capt, 1922, F 25,13:4
Marbury, E, 1933, Ja 23,1:4
Marbury, William B, 1957, N 1,23:3
Marca, Maria, 1948, Ja 11,56:1
Marcadet, Jules Mrs, 1939, Ag 6,37:4
Marcantonio, Edward, 1958, S 23,33:4
Marcantonio, Vito (funl, Ag 13,36:1; will, Ag 19,31:1), 1954, Ag 10,1:8
Marcantonio, Vito Mrs, 1965, Ap 10,29:3
Marcatella, Dominick, 1910, My 16,9:3
Marceau, George J, 1943, D 9,27:2
Marceau, Joseph M, 1948, Je 25,24:2
Marceau, Theodore C Col, 1922, Je 24,13:6
Marceau, Zephyr E, 1948, Jl 16,19:2
Marcel, Alex J, 1954, D 13,27:5
Marcel, Lucille (Mrs Felix Weingartner), 1921, Je 24,15:6
Marceline (Clown), 1927, N 6,1:2
Marcell, Estelle, 1944, Ja 31,17:5
Marcell, Louis L, 1950, O 23,23:4
Marcelle, Emma F C Mrs, 1937, Jl 11,II,4:6
Marcelle, Frank L, 1937, Ap 19,21:5
Marcelle, Pasquale, 1950, Jl 21,19:5
Marcellien Louis, Bro, 1951, My 31,27:4
Marcellus, Cassian, 1948, F 6,23:2
Marcellus, George W, 1921, Mr 9,13:5
Marcellus, John Lawrence, 1916, Ag 11,9:6
Marcellus, Mott V, 1946, N 11,27:2
Marcey, Herbert L, 1960, Ap 9,23:4
March, Alden (por), 1942, S 15,23:1
March, Alden Dr, 1869, Je 20,3:6
March, Alden Mrs, 1957, Ja 3,33:4
March, Arthur W Mrs, 1950, Ag 30,31:4
March, Bertha, 1952, D 7,88:5
March, Charles H (por), 1945, Ag 29,23:5
March, Charles W, 1864, Mr 6,5:3
March, Clement, 1937, Mr 24,25:5
March, David, 1937, F 15,3:5
March, Dr, 1869, Je 18,1:3
March, F A Jr, 1928, F 29,25:3
March, F D, 1903, My 29,9:6
March, Forest O, 1948, Je 8,25:2
March, Francis A, 1967, N 5,86:1
March, Francis A Prof, 1911, S 10,II,13:4
March, Francis J Jr Mrs, 1954, N 27,13:3
March, Frank D. 1966, N 17,47:3
March, Harry A, 1940, Je 11,25:3
March, Harry J, 1946, Mr 2,13:2; 1953, N 17,31:2
March, Harry L, 1939, S 29,23:2
March, Henry, 1964, Ja 15,31:3
March, Henry C Mrs, 1949, F 11,23:3
March, Herbert B, 1939, N 11,15:4
March, James E, 1918, Ag 31,11:3
March, John, 1940, Ja 13,15:1
March, John L, 1952, D 4,35:6
March, Juan, 1962, Mr 10,21:1
March, Juan Sra, 1957, Ap 15,29:6
March, Louis, 1945, Ap 5,23:5
March, Mathias L, 1939, Ja 19,19:1
March, Moncure (por), 1945, N 23,23:3
March, Peyton C (funl plans, Ap 15,23:1; funl, Ap 19,31:4), 1955, Ap 14,29:1
March, Sidney H, 1923, F 5,15:6
March, Thomas S, 1939, Ja 14,17:3
March, William, 1954, My 16,86:3
March, William A, 1963, Jl 6,15:4
March, William A Jr, 1943, Jl 19,15:2
March, William S, 1939, O 5,23:5
Marchais, Jacques, 1948, F 16,21:5
Marchal, Leon, 1956, S 25,33:2
Marchalleck, Franz D, 1959, Je 14,86:1
Marchand, Adolph, 1955, D 1,35:2
Marchand, Almanda, 1949, Ja 5,25:1
Marchand, Damon Mrs (Romany Marie), 1961, F 23,27:4
Marchand, Eugen, 1954, N 24,23:5
Marchand, J B, 1934, Ja 15,15:5
Marchand, Jean, 1941, O 11,17:4; 1952, Mr 7,24:3
Marchand, Johannes M, 1959, Je 28,69:2
Marchand, Jules H, 1951, Je 1,23:4
Marchand, Leopold, 1952, N 27,31:5
Marchand, Richard W Mrs, 1959, Mr 14,23:6
Marchant, A H, 1941, Je 18,21:2
Marchant, Ada Mrs, 1941, O 7,23:1
Marchant, Clarence R, 1937, Mr 30,23:4
Marchant, Frank M, 1942, Ja 14,21:5
Marchant, John H, 1955, Je 22,29:4
Marchant, Luther B, 1957, S 6,21:1
Marchant, M Howard, 1948, Ja 19,23:4
Marchant, Peter D, 1957, F 3,77:1
Marchant, Russell B, 1946, N 3,64:5
Marchant, Stanley, 1949, Mr 1,25:4
Marchant, Thomas M, 1939, N 12,48:8
Marchant, Trelawney E, 1950, Je 4,93:1
Marchant, William A, 1938, Jl 3,13:3
Marchant, William Sidney, 1953, F 3,25:4
Marchat, Nelly, 1953, Ja 13,27:1
Marchbank, John, 1946, Mr 24,46:6
Marchbank, John W, 1947, D 2,29:1
Marchbanks, A J, 1867, Ja 14,8:3
Marchbanks, H, 1934, Ap 14,15:6
Marcher, Benjamin, 1953, Ap 11,17:5
Marchesi, Blanche, 1940, D 16,23:4
Marchesi, Concetto, 1957, F 14,27:6
Marchesi, Mathilde de Castrone, 1913, N 19,9:5
Marchetti, Alberto (por), 1948, O 6,29:2
Marchetti, Carlo, 1937, O 3,II,8:7
Marchetti, Philippe, 1902, Ja 19,6:3
Marchetti, Spyridon, 1943, O 21,27:5
Marchetti-Selvaggiani, Francesco, 1951, Ja 14,84:3
Marchev, Alfred, 1947, N 29,13:4
Marchi, Antonio, 1948, Mr 25,27:4
Marchi, Louis B, 1968, S 3,43:3
Marchi, Louis B Mrs, 1967, Ap 14,39:3
Marchio, Augustino Mrs, 1950, Ja 10,29:1
Marchione, Ralph, 1954, S 3,17:2
Marchiony, Italo, 1954, Jl 29,23:2
Marchiony, Louis S, 1951, Ag 15,27:2
Marchisio, Ercole, 1954, O 15,23:2
Marchisio, Secondo, 1947, Mr 25,25:1
Marchisio, Secondo Mrs, 1956, My 3,31:4
Marchlewski, Leon, 1946, Ja 23,27:3
Marchmont, Arthur W, 1923, Jl 3,13:5
Marchwood, Lord (F G Penny), 1955, Ja 3,27:2
Marcial-Dorado, Carolina, 1941, Jl 26,15:2
Marciante, Louis P, 1961, Mr 31,27:1
Marcil, Charles, 1937, Ja 30,17:2
Marcil, Tancrede, 1955, F 15,27:3
Marcilla, Baldomero, 1940, O 19,17:6
Marcin, Anna Mrs, 1953, S 3,23:3
Marcin, Max (por), 1948, Ap 1,26:2
Marciniak, Raphael, 1947, Ag 15,17:4
Marcinkowski, Peter, 1949, O 12,30:6
Marcinkowski, Vincent A, 1952, Jl 20,52:2
Marck, Siegfried, 1957, F 22,21:3
Marckman, Juan F, 1949, Jl 27,23:1
Marckres, Roland R, 1953, Mr 4,27:6
Marcks, Alfred R, 1966, Ja 5,31:3
Marcks, Eirch C, 1938, N 25,23:5
Marckwald, A Hunt Jr, 1966, Jl 2,23:6

Marckwald, Albert H, 1952, Jl 27,58:5
Marcley, Irving Mrs, 1954, Mr 19,23:1
Marco, C, 1936, F 4,24:3
Marco, Julius L, 1938, N 6,48:8
Marco II Khouzam, Patriarch, 1958, F 4,26:4
Marcojohn, James P, 1946, Mr 13,29:5
Marcolini, Hugo, 1963, S 24,39:3
Marcolongo, Roberto, 1943, My 17,15:2
Marconetti, Arrigo E, 1952, F 19,29:4
Marconi, Giuseppe Mrs, 1920, Je 5,15:4
Marconi, Guglielmo, 1937, Jl 20,1:2
Marcos, Dionisio T, 1938, N 24,18:3
Marcosson, Isaac F, 1961, Mr 15,39:3
Marcosson, Isaac F Mrs, 1937, Ap 7,25:2
Marcosson, Mark, 1957, Jl 30,31:5
Marcotte, Donald, 1964, O 22,32:2
Marcotte, Henry, 1955, Ap 29,23:3
Marcotte, Maurice, 1966, Jl 12,43:4
Marcou, John Belknap, 1912, Jl 20,7:6
Marcoullier, Arthur, 1952, D 13,21:2
Marcoussis, Louis, 1941, O 25,17:5
Marcoux, George E, 1946, Ap 16,25:2
Marcovicci, Eugene E Dr, 1968, Ag 12,35:4
Marcq, Rene, 1947, D 8,25:4
Marcum, Beverly B, 1946, F 2,13:2
Marcum, John A, 1951, My 26,17:4
Marcus, A B, 1950, Ag 8,29:1
Marcus, Abraham, 1949, S 19,23:6
Marcus, Alex, 1954, Ag 3,19:3; 1964, Je 30,33:5
Marcus, Alfred A, 1903, Jl 4,7:6
Marcus, Arthur I, 1949, S 3,13:5
Marcus, Babette Mrs, 1937, Ag 8,II,7:3
Marcus, Ben L, 1952, Ag 31,45:2
Marcus, Bernard K, 1954, Jl 18,57:1
Marcus, Callie K, 1957, F 16,17:5
Marcus, David E, 1940, Ag 13,19:3
Marcus, David R, 1961, N 25,23:5
Marcus, Dorothy E, 1944, Je 7,19:6
Marcus, Edwin, 1961, N 14,39:1
Marcus, Esther Mrs, 1942, N 5,26:3
Marcus, Eugene, 1951, Ag 19,85:1
Marcus, Fred S, 1965, S 1,37:3
Marcus, George I, 1966, O 5,47:2
Marcus, Harold, 1953, Mr 10,29:2
Marcus, Harry, 1961, Je 17,21:1; 1962, F 27,33:1
Marcus, Herbert Sr, 1950, D 14,35:2
Marcus, Isidor, 1954, Ja 2,11:2
Marcus, J Anthony Mrs (por), 1940, F 3,13:4
Marcus, J S, 1927, Jl 4,15:3
Marcus, Jacob, 1942, D 27,34:5
Marcus, Jacob D Mrs, 1963, My 27,29:3
Marcus, Jacob R Mrs, 1953, Jl 28,19:6
Marcus, James, 1950, D 31,42:6
Marcus, James A, 1937, O 16,19:5
Marcus, James H, 1948, O 21,27:4
Marcus, Jay, 1949, Ag 25,19:4
Marcus, Jefferson, 1958, N 2,89:3
Marcus, John, 1956, Ja 11,31:1
Marcus, Joseph A, 1960, N 24,29:4
Marcus, Joseph D, 1964, Jl 9,33:3
Marcus, Joseph H, 1954, Jl 10,13:3
Marcus, Joseph H Mrs, 1957, Mr 27,31:4
Marcus, Julius, 1919, Ap 12,15:3
Marcus, Kurt, 1950, N 30,33:1
Marcus, Louis, 1955, S 9,23:3
Marcus, Louis W Justice, 1923, Ag 19,26:5
Marcus, Mandel, 1964, Ja 19,77:1
Marcus, Moe B, 1951, Je 29,21:1
Marcus, Morris E, 1951, Je 23,15:6
Marcus, Morris I, 1956, S 9,84:2
Marcus, Myer, 1923, N 25,23:2
Marcus, Ralph, 1956, D 27,25:5
Marcus, Richard, 1954, Ag 10,19:4
Marcus, Robert S, 1951, Ja 20,15:1
Marcus, Rose Mrs, 1946, D 11,31:2
Marcus, S Wesley, 1964, D 9,47:2
Marcus, Samuel (por), 1944, My 20,15:3
Marcus, Samuel (will), 1948, Mr 13,17:4
Marcus, William E Mrs, 1956, F 24,25:1
Marcus, William Elder, 1925, Ag 2,5:3
Marcuse, Alex J, 1938, Jl 1,19:5
Marcuse, Alex J Mrs, 1958, Jl 22,28:1
Marcuse, Moses M, 1960, Je 22,35:3
Marcuse, Sidney, 1943, S 23,21:2
Marcuson, Isaac, 1952, S 3,29:3
Marcuson, Jacob M, 1942, S 28,17:5
Marcussen, Marcus, 1941, S 15,17:4
Marcussen, Robert M, 1952, Ap 15,27:4
Marcusson, Peter A, 1966, Ap 7,36:3
Marcy, George E, 1939, Ag 27,34:7
Marcy, George R Mrs, 1878, F 1,1:6
Marcy, Harold C, 1943, Ag 14,11:7
Marcy, Henry Orlando, 1924, Ja 3,17:2
Marcy, John Jr, 1941, S 24,23:6
Marcy, Leonard F, 1943, F 5,21:6
Marcy, Milford M, 1922, O 25,19:5
Marcy, Sherman H, 1939, S 29,23:4
Marcy, Virgil M D Dr, 1904, Ja 22,9:6
Marcy, William J, 1942, Mr 16,15:1
Marcy, William L Sr, 1943, O 9,13:2
Marcy, William N, 1947, F 6,23:5
Marcyes, William E, 1943, O 13,23:5
Marczak, Kazimiarz, 1951, N 23,29:3

Marden, Charles C Mrs, 1967, D 27,34:3
Marden, Charles F, 1949, Mr 4,21:5
Marden, Francis S, 1962, Ap 25,39:3
Marden, George A, 1906, D 20,9:4
Marden, John W, 1946, O 9,27:1
Marden, Martin G, 1941, Je 20,21:4
Marden, Orison Swett, 1924, Mr 11,19:3
Marden, Oscar W, 1947, Jl 16,23:4
Marden, William A, 1964, Je 5,31:4
Marder, Charles Mrs, 1960, F 6,19:2
Marder, Eugene, 1948, D 30,19:2
Marder, John W, 1938, Ap 20,23:4
Mardinly, John, 1968, O 11,47:2
Mardrus, J C, 1949, Mr 28,21:1
Mare, Vito M, 1957, S 13,23:4
Marean, Guy B, 1948, Je 25,24:2
Marechal, Greer, 1960, N 11,31:3
Marechal, Greer Jr, 1968, Je 10,45:2
Marechal, Maurice, 1942, F 17,21:5; 1964, Ap 20,29:1
Marello, Charles M, 1950, O 5,31:1
Maremont, Myer D, 1949, Mr 11,25:3
Maren, Meyer J, 1966, D 13,47:3
Mareness, Fay B, 1954, Ja 26,27:3
Mares, Paul, 1949, Ag 21,69:2
Maresca, Frank, 1945, Mr 6,21:5
Maresca, Samuel J, 1954, Ap 20,29:3
Maresca, Theresa (T Mase), 1966, D 2,39:4
Maresch, Albert L, 1954, S 4,11:5
Maresi, Pompeo M, 1940, Ag 14,19:2
Maret, John H Mrs, 1951, S 3,13:5
Marett, Robert R, 1943, F 20,13:3
Maretzek, Apollonie, 1909, Ja 18,9:4
Maretzek, M, 1897, My 15,7:4
Marfil, Francisco G, 1958, My 22,29:3
Margai, Milton, 1964, Ap 29,41:4
Margal, P y, 1901, N 30,9:5
Margalioth, Mordecai Dr, 1968, Mr 26,46:1
Margalith, Aaron M, 1961, O 22,86:5
Marganella, John Mrs, 1950, Je 22,27:4
Margaret, Sister (Heinbockel), 1951, Ja 4,29:2
Margaret Eustelle, Sister (M Ryan), 1942, Ap 6,15:4
Margaret Irene, Sister, 1958, D 11,13:5
Margaret Mary, Mother, 1944, Jl 2,19:3; 1945, Mr 9, 19:5; 1948, Jl 3,15:3
Margaret Mary, Sister (Fitzpatrick), 1950, O 20,27:4
Margaret Mary, Sister (Sisters of St Joseph), 1951, S 24,27:4
Margaret Maureen, Sister (Dominican), 1959, Ja 31, 19:5
Margaret McKenna, Mother, 1943, Jl 6,21:5
Margaret Teresa, Sister (Sisters of Charity), 1956, Jl 6,21:3
Margareten, Ignatz Mrs, 1959, Ja 15,33:2
Margarethe of Hesse, Princess of Prussia, 1954, Ja 23,13:5
Margarett, Norman A, 1943, S 9,26:3
Margaretta, Dowager Countess of Winchelsea and Nottingham, 1952, D 25,29:6
Margerie, Pierre de, 1942, Je 4,19:2
Margerison, A Ernest, 1954, S 22,29:1
Margerum, Charles E, 1950, O 13,29:2
Margerum, J Fred, 1940, Je 8,15:6
Margerum, Mahlon R Mrs, 1938, Jl 12,19:3
Margeson, John J, 1953, F 10,27:3
Margesson, Henry D R, 1965, D 27,25:3
Marget, Arthur W, 1962, S 8,19:2
Margetson, Arthur, 1951, Ag 14,23:5
Margetson, Edward H, 1962, Ja 24,21:3
Margetts, J Ashton Mrs, 1942, N 20,23:5
Marggraff, Carl C, 1946, S 25,27:2
Marggraff, Frederick C, 1952, F 15,25:3
Marghab, Emile (por), 1947, Jl 29,22:2
Margherita, Queen of Italy, 1926, Ja 5,1:4
Marghiloman, Alexander, 1925, My 11,17:4
Margillo, Eugenio, 1924, Je 9,17:5
Margiotta, Michael D, 1964, O 10,29:5
Margiotti, Charles J, 1956, Ag 26,85:1
Margitan, Stephen, 1951, Ja 24,27:2
Marglis, Bernard A, 1958, Mr 9,86:3
Margold, Nathan R, 1947, D 17,29:5
Margolies, Edward, 1938, Mr 14,16:1
Margolies, Isidore M, 1951, Ag 18,11:3
Margolies, M S, 1936, Ag 26,21:1
Margolies, M S Mrs, 1919, O 15,17:3
Margolies, Moses S Mrs, 1950, S 29,27:5
Margolies, Samuel Mrs, 1963, Ap 27,25:3
Margolies-Davidson, Chaim, 1960, Mr 3,29:4
Margolin, Akiba, 1966, Mr 28,33:5
Margolin, Akiba Mrs, 1959, D 16,41:2
Margolin, Arnold D, 1956, O 31,68:3
Margolin, Ben Mrs, 1968, Je 7,36:3
Margolin, J J, 1943, F 14,48:4
Margolin, Leo J Mrs, 1959, D 24,19:1
Margolin, Louis N, 1942, Mr 31,21:5
Margoliouth, David S, 1940, Mr 24,30:6
Margolis, Albert M, 1954, Ag 29,89:1
Margolis, Benjamin, 1962, S 3,15:6
Margolis, Elias, 1946, N 27,25:3
Margolis, Elias Mrs, 1937, D 10,25:1
Margolis, G W, 1935, S 9,19:3
Margolis, George M, 1966, O 12,43:1
Margolis, George O, 1967, N 28,47:1
Margolis, Jacob H, 1940, O 20,50:1

Margolis, Louis, 1939, My 14,III,7:3
Margolis, Max Mrs, 1959, S 24,37:1
Margolis, Menashe, 1954, Je 3,27:5
Margolis, Morris, 1963, Je 29,23:5
Margolis, Nathan, 1956, O 6,21:5; 1964, F 9,88:4
Margolis, Samuel, 1966, F 7,29:2
Margolis, Sheine E S Mrs, 1941, My 25,36:7
Margolis, William (por), 1942, Jl 21,20:2
Margon, Clarence C, 1943, My 21,19:2
Margon, Irving, 1958, S 24,27:2
Margoshes, Adam, 1966, F 4,31:3
Margoshes, Israel, 1965, S 11,27:3
Margoshes, Joseph, 1955, Ap 11,23:6
Margoshes, Samuel Dr, 1968, Ag 24,29:3
Margoshes, Samuel M Mrs, 1967, My 2,47:2
Margot, Antoinette, 1925, D 29,23:4
Margot, Mary, 1879, N 5,2:7
Margotta, H J, 1954, Ag 19,23:6
Margotti, Carlo, 1951, Ag 1,23:6
Margraf, Walter J, 1951, O 3,33:2
Margrav, H J Gen, 1876, Ja 25,1:5
Margreither, Joseph, 1945, Mr 3,13:2
Margt Mary Hughes, Sister, 1937, D 1,23:4
Marguand, Henry, 1921, Jl 11,11:4
Marguard, Frank F, 1948, Jl 27,25:5
Margucci, Joseph S, 1953, Mr 13,25:5
Marguerite, Julia de Mme, 1866, Je 24,1:7
Marguerite, Victor (por), 1942, Mr 24,19:5
Marguerite d'Orleans, Princess, 1940, F 1,21:5
Margueritte, Paul, 1918, D 31,11:4
Marguess, William H Rev Dr, 1921, Ap 12,17:4
Marguiles, Irvin E, 1959, Mr 14,23:3
Marguilies, Harry, 1968, Ag 3,25:4
Margules, De Hirsh (funl, F 8,26:1; will, F 16,25:1), 1965, F 4,31:1
Margules, DeHirsh Mrs, 1948, Ag 22,60:8
Margules, Edward Mrs, 1968, Mr 11,37:1
Margules, Samuel (Rami-Sami), 1962, Ag 29,29:2
Margules, Samuel Mrs, 1949, My 16,21:5
Margulies, Adele, 1949, Je 7,32:4
Margulies, Carl C, 1965, N 6,29:3
Margulies, Emanuel, 1968, Ag 10,27:4
Margulies, Frank, 1937, Ag 26,22:1
Margulies, Harold, 1962, S 21,29:1
Margulies, Harold L, 1962, Mr 12,31:2
Margulies, Irving, 1963, D 20,26:8
Margulies, John, 1963, Je 16,84:5
Margulies, Morris, 1967, Ag 18,33:1
Margulies, Pincus, 1952, N 15,17:6
Margulies, William Dr, 1937, F 9,23:5
Margulies, Wolf Mrs, 1944, Ag 1,15:6
Margulis, Abraham, 1939, Ag 11,15:5; 1958, D 4,39:2
Margulis, Charlie, 1967, Ap 26,44:6
Margulis, Max, 1938, D 27,17:6
Maria, Alfred J, 1964, Je 17,43:1
Maria, Alicia, 1941, F 15,15:3
Maria, Annemziada Archduchess, 1871, My 6,5:2
Maria, Frederico de, 1954, Ap 2,28:4
Maria, Pietro di Archbishop, 1937, My 4,25:5
Maria, Princess of Greece, 1940, D 14,17:2
Maria, Rev Mother, 1940, Ap 21,42:2
Maria, Sister (F E Marra), 1956, Ag 31,17:1
Maria Annunziatta, Archduchess, 1961, Ap 9,86:5
Maria Augustine, Sister (Flynn), 1955, Jl 6,27:3
Maria Benigna, Sister (J Gillice), 1959, My 5,33:4
Maria Christina, Former Queen Dowager of Spain, 1878, Ag 23,5:3
Maria Concepta, Sister, 1947, F 7,23:5
Maria Concilio, Mother, 1944, Je 8,21:5
Maria Cordes, Sister (Ann T Donahue), 1956, Jl 17, 23:4
Maria Dolorosa, Sister (Sisters of Charity), 1956, Ap 21,17:5
Maria Elena, Sister (McMahon), 1968, O 19,37:4
Maria Ignatia, Sister (Quinn), 1962, Jl 21,19:4
Maria Josepa, Archduchess, 1944, Je 10,15:6
Maria Lucy, Sister (Sisters of Charity), 1955, Mr 16, 33:4
Maria Patrick, Sister (M Manning), 1958, Mr 22,17:1
Maria Pia, Queen Dowager of Portugal (funl, Jl 7,9:4), 1911, Jl 6,9:5
Maria Socorro, Sister (Sisters of Charity), 1959, D 22,31:5
Maria Sophia Amelia, Queen, 1925, Ja 20,21:6
Maria Teresa, Princess, 1912, S 24,13:6
Maria Theresa, Archduchess, 1944, F 16,17:1
Maria Theresa of Bavaria, 1919, F 5,11:1
Maria Thresa, Princess (Archduchess of Austria), 1912, O 25,13:2
Marianette, Sister (Donnelly), 1963, D 4,47:3
Mariani, Domenico (por), 1939, Ag 24,17:1
Mariani, Xavier, 1941, O 1,21:6
Marianne of Jesus, Mother (M F Gurney), 1957, F 11,29:4
Mariano, Henry D, 1947, Jl 8,23:2
Mariano, Nicky, 1968, Je 6,48:1
Marianoff, Dimitri, 1950, F 21,26:2
Mariaux, Henri, 1944, Je 4,41:1
Marie, Dowager Czarina of Russia, 1928, O 14,29:6
Marie, Dowager Queen of Rumania, 1938, Jl 19,1:4
Marie, Empress of Brazil, 1889, D 29,1:7
Marie, Empress of Rusia, 1880, Je 4,3:5
Marie, Ex-Queen of Yugoslavia, 1961, Je 23,29:1

Marie, Grand Duchess of Russia, 1958, D 16,2:5
Marie, John B, 1937, Mr 14,18:4
Marie, Leon Mrs, 1904, S 16,7:7
Marie, Mother, 1940, F 2,17:5
Marie, Peter, 1903, Ja 14,9:3
Marie, Princess of Bourbon-Orleans, 1943, Jl 18,34:4
Marie, Princess of Denmark (trb), 1910, Ap 30,9:5
Marie, Princess of Greece (M Bonaparte),(trb lr, O 13,24:5), 1962, S 22,25:5
Marie, Princess of Hesse, 1878, N 17,7:2
Marie, Sister, 1940, Ja 21,34:6
Marie Adelaide of Luxemburg, 1924, Ja 25,17:5
Marie Agnes, Sister, 1940, Ja 22,15:5
Marie Angel, Sister, 1945, Ag 28,19:2
Marie Anita, Sister (Turner), 1964, Jl 14,33:5
Marie-Anne, Grand Duchess of Luxembourg, 1942, Ag 1,11:5
Marie Antoinette, Princess of Bourbon-Sicily, 1957, Ja 13,32:4
Marie Augustin, Mother Superior, 1941, Ap 19,15:2
Marie Beatrice Therese Charlotte, Princess of Bourbon, 1961, N 2,37:1
Marie Bernard, Mother, 1945, F 27,19:2
Marie Christine, Princess of Prussia, 1966, My 31,26:1
Marie Clotilde, Sister, 1956, F 11,17:3
Marie Consuelo, Sister, 1944, O 5,23:4
Marie De Lourdes, Sister (H Pindar), 1959, S 16,39:3
Marie Dolorosa, Sister (C Potts), 1952, Jl 27,57:2
Marie du Sacre Coeur, Mother (Smith), 1964, Mr 12, 35:4
Marie Eustelle, Sister, 1940, O 20,50:1
Marie Gabriel, sister, 1941, Jl 7,15:2
Marie Gertrude, Mother, 1941, S 13,17:2
Marie Helene, Mother (Cath Sisters of Providence), 1953, N 24,29:5
Marie James, Sister, 1942, Ap 30,19:5
Marie Jose, Duchess of Bavaria, 1943, Mr 12,17:1
Marie Julia, Sister, 1947, F 1,15:1
Marie La Salle, Sister, 1948, N 9,27:2
Marie Louise, Princess (funl plans, D 11,39:1; funl, D 15,25:3), 1956, D 9,88:5
Marie Louise, Sister, 1938, Ag 18,20:3
Marie Louise Ferdinande (Spanish Infanta), 1897, F 3,7:2
Marie Madeline, Sister, 1939, D 15,25:3
Marie Majoux, Mother, 1938, Mr 12,17:4
Marie Malachy, Mother (Cath Curley), 1968, N 11, 47:1
Marie Matilde, Sister, 1938, Ja 12,21:4
Marie Norberta, Sister, 1937, Je 10,23:3
Marie of Belgium, Princess (Countess of Flanders), 1912, N 27,13:5
Marie Redempta, Sister, 1941, Ag 2,15:2
Marie Rosalie, Sister, 1921, Ja 23,22:3
Marie St Jean, Mother (Martin), 1965, Je 30,37:3
Marie Stanislas, Sister (LeMeur), 1949, S 27,27:4
Marie Suzanne, Sister (Marist Order), 1957, N 17, 86:3
Marie Theresa, Sister (Charles), 1967, S 2,22:8
Marie Therese, Sister (Martin), 1954, Ja 3,89:1
Marie Ursulina, Sister (M Foster), 1942, Ja 13,22:4
Marie Valerie Archduchess, 1924, S 8,15:2
Marie Victoire, Sister (Corr), 1957, S 11,33:1
Marie Vincentia, Mother, 1941, D 7,76:1
Marie-Yvonne, Mother (Holy Heart of Mary), 1951, F 8,33:2
Marien, John Mrs, 1953, Mr 1,92:2
Maries, Paul, 1949, Ag 19,17:4
Marietta, Sister (M Murray), 1960, F 8,29:2
Mariette, Pasha (A E), 1881, Ja 20,5:5
Marigold, Dorothy, 1951, N 5,31:5
Marik, Frank E, 1968, Ap 18,47:3
Marik, John A, 1946, Ja 1,28:2
Marikle, Wilson D, 1962, Mr 16,31:2
Maril, Konrad, 1956, Ag 20,21:4
Marilley, Alfred L, 1946, Ap 11,25:2
Marimon, Onofre, 1954, Ag 1,V,7:1
Marin, Edwin L, 1951, My 3,29:5
Marin, Francisco R, 1943, Je 11,19:2
Marin, John Sr, 1953, O 2,21:1
Marin, Joseph, 1966, Ag 23,39:4
Marin, Joseph A, 1948, D 3,25:3
Marin, Louis, 1960, My 24,37:1
Marin, Ned, 1955, N 14,27:4
Marin, William, 1947, Ap 23,25:2
Marina, Princess (Duchess of Kent),(funl, Ag 31,-23:2), 1968, Ag 28,47:1
Marinaro, Francisco S, 1944, Jl 16,31:2
Marinas, Aniceto, 1953, S 25,21:2
Marinbach, Samuel J, 1965, Jl 4,37:1
Marincola di San Floro, Giampaolo, 1960, Mr 27,20:6
Marindin, F Richie Mrs (F Warfield), 1964, S 20,88:4
Marine, Arlando (por), 1944, D 5,23:6
Marine, Arlando Mrs, 1955, My 5,33:5
Marine, Charles, 1941, Ap 9,25:2
Marine, Clarence, 1943, Ag 4,17:5
Marine, David Mrs, 1966, Je 15,47:2
Marinel, Mary, 1948, F 21,13:5
Marinelli, Albert, 1948, Ap 25,70:2
Marinelli, H B, 1924, Ja 8,23:2
Marinelli, Mario, 1962, Mr 18,25:2
Marinello, Vincent A, 1960, Jl 13,35:1
Mariner, Guy C Mrs, 1948, O 24,76:3
Mariner, James J, 1952, Ap 10,29:1
Marinet, Eugene, 1947, S 17,25:5
Marinetti, Filippo T, 1944, D 4,23:5
Maring, Harold R, 1944, My 24,19:4
Marinho, Ireneo, 1925, Ag 22,11:6
Marini, Anna Mrs, 1953, D 27,37:5
Marini, Ernest, 1967, Ap 23,92:5
Marini, Nicolo Cardinal, 1923, Jl 28,7:6
Marinis-Stendardo, Alberto de, 1940, O 14,19:2
Marino, Anthony J, 1958, My 6,35:4
Marino, Joseph B, 1940, Ag 13,19:5
Marino, Louis, 1965, Ag 4,35:3
Marino, Nunzio, 1955, N 24,29:2
Marino, Pasquale, 1958, S 8,29:5
Marinoff, Joseph, 1964, O 28,45:1
Marinoni, Antonio, 1944, Ag 8,17:2
Marinoni, John, 1959, Je 8,27:1
Marinos, Angelos, 1959, F 13,27:3
Marinuzzi, John, 1968, F 9,27:2
Mario, Albert, 1883, Je 18,4:7
Mario, Giuseppe, 1883, D 13,1:1
Mario, Queena, 1951, My 29,25:1
Marion, A Boyce, 1938, F 16,21:5
Marion, Charles, 1954, Je 10,31:3
Marion, Charles H, 1948, O 22,25:1
Marion, Frank J, 1963, Mr 29,7:1
Marion, Frank J Mrs, 1956, N 19,31:5
Marion, George (por), 1945, D 2,46:3
Marion, George, 1955, N 4,30:2
Marion, George Jr, 1968, F 27,39:3
Marion, Julius J Mrs, 1959, Mr 1,86:7
Marion, Kitty, 1944, O 10,23:3
Marion, Lee, 1954, Mr 17,31:3
Marion, Marcel, 1940, Mr 26,21:4
Marion, Marie Diro, 1916, Mr 4,11:6
Marion, Paul, 1954, Mr 3,27:5
Marion, Pierce, 1959, Ja 24,19:5
Marion, Saul, 1951, S 17,21:5
Marion, Susie, 1943, Mr 7,38:6
Marior, George W, 1911, Ap 26,15:4
Mariott, George M, 1949, D 12,33:3
Mariott, Lora L, 1950, Mr 27,23:4
Mariotti, Guido V, 1944, F 13,41:2
Mariotti, Oreste Gen, 1937, F 5,21:6
Mariotti, Vincent H, 1941, D 29,15:4
Marique, Pierre J, 1957, Ap 11,31:4
Maris, Arthur M Mrs, 1945, My 8,34:5
Maris, Bert G, 1948, Ap 19,23:2
Maris, Carroll B, 1955, F 4,19:6
Maris, Herbert L, 1960, S 14,43:4
Maris, James B, 1957, Ja 6,88:2
Mariscal, Ignacio, 1903, D 10,9:5; 1910, Ap 17,II,11:3
Marisillo, Antonio Sr, 1950, D 12,33:4
Marisillo, Antonio Sr Mrs, 1950, D 12,33:4
Marison, Alfred S, 1903, O 8,9:5
Maritain, Jacques Mme, 1960, N 5,23:5
Marius, Emelie A, 1940, Mr 28,23:5
Marix, Adolph Mrs (G Filkins), 1962, S 18,39:1
Marix, Adolph Rear-Adm, 1919, Jl 12,9:7
Marjoribanks, Edward (Baron Tweedmouth), 1909, S 16,9:6
Marjoribanks, George, 1955, Ja 4,21:2
Marjorie Dexter, Mother, 1943, Ja 30,15:1
Mark, Clarence, 1955, S 8,31:1
Mark, Clayton Jr, 1948, Ag 4,21:5
Mark, Edward L, 1946, D 17,38:2
Mark, Harold L, 1962, Jl 12,29:4
Mark, Harry, 1952, My 15,31:1
Mark, Isaac Jr, 1951, My 17,31:6
Mark, Jacob, 1958, Ap 25,27:3
Mark, John G, 1951, Ap 14,16:2
Mark, John William Maj, 1919, My 4,22:5
Mark, Joseph J Mrs, 1939, Ja 11,19:2
Mark, Joseph S, 1962, S 6,31:4
Mark, Julian, 1947, N 30,76:7
Mark, Julius, 1940, Ja 2,20:1; 1959, Mr 7,21:6
Mark, Kenneth L, 1958, Ja 13,29:4
Mark, Le Roy, 1938, D 14,25:2
Mark, Louis, 1942, Mr 19,21:4; 1954, F 26,20:4; 1961, O 28,21:1
Mark, Louis C, 1951, My 9,33:3
Mark, Louis Mrs, 1946, Mr 14,25:5
Mark, Louis W, 1942, N 27,23:1
Mark, M, 1932, N 3,21:3
Mark, Mary, 1945, Ag 30,21:5
Mark, Mitchel H, 1918, Mr 21,13:5
Mark, Moe Mrs, 1954, N 9,27:4
Mark, Phil, 1952, Jl 23,23:2
Mark, Richard E, 1946, Ag 4,45:2
Mark, Richard E Mrs, 1966, S 1,35:3
Mark, Robert W, 1955, F 6,88:2
Mark, Sandor, 1967, Mr 12,86:7
Mark, Stephen, 1949, Mr 29,26:2
Mark, Thomas J, 1951, S 8,17:1
Mark, Walking Elk Chief, 1947, Mr 8,13:2
Markama, Justin, 1954, S 16,21:5
Markart, Hans, 1884, O 4,1:2
Markbreit, Bertha F Mrs, 1937, D 29,21:4
Markbreit, Leopold, 1909, Jl 28,9:4
Markee, Francis J, 1943, Je 27,32:2
Markel, Arnold Mrs, 1957, D 4,39:3
Markel, Harry E, 1950, Ja 15,85:1
Markel, Howard (por), 1947, O 9,25:5
Markel, Jacob L, 1939, D 26,19:3
Markel, John E, 1951, My 3,31:4
Markel, Louis, 1942, Mr 12,19:1
Markel, Max, 1943, S 14,23:6
Markel, Nisson, 1947, Ja 28,23:3
Markel, Samuel A, 1954, F 20,17:3
Markell, John, 1949, Mr 25,24:2
Markels, Lazar, 1962, Mr 26,31:6
Markels, Michael, 1955, Jl 28,23:5
Marker, Abraham, 1943, O 2,13:6; 1954, My 21,27:
Marker, Harold, 1942, Ag 18,21:2
Marker, Samuel Mrs, 1944, Je 21,19:2
Marker, William B, 1951, Ja 5,22:2
Markert, Bertha E Mrs, 1959, Ap 24,27:4
Markert, George J, 1947, D 17,30:3
Markert, John P, 1941, Ja 10,19:2
Markes, Edward E, 1939, Ap 8,15:2
Markes, Lawrence W, 1957, Je 25,29:5
Market, Lena, 1941, Mr 15,17:5
Markewich, Samuel Mrs, 1955, Ap 4,29:4
Markey, Alice W Mrs, 1939, Mr 24,21:4
Markey, Anne M Mrs, 1941, D 16,27:5
Markey, Charles J, 1946, Ap 23,21:2
Markey, Edward J, 1947, N 13,28:2; 1947, D 24,21 1951, Ja 23,27:3
Markey, Eugene L, 1940, Jl 22,17:5
Markey, George W, 1948, Jl 20,23:5
Markey, George W Mrs, 1962, F 26,27:1
Markey, John C, 1968, D 31,27:1
Markey, John L, 1952, S 12,21:1
Markey, John Mrs, 1952, Ja 7,19:5
Markey, L Morris, 1950, Jl 12,30:2
Markey, Michael J, 1948, S 30,27:2
Markey, Peter Mrs, 1952, D 11,33:1
Markey, Richard A, 1941, O 17,23:2
Markey, Thomas J, 1963, Jl 30,29:4
Markgraf, Carl F, 1953, F 18,31:3
Markham, A Rose, 1961, Je 24,21:5
Markham, Alexander W, 1945, Je 12,19:4
Markham, Alton M, 1948, Jl 10,15:1
Markham, Arthur Sir, 1916, Ag 6,17:6
Markham, Baird H, 1968, Jl 18,33:4
Markham, C H, 1930, N 25,27:1
Markham, Charles, 1952, S 9,31:3
Markham, Charles B, 1955, D 4,88:8
Markham, Charles Cole, 1907, O 7,9:6
Markham, Clements Robert Sir, 1916, Ja 31,11:3
Markham, Convas L, 1950, Mr 23,29:2
Markham, Cora Mrs, 1950, N 11,15:6
Markham, Dean, 1963, F 12,7:5
Markham, Dean P, 1966, S 25,1:3
Markham, Edgar C, 1959, S 10,35:4
Markham, Edgar C Mrs, 1949, O 26,27:2
Markham, Edward M, 1950, S 15,25:1
Markham, Edward M Mrs, 1951, Ag 10,15:3
Markham, Edwin, 1940, Mr 8,21:1
Markham, Edwin Mrs (por), 1938, Ap 18,15:5
Markham, George F Mrs (H W Deane), 1966, J 28:5
Markham, George F Sr, 1958, Ap 6,88:7
Markham, Henry V, 1946, D 15,77:2
Markham, John A, 1953, Jl 24,13:5
Markham, L A, 1954, F 7,88:4
Markham, Lemuel A, 1944, N 28,23:5
Markham, Leonard B, 1955, Je 30,25:4
Markham, Osmon G, 1943, Ap 19,19:4
Markham, Pauline, 1919, Mr 21,13:3
Markham, Reginald M, 1948, Jl 16,19:1
Markham, Reuben H, 1949, D 31,15:1
Markham, Reuel F, 1957, Ja 7,25:6
Markham, Thomas A, 1941, N 12,24:2
Markham, Thomas F, 1952, Jl 10,31:2
Markham, Violet (Mrs J Carruthers), 1959, F 4,
Markham, William C, 1961, S 9,19:6
Markham, William G, 1922, My 17,19:4
Markhart, Albert H, 1953, Mr 27,23:1
Markhlevskaya, Bronislava, 1952, F 18,19:1
Markiewicz, Marcus, 1943, Je 16,21:5
Markin, George, 1941, O 10,23:3
Markin, Leonard D, 1949, Je 27,28:4
Markin, Vladimir, 1954, Ap 18,89:1
Markinn, M, 1874, N 26,1:6
Markland, George L Jr, 1941, Ag 15,17:3
Markland, Harry E, 1940, Ja 23,21:4
Markland, John W, 1947, F 11,27:3
Markland, Matthew B, 1958, D 6,23:4
Markland, Morris G, 1923, Ag 15,17:6
Markle, Abraham H, 1953, D 26,13:3
Markle, Alvan Jr Mrs, 1945, My 11,19:3; 1952, Ag 11,15:5
Markle, Alvan Sr Mrs, 1945, Mr 25,38:1
Markle, Arch, 1949, Mr 22,25:2
Markle, Bert C, 1942, N 28,13:2
Markle, Claude, 1951, Jl 31,21:1
Markle, Frank L, 1949, My 14,13:5
Markle, Frederick G, 1946, O 11,23:1
Markle, Frederick G Mrs, 1950, D 19,29:2
Markle, J, 1933, Jl 11,17:3
Markle, Samuel H, 1957, My 29,27:3
Markle, William S, 1942, Ja 31,17:5
Marklew, Ernest, 1939, Je 15,23:5
Markley, Edward A, 1952, Je 3,29:5
Markley, Edward A Judge, 1952, Ja 7,19:4

Markley, Frank A, 1950, Ag 13,76:2
Markley, G Hayes, 1944, Jl 4,19:3
Markley, John A, 1947, Mr 4,25:1
Markley, John M, 1942, Mr 16,15:2
Markley, Mary E, 1954, My 24,27:1
Markley, Phil R, 1953, Mr 14,15:6
Markley, William L, 1950, N 3,27:4
Markman, Sam Mrs, 1960, Ja 2,13:4
Markmann, M Jacob, 1961, Ag 22,29:5
Marko, George A, 1948, Mr 17,25:1
Marko, Paul M, 1940, Ja 14,42:7
Markoe, Bernard, 1940, Je 15,15:3
Markoe, Francis H, 1960, D 30,19:1
Markoe, Francis H Dr, 1907, S 14,9:5
Markoe, J B, 1902, N 30,1:6
Markoe, James W Dr, 1920, Ap 28,11:4
Markoe, Stephen C, 1939, F 11,15:4
Markoe, William, 1956, S 8,17:1
Markoff, Abraham, 1939, Ag 30,17:3
Markoff, Alex, 1957, F 12,27:3
Markoff, Allen, 1963, D 22,34:5
Markoff, Paul F, 1955, Jl 26,25:4
Markoff, Samuel T, 1959, Mr 8,87:1
Markoff, Sol, 1963, D 14,27:4
Markon, Isaac, 1949, Mr 31,25:5
Markovic, Lazar, 1955, Ap 16,19:2
Markovitch, Bozidar Mrs, 1950, My 12,27:1
Markovitch, Ivan, 1944, Jl 12,3:6
Markovitch, Myer, 1954, N 5,21:2
Markovitz, Max Mrs, 1949, Ag 14,68:4
Markow, Harry, 1965, My 14,37:4
Markowitz, A Edward, 1960, F 10,37:1
Markowitz, Abraham, 1960, My 28,21:4
Markowitz, Arthur A, 1962, Ag 30,29:3
Markowitz, Ben, 1956, S 19,37:3
Markowitz, Benjamin F, 1943, Ap 16,22:3
Markowitz, David, 1961, Mr 21,37:1
Markowitz, Harold, 1964, Jl 3,21:4
Markowitz, Harris, 1941, Je 1,40:6
Markowitz, Idel, 1957, Je 22,15:2
Markowitz, Irwin, 1951, O 21,92:6
Markowitz, Jack, 1948, My 7,23:3
Markowitz, Jacob Mrs, 1940, My 16,23:3
Markowitz, Louis H, 1967, Ag 19,25:2
Markowitz, Louis J, 1957, Ag 30,19:2
Markowitz, Mack, 1960, S 25,88:6
Markowitz, Max, 1954, O 12,27:1
Markowitz, Nathan, 1957, N 16,19:5
Markowitz, Sophia Mrs, 1938, O 11,25:1
Markowski, Felix F, 1951, D 25,31:5
Markowski, Joseph J, 1950, O 29,95:2
Marks, Abe L, 1957, Jl 17,27:5
Marks, Abraham, 1919, Je 23,13:4
Marks, Albert B, 1941, Ja 6,15:3
Marks, Alex, 1951, D 13,33:1
Marks, Alfred C, 1954, Ag 10,19:5
Marks, Alice H, 1956, Ap 17,31:4
Marks, Allan E, 1949, Mr 23,27:4
Marks, Alvin B (por), 1955, N 30,33:2
Marks, Arthur D, 1947, F 25,25:2
Marks, Arthur H, 1939, My 2,23:1
Marks, Arthur J, 1937, Je 26,17:4
Marks, Arthur M, 1962, Ja 24,33:2
Marks, August A, 1945, D 14,28:2
Marks, Barney, 1959, My 19,33:2
Marks, Bertram L, 1938, O 6,23:5
Marks, C Perry, 1958, Ap 8,29:5
Marks, Carl, 1961, Ja 14,23:3
Marks, Cecil A, 1942, Ja 16,22:4
Marks, Cecilia A B, 1946, Je 16,40:3
Marks, Chapman, 1948, F 28,15:5
Marks, Charles, 1953, Ag 6,21:6
Marks, Charles E, 1961, My 26,33:4
Marks, Clarence L, 1954, O 28,35:3
Marks, David Mrs, 1922, Je 17,13:6
arks, Edward B (por), 1945, D 18,27:1
arks, Edwin I Mrs, 1959, Ja 12,39:3
arks, Edwin L, 1954, Ag 21,17:4
arks, Emmett, 1945, My 24,19:4
arks, Fred O, 1937, Ap 23,21:4
arks, Frederick W, 1937, F 4,21:3
arks, George, 1956, O 17,35:4
arks, Grauman Mrs, 1958, Ja 18,15:3
arks, Harry F, 1958, Ag 23,15:6
arks, Harry Hananel, 1916, D 23,9:6
arks, Harry M, 1952, Jl 22,25:1; 1964, Jl 18,19:6
arks, Harry M Mrs, 1944, N 18,13:2
arks, Haskell H, 1947, Ag 15,17:4
arks, Henry C, 1949, D 20,32:2
arks, Henry K, 1942, S 5,13:3
arks, Henry W, 1956, My 4,25:2
arks, Herbert S, 1960, N 18,29:1
arks, Irving K, 1962, My 24,35:2
arks, Irwin, 1956, Ap 5,29:5
arks, J Christopher (por), 1946, O 15,25:1
arks, Jack, 1945, Ag 21,21:5
arks, Jacob, 1965, Mr 21,86:3
arks, James L, 1940, Ap 2,25:2
arks, Jeanette, 1964, Mr 16,31:2
arks, Jerome J, 1946, O 23,27:5
rks, Joseph C, 1937, Ag 19,20:1
rks, L Mrs, 1937, N 25,13:4
rks, Laurence M, 1958, Ag 26,29:5

Marks, Lawrence H, 1946, O 23,27:5
Marks, Leo, 1943, Ja 12,24:2
Marks, Leo J, 1941, N 19,23:4
Marks, Leslie V, 1951, Je 1,26:3
Marks, Leslie V Mrs, 1954, D 25,11:6
Marks, Lewis H Mrs, 1961, Mr 25,25:6
Marks, Lionel, 1967, Jl 29,25:5
Marks, Lionel S, 1955, Ja 7,21:1
Marks, Lionel S Mrs, 1922, D 5,19:4
Marks, Lord, 1938, S 25,39:2
Marks, Louis, 1943, Mr 28,24:4
Marks, Louis B, 1939, N 23,27:5
Marks, Louis B Mrs, 1966, Je 20,30:3
Marks, Louis L, 1949, Ap 20,27:2
Marks, M Doyle, 1955, F 7,21:4
Marks, M M, 1934, Ag 27,15:1
Marks, Marcus M Mrs, 1937, Ap 23,21:2
Marks, Maurice, 1952, N 4,29:5
Marks, Max B, 1949, Ja 8,15:6
Marks, Max Mrs, 1958, F 26,27:3
Marks, Melvin M, 1959, My 2,23:5
Marks, Melvin R, 1967, N 1,47:2
Marks, Michael, 1943, F 13,11:5
Marks, Milton, 1950, Ap 10,19:5
Marks, Milton L Mrs, 1956, O 30,34:2
Marks, Mitchell B, 1955, D 23,17:3
Marks, Morris, 1948, Ag 16,19:5; 1952, O 12,89:2
Marks, Mortimer, 1961, F 28,33:3
Marks, Nathan, 1952, O 26,89:1
Marks, Norman L, 1959, S 9,41:4
Marks, O F, 1876, Ap 20,8:4
Marks, Paul S, 1955, N 23,48:7
Marks, Percy, 1956, D 29,15:2
Marks, Phil, 1939, O 28,15:1
Marks, Philip M Lt, 1915, O 9,9:3
Marks, Robert W, 1937, Ag 23,19:2
Marks, Samuel, 1957, Jl 16,25:4
Marks, Shuford B, 1942, D 15,27:5
Marks, Solomon B, 1944, My 2,19:5
Marks, Solomon Dr, 1914, S 30,9:5
Marks, Solomon J, 1909, My 1,9:4
Marks, Theodore, 1965, Jl 9,29:1
Marks, Theodore David (funl, F 12,11:6), 1912, F 10,11:5
Marks, Thomas J, 1958, O 12,87:1
Marks, W Wolcott Maj, 1937, Je 30,23:4
Marks, Walter K, 1967, Je 13,47:1
Marks, Warren, 1943, D 4,13:3
Marks, Wesley, 1966, Mr 15,39:2
Marks, William, 1950, Ag 3,23:5
Marks, William D, 1914, Ja 8,11:4
Marks, William L, 1940, My 24,19:2
Marks, William M, 1951, Ja 1,17:3
Marks, Wirt P Jr, 1963, Je 2,84:2
Marks, Wirt P Jr Mrs, 1941, Mr 19,22:2
Marks of Broughton, Simon Lord, 1964, D 9,47:1
Marksbury, J W, 1925, N 6,23:5
Markson, Eldar, 1941, Ja 19,40:2
Markson, Henry, 1947, Ap 12,17:1
Markson, Henry Mrs, 1957, O 14,27:5
Markson, Isaac, 1948, My 4,26:2
Markson, Malcolm R, 1945, Ja 21,40:2
Markson, Samuel, 1939, Mr 11,17:6
Markstein, Henrietta, 1912, Ap 4,13:4
Markstein, Morris Mrs, 1943, Mr 14,26:4
Markthaler, Edward, 1941, Mr 16,45:3
Markthaler, Henry F, 1946, D 3,32:3
Marku, Samuel, 1953, Mr 14,15:2
Markus, Charles W, 1950, Ap 23,95:2
Markus, Louis, 1960, Je 1,39:3
Markus, Michael Sr, 1952, S 30,31:5
Markus, Roy C, 1965, My 10,33:2
Markuse, Minnie Mrs, 1925, Ag 11,21:4
Markush, Eugene A Dr, 1968, Ap 22,50:7
Markush, Eugene A Mrs, 1952, F 23,11:1
Markush, Fred, 1946, N 1,23:2
Markuson, Gerard O, 1968, Ag 8,33:4
Markvart, Frank, 1956, F 18,19:3
Markward, Billy, 1947, Ag 22,15:5
Markward, William H, 1947, D 23,23:4
Markwart, Arthur H, 1940, Ja 27,13:5
Markwell, Kenneth, 1963, Ag 25,83:1
Markwith, William E, 1916, Ag 3,11:6
Markwood, Wesley Capt, 1913, Ja 18,13:5
Marlaine, Jean Le B, 1941, Mr 23,45:1
Marland, Ernest W, 1941, O 4,15:1
Marland, William C (funl, N 30,41:4), 1965, N 27, 31:1
Marlatt, Abby L, 1943, Je 25,17:2
Marlatt, Charles L, 1954, Mr 4,25:5
Marlatt, Clyde D, 1968, Ja 28,76:4
Marlatt, Edward T, 1937, D 21,23:5
Marlatt, Ernest F, 1947, My 9,21:3
Marlatt, Harry R, 1959, Jl 14,29:5
Marlborough, Duchess of (Mrs J A E W Spencer-Churchill), 1961, My 24,41:3
Marlborough, Duke, 1883, Jl 6,2:1
Marlborough, Duke of, 1892, N 10,1:7; 1934, Jl 1,24:1
Marler, Herbert (por), 1940, F 1,21:1
Marler, William P, 1937, S 5,II,7:2
Marley, George, 1941, Mr 24,17:2
Marley, J Peverell, 1964, F 4,33:3
Marley, Stephen L, 1967, Ja 19,35:1

Marley, Stephen L Mrs, 1962, My 16,41:3
Marley, Thomas D, 1950, S 27,31:3
Marlies, Charles A, 1949, Ja 14,23:1
Marlin, Charles H, 1949, O 15,15:3
Marlin, George Mrs, 1961, My 10,45:2
Marlin, J M, 1901, Jl 2,7:6
Marlin, Mahlon H, 1949, S 15,27:4
Marlin, William, 1963, N 29,34:6
Marlin, William L, 1959, Je 18,31:2
Marling, A E, 1935, My 30,17:1
Marling, C M Lady, 1927, S 13,32:2
Marling, Charles E, 1937, D 28,22:2
Marling, Francis H, 1952, My 19,17:6
Marlow, Charles W Mrs, 1952, Mr 16,91:2
Marlow, Edith A, 1950, Ag 11,19:3
Marlow, Edwin S, 1915, O 26,11:5
Marlow, Ernest W, 1955, My 1,87:5
Marlow, Frank W, 1942, O 6,24:2
Marlow, George, 1947, Ap 11,25:4
Marlow, Harry, 1956, Ja 29,92:2
Marlow, James, 1968, My 3,54:4
Marlow, Mary A, 1943, N 15,19:5
Marlow, Reginald H, 1959, Mr 9,29:1
Marlowe, Alex, 1938, N 30,23:2
Marlowe, Anthony, 1962, Je 30,19:4
Marlowe, Ethel, 1898, N 17,1:7
Marlowe, Helen (por), 1947, Jl 25,17:5
Marlowe, John W, 1952, N 29,17:4
Marlowe, Julia, 1950, N 13,27:1
Marlowe, Julia (est appr), 1954, F 24,23:1
Marlowe, Owen, 1876, My 20,2:1
Marlowe, T, 1935, D 6,25:3
Marmaduke, Harvey C, 1958, F 27,27:2
Marmaduke, Henry H Capt, 1924, N 16,7:2
Marmaduke, J S, 1887, D 29,1:4
Marmaduke, M M, 1864, Ap 11,5:1
Marmaggi, Francesco, 1949, N 4,27:1
Marmein, Anna E Mrs, 1949, Ap 11,25:3
Marmer, Harry A, 1953, N 7,17:3
Marmion, Beatrice C Mrs, 1941, Mr 16,45:3
Marmion, Decatur F, 1951, S 25,29:1
Marmom, Walter C, 1940, Ag 30,19:2
Marmon, H C, 1938, S 20,23:3
Marmon, Howard C, 1943, Ap 5,19:3
Marmon, J A, 1934, D 5,23:1
Marmor, Julius Mrs, 1948, Ag 2,21:1
Marmor, Milton, 1967, F 12,92:1
Marmorek, Oskar, 1947, N 20,29:2
Marmorek, Simon, 1958, Ag 16,17:2
Marmorino, Luigi, 1940, N 7,25:2
Marmottin, Louis, 1960, My 10,37:4
Marmur, Jacob, 1941, Ja 2,23:5
Marnane, James D, 1952, Ap 26,23:2
Marnel, Sarah S Mrs, 1954, O 17,86:6
Marnell, John J, 1941, Ap 26,15:5
Marnell, Nicholas A, 1942, O 28,23:1
Marney, George W, 1940, Ap 5,22:4
Maro, H, 1877, My 27,1:6
Marochetti, Baron, 1868, Ja 3,1:1
Marochetti, George, 1952, Ag 22,21:3
Maroger, Jacques, 1962, Je 30,19:4
Marohn, William F Sr, 1948, My 8,15:3
Maron, French Airman, 1911, S 4,7:2
Marone, Carmine R, 1961, Ag 20,86:5
Marone, John Mrs, 1948, Ag 25,25:3
Marone, Luciano, 1947, Je 3,25:4
Maroney, Daniel C, 1944, O 25,21:4
Maroney, Edward K, 1945, O 12,24:2
Maroney, Frederick W, 1958, O 6,31:3
Maroney, James J, 1945, Mr 21,23:2
Maroney, James M, 1940, D 31,15:2
Maroney, John, 1959, Mr 8,86:8
Maroney, Thomas F, 1944, Jl 3,12:6
Maroney, Thomas P, 1960, N 27,86:1
Maroney, Vincent J, 1949, S 10,17:4
Maroney, William B, 1957, S 3,28:6
Maroni, Fernand, 1945, Ja 24,21:1
Maroon, Samuel Z, 1957, Jl 22,19:4
Maroon, Zacharia J, 1950, D 10,107:3
Marootian, Martin, 1947, Jl 22,24:3
Marot, Helen, 1940, Je 4,24:2
Marott, George J, 1946, F 17,44:2
Marotta, Frank J, 1946, D 10,31:2
Marotta, Giuseppe, 1963, O 12,23:2
Marotte, Agnes Mrs, 1951, Jl 23,17:2
Maroulis, Louis, 1943, D 8,23:4
Marozzi, Antonio, 1940, O 8,25:3
Marple, Allen, 1968, Mr 27,47:4
Marple, Joseph N, 1946, S 30,25:5
Marple, Walter P, 1952, Ag 19,23:3
Marple, Wilbur Bolleau Dr, 1916, Ag 31,9:5
Marquais, Eugene A, 1958, N 4,27:2
Marquand, Allan, 1924, S 25,23:4; 1938, Jl 20,19:3
Marquand, Allan Mrs, 1950, F 28,29:2
Marquand, F, 1882, Jl 15,5:2
Marquand, Fanny, 1951, Je 24,72:3
Marquand, H G, 1902, F 27,9:5
Marquand, John A, 1950, Ap 25,31:4
Marquand, John P (funl plans, Jl 19,29:4; funl, Jl 21,27:2), 1960, Jl 17,1:3
Marquand, Phil, 1954, F 15,23:2
Marquard, A, 1942, O 15,25:3
Marquard, Edward J Mrs, 1937, Mr 9,23:1

Marquard, Fred, 1945, D 18,27:4
Marquard, Otto W G, 1953, S 5,16:4
Marquard, Phil H, 1942, O 15,24:3
Marquard, Richard W Mrs, 1954, Jl 22,23:4
Marquardt, August W, 1950, D 6,33:4
Marquardt, Charles F, 1947, Je 3,25:2
Marquardt, Earl T, 1953, N 12,31:3
Marquardt, Edwin, 1953, O 7,29:3
Marquardt, John J, 1950, Ap 15,15:6
Marquardt, John Mrs, 1943, Ap 24,13:5
Marquardt, Julius C, 1956, Mr 8,29:2
Marquardt, Oswald F, 1952, Je 6,23:3
Marquardt, Walter W, 1962, Je 19,32:1
Marquardt, William H, 1945, Ap 5,23:1
Marquart, Carl A, 1951, D 22,15:4
Marquart, Edward J, 1954, N 6,17:1
Marquart, Gaston J (Bro Defendant Felix), 1955, Ja 16,93:1
Marquart, Louis, 1939, S 2,17:4
Marque, J M De Azevedo, 1943, My 25,23:1
Marques, Anthony D, 1951, Ap 15,92:3
Marqueste, Laurent Honore, 1920, Ap 7,11:5
Marquet, Adrien, 1955, Ap 4,29:4
Marquet, Albert, 1947, Je 15,62:4
Marquet, Eugene, 1956, F 29,3:2
Marquette, Edward F, 1947, Ja 4,15:4
Marquez, Martin E, 1964, Mr 17,35:1
Marquez Sterling y Loret de Mola, M, 1934, D 10,21:3
Marquez Toriz, Ignazio, 1950, Mr 1,27:5
Marquier, Adolph F, 1951, My 15,31:3
Marquina, Eduardo, 1946, N 22,23:4
Marquina, Pablo F, 1955, Ap 29,23:5
Marquis, Albert N (por), 1943, D 22,23:3
Marquis, Bernice M, 1950, S 16,19:6
Marquis, Chalmers C, 1950, F 16,23:1
Marquis, Don, 1937, D 30,19:1
Marquis, Don Mrs, 1923, D 4,21:3
Marquis, Frederick J (Lord Woolton), 1964, D 15, 43:3
Marquis, J A, 1931, Jl 6,17:1
Marquis, James B, 1941, Je 10,23:2
Marquis, John A Mrs, 1947, O 26,70:6
Marquis, John C Mrs, 1937, Ag 31,23:1
Marquis, Joseph E, 1957, My 1,37:4
Marquis, Leonard J, 1952, Ag 18,17:4
Marquis, Neva, 1941, Mr 20,22:2
Marquis, Samuel S, 1948, Je 23,27:3
Marquis, Vivienne, 1966, S 25,84:7
Marquis of Londonderry, 1872, N 27,1:4
Marquisan, Henri Mrs, 1921, O 12,15:5
Marquiss, Walter O, 1957, Ag 13,27:5
Marr, Arthur P, 1943, Jl 22,19:2
Marr, Charlotte M, 1958, Ag 16,17:5
Marr, Del, 1946, D 30,22:3
Marr, George A, 1943, Jl 24,13:5
Marr, George M Mrs, 1962, Ap 3,39:4
Marr, H C, 1936, Je 16,25:3
Marr, James, 1965, Ap 30,35:2
Marr, James P, 1954, Ja 12,23:3
Marr, John, 1940, D 31,15:2
Marr, John D, 1941, My 5,17:4
Marr, Leon H, 1950, Jl 30,61:2
Marr, Ned, 1953, Ap 14,27:4
Marr, Norman, 1954, Ap 22,29:5
Marr, Walter H, 1944, O 26,23:1
Marr, Walter L, 1941, D 12,25:5
Marra, Anthony, 1965, Mr 12,33:2
Marra, Charles, 1961, Jl 11,31:5
Marra, Frances E (Sister Maria), 1956, Ag 31,17:1
Marra, Frank P, 1958, O 26,88:3
Marra, Gerard A, 1967, Ag 24,37:4
Marra, John R, 1954, D 20,29:3
Marra, Roscoe S, 1956, Jl 6,21:4
Marracino, Alessandro, 1941, My 22,21:4
Marrah, Thomas F, 1967, Mr 28,39:4
Marranca, Frank, 1947, Ag 6,23:4
Marren, Nellie E, 1953, Je 1,23:3
Marrener, E, 1876, Ap 20,8:2
Marrero, Domingo, 1960, Ag 22,25:5
Marrero Aristy, Ramon, 1959, Jl 20,1:6
Marrett, Walter H, 1938, Ja 22,15:1
Marrian, Vincent J, 1958, F 4,26:4
Marrin, Charles C, 1950, F 2,27:3
Marrin, Elizabeth Mrs, 1923, Jl 13,15:1
Marrin, John E, 1925, N 9,19:5
Marrin, Joseph J, 1915, Ap 4,14:1
Marrinan, John J, 1959, Mr 14,23:5
Marriner, Alfred W, 1959, D 6,86:6
Marriner, James T, 1937, N 5,23:5
Marriner, Robie D, 1956, Ag 20,21:3
Marriott, Charles, 1957, Jl 17,27:1
Marriott, Harry, 1950, Jl 28,21:5
Marriott, John, 1945, Je 8,19:5
Marriott, Joseph F, 1961, Je 22,31:6
Marriott, Martin R, 1951, S 14,25:2
Marriott, Maud Lady, 1960, O 25,35:2
Marriott, R Elmer, 1952, F 6,29:3
Marriott, Robert H, 1951, N 1,29:1
Marriott, Ross W, 1955, O 21,27:2
Marriott, Thomas S, 1941, Je 21,17:2
Marriott, W T, 1945, Je 11,15:4
Marriott, William, 1941, N 13,27:3
Marris, George, 1952, Ap 7,25:5

Marritt, Henry D, 1950, D 12,28:5
Marro, Carney N, 1951, N 17,17:2
Marro, P Francis, 1946, Je 13,28:2
Marron, Frank J, 1949, F 18,23:2
Marron, James P, 1968, Je 19,47:4
Marron, Joseph Jr, 1954, My 15,15:6
Marron, Joseph P, 1942, Jl 26,30:6
Marron, Louis E, 1966, S 16,37:1
Marron, Owen N, 1945, Ja 4,19:3
Marrone, Joseph, 1925, Ap 25,15:5
Marrone, Joseph M, 1961, Jl 9,76:3
Marrone, Joseph M Mrs, 1960, Jl 2,17:6
Marroquin, J M Dr, 1908, S 22,9:6
Marrow, Alex Mrs, 1948, D 9,33:4
Marrow, Anderson, 1952, N 20,31:1
Marrow, Isidor L, 1947, N 28,27:1
Marrow, Isidor L Mrs, 1968, My 30,25:1
Marrow, Macklin, 1953, Ag 9,77:1
Marryat, Florence, 1899, O 28,7:2
Marryshow, T Albert, 1958, O 21,33:3
Mars, Bruce S, 1958, Jl 5,17:5
Mars, Frank C Mrs, 1945, D 26,19:4
Mars, Grady B, 1965, D 13,48:3
Mars, James C (por), 1944, Jl 27,17:1
Mars, Jesse D, 1951, Je 10,92:3
Mars, John F, 1944, Jl 24,15:6
Mars, Leo, 1912, Ap 9,11:4
Marsa, John, 1955, Ap 16,19:3
Marsac, Charles W, 1944, N 1,23:3
Marsac, Chester D, 1942, Mr 3,24:2
Marsan, Jules, 1939, Je 27,23:6
Marsans, Romulo L Sr, 1955, My 11,31:4
Marsch, John, 1954, Jl 31,13:5
Marschall, Augusta (Mrs A M Schueler), 1942, Jl 8, 23:4
Marschall, Harry L, 1941, Ag 8,15:5
Marschall, Otto, 1940, Je 23,30:7
Marscher, Augustus A, 1943, Je 24,22:2
Marsching, John H, 1948, Je 30,25:2
Marschner, Frank F, 1942, F 4,19:5
Marschner, Fred, 1955, S 3,15:4; 1964, Ag 16,92:7
Marsden, Chris, 1940, Ag 21,19:2
Marsden, Edith D, 1940, S 27,23:5
Marsden, Harry R Mrs, 1952, Ag 28,23:2
Marsden, James H, 1942, F 22,26:4
Marsden, John, 1947, O 4,17:4
Marsden, John N, 1939, Ag 30,17:5
Marsden, Phillips B, 1960, Jl 21,27:4
Marsden, Raymond R, 1942, Mr 12,19:3
Marsden, Robert S, 1960, O 25,35:4
Marsden, Susan E Mrs, 1941, O 23,23:1
Marsel, Charles J, 1964, O 2,37:3
Marsell, Frederic S, 1938, D 3,19:6
Marsell, Frederic S Mrs, 1938, Ag 20,15:2
Marsellis, Arthur S, 1955, D 14,39:4
Marsellus, John, 1941, Ag 28,19:2
Marsellus, John C, 1959, N 15,87:1
Marsh, Adelbert W Mrs, 1949, D 15,35:4
Marsh, Albert C, 1948, Ja 12,19:2
Marsh, Albert E, 1950, S 17,104:6
Marsh, Albert J, 1949, N 24,31:1
Marsh, Albert L, 1944, S 19,21:4
Marsh, Albert Mrs, 1949, Je 29,27:1
Marsh, Alice B, 1960, Jl 15,23:4
Marsh, Allyn Jay, 1968, Je 7,39:1
Marsh, Allyn R, 1950, F 7,28:3
Marsh, Anna W, 1944, Ag 28,11:4
Marsh, Arthur M, 1942, N 23,23:4
Marsh, Arthur R (por), 1937, S 17,25:1
Marsh, Arthur W, 1948, Je 26,17:2
Marsh, Augustus L C, 1942, Je 30,21:4
Marsh, Ben R, 1967, F 23,35:2
Marsh, Benjamin C, 1953, Ja 1,23:1
Marsh, Benjamin F Capt, 1907, N 30,7:4
Marsh, Benjamin O, 1938, O 5,23:4
Marsh, Briant H Mrs, 1945, My 24,19:1
Marsh, C P, 1876, O 19,2:7
Marsh, Carleton L Mrs, 1939, Ap 25,23:5
Marsh, Charles C, 1946, Ap 6,17:5
Marsh, Charles C Mrs, 1946, F 27,25:3
Marsh, Charles E, 1964, D 31,17:1
Marsh, Charles R, 1958, Je 5,31:6
Marsh, Clara S, 1942, O 27,25:4
Marsh, Clarence S, 1962, Jl 8,64:8
Marsh, Clarence W, 1955, O 19,33:6
Marsh, Craig A, 1910, N 13,11:3
Marsh, Daniel L Dr, 1968, My 21,47:2
Marsh, Daniel T Mrs, 1937, Jl 16,19:5
Marsh, Darius A, 1938, Ap 14,23:5
Marsh, David, 1961, Mr 9,29:4
Marsh, David F, 1957, Ap 25,31:1
Marsh, Don R, 1944, D 22,17:3
Marsh, Edith L, 1950, Je 25,68:3
Marsh, Ednor A, 1939, D 13,27:3
Marsh, Edward F, 1945, S 6,25:5
Marsh, Edward F Mrs, 1940, F 24,13:3
Marsh, Edward H, 1953, Ja 14,31:5; 1955, Ja 29,15:2; 1961, D 7,43:1
Marsh, Edward L, 1937, N 22,19:5; 1943, Je 23,21:5
Marsh, Edward S, 1939, Jl 26,19:6
Marsh, Edwin J, 1945, Ap 2,19:3
Marsh, Edythe, 1952, Je 14,15:4
Marsh, Elias J, 1943, S 13,19:5

Marsh, Ephraim, 1864, Ag 31,5:5
Marsh, Ermal W, 1959, Ag 8,36:6
Marsh, Eugene F Mrs, 1954, Ap 10,15:5
Marsh, Fenimore C, 1967, Je 20,39:4
Marsh, Forest E, 1937, Ag 7,15:5
Marsh, Francis B, 1950, Ag 5,15:7
Marsh, Francis B Mrs, 1952, O 30,31:2
Marsh, Francis H, 1949, O 25,27:4
Marsh, Frank, 1951, F 11,88:2
Marsh, Frank B, 1940, Je 2,45:2
Marsh, Frank G, 1956, Je 9,17:4
Marsh, Franklin, 1940, Ap 5,21:5
Marsh, Franklin I, 1942, D 24,28:4
Marsh, Franklin Mrs, 1952, Ag 22,21:5
Marsh, Fred D, 1961, D 21,27:4
Marsh, Fred D Mrs, 1965, Jl 6,33:2
Marsh, Fred T, 1963, Ap 15,29:3
Marsh, Fred T Mrs, 1961, F 12,86:2
Marsh, Frederick Cleveland, 1925, D 12,15:5
Marsh, G P, 1882, Jl 25,2:4
Marsh, George F Mrs, 1958, Je 13,23:2
Marsh, George Hayden, 1920, Ag 16,11:1
Marsh, George J, 1943, D 25,13:5
Marsh, George L, 1964, Je 17,43:2
Marsh, George Mrs, 1951, S 25,29:4
Marsh, George T, 1945, Ag 11,13:4
Marsh, Grace, 1912, S 23,13:2
Marsh, Harold A, 1946, Ap 3,25:1
Marsh, Harold H, 1949, N 13,94:1
Marsh, Harold J, 1950, Ap 30,102:3
Marsh, Harry L, 1921, Ja 14,11:2
Marsh, Harry W, 1938, F 2,19:3
Marsh, Henry W (por), 1943, Ap 14,23:3
Marsh, Herbert, 1941, Je 11,21:6
Marsh, Howard D, 1945, Ag 30,21:5
Marsh, Ina A, 1957, O 23,33:2
Marsh, Ivan D, 1958, O 4,21:4
Marsh, James A, 1946, Mr 25,25:2
Marsh, James J, 1943, Jl 18,34:3
Marsh, James Mrs, 1943, Ap 10,17:3
Marsh, James P, 1941, F 24,15:2
Marsh, John A, 1952, N 6,29:3
Marsh, John A Comdr, 1952, Ap 7,25:3
Marsh, John B, 1967, Mr 23,35:3
Marsh, John Edward, 1914, Mr 23,11:4
Marsh, John L, 1965, N 15,37:4
Marsh, John O, 1958, Ja 1,25:5
Marsh, John O Mrs, 1954, D 7,33:1
Marsh, John P, 1957, Je 5,35:4
Marsh, John R, 1952, My 6,29:3
Marsh, Joseph, 1950, Ap 2,93:1; 1967, N 5,86:1
Marsh, Joseph B Mrs, 1958, F 8,19:5
Marsh, Kendall, 1948, O 14,29:3
Marsh, Leland F, 1957, N 6,35:1
Marsh, Louis S, 1952, Ag 6,21:4
Marsh, M Lewis, 1945, N 13,21:5
Marsh, Mae, 1968, F 14,51:1
Marsh, Marguerite, 1925, D 9,27:4
Marsh, Martha, 1958, Mr 23,89:1
Marsh, Martin L, 1944, S 8,19:4
Marsh, Melvin C, 1949, Ja 7,22:2
Marsh, N J, 1933, N 9,21:4
Marsh, Nathaniel, 1864, Jl 20,8:4; 1924, Ag 12,11:
Marsh, Nelson, 1941, D 16,27:2
Marsh, Noble G, 1938, O 26,23:2
Marsh, Norman F, 1955, S 6,25:1
Marsh, Norman J Mrs, 1946, Ap 5,25:4
Marsh, O C, 1899, Mr 19,6:1
Marsh, Oliver, 1941, My 6,21:1
Marsh, Oliver P, 1948, My 18,24:3
Marsh, Orlando R, 1938, S 9,21:2
Marsh, Owen, 1966, Ja 29,27:5
Marsh, Paul Mrs, 1955, S 1,23:3
Marsh, Peyton C Lt, 1918, F 14,11:5
Marsh, R, 1933, My 21,28:2
Marsh, Reginald (trb lr, Jl 12,18:5), 1954, Jl 4,3
Marsh, Reginald E, 1966, Jl 14,35:3
Marsh, Richard, 1915, Ag 11,9:6
Marsh, Richard B, 1967, Ja 22,77:1
Marsh, Richard F, 1941, Ag 27,19:3
Marsh, Robert M, 1958, S 10,33:3
Marsh, Robert P, 1958, N 11,29:2
Marsh, Rolph Mrs, 1917, Ja 31,11:5
Marsh, Roy K, 1961, S 21,35:1
Marsh, Samuel, 1910, Jl 15,7:6
Marsh, Samuel J, 1958, O 14,37:5
Marsh, Samuel W, 1952, My 23,21:3
Marsh, Spencer S, 1944, D 27,19:6
Marsh, Standish C, 1964, S 9,43:3
Marsh, Stephen Sr, 1951, O 30,29:4
Marsh, Theodore McC, 1964, S 10,35:4
Marsh, Walter R, 1947, F 24,19:2
Marsh, Walter R Mrs, 1953, My 22,27:2
Marsh, Wilbur W Mrs, 1943, S 1,19:3
Marsh, Willard B (cor, Mr 31,27:2), 1961, Mr
Marsh, William, 1944, Jl 26,19:3
Marsh, William L Mrs, 1955, N 18,25:1
Marsh, William M, 1921, Je 25,11:6
Marsh, Wilson, 1939, Mr 26,III,6:6
Marshak, Morton, 1953, Je 2,29:3
Marshak, Samuel D, 1943, S 15,27:5
Marshak, Samuil, 1964, Jl 6,29:4
Marshall, A, 1934, O 1,17:3

Marshall, A W Walton, 1956, D 23,30:8
Marshall, A Winefred, 1952, Ja 5,11:2
Marshall, Alan, 1961, Jl 10,21:4
Marshall, Alan (cor, O 18,39:1), 1962, O 7,82:8
Marshall, Albert, 1947, N 2,73:1
Marshall, Albert E, 1951, S 16,84:4
Marshall, Albert P, 1954, Ag 3,19:4
Marshall, Albert W Mrs, 1952, Ja 27,76:4
Marshall, Alexander Stewart Lt-Col, 1906, Je 23,7:4
Marshall, Alfred, 1907, D 18,9:5
Marshall, Alfred Prof, 1924, Jl 14,15:4
Marshall, Annette, 1943, D 11,15:4
Marshall, Anson S, 1874, Jl 6,1:6
Marshall, Archie D, 1950, D 20,31:3
Marshall, Arthur L (funl O 25,33:4), 1956, O 22,29:5
Marshall, Benjamin H, 1944, Je 20,19:3; 1945, Mr 18, 41:1
Marshall, Benjamin T (por), 1946, Jl 1,31:3
Marshall, Benjamin T Mrs, 1946, O 26,17:1
Marshall, Blanche Mrs, 1948, Ap 30,23:2
Marshall, Boyd, 1950, N 12,94:7
Marshall, C Morgan, 1945, Ap 1,36:5
Marshall, Calvin C, 1953, F 26,25:4
Marshall, Carl B, 1943, Ap 28,23:5
Marshall, Carolyn C Mrs, 1959, Ag 12,29:4
Marshall, Cary A, 1937, My 27,23:6
Marshall, Catherine, 1964, D 23,27:3
Marshall, Cecil, 1948, Ap 18,72:4
Marshall, Charles, 1947, N 11,27:5; 1951, My 11,27:2
Marshall, Charles A, 1942, O 8,27:3; 1957, Mr 26, 33:2; 1962, O 15,29:2
Marshall, Charles B, 1949, D 30,19:5
Marshall, Charles C (por), 1938, Je 10,21:1
Marshall, Charles C, 1950, S 20,31:1
Marshall, Charles C Mrs (Bernice C), 1965, Mr 22, 33:5
Marshall, Charles D (por), 1945, My 17,19:1
Marshall, Charles Dr, 1903, N 14,9:6
Marshall, Charles H, 1912, Jl 3,11:3; 1912, S 24,13:6; 1949, Ja 14,23:4; 1952, N 30,89:1
Marshall, Charles H Capt, 1865, S 25,5:3
Marshall, Charles K Jr, 1953, N 28,15:6
Marshall, Charles M, 1953, F 15,92:4
Marshall, Charles Rhodes, 1968, Ja 2,41:3
Marshall, Charles T, 1938, My 20,19:3
Marshall, Charles W, 1945, O 27,15:3
Marshall, Charlotte A Mrs, 1949, My 29,36:5
Marshall, Chauncey, 1915, F 27,11:6
Marshall, Clare R, 1944, D 26,19:4
Marshall, Clarence G, 1966, Ag 25,37:3
Marshall, Clarence M, 1950, O 18,33:2
Marshall, Clifton N, 1957, D 13,27:1
Marshall, Cloyd, 1942, N 17,26:2
Marshall, Clyde B, 1948, Ap 13,27:3
Marshall, Dexter, 1907, N 14,9:6
Marshall, Donald Mrs, 1952, N 16,89:1
Marshall, Douglas H Mrs, 1954, S 30,31:5
Marshall, Duncan, 1946, Ja 17,23:2
Marshall, E, 1933, F 26,26:1
Marshall, E G Col, 1883, Ag 4,5:5
Marshall, Edison, 1967, O 31,45:1
Marshall, Edward E, 1946, F 12,25:4
Marshall, Edward W, 1959, Ap 22,33:2
Marshall, Edwin C Capt, 1968, Ap 20,33:2
Marshall, Edwin J, 1937, Mr 5,21:5
Marshall, Edwin M, 1952, F 17,84:4
Marshall, Edwin R, 1956, D 2,86:1
Marshall, Eli K Jr, 1966, Ja 12,21:5
Marshall, Elizabeth M, 1937, Ap 22,23:5
Marshall, Emma V P Mrs, 1946, Ja 26,13:2
Marshall, Ernest (por), 1937, F 21,14:1
Marshall, Ernest Mrs, 1962, D 7,34:4
Marshall, Ernest W, 1964, My 31,76:5
Marshall, Erwin E, 1944, S 7,23:6
Marshall, Everett, 1944, My 11,19:5
Marshall, F Stanley Sr, 1950, Mr 10,27:2
Marshall, Fielding L Mrs, 1941, Ag 6,17:1
Marshall, Finis E, 1941, Je 4,23:4
Marshall, Finis E Mrs, 1924, Ap 6,27:2
Marshall, Florence M, 1947, Ja 29,25:3
Marshall, Frank, 1944, N 10,19:1
Marshall, Frank C, 1945, D 26,19:1
Marshall, Frank D, 1949, Ag 17,24:3
Marshall, Frank J Jr, 1963, Je 30,56:2
Marshall, Frank J Mrs, 1956, S 3,13:6
Marshall, Frank Mrs, 1950, Jl 13,25:2
Marshall, Frederick L, 1945, Ja 28,37:1
Marshall, Frederick L Dr, 1925, S 30,23:5
Marshall, Furber I, 1957, S 30,31:5
Marshall, Gabor, 1960, Jl 11,29:1
Marshall, George A, 1958, Jl 18,21:5
Marshall, George B, 1944, Ja 4,17:1
Marshall, George C (funl plans, O 18,43:3), 1959, O 17,1:8
Marshall, George J, 1941, Jl 29,15:2
Marshall, George M, 1951, Jl 28,11:2
Marshall, George Mrs, 1945, S 15,15:3
Marshall, George S, 1942, Ag 15,11:4
Marshall, George W Dr, 1915, Ap 19,9:4
Marshall, George W Jr, 1964, Mr 15,86:5
Marshall, Guy C, 1954, N 15,27:2
Marshall, H Griffen Dr, 1916, S 7,9:2
Marshall, H R, 1927, My 4,25:1
Marshall, H S, 1931, My 30,15:1
Marshall, Harold J, 1964, D 4,40:1
Marshall, Harry A, 1954, Je 26,13:3
Marshall, Harry F, 1938, N 17,25:4
Marshall, Harry H, 1950, Ag 5,15:6
Marshall, Harry W, 1946, S 6,21:2
Marshall, Henoretta, 1903, D 21,3:3
Marshall, Henry, 1938, S 26,17:3; 1960, F 20,23:4
Marshall, Henry A, 1939, Ag 7,15:6
Marshall, Henry I, 1958, Ap 5,15:4
Marshall, Henry M, 1946, Ja 30,25:3
Marshall, Henry Mrs, 1947, Ja 2,28:3; 1957, Mr 1,23:2
Marshall, Henry S, 1959, Jl 22,28:1
Marshall, Henry V, 1955, Ap 15,23:1
Marshall, Henry W, 1951, F 1,25:3
Marshall, Henry W Jr, 1952, My 28,29:4
Marshall, Herbert, 1966, Ja 23,89:1
Marshall, Herbert M, 1946, S 3,19:2
Marshall, Herbert Mrs (Boots Mallory), 1958, D 2, 37:4
Marshall, Herbert Sr, 1944, Ap 2,39:1
Marshall, Howard E, 1939, My 13,15:4
Marshall, Howland G, 1951, Jl 24,25:4
Marshall, Hugh D, 1955, Jl 22,23:5
Marshall, Hugh D Mrs, 1948, Jl 31,15:2
Marshall, Humphrey Gen, 1872, Ap 1,5:1
Marshall, Ingram D, 1947, O 23,25:4
Marshall, J A, 1884, F 14,5:2
Marshall, J G, 1878, Ap 15,1:4
Marshall, J Manuel, 1942, Mr 20,19:5
Marshall, J R, 1881, Ap 22,2:3
Marshall, J Randolph, 1937, Mr 10,23:3
Marshall, J Robert Mrs, 1962, Je 19,35:1
Marshall, J Wallace Mrs, 1963, Jl 20,19:5
Marshall, J Warren, 1953, Je 26,19:3
Marshall, James, 1937, My 19,23:6
Marshall, James A K, 1951, N 6,29:2
Marshall, James C, 1948, Mr 4,25:2
Marshall, James D, 1961, N 4,19:3
Marshall, James E Mrs, 1952, My 29,27:1
Marshall, James F, 1951, Jl 22,60:2
Marshall, James H, 1939, Ap 14,23:6
Marshall, James M, 1946, O 30,27:2; 1955, Mr 10,27:4
Marshall, James William, 1910, F 6,II,11:5
Marshall, James 3d, 1945, D 26,19:1
Marshall, Jessie R, 1944, Jl 20,19:4
Marshall, Jim, 1957, Ja 9,31:4
Marshall, John, 1922, Ag 21,11:4; 1938, Mr 21,16:1; 1949, Ag 30,27:5
Marshall, John (funl, F 2,19:5), 1957, Ja 31,27:3
Marshall, John, 1964, S 15,37:1; 1966, F 4,31:2
Marshall, John Dr, 1925, Ja 6,25:5
Marshall, John F, 1948, F 18,27:4
Marshall, John G, 1953, Je 20,17:5
Marshall, John H, 1943, D 10,27:1; 1958, Ag 19,28:2
Marshall, John J, 1948, O 19,27:2
Marshall, John K, 1945, Ag 4,11:3
Marshall, John L Mrs, 1947, Ap 16,25:3
Marshall, John M, 1966, My 3,44:6
Marshall, John Mrs, 1943, O 15,19:4
Marshall, John P, 1941, Ja 19,40:4
Marshall, John W, 1914, F 20,9:4; 1944, Je 15,19:7; 1950, N 2,31:4
Marshall, John W Col, 1908, F 22,7:5
Marshall, Jonathan, 1904, My 5,9:6
Marshall, Joseph, 1938, S 6,21:4
Marshall, Joseph C, 1942, D 21,23:3
Marshall, Kate Mrs, 1938, N 29,23:3
Marshall, Kenric R, 1962, N 10,25:3
Marshall, Larmar Mrs, 1947, Ap 12,17:2
Marshall, Leon C, 1966, Mr 19,29:4
Marshall, Leroy A, 1950, Jl 23,57:3
Marshall, Lloyd L Sr, 1953, Ja 6,29:1
Marshall, Louis, 1929, S 12,1:1
Marshall, Louis J, 1968, My 8,44:5
Marshall, Louis Mrs, 1916, My 28,17:4
Marshall, Lucile R, 1965, Ap 14,41:1
Marshall, Luke J, 1940, Ja 24,21:1
Marshall, Lyda M, 1948, D 30,19:6
Marshall, M Lee, 1950, Ag 2,25:6
Marshall, M M, 1883, Ja 23,5:2
Marshall, Margaret A, 1961, D 16,25:1
Marshall, Mary E Mrs, 1942, Je 28,32:2
Marshall, Monroe B, 1955, Ap 16,19:1
Marshall, Morrison, 1920, F 27,13:4
Marshall, Newton C, 1968, O 25,47:5
Marshall, Oswald, 1954, Ap 20,29:4
Marshall, Otis M, 1938, My 22,II,7:1
Marshall, Otis Sr, 1951, Ag 13,17:4
Marshall, Pearl Mrs, 1947, N 3,23:4
Marshall, Percy M, 1950, My 16,31:2
Marshall, Ralph T Mrs, 1959, Mr 6,25:3
Marshall, Randolph (funl, D 27,9:4), 1924, D 25,17:4
Marshall, Ray F, 1946, F 23,13:1
Marshall, Ray G, 1960, My 31,31:2
Marshall, Raymond W, 1966, Ap 21,39:5
Marshall, Raymond W Mrs, 1960, Ja 10,86:6
Marshall, Richard C Jr, 1961, Mr 13,29:5
Marshall, Richard H, 1944, S 21,19:3
Marshall, Richard J, 1951, N 14,31:1
Marshall, Robert, 1939, N 12,49:1
Marshall, Robert (will), 1940, N 14,27:8
Marshall, Robert, 1944, Ap 23,43:3
Marshall, Robert B, 1949, Je 23,27:5
Marshall, Robert Capt, 1910, Jl 2,7:6
Marshall, Robert E Rev, 1937, S 23,27:3
Marshall, Robert M, 1941, Jl 31,17:3
Marshall, Robert W, 1962, Je 4,29:3
Marshall, Rodney E, 1955, Mr 31,27:4
Marshall, Rosamond, 1957, N 26,30:1
Marshall, Ross S, 1960, Ag 2,29:4
Marshall, Roy, 1951, F 28,28:2
Marshall, Roy E, 1966, Ag 18,35:2
Marshall, Samuel A Mrs, 1950, Jl 11,31:5
Marshall, Samuel B D, 1946, Ag 17,13:6
Marshall, Samuel W, 1943, N 26,23:4
Marshall, Smith J, 1943, D 2,27:1
Marshall, Stephen, 1942, Ja 23,19:3
Marshall, Stephen Mrs, 1946, Ap 27,17:4
Marshall, Theron Rudd, 1907, Ap 7,9:6
Marshall, Thomas, 1867, O 31,1:5; 1946, Ap 5,25:2
Marshall, Thomas A Col, 1873, N 16,4:6
Marshall, Thomas A Mrs, 1950, Je 20,27:5
Marshall, Thomas C, 1942, O 9,21:1
Marshall, Thomas Dr, 1903, D 15,9:5
Marshall, Thomas F, 1864, O 1,8:2
Marshall, Thomas H, 1941, My 28,25:1
Marshall, Thomas R, 1939, F 14,19:6; 1952, D 11,33:5
Marshall, Thomas R Mrs, 1951, My 24,35:4; 1958, Ja 8,47:3
Marshall, Thomas Riley, 1925, Je 5,17:4
Marshall, Thomas W, 1874, D 12,3:5; 1952, Mr 29, 15:4
Marshall, Thomas W Mrs, 1957, Ag 20,27:5
Marshall, Thurgood Mrs, 1955, F 13,86:5
Marshall, Timothy A, 1903, S 25,7:5
Marshall, Trenholm M, 1951, F 8,33:5
Marshall, Verne, 1965, Mr 27,27:4
Marshall, W, 1934, Mr 30,21:1
Marshall, W Dr, 1885, Ja 23,6:2
Marshall, W Le Roy, 1956, Ja 12,27:3
Marshall, Waldo H (funl, Ag 26,26:4), 1923, Ag 24, 11:6
Marshall, Walter, 1961, Ja 28,19:1
Marshall, Walton H, 1956, Jl 22,61:1
Marshall, Warren F, 1957, Ja 4,23:4
Marshall, Wilbur H, 1967, Ja 4,41:1
Marshall, Wilbur N, 1967, N 22,47:2
Marshall, William, 1912, D 2,11:4; 1930, My 29,23:3; 1943, Mr 6,13:4; 1947, Je 30,19:1
Marshall, William A Sr Mrs, 1961, Ag 12,17:4
Marshall, William C, 1950, Ag 3,23:2; 1953, Mr 25, 31:5
Marshall, William C Mrs, 1959, Mr 21,21:5
Marshall, William D, 1957, Ja 1,23:3
Marshall, William E, 1937, My 27,23:3
Marshall, William E Mrs, 1957, My 30,19:1
Marshall, William Edgar, 1906, Ag 30,7:4
Marshall, William F Mrs, 1952, D 16,31:3
Marshall, William H, 1942, F 12,23:4
Marshall, William J, 1949, F 8,25:2; 1955, Ag 2,23:2
Marshall, William L, 1921, Jl 26,15:6; 1948, Ap 21, 27:3
Marshall, William L Gen, 1920, Jl 4,21:4
Marshall, William Lt-Gen Sir, 1939, Je 1,25:2
Marshall, William Mrs, 1949, Ap 7,29:2; 1951, Mr 16, 31:5
Marshall, Wilson Jr, 1918, Ap 30,13:4
Marshalov, Boris, 1967, O 17,47:2
Marsham, Edward H Bullock, 1913, Ap 8,12:5
Marshman, Bobby, 1964, D 4,52:3
Marshman, William J, 1942, D 10,25:2
Marsi, Pius Rev, 1910, S 10,9:6
Marsicano, Vincent Mrs, 1963, My 31,25:3
Marsiconovo don Luigi Compagna, Prince, 1939, N 22,24:7
Marsiglio, E Frederick, 1951, Mr 24,13:5
Marsillo, Vic, 1961, Ag 14,25:4
Marsillo, Vic Mrs, 1953, F 9,27:4
Marskman, Charles B, 1937, F 14,II,8:5
Marsland, Eugene C, 1955, Jl 27,23:5
Marsland, Horace A Mrs, 1951, Mr 17,15:6
Marsland, John, 1954, Je 4,23:2
Marsland, M E Mrs, 1951, Mr 10,13:3
Marsland, Merwin E, 1960, S 14,43:4
Marsland, Thomas Mrs, 1944, Jl 2,20:2
Marsman, C John, 1968, Ag 27,42:1
Marson, Aileen, 1939, My 6,17:6
Marson, Bert J, 1958, S 1,13:5
Marson, James T, 1950, Ja 24,31:3
Marson, Joseph Mrs, 1944, F 25,17:3
Marson, Thomas M, 1937, Ja 26,21:1
Marstaller, Frederick W, 1953, O 29,31:4
Marsten, Francis Edward Rev Dr, 1915, Ag 25,11:5
Marsters, Arthur A, 1965, Ap 14,41:4
Marsters, Clayton E, 1951, Ja 26,23:3
Marsters, George E, 1938, D 26,24:4
Marsters, Silas M, 1945, S 8,15:2
Marston, Almerin, 1946, Je 1,13:6
Marston, Amos W, 1947, My 9,22:2
Marston, C Harold, 1939, Jl 9,31:2
Marston, Charles (por), 1946, My 23,21:3
Marston, Edgar L Mrs, 1923, D 9,23:2
Marston, Edward, 1914, Ap 7,9:5
Marston, Edwin S, 1922, O 13,17:5
Marston, Ernest L, 1954, O 13,31:3

Marston, Frederic C Jr, 1965, O 25,37:4
Marston, George, 1883, Ag 15,5:4
Marston, John, 1957, N 27,31:2; 1962, S 4,33:3
Marston, John D, 1912, S 28,13:5
Marston, Lady, 1949, My 11,30:4
Marston, Mary T W Mrs, 1940, Je 2,44:8
Marston, Max R (por), 1949, My 8,76:6
Marston, Oliver J, 1944, D 11,23:1
Marston, Richard, 1917, F 17,11:6
Marston, Russell (por), 1948, Ag 28,15:3
Marston, Russell Mrs, 1967, F 25,27:2
Marston, Sylvester W Mrs, 1913, S 18,11:5
Marston, Thomas F, 1942, N 24,25:4
Marston, Trowbridge Mrs, 1964, Jl 13,29:6
Marston, Walter M, 1958, Jl 5,17:3
Marston, William M (por), 1947, My 3,17:3
Mart, Charles E, 1904, Mr 17,9:6
Mart, John A, 1959, S 14,29:4
Marta, Joseph S, 1958, F 27,27:3
Marta, Queen (Mrs G Evans), 1946, S 23,25:4
Martabano, Valerio, 1950, Mr 15,29:4
Martadinata, Eddy, 1966, O 7,12:1
Martakis, Harry, 1966, Mr 22,41:3
Marteaux, Albert, 1949, My 17,26:3
Martel, Charles, 1945, My 18,19:4
Martel, Charles P, 1945, Jl 21,11:6
Martel, Damien De Count (por), 1940, Ja 22,15:6
Martel, Emile G, 1938, D 29,19:4
Martel, F X, 1950, Ag 4,21:2
Martel, Felicien, 1948, Ja 13,25:5
Martel, Frank X, 1955, Ag 30,27:2
Martel, Giffard Sir, 1958, S 4,29:1
Martel, L J, 1882, F 15,5:1
Martel, Speros P Mrs (will), 1956, Mr 18,15:3
Martell, Augustine E Rev, 1937, Ag 29,II,6:6
Martell, Dalmer, 1941, S 10,3:4
Martell, Daniell E (will), 1938, O 5,26:2
Martell, Ezilino S, 1944, Mr 22,19:3
Martell, Forrest J, 1953, Jl 23,11:4
Martell, Frances, 1942, F 15,44:1
Martell, Paul (por), 1949, D 3,15:3
Martell, Romeo C, 1938, S 2,17:3
Martella, Angelo M, 1951, F 13,31:3
Martelli, Carlo, 1964, Ag 28,29:1
Martelli, Francis, 1947, F 19,25:4
Martelli, Victor V, 1956, N 29,35:3
Marten, Francis A, 1950, Mr 16,32:4
Marten, George H, 1947, Je 21,17:1
Marten, Henry, 1948, D 13,23:3
Marten, Manuel E, 1954, Je 21,23:3
Martenis, C J, 1954, S 14,27:1
Martenis, Henry S, 1941, Je 10,23:4
Martens, Arthur, 1960, N 28,31:4
Martens, Charles H, 1955, S 24,19:3
Martens, Charles Mrs, 1947, D 14,80:5; 1953, Je 9,27:3
Martens, Clarence G, 1958, Ag 4,21:4
Martens, Edward A, 1943, F 21,32:8
Martens, Frederick W, 1913, F 21,13:5
Martens, Henry, 1951, O 10,23:5
Martens, Henry W, 1939, N 8,23:2
Martens, John A, 1944, Mr 20,17:3
Martens, John C, 1968, My 3,54:7
Martens, John F Mrs, 1954, Je 12,15:4
Martens, Ludwig K (por), 1948, O 22,26:2
Martens, Maurice, 1958, N 14,27:3
Martens, Paul, 1955, Je 3,23:5
Martens, Preben, 1940, Ap 19,21:2
Martens, William C, 1962, Ja 27,21:4
Martens, William F, 1943, D 18,15:3
Martense, George W Mrs, 1940, Ja 7,48:6
Martensen, Arthur W, 1953, O 9,27:1
Martensen, H L, 1884, F 5,5:3
Martenson, Reinhold, 1939, Mr 25,15:4
Martenstein, Austin W, 1955, F 17,27:2
Marter, Linnaeus E, 1947, S 19,23:2
Martet, Jean, 1940, F 14,21:4
Martha, Alvaro, 1953, Ja 6,29:3
Martha, Crown Princess of Norway (funl, Ap 22,-29:4), 1954, Ap 5,25:1
Martha, Sister, 1941, Ag 6,17:2; 1949, Ja 16,68:2
Martha Eucharia McDonnell, Sister, 1946, O 19,21:5
Marthaler, Ernest, 1961, Ja 21,21:3
Marthaler, Henry F Mrs, 1942, Mr 25,21:6
Marthy, Francis J, 1947, Je 24,23:4
Marti, Amelia, 1944, N 18,13:2
Marti, Charles L, 1961, Je 18,88:8
Marti-Ibanez, Felix Mrs, 1966, F 15,39:3
Marti y Zayas Bazan, Jose, 1945, O 23,17:1
Martianoff, Nicholas Mrs, 1961, S 17,87:1
Martie, Robert B, 1958, Ja 16,29:1
Martignoni, Alex R, 1951, Jl 10,27:5
Martin, A D Lt, 1879, Jl 19,8:1
Martin, A J, 1877, My 22,4:7
Martin, A M, 1941, S 23,23:6
Martin, A Perry, 1949, N 14,27:3
Martin, A Perry Mrs, 1950, Ag 24,27:4
Martin, Adele C, 1964, S 4,29:2
Martin, Adolph H, 1950, Ja 10,29:3
Martin, Adrian B, 1943, Je 12,13:4
Martin, Albert D, 1948, Je 30,25:5
Martin, Albert E, 1950, My 15,21:4
Martin, Albert H, 1959, Ja 17,19:4
Martin, Albert T, 1966, Ja 4,27:3

Martin, Alex R, 1950, S 10,92:6
Martin, Alexander, 1946, Je 15,21:7
Martin, Alexander T Dr, 1968, Ja 16,39:1
Martin, Alfred, 1948, My 23,68:3
Martin, Allan F, 1948, Mr 3,24:2
Martin, Allen S, 1938, Mr 2,19:3
Martin, Alvah H, 1918, Jl 7,21:3
Martin, Anderson M, 1960, O 31,54:5
Martin, Angie S Mrs, 1944, Ja 26,19:4
Martin, Anna, 1917, Mr 2,11:5; 1949, O 5,29:3
Martin, Anne, 1964, Jl 24,27:3
Martin, Archer, 1941, S 3,23:6
Martin, Argalious E, 1960, Ja 10,87:2
Martin, Arnold E (Jake),(funl, Ag 24,19:6), 1956, Ag 21,29:3
Martin, Arthur C, 1948, Jl 30,18:5
Martin, Arthur K, 1942, N 9,23:3
Martin, Arthur Shadwell, 1914, F 26,9:5
Martin, Arthur T, 1946, F 8,19:5
Martin, Asa E, 1962, S 18,39:4
Martin, August L, 1943, F 24,22:3
Martin, August L Mrs, 1957, Ap 25,31:3
Martin, Augustus B, 1907, D 22,9:4
Martin, Augustus J, 1959, Ag 6,27:5
Martin, Augustus J Mrs, 1957, Mr 15,25:2
Martin, B L H, 1883, D 15,2:5
Martin, B N Prof, 1883, D 27,5:4
Martin, Barbara, 1937, S 20,44:5
Martin, Barbara A, 1964, Ag 6,29:2
Martin, Barney, 1914, Ag 11,9:3
Martin, Benjamin, 1957, Je 5,35:6
Martin, Benjamin Ellis, 1909, Ag 16,7:5
Martin, Bernard F, 1954, O 3,87:2
Martin, Bernard J Jr, 1947, N 29,13:5
Martin, Bijie, 1968, F 1,37:2
Martin, Blanche T Mrs, 1941, D 16,27:4
Martin, Bosser, 1952, Ja 24,27:4
Martin, Boston, 1951, S 13,31:4
Martin, Boyd, 1963, Ap 17,41:2
Martin, Bradley, 1913, F 6,11:3; 1963, Je 4,39:4
Martin, Bradley Mrs, 1920, O 25,15:7; 1920, D 14,17:4
Martin, Briton Jr, 1967, Ja 31,31:2
Martin, Burney K, 1967, Je 10,33:5
Martin, Byron E, 1962, Jl 16,23:5
Martin, C, 1926, O 31,1:2
Martin, Cannonball (Eddie), 1966, Ag 28,92:4
Martin, Carl E Dr, 1924, My 15,19:4
Martin, Carl J, 1941, Jl 17,19:4
Martin, Caroline, 1961, Jl 24,23:1
Martin, Carrie, 1955, My 3,31:5
Martin, Celora E Judge, 1909, S 11,9:5
Martin, Charles, 1917, O 30,15:4
Martin, Charles B, 1947, S 27,15:4; 1948, My 14,23:4
Martin, Charles B Jr, 1956, Ja 25,25:7
Martin, Charles C, 1954, F 2,27:3
Martin, Charles Carroll Mrs, 1924, D 28,5:3
Martin, Charles E, 1941, O 29,23:1; 1950, Je 9,23:3; 1968, F 16,1:3
Martin, Charles F, 1953, O 29,31:1; 1955, F 9,25:2
Martin, Charles G, 1965, Je 9,47:2
Martin, Charles H, 1946, S 24,30:2; 1953, Je 13,15:5; 1953, S 6,52:4
Martin, Charles I, 1953, My 10,88:2
Martin, Charles J, 1941, My 28,25:2
Martin, Charles J (por), 1948, S 12,72:1
Martin, Charles J, 1955, Ag 11,21:4
Martin, Charles L, 1942, Jl 11,13:6; 1957, S 9,25:4
Martin, Charles P, 1965, S 13,35:2
Martin, Charles R, 1922, N 4,13:6
Martin, Charles R Mrs, 1941, D 12,25:1
Martin, Charles Tabor, 1915, N 12,11:6
Martin, Charles W, 1943, Je 8,21:5; 1943, N 17,25:5
Martin, Charlie, 1940, Ap 29,15:5
Martin, Chester, 1958, Ap 4,24:1
Martin, Chester Mrs (Louanna Heath), 1958, Ag 6, 25:3
Martin, Chris-Pin, 1953, Je 29,21:4
Martin, Clarence E, 1955, Ap 25,23:5
Martin, Clarence S, 1948, F 22,48:4
Martin, Clayton, 1937, Jl 20,11:6
Martin, Clement L, 1959, Ag 18,30:4
Martin, Cliff E, 1948, Jl 5,15:4
Martin, Clinton G, 1966, My 20,47:4
Martin, Clinton H, 1957, D 20,24:5
Martin, Collier F, 1941, Mr 25,23:6
Martin, Conrad Bp of Paderborn, 1879, Jl 23,2:6
Martin, D Clifford, 1959, F 6,25:2
Martin, Dana M, 1953, O 31,17:4
Martin, Daniel F, 1907, Ja 10,9:5
Martin, Daniel Hoffman Rev Dr, 1920, Ja 3,11:3
Martin, Daniel Strobel, 1925, Ja 5,21:4
Martin, David, 1920, Je 1,15:3
Martin, David J, 1957, D 1,88:6
Martin, Delmer D, 1953, Ja 13,32:4
Martin, DeWitt, 1941, My 25,37:2
Martin, Don, 1943, Je 16,21:6
Martin, Douglas D, 1963, S 27,29:3
Martin, Drelincourt M, 1949, Ja 21,22:2
Martin, E Gwen, 1950, O 7,17:2
Martin, Earle, 1938, My 6,21:5
Martin, Edgar A, 1938, Jl 12,19:3
Martin, Edgar E, 1960, S 1,27:4
Martin, Edgar F, 1961, Ja 12,29:5

Martin, Edgar G, 1949, F 15,23:1
Martin, Edgar H, 1945, My 2,23:3
Martin, Edgar S (por), 1940, Ag 10,13:3
Martin, Edmund J, 1952, Ja 6,93:1
Martin, Edward, 1938, Mr 18,19:5; 1946, Ap 6,17:5; 1967, Mr 20,31:2
Martin, Edward A, 1944, Ja 25,19:2; 1946, Ag 8,21:6 1957, Je 19,35:1
Martin, Edward D, 1967, N 21,48:1
Martin, Edward E I, 1965, Ap 12,35:1
Martin, Edward F Rev, 1903, S 7,7:7
Martin, Edward J Jr, 1953, Ag 1,11:4
Martin, Edward Jr, 1952, F 5,29:1
Martin, Edward K, 1913, My 5,9:2
Martin, Edward L, 1951, Ja 7,76:7
Martin, Edward Mrs, 1937, N 11,25:5; 1967, N 13,4
Martin, Edward R, 1948, My 6,25:4; 1967, S 8,40:2
Martin, Edward S, 1939, Je 14,23:3
Martin, Edward S (will), 1940, Ja 26,9:2
Martin, Edwin C, 1915, Jl 24,9:7
Martin, Edwin G, 1947, Ag 10,53:2
Martin, Edwin H, 1950, F 21,25:4
Martin, Edwin M, 1956, N 23,27:4
Martin, Edwin Thomas Dr, 1968, Ja 24,42:3
Martin, Eliza J, 1938, Jl 9,13:3
Martin, Elizabeth (E Weldon), 1941, Ag 23,13:2
Martin, Elizabeth (Sister Mary Regina), 1943, S 2 25:5
Martin, Elizabeth L, 1945, S 10,19:2
Martin, Ellen W Mrs, 1940, O 15,23:4
Martin, Ernest C, 1951, Je 23,15:6
Martin, Ernest D Mrs, 1953, O 19,21:5
Martin, Ernest J, 1938, Jl 27,17:4
Martin, Erwin S, 1952, Mr 5,29:3
Martin, Eugene F, 1967, Mr 29,45:3
Martin, Everett C, 1964, My 14,35:5
Martin, Everett D, 1941, My 11,44:3
Martin, F H, 1935, Mr 8,21:3
Martin, F Melvin, 1955, Ap 19,31:2
Martin, Florence, 1957, O 29,31:2
Martin, Floyd Mrs, 1940, S 12,13:1
Martin, Frances W, 1955, S 28,35:3
Martin, Francis, 1947, Je 2,25:1
Martin, Francis C, 1924, Je 2,17:6
Martin, Francis S, 1922, Jl 29,7:5
Martin, Francis X, 1943, Ag 31,17:3
Martin, Frank, 1940, F 24,13:3; 1945, D 12,27:3
Martin, Frank B Mrs, 1955, Je 23,29:2
Martin, Frank E, 1905, Ap 2,9:6; 1962, Ja 16,18:5
Martin, Frank F, 1956, My 13,86:6
Martin, Frank G, 1956, O 13,19:5
Martin, Frank J, 1947, My 17,16:2; 1960, F 16,37: 1964, N 5,45:2
Martin, Frank L (por), 1941, Jl 19,13:5
Martin, Frank R Mrs, 1943, F 21,32:4
Martin, Frank V, 1943, Jl 20,19:3
Martin, Frank X, 1950, N 5,92:4
Martin, Fred, 1956, Ap 5,18:5
Martin, Fred C, 1945, Ap 12,23:5
Martin, Fred Mrs, 1952, N 20,31:2
Martin, Fred V, 1940, Jl 9,21:4
Martin, Frederick, 1883, Ja 29,5:6
Martin, Frederick A, 1915, My 21,13:4; 1954, N 3 29:5
Martin, Frederick C, 1944, Ag 21,15:4
Martin, Frederick G, 1939, S 22,23:4
Martin, Frederick L, 1945, S 12,25:3; 1954, F 26,
Martin, Frederick R, 1952, Ap 28,19:3
Martin, Frederick R Mrs, 1940, N 14,23:2
Martin, Frederick Townsend (por),(funl, Mr 18,1 1914, Mr 9,9:2
Martin, Frederick V, 1950, Ap 11,32:2
Martin, George, 1867, D 16,1:4
Martin, George A, 1944, N 2,19:5
Martin, George B, 1945, N 13,21:2; 1947, Je 25,2
Martin, George B Mrs, 1948, Je 9,29:1
Martin, George C, 1943, Je 24,21:2
Martin, George Clement Sir, 1916, F 24,13:4
Martin, George E, 1948, N 16,29:5; 1954, Jl 7,31
Martin, George E Mrs, 1950, Ap 5,31:2
Martin, George F, 1960, Ap 2,23:4
Martin, George H Sr, 1950, D 21,29:4
Martin, George J, 1952, D 9,33:2
Martin, George J Mrs, 1945, Ag 17,17:2
Martin, George K, 1954, D 29,23:2
Martin, George M Mrs, 1946, D 2,25:4
Martin, George R Mrs, 1953, Je 3,31:4
Martin, George T, 1939, Mr 30,23:5
Martin, George T Mrs, 1953, My 10,88:1
Martin, George W, 1948, N 23,30:2; 1953, Je 19 1959, Ja 6,33:1
Martin, George W Mrs, 1959, Mr 12,31:3
Martin, George W Sr, 1951, My 25,27:4
Martin, George Winslow, 1908, My 5,7:5
Martin, Georges P, 1965, Ja 26,37:2
Martin, Gerald, 1937, S 1,19:3
Martin, Gerald Mrs, 1944, F 10,15:2
Martin, Germain, 1948, O 7,29:1
Martin, Gertrude E, 1945, S 9,46:3
Martin, Gervaise G, 1950, Mr 15,29:2
Martin, Glenn, 1954, N 27,13:5
Martin, Glenn L (will, D 16,26:2), 1955, D 5,1
Martin, Glenn L (est appr), 1956, Ja 11,22:3

Martin, Gregory, 1907, Ag 10,7:5
Martin, Gustav, 1945, Jl 20,19:4
Martin, Gustav J, 1967, F 28,37:3
Martin, Gustav M, 1938, Ja 20,24:4
Martin, H, 1883, D 31,3:6
Martin, H J Mrs, 1903, My 3,9:6
Martin, H Walford Mrs, 1944, F 1,20:3
Martin, H Warner, 1945, Ag 14,21:1
Martin, Harlan L, 1968, F 29,37:2
Martin, Harold C, 1948, S 1,23:2
Martin, Harold E, 1961, N 26,88:6
Martin, Harold J, 1956, Ag 13,19:4; 1958, My 9,23:4
Martin, Harold P, 1950, Je 11,92:3
Martin, Harrison J, 1952, Ja 22,29:2
Martin, Harrison S (por), 1937, My 13,25:4
Martin, Harry, 1952, F 26,27:3
Martin, Harry E, 1941, D 25,25:2
Martin, Harry E Mrs, 1949, My 10,25:3
Martin, Harry J, 1947, Ap 17,27:5
Martin, Harry L, 1949, S 13,29:2; 1958, D 24,2:4
Martin, Harry S, 1954, My 19,31:4
Martin, Harry Townsend, 1915, Ag 21,7:6
Martin, Harry W, 1951, Je 25,19:3
Martin, Helen J, 1961, Ap 6,33:3
Martin, Helen R Mrs, 1939, Je 30,19:6
Martin, Henry, 1901, N 20,9:5; 1916, N 5,23:4; 1941, My 27,23:1; 1954, Ja 3,90:5
Martin, Henry B, 1953, Jl 13,25:5
Martin, Henry G, 1949, Ag 14,70:5
Martin, Henry H, 1954, S 23,33:4; 1965, F 8,25:4
Martin, Henry P, 1953, Ap 20,25:6; 1959, Ap 16,33:2
Martin, Henry P Jr Mrs, 1939, My 17,23:3
Martin, Henry Townsend, 1904, My 17,9:6
Martin, Henry W, 1944, My 2,19:4; 1948, My 7,23:5
Martin, Herbert E, 1944, S 20,23:2
Martin, Herbert H, 1954, Ap 1,31:3
Martin, Herbert L, 1938, Ap 10,II,7:1
Martin, Herbert M, 1943, Ja 31,44:7
Martin, Herman F, 1951, D 21,27:2
Martin, Hershey, 1965, Jl 6,33:3
Martin, Hester Brown, 1924, Je 9,17:5
Martin, Hiland W, 1950, Jl 1,15:1
Martin, Hildreth Mrs, 1967, O 14,27:3
Martin, Horace F, 1954, Ap 17,13:4
Martin, Horace G, 1953, Je 6,17:2
Martin, Horace Hawes, 1925, O 21,23:3
Martin, Horace J, 1944, Ja 6,23:5
Martin, Horace L, 1959, S 2,29:5
Martin, Howard D, 1952, F 10,92:2
Martin, Howard J Sr, 1953, Mr 28,17:2
Martin, Howard V, 1941, D 14,69:2
Martin, Hubert (por), 1938, N 18,21:2
Martin, Hugh B, 1954, S 17,27:5
Martin, Hugh C Mrs, 1952, Mr 22,13:4
Martin, Hugh Mrs, 1949, Ja 4,40:3
Martin, I Jack, 1966, N 6,88:3
Martin, I Strevell, 1963, Ap 14,92:8
Martin, Ingla B Mrs, 1955, N 25,27:4
Martin, Ira W, 1960, N 13,89:1
Martin, Irene S Mrs, 1943, Mr 13,13:3
Martin, Irving, 1952, D 9,33:1
Martin, Irving L, 1967, Jl 21,31:3
Martin, Isaac M Mrs, 1954, D 7,33:4
Martin, J A, 1924, Ja 19,13:4; 1949, O 26,27:5
Martin, J Frederick, 1947, S 7,60:5
Martin, J H Talbot, 1941, Jl 1,23:4
Martin, J H Thayer, 1958, Je 28,17:3
Martin, J S, 1876, Ag 17,2:2
Martin, J W, 1939, D 9,15:3
Martin, J W Mrs, 1942, My 9,13:3
Martin, Jack, 1950, S 9,17:5
Martin, Jacob, 1937, F 11,23:1; 1949, N 20,92:5
Martin, James, 1903, Jl 19,1:4; 1910, Mr 16,9:4
Martin, James A, 1950, Je 24,13:3; 1958, Ag 2,17:5
Martin, James A Mrs, 1957, Jl 25,23:2
Martin, James E, 1905, D 25,1:1; 1908, My 21,7:5; 1947, Mr 12,25:5; 1953, O 20,29:4
Martin, James F, 1949, Jl 2,15:6
Martin, James G, 1938, Ja 3,21:5; 1955, Ag 1,19:2
Martin, James J, 1946, Ag 22,27:4; 1951, N 11,90:5
Martin, James J Mrs, 1956, Jl 11,29:4
Martin, James L, 1948, Mr 18,27:5; 1952, D 4,35:4; 1954, My 23,88:7; 1960, Mr 23,37:3
Martin, James L Judge, 1915, Ja 15,11:5
Martin, James M, 1956, N 11,86:3
Martin, James M Mrs, 1944, O 12,27:3
Martin, James R, 1940, Ap 12,23:2; 1943, Je 23,21:1
Martin, James Stewart Gen, 1907, N 21,9:6
Martin, James T, 1939, Jl 18,19:4
Martin, Jane (Sister Mary), 1964, F 5,35:3
Martin, Jean Baptiste, 1918, Je 21,13:4
Martin, Jeremiah N, 1947, Ja 3,21:1
Martin, Jeremiah Neil, 1920, Ag 8,22:5
Martin, Joel P, 1948, D 17,27:3
Martin, John, 1942, O 30,19:5; 1944, Je 29,24:4; 1949, Mr 29,26:2; 1949, Ap 23,13:6; 1954, Mr 22,45:6; 1956, Ap 7,19:2
Martin, John A, 1939, D 23,15:6; 1951, Mr 27,29:4
Martin, John C, 1955, F 18,21:2
Martin, John C Mrs, 1965, Ap 24,29:1
Martin, John C Sr, 1952, Ja 29,25:5
Martin, John Calvin, 1912, S 4,11:3
Martin, John D, 1962, Ap 3,39:3
Martin, John D Sr, 1954, S 3,17:4
Martin, John E, 1941, Ap 7,17:2
Martin, John F, 1918, Mr 29,11:8; 1939, Mr 5,49:1; 1939, N 12,48:6
Martin, John F Jr, 1955, Ja 25,25:3
Martin, John F Mrs, 1938, O 10,19:3
Martin, John H, 1938, Ja 2,41:3; 1951, Mr 29,27:5
Martin, John H Mrs, 1949, Ap 29,23:3
Martin, John J, 1937, My 26,25:5; 1939, Ap 18,23:2; 1945, Ap 3,19:6; 1947, Ag 29,17:5; 1952, O 8,31:2; 1966, Je 4,29:2
Martin, John J Mrs, 1950, S 9,17:6
Martin, John M, 1950, My 27,17:2
Martin, John M Mrs, 1947, S 30,25:4
Martin, John Mrs, 1945, Ap 3,19:1; 1953, Ag 26,27:4; 1957, Ag 21,27:2
Martin, John P, 1939, S 22,23:6; 1950, F 27,19:2
Martin, John P Mrs, 1953, Ja 18,92:6
Martin, John R, 1967, My 29,25:4
Martin, John S, 1942, O 15,23:4; 1954, N 22,23:1; 1968, Je 29,29:3
Martin, John S Mrs, 1965, Ap 1,35:2
Martin, John Sayre, 1905, Ap 19,11:4
Martin, John Sr, 1949, Jl 27,23:3
Martin, John T, 1959, F 23,23:6
Martin, John W, 1949, My 12,31:5; 1952, N 23,88:5; 1958, F 24,19:2
Martin, John W Y, 1954, Je 26,13:5
Martin, John William Capt, 1903, N 23,7:3
Martin, Joseph, 1946, Mr 20,23:4; 1948, Mr 4,25:4
Martin, Joseph B (por), 1941, O 25,17:1
Martin, Joseph B, 1953, N 9,35:2
Martin, Joseph B Jr, 1937, Ap 25,II,8:6
Martin, Joseph C, 1944, Je 19,19:5
Martin, Joseph H, 1914, Mr 26,11:6
Martin, Joseph H Mrs, 1948, D 16,29:3
Martin, Joseph I, 1957, Ap 17,31:4
Martin, Joseph J, 1953, O 9,10:6; 1955, Ja 29,15:1
Martin, Joseph K, 1956, D 6,37:4
Martin, Joseph L, 1950, Ag 6,57:5
Martin, Joseph L Mrs, 1949, S 17,17:2
Martin, Joseph Mrs, 1941, F 28,19:1
Martin, Joseph P, 1937, Ap 21,23:6
Martin, Joseph P (funl, Ja 25,21:3), 1957, Ja 22,29:1
Martin, Joseph Sr, 1945, Ja 13,11:4
Martin, Joseph W, 1938, My 7,15:2; 1948, S 30,27:4; 1952, S 13,17:4
Martin, Joseph W Jr, 1968, Mr 7,1:7
Martin, Joseph W Sr, 1957, S 8,84:8
Martin, Jules T, 1944, D 31,25:2
Martin, Julius, 1948, Mr 13,15:3
Martin, Julius C, 1949, F 10,28:3
Martin, Justin Dr, 1907, D 18,9:5
Martin, Karl A (por), 1942, O 15,23:2
Martin, Karl H, 1954, Jl 8,23:3
Martin, Kathryn B, 1967, Je 6,47:2
Martin, Kenneth C Mrs, 1946, My 3,22:2
Martin, Kingsley G, 1951, O 25,29:3
Martin, Kingsley L, 1947, My 29,21:4
Martin, Lady (Helen Faucit), 1898, N 1,6:6
Martin, Laurence J, 1956, N 12,29:3
Martin, Lawrence, 1955, F 14,20:5
Martin, Lawrence H, 1952, F 18,19:4
Martin, Lawrence N, 1940, Mr 19,25:2
Martin, Lee G, 1950, N 18,15:5
Martin, Leonard J, 1951, My 17,31:4
Martin, Leslie O, 1950, D 24,21:3
Martin, Lester, 1959, Ap 25,21:3
Martin, Lewis J, 1913, My 6,11:3
Martin, Lillien J (por), 1943, Mr 28,25:1
Martin, Linton P, 1954, Mr 13,15:3
Martin, Lloyd B, 1948, Ag 29,56:4
Martin, Lois Sister, 1962, Ja 31,31:1
Martin, Lon E, 1946, F 10,42:1
Martin, Lorenzo W, 1962, Ja 3,33:2
Martin, Loretta A, 1952, Jl 29,21:4
Martin, Louis, 1921, N 17,17:4; 1944, Ag 29,17:4
Martin, Louis (por), 1946, Je 14,22:3
Martin, Louis, 1950, Ja 22,77:1
Martin, Louis A Jr, 1938, Ag 17,19:2
Martin, Louis J, 1938, F 8,21:5
Martin, Louis M, 1940, Mr 2,13:4
Martin, Louise H, 1950, O 19,31:4
Martin, Lowry, 1959, N 3,35:7
Martin, Luther, 1946, Mr 10,47:2
Martin, Luther 3d, 1962, N 28,39:5
Martin, Lydia C, 1943, My 29,13:3
Martin, Lynn A, 1939, Jl 21,19:1
Martin, Lynn C, 1948, Ap 1,25:4
Martin, M G, 1938, O 22,17:5
Martin, Mannesse T Mrs, 1954, Ap 6,30:7
Martin, Manton D, 1950, Ap 10,19:2
Martin, Manuel J, 1939, Jl 28,17:2
Martin, Margaret, 1924, F 4,19:4
Martin, Margaret S Mrs, 1941, S 29,17:4
Martin, Martha Evans Mrs, 1925, Ja 6,25:5
Martin, Mary, 1938, Ap 20,23:5
Martin, Mary E, 1951, N 21,25:4
Martin, Mary Mrs, 1940, Jl 21,29:1
Martin, Matthew R, 1967, N 30,47:1
Martin, Max, 1908, Ap 22,9:5
Martin, Mellen C, 1952, My 7,27:4
Martin, Michael, 1951, D 13,33:1
Martin, Michael J, 1957, Ja 8,31:3
Martin, Michael U, 1922, F 2,17:2
Martin, Mike, 1952, Je 4,21:5
Martin, Minta Mrs, 1953, Mr 15,93:3
Martin, Mungo, 1962, Ag 18,19:5
Martin, Nathan B, 1956, N 9,29:4
Martin, Nathan E, 1968, F 3,29:4
Martin, Newell, 1941, N 16,57:2
Martin, Newell Mrs, 1940, Jl 21,29:3
Martin, Niles, 1951, Jl 29,69:2
Martin, Norman G, 1945, Mr 16,15:1
Martin, Oliver C, 1942, N 19,25:1
Martin, Owen, 1960, My 7,23:4
Martin, Patrick, 1913, N 4,9:7
Martin, Patrick E, 1947, F 7,24:2
Martin, Patrick F, 1945, N 13,22:2
Martin, Patrick H, 1904, Ja 10,7:6
Martin, Paul, 1956, Je 22,23:2
Martin, Paul C, 1939, O 17,25:6
Martin, Paul C F, 1951, Mr 2,25:1
Martin, Pepper (Jno L), 1965, Mr 6,25:4
Martin, Percival D, 1956, Ja 20,23:3
Martin, Percival D Mrs, 1956, Ja 20,23:3
Martin, Percy A, 1942, Mr 10,19:5
Martin, Perry, 1939, Ag 23,21:4
Martin, Peter, 1876, Jl 30,6:7; 1915, Ap 4,14:1
Martin, Peter E, 1944, O 9,23:5
Martin, Phil H, 1954, Mr 30,27:2
Martin, Philip E, 1903, S 23,7:5
Martin, R John, 1958, Ja 17,25:1
Martin, Ralph, 1943, Jl 22,19:4
Martin, Ralph H, 1939, My 9,23:5; 1949, Je 12,76:2
Martin, Rankin, 1965, Mr 25,37:4
Martin, Raymond C, 1956, Je 25,23:1
Martin, Raymond F Sr Mrs, 1957, Ja 9,31:1
Martin, Raymond T, 1955, My 26,31:4
Martin, Reginald E, 1962, S 23,86:6
Martin, Riccardo, 1952, Ag 12,19:1
Martin, Richard Biddulph, 1916, Ag 24,9:3
Martin, Richard L H, 1956, Jl 19,27:1
Martin, Richard M, 1957, Jl 15,19:3
Martin, Richard P, 1944, D 14,23:2
Martin, Richard R, 1947, Ap 22,27:3
Martin, Robert, 1937, Ap 26,19:4; 1947, S 23,25:5
Martin, Robert B, 1938, F 6,II,9:2
Martin, Robert D, 1967, D 30,23:2
Martin, Robert J, 1938, D 23,19:1
Martin, Robert M, 1945, O 7,44:4
Martin, Robert R, 1953, Mr 23,23:4
Martin, Robert V, 1954, My 19,32:3
Martin, Robert W, 1948, D 17,27:4
Martin, Roscoe B, 1951, D 23,22:3
Martin, Rose E, 1959, Ap 16,33:1
Martin, Roy D, 1967, Ag 6,77:2
Martin, Royce G, 1954, My 2,88:6
Martin, Rudolph Mrs, 1940, Ja 23,21:3
Martin, Russell C (por), 1946, Ja 2,19:5
Martin, Ruth, 1952, Ap 10,29:4
Martin, S Sir, 1883, Ja 10,5:4
Martin, Sally H, 1965, My 18,39:4
Martin, Samuel, 1956, My 12,19:3
Martin, Samuel A Mrs, 1949, Ja 7,21:1
Martin, Samuel Albert Rev, 1921, Mr 27,22:3
Martin, Samuel E, 1940, Jl 16,17:4
Martin, Samuel H, 1949, My 15,90:4
Martin, Samuel W, 1958, Jl 11,23:3
Martin, Santford, 1957, Ap 15,29:2
Martin, Selden O, 1942, S 15,24:2
Martin, Shelton E, 1963, Ap 22,27:5
Martin, Stanley G, 1952, Ap 18,25:1
Martin, Stephen A, 1966, N 7,47:4
Martin, Stephen J, 1950, Ap 19,29:3
Martin, Steven, 1903, Ag 30,7:6
Martin, Susanne Mrs (Madame Periwinkle), 1910, F 12,9:4
Martin, Sydney E Mrs, 1950, S 18,23:5
Martin, Sydney Sr Mrs, 1948, F 18,27:1
Martin, T F, 1926, Jl 21,19:3
Martin, Temper C Mrs, 1968, Je 11,44:2
Martin, Terrence B, 1958, Mr 23,88:8
Martin, Theodore D Mrs, 1907, D 19,9:5
Martin, Theodore Sir, 1909, Ag 19,7:5
Martin, Thomas, 1942, Ja 10,15:2; 1951, Ag 16,31:1; 1957, O 26,42:2
Martin, Thomas A, 1941, Je 2,17:2; 1945, Ja 6,11:1; 1945, My 8,19:1
Martin, Thomas B, 1944, Jl 31,13:2
Martin, Thomas C, 1924, My 18,7:1
Martin, Thomas C P, 1961, F 14,37:4
Martin, Thomas D, 1904, Ja 23,9:5
Martin, Thomas E, 1950, Ap 4,29:2; 1959, My 3,87:2
Martin, Thomas F, 1945, F 27,19:5; 1948, O 10,76:3; 1955, Ap 12,29:2
Martin, Thomas G, 1945, F 16,23:3
Martin, Thomas H, 1950, My 11,29:3; 1962, Ap 26, 33:4
Martin, Thomas J, 1941, Ap 4,21:5; 1943, Ja 25,14:2
Martin, Thomas J (por), 1945, D 19,25:1
Martin, Thomas J, 1958, Jl 14,21:4; 1968, D 1,87:1
Martin, Thomas J Mrs (further data, Je 16,43:1), 1967, Je 15,47:1
Martin, Thomas L, 1947, F 23,53:6
Martin, Thomas Mrs, 1943, N 28,69:1

Martin, Thomas S, 1919, N 13,13:1; 1954, My 13,29:4
Martin, Thomas S Maj, 1937, Ag 31,23:3
Martin, Thomas W, 1943, My 13,21:2; 1951, Mr 23, 21:4; 1964, D 11,39:2
Martin, Townsend, 1951, N 24,11:1
Martin, Troy E, 1939, Ag 22,19:3
Martin, V C W Mrs, 1927, Je 11,19:3
Martin, Victor A Mrs, 1954, Je 7,23:4
Martin, Victor H, 1944, Je 24,13:6
Martin, Victoria Mrs, 1948, S 10,23:4
Martin, Vincente L Mrs, 1951, S 16,85:1
Martin, W A Capt (see also D 10), 1877, D 12,8:1
Martin, W H, 1940, D 23,19:4; 1951, Je 11,25:4
Martin, W L, 1907, Mr 4,9:5
Martin, W Linus Mrs, 1952, Mr 28,23:3
Martin, W O, 1942, O 27,25:3
Martin, Wallace Mrs, 1949, D 12,33:3
Martin, Walter, 1938, D 29,19:2
Martin, Walter B, 1966, Ap 24,86:4
Martin, Walter F, 1940, Je 12,25:6; 1949, S 1,21:5
Martin, Walter S Mrs, 1948, Mr 10,27:2
Martin, Walter V, 1939, S 11,19:5
Martin, Walter W, 1951, My 1,29:4; 1966, Mr 18,39:3
Martin, Walton, 1949, Je 19,68:5
Martin, Walton Mrs, 1961, S 19,35:2
Martin, Wayne G Jr, 1959, N 4,35:1
Martin, Whitney Mrs, 1943, My 2,45:1; 1957, Ap 8, 23:5
Martin, Wilfred E, 1953, Mr 24,31:2
Martin, Wilfred T, 1946, F 5,23:5
Martin, Will I, 1954, N 5,21:2
Martin, William, 1916, My 12,11:6; 1925, Jl 14,21:5; 1955, N 11,25:3; 1965, F 3,35:3
Martin, William A, 1908, Ap 13,7:4; 1937, Mr 27,15:3; 1943, Je 25,17:4
Martin, William A Mrs, 1938, Ja 24,23:4
Martin, William Alexander Parsons Rev Dr, 1916, D 24,15:1
Martin, William B, 1940, Jl 9,21:2; 1953, Je 16,27:3
Martin, William C, 1952, My 31,17:2
Martin, William D, 1948, Mr 5,21:3; 1948, Ag 31,26:2
Martin, William D Jr, 1965, N 16,47:3
Martin, William D Mrs, 1957, Ag 18,82:7
Martin, William Dr, 1920, Ap 2,15:1
Martin, William E, 1959, F 26,31:4
Martin, William F, 1942, Ap 16,21:6; 1950, Je 9,23:4
Martin, William G, 1949, S 17,17:2; 1950, F 15,27:3
Martin, William G Mrs, 1948, Jl 2,21:3
Martin, William H, 1937, Mr 26,21:4; 1944, Ap 25, 23:2; 1951, O 5,27:1; 1953, D 17,37:4; 1962, Ja 4, 33:5; 1967, Je 26,33:2
Martin, William H Mrs, 1955, D 14,39:3
Martin, William J, 1938, My 26,25:5; 1943, S 8,23:5; 1950, O 19,31:1
Martin, William J F, 1942, N 25,23:2
Martin, William K, 1943, Je 14,17:3
Martin, William M, 1938, S 10,17:5; 1939, Ag 26,15:6; 1955, Mr 2,27:1
Martin, William Mrs, 1914, Ap 25,15:5
Martin, William P, 1947, Ap 3,25:4
Martin, William R H, 1912, Ja 31,11:5
Martin, William R H (est appr), 1914, My 2,9:4
Martin, William S, 1946, Mr 15,22:3; 1949, Je 13,19:5
Martin, William S Mrs, 1946, O 17,23:2
Martin, William W, 1946, D 27,19:2
Martin, Williams Swift Maj, 1918, F 7,11:5
Martin, Winfred Robert Dr, 1915, F 22,9:4
Martin (Mother Marie St Jean), 1965, Je 30,37:3
Martin Alonso, Pablo, 1964, F 12,33:2
Martin du Gard, Roger, 1958, Ag 24,86:4
Martin-Harvey, John (por), 1944, My 15,19:5
Martin-Harvey, John Mrs, 1949, My 30,13:2
Martin-Leake, Arthur, 1953, Je 24,25:5
Martina, Joe, 1962, Mr 23,33:1
Martina, M Mother, 1940, Ja 17,21:3
Martina, Sister, 1946, Ja 18,19:1
Martindale, Charlotte S Mrs, 1950, Mr 9,29:2
Martindale, Emma Mrs, 1941, Ap 13,38:3
Martindale, George C, 1943, Je 13,45:1
Martindale, Hilda, 1952, Ap 19,15:5
Martindale, J H, 1881, D 14,5:1
Martindale, James Boyd, 1904, My 18,9:6
Martindale, Joseph B (funl, Jl 10,13:5), 1917, Jl 8, 15:1
Martindell, Henry J, 1907, Ag 24,7:4
Martine, Ella L, 1952, F 6,29:3
Martine, James E, 1919, O 17,17:5; 1925, Mr 2,17:6
Martine, R B Judge, 1895, Mr 31,1:5
Martine, Reginald, 1966, S 16,37:3
Martine, S A, 1876, Ja 12,4:7
Martineau, Alfred O, 1937, Ap 17,17:3
Martineau, Clarence R, 1938, N 13,45:1
Martineau, Francis G, 1963, N 19,42:2
Martineau, Harold E, 1951, N 15,29:2
Martineau, Harriet, 1876, Je 29,4:7
Martineau, Hubert M Mrs, 1961, Ag 9,33:5
Martineau, Jean C, 1950, Jl 22,15:3
Martineau, John E (por), 1937, Mr 7,II,8:8
Martineau, Leon, 1909, S 10,9:5
Martineau, Pierre D, 1964, N 3,31:2
Martineck, Joseph Rev, 1937, F 14,II,9:3
Martinek, Frank J, 1948, Mr 4,25:2
Martinek, Thomas C, 1952, S 1,17:4
Martinelli, Antonio, 1957, D 18,35:3
Martinelli, Arthur L, 1944, N 18,13:5
Martinelli, Giuseppe, 1946, N 28,27:2
Martinelli, Raymond C, 1949, Ja 11,31:5
Martinelli, Sebastian Cardinal, 1918, Jl 6,9:6
Martinelli, Silvio, 1955, N 9,33:3
Martinelli, Vito S, 1939, S 14,23:2
Martiner, John, 1940, F 3,30:8
Martines de Pinillos, Carlos, 1947, Je 24,23:3
Martinetti, Carlo D, 1940, D 11,27:4
Martinetti, Carlo D Mrs, 1957, Je 2,86:1
Martinez, Abraham, 1941, Ja 2,23:3
Martinez, Adele Mrs, 1939, Ag 17,21:4
Martinez, Alberto G, 1941, My 22,21:2
Martinez, Antonio, 1951, Je 12,29:4
Martinez, Carlos, 1966, Ag 25,37:2
Martinez, Charles S, 1941, Ja 21,21:3
Martinez, Domingo, 1945, Ap 18,23:6
Martinez, Eduardo, 1938, O 27,23:3; 1942, Mr 10,19:2
Martinez, F N R, 1903, D 28,7:4
Martinez, Frank A, 1952, Mr 12,27:3
Martinez, George Mrs, 1943, Ja 17,44:6
Martinez, John M, 1966, F 24,37:1
Martinez, Juan, 1961, N 29,41:1
Martinez, Juan J, 1960, My 24,38:1
Martinez, Julian, 1943, Mr 8,15:1
Martinez, Luis M (funl plans, F 11,17:5; funl F 12,- 88:7), 1956, F 10,21:3
Martinez, Maximiliano Mrs, 1950, Ja 18,31:4
Martinez, Miguel R, 1914, Jl 29,9:5
Martinez, Orlando Mrs (A Haden-Guest), 1965, D 1,47:5
Martinez, Sebastiana de Mrs, 1951, F 24,13:1
Martinez Aparicio, Carlos, 1959, Ag 29,17:6
Martinez Barrio, Diego, 1962, Ja 2,30:1
Martinez de Irujo y Caro, Pedro Duke of Sotomayor, 1957, S 8,84:7
Martinez Guerrero, Ana R S de Mrs, 1964, S 5,19:1
Martinez-Hernz, Ramon, 1879, N 7,5:5
Martinez Menendez, Antonio, 1939, F 20,17:4
Martinez Mera, Juan de Dios, 1955, O 29,19:4
Martinez Pando, Eladio, 1949, D 25,26:7
Martinez Ruiz, Jose, 1967, Mr 3,35:2
Martinez Sierra, Gregorio (por), 1947, O 2,27:3
Martinez Trueba, Andres, 1959, D 20,60:3
Marting, Edwin O Mrs, 1962, N 25,86:4
Marting, Henry A, 1943, N 27,13:3
Martini, Arturo, 1947, Mr 24,25:6
Martini, Ettore, 1940, Ag 29,19:5
Martini, Eugene R, 1965, Ja 24,80:7
Martini, Ferdinandino, 1953, N 1,86:5
Martini, Giuseppe, 1944, O 26,23:1
Martini, Mary L, 1944, Ap 17,23:3
Martini, Roland, 1966, S 21,47:2
Martinian, Bro, 1959, O 9,29:1
Martinka, Francis J, 1924, N 5,19:4
Martino, Alfredo, 1961, S 14,31:2
Martino, Eduardo de, 1912, My 23,13:5
Martino, Frank, 1941, S 11,23:3
Martino, Gaetano, 1967, Jl 22,26:5
Martino, Giacomo de, 1957, Je 30,68:6
Martino, Italo A, 1952, Mr 4,27:2
Martino, John Mrs, 1953, Jl 26,69:3
Martino, Michelo, 1908, F 10,9:4
Martino, Nicholas, 1916, Jl 24,9:3
Martino, R J, 1951, D 21,27:2
Martino, Yolando, 1950, S 3,42:2
Martinot, Paul J, 1968, Ag 16,33:4
Martinot, Paul J Mrs, 1956, Je 22,23:4
Martinot, Sadie (funl, My 11,17:5), 1923, My 10,19:4
Martinovitch, Nichols N, 1954, S 19,88:6
Martinprey, E C Count, 1883, F 27,5:4
Martins, Francis G, 1944, Je 21,19:2
Martins, Francisco J D, 1952, My 24,19:6
Martins Pereira e Sousa, Carlos, 1965, F 20,25:1
Martinsen, Harry E, 1955, S 24,19:6
Martinsen, Ottocar H (por), 1949, Mr 1,25:5
Martinson, John M, 1949, My 10,25:5
Martinson, Joseph, 1949, Ap 26,25:5
Martinu, Bohuslav, 1959, Ag 30,83:1
Martinuzzi, P Frank, 1965, Ap 13,37:2
Martiny, P, 1927, Je 27,19:5
Martire, Rome A, 1960, O 17,29:4
Martis, George Sr, 1948, Ag 7,15:2
Martland, Harrison S Sr, 1954, My 2,88:4
Martlock, J Frank, 1950, Mr 30,29:4
Martocci, Frank, 1954, Mr 6,15:4
Martocci, Victor, 1959, N 21,23:4
Martoccio, Joseph, 1965, N 2,34:1
Martos, Miguel O, 1942, My 6,19:4
Martow, Julius, 1923, Ap 6,17:4
Marts, Arnaud C Mrs, 1953, Ja 7,31:1
Martsch, John H, 1952, F 12,27:1
Martucci, Alice, 1950, Mr 19,92:7
Martucci, John, 1956, Jl 19,27:2
Martucci, Louis A Dr, 1937, Ag 14,13:2
Martucci, Samuel M, 1958, Ag 26,29:2
Martus, Florence M, 1943, F 10,25:4
Martvon, John, 1948, Mr 24,25:2
Martwick, William Lorimer, 1968, Ag 25,88:8
Marty, Andre, 1956, N 24,19:1
Marty, Frank C, 1950, Ag 8,29:5
Marty, Leon D, 1940, D 22,30:7
Martyn, Charles P, 1939, Ag 30,17:2
Martyn, Edward, 1923, D 7,21:5
Martyn, Gilbert, 1959, Ja 25,92:5
Martyn, Henry H, 1938, F 12,15:2
Martyn, Henry L, 1947, Ja 10,21:2
Martyn, Ida D Mrs, 1952, O 8,31:4
Martyn, James W, 1938, S 12,17:4
Martyn, Marty, 1964, D 28,29:3
Martyn, Montague T, 1948, S 29,29:5
Martyn, Peter, 1955, F 17,27:3
Martz, John G, 1940, N 19,23:6
Maruca, Joseph, 1948, Je 27,52:3
Marucci, Frank, 1956, D 16,86:1
Marucci, Matthew N, 1958, O 20,29:5
Maruchess, Boris (por), 1938, Ap 21,19:2
Maruffi, Paolo, 1938, Mr 8,19:2
Marum, Ludwig, 1952, Jl 31,23:3
Marus, John, 1952, O 28,31:1
Maruzzella, Charles, 1964, D 17,41:4
Maruzzella, Jasper, 1964, Je 15,29:4
Marval, Juan A de, 1948, Je 3,25:4
Marvan, J Arthur, 1964, Mr 17,35:2
Marvel, Frederick Mrs, 1950, F 17,23:3
Marvel, Frederick W, 1938, Ag 22,13:4
Marvel, George E, 1948, F 21,13:3
Marvel, George E Mrs, 1962, Jl 20,25:1
Marvel, Harry A, 1947, Ag 3,53:1
Marvel, I K, 1908, D 16,11:4
Marvel, J, 1930, O 12,II,6:3
Marvel, Jackson, 1942, S 27,49:2
Marvel, Jane, 1941, D 17,27:5
Marvel, Josiah Jr, 1955, D 30,19:4
Marvel, Orin E (por), 1941, Mr 4,23:3
Marvel, Phil, 1938, S 8,26:2
Marvel, Philip H, 1963, My 14,39:4
Marvel, T S, 1916, O 26,11:7
Marvel, Thomas S, 1937, Ja 24,II,8:2
Marvel, Thomas W, 1949, N 20,94:1
Marvel, William P, 1938, Ja 12,21:3
Marvell, George, 1957, Ap 11,31:1
Marvell, George R (por), 1941, N 13,28:2
Marvell, Mary W, 1952, Ag 10,61:2
Marvell, Robert, 1952, F 8,23:5
Marvell, Sumner E, 1953, N 6,27:1
Marvelle, Bernard, 1960, D 29,25:2
Marvelle, Ward B, 1946, Ag 27,27:4
Marvil, J H Gov, 1895, Ap 9,1:1
Marvill, Horace K, 1950, Ja 17,27:3
Marvin, A B, 1875, D 4,4:7
Marvin, Alexander Burr, 1922, Mr 17,17:6
Marvin, Alfred, 1942, Ag 14,17:4
Marvin, Alfred E, 1946, F 13,23:4
Marvin, Arba B 2d, 1960, Ap 29,31:2
Marvin, Arthur L, 1944, Ja 22,13:1
Marvin, Benjamin, 1968, O 5,35:6
Marvin, Bp, 1877, N 30,5:5
Marvin, C R, 1883, Jl 8,7:5
Marvin, Charles F, 1943, Je 6,42:6
Marvin, Claude E, 1940, My 26,35:1
Marvin, Constantine K, 1950, Je 12,27:2
Marvin, Dan Rev, 1915, Jl 26,9:6
Marvin, David M (por), 1949, Ag 23,23:4
Marvin, David M Mrs, 1954, N 18,33:6
Marvin, Dwight E, 1940, F 29,19:5
Marvin, Ezra, 1914, Ap 26,IV,7:6
Marvin, Fred R, 1939, Jl 15,15:6
Marvin, Frederick B, 1958, D 29,15:2
Marvin, George, 1955, D 24,13:4
Marvin, George R, 1937, Ja 20,21:1
Marvin, George S, 1906, Ap 24,11:4
Marvin, Harry N, 1940, Ja 13,15:3
Marvin, J Clifford, 1957, Jl 12,21:4
Marvin, J D, 1877, Ap 13,5:4
Marvin, James S, 1954, Jl 13,23:5
Marvin, Jane Elizabeth, 1925, My 19,21:4
Marvin, Langdon P, 1957, O 15,33:3
Marvin, Louise H Mrs, 1939, Je 16,23:3
Marvin, Mark, 1958, Mr 8,15:3
Marvin, Reignold K, 1948, N 4,30:3
Marvin, Reinold C, 1951, Jl 21,13:5
Marvin, Robert T Mrs, 1953, Je 23,29:4
Marvin, Ross G Prof (mem), 1910, Ap 25,9:4
Marvin, S Webster, 1943, Mr 18,19:2
Marvin, Samuel W, 1923, Ja 3,13:4
Marvin, Selden Erastus, 1907, Jl 2,9:6
Marvin, T R, 1882, My 11,2:4
Marvin, W G, 1932, Ja 6,21:1
Marvin, Walter, 1945, My 2,23:4; 1954, D 21,27:
Marvin, Walter R Jr Mrs, 1957, Mr 30,19:5
Marvin, Walter T (por), 1944, My 27,15:3
Marvin, Walter T Mrs, 1965, F 28,88:5
Marvin, William E, 1938, S 29,25:2
Marvine, W H, 1877, D 19,4:7
Marvingt, Marie, 1963, D 16,33:4
Marwell, Israel, 1940, N 10,57:1
Marwick, Maurice, 1948, Jl 23,19:3
Marwick, Sarah B Mrs, 1945, Ag 23,23:5
Marwig, Carl, 1914, N 18,11:6
Marwood, W, 1883, S 5,5:3
Marx, Aaron H, 1950, Ag 3,23:4
Marx, Alex, 1951, O 20,15:4; 1953, D 27,60:7
Marx, Alex Mrs, 1962, Jl 26,27:4
Marx, Arthur, 1959, S 30,29:6

Marx, Benjamin, 1938, Ag 24,21:5
Marx, Benjamin Mrs, 1958, S 3,33:4
Marx, Charles, 1947, Ja 10,22:3
Marx, Charles D, 1940, Ja 1,24:2
Marx, Dave A, 1944, Ja 30,38:5
Marx, Edward Mrs, 1953, D 18,29:1
Marx, Eliza, 1952, Ap 18,25:2
Marx, Emily, 1966, Je 9,47:4
Marx, Erich A, 1956, F 2,25:4
Marx, Ferdinand, 1946, Ag 22,27:3
Marx, Guido, 1949, S 12,21:5
Marx, Gustav L, 1950, N 22,25:5
Marx, Harpo (Arth),(trb, S 30,42:2; est appr, O 6,-78:6), 1964, S 29,1:2
Marx, Harry S, 1948, Ag 7,15:5
Marx, Henry, 1956, N 17,21:2; 1960, F 10,37:4
Marx, Herman, 1944, Mr 27,19:4
Marx, Hermann Mrs, 1943, O 22,17:3
Marx, Jackson H, 1939, S 15,23:4
Marx, Jacob H, 1957, S 30,31:1
Marx, John W, 1967, Ap 15,31:3
Marx, Joseph L Mrs, 1949, S 20,29:1
Marx, Karl, 1883, Mr 17,3:2; 1966, D 16,47:2
Marx, Karl Dr, 1871, S 6,4:7
Marx, Leo, 1925, Ag 10,13:4
Marx, Leonard (Chico),(funl, O 14,12:4), 1961, O 12,29:2
Marx, Louis, 1943, O 25,15:4
Marx, Marcus, 1921, Ag 5,13:5
Marx, Morris, 1954, F 28,93:1
Marx, Morris H, 1953, S 4,34:2
Marx, Otto Sr, 1963, Je 1,21:5
Marx, Philip, 1913, Je 8,IV,5:6
Marx, Rachel Mrs, 1941, N 23,53:1
Marx, Richard L, 1962, Jl 23,21:4
Marx, Robert S, 1960, S 7,37:5
Marx, Samuel (funl, D 4,17:4), 1922, D 1,17:4
Marx, Samuel A, 1964, Ja 18,23:4
Marx, Simon Dr, 1914, Je 17,11:6
Marx, Valentine J, 1950, My 20,15:2
Marx, Wilhelm, 1946, Ag 7,27:1
Marxhausen, August, 1920, N 3,11:5
Marxhausen, George H, 1939, O 2,17:6
Marxuach, Teofilo, 1939, N 9,23:5
Mary, Cleophas Sister, 1903, My 24,77:4
Mary, Countess of Dartrey, 1939, My 5,23:1
Mary, Jules, 1922, Jl 28,13:5
Mary, Mother (L M Prevost), 1950, Ja 12,28:3
Mary, Mother (S C Dunne), 1953, Ap 30,31:5
Mary, Princess of Baden, 1904, Je 5,4:1
Mary, Princess Royal of G B (Victoria Alexander Alice Mary), 1965, Mr 29,33:1
Mary, Rev Mother, 1938, D 2,23:3
Mary, Sister, 1943, Ja 26,20:2
Mary, Sister (Sisters of Good Shepherd), 1951, N 4, 86:6
Mary, Sister (Sisters of the Good Shepherd), 1951, N 16,25:5
Mary, Sister (J Martin), 1964, F 5,35:3
Mary Adelaide, Sister, 1943, Ap 22,23:4
Mary Adele, Sister, 1922, Je 12,15:6; 1950, Je 22,27:2
Mary Adele, Sister (Doody), 1950, Ag 13,76:3
Mary Agatha, Mother, 1949, My 16,21:2
Mary Agatha, Mother (Browne), 1964, F 8,23:5
Mary Agatha, Sister, 1941, Ag 16,15:4
Mary Agatha, Sister (Sisters of Mercy), 1952, Ja 10, 29:3
Mary Agnes, Mother, 1949, Jl 22,19:5
Mary Agnes, Mother (Franciscan Nuns), 1962, N 4, 88:8
Mary Agnes, Rev Mother, 1905, Mr 10,9:7
Mary Agnes, Sister (M Bigot), 1950, Jl 14,21:5
Mary Agnes Alma, Sister (A S McDonald), 1959, Ap 9,31:4
Mary Agnita, Sister (Reilly), 1963, Jl 20,19:3
Mary Aguinas, Sister (Brady), 1955, Jl 6,27:1
Mary Ahern, Mother, 1949, Je 15,29:5
Mary Aid, Sister, 1942, My 18,15:2
Mary Alain, Sister, 1944, S 8,19:3
Mary Alberta, Sister (Hettel), 1951, Mr 18,89:1
Mary Albertonia, Sister (Congregation of St Agnes), 1957, D 29,49:2
Mary Alcuin, Sister, 1938, Ja 18,23:3
Mary Alexander, Sister, 1948, Jl 23,19:4
Mary Alexandrine, Mother, 1940, D 7,17:4
Mary Alexine, Mother (Gosselin), 1950, Jl 12,29:2
Mary Alexis, Sister (A Gass), 1952, Mr 21,23:2
Mary Alice, Mother (Sisters of the 3d Order),(funl, N 11,31:2), 1960, N 8,29:4
Mary Alice, Sister, 1938, Je 8,23:6
Mary Alicia, Sister, 1947, F 19,25:1
Mary Alinda, Sister, 1939, O 17,25:4
Mary Alodia, Mother (Carmelite), 1959, Ag 16,82:5
Mary Aloyse, Mother (Dominican Order), 1961, Ag 2,29:3
Mary Aloysia, Mother (C A Kelly), 1953, D 30,23:2
Mary Aloysius, Sister, 1939, Ja 22,35:3; 1947, O 11, 17:1; 1948, Ja 13,25:2
Mary Aloysius, Sister (R A Roan), 1951, Ap 29,89:1
Mary Aloysius, Sister (Molloy), 1954, S 30,31:3
Mary Aloysius, Sister (Order of St Dominic), 1966, Ap 19,41:2
Mary Aloysius Blakeley, Sister, 1942, Jl 16,19:2
Mary Alphonsus, Mother, 1943, Je 2,25:2
Mary Alphonsus, Sister, 1944, O 6,23:3
Mary Alphonsus, Sister (McGoldrick), 1961, F 15, 35:4
Mary Ambrose, Mother (Sisters of Mercy), 1951, Ap 14,16:2
Mary Anastasia, Sister, 1942, Ap 22,23:4; 1953, Ag 8, 11:2
Mary Angela, Mother, 1944, Ap 26,19:6
Mary Angela, Mother (Fohs), 1964, S 24,41:1
Mary Angela, Sister (A M Stader), 1952, S 28,77:2
Mary Angela, Sister (M M Walker), 1953, D 14,31:3
Mary Angela, Sister (Sisters of Charity), 1956, F 2, 25:5
Mary Angela, Sister (F R Malone), 1965, My 5,47:4
Mary Angelica, Sister (Gordon), 1949, Jl 6,27:4
Mary Angelica, Sister, 1950, Ap 19,29:3
Mary Angelica, Sister (M Walsh), 1953, My 26,29:6
Mary Angeline, Mother, 1945, D 17,22:2
Mary Aniceta, Sister, 1949, O 2,80:7
Mary Anne, Mother (Sisters of Notre Dame), 1917, Ja 17,9:3
Mary Antoinette, Sister (Sisters of St Joseph), 1952, F 9,13:6
Mary Antonia, Sister (W Sweeney), 1952, Mr 30,94:1
Mary Antonine, Sister, 1945, S 8,15:5
Mary Antonine, Sister (Holy Cross Order), 1951, Ap 14,15:5
Mary Antoninus, Sister, 1948, Jl 2,21:5
Mary Antonio Babb, Sister, 1948, My 20,29:1
Mary Antony, Sister (Community of St Mary), 1960, Ap 25,29:3
Mary Aquinas, Mother (Sisters of St Dominic), 1957, My 11,21:7
Mary Aquinas, Sister (M Doyle), 1940, My 24,19:4
Mary Athanasius, Sister (Caring), 1968, Je 9,84:7
Mary Augusta, Sister, 1942, Ap 23,23:4; 1946, Ap 25, 21:2
Mary Augustine, Mother Superior, 1938, Ja 22,15:5
Mary Augustine, Sister, 1946, F 13,23:5
Mary Augustine, Sister (Sisters of Mercy), 1963, Ap 11,33:1
Mary Austin, Sister (H Coad), 1951, Ap 14,15:4
Mary Austin, Sister (M Stebbins), 1957, Ja 1,8:5
Mary Auxentia, Sister (Sisters of the Poor of St Francis), 1955, O 21,27:3
Mary Avellino, Sister (Sisters of Mercy), 1953, Ja 17,15:3
Mary Basil, Sister, 1950, Jl 23,56:1
Mary Beata, Sister (Sisters of Charity), 1960, Ja 15, 31:2
Mary Beatrice, Sister, 1944, O 17,23:6; 1945, O 7,44:4
Mary Beatrice, Sister (McMullin), 1964, Je 5,31:2
Mary Bellina, Sister, 1938, Mr 19,15:4
Mary Benedict, Sister, 1940, Mr 25,15:2
Mary Benedict Concha, Sister, 1945, D 12,27:4
Mary Benigna McCabe, Sister, 1937, Ap 2,23:4
Mary Benita, Mother (M Kane), 1953, O 4,87:1
Mary Berchmans, Sister, 1962, Ap 18,39:1
Mary Bernadetta, Sister, 1942, S 23,26:2
Mary Bernadette, Sister (Smith), 1950, F 22,29:2
Mary Bernadine, Sister (Caroline Otto), 1956, Jl 12, 23:3
Mary Bernard, Sister (Benedictine Order), 1955, Ap 8,21:3
Mary Bernardetta, Sister, 1938, Je 1,23:2
Mary Bernardine, Sister, 1942, S 2,23:5
Mary Bernardine, Sister (St Joseph), 1952, Jl 23,23:4
Mary Bernardini, Sister, 1939, Ap 11,24:3
Mary Bernice, Mother (Franciscan Sisters), 1951, O 2,28:3
Mary Bertrand, Mother, 1946, My 20,24:3
Mary Bertrand, Sister (O'Neill), 1949, Ap 14,25:2
Mary Blanche, Sister, 1945, Ap 5,23:1
Mary Blandina, Sister, 1939, S 15,23:1
Mary Boleslawa, Sister, 1965, Je 20,72:3
Mary Bonaventure, Sister (Dominican Order), 1955, My 14,19:3
Mary Borgia, Mother, 1937, Mr 23,24:2
Mary Borromeo, Sister (L M O'Brien), 1950, Je 26, 27:5
Mary Bridget, Sister, 1948, Ap 21,27:2
Mary Cajetan, Sister, 1944, Ap 29,15:5
Mary Camillus, Sister, 1945, Jl 18,27:6
Mary Capilano, Indian Princess, 1940, D 17,25:2
Mary Carmel, Sister, 1943, Mr 28,24:5
Mary Carmelita, Mother (M E Hartman), 1952, My 20,25:3
Mary Carmelita, Sister, 1941, Je 13,19:4; 1945, N 13, 22:3; 1947, D 30,23:4; 1948, Ag 25,25:4
Mary Carmita, Sister, 1945, Ja 13,11:4
Mary Cath, Sister (Fitzgerald), 1964, Ag 29,21:6
Mary Catharine, Sister, 1911, Mr 31,11:4
Mary Catherine, Sister (Brett), 1951, Jl 7,13:6
Mary Catherine, Sister, 1958, Ag 26,29:1
Mary Catherine Herbert, Mother, 1944, Mr 29,21:5
Mary Cecelia, Mother (W Norton), 1954, Je 3,27:3
Mary Cecelia, Sister (Sisters of Mercy), 1951, Mr 23,21:2
Mary Cecelia, 1909, N 23,9:5
Mary Cecilia, Mother, 1953, F 3,25:2
Mary Cecilia, Mother (Reed), 1961, F 15,35:3
Mary Cecilia, Sister (M G Fitzgerald), 1950, O 3, 31:1
Mary Cecilia, Sister (Spillane), 1952, D 16,31:3
Mary Cecily, Mother, 1947, My 5,23:3
Mary Celeste, Sister, 1947, Ag 23,13:6
Mary Celestia, Sister (Community of St Joseph), 1951, S 14,25:2
Mary Celestine, Sister, 1923, Ja 6,13:4
Mary Celestine, Sister (Sisters of St Joseph), 1954, Jl 3,11:6
Mary Chaminade, Sister (Dreisoerner), 1958, Ap 14, 25:2
Mary Charles, Mother (Borromeo), 1951, Ja 12,27:4
Mary Cherubim, Sister, 1944, My 10,19:1
Mary Christells, Sister (Sisters of Charity), 1951, Mr 4,93:1
Mary Christine, Sister (Barrett), 1949, Jl 20,25:2
Mary Claire, Mother (M A Barnett), 1956, Ag 28, 27:3
Mary Clara, Sister, 1946, F 20,25:1
Mary Clare, Sister, 1939, D 19,26:2; 1946, F 18,21:2
Mary Clare, Sister (Wiest), 1951, Ag 31,15:2
Mary Clarence, Sister, 1950, Je 14,31:2
Mary Clarissa, Sister, 1938, Ap 8,19:5
Mary Claudia, Mother, 1940, Ap 15,17:1
Mary Claudia, Sister (M A McFadden), 1952, D 27, 9:2
Mary Claudia, Sister (M Carolan), 1965, N 6,47:1
Mary Clemence, Sister (Burns), 1951, S 13,31:3
Mary Clement, Sister (Mary Brennan), 1967, O 27, 45:4
Mary Clement Marie, Sister (Servants of Immaculate Heart, 1957, Ap 18,29:2
Mary Cleophas, Mother, 1946, Ja 7,20:2
Mary Clotilde, Mother (Ursuline Order), 1955, Ap 12,29:2
Mary Colette, Mother (Carmelite Sisters), 1956, Ag 21,29:2
Mary Compassio, Mother (E M Harris), 1951, Ap 10,27:3
Mary Concepta, Mother, 1946, F 2,13:3
Mary Concepta, Sister (J Martin), 1950, S 28,31:1
Mary Concepta, Sister (M Lanigan), 1959, My 20, 35:4
Mary Consilio, Sister (Sisters of Mercy), 1966, Mr 29,41:2
Mary Constance, Sister, 1940, Ag 13,19:1; 1948, Mr 23,25:1
Mary Cora, Mother (Sisters of St Joseph), 1952, My 7,27:3
Mary Coralita, Sister (C Cullinan), 1956, F 5,86:4
Mary Cornelia, Sister (E Roach), 1950, N 4,17:5
Mary Cornelia, Sister (Gallagher), 1962, Ap 19,31:4
Mary Damian, Mother (St Francis Order), 1953, F 28,17:6
Mary Delmatia, Sister (J Finegan), 1949, D 15,35:4
Mary De Lourdes, Sister (M B Hartley), 1951, Ap 15,92:2
Mary Denise, Sister, 1942, Mr 4,19:2
Mary de Paul, Sister (C I Cogan), 1953, N 19,31:5
Mary De Sales, Sister, 1938, O 11,25:5
Mary de Sales, Sister, 1939, Ag 3,19:4
Mary Dolores, Mother (Order of Mercy), 1952, Ag 16,15:2
Mary Dolorosa, Mother (M Farnon), 1952, O 25,17:3
Mary Dominic, Mother (Ward), 1959, Ja 12,39:4
Mary Dominic, Sister, 1948, Ag 31,24:2
Mary Dominic, Sister (Order of Sick and Poor), 1958, F 18,27:2
Mary Dominic, Sister (Congregation of St Catherine De Ricci), 1961, Ag 26,17:6
Mary Dominica, Mother, 1937, Jl 7,23:2
Mary Dominica, Sister, 1942, Je 17,23:3
Mary Domitella, Sister, 1944, N 11,13:5
Mary Domitilla, Sister, 1955, F 19,15:4
Mary Donald, Sister (Sisters of Mercy), 1953, D 10, 48:3
Mary Durkin, Sister (M A Durkin), 1941, Jl 9,21:5
Mary Edilburga, Sister (Puschel), 1965, My 22,31:1
Mary Edmund, Sister (M D Glynn), 1942, Je 17,23:6
Mary Eduardus, Sister, 1942, Ap 7,21:3
Mary Edw, Mother (A McDermott), 1953, F 7,15:5
Mary Edwarda M, Sister, 1937, Ja 15,21:4
Mary Edwards, Mother (Dominican Sisters), 1954, S 1,27:4
Mary Eileen, Sister (Sisters of Charity), 1962, Ja 7, 88:5
Mary Eleanor, Mother (Sisters of St Joseph), 1958, O 10,31:1
Mary Eleanor, Sister (Keogh), 1953, S 2,25:1
Mary Elenita, Mother (E Barry), 1955, Ja 13,27:5
Mary Elias, Mother, 1943, Mr 2,19:1
Mary Elizabeth, sister, 1945, N 3,15:4
Mary Eloise, Sister, 1955, Mr 31,27:5
Mary Emelia, Sister (Benedictine Order), 1955, Mr 7,27:4
Mary Emmanuel, Mother, 1941, N 21,17:2
Mary Emmanuel, Mother (Conlon), 1964, F 15,23:3
Mary Enrica, Sister, 1943, Je 29,19:4
Mary Ephram, Sister (Sisters of Charity), 1957, My 31,19:4
Mary Ernestine, Sister (Reilly), 1952, Ja 24,27:2
Mary Esther, Mother (Order of Missionary Canonesses), 1952, N 3,27:4

Mary Ethelbert, Sister (Cahill), 1949, S 23,24:3
Mary Ethelreda, Sister (Sisters of Mercy), 1953, Ja 2,15:2
Mary Eudosia, Sister (A Godzinski), 1955, N 3,31:5
Mary Eugenia, Sister, 1947, Mr 8,13:4
Mary Eugenia, Sister (Meyer), 1954, Ap 2,27:2
Mary Eugenia, Sister (Servants of Immaculate Heart of Mary), 1967, Ap 8,31:4
Mary Eulalia, Mother, 1946, Ag 8,21:4
Mary Eulalia, Sister (Carroll), 1950, My 11,29:1
Mary Eulalia, Sister (Sisters of Mercy), 1952, Mr 12,27:1
Mary Eulalia Herron, Sister, 1954, Ag 11,25:5
Mary Eunice Joy, Sister (Sinsinawa Order), 1955, Ja 14,21:3
Mary Euphrasia, Sister (Sisters of Mercy), 1952, O 17,27:3
Mary Euphrasia, Sister (St Francis Order), 1955, S 3,15:6
Mary Eustochia, Sister, 1942, F 16,17:4
Mary Evangelist, Sister (M Crotty), 1940, O 19,17:6
Mary Evangelist, Sister, 1946, Jl 3,25:4
Mary Evangelista, Sister (M O'Connell), 1955, Mr 24,31:3
Mary Evaristus, Mother (Sisters of Charity), 1953, O 21,30:6
Mary Evelyn, Mother (K Murphy), 1955, S 13,31:2
Mary Eymard, Sister (M Diamond), 1965, My 7,41:2
Mary Fabian, Sister, 1917, D 11,15:6
Mary Felicitas, Sister, 1949, Je 17,23:3
Mary Felix, Sister (Dominican Order), 1955, Ja 11, 25:2
Mary Ferdinand, Sister (M Calvano), 1952, Ap 23, 29:4
Mary Fidelia, Mother (Sisters of St Joseph), 1952, Mr 26,29:1
Mary Fidelis, Mother, 1946, S 25,27:3
Mary Fidelis, Sister, 1943, S 10,23:3; 1945, O 26,19:3
Mary Fides, Sister (Sisters of St Joseph), 1957, My 6,29:2
Mary Flavia, Sister (Sisters of St Dominic), 1957, N 2,21:1
Mary Florence, Mother (J Brennan), 1940, D 4,27:1
Mary Florence, Sister, 1938, D 20,26:1
Mary Florian, Sister, 1943, Je 2,25:4
Mary Florisenda, Mother (M Egan), 1949, D 5,23:3
Mary Fortunata, Sister (Sisters of Notre Dame), 1954, My 5,31:2
Mary Francesca, Mother, 1947, Ja 1,33:2
Mary Francesca, Sister (D Spaziani), 1950, F 28,29:5
Mary Francesca, Sister, 1953, Ja 22,23:4
Mary Francesca, Sister (McDonough), 1956, Ag 19, 92:5
Mary Francina, Mother, 1944, D 27,19:4
Mary Francis, Sister, 1940, F 12,17:5
Mary Francis, Sister (A Maher), 1940, My 23,23:4
Mary Francis, Sister, 1946, Ag 21,27:6
Mary Francis, Sister (Sisters of St Joseph), 1953, Ap 28,27:2
Mary Francis, Sister (3d Order of St Francis), 1955, Je 8,29:6
Mary Francis, Sister (Spellman), 1957, S 27,19:4
Mary Francis, Sister, 1959, Ag 1,17:3
Mary Francis, Sister (Donnelly), 1960, Jl 24,65:2
Mary Francis Borgia, Sister (Sisters of St Joseph), 1955, Ap 28,29:1
Mary Frederica, Sister, 1949, Ja 8,15:4
Mary Gabriel, Mother (K McNamara), 1956, D 27, 25:4
Mary Gabriel, Sister, 1947, Jl 28,15:3
Mary Gabriel, Sister (Benedictine Order), 1954, Mr 9,27:4
Mary Genevieve, Mother, 1947, N 8,17:6
Mary Genevieve, Sister (Donovan), 1962, Mr 18, 86:4
Mary Genovessa, Sister (Sisters of Charity), 1959, Je 9,37:4
Mary Geraldine, Mother (Sisters of St Dominic), 1964, D 29,27:3
Mary Geraldine, Sister, 1944, Ag 20,34:2
Mary Gerardus, Sister (Lanigan), 1952, Jl 14,17:4
Mary Germaine, Sister, 1945, Mr 16,15:2
Mary Gertrude, Mother, 1959, Ag 16,82:8
Mary Gertrude, Sister (Quinlan), 1949, My 5,28:3
Mary Giles, Sister, 1937, Ja 21,23:3
Mary Godoleva, Sister, 1948, Jl 5,15:5
Mary Gonsolva, Sister (M Burke), 1953, My 13,29:3
Mary Gonzaga, Sister (McDonough), 1951, S 29,17:3
Mary Gonzaga, Sister (Sisters of Mercy), 1959, Ja 18,88:4
Mary Gregoria, Sister, 1941, Mr 4,23:3
Mary Guillelma, Sister, 1946, D 9,25:4
Mary Gwendoline, Sister, 1941, Ap 9,25:6
Mary Helen, Mother, 1944, Jl 19,19:1
Mary Henrica, Sister, 1945, Ap 27,19:2
Mary Hilarion, Sister (M Sullivan), 1957, Mr 29,21:3
Mary Hilda, Sister (Servants of the Immaculate Heart), 1954, Je 1,27:4
Mary Hilda, Sister (Sisters of St Dominic), 1955, Mr 11,25:1
Mary Hildegarde, Sister, 1945, F 12,19:2
Mary Huberta, Sister, 1944, Ag 7,15:5
Mary Hubertine, Sister (L Coolican), 1959, O 13,39:4
Mary Humbeline, Sister, 1947, Ja 8,23:4
Mary Hyacinth, Mother (S A Fitzgerald), 1940, D 20,25:4
Mary Hyacinth, Sister, 1942, Ja 12,15:2
Mary Ignatius, Mother, 1939, Jl 31,13:5
Mary Imelda, Sister, 1943, F 13,11:2
Mary Immaculata, Mother, 1948, Mr 4,25:4
Mary Immaculata, Sister, 1947, O 27,21:2
Mary Immaculata, Sister (E A Roarke), 1949, Mr 18,25:4
Mary Immaculata, Sister (Dillon), 1949, S 16,27:3
Mary Irene, Sister (Cullinane), 1950, Je 8,31:4
Mary Irma, Sister, 1939, My 30,17:3
Mary Irma, Sister (Sisters of Charity), 1958, F 12, 29:2
Mary Irmine, Sister, 1950, My 9,29:4
Mary Ita, Mother, 1949, O 14,27:4
Mary James, Mother, 1917, N 7,13:2; 1948, S 27,23:4
Mary James, Sister (Tower), 1967, O 3,47:1
Mary James Rogers, Mother, 1942, My 26,21:2
Mary Jerome, Sister (C Donovan), 1964, Ap 19,84:8
Mary Joachim, Mother, 1942, Jl 24,20:2
Mary Joan, Sister (Hession), 1966, F 15,36:2
Mary Jodoca, Sister, 1948, Ja 19,23:2
Mary John, Mother (H Considine), 1951, F 2,24:2
Mary John, Sister, 1946, F 10,40:5; 1948, Jl 4,26:8
Mary John, Sister (Berchmans), 1951, My 8,31:3
Mary John, Sister (Presentation Sisters), 1960, Ja 10,86:8
Mary John Berchmans, Sister, 1943, S 25,15:3
Mary Joseph, Mother, 1944, S 29,21:4
Mary Joseph, Mother (M Rogers),(funl plans, O 12,29:1), 1955, O 10,27:1
Mary Joseph, Mother (M Dunn), 1956, Mr 31,15:5
Mary Joseph, Sister (M Friel), 1951, Ag 1,23:4
Mary Joseph, Sister (Sisters of Providence), 1956, Jl 20,17:3
Mary Joseph Sacramentini, Sister, 1947, Mr 24,25:2
Mary Josepha, Mother, 1940, D 5,25:5
Mary Josepha, Sister, 1940, Mr 19,25:5; 1949, O 24, 23:2
Mary Josephine, Mother (Taaffe), 1965, Ja 9,25:5
Mary Josephine, Sister, 1948, Je 2,20:1
Mary Josephine, Sister (Malone), 1959, N 16,31:4
Mary Joy, Sister (D Manzer), 1965, My 5,47:5
Mary Jude Marie, Sister (Benedictine Order), 1955, Ap 26,29:3
Mary Julia, Sister, 1944, My 27,15:4
Mary Just, Sister (F D David), 1959, Je 26,25:2
Mary Kathleen, Mother (Servants of Immaculate Heart of Mary), 1962, F 1,31:1
Mary Kathleen, Sister, 1943, N 25,25:3
Mary Kevin, Mother (Sisters of St Thomas of Villanova), 1962, Mr 4,86:4
Mary Lamberta, Sister (Dowling), 1952, S 17,31:5
Mary Laura, Sister, 1948, Mr 6,13:3
Mary Laurentina, Sister, 1942, O 9,21:2
Mary Laurentine, Sister, 1941, F 2,44:1
Mary Laurietta, Sister (Speddy), 1950, Ag 9,29:4
Mary Laurinda, Sister (Blessed Virgin Mary Order), 1958, My 8,29:1
Mary Lavinia, Sister (J Ash), 1950, N 22,25:2
Mary Lazare, Sister (O'Hare), 1949, Ap 20,27:2
Mary Lelia, Sister, 1954, Jl 4,30:8
Mary Leona, Sister (Franciscan Order), 1955, My 10,29:1
Mary Leona, Sister (A Lawlor), 1963, Ap 19,43:2
Mary Leonita, Sister (Sisters of Charity), 1955, O 19,33:5
Mary Liboria H, Sister, 1937, Ja 15,22:1
Mary Liguori, Sister (A O'Hara), 1954, Je 14,21:4
Mary Liliose, Sister, 1947, O 17,21:3
Mary Lioba, Sister, 1947, O 24,23:3
Mary Liquori, Mother (McHale), 1963, O 17,35:4
Mary Lizette, Sister (Sisters of Charity), 1960, Ap 28,35:4
Mary Longinus, Sister, 1947, F 4,25:5
Mary Loretta, Sister (I McGill), 1954, My 3,25:2
Mary Lorretto, Mother, 1940, D 31,15:5
Mary Louisa, Sister (L Dockwiller), 1954, Jl 17,13:5
Mary Louise, Dowager Marchioness of Queensberry, 1956, Ap 7,19:5
Mary Louise, Sister (Efinger), 1953, Mr 24,31:3
Mary Loyola, Mother (S Gannon), 1957, My 14,35:4
Mary Loyola, Sister (Hayde), 1950, F 7,27:3
Mary Luana, Sister (M Shanley), 1954, D 1,31:4
Mary Lucille, Sister, 1947, D 3,29:5
Mary Lucita, Sister, 1947, Ja 31,23:3
Mary Lucy, Sister (E Abell), 1964, O 2,37:4
Mary Ludwina, Sister, 1938, D 24,15:6
Mary M Dominic, Sister, 1945, Ap 17,23:5
Mary Madeleine, Sister, 1945, D 22,19:1
Mary Madeleva, Sister (M E Wolff), 1964, Jl 26,57:2
Mary Magdalene, Sister, 1937, Jl 21,21:6
Mary Magdalent, Sister, 1945, Mr 25,37:1
Mary Malachy, Sister (E Cody), 1951, D 26,25:5
Mary Mamerta, Sister (Sisters of the Poor), 1965, Ap 21,45:5
Mary Marcella, Mother (Immaculate Heart of Mary), 1955, S 15,33:1
Mary Marcelline, Sister, 1949, Mr 29,25:3
Mary Margaret, Sister (Sisters of Charity), 1955, Ap 5,29:4
Mary Margaret Byrne, Sister, 1948, O 23,15:2
Mary Margarita, Sister (H Whelan), 1959, Je 3,35:2
Mary Margt, Mother, 1948, Mr 23,25:2
Mary Margt, Sister (E Mulligan), 1964, Ag 11,33:4
Mary Maria Ambrosia, Sister, 1944, D 9,15:4
Mary Marion, Sister (Mary Gannon), 1958, Ap 1, 31:1
Mary Mark, Sister (Sisters of St Joseph), 1951, N 19,23:3
Mary Martha, Sister (Sisters of Charity), 1915, Je 23,11:4
Mary Martha, Sister, 1941, Ja 26,36:2; 1944, N 17, 19:1; 1948, Ja 8,25:4
Mary Matthias, Sister (A Gannon), 1949, O 12,30:3
Mary Maurice, Mother (Tobin), 1959, Mr 6,25:2
Mary Mechtilde, Sister, 1939, Je 11,45:2
Mary Mechtildes, Mother, 1950, My 24,30:3
Mary Medulpha Ebner, Mother, 1941, F 20,19:6
Mary Melania, Sister, 1948, Ja 22,27:5
Mary Melician Owens, Sister, 1938, D 31,15:7
Mary Melita Varner, Sister, 1937, D 8,25:4
Mary Mercedes, Mother, 1938, D 17,15:5; 1943, Ja 11,15:4
Mary Mercedes, Sister, 1938, Jl 9,13:3
Mary Mercedes, Sister (Hitchman), 1950, Jl 28,21:6
Mary Michael, Mother, 1948, D 5,92:4
Mary Michaella, Sister, 1937, Ap 10,19:5
Mary Mildred, Sister, 1947, Je 14,15:6
Mary Monica, Sister (M A Cahill), 1951, Jl 10,27:3
Mary Nativa, Sister, 1951, F 7,29:4
Mary Norberta, Sister (M Kelly), 1958, Je 27,25:2
Mary Norine, Sister (Keeshan), 1954, D 9,33:3
Mary Odila, Sister (Sisters of Notre Dame), 1951, O 3,36:2
Mary of Good Counsel, Mother, 1947, Ap 5,19:6
Mary of Nazareth, Sister (Sisters of St Joseph), 1953, Je 5,27:5
Mary of St Felix, Sister (M A Santa Anna), 1960, S 2,23:3
Mary of St John, Sister, 1939, Ag 1,19:6; 1942, My 20 19:1
Mary of St Veronica, Sister (L Cox), 1960, O 25,35:
Mary of St Wilfred, Mother (Soc of Mary Reparatrix), 1961, Ag 24,29:4
Mary of the Desert, Sister, 1939, Je 10,17:5
Mary of the Precious Blood, Mother, 1947, N 3,23:3
Mary Pancratia, Sister, 1944, Ag 23,19:4
Mary Paschal, Mother (Flannigan), 1949, S 17,17:4
Mary Patrice, Sister (Sisters of Mercy), 1957, N 8, 29:3
Mary Patricia, Sister, 1937, F 12,23:4
Mary Patricia, Sister (B Glynn), 1963, My 13,29:2
Mary Paul, Mother, 1921, S 5,11:6
Mary Pauline, Sister (Healey), 1949, F 7,19:5
Mary Pauline, Sister (Powers), 1962, S 18,39:1
Mary Perpetua, Sister, 1948, Ap 17,15:5
Mary Perpetua, Sister (Corcoran), 1959, N 25,29:2
Mary Perpetuum, Sister, 1943, Ag 14,11:1
Mary Petra, Mother, 1940, D 10,26:2
Mary Philip, Sister, 1938, D 29,19:4
Mary Philomena, Sister, 1939, Ap 11,24:3; 1943, Mr 30,21:3; 1944, S 20,13:2
Mary Pierre, Sister, 1946, Ja 10,23:3
Mary Praxedus, Mother Superior (Servants of Jusus Order), 1953, F 21,13:4
Mary Proteria, Sister, 1954, Jl 14,27:5
Mary Raphael, Mother, 1911, Jl 1,11:6
Mary Raphael, Sister, 1939, Ja 26,21:5; 1947, Jl 20, 45:2
Mary Raphael, Sister (Sisters of St Joseph), 1951, S 4,27:1
Mary Raymond, Sister (M Sandiford), 1959, S 1,29:
Mary Rebecca, Sister (M Comerford), 1950, Ag 13, 76:4
Mary Regina, Sister (Eliz Martin), 1943, S 28,25:5
Mary Regina, Sister (B O'Flynn), 1950, Jl 7,19:3
Mary Regina O'Donnell, Mother, 1946, N 26,29:3
Mary Reginald, Mother (Gaffney), 1963, N 27,37:3
Mary Regis, Mother (A Manion), 1962, Je 8,31:5
Mary Regulata, Sister (M Geary), 1961, S 19,35:4
Mary Reparata, Sister (Sisters of St Joseph), 1951, My 1,29:3
Mary Ricardo, Sister (Sisters of Mercy), 1959, Jl 1 19:5
Mary Rita, Very Rev Mother (Rowley), 1963, Jl 2, 29:1
Mary Roberta, Sister, 1938, Je 8,23:3
Mary Robertine, Sister, 1946, O 13,62:5
Mary Romana, Sister, 1949, Ja 8,15:6
Mary Rosa, Mother (McDonough), 1961, Ja 2,25:4
Mary Rosalita, Sister (Gallagher), 1951, Je 29,21:4
Mary Rosaria, Sister (E Georgia), 1958, F 13,29:3
Mary Rosarie, Mother, 1942, Jl 10,17:6
Mary Rose, Mother, 1942, O 1,23:3
Mary Rose, Sister, 1919, My 22,15:6; 1945, F 2,20:2
Mary Rose Alma, Sister (Dominican Order), 1951, Jl 25,23:2
Mary Rose De Lima, Sister, 1948, Jl 12,19:3
Mary Rose Eliz, Mother (Holy Cross Sisters), 196 D 2,47:1
Mary Rosemary, Sister (Malone), 1951, D 15,13:4
Mary Rudolpha, Sister (Rieder), 1961, Jl 26,31:4
Mary Scholastica, Mother, 1937, Je 20,II,7:1

Mary Scholastica, Sister, 1942, F 18,19:5; 1947, My 13,25:3
Mary Sebastian Mitchell, Sister, 1944, Ap 12,21:1
Mary Seraphim, Mother (A Lynch), 1953, N 4,33:2
Mary Seraphim, Sister, 1958, S 27,21:1
Mary Serena, Sister, 1947, D 27,13:2
Mary Servatia, Sister (Madigan), 1963, Jl 13,17:4
Mary Sheridan, Sister (M Sheridan), 1942, F 4,19:1
Mary Sienna, Sister, 1958, S 30,31:5
Mary Sister (Mary Madden), 1915, D 16,15:4
Mary St Anne, Mother (Kelly), 1959, Jl 9,27:3
Mary St Clare, Mother, 1941, Ja 26,37:1
Mary St Helen, Sister (Sisters of Charity), 1955, Ag 6,15:1
Mary St Henry, Sister, 1948, Ap 19,23:4
Mary St Hugh, Mother, 1947, Je 3,26:2
Mary St Jerome, Mother (F S Farrelly), 1942, My 29,17:4
Mary St Lawrence, Sister (Sisters of the Good Shepherd), 1953, Mr 7,15:2
Mary St Peter, Mother, 1942, My 26,21:3
Mary St Remi, Sister, 1946, Ag 13,27:2
Mary Stanislaus, Sister (A Spilker), 1959, Ag 27,27:1
Mary Stanislaus, Sister (Dominican), 1961, O 28, 21:2
Mary Stephen, Sister, 1918, Ap 18,13:8
Mary Sylveria, Sister, 1947, My 24,15:3
Mary Sylvester, Sister (Order of St Francis), 1954, Mr 16,29:2
Mary Sylvia, Sister (Morgan), 1964, Jl 25,19:5
Mary Terence, Sister (A Unhoch), 1956, O 12,29:4
Mary Teresa, Mother, 1942, Ja 12,15:4
Mary Teresa O'Brien, Sister, 1941, Jl 17,19:2
Mary Teresa of Jesus, Rev Mother (M C Foerster), 1959, N 19,39:2
Mary Teresita, Sister (Sisters of Mercy), 1956, D 2, 86:1
Mary Teresita, Sister (Order of St Francis), 1958, O 12,83:3
Mary Thecla, Sister (Hughes), 1951, Jl 22,60:2
Mary Theclan, Sister (E Tierney), 1951, F 21,27:5
Mary Thelca, Sister, 1944, My 24,19:5
Mary Theodora, Sister (Community of St Mary, PE), 1959, O 22,37:6
Mary Theodore, Sister, 1951, D 4,33:3
Mary Theodosia, Sister, 1943, Mr 25,21:5
Mary Theodosia, Sister (Servants of the Immaculate Heart), 1957, O 25,27:4
Mary Theophila, Mother, 1940, N 7,25:5
Mary Theophrista, Sister, 1942, S 13,53:3
Mary Theresa, Mother, 1950, Ja 11,23:6
Mary Theresa, Mother (Sibila), 1950, Mr 8,27:2
Mary Therese, Sister (Mercy Order), 1953, F 13,21:2
Mary Thersa, Sister, 1922, Ja 5,15:4
Mary Thomas, Sister, 1948, D 3,25:2; 1949, Je 21,25:3
Mary Thomas, Sister (Nihil), 1955, Jl 21,23:5
Mary Thomas Aquinas, Sister (Benedictine Order), 1955, Jl 30,17:6
Mary Thos Aquinas, Sister (Sloyan), 1964, Ag 17, 25:2
Mary Tryphosa, Sister (F Sander), 1958, My 27,31:2
Mary Ursula, Sister, 1874, Ap 11,1:6
Mary Ursula, Sister (Sisters of Providence), 1952, Ja 29,25:1
Mary Ursulina, Mother (Franciscan Sisters of Sacred Heart), 1961, Je 11,86:1
Mary Valeria, Sister (Daughters of Divine Redeemer), 1951, Mr 7,33:4
Mary Valerian, Sister, 1943, My 9,40:6
Mary Vera, Mother (Sisters of Notre Dame), 1962, Ap 16,29:5
Mary Veronica, Sister, 1943, D 15,27:5
Mary Veronica, Sister (H Devaney), 1951, N 4,87:2
Mary Veronica, Sister (Sisters of Charity), 1967, Ag 13,80:6
Mary Victoria, sister, 1945, F 23,17:2
Mary Victoria, Sister (H Kraak), 1960, Ja 23,21:5
Mary Victorine, Sister, 1945, S 24,19:3
Mary Vincent, Mother, 1946, Ja 29,25:3
Mary Vincent, Sister, 1941, Je 2,17:4
Mary Vincent, Sister (Hillman), 1962, D 4,41:4
Mary Vincent, Sister (Ralph), 1968, Jl 21,56:7
Mary Vincent de Paul, Sister (H S Giebel), 1955, Je 21,31:3
Mary Vincent de Paul, Sister (M J O'Connell), 1957, F 12,27:2
Mary Vincentia, Mother (E E Fannon), 1949, Ap 10, 76:5
Mary Vincentina, Sister (Louis), 1950, N 2,31:4
Mary Virginia, Mother, 1949, Je 12,76:6
Mary Vivina, Sister (M M Meehan), 1950, Ag 13, 76:4
Mary Winifred, Sister, 1948, Ap 7,25:3
Mary Wm, Sister (Benedictine), 1960, Ag 14,92:8
Mary Xavier, Mother (Sisters of Charity),(funl, Je 29,13:6), 1915, Je 24,11:4
Mary Xavier, Sister, 1923, F 17,13:4; 1943, F 23,21:1
Mary Xavier, Sister (R McCloy), 1951, Jl 29,69:1
Mary Zita, Sister (B Croghan), 1953, F 8,88:4
Mary Zoe, Mother (Sisters of Charity), 1952, D 7, 88:6
Maryatt, W W, 1873, O 13,4:7
Marye, G T, 1933, S 3,17:1
Marye, George T Mrs, 1946, Ja 6,40:3
Maryles, David, 1955, Ag 31,25:5
Maryon-Wilson, Spencer, 1944, My 13,19:4
Marz, Charles Sr, 1950, Jl 23,56:4
Marz, Joseph, 1944, D 16,15:3
Marz, William Mrs, 1947, D 18,30:2
Marzac, M De Carbonnier De, 1875, N 7,1:4
Marzahl, William H, 1939, Ap 29,17:4
Marzall, John A, 1959, Ja 3,17:1
Marzano, Vito, 1940, Ja 23,21:4
Marzec, John A Mrs, 1951, D 18,31:1
Marzo, Clara P Mrs, 1942, Jl 14,20:3
Mas, Jose, 1941, S 21,44:1
Masaryk, Alice G, 1966, N 30,48:1
Masaryk, Antonin, 1957, D 27,20:1
Masaryk, Jan Mrs, 1923, My 14,15:5
Masaryk, Thomas G Dr, 1937, S 14,1:5
Masback, Chester A, 1942, Ag 8,11:2
Masback, Robert J, 1943, Mr 17,21:2
Mascagni, Pietro (por), 1945, Ag 3,17:1
Mascarenhas, Alfredo, 1943, Mr 2,19:5
Mascarenhas de Moraes, Joa Batista Gen, 1968, S 19,47:4
Mascaritolo, George, 1950, Ag 20,76:2
Mascetta, Angelo Mrs, 1950, Ag 7,19:6
Maschal, Charles E, 1954, F 18,31:1
Maschal, Charles S, 1943, S 10,23:2
Mascheroni, Edoardo, 1941, Mr 6,21:5
Maschin, Col, 1910, Ap 20,9:4
Maschmeyer, Edward W, 1953, N 8,89:2
Mascia, Alfred J, 1948, Jl 19,19:2
Mascke, Heinrich Prof, 1908, Mr 2,9:6
Mascord, George W, 1925, S 27,7:3
Mascuch, Jean F, 1943, Ja 6,25:4
Mascuch, John T, 1951, O 27,19:4
Mase, Jacob, 1962, S 4,33:4
Mase, Jacob Dr, 1924, D 21,5:2
Mase, Stanley W, 1964, N 8,88:7
Mase, Tess (T Maresca), 1966, D 2,39:4
Masefield, John (funl, My 17,47:1), 1967, My 13,1:2
Masefield, John Mrs, 1960, F 20,23:4
Maselli, Peter, 1943, Je 8,21:3
Masena, Roy, 1947, S 28,60:3
Maseng, Sigurd, 1952, Ap 21,21:3
Masens, Vilis, 1964, Jl 16,31:4
Maser, Herman A, 1945, Mr 13,23:2
Masham, Samuel Cunliffe Lister Lord, 1906, F 3,9:4
Mashberg, Max, 1959, D 3,37:2
Mashburn, Lloyd A, 1963, D 10,50:7
Mashek, Vojta F, 1940, Ap 25,23:5
Mashey, Harry P Mrs, 1940, My 15,25:4
Mashihin, Ivan T, 1950, Je 17,15:6
Mashioff, Harold H, 1944, D 1,23:2
Mashman, Lillian, 1956, Ag 1,23:5
Mashrigi, Allama E K, 1963, Ag 28,33:1
Mashruwala, Kishorilal G, 1952, S 10,29:3
Masi, Anthony, 1952, Mr 8,13:1
Masie, Frederick W, 1952, My 21,27:3
Masiello, Anthony, 1961, D 14,43:1
Masiello, Joseph J, 1964, D 27,64:4
Masini, Ernest F, 1945, Ag 24,20:3
Masini, Joseph, 1944, Mr 1,19:4
Masius, Leonard M, 1961, Ja 10,47:6
Maske, Gunnar Mrs (mem ser set, S 15,33:3), 1955, Jl 31,39:1
Maskelyne, John Nevil, 1917, My 19,13:7
Masker, James, 1951, My 30,21:4
Masker, James H, 1945, F 2,19:4
Masker, James H Mrs, 1944, F 18,17:3
Masket, Albert V, 1966, D 23,25:2
Masket, Solomon, 1968, F 9,27:2
Masko, John, 1951, F 11,89:1
Maskowitz, Abe J Mrs, 1957, Jl 18,25:2
Maskowitz, Abraham J, 1958, Ag 10,92:2
Masland, Charles H 2d, 1955, Ap 10,88:1
Masland, Frank E, 1951, D 2,90:4
Masland, J Wesley, 1948, Ag 23,17:5
Masland, John W Dr (mem ser set, Ag 15,37:4), 1968, Ag 5,39:1
Masland, Mary E, 1950, Je 27,29:4
Masland, Robert P, 1957, Jl 22,19:5
Maslansky, Herman Mrs, 1964, Jl 18,19:4
Maslansky, Phil (por), 1942, D 20,45:1
Maslaton, Mordecai, 1959, Mr 3,33:4
Maslen, Richard R Mrs, 1952, O 20,23:4
Masley, Michael Jr, 1945, S 11,23:1
Masliansky, Zvi H (por), 1943, Ja 12,24:2
Maslin, Henry, 1953, Ja 28,27:5
Maslin, William R, 1968, Ag 2,33:4
Masline, Samuel D, 1937, Ja 28,25:5
Maslov, Vasily K, 1951, D 23,22:6
Maslow, Joseph, 1958, Jl 8,27:2
Maslow, Saul Mrs, 1963, O 14,29:5
Maslow, William Mrs, 1948, O 21,27:1
Masnicki, Vitus J, 1956, Jl 31,23:1
Maso, Bartolomeo, 1907, Je 15,9:6
Maso, Miguel S, 1939, Mr 25,15:2
Mason, A E W (por), 1948, N 23,29:4
Mason, A Lawrence Mrs, 1908, Ag 4,7:5
Mason, Albert T, 1946, F 20,25:4
Mason, Albert V, 1945, F 15,19:2
Mason, Alex, 1958, Ag 30,15:3
Mason, Alex McC Mrs, 1904, Ag 20,7:6
Mason, Alexander T, 1920, Je 13,22:4
Mason, Alexis I Mrs, 1961, Mr 14,35:4
Mason, Alfred B Mrs, 1945, Ja 21,39:1
Mason, Alfred Bp Mrs, 1912, Ja 18,13:5
Mason, Alfred D, 1945, Mr 13,23:4
Mason, Alfred De Witt, 1923, Ja 28,6:2
Mason, Alfred J, 1946, My 9,21:3
Mason, Alfred S T, 1946, Ag 5,21:3
Mason, Alfred T, 1943, Je 6,44:4
Mason, Amelia Gere, 1923, Ag 12,26:5
Mason, Amos Laurence Dr, 1914, Je 6,9:4
Mason, Andrew, 1909, Ap 29,9:3
Mason, Appleton A, 1938, D 22,21:4
Mason, Arthur C, 1950, My 18,29:4
Mason, Arthur E, 1943, Ap 30,21:5; 1946, Je 2,44:6
Mason, Arthur G, 1946, D 9,25:4
Mason, Arthur H, 1959, Ag 29,17:3
Mason, Arthur L, 1950, Mr 21,22:6
Mason, Arthur Mrs, 1966, O 20,43:6
Mason, Arthur Rev, 1907, My 28,9:6
Mason, Arthur T, 1939, Mr 14,21:2
Mason, Austin B, 1942, F 7,17:6
Mason, Benjamin, 1954, S 3,17:3
Mason, Bernard, 1947, Ag 28,23:4
Mason, Bernard S, 1953, Ap 14,27:6
Mason, Bertram A Mrs, 1951, O 28,85:2
Mason, Broadstreet H, 1942, Ja 2,34:2
Mason, Burdett, 1917, Je 19,13:4
Mason, C E, 1933, Ag 25,15:3
Mason, C W Col, 1913, Jl 22,7:4
Mason, Caroline A Mrs, 1939, My 4,23:1
Mason, Charles, 1879, Je 2,5:4; 1946, Je 5,23:2
Mason, Charles A, 1963, My 30,17:3
Mason, Charles B, 1947, N 3,23:5; 1951, Je 3,95:3
Mason, Charles F, 1947, Mr 2,60:2; 1957, Jl 18,25:1
Mason, Charles J, 1948, Ap 14,27:2
Mason, Charles J Mrs, 1954, Ap 19,23:1
Mason, Charles Kemble (funl), 1875, Jl 14,2:1
Mason, Charles N, 1954, Jl 11,72:2
Mason, Charles P, 1959, My 25,29:1
Mason, Charlotte E, 1939, S 21,23:5
Mason, Colbourne Mrs, 1956, My 6,87:1
Mason, Colbourne O, 1952, S 22,23:2
Mason, Cora L Mrs, 1939, Ja 28,13:6
Mason, D G, 1869, Jl 17,5:2
Mason, Dan O, 1953, Je 13,15:5
Mason, Daniel G, 1953, D 9,11:1
Mason, David, 1967, Jl 4,19:4
Mason, David D, 1942, S 15,23:4
Mason, Earl Potter, 1922, Ag 15,11:5
Mason, Edgar D Jr Mrs, 1958, Ag 7,25:2
Mason, Edward B, 1950, S 28,31:5
Mason, Edward Bereher Rev, 1907, O 22,9:4
Mason, Edward C, 1937, Ap 2,23:5
Mason, Edward G, 1955, Ap 22,25:1
Mason, Edward H, 1939, S 1,17:6; 1948, Ap 21,27:5
Mason, Edward H Mrs, 1948, Je 15,27:3
Mason, Edward M, 1965, Ja 25,37:4
Mason, Edward P, 1940, Jl 18,19:3
Mason, Edward S, 1952, Mr 25,27:1
Mason, Edward S Mrs, 1952, Mr 18,27:2
Mason, Edward W, 1947, Mr 28,24:3
Mason, Edwin C, 1942, Jl 10,17:3
Mason, Eleanor B, 1956, My 24,31:3
Mason, Eliott Mrs, 1944, My 30,21:2
Mason, Elmer K, 1957, My 23,33:2
Mason, Emily Virginia, 1909, F 18,7:5
Mason, Emma E Mrs, 1958, Jl 6,56:5
Mason, Emma G Mrs, 1941, N 25,26:3
Mason, Erskine Dr, 1882, Ap 15,5:4
Mason, Eva B Mrs, 1938, Jl 15,17:5
Mason, F T, 1901, Je 22,9:6
Mason, Fannie P (will, S 4,9:2), 1948, Ag 31,23:1
Mason, Frances V, 1953, Jl 2,23:3
Mason, Francis S, 1951, Ja 22,17:3
Mason, Frank A, 1940, Je 30,32:4
Mason, Frank H, 1948, D 19,76:5; 1959, Ap 25,21:5
Mason, Frank H Capt (funl, Je 24,11:7), 1916, Je 22, 11:6
Mason, Frank H Mrs, 1916, N 26,21:5
Mason, Frank M, 1947, D 16,33:4; 1952, D 29,19:5; 1957, D 15,86:5
Mason, Frank O, 1941, O 11,17:2
Mason, Fred, 1948, Ap 22,27:3
Mason, Frederic Gooding, 1909, F 25,7:5
Mason, Frederick C, 1953, S 3,21:2
Mason, Frederick Thurston, 1917, Mr 8,11:4
Mason, G A Mrs, 1922, My 15,17:7
Mason, G Bartle, 1949, N 6,92:1
Mason, Gabriel R Mrs, 1965, Je 1,39:3
Mason, George, 1941, D 25,25:4; 1942, Ap 2,21:5; 1944, Ap 19,23:5
Mason, George A, 1944, O 23,19:5; 1951, Ja 3,27:2; 1953, N 14,17:5
Mason, George B, 1943, Ap 30,21:2
Mason, George H, 1955, My 2,21:4
Mason, George I, 1962, Ja 18,29:2
Mason, George W, 1954, O 9,17:1
Mason, Georgine R L Mrs, 1937, Jl 12,18:1
Mason, Gregory Dr, 1968, D 1,86:5
Mason, Grover A, 1966, Je 12,86:5
Mason, Guy, 1955, Jl 11,23:2
Mason, H F Randolph, 1964, Ag 12,35:5

Mason, H Raymond, 1945, F 22,27:5
Mason, Harold E, 1950, Ag 2,25:4
Mason, Harold F, 1954, Ap 14,29:1
Mason, Harold W, 1944, N 4,15:3
Mason, Harriet M, 1950, Ap 11,32:3
Mason, Harry H, 1946, Mr 11,25:2
Mason, Harry N, 1968, D 11,47:2
Mason, Harry R Mrs, 1950, Je 21,27:4
Mason, Haven A, 1950, Ap 1,15:4
Mason, Henry, 1873, F 23,8:5
Mason, Henry G, 1958, Mr 24,27:3
Mason, Henry J, 1959, My 26,35:3; 1967, Jl 28,31:3
Mason, Henry L, 1957, O 19,21:4
Mason, Henry Ware, 1924, Ja 3,17:3
Mason, Herbert J, 1946, N 20,34:4
Mason, Herbert W, 1939, Ag 22,19:5
Mason, Herman, 1958, Ja 21,29:1
Mason, Hiram J Mrs, 1875, Jl 28,5:3
Mason, Hobart, 1955, F 24,27:4
Mason, Hobart Mrs, 1962, O 4,39:3
Mason, Howard, 1948, O 25,23:5
Mason, Howard B, 1945, Jl 15,15:6
Mason, Howard H, 1960, My 10,37:4
Mason, J A (Sprague), 1877, D 21,8:3
Mason, J Cooper Col, 1923, Ag 7,17:2
Mason, J Judd, 1943, Jl 26,19:3
Mason, J Leonard, 1942, Ag 11,19:6
Mason, J M (trb), 1871, My 13,2:2
Mason, J Sir, 1881, Je 18,2:4
Mason, J T, 1936, Je 21,II,9:1
Mason, Jack, 1938, My 9,17:6
Mason, Jacob W, 1941, My 1,23:4
Mason, James A, 1952, Ap 27,90:3
Mason, James D, 1948, My 23,70:1
Mason, James F, 1957, Ap 5,27:2
Mason, James Frazier Sr, 1903, O 13,7:6
Mason, James G, 1938, Mr 20,II,8:8
Mason, James J Jr, 1962, Mr 30,33:2
Mason, James Kent, 1915, My 21,13:5
Mason, James M Mrs, 1874, F 17,1:5
Mason, James Murray, 1871, Ap 30,5:2
Mason, James P, 1945, D 12,27:5
Mason, James T A, 1959, Ap 26,86:3
Mason, James W, 1951, D 2,90:5
Mason, James Weir Prof, 1905, Ja 12,7:2
Mason, Jarvis W, 1924, Ag 6,13:4
Mason, John, 1907, N 30,7:5
Mason, John A, 1967, N 9,47:2
Mason, John A Mrs, 1948, O 14,29:3
Mason, John B Mrs, 1953, F 14,17:5
Mason, John C, 1950, Ag 20,77:1
Mason, John D, 1950, N 21,31:5
Mason, John H, 1951, D 24,13:3
Mason, John J B, 1945, Mr 14,19:3
Mason, John J Dr, 1916, N 23,13:5
Mason, John J Jr, 1958, O 25,21:5
Mason, John J Mrs, 1944, Jl 30,36:1
Mason, John Mrs, 1953, S 22,31:1
Mason, John R, 1957, S 13,24:2
Mason, John S Jr Mrs, 1953, F 2,21:1
Mason, John T, 1938, Je 4,15:3
Mason, John Thompson, 1873, Mr 29,12:4
Mason, John W, 1941, Ap 6,48:5; 1965, F 18,33:3
Mason, John W Judge, 1917, Ap 24,11:4
Mason, John Young, 1859, O 17,1:6
Mason, Joseph E, 1950, Ja 8,76:6
Mason, Joseph W T (por), 1941, My 14,21:3
Mason, Joseph W T, 1941, Ag 3,35:1
Mason, Julian Jaquelin, 1914, Mr 30,9:4
Mason, Julian S, 1954, N 9,27:3
Mason, Julian S Mrs, 1956, S 15,17:2
Mason, Kathryn H Mrs, 1961, Ap 10,31:4
Mason, L D, 1927, Je 13,19:5
Mason, Laurence B, 1954, My 18,29:3
Mason, Lawrence, 1939, D 11,23:3
Mason, Leroy, 1947, O 15,27:4
Mason, Lewis F, 1943, Ap 16,21:2
Mason, Louis A, 1946, O 5,17:4
Mason, Louis B Mrs, 1956, Ap 29,87:1
Mason, Louis K, 1943, S 20,21:3
Mason, Lowell Dr, 1872, Ag 13,5:5
Mason, Lucy R, 1959, My 8,27:1
Mason, M C B Mrs, 1953, F 27,21:4
Mason, M Davis, 1947, D 11,33:4
Mason, M Phillips, 1957, Jl 25,23:3
Mason, Madison Charles Butler Rev Dr, 1915, Ag 1, 15:5
Mason, Marie K, 1949, D 10,17:1
Mason, Martha, 1954, My 4,29:4
Mason, Mary, 1951, Ag 14,23:4
Mason, Mary A, 1952, S 10,29:5
Mason, Mary F, 1937, Mr 24,25:4
Mason, Mary R, 1948, Mr 13,25:5
Mason, Mary T, 1957, Ag 15,21:4
Mason, Maud M, 1956, Ag 29,29:6
Mason, Maude O Mrs, 1938, Mr 14,16:1
Mason, Max, 1961, Mr 24,31:2
Mason, Max Mrs, 1944, Ag 9,17:3; 1960, Je 14,37:2
Mason, Morris A, 1953, Mr 5,27:4
Mason, Morris A Mrs, 1948, D 10,25:3
Mason, Myron Mrs, 1949, N 26,15:4
Mason, Noah M, 1965, Mr 30,39:2
Mason, Norman, 1942, F 15,45:2
Mason, Oliver J, 1942, Ja 9,21:3
Mason, Orville J, 1949, F 24,24:3
Mason, Oscar G, 1921, Mr 17,13:4
Mason, Otis T, 1908, N 6,7:4
Mason, Patrick S, 1956, F 17,21:2
Mason, Paul, 1945, Jl 31,19:3
Mason, Peter, 1961, Ja 17,37:4
Mason, R C, 1950, My 13,17:5
Mason, R Osgood, 1903, My 12,9:5
Mason, Randolph F, 1952, Mr 27,29:1
Mason, Redfern, 1941, Ap 17,23:5
Mason, Reginald, 1962, Jl 14,21:4
Mason, Richard H Mrs, 1949, Mr 22,25:5
Mason, Robert, 1906, N 15,9:6
Mason, Robert C, 1938, S 9,21:2
Mason, Robert J Mrs, 1948, Je 10,25:4
Mason, Robert M, 1957, Ag 30,19:5
Mason, Roland K, 1941, D 30,19:5
Mason, Roy H Mrs, 1949, Ap 1,25:2
Mason, S P, 1941, S 21,45:2
Mason, Samuel, 1947, Ap 30,25:3; 1950, Ja 25,27:5
Mason, Samuel H, 1937, Je 23,25:4
Mason, Samuel J, 1938, D 11,61:3
Mason, Sidney J, 1965, S 29,3:5
Mason, Simon J, 1940, N 13,23:6
Mason, Stephen C, 1923, D 13,21:5
Mason, Stephen T Jr, 1937, Ag 3,23:5
Mason, T A Mrs, 1946, S 29,60:6
Mason, T H, 1902, N 16,7:6
Mason, T L, 1882, F 13,5:5
Mason, Thomas, 1918, S 3,11:3
Mason, Thomas A, 1937, F 15,17:2
Mason, Thomas Capt, 1910, N 14,9:5
Mason, Verne R, 1965, N 17,47:3
Mason, Victor L (funl), 1912, My 27,11:4
Mason, Virgil A, 1958, Ag 23,15:5
Mason, W E, 1921, Je 17,13:6
Mason, Wallace E, 1944, Je 15,19:6
Mason, Walt (por), 1939, Je 23,19:3
Mason, Walter, 1960, Jl 3,32:3
Mason, Walter A, 1959, Mr 8,87:1
Mason, Warren P Mrs, 1953, My 20,29:5
Mason, Wilbur N, 1952, D 21,52:8
Mason, William A, 1943, O 21,27:4; 1945, Je 23,13:4
Mason, William B, 1949, Jl 1,19:6
Mason, William B R, 1944, Mr 25,15:2
Mason, William C, 1941, Ja 26,36:1; 1946, N 14,29:4; 1956, Ap 1,88:5; 1957, N 20,35:4
Mason, William D, 1967, D 22,31:2
Mason, William E, 1948, Je 23,27:3
Mason, William E Mrs, 1950, Mr 25,11:8
Mason, William H, 1940, Ag 25,36:5; 1940, S 13,23:4
Mason, William O, 1950, Je 18,76:2
Mason, William P, 1947, D 5,25:2
Mason, William P Dr, 1937, Ja 26,21:5
Mason, William P Jr, 1964, S 9,43:2
Mason, William S, 1939, F 11,15:5; 1961, Ja 12,29:5
Mason, William T, 1938, My 25,23:4
Mason-MacFarlane, Noel, 1953, Ag 13,25:4
Mason-Springgay, Wilfred Henry, 1968, O 4,47:2
Masone, Charles J, 1958, N 4,27:3
Masouras, Constantine, 1949, My 25,30:4
Maspero, Alfredo, 1958, N 2,88:7
Masprone, Alberto, 1964, F 15,23:5
Masquelets, Carlos, 1948, My 18,24:3
Masqueray, Emmanuel Louis, 1917, My 27,19:2
Mass, George W, 1943, My 6,19:5
Mass, Hyman, 1958, F 1,19:3
Mass, Isaac H, 1942, S 6,30:5
Massa, Carl A, 1944, S 7,23:3
Massa, Carl A Mrs, 1953, Jl 24,13:5
Massa, Charles F, 1947, Ja 9,23:5
Massa, William H, 1948, D 12,92:4
Massarene, William G, 1941, F 21,19:2
Massari, Alfonso M, 1949, D 11,92:5
Massari, Ines, 1952, Je 14,15:2
Massaro, Clement, 1949, Mr 24,27:2
Masse, James Mrs, 1960, Ag 22,25:4
Masse, Marie V, 1884, Jl 6,1:6
Masse, Roland J, 1952, Ja 21,16:5
Masseck, Clinton J, 1948, Je 28,19:5
Massee, Margaret Mrs, 1944, N 13,19:5
Massee, May, 1966, D 27,32:5
Massee, W Wellington (por), 1942, Ag 28,19:4
Massel, Edmund S, 1947, N 10,29:4
Massel, Jacob, 1954, S 15,33:4
Masselink, Eugene, 1962, Jl 17,25:4
Masselis, Benedict J Rev, 1913, F 17,11:4
Massell, Alex S, 1964, Ja 29,33:4
Massell, Alex S Mrs, 1958, O 25,21:3
Massell, Benjamin J, 1962, S 11,33:2
Massella, Charles, 1952, My 17,19:6
Massello, Dominick, 1945, N 6,19:1
Massen, John A, 1958, N 17,31:3
Massen, Louis F, 1925, Mr 28,15:4
Massen, Louis Mrs, 1948, Mr 17,25:2
Massena, Victor Prince d'Essling, 1910, O 29,11:6
Massenet, Jules (por), 1912, Ag 14,9:1
Massenet, Jules Mme, 1938, Je 9,23:5
Massengill, Samuel E, 1946, D 17,38:4
Massereene, Viscountess, 1937, D 12,II,8:7
Masserman, Charles, 1954, Ap 22,29:3
Masseth, John E, 1945, O 11,23:5
Massey, Annie G Mrs, 1948, D 22,23:3
Massey, C D, 1926, Je 3,25:4
Massey, Charles R, 1944, Je 19,19:3
Massey, Del (will), 1959, D 15,44:2
Massey, Edmund S, 1947, Ap 12,17:3
Massey, Frank H, 1943, S 9,26:3
Massey, Garrett Mrs, 1951, D 21,27:2
Massey, George, 1915, My 2,20:4
Massey, George V, 1924, O 22,21:4
Massey, Georgiana L, 1943, Jl 16,17:2
Massey, Harry D, 1944, S 22,19:5
Massey, Henry V Jr, 1953, Ap 3,24:4
Massey, Hugh L, 1944, My 17,19:4
Massey, J Floyd Mrs, 1939, S 25,20:1
Massey, John M, 1944, D 19,21:1
Massey, Joseph, 1945, Ap 26,23:2
Massey, Leidia H Mrs, 1958, Je 13,23:4
Massey, Lionel, 1965, Jl 29,27:1
Massey, Peter J, 1956, O 11,39:2
Massey, Richard W, 1949, Ag 6,17:5
Massey, Stephen J, 1950, Ap 12,28:2
Massey, Thomas H, 1957, N 6,35:1
Massey. Vincent, 1967, D 31,44:6
Massey, Vincent (funl plans; funl, Ja 5, 24:4), 1968 Ja 3,40:1
Massey, Vincent Mrs, 1950, Ag 1,23:1
Massey, Walter E H Mrs, 1938, Ja 9,43:1
Massey, Walter F, 1945, N 15,20:2
Massey, William Alexander, 1914, Mr 6,11:5
Massey, William Ferguson, 1925, My 11,17:3
Massey, William H, 1915, D 2,11:6
Massey, William J, 1965, My 14,37:1
Massey, William Mrs, 1944, Jl 1,15:7
Massicot, Phil L, 1940, N 16,17:5
Massie, Arch J, 1938, F 9,19:3
Massie, Arthur, 1914, Je 19,13:4
Massie, Charles C, 1947, D 14,79:3
Massie, Robert W, 1944, Ja 3,21:4
Massie, Thomas L, 1944, D 19,21:3
Massie, Walter Mrs, 1963, Ap 2,48:1
Massimi, Massimo, 1954, Mr 7,91:1
Massimino, Arch J, 1941, Ag 11,13:6
Massimo, Frank, 1949, Je 24,23:4
Massimo, Maria (Princess Colonna), 1916, N 11,9
Massimo, Michael J, 1968, Ag 31,23:4
Massing, John N, 1950, Mr 12,93:1
Massingale, Sam, 1941, Ja 18,15:1
Massingberd, Chancellor, 1872, D 30,5:3
Massingham, H W, 1924, Ag 29,11:5
Massingham, Harold J, 1952, Ag 24,88:4
Massino, Prince, 1873, My 3,6:7
Masslich, C B, 1933, Ja 19,15:5
Masslich, George B, 1941, N 15,17:2
Massman, Frederick H, 1948, N 4,29:2
Massoff, Morris, 1956, Jl 29,65:1
Masson, Carl C, 1962, Ap 20,27:3
Masson, Clement B, 1946, S 7,15:2
Masson, David, 1907, O 8,11:4
Masson, David O Sir, 1937, Ag 11,24:1
Masson, Frederic, 1923, F 20,17:3
Masson, Irenee, 1955, D 10,21:1
Masson, James Harrison, 1907, S 10,7:6
Masson, John M, 1947, Jl 29,21:1
Masson, Milton L, 1967, Mr 26,69:1
Masson, Paul, 1940, O 23,23:5
Masson, Paul L, 1950, Jl 26,25:2
Masson, Pierre, 1959, My 14,33:4
Masson, Robert, 1942, Ja 23,19:1
Masson, T L, 1934, Je 19,19:1
Masson, Thomas L Mrs, 1952, S 5,27:2
Massoneau, Edward Philip, 1904, O 14,7:5
Massonneau, Robert L Jr, 1951, D 28,21:1
Massopust, Anton J, 1945, F 24,11:4
Massopust, Joseph, 1945, Jl 19,23:3
Massoth, Harry P, 1940, Ja 5,19:5
Massoth, Thomas W, 1967, Jl 31,27:4
Massough, Spiridaunaus, 1940, Ja 26,17:4
Massow, Ewald von, 1942, O 15,23:5
Massue, Girard, 1945, Ag 20,19:3
Massy, Hugh H C G, 1958, Mr 22,17:2
Mast, Burdette P Sr, 1964, Ap 25,29:2
Mast, Charles J, 1964, Ap 27,31:3
Mast, Ernest J Mrs, 1946, O 4,23:1
Mast, John S, 1951, Ja 5,21:4
Mast, Samuel O, 1947, F 5,26:1
Mastal, John J, 1948, D 31,15:4
Mastapeter, Antony, 1948, S 3,19:2
Mastbaum, J E, 1926, D 8,27:3
Mastbaum, Jules E Mrs, 1953, O 3,17:6
Mastbaum, Stanley V, 1918, Mr 8,11:5
Masten, A E, 1921, N 24,19:6
Masten, Chester R, 1942, My 14,19:1
Masten, Christine M Mrs, 1937, Je 24,25:4
Masten, Cornelius A, 1942, S 1,19:5
Masten, Edward, 1954, My 30,44:4
Masten, Frank D Mrs, 1953, Mr 26,31:5
Masten, Harold L, 1954, Ja 15,19:1
Masten, J Eugene, 1944, S 21,19:4
Masten, Joseph S Judge, 1871, Ap 15,1:3
Masten, Ralph A, 1959, Ja 30,27:2
Masten, Richard, 1941, Ag 3,35:3
Masten, Stephen E, 1947, Ja 5,53:1
Master, A E, 1881, Ag 27,5:4

Master, Arthur M Mrs, 1967, Ja 31,31:1
Master, David A, 1945, Ja 17,21:4
Master, Henry B, 1955, My 19,29:2
Master, Herbert C, 1951, Jl 17,27:5
Master, Jacob M, 1957, My 2,31:4
Masterjohn, Thomas J, 1949, O 25,27:5
Masterman, John A Mrs, 1958, Mr 8,17:4
Mastern, Everett, 1944, N 18,13:6
Masters, Al (Alf R), 1963, N 22,31:8
Masters, C M Judge, 1914, Mr 15,7:5
Masters, D Nathaniel B, 1952, F 1,21:2
Masters, Dexter Mrs (C Malman), 1959, Ja 15,33:3
Masters, Dorothy (Mrs A E Lee), 1964, D 23,27:2
Masters, E William, 1940, N 30,17:5
Masters, Edgar, 1947, D 1,21:2
Masters, Edgar L, 1950, Mr 6,21:1; 1950, Ap 29,17:4
Masters, Eliza S H D Mrs, 1939, Ap 19,25:2
Masters, Elizabeth W, 1921, Je 10,13:5
Masters, Francis R Mrs, 1943, Mr 1,19:4
Masters, G La Rue, 1938, O 26,23:4
Masters, Hardin W, 1925, N 17,25:3
Masters, Harding W, 1925, N 15,13:1
Masters, Harris K, 1961, N 23,31:5
Masters, Helen J Mrs, 1958, N 28,30:5
Masters, Ira H, 1956, F 20,23:3
Masters, J Edgar, 1954, Ag 7,13:5
Masters, John, 1947, F 8,17:5
Masters, John Marshall, 1907, Ja 28,7:4
Masters, John V, 1954, O 9,17:5
Masters, Joseph G, 1954, My 21,27:3
Masters, Paul V, 1913, D 29,7:4
Masters, Phil, 1950, Ag 8,29:4
Masters, Richard, 1912, Jl 15,9:3
Masters, Robert W, 1940, Ap 19,21:2
Masters, Sarah W, 1943, N 17,25:5
Masters, Victor I, 1954, Jl 2,19:3
Masters, Walter E Mrs, 1946, Ag 17,13:2
Masters, Walter Mrs, 1954, Jl 22,23:2
Masterson, Alonzo, 1942, Ja 1,25:4
Masterson, Alonzo S, 1938, N 12,15:3
Masterson, Bat, 1921, O 27,19:5
Masterson, Bernie, 1963, My 17,33:3
Masterson, Bill, 1968, Ja 16,31:2
Masterson, Edward J, 1941, Ap 3,23:3
Masterson, Everett, 1948, Jl 3,15:5
Masterson, Francis C Sr, 1951, D 12,37:3
Masterson, Frank, 1953, F 26,25:5
Masterson, Frank C, 1955, N 28,31:2
Masterson, Frank J, 1942, Ag 13,19:5
Masterson, Frank Sr, 1945, F 25,37:2
Masterson, Henry, 1938, F 26,30:4
Masterson, Hugh H, 1955, F 11,23:4
Masterson, John, 1903, N 9,7:6
Masterson, John D, 1966, Jl 17,69:1
Masterson, John J, 1954, S 20,15:7; 1962, N 20,35:4
Masterson, John Mrs, 1944, Je 27,19:2
Masterson, John P Jr, 1952, Jl 20,53:2
Masterson, Joseph E, 1941, D 4,25:3
Masterson, Joseph H, 1949, Ag 11,23:4
Masterson, Patrick J, 1953, Je 10,32:1
Masterson, Peter J, 1949, O 14,27:2
Masterson, Robert W, 1960, D 31,17:4
Masterson, Thomas F, 1949, Ag 19,17:3
Masterson, W W, 1922, My 12,19:5
Masterson, Walter J Mrs, 1955, My 3,31:3
Masterson, Walter J Sr, 1952, S 16,29:4
Masterson, William, 1950, Ag 29,27:2
Masterson, William B, 1956, F 14,29:1
Masterson, William F, 1946, Ap 2,27:5
Masterson, William F Mrs, 1958, Ja 20,23:1
Masterson, William H, 1940, S 16,19:4
Masterton, George, 1943, Jl 21,15:3
Masterton, John Mrs, 1966, O 28,31:3
Mastic, Stephen, 1953, Ap 24,24:6
Mastick, George C, 1942, Jl 5,30:2
Mastick, Seabury C Mrs, 1963, N 9,25:5
Mastin, Florence Ripley, 1968, F 24,27:1
Mastin, J Edward, 1917, S 27,13:5
Mastin, James, 1948, Ja 22,35:4
Mastin, William B, 1959, F 26,31:2
Maston, Myer, 1912, Je 28,13:6
Mastriani, Louis, 1937, O 13,23:5
Mastrobattista, Alex J, 1949, Mr 9,25:2
Mastromarino, Joan, 1945, S 19,27:2
Mastromonaco, Anthony Mrs, 1958, D 7,88:2
Mastromonaco, Antonio, 1964, Ap 11,25:2
Masuda, Takashi (por), 1938, D 29,20:2
Masulla, Joseph A, 1946, F 22,25:2
Masur, Sig, 1948, N 21,88:3
Masurel, Edmond F H, 1966, S 30,47:2
Masurovsky, Disraeli S, 1947, My 6,27:4
Masury, Alfred F Mrs, 1955, D 13,39:2
Masury, Fred L M, 1950, N 11,15:2
Masury, J W, 1931, Ag 17,15:5
Mata, Pedro, 1946, D 30,19:3
Mataafa, Ex-King of Samoa, 1912, F 15,11:4
Mataja, Heinrich, 1937, Ja 24,II,8:7
Matarazzo, Francisco Count (will, F 25,16:3), 1937, F 11,23:5
Matas, Rudolph, 1957, S 24,35:3
Matayoshi, Kowa, 1953, S 25,21:3
Match, Pincus, 1944, S 3,26:7
Matchabelli, G V, 1935, Ap 1,19:1
Matchabelli, Norina Princess, 1957, Je 17,23:2
Matchett, Charles Horatio, 1919, O 26,22:3
Matchett, David F, 1946, Jl 26,21:5
Matchett, Theodore, 1950, O 18,33:4
Matchett, Thomas, 1959, S 30,37:4
Matchette, Franklin J, 1943, F 25,21:5
Matecki, Bronislaw E, 1959, D 4,31:2
Mateer, Howard W Mrs, 1949, N 27,104:6
Mateer, John C, 1966, S 4,65:1
Mateer, Madge D, 1939, S 16,17:2
Mateer, Mathew H, 1903, Jl 14,7:6
Matelis, Henry A, 1944, S 29,21:3
Materasso, Alex Mrs, 1959, D 21,48:1
Materne, August, 1964, Ap 1,39:5
Mateucci, Albert, 1950, S 14,31:1
Mateyko, Gladys M Dr, 1968, O 13,84:6
Matfus, Joseph, 1963, My 8,36:5
Math, Anthony J, 1953, My 14,29:3
Math, George A, 1944, N 22,19:5
Math, Nathan W, 1962, Ja 12,23:1
Mathbie, Robert G Sr Mrs, 1961, F 5,80:7
Mathebat, Alfred J Mrs, 1957, Jl 7,61:1
Matheia, Casimer, 1946, Je 3,21:3
Mathein, Hazel K Mrs (death Ap 9 noted), 1967, Ap 20,3:7
Matheis, Jacob, 1939, Ap 20,23:4
Matheke, George A, 1961, My 2,37:4
Matheke, Otto G Sr, 1967, Je 17,31:3
Matheny, Horace B, 1949, Ja 31,19:5
Matheny, Ira C, 1941, D 18,27:5
Matheny, Robert A, 1949, Mr 2,25:6
Matheny, Willard R, 1947, My 31,13:3
Matheo, Wally, 1955, My 13,25:3
Mather, Alonzo C (will, F 15,8:5), 1941, Ja 28,19:1
Mather, Alonzo C Mrs (will, Ap 25,20:3), 1950, Ap 21,23:2
Mather, Arthur G, 1953, Ap 19,90:1
Mather, Aubrey, 1958, Ja 22,27:2
Mather, Bessie F Mrs, 1956, Ap 17,31:2
Mather, Charles C, 1962, Ag 26,82:5
Mather, Charles E, 1950, N 23,35:4
Mather, Charles Milton, 1918, Mr 22,13:4
Mather, Charles S, 1948, My 8,15:5
Mather, Clare V Mrs, 1939, Je 28,21:4
Mather, Cotton A, 1956, Mr 15,31:6
Mather, Dwight Mrs, 1952, N 16,89:1
Mather, Edward O, 1952, O 2,29:3
Mather, Frank H, 1940, Mr 19,25:2
Mather, Frederick Gregory, 1925, S 1,21:5
Mather, George W, 1960, Ag 27,19:4
Mather, Gilbert, 1959, O 24,18:6
Mather, Gordon M, 1955, N 17,35:5
Mather, Hiram F, 1868, Jl 14,4:7
Mather, J C, 1882, Ag 15,5:2
Mather, Jack (Jno E), 1966, Ag 22,33:2
Mather, John A Brig-Gen, 1917, F 13,11:5
Mather, John C, 1938, F 12,15:5
Mather, John C Mrs, 1952, Ja 29,25:1
Mather, John Cotton, 1925, S 3,25:4
Mather, John W, 1961, N 1,43:5
Mather, Joseph S, 1937, Ap 18,II,8:5
Mather, Levi V, 1951, F 8,33:1
Mather, Lillian T Mrs, 1941, F 15,15:2
Mather, Lucius C, 1944, Ag 22,17:5
Mather, Margaret, 1898, Ap 8,7:5
Mather, Maurice W, 1950, D 26,23:2
Mather, Robert (funl, O 27,13:6), 1911, O 25,13:5
Mather, Roland, 1965, Ap 22,33:1
Mather, Roy F, 1954, Mr 6,15:7
Mather, Rufus G, 1952, Ap 28,19:4
Mather, Rufus G Mrs (por), 1945, Je 16,13:1
Mather, S Livingston, 1960, S 12,29:5
Mather, S Livingston (est acctg), 1961, S 3,15:7
Mather, S T, 1930, Ja 23,23:1
Mather, Stephen T Mrs, 1944, Ag 21,15:5
Mather, Thomas Prof, 1937, Je 25,22:1
Mather, Thomas R, 1947, Ag 28,23:4
Mather, Thomas W Mrs, 1943, Mr 12,17:5
Mather, Victor C, 1943, Jl 17,13:4
Mather, Victor C Mrs, 1937, My 18,23:4
Mather, W A, 1961, Ja 3,29:1
Mather, W T Dr, 1937, Je 15,23:2
Mather, William A, 1939, Je 12,17:4; 1957, N 8,29:2
Mather, William A Mrs, 1939, F 22,21:5
Mather, William G, 1951, Ap 7,15:4
Mather, William G Mrs, 1957, N 11,29:5
Mather, William L, 1956, F 13,27:2
Matherly, Walter J, 1954, S 26,86:5
Mathers, Arthur, 1958, Mr 20,29:1
Mathers, Edward P, 1939, F 4,15:5
Mathers, Frank Mrs, 1951, Je 1,23:3
Mathers, Frederick F, 1947, Ap 15,25:1
Mathers, George (Sept 26), 1965, O 11,61:3
Mathers, Helen, 1920, Mr 16,9:4
Matherson, Robert Jr, 1965, D 23,27:4
Mathes, Edward E, 1946, Ag 27,27:4
Mathes, James M, 1957, Ap 29,25:3
Mathes, John, 1940, Ag 17,15:4
Mathes, Mary B Mrs, 1957, N 24,87:3
Mathesius, Frederick, 1963, O 24,33:1
Matheson, A J, 1913, Ja 27,9:4
Matheson, Arnold M, 1959, Je 29,29:4
Matheson, Charles G, 1948, My 26,25:3
Matheson, Donald S, 1943, Je 1,23:2
Matheson, Donald W, 1916, D 23,9:6
Matheson, Duncan, 1942, O 27,26:3
Matheson, Frank F, 1967, F 12,92:2
Matheson, George L, 1952, Jl 21,19:5
Matheson, Gilchrist E, 1965, Je 15,38:1
Matheson, John, 1940, Mr 28,23:6
Matheson, John D, 1953, F 27,21:2
Matheson, John Dr, 1905, D 9,5:1
Matheson, John J, 1937, My 29,17:3; 1940, F 29,19:4
Matheson, K G, 1931, N 30,19:1
Matheson, Murdo, 1954, My 24,27:2
Matheson, Peter M, 1950, Ja 20,25:4
Matheson, Samuel P, 1942, My 20,20:2
Matheson, William Mrs, 1946, Mr 10,46:4
Matheu, Pedro J, 1940, S 1,21:2
Mathew, Francis, 1965, Mr 30,47:2
Mathew, Steere de M, 1966, O 18,45:2
Mathew, Theobald, 1964, Mr 1,83:2
Mathews, Albert, 1903, S 11,7:7
Mathews, Albert F, 1958, S 28,89:1
Mathews, Albert P, 1957, S 23,27:2
Mathews, Alice L, 1960, N 20,87:1
Mathews, Annie, 1959, O 25,85:3
Mathews, Basil J, 1951, Mr 30,23:5
Mathews, C, 1878, Jl 14,7:2
Mathews, C D, 1879, My 24,7:2
Mathews, C H Jr, 1952, Je 26,29:6
Mathews, C T, 1934, Ja 12,23:3
Mathews, Caroline M Mrs, 1941, My 16,23:2
Mathews, Catherine V, 1954, My 11,29:2
Mathews, Charles, 1878, Je 25,5:1
Mathews, Charles E, 1960, Ja 17,86:1
Mathews, Charles H Jr Mrs, 1947, Je 7,13:5
Mathews, Charles Sir, 1920, Je 7,15:2
Mathews, Clifton, 1962, S 9,84:3
Mathews, Daniel A, 1920, Ja 23,13:2
Mathews, Dean C Sr, 1943, N 10,23:1
Mathews, Dorothy, 1958, O 9,37:4
Mathews, Edward B (por), 1944, F 6,41:1
Mathews, Edward L, 1940, Je 9,44:1
Mathews, Ella, 1962, Mr 29,33:1
Mathews, Ernest L, 1958, O 7,35:1
Mathews, Eugene T, 1960, Je 28,31:4
Mathews, F Rockwell, 1945, D 22,19:5
Mathews, F Schuyler, 1938, Ag 21,32:7
Mathews, Floyd D, 1951, Mr 21,33:2
Mathews, Frank, 1871, Jl 27,1:7
Mathews, Frank A Jr, 1964, F 7,31:5
Mathews, Frank H, 1944, D 6,23:3
Mathews, Frank W Mrs, 1942, Ap 24,17:1
Mathews, George B, 1942, F 5,22:2; 1944, F 17,19:5
Mathews, George C, 1946, Jl 14,38:4
Mathews, George S, 1950, D 2,13:5
Mathews, George S Mrs, 1948, Je 17,25:2
Mathews, Gustave X, 1958, S 23,33:4
Mathews, Harold C, 1952, Ap 25,23:1
Mathews, J J, 1947, Ag 1,17:3
Mathews, James W, 1920, D 15,15:4
Mathews, Jane H, 1952, Ap 9,31:5
Mathews, Jerry A, 1955, S 29,33:3
Mathews, John, 1905, Ja 12,7:2
Mathews, John A Mrs, 1949, Ja 7,21:3
Mathews, John E, 1955, My 1,88:8
Mathews, John L, 1947, Mr 29,15:2
Mathews, John Lathrop, 1916, My 28,17:4
Mathews, Joseph P, 1953, Jl 18,13:7
Mathews, Julius, 1943, S 9,26:4
Mathews, Kate R Mrs, 1942, Je 9,23:4
Mathews, Mark, 1946, D 20,23:5
Mathews, Mary, 1950, D 29,19:2
Mathews, Mary C Mrs, 1942, Ja 22,17:2
Mathews, May S Mrs (will, D 6,5:6), 1938, N 28, 15:5
Mathews, Mrs, 1872, Ag 12,1:7
Mathews, Paul, 1954, Ja 18,23:2
Mathews, Philip, 1958, F 20,25:2
Mathews, Poultney, 1961, My 25,37:4
Mathews, Robert F, 1949, Jl 17,58:3; 1951, My 7,25:5
Mathews, Robert F Mrs, 1955, Mr 30,29:4
Mathews, Robert L, 1947, S 2,21:3
Mathews, Ross, 1942, Ja 3,19:2
Mathews, Shailer, 1941, O 24,23:1
Mathews, Shailer Mrs, 1945, D 20,23:2
Mathews, Tartullus Mrs, 1948, Mr 4,25:5
Mathews, Trevor B Mrs, 1955, F 2,27:5
Mathews, Vera L, 1959, S 27,86:7
Mathews, W A Mrs, 1879, Jl 10,8:2
Mathews, Walter J, 1947, N 23,74:6
Mathews, William, 1881, Je 28,5:2; 1909, F 15,7:4; 1921, Ap 4,13:4; 1941, F 20,20:3; 1950, F 7,27:1
Mathews, William B, 1955, N 7,29:3
Mathews, William B Mrs, 1962, N 7,39:2
Mathews, William F, 1960, Mr 15,39:2
Mathews, William H, 1954, N 3,29:2; 1959, F 18,33:4
Mathews, William K, 1951, Ja 9,29:1
Mathewson, Albert M, 1943, S 21,23:4
Mathewson, Allen H, 1964, Ja 2,27:3
Mathewson, Annie E Mrs, 1954, Mr 26,21:1
Mathewson, Charles Frederick, 1915, Mr 25,11:6
Mathewson, Charles H, 1946, Ag 29,27:1
Mathewson, Charles S, 1962, D 3,32:1
Mathewson, Chester A, 1938, N 30,23:5

Mathewson, Christy Jr, 1950, Ag 17,21:2
Mathewson, Christy Mrs, 1967, My 30,19:5
Mathewson, Deyo P, 1941, Ag 20,19:5
Mathewson, Douglas (por), 1948, S 26,76:5
Mathewson, Douglas Mrs, 1940, My 2,23:4
Mathewson, Edward P, 1948, Jl 15,23:3
Mathewson, Edwin H, 1915, Jl 1,11:6
Mathewson, Elmer, 1951, Ap 8,92:5
Mathewson, George A, 1939, D 25,23:4
Mathewson, Henry S Mrs, 1948, Je 19,15:5
Mathewson, Louis C, 1951, O 28,85:2
Mathewson, Ozias D, 1944, Ag 13,36:1
Mathewson, Paul, 1940, Je 12,25:5
Mathewson, Richard D Mrs, 1956, Ap 18,31:2
Mathewson, Richard D Mrs (Pauline), 1966, N 12, 29:1
Mathewson, Rufus W, 1955, N 1,31:5
Mathewson, Stanley B, 1943, Ja 21,21:2
Mathey, Dean Mrs, 1949, Ap 6,29:3; 1965, S 8,47:5
Mathey, Gustave S, 1957, D 10,35:3
Mathey, Henri C, 1961, N 7,33:4
Mathey, William J, 1962, D 7,39:5
Matheys, Henri, 1940, Mr 20,34:7
Matheys, Jacob C, 1939, D 28,23:6
Matheys, John P, 1967, Je 3,31:1
Mathez, Frederick E, 1959, F 25,31:2
Mathez, Samuel Mrs, 1948, F 18,27:2
Mathias, Aaron, 1952, D 26,15:5
Mathias, Benjamin F, 1937, My 4,25:5
Mathias, David B, 1960, N 10,47:3
Mathias, Henry E, 1966, O 9,86:8
Mathias, James F, 1938, O 13,23:4
Mathias, Louis, 1965, Ag 4,35:6
Mathias, Paul, 1942, S 29,23:2
Mathias, Robert D, 1953, Je 23,29:3
Mathiasen, Chrisian, 1949, S 16,27:1
Mathiasen, Conrad, 1960, Mr 12,21:5
Mathiasen, Hans, 1948, Mr 16,27:4
Mathiasen, Metthea E Mrs, 1942, S 24,27:3
Mathiasen, William, 1942, Ag 28,19:4
Mathie, Karl, 1938, D 10,17:1
Mathieson, George S, 1951, F 8,33:3
Mathieson, James R, 1948, D 21,31:3
Mathieson, John K (por), 1941, Ja 11,17:5
Mathieson, Karl, 1920, Ag 3,9:4
Mathieson, R B, 1949, Jl 5,23:4
Mathieu, Albert, 1939, Jl 5,17:5
Mathieu, Charles L, 1950, My 13,17:6
Mathieu, Edward J, 1966, O 18,84:8
Mathieu, Franklin L, 1941, Je 5,23:5
Mathieu, Harriet B Mrs (will), 1938, Mr 3,23:4
Mathieu, Joseph M, 1945, Ap 7,15:4
Mathieu, Pierre, 1949, Ag 22,21:4
Mathieu, Rene, 1960, Jl 18,27:2
Mathiews, Franklin K, 1950, Ag 29,27:3
Mathilde, Bonaparte Princess, 1904, Ja 3,9:3
Mathilde Gravdahl, Sister, 1945, Ap 14,15:5
Mathiot, Orth, 1951, Ag 5,V,1:3
Mathis, Adolph, 1918, D 28,11:5; 1950, N 20,13:5
Mathis, Fernand (cor, Ja 18,43:2), 1942, Ja 17,17:6
Mathis, Henry, 1947, Jl 19,13:6
Mathis, Hiram, 1944, Mr 18,13:6
Mathis, J, 1927, Jl 27,1:6
Mathis, Jennie V, 1942, Mr 10,19:5
Mathis, Jennings, 1905, Ap 27,11:6
Mathis, Lewis, 1944, F 23,19:4
Mathis, Michael, 1960, Mr 11,25:4
Mathis, Robert, 1950, O 23,4:5
Mathis, Sylvester B, 1955, D 7,39:1
Mathis, Thomas A Mrs, 1956, Ap 9,27:3
Mathis, William A, 1947, Jl 16,23:2
Mathis, William H, 1944, N 16,23:5
Mathisen, Arnold G Mrs, 1959, Mr 21,21:2
Mathison, Dave, 1949, Jl 19,29:4
Mathison, J, 1879, Ja 26,8:5
Mathison, Ralph P, 1959, O 7,43:4
Mathon, E C L J, 1951, Ag 1,23:3
Mathot, Leon, 1968, Mr 7,43:3
Mathot, William L, 1907, N 24,9:6
Mathues, W Frank, 1950, Je 3,15:4
Matiez, J D, 1952, S 18,29:2
Matile, Leon A (por), 1938, Ap 11,15:3
Matisse, Henri (funl, N 9,27:3), 1954, N 4,1:2
Matisse, Henri Mme, 1958, N 14,27:5
Matlack, Lewis T, 1962, Ja 21,88:7
Matlack, Samuel D, 1950, F 14,25:3
Matlack, William C, 1956, N 22,33:4
Matlack Jesse B, 1948, My 15,23:2
Matlawski, Adam, 1951, My 17,31:3
Matlocha, John, 1944, Ap 1,13:6
Matlosz, Albert, 1951, O 21,92:3
Matocha, Josef K, 1961, N 15,43:2
Matonti, Felix G, 1959, Je 29,29:5
Matos, Jose M R N de, 1955, Ja 3,27:3
Matos Sequeira, Gustavo de, 1962, Ag 23,29:3
Matowitz, George J, 1951, N 30,23:3
Matray, George, 1947, Je 16,21:5
Matsell, G W (see also Jl 26), 1877, Jl 29,12:4
Matsil, Harry, 1959, Je 27,23:3
Matsil, Regina, 1924, Jl 22,15:4
Matsner, Augusta O Mrs, 1940, Mr 29,22:3
Matsner, William N, 1937, Je 28,19:5
Matson, Aksel A, 1948, Ja 23,23:3
Matson, C C, 1915, S 5,11:4
Matson, Carlton K, 1948, D 14,29:5
Matson, Charles, 1953, S 13,85:2
Matson, Charles E, 1939, Jl 23,29:1
Matson, Clarence H, 1943, O 18,15:3
Matson, Dean R, 1950, My 9,29:2
Matson, George C, 1940, Ja 4,23:5
Matson, Marcus B, 1942, Ja 23,20:2
Matson, Nathaniel Dr, 1916, O 17,13:2
Matson, Norman, 1965, O 19,43:2
Matson, Peter, 1943, Je 1,23:2
Matson, R N, 1933, F 15,21:3
Matson, Robert H, 1957, Ap 6,19:4
Matson, Roy L, 1960, D 4,88:5
Matson, Theodore M, 1954, D 17,31:1
Matson, William A Rev, 1904, Mr 20,7:5
Matsouka, Shizuko Mrs, 1952, Mr 14,23:2
Matsuda, Masahisa, 1914, Mr 5,9:4
Matsudaira, Norio, 1944, Ja 20,19:2
Matsudaira, Tsuneo, 1949, N 15,26:2
Matsudaira, Yorinaga, 1944, S 14,23:6
Matsui, Keishiro, 1946, Je 5,23:1
Matsui, Yasuo, 1962, Ag 12,81:1
Matsukata, Masaoyahi, 1924, F 28,19:5
Matsukata, Masayoshi, 1924, Mr 1,13:6
Matsukata, Masayoshi Prince, 1924, Jl 3,15:6
Matsumoto, Jiichiro, 1966, N 23,39:2
Matsumoto, Takizo, 1958, N 2,89:1
Matsumura, Gen, 1905, F 6,3:2
Matsuno, Tsuruhei, 1962, O 19,20:8
Matsuoka, Komakichi, 1958, Ag 16,17:2
Matsuoka, Yosuke, 1946, Je 27,21:1
Matsuyama, Kinrey, 1953, D 21,31:4
Matt, C David, 1951, D 4,33:5
Matt, David, 1961, Ap 22,25:5
Matt, Frank X Mrs, 1942, D 15,27:2
Mattatal, Carrie Mrs, 1938, Je 1,23:5
Matte, Guillermo E, 1945, Ag 17,17:1
Matte, William L, 1943, Mr 28,24:2
Mattei, Enrico (funl, O 31,2:7; trb lr, N 4,IV,8:6), 1962, O 28,16:2
Mattei, Lawrence, 1948, Je 24,25:4
Mattei, Tite, 1914, Mr 31,11:4
Matteo, Conca, 1951, Ag 24,15:2
Matteo, Dominick A, 1963, S 29,87:2
Matteo, Michael R, 1955, N 24,29:2
Matteossian, Zenas M, 1949, F 11,23:3
Matter, Emil, 1941, Je 28,15:3
Matter, John, 1949, F 22,23:1
Matter, Kate M, 1948, Jl 22,23:1
Matter, Milton, 1947, N 18,29:3
Mattern, Charles, 1957, Je 13,31:2
Mattern, Conrad J, 1938, F 20,II,8:5
Mattern, Frank L, 1943, My 25,23:3
Mattern, George A, 1945, Mr 14,19:3
Mattern, Jacob C Mrs, 1951, S 16,85:2
Mattern, Walter G, 1961, Je 11,86:2
Matternes, James G, 1953, O 30,23:1
Matterson, Martha R Mrs, 1945, Mr 10,17:1
Mattes, Albert L, 1949, Ja 9,72:6
Mattes, Charles, 1951, Ag 7,25:4
Mattes, Charles Mrs, 1959, O 17,23:5
Mattes, Edward C Mrs, 1952, Jl 1,23:5
Mattes, Edward C Mrs (est tax appr), 1956, Ag 31, 15:5
Mattes, Gerard H, 1959, Ap 10,29:1
Mattes, Herman, 1947, Je 8,60:5
Mattes, John C, 1948, Ja 29,23:2
Mattes, M Anthony, 1963, N 14,35:3
Mattes, Otto Dr, 1937, O 26,23:2
Mattes, Samuel S, 1953, My 3,88:3
Matteson, Anson M, 1947, Ag 7,21:2
Matteson, Arch C, 1939, Je 25,36:7
Matteson, Byron, 1948, Je 18,23:4
Matteson, Charles, 1925, Ag 16,5:2
Matteson, Edgar E, 1948, F 12,23:4
Matteson, H C, 1878, F 10,2:1
Matteson, Harry D, 1963, Ag 10,17:1
Matteson, Herbert A, 1952, D 26,15:3
Matteson, Joel A Ex-Gov, 1873, F 1,8:3
Matteson, Leonard J, 1967, Ag 6,77:1
Matteson, Leonard J Mrs, 1960, Ap 14,31:2
Matteson, Walter B, 1956, Ag 15,29:2
Matteson, William A, 1925, S 22,25:4
Mattey, Nicolas, 1955, N 27,88:8
Mattfeld, Julius, 1968, Ag 1,31:4
Matthaei, Raymond D, 1954, D 19,84:3
Matthaeus, Emil R, 1950, My 3,29:1
Matthai, John, 1959, N 3,31:4
Matthai, William H, 1944, Je 25,30:2
Matthay, Tobias, 1945, D 16,40:2
Matthei, Edward, 1955, Ap 14,29:4
Matthes, Francois E, 1948, Je 25,23:5
Matthes, Percy E, 1954, My 1,15:1
Mattheus, Catherine Mrs, 1941, Mr 29,15:4
Matthew, Bro (B Brown), 1959, Ja 31,19:2
Matthew, Schuyler C (por), 1947, O 19,64:3
Matthew, W D, 1930, S 25,25:3
Matthew, W H, 1946, Mr 16,13:3
Matthews, A C Dr, 1911, Je 28,11:5
Matthews, A E, 1960, Jl 26,29:4
Matthews, Albert, 1949, Ag 15,17:5; 1953, O 12,27:5
Matthews, Albert S, 1948, My 7,23:4
Matthews, Alfred H, 1946, Mr 26,29:4
Matthews, Alfred R, 1955, N 1,31:1
Matthews, Allen R, 1957, Jl 27,17:5
Matthews, Archie J, 1945, F 16,23:4
Matthews, Armstrong R, 1960, Ap 4,29:2
Matthews, Arthur, 1941, My 30,15:1
Matthews, Austin R, 1959, Ag 27,27:6
Matthews, Austin R Mrs, 1940, My 10,24:3
Matthews, B, 1929, Ap 1,1:7
Matthews, Belle R Mrs, 1944, Je 25,29:1
Matthews, Ben H, 1952, Ap 9,31:4
Matthews, Benjamin A Mrs, 1962, O 27,25:1
Matthews, Bertha F Mrs, 1940, Jl 31,17:1
Matthews, Brander Mrs (funl, Fe 7,17:5), 1924, F 23:3
Matthews, Bruce, 1944, F 24,15:5
Matthews, Burrows (funl plans), 1955, Ja 1,13:3
Matthews, Burrows Mrs, 1947, Mr 8,14:3
Matthews, Charles A, 1951, Mr 20,29:4
Matthews, Charles B, 1922, Je 18,28:3
Matthews, Charles E Mrs, 1952, Je 24,29:4
Matthews, Charles F, 1955, Ap 6,29:1
Matthews, Charles Henry, 1917, D 12,15:5
Matthews, Charles J, 1949, Ja 1,11:8
Matthews, Chauncey, 1910, S 11,II,11:5
Matthews, Chauncey W, 1947, Je 7,13:2
Matthews, Clarence Com, 1923, Ap 2,17:5
Matthews, David W, 1960, N 13,88:5
Matthews, Donald M, 1948, S 15,31:4
Matthews, Edmund O Rear-Adm, 1911, Ja 31,9:4
Matthews, Edward, 1954, F 22,26:8
Matthews, Edward E, 1941, Je 21,17:5
Matthews, Edward J, 1962, My 9,43:2
Matthews, Edward Mrs, 1903, D 24,9:5
Matthews, Edwin, 1940, N 23,17:6
Matthews, Elijah Mrs, 1950, Ja 5,25:4
Matthews, Emma B Mrs, 1941, D 13,21:5
Matthews, Emma C Mrs, 1940, Ja 14,43:1
Matthews, Everett, 1946, N 23,15:2
Matthews, Florence R, 1947, F 26,25:3
Matthews, Francis P, 1952, O 19,88:1
Matthews, Francis P Sr (est acctg), 1954, F 10,1
Matthews, Frank C, 1961, Ja 17,27:3
Matthews, Franklin Prof (por),(funl, N 29,13:5), 1917, N 27,13:5
Matthews, Fred A, 1958, S 14,84:3
Matthews, Frederick, 1941, Mr 13,21:1
Matthews, Frederick E, 1942, Jl 24,19:6
Matthews, Frederick Mrs, 1951, S 1,11:5
Matthews, G, 1885, F 18,3:5; 1903, S 30,9:6
Matthews, G Mrs, 1885, F 18,3:5
Matthews, Gardiner D, 1920, Je 18,11:4
Matthews, George, 1939, Je 29,23:4
Matthews, George Capt, 1904, My 30,5:6
Matthews, George E, 1938, Mr 11,19:4
Matthews, George H, 1911, Je 12,11:4
Matthews, George Mrs, 1950, My 5,21:2
Matthews, Gifford, 1951, Ag 13,17:5
Matthews, H Freeman Mrs, 1955, O 27,68:6
Matthews, H Freeman Mrs (Helen), 1966, N 10
Matthews, Harold H, 1940, My 13,17:1
Matthews, Harry E, 1944, N 28,23:6
Matthews, Harry G, 1951, Mr 15,29:5
Matthews, Harry W, 1948, F 8,60:7
Matthews, Harvey B, 1961, S 20,29:5
Matthews, Harvey F, 1949, Ap 8,26:2
Matthews, Henry (Viscount Llandaff), 1913, Ap 15:4
Matthews, Henry J, 1945, S 30,46:4
Matthews, Henry P, 1943, Je 18,21:2
Matthews, Henry V, 1961, Ap 7,31:1
Matthews, Herschell P, 1958, O 24,33:1
Matthews, Hettie Mrs, 1948, F 20,27:2
Matthews, Hilliard H, 1957, S 30,31:5
Matthews, Howard B, 1948, N 11,27:5
Matthews, Howard W, 1953, My 28,23:2
Matthews, Hugh, 1943, Ap 10,17:2
Matthews, Isaac G, 1959, Mr 28,17:4
Matthews, J F, 1884, S 1,5:6
Matthews, J M, 1931, O 13,21:3
Matthews, J Mrs, 1877, Je 23,5:4
Matthews, James, 1917, F 27,11:4; 1937, O 25,2
Matthews, James E, 1950, N 25,13:6
Matthews, James H, 1950, N 11,15:4
Matthews, Jason, 1964, D 1,41:2
Matthews, Jennie L Mrs, 1938, N 21,19:3
Matthews, John A, 1960, Ap 21,31:5
Matthews, John F, 1965, N 25,35:4
Matthews, John F Mrs, 1959, S 15,39:4
Matthews, John H, 1955, Ja 26,25:3
Matthews, John H Mrs, 1956, S 9,84:6
Matthews, John H Sr, 1949, D 9,32:2
Matthews, John Mrs, 1957, F 22,21:2
Matthews, John Rev Dr, 1907, S 2,7:7
Matthews, John S, 1949, Je 24,23:2
Matthews, John W, 1941, Ap 24,21:2
Matthews, Joseph, 1956, Ja 16,21:4
Matthews, Joseph B (cor, Jl 18,27:3), 1966, Jl
Matthews, Joseph C, 1956, S 20,33:4
Matthews, Joseph R, 1946, Je 10,21:3
Matthews, Joseph S, 1952, Mr 31,19:5
Matthews, Jules, 1950, Jl 12,29:6
Matthews, Julia, 1876, My 21,6:7

Matthews, Laura, 1907, Jl 30,7:7
Matthews, Laurence H, 1956, F 11,17:2
Matthews, Louis J, 1951, S 26,31:3
Matthews, Louis P, 1942, O 3,15:4
Matthews, Louis P Mrs, 1959, F 23,23:4
Matthews, Luke, 1952, S 14,86:2
Matthews, Luke Mrs, 1948, Mr 25,27:3
Matthews, Mabel R Mrs, 1949, Ja 7,21:5
Matthews, Marianna Mrs (will), 1958, Jl 30,19:2
Matthews, Mark A (por), 1940, F 6,21:5
Matthews, Mary A, 1885, Ja 23,5:2
Matthews, Mary E R Mrs, 1938, S 13,23:4
Matthews, Mary Mrs, 1948, Ja 16,23:1
Matthews, Mary S Mrs, 1937, N 24,23:2
Matthews, Melville T, 1960, S 13,37:5
Matthews, Melvin H, 1940, Ag 1,21:3
Matthews, Murrello O, 1964, Ja 6,47:3
Matthews, N, 1927, D 12,23:3
Matthews, Newman, 1951, N 8,29:1
Matthews, Oliver J, 1947, Ag 3,53:1
Matthews, Orus J, 1964, Jl 25,19:5
Matthews, Oscar C, 1906, S 13,1:2
Matthews, Paul, 1953, Ag 16,77:1
Matthews, Paul Mrs, 1946, Ag 23,19:4
Matthews, Peter, 1958, S 30,31:5
Matthews, Peter P, 1942, Jl 25,13:3
Matthews, Phil, 1949, N 13,92:6
Matthews, Philip S Mrs (Sara E Branham), 1962, N 19,31:2
Matthews, Ralph F, 1962, Jl 22,64:3
Matthews, Richard, 1949, Jl 14,27:2
Matthews, Richard T, 1967, Ap 9,92:7
Matthews, Robert C, 1961, Ja 16,24:2
Matthews, Robert R, 1920, F 7,11:3
Matthews, Robert S, 1942, O 16,19:4
Matthews, Robert W, 1967, N 14,47:3
Matthews, Roger E, 1962, S 5,39:2
Matthews, Ronald, 1967, My 6,31:1
Matthews, Russell V Mrs, 1961, S 16,19:3
Matthews, Samuel, 1946, N 5,25:2
Matthews, Schuyler C Mrs, 1948, O 27,27:4
Matthews, Scott J, 1956, Ap 10,31:4
Matthews, Sherman T, 1940, N 2,15:5
Matthews, Sherrie, 1921, D 9,17:5
Matthews, Sidney T, 1940, S 25,27:3
Matthews, Stanley, 1963, N 21,39:2
Matthews, Stanley G, 1953, Mr 31,31:2
Matthews, Stanley Judge, 1889, Mr 23,1:7
Matthews, Stanley Mrs, 1912, S 20,11:6
Matthews, Star Mrs, 1951, Je 15,23:1
Matthews, Stormont G, 1939, N 20,19:3
Matthews, Thomas Anson, 1914, Ag 17,7:4
Matthews, Thomas C, 1949, Je 21,25:4
Matthews, Thomas Clark Mrs, 1968, My 28,47:2
Matthews, Thomas J, 1957, Je 20,29:4
Matthews, Thomas L, 1959, Ap 12,86:4
Matthews, Thomas Mrs, 1949, D 17,17:5
Matthews, Townsend Mrs, 1949, Je 14,32:4
Matthews, Victor J, 1951, Ag 9,21:3
Matthews, Victory E Mrs, 1907, Mr 11,7:6
Matthews, W D, 1959, Mr 15,88:4
Matthews, Walter J, 1940, Ag 31,13:2
Matthews, Walter W, 1960, F 14,84:5
Matthews, Wid (Oct 4), 1965, O 11,61:3
Matthews, Willard, 1940, O 7,17:1
Matthews, William E, 1948, O 16,15:5; 1964, Ap 8, 43:4
Matthews, William F, 1963, N 17,86:3; 1966, S 17,29:1
Matthews, William H, 1937, S 24,21:2
Matthews, William H (por), 1946, Mr 12,25:3
Matthews, William H, 1946, Je 19,21:3; 1947, S 30, 25:2
Matthews, William H Mrs, 1955, Ja 16,92:6
Matthews, William J, 1951, N 9,27:3
Matthews, William R, 1951, F 22,31:5
Matthews, William T Prof, 1905, Ja 12,7:6
Matthews, Zachariah Keodirelang, 1968, My 12,84:6
Matthewson, Douglas E Sr, 1959, Mr 12,31:5
Matthewson, Frederick, 1907, N 30,7:5
Matthewson, George L, 1943, Je 29,19:2
Matthey, Alice, 1950, Ap 21,23:4
Matthias, Bro (W Comeford), 1952, S 30,31:2
Matthias, Charles, 1908, My 10,9:4
Matthias, Edward S, 1953, N 3,11:4
Matthias, M Paul, 1953, O 1,29:6
Matthias, William W, 1938, Mr 7,17:5
Matthiassen, Anna T Mrs, 1945, Je 6,21:4
Matthies, William H, 1946, O 22,25:1
Matthiesen, Henry M, 1940, F 19,17:2
Matthiesen, John A, 1955, Jl 21,23:1
Matthieson, Charles S Dr, 1937, Mr 4,23:3
Matthiessen, C H Mrs, 1903, Jl 18,7:6
Matthiessen, Conrad H Mrs, 1957, Ap 3,31:2
Matthiessen, Ehrard Adolph, 1905, My 24,9:6
Matthiessen, Frank, 1939, My 4,23:5
Matthieu, Samuel A, 1939, Jl 24,13:6
Matthison, Arthur, 1883, My 22,5:5
Matthison, Edith W, 1955, S 25,93:2
Matthius, George M, 1954, Mr 6,15:3
Mattia, Richard F, 1961, Je 15,43:2
Mattice, Abram Rev, 1904, D 28,7:6
Mattice, Asa M, 1925, Ap 21,21:5
Mattice, Burr Judge, 1903, N 7,9:6
Mattice, Edson H, 1937, F 21,II,10:5
Mattice, Harold A, 1956, Mr 12,27:6
Mattice, Harold A Mrs, 1961, F 25,21:5
Mattiello, Joseph, 1948, My 17,19:4
Mattieson, Henry, 1943, Je 1,23:1
Mattil, William W, 1955, Ap 2,13:8
Mattill, Henry A, 1953, Mr 31,31:5
Mattimiro, Nicholas, 1961, N 29,41:1
Mattimore, James, 1941, F 14,18:3
Mattimore, James S, 1937, Ag 14,13:6
Mattimore, James T, 1938, Ja 29,15:4
Mattingly, Barak T, 1957, Jl 19,19:3
Mattingly, Garrett, 1962, D 20,8:3
Mattingly, George E, 1949, Jl 6,30:1
Mattingly, James F, 1865, Ag 16,1:5
Mattingly, Jesse M, 1955, Ag 31,25:2
Mattingly, Robert E, 1948, S 27,23:5
Mattinson, Frank W, 1955, Ap 28,29:2
Mattioli, Lino, 1949, Ja 24,19:4
Mattirlo, Oreste, 1947, D 6,15:6
Mattis, Doris Mrs, 1940, Ja 13,15:2
Mattis, Ross R, 1945, S 14,23:3
Mattis, Sidney, 1953, Ap 20,25:3
Mattison, Eugene, 1940, Je 15,15:5
Mattison, Hiram Rev, 1868, N 26,8:3
Mattison, Lyle G, 1947, N 20,29:2
Mattison, Samuel J, 1942, O 5,19:4
Mattison, Walter S, 1950, Ag 2,25:4
Mattison, William C (funl, D 2,39:3), 1966, N 29,43:3
Mattison, William C Mrs, 1958, F 20,25:1
Mattlage, Charles F, 1913, Mr 12,11:4
Mattlage, Frederick H, 1942, Ag 22,13:2
Mattle, William, 1942, D 14,23:4
Mattlin, Howard B, 1961, O 27,33:1
Mattlingly, Foster G Sr, 1952, Ja 21,15:2
Mattmann, Carl C, 1961, N 9,35:2
Mattmann, Charles Sr, 1947, Je 20,19:3
Mattocks, Raymond L, 1954, Mr 11,31:3
Mattoon, Albert W, 1937, Je 21,19:4
Mattoon, David, 1939, Jl 25,19:2
Mattoon, Everett W, 1956, Je 6,33:3
Mattoon, Howard V, 1943, Ap 12,23:4
Mattoon, Howard V Mrs, 1966, Ja 20,35:2
Mattoon, John F, 1873, Ag 5,1:5
Mattos Hurtado, Belisario, 1953, My 29,25:5
Mattox, E Tilden, 1951, S 18,31:4
Mattox, Marvin B, 1956, My 7,27:4
Mattox, Norman T, 1960, F 3,33:1
Matts, Reuben Mrs, 1923, D 21,17:4
Mattson, Arthur, 1944, S 17,42:3
Mattson, Axel Mrs, 1958, O 27,27:4
Mattson, Carl M, 1940, D 14,17:6
Mattson, Frank S, 1951, S 6,31:1
Mattson, H Leo, 1949, Je 16,29:1
Mattson, Louis A, 1948, Ap 9,23:5
Mattson, P A, 1944, Ap 5,19:4
Mattson, Peter, 1938, O 26,23:3
Mattsson, Ernest, 1954, Ap 4,88:2
Mattuck, George F, 1941, Ap 3,23:4
Mattuck, Israel I, 1954, Ap 5,25:5
Mattuck, Maxwell S (cor, N 13,35:3), 1957, N 8,29:1
Matturri, Nicola Mrs, 1951, Je 13,29:6
Matuk, Anthony, 1950, Ja 13,24:3
Matulaitis, Wenceslaus V, 1938, D 14,25:4
Matulionis, Teofilo, 1962, Ag 26,83:1
Matullo, Pasquale, 1941, Ja 31,19:3
Mature, Clara P Mrs, 1959, F 5,31:1
Mature, Marcellus G, 1941, O 21,23:3
Maturin, E S, 1881, My 27,2:2
Maturkanics, Michael, 1950, Ja 12,27:1
Matus, Juan de D, 1941, Jl 9,21:4
Matus, Stanley F, 1958, S 23,33:3
Matus, Vega, 1937, D 3,23:1
Matusevich, N N, 1950, Je 8,31:4
Matusoff, Irving, 1966, D 11,88:6
Matusow, Max, 1959, Ag 18,29:1
Matuszewski, Ignacy (por), 1946, Ag 5,21:3
Matyas, Maria (Mrs E C Wilson), 1963, Ap 21,86:6
Matz, Boris B, 1951, D 9,91:1
Matz, Frank H, 1947, D 24,22:2
Matz, Herbert E, 1965, Ag 6,27:1
Matz, Israel, 1950, F 11,15:1
Matz, Israel Mrs, 1948, D 29,21:3
Matz, Nicholas Bp, 1917, Ag 10,9:5
Matzal, Leopold C, 1956, N 24,19:1
Matzen, Harry B Sr, 1955, My 17,29:3
Matzen, Herman N, 1938, Ap 24,II,6:6
Matzenauer, Margaret, 1963, My 20,31:4
Matzka, George, 1883, Je 17,1:3
Matzke, Adele, 1963, S 4,39:2
Matzke, J E Prof, 1910, S 21,9:4
Matzko, John, 1952, Jl 1,23:3
Mau, Cecil T, 1953, Ap 20,25:4
Mau, Henry J, 1958, Jl 13,69:2
Mau, William R H, 1949, Je 25,13:2
Maubert, Gustave, 1960, My 19,37:6
Maubert, Louis, 1949, Mr 26,17:4
Mauceri, Gasper G, 1942, Ag 18,21:1
Mauceri, Joseph C, 1960, N 21,29:4
Mauch, Joseph Bernhard Dr, 1909, F 5,7:4
Mauchel, Robert L, 1962, O 5,33:2
Mauchet, Harry J, 1938, Je 2,23:6
Mauchly, Emanuel C, 1956, My 7,27:2
Maucieri, Anthony J, 1955, F 28,19:5
Mauck, Earl W, 1950, Jl 28,21:5
Mauck, Federico F, 1958, O 20,29:5
Mauck, Frances F, 1958, Ag 24,87:2
Mauck, Joseph W Dr (por), 1937, Jl 8,23:4
Mauck, Victor, 1956, D 4,39:5
Maud, Fred, 1951, N 3,17:6
Maud, W T, 1903, My 13,3:4
Maude, Aylmer, 1938, Ag 26,17:3
Maude, Cyril, 1951, F 21,27:1
Maude, Cyril Mrs, 1924, Jl 16,11:5
Maude, Joseph, 1951, Ja 3,25:2
Maude, Lawrence P, 1952, Ja 30,26:2
Maude, William L, 1966, O 4,47:2
Mauder, Arthur M Mrs, 1964, Ap 1,39:2
Mauder, Edward P, 1951, N 10,17:4
Maud'huy, L E de Gen, 1921, Jl 17,22:4
Maudlin, Arthur S (por), 1946, Je 1,13:4
Maudlin, George H, 1938, N 18,21:1
Maudru, Joseph, 1940, Ja 14,42:5
Mauer, Alfred, 1954, S 21,27:1
Mauer, Carl, 1958, Ag 22,21:1
Mauer, Elizabeth Mrs, 1951, Ag 20,19:4
Mauer, Frederick J, 1960, N 10,47:1
Mauer, Julius M, 1959, Ap 6,27:5
Mauer, Margaret K, 1945, Ag 4,11:4
Mauer, Peter, 1950, Ag 9,29:1
Mauer, William, 1952, Ap 27,91:1
Mauer, William A, 1940, N 14,23:1
Mauff, John R, 1938, Ja 19,23:5
Mauger, Franklin E, 1964, My 4,29:4
Mauger, James E Mrs, 1947, Ap 11,25:4
Mauger, Samuel W, 1949, O 19,29:1
Maugham, Catherine Mrs, 1938, N 4,23:4
Maugham, Frederic H, 1958, Mr 24,27:1
Maugham, Louis F Mrs, 1957, O 5,17:3
Maugham, Sarah V Mrs, 1941, Ag 23,13:2
Maugham, Syrie Mrs, 1955, Jl 27,23:6
Maugham, W Somerset (ashes buried, D 23,28:8), 1965, D 16,1:3
Mauhs, Sharon J, 1964, O 8,43:1
Maujer, Daniel, 1882, Jl 13,2:4
Mauk, Eleanor T, 1952, Ja 15,27:2
Maul, Albert J, 1958, My 5,29:4
Maul, Peter, 1940, Jl 13,13:2
Maul, Theodore R, 1943, O 16,13:2
Maulana Shaukat Ali (por), 1938, N 28,15:5
Maulbetsch, Johnny, 1950, S 15,25:6
Mauldin, Stanley, 1948, S 26,V,5:3
Maule, Charles P, 1950, O 28,17:4
Maule, Frances, 1966, Je 29,47:2
Maule, George A Mrs, 1949, My 14,13:7
Maule, John H, 1955, Ap 22,25:3
M'Auley, Jerry, 1884, S 19,5:3
Maull, Ada E, 1950, Jl 13,25:1
Maull, G Clifton, 1953, My 21,31:3
Maull, Harry M, 1948, D 27,21:1
Maull, R J, 1948, Ag 31,23:3
Maulsby, David L Mrs, 1949, Ja 28,21:3
Maulsby, David Lee, 1924, D 28,5:2
Maun, Marian, 1953, My 9,19:5
Maun, Thomas, 1948, O 2,15:2
Maund, John J, 1944, N 25,13:6
Maund, Loben E H, 1957, Je 21,25:5
Maund, Mary A Mrs, 1952, Jl 31,23:4
Maunder, Frederick Rev, 1947, Je 1,60:3
Maunder, William T, 1942, Jl 7,20:3
Maunders, John, 1944, Ja 18,20:3
Maundrell, David J, 1968, D 31,27:2
Mauney, David H, 1942, D 13,74:3
Mauney, Ernest J, 1959, Ja 29,27:1
Maunoury, Maurice, 1925, My 17,6:1
Maunoury, Michel Joseph Gen, 1923, Mr 29,19:4
Maupai, Ralph G, 1943, Jl 31,13:1
Maupi, Marcel, 1949, Ja 5,25:1
Maupin, R Harry, 1954, F 11,29:5
Maupin, Will, 1948, Je 13,69:1
Maura, Antonio, 1925, D 14,21:5
Maura y Gamazo, Gabriel (Duke of Maura), 1963, Ja 30,9:4
Mauran, Frank, 1954, N 8,21:2
Mauran, William L, 1942, D 7,27:2
Maurao, Ramiro B, 1949, Ag 1,17:3
Maureen, Sister (A Sheedy), 1963, O 19,25:1
Maureen, Sister (Sisters of Mercy), 1965, F 16,35:3
Maurel, Victor, 1923, O 23,21:4
Maurer, Adam C, 1942, Ap 15,23:3
Maurer, Albert Mrs, 1945, D 4,29:5
Maurer, Alex C, 1938, My 1,II,6:6
Maurer, Armand, 1943, Mr 3,23:2
Maurer, Charles F, 1951, O 13,17:4
Maurer, Charles J, 1946, S 4,23:5
Maurer, Charles L, 1958, Jl 6,56:6
Maurer, Edward H, 1952, My 21,27:1
Maurer, Ernst, 1946, F 12,28:1
Maurer, Frank J, 1941, Ag 14,17:2
Maurer, George, 1962, N 20,35:4
Maurer, George E Dr (por), 1937, Mr 19,24:1
Maurer, George J, 1940, D 21,17:5
Maurer, George W, 1939, Mr 11,17:5; 1941, O 4,15:2
Maurer, Godfrey H, 1956, Ag 28,27:4
Maurer, Harry Mrs, 1955, Ap 22,25:2
Maurer, Henry, 1904, Ja 11,7:6

Maurer, Henry B, 1941, N 29,17:5
Maurer, Irving (por), 1942, Mr 1,45:1
Maurer, Jacob, 1942, N 28,13:5
Maurer, James H, 1944, Mr 17,17:4
Maurer, John C, 1937, D 17,25:3
Maurer, John H, 1957, F 1,25:4
Maurer, Keith L (por), 1949, F 25,23:1
Maurer, L, 1932, Jl 20,15:3
Maurer, Lydia S, 1953, O 20,29:4
Maurer, Maurice, 1949, Ap 26,25:3
Maurer, Milton Mrs, 1946, S 20,31:4
Maurer, Murray L, 1967, Mr 6,29:6
Maurer, Oscar E, 1950, D 1,26:2
Maurer, Sascha, 1961, Mr 18,23:4
Maurer, Theodore, 1909, Je 27,7:5
Maurer, Ulrich, 1903, Ag 19,9:6
Maurer, William, 1948, F 5,24:2
Maurette, Fernand, 1937, Ag 2,19:5
Maurette, Rene G, 1948, Mr 18,28:2
Maurey, Max, 1947, F 28,23:4
Maurice, Albert T, 1962, O 5,33:1
Maurice, Arthur B (for), 1946, Je 1,13:1
Maurice, Bro (M H Farrell), 1955, Jl 13,25:5
Maurice, Charles A, 1939, F 15,23:2
Maurice, Countess, 1873, Ap 1,5:5
Maurice, Frank J, 1940, D 6,23:5
Maurice, Frederick, 1951, My 20,88:5
Maurice, Frederick Maj-Gen, 1912, Ja 13,13:4
Maurice, James, 1884, Ag 7,5:2
Maurice, William De Forest, 1903, S 8,7:5
Maurice-Jacquet, Henri, 1954, Je 30,27:5
Maurichi, E V Marchioness, 1928, My 29,5:2
Mauriello, Angelo M, 1962, Ja 20,21:5
Mauriello, Carolina Mrs, 1963, Ag 17,19:4
Mauriello, Louis J Mrs, 1957, Je 18,33:1
Maurier, Louis, 1874, D 8,1:6
Maurilius, Bro, 1947, Ap 25,21:3
Maurin, Frank D, 1960, Jl 16,19:4
Maurin, L J, 1936, N 17,27:2
Maurin, Louis, 1956, Je 7,31:4
Maurin, Peter (por), 1949, My 17,25:3
Mauro, Charles F, 1952, Je 2,22:4
Mauro, Dante, 1950, Ja 18,31:4
Mauro, Filomena Mrs, 1943, My 23,39:2
Mauro, Joseph, 1947, O 24,23:1
Mauro, Phil G, 1959, My 19,33:3
Mauro-Cottone, Melchiorre, 1938, S 30,21:4
Maurocardato, Alex, 1952, F 7,27:2
Maurois, Andre (funl, O 13,39:1), 1967, O 10,1:2
Maurras, Charles, 1952, N 17,25:1
Maurtua, Victor M Dr (por), 1937, My 28,21:3
Maurus, Edward J, 1941, N 27,23:2
Maury, Antonia C, 1952, Ja 10,29:2
Maury, Arthur G Mrs, 1944, S 27,21:4
Maury, Carlotta J, 1938, Ja 4,23:3
Maury, James F Mrs, 1950, D 10,105:2
Maury, M, 1877, S 19,4:6
Maury, M F, 1878, Jl 9,8:4
Maury, Magruder G, 1948, N 24,23:5
Maury, Mather Mrs (funl, F 28,11:4), 1917, F 27,11:4
Maury, Mathew F, 1873, F 2,5:3
Maury, Matthew F Jr Mrs, 1937, My 28,21:5
Maury, Mytton Dr, 1919, Ag 6,9:2
Maury, Philippe, 1967, Je 7,47:1
Maury, Pierre, 1956, Ja 19,33:2
Maury, Rutson (funl), 1882, My 7,10:3
Maury, Sifrein F, 1960, Ag 10,31:2
Maury, Thompson Brooke, 1923, Jl 16,11:5
Maus, M P, 1930, F 10,23:3
Maus, W Donald, 1960, N 18,31:3
Maus, William H, 1948, Ag 10,22:2
Mauser, Frank, 1908, Ap 12,7:7
Mauser, Joseph A, 1947, Ja 9,23:1
Mauser, Paul von Dr, 1914, My 30,11:5
Mauser, Raymond, 1955, My 15,86:4
Mausolff, Paul, 1938, Jl 12,19:4
Mauss, Jacob, 1946, D 10,31:4
Mauss, William G, 1955, Jl 27,23:3
Mausshardt, Edward C, 1944, Jl 18,19:5
Maust, Frederick K, 1963, My 5,86:7
Maust, Robert W, 1952, Ap 24,31:5
Maute, Frederick A, 1957, Ap 28,86:1
Mauterstock, Joseph W, 1925, Ap 11,13:3
Mauthe, J Lester (Pete), 1967, Ja 3,37:3
Mauthe, William, 1942, My 12,19:5
Mauthner, Herbert, 1963, Ap 21,86:7
Mautner, George, 1948, N 12,24:2
Mautner, Isadore, 1945, Mr 15,23:4
Mautner, Samuel, 1944, Ag 17,17:4
Mautner, Sidney, 1955, My 25,33:2
Mauze, J Layton Dr, 1937, Ap 26,19:6
Mavalankar, Ganesh V, 1956, F 28,31:4
Maverick, Maury Sr, 1954, Je 8,27:1
Maves, Arthur E Mrs, 1937, Mr 4,23:5
Mavet, Eugene L, 1955, F 23,27:2
Mavity, John M, 1947, Jl 28,15:5
Mavor, James, 1925, N 2,23:4
Mavor, Preston B, 1962, Ja 5,29:3
Mavrogordato, Theodore M, 1941, Ag 27,19:6
Mavromatis, Demetrios, 1940, O 21,7:2
Mawbey, Frederick R, 1950, D 1,25:2
Mawer, Allen, 1942, Jl 23,19:5
Mawer, Colin D, 1965, Ap 10,29:3
Mawer, John S, 1953, My 26,29:4
Mawer, Lucien, 1947, Jl 9,23:5
Mawhinney, Frances, 1940, Ap 22,17:3
Mawhinney, George S, 1948, D 29,21:5
Mawhinney, George S Mrs, 1957, F 1,25:1
Mawhinney, John A, 1953, Je 30,23:5
Mawhinney, Robert J, 1954, N 19,23:2
Mawhinney, Thomas J Mrs, 1952, O 8,31:2
Mawicke, Henry J, 1953, N 14,17:3
Mawson, C O Sylvester, 1938, N 5,19:2
Mawson, Douglas, 1958, O 15,39:1
Mawson, Edward Robert, 1917, My 22,13:4
Mawwell, Irving, 1950, D 28,25:1
Max, Adolphe, 1939, N 7,25:1
Max, Charles A, 1967, O 16,45:1
Max, Duke of Hohenberg, 1962, Ja 10,47:4
Max, Morris, 1950, O 13,29:1
Max, Prince of Baden, 1929, N 6,25:3
Max, William D, 1954, S 11,17:4
Max-Muller, William G, 1945, My 13,20:4
Max Wilhelm of Saxony, Ex-Prince, 1951, Ja 13,15:3
Maxcy, David Mrs, 1943, Ap 6,21:3
Maxcy, Joseph Francis X Rev (trb, Ja 20,11:4), 1911, Ja 16,11:3
Maxcy, Kenneth F, 1966, D 13,47:1
Maxey, George W, 1950, Mr 21,29:2
Maxey, Paul, 1963, Je 4,39:2
Maxfield, Alvero W, 1954, D 12,88:4
Maxfield, Berton L, 1937, My 27,23:2
Maxfield, Berton L Mrs, 1946, My 12,45:3
Maxfield, Charles H, 1951, Mr 25,73:1
Maxfield, Charles M, 1952, Jl 5,15:6
Maxfield, Clyde J, 1942, S 10,27:4
Maxfield, Edwin R, 1950, Ja 4,35:2
Maxfield, Edwin R Mrs, 1947, D 14,79:1
Maxfield, Ezra K, 1941, Ja 10,19:2
Maxfield, Frank H, 1955, D 30,19:2
Maxfield, Frederick, 1951, D 3,31:3
Maxfield, George D, 1959, Ag 2,81:2
Maxfield, Howard H, 1956, O 28,89:2
Maxfield, Howard W Mrs, 1947, Ag 1,17:2
Maxfield, John G, 1950, Ja 18,31:3
Maxfield, Theodore T, 1961, Ja 22,84:5
Maxfield, Thomas O Sr, 1965, Ja 9,25:5
Maxim, Frederick L, 1941, Ap 13,38:4
Maxim, H, 1927, My 7,17:1
Maxim, H P, 1936, F 18,23:1
Maxim, Hiram Sir, 1916, N 25,13:3
Maxim, Hosea F Mrs, 1953, Mr 24,31:1
Maxim, Leighton L, 1961, N 10,35:4
Maxim, Sarah, 1941, Ag 24,36:4
Maximilian, Archduke of Habsburg, 1952, Ja 19,15:3
Maximilian, Michael, 1953, S 18,23:4
Maximilien, George Henri Baron, 1908, D 13,13:5
Maximillian, Louis Charles (Prince Luitpold), 1914, Ag 28,9:6
Maximoff, Maxim A, 1940, Je 8,15:6
Maximos, Demetrios, 1955, O 17,27:5
Maximov, A A, 1928, D 5,31:3
Maxman, George, 1953, Jl 17,11:6
Maxon, James M, 1948, N 9,28:3
Maxon, Lester H, 1961, Mr 17,24:1
Maxon, William D, 1940, O 4,23:2
Maxon, William R, 1948, F 27,21:1
Maxse, H Sir, 1883, S 9,9:2
Maxse, Ivor, 1958, Ja 30,24:1
Maxse, L J, 1932, Ja 23,15:1
Maxson, Charles P, 1941, Ag 9,15:4
Maxson, Frank T, 1954, S 26,87:1
Maxson, Henry L, 1925, D 17,23:5
Maxson, Henry M Mrs, 1945, Ja 20,11:1
Maxson, Herbert E, 1955, F 12,15:5
Maxson, Julia B Mrs, 1950, Je 17,15:3
Maxson, Louis A, 1957, Je 20,29:2
Maxson, Reuben A, 1949, Ja 20,27:2
Maxson, William E, 1960, F 4,31:4
Maxson, William L, 1947, Jl 15,23:4
Maxson, William S, 1937, Ag 19,20:1
Maxted, Stanley, 1963, My 11,25:3
Maxton, James, 1946, Jl 24,27:1
Maxtone-Graham, James, 1940, O 29,25:5
Maxtone-Graham, James Mrs, 1952, My 15,31:3
Maxudian, Yervant Mrs, 1953, N 16,25:2
Maxwell, A C, 1929, Ja 3,27:3; 1947, Ja 17,23:1
Maxwell, Alex, 1948, F 12,23:3
Maxwell, Allen G, 1943, Ap 25,34:4
Maxwell, Allen J, 1946, D 10,31:2
Maxwell, Arch M, 1949, Ap 19,26:2
Maxwell, Archibald F, 1959, Je 24,31:3
Maxwell, Augustus E, 1903, My 6,9:5
Maxwell, Augustus K, 1945, Ja 30,19:1
Maxwell, Barry, 1917, Jl 20,9:6
Maxwell, Carl A, 1966, Ja 27,33:5
Maxwell, Caroline Mrs, 1948, S 20,25:3
Maxwell, Charles A, 1943, Ag 24,19:4
Maxwell, Charles E, 1941, Ag 25,15:2; 1952, Ap 2,33:3
Maxwell, Charles J, 1945, N 29,23:5
Maxwell, Charles M, 1907, S 28,9:6; 1913, Ag 28,9:3; 1913, S 27,13:4
Maxwell, Charles R, 1939, S 15,23:2
Maxwell, Charles Rev, 1917, Ag 28,7:8
Maxwell, Charles W, 1950, Ag 22,27:2
Maxwell, Clair, 1959, My 12,35:2
Maxwell, Claude W, 1940, Jl 2,22:2
Maxwell, D E Capt, 1908, S 17,7:6
Maxwell, Daniel W, 1946, Jl 18,25:4
Maxwell, Douglas P, 1952, My 11,92:4
Maxwell, Earl P, 1940, D 14,17:6
Maxwell, Edward, 1925, My 31,5:1
Maxwell, Edward H, 1942, Ap 21,23:2
Maxwell, Edwin, 1948, Ag 14,13:6
Maxwell, Elsa (funl plans, N 9,25:3; funl, N 13,41:5), 1963, N 2,25:2
Maxwell, Emerson G, 1962, Mr 11,86:3
Maxwell, Eugene L, 1942, O 17,15:5
Maxwell, Ex-Collector, 1873, Ap 3,8:6
Maxwell, Florence P Mrs (will), 1965, Mr 7,59:1
Maxwell, Francis T, 1942, Mr 24,19:1
Maxwell, Fred F, 1919, O 16,17:2
Maxwell, Frederick R, 1948, D 10,25:2
Maxwell, French T, 1946, Mr 21,25:2
Maxwell, George H, 1946, D 3,31:1
Maxwell, George L, 1947, Ja 4,15:3
Maxwell, George M, 1964, N 3,31:4
Maxwell, Gerald C, 1959, D 19,27:4
Maxwell, Grover, 1955, D 4,88:3
Maxwell, H Elliott, 1946, Jl 29,21:5
Maxwell, H W, 1902, My 13,9:2
Maxwell, Harry, 1952, Ag 13,21:2
Maxwell, Harry T, 1954, S 22,29:5
Maxwell, Henry L, 1951, Ag 12,78:4
Maxwell, Henry L Mrs, 1937, F 23,27:2
Maxwell, Henry Mrs, 1940, Jl 2,21:4
Maxwell, Henry T, 1952, Je 23,19:5
Maxwell, Herbert E Sir, 1937, O 31,II,10:8
Maxwell, Howard W (por), 1947, S 14,60:2
Maxwell, Howard W Mrs, 1956, D 31,14:6; 1958, D 30,32:2
Maxwell, J Alice, 1942, My 4,19:5
Maxwell, J D, 1879, Ja 16,5:6; 1928, Mr 9,25:5
Maxwell, James, 1956, N 29,35:5
Maxwell, James J Mrs, 1959, Jl 26,69:2
Maxwell, John, 1940, O 4,23:6; 1951, Je 3,93:1; 19 My 17,88:5; 1954, Ja 5,27:3
Maxwell, John F Rev, 1937, Ap 15,24:2
Maxwell, John M, 1956, Ap 14,17:6
Maxwell, John W, 1937, Ja 3,II,9:1; 1937, F 16,23
Maxwell, Jonathan D Mrs, 1967, Ag 10,37:2
Maxwell, Joseph S (por), 1945, Jl 11,11:5
Maxwell, Lee W, 1948, O 5,26:2
Maxwell, Lee W Mrs, 1949, Ja 27,23:3
Maxwell, Leslie E, 1951, N 5,31:2
Maxwell, Lillian M, 1956, Je 15,25:3
Maxwell, Lloyd, 1960, N 4,33:2
Maxwell, Manley M, 1940, Jl 8,17:3
Maxwell, Marcuswell, 1938, Ap 22,19:4
Maxwell, Mary, 1942, S 25,21:3
Maxwell, Maxwell C, 1951, Je 15,23:1
Maxwell, Nathaniel Mrs, 1951, S 8,17:5
Maxwell, O Clay Sr, 1950, Je 18,76:2
Maxwell, Perriton, 1947, My 3,17:4
Maxwell, Perriton Mrs, 1939, Ap 30,45:2
Maxwell, Perry D, 1952, N 18,31:3
Maxwell, Priscilla Mrs, 1954, Ag 18,29:3
Maxwell, Richard W, 1954, S 7,25:2
Maxwell, Robert, 1943, O 31,49:1
Maxwell, Robert A Gen, 1912, Je 9,II,15:5
Maxwell, Robert A Mrs, 1924, Ap 3,21:6
Maxwell, Robert C, 1955, Mr 10,27:4
Maxwell, Robert C Jr, 1953, O 11,89:2
Maxwell, Robert L, 1965, D 10,47:2
Maxwell, Robert Mrs, 1948, Ag 15,60:4
Maxwell, Robert W (Tiny), 1922, Jl 1,13:7
Maxwell, Robert W, 1940, Ap 22,17:2
Maxwell, Ross F, 1947, O 29,27:5
Maxwell, Russell L Maj-Gen, 1968, N 25,47:2
Maxwell, S Watson, 1945, Mr 11,39:1
Maxwell, Sara, 1941, N 26,23:4
Maxwell, Seth, 1945, D 6,27:5
Maxwell, Stirling Lady (Mrs Norton), 1877, Je
Maxwell, Stuart B, 1941, Mr 4,23:5
Maxwell, Susan Augusta Mrs, 1923, F 13,21:4
Maxwell, Thomas C, 1951, Ag 11,11:6
Maxwell, Thomas H, 1942, D 13,72:2
Maxwell, Thomas J Mrs, 1948, D 13,23:3
Maxwell, Vera, 1950, My 2,29:5
Maxwell, W J, 1944, Ap 3,21:2
Maxwell, W Kee, 1952, Ap 27,90:4
Maxwell, William, 1942, Ag 12,19:6; 1943, Jl 4, 1947, My 22,27:4
Maxwell, William B, 1938, Ag 5,17:5
Maxwell, William F Mrs, 1954, Jl 6,23:4
Maxwell, William H Dr, 1920, My 6,11:3
Maxwell, William Henry Dr, 1920, My 4,11:3
Maxwell, William J, 1942, Ap 22,23:1
Maxwell, William Joseph, 1919, My 24,13:2
Maxwell, William R, 1946, Mr 17,44:4
Maxwell, William S Mrs, 1940, Mr 3,45:2
Maxwell-Lyte, Henry, 1940, O 30,23:3
Maxwell-Scott, Walter, 1954, Ap 4,88:2
Maxwell-Willshire, Gerard, 1947, Ap 4,23:5
May, A J, 1943, Ap 28,23:1
May, Adolph W, 1942, Je 23,19:4
May, Albert E, 1945, My 14,17:4
May, Albert J, 1955, Ja 25,25:4
May, Alfred A, 1957, D 13,27:3

May, Andrew J (funl, S 9,41:2), 1959, S 7,15:3
May, Andrew J Mrs, 1942, D 28,19:4
May, Ann M, 1961, Je 11,86:4
May, Arthur A, 1963, O 30,39:4
May, Arthur J, 1968, Je 18,47:4
May, Augustus S, 1937, F 12,23:3
May, Benjamin, 1919, Mr 3,13:3
May, Benjamin M Mrs, 1952, N 9,91:1
May, Benjamin Mrs, 1918, D 30,9:2
May, Bernard S, 1951, Mr 30,23:4
May, Calvin Sloane Dr, 1919, Ap 27,22:4
May, Charles, 1941, Je 14,17:2; 1953, Ja 9,21:1
May, Charles A Col, 1864, D 27,5:3
May, Charles C, 1937, S 11,17:6
May, Charles H, 1938, My 8,II,6:6
May, Charles H (por), 1943, D 9,27:3
May, Clarence M, 1951, Ag 19,84:6
May, Clifford H, 1963, Ap 6,19:1
May, D, 1927, Jl 24,24:2
May, David Mrs, 1943, D 21,27:3
May, David T, 1948, Je 25,23:1
May, Earl C, 1960, N 12,21:4
May, Earl C Mrs, 1961, D 13,43:5
May, Earl E, 1946, D 20,23:2
May, Edna (por; will, O 9,11:2), 1948, Ja 3,13:5
May, Edward, 1959, Ag 20,25:1
May, Edward B, 1953, Ag 12,31:4
May, Edward J, 1949, Mr 2,25:1
May, Edward J Jr, 1950, Ap 6,29:3
May, Edward Mrs, 1951, D 29,11:5
May, Edward O, 1941, F 24,15:4
May, Edward P, 1960, Ap 24,88:8
May, Edward Rear-Adm, 1917, F 6,9:3
May, Elizabeth Wenk, 1912, Jl 15,9:6
May, Eric A, 1942, S 9,23:5
May, Ernest Mrs, 1954, Je 8,27:4
May, Ernst A Dr, 1968, Je 1,27:5
May, Erwin G, 1943, F 14,49:2
May, Everett S, 1962, S 5,39:2
May, Evy, 1924, S 12,21:4
May, Foster, 1952, Ap 1,29:3
May, Francis, 1956, Ap 19,31:2
May, Francis Mrs, 1960, F 16,37:1
May, Frank E, 1957, F 1,25:2
May, Frank T, 1950, My 16,25:4
May, Fred J, 1953, Ja 10,17:4
May, Frederic, 1918, Ja 15,13:3
May, Frederick D, 1954, Ag 16,10:7
May, Frederick D Mrs, 1954, Ag 16,10:7
May, Frederick H, 1908, My 11,7:5
May, Frederick T, 1925, S 3,25:5
May, Gene, 1966, D 6,47:3
May, Geoffrey, 1964, F 7,32:1
May, George A, 1948, Mr 29,21:4
May, George H, 1945, My 26,15:4
May, George O, 1961, My 26,33:2
May, George S, 1962, Mr 13,32:1
May, Gerald D Mrs, 1952, F 28,52:6
May, Gerald de C, 1937, Ag 20,17:5
May, H Spencer, 1948, N 20,13:4
May, Hans, 1959, Ja 2,25:2
May, Harry E, 1950, Je 24,13:4
May, Harry F, 1938, Ja 29,15:2
May, Harry O, 1958, Mr 29,17:1
May, Henry, 1866, O 1,2:4; 1944, O 16,19:6
May, Henry C, 1957, O 10,33:5
May, Henry F, 1939, N 15,23:1
May, Henry J, 1939, N 30,21:3
May, Henry R, 1951, O 2,27:4
May, Herbert A, 1966, Mr 13,86:4
May, Herbert L, 1966, F 2,35:1
May, Herbert M, 1942, S 12,13:5
May, Herman Mrs, 1945, Ag 25,11:2
May, Horace P, 1946, F 26,25:2
May, Irving G, 1962, O 2,39:1
May, Isaac, 1953, S 24,33:5
May, Ivar, 1952, Ap 19,15:3
May, Jacob, 1915, Ja 13,9:4
May, James J, 1947, D 28,43:3
May, James S, 1948, Mr 17,25:2
May, James V, 1947, D 25,21:5
May, Jerome, 1922, S 10,28:3
May, John, 1924, Jl 29,15:5; 1951, D 29,11:3
May, John A, 1951, Jl 5,25:4; 1958, Je 1,87:1
May, John C Capt, 1903, O 28,1:6
May, John F, 1944, Ja 13,21:5
May, Joseph M, 1948, D 1,30:3
May, Julia Harris, 1912, My 7,11:6
May, Karl, 1912, Ap 2,12:5
May, Laurence E, 1946, Mr 4,23:5
May, Lawrence, 1951, Je 15,23:2
May, Lewis H, 1945, Mr 31,19:3
May, Lord (por), 1946, Ap 11,25:4
May, Louis H, 1956, My 28,27:3
May, Louis H Mrs, 1937, Ja 12,23:3
May, M B, 1933, Mr 24,17:1
May, M Father Rev, 1895, F 12,3:6
May, M H, 1927, Je 2,25:1
May, Mary, 1937, D 17,25:4
May, Max, 1948, N 14,76:2
May, Max B Mrs, 1914, D 25,11:6
May, Max E, 1946, Ja 31,21:3
May, Mitchell, 1961, Mr 27,31:1
May, Morton J (will, My 22,54:1), 1968, My 18,33:1
May, Morton J Mrs, 1938, N 27,49:1
May, Moses, 1910, Ja 10,9:2
May, Olive (Mrs O M Albaugh), 1938, Jl 27,17:2
May, Otto, 1946, Ag 17,13:2
May, Otto B, 1952, O 27,27:2
May, Otto B Mrs, 1960, D 13,31:3
May, P, 1934, Jl 31,17:1
May, Phil, 1903, Ag 6,7:5; 1953, Ap 22,29:4
May, Phil J, 1954, N 20,17:6
May, R Cameron, 1951, My 6,92:6
May, R H (funl), 1877, Je 30,8:3
May, Rene A, 1958, Mr 10,23:4
May, Richard, 1960, Jl 7,31:5
May, Richard G, 1959, Je 5,27:3
May, Richard Mrs, 1960, Mr 20,86:6
May, Robert E, 1952, D 3,33:4
May, Robert J, 1951, O 18,29:4
May, Ronald W, 1961, Ap 4,37:3
May, Russell J, 1964, F 29,21:1
May, Samuel, 1915, O 2,11:2
May, Samuel C (cor, O 2,87:2), 1955, O 1,19:3
May, Samuel J Rev, 1871, Jl 3,5:6
May, Siegfried Mrs, 1948, N 29,23:2
May, Solomon, 1945, Ja 31,21:4
May, Thomas A, 1937, My 8,19:2
May, Tom, 1968, Ag 28,44:3
May, Walter A, 1943, Ap 22,23:5
May, Walter F W, 1944, D 28,19:5
May, Wilford R, 1952, Je 23,19:6
May, William, 1939, O 3,23:6
May, William B, 1941, Je 29,32:4; 1961, Ap 24,29:4
May, William B Sr, 1941, Ja 31,19:2
May, William Mrs, 1922, Mr 15,19:5
May, William Rev, 1904, O 15,9:5
May Dolorette, Sister (Sisters of Providence), 1953, Jl 21,23:1
May Key Blunt, Mother, 1939, S 2,17:5
Maya, Floyd, 1953, Ag 20,27:3
Mayall, Hershell, 1941, Je 11,21:6
Mayan, Louis S, 1943, Ap 2,21:2
Mayard, Charles H Mrs, 1942, O 17,15:3
Maybach, Karl, 1960, F 9,31:3
Mayback, Albert von, 1904, Ja 22,9:6
Maybank, Burnet R (funl, S 4,11:2), 1954, S 2,21:1
Maybank, Burnet R Mrs, 1947, O 6,21:4
Maybank, John F, 1941, S 10,23:2
Maybank, Joseph, 1942, Ja 3,32:3
Maybarduk, Peter K Dr, 1968, Mr 8,39:4
Maybaum, Alexander, 1903, O 11,7:6
Maybaum, Jacob L, 1951, Je 1,26:2
Maybaum, Milton, 1960, Je 26,72:8
Maybaum, Paul S, 1944, My 21,44:2
Maybaum, William, 1942, O 2,25:6
Maybaum, William H, 1959, O 25,85:5
Maybeck, Bernard, 1957, O 4,21:1
Maybee, Ali D, 1950, Mr 14,25:4
Maybee, Allen F, 1962, Ag 9,25:5
Maybee, Carl M, 1938, Je 11,15:2
Maybee, Louis, 1943, O 5,25:3
Maybee, Sarah, 1944, Ja 10,17:4
Maybee, William J, 1941, F 13,19:1
Mayben, Buell F, 1963, My 6,29:5
Mayberry, George L, 1937, O 19,26:3
Mayberry, Lowell A, 1964, Ja 19,76:5
Maybin, Moses G Jr, 1954, O 14,29:4
Maybo, Andrew, 1949, O 10,23:4
Mayborn, Ward C, 1958, Mr 2,88:7
Maybrick, Florence Mrs, 1941, O 24,1:2
Maybrick, Michael (Steph Adams), 1913, Ag 27,7:6
Maybury, James, 1951, Ja 1,17:4
Maybury, William C, 1909, My 7,9:4
Maybury, William T, 1964, Ja 9,31:4
Maychick, Edward J, 1961, F 28,33:4
Maychick, Theodore, 1944, Ja 6,23:2
Maycock, John F, 1947, D 12,27:1
Maycook, James H, 1953, Ag 4,21:4
Maydan, Vincent, 1953, Jl 7,27:5
Mayden, Thaddeus J Mrs, 1951, My 12,21:1
Maydole, Hugh D, 1949, Jl 29,21:4
Maye, Garrett, 1952, N 29,13:4
Maye, James J Jr, 1967, N 17,47:2
Mayell, Albert J, 1938, Ja 2,41:2
Mayell, Warren, 1966, Mr 5,27:4
Mayer, Abraham Dr, 1915, Ag 21,7:6
Mayer, Adolf, 1961, D 30,19:4
Mayer, Adolph, 1954, Ja 25,19:2
Mayer, Albert D (por), 1949, Jl 30,15:2
Mayer, Albert J, 1956, F 4,19:1
Mayer, Albert J Jr, 1960, Je 6,29:3
Mayer, Alex U, 1937, Ja 16,17:2
Mayer, Alfred, 1956, D 4,39:5
Mayer, Andre (trb lr), 1956, Jl 6,20:7
Mayer, Anton E, 1942, N 27,23:4
Mayer, Arthur D, 1950, D 23,15:4
Mayer, August, 1958, S 20,19:3
Mayer, Augustus C, 1910, N 27,II,13:4
Mayer, Benjamin H, 1958, Jl 30,29:1
Mayer, Benjamin W, 1943, Je 13,44:6
Mayer, Betsy Mrs, 1938, F 2,19:3
Mayer, Brantz Capt, 1937, Je 22,23:4
Mayer, Carl, 1944, Jl 4,19:4
Mayer, Carlos, 1940, N 23,17:1
Mayer, Charles, 1958, Jl 14,21:3
Mayer, Charles F, 1904, F 25,9:4
Mayer, Charles H, 1966, Je 17,45:1
Mayer, Charles S, 1955, Jl 8,23:5
Mayer, Charles W, 1937, My 9,II,11:2
Mayer, Chester, 1945, Ag 21,21:5
Mayer, Clinton O, 1956, Mr 23,27:2
Mayer, Cyril W, 1953, F 24,25:5
Mayer, D, 1928, Ag 24,19:5
Mayer, David, 1914, O 24,13:4; 1943, Ja 19,19:5
Mayer, David Jr, 1961, Ja 5,31:5
Mayer, E, 1931, O 21,23:1
Mayer, Edgar Mrs, 1962, F 16,27:2
Mayer, Edward A, 1949, N 22,29:5
Mayer, Edward B, 1955, Je 11,15:5
Mayer, Edward E, 1957, Je 17,23:2
Mayer, Edward L, 1953, My 14,29:3
Mayer, Edward N, 1941, My 30,15:3
Mayer, Edwin B, 1947, O 30,26:3
Mayer, Edwin C, 1954, Jl 31,13:5
Mayer, Edwin J, 1960, S 12,29:2
Mayer, Edwin Mrs, 1955, Ja 19,27:4
Mayer, Eli Rev, 1920, Jl 30,9:6
Mayer, Elias, 1945, My 6,37:1
Mayer, Emil, 1923, Ap 14,13:5
Mayer, Emil E, 1953, Ja 31,15:3
Mayer, Ernest de Wael, 1968, D 17,47:3
Mayer, Everett H, 1956, O 12,29:3
Mayer, F, 1931, Ag 9,II,4:3
Mayer, Felix S, 1961, Jl 27,31:4
Mayer, Ferdinand, 1940, Mr 28,23:4
Mayer, Frances O M Mrs, 1962, Mr 27,37:3
Mayer, Francis, 1949, Je 24,23:4
Mayer, Francis R, 1951, S 21,23:4
Mayer, Frank D, 1968, N 16,37:2
Mayer, Frank H, 1954, F 14,94:1
Mayer, Franklin E, 1944, My 29,15:5
Mayer, Fred J, 1943, D 3,23:3
Mayer, Frederick C, 1945, Je 21,19:1
Mayer, Frederick E, 1948, Jl 8,23:4
Mayer, George, 1953, F 8,88:2
Mayer, George B (funl, D 11,13:6), 1915, D 10,13:6
Mayer, George C Mrs, 1955, N 20,89:2
Mayer, George F, 1943, Mr 25,21:4
Mayer, George P, 1942, O 2,25:2
Mayer, George R Mrs, 1958, Jl 18,21:1
Mayer, Gerson, 1919, Ag 28,11:3
Mayer, Gustav, 1948, F 24,25:3
Mayer, Gustave C, 1963, Ag 31,17:3
Mayer, Guy, 1952, Mr 17,21:3
Mayer, Harold C, 1963, Ag 14,33:2
Mayer, Harold F, 1948, Je 19,15:4
Mayer, Harriet W (por), 1941, O 4,15:4
Mayer, Harriette H Mrs, 1952, N 2,88:1
Mayer, Harry S, 1952, Jl 13,60:5
Mayer, Harvey A, 1938, Jl 11,17:4
Mayer, Helene, 1953, O 16,27:1
Mayer, Henry, 1950, O 4,31:2; 1954, S 28,29:4
Mayer, Henry A, 1949, D 8,33:1
Mayer, Herbert B, 1957, Mr 16,19:2
Mayer, Herbert G, 1944, Ja 27,19:4
Mayer, Hugo, 1943, Ag 28,11:6
Mayer, Hugo J, 1943, S 18,17:3
Mayer, J G, 1947, S 30,25:3
Mayer, J L, 1933, D 2,13:6
Mayer, J W, 1925, O 13,23:4
Mayer, Jacob, 1959, Jl 11,19:4
Mayer, Jacob N, 1952, My 9,23:3
Mayer, Jacques, 1919, My 7,15:2
Mayer, James J, 1937, N 6,17:7
Mayer, Jerome, 1965, Mr 4,31:1
Mayer, Jerome C, 1967, Ag 19,25:4
Mayer, John, 1912, O 1,13:6; 1924, Ag 25,13:4
Mayer, John A, 1940, Mr 17,51:3
Mayer, John A Mrs (D Quick), 1962, Mr 16,31:5
Mayer, John Lyne Maj, 1919, Ap 9,11:3
Mayer, John M, 1946, Mr 6,27:3
Mayer, Joseph, 1942, N 19,25:2; 1950, S 26,31:5; 1960, Je 29,33:5
Mayer, Joseph B (will, Je 19,18:4), 1951, Ap 7,15:3
Mayer, Joseph B Mrs, 1919, My 21,17:6
Mayer, Joseph Daniel, 1907, Ap 6,7:7
Mayer, Joseph F J, 1961, Ag 30,33:4
Mayer, Joseph L B, 1939, D 5,27:3
Mayer, Joseph Mrs, 1951, Ag 31,15:3
Mayer, Joseph V, 1941, F 18,23:3
Mayer, Juan R, 1940, S 3,17:4
Mayer, Julius M, 1925, D 2,25:4
Mayer, Katherine, 1949, D 16,31:1
Mayer, Laurence, 1943, S 25,15:5
Mayer, Leo K, 1961, F 7,34:1
Mayer, Leo M, 1948, S 14,29:5
Mayer, Leo Mrs, 1954, D 7,33:3
Mayer, Levy, 1922, Ag 15,11:5
Mayer, Levy Mrs, 1943, S 5,29:1
Mayer, Louis, 1941, N 2,52:1
Mayer, Louis B (funl, N 1,27:1), 1957, O 30,29:1
Mayer, Louis H Jr, 1948, Jl 11,52:7
Mayer, Louis Philip, 1952, O 24,23:2
Mayer, Lucius W (por), 1947, Je 12,25:4
Mayer, Ludwig Mrs, 1960, Ja 21,31:4
Mayer, M L, 1903, Ag 6,2:6
Mayer, Marcus, 1918, My 9,13:2

Mayer, Margaret S Mrs, 1955, My 23,23:4
Mayer, Mark A, 1937, N 10,25:3
Mayer, Martin, 1951, F 18,76:5
Mayer, Mary Mrs, 1915, D 12,19:3
Mayer, Max, 1939, S 22,23:4; 1949, Mr 27,76:2; 1961, D 17,82:5
Mayer, Max D, 1913, My 29,13:2
Mayer, Max D Mrs, 1960, Ja 27,33:2
Mayer, Max R (trb, O 6,39:3), 1937, O 5,25:4
Mayer, Max W, 1925, O 9,23:4
Mayer, Maximillian, 1941, N 29,17:4
Mayer, Milton, 1956, N 25,88:3
Mayer, Mortimer G, 1968, Ap 13,25:5
Mayer, Norman C Mrs, 1937, Ap 10,19:2
Mayer, Oscar F, 1955, Mr 12,19:4
Mayer, Oscar G (will, Mr 14,55:6), 1965, Mr 6,25:3
Mayer, Otto G, 1906, Je 26,7:6
Mayer, Paul E Mrs, 1957, Ag 23,19:5
Mayer, Paul M E, 1947, S 20,15:6
Mayer, Pauline H Mrs, 1938, O 15,17:5
Mayer, Phil, 1948, N 18,27:4
Mayer, Pius Rev, 1918, Ap 29,13:5
Mayer, R F, 1952, Ja 20,85:3
Mayer, Ralph E Prof, 1924, Ja 24,17:4
Mayer, Raymond C, 1964, Jl 7,35:2
Mayer, Richard, 1951, Je 9,19:7; 1953, O 29,31:4
Mayer, Richard J L, 1959, Jl 15,29:1
Mayer, Robert, 1939, My 2,23:3
Mayer, Robert G Mrs, 1966, Jl 16,25:2
Mayer, Rudolph W, 1951, Mr 1,32:5
Mayer, Saly, 1950, Ag 1,23:1
Mayer, Sarah Greenspan Mrs, 1968, O 8,47:1
Mayer, Siegel, 1952, N 2,89:1
Mayer, Sigmund, 1964, Ag 19,37:5
Mayer, Sigmund Mrs, 1966, F 6,92:4
Mayer, Simon, 1953, O 8,29:1
Mayer, Stanley, 1953, Ja 14,31:5
Mayer, Stephen K, 1960, Ja 17,86:3
Mayer, Theodore, 1938, Je 14,21:4; 1938, Ag 17,19:3
Mayer, Theodore C, 1958, F 11,25:6
Mayer, Timothy, 1964, F 29,17:8
Mayer, Walter, 1953, F 13,21:4
Mayer, Walter A, 1952, S 12,21:4
Mayer, Walter F, 1940, Je 6,25:3
Mayer, Walter Scott, 1924, N 13,21:4
Mayer, Walther, 1948, S 13,21:3
Mayer, Wilhelm Dr, 1923, Mr 7,15:4
Mayer, William, 1956, D 13,37:3; 1958, Mr 13,29:1
Mayer, William Col, 1906, Ap 18,11:6
Mayer, William E, 1949, N 8,31:5; 1953, Jl 28,19:5
Mayer, William F, 1939, Je 28,21:2
Mayer, William G Capt, 1937, F 26,22:2
Mayer, William H, 1923, O 26,17:4; 1940, Mr 6,23:2
Mayer, William H Mrs, 1913, Jl 25,7:6
Mayer, William T, 1958, O 10,31:3
Mayer, William W, 1943, D 10,28:2
Mayer-Herman, William S, 1945, Je 14,19:3
Mayer-Sommer, Emil, 1961, D 24,37:1
Mayerberg, I Wallace, 1951, My 3,29:5
Mayerberg, Samuel S, 1964, N 23,37:5
Mayeroff, Jacob, 1951, F 28,28:4
Mayers, Ballin Mrs, 1960, Ja 1,19:4
Mayers, Chauncey M, 1961, Ap 1,17:2
Mayers, Chauncey M Mrs, 1956, My 9,33:3
Mayers, Fred O, 1950, F 5,84:8
Mayers, J A, 1931, Ap 25,19:4
Mayers, Jacob, 1943, N 17,25:4
Mayers, Jacob Rabbi, 1921, Ap 21,13:5
Mayers, Joel Mrs (Wilmette K), 1964, My 21,35:5
Mayers, Lawrence S, 1956, D 4,39:3
Mayers, Martin A, 1964, Mr 7,23:4
Mayers, Petties W Mrs, 1965, D 25,13:4
Mayes, Arthur, 1955, N 21,29:5
Mayes, Richard T Mrs, 1959, Ja 2,25:2
Mayes, William H, 1939, Je 27,23:6
Mayfield, Cleo, 1954, N 9,27:1
Mayfield, Earl B, 1964, Je 24,37:4
Mayfield, Irving H, 1963, O 24,33:1
Mayfield, J J, 1927, Ja 2,30:3
Mayfield, John W, 1938, Ja 24,23:2
Mayfield, Melvin Mrs, 1946, D 26,25:4
Mayfield, William A, 1961, O 14,23:5
Mayger, Arthur G, 1948, D 11,15:6
Mayger, William Jr, 1962, S 12,39:3
Mayham, Ray E, 1952, S 15,25:4
Mayhew, Albert S, 1944, My 18,19:5
Mayhew, Augustus, 1875, D 28,1:7
Mayhew, Charles H, 1937, Je 16,24:2
Mayhew, David P Mrs, 1946, Ja 11,21:1
Mayhew, Horace, 1872, My 15,1:6
Mayhew, Jonathan, 1881, D 28,5:2
Mayhew, Karl S, 1944, Ag 11,15:6
Mayhew, Kate (por), 1944, Je 18,35:1
Mayhew, Lloyd D, 1941, Ap 2,23:1
Mayhew, Ulysses E, 1939, F 27,15:5
Mayhew, W Nelson, 1939, Ja 3,18:2
Mayhew, William, 1951, N 18,90:5
Mayhew, William H, 1939, Ag 30,17:4
Mayhoff, Monroe, 1941, Jl 12,13:5
Mayland, Albert H, 1947, Ja 13,21:2
Mayland, Edwin S, 1959, Je 27,23:5
Mayland, Rowland Hill, 1916, O 7,11:3
Mayle, Samuel Bowden, 1912, Mr 13,11:5
Mayles, Arthur, 1941, N 6,23:2
Maylon, Charles, 1958, Je 17,30:6
Maynadier, Gustavus H, 1960, O 14,33:4
Maynadier, T Murray, 1937, Je 26,17:4
Maynadier, William Col, 1871, Jl 4,5:5
Maynard, Albert C Mrs, 1954, Ap 24,17:3
Maynard, Amy B Mrs, 1949, S 1,21:2
Maynard, C Edgar, 1964, Ja 28,31:2
Maynard, Candace E Q Mrs (est tax appr), 1955, S 16,8:3
Maynard, Charles, 1945, Je 30,17:6
Maynard, E W Mrs, 1941, O 28,23:2
Maynard, Edward H Dr, 1922, My 11,17:4
Maynard, Edwin P (por), 1949, N 11,25:1
Maynard, Edwin T, 1953, F 20,19:2
Maynard, Effingham, 1918, Ag 13,9:6
Maynard, Elsie M Mrs, 1941, S 16,23:5
Maynard, Eunice I Mrs, 1942, Je 6,13:3
Maynard, F Alma, 1950, S 19,32:2
Maynard, Frank J, 1942, Je 16,23:4
Maynard, George, 1951, O 28,84:4
Maynard, George A Sr, 1955, F 13,87:1
Maynard, George S, 1939, Ag 28,19:5; 1960, D 15,43:1
Maynard, George William, 1913, F 14,15:5
Maynard, George Willoughby, 1923, Ap 7,13:6
Maynard, Gould, 1967, D 28,32:2
Maynard, Gurdon M (por), 1945, O 8,15:5
Maynard, Gurdon M Mrs, 1950, S 13,27:3
Maynard, H B, 1943, Mr 25,21:1
Maynard, H C, 1882, O 21,4:7
Maynard, Harold B, 1941, N 15,17:5
Maynard, Harold H, 1957, Mr 14,29:4
Maynard, Harold L, 1965, Je 14,33:1
Maynard, Harrison A, 1952, S 13,17:3
Maynard, Harry H, 1948, Ja 10,15:2
Maynard, Harry Mrs, 1951, Jl 7,13:5
Maynard, Hattie Mrs, 1940, Mr 12,23:4
Maynard, Horace, 1882, My 4,1:6
Maynard, Isaac, 1885, F 24,2:3
Maynard, John B, 1945, F 3,11:5
Maynard, John F, 1937, Jl 21,21:3
Maynard, John F Jr, 1945, N 24,19:6
Maynard, John W, 1939, Je 11,44:6; 1957, S 27,19:4
Maynard, John W Mrs, 1950, O 9,25:4
Maynard, Joseph A, 1938, Ja 8,15:1
Maynard, Lasalle A, 1906, N 9,9:6
Maynard, Martin W Mrs, 1941, Jl 25,15:2
Maynard, Mildred Dr, 1968, Jl 27,27:3
Maynard, Morton K, 1938, Ja 10,17:5
Maynard, N Rev, 1901, Jl 3,2:4
Maynard, Naval Apothecary, 1872, Ag 18,8:2
Maynard, Newell C, 1943, F 27,13:3
Maynard, Oswald S, 1953, N 19,31:5
Maynard, Prokofy V, 1950, Ag 28,17:4
Maynard, Reuben, 1945, S 26,23:6
Maynard, Richard S Mrs, 1966, Jl 4,15:4
Maynard, Robert E, 1959, Mr 16,31:3
Maynard, Roger, 1968, Mr 31,81:1
Maynard, Ross H Jr, 1939, My 20,15:6
Maynard, S R Mrs, 1907, O 20,9:6
Maynard, Theodore, 1956, O 19,27:2
Maynard, Theodore Mrs, 1945, N 27,23:5
Maynard, W S, 1866, Je 27,2:3
Maynard, Walter Effingham, 1925, Mr 5,19:5
Maynard, Walter H, 1911, S 3,II,9:4
Maynard, Washburn Adm, 1913, O 26,15:5
Maynard, Washburn Rear-Adm (funl), 1913, O 28, 11:6
Maynard, Westley J, 1939, D 21,23:3
Mayne, David M, 1952, My 28,29:3
Mayne, Earl H, 1949, Je 12,76:5
Mayne, Eric, 1947, F 12,25:5
Mayne, Ernie, 1937, My 16,II,9:2
Mayne, F G Capt, 1908, Mr 25,9:5
Mayne, James D, 1938, My 8,II,7:2
Mayne, Lyle K, 1955, O 9,87:3
Mayne, Mosley, 1955, D 21,29:5
Mayne, Richard Sir, 1868, D 29,4:7
Mayne, Robert B, 1955, D 15,37:4
Maynes, John H, 1949, N 22,30:2
Maynicke, Robert, 1913, O 1,9:5; 1942, D 31,15:3
Maynor, Alice J Mrs, 1946, Ag 22,27:3
Maynz, Emanuel, 1945, Jl 22,37:2
Mayo, Alfred D, 1955, Mr 15,29:1
Mayo, Archie Mrs, 1945, F 27,19:4
Mayo, Benjamin J, 1946, Ag 9,17:4
Mayo, Bocko, 1962, N 26,29:1
Mayo, Charles H, 1939, My 27,15:1
Mayo, Charles H Mrs, 1943, Jl 27,17:5
Mayo, Charles W Dr, 1968, Jl 29,1:1
Mayo, Earl of, 1870, O 3,4:7; 1872, F 13,5:4; 1939, My 8,17:3
Mayo, Earl of (U H Bourke), 1962, D 21,8:6
Mayo, Earl W, 1957, O 11,27:4
Mayo, Earl W Sr, 1962, O 17,39:1
Mayo, Eddie, 1946, F 5,23:1
Mayo, Edmund W, 1949, Jl 24,53:2
Mayo, Elton (por), 1949, S 9,26:4
Mayo, Emerson S, 1941, F 28,19:2
Mayo, Ernest L, 1939, Ap 20,23:3
Mayo, Erskine B Sr, 1962, Mr 22,35:2
Mayo, Frank, 1963, Jl 10,35:4
Mayo, Fred, 1955, O 27,68:7
Mayo, George A, 1951, N 19,23:2
Mayo, Guy B, 1942, Mr 14,15:4
Mayo, Harry P C, 1940, Je 19,23:4
Mayo, Henry R, 1941, Mr 5,21:5
Mayo, Henry T Adm (por), 1937, F 24,23:1
Mayo, Herman S, 1958, S 17,32:5
Mayo, John Ryall Mrs, 1914, My 14,11:5
Mayo, Joseph, 1872, Ag 10,5:2
Mayo, Katherine (por), 1940, O 10,25:1
Mayo, Margaret, 1951, F 26,23:1
Mayo, Maurine, 1939, Mr 8,21:6
Mayo, Mildred Mrs, 1939, O 2,17:5
Mayo, Nanie Wise Mrs, 1909, Mr 25,9:4
Mayo, Nathan, 1960, Ap 15,24:1
Mayo, Nelson S, 1958, Jl 6,56:4
Mayo, Robert M Dr, 1937, O 22,23:1
Mayo, Sam, 1938, Ap 1,23:4
Mayo, Stephen, 1964, My 13,47:4
Mayo, Thomas, 1946, O 26,17:1
Mayo, William B (por), 1944, F 2,21:3
Mayo, William G, 1947, N 25,29:2
Mayo, William G Mrs, 1949, Ap 30,13:3
Mayo, William J, 1939, Jl 29,15:1
Mayo, William J Mrs, 1952, F 2,13:5
Mayo, William W, 1952, Mr 29,15:6
Mayo, William W Mrs, 1958, F 28,13:5
Mayo, Wyndham Jr, 1949, Je 16,29:1
Mayo Gutierrez, Cesar, 1951, Ap 19,31:5
Mayo-Robson, A W, 1933, O 13,19:3
Mayo-Smith, Mabel Mrs, 1938, F 4,21:2
Mayo-Smith, Richmond, 1950, O 8,104:4
Mayock, Minnie Mrs, 1953, Ja 2,10:8
Mayock, Peter P Mrs, 1955, Ja 28,19:1
Mayol, Felix, 1941, O 28,23:2
Mayone, Joseph Sr, 1944, Je 27,19:6
Mayone, Salvatore, 1949, Ja 22,13:2
Mayor, Alfred G Mrs, 1960, D 9,31:2
Mayor, Charles, 1955, Mr 2,27:1
Mayor, Robert H, 1957, Mr 1,23:1
Mayorga, Herbt W, 1937, Jl 17,15:2
Mayorga, Jose W, 1948, S 22,31:4
Mayors, Robert, 1943, Ap 13,25:2
Mayotte, William L, 1956, My 5,19:6
Mayper, Alex A, 1958, N 30,86:6
Mayper, Henry M Mrs, 1942, My 6,19:3
Maypole, John J, 1958, F 9,88:7
Maypole, Robert E, 1950, N 18,15:5
Mayr, Anton, 1922, My 13,13:6
Mayr, Leopold Sr, 1961, N 15,43:4
Mayr, Otto P, 1956, D 17,31:1
Mayrand, Leon T, 1942, My 29,17:1
Mayrand, Oswald Mrs, 1945, F 15,19:3
Mayrose, William, 1948, My 12,27:4
Mayrsohn, Mayr, 1939, D 3,61:1
Mays, De Max, 1957, Ja 25,21:5
Mays, Edward, 1951, O 21,92:4
Mays, Edward L, 1940, Mr 10,51:4
Mays, John W, 1957, Ag 17,15:5
Mays, Livingston T, 1952, D 24,17:3
Mays, Livingston T Mrs, 1943, My 25,23:2
Mays, Samuel W, 1949, My 9,25:1
Mays, Walter, 1953, S 22,31:4
Mayse, A G (Pat), 1955, S 7,31:2
Mayse, Harrison A, 1945, F 21,19:4
Mayser, Charles W, 1967, Jl 16,64:8
Maytag, E H, 1940, Jl 22,17:5
Maytag, E H Mrs, 1963, D 28,23:4
Maytag, Frederick L, 1937, Mr 27,15:5
Maytag, Frederick L 2d (will, N 16,28:8), 1962, N 31:3
Maytag, L B, 1967, Ag 9,39:2
Maytag, Robert E (will, O 28,75:3), 1962, Mr 15,3
Maytham, Thomas E, 1966, My 11,47:1
Maytrott, Fradk J, 1963, S 26,35:3
Maywald, Frederick J, 1937, Jl 5,17:4
Maza, Jocelyn de la, 1945, Ja 20,11:2
Maza, Jose, 1964, My 7,37:3
Mazaki, Jinzaburo, 1956, S 2,56:8
Mazanet, Damaso, 1916, Mr 18,11:4
Mazany, Anna, 1941, Ja 7,23:1
Mazarin, Mariette, 1953, Mr 17,29:4
Maze, Coleman L, 1951, Ag 11,11:4
Maze, Jacob M, 1960, O 29,23:5
Maze, Matthew T, 1940, O 30,23:2
Maze, Montgomery, 1914, Ap 8,13:4
Mazeau, Camille, 1957, D 1,88:8
Mazeine, Raymond, 1947, Jl 18,17:4
Mazenski, Ernest, 1949, Je 16,31:8
Mazer, Abraham, 1953, Mr 28,17:1
Mazer, Abraham Mrs, 1957, My 15,35:3
Mazer, Charles, 1964, F 19,39:1
Mazer, Jacob, 1954, Ap 4,88:4; 1968, Ap 2,47:1
Mazer, Monroe, 1947, Ap 3,27:8
Mazer, Samuel, 1955, My 27,23:6
Mazet, Robert, 1945, D 26,19:2
Mazet, Robert Mrs, 1905, F 23,9:6
Mazillier, Emile A Gen, 1937, S 4,15:2
Mazique, Douglas W, 1964, Jl 11,25:3
Mazkewan, Elizabeth Mrs, 1907, D 26,7:6
Mazliah, Jacob, 1943, Ja 22,19:4
Mazni, Ibrahim A K el, 1949, Ag 11,23:6
Mazoyer, Auguste, 1949, S 5,18:5
Mazuera, Daniel, 1954, Mr 11,18:8

Mazur, Jacob B, 1950, D 24,34:5
Mazur, John A, 1945, O 23,17:3
Mazur, Leo, 1961, Je 18,88:5
Mazur, Stanley, 1948, Ap 8,25:2
Mazure, Maurice M (will), 1951, S 20,25:2
Mazurek, Charles, 1964, S 17,43:1
Mazza, Joseph, 1948, F 4,23:1
Mazza, Joseph E, 1950, S 8,31:3
Mazzali, Guido, 1960, D 26,23:3
Mazzarella, Louis, 1942, Ap 17,17:5
Mazzarella, Nicholas, 1960, Ja 7,29:3
Mazzarelli, Alfred, 1951, My 4,27:4
Mazzei, John E, 1958, Ja 21,29:4
Mazzera, Harry A, 1961, F 28,33:4
Mazzetti, Anthony F, 1953, My 23,15:4
Mazzetti, Frank, 1955, Jl 8,23:4
Mazzia, Edoardo, 1954, Jl 11,72:1
Mazzini, Giuseppe, 1961, N 12,86:7
Mazzini, Joseph (trb, Ap 14,12:1), 1872, Mr 12,5:3
Mazzoleni, Ettore Mrs, 1952, Ap 8,29:2
Mazzolini, Amos E, 1957, S 1,56:4
Mazzolini, Andrew R, 1953, Ja 14,31:3
Mazzolini, Primo D, 1951, Ap 19,31:5
Mazzoni, G, 1880, My 12,2:6
Mazzoni, Mario, 1961, O 8,87:2
Mazzotta, Sebastian G, 1956, N 11,86:4
Mazzucho, Ettore Gen, 1937, S 10,23:1
Mazzuri, Paul (por), 1947, Mr 11,28:2
Mba, Leon, 1967, N 29,47:3
Mdivani, A Prince, 1935, Ag 2,1:2
Meabid, Mohamed A K, 1956, Ja 13,5:6
Meacham, Alfred B, 1944, Ag 23,19:5
Meacham, Benjamin E, 1949, Ag 18,21:4
Meacham, Eugene A, 1946, S 27,23:5
Meacham, Eugene A Mrs, 1950, My 14,106:5
Meacham, Henry G (por), 1955, O 14,27:3
Meacham, Larned E, 1960, Ja 10,86:3
Meacham, Merle R, 1945, Ag 4,11:4
Meacham, Standish, 1949, Ja 4,40:3
Meacham, Thomas O, 1966, Jl 18,27:5
Meacham, Thomas W, 1953, N 26,31:2
Meachamp, A B, 1882, F 17,5:2
Meachem, J C, 1942, S 11,21:5
Meachen, John W, 1949, F 26,15:1
Meachim, Robert, 1953, Jl 1,29:5
Meacle, Edmund X, 1949, My 14,13:4
Mead, Albert H, 1944, Ag 29,17:1
Mead, Albert W, 1949, Mr 7,21:3
Mead, Andrew J, 1904, N 14,7:4
Mead, Arlie C, 1955, S 16,23:1
Mead, Arthur, 1949, Mr 29,25:1
Mead, Augustus I, 1945, F 24,11:5
Mead, Beatrice, 1949, Mr 24,27:5
Mead, Bessie, 1954, O 27,29:3
Mead, C Barry, 1947, D 19,26:3
Mead, Carl A, 1945, Jl 29,11:5
Mead, Charles A, 1951, Mr 30,23:3
Mead, Charles A Mrs, 1954, Je 20,85:2
Mead, Charles G, 1937, Je 7,19:5
Mead, Charles L (por), 1941, My 18,44:1
Mead, Charles L Mrs, 1947, Ja 14,25:5
Mead, Charles M Rev Dr, 1911, F 16,11:5
Mead, Clara L, 1952, O 7,29:5
Mead, Cora P Mrs, 1940, Jl 28,27:2
Mead, David I, 1951, D 1,13:3
Mead, Dewey, 1954, N 27,14:3
Mead, Eddie, 1942, My 26,22:2
Mead, Edward F, 1937, O 10,II,9:4
Mead, Edward S, 1956, Ag 22,29:5
Mead, Edward W, 1937, My 26,25:3
Mead, Edwin D (por), 1937, Ag 18,19:1
Mead, Elizabeth S Mrs, 1938, Je 17,21:5
Mead, Elizabeth Storrs Mrs, 1917, Ap 1,19:2
Mead, Elkanah, 1938, F 10,21:4
Mead, Ella P, 1937, Jl 18,II,7:3
Mead, Elwood Mrs, 1953, Jl 12,65:1
Mead, Emily F, 1950, F 23,27:2
Mead, Emma A, 1939, Ag 11,15:5
Mead, Ephraim, 1937, Ap 13,25:3
Mead, Ernest M, 1949, Jl 5,23:2
Mead, F J Gen, 1901, Ag 28,7:6
Mead, Frances S, 1937, Ag 28,15:2
Mead, Francis L, 1964, N 22,86:6
Mead, Frank, 1937, Jl 24,15:3
Mead, Frank E, 1937, N 4,25:2
Mead, Frank R, 1962, Jl 18,29:1
Mead, Fred J, 1961, Mr 11,21:5
Mead, Frederick, 1918, N 7,15:4
Mead, Frederick A, 1940, N 15,21:2
Mead, Frederick G Mrs, 1948, D 26,52:4
Mead, Frederick Mrs, 1917, Je 10,23:3
Mead, G C, 1883, My 29,8:2
Mead, George B, 1946, F 21,21:4; 1948, N 1,23:5
Mead, George E, 1957, N 2,21:5
Mead, George E Mrs, 1950, N 4,17:4
Mead, George H, 1963, Ja 2,4:8
Mead, George J (por), 1949, Ja 21,21:1
Mead, George L, 1872, N 28,1:4
Mead, George V, 1940, My 18,15:4
Mead, George W, 1938, Ag 14,33:3; 1946, D 20,23:5; 1961, O 3,39:3
Mead, Gideon R Mrs, 1940, Ja 31,19:4
Mead, Gilbert W (por), 1949, Mr 27,76:1
Mead, Giles W, 1937, D 6,27:1
Mead, Glenn C, 1954, My 25,27:3
Mead, Harold, 1949, Mr 14,19:5
Mead, Harold E, 1958, Je 25,29:5
Mead, Harry Mrs, 1941, Ap 30,19:4
Mead, Henry H Mrs, 1946, My 19,42:2
Mead, Henry L Mrs, 1949, Ap 22,23:1
Mead, Herbert Mrs, 1953, F 13,21:3
Mead, Hiram, 1881, My 21,2:6
Mead, Hugh E, 1950, N 1,35:3
Mead, Hunter, 1961, Jl 3,15:4
Mead, I Franklin, 1943, D 31,16:7
Mead, Ivie M, 1950, O 18,33:3
Mead, J Douglass, 1952, F 13,29:5
Mead, James J, 1948, Mr 28,48:2
Mead, James M, 1964, Mr 16,1:6
Mead, James M Mrs, 1964, Ja 14,31:3
Mead, John A Ex-Gov, 1920, Ja 13,13:2
Mead, John F Mrs, 1941, N 14,23:4
Mead, John J, 1949, N 29,29:2
Mead, John J Jr, 1959, O 30,27:1
Mead, John J Sr Mrs, 1957, N 29,29:1
Mead, Kate C, 1941, Ja 2,16:1
Mead, Kent C Capt, 1937, My 13,25:4
Mead, L G, 1933, Mr 8,22:7
Mead, Larkin G, 1910, O 16,II,13:4
Mead, Lawrence M, 1954, S 29,31:5
Mead, Louisa, 1939, Ap 14,23:2
Mead, Martin R, 1940, Ap 27,15:4
Mead, Mary A Mrs, 1938, Mr 20,II,8:8
Mead, Mary R Mrs, 1941, Mr 1,15:2
Mead, Maurice Mrs, 1950, Ag 30,31:4
Mead, Melville Emory, 1921, Je 5,22:2
Mead, Nelson P, 1967, S 27,47:2
Mead, Newell L (will, My 9,II,5:4), 1937, Ag 11,II, 8:2
Mead, Oliver D, 1939, Ja 12,19:4
Mead, Paul E, 1963, O 30,39:1
Mead, Peter F, 1949, S 3,13:3
Mead, Ralph W, 1942, Ag 25,23:3
Mead, Richard B, 1945, Je 17,26:2
Mead, Richard C Sr, 1943, N 12,21:5
Mead, Robert G, 1947, F 27,21:4
Mead, Robert G Mrs (por), 1946, Jl 6,15:4
Mead, Roswell, 1948, Je 12,15:2
Mead, Rufus, 1874, Ap 2,1:4
Mead, S A, 1945, S 30,46:3
Mead, S Christy, 1953, Je 22,21:4
Mead, Sara F Mrs, 1939, Jl 30,29:1
Mead, Seaman, 1915, Jl 1,11:5
Mead, Thomas A Mrs, 1948, N 27,17:5
Mead, W Chester, 1951, D 18,31:3
Mead, W R, 1928, Je 21,25:3
Mead, Walter W, 1949, Mr 8,25:4
Mead, Whitman S Ex-Judge, 1914, Ja 6,13:6
Mead, William, 1954, Je 19,15:4
Mead, William B, 1925, My 6,23:3
Mead, William D Mrs, 1947, D 20,17:3
Mead, William E, 1949, Jl 14,27:2
Mead, William L, 1938, Ap 18,15:4
Mead, William L Mrs, 1937, F 19,19:5
Mead, Winslow M, 1942, Ag 16,45:4
Mead, Winter, 1952, D 11,33:2
Meade, A V Earl of Clanwilliam, 1953, Ja 24,15:5
Meade, Charles A, 1949, S 16,27:4; 1953, Ja 17,15:3
Meade, Charles A Mrs, 1940, O 31,23:4
Meade, Charles E, 1943, Ag 16,15:5
Meade, Charles H B, 1943, S 8,23:4
Meade, Charles W, 1910, My 12,11:4
Meade, Charlotte H, 1967, S 14,47:1
Meade, Clarence W, 1906, Jl 17,7:5
Meade, Edmund J, 1949, Mr 4,21:4
Meade, Edward P, 1949, S 7,29:2
Meade, Elnathan, 1938, N 9,23:3
Meade, Francis L, 1958, F 15,17:4
Meade, Frank B, 1947, Mr 23,60:6
Meade, George G, 1947, S 24,23:5; 1955, Ap 25,23:6
Meade, George G Gen (funl, N 12,5:1; trb, N 8,5:1), 1872, N 7,8:4
Meade, George L, 1925, Ja 12,15:3
Meade, Henrietta, 1944, Mr 22,19:4
Meade, Hugh Allen, 1949, Jl 9,13:5
Meade, J S, 1865, F 24,4:2
Meade, James J, 1949, D 28,25:3
Meade, John F, 1947, Ag 25,17:2
Meade, John J, 1937, Ja 30,17:3; 1958, D 4,39:4
Meade, John P, 1939, Ja 26,21:5
Meade, Joseph F Sr, 1950, N 9,33:6
Meade, Julian, 1945, Jl 26,20:2
Meade, Julian R, 1940, Jl 10,19:1
Meade, Mary I, 1952, My 25,94:4
Meade, Maurice P, 1954, O 5,27:6
Meade, Michael B, 1948, Jl 12,19:4
Meade, Michael G, 1948, Je 30,25:3
Meade, Milo, 1906, Ag 28,7:6
Meade, Morris P, 1951, Ja 4,29:1
Meade, Morris P Mrs, 1953, N 2,25:5
Meade, Nathaniel T Mrs, 1962, Ag 15,31:4
Meade, Norman G, 1924, Mr 1,13:5
Meade, Patrick H Mrs, 1953, My 4,23:4
Meade, R W, 1933, D 4,19:3
Meade, R W Adm, 1897, My 5,9:3
Meade, R W Commodore, 1870, Ap 17,6:6
Meade, Richard Mrs, 1921, D 7,17:6
Meade, Robert L Brig-Gen, 1910, F 12,9:5
Meade, Saunders L Mrs, 1961, Mr 28,35:3
Meade, Sebastian S, 1946, Jl 22,21:5
Meade, Stephen Mrs, 1951, Ap 29,89:1
Meade, William Rev, 1862, Mr 29,6:2
Meade, William S, 1906, F 5,9:4
Meader, Fred M, 1946, Ap 28,42:5
Meader, Lewis H Jr Mrs, 1950, My 16,31:1
Meader, William G, 1955, F 18,21:3
Meaders, Paul L Mrs, 1965, S 8,47:3
Meador, Henry G, 1961, Jl 28,21:5
Meador, James J, 1955, O 12,31:2
Meador, John E D, 1940, Mr 10,51:3
Meadow, Edward, 1948, O 11,23:4
Meadow, Jack, 1967, Ja 19,35:3
Meadow, Noel, 1968, Ag 1,31:4
Meadowcroft, Edward, 1947, F 15,15:2
Meadowcroft, Enid LaM (Mrs D M Wright), 1966, N 24,35:5
Meadowcroft, Frank Mrs, 1959, Jl 28,27:1
Meadowcroft, William, 1956, Ag 7,27:4
Meadowcroft, William H (por), 1937, O 16,19:1
Meadows, Clarence W, 1961, S 13,45:3
Meadows, Dell, 1946, Mr 26,29:3
Meadows, Harold G, 1945, F 3,11:3
Meadows, Henry L (Specs), 1963, Ja 31,7:1
Meadows, J Tyler, 1938, Ja 11,23:3
Meadows, John R, 1946, Mr 15,21:4
Meadows, Kenny, 1874, S 6,4:7
Meadows, Lenore F, 1967, Ap 25,43:1
Meadows, Pal M, 1942, Je 28,32:4
Meadows, Roy, 1955, O 17,27:3
Meadows, Sanford, 1949, S 26,25:4
Meads, Charles, 1942, Ap 25,13:1
Meads, Laurence G (por), 1949, Ja 13,24:2
Meadvin, Louis, 1950, O 28,17:6
Meagher, Bridget Mrs, 1946, Jl 31,27:5
Meagher, Edward T, 1946, N 26,29:3
Meagher, Frank L, 1952, My 22,27:5
Meagher, Frederick J, 1939, Jl 15,15:2
Meagher, Helena A Mrs, 1939, O 2,17:4
Meagher, James Luke Rev, 1920, My 9,22:4
Meagher, James P, 1941, Ap 23,21:4
Meagher, James W Col, 1907, Ag 26,7:7
Meagher, John I, 1955, Ag 2,23:4
Meagher, John J, 1947, Je 13,23:5
Meagher, Joseph, 1947, Ap 2,27:2
Meagher, Mary F Mrs, 1941, D 18,27:6
Meagher, Matthew T, 1953, D 18,29:5
Meagher, Michael Mrs, 1943, N 3,25:3
Meagher, Patrick F, 1967, Ap 6,39:3
Meagher, Patrick Mrs, 1964, Ja 27,23:2
Meagher, Peter, 1939, S 27,25:2
Meagher, Peter Mrs, 1951, S 28,31:3
Meagher, Phil D, 1942, My 1,19:4
Meagher, Raymond, 1954, O 21,27:5
Meagher, Robert A, 1949, My 11,29:5
Meagher, T J N Mrs, 1939, Ja 22,35:2
Meagher, Thomas, 1874, Mr 16,5:6
Meagher, Thomas F Mrs, 1906, Jl 6,7:5
Meagher, Thomas Francis Gen, 1867, Jl 8,5:4
Meagher, William C, 1967, Mr 25,23:4
Meaglia, Samuel, 1947, Jl 6,41:2
Meahl, John H, 1940, Ja 7,48:5
Meaker, Charles G, 1952, S 21,88:6
Meakim, Fletcher, 1953, Ag 30,89:2
Meakin, Bridgett, 1906, Je 28,7:6
Meakin, L H, 1917, Ag 16,11:6
Meakins, John, 1957, F 24,85:2
Meal, William G, 1944, Jl 17,15:5
Mealand, Richard L, 1958, F 21,23:2
Mealey, Carroll E (Feb 23), 1963, Ap 1,36:2
Mealey, John P, 1938, D 13,26:1
Mealey, William E, 1954, Ag 1,85:2
Mealfe, Anthony Mrs, 1952, F 5,29:5
Mealia, James F, 1941, Jl 8,19:2
Mealing, Wade R, 1949, O 11,34:6
Mealio, Lewis, 1882, My 2,2:4
Mealli, Michael, 1939, Jl 25,19:3
Mealor, William G, 1953, O 14,29:3
Meals, Gordon D, 1951, Ja 24,27:5
Meanager, Georges, 1923, S 12,19:5
Meanes, Lenna L, 1942, D 6,76:4
Meaney, James, 1940, Jl 20,15:6
Meaney, John, 1952, Ap 11,23:1
Meaney, Joseph A, 1950, Ag 1,23:5
Meaney, Thomas F Judge, 1968, My 18,34:1
Meaney, Thomas F Sr, 1942, Mr 30,17:3
Meaney, W R, 1871, S 6,1:4
Means, A H, 1946, Je 16,40:3
Means, Earl A, 1952, Ja 6,92:5
Means, Elliott, 1962, Jl 29,60:7
Means, Gaston B, 1938, D 13,8:3
Means, James, 1920, D 4,13:4
Means, James H, 1967, S 6,47:3
Means, John M, 1940, Jl 24,21:2
Means, Laura H Mrs, 1939, Jl 16,31:1
Means, Philip A (por), 1944, N 25,13:4
Means, Rice W, 1949, Ja 31,19:3

Means, Stewart, 1940, Mr 13,23:4
Means, Stewart Mrs, 1949, S 10,17:2
Means, William, 1921, Jl 29,13:4
Means, William M, 1957, O 29,31:2
Meanwell, Walter E, 1953, D 9,11:1
Meany, Edmond S Mrs, 1953, My 17,88:3
Meany, Edward F, 1951, Mr 30,23:2
Meany, Edward F Jr, 1966, F 22,23:1
Meany, Edward F Sr, 1951, O 26,23:3
Meany, Edward P, 1938, N 26,15:4
Meany, Edward Sr, 1937, O 10,II,9:2
Meany, Edwin J, 1950, N 3,27:2
Meany, Edwin J Mrs, 1945, Je 17,26:2
Meany, James C Mrs, 1950, Ja 10,29:4
Meany, Richard W, 1937, Jl 3,15:3
Meany, Walter S, 1945, Ap 9,19:3
Meany, William S Mrs, 1948, My 11,25:1
Meany, William S Sr, 1951, S 2,48:5
Meara, Edward J, 1966, D 16,47:3
Meara, John J, 1956, Mr 7,33:5
Meares, Cecil H Col, 1937, My 14,23:5
Mearns, Edgar A Lt-Col, 1916, N 4,15:3
Mearns, Harry J, 1941, Ag 15,17:5
Mearns, Hughes, 1965, Mr 14,87:1
Mearns, J Gilbert Mrs, 1947, Ag 25,17:3
Mears, Benjamin S, 1952, Ja 31,27:1
Mears, C Mrs (see also N 26), 1877, N 28,2:2
Mears, Charles S, 1940, Ag 25,35:1
Mears, Charles W, 1942, D 10,25:5
Mears, Edward B, 1947, Ja 29,26:2
Mears, Eleanor Mrs, 1937, My 3,19:2
Mears, Eliot G, 1946, My 29,23:5
Mears, Frank, 1953, Ja 26,19:2
Mears, Frederick K, 1942, O 22,21:3
Mears, Frederick Mrs, 1953, D 19,15:5
Mears, Gilbert E, 1962, Ag 29,29:4
Mears, Harry H, 1945, Mr 21,23:1
Mears, Helen F, 1916, F 18,11:5
Mears, Henry W, 1938, D 23,19:2
Mears, Howard R Jr, 1962, F 7,37:3
Mears, J W, 1881, N 11,5:1
Mears, John H, 1956, Jl 27,21:2
Mears, Joseph G, 1961, D 14,43:2
Mears, Joseph H, 1952, N 8,17:2
Mears, Leverett Prof, 1917, Je 24,19:4
Mears, Margot Singleton Dr, 1968, D 4,43:2
Mears, Mary Mrs, 1939, Ag 25,15:5
Mears, O, 1931, Je 26,21:1
Mears, Robert Jr, 1963, Ag 4,80:7
Mears, Thomas, 1948, Jl 5,15:5
Mears, William E, 1945, N 20,21:5
Mears, William E Mrs, 1945, N 20,21:5
Mearson, Lyon, 1966, Ja 10,25:4
Measday, Walter, 1959, O 12,19:4
Measeck, Maria Mrs, 1939, O 22,41:2
Measey, William M, 1967, Jl 1,23:6
Measley, Henry, 1948, D 23,20:4
Measnikoff, Louis Mrs, 1954, D 25,11:5
Measom, E Allan, 1959, Ag 14,21:3
Measure, Charles R, 1953, My 9,19:4
Meath, Earl of, 1929, O 12,19:6
Meath, Earl of (R L Brabazon), 1949, Mr 11,25:1
Meatyard, Florence E, 1949, F 25,23:2
Meatyard, Thomas, 1944, Jl 27,17:4
Meatyard, Thomas Mrs, 1948, Ap 25,68:6
Mebane, Alexander D, 1923, My 2,19:3
Mebane, B Frank Mrs, 1943, Je 16,21:4
Mebane, D C Dr, 1937, N 18,23:1
Mebane, Daniel, 1956, F 10,22:1
Mebane, Frank C, 1952, Mr 6,31:2
Mecabe, Alvaretta, 1948, Ag 8,57:1
Mecca, Leonard, 1964, Ap 27,31:5
Mech, Owen, 1949, F 1,26:3
Mechan, John Col, 1909, Jl 25,7:7
Mechany, Harry, 1908, F 16,11:4
Mechau, Frank A, 1946, Mr 10,45:1
Mechem, F R, 1928, D 12,31:6
Mechem, John C, 1955, S 6,25:4
Mechem, Merritt C (por), 1946, My 26,32:6
Mecherle, George J, 1951, Mr 12,25:3
Mechi, J J, 1880, D 27,1:6
Mechler, Joseph, 1952, Ap 3,36:3
Mechler, Michael A, 1955, Ap 28,29:1
Mechlin, Leila, 1949, My 8,78:1
Mechling, B Franklin, 1961, S 14,31:3
Mechling, Benjamin S, 1945, Jl 9,11:7
Mechling, Edward A, 1938, Ja 13,21:2; 1938, Mr 7, 17:2
Mechtelde, Sister (Scott), 1915, N 14,19:6
Meck, David C, 1939, Ap 7,21:2
Meck, Felix A, 1950, Ag 15,29:4
Meck, Gertrude K, 1947, N 11,28:2
Meck, Robert H Mrs, 1937, Ap 23,21:6
Meckauer, Henry, 1959, Je 9,37:4
Meckauer, Monroe, 1957, Mr 7,29:2
Mecke, J Howard Jr, 1938, Jl 26,19:4
Meckel, Arnold, 1938, Je 28,19:4
Mecklem, Austin M, 1951, O 9,29:4
Mecklenburg, Duke of (Karl Borwin), 1908, Ag 26, 7:6
Mecklenburg, Duke of (Georg), 1963, Jl 8,29:1
Mecklenburg, Marie Duchess, 1922, Ap 23,28:3
Mecklenburg-Strelitz, Frederich William I Grand Duke, 1904, My 31,7:7
Meckler, Louis M Jr, 1948, Je 11,23:4
Mecklin, John M, 1956, Mr 11,88:2
Mecleary, John, 1939, Je 12,17:4
Mecray, Frank B, 1937, F 1,19:2
Mecray, John Sr, 1937, F 5,21:4
Mecum, Ella, 1912, Ja 2,11:5
Meda, Filippo, 1940, Ja 3,22:2
Medalie, George Z, 1946, Mr 6,27:1
Medary, Samuel, 1864, N 13,2:6
Medbery, H Stuart, 1953, Ag 25,21:3
Medbery, James K, 1873, S 27,4:7
Medbury, John P (por), 1947, Je 30,19:2
Medbury, Lewis N C, 1937, N 10,25:5
Medcalf, Florence, 1951, Jl 15,60:5
Medcraft, Russell G, 1962, S 30,40:1
Medd, Henry Dr, 1937, Ap 18,II,9:2
Medd, John C, 1948, Mr 18,27:4
Meddaugh, E W, 1903, D 21,7:5
Meddaugh, Jacob, 1951, N 17,17:6
Medendorp, Alfred, 1954, S 5,1:8
Meder, Albert E, 1961, Ap 19,39:5
Meder, Albert E Mrs, 1955, Ja 12,27:4
Meder, George, 1951, Mr 20,29:1
Meder, John O Mrs, 1951, O 5,27:1
Medford, William L, 1963, D 11,47:4
Medgyes, Ladislas, 1952, Ja 27,76:2
Medhad, Mohsen, 1954, N 26,29:3
Medhurst, Charles, 1954, O 19,27:4
Mediatore, Robert, 1949, O 19,31:3
Medici, Giacomo, 1882, Mr 10,5:1
Medici, Peruzzi de Marchesa, 1917, My 19,13:5
Medick, John E, 1947, D 8,25:4
Medicus, Henry W, 1941, My 14,21:1
Medill, George L, 1942, S 13,53:2
Medill, Joseph, 1899, Mr 17,2:2
Medill, Robert M, 1957, Ja 28,23:4
Medill, S J, 1883, F 21,2:4
Medill, W Ex-Gov, 1865, S 9,5:4
Medina, Duchess of, 1946, S 25,27:3
Medina, Joaquin A Mrs, 1954, Mr 27,17:3
Medina, John F, 1943, D 8,23:4
Medina, Richard A, 1961, Jl 17,21:3
Medina, William B, 1942, F 15,44:1
Medina Angarita, Isaias, 1953, S 16,33:3
Medinaceli, Duke of (L J Fernandez de Cordoba y Salabert), 1956, Jl 15,61:1
Meding, Charles B, 1952, O 16,29:2
Meding, Stewart M, 1940, Jl 1,19:4
Mediz Bolio, Antonio, 1957, S 18,33:5
Medland, Robert E, 1946, Ag 14,25:5
Medlar, Edgar M, 1956, Jl 2,21:3
Medlar, Irvin A, 1938, Ag 25,19:5
Medler, Charles S, 1948, Ag 31,23:1
Medley, Theodore F, 1948, S 12,72:5
Medlicott, William B, 1943, N 1,17:2
Medlock, J Harold, 1956, O 15,25:1
Medovich, Alex J, 1940, S 25,27:5
Medrick, Frank S, 1945, Ap 22,35:1
Medrick, Raphael F, 1940, Mr 25,15:1
Medtner, Nicholas, 1951, N 14,31:2
Medvec, John A, 1950, Mr 22,28:4
Medvecky, Daniel, 1952, N 18,31:5
Medvecsky, Alexis, 1940, N 7,25:1
Medvedev, Dmitry N, 1954, D 17,31:4
Medvedev, Nikolai, 1950, Ja 12,27:3
Medvedieff, Jacques, 1953, Ja 6,29:3
Medvedleff, Jacov, 1919, Ja 3,9:1
Medvene, Charles, 1944, Ap 24,19:4
Medvin, George, 1953, N 2,25:5
Medway, Adam M, 1948, S 16,29:3
Medway, Charles, 1950, D 22,24:2
Medworth, Charles E, 1958, Mr 16,86:6
Medzig, Dikran, 1941, Jl 4,16:5
Mee, Arthur, 1943, My 29,13:5
Mee, John J, 1949, Ja 22,13:3
Mee, Kirk Sr, 1948, Ag 17,21:2
Mee, Patrick J, 1955, Ja 25,25:4
Mee, Walter R, 1941, O 3,23:5
Meech, Clarence L, 1949, F 14,19:4
Meech, Claude E, 1953, Mr 7,15:3
Meech, Frank E, 1954, Ap 1,31:2
Meech, George T, 1941, Mr 30,48:7
Meech, Harold M, 1949, Ag 6,17:4
Meech, Susan B, 1938, O 16,45:3
Meech, T Cox, 1940, O 22,23:5
Meeder, Frederick H, 1944, Mr 7,17:4
Meeder, Philip, 1913, Je 29,5:7
Meeds, Hollyday S Jr, 1962, Je 11,31:4
Meegan, Alice V Mrs, 1938, Ag 18,19:2
Meegan, Edward J Sr, 1947, Je 20,19:3
Meegan, Harold C, 1951, F 27,27:2
Meegan, James E, 1949, Je 8,29:4
Meegan, James P, 1954, Ag 22,93:1
Meegan, John J, 1953, D 8,2:8; 1967, O 16,45:3
Meegan, William G, 1966, Jl 26,35:1
Meegan, William H, 1938, N 18,21:1
Meegeren, Hans van, 1947, D 31,15:5
Meehan, Andrew, 1940, D 8,53:5
Meehan, Annie Mrs, 1947, N 17,23:1
Meehan, Charles G, 1947, Ag 5,23:5
Meehan, Charles L, 1949, F 28,19:5
Meehan, Charles M Mrs, 1953, Ap 22,29:4
Meehan, Edward I, 1953, Jl 14,27:4
Meehan, Francis P, 1968, F 7,47:4
Meehan, Frank J, 1946, Jl 5,19:3
Meehan, George A, 1948, My 24,20:2
Meehan, George E, 1960, Mr 28,29:3
Meehan, George V, 1968, N 11,47:2
Meehan, Hannah F, 1940, My 10,23:1
Meehan, Henry A, 1951, D 2,91:2
Meehan, Hugh, 1945, Ag 17,17:5
Meehan, Irving H, 1948, S 16,29:2
Meehan, J Arthur, 1950, Jl 1,15:2
Meehan, J Franklin, 1938, D 17,15:3
Meehan, James A, 1952, Mr 13,29:2; 1954, O 7,23:2
Meehan, James F, 1945, Jl 18,27:4
Meehan, James T, 1940, Ja 30,19:2
Meehan, James W, 1948, Jl 3,15:3
Meehan, John (funl, O 31,13:5), 1912, O 28,11:3
Meehan, John, 1938, Mr 11,19:2
Meehan, John C, 1948, D 14,29:5
Meehan, John F, 1939, N 14,23:6
Meehan, John H, 1938, Jl 30,13:6; 1945, My 27,26:
Meehan, John J, 1941, Jl 27,31:2; 1944, F 8,15:5; 19 Je 29,48:6; 1952, Jl 19,15:5
Meehan, John M, 1943, Ag 19,19:4
Meehan, John P, 1940, O 9,25:3
Meehan, John R, 1938, Ag 21,33:3; 1944, Je 2,15:5
Meehan, Joseph, 1944, F 17,19:5
Meehan, Joseph A, 1951, F 26,23:3; 1954, D 28,23:
Meehan, Katherine Mrs, 1954, D 3,38:5
Meehan, M Joseph, 1963, Mr 26,9:4
Meehan, Mark V, 1947, Je 6,25:4
Meehan, Martin P, 1940, My 4,17:1
Meehan, Mary, 1950, Ap 25,31:2
Meehan, Michael, 1903, Ag 11,7:7; 1941, S 17,23:4
Mcchan, Michacl J (por), 1948, Ja 3,13:1
Meehan, Michael J, 1948, Mr 4,25:2; 1948, O 18,23
Meehan, Patrick J, 1906, Ap 21,13:5; 1949, D 20,3 1954, Mr 18,31:3
Meehan, Patrick J Mrs, 1949, D 29,25:4
Meehan, Richard H, 1961, Ja 7,19:4
Meehan, Stephen P, 1942, N 20,24:4
Meehan, Thomas, 1901, N 20,9:5
Meehan, Thomas A, 1966, Ag 11,33:3
Meehan, Thomas F, 1942, Jl 9,21:4
Meehan, Thomas P, 1939, Ja 21,15:2
Meehan, Ward, 1949, My 20,28:2
Meehan, William, 1943, Ag 24,19:5; 1950, N 8,29:
Meehan, William F, 1937, O 13,23:4
Meehan, William S, 1962, Mr 16,31:4
Meehan, Willie, 1953, F 11,29:3
Meek, Alex, 1949, N 6,92:1
Meek, Bert B, 1937, S 29,23:3
Meek, Charles E, 1951, Je 7,33:2
Meek, Charles S, 1952, Ap 9,31:3
Meek, Donald, 1946, N 19,31:1
Meek, Dudley H, 1958, Mr 11,29:1
Meek, Fred, 1949, Mr 29,25:1
Meek, Frederick W, 1953, Ap 5,76:6
Meek, Harold P, 1950, O 22,94:6
Meek, James E, 1950, Ap 4,30:2
Meek, John H, 1940, N 24,51:4
Meek, Judge, 1865, N 12,3:6
Meek, Kate, 1925, S 5,13:6
Meek, Robert Col, 1903, D 11,9:5
Meek, Samuel W, 1919, Ja 9,11:3; 1919, Ja 10,13:
Meek, Seth Eugene Prof, 1914, Jl 8,9:7
Meek, Stuart G Mrs, 1948, D 3,26:2
Meek, Thomas S, 1941, D 26,13:4
Meek, William Mrs, 1943, Mr 2,19:3
Meek, William S, 1943, O 1,19:3
Meek, William W Mrs, 1942, F 3,20:2
Meekens, J Austin, 1960, S 27,37:3
Meeker, Alex H, 1950, O 31,27:3
Meeker, Arthur, 1946, F 6,23:6
Meeker, Arthur Mrs, 1948, N 21,88:1
Meeker, Arthur Y, 1961, N 19,88:2
Meeker, Charles A Dr, 1913, S 9,7:6
Meeker, David E, 1964, S 1,35:1
Meeker, E, 1928, D 4,31:3
Meeker, Edward E Mrs, 1944, Ag 18,13:5
Meeker, Edward Percy Capt, 1914, Mr 14,11:5
Meeker, Edward W, 1937, Ap 20,25:4
Meeker, Frank B, 1951, S 5,31:4
Meeker, Frank H, 1955, My 20,25:1
Meeker, Frederick R, 1961, F 26,92:8
Meeker, George H, 1945, S 5,23:6
Meeker, Harold D, 1945, My 28,19:3
Meeker, Henry N, 1914, N 28,13:6
Meeker, Hiram E, 1947, Ja 22,23:5
Meeker, Irving A, 1956, S 17,27:4
Meeker, J E, 1934, Jl 28,13:4
Meeker, Jacob E, 1918, O 17,15:2
Meeker, Jerry C, 1947, Ag 14,23:5
Meeker, John Willard Dr, 1917, Ja 3,11:4
Meeker, Joseph E, 1952, Mr 15,13:4
Meeker, Leland Mrs, 1947, S 30,25:3
Meeker, Lincoln R (por), 1942, Ag 15,11:3
Meeker, Louis E Dr, 1918, My 24,13:7
Meeker, Louise H, 1948, S 23,29:3
Meeker, Mary M, 1941, D 26,14:2
Meeker, Mary O S Mrs, 1940, S 9,15:6
Meeker, Matilda U Mrs, 1950, Ja 10,29:2
Meeker, Robert A, 1947, Ag 17,52:7

Meeker, Royal, 1953, Ag 18,23:6
Meeker, S Merchant, 1952, Mr 4,27:2
Meeker, S Merchant Mrs, 1946, My 22,21:1
Meeker, Samuel M, 1939, F 1,21:5
Meeker, Sidney Dr, 1937, Ja 10,II,10:5
Meeker, W B Sr, 1882, N 24,8:3
Meeker, W H, 1880, O 6,2:7; 1905, Ap 1,11:5
Meeker, Walter H, 1961, Ap 11,37:2
Meeker, Warren H, 1947, Je 3,25:3
Meeker, Wilbur B, 1942, D 18,28:3
Meekin, Jouett, 1944, D 15,19:2
Meekings, William D Mrs, 1948, Ap 9,24:2
Meekins, Isaac M, 1946, N 22,23:2
Meekins, J Austin Mrs, 1954, My 31,13:2
Meekins, Jack, 1950, Ag 8,29:2
Meekins, Katherine W Mrs, 1938, Ap 28,23:1
Meekins, Paul, 1944, Ap 12,21:4
Meeks, Carroll L V, 1966, Ag 28,93:1
Meeks, Clarence G, 1954, S 30,31:4
Meeks, Clarence G Mrs, 1949, O 1,13:5
Meeks, Elmer A, 1945, My 3,23:4
Meeks, Everett V, 1954, O 28,35:1
Meeks, Floyd E, 1941, N 4,26:2
Meeks, Frank H, 1944, Jl 20,19:5
Meeks, George Washington, 1920, Ja 4,23:3
Meeks, Harry E, 1941, Mr 14,21:5
Meeks, James L, 1941, Mr 22,15:3; 1952, F 8,23:5
Meeks, John, 1952, N 22,23:3
Meeks, Robert W, 1919, S 17,13:2
Meeks, Thomas C, 1964, N 7,27:2
Meeks, Thomas C Mrs, 1960, S 9,29:2
Meem, Harry G, 1949, Ja 21,21:2
Meem, James G, 1924, N 22,15:5
Meeman, Edward J, 1966, N 16,47:4
Meenagh, Joseph (Bro Alban), 1961, Je 20,33:5
Meenan, Daniel, 1950, My 15,21:4
Meenan, Harold, 1966, Ja 24,35:5
Meenan, John J, 1958, N 10,29:1
Meenan, John J Mrs, 1962, F 7,37:4
Meenan, Loretta Mrs, 1940, N 14,23:4
Meenan, William T, 1955, Jl 29,17:2
Meengs, John G Rev Dr, 1937, Ap 19,21:3
Meer, Jerome, 1951, Ap 28,15:4
Meer, Sarah Van Buren Mrs, 1917, Mr 19,11:4
Meerbaum, Hyman, 1955, Jl 6,27:2
Meeres, Frank, 1952, O 11,19:4
Meersch, Maxence Van Der, 1951, Ja 16,29:3
Meersehaert, Theophile Bp, 1924, F 22,15:5
Meert, Frederic W, 1951, S 26,31:5
Meert, Virginia L, 1950, Ja 15,84:3
Meerwald, John L, 1939, My 1,23:4
Mees, Arthur Dr, 1923, Ap 27,17:4
Mees, C E Kenneth (est acctg, N 3,48:4), 1960, Ag 17,31:4
Mees, Otto, 1958, Ja 14,33:2
Mees, Theophilus Rev, 1923, Jl 26,15:4
Meese, J W Capt, 1912, D 6,15:5
Meese, William H (por), 1939, Mr 27,15:3
Meeser, Elizabeth Mrs, 1939, F 11,15:6
Meeser, Spencer B, 1939, My 9,23:5
Meester, Theodoor H de, 1946, Je 5,23:3
Meeteer, Henrietta J, 1956, N 21,27:6
Meffert, Anna G Mrs (will), 1943, Ap 27,15:2
Meffert, Henry F, 1957, O 4,23:2
Meffert, William L, 1946, S 28,17:3
Mefford, Earl L, 1945, D 31,17:4
Mega, Attillie E, 1948, Jl 31,15:4
Megaffin, Nelson D, 1948, S 7,25:4
Megan, Charles P, 1947, Je 15,60:4
Megann, James, 1959, Ja 3,17:4
Megargee, Edwin, 1958, Mr 14,25:1
Megargee, Frank S, 1948, Mr 31,26:2
Megaro, Gaudens, 1958, Mr 14,25:2
Megarr, Edward, 1938, Ap 17,II,7:2
Megata, T Baron, 1926, S 11,15:4
Megathlin, Charles W, 1954, D 4,8:8
Megaw, Elmer E, 1955, S 4,56:1
Megaw, John E, 1952, Jl 30,23:2
Megaw, Robert, 1948, Mr 2,23:5
Megear, William B, 1937, Ag 5,23:6
Megeath, Samuel A Mrs, 1953, Je 19,22:3
Meggison, R Marvin, 1939, D 9,15:5
Megibow, Joseph, 1953, Ag 20,27:2
Meginnis, Edward B Mrs, 1941, D 17,27:5
Meglaughlin, Barry F, 1967, Je 22,39:3
Meglia, Cardinal, 1883, Ap 2,5:2
Megowan, Claude H, 1944, F 28,17:2
Megowan, M Jewett Mrs, 1946, Jl 30,23:3
Megowen, Carl R, 1962, Jl 22,64:4
Megowen, Lewis E, 1947, Mr 24,25:3
Megowen, Robert L, 1954, Mr 25,29:3
Megran, Herbert B, 1958, Ap 15,33:4
Megrath, William Alonzo, 1915, My 24,11:5
Megrue, Enoch G, 1954, Ag 28,15:5
Megrue, R C, 1927, F 28,19:4
Megson, Thomas, 1885, F 1,7:3
Meguet, Major, 1942, Ag 14,17:6
Mehaffey, D B, 1949, My 9,25:5
Mehaffey, Harry S, 1963, D 25,33:4
Mehaffey, Robert C, 1943, My 22,13:3
Mehaffy, Thomas M, 1944, O 21,17:7
Mehan, John D Mrs, 1941, F 2,46:4
Mehan, John Dennis, 1920, O 9,15:4

Mehan, Thomas O, 1955, F 7,21:3
Mehard, Churchill B, 1943, S 15,27:6
Meharg, John C, 1947, D 29,17:3
Meherin, Patrick W, 1939, Ap 20,23:5
Meheut, Mathurin, 1958, F 25,27:4
Mehl, Camill H, 1949, Ja 20,27:3
Mehl, George E, 1957, Ag 26,23:4
Mehl, Theodore A, 1950, O 11,33:5
Mehl, William M, 1941, N 29,17:1
Mehlbach, William K, 1955, Jl 2,15:6
Mehldau, Henry, 1966, N 15,47:2
Mehler, Albert J, 1949, Ag 10,21:2
Mehler, Gabriel (Bro Gabriel), 1940, Je 1,15:6
Mehler, Jack, 1948, O 28,29:3
Mehler, Jesse B, 1964, Jl 5,43:2
Mehlhop, Herman A, 1941, D 20,20:3
Mehlhope, Clarence E, 1942, D 27,34:2
Mehlich, William H, 1957, My 6,29:5
Mehlin, Eric W, 1945, My 10,23:2
Mehling, Frank J Sr, 1953, Ap 11,17:6
Mehling, Theodore J, 1961, N 14,39:1
Mehlman, Samuel A Mrs, 1967, Ja 11,25:3
Mehlmann, Casper W, 1952, Jl 7,21:5
Mehlmann, Charles J, 1962, Je 12,37:4
Mehm, Edward C, 1963, N 1,34:1
Mehner, Holger A, 1944, Ag 16,19:2
Mehnert, George N, 1948, Jl 9,19:6
Mehorter, Samuel A, 1959, N 14,21:4
Mehr, Ernest, 1945, D 25,23:4
Mehr, Joseph, 1955, D 28,24:3
Mehr, Morris Mrs, 1950, Mr 15,30:2
Mehrbach, Isidor, 1951, Ja 10,27:2
Mehrback, Albert L Mrs (A Lichter), 1942, D 10, 30:1
Mehrer, Harry, 1945, Mr 20,19:4
Mehrlust, Jacob, 1960, F 10,37:4
Mehrman, George Mrs, 1946, Jl 18,25:2
Mehrtens, Behrend, 1956, N 23,27:1
Mehrtens, Behrend Mrs, 1952, F 25,21:3
Mehrtens, Henry E, 1947, My 28,25:4
Mehrtens, Laura Mrs, 1912, Ja 16,13:3
Mehrtens, Louis D, 1951, Ja 14,84:4
Mehrtens, William, 1944, O 29,43:2
Mehrtens, William Mrs, 1968, Je 4,44:5
Meht, Henry A, 1943, Mr 16,19:4
Mehta, Balwantrai Golpakji, 1965, S 20,7:1
Mehta, Manubhai, 1946, O 15,25:2
Mei, Hua-Chuen, 1953, F 25,27:4
Mei Lan-Fang, 1943, Ag 11,9:5
Mei Lan-fang, 1961, Ag 9,33:1
Mei Yi-chi, 1962, My 20,87:1
Meibauer, Robert, 1959, O 13,39:4
Meidenbauer, John P, 1944, N 15,27:5
Meidman, Harry W, 1966, Mr 24,39:3
Meier, Adolph, 1947, Ja 27,23:5
Meier, Alfred A, 1947, S 28,60:3
Meier, Arthur C, 1940, Jl 3,17:6
Meier, C Augustus, 1939, Je 18,37:2
Meier, Carl Theodore Dr, 1864, F 4,5:1
Meier, Charles A, 1948, D 27,21:2
Meier, Clement R D Mrs, 1960, Ja 5,31:4
Meier, Edward Danile Col, 1914, D 16,15:6
Meier, Edwin A, 1954, Je 8,27:3
Meier, Elizabeth G, 1967, Mr 30,40:3
Meier, Frank, 1956, S 16,84:8
Meier, Frank J, 1948, D 21,31:1
Meier, Fred W, 1954, Ap 18,89:2
Meier, Frederick Mrs, 1951, Mr 6,27:2
Meier, G C H Mrs, 1949, Ap 19,25:4
Meier, George L, 1954, N 21,86:4
Meier, George W, 1954, Mr 12,21:2
Meier, Gottlieb Mrs, 1951, F 25,84:5
Meier, Gregor, 1947, Mr 13,27:1
Meier, Gustav, 1940, O 1,23:1
Meier, Harold C, 1968, Ag 5,39:3
Meier, Herman, 1939, Ap 23,III,6:7
Meier, Julius L (por), 1937, Jl 15,19:3
Meier, Norman C, 1967, N 4,33:3
Meier, Siegfried, 1956, O 11,39:4
Meier, Victor, 1943, Ap 19,19:2
Meiere, Hildreth, 1961, My 3,37:1
Meierhof, Edward L Dr, 1937, O 26,23:2
Meiers, R Dudley, 1961, Ja 7,19:3
Meigel, Caroline W Mrs, 1953, O 1,29:6
Meiggs, H, 1877, O 12,5:4
Meighan, B, 1933, F 7,19:5
Meighan, Bertha S Mrs, 1937, My 24,19:3
Meighan, Burton C Mrs, 1955, S 10,17:6
Meighan, Irene Mrs, 1956, N 6,42:3
Meighan, Lawrence, 1950, Ap 19,29:2
Meighan, Mary E F Q Mrs, 1937, F 25,23:2
Meighan, T, 1936, Jl 9,21:1
Meighan, Thomas Mrs, 1951, Ja 16,29:4
Meighen, Arthur (funl, Ag 9,27:1), 1960, Ag 6,19:3
Meigher, Stephen C, 1960, Jl 28,27:6
Meigs, Arthur Vincent Dr, 1912, Ja 2,11:6
Meigs, C A, 1883, N 9,5:4
Meigs, Charles D Dr, 1869, Je 25,1:4
Meigs, Charles H, 1937, O 28,25:4
Meigs, Edward B Mrs (will Je 10,35:1), 1958, Je 4, 33:4
Meigs, Ferris J, 1943, My 11,21:5
Meigs, Ferris J Mrs, 1965, Ag 20,29:2

Meigs, Ida B Mrs, 1942, D 20,45:1
Meigs, James B, 1945, O 31,23:4
Meigs, James H, 1958, Mr 31,27:4
Meigs, Joe V, 1963, O 26,27:1
Meigs, John Forsyth, 1924, Ap 17,19:4
Meigs, John Mrs, 1946, D 28,15:2
Meigs, John Prof, 1911, N 8,13:5
Meigs, Joseph V, 1959, N 1,86:5
Meigs, Merrill C, 1968, Ja 26,44:8
Meigs, Merrill C Mrs, 1956, Ja 12,27:3
Meigs, William P, 1943, D 23,19:4
Meikle, Arthur F, 1945, Ag 10,15:5
Meikle, G Stanley, 1960, Mr 31,33:2
Meikle, Henry W, 1958, My 25,87:2
Meikle, John K, 1940, My 19,43:2
Meikle, William S, 1945, Ja 23,19:3
Meikleham, William A, 1942, N 13,23:3
Meiklejohn, Alexander, 1964, D 17,41:4
Meiklejohn, Alexander Mrs, 1925, F 14,13:5
Meiklejohn, David, 1942, Ag 12,19:4
Meiklejohn, James T, 1944, N 18,13:4
Meiklejohn, Robert P Mrs, 1958, O 7,35:4
Meiklejohn, William, 1947, F 18,25:2
Meiler, Emil, 1938, S 29,25:6
Meilhac, Henri, 1897, Jl 7,7:1
Meili, Ernest, 1962, Ap 10,43:3
Meilicke, Edward J, 1959, D 3,37:3
Meilinger, Joe, 1955, Ap 7,27:5
Meilink, Charles, 1940, O 10,25:4
Meilink, John G, 1957, S 4,34:2
Meilland, Francois, 1958, Je 16,23:2
Meillet, A, 1936, S 23,25:6
Meillette, Louis J, 1959, D 29,25:1
Meilner, Joseph, 1938, D 9,25:5
Mein, William W, 1964, My 7,37:2
Mein, William W Mrs, 1967, Ag 7,29:4
Meinberg, Alfred, 1961, D 28,27:2
Meinberg, Alfred Mrs, 1962, My 9,43:5
Meinch, William C, 1943, F 13,11:2
Meincke, Albert B, 1944, Je 18,36:2
Meincke, Albert W, 1949, Je 16,30:5
Meincke, Edward Mrs, 1956, O 13,19:2
Meindel, John, 1957, My 25,21:2
Meine, Frank H C, 1940, Je 24,15:7
Meinecke, C William, 1938, Mr 25,19:5
Meinecke, Friedrich, 1954, F 8,23:3
Meinecke, Gerhard E, 1943, Ap 1,23:2
Meineke, William C Mrs, 1958, O 11,23:5
Meinel, Edward Mrs, 1952, Ja 21,15:2
Meinel, Frank A, 1940, Ap 25,23:2
Meinel, William J, 1961, N 18,23:3
Meinell, James Col, 1865, Jl 4,4:6
Meiners, Leo L, 1952, O 7,29:3
Meinersmann, William, 1956, F 18,19:3
Meinert, C J Richard Mrs, 1954, Ap 18,88:6
Meinert, Gustave A, 1942, O 18,52:3
Meinhard, Isaac, 1909, S 19,11:3
Meinhardt, Walter P, 1937, O 14,25:3
Meinhold, Arthur H, 1958, S 24,27:5
Meinhold, Harry, 1949, Jl 21,25:5
Meinholtz, Frederick E, 1961, D 24,36:1
Meinig, E Richard, 1948, Mr 15,23:1
Meininghaus, Charles Mrs, 1951, N 13,29:4
Meinke, William A, 1949, Je 5,92:5
Meinken, Charles F, 1947, N 8,17:6
Meinken, Ernest F, 1942, Mr 12,19:3
Meinken, Ernst A, 1953, Ja 12,27:2
Meinken, Frederick, 1958, My 3,19:2
Meinl, Julius, 1944, Ag 30,17:5
Meinrath, Joseph, 1941, My 16,23:3
Meins, Carroll L, 1953, S 16,33:4
Meints, Harold L, 1965, Ap 22,33:4
Meinzer, Harry V, 1957, N 20,35:2
Meinzer, Henry V, 1950, N 9,33:6
Meinzer, Martin S, 1950, S 16,19:5
Meinzer, Oscar E, 1948, Je 16,29:3
Meir, Jacob, 1939, My 28,III,7:3
Meir, William J, 1948, O 11,23:3
Meire, Julius, 1879, O 15,2:5
Meireles, Manuel C de Q, 1962, Mr 12,31:4
Meirovits, Tilly Mrs, 1941, Jl 17,19:5
Meirowitz, Philip, 1959, Je 21,92:8
Meisdalshagen, Olav, 1959, N 22,86:7
Meise, August H, 1959, Je 14,86:8
Meisel, Carl, 1907, D 28,7:5
Meisel, Frank E Sr, 1950, S 17,105:1
Meisel, Fred, 1915, Jl 3,7:4
Meisel, Harry, 1942, Jl 29,17:5
Meisel, Joseph Mrs, 1939, Ap 28,25:3
Meisel, Louis, 1954, D 7,33:3
Meisel, Nachman, 1966, My 2,37:1
Meisel, Peter, 1939, Mr 5,48:5
Meisel, Phil L, 1953, N 6,28:3
Meisel, Phil Mrs, 1949, D 8,33:4
Meisel, Saul B, 1950, D 13,35:1
Meisels, Charles, 1963, Jl 8,29:3
Meisels, Samuel, 1949, Ap 24,76:5
Meiselwitz, Gertrude E, 1965, Ja 2,19:1
Meisenhelder, Samuel B, 1939, Jl 25,19:6
Meiser, Carl H, 1949, S 28,27:2
Meisky, William H, 1952, My 21,27:1
Meisky, William H Mrs, 1945, S 28,21:2
Meislahn, Albert, 1910, Mr 2,9:4

Meisner, Hans H, 1939, N 24,23:5
Meisner, Harold H, 1948, Ap 5,21:4
Meisner, Henry, 1949, Mr 24,27:3
Meisner, Max W, 1962, S 21,30:1
Meisner, Nelson, 1944, Je 23,19:4
Meiss, Harry, 1954, Ag 9,17:3
Meiss, Milfred D, 1958, S 15,21:5
Meisser, Stanley, 1948, Ag 22,34:4
Meissner, Albert, 1909, O 23,11:2
Meissner, Alfred, 1952, My 24,19:3
Meissner, Alvin R, 1949, Je 26,60:6
Meissner, Charles F, 1952, Je 2,22:4
Meissner, E A, 1902, S 28,5:1
Meissner, Edwin B, 1956, S 11,35:5
Meissner, Fred, 1966, Mr 17,39:1
Meissner, J Elwood, 1941, Ag 15,17:5
Meissner, Otto, 1953, My 28,23:1
Meissonier, J L E, 1891, F 1,9:6
Meister, Carl, 1956, D 23,31:1
Meister, Charles A, 1943, Ja 11,15:1
Meister, Charles A Mrs, 1950, S 22,31:2
Meister, Edward Mrs, 1968, Je 18,47:2
Meister, George S, 1966, S 30,47:2
Meister, Herman O K, 1950, Je 12,27:4
Meister, John, 1960, Mr 20,87:1
Meister, Joseph, 1950, Ag 18,21:3
Meister, Walter F, 1967, F 11,29:1
Meister, Walter F Mrs, 1958, F 15,17:4; 1961, Je 15, 43:5
Meister, William Mrs, 1950, Mr 28,32:3
Meites, Hyman L, 1944, My 4,19:2
Meitin, Abraham, 1952, F 15,26:2
Meitner, Lise Dr, 1968, O 28,1:8
Meixsell, Raymond K Sr Mrs, 1948, Jl 1,23:6
Mejia, Federico, 1937, Je 18,21:5
Mejia, Manuel, 1958, F 12,29:4
Mejia, Rosario Romero Bosque de Mrs, 1954, F 21, 68:5
Mejia Colindres, Vincente, 1966, Ag 25,37:5
Mejia Ricart, Gustavo A, 1962, Je 11,31:5
Mejorada, Carlos S, 1952, Je 26,29:2
Mekeel, Arthur J Mrs, 1952, Ag 13,21:1
Mekeel, H Scudder, 1947, Jl 25,17:3
Mekeel, Van Cortright, 1950, O 27,29:1
Mekhlis, Lev Zakharovich, 1953, F 14,3:6
Mekler, Lev A, 1958, Je 17,29:5
Meklune, Peter, 1950, Ag 16,29:1
Meklune, Peter Mrs, 1950, Ag 16,29:1
Melachrino, George, 1965, Je 19,29:2
Melady, John, 1951, Je 8,27:5
Melady, John F, 1965, Ja 11,45:3
Melahn, Fred L, 1941, N 26,23:2
Melamed, Louis, 1959, F 22,88:4
Melamed, Raphael H, 1948, My 4,25:4
Melamed, Raphael M Mrs, 1954, N 4,31:4
Melamed, Samuel M, 1938, Je 20,15:2
Melamet, Elsa, 1938, N 25,23:2
Melamid, Michael, 1950, Ja 11,23:3
Melamid, Michael Mrs, 1966, Ap 13,43:1
Melan, Ambrose F, 1943, F 23,21:5
Melancon, Joseph A, 1942, O 20,21:4
Melander, Axel, 1962, Ag 15,31:3
Melander, Clifford T, 1968, My 22,47:1
Melandre, Thomas J, 1940, N 30,17:2
Melanson, Gregory H, 1937, S 28,23:1
Melanson, Louis J A, 1941, O 24,24:2
Melba, Midget (Sylvia Willes), 1917, Ap 26,13:6
Melba, N, 1931, F 23,17:1
Melber, Charles P, 1946, My 1,25:1
Melber, Kate Mrs, 1939, O 13,23:3
Melbourne, W F Gen, 1911, F 28,11:4
Melchen, Edward W Sr, 1948, Jl 6,23:4
Melcher, Charles W, 1939, Jl 2,15:2
Melcher, Columbus R, 1947, Mr 24,25:4
Melcher, David A, 1941, O 29,23:1
Melcher, Frederic G, 1963, Mr 11,9:4
Melcher, Harold P, 1953, N 2,25:6
Melcher, Henry J G, 1914, N 11,13:4
Melcher, John, 1956, Jl 29,64:8
Melcher, John H, 1961, S 13,45:1
Melcher, John Loewell Mrs, 1908, S 13,9:5
Melcher, John S, 1945, Jl 29,39:2
Melcher, Josiah R Mrs, 1939, N 7,28:3
Melcher, Martin M, 1968, Ap 21,80:3
Melchers, G, 1932, D 1,21:1
Melchers, Gari Mrs, 1955, Ap 9,13:5
Melchett, Lord, 1930, D 28,26:5; 1949, Ja 23,69:1
Melchinger, Charles F, 1955, Je 9,29:1
Melchionna, Robert H, 1967, Ag 30,43:2
Melchior, C J, 1933, D 31,20:1
Melchior, Montfort, 1956, Ja 26,29:2
Melchior, Oscar G, 1956, Jl 4,19:5
Melchoir, S George, 1948, S 1,23:2
Meldahl, Ferdinand, 1908, F 4,7:5
Meldon, Alfred W, 1956, Ap 21,17:5
Meldon, Phil A, 1942, Ap 11,13:4
Meldrim, P W, 1933, D 14,23:1
Meldrum, Douglas G, 1947, Mr 3,21:3
Meldrum, George G, 1948, Je 5,15:3
Meldrum, James K, 1959, Ja 27,33:1
Meldrum, William B, 1957, Ja 1,23:4
Meldrum, William P, 1947, F 5,26:1
Meldrum, William R, 1953, Ap 14,35:3
Mele, Joseph G, 1964, Ag 25,33:4
Mele, Pasquale E Mrs, 1959, S 16,39:2
Mele, Vincent J Jr, 1954, Mr 13,15:3
Melencio, Jose P, 1952, D 14,91:1
Melendez, Carlos, 1919, O 10,13:3
Melendez, Jorge, 1953, N 3,32:7
Melendy, G B, 1883, F 26,5:6
Melendy, Jesse G, 1954, Je 8,27:3
Meleney, Clarence E (por), 1938, Mr 28,15:1
Meleney, Frank L (Mar 7), 1963, Ap 1,36:2
Meletio, Monroe L Sr, 1956, S 16,84:8
Meletios Metaxakes, Patriarch, 1935, Jl 30,19:4
Melfa, Anthony, 1950, My 8,36:8
Melfi, Domingo, 1946, Ja 12,15:2
Melfi, Marty Mrs, 1967, O 11,47:2
Melford, Mark, 1914, Ja 5,9:6
Melhado, Donald I, 1944, Ag 11,15:2
Melhado, Edmund, 1945, S 25,25:1
Melhado, Vernon K, 1938, Ag 3,19:5
Melhame, Selim P, 1937, D 14,25:4
Melhorn, Nathan R, 1952, F 20,29:4
Melhuish, Edward H, 1951, N 2,23:3
Melhuish, William L, 1954, Ap 21,29:5
Meli, Joseph, 1941, F 13,19:1
Melia, Bartolome, 1939, Je 16,23:3
Melia, Frank A J, 1948, S 27,23:2
Melia, James C, 1965, Ap 10,30:1
Melia, James J, 1937, Ja 19,23:2
Melia, Joseph F, 1949, N 5,13:2
Melican, James P, 1963, S 24,39:3
Melick, Annie M Mrs, 1947, F 3,19:6
Melick, Charles Russell, 1968, D 25,31:3
Melick, George B, 1954, Jl 15,27:3
Melick, Harry C W, 1961, S 23,19:6
Melick, Herbert L, 1941, My 27,23:5
Melick, J Clark, 1944, S 15,19:5
Melick, James S Mrs, 1943, S 5,28:8
Melick, John M, 1955, S 20,31:4
Melick, John W, 1942, D 23,19:2
Melick, Leoni, 1908, Ag 25,7:6
Melick, Phil W, 1941, F 3,20:1
Melick, R Kline, 1951, Ag 21,27:4
Melicov, Dina, 1967, Mr 29,45:1
Melies, Georges, 1938, Ja 23,II,9:2
Melik-Pashayev, Aleksandr S, 1964, Je 19,31:2
Melikian, Saro (S Tellerian), 1960, My 26,33:5
Melikoff, L Gen, 1888, D 27,5:1
Melikoff, Maximilian Prince, 1950, Ap 26,29:2
Melillo, Anthony F, 1968, Jl 1,33:2
Melillo, Oscar, 1963, N 15,35:4
Meline, Frank L, 1944, Ag 19,11:2
Meline, James F Col, 1873, Ag 15,2:4
Meline, Jules Sen, 1925, D 22,21:4
Melinkov, Konstantin, 1954, O 7,23:4
Melioransky, Constantin P, 1957, F 6,25:6
Melish, John H Mrs, 1941, Ag 4,13:2
Melish, John R Mrs, 1960, S 12,29:1
Melish, Thomas G, 1948, F 17,25:3
Melish, Thomas W Rev Dr, 1908, F 24,7:5
Melius, Frederic N, 1941, Ag 1,15:6
Melk, Suzanne, 1951, F 5,23:2
Melkhisedek III, Patriarch (M Pkhaladze), 1960, Ja 17,86:5
Melko, Matthew F, 1958, My 8,29:2
Mell, Augustus, 1939, O 19,23:5
Mell, Charles F, 1944, S 6,19:6
Mell, Clayton D, 1945, Mr 1,21:3
Mellady, James C, 1957, D 15,86:4
Mellana, Ignazio, 1967, Mr 3,35:5
Mellanby, Edward, 1955, Ja 31,19:2
Mellanby, John, 1939, Jl 17,19:3
Mellas, Gregory Mrs, 1946, Ja 1,27:3
Mellberg, Charles, 1957, Jl 26,19:4
Melledge, Edgar C Mrs, 1952, D 13,21:6
Mellen, Albert H, 1942, Ag 13,19:2
Mellen, Arthur W, 1947, Jl 3,21:6
Mellen, Arthur W Jr, 1943, N 17,25:4
Mellen, C S, 1927, N 18,23:1
Mellen, Calvert K, 1945, Jl 6,11:4
Mellen, Chase Mrs, 1950, Ag 6,73:1
Mellen, Chase Sr (por), 1939, Ap 1,19:1
Mellen, Daniel, 1957, S 4,33:2
Mellen, George, 1941, S 12,21:2
Mellen, George A, 1946, Ja 27,42:8
Mellen, George F, 1952, N 11,29:1
Mellen, George Kingsbury, 1909, S 1,9:6
Mellen, George Washington, 1907, My 9,9:5
Mellen, Henry M, 1942, Ja 15,19:4
Mellen, James H, 1910, Je 17,7:4
Mellen, John F H, 1943, S 24,23:4
Mellen, Joseph M, 1961, Jl 5,33:1
Mellen, Rufus H, 1957, N 16,19:5
Mellen, William P, 1953, Jl 16,21:1
Mellenthin, Herman E (por), 1942, Mr 3,23:1
Meller, Abraham H Mrs, 1964, Mr 7,23:4
Meller, Adolf, 1947, D 2,29:6
Meller, Harry B, 1943, Je 29,20:3
Meller, Mischa Mrs, 1966, N 26,36:5
Meller, Raquel (funl, Jl 28,19:6), 1962, Jl 27,25:1
Meller, Richard J, 1940, Je 24,15:6
Mellersh, Francis, 1955, My 26,6:4
Mellett, Homer J, 1949, Mr 7,21:2
Mellett, Lowell, 1960, Ap 7,35:3
Mellett, William J, 1946, O 13,58:6
Melley, Edward, 1951, F 20,25:2
Mellick, Anna C, 1941, Ap 11,21:1
Mellick, George P, 1925, Ag 24,13:7
Mellick, George P Mrs, 1951, Mr 25,74:5
Mellick, John R, 1951, S 6,31:4
Mellick, Roger D, 1968, D 4,47:2
Mellicker, Carl, 1952, Mr 17,21:4
Melliday, John F Mrs, 1937, D 20,27:5
Melliday, S Louis, 1921, Ag 19,13:3
Mellies, Wilhelm, 1958, My 20,34:5
Melliet, Francis Mrs, 1951, S 27,63:8
Mellin, Carl L, 1924, O 16,25:4
Mellin, Nelson F, 1952, Ja 19,15:7
Melling, John R, 1964, O 19,33:4
Melling, O Rodger, 1953, S 5,15:4
Mellinger, Aubrey H, 1960, Ag 9,27:5
Mellino, Gaetano, 1953, Ja 26,19:2
Mellion, Benjamin Mrs, 1955, My 5,33:5
Mellis, Daniel, 1938, D 7,23:1
Mellis, Joseph D, 1948, Ja 11,56:5
Mellish, David B, 1874, My 24,7:2
Mellish, Humphrey, 1937, Je 20,II,6:8
Mellish, William E, 1949, Ja 23,68:4
Mello Franco, Alfranio de, 1943, Ja 2,11:1
Mello Franco, Cairo de, 1955, S 19,12:4
Mellody, John P, 1951, Mr 10,13:2
Mellon, Alfred, 1962, S 1,19:5
Mellon, Andrew, 1937, Ag 27,1:1
Mellon, Ben, 1942, O 31,15:2
Mellon, Charles H, 1943, S 15,27:4; 1962, Je 26,33:3
Mellon, Edward P, 1953, Ap 12,88:8
Mellon, Edward P Mrs, 1938, S 6,21:3
Mellon, George D, 1939, Jl 25,19:5
Mellon, George W, 1943, Ag 8,37:2
Mellon, Jennie K Mrs, 1938, N 16,23:5
Mellon, John H, 1949, Jl 8,19:4
Mellon, John J, 1953, Ja 4,76:6
Mellon, Norman S, 1967, F 14,43:2
Mellon, Paul Mrs (por),(will, D 6,30:4), 1946, O 12 19:1
Mellon, R B, 1933, D 2,13:1
Mellon, Thomas A, 1948, Ap 17,15:4
Mellon, Thomas Judge, 1908, F 4,7:5; 1908, F 6,7:5
Mellon, Thomas 2d, 1946, Ag 20,27:4
Mellon, William, 1952, F 3,84:2
Mellon, William L, 1949, O 9,92:1
Mellon, William L Mrs, 1942, Mr 19,21:3
Mellon, Ziggie, 1947, Jl 10,21:2
Melloninio, Elizabeth C C Mrs, 1939, My 3,23:2
Mellor, Alex S, 1959, S 2,29:4
Mellor, Caroline Mrs, 1951, My 23,35:3
Mellor, Charles E, 1960, Ap 24,88:5
Mellor, Earl G, 1941, Jl 29,15:5
Mellor, Edgar, 1949, D 20,31:4
Mellor, Frederic W, 1954, Ja 24,84:7
Mellor, Geoffrey R, 1960, Ap 29,31:2
Mellor, Gilbert, 1947, Ap 18,22:2
Mellor, Howard A, 1940, F 1,21:3
Mellor, Howard Mrs, 1938, S 30,21:3
Mellor, J Edgar Mrs, 1950, Je 4,92:4
Mellor, John, 1949, Mr 27,76:1
Mellor, Joseph W, 1938, My 28,15:6
Mellor, Norman, 1951, N 5,31:6
Mellor, Richard, 1946, Ap 20,15:2
Mellor, Samuel, 1952, Ag 27,27:4
Mellor, Samuel Mrs, 1950, Je 22,27:1
Mellor, Sigourney, 1949, D 20,31:3
Mellor, Walter, 1940, Ja 12,17:1
Mellor, William, 1942, Je 9,23:5
Mellott, Arthur J, 1957, D 30,23:3
Mellow, Andrew S, 1941, N 6,23:4
Melloy, George G, 1942, D 21,19:6
Mellquist, Jerome, 1963, Ap 13,19:5
Melly, Cornelius, 1937, Ja 23,17:2
Mellyn, James F, 1944, F 17,19:5
Melmo, Onny, 1938, Je 4,15:2
Melms, Alfred J, 1947, F 28,24:3
Melms, Gustave J, 1943, Ap 4,40:3
Melnick, Celia Mrs, 1918, N 5,13:5
Melnick, David, 1955, Jl 1,21:3
Melnick, George, 1952, Ag 29,23:1
Melnick, Joseph, 1942, S 10,27:3
Melnick, Max, 1937, Jl 18,II,7:4
Melniker, Aaron A, 1960, S 11,80:3
Melniker, Louis, 1963, My 17,33:2
Melnikoff, Peter, 1952, Jl 23,23:2
Melnyk, Andrey, 1964, N 7,27:4
Melnyk, Nicholas, 1947, S 29,21:3
Melo y Alcalde, Prudenzio, 1945, N 1,23:3
Meloche, Felice Mrs, 1937, Jl 22,19:5
Melody, John W Msgr, 1925, Mr 9,17:4
Melody, Margaret C, 1966, Je 29,47:4
Melody, Matthew, 1905, Ja 11,9:4
Melody, William E, 1916, My 16,13:7
Melody, William J, 1956, My 12,19:1
Melone, Harry R, 1949, Ja 12,27:3
Meloney, William B Sr Mrs, 1943, Je 24,21:1
Meloney, William Brown Maj (funl, D 11,23:3), 1925, D 8,25:4
Meloon, Frank H Jr, 1942, My 5,21:3
Melosh, Henry J, 1944, Ja 13,21:4
Meloy, G S Jr Mrs, 1959, Ap 26,86:7

Meloy, Guy S Jr Gen, 1968, D 15,86:1
Meloy, Henry J, 1951, Ap 7,15:5; 1954, S 12,85:1
Meloy, W T Rev, 1904, F 21,7:6
Meloy, William W, 1939, Je 20,21:2
Melrose, Gail, 1952, N 24,14:7
Melrose, Henry, 1951, Ja 23,27:3
Melrose, James A, 1948, Mr 4,25:1
Melrose, John C Mrs, 1951, N 1,29:2
Melrose, Walter, 1968, Mr 15,39:2
Mels, Edgar, 1937, N 2,25:2
Melsa, Anthony, 1950, My 7,65:3
Melsa, Mary, 1955, Jl 19,27:3
Melsheimer, Ernst, 1960, Mr 27,86:8
Melsher, Irving, 1962, Mr 4,33:4
Meltabarger, Cecil, 1952, Ag 9,13:5
Meltabarger, Cecil D, 1950, Jl 3,15:4
Meltcher, Simon L, 1968, N 21,47:3
Melton, Andrew J Mrs, 1945, D 20,23:1
Melton, Andrew J Sr, 1960, Jl 25,23:3
Melton, Charles L, 1939, Je 7,23:2
Melton, Charles L Mrs, 1943, Ap 18,48:6
Melton, James Mrs, 1956, N 11,86:4
Melton, James W, 1942, Jl 24,19:3; 1961, Ap 23,86:3
Melton, Sparks W, 1957, Ap 2,31:1
Melton, W D Dr, 1926, My 4,27:3
Melton, Wightman F, 1944, N 14,23:3
Meltsner, Max (por), 1943, Ja 18,15:3
Meltz, Albert D, 1966, O 10,41:1
Meltzer, C H, 1936, Ja 15,19:5
Meltzer, Edward J, 1949, O 22,9:6
Meltzer, Eugene P, 1957, D 22,40:7
Meltzer, Harry C, 1955, My 7,17:2
Meltzer, Hyman, 1966, O 5,42:8
Meltzer, Irving, 1943, Je 18,21:4
Meltzer, James L, 1964, My 25,33:4
Meltzer, Leo I, 1966, Ag 26,33:4
Meltzer, Mark C, 1957, S 16,31:6
Meltzer, Max, 1948, N 5,25:1; 1962, Ja 31,31:4
Meltzer, Morris, 1947, Jl 11,15:3; 1957, Ja 1,23:3
Meltzer, Samuel, 1960, My 7,23:3
Meltzer, Samuel James Dr, 1920, N 8,15:6
Meltzer, Samuel Mrs, 1943, F 5,21:5
Meltzer, Saul W, 1963, My 15,40:1
Melvain, Janet F, 1953, N 6,27:4
Melville, Andrew H, 1946, N 24,78:5
Melville, F H, 1903, O 3,9:6
Melville, F Jr, 1935, F 26,19:1
Melville, Frank Mrs (will, Ag 11,16:5), 1939, Ag 3, 19:5
Melville, Frederick, 1938, Ap 6,23:1; 1940, Ja 13,15:5; 1944, D 28,19:4
Melville, G J W, 1878, D 6,5:3
Melville, George D Mrs, 1915, D 16,15:5
Melville, George Wallace Rear-Adm (trb, Mr 21,-11:4), 1912, Mr 18,11:3
Melville, Harold G, 1951, Ag 15,27:5
Melville, John, 1949, D 20,31:2
Melville, Katherine G, 1939, S 14,23:2
Melville, Park A, 1941, F 10,17:4
Melville, Percy F, 1946, O 15,25:2
Melville, Rose, 1946, O 9,27:1
Melville, T Capt, 1884, Mr 7,5:2
Melville, Walter, 1937, Mr 1,19:2
Melville, William, 1918, F 2,11:5
Melville, William F, 1940, O 25,21:2
Melville, Winnie, 1937, S 20,23:6
Melvin, A D, 1947, Je 27,21:4
Melvin, A D Dr, 1917, D 9,23:1
Melvin, A Warner, 1959, Ja 1,31:4
Melvin, Dennis S, 1951, Mr 1,27:4
Melvin, Edwin F, 1958, D 11,13:6
Melvin, Floyd J Mrs, 1938, Mr 8,19:1
Melvin, Frank W, 1961, Ag 20,86:4
Melvin, Frederick G, 1945, Jl 4,13:7
Melvin, Parker L, 1945, Ja 25,19:5
Melvin, Ridgely P, 1945, D 15,17:6
Melvin, Roland A, 1947, O 3,25:2
Melvin, Valentine A Sr, 1956, Jl 7,13:4
Melvin, W P, 1883, S 9,7:3
Melzer, Roman F, 1943, My 1,15:4
Melzl, Albert J Mrs, 1964, D 19,29:1
Membreno, Don Alberto, 1921, F 6,22:4
Memhard, Allen R, 1957, S 13,24:2
Memminger, C C Mrs, 1948, Ag 16,19:4
Memminger, Willis W Rev Dr, 1937, My 5,25:3
Memmott, Edward F, 1957, My 19,88:4
Memory, Nichol H Mrs, 1949, Ja 15,17:2
Memory, Sarah F Mrs, 1950, My 28,45:1
Memziger, Cologne Dr, 1876, Ja 9,5:7
Menachem, Sabetz Mrs, 1943, My 8,15:4
Menagh, Edward M, 1963, Ag 15,29:1
Menagh, Hugh P, 1939, Ap 12,23:1
Menagh, Louis R, 1947, Ja 27,23:5
Menaker, Michael G, 1967, D 11,47:4
Menapace, Robert B, 1968, S 13,47:4
Menard, Marvin C, 1960, My 29,56:5
Menard, Victor, 1954, Ap 16,21:1
Menasce, Charlotte de, 1947, Mr 8,14:3
Menchen, Joseph L, 1940, O 8,25:6
Mencher, Charles, 1949, S 28,27:5
Mencher, Henry Mrs, 1959, Ag 22,17:5
Mencher, Joel, 1948, S 30,27:5
Mencher, Samuel, 1967, Mr 11,29:3
Mencher, Sidney, 1952, N 10,25:4
Menches, Frank, 1951, O 5,27:2
Mencken, August, 1967, My 21,86:8
Mencken, Harry P, 1957, Ap 22,25:4
Mencken, Henry L (funl plans, Ja 31,29:5; funl, F 1,31:3), 1956, Ja 30,1:2
Mencone, Albert R, 1952, Ja 30,25:3
Menconi, Raffaello E, 1942, Mr 7,17:6
Menczel, Philipp, 1941, O 29,24:2
Mendel, Bernardo, 1967, Je 2,41:1
Mendel, Charles, 1952, Jl 28,15:3
Mendel, Edgar, 1945, Ja 9,23:3
Mendel, Emma, 1956, Mr 21,38:2
Mendel, Ernest, 1957, Ja 19,15:3
Mendel, Harry, 1956, Jl 30,21:2
Mendel, Herman, 1914, Mr 27,11:6
Mendel, Hortense, 1960, O 10,31:2
Mendel, Isador, 1924, My 1,19:5
Mendel, Jacob, 1903, Ap 27,7:5
Mendel, Jules, 1937, S 16,25:2
Mendel, Maurice H, 1942, My 11,15:3
Mendel, Milton, 1957, D 11,32:1
Mendel, Samuel P, 1905, Mr 25,9:6
Mendel, Warner H, 1967, O 24,47:2
Mendel, William H Mrs, 1950, N 10,28:2
Mendeleef, Dmitri Ivanovitch Prof, 1907, F 3,7:5
Mendell, Clara Mrs, 1941, Ag 3,34:2
Mendell, Morris, 1959, Ag 2,81:1
Mendell, Seth, 1922, Jl 29,7:5
Mendelowitz, Abraham, 1966, N 15,41:1
Mendels, Emanuel S, 1911, O 18,11:5
Mendelsohn, Albert, 1949, Je 22,31:1
Mendelsohn, Arthur C, 1937, F 25,23:3
Mendelsohn, Charles J (por), 1939, S 28,25:1
Mendelsohn, David H, 1943, Ap 9,21:3
Mendelsohn, Eric, 1953, S 16,36:7
Mendelsohn, Felix, 1938, O 25,23:3
Mendelsohn, Isaac, 1965, My 22,31:3
Mendelsohn, Jacob J, 1955, Jl 28,23:5
Mendelsohn, Jacques A, 1940, Ja 6,13:3
Mendelsohn, Jerome W Mrs, 1955, F 3,23:4
Mendelsohn, Joseph Mrs, 1961, Ag 31,27:1
Mendelsohn, L J, 1954, Je 5,17:6
Mendelsohn, Lewis, 1939, Ag 27,35:4
Mendelsohn, Louis, 1947, Je 10,27:5
Mendelsohn, Louis Mrs, 1953, Ag 31,17:3
Mendelsohn, Mark, 1941, O 11,17:6
Mendelsohn, Meyer, 1961, F 14,37:2
Mendelsohn, Morris J, 1966, Ag 31,43:1
Mendelsohn, S Felix, 1953, F 28,17:4
Mendelsohn, Samuel, 1966, F 4,31:2
Mendelsohn, Sidney Mrs, 1961, O 10,43:4
Mendelsohn, Sigmund, 1941, Mr 13,21:4
Mendelson, Abraham, 1946, Je 20,23:5
Mendelson, Alan N, 1956, Ag 15,29:4
Mendelson, Herbert A, 1951, Je 25,19:6
Mendelson, Herbert E, 1962, Je 2,19:4
Mendelson, Jacob B Z, 1941, Ag 6,17:2
Mendelson, Joseph Mrs, 1949, F 23,28:2
Mendelson, Jules, 1946, Ja 14,19:2
Mendelson, Jules Mrs, 1959, S 23,35:2
Mendelson, Szlama, 1948, F 11,27:4
Mendelson, Walter, 1940, Ja 20,15:4
Mendelssohn, Eleonora, 1951, Ja 25,26:4
Mendelssohn, F von, 1935, Je 14,23:1
Mendelssohn, Felix, 1952, F 5,29:4
Mendelssohn, Felix R, 1951, My 16,52:3
Mendelssohn, L, 1935, Mr 29,21:4
Mendelssohn, Ludwig Mrs, 1949, Jl 7,25:5
Mendelssohn, Marcus A, 1950, My 19,28:4
Mendelssohn-Bartholdy, Ernest von, 1909, D 26,11:6
Mendelssohn-Bartholdy, Otto von, 1949, Jl 30,15:2
Menden, Elon Herman, 1923, N 11,23:3
Menden, William S (por), 1949, S 28,27:1
Mendenhall, Charles E Mrs (Dorothy), 1964, Ag 1, 21:4
Mendenhall, Earl, 1942, F 17,22:2
Mendenhall, Franklin P, 1955, S 2,17:6
Mendenhall, Harlan G (por), 1940, My 16,23:3
Mendenhall, Priscilla, 1963, Je 16,84:5
Mendenhall, Sterling G, 1942, O 29,23:2
Mendenhall, Walter C, 1957, Je 3,27:5
Mendes, A Piza Mrs, 1959, S 11,27:3
Mendes, Abraham Mrs, 1904, Ap 17,7:6
Mendes, Edward J, 1947, O 28,25:2
Mendes, F de S Rabbi, 1927, O 27,29:1
Mendes, Frank E, 1949, F 25,23:2
Mendes, George A, 1950, F 1,30:3
Mendes, George A Mrs, 1950, F 9,29:5
Mendes, H Pereira Mrs, 1953, F 19,23:2
Mendes, H Pereira Rev Dr, 1937, O 21,23:1
Mendes, Henry E, 1963, D 14,27:5
Mendes, Julius, 1924, S 30,23:1
Mendes, Maria P, 1956, Mr 17,19:7
Mendes, Michael S, 1958, My 30,21:1
Mendes, Norman C, 1961, D 9,27:6
Mendes, William B, 1957, D 10,35:1
Mendes-France, David, 1957, D 2,27:5
Mendes-France, Pierre Mrs, 1967, N 28,47:2
Mendessolle, Evelyn, 1951, Ja 11,25:4
Mendez, Alfredo, 1940, Ap 26,21:4
Mendez, Capote Fernando, 1947, Jl 1,25:3
Mendez, Joaquin, 1943, S 29,21:5; 1957, D 6,29:3
Mendez, Mauro, 1966, Ja 2,72:7
Mendez Pereira, Octavio, 1954, Ag 15,84:3
Mendham, Maurice B, 1912, N 9,11:6
Mendieta, Carlos Mrs, 1942, Jl 22,19:5
Mendieta Montefur, Carlos, 1960, S 29,35:3
Mendieta y Montefor, Pablo, 1951, Jl 25,23:4
Mendinhall, John M, 1938, O 16,44:8
Mendivil, Javier, 1953, Jl 19,56:3
Mendizabal, Ramon Gen, 1921, Mr 8,11:4
Mendl, Charles (will, F 20,51:1), 1958, F 15,17:5
Mendl, Lady (E de Wolfe),(will, Ag 12,14:3), 1950, Jl 13,25:1
Mendl, Lady (Y Steinbach), 1956, D 20,29:4
Mendl, Sigismund F, 1945, Jl 19,23:3
Mendlesen, Marius A, 1966, N 3,39:4
Mendleson, Jerome, 1940, Ag 17,15:4
Mendleson, Leon, 1946, O 21,31:4
Mendlowitz, Herman, 1962, Ap 2,31:2
Mendon, G A, 1879, Ag 9,5:4
Mendonca, Salvador de Dr, 1913, D 7,VIII,19:4
Mendoza, Augustine, 1954, Ap 12,29:4
Mendoza, Carlos, 1916, F 14,13:7
Mendoza, Charles, 1940, Mr 7,23:3
Mendoza, Francisco Archbishop, 1923, Jl 30,13:5
Mendoza, Gen, 1907, Mr 27,9:6
Mendoza, Idelfonso, 1941, Ja 19,40:2
Mendoza, Isaac, 1937, N 4,25:3
Mendoza, Louis D, 1954, Ag 28,15:6
Mendoza, Luis, 1957, Jl 23,27:2
Mendoza, Mario, 1952, D 23,23:1
Mendoza, Maurice A, 1967, Mr 9,39:1
Mendoza, Pablo, 1938, Mr 6,30:6
Mendoza, Rodulfo, 1943, Ja 15,17:5
Mendoza y Freyre de Andrade, Nestor G de, 1954, D 17,31:1
Meneely, A Howard, 1961, My 14,87:2
Meneely, Alfred C, 1952, Jl 31,23:2
Meneely, Andrew E, 1939, Ag 26,15:5
Meneely, Charles Dickinson, 1922, O 24,17:4
Meneely, Chester, 1954, My 6,33:4
Meneely, Chester B, 1957, F 19,31:2
Meneely, Emily F Mrs, 1941, Jl 8,19:3
Meneely, George Rodney, 1915, O 25,9:6
Meneely, Harry W, 1943, Mr 27,14:8
Meneely, Howard R, 1945, S 28,21:5
Meneely, Laurence Y, 1961, Jl 17,21:2
Meneely, William R, 1951, D 10,29:6
Menees, Thomas O Dr, 1937, F 15,17:5
Menefee, Arthur E Mrs, 1944, N 10,19:5
Menefee, Jack (Jock), 1953, Mr 12,27:3
Menefee, Samuel W Jr, 1960, Jl 19,29:4
Menegay, Jules, 1938, Ap 2,15:5
Meneghin, Angelo J, 1964, Ja 22,37:1
Menemencioglu, Numan, 1958, F 16,86:4
Menen, Empress of Ethiopia (funl, F 16,27:3), 1962, F 15,29:5
Menendez, Fernando P, 1968, Jl 13,27:1
Menendez, Joseph C, 1959, Jl 14,29:4
Menendez Behety, Alfonzo, 1945, Je 29,15:3
Menendez Beheyt, Jose, 1951, Ag 10,5:1
Menendez Pidal, Ramon, 1968, N 16,37:2
Meneray, Laura J Mrs, 1949, Ja 8,15:3
Menerth, Edward F Mrs, 1958, Jl 8,27:4
Menet de Agramonte, Juliette de (will), 1952, Ja 1, 13:5
Menfort, Joseph Glaes, 1925, F 8,7:1
Meng, Frederick M, 1950, F 18,15:5
Meng, George E Mrs, 1957, S 22,85:3
Mengarini, Arnaldo Count, 1951, Ap 4,29:4
Mengarini, Ettore, 1952, Ja 20,84:6
Mengarini, Giuseppina P Countess, 1955, Ag 9,26:3
Mengarini, Publio, 1949, Ap 21,26:2
Menge, Edward J von K, 1941, Ja 10,20:2
Menge, Frederick, 1951, Ja 10,28:2
Menge, Frederick L Mrs, 1945, D 8,17:3
Menge, Hermann A, 1939, Ja 14,17:5
Mengebier, William E, 1950, D 23,15:5
Mengel, Jesse M, 1952, Je 6,23:3
Mengel, Levi W, 1941, F 4,21:4
Mengel, Otto H, 1958, Mr 9,86:5
Mengel, Samuel P, 1947, N 12,27:3
Mengelberg, Kaethe Dr, 1968, Ap 24,47:1
Mengelberg, Rudolf, 1959, O 14,43:4
Mengelberg, Willem, 1951, Mr 23,21:3
Menger, Albert C, 1949, N 15,25:3
Menger, Albert C Mrs, 1953, S 1,24:3
Menger, Carl Prof, 1921, F 28,11:4
Menger, Clifford C, 1960, Ja 16,21:2
Menger, Henry L, 1960, S 17,23:3
Menger, John Mrs, 1951, Ag 11,11:6
Menger, Louis C, 1958, Ag 20,27:2
Mengert, Herbert R, 1950, S 17,105:1
Mengert, Ulric J, 1948, Ja 30,24:3
Menges, Ernest H Mrs, 1952, D 11,33:5
Menges, Frederic Mrs, 1939, S 6,23:2
Menges, William A, 1948, Ag 3,25:4
Menghi, Hugh J, 1956, Mr 8,29:5
Mengle, Glenn A, 1968, Ja 19,44:3
Mengoz, Francis, 1946, S 6,21:3
Menick, Louis J, 1949, Ap 8,25:3
Menier, E J, 1881, F 18,2:5
Menier, G, 1934, N 6,25:1
Menier, Henri, 1913, S 7,II,13:6

Menig, Howard M Sr, 1946, F 20,25:2
Menihan, Jeremiah G, 1954, Ja 22,27:3
Menin, Abraham I, 1956, S 22,17:4
Menjinski, V, 1934, My 11,21:1
Menjou, Adolphe J, 1963, O 30,39:2
Menjou, Albert, 1917, O 27,17:5
Menjou, Henry, 1956, Ja 30,27:3
Menk, Walter C, 1956, F 12,89:1
Menke, Bill Capt, 1968, Jl 17,43:2
Menke, Frank G, 1954, My 14,23:3
Menke, Harry, 1953, Ja 27,25:3
Menke, William, 1957, N 11,29:2
Menken, A D Mrs, 1936, Mr 24,23:1
Menken, Adah Isaacs, 1868, Ag 12,4:6
Menken, Helen (Mrs G N Richard),(mem ser set, Ap 7,36:6), 1966, Mr 28,33:2
Menken, Jules, 1957, Jl 23,25:2
Menken, N Davis, 1941, My 23,21:3
Menken, Percival S, 1908, My 18,7:4
Menken, S Stanwood, 1954, Ja 9,16:3
Menken, S Stanwood Mrs, 1938, S 2,17:3
Menkenmeier, George, 1958, Ag 23,7:3
Menkens, Albert, 1941, F 5,19:2
Menkens, Rudolph C, 1960, Ja 15,31:1
Menkes, Jacob, 1952, My 10,21:5
Menkes, Jacob B, 1949, Ap 4,23:5
Menkin, Joshua C, 1948, Ag 3,25:2
Menkin, Valy, 1960, D 24,15:4
Mennan, Eugene W, 1960, Ag 11,27:5
Menne, August C, 1943, Jl 27,17:5
Mennell, James B, 1957, Mr 4,27:4
Mennella, Federico G, 1954, Jl 21,27:4
Mennen, Joseph, 1939, Ap 29,17:4
Mennen, Theophilus L J, 1950, Ag 17,27:3
Mennen, William G, 1968, F 19,39:2
Mennen, William G Mrs, 1959, Ja 28,31:2; 1966, S 26, 41:3
Menner, Robert J M, 1951, Ap 5,29:6
Menner, William C L, 1955, Je 11,15:4
Mennet, Overton H, 1941, Ja 26,37:2
Mennie, William A, 1942, Ag 31,17:2
Menninger, Charles F (late city ed), 1953, N 29,2:8
Menninger, Florian, 1938, F 22,21:3
Menninger, Gus W Mrs, 1951, Ja 28,76:3
Menninger, John, 1881, O 28,5:2
Menninger, William C, 1966, S 7,1:4
Mennis, Cornelius Rev Dr, 1925, Mr 7,13:6
Mennitto, Domenick, 1951, D 12,37:4
Mennitto, Donato, 1950, Jl 17,21:4
Mennweg, Albert, 1950, D 11,25:4
Meno, Fred J, 1941, My 17,15:5
Menocal, Aniceto Garcia, 1908, Jl 21,7:5
Menocal, Fausto, 1940, O 31,23:5
Menocal, Gabriel, 1922, F 14,17:4
Menocal, Gustavo Garcia, 1917, Jl 20,9:6
Menocal, Mariana S de, 1942, Jl 10,17:2
Menocal, Pablo Antonio Garcia Col, 1924, Mr 10,15:4
Menocal y Deop, M G, 1941, S 8,7:1
Menoher, C T, 1930, Ag 12,21:3
Menoher, Pearson, 1958, F 14,24:1
Menold, Charles B, 1951, S 24,27:2
Menon, M Gopola, 1967, Je 12,45:1
Menotti, Carlo Mrs, 1967, Ja 24,28:8
Mensch, Bernard L, 1953, Ag 22,15:4
Mensch, Harold F, 1955, Ja 15,13:5
Mensch, Max, 1967, S 27,47:4
Menschel, Benjamin, 1962, O 8,23:5
Menschel, Victor Dr, 1968, Jl 19,35:3
Mensdorf, Count, 1871, F 16,1:2
Mensdorff, Albert von, 1945, Je 18,19:1
Mensel, Ernst H, 1942, S 8,23:4
Mensen, V H, 1933, Ag 5,11:1
Mensing, Bernard J, 1949, O 15,15:2
Mensing, H D, 1940, D 18,25:1
Mentag, Joseph P, 1949, F 10,28:3
Mentcher, Leo, 1950, Mr 2,27:5
Mente, Joseph, 1958, Ap 15,33:2
Menten, Maud L, 1960, Jl 21,27:3
Menth, Alfred, 1950, O 22,93:1
Menth, Herma, 1968, Mr 1,43:5
Menthon, Jacques de, 1952, N 7,4:2
Menti, Raffaele, 1881, O 19,5:5
Mentiply, George, 1944, F 10,15:5
Menton, James P, 1966, F 1,35:5
Mentrup, Charles J, 1943, O 8,19:2
Mentus, Casmer V, 1964, Ja 23,31:3
Mentz, Frank E Mrs, 1949, My 27,22:2
Mentz, George B, 1947, D 19,25:1
Mentz, George F M, 1957, D 1,88:8
Mentz, John J, 1957, O 5,17:1
Mentz, Joseph W, 1941, My 9,21:3
Mentz, Robert R, 1947, N 8,17:5
Mentzel, Charles, 1949, Je 2,27:3
Mentzel, Eugene J, 1942, D 17,29:6
Mentzendorff, Carl W, 1952, Jl 14,17:6
Mentzendorff, Carl W Mrs, 1963, Ag 11,85:2
Mentzer, Edmund H, 1951, Jl 12,25:5
Mentzer, John F, 1958, Ag 30,15:7
Mentzinger, Charles H, 1947, D 10,38:5
Menuet, Robert L, 1943, My 11,21:2
Menut, Arthur R, 1944, Ag 26,11:4
Menville, Leon J, 1955, Ja 26,25:4
Menville, Raoul L, 1946, Mr 29,23:3
Meny, Leo M, 1942, D 3,25:5
Menz, Albert G, 1947, O 8,25:5
Menz, John E, 1960, F 15,27:3
Menzel, Arthur Mrs, 1964, Jl 10,29:2
Menzel, Frederick, 1946, Mr 6,27:4
Menzel, Paul Rev Dr, 1907, Ap 9,9:6
Menzel, William F, 1945, O 3,19:4
Menzel, William F Mrs, 1950, My 17,29:4
Menzel Adolf von, 1905, F 10,7:3
Menzeli, Lola, 1951, Mr 12,25:2
Menzenwerth, Henry, 1956, Je 21,31:2
Menzer, Bruno, 1958, S 7,87:1
Menzer, Henry, 1950, Je 20,27:2
Menzi, Richard, 1959, O 28,37:4
Menzie, Charles B, 1946, Ja 4,21:1
Menzie, Herbert J, 1942, Je 29,15:6
Menzies, Alan W C, 1966, S 10,29:5
Menzies, Allan Rev Dr, 1916, My 9,11:5
Menzies, Catherine C Mrs, 1944, D 20,23:4
Menzies, Frederick, 1949, My 16,21:2
Menzies, Frederick C G, 1938, Mr 15,23:1
Menzies, G V Maj, 1917, D 16,23:1
Menzies, James L, 1953, O 8,29:3
Menzies, John T, 1965, Ag 2,29:1
Menzies, Peter I, 1944, Ja 11,19:3
Menzies, Robert J Mrs, 1946, D 28,15:2
Menzies, Stewart Graham Maj-Gen Sir, 1968, My 31, 26:1
Menzies, William C, 1957, Mr 7,29:2
Menzies, William G, 1938, N 1,23:5
Menzl, Leon, 1954, N 30,29:4
Meon, Phil C, 1937, Ag 4,19:2
Meore, George P, 1951, Jl 1,51:2
Mepham, Wellington C, 1942, F 16,17:1
Meras, Beatrice, 1958, Ja 25,19:4
Meras, Eward M, 1947, S 10,27:4
Meras, Jean B, 1944, Jl 27,17:3
Meras, Leslie Mrs, 1951, O 14,89:2
Mercadante, Ignatius B, 1952, O 5,89:2
Mercadante, Ignazio Capt, 1919, Ja 16,13:4
Mercadante, Joseph Mrs, 1947, Jl 28,15:5
Mercadante, Saverio, 1871, Ja 3,1:7
Mercado, Carlos, 1952, Mr 28,24:3
Mercado, George, 1952, N 14,23:3
Mercaldi, Nicholas R, 1952, Jl 10,31:1
Mercandino, Julius F Mrs (Julia), 1965, F 25,31:3
Mercati, Alex Countess, 1951, F 5,23:3
Mercati, Alexander Count, 1947, Ap 7,23:1
Mercati, Angelo, 1955, O 5,35:4
Mercati, Giovanni, 1957, Ag 23,19:3
Merce, A, 1936, Jl 20,15:4
Merced Stein, Florentino, 1957, Ap 26,25:4
Mercedes, Dona, 1953, S 13,84:5
Mercedes, Jellinek, 1918, Ja 25,11:8
Mercedes, Queen of Spain, 1878, Je 27,5:5
Mercer, A G, 1945, S 29,15:3
Mercer, Alex G (will), 1940, F 11,15:1
Mercer, Andrew, 1941, Ap 13,38:2
Mercer, Beryl (por), 1939, Jl 29,15:5
Mercer, Cecil W (D Yates), 1960, Mr 6,84:4
Mercer, Charles H, 1953, My 5,29:4
Mercer, Cornelius C, 1952, Ag 6,21:1
Mercer, David D, 1952, N 23,88:1; 1963, O 13,86:6
Mercer, E LeRoy, 1957, Jl 4,19:2
Mercer, Frederic W, 1949, My 27,22:2
Mercer, George W, 1964, N 28,21:4
Mercer, George W Jr, 1951, Jl 21,13:5
Mercer, H W, 1877, Jl 2,8:3
Mercer, Harvey L, 1918, N 15,13:1
Mercer, Henry D, 1954, Je 24,27:5
Mercer, Herbert C, 1951, Mr 5,21:4
Mercer, James S A, 1937, F 6,17:5
Mercer, James W, 1943, O 6,23:1
Mercer, Joel S, 1952, Je 21,15:5
Mercer, John, 1940, Ja 12,17:2
Mercer, John G, 1948, Je 22,25:4
Mercer, John T, 1947, Jl 17,19:4
Mercer, John W, 1949, O 20,29:2
Mercer, Lee D, 1949, Ja 13,24:2
Mercer, Mifflin W, 1953, Ap 18,19:2
Mercer, Ottis, 1953, Jl 8,27:6
Mercer, Robert K, 1949, Je 29,28:2
Mercer, Sid, 1945, Je 19,19:1
Mercer, Thomas J, 1959, Je 10,37:2
Mercer, Thomas L Jr, 1941, Mr 31,15:5
Mercer, Wallace P, 1953, Ja 21,31:1
Mercer, Walter C, 1942, Jl 22,19:5
Mercer, Warren C, 1954, D 19,85:1
Mercer, William F, 1942, Ja 20,20:4
Mercer, William R, 1939, F 28,20:3
Mercer-Henderson, John H (Earl of Buckinghamshire), 1963, Ja 4,2:3
Merchant, Alex, 1952, Jl 29,21:5
Merchant, C S, 1879, D 8,5:2
Merchant, Edward, 1960, O 2,84:1
Merchant, Ernest H, 1956, My 7,27:4
Merchant, George E, 1909, N 24,9:4
Merchant, Huntington Wolcott, 1918, My 22,13:6
Merchant, Louis A, 1950, Ja 22,76:7
Merchant, Mary D Mrs, 1958, S 14,84:2
Merchant, Mary E, 1956, Ag 26,85:2
Merchant, Maude F Mrs, 1951, Ap 20,29:1
Merchant, Orville A, 1938, Ja 16,II,9:1
Merchant, W Alexander Mrs, 1944, Jl 6,15:6
Mercier, Armand T, 1957, N 23,19:2
Mercier, Auguste Gen, 1921, Mr 4,13:3
Mercier, Cardinal, 1926, Ja 24,1:1
Mercier, Honore, 1894, O 31,9:7; 1937, Je 21,19:4
Mercier, Louis J A, 1953, Mr 14,15:3
Mercier, Warren C, 1966, N 29,88:7
Merck, Frederick, 1905, Mr 17,9:4
Merck, George Mrs, 1943, Ag 22,36:8
Merck, George W, 1957, N 10,86:1
Merck, George W (will), 1959, Ja 18,64:6
Merckel, Frederick G, 1960, N 2,39:4
Merckx, Fernand J J, 1940, Ja 9,23:4
Mercogliano, John, 1967, Mr 28,39:3
Mercolino, Michael T, 1945, O 26,19:5
Mercolino, Patrick V, 1953, D 18,29:5
Mercorelli, Louis, 1952, O 10,25:5
Mercouris, Stamatis (mem ser; funl, Jl 16,65:1), 1967, Jl 8,25:1
Mercready, Addison A, 1944, Ja 3,21:4
Mercready, Alex, 1940, F 16,19:5
Mercready, Alex T, 1951, Ag 29,25:1
Mercready, Wallace S, 1951, N 9,27:1
Mercur, Frederic, 1961, S 11,27:4
Mercur, James W, 1941, O 7,23:5
Mercur, Robert S Jr, 1951, Ja 5,21:4
Mercur, Ulysses, 1948, My 29,15:5
Mercure, Pierre, 1966, F 1,31:1
Mercuri, Vincent, 1953, N 8,89:2
Mercurio, John Mrs, 1950, My 2,29:1
Mercurio, Pasquale J, 1959, Ja 12,39:4
Mercy, Frederick Mrs, 1940, F 22,24:2
Merdinger, Abraham, 1961, My 3,37:3
Merdinger, George J, 1960, S 17,23:6
Merean, Ralph B, 1938, Je 16,23:3
Mereand, Louis A Mrs, 1948, O 14,29:4
Merecki, Alexander Mrs, 1944, Mr 19,41:2
Meredith, Albert B (por), 1946, Ap 13,17:1
Meredith, Albert B Mrs, 1938, O 6,23:3
Meredith, Alice V Mrs, 1939, My 4,23:4
Meredith, Ben L, 1946, S 15,9:7
Meredith, Charles A, 1956, Mr 5,23:1
Meredith, Charles H, 1964, D 3,45:3
Meredith, Charles M, 1941, Mr 5,21:2
Meredith, Claude H, 1941, Mr 31,15:4
Meredith, D Webster, 1951, Je 14,27:6
Meredith, E T, 1928, Je 18,19:4
Meredith, Earnest S, 1950, My 16,31:3
Meredith, Edwin T Jr, 1966, Je 6,41:2
Meredith, Edwin T Sr Mrs, 1961, Ja 2,25:2
Meredith, Florence L, 1951, Ag 18,11:4
Meredith, George S, 1949, Jl 14,27:5
Meredith, Howard J, 1960, Ap 29,31:3
Meredith, Isaac H, 1962, N 10,25:5
Meredith, J Llewellyn, 1939, Ag 4,13:2
Meredith, James E (Ted),(funl, N 8,29:3), 1957, N 31:3
Meredith, James V, 1957, D 19,63:2
Meredith, Jane, 1945, F 16,23:2
Meredith, John W, 1952, Je 12,33:4
Meredith, Jonathan, 1872, F 27,5:2
Meredith, Julia Dixon Mrs, 1955, Jl 16,15:6
Meredith, Lida O, 1952, Mr 9,93:2
Meredith, Richard Rev, 1904, Jl 6,9:7
Meredith, Robert R Rev Dr, 1919, N 27,15:3
Meredith, Sol Gen, 1875, O 22,10:4
Meredith, V Sir, 1929, F 25,23:5
Meredith, W M Capt, 1917, D 25,15:4
Meredith, William B, 1947, Ap 6,60:2
Meredith, William F (cor, O 1,19:1), 1943, S 30,
Meredith, William F, 1959, My 15,29:4
Meredith, William M, 1873, Ag 18,1:6; 1937, F 3,
Meredith, William R, 1954, N 4,31:5
Meredith, Wyndham R, 1940, Ja 14,43:3
Meredith, Wynn, 1950, D 23,15:6
Meredity, William M, 1957, Ap 22,25:6
Merejkowski, Dmitri, 1941, D 10,25:4
Mereminsky, Joshua O Mrs, 1944, Je 27,19:4
Mereness, Judson Mrs, 1949, N 29,29:1
Merensky, Hans, 1952, O 23,31:3
Meres, Lloyd M, 1967, Ja 12,39:5
Meresco, Joseph, 1963, O 25,31:3
Merest, M Rev, 1873, N 5,2:3
Merewether, Edward M, 1938, D 29,19:3
Mergaen, Leopold, 1873, Je 6,5:4
Mergendahl, Charles, 1959, Ap 30,31:1
Mergenthaler, Edward F, 1943, O 4,17:1
Mergenthaler, Herman C Mrs, 1962, My 21,33:3
Mergenthaler, William J, 1963, N 5,31:4
Mergentheim, Morton A Sr, 1943, Jl 15,21:4
Mergentime, Marguerita Mrs (por), 1941, My 2 25:4
Mergerum, William B, 1947, N 8,17:4
Mergle, George B, 1955, S 10,17:6
Mergler, Conrad W, 1939, Ap 11,24:4
Mergler, Harry F, 1950, Jl 12,29:4
Mergler, Henry J, 1945, Jl 11,11:5
Mergner, Anthony F, 1961, D 24,36:4
Mergott, Adolph J, 1948, N 28,94:6
Mergott, Helen P, 1958, Ap 25,27:3
Merhige, Amin, 1941, Je 17,21:4
Meriam, Horatio C, 1950, Ap 4,29:2
Meriaux, Renee, 1956, Jl 31,23:5

Merica, Paul D, 1957, O 22,33:1
Merica, Paul D Mrs, 1955, O 21,27:3
Merignac, Emile, 1940, F 11,49:2
Merigold, George E Mrs, 1951, Jl 26,21:3
Merigold, William A, 1956, Ag 10,17:1
Merill, Joshua, 1904, Ja 16,9:5
Merill, R H, 1942, N 1,53:1
Merillat, Louis O, 1941, Je 10,23:5
Merin, Sam, 1943, Ap 20,23:2
Mering, Otto O von, 1963, Je 20,33:4
Merington, Marguerite, 1951, My 21,27:6
Merington, Richard Whiskin Rev, 1916, S 23,7:2
Merio, Eugene, 1946, D 13,23:3
Meritt, Benjamin D Mrs, 1963, S 27,29:2
Merity, Howard E, 1964, Ja 17,40:1
Merivale, Bernard, 1939, My 14,III,7:2
Merivale, Philip, 1946, Mr 14,25:1
Meriweather, A J Capt, 1912, F 22,9:4
Meriwether, Lee (will, Mr 16,88:7), 1966, Mr 14,31:2
Meriwether, Walter S, 1950, O 20,27:3
Merk, Augustin, 1945, Ap 5,23:4
Merk, Otto, 1940, N 28,23:4
Merkel, Andrew D, 1954, Je 26,13:6
Merkel, Bernard R Mrs, 1944, N 11,13:5
Merkel, David, 1955, Mr 15,29:1
Merkel, David Mrs, 1958, Ap 13,84:2
Merkel, Edward A Sr, 1951, Je 15,23:4
Merkel, Emma A Mrs, 1938, S 7,25:1
Merkel, George D, 1949, N 27,104:8
Merkel, George H, 1947, Je 15,62:4
Merkel, Henry, 1954, My 15,15:6
Merkel, Hermann W (por), 1938, Mr 1,21:1
Merkel, Kenneth Mrs, 1953, N 11,31:2
Merkel, Kenneth W, 1957, Mr 6,31:5
Merkel, Michael J, 1941, D 6,17:3
Merkel, Richmond, 1944, My 2,19:3
Merker, August, 1953, Je 2,29:2
Merker, Louis H, 1957, N 5,31:2
Merker, Melvin E, 1940, Ja 16,23:1
Merker, William H, 1943, Ap 12,23:3
Merkert, Marie M, 1955, Ag 1,19:5
Merkin, Arthur J, 1950, Mr 3,25:3
Merkin, Irving, 1968, My 13,43:3
Merkin, Sol, 1940, D 30,17:5
Merkle, Amanda Mrs, 1939, S 15,23:6
Merkle, Fred, 1956, Mr 3,20:1
Merkle, Frederick, 1950, Ja 28,13:4
Merkle, Frederick B, 1961, Ag 24,29:4
Merkle, Frederick G, 1951, My 17,31:6
Merkle, Harry, 1950, N 2,31:3
Merkle, Mary H, 1955, S 14,1:2
Merkle, Theodore C, 1966, Ag 13,25:5
Merklen, Leon, 1949, S 11,95:3
Merkley, James R, 1940, S 1,21:1
Merkley, Walter A, 1948, Ag 15,60:3
Merkley, Walter A Mrs, 1950, My 3,29:2
Merksamer, Julius Mrs, 1945, F 1,23:3
Merkt, Adolph J, 1946, D 22,42:1
Merkt, Oswald L, 1943, Je 23,21:4
Merkt, Theodore B J, 1953, Ag 6,21:3
Merkurov, Sergei D, 1952, Je 11,29:2
Merkyes, Valdes, 1960, Mr 22,24:5
Merlander, John H, 1958, S 4,29:4
Merle, Henry P, 1948, Ag 25,25:2
Merle-Smith, Van S, 1943, N 10,23:1
Merle-Smith, Wilton Rev Dr, 1923, O 4,23:1
Merleau-Ponty, Maurice, 1961, My 5,29:5
Merlehan, Edwin F, 1942, Mr 2,20:2
Merlehan, Joseph P, 1941, Ap 11,21:4
Merlemont, Agnes de, 1943, D 26,32:6
Merlett, John P, 1939, Ja 23,13:5
Merli, Charles J, 1947, My 13,25:2
Merlich, Frederick W, 1941, Ag 16,15:6
Merlika-Kruja, Mustafa, 1958, D 29,15:1
Merlin, Andre, 1960, S 8,35:4
Merlin, Frank, 1968, Mr 4,37:4
Merlin, Henri, 1942, D 12,17:4
Merlin, Kenneth F, 1957, Ag 4,80:5
Merlin, Sidney D, 1958, D 10,4:8
Merlin, Umberto, 1964, My 24,93:2
Merlin, Walter B, 1964, Mr 15,86:6
Merlis, Samuel, 1949, Ap 5,29:3
Merlo, Gaetano, 1951, Je 23,15:4
Merlo, Paul, 1948, Ap 20,27:2
Merlo, Thomas V, 1957, Ap 25,31:2
Merly, William C, 1947, D 2,30:3
Merman, John C, 1960, Ja 7,29:3
Mermel, Stanislas, 1945, Mr 6,21:3
Mermet, Jean B, 1942, F 20,17:1
Mermod, A S, 1903, Ag 25,7:4
Merner, Carl J, 1958, Ap 9,33:3
Mernin, Edward F Mrs, 1943, Je 7,13:2
Mernit, Charles, 1965, Je 18,35:4
Mernit, Murray, 1961, D 21,27:4
Mernit, Robert, 1967, Je 26,33:3
Mernit, Robert Mrs, 1964, O 25,88:2
Mernit, Samuel, 1964, F 27,31:3
Merns, Matthew K, 1946, My 17,21:3
Mernstein, Maxwell H, 1940, My 26,34:2
Mero, Lucia C, 1951, Je 20,27:3
Mero-Irion, Yolanda Mrs, 1963, O 19,25:2
Merode, Cleo de, 1966, O 18,40:3
Merode, Count, 1908, Jl 14,5:6
Merode, Frederic de Prince, 1958, F 5,27:2
Merola, Gaetano, 1953, Ag 31,17:2
Meroni, Eugene V, 1955, Ja 21,23:3
Merovitch, Alexander, 1965, Ag 9,25:2
Merrall, Albert Edward, 1917, F 6,9:3
Merrall, William B, 1910, Ja 4,13:5
Merrall, William B Mrs, 1944, O 22,45:1
Merrall, William John, 1907, Mr 26,9:5
Merredith, William M, 1906, N 12,7:6
Merrell, Alden J, 1941, F 20,19:2
Merrell, Azel F, 1925, D 29,23:6
Merrell, Charles J, 1937, Je 25,21:2
Merrell, Clarence F, 1954, F 12,25:2
Merrell, Clay, 1951, My 9,33:1
Merrell, Edgar S K, 1942, D 7,27:1
Merrell, Edgar S K Mrs, 1953, Jl 19,56:3
Merrell, Frank C, 1950, Ag 28,17:4
Merrell, Frank C Mrs, 1950, Ja 28,13:5
Merrell, George R, 1962, D 18,4:8
Merrell, Gilbert W Mrs, 1961, S 20,29:2
Merrell, John Porter Rear-Adm, 1916, D 9,11:5
Merrell, Lewis C, 1950, Ja 17,27:1
Merrell, Mark Mrs (Clinch Calkins), 1968, D 28,27:3
Merrell, Nellie D Mrs, 1940, Jl 5,13:5
Merrell, Perry, 1956, My 31,27:4
Merrell, Sarah L P, 1966, Je 11,31:5
Merrell, Thurston Mrs, 1948, S 28,27:2
Merrell, William D, 1955, F 12,15:3
Merrett, Isaac B, 1903, S 19,7:6
Merriam, A Wayne, 1949, Ag 12,17:3
Merriam, Alfred B, 1944, Jl 16,31:2
Merriam, Alfred C, 1945, My 9,23:4
Merriam, Arthur L Mrs, 1937, N 12,22:1
Merriam, B W, 1884, Ap 26,5:2
Merriam, Bernard F, 1941, Je 21,17:1
Merriam, Brower G, 1965, Ag 10,29:1
Merriam, C Hart (por), 1942, Mr 21,17:1
Merriam, Carroll B, 1941, D 10,25:4
Merriam, Catherine U Mrs, 1938, My 18,21:2
Merriam, Charles B, 1947, Ja 2,27:1
Merriam, Charles E, 1950, Ag 9,29:4; 1953, Ja 9,21:3
Merriam, David H, 1944, Jl 31,13:6
Merriam, Donald E, 1965, My 2,88:1
Merriam, Eben, 1864, Mr 21,8:1
Merriam, Edward J, 1937, O 9,19:2
Merriam, Eva S Mrs, 1939, Ap 22,17:5
Merriam, F Nixon, 1961, Ja 16,27:3
Merriam, Frank F, 1955, Ap 26,29:3
Merriam, Frank M Mrs, 1948, Jl 14,23:3
Merriam, Franklin A (por), 1937, Ja 24,II,9:1
Merriam, Fredric L Mrs, 1945, Ap 12,23:3
Merriam, G Franklin, 1941, D 9,31:1
Merriam, George, 1941, Ja 8,19:2
Merriam, George E, 1941, Mr 11,23:5
Merriam, George S, 1914, Ja 23,11:5
Merriam, Greenlief A Capt, 1908, S 4,7:4
Merriam, Harold A, 1937, D 22,25:4
Merriam, Henry C Gen, 1912, N 19,15:4
Merriam, Henry F, 1960, Mr 14,29:2
Merriam, Henry M, 1952, O 7,29:5
Merriam, Herman E, 1961, Jl 10,21:3
Merriam, Homer, 1908, My 25,7:6
Merriam, J X, 1926, Ag 4,19:1
Merriam, James R, 1942, N 19,25:6
Merriam, John C (por), 1945, O 31,23:1
Merriam, John D, 1954, D 22,23:5
Merriam, John W, 1939, Ag 6,37:4
Merriam, Joseph, 1945, Ja 12,15:2
Merriam, M C, 1902, Mr 30,7:5
Merriam, Margaret Isabelle, 1914, Ja 10,9:5
Merriam, Mary Jane Mrs, 1908, Ag 22,7:4
Merriam, Maxwell S, 1954, Ag 11,25:5
Merriam, Maxwell S Mrs, 1953, Ag 31,17:2
Merriam, Ned, 1956, Jl 14,15:3
Merriam, Norman, 1944, Ag 18,13:6
Merriam, Rose D W Mrs, 1947, Jl 22,23:5
Merriam, Vera H, 1953, Mr 27,23:3
Merriam, Walter H Mrs, 1943, Mr 25,21:3
Merriam, William S, 1956, O 11,39:5
Merrian, Joseph E, 1961, Ap 9,86:3
Merrick, Agnes R Mrs, 1942, Je 22,15:5
Merrick, Chester W Mrs, 1946, Ja 14,19:4
Merrick, Clarence Mrs, 1948, O 10,76:3
Merrick, Clinton, 1944, Je 29,23:2
Merrick, David A Rev, 1906, Ap 22,11:5
Merrick, Eliza J, 1948, D 15,33:5
Merrick, Elliott T 2d, 1959, Je 19,25:6
Merrick, Ernest, 1950, S 6,30:4
Merrick, Evelyn, 1967, O 18,47:2
Merrick, Frank A (por), 1944, O 27,24:2
Merrick, Frank H, 1944, Ja 19,19:4
Merrick, George E (will, Ap 18,22:7), 1942, Mr 27, 23:3
Merrick, George P, 1938, N 3,23:4
Merrick, George T, 1959, S 12,21:6
Merrick, Harold E, 1967, Ja 22,76:7
Merrick, Harry T, 1947, My 23,24:2
Merrick, Henrietta S, 1944, Je 21,19:2
Merrick, Herbert L, 1938, My 4,23:3
Merrick, J H, 1945, Ap 16,23:1
Merrick, J Hartley (will), 1946, F 2,6:4
Merrick, James H, 1946, Ja 19,13:4
Merrick, John, 1944, Je 4,42:1
Merrick, John H, 1938, Jl 9,13:2
Merrick, John T, 1944, Mr 19,41:2
Merrick, Leonard (por), 1939, Ag 8,17:3
Merrick, Marlowe M, 1948, Mr 5,21:3
Merrick, Mary V, 1955, Ja 12,27:2
Merrick, Pliny Judge, 1867, F 4,2:2
Merrick, R T, 1885, Je 24,5:3
Merrick, Rodney K, 1956, N 15,35:1
Merrick, Russell P, 1959, Ap 27,27:4
Merrick, Wayne, 1950, Jl 16,69:1
Merrick, William, 1907, Ja 10,9:5
Merrifield, Charles E, 1946, F 4,25:3
Merrifield, Don C, 1944, Jl 28,13:6
Merrifield, Fred S, 1953, My 20,29:4
Merrifield, Frederick C, 1948, Ja 7,25:5
Merrifield, Frederick W, 1958, Ja 7,47:1
Merrifield, Mark E, 1941, N 8,19:6
Merrifield, Webster Dr, 1916, Ja 23,17:3
Merrifield, William, 1942, S 21,15:6
Merrigan, J, 1941, O 11,17:2
Merrigan, John T, 1963, My 20,31:1
Merrigan, William J, 1954, Ap 19,23:1
Merrihew, Blanche M Mrs, 1938, Jl 13,21:4
Merrihew, S Wallis Mrs, 1953, F 19,23:1
Merrihew, Stephen W, 1947, Mr 22,14:3
Merrihew, Virgil R, 1942, F 20,17:4
Merrilees, Andy G, 1951, F 25,86:5
Merrill, A Stanton, 1961, Mr 1,33:2
Merrill, Abner Hopkins Brig-Gen, 1923, F 26,13:5
Merrill, Ada F Mrs, 1923, S 30,7:3
Merrill, Albert A, 1952, Je 3,29:3
Merrill, Albert B, 1960, F 26,27:1
Merrill, Alfred E, 1909, Ap 12,7:5
Merrill, Allen H Mrs, 1958, F 11,31:3
Merrill, Ambrose K, 1954, My 18,29:5
Merrill, Arthur R, 1955, O 6,29:4
Merrill, Athel D, 1938, Ja 4,23:2
Merrill, August, 1952, Ag 2,15:6
Merrill, B Winfred, 1954, O 18,25:2
Merrill, Bradford Jr, 1913, D 27,9:5
Merrill, C C, 1949, Ag 7,60:7
Merrill, Charles A, 1951, Jl 9,25:5
Merrill, Charles C, 1961, Ap 2,76:2
Merrill, Charles E, 1944, Ap 20,19:5
Merrill, Charles E (funl plans, O 8,27:1; will, O 10,1:8), 1956, O 7,1:1
Merrill, Charles S Jr (por), 1942, Ja 29,19:1
Merrill, Charles W, 1950, Ja 21,17:2; 1956, F 8,33:4
Merrill, Dana T, 1957, Ag 4,81:1
Merrill, Doane, 1949, Mr 25,23:1
Merrill, Edmund A, 1957, Mr 3,84:5
Merrill, Edward Bagley, 1920, N 9,15:2
Merrill, Edward C, 1949, N 16,29:1
Merrill, Edward K, 1946, Ag 6,25:4
Merrill, Edward Pelton, 1925, Ag 7,15:6
Merrill, Edward S, 1951, Mr 30,23:4
Merrill, Edwin C, 1937, Ag 28,15:4
Merrill, Edwin G (trb lr, Ja 19,26:7), 1950, Ja 17,27:5
Merrill, Edwin G Mrs, 1959, F 13,17:2
Merrill, Edwin S, 1925, Ja 19,17:4
Merrill, Effie A, 1944, O 20,19:3
Merrill, Elmer D, 1956, F 26,88:3
Merrill, Emma M Mrs, 1942, Mr 25,21:5
Merrill, Eugene S Mrs, 1946, Mr 5,25:1
Merrill, Everett F, 1955, Ap 28,29:3
Merrill, Fenimore, 1919, F 21,13:6
Merrill, Floyd, 1943, Ag 29,39:1
Merrill, Francis G, 1941, Je 8,48:4
Merrill, Frank A, 1925, D 22,21:4; 1941, Jl 25,15:1
Merrill, Frank D (funl, D 17,23:2), 1955, D 13,39:1
Merrill, Frank H, 1950, Ap 23,95:6; 1951, O 13,17:7; 1956, Ja 26,29:3
Merrill, Frank Herbert, 1956, F 6,23:3
Merrill, Frank O, 1943, Ap 12,24:2
Merrill, Fred D, 1941, Jl 26,15:5
Merrill, Frederick J M Mrs (trb lr, S 20,30:7), 1951, S 7,29:6
Merrill, Frederick James Hamilton, 1916, D 2,11:5
Merrill, G P, 1929, Ag 16,21:3
Merrill, George A, 1957, S 28,17:3
Merrill, George B Mrs, 1967, My 29,25:3
Merrill, George E Rev Dr (funl, Je 13,7:4), 1908, Je 12,7:3
Merrill, George F, 1941, F 1,17:3; 1950, O 4,31:5
Merrill, George G (por), 1938, Ja 31,19:1
Merrill, George R, 1944, O 31,19:5
Merrill, Grace M, 1957, D 8,88:8
Merrill, Gregor C, 1965, My 21,35:3
Merrill, Gretchen Van Z, 1965, Ap 23,35:1
Merrill, Gyles, 1954, Jl 13,23:2
Merrill, H Augustus, 1954, D 8,35:4
Merrill, Harry F, 1951, Je 27,29:6
Merrill, Helen A, 1949, My 3,25:5
Merrill, Helen M Mrs, 1942, Jl 15,19:3
Merrill, Henry, 1940, Mr 6,2:2
Merrill, Henry C, 1940, Ja 1,23:2
Merrill, Henry F, 1956, Ap 13,25:4
Merrill, Henry W, 1922, Jl 16,26:4; 1944, Je 2,15:3
Merrill, Herbert M, 1956, Mr 7,33:3
Merrill, Howard R, 1968, Ja 5,35:2
Merrill, J B, 1930, Mr 24,6:3
Merrill, James A, 1938, Je 24,19:4; 1945, D 12,27:2
Merrill, James E, 1939, D 20,25:1

Merrill, James W, 1947, N 14,23:3
Merrill, John C, 1954, Ja 24,84:3
Merrill, John D, 1940, Ja 10,21:2
Merrill, John E, 1960, S 24,23:5
Merrill, John F A, 1944, Ja 3,22:2
Merrill, John J, 1951, Ap 20,29:4
Merrill, John J Mrs, 1939, Jl 12,19:4
Merrill, John L, 1903, D 8,9:5; 1949, D 19,27:3; 1953, Ag 20,27:2
Merrill, Joseph F, 1952, F 4,17:2
Merrill, Joseph J, 1952, Ag 4,15:4
Merrill, Joseph M, 1941, Mr 26,23:3
Merrill, Keith, 1959, Je 10,37:1
Merrill, Kenneth A, 1956, Ap 18,31:1
Merrill, Kenneth R, 1960, Ja 3,88:8
Merrill, Lewis, 1965, Je 20,72:5
Merrill, Louis T, 1960, S 4,68:8
Merrill, Marriner W, 1906, F 8,1:2
Merrill, Mary T, 1959, Mr 1,86:1
Merrill, Maud V, 1940, Jl 14,30:7
Merrill, Mildred S, 1956, F 12,88:7
Merrill, Millard W, 1965, My 11,39:3
Merrill, Minnie E Mrs, 1938, My 6,21:5
Merrill, Moody (Grayson), 1903, D 25,7:5
Merrill, Nathaniel P, 1945, Jl 15,15:5
Merrill, O C, 1865, Ap 22,4:2
Merrill, Oliver B (por), 1944, Mr 23,19:3
Merrill, Oscar C, 1951, Ja 16,29:2
Merrill, Paul W, 1961, Jl 21,23:3
Merrill, Portland, 1965, N 24,39:1
Merrill, Robert D (more details, F 18,29:4), 1967, F 16,44:8
Merrill, Robini F (will, F 27,23:6), 1945, F 10,11:5
Merrill, Roger, 1947, Ja 24,21:2
Merrill, S S, 1885, F 9,2:3
Merrill, Samuel Col, 1924, S 4,19:4
Merrill, Samuel H, 1956, D 30,32:7
Merrill, Solon W Mrs, 1955, O 16,86:2
Merrill, Theodore C, 1965, O 5,6:1
Merrill, Thomas S (por), 1937, D 26,II,6:8
Merrill, W B, 1928, N 27,31:3
Merrill, Walter H, 1952, Jl 25,18:8
Merrill, Whitney, 1957, F 12,27:5
Merrill, Whitney W, 1967, F 13,33:1
Merrill, Wilford J, 1941, Ap 11,21:2
Merrill, William A, 1951, F 25,84:8
Merrill, William B Mrs, 1945, N 29,23:4
Merrill, William C, 1938, Jl 20,19:1; 1964, S 1,36:4
Merrill, William D, 1950, F 16,23:1
Merrill, William H, 1907, S 8,7:6; 1907, S 10,7:4
Merrill, William M, 1957, O 25,27:3
Merrill, William P, 1954, Je 21,23:1
Merrill, William Willis, 1921, D 7,17:6
Merrill, Zadoc E, 1956, N 28,35:4
Merrills, Leo, 1949, F 9,27:3
Merriman, Buckingham P, 1953, F 3,25:2
Merriman, Charles H, 1920, Mr 15,15:6; 1950, F 7,27:1
Merriman, Dana S, 1960, Jl 9,41:5
Merriman, Daniel Mrs, 1968, F 21,47:2
Merriman, Daniel Rev Dr, 1912, S 19,11:6
Merriman, Elsie A, 1954, Ja 20,27:3
Merriman, Frank B, 1962, Ja 19,31:3
Merriman, Frank W, 1961, Jl 17,21:5
Merriman, H Morton, 1954, D 31,13:2
Merriman, H Morton Mrs, 1957, N 28,31:4
Merriman, Harold T, 1941, Ap 12,15:6
Merriman, Harvey M, 1945, O 25,21:2
Merriman, Henry M, 1942, Ag 18,21:2
Merriman, Henry Seton, 1903, N 20,9:5
Merriman, John A, 1968, Jl 25,33:4
Merriman, L F Dr, 1925, Jl 9,19:4
Merriman, Mansfield Mrs, 1944, O 16,19:4
Merriman, Mansfield Prof, 1925, Je 9,21:4
Merriman, Myra Kingman Mrs, 1922, Jl 1,13:6
Merriman, Robert L Capt, 1903, D 22,9:5
Merriman, Robert N, 1949, Ap 22,23:1
Merriman, Roger B, 1945, S 8,15:6
Merriman, Thaddeus (por), 1939, S 27,25:3
Merriman, Thaddeus Mrs, 1960, Ja 16,21:1
Merriman, Willis E, 1911, Mr 23,9:4
Merrin, Joseph Mrs, 1958, Mr 2,89:1
Merrion, J Leo, 1954, Ag 7,13:5
Merriss, Marion H, 1939, Ja 21,15:1
Merrit, Charles P W Mrs, 1937, Ja 22,21:3
Merrit, Francis E, 1947, Ja 3,21:1
Merrit, William H, 1940, Ja 3,21:4; 1953, Jl 5,49:2
Merritt, Abraham (por), 1943, Ag 22,36:6
Merritt, Abraham L, 1950, Ap 30,102:4
Merritt, Alexander, 1922, Mr 27,15:5
Merritt, Alexander S Col, 1915, Je 8,13:6
Merritt, Alfred H, 1947, Ag 15,18:2
Merritt, Alfred K, 1943, Mr 30,26:4
Merritt. Alfred L, 1956, F 25,19:6
Merritt, Anna V Mrs, 1942, Mr 4,19:4
Merritt, Annie M, 1945, My 22,19:6
Merritt, Arthur H, 1961, F 10,27:3
Merritt, Benjamin B, 1937, O 5,25:4
Merritt, C H Mrs, 1903, Ap 18,9:5
Merritt, C Wesley, 1962, Je 1,27:1
Merritt, Carrie L Mrs, 1943, Ap 14,23:1
Merritt, Charles, 1947, Mr 29,15:2
Merritt, Charles D, 1940, Mr 26,21:5
Merritt, Charles E, 1938, D 5,23:4
Merritt, Charles Evan Capt, 1912, Ja 15,13:4
Merritt, Charles F, 1957, S 1,56:6
Merritt, Charles T Mrs (E B Evans), 1964, Je 20,25:2
Merritt, Charles W D, 1950, Ja 25,27:4
Merritt, Chester A Mrs, 1939, O 23,19:4
Merritt, Clarence C, 1967, Mr 7,41:4
Merritt, Clarence E, 1948, Ap 1,25:2
Merritt, Cora B Mrs, 1943, My 2,45:2
Merritt, Donald G, 1967, Mr 10,36:3
Merritt, E G, 1939, My 1,23:5
Merritt, E Lester, 1956, My 5,19:5
Merritt, E M, 1878, Jl 31,8:6
Merritt, Edgar B, 1944, Mr 14,19:1
Merritt, Edgar B Mrs, 1945, Mr 17,13:6
Merritt, Edward, 1911, F 12,12:2
Merritt, Edward C, 1939, O 2,17:2
Merritt, Edward K, 1958, Jl 30,29:3
Merritt, Edwin A, 1914, D 5,13:5
Merritt, Edwin A Gen, 1916, D 27,9:5
Merritt, Edwin B, 1943, Mr 7,38:3
Merritt, Eli B, 1949, N 1,27:6
Merritt, Elizabeth C, 1941, F 16,41:2
Merritt, Ellsworth, 1943, Je 27,32:1
Merritt, Ernest, 1948, Je 6,73:1
Merritt, Ethel D, 1952, Ap 26,23:3
Merritt, Florence A Mrs, 1937, Ja 3,II,8:3
Merritt, Florence D, 1944, O 31,18:3
Merritt, Frank B, 1947, Ag 16,13:2
Merritt, G Hunter, 1951, N 2,23:3
Merritt, George, 1876, F 18,8:6; 1938, F 22,21:1
Merritt, George F, 1937, Je 30,23:6
Merritt, George Sumner, 1925, O 18,5:1
Merritt, Gertrude Mrs, 1922, Ap 12,21:5
Merritt, Harold, 1955, N 10,35:3
Merritt, Harry A, 1946, Ap 30,21:4
Merritt, Harry C, 1943, N 18,23:4
Merritt, Henry Capt, 1911, Ja 4,9:2
Merritt, Henry N, 1956, D 16,86:2
Merritt, Henry N Mrs, 1944, Ja 27,19:3
Merritt, Henry W, 1938, O 9,45:2
Merritt, Herbert L, 1940, Jl 11,19:4
Merritt, Hubert L, 1948, O 15,23:2
Merritt, Hulett C, 1956, Ja 15,92:1
Merritt, Hulett C Mrs, 1954, My 27,27:1
Merritt, Israel John Capt, 1911, D 15,13:6
Merritt, J A, 1876, Ap 29,5:2
Merritt, James C, 1954, N 8,21:2
Merritt, James S, 1937, D 1,23:6
Merritt, Jerome S, 1955, N 4,29:3
Merritt, Jesse, 1957, Je 4,35:5
Merritt, John A, 1919, O 17,17:5
Merritt, John B, 1938, D 12,19:4
Merritt, John E, 1964, Ag 26,39:6
Merritt, John I, 1954, D 13,27:6
Merritt, John S, 1951, N 17,17:6
Merritt, John V, 1947, Je 20,20:2
Merritt, Joseph, 1950, Ja 4,35:3; 1954, N 28,86:3
Merritt, Joseph E, 1940, Jl 20,15:2
Merritt, Joseph Mrs, 1950, O 18,33:3
Merritt, Kinsey N, 1967, Je 20,39:1
Merritt, Leslie, 1948, S 4,15:3
Merritt, Lewis N, 1940, Ja 16,23:5
Merritt, Lucius R, 1941, Mr 10,17:1
Merritt, Mable V Mrs (est tax appr), 1955, O 28,13:4
Merritt, Maey Mrs, 1947, Je 14,15:2
Merritt, Malcolm H, 1948, D 29,21:2
Merritt, Matthew J (por), 1946, S 30,25:3
Merritt, Morris H, 1955, Je 14,29:3
Merritt, Mortimer G, 1941, My 23,21:5
Merritt, N Maj, 1922, N 13,15:5
Merritt, Norma, 1953, O 6,29:3
Merritt, Robert N, 1947, Ja 26,53:3
Merritt, Roland E Prof, 1937, Ja 7,22:1
Merritt, S Virgil, 1950, Ag 17,28:4
Merritt, Sadie T Mrs, 1938, S 3,13:5
Merritt, Schuyler (will, Ap 15,20:4), 1953, Ap 2,27:1
Merritt, Sidney Mrs, 1944, D 23,13:6
Merritt, Stephen, 1945, D 24,15:2
Merritt, Stephen Rev, 1917, Ja 30,9:5
Merritt, Thomas A Mrs, 1950, Ap 4,29:3
Merritt, Thomas E Maj, 1904, Ag 27,2:6
Merritt, Walter Gordon, 1968, S 14,31:1
Merritt, Walter H, 1956, Je 30,17:5
Merritt, Wesley Gen (funl, D 5,9:4), 1910, D 5,13:3
Merritt, Wilbur J, 1939, S 17,48:7
Merritt, William B Mrs, 1955, D 2,27:3
Merritt, William E, 1944, Je 11,45:2
Merritt, William E Mrs, 1938, Ja 31,19:3
Merritt, William H, 1937, N 13,23:4; 1949, Ag 4,23:4
Merritt, William Hamilton Lt-Col, 1924, Ap 23,21:4
Merritt, William J W, 1957, Je 11,35:1
Merritt, William Jenks, 1922, N 17,17:5
Merritt, Winfield, 1921, S 27,19:4
Merrivale, Lord, 1939, My 22,17:3
Merron, Michael F Mrs, 1956, Ap 6,25:3
Merrow, John G F (cor, O 21,43:3), 1959, O 19,29:1
Merrow, Joseph M, 1947, Mr 28,24:3
Merry, E Remington Jr, 1951, D 5,35:2
Merry, English Turfman, 1877, F 20,2:4
Merry, Fred H, 1948, Ag 20,17:1
Merry, George E, 1949, Mr 22,25:4
Merry, Harley, 1911, S 3,II,9:4
Merry, James, 1953, Jl 8,27:3
Merry, John, 1950, Ja 24,31:1
Merry, John F Rear-Adm, 1916, My 31,13:3
Merry, Joseph J, 1968, My 19,86:4
Merry, William Lawrence, 1911, D 16,13:5
Merry del Val, R, 1930, F 27,23:1
Merry del Val y Zulueta, Alfonso, 1943, My 28,21:
Merryman, David B Mrs, 1964, N 29,87:1
Merryman, Nicholas B Jr, 1939, N 17,21:3
Merryman, Ridgaway, 1937, Mr 21,II,8:3
Merryman, William C, 1941, My 31,11:7
Merryweather, Almon S, 1947, Jl 4,13:5
Merryweather, Charles E, 1944, F 23,19:5
Merryweather, Hubert, 1949, Je 9,31:3
Merscher, Washington, 1947, Je 17,28:2
Merschersky, Vladimir Rev, 1937, Jl 29,19:6
Merschrod, Frank Sr, 1957, Mr 21,31:1
Merseles, T F, 1929, Mr 8,25:1
Merseles, Theodore I, 1968, Mr 16,31:3
Merselis, Stephen, 1946, Mr 29,23:1
Mersereau, Elizabeth Y Mrs, 1941, Mr 31,15:3
Mersereau, Henry C, 1955, Ja 18,27:2
Mersereau, Samuel F, 1942, Mr 5,23:5
Mersereau, Truman S, 1957, Jl 13,17:2
Mersereau, William T R, 1957, D 22,40:5
Mersey, Lord (C C Bigham), 1956, N 22,33:4
Mersfelder, Albert, 1952, O 30,31:4
Mershon, Albert L Rev, 1920, Jl 16,11:4
Mershon, Claude A, 1944, D 27,19:3
Mershon, Cornelius C, 1951, F 8,33:2
Mershon, James B, 1954, F 18,31:4
Mershon, James B Mrs, 1959, Mr 11,35:1
Mershon, John V, 1953, F 20,19:4
Mershon, Joseph V D Mrs, 1953, Je 13,15:6
Mershon, L Stephen, 1938, Ja 25,22:2
Mershon, Leroy A, 1942, Ja 17,17:4
Mershon, Oliver F, 1953, F 24,25:5
Mershon, Ralph D, 1952, F 16,13:1
Mershon, Robert H, 1947, My 8,25:3
Mershon, Samuel D, 1949, Mr 23,27:2
Mershon, Stephen L Rev, 1874, Ap 30,3:3
Mershon, William B, 1943, Jl 14,19:2
Mershon, William L, 1942, My 8,21:2
Mersman, Marguerite Mrs, 1946, Jl 12,17:1
Merson, Billy, 1947, Je 26,23:4
Merson, Henry, 1943, O 25,15:5
Merson, Jules, 1952, Jl 19,15:4
Merta, Frank J, 1968, Mr 7,43:4
Mertching, Reinhold A, 1943, N 24,21:1
Merte, George J, 1942, N 14,15:5
Merte, George J Mrs, 1953, F 21,13:6
Merte, Valentine J, 1945, D 26,19:1
Merte, Willie, 1948, My 20,29:2
Mertel, Henry P, 1949, Je 8,29:5
Merten, Cort Sr, 1951, Mr 13,31:3
Merten, Eugene Mrs, 1951, N 21,25:2
Merten, Joseph F Sr, 1958, Ag 11,21:2
Merten, William H, 1951, O 27,19:3
Mertens, Andre, 1963, Jl 10,35:2
Mertens, Frederick H, 1958, My 24,21:6
Mertens, Hermann Joseph Rev, 1920, F 4,11:4
Mertens, Robert A, 1949, Ja 5,25:2
Mertes, George F, 1951, My 3,29:5
Mertes, Joseph, 1950, Mr 9,29:3
Mertes, Martin, 1944, Je 26,15:4
Mertes, William Mrs, 1944, Ja 13,21:5
Merthyr, Baron (Wm Thos Lewis), 1914, Ag 28,
Mertine, Alvin, 1951, Je 24,72:2
Merton, Holmes W, 1948, Ja 19,23:4
Merton, M, 1874, F 6,3:1
Merton, Thomas, 1968, D 11,1:3
Mertz, Louis C, 1923, Ap 27,17:5
Mertz, Peter, 1954, Mr 7,57:5
Mertz, Philip, 1918, D 9,13:4
Mertzanoff, Christopher E, 1945, F 17,13:3
Merville, Ernest E, 1948, My 6,25:4
Mervin, T T, 1885, Ja 17,2:3
Mervine, Arthur E Mrs, 1948, O 9,19:4
Merwe, N J Van Der, 1940, Ag 12,15:1
Merwede, John, 1945, D 30,14:6
Merwin, Berkley R, 1918, Je 12,13:5
Merwin, Earl J, 1950, Mr 22,27:5
Merwin, Edward Payson, 1907, Jl 7,7:6
Merwin, H C, 1929, Ja 23,23:2
Merwin, Henry W, 1943, O 9,13:3
Merwin, Horace B, 1948, Jl 25,48:3
Merwin, Lucy M Mrs, 1941, S 20,17:3
Merwin, Lyman A, 1948, O 26,31:3
Merwin, Miles T, 1943, Ja 22,19:2
Merwin, Orange, 1907, N 22,9:5
Merwin, Orange F, 1952, F 20,30:3
Merwin, Orland H, 1910, Mr 18,11:5
Merwin, Robert E Mrs, 1958, N 29,21:3
Merwin, S, 1936, O 18,II,8:1
Merwin, Samuel E, 1907, Mr 6,9:6
Merwin, Timothy Dwight, 1920, Mr 7,22:3
Merwin, William M, 1903, S 5,7:7
Meryman, Richard S, 1963, O 1,39:2
Merz, Adolph S, 1954, Ag 24,21:6
Merz, Albert R, 1950, Jl 16,69:1
Merz, Charles F, 1964, Ja 10,43:2
Merz, Charles G, 1952, Jl 9,27:6
Merz, Charles H, 1947, O 15,27:3
Merz, Charles H Mrs, 1958, S 1,13:4

Merz, Eugene, 1937, S 6,17:5
Merz, Frank, 1939, O 5,23:6
Merz, Harry J, 1956, Ja 6,24:4
Merz, Herman J, 1951, Jl 29,69:3
Merz, Leon, 1957, F 3,76:3
Merz, Oscar H, 1952, Ja 24,27:5
Merz, Oscar H Mrs, 1944, F 29,17:2
Merz, Richard E Mrs, 1963, D 24,17:2
Merz, Werner F, 1938, D 28,26:2
Merz, William A, 1939, N 7,25:4
Merz, William H, 1946, S 22,62:4
Merzbach, Joseph Dr, 1919, Ap 29,15:4
Merzbach, Lou, 1945, F 16,23:3
Merzon, Sam M, 1964, Ja 11,23:2
Mesalo, John, 1924, F 4,19:4
Mesard, Harry, 1966, Je 30,39:4
Mescall, Edward J, 1959, My 18,27:5
Meschter, Charles K, 1942, Ja 23,19:6
Meschter, Eugene F, 1955, S 3,15:6
Meschutt, Joseph M, 1879, N 16,7:2
Meschutt, Stephen F Mrs, 1962, Mr 26,31:1
Meseck, Joseph Sr, 1965, Ag 27,29:4
Mesenholl, Ferdinand, 1946, Mr 14,25:2
Meserole, Abraham, 1912, O 19,11:5
Meserole, Adrian, 1913, S 27,13:5
Meserole, Clinton V, 1951, Ja 9,29:2
Meserole, Cornelia P Mrs (will), 1946, Jl 20,15:6
Meserole, Darwin J, 1952, My 22,27:2
Meserole, Frank D, 1946, Je 19,21:1
Meserole, Jeremiah V (funl, Ag 15,7:4), 1908, Ag 14, 7:4
Meserole, Nicholas Mrs, 1944, Je 28,23:5
Meserve, Donald R, 1964, Jl 2,31:2
Meserve, Elmon L, 1946, Je 20,23:4
Meserve, F Leighton, 1968, Ap 11,45:1
Meserve, Faith L, 1946, Jl 20,13:6
Meserve, Frederick H, 1962, Je 26,33:1
Meserve, Frederick H Mrs, 1965, Ag 29,84:5
Meserve, H F, 1941, Ap 6,48:6
Meserve, Harry C Maj, 1925, O 23,23:5
Meserve, Perley J, 1953, My 3,88:8
Meservey, Arthur B, 1952, My 10,21:6
Mesevich, William, 1952, Ag 25,17:3
Meshaloff, Moses, 1956, N 7,31:2
Meshel, Morris L, 1963, Ap 30,35:4
Mesick, Edward K, 1955, N 15,29:5
Mesick, Edward K Mrs, 1955, D 19,27:5
Mesick, Herbert S, 1952, D 1,23:4
Mesick, John F Dr, 1915, Jl 1,11:6
Mesick, John Mrs, 1937, Ja 13,23:1
Mesick, Warren C, 1950, My 27,17:3
Mesier, Louis, 1905, Ap 23,9:6
Mesinger, Frederick, 1946, Ja 18,19:4
Mesinger, Henry, 1946, O 5,17:5
Mesjian, Harry A, 1953, Ag 1,11:7
Meskell, Patrick E, 1961, Jl 22,21:7
Mesker, Raymond T, 1950, Ap 10,19:5
Meskill, Thomas H Mrs, 1947, Je 1,62:3
Meskill Wm H, 1957, Ag 15,21:1
Meskin, Jacob, 1956, F 26,88:2
Meslar, Ira E, 1953, S 26,17:3
Meslar, Orville V, 1963, O 8,43:4
Meslar, Thomas V, 1949, N 23,29:5
Mesler, William J Sr, 1955, O 9,87:1
Meslin, Dominick Mrs, 1952, S 11,31:4
Meslin, Elmer C, 1960, Je 14,37:1
Mesloh, Ch W Prof, 1904, Mr 16,1:2
Mesnard-Lyons, Julie, 1946, Ap 28,44:5
Mesner, Charles W, 1953, O 20,29:4
Mesny, Henry W G Rev, 1914, Je 23,11:5
Mespoulet, Marguerite, 1965, Ja 3,84:7
Mess, Gabriel, 1921, Ap 9,11:4
Message, John S, 1961, O 4,45:4
Messager, Andre Mrs, 1938, My 11,19:2
Messal, Lucyna, 1953, D 12,19:5
Messant, Paul, 1873, Ja 27,8:3
Messayeh, Alex D, 1942, F 25,20:3
Messbauer, John A, 1961, D 13,43:5
Messe, Giovanni Gen, 1968, D 19,47:1
Messel, Alfred Prof, 1909, Mr 25,9:5
Messel, L C R Mrs, 1960, Mr 9,33:3
Messemer, J Francis, 1947, Ap 17,27:3
Messenger, Charles W, 1951, Jl 11,23:5
Messenger, Hiram J Prof, 1913, D 16,11:6
Messenger, James W, 1959, Ap 2,31:4
Messenger, Joseph E Dr, 1921, Ja 7,13:5
Messenger, Maria G, 1937, My 29,17:5
Messenger, Max, 1925, My 4,19:5
Messenger, North Overton, 1925, Je 16,21:6
Messenger, Otis G, 1954, Ag 5,23:5
Messenger, Robert W Mrs, 1955, Je 30,25:4
Messenger, Ruth E, 1964, Mr 4,37:1
Messenger, Samuel, 1960, S 28,39:5
Messenkopf, John P, 1953, F 3,25:2
Messer, Charles W, 1952, Jl 24,27:4
Messer, Frank, 1937, F 26,21:3
Messer, Frederick, 1907, F 21,9:6
Messer, Irving W, 1955, Ag 11,21:3
Messer, Ivan V, 1952, D 18,29:2
Messer, Paul Mrs, 1954, N 6,17:3
Messer, Stanley D, 1950, Je 27,29:1
Messer, Wilbur, 1923, Jl 16,11:5
Messer, William S, 1960, D 22,23:4
Messer, Wilson, 1958, S 10,33:1
Messerly, Christian, 1946, N 28,27:3
Messerly, George D, 1961, Ap 17,29:5
Messerole, Benjamin R, 1939, N 6,23:5
Messerschmitt, Christopher F, 1958, S 9,35:3
Messersmith, George S (funl, F 2,35:2), 1960, Ja 30, 21:2
Messersmith, George S Mrs, 1966, N 18,43:4
Messersmith, S B Mrs, 1938, Jl 9,13:6
Messersmith, Wesley M, 1948, N 7,88:7
Messersmith, Wesley M Mrs, 1948, S 30,27:5
Messervy, Harriet C Mrs (will), 1938, Ap 27,3:2
Messick, Charles, 1907, Je 4,7:6; 1939, My 27,15:6
Messick, Charlton, 1945, Jl 3,13:6
Messick, George V, 1952, Je 6,23:3
Messick, Lena Mrs, 1940, Ag 10,13:1
Messick, William R, 1956, Je 18,25:1
Messick, William R Mrs, 1945, Ja 29,13:1
Messier, Charles, 1948, Mr 13,15:2
Messier, Henri, 1948, Mr 13,15:2
Messina, Angelina Rose, 1968, N 21,47:2
Messina, Frank E, 1963, N 30,27:4
Messina, Frank R, 1953, Ag 27,25:3
Messina, Salvatore, 1948, S 1,23:1
Messing, Alfred H, 1943, Mr 30,21:4
Messing, Arnold, 1958, Mr 21,21:3
Messing, David L, 1966, Ja 16,82:3
Messing, David L Mrs, 1957, Je 10,27:5
Messing, Frederick G C, 1947, Mr 24,25:1
Messing, George J, 1960, Ap 1,33:3
Messing, Jacob, 1940, Ja 20,15:4
Messing, Morris B Mrs, 1966, My 29,56:7
Messing, Nat, 1964, Ap 26,88:3
Messing, Nuchem (cor, O 12,19:3), 1946, O 11,23:1
Messinger, Abe, 1957, Ap 25,31:5
Messinger, Charles H, 1943, O 14,21:3
Messinger, Charles R, 1941, F 6,21:4
Messinger, Edwin J, 1965, Ja 29,29:3
Messinger, Elmer S, 1904, Ja 5,9:6
Messinger, Harry C, 1950, Ag 3,23:4
Messinger, Helen B Mrs, 1938, Ap 19,21:2
Messinger, J Prout, 1965, Ja 27,35:2
Messinger, Zane S, 1966, Ag 16,39:5
Messinmer, Robert L, 1945, O 14,44:3
Messiter, Arthur Henry, 1916, Jl 3,9:7
Messiter, Margaret G Mrs, 1938, F 6,II,8:2
Messiter, Richard P, 1914, F 3,11:6
Messler, Benjamin E, 1952, Ja 26,13:4
Messler, Benjamin E Mrs, 1957, S 4,34:4
Messler, Daniel I, 1954, Ja 3,88:1
Messler, Eugene L, 1950, Mr 2,27:1
Messler, Isaac Mrs, 1949, Mr 16,27:5
Messler, John J, 1943, S 27,19:1
Messler, John J Mrs, 1949, O 27,27:3
Messler, W Allen, 1956, Ja 9,25:3
Messmer, S G, 1930, Ag 5,23:5
Messmore, George H, 1961, F 16,31:4
Messmore, Max J, 1947, S 25,25:6
Messmore, Samuel (funl), 1906, Mr 14,4:3
Messner, Daniel A, 1938, Ja 15,15:1
Messner, E B, 1940, Ap 20,17:5
Messner, Emile, 1942, Je 1,13:5
Messner, George H, 1946, Mr 1,21:3
Messner, Henry L, 1955, Ag 10,25:4
Messner, Jacob, 1937, S 21,25:1
Messner, Julian (por), 1948, F 9,17:1
Messner, Julian Mrs (Kathryn G), 1964, Ag 5,33:4
Messner, Karl, 1957, D 8,88:5
Messner, Manfred, 1968, Ap 7,92:6
Messolonghites, Constantine N, 1959, Ag 16,82:4
Messuri, Philip A, 1944, Ja 25,19:5
Mesta, L W, 1953, D 31,19:2
Mestayer, Louis, 1880, O 1,5:4
Mestchersky, Boris A, 1957, Je 30,68:3
Mestchersky, Boris A Mrs, 1957, Je 30,68:3
Mestchersky, Vladimir Petrovitsch Prince, 1914, Jl 24, 9:5
Mestechin, Jacob Mrs, 1963, Jl 31,29:4
Mestechkin, Jacob, 1953, Mr 16,19:5
Mestel, Jacob, 1958, Ag 8,17:7
Mestel, Morris, 1961, Jl 24,23:2; 1964, My 11,31:4
Mestel, Nathan, 1960, Je 19,88:5
Mester, Arthur C, 1939, Ja 16,15:1
Mestern, Armand E, 1964, O 8,43:5
Mestice, P Francis, 1960, Jl 19,29:5
Meston, Arch F, 1948, S 29,29:3
Meston, Lord, 1943, O 8,19:5
Mestre, Harold, 1939, S 11,19:4
Mestres, Ricardo A Mrs, 1961, Jl 17,21:4
Mestrovic, Ivan (funl, Ja 25,31:4), 1962, Ja 17,33:1
Meszar, John, 1966, Mr 5,27:1
Meszaros, John A, 1955, Ja 23,85:2
Meszlenyi, Zoltan L, 1952, Mr 18,3:6
Metalious, Grace (Mrs Geo Matalious),(funl, F 28,29:1), 1964, F 26,35:2
Metaluna, Nicanor O, 1960, Ag 13,15:7
Metaxa, Georges, 1950, D 11,25:2
Metaxas, Angelo S (will), 1955, Mr 5,5:2
Metaxas, John Premier, 1941, Ja 30,1:3
Metc, Anna, 1923, Ag 6,11:2
Metcalf, Albert, 1912, Ja 4,13:4
Metcalf, Antoinette B P, 1962, Mr 3,21:4
Metcalf, Arthur, 1953, F 7,15:3
Metcalf, Bryce, 1951, O 26,23:4
Metcalf, Charles H, 1948, F 2,19:3
Metcalf, Clell L, 1948, Ag 23,17:5
Metcalf, David B Mrs, 1951, Ja 9,29:4
Metcalf, Edward B, 1875, Je 9,7:3
Metcalf, Edwin F, 1949, O 1,13:3
Metcalf, Ernest T H, 1941, N 6,23:4
Metcalf, Francis M 2d, 1963, S 2,15:5
Metcalf, Frank H, 1938, Ja 12,21:5
Metcalf, Frank J, 1945, F 27,19:4
Metcalf, Franklin P Mrs, 1949, Je 9,31:2
Metcalf, George P, 1939, Je 11,44:7; 1957, Jl 28,60:5
Metcalf, George W, 1948, Jl 5,15:1
Metcalf, Harry B, 1947, S 1,19:2
Metcalf, Henry, 1881, F 9,2:5
Metcalf, Henry B, 1904, O 11,9:6
Metcalf, Henry C (lr, O 27,24:7), 1942, Ag 30,42:4
Metcalf, Henry K, 1964, N 30,33:5
Metcalf, Henry K Mrs, 1964, Ap 25,29:5
Metcalf, Henry M, 1955, Jl 21,23:5
Metcalf, Houghton P, 1958, Ja 31,22:7
Metcalf, Irving W, 1938, F 15,26:6
Metcalf, Isabel H Mrs, 1943, My 17,15:2
Metcalf, James A, 1913, Ja 18,13:5
Metcalf, Jesse H (por),(will, O 17,16:8), 1942, O 10, 15:1
Metcalf, Joel H Mrs, 1955, Mr 3,27:5
Metcalf, Joel Hastings Rev, 1925, F 22,19:2
Metcalf, John C, 1949, S 11,96:1
Metcalf, Keyes D Mrs, 1938, Ag 6,13:5
Metcalf, Lorettus S Mrs, 1912, Ja 13,13:4
Metcalf, Lorettus Sutton, 1920, Ja 17;11:4
Metcalf, Manton B, 1923, O 13,15:4
Metcalf, Manton B Mrs, 1945, My 20,32:4
Metcalf, Nelson C, 1939, My 10,23:4
Metcalf, Ralph, 1939, Ap 16,III,6:7
Metcalf, Richard B, 1965, S 5,57:2
Metcalf, Samuel G, 1942, Ja 2,34:2
Metcalf, Stanley W Mrs (funl plans, Jl 20,55:2), 1961, Jl 19,14:5
Metcalf, Stephen Olney Mrs, 1925, Mr 31,19:5
Metcalf, Thomas N, 1951, Ag 23,23:5
Metcalf, V H, 1936, F 21,17:3
Metcalf, Walter C Mrs, 1952, D 18,29:1
Metcalf, Walter W, 1953, O 24,15:1
Metcalf, Walter W Mrs, 1948, F 14,13:3
Metcalf, Willard L (funl, Mr 11,21:4), 1925, Mr 10, 21:1
Metcalf, William, 1909, D 7,9:4
Metcalf, Zeno P, 1956, Ja 7,17:6
Metcalfe, A R Mrs, 1957, Mr 11,25:5
Metcalfe, Alexandria I Mrs, 1966, D 30,26:1
Metcalfe, Alexandria I Mrs (inquest), 1967, Ja 3,16:6
Metcalfe, Alfred, 1941, O 16,21:6
Metcalfe, Edward D (funl, D 4,14:3), 1957, N 20,32:1
Metcalfe, Ex-Judge, 1875, N 14,6:5
Metcalfe, Fred, 1951, Ja 12,27:1
Metcalfe, G T Judge, 1871, Jl 14,5:5
Metcalfe, Henry D, 1954, F 27,13:3
Metcalfe, Herbert, 1940, N 1,25:4
Metcalfe, J S, 1927, My 27,23:1
Metcalfe, Jacob T, 1915, S 1,9:5
Metcalfe, James, 1943, Je 22,19:1
Metcalfe, James J, 1960, Mr 20,86:5
Metcalfe, James S Mrs, 1952, Ag 9,13:2
Metcalfe, Katharine E C H Mrs, 1942, Ag 6,19:4
Metcalfe, Louis R, 1946, O 27,62:5
Metcalfe, Mortimer D, 1957, F 20,33:5
Metcalfe, Rachel A, 1955, F 28,19:4
Metcalfe, Raymond F, 1957, My 9,31:5
Metcalfe, Richard L, 1954, Ap 1,31:4
Metcalfe, Tristam W, 1952, F 25,21:1
Metcalfe, Tristram W Mrs, 1952, Ag 13,21:3
Metchik, Isaac W, 1953, Ja 26,19:5
Metchik, M Judah, 1967, Je 5,43:2
MetchnikofF, Elie Prof, 1916, Jl 16,17:6
Meth, Arthur, 1963, Ap 16,35:3
Meth, Jason, 1963, N 23,29:6
Metha, Jomnades, 1955, F 8,27:4
Metheany, Richard R, 1947, Ja 17,23:2
Metheny, Harry E, 1940, Jl 7,25:5
Metheny, James P, 1948, My 4,25:4
Metherall, Astley, 1937, Ap 8,23:1
Methfessel, Elvira A, 1949, F 9,28:2
Methfessel, Herman, 1963, Jl 9,31:2
Methot, Edward Wenceslas, 1914, Je 2,11:3
Methot, Homer C, 1954, Jl 20,19:5
Methot, Mayo, 1951, Je 10,93:1
Methuen, Algernon Sir, 1924, S 22,19:5
Methuen, Lord, 1932, O 31,15:1
Methven, Huston F, 1944, Ap 2,39:1
Methvin, John, 1940, Ja 23,21:1
Metin, Albert, 1918, Ag 17,7:5
Metivier, George D, 1947, Mr 4,25:1
Metlin, Paul Dr, 1968, Ap 2,47:1
Metras, Felix, 1946, Ag 28,27:3
Metro, Francis C, 1957, Ap 5,27:1
Metsch, Lester M, 1957, Ag 25,86:8
Metsker, Clay W, 1949, Ag 23,23:3
Metson, Charles R, 1943, O 5,25:3
Mettam, George H (por), 1945, F 7,21:3
Metten, John F, 1968, S 19,47:1
Metten, William F, 1951, Ag 13,17:5

Metterhouse, Charles F, 1945, O 24,21:4
Metternich, Klemens Wenzel Prince, 1859, Je 27,8:1
Metternich, Pauline Princess, 1921, S 30,15:5
Metternich-Sandor, Clementine von Princess, 1963, O 26,27:3
Mettgenberg, Wolfgang, 1950, Ap 8,5:3
Mettke, Emil G, 1952, My 31,17:5
Mettlach, Herman G, 1945, N 18,44:2
Mettler, Alex, 1959, Mr 17,33:3
Mettler, John J, 1940, Je 2,44:6
Mettler, John W (will, F 26,29:6), 1952, F 14,27:4
Mettler, L Harrison, 1939, Mr 22,23:5
Mettler, Maude C, 1911, Jl 19,9:2
Mettler, Thomas H, 1957, D 31,18:3
Metz, Adam, 1940, Je 26,23:4; 1959, Ag 19,30:1
Metz, Albert F, 1967, Ja 29,77:1
Metz, Aug C, 1939, F 4,15:4
Metz, Charles E, 1946, Jl 6,15:6
Metz, Earle C, 1950, D 31,42:3
Metz, Edward J, 1913, Ag 30,7:6
Metz, Emma (Sister Aloysius Marie), 1961, S 4,15:4
Metz, Frederick C Jr, 1948, N 30,27:3
Metz, Frederick E Col, 1937, D 29,21:3
Metz, Gustave P, 1944, Ap 8,13:4
Metz, H A, 1934, My 18,23:4
Metz, Harry E, 1958, F 25,27:1
Metz, Herbert, 1956, D 6,37:4
Metz, Herman A Mrs, 1966, Jl 17,69:1
Metz, Hugo L M Mrs, 1945, N 23,23:4
Metz, John, 1946, Ag 21,27:5
Metz, Karl H Mrs, 1941, S 25,25:6
Metz, Kenneth L, 1947, Je 7,13:4
Metz, Myron M, 1942, Ap 8,19:3
Metz, Phil F, 1941, Jl 15,20:3
Metz, Robert Mrs, 1942, Ag 14,17:5
Metz, Stephanie, 1925, S 5,13:6
Metz, T A, 1936, Ja 13,17:1
Metz, William, 1957, Jl 13,17:2
Metz, William F, 1963, Ap 20,27:4
Metzdorf, August E, 1955, My 21,17:4
Metzdorf, Jack R, 1966, My 2,37:1
Metze, Erich, 1952, Jl 30,23:3
Metzel, Alex L, 1948, Ap 1,25:2
Metzel, Edward C Sr, 1953, S 1,23:4
Metzel, George W, 1941, Ja 3,20:2
Metzelthin, Theodor Mrs, 1948, Ja 2,24:1
Metzenbaum, James, 1961, Ja 1,48:3
Metzenbaum, Myron, 1944, Ja 27,19:5
Metzendorf, Adolph M, 1948, Mr 16,27:1
Metzer, Joseph F, 1954, D 1,31:2
Metzerott, Frank R, 1921, D 8,19:5
Metzgar, A D, 1944, O 3,23:3
Metzger, Alfred, 1943, Je 30,21:4
Metzger, Charles, 1942, S 27,48:6
Metzger, Clark W, 1946, Ap 17,25:4
Metzger, Conrad E Mrs, 1949, Ap 19,25:2
Metzger, D Ross Mrs, 1950, N 29,33:4
Metzger, David, 1903, S 22,7:4
Metzger, Delbert E, 1967, Ap 26,47:4
Metzger, Edward W, 1955, N 18,25:2
Metzger, Emy A, 1966, Ap 6,43:1
Metzger, Ethel, 1952, Ap 6,88:3
Metzger, Floyd J, 1961, O 15,88:7
Metzger, Frank K, 1955, N 19,19:2
Metzger, Fraser, 1954, My 30,44:3
Metzger, Fred Sr, 1946, My 15,21:5
Metzger, G, 1879, Je 12,2:2
Metzger, George A, 1949, Jl 22,20:2
Metzger, George H, 1943, Mr 15,13:1
Metzger, George P, 1958, S 19,27:2
Metzger, George R, 1944, N 16,23:5
Metzger, Herman, 1912, Jl 16,9:6
Metzger, Homer P Mrs (C D Owen), 1965, S 8,47:1
Metzger, Irvin D, 1947, Ap 3,25:1
Metzger, Jacob A, 1937, Mr 1,19:1
Metzger, Joe, 1965, My 7,41:3
Metzger, John, 1948, Ja 25,56:4
Metzger, John F, 1960, N 2,39:2
Metzger, Kern D, 1955, Ag 18,35:6
Metzger, Kurt A, 1963, D 8,86:5
Metzger, Max, 1938, O 3,15:3
Metzger, Morris M, 1956, Ap 5,29:3
Metzger, Nordyke, 1948, N 2,25:5
Metzger, Otto (por), 1946, Mr 11,25:4
Metzger, Paul A, 1959, Ag 7,23:3
Metzger, Ralph S, 1952, Ja 12,13:4
Metzger, Robert W, 1965, My 12,47:5
Metzger, Samuel, 1952, O 24,23:2
Metzger, Samuel P Jr, 1966, Jl 31,72:3
Metzger, T Warren, 1949, F 17,23:4
Metzger, Theodor, 1952, Ja 12,13:5
Metzger, William F, 1956, Ja 14,19:6
Metzinger, Jean, 1956, N 4,87:3
Metzl, Ervine, 1963, N 24,22:6
Metzler, Charles M, 1951, My 5,17:3
Metzler, Fred L, 1964, N 5,45:1
Metzler, George A, 1949, Je 4,16:8
Metzler, Henry Mrs, 1952, O 21,29:1
Metzler, Herman J Mrs, 1948, O 21,27:1
Metzler, Walter, 1945, O 24,21:2
Metzler, Warren A, 1958, O 2,37:3
Metzler, William H, 1943, Ap 20,23:1
Metzler, William Mrs, 1951, Ja 21,78:2
Metzman, Gustav, 1960, Ap 12,33:3
Metzman, Louis Mrs, 1960, O 4,43:4
Metzner, Edward, 1950, Mr 9,29:1
Metzner, Martin A, 1925, My 5,21:3
Metzner, Russel W, 1948, Jl 19,19:3
Metzrath, Frank A, 1944, Ap 28,19:5
Meub, Walter E, 1944, N 29,23:4
Meuche, Arthur J, 1962, Jl 21,19:5
Meuer, Arthur J, 1951, Ja 16,29:2
Meuer, Charles A, 1955, Mr 15,29:1
Meuer, Fred W, 1953, S 24,33:1
Meugel, Harry R Mrs, 1937, My 19,23:5
Meulemeester, Adolphe de, 1944, Jl 7,15:4
Meumann, Ernst Prof, 1915, Jl 5,7:6
Meurer, Edward C, 1964, Jl 21,33:4
Meurer, Edward J, 1943, Je 8,21:2
Meurer, Margaret Mrs, 1950, F 23,21:2
Meurer, Otto, 1902, Mr 26,9:6
Meurer, William, 1939, Je 22,23:4
Meurice, Francois P, 1905, D 12,9:3
Meurich, Bernard C, 1960, O 10,31:2
Meurs, Henry, 1958, Je 30,19:1
Meurthe, Emile Deutsch de la, 1924, My 19,17:3
Meury, Emil A Rev Dr (funl, Mr 18,11:5), 1912, Mr 14,11:5
Meury, Emilie J, 1912, Ag 27,9:6
Meusel, Herbert E, 1948, S 30,27:2
Meusel, Irish (Emil F), 1963, Mr 2,7:4
Meuser, Edwin H, 1949, N 14,27:5
Meuthen, Joseph, 1951, Jl 8,60:2
Meuwissen, Juul, 1952, O 1,33:4
Meux, H Sir, 1929, S 21,19:3
Meux, Henry Mrs, 1910, D 22,13:5
Meux, Thomas, 1940, F 8,23:5
Mevas, Nathan, 1964, Ag 23,87:1
Mevi, George G, 1948, Ag 31,26:2
Mevitsky, Charles, 1953, Mr 6,14:4
Mewes, Henry J, 1956, Je 1,23:4
Mewett, Alfred, 1955, Je 30,25:4
Mews, Arthur, 1947, D 28,40:5
Mewshaw, Thomas E, 1940, Jl 6,15:5
Mexia, Ynez, 1938, Jl 14,21:2
Meyendorff, Alex, 1964, F 21,29:1
Meyer, A O, 1950, N 21,31:2
Meyer, Abraham I, 1953, Ag 24,23:6
Meyer, Abraham P, 1951, Jl 4,17:6
Meyer, Adalbert E, 1963, Ap 15,29:3
Meyer, Adolf Mrs, 1967, Ja 13,23:1
Meyer, Adolf W Rev Dr (por), 1937, My 27,23:1
Meyer, Adolph, 1908, Mr 9,7:4; 1947, Ja 5,53:3; 1950, Mr 18,13:6
Meyer, Adolph W, 1943, Ag 21,11:6
Meyer, Albert A, 1966, My 12,45:3
Meyer, Albert Cardinal (funl, Ap 14,41:1), 1965, Ap 10,29:1
Meyer, Albert P, 1940, Ja 28,32:3
Meyer, Alfred E, 1944, Jl 31,13:5
Meyer, Alfred H, 1944, D 31,26:4
Meyer, Alfred L, 1962, Mr 1,31:3
Meyer, Alfred Mrs, 1951, S 24,27:1
Meyer, Allan E, 1953, Ja 17,15:2
Meyer, Alois, 1952, My 6,29:4
Meyer, Andrew C Mrs (P H Joyce),(funl plans, Je 14,25:5), 1957, Je 13,31:4
Meyer, Andrew C Mrs (P H Joyce),(est tax appr), 1959, Ap 21,37:1
Meyer, Andrew J, 1962, Ap 12,35:4
Meyer, Anna E H, 1967, S 9,31:2
Meyer, Arthur, 1924, F 3,23:1
Meyer, Arthur S, 1955, Ag 8,21:1
Meyer, Arthur S (est tax appr), 1958, N 26,6:6
Meyer, Aug H, 1941, F 25,23:2
Meyer, Aug P, 1952, O 17,27:4
Meyer, Aug W, 1940, Ap 12,23:3
Meyer, August B, 1964, Ap 27,31:3
Meyer, August F Mrs, 1951, Mr 25,72:4
Meyer, August P, 1948, N 30,27:3
Meyer, Balthasar H, 1954, F 10,29:3
Meyer, Ben F, 1949, Ja 16,69:1
Meyer, Ben R, 1957, Mr 8,25:1
Meyer, Bernard, 1937, Jl 24,15:4; 1959, Jl 23,27:4
Meyer, Bernard C Mrs (E Kassman), 1960, My 26, 33:2
Meyer, Bernard L, 1954, My 30,45:2
Meyer, Bernhardt G, 1949, Ag 27,13:5
Meyer, Bjarne, 1949, Jl 19,29:2
Meyer, Blakeman Q, 1952, Ag 9,13:4
Meyer, Blanche W Mrs, 1940, O 15,23:1
Meyer, C E (Clarence E), 1965, Mr 17,45:4
Meyer, Carl, 1954, My 29,15:7
Meyer, Carl B, 1948, Je 8,25:5
Meyer, Carl J, 1940, O 15,23:5
Meyer, Carleton W, 1953, F 17,27:4
Meyer, Carrie S Mrs, 1953, O 31,17:1
Meyer, Cassius J, 1903, My 9,9:6
Meyer, Charles A, 1938, Ap 17,II,7:2; 1943, Ja 17, 45:2; 1953, Ap 16,29:1; 1966, Ja 8,26:3
Meyer, Charles Barnard, 1923, Ag 2,15:5
Meyer, Charles F, 1948, O 14,29:2
Meyer, Charles G, 1950, Ap 10,19:1
Meyer, Charles G Mrs, 1939, Ap 1,19:1; 1959, F 28, 19:5
Meyer, Charles H, 1937, Ap 13,25:2; 1952, My 4,91:1; 1952, Jl 14,17:2; 1958, Je 27,25:2; 1962, Jl 20,25:4
Meyer, Charles H Mrs, 1944, F 29,17:5; 1952, O 10, 25:2
Meyer, Charles H Sr, 1952, My 13,23:2
Meyer, Charles J, 1951, D 22,15:5; 1964, S 26,23:4
Meyer, Charles Mrs, 1937, Mr 20,19:3
Meyer, Charles P, 1937, My 21,21:2
Meyer, Christian H, 1941, Ja 13,15:5
Meyer, Christian Moller, 1925, Ag 31,15:7
Meyer, Clarence D, 1957, Mr 19,37:3
Meyer, Clarence H, 1943, Mr 8,15:3
Meyer, Cord, 1910, O 15,11:5; 1964, Je 21,84:7
Meyer, Cornelia M C Mrs, 1939, Mr 24,21:1
Meyer, David, 1904, Ja 4,9:6; 1966, Mr 26,29:2
Meyer, David G, 1941, S 6,15:1
Meyer, Delbert C, 1943, F 4,23:5
Meyer, Diedrick R, 1945, Ag 6,15:3
Meyer, Dietrich, 1945, My 10,23:3
Meyer, Dorrien R, 1943, O 16,13:4
Meyer, E Alvin, 1949, Je 18,13:5
Meyer, E Lloyd, 1957, N 27,31:4
Meyer, Edward A, 1947, Jl 25,17:4
Meyer, Edward B (por), 1937, Ja 31,II,9:1
Meyer, Edward F, 1952, D 20,17:6
Meyer, Edward M, 1953, Ag 17,15:1
Meyer, Edward Sr, 1943, Mr 10,19:4
Meyer, Edwin A, 1958, F 25,27:2
Meyer, Edwin C Mrs, 1940, D 1,62:2
Meyer, Edwin J, 1948, N 11,27:2
Meyer, Emil, 1943, F 1,15:2
Meyer, Emilie J (will), 1949, D 30,21:4
Meyer, Ernest A, 1959, F 10,33:4
Meyer, Ernest G (funl, S 27,7:3), 1925, S 26,17:5
Meyer, Ernest G Mrs, 1949, Ja 30,60:3
Meyer, Ernest L, 1952, F 4,17:2
Meyer, Ethel, 1948, My 29,15:5
Meyer, Eugene, 1925, Ja 18,7:2
Meyer, Eugene (funl plans, Jl 19,69:3; mem ser, Jl 22,27:4), 1959, Jl 18,1:5
Meyer, Everett K, 1947, Jl 8,23:2
Meyer, F B, 1929, Mr 29,23:1
Meyer, Fanny, 1954, Ag 25,27:1
Meyer, Felix Dr, 1925, Ja 5,21:4
Meyer, Francis I T, 1950, Ap 3,23:4
Meyer, Francis J Rev, 1937, Ag 15,II,7:2
Meyer, Frank, 1956, Ag 17,19:2
Meyer, Frank C, 1954, Jl 26,17:1
Meyer, Frank Mrs, 1966, Jl 20,41:4
Meyer, Frank N, 1918, Je 19,11:6
Meyer, Frank W, 1950, Ap 30,102:3
Meyer, Fred (Fritz), 1957, D 15,86:3
Meyer, Fred L, 1952, Mr 26,29:5
Meyer, Fred M, 1952, Jl 4,13:4
Meyer, Fred S, 1957, D 10,35:2
Meyer, Fred W, 1958, Mr 3,27:4
Meyer, Frederick F, 1913, Jl 21,7:6
Meyer, Frederick H, 1948, Ap 16,23:1
Meyer, Frederick H Mrs, 1951, S 8,17:3
Meyer, Frederick W, 1912, Jl 20,7:6
Meyer, Frederick W C, 1942, N 16,19:4
Meyer, Gabriel, 1952, F 2,13:2
Meyer, George, 1940, Ap 9,24:4
Meyer, George C, 1945, N 23,23:4; 1949, D 20,31 1956, S 25,18:4
Meyer, George F, 1905, Mr 23,9:6
Meyer, George H, 1946, D 10,31:5
Meyer, George J, 1945, Jl 31,19:3
Meyer, George Mrs (will), 1952, My 14,32:5
Meyer, George R, 1951, N 25,87:1
Meyer, George von L, 1918, Mr 11,11:5
Meyer, George W, 1937, Ag 22,II,7:3; 1959, Ag 2[illegible] 38:2
Meyer, Gerald O, 1950, O 25,35:3
Meyer, Gertrude C Mrs, 1950, Ap 29,15:5
Meyer, Guenther, 1963, D 29,42:7
Meyer, Gustave, 1944, Ag 18,13:3
Meyer, Gustave (cor, Mr 24,25:4), 1947, Mr 23,[illegible]
Meyer, Gustave M, 1945, My 10,23:3
Meyer, Gustave Mrs, 1950, Jl 7,19:2
Meyer, H Conrad, 1957, Je 11,35:1
Meyer, H D Jr, 1904, D 21,1:2
Meyer, H Kenneth, 1964, F 10,27:3
Meyer, Hans E Mrs, 1952, Mr 19,29:3
Meyer, Hans J, 1964, Je 24,37:3; 1968, Je 28,41:2
Meyer, Harold R, 1965, Ag 27,29:2
Meyer, Harry, 1944, F 24,15:3; 1944, Ag 5,4:5
Meyer, Harry A, 1950, Ja 4,35:5
Meyer, Harry D, 1944, F 25,17:3
Meyer, Harry E, 1949, S 25,92:6
Meyer, Harry H, 1960, Ja 15,31:3
Meyer, Harry V, 1951, My 18,27:1
Meyer, Helen, 1955, Ap 26,36:6
Meyer, Heloise, 1952, F 26,27:4
Meyer, Henrietta Mrs, 1937, D 19,II,9:2
Meyer, Henry, 1918, Ap 3,13:4; 1940, Mr 29,21:4 1951, F 20,25:1; 1958, Jl 27,61:3
Meyer, Henry A, 1940, Ag 21,21:4
Meyer, Henry C, 1939, D 31,18:7
Meyer, Henry C E, 1955, Ag 20,17:7
Meyer, Henry C Jr, 1957, Je 18,33:2
Meyer, Henry C Jr Mrs, 1963, My 6,29:4
Meyer, Henry H, 1951, O 8,21:5
Meyer, Henry H Mrs, 1963, Ag 28,33:4

Meyer, Henry L G, 1961, My 30,17:5
Meyer, Henry Sr Mrs, 1954, N 13,15:6
Meyer, Henry von L, 1950, Jl 2,24:5
Meyer, Herbert, 1960, Mr 31,86:7; 1968, Mr 26,45:1
Meyer, Herbert A, 1950, O 3,31:2
Meyer, Herbert R, 1967, Je 5,43:2
Meyer, Herbert W Mrs, 1958, Je 17,30:4
Meyer, Herman, 1949, F 23,27:1; 1952, F 5,29:5
Meyer, Herman H B, 1937, Ja 17,II,8:2
Meyer, Hermann A Mrs, 1949, Ag 14,68:8
Meyer, Hugo E, 1947, O 4,17:6
Meyer, Ida (will), 1939, Mr 30,8:4
Meyer, Ira R, 1949, D 29,25:3
Meyer, Irving H, 1964, S 13,86:6
Meyer, Isaac, 1882, D 4,5:3
Meyer, Isaac Mrs, 1959, F 2,25:2
Meyer, Isidore, 1950, Jl 27,25:1
Meyer, J Capt, 1881, My 12,5:4
Meyer, J Edward, 1964, Jl 12,68:4
Meyer, J Henry, 1959, F 15,86:3
Meyer, J Louis, 1965, Ja 28,30:8
Meyer, Jacob, 1955, D 19,27:2
Meyer, Jacob F, 1941, F 25,23:5
Meyer, Jacob Mrs, 1945, Mr 13,23:3
Meyer, Jacob T, 1944, Ag 12,11:1
Meyer, James, 1955, Ap 23,19:6
Meyer, James K, 1948, Ap 24,15:5
Meyer, Jane F, 1962, F 11,86:4
Meyer, Jerome, 1937, Ja 3,II,8:2
Meyer, Jim (Rudolph A), 1966, My 22,V,6:6
Meyer, Joachim H, 1964, D 3,45:5
Meyer, John, 1947, D 1,21:3
Meyer, John C Mrs, 1944, D 3,58:3
Meyer, John D, 1939, Jl 13,19:5
Meyer, John D Mrs, 1956, My 19,19:4
Meyer, John E A, 1951, D 20,31:3
Meyer, John H, 1939, Ag 18,19:3; 1946, My 30,21:4
Meyer, John H W, 1948, S 24,25:3
Meyer, John J, 1948, Mr 9,69:2
Meyer, John J Mrs, 1951, D 11,33:4
Meyer, John L, 1953, Mr 21,17:4
Meyer, John W, 1953, Jl 12,65:2
Meyer, Jonas A, 1955, Ja 22,11:2
Meyer, Joseph, 1948, N 30,27:2
Meyer, Joseph B, 1965, Mr 29,33:1
Meyer, Joseph H Mrs, 1948, Je 1,23:3
Meyer, Jule, 1937, Ag 22,II,7:2
Meyer, Julius G, 1925, S 22,25:4
Meyer, Julius P, 1945, Jl 10,11:6
Meyer, Julius W, 1941, O 12,52:2
Meyer, Jurgen F H, 1913, F 5,11:4
Meyer, Kenneth, 1953, D 25,17:4
Meyer, Kuno Dr, 1919, O 16,17:2
Meyer, Kurt, 1961, D 26,25:4
Meyer, Kurt A, 1943, S 22,23:4
Meyer, Kurt E, 1961, Ap 2,76:2
Meyer, Leo B, 1943, Jl 4,21:2
Meyer, Leon, 1948, Ja 23,23:3
Meyer, Leonard J, 1939, My 30,17:5
Meyer, Leopold S, 1946, Ag 4,45:2
Meyer, Leopold S Mrs, 1944, D 13,23:3
Meyer, Lester, 1965, N 15,37:3
Meyer, Lillian, 1953, Je 16,22:8
eyer, Lou, 1952, O 20,23:4
eyer, Louis, 1915, F 2,7:6; 1945, Mr 24,17:5; 1946, Ap 13,17:3; 1965, S 3,27:1
eyer, Louis A, 1951, Ag 5,72:4
eyer, Louis Mrs, 1945, F 27,19:4
eyer, Louise S Mrs, 1942, Je 12,21:2
eyer, Lucas Gen, 1902, Ag 9,9:6
eyer, M James, 1941, S 30,23:4
eyer, Malvin, 1949, Ag 20,11:3
eyer, Marcus, 1938, S 16,22:2
eyer, Martin, 1956, Ag 1,23:3
eyer, Martin A Dr, 1923, Je 28,15:5
eyer, Maurice, 1961, N 1,43:4
eyer, Max, 1953, F 1,89:1
eyer, Max J, 1945, Ja 28,38:2
eyer, Max Mrs, 1948, Je 15,27:2; 1967, Je 3,31:4
eyer, Milton A, 1959, F 21,21:6
eyer, Milton J, 1940, My 21,23:2
eyer, Milton J Mrs, 1943, O 13,23:1
eyer, Milton S, 1965, My 22,32:5
eyer, Net, 1955, Mr 20,89:2
eyer, Nicholas, 1952, Je 1,84:5
eyer, O Charles, 1954, S 14,27:5
eyer, O Jackson, 1939, Jl 8,15:3
yer, Oscar, 1939, Ap 30,44:7
yer, Oscar R, 1938, D 15,27:2
eyer, Otto, 1950, My 21,31:3; 1959, N 28,21:5
yer, Otto A, 1945, N 27,23:1
yer, Otto E, 1966, Je 15,47:4
yer, Otto Mrs, 1955, Jl 2,15:6
yer, Otto T, 1939, Je 16,23:5
yer, P F, 1927, Mr 11,21:1
yer, P J, 1952, Ap 7,25:4
yer, Paul A, 1953, Jl 14,27:2
yer, Paul H, 1964, Ja 22,37:4
yer, Pierre H, 1948, Je 13,69:1
yer, Raymond F, 1937, N 10,25:6
yer, Richard, 1942, D 11,23:3; 1951, Je 10,92:4; 55, N 19,19:1
yer, Richard J Mrs, 1949, N 10,31:4

Meyer, Richard Mrs, 1956, O 26,29:1
Meyer, Richard N, 1957, Jl 30,23:2
Meyer, Richard Prof, 1914, O 10,11:5
Meyer, Robert, 1947, D 14,76:5
Meyer, Robert B, 1951, Ag 22,23:1
Meyer, Robert C, 1952, Ag 12,19:4
Meyer, Robert R, 1947, O 31,23:4
Meyer, Robert R Mrs, 1947, Ja 4,15:3
Meyer, Rudolf, 1961, S 24,86:3
Meyer, Rudolph J Rev, 1912, D 2,11:4
Meyer, Ruth R Mrs, 1965, My 5,47:3
Meyer, Sam, 1944, Jl 15,13:4
Meyer, Samuel, 1953, Ag 4,21:4; 1958, Ja 30,23:3
Meyer, Sarah E Mrs, 1937, Je 21,19:6
Meyer, Selma, 1958, N 14,27:4
Meyer, Severin, 1949, O 9,92:2
Meyer, Seymour R, 1968, N 2,37:4
Meyer, Sigmund T, 1915, O 12,11:5
Meyer, Simon Mrs, 1940, F 29,19:3
Meyer, Theodore R, 1951, F 15,31:3
Meyer, Theresa, 1945, Jl 20,21:6
Meyer, Victor E, 1942, Ja 4,48:4
Meyer, Victor H, 1956, Mr 15,31:5
Meyer, W, 1932, F 25,28:2
Meyer, Walter, 1912, Ag 4,II,11:4; 1950, Ja 30,17:2
Meyer, Walter E, 1957, Ja 11,23:4
Meyer, Walter Mrs, 1957, Ap 24,33:2
Meyer, Werner, 1955, N 9,33:2
Meyer, William, 1916, Jl 10,11:4; 1959, N 17,35:1
Meyer, William A, 1941, Jl 29,15:2
Meyer, William C, 1955, Ja 8,13:1
Meyer, William D, 1943, N 25,25:2
Meyer, William E, 1925, O 13,23:5; 1942, Mr 1,45:2; 1950, O 10,31:1
Meyer, William F, 1948, Ag 31,26:1
Meyer, William H, 1951, O 18,29:6; 1961, Je 15,43:3
Meyer, William H Mrs, 1951, Ag 4,15:5
Meyer, William J, 1946, O 11,23:3; 1948, O 6,30:3
Meyer, William J L, 1944, S 29,21:5
Meyer, William M, 1958, Ja 14,33:4
Meyer, William P, 1955, N 6,86:8
Meyer-Kassel, Hans, 1952, Ag 31,45:1
Meyerbeer, Giacomo, 1864, My 22,2:5
Meyercord, George R, 1941, F 23,40:1
Meyercord, Herman A, 1947, My 16,23:4
Meyerding, Edward H, 1961, O 9,40:4
Meyerer, Frederick H, 1941, Ap 2,23:5
Meyerheim, Frederick, 1945, Ap 3,19:2
Meyerheim, Paul F, 1915, S 15,9:3
Meyerherm, Charles F, 1947, Jl 28,15:5
Meyerhof, Max, 1945, Ap 25,23:4
Meyerhof, Otto, 1951, O 8,21:4
Meyerhof, Otto Mrs, 1954, Mr 24,14:6
Meyerhoff, John C, 1940, F 17,13:5
Meyerholz, Frederick G, 1953, N 10,31:2
Meyerholz, John C Sr, 1955, Je 26,76:8
Meyerholz, John H (por), 1943, F 11,20:3
Meyering, Aloysius G, 1940, D 17,25:4
Meyering, Herman, 1942, Ag 21,19:5
Meyerovitz, Morris Dr, 1937, Mr 4,23:5
Meyerowich, Isaac, 1948, Ja 30,26:3
Meyerowitz, Arthur, 1964, O 12,29:1
Meyerowitz, Harry A, 1960, S 16,28:6
Meyerowitz, Martin, 1966, N 18,43:1
Meyerowitz, Menashe H, 1949, Jl 11,17:3
Meyerrose, Joseph, 1940, F 3,13:3
Meyers, Alfred H, 1957, Ja 27,84:8
Meyers, Arthur, 1947, F 3,19:3
Meyers, Arthur C, 1949, My 17,25:4
Meyers, Arthur D, 1949, S 12,21:3
Meyers, C K Mrs, 1943, D 9,28:2
Meyers, Carl G, 1937, Jl 20,23:2
Meyers, Catherine D Mrs, 1942, F 7,30:4
Meyers, Charles A, 1950, S 11,23:5
Meyers, Charles B, 1958, O 23,31:3
Meyers, Charles B Mrs, 1967, S 21,47:2
Meyers, Charles C, 1944, Ja 23,37:2
Meyers, Charles N, 1947, N 14,23:2
Meyers, Charles P, 1944, S 8,19:4
Meyers, Clifford P, 1944, F 25,17:3
Meyers, Edward P, 1938, Ag 26,17:4
Meyers, Ellis W, 1964, Ap 13,29:3
Meyers, Ernest, 1945, Jl 30,19:4
Meyers, F W H Mrs, 1937, Mr 14,37:5
Meyers, Frank R, 1944, Ja 22,13:4
Meyers, Fred, 1955, O 26,31:4
Meyers, George H, 1949, Jl 20,25:2
Meyers, George J, 1939, D 8,25:3
Meyers, Harry, 1948, N 10,29:6; 1951, My 27,68:3; 1960, O 4,43:3; 1963, Jl 28,65:2
Meyers, Henry H, 1943, My 28,21:3
Meyers, Henry Mrs, 1946, S 16,5:5
Meyers, Herman, 1941, F 16,39:6; 1952, Mr 11,27:6
Meyers, Herman Mrs, 1957, Je 10,27:4
Meyers, I S, 1945, D 15,17:4
Meyers, Isaac, 1948, Je 20,60:6
Meyers, James F, 1965, My 8,31:5
Meyers, Jerome, 1955, S 12,25:2
Meyers, John M, 1956, F 19,92:4
Meyers, John W, 1950, Mr 10,27:1
Meyers, Joseph, 1941, Ja 18,15:5; 1957, N 4,29:2; 1965, D 24,17:2
Meyers, Lawrence F, 1946, Ag 11,46:2

Meyers, Louis, 1904, Ag 30,7:6; 1952, Jl 2,25:2
Meyers, Malvina Hyman Mrs, 1925, Je 2,23:2
Meyers, Matthew G, 1938, Ag 16,19:3
Meyers, Max, 1959, O 2,29:1
Meyers, Meredith, 1945, D 23,18:6
Meyers, Meyer, 1967, N 18,37:4
Meyers, Michael Mrs, 1953, Ag 10,23:5
Meyers, Milton K, 1954, Ja 27,27:2
Meyers, Mitchell, 1959, S 16,39:5
Meyers, Mitchell Mrs, 1960, Jl 2,17:6
Meyers, Morris, 1947, Mr 8,13:2; 1956, Ja 13,23:3
Meyers, Moses S Mrs, 1949, F 1,25:5
Meyers, Myron A, 1942, Ap 24,17:2
Meyers, Paul D, 1966, Jl 3,34:8
Meyers, Paul D Mrs, 1948, N 26,23:2
Meyers, Richard Wain, 1917, Ap 21,13:4
Meyers, Sylvester J Mrs, 1953, Ap 5,77:1
Meyers, Walter S Mrs, 1945, O 20,11:5
Meyers, William B, 1958, Mr 4,29:2
Meyers, William K, 1944, N 12,48:5
Meyersburg, Harry, 1962, S 16,86:6
Meyerson, Daniel C, 1964, S 9,43:2
Meyerson, Harry, 1966, Mr 24,39:5
Meyerson, Herman, 1961, Jl 26,31:1
Meyerson, Hyman, 1959, S 22,35:4
Meyerson, Louisa Mrs, 1953, Jl 25,11:6
Meyerson, Oscar L, 1956, N 30,23:2
Meyerson, Samuel C, 1962, Ap 25,39:2
Meyerson, William S, 1955, Mr 8,27:4
Meyerstein, E H W, 1952, S 13,17:2
Meyerstein, Edward, 1942, F 2,15:4
Meyfarth, John L Mrs, 1947, O 27,21:4
Meyfohrt, William M, 1966, O 5,47:1
Meyier, Fenna de, 1944, Ja 9,42:3
Meylan, George L, 1960, F 16,37:3
Meylan, Paul J, 1961, Ap 3,33:4
Meyn, Albert W, 1960, S 11,81:3
Meyn, Carl V, 1956, Ap 11,33:3
Meyn, Ernest G, 1951, Je 9,19:4
Meyn, Gustav L, 1942, S 22,21:3
Meynell, Wilfred, 1948, O 22,25:4
Meynell, Wilfred Mrs, 1922, N 28,21:4
Meynen, George K, 1939, Ap 8,15:2
Meynen, George K Mrs, 1939, F 14,19:5
Meyner, Gustave H, 1950, Mr 19,95:6
Meyner, Gustave H Mrs, 1968, My 3,47:1
Meyner, Walter, 1938, Ja 7,19:2
Meyran, Louis A, 1941, O 11,17:2
Meyrowitz, Emil B (por), 1937, D 11,9:6
Meyrowitz, Evelyn C Mrs, 1939, Jl 13,19:4
Meyrowitz, George, 1951, S 4,27:3
Meyrowitz, Paul A, 1946, Mr 22,22:3
Meyrowitz, Phil, 1941, My 28,25:3
Meystre, Frederick J, 1960, Ja 27,33:2
Meyszner, Rudolf von Mrs, 1945, N 16,19:3
Meysztowicz, Alexander, 1943, F 20,13:3
Meytrott, Charles C, 1951, O 21,93:2
Meytrott, Charles C Mrs, 1952, Je 29,56:5
Mezes, S E, 1931, S 12,17:1
Mezey, Albert E, 1966, F 2,32:6
Mezey, John B, 1957, My 12,87:3
Mezhitsan, Ivan, 1950, Je 11,92:1
Mezieres, Alfred, 1915, O 14,11:6
Mezierres, Bonel de, 1942, S 16,23:3
Mezo, Ferenc, 1961, N 23,31:2
Mezullo, Marcello, 1942, Ja 2,34:2
Mezzatesta, Henry, 1953, Ap 1,29:4
Mezzullo, Raffaele, 1944, Mr 28,19:6
Miaco, Alfred, 1923, Jl 22,24:4
Miaja, Jose, 1958, Ja 14,33:5
Mial, Bennett T, 1963, Ag 3,17:5
Mial, Leonidas I Dr (will, S 16,28:4), 1937, Ag 21, 15:6
Mial, Thomas K, 1950, F 6,25:5
Miall, E, 1881, My 1,2:5
Mialotsky, Col, 1864, Mr 21,1:5
Mianny, Eugenie Mrs, 1967, Ap 11,41:5
Miano, Joseph, 1925, Ag 17,15:5
Miaskovsky, Nikolai Y, 1950, Ag 10,25:3
Mibaya, Sagazeen Queen, 1925, Ap 30,21:4
Micara, Clemente Cardinal (requiem mass, Mr 16,-39:4), 1965, Mr 12,33:1
Micari, Vincent, 1956, Mr 4,89:1
Micco, Huputta, 1905, Mr 27,9:3
Miceli, Anthony, 1951, D 25,31:2
Micelli, Ralph, 1944, Ap 29,19:5
Micelotta, Frank, 1963, Je 3,9:3
Mich, Dan D, 1965, N 23,45:3
Michael, Archbishop (trb; funl plans, Jl 15,25:4), 1958, Jl 14,21:4
Michael, Arthur, 1942, F 12,23:6
Michael, Benjamin R, 1956, S 20,33:3
Michael, Bro (E F Kiernan), 1964, Ag 5,33:1
Michael, Charles R, 1954, Je 21,23:4
Michael, Charles R Mrs, 1958, S 14,84:3
Michael, Edward, 1951, O 25,29:4
Michael, Elias, 1913, S 16,11:4
Michael, Fred, 1949, N 9,27:2
Michael, Gertrude, 1965, Ja 2,19:4
Michael, Grand Duke of Russia, 1929, Ap 27,19:3
Michael, Harry D, 1942, O 18,52:8
Michael, Harvey C, 1950, D 1,26:3
Michael, Herbert H, 1948, F 19,23:1

Michael, Ike, 1952, Mr 25,27:4
Michael, Jacob Mrs, 1964, D 31,19:1
Michael, James R Col, 1908, D 14,9:5
Michael, Jerome, 1953, Ja 12,27:3
Michael, Jimmie, 1904, N 26,5:2
Michael, Joseph (por), 1944, Jl 23,36:2
Michael, Jules H, 1938, Mr 28,15:3
Michael, Leonard, 1951, Ag 9,21:5
Michael, Lionel B, 1950, Ap 13,29:5
Michael, Louis W, 1959, Ja 28,31:3
Michael, Moina (por), 1944, My 11,19:5
Michael, Oscar S, 1942, My 12,19:4
Michael, Robert W, 1953, D 24,15:1
Michael, William H, 1916, My 18,11:6; 1948, Ap 21, 27:3
Michael, William J, 1944, Ap 29,15:3
Michael Damian, Bro (Saraz), 1958, N 30,86:4
Michaeli, Felix, 1942, Ja 30,8:2
Michaelian, G George Mrs, 1962, Je 14,33:4
Michaelis, Alfred, 1938, Ja 28,21:2
Michaelis, Curt, 1950, S 15,26:3
Michaelis, Emil B, 1939, N 9,23:5
Michaelis, G, 1936, Jl 25,13:1
Michaelis, Harry, 1967, Je 25,69:2
Michaelis, Joseph Mrs, 1958, D 31,19:2
Michaelis, Julius, 1941, S 22,15:3
Michaelis, Karin Mrs, 1950, Ja 12,28:2
Michaelis, Leonor (por), 1949, O 10,23:1
Michaelis, Leonor Mrs, 1964, D 16,44:8
Michaelis, M, 1883, Je 24,7:4
Michaelis, S, 1932, Ja 29,17:3
Michaels, Arthur J Mrs, 1967, D 7,47:1
Michaels, Belle J Mrs, 1941, Mr 29,15:2
Michaels, C A, 1941, F 23,41:3
Michaels, Charles D, 1942, O 17,15:5
Michaels, Charles F (por), 1944, F 22,23:3
Michaels, Charles J, 1947, Je 24,23:5
Michaels, Charles S, 1954, O 19,27:5
Michaels, Harry, 1949, Jl 7,25:2
Michaels, Henry, 1951, F 24,13:3
Michaels, Irving Mrs, 1954, D 12,88:5
Michaels, Isaac, 1940, My 19,43:3
Michaels, John L, 1874, N 19,4:6; 1943, Ap 11,49:1
Michaels, Joseph, 1938, Mr 20,II,8:3
Michaels, Joseph J, 1966, N 21,45:2
Michaels, Joseph Jr, 1953, S 5,15:4
Michaels, Joseph Mrs, 1950, My 4,27:4
Michaels, Leo, 1957, S 22,86:2
Michaels, Louis, 1945, O 15,17:5
Michaels, Mickey, 1965, Je 21,29:2
Michaels, Myer, 1937, N 24,23:3
Michaels, Philip H, 1968, F 15,43:2
Michaelsen, Carl J, 1968, Je 16,60:4
Michaelson, Ben J, 1962, Ja 21,89:1
Michaelson, Charles D Mrs, 1965, Ag 14,23:4
Michaelson, Clifford J, 1954, N 18,33:1
Michaelson, Ephraim, 1955, D 28,23:4
Michaelson, Henry, 1904, F 20,9:5
Michaelson, Lewis B (por), 1944, Ap 15,11:6
Michaelson, M Alfred, 1949, O 27,27:2
Michaelson, Max, 1967, S 23,31:4
Michaelson, Sidney, 1950, F 28,29:2
Michaelyan, Harutune, 1955, My 23,23:4
Michailovsky, Michael, 1963, D 10,50:8
Michalakopoulos, Andrew (por), 1938, Mr 28,15:4
Michalesko, Michal, 1957, Ap 30,29:4
Michalove, Dan, 1949, D 24,15:2
Michals, Maxim, 1962, Ja 14,84:8
Michalski, Joseph J, 1967, Ag 22,34:4
Michalski, Marianne (G Gray), 1959, D 23,27:4
Michalson, Harry J, 1957, Ap 3,31:2
Michaud, Benoit, 1949, Ag 30,27:3
Michaud, F X J Rev, 1903, O 18,7:6
Michaud, J Omer, 1937, D 13,27:4
Michaud, John Stephen Rev, 1908, D 23,9:6
Michaud, Regis, 1939, F 8,23:4
Michaux, Solomon Lightfoot, 1968, O 21,47:2
Miche, Rudolph, 1950, F 3,23:1
Michel, A Eugene, 1939, N 10,23:5
Michel, Albin, 1943, Mr 5,17:3
Michel, Alfred E, 1957, O 5,17:5
Michel, Alfred F, 1950, N 26,90:6
Michel, Arthur, 1946, N 17,68:3
Michel, Arthur S, 1941, Ap 1,23:4
Michel, Carl (por), 1946, Ja 4,22:2
Michel, Clarence W, 1958, Ja 12,86:4
Michel, Firmin, 1942, N 9,23:2
Michel, Francois Emile, 1909, My 25,9:4
Michel, Frederick P, 1946, N 12,29:1
Michel, George L, 1942, Mr 8,42:4
Michel, James F, 1938, Ja 22,15:4
Michel, John, 1940, Ja 26,17:5
Michel, John R, 1956, Ja 31,29:1
Michel, Joseph E, 1961, S 5,16:5
Michel, Julius, 1946, Mr 13,29:3
Michel, Leo L, 1960, O 30,86:2
Michel, Louis, 1950, F 13,21:5
Michel, Louise, 1905, Ja 10,9:3
Michel, Ludwig R, 1951, Ap 29,88:7
Michel, Raymond, 1952, My 1,29:5
Michel, Victor C Gen, 1937, N 10,25:2
Michel, Virgil, 1938, N 27,48:8
Michela, Joseph A, 1949, Je 13,19:6
Michelena, Beatriz, 1942, O 12,17:4
Michelena, Vera (Mrs F Hillebrend), 1961, Ag 27, 85:1
Michelet, Jules, 1874, F 11,1:7
Michelet, R H, 1934, Mr 15,24:3
Michelet, Simon T, 1956, Ag 9,25:2
Michelfelder, Sylvester C, 1951, O 1,23:3
Michelham, Baron (Herbert Stern), 1919, Ja 8,11:2
Micheli, Alfred de, 1940, Ag 14,19:4
Micheli, Bruno, 1954, My 2,88:4
Micheli, Giuseppe, 1948, O 18,23:6
Michelin, A J, 1931, Ap 5,26:5
Michelin, Edouard, 1940, Ag 26,15:6
Michelin, Edouard Mrs, 1953, N 26,31:1
Michelin, Jules H, 1937, D 4,17:3
Michell, Arthur A, 1943, Je 22,19:2
Michell, Bernard S, 1938, O 22,17:5
Michell, Frederick M, 1938, Ag 28,33:4
Michell, H W Col, 1908, S 23,9:5
Michell, Henry F Mrs, 1948, Ja 27,26:2
Michelman, Abraham M, 1939, F 5,40:3
Michelman, Louis I, 1953, My 30,15:3
Michelmore, Thomas G Mrs, 1961, Ja 28,19:4
Michelotti, Virgilio, 1942, S 15,23:2
Michels, Casper, 1945, F 14,19:4
Michels, Emmanuel, 1938, Je 22,23:2
Michels, Fred F, 1941, Ag 29,17:3
Michels, Gustav, 1909, Jl 25,7:7
Michels, Hermann S A, 1939, N 18,17:2
Michels, Louis M, 1910, Je 9,7:5
Michels, Nicholas A Mrs, 1939, N 12,49:2
Michels, Walter C Mrs, 1940, Mr 10,51:4
Michelsen, Carl J, 1947, O 21,24:3
Michelsen, Charles C, 1945, Mr 22,23:5
Michelsen, Christian, 1925, Je 30,19:6
Michelsen, Ernesto, 1945, Je 27,9:1
Michelsen, George J, 1944, Ap 15,11:4
Michelsen, Gustave R, 1948, Je 25,23:4
Michelsen, John H, 1955, N 22,35:3
Michelson, A A, 1931, My 10,1:4
Michelson, Aaron, 1967, N 27,47:3
Michelson, Albert, 1954, D 14,33:4
Michelson, Albert G, 1938, N 30,23:4
Michelson, Albert Heminway, 1915, Je 11,15:6
Michelson, Charles, 1948, Ja 9,21:1
Michelson, Gustav, 1964, Mr 8,86:5
Michelson, Henriette, 1958, My 6,35:1
Michelson, Zella Mrs, 1940, F 21,19:3
Michener, Annie M Mrs, 1938, Ap 1,23:6
Michener, Charles C, 1938, O 7,23:6
Michener, Charles W, 1953, S 2,25:2
Michener, Earl C, 1957, Jl 6,15:2
Michener, Edgar C Jr, 1941, Jl 29,15:3
Michener, Edward, 1947, Je 17,28:3
Michener, Evan W Dr, 1937, O 14,25:3
Michener, John H Jr Mrs, 1956, F 8,33:1
Michener, William J, 1952, S 28,77:2
Michie, Andrew Y, 1948, Mr 6,13:6
Michie, Charles C Sr, 1949, D 14,31:5
Michie, George, 1947, Mr 16,60:2
Michie, H Stuart, 1943, Jl 22,19:2
Michie, Robert W, 1963, Ap 18,35:4
Michill, Robert M Mrs, 1943, Ag 18,19:1
Michl, Francis S, 1951, Ag 23,23:4
Michler, A K, 1927, S 16,23:5
Michler, Francis Col, 1901, My 30,7:5
Michler, Frederick W Mrs, 1945, Ag 18,11:6
Michler, Nathaniel Lt-Col, 1881, Jl 19,5:3
Michler, William M, 1948, Ap 8,25:4
Michlin, Samuel G, 1940, N 1,25:1
Michon, Alfred E, 1956, S 29,19:5
Michon, George, 1950, O 7,9:4
Michotte, Joseph E V, 1964, My 17,87:3
Michtom, Joseph S (will filed, Jl 25,21:2), 1951, Je 22,25:5
Michtom, Morris, 1938, Jl 22,17:5
Michton, Morris Mrs, 1937, Ag 29,II,6:8
Michurin, I V, 1935, Je 8,15:1
Michurina-Samoilova, Vera, 1948, N 4,29:2
Miciak, John, 1948, Ja 16,21:3
Mick, Edwin C, 1955, Mr 30,29:3
Mickel, Ben L, 1939, D 19,26:3
Mickel, Ben L Mrs, 1950, F 4,15:5
Mickelberry, Charles E, 1954, Mr 5,19:1
Mickelburgh, Henry W, 1964, Jl 22,33:2
Mickelsen, Jens Mrs, 1967, N 27,47:3
Mickelsen, Stanley R, 1966, Mr 30,45:1
Mickelson, George T, 1965, Mr 1,27:2
Mickelson, Iver Mrs, 1945, D 25,23:4
Mickelson, Paul R, 1958, N 22,21:1
Mickevicius, Julius, 1938, Mr 9,23:3
Mickey, John H Ex-Gov, 1910, Je 3,7:4
Mickey, Karl B, 1946, My 30,21:3
Mickle, Will, 1961, Ja 30,23:3
Mickle, William K Gen, 1920, F 19,11:4
Mickleborough, Fernando H, 1944, Mr 21,19:3
Micklem, Nathaniel, 1954, Mr 20,15:6
Micklem, Robert, 1952, My 14,27:4
Mickley, James J, 1964, Mr 13,33:2
Mickley, Thomas B, 1941, Ja 15,12:5
Micocci, Antonio A, 1966, My 22,86:8
Micou, Creswell M, 1945, D 13,29:5
Micou, James R, 1939, S 29,23:4
Micou, Paul, 1920, F 12,11:4
Micou, Richard Wilde, 1912, Je 5,11:6
Midaglia, Salvatore, 1942, D 8,26:3
Midas, Julius, 1938, Ja 18,23:4
Middagh, Joseph Mrs, 1946, My 28,21:2
Middagh, Simon S, 1942, Ag 30,43:2
Middaugh, Alice M Mrs, 1941, My 13,23:3
Middaugh, M G, 1954, S 19,89:2
Middaugh, Theodore D, 1942, S 10,27:1
Middaugh, W Clay, 1952, F 10,92:2
Middendorf, G Frederick Jr, 1957, My 8,37:3
Middendorf, Harry S Mrs, 1958, S 20,19:2
Middlebrook, Charles F, 1942, F 2,15:2
Middlebrook, D N, 1904, S 4,3:5
Middlebrook, Eleanor, 1948, O 12,25:6
Middlebrook, Louis F, 1937, F 2,23:4
Middlebrook, Robert, 1957, Ja 21,25:6
Middlecoff, Herman F, 1964, N 14,29:4
Middleditch, Margaret A, 1953, D 19,15:2
Middlekauf, Edison B, 1946, D 7,21:5
Middleman, I C Dr, 1968, S 22,88:6
Middlemas, Raymond L, 1946, N 30,15:2
Middlemas, Roy S, 1958, Mr 22,17:1
Middlemass, Susan C Mrs, 1937, F 13,13:1
Middlemiss, George H, 1946, Je 19,21:5
Middlesteadt, Ernest Mrs, 1947, O 30,25:4
Middlesteadt, Frank H, 1949, Je 30,23:4
Middlesworth, Harry, 1915, Ag 17,9:5
Middleton, A Safroni, 1950, N 8,29:6
Middleton, A W, 1933, N 16,23:5
Middleton, Albert C, 1939, Mr 5,48:5
Middleton, Alfredo (A Morelli), 1967, Ap 10,35
Middleton, Allen C, 1952, F 3,85:2
Middleton, Almor C, 1947, Ag 12,23:2
Middleton, Anne Mrs, 1952, F 25,21:3
Middleton, Arthur, 1953, O 20,29:5
Middleton, Arthur R, 1944, F 8,15:2
Middleton, Austin Dickinson, 1917, My 31,11:4
Middleton, Benjamin P, 1952, Jl 11,17:4
Middleton, C Lloyd, 1946, N 11,27:4
Middleton, Cecil H, 1945, S 19,25:2
Middleton, Charles, 1951, Mr 2,25:4
Middleton, Charles B, 1949, Ap 25,23:2
Middleton, Cornelius W, 1966, D 17,33:1
Middleton, D W, 1880, Ap 29,5:6
Middleton, E, 1883, Ap 29,9:2
Middleton, E Willoughby, 1949, Ag 8,15:3
Middleton, Edgar, 1939, Ap 11,23:4
Middleton, Eduardo, 1950, O 27,29:5
Middleton, Elliott, 1959, Ag 26,29:4
Middleton, Ellis G, 1960, O 29,23:6
Middleton, Ethelyn F Mrs, 1938, Je 17,21:4
Middleton, Frank B, 1942, O 10,15:4
Middleton, G P, 1954, Ag 20,19:5
Middleton, George, 1875, Jl 6,8:6; 1916, Ja 26,1 1938, O 26,23:3; 1967, D 24,49:1
Middleton, George W, 1950, Ag 2,25:2
Middleton, Herbert P, 1925, F 25,19:2
Middleton, Howard A, 1956, N 3,23:6
Middleton, J Raeburn, 1940, Ap 11,25:1
Middleton, Jack A, 1952, Je 17,27:4
Middleton, James, 1937, N 9,24:4
Middleton, James E, 1941, Ag 22,15:3
Middleton, John, 1938, Ja 18,23:2; 1954, N 7,88
Middleton, John I, 1964, N 8,88:5
Middleton, John Jr, 1951, Ap 4,29:2
Middleton, John S, 1963, My 15,39:1
Middleton, Joseph W Mrs, 1943, Je 20,34:5
Middleton, Lewis L, 1949, S 21,31:2
Middleton, M F Jr, 1951, Ja 3,25:2
Middleton, Milton T, 1938, Je 12,39:2
Middleton, Monta W J, 1942, Ap 7,21:5
Middleton, Mortimer, 1946, F 8,19:2
Middleton, O F, 1905, D 27,9:6
Middleton, Orley B, 1952, D 28,50:7
Middleton, P Harvey Mrs (will), 1937, D 24,1
Middleton, Paul, 1956, Mr 31,11:1
Middleton, Ray T, 1957, My 6,29:2
Middleton, Richard L, 1954, O 29,21:1
Middleton, Samuel, 1948, Mr 23,25:1
Middleton, Scudder, 1959, F 27,25:1
Middleton, Stuart G, 1942, S 22,21:4
Middleton, Theodore R, 1949, Ja 30,60:7
Middleton, Thomas G Rev, 1923, N 20,19:4
Middleton, Thomas H, 1961, F 3,25:1
Middleton, Velma, 1961, F 11,23:4
Middleton, W Vernon, 1965, N 14,89:2
Middleton, William H, 1939, F 25,15:3
Middleton, William J, 1942, D 14,23:2
Middleworth, Leroy E, 1948, Mr 4,25:1
Midgely, Harry C, 1952, S 3,29:4
Midgette, Harry J, 1960, Ag 28,83:1
Midgley, Alfred E, 1955, S 10,17:2
Midgley, Charles E Jr, 1957, O 2,33:2
Midgley, Charles E Mrs, 1948, O 2,15:4
Midgley, David M Sr Mrs, 1954, Ag 6,17:5
Midgley, Frederick W, 1940, Mr 21,25:4; 196(69:2
Midgley, James A Rev, 1953, F 24,25:2
Midgley, Leslie Mrs, 1965, Ag 16,49:4
Midgley, Richard A, 1956, D 2,86:6
Midgley, Robert C, 1951, Ap 8,92:4
Midgley, Wilfred A, 1947, D 11,34:3

Midgley, William D, 1961, Ag 10,27:1
Midhat, Pasha, 1884, My 12,5:4
Midkiff, T W, 1949, F 26,15:4
Midlam, H Clayton, 1940, N 19,23:1
Midlam, S C, 1915, Je 3,11:6
Midlane, Albert, 1909, Mr 1,9:2
Midler, Harry, 1959, Je 25,29:4
Midleton, Earl of, 1942, F 15,45:1
Midleton, Viscount (Wm Brodrick), 1907, Ap 19,9:5
Midworth, John B, 1961, Mr 22,41:4
Miegel, Emliy L, 1953, Mr 24,31:4
Miegemolle, Luis B, 1942, Jl 1,25:3
Miehe, Emma Mrs, 1951, N 29,33:2
Miehling, Charles Jr, 1905, Mr 1,16:5
Miel, George A, 1956, F 25,19:7
Mielatz, Charles Frederick William, 1919, Je 5,13:2
Miele, Angelo J, 1952, Ag 7,21:3
Miele, Anthony, 1946, My 29,24:2
Miele, Frank, 1961, Ja 26,29:2
Miele, Humbert, 1943, Je 11,19:3
Miele, Jene G, 1968, My 22,47:2
Miele, John G Mrs, 1967, My 24,32:1
Miele, Ralph, 1948, O 17,76:2
Miele, Ralph J Mrs, 1950, Mr 1,27:5
Miele, Stephen, 1947, Ja 21,23:2
Miele, Theresa P Mrs, 1954, My 13,29:5
Mielenz, Charles L Mrs, 1946, Ap 30,21:1
Mielke, Carl F, 1963, D 28,23:5
Mielke, Otto W, 1951, D 26,25:3
Mielziner, Leo Mrs, 1968, F 4,81:1
Mielziner, Moses Rabbi, 1903, F 20,9:6
Mielziner, William J, 1944, Ap 28,19:3
Mier, Sebastian, 1916, Mr 16,13:3
Mier, Sol, 1910, F 22,9:3
Mier, Ynacio, 1918, Ap 2,13:5
Mierau, Ernest W, 1955, My 5,33:2
Mierendorff, Carl, 1944, F 5,4:8
Mieroslawski, Gen, 1878, D 8,5:2
Miers, Henry, 1942, D 12,17:3
Miersch, Paul F T, 1956, Mr 4,89:1
Mierson, Feodor Dr, 1884, Mr 14,5:5
Mieschberger, Maurice E, 1955, F 18,21:2
Miese, William H Mrs, 1943, Jl 29,19:3
Mieses, Jacques, 1954, F 25,31:4
Miesse, Clifton H Mrs, 1952, Jl 12,13:4
Miestchaninoff, Oscar, 1956, Jl 16,21:3
Mieszkowski, Matthew, 1960, Ag 23,58:6
Mieszkowski, Walter, 1960, Ag 23,58:6
Miethe, A, 1927, My 6,23:5
Mietzelfeld, Otto E, 1954, My 26,29:1
Mieville, Roberto (funl, Ap 14,2:4), 1955, Ap 12,3:3
Miffert, Frank W, 1940, Ap 5,22:2
Mifflin, Benjamin, 1866, Je 17,4:7
Mifflin, Edward L, 1959, S 26,23:1
Mifflin, George Harris, 1921, Ap 6,15:5
Mifflin, Lloyd, 1921, Jl 17,22:4
Mifflin, Samuel W, 1959, Mr 24,39:2
Mifsud, Ugo P, 1942, F 13,21:5
Migel, M C, 1958, O 25,21:1
Migel, M C Mrs, 1967, My 19,39:3
Migely, Walter L, 1942, S 14,15:4
Miggins, Thomas J, 1946, Ag 21,27:6
Mighels, Harry M, 1879, My 30,4:7
Might, H Kenneth, 1956, O 6,21:5
Migliaccio, Edward, 1946, Mr 29,24:3
Miglietta, Romeo Mrs, 1913, S 27,13:4
Miglioli, Guido, 1954, O 26,27:4
Migliore, Nicholas, 1955, Mr 10,27:4
Migliore, Thomas, 1951, Jl 29,68:3
Miglorie, John J, 1955, F 3,23:2
Mignault, Arthur Dr, 1937, Ap 27,23:3
Mignault, Pierre B, 1945, O 16,23:5
Mignen, Msgr, 1939, N 2,9:4
Mignet, F, 1884, Mr 25,5:3
Miguel, D Duke of Braganza, 1927, O 13,25:5
Miguel, J Dr (funl, S 12,7:2), 1901, S 9,7:6
Mihail, John, 1952, S 10,29:6
Mihalik, John M, 1962, My 7,31:1
Mihalik, Julius C, 1943, Ja 14,21:3
Mihaliska, Michael Mrs, 1912, My 17,13:4
Mihalkovitz, Isadore, 1946, My 23,21:3
Mihas, Nicholas, 1952, D 2,31:4
Mihaylovitch, Bogdan, 1962, Jl 29,61:1
Mihic, Hubert L, 1955, Ag 18,23:4
Mihm, Rose Mrs, 1949, My 13,23:3
Mihm, Theodore W, 1951, Ag 26,77:1
Mihoels, Sol, 1948, Ja 14,25:4
Mijana, Marquis de (Carlos Alastaire Raoul Gotesmani), 1912, Ja 26,11:5
Mika, Joseph F, 1952, D 16,31:5
Mikades, Constantinos, 1939, Ja 11,10:4
Mikan, Joseph G, 1961, N 9,35:2
Mikel, William, 1948, My 12,27:3
Mikell, Henry J (por), 1942, F 21,19:1
Mikell, William E, 1944, Ja 21,17:5; 1944, Je 30,21:2
Mikels, W S, 1883, Je 25,5:6
Mikesh, James S, 1949, F 1,25:2
Mikhalenkoff, Karp P, 1940, Je 16,38:8
Mikhalevsky, Faddei I, 1952, N 21,26:3
Miki, Bukichi, 1956, Jl 4,19:3
Miki, Kiyoshi, 1945, O 1,4:7
Mikimoto, Kokichi, 1954, S 22,29:1
Mikionis, Joseph, 1949, S 26,20:6
Mikita, John, 1946, N 27,25:4
Mikkelsen, Aksel H, 1954, N 30,29:2
Mikkelsen, George, 1955, Ja 25,25:5
Mikkelsen, John Mrs, 1953, Ag 8,11:4
Mikkelsen, Michael, 1941, F 9,49:2
Mikkelsen, N Peter, 1958, O 10,31:4
Mikkelsen, Oluf, 1952, Jl 21,19:3
Mikkelson, Roy, 1967, O 31,49:2
Mikkola, Jaakko J, 1952, My 31,17:4
Miklas, Wilhelm, 1956, Mr 21,37:3
Miklasavige, Peter A, 1952, My 3,21:4
Miklos, Bela D, 1948, N 25,32:2
Mikolajczak, John A, 1939, S 12,25:5
Mikolajczak, Joseph F, 1954, Jl 14,27:5
Mikolajczyk, Alex, 1951, Je 30,15:5
Mikolajczyk, Stanislaw, 1966, D 14,47:1
Mikolajczyk, Stanislaw Mrs, 1951, S 25,29:4
Mikoyan, Anastas I Mrs (funl, N 10,2:6), 1962, N 4, 1:6
Miksa, Ludwig, 1956, Jl 21,15:1
Miksche, David M, 1964, Ag 8,19:4
Mikuta, Charles F, 1949, D 5,23:3
Milam, Arthur Y, 1956, Mr 28,31:3
Milam, Carl H, 1963, Ag 28,33:3
Milam, D Franklin, 1965, Ap 8,39:2
Milam, F B, 1949, Ag 21,69:1
Milam, J Cal, 1949, F 12,17:4
Milam, Robert R, 1950, S 25,23:4
Milan, Clyde, 1953, Mr 4,27:1
Milan, ex-King of Servia, 1901, F 12,9:5
Milan, H Robert Jr, 1946, Ja 9,23:3
Milan, Thomas J, 1939, F 27,15:4; 1961, My 28,65:1
Milanese, Clarence C, 1951, Mr 29,27:3
Milanese, Edward J (Milla), 1959, S 26,23:6
Milanese, Mariano, 1952, S 27,17:1
Milanesi, Guido, 1956, D 17,31:4
Milani, Augusto, 1952, S 26,21:2
Milani, George E Sr, 1961, Ja 17,37:4
Milani, Giovanni B, 1940, Je 27,23:6
Milani, Joseph L, 1965, D 1,47:1
Milano, Joseph, 1922, Jl 10,13:3
Milans, Henry F, 1946, O 6,59:6
Milar, John T, 1940, N 29,21:2
Milar, Robert F, 1967, O 13,39:4
Milasch, Robert E, 1954, N 18,33:5
Milau, Edward C, 1967, My 10,47:4
Milbank, Albert G (trb lr, S 10,16:3), 1949, S 8,29:1
Milbank, Albert G (will), 1949, S 22,17:4
Milbank, C E, 1879, D 18,5:4
Milbank, Dunlevy (will, O 23,13:7), 1959, O 17,23:6
Milbank, Dunlevy Mrs, 1967, Ap 13,43:3
Milbank, J, 1884, Je 2,5:4
Milbank, Joseph, 1914, S 8,11:6
Milbank, Robbins Mrs, 1952, N 21,25:5
Milbauer, Charles, 1947, F 26,25:4
Milbauer, Frank W Mrs, 1954, D 4,17:5
Milbauer, Nathaniel, 1957, S 24,35:1
Milberg, Benjamin, 1950, F 24,23:2
Milberg, Henry, 1966, Je 18,31:5
Milberg, Joseph M, 1957, N 24,87:2
Milberg, Samuel, 1962, S 15,25:5
Milberg, Samuel Mrs, 1963, Ap 23,37:3
Milbourne, Howard V, 1951, Ap 6,25:3
Milbourne, Leander B, 1947, Ap 20,63:3
Milburn, Arthur W, 1937, O 12,25:1
Milburn, Benedict Arell, 1906, Ap 21,13:5
Milburn, Devereux (por), 1942, Ag 16,45:1
Milburn, Devereux Mrs, 1955, N 10,35:3
Milburn, Frank, 1962, O 26,31:2
Milburn, George, 1966, S 23,37:2
Milburn, J G, 1930, Ag 12,21:1
Milburn, Otto A, 1948, Ag 4,21:3
Milburn, Thomas E, 1945, F 26,19:1
Milburn, W H Rev, 1903, Ap 11,9:5
Milburn, Walter F, 1954, D 25,11:6
Milbury, Herbert J, 1950, Ja 3,25:1
Milch, Albert, 1951, O 22,23:2
Milch, Albert Mrs, 1946, My 27,23:1
Milch, Bernard, 1954, D 17,31:2
Milch, David, 1962, Je 27,32:6
Milch, Edward, 1953, Ap 12,88:2
Milch, Eugene C, 1957, Ja 9,31:2
Milch, Henry, 1964, Mr 5,33:1
Milch, Jacob, 1945, Ag 19,39:3
Milchman, Daniel F, 1966, My 4,47:4
Milcinovic, Andrea Mrs (Adela), 1968, Je 21,41:4
Milcke, Franz, 1944, Ja 22,13:1
Milde, James F, 1942, Ag 19,38:1
Mildeberger, Elwood, 1943, Ja 22,19:3
Milden, Alfred W, 1944, F 17,19:5
Mildenberg, Albert Dr, 1918, Jl 4,13:2
Mildenberg, Samuel H Col, 1918, Je 25,13:7
Mildenberg, Victor Dr, 1937, Ag 15,23:5
Milder, Maurice, 1953, Ja 17,32:5
Milder, Max (por), 1948, Ag 3,25:5
Mildmay, Francis B, 1947, F 9,63:4
Mildmay, Lord, 1950, Je 7,2:5
Mildon, R B, 1952, Ag 7,21:5
Mildram, Samuel H, 1950, Ja 20,26:3
Mildrum, Roy F, 1956, Ap 10,31:3
Mildwurm, Samuel, 1961, Ag 28,25:3
Milem, George H, 1941, Ap 23,21:2
Milenberger, Anthony W Mrs, 1949, Ja 13,23:5
Milener, Eugene D, 1952, N 23,88:5
Milenky, Joseph D, 1967, F 26,33:1
Milenov, Alex, 1956, Ja 9,25:1
Milenthal, Jacob Mrs, 1953, Ap 24,23:2
Miler, Frank L, 1946, F 13,23:4
Miles, Agnes T, 1944, Mr 31,21:3
Miles, Alfred H, 1956, O 8,21:3
Miles, Alfred W, 1962, F 19,31:4
Miles, Arnold, 1957, Ap 20,17:6
Miles, Arthur T Sr, 1952, N 1,21:6
Miles, C Austin, 1946, Mr 12,25:1
Miles, Carlton, 1954, S 20,23:5
Miles, Charles, 1945, O 16,23:2
Miles, Charles G Mrs, 1950, My 24,30:2
Miles, Charles H, 1956, D 26,27:5
Miles, Charles H Mrs, 1945, F 15,19:1
Miles, Charles S, 1939, My 20,15:3
Miles, Charles W, 1947, D 23,23:2
Miles, David H, 1960, Jl 24,64:4
Miles, E C Rev, 1905, Ap 9,9:6
Miles, Edward B, 1949, My 30,13:5
Miles, Egbert J, 1964, N 5,45:3
Miles, Evan Brig-Gen, 1908, My 25,7:6
Miles, Fordham C, 1957, D 27,19:2
Miles, Francis A Mrs, 1951, S 24,1:6
Miles, FRanklin H, 1954, N 24,23:1
Miles, Fred E, 1953, Ag 8,11:2
Miles, Frederick, 1948, S 6,13:6
Miles, George A, 1951, D 16,89:3
Miles, George Elmer, 1919, Ag 20,15:2
Miles, George F, 1955, F 11,23:2
Miles, George F Mrs, 1955, F 8,27:4
Miles, George Mrs, 1958, F 16,86:5
Miles, George R, 1951, F 20,25:5
Miles, Grace F Mrs, 1941, F 14,17:1
Miles, Harry R, 1951, D 2,91:1
Miles, Harry R Mrs, 1949, S 12,21:5
Miles, Henry D, 1945, Jl 7,13:5
Miles, Herbert E, 1939, Ag 8,17:1
Miles, Homer A, 1940, S 14,17:6
Miles, Hooper S, 1964, Mr 9,29:4
Miles, Howard E, 1954, O 14,29:3
Miles, J B Rev, 1875, N 14,6:5
Miles, J Corwin, 1939, Ag 4,13:3
Miles, J Fred, 1963, Ag 23,25:5
Miles, Jackie, 1968, Ap 27,39:3
Miles, James (lr), 1938, Ap 3,IV,9:7
Miles, James, 1958, F 3,23:1
Miles, James (Mother), 1966, Ja 14,36:4
Miles, James E, 1937, D 29,21:2
Miles, James Mrs, 1955, Mr 14,23:1
Miles, John E, 1946, Ja 5,13:3
Miles, John H, 1960, Jl 18,27:2
Miles, John P, 1943, Ap 9,21:1
Miles, Joseph Elmslie, 1919, Mr 5,11:3
Miles, Ken, 1966, Ag 18,43:1
Miles, L Wardlaw, 1944, Je 29,23:3
Miles, Lester F, 1949, Ag 15,17:4
Miles, Lewis W, 1943, N 9,21:4
Miles, Lovick P, 1953, Ja 18,93:2
Miles, M H (Capt Wm Hudson), 1903, F 12,2:1
Miles, Matt J, 1937, D 1,23:4
Miles, Mildred L, 1953, Ap 21,27:2
Miles, Milton E, 1961, Mr 26,93:1
Miles, Nelson Gen, 1925, My 20,23:4
Miles, Oliver E, 1964, Je 3,43:1
Miles, Pliny, 1865, My 4,8:1
Miles, Raymond B, 1944, F 18,17:5
Miles, Raymond T, 1944, Ap 9,34:3
Miles, Richard W Mrs, 1959, D 3,37:2
Miles, Robert M, 1951, O 24,32:2
Miles, Robert P, 1940, D 29,24:7
Miles, Robert W, 1952, Ja 10,29:4
Miles, Russell L, 1947, Je 27,22:2
Miles, Samuel T, 1924, My 1,19:3
Miles, Sherman, 1966, O 8,31:1
Miles, Sherman Mrs, 1953, F 23,25:4
Miles, Southey F, 1948, Mr 6,13:1
Miles, Susan S, 1937, D 13,27:3
Miles, T Foster, 1950, My 24,29:2
Miles, Vincent M (por), 1947, Ag 22,15:1
Miles, Vincent T, 1961, Ag 2,29:1
Miles, Walter A, 1948, F 25,23:5
Miles, Walter A Mrs, 1937, Ja 10,II,10:5
Miles, Walter D Mrs, 1945, F 7,22:2
Miles, Walter E, 1961, My 11,37:2
Miles, William, 1902, Jl 17,9:5
Miles, William A, 1938, D 4,60:8; 1955, S 18,87:1
Miles, William B, 1949, Jl 30,15:4
Miles, William C, 1953, Je 4,29:3
Miles, William E, 1940, Ag 6,19:5; 1949, F 7,19:4
Miles, William M, 1938, Je 7,23:3
Miles, William O Mrs, 1948, Mr 13,15:5
Mileski, Anthony S, 1961, Jl 27,31:5
Milette, Harry B, 1941, O 11,17:4
Miletti, Frank J, 1950, Je 26,27:4
Miletti, Phillip, 1944, My 22,19:6
Miley, Frank S, 1950, Ap 20,29:2
Miley, George W, 1957, Je 25,29:4
Miley, J Frank, 1939, S 11,19:1
Miley, Jack, 1945, Je 18,19:4
Miley, Levi E, 1953, Jl 19,56:4
Miley, Thomas H, 1939, O 15,49:3

Miley, William R, 1959, F 12,27:3
Milford, Daniel, 1952, F 19,29:3
Milford, David H, 1871, D 2,1:4
Milford, Eugene M, 1953, Ja 31,15:4
Milford, Humphrey S, 1952, S 10,29:3
Milford, Morton M, 1938, Jl 19,21:5
Milford Haven, Dowager Marchioness of, 1950, S 25, 23:1
Milford-Haven, Dowager Marchioness of, 1963, Ja 23,7:6
Milford Haven, Marquess of (por), 1938, Ap 9,17:3
Milford Haven, Marquis of, 1921, S 12,13:1
Milgram, Harry N, 1957, D 12,30:2
Milgram, Isadore, 1946, Ja 24,21:4
Milgrim, Charles, 1967, F 18,29:6
Milgrim, Herman, 1956, O 30,37:5
Milgrim, Irving, 1961, N 22,33:4
Milgrim, Louis Mrs, 1951, Ja 14,84:4
Milgrom, Louis, 1950, S 13,27:5
Milgroom, Herman Mrs, 1944, F 22,23:4
Milham, Charles O, 1952, S 29,23:3
Milham, Charlotte M C Mrs, 1938, S 22,23:1
Milham, Willis I, 1957, Mr 24,86:6
Milhau, John, 1874, D 24,5:2
Milholin, Harry B, 1940, D 3,25:5
Milholin, Harry D Mrs, 1951, My 18,27:4
Milholland, George V, 1944, Ja 29,13:2
Milholland, Harry C, 1939, My 28,III,7:2
Milholland, Harry C Mrs, 1959, Ap 14,35:1
Milholland, Harry S Sr, 1968, Ja 14,84:1
Milholland, Howard I, 1941, O 22,23:2
Milholland, James, 1956, F 16,29:5
Milholland, Jean T Mrs, 1939, F 16,21:4
Milholland, John A, 1949, Ap 3,77:1
Milholland, John Elmer, 1925, Jl 1,23:4
Milholland, Vida, 1952, D 2,36:6
Milholland, W Carroll, 1944, Ja 29,13:2
Milholland, William H, 1948, My 27,25:1
Milici, Attilio, 1965, N 3,35:5
Milillo, Giuseppe, 1953, My 16,19:2
Milillo, Giuseppe Mrs, 1953, My 16,19:2
Milinowski, Arthur S, 1966, D 29,31:2
Milinowski, Carlton R, 1964, O 3,29:1
Milione, Louis G, 1955, Mr 29,29:3
Militza, Grand Duchess, 1951, S 7,29:3
Miliukoff, Paul N, 1943, Ap 16,21:3
Milius, Fred A, 1925, Ap 6,19:5
Milius, Gay E, 1959, My 13,37:4
Miljan, John, 1960, Ja 25,27:2
Milk, Arthur L, 1962, O 12,31:1
Milk, Morris, 1947, My 3,17:6
Milklowitz, Harry, 1967, Ap 15,31:2
Milkman, Walter B, 1945, Jl 5,13:5
Mill, Hugh R, 1950, Ap 7,25:2
Mill, John, 1952, O 4,17:2
Mill, John C F, 1938, D 12,19:4
Mill, John S, 1954, My 18,30:3
Mill, John Stuart, 1873, My 10,6:4
Mill, Robert R, 1942, Je 19,23:4
Mill, William, 1966, My 30,19:4
Milla (E J Milanese), 1959, S 26,23:6
Millais, J E Sir, 1896, Ag 14,9:3
Millais, Lady, 1897, D 24,7:2
Millan, Gabriel R, 1949, S 28,30:5
Millan, Henry B, 1964, My 4,29:2
Millan, Ignacio, 1963, Jl 20,19:1
Milland, M, 1871, N 1,2:2
Millar, Adelqui, 1956, Ag 7,27:5
Millar, Albert S C (por), 1939, D 4,23:4
Millar, Alex C, 1940, N 10,57:1
Millar, Charles, 1953, Je 22,21:3
Millar, Charles E, 1955, Mr 28,27:1
Millar, David P, 1937, Ap 10,19:5
Millar, Donald G Mrs, 1962, Mr 14,29:3
Millar, George A, 1957, Mr 12,33:4
Millar, Gertie Countess of Dudley, 1952, Ap 26,23:5
Millar, H Percye, 1949, N 26,15:3
Millar, James, 1956, Ag 21,29:2
Millar, John C, 1942, My 28,17:1
Millar, John R, 1959, D 3,37:1
Millar, Joseph H Jr, 1938, Ap 5,21:5
Millar, Mack, 1962, N 10,25:5
Millar, Malvina W H Mrs, 1940, O 12,17:5
Millar, Moorhouse F X, 1956, N 16,28:1
Millar, Preston S (por), 1949, Je 19,71:3
Millar, Richard von, 1915, Ag 10,11:5
Millar, Robert W, 1959, F 12,27:2
Millar, Ronald, 1946, My 27,23:5
Millar, Samuel D B, 1949, Ja 24,19:2
Millar, Tag, 1949, O 22,17:5
Millar, W Howard, 1944, Jl 9,35:2
Millar, William, 1940, Jl 22,17:3
Millar, William B (por), 1939, My 31,23:3
Millar, William C, 1940, D 22,31:2
Millar, William D, 1939, Ja 10,19:3
Millard, Almon H Sr, 1953, My 1,22:3
Millard, Arthur C, 1956, D 20,29:5
Millard, Arthur N, 1946, D 9,25:2
Millard, Austin J, 1964, Ap 27,31:2
Millard, Bailey, 1941, Mr 21,21:3
Millard, Benjamin H, 1940, Ag 11,31:1
Millard, Benjamin Lyman, 1872, Mr 11,2:5
Millard, Charles, 1942, Ag 6,19:4
Millard, Charles S, 1942, Je 6,13:4
Millard, Charles S Mrs, 1947, D 27,13:5
Millard, Charles W Mrs, 1956, S 15,17:2
Millard, Charles W Sr, 1948, Je 26,17:4
Millard, Clara L D Mrs, 1942, My 6,19:3
Millard, Clarence L, 1946, F 25,25:4
Millard, Elizabeth L, 1958, Mr 27,33:1
Millard, Ernest B, 1941, Je 8,48:3
Millard, Flora, 1960, F 4,31:3
Millard, Francis E, 1958, Jl 16,29:4
Millard, Frank V Mrs, 1952, S 24,33:4
Millard, George A, 1947, My 21,25:3
Millard, Harriet S, 1924, Je 25,23:5
Millard, Homer B, 1962, My 26,25:2
Millard, Homer Mrs, 1944, F 10,15:2
Millard, Hugh Mrs, 1951, Jl 12,25:3
Millard, Jacob, 1942, O 1,23:5
Millard, James C B (por), 1949, Ja 29,13:6
Millard, Jesse C, 1955, Mr 12,19:5
Millard, John R, 1945, Ap 3,19:1
Millard, Joseph H Ex-Sen, 1922, Ja 14,11:5
Millard, Joseph M Mrs, 1940, Mr 25,15:2
Millard, Katherine, 1940, Ap 14,44:8
Millard, Phillip Mrs, 1964, Mr 9,29:2
Millard, R G, 1877, D 31,2:3
Millard, Stephen H, 1962, Je 27,32:7
Millard, Thomas F (por), 1942, S 9,23:1
Millard, Wallace M, 1950, O 17,31:3
Millard, Walter J, 1951, F 1,25:2
Millard, William J, 1939, Ja 30,13:3
Millard, William J Mrs, 1946, O 19,21:1
Millay, Edna S, 1950, O 20,27:1
Millay, Kathleen (Mrs Howard I Young), 1943, S 23,21:3
Millbank, Harry D, 1947, F 1,15:3
Mille, Pierre, 1941, Ja 16,21:4
Millea, Thomas C, 1952, D 5,28:3
Millegan, Robert Wiley Rear-Adm, 1909, O 15,11:4
Milleman, Jere, 1949, F 15,24:2
Millen, Arthur, 1947, D 14,80:3
Millen, Edmund Mrs, 1950, Jl 27,25:6
Millen, Edwin R, 1943, O 3,48:5
Millen, Frederick H, 1954, My 7,23:5
Millen, Gilmore, 1937, Je 6,II,8:5
Millen, Herbert, 1959, Jl 26,68:2
Millen, John T, 1956, D 8,19:1
Millen, Kenneth R Mrs, 1954, Jl 29,23:5
Millen, William B, 1956, Mr 11,89:1
Millender, Marion C, 1963, Ag 13,31:4
Millener, F H Dr, 1925, My 1,19:4
Miller, A Bertha, 1962, Ag 6,25:5
Miller, A Lincoln J, 1948, F 17,25:3
Miller, A Mathilde, 1958, F 23,92:6
Miller, A Q Sr, 1959, D 31,21:4
Miller, Aaron, 1960, Ag 1,23:5
Miller, Abbie L Mrs, 1939, Jl 26,19:1
Miller, Abraham, 1940, Ja 11,23:3; 1942, D 13,74:3; 1949, Jl 6,27:2; 1963, S 12,37:4
Miller, Abraham J, 1951, N 21,25:2
Miller, Abraham S, 1964, S 9,43:2
Miller, Abram Mrs, 1964, Jl 25,19:3
Miller, Addison F, 1958, S 9,35:3
Miller, Admer D, 1942, Ap 22,23:3
Miller, Adolf L, 1944, N 24,24:3
Miller, Adolph, 1940, My 15,25:2
Miller, Adolph C, 1953, F 12,28:3
Miller, Adolph C Mrs, 1957, Ja 12,19:2
Miller, Agnes, 1951, N 19,23:2
Miller, Al, 1967, Ag 20,88:2
Miller, Alan H, 1955, Ja 17,23:5
Miller, Albert, 1950, Jl 4,17:1; 1966, D 22,33:4
Miller, Albert C, 1959, O 25,85:6
Miller, Albert C Mrs, 1954, Jl 14,27:5
Miller, Albert E, 1943, O 8,19:2
Miller, Albert F, 1949, Ag 13,11:4
Miller, Albert H, 1947, My 2,22:2; 1959, Ag 1,17:3; 1959, N 1,86:6
Miller, Albert J, 1954, D 11,13:5
Miller, Albert L, 1945, Ja 28,37:2; 1958, Ap 27,86:5
Miller, Albert L Mrs, 1950, D 9,15:5
Miller, Albert M, 1949, Ap 14,25:4
Miller, Albert W, 1940, S 4,23:2
Miller, Alex M Jr, 1939, D 3,61:2
Miller, Alex Mrs, 1937, Ja 25,19:3
Miller, Alex R, 1961, Ag 16,29:5
Miller, Alex R G, 1940, Ja 3,22:2
Miller, Alexander F, 1967, Mr 27,33:3
Miller, Alfred, 1943, N 29,19:5
Miller, Alfred E, 1952, Jl 6,48:8
Miller, Alfred J, 1949, Ag 11,23:5; 1950, Ag 13,76:3
Miller, Alfred J Mrs, 1947, S 16,23:3
Miller, Alfred R, 1957, N 14,34:1
Miller, Alice D Mrs, 1942, Ag 23,42:1
Miller, Allan A, 1957, D 4,39:5
Miller, Allan D, 1949, S 13,30:4
Miller, Allister, 1951, N 6,29:1
Miller, Alphonse B, 1959, S 24,37:4
Miller, Alten S, 1967, Ja 31,31:2
Miller, Althea F Mrs, 1938, F 28,15:4
Miller, Alvah L, 1950, O 11,33:6; 1966, Ja 12,21:2
Miller, Amos C, 1949, O 19,29:5
Miller, Amy Mrs, 1963, N 1,34:4
Miller, Amy P, 1940, Ap 6,17:4
Miller, Andrew, 1920, Ja 1,15:1
Miller, Andrew J (por), 1937, N 2,25:4
Miller, Andrew J, 1938, My 20,19:2
Miller, Andrew J Mrs, 1944, Jl 22,15:5
Miller, Andrew Mrs, 1944, My 4,19:3
Miller, Andrew N, 1958, O 13,29:4
Miller, Andrew O, 1943, My 14,19:2
Miller, Andrew T, 1957, N 12,34:2
Miller, Anna K, 1952, N 21,25:2
Miller, Anne R Mrs, 1949, D 13,31:4
Miller, Annie (will), 1938, Ja 11,23:2
Miller, Arabella H, 1950, Je 6,29:1
Miller, Arbie J Mrs, 1949, Ap 22,23:1
Miller, Archibald L, 1956, Mr 3,19:4
Miller, Archie H, 1958, F 12,29:5
Miller, Armenia Mrs, 1940, Ap 13,17:6
Miller, Armina, 1942, S 2,23:4
Miller, Arnold H, 1962, Mr 4,86:7
Miller, Arnon P, 1922, Ag 30,15:6
Miller, Arthur, 1967, Je 27,39:1
Miller, Arthur A, 1966, Ja 26,37:3
Miller, Arthur B, 1957, Ja 29,31:1; 1966, Ja 18,34:2
Miller, Arthur D, 1952, Je 12,34:5
Miller, Arthur E, 1956, Ja 5,33:2
Miller, Arthur F, 1961, Jl 3,15:4
Miller, Arthur I, 1947, N 7,23:4
Miller, Arthur L, 1955, Je 20,21:4; 1967, Mr 17,41:
Miller, Arthur O Jr Dr, 1924, Ag 9,11:6
Miller, Arthur W, 1955, S 1,23:5
Miller, Arvilla, 1951, My 12,21:2
Miller, Atwood H, 1959, My 19,33:3
Miller, August, 1922, Jl 8,11:7
Miller, August C, 1947, Ja 27,23:4
Miller, August Mrs, 1955, Je 18,17:6
Miller, Austin H, 1950, Mr 19,95:4
Miller, Barbara Mrs, 1925, F 6,17:5
Miller, Barton D, 1952, Ja 25,21:5
Miller, Belle C, 1960, D 6,37:1
Miller, Benjamin, 1951, S 26,31:3
Miller, Benjamin F, 1949, Je 21,25:4; 1951, Jl 25,2
Miller, Benjamin G, 1941, Je 30,17:1
Miller, Benjamin H, 1942, Jl 4,17:2; 1947, Ag 19,2
Miller, Benjamin L, 1944, Mr 24,19:2; 1949, O 30,
Miller, Benjamin M, 1944, F 7,15:2
Miller, Benjamin R, 1966, F 20,88:3
Miller, Bennett, 1948, Ag 29,59:5
Miller, Bernard, 1951, D 30,24:5; 1966, F 14,29:2
Miller, Bernard A Maj, 1921, D 19,15:5
Miller, Bernard L, 1960, F 24,37:4
Miller, Bernard T, 1949, Je 15,29:5
Miller, Bernard W, 1955, Ag 1,19:2
Miller, Bert H, 1949, O 9,93:1
Miller, Bert W, 1941, D 1,19:3
Miller, Bertram B, 1960, My 26,33:5
Miller, Bijou H Mrs, 1937, Mr 20,19:5
Miller, Billy (Wade), 1961, Ag 23,33:6
Miller, Bing (Edmund J Miller), 1966, My 8,82:
Miller, Bloomfield J, 1905, Ap 12,9:4
Miller, Bob, 1955, Ag 27,15:2
Miller, Branch M Mrs, 1960, Mr 26,21:2
Miller, Burr C, 1958, O 11,23:2
Miller, Byron D, 1960, My 20,31:2
Miller, Byron De W Mrs, 1961, N 20,31:5
Miller, C A Col, 1904, S 16,7:7
Miller, C Armand Rev Dr, 1917, S 12,11:3
Miller, C Blackbum, 1957, Ja 1,23:3
Miller, C M, 1933, Ag 21,13:3
Miller, C R, 1927, S 19,25:5
Miller, C S S, 1934, Ap 13,19:4
Miller, C Wilbur, 1955, S 23,26:3
Miller, Calvin E, 1950, O 2,23:3
Miller, Cap E, 1957, D 22,40:4
Miller, Carl, 1946, Mr 19,27:2
Miller, Carl A, 1949, Mr 1,26:2; 1953, Ag 25,21: 1955, My 26,31:4
Miller, Carl H, 1956, F 26,88:4
Miller, Carl J, 1947, My 16,24:2
Miller, Carl L, 1957, Ag 3,15:3
Miller, Carl N, 1944, D 21,21:2
Miller, Carlton O, 1962, S 24,29:3
Miller, Caro G, 1953, O 14,29:5
Miller, Caro Mrs, 1942, Mr 20,19:2
Miller, Carroll, 1949, D 25,26:8
Miller, Caspar W, 1940, Je 27,23:5
Miller, Casper J Mrs, 1951, My 26,17:4
Miller, Catherine C, 1917, Ag 4,7:2
Miller, Chalmers B, 1951, D 7,28:2
Miller, Chapman A, 1950, Ja 17,27:3
Miller, Charles, 1937, Jl 19,6:6; 1944, N 25,13:4 N 17,17:4; 1951, My 27,17:1
Miller, Charles (Bronco Charlie),(funl, Ja 20,31: 1955, Ja 16,93:1
Miller, Charles, 1955, Ag 20,17:5; 1966, N 20,8
Miller, Charles A, 1916, Ja 27,11:2; 1940, Jl 4,
Miller, Charles A (por), 1944, N 24,23:1
Miller, Charles A, 1945, My 29,15:3; 1949, Mr
Miller, Charles A A J, 1948, Jl 7,23:1
Miller, Charles A Gen, 1908, S 21,7:6
Miller, Charles A Jr, 1948, My 11,25:5
Miller, Charles Augustus, 1904, Ja 29,9:6
Miller, Charles C, 1953, F 23,25:5
Miller, Charles C Mrs, 1942, S 13,53:2; 1955, 15:4

Miller, Charles Carroll Rev, 1907, Ag 18,7:5
Miller, Charles Coleman, 1953, N 4,33:2
Miller, Charles D, 1945, S 15,15:4; 1951, D 23,22:8; 1952, Mr 2,92:1
Miller, Charles Dexter, 1903, O 25,7:6
Miller, Charles E, 1906, D 21,9:4; 1939, Ja 12,19:5; 1940, Ja 22,15:2; 1940, Ag 18,37:4; 1941, Mr 20,21:3; 1948, S 15,31:2; 1950, F 8,27:2
Miller, Charles F, 1949, O 1,13:4; 1949, N 11,25:2
Miller, Charles G, 1942, S 4,24:3
Miller, Charles G Mrs, 1939, O 7,17:3; 1945, My 16, 19:3; 1955, D 8,37:4
Miller, Charles H, 1921, S 21,15:4; 1946, F 23,13:5
Miller, Charles H Dr, 1922, Ja 22,22:3
Miller, Charles J, 1938, S 6,21:2; 1950, My 10,31:3; 1953, Jl 23,23:3
Miller, Charles L, 1945, Ap 11,23:3; 1950, Je 14,31:5; 1967, Ja 15,85:1; 1967, N 16,47:2
Miller, Charles Mrs, 1945, N 16,19:4; 1948, N 20,13:5
Miller, Charles N, 1940, Mr 28,23:2
Miller, Charles O Jr Mrs, 1966, D 13,47:1
Miller, Charles P, 1951, D 1,13:4
Miller, Charles P Mrs, 1945, O 26,19:4
Miller, Charles R, 1949, D 10,17:2; 1963, My 30,17:3
Miller, Charles R D, 1964, Je 18,35:4
Miller, Charles R Maj, 1916, D 20,13:5
Miller, Charles R Mrs, 1906, D 10,7:5; 1943, Jl 26,19:5
Miller, Charles Ransom (por), 1915, Jl 8,13:1
Miller, Charles S, 1945, S 9,45:2; 1966, D 5,45:4
Miller, Charles T K, 1911, F 10,9:4
Miller, Charles V (por), 1943, N 3,25:2
Miller, Charles W, 1940, N 5,25:4; 1951, Ag 15,27:1; 1951, O 26,23:1
Miller, Charles W Mrs, 1951, Ap 25,29:5; 1963, Jl 12, 25:3
Miller, Charlie, 1940, Ja 28,33:1
Miller, Charlotte, 1943, O 29,19:3
Miller, Charlotte G Mrs, 1937, My 13,25:4
Miller, Charlotte R Mrs, 1937, F 17,21:4
Miller, Chester L, 1943, My 7,19:1
Miller, Chet, 1953, My 16,14:6
Miller, Christian, 1966, Jl 23,25:2
Miller, Christian O G, 1952, Ap 24,32:3
Miller, Christopher, 1952, Ja 31,27:4; 1955, Ap 20,33:2
Miller, Clara E, 1945, N 12,21:4
Miller, Clarence A, 1953, N 24,29:4; 1963, Ag 26,27:4
Miller, Clarence B (funl, Ja 12,17:5), 1922, Ja 11,21:6
Miller, Clarence B Mrs, 1954, O 16,17:4
Miller, Clarence C, 1951, O 10,23:7
Miller, Clarence E, 1952, Ag 23,13:5
Miller, Clarence L, 1965, Ja 31,89:1; 1965, F 1,23:2
Miller, Clarence S, 1941, Ja 23,22:2
Miller, Claude E, 1951, Ap 28,15:2
Miller, Claude H, 1950, O 11,33:1
Miller, Clayton I, 1956, O 3,33:4
Miller, Clement W (Clem), 1962, O 9,30:2
Miller, Clifton M, 1943, F 27,13:5
Miller, Clifton M Mrs, 1940, Ap 6,17:6
Miller, Clinton T, 1960, Ap 13,39:2
Miller, Clyde R Mrs, 1964, N 16,31:4
Miller, Clyde W, 1940, Ap 17,23:3
Miller, Conrad H, 1952, N 7,23:2
Miller, Cora Mrs, 1941, Jl 2,21:3
Miller, Cornelius H, 1956, Ag 7,27:1
Miller, Cornelius T (por), 1940, O 3,25:5
Miller, Courtland, 1939, Jl 27,19:4
Miller, Craig C Mrs, 1941, S 8,15:5
Miller, Curt W, 1943, Jl 27,17:5
Miller, Cyrus C, 1956, Ja 23,25:1
Miller, Cyrus R, 1947, My 30,21:3
Miller, Cyrus W, 1951, Ag 15,27:1
Miller, D Leeds Jr, 1942, Ag 14,17:4
Miller, D Newton, 1949, S 4,40:4
Miller, D Sheldon, 1941, F 11,23:2
Miller, D W, 1903, My 29,9:5
Miller, Daisy O Mrs, 1955, D 7,39:4
Miller, Danforth, 1952, N 8,17:5
Miller, Daniel C, 1951, S 20,31:2
Miller, Daniel E, 1939, O 25,23:6
Miller, Daniel K, 1958, My 24,21:7
Miller, Darius, 1914, Ag 24,9:4
Miller, Dave, 1937, Ag 26,21:6
Miller, David, 1941, Ap 14,17:4; 1958, My 22,29:5; 1965, Ag 7,21:3
Miller, David A, 1958, Ja 23,27:2
Miller, David B Mrs, 1952, Jl 12,13:4
Miller, David D, 1947, F 14,21:4
Miller, David H, 1954, F 9,27:1; 1961, Jl 24,23:1
Miller, David H Maj, 1915, Ap 7,13:4
Miller, David H Mrs, 1964, Ag 7,29:4
Miller, David K, 1950, Jl 2,25:1
Miller, David Mrs, 1959, Ja 12,39:2
Miller, David S Capt, 1924, N 4,21:3
Miller, Dayton C (por), 1941, F 23,41:1
Miller, Delia A Mrs, 1939, O 13,23:3
Miller, Dick, 1953, Ap 22,40:5
Miller, Dickinson S, 1963, N 14,35:1
Miller, Don H, 1968, Ap 8,47:2
Miller, Donald T, 1952, Ag 2,15:3
Miller, Donnell D, 1958, Mr 4,29:3
Miller, Dora, 1913, Je 20,9:4; 1938, Ja 17,19:2
Miller, Dora Loues Mrs (Mrs Allan Updegraff), 1968, F 17,29:4
Miller, Dorsey N, 1938, Mr 22,21:5
Miller, Douglas C, 1950, Ag 31,25:2
Miller, Douglas J, 1948, D 28,21:5
Miller, Durando, 1962, O 9,42:1
Miller, E Clarence (por), 1944, Mr 4,13:1
Miller, E F, 1933, Je 13,19:6
Miller, E Freeman (Sept 30), 1965, O 11,61:4
Miller, E Howard, 1938, S 7,25:1
Miller, E L, 1934, Ag 22,17:3
Miller, E Spencer, 1941, Ag 11,13:4
Miller, Earl, 1940, Jl 5,13:4
Miller, Earl A, 1949, Je 27,27:2
Miller, Earl H, 1939, D 3,60:8
Miller, Earl W, 1951, My 16,35:4
Miller, Ed, 1952, Ap 28,19:5
Miller, Edgar G Jr, 1955, Je 29,29:3
Miller, Edgar G Mrs, 1953, O 15,33:5
Miller, Edgar M, 1955, Ap 3,86:4
Miller, Edgar P, 1942, Ap 5,42:2
Miller, Edgar W Jr, 1955, F 9,27:4
Miller, Edgar W Mrs, 1956, F 4,19:3
Miller, Edmund C, 1942, Mr 5,23:5
Miller, Edmund H Prof, 1906, N 9,9:6
Miller, Edmund T, 1945, D 19,25:1
Miller, Edson W, 1952, Jl 4,13:3
Miller, Edward, 1940, N 16,17:6; 1943, F 10,25:2; 1951, Ja 15,17:3
Miller, Edward A, 1942, Jl 29,17:5; 1946, Ja 3,19:3
Miller, Edward C, 1963, Ag 15,29:4
Miller, Edward E, 1946, Ag 3,15:3
Miller, Edward F, 1945, N 23,23:2
Miller, Edward G, 1951, S 23,86:1; 1953, Ja 19,23:3
Miller, Edward G Jr, 1968, Ap 16,47:1
Miller, Edward H, 1950, Je 23,25:5
Miller, Edward I, 1961, S 24,87:1
Miller, Edward J Sr, 1952, Ja 24,27:1
Miller, Edward M, 1942, F 16,17:3; 1942, Ap 23,24:2
Miller, Edward M F, 1914, D 2,13:6
Miller, Edward Mrs, 1947, Ja 10,22:3
Miller, Edward R, 1942, N 28,13:6
Miller, Edward S, 1957, Je 27,25:4
Miller, Edward T, 1938, Ag 12,17:4; 1968, Ja 21,76:4
Miller, Edward Whitney, 1968, O 6,85:1
Miller, Edwell B, 1942, Jl 29,17:4
Miller, Edwin B, 1955, Je 4,15:3
Miller, Edwin E, 1949, Je 9,31:4
Miller, Edwin H, 1955, Ag 13,13:1
Miller, Edwin L, 1943, O 8,19:1
Miller, Eleanor Mrs, 1962, O 3,41:4
Miller, Elihu S, 1940, N 19,23:1
Miller, Elihu S Mrs, 1938, My 16,17:3
Miller, Elizabeth N Mrs, 1937, Jl 7,23:1
Miller, Elmer, 1961, D 16,25:6
Miller, Elsie L, 1953, Ag 8,11:5
Miller, Elton H, 1942, Ag 7,17:5
Miller, Elvira H, 1955, Jl 25,19:3
Miller, Elwood W, 1948, My 12,27:2
Miller, Emil C, 1938, F 17,21:2
Miller, Emily, 1947, Ja 7,27:1
Miller, Emily Huntington Mrs, 1913, N 5,13:7
Miller, Emily J Mrs, 1937, Mr 25,25:5
Miller, Emma E, 1955, Ja 25,25:3
Miller, Emma G Mrs, 1948, O 9,19:1
Miller, Ernest B, 1959, F 22,88:4
Miller, Ernest H, 1958, My 17,19:4
Miller, Ernest Sir, 1939, Mr 24,21:4
Miller, Erskine J, 1937, F 7,II,8:8
Miller, Ethel B (Sept 22), 1965, O 11,61:4
Miller, Etta L, 1958, D 10,39:2
Miller, Eugene D, 1925, Ap 29,21:5
Miller, Eugene D Mrs, 1951, F 13,31:3
Miller, Eugenie, 1955, My 3,42:3
Miller, Eustace P, 1940, Je 23,30:8
Miller, Everard P, 1940, Ja 21,34:5
Miller, Everett H, 1954, Je 7,23:5
Miller, Everett H Jr, 1950, Jl 10,21:4
Miller, Everett H Mrs, 1948, Mr 29,21:5
Miller, Everett W, 1948, Ag 19,21:4
Miller, Ewing L Jr, 1955, S 18,87:2
Miller, Ezra E, 1948, O 14,30:2
Miller, F A, 1931, Je 26,23:5
Miller, F D, 1939, Jl 17,19:1
Miller, F E, 1932, Ap 16,15:1
Miller, F Frank Col, 1873, D 13,6:6
Miller, Fannie E C Mrs, 1938, S 17,17:3
Miller, Ferdinand W, 1945, Ja 11,23:2
Miller, Florence P Mrs, 1939, My 17,23:3
Miller, Floyd, 1962, My 28,29:4
Miller, Floyd H, 1945, Ja 22,17:5
Miller, Floyd J, 1954, S 17,27:2
Miller, Forrest A, 1950, Ag 24,27:3
Miller, Francis, 1947, Mr 1,15:4
Miller, Francis H Dr, 1925, My 3,5:1
Miller, Francis P, 1941, Je 5,24:4
Miller, Francis T, 1959, N 8,88:4
Miller, Francis X, 1919, F 27,11:2
Miller, Frank, 1921, Ag 15,13:6; 1923, Je 1,19:5; 1945, Je 9,13:4; 1949, D 4,108:8; 1950, N 8,29:3; 1952, O 28,31:2; 1954, N 12,15:2
Miller, Frank B, 1941, O 23,23:2; 1962, Je 2,19:2
Miller, Frank C, 1953, N 22,88:2
Miller, Frank D, 1938, D 7,23:5
Miller, Frank E, 1947, Ja 11,19:5; 1947, F 24,19:2; 1954, Ap 6,30:7
Miller, Frank G, 1939, My 16,23:5
Miller, Frank H, 1942, F 6,19:4; 1942, D 21,23:4
Miller, Frank J, 1938, Ap 25,15:6; 1939, F 6,13:3
Miller, Frank L, 1951, Ag 8,25:5
Miller, Frank L Jr (will, F 8,10:5), 1958, Ja 29,27:3
Miller, Frank M, 1945, O 31,23:4; 1949, Ap 30,13:4
Miller, Frank Mrs, 1944, O 18,21:3
Miller, Frank O, 1945, Ja 3,17:1
Miller, Frank S, 1938, O 15,22:8
Miller, Frank W, 1940, Ag 27,21:5
Miller, Franklin A, 1960, My 20,29:1
Miller, Franklin P, 1954, Ag 25,27:5
Miller, Franklin T, 1940, Ja 30,19:4
Miller, Franz, 1963, F 8,18:2
Miller, Fred E, 1948, F 23,25:5
Miller, Fred J, 1939, N 27,17:6
Miller, Fred J Mrs, 1938, D 5,23:5
Miller, Fred M, 1956, Je 7,31:4
Miller, Fred Mrs, 1952, My 12,25:4
Miller, Freddie, 1962, My 9,43:3
Miller, Frederic H, 1964, Ja 12,93:1
Miller, Frederic M, 1958, Je 9,23:5
Miller, Frederick, 1924, N 6,19:4; 1944, Ja 23,38:1
Miller, Frederick A, 1948, Je 25,24:2; 1954, N 30,29:4
Miller, Frederick C, 1952, Ja 8,27:5
Miller, Frederick C (will D 25,14:4), 1954, D 18,16:1
Miller, Frederick C, 1960, O 14,33:1
Miller, Frederick C Jr, 1954, D 18,16:1
Miller, Frederick E, 1937, Mr 17,25:3
Miller, Frederick F, 1937, O 30,19:4
Miller, Frederick L, 1950, Je 10,17:1
Miller, Frederick M, 1947, Jl 10,21:2
Miller, Frederick P, 1940, D 13,23:5
Miller, Frederick S, 1948, Mr 5,21:4; 1961, My 25,37:5
Miller, Frederick S Rev, 1937, O 8,23:3
Miller, Frederick W, 1942, O 7,25:3; 1950, Je 30,23:4
Miller, Freeman M, 1945, Mr 18,41:1
Miller, G Clinton, 1940, S 19,23:4
Miller, G E, 1934, Ja 16,22:1
MilleR, George, 1937, O 29,22:3
Miller, George, 1940, N 14,23:1; 1948, N 30,27:1; 1949, Ja 16,68:3; 1949, F 25,23:4; 1950, My 21, 104:5; 1950, O 5,31:1; 1957, Jl 22,19:5; 1957, Ag 14, 25:3; 1960, F 21,92:7
Miller, George A (will), 1951, F 20,27:6
Miller, George A, 1954, D 29,23:1
Miller, George A Dr, 1925, Mr 12,19:4
Miller, George B, 1948, D 8,31:4; 1957, O 25,27:2; 1968, Ap 16,44:1
Miller, George C, 1939, My 11,25:6; 1951, F 25,84:6
Miller, George E, 1938, Mr 11,19:5; 1950, S 5,27:4
Miller, George F, 1943, My 11,21:2; 1954, F 15,23:3; 1961, F 15,35:4
Miller, George H, 1943, My 18,23:5
Miller, George H (will), 1955, Ja 21,21:6
Miller, George H, 1961, Je 29,33:3; 1962, Ap 23,29:4
Miller, George H Rev, 1903, N 5,9:6
Miller, George I, 1947, Mr 18,27:4
Miller, George J, 1938, F 22,21:2; 1939, Jl 5,17:5; 1944, N 28,23:2
Miller, George J Mrs, 1948, Ap 24,15:3
Miller, George J Sr, 1947, Je 21,17:2
Miller, George L, 1941, O 12,53:2
Miller, George L Dr, 1920, Ag 31,9:3
Miller, George L Mrs, 1953, O 22,29:3
Miller, George M, 1948, Ja 7,26:2; 1955, Ap 26,29:2
Miller, George M Mrs, 1940, O 8,25:5
Miller, George M Prof, 1937, Ja 17,II,8:4
Miller, George Macculloch, 1917, N 15,13:5
Miller, George Mrs, 1952, Jl 6,48:8
Miller, George O, 1944, Je 8,21:5; 1961, Je 5,31:4
Miller, George R, 1953, Ap 29,29:3
Miller, George R Sr, 1954, Ag 27,21:3
Miller, George S, 1959, Ap 4,19:5
Miller, George S Mrs, 1956, Mr 26,29:3
Miller, George U, 1950, D 30,13:5
Miller, George V Mrs, 1944, Jl 26,19:3
Miller, George W, 1950, Ja 14,15:2; 1956, S 7,23:2
Miller, George W Mrs, 1941, O 30,23:2; 1954, Ap 20, 29:5
Miller, George Walbridge, 1923, Mr 13,22:5
Miller, George Washington, 1911, Ja 7,9:5
Miller, Gerald, 1947, N 8,17:5
Miller, Gerald F Sr, 1958, Ap 5,15:4
Miller, Gerardus L, 1947, Je 30,19:4
Miller, Gerardus L Mrs, 1940, S 25,27:3
Miller, Gerrit S, 1937, Mr 11,24:1
Miller, Gerritt S Jr, 1956, F 26,88:5
Miller, Gertrude, 1962, S 21,29:2
Miller, Gertrude K Mrs, 1938, N 24,27:4
Miller, Gilbert E, 1949, Ag 17,23:5
Miller, Glenn Mrs, 1966, Je 5,85:1
Miller, Gordon Mrs, 1949, N 10,31:3
Miller, Grace G Mrs, 1948, Je 6,72:4
Miller, Grace H, 1952, My 31,17:2
Miller, Grace M, 1945, Je 14,19:5
Miller, Grace S, 1938, Je 8,23:2
Miller, Gray, 1947, My 12,21:6
Miller, Guerdon B Mrs, 1947, N 16,76:3
Miller, Gustave, 1943, F 14,48:5; 1946, Mr 11,25:4
Miller, Guy P, 1950, Ag 18,21:4
Miller, H Clay, 1938, N 12,15:1

Miller, H Eugene, 1964, Ag 8,19:4
Miller, H Garver, 1964, My 27,39:4
Miller, H Gregory, 1953, S 27,87:2
Miller, Hannah, 1949, Jl 20,25:3
Miller, Hans J, 1955, F 15,27:4
Miller, Harlan, 1968, Ag 8,33:2
Miller, Harold A, 1953, N 25,23:3
Miller, Harold A Sr, 1952, S 24,33:5
Miller, Harold B, 1948, N 16,29:4
Miller, Harold F, 1956, Ja 30,27:2
Miller, Harold G, 1960, My 3,39:3
Miller, Harold L, 1938, N 23,21:4
Miller, Harold P, 1951, Je 12,29:2
Miller, Harold R, 1940, O 2,23:5; 1957, D 11,31:1
Miller, Harold S Rev Dr, 1968, Mr 19,47:2
Miller, Harry, 1945, Mr 8,23:4; 1954, Ja 26,27:3; 1956, Mr 24,19:5; 1958, Ja 4,15:6
Miller, Harry A, 1943, My 4,23:5; 1954, O 13,31:4
Miller, Harry B, 1949, Ag 18,21:4
Miller, Harry C, 1954, Mr 13,15:6
Miller, Harry E, 1952, Ap 13,76:4
Miller, Harry E Prof, 1937, N 15,23:4
Miller, Harry G, 1947, Ap 6,60:1; 1950, My 8,23:3
Miller, Harry H, 1947, O 18,15:2
Miller, Harry I Mrs, 1960, Ja 21,31:1
Miller, Harry K, 1957, Ap 11,31:4
Miller, Harry K Mrs, 1949, My 12,31:5
Miller, Harry L Mrs, 1942, My 12,19:1
Miller, Harry M, 1947, Ag 24,56:2; 1949, F 15,23:4
Miller, Harry Mrs, 1947, My 12,21:5
Miller, Harry N, 1959, O 9,21:3
Miller, Harry R, 1960, O 25,35:2
Miller, Harry S, 1937, S 19,6:7; 1944, Jl 5,17:3
Miller, Harry T, 1948, Jl 2,21:6; 1955, Ja 17,23:1
Miller, Harvey, 1954, F 27,13:2
Miller, Harvey A, 1952, S 15,25:3
Miller, Harvey H, 1950, My 20,15:4
Miller, Harvey L, 1941, Jl 18,19:4
Miller, Harvey Mrs, 1948, O 20,29:3
Miller, Heber J C, 1959, Ap 23,31:4
Miller, Helen T, 1960, F 5,27:2
Miller, Henry, 1901, Ag 3,7:6; 1912, F 12,11:5; 1926, Ap 10,1:4; 1948, F 14,13:3; 1949, My 12,31:5; 1956, Ap 23,27:5
Miller, Henry A, 1939, My 25,25:4; 1945, Jl 16,11:6
Miller, Henry C, 1940, My 8,23:4; 1944, F 29,17:1; 1952, Je 12,33:3
Miller, Henry C Mrs, 1937, Mr 2,21:1
Miller, Henry C Mrs (will), 1948, N 20,13:1
Miller, Henry D Jr, 1968, Jl 3,32:3
Miller, Henry D Sr, 1946, Jl 11,23:3
Miller, Henry E, 1944, Ja 11,19:4
Miller, Henry F, 1951, Ag 30,23:2
Miller, Henry H, 1965, My 11,39:4
Miller, Henry J, 1945, My 28,19:5; 1958, D 29,15:3; 1964, Je 10,45:3
Miller, Henry J Dr, 1968, Mr 3,88:8
Miller, Henry K, 1950, N 21,31:6
Miller, Henry L, 1952, D 29,19:1
Miller, Henry N, 1952, N 14,23:3
Miller, Henry P, 1940, Ja 6,13:2; 1948, My 21,23:4
Miller, Henry R, 1955, D 18,93:1
Miller, Henry S, 1948, N 29,23:3
Miller, Henry W, 1954, S 16,29:6; 1960, Je 23,29:2
Miller, Henry William, 1904, Ja 31,7:6
Miller, Herbert A, 1951, My 7,25:5
Miller, Herbert H, 1955, Je 3,23:5
Miller, Herbert J, 1966, N 22,41:3
Miller, Herbert M, 1955, My 12,29:5
Miller, Herbert Mrs, 1963, Ag 15,29:2
Miller, Herbert S, 1947, Ja 10,21:4; 1953, My 22,27:1
Miller, Herman, 1946, Je 27,21:4
Miller, Herman A, 1939, Jl 24,13:5
Miller, Herman D, 1967, Jl 5,39:7
Miller, Heyman R, 1952, Ag 25,17:2
Miller, Hilliard E, 1945, Ap 21,13:6
Miller, Hiram C, 1941, Jl 2,21:4
Miller, Hoffman, 1917, Ag 14,9:4
Miller, Hortense A Dr, 1903, N 13,9:7
Miller, Howard C, 1950, My 20,15:5
Miller, Howard M, 1937, D 28,21:3
Miller, Howard U, 1952, S 29,23:3
Miller, Howard V, 1948, D 30,19:4
Miller, Hoyt (cor, Ag 9,19:4; funl, Ag 10,15:5), 1957, Ag 8,23:1
Miller, Hubert F, 1951, Je 19,29:2
Miller, Hugh, 1871, Ap 29,2:6; 1941, O 15,21:3
Miller, Hugh G, 1962, Ag 3,23:1
Miller, Hugh R, 1942, D 16,25:5
Miller, Hugh S, 1945, D 26,19:3; 1950, My 28,44:4
Miller, Hugh T, 1947, My 28,25:2
Miller, I, 1929, Ag 14,23:5
Miller, Irvin, 1959, Ja 28,31:2
Miller, Irving, 1958, Mr 26,37:5
Miller, Irwin Mrs, 1951, Jl 8,61:1
Miller, Isabelle M Mrs, 1942, Mr 20,19:2
Miller, Isadore, 1957, D 17,35:2
Miller, Isadore Mrs, 1961, Mr 7,35:3
Miller, Isidore (cor, Ja 3,88:3), 1960, Ja 1,19:4
Miller, Israel Mrs, 1953, S 13,84:8
Miller, Israel S, 1954, My 22,15:5
Miller, Ivan, 1948, Je 1,23:4
Miller, Iver M, 1952, Je 17,27:3

Miller, J C, 1880, Jl 13,5:4
Miller, J Clare, 1962, Ja 5,29:1
Miller, J Edmund, 1944, Ja 29,13:2
Miller, J Edward Mrs, 1952, S 30,31:5
Miller, J F Sen, 1886, Mr 9,2:2
Miller, J Frank, 1950, F 20,25:4
Miller, J French, 1956, Ap 17,31:1
Miller, J Harold, 1954, Ja 14,29:3
Miller, J Herbert, 1954, Ja 19,25:3
Miller, J Hillis, 1953, N 15,88:4; 1955, Mr 20,57:2
Miller, J L (see also N 29), 1876, N 30,8:2
Miller, J Lane, 1954, Ja 4,19:3
Miller, J Leroy, 1964, Je 28,57:1
Miller, J M, 1939, Jl 7,17:3
Miller, J Paul, 1953, Jl 22,27:4
Miller, J Quinter Mrs, 1945, N 20,21:2
Miller, J Robert, 1942, My 17,47:4
Miller, J Smith, 1961, F 6,23:4
Miller, J Strother Jr, 1952, Ag 28,23:1
Miller, Jack B, 1953, Ag 29,17:6
Miller, Jackson, 1938, Ag 3,19:5
Miller, Jacob, 1952, S 26,21:1
Miller, Jacob F, 1906, D 13,9:4
Miller, Jacob G Mrs, 1951, O 11,37:2
Miller, Jacob J, 1949, O 21,25:4
Miller, Jacob K, 1951, Je 9,19:3
Miller, Jacob R, 1942, Ag 30,42:3
Miller, Jacob W Com, 1918, Mr 9,13:5
Miller, Jake, 1953, Ja 4,76:4
Miller, James, 1909, My 26,9:5; 1943, S 12,53:2; 1952, Ja 5,11:5; 1955, N 3,31:1
Miller, James A, 1940, Ag 12,15:5; 1948, Jl 30,17:6
Miller, James Alexander Mrs, 1968, Mr 26,45:2
Miller, James B, 1944, O 1,45:2; 1951, My 19,15:6
Miller, James Brig-Gen, 1916, D 14,15:5
Miller, James C, 1940, O 3,25:6; 1956, N 18,89:1
Miller, James D Mrs, 1956, S 7,23:2
Miller, James E, 1947, Ag 11,23:5; 1963, Ap 8,47:3
Miller, James G, 1941, Jl 31,17:4; 1950, S 13,28:2; 1954, Mr 26,21:1
Miller, James H, 1948, Ag 16,19:4; 1962, Jl 21,19:5
Miller, James I, 1964, D 23,30:2
Miller, James K, 1953, O 24,15:5
Miller, James L, 1925, Jl 4,11:5; 1945, S 14,23:1
Miller, James M, 1939, Ag 20,33:3
Miller, James M Rear-Adm, 1908, N 12,9:5
Miller, James Mrs, 1968, O 17,47:2
Miller, James P, 1959, F 2,25:2
Miller, James P Sir, 1906, Ja 22,7:6
Miller, James R Mrs, 1949, F 24,24:3
Miller, James Sr, 1953, Ja 17,15:3
Miller, James Sr Mrs, 1953, Ja 17,15:3
Miller, James W, 1937, Je 29,21:3; 1953, Je 26,19:5
Miller, Janice, 1953, Ag 13,15:8
Miller, Jasper, 1948, Ag 4,21:2
Miller, Jay, 1947, Mr 24,25:2
Miller, Jay E, 1943, D 22,23:2
Miller, Jean, 1956, My 25,23:4
Miller, Jennie C Mrs, 1914, Je 17,11:4
Miller, Jesse I, 1949, N 10,31:2
Miller, Joaquin, 1913, F 18,13:5
Miller, Joe, 1958, Mr 7,24:1
Miller, Joe D, 1941, Je 22,32:6
Miller, Joe J, 1948, Je 2,29:2
Miller, John, 1919, Ag 30,7:6; 1946, O 23,27:1; 1948, Ag 23,17:5; 1949, Jl 9,13:1; 1951, Ja 16,29:4; 1951, F 27,27:4; 1956, O 11,39:1; 1964, S 5,19:5
Miller, John A, 1942, Ja 19,20:1; 1946, Je 17,21:4; 1956, Jl 26,25:4; 1959, Ag 25,31:2; 1961, Ap 13,35:2; 1964, F 27,31:3
Miller, John B, 1908, N 12,9:4; 1944, Ag 30,17:5; 1947, F 1,15:2; 1947, Ap 9,25:1
Miller, John Bleecker (funl, Je 15,19:6), 1922, Je 13, 19:6
Miller, John C, 1948, O 4,23:6; 1951, O 10,23:5
Miller, John D, 1941, F 20,19:5
Miller, John D (por), 1946, N 28,27:1
Miller, John D Mrs, 1948, My 2,76:3
Miller, John E, 1943, Je 19,13:7; 1945, Ag 25,11:4; 1960, N 10,47:1
Miller, John E (Bing), 1964, O 13,43:1
Miller, John E Sr Mrs, 1955, D 30,19:4
Miller, John Ex-Gov, 1908, O 27,9:6
Miller, John F, 1939, My 25,25:4
Miller, John F (will, S 24,12:3), 1939, S 18,19:1
Miller, John F G, 1939, D 10,69:2
Miller, John Ford, 1916, Mr 20,11:3
Miller, John G, 1938, Je 26,27:2
Miller, John G Mrs, 1944, N 9,27:5
Miller, John H, 1910, Ap 25,9:6; 1917, S 10,13:5; 1940, Jl 19,19:5; 1943, D 1,21:2; 1951, Ap 5,29:3; 1956, Mr 3,19:4
Miller, John J, 1937, Je 21,19:4; 1948, Je 24,26:2; 1950, F 14,25:4
Miller, John J Mrs, 1950, D 13,35:1
Miller, John L, 1943, Jl 23,17:1; 1946, My 25,15:3; 1965, Ag 2,29:4
Miller, John M, 1938, S 23,27:1; 1944, D 27,19:3; 1950, F 22,29:3; 1962, My 19,27:2
Miller, John M Jr, 1948, O 10,76:2
Miller, John Morris Mrs, 1968, Mr 28,47:3
Miller, John Mrs, 1943, Ja 8,19:5; 1948, O 28,30:2
Miller, John Mrs (Kath), 1964, Ap 10,35:3

Miller, John O Mrs, 1962, Jl 1,56:3
Miller, John P, 1945, Mr 16,15:3
Miller, John R, 1945, Mr 16,15:4; 1945, Jl 5,13:5; 1955, Ap 29,23:2
Miller, John R Jr, 1966, Ja 9,56:5
Miller, John S, 1922, F 17,15:5; 1965, O 27,47:4
Miller, John S Mrs, 1949, Ap 19,25:4
Miller, John T, 1941, Je 30,17:3
Miller, John V (por), 1940, Ag 17,15:3
Miller, John V Mrs, 1943, Jl 20,19:2
Miller, John V W, 1949, Ja 26,25:4
Miller, John V W Mrs, 1946, Mr 21,25:2
Miller, John W, 1938, O 30,40:7
Miller, John W (por), 1949, Mr 5,17:5
Miller, John W, 1959, N 26,37:4
Miller, John Z, 1958, O 5,86:7
Miller, Jonas S, 1942, My 12,19:3
Miller, Jonathan M, 1912, Jl 15,9:6
Miller, Joseph, 1938, S 28,25:4; 1951, Ja 25,25:4; 1 S 11,21:4; 1965, F 23,33:2; 1967, Je 19,35:1
Miller, Joseph Baynes, 1874, Jl 24,5:2
Miller, Joseph C, 1949, D 30,19:2; 1950, Ja 1,42:4
Miller, Joseph D, 1939, My 9,23:3
Miller, Joseph E, 1951, D 28,21:5
Miller, Joseph H, 1955, Ja 4,21:4
Miller, Joseph L, 1939, Ag 20,32:5; 1951, Mr 9,25:
Miller, Joseph L Dr, 1937, Ag 8,II,6:8
Miller, Joseph Mrs, 1943, Je 30,21:4; 1950, Je 3,1 1951, Je 15,23:1; 1966, N 26,36:8
Miller, Joseph Nelson Rear-Adm, 1909, Ap 27,11:
Miller, Joseph P, 1946, N 7,31:4
Miller, Joseph R, 1951, O 21,92:4
Miller, Joseph S, 1942, N 30,23:4; 1959, Ja 18,88:
Miller, Joseph W Mrs, 1941, Ap 11,21:3
Miller, Joshua, 1956, Ja 27,23:3
Miller, Jotham E, 1950, Jl 19,31:3
Miller, Judson J, 1950, Ja 6,22:4
Miller, Julian S, 1946, Jl 29,21:4
Miller, Julius, 1950, F 12,84:2
Miller, Julius (funl plans, F 5,15:3; funl, F 7,21:4), 1955, F 4,21:3
Miller, Julius, 1968, Ap 30,47:1
Miller, K B, 1933, N 24,22:1
Miller, Karl P, 1965, O 26,45:4
Miller, Kelly, 1939, D 30,15:5
Miller, Kelton B, 1941, D 3,26:2
Miller, Kelton B Mrs, 1953, Jl 1,29:3
Miller, Kenneth Dexter Rev Dr, 1968, Jl 7,52:6
Miller, Kenneth H, 1952, Ja 3,27:1
Miller, Kenneth R, 1960, O 25,35:2
Miller, L E, 1927, My 23,21:1
Miller, L H (will), 1939, F 23,13:6
Miller, L W, 1880, My 2,5:4
Miller, Landes F, 1950, Je 14,31:2
Miller, Lawrence S, 1945, Mr 21,23:2
Miller, Lee G, 1961, F 19,86:8
Miller, Lee P, 1962, N 26,29:4
Miller, Lee R, 1941, S 29,17:6
Miller, Leo, 1951, Mr 13,31:4
Miller, Leo E, 1952, O 7,29:1
Miller, Leo T, 1962, Ap 5,33:2
Miller, Leon A, 1961, Ag 14,25:2
Miller, Leon L Mrs, 1949, Je 7,31:3
Miller, Leon Mrs, 1966, Mr 14,31:4
Miller, Leonard, 1955, Ap 11,23:5
Miller, Leonard W, 1966, Ap 2,29:2
Miller, Leonidas G, 1943, Ap 30,21:3
Miller, Leroy, 1952, D 30,19:1
Miller, Leroy Mrs, 1946, Ja 12,15:4
Miller, Lester S, 1946, S 8,44:7
Miller, Lewis, 1909, Ap 3,9:5; 1950, O 3,23:1
Miller, Lewis H, 1963, Ap 9,31:1
Miller, Lewis K, 1942, My 23,13:5
Miller, Lewis Mrs, 1912, O 21,11:5
Miller, Lida W Mrs, 1939, N 24,23:2
Miller, Lingard, 1949, Ap 14,25:6
Miller, Linwood A, 1953, Ag 4,21:3
Miller, Logan C, 1958, F 28,21:4
Miller, Loren, 1967, Jl 16,64:7
Miller, Louis, 1938, Ja 3,22:1; 1939, F 12,45:3; Ag 31,13:4; 1944, Ap 6,23:3; 1946, S 27,23:4; F 15,39:1
Miller, Louis D, 1947, Jl 13,44:1
Miller, Louis F, 1937, Ap 1,23:3
Miller, Louis H, 1963, S 4,39:2
Miller, Louis L, 1937, N 26,21:5
Miller, Louis M Rev Dr, 1909, S 11,9:4
Miller, Louis Mrs, 1937, N 16,23:5
Miller, Louis P, 1949, D 4,108:8; 1952, Ja 31,2
Miller, Louis R, 1951, N 27,31:3
Miller, Louise S, 1948, N 14,76:2
Miller, Lucille F, 1947, S 11,27:4
Miller, Lucius H, 1949, F 2,28:2
Miller, Luther H, 1940, N 17,50:8
Miller, Lyman Mrs, 1945, O 12,23:4
Miller, Lynn H, 1962, Ag 28,31:2
Miller, Lynn S, 1962, Ja 28,76:8
Miller, M, 1936, Ap 8,23:4
Miller, M O Mrs (Faith Latimer), 1903, My
Miller, M Valentine, 1963, N 19,41:2
Miller, Manasseh (por), 1938, Mr 11,19:3
Miller, Marcus P Gen, 1906, D 31,7:5
Miller, Marcus P Mrs, 1925, Ag 28,13:4

Miller, Margaret, 1942, F 10,20:3
Miller, Mark, 1963, N 29,34:6
Miller, Martha, 1943, F 1,15:1
Miller, Martha T, 1923, O 24,19:5
Miller, Martin G, 1962, O 2,39:1
Miller, Martin O, 1961, N 18,23:4
Miller, Mary, 1953, Jl 3,19:5
Miller, Mary A, 1962, O 25,39:5
Miller, Mary A H Mrs, 1942, N 6,23:3
Miller, Mary E Mrs, 1955, Je 1,33:3
Miller, Mary Mrs, 1909, Mr 15,9:3; 1949, S 17,17:4
Miller, Mary W Mrs (will), 1964, Ag 8,16:6
Miller, Matthew F Mrs, 1944, N 7,27:4
Miller, Matthias, 1948, Ja 27,25:3
Miller, Matthias Mrs, 1950, My 12,27:1
Miller, Maurice, 1963, D 15,87:1
Miller, Maurice B, 1959, Jl 16,27:5
Miller, Max, 1910, Jl 21,7:4; 1967, D 28,32:3
Miller, Max B, 1951, Ap 1,92:7
Miller, Max C, 1949, Mr 1,25:5
Miller, Maximilian, 1962, N 6,33:3
Miller, Maxine A, 1960, Ag 14,55:4
Miller, Maxwell V, 1951, Ag 29,25:5
Miller, Mayer, 1962, S 28,33:2
Miller, McGowan, 1941, Ap 15,1:3
Miller, McNaughton, 1943, D 5,66:4
Miller, Melvin, 1944, Ja 19,19:3
Miller, Melvin J, 1941, N 11,23:6
Miller, Merton L, 1953, Ja 29,27:4
Miller, Michael A, 1960, D 3,23:1
Miller, Mills, 1960, N 7,35:4
Miller, Milo G Jr, 1938, F 26,15:5
Miller, Milton A, 1950, Ja 19,27:3
Miller, Milton G, 1964, Ja 16,25:2
Miller, Milton P, 1955, Ja 26,25:1
Miller, Milton R, 1959, O 14,43:2
Miller, Minetta Mrs, 1941, Je 17,21:5
Miller, Morris, 1918, My 23,13:5; 1946, Je 10,21:3; 1954, O 6,25:2
Miller, Morris Booth, 1924, N 6,19:4
Miller, Morris M, 1955, My 21,17:3
Miller, Morris Mrs, 1949, Mr 25,23:4
Miller, Morris S Gen, 1870, Mr 13,4:7
Miller, Morrow C, 1965, S 7,39:4
Miller, Mortimer R, 1938, F 7,15:4
Miller, Morton B, 1951, Jl 26,21:3
Miller, Murray H, 1968, Je 6,48:1
Miller, Myer, 1961, F 16,31:4
Miller, Myron D, 1959, N 26,37:4
Miller, Myron V, 1961, N 29,41:2
Miller, Nancy, 1966, F 28,27:3
Miller, Nancy Dr, 1915, Mr 18,11:6
Miller, Nathan, 1955, My 5,33:5
Miller, Nathan A, 1941, Jl 24,17:5
Miller, Nathan L, 1953, Je 27,1:1
Miller, Nathan L Mrs, 1959, Jl 12,73:1
Miller, Neville D, 1950, D 21,29:5
Miller, Nicholas E, 1951, Mr 25,72:3
Miller, Nicholas P, 1955, Jl 1,21:1
Miller, Nicolai, 1961, Ag 17,27:2
Miller, Norman A, 1968, My 30,25:3
Miller, Norman M, 1946, My 22,21:3
Miller, O R Mrs, 1937, F 9,23:3
Miller, Oakley, 1952, Je 11,29:2
Miller, Oliver Jr, 1943, Je 13,44:6
Miller, Orlando A, 1949, Ja 25,23:1
Miller, Orlando E, 1947, Ap 8,27:3
Miller, Ormal, 1948, Je 7,19:5
Miller, Oscar (Jan 7), 1963, Ap 1,36:2
Miller, Oscar G, 1951, Jl 9,25:5
Miller, Oswald Otto Capt, 1912, N 20,15:6
Miller, Otis L, 1959, Jl 27,25:2
Miller, Otto L, 1962, Mr 30,23:4
Miller, Otto M Mrs, 1947, N 4,25:5
Miller, P, 1945, S 5,23:1
Miller, P Compton, 1942, D 16,25:3
Miller, P Compton Mrs, 1959, Mr 3,33:4
Miller, Paul, 1945, D 1,23:4
Miller, Paul B, 1949, Jl 8,19:1
Miller, Paul D, 1965, F 17,43:1
Miller, Paul E, 1954, O 22,27:2
Miller, Paul G, 1952, My 22,27:1
Miller, Paul H, 1949, Ag 13,11:6
Miller, Paul R, 1953, S 5,15:3
Miller, Percey E, 1958, Ja 28,27:3
Miller, Percival, 1955, Mr 5,17:2
Miller, Percival W Mrs, 1945, O 15,17:4
Miller, Percy C, 1955, Je 25,15:5
Miller, Percy W, 1952, Ap 3,35:4
Miller, Perry G E (trb lr, D 14,26:4), 1963, D 10,43:1
Miller, Persis K, 1941, S 3,23:5
Miller, Peter, 1954, Mr 9,27:2
Miller, Peter W, 1957, Mr 10,89:1
Miller, Phil, 1954, D 30,17:4
Miller, Phil Mrs, 1950, S 22,31:1
Miller, Phil N, 1937, My 29,17:2
Miller, Phil R, 1950, D 24,35:1
Miller, Phil S, 1955, Je 9,29:5
Miller, Philip, 1947, Ag 28,23:5
Miller, Philip L, 1945, N 4,44:3
Miller, Philip L Mrs, 1966, Je 8,47:2
Miller, Philippus W, 1941, F 5,19:4
Miller, Pitser, 1966, S 6,48:1
Miller, Pitser Jr Mrs, 1960, Jl 26,29:2
Miller, Porter W, 1947, Ja 18,15:5
Miller, R Bruce, 1952, D 27,9:2
Miller, R Paul, 1962, Ap 20,27:1
Miller, R T Jr, 1958, Jl 29,23:4
Miller, Rachel A, 1946, N 8,23:3; 1949, Ap 4,23:2
Miller, Ralph, 1903, Ag 14,7:7; 1939, Mr 19,III,7:1; 1959, Ap 10,29:1
Miller, Ralph C (por), 1945, D 12,27:3
Miller, Ralph D, 1945, D 17,21:5
Miller, Ralph E, 1945, Ag 3,17:3; 1948, D 15,34:3; 1959, My 7,17:1
Miller, Ralph F, 1949, N 3,3:1
Miller, Ralph F Mrs, 1949, N 3,3:1
Miller, Ralph M, 1958, F 25,27:4
Miller, Raphael H, 1963, My 17,33:2
Miller, Ray, 1961, Je 30,25:3
Miller, Ray E, 1954, N 18,33:3
Miller, Ray Mrs, 1968, O 25,47:4
Miller, Ray S, 1961, Je 2,32:8
Miller, Ray T Sr, 1966, Jl 14,35:1
Miller, Raymond, 1945, Ag 29,23:4
Miller, Raymond G, 1949, O 21,25:3
Miller, Raymond O, 1940, D 31,15:3
Miller, Raymond Van V, 1967, N 9,47:2
Miller, Reed, 1923, D 30,20:1
Miller, Reed (funl), 1924, Ja 1,23:1
Miller, Reuben, 1917, Mr 15,11:5
Miller, Rheua Mrs, 1908, Mr 10,7:5
Miller, Richard C, 1963, S 9,27:2
Miller, Richard E, 1943, Ja 24,44:1
Miller, Richard H, 1952, Je 4,27:3
Miller, Richard R, 1960, O 26,39:3
Miller, Robert, 1946, Je 21,23:5
Miller, Robert (Moose), 1956, N 21,27:5
Miller, Robert B, 1968, Je 1,27:5
Miller, Robert C, 1954, Jl 25,69:1; 1959, Ja 21,31:3
Miller, Robert E, 1942, Ag 30,43:3; 1945, Mr 15,23:1
Miller, Robert F, 1943, Je 27,32:2
Miller, Robert J, 1959, O 16,31:2; 1964, S 13,86:6
Miller, Robert K, 1964, Ag 17,25:5
Miller, Robert M, 1951, F 21,27:3; 1966, D 30,25:5
Miller, Robert Mrs, 1954, D 25,11:6
Miller, Robert N, 1968, Ja 2,41:3
Miller, Robert S, 1950, Ag 31,25:2
Miller, Robert T, 1914, Ap 24,13:4; 1962, My 1,37:4
Miller, Robert W, 1940, Ag 7,19:5; 1947, O 9,25:3; 1954, D 11,13:3
Miller, Roland E, 1957, Ja 22,29:1
Miller, Roland H, 1937, My 5,25:2
Miller, Rome, 1941, F 22,15:1
Miller, Roswell D, 1949, My 11,29:6
Miller, Roswell Sr Mrs, 1955, D 26,19:2
Miller, Roy, 1946, Ap 29,21:4; 1952, My 16,23:2
Miller, Rudolph, 1944, My 9,19:1
Miller, Rudolph N Mrs, 1948, Jl 17,16:8
Miller, Rudolph P, 1947, Ja 19,53:3
Miller, Rudolph P Mrs, 1944, Je 23,19:4
Miller, Rufus E, 1949, Ag 6,17:1
Miller, Rufus W Rev, 1925, O 12,21:3
Miller, Russell G, 1954, Jl 23,17:6
Miller, Russell K, 1939, My 4,23:2
Miller, Rutger B, 1947, Ap 15,25:4
Miller, S D Mrs, 1943, Ja 21,21:4
Miller, S Eugene, 1942, F 7,17:5
Miller, S F Justice, 1890, O 14,1:3
Miller, S Fisher, 1939, S 5,23:4
Miller, S Gale, 1951, Je 22,25:5
Miller, S S, 1938, Ja 30,II,8:7
Miller, Samuel, 1902, Je 9,9:3; 1946, Ag 7,27:5; 1950, Je 26,27:3; 1962, My 18,31:1; 1965, Ap 30,35:5
Miller, Samuel C, 1954, Ja 8,22:3; 1958, F 9,88:3
Miller, Samuel D, 1939, S 8,23:4
Miller, Samuel E, 1960, Je 11,21:6
Miller, Samuel H, 1937, Ag 5,23:4; 1953, N 10,31:4
Miller, Samuel H Rev Dr, 1968, Mr 21,53:1
Miller, Samuel J, 1943, N 11,23:3
Miller, Samuel J Sr, 1944, F 3,19:4
Miller, Samuel J Sr Mrs, 1948, Mr 9,23:1
Miller, Samuel L, 1957, Ag 9,19:3
Miller, Samuel Mrs, 1951, S 6,31:3
Miller, Samuel O, 1942, Mr 28,17:6
Miller, Samuel W, 1940, Ap 23,23:2; 1949, O 4,27:3
Miller, Sarah M, 1960, Ag 6,19:6
Miller, Sarah Mrs, 1923, O 26,17:4
Miller, Seaman, 1939, Jl 16,30:8
Miller, Seward A, 1953, Ja 2,15:2
Miller, Shackelford Jr, 1965, N 26,37:2
Miller, Sherman (por), 1949, S 26,25:3
Miller, Sherman R 3d, 1968, Ja 26,47:3
Miller, Sidney L, 1957, N 10,86:5
Miller, Sidney T, 1940, My 20,17:2
Miller, Simon, 1944, Jl 28,13:4; 1945, Ag 13,19:2
Miller, Solomon J, 1966, O 18,45:2
Miller, Spencer Jr Dr, 1968, N 7,47:2
Miller, Spencer Jr Mrs, 1955, S 9,23:4; 1957, O 3,29:4
Miller, Spencer Sr, 1953, Je 18,29:3
Miller, Stanley, 1950, Ja 2,23:4
Miller, Stanley Mrs, 1960, My 9,29:2
Miller, Staunton M, 1941, O 12,52:1
Miller, Stephen, 1947, D 3,29:4
Miller, Stewart W, 1962, Ja 31,31:3
Miller, Sydney Mrs, 1923, D 5,19:4
Miller, Sydney R, 1949, My 26,29:4
Miller, T Gordon, 1942, Ag 24,15:3
Miller, T H Mrs, 1941, My 7,25:6
Miller, T H Rev, 1870, Mr 31,2:5
Miller, T J Capt, 1903, Mr 29,8:4
Miller, Theodora, 1920, Ag 9,9:1
Miller, Theodore Frelinghuysen, 1913, My 20,11:5
Miller, Theodore G (por), 1946, N 30,15:1
Miller, Theodore J, 1903, D 7,1:7; 1959, D 8,45:4
Miller, Theodore J Mrs, 1942, N 3,23:4
Miller, Theodore L, 1948, Ag 12,22:2
Miller, Theodore S Jr, 1958, Jl 29,23:5
Miller, Thomas, 1945, Je 21,19:5; 1952, Ag 11,15:4
Miller, Thomas B, 1951, N 5,31:5
Miller, Thomas C, 1947, Je 12,25:3
Miller, Thomas D, 1954, Jl 22,23:3
Miller, Thomas D Jr, 1944, Mr 14,19:3
Miller, Thomas E, 1938, Ap 10,II,7:2
Miller, Thomas E (por), 1948, S 23,29:2
Miller, Thomas F, 1939, F 14,19:4
Miller, Thomas I, 1948, My 30,34:4
Miller, Thomas I Mrs, 1950, S 8,31:1
Miller, Thomas N, 1911, D 17,II,13:4
Miller, Thomas S Mrs, 1951, Ap 26,29:3
Miller, Thomas Sr, 1949, D 10,17:4
Miller, Thomas W, 1945, Ag 30,21:2
Miller, Thomas W Mrs, 1945, Ap 27,19:4
Miller, Tobias F, 1950, F 9,29:2
Miller, Tom Mrs (funl), 1963, D 31,7:1
Miller, Towne L, 1946, My 28,21:2
Miller, Trelford S, 1948, D 25,17:4
Miller, Troup, 1957, Ja 29,31:1
Miller, Valentine F, 1956, Ap 10,31:4
Miller, Verne E, 1943, Mr 3,23:1
Miller, Vernon J, 1939, D 7,27:2
Miller, Victor B Mrs, 1946, S 5,27:5
Miller, Victor G, 1951, My 27,68:5
Miller, Victor J, 1955, Ja 7,22:2
Miller, Virgil R Col, 1968, Ap 8,33:1
Miller, Virgil W, 1940, D 5,25:3
Miller, W B, 1884, Mr 27,4:6
Miller, W F, 1881, Jl 29,5:1; 1883, Ja 15,5:4
Miller, W H, 1880, My 22,5:3; 1882, Mr 11,5:3
Miller, Wallace H, 1938, S 8,23:3
Miller, Wallace J, 1951, N 24,11:4
Miller, Walter, 1949, Ap 27,27:6; 1949, Je 10,27:5; 1949, Jl 29,22:2; 1950, Mr 2,27:2
Miller, Walter A, 1950, My 21,107:3
Miller, Walter A Jr, 1956, O 3,33:4
Miller, Walter D, 1951, N 10,17:6
Miller, Walter E, 1945, Ap 4,21:3; 1962, Jl 26,27:5
Miller, Walter G, 1940, My 11,19:2
Miller, Walter H, 1941, My 27,23:6; 1947, Je 5,25:4
Miller, Walter J, 1957, Ap 1,25:5; 1959, Mr 24,39:1
Miller, Walter L, 1942, S 15,23:5
Miller, Walter M, 1947, Ja 3,21:2
Miller, Walter Mrs, 1949, Je 23,27:1
Miller, Walter R C, 1955, D 28,23:3
Miller, Walter S, 1956, S 19,37:1
Miller, Waltron J, 1911, D 25,7:5
Miller, Ward A, 1945, Mr 31,19:5
Miller, Warner Ex-Sen, 1918, Mr 22,13:3
Miller, Warner Mrs, 1903, Ja 16,9:7
Miller, Warren, 1966, Ap 21,39:3
Miller, Warren H, 1960, Jl 15,23:4
Miller, Warren J, 1946, Ja 17,23:1
Miller, Warren V, 1947, Je 23,23:3
Miller, Watson B, 1961, F 12,86:1
Miller, Wentworth E, 1957, Ap 12,25:2
Miller, Westley T, 1964, Ap 22,47:1
Miller, Wilbur C Mrs, 1952, Ja 21,16:2
Miller, Wilbur G, 1950, S 25,23:1
Miller, Willard W, 1946, F 11,29:5
Miller, Willard W Mrs, 1957, Ap 12,25:3
Miller, Willet G Dr, 1925, F 5,19:4
Miller, William, 1915, Je 18,11:6; 1939, Mr 13,17:4; 1940, My 26,34:2; 1941, F 23,41:3; 1946, Ja 9,23:2; 1947, O 29,27:3; 1953, S 14,27:4; 1953, N 24,29:2; 1960, Je 4,23:4
Miller, William A, 1944, F 17,19:4; 1949, O 8,13:6; 1950, F 1,29:2; 1953, My 5,29:5; 1958, S 29,27:4; 1962, Jl 17,25:3
Miller, William B, 1944, Jl 14,13:3; 1944, Jl 29,13:3; 1950, Ja 9,25:5
Miller, William B M, 1947, O 25,19:5
Miller, William B Mrs, 1942, N 17,25:3
Miller, William C, 1939, Je 17,15:3; 1939, O 6,25:5; 1950, My 19,27:1; 1967, Ap 2,54:2
Miller, William C Dr, 1937, Mr 17,25:5
Miller, William D, 1964, O 2,37:1
Miller, William De Witt Maj, 1914, Je 30,11:6
Miller, William E, 1941, My 18,45:3; 1941, O 23,23:4; 1946, D 1,78:4; 1953, S 17,29:2; 1963, Jl 29,41:1
Miller, William F, 1939, D 19,26:3; 1944, Ap 19,23:3
Miller, William G, 1948, My 29,15:4
Miller, William H, 1938, Ap 22,19:1; 1938, O 26,23:4; 1944, S 19,15:5; 1945, Ap 25,23:2; 1950, Mr 13,21:1; 1958, Je 22,77:1; 1960, Ag 13,15:4; 1963, D 19,33:1
Miller, William H H, 1917, My 26,13:4; 1940, Ap 12, 23:1
Miller, William H Mrs, 1950, My 23,29:2
Miller, William H Rev, 1914, S 15,11:6; 1925, F 23, 17:6

Miller, William J, 1937, N 13,23:4; 1939, N 14,23:5; 1944, S 30,13:4; 1950, N 23,35:1
Miller, William J Jr, 1967, Ap 28,41:3
Miller, William L, 1940, S 2,15:5
Miller, William M, 1956, O 4,33:3; 1967, Je 16,43:1
Miller, William Mrs, 1944, D 30,11:6; 1964, N 11,48:5
Miller, William N, 1913, Ja 10,11:4
Miller, William R, 1958, N 19,37:5
Miller, William S, 1939, O 5,23:3; 1939, D 28,21:5; 1948, O 10,76:3; 1953, Jl 28,19:3
Miller, William T, 1944, My 15,19:4
Miller, William W, 1919, My 30,9:6; 1940, Jl 17,21:5; 1954, Mr 20,15:6; 1962, Mr 10,22:1
Miller, Willis D, 1960, D 21,31:4
Miller, Worthington L, 1949, O 26,27:2
Miller, Zachariah Taylor, 1913, N 15,11:7
Miller, Zack T, 1952, Ja 4,40:2
Miller-Jones, Henry A, 1962, Ag 25,22:2
Millerand, Alexandre E, 1943, Ap 7,25:1
Millerand, Alexandre Mrs, 1950, O 26,31:4
Millerd, George H Jr, 1949, N 19,17:4
Millers, Edward W, 1939, F 8,23:5
Milles, Carl, 1955, S 20,31:2
Milles, Lewis A, 1941, Ja 21,21:4
Milles, Solomon Rabbi, 1924, S 8,15:5
Millet, Arthur, 1943, Ap 9,21:3
Millet, Francois Mrs, 1945, F 26,19:5
Millet, Gardner W Mrs, 1966, Ag 22,33:5
Millet, Jean Francois, 1917, Ap 21,13:6
Millet, Josiah B (cor, Je 11,15:5), 1938, Ja 28,21:1
Millet, Laurence, 1945, D 10,21:3
Millet, Luis (lr), 1942, Ap 19,VIII,6:6
Millet, Philippe, 1923, O 26,17:4
Millet, Rene, 1919, D 2,13:2
Millett, Gardner W, 1947, D 23,23:4
Millett, George V, 1955, N 10,35:4
Millett, Harry H, 1950, Ap 25,31:2
Millett, Joseph, 1966, S 14,47:1
Millett, Ralph L, 1954, N 25,29:2
Millett, William F, 1967, Ag 21,31:4
Milley, Herbert Mrs, 1963, D 24,17:4
Millham, Jesse B, 1949, Mr 2,26:2
Millham, Lewis F, 1956, Jl 28,17:6
Millhau, E L, 1903, My 27,9:3
Millhauser, Arthur W, 1937, S 3,17:2
Millhauser, Bertram, 1958, D 4,39:1
Millhauser, De Witt (por), 1946, Ap 15,27:3
Millhiser, Clarence, 1919, My 22,15:6
Millhiser, Clarence Mrs, 1965, Mr 26,35:5
Millhiser, Emanuel Mrs, 1953, S 1,23:4
Millholland, Raymond, 1956, My 3,31:1
Millholland, William K, 1948, F 4,23:4
Millhouse, Frederick, 1938, D 14,25:6
Millian, John C, 1953, Jl 9,25:3
Milliard, Ferdinand J, 1950, S 2,15:6
Millican, Harry N, 1963, O 2,41:3
Millican, James, 1955, N 25,27:1
Milligan, A F C Capt, 1919, Ag 6,9:2
Milligan, Carl G, 1941, Je 19,21:5
Milligan, Caroline A Mrs, 1937, Ja 31,II,8:3
Milligan, Charles C, 1954, S 15,33:3
Milligan, Edward, 1937, My 2,II,9:1
Milligan, Frederick G, 1942, N 13,23:5
Milligan, George, 1946, Je 15,21:4
Milligan, George H, 1950, N 29,33:3
Milligan, George Seaton, 1914, Je 19,13:6
Milligan, Grace L B, 1952, N 2,88:1
Milligan, Harold V, 1951, Ap 14,15:3
Milligan, Harold V Mrs, 1967, Ag 31,33:3
Milligan, Henry C, 1940, Mr 9,15:5
Milligan, Jacob L, 1951, Mr 11,92:7
Milligan, James, 1961, N 29,41:1
Milligan, Jane Mrs, 1947, My 25,60:2
Milligan, John D, 1953, Ja 17,15:5
Milligan, John H, 1943, Jl 12,15:2
Milligan, John J, 1959, Ag 23,92:5
Milligan, John R, 1959, N 19,39:4
Milligan, John R Mrs, 1938, N 11,25:3
Milligan, Josephine, 1946, Ag 29,27:3
Milligan, Lee B, 1947, Ap 19,15:5
Milligan, Margaret R, 1951, S 24,27:2
Milligan, Maurice M, 1959, Je 17,35:4
Milligan, Peter J, 1946, Mr 30,15:6
Milligan, Robert F, 1937, S 11,17:5
Milligan, Robert W, 1953, S 14,27:2
Milligan, Samuel, 1965, Ag 9,25:3
Milligan, Samuel C, 1947, Ja 6,23:2
Milligan, Samuel Judge, 1874, Ap 21,1:4
Milligan, Sidney J, 1956, N 19,31:2
Milligan, Stephen W, 1941, Ja 31,19:1
Milligan, Thomas H, 1942, O 15,23:5
Milligan, William, 1916, Je 28,11:3; 1947, Ag 16,13:1; 1957, Je 18,29:3
Milligan, William G, 1904, Ja 10,7:6
Milligan, William J, 1943, N 28,68:3
Millikan, Charles E, 1949, Je 29,28:2
Millikan, Clark B, 1966, Ja 3,27:1
Millikan, Mervyn M, 1955, Mr 5,17:5
Millikan, Michael F, 1940, N 24,49:2
Millikan, Robert A, 1953, D 20,1:4
Millikan, Robert A Mrs (will, N 3,29:7), 1953, O 11, 89:1
Millikan, Robert S, 1951, D 31,13:3

Milliken, Arnold W, 1964, N 27,35:1
Milliken, Carl E, 1961, My 2,37:3
Milliken, Charles H, 1909, F 14,11:5
Milliken, Charles N Mrs, 1949, Je 12,76:5
Milliken, Charles S Mrs, 1939, Ja 29,33:2
Milliken, Cornelius J, 1956, Ja 9,25:4
Milliken, Earle, 1955, F 14,19:4
Milliken, Edward Fullerton, 1906, N 11,9:6
Milliken, Edwin H, 1952, Ja 21,15:2
Milliken, Elias Col, 1902, Je 19,9:6
Milliken, Gerrish H, 1947, Je 12,27:6
Milliken, Harry N Mrs, 1924, D 13,15:3
Milliken, Henry O, 1945, Ag 7,23:4
Milliken, Hugh K, 1952, N 7,23:3
Milliken, J E, 1884, Mr 8,4:7
Milliken, James Foster Col, 1917, S 27,13:5
Milliken, James M, 1941, Ap 4,21:2
Milliken, James W, 1908, Je 20,9:6
Milliken, John F (por), 1938, S 19,19:3
Milliken, John T, 1919, F 1,13:4
Milliken, Joseph K, 1961, My 28,64:3
Milliken, Nathan T, 1953, Ag 10,23:4
Milliken, Norman I, 1948, My 5,25:1
Milliken, Peter H, 1940, O 2,23:5
Milliken, Richard P, 1954, S 10,23:2
Milliken, Robert M, 1947, D 25,21:5
Milliken, Roy S, 1951, Ja 20,15:2
Milliken, Samuel H, 1915, My 22,11:4
Milliken, Seth M, 1957, N 19,33:1
Milliken, Seth Mellen, 1920, Mr 6,11:6
Milliken, Stanley T, 1954, F 19,27:4
Milliken, William H, 1942, Ja 13,19:1
Millikin, Benjamin L Mrs, 1950, Ag 20,77:1
Millikin, Charles H, 1945, O 8,15:5
Millikin, Eugene D (funl plans, Jl 28,23:1; trb, Jl 29,23:2), 1958, Jl 27,61:1
Milliman, Elmer E, 1947, Ja 2,28:3
Milliman, Henry J, 1955, F 26,15:5
Milliman, Susan, 1941, Ag 14,17:5
Milliman, William H, 1940, D 23,19:4
Millin, Phil, 1952, Ap 16,27:5
Millin, Raymond J, 1956, S 30,87:1
Millin, Sarah Gertrude (Mrs Philip), 1968, Jl 12,31:2
Millinder, Lucky (Lucius), 1966, S 30,47:1
Milling, Thomas D, 1960, N 27,86:4
Millingen, Lord Byron's Dr, 1878, D 26,6:1
Millinger, Henry, 1925, Ja 19,17:5
Millington, Charles S, 1913, O 26,15:5
Millington, Ernest J, 1958, Mr 11,29:1
Million, Helen L L Mrs, 1941, D 6,17:5
Million, John W (por), 1941, S 7,49:1
Milliot, Fannie, 1957, My 8,37:2
Milliot, Leon, 1950, Je 1,27:4
Milliot, Louis, 1962, Ja 13,21:5
Milliot, William, 1942, Ja 7,19:5
Millis, Fred C, 1951, My 28,21:2
Millis, Harry A, 1948, Je 26,17:1
Millis, John, 1952, Mr 21,24:3
Millis, Walter, 1968, Mr 18,45:2
Millman, David, 1953, N 25,23:2
Millman, Edward, 1964, F 14,29:1
Millman, Joseph, 1958, Ag 23,15:6
Millman, Morris, 1962, Ja 12,23:5
Millman, Peter Carl, 1917, Mr 20,11:6
Millman, William L, 1937, Jl 20,23:1
Millmann, Karl, 1961, Ja 6,27:1
Millmore, Martin, 1883, Jl 22,2:6
Millner, George W, 1946, Jl 11,23:1
Millner, Isaac A, 1964, N 3,31:3
Millner, Simon, 1952, Ja 15,27:2
Millon, John P, 1956, Mr 3,19:1
Millonig, Henry, 1942, N 14,16:3
Millonig, Henry Mrs, 1948, Je 5,15:3
Millosevich, Elizabeth Prof, 1919, D 6,11:5
Millot, John, 1903, Ap 19,7:4
Millroy, Alfred T, 1942, Ja 7,19:4
Mills, A, 1929, Ag 28,25:3; 1936, S 25,23:3
Mills, A Harold, 1961, Mr 17,31:1
Mills, Addie B Mrs, 1939, O 22,41:2
Mills, Addison, 1954, My 30,45:2
Mills, Adelbert G, 1944, N 12,49:2
Mills, Adelbert G Sr Mrs, 1958, Ap 13,84:8
Mills, Albert E, 1949, My 11,29:4
Mills, Albert L Gen (funl, S 21,11:2), 1916, S 19,11:3
Mills, Alfred, 1913, D 14,III,15:5
Mills, Andrew, 1879, Je 24,5:2
Mills, Andrew Jr, 1962, Ag 7,29:3
Mills, Andrew Mrs, 1960, N 7,35:4
Mills, Anna E, 1952, Je 6,23:4
Mills, Annette, 1955, Ja 11,25:4
Mills, Annie H Mrs, 1957, S 27,19:2
Mills, Anson Gen, 1924, N 6,19:4
Mills, Arthur, 1954, D 31,14:7
Mills, Augustus K, 1954, S 13,23:2
Mills, Barrett V, 1925, Mr 10,21:3
Mills, Ben, 1950, Ag 11,19:2
Mills, Benjamin F, 1941, N 6,23:5
Mills, Benjamin Fay Rev, 1916, My 2,13:7
Mills, Benjamin W, 1947, F 8,17:5
Mills, Bert N, 1951, Ap 5,29:2
Mills, Bertram W, 1938, Ap 17,II,6:8
Mills, Beverly G, 1940, O 27,45:1
Mills, Bob (Frank W Stilwell), 1968, F 7,47:3

Mills, C K, 1931, My 29,21:3
Mills, C Wright, 1962, Mr 21,39:3
Mills, Calvert, 1966, N 9,39:1
Mills, Cara M B Mrs, 1940, Jl 23,19:2
Mills, Carley, 1962, O 22,29:5
Mills, Caswell L, 1909, S 14,9:6
Mills, Cecil R, 1955, Mr 29,29:3
Mills, Charles, 1874, Ap 12,1:4
Mills, Charles E, 1954, Ja 5,27:4
Mills, Charles F, 1943, Ap 14,23:4
Mills, Charles H, 1948, O 31,88:4
Mills, Charles H Dr, 1937, Jl 23,19:6
Mills, Charles H Mrs, 1961, Mr 4,23:3; 1966, F 26,2
Mills, Charles M, 1950, O 14,19:5
Mills, Charles P, 1949, S 16,28:2
Mills, Charles S (por), 1942, Mr 6,21:5
Mills, Charles S, 1954, Ap 8,27:2
Mills, Charles S Mrs, 1937, My 25,28:2
Mills, Charles W, 1925, Ag 11,21:4; 1938, Ap 20,23: 1947, Jl 8,23:2; 1948, Jl 1,23:2
Mills, Charlotte, 1952, F 4,11:4
Mills, Chester P, 1947, S 16,23:2
Mills, Chester R, 1954, Ap 13,31:2
Mills, Christopher Mrs, 1942, Ap 7,21:5
Mills, Clark, 1883, Ja 13,5:3
Mills, Clifford, 1952, O 16,29:3
Mills, Clifford E, 1942, Jl 18,13:1
Mills, Cuthbert, 1904, F 17,9:7
Mills, D M Mrs, 1902, Jl 28,9:6
Mills, Daniel, 1905, F 26,7:2
Mills, Daniel C, 1960, S 8,35:3
Mills, Darfus O (funl), 1910, Ja 8,9:4
Mills, David B, 1944, F 26,13:6; 1954, D 3,28:2
Mills, Don P, 1948, Jl 31,15:5
Mills, E Edwin, 1946, Mr 14,25:2
Mills, Earl H, 1944, Je 27,19:3
Mills, Earle W Vice-Adm, 1968, Ag 28,47:3
Mills, Edgar R, 1955, F 20,89:1
Mills, Edward C, 1962, My 25,33:4
Mills, Edward H, 1950, Ap 16,104:6
Mills, Edward K (por), 1938, Mr 11,19:1
Mills, Edward K Jr, 1964, Ag 9,76:6
Mills, Edward K Mrs, 1955, Ag 10,25:3
Mills, Edward M, 1950, O 12,31:1
Mills, Edward N, 1948, F 7,15:3
Mills, Edwin C, 1959, Mr 15,88:6
Mills, Edwin S Sr, 1951, N 12,25:2
Mills, Elden, 1965, My 10,33:3
Mills, Ella A, 1940, Ag 10,13:1
Mills, Ellsworth L, 1959, D 8,45:2
Mills, Emma, 1956, Je 14,33:5
Mills, Emma H Mrs, 1940, Je 21,21:6
Mills, Enos, 1922, S 22,15:5
Mills, Ernest A, 1947, My 10,13:6
Mills, Ernest C Mrs (L Stibal), 1960, N 26,21:4
Mills, Ethelbert S, 1873, Jl 16,8:5
Mills, Evelyn J Mrs, 1960, Je 10,31:3
Mills, Everett E, 1953, My 9,19:3
Mills, Florence T Mrs, 1942, N 23,23:3
Mills, Frank, 1921, Je 12,22:3; 1939, Ag 20,32:5; 1 D 31,15:5
Mills, Frank F Mrs, 1950, Ap 16,104:4
Mills, Frank H Mrs, 1954, O 13,31:2
Mills, Frank L, 1953, Ag 29,17:6
Mills, Franklin H, 1940, F 18,41:1
Mills, Fred L, 1944, Jl 6,15:6
Mills, Frederick, 1954, Ja 2,11:4
Mills, Frederick A, 1948, D 7,31:2
Mills, Frederick W Mrs, 1940, D 29,24:7
Mills, George, 1944, Ap 10,19:2; 1949, F 16,25:5
Mills, George A, 1950, Je 5,23:3
Mills, George A H, 1950, Jl 14,21:4
Mills, George F, 1914, O 29,11:4
Mills, George G, 1947, N 18,29:2
Mills, George H Mrs, 1943, My 21,19:2
Mills, George O, 1918, Je 5,11:5
Mills, George S, 1939, D 28,22:2; 1966, Ja 3,27:4
Mills, George W T, 1948, My 9,68:7
Mills, H Brooker, 1948, Ja 1,23:5
Mills, H L, 1882, Ap 1,5:2
Mills, H M, 1935, My 17,21:1
Mills, Harmon J, 1958, My 4,89:1
Mills, Harold H, 1965, D 16,47:2
Mills, Harold P Mrs, 1941, My 21,23:5
Mills, Harriet E, 1943, D 11,15:5
Mills, Harry C, 1952, N 11,30:3
Mills, Harry E, 1941, D 3,25:3
Mills, Harry H, 1939, My 23,23:2
Mills, Henry, 1941, Mr 18,23:4
Mills, Henry D, 1946, My 26,32:7
Mills, Henry J, 1937, Ap 6,23:4
Mills, Henry M, 1940, Ap 27,15:4; 1961, Jl 29,19
Mills, Henry P, 1951, F 15,31:3
Mills, Herbert E, 1946, Mr 10,46:4
Mills, Herbert F, 1938, Jl 6,23:3
Mills, Herbert L, 1945, F 27,20:2
Mills, Hillis, 1965, Mr 2,35:1
Mills, Hilton E, 1950, Mr 30,29:4
Mills, Hiram, 1882, Ag 4,2:1
Mills, Hiram F, 1965, Ag 25,39:1
Mills, I N, 1929, Jl 15,21:3
Mills, I Tracy, 1943, Je 16,21:3
Mills, Ian D, 1961, O 10,43:5

Mills, Ira B Judge, 1921, My 5,17:4
Mills, Irving P Mrs, 1960, Ja 29,25:2
Mills, J Clawson (will), 1940, My 9,21:4
Mills, J Doremus, 1905, Ap 27,11:6
Mills, J Emory, 1948, Mr 18,27:3
Mills, J Evan, 1944, Mr 29,21:2
Mills, J G, 1884, Je 2,5:3
Mills, J W, 1882, S 26,8:4
Mills, Jackson M, 1943, Mr 21,26:4
Mills, James, 1906, My 6,9:6; 1965, N 9,43:4
Mills, James A (por), 1942, Mr 28,17:1
Mills, James A, 1942, Ap 2,21:1
Mills, James O, 1939, O 13,23:4
Mills, James P, 1948, S 8,29:2
Mills, James R, 1955, D 14,39:3
Mills, Jay, 1951, Mr 7,33:4
Mills, Jay G, 1960, O 12,43:2
Mills, Jesse T Mrs, 1953, F 29,23:5
Mills, Job S Rev Dr, 1909, S 17,9:6
Mills, John (por), 1948, Je 16,29:1
Mills, John A, 1961, F 22,25:5
Mills, John H, 1938, Mr 13,II,8:4; 1967, D 10,87:1
Mills, John J, 1948, N 6,13:5
Mills, John K, 1957, Ag 9,19:2
Mills, John K Mrs, 1959, D 19,27:5
Mills, John Lt, 1867, Je 28,2:3
Mills, John M, 1937, Ja 21,23:4
Mills, John T, 1910, My 19,9:4
Mills, John W Sr, 1954, F 27,13:4
Mills, Johnny, 1949, Mr 27,76:8
Mills, Joseph, 1941, N 15,17:2; 1944, Jl 14,13:6; 1958, Je 24,31:5
Mills, Joseph S, 1952, Ja 22,29:4
Mills, Joseph S Mrs, 1950, S 28,31:4
Mills, Kermit J, 1953, D 29,23:3
Mills, Knower, 1956, S 13,35:4
Mills, Lawrence H, 1944, F 12,13:5
Mills, Lawrence Heyworth Prof, 1918, F 1,9:5
Mills, Lelia D, 1948, O 15,24:3
Mills, Leroy N, 1938, O 10,19:1
Mills, Luther Laflin, 1909, Ja 20,9:4
Mills, Margaret D Mrs, 1941, Jl 15,20:2
Mills, Mark M, 1958, Ap 8,1:5
Mills, Mary C H Mrs, 1937, Je 11,23:4
Mills, Mary E, 1946, D 3,32:2
Mills, Mason, 1943, Ag 16,15:5
Mills, Maura, 1955, Mr 7,27:4
Mills, Michael Keyfor, 1922, Ja 21,13:4
Mills, Morgan R, 1939, Mr 7,21:2
Mills, Mountfort, 1949, Ap 25,23:2
Mills, Nancy H Mrs, 1951, Jl 17,27:3
Mills, Nat Mrs, 1955, Ja 22,11:4
Mills, Nathan, 1937, Je 15,23:2
Mills, O, 1929, Ja 29,8:1
Mills, Ogden, 1937, O 12,1:2
Mills, Ogden Livingston Mrs, 1968, My 2,48:1
Mills, Ogden Mrs, 1920, O 14,13:3
Mills, Ogden Mrs (funl, N 5,15:6), 1920, N 1,15:6
Mills, Paul D, 1954, Jl 12,19:4
Mills, Percy E, 1952, My 29,27:3
Mills, Percy Herbert Viscount, 1968, S 11,47:1
Mills, Perry R, 1949, My 30,13:4
Mills, Ray C, 1962, Mr 7,35:3
Mills, Raymond T, 1958, Je 18,33:5
Mills, Richard M, 1961, O 17,39:3
Mills, Robert B, 1950, Je 20,27:5
Mills, Robert H, 1947, Ag 11,23:5
Mills, Robert J, 1918, O 23,13:1
Mills, Roger F, 1966, Ja 19,41:2
Mills, Roger Quarles Ex-Sen, 1911, S 3,II,9:4
Mills, Roy R, 1968, Ja 18,39:3
Mills, Samuel A, 1956, Ja 4,27:1
Mills, Samuel J, 1947, Mr 10,22:2
Mills, Samuel J Mrs, 1952, F 12,27:4
Mills, Samuel M, 1906, Ja 2,9:6
Mills, Samuel M Brig-Gen, 1907, S 19,7:6
Mills, Samuel Myers Gen, 1907, S 9,7:6
Mills, Samuel W, 1965, D 25,13:2
Mills, Sherman O H Mrs, 1947, Ag 19,23:2
Mills, Sophie D Mrs, 1945, Jl 22,37:1
Mills, Stephen Col, 1914, Ag 4,11:6
Mills, Stephen R, 1946, Jl 27,17:5
Mills, Susan Lincoln, 1912, D 14,15:3
Mills, T M K Maj, 1915, F 8,7:4
Mills, Thomas E, 1944, F 26,13:5
Mills, Thomas R Mrs, 1951, Jl 22,61:2
Mills, Van Strycker, 1957, N 30,21:4
Mills, Victor, 1959, Ag 24,21:2
Mills, Victor G, 1956, Ja 16,21:2
Mills, W F, 1883, My 1,4:7
Mills, W Plumer, 1959, F 27,25:2
Mills, W S, 1934, Ja 6,15:1
Mills, Walter, 1943, Jl 21,15:3
Mills, Walter R, 1948, S 16,29:2
Mills, Walter S, 1947, Ja 17,23:2
Mills, Walter Sands, 1925, Ap 20,17:4
Mills, Walter T, 1942, My 9,13:2
Mills, Weymer J, 1938, My 26,25:4
Mills, William, 1952, Jl 14,17:5
Mills, William A, 1942, My 25,15:2
Mills, William A Sr, 1940, Ap 22,17:4
Mills, William H, 1940, N 12,24:2
Mills, William H A Jr, 1965, Jl 27,33:3
Mills, William Harrison, 1907, My 25,9:4
Mills, William J, 1915, D 27,9:5; 1940, My 20,17:1; 1949, Je 24,23:1
Mills, William M, 1949, F 15,23:1
Mills, William W, 1916, Mr 1,11:4; 1946, Ja 31,21:1
Millson, John S, 1874, Mr 2,1:5
Millsop, Thomas E, 1967, S 13,47:1
Millspaugh, Arthur C, 1955, S 26,23:4
Millspaugh, Charles F Dr, 1923, S 17,15:3
Millspaugh, Clarence A, 1961, Jl 19,29:3
Millspaugh, Frank A Rev, 1916, N 23,13:5
Millspaugh, George V, 1952, N 13,31:2
Millspaugh, Harriet S, 1942, D 21,23:3
Millspaugh, Isaac L Dr, 1908, Ag 28,7:5
Millspaugh, Jane Mrs, 1947, D 10,31:1
Millspaugh, M Laurance, 1964, Mr 9,29:3
Millspaugh, Mabel K, 1961, Ap 13,35:4
Millspaugh, Stanley, 1943, F 24,22:2
Millspaugh, Stanley H, 1948, Ap 11,72:2
Millspaugh, Willard P Dr, 1937, O 30,19:6
Millstein, Benjamin, 1952, My 30,15:1
Millstein, Joseph (will), 1947, Mr 14,14:6
Millstein, William H, 1958, My 18,86:7
Millus, Felix L, 1960, F 9,31:2
Millus, Frederic, 1947, Jl 27,45:1
Millward, Arthur, 1937, F 10,8:2
Millward, Harry, 1909, Ja 3,11:1
Millward, W, 1871, N 29,1:5
Milman, Barnet S, 1952, Mr 10,21:5
Milman, George Bryan Lt-Gen, 1915, Ja 31,3:6
Milman, H H, 1868, S 26,1:5
Milman, Robert, 1876, Mr 16,2:2
Milmine, Charles Edward, 1924, Ap 28,15:4
Milmine, Elmer L, 1937, F 18,21:4
Milmoe, M J, 1938, Mr 23,23:1
Milmoe, Mary E, 1958, Je 19,31:5
Milne, Alan A (will, Ap 17,29:4), 1956, F 1,31:1
Milne, Alex Sr, 1951, Ap 22,88:3
Milne, Alexander, 1915, Ag 3,9:7
Milne, Alexander Boland, 1904, Ja 19,9:6
Milne, Alexander M, 1943, S 20,21:4
Milne, Andrew J Rev, 1907, Ag 24,7:4
Milne, Arch N, 1937, Ap 20,25:2
Milne, Arthur Mrs, 1945, S 1,11:3
Milne, Berkeley, 1938, Jl 6,23:4
Milne, Caleb J Jr, 1941, My 24,15:6
Milne, Caleb J 3d, 1961, Jl 1,17:4
Milne, Clyde, 1953, Je 29,21:5
Milne, David, 1954, F 16,25:2
Milne, David L, 1962, Ja 24,33:4
Milne, David Mrs, 1956, O 10,39:4
Milne, Don L Mrs, 1949, N 26,15:5
Milne, Edward A, 1950, S 23,17:1
Milne, Edward J, 1960, N 20,86:8
Milne, George D, 1925, Ag 13,19:6
Milne, George F, 1948, Mr 24,25:1
Milne, George G Jr, 1955, N 3,31:4
Milne, George H, 1945, D 29,13:4
Milne, George M, 1937, O 1,21:2
Milne, George O, 1950, Ja 30,17:2
Milne, J Scott, 1955, Jl 21,23:5
Milne, James, 1953, Ja 10,17:4
Milne, James M Dr, 1903, N 6,9:6
Milne, James Y, 1947, My 19,21:5
Milne, John D, 1951, S 29,17:5
Milne, John H, 1949, Jl 21,26:5
Milne, John Prof, 1913, Ag 1,7:6
Milne, John W, 1945, Ja 1,21:4
Milne, Joseph D Mrs, 1947, O 11,17:4
Milne, Lorne A, 1946, D 4,31:1
Milne, Louis A, 1943, Mr 8,15:1
Milne, Margaret Mrs, 1937, Jl 29,19:3
Milne, Nelson A, 1938, Jl 21,21:3
Milne, Robert S Jr, 1946, Jl 30,23:5
Milne, Ross, 1964, Ja 26,V,1:5
Milne, Theodore R, 1962, N 22,29:5
Milne, William J Dr, 1914, S 5,7:4
Milne-Watson, David, 1945, O 4,23:2
Milner, Alfred Viscount (por), 1925, My 14,19:4
Milner, Edward J, 1949, Ag 4,23:5
Milner, Edwin, 1914, F 20,9:4
Milner, Frederic, 1957, S 6,21:1
Milner, Harry R, 1950, Je 20,27:2
Milner, Isaac J, 1905, Ag 29,7:4
Milner, J W, 1880, Ja 18,7:4
Milner, James F, 1959, Ja 1,31:4
Milner, Viscountess, 1958, O 11,23:1
Milner, William Mrs, 1947, Je 28,14:3
Milnes, Albert, 1966, Ap 6,43:2
Milnes, Charles, 1939, Ap 2,III,6:7
Milnes, Clarence S, 1953, O 22,29:5
Milnes, Mark Mrs, 1952, Je 23,19:2
Milnes, R M (Lord Houghton), 1885, Ag 12,5:3
Milnes, T Edgar, 1954, Ap 10,15:4
Milnes, William, 1947, Ja 25,17:5
Milnor, Bennett Mrs, 1957, Je 30,68:5
Milnor, Frank R, 1938, Je 8,23:4
Milnor, Joseph W, 1949, Mr 31,25:2
Milnor, Leland T, 1949, O 19,29:3
Milnor, William H, 1938, My 20,19:1
Milon, Gen, 1881, Mr 21,5:3
Milone, Salvatore Mrs, 1966, Mr 18,39:4
Milos, Joseph, 1948, Je 12,15:6
Miloslavich, Edward L, 1952, N 13,31:1
Milosy, Stephen G, 1947, My 23,23:3
Milot, Hubert C, 1950, D 20,31:3
Milowitz, William J, 1959, Jl 24,25:2
Milroy, James, 1941, S 25,25:3
Milroy, Lafayette J, 1951, Je 28,25:3
Milroy, Robert A, 1942, D 20,44:6
Milroy, William S, 1942, S 22,21:4
Milsner, Jacob J, 1950, O 11,33:3
Milsom, Grace E, 1944, O 11,21:6
Milsop, Earl T, 1955, Ja 28,20:2
Milstead, Century A, 1963, Je 3,29:4
Milstead, Lavier C, 1941, S 25,25:4
Milstead, William, 1961, Ap 4,37:2
Miltenberg, Emil, 1939, Mr 24,21:3
Miltner, Frank, 1942, Mr 3,23:4
Milton, Deborah A, 1946, Ap 3,25:5
Milton, Emily Mrs, 1939, Mr 24,21:2
Milton, Ernest Mrs (N R Smith), 1964, Jl 29,33:1
Milton, George A, 1961, S 30,25:1
Milton, George F, 1924, Ap 24,19:4; 1955, N 13,88:5
Milton, James, 1945, F 11,38:3
Milton, Jeff D, 1947, My 8,25:2
Milton, Jim, 1949, Ag 3,23:5
Milton, John Mrs, 1945, N 22,35:2
Milton, John P, 1940, My 19,42:6
Milton, Joseph J, 1950, Ja 13,23:3
Milton, Michael, 1957, Jl 9,29:1
Milton, Nolan S Mrs, 1946, O 8,23:4
Milton, Tommy, 1962, Jl 11,25:5
Milton, Vera, 1952, Ag 4,15:5
Milton, William H, 1942, Ja 5,17:3
Milward, Henry Townsend, 1919, S 5,11:1
Milward, Luke U, 1943, Je 11,19:2
Milwitzky, William, 1956, Je 9,17:5
Milyko, Andrew, 1953, Jl 2,25:3
Milzner, Richard, 1940, Ja 9,23:2
Mimi (Gypsy Queen), 1958, Ap 25,8:2
Mimmi, Marcello Cardinal (funl, Mr 10,27:1), 1961, Mr 7,35:1
Mimnagh, Catherine E R Mrs, 1939, My 6,17:4
Mimnagh, William P, 1952, My 10,21:5
Mimnaugh, Thomas F Mrs, 1945, Mr 15,23:3
Mimne, Edmund T, 1949, My 18,27:4
Mims, Edwin, 1959, S 17,39:5
Mims, G L, 1958, Ja 22,28:1
Mims, Henry, 1925, D 28,15:3
Mims, Joseph S, 1955, S 3,15:6
Mims, Livingston Maj, 1906, Mr 6,9:6
Mims, Marion R, 1954, Mr 5,19:3
Mims, Morrill P, 1948, D 5,92:2
Mims, Stewart L, 1961, S 24,86:4
Mims, Stewart L Mrs, 1957, Ja 18,21:2
Minahan, Daniel F, 1947, Ap 30,26:3
Minahan, Edmund J, 1958, My 22,29:3
Minahan, Katharine, 1953, S 4,15:2
Minahan, Victor I, 1954, Ag 6,17:4
Minami, Jiro, 1955, D 7,39:3
Minami, Naoyuki, 1960, Ap 7,35:5
Minan, Daniel J Jr, 1948, D 19,76:3
Minar, Mina, 1911, Ag 9,9:4
Minard, Archilbald E, 1950, My 10,31:2
Minard, Duane H, 1964, Jl 11,25:4
Minard, Florence V, 1948, Je 22,25:1
Minard, George C, 1940, Jl 4,15:5
Minard, George W, 1939, D 3,60:7
Minard, Harold, 1953, N 13,27:3
Minard, Ira D, 1942, Mr 26,23:4
Minard, Laura A Mrs, 1940, My 30,17:4
Minard, Sadie M, 1948, Je 8,25:3
Minard, William E, 1951, Ag 27,19:2
Minas, Edward C, 1950, Ja 1,42:3
Minassian, Kirkor, 1944, My 9,19:5
Minault, Francis H Jr, 1967, My 5,39:4
Mince, H A, 1938, N 15,23:1
Mincer, Arthur, 1954, Ap 21,29:1
Minch, Emil L, 1949, Mr 29,25:3
Minch, Philip, 1944, Ap 15,11:2
Minch, Walter B, 1944, N 10,19:3
Minches, Samuel, 1954, F 18,31:5
Minchin, Harry W, 1952, Je 25,29:2
Minchin, James, 1942, S 22,21:5
Minchin, James A, 1965, Ja 2,19:1
Minciotti, Silvio Mrs (Esther), 1962, Ap 16,29:2
Minck, Franklin J Mrs, 1950, S 25,23:3
Minck, Henry, 1925, Ap 25,15:5
Minckler, Edward G, 1959, Ap 8,37:3
Minckler, Robert L, 1963, Ag 7,33:5
Mindala, Joseph Mrs, 1949, My 28,15:5
Mindell, Louis Mrs, 1966, Ja 27,33:3
Minder, Andy, 1943, My 7,25:5
Minder, Paul L, 1949, Ja 23,69:1
Minder, Walter C, 1952, N 18,31:4
Mindermann, Frederick H, 1939, N 21,26:2
Mindermann, Henry J F, 1947, Ap 2,27:1
Mindil, George W Gen, 1907, Jl 21,7:6
Mindil, Philip Kearny, 1920, O 23,13:6
Mindlin, Max, 1950, S 9,17:3
Mindlin, Max Mrs, 1959, N 19,39:4
Mindlin, Michael, 1946, S 14,7:4
Mindnich, Charles G, 1954, Ap 18,89:1
Mindorff, Elgar, 1950, My 30,17:2
Minds, John H, 1964, Ja 1,25:4

Minds, William R, 1946, My 4,15:5
Minehan, Andrew F Mrs, 1956, N 5,31:5
Minehan, Michael, 1943, Je 2,25:2
Minehart, Anna W Mrs, 1948, Je 19,15:5
Miner, Alex S, 1964, S 30,43:5
Miner, Amos T, 1945, Ag 22,23:4
Miner, Antonia S S Mrs, 1941, S 6,15:2
Miner, Asher Gen, 1924, S 3,17:2
Miner, Charles A, 1903, Jl 26,7:6
Miner, Charles H, 1959, Jl 14,29:1
Miner, Clarence A, 1940, Mr 15,23:4
Miner, Daniel B, 1956, N 12,29:4
Miner, Donald, 1942, S 14,15:4
Miner, Douglas C, 1966, Mr 15,39:1
Miner, Edmund C, 1903, S 11,7:7
Miner, Edward G, 1955, O 11,39:4
Miner, Edward H, 1941, O 11,17:6
Miner, Edward H Mrs, 1941, S 13,17:3
Miner, Edward S, 1951, My 12,21:3
Miner, Edwin D, 1916, Jl 10,11:5
Miner, Edwin H Mrs, 1954, Ap 8,27:4
Miner, Floyd B, 1943, Ag 31,17:5
Miner, George E, 1941, O 14,23:2
Miner, George E Mrs, 1940, N 20,21:2
Miner, George F, 1939, S 17,49:1
Miner, George H, 1949, D 13,38:2
Miner, George H Mrs, 1940, Jl 10,19:5
Miner, George R Mrs, 1953, Mr 5,27:5
Miner, H Clay, 1950, Ag 11,19:4
Miner, H Clay Mrs, 1953, S 23,31:2
Miner, Harlan S, 1938, Ap 15,19:4
Miner, Harry T, 1939, F 12,44:6
Miner, Herbert J, 1946, N 30,15:1
Miner, Herbert J Mrs, 1950, N 16,31:4
Miner, Ira J, 1959, N 14,21:6
Miner, J W, 1943, Ap 27,24:2
Miner, Jack (por), 1944, N 4,15:2
Miner, James A, 1904, S 20,9:6
Miner, James B, 1943, Mr 25,21:1
Miner, James Dr, 1925, S 19,15:4
Miner, James F, 1939, Jl 31,13:4
Miner, James H, 1943, Je 2,25:4
Miner, James S, 1954, F 21,68:1
Miner, John D, 1906, Mr 24,9:6
Miner, John L, 1940, N 21,30:2
Miner, Joshua L, 1949, O 9,92:5
Miner, Karl R, 1947, Ag 29,17:6
Miner, L Amelia Mrs, 1948, D 23,20:2
Miner, Louie M, 1964, Ap 17,35:1
Miner, Pierre A, 1960, Mr 11,25:3
Miner, Randall W Mrs, 1959, Je 19,25:1
Miner, Randolph H Mrs, 1957, F 20,33:3
Miner, Ranlet, 1968, Ag 10,27:5
Miner, Roy W, 1955, D 14,39:5
Miner, Samuel A, 1946, My 27,23:5
Miner, Sidney H, 1937, N 21,II,9:2
Miner, Sidney L, 1944, O 26,23:2
Miner, Stanley G, 1942, Je 30,21:1
Miner, T W, 1928, Ja 19,23:5
Miner, Torry G, 1959, O 13,39:3
Miner, Vincent B, 1956, F 24,25:3
Miner, W H Mrs, 1950, Mr 30,29:4
Miner, Walter N, 1948, Jl 18,52:4
Miner, Willard M, 1938, D 14,25:4
Minerd, David E, 1943, Ap 21,26:2
Minervini, Ettore Mrs, 1955, F 17,27:3
Mines, Abraham S, 1957, Jl 2,27:2
Mines, Benjamin, 1950, Mr 19,92:3
Minett, Henry, 1952, D 21,53:2
Minetti, G Joseph Mrs, 1957, Je 6,31:3
Minetti, Richard L, 1962, S 12,39:4
Minevitch, Borrah, 1955, Je 27,21:4
Minevitch, Joseph R, 1957, Jl 5,17:4
Minford, Agnes A, 1938, Ja 9,42:2
Minford, Hugh, 1950, D 20,31:1
Minford, Levis W Jr, 1946, N 11,27:4
Ming, Fred R, 1943, F 23,21:4
Ming, William E, 1950, S 26,31:1
Ming-Chen Hsu, 1963, N 10,86:5
Mingana, Alphonse, 1937, D 6,27:2
Mingay, Henry M, 1947, Ap 24,25:4
Minger, Rudolf, 1955, Ag 24,27:1
Minges, Arthur S, 1938, Mr 12,17:2
Mingey, Edward J, 1961, O 29,88:5
Minghini, William E, 1949, Mr 11,26:2
Mingle, James D, 1957, S 10,33:4
Mingle, Sampson Q, 1903, S 16,9:5
Mingle, William, 1923, Mr 31,13:3
Mingo, Joseph W Mrs, 1948, O 15,23:4
Mingos, Howard L, 1955, D 30,19:6
Mingus, George, 1961, Mr 9,29:2
Mini, James H, 1963, D 8,86:3
Minich, Henry D, 1952, Mr 23,92:3
Minich, Mary J Mrs, 1938, Je 8,23:4
Minichink, Carmine, 1924, F 10,23:1
Minico, Lorenzo del, 1949, Ag 14,70:6
Minicus, George C, 1949, D 12,33:3
Minier, Ernest A, 1958, Je 10,33:6
Miniger, Clement O, 1944, Ap 24,19:4
Minihan, Daniel J, 1949, Mr 25,23:4
Minikes, Jesse, 1967, My 3,45:2
Minikin, J Harris, 1964, O 17,29:4
Minisi, Anthony F, 1958, Ap 1,31:5
Miniter, Francis G Dr, 1937, Ap 11,II,8:4
Miniter, John J, 1939, N 5,49:2
Miniter, Thomas B, 1920, O 3,22:4
Mink, Casper L, 1938, Jl 23,13:5
Mink, George W Jr, 1949, Ap 30,13:2
Minke, Jacob J, 1939, O 3,23:5
Minker, George J Mrs, 1950, My 16,31:2
Minker, Roger R, 1952, Ja 23,27:3
Minkin, Jacob S, 1962, Mr 15,35:2
Minkin, Leopold, 1924, O 16,25:4
Minkin, William, 1941, Ap 10,23:4
Minkler, David L, 1949, N 2,27:1
Minkler, Frederick Sr, 1950, Ag 25,21:5
Minkoff, Nochum B, 1958, Mr 15,17:6
Minkoff, Saul N, 1939, Ap 29,17:6
Minkowitz, Michael, 1962, Ja 16,33:1
Minkowski, Giacomo, 1941, My 6,21:4
Minkowsky, Pincus Rev (funl, Ja 22,17:2), 1924, Ja 19,13:4
Minne, George, 1941, Mr 9,40:5
Minner, Delbert M, 1961, My 29,19:3
Minner, Jeremiah Mrs, 1941, My 13,23:4
Minnerly, Arthur G, 1956, My 24,31:4
Minnerly, Charles S, 1952, Je 10,27:4
Minnerly, Frank, 1938, Mr 2,19:5
Minnerly, Isaac Mrs, 1948, D 14,29:3
Minnerly, Issac R, 1938, D 17,15:6
Minnerly, Katherine B Mrs, 1939, S 11,19:1
Minnerly, William A, 1944, Jl 9,35:1
Minnich, Arthur O, 1937, F 26,21:2
Minnich, Harvey C, 1952, My 14,28:4
Minnick, Guy F, 1956, O 31,33:4
Minnick, Jim H, 1947, My 1,25:5
Minnick, Maurice M, 1945, S 27,21:4
Minnick, Nathan R, 1948, D 6,25:1
Minnick, Paul W, 1954, Je 23,26:4
Minnick, Thomas J Jr, 1951, My 22,31:4
Minnie, Etienne, 1879, D 16,2:3
Minnigerode, C Powell, 1951, Mr 2,25:3
Minnigerode, Fitzhugh L, 1948, Mr 9,23:1
Minnigerode, L, 1935, Mr 25,15:4
Minnigerode, Meade, 1967, O 29,84:7
Minnihan, John F, 1945, My 23,19:3
Minns, Ellis H, 1953, Je 16,27:1
Minns, Mrs, 1871, My 4,2:2
Minns, Susan, 1938, Ag 3,19:3
Minobe, Tatsukichi (por), 1948, My 25,27:3
Minogue, Rich F, 1951, D 25,31:5
Minogue, William J, 1954, Ag 12,25:5
Minoka-Hill, Lillie R, 1952, Mr 19,29:1
Minor, Benjamin S, 1946, S 28,17:3
Minor, Catherine Mrs, 1925, F 21,11:5
Minor, Charles L, 1950, D 13,35:4
Minor, Clark H, 1967, F 5,89:1
Minor, Clark H Mrs, 1964, D 15,44:1
Minor, Clifford E Mrs, 1941, S 3,23:3
Minor, Cornelius, 1882, Ag 13,7:6
Minor, Doug, 1959, Ap 27,27:5
Minor, Dwight J, 1960, F 25,29:4
Minor, Edna V, 1957, Je 11,35:3
Minor, Edward E, 1953, My 15,23:2
Minor, Edward G, 1942, S 10,27:5
Minor, Emily T, 1938, Ja 21,19:4
Minor, Emma H Mrs, 1939, Mr 30,23:6
Minor, Frank M, 1948, Jl 30,17:3
Minor, Frederick W, 1952, N 22,23:5
Minor, George H, 1937, Mr 23,23:2
Minor, George Mrs, 1947, O 25,19:4
Minor, Guy H Mrs, 1946, Jl 8,29:3
Minor, Henrietta J, 1942, F 16,17:3
Minor, James H, 1943, Ap 8,23:5
Minor, John B, 1947, Je 3,26:2
Minor, John Crannell Dr, 1913, Ag 17,II,9:3
Minor, John Mrs, 1946, F 28,23:5
Minor, Kathryn, 1939, F 27,15:3
Minor, Norris E, 1954, O 22,27:2
Minor, Robert, 1952, N 28,25:3
Minor, Robert Crannell, 1904, Ag 5,7:6
Minor, S Carrington Dr, 1916, Je 17,11:6
Minor, Ward A, 1951, D 11,33:2
Minor, Wilfred C, 1945, N 2,20:2
Minore, Joseph L, 1967, Jl 10,28:7
Minoretti, Carlo D (por), 1938, Mr 14,16:2
Minot, Alice H, 1950, Ag 25,21:4
Minot, Charles Sedgwick Dr, 1914, N 21,13:6
Minot, Francis, 1960, Mr 13,4:1
Minot, George R, 1950, F 26,76:3
Minot, Grafton W Mrs (cor, Jl 10,27:3), 1952, Je 9, 23:4
Minot, James J, 1938, My 1,II,6:6
Minot, Joseph G, 1939, Je 20,21:2
Minot, Laurence, 1921, Je 5,22:2
Minot, William, 1937, Mr 17,25:5
Minot, William A G, 1963, Jl 2,30:1
Minott, Frederick S, 1942, Mr 2,19:5
Minott, George H, 1957, Je 23,85:2
Minott, Harold, 1949, Ag 17,23:5
Minott, Nellie R, 1937, N 2,25:4
Minotto, A Dowager Countess, 1927, F 12,15:5
Minotto, Demetrius Count, 1920, My 18,11:5
Minotto, James Mrs, 1943, O 19,19:3
Minrath, Ferdinand Richard, 1923, Ap 22,8:2
Minsch, William J, 1954, O 26,27:4
Minshall, Robert J, 1954, S 8,31:2
Minshall, Stanley C, 1967, Ja 25,43:4
Minshall, T Ellis Mrs (will), 1966, Mr 25,42:8
Minshall Robt E, 1958, Ag 16,17:2
Minskoff, Sam, 1950, D 27,27:1
Minsky, Abraham B, 1949, S 5,17:4
Minsky, Abraham B Mrs, 1964, My 15,35:2
Minsky, Henry, 1954, My 24,27:4
Minsky, Herbert K, 1959, D 22,31:2
Minsky, Isaac, 1950, Ap 27,33:1
Minsky, Jacob, 1954, Ag 20,19:3
Minsky, Louis, 1957, D 31,17:1
Minsky, M W, 1932, Je 13,15:5
Minster, Henry W, 1949, Je 1,32:3
Minsterer, Charles J, 1937, Je 27,II,6:7
Minteer, James I, 1953, F 26,25:5
Mintel, August L Mrs, 1944, S 30,13:5
Mintel, Frederick L, 1956, N 8,39:5
Mintel, George M, 1945, Ag 9,21:6
Mintel, Leonard C Sr, 1951, Je 9,19:6
Minter, Billy, 1940, My 21,23:3
Minter, James M, 1943, My 13,21:2
Minter, Thomas K Mrs, 1962, Ag 28,31:4
Mintern, Michael J, 1961, Jl 12,32:5
Minthorn, H J Dr, 1922, O 12,19:5
Minthorn, Pennington W, 1940, Mr 15,23:2
Mintier, Arthur M, 1965, Ag 26,33:5
Minto, Mary Countess, 1940, Jl 16,17:3
Minton, Alton J, 1946, S 8,44:8
Minton, August M, 1947, S 10,27:1
Minton, Benjamin, 1944, Je 29,23:6
Minton, Charles A, 1940, My 9,23:4
Minton, David M, 1943, Ap 20,23:4
Minton, David M Jr, 1967, N 14,47:1
Minton, Francis L, 1924, My 13,21:3
Minton, George D, 1950, Jl 4,17:3
Minton, Henry C Jr, 1967, Ap 26,47:3
Minton, Hugh, 1963, Ag 17,19:1
Minton, John E, 1939, F 2,19:3
Minton, John M Sr, 1944, Je 16,19:1
Minton, Joseph D, 1954, Jl 25,69:3
Minton, Lavinia M Mrs (por), 1948, My 30,34:5
Minton, Melville, 1955, Ag 2,23:1
Minton, Ogden, 1944, D 28,19:4
Minton, R Elmer, 1956, Ap 29,86:1
Minton, Ralph H, 1955, O 28,25:4
Minton, Robert P, 1945, N 8,19:4
Minton, Roger M, 1954, N 24,23:5
Minton, Rosco, 1968, Jl 5,25:1
Minton, Sherman, 1965, Ap 10,29:4
Minton, W J, 1949, D 14,31:3
Minton, William H, 1942, N 24,25:2
Mintrop, Ludger, 1956, Ja 4,27:4
Minturn, Harry L, 1963, Mr 9,7:5
Minturn, Hugh, 1915, F 11,9:6; 1941, D 29,15:4
Minturn, John C, 1941, O 27,17:5
Minturn, John W Mrs, 1913, O 5,IV,17:5
Minturn, Jonas, 1884, Ag 13,5:6
Minturn, Robert B, 1866, Ja 10,4:7
Minturn, Thomas J, 1956, Ag 9,25:5
Minty, John R, 1945, F 18,33:2
Mintz, Benjamin, 1940, S 12,25:5
Mintz, Benjamin Mrs, 1954, Ap 22,29:2
Mintz, Benyamin, 1961, My 31,33:4
Mintz, Charles, 1953, N 1,86:8
Mintz, Charles B, 1939, D 31,19:1
Mintz, David, 1960, S 10,21:6
Mintz, Eugene G, 1946, F 5,23:5
Mintz, Harry, 1945, Ag 26,43:3
Mintz, Harry A, 1959, Je 10,37:4
Mintz, Harry B, 1940, F 1,21:2
Mintz, Hyman E, 1966, Mr 26,29:2
Mintz, Israel, 1959, Ag 10,27:2
Mintz, Jack E, 1964, Ag 20,29:4
Mintz, Jake, 1947, O 24,23:5; 1957, Je 9,88:5
Mintz, Joseph Mrs, 1958, Ag 13,27:3
Mintz, Lawrence M, 1944, Ap 15,11:1
Mintz, Mary Mrs, 1937, O 6,25:3
Mintz, Maurice E, 1958, S 12,25:3
Mintz, Max Mrs, 1962, Je 19,35:3
Mintz, Nathan, 1962, Ap 21,19:5
Mintz, William L, 1957, Ag 8,23:2
Mintzer, George S, 1957, Je 14,25:4
Mintzer, Joseph, 1967, S 1,31:3
Mintzer, Nat, 1960, F 2,35:1
Mintzer, William B, 1962, Jl 4,21:3
Minuse, Alfred W, 1941, My 26,19:2
Minuse, Frank M, 1964, O 30,37:4
Minuse, John M, 1955, Ag 18,23:3
Minuskin, Nick, 1950, Je 16,25:3
Minzesheimer, Clarence C, 1910, My 5,11:4
Minzesheimer, Max, 1958, Jl 1,31:5
Minzesheimer, Max Mrs, 1948, O 2,15:2
Minzey, Frank, 1949, N 14,27:2
Mioduski, Adam, 1960, Je 3,31:2
Miotte, Joseph Mrs, 1961, F 16,31:4
Miquelarena, Jacinto, 1962, Ag 11,4:1
Mir, Joacquin, 1940, Ap 28,36:8
Mira Fernandes, Aureliano, 1958, Ap 21,23:5
Mirabella, Anthony, 1949, Jl 23,11:4
Mirabelli, August, 1945, O 25,21:3
Mirabelli, Michael A, 1949, N 15,25:2
Mirabelli, Michael A Mrs, 1946, Ja 24,21:4

Mirabito, Nicholas V, 1956, Ag 16,25:4
Miraglia, Donald, 1945, Je 20,25:4
Miraglia, Gary, 1945, Je 20,25:4
Miraglia, Louis, 1965, Ag 16,27:5
Miralles, Jose, 1947, D 24,21:1
Mirand, Duke de, 1935, Mr 7,24:2
Miranda, Carlos E, 1945, N 9,19:2
Miranda, Carmen (rites, Ag 9,25:1; trb, Ag 13,13:6), 1955, Ag 6,15:2
Miranda, Fred, 1957, Jl 7,61:1
Miranda, Jerry, 1961, Je 15,43:4
Miranda, Julius C de, 1956, N 29,35:1
Miranda, Luis, 1952, My 3,21:3
Miranda, Miguel (funl, F 23,25:3), 1953, F 22,60:3
Miranda, Pasquale Jr, 1960, Ja 22,27:3
Miranda, Ramon Dr, 1910, Ja 29,9:4
Miranda Cabral, P C O, 1949, Ap 7,29:4
Miranda Vincente, Francisco, 1960, Mr 14,8:6
Mirandi, Frank, 1944, Ja 5,17:2
Mirandon, Joseph E, 1954, Jl 15,27:5
Mirandy, Samuel F, 1961, Ap 7,31:2
Miratti, Frank, 1945, My 3,23:3
Mirbach, H Henry, 1949, Mr 24,27:2
Mirbeau, Octave, 1917, F 17,11:6
Mircoff, Jacob, 1950, O 1,105:1
Mireles, Gustavo E, 1939, My 5,23:2
Mires, Jules, 1871, Je 9,5:5
Mirfield, Arthur W, 1948, O 16,15:3
Miriam, Alice, 1922, Jl 24,15:5
Miriam, Sister (Parthenia Mary Mulry), 1910, Ap 19,9:5
Miriam Daniels, Sister, 1945, Ag 5,38:4
Miriam Francis, Sister (Florence McCarthy), 1968, Ja 25,37:2
Miriam Gabriel, Sister (Sisters of Charity), 1961, Ja 28,19:5
Miriam Margaret, Sister (Soc of St Margaret), 1953, My 14,29:5
Miriam Vincetta, Sister (Donachie), 1964, Ap 25,29:5
Mirick, George A, 1938, Ja 21,19:5
Mirisch, Harold J, 1968, D 7,47:1
Mirkil, I Hazelton, 1944, Je 24,13:5
Mirkin, Charles S, 1956, My 16,35:3
Mirkin, Joseph, 1956, Ja 16,21:2
Mirkine-Guetzevitch, Boris, 1955, Ap 7,27:2
Mirko, Prince, 1918, Mr 5,11:4
Mirman, Leon, 1941, N 16,57:2
Miro, Ricardo, 1940, Mr 3,44:4
Miro Quesada, Aurelio, 1950, My 16,31:3
Miro y Argenter, Jose Gen, 1925, My 3,5:1
Miron, Abraham, 1963, Jl 14,61:2
Miron, Joseph, 1941, Ap 13,39:1
Miron, Morris, 1956, Jl 3,25:5
Mironoff, Peter A, 1938, Je 21,19:3
Mirosevitch-Sorgo, Nico, 1966, S 15,43:6
Mirovitch, Alfred, 1959, Ag 4,27:2
Mirow, Martha M, 1948, Je 6,72:5
Mirrielees, Edith R, 1962, Je 5,41:4
Mirsky, Alfred E Mrs (Reba), 1966, N 23,39:2
Mirsky, Harrison B, 1959, Ap 8,37:1
Mirsky, Leo, 1967, Ap 10,35:2
Mirsky, Michael D, 1938, F 16,21:3
Mirsky, Peter Sviatopolk Prince, 1914, My 31,5:6
Mirsky, Rose, 1948, Ag 22,60:5
Mirsky, Samuel K, 1967, O 2,47:3
Mirsky, Samuel Mrs, 1964, D 4,39:1
Mirto, Nicholas (est appr, Ja 25,10:5), 1964, Ja 20, 43:4
Mirtz, Charles J, 1940, My 26,34:3
Mirza, Riza K Prince, 1941, My 6,9:3
Mirza, Youel B, 1947, O 1,29:6
Mirzaoff, August N Mrs, 1945, D 3,21:4
Miscall, Jack, 1966, Ja 6,27:2
Misch, Ludwig, 1967, Ap 24,33:5
Misch, Marion L Mrs, 1941, Ja 20,17:4
Misch, Paul, 1945, Ap 1,36:3
Misener, H R, 1945, Ag 13,19:4
Misener, Mary L Mrs, 1948, O 19,27:3
Misener, Robert, 1963, Je 5,41:4
Misenti, Santi, 1950, Ja 1,42:3
Miserendino, Vincenzo, 1943, D 28,17:4
Miserocchi, Teresita Mrs, 1937, Mr 16,23:3
Mishell, Boris, 1943, Jl 20,19:2
Mishima, Michiharu, 1965, Ap 22,33:4
Mishkin, Herman, 1948, F 7,15:2
Mishkin, Leo I Dr, 1937, Mr 5,21:4
Mishkin, Samuel, 1951, Je 8,27:2
Mishler, Isaac C, 1944, My 9,19:6
Mishler, Robert L, 1949, My 26,29:2
Misicka, Rudolph J Mrs, 1956, D 4,39:1
Miskell, Katherine Mrs, 1938, Ag 13,3:4
Miskewicz, Adolph, 1950, Ja 29,69:2
Miskey, John A Dr, 1911, Ap 16,II,11:4
Miskey, W F Jr, 1882, Mr 30,5:5
Miskimen, William A, 1956, S 1,15:5
Miskimin, Harry A, 1957, Mr 17,86:2
Miskin, Frederick, 1943, Mr 19,19:3
Miskin, Frederick Mrs, 1946, My 7,21:3
Miskus, Anna Mrs, 1908, Ag 2,7:7
Misner, Arthur L, 1948, My 28,23:4
Misner, Henry Mrs, 1949, D 7,31:5
Misner, John Mrs, 1952, Ag 19,23:2
Missbach, George A, 1959, My 23,25:4
Missbach, Joseph W, 1947, S 24,23:6
Missbach, William, 1960, Je 26,72:7
Missett, Margaret B Mrs, 1940, Je 23,31:3
Missia, Cardinal, 1902, Mr 25,9:3
Missik, William Mrs, 1947, Jl 8,27:1
Misson, Thomas, 1967, Jl 3,22:1
Missud, Jean, 1941, Jl 18,19:4
Mistinquett (funl plans, Ja 7,17:3), 1956, Ja 6,23:2
Mistler, Arthur O, 1948, O 30,15:4
Mistral, Frederic, 1914, Mr 26,11:3
Mistral, Frederic Mrs, 1943, F 9,23:1
Mistral, Gabriela, 1957, Ja 11,23:2
Mistrangelo, A M, 1930, N 8,17:3
Mistretta, Joseph, 1960, Ap 16,17:5
Mistri, N R, 1953, O 30,23:3
Mistruzzi, Aurelio, 1960, D 27,29:1
Misuraca, Giuseppe, 1962, Je 5,8:3
Misurata, Giuseppe V di, 1947, N 17,21:3
Misurell, Edwin, 1966, D 15,47:2
Mitcham, Edward H Mrs, 1947, Mr 20,15:5
Mitcham, William M, 1957, F 16,17:2
Mitchel, Charles A T, 1939, D 16,17:4
Mitchel, Elizabeth P Mrs, 1942, Jl 2,21:1
Mitchel, Eric, 1960, S 7,42:1
Mitchel, J H Chris, 1964, N 5,45:2
Mitchel, James J Mrs, 1963, Ag 12,21:5
Mitchel, John Purroy, 1925, Jl 20,15:5
Mitchel, John Purroy Mrs, 1918, Jl 8,11:3
Mitchel, Ormsby MacKnight Maj Gen, 1862, N 5,8:5
Mitchell, A B Mrs, 1948, S 1,24:2
Mitchell, A D, 1882, Mr 30,5:5
Mitchell, A S, 1881, F 25,5:3
Mitchell, Abbie (Mrs W M Cook), 1960, Mr 20,86:4
Mitchell, Abe (por), 1947, Je 12,25:5
Mitchell, Adalaide, 1963, Ap 2,47:2
Mitchell, Albert, 1952, Ag 27,27:3; 1954, O 5,27:3
Mitchell, Albert E, 1937, D 28,22:4; 1945, Mr 16,15:1
Mitchell, Albert G, 1941, Je 2,17:4
Mitchell, Alex, 1903, N 10,9:5; 1951, N 20,31:4
Mitchell, Alex C, 1911, Jl 8,9:4
Mitchell, Alex F, 1952, Jl 8,27:5
Mitchell, Alexander, 1887, Ap 20,1:5
Mitchell, Alfred, 1911, Ap 28,13:4; 1952, Je 17,12:3
Mitchell, Alfred Dr, 1915, Je 14,9:4
Mitchell, Alfred F, 1952, N 29,17:5
Mitchell, Alfred J, 1947, Ap 14,27:3
Mitchell, Alice H, 1953, Je 11,29:1
Mitchell, Allan C G, 1963, N 8,31:4
Mitchell, Allison H Mrs, 1954, Je 24,27:2
Mitchell, Allister F, 1950, S 17,105:1
Mitchell, Americus, 1938, S 3,13:5
Mitchell, Amy E, 1944, Ag 24,19:2
Mitchell, Andrew E, 1945, My 9,23:5
Mitchell, Andrew L Mrs, 1959, Ap 2,31:4
Mitchell, Anne A, 1943, O 26,23:3
Mitchell, Annie O T Mrs (will, F 25,16:6), 1937, Ja 3,II,8:4
Mitchell, Anthony Rev, 1917, Ja 19,7:3
Mitchell, Archibald, 1923, Ag 3,15:4
Mitchell, Arthur, 1953, Ja 13,32:3
Mitchell, Arthur H, 1954, D 1,31:4
Mitchell, Arthur L, 1939, My 14,III,7:2
Mitchell, Arthur Mrs, 1920, O 4,13:2
Mitchell, Arthur W, 1968, My 10,47:4
Mitchell, Arthur Y, 1941, Ag 15,17:3
Mitchell, Asahel W, 1948, Ag 28,16:2
Mitchell, Ashmore L L Mrs, 1967, Mr 19,93:1
Mitchell, Augustus M Mrs, 1938, F 7,15:2
Mitchell, Austin B, 1943, S 30,21:3
Mitchell, Baird, 1938, D 25,14:6
Mitchell, Barrett D, 1912, My 16,11:4
Mitchell, Benjamin F, 1912, F 14,11:4
Mitchell, Billy, 1952, Ag 31,44:6
Mitchell, Bruce, 1963, S 14,25:5
Mitchell, Burton J, 1941, Je 17,21:3
Mitchell, Butler C, 1948, Ja 18,60:2
Mitchell, Byron R, 1955, Ja 19,27:4
Mitchell, C Halsey, 1947, S 23,25:4
Mitchell, C S, 1935, Ag 15,19:3
Mitchell, C Stanley, 1945, Ap 8,20:7
Mitchell, Catherine, 1938, Ag 25,19:1
Mitchell, Charles B, 1942, F 25,20:2
Mitchell, Charles C, 1947, Mr 24,25:5
Mitchell, Charles D, 1940, Ap 2,26:2; 1960, F 18,33:3; 1964, My 18,29:3
Mitchell, Charles D Mrs (Mildred), 1965, Jl 2,29:4
Mitchell, Charles E, 1937, Mr 30,23:4; 1940, O 14,19:4
Mitchell, Charles E (funl plans, D 16,29:2), 1955, D 15,37:1
Mitchell, Charles E Mrs, 1953, N 15,88:1
Mitchell, Charles Elliott, 1911, Mr 18,13:6
Mitchell, Charles F, 1962, Jl 6,25:4
Mitchell, Charles F Mrs, 1959, My 30,17:2
Mitchell, Charles H, 1941, Ag 27,19:5; 1958, Ap 30, 33:3
Mitchell, Charles L, 1946, Je 5,23:5
Mitchell, Charles S, 1922, Ja 10,19:2; 1943, Ag 22,36:4
Mitchell, Charles W, 1958, Je 6,23:2
Mitchell, Charles W Dr, 1917, D 29,11:4
Mitchell, Chauncey L, 1940, F 5,17:2
Mitchell, Clara Van Kirk Mrs, 1923, Jl 21,9:7
Mitchell, Clarence, 1963, N 7,37:2
Mitchell, Clarence B, 1956, S 27,35:2
Mitchell, Clarence B Mrs, 1967, Ja 6,35:4
Mitchell, Clarence V S, 1966, F 23,39:4
Mitchell, Clifford, 1939, O 20,23:4
Mitchell, Cornelius B, 1910, My 26,9:4
Mitchell, Cornelius Berrien Mrs, 1921, S 29,17:5
Mitchell, Cornelius von E, 1966, F 22,23:4
Mitchell, Dale G, 1949, My 20,28:5
Mitchell, Dana P, 1966, F 8,80:1
Mitchell, Dana P Mrs, 1966, F 8,80:1
Mitchell, David, 1956, Jl 15,60:4
Mitchell, David F, 1950, D 28,25:2
Mitchell, David J, 1874, S 23,4:7
Mitchell, David R, 1959, Ja 27,33:2
Mitchell, Dennis H Mrs, 1943, Ag 20,15:5
Mitchell, Dodson L, 1939, Je 3,15:4
Mitchell, Donald, 1913, N 22,15:5
Mitchell, Donald D, 1938, Ag 2,19:5
Mitchell, Donald G, 1908, D 18,9:4
Mitchell, Donald W, 1962, N 6,33:4
Mitchell, Douglas Mrs, 1951, F 3,15:3
Mitchell, Douglas T, 1955, Ag 3,23:4
Mitchell, E A, 1937, S 4,15:3
Mitchell, E K, 1934, O 6,15:4
Mitchell, Earle (por), 1946, F 18,21:3
Mitchell, Earle E Mrs, 1946, Mr 30,15:2
Mitchell, Ed Gen, 1871, Mr 9,2:3
Mitchell, Edgar, 1953, Je 25,27:4
Mitchell, Edgar O Mrs, 1944, Ap 12,21:2
Mitchell, Edmund, 1917, Ap 1,19:3; 1944, N 11,13:2
Mitchell, Edward, 1909, F 16,9:5
Mitchell, Edward Bedinger Lt, 1918, Ja 26,13:8
Mitchell, Edward E, 1946, Ag 27,27:5
Mitchell, Edward F, 1941, My 8,23:4
Mitchell, Edward J, 1956, Ag 21,29:3
Mitchell, Edward J Col, 1923, Ja 16,21:3
Mitchell, Edward S, 1945, My 19,19:5
Mitchell, Edward S Mrs, 1957, Je 14,25:1
Mitchell, Edward T, 1944, F 16,17:2
Mitchell, Edward W, 1905, Ap 9,4:4
Mitchell, Edwin H, 1953, F 6,19:3
Mitchell, Edwin T, 1953, Ap 4,13:5
Mitchell, Edwin W, 1953, Ap 22,29:2
Mitchell, Elizabeth G, 1939, Ap 12,23:4
Mitchell, Elizabeth W, 1945, Ap 7,15:5
Mitchell, Ella G, 1956, My 29,27:2
Mitchell, Elwood H, 1947, N 5,27:4
Mitchell, Emil, 1942, O 21,21:4
Mitchell, Ernest, 1966, Jl 5,37:2
Mitchell, Esther Mrs, 1953, N 27,27:5
Mitchell, Eugene M, 1944, Je 18,36:2
Mitchell, Ewing Y, 1954, Ag 30,17:4
Mitchell, F L Sen, 1904, Je 30,9:6
Mitchell, Frances, 1940, My 7,25:4
Mitchell, Frank J, 1949, O 6,31:5
Mitchell, Frank J R, 1937, My 12,23:2
Mitchell, Frank J R Mrs, 1954, S 21,27:1
Mitchell, Frank T, 1941, My 22,21:4
Mitchell, Fred, 1944, Ap 6,23:5; 1946, N 29,25:2
Mitchell, Fred G, 1939, Ja 14,17:2
Mitchell, Frederick, 1941, S 17,23:6; 1956, F 12,88:7
Mitchell, Frederick D, 1950, Jl 21,19:5
Mitchell, Frederick L Mrs, 1967, F 12,92:8
Mitchell, Frederick M, 1960, Mr 28,29:1
Mitchell, Frederick T, 1948, N 23,29:1
Mitchell, Frederick W, 1943, S 7,23:4
Mitchell, George, 1937, Jl 5,17:4; 1948, Mr 1,23:1; 1967, S 7,45:4
Mitchell, George A, 1943, My 4,23:4; 1950, S 29,27:3
Mitchell, George A Mrs, 1958, O 9,37:2
Mitchell, George A Sr, 1955, Je 24,21:4
Mitchell, George D, 1950, Ja 4,46:4
Mitchell, George E Mrs, 1951, Ja 2,23:2
Mitchell, George F, 1952, Mr 27,30:4
Mitchell, George H, 1949, S 27,27:3; 1951, Je 7,33:2
Mitchell, George Mrs, 1947, Je 24,23:2
Mitchell, George R, 1951, Ja 9,30:2
Mitchell, George T, 1963, Ap 6,19:5
Mitchell, George W, 1943, Ja 27,21:3; 1943, O 23,13:3
Mitchell, Glen L, 1952, O 29,29:6
Mitchell, Grace, 1941, Mr 25,23:3
Mitchell, Grant, 1957, My 2,31:3
Mitchell, Guernsey, 1921, Ag 2,9:4
Mitchell, H Prof, 1902, D 2,9:4
Mitchell, H Walton, 1943, O 12,27:3
Mitchell, Hal, 1956, Ag 9,25:5
Mitchell, Harbour, 1947, Mr 25,26:3
Mitchell, Harold, 1961, Je 2,31:2
Mitchell, Harold C, 1938, F 23,23:6
Mitchell, Harold E, 1947, Jl 27,45:2; 1950, Je 20,27:1
Mitchell, Harold E Sr, 1967, Ag 5,21:8
Mitchell, Harold J, 1966, Je 18,31:5
Mitchell, Harold L, 1946, Je 17,21:3
Mitchell, Harry B, 1955, O 1,19:6
Mitchell, Harry B Mrs, 1951, S 7,29:1
Mitchell, Harry H, 1944, D 12,23:1
Mitchell, Harry L, 1948, S 11,16:8
Mitchell, Harvey R, 1912, F 24,11:5
Mitchell, Henry B, 1956, Jl 31,23:4
Mitchell, Henry C, 1946, F 13,23:2
Mitchell, Henry George, 1911, Je 1,11:5
Mitchell, Henry H, 1955, Ap 7,27:5
Mitchell, Henry J, 1945, Ap 8,35:1
Mitchell, Henry T, 1903, O 15,9:7

Mitchell, Herbert E, 1953, Ap 9,27:3
Mitchell, Herbert L Rev, 1909, Ag 4,7:3
Mitchell, Herman G, 1937, Ja 27,21:1
Mitchell, Howard C, 1951, Je 23,15:2
Mitchell, Howard H, 1943, Mr 14,24:6
Mitchell, Hubert S, 1955, F 21,21:4
Mitchell, Humphrey, 1950, Ag 2,25:2
Mitchell, I Allen, 1960, Mr 14,30:1
Mitchell, Isabel S, 1946, O 29,25:5
Mitchell, J, 1926, Je 24,21:4
Mitchell, J F Rev, 1881, O 10,5:6
Mitchell, J L, 1880, Ap 15,5:5; 1882, Jl 5,8:4
Mitchell, J R, 1933, F 1,18:3
Mitchell, J W, 1878, Ag 1,2:6
Mitchell, Jack M, 1965, Je 1,39:2
Mitchell, Jacques A, 1938, Mr 24,23:5
Mitchell, James, 1920, Jl 24,9:6; 1946, My 30,21:2; 1951, Jl 27,19:2
Mitchell, James A, 1962, Mr 20,37:3; 1967, Mr 23,35:1
Mitchell, James B, 1954, My 1,15:6
Mitchell, James H Jr Mrs, 1949, Ja 25,23:2
Mitchell, James J, 1940, Ag 25,35:3; 1959, F 11,39:4
Mitchell, James L, 1916, O 11,11:4; 1941, Jl 15,20:3
Mitchell, James M (por), 1948, O 15,23:1
Mitchell, James M, 1958, S 25,33:1
Mitchell, James M Mrs, 1959, Jl 25,17:7
Mitchell, James N, 1942, N 26,27:5
Mitchell, James P (funl, O 24,29:6), 1964, O 20,37:1
Mitchell, James S, 1942, F 19,19:2
Mitchell, James S Mrs, 1955, O 24,27:4
Mitchell, James T, 1951, D 24,1:1
Mitchell, James Tyndale, 1915, Jl 5,7:7
Mitchell, Jesse H, 1955, Mr 6,88:8
Mitchell, Jessie A, 1964, Mr 10,37:2
Mitchell, Joe, 1938, S 18,44:5
Mitchell, John, 1867, Mr 17,4:6; 1874, D 31,4:6; 1912, Mr 31,15:3
Mitchell, John (funl), 1919, S 11,15:4
Mitchell, John, 1950, Je 8,31:2; 1960, S 12,29:1; 1967, Mr 18,29:1
Mitchell, John A, 1918, Je 30,19:1; 1938, S 22,23:3
Mitchell, John A Mrs, 1954, Ap 13,31:4; 1963, My 23, 37:3
Mitchell, John A Sr, 1951, F 20,25:2
Mitchell, John C Mrs, 1921, N 26,13:6; 1944, Je 4,42:4
Mitchell, John F, 1939, Ap 4,25:1; 1956, F 15,31:3
Mitchell, John Fulton, 1910, Ag 5,9:5
Mitchell, John G, 1942, Ja 6,23:1
Mitchell, John G Jr, 1948, Ap 11,73:1
Mitchell, John H, 1905, D 9,6:4; 1961, D 20,33:2
Mitchell, John H Mrs, 1961, Je 20,33:4
Mitchell, John J, 1925, S 14,19:4; 1944, O 16,19:5; 1947, Ja 15,25:3
Mitchell, John J Jr, 1954, S 17,27:1
Mitchell, John K, 1949, D 1,31:4
Mitchell, John K Dr, 1917, Ap 11,13:6
Mitchell, John K Mrs, 1950, O 15,104:5
Mitchell, John L, 1942, O 28,14:3
Mitchell, John M, 1950, Mr 2,27:3; 1950, Mr 11,15:1
Mitchell, John Mrs, 1956, F 28,31:2
Mitchell, John R, 1939, Mr 25,15:3; 1949, S 26,25:2
Mitchell, John R Mrs, 1958, O 22,35:1; 1966, Jl 25,27:2
Mitchell, John T H Mrs, 1967, Ap 29,35:4
Mitchell, John W, 1915, Je 20,15:4
Mitchell, John W Mrs, 1958, Je 19,31:5
Mitchell, John W W, 1939, O 1,53:1
Mitchell, John William, 1925, Jl 3,13:6
Mitchell, Joseph, 1925, S 6,13:3; 1958, D 3,37:4
Mitchell, Joseph A, 1956, My 22,42:6; 1959, N 17,35:2
Mitchell, Joseph B, 1950, O 31,27:4
Mitchell, Joseph E, 1952, D 18,29:5
Mitchell, Joseph J, 1940, Ag 19,17:6
Mitchell, Joseph J Mrs, 1950, Ag 4,21:2
Mitchell, L E, 1935, O 22,22:4
Mitchell, L R C Mrs (por), 1941, Je 22,32:6
Mitchell, Langdon E Mrs, 1944, Je 9,15:5
Mitchell, Lanier C Mrs, 1950, Ap 3,23:1
Mitchell, Leander P, 1912, D 7,15:5
Mitchell, Leeds, 1957, Jl 27,17:2
Mitchell, Lennard H, 1944, D 23,13:4
Mitchell, Leon A, 1950, F 15,27:2
Mitchell, Leonard C, 1956, Mr 31,15:5
Mitchell, Leonard J, 1966, Ag 16,39:5
Mitchell, Lester F, 1957, Ap 18,29:4
Mitchell, Louis, 1943, O 17,49:1; 1957, S 13,23:3
Mitchell, Lt-Com, 1873, S 16,4:7
Mitchell, Lucille Mrs, 1957, N 17,87:1
Mitchell, Lucy S (Mrs Wesley C), 1967, O 17,44:2
Mitchell, Macgregor, 1938, Ap 26,21:1
Mitchell, Maggie (funl, Mr 25,13:3), 1918, Mr 23, 13:3
Mitchell, Margaret, 1949, Ag 17,23:1
Mitchell, Margaret A, 1953, O 31,17:6
Mitchell, Margaret D Mrs, 1940, Mr 20,27:3
Mitchell, Margaret W, 1941, N 27,23:5
Mitchell, Maria, 1889, Je 29,5:5
Mitchell, Marion, 1958, S 28,89:1
Mitchell, Mary A, 1947, My 9,21:3
Mitchell, Matthias O, 1950, Ap 29,15:2
Mitchell, Maxwell L, 1965, Mr 28,92:6
Mitchell, Meldon, 1967, F 14,43:1
Mitchell, Melviva, 1948, S 13,21:2
Mitchell, Michael, 1959, Ag 23,95:5
Mitchell, Michael Mrs, 1952, Je 21,15:2
Mitchell, Millard, 1953, O 14,29:1
Mitchell, Miller, 1954, S 16,29:5
Mitchell, Mother (C S Mitchell), 1949, Mr 25,23:3
Mitchell, Muriel E, 1946, F 4,25:2
Mitchell, Myron C, 1953, Mr 27,23:3
Mitchell, Myron S, 1956, My 16,35:4
Mitchell, Nathan J, 1919, My 15,17:6
Mitchell, Nathaniel M, 1965, Ap 17,19:5
Mitchell, Nathaniel Sr, 1950, F 14,26:5
Mitchell, Neville, 1954, S 17,27:3
Mitchell, Norma (Mrs W D Steele), 1967, My 30, 19:5
Mitchell, Oliver W, 1948, D 21,31:3
Mitchell, Orville J, 1950, Jl 29,13:4
Mitchell, Oswald, 1949, Ap 28,31:3
Mitchell, P Lincoln Mrs, 1956, Jl 5,25:4
Mitchell, Patrick C, 1946, O 15,26:2
Mitchell, Paul C, 1964, Ja 4,23:4
Mitchell, Paul G Mrs, 1955, O 12,29:1
Mitchell, Percy, 1944, Ap 16,42:1
Mitchell, Percy Van G, 1967, F 2,36:1
Mitchell, Peter C, 1945, Jl 3,13:7
Mitchell, Peter H, 1950, F 15,27:2
Mitchell, Phil A, 1951, My 25,27:4
Mitchell, Phil J, 1957, Mr 3,84:4
Mitchell, Philip A, 1967, Mr 23,35:4
Mitchell, R H, 1933, F 13,15:1
Mitchell, R Paul, 1959, Ag 28,23:3
Mitchell, R Verne, 1955, Ja 3,27:5
Mitchell, Ralph W, 1951, F 11,88:1
Mitchell, Reginald J (por), 1937, Je 12,15:3
Mitchell, Reuben A, 1937, Ja 11,19:5
Mitchell, Richard, 1946, F 12,28:1
Mitchell, Richard A, 1956, Jl 22,61:1
Mitchell, Richard B, 1961, Mr 9,29:5
Mitchell, Richie, 1949, Je 27,27:5
Mitchell, Rob G Col, 1904, My 21,6:2
Mitchell, Robert, 1965, N 13,29:5
Mitchell, Robert B, 1938, Jl 22,17:4
Mitchell, Robert C, 1942, Ja 9,21:2
Mitchell, Robert J, 1947, S 17,25:2; 1949, Ja 11,27:2; 1965, D 24,17:3
Mitchell, Robert J Mrs, 1962, Jl 12,29:4
Mitchell, Robert L, 1958, N 4,27:4
Mitchell, Robert M, 1948, N 16,29:1
Mitchell, Robert S, 1942, Ja 12,15:4
Mitchell, Robert W Mrs, 1945, Ag 18,11:6
Mitchell, Robie L, 1968, F 9,27:2
Mitchell, Roy, 1944, Jl 28,13:4
Mitchell, Ruth B Mrs, 1940, Jl 28,27:4
Mitchell, Ruth C, 1954, F 19,34:1
Mitchell, S K Rev, 1903, D 9,9:5
Mitchell, S Louise, 1946, D 14,15:5
Mitchell, S Weir Dr, 1914, Ja 5,9:3
Mitchell, S Weir Mrs, 1914, Ja 16,9:5
Mitchell, Samuel, 1967, My 20,35:3
Mitchell, Samuel A, 1960, F 23,31:1
Mitchell, Samuel A Mrs, 1955, N 22,35:1
Mitchell, Samuel C (por), 1948, Ag 21,15:4
Mitchell, Samuel J, 1937, Mr 30,23:4
Mitchell, Samuel P (will), 1940, F 21,21:1
Mitchell, Samuel S, 1940, Ag 15,19:2
Mitchell, Sidney, 1938, F 26,15:4
Mitchell, Sidney A, 1966, N 29,43:2
Mitchell, Sidney J, 1949, S 15,27:4
Mitchell, Sidney Z, 1944, F 19,13:2
Mitchell, Sidney Z Mrs, 1944, Ap 22,13:6
Mitchell, Spencer T, 1939, F 24,19:5
Mitchell, Stanley, 1958, Jl 28,23:3
Mitchell, Suder Q, 1947, Mr 29,15:4
Mitchell, Sydney B, 1951, S 23,86:2
Mitchell, Sydney K, 1948, Ja 24,15:6
Mitchell, T Carlisle, 1949, Ap 26,25:1
Mitchell, T L John M, 1940, D 28,15:4
Mitchell, Terrence, 1951, My 11,17:2
Mitchell, Thomas, 1962, D 18,4:6
Mitchell, Thomas E Mrs, 1967, O 26,47:2
Mitchell, Thomas F, 1951, S 8,19:8
Mitchell, Thomas Mrs, 1955, O 3,27:5; 1965, Jl 24,21:3
Mitchell, Thomas S, 1940, Ja 10,21:4
Mitchell, Victor, 1940, N 8,21:4
Mitchell, Victor W, 1946, My 23,21:5
Mitchell, Vinton W, 1941, F 5,20:2
Mitchell, W A, 1941, Mr 7,21:2
Mitchell, W G Gen, 1883, My 31,5:5
Mitchell, W L, 1936, F 20,19:1
Mitchell, W Robert, 1961, Ja 18,33:2
Mitchell, W Sir, 1878, My 3,5:4
Mitchell, Walter B J, 1966, My 20,47:3
Mitchell, Walter H, 1955, Je 12,87:1
Mitchell, Walter L, 1961, D 11,31:2; 1968, S 20,47:4
Mitchell, Walter M, 1947, Mr 27,27:2
Mitchell, Wesley C, 1948, O 30,15:3
Mitchell, Willard A (por), 1942, D 21,23:3
Mitchell, Willard A Mrs, 1946, S 26,25:2
Mitchell, William, 1921, O 19,19:4; 1939, Ap 14,23:4; 1954, Je 1,27:3
Mitchell, William A, 1957, Ap 14,86:8
Mitchell, William Anderson Dr, 1913, S 27,13:5
Mitchell, William C, 1937, Ja 10,II,9:4
Mitchell, William Com, 1871, Jl 19,8:2
Mitchell, William D, 1955, Ag 25,23:4; 1962, F 24,27:4
Mitchell, William D Mrs, 1952, O 4,17:2
Mitchell, William E, 1960, Ag 2,29:5
Mitchell, William E G, 1944, N 12,49:2
Mitchell, William E G Mrs, 1956, Ja 12,27:3
Mitchell, William F, 1955, Ag 5,19:5
Mitchell, William F Mrs, 1957, O 15,30:3
Mitchell, William G, 1944, Ag 17,17:4; 1951, Mr 27 29:2; 1955, D 2,27:4
Mitchell, William G Mrs, 1952, Jl 4,13:6
Mitchell, William H, 1910, Mr 9,9:3; 1949, N 3,29:5 1958, S 18,31:4
Mitchell, William J, 1945, Ja 16,19:1; 1954, Ja 17,92
Mitchell, William L, 1940, D 19,25:5; 1964, My 20, 43:4
Mitchell, William Mrs, 1946, Je 5,23:6; 1952, Jl 5,1 1953, Mr 22,86:2
Mitchell, William S, 1921, Ja 1,9:4; 1940, My 21,23 1941, O 4,15:5; 1947, Ag 26,23:2
Mitchell, William T B, 1941, Jl 9,21:6
Mitchell, William W, 1938, Ag 21,32:6
Mitchell, Willis G, 1960, F 4,31:2
Mitchell, Willis G Mrs, 1960, Jl 28,27:3
Mitchell, Willis H, 1955, Ap 8,21:3
Mitchell, Wilmot B, 1962, Ap 24,37:3
Mitchell, Wirt, 1955, Ja 5,23:5
Mitchell-Hedges, Frederick A, 1959, Je 13,21:3
Mitchelson, Archibald, 1945, D 31,17:2
Mitchelson, Joseph C, 1911, S 27,13:5
Mitchem, Horace F Mrs, 1952, D 2,36:4
Mitchener, R W, 1925, Ap 4,17:5
Mitchill, S L, 1881, N 6,7:4
Mitchill, W H Mrs, 1917, Mr 27,11:4
Mite, Louis, 1962, Je 14,33:2
Miter, Harry F, 1951, O 6,19:6
Mithoefer, James, 1963, Jl 29,1:1
Mithouard, Adrien, 1919, Mr 29,13:2
Mitin, Alex M, 1953, Mr 5,10:2
Mitkevich, Vladimir, 1951, Je 3,93:1
Mitler, Bernhardt E, 1965, My 6,39:2
Mitler, Herbert E Mrs, 1950, Ap 2,92:3
Mitlitzky, Samuel E Mrs, 1954, Ja 8,21:2
Mitman, Wesley L, 1949, D 6,31:5
Mitnick, Isadore, 1942, Ja 2,23:2
Mitnitsky, Isaac, 1903, N 30,1:1
Mitosky, Joseph, 1953, Ja 12,27:4
Mitra, Ajai K, 1961, D 14,14:8
Mitra, Bhupendra N Sir (por), 1937, F 26,21:4
Mitra, Sisir K, 1963, Ag 14,33:5
Mitrani, Solomon H, 1951, D 21,27:4
Mitre, Bartolome Gen, 1906, Ja 20,4:2
Mitre, Jorge A, 1966, Je 5,85:1
Mitre, Luis, 1950, N 9,33:1
Mitri, Leonardo de, 1956, Jl 16,21:1
Mitropoulos, Dimitri (trb, N 3,48:1; will, N 10,57 1960, N 3,1:3
Mitscher, Marc A, 1947, F 4,5:1
Mitscher, Myrta S Mrs, 1948, S 13,21:2
Mitsui, Benzo, 1941, My 23,21:3
Mitsui, Takasue, 1945, Je 7,19:5
Mitsui, Takayasu Baron, 1922, Ja 6,17:5
Mittag, Winfred G, 1968, F 27,43:3
Mittaine, Paul M, 1955, Ja 29,15:2
Mittasch, Ernest J, 1958, O 18,21:5
Mittelholzer, Edgar, 1965, My 7,8:5
Mittelhouser, Eugene, 1949, D 22,23:5
Mittell, Philip, 1943, Ja 28,19:3
Mittell, Sherman, 1942, Jl 23,19:2
Mittelman, Samuel, 1943, D 17,27:4
Mittelmark, Seymour, 1944, D 28,19:2
Mittelsdorf, George, 1940, O 12,17:4
Mittelstaedt, Bernard F, 1945, Je 3,31:1
Mittelstaedt, Charles B J, 1941, Jl 27,31:2
Mittelstaedt, Emma T, 1949, O 22,17:2
Mittelstaedt, Harriet, 1964, Mr 14,23:5
Mittelstaedt, William E, 1940, S 4,23:3
Mitten, Arthur G, 1938, N 25,23:3
Mitten, Frank S, 1943, Je 24,21:1
Mitten, Fred Mrs, 1938, Ja 24,23:4
Mitten, Peter F Sr, 1948, D 12,92:6
Mittendorf, Albert E, 1949, Ap 4,23:5
Mittendorf, Alfred D Mrs, 1960, Jl 7,31:5
Mittendorf, George S, 1952, N 12,27:3
Mittendorf, George S Mrs, 1962, S 21,30:1
Mittendorf, William, 1952, O 11,19:6
Mittendorf, William K, 1957, D 8,88:3
Mittenmeyer, William E, 1952, Mr 12,27:1
Mittenthal, Abraham, 1954, D 31,13:5
Mitterling, Ralph, 1956, Ja 23,25:5
Mitterling, Stephen, 1950, Mr 22,27:2
Mittiga, Agostino, 1949, Ja 6,23:5
Mittle, Theodore I, 1953, F 24,25:3
Mittleman, Armine H, 1950, S 28,32:3
Mittleman, Chaim, 1940, D 1,62:2
Mittleman, Edward B, 1949, S 27,27:1
Mittleman, Harry S, 1959, D 10,39:1
Mittleman, Isaac, 1941, Ap 19,15:3
Mittleman, Meyer, 1957, D 4,39:5
Mittlemann, Bela, 1959, O 5,31:2
Mittler, Benjamin B, 1948, F 29,60:8
Mittler, Harold M, 1953, Jl 28,19:6
Mittler, Leo, 1958, My 18,86:3
Mitton, Arthur G, 1952, My 20,25:2
Mitton, George W, 1947, N 15,17:6

Mitton, Richard, 1945, Je 23,13:5
Mitty, John J (funl, O 21,21:3), 1961, O 16,29:4
Mitty, William F, 1967, N 28,51:4
Mitubatuba, Chief, 1954, D 4,17:5
Mitzian, Frank, 1950, Je 16,25:4
Miugala, Tony, 1950, O 24,29:1
Miura, Tamaki, 1946, My 27,23:1
Mivart, St G Dr, 1900, Ap 2,1:6
Miville-Deschenes, Elzear, 1956, Je 15,25:4
Mix, Charles M Mrs, 1951, O 29,23:4
Mix, Charles W, 1944, N 11,13:4
Mix, Clifton H Rev, 1937, Ag 24,21:3
Mix, E, 1930, F 19,25:1
Mix, Edward T Sr, 1949, My 8,76:7
Mix, Elizabeth Mrs, 1937, Jl 25,II,7:3
Mix, Emil, 1954, D 20,29:2
Mix, Emil Mrs, 1961, Mr 27,31:4
Mix, Florence, 1922, N 7,17:4
Mix, James E, 1954, Mr 6,15:4
Mix, James T, 1945, Ja 2,19:5
Mix, John Maj, 1881, O 27,5:4
Mix, M Emma, 1942, Ap 4,13:3
Mix, Robert Johnson, 1918, O 18,13:2
Mix, William, 1943, Jl 28,15:2
Mixer, Charles A, 1947, O 26,70:3
Mixer, Edwin R Mrs, 1952, Jl 9,27:4
Mixer, S F, 1883, S 18,4:6
Mixsell, Austin D, 1916, Ja 16,17:5
Mixsell, Donald G, 1947, N 21,27:2
Mixsell, Harold R, 1958, F 15,17:4
Mixsell, Raymond B, 1949, D 28,25:3
Mixter, Florence K Mrs, 1949, Mr 22,25:5
Mixter, George, 1968, N 16,37:4
Mixter, George W, 1947, Ja 30,25:5
Mixter, William J, 1958, Mr 17,29:1
Miyagi, Michio, 1956, Je 26,13:4
Miyajima, Toshio, 1954, Ap 14,3:2
Miyakawa, Masuji, 1916, Mr 6,13:4
Mize, Johnny Mrs, 1957, Jl 15,19:4
Mize, Sidney C, 1965, Ap 27,37:2
Mizell, Horace W, 1947, Ap 3,25:4
Mizen, George E, 1942, S 6,30:6
Mizner, Henry Rutgeras Brig-Gen, 1915, Ja 6,13:4
Mizner, W, 1933, Ap 4,17:3
Mizuno, Kokichi, 1914, My 24,IV,7:4
Mizzi, Enrico, 1950, D 21,29:4
Mizzy, Albert D, 1964, Ja 23,31:1
Mjaaland, Olav, 1961, Je 10,23:4
Mketko, Karol, 1948, D 24,17:2
Mkitarian, Luther M, 1958, O 1,37:4
Mkoba, Krimples, 1951, Ap 26,29:2
Mlynarski, Emil Mrs, 1960, Jl 5,31:2
Mnich, John J Sr, 1950, F 28,29:2
Mnuchin, Leon A, 1966, Ag 10,41:3
Mo Teh-hui, 1968, Ap 20,33:5
Moak, Franz H, 1949, Je 9,31:5
Moakley, Arthur I, 1963, Je 19,37:3
Moakley, James I, 1945, N 5,19:3
Moakley, John F, 1955, My 23,23:1
Moale, Edward Brig-Gen, 1913, S 28,7:6
Moar, David W, 1957, N 13,32:3
Moasili, Mustapha Bin Hakim, 1964, Ja 19,76:5
Moat, Howard B Mrs, 1953, Ag 2,72:5
Moate, John W, 1947, Je 15,60:1
Mobb, Hunter Mrs, 1910, Ap 17,II,11:4
Moberg, Edward J, 1946, O 31,25:2
Moberg, Goesta Mrs, 1946, Mr 16,13:5
Moberly, Annie, 1937, My 7,25:1
Moberly, Edward E, 1948, O 15,23:2
Mobley, Mary E, 1948, D 30,19:3
Mobley, Nathan Mrs, 1964, D 24,19:5
Mobley, Thomas E, 1949, Jl 3,26:8
Mobus, Edward, 1955, Mr 29,29:2
Mocenni, Cardinal, 1904, N 15,5:3
Moch, Eugene W, 1939, My 17,23:6
Moch, Jules Mme, 1962, Jl 27,2:1
Mochales, Marquis de, 1919, Jl 22,9:5
Mochizuki, Keisuke (por), 1941, Ja 2,23:4
Mock, Bernard L, 1948, Jl 3,15:7
Mock, Charles, 1950, Mr 9,29:2
Mock, Charles R, 1941, Jl 25,15:2
Mock, Ervin C, 1954, Mr 10,25:2
Mock, Eugene Sr, 1954, F 2,27:1
Mock, Frank C, 1964, N 15,86:6
Mock, Harry E, 1959, Jl 1,25:7
Mock, Henry, 1942, My 27,23:5
Mock, Henry C, 1958, My 16,25:3
Mock, Hugo, 1955, Mr 25,23:2
Mock, J Ernest, 1944, S 7,23:2
Mock, James C, 1961, Jl 8,19:6
Mock, John, 1952, O 22,27:5; 1957, My 11,21:5
Mock, Joseph, 1953, D 15,44:8
Mock, Nicholas J, 1924, Ap 19,13:5
Mock, Richard, 1905, Ja 7,7:5
Mock, Ruth, 1938, Ja 15,15:3
Mockaitis, John B, 1958, Jl 22,27:1
Mockel, Marie, 1947, Mr 18,27:3
Mockett, E E, 1954, F 4,25:4
Mockler, Martin J Jr, 1942, Ag 29,15:3
Mockler, Minnie R Mrs, 1940, S 7,15:3
Mockler, Robert D, 1968, Je 10,45:2
Mockler, Stanton G, 1968, F 24,27:2
Mockler, Thomas W, 1948, Mr 7,68:4
Mockridge, Frank W, 1946, S 25,27:1
Mockridge, Frank W Mrs, 1951, Jl 2,23:5
Mockridge, John Mrs, 1942, My 30,15:3
Mockridge, Lavinia I, 1959, S 18,31:2
Mockridge, Oscar A (por), 1941, Ja 27,15:1
Mockridge, Oscar A Jr, 1963, Ap 3,47:1
Modak, Ramakrishna Shahu Archbishop, 1968, Ap 15,43:3
Modance, Abraham M, 1959, N 26,37:1
Modard, M J M, 1947, D 27,13:2
Modarelli, Alfred E, 1957, S 23,27:6
Modarelli, Antonio, 1954, Ap 3,15:3
Modave, Jeanne, 1953, Ja 7,31:6
Modavis, Howard, 1968, Ag 9,35:4
Modavis, Howard R Sr, 1947, N 6,27:4
Modder, Montagu F, 1958, Je 2,27:4
Moddrel, Charles A, 1942, O 6,23:2
Mode, Douglas E, 1962, O 23,37:3
Mode, Joseph H Capt, 1937, Mr 31,23:1
Model, Jean, 1955, My 31,27:5
Model, Jean Mrs, 1960, Jl 3,32:3
Model, Max, 1950, S 12,28:3
Modell, Boris Mrs, 1949, O 3,17:6
Modell, Celia Mrs, 1942, My 27,23:5
Modell, George L Mrs, 1968, Ap 8,47:2
Modelski, Izydor R, 1962, S 28,25:6
Modemann, Eugene M, 1940, Jl 30,19:3
Moderno, Alice, 1946, F 22,25:3
Moderski, Seigfried L, 1953, Ja 1,23:2
Moderwell, Charles M, 1955, D 21,29:2
Modesta, Mother, 1948, Ap 3,15:5
Modesta, Sister (A Nolte), 1954, Mr 2,25:1
Modestus, Bro, 1948, My 20,29:2
Modica, Anthony N, 1966, F 16,43:4
Modica, Charles, 1953, Ap 7,29:1
Modica, Santo G, 1947, Jl 25,18:2
Modigliani, Giuseppe, 1947, O 9,25:2
Modjeska, Helena, 1909, Ap 9,9:1
Modjeski, Charles E J, 1944, O 2,19:5
Modjeski, Ralph (por), 1940, Je 28,19:1
Modlin, Earl H, 1950, Ag 15,29:2
Modne, Edythe H, 1957, Ja 11,23:1
Modra, Rodman L, 1944, Mr 19,42:1
Modzelewski, Zygmunt, 1954, Je 20,85:1
Moe, Alfred K, 1950, D 13,35:1
Moe, Alfred K Mrs, 1939, Ja 26,21:5
Moe, Kenneth W, 1961, N 16,39:2
Moe, Mathias J, 1958, Je 3,31:5
Moe, Ray W Mrs, 1948, N 7,88:6
Moe, Raymond W, 1941, O 28,23:4
Moebus, August Mrs, 1947, S 18,25:2
Moebus, Harry, 1966, O 23,88:8
Moeckel, Otto, 1937, Ja 24,II,8:2
Moehlenpah, Henry A, 1944, N 11,13:4
Moehlenpah, William F Mrs, 1952, Mr 21,23:2
Moehlig, Jacob, 1950, Jl 20,25:5
Moehlman, Conrad A, 1961, S 21,35:2
Moehring, Charles F, 1945, Ja 29,13:1
Moehring, Edward, 1937, F 24,23:5
Moehring, Lester A (por), 1947, Ap 12,17:3
Moehringer, Francis J, 1959, My 11,27:4
Moehrke, Henry E Mrs, 1949, Ja 28,22:3
Moeller, Albert J, 1950, N 23,35:1
Moeller, Alfred L, 1952, F 16,13:1
Moeller, Arnold P, 1965, Je 14,33:1
Moeller, August J, 1943, Ag 28,11:6
Moeller, Carl F, 1937, My 20,21:2
Moeller, Edgar J, 1954, My 26,29:3
Moeller, Ferdinand A, 1946, D 18,30:2
Moeller, Hans W, 1949, D 17,17:4
Moeller, Harold F, 1967, My 9,40:8
Moeller, Henry, 1946, Jl 28,40:4
Moeller, Henry Archbishop (funl, Ja 8,25:5), 1925, Ja 6,25:5
Moeller, Henry D, 1959, S 24,37:3
Moeller, Henry Dr, 1924, Ag 7,15:6
Moeller, Henry L, 1956, S 19,37:4
Moeller, Herbert L, 1940, Ag 13,19:3
Moeller, J Christmas, 1948, Ap 14,27:1
Moeller, Mathias P (por), 1937, Ap 14,25:5
Moeller, Max Capt, 1937, Jl 10,15:3
Moeller, Paul G, 1967, Jl 12,43:4
Moeller, Phil, 1958, Ap 27,86:8
Moeller, William, 1943, S 12,52:6
Moeller, Winton L, 1959, Ag 25,31:3
Moellhausen, Rene, 1940, Ja 14,43:3
Moellmann, Carl F, 1950, Jl 5,31:2
Moen, Arnold, 1951, Ag 15,27:5
Moen, C J, 1951, Jl 11,23:4
Moen, Edward Arthur, 1903, D 6,7:6
Moen, Edward Calvin, 1920, O 21,13:5
Moen, James F, 1948, My 26,25:3
Moen, LeClanche, 1957, N 25,31:5
Moen, Levi W, 1947, My 10,13:3
Moen, Philip W, 1904, S 13,1:6
Moen, Thomas, 1962, S 3,15:3
Moench, Charles F, 1951, Mr 4,94:2
Moench, John C, 1941, S 15,17:2
Moench, L Mary, 1958, Mr 28,25:2
Moennig, William H, 1962, Mr 10,37:4
Moer, Samuel H Judge, 1909, N 30,9:4
Moeran, Edward H, 1904, D 6,9:2
Moeran, Ernest J, 1950, D 2,13:4
Moeri, Charles A, 1963, N 30,27:2
Moering, Alex K, 1952, N 18,31:3
Moerk, Frank X, 1945, N 23,23:3
Moerler, Charles E, 1948, Ja 1,23:3
Moers, Theresa Mrs, 1924, Ag 28,17:6
Moers, Walter N, 1949, S 3,13:4
Moersch, John, 1915, N 15,11:5
Moeser, Jeremiah, 1954, My 29,15:5
Moeslein, Mark (por), 1946, O 29,25:3
Moesser, Frederick, 1953, Ap 11,17:6
Moessinger, H, 1881, F 23,5:3
Moeur, B B Dr, 1937, Mr 17,25:3
Moff, Edwin, 1952, D 23,23:4
Moffa, Thomas, 1951, My 5,17:6
Moffat, Adelene, 1956, F 12,88:6
Moffat, Alexander, 1914, F 25,9:5
Moffat, Almet S, 1941, O 1,21:1
Moffat, Arthur R, 1955, S 25,16:4
Moffat, Barclay W, 1942, O 29,23:5
Moffat, Beverly T, 1958, Je 17,29:2
Moffat, Beverly T Mrs, 1958, Je 23,23:5
Moffat, David H (funl, Mr 20,9:4), 1911, Mr 19,II, 11:3
Moffat, David W, 1944, Mr 6,19:4
Moffat, Donald, 1958, My 5,29:3
Moffat, Douglas M (mem ser, S 27,35:4), 1956, Ag 30,25:1
Moffat, Douglas M (est tax appr), 1959, N 18,35:6
Moffat, E Curtis, 1949, F 16,25:4
Moffat, Frank C, 1961, O 17,39:3
Moffat, Fraser M Mrs, 1957, O 21,25:3
Moffat, George H, 1966, Ap 17,79:3
Moffat, James E, 1957, Ja 11,23:2
Moffat, Jay P (por),(will, F 21,20:8), 1943, Ja 25,13:3
Moffat, John, 1863, N 7,4:4
Moffat, John B, 1943, Jl 2,19:5
Moffat, John B Mrs, 1952, O 16,29:3
Moffat, John G Mrs, 1961, N 6,37:3
Moffat, John L Dr, 1917, F 20,9:5
Moffat, Mary C, 1949, F 22,23:5
Moffat, Nelson, 1948, D 7,32:2
Moffat, R Burnham, 1916, Je 22,11:3
Moffat, R Burnham Mrs, 1960, Ja 4,29:4
Moffat, Robert, 1883, Ag 11,5:6
Moffat, Samuel A, 1948, O 17,76:1
Moffat, Stanley M Mrs, 1968, D 25,31:3
Moffat, Thomas L, 1960, N 24,29:5
Moffat, Tom, 1939, D 14,27:6
Moffat, Warren H, 1937, S 12,II,7:1
Moffat, Will Y Mrs, 1946, D 25,29:4
Moffat, William D, 1946, O 1,23:4
Moffat, William L, 1946, Ap 17,25:4
Moffatt, Alfred, 1967, Jl 12,43:4
Moffatt, Alfred F, 1959, My 19,34:1
Moffatt, Arthur H, 1943, My 9,40:4
Moffatt, Benjamin T, 1962, Jl 6,25:1
Moffatt, Clinton W, 1918, Je 7,13:6
Moffatt, Davis T, 1947, D 10,31:3
Moffatt, Earl B, 1953, N 17,31:1
Moffatt, Elbert M Mrs, 1950, Je 17,15:2
Moffatt, Fred C, 1949, D 17,17:3
Moffatt, James, 1939, Ag 1,19:3; 1944, Je 28,23:1
Moffatt, James David Rev Dr, 1916, N 5,23:4
Moffatt, James Mrs, 1947, Mr 27,27:4
Moffatt, Jennie Mrs, 1940, Jl 30,19:4
Moffatt, John W, 1947, D 24,22:3
Moffatt, Lester E, 1948, Ap 2,23:4
Moffatt, Miles R, 1941, Ja 21,22:3
Moffatt, R Gordon, 1940, Jl 6,15:5
Moffatt, Thomas C Dr, 1869, D 27,5:2
Moffatt, William, 1943, My 12,25:1
Moffatt, William J, 1937, Ja 21,23:4
Moffet, Francis H, 1942, O 24,15:4
Moffet, Harold L, 1938, N 8,23:3
Moffet, Hugh R, 1957, N 25,31:2
Moffett, Blanche Mrs, 1962, S 25,37:1
Moffett, C, 1926, O 16,17:6
Moffett, Charles A, 1949, D 29,26:2
Moffett, Charles L, 1952, My 2,25:1
Moffett, Charles Mrs, 1947, Ag 8,17:5
Moffett, Charles T, 1950, N 16,31:2
Moffett, Cleveland Mrs, 1946, Ap 27,17:5
Moffett, Donovan C, 1963, Ap 17,41:4
Moffett, Edna V, 1962, Mr 2,29:2
Moffett, Edward Montgomery, 1909, Je 14,7:4
Moffett, Francis, 1938, S 16,21:2
Moffett, George H Capt, 1912, S 1,II,9:4
Moffett, George M, 1951, D 23,22:4
Moffett, George M (will), 1952, Ja 9,24:7
Moffett, George M Mrs, 1956, N 18,89:1
Moffett, George W, 1943, My 4,23:5
Moffett, Guy A, 1951, Mr 28,29:2
Moffett, Harold T, 1957, Mr 30,19:4
Moffett, Herbert N, 1942, D 4,25:6
Moffett, Howard J, 1949, Ja 25,23:2
Moffett, James, 1914, D 12,15:7; 1961, Ag 12,17:1
Moffett, James A, 1953, Mr 26,31:1
Moffett, James Andrew (funl, Mr 2,7:4), 1913, F 27, 13:3
Moffett, John B, 1959, Mr 10,35:4
Moffett, John K, 1965, D 18,29:3
Moffett, Mary E Mrs, 1940, O 3,25:2
Moffett, Paul G, 1948, Ap 8,25:4

Moffett, Phyllis S Mrs, 1964, Mr 1,83:3
Moffett, Robert E, 1941, O 5,48:3
Moffett, Rudolph D, 1962, Ag 6,25:5
Moffett, Samuel A, 1939, O 26,23:2
Moffett, Samuel A Mrs, 1962, Mr 17,25:5
Moffett, Samuel H Mrs, 1955, Ja 18,27:5
Moffett, Thomas C, 1945, N 14,19:4
Moffett, Thomas K, 1909, Ag 9,7:6
Moffett, Webster V, 1940, Jl 26,17:4
Moffett, Wilbur K, 1942, Je 17,23:2
Moffett, William W, 1950, My 9,30:2
Moffett, William W Mrs, 1942, D 30,17:4
Moffit, Albert R, 1944, Mr 22,19:5
Moffit, James K Mrs, 1948, Je 25,23:2
Moffit, John A (por), 1942, Je 8,15:5
Moffit, John T, 1947, N 12,27:3
Moffit, Samuel P, 1950, Mr 15,29:4
Moffitt, Edward C, 1959, Mr 9,29:3
Moffitt, Emmett L, 1941, Mr 30,49:1
Moffitt, Frank X, 1946, Jl 11,23:5
Moffitt, Herbert C Sr, 1951, F 6,27:3
Moffitt, Hopkins, 1937, N 16,23:4
Moffitt, James K, 1955, Ag 18,23:5
Moffitt, John B, 1953, Ja 28,27:4
Moffitt, John R, 1909, N 16,9:5
Moffitt, Mary A Mrs, 1941, Je 28,15:1
Moffitt, Stephen Gen, 1904, Ja 4,9:5
Moffitt, Walter Volentine, 1968, Ap 16,44:1
Moffitt, William A, 1954, Ag 12,25:4
Moffitt, William A Mrs, 1952, My 19,17:4
Moffitt, William E, 1958, D 29,15:5
Moffitt, William P, 1966, My 17,47:3
Mogador, Celeste (Celeste Venard), 1909, F 20,7:4
Mogan, Edmund F, 1948, D 12,92:4
Mogan, J P Mrs (funl), 1925, Ag 18,19:3
Mogan, John M Msgr, 1937, My 31,16:2
Mogavero, Francesco, 1956, Jl 24,25:3
Mogee, John A, 1948, Ja 7,26:2
Mogelever, Barnet, 1940, S 17,23:5
Mogelever, Bernard Mrs, 1948, S 30,27:4
Mogensen, Walter A, 1965, Ja 4,29:2
Moger, Daniel W, 1949, F 19,15:4
Moger, George E, 1951, Ja 11,26:2
Mogerley, Albert, 1947, Je 29,48:7
Mogey, William, 1938, S 14,23:4
Mogge, Ernest L, 1941, Mr 4,23:5
Moggridge, Arthur Y, 1946, N 16,19:5
Moghannam, Moghannam E, 1944, S 8,19:5
Moghtader, Mansur J, 1947, S 16,23:2
Mogil, Isidore, 1939, Je 16,23:6
Mogilesky, Bernard (por), 1939, D 7,27:3
Mogilesky, Bernard (will), 1940, Je 1,31:6
Mogilesky, Sarah B Mrs, 1938, My 27,17:2
Mogilewsky, Rubin, 1906, My 7,4:3
Mogueres, Louis, 1956, My 6,87:1
Mogulesco, Sigmund (funl, F 7,11:6), 1914, F 5,9:5
Mogull, Peter, 1964, N 29,87:1
Mohaghan, Norman, 1937, D 4,17:3
Mohamed, Molay B, 1945, D 27,19:2
Mohamed Abul Asad el Alem, Sheik, 1964, Ag 18,31:4
Mohammed, Ghulam, 1956, Ag 30,25:4
Mohammed el Amin Pasha, Sidi Bey of Tumis, 1962, O 2,39:1
Mohammed Rida Mahdi el Senussi, Crown Prince, 1955, Jl 30,17:5
Mohammed Tewtik, Khedive of Egypt, 1892, Ja 8,8:1
Mohammed V, King of Morocco (funl, Mr 1,4:6), 1961, F 27,1:6
Mohammed V, 1918, Jl 5,11:3
Mohammed VI, former Sultan of Turkey, 1926, My 17,21:4
Mohan, Arthur J Sr, 1956, My 19,19:5
Mohan, John J, 1948, My 1,15:5; 1952, Je 18,27:1
Mohan, William, 1940, N 8,21:3
Mohan, William F, 1943, Je 6,44:5; 1954, Jl 17,13:6
Mohaupt, Arthur G, 1950, Ja 13,23:2
Mohaupt, Richard Mrs, 1952, S 26,21:1
Mohen, James F, 1945, F 6,19:1
Mohen, Marion C, 1944, My 3,19:2
Mohill, Leon, 1967, Jl 4,19:3
Mohl, Emanuel N Mrs, 1958, Jl 2,29:3
Mohl, M Jules de, 1876, Je 6,4:7
Mohle, Adolphe, 1907, Mr 12,9:6
Mohler, A L, 1930, Je 7,17:5
Mohler, Frank L, 1937, Ja 26,21:3
Mohler, Henry D, 1941, My 17,15:3
Mohler, Lily A B Mrs, 1937, Ap 25,II,8:1
Mohler, Orville E, 1949, N 28,44:2
Mohler, Richard H, 1955, Je 13,23:2
Mohler, Roy W, 1964, Ag 7,29:5
Mohlte, J Albert, 1957, N 17,86:7
Mohlte, John A Mrs, 1949, D 30,19:3
Mohme, Otto M, 1948, Ap 20,27:1
Mohn, Charles A, 1940, Jl 11,19:2
Mohn, Otto L F, 1949, Je 9,31:3
Mohnacky, Stephen, 1955, Ja 21,23:1
Moholy-Nagy, Laszlo, 1946, N 25,27:4
Mohor, Albert, 1941, Ag 13,17:2
Mohor, L V, 1903, My 28,5:4
Mohor, Robert D, 1948, D 13,23:5
Mohor, Robert V J, 1949, Ja 13,23:5
Mohorovicic, Joseph, 1964, Ag 2,77:2
Mohr, August, 1904, N 29,9:1
Mohr, Charles, 1960, Ap 18,40:6
Mohr, Charles H, 1962, Ag 29,29:2
Mohr, Charles L, 1941, Ja 16,23:2
Mohr, Claude M, 1947, Ag 2,13:2
Mohr, Francis J, 1952, Ja 23,27:3
Mohr, Franz J, 1944, Jl 13,17:5
Mohr, Frederick A, 1943, F 7,48:2
Mohr, George J, 1965, Mr 8,29:4
Mohr, Gerald, 1968, N 11,47:1
Mohr, Gordon S, 1960, Ap 2,23:7
Mohr, Henry W Mrs, 1958, Ag 2,17:6
Mohr, Herman M, 1944, Jl 13,17:3
Mohr, J M, 1903, Ag 21,9:6
Mohr, Jean G, 1951, Ag 26,79:3
Mohr, John, 1946, My 9,21:4
Mohr, John R, 1938, N 22,24:6
Mohr, Louis F Sr, 1949, D 18,88:4
Mohr, Mark, 1953, Ja 7,31:4
Mohr, Michael J, 1956, Jl 19,27:2
Mohr, Morris, 1956, S 22,17:2
Mohr, Phil, 1949, Je 10,27:3
Mohr, Thomas, 1957, Mr 15,16:2
Mohr, Walter M, 1955, Ja 5,23:2
Mohr, William J, 1964, My 19,37:2
Mohr, William L, 1963, Ag 13,31:4
Mohr, William R, 1939, O 14,19:4
Mohrhardt, Fred M, 1953, N 16,25:5
Mohrhardt, John S, 1953, Jl 24,13:6
Mohring, Harry H, 1947, D 19,25:1
Mohrmann, Frederick, 1955, D 28,23:5
Mohrmann, Henry F W, 1949, O 9,93:1
Mohrmann, Margaret L Mrs, 1937, My 23,II,11:2
Mohun, John L, 1947, Ap 28,23:3
Mohun, Richard Dorsey, 1915, Jl 15,9:6
Moi Nai Gam (funl), 1954, O 27,31:3
Moidel, Isadore, 1960, My 5,35:4
Moinard, August, 1951, F 16,25:5
Moinet, Edward J, 1952, D 24,17:6
Moinet, Edward J Mrs, 1942, Je 27,13:5
Moir, Alex, 1956, Jl 24,25:5
Moir, Alex G, 1938, My 16,17:2
Moir, Arthur D, 1942, Je 9,23:4
Moir, David, 1939, Ap 20,23:3
Moir, E, 1933, Je 16,17:4
Moir, Emma T Mrs, 1951, Ap 11,29:5
Moir, Henry (por), 1937, Je 10,23:1
Moir, Henry Mrs, 1958, O 7,35:1
Moir, James (Gunner), 1939, Je 13,23:5
Moir, James D, 1946, Ag 20,28:3
Moir, James R, 1944, F 26,13:3
Moir, Jesse T, 1945, D 7,22:2
Moir, John, 1938, S 21,25:1
Moir, Martha, 1952, Mr 23,92:3
Moisan, Calixa N, 1954, Mr 6,15:4
Moisant, Matilde, 1964, F 7,31:2
Moise, Albert L, 1940, My 27,19:5
Moise, Anna F Mrs, 1948, My 7,23:3
Moise, Isaac R Col, 1907, Ap 8,9:6
Moise, Lionel C, 1952, Ap 10,60:4
Moise, Michael, 1963, D 14,27:1
Moise, W H, 1939, O 31,23:4
Moiseiwitsch, Benno, 1963, Ap 10,39:3
Moisseiff, Leon S (por), 1943, S 4,13:1
Moisseiff, Leon S Mrs, 1948, F 14,13:6
Moissi, A, 1935, Mr 23,15:5
Moister, Roger W, 1941, Mr 11,23:6
Moitrier, William Jr, 1961, S 25,33:6
Moizo, Riccardo, 1962, Mr 1,31:5
Mojecki, John F, 1952, Ja 1,25:2
Mojica, John, 1955, Ap 2,38:4
Mok, Henry J, 1941, Ag 22,15:6
Mok, Michael, 1961, F 3,25:4
Mok, S, 1948, F 26,23:2
Mokarzel, S A, 1952, Ja 3,27:5
Mokri, Hadj Mohammed el, 1957, S 10,33:2
Moktar, Nemat, 1945, Je 22,15:5
Molanari, Robert, 1939, Ag 24,19:2
Molander, Julia C, 1965, Mr 30,47:4
Molanphy, John P, 1949, F 17,23:2
Molanphy, Thomas N, 1950, Jl 13,25:2
Molarsky, Maurice, 1950, Ja 3,25:4
Molas Lopez, Felipe, 1954, Mr 3,27:5
Mold, Harry J, 1942, Ag 8,11:6; 1947, Ja 25,17:2
Molday, Sonia, 1967, S 5,43:2
Molden, Ernest, 1953, Ag 13,25:3
Moldenhawer, Julius V (por), 1948, Ap 1,25:1
Moldenhawer, Thora E, 1957, Je 26,31:1
Moldenhour, Paul, 1947, F 20,25:2
Moldenke, Alfred B (por), 1943, Ap 7,25:3
Moldenke, Alfred B, 1943, D 6,19:5
Moldenke, Edward F Rev, 1904, Je 26,3:3
Moldenke, Theodore V, 1960, F 15,27:1
Mole, George A, 1950, D 26,23:4
Mole, George A Mrs, 1954, D 13,27:5
Mole, Harvey E, 1957, Ap 10,33:5
Mole, Harvey E Mrs, 1953, N 3,31:3
Mole, Irving M (Miff), 1961, Ap 30,87:1
Mole, Peter, 1960, Ag 4,25:4
Mole, Samuel, 1940, Ap 17,23:4
Moler, Jacob A O, 1939, O 6,25:1
Moler, William F, 1942, S 14,15:5
Moles, Enrique, 1953, Mr 31,31:3
Moles, Thomas, 1937, F 4,21:6
Moles, William F, 1947, D 8,25:2
Molesky, Frank J, 1951, Je 2,19:5
Molesphini, Charles B, 1939, Mr 1,21:2
Molesworth, Guilford Lindsey, 1925, Ja 22,19:5
Molesworth, Keith, 1966, Mr 14,31:4
Molesworth, Keith Mrs, 1947, Ag 26,23:5
Molesworth, Lewis W Sir, 1912, My 30,11:6
Molesworth, Mary Louisa Mrs, 1921, Jl 22,11:6
Molev, Mikhail, 1952, My 1,29:5
Moley, Agnes F Mrs, 1937, F 21,10:7
Moley, James P, 1948, Je 17,25:3
Molgno, Abbe F N M, 1884, Jl 16,5:1
Molin, George C, 1943, O 3,49:1
Molin, Ivan, 1950, Mr 20,22:2
Molina, Edward C, 1964, Ap 30,35:4
Molina, Henry G, 1957, O 21,25:4
Molina, Santos M, 1966, Ag 5,31:3
Molina Campos, Florencio, 1959, N 18,41:2
Molina Garces, Ciro, 1953, S 26,17:2
Molinari, Bernardino, 1952, D 26,15:5
Molinari, Gustave de, 1912, Ja 30,9:4
Molinari, Louis (Gigi), 1959, Ja 31,19:1
Molinari, S Robert, 1957, Je 2,86:6
Molinelli, Anthony, 1940, Jl 18,19:5
Molinelli, Emil E, 1961, N 6,37:5
Molinet, Eugenio, 1959, My 24,88:5
Molinet, William F, 1954, Jl 13,23:2
Molineux, Cecil Sefton, 1923, S 30,7:3
Molineux, Edward L Mrs, 1914, F 6,9:5
Molineux, Leslie E, 1943, S 8,23:6
Molineux, Marie A, 1938, My 16,17:2
Molineux, Roland B, 1917, N 3,15:6
Molini, Andrew, 1951, Jl 31,21:1
Molino, Lelio M, 1943, S 2,19:5
Molins, Hugo, 1943, F 10,25:4
Molisani, Edward, 1957, Ja 14,23:2
Molisch, Hans Dr, 1937, D 9,25:2
Molitch, Louis, 1966, Ja 15,27:5
Moliter, Edward, 1952, Ja 11,21:1
Molitor, Frederic A (por),(will, Ap 14,11:2), 1938, Mr 13,II,9:1
Molitor, Harry, 1947, D 4,31:2
Molitor, William C, 1965, Mr 9,35:3
Molkenthin, Henry H, 1955, My 5,33:4
Moll, Hilmar F, 1949, Ap 12,29:4
Moll, Jewell T, 1963, My 4,25:3
Moll, Louis H, 1940, F 7,21:6
Moll, Sadie, 1915, F 26,9:5
Mollaber, Mary Mrs, 1953, Jl 25,11:7
Mollan, Malcolm J, 1947, Mr 3,21:4
Mollander, Sven O, 1950, Je 1,27:1
Mollat, Henri, 1937, F 24,23:3
Mollath, J George, 1948, Ap 11,72:1
Mollath, J George Mrs, 1938, S 14,23:2
Mollema, J C, 1946, N 3,63:1
Mollenauer, Ernest J Mrs, 1957, Jl 13,17:5
Mollenauer, Vernon S, 1953, N 21,13:4
Mollenberg, Henry J, 1943, Jl 13,21:3
Mollenhauer, Chris C Mrs, 1939, F 16,21:5
Mollenhauer, Christopher C, 1952, S 19,23:3
Mollenhauer, E, 1927, D 11,31:4
Mollenhauer, Frederick D, 1914, N 21,13:5
Mollenhauer, Henry, 1953, My 24,89:2
Mollenhauer, Ida A, 1940, S 7,15:3
Mollenhauer, John, 1905, Ja 1,7:6
Mollenhauer, John Mrs, 1915, Mr 20,13:5
Mollenhauer, Otto, 1949, Je 9,31:3
Mollenhauer, Richard, 1946, Ap 19,29:2
Mollenhauer, 1926, Mr 7,II,9:1
Mollenkamp, Fred, 1948, N 2,25:4
Mollenkopf, Fred L, 1958, My 14,33:5
Mollenkopf, Rodney E, 1954, F 13,13:6
Moller, Charles G, 1917, Mr 3,9:3
Moller, Christian Henry, 1915, Je 2,13:6
Moller, Christopher, 1913, S 16,11:5
Moller, Ernest F, 1954, Ag 21,17:5
Moller, Francis S, 1948, Ja 19,23:3
Moller, Frederick C, 1947, Ag 30,15:2
Moller, G Harold, 1915, N 24,13:6
Moller, George L, 1967, O 25,47:1
Moller, Honora A Mrs, 1949, Ap 25,23:3
Moller, Jacob A L, 1957, F 19,31:4
Moller, John, 1923, O 2,7:3
Moller, John G, 1950, F 20,25:3
Moller, Lester J, 1944, My 27,15:5
Moller, Louise Mrs, 1911, Je 26,9:6
Moller, Martha, 1952, My 6,29:4
Moller, Mathias P Jr, 1961, O 21,21:3
Moller, Peter, 1879, F 19,8:3
Moller, Peter Jr, 1907, My 17,9:5
Moller, Peter Mrs, 1917, My 29,13:4
Moller, William Jr, 1946, Ag 30,18:2
Moller, William R, 1951, Ja 2,23:2
Molleson, Dean C Mrs, 1963, N 23,29:2
Molleson, George A, 1962, Mr 17,25:6
Molleson, Stanley H, 1951, Mr 6,27:5
Molleson, Stanley H Mrs, 1961, D 14,43:2
Mollier, Eleanor, 1954, S 20,15:7
Mollin, F E, 1958, O 18,21:2
Mollis, Edward L, 1960, Jl 31,68:6
Mollison, A P (A Pincus), 1956, S 22,17:6
Mollison, Ethel K, 1949, S 23,23:2
Mollison, Howard E Mrs, 1953, Je 20,17:5

Mollison, Irvin C, 1962, My 6,88:5
Mollison, James A, 1959, N 1,86:1
Mollison, James S, 1950, My 18,29:1
Mollmann, Augustus L Mrs, 1940, Ag 24,13:7
Mollod, Harry I, 1965, Je 22,35:3
Mollow, J Edward, 1944, My 12,19:3
Molloy, Catherine L, 1955, My 14,19:5
Molloy, Cornelius J, 1950, O 3,31:2
Molloy, Daniel M, 1944, Ja 30,37:1
Molloy, Edmond J, 1956, Ag 11,13:5
Molloy, Frances Mother, 1916, N 27,11:2
Molloy, Francis J, 1911, Je 19,9:5
Molloy, George P Mrs, 1958, Je 14,21:6
Molloy, J Carroll Jr Mrs, 1952, S 1,17:5
Molloy, Jacqueline J Mrs, 1940, My 28,23:2
Molloy, James, 1939, Ja 21,15:3
Molloy, James F, 1953, N 1,87:1; 1954, F 20,17:5
Molloy, James H, 1950, S 21,31:4
Molloy, John A Mrs, 1952, Ap 21,21:3
Molloy, John J, 1940, F 13,23:4; 1957, Mr 16,19:5
Molloy, John M, 1957, Mr 12,33:3
Molloy, John T Mrs, 1950, Mr 15,29:5
Molloy, Joseph A, 1961, F 28,33:4
Molloy, Joseph J, 1956, Ag 4,15:5; 1961, Jl 2,32:8
Molloy, Joseph P, 1954, Je 1,27:3
Molloy, Minnie M, 1942, My 26,21:5
Molloy, Thomas E (funl plans, N 28,35:1; funl, D 1,21:6), 1956, N 27,37:2
Molloy, Thomas F, 1945, Ap 18,23:3
Molloy, Thomas M, 1945, O 12,23:2
Molloy, William, 1905, Ja 29,7:6; 1945, N 7,23:2
Molloy, William A, 1943, F 2,20:3
Molloy, William M, 1952, D 24,17:5
Molloy, William P, 1949, Ja 14,23:3
Molloy, William R, 1943, My 30,27:1
Molnar, Alex J, 1958, O 14,37:5
Molnar, Erik, 1966, Ag 9,37:1
Molnar, Ferenc, 1952, Ap 2,33:1
Molnar, Jacob, 1948, O 5,25:4
Molnar, Jacob Mrs, 1958, O 18,21:7
Molnar, Julius, 1960, S 19,31:4
Molnar, Lewis, 1957, My 17,25:3
Molnar, Marta, 1966, Ag 11,33:1
Molner, Joseph Dr, 1968, N 18,47:4
Molodykh, Terenty, 1950, Je 5,23:3
Moloney, Edward F, 1952, Je 28,19:1
Moloney, Frank A, 1960, F 14,84:1
Moloney, Frank F, 1960, Ja 24,88:8
Moloney, Herbert W Sr, 1967, S 28,57:3
Moloney, James, 1916, Ag 1,9:6; 1953, Ap 14,27:2
Moloney, James J, 1957, Ap 14,86:2; 1959, My 14,33:4
Moloney, John J, 1966, N 7,47:2
Moloney, Stephen J, 1951, Ap 13,23:4
Moloney, Thomas F, 1947, Je 22,52:7
Moloney, Thomas J, 1959, D 14,31:3
Moloney, William R, 1945, F 26,19:4
Molony, Clement, 1949, Mr 12,17:4
Molony, Clement J, 1954, D 6,27:6
Molony, Frank T, 1957, My 4,21:6
Molony, George A Mrs, 1945, O 9,22:2
Molony, Isaac W, 1947, Je 5,25:4
Molony, Isaac W Mrs, 1945, D 22,19:4
Molony, John E, 1958, S 18,31:3
Molony, Justin J, 1943, N 2,25:4
Molony, Noblett J, 1961, O 18,43:1
Molony, Thomas, 1949, S 4,40:8
Molossi, Umberto Mrs, 1940, N 26,23:2
Molowitz, Samuel, 1946, S 1,36:1
Moloy, Howard C, 1953, Mr 14,15:4
Molson, George L, 1946, Ja 8,24:2
Molson, Herbert, 1938, Mr 22,21:5
Molson, Herbert W, 1955, Ap 16,19:2
Molson, John J, 1941, Je 10,23:4
Molson, Percival Talbot, 1966, S 14,9:6
Molson, Walter, 1953, Mr 6,23:3
Molt, Albert H, 1950, Ag 26,13:4
Moltasch, Boris, 1953, Ap 28,27:5
Molten, Robert P, 1940, My 30,18:2
Molteno, Percy A, 1937, S 21,35:5
Molter, Augustus A, 1950, D 10,104:3
Molter, John N Mrs, 1944, S 21,19:3
Molter, William, 1960, Ap 3,86:3
Molthan, E Henry, 1952, Jl 28,15:6
Moltke, Cornelia Countess, 1960, Je 16,33:6
Moltke, Detler von, 1944, My 21,44:7
Moltke, Doris Countess, 1965, Je 15,41:1
Moltke, Hans A von, 1943, Mr 23,19:3
Moltke, Lt-Gen von, 1916, Je 20,11:7
Moltke, von Count, 1891, Ap 25,1:7
Moltke-Bregentved, Count, 1875, O 2,1:5
Moltke-Huitfeldt, Adam de Countess, 1923, Ja 23,21:5
Moltrasio, Joseph, 1914, Ag 16,15:6
Moltz, Reuben M, 1956, S 17,27:4
Moltzer, Jan H, 1951, D 5,35:4
Molumby, Loy J, 1939, Ja 31,21:5
Molyneaux, Abram F, 1951, F 3,15:5
Molyneaux, Albert J, 1960, O 20,35:2
Molyneaux, John, 1945, Jl 20,19:6
Molyneaux, John J, 1948, Ap 13,27:2
Molyneaux, Joseph W, 1940, Ja 25,21:3
Molyneaux, Peter, 1953, Ja 11,91:3
Molyneux, Edward F, 1958, Mr 26,37:3
Molyneux, George E, 1941, F 7,19:3
Molyneux, Richard, 1954, Ja 21,31:5
Molyneux, Robert E, 1968, S 19,47:3
Molyneux, William Mrs, 1938, O 29,19:5
Molz, Linus C, 1955, F 21,21:3
Momat, Solomor, 1952, S 15,25:3
Mombert, Adolph Mrs, 1950, Je 10,17:4
Mombert, Jacob Isadore Rev, 1913, O 8,11:6
Moment, Alfred H Dr, 1907, O 10,9:4
Moment, John J, 1959, My 12,35:3
Momeyer, Alvy Wilson, 1919, D 9,17:4
Momigiiano, Attilio, 1952, Ap 7,25:5
Momm, Walter, 1952, D 20,17:6
Mommer, Paul (Mar 14), 1963, Ap 1,36:3
Momsen, Charles B, 1967, My 26,47:1
Momsen, Richard P, 1964, F 21,27:1
Momsen, William H, 1939, Ja 25,21:2
Monaca, Francis La, 1937, F 6,17:3
Monaco, A M, 1959, Mr 6,25:2
Monaco, James V, 1945, O 18,23:3
Monaco, Joseph, 1952, S 3,29:4
Monaelesser, A, 1935, Mr 28,21:4
Monaelesser, Mozart Dr, 1941, Ag 10,37:1
Monaghan, Bartholomew F, 1940, Ja 1,23:2
Monaghan, Charles, 1955, Ja 20,31:1
Monaghan, Conor, 1952, My 3,21:5
Monaghan, Daniel E, 1949, Mr 1,25:4
Monaghan, Francis A, 1963, O 12,23:3
Monaghan, Francis J (por), 1942, N 14,15:4
Monaghan, Frank A, 1948, D 2,29:4
Monaghan, Frank J, 1941, Jl 27,30:1
Monaghan, Hugh, 1950, Ja 11,23:4
Monaghan, James, 1946, O 15,25:5; 1947, D 17,30:2; 1949, Ap 7,29:4
Monaghan, James C Prof, 1917, N 13,13:4
Monaghan, John, 1954, D 28,23:5
Monaghan, John F, 1950, Je 26,27:5
Monaghan, John P, 1961, Jl 27,31:1
Monaghan, John S A, 1948, My 24,19:5
Monaghan, Joseph A, 1949, D 15,35:5
Monaghan, Katherine A, 1958, F 21,24:1
Monaghan, Marcus A, 1951, S 19,31:5
Monaghan, Margaret R, 1945, My 25,19:3
Monaghan, Mary E Mrs, 1941, O 30,23:1
Monaghan, Mary K Mrs (May), 1966, D 13,47:3
Monaghan, Peter J, 1942, Ag 15,11:4
Monaghan, Richard H, 1958, N 11,30:6
Monaghan, T Francis Mrs, 1946, Je 9,40:6
Monaghan, Thomas E, 1967, O 20,47:2
Monaghan, Thomas F, 1958, Mr 28,25:4
Monaghan, William A, 1940, S 17,23:2
Monaghan, William J (por), 1938, N 27,49:1
Monaghan, William J, 1943, Je 28,21:2
Monagle, Alonzo C (por), 1943, Ag 30,15:3
Monagus, Lionel, 1945, S 5,23:6
Monahan, Alfred E, 1945, Ag 12,39:2
Monahan, Arthur C, 1953, Jl 4,11:6
Monahan, Doris M, 1953, D 15,39:1
Monahan, Frank, 1939, D 11,23:2
Monahan, George E, 1961, Ap 24,29:2
Monahan, Harry V (cor, Mr 18,29:4), 1958, Mr 17, 29:2
Monahan, Herbert E, 1964, Mr 26,35:4
Monahan, Hugh, 1952, N 12,27:5
Monahan, Humphrey J, 1964, Ja 23,31:1
Monahan, Humphrey J Mrs, 1946, Ja 1,27:1
Monahan, James, 1917, Je 29,9:6
Monahan, James F (Boston Billy Williams), 1960, O 25,18:5
Monahan, James J, 1937, N 13,23:4; 1952, Ag 15,15:2
Monahan, James Mrs, 1948, Mr 30,23:2
Monahan, Jane E, 1946, Je 5,23:3
Monahan, Jeremiah J, 1968, O 27,82:3
Monahan, Jerry, 1947, Ja 12,59:2
Monahan, John F, 1944, D 9,15:5; 1949, Jl 7,25:2
Monahan, John G, 1949, O 17,23:5
Monahan, John H, 1941, Ja 23,21:5
Monahan, John Mrs, 1950, Je 13,27:4
Monahan, Joseph, 1943, N 29,19:5
Monahan, Joseph F, 1966, F 13,84:4
Monahan, Joseph J, 1941, Mr 1,15:5
Monahan, Lawrence, 1940, S 7,15:3
Monahan, Lawrence J, 1949, D 25,26:3
Monahan, Leonard C, 1946, Ap 5,25:2
Monahan, Linus, 1967, O 26,47:5
Monahan, M, 1933, N 23,21:3
Monahan, M Edward, 1961, My 21,86:4
Monahan, Maurice F, 1956, Ag 22,29:4
Monahan, Michael Mrs, 1948, Ap 16,23:1
Monahan, Otto F, 1942, Je 7,42:2
Monahan, Owen, 1924, S 20,15:6
Monahan, Paul A, 1937, Ap 10,19:2
Monahan, Peter J, 1947, My 7,27:4; 1960, F 21,92:4
Monahan, Tom, 1948, My 24,19:4
Monahan, Vincent M, 1940, Ag 23,15:3
Monahan, William A, 1952, My 3,21:5
Monahan, William F, 1953, My 8,25:3
Monahan, William L, 1967, Ja 3,37:3
Monahon, Arthur T, 1948, S 10,23:2
Monarque, George H, 1949, F 3,23:2
Monas, David J Mrs, 1958, O 8,35:1
Monash, J, 1931, O 8,25:5
Monash, Leon, 1956, Ap 29,86:3
Monasterio, Joseph, 1952, D 5,28:3
Monastero, Victor J Mrs, 1952, Ag 24,88:1
Monat, Peter, 1944, Jl 8,11:7
Monath, Hortense, 1956, My 22,33:2
Moncada, Jose M, 1945, F 24,11:6
Moncado, Hilario C, 1956, Ap 10,31:2
Moncado, Pietro S, 1965, Je 22,35:2
Moncaya, Jose P, 1958, Je 17,29:1
Moncef, Sidi Mohamed al-, 1948, S 2,10:3
Moncelle, Frank P, 1953, S 9,29:1
Monchow, Helen C, 1950, D 25,19:3
Monchy, Willem Hugo de, 1968, D 25,31:2
Monck, Edward P, 1940, D 3,25:4
Monck, Solomon J, 1950, Ja 13,23:4
Monckton of Brenchley, Viscount (Walter Monckton), 1965, Ja 10,92:1
Monclar, Ralph (R C Magrin-Vernery), 1964, Je 4, 37:4
Moncrief, Albert, 1943, D 22,23:5
Moncrief, J W Mrs, 1947, F 26,25:1
Moncrieff, Ernest V, 1950, N 7,27:4
Moncrieff, J J, 1939, Ap 12,24:4
Moncrieff, John N, 1940, S 21,19:2
Moncrieff, Ray A, 1953, S 29,29:5
Moncure, R C L, 1882, Ag 26,5:5
Moncure, William A, 1954, N 3,29:4
Mond, Emile, 1938, D 31,15:2
Mond, Ludwig Dr, 1909, D 11,11:3
Mond, Robert, 1938, O 23,40:6
Mondadori, Valmiro, 1944, N 6,19:2
Mondale, T S Mrs, 1967, Ap 1,31:3
Mondell, Frank W (por), 1939, Ag 7,15:3
Mondello, Ugo, 1939, D 4,23:4
Mondini, Cesare, 1940, S 25,27:5
Mondloch, Arnold, 1944, N 16,23:6
Mondor, Henri, 1962, Ap 8,87:3
Mondragon, Guerra, 1947, Ap 11,25:4
Mondrian, Piet, 1944, F 2,21:4
Mondschein, Wallace, 1966, N 15,41:6
Mondt, Ralph, 1949, F 26,15:1
Mone, Edward J, 1925, Jl 21,21:5
Monell, Ambrose, 1921, My 3,17:5
Monell, Charles H, 1903, D 29,9:2
Monell, Charles Mrs, 1949, Jl 30,15:2
Monell, Claudius I Mrs, 1907, Je 20,7:5
Monell, Frances, 1940, Jl 14,31:2
Monell, Frank D, 1940, Jl 1,19:5
Monell, Ralph, 1940, Ap 30,21:1
Monell, Theodore, 1950, D 18,31:2
Mones, Jacob B, 1952, O 20,23:3
Monestersky, Lewis, 1968, Ap 4,47:1
Monet, C, 1926, D 6,23:3
Monet, Dominique Justice, 1923, F 8,19:5
Moneta, Cesare A (por), 1948, Je 13,68:3
Moneta, Ernesto Teodoro, 1918, F 28,9:4
Moneuse, Alphonse E, 1955, F 26,15:4
Moneuse, Alphonse F, 1947, Ap 24,25:2
Money, George P, 1951, Mr 8,29:2
Money, Harold Mrs, 1947, Je 23,23:2
Money, Hernando de Soto Ex-Sen, 1912, S 19,11:6
Money, Leo C, 1944, O 1,45:3
Moneypenny, Nelson Mrs, 1945, O 19,23:2
Moneypenny, Walter V, 1967, Ja 4,43:3
Monfort, Elias R Capt, 1920, Jl 30,9:4
Monfort, F C, 1928, O 2,31:3
Monfort, Reid, 1943, My 19,25:2
Monfreiffe, Malcolm, 1948, Je 16,29:1
Monfried, Max, 1951, Jl 25,23:2
Monfried, Richard M, 1957, Je 12,35:3
Mong, William V, 1940, D 14,17:4
Mongan, Charles E, 1952, Ap 14,19:6
Mongan, Rauley O, 1945, My 24,19:2
Mongan, Thomas F, 1965, N 26,37:1
Mongeau, Alfred C, 1951, N 2,24:3
Mongel, Ernest B, 1952, My 14,27:3
Mongelli, Giuseppe A, 1957, My 26,92:5
Mongendre, Maxime, 1951, N 11,89:4
Mongeon, Michael J Mrs, 1953, Je 16,27:2
Monges, Henry B, 1954, Jl 21,27:3
Monghan, Thomas P, 1944, Je 22,19:5
Mongibeaux, Paul, 1950, S 24,104:7
Mongini, Mario, 1958, S 8,29:4
Mongini, Signor, 1874, My 21,5:5
Mongovan, Edward J, 1954, N 28,87:1
Monheimer, Jonas, 1938, Ag 10,19:6
Monheimer, Maurice W, 1938, Ag 21,33:3
Monias, Bruno L, 1948, F 21,13:4
Monica, Mother, 1947, Je 14,15:3
Monica, Mother (M Gallagher), 1953, Ja 13,27:4
Monier, Fernand, 1919, D 15,15:3
Monier-Williams, Montague Mrs, 1925, N 23,21:5
Monies, W N, 1881, Ja 11,2:2
Monighan, John, 1941, Mr 26,23:2
Monihan, James L, 1947, D 24,21:1
Monihan, Joseph P Mrs, 1958, Jl 21,21:1
Moninger, Margaret, 1950, Mr 24,25:3
Monitz, Constantin, 1948, Ag 21,15:5
Moniz, Raymond T, 1961, S 4,15:1
Monje-Gutierrez, Tomas, 1954, Jl 2,19:5
Monjo, Arthur, 1954, D 20,29:4
Monjo, Ferdinand N Mrs, 1960, S 22,27:5
Monjo, Luis, 1950, Ja 10,29:2
Monk, Alice M, 1952, Jl 3,25:1
Monk, Frederick D, 1914, My 16,11:6

Monk, J E, 1930, Jl 21,15:5
Monk, James A, 1943, Mr 11,21:4
Monk, John Mrs, 1950, D 3,89:2
Monk, Minnie, 1904, Mr 23,9:3
Monk, William, 1937, Ap 9,21:3
Monkiewicz, Boleslaus J Mrs, 1952, D 29,19:5
Monkiewicz, Metchislav, 1946, Je 5,23:3
Monkman, John A, 1965, F 28,88:4
Monks, George F, 1952, Ag 8,17:3
Monks, George H Mrs, 1944, Ap 24,19:6
Monks, George V, 1962, S 6,31:1
Monks, Harvey W, 1957, Je 12,35:4
Monks, James E, 1943, Ap 5,19:1
Monks, Jerome, 1946, N 13,27:3
Monks, Jerome Mrs, 1938, Ap 22,19:5
Monks, John, 1917, My 26,13:5; 1938, S 27,44:3; 1939, O 18,25:1; 1940, Ag 8,19:5
Monks, John P, 1956, Mr 5,23:1
Monks, Raphael I, 1952, Ja 11,22:2
Monks, Richard A, 1942, Mr 11,20:2
Monkswell, Lord (Robt Collier), 1909, D 23,9:5
Monnett, James C, 1943, Je 9,21:4
Monnett, Osborn, 1951, My 14,25:5
Monnett, Richard J, 1946, O 19,21:2
Monnier, France X, 1912, Ap 6,11:6
Monnier, H (J Prudhomme), 1877, F 3,5:1
Monnier, Henri, 1941, Ag 23,13:6
Monnier, Mathilde, 1954, Ap 25,87:3
Monnier, Victor G, 1954, Jl 10,13:5
Monniger, Louis, 1944, Ag 9,17:3
Monnot, Marguerite, 1961, O 13,35:4
Monod, Gabriel Jacque Jean, 1912, Ap 11,11:5
Monod, Wilfred, 1943, My 6,19:5
Monoghan, James P, 1941, My 6,21:5
Monoghan, Walter C, 1953, O 13,29:4
Monohan, Julia Mrs, 1937, Mr 29,3:2
Monolulu, Ras Prince (P C Mackay), 1965, F 16,28:4
Monory, Leon O Dr, 1915, Je 17,11:5
Monro, George N Jr, 1948, Je 9,29:5
Monro, Hugh R, 1954, N 22,23:5
Monro, Hugh R Jr, 1937, F 12,23:1
Monro, Walter J, 1958, O 9,37:1
Monro, William L, 1945, Jl 28,11:3
Monro, William L Jr, 1942, Je 11,23:5
Monro, William L Mrs, 1942, D 22,25:5
Monroe, Alex R, 1941, Je 18,21:4
Monroe, Andrew P Sr (Oct 7), 1965, O 11,61:4
Monroe, Andrew T Mrs, 1959. Mr 29,80:7
Monroe, Anne S, 1942, O 20,21:2
Monroe, Augustin, 1904, Je 28,3:6
Monroe, Belle M, 1943, N 9,21:5
Monroe, Charles E, 1942, Jl 16,19:5
Monroe, Charles S, 1960, D 28,27:4
Monroe, Cyrus, 1957, Mr 11,25:5
Monroe, Douglas D, 1949, Ag 15,17:4
Monroe, E N, 1951, Jl 27,19:6
Monroe, Edward, 1915, F 11,9:5
Monroe, Edwin S, 1940, N 3,57:3
Monroe, Frank, 1937, Jl 20,23:2
Monroe, Frazier F, 1951, S 9,89:2
Monroe, George E, 1949, O 12,30:3
Monroe, H, 1936, S 27,15:3
Monroe, Harris G Mrs, 1946, D 2,25:2
Monroe, Harry Mrs, 1945, D 29,14:3
Monroe, Harry R, 1940, S 12,25:5
Monroe, Henry, 1916, Ag 2,9:6
Monroe, Henry C Mrs, 1960, O 4,43:1
Monroe, Henry E, 1940, D 10,25:5
Monroe, Howard A, 1947, D 27,14:2
Monroe, James A, 1952, O 14,3:6
Monroe, Jay R, 1937, Ap 30,22:3
Monroe, John C, 1964, Je 9,35:2
Monroe, John D, 1953, Ap 2,27:1
Monroe, Kathryn B, 1951, Je 3,92:8
Monroe, Leslie R, 1955, O 11,39:4
Monroe, Louis G, 1940, S 28,17:5
Monroe, Marilyn, 1939, N 5,49:1
Monroe, Marilyn (funl plans, Ag 7,35:1; funl, Ag 9,22:5), 1962, Ag 6,1:2
Monroe, Nelson Gen, 1924, My 9,19:4
Monroe, Paul (por), 1947, D 7,76:3
Monroe, Pete, 1937, D 21,23:2
Monroe, Ralph R, 1950, D 27,27:4
Monroe, Robert Grier, 1924, N 26,19:5
Monroe, Rolland G, 1939, My 18,25:3
Monroe, Samuel F, 1956, My 19,19:4
Monroe, Seymour, 1959, Ja 17,19:4
Monroe, Stephen B, 1946, Mr 14,25:1
Monroe, Thomas A, 1959, D 11,33:2
Monroe, W Raymond, 1953, Ja 12,27:2
Monroe, W S, 1952, O 8,31:3
Monroe, Will S, 1939, Ja 30,13:4
Monroe, William H, 1940, Ja 15,15:3
Monroe, William S, 1953, S 14,27:5
Monroe, William S Mrs, 1944, My 23,23:2
Monsanto, H M, 1883, N 11,9:5
Monsarrat, Nicholas, 1910, O 1,13:3
Monsees, Henry J, 1962, Ja 11,33:2
Monsees, John C A, 1944, Ag 5,11:4
Monsell, George H, 1951, Ap 13,24:2
Monsell, J A, 1882, Je 6,5:2
Monsell, Samuel W, 1948, N 14,76:7
Monsell, Willard B, 1948, O 20,29:3
Monsey, John J, 1952, Jl 12,13:5
Monsky, Henry, 1947, My 3,17:1
Monsky, Leo, 1966, Ja 8,25:5
Monsky, Milton E, 1948, S 26,76:6
Monson, Edmund John, 1909, O 30,9:5
Monson, Harold Mrs, 1959, F 25,31:4
Monson, Lady, 1943, Ja 2,11:1
Monson, Lord, 1940, O 12,17:4
Monson, Sven, 1950, N 16,31:3
Monson, William O, 1948, S 9,27:4
Mont, Frederic Mrs, 1953, S 14,27:5
Mont, Lemuel, 1951, F 24,13:6
Montabert, Fred G Mrs, 1961, S 28,41:3
Montafiore, Leonard, 1879, S 7,2:7
Montag, Frank G, 1956, N 8,39:3
Montagne, Annie Davis La, 1924, Ja 30,19:4
Montagne, Augustus A, 1942, Je 28,32:4
Montagne, Ernesto, 1954, Ag 30,17:6
Montagne, Prosper, 1948, Ap 24,15:2
Montagne, Robert, 1954, N 27,14:3
Montagnini, Msgr, 1913, O 26,15:5
Montagriff, Charles B, 1943, Ja 19,19:4
Montagu, Charles Lord, 1939, N 12,49:1
Montagu, Edward E F, 1954, My 19,31:5
Montagu, Edwin S, 1924, N 16,7:3
Montagu, Ernest, 1952, N 21,25:4
Montagu, G F, 1882, Mr 15,5:5
Montagu, George C Earl of Sandwich, 1962, Je 17,81:2
Montagu, Lord, 1929, Mr 31,26:3
Montagu, William A D, 1947, F 10,29:3
Montagu-Douglas-Scott, Herbert, 1944, Je 19,19:5
Montagu-Douglas-Scott, William Henry (Duke of Buccleuch), 1914, N 6,11:5
Montagu-White, O G, 1916, Ap 22,11:5
Montagu y Vivero, Guillermo de, 1952, S 2,5:3
Montague, Abe, 1962, F 14,35:1
Montague, Allison, 1961, O 22,57:1
Montague, Andrew J (por), 1937, Ja 25,19:1
Montague, Andrew J Mrs, 1951, Ap 26,29:5
Montague, Arthur, 1943, O 10,48:6
Montague, C E, 1928, My 29,25:5
Montague, David T, 1945, O 19,23:4
Montague, Dwight, 1921, My 26,13:2
Montague, Evelyn A, 1948, F 2,19:2
Montague, Everett L, 1955, Ja 7,21:3
Montague, Gilbert H, 1961, F 6,23:2
Montague, Gilbert H Mrs, 1941, S 23,23:4
Montague, H J, 1878, Ag 13,5:1
Montague, Harry E, 1944, N 5,54:2
Montague, Henry B, 1951, Ag 14,23:2
Montague, Henry W, 1942, F 24,22:2
Montague, J Harold, 1950, My 1,25:2
Montague, James, 1965, Ap 29,35:3
Montague, James J (por), 1941, D 17,27:1
Montague, James J Mrs, 1937, Ja 22,21:2
Montague, John J Mrs, 1951, My 15,31:5
Montague, John J Sr, 1964, Jl 22,33:5
Montague, John V, 1960, Ag 17,31:2
Montague, Joseph E, 1939, N 27,17:4
Montague, Margaret P, 1955, S 27,35:4
Montague, Mary Mrs, 1946, O 21,33:5
Montague, N Thayer, 1923, F 18,19:2
Montague, Percy Jr, 1947, N 4,26:3
Montague, Richard Mrs, 1951, O 22,23:3
Montague, Robert M, 1958, F 21,23:4
Montague, Theodore G, 1910, S 4,9:6; 1967, Ag 14, 31:4
Montague, Victor A Rear-Adm, 1915, F 1,9:4
Montague, W H Dr, 1915, N 14,19:6
Montague, Wallace R Mrs, 1954, Ja 29,19:2
Montague, Wallace T, 1952, Jl 31,23:3
Montague, Warner J, 1959, Mr 26,31:3
Montague, William, 1951, Ag 31,15:2
Montague, William P, 1953, Ag 2,72:3; 1957, O 6,85:2
Montague, William P Mrs (Helen R), 1964, O 30, 38:1
Montague, Winetta, 1877, My 30,8:4
Montaigne, Arthur (Bozo the Clown), 1956, D 19, 31:3
Montaigne, Gerald, 1950, Ag 8,30:2
Montalban, Leonardo, 1946, S 18,31:2
Montaldo, Pedro, 1884, F 24,7:4
Montalembert, Count, 1870, Mr 14,5:1
Montalivet, Count, 1880, Ja 6,5:2
Montalvao, Justino, 1949, F 26,15:3
Montalvo, Evaristo V de, 1938, N 3,23:5
Montalvo, Mario M, 1937, Ag 24,22:2
Montalvo y Morales, Rafael, 1947, N 30,76:4
Montamat, Leo, 1966, Jl 3,35:3
Montana, John C, 1964, Mr 19,67:1
Montana, Louis (Bull), 1950, Ja 25,27:1
Montana, Louis Mrs, 1962, Mr 14,39:4
Montanari, Luigi Lt-Gen, 1937, Mr 3,23:3
Montanaro, Manuel E, 1959, Ag 26,29:1
Montani, Nicola A, 1948, Ja 12,19:5
Montano, Walker M Mrs, 1955, My 4,29:5
Montant, Auguste P, 1909, N 26,9:5
Montant, Jules A, 1915, Je 3,11:6; 1923, D 6,19:3
Montant, L B (see also Ap 6), 1877, Ap 8,12:1
Montany, Charles A, 1942, N 15,58:2
Montanye, Carlton S, 1948, Ag 4,21:2
Montanye, Lillian M Mrs, 1939, Ja 20,19:2
Montanye, William C, 1948, My 14,23:4
Montanye, William J, 1952, My 29,27:1
Montara, Edgardo L, 1940, Ap 21,43:1
Montavani, Albert A, 1963, Ag 8,27:4
Montavon, William F, 1959, F 18,33:4
Montayne, Frederick W, 1950, D 28,26:5
Montchar, Isidor, 1961, F 26,92:3
Montchyk, Edward, 1948, Ja 18,60:2
Monte, Louis G, 1955, Je 12,86:7
Monte, Salvatore, 1950, N 30,33:3
Monteagle, Louis F, 1940, Jl 17,21:2
Monteagle of Brandon, Lord, 1937, D 23,22:4
Monteagudo, Jose Jesus Gen, 1914, D 15,13:5
Montealegre, Edgar, 1940, N 2,15:2
Montebello, Duke of, 1874, Jl 21,5:3
Montechio, Marthia, 1871, Mr 31,1:3
Montedoro, Marco, 1947, S 6,17:3
Montefiore, Moses Sir, 1885, Jl 29,5:6
Montefiori, Luigi, 1951, S 25,29:1
Monteith, Ethel R, 1948, D 18,19:3
Monteith, Mary H, 1951, Je 19,29:5
Monteith, Robert, 1956, F 20,23:3
Monteith, Stephen R, 1949, D 10,17:3
Monteith, William, 1948, Jl 22,23:6
Monteleone, Ernest J, 1955, My 21,17:3
Monteleone, Giovanni, 1947, F 3,19:5
Montell, Edwin, 1939, Mr 28,24:2
Montell, Eleanor, 1949, Mr 26,17:1
Montell, F T, 1883, My 13,9:2
Montelli, Anthony L, 1946, Ag 14,25:5
Montells, Joseph E, 1925, O 3,15:4
Montemarano, Rocco, 1960, My 21,35:3
Montemezzi, Italo, 1952, My 16,24:3
Montenaro, Peter L, 1966, My 4,47:2
Montenecourt, Edward Jr Mrs, 1965, Mr 18,33:5
Montenecourt, Edward Mrs, 1942, D 5,15:4
Montenegro, Adolfo, 1951, D 22,15:3
Montenegro, Carlos, 1953, Mr 12,27:2
Montenyohl, Victor I, 1945, O 28,44:3
Montepin, X de, 1902, My 2,9:2
Monterio, Manuel, 1952, Ja 20,84:2
Montero, Juan, 1948, F 26,23:6
Montero-Rios, Eugenio, 1914, My 13,11:6
Montero y Baldarrain, Mario E, 1952, S 2,23:5
Montes, Armando, 1948, Jl 18,52:6
Montes, Felix, 1942, O 28,23:4
Montes, I, 1933, N 19,36:1
Montesani, Frank, 1954, O 15,23:4
Montesano, Michael J, 1961, Ag 25,25:2
Montesano, Nicholas A, 1961, S 22,34:1
Montesanto, Luigi, 1954, Je 15,29:5
Monteser, Frederick, 1915, D 6,9:3
Montesguion-Fezensac, Robert de, 1921, D 16,17:
Montesi, Anthony E, 1950, Mr 29,29:3
Montesi, Anthony Mrs, 1950, Jl 4,17:2
Montesi, Pamelia A, 1953, D 23,23:2
Montesquiou-Fezensac, Lionel de Count, 1941, Je 32:7
Montessori, Maria, 1952, My 7,27:1
Montet, Pierre, 1966, Je 21,43:2
Monteux, Pierre (funl, Jl 5,43:3), 1964, Jl 2,1:2
Montez, Lola (funl), 1861, Ja 21,8:1
Montez, Maria, 1951, S 8,8:3
Montford, Abram E, 1938, Je 9,23:5
Montford, Paul R, 1938, Ja 16,II,8:4
Montfort, Barret, 1962, S 3,15:5
Montfort, Ralph A, 1948, Mr 31,25:1
Montfort, Robert J, 1943, Ap 6,21:2
Montfort, Walter J, 1952, Mr 28,24:5
Montgelas, Adolph von Count, 1924, Ap 24,19:5
Montglyon, Princess (Mercy D Argenteau), 192 Jl 28,13:6
Montgmoery, George (will), 1940, Je 12,47:1
Montgomery, A J, 1955, N 9,33:3
Montgomery, Agnes, 1955, Mr 21,11:6
Montgomery, Albert H, 1948, F 2,19:4
Montgomery, Alfred, 1922, Ap 22,9:5
Montgomery, Alice M, 1943, N 28,68:7
Montgomery, Andrew, 1952, D 23,23:2
Montgomery, Andrew H, 1960, Mr 19,21:4
Montgomery, Andrew H Mrs, 1956, Mr 26,29:1
Montgomery, Andrew J, 1961, Ag 3,23:4
Montgomery, Archibald, 1952, Mr 24,25:3
Montgomery, Archibald E, 1947, Jl 24,21:5
Montgomery, Arthur, 1940, S 6,21:5
Montgomery, Arthur L, 1954, N 11,31:2
Montgomery, Bella R Mrs, 1939, Je 27,23:6
Montgomery, Bernard A, 1955, Je 17,23:4
Montgomery, Blinn C, 1941, Jl 27,30:1
Montgomery, C S Capt, 1865, F 25,8:5
Montgomery, Carl F, 1960, Ap 17,92:6
Montgomery, Carol G, 1950, D 4,29:2
Montgomery, Chandler Capt, 1919, S 18,13:6
Montgomery, Charles, 1951, S 17,21:3
Montgomery, Charles D, 1943, Mr 23,20:3
Montgomery, Charles H, 1945, Jl 14,5:8
Montgomery, Charles S, 1950, Ap 1,15:6
Montgomery, Colvin R, 1959, Ag 30,82:5
Montgomery, David (funl, Ap 24,11:4), 1917, A 13:3
Montgomery, Donald H, 1953, Ag 15,15:7
Montgomery, Donald Mrs (M Taylor), 1957, A 19:6
Montgomery, Donald S, 1949, My 21,13:4

Montgomery, E E, 1927, Ap 19,27:3
Montgomery, Edmund B, 1954, D 9,33:4
Montgomery, Edward, 1962, F 5,31:2
Montgomery, Edward L, 1946, My 5,46:3
Montgomery, Edward W, 1946, D 9,25:3
Montgomery, Elizabeth Shaw Mrs, 1968, D 23,39:1
Montgomery, Ewan Mrs, 1942, Ap 25,13:4
Montgomery, Finis E, 1946, Je 17,21:2
Montgomery, Finis E Mrs, 1966, D 7,47:1
Montgomery, Fletcher H (por), 1948, O 16,15:4
Montgomery, Frances Trego Mrs, 1925, Ap 7,19:5
Montgomery, Francis L, 1948, O 2,15:5
Montgomery, Frank B, 1919, N 25,11:2
Montgomery, Frank P, 1942, Mr 13,19:1
Montgomery, Frederick, 1941, D 29,15:5
Montgomery, George, 1938, D 9,26:1
Montgomery, George Archbishop, 1907, Ja 11,9:6
Montgomery, George B, 1938, Mr 17,21:3
Montgomery, George I, 1922, N 9,19:4
Montgomery, George M, 1947, Je 29,48:5
Montgomery, George R, 1945, D 1,23:3
Montgomery, George S Jr, 1966, Ja 8,26:4
Montgomery, George Washington, 1913, D 24,11:6
Montgomery, Gertrude M Mrs, 1954, Jl 21,27:4
Montgomery, Gilbert M, 1956, Mr 31,15:3
Montgomery, Grace, 1882, N 26,1:6
Montgomery, Guy, 1951, S 25,29:2
Montgomery, H E Rev, 1874, O 17,2:6
Montgomery, Hale L, 1967, Jl 17,29:5
Montgomery, Harry, 1911, Jl 9,11:4
Montgomery, Harry A, 1951, Mr 24,13:3
Montgomery, Harry E, 1954, My 23,88:5
Montgomery, Helen B, 1967, Ag 6,76:2
Montgomery, Henry A, 1957, Mr 31,89:1
Montgomery, Henry E, 1939, Jl 14,19:4
Montgomery, Henry E (por), 1941, Mr 17,17:5
Montgomery, Henry G, 1945, Mr 24,17:3
Montgomery, Henry H, 1943, D 30,17:2
Montgomery, Henry Mrs (por), 1949, Jl 10,57:1
Montgomery, Hugh L, 1942, S 5,13:4
Montgomery, James A, 1914, O 12,9:4; 1949, F 8,26:3
Montgomery, James B, 1939, Ap 15,19:6
Montgomery, James C, 1953, F 16,21:1
Montgomery, James C Mrs, 1945, O 25,21:4
Montgomery, James E, 1946, Ag 4,45:2; 1949, Mr 28, 21:3
Montgomery, James H, 1966, Je 19,84:8
Montgomery, James J Lt, 1937, F 6,21:4
Montgomery, James M Mrs, 1945, Mr 27,19:3
Montgomery, James Rev, 1904, My 26,7:6
Montgomery, James S, 1952, Jl 1,23:2; 1955, N 11,25:2
Montgomery, James T, 1945, F 8,19:2
Montgomery, James W, 1949, N 9,27:3
Montgomery, Jay H, 1953, N 24,29:3
Montgomery, Jennie, 1961, Ag 31,27:2
Montgomery, Job H, 1941, N 6,23:2
Montgomery, John A, 1949, My 6,25:2
Montgomery, John A Judge, 1922, Jl 29,7:5
Montgomery, John B Rear-Adm, 1873, Mr 28,5:5
Montgomery, John C, 1867, Ag 21,5:6; 1948, Je 9,29:6
Montgomery, John F, 1953, Ap 23,29:5; 1954, N 8,21:3
Montgomery, John F Mrs, 1953, Ap 8,29:1
Montgomery, John H, 1915, Ja 23,11:6; 1957, Ag 4, 80:4
Montgomery, John L, 1960, F 9,31:2; 1962, Jl 7,17:4
Montgomery, John L Mrs, 1946, O 9,27:2
Montgomery, John R, 1946, My 12,43:1
Montgomery, John R Sr, 1937, Mr 6,17:1
Montgomery, John S, 1940, F 3,13:4
Montgomery, Joseph W Mrs, 1953, My 13,29:4
Montgomery, Kingsley, 1937, My 22,15:1
Montgomery, Lawrence J, 1941, Ja 22,21:1
Montgomery, Lee A, 1961, Ag 2,29:2
Montgomery, Leila Y Mrs, 1940, Ap 29,15:4
Montgomery, LeRoy, 1956, Ja 9,25:4
Montgomery, Leslie A (L Doyle), 1961, Ag 14,25:4
Montgomery, Lois, 1954, O 30,17:2
Montgomery, Louis, 1958, S 4,29:4
Montgomery, Louis A, 1950, N 13,27:4
Montgomery, Mabel (Mrs J Mooney), 1942, Jl 24, 19:4
Montgomery, Marshall F, 1956, N 28,35:4
Montgomery, Matthew J, 1944, F 18,17:1
Montgomery, Melvin, 1938, Ag 2,19:2
Montgomery, Mortimer L, 1957, Je 4,35:3
Montgomery, O M, 1940, D 5,25:4
Montgomery, Oliver, 1944, N 24,23:4
Montgomery, Ora C, 1940, N 11,19:3
Montgomery, Oscar H, 1924, N 29,13:4
Montgomery, Phelps, 1954, N 15,27:6
Montgomery, R Ames Mrs, 1940, Jl 22,17:2
Montgomery, Richard D, 1952, D 11,33:3
Montgomery, Richard M, 1942, Ap 24,17:5
Montgomery, Richard M Jr, 1938, Jl 7,19:2
Montgomery, Richard W, 1950, Jl 11,31:2
Montgomery, Richmond A, 1950, Jl 18,29:4
Montgomery, Robert A K, 1951, N 21,25:1
Montgomery, Robert C, 1950, Ja 9,25:5
Montgomery, Robert Craig, 1968, Je 5,47:3
Montgomery, Robert H, 1943, Ap 1,23:4; 1953, My 4, 23:3
Montgomery, Robert J, 1951, Ja 16,29:2
Montgomery, Robert L, 1947, My 30,21:2
Montgomery, Robert L (will, Ja 29,15:5), 1949, Ja 24,19:4
Montgomery, Robert M, 1920, Je 29,11:4
Montgomery, Robert N, 1967, Ap 23,92:7
Montgomery, Robert O, 1946, Ag 15,25:6
Montgomery, Robert T, 1947, My 31,13:5
Montgomery, S G Morton, 1948, My 19,27:1
Montgomery, Samuel D, 1958, O 15,39:4
Montgomery, Stephen C, 1953, F 8,88:4
Montgomery, T Ewing, 1962, F 10,23:3
Montgomery, Thomas Harrison Prof, 1912, Mr 20,13:5
Montgomery, Thomas Mrs, 1947, Ag 15,17:3
Montgomery, Thomas P, 1937, S 28,23:5
Montgomery, Vaughan E, 1948, S 29,29:3
Montgomery, Victoria, 1882, N 26,1:6
Montgomery, Virgil, 1945, Mr 26,19:4
Montgomery, W Jr, 1880, Je 20,2:6
Montgomery, W Ray, 1953, Ag 2,72:8
Montgomery, Walter, 1871, S 3,5:5
Montgomery, Walter A, 1949, Ja 8,15:4
Montgomery, Walter B, 1953, Ag 11,27:4
Montgomery, Walter C, 1940, Ja 16,23:3
Montgomery, Walter S, 1937, N 13,19:4
Montgomery, Warren T, 1940, S 19,23:2
Montgomery, Wes, 1968, Je 16,68:5
Montgomery, William, 1953, N 23,27:4; 1955, S 5,11:1
Montgomery, William B, 1940, Ag 26,15:5; 1960, Ag 13,15:5
Montgomery, William H, 1958, Mr 22,17:5; 1964, Ag 18,31:4
Montgomery, William P, 1941, Mr 5,21:5
Montgomery, William R, 1945, Ja 7,38:1
Montgomery, William R Mrs, 1948, D 21,25:2
Montgomery, William S, 1912, Ja 21,II,13:2
Montgomery, William W, 1962, Mr 28,39:1
Montgomery, William W Jr, 1949, Ag 10,21:4
Montgomery, William Watts, 1910, Ja 3,9:4
Montgomery-Massingberd, Archibald, 1947, O 14,28:2
Monti, Carlo, 1949, O 23,84:3
Monti, Guglielmo, 1951, Ja 29,19:5
Montieth, John Rev Dr, 1918, My 6,13:8
Montieth, May G, 1948, D 16,29:3
Montieth, Percy L, 1941, Jl 27,30:5
Montigny, John W, 1946, O 18,23:2
Montigny, Manager of the Gymnase Theatre, 1880, Mr 22,5:2
Montijo, Comtesse de, 1879, D 8,3:7
Montillot, Robert, 1956, Mr 20,23:5
Montinola, Ruperto, 1940, F 10,15:6
Montjoie, Fina, 1951, F 27,27:4
Montmasson, Rosalia, 1904, S 10,8:5
Montmorency, Luxemberg de Prince, 1878, F 3,4:6
Montmoreney, Duke de, 1915, Mr 27,11:4
Monton, Robert R (ed), 1940, Je 3,14:3
Montonna, Ralph E, 1952, Ja 9,29:6
Montour, Monsignor, 1874, O 22,1:7
Montowne, Russ, 1950, S 10,93:1
Montoya, Nestor, 1923, Ja 14,6:2
Montpensier, Duchess of, 1958, Jl 12,15:1
Montpensier, Duke of, 1890, F 5,5:4
Montpensier, Isabelle de (Countess of Paris), 1919, Ap 25,15:4
Montreuil, Antoine, 1940, Jl 2,21:3
Montrose, Belle (Mrs B Allen), 1964, O 27,39:2
Montrose, Dowager Duchess of, 1940, N 24,49:2
Montrose, Duke of (Douglas Beresford Malise Ronald Graham), 1925, D 11,23:4
Montrose, Duke of (J Graham), 1954, Ja 21,31:4
Montrose, Otis, 1937, S 3,17:5
Montrose, Paris, 1961, F 15,35:5
Montrose, William H Jr, 1952, Ja 3,27:2
Montross, Charles, 1943, O 7,23:2
Montross, Edward B, 1937, N 27,17:4
Montross, Franklin, 1952, Ag 26,25:1
Montross, Franklin Mrs, 1943, My 7,19:3
Montross, Harry L, 1958, Ja 17,25:3
Montross, Lois (Mrs J Ford), 1961, S 18,29:2
Montross, Lynn, 1961, Ja 30,23:1
Montross, N E, 1932, D 11,34:1
Montross, Robert H, 1963, O 31,33:1
Montroy, Robert H, 1949, Ja 9,72:7
Montselos, Constantine, 1955, Ja 26,25:2
Montsko, Charles W, 1945, N 7,23:5
Montstiers-Merinville, Marquise des, 1909, O 6,9:3
Montt, Jorge, 1922, O 9,15:6
Montt, Luis, 1909, N 26,9:7
Montulet, August Mrs, 1946, Je 17,21:2
Montuori, Francesco, 1940, D 5,25:2
Montuori, Luca, 1952, Mr 10,21:5
Montus, Gerard, 1957, My 1,37:1
Monty, Amedee Mrs, 1945, Mr 23,19:4
Monty, Grace E, 1946, Ag 27,27:2
Monvel, Bernard B de, 1949, O 29,1:8
Monville, Joseph P, 1950, My 4,27:3
Monyek, Herbert A, 1962, S 16,86:1
Monypenny, Thomas L Mrs, 1946, D 15,77:5
Monypenny, William Flavelle, 1912, N 25,13:5
Monzani, Pietro D, 1951, Ja 31,25:3
Mooberry, Henry E, 1965, Ja 10,92:5
Moock, Russell H, 1966, D 27,32:8
Mood, James R, 1956, Ap 23,27:2
Mood, Orlondo C, 1953, My 3,88:2
Mood, Raymond, 1952, Ag 2,15:2
Moodey, William, 1937, N 5,23:2
Moodie, Alexander, 1944, My 20,15:2
Moodie, Arthur J, 1954, Ap 17,13:4
Moodie, E R Capt, 1881, Ag 28,1:2
Moodie, Thomas H (por), 1948, Mr 4,25:3
Moodie, Walter C, 1939, My 8,17:5
Moodnik, Benjamin Mrs, 1953, Ja 29,28:3
Moody, A Gordon, 1962, Ag 31,21:3
Moody, Alfred J F, 1967, Mr 21,46:2
Moody, Ambert G, 1945, N 12,22:2
Moody, Ambert G Mrs, 1952, N 4,30:3
Moody, Ambrose A, 1950, F 26,76:7
Moody, Arthur W, 1959, Je 15,27:5
Moody, Aunt Agnes, 1903, Ap 11,9:6
Moody, Blair (funl, Jl 25,68:6), 1954, Jl 21,27:1
Moody, Blair Mrs, 1961, Je 23,29:4
Moody, C E, 1944, F 17,19:5
Moody, Charles P, 1955, F 12,15:2
Moody, Clarence L, 1944, N 21,25:2
Moody, Cleveland E, 1948, Mr 6,13:2
Moody, Dan, 1966, My 23,41:1
Moody, Dwight L, 1899, D 23,4:4; 1951, Je 11,25:4; 1968, S 10,47:1
Moody, Dwight L Mrs, 1903, O 11,7:6
Moody, Elizabeth E Mrs, 1941, Je 9,19:1
Moody, Ethel M, 1949, S 23,23:3
Moody, Fanny, 1945, Jl 23,19:5
Moody, Frank R, 1950, D 31,42:6
Moody, H A, 1926, Jl 24,11:5
Moody, H J, 1880, My 21,5:4
Moody, Harold, 1947, Ap 25,21:2
Moody, Harry, 1943, My 17,15:2
Moody, Henry L, 1954, Mr 25,29:2
Moody, Herbert R (por), 1947, O 21,23:5
Moody, Horace W Mrs, 1950, My 15,21:2
Moody, Hunter C, 1962, Mr 17,37:2
Moody, J M, 1903, F 6,9:6
Moody, John, 1958, F 17,23:1
Moody, John S, 1952, D 9,33:4
Moody, John Sr, 1966, S 15,43:3
Moody, Julia E, 1959, O 17,23:5
Moody, Leonard, 1905, F 23,9:7
Moody, Lewis F, 1953, Ap 20,25:4
Moody, Lewis F Mrs, 1937, Ja 7,21:3
Moody, Martha L Mrs, 1942, D 15,27:3
Moody, Nancy Elizabeth Mrs, 1914, My 3,13:5
Moody, Nelson K, 1944, D 31,26:8
Moody, Paul D, 1947, Ag 20,21:1
Moody, Rollin H, 1949, F 22,23:5
Moody, S Irving, 1942, S 11,21:2
Moody, Samuel, 1876, O 7,2:3
Moody, Samuel A, 1947, Mr 11,27:2
Moody, Thomas, 1952, Mr 25,27:4
Moody, Virginius D, 1940, Je 1,15:2
Moody, W Howard, 1953, Je 15,29:5
Moody, W L Jr (will, Jl 29,15:6), 1954, Jl 22,23:4
Moody, W S Mrs, 1928, D 15,19:4
Moody, Walter D, 1920, N 22,15:4
Moody, Walter S (por), 1938, N 8,23:1
Moody, William A, 1946, Ag 25,45:1; 1947, F 3,19:2
Moody, William F, 1958, Ja 12,87:1
Moody, William F Mrs, 1943, S 20,21:2
Moody, William H Ex-Justice (funl, Jl 6,9:6), 1917, Jl 2,9:5
Moody, William Vaughn, 1910, O 18,9:3
Moody, Winfield Scott Mrs, 1922, D 29,13:5
Mooers, Clifford, 1956, N 14,35:2
Mooers, De Sacia (Mrs H L Lewis), 1960, Ja 13,47:3
Mooers, Louis P, 1962, Je 23,23:3
Moog, William C Sr, 1958, Ja 13,29:3
Moog, William T, 1953, Ja 9,21:2
Mook, Ann E Mrs, 1953, Ap 6,19:5
Mook, Charles C, 1966, O 11,43:7
Mook, De Lo, 1949, Jl 6,30:3
Mook, Hubertus J van, 1965, My 15,31:4
Mookerjee, Syama P, 1953, Je 23,3:8
Moolten, Ralph R, 1959, Jl 22,27:3
Moomau, Laurence P, 1957, D 13,27:4
Moomaw, Mary, 1957, F 7,27:4
Moon, Bucklin Mrs (A Curtis Brown), 1965, D 8,47:2
Moon, Carl, 1948, Je 26,17:6
Moon, Carl Mrs, 1947, S 8,21:5
Moon, Cary B, 1951, Jl 31,21:2
Moon, Charles, 1953, F 1,59:2
Moon, David H, 1939, Ja 23,13:3
Moon, Dewitt C, 1939, S 7,25:2
Moon, Frederic R, 1942, O 23,22:4
Moon, George C (por), 1947, Mr 9,60:3
Moon, George W, 1952, F 26,27:2
Moon, Guy H, 1948, Mr 22,23:3
Moon, Harold P, 1966, Ag 12,31:4
Moon, Harriett A, 1942, D 7,27:3
Moon, Harry Barber, 1909, Mr 26,9:4
Moon, John A, 1921, Je 27,13:5
Moon, Le Roy H, 1950, Ap 8,13:3
Moon, Nicholas L, 1943, D 30,17:3
Moon, Odas Capt, 1937, N 21,II,9:2
Moon, Owen, 1947, Ap 14,27:3
Moon, P T, 1936, Je 13,17:3
Moon, Parker T Mrs, 1940, F 25,38:3
Moon, Raymond E, 1956, Jl 8,65:2
Moon, Reuben O, 1919, O 27,11:5
Moon, Ridgway F, 1963, My 12,86:4

Moon, Robert C Dr, 1914, F 14,11:5
Moon, Robert E, 1948, S 20,25:4
Moon, S S, 1879, My 2,4:6
Moon, Truman J, 1946, Jl 17,23:4
Moon, W R, 1933, N 24,21:5
Moon, Ward C, 1947, D 28,40:3
Moon, William D, 1943, Ja 16,13:2
Moon, William T, 1942, My 1,19:4
Moone, John I, 1959, My 8,27:1
Moone, Luke, 1905, Mr 19,9:4
Mooney, A Hulse Mrs, 1964, My 1,35:1
Mooney, Alex Mrs, 1952, F 13,29:4
Mooney, Anna Mrs, 1911, Ag 1,9:6
Mooney, C A, 1931, My 30,15:5
Mooney, C P J, 1926, N 23,29:3
Mooney, Charles E, 1954, Jl 23,17:2
Mooney, Charles J, 1947, N 7,23:1
Mooney, Charles L, 1942, O 18,52:4
Mooney, Charles P, 1952, Ap 30,27:3
Mooney, Christopher G, 1957, My 30,19:5
Mooney, Clarence V, 1944, Ja 14,19:3
Mooney, Daniel, 1911, O 1,13:5
Mooney, Daniel J, 1957, F 1,25:1
Mooney, Denis, 1966, Ag 21,93:2
Mooney, Doris E, 1949, Je 2,28:3
Mooney, E L, 1933, O 16,17:6
Mooney, Edmund S, 1953, Ja 29,28:5
Mooney, Edward (funl, N 1,19:2), 1958, O 26,1:7
Mooney, Edward S Jr, 1959, F 19,31:1
Mooney, Edwin J Mrs, 1959, My 20,35:3
Mooney, Frances D Mrs, 1940, Jl 21,28:7
Mooney, Francis I, 1940, N 26,23:4
Mooney, Frank, 1942, D 1,25:2
Mooney, Frank J, 1949, Ag 17,23:6
Mooney, Franklin D, 1966, F 3,31:1
Mooney, Frederick C, 1951, D 13,33:2
Mooney, George S Mrs, 1950, Ap 19,29:3
Mooney, Harold M, 1961, O 26,17:4
Mooney, Harry R, 1957, My 24,25:2
Mooney, Henry W, 1938, Jl 18,13:5
Mooney, Herbert F Mrs, 1952, D 7,89:1
Mooney, Ila, 1911, Ag 3,7:5
Mooney, J Boyce Mrs, 1947, O 29,27:2
Mooney, James, 1937, N 6,17:6; 1951, S 28,31:5
Mooney, James (will), 1953, Ap 24,30:1
Mooney, James B, 1945, Ag 25,11:4
Mooney, James D, 1957, S 22,85:1
Mooney, James F, 1951, Ja 20,15:4; 1953, D 9,11:2
Mooney, James H, 1956, Ag 21,29:2
Mooney, James J, 1948, Ja 6,23:5; 1949, My 10,25:2; 1959, D 14,31:2
Mooney, James M, 1914, D 3,13:3
Mooney, James Mrs (M Montgomery), 1942, Jl 24, 19:4
Mooney, James X Sr, 1949, N 18,29:2
Mooney, Joachim J, 1955, Jl 8,23:1
Mooney, John, 1952, S 15,25:3
Mooney, John B, 1956, D 4,39:5
Mooney, John D, 1962, Ag 22,34:4
Mooney, John E, 1940, Ap 5,21:1; 1954, F 18,31:5
Mooney, John G, 1951, Jl 1,51:1
Mooney, John H, 1906, Je 5,9:6
Mooney, John J, 1940, Ap 23,24:3; 1950, Ap 5,31:1
Mooney, John J Sr, 1945, Je 25,17:5
Mooney, John R, 1955, Jl 23,17:2
Mooney, John W, 1942, Je 8,15:1
Mooney, Joseph B, 1964, Mr 18,41:4
Mooney, Joseph F, 1944, My 2,19:3
Mooney, Joseph F Msgr, 1923, My 14,15:4
Mooney, Joseph J, 1938, Ag 17,19:2; 1940, D 27,20:2; 1945, Je 3,32:4
Mooney, Joseph T Jr, 1963, N 19,41:1
Mooney, Joseph W, 1961, Ap 5,37:4; 1965, Ja 8,27:1
Mooney, Lawrence, 1954, Jl 18,56:2
Mooney, Louis M, 1949, Ja 21,21:2
Mooney, Louisa A Mrs, 1940, O 23,23:4
Mooney, Luis Walton, 1911, Jl 13,9:4
Mooney, M Mrs, 1934, S 3,13:1
Mooney, Mary T, 1946, Mr 27,27:3
Mooney, Michael J, 1946, O 10,27:6
Mooney, Miriam L Mrs (will, Je 18,47:1), 1940, Je 9,44:8
Mooney, Neil A, 1942, Jl 11,13:2
Mooney, Neil Mrs, 1952, Ap 21,21:3
Mooney, Patrick H, 1919, O 11,9:2
Mooney, Patrick J, 1943, My 15,15:4
Mooney, Paul C, 1941, My 1,23:6
Mooney, Peter T, 1948, F 1,60:7
Mooney, Phil, 1938, My 29,II,6:6
Mooney, Philip, 1947, N 5,27:6
Mooney, Raymond M, 1954, Ap 13,31:3
Mooney, Richard A, 1962, S 26,39:2
Mooney, Richard J, 1943, N 18,23:2
Mooney, Robert C, 1943, O 6,23:4
Mooney, Robert H, 1958, Ap 29,29:1
Mooney, Seymour Mrs, 1952, Ap 6,90:4
Mooney, T J Rev (see also S 14,15), 1877, S 16,12:1
Mooney, Thomas P, 1948, N 20,13:3
Mooney, Thomas R, 1961, Jl 10,21:4
Mooney, Timothy, 1905, Mr 4,7:3
Mooney, Timothy C, 1945, O 29,19:2
Mooney, Tom, 1942, Mr 7,18:2
Mooney, Tom Mrs, 1952, Ag 12,12:3
Mooney, Volney P, 1945, Ag 4,11:5
Mooney, Walter J, 1955, My 13,25:1
Mooney, William J, 1941, O 8,23:1; 1954, Mr 16,29:2
Mooney, William L, 1948, O 23,15:3
Mooney, William M, 1960, Ap 12,33:2
Mooney, William Mrs, 1955, Jl 19,27:4
Mooney, William T, 1948, D 2,29:5; 1952, Ja 17,27:4; 1954, D 9,33:4
Moons, Frank A, 1952, O 29,29:5
Moons, Theodore, 1962, Ja 13,21:5
Moor, Dmitri, 1946, O 28,27:2
Moor, George C, 1957, Jl 18,25:4
Moor, Jan M de (por), 1945, Je 1,15:2
Moor, Lee Mrs (will), 1952, F 1,8:4
Moor, Otto C, 1967, S 4,21:4
Moor, Ralph Denham Rayment Sir, 1909, S 15,9:5
Moora, Godfrey, 1945, N 15,19:2
Moora, John C, 1937, My 26,25:5
Moora, Louise W, 1940, My 12,48:1
Moorad, George, 1949, Jl 13,1:8
Moorcroft, Walter B, 1915, Je 17,11:6
Moore, A Capt, 1881, F 27,7:3
Moore, A G, 1934, Ap 5,21:1
Moore, A Harry, 1952, N 19,1:2
Moore, A M Dr, 1910, Ja 14,9:4
Moore, A Maurice, 1959, O 3,19:2
Moore, A P (por), 1930, F 18,1:4
Moore, Abigail W Mrs, 1945, D 23,18:2
Moore, Addison U, 1952, Mr 21,23:4
Moore, Albert B, 1967, Ap 22,31:4
Moore, Albert E, 1939, Mr 7,22:2
Moore, Albert H, 1908, Je 22,7:4
Moore, Albert R Jr, 1947, Ap 27,60:6
Moore, Albert V (will, F 6,26:1), 1953, Ja 9,21:1
Moore, Albert W, 1940, Ja 22,15:5; 1940, N 19,23:3
Moore, Albert W Sr, 1957, Ap 26,26:1
Moore, Albertus A, 1942, Mr 24,19:3
Moore, Alex J, 1962, Ag 28,31:2
Moore, Alex P, 1961, Je 19,27:1
Moore, Alfred C, 1942, O 31,15:5
Moore, Alfred P, 1946, S 23,23:5
Moore, Alfred T, 1942, O 7,25:6
Moore, Alfred W, 1950, Je 29,29:4
Moore, Alice M, 1925, D 11,23:2
Moore, Alvin, 1947, Je 17,25:2
Moore, Amada Mrs, 1953, O 15,33:5
Moore, Amos (G B Hubbard), 1958, Jl 7,27:2
Moore, Andrew B, 1955, Jl 26,25:4
Moore, Ann, 1955, S 1,23:3
Moore, Anna P, 1950, Ag 10,25:5
Moore, Anne C, 1961, Ja 21,21:3
Moore, Annie, 1924, Ap 15,21:2
Moore, Annie E, 1958, S 7,87:3
Moore, Arch C, 1942, S 29,23:4
Moore, Arthur E, 1950, O 6,27:2; 1963, Ja 9,8:3
Moore, Arthur F, 1966, Ap 11,35:2
Moore, Arthur G, 1946, Ja 9,23:2
Moore, Arthur H, 1964, N 7,27:6
Moore, Arthur J, 1949, N 24,31:6
Moore, Arthur L, 1940, O 17,25:1
Moore, Arthur M, 1945, S 6,25:3
Moore, Arthur R, 1947, My 30,21:1
Moore, Arthur S, 1956, Ap 23,27:2
Moore, Aubrey S, 1955, D 14,39:3
Moore, B F, 1878, N 28,5:3
Moore, B H, 1878, Jl 10,3:1
Moore, Baker, 1947, D 4,31:4
Moore, Banton, 1954, Ja 4,19:2
Moore, Benjamin, 1938, Mr 14,15:4; 1939, Ap 16,III, 6:8; 1950, O 13,29:2
Moore, Benjamin H, 1937, Je 4,23:1
Moore, Benjamin Mrs, 1942, Ja 7,20:2
Moore, Benjamin W, 1950, Ja 19,27:2
Moore, Benoni, 1955, Ja 1,13:4
Moore, Bernie, 1967, N 7,43:2
Moore, Bertha Pearl, 1925, My 3,5:1
Moore, Bessie V, 1949, D 22,23:2
Moore, Beveridge H, 1944, Mr 1,19:6
Moore, Blaine F, 1941, F 16,15:2
Moore, Burress, 1952, Jl 9,27:3
Moore, C E, 1941, Ap 3,23:3
Moore, C Oscar Prof, 1925, Mr 23,17:4
Moore, Caleb C, 1949, D 22,23:1
Moore, Carl E, 1954, Ap 16,21:5
Moore, Carl R, 1955, O 17,27:3
Moore, Caroline A Mrs, 1951, Ja 16,29:1
Moore, Carroll Sr Mrs, 1943, D 24,13:1
Moore, Casimir de Rham, 1925, My 11,17:4
Moore, Catherine, 1944, My 7,46:1
Moore, Catherine M, 1949, Jl 8,19:3
Moore, Charles, 1959, Mr 27,24:5
Moore, Charles A, 1914, D 10,13:4; 1923, Jl 7,11:6; 1940, My 23,23:4; 1949, Ag 24,25:3; 1953, Je 25, 27:2; 1967, Ap 15,31:3
Moore, Charles A Mrs, 1944, Mr 25,15:6
Moore, Charles B, 1946, O 20,60:3
Moore, Charles Brainard Taylor Rear-Adm, 1923, Ap 5,19:6
Moore, Charles E, 1939, N 18,17:6; 1953, Je 21,84:8; 1961, N 28,37:2
Moore, Charles E Dr, 1922, S 23,15:4
Moore, Charles F, 1938, Jl 26,19:3; 1959, My 23,25:5
Moore, Charles G, 1949, My 12,31:6; 1958, Mr 22,17:4
Moore, Charles H, 1941, F 1,17:5; 1942, S 12,13:5
Moore, Charles H Jr, 1942, Ap 28,21:5
Moore, Charles J, 1950, Ja 26,27:5
Moore, Charles L, 1945, S 26,23:5; 1960, O 27,37:3
Moore, Charles R, 1951, Mr 19,27:5
Moore, Charles S, 1958, D 16,2:5; 1964, Je 10,45:2
Moore, Charles S Mrs, 1966, Je 18,31:5
Moore, Charlotte M Mrs, 1908, Ap 21,9:5
Moore, Christopher C, 1946, N 13,28:3
Moore, Christopher C Mrs, 1951, Ap 8,92:8
Moore, Churchill, 1945, Mr 13,23:3
Moore, Clarence E, 1941, N 27,23:5
Moore, Clarence S, 1918, Jl 24,11:4
Moore, Clement, 1937, Ag 4,19:2
Moore, Clement Clarke Maj, 1910, D 16,11:5
Moore, Clement Mrs, 1919, Ag 7,7:4
Moore, Clifford B, 1944, Mr 13,15:3
Moore, Clifford H Mrs, 1949, Ja 2,63:1
Moore, Clifford R, 1956, Jl 16,8:5
Moore, Cy (Wm W), 1963, Ap 1,27:4
Moore, D C Y, 1947, S 5,19:4
Moore, Dale, 1954, N 2,27:4
Moore, Dan T, 1941, Ap 17,23:3
Moore, Daniel D, 1938, D 20,25:3
Moore, Davey (funl plans, Mr 28,15:2), 1963, Mr 26,1:3
Moore, David H, 1942, D 2,25:1
Moore, David H Bp, 1915, N 27,15:6
Moore, David T, 1946, Ap 16,25:2; 1951, Ja 2,23:4
Moore, David V, 1951, Ag 18,11:5
Moore, David W Jr, 1937, F 24,23:2
Moore, Dean Crawford Dr, 1968, Je 27,43:3
Moore, Dean H, 1958, Jl 16,29:4
Moore, Don L, 1965, Ja 28,30:5
Moore, Dudley W, 1948, Ap 18,68:4
Moore, E, 1877, Ja 13,2:3; 1938, Jl 12,20:3
Moore, E A, 1941, My 27,23:1; 1955, My 27,23:5
Moore, E C, 1877, Mr 6,5:6
Moore, E Clifton, 1949, O 12,29:4
Moore, E Earl, 1965, Ap 18,80:5
Moore, E H, 1932, D 31,15:3
Moore, E W, 1938, Ag 9,19:5
Moore, Earl F, 1958, Mr 14,25:3
Moore, Edgar B (por), 1946, Ja 28,19:3
Moore, Edgar B Mrs, 1953, N 3,32:7
Moore, Edith J Mrs, 1949, F 26,15:6
Moore, Edmund J, 1952, O 23,31:3
Moore, Eduardo, 1941, N 8,19:1
Moore, Edward, 1938, Ag 31,36:3
Moore, Edward B, 1915, S 8,13:6
Moore, Edward C, 1937, Ag 16,19:3; 1943, Mr 28,24
Moore, Edward C Mrs, 1944, Mr 29,21:4; 1959, N 2 37:1
Moore, Edward E, 1940, O 26,15:5; 1945, Jl 8,11:5
Moore, Edward G, 1963, S 20,33:2
Moore, Edward H, 1950, S 3,39:1
Moore, Edward J, 1937, Jl 19,16:1; 1939, Je 10,17:3; 1948, Mr 13,15:4; 1955, S 29,33:4
Moore, Edward Mrs, 1941, Ag 5,19:2; 1964, Jl 1,35:
Moore, Edward R, 1952, Je 3,29:1
Moore, Edward S, 1944, My 18,19:6; 1948, Mr 16,2
Moore, Edward S (por), 1948, S 28,27:3
Moore, Edward S Jr, 1959, O 25,86:3
Moore, Edward Small 3d, 1968, S 16,47:3
Moore, Edwin A, 1954, F 10,29:3
Moore, Edwin A Mrs, 1944, Je 11,45:2
Moore, Edwin J Mrs, 1948, N 25,31:2
Moore, Edwin L, 1954, S 22,29:4
Moore, Edwin R, 1950, O 27,29:1
Moore, Edwin R Mrs, 1938, Je 5,44:8
Moore, Edwin W Maj, 1937, Mr 18,25:1
Moore, Edwin W Mrs, 1956, My 14,25:5
Moore, Egbert H Mrs, 1944, Mr 7,17:3
Moore, Egbert J, 1944, F 2,21:6
Moore, Egbert J Mrs, 1948, Je 22,25:3
Moore, Eleanor P Mrs, 1941, F 4,22:2
Moore, Eliot D, 1946, D 7,21:4
Moore, Eliza A Mrs, 1942, D 4,25:5
Moore, Elizabeth C Mrs, 1953, Ja 3,15:4
Moore, Elizabeth H M, 1959, Ja 24,19:1
Moore, Elizabeth M Mrs, 1921, Jl 13,9:4
Moore, Elizabeth P Mrs, 1938, Ap 4,17:3
Moore, Ellen, 1941, F 3,20:2
Moore, Elmer W, 1920, S 17,11:5
Moore, Emily C Mrs, 1946, D 14,15:5
Moore, Emmeline, 1963, S 14,25:2
Moore, Emmet K, 1958, Ag 9,13:3
Moore, Enoch Jr, 1944, Je 6,17:1
Moore, Eric C Mrs, 1942, Ag 20,19:1
Moore, Ernest C, 1938, Ap 19,21:5; 1955, Ja 25,25
Moore, Ernest E, 1962, Mr 17,37:3
Moore, Ernest M, 1948, Mr 6,13:2; 1949, F 7,19:3
Moore, Ethel, 1946, Jl 9,21:4
Moore, Ethelbert A, 1956, F 15,31:1
Moore, Eurene F 2d, 1953, Jl 25,11:3
Moore, Eva G Mrs, 1940, Ag 2,15:3
Moore, Everett F, 1938, S 21,25:5
Moore, F D, 1884, Ap 2,4:7
Moore, F L, 1935, Mr 29,21:1
Moore, F W, 1927, My 31,21:3
Moore, Faith, 1944, Mr 17,17:6
Moore, Fannie L, 1949, F 5,15:1
Moore, Francis, 1946, Jl 12,17:4

Moore, Francis C, 1912, Mr 18,11:5
Moore, Francis V, 1949, Ag 21,69:2
Moore, Francis William, 1908, D 26,7:6
Moore, Frank, 1939, D 28,21:3; 1960, My 9,29:4
Moore, Frank B, 1912, Ja 16,13:4
Moore, Frank C Mrs, 1961, Mr 30,29:3
Moore, Frank E Mrs, 1938, Mr 23,23:3
Moore, Frank G, 1955, N 19,19:6
Moore, Frank G Mrs, 1943, S 24,23:2
Moore, Frank J, 1938, N 1,23:4; 1949, S 20,29:2
Moore, Frank L, 1938, Ja 26,23:5
Moore, Frank Mrs, 1956, Mr 6,31:1
Moore, Frank R, 1946, Mr 16,13:4; 1949, Mr 7,21:2; 1949, O 18,27:1
Moore, Frank S, 1960, Ap 16,17:4
Moore, Frank Sr, 1956, N 27,38:1
Moore, Frank W, 1947, Je 18,25:4
Moore, Fred A, 1951, S 27,31:6
Moore, Fred E Jr, 1953, Jl 24,13:5
Moore, Fred R (por), 1943, Mr 3,24:3
Moore, Fred R Mrs, 1939, Jl 15,15:5
Moore, Frederic L, 1946, Ap 26,21:3
Moore, Frederic P (por),(will, Ja 13,12:2), 1937, Ja 2,14:3
Moore, Frederick A, 1940, Ap 10,25:3
Moore, Frederick C, 1951, S 17,21:4; 1959, Je 14,86:5
Moore, Frederick E, 1924, D 12,21:3
Moore, Frederick H, 1940, N 25,17:5
Moore, Frederick T, 1938, Ap 1,23:3
Moore, Frederick W (por), 1949, Ag 25,23:3
Moore, G, 1933, Ja 22,24:1
Moore, G F, 1883, Ag 31,4:7; 1931, My 17,31:5
Moore, G Roland, 1960, D 14,35:6
Moore, Gene, 1938, S 1,23:3
Moore, Geoffrey L, 1940, Mr 4,15:4
Moore, George, 1939, Jl 29,15:7; 1952, Mr 25,27:3
Moore, George A, 1945, O 7,45:1; 1953, Jl 10,19:1
Moore, George A Mrs, 1958, S 14,84:4
Moore, George B, 1924, S 4,19:4
Moore, George C, 1938, F 16,21:2
Moore, George D, 1951, Ap 26,29:3
Moore, George E, 1958, O 26,88:7; 1967, My 31,43:4
Moore, George E Mrs, 1950, Je 6,30:2; 1961, Ap 4,37:2
Moore, George G, 1939, Mr 17,21:2
Moore, George H, 1924, Ag 6,13:4; 1962, N 6,33:4; 1965, F 5,31:2
Moore, George J, 1949, O 17,23:4
Moore, George L, 1945, Ap 14,15:2
Moore, George N, 1950, F 12,85:1
Moore, George P, 1938, Je 27,17:2
Moore, George R, 1948, N 18,27:4
Moore, George T, 1938, S 1,23:2; 1956, N 29,35:1; 1966, Ja 11,29:1
Moore, George V, 1947, F 10,29:4
Moore, George Washington, 1909, O 2,9:4; 1912, My 25,13:6
Moore, Gertrude, 1953, My 4,23:3
Moore, Gladys C Mrs, 1937, S 8,23:4
Moore, Graves, 1943, D 3,23:4
Moore, Guernsey, 1925, Ja 7,25:4
Moore, Guy B, 1941, F 7,19:5
Moore, Guy W, 1957, Je 18,29:3
Moore, H, 1929, My 19,27:6
Moore, H Andrew Mrs, 1952, S 29,23:4
Moore, H D, 1930, Mr 26,27:3
Moore, H Napier, 1963, Ap 5,48:1
Moore, H Napier Mrs, 1951, S 21,23:2
Moore, H S, 1885, F 17,2:5
Moore, Hannah T Mrs, 1942, Jl 30,21:5
Moore, Harold A, 1945, O 26,19:2; 1951, Ap 17,30:3
Moore, Harold B Mrs, 1943, My 15,15:6
Moore, Harold F, 1951, Je 12,29:1
Moore, Harold J, 1964, O 7,47:2
Moore, Harold L, 1953, Ja 11,90:3
Moore, Harriot V Col (por), 1937, Ap 1,23:3
Moore, Harrison Bray, 1915, Mr 5,9:4
Moore, Harry A, 1955, S 14,35:5; 1959, Ap 8,37:4
Moore, Harry H, 1947, Jl 9,23:2; 1949, D 28,32:1; 1950, O 22,94:3
Moore, Harry M, 1924, Ag 9,11:5
Moore, Harry N, 1937, Je 10,23:6
Moore, Harry R (Tim), 1958, D 14,2:5
Moore, Harry S, 1946, Ap 20,13:3; 1954, N 26,29:5
Moore, Harry T Col, 1937, S 8,23:1
Moore, Harvey A, 1949, N 8,31:2
Moore, Helen, 1954, Ag 3,19:1
Moore, Henry C P Earl of Drogheda, 1957, N 23,19:7
Moore, Henry F, 1948, Ja 11,56:4; 1954, Ja 26,27:4
Moore, Henry H, 1946, O 3,27:2
Moore, Henry J, 1946, S 22,62:7
Moore, Henry T, 1967, My 16,45:3
Moore, Herbert, 1943, Jl 8,19:2
Moore, Herbert A, 1951, S 23,87:1
Moore, Herbert E, 1952, Ap 2,33:3
Moore, Herbert H, 1949, Je 8,29:1
Moore, Herbert L, 1950, D 12,33:2
Moore, Herbert M, 1942, Ap 25,13:1; 1942, My 8,21:4
Moore, Herman A, 1948, Ja 13,25:6
Moore, Hervey S, 1947, D 11,33:1
Moore, Hobart, 1904, Mr 4,9:5
Moore, Homer H, 1925, D 31,15:5
Moore, Houston P, 1953, O 7,29:1
Moore, Howard, 1944, D 31,26:2
Moore, Howard B, 1939, Ap 16,III,7:3
Moore, Howard E, 1953, Jl 24,13:5
Moore, Howard E Mrs, 1956, O 13,19:4
Moore, Howard F, 1957, Ap 7,88:5
Moore, Howard G, 1949, Ja 5,25:2
Moore, Howard P, 1954, N 29,25:1
Moore, Hoyt A, 1958, N 19,37:5
Moore, Hugh K, 1939, D 19,23:4
Moore, Hyland R, 1953, D 19,15:3
Moore, Irving H, 1947, F 9,62:5
Moore, Isaac Rev, 1884, N 19,2:3
Moore, J Burns, 1951, N 3,17:5
Moore, J Clark, 1943, Mr 6,13:2
Moore, J Hampton, 1950, My 3,29:1
Moore, J Hampton Mrs, 1953, S 13,85:1
Moore, J Kenneth, 1955, D 12,31:4
Moore, J Lee, 1949, O 5,29:4
Moore, J M Gen, 1905, Ap 22,11:5
Moore, J P, 1881, Ag 31,8:2
Moore, J Preston, 1961, S 28,41:5
Moore, J Ridgway, 1901, S 28,9:6
Moore, J Ross, 1963, Ap 9,32:1
Moore, J T, 1876, Jl 23,12:6
Moore, J Thomas Mrs, 1937, O 6,25:3
Moore, J Vreeland Gen, 1903, Jl 9,7:6
Moore, J W, 1939, F 12,44:6
Moore, Jacob T, 1949, D 15,35:5
Moore, James (Soldier of Fort Sumter), 1872, Jl 13, 8:5
Moore, James (Dinty), 1952, D 26,15:1
Moore, James (Dinty),(will), 1953, Ja 9,16:1
Moore, James, 1966, D 27,35:1
Moore, James A, 1959, Je 11,33:5; 1963, O 29,36:4
Moore, James C, 1961, Ag 20,87:1
Moore, James Capt, 1909, Jl 4,7:4
Moore, James F Mrs, 1943, N 4,23:4
Moore, James G, 1960, Jl 4,15:5
Moore, James H, 1924, My 19,17:3; 1968, Ap 16,44:3
Moore, James Hobart (funl, Jl 20,11:6), 1916, Jl 19, 9:6
Moore, James J, 1960, Mr 15,39:3
Moore, James K Mrs, 1944, My 21,44:1
Moore, James L, 1957, Jl 6,15:5
Moore, James M, 1904, Ap 5,16:2; 1938, F 24,19:1; 1952, F 4,17:1
Moore, James Mrs, 1957, Ap 9,33:5
Moore, James O Sr (por), 1947, F 25,25:4
Moore, James R, 1946, My 25,15:4
Moore, James S, 1945, D 24,15:4
Moore, James T, 1938, N 6,49:1; 1948, F 26,23:5
Moore, James T Maj, 1916, My 15,9:7
Moore, James W, 1948, Ja 4,52:4; 1951, F 27,28:3
Moore, James W Mrs, 1949, Jl 26,27:3
Moore, Jared S, 1951, Ap 11,29:3
Moore, Jennie Mrs, 1940, Ap 23,24:2
Moore, Jesse C, 1957, My 11,21:6
Moore, John, 1866, O 1,2:4; 1904, F 28,12:5; 1940, Ap 4,23:4; 1946, My 29,23:5
Moore, John A, 1947, Jl 13,44:2; 1950, Ja 17,27:3; 1955, Mr 4,23:4
Moore, John B, 1947, N 13,27:1
Moore, John B Mrs, 1958, Ag 3,80:5
Moore, John C, 1947, Ag 29,17:2
Moore, John C Col, 1915, O 28,11:5
Moore, John C Mrs, 1942, O 11,56:2
Moore, John D, 1940, My 14,23:3
Moore, John D J (por), 1940, O 2,23:1
Moore, John D Mrs, 1943, F 18,23:4
Moore, John E, 1955, Ja 28,20:1
Moore, John E (C Maddox), 1958, Je 23,31:6
Moore, John E, 1959, O 4,87:1
Moore, John F, 1907, D 27,7:6; 1948, F 27,22:3; 1948, O 15,24:2
Moore, John F Mrs, 1950, Ja 14,15:3
Moore, John G, 1941, My 30,15:4
Moore, John Gen, 1907, Mr 20,9:6
Moore, John H, 1967, Jl 18,37:4
Moore, John H Mrs, 1957, Je 4,35:2
Moore, John J, 1940, S 12,25:6; 1941, O 15,21:3; 1945, Ap 23,19:5; 1953, N 21,13:5
Moore, John L, 1939, My 9,23:3
Moore, John M, 1947, F 12,25:4
Moore, John M (por), 1948, Ag 1,57:1
Moore, John M, 1950, Jl 26,25:4
Moore, John N, 1940, O 16,23:2
Moore, John P, 1955, Ja 24,1:6
Moore, John R, 1954, Ap 18,89:2
Moore, John Robert, 1916, N 16,11:4
Moore, John T, 1944, Mr 9,17:5
Moore, John W, 1941, D 24,17:4; 1944, Ag 15,17:6; 1945, Ag 24,19:4
Moore, John W Dr, 1925, Je 4,19:5
Moore, John W Mrs, 1945, Ja 28,38:1
Moore, John W Msgr, 1925, Je 6,15:5
Moore, John W Rear-Adm, 1913, Ap 1,11:5
Moore, John W Sir, 1937, O 12,25:1
Moore, Jonathan, 1943, My 17,15:2
Moore, Joseph, 1954, S 25,15:6
Moore, Joseph A, 1937, Je 20,II,5:4
Moore, Joseph A Sr, 1956, Jl 1,57:1
Moore, Joseph B, 1967, N 25,39:4
Moore, Joseph Clifford Dr, 1909, Mr 20,9:4
Moore, Joseph E, 1957, D 8,88:6
Moore, Joseph H, 1949, Mr 16,27:2
Moore, Joseph L, 1944, F 29,17:1; 1957, Jl 19,19:4
Moore, Joseph P, 1959, Je 8,27:3
Moore, Joseph T, 1914, D 12,15:4
Moore, Joseph W, 1967, O 15,85:2
Moore, Joseph W Mrs, 1944, Jl 29,13:4
Moore, Joshua N Mrs, 1948, S 3,19:2
Moore, Josiah J, 1964, My 6,47:1
Moore, Kneeland, 1942, Jl 11,13:1
Moore, L H (Lou), 1956, Mr 26,29:5
Moore, L M, 1934, N 9,21:4
Moore, L Mrs, 1950, O 21,17:4
Moore, L Roy, 1951, Ag 12,76:7
Moore, Lansing C, 1873, Je 1,5:3
Moore, Laurence L, 1955, My 26,31:2
Moore, Lauriston G, 1950, Ap 12,27:3
Moore, Lawrence E, 1960, My 23,29:4
Moore, Leo M, 1946, Ja 9,23:2
Moore, LeRoy Mrs (L Beavers), 1962, O 27,25:2
Moore, Lewis K, 1939, O 28,15:3
Moore, Lewis W, 1951, Ag 21,27:4
Moore, Lillian, 1967, Jl 29,25:2
Moore, Lina W Mrs, 1939, Ja 28,13:5
Moore, Livingston P, 1942, D 25,17:2
Moore, Livingston P Mrs, 1965, D 1,47:4
Moore, Loring, 1948, D 31,16:3
Moore, Lory M, 1940, N 16,17:5
Moore, Louis A, 1948, Mr 2,23:4
Moore, Louis J F, 1960, F 18,33:5
Moore, Louise, 1915, Je 19,9:5
Moore, Luther B, 1949, D 3,15:1
Moore, Lyman S, 1952, Ag 6,21:3
Moore, M C, 1952, My 29,27:5
Moore, Mabel R Mrs, 1941, Ap 19,15:5
Moore, Maggie, 1926, Mr 17,25:3
Moore, Marcia, 1958, My 12,49:4
Moore, Marcus H, 1937, Je 2,23:1
Moore, Margaret, 1912, My 23,13:6
Moore, Margaret W Mrs, 1941, N 19,23:5
Moore, Mark, 1922, Ja 7,13:4
Moore, Martin A, 1964, Ap 18,29:2
Moore, Martin F, 1939, O 30,17:5
Moore, Martin J, 1939, O 13,21:6
Moore, Martin J Sr, 1952, Je 22,68:4
Moore, Martin Rev, 1866, Mr 13,8:1
Moore, Mary E, 1912, My 23,13:6
Moore, Mary F, 1943, Ag 4,17:4
Moore, Matilda Mrs, 1905, F 27,12:5
Moore, Maurice, 1945, D 23,22:6
Moore, Melville L, 1960, Ap 12,33:4
Moore, Michael Mrs, 1948, S 18,17:5
Moore, Milton E, 1951, Jl 9,25:3
Moore, Minnie B Mrs, 1937, Je 21,19:5
Moore, Minnie L, 1940, S 10,23:4
Moore, Minor, 1958, Ja 6,39:4
Moore, Mitchell B, 1957, Je 1,17:5
Moore, Morris P, 1949, Ap 27,27:2
Moore, Nathanial D, 1940, My 19,42:5
Moore, Nelson, 1918, My 9,13:5
Moore, Newton H, 1941, D 24,17:5
Moore, Otis H, 1955, Mr 24,31:3
Moore, Owen, 1939, Je 10,36:2
Moore, P Harry W, 1948, Ja 17,18:3
Moore, P T, 1883, F 21,2:4
Moore, Pal, 1953, Mr 16,19:2
Moore, Pamela (Mrs A Kanarek), 1964, Je 8,59:5
Moore, Patrick M, 1954, Ag 29,89:1
Moore, Patrick T, 1943, Ap 21,25:2
Moore, Patrick W (por), 1955, O 31,25:3
Moore, Paul, 1943, D 22,23:3; 1959, D 20,60:4
Moore, Paul J, 1938, Ja 11,23:5
Moore, Paul O, 1941, Ap 12,15:4
Moore, Percy, 1945, Ap 9,19:4
Moore, Peter, 1942, Ja 23,19:5
Moore, Phil A, 1951, N 3,17:3
Moore, Phillip, 1946, My 31,23:3
Moore, Pierce, 1938, Ap 24,II,7:3
Moore, Pius L, 1950, O 14,19:1
Moore, R B, 1931, Ja 21,19:1
Moore, R L Mrs, 1950, Jl 26,25:2
Moore, R Walton (por), 1941, F 9,49:1
Moore, Ralph D, 1937, Ja 20,21:2
Moore, Ralph H Mrs, 1968, Mr 29,41:3
Moore, Ralph L, 1947, Jl 30,21:3
Moore, Ralph W, 1953, Ja 11,90:2
Moore, Ransom A, 1941, F 27,19:3
Moore, Raymond (will, Mr 15,26:4), 1940, Mr 10, 51:5
Moore, Raymond B, 1945, F 17,13:2
Moore, Raymond C, 1952, Ap 26,23:4
Moore, Reginald H, 1959, S 16,39:4
Moore, Richard C, 1966, Ag 23,39:1
Moore, Richard Channing, 1909, F 14,11:3
Moore, Richard E, 1947, Ja 24,22:3
Moore, Richard L, 1944, N 28,23:1
Moore, Richard T, 1952, S 23,33:5
Moore, Robert, 1914, F 15,5:5; 1950, D 15,32:4; 1954, Ag 29,50:3; 1965, Ag 13,29:5
Moore, Robert A, 1952, Mr 24,43:6
Moore, Robert C, 1950, S 7,31:2
Moore, Robert D, 1939, O 27,23:4
Moore, Robert E, 1951, Jl 1,51:2; 1954, Je 29,27:5; 1961, N 7,33:2; 1966, Ap 22,41:2

Moore, Robert F, 1939, D 1,23:4; 1964, F 27,31:4; 1964, Ag 11,33:3
Moore, Robert F Jr, 1948, S 17,25:3
Moore, Robert J, 1947, Ja 8,24:3; 1950, My 27,17:5
Moore, Robert L, 1966, Ja 29,27:1
Moore, Robert M, 1940, F 7,21:3
Moore, Robert R, 1951, Ja 26,23:3
Moore, Robert Sr, 1952, Ag 20,25:4
Moore, Robert T, 1958, N 3,37:3
Moore, Robert W, 1942, N 23,23:1
Moore, Robert W Mrs, 1938, F 21,19:3
Moore, Roland, 1962, My 25,33:6
Moore, Rolland B, 1953, S 12,17:3
Moore, Roscoe L, 1940, Ap 7,45:2
Moore, Roy D, 1954, My 2,89:1
Moore, Roy D Mrs, 1964, N 20,37:1
Moore, Roy E, 1957, F 10,86:7
Moore, Rufus Ellis, 1918, Mr 30,13:4
Moore, Russell, 1958, D 2,45:3
Moore, Russell Wellman, 1920, Ag 1,22:5
Moore, Ryan S, 1940, Ag 7,19:5
Moore, Samuel A, 1959, O 13,39:4
Moore, Samuel B, 1954, Ja 18,23:4
Moore, Samuel C, 1946, O 23,28:2; 1953, My 10,88:3
Moore, Samuel H, 1959, Ap 5,86:4
Moore, Samuel J, 1938, Ag 6,13:4; 1948, Ap 24,15:6
Moore, Samuel J Mrs, 1944, Jl 28,13:5
Moore, Samuel Preston Mrs, 1912, Ja 3,13:4
Moore, Samuel S, 1914, Ja 7,11:5; 1947, O 19,66:3
Moore, Sanford K Mrs, 1948, Je 27,52:4
Moore, Seth E Mrs (will), 1952, Ag 17,42:6
Moore, Sherwood, 1963, Jl 11,29:2
Moore, Silas H, 1916, Mr 24,11:5
Moore, Simon, 1954, Ag 26,27:2
Moore, Stewart L, 1903, Ap 22,9:5
Moore, T Albert, 1940, Ap 1,19:3
Moore, T Channing Mrs, 1959, O 23,17:4
Moore, T O, 1876, Jl 4,4:6
Moore, T W C, 1873, N 25,8:5
Moore, Ted, 1945, Ag 15,19:2
Moore, Theodore, 1917, N 22,13:4
Moore, Thomas, 1952, Mr 23,92:2
Moore, Thomas A, 1957, Ap 14,86:1
Moore, Thomas A Mrs, 1966, Jl 8,36:1
Moore, Thomas C, 1945, F 22,27:2
Moore, Thomas E, 1950, Ap 2,92:5
Moore, Thomas F, 1945, Jl 17,13:6
Moore, Thomas F Sr, 1937, Je 24,25:1
Moore, Thomas H, 1950, Ag 4,21:3
Moore, Thomas L Mrs, 1945, Je 17,26:4
Moore, Thomas M, 1906, F 4,7:6
Moore, Thomas M Mrs, 1967, Jl 13,37:1
Moore, Thomas Mrs, 1865, S 21,1:5
Moore, Thomas R, 1942, Mr 30,17:4
Moore, Thomas R Dr, 1937, Ag 18,19:2
Moore, Thomas S, 1944, Jl 21,19:1
Moore, Thomas S Mrs, 1923, Mr 9,15:4
Moore, Thornton C, 1948, Ap 25,68:4
Moore, Tom, 1946, Jl 8,29:5; 1955, F 14,19:4
Moore, Tommy, 1955, Je 13,23:5
Moore, Tredwell, 1876, Je 4,5:2
Moore, Underhill, 1949, Ja 27,23:2
Moore, V A, 1931, F 12,21:3
Moore, Victor (funl, Jl 27,25:1), 1962, Jl 24,27:1
Moore, Vida F Dr, 1915, Je 12,11:6
Moore, W A, 1871, Ap 25,8:4; 1877, Jl 17,5:5; 1928, D 13,29:5
Moore, W B S, 1869, Mr 2,7:3
Moore, W Bedford Jr, 1953, Ap 29,29:5
Moore, W Carter, 1953, F 1,88:1
Moore, W Gerald, 1957, O 19,21:4
Moore, W H Rev, 1903, Ag 23,7:5
Moore, W Maxwell, 1946, S 15,10:1
Moore, W W Dr, 1926, Je 15,25:4
Moore, Walter, 1912, F 19,9:6
Moore, Walter Burritt, 1907, Je 9,9:5
Moore, Walter J, 1943, Mr 1,19:5; 1960, Ja 22,25:5
Moore, Walter J Mrs, 1952, My 3,21:6
Moore, Walter L, 1945, Mr 18,42:1
Moore, Walter R, 1948, Ag 4,21:3
Moore, Walter V, 1962, F 21,45:2
Moore, Walter 2d, 1960, S 24,23:3
Moore, Walton N, 1946, Ja 27,42:4
Moore, Warren J, 1925, Ag 9,5:2
Moore, Wendell W, 1960, Ja 20,31:4
Moore, Wiley L, 1956, D 31,13:5
Moore, Will C, 1948, N 19,28:3
Moore, Willfred, 1939, Jl 15,15:4
Moore, William, 1907, Mr 1,9:6; 1941, Mr 22,15:2
Moore, William A, 1912, My 17,13:5; 1956, D 3,29:4
Moore, William Arthur Dr, 1918, Ap 27,15:8
Moore, William D, 1942, Mr 2,19:4; 1950, N 12,92:4
Moore, William E (por), 1941, D 28,28:1
Moore, William E Mrs, 1944, Mr 28,19:2
Moore, William F, 1938, Ap 26,21:2; 1946, My 11, 27:1; 1954, Je 29,27:3; 1959, Jl 29,29:2
Moore, William F Mrs, 1924, Je 14,11:6; 1943, F 13, 11:4
Moore, William G, 1953, My 12,27:4; 1965, N 6,29:5
Moore, William G Mrs, 1961, Ap 10,31:6
Moore, William H, 1916, My 17,11:4
Moore, William H (por),(funl, Ja 13,13:5), 1923, Ja 12,15:3
Moore, William H, 1939, D 1,23:4; 1940, Je 8,15:2; 1946, Mr 26,29:6; 1957, Je 18,33:3; 1964, Je 18,35:2
Moore, William H Helme, 1910, Ja 5,11:3
Moore, William H Mrs, 1955, Ja 31,19:3
Moore, William H Mrs (est tax appr), 1958, My 22, 60:6
Moore, William I, 1941, D 5,23:3
Moore, William I Mrs, 1940, Ap 7,45:3
Moore, William J, 1940, Ja 19,19:2; 1942, F 24,21:2; 1949, My 13,23:3; 1951, My 24,35:2; 1960, Ag 31, 29:3
Moore, William J Mrs, 1955, Mr 9,27:5
Moore, William Jr, 1965, Je 4,35:5
Moore, William L, 1949, Ja 17,19:2
Moore, William L Sr, 1957, D 8,87:4
Moore, William M, 1966, Mr 24,39:4
Moore, William R, 1909, Je 15,7:4; 1940, Mr 12,23:5
Moore, William R Mrs, 1907, Mr 17,9:5
Moore, William S, 1938, S 14,23:5; 1942, Ap 14,21:6; 1944, Mr 30,21:3; 1949, Ag 20,11:2; 1950, My 21, 104:5; 1950, Je 14,31:4; 1953, Ja 2,16:4
Moore, William T, 1958, Jl 17,27:2
Moore, William W, 1940, F 24,13:5
Moore, Willis M Mrs, 1941, S 20,17:4
Moore, Ziba T, 1914, Ag 21,9:6
Moore-Brabazon, Jno-Theodore C (Lord Brabazon of Tara), 1964, My 18,29:3
Moore-Smith, Jeanette, 1946, O 31,25:4
Moorefield, Nancy, 1944, Ap 19,23:4
Moorehead, A L Mrs, 1939, Ja 30,13:4
Moorehead, Frederick B, 1944, Ag 30,17:4
Moorehead, J Dr, 1884, Ja 20,2:4
Moorehead, John C, 1904, Jl 20,7:7
Moorehead, John J, 1957, Jl 2,27:5
Moorehead, Joseph E, 1942, Ag 10,19:4
Moorehead, Mary Elizabeth, 1903, N 21,9:6
Moorehead, Singleton P, 1964, D 13,86:5
Moorehead, Singleton P Mrs, 1962, My 9,43:3
Moorehead, Warren K Mrs, 1939, Ja 6,21:5
Moorehouse, Claude E, 1950, Mr 12,92:3
Moorehouse, George, 1943, O 13,23:2
Moores, Charles W, 1923, D 8,13:5
Moorfield, Amelia Mrs, 1950, F 27,19:1
Moorhead, Edward V, 1946, Mr 21,25:6
Moorhead, Eugene W, 1963, My 13,29:3
Moorhead, Harley G, 1944, My 23,23:2
Moorhead, Harry M, 1939, O 6,25:1
Moorhead, Helen H Mrs, 1950, Mr 10,27:3
Moorhead, Horace R, 1944, F 25,17:4
Moorhead, Horace R Mrs, 1958, O 25,21:1
Moorhead, J K Gen, 1884, Mr 7,5:2
Moorhead, Jean, 1953, N 2,25:5
Moorhead, John M, 1959, O 23,29:3
Moorhead, Louis D, 1951, S 15,15:3
Moorhead, Raynolds G, 1947, D 14,76:6
Moorhead, Robert L, 1960, Ag 3,29:6
Moorhead, Rutherford S, 1958, Ag 7,25:4
Moorhouse, A P, 1907, My 16,7:6
Moorhouse, Glen E, 1963, Jl 25,25:1
Moorhouse, Robert T, 1952, N 27,31:3
Moorhouse, Walter V, 1953, My 12,27:5
Moorhouse, William L, 1945, Mr 16,15:3
Moorhouse, William R, 1925, Ag 18,19:5
Moorland, Jesse E, 1940, My 2,24:3
Moorman, Charles H, 1938, Ja 27,21:3
Moorman, Edgar V, 1942, Ag 10,19:6
Moorman, Edna N, 1950, Ja 20,25:4
Moorman, Frederick William Prof, 1919, S 11,15:2
Moorman, George Gen, 1902, D 17,9:6
Moorman, Herbert R, 1955, D 3,17:4
Moorman, L J, 1954, Ag 3,19:4
Moormann, James P, 1925, Ag 10,13:6
Moors, Arthur W, 1949, Ja 9,72:2
Moors, John F (will, Jl 9,19:3), 1953, Mr 24,31:5
Moorshead, Frank A, 1954, Ap 17,13:5
Moos, Joseph B, 1946, O 27,63:3
Moos, Louis H, 1942, S 3,19:2
Moos, Paul B, 1940, My 7,25:3
Moosbrugger, Frederick, 1949, Ap 24,76:1
Mooser, Leon, 1915, Jl 12,7:5
Mootz, Herman E, 1949, Mr 3,25:3
Mooyer, Herbert, 1959, O 2,29:1
Mopper, Abraham, 1953, D 23,25:5
Mopsick, Samuel Mrs, 1961, Jl 24,23:5
Mor, Kraus, 1916, F 27,17:4
Mora, Bernardo, 1951, D 29,11:2
Mora, Constancia de la, 1950, Ja 29,22:3
Mora, Countess of, 1943, Ja 14,21:3
Mora, F Luis, 1940, Je 6,25:4
Mora, Helena, 1903, Jl 21,9:5
Mora, Jo (por), 1947, O 11,17:4
Mora, Jose de la, 1949, N 30,1:8
Mora, Joseph M, 1904, D 14,9:4
Mora Figueroa, Manuel, 1964, Ja 14,31:1
Mora-Silva, Franc, 1904, Je 14,7:6
Mora y del Rio, J Archbishop, 1928, Ap 23,23:3
Mora y Varona, Gaston, 1938, My 22,II,7:1
Morabito, Anthony J, 1957, O 28,27:2
Morabito, Vic, 1964, My 11,31:2
Moraghan, Martin J Sr, 1958, Ap 1,31:4
Morahan, Elizabeth, 1943, Ap 11,48:2
Morahan, Eugene H, 1949, N 16,29:5
Morahan, Grace S, 1948, F 25,23:4
Morahan, John M, 1960, Ag 9,27:4
Morahan, John T Sr Mrs, 1951, O 19,27:1
Morahan, Joseph E, 1962, S 27,37:4
Morain, Alfred, 1938, D 25,15:1
Morais, Herbert Mrs, 1957, D 12,29:5
Moraitinis, Timos, 1952, S 23,33:4
Morales, A J Prof, 1885, My 15,2:2
Morales, Angel, 1959, Ja 14,27:3
Morales, Antoinette, 1919, Jl 16,13:3
Morales, Carlos A, 1947, D 13,15:1
Morales, Carlos F Gen, 1914, Mr 3,9:4
Morales, E A, 1914, Ag 3,11:6
Morales, Eduardo G, 1953, Ap 9,27:3
Morales, Franklin E, 1962, Jl 21,19:5
Morales, Ismael (Esy), 1950, N 4,17:7
Morales, Jocelyn S, 1940, Ap 13,17:1
Morales, L S, 1934, Mr 29,23:3
Morales, Manuel H Mrs, 1965, Ag 7,21:4
Morales, Noro (Norberto), 1964, Ja 16,25:2
Morales, Raul, 1946, F 13,23:4
Morales Duval, Oscar, 1966, O 4,3:4
Morales Montserrat, Ricordo, 1966, D 29,10:6
Morales Ortiz, Jesus, 1953, S 5,8:5
Moraller, Erich L, 1955, S 28,35:4
Moralt, Rudolf, 1958, D 29,15:5
Moran, Agnes, 1946, D 16,23:4
Moran, Alfred B, 1942, Ja 23,19:5
Moran, Alfred Capt, 1903, Je 8,7:6
Moran, Ambrose W P, 1959, D 18,30:1
Moran, Amedee Depau, 1915, Ap 9,11:5
Moran, Annie A, 1951, D 15,13:7
Moran, Anson B, 1941, S 22,15:6
Moran, Anthony A, 1954, Je 17,29:2
Moran, Bernard, 1965, Je 1,27:6
Moran, Bernard A, 1967, Ap 3,33:4
Moran, Bernard J, 1941, N 6,23:3
Moran, Charles B, 1949, Je 15,29:3
Moran, Charles H, 1952, Ap 8,29:2
Moran, Charles J, 1952, Jl 18,19:2
Moran, Charles Mrs, 1940, N 27,23:1; 1943, Ja 30,1
Moran, Christopher P, 1952, Mr 12,27:2
Moran, Dan J, 1948, Ap 4,60:2
Moran, Daniel A, 1917, My 12,11:6; 1961, Ag 2,29:
Moran, Daniel E (por), 1937, Jl 4,II,7:3
Moran, Daniel E Mrs, 1947, D 13,15:3
Moran, Daniel J, 1962, Je 1,27:3
Moran, Daniel O, 1941, Ja 3,19:3
Moran, Daniel P Sr, 1953, Mr 25,31:2
Moran, David J, 1963, S 17,35:3
Moran, Derby W, 1965, Ag 16,27:6
Moran, Edward, 1901, Je 10,7:5
Moran, Edward A Mrs, 1965, My 31,17:4
Moran, Edward C Jr, 1967, Jl 13,37:2
Moran, Edward F, 1947, Ja 19,53:3
Moran, Edward J, 1957, Ap 25,31:1
Moran, Edward J Sr, 1951, S 21,23:2
Moran, Edward Mrs, 1904, N 11,9:2
Moran, Edwin L, 1946, D 5,31:2
Moran, Ellsworth E Rev, 1925, Ja 14,21:4
Moran, Emanuel J Mrs, 1946, Ag 15,25:2
Moran, Eugene F, 1961, Ap 14,29:1
Moran, Eugene F Mrs, 1939, N 15,23:6
Moran, Eugenie E, 1949, My 12,31:6
Moran, Fenton, 1958, Ag 18,19:2
Moran, Fillan J, 1963, N 10,86:2
Moran, Francis E, 1955, S 26,23:5
Moran, Francis J Clay Rev, 1910, Ag 13,7:6
Moran, Frank, 1967, D 16,41:4
Moran, Frank T, 1949, Ag 25,23:2
Moran, Fred, 1925, Ja 1,27:3
Moran, Frederick A, 1952, F 10,92:1
Moran, George, 1941, N 7,24:3
Moran, George (por), 1949, Ag 2,19:1
Moran, George C (Bugs),(funl, F 28,12:4), 1957, F 26,59:2
Moran, George H, 1965, N 7,88:6
Moran, George J, 1939, F 22,21:6
Moran, Gregory, 1950, S 8,52:8
Moran, Harry, 1950, Jl 4,17:4
Moran, Harry J, 1938, Je 12,39:2
Moran, Horace, 1941, Mr 10,17:4
Moran, J Herbert, 1954, S 23,33:5
Moran, James, 1907, My 22,9:4
Moran, James A, 1948, Ag 14,13:4
Moran, James C, 1943, Ap 29,21:2
Moran, James H (por), 1943, Ap 1,23:3
Moran, James H, 1947, My 19,21:4
Moran, James H Mrs, 1951, O 23,29:1
Moran, James J, 1968, Ja 6,29:1
Moran, James L, 1940, F 9,19:3
Moran, James P, 1940, D 16,23:5; 1946, Ap 1,27: 1961, My 18,35:4
Moran, James T, 1946, Ap 10,27:3
Moran, James V, 1953, Ap 7,29:3
Moran, Jeremiah Mrs, 1958, Jl 19,15:3
Moran, Jim (Jas Brocato), 1958, Ap 14,25:1
Moran, John, 1952, S 23,33:4
Moran, John A, 1948, O 31,88:5; 1952, N 2,88:3; O 1,86:2
Moran, John D, 1947, Ap 19,15:1
Moran, John F, 1953, S 4,15:3
Moran, John G, 1946, Ja 4,21:2
Moran, John J, 1949, Ap 12,30:3; 1949, N 6,92:3; 1950, S 30,17:4

Moran, John J Sr, 1964, F 24,25:4
Moran, John L, 1941, Ag 6,17:6; 1964, Ag 18,31:5
Moran, John M, 1952, Ag 18,17:4
Moran, John Mrs, 1946, Je 11,23:3
Moran, John S, 1953, Ja 10,17:1
Moran, John T Jr, 1968, D 27,33:1
Moran, John V, 1952, Jl 12,13:5
Moran, John W, 1953, F 4,27:1
Moran, Joseph A, 1968, Ja 6,29:3
Moran, Joseph F, 1959, S 16,39:5
Moran, Joseph H, 1940, D 28,15:6
Moran, Joseph P, 1941, Jl 27,31:1
Moran, Joseph Thomas, 1923, S 6,15:3
Moran, Joseph W, 1947, O 6,21:6
Moran, Leo, 1941, F 24,15:5
Moran, Louis J, 1967, S 27,47:2
Moran, Mae C, 1948, N 12,23:4
Moran, Margaret, 1946, Jl 16,23:2
Moran, Marie L, 1943, Ja 11,15:4
Moran, Martin H, 1949, N 10,32:2
Moran, Meyer Mrs, 1965, S 11,27:4
Moran, Michael Capt, 1906, Je 29,9:7
Moran, Michael F, 1954, Je 18,23:6
Moran, Owen, 1949, Mr 18,26:2
Moran, P, 1935, Mr 26,19:3
Moran, Patrick Francis Cardinal, 1911, Ag 17,7:7
Moran, Patrick J, 1940, Ag 14,19:5; 1946, F 6,23:4
Moran, Patrick Rev, 1866, Jl 26,5:4
Moran, Paul Nimms, 1907, My 27,7:6
Moran, Pete (P Mangini), 1961, Ag 25,25:2
Moran, Peter, 1941, Je 22,32:5
Moran, Polly, 1952, Ja 26,13:3
Moran, Raymond H, 1959, Ag 2,81:2
Moran, Richard A, 1956, O 17,41:1
Moran, Richard E Mrs, 1952, N 6,29:4
Moran, Richard J Mrs, 1941, Ag 30,13:5; 1952, S 9, 31:3
Moran, Robert, 1943, Mr 30,26:4
Moran, Robert C, 1944, Ja 14,19:6
Moran, Robert G Mrs, 1950, O 17,31:3
Moran, Robert L, 1954, Ag 19,23:3
Moran, Ruth S, 1948, My 12,27:2
Moran, S F, 1928, Mr 21,27:5
Moran, Stephen J, 1955, Jl 31,69:2
Moran, T, 1926, Ag 27,17:5
Moran, Terry, 1965, Je 1,27:6
Moran, Thomas, 1911, F 24,9:4
Moran, Thomas A, 1945, Ja 5,15:5; 1953, Ag 28,17:1
Moran, Thomas A Ex-Judge, 1904, N 19,7:2
Moran, Thomas E, 1944, Je 11,45:1
Moran, Thomas F, 1938, Ag 20,15:2; 1943, D 5,66:8; 1950, Mr 26,95:3; 1950, N 1,35:3; 1964, S 16,31:5
Moran, Thomas J, 1945, D 23,18:7; 1954, Ap 27,29:4
Moran, Thomas J Rev Father, 1917, F 4,19:3
Moran, Thomas M, 1949, N 28,27:5
Moran, Ursula M, 1964, Jl 9,33:3
Moran, Victor, 1949, S 13,29:2
Moran, William, 1884, S 7,6:7; 1939, Je 8,25:5
Moran, William C, 1944, F 3,19:5
Moran, William E, 1961, Jl 27,31:4
Moran, William F Mrs, 1962, Ja 9,47:1
Moran, William J, 1943, Jl 4,20:3; 1948, N 10,29:1; 1949, O 25,27:3; 1949, N 10,32:4; 1960, Ap 2,23:6
Moran, William L, 1941, Je 10,23:4; 1953, Ap 19,91:2
Moran, William L Mrs, 1946, Ja 11,21:1
Moran, William T, 1942, N 18,26:4
Moran-Olden, Fanny, 1905, F 14,7:4
Morandi, Giorgio, 1964, Je 19,31:1
Morandi, Rodolfo, 1955, Jl 27,23:2
Morando, Otto, 1953, N 19,31:3
Morane, Leon, 1918, O 21,15:4
Morang, George N, 1937, O 6,25:2
Morang, Lemer H, 1939, Ap 25,23:2
Morang, Ralph W, 1946, Ap 9,27:4
Morange, Edward A, 1955, My 20,25:5
Morani, Salvatore, 1964, Je 27,25:6
Morano, Ettore P, 1951, N 3,17:2
Morano, Francesco Cardinal, 1968, Jl 13,27:1
Morante, Valentin G, 1952, Je 9,23:5
Moranti, Paul J, 1951, Ag 15,27:1
Moranz, Vincent J, 1963, Jl 31,29:4
Moranzoni, Roberto, 1959, D 15,39:2
Moras, Daniel E Mrs, 1947, D 13,15:3
Moras, Ernesto de, 1949, Jl 29,21:5
Morash, A Urban, 1953, Jl 1,29:2
Morash, Albert V, 1941, Mr 9,41:3
Moraski, Joseph, 1953, Ja 27,25:3
Moravec, Frantisek, 1966, Jl 28,33:4
Morawetz, Victor (por),(will, My 28,15:3), 1938, My 19,21:4
Morawetz, Victor (est acctg), 1957, O 18,24:1
Morawetz, Victor Mrs, 1918, D 16,15:2; 1957, Ja 4, 23:2
Moray, Earl of, 1901, Je 12,9:6
Moray, Earl of (por), 1943, Jl 10,13:4
Moray, Norman R (por), 1940, My 20,17:1
Morber, John G Jr, 1950, Je 10,17:3
Morch, Thomas, 1944, Jl 12,19:4
Morck, Aug C Mrs, 1948, D 29,21:1
Morck, Hugo, 1960, Ap 4,29:4
Morcom, Clifford B, 1951, S 27,31:4
Morcom, Thomas H, 1942, Ja 12,15:2
Morcom, William J, 1937, N 9,24:8
Morcombe, Joseph E, 1942, O 23,21:4
Mord, Reuben Mrs, 1945, Mr 20,19:3
Mordanier, Louis, 1945, D 29,18:4
Mordant, Edwin, 1942, F 17,21:2
Mordaunt, Sarah M Mrs, 1939, N 27,17:3
Mordecai, Alfred Brig-Gen, 1920, Ja 21,7:2
Mordecai, Allen L, 1908, F 9,11:5; 1954, My 24,27:4
Mordecai, Benjamin (por), 1943, Ag 5,15:3
Mordecai, David, 1949, S 13,29:2
Mordecai, Goodman L, 1922, Ap 27,17:4
Mordecai, John B, 1873, Mr 15,1:2
Mordecai, Joseph, 1941, Ja 3,20:2
Mordecai, Walter C, 1953, N 25,23:1
Morden, Earle B Col, 1937, D 8,25:4
Morden, Gilbert W, 1951, Mr 9,25:4
Morden, Harold M, 1947, Ag 24,58:2
Morden, K G, 1961, Jl 16,69:1
Morden, William J, 1958, Ja 24,23:3
Mordey, William M, 1938, Jl 2,13:3
Mordinov, Nikolai, 1966, Ja 28,47:5
Mordkin, Mikhail M, 1944, Jl 16,31:4
Mordoff, Fred C, 1948, Ja 3,13:4
Mordue, Allison K, 1951, Jl 10,27:4
Mordvinov, Arkadi G, 1964, Jl 31,23:4
More, Charles H, 1954, My 23,89:1
More, Charles H Mrs, 1945, O 26,19:2
More, G Roberts, 1952, D 23,23:5
More, George C Mrs, 1952, Jl 24,27:3
More, Harry G, 1954, Ja 27,27:3
More, Hermon, 1968, D 2,47:1
More, John G, 1949, Ap 19,26:6
More, Paul E Dr, 1937, Mr 10,23:1
More, Robert, 1938, S 17,17:4
More, Roderick D M, 1951, Mr 30,23:4
More, William G, 1954, Je 1,27:2
Morean, Dudley R, 1943, Ap 29,21:2
Moreau, Adrian E, 1942, D 25,18:3
Moreau, Charles T, 1925, Ap 30,21:3
Moreau, Daniel H, 1963, Je 8,25:5
Moreau, Emile, 1950, N 10,27:4
Moreau, Ernest, 1953, D 12,19:4
Moreau, Jack, 1941, D 7,76:1
Moreau, Jacques, 1962, Mr 7,4:3
Moreau, Joseph T, 1947, S 1,19:4
Moreault, L J, 1943, Ja 2,11:4
Morecraft, Harry, 1942, Ja 15,19:3
Moreel, Ben Mrs, 1958, D 26,2:6
Moreford, William B, 1952, N 5,27:3
Morehead, Albert H, 1966, O 6,47:2
Morehead, Albert Mrs, 1945, Jl 28,11:6
Morehead, J A, 1936, Je 2,27:5
Morehead, John H, 1942, Je 2,24:2
Morehead, John L, 1964, N 10,47:3
Morehead, John M, 1866, Ag 30,4:6
Morehead, John M (funl, Ja 10,92:6), 1965, Ja 8,29:1
Morehead, John M Mrs, 1945, Ap 17,23:2; 1961, O 23,29:1
Morehead, Kenneth P, 1964, N 26,33:4
Morehead, R Gould, 1967, My 24,47:3
Morehouse, A C Rev, 1903, Jl 27,7:6
Morehouse, Albert K, 1955, D 19,27:1
Morehouse, Alexander, 1907, S 1,7:6
Morehouse, Andrew R, 1953, Ap 20,25:5
Morehouse, Anne O, 1952, F 11,25:4
Morehouse, Augustus W Mrs, 1939, Mr 20,17:4
Morehouse, D Page Jr Mrs, 1951, N 11,89:4
Morehouse, Daniel W, 1941, Ja 22,21:1
Morehouse, David, 1940, Mr 16,15:6
Morehouse, David P, 1958, S 20,19:4
Morehouse, Edith T, 1942, D 15,27:4
Morehouse, Eugene, 1950, Jl 6,27:5
Morehouse, F C, 1932, Je 27,17:1
Morehouse, Frances M, 1945, Mr 22,23:4
Morehouse, H Livingston, 1958, Jl 21,21:5
Morehouse, Henry, 1943, S 30,21:5
Morehouse, Henry B, 1968, My 17,47:1
Morehouse, Henry B Jr, 1966, My 7,31:4
Morehouse, Henry G, 1948, D 27,21:1
Morehouse, Henry Lyman Rev, 1917, My 6,19:4
Morehouse, Henry P, 1958, Ap 26,19:5
Morehouse, J Stanley, 1961, Jl 13,29:5
Morehouse, James Dr, 1920, D 22,11:4
Morehouse, John Newton, 1908, N 13,9:3
Morehouse, Josiah H, 1947, Mr 11,27:5
Morehouse, Linden H, 1967, Ap 7,37:3
Morehouse, Lyman A, 1948, Je 18,23:3
Morehouse, Lyman F, 1947, My 3,17:2
Morehouse, M W Mrs, 1953, Mr 5,27:5
Morehouse, Noyes, 1904, D 18,7:6
Morehouse, Sallie M Mrs, 1951, Ap 30,21:3
Morehouse, Samuel, 1907, S 20,9:7
Morehouse, Theodore C Mrs, 1965, Ap 13,37:3
Morehouse, Vernon S, 1951, Mr 19,27:1
Morehouse, Ward, 1966, D 9,47:2
Morehouse, William H, 1941, Jl 26,15:2
Morehouse, William R, 1937, D 8,25:1
Morehouse, Wilmot L, 1948, O 17,76:6
Moreing, Adrian C, 1940, Jl 12,15:2
Moreira, Delfin, 1920, Jl 2,11:4
Moreira, Manuel A, 1953, Mr 19,29:5
Morel, Charles A, 1952, Ag 9,13:4
Morel, Compere, 1941, Ag 5,19:1
Morel, Edmund Dene, 1924, N 14,19:6; 1925, Ja 26, 17:3
Moreland, Arthur C, 1915, N 18,9:5
Moreland, Edward L, 1951, Je 18,23:4
Moreland, Gray M, 1951, F 12,23:4
Moreland, Harry C, 1938, My 12,23:5
Moreland, Henry A, 1942, Ap 28,21:4
Moreland, Hugh D, 1925, O 5,21:4
Moreland, James, 1951, My 28,21:5
Moreland, John H, 1946, My 23,21:3
Moreland, Robert E, 1959, S 3,27:4
Moreland, Sherman P, 1951, D 28,21:1
Moreland, William C, 1952, F 17,84:4
Moreland, William H, 1938, S 30,21:4; 1945, S 28,21:3
Moreland, William H (por), 1946, O 28,27:5
Morell, Alfred, 1943, Mr 19,19:2
Morell, Anthony, 1958, Je 16,23:3
Morell, Benjamin, 1950, O 22,68:4
Morell, Frank, 1952, Mr 17,21:3
Morell, G W Gen, 1883, F 13,2:4
Morell, James, 1944, Mr 18,13:2
Morell, Thomas D, 1957, S 15,84:4
Morell, Werner H, 1964, F 18,35:4
Morella, Annata , 1871, Mr 2,1:2
Morelli, Alfredo (A Middleton), 1967, Ap 10,35:4
Morelli, Joseph, 1950, Ag 28,11:2
Morelli, Lorenzo, 1950, Ag 9,29:2
Morelli, Luigi R, 1940, D 4,27:4
Morelock, Sterling L, 1964, S 3,26:3
Moren, Frank H Sr, 1942, F 6,19:1
Morena, Berta, 1952, O 17,27:5
Morena, Joseph, 1941, My 11,44:6
Moreng, George E, 1965, S 1,37:1
Moreno, Alfredo B, 1951, Mr 21,33:2
Moreno, Antonio (will, Mr 4,25:8), 1967, F 16,35:3
Moreno, Aristides, 1955, O 9,86:6
Moreno, Marguerite, 1948, Jl 15,23:5
Moreno, Mario Mrs, 1966, Ja 6,27:2
Moreno, Martin, 1941, Ap 24,21:3
Moreno, Rodolfo, 1953, N 20,23:4
Moreno, Thomas B, 1938, O 29,19:6
Moreno Duran, Gustavo, 1951, Je 30,15:4
Moreno-Lacalle, Julian, 1945, Je 19,19:5
Morenski, Jacob, 1947, Ja 28,23:2
Morentz, Paul I, 1938, Jl 17,26:6
Morenz, Donald, 1939, Ja 16,15:3
Morenz, Howie, 1937, Mr 9,23:3
Morenz, William F, 1942, S 24,27:2
Morera, Enric (lr), 1942, Ap 19,VIII,6:6
Mores, Marquise de, 1921, Mr 5,13:6
Moresby, John Adm, 1922, Jl 13,13:2
Moreschauser, Joseph (por), 1947, N 4,25:1
Moresco, A, 1945, Jl 26,20:2
Moresco, Bartolomeo F, 1939, S 24,44:1
Moresco, Joseph, 1938, Mr 10,21:3
Moress, Ignace, 1952, Jl 6,48:8
Moress, Ignace Mrs, 1942, F 25,20:2
Moret, Alexandre, 1938, F 3,23:3
Moreton, Edward F, 1941, Je 13,19:4
Moreton, Henry John (Earl of Ducie), 1921, O 29, 13:6
Moretti, Marcello, 1961, Ja 21,21:5
Moretti, Onorio, 1939, O 24,23:4
Moretti, Raoul, 1954, Mr 10,25:4
Moretti, Salvatore, 1952, Je 9,23:2
Moretti, Stefano, 1906, F 1,9:5
Moreux, Theophile, 1954, Jl 14,27:4
Morewood, J R, 1903, Ja 26,1:6
Morey, Addie C Mrs, 1939, Mr 18,17:4
Morey, Agnes Mrs, 1924, Mr 30,X,8:2
Morey, Anna, 1954, S 2,21:4
Morey, C P, 1881, F 22,4:7
Morey, Charles H Mrs, 1941, Ap 28,15:3
Morey, Charles R, 1955, Ag 30,27:3
Morey, Clarence G, 1952, Ap 19,15:5
Morey, Daniel H, 1950, Jl 7,19:1
Morey, Edmond, 1947, S 30,25:1
Morey, Ernest Mrs, 1943, S 6,17:5
Morey, Eugene S, 1938, My 26,25:2
Morey, Florence K Mrs, 1958, S 4,29:5
Morey, Francis L, 1939, F 19,39:1
Morey, Frank A Mrs, 1959, Jl 7,33:5
Morey, George T Mrs, 1950, Ap 5,31:4
Morey, Isaac H Sr, 1948, N 1,23:5
Morey, James S, 1943, F 21,32:8
Morey, John D, 1941, N 13,27:1
Morey, John W, 1945, S 17,19:5
Morey, L, 1884, Ag 24,12:3
Morey, Leon K, 1954, F 20,17:4
Morey, Lewis S, 1948, Ap 16;23:5
Morey, Lloyd (Sept 29), 1965, O 11,61:4
Morey, Mahlon, 1921, F 8,11:5
Morey, Mahlon Mrs, 1948, My 9,68:7
Morey, Marcus W, 1952, F 29,23:3
Morey, Russell C, 1949, Ag 27,13:6
Morey, Samuel, 1962, Je 13,41:4
Morey, Sigmund M, 1965, Jl 29,27:4
Morey, Victor P, 1951, My 19,15:2
Morey, Walter W, 1952, Mr 11,27:5
Morey, Warren S, 1944, Ap 5,19:4
Morey, William C, 1925, Ja 21,21:3
Morey, William H S Mrs, 1950, My 4,106:4
Morey, William S, 1952, Mr 15,13:4

Morf, Heinrich Prof, 1921, Ja 27,13:4
Morfa, Raymond J, 1952, O 20,23:3
Morfit, Clarence M Jr, 1962, N 22,29:4
Morfit, Clarence O Mrs, 1945, Mr 7,22:3
Morfit, Mason P, 1954, Mr 31,27:5
Morfogen, Paul G, 1955, S 22,31:2
Morford, Charles A, 1907, O 15,9:4
Morford, Harold C, 1956, S 30,86:4
Morford, Harry, 1959, N 9,31:1
Morford, Henry, 1881, Ag 7,2:2
Morford, Rex H, 1964, My 20,43:3
Morford, Theodore, 1908, My 28,7:6
Morg, John, 1912, F 24,11:4
Morgan, A C, 1949, O 7,31:3
Morgan, A Maurice, 1938, Mr 2,19:2
Morgan, A N Mrs, 1934, D 4,19:1
Morgan, A Rees, 1946, D 31,18:2
Morgan, Ada J Mrs, 1947, S 17,25:4
Morgan, Agnes Fay Dr, 1968, Jl 23,36:3
Morgan, Albert E, 1946, Mr 21,25:3
Morgan, Albert E Mrs (Edytha Johnston), 1958, Mr 20,29:3
Morgan, Albert H, 1953, Ja 7,31:2
Morgan, Albert W (por), 1938, Jl 3,13:3
Morgan, Alexander Perry, 1968, D 20,42:5
Morgan, Alfred, 1944, Je 29,23:5
Morgan, Alfred J, 1954, My 10,23:3
Morgan, Alfred Lee Prof, 1925, Jl 6,11:6
Morgan, Algernon R, 1937, O 11,21:2
Morgan, Alice B Mrs, 1958, My 31,15:2
Morgan, Alonzo D, 1873, Ja 3,5:1
Morgan, Andrew C, 1941, Ag 6,17:5
Morgan, Angela, 1957, Ja 25,21:4
Morgan, Ann H, 1966, Je 6,41:3
Morgan, Anne, 1952, Ja 30,25:1
Morgan, Anne (est tax appr), 1954, Ag 31,23:2
Morgan, Arthur C, 1940, O 22,23:3
Morgan, Arthur H Mrs, 1963, D 31,19:2
Morgan, Arthur J Mrs, 1952, Ja 24,27:4
Morgan, Arthur M, 1948, Ja 27,25:1
Morgan, Arthur R, 1938, Jl 31,32:8
Morgan, Arthur W, 1956, S 26,33:3
Morgan, Augustine H, 1948, Ja 20,23:4
Morgan, Bankson Taylor, 1913, Mr 30,IV,7:5; 1916, Je 4,21:5
Morgan, Barney N, 1958, S 10,33:2
Morgan, Belden, 1958, Mr 19,31:2
Morgan, Ben C, 1949, Mr 11,25:4
Morgan, Benjamin F, 1950, Ag 14,17:4
Morgan, Benjamin H Sir, 1937, Jl 17,15:5
Morgan, Bertha A, 1951, Jl 29,68:4
Morgan, Bertha D, 1947, My 4,60:5
Morgan, Bradley D Mrs, 1948, Ja 24,16:2
Morgan, Brewster B, 1960, D 29,25:4
Morgan, Brockholst Rev, 1920, F 25,11:4
Morgan, Bronson, 1955, S 20,31:1
Morgan, Browne, 1953, My 29,25:5
Morgan, C, 1877, Ap 4,4:7
Morgan, C (see also My 9), 1878, My 12,2:3
Morgan, C A Sr, 1882, F 12,2:6
Morgan, C B, 1933, Ag 18,15:1
Morgan, C Brinley Rev Dr, 1909, Ap 7,11:6
Morgan, C Daniel, 1956, O 27,21:5
Morgan, C H, 1901, N 3,7:5
Morgan, C H Gen, 1875, D 23,2:5
Morgan, C Powell, 1966, O 18,40:6
Morgan, Carey, 1960, Ja 7,30:1
Morgan, Carey E Dr, 1925, My 11,17:5
Morgan, Caroline L, 1942, Ja 15,19:2
Morgan, Charles, 1937, F 23,27:4; 1946, F 24,44:7; 1959, My 8,28:3
Morgan, Charles C, 1962, O 8,23:6
Morgan, Charles D, 1948, Mr 6,13:5
Morgan, Charles E, 1917, Mr 6,11:6; 1960, F 21,92:2
Morgan, Charles E 3d, 1947, Ap 17,27:4
Morgan, Charles H Sr, 1949, N 13,92:8
Morgan, Charles Henry, 1912, Ja 5,13:4
Morgan, Charles Hill, 1911, Ja 11,13:5
Morgan, Charles Jr, 1947, F 5,23:2
Morgan, Charles L, 1954, Mr 9,27:2; 1958, F 7,21:1
Morgan, Charles L Mrs, 1952, F 26,27:2; 1961, Jl 27, 31:3
Morgan, Charles N, 1960, F 4,31:3
Morgan, Charles S, 1950, N 29,36:5; 1951, Ap 30,21:4
Morgan, Charlotte E, 1961, Jl 25,27:3
Morgan, Charlotte F, 1879, D 19,4:7
Morgan, Christian D Mrs, 1956, My 2,31:4
Morgan, Clara E, 1943, My 21,19:3
Morgan, Clara W Mrs, 1939, Ja 19,19:1
Morgan, Clarence, 1937, N 17,23:5
Morgan, Clayland T, 1954, Jl 27,21:3
Morgan, Clifford L, 1951, N 16,25:3
Morgan, Clifford V, 1954, O 5,27:2
Morgan, Clinton E, 1956, Jl 12,23:4
Morgan, Cole E, 1946, Mr 5,25:5
Morgan, D Parker Rev Dr, 1915, S 27,9:4
Morgan, Daniel C, 1949, My 12,31:6
Morgan, Daniel D, 1960, D 29,25:3
Morgan, Daniel Dr, 1937, D 29,22:1
Morgan, Daniel E, 1949, My 2,25:4
Morgan, Daniel F (Dumb Dan), 1955, Jl 8,23:2
Morgan, Daniel J, 1961, N 16,39:1
Morgan, David B, 1954, Mr 27,17:4
Morgan, David Pierce Mrs, 1914, Ag 5,13:6
Morgan, David R, 1938, Je 15,23:6
Morgan, David Sir, 1939, O 7,17:4
Morgan, David W, 1946, Ja 31,21:3
Morgan, Davy, 1938, Jl 7,19:4
Morgan, Dessa A J Mrs, 1940, S 2,15:4
Morgan, Dick I, 1920, Jl 6,15:2
Morgan, Don C Mrs, 1946, Ja 5,14:2
Morgan, Douglas M, 1964, Ja 7,33:4
Morgan, E B, 1881, O 14,4:7
Morgan, E D, 1883, F 15,1:7; 1933, Je 14,19:3
Morgan, E D Jr, 1879, Ag 16,8:3
Morgan, E D Mrs, 1885, Mr 27,5:5
Morgan, E Louise, 1959, Je 17,35:4
Morgan, E V, 1934, Ap 17,21:3
Morgan, E W Col, 1869, Ap 17,3:1
Morgan, Earl B, 1968, Ap 9,47:1
Morgan, Earle G, 1951, Ap 24,29:1
Morgan, Eddie, 1937, Jl 19,15:5
Morgan, Edith P, 1951, Ja 28,77:2
Morgan, Edith P Mrs, 1942, My 20,19:5
Morgan, Edmund M, 1966, F 1,35:3
Morgan, Edward J, 1906, Mr 11,9:5
Morgan, Edward S, 1925, Ja 12,15:3
Morgan, Edward W, 1953, My 16,19:2
Morgan, Edwin, 1957, O 25,27:2
Morgan, Edwin A, 1959, O 5,31:2
Morgan, Edwin B, 1940, D 12,27:5
Morgan, Edwin D, 1954, O 19,27:4
Morgan, Edwin D Mrs, 1948, O 18,23:6
Morgan, Egbert P, 1960, Jl 11,29:2
Morgan, Eilsha, 1903, F 2,8:6
Morgan, Elizabeth, 1949, O 25,28:4
Morgan, Ella Mrs, 1937, F 1,4:4
Morgan, Ellen K H, 1956, Ja 25,31:4
Morgan, Emily, 1909, Jl 7,9:4
Morgan, Ephraim F, 1950, Ja 17,27:4
Morgan, Ernest J, 1955, D 23,17:2
Morgan, Evelyn V, 1951, Ja 30,25:4
Morgan, Everett L, 1951, Ap 17,29:4
Morgan, F A Mrs, 1954, N 1,27:3
Morgan, F Allan Mrs, 1955, My 12,29:5
Morgan, F Bruce, 1947, Ap 22,27:2
Morgan, F Corlies, 1939, Je 14,23:2
Morgan, F R, 1905, Je 23,2:2
Morgan, Farran M, 1941, Ja 5,45:1
Morgan, Florence H Mrs, 1941, Ja 13,15:1
Morgan, Forde, 1938, O 10,19:4
Morgan, Frank (por),(will, S 22,31:2), 1949, S 19,23:1
Morgan, Frank (will), 1949, O 13,21:6
Morgan, Frank B, 1956, S 10,27:4; 1958, O 9,37:5
Morgan, Frank J, 1954, Ag 28,15:3
Morgan, Frank M, 1966, Je 30,39:6
Morgan, Frank P, 1940, O 26,15:3
Morgan, Frank V Dr, 1922, S 23,15:4
Morgan, Fred C Mrs, 1958, Ag 26,29:4
Morgan, Fred R, 1947, S 16,23:6
Morgan, Frederick E, 1967, Mr 21,43:2
Morgan, Frederick J, 1950, Mr 11,15:6
Morgan, Frederick N, 1946, Ja 23,27:5
Morgan, G Campbell (por), 1945, My 18,19:3
Morgan, G Walter, 1946, Ap 18,29:3
Morgan, Garfield, 1950, Ap 6,29:5
Morgan, Gene (E Kenney), 1940, Ag 16,15:5
Morgan, Gene, 1953, D 31,19:4
Morgan, George, 1939, Ap 9,III,6:7
Morgan, George A, 1955, S 16,23:1
Morgan, George D, 1915, Jl 11,15:5; 1937, N 19,23:5
Morgan, George F Mrs, 1945, F 6,19:4
Morgan, George Frederick, 1925, F 8,7:2
Morgan, George H (por), 1948, F 15,60:4
Morgan, George Halle, 1911, Ap 29,13:6
Morgan, George J, 1952, Mr 13,29:2
Morgan, George N Gen, 1866, Ag 3,6:2
Morgan, George O, 1958, N 9,88:2
Morgan, George R, 1950, D 23,15:4
Morgan, George Sr, 1947, Ap 2,27:3
Morgan, George T, 1925, Ja 6,25:5; 1957, Ja 28,23:5
Morgan, George W Mrs, 1952, Ag 12,19:2
Morgan, Gerald, 1948, O 14,30:3; 1953, N 21,13:4
Morgan, Gifford, 1944, F 5,15:1
Morgan, Gilbert Rev Dr, 1875, My 30,7:1
Morgan, Gilbert T, 1940, F 2,17:2
Morgan, Gorton P, 1960, My 30,17:6
Morgan, Grace B, 1959, F 5,31:3
Morgan, Guion C, 1963, Je 11,37:1
Morgan, Gwilyn S, 1947, Ag 8,17:4
Morgan, H A, 1903, Mr 22,7:5
Morgan, H Carey (funl, Jl 27,13:6), 1923, Jl 25,11:6
Morgan, H H, 1933, Mr 20,15:1
Morgan, H T, 1883, Ja 28,5:5
Morgan, Hamilton R, 1949, Je 10,27:4
Morgan, Harcourt A, 1950, Ag 26,13:1
Morgan, Harold L Jr, 1958, Mr 25,31:1
Morgan, Harry A, 1947, My 18,60:4
Morgan, Harry B, 1946, O 5,17:2
Morgan, Harry C, 1962, Je 30,19:4
Morgan, Harry H Mrs, 1948, My 3,21:5
Morgan, Harry H Mrs (will, F 17,26:6), 1956, F 6, 23:5
Morgan, Harry S, 1946, Ag 31,15:5
Morgan, Harry V, 1943, O 28,23:5
Morgan, Helen, 1941, O 9,24:2
Morgan, Helen C Mrs, 1955, Jl 20,27:3
Morgan, Henry, 1942, D 13,74:5; 1961, My 11,37:1
Morgan, Henry J Dr, 1913, D 28,II,15:5
Morgan, Henry Mrs, 1948, Ja 1,23:4
Morgan, Henry S, 1959, My 2,23:5
Morgan, Henry W, 1937, Je 18,21:4
Morgan, Herbert, 1951, Jl 5,25:2
Morgan, Herbert R, 1957, Je 13,31:3
Morgan, Homer Bartlett Rev, 1865, S 23,1:6
Morgan, Hugh, 1916, Je 22,11:6
Morgan, Hugh C, 1957, My 20,25:3
Morgan, Hugh J, 1961, D 25,23:2
Morgan, Hugh Jr, 1956, Ag 20,21:2
Morgan, Humphrey F, 1942, Ap 9,19:2
Morgan, Ida Mrs, 1960, My 24,37:4
Morgan, Ike, 1913, S 13,11:5
Morgan, Isaac G, 1961, Ja 20,29:1
Morgan, Ivan C, 1949, F 27,69:1
Morgan, Ivor O Mrs, 1937, Jl 9,21:2
Morgan, J A, 1928, Ag 16,21:4
Morgan, J Earl, 1945, S 16,44:2
Morgan, J Edward, 1947, Ag 17,53:1
Morgan, J F Rev, 1917, My 27,19:5
Morgan, J M, 1928, Ap 23,23:1
Morgan, J Maynard, 1957, My 16,31:3
Morgan, J P Mrs, 1925, Ag 16,5:1
Morgan, J Pierpont (funl plans), 1913, Ap 14,9:1
Morgan, J Pierpont Mrs (funl, N 21,19:5), 1924, N 18,25:3
Morgan, J S, 1890, Ap 6,1:7; 1932, Ag 19,17:1
Morgan, J W, 1881, Jl 20,5:4
Morgan, J W Mrs, 1961, D 13,43:2
Morgan, J Willard, 1912, F 25,II,11:3
Morgan, James, 1955, Mr 14,19:4
Morgan, James C, 1959, Jl 18,15:4
Morgan, James G, 1920, D 3,15:4; 1950, Ap 15,15:5
Morgan, James H, 1939, O 18,25:1
Morgan, James J (por), 1949, Ag 18,21:1
Morgan, James J, 1960, D 11,88:8
Morgan, James Lancaster, 1925, O 28,25:4
Morgan, James W, 1957, F 2,19:5
Morgan, Jasper, 1964, O 10,29:3
Morgan, Jasper Deacon, 1869, Ag 29,1:4
Morgan, Jay H, 1937, Je 8,25:1
Morgan, Jeanette Mrs, 1944, Mr 28,19:3
Morgan, Jerome J, 1967, Ap 21,39:3
Morgan, Jerome J Mrs, 1962, Mr 11,87:1
Morgan, Jesse G, 1937, Mr 2,21:5
Morgan, John, 1940, D 5,25:4; 1957, Je 27,26:5
Morgan, John A, 1949, Jl 14,27:2; 1949, O 1,13:6; 1953, F 4,27:2
Morgan, John A (Oct 1), 1965, O 11,61:3
Morgan, John A Mrs, 1949, Je 30,23:5
Morgan, John B Mrs, 1923, Ap 3,23:4
Morgan, John C, 1956, Ja 31,29:2
Morgan, John D, 1939, My 25,25:6
Morgan, John G, 1946, N 9,17:5
Morgan, John H, 1939, D 1,23:5; 1942, F 8,49:2; 194 Jl 18,27:3; 1955, Ap 9,13:3
Morgan, John Howard Dr, 1913, Je 22,IV,5:6
Morgan, John J (died Mar 16; will), 1949, Ap 15,28
Morgan, John J B, 1945, Ag 18,11:6
Morgan, John L, 1941, F 20,19:2
Morgan, John P, 1943, Mr 13,1:3
Morgan, John T (funl, Je 14,7:7), 1907, Je 13,7:5
Morgan, John T, 1924, Je 10,11:4
Morgan, John W, 1964, My 21,35:1
Morgan, Joseph, 1942, Ag 15,9:7; 1946, Je 19,21:2
Morgan, Joseph B, 1939, D 6,25:5
Morgan, Joseph La Motte, 1904, Ja 30,9:5
Morgan, Joseph Mrs, 1945, Jl 20,19:5
Morgan, Joseph S, 1951, D 27,21:3
Morgan, Julia, 1948, Ja 28,23:6
Morgan, Junius S (funl plans, O 21,33:1; funl, O 23,88:1), 1960, O 20,1:7
Morgan, Junius S Mrs, 1963, Ap 27,25:5
Morgan, Justin C, 1959, My 25,29:5
Morgan, Kays R, 1964, D 27,64:3
Morgan, L H, 1881, D 19,2:5
Morgan, Lancaster (por), 1946, Jl 23,25:4
Morgan, Lancaster Mrs, 1957, My 16,31:4
Morgan, Lee H Mrs, 1948, Ag 17,21:2
Morgan, Lee P, 1961, N 15,31:4
Morgan, Len, 1957, F 7,27:1
Morgan, Lewis V, 1953, N 28,15:7
Morgan, Lissa J Mrs, 1947, D 14,76:4
Morgan, Loren S, 1955, Je 12,86:6
Morgan, Lorne T Mrs, 1960, D 8,35:2
Morgan, Lucy P, 1906, F 4,7:6
Morgan, Lulu St Clair Mrs, 1903, Jl 21,9:6
Morgan, Margaret M, 1946, My 29,24:2
Morgan, Mary A Mrs, 1941, Ag 27,19:6
Morgan, Mary E Mrs, 1942, Mr 22,48:6
Morgan, Mary J, 1923, O 16,21:4
Morgan, Mary Mrs, 1942, My 17,47:2
Morgan, Maud (por), 1941, D 4,25:1
Morgan, Michael D, 1940, N 26,23:3
Morgan, Minot C, 1955, Ag 15,6:3
Morgan, Mona, 1959, S 9,41:1
Morgan, N H, 1881, Jl 13,5:4
Morgan, N J B Rev, 1872, Ap 9,5:1
Morgan, Nathan A, 1940, Ap 16,23:3
Morgan, Nellie S, 1951, Je 26,29:2
Morgan, Nicholas G, 1965, Mr 13,25:3

Morgan, Olive (Mrs E C Bryan), 1961, Mr 5,86:5
Morgan, Ora S, 1961, Ag 16,29:6
Morgan, Oscar, 1958, My 1,31:4
Morgan, Oyuki (Mrs Geo D), 1963, My 20,31:3
Morgan, Paul, 1939, Ja 5,23:2
Morgan, Paul B, 1952, N 6,29:1
Morgan, Peter, 1950, Mr 23,36:2
Morgan, Philip M, 1965, N 20,35:6
Morgan, Porter S, 1957, Ag 15,21:5
Morgan, R, 1926, Mr 21,II,9:1; 1934, Mr 12,17:3
Morgan, R C, 1884, F 29,5:4; 1940, N 20,21:1
Morgan, Ralph, 1956, Je 13,37:1; 1965, Ja 6,39:3
Morgan, Ralph Mrs, 1940, Mr 5,24:4; 1948, My 10, 21:3
Morgan, Randall Jr, 1907, Jl 2,9:5
Morgan, Ray, 1940, F 16,19:5
Morgan, Raymond B, 1921, S 19,15:4
Morgan, Raymond G, 1955, Je 25,15:2
Morgan, Raymond R Sr, 1958, O 5,87:1
Morgan, Reed A, 1959, My 17,84:1
Morgan, Reginald H, 1944, D 29,15:3
Morgan, Rhys, 1961, Ag 26,17:4
Morgan, Richard C, 1940, N 14,23:4
Morgan, Richard J, 1940, Ag 20,19:1
Morgan, Richard P, 1951, Je 1,23:4
Morgan, Robert D, 1939, Ja 17,22:4; 1950, S 5,27:3
Morgan, Robert M, 1959, O 31,23:5
Morgan, Robert W, 1960, Jl 30,17:6
Morgan, Rodney D, 1954, Jl 19,19:4
Morgan, Rodney L, 1938, Ap 21,19:5
Morgan, Rodney M Mrs, 1960, Ap 5,37:4
Morgan, Roy, 1951, N 2,23:2
Morgan, Russell E, 1958, My 25,87:1
Morgan, Ruth B, 1955, Mr 12,19:6
Morgan, S A L, 1954, D 5,88:2
Morgan, Samuel, 1949, O 8,13:5
Morgan, Samuel Maurice, 1925, Ja 9,17:3
Morgan, Samuel T Sr, 1959, D 3,37:5
Morgan, Samuel Tate, 1920, Ap 17,15:3
Morgan, Sarah L, 1943, Je 8,22:2
Morgan, Sheldon, 1947, O 20,23:2
Morgan, Shepard, 1968, N 18,47:3
Morgan, Stokeley W, 1963, S 11,43:2
Morgan, Susan E Mrs, 1951, My 29,25:3
Morgan, Sydney Lady, 1859, Ap 30,5:1
Morgan, Tali E, 1941, Jl 2,21:5
Morgan, Theodore R, 1946, Ja 6,40:6
Morgan, Thomas, 1944, Ja 19,19:2; 1965, Jl 19,21:3
Morgan, Thomas A, 1967, O 30,45:1
Morgan, Thomas F, 1939, Ag 11,15:3; 1950, Mr 6,22:2
Morgan, Thomas H (lr on obituary, D 14,26:6), 1945, D 5,25:1
Morgan, Thomas H Mrs, 1946, My 14,21:2; 1952, D 8,41:2
Morgan, Thomas J, 1943, N 13,13:5; 1949, Je 7,31:1
Morgan, Thomas Mrs, 1938, Mr 15,23:6
Morgan, Thomas P Jr, 1949, S 10,17:2
Morgan, Tod, 1953, Ag 4,21:4
Morgan, Townsend, 1939, Je 30,19:3
Morgan, Truman Mrs, 1947, Ap 9,25:2
Morgan, Truman S, 1940, D 22,30:8
Morgan, Victor H, 1946, O 3,27:2
Morgan, Vincent E, 1939, Ap 25,23:3
Morgan, Vincent Prof, 1968, Ja 28,76:6
Morgan, W A, 1953, Ag 25,21:4
Morgan, W F Rev Dr, 1888, My 20,4:7
Morgan, W Forbes, 1916, D 19,11:3; 1937, Ap 21,23:1
Morgan, W H Mrs, 1954, My 7,23:3
Morgan, Wallace (por), 1948, Ap 25,68:5
Morgan, Wiley L, 1960, Jl 18,27:4
Morgan, Willard D, 1967, S 19,51:3
Morgan, William, 1937, O 18,17:1
Morgan, William A, 1947, My 29,21:1; 1948, My 7, 23:3
Morgan, William B, 1944, Jl 24,15:4
Morgan, William C, 1940, F 10,15:3; 1948, Ag 3,25:4; 1958, D 29,15:5
Morgan, William C Mrs, 1958, Mr 19,31:3
Morgan, William E, 1939, Ap 27,25:1
Morgan, William E Mrs, 1948, O 14,29:4; 1949, N 30, 27:4
Morgan, William F, 1945, O 20,13:4; 1946, Ja 25,23:2
Morgan, William F Jr Mrs, 1948, Ap 19,23:2
Morgan, William F Mrs, 1952, D 4,35:5; 1956, D 30, 32:5
Morgan, William F Sr (will, My 8,18:5), 1943, My 3, 17:1
Morgan, William G, 1942, D 28,19:5
Morgan, William G (por), 1949, Jl 9,13:1
Morgan, William H, 1944, S 9,15:7; 1958, F 24,19:3
Morgan, William H Mrs, 1941, Ja 4,13:5
Morgan, William J, 1948, O 3,65:1; 1966, N 25,37:3
Morgan, William J Jr, 1948, D 25,17:6
Morgan, William J Mrs, 1950, O 7,19:1
Morgan, William L (por), 1942, S 20,40:1
Morgan, William L Mrs, 1943, My 8,15:2
Morgan, William M, 1942, O 18,52:5
Morgan, William Mrs, 1947, My 29,21:4
Morgan, William N, 1948, O 19,27:2
Morgan, William O, 1966, N 25,37:2
Morgan, William O Mrs, 1946, My 14,21:4
Morgan, William O P Mrs, 1967, Mr 17,41:3
Morgan, William R, 1950, Je 6,29:1
Morgan, William T, 1940, S 24,23:5; 1941, F 3,17:2; 1945, Ag 24,19:2; 1946, Je 10,21:2; 1951, Ap 4,29:3
Morgan, William W, 1947, Mr 29,15:3
Morgan (Sister Mary Sylvia), 1964, Jl 25,19:5
Morgan-Powell, Samuel, 1962, Je 5,41:2
Morganroth, Lee C, 1940, My 7,25:4
Morgans, Lillian, 1948, Ap 9,23:2
Morgans, Maud J, 1952, Mr 12,28:4
Morgans, W T, 1882, Ap 16,2:7
Morganstern, David A, 1957, Mr 31,88:1
Morganstern, Jacob, 1967, Jl 9,61:1
Morganthaler, Henry W, 1937, F 28,II,8:8
Morgart, William A, 1944, Ag 14,15:5
Morgen, Lewis, 1947, Jl 4,13:4
Morgensen, Jens, 1944, Ja 19,19:5
Morgenson, Olaf J, 1949, Ap 23,13:3
Morgenstern, Adolph, 1953, Mr 29,95:3
Morgenstern, David, 1953, S 8,31:1
Morgenstern, George, 1961, D 17,83:1
Morgenstern, Henry, 1953, O 11,88:4
Morgenstern, James A, 1951, S 6,31:2
Morgenstern, Mark E, 1956, O 15,25:3
Morgenstern, Morris Mrs, 1956, D 16,86:2
Morgenstern, Nathan, 1955, Jl 26,25:1
Morgenstierne, Wilhelm M de, 1963, Jl 16,31:2
Morgenthal, Jacob H, 1951, Mr 20,29:1
Morgenthaler, Elizabeth, 1955, O 5,35:5
Morgenthaler, Jacob, 1916, Jl 11,9:7
Morgenthaler, William, 1945, O 24,21:5
Morgenthau, Alma Mrs, 1953, D 26,13:6
Morgenthau, Beatrice F, 1943, Je 7,13:2
Morgenthau, Henry Jr (funl plans, F 8,31:2; funl, F 10,35:3), 1967, F 7,1:2
Morgenthau, Henry Sr, 1946, N 26,18:3
Morgenthau, Henry Sr Mrs, 1953, F 20,19:1
Morgenthau, M, 1936, D 14,23:3
Morgenthau, M L, 1927, My 22,28:1
Morgenthau, Max Jr Mrs, 1964, Ap 9,31:2
Morgenthau, Maximilian Jr, 1938, Ja 25,21:5
Morgenthau, Mengo L Mrs, 1945, D 1,23:2
Morgere, Frank, 1960, N 7,35:5
Morginson, Frank L, 1954, Ap 8,27:5
Morgner, Arthur A, 1951, Je 19,29:3
Morgrage, Richard J, 1956, My 30,21:6
Morhart, Adam, 1952, F 14,27:1
Morhart, Frederick J, 1951, My 5,17:3
Morhous, Charles M, 1956, Ja 18,31:3
Morhous, John A, 1967, Ja 4,41:1
Morhous, Oakley A, 1957, Ap 22,25:3
Mori, Cesare, 1942, Jl 6,15:6
Mori, Edmund, 1963, Je 29,23:5
Mori, Hirozo, 1944, Ja 13,21:4
Morian, Florence G Mrs, 1949, Mr 27,76:6
Moriana, Count, 1914, Mr 9,9:4
Moriarity, Edward J Msgr, 1951, Mr 30,24:3
Moriarity, Harris, 1938, O 16,44:6
Moriarity, Joseph P, 1942, Je 9,24:2
Moriarta, Douglas C, 1944, S 14,23:5
Moriarta, Douglas C Mrs, 1940, Ag 6,19:5
Moriarty, Alfred I, 1955, Je 4,15:5
Moriarty, Ambrose J, 1949, Je 4,13:4
Moriarty, E J, 1932, Mr 21,15:2
Moriarty, Edward J, 1951, My 6,92:4; 1965, O 24,86:7
Moriarty, George H, 1957, Mr 11,25:5
Moriarty, George J, 1964, Ap 9,32:1
Moriarty, J Arthur, 1956, Ap 24,31:2
Moriarty, James D, 1922, D 23,13:6
Moriarty, James L, 1940, D 1,61:3
Moriarty, James M, 1946, Je 18,25:1
Moriarty, James T, 1950, Ap 6,29:5
Moriarty, John F, 1966, My 29,56:3
Moriarty, John Francis, 1915, My 3,11:2
Moriarty, John J, 1961, N 22,33:2
Moriarty, Joseph B Sr, 1959, N 8,88:3
Moriarty, Joseph F Sr, 1965, D 13,39:2
Moriarty, Kenneth L, 1956, Ag 14,25:3
Moriarty, Michael E, 1941, O 12,V,11:2; 1941, D 31, 17:3
Moriarty, Nellie, 1951, Mr 30,23:2
Moriarty, P E Rev Dr, 1875, Jl 11,7:6
Moriarty, Patrick M, 1955, Ag 5,19:5
Moriarty, Patrick S, 1945, Jl 26,20:2
Moriarty, Richard T Mrs, 1960, N 3,39:3
Moriarty, Rose, 1950, D 26,23:1
Moriarty, Thaddeus, 1904, D 3,9:4
Moriarty, Thomas A, 1961, Ap 22,25:2
Moriarty, Timothy J, 1944, Je 6,17:4
Moriarty, Timothy J 2d, 1948, Ag 11,21:3
Morice, Adrien G, 1938, Ap 23,15:3
Morichard, Joseph E, 1944, Ag 31,17:3
Morichini, Ettore, 1940, D 21,17:5
Morie, Jesse S Sr, 1956, Ja 26,29:5
Morie, Richard P Maj, 1914, Ja 20,9:6
Morill, Joaquin Dr, 1908, Ja 15,9:4
Morill, Oscar, 1944, F 15,17:6
Morimoto, Andrew, 1968, S 21,33:2
Morimoto, Gitchi, 1944, Mr 5,35:1
Morimura, Ichizayemon Baron, 1919, S 13,11:5
Morin, A J, 1880, F 8,6:7
Morin, Charles R, 1947, Jl 6,41:3
Morin, E A, 1882, Ag 22,5:1
Morin, George A, 1944, Mr 17,17:2
Morin, George F, 1945, F 15,19:6
Morin, Guillame J, 1953, Jl 13,25:5
Morin, John B, 1950, N 4,17:6
Morin, Joseph A, 1953, My 2,15:4
Morin, Joseph P, 1942, Ag 18,21:7
Morin, Leo P, 1949, F 28,21:8
Morin, Louis, 1967, F 1,39:1
Morin, Mary E Mrs, 1940, Mr 3,45:1
Morin, Oscar, 1952, Ap 7,25:3
Morin, Philip J Mrs, 1960, Jl 31,69:1
Morinaga, Tiachiro, 1937, Ja 26,21:3
Morine, Alfred B, 1944, D 19,21:6
Morine, Leon H, 1963, Jl 20,19:3
Morini, Oscar, 1953, Mr 12,27:3
Morinigo, Juan, 1960, Ag 19,12:5
Morino, Samuel M, 1953, Ap 23,29:4
Morishita, Masaichi, 1957, Mr 6,31:3
Morison, Alexander, 1925, Je 2,23:3
Morison, Andrew, 1914, Jl 20,7:4
Morison, Archibald J, 1962, Je 10,86:3
Morison, Binnie, 1959, D 17,37:4
Morison, George H, 1962, N 6,33:1
Morison, George Shattuck, 1903, Jl 3,9:5
Morison, Hector, 1939, Je 5,17:2
Morison, James Dr, 1882, My 22,5:3
Morison, John A, 1940, O 15,23:2
Morison, Lord, 1945, Ag 2,19:4
Morison, Malcolm J, 1941, O 22,23:2
Morison, Rufus A, 1957, N 24,86:8
Morison, Samuel E Mrs, 1945, Ag 21,21:2
Morison, Samuel Lord, 1907, My 22,9:4
Morison, Stanley, 1967, O 13,39:1
Morison, T, 1936, F 15,15:6
Morison, William (N Rainey), 1960, S 13,37:1
Morison, William L, 1963, S 23,29:5
Morissette, Ralph J, 1953, O 11,89:2
Moritsch, Hans, 1965, N 13,29:2
Moritz, Albert, 1941, Ja 17,17:4; 1952, Ja 8,27:2
Moritz, Benjamin, 1947, Mr 25,25:2
Moritz, Charles H, 1948, Je 29,23:4
Moritz, Fred, 1959, Jl 19,69:1
Moritz, John A, 1943, Ja 22,19:4
Moritz, Joseph J, 1946, D 31,18:5
Moritz, Martin, 1946, S 4,23:2
Moritz, Max, 1941, My 17,15:4
Moritz, Paul W, 1968, Mr 29,45:2
Moritz, Rudy A, 1962, N 21,33:1
Moritz, William, 1948, D 23,19:3
Moritzen, Julius, 1946, Je 25,21:4
Moriya, Shizu (Mrs C L O'Brien), 1961, My 13,29:4
Morize, Andre, 1957, O 5,17:4
Morize, Paul, 1938, D 6,23:1
Mork, Donald, 1964, Ap 26,80:6
Mork, E Clifford, 1962, Ag 15,31:1
Mork, Seymour, 1943, D 5,66:6
Mork, Waldo H Dr, 1953, F 13,21:4
Morlan, A F, 1940, Ap 16,23:5
Morlan, Chauncey Mrs, 1904, Mr 31,9:4
Morland, David F, 1944, My 20,15:6
Morland, Jules A, 1966, Ap 4,31:3
Morlang, Cora Mrs, 1938, F 28,16:2
Morlang, William C, 1943, Je 5,15:5
Morlay, Edward, 1918, My 18,13:6
Morlay, Gaby (B Fumoleau), 1964, Jl 5,43:1
Morley, Albert W Jr Mrs, 1948, Mr 3,23:4
Morley, Alonzo B, 1938, Jl 11,17:2
Morley, Arnold, 1916, Ja 18,11:4
Morley, Arnold Mrs, 1912, O 5,13:5
Morley, Charles A, 1942, Ja 28,19:3
Morley, Charles F (por), 1940, N 1,25:1
Morley, Charles M, 1951, S 14,26:3
Morley, Charles S, 1959, N 26,37:2
Morley, Christopher, 1957, Mr 29,1:3
Morley, Christopher Mrs, 1966, S 2,31:2
Morley, Clair L, 1945, Je 19,19:4
Morley, Clarence H, 1947, F 25,25:1
Morley, Earl of, 1905, F 27,7:5
Morley, Earl of (E R Parker), 1951, O 12,27:1
Morley, Edward J, 1944, O 1,45:1
Morley, Elbert F, 1950, D 27,27:3
Morley, Evelyn Mrs, 1962, Ag 21,33:4
Morley, Felix W, 1952, Jl 7,21:4
Morley, Frank Dr, 1937, O 18,17:4
Morley, Franklin A, 1944, Ag 16,19:5
Morley, Frederic A, 1952, Mr 3,21:3
Morley, Frederick W, 1941, Jl 20,30:2
Morley, George F, 1952, Mr 29,15:6
Morley, George M Mrs, 1955, Je 8,29:5
Morley, Henry, 1955, Jl 13,25:3
Morley, James, 1940, D 24,15:4
Morley, Jeremiah, 1950, S 11,23:5
Morley, John, 1946, Ap 27,17:3
Morley, John A, 1966, O 30,88:6
Morley, John Viscount, 1923, S 22,4:6
Morley, Lady, 1908, F 11,7:5
Morley, Lillian J Mrs, 1939, My 25,25:4
Morley, Margaret Warner, 1923, D 15,13:4
Morley, Robert, 1949, Ja 5,25:5
Morley, Sidney T Sr, 1953, Jl 21,23:3
Morley, Syvanus G, 1948, S 3,19:2
Morley, Victor, 1953, Je 30,23:4
Morley, Viscountess, 1923, N 28,17:2
Morley, William L Mrs, 1949, D 19,27:1

Morlock, Henry F, 1941, Ap 30,19:2
Morlock, John C, 1959, My 15,29:3
Morlock, Sophie Mrs, 1947, O 15,27:4
Morlock, William J, 1959, My 25,29:2
Morner, Ethel G Countess, 1960, Ja 31,92:8
Morner, Gosta (por), 1947, D 2,29:4
Morner, Gosta Mrs (G Fitch), 1963, N 22,31:5
Morner de Morlanda, Hans-Georg Count, 1958, Jl 6, 56:4
Mornet, Andre, 1955, Jl 23,17:3
Morning, Joseph B, 1945, My 1,23:4
Morningstar, Carter, 1964, F 22,21:2
Morningstar, Joseph, 1916, Ap 1,13:7
Morningstar, Ora, 1945, My 30,19:5
Morningstar, Thomas W, 1964, Je 12,21:2
Morny, Duke de, 1865, Mr 24,4:5; 1920, Jl 16,11:3
Morny, Louis O (por), 1949, O 3,17:4
Moro-Giafferi, Vincent de, 1956, N 23,27:2
Moro Raba Kom Kom, Emperor, 1942, Mr 18,23:2
Morocco, Benjamin P. 1950, Jl 12,29:2
Morocco, Sultan of, 1887, O 8,1:3
Moroch, Basil, 1947, F 18,26:3
Moroch, George, 1950, D 20,31:4
Moroney, Carl J, 1951, N 28,31:4
Moroney, Edward F, 1942, My 10,43:1
Moroney, James A, 1942, D 31,15:4
Moroney, James M, 1968, S 25,43:3
Moroney, John, 1948, Je 27,52:7
Moroney, Kenneth W, 1968, O 26,37:4
Moroney, Margaret Mrs, 1939, D 31,18:8
Moroni, Byron P, 1963, O 23,42:4
Moroni, Harry, 1966, Ja 21,47:3
Morosco, Walter, 1948, D 31,15:2
Morosine, Ernest Mrs, 1964, My 6,47:4
Morosini, Amalia, 1937, Mr 15,24:1
Morosini, Attilio P, 1924, My 20,21:4
Morosini, Attilio P Mrs, 1954, D 16,37:5
Morosini, Countess Annina, 1954, Ap 12,29:5
Morosini, Emil Jr, 1962, D 2,88:8
Morosini, G P, 1932, F 5,21:3; 1935, S 14,15:4
Moroso, John A, 1957, Je 7,23:3
Moroso, John A Mrs, 1946, Ag 23,19:4
Morosoff, Serge P, 1954, Ag 27,21:2
Moross, Ernest, 1949, Ap 5,29:1
Morozov, Ivan I, 1958, O 17,29:1
Morozov, Mikhail, 1952, My 11,93:2
Morozov, Stephan, 1950, O 5,31:5
Morozow, William, 1965, Mr 19,35:2
Morpeth, Clarence R, 1948, Ja 30,23:1
Morpeth, William R, 1954, Je 23,26:7
Morphy, M William, 1939, N 22,24:7
Morphy, Paul, 1884, Jl 11,4:7
Morpurgo, Louis, 1940, N 22,23:1
Morra, Gennaro Mrs, 1951, Jl 21,13:6
Morreale, Vincent F, 1965, Mr 10,41:3
Morreau, Albert Mrs, 1947, Je 3,25:4
Morrell, A J, 1938, F 5,15:3
Morrell, Ben, 1950, O 18,35:6
Morrell, Blanche A, 1945, O 31,23:4
Morrell, C L (funl, Ag 5,8:2), 1876, Ag 2,4:7
Morrell, Charles A, 1953, F 25,27:2
Morrell, Clarence P, 1941, F 24,15:4
Morrell, Clarence P Mrs, 1949, Jl 23,11:5
Morrell, Edmund B Mrs, 1953, Ap 26,85:1
Morrell, Franklin W, 1965, Mr 27,27:4
Morrell, Frederick E Mrs, 1938, Jl 20,19:3
Morrell, Henry B, 1945, S 14,23:2
Morrell, Herbert K, 1968, N 3,89:1
Morrell, Herbert P, 1938, D 8,27:4
Morrell, Imogene Robinson Mrs, 1908, N 23,9:5
Morrell, John H Mrs, 1943, Je 5,15:3
Morrell, Joseph C Mrs, 1947, Jl 12,13:5
Morrell, Linda L Mrs, 1941, D 15,19:4
Morrell, Louis, 1938, Je 17,21:5
Morrell, Louise B D Mrs (cor, N 9,19:4), 1945, N 6, 20:2
Morrell, Malcolm E, 1968, O 20,86:5
Morrell, Michael J Lt, 1937, Je 20,II,7:1
Morrell, Newton B Sr, 1955, O 21,55:4
Morrell, Richard B, 1938, Ag 14,32:5
Morrell, Robert, 1939, Jl 7,17:1
Morrell, Robert E L Mrs, 1956, Je 24,77:1
Morrell, Robert W, 1955, N 19,19:5
Morrell, Samuel, 1960, My 24,38:1
Morrell, Theodore, 1948, Je 2,29:3
Morrell, William A, 1961, My 3,37:1
Morrell, William A Mrs, 1904, Ja 26,9:6
Morrell, William W (H Hough), 1942, O 16,19:2
Morrey, Charles B, 1954, Ap 23,27:1
Morrey, William T, 1942, Ja 22,17:2
Morriello, Anthony, 1962, O 8,23:5
Morrill, Albert H, 1942, S 14,15:1
Morrill, Albro D, 1943, Je 9,21:5
Morrill, Alice, 1942, S 5,13:6
Morrill, Asa H, 1938, D 21,23:5
Morrill, Ashley Baker Dr, 1968, S 30,47:3
Morrill, C H, 1928, D 13,29:4
Morrill, Charles W, 1941, Ag 23,13:6
Morrill, Clyde G, 1948, F 6,23:3
Morrill, Donald L Judge, 1923, Mr 26,13:4
Morrill, Donald M, 1964, D 19,29:4
Morrill, Edmund M, 1943, My 19,25:4
Morrill, Edward H, 1950, Ap 5,31:4
Morrill, Edward T, 1958, My 2,27:1
Morrill, Ernest J, 1938, Ja 9,42:1
Morrill, F Whitney, 1937, N 28,II,9:1
Morrill, Frank A, 1946, Ja 1,27:1
Morrill, Guy L, 1966, Mr 19,29:1
Morrill, Harley W, 1943, Ap 4,40:8
Morrill, Harley W Mrs, 1952, Ja 31,27:1
Morrill, Harold B, 1949, O 6,31:2
Morrill, J Lee Dr, 1916, Ja 17,11:4
Morrill, J S Sen, 1898, D 28,1:3
Morrill, James P Sr, 1941, D 16,27:6
Morrill, L M, 1883, Ja 11,5:4
Morrill, Lowell, 1958, My 20,34:4
Morrill, Mendon, 1961, Mr 13,29:5
Morrill, Russell D, 1961, Jl 18,29:4
Morrill, Stanwood A, 1956, O 17,35:2
Morrill, Warren P, 1947, S 29,21:2
Morrill, William C, 1940, O 12,17:6
Morrin, Father, 1903, Ap 18,9:5
Morrin, Frances, 1953, Je 28,60:8
Morrin, John S Mrs, 1945, O 11,23:1
Morris, A Fred, 1948, My 4,25:4
Morris, Abner, 1950, D 11,25:5
Morris, Adrian M, 1941, D 1,19:4
Morris, Albert E, 1941, Je 16,15:6
Morris, Albert T, 1957, F 23,17:4
Morris, Albert W, 1954, Ap 5,25:5
Morris, Alex H, 1959, Mr 5,31:5
Morris, Alex Mrs, 1938, Mr 22,21:4
Morris, Alfred D, 1951, D 3,31:5
Morris, Alfred F, 1939, F 24,19:3
Morris, Alfred H, 1959, Jl 10,25:1
Morris, Allan B, 1965, S 6,15:4
Morris, Allston J, 1949, My 18,27:5
Morris, Annie Revere Mrs, 1907, F 22,9:5
Morris, Archibald M, 1964, N 12,37:3
Morris, Arthur J, 1965, Ap 14,41:2
Morris, Arthur J Mrs, 1960, F 29,27:5
Morris, Arthur W, 1961, Ap 24,29:3
Morris, Augustus Newbold (will, S 19,9:3), 1906, S 3,7:6
Morris, Bella, 1909, D 27,7:4
Morris, Benjamin B, 1961, F 24,29:2
Morris, Benjamin H, 1944, Mr 18,13:3
Morris, Benjamin P, 1937, F 21,II,11:2
Morris, Benjamin W, 1944, D 5,23:1
Morris, Benjamin W Mrs, 1947, Ap 6,60:4
Morris, Benjamin Wister Bp, 1906, Ap 9,9:4
Morris, Bernard L, 1938, Ja 30,II,8:6
Morris, Bernhard, 1968, F 10,33:1
Morris, Brig-Gen, 1865, D 13,1:4
Morris, C Rosalie, 1919, S 27,13:6
Morris, Carl E, 1951, Jl 12,25:2
Morris, Carlyle, 1958, Ap 12,19:4
Morris, Casper, 1944, Mr 2,17:4
Morris, Catherine C Mrs, 1942, S 20,40:4
Morris, Charles, 1953, D 20,77:1
Morris, Charles A, 1922, Ap 20,17:5
Morris, Charles A Capt, 1914, Mr 10,9:4
Morris, Charles B Mrs, 1947, Jl 31,21:4
Morris, Charles Barrett, 1903, Jl 1,9:6
Morris, Charles Brig-Gen, 1912, O 28,11:4
Morris, Charles D, 1940, Ap 30,21:2; 1940, N 10,56:3; 1954, My 22,15:3
Morris, Charles D Jr, 1956, Mr 25,92:1
Morris, Charles D Mrs, 1943, Ja 6,25:4
Morris, Charles E, 1949, D 30,19:2; 1953, O 22,29:4
Morris, Charles G, 1961, F 10,24:1
Morris, Charles G Mrs, 1964, Ap 3,33:2
Morris, Charles H, 1939, Jl 21,19:2
Morris, Charles J, 1943, Ja 27,21:3
Morris, Charles L, 1958, Mr 5,31:2
Morris, Charles M, 1944, Je 8,21:4; 1947, Ja 13,21:4; 1961, Mr 2,27:2
Morris, Charles O, 1903, N 20,9:5
Morris, Charles R, 1942, N 9,23:3
Morris, Charles R Mrs, 1954, Jl 7,31:4
Morris, Charles S, 1938, Ja 8,15:4; 1952, F 25,21:4
Morris, Christopher M, 1946, Ja 2,19:3
Morris, Clara, 1925, N 22,9:1
Morris, Claremont R, 1947, N 4,25:1
Morris, Claude E, 1941, N 7,23:4
Morris, Clement L, 1943, N 23,26:3
Morris, Clinton P, 1938, O 17,15:6
Morris, Cobb, 1939, S 6,23:5
Morris, Courtland P, 1951, Mr 28,29:1
Morris, Daniel L, 1966, D 27,32:8
Morris, Daniel L Mrs, 1958, Ja 11,17:5
Morris, Dave H (por), 1944, My 5,19:4
Morris, Dave H Mrs, 1950, Ag 16,29:1
Morris, David, 1940, O 20,49:3; 1943, O 15,19:4
Morris, David Mrs, 1944, S 11,17:6
Morris, David R, 1947, Ja 11,19:6
Morris, David V, 1942, My 14,19:3
Morris, Delmar, 1961, S 10,86:1
Morris, Donald F, 1963, N 19,41:4
Morris, DuBois S, 1956, S 5,27:3
Morris, DuBois S Mrs, 1966, Mr 10,33:1
Morris, E J, 1882, Ja 1,7:4
Morris, Ed C, 1949, S 6,27:3
Morris, Edgar, 1967, N 27,47:2
Morris, Edgar Colt Prof, 1916, D 26,11:4
Morris, Edgar L, 1963, F 20,12:2
Morris, Edgar Mrs, 1954, Jl 5,11:6
Morris, Edmund M, 1939, Ja 3,17:5
Morris, Edward, 1874, My 6,4:7; 1913, N 4,9:5; 1946, O 25,23:3
Morris, Edward B, 1948, S 11,15:5
Morris, Edward F, 1958, S 27,21:2
Morris, Edward G, 1950, S 7,31:4; 1959, Je 25,29:5
Morris, Edward J, 1939, Mr 6,15:3; 1945, Ag 15,19:3; 1960, My 28,21:6
Morris, Edward Lyman, 1913, S 15,9:3
Morris, Edward P, 1938, N 18,22:2
Morris, Edward S, 1959, My 16,23:2
Morris, Edward S Mrs, 1962, Jl 12,29:5
Morris, Edwin, 1938, Jl 10,29:6; 1943, My 25,23:3
Morris, Effingham B, 1937, Ja 23,17:1
Morris, Effingham B Jr, 1955, Ag 17,27:3
Morris, Eleanor Colford Mrs, 1906, Ap 27,11:5
Morris, Elizabeth M, 1910, S 27,13:6
Morris, Ellis, 1914, N 19,11:7
Morris, Elliston J Mrs, 1907, F 9,9:6
Morris, Emma, 1955, Ja 26,25:3
Morris, Ernest M, 1951, My 4,27:3; 1954, Mr 7,91:2
Morris, Evan J, 1939, Jl 6,23:5
Morris, Everett B, 1967, F 15,41:1
Morris, Ex-Police Capt, 1882, Jl 4,8:6
Morris, Felix Mrs, 1954, Ap 19,23:4
Morris, Fordham, 1909, Jl 7,9:5
Morris, Frances, 1955, Ja 27,23:4
Morris, Francis, 1947, F 15,15:3
Morris, Francis C P, 1949, D 20,31:1
Morris, Francis Com, 1923, Je 16,11:5
Morris, Francis E, 1965, Ag 29,84:7
Morris, Francis Lt, 1883, F 13,2:4
Morris, Francis Mrs, 1923, Je 18,13:6
Morris, Frank, 1949, Ag 13,11:5; 1957, Jl 2,27:5
Morris, Frank A Mrs, 1947, Ag 3,52:5
Morris, Frank E, 1963, O 1,40:1
Morris, Frank J, 1937, N 11,25:5; 1960, Jl 17,21:1
Morris, Frank L, 1938, Jl 31,33:5
Morris, Frank M, 1925, Mr 28,15:5
Morris, Frank P Mrs, 1949, O 25,27:5
Morris, Frank R Mrs, 1961, Je 12,29:4
Morris, Fred A, 1947, Ap 29,27:1
Morris, Frederick Parry, 1915, D 2,11:6
Morris, Frederick S, 1943, S 23,21:5
Morris, G Michael (death laid to natural causes, F 16,37:2), 1968, F 16,29:6
Morris, Galloway C, 1951, My 18,27:4
Morris, George, 1944, Ap 26,19:5; 1952, Ag 3,60:1
Morris, George A, 1951, Jl 12,25:5
Morris, George D (por), 1942, My 1,19:1
Morris, George D Mrs (Dorothy Craigie Morris), 1924, D 18,21:4
Morris, George F, 1960, Je 22,35:2
Morris, George F Dr, 1918, F 26,13:5
Morris, George H, 1965, Mr 4,31:2
Morris, George I, 1960, N 18,31:2
Morris, George Kenneth Rev Dr, 1918, D 25,15:6
Morris, George L, 1947, N 26,23:3
Morris, George M, 1905, Je 16,9:6; 1954, Ag 22,93:
Morris, George Mrs, 1951, Mr 11,94:5
Morris, George P Gen, 1864, Jl 8,4:6
Morris, George Q, 1962, Ap 24,37:2
Morris, George R Jr, 1944, My 13,19:2
Morris, George U Com, 1875, Ag 17,4:5
Morris, George W, 1939, My 2,23:3; 1940, Ag 25,3
Morris, Gertrude P Mrs, 1939, Ap 14,23:5
Morris, Gilbert A, 1947, My 3,17:4
Morris, Glenn K, 1953, Mr 2,23:5
Morris, Gordon, 1940, Ap 8,19:1
Morris, Gouverneur, 1953, Ag 15,15:3
Morris, Gouverneur Mrs, 1939, Ap 20,23:3
Morris, Grace H Mrs, 1939, Mr 9,21:3
Morris, H Sir, 1926, Je 15,25:4
Morris, Harold, 1964, My 7,37:4
Morris, Harold A, 1947, Ja 18,15:3
Morris, Harold H Mrs, 1950, N 18,15:3
Morris, Harold T, 1963, Ap 4,47:4
Morris, Harold W, 1962, S 23,86:8
Morris, Harrison S, 1948, Ap 13,27:5
Morris, Harrison S Mrs, 1957, Je 24,23:5
Morris, Harry, 1948, Ja 29,24:3; 1968, Ja 5,24:1
Morris, Harry Lord, 1954, Jl 2,19:5
Morris, Harvey D, 1944, Ap 13,19:2
Morris, Henrietta Baldwin Mrs, 1924, O 25,15:6
Morris, Henry, 1905, F 28,9:6
Morris, Henry C (will), 1948, Ag 10,24:4
Morris, Henry J, 1942, F 25,20:3
Morris, Henry L Mrs, 1947, Je 27,21:3
Morris, Henry Lewis Mrs, 1923, N 1,21:4
Morris, Henry W Commodore, 1863, Ag 15,4:6
Morris, Herbert C, 1960, Ap 5,37:2
Morris, Herbert Jacques, 1968, Mr 18,45:4
Morris, Herbert N, 1949, Mr 2,25:4
Morris, Herbert R Mrs, 1960, O 22,23:5
Morris, Herman W, 1943, My 8,15:2
Morris, Hilda, 1947, Je 13,23:4
Morris, Hixon, 1947, D 24,21:3
Morris, Homa L, 1942, S 23,25:4
Morris, Homer L, 1951, N 29,33:4
Morris, Howard, 1939, Ja 29,33:1; 1954, My 2,88:5
Morris, Howard B, 1952, Je 25,29:3
Morris, Howard K, 1956, N 27,37:3

Morris, Hugh M, 1966, Mr 20,86:7
Morris, Hugo, 1950, Ag 10,25:2
Morris, I N, 1879, O 30,5:2
Morris, I Wistar, 1950, D 2,13:6
Morris, Ira K, 1921, Ap 5,19:4
Morris, Ira N (por), 1942, Ja 16,21:1
Morris, Ira N Mrs, 1954, My 15,15:5
Morris, Irving J, 1949, O 20,29:3
Morris, Isaac, 1944, Je 2,15:3
Morris, Isaac J Mrs, 1956, N 6,35:3
Morris, Isaiah S, 1942, F 17,21:5
Morris, J Oliver Mrs (will), 1960, Jl 2,37:1
Morris, J R, 1882, S 26,8:5; 1903, My 25,9:6
Morris, J Vincent, 1942, N 2,21:5
Morris, J W Mrs, 1944, Ap 14,19:3
Morris, J Walter, 1961, Ag 3,23:3
Morris, Jack, 1964, My 30,17:5
Morris, Jack K, 1952, N 1,21:4
Morris, Jacob E K, 1939, Ja 26,21:3
Morris, Jacob H, 1939, Jl 7,17:2
Morris, James B, 1953, My 13,29:2
Morris, James C, 1944, My 6,19:6
Morris, James C Jr, 1954, My 6,33:3
Morris, James E, 1903, O 18,7:6
Morris, James T, 1947, Je 5,25:6
Morris, Jennie Mixer Mrs, 1924, Ja 28,15:4
Morris, Jenny H, 1949, My 1,89:1
Morris, John, 1908, Ag 31,7:6; 1946, Jl 31,27:5; 1947, O 31,23:2; 1955, S 5,11:3
Morris, John A Mrs, 1922, Ap 13,19:6
Morris, John B, 1915, Jl 21,11:4; 1940, N 24,51:4; 1946, O 23,27:3; 1957, Jl 6,15:1
Morris, John C, 1940, N 30,17:1
Morris, John F, 1964, Jl 18,19:4
Morris, John F L, 1939, Ja 28,15:5
Morris, John H, 1942, N 25,23:5; 1948, Ag 4,21:5; 1955, Ag 10,25:4
Morris, John H M, 1910, F 28,9:4
Morris, John Henry, 1910, D 27,9:4
Morris, John J, 1964, Ja 18,23:5
Morris, John L S, 1957, Ag 24,15:1
Morris, John M, 1873, N 29,1:7
Morris, John M Sr, 1950, D 23,15:2
Morris, John Mrs, 1948, Je 5,15:4
Morris, John R, 1945, Mr 14,19:5; 1947, Ag 7,21:2
Morris, John R J, 1942, Ap 11,13:2
Morris, John S, 1938, My 9,17:5; 1947, Ja 4,15:2
Morris, John T, 1915, Ag 16,9:6; 1960, Je 1,39:5
Morris, John W, 1961, F 12,86:3
Morris, John W Mrs, 1949, O 9,92:2
Morris, John W Sr, 1950, My 14,106:5
Morris, Jonas H Mrs, 1948, Ja 3,13:4
Morris, Joseph, 1951, Mr 24,13:6
Morris, Joseph A, 1958, Ag 28,27:1
Morris, Joseph C, 1904, D 11,7:6
Morris, Joseph E, 1961, Mr 16,37:2; 1962, Mr 1,31:4
Morris, Joseph F, 1965, S 7,39:3
Morris, Joseph H Sr, 1952, Mr 16,91:2
Morris, Joseph T, 1950, Jl 1,15:4
Morris, Josephine, 1945, S 8,15:4
Morris, Judson H R Mrs, 1943, D 19,49:2
Morris, Julius A, 1944, F 4,15:1
Morris, L B, 1895, Ag 23,8:5
Morris, L C C, 1909, Je 20,9:4
Morris, L Howard, 1948, Ag 3,26:2
Morris, Langdon E Mrs, 1957, F 1,25:3
Morris, Lardner V, 1941, N 17,19:6
Morris, Lawrence, 1967, N 25,39:1
Morris, Lawrence J, 1949, N 19,17:2
Morris, Leland B, 1950, Jl 5,31:2
Morris, Leo M Sr, 1948, F 24,25:2
Morris, Leonard A, 1940, Ag 29,19:5
Morris, Leroy, 1946, Ja 10,23:2
Morris, Leslie, 1964, N 14,29:3
Morris, Levi H, 1951, My 12,21:2
Morris, Lewis (por), 1940, N 16,17:4
Morris, Lewis G, 1942, N 7,15:1; 1967, Ag 15,36:4
Morris, Lewis Lowndes, 1921, N 13,22:3
Morris, Lewis Mrs, 1953, Ja 11,91:1
Morris, Lewis O Col, 1864, Je 9,2:3
Morris, Lewis S (por), 1944, N 30,23:1
Morris, Lily (Mrs L McDougall), 1952, O 4,17:5
Morris, Llewellyn K, 1946, O 10,27:6
Morris, Lloyd, 1954, Ag 10,19:3
Morris, Lorenzo, 1903, O 3,9:6
Morris, Louis B, 1944, Mr 19,41:2; 1952, Je 29,59:4
Morris, Louis H, 1940, S 8,49:1
Morris, Louis J, 1955, Ap 24,87:1
Morris, Louis Mrs, 1909, Je 17,7:6
Morris, Mabel M, 1938, Mr 3,21:3
Morris, Malcolm Sir, 1924, F 21,17:6
Morris, Manny, 1949, Ap 12,29:2
Morris, Margaret, 1966, Je 9,47:4
Morris, Marion Longfellow, 1924, Ja 24,17:4
Morris, Mark, 1949, N 16,29:2
Morris, Mark L, 1939, My 29,15:4
Morris, Marriott C, 1948, Mr 4,25:5
Morris, Marriott C Mrs, 1950, Mr 26,95:3
Morris, Martha J Mrs, 1943, D 5,49:4
Morris, Martin B, 1965, O 16,27:2
Morris, Martin F Judge, 1909, S 14,9:5
Morris, Mary, 1959, Ja 7,33:1
Morris, Mary B, 1884, O 20,4:6
Morris, Mary F Mrs, 1939, O 27,23:4
Morris, Mary Mrs, 1940, F 28,21:2
Morris, Matthew, 1954, D 17,31:2
Morris, May, 1938, O 18,25:2
Morris, Maynard, 1964, Ja 28,31:4
Morris, McKay, 1955, O 4,28:8
Morris, Michael, 1959, Ap 25,21:4
Morris, Monson Mrs, 1914, Mr 19,9:5
Morris, Montrose W, 1916, Ap 16,21:4
Morris, Moreau Dr, 1904, Mr 18,9:1
Morris, Morgan F Mrs, 1945, My 1,23:3
Morris, Mowbray, 1874, My 17,7:4
Morris, Myron B, 1949, Ja 5,25:3
Morris, Myron I, 1962, Jl 30,23:5
Morris, Myron L, 1963, My 6,29:5
Morris, Nellie Mrs, 1940, D 15,60:2
Morris, Nelson, 1907, Ag 28,7:6
Morris, Nelson Mrs, 1909, S 17,9:5
Morris, Newbold, 1928, D 21,27:5
Morris, Newbold (funl, Ap 3,84:6; will, Ap 16,33:2), 1966, Ap 1,1:7
Morris, Newbold Mrs (Helensk), 1956, Ap 13,25:2
Morris, O W Prof (see also Ag 10), 1877, Ag 13,8:2
Morris, O Wolcott, 1957, D 29,48:7
Morris, Oliver B Judge, 1871, Ap 10,1:3
Morris, Oliver S, 1939, D 31,18:7
Morris, Oregon E Mrs, 1950, D 8,29:4
Morris, Orlando H Col, 1864, Je 9,2:3
Morris, Oscar, 1951, Ag 17,17:4
Morris, Oscar H, 1939, Ja 3,18:1
Morris, Othniel J Jr, 1960, F 25,29:4
Morris, Otto M, 1959, O 4,86:1
Morris, P Hollingsworth, 1940, F 24,13:4
Morris, Pattie C K Mrs, 1939, Mr 7,21:2
Morris, Paul, 1957, Ja 4,23:3
Morris, Percival E, 1952, N 2,88:1
Morris, Philip, 1947, S 10,27:3
Morris, R R, 1881, S 7,2:4
Morris, Ralph S, 1945, Jl 18,27:6
Morris, Ray, 1961, My 20,23:2
Morris, Raymond A, 1944, Mr 3,15:1
Morris, Rbot F Mrs, 1966, Ap 30,31:3
Morris, Reginald O, 1961, Ag 25,25:4
Morris, Rhys H, 1956, N 23,27:3
Morris, Richard, 1865, F 19,6:4; 1951, S 20,31:2
Morris, Richard H, 1941, Ap 10,23:5
Morris, Richard J, 1945, Ap 17,23:3
Morris, Richard L, 1954, Jl 5,11:4
Morris, Richard Mrs, 1954, Ap 2,27:4; 1962, O 14,86:1
Morris, Robert, 1874, My 4,1:7; 1951, O 24,31:1; 1954, My 8,17:6
Morris, Robert C (por), 1938, O 14,23:1
Morris, Robert C (will), 1939, Ja 31,19:1
Morris, Robert C, 1953, D 20,77:1
Morris, Robert C Mrs, 1958, O 11,23:1
Morris, Robert F, 1939, F 8,23:5; 1950, Jl 3,17:7
Morris, Robert H, 1865, O 23,5:1; 1942, O 20,21:4
Morris, Robert Mrs, 1950, Mr 10,28:4
Morris, Robert Sylvester Dr, 1925, Je 19,19:7
Morris, Robert T (por), 1945, Ja 10,23:1
Morris, Robert W, 1945, My 28,19:6
Morris, Roland S (por), 1945, N 24,19:1
Morris, Roland S Mrs, 1950, F 23,28:2
Morris, Rudolph E Mrs (Marketa), 1965, My 26,47:1
Morris, Russell G, 1960, O 13,37:4
Morris, S Arthur, 1942, Ja 6,23:6
Morris, S Arthur Mrs, 1939, Ja 18,20:2
Morris, Sallie W B Mrs, 1915, D 20,11:5
Morris, Samuel, 1908, O 25,13:6; 1947, F 8,17:3; 1947, Mr 21,21:3
Morris, Samuel B, 1962, Mr 7,35:1
Morris, Samuel D Ex-Judge, 1909, N 1,11:4
Morris, Samuel E, 1954, Ag 24,21:3
Morris, Samuel L Rev Dr, 1937, My 11,25:2
Morris, Samuel Mrs, 1958, D 3,37:3
Morris, Samuel R, 1923, F 5,15:6
Morris, Samuel R Mrs, 1946, N 4,25:5
Morris, Samuel W, 1941, N 30,68:3
Morris, Seymour, 1921, S 28,19:5
Morris, Sophia S Mrs, 1940, Ap 6,17:3
Morris, Stanley P, 1948, Ag 23,17:3
Morris, Stephen P, 1951, Ap 17,29:3
Morris, Stewart E, 1947, Je 11,27:5
Morris, Stuyvesant F, 1948, Mr 23,25:2
Morris, Stuyvesant F Jr, 1925, Ap 10,19:5
Morris, T W Mrs, 1938, My 21,15:2
Morris, Theodore B, 1944, Jl 11,15:1
Morris, Thomas, 1912, Ja 14,II,16:2; 1916, F 2,11:4; 1920, My 4,11:1; 1939, Mr 24,21:5; 1950, S 5,27:3
Morris, Thomas F, 1943, D 9,27:5; 1944, Ap 7,19:4; 1944, N 21,25:3
Morris, Thomas Francis Xavier, 1907, Mr 14,7:5
Morris, Thomas H, 1949, Jl 26,27:3
Morris, Thomas H Bp, 1874, S 3,4:7
Morris, Thomas J, 1944, My 20,15:6; 1945, Jl 1,17:2
Morris, Thomas J Mrs (C Finnell), 1963, N 16,27:1
Morris, Thomas M Rev, 1968, F 25,77:1
Morris, Thomas Mrs, 1943, Ap 27,23:4
Morris, Thomas P, 1951, N 7,29:5
Morris, Thomas Watkin, 1924, Ap 16,23:5
Morris, Thomas Y, 1872, F 18,1:6
Morris, Tom, 1908, My 25,7:2
Morris, Uncle Benny, 1904, Ja 23,9:5
Morris, Victoria Mrs (will), 1938, S 30,23:7
Morris, W E, 1878, O 12,5:4; 1933, N 27,17:3
Morris, W G Maj, 1884, F 19,5:5
Morris, W H Mrs, 1881, N 22,8:3
Morris, W L, 1880, Jl 8,8:3
Morris, W Norman, 1939, S 7,25:4
Morris, W Reed, 1953, Mr 3,27:4
Morris, W V, 1931, Jl 18,13:1
Morris, Walter, 1955, Ja 18,27:5
Morris, Walter A, 1964, My 23,23:4
Morris, Walter A Mrs (I Patricola), 1965, My 25, 41:4
Morris, Walter G, 1940, N 14,23:4
Morris, Walter S Mrs, 1966, Jl 27,39:3
Morris, Watson B, 1956, Mr 20,23:5
Morris, Wayne, 1959, S 15,39:3
Morris, William (por), 1896, O 4,9:3
Morris, William, 1945, Ap 3,19:3; 1946, Ag 8,21:4
Morris, William A, 1946, F 21,21:5
Morris, William A Sr, 1951, S 1,11:2
Morris, William C, 1940, Ap 11,25:4; 1954, N 17,31:2
Morris, William C F, 1960, Ap 30,23:6
Morris, William D, 1940, Je 5,25:3
Morris, William E, 1937, Mr 23,23:1; 1948, S 23,29:4; 1949, Ja 21,21:2
Morris, William F, 1952, F 6,29:5; 1955, D 27,23:3
Morris, William F Gen, 1921, F 8,7:4
Morris, William F Jr Mrs, 1947, My 18,60:2
Morris, William H, 1916, My 26,11:4; 1937, N 22, 19:6; 1941, D 10,25:5; 1944, Ag 31,17:1; 1948, O 9, 17:4; 1949, O 9,94:3; 1965, Ag 28,21:3
Morris, William J, 1937, Ap 14,25:5; 1950, F 7,27:4; 1958, N 5,39:1
Morris, William J Jr, 1958, O 26,89:1
Morris, William J Jr Mrs, 1941, My 7,25:6
Morris, William L, 1945, D 11,25:4
Morris, William Mrs, 1945, Jl 15,15:3; 1954, N 9,27:2; 1959, Mr 8,87:2
Morris, William P, 1942, D 17,29:2
Morris, William P Mrs, 1957, My 23,33:3
Morris, William R (Viscount Nuffield),(will, O 3,-71:5), 1963, Ag 22,27:1
Morris, William R Mrs, 1937, Je 23,25:2
Morris, William S, 1955, Ap 12,29:4; 1967, Ap 12,47:3
Morris, William T, 1946, F 7,23:2; 1950, Ja 8,77:1
Morris, William V Mrs, 1947, Ag 28,23:4
Morris, Wilson Cooper, 1921, D 14,17:6
Morris & Killanin, Lord, 1901, S 9,7:6
Morris-Roe, Elizabeth Mrs, 1907, D 27,7:6
Morrisette, Frank O, 1951, N 20,31:2
Morrisette, Kenneth Capt, 1949, Je 13,37:4
Morrisey, Francis J, 1949, Mr 17,25:3
Morrisey, Helen (Sister Aloysia Concepta), 1954, F 7,88:2
Morrisey, John H, 1957, Ap 6,19:6
Morrisey, Richard C, 1968, Jl 10,40:1
Morrisey, William G Jr, 1953, Ap 4,13:3
Morrish, Will F, 1955, Ap 27,31:2
Morrisine, A (Mrs N H Van Sauter), 1942, My 15, 19:3
Morrison, A Cressy, 1951, Ja 10,27:2
Morrison, A Cressy Mrs, 1946, My 5,46:4
Morrison, Adriene Mrs, 1940, N 21,29:3
Morrison, Alice W Mrs, 1940, Je 29,15:6
Morrison, Allan, 1968, My 24,47:3
Morrison, Amos C Mrs, 1963, O 9,40:4
Morrison, Andrew, 1943, O 23,13:3
Morrison, Anna V, 1943, Ja 13,23:2
Morrison, Anna W, 1950, Mr 13,21:5
Morrison, Archie B, 1958, Ja 25,19:2
Morrison, Arthur B, 1951, O 10,23:4
Morrison, Arthur J, 1947, Ja 10,22:2
Morrison, Augusta Lady, 1905, F 18,6:1
Morrison, Aulay, 1942, F 28,17:5
Morrison, Bartholomew J, 1962, Je 7,35:2
Morrison, Benjamin Y, 1966, Ja 26,37:5
Morrison, Cameron, 1953, Ag 21,17:4
Morrison, Cameron Mrs, 1950, My 27,17:4
Morrison, Carl F, 1954, My 6,33:4
Morrison, Caroline T, 1954, O 30,17:5
Morrison, Charles, 1950, Jl 27,25:5; 1957, Mr 23,19:3
Morrison, Charles A, 1941, Ap 20,43:1
Morrison, Charles C, 1966, Mr 4,33:1
Morrison, Charles E, 1957, Jl 2,27:3
Morrison, Charles H, 1947, Je 5,25:2
Morrison, Charles King, 1920, O 19,11:3
Morrison, Charles L, 1960, Jl 5,31:5
Morrison, Charles L Mrs, 1959, Ap 25,21:5
Morrison, Charles M, 1950, Ja 15,84:4
Morrison, Charles Mrs, 1940, N 13,23:4
Morrison, Charles R, 1942, Je 27,13:4
Morrison, Charles S, 1948, N 26,23:4
Morrison, Charles W, 1959, D 9,45:4
Morrison, Chester B, 1959, My 9,21:2
Morrison, Chester L, 1966, Je 22,47:5
Morrison, Clark Jr, 1957, Mr 9,19:5
Morrison, D, 1878, N 10,6:7
Morrison, D W, 1951, Ag 11,11:4
Morrison, Daniel, 1870, Ap 12,4:7
Morrison, Daniel L, 1940, Ap 3,23:5
Morrison, Daniel S, 1945, Mr 21,24:2
Morrison, David Mrs, 1953, O 7,29:2
Morrison, deLesseps Mrs, 1959, F 27,25:4

Morrison, deLesseps S (funl, My 27,39:1), 1964, My 24,1:6
Morrison, Dennia A, 1966, S 26,41:3
Morrison, Dennis J, 1925, Mr 3,23:5
Morrison, Donald A, 1948, Ag 6,17:3
Morrison, Donald H, 1959, Mr 18,37:2
Morrison, Dorothy J, 1953, N 5,34:6
Morrison, Edward A, 1950, O 14,19:3
Morrison, Edward L, 1938, O 25,23:3
Morrison, Edward O, 1940, N 21,29:3
Morrison, Edward W, 1939, N 25,17:4
Morrison, Edward Whipple Bancroft Sir, 1925, My 29, 17:4
Morrison, Edwin Vedder Dr, 1968, Ag 7,43:2
Morrison, Eleanor V Mrs, 1938, My 26,25:3
Morrison, Ella, 1913, F 10,11:4
Morrison, Elmer J, 1948, N 7,89:1
Morrison, Ernest W, 1940, Ja 5,20:3
Morrison, Frank (por), 1949, Mr 13,76:3
Morrison, Frank A, 1947, Ap 19,15:5
Morrison, Frank B, 1958, Ap 8,29:4
Morrison, Frank E, 1949, S 5,17:2
Morrison, Frank S, 1945, Jl 24,23:2
Morrison, Frank W, 1952, Ag 12,19:4
Morrison, Franklin J, 1952, Mr 5,29:1
Morrison, Fred B, 1959, O 23,29:2
Morrison, Frederick J, 1938, My 25,23:1
Morrison, Frederick J Mrs, 1957, N 19,33:4
Morrison, G Elliott, 1938, D 2,23:4
Morrison, George, 1950, Ag 12,13:1
Morrison, George A, 1947, S 8,21:4
Morrison, George A E, 1939, Mr 4,15:3
Morrison, George Austin, 1916, F 27,17:5
Morrison, George D, 1957, Ag 9,19:1
Morrison, George Dr, 1920, My 31,11:3
Morrison, George E, 1945, Jl 4,13:6
Morrison, George F, 1943, O 22,17:3
Morrison, George M, 1960, My 21,23:5
Morrison, Harley J, 1950, O 9,25:4
Morrison, Harold A, 1953, N 13,27:1
Morrison, Harold F Mrs, 1950, S 29,27:1
Morrison, Harry F, 1957, Ag 17,15:4
Morrison, Hazel, 1968, Ja 11,37:1
Morrison, Helen A, 1908, Jl 30,5:6
Morrison, Henrietta L, 1949, Ja 1,11:8
Morrison, Henry C, 1942, Mr 25,21:1; 1945, Mr 20, 19:5
Morrison, Henry Clay Bp, 1921, D 22,15:5
Morrison, Henry Prentiss, 1918, D 18,15:4
Morrison, Herbert B, 1956, My 1,33:4
Morrison, Herbert Mrs, 1953, Jl 12,65:4
Morrison, Herbert W, 1964, N 18,47:3
Morrison, Horace B, 1937, Ja 28,6:3
Morrison, Howard, 1967, My 5,39:3
Morrison, Howard Mrs, 1959, N 8,89:1
Morrison, Hugh, 1946, D 29,35:5
Morrison, Hugh F Mrs, 1953, Mr 2,23:1
Morrison, Hugh T Mrs, 1939, Je 16,23:5
Morrison, Irving, 1924, Ag 28,17:6
Morrison, Isidore D (por), 1938, O 3,15:1
Morrison, Isidore D Mrs, 1944, N 27,23:3
Morrison, J Rutherford, 1939, Ja 10,19:5
Morrison, James, 1939, Je 5,12:6; 1957, My 22,33:3
Morrison, James A, 1950, Mr 19,92:3
Morrison, James C Mrs, 1946, My 25,15:5
Morrison, James D, 1950, Ap 7,25:3
Morrison, James F, 1957, Mr 24,86:1
Morrison, James F Mrs, 1956, F 29,31:4
Morrison, James F Rev, 1916, Ag 27,17:5
Morrison, James H, 1949, Ja 19,27:2
Morrison, James L, 1959, Jl 21,29:4
Morrison, James M, 1880, D 20,8:2
Morrison, James Mrs, 1960, Ag 27,19:7
Morrison, James P, 1941, F 21,19:5
Morrison, John, 1916, Ja 31,11:3; 1938, Je 20,15:4; 1956, S 15,17:3
Morrison, John B, 1952, F 16,13:5
Morrison, John D, 1943, D 19,49:1
Morrison, John E Jr, 1966, N 24,35:3
Morrison, John G Mrs, 1962, Je 26,33:4
Morrison, John H, 1949, Ag 27,13:4
Morrison, John Harrison, 1917, Ag 29,9:6
Morrison, John J, 1939, D 17,49:3; 1952, Ja 6,92:6
Morrison, John J H, 1947, O 30,25:3
Morrison, John L, 1957, N 22,25:3
Morrison, John W, 1945, S 11,23:2; 1952, Jl 28,15:4; 1955, S 7,31:2
Morrison, Joseph, 1954, D 26,25:6
Morrison, Joseph A, 1938, O 26,23:5
Morrison, Joseph E, 1943, F 23,21:2
Morrison, Joseph G, 1939, N 24,23:5
Morrison, Joseph M, 1938, My 23,17:5
Morrison, Joseph P, 1957, Ag 15,21:4
Morrison, Kenneth L, 1959, D 18,29:2
Morrison, Lacey H, 1941, S 22,15:5
Morrison, Lacey Mrs, 1948, Je 19,15:3
Morrison, Lawrence R, 1950, Ag 14,17:6
Morrison, Lee, 1941, Ap 1,23:2
Morrison, Lewis, 1906, Ag 20,6:6
Morrison, Mark, 1964, O 18,89:2
Morrison, Mark S Mrs, 1964, Ja 23,31:5
Morrison, Martin D, 1944, Jl 11,15:2
Morrison, Marvin B, 1958, S 29,27:5
Morrison, Mary Mrs, 1938, D 8,5:4
Morrison, Matthew A, 1949, N 5,13:5
Morrison, Maurice, 1917, Ag 29,9:4
Morrison, Max, 1951, Ag 19,86:4
Morrison, Merlin C, 1943, O 14,21:4
Morrison, Michael J, 1944, D 26,19:3
Morrison, Michael J Mrs, 1952, N 30,88:7
Morrison, Morris, 1917, Ag 31,7:4; 1947, Jl 25,18:2
Morrison, Morris Mrs, 1943, Je 29,19:1
Morrison, Murray, 1948, My 24,19:2; 1957, Ja 11,23:2
Morrison, Murray C, 1949, N 28,27:5
Morrison, Norman, 1949, Ap 5,29:1
Morrison, Phoebe Dr, 1968, O 2,39:2
Morrison, Priestly (por), 1938, Ja 27,21:1
Morrison, Ralph W, 1948, Ap 5,21:3
Morrison, Raymond, 1961, Ap 29,23:5
Morrison, Richard J, 1924, N 14,19:5
Morrison, Richard James, 1874, My 25,2:6
Morrison, Richard M, 1954, Je 27,68:3
Morrison, Robert B, 1958, Je 27,25:6
Morrison, Robert F, 1943, O 17,49:2
Morrison, Robert H, 1956, My 29,27:2
Morrison, Robert J, 1916, Ja 10,11:4; 1942, Je 10,21:2
Morrison, Robert Lord, 1953, D 26,13:3
Morrison, Roger L, 1952, Mr 25,27:2
Morrison, Rosabelle, 1911, D 20,13:5
Morrison, Russell, 1956, Ag 14,25:3
Morrison, Russell D, 1947, Je 17,28:4
Morrison, Samuel A, 1947, Ap 25,21:3; 1956, Ap 7,19:6
Morrison, Samuel A Mrs, 1962, O 23,37:1
Morrison, Samuel O, 1949, Jl 29,21:3
Morrison, Staats D, 1967, Mr 3,35:3
Morrison, Stanley, 1955, Jl 25,19:5
Morrison, Thomas, 1946, O 27,60:7; 1950, S 24,104:5
Morrison, Thomas H, 1914, Mr 7,11:6
Morrison, Thomas J, 1942, Jl 30,21:4; 1946, Ag 1,23:4
Morrison, Thomas V, 1948, F 27,21:1
Morrison, Wilbur L Mrs, 1946, My 10,19:4
Morrison, William, 1866, Ag 21,6:1; 1944, S 16,13:6; 1947, F 2,57:2; 1947, My 4,60:6; 1951, S 10,21:4; 1965, Jl 22,31:4
Morrison, William E, 1958, Ag 10,93:3
Morrison, William E Mrs, 1961, Ja 14,23:1
Morrison, William F, 1953, Ap 25,15:4; 1956, Mr 4, 88:1
Morrison, William H, 1942, Mr 8,42:3
Morrison, William J, 1951, Je 4,27:4
Morrison, William J Jr, 1954, Mr 2,25:6
Morrison, William John Dr, 1914, My 23,11:6
Morrison, William Mrs, 1940, S 8,49:1
Morrison, William Norman, 1921, S 1,15:4
Morrison, William P, 1950, Ap 13,29:4
Morrison, William R, 1944, O 17,23:4
Morrison, William R Mrs, 1946, Ap 28,44:3
Morrison, William Ralls Col, 1909, S 30,9:4
Morrison, William Rev, 1915, Ja 8,11:4
Morrison, William S, 1954, S 7,25:1
Morrison, William S (Viscount Dunrossil), 1961, F 3, 25:1
Morrison, William T, 1912, Jl 23,9:4; 1948, My 4,25:1
Morrison, William W, 1960, Ap 19,37:1
Morrison, wm W Mrs (H Stewart), 1961, My 7,87:1
Morrison, Zaidee L, 1953, Ag 31,17:4
Morrison of Lambeth, Lord (Herbert Morrison), 1965, Mr 7,82:2
Morrisroe, Patrick, 1946, My 29,23:4
Morriss, Clarence T, 1952, Jl 8,27:4
Morriss, Ruth M, 1961, Jl 14,23:6
Morriss, T G B, 1944, Ag 6,38:3
Morriss, William H, 1939, D 1,23:3; 1961, Ag 12,17:3
Morriss, William H Mrs, 1951, Mr 15,29:2
Morrissey, Andrew Rev Dr, 1921, My 29,22:4
Morrissey, Augustine, 1951, Mr 24,13:4
Morrissey, Clara Mrs, 1953, My 22,27:2
Morrissey, Daniel C, 1944, Je 15,19:5
Morrissey, Daniel E, 1949, O 28,24:2
Morrissey, David A, 1947, O 21,23:4
Morrissey, Edward M, 1958, My 17,19:1
Morrissey, George F, 1950, Ap 4,29:3
Morrissey, Harry, 1937, N 3,24:2
Morrissey, Helen, 1941, O 24,24:2
Morrissey, Helen Sister, 1953, Ap 10,21:3
Morrissey, Hugh C, 1951, D 6,33:1
Morrissey, James C, 1945, O 7,45:1
Morrissey, James G, 1943, O 7,23:3
Morrissey, James J, 1947, Ja 21,23:3
Morrissey, James R, 1953, Ap 4,13:4
Morrissey, James W, 1917, Mr 30,11:6
Morrissey, John, 1878, My 2,1:7
Morrissey, John D, 1925, N 2,23:4
Morrissey, John F, 1941, O 8,23:5
Morrissey, John J, 1946, Jl 31,27:1; 1961, Ja 30,23:4; 1963, My 18,27:3
Morrissey, John L, 1943, N 22,19:2
Morrissey, John P, 1946, Je 7,21:8; 1958, N 22,21:3; 1960, N 22,35:4; 1966, O 31,35:1
Morrissey, John R, 1940, My 31,19:3
Morrissey, Joseph A, 1950, My 4,27:3
Morrissey, Joseph L, 1939, S 14,23:2
Morrissey, Mary C Mrs, 1941, S 5,21:4
Morrissey, Maurice, 1945, Ap 9,19:2
Morrissey, Michael A, 1955, Ja 7,21:4; 1964, Ap 20, 29:3
Morrissey, Michael J, 1942, Ja 13,19:2
Morrissey, Michael Mrs, 1948, F 17,26:3
Morrissey, Michael N, 1937, Jl 31,15:5
Morrissey, Patrick H, 1916, N 29,11:5
Morrissey, Paul C, 1965, Je 12,31:4
Morrissey, Peter J, 1946, N 15,24:3; 1950, Mr 17,24:
Morrissey, Peter J Mrs, 1948, My 18,23:4
Morrissey, Raymond L, 1958, F 19,27:3
Morrissey, Richard, 1942, S 6,30:7
Morrissey, Thomas E Sr, 1940, Ja 4,23:5
Morrissey, Thomas F, 1961, Ap 28,31:1
Morrissey, Thomas Mrs, 1954, My 11,29:5
Morrissey, Will, 1957, D 18,35:1
Morrissey, William, 1946, S 27,23:3
Morrissey, William H Sr, 1947, My 20,25:6
Morrissey, William J Mrs, 1944, My 19,19:6
Morrissey, William T, 1941, O 24,24:2; 1951, N 7,29:
Morrissey, William T Mrs, 1948, Ag 29,56:4
Morrisson, Norman J, 1960, S 27,37:2
Morrissy, John L, 1951, Ja 24,27:1
Morritt, Walter, 1942, Je 11,23:4
Morrix, Marie G Mrs, 1937, F 25,23:4
Morron, John H Rev, 1923, F 12,13:4
Morron, John R, 1950, Je 26,27:2
Morrongiello, Sal Mrs, 1958, Ja 20,23:4
Morros, Boris M, 1963, Ja 10,15:6
Morrow, A J, 1877, Jl 3,8:1
Morrow, Albert S, 1960, F 28,83:1
Morrow, Alice, 1940, My 10,23:4
Morrow, Arthur R, 1942, Ag 14,17:6
Morrow, Benjamin F, 1958, O 28,35:2
Morrow, Caroline Mrs, 1909, N 23,9:4
Morrow, Charles A, 1939, Ja 12,19:2
Morrow, Charles E Rev, 1920, Ag 10,13:5; 1920, Ag 13,9:5
Morrow, Charles S Mrs, 1943, Ag 11,19:3
Morrow, Christopher R, 1953, F 4,27:1
Morrow, Clarence E, 1937, Je 7,19:4
Morrow, Cornelius Wortendyke Dr, 1923, Mr 30,17:
Morrow, Curtis G, 1945, My 18,19:5
Morrow, D W, 1931, O 6,1:8
Morrow, David W, 1951, F 8,23:7
Morrow, Doretta, 1968, F 29,37:4
Morrow, Dwight W Mrs (funl plans, Ja 25,25:2; funl Ja 27,23:5), 1955, Ja 24,23:2
Morrow, Dwight W Mrs (est tax appr filed), 1956, O 12,32:2
Morrow, E Boyd, 1946, Jl 14,37:2
Morrow, Edgar S, 1946, O 1,23:4
Morrow, Edwin P Mrs, 1957, S 9,25:4
Morrow, Francis J, 1941, S 15,17:6
Morrow, Frederick A, 1948, F 14,13:3
Morrow, Frederick K, 1953, My 31,72:6
Morrow, G H Judge, 1877, Jl 10,4:7
Morrow, George, 1955, Ja 20,31:3
Morrow, George K (por), 1941, My 18,43:1
Morrow, George S, 1942, My 16,15:4
Morrow, Harry Smith, 1918, Mr 5,11:5
Morrow, Helen H, 1953, N 8,89:1
Morrow, Henry W, 1946, Jl 21,40:2
Morrow, Honore W (por), 1940, Ap 13,17:3
Morrow, Isabelle, 1940, Ap 5,21:2
Morrow, Jack A, 1945, S 5,23:2
Morrow, James A, 1941, N 29,17:2
Morrow, James A Sr, 1945, D 13,29:1
Morrow, James E, 1948, Ja 15,23:1
Morrow, James E Mrs, 1940, Jl 8,17:4
Morrow, James McClintock, 1906, D 3,9:4
Morrow, Jay J Brig-Gen, 1937, Ap 18,II,9:1
Morrow, John B, 1956, Ap 11,33:2
Morrow, John C, 1955, Je 29,29:4
Morrow, John H H, 1957, Je 1,17:2
Morrow, John T, 1924, Ap 20,22:1
Morrow, John W, 1963, Ag 11,85:1
Morrow, Joseph A, 1948, Ag 25,25:2
Morrow, Joseph R, 1962, Ap 21,20:6
Morrow, Lester W W (por), 1942, N 17,25:2
Morrow, Owen J, 1956, Ap 26,33:5
Morrow, Prince A Dr (est), 1913, N 6,11:5
Morrow, Ralph L, 1947, Ja 22,23:5
Morrow, Rising L, 1944, Ap 1,13:2
Morrow, Robert H, 1947, Jl 25,17:2
Morrow, Robert L, 1960, Jl 8,21:5
Morrow, Samuel T, 1939, Je 27,23:5
Morrow, Thomas, 1967, F 27,29:2
Morrow, Thomas H, 1950, Mr 1,27:3
Morrow, W, 1931, N 12,25:1
Morrow, Walter, 1949, Jl 16,13:1
Morrow, William, 1940, Jl 19,19:6
Morrow, William Bryce Rev, 1908, My 2,9:4
Morrow, William M, 1944, Jl 23,35:2
Morrow, William O Jr, 1966, O 18,45:2
Morsbach, Frederick Mrs, 1950, F 7,27:3
Morsch, Edwin C, 1960, Ag 31,29:1
Morsch, Henry W, 1940, Jl 31,17:4
Morschauser, Joseph J Mrs, 1939, My 30,17:3
Morschhauser, William A, 1940, D 5,25:4
Morse, A B (see also Jl 18), 1876, Jl 24,3:3
Morse, Albert S, 1958, Jl 27,61:4
Morse, Albert W, 1947, D 13,15:4; 1950, N 26,90:
Morse, Alfred A, 1954, Je 12,15:3
Morse, Allan Fuller Mrs, 1915, O 11,9:5
Morse, Amalia F Mrs (will), 1939, Ja 13,20:2

Morse, Amasa, 1918, Mr 15,13:5
Morse, Anson D Prof, 1916, Mr 15,11:5
Morse, Anson E, 1966, My 13,41:4
Morse, Anthony W, 1942, Ag 30,43:2
Morse, Arthur, 1967, My 17,47:2
Morse, Arthur E Sr, 1953, F 21,13:2
Morse, Arthur G, 1938, N 8,23:4
Morse, Arthur H, 1950, Ja 27,24:2
Morse, Arthur W, 1954, O 21,27:5
Morse, B G, 1884, S 16,2:3
Morse, Benjamin F, 1948, Ag 10,21:2
Morse, Bernard J, 1949, O 7,27:5
Morse, Bryan, 1939, Ja 24,19:4
Morse, C Frederick, 1957, My 26,92:3
Morse, C H, 1927, Je 6,21:3
Morse, C W, 1933, Ja 13,15:1
Morse, Cady R, 1941, O 14,23:2
Morse, Cecelia F, 1939, My 2,23:1
Morse, Charles A, 1940, My 21,23:3
Morse, Charles C, 1939, Ap 13,23:5; 1949, Je 7,31:1
Morse, Charles F, 1956, Ag 6,23:3
Morse, Charles F Dr, 1920, O 10,22:3
Morse, Charles H, 1921, My 6,13:4; 1938, F 11,24:3; 1948, Jl 2,21:6
Morse, Charles H Sr, 1959, Ag 25,31:5
Morse, Charles H 3d, 1949, Jl 10,60:1
Morse, Charles L, 1962, Jl 16,23:4
Morse, Charles L Mrs, 1940, Jl 18,19:5
Morse, Charles O, 1938, D 4,60:7
Morse, Clark T, 1953, S 20,86:4
Morse, Clinton R, 1942, D 27,34:5
Morse, Donald H, 1955, F 17,27:1
Morse, E Rollins Mrs, 1920, My 2,22:3
Morse, Edmond S, 1959, Ja 29,27:5
Morse, Edward Fleet, 1913, N 12,9:7
Morse, Edward H, 1938, Ag 9,19:5
Morse, Edward K, 1947, My 10,13:5
Morse, Edward Lind, 1923, Je 11,13:4
Morse, Edward Sylvester (funl D 23,19:4), 1925, D 21,21:4
Morse, Edwin F, 1953, My 5,29:2
Morse, Edwin H, 1951, Ag 24,15:3
Morse, Edwin K, 1942, My 30,15:6
Morse, Ella J Mrs, 1940, My 19,43:3
Morse, Ella P Mrs, 1937, F 17,21:1
Morse, Ellsworth B, 1954, D 8,35:1
Morse, Ernest C, 1938, O 19,23:3
Morse, Frank C, 1956, S 2,56:5
Morse, Frank H, 1953, Mr 8,91:1
Morse, Frank H Mrs, 1937, Ag 2,19:3
Morse, Frank L, 1952, My 9,23:2; 1954, My 22,15:3
Morse, Frank R rev, 1904, Mr 31,9:6
Morse, Frederick A, 1968, N 26,47:3
Morse, Frederick E Mrs, 1963, Ja 5,8:2
Morse, Frederick R, 1943, Ag 7,11:3
Morse, George D, 1910, D 24,9:6
Morse, George H, 1905, Mr 6,7:5; 1949, Je 5,92:3
Morse, George J, 1951, Ag 2,21:4
Morse, George L, 1924, N 9,7:2
Morse, George P, 1959, Ap 18,23:5
Morse, George S, 1942, Ag 29,15:1; 1942, S 7,19:5
Morse, George W (por), 1941, Jl 22,20:2
Morse, Glenn R, 1956, Jl 23,23:5
Morse, Glenn T, 1950, Je 23,25:3
Morse, H G, 1903, Je 3,9:5
Morse, Harmar, 1947, Jl 17,19:3
Morse, Harmon Northrop Dr, 1920, S 9,11:2
Morse, Harold J, 1952, My 1,29:4
Morse, Harold R Mrs, 1947, F 5,26:1
Morse, Harold S Mrs, 1943, O 2,13:5
Morse, Harriet B H Mrs, 1937, Je 8,25:5
Morse, Harry F, 1919, O 10,13:3
Morse, Haven H, 1950, Je 7,58:2
Morse, Henry F Mrs, 1924, D 13,15:3
Morse, Herbert J, 1940, F 20,21:3
Morse, Herbert R, 1953, F 22,60:4
Morse, Herbert W, 1948, D 10,25:2
Morse, Hermann N Mrs, 1962, Mr 3,21:3
Morse, Hiram B, 1952, S 14,86:7
Morse, Horace H, 1959, Je 18,31:4
Morse, Howard H, 1912, Ja 3,13:5
Morse, Howard M, 1963, Je 2,84:8
Morse, Irving H, 1953, S 10,25:2
Morse, J B, 1883, S 17,5:5
Morse, Jacob C, 1937, Ap 13,25:2
Morse, James Edwards Finley, 1914, S 10,9:5
Morse, James F, 1925, My 2,15:5
Morse, James H, 1943, Je 15,21:5
Morse, James R, 1943, S 5,28:7
Morse, James Rolland, 1921, D 24,11:5
Morse, Jamin S, 1945, O 5,23:2
Morse, Jay C, 1906, Ag 23,7:7
Morse, Jerome Edward Lt-Com, 1923, N 1,21:4
Morse, John A, 1955, Ja 26,25:5
Morse, John H, 1950, O 1,104:7
Morse, John L, 1940, Ap 4,23:3
Morse, John Milton, 1916, S 13,9:6
Morse, John P, 1944, D 25,19:2
Morse, John R, 1946, Je 15,21:1
Morse, John T Jr, 1937, Mr 28,II,8:4
Morse, Joseph H, 1953, Ag 11,27:2
Morse, Joseph M, 1949, D 31,15:3
Morse, Josiah, 1946, Mr 23,13:4
Morse, Katherine, 1937, D 6,27:1
Morse, L C, 1936, Jl 15,19:4
Morse, Lady, 1946, S 21,15:3
Morse, Lawrence B, 1963, My 7,43:3
Morse, Lee, 1954, D 17,31:2
Morse, Lester L, 1953, N 7,17:2
Morse, Lewis C, 1964, Je 9,35:4
Morse, Lynn E, 1944, N 15,27:1
Morse, Magham Mrs, 1943, Je 17,21:3
Morse, Marshall S, 1958, Ja 21,26:6
Morse, Merton D, 1968, My 17,47:2
Morse, Michael J, 1968, S 25,47:1
Morse, Oliver Cromwell Rev, 1922, My 7,28:2
Morse, Perley (will, My 23,11:5), 1942, Ap 26,39:1
Morse, Perley Mrs, 1937, O 22,19:5
Morse, Philip S, 1953, Mr 2,23:5
Morse, R C, 1926, D 26,II,7:1
Morse, Richard C, 1963, S 15,86:1
Morse, Richard W, 1955, Ja 28,19:2
Morse, Robert, 1947, Je 27,21:4
Morse, Robert F, 1947, Ja 25,17:4
Morse, Robert H, 1964, Ap 13,29:4
Morse, Robert H Mrs, 1948, Je 27,52:5
Morse, Robert J, 1945, Mr 1,21:5
Morse, Robert T, 1964, F 20,29:4
Morse, Robert W, 1967, Je 24,29:4
Morse, Roland E, 1966, Je 23,39:3
Morse, Roy B, 1953, O 15,33:2
Morse, S F B Prof (trb, Ap 5,8:3), 1872, Ap 3,5:2
Morse, Samuel, 1946, Je 22,19:3; 1957, Jl 7,60:7
Morse, Samuel F, 1943, Ap 22,23:3
Morse, Samuel F B Jr, 1956, O 29,20:7
Morse, Sherman, 1963, O 16,45:4
Morse, Sidney E, 1948, Ja 1,23:3
Morse, Sidney Edward, 1871, D 24,3:5
Morse, Simon, 1945, Ja 3,17:4
Morse, Sterne, 1960, Jl 4,15:5
Morse, Theodore, 1924, My 27,21:5
Morse, Theodore Mrs, 1953, N 11,31:5
Morse, Verranus Dr, 1904, Mr 12,9:4
Morse, Walter E Mrs, 1944, Ja 30,38:4
Morse, Walter G, 1919, N 14,13:2
Morse, Walter L, 1954, Mr 12,21:5
Morse, Wilbur A, 1949, My 24,28:5
Morse, Wilbur Jr, 1955, Mr 2,27:5
Morse, William A, 1925, Ja 27,13:2
Morse, William F, 1958, F 18,27:4; 1966, O 22,31:1
Morse, William I, 1952, Je 6,23:5
Morse, William I Mrs, 1951, Je 11,25:4
Morse, William R, 1939, N 12,48:6
Morse, Willis E, 1949, Ap 25,23:4
Morse, Winfield L, 1959, Je 23,33:2
Morse, Withrow, 1951, F 11,88:6
Morsell, Herndon, 1937, S 19,II,6:5
Morsell, Samuel R (cor, Jl 17,60:8), 1955, Jl 13,25:2
Morshauser, C, 1926, D 31,13:1
Morshead, Leslie J, 1959, S 26,23:2
Morsheimer, C G, 1941, Ag 30,13:5
Morsman, Edgar M Jr, 1951, Ja 22,17:1
Morss, C A, 1927, Jl 6,25:3
Morss, Charles Anthony, 1903, Jl 28,7:6
Morss, Franklin C, 1940, D 14,17:2
Morss, Herbert R, 1945, F 13,23:5
Morss, Herbert R Mrs, 1961, Je 7,41:1
Morss, Jeannette Mrs, 1942, My 20,19:3
Morss, John W, 1939, Je 5,17:3
Morss, Samuel E, 1903, O 22,1:6
Morss, Stephen B, 1939, Mr 7,21:2
Morsztyn, Helena, 1954, My 23,89:2
Mort, Paul R, 1962, Mr 13,88:4
Morta, Carlo C, 1954, O 9,17:2
Mortati, Frederick, 1968, Mr 28,47:2
Mortel, Jan C A M van de, 1947, D 23,23:1
Mortell, John T, 1940, My 28,23:1
Morten Alex Mrs, 1958, O 24,33:4
Mortensen, Carsten P, 1952, S 23,33:5
Mortensen, Hans F, 1943, My 14,19:2
Mortensen, Jess, 1962, F 20,36:1
Mortensen, William, 1965, Ag 14,23:4
Mortenson, Karine Mrs, 1946, Ja 1,28:2
Mortenson, Peter M, 1959, N 9,31:5
Mortera, David R, 1957, Je 12,35:4
Morterud, Bernt G, 1960, Ag 2,10:6
Morthimer, Guy V, 1942, Mr 21,17:2
Mortier, Arnold, 1885, Ja 25,10:3
Mortimer, Charles W, 1958, S 15,21:5
Mortimer, Clarence L, 1964, O 8,43:4
Mortimer, Edmund, 1944, My 25,21:6
Mortimer, Ernest, 1937, D 21,23:2
Mortimer, F C, 1936, Ja 28,19:1
Mortimer, Francis J, 1944, Ag 1,15:2
Mortimer, Frank C, 1955, Ap 8,21:4
Mortimer, Frederick E, 1944, My 31,19:2
Mortimer, George N, 1960, Jl 26,29:3
Mortimer, Harry, 1958, S 21,87:1
Mortimer, Henry Colt, 1912, O 1,13:5
Mortimer, J K, 1878, S 19,8:2
Mortimer, James, 1911, F 25,11:6
Mortimer, James D, 1950, Jl 23,56:4
Mortimer, James S, 1944, My 23,23:3
Mortimer, John H, 1939, Jl 20,19:2
Mortimer, John N, 1951, N 29,33:3
Mortimer, Joseph P, 1961, N 28,32:7
Mortimer, Lee, 1963, Mr 2,7:5
Mortimer, Lee Mrs, 1954, D 19,84:1
Mortimer, Lillian, 1946, D 20,23:3
Mortimer, Richard, 1882, My 31,5:4
Mortimer, S, 1932, Mr 25,17:2
Mortimer, Stanley G (por), 1947, Ap 6,60:1
Mortimer, Stanley Mrs, 1944, D 18,19:5
Mortimer, Walter M, 1945, My 24,19:3
Mortimer, William M, 1956, Ja 18,31:5
Mortimer, Wyndham, 1966, Ag 27,29:1
Mortimore, Edwin B Mrs, 1957, Mr 4,27:4
Mortimore, Pauline, 1903, Ag 19,2:3
Mortison, Carl L, 1963, My 12,87:1
Mortland, Walter G, 1956, Je 16,19:5
Mortlock, Bertram J, 1967, Mr 1,43:4
Mortola, Albert J Mrs, 1960, Ag 19,23:5
Mortola, Alexis J, 1964, Ap 23,39:4
Morton, A, 1869, O 20,5:4; 1885, F 14,5:3
Morton, A C, 1876, Ja 16,2:7
Morton, Ada, 1922, Ag 17,13:4
Morton, Albert I, 1944, Je 2,15:2
Morton, Alvin C, 1871, F 27,4:7
Morton, Alvin D, 1940, S 26,23:5
Morton, Annie R, 1924, N 22,15:5
Morton, Arthur C, 1959, Ag 22,17:3
Morton, Arthur S, 1950, D 14,35:5
Morton, Arthur V, 1949, Mr 29,25:4
Morton, Benjamin A, 1955, S 26,23:5
Morton, Byron B Sr, 1959, Ag 15,17:4
Morton, Charles, 1939, Jl 19,19:6; 1943, F 9,23:4; 1950, F 11,15:5
Morton, Charles Beatty Col, 1922, Ja 17,17:3
Morton, Charles Brig-Gen, 1914, D 21,9:4
Morton, Charles I, 1961, Jl 25,27:4
Morton, Charles R, 1964, O 1,35:3
Morton, Charles R Mrs, 1957, N 9,27:6
Morton, Charles W, 1967, S 24,84:1
Morton, Charlotte G Mrs, 1938, D 29,19:3
Morton, Chester S, 1962, Je 21,31:4
Morton, Clifford A, 1947, F 11,27:5
Morton, Commodore, 1873, O 20,2:2
Morton, D Walter, 1941, Jl 7,15:3
Morton, Daniel O, 1957, Je 12,35:2
Morton, David (trb lr, Je 19,34:7), 1957, Je 14,25:1
Morton, David C, 1949, O 14,27:4
Morton, David J, 1949, Mr 31,25:2
Morton, DeWitt P, 1952, S 24,33:5
Morton, Donald R, 1951, Ja 4,29:5
Morton, Donald W, 1954, Ja 5,27:5
Morton, Dudley J, 1960, My 23,29:3
Morton, Duncan R, 1949, F 14,19:2
Morton, Edmund R, 1951, F 21,27:4
Morton, Edward, 1952, Jl 22,25:3
Morton, Eleanor (Mrs E G Stem), 1954, Ja 10,86:1
Morton, Elmer J, 1952, N 15,17:3
Morton, Eugene E, 1951, Ja 29,19:5
Morton, F, 1937, N 2,16:2
Morton, Ferdinand, 1941, Jl 12,13:1
Morton, Ferdinand Q (cor, N 10,31:3), 1949, N 9,27:5
Morton, Frank F, 1945, Ag 1,19:4
Morton, Frederick J, 1941, Je 2,17:5
Morton, Frederick Mrs, 1949, Je 10,27:4
Morton, G Nash, 1925, D 15,25:2
Morton, Gary, 1957, Mr 28,31:5
Morton, Gaylord S, 1939, My 7,III,6:7
Morton, George E, 1953, Ap 10,21:6
Morton, George H L, 1944, Je 10,15:6
Morton, George Mrs (Louise Hawthorne), 1876, Je 29,4:7
Morton, George V Mrs, 1968, My 18,33:1
Morton, Harry K, 1956, My 11,27:3
Morton, Harry M, 1946, My 11,27:2
Morton, Heber, 1954, Ag 10,9:4
Morton, Helen S Mrs, 1952, S 7,87:1
Morton, Henry, 1902, My 10,9:5
Morton, Henry H, 1940, My 4,17:2
Morton, Howard, 1949, My 2,25:5
Morton, Howard E, 1938, D 25,15:2
Morton, Howard M, 1939, Jl 20,19:2
Morton, Hugh H F, 1961, Ap 6,33:4
Morton, J M, 1883, Ap 6,4:7
Morton, J S, 1902, Ap 28,9:4
Morton, James, 1939, Ag 24,19:2
Morton, James (por), 1943, Ag 26,17:1
Morton, James F (por), 1941, O 8,23:1
Morton, James G, 1941, S 27,17:6
Morton, James J (cor, Ap 12,23:2), 1938, Ap 11,15:5
Morton, James M (por), 1940, Je 27,23:1
Morton, James M Ex-Justice, 1923, Ap 21,11:4
Morton, James R, 1939, O 9,19:4
Morton, Jane, 1945, Mr 23,20:2
Morton, John, 1962, O 3,41:4
Morton, John Clark, 1914, Je 30,11:6
Morton, John E, 1947, O 19,66:3
Morton, John E C, 1937, O 16,19:2
Morton, John H, 1949, F 8,26:2
Morton, John S, 1909, S 6,7:6
Morton, John T, 1951, S 2,49:2
Morton, Joseph W, 1959, Ap 10,26:7
Morton, Joy 2d, 1957, Ag 7,27:6
Morton, Lane, 1949, S 13,29:4
Morton, Lawrence J, 1939, F 28,19:5
Morton, Lena, 1904, Je 11,9:7

Morton, Lethia Mrs, 1952, Mr 12,27:2
Morton, Levi P (funl, My 18,11:1), 1920, My 17,15:2
Morton, Levi P Mrs, 1918, Ag 15,11:6
Morton, Lewis E, 1949, D 19,27:5
Morton, Lucy Kimball, 1871, Jl 31,5:7
Morton, M, 1931, Ja 13,27:1
Morton, Manuella D, 1937, O 3,II,8:8
Morton, Marcus, 1939, Mr 21,23:4
Morton, Marcus Gov, 1864, F 7,1:3
Morton, Mark, 1951, Je 26,29:3
Morton, Marmaduke B, 1943, Ap 18,48:7
Morton, Martha, 1925, F 20,17:4
Morton, Mary (will), 1937, D 14,16:6
Morton, O P Sen, 1877, N 2,1:5
Morton, Oliver, 1951, F 3,15:6
Morton, Oliver S, 1957, S 3,27:3
Morton, Oscar G, 1938, Ap 6,23:5
Morton, Paul (funl), 1911, Ja 22,II,11:3
Morton, Paul C Mrs, 1960, Mr 16,37:4
Morton, Paul Mrs, 1968, Jl 4,19:2
Morton, Percy, 1956, D 10,31:4
Morton, Perry W, 1967, Ja 16,41:1
Morton, Phil, 1941, My 31,11:1
Morton, Quinn, 1925, Mr 12,19:4
Morton, Ralph O, 1961, N 19,88:5
Morton, Richard J, 1941, O 30,23:2
Morton, Robert C, 1959, D 18,29:1
Morton, Robert K, 1943, Jl 28,15:3
Morton, Robert W, 1949, N 8,31:3
Morton, Roger W, 1956, Jl 27,21:3
Morton, Samuel F, 1904, Jl 30,7:5
Morton, Samuel P Jr, 1946, N 7,31:5
Morton, Samuel R, 1954, Ap 14,29:5
Morton, Seaborn Mrs, 1952, Ap 26,23:1
Morton, Seth W, 1952, Jl 26,13:6
Morton, Sterling, 1961, F 25,21:4
Morton, Sterling (est tax appr), 1962, N 16,19:2
Morton, T G Dr, 1903, My 21,9:3
Morton, Tom, 1954, Ap 21,29:3
Morton, Vance M, 1959, Ap 21,35:5
Morton, W Brown, 1968, Ja 12,34:6
Morton, W T Dr Mrs, 1904, Ap 22,16:2
Morton, W T G Prof, 1868, Jl 17,5:4
Morton, William, 1943, My 19,25:1
Morton, William C, 1948, N 11,27:5
Morton, William H, 1962, My 17,37:2
Morton, William J, 1942, S 19,15:6; 1956, My 19,19:4
Morton, William James Dr, 1920, Ap 4,22:2
Morton, William M Col, 1917, N 29,13:5
Morton, William S, 1946, Mr 10,46:5
Morton, William T, 1940, S 26,23:5
Morton, William W, 1943, Ja 5,19:4; 1961, N 11,23:3
Moruzi, Alexandre D, 1957, My 4,21:4
Morvay, Sigmond M, 1966, Ja 23,89:3
Morvi, Maharaja of (Yuvral Shri Mahendrasinhji), 1957, Ag 19,19:4
Mory, Austin Van Hoesen, 1953, F 24,25:5
Mosbach, Eric, 1947, Ja 22,23:1
Mosberg, Sammy, 1967, S 1,31:4
Mosby, A T Mrs, 1874, O 29,5:1
Mosby, Ada, 1937, My 4,25:5
Mosby, Charles V, 1942, N 11,25:4
Mosby, Gilbert, 1944, Je 3,13:3
Mosby, Hal B, 1920, D 28,11:4
Mosby, John S Jr, 1915, Ag 27,9:6
Mosby, John Singleton (por), 1916, My 31,13:3
Mosca, Bianca, 1950, Je 20,27:4
Mosca, Enrique, 1950, Jl 7,19:2
Mosca, Gaetano, 1941, N 10,17:4
Mosca, Patsy A, 1957, Je 8,19:6
Moscardo, Jose, 1956, Ap 13,25:3
Moscardo, Jose Mrs, 1964, D 23,30:3
Moscatelli, Joseph J, 1958, Jl 30,29:2
Moschcowitz, Eli, 1964, F 24,25:1
Moschcowitz, Paul, 1942, Ja 6,23:5
Moscheles, Felix, 1917, D 25,15:4
Moschella, Janice, 1946, S 3,21:4
Moschen Hassan, Prince, 1949, O 11,34:2
Moschenross, Antoine Mrs, 1947, N 6,27:3
Moschowitz, Leopold L Mrs, 1945, F 1,23:5
Moscicki, Ignace, 1946, O 3,27:1
Moscicki, Michal, 1961, Mr 5,86:3
Moscos, Constantine J, 1954, S 16,29:5
Moscosco, A A Gen, 1904, Jl 30,7:4
Moscovich, Maurice (por), 1940, Je 19,23:3
Moscovitz, Max, 1940, N 4,19:5
Moscovitz, Morris, 1937, N 7,II,9:3
Moscovitz, Morris Mrs, 1952, Mr 14,23:1
Moscow, Daniel, 1950, D 8,29:4
Moscow, Jacob H, 1955, Ja 10,23:5
Moscow, Samuel H, 1944, My 12,19:5
Moscowitz, Abraham, 1958, F 13,29:5
Moscowitz, Benjamin, 1964, Ja 12,92:3
Moscowitz, Benjamin Rabbi, 1879, N 9,6:7
Moscowitz, Grover M, 1947, Ap 1,27:1
Moscowitz, Jacob, 1948, Ap 8,25:4
Moscowitz, Jennie Mrs, 1953, Jl 27,19:5
Moscowitz, Max, 1947, Ja 13,21:5; 1949, Ag 19,17:1
Moscowitz, Stephen H, 1953, My 16,19:4
Moscrip, Amos D, 1955, S 10,17:2
Moscrip, F A, 1941, Ap 21,19:5
Moscrip, William S, 1959, N 2,63:2
Mose, Billie, 1951, D 28,21:2
Mosedale, Dora A, 1941, O 26,43:1
Mosehart, Henry C, 1947, Ag 10,53:2
Mosel, George A, 1967, D 21,37:2
Moseley, Edward A, 1911, Ap 19,11:5
Moseley, Edwin L, 1948, Je 7,19:4
Moseley, Emma W Mrs, 1941, My 28,25:4
Moseley, Frederick S, 1938, Je 4,15:5
Moseley, Frederick S Jr Mrs, 1958, S 5,27:2
Moseley, George B, 1908, Ja 18,9:6
Moseley, George V, 1960, N 8,29:1
Moseley, George V Mrs, 1950, N 6,27:4
Moseley, Harry L, 1942, O 17,15:1
Moseley, Henry P Dr (will, Ja 17,II,2:2), 1937, Ja 6, 23:5
Moseley, J Rufus, 1954, S 28,29:3
Moseley, John O, 1955, O 12,31:4
Moseley, M P, 1928, Ap 26,27:5
Moseley, M U, 1940, Ja 24,21:4
Moseley, Robert R, 1952, Ja 23,27:3
Moseley, Susan, 1951, O 13,20:1
Moseley, Sydney A, 1961, D 6,47:4
Moseley, William, 1950, N 20,25:4
Moseley, William B Dr, 1914, Je 27,7:6
Moselle, Charles M, 1953, Je 18,32:2
Moselli, Jose, 1941, Jl 23,19:3
Moselsio, Simon, 1963, D 29,43:1
Mosely, Alex, 1881, S 1,2:3
Mosely, Alfred, 1917, Jl 24,11:7
Mosely, Edmund S, 1873, Je 24,1:6
Mosely, Edward B Gen, 1923, Ag 6,11:2
Mosely, Frederick S Mrs, 1952, O 30,31:1
Moseman, Milo C, 1958, O 29,35:5
Mosena, Roscoe L, 1940, Jl 30,19:2
Mosenthal, H, 1877, F 19,5:5
Mosenthal, Herman O, 1954, Ap 25,87:1
Mosenthal, Philip J, 1924, N 19,21:4
Mosenthal, Walter J, 1946, Je 2,44:3
Moser, Alfred A Mrs, 1953, D 30,23:2
Moser, Alfred S, 1967, F 13,33:4
Moser, Annie Mrs, 1907, D 9,7:2
Moser, Arnold, 1937, Ag 31,23:6
Moser, Charles A, 1947, N 7,23:1
Moser, Charles A Mrs, 1946, Ja 23,27:4
Moser, Charles G, 1941, Ap 13,38:4
Moser, Clarence J, 1950, Ag 19,13:5
Moser, Ellsworth, 1965, N 27,31:1
Moser, Frank H, 1964, O 2,37:5
Moser, Frank W, 1959, D 29,26:1
Moser, Guy L, 1961, My 10,45:2
Moser, Hanns, 1953, Jl 16,21:4
Moser, Harry, 1952, S 14,86:2
Moser, Harvey W, 1948, O 30,15:5
Moser, Henry L, 1961, N 4,19:2
Moser, Jacob L, 1946, Ap 7,46:2
Moser, Jacob Mrs, 1946, Ap 10,27:2
Moser, James H, 1913, N 11,13:6
Moser, James H Mrs, 1941, O 1,21:6
Moser, Jeanette K Mrs (por), 1949, O 21,25:2
Moser, O A, 1953, N 11,31:5
Moser, Paul, 1958, Je 18,33:4
Moser, Rudolf, 1960, Ag 22,13:7
Moser, Sol, 1952, D 28,48:4
Moser, Theodore E, 1943, N 19,19:4
Moser, Walter J, 1924, Je 30,15:3
Moser, William, 1947, S 13,11:5
Moser, William J (Mike), 1953, Ap 25,10:6
Moses, Alfred J Mrs, 1948, O 31,88:7
Moses, Andrew (por), 1946, D 24,17:4
Moses, Anna M R Mrs (Grandma Moses),(trb; funl plans, D 15,37:3), 1961, D 14,1:3
Moses, Arthur C, 1949, Mr 13,76:2
Moses, Bernard, 1920, S 24,15:4
Moses, Blanche, 1883, O 27,1:7; 1946, Ag 23,19:3
Moses, Brice J Mrs, 1958, O 20,29:1
Moses, C Hamilton, 1966, Jl 27,39:1
Moses, Carl A, 1964, Ja 26,81:1
Moses, Charles G, 1953, O 10,17:4
Moses, Charles H, 1923, D 27,13:3; 1965, Ja 21,31:1
Moses, David, 1925, My 9,15:3
Moses, Edgar W Mrs, 1957, Je 19,35:1
Moses, Edith W, 1955, N 5,19:1
Moses, Edmund Q, 1966, Ja 2,73:1
Moses, Edward P, 1948, N 10,29:3
Moses, Elisabeth, 1957, D 23,23:1
Moses, Elliott S, 1947, Ja 20,25:4
Moses, Eugene, 1948, O 2,15:2; 1955, Ag 7,72:8
Moses, F J, 1877, Mr 7,5:2
Moses, Frank R, 1944, O 31,19:5
Moses, Franklin J, 1906, D 12,6:2
Moses, Franklin James Col, 1914, S 27,15:6
Moses, Fred C Mrs, 1967, My 23,47:1
Moses, Frederick J, 1950, Ja 24,31:2
Moses, Frederick T, 1959, Ap 8,37:3
Moses, George, 1941, S 14,51:8
Moses, George H (por), 1944, D 21,21:1
Moses, Gustave H, 1906, Ag 18,5:6
Moses, Harry, 1937, S 1,19:3
Moses, Harry M, 1956, Ap 2,23:3
Moses, Harry Mrs, 1956, My 23,31:5
Moses, Henry C, 1950, S 29,27:1; 1954, Ap 28,31:4
Moses, Henry L, 1961, F 19,86:1
Moses, Henry M, 1958, Ja 12,86:3
Moses, Horace A (por), 1947, Ap 23,25:4
Moses, Horace A Mrs, 1962, My 24,35:4
Moses, Horace C, 1940, Ag 16,15:6
Moses, Howard V, 1955, Ja 25,25:1
Moses, Hugh W, 1949, F 12,17:6
Moses, I S Rev, 1926, D 4,17:4
Moses, Isaac, 1955, Ag 26,19:2
Moses, J Arthur, 1949, Mr 8,25:3
Moses, J Morris, 1945, Ja 30,19:3
Moses, James M, 1961, F 26,92:5
Moses, Joel, 1943, My 1,15:2
Moses, John, 1945, Mr 4,38:3; 1967, Ap 3,33:3
Moses, John A, 1949, Ap 2,15:5
Moses, John Robert Rev, 1916, Ap 12,13:4
Moses, John V, 1957, My 31,19:2
Moses, John V Mrs, 1958, Jl 7,27:2
Moses, Julius A, 1938, My 18,21:3
Moses, Karl, 1938, Mr 4,23:2
Moses, Leonard, 1960, Ag 28,83:3
Moses, Lewis, 1945, O 10,21:3
Moses, Lorenzo, 1944, Ja 3,21:1
Moses, Louis, 1941, F 25,23:3
Moses, Louis A, 1952, Mr 27,29:3
Moses, M J, 1934, Mr 30,21:3
Moses, Maurice, 1915, Mr 29,9:4
Moses, Michael, 1962, F 5,31:4
Moses, Morton, 1961, Jl 31,19:3
Moses, Moses H, 1919, O 15,17:3
Moses, Nicholas P, 1952, Ag 15,15:4
Moses, Otto A, 1906, Ja 6,9:4
Moses, Percival R, 1962, Ag 24,25:1
Moses, Raphael J, 1909, D 14,11:4
Moses, Richard C Rev, 1906, Ja 28,7:6
Moses, Robert H Mrs, 1937, My 19,23:6
Moses, Robert Mrs, 1966, S 7,47:2
Moses, Samuel, 1963, My 16,35:5
Moses, Thomas, 1948, F 21,13:3
Moses, Vivian M, 1957, Ja 8,31:1
Moses, William H, 1940, Ag 20,19:5
Moses, William J, 1946, Je 18,25:4
Mosesco, Filippus Mrs (L Doris), 1966, Mr 17,43:7
Moseson, Chaim E, 1955, My 2,21:3
Moseson, Solomon, 1962, Ap 23,29:3
Mosessohn, Moses D (por), 1940, Ag 3,15:3
Mosessohn, N Rev, 1926, D 11,17:4
Mosesson, David S, 1947, Ja 24,21:3
Mosetig-Moorhof, Albert Ritter von Prof, 1907, Ap 27,9:6
Mosettig, Erich, 1962, Je 7,35:3
Mosgrove, George F, 1944, Ja 19,19:3
Mosheim, Albert C, 1966, F 14,29:4
Mosher, A R, 1959, S 27,86:6
Mosher, Alfred F, 1967, F 10,36:1
Mosher, Asa H, 1960, O 6,41:5
Mosher, Burr Burton Dr, 1921, F 1,11:2
Mosher, Charles A, 1943, N 22,19:2
Mosher, Charles F, 1942, My 15,19:3
Mosher, Charles L, 1946, Jl 31,27:4
Mosher, Clelia D, 1940, D 24,15:2
Mosher, Clinton E, 1964, Ja 16,26:1
Mosher, Clure, 1966, Jl 24,60:4
Mosher, E M, 1928, O 17,29:5
Mosher, Edgar S, 1939, O 29,40:7
Mosher, Esek R, 1944, O 31,19:4
Mosher, Frank, 1918, Ag 25,19:1
Mosher, Frank A, 1945, D 1,23:4
Mosher, Frank D, 1952, Je 20,23:5
Mosher, Frank E, 1941, O 23,23:3
Mosher, Frederick F Mrs, 1948, Ap 14,27:5
Mosher, George I Mrs, 1946, Ag 22,27:4
Mosher, Gibson C, 1944, S 28,19:4
Mosher, Gilbert E, 1948, Ag 26,21:2
Mosher, Gouverneur F, 1941, Jl 20,31:1
Mosher, Grace D, 1951, N 5,31:2
Mosher, Harlow B, 1947, Jl 1,25:3
Mosher, Harris P, 1954, N 6,17:5
Mosher, Harry A, 1949, F 12,18:2
Mosher, Herbert S, 1963, D 17,39:1
Mosher, Howard D, 1944, My 28,33:2
Mosher, Howard T, 1919, F 16,20:4
Mosher, Ira, 1968, Mr 10,92:7
Mosher, J Montgomery Dr, 1922, D 8,17:4
Mosher, John C, 1942, S 4,24:2
Mosher, John L, 1944, O 15,45:1
Mosher, Lewis E, 1938, Jl 15,17:3
Mosher, Mary, 1937, F 10,23:3
Mosher, Mary M Mrs, 1938, Mr 5,17:4
Mosher, Matthew V, 1949, My 21,13:2
Mosher, Max, 1958, D 7,88:1
Mosher, Raymond Sr Mrs, 1956, Ja 27,23:3
Mosher, Ten Eyck T, 1949, Ag 8,15:3
Mosher, Theodore D Mrs, 1944, N 22,19:2
Mosher, Thomas Bird, 1923, S 3,13:5
Mosher, W S, 1948, Ja 9,21:2
Mosher, Whiting C, 1951, Ja 2,23:2
Mosher, William B, 1945, D 7,22:3
Mosher, William E (por), 1945, Je 2,15:5
Mosher, William J, 1945, D 27,20:3
Moshier, George I, 1943, O 18,15:5
Moshier, George W, 1939, My 21,III,7:3
Moshinsky, Alex L, 1959, Mr 27,23:1
Mosick, 1950, Je 24,13:2
Mosier, Carl, 1939, Jl 18,19:5
Mosier, Charles I, 1951, Ja 18,27:3

Mosier, Earl F, 1965, Jl 3,19:4
Mosier, Martin H Mrs, 1954, My 28,23:2
Mosier, O M, 1967, F 10,36:1
Mosier, Watson J, 1940, S 1,21:2
Mosiman, S K, 1940, Ja 25,21:4
Mosjoukine, Ivan, 1939, Ja 19,19:4
Mosk, Sanford A, 1960, Jl 9,19:2
Moskaluk, Nicholas, 1952, Jl 4,13:6
Moskin, Charles H, 1940, F 9,19:1
Moskin, Morris Mrs, 1940, My 20,17:2
Moskin, Richard, 1949, D 17,17:1
Mosko, Paul P, 1946, N 17,70:4
Moskovics, Frederick E, 1967, F 19,88:8
Moskovit, Adolph Mrs, 1952, Ag 13,21:5
Moskowa, Princess de la, 1881, Mr 6,10:4
Moskowa, Princess de la (E Bonaparte), 1949, Jl 5, 23:2
Moskowitz, Adolf, 1924, D 2,25:4
Moskowitz, Anna Mrs, 1944, Jl 21,19:2
Moskowitz, Benjamin, 1954, S 13,23:4
Moskowitz, David H, 1962, Ja 21,88:7
Moskowitz, Emanuel J, 1967, Je 5,43:2
Moskowitz, H Leo, 1939, N 1,23:2
Moskowitz, H Mrs, 1933, Ja 3,1:4
Moskowitz, Harry, 1962, Ap 10,43:2; 1966, Ag 9,37:2
Moskowitz, Henry (will), 1938, Ap 27,3:2
Moskowitz, Henry, 1941, Ap 25,19:4
Moskowitz, Herman, 1949, Jl 15,19:5
Moskowitz, Israel, 1954, Mr 24,27:2
Moskowitz, Israel Mrs, 1951, My 18,27:5
Moskowitz, Joseph, 1951, Ja 30,25:2
Moskowitz, Joseph E, 1959, Ap 4,19:3
Moskowitz, Leo, 1953, F 21,13:6
Moskowitz, Louis A, 1947, D 15,25:2
Moskowitz, Louis C, 1958, My 14,33:5
Moskowitz, Max, 1952, S 7,83:1
Moskowitz, Samuel H Mrs, 1963, Je 22,23:5
Moskowitz, Samuel N, 1964, O 15,39:1
Moskvin, Ivan M, 1946, F 18,21:5
Moskvitinoff, Ivan, 1963, Jl 28,65:2
Mosle, A Henry, 1957, My 30,19:2
Mosle, A Henry Mrs, 1963, N 9,25:5
Mosler, Abram, 1944, O 5,23:2
Mosler, Arthur R, 1953, F 27,21:2
Mosler, Edwin H Mrs, 1957, O 26,21:2
Mosler, Edwin H Sr, 1952, Jl 30,24:3
Mosler, Ernest, 1950, S 22,31:5
Mosler, Gustave M, 1946, Je 12,27:2
Mosler, Henry, 1920, Ap 22,11:4
Mosler, Henry Mrs, 1903, My 6,9:5
Mosler, Moses, 1922, Ja 22,22:1
Mosley, Arthur, 1918, My 3,15:5
Mosley, C Lady, 1933, My 17,17:1
Mosley, Dowager Lady, 1938, N 14,19:5
Mosley, Eleanor S, 1947, N 12,27:3
Mosley, James M, 1879, D 14,7:1
Mosley, Juel, 1961, Jl 26,31:1
Mosley, Maud, 1948, Je 21,21:5
Mosley, Richard K, 1951, Ja 20,15:5
Mosley, Thomas J, 1940, Ja 7,48:5
Mosley, William P, 1948, Ja 10,15:4
Moslovitz, Harry S, 1956, My 2,31:5
Mosman, Harry T, 1949, O 25,27:3
Mosman, Herbert, 1948, N 2,25:3
Mosman, M H, 1926, Ja 13,27:2
Mosolov, Vassili P, 1951, F 12,23:4
Mosolov, Victor F, 1949, Je 6,19:4
Mosquera, Bernardino Dr, 1923, O 3,15:3
Mosquera Narvaez, Aurelio Pres, 1939, N 18,17:1
Moss, Abraham L, 1955, D 4,88:4
Moss, Albert, 1943, Ag 16,15:4
Moss, Anton (E Clarke), 1960, Ag 9,27:2
Moss, Arch W, 1941, Mr 17,17:5
Moss, B Franklin, 1947, F 12,25:5
Moss, B S, 1951, D 13,33:2
Moss, Benjamin, 1940, Ja 11,23:4
Moss, Castle P, 1955, F 11,23:4
Moss, Charles Sir, 1912, O 12,11:6
Moss, Clyde S, 1949, N 1,27:5
Moss, Courtlandt D, 1955, Ja 15,13:6
Moss, Courtlandt D Mrs, 1960, S 1,27:3
Moss, David, 1959, My 17,84:5; 1966, F 24,37:1
Moss, Edgar E, 1961, Je 21,37:2
Moss, Edward B (por), 1948, S 24,26:2
Moss, Edward B Mrs, 1958, S 20,19:3
Moss, Edward S, 1964, Je 21,30:3
Moss, Emily Lady, 1941, Mr 23,44:1
Moss, Erving A, 1950, My 15,21:5
Moss, Frank, 1919, N 15,11:3
Moss, Frank (funl), 1920, Je 8,11:3
Moss, Frank H, 1953, Ja 22,23:3
Moss, George A, 1903, S 12,9:6; 1957, F 5,23:1
Moss, George F, 1940, Mr 9,15:3; 1941, Je 10,23:2
Moss, Harry, 1947, D 20,17:1
Moss, Harry M, 1948, S 10,23:3
Moss, Henri, 1952, Ag 24,89:2
Moss, Henry, 1875, Ag 17,4:6
Moss, Herbert J, 1955, Je 26,76:6
Moss, Issac H, 1938, My 31,19:3
Moss, J Calvin, 1937, My 15,19:5
Moss, J Franklin, 1938, F 20,II,8:7
Moss, James E, 1961, S 16,19:3
Moss, Jim Mrs, 1961, D 26,25:2
Moss, Johanna Mrs, 1947, Jl 13,44:8
Moss, John A, 1921, My 6,13:4; 1954, My 23,90:1
Moss, John B, 1950, Mr 18,13:4; 1961, F 1,35:3
Moss, John H, 1941, Mr 11,23:1; 1941, Ap 1,23:5
Moss, John K, 1955, Ja 10,23:3
Moss, John M, 1947, O 1,29:3
Moss, Joseph, 1955, F 18,22:2; 1959, D 31,21:4
Moss, Joseph F (por), 1937, Jl 10,15:5
Moss, Joseph H, 1967, F 13,33:1
Moss, Joseph L, 1905, Ap 22,11:7; 1955, Ja 18,27:1
Moss, L Howard, 1966, N 21,45:2
Moss, Lemuel Rev, 1904, Jl 13,5:5
Moss, Leon V, 1958, Je 8,88:5
Moss, Leonard Mrs, 1945, Je 14,19:2
Moss, Leslie B (por), 1949, Ap 3,76:3
Moss, Leslie B Mrs, 1949, Ap 1,25:3
Moss, Lincoln D, 1945, Je 16,13:4
Moss, Louis J (por), 1948, Mr 19,24:2
Moss, Margaret S, 1964, Ag 1,21:3
Moss, Marvin S, 1946, S 25,27:1
Moss, Mary A Mrs, 1938, Ja 14,23:2
Moss, Maximilian, 1964, Ap 20,29:1
Moss, Mike M, 1947, D 10,31:1
Moss, Neil, 1959, Mr 25,13:2
Moss, Nelson A Mrs, 1951, Je 25,19:5
Moss, Paul, 1950, F 26,76:1
Moss, Paul F, 1954, Je 15,29:5
Moss, Richard J, 1939, Je 12,17:4
Moss, Richard M, 1958, N 9,89:2
Moss, Robert, 1940, Ag 20,19:2
Moss, Robert F, 1964, Ap 24,33:2
Moss, Robert T W, 1949, Ja 6,23:3
Moss, Russell M, 1967, Ja 17,39:2
Moss, S C, 1934, F 24,14:1
Moss, Samuel A, 1960, F 22,17:2
Moss, Sanford A (por), 1946, N 11,27:1
Moss, Sanford A Jr, 1949, Je 19,68:6
Moss, Sidney H, 1949, Ag 9,25:2
Moss, T E, 1942, My 9,13:2
Moss, Theodore Mrs, 1910, Ja 16,II,11:4
Moss, Thomas J, 1941, Jl 26,15:5
Moss, Thomas O, 1939, Je 24,17:1
Moss, Walter E, 1945, Je 23,13:2
Moss, William, 1945, F 20,19:4; 1960, Jl 24,64:5
Moss, William C, 1949, S 20,29:2
Moss, William L, 1957, Ag 14,25:2
Moss, William W, 1939, D 19,26:2; 1949, D 17,17:2
Moss, William W Jr, 1959, Ja 10,17:4
Moss, William W Mrs, 1957, Ag 16,19:5
Mossadegh, Mohammed (other biog details, Mr 6,33:1), 1967, Mr 5,87:1
Mossberg, Frank, 1953, O 16,27:3
Mossberg, Iver O, 1945, F 20,19:4
Mossberg, Joel, 1943, O 18,15:5
Mossbrugger, Herman F, 1938, Ag 20,15:6
Mossburger, Edward, 1924, N 18,25:4
Mosscrop, Alfred M, 1941, Mr 28,23:4
Mosse, Eric P, 1963, Je 20,33:4
Mossell, Nathan F, 1946, O 29,25:4
Mossell, Nathan F Mrs, 1948, Ja 25,56:4
Mosser, Benjamin D, 1948, Jl 21,23:5
Mosser, Charles M, 1952, My 16,23:1
Mosser, Frederick L, 1963, Je 30,56:6
Mosser, J Belmont, 1950, F 14,25:3
Mosser, James K, 1905, F 7,9:5
Mosser, Jean Henri, 1874, N 23,2:4
Mossinsohn, Ben Z, 1942, N 23,23:5
Mossly, Rene, 1947, F 16,57:2
Mossman, Alex H Mrs (Maria M), 1965, Ag 24,31:3
Mossman, Arthur, 1955, Jl 17,60:8
Mossman, Chesley D, 1953, F 14,17:4
Mossman, Donald P Mrs, 1950, Mr 16,31:5
Mossman, Frank E, 1945, Je 13,23:2
Mossman, G Elmer, 1951, Ap 1,93:1
Mossman, Guy M, 1941, N 21,17:2
Mossman, John Malcolm, 1912, Mr 7,11:4
Mossman, John P, 1942, Ap 6,15:1
Mossman, Paul B, 1950, Jl 9,69:3
Mossman, Trevor Mrs, 1955, F 21,2:3
Mossman, William T, 1949, My 6,25:1
Most, August F, 1955, Ap 3,86:5
Most, Johann, 1906, Mr 18,11:5
Most, Philip, 1960, Mr 1,33:1
Mostar, Munir, 1963, N 6,41:3
Mosteller, James B, 1953, Ap 4,13:4
Mostow, Harry L, 1961, Jl 2,33:2
Moszkowski, George A, 1952, F 12,27:4
Moszowski, Moritz, 1925, Mr 10,21:2
Motch, E Franklin, 1955, Ja 7,21:5
Motch, Edwin R, 1947, Je 10,27:5; 1953, Ja 24,15:2
Mote, Carl H, 1946, Ap 30,21:4
Mote, Walter H Sr, 1945, Je 1,15:3
Motenko, Alex B, 1958, N 4,27:2
Motheral, Charles D, 1945, N 11,42:3
Motheral, Theodore A, 1942, Ja 6,13:5
Mothersbaugh, Roland E, 1968, Je 11,44:5
Motherwell, Hiram (por), 1945, D 3,21:3
Motherwell, Larry L, 1966, Mr 1,13:1
Motherwell, W R, 1943, My 25,23:4
Mothner, Flora Mrs, 1925, Jl 17,15:6
Mothner, Samuel H, 1925, Mr 7,13:6
Motl, Emil, 1953, F 21,13:3
Motley, Guy C, 1949, D 29,25:2
Motley, J L (funl, Je 5,1:7), 1877, Mr 31,5:1
Motley, James M Mrs, 1909, N 15,9:3
Motley, John J, 1952, Je 1,84:5
Motley, John L, 1959, Jl 27,25:5
Motley, Lucy B Mrs, 1960, F 12,27:1
Motley, Patrick J, 1952, O 29,31:7
Motley, Patrick J Mrs, 1952, O 29,31:7
Motley, Willard, 1965, Mr 5,30:1
Moton, Jennie B Mrs, 1942, D 27,34:2
Moton, Robert R (por), 1940, Je 1,15:1
Motono, Ichiro Viscount, 1918, S 19,13:7
Motoyama, H, 1932, D 31,15:1
Motsch, George, 1949, Ap 9,17:3
Mott, Abram C Jr, 1953, F 27,21:2
Mott, Albert A Mrs, 1954, Jl 30,17:4
Mott, Alice L, 1943, O 4,17:4
Mott, Basil, 1938, S 8,24:2
Mott, Benjamin B, 1905, Ja 21,9:4
Mott, Benjamin Mrs, 1909, Je 17,7:6
Mott, Bessie Q Mrs, 1957, D 25,31:5
Mott, Charles S, 1943, S 18,17:2
Mott, Chester D, 1952, Ap 2,33:4
Mott, Clarence I, 1952, D 10,35:3
Mott, E Bertram, 1961, S 25,33:6
Mott, Edward Harold, 1920, Ap 8,11:4
Mott, Edwin C, 1937, F 26,21:2
Mott, Elliott B, 1957, Ja 6,88:7
Mott, Francis L, 1944, Ag 26,11:4
Mott, Frank L, 1964, O 24,29:1
Mott, Frank P, 1907, Ag 23,7:4
Mott, Frank S, 1944, Ja 25,19:6
Mott, Frederick Sir, 1926, Je 9,23:3
Mott, G Gen, 1884, N 30,9:1
Mott, Garret, 1946, Mr 14,25:4
Mott, Garret Schenck, 1920, D 5,22:4
Mott, George F, 1947, N 8,17:3
Mott, George Mrs, 1955, Ap 24,86:5
Mott, George W Mrs, 1947, Je 24,23:3
Mott, Guy C Mrs, 1948, Ag 28,15:5
Mott, H S, 1877, Je 9,4:7
Mott, Harold B, 1946, My 15,21:5
Mott, Harvey L, 1960, F 4,31:4
Mott, Henry H Col, 1916, Je 4,21:5
Mott, Henry W Mrs, 1954, Jl 4,30:7
Mott, Herbert A, 1944, Ap 18,21:6
Mott, Hopper S Mrs, 1954, Ap 28,31:3
Mott, Howard S, 1937, Ja 15,22:2
Mott, Isabella T S Mrs, 1941, Jl 31,17:3
Mott, J O Mrs, 1902, Jl 31,9:6
Mott, J Varnum Dr, 1904, Ja 24,6:6
Mott, James W, 1945, N 13,21:1
Mott, Jesse, 1941, F 1,17:5
Mott, Jesse W, 1947, My 14,25:4
Mott, John C, 1872, Ja 2,5:6
Mott, John G, 1942, Jl 24,20:2
Mott, John Owen, 1905, Ag 12,7:5
Mott, John R (funl plans, F 2,27:2; funl, F 8,27:4), 1955, F 1,29:1
Mott, John R Mrs, 1952, S 30,31:5
Mott, John W, 1913, N 11,13:6
Mott, Jordan L Mrs, 1949, Jl 13,27:3
Mott, Jordan Lawrence, 1915, Jl 27,9:5
Mott, Joseph W, 1956, F 10,22:1
Mott, Kenneth, 1951, Jl 8,61:1
Mott, Lawrence S, 1910, Mr 30,12:3
Mott, Lewis C, 1951, O 24,31:2
Mott, Lewis F (por), 1941, N 21,17:1
Mott, Lewis F Mrs, 1948, Je 2,29:2
Mott, Lucretia, 1880, N 12,5:4
Mott, Luther W, 1923, Jl 11,19:6
Mott, Marshall E, 1947, Je 3,25:3
Mott, Morrison, 1940, Ag 16,15:4
Mott, Nathaniel, 1963, O 2,41:1
Mott, Richard W, 1938, Ap 21,19:1
Mott, Robert G, 1904, Jl 8,9:6
Mott, Samuel J, 1942, O 30,19:3
Mott, Sara E, 1937, Ap 1,23:4
Mott, Sarah M, 1952, Ap 28,19:2
Mott, Stephen D, 1944, F 23,19:3
Mott, Thomas B, 1952, D 19,31:1
Mott, Valentine Dr, 1865, Ap 27,4:4; 1918, Je 20,11:5
Mott, W F, 1867, My 4,2:5; 1882, My 26,4:7
Mott, Wallace Capt, 1925, Mr 30,17:4
Mott, Walter H, 1947, F 1,15:2
Mott, William C, 1938, Ap 9,17:2
Mott, William E, 1938, D 7,23:4; 1945, O 7,44:7
Mott, William H, 1904, Ja 24,6:6; 1942, N 10,28:3
Mott-Smith, Geoffrey A, 1960, Ag 20,19:5
Mott-Smith, Harold M, 1948, Mr 29,21:5
Mott-Smith, May, 1952, Je 7,19:6
Mott-Smith, Morton C, 1944, Je 12,19:6
Motta, Angelo, 1957, D 27,19:2
Motta, Giuseppe, 1942, Ja 3,19:6
Motta, Giuseppi, 1940, Ja 23,22:2
Motte, William E Ernest Ludwig de la Count, 1923, S 18,21:5
Mottelay, Paul F, 1907, Mr 20,9:6
Motten, Roger H, 1951, F 8,33:3
Motter, Murray G Mrs, 1952, F 1,21:4
Motter, Orton B, 1953, Ag 6,21:5
Motter, William D B Jr, 1947, Mr 20,27:3
Mottershead, James O, 1948, Jl 26,17:1
Mottet, Henry, 1929, Je 21,25:3

Mottistone, Lord, 1947, N 8,17:3
Mottl, Felix, 1911, Jl 3,7:3
Mottley, William M, 1943, Ag 11,19:4
Mottola, Joseph K, 1947, O 21,23:3
Mottole, Frank R, 1947, My 7,30:4
Mottram, Marjorie, 1950, Ap 8,13:5
Mottram, Thomas Sir, 1937, Mr 25,25:3
Motts, Charles W, 1951, O 23,29:3
Mottur, J Preston, 1964, D 19,29:4
Motz, Albert N, 1937, Ap 6,23:1
Motz, C Henry, 1925, N 15,13:1
Motz, Fred P, 1958, Jl 9,27:3
Motz, George M, 1950, F 18,15:1
Motz, Roger, 1964, Mr 28,19:4
Motz, William J, 1946, Jl 12,17:2
Motzan, Otto, 1937, Ja 16,17:4
Motzenbecker, Peter F, 1951, F 10,13:2
Motzenbecker, William J, 1961, Jl 19,29:1
Motzer, Carlyle E, 1942, Ja 17,17:3
Motzkin, L, 1933, N 8,21:3
Mouakad, George, 1953, S 17,29:5
Mouat, Malcolm O, 1943, Ja 4,15:4
Mouatt, Gerald L, 1949, Mr 24,27:1
Mouery, Frank W, 1950, N 3,27:1
Mouget, Georges Vice-Adm, 1937, Ap 8,23:3
Mougey, Gordon P, 1939, O 10,23:4
Mouk, Robert L, 1943, Jl 25,30:7
Moul, Harry A, 1938, D 31,15:3
Moulan, Frank, 1939, My 14,III,6:7
Moulay Joussef, Sultan of Morocco, 1927, N 18,9:2
Mould, Elmer K, 1950, N 16,31:5
Mould, Elmer W K Mrs, 1955, D 18,92:5
Mould, J W, 1886, Je 16,5:2
Mould, William L, 1949, F 8,25:3
Moulden, Jarvis Mrs, 1961, Ja 25,33:5
Moulder, Walter C, 1967, Je 29,43:2
Moulder, Walter J, 1944, My 31,19:4
Moule, Handley Carr Glyn, 1920, My 9,22:4
Moule, Henry Rev, 1880, F 4,3:4
Moulin, Bp of, 1942, Ap 23,24:3
Moulin, Gabriel, 1945, Ap 11,23:5
Moulin de la Barthete, Henri du, 1948, O 13,25:1
Moulinet, Aline D Mrs, 1955, Ag 12,19:4
Moulinier, Edward P, 1952, Mr 2,93:2
Moulson, George D, 1968, Ap 4,47:3
Moultin, Baron, 1921, Mr 10,13:6
Moulton, Arthur G, 1942, Ap 1,21:5
Moulton, Arthur W, 1962, Ag 19,88:4
Moulton, Benjamin P, 1947, D 2,29:3
Moulton, Charles A, 1946, D 9,25:3
Moulton, Charles D, 1942, Ap 12,45:2
Moulton, Charles R, 1949, D 5,23:4
Moulton, Clinton A, 1954, N 30,29:5
Moulton, David E, 1951, Ap 23,25:4
Moulton, Diana B, 1962, Ag 12,80:1
Moulton, Edith P Mrs, 1952, Je 28,19:3
Moulton, Edward Q, 1941, My 10,15:5
Moulton, Edward S Dr, 1937, D 31,15:2
Moulton, Edward W, 1922, Jl 21,11:6
Moulton, Eliza, 1914, O 9,9:4
Moulton, Emma C, 1910, D 3,11:5
Moulton, F D, 1884, D 5,8:2
Moulton, Forest R, 1952, D 9,33:3
Moulton, Frank I, 1941, S 15,17:2
Moulton, G S, 1882, Je 8,5:4
Moulton, Gilman L, 1953, Je 30,23:1
Moulton, Harold G, 1965, D 15,48:1
Moulton, Harold M, 1960, N 16,41:1
Moulton, Henry H, 1939, F 10,23:1
Moulton, James Eagen Dr, 1909, Je 12,7:4
Moulton, John B, 1946, F 28,23:4
Moulton, John Fletcher Mrs, 1909, Ja 26,9:3
Moulton, LeRoy D, 1952, O 20,33:5
Moulton, Leroy D Mrs, 1959, Ap 21,35:4
Moulton, Louise Chandler Mrs, 1908, Ag 11,5:6
Moulton, Mary A Mrs, 1945, O 2,23:4
Moulton, Onsville J, 1955, Ja 28,20:2
Moulton, Powers, 1953, Ja 26,22:8
Moulton, Richard Green Prof, 1924, Ag 16,11:6
Moulton, Robert E, 1952, Ja 16,25:1
Moulton, Robert H, 1945, D 13,29:5
Moulton, S D (see also Ap 20), 1878, Ap 22,5:4
Moulton, Sherman R, 1949, Je 17,23:1
Moulton, Stanley C, 1951, Je 15,23:4
Moulton, Warren J, 1947, My 8,25:6
Moulton, William H, 1961, D 10,88:5
Moulton, William Sr, 1947, S 5,20:3
Moumie, Felix, 1960, N 4,5:4
Mouncey, Arthur L, 1944, Ag 25,13:5
Mounet-Sully, Jean, 1916, Mr 4,11:3
Mounfort, George C, 1956, Ag 7,27:2
Mounier, Emmanuel, 1950, Mr 24,25:3
Mounier, Henry, 1953, Ag 19,29:5
Mounsey, William R, 1952, Je 20,23:3
Mount, Arnold J, 1942, D 18,27:2
Mount, C H, 1884, D 24,8:2
Mount, Charles A Jr, 1944, Ap 9,34:2
Mount, Elmer M, 1956, My 18,25:3
Mount, Finley P, 1938, Ag 8,13:6
Mount, Frank D, 1944, N 29,23:3
Mount, George A, 1963, Mr 14,39:3
Mount, Helen Mrs, 1921, Ap 4,13:4
Mount, James R, 1953, Ag 19,29:3
Mount, James R Mrs, 1940, Ap 8,19:1
Mount, Judson S, 1950, Mr 26,92:4
Mount, Lillian G, 1945, Ja 7,38:1
Mount, Louise I Mrs, 1937, D 18,21:1
Mount, Mary E Mrs, 1937, D 15,27:4
Mount, Oliver E, 1965, My 3,33:4
Mount, R E, 1880, Ap 2,2:4
Mount, Russell T, 1962, Je 1,28:1
Mount, Russell T Mrs, 1954, Ja 21,31:4
Mount, Sidney, 1868, N 21,4:7
Mount, Walter B, 1948, F 12,23:4
Mount, Wendell H, 1950, Jl 5,31:4
Mount, William E Sr, 1943, S 30,21:3
Mount, William H H Mrs, 1961, O 13,35:1
Mount Edgcumbe, Earl of (Kenelm W E Edgcumbe), 1965, F 12,29:1
Mount Passillo, Count of (A C Nobili), 1950, F 17, 24:2
Mount Pleasant, Frank, 1937, Ap 13,52:3
Mount Pleasant, William, 1954, Ap 18,89:2
Mount Temple, Lord (por), 1939, Jl 4,13:2
Mountain, Arthur R, 1940, Ag 21,19:2
Mountain, David J Mrs, 1943, Ag 20,15:3
Mountain, Edward John Dr, 1924, S 3,17:1
Mountain, Edward M, 1948, Je 24,25:2
Mountain, Elsie, 1945, Ap 22,36:2
Mountain, Frank H, 1939, N 21,26:4
Mountain, George E, 1948, Ja 15,23:1
Mountain, Harold C, 1940, Je 10,17:4
Mountain, Jacob Bishop, 1863, Ja 18,3:1
Mountain, John H, 1967, O 29,85:1
Mountain, Milton T, 1955, Ap 2,17:4
Mountain Chief (lr, Mr 8,IV,9:4), 1942, F 6,7:5
Mountbatten, Alex A (Marquess of Carisbrocke), 1960, F 24,37:2
Mountbatten, Irene Lady (Marchioness of Carisbrooke), 1956, Jl 17,23:5
Mountbatten, Leopold Lord, 1922, Ap 24,15:4
Mountbatten of Burma, Edwina C A A Countess, 1960, F 21,92:5
Mountcastle, R E L, 1913, Ag 10,II,11:5
Mountel, Edward Sr, 1937, F 4,21:4
Mountevans, Adm Lord (E R G R Evans), 1957, Ag 22,27:2
Mountford, Frank T, 1944, O 4,19:1
Mountford, Harry, 1950, Je 5,23:4
Mountford, Thomas A, 1943, F 24,21:2
Mountfort, Arnold G, 1942, Ag 14,17:1
Mountfort, N B, 1883, N 24,5:2
Mountfortt, Wade, 1941, F 19,21:5
Mountifield, Alfred, 1939, My 23,23:6
Mountin, Joseph W, 1952, Ap 28,19:5
Mountjoy, Michael C, 1950, Ap 1,32:1
Mouquin, H, 1933, D 25,1:4
Mouquin, Henri Mrs, 1925, Mr 27,19:6
Mouquin, Henry, 1957, N 13,35:2
Mouquin, Henry F, 1944, Jl 13,17:6
Mouquin, Henry Mrs, 1951, D 11,33:4
Mouquin, John L, 1939, Mr 23,23:5
Mouquin, John L Mrs, 1943, O 20,21:4
Mouquin, Louis G, 1938, D 7,23:6
Mourad, Zade A A, 1953, Mr 30,21:4
Mouradian, Michael K, 1954, Ap 18,89:1
Mourawieff, N Gen, 1881, D 16,5:2
Moure, Jean G E, 1941, D 3,25:5
Mourik-Broekman, Gerrit H van, 1948, Mr 16,27:4
Mouritzen, Einar M, 1952, O 22,27:3
Mouromtseff, Ilia, 1954, My 19,31:4
Mouromtseff, Serge A Prof, 1910, O 21,11:4
Moursund, Walter H, 1959, Ap 4,19:6
Moursund, Walter H Jr, 1959, N 21,23:2
Mousel, Russell C, 1968, D 2,47:2
Mouser, Grant E, 1949, My 7,13:2
Mousette, Alphonse, 1951, S 14,25:4
Mousharrafa, Ali M, 1950, Ja 17,27:4
Mouskos, Christodoulos, 1967, Ja 6,35:4
Mousley, Franklin, 1961, Je 15,43:1
Mousley, George E, 1940, Ag 18,37:3
Mousley, Howard M, 1947, S 26,23:3
Moussman, Boris Mrs (Ex-Princess Galitzin), 1950, N 23,35:3
Moussou, Rene A, 1945, Jl 20,19:5
Moussu, Lucie, 1947, N 4,17:2
Moutenot, Edmond Mrs, 1945, D 1,23:2
Moutet, Marius, 1968, O 30,47:1
Mouthberger, John, 1937, Mr 10,23:4
Moutier, Pierre, 1946, Ag 30,17:5
Mouton, Mark M, 1944, Ag 22,17:6
Mouton, Mother Matilde, 1943, F 8,19:4
Mouton, the Clown, 1941, O 17,23:2
Moutran, Khalil, 1949, Jl 1,19:5
Mouvet, M, 1927, My 19,27:5
Mouvet, Robert J, 1966, Je 25,31:4
Mouw, Hendrik Mrs, 1949, Ja 24,19:2
Mouzilly, Countess de, 1905, My 23,9:6
Mouzinho de Albuquerque, Mecia, 1961, F 12,87:1
Mouzon, Edwin D Bp, 1937, F 11,23:3
Movich, Jacob, 1954, F 13,15:6
Movius, Alice L W Mrs, 1944, D 25,19:5
Movius, Gerald W, 1961, Ja 26,29:4
Mow, William, 1951, Ja 12,27:2
Mowat, Harold J, 1949, Ja 26,25:5
Mowat, Oliver Sir, 1903, Ap 20,7:5
Mowatt, Anna Cora, 1870, Jl 30,1:7
Mowbray, Albert H, 1949, Ja 9,72:1
Mowbray, Edwin T, 1948, Mr 23,25:4
Mowbray, George A, 1959, O 23,29:4
Mowbray, James Edward, 1925, Jl 18,13:5
Mowbray, James N, 1941, N 24,23:6
Mowbray, Louis L, 1952, Je 6,23:2
Mowbray, William R, 1939, Ap 27,25:3
Mowbray and Stourton, Lord (W M Stourton), 196 My 8,31:5
Mowbray-Clarke, John F Mrs (Mary), 1962, N 21, 33:2
Mowel, Abram V, 1948, Ap 5,21:4
Mowell, Abraham S, 1949, F 22,23:2
Mowen, John Henry, 1914, D 29,11:6
Mowen, William H, 1941, Ja 7,23:5
Mower, Arthur C Mrs, 1943, Ja 28,19:4
Mower, Charles D, 1942, Ja 19,17:3
Mower, Edmund C, 1940, Ap 26,21:5
Mower, Edward, 1938, D 1,23:1
Mower, Frank E, 1956, D 14,29:2
Mower, H H, 1943, S 12,52:3
Mower, Penfield Mrs (S M Jordan), 1959, N 22,86
Mower, William D, 1946, Ap 9,27:1
Mowers, Milford, 1942, Ag 28,19:5
Mowers, Raymond A, 1943, Je 8,21:5
Mowerson, Archer J, 1955, O 28,25:2
Mowinckel, Jens G, 1950, Ja 13,23:4
Mowinckel, Johan L, 1943, O 1,19:1
Mowles, Henry J, 1955, My 24,31:4
Mowll, William L, 1948, S 8,29:4
Mowrer, Rufus, 1942, Ja 1,25:4
Mowrey, Burtis E, 1960, S 29,35:4
Mowrey, Harry H, 1947, Mr 21,22:2
Mowrey, Paul Mrs, 1952, F 18,19:3
Mowry, Daniel P, 1955, Ag 3,23:4
Mowry, Harry, 1939, D 14,27:3
Mowshowitz, Samuel J, 1966, My 5,47:1
Mowton, Edward P Mrs, 1950, Je 17,15:4
Mowton, John, 1865, My 13,4:6
Moxey, Albert F, 1953, S 23,32:3
Moxey, Edward P, 1943, Ap 8,23:3
Moxham, Egbert, 1956, Je 19,29:1
Moxham, George, 1944, My 26,3:8
Moxley, Frank W, 1937, O 8,24:2
Moxley, George B, 1955, Mr 17,45:5
Moxley, George W Capt, 1921, Ag 7,22:5
Moxley, Richard I, 1946, O 16,27:5
Moxley, Wiley M, 1957, Ja 29,31:3
Moxley, William F, 1950, Ag 6,73:1
Moxley, William J, 1938, Ag 6,13:4
Moxly, Francis J, 1949, N 22,29:4
Moxom, Howard Osgood Dr, 1919, Mr 10,11:4
Moxom, Jessie B Mrs, 1939, Jl 20,19:7
Moxom, Philip Stafford Rev (funl, Ag 15,17:6), 1923, Ag 14,15:5
Moxom, Walter J, 1959, Ja 14,27:2
Moxon, John R Mrs, 1953, Jl 3,19:5
Moxter, James, 1954, Je 10,31:2
Moy, Dong H, 1948, D 29,22:2
Moy, Frank, 1937, S 18,19:6
Moy, George W V, 1949, F 27,68:8
Moy, William Mrs, 1945, O 26,19:4
Moya, Miguel, 1920, Ag 22,20:5
Moyar, Samuel N, 1952, D 14,91:1
Moye, Donald, 1950, My 5,21:2
Moyer, Albert, 1953, O 14,29:5
Moyer, Andrew J, 1959, F 19,31:4
Moyer, Arthur C, 1943, Ap 5,19:1
Moyer, Ben L, 1964, F 21,27:4
Moyer, Charles S Maj, 1937, O 4,21:5
Moyer, Clarence L, 1950, Je 15,31:3
Moyer, Earl J, 1962, F 21,45:3
Moyer, Elmer L Mrs, 1962, Jl 10,33:1
Moyer, Erwin B, 1951, Ja 14,85:1
Moyer, Fayette E, 1938, Mr 19,15:5
Moyer, Ford, 1948, My 20,29:3
Moyer, Gabriel H, 1939, My 9,23:5
Moyer, George J, 1943, Ap 18,49:1
Moyer, H Allen, 1944, Ja 7,17:2
Moyer, Harry B, 1950, O 10,17:2
Moyer, Harry J, 1961, S 16,19:1
Moyer, Harvey V, 1959, Ag 8,17:5
Moyer, J Cooper, 1955, Ja 22,11:4
Moyer, J W, 1912, Ag 23,9:4
Moyer, James A, 1945, N 30,23:3
Moyer, Luther M, 1944, Ja 26,19:4
Moyer, Melbourne S, 1960, Ap 28,35:2
Moyer, Morris, 1948, My 21,23:4
Moyer, Myron R, 1951, F 27,27:3
Moyer, Purdy B, 1955, Ja 17,23:4
Moyer, Ray E, 1957, N 7,35:4
Moyer, S Russell, 1950, Ag 23,29:4
Moyer, Walter O, 1950, Je 29,29:1
Moyer, Walter W, 1945, Mr 9,19:2
Moyer, William B, 1955, Ag 6,15:5
Moyer, William U, 1938, D 6,23:2
Moyers, James H (funl, S 20,47:3), 1966, S 18,84
Moyers, Leon Mrs, 1959, Ag 29,17:5
Moyes, Emanuel, 1940, Ja 20,15:3
Moylan, Cornelius A, 1946, D 25,29:5
Moylan, David, 1942, My 17,47:4
Moylan, Helen S, 1941, S 24,23:5

Moylan, James R, 1943, O 28,23:3
Moylan, John J, 1955, Jl 12,25:4
Moylan, Patrick, 1945, My 19,19:2
Moylan, Sean, 1957, N 17,86:8
Moyland, John J, 1943, Ag 3,19:3
Moyle, Anselm, 1943, Je 28,21:3
Moyle, Henry D, 1963, S 19,27:2
Moyle, James H (por), 1946, F 21,21:3
Moyle, Richard, 1950, F 7,28:2
Moyle, Richard L, 1950, Ap 26,29:3
Moyle, Wilbert Mrs, 1951, N 6,29:3
Moyles, William P, 1942, Ja 12,15:5
Moynahan, Daniel, 1918, Ap 1,11:5
Moynahan, John J, 1939, F 1,21:5
Moynahan, Lawrence, 1956, Mr 8,8:3
Moynahan, Maurice A, 1957, Mr 14,29:5
Moynahan, Patrick A, 1938, My 2,17:6
Moynahan, Timothy J Jr, 1960, F 22,17:5
Moynehan, Dennis B, 1946, S 26,25:4
Moynier, Gustave, 1910, Ag 23,9:6
Moynihan, Andrew M, 1947, Jl 30,21:3
Moynihan, Daniel C, 1912, S 26,11:4
Moynihan, Edward A, 1959, O 12,19:2
Moynihan, Edward F, 1907, Mr 9,9:6
Moynihan, Edward P, 1940, N 14,23:3
Moynihan, Eugene F, 1960, O 27,37:4
Moynihan, Humphrey Mrs, 1945, F 4,38:2
Moynihan, J Oscar, 1960, F 3,33:1
Moynihan, James H, 1947, Ap 4,23:4
Moynihan, John Mrs, 1963, Jl 21,64:4
Moynihan, Lord, 1936, S 8,27:5
Moynihan, Manus J, 1950, Ap 5,31:1
Moynihan, Margaret N, 1959, Jl 11,19:5
Moynihan, Michael W, 1942, O 5,19:3
Moynihan, Patrick B Lord, 1965, Ap 30,36:7
Moynihan, Patrick H, 1946, My 22,21:3
Moynihan, Richard K, 1953, F 6,20:6
Moynihan, Tim, 1952, Ap 5,15:6
Moyse, Charles Ebenezer, 1924, Je 30,15:3
Moyse, George G, 1951, Mr 16,31:3
Moysey, Arthur E, 1943, F 6,13:5
Moyston, John G, 1962, My 3,33:3
Mozart, George, 1947, D 11,33:5
Mozart, Karl Thomas (Oct 30), 1858, N 24,1:5
Mozdof, Elhanen (Choneh), 1966, Ag 8,27:5
Mozes, Mendel, 1966, Mr 5,27:2
Mozian, Vahan, 1945, Jl 17,13:6
Mozier, Joseph, 1870, O 30,3:6
Mozur, Charles James, 1968, Ap 21,80:4
Mracek, John J Sr, 1948, Jl 1,23:3
Mravlag, V, 1934, My 16,19:1
Mrkvicka, Gustavus A, 1957, Jl 15,19:4
Mrlik, Joseph Mrs, 1947, F 14,21:4
Mroczkowski, Stanley A, 1963, N 8,31:2
Muccia, Carrol A, 1963, Ap 8,47:1
Muccia, Michael R, 1966, D 30,25:2
Muccini, Corrado, 1959, Ap 1,37:2
Mucelli, Louis, 1941, F 24,15:2
Mucerino, John V Mrs, 1962, N 14,39:1
Mucha, Artist, 1939, Jl 18,19:4
Mucha, Caroline, 1958, Ap 3,31:2
Muche, William J, 1947, Mr 30,56:4
Muchmore, G Burton, 1957, Je 1,17:3
Muchmore, George V, 1937, Je 11,23:3
Muchmore, Guy B, 1948, My 22,15:4
Muchmore, James H, 1959, Mr 31,29:3
Muchmore, Willard S (por), 1940, S 23,17:6
Muchnic, Charles M, 1958, N 21,29:3
Muchnick, Edward, 1951, S 17,21:6
Muchow, Albert J, 1950, O 26,31:6
Muck, Ernest F, 1956, N 10,19:5
Muckenfuss, A M, 1941, Ap 18,21:2
Muckenhoupt, Anna, 1939, S 20,27:3
Muckenhoupt, Charlotte F, 1946, N 8,23:3
Muckenhoupt, John L, 1937, Mr 3,23:4
Muckenhoupt, L Brandt, 1945, S 26,23:5
Muckerman, Richard C, 1959, Mr 17,30:5
Muckian, James J, 1947, N 27,31:4
Muckle, Leo A, 1942, Mr 30,17:5
Muckle, M Richard Col, 1915, Mr 31,11:4
Muckley, Ralph W, 1958, Jl 20,65:1
Mucklow, William B, 1943, Je 9,21:2
Mudd, Arthur, 1946, Mr 1,21:3
Mudd, Della M Mrs, 1941, Ja 28,19:4
Mudd, Edward J, 1946, D 24,18:3
Mudd, Harvey S (will, Ap 24,88:1), 1955, Ap 13,29:3
Mudd, Harvey S Mrs, 1958, Ag 25,21:1
Mudd, John P, 1955, My 3,31:5
Mudd, Samuel A Jr Mrs, 1961, F 5,80:3
Mudd, Seely G Dr (will), 1968, Mr 20,15:1
Mudd, Sydney E, 1911, O 22,II,15:4
Mudd, William S, 1942, S 20,40:7
Muddell, Chester M, 1948, O 13,25:2
Muddell, Irving, 1949, O 22,17:6
Muddell Gilbert L, 1950, Je 9,23:6
Mudge, Alden A Jr, 1965, S 11,27:2
Mudge, Alfred E, 1945, Ag 24,20:2
Mudge, Alfred E Mrs, 1963, Ap 29,31:2
Mudge, Alfred Eugene, 1903, Ap 29,9:5
Mudge, E R, 1881, O 2,5:4
Mudge, Edmund W, 1949, Jl 2,15:7
Mudge, Edwin B, 1953, My 24,88:3
Mudge, Frederick P, 1956, Mr 5,23:4
Mudge, Henry U, 1920, Ja 31,11:4
Mudge, John B, 1939, Je 6,23:6
Mudge, Lewis S (por), 1945, Ap 30,19:1
Mudge, Louis J, 1967, Mr 19,92:5
Mudge, Verne D, 1957, Ja 30,29:3
Mudge, William J Mrs, 1942, Jl 14,20:2
Mudge, William L, 1956, Ag 10,17:3
Mudge, William L Jr, 1944, Ag 25,13:5
Mudgett, William C Mrs, 1948, D 10,25:2
Mudrick, Louis, 1952, Je 28,19:1
Mudry, Vasyl, 1966, Mr 21,33:3
Mueck, Otto F, 1952, My 20,25:5
Muecke, Charles, 1947, Ap 28,23:4
Muecke, Edward, 1956, Je 19,29:1
Mueden, Emma, 1958, N 9,88:1
Mueden, George F, 1951, Ag 20,19:4
Muehlberg, Clarence E, 1964, N 18,47:1
Muehlebach, George E, 1955, Ja 12,27:1
Muehlens, Peter, 1943, Je 9,21:5
Muehlhof, C Frank, 1949, Ja 1,13:1
Muehling, John A (por), 1944, Ap 20,19:6
Muehling, Lawrence G Mrs, 1952, Ja 13,88:7
Muehlsiepen, Henry, 1903, Jl 22,7:2
Muehlstein, Herman, 1962, Jl 31,27:4
Muehlstein, Julius, 1950, Je 16,25:3
Muehsam, Alice Freimark Dr, 1968, F 29,37:3
Muehsam, George, 1962, Ap 21,19:5
Muelchi, Frederick, 1961, O 6,35:1
Muelders, Martin Rev, 1925, D 21,21:5
Mueller, Alfred G, 1966, D 20,43:2
Mueller, Alios E, 1956, N 28,35:1
Mueller, Anthony J, 1958, O 21,33:3
Mueller, Armand Dr, 1915, Jl 22,9:4
Mueller, Arthur H, 1941, D 8,23:3
Mueller, Arthur M, 1956, Jl 14,15:2
Mueller, Arthur S Mrs, 1954, Mr 11,31:2
Mueller, Aug H, 1937, F 14,II,9:2
Mueller, August, 1951, My 29,25:4
Mueller, August G, 1946, O 17,23:4
Mueller, Benedict, 1949, D 27,23:2
Mueller, Carl, 1925, Jl 13,17:6
Mueller, Carl F, 1947, Ag 4,17:2
Mueller, Carl H, 1964, Mr 28,19:5
Mueller, Charles, 1944, Je 24,13:2; 1958, N 3,37:1
Mueller, Charles R, 1963, Ja 16,16:1
Mueller, Clifford W, 1950, Ag 19,13:2
Mueller, Edward, 1956, N 8,39:6
Mueller, Edward A, 1951, F 20,25:5; 1958, S 1,13:5
Mueller, Edwin, 1962, O 5,33:3
Mueller, Emil, 1937, Je 9,25:5; 1942, Je 27,13:4
Mueller, Emil Mrs, 1945, My 11,19:2
Mueller, Ernest W, 1950, Mr 29,29:4
Mueller, Ferdinand F, 1948, Je 13,69:1
Mueller, Frank, 1949, O 13,27:1
Mueller, Fred H Mrs, 1958, Ap 18,23:3
Mueller, Fred W, 1955, Ja 31,19:3
Mueller, Frederick R, 1942, S 11,21:2
Mueller, Friedrich, 1942, N 15,45:2
Mueller, Georg A von, 1940, Ap 20,17:4
Mueller, George, 1951, My 8,31:3
Mueller, Gerda, 1951, Ap 30,21:4
Mueller, Gustav Prof, 1925, Jl 11,11:6
Mueller, H, 1931, Mr 21,17:1
Mueller, Hans A, 1962, Jl 25,33:2
Mueller, Harry, 1951, Jl 9,25:6
Mueller, Helen I, 1937, F 26,22:2
Mueller, Henry, 1946, N 12,29:4; 1947, Mr 28,25:6; 1951, N 12,25:5
Mueller, Henry A, 1949, Mr 16,27:2
Mueller, Henry F, 1946, Je 1,13:5
Mueller, Henry J, 1953, F 7,15:3
Mueller, Henry R Dr, 1937, My 4,25:3
Mueller, Herman, 1937, Jl 31,15:6
Mueller, Herman C, 1941, S 23,23:1
Mueller, Hugo A, 1951, My 2,13:4
Mueller, Ignatius Rabbi, 1925, S 9,25:5
Mueller, J George Mrs, 1952, Jl 4,13:4
Mueller, Jacob P, 1943, My 26,23:4
Mueller, John, 1944, Ja 12,23:3; 1946, My 30,21:4
Mueller, John H, 1954, F 18,31:1; 1965, S 2,31:1
Mueller, Joseph E, 1950, F 24,24:1
Mueller, Joseph P Mrs, 1948, Mr 18,27:1
Mueller, Logan E, 1940, F 19,17:1
Mueller, Louis Mrs, 1951, Mr 3,13:3
Mueller, Lucien W, 1953, O 8,29:2
Mueller, Matthew, 1953, O 25,39:5
Mueller, Max, 1938, Ap 20,23:6
Mueller, Max B, 1957, Je 5,35:3
Mueller, Max Prof, 1900, O 29,7:1
Mueller, Michael A, 1950, Mr 30,29:3
Mueller, Nanette L, 1958, Ja 19,87:1
Mueller, Nicholas G, 1949, Ag 22,21:1
Mueller, Oscar, 1941, Ap 25,19:3
Mueller, Otto, 1942, S 14,15:4; 1946, Ag 11,45:1; 1960, Jl 1,25:3
Mueller, Pablo P, 1960, Mr 2,37:1
Mueller, Paul A, 1956, N 9,29:4
Mueller, Paul F, 1945, Ap 9,19:1
Mueller, Peter, 1951, Ja 3,27:4
Mueller, Pius, 1956, Ag 31,17:3
Mueller, R Sterling Dr, 1968, S 30,47:2
Mueller, Renate, 1937, O 26,23:3
Mueller, Richard H, 1947, Mr 22,13:2
Mueller, Robert F, 1959, Ja 7,33:2
Mueller, Rudolph, 1967, F 19,88:8
Mueller, Samuel, 1957, O 20,86:5
Mueller, Sebastian, 1938, N 18,22:3
Mueller, Theodore F, 1958, Ap 2,31:1
Mueller, Theophil H, 1961, Jl 29,19:5
Mueller, Trugott J, 1948, Mr 10,28:2
Mueller, W, 1928, Ag 24,19:4
Mueller, Wilhelm, 1945, O 19,23:2
Mueller, William, 1952, Je 17,27:2
Mueller, William A, 1960, O 11,45:2
Mueller, William E, 1947, S 23,25:2
Muellner, Adolph F, 1942, D 17,37:4
Muench, Albert A, 1955, Ap 15,23:3
Muench, Aloisius J Cardinal (funl, F 20,35:1), 1962, F 16,29:1
Muench, C Lawrence, 1950, Mr 7,27:6
Muench, Emily E J Mrs, 1937, My 25,27:2
Muench, Frank B, 1952, Jl 4,13:6
Muench, Joseph C, 1942, Je 1,13:3
Muench, Julius T, 1950, S 17,104:3
Muench, Theresa B Mrs, 1955, My 26,31:3
Muenchinger, Gustave, 1915, F 12,9:6
Muenchinger, Gustave A Mrs, 1921, Ja 17,11:4
Muennick, John, 1942, Ja 20,19:2
Muensterberg, Hugo Prof (por), 1916, D 17,19:1
Muenzen, Charles J, 1949, D 10,17:1
Muenzen, Joseph B, 1964, Je 3,43:4
Mues, A William, 1946, S 16,5:4
Mueser, William, 1950, Ag 5,15:5
Mufson, Abraham, 1963, My 26,92:6
Mufson, Samuel, 1957, Ja 15,29:4; 1964, Ap 15,39:3
Mugavero, Angelo Mrs, 1952, Je 14,15:2
Mugnier, Arthur, 1944, Mr 12,38:4
Muhammad Ali, M, 1931, Ja 5,7:3
Muhlbach, Louise, 1873, S 29,1:7
Muhlbacher, Anthony, 1941, Mr 4,10:3
Muhleman, Donald C, 1947, N 20,29:2
Muhleman, Elis M, 1942, My 27,23:5
Muhleman, Maurice L, 1913, Je 13,9:5
Muhlenberg, Charles R, 1953, Jl 17,17:3
Muhlenberg, E D Maj, 1883, Mr 12,4:7
Muhlenberg, F A Dr, 1867, Jl 12,2:6
Muhlenberg, George F, 1958, S 26,28:1
Muhlenberg, John Cameron Brig-Gen, 1916, Mr 15, 11:5
Muhlenberg, W A, 1877, Ap 9,5:4
Muhlenberg, William F Dr, 1915, Ag 26,9:6
Muhlenbrock, Herman J H, 1953, Ag 4,21:4
Muhlenfeld, August, 1946, Ja 23,27:5
Muhlethaler, Paul, 1959, F 7,19:1
Muhlfeld, Frank J, 1954, Mr 24,27:4
Muhlfeld, George O (por), 1948, Jl 9,19:1
Muhlfeld, George O Mrs, 1961, N 3,35:1
Muhlfeld, John E, 1941, Je 20,21:3
Muhlfelder, Joseph L, 1938, Ap 30,15:3
Muhlhofer, Elizabeth, 1950, Ap 13,29:5
Muhlig, Paul, 1946, Jl 31,27:4
Muhling, Francis J, 1944, Ap 10,19:3
Muhlker, Herbert, 1942, Mr 2,19:5
Muhlmann, Ulrich, 1952, F 28,27:5
Muhlstock, David, 1967, S 26,47:1
Muhlstock, Rudolph, 1964, Jl 10,29:3
Muhs, Frederick R, 1949, F 10,27:3
Muhs, Henry Lewis, 1913, D 22,9:5
Muhtar Bey , A, 1934, Jl 4,16:6
Muilenburg, Cornelius W, 1954, O 3,35:3
Muir, Alex J, 1941, O 25,17:1
Muir, Alexander, 1906, Je 28,7:6; 1947, S 28,60:3
Muir, Arthur T Mrs, 1959, Ap 1,37:2
Muir, C H, 1933, D 9,15:1
Muir, Charles S Mrs, 1944, Ap 25,23:4
Muir, David, 1943, Mr 7,38:2
Muir, Edward J, 1947, O 15,28:3
Muir, Edwin, 1959, Ja 5,29:4
Muir, Edwin H, 1959, Ja 16,27:3
Muir, George A, 1941, D 20,19:2
Muir, George W, 1924, My 22,17:6
Muir, Harry B, 1939, Ja 26,21:2
Muir, Hugh Sir, 1906, Ja 2,9:6
Muir, J, 1935, Ja 24,19:4
Muir, James, 1918, Ap 19,13:6; 1960, Ap 11,31:1
Muir, James A, 1953, Ap 21,27:4
Muir, James I, 1964, My 10,83:2
Muir, John, 1882, Mr 9,5:2; 1914, D 25,11:5; 1947, Ag 5,25:8
Muir, John D, 1952, D 21,52:7
Muir, John W, 1960, Ja 10,86:1
Muir, Joseph, 1903, Mr 6,9:5
Muir, Joseph Dr Mrs, 1901, D 31,7:5
Muir, Lida K Mrs, 1958, My 6,35:2
Muir, Ownie D Jr, 1937, O 24,II,9:2
Muir, Ralph D Mrs, 1952, Ap 2,33:6
Muir, Ramsay (por), 1941, My 5,17:4
Muir, Raymond D, 1954, Je 24,27:4
Muir, Robert, 1959, Ap 1,37:4
Muir, Robert W, 1938, D 2,23:3
Muir, Thomas M, 1955, F 24,27:1
Muir, Wallace, 1947, Ap 20,60:3
Muir, William, 1965, D 20,35:3
Muir, William H, 1964, Mr 10,37:2
Muir, William W, 1954, Mr 27,17:2
Muirhead, Anthony J, 1939, O 30,17:2

Muirhead, Brian R, 1949, O 21,25:1
Muirhead, Charles, 1949, S 25,92:6
Muirhead, J F, 1934, Ap 7,15:4
Muirhead, James H H, 1954, N 22,23:4
Muirhead, John, 1905, Ap 8,9:5
Muirhead, John E, 1958, O 21,33:4
Muirhead, Stanley N, 1942, S 16,23:3
Muirhead, Walter G, 1921, Ja 13,13:5
Muirhead, William, 1939, O 6,25:2
Muirhead, William B, 1958, Mr 25,33:4
Muirhead, William B Mrs, 1952, N 4,29:2
Muirhead, William P, 1960, My 29,56:3
Muirhead, William Y, 1939, S 5,23:5
Muirhead-Gould, G C, 1945, Je 30,17:6
Muirheid, C H, 1883, My 9,4:7
Muirheid, Charles H, 1942, Ap 17,17:3
Muirheil, Benjamin C, 1945, My 19,19:1
Muiry, James M, 1961, Jl 11,31:2
Mujica, Francisco J, 1954, Ap 14,29:2
Mujica, Jacques, 1950, N 14,14:5
Mukerjee, Subroto, 1960, N 10,7:1
Mukhina, Vera I, 1953, O 8,29:2
Mulane, Phil H, 1948, Jl 21,23:4
Mulcahey, James J, 1949, My 23,23:2; 1960, Ja 17, 86:4
Mulcahey, Mary O Mrs, 1942, My 27,23:4
Mulcahy, Bernard J, 1948, Ag 23,17:1
Mulcahy, Cornelius, 1940, Jl 20,15:5
Mulcahy, Edmond L, 1942, Ag 4,19:4
Mulcahy, Edward J, 1949, My 27,21:5
Mulcahy, Frank H Sr, 1967, F 12,92:7
Mulcahy, James E (funl, Jl 10,33:3), 1962, Jl 7,17:3
Mulcahy, James J Mrs, 1943, Ap 23,17:3
Mulcahy, John C, 1950, Ag 10,25:5
Mulcahy, John J, 1942, N 20,24:3
Mulcahy, John J (por), 1948, S 21,27:2
Mulcahy, John J Mrs, 1950, Ag 8,29:3
Mulcahy, John S, 1946, S 8,46:4
Mulcahy, John V, 1944, Ag 4,13:6
Mulcahy, Joseph A (por), 1944, S 7,23:4
Mulcahy, Joseph J, 1952, D 13,21:4
Mulcahy, Mary, 1961, My 26,33:3
Mulcahy, Maurice A, 1941, Jl 1,23:4
Mulcahy, Michael, 1947, D 26,15:3
Mulcahy, Michael J, 1938, Jl 25,5:6; 1942, F 11,21:4
Mulcahy, Michael Mrs, 1955, Ja 27,23:1
Mulcahy, Patrick J, 1953, Ja 15,27:5
Mulcahy, Robert E, 1952, Ja 17,27:3
Mulcahy, Thomas A, 1941, Mr 6,21:4
Mulcahy, Thomas R, 1957, Ap 28,86:1
Mulcahy, Timothy J Mrs, 1948, Ag 28,15:1
Mulcahy, William F, 1957, N 13,35:1
Mulcahy, William J Rev, 1919, Ag 22,11:6
Mulcahy, William L, 1940, Ap 22,17:6
Mulcahy, William R, 1951, S 15,15:5
Mulchinock, Dennis, 1948, Ag 18,25:5
Mulcox, Frederick S, 1938, D 8,27:1
Mulculsky, Roman, 1922, Ag 22,17:5
Muldaur, Barton Mrs, 1967, Jl 11,37:3
Muldaur, Charles E A Mrs, 1959, Je 6,21:6
Muldaur, George B, 1943, Ja 29,19:4
Muldavin, Leon F, 1948, Ap 25,69:1
Muldberg, Moritz, 1942, Ap 15,21:2
Muldener, Louise, 1938, My 11,19:3
Mulder, Arnold, 1959, Mr 29,80:5
Mulder, Arthur G, 1953, Ag 14,19:2
Mulder, Fabri Richard, 1874, D 31,4:6
Mulder, Henry J, 1943, Ag 2,15:5
Mulderry, Patrick W, 1942, Jl 8,23:4
Muldoon, Annie Mrs, 1937, Je 3,28:3
Muldoon, Bernard F, 1947, Ag 21,23:5
Muldoon, Charles W, 1953, Ag 26,27:1
Muldoon, Felix A, 1968, N 24,87:2
Muldoon, Felix A Mrs, 1962, Jl 23,21:1
Muldoon, Hugh, 1943, N 14,56:4
Muldoon, Joseph A Sr, 1945, N 5,19:3
Muldoon, Martin M, 1955, D 5,31:3
Muldoon, Mary, 1958, Mr 13,29:2
Muldoon, Mary T (will), 1938, Ag 30,15:3
Muldoon, P J Bishop, 1927, O 9,30:5
Muldoon, Theodore J, 1967, D 14,47:2
Muldoon, W, 1933, Je 4,32:1
Muldoon, William H (funl, Jl 5,9:3), 1920, Jl 3,15:6
Muldowney, Joseph D Jr, 1950, Ag 17,27:2
Muldowney, Michael J, 1947, Mr 31,23:2
Muldowney, Robert J, 1946, F 16,13:4
Muldowney, Thomas J, 1967, My 18,47:2
Muldrow, H L Chancellor, 1905, Mr 5,9:3
Mule, Giuseppe, 1951, S 11,29:2
Muley, Abdul Aziz Sultan of Morocco, 1898, Ag 14,7:2
Muley-Hassan, Sultan of Morocco, 1878, Mr 26,4:7
Muley Hassan, Sultan of Morocco, 1894, Je 12,5:1
Muleya, Yotham, 1959, N 24,25:5
Mulford, Allen, 1954, Ag 23,17:5
Mulford, Allen Mrs, 1951, Mr 18,88:5
Mulford, Anna I, 1943, Je 17,21:5
Mulford, Charles W, 1949, F 13,76:6
Mulford, Clare H, 1947, Ja 11,19:6
Mulford, Clarence E, 1956, My 12,19:1
Mulford, E W, 1903, Je 14,7:6
Mulford, Edwin H, 1945, Ag 25,11:3
Mulford, Elizabeth Mrs, 1950, N 28,31:1
Mulford, Ephraim R, 1939, Mr 12,III,6:7
Mulford, Florence, 1962, S 10,29:3
Mulford, Frank E, 1951, Ap 2,25:6
Mulford, George, 1955, O 29,19:5
Mulford, Henry, 1939, N 23,27:5
Mulford, Henry K, 1937, O 16,19:4
Mulford, Jesse G, 1940, S 30,17:3
Mulford, John B, 1949, D 5,23:4
Mulford, John E Brig-Gen, 1908, O 20,9:6
Mulford, John W, 1953, N 7,17:3; 1964, Je 4,37:1
Mulford, L J, 1927, S 14,31:3
Mulford, Leslie F Dr, 1937, Mr 7,II,8:3
Mulford, Mary, 1951, Jl 31,21:4
Mulford, O J, 1943, Ag 4,17:2
Mulford, Roland J, 1951, My 12,21:6
Mulford, Thomas J, 1924, Mr 21,19:4
Mulford, Vincent S, 1925, S 23,25:4; 1960, F 18,33:3
Mulford, William R, 1940, D 26,19:5
Mulgrave, Dorothy I, 1960, Jl 9,19:5
Mulgrave, Thomas J, 1937, Mr 23,23:3
Mulgrew, John F Mrs, 1951, S 19,31:6
Mulhaley, John, 1938, O 7,23:6
Mulhall, Edward, 1943, Jl 11,34:7
Mulhall, James J, 1942, Je 15,19:3; 1962, Jl 25,33:5
Mulhall, James P, 1952, O 15,31:5
Mulhall, John Dillon, 1903, Jl 8,9:7
Mulhall, Margaret Mrs, 1944, D 24,26:2
Mulhall, Martin J, 1955, Ag 13,13:2
Mulhall, Michael J Lt, 1922, N 22,21:3
Mulhall, Sylvanus C, 1943, Ja 11,15:1
Mulhall, Walter F, 1966, Je 25,31:5
Mulhane, Charles A, 1958, My 30,22:1
Mulhare, Hugh E, 1961, Ja 24,29:2
Mulhare, Robert A, 1957, My 22,33:1
Mulhaupt, Fred J, 1938, Ja 11,23:5
Mulhauser, Frank A, 1946, Ap 29,22:2
Mulhearn, Charles J, 1963, Ag 27,31:2
Mulhearn, Michael J, 1937, Ag 17,19:3
Mulhearn, Michael T Mrs, 1951, N 16,25:3
Mulhearn, William T, 1946, Ag 27,27:5
Mulhern, Edward J Sr, 1948, Jl 31,15:6
Mulhern, James O, 1948, Ja 15,23:3
Mulhern, Mary Mrs, 1940, S 1,20:7
Mulhern, Michael J Rev (funl, Jl 18,11:4), 1919, Jl 15,11:2
Mulheron, James H, 1925, Je 18,21:5
Mulholland, Bert, 1968, Jl 13,27:2
Mulholland, Daniel J Mrs, 1945, Jl 13,11:7
Mulholland, Daniel J Sr, 1943, Ja 14,21:5
Mulholland, David A, 1962, Je 11,31:5
Mulholland, Donald C, 1960, Ag 25,29:6
Mulholland, Edward J, 1955, My 26,31:1
Mulholland, Edward Mrs, 1962, Ag 23,29:4
Mulholland, Edwin M, 1961, Mr 7,35:2
Mulholland, Eliza B Mrs (will), 1938, My 22,20:2
Mulholland, Frank L (por), 1949, Je 8,29:5
Mulholland, George W, 1947, Je 20,19:4
Mulholland, Henry B, 1966, O 31,35:3
Mulholland, Henry W, 1959, Mr 15,88:7
Mulholland, James E, 1940, D 23,19:6
Mulholland, James V, 1958, My 8,29:2
Mulholland, John A, 1951, Jl 12,25:1
Mulholland, John J, 1954, Ag 5,23:3
Mulholland, Leo F, 1948, Ap 22,27:1
Mulholland, Rosa (Lady Gilbert), 1921, Ap 27,17:4
Mulholland, Thomas F, 1961, Ap 28,31:3
Mulholland, William R, 1959, Je 9,37:5
Mulich, Edward J, 1941, S 8,15:4
Mulinari, Luigi, 1954, S 15,33:1
Mulkeen, Patrick J, 1964, F 24,25:2
Mulkeen, William J, 1964, My 28,37:5
Mulkern, Frank, 1956, O 4,33:3
Mulkern, John M, 1951, S 10,21:4
Mulkern, Pat, 1948, Je 27,52:5
Mulkey, Frederick W, 1924, My 6,21:5
Mulki, Fawzi el-, 1962, Ja 11,33:1
Mulkins, Henry L, 1945, S 16,43:2
Mull, Harry E, 1941, D 21,41:2
Mull, J H, 1936, Jl 28,19:6
Mull, Richard, 1938, S 22,23:4
Mullady, Agnes C, 1941, N 18,25:6
Mullady, Patrick, 1952, N 4,29:1
Mullady, Patrick Mrs, 1949, Je 1,32:2
Mullahy, T Vincent, 1962, F 2,29:1
Mullahy, Thomas F, 1949, Jl 21,26:2
Mullally, Francis P Rev Dr, 1904, Ja 20,9:5
Mullally, John, 1915, Ja 5,15:4
Mullally, John P Mrs, 1947, My 15,25:1
Mullally, Joseph W, 1952, Je 12,33:2
Mullally, Mandeville, 1957, O 28,27:4
Mullally, Thornwell (por), 1943, Mr 18,19:1
Mullally, William T, 1957, N 25,31:2
Mullaly, Arthur L, 1949, Ap 21,25:1
Mullaly, Charles J, 1949, O 26,27:2
Mullaly, Charles J Mrs, 1937, Jl 27,21:1
Mullan, Donald G, 1954, Je 27,69:3
Mullan, Eugene H, 1965, My 27,37:3
Mullan, Eugene H Mrs, 1964, My 4,29:4
Mullan, G V, 1931, D 30,19:1
Mullan, J M, 1933, Ag 23,17:5
Mullan, John B, 1955, Ag 16,49:2
Mullan, Joseph J, 1938, F 16,21:4
Mullan, Joseph J Mrs, 1950, Ag 24,27:6
Mullan, W G R Rev, 1910, Ja 26,9:5
Mullanaphy, James A, 1966, D 28,43:7
Mullane, Dennis J, 1957, N 3,88:8
Mullane, Frank A, 1946, Je 26,25:5
Mullane, Harvey T, 1951, Mr 15,29:6
Mullane, Jerome, 1954, N 26,29:2
Mullane, John D, 1946, N 7,31:3
Mullane, Robert E, 1951, Mr 23,21:4
Mullane, Tony, 1944, Ap 27,23:2
Mullaney, Anthony J, 1960, N 29,37:4
Mullaney, Bernard J, 1949, S 3,13:3
Mullaney, Frank R, 1953, Ja 24,15:3
Mullaney, James, 1965, O 20,47:2
Mullaney, James T, 1950, N 7,27:2
Mullaney, James V, 1963, Ag 1,27:2
Mullaney, John H, 1950, Je 20,29:3
Mullaney, John J, 1951, S 25,29:4; 1955, Mr 3,27:4
Mullaney, Joseph A, 1954, D 25,11:3
Mullaney, Mary Gratta Mother, 1939, N 10,23:6
Mullaney, Robert B Mrs, 1954, Ag 4,21:3
Mullaney, Thomas F, 1950, N 7,19:2
Mullaney, Thomas W, 1948, My 28,23:5
Mullaney, William J Mrs (L Carver), 1955, Ag 13, 13:2
Mullany, Ethel M, 1965, Mr 16,39:1
Mullany, James J, 1955, Ag 2,23:1
Mullany, John F Rev Dr, 1916, S 25,9:3
Mullany, Leo, 1940, N 9,17:2
Mullarkey, John P, 1937, Ja 1,23:4
Mullarney, Thomas, 1939, Ap 15,19:2
Mullay, J Frank, 1951, D 9,91:2
Mullee, John J, 1957, Ja 10,29:1
Mullee, Raymond G, 1963, O 31,33:4
Mullegg, Gaston, 1958, Ag 4,12:3
Mullen, Albert E, 1951, O 30,29:2
Mullen, Alice M, 1949, D 8,33:2
Mullen, Arthur C, 1964, D 29,27:1
Mullen, Arthur D, 1942, O 15,23:1
Mullen, Arthur F (por), 1938, Jl 15,17:1
Mullen, Arthur F Mrs, 1958, Je 10,33:2
Mullen, Arthur J, 1959, Jl 21,30:3
Mullen, Carroll R, 1961, F 2,29:3
Mullen, Charles F Mrs, 1952, N 4,29:4
Mullen, Edgar C, 1949, Je 8,29:2
Mullen, Edward, 1962, Ja 18,29:2
Mullen, Edward C, 1944, Ag 12,11:4
Mullen, Edward J, 1955, N 6,86:3
Mullen, Frank A, 1945, S 28,21:4
Mullen, Frank B, 1940, Jl 12,15:6
Mullen, Frederick S, 1921, F 19,11:5
Mullen, George B Mrs, 1945, N 22,35:4
Mullen, George D, 1945, F 10,11:4
Mullen, Gordon M, 1949, Jl 13,27:4
Mullen, Grace M Sister, 1954, Ja 21,31:6
Mullen, Harold, 1948, O 27,27:5
Mullen, Harvey J, 1950, Mr 29,29:2
Mullen, Henry J, 1922, Ap 25,17:5; 1943, Mr 30,21:
Mullen, J W, 1903, My 13,9:5
Mullen, J W Mrs, 1954, Ag 26,27:2
Mullen, James, 1925, My 2,15:6
Mullen, James B Sen, 1911, Ja 6,9:2
Mullen, James C, 1945, Je 6,21:5
Mullen, James Ignatius Father, 1866, S 23,1:6
Mullen, James P, 1944, D 24,25:1
Mullen, John A, 1959, S 27,86:4
Mullen, John A Mrs, 1950, S 6,29:3
Mullen, John C, 1943, Ag 9,13:7; 1945, Jl 22,38:1
Mullen, John Capt, 1909, D 31,9:4
Mullen, John E, 1942, D 28,19:4
Mullen, John J, 1945, Mr 29,23:2; 1952, Ag 20,25:4; 1955, Ap 28,29:2
Mullen, John P, 1959, N 9,62:2
Mullen, Joseph, 1882, My 18,5:6
Mullen, Joseph A, 1948, Je 9,29:3
Mullen, Joseph D, 1948, D 1,29:4
Mullen, Joseph W, 1943, Jl 13,21:2; 1964, Ap 14,37:
Mullen, Martin A, 1953, Je 9,27:2
Mullen, Martin E Sr, 1939, S 20,27:5
Mullen, Merritt D, 1957, Ap 10,33:3
Mullen, Myles J, 1952, My 18,92:6
Mullen, Patrick J, 1950, D 17,85:1
Mullen, Ralph W, 1951, My 23,35:1
Mullen, Rosemary F, 1950, Ja 12,28:3
Mullen, Terence J, 1957, My 11,21:5
Mullen, Thomas, 1921, S 15,15:1
Mullen, Thomas A, 1943, Ap 24,13:4
Mullen, Thomas A Rev, 1920, F 6,13:3
Mullen, Thomas F, 1952, Ja 5,11:4; 1952, Mr 20,29:
Mullen, Thomas R, 1958, D 3,37:3
Mullen, Thomas R Jr, 1948, N 17,27:3
Mullen, W J (see also Jl 27), 1882, Jl 30,8:5
Mullen, Wallace, 1945, F 1,23:2
Mullen, William, 1950, D 8,29:3
Mullen, William J, 1945, O 9,21:4
Mullendore, Havre, 1950, N 17,27:2
Mullenix, Charles A, 1953, N 10,31:2
Mullens, John C, 1949, Ja 12,27:6
Mullens, John Sir, 1937, D 31,15:1
Mullens, Joseph (Fenian), 1875, My 10,1:7
Mullens, Patrick A, 1941, Jl 3,19:1
Muller, Adam G, 1960, Jl 28,27:5
Muller, Adolf, 1943, Jl 31,13:5
Muller, Albert, 1953, My 4,23:4
Muller, Alex, 1949, F 18,23:2

Muller, Anthony, 1941, Mr 10,19:3
Muller, Arthur E, 1963, S 3,33:3
Muller, Arthur Jr Mrs, 1948, S 26,76:4
Muller, Arthur W, 1964, Jl 4,13:4
Muller, August R Mrs, 1947, Ap 24,25:5
Muller, Bernhard, 1948, S 22,32:2
Muller, Carl, 1947, Ja 30,25:6; 1966, Je 5,85:1
Muller, Carl Christian, 1914, Je 5,11:4
Muller, Charles A, 1952, Mr 10,21:6
Muller, Charles F, 1956, Mr 12,27:4; 1959, Je 21,92:5
Muller, Charles P, 1945, Mr 6,21:2
Muller, Clarence T, 1954, Jl 4,31:1
Muller, E Lester, 1953, O 21,30:6
Muller, Edgar E, 1942, D 29,21:4
Muller, Edouard (por), 1948, S 29,29:1
Muller, Edward A, 1960, Ja 15,31:3
Muller, Edward F, 1940, D 29,25:1
Muller, Edward J, 1960, D 17,23:4
Muller, Edward M, 1945, Mr 2,19:3
Muller, Edwin, 1963, S 21,21:3
Muller, Elizabeth Mrs, 1952, F 28,27:2
Muller, Elizabeth S Mrs, 1940, O 30,23:1
Muller, Eric T, 1963, Ag 4,80:4
Muller, Ernest W, 1943, Ap 9,21:1
Muller, Ernest W Mrs, 1942, Ap 24,17:3
Muller, F B, 1882, Je 2,2:6
Muller, F Joseph, 1959, D 30,21:4
Muller, Frank, 1955, Ja 29,15:1
Muller, Frank B, 1948, D 28,21:3
Muller, Frank J, 1948, F 8,61:1
Muller, Fred, 1956, F 9,31:1
Muller, Fred H, 1937, Ag 4,19:3
Muller, Frederic A, 1937, F 2,23:5
Muller, Frederick, 1948, My 2,76:4
Muller, Frederick H, 1963, Jl 7,52:7
Muller, Frederick W, 1947, Je 13,23:5
Muller, George, 1898, Mr 11,7:4; 1903, Ag 30,7:6; 1941, N 5,23:5
Muller, George F, 1958, Ag 6,25:5
Muller, George Mrs, 1948, Ag 3,25:2
Muller, George O, 1950, Ag 18,21:2
Muller, George P, 1947, F 20,25:5; 1948, O 2,15:4
Muller, Geza, 1947, N 30,76:4
Muller, Gustav, 1940, O 3,25:4
Muller, Gustave H, 1948, O 21,27:1
Muller, Harold C, 1947, N 21,27:3
Muller, Harold P, 1962, My 19,27:6
Muller, Harry C Mrs, 1949, My 5,27:3
Muller, Harry Mrs, 1942, Ag 21,21:7
Muller, Hendrik A S, 1955, Mr 11,25:4
Muller, Henri F, 1959, S 12,21:4
Muller, Henry D, 1939, Ag 3,19:7
Muller, Henry Jr, 1961, O 20,33:4
Muller, Herman E, 1965, O 24,83:6
Muller, Herman E Mrs, 1965, O 24,83:6
Muller, Herman J, 1939, Ap 5,25:5
Muller, Herman N Mrs, 1962, Jl 18,29:4
Muller, Hermann J, 1967, Ap 6,39:1
Muller, Homer R Mrs, 1949, My 19,29:3
Muller, Isador J (por), 1943, Mr 22,19:3
Muller, J Herman, 1947, S 2,21:2
Muller, J P, 1938, N 18,21:3
Muller, Jacob F, 1942, S 18,22:2
Muller, Jacob Mrs, 1964, Ag 18,31:1
Muller, Jacob P (por), 1937, Jl 12,17:4
Muller, James A, 1945, S 8,15:5
Muller, Jan, 1958, Ja 31,22:5
Muller, Johannes, 1943, D 31,16:5
Muller, John, 1925, O 3,15:5; 1964, D 2,50:4
Muller, John D, 1945, Ja 5,15:5
Muller, John F, 1953, O 31,17:1
Muller, John H, 1943, My 16,42:5; 1957, Ap 30,29:4
Muller, John J, 1951, Ag 17,17:5
Muller, John M, 1957, N 4,29:2
Muller, John O, 1948, D 29,21:1
Muller, John V, 1958, Je 8,88:6
Muller, Joseph A, 1956, Ja 17,33:1
Muller, Joseph H, 1952, N 27,31:1
Muller, Joseph I, 1950, O 3,31:4
Muller, Joseph Mrs, 1948, Ap 22,27:4
Muller, Joseph Msgr, 1913, N 25,11:6
Muller, Josephine, 1952, N 2,88:1
Muller, Juan, 1952, O 4,17:6
Muller, Jules (por), 1944, My 18,19:2
Muller, Jules Mrs, 1962, F 14,35:1
Muller, Julius, 1939, Ag 28,19:5
Muller, Lillie H, 1948, S 15,31:3
Muller, M Gladys, 1950, N 7,27:3
Muller, Michael N, 1944, Je 4,42:3
Muller, Nicholas, 1917, D 13,13:4; 1944, Mr 31,21:3
Muller, Nicholas W (por), 1943, Je 19,13:4
Muller, Oscar F, 1964, Mr 15,86:5
Muller, Otto, 1962, My 1,38:1
Muller, Paul, 1941, S 26,23:2; 1950, Jl 9,69:2
Muller, Paul H, 1965, O 14,47:1
Muller, Peter, 1941, Ap 21,19:4
Muller, Phil P, 1948, F 23,17:4
Muller, Richard J, 1958, Mr 27,33:4
Muller, Richard W Dr, 1920, Je 4,13:4
Muller, Robert A, 1959, Ja 13,47:3
Muller, Robert O, 1957, N 10,86:6
Muller, Siegfried H, 1965, Je 13,85:1
Muller, Valentine, 1945, O 19,23:5
Muller, Walter J, 1967, N 17,47:3
Muller, Walter Mrs, 1957, Je 23,85:1
Muller, Werner, 1949, Jl 27,23:1
Muller, William A, 1941, My 12,17:3
Muller, William C, 1949, N 2,27:2
Muller, William F, 1944, S 5,19:5
Muller, William G, 1958, S 28,89:1
Muller, William J, 1953, Mr 17,29:2
Muller, William S, 1959, D 11,33:3
Muller, William S Mrs, 1962, My 14,29:4
Muller, William V, 1945, F 6,19:3
Muller-Ury, Adolph, 1947, Jl 8,23:5
Mullery, Richard Sr, 1951, Je 13,29:5
Mullette, Jesse, 1946, Jl 21,39:1
Mullgardt, Louis C, 1942, Ja 16,21:5
Mullican, Aubrey (Moon), 1967, Ja 2,19:4
Mulligan, Andrew R, 1952, N 2,88:3
Mulligan, Anna, 1952, Ap 17,29:1
Mulligan, Arthur G, 1965, Mr 13,25:4
Mulligan, Bernard E, 1951, S 24,27:2
Mulligan, Bernard E Mrs, 1939, Mr 24,21:1
Mulligan, Bernard F, 1942, Ag 11,19:5
Mulligan, Charles A Sr, 1951, Ja 21,78:2
Mulligan, Charles H, 1940, Ap 10,25:3
Mulligan, Charles L, 1957, Ap 7,88:7
Mulligan, David, 1941, Mr 2,42:6
Mulligan, David B, 1954, D 28,23:1
Mulligan, David G, 1942, N 1,52:4
Mulligan, Edward F, 1955, N 24,29:2
Mulligan, Edward J, 1945, F 9,15:4
Mulligan, Edwin C, 1955, D 6,37:3
Mulligan, Eleanor, 1949, N 12,15:3
Mulligan, Ellen (Sister Mary Margt), 1964, Ag 11, 33:4
Mulligan, Francis J, 1953, D 19,15:4; 1954, My 18,29:3
Mulligan, Frank J, 1952, Mr 23,94:5
Mulligan, George D, 1955, Jl 28,23:2; 1959, Jl 8,29:4
Mulligan, George F Jr, 1962, My 16,41:3
Mulligan, Henry A, 1956, D 27,25:2
Mulligan, James, 1903, S 18,7:3; 1949, Je 10,27:3
Mulligan, James A, 1954, Je 6,86:4
Mulligan, James B Col, 1912, Mr 30,13:5
Mulligan, James Col, 1864, Ag 2,2:6
Mulligan, James J, 1956, D 30,33:1
Mulligan, James V, 1950, Je 2,23:5
Mulligan, John, 1938, Jl 15,17:3; 1941, O 23,23:2; 1949, N 12,15:5; 1957, Mr 20,37:6
Mulligan, John F, 1941, F 7,40:1
Mulligan, John H, 1951, Ja 30,25:2
Mulligan, John J, 1961, Ja 14,23:6
Mulligan, John J Mrs, 1948, N 6,13:2
Mulligan, John L, 1939, Ag 3,19:5
Mulligan, Joseph H, 1939, My 21,III,6:5
Mulligan, Joseph M, 1956, Mr 10,17:1
Mulligan, Joseph T, 1944, N 20,21:5
Mulligan, Joseph T Mrs, 1959, Ja 31,19:5
Mulligan, Margaret (Sister Jean Agnes), 1960, My 7,23:4
Mulligan, Mary L, 1959, Mr 3,33:4
Mulligan, Michael J, 1967, S 25,45:3
Mulligan, Paul B, 1958, My 5,29:1
Mulligan, Ralph F, 1941, D 9,31:4
Mulligan, Ralph R, 1947, My 2,21:4
Mulligan, Ralph R Mrs, 1937, Jl 30,19:5
Mulligan, Raymond J, 1957, D 13,27:4
Mulligan, Richard T Mrs, 1914, Ap 6,9:6
Mulligan, Richard Thomas, 1917, F 24,9:6
Mulligan, Stephen J, 1956, D 25,25:2
Mulligan, Sylvester, 1950, O 25,35:4
Mulligan, Thomas C, 1960, Je 9,33:5
Mulligan, Thomas F (por), 1949, Ja 24,19:5
Mulligan, Thomas F, 1952, D 11,33:4
Mulligan, Thomas J, 1941, O 28,23:3
Mulligan, Timothy A, 1948, O 2,15:2
Mulligan, William, 1953, F 9,27:4
Mulligan, William A, 1944, Ap 5,19:5
Mulligan, William Edward, 1913, O 24,11:5
Mulligan, William G Mrs (por), 1943, Ap 24,13:4
Mullikan, James C, 1964, O 5,33:1
Mulliken, Albert E, 1947, Mr 13,27:3
Mulliken, David B, 1958, Jl 21,21:5
Mulliken, Edward A, 1921, My 15,22:3
Mulliken, Harry B, 1952, Je 21,15:6
Mulliken, John, 1939, My 28,III,7:2
Mullikin, Percival, 1937, Ag 6,17:2
Mullin, Basil A, 1943, Ap 7,26:3
Mullin, Bernard, 1959, Ja 11,88:1
Mullin, C Donald, 1949, O 23,86:3
Mullin, Charles A, 1946, S 22,60:5
Mullin, Charles C, 1939, Ap 16,III,6:8
Mullin, Esther (Mrs H Pollock), 1953, F 21,13:2
Mullin, Francis B, 1920, Ag 15,20:5
Mullin, Francis E, 1945, Jl 16,11:8
Mullin, Francis R, 1942, Ag 10,19:7
Mullin, Francis T, 1951, Ap 25,29:4
Mullin, George, 1944, Ja 8,13:6
Mullin, Glen, 1952, D 15,25:5
Mullin, Harry J Jr, 1960, S 24,11:8
Mullin, J William, 1940, O 12,17:4
Mullin, James A, 1941, Mr 2,42:7; 1950, Jl 25,27:1
Mullin, James A E, 1937, D 29,21:2
Mullin, John B, 1963, D 4,47:4
Mullin, John H, 1939, D 22,19:1
Mullin, John M, 1966, My 7,31:3
Mullin, Joseph A, 1944, Jl 13,17:5
Mullin, June T, 1939, D 22,19:5
Mullin, Leo C, 1954, Ja 4,19:2
Mullin, Lester S Dr, 1968, F 20,44:1
Mullin, Michael A, 1903, Je 27,9:6
Mullin, Raymond J, 1954, Ap 20,29:2
Mullin, Walter J Dr, 1937, Ja 6,23:3
Mullin, William A, 1955, F 15,27:4
Mullin, William J, 1950, Ag 10,25:4
Mullineaux, Edward H, 1951, Ag 9,21:5
Mullineaux, Mary H Mrs, 1939, N 9,23:3
Mulliner, Alexander C, 1907, Mr 9,9:6
Mulliner, Harold G, 1946, Jl 3,25:6
Mulliner, Walter G, 1919, Je 30,11:3
Mullins, Annie M Mrs, 1937, Ja 2,11:4
Mullins, Charles Mrs, 1925, S 7,11:5
Mullins, Claude S, 1952, D 14,91:1
Mullins, E V, 1928, N 24,17:5
Mullins, Edward (funl, N 20,17:3), 1954, N 18,33:4
Mullins, Flavian, 1939, Je 20,21:6
Mullins, Francis D, 1949, Ag 30,27:3
Mullins, George W (mem plans), 1956, Mr 21,37:3
Mullins, Gordon R, 1959, My 21,31:5
Mullins, Henry A, 1952, Jl 10,31:4
Mullins, Hugh A, 1958, My 2,27:2
Mullins, James F, 1947, Mr 8,13:6
Mullins, John E, 1937, Jl 3,15:3; 1952, S 5,27:4
Mullins, Joseph J Mrs, 1950, O 11,33:5
Mullins, Lillian, 1956, S 13,70:8
Mullins, Michael Mrs, 1954, D 29,23:2
Mullins, Moon (Lawrence A Mullins), 1968, Ag 12, 35:2
Mullins, Roy, 1941, F 19,21:4
Mullins, Samuel F, 1949, D 19,27:4
Mullins, Thomas C, 1954, Jl 27,21:2
Mullins, William E, 1948, S 13,21:4; 1958, O 2,37:3
Mullison, Olin R, 1956, Je 8,25:5
Mulliss, George W F, 1953, D 12,19:2
Mulloly, Mary, 1950, O 11,33:5
Mullon, Charles, 1950, O 8,104:3
Mullon, Edgar P, 1951, Jl 10,35:8
Mullowney, Edward, 1956, Mr 7,33:4
Mulloy, Robin B, 1956, Ap 14,17:5
Mulloy, William T, 1959, Je 2,35:5
Mulnick, Morris, 1960, My 9,29:4
Mulock, Herman, 1939, O 7,17:5
Mulock, Percy, 1955, N 17,35:3
Mulock, William (por), 1944, O 2,19:4
Mulock, William P, 1954, Ag 27,21:5
Mulot, Otto L, 1943, Je 23,21:6
Mulqueen, Bruce A, 1957, Jl 13,17:2
Mulqueen, Carr, 1955, D 20,31:2
Mulqueen, John J, 1958, Ap 10,29:2
Mulqueen, Joseph F, 1940, Ag 16,15:3; 1960, My 29, 57:1
Mulqueen, Mary Mrs, 1938, Ja 22,15:2
Mulqueen, Michael J (funl, O 20,17:6), 1924, O 11, 25:3
Mulqueeney, John P, 1953, F 24,25:2
Mulrain, Andrew J, 1960, Mr 23,37:2
Mulrain, Martin J Mrs, 1952, Ja 1,25:1
Mulrean, Francis X, 1958, Je 24,31:2
Mulrenan, Luke, 1946, Ja 3,19:4
Mulrenin, Edward F, 1952, My 21,27:4
Mulrey, Helen V Mrs, 1943, My 10,19:2
Mulrone, Sadie H, 1956, Ja 3,31:3
Mulroney, A J, 1943, Ag 3,19:4
Mulrooney, Edward Mrs, 1942, Ap 16,21:3
Mulrooney, Edward P (trb, My 3,33:3; funl, My 4,45:2), 1960, My 1,86:5
Mulrooney, John J, 1947, N 11,27:2
Mulrooney, Patrick R, 1943, Jl 10,13:5
Mulrooney, Walter S, 1960, Mr 5,19:1
Mulroy, James, 1955, Ag 4,25:3
Mulroy, James R Mrs, 1952, My 15,31:5
Mulroy, James W, 1952, Ap 30,27:2
Mulroy, John R, 1965, Je 20,72:6
Mulroy, Patrick J, 1954, O 30,17:2
Mulry, Joseph A, 1945, Mr 14,19:3
Mulry, Joseph A Rev, 1921, S 1,15:4
Mulry, Parthenia Mary (Sister Miriam), 1910, Ap 19,9:5
Mulry, Patrick F X Rev, 1922, N 3,17:5
Mulry, Thomas M (funl, Mr 14,11:4), 1916, Mr 11, 11:5
Mulry, William P, 1949, Mr 29,25:3
Mulster, Daniel J, 1939, Je 26,15:5
Multer, Max Mrs, 1952, My 17,19:5
Multer, Samuel S, 1966, F 6,92:5
Multer, Smith L, 1952, Jl 17,23:6
Multer, Smith L Mrs, 1944, N 2,19:4
Multer, William W, 1940, Je 22,15:4
Mulva, James B, 1948, Je 16,29:2
Mulvaney, Francis E Mrs, 1964, Je 1,29:5
Mulvaney, Joseph E, 1951, Je 30,15:6
Mulvaney, Lewis J, 1947, Mr 26,25:4
Mulvany, Thomas, 1943, Je 17,21:3
Mulvehill, Edward L, 1961, Ja 5,31:5
Mulvehill, Peter H, 1919, F 26,11:4
Mulvey, Bridget Mrs, 1947, Mr 4,25:2
Mulvey, Everett N, 1952, Jl 26,13:6
Mulvey, Frank, 1943, N 27,13:5

Mulvey, Henry S, 1948, F 29,60:5
Mulvey, James A Mrs, 1968, N 25,47:3
Mulvey, John M, 1943, S 22,23:5
Mulvey, Joseph E, 1951, Je 9,19:6
Mulvey, Peter J, 1944, D 13,23:3
Mulvey, Richard W, 1956, S 16,84:7
Mulvey, Thomas, 1915, O 16,11:6
Mulvey, Thomas J, 1952, Ag 29,23:2
Mulvey, William A, 1948, D 26,52:3
Mulvihill, Cornelius F, 1963, S 28,19:5
Mulvihill, James V, 1937, Ap 1,23:1
Mulvihill, Nancy Mrs, 1924, Ag 27,17:6
Mulvihill, Thomas J, 1940, D 31,15:5
Mulvihill, William J Jr, 1967, Ag 16,41:4
Mulville, Donald, 1944, N 6,19:3
Muma, Jasper C, 1942, O 19,19:4
Mumberg, W F, 1938, Je 10,21:4
Mumchausen, Martha Mrs, 1945, N 12,35:7
Mumford, Bryant, 1951, Ja 29,19:4
Mumford, Eben, 1942, O 20,21:6
Mumford, Edward R, 1941, Ap 22,21:1
Mumford, Frederick A, 1959, Jl 9,27:1
Mumford, George D Mrs, 1944, O 23,19:6
Mumford, George II, 1875, Jl 27,4:6
Mumford, George S, 1946, Jl 16,23:1
Mumford, Gertrude C Mrs, 1942, Ap 18,15:6
Mumford, Herbert W, 1938, Je 1,23:5; 1945, Ag 19, 40:4
Mumford, Herbert W Mrs, 1952, S 30,31:5
Mumford, James D Sr, 1957, Ag 24,15:4
Mumford, John I, 1946, O 6,56:2
Mumford, John K Mrs, 1949, Je 28,27:4
Mumford, L Quincy Mrs, 1961, Ap 26,39:3
Mumford, Manly J, 1950, Ap 29,15:4
Mumford, O R, 1883, Ja 27,2:2
Mumford, Phil G, 1951, O 29,23:3
Mumford, Thomas D, 1955, N 26,19:3
Mumford, Thomas S, 1941, Ag 21,17:2
Mumm, George F Mrs, 1954, Ja 9,15:3
Mumm, Walter de Mrs, 1920, My 6,11:3
Mumm, William M, 1960, My 16,31:3
Mumma, Morton C, 1945, Je 1,15:4
Mumma, Paul F, 1954, Ap 17,13:6
Mumma, Walter M, 1961, F 26,92:5
Mummert, Harvey, 1939, My 4,23:5
Mummery, Frederick J, 1950, Jl 10,21:3
Mumper, J Harold, 1949, Ag 5,19:4
Mun, Adrian Albey Marie de, 1914, O 7,9:6
Munafo, Joseph C, 1959, Ag 20,25:1
Munce, Clifford J, 1942, Ja 27,21:5
Muncey, Frank D, 1940, F 6,21:5
Munch, Adam W, 1941, S 18,25:1
Munch, Benjamin S Mrs, 1951, F 10,13:4
Munch, Charles (funl plans, N 9,33:2; mem ser, N 14,47:1), 1968, N 7,50:1
Munch, Charles J, 1959, Je 17,35:3
Munch, Charles Mrs, 1956, Ag 25,15:1
Munch, Edvard, 1944, Ja 25,19:3
Munch, Edward A, 1944, Jl 10,15:6
Munch, Peter D (por), 1948, Ja 13,25:4
Muncie, Elizabeth H, 1953, Mr 16,19:3
Muncie, Samuel, 1914, Ap 20,9:2
Muncie, William, 1915, F 8,7:4
Munck, Ernest de, 1915, F 6,11:6
Munday, Bill, 1965, F 27,25:2
Munday, Charles B, 1938, Je 14,21:1
Munday, John L, 1958, F 5,28:1
Munday, Perry, 1925, D 20,11:1
Munday, William F, 1950, N 3,27:1
Munde, Erich Dr, 1914, F 28,9:4
Munde, P F Dr, 1902, F 8,9:5
Mundelein, George Cardinal, 1939, O 3,1:6
Munder, Charles F, 1952, D 29,19:3
Munder, Norman T A, 1953, Ap 29,29:4
Mundheim, Samuel, 1940, Mr 17,48:8
Mundheim, Samuel Mrs, 1952, Mr 27,29:4
Mundheim, Sidney K, 1954, S 18,15:1
Mundhenk, Russell L, 1946, F 19,25:5
Mundie, William B, 1939, Mr 28,23:1
Mundle, Arthur C, 1963, S 1,57:1
Mundorff, Harry A, 1939, Jl 11,20:4
Mundrane, Maude E, 1944, N 15,27:4
Munds, Anne, 1940, D 28,15:5
Munds, J Theus, 1938, Ap 20,23:6
Munds, Louis D, 1952, Mr 2,92:3
Mundsen, James N, 1938, Mr 8,19:4
Mundstock, Curt A, 1966, Ag 17,36:4
Mundt, F J, 1947, D 30,23:2
Mundt, Frederick, 1941, Ap 28,15:5
Mundy, Ambrose, 1962, Je 2,19:4
Mundy, Charles R, 1951, My 3,29:5
Mundy, Floyd W, 1953, N 17,31:2
Mundy, James F, 1938, D 28,26:2
Mundy, John Mrs, 1951, N 4,87:1
Mundy, Joseph A S, 1954, F 5,19:4
Mundy, Lawrence, 1962, Mr 14,39:4
Mundy, Leo C, 1944, Je 12,19:4
Mundy, Maynard T, 1945, Ap 11,23:5
Mundy, Norris H, 1943, Ja 6,25:4
Mundy, Raymond W, 1945, O 11,23:4
Mundy, Talbot C, 1940, Ag 6,20:2
Mundy, William G Mrs, 1955, Mr 3,27:1
Mundy, William N, 1946, Mr 2,13:3
Munford, Mary C B Mrs, 1938, Jl 4,13:6
Munford, Walter F (funl, O 2,29:1), 1959, S 29,35:2
Mungall, Daniel Mrs, 1948, S 28,27:2
Mungar, J Edward, 1937, S 3,17:3
Mungeer, Hollis J, 1943, Ag 15,39:2
Mungen, Theodore, 1952, D 24,17:4
Munger, Clarence B, 1947, Jl 2,23:2
Munger, Claude W, 1950, F 4,15:4
Munger, Divine M, 1912, Je 17,9:6
Munger, Dudley B, 1940, Mr 1,21:5
Munger, Earl A, 1946, Ja 30,25:2
Munger, Edgar O, 1948, Ap 1,25:5
Munger, Edwin Thomas, 1915, N 17,11:6
Munger, George W, 1947, O 29,27:5
Munger, H A, 1903, S 8,7:6
Munger, Henry J, 1950, Ag 20,77:2
Munger, Jessie D, 1957, S 20,25:1
Munger, Lewis E, 1941, D 25,25:3
Munger, Margaret E Mrs, 1946, Ag 22,27:5
Munger, Mary W Mrs, 1942, S 17,25:6
Munger, Ray T, 1948, S 20,25:4
Munger, Ray T Mrs, 1954, Jl 1,25:5
Munger, T C, 1941, N 30,68:2
Munger, William L, 1948, D 4,13:5
Mungia, Enrique, 1940, F 8,23:2
Mungle, Alex, 1938, Ja 3,21:2
Mungovan, Thomas M, 1956, N 20,37:4
Munhall, George W, 1943, Je 22,19:1
Munhall, Horace E, 1952, My 4,90:4
Munhall, John, 1904, Je 10,9:7
Munhall, Katharine S, 1946, Ap 16,25:6
Munholland, John J, 1938, F 15,26:5
Muni, Marquis del (Fernando Leon y Castillo), 1918, Mr 13,11:4
Muni, Paul, 1967, Ag 26,1:5
Munier, Ferdinand, 1945, My 29,15:6
Munier, Leon L, 1966, S 25,84:5
Munier, Leon L Mrs, 1967, My 29,25:4
Munier, Vincent M, 1949, N 4,28:4
Munier, Vincent M Mrs, 1957, D 16,29:4
Muniz, Joao C, 1960, Je 20,31:2
Muniz, Ricardo, 1962, N 19,31:4
Munk, Alex, 1937, Ap 8,23:3
Munk, Andrew W, 1944, Je 29,23:1
Munk, Arnold H, 1957, Ag 7,27:6
Munk, Eugene, 1950, Ap 16,104:5
Munk, Fritz, 1950, N 19,93:3
Munkacsy, Arthur Mrs, 1944, S 13,19:4
Munkacsy, John Mrs, 1966, My 18,47:4
Munkacsy, Mihaly, 1900, My 2,8:7
Munkel, Charles, 1938, N 5,19:1
Munkel, Frank C, 1957, S 29,86:4
Munkelwitz, Amelia R, 1941, Mr 13,21:5
Munkenbeck, August, 1952, Je 12,33:2
Munkittrick, Richard Kendall, 1911, O 20,13:4
Munkwitz, Frank H, 1947, O 20,23:5
Munley, John A, 1954, S 24,24:3
Munley, Joseph H, 1955, Ja 21,23:5
Munley, Robert W, 1947, Ja 26,53:4
Munley, William J, 1938, Mr 10,21:4
Munn, Albert Courtlandt, 1905, Ap 19,11:4
Munn, Charles A Jr, 1957, S 6,21:3
Munn, Charles Allen (funl, Ap 6,27:2), 1924, Ap 4, 19:5
Munn, Edward, 1903, Jl 2,9:6
Munn, Eugene H, 1952, Ja 10,30:2
Munn, Eugene L, 1908, N 2,7:5
Munn, Fernanda W Mrs, 1958, O 1,37:2
Munn, Frank, 1953, O 2,21:5
Munn, Franklin S, 1941, Jl 17,19:1
Munn, George F Mrs, 1946, My 22,21:1
Munn, Gurnee, 1960, My 8,88:6
Munn, Henry T, 1952, Mr 26,29:2
Munn, J P, 1931, Ag 16,26:5
Munn, James, 1939, Ap 30,44:7
Munn, James B, 1967, F 15,41:2
Munn, Jessie I, 1943, Ag 2,15:2
Munn, John O, 1957, S 28,17:5
Munn, John P, 1944, Je 13,19:6
Munn, John R, 1966, Ap 30,31:2
Munn, Leslie S, 1941, F 10,17:4
Munn, Mortimer A, 1955, F 13,86:1
Munn, Orson D, 1907, Mr 2,9:6; 1958, D 23,2:6
Munn, Richard E, 1951, Mr 6,27:3
Munn, Stewart Mrs, 1952, My 2,8:6
Munn, Walter A Sr, 1961, Mr 20,29:6
Munn, Wilbur, 1943, Ag 10,19:3
Munn, Wilbur Mrs, 1949, N 23,29:1
Munn, William H Col, 1915, Je 8,13:6
Munn, William O, 1949, O 4,27:2
Munnell, Franklyn, 1937, Mr 23,23:4
Munnich, Ferenc, 1967, N 30,47:2
Munnikhuysen, Walter F, 1964, Ag 30,93:1
Munning, Aug P, 1941, O 30,23:2
Munning, August P Mrs, 1943, Je 5,15:3
Munnings, Alfred J, 1959, Jl 18,15:1
Munns, I Bernard, 1942, Ja 14,21:4
Munns, Margaret C Mrs, 1957, S 6,21:4
Munoyerro, Luis Alonso Archbishop, 1968, S 24,44:7
Munoz, Cecil M, 1949, Jl 8,19:5
Munoz, Fernando Duke of Rianzares, 1873, S 16,4:7
Munoz, Francisco O, 1950, Mr 9,29:4
Munoz, James R, 1968, O 31,47:4
Munoz, Manuel, 1944, F 19,13:2
Munoz, Rafael C, 1943, Je 16,21:3
Munoz, Sigmono C Mrs, 1941, Ap 7,17:1
Munoz, Signono C, 1942, Ap 9,20:3
Munoz Meany, Enrique, 1952, Ja 17,27:5
Munoz Rivera, Amalia de Mrs, 1957, My 6,29:3
Munoz Vernaza, Alberto, 1941, My 7,25:2
Munro, Annette G, 1955, O 4,35:4
Munro, Archibald, 1958, My 9,23:3
Munro, Charles G, 1946, S 5,27:2
Munro, Dana C Mrs, 1956, Mr 28,31:4
Munro, David A, 1910, Mr 10,9:3
Munro, Frederick W, 1941, S 16,23:2
Munro, George, 1923, Je 7,19:5
Munro, George C, 1963, D 6,35:4
Munro, George Mrs, 1912, F 5,9:6
Munro, Gordon, 1967, O 6,39:4
Munro, Grace E, 1949, Mr 9,25:5
Munro, Henry F, 1949, Ja 19,27:5
Munro, Henry H, 1942, F 24,22:2
Munro, Hugh F, 1964, O 16,39:3
Munro, J, 1931, Ag 4,21:5
Munro, James Mrs, 1954, Mr 21,89:3
Munro, John, 1947, Ag 27,23:2
Munro, John A, 1966, N 28,39:1
Munro, John K, 1941, Ap 23,21:6
Munro, John R H (S Hale), 1959, Je 10,37:3
Munro, Keith, 1957, S 27,19:4
Munro, Louis W Jr, 1960, N 7,39:1
Munro, Melville S, 1945, Je 2,15:3
Munro, Muriel P, 1953, Jl 14,27:3
Munro, Patrick (por), 1942, My 4,4:8
Munro, Robert F, 1950, S 28,31:2
Munro, Thomas H, 1939, F 20,17:3
Munro, W H, 1934, Ag 10,17:1
Munro, W Thow, 1948, O 26,31:4
Munro, Wallace (por), 1948, Ja 23,23:3
Munro, Walter L, 1939, O 24,23:4
Munro, William B, 1957, S 5,29:3
Munro, William D, 1959, S 27,86:8
Munro, William G, 1959, Je 18,31:3
Munroe, Abby, 1962, Ja 9,47:1
Munroe, Addison P, 1955, O 27,33:4
Munroe, Albert E, 1950, Ja 28,13:2
Munroe, Alice K Mrs, 1940, O 2,23:7
Munroe, Charles A, 1957, D 29,48:4
Munroe, Charles E, 1938, D 8,27:5
Munroe, Donald M, 1952, D 24,17:6
Munroe, Elward S, 1940, My 17,19:3
Munroe, Frederick C Mrs, 1954, My 19,31:4
Munroe, Frederick G, 1955, N 22,35:5
Munroe, Frederick M, 1938, Ag 30,17:2
Munroe, George Peabody, 1921, S 20,17:5
Munroe, George R, 1938, My 20,19:2
Munroe, Gordon T, 1952, Ja 16,25:2
Munroe, Harold, 1948, O 21,27:1
Munroe, Hugh E, 1947, Mr 13,27:5
Munroe, James M, 1937, Ja 4,29:3
Munroe, John, 1904, D 2,9:4; 1949, Mr 29,25:5
Munroe, John A, 1942, F 15,44:1
Munroe, John E Col, 1937, Mr 10,23:4
Munroe, Louis Mrs, 1944, Ag 31,17:3
Munroe, Martha O Mrs, 1938, Ap 14,23:1
Munroe, Ned, 1941, S 3,23:2
Munroe, Richard A, 1944, Ag 11,15:2
Munroe, Robert K, 1968, O 6,84:6
Munroe, Ruth L (Mrs H B Parkes), 1963, O 16,4
Munroe, S Y Rev, 1867, F 11,5:5
Munroe, Thomas B, 1866, Ja 8,4:2
Munroe, Thomas F, 1953, Mr 7,15:5
Munroe, Vernon, 1957, Jl 16,26:1
Munroe, William D, 1943, F 27,13:2
Munroe, William R, 1966, Mr 3,33:3
Muns, Robert W, 1960, O 1,19:1
Muns, Spencer, 1962, S 15,25:5
Munsch, Charles M, 1937, My 18,23:1
Munschauer, George R, 1941, Ap 25,19:4
Munsell, Albert H, 1918, Je 29,11:5
Munsell, Albert H Mrs, 1948, S 3,19:5
Munsell, Albert W, 1941, S 25,25:4
Munsell, Frank, 1940, Ag 10,13:1
Munsell, Harriet S Mrs, 1939, Ap 14,23:1
Munsell, Harry B, 1961, Ap 17,29:5
Munsell, Warren P Jr, 1952, Jl 29,21:4
Munsey, Alice C, 1948, Ap 2,23:2
Munsey, Andrew C, 1907, Jl 2,9:6
Munsey, Hilson, 1948, F 10,23:2
Munsey, Percy F, 1948, My 31,19:4
Munsick, Donald B, 1958, Mr 26,37:1
Munsick, George, 1966, O 24,39:5
Munsick, George W, 1945, Mr 20,19:5
Munsick, George W Mrs, 1958, Je 29,68:8
Munsie, Malcolm L, 1959, O 11,86:8
Munsie, S W, 1938, Mr 14,15:3
Munsil, Charles D, 1945, D 2,45:2
Munsill, Eva M Mrs, 1953, Mr 9,29:1
Munsill, Marcus M, 1956, My 18,25:1
Munson, Agnes McNamara, 1916, Je 20,11:5
Munson, Carlos W (will, Jl 20,26:1), 1940, Jl 9,
Munson, Charles E, 1956, O 2,35:4
Munson, Clarence L, 1961, My 31,33:4
Munson, Edmund L, 1940, D 10,25:4
Munson, Edward H, 1939, D 27,21:4

Munson, Edward L, 1947, Jl 9,23:3
Munson, Edward L Mrs, 1954, O 18,25:2
Munson, Edwin S, 1958, F 4,29:4
Munson, Edwin S Mrs, 1945, Ap 5,23:5
Munson, Erastus H, 1958, O 28,35:2
Munson, F C, 1936, S 25,23:1
Munson, Frank C Mrs, 1908, Mr 22,9:6; 1955, Je 22, 30:1
Munson, Frank G (will), 1938, O 8,9:2
Munson, Garry W, 1942, Je 16,23:5
Munson, George C, 1940, F 21,19:1
Munson, George D Mrs, 1949, Ag 3,23:3
Munson, George W, 1941, Mr 4,23:6
Munson, Halsey J, 1952, O 22,27:4
Munson, Halsey J 3d, 1960, S 1,27:2
Munson, Henry G, 1946, Ap 10,27:2
Munson, Hubert B, 1955, S 4,56:5
Munson, John G, 1952, Mr 30,29:3
Munson, John M, 1950, Je 24,13:3
Munson, John N, 1944, F 10,15:2
Munson, John N Capt, 1911, S 6,9:6
Munson, John W, 1908, Mr 13,7:4; 1946, My 30,21:2
Munson, Lawrence J, 1950, Je 12,27:4
Munson, Lawrence J Mrs, 1944, Ag 3,19:3
Munson, Lester D, 1944, Jl 6,15:3
Munson, Loveland Ex-Justice, 1921, Mr 26,13:6
Munson, M Webster, 1940, Jl 7,25:4
Munson, Niels F, 1948, O 16,15:5
Munson, Ona, 1955, F 12,16:1
Munson, Oscar, 1960, N 21,29:4
Munson, Oscar P, 1940, Je 1,15:5
Munson, Ralph, 1947, Jl 30,21:4
Munson, Raymond B, 1958, D 7,88:1
Munson, Robert H, 1943, D 26,33:1
Munson, Robert P, 1940, S 12,25:4
Munson, Ruth W, 1958, Mr 13,29:2
Munson, S Lyman Mrs, 1959, Mr 25,35:1
Munson, W Donald Sr, 1960, Mr 12,21:3
Munson, Walter D, 1908, Ap 25,9:4
Munson, Walter D Mrs, 1925, D 27,7:1
Munson, William, 1942, N 6,23:5
Munson, William C Sr, 1949, Ap 22,24:6
Munson, William H, 1968, Jl 13,27:4
Munson, William R, 1944, F 19,14:7
Munson, William S Col, 1917, D 30,19:1
Munster, August W, 1958, Ja 15,29:2
Munster, Earl of, 1902, F 4,1:1
Munster, W F, 1877, Ap 13,1:2
Munsterberg, Emil Dr, 1911, Ja 26,11:3
Munteanu, George Mrs, 1948, N 15,25:2
Munter, Charles, 1944, Ap 15,11:6
Munter, William M, 1957, Jl 18,25:5
Munthe, Axel M F (por), 1949, F 12,17:3
Munther, Henry D, 1905, Ap 11,11:6
Munton, John D, 1951, S 1,11:6
Muntrick, Charles, 1942, Mr 26,23:2
Muntz, Earl E, 1965, Mr 28,92:7
Muntz, Earl W Mrs (P Stevens), 1959, Je 26,25:5
Muntz, Henry, 1940, N 19,23:1
Munves, Edward Mrs, 1960, D 25,42:1
Munyon, David C, 1947, D 5,25:2
Munyon, James M Dr, 1918, Mr 11,11:6
Munz, Frederick, 1938, F 14,17:5
Munz, Jacob, 1945, Ag 18,11:5
Munzer, Egbert L, 1948, Ag 3,25:4
Munzer, Jan, 1950, Jl 13,25:6
Munzert, Edwin L, 1960, D 17,23:4
Munzig, George Chickering, 1908, Mr 7,7:6
Muoio, John R Mrs, 1967, S 4,21:1
Muprhy, Michael, 1937, Ag 11,24:1
Mura, August M, 1959, Jl 12,72:5
Murafski, Andre Mrs, 1948, Ap 20,27:1
Muraji, Koichi, 1961, O 14,23:5
Muranyi, Gustave Count, 1961, D 5,39:3
Muraszko, Nicholas (por), 1949, Ag 5,19:5
Murat, Amelie, 1940, Mr 11,15:5
Murat, Eugene Michel Joachim Napoleon Prince, 1906, Jl 27,1:4
Murat, J Prince, 1932, N 3,21:4
Murat, Jean, 1968, Ja 6,29:4
Murat, Joachim Prince (por), 1938, My 13,20:3
Murat, Lessaril W, 1955, O 30,88:2
Murat, Prince, 1878, Ap 12,4:6; 1901, O 25,1:4
Murat, Ronald (funl plans), 1957, Jl 17,27:6
Murata, Goro, 1956, Ag 12,84:4
Murata, Shozo, 1957, Mr 16,19:2
Muratore, Lucien, 1954, Ag 4,21:1
Muravchik, Chaim, 1950, Ap 8,13:2
Muravchik, Chaim Mrs, 1953, Ap 10,21:2
Muravieff, Count, 1900, Je 22,6:6
Muravieff, Countess (Mrs Vera F Komisarzhevsky), 1910, F 24,9:3
Muravieff, Nicholas, 1908, D 15,9:5
Muraviev, Anatoly, 1954, Je 30,27:3
Muraviev-Volkonsky, Nikolai O, 1948, Ap 13,27:4
Muray, Arthur, 1956, Jl 31,23:5
Muray, Nickolas, 1965, N 3,39:3
Murayama, R, 1933, N 24,21:1
Murayasu, Shinkuro, 1952, Jl 12,13:3
Murbarger, Samuel L, 1944, D 14,23:5
Murch, Abraham J, 1953, F 14,17:2
Murch, Chauncey Rev, 1907, O 21,7:5
Murch, Elmer F, 1949, N 7,27:5
Murch, Harry H, 1953, S 11,21:3
Murch, J Harold, 1951, F 27,27:4
Murch, J Howard, 1947, Je 16,21:5
Murch, John H, 1944, Je 2,15:5
Murch, Leslie F, 1965, My 15,31:6
Murch, Walter T, 1967, D 13,47:2
Murcherson, Lnagston Mrs, 1966, S 8,47:1
Murchie, Frank W, 1942, My 14,19:1
Murchie, Harold H, 1953, Mr 8,90:6
Murchie, John C, 1966, Mr 8,39:3
Murchio, Joseph J, 1961, D 12,57:7
Murchison, Carl A, 1961, My 22,31:2
Murchison, Claudius Temple Dr, 1968, Ag 20,41:2
Murchison, D R, 1882, Mr 1,5:2
Murchison, David W Mrs, 1946, Je 16,40:7
Murchison, Kenneth M, 1938, D 16,26:1
Murchison, Roderick Impey Sir, 1871, O 24,1:7
Murchison, Thomas E, 1952, D 25,29:5
Murck, Knud, 1943, Je 9,21:1
Murdaugh, J E Dandridge, 1939, F 11,15:3
Murden, Alfred T, 1937, Ja 24,II,8:1
Murden, David S, 1958, F 16,86:3
Murden, Robert Mrs, 1942, S 26,15:3
Murden, Robert P, 1954, N 3,29:3
Murdick, P H, 1938, Ap 20,23:3
Murdoch, Alex, 1938, My 29,II,6:8
Murdoch, Donald H, 1966, Ag 17,36:5
Murdoch, Francis V, 1963, My 26,67:5
Murdoch, H J Sr, 1903, My 21,9:4
Murdoch, H S (see also D 7), 1876, D 12,8:1
Murdoch, James, 1939, N 8,23:6
Murdoch, James M, 1944, O 11,21:6
Murdoch, James W, 1958, S 18,31:3
Murdoch, James Y, 1962, Ap 19,31:2
Murdoch, John M, 1904, Ja 10,7:6
Murdoch, John W, 1938, N 17,25:1
Murdoch, Katherine (K M Cooper-Ellis), 1962, Jl 4, 21:3
Murdoch, Keith A, 1952, O 6,25:1
Murdoch, Kenneth J, 1948, Ja 12,19:4
Murdoch, Robert R, 1940, D 1,62:2
Murdoch, Walter B, 1916, Mr 8,11:6
Murdoch, William, 1939, F 17,19:4
Murdock, A Gordon, 1937, O 31,II,11:1
Murdock, Archibald H, 1945, Mr 1,21:1
Murdock, Arthur E, 1944, My 31,19:4
Murdock, Arthur W, 1947, S 12,21:4
Murdock, B Frank Jr, 1938, F 3,23:1
Murdock, C Joseph, 1958, O 5,87:1
Murdock, Charles L, 1961, Ag 18,21:4
Murdock, E A, 1920, Jl 25,20:5
Murdock, Frank C, 1955, Jl 6,27:2
Murdock, Fred A, 1954, Ag 7,13:6
Murdock, George D, 1956, D 25,25:3
Murdock, George G, 1961, S 8,31:1
Murdock, George J, 1942, Jl 28,17:6
Murdock, George R, 1956, My 19,19:6
Murdock, George W, 1940, N 6,23:5
Murdock, H, 1934, Ap 6,23:3
Murdock, Harriett S Mrs, 1942, N 18,26:2
Murdock, Harris H, 1959, My 11,27:1
Murdock, Harvey, 1922, Jl 16,26:4
Murdock, J B, 1931, Mr 21,17:5
Murdock, James, 1949, My 17,26:2
Murdock, James Paulding Com, 1920, Ap 5,15:4
Murdock, John J, 1948, D 9,33:5
Murdock, John S, 1946, D 19,30:3
Murdock, Katherine H Mrs, 1937, Ag 8,II,7:2
Murdock, Leonard, 1938, D 27,17:1
Murdock, Leonard W, 1950, My 23,29:3
Murdock, Lewis Champlin, 1921, Jl 9,9:6
Murdock, Louis R, 1938, Mr 3,21:3
Murdock, Marcellus M Mrs, 1938, My 23,17:3
Murdock, Marguerita G, 1943, Jl 12,15:5
Murdock, Mary C, 1960, Je 10,31:4
Murdock, Max, 1950, Mr 11,15:1
Murdock, Mortimer, 1908, Ap 2,7:6
Murdock, Paul E Mrs, 1945, Mr 30,15:3
Murdock, Samuel B, 1947, O 17,22:6
Murdock, Samuel F, 1921, Mr 23,13:5
Murdock, Solomon Mrs, 1957, My 11,21:5
Murdock, Symes M, 1942, Ja 18,43:2
Murdock, Victor (por), 1945, Jl 9,11:5
Murdock, Victor Mrs, 1940, Ap 23,24:3
Murdock, William D, 1940, O 14,19:4
Murdock, Willis J, 1957, O 15,33:2
Murdy, Mary C Mrs, 1940, O 11,21:2
Murdy, William, 1943, My 26,23:1
Mure, William, 1880, N 10,5:4
Mure, William Col, 1860, Ap 19,4:5
Murer, Harvey, 1960, Ag 16,4:6
Muret, Charlotte T, 1954, N 28,87:1
Murfin, James O, 1940, Jl 12,15:5
Murfin, Orin G, 1956, O 24,37:3
Murfit, Wallace G, 1953, Ap 1,29:4
Murgatroyd, Austin E, 1946, S 17,7:3
Murgatroyd, Everett F, 1946, Ja 28,19:2
Murgatroyd, George F, 1945, Mr 29,23:3
Murias, Manuel, 1960, Jl 25,23:5
Murie, James Dr, 1925, D 22,21:4
Murie, Olaus J, 1963, O 24,33:3
Murillo, Andres, 1955, My 24,31:4
Murillo, Gerardo, 1964, Ag 16,92:6
Murken, Gustave, 1937, S 9,23:2
Murken, Willy, 1920, Jl 20,7:1
Murkin, H Mrs, 1947, Ja 14,26:2
Murkland, C S Rev, 1926, N 12,23:3
Murkland, Harry B, 1966, Ja 28,47:5
Murkland, Phillip A, 1944, Jl 26,19:6
Murkland, S Wallace (por), 1955, N 16,35:2
Murless, Frederick T Jr, 1948, Mr 13,15:2
Murlin, Edgar L, 1937, O 9,19:6
Murlin, Ermina F Mrs, 1939, S 30,17:5
Murnane, Allan L, 1950, Ap 4,29:4
Murnane, Charles F, 1939, Ag 21,13:1
Murnane, Dennis, 1943, F 6,13:6
Murnane, Harald E, 1942, F 22,26:5
Murnane, Johanna, 1939, Ap 11,13:1
Murnane, John H, 1948, N 10,29:2
Murnane, Margaret, 1939, Ap 11,13:1
Murnane, Mary, 1939, Ap 11,13:1
Murnen, Owen F, 1952, Jl 2,25:2
Murner, James J Sr, 1965, Je 17,33:2
Murney, John J Mrs, 1941, O 30,23:3
Murnin, High H, 1947, Ja 9,23:1
Murnin, Tim, 1909, S 9,9:7
Murnos, Edward P, 1965, N 15,37:3
Muro, Bernardo de, 1955, O 29,19:4
Muro, Carmen, 1955, Mr 2,27:5
Murolo, Ernesto, 1940, Ja 7,IX,8:5
Murphey, Elmer R, 1951, Jl 7,13:5
Murphey, J Griffin Jr, 1950, Mr 23,29:4
Murphree, Dennis, 1949, F 10,27:5
Murphree, Eger V, 1962, O 30,35:4
Murphree, Thomas A, 1945, S 6,25:6
Murphy, A L, 1945, My 31,15:4
Murphy, A Stanwood, 1963, Ap 11,33:2
Murphy, A Watkins, 1961, My 28,64:2
Murphy, Albert J, 1957, O 7,27:3
Murphy, Albert T, 1947, My 17,15:2
Murphy, Althea, 1952, O 25,17:1
Murphy, Ambrose P, 1963, D 28,23:2
Murphy, Andrew J Jr, 1954, Jl 25,69:1
Murphy, Andrew L Mrs, 1966, Ag 11,33:3
Murphy, Anna F O Mrs, 1940, F 11,48:2
Murphy, Anna M Mrs, 1943, D 29,17:4
Murphy, Anna Mrs, 1952, O 8,31:5
Murphy, Anna V, 1950, My 18,29:1
Murphy, Annie B Mrs, 1956, S 27,35:5
Murphy, Annie E, 1949, Ap 15,24:3
Murphy, Annie M, 1941, Ap 25,19:3
Murphy, Anson, 1939, F 7,20:1
Murphy, Arthur, 1949, Ap 6,29:4
Murphy, Arthur E, 1959, Jl 15,29:3; 1962, My 13,88:6
Murphy, Arthur H (funl, F 10,15:4), 1922, F 7,17:3
Murphy, Arthur I, 1943, Ja 19,19:5
Murphy, Arthur J, 1956, Ja 8,87:1; 1967, F 2,35:3
Murphy, Arthur Mrs (Celli Faith), 1942, D 18,28:3
Murphy, Arthur Mrs, 1951, S 18,31:3
Murphy, Benjamin, 1909, Ja 4,9:6
Murphy, Benjamin J, 1955, Jl 20,27:1
Murphy, Benjamin Mrs, 1950, Jl 14,21:3
Murphy, Bernard F, 1939, Ap 4,25:3
Murphy, Bernard J, 1962, Mr 19,29:2
Murphy, Bernard P, 1940, D 15,60:2
Murphy, Bob, 1948, Ag 6,17:1
Murphy, Brian T, 1967, Mr 14,47:1
Murphy, C, 1931, D 3,6:2
Murphy, C F, 1907, Jl 28,7:6; 1934, Je 20,21:1
Murphy, C Francis, 1944, Jl 4,19:5
Murphy, C J Mrs, 1903, Mr 6,9:5
Murphy, C W, 1931, O 17,15:2
Murphy, C W Mrs, 1954, My 4,29:4
Murphy, Carl, 1967, F 26,84:2
Murphy, Carroll B, 1953, O 7,29:4
Murphy, Catherine M, 1953, Ag 8,11:4
Murphy, Catherine T, 1957, Jl 28,28:1
Murphy, Charles, 1918, Ja 10,13:1
Murphy, Charles A, 1938, S 13,23:1; 1945, Je 17,26:1
Murphy, Charles C, 1913, Ap 28,11:5; 1945, Je 20, 23:2; 1950, Mr 31,31:3
Murphy, Charles E, 1949, D 22,23:2; 1950, N 8,29:2
Murphy, Charles E (funl, N 25,29:3), 1959, N 23,31:1
Murphy, Charles F, 1944, Ap 25,23:4
Murphy, Charles F Jr, 1939, O 10,23:5
Murphy, Charles H, 1938, My 10,21:3; 1945, D 29, 13:2; 1954, Ap 5,25:2
Murphy, Charles J, 1941, Jl 23,19:6
Murphy, Charles J Mrs, 1941, My 26,19:5
Murphy, Charles W, 1937, D 11,19:2; 1938, N 26,16:2; 1947, Je 29,48:8
Murphy, Charlie M, 1950, F 18,15:3
Murphy, Charlton L, 1951, Mr 1,28:2
Murphy, Charlton L Jr, 1961, D 7,43:5
Murphy, Christopher S, 1965, Jl 31,21:4
Murphy, Clarence, 1939, Mr 29,23:5
Murphy, Clarence A, 1951, Je 11,25:2
Murphy, Clarence E, 1951, My 11,27:3
Murphy, Clarence L, 1948, Ap 26,23:4
Murphy, Claudia Q Mrs, 1941, O 3,23:4
Murphy, Clement, 1951, Ja 17,28:2
Murphy, Clement P, 1955, D 11,89:1
Murphy, Cornelius E, 1954, Ap 26,25:4
Murphy, Cornelius S, 1956, My 22,33:2
Murphy, D J, 1957, Ja 15,29:1
Murphy, D T, 1885, Je 4,5:6

Murphy, Dan S, 1950, S 8,31:2
Murphy, Daniel, 1955, N 23,23:1
Murphy, Daniel C, 1952, Mr 19,29:1
Murphy, Daniel D, 1941, Ag 10,36:6
Murphy, Daniel F, 1937, My 24,19:3; 1949, O 18,27:2; 1959, My 30,17:6
Murphy, Daniel J, 1941, F 22,15:1; 1941, My 23,21:1; 1944, Je 17,13:5; 1946, O 22,25:1; 1955, Ap 24,87:1
Murphy, Daniel J Mrs, 1947, F 14,21:3
Murphy, Daniel J Sr, 1941, My 15,23:3
Murphy, Daniel P Dr, 1920, Ag 18,9:5
Murphy, Daniel Rev, 1907, D 30,7:6
Murphy, Daniel S, 1952, Jl 1,23:3
Murphy, Daniel W, 1874, Mr 17,2:7
Murphy, Danny (D Laub), 1967, Ja 1,52:1
Murphy, David E Mrs, 1967, My 13,33:5
Murphy, David F, 1954, Jl 22,23:5
Murphy, David Mrs, 1952, Ag 21,19:5
Murphy, David W, 1912, S 7,11:5
Murphy, Deacon, 1968, Ag 1,31:3
Murphy, Denis C, 1952, F 12,27:3
Murphy, Dennis J, 1949, Ag 14,69:1; 1951, N 6,29:4; 1958, Jl 22,27:1
Murphy, Dennis Mrs, 1959, My 10,70:4
Murphy, Dorothy Mrs, 1958, Ap 16,33:2
Murphy, Dwight, 1968, Ap 2,47:3
Murphy, E H Col, 1903, Ap 11,9:5
Murphy, Edgar G, 1948, Mr 5,21:5
Murphy, Edgar G Mrs, 1957, My 12,86:3
Murphy, Edgar Gardner Rev, 1913, Je 24,11:6
Murphy, Edgar L, 1954, Jl 5,11:2
Murphy, Edgar O, 1959, My 6,39:1
Murphy, Edward A, 1957, O 6,86:8
Murphy, Edward A Dr, 1924, Ag 16,11:6
Murphy, Edward D, 1957, Mr 30,19:6
Murphy, Edward F, 1941, Ja 19,40:6; 1952, F 11,25:4; 1953, Je 23,29:2
Murphy, Edward F Mrs, 1944, Ja 31,17:5; 1951, O 27, 19:6
Murphy, Edward F Sr, 1965, Mr 31,39:4
Murphy, Edward G, 1957, Mr 8,25:2
Murphy, Edward H, 1949, S 21,31:2; 1964, O 14,45:4
Murphy, Edward J, 1937, Jl 12,17:3; 1942, My 11, 15:4; 1952, D 26,15:4
Murphy, Edward J Sr, 1952, Ap 5,15:6
Murphy, Edward L, 1951, N 17,17:4
Murphy, Edward M-P, 1962, S 12,39:1
Murphy, Edward Mrs, 1915, Je 10,11:5; 1963, My 28, 28:8
Murphy, Edward P, 1950, Mr 26,96:2; 1958, D 15,2:5
Murphy, Edward S, 1945, D 5,25:6
Murphy, Edward T, 1937, Ja 12,23:4; 1965, Ja 6,39:1
Murphy, Edward V, 1919, Jl 18,11:4; 1941, O 27,17:3
Murphy, Edward W, 1940, D 2,23:5
Murphy, Edwin S, 1962, Jl 17,25:2
Murphy, Elbert D, 1944, Ag 3,19:2
Murphy, Elijah, 1942, D 25,17:4
Murphy, Elizabeth, 1945, Ag 4,11:3; 1946, Mr 3,44:6
Murphy, Ellen Mrs, 1905, Je 23,7:5
Murphy, Elliot J, 1965, O 22,43:3
Murphy, Elmer B, 1950, O 27,30:2
Murphy, Elmer J, 1962, Ap 23,29:4
Murphy, Emmet J, 1950, Ja 4,35:3
Murphy, Emmett P, 1960, Je 18,23:3
Murphy, Ernest, 1951, Mr 5,21:3
Murphy, Eugene, 1938, My 2,17:4
Murphy, Eugene C, 1941, N 9,52:4; 1953, Jl 11,11:4
Murphy, Eugene E, 1965, Jl 11,68:6
Murphy, Eugene P, 1908, Je 17,9:5; 1949, Je 24,23:5
Murphy, Evelyn H (will), 1952, S 11,38:2
Murphy, Francis, 1907, Jl 1,7:6; 1961, O 28,21:2
Murphy, Francis C X, 1958, My 31,15:3
Murphy, Francis F, 1938, Ap 26,21:5
Murphy, Francis H, 1954, N 16,29:1
Murphy, Francis J, 1953, My 6,31:4; 1954, Ap 18,64:1; 1956, O 5,25:2
Murphy, Francis M, 1941, Ag 1,15:1
Murphy, Francis P, 1942, Ag 4,13:3; 1958, D 20,2:5
Murphy, Francis P Mrs, 1957, My 6,29:4
Murphy, Frank, 1904, D 13,9:3; 1940, Mr 1,21:2; 1944, D 26,19:2
Murphy, Frank (funl, D 16,86:6), 1956, D 14,29:3
Murphy, Frank C Mrs, 1968, N 24,87:2
Murphy, Frank J, 1944, My 24,19:6; 1944, Ag 5,11:4; 1948, Ja 4,52:6; 1965, F 27,25:2
Murphy, Frank Justice, 1949, Jl 20,1:2
Murphy, Frank M, 1942, F 3,19:5; 1947, S 25,29:3; 1965, Je 21,29:2
Murphy, Frank W (por), 1940, N 23,17:3
Murphy, Franklin (funl, F 26,11:4), 1920, F 25,11:5
Murphy, Franklin Mrs, 1904, F 11,9:7
Murphy, Fred J, 1956, D 21,23:1
Murphy, Fred T, 1948, Ja 11,58:3
Murphy, Frederick, 1951, O 10,23:4
Murphy, Frederick A, 1942, Ap 12,44:4
Murphy, Frederick C, 1957, Jl 27,17:1
Murphy, Frederick D, 1961, S 6,37:3
Murphy, Frederick D Mrs, 1964, My 14,35:3
Murphy, Frederick E (por), 1940, F 15,19:1
Murphy, Frederick E, 1955, Ap 9,25:3
Murphy, Frederick J, 1949, F 18,23:2
Murphy, Frederick Lt, 1924, My 24,15:4
Murphy, Frederick S, 1950, Je 23,25:5

Murphy, Frederick W, 1937, Ja 23,17:5
Murphy, George, 1938, Je 16,23:1; 1961, Jl 13,29:1
Murphy, George B, 1955, F 14,12:7
Murphy, George E, 1952, N 25,29:3; 1961, Mr 17,31:1
Murphy, George F, 1942, Jl 26,30:6
Murphy, George H, 1924, O 18,15:6
Murphy, George Moseley Dr, 1968, D 8,86:7
Murphy, George Mrs, 1943, D 9,27:2
Murphy, George N, 1948, D 1,29:4
Murphy, George S, 1944, Ja 18,19:3
Murphy, George V, 1962, My 10,37:4
Murphy, George W, 1952, O 24,23:5
Murphy, Gerald, 1964, O 18,89:1
Murphy, Gilbert P, 1949, Je 16,29:3
Murphy, Grayson M Col (por), 1937, O 19,25:1
Murphy, Griffin, 1940, Ag 24,13:5
Murphy, H C, 1882, D 2,8:1
Murphy, Harold (por), 1946, O 22,25:4
Murphy, Harold J, 1953, Ja 25,86:3
Murphy, Harold P, 1958, F 4,29:2
Murphy, Harold W, 1952, Je 14,15:1
Murphy, Harry, 1937, O 12,25:4
Murphy, Harry C, 1967, Mr 5,87:3
Murphy, Harry J, 1944, S 15,19:3
Murphy, Hayward, 1941, Ap 14,17:2
Murphy, Helen A, 1945, Ag 31,17:2
Murphy, Helen C Sister, 1951, Ag 15,27:4
Murphy, Henry, 1964, N 23,37:2
Murphy, Henry A, 1950, Ap 1,15:4
Murphy, Henry C, 1947, Mr 2,60:7; 1948, D 5,92:4
Murphy, Henry C Mrs, 1949, Mr 1,25:2
Murphy, Henry F, 1955, Jl 12,25:1
Murphy, Henry F Mrs, 1942, N 19,25:3
Murphy, Henry K, 1954, O 14,29:1
Murphy, Henry P, 1949, D 9,31:4
Murphy, Henry R, 1963, S 3,33:3
Murphy, Henry V, 1944, Mr 25,15:4; 1960, My 19,37:1
Murphy, Herbert C, 1948, S 14,30:3
Murphy, Herbert H, 1951, Ja 6,15:4
Murphy, Herbert H Mrs, 1943, Ap 27,23:3
Murphy, Herbert S, 1947, My 25,60:2
Murphy, Hermann D, 1945, Ap 17,23:3
Murphy, Hobart A, 1951, Mr 28,29:2
Murphy, Homer G, 1953, O 3,17:2
Murphy, Horatio H Jr, 1948, Ja 18,61:1
Murphy, Howard A, 1962, F 26,27:1
Murphy, Howard J, 1938, Ap 11,15:3
Murphy, Howard N, 1950, My 19,27:2
Murphy, Howard W, 1943, S 9,25:1
Murphy, Hugh J, 1938, Jl 6,23:3; 1945, Je 16,13:6
Murphy, Hugh Rev, 1905, Je 6,9:5
Murphy, Ida S (will), 1940, S 17,21:4
Murphy, J A, 1876, Jl 2,5:3
Murphy, J D, 1942, N 14,15:4
Murphy, J Edward, 1954, Mr 6,15:6
Murphy, J Edwin, 1943, Mr 30,21:2
Murphy, J Harvey, 1941, S 20,17:6
Murphy, J J, 1936, D 8,25:3
Murphy, J K, 1876, F 11,1:2
Murphy, J McLeod Col, 1871, Je 2,8:3
Murphy, J P, 1933, F 23,17:6; 1936, F 3,17:4
Murphy, J Prentice Mrs, 1951, Mr 24,13:6
Murphy, J R, 1932, D 29,19:1
Murphy, Jack Mrs, 1968, S 26,55:1
Murphy, James, 1875, Ag 21,4:6; 1905, Ap 15,8:4
Murphy, James (Jas Balnau), 1908, My 25,7:2
Murphy, James B, 1950, Ag 25,21:4
Murphy, James C, 1943, Ja 16,13:4
Murphy, James D, 1950, N 18,15:5; 1957, Ja 27,84:1
Murphy, James E, 1939, N 1,23:5
Murphy, James E Sr, 1956, Mr 27,35:4
Murphy, James F, 1949, Ja 20,27:5
Murphy, James J, 1950, Ap 18,31:3; 1962, O 20,25:3
Murphy, James J Jr (por), 1941, Ja 8,19:2
Murphy, James J Mrs, 1953, N 11,31:4
Murphy, James L, 1961, Ag 13,89:1
Murphy, James M, 1946, Mr 2,13:4; 1947, D 27,13:2
Murphy, James N, 1946, Mr 22,21:2
Murphy, James P, 1947, D 2,29:1
Murphy, James R (por), 1945, N 1,23:5
Murphy, James S, 1949, S 1,21:3
Murphy, James S Mrs, 1963, Je 26,39:2
Murphy, James W, 1960, Ap 12,33:1
Murphy, Jeremiah, 1938, Je 30,23:5; 1953, F 18,31:4; 1955, Mr 15,29:3
Murphy, Jeremiah J, 1937, D 19,II,8:5
Murphy, Jeremiah L, 1951, Jl 14,13:5
Murphy, Jerome F, 1961, Je 23,29:1
Murphy, Jerry, 1945, S 30,46:6
Murphy, Jimmy, 1947, D 26,15:2; 1965, Mr 11,33:4
Murphy, Joe, 1916, Ja 1,11:5
Murphy, John, 1925, Ap 28,21:4; 1941, F 17,15:2; 1944, F 28,17:5; 1949, S 25,92:4; 1950, Mr 14,25:1; 1958, Ja 10,26:3
Murphy, John A, 1922, Ap 13,19:6; 1922, My 1,17:2; 1939, My 31,23:2; 1939, Je 14,23:4; 1947, Jl 22,23:2; 1948, Je 2,29:3; 1948, Je 6,47:5; 1952, My 11,93:1
Murphy, John B, 1943, Mr 19,19:5
Murphy, John B Dr (est, Ag 15,9:6), 1916, Ag 12,9:3
Murphy, John C Dr, 1937, Ag 19,19:4
Murphy, John Capt, 1907, D 29,9:5
Murphy, John D, 1941, Mr 9,40:6
Murphy, John D (por), 1949, Ag 4,23:4

Murphy, John D Mrs, 1950, N 5,92:5
Murphy, John E, 1941, Ap 10,24:2; 1941, S 26,23:4
Murphy, John F, 1937, Ja 7,21:5; 1941, Ag 17,39:2; 1945, F 15,19:3; 1948, Jl 15,23:4; 1953, Ag 31,17:2
Murphy, John F Sr, 1959, Jl 4,15:5
Murphy, John Francis, 1921, Ja 31,9:4
Murphy, John G, 1947, S 5,20:3; 1957, My 25,21:2
Murphy, John H, 1922, Ap 6,17:4; 1956, Ja 15,93:1; 1961, My 20,23:4
Murphy, John J (funl, S 26,9:5), 1911, S 22,11:6
Murphy, John J, 1944, F 8,15:4; 1947, Mr 15,13:2; 1947, My 2,21:1; 1950, Ap 4,29:2; 1950, Jl 2,24:6; 1952, Je 29,56:6; 1953, Ja 22,23:2; 1955, Ap 20,33: 1957, Jl 21,61:2; 1959, Jl 31,23:4; 1960, F 13,19:5; 1964, S 25,41:3; 1965, My 18,39:3
Murphy, John J A, 1967, Ja 25,43:1
Murphy, John J Mrs, 1948, D 17,27:2; 1954, Je 4,23 1966, Ap 12,35:3
Murphy, John L, 1965, Mr 11,33:3
Murphy, John M, 1949, Mr 9,25:5
Murphy, John M Sr, 1950, O 30,27:4
Murphy, John O, 1961, O 21,21:2
Murphy, John P, 1945, S 5,23:3; 1955, Ja 9,87:3
Murphy, John P Mrs, 1943, Mr 27,13:3
Murphy, John P Sr, 1939, D 24,14:5
Murphy, John R, 1968, D 16,47:6
Murphy, John S, 1946, Jl 20,13:4
Murphy, John S Mrs, 1951, O 27,19:4
Murphy, John T, 1941, Ag 4,15:1; 1942, N 6,23:5; 1944, Je 16,19:1; 1952, Ap 22,23:2
Murphy, John T Jr, 1939, Je 30,19:5
Murphy, John T Mrs, 1948, D 10,25:3
Murphy, John W, 1942, N 22,52:6; 1947, Ap 11,25: 1952, Je 12,33:1; 1962, Mr 29,33:1; 1963, D 10,50
Murphy, John W Dr, 1923, Ag 4,13:4
Murphy, Joseph, 1941, O 29,23:3; 1942, Jl 17,15:4; 1949, My 24,28:2
Murphy, Joseph A, 1939, N 26,42:7; 1940, D 17,25 1941, Ja 25,15:6; 1944, Ap 15,11:6; 1946, Je 9,42: 1946, S 6,22:2; 1950, Mr 25,13:5; 1951, Mr 29,27: 1952, Ap 13,76:4; 1955, Ap 23,19:4
Murphy, Joseph A Rev, 1952, D 14,90:8
Murphy, Joseph D E, 1953, Ja 3,15:2
Murphy, Joseph E, 1945, Je 19,19:3
Murphy, Joseph E (por), 1946, My 23,21:1
Murphy, Joseph E, 1948, Ap 19,23:4; 1952, Mr 11, 27:5; 1955, F 28,19:5
Murphy, Joseph F, 1939, F 5,40:3; 1941, Ag 8,15:4 1942, My 12,19:4
Murphy, Joseph J, 1939, My 8,17:3; 1960, My 21, 1961, Ag 1,31:1
Murphy, Joseph L, 1957, Ag 10,15:3
Murphy, Joseph M Sr, 1968, Je 28,41:2
Murphy, Joseph N, 1966, F 25,31:3
Murphy, Joseph P, 1941, S 25,25:4; 1949, D 14,31
Murphy, Joseph R, 1948, S 9,27:4
Murphy, Joseph T, 1955, F 25,21:3
Murphy, Joseph T Rev, 1955, Ja 20,31:1
Murphy, Josephine V, 1943, S 5,28:6
Murphy, Julia J, 1965, S 15,47:2
Murphy, Katherine (Mother Mary Evelyn), 1955 S 13,31:2
Murphy, Katherine T, 1966, Mr 29,41:4
Murphy, Kid (P Frascella), 1963, O 30,39:4
Murphy, Kieran T, 1961, F 3,23:1
Murphy, Kingsley H, 1953, Mr 5,27:4
Murphy, Lambert, 1954, Jl 26,17:3
Murphy, Laurence A, 1961, Ag 9,33:1
Murphy, Lawrence C, 1957, N 27,31:3
Murphy, Lawrence J, 1914, Ja 23,11:5
Murphy, Lecturer, 1872, Mr 14,1:5
Murphy, Leo, 1945, F 11,40:4
Murphy, Leslie H, 1943, D 5,45:3
Murphy, Lillian, 1940, My 10,23:4
Murphy, Louis E, 1940, Je 29,15:4
Murphy, Louise B, 1938, S 4,17:3
Murphy, Luke J, 1952, S 13,17:4
Murphy, Luther Mrs, 1946, Mr 24,44:4
Murphy, M William Mrs, 1962, Jl 15,60:3
Murphy, Malvern-Hill, 1964, N 5,45:3
Murphy, Margaret, 1955, Jl 1,21:4
Murphy, Margaret K Mrs, 1941, Ja 19,40:1
Murphy, Margaret Mrs, 1940, N 9,17:4
Murphy, Marguerite B, 1946, Ja 18,19:4
Murphy, Maria Mrs, 1942, Ja 30,20:2
Murphy, Mark, 1917, Ja 11,15:4; 1952, Ag 1,17:2
Murphy, Martin, 1944, Mr 16,19:4
Murphy, Martin A, 1953, Jl 11,11:5
Murphy, Martin J, 1939, Mr 8,21:1; 1949, My 1 1964, Jl 6,29:2
Murphy, Martin W, 1943, Ja 19,19:1
Murphy, Mary, 1944, Ag 22,17:4
Murphy, Mary A (will), 1939, F 19,37:3
Murphy, Mary A, 1944, Ja 7,17:3; 1962, Jl 10,33
Murphy, Mary H, 1945, N 27,23:2
Murphy, Mary H R, 1943, Ap 13,25:5
Murphy, Mary J, 1940, Jl 14,31:2
Murphy, Mary M Mrs, 1956, Ja 4,27:1
Murphy, Matt H, 1959, D 19,27:4
Murphy, Matt H Jr (funl, Ag 23,18:7), 1965, A 9:6
Murphy, Matthew J, 1943, Jl 10,13:2; 1951, D
Murphy, Maude K, 1942, Je 5,17:5

Murphy, Maurice, 1949, Mr 27,76:8
Murphy, Maurice J, 1947, Mr 6,25:5
Murphy, Maurice K M, 1963, Ap 27,25:2
Murphy, May D Mrs, 1941, F 8,15:5
Murphy, Merle B Sr, 1961, Ap 20,33:4
Murphy, Michael, 1912, Ja 2,11:5; 1940, N 22,23:5; 1951, S 11,31:8
Murphy, Michael C, 1913, Je 5,11:3
Murphy, Michael F, 1945, F 1,23:2
Murphy, Michael F Mrs, 1954, N 14,89:2
Murphy, Michael J, 1939, S 9,17:5; 1945, Ja 19,19:2; 1947, S 10,27:5; 1949, Ja 15,17:1; 1951, Mr 4,93:1; 1952, O 29,29:4; 1956, S 2,57:1; 1958, Ag 18,19:4
Murphy, Michael J Dr, 1937, S 27,21:3
Murphy, Michael J J, 1954, Jl 24,13:1
Murphy, Michael J Mrs, 1945, O 3,19:5
Murphy, Michelle C Mrs, 1954, Ag 22,93:1
Murphy, Miles S, 1958, O 4,21:6
Murphy, Nathan, 1908, Ag 24,7:7
Murphy, Neil D, 1948, Ja 11,56:6
Murphy, Nellie Mrs, 1950, S 27,31:2
Murphy, Nicholas J, 1941, Jl 2,21:2; 1953, N 5,31:5
Murphy, Nicholas J Rev, 1917, F 20,9:5
Murphy, Owen, 1965, Ap 4,87:1
Murphy, Owen K, 1968, Ag 27,42:1
Murphy, P C Sen, 1925, Mr 7,13:7
Murphy, P F, 1931, N 24,25:1
Murphy, Parker, 1944, D 19,21:4
Murphy, Patrick, 1947, Mr 26,25:4
Murphy, Patrick A, 1943, My 10,19:2
Murphy, Patrick F 2d, 1937, Ja 31,II,9:2
Murphy, Patrick H, 1938, Mr 24,23:1
Murphy, Paul A, 1948, D 7,31:1
Murphy, Paul D, 1959, Mr 23,31:4
Murphy, Paul E, 1957, D 12,29:1
Murphy, Paul V, 1954, Ag 18,29:5
Murphy, Peter, 1941, My 12,17:4; 1945, Ap 28,15:1
Murphy, Peter A, 1908, My 8,7:5
Murphy, Peter J, 1949, F 18,23:2; 1955, Jl 11,23:5; 1968, Ap 4,47:2
Murphy, Peter M, 1943, Ap 20,24:3
Murphy, Ray D, 1964, F 25,31:1
Murphy, Ray L, 1953, F 1,88:5
Murphy, Raymond M, 1951, My 8,31:3
Murphy, Raymond P, 1952, N 27,31:2
Murphy, Raymond W, 1960, O 17,29:2
Murphy, Reginald J, 1947, O 21,23:1
Murphy, Rich F, 1924, Mr 6,17:4
Murphy, Richard C, 1965, D 25,13:4
Murphy, Richard D, 1959, Ap 19,86:5
Murphy, Richard F, 1958, My 21,33:4
Murphy, Richard J, 1944, Ja 5,18:3; 1948, Ja 20,23:4; 1966, Jl 7,37:2
Murphy, Robert E, 1956, Je 5,35:2
Murphy, Robert J, 1942, D 6,76:2
Murphy, Robert M (Irish Bob), 1961, Ag 18,48:7
Murphy, Robert S, 1912, Je 25,11:4; 1940, Jl 3,17:5
Murphy, Robert T Jr, 1937, D 5,II,8:7
Murphy, Roy, 1940, Mr 16,15:5
Murphy, Russell W, 1953, Jl 26,69:3
Murphy, S Edward, 1949, Jl 19,29:3
Murphy, Samuel G Mrs, 1945, N 7,23:4
Murphy, Samuel W (por), 1944, N 20,21:3
Murphy, Sarah Mrs, 1954, My 18,29:2
Murphy, Seymour N, 1949, S 21,31:3
Murphy, Starr J, 1921, Ap 5,19:5
Murphy, Stephen J, 1949, Je 22,31:5
Murphy, Stephen L, 1939, Ag 18,19:2
Murphy, T, 1929, Ja 12,17:3
Murphy, T E, 1933, D 16,15:6
Murphy, T J, 1871, Ag 6,8:6; 1885, Ja 25,7:5
Murphy, T P, 1948, F 3,25:1
Murphy, Terence E Col, 1937, Ja 31,II,9:3
Murphy, Thomas, 1904, Je 29,7:7; 1906, My 21,9:3; 1917, S 14,9:4; 1923, Mr 17,13:2; 1943, O 18,15:2; 1955, Je 29,29:4; 1967, D 27,37:2
Murphy, Thomas A, 1940, Jl 27,13:5; 1946, N 10,64:3; 1950, N 25,13:5
Murphy, Thomas C, 1958, N 21,29:3
Murphy, Thomas D, 1925, Ja 28,17:4
Murphy, Thomas E, 1937, D 20,27:2; 1953, D 27,60:7; 1957, Mr 20,37:2; 1960, Ap 10,85:3
Murphy, Thomas E Mrs, 1964, Jl 14,33:3
Murphy, Thomas E Sr, 1951, D 5,35:2
Murphy, Thomas F, 1944, S 11,17:5; 1958, My 9,23:4
Murphy, Thomas F Mrs, 1956, D 9,87:3; 1964, N 4, 39:4
Murphy, Thomas H, 1942, Jl 4,17:6; 1966, O 24,39:4
Murphy, Thomas I, 1942, F 15,44:3
Murphy, Thomas J, 1938, Ag 3,19:2; 1952, F 22,2:1; 1952, Je 12,33:2
Murphy, Thomas L, 1945, My 20,32:3
Murphy, Thomas M, 1946, My 21,23:4
Murphy, Thomas P, 1949, Jl 29,21:4
Murphy, Thomas P Mrs, 1938, Jl 9,13:7; 1949, F 11, 24:3
Murphy, Thomas V, 1960, Ap 29,31:5
Murphy, Thomas W, 1967, Mr 22,47:3
Murphy, Timothy, 1941, S 17,23:3; 1949, Ap 30,13:6
Murphy, Timothy A, 1943, Ap 2,21:5
Murphy, Timothy J, 1949, Ap 12,30:2; 1949, D 17,17:1
Murphy, Timothy P, 1937, Mr 6,17:1
Murphy, Truman O, 1938, S 3,13:5
Murphy, Vincent B, 1954, Jl 10,13:3; 1956, F 27,23:3
Murphy, Virginia, 1950, Je 8,31:4
Murphy, W Arthur, 1949, Ap 18,25:2
Murphy, W D, 1877, Ag 29,4:7
Murphy, W Gordon, 1954, O 27,29:3
Murphy, W J, 1908, My 11,7:5
Murphy, W Tayloe, 1962, N 17,25:1
Murphy, Walter, 1939, S 6,23:4
Murphy, Walter G, 1938, D 11,60:8; 1948, Je 11,23:5
Murphy, Walter H, 1949, N 2,27:1
Murphy, Walter J, 1959, N 27,29:1
Murphy, Walter M, 1952, Ag 15,16:4
Murphy, Walter P (por),(will, D 31,17:5), 1942, D 17,29:1
Murphy, Walter P (will), 1943, Ja 1,26:2
Murphy, Walter W, 1962, F 10,23:2
Murphy, Wilbur J, 1953, Jl 4,11:5
Murphy, William A, 1940, Jl 3,17:1; 1945, Ap 9,19:6; 1946, D 17,31:3
Murphy, William A Sr, 1963, D 27,25:1
Murphy, William C, 1945, F 22,27:2
Murphy, William C Jr, 1949, N 27,104:5
Murphy, William D, 1908, O 11,11:5; 1948, Jl 6,23:5
Murphy, William E, 1925, N 23,21:4
Murphy, William F, 1939, Ap 13,23:2; 1939, O 10, 23:5; 1940, D 15,62:2; 1950, F 8,27:2; 1950, O 5,31:3; 1953, Mr 15,93:1; 1964, N 26,33:1
Murphy, William G, 1940, Ja 3,21:2; 1951, D 5,35:5
Murphy, William H, 1948, My 17,19:2; 1954, N 17, 31:2; 1957, My 20,25:1
Murphy, William H Rev, 1917, O 25,15:4
Murphy, William J, 1937, Ja 5,23:3; 1940, S 26,23:5; 1942, F 28,17:6; 1942, S 23,25:5; 1944, F 9,19:3; 1953, My 9,19:3; 1954, Ap 26,25:2; 1955, D 12,31:5; 1956, Mr 24,19:5; 1959, F 26,31:4; 1961, N 28,32:5; 1967, F 3,28:6; 1967, D 21,37:3
Murphy, William J Mrs (H Essary), 1951, Ag 16, 27:3
Murphy, William J Mrs, 1951, D 15,13:5
Murphy, William James, 1918, O 25,13:5
Murphy, William L, 1943, Ja 10,50:2; 1957, My 24, 25:1
Murphy, William M, 1943, O 22,17:4
Murphy, William Mrs, 1944, Jl 10,15:4
Murphy, William P, 1946, My 16,21:3; 1957, Ag 10, 15:2
Murphy, William T, 1948, O 3,67:3; 1965, D 7,47:1
Murphy, William W, 1939, O 4,25:3
Murr, Samuel Mrs, 1947, Mr 2,60:6
Murrah, William B Bp, 1925, Mr 6,19:5
Murray, A Gordon, 1951, D 3,31:3
Murray, Achols J, 1925, Ap 21,21:6
Murray, Adrian O Mrs, 1945, D 21,21:3
Murray, Albert A, 1964, F 27,31:1
Murray, Alex, 1959, D 13,86:6
Murray, Alexander William Charles Baron, 1920, S 14,11:1
Murray, Alice H Mrs, 1937, Jl 24,15:5
Murray, Alice Mrs, 1914, N 9,9:5
Murray, Ambrose S 3d, 1939, Je 15,23:2
Murray, Ambrose Spencer Jr, 1924, Je 3,17:3
Murray, Amy, 1947, Ja 18,15:2
Murray, Andrew Dr, 1903, Ag 23,1:2
Murray, Anna Mrs, 1961, Ag 30,33:5
Murray, Annie A Mrs, 1941, D 15,19:2
Murray, Anthony Shorbe, 1907, Jl 13,7:6
Murray, Arch, 1961, D 21,27:2
Murray, Archibald (por), 1945, Ja 26,21:3
Murray, Archibald, 1945, F 11,38:3
Murray, Arnold, 1952, D 1,23:3
Murray, Arthur B, 1965, Ja 24,81:1
Murray, Arthur C (Viscount Elibank), 1962, D 6,43:5
Murray, Arthur E, 1946, Ja 5,13:5
Murray, Arthur E Mrs, 1944, Jl 21,19:4
Murray, Arthur F, 1961, My 12,29:4
Murray, Arthur Gen, 1925, My 13,21:3
Murray, Arthur J, 1956, S 17,27:5
Murray, Arthur S, 1941, Ja 3,19:1; 1955, Ap 14,36:5
Murray, Arthur T, 1962, N 26,29:4
Murray, Athole Mrs, 1959, Ag 25,31:3
Murray, Augustus T (por), 1940, Mr 10,48:1
Murray, Austin S, 1949, O 12,29:3
Murray, Basil, 1937, Ap 2,23:2
Murray, Benjamin A, 1942, D 25,17:5
Murray, Benjamin B Gen, 1906, Mr 2,9:6
Murray, Benjamin H R Mrs, 1963, Ag 15,33:6
Murray, Billy, 1954, Ag 19,23:5
Murray, Bob, 1950, O 7,14:4
Murray, C Athey, 1944, Jl 26,19:1
Murray, C Edward, 1943, Ja 13,23:5
Murray, C Morton Rev Dr, 1937, Je 20,II,7:2
Murray, Carl T, 1940, S 13,23:3
Murray, Catherine, 1941, Ap 8,25:6
Murray, Charles, 1924, Ap 30,19:3; 1941, My 3,15:5
Murray, Charles A, 1952, O 20,23:5
Murray, Charles A H Sir, 1915, Jl 27,9:6
Murray, Charles B (por), 1938, Ap 1,23:2
Murray, Charles D, 1945, Ap 17,23:4
Murray, Charles F Mrs, 1943, My 14,19:4
Murray, Charles H Ex-Judge, 1916, S 7,9:3
Murray, Charles J, 1943, Ja 4,15:2; 1950, Mr 23,36:2
Murray, Charles L Mrs, 1946, D 10,32:2
Murray, Charles M Sr, 1940, N 1,25:1
Murray, Charles Mrs, 1961, Ap 21,33:4
Murray, Charles Mrs (L A Westman), 1965, N 15, 37:3
Murray, Charles R, 1938, Je 24,19:2; 1953, O 28,29:3
Murray, Charles Theodore Maj, 1924, N 21,19:5
Murray, Charles W, 1950, Jl 27,25:4
Murray, Charles W Mrs, 1961, My 13,19:3
Murray, Charlie (por), 1941, Jl 30,17:3
Murray, Charnley L, 1940, Jl 11,19:3
Murray, Cicero I, 1959, S 16,39:1
Murray, Clarke L, 1957, Ag 21,27:4
Murray, Clay R (por), 1947, Je 16,21:3
Murray, Cleon B, 1943, N 25,25:3
Murray, Clifford J, 1958, My 21,33:3
Murray, Cornelius J, 1953, O 24,15:5
Murray, Dan T, 1924, Ap 28,15:4
Murray, Daniel F, 1950, Jl 14,21:4
Murray, Daniel F Mrs, 1941, D 20,19:6
Murray, David, 1938, N 18,21:5
Murray, David A, 1949, O 1,13:2
Murray, David C, 1907, Ag 2,7:5; 1943, Mr 2,19:2
Murray, David Dr, 1905, Mr 7,9:6
Murray, David K, 1871, My 29,1:3
Murray, David L, 1962, Ag 31,21:3
Murray, Dennis, 1946, Ap 23,21:4
Murray, Donald C L, 1938, O 9,45:1
Murray, Donald W, 1949, S 7,29:3
Murray, Douglas Jr, 1940, Je 18,23:4
Murray, E G, 1932, Ag 30,18:1
Murray, Earle W, 1957, Mr 28,31:5
Murray, Edward B, 1940, Jl 2,21:4; 1942, My 13,19:4
Murray, Edward E, 1965, Ap 11,92:8
Murray, Edward F, 1924, My 23,19:5
Murray, Edward G Mrs, 1957, Mr 8,48:5
Murray, Edward J, 1944, My 26,19:6; 1957, Ag 16, 19:3
Murray, Edward J B, 1950, F 4,15:6
Murray, Edward Jr, 1944, D 6,23:5
Murray, Edward S, 1939, Mr 8,21:5
Murray, Edwin C, 1957, F 13,35:4
Murray, Edwin C Mrs, 1951, Ap 17,29:6
Murray, Effingham C, 1948, S 23,29:6
Murray, Elizabeth, 1882, D 9,2:5
Murray, Elizabeth M Mrs, 1946, Mr 29,23:1
Murray, Eric W, 1947, O 1,29:5
Murray, Ernest M, 1943, Ja 19,19:3
Murray, Eugene F, 1952, Jl 26,13:7
Murray, Evelyn, 1947, Mr 31,23:2
Murray, Everett B, 1945, Jl 25,23:5
Murray, F A, 1923, Ap 18,21:5
Murray, F K Capt, 1868, Ag 4,2:3
Murray, Fannie M Mrs, 1940, Je 3,15:4
Murray, Fay L, 1941, Mr 5,21:5
Murray, Francis A, 1959, N 18,41:3; 1967, Ag 22,39:2
Murray, Francis D, 1962, Mr 17,25:6
Murray, Francis J, 1939, F 22,21:2; 1939, N 17,21:2
Murray, Francis J Mrs, 1948, Jl 13,27:5
Murray, Francis X, 1960, S 6,35:4
Murray, Frank, 1951, S 14,26:3
Murray, Frank E, 1939, F 25,15:4; 1957, My 24,25:4
Murray, Frank J, 1953, Je 2,29:4; 1959, O 19,29:2
Murray, Frank L, 1954, D 29,23:1
Murray, Frank Prof, 1951, Ag 31,15:3
Murray, Fred J, 1947, Ap 2,27:6
Murray, Frederick H, 1954, N 17,31:5
Murray, G Donald, 1957, Jl 6,15:3
Murray, G H, 1929, Ja 7,29:4
Murray, George, 1942, F 19,19:4; 1951, Ag 28,24:2; 1961, Ag 21,23:5
Murray, George A, 1968, Ag 8,33:4
Murray, George D, 1956, Je 20,31:1
Murray, George J, 1941, Ag 20,19:4
Murray, George L, 1942, My 25,15:5; 1956, D 10,31:2
Murray, George M, 1958, Ap 26,19:1
Murray, George R, 1938, Ap 15,19:1; 1939, S 24,43:2
Murray, George W, 1943, Ap 26,19:3
Murray, George W Mrs, 1954, S 16,29:4
Murray, George Wellwood, 1925, D 5,19:4
Murray, Gerald, 1951, Je 4,27:4
Murray, Gerald D, 1959, O 18,86:1
Murray, Gilbert (mem ser set, Je 23,84:4), 1957, My 21,35:2
Murray, Gilbert D, 1938, My 24,19:1
Murray, Gilbert M, 1949, D 18,88:3
Murray, Grenville, 1881, D 24,2:5
Murray, H Loomis, 1948, F 29,60:4
Murray, Harold G, 1942, S 5,13:4
Murray, Harry L, 1948, Jl 31,15:6
Murray, Harry R, 1951, O 4,33:5
Murray, Helen C, 1955, Je 1,33:3
Murray, Helen J Mrs, 1940, My 10,23:4
Murray, Henry, 1923, D 24,11:6
Murray, Henry F Rev, 1923, Ap 21,11:4
Murray, Henry R, 1945, Mr 14,19:4
Murray, Herman S, 1965, Je 15,41:4
Murray, Herschel, 1967, My 22,38:5
Murray, Hervey J Mrs, 1951, Ap 25,29:3
Murray, Howell W, 1958, N 30,87:1
Murray, Hubert, 1940, F 28,22:2
Murray, Hugh E, 1945, My 4,19:4
Murray, Hugh J, 1948, Ja 2,23:3
Murray, Hugo, 1955, O 12,31:2
Murray, J Archibald, 1954, F 27,13:6

Murray, J Edward, 1938, Ag 15,15:5
Murray, J Emmett, 1952, Je 6,23:4
Murray, J G, 1929, O 4,1:2
Murray, J H, 1881, D 28,2:7
Murray, J Harold, 1940, D 13,23:3
Murray, J J Rev Dr, 1905, Ap 12,9:4
Murray, J Lovell, 1955, My 2,21:5
Murray, J M, 1966, Ag 9,37:3
Murray, J R, 1881, N 2,5:1
Murray, J S Mrs, 1923, Ja 8,17:6
Murray, J Sir, 1928, D 1,17:5
Murray, J Warren, 1942, O 5,19:3
Murray, James, 1947, Mr 2,60:2; 1950, O 24,29:1; 1952, Ja 26,13:2; 1957, Ja 30,29:6
Murray, James A, 1939, N 11,15:2; 1960, Mr 7,29:4
Murray, James A Mrs, 1944, Ap 22,15:4
Murray, James B, 1937, D 9,25:5; 1948, My 11,25:4
Murray, James B Mrs, 1946, F 25,25:3
Murray, James C, 1940, Mr 4,15:4; 1943, Mr 28,25:1; 1951, Ap 7,15:4
Murray, James D, 1954, N 27,13:4
Murray, James D C, 1967, O 15,85:2
Murray, James D C Mrs, 1957, D 29,48:4
Murray, James E, 1938, S 28,25:2; 1961, Mr 24,31:1
Murray, James E Mrs, 1950, Ap 12,27:2
Murray, James F, 1943, Je 11,19:1; 1944, D 4,23:4; 1957, F 23,17:5
Murray, James F Jr, 1965, Mr 13,25:3
Murray, James F Sr, 1952, S 30,31:3
Murray, James F Sr Mrs, 1968, Ap 13,25:4
Murray, James G, 1966, My 31,43:1
Murray, James H, 1947, F 19,25:3; 1949, D 17,17:6
Murray, James J, 1947, D 29,17:4; 1948, F 22,48:2; 1948, Jl 16,19:4; 1958, N 27,29:4
Murray, James L, 1966, Mr 25,41:2
Murray, James M, 1865, Ag 14,8:2; 1949, D 27,23:4
Murray, James N, 1943, Ap 30,21:3
Murray, James O, 1941, Ja 20,17:2; 1945, Ap 26,23:3
Murray, James P, 1937, D 22,25:1; 1946, F 28,23:5
Murray, James R, 1941, Je 29,32:7; 1963, Ag 24,19:6
Murray, James R Mrs, 1938, O 1,17:3
Murray, James S (cor, O 20,23:1), 1939, O 19,23:5
Murray, James T, 1940, Ap 16,23:2; 1959, O 15,39:4; 1968, N 14,47:2
Murray, James V, 1942, S 3,19:3; 1952, D 27,7:8
Murray, James W, 1942, Ap 29,21:6
Murray, James W Mrs, 1962, Mr 8,31:3
Murray, Janette S (Mrs F G Murray), 1967, D 25, 21:3
Murray, Jennie E, 1952, Mr 13,30:3
Murray, John, 1912, O 1,13:5; 1914, Jl 7,9:6; 1938, Ag 27,28:3
Murray, John (Red), 1958, D 5,31:4
Murray, John, 1967, O 26,47:4
Murray, John A, 1939, F 9,21:4; 1940, Ag 4,33:1; 1954, F 13,13:2; 1957, D 27,19:3
Murray, John A Mrs, 1950, Mr 11,15:1
Murray, John B, 1951, Jl 7,13:6
Murray, John C, 1952, Ja 1,25:5; 1959, Mr 22,87:1; 1963, N 21,39:4
Murray, John C (trb, Ag 18,33:3; funl, Ag 22,34:1), 1967, Ag 17,37:1
Murray, John Clark Dr, 1917, N 22,13:5
Murray, John E, 1940, N 14,23:4
Murray, John E Mrs, 1940, Mr 10,48:8
Murray, John F (por), 1937, Mr 28,II,8:6
Murray, John F, 1942, Mr 17,22:3; 1944, Ap 8,13:2; 1944, Ag 12,11:3
Murray, John F Mrs, 1950, Mr 21,29:4
Murray, John F Mrs (L Corder), 1956, Ag 13,19:5
Murray, John F Mrs, 1962, My 16,41:2
Murray, John G (trb, O 17,20:3), 1956, O 12,29:1
Murray, John G, 1961, Ja 27,23:1
Murray, John H, 1945, Ja 16,19:3
Murray, John H Jr, 1961, F 28,33:2
Murray, John H Mrs, 1947, O 20,23:2
Murray, John Harry Mrs, 1910, Ap 9,11:4
Murray, John J, 1949, D 14,31:3; 1952, F 1,22:2; 1955, F 2,27:3; 1958, Ag 1,21:4; 1960, S 17,23:2
Murray, John J Mrs, 1946, D 26,25:2
Murray, John L (funl, S 4,11:5), 1917, Ag 31,7:7
Murray, John M, 1940, Ja 5,20:4; 1950, S 27,31:2
Murray, John M Mrs, 1952, N 22,23:6
Murray, John Mrs, 1955, My 4,29:3
Murray, John P Sr, 1948, Ag 20,17:5
Murray, John R Mrs, 1940, Ja 21,35:1
Murray, John V, 1962, My 6,88:3
Murray, John W, 1918, Jl 13,9:5; 1938, O 12,27:4; 1968, D 23,39:1
Murray, John W Mrs, 1958, F 7,21:4
Murray, Joseph, 1967, Mr 9,39:2
Murray, Joseph A, 1949, Ag 8,15:4
Murray, Joseph A F, 1957, Mr 14,29:6
Murray, Joseph B, 1961, S 15,33:1
Murray, Joseph D, 1959, Ja 4,88:3
Murray, Joseph E, 1960, F 6,19:4; 1960, O 12,39:2
Murray, Joseph E Mrs, 1950, My 18,29:3
Murray, Joseph F, 1940, Ap 2,25:5; 1951, Ja 25,25:4; 1954, Jl 26,17:5
Murray, Joseph G, 1941, D 13,21:5
Murray, Joseph H, 1944, Je 23,19:5
Murray, Joseph J, 1950, F 16,23:3
Murray, Joseph L, 1937, Je 24,25:1
Murray, Joseph M, 1955, F 12,15:5
Murray, Joseph P, 1962, Ja 10,47:3
Murray, Joseph T, 1907, Ja 28,7:4; 1943, My 27,25:2
Murray, Joseph V, 1961, F 12,86:1
Murray, Katherine S Mrs, 1939, Ap 4,25:2
Murray, Kenneth P, 1939, F 21,19:3
Murray, L O, 1926, Je 11,21:5
Murray, Lawrence E Rev, 1920, Ag 8,22:5
Murray, Lemuel M, 1952, O 30,31:2
Murray, Leo A, 1949, D 13,38:3
Murray, Leonard J, 1945, S 1,11:1
Murray, Lewis N, 1957, Ap 30,30:1
Murray, Lewis R, 1940, D 25,27:5
Murray, Lindley, 1906, D 31,7:5
Murray, Logan C, 1924, Je 2,17:6
Murray, Lucy E, 1948, N 26,23:3
Murray, Lula M Mrs, 1940, Jl 9,21:3
Murray, Mabel C, 1947, Ag 31,37:1
Murray, Mae, 1965, Mr 24,43:2
Murray, Malachy T, 1966, O 10,41:1
Murray, Margaret, 1963, N 15,35:1
Murray, Marion, 1949, N 23,29:5
Murray, Marion E, 1951, Ap 10,27:2
Murray, Martin J, 1960, O 30,86:8
Murray, Martin L, 1948, O 13,25:3
Murray, Martin M, 1949, F 5,15:5
Murray, Mary (Sister Marietta), 1960, F 8,29:2
Murray, Mary A Mrs, 1952, My 14,27:2
Murray, Mary Lady, 1956, S 3,13:2
Murray, Mary S (will), 1939, Ag 2,4:4
Murray, Matthew H Mrs, 1944, Ap 8,13:5
Murray, Maxwell (por), 1948, Ag 5,21:5
Murray, Melville I Lt, 1924, F 18,13:1
Murray, Meredith J, 1940, N 3,57:1
Murray, Michael, 1913, S 20,11:5
Murray, Michael J, 1944, O 17,23:3
Murray, Nat C, 1952, Ag 28,23:5
Murray, Neil R, 1959, Mr 6,25:2
Murray, Nellie B Mrs, 1942, My 19,20:2
Murray, Nicholas, 1918, D 10,13:2
Murray, Nina B Mrs, 1939, Ag 8,17:5
Murray, Norbury C, 1961, Ap 8,19:1
Murray, Oscar G, 1917, Mr 15,11:4
Murray, Oscar H, 1957, Ap 26,25:3
Murray, Patrick H, 1937, D 5,II,9:3; 1956, N 26,27:4
Murray, Patrick J, 1942, O 10,15:2; 1946, Ap 3,25:4
Murray, Patrick Rev, 1911, N 14,13:5
Murray, Paul, 1951, O 29,23:3; 1962, Mr 27,37:4
Murray, Percy, 1961, S 27,41:3
Murray, Peter, 1940, D 28,15:2; 1952, N 22,23:5
Murray, Peter A, 1942, Ag 15,11:6
Murray, Peter J, 1949, Jl 10,56:5
Murray, Peter J Mrs, 1961, S 19,35:1
Murray, Peter Mrs, 1941, My 29,19:5
Murray, Philip, 1952, N 10,1:2
Murray, Philip A, 1963, My 15,40:2
Murray, Poyntz M, 1946, Mr 19,27:1
Murray, R D Dr, 1903, N 23,2:3
Murray, R Lindley Mrs, 1951, Je 25,19:4; 1965, Ap 3, 29:3
Murray, Ray, 1960, Mr 10,31:2
Murray, Raymond B, 1945, Ja 4,19:5
Murray, Raymond H, 1950, N 29,33:2
Murray, Raymond J, 1944, F 3,19:4
Murray, Rear-Adm, 1884, N 11,2:4
Murray, Reid F, 1952, Ap 30,27:4
Murray, Richard, 1950, N 12,93:2
Murray, Richard F, 1940, My 12,49:1
Murray, Richard J, 1958, Ap 13,84:6
Murray, Richard R, 1967, Ap 28,41:4
Murray, Robert, 1940, F 19,17:1; 1949, Je 15,29:1; 1949, Ag 2,19:4
Murray, Robert A Dr, 1909, F 28,11:4
Murray, Robert B, 1954, Ag 14,15:4
Murray, Robert Gen, 1913, Ja 2,11:4
Murray, Robert H, 1942, N 4,23:4
Murray, Robert J, 1938, My 26,25:4; 1948, F 24,25:4; 1950, Ap 18,31:4
Murray, Robert J Mrs, 1950, Ap 2,92:3
Murray, Robert Jr, 1882, Ag 30,8:3
Murray, Robert L, 1945, F 14,19:4
Murray, Robert Lindley Mrs, 1908, O 24,9:4
Murray, Robert T, 1953, Ja 31,15:2
Murray, Roger F, 1941, Ap 16,25:4; 1958, Je 27,25:1
Murray, Roger F Mrs, 1947, F 7,23:3
Murray, Rose, 1946, Ja 3,19:1
Murray, Roy I, 1951, O 26,23:2
Murray, Rufus E, 1943, Je 17,22:3
Murray, Samuel, 1941, N 4,26:6
Murray, Samuel T Mrs, 1949, O 21,25:4
Murray, Sidney C, 1954, Je 3,27:2
Murray, Stanley C, 1962, S 6,31:4
Murray, Stanley G, 1937, D 3,23:1
Murray, Stephen G, 1950, My 5,22:3
Murray, Stephen J, 1939, Ag 30,17:2
Murray, T E, 1929, Jl 22,19:5
Murray, Thomas, 1903, O 13,7:2; 1921, D 28,15:6
Murray, Thomas A, 1946, D 26,25:5; 1958, My 3,1:1
Murray, Thomas B, 1958, Ja 26,88:3
Murray, Thomas C, 1959, Mr 8,86:7
Murray, Thomas E (funl plans, My 28,64:6; funl, My 30,17:3), 1961, My 27,23:1
Murray, Thomas E Mrs, 1943, D 1,21:4
Murray, Thomas F, 1937, N 9,23:3; 1942, D 28,20:2
Murray, Thomas G, 1941, D 24,17:2
Murray, Thomas H, 1941, Ag 5,19:3
Murray, Thomas J, 1941, S 21,42:2; 1947, S 23,25:2; 1952, Jl 29,21:5
Murray, Thomas J Mrs, 1947, My 19,22:3
Murray, Thomas V, 1940, O 4,23:4
Murray, Thomas W, 1948, D 21,31:2
Murray, Timothy, 1944, Je 1,19:2
Murray, Timothy F, 1951, Ap 16,25:4
Murray, Valentine, 1942, Ap 11,13:2
Murray, Vera M, 1956, Jl 1,57:2
Murray, Verne L, 1958, Jl 19,15:3
Murray, Virgil F Mrs, 1950, Jl 12,29:4
Murray, Virginia M (por), 1941, D 23,21:4
Murray, W H Rev, 1904, Mr 4,9:5
Murray, W John Rev, 1925, Je 17,21:5
Murray, Wallace S, 1965, Ap 28,45:2
Murray, Walter C, 1945, Mr 24,17:6
Murray, Walter F, 1956, S 3,13:5; 1960, Jl 2,7:5
Murray, Walter J Mrs, 1947, Mr 8,13:1
Murray, Walter M, 1953, Ja 7,31:5
Murray, Wendell P, 1946, Mr 1,21:4
Murray, Will, 1955, Mr 18,28:4
Murray, William, 1904, F 7,7:6; 1908, S 10,9:5; 19(S 13,9:5; 1914, N 3,11:5; 1937, N 23,23:5; 1946, My 15,21:5; 1959, Ja 6,33:3
Murray, William A, 1953, O 8,29:2
Murray, William B (por), 1949, Mr 11,25:1
Murray, William C R, 1941, Ag 1,15:4
Murray, William D (por), 1939, N 21,23:1
Murray, William D, 1943, My 3,17:5; 1946, F 5,23
Murray, William F, 1919, Je 11,15:4
Murray, William H, 1921, N 30,17:4; 1943, Ja 26, 1950, S 21,31:1
Murray, William H (Alfalfa Bill), 1956, O 16,33:
Murray, William H Mrs, 1938, Ag 29,13:6
Murray, William Houghton Dr, 1925, S 2,23:5
Murray, William I, 1952, Ag 22,21:1
Murray, William J, 1937, Mr 23,23:2; 1940, Ja 21, 35:1; 1942, Jl 19,30:7; 1946, My 18,19:4; 1959, D 27:3; 1959, D 25,21:3; 1966, Ag 21,93:1
Murray, William L, 1947, Jl 16,23:4
Murray, William M Col, 1908, Ap 5,11:4
Murray, William Mrs, 1946, Ag 14,26:3
Murray, William P, 1950, Ja 4,46:2
Murray, William S, 1939, My 10,23:2; 1942, Ja 1C 15:1; 1962, N 14,40:1
Murray, William S Mrs, 1943, Mr 28,24:2
Murray, William W, 1950, Ja 17,27:4; 1956, Ag 3,
Murray, Winifred, 1949, F 5,15:5
Murray, Wynn, 1957, F 8,23:2
Murrel, John R, 1951, O 8,21:3
Murrell, Cyrus A, 1944, Ap 6,23:4
Murrell, Frederick W H, 1916, Je 10,11:7
Murrell, Ralph E, 1942, F 4,19:2
Murrer, Nellie E, 1945, My 31,15:4
Murrie, William F R, 1950, S 9,17:1
Murrill, Herbert H J, 1952, Jl 26,13:7
Murrill, James L, 1937, Ap 26,19:5
Murrill, William A, 1957, D 27,20:1
Murrin, Christina, 1949, O 25,27:5
Murrin, Edward, 1943, D 20,23:3
Murrin, Gale F, 1958, Ag 13,27:5
Murrin, Robert E, 1940, D 21,17:4
Murrow, Edward R (funl plans, Ap 30,35:3; funl, 1,31:3), 1965, Ap 28,1:4
Murrow, J, 1881, Je 30,1:4
Murrow, Roscoe C, 1955, Ap 3,86:5
Murrow, Roscoe Mrs, 1962, Ja 1,23:5
Murry, John M, 1957, Mr 14,29:4
Murry, Jules, 1939, D 31,19:2
Murscoe, Matthews, 1945, Jl 8,11:5
Murska, Ilma Di, 1889, Ja 18,5:3
Murt, M Mrs, 1946, N 27,45:5
Murta, Albert, 1951, Mr 7,34:4
Murta, John P, 1946, D 20,24:2
Murtagh, J Charles, 1957, My 12,86:3
Murtagh, Michael J, 1958, Ja 28,28:1
Murtagh, Thomas F, 1937, Mr 9,23:4
Murtagh, Thomas P Mrs, 1966, S 22,47:2
Murtagh, William J, 1942, Ap 29,21:3; 1956, D
Murtaugh, Bartholomew, 1910, Ap 10,13:2
Murtaugh, Camilla A, 1945, Ja 12,15:4
Murtaugh, Daniel J, 1941, Mr 19,15:7
Murtaugh, Edward J, 1951, Mr 6,27:3
Murtaugh, Emily Mrs, 1939, Ja 16,15:3
Murtaugh, H Frank, 1949, O 3,17:5
Murtaugh, Marie R, 1942, My 16,13:3
Murtaugh, T Edward, 1950, Jl 18,30:2
Murtfeldt, Edward W, 1964, Ap 6,31:4
Murtfeldt, Frank W, 1962, F 5,31:3
Murth, Annie Mrs, 1944, F 4,15:3
Murtha, Charles A, 1938, N 30,23:4
Murtha, Edward J, 1954, Mr 8,27:3
Murtha, Frank B, 1903, Ag 12,9:6
Murtha, James A Sr, 1918, Ag 3,9:6
Murtha, James J, 1947, O 16,28:2
Murtha, James L, 1952, Jl 31,23:3
Murtha, John J, 1918, My 27,13:5
Murtha, Joseph A, 1948, N 2,25:2
Murtha, Manus F Sr, 1947, Ag 19,23:2
Murtha, Marie, 1922, My 5,17:5

Murtha, Matthew J, 1960, Ja 22,27:1
Murther, Stuart R, 1945, N 14,19:4
Murthey, Elmore S, 1951, Mr 18,88:4
Murtland, Anna A Mrs, 1939, F 23,23:5
Murtland, Samuel Dr, 1916, Je 17,11:5
Murton, George Mrs, 1951, Mr 17,15:3
Murton, Walter T, 1958, S 14,84:3
Murty, J Thomas, 1961, Ap 24,29:3
Murzin, Nathan C, 1962, Ag 22,33:1
Musacchio, Frederick A, 1964, My 16,25:6
Musard, Napoleon, 1859, Ap 22,2:2
Musaus, John, 1942, F 28,17:3
Musbah, Queen of Jordan, 1961, Mr 19,89:1
Muscanto, Mischa, 1946, My 21,23:2
Muscarella, Anthony, 1952, D 8,41:1
Muscat, Benjamin, 1966, D 9,47:1
Muscat, Lazarus, 1944, S 16,13:6
Muscatell, Dominic, 1941, F 13,19:5
Muscente, Frank Mrs, 1944, Ag 10,17:6
Muschel, William Mrs, 1961, D 1,30:3
Muschell, Charles S, 1963, My 12,86:2
Muschenheim, Frederick A, 1956, D 19,31:4
Muschenheim, William C, 1918, O 26,11:1
Musco, Angelo, 1937, O 7,27:3
Muse, Ban T, 1950, F 6,25:3
Muse, Charles A, 1951, Ag 28,23:1
Muse, Harry R Sr, 1965, N 29,35:3
Muselier, Emile H, 1965, S 3,27:1
Muser, Max, 1951, S 8,17:2
Musgrave, Anthony Lady, 1920, O 29,15:5
Musgrave, Christopher James Dr, 1921, Jl 30,9:6
Musgrave, Curt A, 1938, N 5,19:5
Musgrave, Darwin Mrs, 1951, O 19,27:5
Musgrave, Edith P Mrs, 1939, Ag 4,13:4
Musgrave, Everett A, 1945, Je 8,19:5
Musgrave, George W S, 1947, Ag 13,23:4
Musgrave, Herbert Mrs, 1943, Ja 14,21:2
Musgrave, Jennye Lucinda Lady, 1920, Ag 27,11:4
Musgrave, Maurice D, 1944, O 22,45:2
Musgrave, S B, 1884, N 13,5:5
Musgrave, T B, 1903, My 1,9:4
Musgrave, Thomas Archbishop, 1860, My 21,1:6
Musgrave, Walter E, 1950, My 9,30:3
Musgrave, Wayne M, 1941, Jl 24,17:4
Musgrove, Frederick E, 1953, Mr 22,86:2
Musgrove, Mary L, 1945, Je 12,19:3
Mushanoff, Nicolas, 1951, Ag 8,14:2
Mushett, Thomas H, 1965, Jl 26,23:2
Mushkin, Julius, 1958, O 19,86:5
Musial, Lakasz, 1948, D 21,31:1
Musil, L F, 1936, O 2,25:3
Musil, Rudolph F, 1945, Ap 18,23:6
Musinyants, Gurgen M, 1967, My 16,45:4
Muskat, G Fred Mrs, 1953, Ag 8,11:4
Muskin, Elazer R, 1950, Ag 3,23:5
Musmanno, Michael A Justice, 1968, O 13,84:1
Muss, Isaac, 1954, O 25,27:3
Muss, Louis, 1962, My 17,37:2
Mussaeus, Henry Mrs, 1939, F 1,21:6
Mussayassul, Halio Prince, 1949, Je 20,19:5
Musselman, Alvin J, 1950, O 12,31:5
Musselman, B Ovid, 1938, My 1,II,6:4
Musselman, C A, 1946, Ja 4,21:3
Musselman, Morris M, 1952, Ap 24,31:1
Musselman, Norman B Mrs, 1947, S 24,23:6
Musselwhite, Harry W, 1955, D 15,37:5
Musser, Alfred J, 1945, N 10,15:3
Musser, Charles E, 1952, O 4,17:5
Musser, Charles S, 1951, Ag 14,23:2
Musser, Clayton A Mrs, 1954, N 25,29:6
Musser, Frederic O, 1950, Ja 21,17:1
Musser, Harold W, 1961, N 23,31:2
Musser, John (por), 1949, Mr 23,27:5
Musser, John H, 1947, S 7,60:5
Musser, John H Dr, 1912, Ap 4,13:4
Musser, Paul H, 1951, N 22,31:1
Musser, R Drew, 1958, Jl 31,23:1
Musser, Robert S Mrs, 1958, N 20,35:3
Mussett, Charles, 1939, D 11,23:1
Mussey, Henry R, 1940, F 11,48:1
Mussey, Kendall K (por), 1940, Ja 19,19:3
Mussey, W H Dr, 1882, Ag 2,5:6
Mussey, William H, 1939, Ag 24,19:2
ussig, Phil, 1951, Je 26,29:5
ussinan, Oscar L, 1951, Ap 17,29:4
usso, Alfred, 1942, D 5,15:6
usso, Luigi, 1958, Jl 7,32:1
ussolini, A, 1931, D 22,23:1
ussolini, Vito, 1963, O 6,89:1
usson, Arthur G, 1942, My 16,13:5
usson, Bennet, 1946, F 19,25:3
usson, Charles J, 1947, Ap 15,25:2
usson, Emma E Dr, 1913, D 30,9:5
usson, George T Maj, 1925, Ja 23,19:4
usson, Ron, 1966, Je 20,45:1
ussulli, Boots, 1967, S 25,45:4
ustaine, William W H, 1937, Ja 6,23:3
ustapha El Maraghi, Sheik, 1945, Ag 23,23:4
ustard, Edgar Mrs, 1948, D 10,26:3
ustard, Elmer, 1940, Mr 2,13:3
uste, Abraham J (mem ser plans, F 13,33:4; ser, F 4,14:1), 1967, F 12,92:4
usterman, Henry H, 1946, D 2,25:3

Mustin, Gilbert B, 1948, O 31,88:3
Mustin, Henry C Capt, 1923, Ag 24,11:6
Mustin, J Burton, 1953, Ag 25,21:2
Musto, Fannie Mrs, 1946, O 13,62:5
Musto, Frank A, 1966, F 15,36:4
Musy, Jean-Marie, 1952, Ap 20,94:6
Muszynski, John J, 1946, Jl 13,15:3
Muta, Samuel A, 1946, Mr 23,21:3
Mutaguchi, Renyu, 1966, Ag 4,33:5
Mutch, Andrew, 1964, O 8,43:4
Mutch, John, 1946, Ja 10,23:4
Mutchler, Harry W, 1944, Je 13,19:3
Mutchler, James E, 1950, F 28,29:2
Mutchler, Julia C, 1943, Jl 18,35:2
Mutchler, Morris E, 1940, Jl 24,21:5
Mutchler, Thomas T Rev Dr, 1937, D 14,25:2
Mutell, Alfred J, 1956, S 29,19:5
Muter, John M, 1942, Mr 22,49:4
Muth, Arthur E, 1942, Mr 15,42:8
Muth, Charles, 1952, Ja 11,22:2
Muth, Elizabeth Mrs, 1941, S 21,44:1
Muth, George J, 1949, Ja 12,27:2
Muth, John C, 1937, Mr 6,17:6; 1950, F 3,23:1
Muth, John E, 1950, Jl 12,29:4
Muth, Peter (Bro Clementian), 1912, D 3,15:5
Muth, Russell, 1961, Ap 23,86:6
Muther, Jeannette E, 1962, Ag 31,21:2
Muthig, Frank W, 1943, F 19,19:2
Muti, Ettore, 1943, Ag 25,19:3
Mutiz, Manuel, 1957, D 17,35:1
Mutner, Samuel, 1945, Mr 1,21:5
Mutnick, Joseph J Jr, 1962, N 29,38:8
Mutnick, Louis B, 1945, D 3,21:5
Muto, Anthony, 1964, My 26,39:2
Muto, N, 1933, Jl 28,15:4
Mutrie, James (por), 1938, Ja 25,21:3
Mutrie, Joseph A, 1959, N 18,41:3
Mutschler, Frederick, 1941, Ja 14,21:1
Mutschler, George A, 1940, D 29,24:6
Mutschler, Louis H, 1950, O 4,31:3
Mutsu, Count, 1897, Ag 26,5:2
Mutsuhito, Emperor, 1912, S 13,9:3
Muttart, Charles J Dr, 1937, Ja 22,22:3
Mutter, Alfred A, 1955, S 28,35:5
Mutterperl, Sol, 1968, O 15,47:3
Mutterperl, Sol Mrs, 1964, Ja 20,43:2
Muttkowski, Richard A, 1943, Ap 17,17:5
Mutton, Frank E, 1937, Ap 13,25:4
Mutuell, George H, 1947, S 9,31:4
Muxoll, Harold W Sr, 1951, Ag 12,77:2
Muyskens, John, 1948, F 20,28:3
Muyskens, John D, 1963, O 6,89:1
Muzakkar, Kahar, 1954, My 23,35:5
Muzik, Jacob, 1950, Ap 16,104:3
Muzio, C, 1936, My 25,19:3
Muzio, Carlo, 1917, Ag 3,9:2
Muzslay, Joseph, 1955, F 16,29:4
Muzzey, David S, 1965, Ap 15,33:1
Muzzey, Frank S, 1950, Je 5,23:5
Muzzicato, Charles Dr, 1968, D 22,53:1
Muzzio, Joseph P, 1951, S 5,31:4
Muzzy, Adrienne F (will), 1949, Je 22,33:8
Muzzy, Edward W, 1950, N 3,27:2
Muzzy, Henry, 1939, My 22,17:2
Muzzy, Samuel V, 1937, S 24,21:4
Muzzy, William H, 1938, Ag 14,32:6
Myasnikov, Aleksandr L, 1965, N 22,37:5
Myatt, Harold S, 1945, O 13,15:2
Myatt, John W Mrs, 1943, Ja 4,15:5
Myburgh, Philip, 1946, Jl 2,25:1
Mydaek, Joseph, 1937, Jl 20,7:4
Myddelton, Robert E, 1949, Ag 17,23:3
Myell, John, 1871, My 17,8:4
Myer, A J, 1880, Ag 25,5:1
Myer, Anna B Mrs, 1941, Ja 9,21:2
Myer, Augustus Mrs, 1947, Mr 16,60:2
Myer, Earl C, 1944, D 16,15:6
Myer, Francis A, 1952, Je 4,27:1
Myer, Frank H, 1937, D 16,27:4
Myer, H B, 1882, Mr 30,5:5
Myer, H Leslie, 1943, My 31,17:5
Myer, J C, 1934, Ap 6,23:1
Myer, John M, 1953, Mr 4,27:1
Myer, Millard B, 1958, S 9,35:5
Myer, Robert R, 1953, Ag 22,15:2
Myer, Thomas J Sr, 1954, Mr 2,25:4
Myer, Walter E, 1955, O 26,31:5
Myer, William A, 1942, Ag 28,19:2
Myer, William C Mrs, 1944, Jl 9,36:2
Myerle, Ellis C, 1956, Mr 9,23:2
Myers, Abe C, 1965, Ap 7,43:4
Myers, Albert, 1959, O 12,19:5
Myers, Albert C, 1960, Ap 3,86:7
Myers, Alex J, 1962, Ag 14,31:5
Myers, Alfred E Rev Dr, 1915, S 17,7:6
Myers, Allen F, 1968, N 10,88:5
Myers, Allen O, 1910, Jl 3,II,7:4
Myers, Alva D, 1949, O 18,27:5
Myers, Alva F, 1956, Ag 15,29:4
Myers, Angelo, 1907, S 21,9:4
Myers, Arthur L, 1953, Ag 26,27:3
Myers, Arthur L Mrs, 1967, Ja 4,43:3
Myers, Arthur W, 1939, Je 17,15:4; 1943, Ja 21,21:3

Myers, Barton A, 1955, Ag 29,19:6
Myers, Barton A Mrs, 1947, D 9,29:4
Myers, Benjamin F, 1937, N 30,23:4
Myers, Burton D, 1951, Mr 1,28:2
Myers, C G, 1881, D 30,5:4
Myers, C Leland, 1950, N 25,13:5
Myers, Calvin D, 1958, F 28,13:4
Myers, Carl E, 1925, D 1,25:5
Myers, Charles A, 1955, Jl 30,17:3; 1958, Ja 2,27:2
Myers, Charles E, 1957, Jl 11,25:3; 1958, Ja 28,27:3
Myers, Charles F, 1948, Jl 21,23:6
Myers, Charles K, 1942, D 15,27:2
Myers, Charles M (por), 1940, F 6,21:3
Myers, Charles M Mrs, 1950, Ap 1,15:3
Myers, Charles Mrs, 1951, Jl 6,23:5
Myers, Charles W, 1941, F 24,15:4; 1947, N 4,25:3
Myers, Chester N, 1954, My 5,31:3
Myers, Clara L, 1945, N 21,21:2
Myers, Clay, 1952, N 4,29:3
Myers, Clinton N, 1954, Jl 24,13:1
Myers, Clyde H, 1944, Ag 6,37:2
Myers, Cortland, 1941, D 27,20:2
Myers, David A, 1955, Jl 3,32:8; 1957, S 28,17:3
Myers, David M, 1954, Ja 22,28:3
Myers, David S, 1961, D 7,43:3
Myers, Dennis E, 1957, My 31,19:2
Myers, Diller S, 1947, My 14,25:4
Myers, Don W, 1949, S 10,17:6
Myers, Donald L V, 1952, O 7,5:4
Myers, Earl D, 1951, N 24,11:2
Myers, Edgar, 1956, Ag 3,20:2
Myers, Edmund, 1957, S 6,21:3
Myers, Edward, 1956, S 14,23:3
Myers, Edward E Dr, 1925, Mr 23,17:4
Myers, Edward H Mrs, 1958, Ap 30,33:4
Myers, Edward L Mrs, 1952, Jl 22,25:4
Myers, Elias, 1964, S 8,29:2
Myers, Elijah E Col, 1909, Mr 6,7:4
Myers, Elken R, 1963, D 12,39:1
Myers, Ella B (Mrs R N Dagg), 1950, D 27,28:3
Myers, Ellsworth, 1939, My 4,23:5
Myers, Emery D, 1948, Ap 2,23:3
Myers, Erskine R, 1949, Ap 27,27:4
Myers, Eugene V A, 1943, N 2,25:5
Myers, Fenton, 1947, N 20,29:1
Myers, Floyd B, 1955, Ap 16,19:4
Myers, Ford S, 1944, Mr 30,21:4
Myers, Fran (Mrs Edw E Bauer), 1964, My 30,17:5
Myers, Frances Merriam Dr, 1916, S 15,11:4
Myers, Francis A, 1946, D 1,76:3
Myers, Francis B, 1923, D 4,21:2
Myers, Francis J (will, Ag 11,32:3), 1956, Jl 6,21:1
Myers, Frank, 1939, Mr 24,21:2
Myers, Frank B Prof, 1937, F 15,17:3
Myers, Frank C, 1950, Je 15,31:1
Myers, Frank K, 1940, Ag 3,15:4
Myers, Frank W, 1966, N 2,45:4
Myers, Fred, 1963, D 3,43:3
Myers, Frederick Gen, 1874, Jl 10,4:6
Myers, Frederick M, 1963, Ag 13,31:2
Myers, George A, 1945, S 16,44:2
Myers, George E, 1946, Je 12,27:4
Myers, George E Mrs, 1951, S 12,31:2
Myers, George F, 1961, Ap 6,26:3
Myers, George H, 1957, D 25,31:2
Myers, George L, 1951, Ap 2,25:4
Myers, George S, 1940, My 10,23:2
Myers, Gustavus, 1942, D 9,27:4
Myers, Hannah R Mrs, 1943, Ap 14,23:4
Myers, Harold A, 1964, Jl 9,33:4
Myers, Harry, 1938, D 26,23:3; 1948, S 23,29:3
Myers, Harry C, 1939, Jl 24,13:5
Myers, Harry E, 1958, F 25,27:2
Myers, Harry J, 1918, My 11,13:4
Myers, Harry S, 1963, N 27,37:1
Myers, Harry W, 1945, Ag 7,23:3
Myers, Harry W Jr, 1955, O 24,27:4
Myers, Hattie D Mrs, 1941, Ag 7,17:2
Myers, Henry A, 1955, My 3,31:5
Myers, Henry L Mrs, 1942, My 9,13:3
Myers, Henry Mrs, 1954, Mr 14,88:6
Myers, Henry T Col, 1968, D 10,47:2
Myers, Herbert F Jr, 1966, Ap 15,39:3
Myers, Herbert M, 1943, Jl 25,30:8
Myers, Horace V (por), 1944, F 26,13:7
Myers, Howard (por), 1947, S 20,15:5
Myers, Howard B, 1956, Mr 10,17:1
Myers, Howard G Mrs, 1954, N 6,17:5
Myers, Howard W, 1945, N 22,35:4
Myers, Irene T, 1941, F 1,17:5
Myers, Irving T, 1948, F 11,27:1
Myers, Isaac L, 1960, S 25,88:1
Myers, J Ross Jr, 1957, Jl 14,73:2
Myers, Jacob Mrs, 1940, My 21,23:5
Myers, James, 1967, My 13,33:4
Myers, James L Mrs, 1947, S 13,11:2
Myers, James S, 1953, O 22,29:3
Myers, Jared Kirtland, 1906, N 27,9:5
Myers, Jennie S Mrs, 1908, D 19,9:5
Myers, Jerome, 1940, Je 20,23:3
Myers, Jerome Mrs, 1960, My 25,39:3
Myers, John A, 1938, S 6,21:4
Myers, John C (por), 1944, S 19,21:4

Myers, John C, 1952, Mr 3,21:3
Myers, John C Mrs, 1937, Ap 3,19:4
Myers, John D, 1964, S 13,86:5
Myers, John E, 1953, O 14,29:3
Myers, John F, 1942, D 28,19:3; 1945, Ap 23,19:4; 1962, F 18,93:1
Myers, John G Mrs, 1904, F 10,9:6
Myers, John H, 1955, Mr 30,29:2
Myers, John K, 1951, F 14,29:3
Myers, John M, 1951, Ja 11,25:5
Myers, John P, 1966, Ap 4,24:7
Myers, John T, 1937, My 13,25:5
Myers, Joseph, 1942, Je 25,23:3
Myers, Joseph A, 1949, F 24,23:3
Myers, Joseph M, 1947, Mr 1,15:2
Myers, Joseph S, 1953, O 18,87:1
Myers, Karl R, 1946, Je 26,25:5
Myers, Keziah J Mrs, 1943, Ja 1,23:4
Myers, Lanning, 1945, Ag 21,21:3
Myers, Lawrence, 1905, Je 15,9:6; 1957, Ag 11,81:2
Myers, Lena P Mrs, 1940, D 31,15:1
Myers, Leopold H (por), 1944, Ap 11,19:4
Myers, Lewis C, 1951, My 23,35:4
Myers, Lewis E, 1945, F 6,19:5
Myers, Lewis J, 1955, N 11,25:5
Myers, Lewis R, 1938, S 12,17:3
Myers, Lindol R, 1952, Mr 25,27:1
Myers, Louis, 1938, N 9,23:5; 1953, Ja 5,21:2
Myers, Louis G Mrs, 1951, N 9,27:1
Myers, Louis Mrs, 1944, F 17,19:5
Myers, Louis S, 1951, My 31,19:2
Myers, Louis W, 1960, F 17,35:1
Myers, Louis W Mrs, 1943, My 2,44:5
Myers, Lydia S Mrs, 1940, Jl 24,21:1
Myers, Lyndon F M, 1940, Mr 3,44:2
Myers, Marie A Mrs, 1950, Jl 25,27:2
Myers, Maurice, 1945, Jl 10,11:4
Myers, Max, 1954, Ap 8,27:2; 1954, Ag 31,21:2
Myers, Meyer Mrs, 1949, Mr 17,25:2
Myers, Michael, 1950, Ap 9,85:1
Myers, Milton H, 1942, N 11,25:5
Myers, Mordecai Maj, 1871, Ja 22,1:5
Myers, Moss S, 1944, My 6,19:5
Myers, Nathan, 1937, Ag 14,13:4
Myers, Nathaniel, 1921, Ag 31,13:3
Myers, Oliver, 1952, D 12,29:1
Myers, Oscar P, 1962, N 15,37:2
Myers, Otto L, 1958, S 1,13:1
Myers, Percy H, 1944, D 11,23:4
Myers, Phil V Prof, 1937, S 21,25:6
Myers, Priscilla N, 1949, N 15,25:1
Myers, Ralph E, 1953, My 5,29:3
Myers, Ralph W, 1948, D 30,19:6
Myers, Ralph W Mrs, 1945, Ja 6,11:2
Myers, Richard E, 1958, Ag 9,13:6
Myers, Richard W Mrs, 1948, F 28,15:4
Myers, Rita C, 1953, O 29,31:3
Myers, Robert H, 1942, Je 27,13:5
Myers, Robert L, 1953, My 7,31:2
Myers, Rodes K, 1960, Mr 13,85:2
Myers, Sam, 1940, Jl 14,30:7
Myers, Samuel R, 1915, Mr 5,9:6
Myers, Sarah A Mrs, 1937, Ag 10,19:4
Myers, Saul S, 1938, Je 27,17:2
Myers, Silas, 1948, Ap 12,21:5
Myers, Stewart C Mrs, 1955, O 2,87:1
Myers, Susan Mrs, 1942, N 1,53:2
Myers, T B (will), 1966, Ap 13,24:3
Myers, T E (Pop), 1954, Mr 14,89:2
Myers, Thaddeus H Dr, 1925, D 25,17:6
Myers, Theodore Mrs, 1909, Mr 29,7:4
Myers, Theodore R, 1939, O 13,23:3
Myers, Theodore W, 1918, Mr 21,13:1
Myers, Thomas C Mrs, 1945, F 2,19:3
Myers, Thomas J, 1943, Jl 18,34:2; 1944, Jl 2,19:2
Myers, Victor C, 1948, O 9,19:4
Myers, W Heyward, 1923, My 2,19:3
Myers, W J, 1940, My 4,17:3
Myers, Walter, 1950, Je 19,21:4
Myers, Walter E, 1949, Mr 20,76:5
Myers, Walter E (will), 1957, F 26,31:3
Myers, Walter K, 1964, S 1,35:2
Myers, Walter M, 1949, Mr 15,27:2
Myers, Walter P, 1949, F 22,23:2
Myers, William, 1951, Ap 17,29:5; 1961, Ja 1,49:1
Myers, William A Dr, 1920, F 17,9:4
Myers, William Baxter, 1921, S 3,9:6
Myers, William C Lt, 1916, O 28,13:3
Myers, William Gen, 1887, N 16,2:5
Myers, William H, 1947, Jl 14,21:4
Myers, William J G, 1953, N 20,23:2
Myers, William M K, 1953, S 9,29:5
Myers, William M Mrs, 1943, Ap 18,48:6
Myers, William S, 1945, Ja 12,15:5; 1956, Ja 29,92:5; 1965, Ja 21,31:3
Myerson, Abraham, 1948, S 4,15:1
Myerson, Jonas, 1941, Je 24,20:3
Myerson, Meir, 1951, My 28,21:5
Mygatt, Frederic E Mrs, 1947, Mr 8,13:2
Mygatt, Gerald, 1955, Je 3,23:1
Mygatt, J P K Lt, 1866, O 30,5:3
Mygatt, John Tracey Mrs, 1915, Mr 18,11:6
Mygatt, Kenneth, 1965, Jl 8,28:1
Mygatt, Royal E, 1948, Je 1,23:4
Myhan, Thomas F Father, 1916, O 9,11:6
Myhrum, Arthur, 1955, Jl 15,21:3
Myklebost, Tor Ambassador, 1968, S 23,35:4
Mylander, Charles H, 1949, Jl 13,28:2
Mylchreest, Joseph W, 1952, Jl 28,15:6
Mylchreest, William, 1950, Jl 23,57:2
Mylecraine, Earl, 1964, O 3,29:2
Myler, Ernest W, 1956, Ap 14,17:6
Myler, Joseph J, 1965, Je 1,39:1
Myler, Paul J, 1945, Ap 21,13:4
Myles, Arthur, 1945, Mr 2,19:3
Myles, Beverly R, 1951, F 20,25:4
Myles, Fred K, 1947, D 3,29:5
Myles, Frederick G, 1955, Ja 29,15:3
Myles, George C, 1948, My 13,25:3
Myles, George T, 1960, Ap 6,41:1
Myles, Mary Sister, 1952, Ap 10,29:5
Myles, Robert C Dr (por), 1937, Ja 3,II,8:8
Myles, Robert C Mrs, 1959, Ag 25,31:5
Myles, Thomas Sir, 1937, Jl 15,19:1
Myller, Ernest, 1953, O 24,15:4
Myllykangas, Lauri E, 1954, D 24,13:3
Mylod, John F, 1967, Ja 26,33:4
Mylod, Phil A, 1940, Mr 24,31:1; 1956, Ja 8,87:1
Mylod, Thomas F, 1954, Ap 16,22:3
Mylott, Francis T, 1966, My 7,31:2
Mylott, Frank E, 1937, Ja 3,II,9:1
Mylrea, Thomas D, 1949, Ja 20,27:1
Mynard, E Stanley, 1940, N 15,21:1
Mynders, Seymour A Mrs, 1946, Ag 6,25:2
Mynderse, Helen L D Mrs, 1942, F 5,22:2
Mynderse, Wilhelmus, 1906, N 16,9:6
Mynotte, William T Maj, 1914, Jl 1,11:5
Myo Mook Lee, 1957, F 28,27:3
Myrddin-Evans, Guildhaume, 1964, F 18,35:2
Myren, Alben T, 1939, O 4,25:4
Myrick, Eugene, 1945, D 1,23:3
Myrick, Franklin A Mrs, 1942, S 2,23:3
Myrick, Gardner A, 1952, F 3,84:6
Myrick, Hartley, 1950, Jl 21,19:3
Myrick, Henry L Rev, 1914, Ja 1,15:5
Myrick, John R Brig-Gen, 1909, S 1,9:6
Myrin, William S, 1961, Ag 5,17:6
Myron, Charles W, 1964, Jl 5,43:2
Myron, John F, 1939, Ja 27,19:3
Myrose, Claude W, 1939, O 2,17:6
Myrra, Onni, 1955, Ja 27,23:1
Myrup, Andrew A, 1943, O 2,13:6
Myrvold, Petter, 1952, N 6,29:3
Myshuha, Luke, 1955, F 9,25:3
Myskov, Pedersen, 1922, Mr 31,17:4
Myslik, Otto (por), 1955, My 26,31:4
Mysore, Maharajah of (K W Bahadur),(por), 1940, Ag 4,33:4
Mysore, Yuvaraja of (K N W Bahadur), 1940, Mr 11,15:3
Mysz-Gmeiner, Lula, 1948, Ag 11,21:4
Myton, John D, 1939, Ap 5,25:3
Mytton, H F, 1937, N 26,26:3
Myzie, Raymond J, 1957, My 14,35:4

N

Naab, John F Rev, 1937, Jl 3,15:7
Naab, Joseph M, 1966, Jl 29,31:4
Naame, George T, 1965, My 16,88:4
Naar, Cornelis W, 1944, Ap 4,21:4
Naar, David, 1880, F 25,5:6
Naar, Joseph L, 1905, S 20,9:6
Naar, Josephine, 1953, Mr 27,23:4
Naar, M D, 1885, Ja 11,2:2
Naar, Sarah R, 1948, N 3,27:2
Nabeshima, Nachiro Marquis, 1921, Je 19,22:4
Nabors, William D, 1960, Jl 13,35:1
Nabried, Thomas, 1965, Ja 22,43:1
Nabuco, Joaquim, 1910, Ja 18,11:4
Nace, I George Mrs, 1955, O 8,19:7
Nace, Irwin K, 1945, Jl 28,11:5
Nace, Robert R, 1947, My 20,25:5
Nachamie, Irving Mrs (H M Levin), 1965, Ja 27,35:3
Nachamie, Max, 1961, Ap 17,29:4
Nachbar, Caroline Mrs, 1949, Ja 22,13:1
Nachbar, Daniel, 1960, O 18,39:2
Nachlas, William, 1958, Ap 22,33:4
Nachman, David Mrs, 1959, Ag 11,27:5
Nachman, George G, 1903, D 12,9:6
Nachman, Henry, 1916, Ag 28,9:5
Nachmani, Isaac, 1952, Ja 31,27:2
Nachmann, Benjamin, 1910, N 4,9:4; 1955, N 10,35:1
Nachmann, George W, 1950, Mr 19,92:5
Nachod, George, 1945, D 21,21:1
Nachod, Hans, 1958, Jl 25,19:5
Nachtigal, G Dr, 1885, My 6,5:3
Nachtigall, Simon N Mrs, 1949, Ag 24,25:3
Nachtman, Martin T, 1944, Je 21,19:2
Nachtrieb, Henry F, 1942, Jl 19,31:3
Naci Karacan, Ali, 1955, Jl 9,15:2
Nack, Matthias, 1948, S 22,31:4
Nack, Walter E, 1948, Jl 12,19:5
Nacy, Richard R, 1961, Ja 11,47:2
Nadal, B H Rev Dr, 1870, Je 21,5:3
Nadal, Bautista, 1946, Je 12,27:1
Nadal, Charles C Mrs, 1943, S 11,13:3
Nadal, Ehrman S, 1922, Jl 28,13:4
Nadal, Herbert, 1957, Ja 28,23:6
Nadal, James, 1946, Mr 16,13:6
Nadal, Rafael M, 1941, Jl 8,19:6
Nadal, Ramon, 1949, Ap 11,25:4
Nadeau, Elzear Mrs, 1957, My 23,33:5
Nadel, Benjamin, 1938, Ap 4,17:5
Nadel, Harry H, 1966, O 10,41:1
Nadel, Harry N Mrs, 1962, O 12,32:8
Nadel, Irving N, 1949, Ap 26,25:5
Nadel, Joseph H, 1950, N 21,31:2
Nadel, Leo Mrs, 1961, D 21,27:1
Nadel, Samuel, 1944, My 5,19:5; 1955, Ap 1,27:4
Nadelhoffer, Luella E (Mrs O R O'Neill), 1964, Je 9,35:2
Nadell, David A, 1953, My 4,23:4
Nadell, Irving, 1946, Je 18,25:1
Nadelman, Elie, 1946, D 30,19:5
Nadelman, Elie Mrs, 1962, Mr 2,29:1
Nadelstein, Adolph, 1943, D 22,23:4
Nadelstein, Adolph Mrs, 1958, My 9,23:1
Nadi, Aldo, 1965, N 13,29:4
Nadi, Nedo (por), 1940, Ja 29,15:4
Nadig, Francis H, 1964, N 22,86:8
Nadle, Lawrence, 1963, D 28,23:2
Nadler, Carl S, 1953, O 15,33:5
Nadler, Harry A, 1944, Mr 24,19:4
Nadler, Jacob, 1953, Ap 2,27:4
Nadler, Joseph J, 1959, Mr 26,31:3
Nadler, Marcus, 1965, Ap 25,88:2
Nadler, Max, 1944, S 1,13:4
Nadolny, Rudolph, 1953, My 20,29:4
Nadolny, Theodore, 1948, Mr 3,23:1
Nadolny, Walter B, 1955, D 15,37:2
Nadon, J C, 1953, D 18,29:2
Nadon, Leo Mrs, 1961, O 17,39:2
Nadvornik, John, 1942, Ja 11,45:2
Nadworney, Devora, 1948, Ja 8,25:2
Nadzan, John A, 1960, My 19,37:5
Naeder, Rose A Mrs, 1940, Ap 15,17:1
Naeff, Johan A, 1942, D 31,4:3
Naegele, Charles, 1962, O 27,25:6
Naegele, Charles F, 1944, Ja 29,13:5
Naegele, George J, 1937, S 23,27:4
Naegele, John, 1942, O 31,15:1
Naegeli, Harry C, 1960, N 7,35:5
Naegeli, Harry C Mrs, 1948, S 20,25:5
Naegle, F W Dr, 1918, Ja 25,11:8
Naeher, Charles Ex-Justice, 1909, S 14,9:5
Naeher, Charles Judge Mrs, 1903, N 7,9:6
Naeser, Vincent Dr, 1968, D 6,47:3
Naesmith, Andrew, 1961, O 24,37:2
Naess, John A E, 1955, Ag 17,27:4
Naeter, George A, 1956, N 12,29:5
Naething, Charles F, 1913, Ja 31,11:4
Naething, W H, 1903, F 24,9:6
Naeyer, de Smet de Count, 1913, S 11,11:6
Nafey, Herbert W, 1951, O 27,19:5
Nafey, Herbert W Mrs, 1944, Mr 23,19:6
Naff, George T, 1968, Je 19,47:4
Naffziger, Howard C, 1961, Mr 23,33:2
Naft, Stephen, 1956, D 13,37:4
Naftal, Henry, 1923, O 5,19:2
Naftali, Valentine, 1963, My 1,39:5
Naftalowitz, Joseph, 1941, S 5,21:4
Naftzger, Roy E, 1952, Je 3,29:1
Nagai, Takashi, 1951, My 2,31:3
Nagal, Anne, 1966, Jl 8,35:1
Nagano, Osami, 1947, Ja 6,5:6
Naganoka, Kokugyo, 1945, Ag 6,15:3
Nagata, Hidejirp, 1943, S 18,17:2
Nagatsuka, Keili Dr, 1937, F 14,II,9:2
Nagayo, Matao, 1941, Ag 16,15:2
Nagel, Albert C, 1954, F 21,68:5
Nagel, Charles (por), 1940, Ja 6,13:3
Nagel, Charles E, 1967, O 18,47:1
Nagel, Charles von Mrs, 1944, Ap 29,15:6
Nagel, Conrad F Jr, 1957, Jl 6,15:3
Nagel, David G, 1960, S 24,23:6
Nagel, Frank Dr, 1937, Ap 16,24:1
Nagel, Germain, 1921, S 29,17:1
Nagel, Henry H, 1945, N 3,15:2
Nagel, Henry Mrs, 1948, Jl 24,15:6
Nagel, Hugo, 1953, Ap 25,15:5
Nagel, Isidor, 1951, Ja 25,25:4
Nagel, Jacob, 1949, Ap 21,26:3
Nagel, James, 1947, N 17,21:4
Nagel, John C W, 1960, My 12,35:4
Nagel, John P, 1948, My 14,23:3
Nagel, Joseph D, 1961, Ag 14,25:5
Nagel, Otto, 1955, S 21,33:2
Nagel, William H, 1937, Ja 2,14:3
Nagele, Frank, 1944, Mr 2,17:4
Nagele, Frank J, 1954, Mr 16,29:4
Nageleisen, John, 1952, My 7,27:4
Nageleisen, Urban C, 1950, My 20,15:6
Nageli, Joseph, 1947, Mr 5,25:1
Nagell, George, 1906, Jl 7,7:7
Nagell, Wilbur E, 1951, Jl 11,23:4
Naghel, Charles E, 1945, O 1,19:2
Naghten, James I Mrs, 1944, O 25,21:6
Nagin, Charles, 1938, Jl 10,29:4
Nagin, William, 1943, S 21,24:2
Nagle, Allen W, 1937, Mr 13,19:2
Nagle, Charles Francis Lt-Com, 1914, My 28,13:6
Nagle, Charles H Mrs, 1949, Je 26,60:2
Nagle, D A, 1878, Mr 19,4:7
Nagle, Daniel F, 1939, Ag 2,19:6
Nagle, Edward C, 1954, Mr 19,23:4
Nagle, Edward C Mrs, 1968, N 25,47:2
Nagle, Emma L Mrs, 1946, N 27,25:5
Nagle, Frank L, 1951, Jl 2,23:4
Nagle, Fred T, 1955, Ap 2,17:6
Nagle, Garrett Col, 1911, N 9,11:4
Nagle, Isaac, 1954, Jl 24,13:2
Nagle, James F Dr, 1924, Jl 28,11:4
Nagle, James Gen, 1866, Ag 25,3:2
Nagle, James J, 1939, O 20,23:1
Nagle, John J, 1961, N 6,43:1
Nagle, John R, 1954, Ja 19,25:1
Nagle, John T Dr, 1919, Je 15,22:3
Nagle, Kate, 1911, My 31,11:4
Nagle, Michael J, 1938, O 5,23:3
Nagle, Oscar, 1948, Ag 26,21:3
Nagle, P E, 1881, S 18,7:5
Nagle, Percival E (funl, D 30,20:1), 1923, D 29,13:5
Nagle, Percival E D, 1957, My 17,25:3
Nagle, Raymond T, 1950, Mr 7,27:4
Nagle, Robert A, 1950, O 9,25:1
Nagle, Urban, 1965, Mr 12,33:4
Nagle, William J, 1942, N 30,23:5
Nagler, Harris, 1947, Mr 13,27:2
Nagler, Herbert B, 1963, Ap 26,35:2
Nagler, Isidore (funl, S 24,37:5), 1959, S 22,39:1
Nagler, Maurice, 1961, Jl 12,32:6
Nagler, Russell A, 1952, D 26,15:4
Nagley, William Sr, 1949, D 30,19:3
Nagoski, Joseph, 1959, O 25,86:5
Nagrin, Daniel Mrs (H Tamiris), 1966, Ag 5,31:1
Nagry, Frank, 1914, Jl 23,9:2
Nagurski, Michael G, 1956, F 6,23:3
Nagy, Carl, 1953, Mr 11,29:3
Nagy, Desiderius, 1941, Ap 15,23:2
Nagy, Ethel Mrs, 1950, F 14,8:4
Nagy, Ladislaus, 1956, D 24,13:2
Nagy, Paul L Sr, 1951, Ja 14,84:3
Nagy, Steve, 1966, N 13,89:2
Nagy, Vince, 1964, Je 2,37:1
Nahas, Abdel-Aziz, 1951, F 12,23:3
Nahas, Mustafa (funl, Ag 25,39:3), 1965, Ag 24,31:3
Nahigian, Hovsep C, 1952, S 20,15:2
Nahigian, Mihran H, 1957, S 22,86:2
Nahigian, Sarkis H, 1948, S 13,21:4
Nahin, Louis M, 1941, F 25,23:1
Nahler, Eugene G, 1953, Ja 22,23:3
Nahm, Eric H, 1967, N 16,47:4
Nahm, Eugene A, 1954, Mr 4,25:6
Nahm, Ida C Dr, 1922, N 3,17:6
Nahon, Abraham, 1911, Ap 11,11:5
Nahon, Edward E, 1940, S 20,23:4
Nahum, Haim, 1960, N 14,31:5
Nahum, Jacques, 1959, N 11,35:5
Nahum, Stirling H, 1956, S 6,25:2
Naiditch, Isaac, 1949, D 23,22:6
Naidoo, P K Mrs, 1950, S 13,27:2
Naidu, Dwaram, 1964, N 26,33:3
Naidu, Sarojini (por), 1949, Mr 3,25:2
Naigus, Vlades, 1954, S 17,27:3
Nail, James B, 1942, F 15,45:2
Nail, John E, 1947, Mr 6,25:2
Naile, Frederick R Capt, 1937, N 7,II,9:3
Naiman, Samuel H, 1949, My 5,27:5
Naimska, Zofia, 1958, Ja 14,33:3
Nair, David L, 1950, Ap 8,13:6
Nairn, Michael Baker Sir, 1915, D 1,13:5
Nairn, Norman, 1953, My 25,25:3
Nairne, C M, 1882, My 30,5:5
Nairne, Elizabeth, 1944, N 9,27:6
Nairne, Frank B, 1954, D 27,17:1
Nairne, Gordon, 1945, F 10,11:2
Nairne, Harriet D, 1947, N 26,23:1
Naismith, James A, 1939, N 28,25:4
Naismith, James A Mrs, 1937, Mr 5,21:3
Naitove, Jack, 1950, F 16,23:4
Naitove, Samuel, 1944, F 6,41:1
Naive, Smith P, 1942, My 21,19:2
Naives, L G de Viscountess, 1943, O 5,25:4
Najimy, Justin Bp, 1968, Je 13,47:4
Najman, Josef W, 1937, D 5,II,9:3
Nakabayashi, Tomako, 1956, My 25,6:3
Nakachidse, Nikolaus Prince, 1966, My 26,13:1
Nakae, Kiyose, 1962, Ag 31,21:4
Nakajima, Chikuhei, 1949, O 31,25:3
Nakamura, Juzo, 1910, Jl 10,II,9:5
Nakamura, Kotaro, 1947, S 4,25:5
Nakamura, Ryozo, 1945, Mr 2,19:2
Nakamura, Satoru Gen, 1925, Ja 29,19:4
Nakamura, Tokizo, 1959, Jl 13,27:1
Nakamura, Utaemon, 1940, S 12,25:5
Nakano, Eijaro, 1906, My 8,9:1
Nakano, Yosuke W, 1961, Ap 8,19:4
Nakashian, Avedis, 1943, Mr 31,19:2
Nakashoji, Ren, 1924, Ja 19,13:4
Nakayama, Toshihiko, 1957, N 27,31:2
Nakazawa, Ken, 1953, S 30,31:4
Nakoneczny, Joseph, 1954, Ap 12,29:3
Nakshabandi, Khaled al, 1961, N 28,37:1
Nalbantian, Haig Mrs, 1965, Ag 3,31:2
Naldi, Nita (N Dooley), 1961, F 18,19:3
Nalepa, Harry, 1949, S 4,40:4
Naley, Ragnvald M, 1961, S 8,31:1
Nalibotsky, Albert, 1953, Mr 22,87:1
Nalkowska, Zofia, 1954, D 29,23:4
Nall, Russell J, 1948, Ag 22,62:3
Nallin, Richard F, 1956, S 8,17:3
Nallino, Carlo A, 1938, Jl 26,19:3
Nally, Edward J, 1953, S 23,31:1
Nally, Edward J Mrs, 1959, O 17,23:6
Nally, James J (funl, Ag 23,7:4), 1907, Ag 20,7:5
Nally, James Sr, 1943, F 19,19:2
Nally, Thomas F, 1948, Mr 22,23:2
Nally, William F, 1952, Ap 7,25:2
Nam Phuong, Ex-Empress of Annam, 1963, S 17,35:4
Namack, Thomas, 1949, Ja 5,25:4
Namatjira, Albert, 1959, Ag 9,88:2
Nametkin, Sergei, 1950, Ag 7,19:6
Namgyal, Tashi Maharaja of Sikkim, 1963, D 3,3:1
Namias, Elie D, 1947, Mr 19,26:2
Namier, Lewis, 1960, Ag 22,25:5
Namik, Shevket Mrs, 1958, N 1,19:2
Namiot, Leo Sr Mrs, 1957, Je 6,31:4
Namkoong, David Y, 1961, D 2,23:1
Namm, Adolph I, 1920, O 27,11:4
Nammack, C E Dr, 1926, O 5,29:5
Nammack, Charles H, 1956, S 30,87:1
Nammack. Elizabeth F, 1940, N 25,17:6
Nammack, Griswold D, 1965, N 28,88:4
Nammack, William H Mrs, 1949, N 7,27:1
Nana Sahib (Dandhu Panth), 1860, F 15,1:5
Nanabush, James, 1938, Ja 24,23:5
Nance, A Steve, 1938, Ap 4,17:4
Nance, Clement A, 1959, S 21,31:5
Nance, Ellwood C, 1965, My 29,27:5
Nance, Grover C, 1955, My 25,33:3
Nance, Henry H, 1949, D 19,28:2
Nance, Joseph N, 1948, N 25,31:1
Nance, Owen H, 1948, Je 29,23:5
Nance, Walter B, 1964, Jl 17,27:3
Nance, Walter B Mrs, 1940, D 17,25:3
Nance, Willis O, 1948, Ja 17,17:4
Nancrede, Harry W G de Rev Canon, 1937, D 1,23:1
Nancrede, William H, 1954, Ja 3,89:1
Nanes, Phil, 1957, Mr 3,84:3
Nangle, Bernard A, 1945, Ap 26,23:5
Nangle, Frederick J, 1959, Ja 19,27:5
Nangle, Harvey P, 1949, Jl 19,29:5
Nangle, John J, 1960, Ag 25,29:4

Nanini, Ron, 1951, N 3,13:5
Nanjee, Pranlal D, 1956, Jl 26,25:2
Nankivell, Frank A, 1959, Jl 8,29:2
Nannetti, Joseph P, 1915, Ap 27,13:4
Nanry, John J, 1955, Mr 16,33:4
Nanry, Joseph J Sr, 1950, O 10,31:4
Nansen, Betty, 1943, Mr 16,19:4
Nansen, F, 1930, My 14,1:2
Nantel, W Bruno, 1940, My 24,19:5
Nanton, Augustus Sir, 1925, Ap 25,15:5
Nantz, Davis S, 1950, D 24,34:7
Nanz, Charles, 1947, My 11,60:4
Nanz, Charles A Mrs, 1947, S 25,29:5
Nanz, Robert H, 1957, N 24,86:2
Naon, Romulo S, 1941, D 31,17:3
Napal, Dionisio Msgr, 1940, Mr 31,44:1
Napaporn Prapha Kromluang Dipsarat, Princess, 1958, Jl 29,23:4
Napear, Matthew, 1968, Ap 16,47:3
Naphen, George F, 1944, N 14,23:5
Naphen, Henry F, 1905, Je 9,9:5
Naphen, William J, 1942, S 23,25:4
Naphey, John H, 1942, Mr 11,19:2
Naphtali, Peretz, 1961, My 1,29:5
Napier, Arthur Sampson Prof, 1916, My 12,11:6
Napier, Baron of Magdala, 1890, Ja 15,2:2
Napier, Charles S, 1946, Je 19,21:2
Napier, Charles Sir, 1860, N 19,2:2
Napier, Germal, 1911, Ag 2,7:3
Napier, J, 1879, Je 24,2:7
Napier, J C, 1940, Ap 22,17:4
Napier, James C, 1954, Jl 23,17:5
Napier, James H, 1960, F 9,31:4
Napier, Joseph A Capt, 1914, Je 13,9:4
Napier, Lila, 1967, D 11,47:4
Napier, Mark Francis, 1919, Ag 21,11:4
Napier, Sam H, 1902, S 10,2:1
Napier, Trevylyan D W Vice-Adm, 1920, Jl 31,7:6
Napier, William, 1951, Ja 2,23:4
Napier, William C, 1948, Mr 19,23:4
Napier, William C Mrs, 1948, N 23,29:5
Napier, William E, 1952, S 8,21:3
Napier, William F C J H Lord, 1954, Ag 24,21:5
Napier, William Francis Patrick Sir (funl, Mr 5,1:4), 1860, Mr 2,1:6
Napisa, M E Pool Mrs, 1950, D 14,35:2
Naples, Peter J, 1947, Jl 8,23:3
Naples, S James, 1952, Mr 14,20:5
Napoleon, Louis Prince, 1879, Jl 5,2:1
Napoleon, Prince Jerome (Plon Plon), 1891, Mr 18, 4:7
Napoleon, Princess, 1955, Mr 9,27:5
Napoleon, Teddy, 1964, Jl 7,32:7
Napoleon, Victor Prince, 1926, My 4,27:1
Napoleon, Walter, 1966, Ja 31,39:3
Napoleon III, Ex-Emperor of the French, 1873, Ja 10, 4:3
Napoli, Charles, 1953, Mr 3,27:1
Napoli, Richard V, 1962, O 26,31:1
Napoliello, R Rosino, 1959, Ap 17,25:1
Napoliello, Vincent, 1952, N 17,25:2
Napolino, George, 1965, Je 29,32:5
Napolitano, Victor, 1948, O 24,78:5
Napp, Frank S, 1963, Jl 27,17:5
Napp, John A, 1951, My 5,17:4
Nappe, Joseph C, 1943, N 9,21:2
Nappe, William D, 1950, Ja 15,84:5
Nappen, Edward, 1957, Jl 29,19:3
Napton, W B, 1883, Ja 10,5:4
Napurski, Albert P, 1948, Mr 16,27:4
Narahara, Sanji, 1944, Jl 15,13:4
Narajowski, Waclaw J, 1960, O 21,33:1
Naramore, Chester, 1961, Ja 31,29:4
Naramore, Elisabeth, 1952, Ap 19,15:5
Naramore, Harold B, 1957, S 28,17:5
Narancio, Atilio, 1952, F 23,11:2
Naranjo, Jose, 1951, Jl 30,8:3
Narath, Peter, 1962, Ja 4,33:1
Narayanan, Teralandur G (trb, Mr 27,3:5; funl, Mr 30,33:4), 1962, Mr 27,37:1
Narbeth, John H, 1944, My 23,23:2
Narbeth, Octavius, 1952, Ap 11,23:2
Narcho, Agnes, 1939, Je 11,44:8
Narcotte, George N, 1958, Jl 7,27:4
Nardi, Bruno, 1958, N 24,29:3
Nardi, Julian Mrs, 1947, Ag 12,23:4
Nardiello, Anthony J, 1956, Je 20,31:3
Nardiello, Vincent A, 1965, Ja 18,35:1
Nardin, William T, 1954, O 27,29:6
Nardis, Camillo de, 1951, Ag 6,21:4
Nardizzi, Louis, 1951, O 5,27:1
Nardone, Beniamino, 1963, F 21,9:7
Nardone, Charles J, 1958, My 6,35:1
Nardone, Joseph Mrs, 1950, Jl 25,27:3
Nardy, Ralph L, 1951, Mr 11,95:1
Nardyz, Mark L Dr, 1907, O 31,9:6
Nareff, Max Mrs, 1956, Ap 3,35:1
Narelle-Currie, Marie (por), 1941, Ja 29,17:6
Nares, Eric P, 1947, Je 19,21:3
Nares, George S Adm, 1915, Ja 16,9:4
Nares, Owen (por), 1943, Ag 2,15:4
Narey, William J, 1944, O 16,19:4
Narey, William J Mrs, 1938, Mr 29,21:3
Narfon, Julien de, 1919, My 5,13:6
Narganes, Ricardo, 1917, O 4,13:4
Nargizian, Vahan H, 1954, Ag 3,19:5
Narimanoff, Nariman, 1925, Mr 21,13:4
Narins, Lester M, 1960, Ja 24,88:1
Narins, William, 1955, Ap 10,89:1
Narizzano, Mario F, 1967, Mr 28,39:5
Narkiss, Mordechai, 1957, Mr 28,31:1
Narodny, Ivan, 1953, S 30,31:4
Narr, Grace, 1952, Ag 14,23:6
Narr, Grace E, 1952, O 18,19:6
Narracott, Arthur H, 1967, My 18,47:3
Narvaez, Prime Minister of Spain, 1868, Ap 24,5:2
Narvye, Nathan Mrs, 1960, N 13,88:5
Nasalli-Rocca, Giovanni B, 1952, Mr 14,23:3
Nasanow, David L, 1951, Ja 16,29:1
Naschke, Harry C, 1955, Ag 2,23:2
Nase, Stewart, 1946, Ap 26,21:2
Nasedkin, Viktor G, 1950, Ap 21,23:3
Nash, A, 1927, O 31,19:1
Nash, A Douglas, 1940, Mr 31,44:8
Nash, Abraham B, 1961, N 23,31:4
Nash, Alanson, 1874, Ag 13,4:7
Nash, Alex V, 1925, S 3,25:5
Nash, Amelia R, 1954, N 10,33:1
Nash, Arthur J Mrs, 1938, My 26,25:5
Nash, Arthur Mrs, 1944, Ap 5,19:1
Nash, Augustus C, 1957, Mr 20,37:5
Nash, Ben, 1951, S 23,85:4
Nash, Benjamin C Mrs, 1948, O 16,15:4
Nash, Charles B, 1945, Ap 18,23:4
Nash, Charles E, 1953, Mr 25,31:3
Nash, Charles F Mrs, 1963, O 19,25:4
Nash, Charles Mrs, 1943, Ja 16,13:2; 1952, Jl 30,23:3
Nash, Charles W, 1938, D 23,19:3; 1944, My 17,19:2; 1948, Je 7,19:1
Nash, Charles W Mrs, 1947, Ag 20,25:2
Nash, Charles W Mrs (will), 1947, S 26,21:2
Nash, Chester A, 1949, Mr 27,76:5
Nash, Clement W, 1943, S 30,21:2
Nash, E Briggs, 1938, Je 24,19:4
Nash, Edith, 1952, F 12,27:2
Nash, Edmond H, 1949, Ag 19,17:5
Nash, Edmund W Sr, 1947, Jl 28,15:5
Nash, Edward A, 1967, O 29,85:2
Nash, Edward L, 1943, O 4,17:6
Nash, Edward M, 1957, S 18,33:5
Nash, Edwin A Ex-Justice, 1911, Jl 25,7:5
Nash, Eveleigh, 1956, Jl 11,29:4
Nash, Florence, 1950, Ap 3,23:2
Nash, Francis B Mrs, 1949, Ap 20,27:1
Nash, Francis C (trb lr), 1958, Ja 4,14:7
Nash, Francis H, 1941, D 4,25:1
Nash, Francis Philip, 1911, F 6,9:5
Nash, Frank C, 1957, D 12,29:4
Nash, Frank W, 1937, Ja 21,24:1
Nash, Frederick H, 1946, F 4,25:6
Nash, Frederick O, 1958, F 3,23:1
Nash, Frederick W, 1943, O 11,19:4
Nash, G K Ex-Gov, 1904, O 29,9:4
Nash, George, 1915, N 30,13:5
Nash, George F, 1945, Ja 1,21:5
Nash, Harold E, 1948, D 10,25:1
Nash, Harry, 1952, D 12,29:2
Nash, Harry D, 1954, Mr 20,15:5
Nash, Helen, 1885, Mr 24,8:2
Nash, Henry, 1948, Ap 30,23:4
Nash, Henry Fontaine, 1915, N 27,15:6
Nash, Henry S Rev Dr, 1912, N 7,13:4
Nash, Herbert A, 1958, Mr 4,29:4
Nash, Herman S (more details, Ja 15,84:6), 1967, Ja 14,31:2
Nash, Howard P, 1961, Ag 29,31:3
Nash, Isabelle T Mrs, 1941, S 26,24:2
Nash, J Newton, 1959, Jl 13,27:3
Nash, James, 1867, Ag 26,5:6
Nash, James B, 1964, Mr 11,39:2
Nash, James G, 1950, D 14,35:2
Nash, James H, 1960, Mr 6,86:3
Nash, James J, 1946, D 14,15:2
Nash, James W, 1940, My 7,26:2
Nash, Jay B (Sept 20), 1965, O 11,61:4
Nash, John B, 1939, Ag 15,19:2
Nash, John B Mrs, 1952, S 29,23:3
Nash, John F Rev Father, 1913, F 12,15:4
Nash, John H, 1947, My 25,60:4
Nash, John J, 1953, D 9,11:2
Nash, John McLean, 1916, Mr 9,13:8
Nash, Joseph, 1943, Mr 3,23:4; 1952, Jl 26,13:6
Nash, Joseph A, 1952, Mr 13,29:2
Nash, Joseph E, 1946, S 7,15:5
Nash, Joseph P, 1951, D 17,23:4
Nash, Joseph W, 1951, O 27,19:4
Nash, Kenneth G Sr, 1957, Je 14,25:2
Nash, Latinous J, 1948, My 5,25:1
Nash, Leslie H, 1958, F 11,31:4
Nash, Leslie H Mrs, 1959, F 21,21:4
Nash, Luther R, 1947, Ag 11,23:6
Nash, Luther R Mrs, 1937, D 27,15:4
Nash, Mary E (died Je 28; funl), 1965, Jl 3,19:2
Nash, Maurice R, 1938, F 24,19:5
Nash, Miles Henry Dr, 1907, Ag 17,7:6
Nash, Morris, 1943, Ap 25,34:7
Nash, Norman (por), 1955, N 18,25:4
Nash, Norman B, 1963, Ja 5,8:4
Nash, Patrick A, 1943, O 7,23:5
Nash, Paul, 1913, Ja 8,11:4; 1946, Jl 13,15:5
Nash, Phil I, 1956, Ap 26,33:3
Nash, Philip, 1914, O 5,11:5
Nash, Philip C, 1947, My 7,27:5
Nash, Philip Mrs, 1946, D 7,21:5
Nash, Richard, 1951, D 13,34:3
Nash, Richard J, 1949, My 8,76:6
Nash, Robert C, 1937, Ja 23,17:3
Nash, Robert J, 1939, O 28,15:4
Nash, Robert T, 1951, N 16,36:1
Nash, Robert T Mrs, 1949, Ap 3,76:3
Nash, Roger H, 1952, O 22,27:5
Nash, Samuel O, 1937, N 12,21:2
Nash, Samuel W, 1949, S 25,92:5
Nash, Sarah A, 1937, My 16,II,8:4
Nash, Stephen P, 1959, Ja 18,88:2
Nash, Timothy Mrs, 1955, Ap 15,23:2
Nash, W H (funl), 1875, S 18,10:1
Nash, W T, 1903, Ap 22,9:5
Nash, Walter A Mrs, 1945, D 17,21:3
Nash, Walter Sir, 1968, Je 5,47:1
Nash, Warren B, 1962, Ja 14,84:8
Nash, Willard, 1942, S 3,19:4
Nash, William, 1942, S 11,21:1
Nash, William Alexander, 1922, S 1,13:4
Nash, William B, 1937, D 23,22:2; 1940, Mr 23,13:
Nash, William L, 1959, Ag 13,27:5
Nash, William P, 1945, S 6,25:6
Nash, Willis G, 1942, Ap 30,19:3
Nash, Willis G Mrs, 1944, O 21,17:6
Nashashibi Pasha, Raghed, 1951, Ap 11,29:4
Nashelsky, Harry, 1952, F 17,84:6
Nashimoto, Morimasa Prince, 1951, Ja 2,23:1
Nasibu, Ras, 1936, O 17,17:1
Nasium, Jim (Edgar F Wolfe), 1958, Ag 10,93:2
Nasmyth, George Dr, 1920, S 22,15:1
Naso, Stephen, 1957, S 16,31:2
Nason, Arthur H, 1944, Ap 23,43:3
Nason, Carlton Walworth, 1906, N 6,9:5
Nason, Charles P H Rev Dr, 1937, Ja 17,II,8:8
Nason, Daniel, 1911, Mr 15,13:5
Nason, Daniel Mrs, 1943, Ja 15,17:4
Nason, Frank L, 1955, Jl 18,21:4
Nason, Frederick F H, 1951, Mr 27,29:2
Nason, H T Judge, 1903, Ap 4,7:3
Nason, Harold Mrs, 1946, F 24,44:4
Nason, Harry B Sr Mrs, 1945, S 12,25:3
Nason, John W Mrs, 1955, D 17,42:3
Nason, Leonard M, 1942, Mr 7,17:2
Nason, Lindsay B, 1951, F 5,23:4
Nason, Merton D, 1952, Ja 23,27:5
Nass, Max, 1945, Je 9,13:6
Nass, Max Mrs, 1948, F 6,26:6
Nass, Odin F, 1941, Ap 27,38:3
Nassau, Charles F, 1940, Ag 12,15:2
Nassau, James A, 1950, F 27,19:4
Nassau, Jason J, 1965, My 13,37:3
Nassau, Joseph M, 1951, S 3,13:3
Nassoit, Joseph H, 1964, Je 3,43:2
Nassokin, Carl, 1937, D 19,II,9:3
Nassow, Harris, 1946, D 22,13:6
Nast, Conde (por),(will, O 2,9:1), 1942, S 20,39:
Nast, Cyril Mrs, 1954, Jl 27,21:3
Nast, Max, 1939, Ja 12,19:3
Nast, Peter C, 1958, F 25,16:5
Nast, Phil M, 1942, My 6,19:2
Nast, Richard G, 1940, Je 21,21:5
Nast, Samuel M, 1948, O 30,15:2
Nast, Thomas Jr Mrs, 1942, D 20,44:5
Nastal, Stanley, 1947, S 9,31:2
Nastick, Vojislav V, 1964, N 16,31:4
Nastorg, Lionel, 1940, Ap 9,23:4
Nastvogel, Albert J, 1950, O 19,31:4
Nastvogel, William, 1951, My 23,35:3
Nat, Yves O, 1956, S 2,57:1
Natal, Robert L, 1967, Ap 26,44:5
Natale, James, 1965, F 1,23:5
Natale, Louis, 1960, F 1,27:2
Natale, Peter, 1956, Ja 13,23:2
Natalia, Former Queen of Serbia, 1941, My 9,21:
Natalish, Vincent, 1922, O 6,23:4
Natanson, Alex S, 1961, Jl 4,19:5
Natanson, Bertha S Mrs, 1939, Je 13,23:4
Natanson, Max N Mrs, 1959, Mr 17,33:3
Natanson, Sigmund I, 1955, N 9,33:4
Natarianni (Sister Thos Francis), 1962, O 29,29
Natelson, Albert L, 1968, Je 6,47:2
Natelson, Maurice L, 1948, Ag 25,25:2
Natelson, Nathan Mrs, 1946, N 26,29:4
Natelson, Rachel, 1943, My 9,40:6
Nath, Walter J, 1953, O 12,27:6
Nathan, Albert F, 1945, Ap 5,23:1
Nathan, Alfred B, 1958, Ja 21,29:4
Nathan, Benjamin M Mrs, 1938, Je 3,21:5
Nathan, Bernard F, 1964, F 29,21:4
Nathan, Caroline C Mrs, 1872, Ag 22,8:6
Nathan, Clarence C, 1967, Jl 24,27:3
Nathan, Clarence S, 1924, My 13,21:4
Nathan, Clarence S Mrs, 1950, Mr 16,31:3
Nathan, David S, 1957, Jl 2,27:3

Nathan, Edgar J Jr, 1965, My 2,88:4
Nathan, Edward, 1948, Ja 13,25:3; 1951, D 18,31:2
Nathan, Eli M Mrs, 1961, F 26,93:1
Nathan, Ernest, 1915, S 5,11:5
Nathan, Ernest A, 1941, S 13,17:5
Nathan, Ernesto, 1921, Ap 11,11:1
Nathan, Frederic A Mrs, 1955, Mr 7,27:4
Nathan, Frederick, 1918, Ja 30,9:8
Nathan, Frederick Mrs (por),(will, D 31,12:2), 1946, D 16,23:3
Nathan, Fritz, 1960, N 4,33:2
Nathan, George, 1948, Ja 31,19:1
Nathan, George J (funl plans, Ap 9,36:2; funl;will, Ap 12,21:6), 1958, Ap 8,1:2
Nathan, George J (est acctg), 1959, Ja 1,29:4
Nathan, Hannah Mrs, 1945, Ap 16,23:3
Nathan, Harold (por), 1941, Je 21,17:1
Nathan, Harold B, 1963, Jl 11,29:3
Nathan, Harold Mrs, 1954, N 17,31:1
Nathan, Harry, 1944, F 14,17:3; 1949, Mr 7,21:5
Nathan, Henry, 1938, F 13,II,7:1
Nathan, Horace L, 1956, Ag 19,92:3
Nathan, Hyman H Mrs, 1965, Je 3,35:2
Nathan, J F Mrs, 1923, Ag 16,15:5
Nathan, Jack J, 1950, D 27,27:3
Nathan, Jacob, 1939, O 10,23:3
Nathan, Jacob P, 1954, Jl 25,69:2
Nathan, James F, 1952, S 3,29:4
Nathan, John B, 1963, Ap 11,33:2
Nathan, Karl, 1964, F 17,31:3
Nathan, Leo R Dr, 1916, Ja 12,13:3
Nathan, Louis T, 1950, Jl 8,13:5
Nathan, Martha A, 1963, N 18,33:3
Nathan, Matthew Sir, 1939, Ap 19,23:2
Nathan, Max, 1922, Ap 20,17:4
Nathan, Michael, 1924, F 3,23:1
Nathan, Michael H Mrs, 1949, F 22,24:2
Nathan, Milford, 1953, Ja 11,91:2
Nathan, Murray R (Oct 4), 1965, O 11,61:4
Nathan, Myron B, 1965, Ap 24,29:5
Nathan, Paul S Mrs, 1966, D 23,25:3
Nathan, Reuben S Mrs, 1961, S 7,35:3
Nathan, Samuel F, 1952, Ag 8,17:4
Nathan, Samuel Mrs, 1919, S 22,11:3
Nathan, Sara S Mrs, 1937, Ag 11,23:2
Nathan, Sigurd, 1961, Je 23,29:1
Nathan of Churt, Harry L Lord, 1963, O 25,31:1
Nathans, I Elkin, 1962, My 16,41:4
Nathans, Robert Mrs, 1955, Ja 12,27:1
Nathans, Sol P, 1941, Ag 6,17:4
Nathanson, Albert J, 1965, F 2,33:1
Nathanson, Ben Z, 1944, O 30,19:4
Nathanson, George, 1967, My 27,31:3
Nathanson, Harry Mrs, 1954, Jl 7,31:1
Nathanson, Henry, 1945, Ag 28,19:2
Nathanson, Ira T, 1954, My 4,29:6
Nathanson, Jack, 1946, Ap 24,25:3
Nathanson, Jerome Mrs, 1968, Ap 14,76:6
Nathanson, Louis Dr, 1968, O 28,47:1
Nathanson, Morris H, 1952, Ap 28,19:3
Nathanson, Nathan, 1943, My 28,21:2; 1954, Ja 5,27:1
Nathanson, Pauline, 1947, D 7,76:7
Nathanson, Samuel S Mrs, 1942, N 1,52:5
Nathorff, Eric H, 1954, Je 30,27:3
Naticchdone, Nello, 1954, S 20,23:3
Natili, Randolphe, 1915, My 11,15:5
Nation, Carrie, 1911, Je 10,13:6
Nations, Gilbert O, 1950, F 14,26:4
Natkin, Benjamin, 1940, Ja 3,21:1
Natkin, Bertram M, 1960, O 26,39:4
Natoli, Anthony J, 1953, Jl 30,23:3
Natoli, Ernest J, 1941, Ag 27,19:5
Natonek, Hans, 1963, O 25,32:1
Natt, Bernard, 1948, Jl 8,23:4
Natt, Rodina, 1909, S 23,11:2
Nattan, Robert F, 1949, N 18,29:1
Nattell, Anna Mrs, 1912, Ja 2,11:4
Nattuzik, John, 1916, Jl 24,9:3
Natzka, Oscar, 1951, N 6,29:5
Nau, Carl A, 1944, Ja 18,19:2
Nau, Carl H, 1950, F 2,27:2
Nau, Fred C, 1944, Jl 2,19:1
Naudain, May, 1923, F 11,6:2
Naudeau, Ludovic, 1949, S 6,27:5
Naudin, John, 1959, Je 6,21:4
Naudin, Kenneth, 1959, Ag 11,12:5
Naue, Henry, 1953, Ag 23,88:2
Naue, William F, 1951, Mr 18,88:3
Nauer, Henry J, 1957, N 5,39:4
Naughright, Lena, 1962, Je 15,27:3
Naughright, W Stanley, 1953, O 9,27:2
Naught, George L (por), 1942, S 20,40:3
Naughton, Bernard, 1941, D 9,31:3
Naughton, Frederick J, 1950, Ja 27,23:3
Naughton, James, 1950, F 18,15:3
Naughton, James W, 1925, O 4,5:3
Naughton, John J, 1941, Jl 6,27:3; 1948, D 8,31:2; 1961, Ag 4,21:5
Naughton, Leo F, 1949, O 14,27:1
Naughton, Martin F, 1939, Jl 30,29:1
Naughton, Michael, 1944, Jl 29,13:5
Naughton, Michael A, 1960, My 5,35:3
Naughton, Michael Mrs, 1950, D 8,30:3
Naughton, Mortimer J (Jack Norton), 1958, O 16, 37:2
Naughton, Thomas J, 1959, Ag 13,27:3
Naughton, Walter, 1951, Mr 8,29:4
Naughton, William J Sr, 1959, O 25,87:1
Naughton, William Walter, 1914, Mr 11,11:5
Naugle, Edwin E, 1942, N 22,52:2
Naugle, George, 1952, Ap 15,27:3
Naugle, Harry, 1959, Jl 16,27:5
Naugle, Karl, 1951, Ap 26,29:4
Naugle, William H, 1937, N 30,23:2
Naugles, George, 1948, S 27,23:4
Nauheim, Elias Mrs, 1968, N 22,47:4
Nauke, Mary F, 1955, Jl 17,61:1
Naul, Arthur, 1950, F 5,84:6
Naul, James M, 1956, Je 26,29:5
Nault, James T Mrs, 1952, S 28,77:1
Nault, S A, 1944, Je 5,19:5
Naulty, Edwin F Mrs, 1951, Ja 4,29:3
Naulty, George A, 1937, Mr 17,26:2
Naulty, James N, 1923, Ja 18,15:4
Nauman, Charles W, 1941, My 6,21:6
Nauman, Luther, 1950, F 26,69:8
Naumann, John H, 1964, D 8,45:2
Naumann, Joseph Friedrich, 1919, Ag 26,13:6
Naumann, May B Mrs, 1937, O 22,24:3
Naumann, Oscar C, 1922, O 18,19:4
Naumberg, Edward S Mrs, 1945, Ap 4,21:6
Naumberg, Robert E, 1953, Ja 31,15:5
Naumberg, Walter W Mrs, 1953, N 26,31:3
Naumburg, A, 1928, Jl 1,25:5
Naumburg, C Frank Mrs, 1956, Ja 26,29:5
Naumburg, Elkan (funl, Ag 2,9:7), 1924, Ag 1,11:5
Naumburg, Walter W (mem ser set, O 24,21:6; ser, O 27,41:4), 1959, O 18,86:4
Naumburg, William (por), 1944, Je 29,23:2
Naumburg, William Jr, 1960, Ap 18,29:4
Naumburg, William Mrs, 1941, N 15,17:5
Naumer, John, 1917, D 6,13:4
Naumov, Nikolai G, 1951, Ja 12,27:3
Naundorff, Adalbart, 1887, N 16,7:2
Nauss, Earl F, 1950, Ag 6,73:2
Nauss, Ralph W, 1958, D 19,2:6
Nauts, Merritt Mrs, 1954, D 12,89:1
Nava, Giuseppe de, 1924, F 28,19:5
Navagh, James J, 1965, O 4,4:1
Navaire, Peter, 1874, Mr 22,4:7
Navarette, Wesley, 1959, N 4,41:6
Navarra, Henry G, 1954, Ja 7,31:2
Navarrete, Sarvelio, 1952, Je 3,29:1
Navarro, Ade, 1932, O 12,23:1
Navarro, Armando, 1938, F 8,22:2
Navarro, Francisco, 1949, Ag 18,21:1
Navarro, Pasquale, 1946, Jl 19,19:6
Navarro, Ralph, 1939, Mr 17,21:5
Navarro, Salvador V, 1937, My 5,25:4
Navas, Rafael, 1939, Ap 21,23:4
Navassardian, Vahan, 1956, Je 27,31:4
Navatto, Joseph Sr, 1954, Je 3,27:3
Navazio, Alfred A, 1960, Ag 25,29:1
Navelet, Jean-Marie, 1967, Je 28,21:2
Naville, E Prof, 1926, O 18,21:1
Navillio, Antonio, 1948, Ja 1,23:4
Navin, Charles F, 1950, Ja 26,28:2
Navin, F J, 1935, N 14,21:1
Navin, Frank Mrs, 1960, O 29,23:5
Navin, William E, 1951, Jl 30,17:4
Navizowsky, John, 1954, My 1,15:6
Nawanagar, Maharajah of, 1933, Ap 3,15:3
Nawn, Henry P, 1922, Mr 29,17:5
Nawrocki, Adalbert, 1940, F 15,19:3
Nax, Charles W, 1951, Ja 6,15:4
Nay, Ira A, 1946, D 9,25:3
Nay, J Henry, 1937, Mr 28,II,9:1
Nayer, William, 1946, Ja 16,23:2
Nayfack, Nicholas, 1958, Ap 1,31:3
Nayfack, Saul J, 1959, F 25,31:1
Naylon, Daniel, 1939, N 19,39:1
Naylon, William J, 1942, Ap 3,21:3
Naylor, Alex D, 1938, Mr 9,23:2
Naylor, C Calvin, 1964, D 26,17:5
Naylor, Charles W, 1965, Mr 17,45:2
Naylor, Edwin J, 1945, Mr 18,42:3
Naylor, Emmett H, 1938, Jl 29,17:4
Naylor, Frederick W, 1945, Ja 11,23:1
Naylor, George, 1968, Ag 20,41:2
Naylor, George M, 1955, Ap 16,19:4
Naylor, George M Mrs, 1948, Je 24,25:2
Naylor, George W, 1943, Jl 31,13:4
Naylor, George W Mrs, 1941, Jl 15,19:3
Naylor, George 2d, 1964, S 13,86:8
Naylor, James B, 1945, Ap 3,19:4
Naylor, James E, 1954, Ap 6,30:6
Naylor, John, 1941, Ap 2,23:1
Naylor, John H, 1950, D 15,31:4
Naylor, John J Mrs, 1948, S 11,16:7
Naylor, John W, 1952, O 6,25:1
Naylor, Joseph R, 1948, Mr 9,23:3
Naylor, Lawrence P, 1937, Jl 10,15:4
Naylor, Louise, 1951, Mr 27,29:4
Naylor, Peter, 1903, O 30,9:6
Naylor, Robert B Mrs, 1945, N 2,19:3
Naylor, Robert D Mrs, 1951, F 24,13:3
Naylor, Robert J, 1939, F 25,15:3; 1944, Je 5,19:4
Naylor, Thomas E, 1958, D 29,15:2
Naylor, William G, 1947, My 21,25:5
Naylor, William K (por), 1942, Ag 4,19:3
Nayor, Harry, 1939, Je 9,21:4
Nazarene Gervasi, Bro, 1954, Mr 30,9:5
Nazaruk, Mike, 1955, My 2,8:6
Nazer, Harry O B, 1941, D 23,21:3
Nazey, Willis Bp, 1875, Ag 25,4:7
Nazimova, Alla (por), 1945, Jl 14,11:5
Nazimuddin, Khwaja, 1964, O 23,39:1
Nazitoff, Vice Adm, 1905, My 14,1:3
Nazro, Arthur P, 1911, F 17,9:4
Nazro, Mary E G Mrs, 1940, My 6,17:2
Nazzaro, Anthony D, 1949, Je 2,27:3
Nazzaro, Felice, 1940, Mr 23,26:8
Neach, Harry D, 1937, Ag 30,21:5
Nead, Gustaf S, 1950, Ag 27,89:2
Neaderland, Herman, 1952, S 14,86:1
Neafie, Harry Jr, 1957, My 25,21:2
Neafle, Charles F, 1950, N 23,35:1
Neafle, Walter A Mrs, 1948, Je 28,19:4
Neafsey, Edward M, 1952, Ja 3,27:2
Neafsey, James G, 1956, Ag 13,19:5
Neafsey, James J, 1945, Ap 4,21:5
Neafsey, James J Mrs, 1948, S 17,26:2
Neafsey, John A, 1952, S 18,29:3
Neafsey, John A Mrs, 1949, F 21,23:3
Neafsey, William P, 1939, My 1,23:5
Neagle, Elmer F, 1946, N 10,62:4
Neagle, Harry B, 1944, Ap 12,21:4
Neagle, Richard, 1943, Je 19,13:2
Neal, Alan D, 1948, O 14,29:4
Neal, Ambrose Orville, 1923, F 23,13:4
Neal, Anna Mrs, 1940, Ag 16,15:4
Neal, Austin E, 1941, Mr 16,45:2
Neal, Benjamin E, 1957, O 22,33:5
Neal, Brent B, 1941, O 17,23:5
Neal, C S Mrs, 1949, Ag 4,23:5
Neal, Charles A, 1950, Je 14,31:3
Neal, Charles T, 1921, N 11,13:4
Neal, Clarence B, 1965, Je 3,35:3
Neal, Clarence H Jr, 1957, Ja 17,29:3
Neal, Edward E, 1951, O 14,88:5
Neal, Ernest, 1943, Ja 25,13:4
Neal, Frank, 1955, My 11,31:4
Neal, George C, 1938, Mr 23,23:2
Neal, George F, 1955, O 11,39:2
Neal, George I, 1946, F 4,25:3
Neal, Guy K, 1944, Mr 12,38:3
Neal, Harry D, 1952, O 16,29:3
Neal, Henry, 1921, S 28,19:5
Neal, J Frank, 1949, S 8,29:3
Neal, James Erskine Col, 1908, Ap 20,7:4
Neal, John K, 1908, Je 3,7:6
Neal, John R, 1941, Jl 3,19:3; 1959, N 24,37:1
Neal, Josephine B, 1955, Mr 20,88:5
Neal, Kenneth S, 1960, Ja 2,13:6
Neal, Lex, 1940, Jl 5,13:6
Neal, Mary A Mrs, 1942, N 28,13:3
Neal, Moses P, 1954, S 29,27:1
Neal, Nathaniel J, 1948, F 27,21:2
Neal, Phene, 1942, Jl 8,23:6
Neal, Phil H, 1941, Ja 23,21:1
Neal, Ray L, 1948, Ag 11,21:2
Neal, Robert R, 1967, D 10,87:2
Neal, Robert W, 1939, My 7,III,7:2
Neal, Stanley S, 1953, O 23,23:4
Neal, T Hopkins, 1952, D 13,21:4
Neal, Thomas, 1940, O 7,17:1
Neal, Warren K, 1947, O 7,27:4
Neal, Will E, 1959, N 13,29:3
Neal, Willard, 1940, Ag 25,35:2
Neal, William E, 1962, F 13,35:3
Neal, William E Mrs, 1951, D 24,13:5
Neal, William H, 1939, Je 8,25:2
Neal, William H H, 1923, Ja 4,19:4
Neal, William M, 1961, O 21,21:4
Neal, William S, 1939, S 6,23:2
Neal, William T, 1950, Jl 25,27:4
Neale, Alfred W, 1943, S 5,28:5
Neale, Benjamin A, 1950, F 10,23:2
Neale, Earle Mrs, 1951, Ap 16,25:3
Neale, Emma J, 1943, N 30,27:4
Neale, Floyd J, 1941, Ag 25,15:2
Neale, George Henry, 1905, O 12,9:4
Neale, Harold H, 1948, Je 30,25:2
Neale, Henry M Dr, 1937, Je 18,21:1
Neale, James B, 1943, F 13,11:3
Neale, Joseph C, 1941, Ag 8,15:4
Neale, Laurence I, 1956, Ap 1,88:4
Neale, Mervin G, 1963, Je 28,29:4
Neale, Millard F, 1947, O 21,23:3
Neale, Ralph, 1940, Mr 23,26:7
Neale, S A, 1880, Ag 18,2:6
Neale, Sadie, 1948, F 18,27:2
Neale, Stephen Judge, 1905, Je 24,9:5
Neale, Thomas A, 1940, D 16,23:2
Neale, Walter, 1967, Ag 9,39:1
Neales, Stanley C, 1952, Ag 28,23:5
Nealey, James B, 1957, Jl 13,17:1
Nealis, Edward F, 1919, My 18,22:5
Nealis, James J, 1908, D 5,9:2

Nealis, W T Dr, 1879, Ja 19,12:2
Neall, Adelaide W, 1957, Je 29,17:5
Neall, E Percival, 1953, O 18,86:6
Neall, Robert W, 1957, Je 15,17:6
Nealley, Calvin H, 1958, Ap 29,29:4
Nealley, Willis G, 1948, Ja 9,21:5
Nealley, Willis G Mrs, 1955, Jl 17,61:1
Nealon, George L, 1951, Ap 26,29:2
Nealon, John J, 1940, My 30,17:2
Nealon, William A, 1946, O 11,23:5
Neaman, Pearson E, 1961, Ag 11,24:1
Neame, Laurence, 1964, Jl 1,35:4
Neamy, Nicholas J, 1950, Ja 23,23:4
Neander, John, 1952, Ja 17,27:2
Near, Albert H, 1951, My 28,21:4
Near, William K, 1950, Jl 22,15:5
Nearbor, Daniel Sr, 1947, F 12,25:5
Neare, Clifford R, 1942, N 11,25:4
Nearey, James F, 1939, Mr 31,21:5
Nearing, Florence, 1950, Ag 7,19:4
Nearing, Helen E, 1943, My 19,25:3
Nearing, Minnie Z Mrs, 1942, F 9,15:1
Nearing, Scott Mrs, 1946, D 5,31:4
Nearing, William W, 1946, D 29,35:2
Nearpass, B F, 1947, Jl 2,23:5
Nearpass, Egbert E, 1938, Ag 5,17:2
Nearpass, F G, 1947, Jl 2,23:5
NearpasS, Homer, 1940, Ap 27,15:5
Neary, Alcott, 1941, Jl 29,7:1
Neary, Augustus, 1947, O 27,21:5
Neary, Daniel J, 1940, My 15,25:1
Neary, Edward H, 1965, My 22,31:1
Neary, Edward J, 1960, O 2,84:8; 1966, Ja 3,27:3
Neary, Frank A, 1944, Mr 21,19:4
Neary, George A, 1961, D 27,27:3
Neary, Hugh G, 1942, My 19,19:3
Neary, J Madison, 1941, Jl 11,15:3
Neary, James, 1944, Ap 5,19:5
Neary, James C, 1959, S 20,86:3
Neary, James T, 1962, Ap 2,31:2
Neary, James W, 1952, Je 5,31:5
Neary, John E Sr, 1959, Mr 3,33:4
Neary, John F (por), 1938, Ag 6,13:3
Neary, John F, 1961, Je 23,29:4
Neary, Joseph, 1959, Je 12,27:3
Neary, Joseph A, 1953, D 23,25:4
Neary, Peter J, 1945, Mr 1,21:3
Neas, Alfred C Sr, 1954, Ag 5,23:3
Neasmith, John I, 1947, F 15,15:1
Neason, Eric W, 1959, My 27,35:3
Neath, J A, 1957, N 17,86:6
Neave, Charles, 1937, S 11,17:6
Neave, Charles F, 1961, Je 21,37:3
Neaves, Edward, 1944, Mr 26,42:1
Neaves, Thomas G, 1940, Ja 17,21:2
Nebecker, Enos H, 1913, Ja 7,11:6
Nebel, Arthur J Sr, 1941, S 30,23:5
Nebel, Berthold, 1964, Ap 5,86:8
Nebel, Edward, 1939, Mr 15,25:1
Nebenzahl, A Louis, 1943, D 9,27:3
Nebenzahl, Meyer, 1938, D 5,23:3
Nebenzal, Seymour, 1961, S 28,41:4
Nebiolo, John F, 1949, D 31,15:2
Neblo, Emil, 1940, D 6,23:2
Nebo, Burkhardt C Jr, 1961, My 16,37:1
Nebolsin, Vasily, 1959, D 1,39:3
Nebolsine, Arcadi Mrs, 1948, Ja 6,23:4
Nebolsine, Eugene A, 1966, Ap 30,31:1
Nebolsine, George, 1964, Mr 25,41:4
Nebout, Albert, 1939, S 27,25:5
Necarsulmer, Edward, 1959, D 8,45:2
Necarsulmer, Henry, 1938, S 2,17:4
Necas, Jaromir (por), 1945, F 4,38:5
Necas, Joseph V Jr, 1950, Ag 22,27:5
Neches, Solomon M, 1954, F 13,13:5
Necker, William, 1916, S 13,9:6
Neckere, Felix de Msgr, 1903, F 1,10:3
Neckermann, Leopold M, 1956, N 11,86:3
Neckritz, Jacob, 1937, Ag 30,24:5
Necollins, John E, 1942, My 24,42:3
Necollins, John Elmer Mrs, 1968, Mr 29,45:4
Nedden, Harry E, 1952, Mr 11,27:4
Neddham, Maurice H, 1966, Je 13,39:1
Neddo, Henry E (funl, Ja 16,31:4), 1957, Ja 12,19:3
Neddo, William J, 1949, N 26,15:1
Nedelec, Anne M, 1957, Ag 18,82:3
Nedelin, Mitrofan I (funl, O 28,31:1), 1960, O 26,22:1
Nederhoed, William L, 1957, S 17,35:1
Nederlander, David T, 1967, O 17,44:2
Nedley, Mary J Mrs, 1939, Jl 6,23:4
Nedowitz, Gustave, 1957, Ap 27,19:4
Nee, George H, 1952, Mr 5,29:2
Nee, John C, 1957, Ap 23,63:3
Nee, Maurice L, 1964, Je 4,37:3
Nee, Michael J, 1940, Je 9,44:6
Neeb, Lawrence Mrs, 1962, Jl 22,64:4
Needell, Meyer, 1951, Jl 11,23:6
Needell, William L, 1951, Jl 1,51:1
Needes, Ralph, 1944, N 11,13:2
Needes, Ralph Mrs, 1948, N 23,29:3
Needham, Alfred C, 1952, O 7,29:3
Needham, Charles Austin, 1922, N 25,13:5
Needham, Charles Francis (Earl of Kilmorey), 1915, Jl 29,9:6
Needham, Edmund F, 1944, My 31,19:5
Needham, G C Rev, 1902, F 17,3:5
Needham, George A, 1942, My 24,43:1
Needham, Helene, 1903, Ag 24,7:7
Needham, Henry G, 1939, Mr 26,III,7:1
Needham, James G, 1957, Jl 26,19:6
Needham, James P, 1960, S 15,37:1
Needham, James P Mrs, 1944, Ap 8,13:6
Needham, Thomas C Rev Dr, 1916, O 2,11:6
Needham, Thomas J, 1964, N 24,39:2
Needham, William R, 1939, Je 29,23:3
Needleman, Sam, 1951, S 1,11:5
Needles, A C, 1936, O 26,17:1
Needles, Harry H, 1950, Je 19,21:6
Needles, John O, 1961, D 21,27:3
Needles, Sol Jr, 1958, F 5,27:2
Needles, William B, 1948, Je 6,72:4
Neef, Francis A (mem ser set), 1956, D 7,27:4
Neef, Frederick E, 1958, Mr 25,33:2
Neef, Joseph N, 1953, Ja 9,21:4
Neeff, George E, 1945, My 8,34:6
Neefus, Lester W Mrs, 1948, O 27,27:3
Neefus, Wendover, 1945, Ag 13,19:2
Neefus, William F, 1907, Ja 24,9:4
Neel, Harrell H (por), 1949, F 24,23:3
Neel, Henri C, 1957, N 24,87:1
Neeland, M W, 1927, O 25,29:5
Neelands, Ernest V, 1957, My 26,92:5
Neeld, Charles M, 1945, D 27,19:2
Neeld, Charles W, 1940, Ag 27,21:2
Neeld, Reginald R, 1939, Ag 2,19:5
Neeley, Arthur H, 1965, Jl 20,33:4
Neely, A Howard, 1960, N 16,41:3
Neely, Ann E, 1966, N 1,41:3
Neely, Carie B, 1938, N 30,23:4
Neely, Charles W, 1943, Ja 23,13:2
Neely, Harry C, 1943, O 31,48:5
Neely, Henry M, 1963, My 2,35:3
Neely, James M, 1946, Ja 27,42:4
Neely, Marvin Y, 1956, Ja 18,31:6
Neely, Matthew M, 1958, Ja 19,1:2
Neely, Nathaniel J, 1949, O 5,29:6
Neely, Richard A Mrs, 1950, F 16,23:1
Neely, Robert C Mrs, 1942, Ja 30,19:4
Neely, Robert G Mrs, 1943, My 9,40:8
Neely, Robert T, 1962, N 6,33:1
Neemes, Oscar, 1948, Ag 19,21:4
Neer, Charles H, 1950, Ap 2,92:5
Neer, William A, 1955, Mr 5,17:2
Neergaard, Charles F, 1961, Mr 6,25:3
Neergaard, Charles F Mrs, 1961, Jl 12,31:5
Neergaard, J W, 1880, My 27,5:6
Neergaard, William B, 1963, Je 22,23:5
Nees, John L, 1946, Je 2,44:5
Neesan, Azley Mrs, 1941, D 10,25:3
Neesan, Yaroo M Rev, 1937, S 25,17:5
Neese, Albert M Mrs, 1951, Ja 21,77:1
Neese, Elbert H Sr, 1961, S 18,29:4
Neese, Frederick W J, 1947, Mr 20,27:4
Neeson, Edward Joseph, 1918, Mr 7,11:5
Neeson, John H, 1945, S 2,32:1
Neevel, Alvin J, 1965, My 1,31:5
Neff, Bentley P, 1943, S 3,19:3
Neff, Charles D, 1941, F 10,17:5
Neff, Edward L, 1943, Je 17,21:2
Neff, Elmer H, 1946, Ja 27,42:7
Neff, Emery Mrs, 1961, Ja 12,29:6
Neff, H Clifton, 1963, My 5,86:5
Neff, Henry, 1949, Ag 17,23:5
Neff, Irwin H, 1942, My 12,19:2
Neff, John P, 1947, Ja 19,53:4
Neff, John P Mrs, 1946, Jl 31,27:2
Neff, John R, 1942, D 3,25:2
Neff, Lewis K (por), 1943, My 7,19:3
Neff, Pat M, 1952, Ja 21,16:2
Neff, Pat M Mrs, 1953, Jl 21,23:5
Neff, Paul J, 1952, Ja 11,21:4; 1957, Je 10,27:3
Neff, Peter A, 1951, My 28,21:2
Neff, Silas S Dr, 1937, O 22,24:3
Neff, W B Mrs, 1942, Ag 2,38:8
Neff, Walter P, 1950, F 14,26:3
Neff, Ward A, 1959, Jl 13,27:2
Neff, Warren R, 1945, F 5,15:5
Neff, Warren R Mrs, 1945, Mr 8,23:3
Neff, William R, 1950, Ja 9,26:3
Neff, Xavier, 1905, Ap 10,1:6
Neftel, William B Dr, 1906, Ja 22,7:6
Neftel, William B Mrs, 1908, Je 22,7:3
Negbaur, Jacob, 1904, D 16,9:5
Negelstad, Ole T, 1946, Ja 19,13:5
Neger, August J, 1954, N 5,15:1
Neger, Max, 1951, Mr 9,25:1
Neger, Sam, 1959, Ag 13,27:1
Neggersmith, Ignatius, 1910, Jl 8,7:4
Negin, Aaron S, 1951, D 8,11:3
Negley, Alice M, 1943, S 7,23:5
Negley, J S Gen, 1901, Ag 8,7:6
Negley, John L, 1953, O 25,88:8
Negoescu, Stephen, 1956, Ag 9,25:5
Negreponte, Michel Mrs, 1941, D 3,25:2
Negrete, Jorge, 1953, D 9,11:2
Negrey, Stephen J Mrs, 1961, O 21,21:5
Negrey, Stephen J Sr, 1960, D 22,23:2
Negri, Ada, 1945, Ja 14,39:2
Negri, Angelo, 1947, D 17,29:3
Negri, Anton C, 1955, F 5,15:5
Negri, Frank Mrs, 1963, Ap 5,47:2
Negri, Giuseppe Mrs (Anna Maria Mussolini),(funl, Ap 27,8:4), 1968, Ap 26,43:1
Negri, Guido, 1942, Ag 28,19:1
Negrin, Juan, 1956, N 15,35:1
Negrini, Matthew, 1950, Ap 23,92:5
Negus, John C, 1961, D 15,37:4
Negus, John S, 1944, Jl 14,13:5
Negus, Sidney S, 1963, My 19,86:4
Negus, William Shippen, 1914, My 12,11:5
Negus, William V, 1958, Jl 20,65:2
Nehemiah, Samuel, 1960, Ja 14,33:2
Neher, Harriet H Mrs, 1940, N 28,23:2
Neher, William F, 1946, S 12,7:4
Nehf, Arthur N (Art), 1960, D 20,33:3
Nehf, Charles T, 1954, F 13,13:4
Nehill, Edward, 1955, D 3,17:1
Nehill, Edward T, 1963, N 3,88:2
Nehill, L M, 1955, D 3,17:1
Nehls, Herbert, 1960, Ag 16,29:4
Nehls, Herbert H Mrs, 1946, S 4,23:2
Nehls, John H, 1950, Ja 10,29:3
Nehrbas, Anton Mrs, 1945, Mr 23,19:4
Nehring, August F, 1951, S 14,26:2
Nehring, Ernest Mrs, 1949, My 14,13:4
Nehring, Frederick W, 1962, Jl 16,23:3
Nehring, Gustav, 1950, Mr 11,15:5
Nehru, Jawaharlal (funl, My 29,1:4; will; excerpts, J 4,14:4,5), 1964, My 27,1:7
Nehru, Motilal Mrs, 1938, Ja 11,23:6
Nehru, Rameshwari Mrs, 1966, N 9,39:2
Neibaur, Thomas C (por), 1942, D 26,11:1
Neichev, Mincho, 1956, Ag 13,19:3
Neide, George Little Rev, 1903, N 18,9:3
Neidel, Louis F, 1950, My 3,29:1
Neider, Charles W Mrs, 1949, D 28,32:1
Neider, Rudolf, 1940, Ja 17,21:5
Neidermeyer, Adolph C, 1948, Ap 19,23:5
Neidhardt, Augusta W, 1962, My 18,31:1
Neidhardt, Walter R Mrs, 1950, N 17,27:2
Neidich, Samuel A, 1961, F 13,27:5
Neidig, Robert T, 1955, My 19,29:4
Neidle, Marks, 1954, Jl 5,11:5
Neidlinger, Newell, 1952, Ag 13,21:1
Neidlinger, Samuel C Mrs, 1948, Ap 30,23:5
Neidlinger, William, 1903, N 9,7:6; 1957, Ag 5,21:
Neidlinger, William H, 1924, D 7,7:2
Neier, Charles E, 1949, N 9,27:2
Neifeld, Harold, 1955, Mr 24,31:4
Neifeld, Morris R, 1968, F 2,35:3
Neifert, J M Rev, 1920, Jl 29,9:3
Neigauz, Genrikh G, 1964, O 11,85:7
Neighbor, Edson J, 1939, S 26,23:3
Neighbors, James E, 1938, S 16,21:4
Neighbour, Grace P Mrs, 1954, My 8,17:5
Neighmond, Frederick, 1944, Jl 11,15:4
Neikov, Dimiter, 1949, F 17,23:2
Neikrug, Edward, 1945, N 7,23:1
Neikrug, Lewis, 1953, Ap 9,27:3
Neikrug, Samuel E, 1965, F 28,89:1
Neil, Charles E, 1951, Je 16,15:4
Neil, Edward J, 1942, Jl 14,19:6
Neil, Edward J Mrs, 1958, F 9,88:5
Neil, Edward Wallace Rev (mem, Ag 7,5:4), 190 Ag 6,5:4
Neil, George, 1937, D 6,27:5
Neil, George M, 1957, N 5,31:5
Neil, Harry, 1861, N 8,4:6
Neil, Helen N (Mrs Edw J), 1964, S 2,37:4
Neil, Henry, 1939, Ag 16,23:4
Neil, James Dr, 1914, S 30,9:5
Neil, John W, 1944, Ja 19,19:2
Neil, Mary P, 1956, Mr 14,33:3
Neil, Richard J, 1954, Mr 19,23:1
Neil, S Montaudevert, 1947, Mr 12,25:3
Neil, Thomas, 1952, Ag 15,15:3
Neil, Thomas R, 1940, Jl 10,19:1
Neilan, James A, 1964, Ag 19,37:4
Neilan, James P, 1943, S 8,23:4
Neilan, Marshall, 1958, O 28,35:3
Neilans, Alison R, 1942, Jl 21,20:3
Neild, Edward F Sr, 1955, Jl 7,27:4
Neild, Frank, 1945, Ap 10,3:7
Neiley, Charles F, 1941, O 28,23:1
Neiley, Edward A, 1963, Je 24,27:4
Neill, A W, 1948, N 1,23:3
Neill, Abby W Mrs, 1942, Mr 11,19:4
Neill, Al, 1937, N 7,II,9:3
Neill, Alex B, 1950, Mr 10,27:4
Neill, Alexander S Mrs, 1944, My 4,19:4
Neill, Allan P S, 1949, F 26,15:2
Neill, Archie T, 1958, Ja 10,26:3
Neill, C E, 1931, D 17,23:1
Neill, Charles L, 1954, My 29,15:5
Neill, Charles P, 1942, O 4,53:1
Neill, Edward M Col, 1907, Jl 23,7:6; 1907, Jl 2:
Neill, Edythe C, 1948, O 16,15:2
Neill, Francis I (will), 1940, My 18,13:4
Neill, George G, 1947, D 24,22:2

Neill, Henry Harmon, 1909, Jl 20,7:6
Neill, Henry M, 1906, S 13,7:3
Neill, James H, 1948, Ap 9,23:3
Neill, James M, 1964, S 17,43:1
Neill, Jerry F, 1955, Ja 8,13:3
Neill, John B Jr, 1941, Ag 14,17:6
Neill, John R, 1943, S 21,23:4
Neill, Joseph H, 1953, D 16,35:3
Neill, Joseph R, 1961, Je 1,35:3
Neill, Paul, 1940, Mr 10,49:1
Neill, Robert I, 1954, Ap 22,29:6
Neill, Roy W, 1946, D 17,38:4
Neill, T H Gen, 1885, Mr 14,5:2
Neill, Thomas, 1948, D 7,32:3
Neill, Thomas E Dr, 1948, F 24,25:4
Neill, Thomas Sir, 1937, Je 1,23:5
Neill, William G, 1961, Ap 10,31:4
Neill, William Jr, 1956, Je 25,23:4
Neilly, Balmer, 1956, F 4,19:5
Neilsen, Christian, 1938, Je 19,29:1
Neilsen, James P, 1962, Jl 8,65:1
Neilsen, John C, 1951, My 1,29:5
Neilsen, William H Rev Dr, 1922, D 9,13:4
Neilson, Albert, 1912, Je 12,13:6
Neilson, C Frederic, 1941, Ja 12,44:2
Neilson, C Frederic Jr, 1959, Ag 15,17:5
Neilson, C Frederic Mrs, 1938, D 13,25:2
Neilson, Charles E, 1958, Mr 18,29:2
Neilson, Edward N, 1938, Je 28,19:3
Neilson, Edward S, 1947, N 22,15:4
Neilson, Francis, 1961, Ap 14,29:3
Neilson, Francis Mrs, 1945, Je 19,19:2
Neilson, Franz, 1951, Je 15,23:1
Neilson, Frederic W G, 1937, Ag 23,19:2
Neilson, Frederic W Mrs, 1949, Ja 30,60:3
Neilson, Frederick W, 1938, Je 13,19:5
Neilson, Harry R, 1949, S 28,27:1
Neilson, Harry R Mrs, 1938, S 20,23:5
Neilson, Helen S Mrs (will), 1945, Je 21,21:7
Neilson, Henry A, 1912, My 7,11:4
Neilson, Howard S, 1957, D 27,19:4
Neilson, Hugh, 1938, Ja 14,23:5
Neilson, James (por),(will, Mr 3,43:3), 1937, F 20, 17:1
Neilson, James, 1967, Ag 2,37:4
Neilson, Jason A, 1940, Jl 25,17:4
Neilson, John, 1903, D 29,9:6; 1950, N 26,90:4
Neilson, John S, 1942, My 13,19:2
Neilson, L A, 1880, Ag 16,5:3
Neilson, Lewis, 1952, F 27,27:5
Neilson, London Times Reporter, 1881, Ag 12,3:7
Neilson, Margaret Mrs, 1942, Ap 26,40:8
Neilson, Morden, 1947, Ag 27,23:5
Neilson, Moses Rev, 1937, N 30,23:2
Neilson, Nellie (por), 1947, My 27,25:1
Neilson, Nicholas B, 1937, Ag 1,II,7:2
Neilson, Preston M, 1960, Ap 28,35:5
Neilson, Raymond P R, 1964, Mr 2,27:5
Neilson, Robert H (por), 1940, Jl 17,21:3
Neilson, Theodore T, 1943, O 13,23:2
Neilson, Thomas Hall, 1921, O 18,17:4
Neilson, Thomas R, 1939, O 26,23:2
Neilson, William, 1882, My 27,5:3
Neilson, William A, 1946, F 14,25:1
Neilson, William Allan Mrs (Elisabeth), 1968, O 10, 47:4
Neilson, William H, 1941, Ag 19,21:3
Neilson, William J, 1949, F 24,23:6
Neilson, William L, 1957, Mr 7,29:4
Neilson, Winthrop C (por), 1938, Mr 13,II,8:3
Neilson, Winthrop C Mrs, 1952, F 1,21:2
Neilson-Terry, Julia Mrs, 1957, My 28,34:2
Neiman, Benjamin, 1948, S 29,29:5
Neiman, Benjamin Mrs, 1945, O 1,19:5
Neiman, Carrie Mrs, 1953, Mr 8,89:4
Neiman, Howard S (por), 1947, N 2,73:1
Neiman, Morris Mrs (D Wagner), 1967, Jl 25,32:4
Neimeth, Albert, 1955, O 13,31:5
Neimeyer, Lewis H, 1948, Je 17,25:3
Neinken, Jacob, 1957, Mr 21,31:5
Neinken, Maurice, 1962, Je 17,80:8
Neinken, Morris, 1955, D 11,89:1
Neinken, Morris Mrs, 1952, O 10,25:2
Neinken, Samuel, 1944, N 14,23:3
Neira, Ignacio, 1907, Jl 14,7:2
Neis, L A, 1942, Je 11,23:2
Neish, John M, 1940, F 22,23:1
Neisloss, Benjamin, 1960, F 5,27:4
Neisner, Joseph M, 1942, N 10,27:3
Neisner, Joseph M Mrs, 1949, Jl 25,15:4
Neisser, L Albert Prof, 1916, Ag 1,9:5
Neisz, William, 1948, My 1,15:5
Neithercut, Richard J, 1950, Ap 3,24:2
Neitz, John D, 1968, Je 13,47:4
Neivert, Harry, 1961, Je 3,23:6
Neivert, Samuel, 1967, Ap 23,94:2
Nejako, Frances T, 1957, D 22,42:3
Nejame, Fareed B, 1957, Jl 2,27:1
Nejedly, Joseph E, 1918, Ap 5,15:5
Nejedly, Zdenek, 1962, Mr 10,21:5
Nejedlya, Zdenek Mrs, 1953, Jl 18,13:5
Nelan, Charles (see also N 23), 1904, D 8,9:2
Nelan, Frederick A, 1964, O 4,88:8
Nelaton, Auguste Dr, 1873, S 22,5:4
Nelde, Horace Brig-Gen, 1915, D 4,15:6
Nelden, Robert J, 1943, N 15,19:4
Nelen, Christina Mrs, 1951, Ag 21,27:2
Nelidow, Alexander A, 1947, N 4,26:2
Nelis, Joseph J, 1958, Je 5,31:5
Nell, Duncan F D, 1938, Ap 21,19:4
Nell, Edward J, 1957, Ap 24,33:1
Nell, May Mrs, 1946, Jl 5,7:6
Nell, Richard C, 1966, D 9,47:3
Nellagan, Ada, 1955, Ap 15,23:4
Nellans, Byron H, 1949, O 5,29:4
Nelles, Henry J, 1948, Ja 25,57:1
Nelles, John H, 1952, S 3,29:1
Nelles, Percy W, 1951, Je 15,23:2
Nelles, Valerius Rev, 1937, Ja 4,29:5
Nelles, Walter Prof, 1937, Ap 1,23:5
Nelligan, Arthur M, 1941, Mr 8,19:2
Nelligan, Clifford D Mrs, 1955, Ag 8,21:1
Nelligan, H Paul, 1952, My 18,93:2
Nelligan, James A Sr, 1955, S 23,25:4
Nelligan, John P, 1954, My 31,13:7
Nelligan, John S, 1960, Mr 1,33:4
Nelligan, Richard F, 1945, Mr 11,40:1
Nellis, Abram Fox, 1923, Je 11,13:4
Nellis, Benjamin F, 1944, Jl 25,19:3
Nellis, Fred W, 1956, My 2,31:3
Nellis, S K G, 1866, Ap 9,8:5
Nellson, Walter S Mrs, 1912, Jl 7,II,11:5
Nelmes, Harry B, 1960, Ja 6,35:2
Nelms, Homer L Dr, 1968, O 31,43:4
Nelsen, Nels, 1943, Je 10,21:2
Nelsen, Nicholai, 1952, Ap 13,76:5
Nelson, Abraham, 1953, S 6,52:6
Nelson, Abram G, 1942, Jl 30,21:2
Nelson, Albert J Lt, 1968, Ja 20,26:5
Nelson, Alex, 1923, Jl 31,17:4
Nelson, Alex C, 1940, O 22,23:4
Nelson, Alfred B Mrs, 1949, D 25,26:5
Nelson, Alfred Mrs, 1923, Ag 4,13:4
Nelson, Alfred 2d, 1952, Mr 27,29:4
Nelson, Allan S, 1965, Ag 20,29:4
Nelson, Allen H, 1944, Ap 30,46:2
Nelson, Allen H Mrs, 1941, Jl 31,17:5
Nelson, Allen Jr, 1957, Mr 24,26:5
Nelson, Alphonso F, 1967, Jl 6,35:2
Nelson, Alvin E, 1950, My 5,22:3
Nelson, Amos, 1947, Ag 14,23:1
Nelson, Andrew, 1964, Jl 8,35:4
Nelson, Andrew E, 1945, F 11,38:5
Nelson, Andrew L, 1958, Ag 28,27:2
Nelson, Andrew P, 1964, N 15,86:5
Nelson, Andrew R, 1961, Je 15,43:2
Nelson, Arthur, 1915, Ag 17,9:5
Nelson, Arthur A, 1958, Ag 3,80:5
Nelson, Arthur E, 1955, Ap 13,29:2
Nelson, Arthur M, 1960, S 2,23:3
Nelson, Arthur W, 1948, O 23,15:3
Nelson, Aubrey G, 1953, D 31,19:3
Nelson, August Mrs, 1946, Mr 12,25:5
Nelson, Augustus, 1949, Je 19,68:1
Nelson, Axel, 1943, Mr 1,19:5; 1960, Mr 18,26:5
Nelson, Axel H, 1962, O 12,31:3
Nelson, Axel N, 1947, F 15,15:2
Nelson, Bernat, 1968, Ja 31,41:1
Nelson, Bernhardt, 1955, Je 17,23:2
Nelson, Bertram G, 1938, D 30,15:1
Nelson, C A, 1934, O 22,15:5
Nelson, C Gustave, 1955, Ja 29,15:3
Nelson, Carl, 1953, D 19,9:2
Nelson, Carl E, 1955, Ap 28,29:1
Nelson, Carl Mrs, 1946, My 2,21:3; 1955, F 9,27:2
Nelson, Carl P, 1947, My 29,21:2
Nelson, Carl V, 1939, S 3,19:2
Nelson, Charles, 1910, Mr 31,11:4; 1946, Jl 30,23:4
Nelson, Charles A, 1945, S 20,23:2
Nelson, Charles B, 1953, D 23,25:3
Nelson, Charles J, 1940, N 10,57:2
Nelson, Charles N Mrs, 1946, S 12,7:1
Nelson, Charles O, 1961, Ap 4,37:1
Nelson, Charles P, 1962, Je 9,25:4
Nelson, Charles P Mrs, 1953, N 12,31:3
Nelson, Charles Rev, 1912, O 25,13:2
Nelson, Charles S, 1953, Je 27,15:2
Nelson, Charles T, 1944, Jl 2,19:1
Nelson, Charles W, 1949, N 2,27:1; 1966, Ja 4,31:3
Nelson, Clarence L, 1903, O 31,9:6
Nelson, Claud D, 1967, O 26,47:1
Nelson, Clyde, 1949, Jl 27,32:2
Nelson, Crescent F, 1967, Jl 22,26:3
Nelson, D Horace, 1955, Ja 15,13:2
Nelson, Daniel I, 1953, Ap 14,35:3
Nelson, David C, 1950, My 20,15:5
Nelson, David J, 1953, My 8,25:3
Nelson, De Wayne, 1960, D 29,25:3
Nelson, Donald M (funl plans, O 1,35:4; will, O 29,67:5), 1959, S 30,37:1
Nelson, Donald M Mrs, 1947, F 13,23:3
Nelson, Dorothy, 1949, F 4,23:1
Nelson, Douglas C, 1948, Ja 16,21:4
Nelson, E D, 1871, N 4,9:2
Nelson, E William, 1934, My 20,31:1
Nelson, E Wilmer, 1956, Mr 28,31:4
Nelson, Earl, 1947, O 1,30:2
Nelson, Earl W, 1954, Ap 9,23:2
Nelson, Edgar A, 1959, Jl 12,72:7
Nelson, Edgar R, 1951, Ap 15,93:1
Nelson, Edgar S, 1967, D 15,94:4
Nelson, Edmund (Gunner), 1957, My 13,1:5
Nelson, Edward A H Lord, 1951, Ja 31,26:2
Nelson, Edward E, 1959, F 26,31:3
Nelson, Edward F, 1949, Ag 25,23:4
Nelson, Edward L, 1955, S 22,31:3
Nelson, Edward M, 1938, Jl 21,21:3
Nelson, Edward Mrs, 1940, My 2,23:2
Nelson, Edward T, 1946, O 6,58:4
Nelson, Edwin J, 1938, Ag 6,13:2
Nelson, Egbert V Mrs, 1948, Ag 14,13:5
Nelson, Elba C Mrs, 1967, Ap 4,43:4
Nelson, Eleanor Taylor Mrs, 1968, D 9,47:1
Nelson, Elmer M, 1958, D 26,2:6
Nelson, Elmer W, 1967, Jl 10,28:4
Nelson, Elnathan K, 1940, N 10,56:2
Nelson, Erling G, 1958, Mr 26,37:1
Nelson, Erwin, 1945, My 1,23:1
Nelson, Esther O Mrs, 1941, Ag 30,13:5
Nelson, Everit E, 1964, Mr 3,35:2
Nelson, Fayette, 1938, Jl 10,27:1
Nelson, Francis A, 1950, Mr 30,29:2
Nelson, Francis K, 1944, Je 17,13:5
Nelson, Francis K Mrs, 1950, O 22,92:1
Nelson, Frank, 1951, Ja 22,17:3; 1952, Jl 12,13:1
Nelson, Frank H, 1939, N 1,23:3
Nelson, Frank H Mrs, 1948, O 23,15:5
Nelson, Frank L, 1947, F 5,26:2
Nelson, Frank L Mrs, 1938, Jl 7,19:2
Nelson, Franklin S, 1959, Ja 4,88:4
Nelson, Frederic T Mrs, 1963, Jl 4,17:1
Nelson, Frederick B, 1947, Ja 24,21:1
Nelson, Frederick T, 1960, N 10,47:3
Nelson, G F Rev Dr, 1932, Mr 17,21:3
Nelson, G Harry, 1950, S 27,31:4
Nelson, G S, 1880, F 8,2:4
Nelson, G W, 1903, Ag 24,7:7
Nelson, Gaylord, 1947, Mr 25,25:2
Nelson, George, 1915, Ag 14,7:5
Nelson, George A, 1946, Ja 1,27:1
Nelson, George D, 1910, F 9,7:4
Nelson, George D (Geo Nelson Dunn), 1910, F 21, 9:5
Nelson, George E, 1953, Mr 23,23:4; 1966, Ja 16,82:6
Nelson, George H, 1962, Jl 17,25:2
Nelson, George M, 1912, O 4,13:4; 1946, F 23,13:2
Nelson, George P, 1905, S 28,9:6
Nelson, George S Mrs, 1944, N 11,13:4
Nelson, George V, 1952, Ja 28,17:2
Nelson, George W, 1939, Jl 24,13:6; 1959, Ja 19,27:2
Nelson, Godfrey N (funl, N 7,86:1), 1954, N 5,21:1
Nelson, Gordon, 1956, F 20,23:4
Nelson, Gordon W Capt, 1968, S 12,47:2
Nelson, Grace R Mrs, 1966, D 7,47:3
Nelson, Guy A, 1957, Ja 30,29:5
Nelson, H Ogden, 1945, My 10,23:2
Nelson, Hannah Mrs, 1905, Ap 18,11:5
Nelson, Harold, 1942, Ap 8,19:5
Nelson, Harold G, 1946, Jl 25,21:5
Nelson, Harold H, 1954, Ja 25,19:5
Nelson, Harold Lt, 1918, Ja 24,9:5
Nelson, Harold R, 1960, Ap 4,29:6; 1968, My 13,43:2
Nelson, Harriet S A Mrs, 1939, O 26,23:5
Nelson, Harry, 1964, O 28,45:3; 1967, Mr 28,39:4
Nelson, Harry J, 1944, Je 3,13:4
Nelson, Harry L, 1939, Mr 12,III,7:2
Nelson, Harvey B Jr, 1957, Je 11,35:4
Nelson, Henry, 1952, Jl 25,17:3
Nelson, Henry A, 1948, Ag 31,26:2
Nelson, Henry Clay Ex-Sen, 1909, Ap 18,11:4
Nelson, Henry Knute, 1908, Mr 18,7:6
Nelson, Henry L, 1942, Je 3,24:3
Nelson, Henry L Mrs, 1949, My 15,90:3
Nelson, Henry Loomis Prof, 1908, Mr 1,9:4
Nelson, Henry P Mrs, 1947, Mr 18,27:3; 1950, Ag 28, 17:3; 1956, Ap 11,33:4
Nelson, Henry R, 1940, D 31,15:6
Nelson, Henry W, 1961, Ja 16,27:3
Nelson, Herbert U, 1956, N 21,27:3
Nelson, Hilmer M, 1948, S 6,13:3
Nelson, Horation Earl, 1913, F 26,13:4
Nelson, Hugh, 1954, N 23,35:3
Nelson, Irma Mrs, 1949, D 27,24:2
Nelson, Irving M Mrs, 1952, D 3,33:3
Nelson, Isaac, 1948, Jl 19,19:1
Nelson, J A, 1883, Je 14,4:7
Nelson, J Eugene Dr, 1949, My 23,19:7
Nelson, J Eugene Mrs, 1949, My 23,19:7
Nelson, J Homer, 1952, N 30,88:4
Nelson, J R, 1956, My 20,86:6
Nelson, J Raleigh, 1961, Ja 3,29:4
Nelson, Jabez C, 1952, Ja 24,28:2
Nelson, Jacob, 1950, Ap 11,31:4
Nelson, James, 1939, Je 16,48:7; 1949, F 17,23:1; 1951, N 29,33:3
Nelson, James A, 1942, F 18,19:4
Nelson, James M Jr, 1954, F 23,27:4
Nelson, James R, 1938, Ag 27,13:4
Nelson, John, 1860, Ja 21,5:3; 1924, Jl 27,23:3; 1940, Je 15,15:3

Nelson, John A, 1942, O 14,14:5; 1964, S 6,56:5
Nelson, John B, 1965, D 19,84:1
Nelson, John C, 1920, Ag 23,11:4
Nelson, John E, 1951, O 8,21:1; 1955, Ap 12,29:1
Nelson, John E Mrs, 1945, Ja 22,17:3
Nelson, John G, 1955, Mr 15,29:3; 1961, Ja 18,33:4
Nelson, John H, 1952, N 11,30:3
Nelson, John J, 1874, N 14,3:6
Nelson, John M, 1955, Ja 30,84:6; 1965, N 16,43:5
Nelson, John R Rev, 1924, Ap 23,21:4
Nelson, John Rev, 1871, D 9,2:7
Nelson, John T, 1946, My 31,24:3; 1949, Ja 21,21:3
Nelson, John W, 1954, O 10,61:1
Nelson, Jordan, 1922, D 15,19:5
Nelson, Joseph A, 1963, N 10,86:4
Nelson, Joseph Capt, 1903, N 3,7:7
Nelson, Joseph E, 1961, Ja 1,49:2
Nelson, Joseph J, 1937, Ap 11,17:4
Nelson, Joseph M, 1947, S 26,23:5
Nelson, Josephine M Mrs, 1941, D 24,17:3
Nelson, Judith M, 1955, Ja 21,23:5
Nelson, Julia Mrs, 1923, Ag 3,15:4
Nelson, Julian H, 1957, Mr 29,21:2
Nelson, Julius L Mrs, 1964, My 21,35:1
Nelson, Julius Prof, 1916, F 17,11:7
Nelson, Karl L, 1947, N 19,27:2
Nelson, Kent, 1944, N 12,48:4
Nelson, L Raymond, 1944, S 16,13:6
Nelson, Leon M, 1941, My 3,15:6
Nelson, Leroy, 1956, Ja 13,30:5
Nelson, Leroy E, 1957, D 23,23:5
Nelson, Lord (A F J H Nelson), 1957, Je 25,29:4
Nelson, Louis, 1912, Ap 27,13:5; 1946, O 12,19:5
Nelson, Louis M, 1942, Ag 25,23:2
Nelson, Lusha, 1938, My 5,23:3
Nelson, Luther, 1957, O 7,27:4
Nelson, Luther Mrs, 1958, Je 15,26:6
Nelson, Lynn, 1955, F 17,27:1
Nelson, Marie, 1943, My 13,21:5
Nelson, Marjorie M, 1962, D 1,25:4
Nelson, Marks, 1948, D 13,23:3
Nelson, Marshall V, 1964, N 16,31:4
Nelson, Martha F, 1940, Mr 29,21:4
Nelson, Martha H Mrs, 1942, My 27,23:5
Nelson, Martin E, 1953, F 5,23:1
Nelson, Martin P, 1966, O 21,41:3
Nelson, Maurice Horatio Rear-Adm, 1914, S 9,9:6
Nelson, Moses Mrs, 1943, Mr 21,26:7
Nelson, Mrs, 1872, Ap 8,1:7
Nelson, Nels, 1950, Jl 5,1:6
Nelson, Nels B, 1953, Ja 22,23:1
Nelson, Nels C, 1951, Mr 14,33:4; 1964, Mr 6,31:1
Nelson, Nelson B, 1949, S 14,31:3
Nelson, Nicholine J Mrs, 1922, Ag 10,11:6
Nelson, Noel, 1947, N 7,23:1
Nelson, Norman F, 1954, Jl 14,27:5
Nelson, O T Capt, 1937, F 16,23:3
Nelson, Ole C, 1954, Ja 18,23:3
Nelson, Oley (por), 1938, Ap 16,13:4
Nelson, Oscar, 1943, Jl 15,21:4; 1951, Ap 3,27:5; 1953, N 28,15:5
Nelson, Oscar (Battling), 1954, F 8,23:1
Nelson, Paul D Mrs, 1951, Ag 16,27:5
Nelson, Pauline K Mrs, 1949, Jl 15,19:5
Nelson, Per, 1947, Jl 18,17:1
Nelson, Peter, 1944, Ja 28,17:1
Nelson, Peter B, 1960, O 6,41:4
Nelson, Peter C, 1947, O 3,25:3
Nelson, Phillips R, 1968, D 5,47:2
Nelson, R R Judge, 1904, O 16,9:7
Nelson, R Rev, 1879, F 20,5:4
Nelson, R W, 1926, Jl 30,17:5
Nelson, Ray S, 1948, Je 19,15:2
Nelson, Raymond E, 1959, S 26,23:5
Nelson, Reuben E, 1960, Ja 7,29:5
Nelson, Richard A, 1961, Mr 8,33:5
Nelson, Rinico, 1958, S 3,33:1
Nelson, Robert, 1947, Jl 21,17:4
Nelson, Robert J, 1949, F 5,15:6
Nelson, Robert J Mrs, 1943, Ag 26,17:5
Nelson, Robert W, 1951, Je 13,29:3
Nelson, Roland E (Chief Needahbeh), 1954, Ag 6, 17:4
Nelson, Ronald R, 1960, O 23,88:6
Nelson, Roscoe, 1961, N 11,23:5
Nelson, Ross S, 1959, N 30,19:6
Nelson, Rowe H, 1945, Ag 19,40:8
Nelson, Roy C, 1948, O 12,25:4
Nelson, Salome D Mrs, 1942, Ja 6,23:3
Nelson, Samuel, 1937, Ap 4,II,10:8; 1948, Ag 3,26:2; 1959, N 15,86:8
Nelson, Samuel Armstrong, 1907, O 31,9:6
Nelson, Samuel Ex-Judge (trb, D 16,2:5), 1873, D 14,4:7
Nelson, Samuel W, 1955, Ag 24,27:3
Nelson, Saxby B, 1946, Jl 4,19:4
Nelson, Simon L, 1949, F 24,23:5
Nelson, Starr, 1949, Ag 29,17:6
Nelson, Stephen H, 1947, Je 20,19:5
Nelson, Stuart Greenleaf, 1919, D 5,15:2
Nelson, Theodore, 1945, D 13,29:2
Nelson, Theodore Dr, 1872, Ap 5,1:3
Nelson, Theophilus, 1947, Ap 20,60:7
Nelson, Thomas, 1907, Jl 27,7:6; 1952, Jl 5,4:4; 1953, Jl 24,13:4
Nelson, Thomas A R, 1938, Ja 7,19:3
Nelson, Thomas A R Judge, 1873, Ag 25,5:3
Nelson, Thomas A Rev, 1906, Je 17,9:6
Nelson, Thomas Mrs, 1940, D 13,26:5
Nelson, Thurlow C, 1960, S 13,26:3
Nelson, Victor, 1956, Ag 29,29:4; 1959, Ap 25,21:2
Nelson, W A Dr, 1902, Je 6,9:6
Nelson, W C, 1957, Ag 4,81:2
Nelson, Walter Alvin Dr, 1968, Jl 24,41:2
Nelson, Walter G Jr, 1963, S 24,39:3
Nelson, Warren O, 1964, O 20,32:1
Nelson, Willard B Mrs, 1952, Mr 24,25:2
Nelson, William, 1903, O 4,1:6; 1905, Ap 4,11:6; 1914, Ag 11,9:6
Nelson, William A, 1954, S 11,17:4; 1955, F 16,29:4; 1964, Ap 13,29:4
Nelson, William C, 1950, S 19,31:3; 1954, Je 9,31:5
Nelson, William Col, 1916, Ap 12,13:5
Nelson, William E, 1953, My 11,27:5
Nelson, William G, 1965, My 5,47:4
Nelson, William H, 1962, O 4,39:4
Nelson, William H de Beau, 1920, S 28,13:2
Nelson, William L, 1947, Ja 1,33:5; 1949, Ja 11,31:1
Nelson, William M, 1958, Jl 10,27:2
Nelson, William R, 1915, Ap 14,13:4; 1960, O 26,39:4
Nelson, William R Mrs, 1921, O 7,17:4
Nelson, William Sir, 1922, Jl 8,11:7
Nelson, William T, 1952, Ja 30,25:4
Nelson, Wolfred Dr, 1913, Ja 16,17:5
Nelson, York, 1961, Jl 23,69:1
Nemac, Francis T, 1956, Mr 15,31:3
Nemanoff, Richard, 1937, S 27,21:6
Nemchinov, Vasily S, 1964, N 6,37:2
Nemcsik, John M Sr, 1952, O 30,31:5
Nemec, Edward W, 1949, My 6,25:4
Nemec, Steven G, 1942, N 20,23:3
Nemecek, Zdenek (trb lr, Jl 15,18:7), 1957, Jl 9,27:2
Nemens, Harry S, 1956, Ja 11,31:1
Nemenyi, Ernest N, 1941, S 29,17:1
Nemeroff, Herbert S Mrs, 1967, Je 29,43:4
Nemerov, David, 1963, My 24,31:1
Nemerov, Joseph (por), 1949, Je 3,25:3
Nemerov, Meyer, 1939, N 20,19:5
Nemerov, Meyer Mrs, 1939, Jl 1,17:5
Nemerov, William T, 1966, Jl 25,27:1
Nemeth, John, 1938, S 5,2:7
Nemeth, Julia Mrs, 1909, Ag 4,7:3
Nemeth, Steven F, 1950, Mr 14,25:4
Nemire, Aug Mrs, 1940, Ja 28,33:2
Nemirow, Martin, 1958, Ap 19,21:5
Nemirow, Phillip, 1966, N 9,39:4
Nemirowski, Abraham, 1939, S 2,17:6
Nemirowsky, Abraham Mrs, 1951, My 19,15:4
Nemmers, Irwin P, 1944, D 23,13:2
Nemmert, Edmund L, 1946, Ap 4,25:3
Nemmert, P J Max, 1943, S 8,24:3
Nemmert, Paul, 1964, Ja 19,76:8
Nemser, Charles, 1967, N 11,33:4
Nemser, David A, 1949, Ja 8,15:5
Nemser, Herman, 1950, Je 22,27:3
Nemser, Hyman Mrs, 1967, My 11,54:6
Nemser, Joseph, 1940, Ag 1,21:3
Nemser, Saul, 1946, D 4,31:1
Neneman, Albert G, 1952, Ja 5,11:1
Nenna, Albert N, 1968, N 5,47:1
Nenner, George, 1957, Mr 26,33:1
Nenonen, Vilho, 1960, F 18,33:2
Nepivoda, Edward, 1925, Ag 27,19:5
Nepo, Arik, 1961, Mr 24,27:4
Nepokoitschitzky, Gen, 1881, N 24,3:1
Nepola, Thomas, 1963, Ap 30,35:2
Nepomuk, Johann, 1938, O 2,48:8
Nepoti, Teresa, 1942, N 28,8:6
Neprash, Ivan V, 1957, Ap 15,29:5
Neprash, Jerry A, 1955, F 11,23:1
Neptun, Rudolph P, 1966, N 12,29:6
Neptune, Edgar M Mrs, 1949, S 17,17:5
Neptune, Robert L, 1941, O 9,23:6
Nerenberg, Charles I, 1954, N 7,87:4
Nerges, John G, 1960, Jl 31,69:2
Neri, Frank, 1957, O 4,23:3
Neri, Giulio, 1958, Ap 22,33:1
Neri, Sylvester, 1950, O 27,29:5
Nering, Albert, 1951, Ja 23,27:4
Nerlinger, Michael J, 1945, Jl 22,37:1
Nerney, Dennis J, 1961, F 28,33:2
Nerney, Mary C, 1959, D 19,27:2
Nernst, Walter H (por), 1941, N 19,23:3
Nero, Frank, 1948, F 9,17:4
Nero, Joyce, 1959, Ap 12,86:4
Nersesian, Arshak, 1940, Ag 4,33:2
Neruda, Norman Mrs (Lady Halle), 1911, Ap 16,II, 11:4
Nervo, Amado, 1919, My 25,20:5
Nes, H M van, 1946, Ag 20,27:5
Nesbit, Evelyn (funl, Ja 21,31:3), 1967, Ja 19,1:3
Nesbit, Fred T, 1949, Ap 28,31:5
Nesbit, George H, 1942, F 28,17:3
Nesbit, Isabel D, 1941, My 12,17:3
Nesbit, John L, 1961, Mr 5,86:6
Nesbit, Thorpe Mrs, 1943, Ja 3,43:1
Nesbitt, A Hamilton (por), 1949, Je 4,13:5
Nesbitt, Arthur J, 1954, O 26,27:2
Nesbitt, Arthur P, 1963, Jl 17,31:3
Nesbitt, Benjamin F, 1942, S 1,19:4
Nesbitt, Charles M, 1954, My 6,33:4
Nesbitt, Chester L, 1942, N 19,25:2
Nesbitt, Clarence B, 1950, Ap 3,24:2
Nesbitt, Elizabeth H Mrs, 1940, Mr 24,31:2
Nesbitt, G T, 1869, Ap 8,5:5
Nesbitt, Harry, 1938, Ja 13,21:1
Nesbitt, Henry (por), 1938, Ja 7,19:2
Nesbitt, Henry Mrs, 1963, Je 17,25:4
Nesbitt, Hugh, 1914, N 2,9:5
Nesbitt, James L, 1950, N 14,31:2
Nesbitt, John A Rev, 1937, My 25,27:5
Nesbitt, John J, 1941, S 12,21:2
Nesbitt, N, 1884, O 22,5:6
Nesbitt, William, 1915, Ag 3,9:6
Nesbitt, William B (por), 1938, D 8,27:4
Nesbitt, William M, 1953, My 8,25:2
Nesensohn, J A, 1938, Ja 27,21:2
Neshanian, Mersrob, 1944, Jl 28,13:3
Nesi, William H Rev, 1925, Ap 16,21:5
Nesin, Benjamin C, 1964, Ja 29,33:4
Neskovits, Andrew, 1951, Ja 8,17:4
Neslin, Samuel J, 1937, Jl 16,19:5
Nesmith, I E Mrs, 1937, Je 6,5:3
Nesmith, Mary B, 1964, Je 3,43:1
Nesmith, Otto A Capt, 1923, F 26,13:5
Nesmith, Robert, 1880, D 29,5:1
Nesmith, Thomas, 1948, Ap 27,25:1
Nespece, James V, 1950, Mr 2,27:1
Nesper, Paul W, 1960, N 23,29:4
Ness, Affie, 1950, N 1,35:4
Ness, Charles M, 1938, Mr 28,15:4
Ness, Zenobia B, 1943, Je 28,21:2
Nesselhous, William E, 1937, Ja 4,29:3
Nesselrode, Clifford C, 1959, Jl 19,68:3
Nesselrode, Karl Robert Count, 1862, Ap 8,4:6
Nessen, Walter von, 1943, S 5,28:7
Nessim, Simon S, 1968, D 31,27:2
Nessle, Charles E, 1941, Jl 10,19:3
Nessler, Charles, 1951, Ja 24,27:3
Nessler, Herman D, 1922, Je 18,28:3
Nessly, William V Mrs, 1947, Mr 5,25:5
Nestel, Walter, 1967, N 7,39:3
Nester, Elizabeth Mrs, 1941, Mr 26,23:3
Nester, Joseph M, 1955, Ag 24,27:5
Nesterov, Mikhael, 1942, O 21,21:6
Nesterov, Nikolai E, 1957, O 7,27:1
Nesterowicz, Melania Mrs, 1951, F 22,31:1
Nestler, John P Dr, 1937, D 31,15:2
Nestler, William L, 1953, Je 10,29:3
Nestor, Agnes, 1948, D 29,21:3
Nestor, Archbishop, 1882, Ag 15,5:4
Nestor, Cornelius E, 1953, S 15,31:1
Nestor, John J, 1939, Ja 31,21:4
Nestor, Michael J, 1949, Ja 10,25:2
Nestor, William C, 1954, My 4,29:5
Nestos, Ragnvald A (por), 1942, Jl 16,19:3
Netcher, Fred C, 1951, Ap 9,25:5
Netcher, Irving (will, Jl 8,29:7), 1953, Je 27,15:2
Netcher, Irving (est acctg), 1954, Mr 17,33:1
Netcher, Townsend, 1955, Ja 8,13:2
Nethanel, Aharon, 1957, Ag 10,15:2
Netheim, Herman, 1957, F 14,27:4
Nethercut, William R, 1940, Je 18,23:3
Netherland, William R Mrs, 1948, O 6,29:1
Netherland, Wood (por), 1943, N 8,19:3
Nethersole, Olga, 1951, Ja 11,25:1
Netherwood, Charles W, 1938, Jl 5,17:3
Netherwood, Joseph H, 1944, Ag 21,15:3
Netherwood, William R, 1943, Je 14,17:4
Nett, Mathias Rev, 1937, S 21,35:5
Nett, Richard F, 1957, Ag 7,27:5
Netter, Anna V M Mrs, 1942, Jl 23,19:4
Netter, Charles A, 1950, N 28,33:7
Netter, Jacob, 1941, Ja 27,15:4
Netter, Louis, 1951, O 5,27:4
Netter, Martin F, 1939, Ja 11,19:5
Netter, William, 1956, D 30,33:1
Netterville, James J, 1938, Jl 13,21:5
Netting, S C, 1938, Ag 22,13:4
Nettl, Paul Mrs, 1952, S 19,23:3
Nettleford, Archibald, 1944, D 2,13:3
Nettles, Hugh, 1947, Je 20,19:2
Nettleship, Charles F, 1955, O 28,25:4
Nettleship, William C, 1950, O 10,31:5
Nettleton, Albert E, 1939, N 3,21:6
Nettleton, Alvred Bayard Gen, 1911, Ag 12,9:6
Nettleton, Arthur T, 1951, Ag 13,17:3
Nettleton, Clark, 1943, Je 9,21:4
Nettleton, Edward L Mrs, 1949, D 18,88:4
Nettleton, Francis I, 1938, Mr 20,II,8:2
Nettleton, Francis S, 1949, Ag 14,68:1
Nettleton, George H, 1959, F 6,25:2
Nettleton, George H Mrs, 1964, My 7,37:5
Nettleton, Irving L, 1955, Ap 23,19:1
Nettleton, Katharine A, 1939, Jl 25,19:5
Nettleton, Mary G Mrs, 1965, Ja 15,43:4
Nettleton, Ralph B, 1940, Ap 27,15:5
Nettrour, Charles F, 1950, Ja 9,25:1

Netzel, Charles F, 1952, Ja 18,27:4
Netzhammer, Raymund, 1945, S 19,25:2
Netzorg, Morton I, 1946, O 22,25:5
Netzorg, Sidney M, 1949, Ag 23,23:4
Neu, Edward A, 1964, Ja 30,29:4
Neu, Jacob, 1917, Ap 24,11:3
Neu, Jacobina Mrs, 1939, D 8,25:2
Neu, John P, 1951, Je 21,27:6
Neu, Oscar F, 1957, Ag 28,27:5
Neubauer, David, 1943, O 18,15:4
Neubauer, Ferdinand J, 1952, S 17,31:4
Neubauer, Frank N, 1947, Ap 29,27:2
Neubauer, Frederick, 1946, Ja 31,21:3
Neubauer, Harold, 1949, S 11,96:5
Neubauer, John G, 1940, Je 10,17:4
Neubauer, Joseph L, 1961, N 8,35:3
Neubauer, Paul, 1954, Ja 21,31:2
Neubauer, Richard, 1968, Je 19,47:2
Neubauer, William A, 1949, S 4,40:6
Neubeck, Henry W, 1921, Ag 25,13:5
Neubecker, William, 1949, D 30,19:3
Neuber, Charles F, 1940, Mr 11,15:6
Neuberg, Carl, 1956, My 31,27:3
Neuberg, Frank J, 1961, My 11,37:2
Neuberg, Hugo, 1945, F 27,19:3
Neuberg, Louis, 1957, Ag 1,25:3
Neuberger, Benno, 1914, Jl 8,9:5
Neuberger, David M, 1957, O 4,23:5
Neuberger, Harold S, 1940, D 14,17:6
Neuberger, Julius F Mrs, 1950, O 20,28:3
Neuberger, Leslie L, 1951, Mr 10,13:5
Neuberger, Moritz, 1937, My 11,25:4
Neuberger, Raymond J, 1965, My 1,31:3
Neuberger, Richard L (trb, Mr 10,31:3; funl, Mr 14,29:1), 1960, Mr 10,1:3
Neuberger, Rudolf, 1958, F 17,23:3
Neuberger, Seymour, 1943, Mr 31,19:2
Neubert, Charles G, 1948, D 26,52:4
Neubert, H Norman (por), 1955, My 20,25:4
Neubert, John V (por), 1940, Je 5,25:5
Neubrand, Edward W, 1947, Je 1,60:4
Neuburger, Charles, 1941, Jl 19,13:6
Neuburger, Emil, 1946, D 29,37:3
Neuburger, Ralph S (will, Ap 13,45:2), 1938, Mr 3, 21:5
Neuburger, Selig B, 1920, O 6,15:5
Neudeck, Joseph E, 1958, O 1,37:5
Neuendorffer, Rudolph C, 1962, Jl 13,23:3
Neuendorffer, Rudolph C Mrs, 1960, S 6,35:3
Neuer, Berthold (por), 1938, Jl 1,19:5
Neuer, David, 1945, S 26,23:5
Neufeld, Boris, 1958, Ap 28,23:4
Neufeld, Karl, 1918, Jl 13,9:5
Neufeld, Maurice A, 1939, O 22,40:8
Neufeld, Maxwell, 1958, My 5,29:2
Neufeld, Oscar, 1954, Ap 29,31:2
Neuffer, Herman A, 1949, Jl 18,17:5
Neufield, Albert W, 1909, Ap 13,9:5
Neuflitze, Jacques de, 1953, Ja 17,15:4
Neuflize, J de Baron, 1928, S 22,19:4
Neufville, Jacob Jules, 1915, N 13,11:6
Neufville, Stephanie de, 1957, F 15,23:2
Neugass, James I N, 1949, S 10,17:4
Neugebauer, Alfred, 1957, S 16,31:5
Neuhardt, John Prof, 1912, Ag 16,9:5
Neuhaus, David, 1961, N 15,43:3
Neuhaus, Henriette A, 1959, N 24,37:4
Neuhaus, Hugo, 1959, N 26,37:5
Neuhaus, Hugo V, 1947, O 12,76:3
Neuhaus, Max (por), 1955, N 9,33:4
Neuhauser, Frank A, 1961, Ag 24,29:4
Neuhauser, Max G, 1952, D 10,35:4
Neuhof, Harold, 1964, Ja 9,31:4
Neuhof, Selian Dr, 1924, O 9,23:6
Neuhoff, Karl W (will), 1939, F 24,21:7
Neuhs, William, 1950, Ap 26,29:3
Neuhuys, Albert, 1914, F 8,15:4; 1914, F 28,9:4
Neukirch, Charles, 1916, Mr 28,13:6
Neukirk, Philip F, 1946, Jl 4,19:5
Neulander, Joseph, 1952, Je 27,23:4
Neulist, Charles J D, 1964, My 5,43:3
Neuman, David L, 1944, N 27,23:5
Neuman, Diana K Mrs, 1937, My 24,19:3
Neuman, Donald G, 1951, O 16,31:1
Neuman, Henry Mrs, 1959, N 14,21:6
Neuman, Joseph W, 1942, Jl 14,20:2
Neuman, Joseph W Mrs, 1965, Je 23,41:4
Neuman, Leo H, 1941, Mr 16,45:3
Neuman, Max Mrs, 1949, S 13,29:1
Neuman, Moritz Mrs, 1946, Jl 9,21:2
Neuman, Mortimer Mrs, 1946, Jl 23,25:5
Neuman, Samuel, 1952, F 9,13:3
Neuman, Theresa, 1939, S 12,25:5
Neuman, Wladyslaw, 1945, Ja 25,19:3
Neuman de Vegvar, Charles, 1959, Ap 28,36:1
Neuman de Vegvar, Edward Mrs, 1955, F 27,87:1
Neumann, Alfred, 1952, O 4,17:4
Neumann, Arthur F, 1960, Ap 22,31:3
Neumann, August C, 1950, D 30,13:6
Neumann, August W, 1915, My 18,13:5
Neumann, Camilla, 1946, Je 30,38:7
Neumann, Carl S, 1945, S 14,23:1
Neumann, Charles H Mrs, 1942, F 12,23:3
Neumann, Christian, 1942, Mr 7,17:3
Neumann, Eduard, 1942, Mr 20,19:5
Neumann, Ernst V, 1945, Ag 15,19:5
Neumann, F Wight, 1924, O 23,21:4
Neumann, Frank, 1964, My 23,23:6
Neumann, Franz L, 1954, S 3,18:3
Neumann, Frederic Mrs, 1952, My 12,25:5
Neumann, Frederick, 1967, My 15,43:4
Neumann, Frederick W, 1938, Jl 27,17:4
Neumann, George E, 1949, N 24,31:4
Neumann, Gottfried, 1959, S 27,86:4
Neumann, Harry, 1952, Ag 18,17:3
Neumann, Heinrich, 1939, N 7,28:2
Neumann, Helen M, 1944, F 23,19:3
Neumann, Henry, 1966, N 3,39:4
Neumann, Henry Mrs, 1956, O 19,27:4
Neumann, Henry R, 1941, F 16,39:6
Neumann, Ignac, 1942, O 3,15:3
Neumann, J B, 1961, Ap 29,23:3
Neumann, John H, 1947, Ag 29,17:5
Neumann, John P, 1943, N 19,19:6
Neumann, Joseph, 1964, Je 28,57:2
Neumann, Kurt, 1958, Ag 22,40:7
Neumann, Meyer, 1959, N 6,30:2
Neumann, Moses, 1914, N 8,9:6
Neumann, Paul E Mrs, 1958, Jl 10,27:5
Neumann, Paul E Sr, 1946, My 16,21:5
Neumann, Rudolph R Mrs, 1940, D 18,25:4
Neumann, S K, 1947, Je 29,48:7
Neumann, Samuel, 1940, N 25,17:5
Neumann, Sigmund, 1962, O 23,37:2
Neumann, Sigmund Sir, 1916, S 14,7:6
Neumann, Theodore W, 1958, Jl 29,23:2
Neumann, Therese, 1962, S 19,39:2
Neumann, Wilhelm, 1939, D 31,19:1
Neumann, William F, 1947, My 18,60:8
Neumark, Arthur J, 1966, Jl 8,35:3
Neumark, David Prof, 1924, D 17,21:3
Neumer, Arthur E, 1957, N 22,26:1
Neumeyer, William E, 1959, Ja 4,88:4
Neumoegen, Manfred L, 1953, S 29,29:3
Neumuller, Walter, 1924, Ap 10,23:4
Neun, Emelie U Mrs, 1949, S 15,27:1
Neun, John G, 1940, D 22,31:2
Neunert, Joseph T Mrs, 1958, Jl 5,17:2
Neunert, Paul, 1949, S 7,30:3
Neurath, Constantin von, 1956, Ag 16,25:1
Neurath, Otto (por), 1945, D 27,20:2
Neurath, Walter, 1967, S 27,47:4
Neureuter, Clarence H, 1948, My 24,19:4
Neurohr, Ferdinand G, 1948, Je 26,18:2
Neus, Engelbert (por), 1943, Ja 26,19:1
Neuschaefer, Franz L, 1942, N 7,15:2
Neuschaefer, Franz L Mrs, 1961, O 10,43:4
Neuschatz, Gerald, 1966, Mr 28,33:4
Neuscheler, Albert F, 1954, Ap 11,87:1
Neuschutz, Louise M, 1960, Je 6,29:5
Neuschwander, Ernst P, 1959, Je 18,31:5
Neuse, August, 1944, F 9,19:4
Neusel, Walter, 1964, O 10,29:4
Neushul, Ilya S, 1945, Jl 10,11:7
Neuss, Gustave Sr, 1944, N 15,27:4
Neuss, Hyman, 1961, S 21,35:4
Neuss, Jack F, 1956, Mr 9,23:2
Neuss, William Dr, 1937, S 23,27:4
Neussell, Conrado, 1939, S 7,25:4
Neustadt, Egon Mrs, 1961, Ag 9,33:2
Neustadt, George, 1968, Ja 31,41:3
Neustadt, Hanna Mrs, 1903, Jl 5,7:5
Neustadt, Otto, 1908, Ja 10,7:5
Neustadt, Richard M, 1946, My 29,24:2
Neustadt, Sigmund, 1949, D 27,23:3
Neustadter, Josephine D Mrs, 1937, S 16,25:2
Neustadtl, Victor, 1941, Mr 19,21:5
Neustaedter, Florence B, 1953, N 14,17:5
Neustaedter, Joseph C, 1937, Ap 27,23:4
Neustaedter, Marcus, 1947, Je 18,25:2
Neustein, Dudley H, 1953, D 29,23:2
Neutra, William V, 1947, Jl 18,17:2
Neutzenholzer, Edward A, 1948, N 20,13:2
Neuville, A de, 1885, My 20,5:4
Neuville, Rene, 1952, Je 24,29:4
Neuville, Rosina, 1916, Je 3,13:4
Neuweiler, Charles F, 1947, N 27,31:2
Neuwelt, Louis, 1942, Mr 14,15:3
Neuwirth, Harold, 1960, D 12,29:5
Neuwirth, J Paul, 1954, N 20,17:4
Neuwirth, Milton, 1953, Ja 22,23:2
Neuzil, Procopius C, 1946, D 3,31:2
Nevada, Emma Mrs, 1940, Je 22,15:3
Nevanas, H H, 1943, Mr 19,20:3
Nevard, William J, 1942, Ag 30,42:5
Nevas, Bernard A, 1942, F 25,19:3
Neve, Frederick W, 1948, N 17,28:3
Neve, Marg Mrs (see also Ap 5), 1903, Ap 19,4:3
Neve, Willard E, 1948, Ja 19,23:2
Neve de Roden, Max de, 1952, Ag 3,60:8
Nevel, Charles O, 1951, N 21,25:2
Nevengood, James, 1943, My 20,21:5
Nevers, B M (see also N 20), 1877, N 21,8:3
Neves, Carlo, 1949, My 17,26:2
Neves, Charles S, 1938, N 6,48:8
Neves da Fontoura, Joao, 1963, Ap 2,48:1
Neveu, Ginette (por), 1949, O 29,1:8
Neveu, Romeo, 1938, N 9,23:2
Nevill, Edmund N, 1940, Ja 18,23:2
Nevill, Henry J M Earl of Lewes, 1965, Ap 3,29:4
Nevill, Hugh E, 1945, F 6,19:1
Nevill, John H, 1950, Jl 29,13:6
Nevill, Richard P Lord, 1939, D 4,23:2
Nevill, Timothy J, 1941, O 8,24:3
Nevill, William B Lord, 1939, My 14,19:1
Neville, Alfred G, 1955, Mr 5,17:4
Neville, Edwin L (por), 1944, Ap 9,33:1
Neville, Edwin L Mrs, 1941, D 23,21:2
Neville, George Wilder, 1914, F 19,9:6
Neville, Glenn, 1965, Je 3,35:1
Neville, Harry, 1945, Ja 27,11:4
Neville, Henry, 1910, Je 20,7:5
Neville, James C, 1941, Ap 5,17:4
Neville, James H, 1941, F 16,40:1
Neville, James L, 1949, Je 20,19:3
Neville, John, 1901, O 2,3:2; 1944, Ag 30,17:5
Neville, John W, 1961, Jl 20,27:1
Neville, Joseph A, 1960, F 15,27:5
Neville, Julian, 1882, Jl 20,5:4
Neville, Keith, 1959, D 5,23:6
Neville, Louis G, 1945, F 3,11:4
Neville, Richard, 1945, Jl 24,23:2
Neville, Richard Capt, 1903, S 27,7:6
Neville, Richard S, 1945, Ag 6,15:4
Neville, Robert Col, 1910, F 19,11:4
Neville, Robert H, 1944, Ap 21,19:5
Neville, Robert N, 1948, S 22,32:3
Neville, Rosalind H, 1952, Je 3,29:1
Neville, Russell T, 1950, My 19,27:1
Neville, Samuel, 1954, Je 15,29:3
Neville, Thomas A, 1954, Ap 22,29:4
Neville, Thomas F, 1939, Jl 30,29:4
Neville, Thomas H, 1952, Je 11,29:4
Neville, W C, 1930, Jl 9,23:1
Neville, William, 1944, F 23,19:3
Neville, William H H, 1952, Jl 5,15:3
Nevills, Norman D, 1949, S 20,30:2
Nevils, W Coleman (funl plans, O 14,27:4; funl, O 16,86:2), 1955, O 13,31:5
Nevin, Anne P Mrs, 1942, My 16,13:4
Nevin, Arthur F, 1943, Jl 12,15:2
Nevin, Arthur Mrs, 1941, N 18,25:5
Nevin, Blanche, 1925, Ap 22,23:5
Nevin, Bruce E, 1947, Ag 17,53:1
Nevin, Daniel E, 1947, D 16,33:2
Nevin, David W, 1945, Ap 1,36:2
Nevin, Edward V, 1956, Jl 23,23:5
Nevin, Edwin H, 1908, Mr 15,9:4
Nevin, Gordon B, 1943, N 17,25:2
Nevin, Hardwick, 1965, Jl 11,68:4
Nevin, Henry W, 1943, Ag 13,17:6
Nevin, J B, 1948, Ag 20,17:5
Nevin, J I, 1884, Ja 6,5:2
Nevin, John D, 1949, Je 24,23:3
Nevin, Leo J, 1961, N 17,35:2
Nevin, Lillian C D Mrs, 1942, D 6,77:2
Nevin, Mendel, 1950, N 11,15:4
Nevin, Paul, 1950, Ag 19,13:2
Nevin, Robert D Mrs, 1950, D 30,13:4
Nevin, Robert J Rev Dr, 1906, S 21,9:4
Nevin, Robert M, 1912, D 18,15:4
Nevin, Robert R, 1953, Ja 1,23:4
Nevin, Vincent, 1942, D 8,25:1
Nevin, W Scott Mrs, 1953, Jl 13,25:5
Nevin, William A, 1940, Ja 5,19:4
Nevin, William L (por), 1943, Ap 14,23:1
Nevin, William M, 1963, S 10,39:3
Nevinny, Daniel, 1955, Ap 29,23:3
Nevins, Bert, 1966, Jl 20,41:2
Nevins, Frank J, 1957, N 25,31:2
Nevins, Frank M, 1945, N 8,19:4
Nevins, Frank W, 1946, S 4,23:6
Nevins, Gertrude M, 1960, Ap 2,23:6
Nevins, Henry B, 1950, Ja 7,18:2
Nevins, Henry P Sr, 1940, Ag 17,15:6
Nevins, John T, 1948, Je 23,27:5
Nevins, Joseph H Mrs, 1939, N 1,23:1
Nevins, Julius, 1954, Ap 12,29:4
Nevins, Ken, 1951, My 19,15:4
Nevins, Matthew J, 1951, Jl 2,23:5
Nevins, Richard Jr, 1902, Ap 6,1:4
Nevins, Russell H, 1951, Jl 15,61:3
Nevins, Samuel, 1952, My 26,23:4
Nevins, Thomas A, 1939, Ja 11,19:2
Nevins, Thomas F, 1924, My 10,13:4
Nevins, Thomas Mrs, 1907, D 5,9:4
Nevins, Walter H, 1942, Je 3,23:4
Nevins, Willard I, 1962, S 17,31:3
Nevins, William F, 1960, O 12,39:1
Nevinson, Christopher R W (por), 1946, O 8,23:1
Nevinson, Henry W (por), 1941, N 10,17:1
Nevius, A Layton, 1953, N 6,27:2
Nevius, D Barclay, 1943, F 2,20:3
Nevius, Franklin C, 1965, Mr 1,27:2
Nevius, Garrett W Mrs, 1959, Ap 29,33:1
Nevius, George M, 1960, Je 14,37:4
Nevius, George M Mrs, 1962, Mr 20,37:1
Nevius, Harold Mrs, 1951, F 18,78:5
Nevius, Henry M, 1911, Ja 30,9:4

Nevius, J Howard, 1955, My 10,29:2
Nevius, John M, 1948, D 5,92:3
Nevius, P I, 1883, Jl 10,5:2
Nevius, Reuben D Rev, 1913, D 16,11:5
Nevius, Warren N, 1951, N 13,29:5
Nevseta, Joseph, 1948, N 4,29:4
New, Amelia L, 1949, My 7,13:7
New, Burt, 1944, S 6,19:3
New, C H, 1933, Ja 10,24:3
New, Chester W, 1960, S 2,23:3
New, Francis, 1952, Ja 28,17:2
New, Frank J, 1939, My 20,15:5
New, Frank J Mrs, 1944, F 22,23:2
New, Gabriel B, 1954, F 22,19:5
New, George H Mrs, 1948, S 11,16:7
New, Gordon B, 1954, O 30,17:4
New, Harry S, 1937, My 10,19:1
New, Harry S Mrs, 1953, Ap 6,19:4
New, John C, 1906, Je 5,9:6
New, Mary C, 1961, Ja 26,29:1
New, Milton, 1946, N 10,62:3
New, Norman R, 1942, O 31,15:4
New, Ronald H, 1952, F 11,25:4
New, W Ambrose Mrs, 1946, S 11,7:2
New, Way Sung Dr, 1937, My 4,25:2
New Yung-chien, 1965, D 26,68:4
Newall, Cyril L N Lord, 1963, D 1,84:1
Newall, Guy, 1937, F 28,II,9:2
Newbauer, Emmett C, 1954, O 8,23:4
Newbauer, George H, 1940, F 24,14:6
Newberg, Morris, 1964, My 8,33:2
Newberg, Nils A, 1947, O 31,23:2
Newberger, Charles, 1953, S 26,17:1
Newberger, Emanuel, 1939, O 15,49:3
Newberger, Monroe, 1938, O 20,23:4
Newbern, John, 1950, Ap 6,29:1
Newberry, Alfred Dr, 1937, Ag 19,19:4
Newberry, Charles T, 1939, N 9,23:3; 1966, D 28,37:1
Newberry, Charles T Mrs, 1966, F 2,35:1
Newberry, Edgar A, 1962, Ja 27,21:3
Newberry, Fannie S, 1942, Ja 25,41:2
Newberry, Farrar, 1968, Ag 2,33:1
Newberry, Frank E, 1937, My 21,21:2
Newberry, Frederick M, 1939, F 9,21:3
Newberry, Howard B, 1952, D 20,17:4
Newberry, John J, 1954, Mr 8,27:2
Newberry, John J Mrs, 1944, My 10,19:6
Newberry, John S, 1937, Ag 24,22:1; 1953, Ap 14,27:4; 1964, O 25,88:3
Newberry, Percy E, 1949, Ag 8,15:1
Newberry, Perry, 1938, D 8,27:3
Newberry, Phelps, 1949, Jl 9,13:2
Newberry, Raymond J, 1951, My 15,31:4
Newberry, Truman H (por), 1945, O 4,23:3
Newberry, Truman H Mrs, 1943, Ja 19,20:2
Newberry, Walter Casa Gen, 1912, Jl 21,II,11:4
Newberry, William F, 1948, D 8,31:5
Newberry, William F Mrs, 1941, Mr 16,45:2
Newbery, Beverley R, 1962, S 13,37:2
Newbery, Fred G, 1940, S 16,19:4
Newbill, Willard D, 1947, N 29,13:4
Newbold, Arthur E Jr, 1946, S 4,23:3
Newbold, Arthur Emlen, 1920, Je 11,13:5
Newbold, Clement B Mrs, 1905, My 3,9:5
Newbold, David M, 1952, Ap 12,11:5
Newbold, Eugene S, 1941, Mr 5,21:6
Newbold, Fleming, 1949, F 1,25:1
Newbold, Fleming Mrs, 1946, S 23,23:3
Newbold, John, 1950, F 16,23:3
Newbold, John S, 1937, Ap 2,23:4
Newbold, Richard C, 1941, My 2,21:5
Newbold, Robert, 1948, Je 19,15:2
Newbold, Thomas J, 1939, Jl 6,23:3
Newbold, Trenchard E, 1938, Ja 19,23:6
Newbold, Trenchard E Jr, 1942, O 20,21:5
Newbold, W R Dr, 1926, S 27,21:2
Newbold, William B Mrs, 1959, N 10,47:4
Newbold, William H, 1944, Ap 30,45:1
Newbolt, Francis G, 1940, D 8,69:3
Newbolt, Henry, 1938, Ap 21,19:5
Newborg, Leopold, 1938, Mr 23,23:4
Newborg, Moses, 1945, Ja 19,19:4
Newborg, Sidney, 1958, My 2,27:1
Newborough, Lord (Wm Chas Wynn), 1916, Jl 20, 11:5
Newborough, Lord (T J Wynn), 1957, Ap 29,25:1
Newboult, Robert, 1939, Ja 3,18:2
Newbourg, Florence E Mrs, 1953, Jl 25,11:7
Newbranch, Harvey E, 1959, Ja 28,31:3
Newbrand, Edward C, 1938, Mr 26,15:1
Newburger, Alex, 1904, O 31,9:6
Newburger, Alfred H, 1964, Ja 1,25:4
Newburger, Frank L Sr, 1946, Ag 7,27:5
Newburger, Frank L Sr Mrs, 1950, N 30,33:5
Newburger, Harry W, 1941, Mr 19,21:3
Newburger, J, 1926, D 18,17:3; 1931, Jl 20,17:3
Newburger, Lester M, 1965, O 11,39:1
Newburger, Morris, 1917, Jl 17,9:5; 1968, S 13,47:4
Newburger, Morton J Mrs, 1965, My 24,31:6
Newburger, Samuel M (por), 1944, Ap 15,11:5
Newburger, William S, 1951, N 25,87:2
Newburgher, G F, 1939, Ag 2,19:1
Newburn, Charles Mrs, 1953, My 10,88:5
Newbury, Allan A, 1948, My 24,20:2
Newbury, Andrew J Capt, 1919, Mr 25,13:4
Newbury, Edwin H Mrs, 1937, O 18,17:4
Newbury, Frederick M, 1941, S 21,42:2
Newbury, Nelson E, 1957, Jl 22,19:5
Newbury, Saul, 1950, F 3,23:3
Newbury, Saul Mrs (will, D 14,39:4), 1954, D 13, 27:3
Newby, Alva W, 1948, F 18,27:2
Newby, Henry H, 1961, My 23,39:4
Newby, Henry Mrs, 1938, F 2,19:4
Newby, Jerry O H, 1939, Jl 10,19:5
Newby, Mary Mrs, 1951, O 25,29:5
Newcastle, Duke of, 1864, O 31,8:3
Newcastle, H A D P-C Duke of, 1928, My 31,23:3
Newcomb, A C Mrs, 1903, Ap 25,9:5
Newcomb, Arthur T, 1938, Jl 19,21:5
Newcomb, Arthur W, 1957, N 22,19:2
Newcomb, Charles H, 1947, D 21,52:7
Newcomb, Charles J, 1950, Jl 22,15:2
Newcomb, Charles S Mrs, 1944, Ap 3,21:4
Newcomb, Edward T, 1943, D 2,27:4
Newcomb, Edwin L, 1950, S 3,38:5
Newcomb, Edwin R Mrs, 1948, Ap 7,25:5
Newcomb, Elizabeth W Mrs (por),(will, Je 23,23:3), 1938, My 31,19:5
Newcomb, Elrie P, 1948, Mr 7,70:3
Newcomb, Ethel, 1959, Jl 5,56:5
Newcomb, Florence A, 1943, Ap 16,21:5
Newcomb, Frances H, 1956, O 26,29:2
Newcomb, Frank H, 1922, D 7,19:6
Newcomb, Harry T, 1944, O 8,42:7
Newcomb, Horatio Victor, 1911, N 4,13:4
Newcomb, James E Dr, 1912, Ag 28,9:6
Newcomb, James F (por), 1948, Je 16,29:4
Newcomb, James G Mrs, 1961, Ja 14,23:5
Newcomb, James L Sr, 1950, Ja 31,23:2
Newcomb, John E, 1954, Ag 27,21:4
Newcomb, John L, 1954, F 24,25:1
Newcomb, John L Mrs, 1941, O 11,17:3
Newcomb, Joseph P, 1952, Ja 5,11:2
Newcomb, Josiah T, 1944, Ja 4,18:2; 1958, My 7,35:4
Newcomb, Kate P, 1956, My 31,27:4
Newcomb, Leila T, 1958, D 3,37:2
Newcomb, Leslie W, 1952, Ja 2,25:3
Newcomb, Marcus W, 1957, Ja 19,15:2
Newcomb, Mary S Mrs, 1946, Ap 17,25:3
Newcomb, Norton, 1937, D 8,25:4
Newcomb, Robert E, 1948, Jl 25,49:3
Newcomb, Rush F, 1955, N 27,88:4
Newcomb, Rush F Mrs, 1953, Ag 26,27:3
Newcomb, Sarah Mrs, 1944, N 27,23:5
Newcomb, Simon Prof (funl), 1909, Jl 15,7:4
Newcomb, T James, 1961, Ja 13,29:2
Newcomb, Thomas E, 1949, Ap 12,29:2
Newcomb, Victor E, 1961, D 12,43:2
Newcomb, Victor E Mrs, 1954, Ja 24,84:5
Newcomb, W W (see also My 3), 1877, My 4,8:1
Newcomb, William Wallace Capt, 1918, O 30,11:2
Newcomb, Willis H, 1943, Jl 12,15:4
Newcomb, Wyllys S, 1968, Ag 31,23:4
Newcombe, Albert (por), 1948, S 3,19:3
Newcombe, Andrew B, 1962, Mr 13,32:2
Newcombe, C M, 1927, O 29,17:5
Newcombe, Caroline, 1941, D 18,27:5
Newcombe, Charles, 1940, Ap 23,24:3
Newcombe, Edward R, 1958, My 18,86:3
Newcombe, George, 1943, Jl 7,19:5
Newcombe, George E, 1915, Mr 4,9:6
Newcombe, Havelock H, 1952, Jl 30,24:6
Newcombe, James Mrs, 1965, F 2,33:4
Newcombe, Martha K E Mrs, 1959, O 25,86:5
Newcombe, William A, 1940, Ja 5,20:2
Newcomber, Benjamin B, 1953, Mr 17,35:5
Newcomber, Richard, 1951, O 9,29:2
Newcomer, Alfonso G Prof, 1913, S 18,11:5
Newcomer, David A Mrs, 1965, Ja 20,39:4
Newcomer, Francis K, 1967, Ag 17,37:4
Newcomer, Harlan G, 1952, S 22,23:1
Newcomer, Harvey, 1941, N 29,17:2
Newcomer, Henry C, 1952, D 6,21:5
Newcomer, Mae, 1955, F 27,87:1
Newcomer, Marian A S, 1949, D 31,15:4
Newcomer, Marin, 1948, F 26,23:2
Newcomet, Horace E, 1944, Ja 15,13:6
Newcorn, Harry, 1940, Ag 28,19:1
Newcorn, William, 1946, N 12,29:3
Newcorn, William Mrs, 1942, My 16,13:2
Newdigate, Lady, 1941, Ja 2,23:1
Newell, Albert S, 1939, Ja 7,15:2
Newell, Alfiretta, 1949, Ap 27,27:2
Newell, Alfred C, 1952, D 27,9:2
Newell, Alfred C Mrs, 1959, Ja 27,33:2
Newell, Ashbel B Sr, 1950, Ag 28,17:6
Newell, Carroll D, 1968, D 25,31:3
Newell, Charles E Mrs, 1942, N 19,25:1
Newell, Clarence D, 1967, N 28,51:4
Newell, Daniel E, 1937, F 12,23:5
Newell, Darius E, 1906, Ja 22,7:6
Newell, E R, 1931, S 24,25:5
Newell, E T, 1950, Ap 29,15:5
Newell, Edgar A, 1920, Ag 21,7:6
Newell, Edmund Jr, 1916, F 14,13:7
Newell, Edward J, 1940, D 20,25:4
Newell, Edward Jackson, 1922, F 25,13:4
Newell, Edward S, 1938, D 13,25:5
Newell, Edward T (will, Mr 19,18:2), 1941, F 20,19
Newell, Elsie S, 1950, D 14,35:3
Newell, Ernest P, 1948, Ap 13,27:1
Newell, Etta M, 1940, Ap 5,21:5
Newell, Frank B, 1943, Mr 8,15:2
Newell, Frank J, 1952, S 23,33:3
Newell, Frank S Mrs, 1946, F 13,23:4
Newell, Franklin S, 1949, Mr 5,17:4
Newell, Frederick C, 1946, N 2,15:6
Newell, G Glenn, 1947, My 9,21:3
Newell, Gad Rev, 1859, Mr 12,8:1
Newell, George H, 1939, O 10,23:3
Newell, George R, 1939, D 14,27:4
Newell, Gerrish, 1941, O 11,17:5
Newell, Harlow C, 1948, My 25,27:2
Newell, Harmon F, 1961, Ap 21,33:2
Newell, Harrison L, 1949, F 15,23:6
Newell, Harry E, 1958, Je 11,35:3
Newell, Henry C, 1953, N 21,13:4
Newell, Herbert C, 1951, D 4,33:5
Newell, Herbert C Mrs, 1955, N 16,35:3
Newell, Herman W, 1954, D 20,29:5
Newell, Herman W Mrs, 1958, Je 28,17:6
Newell, Horatio B, 1943, Ag 19,19:5
Newell, Howe S, 1960, My 31,31:1
Newell, Isaac, 1960, D 4,89:1
Newell, Isaac Mrs, 1949, Je 8,29:1
Newell, James M Mrs (Hope), 1965, F 6,53:3
Newell, James P, 1940, My 19,42:2
Newell, John Mrs, 1910, My 14,9:4
Newell, John R, 1924, Jl 2,19:5
Newell, John Stark Mrs, 1915, F 20,11:5
Newell, Joseph S, 1952, My 6,29:3
Newell, Louise L, 1954, N 15,27:4
Newell, Mary C Mrs, 1938, O 29,19:5
Newell, Mary O Mrs, 1954, S 15,33:2
Newell, Moyca, 1968, F 26,37:2
Newell, Oliver S, 1956, O 7,87:1
Newell, Oliver S Mrs, 1949, F 11,23:3
Newell, Oscar Mapes, 1910, Ag 7,II,9:4
Newell, Otis K Dr, 1924, S 29,15:2
Newell, Patrick J, 1952, N 7,23:1
Newell, Peter, 1924, Ja 16,19:5
Newell, Peter Mrs, 1954, O 27,29:2
Newell, R H, 1901, Jl 13,7:6
Newell, Richard M, 1950, Ap 6,29:2
Newell, Robert B, 1947, S 16,24:2
Newell, Robert H, 1945, My 11,19:3
Newell, Robert R, 1965, Ag 30,25:5
Newell, Roberta, 1949, Je 10,27:3
Newell, Roger S, 1942, D 31,15:2
Newell, Roger S (will), 1943, Ja 10,25:1
Newell, Sibyl G Mrs, 1946, My 30,21:2
Newell, Stanford, 1907, Ap 9,9:5
Newell, T J Mrs, 1953, Jl 1,29:5
Newell, Ursula B, 1937, Je 5,17:4
Newell, W A Ex-Gov, 1901, Ag 9,7:6
Newell, W Allan Mrs, 1954, O 27,29:3
Newell, W Wirt, 1937, Ap 25,II,8:8
Newell, Wilbur C, 1947, Ja 4,15:2
Newell, William, 1881, Ja 24,3:6
Newell, William C, 1952, Mr 14,20:5
Newell, William C Mrs, 1953, My 27,31:4
Newell, William G, 1949, D 15,35:5
Newell, William S (trb lr, Ap 28,30:7), 1954, Ap 23:1
Newell, William S Mrs, 1950, Ap 15,15:4
Newell, Wilmon, 1943, O 27,23:5
Newell, Zenas E, 1912, D 21,13:4
Newer, Bernard S, 1963, Ap 15,29:3
Newey, Frederick J, 1944, Ja 11,19:3
Newey, Samuel W, 1949, N 29,29:3
Newfang, Carl A Mrs, 1953, D 11,34:2
Newfang, Oscar, 1943, F 15,15:5
Newfeld, Israel, 1903, D 19,5:2
Newfield, Albert, 1957, N 30,21:3
Newfield, Stanley, 1968, Ap 6,39:3
Newgass, George W, 1954, S 3,17:3
Newgeon, W B, 1903, Ag 1,7:6
Newgold, Pauli Mrs, 1938, Jl 13,21:4
Newhall, Almer Mrs, 1950, Ap 15,15:5
Newhall, Annette W Mrs, 1940, F 22,23:2
Newhall, Arthur B, 1954, Mr 13,15:3
Newhall, Benjamin F, 1938, Ja 11,23:3
Newhall, Campbell, 1963, My 9,37:2
Newhall, Charles A Mrs, 1912, S 8,II,13:4
Newhall, Charles Mrs, 1947, Mr 13,27:1
Newhall, Cushman, 1939, My 20,15:3
Newhall, Daniel H Mrs, 1945, Ap 4,21:3
Newhall, David Sr, 1957, Ag 29,27:5
Newhall, G Stevenson, 1950, D 16,17:4
Newhall, George T, 1950, Ja 12,27:3
Newhall, Harriet M, 1960, Ja 18,27:4
Newhall, John B, 1944, Ag 19,11:5
Newhall, John K, 1952, Ag 18,17:3
Newhall, Katherine C Mrs, 1955, Ap 24,86:5
Newhall, Parker, 1965, S 9,41:4
Newhall, R Kenneth, 1962, Ap 23,29:3
Newhall, Thomas Mrs, 1946, D 27,19:1
Newhall, Walter S, 1947, S 3,25:3

Newhall, William P, 1950, Ja 4,35:1
Newham, Ed, 1959, O 25,87:1
Newham, Herbert S, 1939, D 26,19:3
Newham-Davis, Nathaniel Col, 1917, My 30,9:5
Newhoss, Morton L, 1949, S 12,21:2
Newhouse, Charles R, 1942, S 12,13:5
Newhouse, Dean S, 1955, Ap 15,23:3
Newhouse, Edgar L Mrs, 1945, O 25,21:4
Newhouse, Edgar L Sr (por), 1937, Jl 14,21:2
Newhouse, Gerald D, 1955, Je 1,33:3
Newhouse, Isaac Mrs, 1916, Mr 16,13:7
Newhouse, Jonathan, 1874, Jl 10,8:6
Newhouse, Louis, 1958, Je 12,31:2
Newhouse, Louis Mrs, 1953, Mr 24,31:3
Newhouse, M R, 1945, Je 21,19:4
Newhouse, M R Mrs, 1947, Mr 6,26:1
Newhouse, Mott, 1910, Ap 23,11:6
Newhouse, Robert J, 1953, Mr 18,31:2
Newhouse, S, 1930, S 25,25:5
Newhouse, Theodore Mrs, 1955, Mr 1,25:4
Newhouse, W Darst Mrs, 1958, My 6,35:2
Newhouse, Walter S, 1964, Mr 10,34:4
Newick, Ira A, 1951, O 10,23:6
Newing, Charles, 1943, Ag 8,37:2
Newing, De Witt, 1944, N 5,54:4
Newington, Harry M, 1945, Ap 30,19:5
Newins, Fred B, 1951, Ag 13,17:3
Newins, H Dewitt, 1944, Ja 4,17:2
Newins, Robert, 1964, Ag 15,21:5
Newins, W Lawrence Mrs, 1950, S 14,32:2
Newins, Wilfred O, 1947, N 14,23:2
Newitts, Theodore P Mrs, 1966, N 27,86:6
Newkirk, Anna C, 1943, Je 13,45:2
Newkirk, Arthur T E, 1966, Ja 17,47:3
Newkirk, Bryan W, 1966, Ja 11,29:3
Newkirk, Charles M, 1952, Ja 30,26:3
Newkirk, Clyde C, 1938, My 17,23:5
Newkirk, Edgar W, 1948, Ap 3,15:6
Newkirk, H Wirt, 1946, Ap 2,28:2
Newkirk, James S, 1938, Je 1,23:4
Newkirk, Jane B Mrs, 1906, O 6,9:6
Newkirk, John L, 1952, D 29,19:2
Newkirk, Louis H, 1950, S 10,94:1
Newkirk, Mary K, 1954, Ja 28,27:3
Newkirk, Moses Dr, 1925, Ag 6,19:6
Newland, Alice S, 1942, Je 14,46:4
Newland, David J, 1943, O 20,21:5
Newland, Harrod C, 1944, Ja 21,17:3
Newland, Russ, 1955, Ja 7,21:3
Newland, William C, 1951, N 13,29:5
Newlands, Alex, 1938, Ag 29,13:5
Newlands, Mary R, 1937, Jl 6,19:3
Newlin, Albert J, 1952, Ag 15,15:4
Newlin, Claude M, 1962, O 2,39:3
Newlin, Frank, 1957, Ag 19,19:6
Newlin, Gurney E, 1955, My 5,33:6
Newlin, John A, 1943, Mr 28,24:7
Newlin, Mary H B Mrs, 1937, F 26,21:5
Newlin, William J, 1958, Jl 25,19:1
Newlinger, Arnold J, 1955, F 6,88:1
Newlon, Jesse H, 1941, S 2,17:1
Newman, A J Mrs, 1952, O 15,31:1
Newman, Abraham Mrs, 1965, N 11,47:2
Newman, Abram, 1968, Mr 5,41:1
Newman, Abram Mrs, 1963, Ap 21,86:7
Newman, Adolph, 1939, Je 20,21:2
Newman, Albert B, 1952, My 10,21:4
Newman, Albert H Mrs, 1952, Ap 14,19:5
Newman, Albert S, 1938, Mr 13,II,8:6
Newman, Alex T Rev, 1937, Ja 27,21:3
Newman, Allen G, 1940, F 4,40:4
Newman, Allen Jr Mrs, 1948, N 18,27:5
Newman, Alvin, 1950, D 20,32:3
Newman, Arthur, 1960, Mr 6,86:2; 1964, D 2,50:5
Newman, Arthur Rev, 1924, D 9,25:4
Newman, Athol C Mrs, 1959, Ja 14,27:2
Newman, Bernard, 1966, D 1,47:2; 1968, F 20,44:1
Newman, Bernard J, 1941, O 8,23:3
Newman, Bernard J Mrs, 1951, Ag 21,27:2
Newman, Bessie C Mrs, 1940, O 9,25:2
Newman, Carol S Hersh, 1937, S 18,5:8
Newman, Cecil, 1952, Je 5,31:4
Newman, Charles, 1948, Ap 9,23:3
Newman, Charles F, 1961, Ag 5,17:2
Newman, Charles G, 1937, Mr 1,4:6
Newman, Charles H, 1963, S 4,40:3
Newman, Charles Israel, 1914, N 6,11:5
Newman, Charles J Mrs, 1946, Ap 25,21:5
Newman, Charles M Sr, 1958, Ag 14,29:3
Newman, Chester Sr Mrs, 1947, Ja 25,17:3
Newman, Chester W, 1939, N 27,17:5; 1963, My 8, 39:5
Newman, Christian M, 1939, S 29,23:6
Newman, Clarence B, 1962, Ap 14,25:6
Newman, Clarence E, 1944, Jl 16,31:3
Newman, Claude S, 1947, My 8,25:1
Newman, Cleveland A (por), 1945, S 18,24:3
Newman, Daniel A, 1951, Jl 1,51:1
Newman, Daniel J, 1961, S 6,37:1
Newman, David, 1949, F 12,17:6
Newman, David A, 1964, Je 14,85:1
Newman, David B, 1949, My 12,31:4
Newman, Delbert F, 1957, Ap 15,29:5
Newman, Donald O Mrs, 1966, Ap 10,76:8
Newman, E M, 1953, Ap 19,91:1
Newman, Edward, 1953, Jl 7,27:2; 1966, Jl 29,31:4
Newman, Edward L, 1956, Ag 22,29:5
Newman, Edwin D, 1947, D 21,52:3
Newman, Edwin J, 1959, Ap 8,37:1
Newman, Elizabeth, 1946, D 3,31:5
Newman, Ellen, 1908, N 13,9:6
Newman, Emanuel, 1957, Ag 13,27:5
Newman, Ernest (trb, Jl 19,II,7:2), 1959, Jl 8,29:3
Newman, Eva G Mrs, 1962, Je 2,19:5
Newman, F W Prof, 1897, O 6,7:2
Newman, Frank E, 1953, N 27,27:4
Newman, Frank T, 1940, Ja 30,20:4
Newman, Franklin D, 1952, Ap 1,29:3
Newman, Fred B, 1958, Jl 9,27:3
Newman, Fred B Mrs, 1950, O 31,27:3
Newman, Fred O, 1963, Ag 15,29:3
Newman, Frederick F Mrs, 1964, O 26,31:5
Newman, G, 1871, My 25,4:2
Newman, Gabrielle L Mrs, 1957, S 13,23:2
Newman, George, 1948, My 27,25:5
Newman, George A, 1948, Mr 31,25:5
Newman, George B, 1951, Mr 27,29:4
Newman, George H, 1947, Ap 10,26:2
Newman, George S, 1961, F 2,29:2
Newman, George W Dr, 1914, Je 14,15:5
Newman, Gwendall B, 1920, F 3,15:2
Newman, Harry, 1968, Ag 23,39:1
Newman, Harry A, 1948, Mr 31,25:5
Newman, Harry E, 1964, F 3,27:4
Newman, Harry L, 1942, Mr 5,23:2
Newman, Harry Mrs, 1958, Ja 19,87:1
Newman, Harry S, 1949, Mr 15,27:3; 1966, Ag 13,25:1
Newman, Harry T Sr, 1950, Mr 8,25:2
Newman, Helen C, 1965, Jl 22,31:5
Newman, Henrietta H Mrs, 1942, D 18,27:3
Newman, Henry, 1918, Ja 31,9:5
Newman, Henry W, 1959, S 20,86:7
Newman, Horace, 1947, N 14,23:2
Newman, Horatio H, 1957, Ag 30,19:6
Newman, Howard, 1945, Ap 18,23:5; 1950, Ap 30, 102:7
Newman, Howard B, 1948, S 13,21:4
Newman, Howard H, 1948, Ja 4,52:2
Newman, Hugo, 1951, O 18,29:3
Newman, Irene M Mrs, 1958, N 17,31:5
Newman, Irving, 1966, Mr 11,33:4
Newman, Isidor J, 1955, S 23,25:3
Newman, Isidor Mrs, 1967, F 18,29:2
Newman, J H Cardinal, 1890, Ag 12,1:5
Newman, J Kiefer Jr, 1962, Ap 24,37:2
Newman, Jack E, 1958, O 6,31:3
Newman, Jacob, 1953, Ag 14,19:5
Newman, Jacob K, 1943, Ap 7,25:4
Newman, Jacob L, 1960, Ja 21,31:5
Newman, James B, 1959, F 9,26:1
Newman, James E, 1945, Ag 4,13:4
Newman, James J, 1937, S 28,23:2
Newman, James L, 1938, Je 21,19:6
Newman, James R, 1966, My 29,56:4
Newman, Jerome A Mrs, 1964, Jl 11,25:2
Newman, Jerome J, 1951, S 11,23:5
Newman, John, 1904, Ja 10,10:2; 1953, S 15,31:5
Newman, John D, 1940, D 10,25:3
Newman, John E, 1950, Je 6,29:4; 1960, F 28,82:8
Newman, John F, 1966, Mr 10,33:3
Newman, John G, 1956, S 29,19:3
Newman, John H, 1938, O 12,27:2
Newman, John J, 1953, O 9,27:2; 1964, N 25,37:1
Newman, John L, 1946, D 31,18:4
Newman, John Ludlow Maj, 1913, S 8,7:2
Newman, John P Bishop, 1899, Jl 6,7:5
Newman, John P Bp, 1909, S 16,9:4
Newman, John S, 1940, Jl 24,21:5
Newman, John V, 1956, F 18,19:3
Newman, John V Mrs, 1967, Jl 16,64:8
Newman, John W, 1938, Je 7,23:1; 1946, Ap 27,17:5
Newman, Jonas, 1961, Jl 9,77:2
Newman, Joseph J, 1967, N 22,47:1
Newman, Joseph J Mrs, 1963, Jl 7,52:1
Newman, Julian C Mrs, 1959, S 3,27:5
Newman, Julius, 1958, Jl 16,29:3; 1964, F 22,21:1
Newman, Julius F, 1940, Mr 5,23:4
Newman, Kenneth C, 1953, N 10,31:4
Newman, L, 1928, Jl 2,19:5
Newman, Leander A Mrs, 1960, S 4,69:1
Newman, Lee, 1950, S 6,29:4
Newman, Leon A, 1959, S 5,15:5
Newman, Leona, 1948, O 23,15:4
Newman, Lewis, 1963, Je 10,31:3
Newman, Louis, 1941, Ag 3,35:3; 1950, F 18,15:5; 1954, F 9,27:2
Newman, Louis A, 1955, Ag 9,25:1
Newman, Louis G, 1940, S 11,25:2
Newman, Louise M, 1937, S 28,23:2
Newman, Luna Mrs, 1906, Ja 20,9:5
Newman, M H, 1959, S 1,29:2
Newman, Max, 1949, Ja 20,27:3; 1966, Jl 20,41:5
Newman, Max H, 1951, My 15,31:2
Newman, Milton, 1938, O 2,48:8
Newman, Milton D Mrs, 1954, Mr 5,19:2
Newman, Morris, 1955, O 23,86:6; 1956, Ag 23,27:3
Newman, Morton W Mrs, 1946, D 25,29:5
Newman, Nathan, 1960, F 17,35:4; 1963, S 27,29:4
Newman, Nathan E, 1945, Mr 15,23:2
Newman, Nathan J, 1948, Jl 6,23:2
Newman, Neil, 1951, O 20,15:3
Newman, Norman N Mrs (Frances), 1968, O 2,39:5
Newman, Oliver P, 1956, S 27,35:2
Newman, Philip N, 1950, Jl 26,25:4
Newman, Pinkus A, 1950, S 13,27:6
Newman, Prentice A, 1964, Je 30,33:2
Newman, Raymond, 1964, Mr 10,34:4
Newman, Richard D, 1939, S 21,23:2
Newman, Richard E, 1953, Ap 19,90:1
Newman, Robert James, 1922, My 11,17:4
Newman, Robert W, 1954, My 7,23:3
Newman, Rose Mrs, 1937, My 16,II,9:1
Newman, Samuel, 1952, Je 19,27:5
Newman, Samuel B, 1942, Ja 2,34:3
Newman, Samuel J, 1961, F 12,87:1
Newman, Samuel L, 1964, N 20,37:1
Newman, Samuel W, 1947, Mr 25,25:4
Newman, Simon, 1958, My 30,21:4
Newman, Sol, 1964, Ag 17,25:4
Newman, Stephen L, 1951, My 29,25:2
Newman, Stephen M Rev Dr, 1924, N 22,15:5
Newman, Steve B, 1960, Je 30,29:3
Newman, Thomas, 1943, O 1,19:5
Newman, Thomas A, 1949, O 19,29:5
Newman, Thomas F, 1941, N 7,23:5
Newman, Thomas F Mrs, 1942, Ag 28,19:2
Newman, Wallace F, 1951, N 23,29:4
Newman, Walter B, 1937, Ja 12,24:2
Newman, Wilford M, 1957, Jl 20,15:3
Newman, Willard L, 1944, N 2,19:5
Newman, William A Mrs, 1954, O 20,29:4
Newman, William B Lt-Com, 1912, Ag 12,9:6
Newman, William C, 1940, Ja 12,17:2; 1956, Ap 5,29:2
Newman, William J, 1943, Je 3,21:4; 1958, Mr 14,25:1
Newman, William T, 1920, F 15,22:3
Newmann, Gustav A, 1946, My 23,21:1
Newmann, John, 1903, Je 13,9:1
Newmarch, William, 1882, Ap 12,4:7
Newmark, Arnold, 1951, Ap 2,22:2
Newmark, Benjamin M, 1950, S 5,19:6
Newmark, Charles, 1961, S 17,86:5
Newmark, Howard J, 1964, Je 19,31:2
Newmark, Hyman, 1941, O 13,17:4
Newmark, Isidore, 1951, D 27,21:3
Newmark, Louis, 1952, Mr 5,31:3
Newmark, Maurice B, 1950, Ja 14,15:6
Newmark, R R, 1949, S 13,29:3
Newmark, S Fred, 1957, Ag 31,15:5
Newmark, Samuel, 1952, Ag 30,13:5
Newmark, Saul, 1965, Jl 19,27:5
Newmark, Stanley J, 1955, Ag 30,27:1
Newmaster, Herbert, 1956, Ap 19,31:4
Newmeyer, C Joseph, 1954, F 28,92:3
Newmiller, Charles L, 1955, N 22,35:4
Newmiller, Phil J, 1952, Ag 5,19:5
Newmyer, Arthur G, 1955, O 13,32:1
Newnes, Frank H, 1955, Jl 11,23:6
Newnes, George Sir, 1910, Je 10,9:4
Newnes, Lady, 1939, O 9,19:4
Newport, Baronet of (Sir Chas Christian Waller), 1912, My 29,11:5
Newport, Carl T, 1949, F 9,27:2
Newport, Clara P Mrs, 1949, F 7,19:3
Newport, Dwight, 1937, Jl 1,27:4
Newport, Edward, 1912, Ag 23,9:3
Newport, Reece Marshall Gen, 1912, N 4,11:6
Newry, Edwin L, 1942, Je 3,23:5
Newschafer, William H, 1908, Ja 7,7:6
Newsham, Harold G, 1961, My 17,37:1
Newsholme, Arthur, 1943, Je 19,13:4
Newsom, Bobo (Louis N), 1962, D 8,27:4
Newsom, John D, 1954, Ap 27,29:5
Newsom, Marion E, 1948, S 15,32:3
Newsom, Reeves J, 1967, My 1,37:4
Newsom, William M, 1942, F 3,19:2
Newsom. William P, 1942, F 2,10:2
Newsome, Albert R, 1951, Ag 7,25:5
Newsome, James, 1873, Je 12,4:7
Newsome, John H, 1949, Ja 12,28:3; 1963, Ag 6,31:2
Newsome, Lillian Mrs, 1952, O 4,17:4
Newsome, Mary P, 1939, F 12,44:7
Newsome, Milton P Mrs, 1957, S 19,29:1
Newson, H Dorsey, 1956, Ag 6,23:6
Newstead, Arthur E, 1952, Ap 2,33:2
Newstead, Jacob, 1910, Mr 21,9:3
Newstead, Jacob A, 1910, Mr 18,11:5
Newstead, Robert, 1947, F 18,26:2
Newstedt, George H, 1953, F 24,25:2
Newswander, Fred A, 1948, D 14,29:2
Newswander, Fred A Jr, 1950, My 25,29:3
Newte, Horace W C, 1949, D 31,15:4
Newton, A Clinton Mrs, 1951, N 27,31:2
Newton, Adella M Mrs, 1949, Ap 7,29:2
Newton, Albert W, 1950, O 11,33:4
Newton, Albro J, 1919, S 25,15:5
Newton, Alfred E (por), 1940, S 30,17:5
Newton, Alfred Prof, 1907, Je 9,9:5
Newton, Almira G, 1947, Ja 4,15:2
Newton, Arch M, 1952, Jl 28,15:4

Newton, Arthur E, 1952, S 16,29:2
Newton, Arthur G, 1955, Mr 4,23:3
Newton, Arthur L, 1956, My 22,33:4
Newton, Arthur U Mrs, 1958, Ag 6,25:4
Newton, Arthur U Mrs (M White), 1960, D 27,29:5
Newton, Babette E Mrs, 1941, Ja 18,15:1
Newton, Bert W, 1953, S 23,31:2
Newton, Billy (W N Smeltz), 1954, F 16,25:5
Newton, Byron R, 1938, Mr 21,15:3
Newton, Carolyn Mrs, 1940, My 31,19:5
Newton, Charles B Mrs, 1952, Ap 5,15:5
Newton, Charles D, 1930, O 31,23:1
Newton, Charles H, 1959, F 24,29:3
Newton, Charles W, 1948, S 5,40:6
Newton, Cuthbert P, 1942, O 28,23:6
Newton, Don W, 1952, Jl 31,23:2
Newton, E Swift Mrs, 1965, N 4,47:3
Newton, Edward G, 1950, Jl 12,29:2
Newton, Edwin M, 1957, F 16,17:6
Newton, Elbridge W, 1940, My 7,26:2
Newton, Elmer, 1953, Ap 6,19:3
Newton, Elsie E Mrs, 1941, Ja 13,15:4
Newton, Emily, 1940, F 5,17:4
Newton, Emmet F, 1940, F 10,15:5
Newton, Emmett, 1940, My 26,35:2
Newton, Eric, 1965, Mr 11,33:3
Newton, Ethel B, 1944, Ja 19,19:5
Newton, Francis C, 1946, Ag 5,21:4
Newton, Francis J, 1948, My 10,21:1
Newton, Francis Mrs, 1949, F 7,19:5
Newton, Frank A (por), 1945, N 17,17:5
Newton, Frank C, 1943, Ap 29,22:3
Newton, Frank L, 1940, O 3,25:2
Newton, Frank Mrs, 1907, Ap 2,11:5
Newton, Fred J, 1965, F 20,25:4
Newton, Frederic, 1942, Ag 13,19:2
Newton, Frederic J, 1941, My 4,52:5
Newton, George A, 1956, Mr 22,35:3
Newton, George D, 1965, Mr 25,37:2
Newton, H Prof, 1877, Ag 21,4:6
Newton, Harry J, 1955, Ap 12,29:1
Newton, Hattie M Mrs, 1954, S 9,31:4
Newton, Henry G, 1914, Mr 22,15:4
Newton, Henry W, 1937, Mr 25,25:5
Newton, Homer C, 1957, Je 22,15:2
Newton, Howard D, 1916, N 25,13:4
Newton, Howard D Mrs, 1947, N 16,76:5
Newton, Howard W, 1951, Ja 10,28:2
Newton, Hugh S Mrs, 1957, Ag 23,19:2
Newton, Isaac, 1858, N 24,1:5
Newton, Isaac Sir, 1924, Mr 23,X,8:2
Newton, J Edward, 1947, My 14,25:4
Newton, J S, 1876, F 7,5:6
Newton, Jacob C, 1946, Ag 27,27:5
Newton, James B Mrs, 1954, F 24,25:2
Newton, James H, 1964, D 17,41:3
Newton, James R, 1956, Ja 8,87:2
Newton, Jean (Mrs H J Stich), 1954, S 3,17:5
Newton, John, 1957, Je 9,88:5
Newton, John E (por), 1943, Jl 8,19:5
Newton, John Gen, 1895, My 2,3:6
Newton, John H, 1948, My 5,25:1
Newton, John Mrs, 1914, Je 29,9:6
Newton, John R, 1949, Ja 2,60:6
Newton, Joseph F, 1950, Ja 26,27:1
Newton, Kate, 1873, O 13,4:7
Newton, L V, 1880, Jl 12,5:4
Newton, Lord, 1942, Mr 22,49:3
Newton, Louis, 1952, O 19,88:8
Newton, M W, 1925, N 30,19:6
Newton, Mabel D Mrs, 1937, D 31,16:2
Newton, Margaret, 1942, Ja 2,23:4
Newton, Marshall E Mrs, 1967, My 9,47:4
Newton, Mary W, 1960, N 24,29:5
Newton, Maurice, 1968, Ap 27,39:6
Newton, Mildred W Mrs, 1948, D 15,33:6
Newton, Minnie E, 1944, Ja 26,19:5
Newton, Minor, 1951, Jl 2,23:4
Newton, Oliver A, 1949, Ap 16,15:2
Newton, Oscar, 1939, F 14,20:2
Newton, Phil, 1950, Je 21,27:5
Newton, Phineas S, 1948, Ap 19,23:5
Newton, R, 1902, My 15,9:5
Newton, R G, 1881, O 11,4:7
Newton, R S Dr, 1903, Mr 26,9:6
Newton, Ralph A, 1947, Ja 11,19:2
Newton, Ray L, 1955, My 18,31:1
Newton, Raymond A, 1943, Ap 15,25:5
Newton, Richard B, 1945, Mr 19,19:4
Newton, Richard Heber, 1914, D 20,15:5
Newton, Richard Jr, 1951, Ap 21,17:3
Newton, Richard T, 1950, Jl 14,21:3
Newton, Robert, 1956, Mr 26,29:3
Newton, Robert E, 1954, My 26,29:3
Newton, Robert P, 1967, Ja 25,43:2
Newton, Samuel E, 1950, D 2,13:3
Newton, Samuel P S, 1960, Ja 4,29:2
Newton, Samuel P S Mrs, 1951, Mr 24,13:2
Newton, Theodore, 1963, F 26,7:1
Newton, Thomas J, 1937, Mr 4,23:5; 1949, D 21,29:4
Newton, Thomas M, 1924, D 6,15:6
Newton, Vancott, 1943, Jl 9,17:4
Newton, Wallace H, 1948, My 24,19:1
Newton, Walter A, 1948, Ag 24,23:1
Newton, Walter H (por), 1941, Ag 11,13:3
Newton, Walter R, 1938, Ag 29,21:5
Newton, William, 1916, Ja 15,9:4; 1949, Jl 13,1:8
Newton, William Kelley Dr, 1909, D 21,9:3
Newton, William V (por), 1949, N 8,31:2
Newton, William W (por), 1946, D 28,15:4
Newton, William W, 1948, Ap 27,25:1
Newton, Zachariah B, 1960, My 21,23:6
Nexon, Robert de, 1967, S 16,33:3
Nexsen, Randolph H, 1961, Ap 1,17:5
Ney, Elizabeth, 1907, Jl 1,7:6
Ney, Elly, 1968, Ap 1,45:2
Ney, John M, 1907, S 27,9:6
Ney, Karl W, 1949, Je 1,31:5
Ney, Lloyd R, 1965, My 12,47:3
Ney, M A Gen, 1881, F 25,5:3
Ney, Napoleon Count, 1882, O 15,9:3
Ney, Paul Sprague, 1924, D 30,17:6
Neyer, S, 1877, N 11,2:7
Neylan, Agnes, 1951, Ja 29,11:5
Neylan, John F, 1952, F 16,13:5; 1960, Ag 20,19:3
Neyland, Harry A, 1958, O 24,33:1
Neyland, Helen R, 1956, D 10,31:3
Neyland, Robert R (funl, Mr 31,25:3), 1962, Mr 29, 33:4
Neylon, Patrick M, 1939, O 11,27:3
Neymann, Clarence A, 1951, Ja 15,17:4
Neymann, Emma H Mrs, 1942, O 20,21:5
Nezhdanova, Antonina, 1950, Je 28,27:1
Nezu, Kaichiro, 1940, Ja 5,19:4
Nguyen, Van Le Mrs, 1959, S 13,84:7
Nguyen Chi Thanh, 1967, Jl 9,61:1
Nguyen Cuong De Prince, 1951, Ap 7,15:2
Nguyen Huu Tri, 1954, Jl 27,21:2
Nguyen Phan Long (funl), 1960, Jl 19,29:1
Nhlapo, J M, 1957, My 26,93:2
Nhouy, Abhay, 1963, O 2,41:1
Nial, Michael E, 1940, O 31,10:4
Nias, Henry, 1955, Ag 23,23:5
Nias, Maurice, 1954, Je 23,17:2
Nibecker, Bell S Mrs, 1937, My 30,19:2
Niblack, A P, 1929, Ag 21,27:3
Niblo, Fred (will, D 3,32:2),(por), 1948, N 12,23:1
Niblo, Fred Mrs (funl), 1916, Jl 15,9:7
Niblo, James, 1903, Je 28,7:5
Niblo, Mons, 1905, Mr 16,9:6
Niblo, Urban, 1957, Ag 14,25:1
Niblo, W, 1878, Ag 22,5:5
Nicachi, Stephen C, 1939, My 2,23:1
Nicander, Edwin (N E Rau), 1951, Ja 3,27:5
Nicastri, Daniel Mrs, 1960, S 19,31:3
Nicastro, Michael, 1944, Je 15,19:3
Nicastro, Orestes J, 1951, Ap 23,25:3
Nicchia, J P Mrs, 1945, Je 21,19:3
Nice, Harry W (por), 1941, F 26,21:3
Nice, J Charles Jr, 1956, Ap 8,84:2
Nice, John, 1880, Ap 14,4:7
Nice, Samuel V W, 1939, S 28,25:2
Nice, William F, 1965, O 31,86:8
Nicely, Harold E, 1954, Je 9,31:5
Nicely, John W Mrs, 1953, Ap 3,24:3
Nicewanger, William B, 1956, Ag 3,19:5
Nicewonger, Olney W, 1952, Ag 20,25:3
Nichel, Frank H, 1948, My 8,15:4
Nichiporchik, Mary, 1951, O 14,80:3
Nichlos, Salem, 1959, Ap 19,87:1
Nichoalds, Harry W, 1940, D 14,17:4
Nichol, Archibald J, 1955, Ap 19,31:3
Nichol, Charles H, 1947, My 4,60:4
Nichol, F B, 1878, Ja 7,5:3
Nichol, Frederick W, 1955, O 28,26:1
Nichol, George A Jr, 1951, D 17,31:2
Nichol, John B, 1955, Je 2,29:2
Nichol, John Pringle Prof, 1859, O 13,5:3
Nichol, Kenneth D, 1962, F 13,35:4
Nichol, Thomas, 1905, Je 23,7:1
Nichol, Thomas Mrs, 1957, Je 15,17:3
Nicholaieff, Nicholas, 1950, O 15,104:2
Nicholaievitch, Michael Duke, 1909, D 19,11:6
Nicholas, Acosta, 1945, F 9,15:5
Nicholas, Blaine J Mrs, 1947, Ag 19,23:3
Nicholas, Charles B, 1951, My 31,27:5
Nicholas, Charles J, 1951, Ag 15,27:2
Nicholas, Charles Mrs, 1956, O 15,25:2
Nicholas, de George Count, 1864, N 12,8:4
Nicholas, Edwin A, 1953, Ja 29,27:3
Nicholas, Elizabeth T, 1955, Jl 11,23:5
Nicholas, Ella B Mrs, 1939, Ap 5,25:5
Nicholas, Francis G, 1938, Ap 14,23:3
Nicholas, Frank J, 1950, Mr 15,29:1
Nicholas, George, 1919, My 19,17:5
Nicholas, George R, 1960, S 21,37:1
Nicholas, George S, 1952, D 11,33:1
Nicholas, Grosvenor, 1955, Mr 8,27:1
Nicholas, Harry D, 1951, F 5,23:2
Nicholas, Harry E, 1963, D 25,33:6
Nicholas, Harry I, 1961, Je 26,31:4
Nicholas, Henry B Mrs, 1955, Ag 29,37:1
Nicholas, Herrmann, 1954, O 23,15:6
Nicholas, Hiram C, 1950, Ap 25,31:2
Nicholas, Ira C, 1942, Ap 3,21:4
Nicholas, James L, 1945, D 21,21:2
Nicholas, Joe (funl), 1967, Jl 5,17:1
Nicholas, John P, 1938, S 28,25:2
Nicholas, John S, 1960, My 15,86:8; 1963, S 12,37:3
Nicholas, Leslie R, 1948, D 18,19:4
Nicholas, Lewis A, 1940, Ap 23,23:6
Nicholas, Merton A, 1944, Jl 19,19:2
Nicholas, Peter H Mrs, 1966, Jl 23,25:3
Nicholas, Prince of Yugoslavia (funl plans, Ap 17,- 13:6), 1954, Ap 13,6:4
Nicholas, Princess of Greece, 1957, Mr 15,25:2
Nicholas, Ridgely, 1954, Ja 21,31:5
Nicholas, Robert C, 1941, S 1,15:5
Nicholas, T J Randolph, 1938, Ja 2,40:4
Nicholas, William, 1913, Jl 6,II,11:2; 1950, D 17,84:
Nicholas, William H, 1952, F 8,23:4
Nicholas, William Rev, 1912, S 25,13:6
Nicholas Mary, Bro (N Whiteside), 1957, O 21,25:
Nicholas Nicolaievitch, Grand Duke of Russia, 192 Ja 7,3:1
Nicholas of Montenegro, King, 1921, Mr 2,9:4
Nicholason, Mack, 1947, My 15,26:2
Nicholason, Matthew, 1950, F 23,27:1
Nicholay, Paul, 1950, Ag 8,29:3
Nicholds, Joseph V, 1960, Jl 27,29:1
Nicholes, Postell M Jr, 1960, Ag 14,93:2
Nicholl, Charles, 1950, O 12,31:3
Nicholl, Charles L, 1965, Ap 11,92:8
Nicholl, Edward Sir, 1939, Ap 1,19:3
Nicholl, Thomas H, 1956, My 23,31:4
Nicholl, William, 1949, S 30,23:1
Nicholls, Arthur Bell Rev, 1906, D 5,1:6
Nicholls, Charles C Jr, 1968, O 14,47:4
Nicholls, Charles W De Lyon, 1923, My 30,15:4
Nicholls, Francis, 1937, S 22,27:2
Nicholls, Francis Tillon Ex-Gov, 1912, Ja 6,13:4
Nicholls, Gil, 1950, Ja 18,31:2
Nicholls, Harriet H Mrs, 1937, F 25,23:5
Nicholls, Isabelle Mrs, 1938, N 22,24:2
Nicholls, J Shane, 1942, My 14,19:4
Nicholls, John C, 1952, My 29,27:2
Nicholls, John H, 1943, N 19,19:1
Nicholls, Percy, 1942, F 14,15:5
Nicholls, Robert E, 1945, Ap 24,19:4
Nicholls, Thomas E, 1945, Jl 1,18:3
Nicholls, Walter A, 1968, S 3,43:3
Nicholls, William E, 1953, Je 2,29:5
Nicholls, William H, 1937, Mr 21,II,8:7
Nichols, A Donald Mrs, 1966, My 17,47:5
Nichols, A P, 1880, My 31,1:6
Nichols, Abram J, 1939, My 29,15:5
Nichols, Abram T, 1944, N 11,13:3
Nichols, Acosta Mrs, 1950, Ja 29,68:3
Nichols, Alfred S, 1938, Mr 26,15:6
Nichols, Alice, 1958, Jl 19,15:5
Nichols, Alice Mrs, 1939, Mr 4,15:3
Nichols, Alvah E, 1955, D 29,23:4
Nichols, Alvin H, 1943, F 6,13:5
Nichols, Amos, 1940, Ja 17,21:5
Nichols, Ann R, 1952, F 17,86:3
Nichols, Anne, 1966, S 16,37:2
Nichols, Arthur, 1945, My 15,19:2
Nichols, Arthur A, 1950, N 3,27:4
Nichols, Arthur B, 1955, My 7,17:3
Nichols, Arthur C, 1965, F 27,25:2
Nichols, Arthur F, 1947, O 9,25:5
Nichols, Benjamin H, 1939, Ap 26,23:4
Nichols, Blanche, 1947, Jl 18,17:5
Nichols, Burt F Mrs, 1943, Mr 20,15:4
Nichols, C Arlene, 1942, Ja 18,44:4
Nichols, C Walter, 1963, Ap 28,88:5
Nichols, C Walter Mrs, 1960, Ja 28,31:1
Nichols, Caroline B Mrs, 1939, Ag 17,21:2
Nichols, Caroll L, 1938, Je 11,15:4
Nichols, Charles, 1865, Je 13,2:5; 1951, Mr 23,21:
Nichols, Charles A, 1920, Ap 26,13:4
Nichols, Charles A (Kid), 1953, Ap 12,88:5
Nichols, Charles C, 1937, O 24,II,8:5
Nichols, Charles D Sr, 1952, Ag 24,89:2
Nichols, Charles E, 1946, Je 28,21:4
Nichols, Charles F, 1951, Je 29,21:2; 1955, Ja 12,
Nichols, Charles G, 1959, Ap 29,33:1
Nichols, Charles H, 1950, D 4,29:3
Nichols, Charles H Jr, 1961, Ja 28,19:4
Nichols, Charles K, 1962, Ag 27,23:1
Nichols, Charles M Capt, 1937, Ap 6,23:5
Nichols, Charles S, 1946, Ap 20,13:3
Nichols, Charles W, 1943, D 18,15:1
Nichols, Charles W Mrs, 1961, Ag 27,84:7
Nichols, Chester R Mrs, 1948, Je 16,29:3
Nichols, Cicero, 1943, Ag 15,39:1
Nichols, Clarence, 1942, D 13,73:2
Nichols, Clarence H, 1948, My 31,19:4
Nichols, Clark S, 1966, S 12,45:5
Nichols, Clement H Mrs, 1955, Ap 19,31:1
Nichols, D P, 1882, Ja 3,5:5
Nichols, David F, 1940, Ja 20,15:5
Nichols, Dudley, 1960, Ja 6,35:1
Nichols, E W, 1939, Ag 29,21:2
Nichols, Edgar D, 1956, Mr 3,19:2
Nichols, Edith L, 1966, S 30,47:1
Nichols, Edward L Dr, 1937, N 11,25:4
Nichols, Edward T, 1942, Ag 13,19:3
Nichols, Elias, 1948, Jl 28,23:3

Nichols, Elizabeth C, 1937, Ag 31,23:7
Nichols, Erickson N, 1937, My 11,25:3
Nichols, Ernest Mrs, 1950, F 11,15:6
Nichols, Ernest R, 1938, N 27,49:2
Nichols, Estes, 1944, D 13,23:2
Nichols, F Harris, 1953, Jl 14,27:5
Nichols, Finette B, 1948, F 12,24:3
Nichols, Francis A Mrs, 1957, My 12,86:4
Nichols, Francis H, 1905, F 3,7:2
Nichols, Francis T Jr, 1953, N 3,28:4
Nichols, Frank, 1938, F 1,21:2
Nichols, Frank B, 1960, Ag 13,15:6
Nichols, Frank C, 1937, Ja 10,II,9:2
Nichols, Frank I, 1952, N 11,30:3
Nichols, Frank R, 1947, D 18,29:2; 1956, Ap 8,84:4
Nichols, Franklin O, 1955, F 4,19:7
Nichols, Frederick G, 1954, Je 4,23:3
Nichols, Frederick H, 1965, My 16,88:5
Nichols, Frederick Mrs, 1948, O 17,76:7
Nichols, Frederick W, 1944, Ap 16,41:2
Nichols, G L Mrs, 1885, F 3,2:3
Nichols, G Louis, 1943, D 16,27:2
Nichols, George, 1903, Ja 9,9:5; 1950, Ag 15,29:1
Nichols, George A, 1958, Mr 25,33:3
Nichols, George Dana, 1908, My 7,7:6
Nichols, George E, 1939, Je 21,23:2
Nichols, George F, 1947, D 4,31:2
Nichols, George F Brig-Gen, 1916, Ja 19,11:5
Nichols, George G, 1943, O 14,22:2
Nichols, George L, 1948, S 24,25:5
Nichols, George P, 1939, Jl 22,15:5; 1954, F 10,29:3
Nichols, George S Gen, 1916, My 30,9:3
Nichols, Gilbert E, 1942, Ag 31,17:4
Nichols, H Alden, 1942, N 5,26:2
Nichols, H C, 1903, Je 2,9:7
Nichols, H Janney Jr, 1957, Ja 5,17:2
Nichols, Hal M, 1947, Je 5,25:3
Nichols, Harold E, 1960, O 14,33:3
Nichols, Harold S, 1957, N 6,35:1
Nichols, Harry G, 1962, S 12,39:3
Nichols, Harry P, 1940, N 16,17:6; 1946, Ag 16,21:5
Nichols, Harry Pierce Rev Dr, 1915, Mr 1,9:5
Nichols, Harry S, 1949, Ja 3,23:3
Nichols, Henry, 1951, Jl 26,21:2
Nichols, Henry J, 1942, F 10,19:5
Nichols, Henry W, 1945, Jl 3,13:6; 1950, Je 13,27:4
Nichols, Herbert L, 1951, Ag 17,17:3; 1964, D 5,31:5
Nichols, Hobart, 1962, Ag 15,31:1
Nichols, Hobart Mrs, 1954, Mr 23,27:2
Nichols, Howard W, 1916, My 10,13:7
Nichols, Hugh L, 1942, D 30,23:1
Nichols, Humphrey T, 1948, N 24,24:2
Nichols, Irving H, 1955, N 1,31:1
Nichols, Isabel M Mrs, 1941, N 16,57:3
Nichols, J C, 1950, F 17,23:4
Nichols, J Osgood, 1950, Jl 11,31:3
Nichols, J Osgood Mrs, 1968, S 22,88:4
Nichols, James, 1938, Ap 11,15:3
Nichols, James A, 1946, O 31,25:3
Nichols, James Allen Dr, 1917, Jl 30,9:5
Nichols, James E, 1914, Jl 22,9:5
Nichols, James Edward Mrs, 1915, S 13,9:7
Nichols, James L, 1941, Ap 4,21:2
Nichols, Jarvis Z, 1881, Ag 16,2:1
Nichols, Jay T Mrs, 1957, Jl 18,25:5
Nichols, Jeremiah, 1869, Ag 13,1:7
Nichols, Jesse C, 1961, Jl 28,21:5
Nichols, Joel M, 1950, Mr 7,28:2
Nichols, John A, 1905, D 24,7:1; 1950, Ja 1,43:1
Nichols, John A Ex-Sen, 1924, Ap 2,19:4
Nichols, John A Prof, 1868, N 29,5:5
Nichols, John C, 1941, Mr 3,15:1
Nichols, John E, 1947, My 24,15:6
Nichols, John F, 1940, Mr 10,51:2
Nichols, John G, 1941, N 12,23:2; 1960, D 23,19:3
Nichols, John H, 1940, My 24,19:4
Nichols, John M, 1942, D 30,23:5
Nichols, John R Dr, 1968, My 7,41:4
Nichols, John S, 1947, D 20,17:2
Nichols, John T, 1958, N 11,29:1
Nichols, John W, 1920, Ap 27,9:2; 1940, S 11,26:2
Nichols, John W Mrs, 1943, Je 20,34:7
Nichols, John W T Mrs, 1943, S 9,26:3
Nichols, Joseph, 1955, Ja 19,53:3
Nichols, Joseph O, 1905, Mr 22,9:6
Nichols, Joseph V, 1938, Ag 11,17:3
Nichols, Kenneth, 1946, S 15,9:7
Nichols, Kenneth E, 1952, Ja 15,27:4
Nichols, Kenneth R Mrs, 1964, My 28,37:5
Nichols, L Nelson, 1953, Ag 5,23:4
Nichols, Lester J, 1947, Ja 31,23:2
Nichols, Lewis Rev Dr, 1937, S 18,19:5
Nichols, Lloyd W Mrs, 1938, Mr 15,23:2
Nichols, Lucius T, 1942, D 27,34:7
Nichols, M E, 1961, My 2,37:2
Nichols, M Louise Dr, 1953, F 24,25:4
Nichols, Malcolm E, 1951, F 8,33:4
Nichols, Marie, 1954, N 23,33:1
Nichols, Marjorie Minot, 1916, O 17,13:6
Nichols, Mary A Mrs, 1939, My 16,23:4
Nichols, Mary L, 1954, Mr 30,27:2
Nichols, Michael Mrs, 1963, Je 26,39:3
Nichols, Milton H, 1958, My 13,29:5
Nichols, Milton J, 1937, Ag 17,19:4
Nichols, Neil E, 1943, Je 25,17:6
Nichols, Orlando, 1940, Je 26,23:5
Nichols, Oscar A, 1949, My 31,23:3
Nichols, Oscar J, 1937, F 5,21:3
Nichols, Othniel Foster, 1908, F 5,7:5
Nichols, Paul, 1944, Jl 1,15:3
Nichols, Philip, 1962, D 8,27:6
Nichols, Pomeroy, 1958, Ap 6,88:1
Nichols, Ralph H, 1940, O 22,23:3
Nichols, Ray A, 1956, D 21,9:6
Nichols, Raymond F, 1941, Je 4,23:2
Nichols, Red (Ernest L), 1965, Je 29,35:1
Nichols, Robert, 1916, Ja 27,11:2; 1944, D 19,21:6
Nichols, Robert C Mrs, 1964, Je 22,27:1
Nichols, Robert H, 1955, Jl 20,27:3
Nichols, Robert M, 1953, Jl 20,17:4
Nichols, Rodman A, 1940, My 28,23:3
Nichols, Roger S, 1944, Jl 25,19:3
Nichols, Roswell S, 1959, D 27,61:1
Nichols, Ruth R, 1960, S 26,28:1
Nichols, S P (funl), 1884, O 21,2:4
Nichols, Samuel J, 1937, N 24,23:2
Nichols, Sarah P, 1881, Ag 16,2:1
Nichols, Sayres O, 1937, Je 20,II,5:5
Nichols, Shirley H, 1964, F 28,27:5
Nichols, Sillick, 1876, Ja 16,2:7
Nichols, Smith W Capt, 1915, N 19,11:6
Nichols, Spencer B, 1950, Ag 29,27:1
Nichols, Spencer B Mrs, 1953, F 25,27:3
Nichols, Spencer V, 1947, Jl 1,25:5
Nichols, Susan P, 1942, D 7,27:3
Nichols, T McBride, 1939, N 11,15:4
Nichols, Thomas B, 1953, Ja 31,15:4
Nichols, Thomas C, 1962, S 22,25:2
Nichols, Viola, 1951, S 8,17:2
Nichols, Virginia I, 1959, N 10,47:2
Nichols, Vivian J, 1938, Ap 2,15:4
Nichols, W A Maj Gen, 1869, Ap 12,1:3
Nichols, W H Jr, 1928, My 27,II,7:1
Nichols, Walter, 1951, S 5,31:2
Nichols, Walter J, 1946, S 21,15:2
Nichols, Warren M, 1945, Ja 3,17:1
Nichols, William, 1946, Ja 23,27:4
Nichols, William A, 1947, F 7,23:2
Nichols, William B, 1967, S 10,82:7
Nichols, William De Nyse, 1905, Ap 6,11:6
Nichols, William E, 1957, N 11,29:5
Nichols, William E Mrs, 1949, Ap 5,30:2
Nichols, William Ford Bp, 1924, Je 6,17:5
Nichols, William H, 1930, F 23,30:1
Nichols, William H Jr Mrs, 1943, Jl 29,19:3
Nichols, William Hayward, 1907, D 28,7:6
Nichols, William I Mrs, 1949, N 20,94:3
Nichols, William Jr, 1951, D 11,33:4
Nichols, William P Mrs, 1950, O 2,23:5
Nichols, William W, 1938, Ja 12,21:1; 1948, Ag 15, 61:1
Nichols, William W Mrs, 1946, N 23,15:5
Nicholsen, Christian, 1943, F 1,15:4
Nicholsen, Elias, 1944, Je 14,19:3
Nicholson, A O P, 1876, Mr 24,4:7
Nicholson, Alfred, 1940, F 29,19:2
Nicholson, Ann Mrs, 1941, Ja 1,23:3
Nicholson, Arch K, 1937, F 27,17:4
Nicholson, Arthur E, 1951, Ja 24,27:1
Nicholson, Arthur P, 1940, Ja 26,17:2
Nicholson, Arthur T, 1920, F 28,11:4
Nicholson, Carl M, 1943, My 9,40:5
Nicholson, Charles B, 1964, Ap 8,43:1
Nicholson, Charles E, 1954, F 28,93:1
Nicholson, Charles F, 1947, F 23,54:5
Nicholson, Charles J, 1940, S 18,23:5
Nicholson, Daniel, 1949, Jl 25,15:6
Nicholson, Daniel F, 1958, Ja 29,27:4
Nicholson, David E, 1940, F 23,15:2
Nicholson, Donald W, 1968, F 18,80:5
Nicholson, Douglas, 1953, S 26,17:7
Nicholson, Edgar W, 1951, Ap 24,29:4
Nicholson, Ernest, 1957, F 22,21:3
Nicholson, Ernest K, 1967, D 25,21:3
Nicholson, Ethel F Mrs, 1942, Ag 7,8:3
Nicholson, Francis G, 1954, Mr 24,27:1
Nicholson, Frank Mrs (A C Hewitt), 1956, F 11,13:3
Nicholson, Frank S, 1953, D 31,19:5
Nicholson, G J Guthrie, 1950, D 26,23:5
Nicholson, G J Guthrie Mrs, 1959, Ja 9,25:1
Nicholson, G P, 1929, Ap 2,31:1
Nicholson, George E, 1937, Ap 11,II,8:5; 1952, My 2, 25:2
Nicholson, George R H, 1947, N 28,27:4
Nicholson, George T, 1913, Mr 31,13:4
Nicholson, George W, 1938, O 4,25:1
Nicholson, George W Rev, 1920, O 10,22:3
Nicholson, Gertrude E Mrs, 1940, D 12,27:3
Nicholson, Gordon W, 1955, N 29,29:1
Nicholson, Grace, 1948, S 2,23:2
Nicholson, Grimes J, 1950, Mr 10,27:1
Nicholson, Hammond B, 1961, Je 6,37:4
Nicholson, Harold H, 1940, N 11,19:4
Nicholson, Henry H, 1940, Ag 18,37:4
Nicholson, Hugh P, 1962, F 6,35:4
Nicholson, Ida H Mrs, 1938, Mr 5,17:4
Nicholson, Ivor, 1937, S 10,23:4
Nicholson, J B, 1879, My 20,5:3
Nicholson, J Elliott, 1956, N 2,27:2
Nicholson, J Lee Maj, 1924, N 6,19:3
Nicholson, J T, 1931, Jl 18,13:3
Nicholson, J W A Rear Adm, 1887, O 29,3:4
Nicholson, James A, 1940, My 1,24:3
Nicholson, James B, 1937, Mr 27,15:3
Nicholson, James J (Bro Christopher Xavier), 1957, N 21,30:1
Nicholson, James J Mrs, 1958, Ag 13,27:3
Nicholson, James Mrs, 1944, Jl 21,19:4
Nicholson, James R, 1965, S 1,37:5
Nicholson, John A, 1961, Je 3,23:3
Nicholson, John B, 1942, Ag 9,43:2
Nicholson, John H, 1937, Je 22,23:6; 1946, O 28,27:3
Nicholson, John J, 1948, Jl 14,23:3
Nicholson, John M, 1956, Ja 9,25:4
Nicholson, John P, 1940, Ap 3,24:2; 1962, N 13,38:1
Nicholson, John P Col, 1922, Mr 9,17:2
Nicholson, John R, 1903, D 20,7:6; 1937, D 8,25:4
Nicholson, John T, 1953, O 20,29:6
Nicholson, John W, 1939, Ja 9,15:1
Nicholson, Katherine N Mrs, 1941, Ag 28,19:6
Nicholson, Leonard K, 1952, O 20,23:1
Nicholson, Leonard K Mrs, 1945, D 22,19:5
Nicholson, Martin R, 1941, N 11,23:2
Nicholson, Mary, 1907, Ja 10,9:4
Nicholson, Meredith, 1947, D 22,21:1
Nicholson, Mrs (funl), 1871, My 16,8:4
Nicholson, Norman C, 1966, D 11,88:8
Nicholson, Paul C, 1956, Je 30,17:6
Nicholson, Paul C Mrs, 1955, Ja 18,27:4
Nicholson, Percival, 1962, Ap 12,35:3
Nicholson, Peter J, 1944, S 3,26:6
Nicholson, Rebecca B Mrs, 1941, F 4,21:5
Nicholson, Reginald F, 1939, D 20,28:5
Nicholson, Reynolds A, 1945, S 1,11:6
Nicholson, Rhoda E Mrs, 1940, S 10,23:4
Nicholson, S E, 1934, Ap 18,19:5
Nicholson, Samuel D Sen, 1923, Mr 25,6:3
Nicholson, Samuel M, 1939, Ap 8,23:8
Nicholson, Samuel T, 1948, N 23,29:2
Nicholson, Seth B, 1963, Jl 3,25:2
Nicholson, Somerville Commodore, 1905, My 2,11:6
Nicholson, Sydney H, 1947, My 31,13:5
Nicholson, T B, 1939, O 5,23:5
Nicholson, Thomas (por), 1944, Mr 9,17:1
Nicholson, Thomas B, 1962, O 9,41:3
Nicholson, Thomas T, 1953, O 15,33:5
Nicholson, Thomas W, 1943, Ag 25,19:4
Nicholson, W Curtis, 1944, N 19,50:2
Nicholson, W R, 1928, F 23,21:3
Nicholson, W S, 1951, My 12,21:3
Nicholson, Walter W, 1954, Ag 31,21:4
Nicholson, William, 1910, Mr 30,12:2; 1949, My 17, 26:2
Nicholson, William A, 1968, Ag 23,39:3
Nicholson, William C Commodore, 1872, Jl 27,5:3
Nicholson, William G, 1951, Je 5,31:4
Nicholson, William R, 1951, F 20,25:4
Nicholson, William T, 1939, O 7,17:6
Nicholson, Yorke P, 1948, F 24,25:5
Nicht, Frank J, 1964, F 19,39:2
Nichter, Frank H, 1950, O 8,104:2
Nick the Greek (Nicholas Andrea Dandalos), 1966, D 27,35:3
Nickalls, Cecil P Col, 1925, Ap 9,23:5
Nickel, Adam, 1912, My 22,13:6
Nickel, August, 1938, Ag 12,17:6
Nickel, Isabel Mrs, 1951, F 28,27:1
Nickel, William F, 1965, Ag 22,82:7
Nickel, William F Jr, 1952, Jl 10,31:3
Nickell, Joseph H, 1953, Je 29,21:5
Nickels, Clarence L, 1951, My 8,31:3
Nickels, John A Commodore, 1910, My 20,9:6
Nickels, John J, 1941, Ap 24,21:4
Nickels, Walter G, 1943, Jl 12,15:1
Nickelsburg, Julius F E, 1967, My 19,39:1
Nickelsburg, Julius F E Mrs, 1955, Ag 3,23:4
Nickelsburg, Max C, 1938, Mr 17,21:5
Nickenig, Charles W, 1950, D 30,13:2
Nickerson, Arno W, 1953, My 28,23:4
Nickerson, Carleton B, 1940, D 31,15:5
Nickerson, Charles, 1955, My 6,24:6
Nickerson, Charles L, 1948, D 4,13:3
Nickerson, Charles R, 1965, N 15,37:4
Nickerson, Clifford A, 1968, O 8,44:2
Nickerson, Cornelius L, 1950, My 22,21:2
Nickerson, D W, 1909, Je 20,9:4
Nickerson, David, 1947, Jl 8,23:2
Nickerson, E Graham, 1959, My 4,29:4
Nickerson, Franklin H (por), 1945, Mr 31,19:5
Nickerson, Franklin H Mrs, 1950, F 17,23:2
Nickerson, Guy H, 1948, Ja 20,23:3
Nickerson, Harold E, 1953, D 15,39:4
Nickerson, Harry L (por), 1948, Mr 26,22:2
Nickerson, Harry L, 1952, Jl 3,25:5
Nickerson, Herman, 1954, Je 12,15:6
Nickerson, Hoffman, 1965, Mr 25,37:2
Nickerson, Howard A, 1951, N 29,33:5
Nickerson, Ira L, 1952, Ap 5,15:3
Nickerson, John, 1925, Je 13,15:5; 1956, O 27,21:4

Nickerson, John C, 1964, Mr 3,30:2
Nickerson, John C Mrs, 1964, Mr 3,30:2
Nickerson, Kingsbury S, 1967, D 23,23:1
Nickerson, Leo E, 1957, Jl 27,17:5
Nickerson, Leonard J (will, My 4,17:2), 1937, F 12, 23:2
Nickerson, Lyra, 1916, Ag 31,9:4
Nickerson, Paul S, 1955, My 17,29:1
Nickerson, Stewart H, 1938, Ja 29,15:5
Nickerson, Theodore C Mrs, 1947, D 28,43:3
Nickerson, Thomas J, 1941, Je 15,36:6
Nickerson, Thomas W Mrs, 1911, O 6,13:6
Nickerson, V A, 1903, F 2,1:2
Nickerson, Wallace T, 1949, N 2,27:4
Nickerson, William A, 1946, Ag 5,21:4
Nickerson, William H, 1955, N 25,27:2
Nickerson, Winfred M, 1958, O 1,37:2
Nickham, John J Mrs, 1911, D 9,13:4
Nicklas, C Aubrey, 1942, Mr 8,42:6
Nicklas, Victor C, 1956, D 6,37:2
Nickle, Clifford A, 1942, D 10,25:4
Nickle, William F, 1957, N 16,19:5
Nickles, Charles, 1946, Ag 1,23:2
Nickles, Robert E, 1950, N 3,27:3
Nickles, Theophilis A, 1965, Je 8,41:2
Nickless, Percy H, 1948, S 4,15:4
Nickoley, Edward F, 1937, Mr 14,II,8:7
Nickols, D F, 1951, S 27,31:5
Nickols, W, 1927, D 25,19:6
Nickos, George, 1953, D 27,52:2
Nickowal, Stanley, 1946, D 15,77:2
Niclas, Julius, 1944, Jl 19,19:5
Nicodemus, Frank C, 1957, N 18,31:5
Nicodemus, Frank C Jr Mrs, 1955, D 14,39:5
Nicodemus, Harry, 1937, O 23,15:6
Nicodemus, John D, 1938, Ap 11,15:2
Nicodim, Patriarch, 1948, F 28,15:2
Nicol, Charles W, 1959, D 4,32:2
Nicol, Harold J, 1950, Je 1,27:3
Nicol, Harold J Mrs, 1954, F 24,25:4
Nicol, Irene W Mrs, 1937, Ap 11,II,8:6
Nicol, James M, 1945, Jl 10,11:5
Nicol, James S, 1955, F 17,27:3
Nicol, John, 1950, Jl 23,56:2
Nicol, Lucille, 1958, O 4,21:4
Nicol, Margaret Mrs, 1937, Je 8,25:3
Nicol, R, 1879, Ja 18,3:3
Nicol, Robert A, 1960, Jl 22,23:1
Nicol, William A, 1955, Jl 24,65:3
Nicol, William M (por), 1946, F 2,13:5
Nicol, William O, 1963, Jl 12,25:1
Nicola, Enrico de (funl, O 3,19:3), 1959, O 1,35:3
Nicolaevsky, Boris J, 1966, F 23,39:2
Nicolai, Ernest, 1949, N 11,25:2
Nicolai, Frank, 1966, Ja 27,33:3
Nicolai, George H, 1945, Ap 5,23:5
Nicolai, Harold E, 1967, Ag 14,31:1
Nicolai, Lawrence G, 1966, Jl 8,36:1
Nicolai, Martha, 1958, Jl 13,69:2
Nicolaides, Kimon, 1938, Jl 20,19:2
Nicolaievna, Maria Grand Duchess of Russia, 1876, F 22,5:6
Nicolaison, Henry Mrs, 1937, N 6,17:5
Nicolari, George, 1937, Ap 10,19:3
Nicolas, J H Dr, 1937, O 3,9:1
Nicolas, Kean H Dr, 1937, S 26,II,8:5
Nicolas, Prince of Greece (por), 1938, F 9,19:1
Nicolas V Patriach of Alexandria, 1939, Mr 4,15:5
Nicolaus, Charles A, 1940, Ja 30,19:2
Nicolay, Alex, 1959, Mr 17,33:2
Nicolay, Helen, 1954, S 14,27:1
Nicolay, J G, 1901, S 27,7:6
Nicolaysen, Erik Mrs, 1954, F 12,25:1
Nicolesco, Emma Wizjak de, 1913, F 27,13:4
Nicolescu-Buzesti, Grigore (por), 1949, O 5,29:5
Nicolet, Ben H, 1959, My 18,27:4
Nicolet, C C, 1943, Ja 23,13:3
Nicolet, Flora C Mrs, 1940, D 21,17:6
Nicolet, Harry L, 1937, F 2,23:2
Nicolet, Jules, 1880, S 11,2:6
Nicoletti, Alberto, 1949, O 23,86:4
Nicoletti, Ettore, 1961, O 18,43:3
Nicoletti, Henry, 1945, O 23,17:4
Nicoletto, John, 1952, Je 18,27:5
Nicolini, E, 1898, Ja 19,7:2
Nicolini, Oscar L, 1956, Je 9,17:4
Nicoll, Alex, 1956, S 25,33:2
Nicoll, Alfred H Mrs, 1951, Ja 7,76:3
Nicoll, Amelia Mrs, 1903, Ag 13,9:7
Nicoll, Benjamin, 1921, Jl 4,9:7
Nicoll, Courtlandt (por),(will, S 28,22:6), 1938, S 21, 25:3
Nicoll, Daisy, 1937, Jl 3,15:6
Nicoll, Daniel, 1963, Ag 19,25:4
Nicoll, Daniel Mrs, 1961, Ag 12,17:2
Nicoll, David T, 1954, Jl 13,23:3
Nicoll, David T Mrs, 1958, Ja 23,27:1
Nicoll, De L, 1931, Ap 1,29:1
Nicoll, De Lancey Mrs, 1924, F 17,23:1
Nicoll, Delancey Jr, 1957, S 16,31:4
Nicoll, Emanuel, 1956, My 15,31:3
Nicoll, Gilbert L, 1954, Mr 25,29:1
Nicoll, Henry Denton Dr, 1908, O 28,7:5
Nicoll, Jack L, 1968, My 18,34:1
Nicoll, James C, 1944, Ag 30,17:5
Nicoll, James Craig, 1918, Jl 27,9:6
Nicoll, Josephine, 1915, Ap 27,13:4
Nicoll, Matthias Jr (por), 1941, My 14,21:1
Nicoll, William C Mrs, 1947, Mr 11,27:2
Nicoll, William Greenley, 1919, Mr 22,15:3
Nicoll, William Robertson Sir, 1923, My 5,11:6
Nicoll, William W, 1922, Ag 25,13:5
Nicolle, C J H, 1936, F 29,15:3
Nicollet, Edouard A, 1958, D 3,37:1
Nicolls, Arthur Sr Mrs, 1949, F 19,15:4
Nicolls, William Jasper, 1916, F 15,11:7
Nicolosi, Joseph, 1961, Jl 15,19:4
Nicols, Lowell, 1940, Ag 2,15:3
Nicolson, Alex M, 1950, F 4,15:2
Nicolson, Charles B, 1950, Ja 24,31:2
Nicolson, Elizabeth W Mrs, 1953, Ag 17,15:4
Nicolson, Frank W (por), 1946, D 22,42:1
Nicolson, Harold Mrs (V Sackville-West), 1962, Je 3,88:3
Nicolson, Harold Sir, 1968, My 2,47:1
Nicolson, John W, 1953, Mr 24,89:3
Nicolson, Katherine I, 1938, D 19,23:5
Nicosia, Joseph Sr, 1950, Jl 16,69:2
Nicosia, Richard, 1923, N 9,17:5
Nicosia, Robert, 1958, Ag 31,56:1
Nicotri, Gaspare, 1955, O 14,27:2
Nicotri, Gaspare Mrs, 1958, F 20,25:3
Nidecker, Johann E Rev Dr, 1937, Je 1,23:2
Niditch, Samuel B, 1956, S 17,27:4
Nie, Leslie N, 1941, O 6,17:5
Niebecker, Karl, 1957, My 12,86:2
Nieber, Stanley J, 1962, My 20,87:1
Nieberg, Harry, 1940, N 8,21:6
Niebergall, Gerald C, 1959, Ag 2,81:2
Niebergall, Wesley J, 1943, Ja 24,42:4
Niebling, August, 1937, Jl 24,15:2
Niebling, Charles, 1960, Jl 14,27:3
Niebling, Charles Mrs, 1955, Ja 8,13:2
Niebling, George F Sr Mrs, 1959, D 16,41:3
Niebrugge, William P, 1952, Ja 5,11:6
Niebuhr, H Richard, 1962, Jl 6,25:2
Niebuhr, Hulda, 1959, Ap 18,23:2
Niebuhr, Malcolm, 1943, Jl 30,15:1
Niece, Frederick E, 1918, O 28,11:3
Niece, George W, 1941, D 17,27:2
Niecko, Joseph, 1953, N 21,13:5
Nied, Frank, 1873, F 12,2:5
Niede, William F, 1941, Ap 15,23:5
Niedelman, Samuel, 1956, Je 15,25:5
Niedenthal, Noah, 1956, O 18,33:2
Nieder, Berthold F, 1951, F 18,77:1
Nieder, Frederick W, 1956, D 7,27:2
Nieder, George P, 1944, N 29,23:2
Nieder, Philip G, 1945, N 30,23:4
Niederauer, Edward H, 1964, Ap 18,29:4
Niederer, John G, 1957, Ja 16,31:4
Niederlander, Daniel B, 1964, Mr 3,35:1
Niedermeyer, Frederick D, 1951, Mr 17,15:3
Niederstein, John, 1910, Ap 9,11:4
Niedert, George T, 1956, Mr 12,27:6
Niedfeld, Henry W, 1938, Jl 6,23:2
Niedhammer, Frederick Mrs, 1957, Ap 11,31:2
Nieding, John A, 1948, Ag 28,15:1
Niedner, William, 1947, My 2,22:2
Niedrach, Robert W, 1959, My 29,23:1
Niedringhaus, Frederick G, 1922, N 27,15:3
Niedringhaus, Frederick William, 1913, Ag 30,7:6
Niedringhaus, Henry F, 1941, Ag 4,13:2
Niedringhaus, Ralph E, 1964, N 5,45:4
Niedringhaus, Thomas K Mrs, 1949, D 28,32:3
Niedzwiecki, Wladislaw, 1923, F 15,19:4
Niehaus, Charles H Mrs, 1950, Mr 9,30:3
Niehaus, Herbert I, 1950, D 15,31:1
Niehoff, Harry R, 1955, My 17,29:4
Niel, Herms, 1954, Jl 17,13:5
Niel, Marshal, 1869, Ag 15,5:4
Nield, Charles F, 1941, Ja 19,41:1
Nield, Edward L, 1952, My 13,23:2
Nields, Benjamin 3d, 1960, F 26,27:3
Nields, H C, 1880, D 14,2:4
Nields, John P, 1943, Ag 27,17:6
Nielsen, Aksel Mrs, 1962, My 25,33:2
Nielsen, Alex T Sr, 1946, D 9,25:2
Nielsen, Alfred M, 1965, Ap 2,35:4
Nielsen, Alice, 1943, Mr 9,23:1
Nielsen, Charles I, 1942, Mr 30,17:6
Nielsen, Charles J, 1920, Mr 10,11:4
Nielsen, Edwin, 1960, N 30,37:4
Nielsen, Einar C Mrs, 1962, Je 7,35:2
Nielsen, Einar W, 1954, F 4,25:4
Nielsen, Eleanor Mrs, 1949, Mr 4,21:4
Nielsen, Gerald B, 1953, Je 15,29:5
Nielsen, Gerard, 1947, F 14,21:2
Nielsen, Hans, 1952, O 7,29:4
Nielsen, Hans Mrs, 1943, O 5,25:3
Nielsen, Helge, 1950, My 11,29:2
Nielsen, Holger, 1955, F 1,29:2
Nielsen, Jack T Mrs (A Bollinger), 1962, Jl 17,25:3
Nielsen, James, 1940, My 10,23:2
Nielsen, Joseph, 1943, D 27,19:5
Nielsen, Kay, 1957, Je 23,84:6
Nielsen, Mads K, 1947, F 11,27:4
Nielsen, Martin, 1949, Mr 24,27:2
Nielsen, Morris, 1955, Ja 18,27:5
Nielsen, Niels O, 1951, My 11,27:2
Nielsen, Parker E, 1941, F 1,17:2
Nielsen, Peer, 1946, Mr 2,13:6
Nielsen, Rasmus, 1944, Jl 21,19:2
Nielsen, Soren N, 1948, O 20,29:4
Nielsen, Thorlief S B Mrs, 1951, Ag 7,25:6
Nielson, Christen, 1906, Ja 8,9:6
Nielson, Joseph L Mrs, 1941, My 13,23:5
Nielson, Oscar, 1912, Ag 24,9:3
Nielson, Ove H, 1961, N 22,33:2
Nielson, Paul A, 1960, O 29,23:6
Nielson, Peter C, 1958, Mr 5,31:3
Nielson, Thomas A, 1967, Ap 22,31:3
Nieman, Elmer G, 1951, Ja 24,27:4
Nieman, L W, 1935, O 2,23:3
Nieman, Mary Mrs, 1909, F 14,11:5
Niemann, Albert, 1917, F 6,9:3
Niemann, Charles F, 1944, F 7,15:6
Niemann, Jacob, 1941, Ap 28,15:3
Niemeir, Edward, 1940, Jl 29,9:2
Niemetz, Henry S, 1957, D 7,21:5
Niemeyer, Alfred H, 1965, Ap 16,29:1
Niemeyer, August, 1960, O 23,88:4
Niemeyer, Charles V Dr, 1937, Ja 12,24:2
Niemeyer, E H, 1956, Jl 5,25:3
Niemeyer, F J, 1933, D 18,19:5
Niemeyer, Grover C, 1960, Ag 10,31:3
Niemeyer, Gustav H, 1967, O 19,47:3
Niemeyer, Gustave J, 1943, F 28,47:6
Niemeyer, Harry H, 1940, Jl 28,27:3
Niemeyer, J H, 1932, D 8,21:1
Niemeyer, John C, 1946, Ag 24,11:3
Niemeyer, Karl G, 1950, Je 5,23:4
Niemeyer, William A, 1939, Mr 28,23:2
Niemi, Robert A, 1962, S 5,39:3
Niemirower, Jacob, 1939, N 19,38:8
Niemoeller, Heinrich, 1941, Mr 27,23:5
Niemoeller, Martin Mrs, 1961, Ag 8,2:3
Nienhuser, F M, 1947, Ap 24,25:5
Niepoth, George W, 1941, O 19,45:3
Nierenberg, Albert, 1950, Jl 3,15:3
Nierenberg, Daniel, 1946, Je 23,40:4
Nierenberg, David, 1944, Mr 8,19:1
Nierenberg, Julius R, 1948, Ja 1,23:4
Nierenberg, Lou Mrs, 1959, Ap 18,23:1
Nierendorf, Karl, 1947, O 29,27:5
Niergarth, Omer O, 1964, Ag 22,21:4
Niermann, Antonio Msgr, 1914, D 11,13:5
Nies, Ada V Mrs, 1939, O 18,26:3
Nies, Albert B, 1955, S 26,23:5
Nies, Frederick H Dr, 1937, S 2,21:5
Nies, James B Rev Dr, 1922, Je 20,19:6
Nieschlag, Frederick K, 1963, D 16,33:4
Niese, Alfred M, 1951, N 22,31:2
Niese, Benedictus E, 1962, Ap 11,43:5
Niese, Harriette E, 1961, My 2,37:2
Niese, Henry C, 1943, Ag 27,17:6
Niesen, Claire (Mrs M Ruick), 1963, O 6,88:8
Niesley, Paul, 1956, Ap 1,88:5
Niessen, Richard Jr, 1942, N 14,15:4
Niestrom, Victor J, 1953, Mr 12,27:3
Nieswandt, Edward, 1948, Ja 10,15:4
Niesz, John Sr, 1954, My 25,21:5
Nietert, Henry, 1906, Je 9,9:4
Nieto, Ricardo, 1952, Ag 24,89:1
Nieto del Rio, Felix, 1953, Ja 13,27:1
Nieukirk, Raymond B, 1940, Ja 10,21:2
Nieuwland, J A, 1936, Je 12,23:1
Niezychowski, Alfred, 1964, Je 17,43:5
Nifenecker, Eugene A, 1960, Ag 26,26:1
Niflot, Isidor (Jack), 1950, Mr 31,31:4
Niger, Frank C, 1956, Ja 29,92:4
Nigey, William N, 1962, Mr 13,32:2
Nigg, Ferdinand, 1957, Jl 15,19:6
Nigh, George W Mrs, 1957, Ag 30,19:2
Nightengale, Garrard P, 1954, Jl 17,13:6
Nightingale, Augustus Frederick, 1925, D 5,19:6
Nightingale, Eleanor M, 1945, O 12,24:3
Nightingale, Eva, 1945, F 1,23:5
Nightingale, Florence, 1910, Ag 15,7:1
Nightingale, Frances N, 1948, N 16,29:5
Nightingale, John, 1903, My 30,7:5
Nightingale, John T, 1954, Ag 19,23:2
Nightingale, Lester M, 1951, F 27,27:2
Nightingale, Robert M Mrs, 1948, Je 30,26:2
Nightingale, William T, 1964, My 6,47:2
Nightingale, Winthrop E, 1953, Ap 17,25:2
Nigio, Michael, 1956, Mr 28,10:5
Nigra, Constantino Count, 1907, Jl 2,9:5
Nigrosh, Max, 1956, F 27,7:5
Niiniluoto, Yrjo E, 1961, N 5,88:7
Nijgh, Eduard, 1949, My 31,23:2
Nijinsky, Vaslav, 1950, Ap 9,84:1
Nijland, G J, 1946, O 29,25:1
Nikijuluw, Karel J V, 1962, N 29,38:1
Nikisch, Arthur, 1922, Ja 25,15:6
Nikitcheno, Iola T, 1967, Ap 23,92:1
Nikitin, Boris, 1952, Jl 24,27:6
Nikitin, Pyotr V, 1959, Ja 28,31:1
Nikitine, Mrs, 1885, Ja 2,5:6

Niklad, James S Mrs, 1963, Jl 24,31:4
Niklas, Rudolf, 1957, Ap 14,86:8
Nikliborc, John E, 1947, Je 25,25:5
Nikly, Otto, 1939, F 28,19:3
Nikola, William H, 1953, D 19,15:2
Nikolaevich, Ivan, 1951, S 1,11:4
Nikolai (Met), 1961, D 14,43:2
Nikolaieff, Alexander M, 1967, Ap 7,37:1
Nikolajeff, Danail, 1942, Ag 30,42:3
Nikolaus, Count of Dohna, 1956, Ag 23,27:4
Nikolaus, Frederick, 1941, Ja 20,17:3
Nikolaus, Frederick J Mrs, 1966, My 20,44:2
Nikolaus, John, 1952, Ag 5,19:2
Nikolaus, John F Mrs, 1949, D 11,92:6
Nikolaus, Otto, 1950, Ag 27,47:4
Nikolayev, Alex A, 1949, O 12,29:2
Nikolayeva, Galina, 1963, O 23,42:5
Nikolsky, Alex A, 1963, F 18,17:7
Nikrent, Joseph A, 1958, Jl 28,23:2
Nikulin, Lev V, 1967, Mr 10,39:4
Nilan, Edward C, 1967, O 25,47:3
Nilan, J J, 1934, Ap 14,15:1
Nilan, James F, 1963, S 22,86:8
Nilan, James P, 1943, D 9,27:3
Nilan, John J, 1963, S 4,39:2
Nilan, Martin H, 1942, D 5,15:5
Nilan, Stephen F, 1943, Jl 29,19:3
Niland, James L, 1965, O 29,43:2
Niland, Thomas J Mrs, 1966, Mr 1,37:2
Niles, Albert R, 1939, My 26,23:5
Niles, Alva J, 1950, Ja 21,17:4
Niles, Arthur L, 1951, Mr 15,29:3
Niles, Arthur L Jr, 1919, Je 21,15:7
Niles, Arthur L Mrs, 1938, N 25,23:3
Niles, David K, 1952, S 29,23:1
Niles, David S, 1960, Mr 30,37:4
Niles, Edgar C, 1945, S 19,25:4
Niles, Edward A, 1963, S 3,33:2
Niles, Edwin Glover, 1908, Ag 18,9:6
Niles, Edwin J, 1947, F 6,23:2
Niles, Frank S, 1951, Ja 18,27:3
Niles, Harold H, 1955, O 29,19:5
Niles, Harriet W, 1952, My 20,25:4
Niles, Harry, 1953, Ap 19,91:1
Niles, Henry C, 1939, Jl 15,15:5
Niles, J, 1877, Ap 6,5:2
Niles, J M, 1881, Ag 9,5:2
Niles, James B, 1942, D 19,19:4
Niles, Jean M, 1953, Je 15,29:4
Niles, John S Sr, 1947, Mr 22,13:2
Niles, Joseph S, 1961, Ag 11,24:1
Niles, Kossuth Rear-Adm, 1913, D 7,VIII,19:4
Niles, Lotus Col, 1925, Mr 1,5:1
Niles, Nathaniel W Mrs, 1947, Ag 7,21:4
Niles, Perley L, 1923, Ap 11,21:5
Niles, Philip B, 1958, S 25,33:3
Niles, Robert L Mrs (Blair), 1959, Ap 15,33:1
Niles, Susan Mrs, 1937, Mr 16,23:1
Niles, T E Mrs, 1959, Mr 5,31:5
Niles, Theophilus E (funl, N 11,23:4), 1925, N 9,19:5
Niles, Thomas J, 1950, Mr 23,36:3
Niles, Walter L, 1941, D 23,21:3
Niles, William Woodruff Bp (funl, Ap 4,15:5), 1914, Ap 1,13:6
Nillson, Carlotta, 1952, Ja 1,25:6
Nilon, Michael J, 1941, D 27,19:5
Nilsen, Albert L, 1960, My 4,45:3
Nilsen, Carl, 1958, O 19,87:2
Nilsen, Clifford O, 1951, My 10,31:5
Nilson, Alfred, 1966, Je 14,48:1
Nilson, Einar, 1964, Ap 22,47:4
Nilson, Siegfried J, 1960, Ap 26,37:2
Nilson, Siegfried J Mrs, 1952, O 31,25:1
Nilson, Swen, 1883, D 1,5:4
Nilson, Victor J, 1937, D 11,19:6
Nilson, Walter F, 1961, D 31,48:4
Nilsson, Bert, 1954, S 8,45:2
Nilsson, Christine, 1921, N 23,15:2
Nilsson, Janne, 1938, D 10,17:6
Nilsson, John R, 1952, D 6,21:5
Nilsson, Oscar F, 1959, F 5,31:4
Niman, M Robert, 1965, S 2,31:4
Niman, Max G, 1942, S 10,27:4
Nimick, T Howe, 1947, Ag 26,23:4
Nimick, William H Mrs, 1949, D 8,34:3
Nimier, Roger, 1962, S 30,87:1
Nimitz, Chester W (funl, F 25,31:1), 1966, F 21,1:5
Nimitz, Otto, 1960, F 11,36:1
Nimkoff, Louis H, 1944, O 24,23:2
Nimkofsky, Morris, 1920, My 10,13:5
Nimmo, Adam Sir, 1939, Ag 12,13:6
Nimmo, Harry M, 1937, My 1,19:5
Nimmo, Herbert M, 1952, Ap 21,21:3
Nimmo, Joseph N, 1909, Je 16,7:5
Nimmo, Robert H (funl, Ja 14,39:4), 1966, Ja 5,31:1
Nimmo, W H D Capt, 1909, F 22,9:5
Nimmons, William J, 1960, Ja 15,31:1
Nimphius, August C, 1951, Je 11,25:5
Nimphius, Harry F, 1944, S 28,19:6
Nimr Pasha, Faris, 1951, D 18,31:4
Nims, Arthur V, 1961, Je 29,33:6
Nims, Brainerd, 1954, Je 9,31:2
Nims, Charles W, 1941, My 16,23:4
Nims, Clarence R, 1956, F 28,31:1
Nims, Eugene D, 1954, Ja 31,88:1
Nims, Frederick D, 1944, Mr 3,16:3
Nims, Harold D, 1950, O 16,27:2
Nims, Harry D Mrs, 1965, Ag 14,23:3
Nims, Harry Dwight, 1968, Ja 2,37:4
Nims, O F Col, 1911, My 24,11:5
Nims, Thomas L, 1965, My 20,43:1
Nina, Duchess of Hamilton, 1951, Ja 14,84:4
Nincitch, Momcilo, 1949, D 24,15:5
Nind, J Newton, 1921, Mr 7,11:6
Ninde, Albert E Mrs, 1947, Ap 12,17:5
Ninde, Lee J, 1953, D 25,17:5
Nindeman, Ernst N, 1949, Ja 27,23:4
Nindeman, William F C, 1913, My 8,11:6
Niner, Isidor, 1962, S 30,86:8
Ninesling, Herbert R, 1942, Ag 10,19:6
Ninesling, Raymond, 1964, Ag 21,30:7
Ninesling, William H, 1939, Je 30,19:3
Ninfo, Salvatore, 1960, Ja 5,31:1
Nininger, Sigourney F, 1943, O 6,23:6
Ninivaggio, Frank, 1951, Ag 15,27:4
Ninnemann, Herman K, 1953, N 4,33:2
Ninogue, John A, 1946, S 2,17:5
Ninomiya, Harushige, 1945, F 18,33:1
Niosi, Francesco, 1948, O 6,29:5
Niox, Gen, 1921, O 27,19:6
Niper, George, 1916, Mr 9,13:8
Niper, William D, 1940, N 22,23:5
Nipher, E E Prof, 1926, O 7,27:2
Nipkow, Paul, 1940, Ag 25,35:2; 1953, Ag 5,23:3
Nippert, Alfred K, 1956, Ag 8,25:6
Nippert, Alfred K Mrs, 1937, O 14,25:4
Nirdinger, Samuel F (Saml F Nixon), 1918, N 14,13:2
Nirdlinger, Charles F, 1940, My 14,23:3
Nirdlinger, Sidney, 1944, Jl 4,19:6
Nirenberg, Bertram Mrs, 1938, Mr 1,21:4
Nirenberg, David, 1949, Je 16,29:3
Nirenberg, Louis, 1939, Ap 23,III,6:6
Nirenstein, Samuel Mrs, 1968, Ja 4,34:4
Nires, Henry, 1940, Jl 5,13:3
Nisbet, James, 1865, O 8,5:4
Nisbet, James D Mrs, 1960, Je 30,29:2
Nisbet, John S, 1949, D 21,29:4
Nisbet, Robert H, 1961, Ap 21,33:2
Nisbet, William, 1960, F 27,19:5
Nisbet, William F, 1906, F 6,9:6
Nisbeth, Clyde M, 1946, Jl 15,25:6
Nisbett, James A, 1873, F 19,1:6
Nisenson, Charles, 1950, Jl 13,25:2
Nisenson, Samuel, 1968, Ag 3,25:5
Nishida, Ikutaro, 1945, Je 9,13:4
Nishina, Yoshio, 1951, Ja 11,26:2
Nishio, Toshizo, 1960, O 28,31:1
Nishiyama, Tsutomu, 1960, S 23,29:4
Nishtar, Sardar Abdur Rab, 1958, F 15,17:1
Nisita, Giovanni, 1962, N 26,29:3
Nisley, Harold A, 1963, D 25,33:3
Nislick, Aaron, 1956, Ap 8,84:2
Nislow, Lena, 1947, Ag 14,23:4
Nison, Charles, 1945, D 1,23:6
Nisonoff, Herman, 1962, N 29,40:6
Niss, Clarence C, 1948, My 23,68:4
Nisselson, Max, 1958, My 13,29:6
Nissen, Alphonse, 1942, F 9,15:4
Nissen, Egede, 1953, Ap 5,76:4
Nissen, Ferdinand, 1952, O 17,27:2
Nissen, Hartvig Dr, 1924, Ap 23,21:4
Nissen, Henry W, 1958, Ap 30,33:5
Nissen, Louis P, 1962, Ja 9,47:1
Nissen, Ludwig, 1924, O 27,19:5
Nissen, William C, 1960, Mr 28,29:4
Nissenbaum, Samuel, 1964, My 4,29:3
Nissenson, Asron, 1964, My 2,27:6
Nissenson, Samuel G, 1953, Je 28,25:6
Nissler, Christian W, 1953, Je 2,29:4
Nissley, John K, 1956, F 5,86:3
Nissley, Warren W, 1950, Ja 19,27:1
Nist, Martin, 1960, O 28,31:3
Nistal, Adalaide K K Mrs, 1955, Ja 29,15:4
Niswander, George R Mrs, 1950, D 8,29:2
Nitchie, Edward B Mrs, 1961, F 18,19:5
Nitchle, Edward Bartlett, 1917, O 6,13:6
Nithart, Legon T, 1951, Ap 19,31:3
Nitobe, I, 1933, O 16,17:3
Nitobe, Marico Mrs, 1938, S 23,27:4
Nitsche, Robert F, 1949, Ag 1,17:3
Nitschke, George A, 1946, Ap 15,27:4
Nitschke, Oswald Mrs, 1952, Ap 6,89:1
Nitsunaga, Hoshio, 1945, F 24,11:5
Nittel, William, 1956, D 15,25:4
Nitti, Federico, 1947, Mr 3,21:3
Nitti, Francesco S Mrs, 1948, F 20,27:1
Nitti, Francesco Saverio, 1953, F 21,13:1
Nittoli, Agnes Mrs, 1947, F 18,25:4
Nittoli, Rocco M Dr, 1968, F 13,43:3
Nitzberg, Jacob, 1953, Ja 23,19:3
Nitzburg, Abraham, 1952, My 20,29:5
Nitzchke, Frederick Mrs, 1953, N 6,27:4
Nitze, William A, 1957, Jl 6,15:5
Nitzsche, Elsa K, 1952, Mr 20,29:5
Nitzsche, George E, 1961, Jl 30,68:4
Nitzschke, Frederick R, 1944, F 16,17:2
Nivelle, George Robert Gen, 1924, Mr 23,X,8:1
Niven, Allan, 1917, N 24,13:6
Niven, Archibald C, 1943, Mr 31,20:3
Niven, Burton E, 1960, S 19,31:4
Niven, Frederick, 1944, Ja 31,17:2
Niven, George, 1903, Je 2,9:5
Niven, George M, 1953, Ja 7,31:5
Niven, John, 1954, My 30,45:2
Niven, John B, 1954, N 18,33:1
Niven, John K, 1938, My 12,23:4
Niven, Max, 1953, Mr 26,31:4
Niven, Thomas, 1940, Jl 6,15:4
Niven, William Prof, 1937, Je 4,23:1
Niver, Absolam Mrs, 1955, Ja 14,21:1
Niver, Edward Barnes, 1940, S 12,25:4
Niver, Ernest W, 1956, My 25,23:1
Niver, Eugene J, 1946, Ap 15,27:4
Niver, Norman H, 1908, N 30,9:4
Niver, W R, 1952, Je 11,29:1
Niver, Walder D Mrs, 1949, Ap 24,76:3
Niver, William K, 1907, Ap 1,9:7
Nivison, Theodore E, 1951, Je 24,72:6
Nivison, William, 1944, O 19,23:2
Nivling, Samuel T, 1960, My 19,37:4
Niwes, Jan, 1964, Jl 21,33:3
Nix, Edward, 1947, My 25,60:4
Nix, Edward D, 1945, Ap 7,15:3
Nix, Fred P Jr, 1942, Mr 24,19:3
Nix, George W, 1943, F 11,19:3
Nix, John W, 1922, F 26,26:3
Nix, Nelson C, 1944, D 24,25:2
Nix, Phil F Mrs, 1948, Ag 22,60:4
Nix, Philip F, 1944, Ap 13,19:6
Nixdorf, Ralph A, 1954, Je 7,41:7
Nixdorff, Frank B, 1960, Mr 14,29:3
Nixon, Albert B (por), 1948, Je 15,27:5
Nixon, Allen Mrs (H Bard), 1967, Ap 25,43:1
Nixon, Am, 1902, F 2,1:5
Nixon, Arthur H, 1949, D 31,15:6
Nixon, Arthur V, 1968, Jl 6,21:3
Nixon, Boyd, 1958, Ap 22,33:1
Nixon, Charles E, 1941, D 6,17:6
Nixon, Christopher, 1945, Ap 25,23:3
Nixon, Christopher John, 1914, Jl 21,9:5
Nixon, Edward A, 1939, Mr 27,15:5
Nixon, Edward L, 1949, F 28,19:4
Nixon, Edwin C, 1951, Je 3,92:2
Nixon, Elliot B, 1952, Ag 9,13:7
Nixon, Florence Mrs, 1956, Jl 2,21:5
Nixon, Francis A (funl, S 8,17:5), 1956, S 5,27:1
Nixon, Francis A Mrs, 1967, O 1,84:5
Nixon, Francis E, 1944, D 23,13:3
Nixon, Frederick J, 1949, F 14,19:3
Nixon, Frederick K (por), 1941, Ap 12,15:3
Nixon, George E, 1968, My 25,35:3
Nixon, Gouverneur H, 1944, Jl 26,19:6
Nixon, Harry C, 1961, O 24,37:3
Nixon, Harry E, 1951, S 3,13:5
Nixon, Harry L, 1937, N 24,23:6
Nixon, Henry D, 1904, Ja 17,7:6
Nixon, Howard C, 1955, O 14,27:3
Nixon, Howard K, 1963, Je 11,37:4
Nixon, Hugh H Mrs, 1960, Ap 12,33:4
Nixon, Ivan L, 1949, Je 26,60:3
Nixon, J Fred, 1948, My 29,15:4
Nixon, J Fred Mrs, 1953, D 14,31:3
Nixon, James H Judge, 1903, N 23,7:3
Nixon, James W, 1948, Ag 16,19:4
Nixon, Job, 1938, Jl 28,19:5
Nixon, John Eccles Gen, 1921, D 17,13:4
Nixon, John J, 1939, Ag 10,19:1
Nixon, Justin W, 1958, Jl 12,15:6
Nixon, Kate I Mrs, 1939, O 29,40:5
Nixon, Kenneth J, 1952, N 2,88:2
Nixon, Larry, 1953, Je 6,17:1
Nixon, Lester, 1962, Ag 31,21:1
Nixon, Lewis, 1940, S 24,23:1
Nixon, Lewis Mrs, 1937, Je 16,24:2
Nixon, Liston, 1938, Ag 30,17:4
Nixon, Loren H, 1954, My 31,13:5
Nixon, Mabel, 1957, N 29,29:1
Nixon, Mary I Mrs, 1937, F 22,17:2
Nixon, Morris B Mrs, 1948, Ja 31,19:2
Nixon, Paul, 1956, O 28,89:1
Nixon, Russell T, 1940, Mr 30,15:2
Nixon, Russell T Mrs, 1967, Jl 1,23:4
Nixon, S Fred (funl plans, O 12,9:3; est appr, O 20,1:3), 1905, O 11,11:1
Nixon, Stanhope W, 1958, Ja 12,86:6
Nixon, W N, 1938, Ag 30,17:4
Nixon, W N Mrs, 1938, Ag 30,17:4
Nixon, W Sargent, 1962, S 19,39:4
Nixon, Walter R Mrs, 1950, N 18,15:3
Nixon, William, 1909, D 30,9:5
Nixon, William C, 1916, D 16,13:6
Nixon, William J, 1958, N 7,28:1
Nixon, Wilson K, 1952, Mr 31,19:4
Nizer, Joseph, 1955, N 13,89:2
Noa, Julian, 1958, N 28,30:3
Noack, Harold Q, 1951, My 28,10:3
Noack, Sylvain, 1953, O 28,29:5
Noah, Benjamin, 1938, Ja 11,23:2
Noah, Lionel J, 1962, S 24,29:2

Noah, M M, 1873, F 15,1:2
Noailles, A de, 1933, My 1,15:3
Noailles, Emmanuel Henri V de, 1909, F 17,9:6
Noakes, Edward B, 1958, D 25,2:6
Noakes, George, 1941, Ap 9,25:6
Noakes, James G, 1941, N 3,19:2
Noakes, Louise E G Mrs, 1941, Ap 15,23:5
Noakes, Mary A Mrs, 1946, My 25,15:4
Noakes, Mary E Mrs, 1937, Jl 4,II,7:4
Noakes, William, 1953, D 28,21:4
Noback, Charles V Dr, 1937, Ja 17,II,8:6
Noback, Gustave J, 1955, S 10,17:6
Nobb, Thomas S, 1907, Ap 29,9:6
Nobbe, Edward O, 1956, O 24,26:4
Nobbe, Frederick G, 1962, Ja 21,88:8
Nobbe, George, 1963, Ag 21,33:4
Nobbe, Henry, 1940, F 24,13:6
Nobbs, Henry A Sr, 1955, Mr 15,29:2
Nobbs, William H, 1948, Ap 10,13:4
Nobel, Fred W, 1947, Mr 25,25:4
Nobel, Goesta, 1955, O 18,37:1
Nobel, Henry G S, 1946, F 7,23:1
Nobel, John, 1940, Ap 28,37:2
Nobel, Nicolson, 1942, N 11,25:4
Nobile, Alessandro, 1941, Jl 21,15:3
Nobiletti, Frank A, 1945, Ap 22,36:2
Nobili, Marchese de, 1947, D 12,27:2
Nobis, Walter S, 1965, Je 18,35:5
Noble, A Grant Mrs, 1962, O 20,25:5
Noble, Albert F, 1944, D 2,13:2
Noble, Albert J, 1944, D 30,11:6
Noble, Alden C, 1942, Je 16,23:3
Noble, Alfred, 1914, Ap 20,9:3
Noble, Andrew Sir, 1915, O 23,11:5
Noble, Annie L Mrs, 1965, Jl 5,17:5
Noble, Arthur G, 1953, Ja 13,27:1
Noble, Augustus V, 1949, Ap 10,78:8
Noble, Belle L Mrs, 1946, F 6,23:3
Noble, Charles, 1938, O 7,23:4
Noble, Charles H, 1944, Ap 22,15:6
Noble, Charles H Gen, 1916, Mr 5,21:6
Noble, Charles S, 1957, Jl 6,16:1
Noble, Charles W, 1946, D 9,25:5; 1948, Je 7,19:2
Noble, Clarence W, 1945, N 11,42:5
Noble, Clem (Uncle Pike), 1954, Mr 23,27:1
Noble, Clifford R, 1954, S 8,31:2
Noble, Clinton, 1952, F 3,84:1
Noble, Crawford, 1950, F 4,15:4
Noble, D A, 1939, Ap 9,III,7:1
Noble, Daniel, 1937, My 31,16:1; 1948, Mr 30,23:1
Noble, Edmund, 1937, Ja 9,17:5
Noble, Edward E, 1949, Ag 22,21:4
Noble, Edward J, 1958, D 29,15:1
Noble, Edward J (will), 1959, Ja 7,18:1
Noble, Emily Dr, 1923, Je 7,19:4
Noble, Estelle H, 1953, Ag 20,27:3
Noble, Eugene A (por), 1948, Je 29,23:1
Noble, Floyd C Mrs, 1946, Mr 21,25:5
Noble, Francis L H, 1948, F 4,24:2
Noble, Francis O, 1950, My 12,28:2
Noble, Frank S, 1921, Jl 6,15:6
Noble, Frederick C, 1946, D 19,29:3
Noble, G Clifford Mrs, 1955, Mr 26,15:5
Noble, G W C, 1919, Je 8,20:4
Noble, George, 1937, O 1,21:2
Noble, George H Sr, 1962, N 14,39:1
Noble, George Sir, 1937, Jl 30,19:4
Noble, Gifford J, 1948, S 15,32:3
Noble, Gladwyn K (por), 1940, D 10,25:1
Noble, Guy H, 1943, Ap 30,15:4
Noble, H Joseph, 1955, N 25,27:2
Noble, Harold J, 1953, D 24,15:1
Noble, Harriet I Dr, 1920, O 12,15:2
Noble, Harry L, 1937, Mr 14,II,8:4
Noble, Harry M, 1939, S 27,25:3
Noble, Harry S, 1953, Jl 11,11:4
Noble, Harry W, 1943, Mr 21,26:8
Noble, Herbert Mrs, 1944, Ag 23,19:4
Noble, Herbert W, 1941, D 10,25:1
Noble, Howard A, 1943, Mr 1,19:3
Noble, Howard G, 1943, Ag 26,17:4
Noble, Israel, 1952, Mr 18,27:1
Noble, J, 1934, Ja 7,31:2
Noble, J C Col, 1901, D 22,7:5
Noble, J H, 1957, Ag 20,27:3
Noble, James, 1865, F 4,4:1
Noble, James A, 1944, O 21,17:5
Noble, John, 1938, Ja 9,43:2; 1943, N 1,17:5; 1964, My 3,87:1
Noble, John B, 1908, Jl 28,5:4
Noble, John J, 1949, O 4,27:4
Noble, John Mrs, 1951, Ap 22,89:2; 1959, Je 26,25:4
Noble, John W, 1950, Ag 9,29:5
Noble, John W Gen, 1912, Mr 23,13:5
Noble, John W Mrs, 1947, Ap 10,26:2; 1959, Je 30,31:3
Noble, John W Sr, 1937, My 22,18:1
Noble, Johnny, 1944, Ja 15,13:1
Noble, Joseph W, 1949, Jl 4,13:6
Noble, Julio A, 1960, O 30,86:7
Noble, Leroy B, 1963, Je 7,31:3
Noble, Liston, 1966, O 30,89:1
Noble, Lloyd, 1950, F 15,27:5
Noble, Loren R, 1952, D 3,33:5
Noble, M A, 1940, Je 23,31:2
Noble, Marcus C S, 1942, Je 3,24:5
Noble, Mark A, 1950, N 4,17:6
Noble, Matthew, 1876, Je 25,2:2
Noble, Melville E, 1958, Ap 20,84:6
Noble, Michael, 1947, F 23,54:3
Noble, Newton A, 1967, N 1,47:4
Noble, Percy, 1955, Jl 26,25:3
Noble, Percy W, 1960, S 19,31:4
Noble, Philip Brocon Rev, 1915, Ag 6,9:6
Noble, Raymond G, 1945, Ag 2,19:6
Noble, Reginald, 1962, Ja 21,88:5
Noble, Richard H, 1937, Ja 17,II,9:2
Noble, Robert, 1956, S 20,33:2
Noble, Robert E, 1956, O 16,33:2
Noble, Robert H, 1939, O 28,15:4; 1949, Ja 28,21:4
Noble, Robert H Mrs, 1944, Jl 13,17:5
Noble, Robert P Mrs, 1956, Mr 2,23:4; 1963, My 2, 35:4
Noble, Sally, 1944, F 10,15:3
Noble, Stephen E, 1947, Ja 7,27:4
Noble, Stephen E Mrs, 1948, Mr 22,23:5
Noble, T Tertius, 1953, My 5,29:1
Noble, Urbane A, 1946, O 11,23:4
Noble, W Carey, 1960, Ja 18,27:1
Noble, W Clark Mrs, 1959, Ap 2,31:3
Noble, Walter J, 1962, Je 23,23:5
Noble, Warren, 1950, Jl 4,17:6
Noble, Warren P, 1903, Jl 9,7:6
Noble, William C (por), 1938, My 12,23:4
Noble, William D, 1940, Jl 24,21:5
Noble, William F, 1950, D 13,35:2
Noble, William L Dr, 1937, O 16,19:2
Noble, Willis C Jr, 1956, My 26,17:4
Noble, Wilson, 1917, N 2,15:6
Nobles, Andrew J, 1962, D 5,47:3
Nobles, Byron O, 1940, Mr 26,21:3
Nobles, Elon B Mrs, 1949, Mr 16,27:4
Nobles, Milton, 1924, Je 15,23:2
Nobles, William, 1956, My 25,23:5
Noblitt, Quintin G, 1954, Jl 4,31:3
Nobmann, Clarence J, 1959, F 1,84:6
Nobre, Augusto, 1946, S 15,9:8
Nobriga, J P, 1881, Jl 22,5:6
Nobs, Ernest, 1957, Mr 15,25:4
Noc, Ivan, 1951, Ja 27,10:2
Nocar, Stanley Sr, 1950, Ja 17,27:4
Noci, Arturo, 1953, Ag 25,21:5
Nocilla, Benjamin, 1954, O 6,25:5
Nock, Albert J (por), 1945, Ag 20,19:3
Nock, E, 1883, Ap 23,1:4
Nock, Frederic B (funl, My 19,21:4), 1925, My 18, 15:5
Nock, Robert, 1949, F 23,27:5
Nock, Robert Mrs, 1938, Ag 24,21:4
Nock, Rupert A, 1943, D 6,23:3
Nock, Rupert A Mrs, 1960, F 6,19:6
Nockels, Edward N, 1937, F 28,II,9:2
Nocton, Edward J, 1947, Ag 3,52:6
Nocton, James A, 1915, S 12,17:6
Noctor, Thomas J, 1925, Jl 15,17:5
Noda, Hideo, 1939, Ja 14,17:5
Noddack, Walter, 1960, D 9,31:3
Nodel, Mordecai, 1962, Jl 2,29:4
Nodge, Joseph F Sr, 1952, F 7,27:4
Nodine, Charles C, 1950, S 29,27:4
Nodine, Edgar C Mrs, 1953, F 6,19:2
Nodine, Oscar L Jr, 1952, D 1,23:5
Nodine, Ralph H, 1938, Ag 23,17:6
Nodine, Wright A, 1966, Ja 22,29:4
Nodop, Jacob, 1947, Mr 15,13:3
Nodzu, Michitsura Count, 1908, O 18,VII,11:5
Noe, Adolf C, 1939, Ap 11,24:4
Noe, Albert D Jr, 1947, S 29,21:1
Noe, Amedee de Count (Cham), 1879, S 20,2:6
Noe, Amon T, 1947, Ag 19,23:3
Noe, Charles D, 1925, My 12,23:3
Noe, Charles L, 1948, O 22,26:2
Noe, Charles S, 1923, O 19,19:5
Noe, Edward A, 1951, Ja 23,27:3
Noe, Ella M, 1953, Ag 7,19:3
Noe, Elzer C, 1940, N 29,21:4
Noe, Floyd A, 1939, Ag 6,36:7
Noe, Frederick, 1903, O 4,7:6
Noe, Harold C, 1968, Jl 6,21:3
Noe, Israel H, 1960, Jl 4,15:6
Noe, James B, 1953, Jl 9,25:5
Noe, James T C, 1953, N 11,31:2
Noe, John A, 1954, O 30,17:3
Noe, Louis M, 1909, Mr 12,7:4
Noe, Ralph W, 1968, Mr 29,45:3
Noe, Theodore Cuyler, 1909, Ja 19,9:5
Noecker, John M, 1955, Mr 31,27:1
Noecker, Samuel M, 1959, O 3,19:4
Noehren, Alfred H, 1959, N 15,87:1
Noehren, Arthur G Dr, 1937, S 18,19:2
Noehren, Carl, 1940, Mr 5,24:3
Noel, Auguste L, 1964, Mr 15,86:4
Noel, Baptist Rev, 1873, Ja 21,5:2
Noel, Carlos M, 1941, Ja 4,13:1
Noel, Charles V, 1937, D 27,32:2
Noel, Conrad le D R, 1942, Jl 24,19:2
Noel, Edmond P, 1958, Ap 9,36:1
Noel, Ernest S Mrs, 1949, N 23,29:5
Noel, James W, 1944, Ap 7,19:4
Noel, John H, 1939, N 5,49:2
Noel, John V, 1960, S 27,38:1
Noel, John V Mrs, 1904, S 23,2:5
Noel, Joseph, 1946, Ag 8,21:5
Noel, Joseph R, 1940, Mr 11,15:6
Noel, Layton C Mrs, 1953, D 10,47:4
Noel, Lionel S, 1960, D 17,23:5
Noel, Louis W, 1966, Je 30,39:4
Noel, M G, 1945, My 31,15:4
Noel, Pappy (Frank E), 1966, N 30,47:3
Noel, Rene, 1959, Ag 20,25:3
Noel, Rose F Mrs, 1950, Je 18,76:5
Noel, Victor A (por), 1955, N 17,35:3
Noel, William F, 1958, O 30,31:3
Noel-Buxton, Baron (por), 1948, S 14,29:4
Noel-Buxton, Lucy Lady, 1960, D 12,29:4
Noelker, Albert H, 1950, D 14,35:4
Noelker, Robert, 1953, Mr 3,27:2
Noell, J W, 1961, Ja 17,37:5
Noell, Thomas E, 1867, O 4,5:3
Noelte, Albert, 1946, Mr 3,46:4
Noelte, Albert E, 1957, Ag 14,25:4
Noelting, Erik, 1953, Jl 17,17:5
Noennich, Louis H, 1949, O 13,27:4
Noerdlinger, Victo, 1961, Je 15,43:1
Noerling, Henry J, 1944, F 5,15:6
Noeth, Vincent G, 1948, N 7,89:1
Nofer, Edward J, 1958, Mr 6,27:2
Noffsinger, John S, 1966, My 5,47:1
Noffsinger, W N, 1924, F 4,19:5
Nogara, Bartolomeo, 1954, Je 20,84:5
Nogara, Bernardino, 1958, N 16,88:1
Nogara, Giuseppe, 1955, D 10,21:2
Nogas, Edward, 1949, Je 20,19:5
Nogay, Francis X, 1952, N 8,17:4
Noge, John F Sr Mrs, 1952, My 2,25:3
Nogent-St Laurens, M, 1882, F 26,4:5
Noggle, David, 1878, Jl 28,10:6
Nogin, Victor Pavlovitch (funl, My 26,17:6), 1924, My 23,19:5
Noglows, William S, 1961, Ja 25,33:1
Noguchi, H, 1928, My 22,1:2
Noguchi, Toru, 1944, Ja 16,43:2
Noguchi, Yone, 1947, Jl 15,23:1
Nogueira, Bento D S, 1947, F 5,26:1
Nogueres, Louis, 1956, My 8,33:2
Nogues, Pablo, 1943, Ja 16,13:3
Nohl, Max W, 1943, Mr 28,24:2
Noithcliffe, Lord (funl), 1922, Ag 18,13:1
Nojunas, John, 1954, N 1,20:6
Noke, G Harold, 1965, Mr 29,33:1
Nolan, Aloysius V, 1958, My 27,31:4
Nolan, Andrew F, 1945, Ap 29,37:2
Nolan, Anna M, 1954, Ap 2,27:3
Nolan, Anthanasius, 1947, Je 3,25:3
Nolan, Catherine E, 1966, Ag 14,89:1
Nolan, Charles F, 1924, O 10,19:5
Nolan, Charles W, 1940, O 7,17:4
Nolan, Clarence D, 1948, O 28,29:2
Nolan, Daniel C Jr, 1957, Jl 29,19:4
Nolan, Dennis E, 1956, F 25,19:3
Nolan, Edward C, 1938, Je 15,23:4
Nolan, Edward J, 1957, F 5,23:3
Nolan, Edward P, 1942, My 21,19:1
Nolan, Ezra L, 1962, Mr 27,37:3
Nolan, Felix, 1947, Ag 11,25:6
Nolan, Florence N, 1946, Je 7,19:5
Nolan, Francis, 1938, F 20,II,8:7
Nolan, Francis P, 1938, N 24,27:4
Nolan, Frank A, 1960, My 21,23:6
Nolan, Frank J, 1954, S 21,27:1
Nolan, Fred A, 1946, D 13,23:3
Nolan, George E, 1955, S 6,25:3
Nolan, George F, 1956, Ap 6,25:4; 1957, Je 22,15:4
Nolan, George H, 1953, S 7,19:5
Nolan, George M, 1906, N 10,9:4
Nolan, Gerard J, 1959, My 6,39:2
Nolan, Henry G, 1957, Jl 9,29:1
Nolan, Henry J, 1949, My 27,21:3
Nolan, James, 1917, Jl 30,9:5; 1941, My 12,17:3; 1952, Je 29,58:5
Nolan, James A, 1944, Ja 19,19:3; 1952, O 20,23:2; 1955, My 13,25:2
Nolan, James B Mrs, 1949, Mr 10,27:4
Nolan, James C, 1944, D 20,23:5
Nolan, James F, 1952, S 5,27:4
Nolan, James G, 1924, My 4,23:2
Nolan, James J, 1939, Mr 10,23:4; 1943, N 30,27:4; 1946, Ja 10,23:4; 1950, Mr 5,92:6
Nolan, James L, 1950, Je 28,27:2
Nolan, James Mrs, 1948, My 18,24:2; 1965, Ja 14,3
Nolan, James P, 1945, My 2,23:5; 1960, Je 28,31:3
Nolan, John A, 1947, D 13,15:4
Nolan, John Col, 1924, My 6,21:5
Nolan, John F, 1957, Jl 29,19:4
Nolan, John F Mrs, 1950, Ap 18,32:2
Nolan, John H, 1950, Ap 26,30:2; 1967, N 4,33:2
Nolan, John H Mrs, 1965, Jl 26,23:4
Nolan, John I, 1922, N 19,6:4
Nolan, John J, 1912, Je 14,11:5; 1940, F 16,19:1; 19 N 20,23:3; 1946, Ag 14,25:1; 1948, My 27,25:5; 1 Ag 12,31:2; 1954, My 25,27:1

Nolan, John P, 1954, F 9,27:3
Nolan, John R, 1948, N 23,29:1
Nolan, John T, 1915, O 22,11:5; 1964, Ja 8,37:2
Nolan, John W, 1953, Mr 26,31:4
Nolan, Joseph, 1949, S 10,17:5; 1960, D 15,43:1
Nolan, Joseph E, 1946, Je 6,21:5; 1948, Ag 30,17:3
Nolan, Katherine M Mrs, 1938, F 23,23:4
Nolan, Katie L Mrs, 1948, N 10,29:4
Nolan, Lawrence A Dr, 1937, Mr 24,25:4
Nolan, Leo V Mrs, 1941, Ap 11,21:3
Nolan, Louis W, 1955, O 5,35:5
Nolan, Margaret M, 1954, Ag 17,21:4
Nolan, Mary, 1948, N 1,29:2
Nolan, Mary F Mrs, 1939, Ag 19,15:5
Nolan, Mary Mrs, 1937, S 28,23:3
Nolan, Michael E, 1966, Ag 1,27:2
Nolan, Michael J, 1943, Ja 5,19:4
Nolan, Michael Mrs, 1944, Jl 11,15:5
Nolan, Patrick J, 1941, Ja 12,44:4; 1949, S 16,27:2
Nolan, Phil G, 1951, Jl 26,46:5
Nolan, Philip F Jr, 1960, Jl 8,21:2
Nolan, Robert E, 1964, Ap 22,47:4
Nolan, Stephen J, 1955, Ag 30,27:4
Nolan, Sylvester F, 1956, Ag 14,25:5
Nolan, Thomas, 1944, F 1,19:4; 1947, N 21,27:3
Nolan, Thomas A, 1937, Ja 12,23:3; 1938, Ag 24,21:4; 1960, S 21,32:3
Nolan, Thomas F, 1948, My 29,15:6; 1963, S 25,43:5
Nolan, Thomas J, 1940, Mr 18,18:2; 1955, My 28, 15:2; 1960, Ap 20,39:3
Nolan, Thomas J Justice, 1937, Ja 24,II,8:6
Nolan, Thomas M, 1941, My 10,15:4
Nolan, Thomas Mrs, 1943, My 19,25:3
Nolan, Thomas S, 1961, Ja 3,29:4
Nolan, Timothy A, 1939, F 28,19:5
Nolan, Val, 1940, O 12,17:4
Nolan, W I, 1943, Ag 4,17:2
Nolan, Walter F, 1965, Mr 17,45:3
Nolan, William A, 1960, N 12,21:3
Nolan, William C, 1964, F 9,88:5
Nolan, William D, 1938, Mr 22,21:4
Nolan, William H, 1939, Ap 4,25:2; 1943, Mr 20,15:4
Nolan, William H Mrs, 1944, N 4,15:5
Nolan, William L, 1945, Jl 18,27:4
Nolan, William P, 1968, Mr 12,43:2
Nolan, William Whiting, 1923, Je 7,19:4
Noland, Ellen T, 1958, Ag 9,13:5
Noland, Joseph T Mrs, 1948, O 2,15:3
Noland, Lloyd, 1949, N 28,27:4
Noland, Lloyd U, 1952, O 30,31:4
Noland, William C, 1951, Ag 19,86:1
Nold, George J, 1962, Je 3,89:1
Nolde, Emil, 1956, Ap 16,27:5
Nolde, O Frederick Mrs, 1961, Ag 1,31:2
Nolder, James E, 1953, D 28,21:4
Nolen, James R, 1959, Jl 20,25:5
Nolen, John Dr, 1937, F 19,19:3
Nolen, John Mrs, 1954, D 12,88:6
Nolen, Mary H, 1948, Mr 25,27:3
Nolen, William W, 1952, S 14,86:1
Nolf, John T, 1950, My 30,17:3
Nolf, Pierre, 1953, S 15,31:1
Nolfo, Frank C, 1958, Ag 13,27:5
Noli, Fan S, 1965, Mr 16,39:3
Noling, Isaac O, 1950, Je 5,23:5
Noll, A Robert, 1968, S 24,47:1
Noll, Anthony F Mrs, 1954, N 7,88:1
Noll, Carl V, 1960, F 27,19:2
Noll, Charles, 1952, Ap 21,21:4
Noll, Charles F, 1951, D 19,31:3
Noll, Chris W Mrs, 1945, F 17,13:4
Noll, Christian W, 1942, N 19,25:6
Noll, Edward N, 1950, Je 1,27:4
Noll, Elizabeth Mrs, 1940, F 22,23:4
Noll, Henry D, 1937, Ag 26,21:5
Noll, I Martin, 1963, Jl 31,29:4
Noll, Isidore M Mrs, 1947, Ag 12,23:4
Noll, John F, 1956, Ag 1,23:1
Noll, Joseph A, 1948, Ja 2,23:3
Noll, Joseph J Dr, 1915, O 18,9:6
Noll, Margaret M, 1957, O 1,33:3
Noll, Michael A, 1947, Ag 16,13:5
Noll, Paul Mrs, 1950, Ap 6,29:2
Noll, Thomas J, 1943, S 2,19:6
Noll, Walter J, 1968, Ja 29,31:2
Noll, William H, 1941, Ap 10,24:2
Nollau, Edgar H, 1945, My 9,23:2
Nolle, William J, 1965, Jl 26,23:5
Nollen, Gerard S, 1965, S 6,15:4
Nollen, John S, 1952, Mr 14,20:5
Nollet, Edouard, 1941, Ja 29,17:3
Nolte, Anna (Sister Modesta), 1954, Mr 2,25:1
Nolte, Bernhardt, 1955, Ja 12,27:1
Nolte, Charles B (por), 1941, Ap 30,19:3
Nolte, George F, 1960, My 18,41:3
Nolte, George H, 1954, Ja 24,85:2
Nolte, Henry K, 1942, Ag 20,19:2
Nolte, Joseph, 1904, F 14,7:6
Nolte, Joseph H, 1947, Mr 16,60:8
Nolte, Lewis G, 1942, F 16,17:5
Nolte, Louis H, 1950, Je 2,23:5
Noltein, George F, 1961, Ag 5,17:3
Noltie, William A, 1950, F 15,27:3
Nolting, Frederick E, 1955, Ja 7,21:3
Nolting, William G, 1940, N 26,23:3
Noma, Seiji, 1938, O 18,26:3
Noma, Tsune, 1938, N 9,20:3
Nomikos, Van A, 1958, F 3,23:5
Nommenson, Clara P Mrs, 1938, D 2,24:1
Nomura, Kichisaburo, 1964, My 8,33:1
Noneman, Harold F, 1961, Mr 7,35:5
Noneman, Harry W, 1950, Mr 15,29:3
Nones, Alexandre, 1908, N 25,9:5
Nones, H B Capt, 1868, Ag 28,2:3
Nones, Walter M, 1942, Mr 13,19:4
Nonidez, Jose F, 1947, S 29,21:4
Nonn, Otto E, 1954, Ja 17,93:1
Noon, Henry J, 1947, Mr 10,21:4
Noon, Henry S, 1947, Jl 23,23:5
Noon, Martin M, 1956, Mr 15,31:2
Noon, T F, 1882, Ap 6,2:6
Noon, William D, 1952, Jl 6,48:7
Noonan, Augustin A Mrs, 1953, My 26,29:4
Noonan, Bernard J, 1943, D 9,27:4
Noonan, Billy, 1957, F 14,27:3
Noonan, Chester J, 1962, O 25,39:1
Noonan, Cornelius J, 1944, S 11,17:5; 1964, N 18,47:2
Noonan, Daniel, 1951, Jl 29,69:2
Noonan, Daniel A, 1915, Jl 7,11:6
Noonan, David A Mrs, 1951, S 30,72:3
Noonan, Denis T, 1952, N 19,29:1
Noonan, Elizabeth A, 1948, Ja 10,15:3
Noonan, Ernest E, 1948, Ap 16,23:5
Noonan, Felix E, 1944, Mr 4,13:1
Noonan, Gregory F, 1964, My 2,27:4
Noonan, Harry, 1948, F 3,25:2
Noonan, Helen M, 1956, Jl 4,19:6
Noonan, Herbert C, 1956, Jl 7,13:3
Noonan, Jeremiah Mrs, 1950, S 16,19:2
Noonan, Jerome, 1951, N 30,23:1
Noonan, John, 1942, My 31,38:5
Noonan, John A, 1955, Ap 3,86:8
Noonan, John C, 1961, Je 7,41:3
Noonan, John J, 1911, F 26,II,11:3; 1952, Jl 19,15:3
Noonan, John P, 1938, O 28,23:5
Noonan, John T, 1961, O 9,35:4
Noonan, Joseph, 1949, Jl 19,29:4
Noonan, Joseph M, 1959, O 1,35:4
Noonan, Joseph P, 1950, N 3,28:5
Noonan, Leo P, 1960, N 10,47:2
Noonan, Martin A, 1949, Je 2,27:1; 1951, F 4,76:6
Noonan, Mary F, 1957, F 14,27:4
Noonan, Michael, 1904, My 8,3:2
Noonan, Michael H, 1943, Jl 11,35:3
Noonan, Michael J, 1951, Jl 4,17:5
Noonan, Nicholas, 1902, N 1,1:6
Noonan, Ottilia G Mrs, 1939, Jl 15,15:5
Noonan, Peter J, 1965, F 12,29:3
Noonan, Raymond E, 1953, S 5,15:5
Noonan, Robert E, 1960, O 5,41:2; 1965, My 28,33:2
Noonan, T, 1935, Jl 26,15:3
Noonan, Theodore Rev, 1953, F 5,23:3
Noonan, Thomas F (por), 1940, D 7,17:1
Noonan, Thomas H, 1957, S 1,57:2
Noonan, Thomas P, 1937, D 20,27:2; 1938, Ag 12, 17:4; 1949, Je 5,92:4
Noonan, Tommy, 1968, Ap 25,47:2
Noonan, William D, 1959, F 22,88:5
Noonan, William E, 1961, F 7,33:3
Noonan, William F, 1941, F 15,15:2
Noonan, William J (por), 1946, Mr 18,21:6
Noonan, William J, 1952, Ja 13,88:2; 1959, N 25,29:4
Noonan, William T, 1952, Jl 23,23:4
Noone, Byron M, 1964, Ag 6,29:4
Noone, Jimmie, 1944, Ap 21,19:4
Noone, Luke, 1905, Mr 21,11:4
Nooney, Robert, 1911, Mr 19,II,11:2
Noorden, Carl von, 1944, N 18,13:5
Noorduyn, Robert B C, 1959, F 24,29:3
Noorian, D, 1929, Ja 11,23:1
Noort, Gerardus C van, 1946, S 17,7:3
Nootbaar, Max, 1939, Je 11,45:2
Noothoven van Goor, G B, 1942, Mr 13,20:3
Nooy, Cornelius N, 1958, Mr 14,25:3
Nops, Jere, 1937, Mr 28,II,8:8
Norbeck, P, 1936, D 21,23:1
Norberg, Carl F, 1959, My 21,31:2
Norberg, Rudolph C, 1958, S 7,86:5
Norberg, Stephen A, 1961, D 24,36:4
Norbert, Bro, 1937, F 17,22:2
Norbert, Bro (Bros of St Francis Xavier), 1962, Ap 14,25:4
Norblad, Albin, 1960, Ap 19,37:3
Norblad, Walter, 1964, S 21,31:4
Norbury, Frank P, 1939, Mr 16,23:3
Norbury, T S Dr, 1885, Mr 18,5:4
Norby, Charles W, 1948, O 17,76:1
Norby, May W Mrs, 1965, Jl 12,27:1
Norcom, William P, 1948, Ja 23,24:2
Norcross, Alvin C Capt, 1912, Je 9,II,15:6
Norcross, Cleveland, 1949, Mr 22,25:6
Norcross, Frank H, 1952, N 5,27:5
Norcross, Greenville H, 1937, F 13,13:5
Norcross, Hale, 1947, O 17,21:2
Norcross, J Arnold, 1940, Ag 21,19:2
Norcross, James A, 1903, Ag 5,7:6
Norcross, Josiah, 1942, Ap 16,21:4
Norcross, Orlando W, 1920, F 28,11:5
Norcross, Sherman B, 1942, F 7,17:4
Norcross, Wilbur H (por), 1941, Je 12,23:4
Norcross, Wilbur H Mrs, 1953, Je 12,27:2
Norcross, Winfred Mrs, 1946, Je 19,21:4
Nord, Count du, 1881, Je 14,5:4
Nord, Henry, 1955, F 9,25:2
Nordau, Max, 1923, Ja 23,21:4
Nordberg, Bruno V E, 1946, Ag 21,28:3
Nordberg, Gustav S, 1956, N 17,21:6
Nordberg, Harry M, 1963, My 21,37:3
Nordblom, Robert A, 1952, Ap 14,19:5
Nordburg, William S, 1960, Ag 12,19:5
Nordeck, John P, 1957, Ag 28,27:5
Nordegg, Martin (por), 1948, S 14,29:2
Nordell, Edward F, 1962, S 10,29:1
Nordell, Frank, 1938, Ap 6,23:2
Nordell, Harry W, 1941, Ap 21,19:3
Nordeman, Herman F Mrs, 1946, Ag 14,25:1
Nordeman, Jacques C Sr, 1953, Ag 29,17:4
Nordemann, Felix Dr, 1907, S 17,11:6
Norden, Carl L, 1965, Je 16,43:4
Norden, Ira B, 1955, Ap 7,27:4
Norden, Lee, 1941, N 13,27:3
Norden, Mortimer, 1962, O 28,88:8
Norden, Norris L, 1956, N 6,35:3
Nordenholt, George D, 1949, My 25,29:1
Nordenholz, Albert, 1950, Mr 16,31:2
Nordenskjoeld, O, 1928, Je 3,25:4
Nordenskjold, A E Baron, 1901, Ag 14,7:6
Nordfeldt, Bror J O, 1955, Ap 22,25:1
Nordfeldt, Margaret Doolittle Dr, 1968, Je 12,47:1
Nordgaard, Morton A, 1952, O 21,29:1
Nordgren, J Vincent, 1966, Mr 10,33:4
Nordhausen, Henry Mrs, 1952, O 8,31:5
Nordheim, John C, 1943, Jl 31,13:6
Nordhoff, Charles, 1901, Jl 16,7:5
Nordhoff, Charles B, 1947, Ap 12,17:1
Nordhoff, Franklin W, 1956, Ap 18,62:3
Nordhoff, Heinz, 1968, Ap 13,25:1
Nordhoff, Walter Mrs, 1951, N 13,29:3
Nordhouse, John, 1961, Jl 31,19:4
Nordica, Lillian (will, My 15,11:5), 1914, My 11,11:4
Nordlicht, Stephen Mrs (C Mann), 1960, Ja 2,13:6
Nordlie, Charles S, 1952, Je 4,27:2
Nordling, Raoul, 1962, O 2,39:3
Nordlinger, Louis S, 1940, Je 10,17:3
Nordlinger, Melville, 1938, N 4,3:6
Nordlinger, Sidney, 1940, Mr 27,21:3
Nordlund, Anders L, 1944, N 25,13:2
Nordman, Joseph, 1951, O 24,31:1
Nordmann, Charles, 1940, N 16,17:3
Nordmeyer, Charles E, 1966, F 28,27:4
Nordon, Otto N, 1956, D 8,19:1
Nordsieck, Charles L, 1937, Mr 10,23:6
Nordskog, Lars J, 1946, Ag 15,25:6
Nordstrom, Clarence A, 1968, D 15,86:3
Nordstrom, Ludvig, 1942, Ap 17,17:4
Nordstrom, Morris D, 1960, O 19,45:4
Nordstrom, N J, 1943, Ja 7,20:2
Nordt, Carl H, 1959, N 12,35:3
Nordt, William A Rev Dr, 1937, O 13,23:2
Norducci, William, 1953, N 25,32:1
Norek, A W, 1933, Ap 10,13:5
Norelli, Jenny, 1942, F 4,20:2
Noren, Robert J, 1942, My 21,19:6
Norfleet, A L Dr, 1937, Ap 27,23:3
Norfleet, Catherine, 1957, D 14,21:1
Norfolk, Charles, 1944, Mr 10,32:3
Norfolk, Duchess of, 1945, Ag 29,23:4
Norfolk, Duke of (Hy Fitzalan-Howard), 1917, F 12, 9:4
Norfolk, Henrietta M Mrs, 1937, My 15,19:2
Norgaard, Hookon R, 1950, Ap 17,23:3
Norgan, George, 1964, S 15,37:3
Norgard, George F, 1960, Ja 15,31:3
Norgord, Christian P, 1962, My 2,37:1
Norhtrop, Charles P, 1938, Je 10,21:4
Noria, Jane, 1924, Mr 31,17:1
Norie-Miller, Francis, 1947, Jl 5,11:7
Norins, Michael, 1938, Jl 4,13:5
Norlander, Everett C Mrs, 1960, My 15,85:4
Norli, Erling, 1950, F 7,28:2
Norlin, George, 1942, Mr 31,21:3
Norling, John A, 1957, My 25,21:2
Norloff, Carl, 1948, Ag 21,15:4
Norloff, Carl Mrs, 1950, N 10,27:2
Norlund, Poul, 1951, Je 1,26:1
Norman, A E, 1936, Jl 2,21:3
Norman, Adolphus Mrs, 1943, N 3,25:5
Norman, Alpheus J, 1965, N 19,39:1
Norman, Arthur R, 1968, Ag 1,31:3
Norman, Bill, 1962, Ap 22,80:8
Norman, Bradford, 1950, Ap 7,25:6
Norman, Bradford Jr, 1951, N 7,29:5
Norman, Charles T, 1939, Ap 13,23:4
Norman, Christian G, 1955, Mr 17,45:1
Norman, Christian G Mrs, 1938, Je 3,21:3
Norman, Dan, 1947, Ja 25,17:1
Norman, Edward A, 1955, Je 21,31:1; 1956, N 21,27:4
Norman, Edward H, 1947, D 30,24:3

Norman, Ella M J, 1946, Ag 27,27:1
Norman, Ferdinand S, 1968, F 3,29:5
Norman, Francis Capt, 1918, S 27,13:7
Norman, Francis K, 1939, Je 1,25:3
Norman, Fred, 1947, Ap 19,15:3
Norman, Fred G, 1945, F 22,27:1
Norman, Fred Mrs, 1944, F 11,19:2
Norman, Fred R J, 1937, Ap 10,19:4
Norman, Frederick F, 1951, Mr 1,27:3
Norman, Frederick Prof, 1968, D 11,47:3
Norman, George H Lt, 1908, F 14,7:5
Norman, George H Mrs, 1915, S 7,13:6
Norman, Gustave H, 1956, Mr 20,23:4
Norman, Guy Lt, 1918, Je 4,13:4
Norman, Henry G, 1967, N 29,40:3
Norman, Henry Sir, 1904, O 27,9:5
Norman, Henry Sir (por), 1939, Je 5,17:5
Norman, Hugart F, 1951, S 2,48:6
Norman, Irwin L, 1965, Mr 6,25:1
Norman, J B, 1956, S 20,33:3
Norman, John E Mrs, 1948, S 13,21:4
Norman, Jonathan V Sr, 1952, N 19,29:1
Norman, Leonard, 1964, N 1,89:1
Norman, Lottie R Mrs, 1939, My 4,23:4
Norman, Mark W, 1951, Jl 6,23:4
Norman, Mark W Mrs, 1963, My 26,92:7
Norman, Max M, 1915, N 22,15:5
Norman, Montagu C Lord, 1950, F 5,84:3
Norman, Norman J, 1941, O 11,17:5
Norman, Perry, 1945, Ag 28,19:4
Norman, R, 1880, Ap 24,8:3
Norman, Reginald, 1951, My 10,31:5
Norman, Reginald Mrs, 1965, Jl 22,31:4
Norman, Robert C, 1937, Ap 10,19:2
Norman, Robert C Mrs, 1946, N 24,79:5
Norman, Robert S, 1952, F 10,92:1
Norman, Samuel L, 1953, N 5,31:4
Norman, Sidney, 1956, Je 30,17:6
Norman, Thomas S, 1949, F 2,27:1
Norman, Wayne, 1938, O 6,23:4
Norman, Wellington J, 1949, My 13,24:2
Norman, William, 1940, F 15,19:4; 1951, Ap 2,22:2
Norman, William B, 1906, Ag 17,7:6
Norman-Hansen, C M, 1947, Ap 28,23:1
Normanbrook, Lord (Norman C Brook), 1967, Je 16, 43:2
Normanby, Marquis of, 1863, Ag 12,3:5
Normand, George, 1938, My 22,II,7:1
Normand, Jacques, 1941, Ag 3,35:2
Normand, Jean N, 1950, My 6,15:5
Normand, M, 1930, F 24,1:7
Normandie, Robert L D, 1953, Ap 21,27:2
Normandin, A L, 1945, S 1,11:4
Normandin, Fortunat E, 1967, My 13,33:2
Normanly, James P (por), 1947, My 11,60:5
Normann, Arthur Frederick Rudolph Baron, 1910, D 7,13:3
Normann, Axel A, 1962, My 9,43:2
Normano, John F, 1945, Ap 26,23:3
Normanton, Helena Mrs, 1957, O 17,33:2
Norment, Clarence F Jr, 1956, Je 4,29:6
Norment, E Virginia, 1943, N 16,23:2
Norment, W M Rev, 1924, Mr 22,15:6
Normile, Gene, 1963, Je 6,35:4
Normile, Nicholas J, 1960, Ap 30,23:5
Normoyle, James E Maj, 1916, F 12,11:3
Normoyle, James E Mrs, 1944, Ja 12,24:3
Nornabell, Harry M Mrs, 1953, Ag 12,31:5
Norodom Suramarit, King of Cambodia (funl, Ag 21,9:6), 1960, Ap 4,29:2
Noronha, Eduardo de, 1948, S 27,23:2
Noronha, Silvio de, 1957, Je 21,25:3
Norr, Anna A, 1953, Mr 17,29:4
Norr, Isroy M, 1962, Mr 20,37:4
Norrell, W F, 1961, F 16,31:3
Norrie, Adam, 1882, Je 8,5:4
Norrie, Adam Gordon Mrs, 1921, Ja 30,22:4
Norrie, Gordon, 1909, N 9,9:5
Norrie, Lewis G, 1923, S 22,4:4
Norris, Alfred E, 1946, N 10,62:6
Norris, Alfred E Sr, 1946, Jl 28,40:4
Norris, Alfred L Mrs, 1961, D 13,43:3
Norris, B W, 1873, Ja 28,1:6
Norris, Bessie P Mrs, 1944, Ja 26,19:3
Norris, C, 1935, S 12,1:2
Norris, Carlton B, 1963, S 8,86:8
Norris, Ch E, 1904, Ag 28,1:5
Norris, Charles C, 1961, F 28,33:3
Norris, Charles E, 1941, N 2,55:3; 1950, Ja 17,28:3
Norris, Charles G, 1945, Jl 26,19:5
Norris, Clarence E, 1945, N 19,21:4
Norris, D W, 1949, O 6,31:2
Norris, Daniel L, 1922, Mr 23,13:4
Norris, David, 1950, N 20,25:3
Norris, Donald L, 1967, Jl 27,35:3
Norris, Earl R, 1952, Mr 31,19:3
Norris, Eben H, 1943, My 14,19:2
Norris, Edmond, 1942, Ag 21,19:1
Norris, Edson R, 1946, Ap 30,22:2
Norris, Edward, 1941, Ja 15,23:1; 1956, Ja 26,29:5
Norris, Edward O, 1968, S 22,88:6
Norris, Edwin, 1872, D 30,5:3
Norris, Edwin Lee, 1924, Ap 26,15:4
Norris, Edwin M, 1925, Ap 20,17:6
Norris, Edwin M Mrs, 1947, Jl 31,21:2
Norris, Emilie K, 1950, N 3,27:2
Norris, Emma D (will), 1956, Je 20,29:1
Norris, Ernest E, 1958, Ap 24,31:3
Norris, F L, 1926, Mr 15,21:3
Norris, Fanny (will), 1940, Jl 17,24:5
Norris, Fleming H Jr, 1967, Mr 10,39:3
Norris, Florence B, 1946, O 24,27:4
Norris, Francis H, 1937, F 16,23:1
Norris, Francis L, 1945, Jl 24,23:6
Norris, Francis W, 1946, S 12,7:1
Norris, Frank, 1902, O 26,7:5; 1950, Ja 27,23:4
Norris, Frank A, 1939, S 6,23:4
Norris, Frank C, 1967, Ag 9,39:1
Norris, Fred A, 1952, Jl 4,13:4
Norris, Fred B, 1941, Mr 9,41:2
Norris, Fred J, 1949, Ap 19,26:7
Norris, Frederick A, 1948, N 25,31:1
Norris, Frederick J Sr Mrs, 1948, Jl 9,19:5
Norris, George, 1966, My 4,47:1
Norris, George H, 1942, S 7,19:4
Norris, George W, 1942, My 14,19:1; 1944, S 3,1:2
Norris, H Claude, 1956, S 8,17:4
Norris, Harlie Mrs, 1951, O 19,27:2
Norris, Henry, 1941, O 7,24:3
Norris, Henry Dole, 1917, O 21,23:3
Norris, Henry H, 1940, Ap 15,17:2
Norris, Henry L Mrs, 1962, D 7,39:1
Norris, Henry M, 1943, Ja 31,46:1
Norris, Henry McCoy, 1925, D 27,7:1
Norris, Henry S, 1947, S 19,23:1
Norris, Homer, 1920, Ag 16,11:5
Norris, Howard D, 1951, O 15,25:3
Norris, Ida M Mrs, 1937, S 9,23:4
Norris, J B (see also F 19), 1878, F 20,2:4
Norris, J Frank, 1952, Ag 21,19:5
Norris, J Frank Mrs, 1940, My 14,24:2; 1955, Ja 1,13:5
Norris, J W, 1928, My 9,25:3
Norris, James, 1952, D 5,27:3
Norris, James D (will, Mr 8,22:7), 1966, F 26,25:2
Norris, James D Jr Mrs, 1952, Je 12,33:4
Norris, James F (por), 1940, Ag 5,13:5
Norris, James F Mrs, 1948, Je 2,29:5
Norris, James L, 1910, Mr 6,II,11:3
Norris, James Newton, 1925, N 11,23:4
Norris, John (por),(funl, Mr 23,11:4), 1914, Mr 22, 15:1
Norris, John, 1917, Ja 14,19:1
Norris, John C, 1953, My 23,15:4
Norris, John Mrs, 1947, My 24,15:7
Norris, John N, 1957, Ja 4,23:1
Norris, Joseph F P, 1938, Ja 21,19:5
Norris, Joseph Mrs, 1940, Ag 29,19:4
Norris, Joseph Parker Jr, 1916, Mr 18,11:7
Norris, Julian R, 1950, Mr 1,27:3
Norris, Kathleen (Mrs Chas G),(est appr, Jl 15,17:2), 1966, Ja 19,41:1
Norris, Lee (Mrs Jas W Elder), 1964, Mr 2,27:4
Norris, Lloyd B, 1951, N 24,11:5
Norris, Maria C, 1946, Ja 8,23:3
Norris, Mark (por), 1943, Je 1,23:1
Norris, Nathaniel R Mrs, 1957, Mr 17,87:1
Norris, Olivia J, 1962, Je 6,41:3
Norris, Ralph T, 1938, Mr 3,21:1
Norris, Richard, 1874, Je 5,4:6
Norris, Richard C Dr, 1937, Je 15,23:2
Norris, Richard J, 1913, Ag 1,7:6
Norris, Robert A, 1940, Mr 6,23:4
Norris, Robert B, 1942, Ja 24,15:7
Norris, Robert P, 1961, Ja 31,29:4
Norris, Robert V, 1937, Ja 19,17:4
Norris, Rollin, 1951, Jl 19,23:3
Norris, Russell, 1942, Ja 27,21:4
Norris, Samuel, 1941, S 26,23:2
Norris, Samuel E, 1948, O 29,25:2
Norris, Sarah Goodhue, 1921, O 20,17:5
Norris, Thomas J Jr, 1953, O 9,29:6
Norris, Thomas M, 1946, N 30,15:3
Norris, True L Col, 1920, D 5,22:3
Norris, W A, 1948, D 24,17:1
Norris, W E, 1925, N 21,17:4
Norris, Walter H, 1942, Jl 12,35:2
Norris, Walter J, 1965, Jl 8,31:2
Norris, William C, 1954, My 11,29:4
Norris, William F Dean (por), 1937, S 29,23:3
Norris, William K, 1951, My 4,27:2
Norris, William M, 1938, D 3,20:2
Norris, William M Mrs, 1945, Ag 5,38:8
Norris, Zoe Anderson Mrs, 1914, F 14,11:5
Norrle, A Lanfear, 1910, D 23,13:4
Norseen, Wilbur H, 1953, D 23,25:1
Norsk, John C Mrs, 1951, N 19,23:3
Norstad, Martin Mrs, 1961, Mr 2,27:2
Norsworthy, Clarence F, 1958, Mr 22,17:5
Norsworthy, Howard R, 1948, My 21,23:4
Norsworthy, Naomi Dr, 1916, D 26,11:5
North, Alfred B, 1957, Ja 2,27:4
North, Arthur A, 1966, Ja 30,84:7
North, Cecil B Mrs, 1947, N 22,15:4
North, Charles E, 1961, Jl 28,21:4
North, Charles T, 1950, Ja 9,25:4
North, Dexter Mrs, 1950, My 6,15:3
North, Edgerton G, 1967, F 17,37:3
North, Edward Dr, 1903, S 14,7:5
North, Edward P, 1911, Jl 21,9:6
North, Elizabeth P Mrs, 1957, Mr 19,37:4
North, Emerson A, 1953, Ag 23,89:1
North, Ernest D, 1945, Mr 18,42:1
North, Francis R, 1945, Mr 1,21:3
North, Frank A, 1951, Mr 16,31:1
North, George R, 1946, O 23,27:4
North, Harold F, 1965, Jl 24,21:5
North, Harry C, 1954, O 26,27:1
North, Hart H, 1950, Ap 18,31:2
North, Henry E, 1962, F 27,33:1
North, Henry W Mrs, 1950, D 21,29:1
North, Herbert S, 1945, Ja 11,23:5
North, Herman H, 1950, My 19,28:4
North, Howard A Mrs, 1944, O 22,46:5
North, Isabelle A Mrs, 1942, Jl 25,13:6
North, J T Col, 1896, My 6,5:3
North, Jack E, 1953, Jl 2,23:1
North, James H Jr, 1945, D 3,21:5
North, James M, 1956, O 17,35:3
North, John H, 1950, D 28,25:4
North, John K, 1953, Je 29,21:4
North, John S, 1940, S 14,17:3
North, Joseph E, 1939, O 23,19:3; 1967, Ja 11,25:3
North, Lillian S C Mrs, 1937, Mr 29,19:4
North, Lord, 1938, D 11,60:8
North, Mary, 1952, My 29,27:6
North, Mortimer C, 1937, O 28,25:1
North, Ralph M Jr, 1942, S 22,21:5
North, Robert E, 1955, Ap 22,25:4
North, Robert Mrs, 1944, Ja 9,42:4
North, S Rev, 1884, F 11,2:6
North, Simon Newton Dexter Dr, 1924, Ag 4,13:4
North, Stanley G, 1965, O 28,43:3
North, Walter S, 1940, Jl 13,13:5
North, William B, 1959, Je 23,33:4
North, William P, 1937, S 14,23:6
North, William S 3d, 1955, D 22,1:7
Northall, Henrietta, 1909, D 11,11:5
Northam, C H, 1881, N 13,9:5
Northam, Charles H, 1916, Je 7,13:5
Northam, George H, 1950, O 17,31:2
Northam, William B, 1937, S 7,21:5
Northam, William E, 1959, Mr 12,31:5
Northbacker, Howard A, 1967, S 13,47:2
Northbrook, Earl of, 1904, N 16,9:3
Northcote, Geoffrey A, 1948, Jl 12,19:6
Northcote, Henry Stafford Baron, 1911, S 30,13:6
Northcote, James, 1904, F 7,7:6
Northcote, Stafford M, 1949, N 18,29:1
Northcote (Son of Sir Clifford Northcote), 1872, O 1:6
Northcott, Elliott, 1946, Ja 5,13:2
Northcott, Elliott Mrs, 1942, Jl 3,17:6
Northcott, Gustavus A, 1938, D 9,25:1
Northcroft, George, 1943, N 20,13:6
Northcutt, Robert, 1947, S 16,23:2
Northen, Charles S, 1950, My 19,28:3
Northern, Herbert E, 1947, O 2,27:2
Northesk, Earl of (D L G H Carnegie), 1963, N 8 32:1
Northey, Carrie, 1937, S 24,21:2
Northey, Edward, 1953, D 30,23:2
Northey, John P, 1939, Mr 6,15:2
Northey, William C, 1951, Jl 24,25:4
Northey, Winifred L, 1942, O 14,25:5
Northington, Merrill P, 1938, Mr 6,II,9:2
Northridge, Edward C, 1949, Jl 26,27:4
Northridge, John A, 1961, Je 9,33:4
Northridge, Laddie, 1959, D 25,21:5
Northrip, James Mrs, 1948, Ja 23,23:2
Northrop, Absalom, 1905, Mr 18,11:5
Northrop, Adelbert, 1959, My 25,29:2
Northrop, Allan P Prof, 1916, Ap 14,9:5
Northrop, Amanda C, 1955, O 15,15:1
Northrop, B K, 1957, O 26,21:5
Northrop, Caro H, 1941, O 14,23:5
Northrop, Cecil P, 1949, My 22,88:1
Northrop, Charles P Mrs, 1950, F 22,29:4
Northrop, Cyrus Dr, 1922, Ap 4,17:5
Northrop, David D, 1959, My 26,29:5
Northrop, Earl C, 1946, Ja 11,21:3
Northrop, Edwin C, 1960, Ag 4,25:4
Northrop, Ellis R, 1942, My 14,19:2
Northrop, Frank A Mrs, 1952, Je 1,84:4
Northrop, George N, 1964, Ag 1,21:6
Northrop, George P, 1938, S 21,25:6; 1950, Ap 24,
Northrop, Harry Mrs, 1950, My 9,29:2
Northrop, Henry Evans, 1921, N 29,17:3
Northrop, Horace W, 1941, Ja 24,17:5
Northrop, James H, 1940, D 14,17:2
Northrop, Joe E, 1951, Ap 28,15:5
Northrop, John B, 1964, Mr 25,41:2
Northrop, Mary L, 1954, N 26,29:2
Northrop, Maurice E, 1945, Jl 23,19:4
Northrop, Mildred B, 1963, N 20,43:5
Northrop, Reid, 1909, Jl 8,7:6
Northrop, Richard D, 1957, Ja 20,92:4
Northrop, Richard F, 1944, Mr 13,15:4
Northrop, Ruth E Mrs, 1951, Jl 16,21:4
Northrop, Sarah L Mrs, 1940, Mr 7,23:4

Northrop, William B, 1965, D 16,47:3
Northrup, A M, 1939, O 4,25:4
Northrup, Agnes, 1953, S 15,31:6
Northrup, Ansel J, 1919, N 24,15:2
Northrup, Benjamin K, 1952, O 4,17:6
Northrup, Charles E, 1938, My 13,19:1
Northrup, Edwin F, 1940, My 2,24:2
Northrup, Frederick, 1939, Mr 19,III,7:2
Northrup, Frederick L, 1943, Ap 4,40:4
Northrup, George A, 1945, My 17,19:5
Northrup, H B (see also N 15), 1877, N 18,10:6
Northrup, Herbert E, 1946, Ag 13,27:2
Northrup, James A, 1922, Ja 29,22:2
Northrup, James L, 1941, S 5,22:3
Northrup, John H, 1941, O 24,23:4
Northrup, Lillian A Mrs, 1942, Jl 30,21:4
Northrup, W C, 1905, Mr 8,3:7
Northrup, Walter J, 1939, Mr 26,III,6:7
Northrup, William, 1912, Je 12,13:6
Northrup, William F, 1951, D 30,25:1
Northumberland, Dowager Duchess of (Helen), 1965, Je 14,33:3
Northumberland, Duke of (Hy Geo Percy), 1918, My 16,13:6
Northumberland, Duke of, 1930, Ag 23,13:5
Northup, Charles F, 1950, Ap 5,31:2
Northup, Daniel W, 1961, Ap 14,29:3
Northup, Robert C Mrs, 1947, F 5,23:5
Northup, Royal, 1949, D 22,23:1
Northway, John K, 1966, Je 29,47:1
Northway, Ralph E, 1940, D 6,27:2
Northwood, Arthur, 1963, Je 20,33:5
Northwood, Arthur Mrs, 1968, Ap 21,80:5
Nortn, Robert L, 1948, Ja 8,25:4
Norton, Adelaide I Mrs, 1950, N 26,90:7
Norton, Albert G, 1939, S 13,25:5
Norton, Albert H, 1940, Mr 26,21:5
Norton, Alfred V, 1958, Ag 13,27:2
Norton, Algernon Sidney, 1920, D 9,13:3
Norton, Allen T, 1951, S 8,17:6
Norton, Alston C Mrs, 1960, Mr 9,33:3
Norton, Arden L, 1949, Ag 14,68:2
Norton, Arie R, 1944, My 3,19:4
Norton, Arthur Brigham, 1919, Je 19,13:5
Norton, Arthur E, 1940, F 25,39:3
Norton, Arthur H, 1939, My 1,23:5
Norton, Arthur O, 1959, Ag 26,29:5
Norton, Arthur W, 1938, D 2,23:6
Norton, Bayes, 1967, O 28,31:4
Norton, Belle, 1938, Mr 23,23:4
Norton, Benjamin, 1924, My 22,17:6
Norton, Benjamin V, 1946, F 13,23:5
Norton, Brownrigg L, 1946, S 17,7:2
Norton, Carleton G, 1948, N 20,13:2
Norton, Carol, 1904, Ap 8,2:2
Norton, Carroll F, 1938, Mr 20,II,8:7
Norton, Cedric Mrs, 1967, My 29,25:1
Norton, Charles D, 1916, Jl 22,9:6
Norton, Charles D Mrs, 1948, F 10,23:2
Norton, Charles Dyer (funl, Mr 9,15:4), 1923, Mr 7, 15:3
Norton, Charles E, 1940, N 2,15:4; 1952, Ap 14,19:3
Norton, Charles H, 1942, O 28,23:4
Norton, Charles L, 1872, Mr 24,8:2; 1939, S 9,17:6
Norton, Charles Stuart Rear-Adm, 1911, Je 25,11:4
Norton, Charles W, 1952, My 6,29:4
Norton, Chester A, 1946, D 12,29:5
Norton, Chester H, 1946, O 19,21:4
Norton, Clara M, 1941, Jl 24,17:2
Norton, Daniel F, 1937, O 6,25:1; 1956, Ja 16,21:3
Norton, Daniel S, 1870, Jl 15,5:5; 1951, O 28,84:6
Norton, Dennis F Sr, 1953, S 15,31:4
Norton, Donald H, 1950, Je 1,27:2
Norton, Dudley S, 1967, Je 12,53:6
Norton, Dwight F, 1937, Ap 8,23:3
Norton, E Hope, 1961, Ap 6,33:2
Norton, Eben D, 1945, Mr 20,19:4
Norton, Edward F, 1954, N 6,17:2
Norton, Edward Mrs, 1937, Ap 29,21:6
Norton, Edward V, 1956, Jl 19,27:2
Norton, Edwin C, 1943, O 8,19:5
Norton, Edwin L, 1959, Ja 9,27:3
Norton, Elijah Hise Ex-Justice, 1914, Ag 7,11:6
Norton, Elizabeth G, 1958, My 20,33:4
Norton, Ella M, 1937, F 11,23:4
Norton, Emily R Mrs, 1942, My 13,19:4
Norton, Eugene B, 1950, S 30,17:5
Norton, Eugene G, 1942, My 28,17:4
Norton, Eugene L, 1960, Jl 21,27:5
Norton, Everett, 1912, F 23,11:4
Norton, Francis C Mrs, 1962, Ja 6,19:4
Norton, Frank D, 1960, Ag 21,84:3
Norton, Frank E, 1940, Ap 27,15:2
Norton, Frank H Col, 1921, F 21,11:6
Norton, Fred A, 1940, My 18,15:6
Norton, Fred E, 1941, Ap 20,42:4
Norton, Fred H, 1945, F 22,28:2
Norton, Frederick C, 1940, D 17,25:4
Norton, Frederick Dr, 1924, Mr 1,13:6
Norton, Frederick E, 1943, O 24,45:2
Norton, George C, 1953, O 19,21:5
Norton, George F, 1946, D 16,23:2
Norton, George H, 1938, O 19,23:4
Norton, George L Capt, 1923, Mr 25,6:3
Norton, George L Mrs (Isabel Freeman), 1911, Jl 9, 11:5
Norton, George W, 1920, O 23,13:6; 1924, D 11,23:4
Norton, Grady, 1954, O 10,87:2
Norton, Guy P, 1952, F 10,93:1
Norton, Guy W Sr, 1960, F 2,35:1
Norton, H J Lt, 1926, S 14,3:3
Norton, Harry N, 1941, S 16,23:4
Norton, Harry T, 1946, Mr 2,13:4
Norton, Hastings, 1953, S 26,17:1
Norton, Henry K, 1965, O 13,47:1
Norton, Henry M Mrs, 1946, My 16,21:4
Norton, Homer H, 1965, My 27,37:4
Norton, Horace G Dr, 1915, O 28,11:5
Norton, Horace S, 1947, Ag 6,23:3
Norton, Huntington, 1958, O 17,30:1
Norton, J A, 1880, Ja 10,5:2
Norton, J S (see also Ap 22), 1878, Ap 23,8:5
Norton, J T, 1865, S 2,2:6
Norton, Jack (M J Naughton), 1958, O 16,37:2
Norton, James A (por), 1949, My 25,29:3
Norton, James C, 1948, Ja 29,24:2
Norton, James E, 1950, S 5,27:5
Norton, James Ex-Sen, 1915, N 5,13:4
Norton, James F, 1930, Ja 21,25:5; 1950, S 28,31:5
Norton, James J, 1939, D 14,27:4; 1940, D 13,23:4
Norton, Jeannette Y Mrs, 1941, F 23,39:6
Norton, Jesse B, 1938, Je 10,21:6
Norton, Jesse O, 1875, Ag 5,1:5
Norton, John A, 1959, Jl 2,25:1
Norton, John A Mrs, 1945, Ja 27,11:5
Norton, John J, 1943, Jl 13,21:3
Norton, John L, 1950, My 27,17:7
Norton, John P, 1950, Jl 13,25:4
Norton, John S, 1942, F 5,21:4
Norton, John T, 1942, Ap 17,17:5
Norton, John W, 1950, Ja 28,13:5
Norton, John W Mrs, 1938, D 30,16:1
Norton, John Z, 1947, Ja 1,33:3
Norton, Joseph A Mrs, 1951, N 20,31:2
Norton, Joseph C, 1945, N 24,20:2
Norton, Karl B Mrs, 1949, O 17,23:4
Norton, Kenneth B Mrs, 1968, Ja 24,45:3
Norton, Laurence H, 1960, Je 12,86:7
Norton, Laurence J, 1956, F 4,19:7
Norton, Lawrence A, 1953, Je 25,27:6
Norton, Lawrence D, 1941, N 10,17:4
Norton, Leland B, 1953, Je 12,27:5
Norton, Lord, 1905, Mr 29,9:2; 1945, Ja 4,19:3
Norton, Louise Z, 1946, F 20,25:2
Norton, Madge Mrs, 1945, Ja 26,21:4
Norton, Marie T Mrs, 1940, S 30,17:4
Norton, Martin E, 1967, Ap 1,32:4
Norton, Mary T Mrs (trb, Ag 5,9:8; funl, Ag 6,27:4), 1959, Ag 3,25:3
Norton, Matthew F, 1950, O 23,23:3
Norton, Mrs (Lady Stirling Maxwell), 1877, Je 16,2:6
Norton, Nathaniel R (por), 1948, O 3,64:5
Norton, Norris Randal, 1870, D 19,1:7
Norton, P S, 1949, Ag 11,24:7
Norton, Patrick J, 1951, Ja 26,23:2; 1962, Mr 4,86:7
Norton, Peter J Sr, 1937, Jl 18,II,7:2
Norton, Ralph, 1952, Mr 3,21:2
Norton, Ralph H Mrs, 1947, Mr 18,27:2
Norton, Ralph Jr, 1954, D 6,27:6
Norton, Richard W, 1940, Jl 18,19:2
Norton, Robert A, 1964, S 1,36:1
Norton, Robert C, 1959, N 23,31:4
Norton, Robert H, 1958, N 15,23:6
Norton, Roscoe G, 1937, Jl 23,19:6
Norton, Roy, 1917, Jl 16,9:4
Norton, Roy E, 1942, Je 30,21:3
Norton, Sheridan S Mrs, 1968, S 14,31:3
Norton, Skeffington S Sr Mrs, 1953, Je 14,84:1
Norton, Stephen A, 1951, Ja 4,29:4
Norton, Sybil (Mrs J Cournos), 1959, Ag 16,31:4
Norton, Thomas H (por), 1941, D 3,25:1
Norton, Thomas J, 1943, Mr 2,19:3
Norton, Vernon C, 1950, Ap 19,29:2
Norton, W A, 1883, S 23,3:6
Norton, W Kenneth (por), 1942, Ja 10,15:4
Norton, Wallace M, 1958, Mr 12,31:1
Norton, Washington F, 1938, D 26,23:4
Norton, Wendell P, 1955, Ag 11,21:2
Norton, Wilbur H, 1963, Ap 4,47:1
Norton, William, 1948, O 26,31:5; 1963, D 5,45:2
Norton, William A, 1940, Mr 22,19:4
Norton, William B, 1943, O 14,21:3; 1948, Ag 23,17:1
Norton, William E, 1948, F 26,23:5
Norton, William Edward, 1916, F 29,11:5
Norton, William G, 1959, Je 28,68:7
Norton, William H, 1946, D 12,29:1; 1950, F 3,23:3
Norton, William J, 1949, Ap 28,31:6; 1958, Mr 6,27:6; 1958, Jl 13,68:8
Norton, William R Mrs, 1937, Mr 1,19:3
Norton, William S, 1966, Ag 30,36:4
Norton, William W, 1941, O 11,17:6
Norton, William W (por), 1945, N 9,19:1
Norton, Winifred (Mother Mary Cecelia), 1954, Je 3,27:3
Norulak, Ludwig A, 1959, Jl 29,29:3
Norval, James, 1947, D 15,25:4
Norval, Theophilus L, 1942, F 11,21:2
Norvell, Charles H, 1938, N 20,38:8
Norvell, Saunders, 1949, Ag 26,20:6
Norvell, Saunders Mrs, 1946, N 27,25:5
Norway, Nevil S (N Shute), 1960, Ja 13,47:1
Norweb, Henry Mrs, 1955, Ap 17,87:1
Norweb, John H, 1960, Ap 30,23:6
Norwell, Woodson E, 1950, Ja 2,23:2
Norwich, Lord (Sir A D Cooper), 1954, Ja 2,11:1
Norwick, Harry A, 1948, F 15,60:6
Norwitz, Mary R, 1937, Je 23,25:5
Norwood, A G, 1879, Mr 13,3:1
Norwood, Benjamin F, 1942, Ja 14,21:6
Norwood, C, 1936, N 20,23:1
Norwood, Charles A, 1940, My 26,35:2
Norwood, Cornelius H, 1949, Mr 18,25:2
Norwood, Edward R, 1942, N 26,27:3
Norwood, Edwin P, 1940, O 15,23:5
Norwood, George W, 1946, Je 25,21:2
Norwood, Gilbert, 1954, O 19,27:2
Norwood, Harry V, 1955, Jl 30,17:6
Norwood, Leslie E, 1958, Mr 1,17:5
Norwood, R, 1932, S 30,19:1
Norwood, Robert, 1903, My 23,9:3
Norwood, Robert Mrs, 1959, F 12,27:1
Norwood, Thomas M Ex-Sen, 1913, Je 21,9:5
Norworth, Jack, 1959, S 2,29:1
Norz, Charles, 1948, Ag 29,56:3
Nosakova, Eliska, 1948, Ag 15,V,3:7
Nosek, Vaclav, 1955, Jl 23,17:5
Nosenko, Ivan I, 1956, Ag 4,15:2
Noseworthy, Frederick, 1942, F 26,19:6
Noseworthy, Joseph W, 1956, Ap 2,23:3
Noska, Elliot V, 1946, Mr 23,13:2
Noske, Gustav, 1946, D 1,76:4
Nosler, Don S, 1950, N 25,13:4
Nosov, Grigori I, 1951, Ag 11,11:2
Nossen, Herbert L, 1951, Je 5,31:1
Nossiter, George, 1948, S 2,23:4
Nossitter, Charles E Mrs, 1946, Je 4,23:3
Nostitz, Ethelene von, 1944, Jl 30,35:3
Nostrand, Alfred E C, 1951, Je 7,33:1
Nostrand, George E, 1938, N 26,15:4
Nostrand, Howard O, 1956, Je 13,37:5
Nosworthy, Arthur, 1937, My 11,25:1
Nosworthy, Richard, 1946, Ap 1,27:5
Nosworthy, T Arthur, 1967, Ap 11,41:2
Nosworthy, T Arthur Mrs, 1958, F 1,19:1
Note, Jean, 1922, Ap 2,29:4
Noteman, Norman L, 1944, My 27,15:6
Noteman, Norman L (will), 1944, Je 4,35:6
Noteman, Norman L Mrs, 1942, D 6,77:2
Noterup, George, 1948, Je 27,52:5
Noth, Charles J, 1966, Mr 15,39:4
Nothenberg, Oscar J, 1948, N 11,27:3
Nothnagel, Peter, 1957, N 19,33:4
Nothnagel, William, 1943, Je 2,25:3
Notkin, Meyer, 1956, Ap 27,27:3
Notman, Arthur, 1961, Jl 21,23:1
Notman, George Mrs, 1946, Ja 31,21:4
Notman, Grant, 1918, Ja 14,11:4
Notman, John, 1907, Ja 7,7:4
Notman, W Robson Rev, 1909, Ja 1,11:5
Notman, William A, 1945, F 23,17:3
Noto, Joseph, 1944, Jl 26,19:4
Noto, Nellie F Mrs, 1950, Ja 2,23:5
Notopoulos, James A, 1967, O 19,47:2
Notre Dame, sister of (Mother Mary Anne), 1917, Ja 17,9:3
Nott, Benjamin C, 1943, Ap 18,48:7
Nott, C C, 1881, Ja 12,5:4
Nott, C D Rev, 1904, My 19,9:1
Nott, Charles C Jr, 1957, My 11,21:3
Nott, Charles C Sr, 1915, Ap 5,11:4
Nott, Charles Cooper, 1916, Mr 7,11:4
Nott, Claude R, 1944, Ja 31,17:4
Nott, Eliphalet Dr, 1866, Ja 30,4:6
Nott, Francis A, 1942, F 22,26:4
Nott, Hiram, 1882, S 10,7:4
Nott, J Frederick Dr, 1904, Ag 10,7:6
Nott, Stanley C, 1957, My 26,93:2
Nott-Bower, William, 1939, F 5,40:5
Nottage, G S Lord Mayor, 1885, Ap 12,2:5
Nottbohm, Otto, 1948, N 10,29:5
Nottebaum, Ralph L, 1941, F 28,19:2
Nottenberg, Arthur A, 1964, Je 13,23:5
Notter, Harley A, 1950, Je 20,27:6
Nottingham, Charles A, 1961, Ja 4,33:1
Nottingham, Charles A Mrs, 1944, D 15,19:4
Nottingham, Eloise H Mrs, 1939, O 16,19:6
Nottingham, Leon J, 1947, Ap 3,25:3
Nottingham, William, 1921, Ja 24,11:4
Notz, Felix J, 1946, Ag 18,44:3
Notz, W F, 1935, Je 5,19:3
Noue, Jehan de Countess, 1968, D 1,86:1
Nouel, Adolfo A Dr (por), 1937, Je 27,II,6:6
Nounnan, Joseph F, 1962, O 28,88:5
Nourjian, Nihran H, 1953, Ap 1,29:3
Nourse, Charles E, 1939, Ap 3,15:6
Nourse, Charles James, 1907, N 19,9:5
Nourse, Dave, 1948, Jl 9,19:4
Nourse, Elizabeth, 1938, O 10,19:6
Nourse, Henry, 1942, O 7,25:4

Nourse, Henry S, 1903, N 15,7:5
Nourse, John C, 1940, N 25,17:2
Nourse, John D, 1956, Ap 8,84:8
Nourse, John V, 1958, Ja 14,33:3
Nourse, John V Mrs, 1955, O 2,86:8
Nourse, Joseph P, 1954, F 18,31:3
Nova, Algernon I, 1953, My 7,31:3
Nova, Algernon I Mrs, 1939, Ap 14,14:4
Nova, Guillermo, 1952, Je 23,19:5
Nova, Pauline Mrs, 1941, Jl 9,21:6
Novac, Frantisek, 1940, Ap 28,37:2
Novack, Herschel, 1952, Ag 9,13:5
Novack, Hyman, 1955, My 28,15:5
Novack, Joseph, 1956, S 10,27:1
Novack, Joseph Mrs, 1962, S 3,15:4
Novack, Max D (por), 1946, Jl 7,35:1
Novack, Paul, 1966, F 10,34:2
Novak, Edward J, 1965, D 9,47:1
Novak, Jaroslav, 1942, F 3,20:2
Novak, John W, 1954, Ap 29,31:2
Novak, Joseph, 1952, Jl 25,18:5
Novak, Leo V, 1961, S 19,35:4
Novak, Michael Mrs, 1943, My 18,23:3
Novak, Stephen S, 1955, Ag 25,23:5
Novak, Vitezslav, 1949, Jl 19,29:3
Novak, Wenceslas, 1953, Mr 8,91:2
Novakovitch, Uros, 1950, F 15,8:4
Novaro, Angiolo S, 1938, Mr 11,19:4
Novarro, Ramon (will), 1968, N 15,47:2
Novasio, Pietro, 1952, F 21,27:3
Novatschek, Carl M, 1910, Jl 4,7:4
Novelli, Ermete, 1919, Ja 31,11:5
Novelli, Joseph A, 1947, Ja 16,25:3
Novello, Armando (Toto the Clown),(por), 1938, D 16,2:3
Novello, George, 1942, Ap 15,21:4
Novello, Ivor, 1951, Mr 6,27:1
Novello, Joseph A, 1958, Ag 7,25:1
Novello, Leonard Mrs, 1944, Ag 2,15:4
November, Norman, 1966, S 13,47:3
November, Norman Mrs (D Green), 1963, N 18,33:5
Novey, Alex, 1949, Jl 17,56:4
Novich, Solomon, 1939, N 1,23:5
Novick, Abraham, 1965, Ja 14,35:1
Novick, Constantine Mrs, 1946, Mr 14,25:1
Novick, Harry (cor, Ja 22,29:3), 1957, Ja 20,93:1
Novick, Jacob, 1949, Jl 31,61:1
Novick, Louis P, 1954, O 23,15:1
Novick, Sam, 1968, Jl 5,25:3
Novik, Sam, 1959, Ap 13,31:5
Novikoff, Jacob, 1937, F 4,21:5
Novikoff, Laurent, 1956, Je 29,21:3
Novikoff, Olga, 1925, Ap 22,23:4
Novikov-Priboy, Alexei, 1944, My 1,15:6
Novikova, Paola (Mrs W Singer), 1967, Ag 24,37:3
Novins, J K, 1953, My 12,27:2
Novis, Donald, 1966, Jl 24,60:6
Novitsky, Fedor F, 1944, Ap 9,34:2
Novoa, Andres, 1947, S 18,25:1
Novoa, Fidel Antonio Dr, 1922, N 17,17:5
Novod, Gordon I, 1963, O 27,88:2
Novokovsky, Gertrude D, 1955, Jl 20,27:1
Novomeysky, Moshe, 1961, Ap 3,33:1
Novoseller, Davis S, 1966, Ap 30,31:4
Novotny, Adolph Mrs, 1943, N 30,27:2
Novotny, Edward L, 1949, Ag 27,13:4
Novotny, Joseph, 1966, D 2,39:5
Novotny, Louis C, 1950, Ja 17,28:3
Novy, Frederick G, 1957, Ag 10,15:1
Nowak, Abraham Mrs, 1943, My 20,21:3
Nowak, Andrew J Mrs, 1949, O 21,25:1
Nowak, Charles A, 1943, Jl 11,34:6
Nowak, Edward, 1945, Jl 2,15:4
Nowak, Joseph F, 1952, S 25,31:4
Nowak, Julian, 1946, N 11,27:3
Nowak, Walter, 1958, D 29,15:5
Nowak, Walter Mrs, 1953, O 27,27:3
Nowak, William, 1957, N 13,32:4
Nowakoski, Alfred G, 1966, Je 25,31:2
Nowell, Elizabeth, 1958, Ag 25,21:2
Nowell, Herbert E, 1951, Ag 20,19:4
Nowell, Irma S Mrs, 1951, Mr 19,27:5
Nowell, Robert V, 1949, O 28,23:3
Nowicki, Ignace F, 1967, O 8,83:3
Nowicki, Joseph, 1945, D 20,3:4
Nowicki, Valentine J, 1946, Ja 17,23:3
Nowicki, Valentine Sr Mrs, 1953, N 10,31:4
Nowikas, Louis, 1956, S 18,35:1
Nowill, Walter, 1942, N 28,13:1
Nowinski, Lucian, 1958, N 24,29:5
Nowinski, Miczyslaw M, 1950, D 5,31:4
Nowka, Frederick W, 1943, Ap 20,23:4
Nowlan, Francis P, 1952, Mr 12,27:4
Nowlan, George, 1965, Je 1,39:1
Nowlan, Phil F, 1940, F 4,41:1
Nowland, John W, 1948, F 20,27:2
Nowland, Otho, 1951, O 30,29:5
Nowlen, Joseph C, 1941, Je 10,23:5
Nowlen, Joseph P, 1939, Jl 11,20:2
Nowlin, Christopher P Mrs, 1912, Mr 31,15:3
Nowlin, Sid, 1951, Jl 16,21:4
Nowodworski, Leon, 1942, Ja 26,15:5
Nowogrodsky, Emanuel, 1967, Ag 11,31:4
Nowowiejski, Feliks, 1946, Ja 25,23:2
Nowrey, John E Mrs, 1950, Ap 2,93:1
Nowrey, Joseph E, 1937, My 31,16:1
Noxon, Ellsworth, 1952, S 15,25:4
Noxon, Frank W, 1945, Mr 22,23:6
Noxon, Henry C, 1950, My 14,106:5
Noxon, James, 1881, Ja 7,5:4
Noxon, Olive F Mrs, 1942, F 13,21:5
Noyce, Wilfrid, 1962, Jl 31,8:1
Noyes, A A, 1936, Je 4,23:5
Noyes, A C, 1880, S 5,7:3
Noyes, Alexander D, 1945, Ap 23,19:1
Noyes, Alfred (funl, Jl 3,25:5), 1958, Je 29,1:3
Noyes, Alfred C, 1962, S 11,33:2
Noyes, Arthur A, 1954, Ap 7,31:1
Noyes, Arthur P, 1963, Ag 23,25:2
Noyes, B Lake, 1945, O 17,19:3
Noyes, C D, 1936, Je 4,23:3
Noyes, C Reinold, 1954, Jl 6,23:6
Noyes, C Reinold Mrs, 1967, Ap 2,93:2
Noyes, Charles D (por), 1940, F 17,13:5
Noyes, Charles Prentiss Mrs, 1924, Jl 12,9:7
Noyes, Charles R Mrs, 1951, Ap 27,23:3
Noyes, Clarence T, 1952, My 16,24:3
Noyes, Crosby Everett, 1908, F 22,7:6
Noyes, D Raymond, 1940, N 22,23:4
Noyes, David A, 1946, D 18,29:4
Noyes, David C, 1954, Mr 30,27:2
Noyes, DeWitt C, 1939, D 21,23:4
Noyes, Douglas K, 1952, S 11,31:6
Noyes, Edward A, 1963, Jl 26,25:1
Noyes, Edward S, 1967, D 19,47:1
Noyes, Edward S Mrs, 1956, Mr 23,28:2
Noyes, Eugene J, 1961, Mr 16,37:4
Noyes, Frank, 1965, Ja 4,29:1
Noyes, Frank B, 1948, D 1,29:1
Noyes, Frank B Mrs, 1942, N 9,23:5
Noyes, Frank E, 1941, N 29,17:4
Noyes, Frank E Mrs, 1940, Je 25,23:2
Noyes, Frederick C Mrs, 1959, F 25,31:2
Noyes, Frederick K, 1941, D 20,19:4
Noyes, George B, 1949, Ap 17,76:6
Noyes, George C, 1958, My 13,29:1
Noyes, George E, 1945, Ja 8,17:4
Noyes, George F, 1868, Ja 11,4:6
Noyes, George H Ex-Judge, 1916, Ja 11,11:5
Noyes, George L, 1954, S 13,23:5
Noyes, H T Gen, 1903, O 17,9:6
Noyes, Halbert H, 1940, N 1,25:2
Noyes, Harley H, 1954, Mr 26,21:3
Noyes, Harold G, 1967, S 20,47:2
Noyes, Harry C, 1959, Mr 25,35:4
Noyes, Harry L, 1959, Mr 16,31:4
Noyes, Haskell, 1948, D 9,33:1
Noyes, Henry Frothingham, 1922, Ja 16,13:4
Noyes, Hilton L Sr Mrs, 1960, D 31,17:5
Noyes, Holton V Mrs, 1940, Ja 28,32:4
Noyes, Horatio T, 1949, My 9,25:4
Noyes, Horton V, 1953, Mr 18,31:3
Noyes, Isabelle H, 1946, Ag 3,15:4
Noyes, J R, 1879, Mr 15,3:4
Noyes, James B, 1948, N 4,29:2; 1949, My 1,88:3
Noyes, James H, 1948, My 23,70:2
Noyes, Jane D, 1939, Mr 15,23:4
Noyes, John H, 1940, My 4,17:2
Noyes, John R, 1956, F 1,14:4
Noyes, Julius W (funl plans, Ja 16,31:1), 1957, Ja 15,29:4
Noyes, Katharine C, 1944, N 9,27:5
Noyes, La Verne W, 1919, Jl 25,11:5
Noyes, Lawrence G, 1954, Je 6,86:5
Noyes, Leigh Mrs, 1952, Ap 22,29:2
Noyes, Linwood I, 1964, Ap 21,37:1
Noyes, Nathaniel K, 1945, Ap 14,15:4
Noyes, Newbold (por), 1942, Ap 17,17:1
Noyes, Pauline R Mrs, 1942, O 14,25:4
Noyes, Pierrepont B, 1959, Ap 16,33:4
Noyes, Pierrepont B Mrs, 1968, Je 20,45:2
Noyes, Robert A, 1956, Ja 18,31:4
Noyes, Robert B, 1938, Ja 2,41:3
Noyes, Robert G, 1961, Mr 26,92:6
Noyes, S B, 1885, Mr 12,5:6
Noyes, Theodore W, 1946, Jl 5,19:3
Noyes, Thomas C, 1912, Ag 22,9:5
Noyes, W C, 1865, Ja 2,8:3
Noyes, Weller H, 1947, Jl 21,17:5
Noyes, William, 1953, Je 22,21:3; 1958, Ag 3,81:2
Noyes, William A (por), 1941, O 25,17:4
Noyes, William Curtis (funl, D 29,8:3), 1864, D 26, 5:3
Noyes, William Dr, 1915, O 21,11:5
Noyes, Winchester, 1954, Ap 4,88:1
Nozick, Gerald, 1949, Jl 14,27:1; 1949, Jl 16,13:3
Nubel, John F, 1947, S 16,23:4
Nuber, Albert C Jr, 1961, Mr 10,27:1
Nuberg, John B, 1951, Jl 31,21:2
Nuberg, John B Mrs, 1948, O 9,19:2
Nuccio, John Mrs, 1965, N 8,35:4
Nuckolls, Asa H, 1951, S 2,48:7
Nuckols, Claude C, 1939, Je 21,23:5
Nuckols, Henry W, 1959, Jl 17,21:4
Nuckols, Henry W Mrs (will), 1958, F 1,24:5
Nuckols, Marvin E, 1942, Jl 22,19:3
Nuckols, Samuel, 1942, F 6,21:7
Nuckols, Walter S Mrs, 1960, My 4,45:1
Nudant, Pierre, 1952, Ja 17,27:4
Nudd, Howard W, 1966, D 29,31:3
Nudelman, Charles W, 1960, Je 23,29:1
Nudelman, Mosze, 1967, Jl 26,39:1
Nuebling, Edward T, 1949, Ag 25,23:3
Nuebling, John G, 1951, Ag 20,19:6
Nuelle, Joseph H, 1964, Ap 11,25:6
Nuelsen, John L, 1946, Je 27,21:2
Nuese, Harry L, 1944, Ja 20,19:1
Nueske, Frederick W, 1947, Ja 31,23:2
Nuesseler, Charles T, 1940, My 2,23:1
Nufer, Albert F (funl plans, N 8,39:2; funl, N 14,35:2) 1956, N 6,35:1
Nuffer, Joseph H, 1968, N 14,47:3
Nuffield, Viscount (Wm R Morris),(will, O 3,71:5), 1963, Ag 22,27:1
Nuffort, F William, 1961, Ag 17,27:5
Nugent, Allen H, 1944, Je 25,30:1
Nugent, Arthur J, 1953, S 7,19:4
Nugent, Arthur W Mrs, 1947, Ap 9,25:3
Nugent, Byron, 1908, Ap 5,11:4
Nugent, Charles W, 1911, Jl 29,7:5
Nugent, Cornelius H Mrs, 1961, Ap 11,37:2
Nugent, Cornelius J, 1946, Ja 5,13:5
Nugent, Daniel F, 1968, D 10,77:5
Nugent, Edmund B Mrs, 1948, Ja 27,25:4
Nugent, Edmund M (death ruled accidental, F 20,-21:4), 1964, F 12,41:2
Nugent, Edward C (por), 1943, D 30,17:1
Nugent, Edward C, 1944, Ja 4,17:1
Nugent, Edward F Mrs, 1951, My 9,33:2
Nugent, Edward G Dr, 1937, My 10,19:5
Nugent, Edward J, 1947, O 10,25:3
Nugent, Edward L, 1946, Ag 28,27:4
Nugent, Edward P, 1948, D 20,25:4
Nugent, Edward R Jr Mrs, 1952, O 17,27:2
Nugent, Edward Sr, 1939, S 17,49:2
Nugent, Edward T, 1949, Jl 22,19:2
Nugent, Frank H, 1955, Je 4,15:4
Nugent, Frank S, 1965, D 31,21:2
Nugent, George A, 1958, Ja 6,39:2
Nugent, Hanna, 1903, Ja 4,2:3
Nugent, Harry B, 1966, My 19,47:4
Nugent, Homer H, 1945, My 29,15:3
Nugent, Horace Sir, 1924, My 6,21:5
Nugent, Howard M, 1959, D 16,41:2
Nugent, J C, 1947, Ap 22,27:1
Nugent, J F, 1931, S 19,17:3
Nugent, J R, 1927, Ap 27,25:3
Nugent, James, 1910, Je 30,7:4
Nugent, James A, 1946, D 25,29:1
Nugent, James B, 1948, D 14,29:2
Nugent, James C, 1938, O 31,15:3
Nugent, James E, 1942, My 13,19:5
Nugent, James F, 1950, Ja 10,29:2
Nugent, James J, 1946, N 21,31:3
Nugent, James T, 1949, O 26,27:2
Nugent, John, 1962, F 18,93:1
Nugent, John F, 1938, Je 13,19:4
Nugent, John F Mrs, 1945, Je 13,23:5
Nugent, John Mrs, 1943, Jl 25,31:1; 1951, F 22,31:4; 1955, My 16,23:6
Nugent, John P, 1944, O 3,23:3; 1945, O 6,13:5
Nugent, John Sr, 1944, Ja 19,19:2
Nugent, John W, 1951, Ag 25,11:2
Nugent, Joseph F, 1964, F 6,29:1
Nugent, Joseph R Mrs, 1953, Je 23,29:4
Nugent, Julian J, 1955, Je 2,29:4
Nugent, Martin P, 1958, Mr 27,33:1
Nugent, Maude (Mrs W Jerome), 1958, Je 4,31:1
Nugent, Maurice A, 1938, Ag 16,19:3
Nugent, Michael J, 1938, S 8,23:2
Nugent, Moya, 1954, Ja 27,27:2
Nugent, Oliver, 1938, Ag 13,13:5
Nugent, Paul L Mrs, 1959, S 19,23:5
Nugent, R H, 1903, Je 10,9:6
Nugent, Rob Gen, 1901, Je 21,7:6
Nugent, Robert G, 1953, Ja 16,24:3
Nugent, Robert L, 1963, Je 24,27:4
Nugent, Robert M, 1946, O 22,25:5
Nugent, Rolf, 1946, Jl 28,40:3
Nugent, Stephen A, 1923, N 1,21:4
Nugent, Thomas F, 1952, F 7,27:2
Nugent, Thomas J, 1955, N 10,35:4
Nugent, Thomas Mrs, 1948, Je 4,23:2
Nugent, William D, 1950, Jl 21,19:4
Nugent, William E, 1942, Je 30,21:6
Nuhn, Ferner Mrs (R Suckow), 1960, Ja 24,88:1
Nuland, Lester H, 1967, My 2,47:4
Null, Miriam E, 1956, Ag 14,25:4
Null, Samuel, 1949, D 11,91:1
Null, William T, 1950, N 12,93:2
Nulle, Augustus, 1948, Mr 2,24:3
Nulle, Richard (por), 1949, N 20,92:6
Nullet, Samuel G, 1957, Jl 17,27:3
Nulman, Samuel, 1966, Ap 13,43:1
Nulton, Louis M, 1954, N 12,21:2
Nulton, Nathaniel C, 1946, Ja 8,24:2
Nulty, Francis J, 1967, Ag 3,33:3
Nulty, James, 1950, S 12,28:5
Nulty, John F, 1954, Jl 31,13:4

Numan, Donald, 1951, My 8,63:3
Number, Albert C, 1955, D 23,17:1
Numbers, Charles Mrs, 1948, Ap 2,24:2
Nummey, Thomas A, 1950, Ja 24,31:2
Nummey, William J, 1925, O 7,27:5
Nun, A H (Al), 1952, Ja 19,15:4
Nunamaker, Blair E, 1944, Jl 1,15:2
Nunamaker, Leslie G, 1938, N 15,23:2
Nunan, Andrew L, 1953, D 9,11:4
Nunan, Dennis, 1912, D 23,9:4
Nunan, Joseph D Jr, 1968, F 23,33:3
Nunan, Marie, 1938, Je 13,19:2
Nunberg, Ralph M, 1949, Mr 27,76:5
Nunburnholme, Lord (Chas Hy Wilson), 1907, O 28, 9:5
Nunemaker, Guy E, 1946, Mr 31,46:2
Nunes, George P, 1956, Ag 25,15:2
Nunez, Emilio Gen, 1922, My 6,11:6
Nunez, Juan, 1943, Ja 10,48:2
Nunez Mesa, Delio, 1951, Ag 29,25:1
Nunez y Dominguez, Jose de J, 1959, Ap 1,37:2
Nungezer, Edwin, 1950, Jl 12,29:4
Nunley, Thomas, 1954, Ap 14,29:4
Nunley, William T, 1964, Jl 11,25:3
Nunley, William T Mrs, 1960, Mr 15,39:2
Nunn, Curtis P, 1959, S 19,23:6
Nunn, Frank, 1957, Ag 22,27:2
Nunn, Herman C, 1943, Je 7,13:4
Nunn, Joseph E, 1938, My 3,23:2
Nunn, Loftus J Mrs, 1944, Ag 31,17:3
Nunn, Marshall E, 1950, Je 4,92:4
Nunn, Shepard W, 1947, D 19,26:3
Nunn, Thomas H, 1937, Je 24,25:3
Nunn, William H, 1956, F 2,25:3
Nunnally, William J Jr, 1941, S 11,23:1
Nunnink, Leo A, 1947, Ja 27,23:5
Nunnis, Arthur L Mrs (will), 1959, My 6,22:6
Nuno, Christine M (por), 1946, F 12,25:3
Nunoi, Ryosuke, 1946, N 2,15:4
Nunziante, Ferdinando, 1941, F 27,19:2
Nunziato, Carlo, 1938, My 10,21:4
Nurczyk, Paulin, 1948, My 28,23:1
Nurkin, Louis, 1964, F 27,31:4
Nurkin, Sidney Mrs, 1954, Ag 21,17:3
Nurkse, Ragnar, 1959, My 7,33:1
Nurnberg, Charles, 1945, Je 29,15:2
Nurnberg, Joseph Mrs, 1952, Mr 17,21:2
Nurre, Joseph M, 1943, F 23,21:4
Nurse, Godfrey Dr, 1968, D 23,39:4
Nursi, Saidi, 1960, Mr 24,33:1
Nury de Restrepo, Echevania Mrs, 1939, O 12,14:6
Nusbaum, Daniel, 1950, Mr 8,25:1
Nusbaum, Harris, 1951, D 5,35:1
Nusbaum, Jacob (will), 1951, F 21,24:7
Nusbaum, Jacob, 1951, S 5,31:1
Nusbaum, Joseph H, 1952, Je 9,23:5
Nusbaum, Louis, 1954, O 22,27:2; 1955, N 14,27:4
Nusbaum, Maxwell O, 1949, D 6,32:3
Nusbaum, Morris, 1951, Mr 2,25:3
Nusbaum, Samuel L, 1940, S 14,17:6
Nuschke, Otto (funl, D 31,18:5), 1957, D 28,17:1
Nussa, Rafael L, 1943, Mr 5,17:4
Nussbaum, Abraham, 1913, D 5,11:6
Nussbaum, Adolph, 1954, Ap 5,25:3
Nussbaum, Arthur, 1964, N 23,37:2
Nussbaum, Berthold M, 1941, D 2,23:4
Nussbaum, E Phil, 1938, N 30,24:1
Nussbaum, Howard L, 1958, D 1,29:5
Nussbaum, Martin Mrs, 1962, Mr 4,86:7
Nussbaum, Sydney, 1961, O 5,37:2
Nussbaum, William, 1947, S 3,25:5
Nusse, William H Sr Mrs, 1955, F 26,15:5
Nussenfeld, Sidney R Mrs, 1956, Mr 2,49:5
Nussey, Herbert F, 1958, F 27,27:2
Nussman, George, 1947, O 3,25:4
Nute, Alfred, 1954, Ag 14,15:2
Nute, John W Mrs, 1954, N 8,21:5
Nute, Joseph E, 1949, S 16,27:4
Nute, William L Jr Mrs, 1968, Je 25,41:4
Nutley, Rose, 1949, O 20,29:2
Nutley, William B, 1953, S 12,17:5
Nutt, Commodore, 1881, My 26,8:3
Nutt, Cyrus Rev Dr, 1875, Ag 24,4:7
Nutt, George S, 1957, D 27,20:1
Nutt, Henry C, 1942, S 29,23:4
Nutt, Henry H, 1961, Ap 7,31:1
Nutt, John J (por), 1943, N 17,25:2
Nutt, John J Mrs, 1938, Ja 26,23:4
Nutt, Joseph H, 1948, F 1,60:5
Nutt, Joseph R (por), 1945, D 19,25:3
Nutt, Levi G, 1938, Ap 17,II,6:7
Nutt, Philip S, 1947, Ag 3,53:2
Nutt, Robert L, 1943, Ap 19,19:4
Nutt, Robert L Mrs, 1950, Ja 21,17:4
Nutt, W Lester, 1966, D 31,19:2
Nutt, Walter E Mrs, 1950, Jl 11,31:2
Nutt, Walter F, 1953, Mr 10,29:4
Nuttall, Dan E, 1942, N 15,58:2
Nuttall, Enos Rev Dr, 1916, Je 1,11:6
Nuttall, G H F Dr, 1937, D 17,25:4
Nuttall, Keith, 1941, S 2,17:4
Nuttall, Raymond P Rev, 1968, My 22,47:3
Nuttall, Walter, 1946, My 4,15:2
Nutter, Donald G (funl plans, Ja 28,12:4), 1962, Ja 26,1:4
Nutter, George R, 1937, F 22,17:2
Nutter, John E, 1943, Ap 30,21:3
Nutter, Joseph W, 1948, F 17,25:2
Nutter, Nelson C, 1946, Ja 7,19:1
Nutter, Ralph W, 1940, F 27,21:3
Nutter, Roy B, 1948, Ag 9,20:3
Nutter, Walter E, 1947, My 6,27:2
Nutter& Wm H, 1941, Mr 20,21:6
Nutting, Andrew Jackson, 1924, S 5,17:4
Nutting, Ernest S, 1950, Ja 3,25:4
Nutting, Floyd L, 1954, Ag 10,19:4
Nutting, John D, 1949, O 6,31:3
Nutting, Mary A (por), 1948, N 5,25:3
Nutting, Perley G, 1949, Ag 9,25:4
Nutting, Wallace, 1941, Jl 20,30:3
Nutting, Wallace A Mrs, 1944, S 1,13:3
Nuttle, Elbert R, 1939, Mr 17,21:3
Nutty, Gale R, 1939, Je 1,25:1
Nutze, Frank T, 1939, Ap 24,17:4
Nutzhorn, Carl W, 1958, Ap 15,34:1
Nuveen, John, 1948, N 16,29:6; 1968, Ag 9,35:4
Nuvius, Walter I, 1951, Mr 26,23:2
Nuvolari, Tazio, 1953, Ag 12,31:3
Nuyttens, Pierre, 1960, Ja 10,78:3
Nuzum, John W, 1953, Je 16,27:3
Nuzum, Will P, 1948, Ja 20,23:2
Nuzzetti, Pasquale, 1947, Ap 25,21:2
Nyary, Alec S, 1957, S 1,56:8
Nyberg, Charles A, 1949, Ap 24,76:1
Nybloc, Margaret (Mrs A B Smith), 1962, Ja 15,27:2
Nyburg, Simon Mrs, 1939, Ag 30,17:3
Nyce, George M, 1941, D 4,25:5
Nyce, William G, 1958, N 23,88:4
Nydegger, Paul F, 1952, Ag 15,16:4
Nydele, Victor T, 1955, S 1,23:5
Nydes, Jule, 1967, Mr 23,35:1
Nye, Archibald, 1967, N 15,47:3
Nye, Bernard B Mrs, 1949, My 24,27:2
Nye, Berthold H, 1943, N 21,57:2
Nye, Bertrand W, 1943, D 8,23:3
Nye, Bill Mrs, 1906, N 5,7:4
Nye, Carl M, 1952, Jl 29,21:2
Nye, Charles G, 1948, F 18,27:2
Nye, Clement D, 1963, Ag 31,17:5
Nye, E G, 1881, Ja 9,12:2
Nye, Ezra Capt, 1866, Ap 22,3:5
Nye, Frank E Col, 1905, O 8,9:6
Nye, Frank W, 1963, Jl 8,29:2
Nye, Gertrude H, 1940, Ja 1,23:2
Nye, Gordon, 1950, Mr 29,29:3
Nye, Howard H, 1947, D 30,24:2
Nye, Isaac, 1871, My 1,2:7
Nye, J W, 1876, D 28,4:6
Nye, James Warren, 1925, F 5,19:4
Nye, John Capt, 1871, Jl 8,8:4
Nye, Joseph M, 1948, My 18,23:3
Nye, Loyal S, 1913, Ja 13,11:4
Nye, Olin S, 1967, D 11,47:4
Nye, Phila C Mrs, 1959, My 14,33:4
Nye, Richard S Mrs, 1965, S 5,57:1
Nye, Robert N, 1947, S 11,27:5
Nye, Sylvanus B, 1941, O 19,44:1
Nye, Thomas M, 1948, Mr 9,23:3
Nyegaard, Edward A, 1963, Ja 28,9:8
Nygaard, Hjalmar, 1963, Jl 19,25:4
Nygaardsvold, Johann, 1952, Mr 14,23:2
Nygren, Alfred M, 1954, S 15,33:5
Nygren, John H, 1949, Jl 5,23:3
Nyhen, E MacDonald Mrs, 1964, Je 20,25:1
Nyhoff, Henry E, 1956, Ap 4,29:2
Nyhoff, John J, 1939, N 19,39:3
Nyhus, Paul Mrs, 1938, D 22,21:5
Nyikos, Michael J, 1947, Je 5,25:4
Nyka, Leon C, 1957, Je 21,25:1
Nyland, Anne C H, 1921, Ja 6,11:3
Nylander, Elise, 1949, N 10,32:2
Nylander, Lennart K, 1966, Jl 16,25:4
Nylander, Lennart Mrs, 1967, F 13,33:3
Nylander, Olaf O, 1943, Jl 30,15:5
Nylin, Gustav, 1961, Ag 10,27:1
Nylin, Josef B, 1945, Je 26,19:3
Nyman, George, 1940, Je 17,15:4
Nyman, Richmond C, 1951, Je 28,25:5
Nymeyer, Fred H, 1944, N 29,23:5
Nyri-Szabo, Nicholas, 1957, Ap 23,31:4
Nys, Odilo A, 1942, D 30,23:5
Nyse, William H, 1907, Ag 22,7:5
Nyson, Benedict W, 1942, Ja 3,19:3
Nystad, Josef H, 1948, Ap 17,15:2
Nystrom, Albert J, 1956, D 25,25:5
Nystrom, Andrew G, 1953, My 13,29:2
Nystrom, Charles G, 1950, O 7,19:3
Nyswander, Reuben E, 1941, Ap 10,23:4
Nyvall, David, 1946, F 8,19:3

O

Oak, Calvin, 1952, D 10,35:2
Oak, David E, 1943, Ag 6,15:2
Oake, George Mrs, 1947, S 12,21:3
Oakeley, F Canon, 1880, Ja 31,2:6
Oakes, Alec E, 1962, Ap 21,19:1
Oakes, Alfred E, 1938, D 22,21:5
Oakes, Augustin F, 1940, O 19,17:5
Oakes, Carl C Mrs, 1955, Mr 20,88:4
Oakes, Chester A, 1943, N 30,27:3
Oakes, Clarissa S, 1955, Mr 13,87:1
Oakes, David, 1947, Jl 11,15:3
Oakes, Elbert, 1968, Ja 16,39:2
Oakes, Elizabeth B, 1941, Je 13,19:5
Oakes, Francis J, 1919, D 23,9:2
Oakes, Frank C, 1947, Jl 6,40:3
Oakes, Frederick W Mrs, 1941, N 2,53:2
Oakes, G W O, 1931, O 27,25:3
Oakes, George A, 1949, S 23,24:2
Oakes, George F, 1956, Jl 13,19:2
Oakes, George W (funl plans, Ja 7,31:4), 1965, Ja 6, 27:1
Oakes, George W Mrs, 1965, Ja 6,27:1
Oakes, James, 1965, Ja 6,27:1
Oakes, James Gen, 1910, N 28,9:5
Oakes, James H, 1961, Jl 22,21:6
Oakes, James L Jr, 1959, O 18,86:1
Oakes, Jeanne S Mrs, 1942, D 13,60:5
Oakes, John C, 1950, N 12,94:3
Oakes, Josiah, 1873, D 4,8:5
Oakes, Louis, 1964, N 7,27:4
Oakes, Mervin E Dr, 1968, F 21,47:4
Oakes, Myrtice, 1957, O 26,25:2
Oakes, Russell E, 1961, Jl 19,29:2
Oakes, Sydney, 1966, Ag 9,37:3
Oakes, Thomas, 1924, Je 14,11:6
Oakes, Thomas Fletcher, 1919, Mr 15,15:4
Oakes, Walter Mrs, 1948, Ap 8,25:1
Oakes, Warren D, 1952, N 16,88:8
Oakes, Warren Mrs, 1958, Je 7,19:4
Oakes, William P, 1958, Ap 28,23:2
Oakey, Francis, 1950, D 7,33:1
Oakey, John M, 1954, O 7,23:6
Oakey, P Davis, 1920, N 19,15:4
Oakford, Charles W, 1956, Ap 27,28:1
Oakhill, Frederic, 1953, Ja 28,27:6
Oakland, Henry M, 1955, Mr 2,27:2
Oakland, Will, 1956, My 16,35:2
Oakley, A, 1926, N 5,21:3
Oakley, Alonzo G (will, Ap 24,10:7), 1948, Ap 9,24:2
Oakley, C Arthur, 1966, Mr 19,29:5
Oakley, C Arthur Mrs, 1951, My 26,17:6
Oakley, Charles, 1884, O 10,2:4
Oakley, Charles R, 1940, My 27,19:4
Oakley, Charles S, 1954, O 30,17:4
Oakley, Charles S Mrs, 1950, Mr 5,92:6
Oakley, Clarence A, 1946, N 2,15:2
Oakley, Clifford B, 1948, S 2,23:2
Oakley, Ferris D, 1948, Ja 14,25:2
Oakley, Frank E, 1949, Jl 22,19:3
Oakley, Fred, 1949, Mr 1,25:4
Oakley, George, 1947, F 10,29:1
Oakley, George A, 1944, Ag 3,19:4
Oakley, George C, 1956, Jl 26,25:4
Oakley, Gilbert, 1939, Ap 30,45:4
Oakley, Grace C Mrs, 1956, Ap 28,17:4
Oakley, H Ward, 1941, N 30,68:5
Oakley, H Wayne, 1965, S 10,35:4
Oakley, Harold, 1951, Ap 26,29:1
Oakley, Henry Cruger, 1906, My 26,11:6
Oakley, Henry W Mrs, 1955, Ag 23,23:3
Oakley, James W, 1954, Ag 12,25:4
Oakley, John, 1960, Ja 23,21:1
Oakley, John A, 1937, F 21,II,10:5
Oakley, John Greenleaf Rev Dr, 1922, Ag 24,15:5
Oakley, John T (funl, Mr 4,13:4), 1913, F 28,13:5
Oakley, John T, 1960, Ap 2,23:6
Oakley, John T Mrs, 1905, Mr 7,9:6
Oakley, Kenneth, 1940, F 20,15:6
Oakley, Lauretta I, 1945, O 1,19:2
Oakley, M C, 1940, N 6,23:5
Oakley, Norman F, 1955, N 6,87:1
Oakley, Owen H Mrs, 1954, Ag 27,21:2
Oakley, Owen Horace Lt-Com, 1916, Ja 17,11:4
Oakley, R Lawrence, 1963, Ap 9,31:3
Oakley, Ralph, 1907, My 14,11:4
Oakley, Ray M, 1948, My 13,26:3
Oakley, Raymond E, 1950, Ja 19,28:2
Oakley, Robert S, 1949, Ag 31,23:4
Oakley, Thomas B, 1959, Mr 14,23:6
Oakley, Thomas P, 1943, Ja 12,24:3
Oakley, Thomas R, 1949, Jl 7,25:4
Oakley, Thornton, 1953, Ap 5,76:3
Oakley, Violet, 1961, F 26,93:1
Oakley, W M, 1871, Jl 17,8:6
Oakley, Walton L, 1964, F 15,23:5
Oakley, Wiley, 1954, N 20,17:5
Oakman, Edward C, 1947, S 3,25:5
Oakman, John, 1963, D 23,25:1
Oakman, John Mrs, 1948, Ja 31,19:3
Oakman, Robert, 1942, O 4,52:5
Oakman, Thomas Campbell, 1909, F 14,11:5
Oakman, Walter G, 1922, Mr 19,28:3
Oakman, Wheeler, 1949, Mr 20,76:3
Oaks, Fred L, 1938, Je 6,17:4
Oaks, Orion O, 1960, Mr 17,33:4
Oaks, Wesley L Mrs, 1958, Je 5,31:3
Oaks, Wilbur W, 1950, D 21,29:1
Oakwood, John W, 1947, F 7,23:4
Oasa, Tadao, 1957, F 21,27:4
Oast, Samuel P Jr, 1942, O 17,15:5
Oastler, Frank R (will), 1938, S 30,21:1
Oastler, Frank R Mrs, 1962, F 26,27:4
Oastler, James, 1962, Ag 15,31:1
Oastler, William C, 1914, Mr 31,11:2
Oat, William H, 1947, O 19,64:2
Oaten, Charles R, 1942, O 5,19:5
Oates, Alfred B Rev, 1937, D 3,23:5
Oates, Caroline Mrs, 1937, D 1,23:6
Oates, Frank, 1875, Je 7,5:2
Oates, James A (funl), 1871, Jl 17,8:5
Oates, James F, 1954, D 5,88:6
Oates, John D Mrs, 1945, S 26,23:4
Oates, Peter J, 1942, Ag 14,17:3
Oates, Theodore K, 1951, F 6,27:4
Oates, William Calvin Gen, 1910, S 10,9:6
Oathout, Mary Mrs, 1951, F 19,23:1
Oathout, William J, 1948, Jl 1,23:2
Oatis, J H, 1938, N 12,8:6
Oatley, Donald B, 1961, Ag 8,29:2
Oatley, Henry B, 1962, D 4,41:3
Oatley, Henry B Mrs, 1942, S 29,23:5
Oatman, Edward L Dr, 1912, D 27,9:5
Oatman, Frederic, 1960, F 7,84:1
Oatman, Frederic A, 1954, Ag 12,25:5
Oatman, Harold F, 1938, F 27,13:1
Oatman, J S, 1876, O 8,6:7
Oatman, Joseph, 1948, Je 9,29:3
Oatman, Lewis R Mrs, 1953, F 24,25:6
Oatman, Louis M, 1958, Ap 19,21:4
Oatman, William F Mrs, 1948, S 14,29:2
Obach, Philip, 1944, Ap 28,19:4
Obaldia, Jose Domino de, 1910, Mr 2,9:3
O'Bannon, Hanna S Mrs, 1942, Je 4,19:4
O'Banyoun, Simon E, 1957, Ap 10,33:3
Obbink, Herman T, 1947, D 31,15:2
Obdyke, George, 1941, My 21,23:3
Obdyke, William A, 1948, Ag 31,24:3
Obeck, John A, 1952, F 3,84:4
Obedin, Nathan, 1964, Je 12,35:2
O'Beirne, Edward J, 1940, Jl 30,19:3
O'Beirne, James Rowan Brig-Gen (funl, F 19,11:4), 1917, F 18,17:3
O'Beirne, Owen, 1956, Jl 15,61:2
O'Beirne, Patrick J Mrs, 1946, Je 9,40:3
O'Beirne, R D, 1905, Mr 24,9:6
O'Beirne, Richard Mrs, 1938, F 25,17:5
O'Beirne, Thomas, 1905, My 7,3:3
O'Beirne, William H, 1949, S 14,31:3
Obenchain, Ralph R, 1939, S 21,23:5
Obenchain, William A Maj, 1916, Ag 18,9:4
Obendorfer, Marx, 1962, O 7,83:1
Obenhuber, Phil, 1939, F 5,41:3
Ober, Beverly, 1955, Ap 9,13:5
Ober, Byron, 1961, Jl 1,17:5
Ober, Charles K (por), 1948, Jl 15,23:1
Ober, Emil H, 1961, Jl 18,29:5
Ober, Frank R, 1960, D 28,27:4
Ober, Frank S Mrs, 1952, Ap 9,31:5
Ober, Frank W, 1949, F 2,27:5
Ober, Frank W Mrs, 1947, Je 25,25:4
Ober, Frederick Albion, 1913, Je 2,7:5
Ober, George, 1912, N 18,11:4
Ober, George Mrs, 1922, F 9,17:4
Ober, Harold, 1959, N 1,85:6
Ober, Harrie L, 1940, Ja 9,23:2
Ober, Joseph, 1946, Ag 18,44:5
Ober, Robert, 1912, S 2,9:6; 1950, D 8,30:2
Oberdorf, Winfield S, 1948, Je 13,68:3
Oberdorfer, Archie L, 1945, Mr 13,23:3
Oberdorfer, J P Dr, 1907, D 2,9:4
Oberdorfer, Max, 1952, Jl 27,56:3
Oberfelder, Arthur M, 1954, Ja 31,88:4
Oberfelder, Irving M, 1937, Je 3,25:6
Oberfelder, Simon, 1925, Mr 19,21:3
Oberg, Charles F, 1940, S 15,48:2
Oberg, Erik, 1951, O 24,25:3
Oberg, George W, 1917, D 17,13:4
Oberg, John, 1940, D 12,27:2
Oberg, John L, 1906, N 10,9:4
Obergfell, Herbert, 1943, D 30,18:3
Obergfell, Joseph, 1945, N 4,44:3
Oberhardt, William, 1958, Jl 23,27:2
Oberhoffer, E, 1933, My 23,19:1
Oberholser, Harry C, 1963, D 26,28:4
Oberholtzer, E E, 1954, Je 19,15:7
Oberholtzer, Horace M, 1944, Ja 10,17:3
Oberholtzer, John C, 1949, Je 3,25:3
Oberholzer, Emil, 1958, My 5,29:4
Oberholzer, Mira M, 1949, D 13,38:4
Oberhummer, Eugen, 1944, O 12,27:4
Oberkircher, Edward C, 1952, F 21,27:4
Oberkircher, Jacob, 1939, Ag 13,29:3
Oberlaender, Alice Mrs, 1939, F 2,19:2
Oberlaender, Ernest J, 1967, Ap 13,43:2
Oberlaender, G, 1936, D 1,25:1
Oberlander, Alex E, 1942, My 7,19:4
Oberlander, Andrew James (Swede), 1968, Ja 3,40:
Oberlander, Fridolin E, 1938, Ja 24,23:3
Oberlander, Fridolin E Rev Dr, 1937, D 6,27:4
Oberlander, George J, 1954, D 18,15:3
Oberle, Florence Mrs, 1943, Jl 11,34:7
Oberleder, William, 1925, Ap 10,19:2
Oberlies, Herbert H, 1960, F 12,28:1
Oberlin, A Frederick, 1938, Jl 12,19:4
Oberlin, A J, 1921, My 16,15:3
Oberling, Charles, 1960, Mr 13,85:4
Oberly, H Sherman, 1967, Mr 26,68:6
Oberly, Henry Harrison Rev Dr, 1914, Mr 20,11:4
Oberly, John, 1951, F 20,25:3
Oberman, Philip, 1966, Ap 16,33:3
Oberman, Samuel, 1961, Ja 9,39:4
Obermann, Julian J, 1956, O 18,33:1
Obermayer, Charles J, 1925, D 25,17:4
Obermayer, Frederik, 1951, Je 29,21:6
Obermayer, W, 1934, N 27,21:3
Obermeier, Leonard J, 1963, Ag 14,33:3
Obermeier, Mich J, 1960, My 21,23:5
Obermeyer, David H, 1953, Je 23,29:4
Obermeyer, Ernest, 1937, F 19,19:6
Obermeyer, George, 1903, Ja 31,8:2
Obermeyer, Joseph, 1943, Ja 18,19:2
Obermyer, John B, 1907, D 1,11:6
Oberndorf, Clarence P, 1954, My 31,13:3
Oberndorf, Ludwig, 1966, F 25,31:5
Oberndorfer, Ira H, 1961, F 4,19:5
Obernier, Frank, 1939, Je 28,21:6
O'Berry, Audrey, 1939, Jl 1,17:6
Oberski, John, 1952, Je 13,23:4
Oberson, Samuel Mrs, 1940, O 26,15:5
Oberst, Andrew, 1942, O 20,21:2
Oberst, Bonaventure, 1948, N 17,27:5
Oberstein, Eli E, 1960, Je 14,37:4
Obert, Gustavus Jr, 1946, N 11,27:2
Obert, Laura D, 1944, My 31,19:2
Obert, Willie, 1948, Ap 2,23:4
Oberteuffer, George, 1940, My 14,24:2
Oberteuffer, George Mrs, 1962, N 5,31:5
Obertubbesing, Herman, 1947, My 29,21:2
Oberwager, Charles A (por), 1945, Jl 18,27:2
Oberwager, Edwin R Mrs, 1948, S 5,40:5
Oberwager, John, 1960, Ja 3,88:2
Oberwarth, Leo L, 1939, My 25,26:3
Obester, Gabriel E, 1962, S 18,39:2
Obey, J Edward, 1964, Jl 3,21:3
Obici, Amedeo (will, My 28,19:6), 1947, My 22,27
Obici, Amedeo Mrs, 1938, Ag 31,15:4
O'Bierne, Richard J, 1940, O 2,23:4
Oblatt, Rudolph, 1939, O 4,25:5
Obletz, Samuel Mrs, 1952, F 2,13:4
Oblinger, Daniel B, 1945, O 23,17:6
Oblinski, Valentine, 1952, Ag 24,89:2
Obolensky, Alexis A (por),(funl plans, Ag 19,19:3), 1942, Ag 18,21:3
Obolensky, Lydia Princess, 1963, Jl 4,17:1
Obolensky, Serge Prince, 1960, D 6,41:2
Oboukhoff, Anatole, 1962, F 26,27:2
O'Boyle, Edmund J, 1960, N 12,21:2
O'Boyle, Francis E, 1950, My 26,23:6
O'Boyle, Frank H Sr, 1947, S 5,19:2
O'Boyle, Patricia, 1945, N 2,12:3
O'Boyle, Peter A Mrs, 1949, N 17,29:2
O'Boyle, Robert E Mrs, 1937, S 2,21:2
Obradovich, Milan, 1955, O 30,88:6
Obraztsov, Vladimir B, 1949, N 30,27:1
Obre, Arthur L, 1951, Jl 17,27:4
Obrecht, E M, 1935, Ja 5,17:4
Obrecht, Herman, 1940, Ag 22,19:4
Obregon, Alfonso, 1922, My 17,19:4
Obregon, Carmen Mrs, 1923, Je 27,19:4
Obregon, Luis G, 1938, Je 20,15:3
Obregon, Manuel Gen, 1922, S 30,13:5
O'Brein, James J, 1944, Ja 31,17:5
O'Brein, John A, 1940, S 15,48:3
O'Brein, Joseph W, 1943, Je 26,13:3
O'Brein, Patrick M, 1944, Je 1,19:2
O'Brein, Thomas E, 1944, Mr 7,17:4
O'Brein, Timothy W, 1944, Ag 10,17:3
O'Brein, William J, 1947, F 6,23:5
Obreshkove, Vasil, 1950, Jl 16,68:5
O'Briain, Art P, 1949, Ag 13,11:4
O'Brian, Dennis Mrs, 1951, Ag 5,73:1
O'Brian, George R, 1949, Jl 28,23:2
O'Brian, L Etienne, 1961, O 24,37:3
O'Brian, Lewis Atwell Dr, 1918, Je 5,11:2
O'Brian, Thomas F, 1943, Ap 16,22:2

O'Brian, William J, 1946, S 15,9:8
O'Brien, Aileen Mrs, 1955, Ap 14,29:3
O'Brien, Albert C Rev, 1937, Jl 13,20:1
O'Brien, Alfred A, 1939, Jl 16,17:1
O'Brien, Alfred J, 1961, D 24,37:1
O'Brien, Alfred S, 1951, Ja 30,25:6
O'Brien, Anna Mrs, 1908, Ap 11,7:4
O'Brien, Anne C, 1940, Ap 13,17:5
O'Brien, Arthur J, 1953, Jl 8,27:4
O'Brien, Arthur R, 1947, Ja 8,23:4
O'Brien, Arthur S, 1949, Je 24,23:4
O'Brien, Aubrey M, 1959, Je 29,29:2
O'Brien, Baron, 1914, S 10,9:5
O'Brien, Branch, 1922, Ap 13,19:6
O'Brien, Brian Mrs, 1954, F 3,23:4
O'Brien, Bridget, 1952, Je 8,39:1
O'Brien, Bruce, 1954, Ap 5,25:2
O'Brien, Charles, 1950, S 4,17:6
O'Brien, Charles E, 1914, Ag 30,15:6
O'Brien, Charles F Mrs, 1944, S 16,13:4
O'Brien, Charles F X (por), 1940, N 15,21:3
O'Brien, Charles L, 1939, Ap 30,45:1
O'Brien, Charles S, 1958, Ja 30,23:4
O'Brien, Charles V, 1941, Je 19,21:4
O'Brien, Chester L Mrs (S Moriya), 1961, Mr 13,29:4
O'Brien, Conon, 1964, Ja 15,31:4
O'Brien, Cornelius, 1941, N 27,23:3; 1953, Jl 18,13:6
O'Brien, Cornelius C Sr, 1955, O 7,25:1
O'Brien, Cornelius J (Neil), 1954, Ja 14,29:5
O'Brien, Cornelius J, 1962, F 12,23:1
O'Brien, D P, 1938, Ag 8,13:4; 1954, N 8,21:5
O'Brien, Daniel, 1945, N 23,23:4
O'Brien, Daniel E, 1943, D 24,13:4
O'Brien, Daniel J, 1965, N 6,29:4
O'Brien, Daniel P, 1958, Ag 20,27:2
O'Brien, Daniel W, 1944, Ja 27,19:5
O'Brien, David H, 1965, Mr 17,45:1
O'Brien, Denis Ex-Judge, 1909, My 19,9:5
O'Brien, Denis F, 1945, F 1,23:3
O'Brien, Dennis, 1938, S 12,17:3; 1941, O 7,23:4
O'Brien, Dennis F, 1946, O 3,27:3
O'Brien, Dennis F Mrs, 1937, Ja 12,24:1
O'Brien, Dennis F X, 1950, Ag 1,23:3
O'Brien, Dennis Mrs, 1953, F 16,21:1
O'Brien, Donough Edward Foster (Baron of Inchiquin), 1968, O 20,86:3
O'Brien, Duncan Mrs (Harriet), 1968, Je 3,41:4
O'Brien, Duncan T, 1938, S 14,23:5
O'Brien, Duncan T Mrs, 1961, Jl 2,32:6
O'Brien, E Vincent, 1967, Ag 22,39:1
O'Brien, Earle P, 1944, D 18,19:5
O'Brien, Edna V, 1959, Mr 21,12:2
O'Brien, Edward, 1940, Je 26,23:2; 1947, O 2,27:3
O'Brien, Edward A Mrs, 1944, Jl 8,11:6
O'Brien, Edward C, 1952, Ap 20,92:5
O'Brien, Edward E, 1949, Ja 14,23:1
O'Brien, Edward F, 1945, Ja 20,11:4; 1946, Je 5,23:1
O'Brien, Edward F Mrs, 1953, Ja 7,31:5
O'Brien, Edward J, 1939, Jl 27,19:4; 1941, F 26,21:2; 1941, Mr 7,19:6; 1948, F 16,21:4; 1951, Ja 16,29:5; 1955, Ja 9,86:7; 1966, Ag 1,27:5
O'Brien, Edward N, 1943, N 27,13:4
O'Brien, Edward R, 1955, S 30,25:2
O'Brien, Edward T, 1957, Ag 30,19:1
O'Brien, Edward V, 1959, Jl 16,27:3; 1964, Jl 21,33:4
O'Brien, Edward W, 1943, Ap 14,23:5
O'Brien, Edward W Mrs, 1944, O 22,46:3
O'Brien, Edwin J, 1952, Ja 22,29:4
O'Brien, Eliza, 1882, F 27,8:5
O'Brien, Elizabeth T Mrs, 1925, Ag 22,11:6
O'Brien, Ellen, 1952, My 25,92:5
O'Brien, Ernest A, 1948, O 10,78:1
O'Brien, Esmond P, 1960, My 14,23:5
O'Brien, Esmonde M, 1966, O 1,31:3
O'Brien, Eugene, 1966, My 1,89:1
O'Brien, Eugene G, 1947, Jl 16,23:4
O'Brien, Eugene H, 1941, F 13,19:3
O'Brien, Eugene J, 1957, F 26,29:5
O'Brien, Fitzpatrick C, 1942, O 11,56:3
O'Brien, Flann (B O'Nolan), 1966, Ap 2,29:1
O'Brien, Francis D, 1956, Jl 9,23:3
O'Brien, Francis E, 1952, F 16,13:5
O'Brien, Francis J, 1946, D 8,77:3
O'Brien, Francis R, 1944, N 29,23:5
O'Brien, Francis W, 1949, Ja 25,23:1; 1958, F 23,93:1
O'Brien, Francis W Mrs, 1948, N 19,28:3
O'Brien, Frank, 1960, Ja 20,31:2
O'Brien, Frank A, 1944, Ap 18,21:2
O'Brien, Frank C, 1953, N 25,23:5
O'Brien, Frank E, 1956, N 11,87:2
O'Brien, Frank J, 1956, F 13,27:5; 1956, Mr 14,33:1; 1958, My 19,25:4; 1964, Je 20,25:2
O'Brien, Frank M (por), 1943, S 23,21:1
O'Brien, Frederick W, 1965, D 22,31:1
O'Brien, Gene D Mrs, 1941, Ap 6,48:5
O'Brien, George, 1951, Ja 10,27:2
O'Brien, George A, 1937, Mr 17,25:5
O'Brien, George C, 1965, My 15,31:2
O'Brien, George D, 1954, Je 18,48:1; 1957, O 26,21:2
O'Brien, George E, 1957, Jl 11,25:2
O'Brien, George F, 1956, Jl 11,29:4
O'Brien, Gerald F, 1959, S 20,87:1
O'Brien, Gerald R, 1960, D 1,35:5
O'Brien, Gladys Mrs, 1958, Ag 29,23:3
O'Brien, Greg, 1954, F 17,31:2
O'Brien, Guy E, 1967, Je 13,47:2
O'Brien, Harold I, 1957, D 30,23:2
O'Brien, Harold S, 1958, Ap 30,33:3
O'Brien, Harriett H Mrs, 1937, Ag 23,19:5
O'Brien, Harry, 1944, O 4,19:1
O'Brien, Harry F, 1941, D 12,26:2; 1961, Jl 20,27:4
O'Brien, Harry J, 1964, Ap 25,29:5
O'Brien, Helen D, 1952, O 6,25:5
O'Brien, Henry L Jr, 1949, Ag 30,27:1
O'Brien, Henry Stanton, 1912, Ag 5,9:6
O'Brien, Herbert A, 1966, Mr 17,43:4
O'Brien, Herbert A Mrs, 1966, Jl 15,31:3
O'Brien, Herbert R, 1957, Jl 26,19:1
O'Brien, Howard, 1952, Jl 29,21:3
O'Brien, Howard V, 1947, O 1,29:5
O'Brien, Hugh, 1875, My 14,6:6
O'Brien, Hugh J, 1943, D 30,17:1
O'Brien, Hugh M, 1960, My 11,39:3
O'Brien, Isadore, 1953, O 29,31:2
O'Brien, J C, 1902, Ja 7,7:5
O'Brien, J Charles, 1945, Ap 18,23:2
O'Brien, J Edmund, 1953, Ja 25,86:4
O'Brien, J G, 1931, N 20,23:3
O'Brien, J J, 1890, Ap 28,1:3
O'Brien, J Jay (por), 1940, Ap 6,17:3
O'Brien, J M, 1950, Ja 18,32:3
O'Brien, J Robert, 1965, My 29,27:5
O'Brien, J Vincent, 1937, Ap 15,23:3
O'Brien, J William, 1946, O 1,23:4
O'Brien, Jack, 1938, D 7,23:1
O'Brien, Jack (F J Hagan), 1942, N 12,23:1
O'Brien, Jack, 1954, D 27,17:3
O'Brien, Jack Mrs (L Lorraine), 1955, Ap 21,29:2
O'Brien, James, 1907, Mr 6,9:5; 1943, Ap 20,24:2; 1945, O 9,21:3; 1947, S 29,21:5; 1949, S 2,17:5
O'Brien, James A, 1951, Ja 2,23:3
O'Brien, James B, 1945, O 21,46:1
O'Brien, James C, 1949, F 2,27:3; 1952, D 5,27:3
O'Brien, James E, 1950, Mr 3,25:1
O'Brien, James F, 1940, O 14,19:3
O'Brien, James F Mrs, 1937, Jl 27,21:3
O'Brien, James H, 1924, S 4,19:5; 1944, Mr 25,15:5
O'Brien, James J, 1907, Mr 9,9:5; 1940, Ap 20,17:5; 1940, N 24,51:1; 1943, My 13,21:4; 1943, D 29,17:2; 1945, Mr 6,21:2; 1947, Ja 2,27:1; 1950, Jl 30,61:2
O'Brien, James J (mem mass set, Je 26,47:5), 1968, Je 4,44:1
O'Brien, James M, 1963, D 18,41:2
O'Brien, James P, 1963, N 7,34:2
O'Brien, James P Msgr, 1937, My 30,18:7
O'Brien, Jay J, 1960, N 29,37:2
O'Brien, Jay J Mrs, 1965, Ja 13,25:5
O'Brien, Jeremiah J, 1951, O 12,27:2
O'Brien, Jeremiah M, 1960, D 23,19:3
O'Brien, Joachim Rev, 1925, D 24,13:6
O'Brien, John (funl), 1871, Ap 10,1:2
O'Brien, John, 1881, O 30,9:3; 1906, N 19,3:7; 1950, Jl 22,15:5; 1951, Ja 10,27:3; 1952, Ja 15,27:4
O'Brien, John (funl, F 16,25:4), 1954, F 12,25:1
O'Brien, John, 1955, F 19,15:3
O'Brien, John A, 1943, Ag 29,38:5; 1948, Je 8,25:4; 1951, N 27,31:4; 1963, N 23,29:3
O'Brien, John B, 1967, Mr 15,47:1
O'Brien, John C, 1967, Ap 11,41:2
O'Brien, John Capt (Dynamite Johnny), 1917, Je 22, 13:3
O'Brien, John D, 1943, S 18,17:3; 1952, Jl 18,19:2
O'Brien, John F, 1938, S 20,23:4; 1939, D 18,23:4
O'Brien, John F (por), 1939, D 26,19:1
O'Brien, John H, 1941, F 5,19:1; 1945, Ja 6,11:1; 1949, F 18,23:1
O'Brien, John H S Dr, 1937, Ja 10,II,10:5
O'Brien, John J, 1937, N 6,17:5; 1938, O 19,23:5; 1941, N 25,25:6; 1942, Ja 22,18:3; 1942, Je 12,21:1; 1948, N 21,88:3; 1949, Ja 24,19:5; 1949, Jl 9,13:1; 1950, Ja 5,25:2; 1950, Jl 14,21:5; 1951, My 17,31:2; 1953, Ja 9,21:1; 1955, Jl 28,23:4; 1965, Mr 2,35:4; 1966, My 31,43:3; 1967, D 11,47:4
O'Brien, John J E, 1951, S 26,31:3
O'Brien, John J Mrs, 1953, S 5,15:2; 1967, S 13,47:4
O'Brien, John J P, 1950, O 15,104:5
O'Brien, John L, 1949, My 5,27:5
O'Brien, John M, 1964, D 13,86:3
O'Brien, John Msgr, 1917, Jl 20,9:6
O'Brien, John P, 1943, Ap 4,41:1; 1945, Ag 1,19:5; 1951, Je 9,19:5; 1951, S 23,1:4; 1951, D 17,31:3; 1956, Jl 2,21:3
O'Brien, John P Dr, 1937, Jl 23,19:3
O'Brien, John P Mrs, 1950, Jl 14,21:4
O'Brien, John R, 1962, My 15,39:4
O'Brien, John T, 1967, Ap 1,31:3
O'Brien, John T Mrs, 1946, Ap 8,27:2
O'Brien, John T Rev, 1968, Ap 16,44:1
O'Brien, John W, 1939, Ja 8,42:6; 1941, S 5,21:4; 1955, Je 12,87:1
O'Brien, Joseph, 1945, Mr 30,15:3; 1949, N 3,29:3; 1953, Je 25,27:5; 1957, O 8,35:1
O'Brien, Joseph A, 1942, Ag 2,38:8
O'Brien, Joseph A Mrs, 1941, N 2,53:2
O'Brien, Joseph F, 1941, Ap 23,21:5; 1958, F 16,85:1; 1960, My 6,31:2; 1967, Mr 28,39:4
O'Brien, Joseph H, 1947, S 1,19:1
O'Brien, Joseph H Mrs, 1947, F 14,22:2
O'Brien, Joseph I, 1946, F 13,23:4
O'Brien, Joseph J, 1948, F 9,17:1; 1951, Mr 4,92:6; 1953, Ja 25,85:1
O'Brien, Joseph L, 1952, Mr 4,27:2
O'Brien, Joseph P, 1946, Jl 30,23:2
O'Brien, Joseph S, 1948, F 2,19:5
O'Brien, Joseph T, 1947, D 11,33:2; 1953, Ag 18,23:1
O'Brien, Joseph V, 1949, Ag 9,25:4
O'Brien, Joseph X, 1965, Je 19,29:4
O'Brien, Josephine, 1937, N 19,23:2
O'Brien, Julia A, 1945, Jl 13,11:5
O'Brien, Julia Mrs, 1908, N 7,7:3
O'Brien, Justin C, 1957, Je 14,25:3
O'Brien, Justin Prof, 1968, D 8,86:4
O'Brien, Justus R, 1945, Ag 11,13:3
O'Brien, Kate W, 1938, Ap 7,23:4
O'Brien, Katherine E, 1949, Je 21,25:5
O'Brien, Kennedy, 1940, Ap 8,19:6
O'Brien, Kenneth (funl, Ja 24,84:4; mem ser, Ja 26,-27:2), 1954, Ja 21,31:1
O'Brien, L Frank, 1957, Ap 29,25:5
O'Brien, Leo F, 1942, O 26,15:3
O'Brien, Lewis Ogden, 1908, D 22,9:6
O'Brien, Lewis P, 1945, D 21,21:1
O'Brien, M Hubert, 1943, Mr 12,17:1
O'Brien, Madeline Sister, 1911, Jl 10,7:5
O'Brien, Mae Mrs, 1937, My 2,II,8:8
O'Brien, Margarita, 1954, Ag 31,21:3
O'Brien, Marie S Mrs, 1940, S 24,23:4
O'Brien, Mark J, 1910, F 15,9:5
O'Brien, Martin, 1911, Jl 30,9:5
O'Brien, Martin J, 1940, Jl 7,2:5; 1950, N 27,25:1; 1955, Jl 9,15:2
O'Brien, Martin V, 1947, Ja 7,27:3
O'Brien, Mary A Mrs, 1937, Jl 7,23:3
O'Brien, Mary E, 1955, Ap 23,19:4
O'Brien, Mary H, 1956, D 8,19:5
O'Brien, Mary I, 1952, Ap 28,19:2
O'Brien, Mary J, 1949, O 19,29:1
O'Brien, Mary M Mrs, 1952, Ag 3,61:1
O'Brien, Matthew H, 1966, My 25,47:4
O'Brien, Maurice F, 1938, S 20,23:4
O'Brien, Maurice W, 1941, O 25,17:5
O'Brien, Michael, 1906, My 7,5:3
O'Brien, Michael C Mrs, 1962, Je 11,31:5
O'Brien, Michael J, 1940, N 27,23:2; 1943, Ag 31,17:2; 1951, F 25,87:1; 1951, Je 14,27:4; 1960, N 13,88:3
O'Brien, Michael J Col (funl, S 14,9:6; will, S 25,11:5), 1909, S 12,9:5
O'Brien, Michael J Jr, 1950, N 15,32:2
O'Brien, Michael S, 1939, Je 11,45:3
O'Brien, Michael W, 1960, S 28,39:2
O'Brien, Mildred L, 1965, N 15,37:2
O'Brien, Miles M (funl, D 25,9:4), 1910, D 22,13:4
O'Brien, Miles M, 1959, My 13,37:4
O'Brien, Millionaire, 1878, N 3,10:5
O'Brien, Morgan J (por), 1937, Je 17,23:1
O'Brien, Morgan J, 1949, Mr 18,27:5; 1954, Ag 30,17:5
O'Brien, Morgan J Jr, 1958, Je 1,86:2
O'Brien, Morgan J 2d, 1940, Je 20,23:5
O'Brien, Mrs, 1874, Ag 3,8:3
O'Brien, Nancy Mrs, 1924, D 5,21:5
O'Brien, Norman A Mrs, 1941, Ja 5,44:5
O'Brien, P J, 1940, F 28,22:2
O'Brien, Patrick, 1917, Jl 13,9:5; 1952, N 28,26:3
O'Brien, Patrick A, 1950, D 26,23:3
O'Brien, Patrick E, 1940, Ag 15,19:2
O'Brien, Patrick F, 1944, N 17,19:2
O'Brien, Patrick J, 1937, Mr 19,12:4; 1937, Je 8,25:5; 1938, Je 11,15:4; 1943, Ap 10,17:2
O'Brien, Patrick M, 1967, Mr 31,37:4
O'Brien, Patrick Mrs, 1965, Je 4,35:2
O'Brien, Patrick S, 1939, Ap 2,III,7:2
O'Brien, Pearl Mrs, 1961, F 15,35:2
O'Brien, Peter J, 1954, Ag 21,17:3
O'Brien, Phil J Mrs, 1956, My 22,33:1
O'Brien, Phil R, 1954, Ja 1,23:4
O'Brien, Philip, 1958, My 30,21:1
O'Brien, Raymond A, 1958, Jl 16,29:5
O'Brien, Raymond F, 1954, Ag 10,19:5
O'Brien, Reuben, 1951, D 7,28:3
O'Brien, Richard, 1923, Ja 23,21:5
O'Brien, Richard A, 1948, Jl 14,23:3
O'Brien, Richard B, 1960, My 4,45:3
O'Brien, Richard C, 1957, N 18,31:1
O'Brien, Richard J Mrs, 1947, Jl 9,23:3
O'Brien, Richard P Mrs, 1942, S 3,19:1
O'Brien, Richard P Sr, 1947, Ag 2,13:2
O'Brien, Robert E, 1948, D 29,21:6
O'Brien, Robert H, 1955, S 11,85:2
O'Brien, Robert J, 1948, My 11,25:5
O'Brien, Robert L, 1955, N 24,29:1; 1959, Ag 1,17:5
O'Brien, Robert L Mrs, 1945, Ja 24,22:2
O'Brien, Robert R, 1955, My 24,31:4
O'Brien, Rose L, 1951, My 22,31:4
O'Brien, Rose M C Mrs (por),(will, D 28,13:2), 1940, D 17,26:3
O'Brien, S Weldon, 1967, O 25,47:2
O'Brien, Smith, 1941, Mr 1,15:4
O'Brien, Stephen, 1944, F 3,19:4
O'Brien, Stephen A, 1913, Jl 31,7:5

O'Brien, Stephen E, 1938, Ag 24,21:4
O'Brien, Stephen J, 1943, D 23,19:2; 1950, Ag 12,13:4
O'Brien, Stephen V, 1965, F 5,31:5
O'Brien, Susan M, 1959, Jl 7,33:5
O'Brien, T Carroll, 1947, Mr 28,24:3
O'Brien, T E, 1932, F 14,II,6:1
O'Brien, T J, 1933, My 20,13:3
O'Brien, Thomas, 1904, Mr 31,9:6; 1943, N 12,22:3; 1943, D 29,17:3
O'Brien, Thomas A, 1941, Je 23,18:3; 1942, D 1,25:4; 1943, N 6,13:3
O'Brien, Thomas B, 1957, My 31,19:4
O'Brien, Thomas C, 1946, Jl 9,21:4; 1951, N 23,30:2; 1954, Jl 19,19:4; 1958, Ja 22,27:3
O'Brien, Thomas D Jr, 1965, N 18,47:4
O'Brien, Thomas F, 1938, My 13,19:5; 1947, N 5,27:5; 1949, Jl 3,26:4; 1951, D 6,34:3
O'Brien, Thomas F Mrs, 1941, D 10,25:1; 1958, D 7, 88:6
O'Brien, Thomas G Mrs, 1957, D 11,32:1
O'Brien, Thomas J (por), 1939, Ag 27,35:1
O'Brien, Thomas J, 1943, Mr 1,19:3; 1951, Ap 13,23:2; 1953, Jl 8,27:5; 1953, O 6,29:2; 1955, Mr 13,86:1
O'Brien, Thomas J (Buck), 1959, Jl 26,68:4
O'Brien, Thomas J, 1964, Ap 15,39:2
O'Brien, Thomas J Jr Mrs, 1949, S 17,17:5
O'Brien, Thomas K, 1941, S 24,23:3
O'Brien, Thomas K Mrs, 1950, My 25,29:4
O'Brien, Thomas M Jr, 1953, Ag 16,77:2
O'Brien, Thomas M Sr, 1941, Jl 3,19:3
O'Brien, Thomas S, 1920, My 21,15:4; 1947, D 8,25:5
O'Brien, Thomas T, 1940, D 30,17:2
O'Brien, Thomas W, 1940, Je 8,15:3
O'Brien, Timothy E, 1950, Ja 25,27:5
O'Brien, Timothy J Mrs, 1955, N 3,31:1
O'Brien, Vincent, 1948, Je 22,25:2
O'Brien, W, 1928, F 27,19:5
O'Brien, W Howard, 1944, Ag 8,17:2
O'Brien, W Howard Mrs, 1945, Jl 30,19:5
O'Brien, W S, 1878, My 3,5:4
O'Brien, W W, 1885, Ja 14,5:5
O'Brien, Walter J, 1949, Ap 9,17:5
O'Brien, William, 1885, Ja 4,2:1; 1940, O 26,15:5; 1944, S 8,14:2; 1946, N 18,23:1; 1947, Ag 22,15:2; 1951, Ja 24,27:3
O'Brien, William A, 1938, O 15,17:4; 1941, Je 25,21:1; 1947, N 17,21:2
O'Brien, William D, 1951, Jl 31,21:5; 1962, F 20,35:2
O'Brien, William E, 1956, F 8,33:3; 1957, My 15,35:2
O'Brien, William F, 1937, N 19,23:2; 1942, S 3,19:5
O'Brien, William F Mrs, 1951, Je 29,21:5
O'Brien, William G, 1956, F 10,21:1
O'Brien, William G Mrs, 1951, Ag 18,11:4
O'Brien, William H, 1940, Mr 7,23:5; 1954, F 12,25:2; 1960, Ap 6,41:3
O'Brien, William J, 1917, D 12,15:6; 1939, Ap 25,23:2
O'Brien, William J (will, Mr 14,29:1), 1940, Mr 7, 23:4
O'Brien, William J, 1943, D 10,27:3; 1945, Je 10,32:3; 1945, N 5,19:4; 1952, S 20,15:1; 1953, Je 26,19:5; 1965, N 24,39:4; 1966, D 28,43:7
O'Brien, William J Mrs, 1949, Ja 17,19:3; 1956, S 20, 33:5; 1960, Ja 6,35:4; 1963, My 2,35:5
O'Brien, William Mrs, 1957, N 21,33:4
O'Brien, William P, 1958, Ag 17,87:2; 1960, D 18,85:1
O'Brien, William R, 1942, Ja 22,17:4
O'Brien, William S, 1946, O 22,25:6; 1951, S 14,25:4
O'Brien, William Smith, 1864, Jl 2,8:3
O'Brien, William T, 1954, Ap 5,25:3
O'Brien, Willis, 1941, Jl 15,19:3
O'Brien, Willis H, 1962, N 12,29:2
O'Brien-Moore, J B L Mrs, 1964, My 19,37:3
Obrig, Adolph, 1917, Mr 3,9:2
Obrig, Elwood M, 1958, My 20,34:4
Obrig, J A Theodore, 1955, N 4,30:3
Obrig, J K Theodore Mrs, 1957, Ap 14,86:5
Obrig, Theodore E, 1967, F 25,28:2
O'Brion, Clarence R, 1958, My 22,29:2
Obrist, Jacob, 1937, My 13,II,10:7
Obrock, August J, 1937, Ag 4,19:4
Obruchev, Vladimir A, 1956, Je 27,31:4
O'Bryan, A Wood, 1950, Ag 24,27:4
O'Bryan, Francis E, 1948, Ap 17,15:3
O'Bryan, Leonel C Mrs, 1938, Jl 17,26:8
O'Bryen, Roland F, 1955, Ja 7,22:2
Obst, Bertram, 1948, Jl 14,24:2
Obus, Nathan, 1949, Ja 8,15:1
O'Byrne, Augusta Mrs, 1938, F 5,15:4
O'Byrne, Charles C, 1946, Jl 13,15:3
O'Byrne, Edward, 1941, O 14,23:5
O'Byrne, Frederick (por), 1937, Je 18,21:3
O'Byrne, James J, 1953, N 24,29:3
O'Byrne, Roscoe C, 1950, Ag 3,23:1
O'Byrne, William J Dr, 1914, Jl 20,7:4
Oca, Souza d', 1945, My 22,19:5
Oca y Obregon, Ignacio Montes de Archbishop, 1921, Ag 19,13:5
O'Callaghan, E B, 1880, My 31,5:4
O'Callaghan, Jerome H, 1963, Je 21,29:4
O'Callaghan, John, 1913, Jl 28,7:6
O'Callaghan, Michael P Adm, 1937, Je 10,23:4
O'Callaghan, P J, 1931, Ag 12,19:5
O'Callaghan, Patrick R, 1966, F 3,31:2
O'Callaghan, Roger O, 1954, Mr 7,24:3
O'Callaghan, Thomas A Rev, 1916, Je 15,11:6
O'Callaghan, William J, 1942, S 5,13:2; 1950, Ag 17, 27:3
O'Callaghan-Westropp, George, 1944, Ag 14,15:4
O'Callahan, Joseph T, 1964, Mr 19,33:1
O'Callahan, Mary, 1955, N 8,31:1
Ocampo, Pablo, 1925, F 7,15:5
Ocampos, Bernardo, 1953, Jl 18,13:6
O'Carroll, Henry, 1957, My 11,21:6
O'Casey, Niall, 1957, Ja 8,31:5
O'Casey, Sean (funl plans, S 20,88:8), 1964, S 19,1:4
Occhiuzzi, Virgilio, 1962, Ja 1,23:4
Oceansek, Otto G, 1942, Jl 21,20:3
Ocenasek, Ludvik, 1949, Ag 13,11:7
Ochacher, Morris, 1950, Jl 8,13:6
Ochberg, Isaac (will), 1937, D 16,24:6
Ocheltree, John B Mrs, 1952, Ag 3,61:1
Ochiltree, Robert, 1948, Ja 29,24:3
Ochiltree, T P Col, 1902, N 26,9:5
Ochiltree, Thomas E, 1942, Jl 26,31:2
Ochiltree, William, 1938, My 23,17:3
Ochmann, Leonard K, 1960, Je 25,21:4
Ochner, George F, 1948, My 11,25:5
Ochs, A S, 1935, Ap 9,1:3
Ochs, Adolph S Mrs, 1937, My 7,25:1
Ochs, Arthur, 1962, My 5,27:5
Ochs, Bertha Mrs, 1908, F 1,9:5
Ochs, Bertram, 1945, F 21,19:2
Ochs, Carrie B Mrs, 1937, Jl 27,21:5
Ochs, Chris J, 1951, Ag 4,15:5
Ochs, Clarence H Mrs, 1941, Mr 13,21:5
Ochs, Edward C, 1949, Mr 15,27:6
Ochs, Ernest, 1963, Ap 24,35:2
Ochs, Ernest Mrs, 1937, My 5,25:3
Ochs, George C, 1958, Mr 2,88:8
Ochs, George W Mrs (funl, My 3,11:6), 1913, My 1, 11:4
Ochs, I Julius, 1965, F 16,35:4
Ochs, John N, 1942, My 12,19:4
Ochs, Louis, 1938, Jl 9,13:5
Ochs, Milton, 1925, Mr 8,5:3
Ochs, Milton B, 1955, My 1,89:1
Ochs, Milton B Mrs, 1965, Ag 15,83:3
Ochs, Nannie, 1947, D 12,28:3
Ochs, Peter W, 1950, Mr 7,27:5
Ochs, Rose K Martin Mrs, 1952, D 11,33:3
Ochs, William, 1940, O 25,21:3
Ochsen, George A, 1949, Ap 25,23:2
Ochsenhirt, Norman C, 1952, Jl 26,13:4
Ochsner, Albert John Dr, 1925, Jl 26,5:3
Ochsner, Gustave A, 1952, Ap 1,29:3
Ochsner, Paul O, 1937, Jl 18,II,7:1
Ockenden, Albion C, 1938, Ag 6,13:2
Ockendon, Harvey G, 1966, S 18,84:7
Ockendon, William T, 1961, O 16,29:2
Ockendon, William T Mrs, 1967, My 14,87:1
Ockenlander, Laurence, 1940, O 2,23:2
Ocker, William C (por), 1942, S 18,22:2
Ockers, Jacob Capt, 1918, D 5,13:2
Ockershausen, H J, 1882, My 17,5:5
Ockershauson, A F (see also Ap 25), 1877, Ap 27,8:3
O'Cone, Michael, 1953, Mr 18,31:4
O'Connel, Daniel G, 1956, S 3,13:6
O'Connell, Ambrose, 1962, O 14,86:7
O'Connell, Arthur, 1954, O 6,25:3
O'Connell, Bernard J, 1949, S 26,25:2
O'Connell, Bernard T Msgr, 1917, Mr 1,13:4
O'Connell, Bill, 1942, D 15,27:4
O'Connell, C A, 1951, Ja 9,30:3
O'Connell, Catherine, 1942, Ap 7,21:4
O'Connell, Charles, 1962, S 3,15:4
O'Connell, Charles J, 1958, My 11,86:7
O'Connell, Charles K, 1957, Ja 12,19:5
O'Connell, Conrad W, 1959, S 13,84:5
O'Connell, Cornelius P, 1950, S 29,27:2
O'Connell, D J Bishop, 1927, Ja 2,II,9:1
O'Connell, Daniel, 1872, Ja 17,8:5; 1907, Ag 22,7:5; 1914, Mr 15,7:5; 1948, Ja 4,52:8
O'Connell, Daniel J, 1938, Je 28,19:5
O'Connell, Daniel M, 1958, Jl 31,23:5
O'Connell, Daniel T, 1964, Mr 12,35:2
O'Connell, Dannis J, 1937, Ag 1,II,7:1
O'Connell, David F, 1923, Ag 13,13:3
O'Connell, David J, 1945, O 7,44:8
O'Connell, Edward C, 1946, Je 10,21:2
O'Connell, Edward D, 1948, F 9,17:5
O'Connell, Edward J, 1939, Je 5,17:2; 1939, Je 7,1:2
O'Connell, Edward W, 1942, F 9,15:4
O'Connell, Emmett R, 1960, Jl 7,31:5
O'Connell, Eugene, 1942, Ag 30,42:7
O'Connell, F Claude, 1950, S 29,27:1
O'Connell, Frances R Mrs, 1956, Je 7,31:2
O'Connell, Francis A Mrs, 1941, Mr 4,23:1
O'Connell, Frank, 1952, Jl 28,15:2
O'Connell, Frank L, 1950, N 10,28:3
O'Connell, Frank M, 1959, Jl 13,27:4
O'Connell, Frederick W, 1954, Jl 22,23:4
O'Connell, George B, 1941, D 3,25:2
O'Connell, Harold J, 1964, Jl 15,35:4
O'Connell, Harold V, 1959, Jl 19,68:5
O'Connell, Henry L, 1959, My 7,33:3
O'Connell, Hugh (por), 1943, Ja 21,21:3
O'Connell, J J, 1944, F 21,15:4
O'Connell, J S, 1927, Ap 4,23:3
O'Connell, J William, 1961, Jl 17,21:3
O'Connell, Jack, 1955, Ap 9,13:5
O'Connell, James, 1948, S 28,27:5
O'Connell, James A, 1937, Mr 29,19:3; 1954, D 16,
O'Connell, James D Mrs, 1965, S 12,87:1
O'Connell, James E, 1948, F 16,21:1
O'Connell, James H, 1952, O 12,89:2
O'Connell, James J, 1944, S 25,17:3
O'Connell, James Sir, 1872, Jl 30,1:6
O'Connell, James T, 1966, O 13,45:1
O'Connell, Jerome A, 1921, F 24,13:6
O'Connell, Jerry J, 1956, Ja 19,33:2
O'Connell, John, 1913, N 25,11:6; 1924, F 11,15:3
O'Connell, John B, 1944, Je 17,13:1; 1948, F 10,23
O'Connell, John C (por), 1945, Ap 1,35:1
O'Connell, John C Mrs, 1954, Je 27,69:2
O'Connell, John D, 1940, Je 1,15:2
O'Connell, John E, 1954, Jl 27,21:3
O'Connell, John H, 1921, Je 25,11:6; 1955, Ap 7,2
O'Connell, John I, 1942, Mr 15,42:7
O'Connell, John J, 1923, F 17,13:4
O'Connell, John J (por), 1946, O 19,21:1
O'Connell, John J, 1949, D 17,17:2; 1953, My 29,2 1959, My 15,39:1
O'Connell, John J Jr, 1954, S 5,50:3; 1955, Je 28,2 1961, Je 2,32:4
O'Connell, John J Mrs, 1947, Ja 30,25:3
O'Connell, John K, 1965, O 23,31:3
O'Connell, John M (por), 1941, D 7,77:2
O'Connell, John M Jr, 1954, N 20,17:6
O'Connell, John Mrs, 1945, O 2,23:2
O'Connell, John P, 1953, O 22,29:3; 1960, F 22,17
O'Connell, John R, 1943, D 30,17:5; 1945, F 15,20 1950, Je 24,13:1
O'Connell, John R Mrs, 1958, Ag 2,17:6
O'Connell, John T, 1957, Je 8,19:5
O'Connell, Joseph B Rev, 1968, Ja 7,84:8
O'Connell, Joseph C, 1955, Mr 5,17:6
O'Connell, Joseph E, 1960, Jl 9,19:3
O'Connell, Joseph F, 1942, D 11,23:2
O'Connell, Joseph H Dr, 1924, My 20,21:5
O'Connell, Joseph J, 1949, Jl 19,29:6
O'Connell, Joseph P, 1942, F 6,19:3
O'Connell, Joseph P Msgr, 1915, Mr 11,11:4
O'Connell, Joseph S, 1954, Ap 9,23:6
O'Connell, Katherine L, 1956, D 13,37:4
O'Connell, Kathleen, 1956, Ap 8,84:1
O'Connell, Louis A, 1949, Je 16,29:4
O'Connell, M Phil, 1954, My 18,29:2
O'Connell, Margaret F (funl, Mr 30,17:5), 1925, Mr 28,15:4
O'Connell, Margaret J (Sister Mary Vincent de Pa 1957, F 12,27:2
O'Connell, Margaret Mrs, 1940, D 22,31:1
O'Connell, Marion E, 1937, Jl 31,15:3
O'Connell, Mary (Sister Mary Evangelista), 195 Mr 24,31:3
O'Connell, Mary Elizabeth, 1953, F 14,17:2
O'Connell, Matt F, 1957, Jl 17,27:2
O'Connell, Maurice D, 1922, Ag 27,28:5; 1946, M 21:5
O'Connell, Michael G, 1940, D 3,25:4
O'Connell, Milton V (Jan 20), 1963, Ap 1,36:3
O'Connell, Milton V Mrs, 1947, My 31,13:4
O'Connell, Mort L, 1962, O 13,25:4
O'Connell, Mort L Jr, 1945, Ap 3,8:4
O'Connell, Mort L Mrs, 1939, D 3,60:5
O'Connell, P A, 1958, Mr 8,17:6
O'Connell, Patrick J, 1950, F 16,23:2; 1950, Ag 1 13:1; 1951, Jl 4,17:6
O'Connell, Paul B, 1947, Mr 25,25:1
O'Connell, Percy D, 1960, O 29,23:4
O'Connell, Raymond D (por), 1945, O 10,21:5
O'Connell, Raymond G, 1951, O 6,19:3
O'Connell, Raymond T, 1966, O 7,43:3
O'Connell, Raymond T Mrs, 1967, Je 20,39:1
O'Connell, Richard J, 1943, Ag 23,15:5
O'Connell, Robert C, 1942, Ap 1,21:5
O'Connell, Robert S, 1944, F 11,19:4
O'Connell, Thomas E, 1912, Je 18,11:5; 1942, Jl 19:4; 1965, Ja 6,39:3
O'Connell, Thomas J, 1961, Ja 3,33:2; 1966, Ap 76:5
O'Connell, Thomas W, 1939, Ja 18,20:4
O'Connell, Timothy, 1953, Ja 12,27:4
O'Connell, Timothy J, 1947, Mr 22,13:3
O'Connell, Timothy Mrs, 1957, Ag 29,27:2
O'Connell, Valentine G, 1962, Je 15,27:5
O'Connell, Vincent P, 1954, Ja 9,15:6
O'Connell, Walter C, 1949, Ja 1,13:4
O'Connell, Walter J, 1960, N 12,21:2
O'Connell, William, 1944, Ap 23,1:2; 1953, Ap 1
O'Connell, William A, 1945, D 2,45:1
O'Connell, William J, 1950, Je 11,92:3
O'Connell, William K, 1950, D 5,31:2
O'Connell, William P, 1949, D 28,25:3
O'Connoer, John F, 1938, S 29,25:2
O'Connor, Alice M, 1944, F 1,19:4
O'Connor, Andrew, 1941, Je 11,21:2
O'Connor, Andrew J, 1950, Mr 14,25:2
O'Connor, Anna B Mrs, 1939, S 16,17:4

O'Connor, Annie Mrs, 1925, O 28,25:5
O'Connor, Arthur Rev, 1911, Mr 6,7:6
O'Connor, Augustine R, 1949, Ag 2,19:1
O'Connor, Basil Mrs, 1955, Jl 27,23:3
O'Connor, Bernard A, 1953, F 17,27:4
O'Connor, C T, 1875, D 4,4:7
O'Connor, Caleb W, 1956, Ap 7,19:4
O'Connor, Catherine E, 1949, My 29,36:5
O'Connor, Catherine Mother, 1939, Mr 13,17:3
O'Connor, Cecilia T, 1948, Mr 28,48:4
O'Connor, Charles, 1948, Ag 1,59:1; 1953, Ap 21,27:2
O'Connor, Charles A, 1940, S 22,49:1
O'Connor, Charles A Mrs, 1957, Mr 29,21:2
O'Connor, Charles A Rev, 1907, S 23,9:4
O'Connor, Charles E, 1951, Mr 31,15:5
O'Connor, Charles H, 1946, Ja 21,23:4
O'Connor, Charles J, 1952, My 7,27:2; 1957, Ap 14, 86:5
O'Connor, Charles L, 1937, Ja 26,21:5; 1952, Mr 12, 27:4
O'Connor, Charles R, 1940, O 23,23:5; 1946, Ag 7,27:3
O'Connor, Charles T, 1955, Je 14,29:1
O'Connor, Clarence J, 1958, S 19,28:1
O'Connor, Clarence J Mrs, 1941, My 9,21:6
O'Connor, Cornelius, 1939, O 10,23:4
O'Connor, Cornelius J, 1946, D 12,29:2
O'Connor, Daniel, 1945, S 2,31:1
O'Connor, Daniel C, 1949, Mr 4,21:2
O'Connor, Daniel F, 1938, Mr 23,23:2
O'Connor, Daniel J, 1950, F 7,27:2
O'Connor, Daniel J Rev, 1937, Ap 4,II,11:1
O'Connor, Daniel Rev, 1903, D 17,9:4
O'Connor, Darcy, 1941, Ap 16,25:3
O'Connor, David, 1942, O 22,21:2
O'Connor, David G, 1949, Je 8,29:2
O'Connor, David P, 1961, N 12,86:8
O'Connor, David P Mrs, 1957, O 10,33:4
O'Connor, Denis S, 1943, My 22,13:6
O'Connor, Dennis Archbishop, 1911, Jl 1,11:5
O'Connor, Dennis F, 1957, N 4,29:1
O'Connor, Dennis Finbar Rev, 1924, Mr 2,22:2
O'Connor, Deno F, 1944, Ap 20,19:4
O'Connor, Donal, 1942, Ja 11,44:1
O'Connor, Donald C, 1952, My 26,23:5
O'Connor, E F, 1928, Mr 27,27:3
O'Connor, Edmund, 1941, Ap 1,23:3
O'Connor, Edmund A, 1938, F 3,23:3
O'Connor, Edmund E, 1960, D 1,35:2
O'Connor, Edward, 1940, Ap 22,17:5
O'Connor, Edward F, 1959, D 15,39:1; 1960, Ja 29, 25:3
O'Connor, Edward F Mrs, 1950, F 25,17:4
O'Connor, Edward M, 1957, F 20,33:5
O'Connor, Edward M Sr, 1950, N 11,15:4
O'Connor, Edward Mrs, 1948, F 3,25:2
O'Connor, Edward P, 1925, Ag 28,13:6
O'Connor, Edward S, 1937, Ag 29,II,7:4
O'Connor, Edwin, 1968, Mr 24,92:5
O'Connor, Eugene F Jr, 1945, Je 27,19:2
O'Connor, Eugene J, 1952, N 9,80:4
O'Connor, Eugene T, 1943, Ag 7,11:6; 1947, Ag 9,13:6
O'Connor, F Barnard, 1953, My 28,23:2
O'Connor, Flannery (funl, Ag 5,33:2), 1964, Ag 4, 29:4
O'Connor, Francis E, 1957, S 14,19:3
O'Connor, Francis J, 1921, Ag 9,9:5; 1966, Mr 14,10:6
O'Connor, Francis W Dr, 1937, O 4,21:6
O'Connor, Francis X, 1958, F 11,31:1
O'Connor, Francis X Rev, 1920, F 1,22:2
O'Connor, Frank (por), 1939, Ag 22,19:3
O'Connor, Frank, 1943, Ja 17,44:6; 1954, N 15,27:4
O'Connor, Frank (Bucky), 1958, Ap 23,22:5
O'Connor, Frank, 1966, Mr 11,33:1
O'Connor, Frank A, 1954, Je 22,27:2; 1957, Mr 17,87:2
O'Connor, Frank V, 1941, N 16,56:4
O'Connor, Frank X, 1948, O 28,29:3
O'Connor, Frederick G, 1952, Je 12,33:5
O'Connor, George B, 1957, Ja 14,23:6
O'Connor, George D, 1954, Ja 5,27:4
O'Connor, George H, 1946, S 29,61:1
O'Connor, George T, 1959, O 11,87:1
O'Connor, Harold H, 1951, Ag 6,21:5
O'Connor, Harry F Mrs, 1942, Mr 15,43:1
O'Connor, Harry J, 1919, Ja 1,17:2
O'Connor, Henry G, 1951, Ag 16,27:6
O'Connor, Hugh, 1967, Jl 4,19:1
O'Connor, Hugh B, 1945, Ap 7,15:5
O'Connor, J F Dr (see also Je 26), 1878, Je 27,2:7
O'Connor, J J Bishop, 1927, My 21,19:4
O'Connor, J Leo, 1956, Jl 13,19:3
O'Connor, J Vincent, 1956, My 28,27:6
O'Connor, Jack, 1937, N 15,23:3
O'Connor, James, 1910, Mr 13,II,11:2; 1940, Ag 23, 15:4
O'Connor, James A, 1946, Ap 10,27:1; 1959, Je 11,33:4
O'Connor, James A Rev, 1911, Jl 26,9:6
O'Connor, James C, 1952, Je 26,29:2
O'Connor, James C Mrs, 1961, N 11,23:4
O'Connor, James F, 1938, O 16,45:1; 1939, Mr 5,49:2; 1945, Ja 16,19:4; 1963, Mr 19,7:6
O'Connor, James F T, 1949, S 29,29:1
O'Connor, James I R, 1937, Ag 29,II,7:2
O'Connor, James J, 1919, Ja 21,9:4; 1947, Jl 1,25:4; 1950, Ja 29,68:8; 1959, F 18,33:3
O'Connor, James K, 1922, F 14,17:4
O'Connor, James M, 1963, O 14,29:2
O'Connor, James Mrs, 1958, My 24,21:6
O'Connor, James P, 1941, D 21,40:7; 1955, Ap 20, 33:4; 1955, Ag 15,15:5
O'Connor, James P Msgr, 1915, Mr 17,11:5
O'Connor, James R, 1946, D 11,31:2
O'Connor, James Sr, 1941, Ja 9,21:5
O'Connor, James T, 1944, S 4,19:5
O'Connor, James V, 1968, My 13,43:2
O'Connor, James W, 1950, O 12,31:5; 1952, N 18,31:1
O'Connor, Jeremiah T Mrs, 1949, Je 10,27:2
O'Connor, John (Bro Clement), 1910, S 26,13:6
O'Connor, John, 1939, S 27,25:5; 1941, N 9,52:4; 1945, F 26,19:4; 1951, F 23,27:3; 1952, F 8,23:5; 1960, Je 6, 29:6
O'Connor, John A, 1939, F 12,44:7; 1951, O 9,29:4; 1953, Ja 29,27:1; 1958, Ap 22,33:4
O'Connor, John B, 1949, Ag 24,25:5; 1965, Ap 18,81:1
O'Connor, John C, 1946, O 7,31:2
O'Connor, John C Mrs, 1952, Je 13,23:2
O'Connor, John E, 1938, F 8,21:4; 1943, F 20,13:5
O'Connor, John F, 1916, Mr 18,11:6; 1951, Jl 12,25:5; 1957, Ap 14,87:1; 1958, Je 7,19:6; 1965, Mr 4,31:3
O'Connor, John F X, 1953, F 17,34:3
O'Connor, John G, 1943, S 21,24:3
O'Connor, John J, 1938, O 7,23:5; 1941, O 5,48:2; 1941, D 31,18:2; 1946, N 3,64:4; 1948, Ja 2,23:1; 1948, Jl 5,15:2; 1950, Mr 20,21:1; 1950, My 22,21:4; 1957, S 17,35:1; 1960, Ja 27,33:1
O'Connor, John J (cor, F 21,35:3), 1961, F 20,27:2
O'Connor, John J, 1962, Mr 27,37:1; 1965, Mr 17,45:4
O'Connor, John J A, 1961, My 15,31:3
O'Connor, John J Mrs, 1945, Jl 27,15:4; 1946, N 29, 25:1; 1951, Jl 31,22:2; 1952, D 1,23:4; 1956, Jl 31, 23:1; 1962, Ja 10,47:1
O'Connor, John K, 1945, Mr 24,17:5
O'Connor, John M, 1945, O 14,42:7; 1948, Ap 23,23:2
O'Connor, John P, 1965, D 3,35:2
O'Connor, John P Mrs, 1943, O 23,13:6
O'Connor, John R, 1960, Mr 3,29:1
O'Connor, John T, 1945, Ja 20,11:2
O'Connor, John T Mrs, 1941, Mr 11,23:3
O'Connor, John V, 1940, Jl 4,15:6; 1956, S 16,85:1
O'Connor, Joseph, 1908, O 11,11:6
O'Connor, Joseph A, 1938, Je 16,23:6; 1942, Je 13, 15:3; 1951, Ap 14,31:2; 1964, D 1,41:1
O'Connor, Joseph F, 1951, Ag 17,17:2
O'Connor, Joseph V, 1967, F 7,39:3
O'Connor, Julia L, 1945, O 4,23:4
O'Connor, Kate F (por), 1945, My 26,15:5
O'Connor, Kathleen, 1920, N 13,11:3
O'Connor, Keyram J (funl, Mr 22,13:4), 1913, Mr 18,11:5
O'Connor, Leo P, 1954, O 13,31:5
O'Connor, Leslie M, 1966, Ja 22,29:4
O'Connor, Lester T, 1958, Mr 13,29:4
O'Connor, Lillian M, 1955, Ja 19,27:1
O'Connor, Lucille M, 1962, F 18,92:6
O'Connor, Luke Gen, 1915, F 2,7:6
O'Connor, M P, 1881, Ap 27,5:5
O'Connor, Mae E, 1955, Mr 29,30:4
O'Connor, Manning, 1955, Ja 12,27:1
O'Connor, Margaret, 1945, Jl 10,11:3; 1947, Jl 14,21:4; 1967, My 5,39:2
O'Connor, Margaret W, 1937, Ag 15,II,7:2
O'Connor, Martin D, 1946, O 8,23:4
O'Connor, Martin P, 1946, S 19,31:2; 1959, My 8,27:2
O'Connor, Mary A, 1948, Ag 1,58:1
O'Connor, Mary E, 1948, Ap 18,69:1
O'Connor, Mary H Mrs, 1950, My 26,23:4
O'Connor, Mary J, 1959, D 7,31:5
O'Connor, Maurice J, 1951, D 2,90:1; 1963, Ag 23,25:5
O'Connor, Maurice J Mrs, 1951, D 2,90:1
O'Connor, Maurice P Rev, 1913, D 13,13:5
O'Connor, Michael, 1938, N 1,23:5
O'Connor, Michael (Uncle Mike), 1953, Je 30,23:3
O'Connor, Michael A, 1957, S 16,31:5
O'Connor, Michael F, 1938, Ag 28,33:3; 1942, Ap 30, 19:4
O'Connor, Michael J, 1944, S 27,21:4; 1959, Ap 20, 31:4; 1961, Je 3,23:3
O'Connor, Michael Mrs, 1957, Ja 11,23:1
O'Connor, Michael P, 1916, Jl 9,19:5
O'Connor, Owen J, 1961, Jl 1,17:1
O'Connor, Owen W, 1943, S 3,19:6
O'Connor, Owen W Mrs, 1949, Mr 30,25:3
O'Connor, Pat (funl, Je 2,32:6), 1958, My 31,1:3
O'Connor, Patrick Capt, 1922, F 16,15:3
O'Connor, Patrick F (por), 1943, Mr 23,19:4
O'Connor, Patrick F, 1950, Ag 18,21:2; 1952, Ag 7,21:4
O'Connor, Patrick H Mrs, 1947, F 13,23:3
O'Connor, Patrick J, 1938, Ja 4,23:1
O'Connor, Patrick Mrs, 1959, F 28,19:5
O'Connor, Peter B, 1961, N 24,31:2
O'Connor, Peter C, 1946, Ja 20,43:1
O'Connor, Peter J, 1942, D 7,27:5
O'Connor, Peter Mrs, 1955, My 23,23:3; 1966, F 25, 31:4
O'Connor, Peter P, 1952, D 12,29:1
O'Connor, Phil, 1952, O 9,31:3
O'Connor, Raymond A, 1966, Ag 20,25:3
O'Connor, Rena M Mrs, 1938, N 10,27:2
O'Connor, Richard, 1907, F 7,9:5; 1950, F 24,23:3; 1952, N 23,88:1
O'Connor, Richard B, 1956, N 16,28:1
O'Connor, Robert, 1947, Mr 6,25:5
O'Connor, Robert A Dr, 1968, Mr 15,39:3
O'Connor, Robert E, 1950, Je 10,17:3; 1962, S 7,29:2
O'Connor, Robert F, 1961, Jl 4,19:3
O'Connor, Robert K, 1940, Ap 30,21:5
O'Connor, Roderick, 1950, Jl 28,38:3
O'Connor, Sarah C Mrs, 1942, O 31,15:6
O'Connor, Sheelagh, 1966, Mr 13,87:2
O'Connor, Susan A, 1965, S 13,35:3
O'Connor, T Maj, 1883, Ag 21,2:6
O'Connor, T P, 1929, N 18,1:7
O'Connor, T V, 1935, O 18,23:1
O'Connor, Terence (por), 1940, My 9,23:2
O'Connor, Terrence D, 1951, My 12,21:3
O'Connor, Thomas, 1938, Je 27,19:1; 1938, Je 28,19:4; 1952, Jl 25,18:7
O'Connor, Thomas D, 1955, Ja 7,21:6
O'Connor, Thomas D Rev, 1968, Je 22,33:5
O'Connor, Thomas F, 1915, Ap 4,14:1; 1943, D 1,21:5; 1945, D 10,21:5; 1950, S 19,31:3
O'Connor, Thomas F Mrs, 1955, N 19,19:6
O'Connor, Thomas Henry, 1916, F 6,15:4
O'Connor, Thomas J, 1868, Ag 15,5:5; 1943, My 6, 19:4; 1951, N 20,31:2; 1955, Ja 4,21:4
O'Connor, Thomas K, 1948, O 27,27:4
O'Connor, Thomas M, 1949, Je 1,31:5
O'Connor, Thomas V Mrs, 1956, Ap 26,33:2
O'Connor, Timothy M Mrs, 1954, Jl 21,27:3
O'Connor, Una (A T McGlade), 1959, F 6,25:3
O'Connor, Valentine J, 1954, Ag 13,15:5
O'Connor, Valeria, 1964, Mr 14,23:4
O'Connor, W F, 1940, D 17,26:3
O'Connor, Walter J, 1946, Mr 3,46:6
O'Connor, William, 1924, Ap 28,15:4; 1939, Ja 31, 21:3; 1939, S 27,25:4
O'Connor, William (Okie), 1956, O 6,21:3
O'Connor, William A, 1950, F 5,84:5
O'Connor, William E Mrs, 1954, Je 12,15:2
O'Connor, William F, 1943, Jl 1,19:3; 1945, F 19,17:3; 1956, Je 29,21:3
O'Connor, William H, 1949, S 7,29:1
O'Connor, William J, 1943, Jl 1,19:4; 1956, F 14,29:1; 1956, O 16,34:1; 1957, Jl 30,23:5; 1958, Jl 5,17:5
O'Connor, William M, 1946, Ja 18,19:3
O'Connor, William P, 1949, N 2,27:3
O'Connor, William R, 1962, O 6,25:6
O'Connor, William S (will), 1940, Ag 10,13:1
O'Connor, William T, 1951, O 27,19:6
O'Connor, William V, 1959, Ag 28,23:4
O'Connor, Winfield S, 1947, Mr 7,26:3
O'Conor, Charles (funl), 1884, My 14,5:1
O'Conor, Charles Mrs, 1874, My 15,8:5
O'Conor, Daniel J, 1918, My 11,13:8
O'Conor, Daniel J Sr, 1968, D 20,47:3
O'Conor, George T, 1943, Ja 28,19:2
O'Conor, Herbert R, 1960, Mr 5,19:5
O'Conor, James P A Mrs, 1949, Ja 5,25:2
O'Conor, John C Mrs, 1948, Jl 9,19:5
O'Conor, John W, 1950, Ja 7,17:5
O'Conor, Justin V, 1948, D 25,17:3
O'Conor, Nicholas Sir, 1908, Mr 20,7:5
O'Conor, Patrick H, 1938, Mr 28,15:1
Ocorr, Violet Mrs, 1947, Jl 31,21:6
O'Crowley, Clarence R, 1959, Mr 30,31:2
Octavio, Rodrigo, 1944, Mr 1,19:4
Ocumpaugh, Edmund 3d, 1964, D 3,49:2
Odachi, Shigeo, 1955, S 27,35:3
O'Daniel, Edgar V, 1943, N 6,13:5
O'Daniel, Edgar V Mrs, 1951, F 2,23:1
O'Dare, Hugh, 1953, My 12,27:2
O'Dare, James J, 1950, Ja 9,25:3
O'Day, Bernard V, 1950, Je 4,92:3
O'Day, Daniel (funl, O 16,9:6), 1906, S 14,7:1
O'Day, Daniel, 1916, Je 1,11:6
O'Day, Daniel T Mrs (por), 1943, Ja 5,19:3
O'Day, James A, 1951, Jl 17,27:5
O'Day, John H, 1938, D 19,23:4
O'Day, John M, 1946, O 11,23:5
O'Day, Joseph F, 1937, S 16,25:4
Oddie, Clarence M, 1961, Ag 7,23:5
Oddie, J V S, 1902, Ja 17,14:1
Oddie, Orville Capt, 1912, N 25,13:5
Oddie, Samuel I, 1945, My 12,13:6
Oddie, Tasker L, 1950, F 18,15:2
Oddie, William E (funl, My 25,20:4), 1919, My 23, 13:4
Oddone, Andrea, 1950, O 31,27:2
Oddy, Christine, 1947, Ag 13,23:5
Oddy, W Harold, 1955, O 4,35:4
O'Dea, E J, 1932, D 27,13:3
O'Dea, Francis, 1942, Ja 3,19:4
O'Dea, Francis J, 1951, Jl 15,60:3
O'Dea, James, 1914, Ap 13,11:4
O'Dea, John, 1937, D 23,21:3
O'Dea, John H, 1957, F 25,25:5
O'Dea, Michael, 1938, Ja 24,23:5
O'Dea, Patrick J, 1962, Ap 5,33:3
O'Dea, Richard E, 1956, F 26,88:1
O'Dee, Thomas J, 1961, Mr 15,39:6

Odegard, Peter H, 1966, D 7,47:1
Odell, Abram B, 1938, F 20,II,8:4
Odell, Albert G, 1947, My 20,25:2
Odell, Albert S, 1947, S 16,23:4
Odell, Allan F Dr, 1937, Ap 12,18:1
Odell, Allen G, 1954, D 7,33:2
Odell, Andrew J, 1903, N 24,9:5
Odell, Arthur R, 1950, O 27,29:1
Odell, B B, 1926, My 10,21:1
Odell, B Bryant, 1945, Ja 26,21:4
Odell, Benjamin Barker, 1916, Jl 22,9:7
O'Dell, Benjamin L, 1946, Jl 10,23:3
Odell, Berton E, 1945, D 6,27:3
Odell, Caleb H, 1944, O 5,23:5
Odell, Charles, 1947, My 4,60:3
Odell, Charles F, 1945, My 1,23:5
Odell, Charles F Mrs, 1947, Ap 12,17:2
Odell, Charles J, 1946, Ap 22,21:5
Odell, Charles Mortimer, 1925, F 19,19:4
Odell, Charles N, 1952, Ag 21,19:6
Odell, Chester V, 1959, F 17,31:4
Odell, Clara, 1948, Jl 1,23:5
Odell, Clarence P Mrs, 1956, Ag 20,21:2
Odell, D D Rev, 1902, Ap 3,9:7
O'Dell, Daniel, 1920, N 26,13:2
Odell, David D Mrs (Eliz), 1965, Jl 19,27:4
O'Dell, DeForest, 1958, Je 20,23:3
O'Dell, Delancey, 1939, My 6,17:6
Odell, Dolph H, 1955, Je 30,25:4
Odell, Dyckman, 1907, Ja 6,II,9:6
Odell, Edward, 1940, Jl 30,19:1
Odell, Edward A, 1965, Mr 30,39:6
Odell, Elbridge H, 1944, Mr 12,38:2
Odell, Emery, 1953, Ja 19,23:5
Odell, Emery A Mrs, 1948, O 8,25:3
Odell, Frank L, 1945, D 4,30:2
Odell, George, 1922, D 29,13:4
Odell, George C D, 1949, O 18,27:1
O'Dell, George T, 1946, Jl 11,23:2
Odell, George T, 1947, My 21,25:5
Odell, George W, 1941, Je 8,48:4
O'Dell, Harrison M Mrs, 1946, Mr 11,25:2
Odell, Harry, 1938, My 6,21:4
Odell, Harry A, 1952, Ja 6,93:2
Odell, Harry H, 1949, My 5,28:3
Odell, Herbert R, 1957, O 9,35:1
Odell, Hiram B, 1952, S 21,89:1
Odell, Horace, 1945, Mr 19,19:5
Odell, Howard L, 1947, Mr 1,15:5
Odell, I Herbert Jr, 1938, S 24,17:5
Odell, Isaac H, 1947, Jl 14,21:3
Odell, James E, 1939, Ag 28,19:4
O'Dell, John E, 1950, N 6,27:2
Odell, Joseph Rev, 1923, My 16,19:5
Odell, LeRoy L, 1963, S 21,21:1
Odell, Lewis C Mrs, 1944, S 13,19:6
Odell, Lewis E, 1946, Ap 26,21:5
Odell, Linda C Mrs, 1940, Ja 29,15:3
Odell, Lyman, 1880, Mr 9,8:2
Odell, Mary F Mrs, 1943, My 17,15:2
Odell, Maude (will, Mr 3,43:4), 1937, F 28,1:4
Odell, Michael, 1925, Jl 14,21:5
Odell, Moses F, 1866, Je 14,5:3
Odell, Oliver, 1940, F 1,21:3
Odell, Orlando H, 1947, O 3,25:2
Odell, Otis, 1946, Ja 4,22:2
O'Dell, Owen H, 1914, My 17,IV,7:6
Odell, Paul E, 1948, S 11,15:3
Odell, Preston, 1949, O 12,29:4
Odell, Randolph, 1961, F 23,27:4
Odell, Reuben, 1944, Ag 2,15:5
Odell, Reuben Mrs, 1958, N 26,29:6
Odell, Rutledge Mrs, 1953, N 22,89:1
Odell, S H F, 1875, My 8,4:6
Odell, Samuel W, 1948, O 12,25:6
Odell, Theodore F, 1964, Ja 22,37:3
O'Dell, Thomas, 1924, Je 8,26:1
O'Dell, Wallace Mrs, 1964, F 9,88:5
O'Dell, Walter T, 1960, O 23,89:1
Odell, Walter T Mrs, 1962, Je 27,32:6
Odell, William L Mrs, 1960, O 19,45:3
Odell, William R, 1938, Mr 26,15:2
Odell, William R Sr, 1949, Je 28,28:2
Odell, William W, 1949, Mr 22,25:4
Odell, Willis P Mrs, 1904, Mr 28,9:7
Oden, Charles R Jr Mrs, 1963, Ag 12,21:5
Oden, Charles V, 1925, Jl 25,11:6
Oden, J Howard, 1954, Ja 28,27:4
Oden, Minnie B G Mrs, 1951, Ja 6,15:2
Oden, Redmond S Jr, 1940, Ja 25,21:5
Oden, Walter P, 1957, Jl 26,19:4
Odenbach, F L, 1933, Mr 16,17:1
Odenbach, Joseph F, 1962, O 20,25:4
Odence, Josiah, 1948, Ag 25,25:1
Odendahl, Martin P Jr, 1949, Ag 14,25:5
Odenheimer, Sigmund, 1945, Mr 21,23:2
Odenheimer, Sigmund Mrs, 1962, Ag 13,25:4
Odenheimer, W H Bp, 1879, Ag 15,5:4
Odenkirk, Harry C, 1953, Mr 17,35:6
Odenrick, Rolf, 1951, Ja 8,21:6
Oderkirk, Burt, 1949, Ja 2,60:8
Odermatt, Basil, 1952, Je 2,21:6
Oderwald, William F Mrs, 1943, My 8,15:1
Odes, Israel, 1956, O 17,35:5
Odescalchi, B Gialma, 1957, Jl 15,19:2
Odets, Clifford (funl, Ag 18,81:2; trb, Ag 25,II,1:1), 1963, Ag 16,27:1
Odette, Edmond G, 1939, Ap 1,19:4
Odgen, Benjamin W, 1958, Ag 20,27:3
Odgen, H A, 1936, Je 16,25:3
Odgen, Wilson L, 1918, Jl 28,19:3
Odger, George, 1877, Mr 11,7:2
Odgers, Arthur J, 1965, My 11,39:2
Odgers, Elizabeth R Mrs, 1945, N 21,21:5
Odgers, William Blake, 1924, D 17,21:3
Odierno, Errico, 1942, F 20,17:2
Odilon, Helene, 1939, F 10,23:4
Odio Herrera, Ruben, 1959, Ag 22,17:4
Odiorne, Howard E, 1954, Mr 29,19:4
Odiorne, Thomas H Mrs, 1943, Ag 25,19:5
Odishoo, Jacob, 1949, D 8,33:5
Odlin, Lawrence A, 1961, N 9,31:6
Odlin, William S, 1955, O 31,25:2
Odlin, William S Mrs, 1953, Ja 10,17:1
Odlum, Arnold A, 1957, Ag 14,25:2
Odlum, Jerome, 1954, Mr 5,20:3
Odlum, Stanley A (funl, Mr 18,27:1), 1957, Mr 16, 19:5
O'Doherty, Dominick, 1960, My 26,33:4
O'Doherty, Michael J, 1949, O 14,27:3
O'Doherty, W Archdall, 1873, My 19,8:3
Odom, Allen, 1947, Ag 23,13:5
Odom, George M, 1964, Jl 31,23:1
Odom, Peter C, 1953, Mr 17,29:3
Odom, Robert B, 1954, My 10,23:4
Odom, William M, 1942, Ja 31,17:4
Odom, William P, 1949, S 6,1:2
O'Donnel, Frank A, 1906, Jl 7,7:6
O'Donnel, Richard Lincoln, 1920, S 29,9:2
O'Donnell, Adrian V, 1947, Jl 28,15:4
O'Donnell, Alan E, 1950, Mr 4,17:4
O'Donnell, Alex, 1949, My 1,88:4
O'Donnell, Alex C, 1940, F 11,48:2
O'Donnell, Alice, 1953, D 15,39:3
O'Donnell, Anthony C, 1945, Ja 9,19:5
O'Donnell, Arthur F, 1947, Ap 17,27:4
O'Donnell, Barnard J, 1953, Mr 28,17:5
O'Donnell, Bernard, 1916, N 12,23:2
O'Donnell, Bernard L, 1938, Jl 20,19:4
O'Donnell, C (Billy Gray), 1882, N 22,5:2
O'Donnell, C L, 1934, Je 5,23:1
O'Donnell, Charles (Dixieland), 1951, S 20,16:2
O'Donnell, Charles B, 1951, N 15,29:4
O'Donnell, Charles E, 1959, O 5,31:1
O'Donnell, Charles F, 1938, Ap 1,23:5
O'Donnell, Charles H, 1940, My 24,19:2
O'Donnell, Charles J, 1965, N 26,37:2
O'Donnell, Charles O, 1941, Ja 19,40:2
O'Donnell, Charles S, 1958, Mr 17,29:4
O'Donnell, Charles V, 1940, N 25,17:3
O'Donnell, Cleo, 1953, F 15,92:2
O'Donnell, Columbus, 1873, My 26,1:6
O'Donnell, Cornelius, 1946, Ag 24,11:6
O'Donnell, Cornelius A, 1953, Je 15,29:4
O'Donnell, Cornelius Mrs, 1954, Ag 4,21:3
O'Donnell, Daniel Kane, 1871, S 9,1:6
O'Donnell, Davis S, 1948, D 25,18:2
O'Donnell, Donald, 1967, Ja 10,43:2
O'Donnell, E E, 1933, Ap 11,22:1
O'Donnell, Edward F, 1956, Ap 8,84:2
O'Donnell, Edward L, 1946, S 21,15:4
O'Donnell, Ellen M, 1950, S 17,104:5
O'Donnell, Ellsworth Mrs, 1949, S 22,31:3
O'Donnell, Emmett, 1960, F 19,28:1
O'Donnell, Eric H, 1950, Jl 6,27:2
O'Donnell, Francis J, 1959, O 6,39:3
O'Donnell, Francis P, 1962, Je 27,37:8
O'Donnell, Francis V, 1964, Ap 16,37:4
O'Donnell, Frank, 1951, Jl 25,23:3
O'Donnell, Frank P, 1939, O 4,25:2
O'Donnell, Frank X, 1960, S 3,17:5
O'Donnell, George A, 1952, Ja 2,25:4
O'Donnell, George T, 1955, O 5,36:5
O'Donnell, Harry, 1952, Je 25,29:4
O'Donnell, Henry G, 1943, N 11,23:5
O'Donnell, Howard J, 1948, S 2,23:3
O'Donnell, Hugh A (por),(will, Ag 27,14:1), 1941, Ag 24,35:1
O'Donnell, J A, 1928, Jl 26,21:5
O'Donnell, J Hugh, 1947, Je 13,23:1
O'Donnell, James, 1946, F 21,21:5
O'Donnell, James A, 1957, Ja 19,15:3
O'Donnell, James B, 1956, Mr 3,20:3
O'Donnell, James E, 1941, Ap 13,39:1; 1944, F 25,17:4
O'Donnell, James E (Spike), 1962, Ag 28,32:5
O'Donnell, James F, 1962, Ap 25,39:1
O'Donnell, James G, 1949, Ag 21,68:5
O'Donnell, James H, 1956, O 6,21:4
O'Donnell, James W, 1959, D 31,21:1
O'Donnell, John, 1914, Ap 21,11:5; 1944, Ja 7,17:3; 1954, Mr 2,25:3; 1961, D 18,35:3
O'Donnell, John E, 1949, My 10,26:3
O'Donnell, John J, 1945, Mr 8,23:2; 1965, Ap 8,39:2; 1967, O 10,47:3
O'Donnell, John R, 1909, O 6,9:4; 1960, Ja 12,47:4
O'Donnell, John T, 1940, Ag 14,19:4
O'Donnell, John Z, 1939, Jl 6,23:5
O'Donnell, Joseph D (Joe Darcey), 1963, Ag 23,2
O'Donnell, Joseph F A, 1938, Ag 21,32:7
O'Donnell, Joseph R, 1958, Ja 31,22:6
O'Donnell, Laurence W Sr, 1943, Ja 7,19:4
O'Donnell, Leo J, 1959, F 8,87:1
O'Donnell, Manus T, 1954, S 2,21:6
O'Donnell, Marshal Duke, 1867, N 18,1:5
O'Donnell, Martin J (funl, Ag 8,19:2), 1958, Ag 5, 27:4
O'Donnell, Martin J Sr, 1949, Ap 13,29:1
O'Donnell, Mary A, 1938, My 27,17:5
O'Donnell, Mary P, 1961, O 28,21:6
O'Donnell, Michael F, 1945, S 6,25:5; 1956, My 6,8
O'Donnell, Michael J, 1941, S 30,23:5; 1966, Ag 22 33:4
O'Donnell, Michael Msgr, 1937, My 18,23:6
O'Donnell, Nancy A, 1943, Je 9,11:1
O'Donnell, P Cardinal, 1927, O 23,31:1
O'Donnell, Pat, 1943, Ap 21,25:5
O'Donnell, Patrick J, 1958, Je 22,76:5; 1959, Ja 21,
O'Donnell, Paul F, 1950, F 1,29:4
O'Donnell, Peter, 1938, D 6,23:4
O'Donnell, Peter R, 1950, Ja 13,23:4
O'Donnell, Richard A, 1945, Je 28,19:4
O'Donnell, Robert J, 1959, N 12,35:5
O'Donnell, Robert M, 1965, F 27,25:3
O'Donnell, Rodger J, 1945, Mr 18,42:3
O'Donnell, Terrence H, 1967, My 9,40:7
O'Donnell, Thomas A, 1945, F 22,28:2
O'Donnell, Thomas C, 1962, N 13,38:1
O'Donnell, Thomas E, 1966, Ag 8,27:4
O'Donnell, Thomas F, 1945, Mr 20,19:2; 1951, D 1 31:2; 1963, Ag 1,27:4
O'Donnell, Thomas F Mrs, 1948, Jl 24,15:5; 1954, Mr 28,88:5
O'Donnell, Thomas J Rev, 1920, Ag 20,9:6
O'Donnell, Thomas Mrs, 1949, Je 11,17:4
O'Donnell, Vincent H, 1962, N 17,25:6
O'Donnell, Walter B, 1951, Ap 14,15:4
O'Donnell, William A, 1947, Mr 3,21:4; 1951, My 35:3
O'Donnell, William F, 1943, N 6,13:5; 1953, Je 6,1
O'Donnell, William H, 1923, D 13,21:5
O'Donnell, William J, 1937, N 7,II,9:3; 1948, O 17
O'Donnell, William Mrs, 1948, F 13,21:4
O'Donnell, William R, 1947, Ja 19,53:1
O'Donnell, William T, 1946, My 12,44:2
O'Donnoghue, F Capt, 1882, Jl 2,6:4
O'Donnohue, William, 1943, Mr 21,27:1
O'Donoghue, Cornelius, 1946, Ja 10,23:3
O'Donoghue, Roderick, 1962, Jl 12,29:3
O'Donoghue, Sidney E, 1964, Jl 29,33:5
O'Donoghue, Tadhgh, 1949, O 22,17:6
O'Donohoe, James J (por), 1943, Ag 27,17:3
O'Donohue, J J, 1897, Je 26,5:1
O'Donohue, J Sir, 1933, N 21,19:4
O'Donohue, John J, 1949, Ag 6,17:1
O'Donohue, Joseph J, 1937, O 31,II,11:3
O'Donohue, Joseph J Mrs, 1918, Ja 8,15:8
O'Donohue, Teresa (por),(will, S 23,25:2), 1937, Ag 18,19:5
O'Donohue, Thomas J Col, 1909, S 29,11:4
O'Donovan, Daniel J, 1947, Ja 30,25:5
O'Donovan, Dennis Rev, 1911, Ja 23,7:4
O'Donovan, Fred, 1952, Jl 22,25:3
O'Donovan, Jeremiah (O'Donovan Rossa), 1915 Je 30,11:5
O'Donovan, Thomas P, 1953, F 16,21:4
O'Donovan, William Rudolf, 1920, Ap 21,9:4
Odor, Theodore, 1921, D 9,17:5
O'Doran, John J, 1941, Ag 26,19:5
O'Doran, Marie Louise, 1967, Jl 7,33:3
O'Dougherty, Harold S L, 1948, F 11,27:3
O'Dowd, Charles H, 1950, S 14,31:3
O'Dowd, Eddie, 1966, Je 9,47:2
O'Dowd, Edwyn W, 1962, My 30,19:5
O'Dowd, Henry W, 1949, F 26,15:2
O'Dowd, James T, 1950, F 6,25:5
O'Dowd, Joseph, 1958, S 21,86:2
O'Dowd, Maurice D F (Mike), 1953, D 19,15:4
O'Dowd, Mike, 1957, Jl 29,19:5
Odquist, Victor Mrs, 1959, Ap 9,31:1
Odria, Zoila A V Mrs, 1949, O 6,31:2
O'Driscoll, Daniel, 1940, Mr 5,23:3
O'Driscoll, Frank, 1954, My 26,29:1
O'Driscoll, William V, 1956, O 9,35:2
O'Duffy, Eion (por), 1944, D 1,23:3
Odum, Howard W, 1954, N 9,27:4
O'Dunne, Eugene Jr, 1959, N 23,31:2
O'Dwyer, Daniel H Rev Father, 1909, N 15,9:3
O'Dwyer, David T (por), 1944, O 6,23:4
O'Dwyer, David W, 1964, D 3,49:3
O'Dwyer, Denis P, 1958, Mr 4,29:2
O'Dwyer, Edward F (funl, O 12,19:5), 1922, O 21:3
O'Dwyer, Edward F Mrs, 1952, O 13,21:2
O'Dwyer, Edward Thomas (Bp of Limerick), 1 Ag 20,9:4
O'Dwyer, Joseph, 1953, O 21,29:4
O'Dwyer, William (funl plans, N 27,36:5; funl, N 28,21:2), 1964, N 25,1:4
O'Dwyer, William Mrs, 1946, O 13,58:3
Odzer, Harry, 1966, Mr 27,86:5

Oechler, Walter G, 1958, S 11,33:1
Oechsler, Adam J, 1964, My 1,35:1
Oechsler, Francis A Mrs, 1945, Ja 20,11:3
Oechsler, Francis J, 1966, S 7,47:1
Oedenkovn, Fernand, 1949, F 18,23:4
Oeder, Andrew H, 1955, D 8,37:2
Oefinger, Frederick C, 1942, D 21,23:5
Oefinger, Hugh S, 1945, D 13,29:2
Oefinger, Walt C, 1952, O 24,23:2
Oehler, Christian, 1957, Je 9,88:6
Oehler, Karl F, 1950, Je 12,27:5
Oehler, Kathleen V, 1950, Mr 23,29:5
Oehlers, Herbert C, 1937, Ag 26,21:6
Oehley, Charles F, 1957, Ag 6,27:2
Oehlke, Anna Kost Mrs, 1945, Ag 1,12:7
Oehm, Charles A, 1951, N 4,87:2
Oehme, William Mrs, 1950, Ja 31,24:2
Oehmichen, Etienne, 1955, Jl 12,25:3
Oehrle, Albert C, 1955, D 21,29:5
Oehrle, Walter W, 1957, Jl 5,18:7
Oehser, Nina B, 1941, F 25,23:4
Oei Tiong Ham, Mrs, 1947, F 1,15:2
Oeland, Isaac R, 1941, Mr 10,17:3
Oelkers, Henry J, 1949, F 5,15:1
Oelkers, Richard Jr, 1948, D 29,21:2
Oelkers, William I Mrs, 1937, D 21,23:2
Oelkers, William R, 1943, Mr 24,23:4
Oelkers, William R Jr, 1963, N 19,41:4
Oelrichs, C M, 1932, Ja 16,15:1
Oelrichs, H Mrs, 1926, N 23,29:5
Oelrichs, Harry, 1902, My 29,9:4
Oelrichs, Henry, 1875, Je 29,3:7
Oelrichs, Henry E, 1944, My 12,19:1
Oelrichs, Hermann (funl, S 6,9:7; will, S 11,7:3), 1906, S 4,1:1
Oelrichs, Hermann (por), 1948, Ag 6,17:1
Oelrichs, Marjorie T Mrs, 1952, Je 2,21:4
Oels, Edward H, 1964, Ap 26,88:4
Oenslager, George, 1956, F 7,31:1
Oeri, Albert, 1950, D 23,15:6
Oeri, Felix, 1941, Jl 28,13:4
Oeri, Georgine, 1968, Jl 16,39:4
Oertel, Abraham L, 1938, O 29,19:5
Oertel, Ernest G Dr, 1916, Jl 25,9:6
Oerter, John Henry Rev, 1915, Ja 25,9:4
Oerther, Lucie Mrs, 1948, Je 22,3:7
Oesch, Ernest H, 1941, Ap 23,21:3
Oeslby, Signard R, 1942, F 19,19:5
Oesper, E William, 1951, Ag 23,23:6
Oest, William R, 1955, Ap 22,25:4
Oestensson, Nils, 1949, Jl 26,34:6
Oestereich, Charles F, 1967, N 14,47:1
Oesterreicher, Sandor I, 1947, N 1,15:6
Oesterrich, Fred Mrs, 1961, Ag 15,10:6
Oestnaes, Victor L, 1952, Ap 22,29:4
Oestreich, Arthur J, 1966, Je 17,45:2
Oestreich, George E, 1964, My 3,87:2
Oestreich, Henry L, 1914, Ag 14,11:6
Oestreicher, Carl, 1960, N 23,29:3
Oestreicher, John C, 1951, D 17,31:2
Oestreicher, Louis, 1957, Mr 10,89:1
Oestricher, Walter M Mrs, 1964, N 17,41:3
Oeters, Edgar O, 1957, D 29,49:1
Oetjen, Lloyd H, 1941, My 24,15:4
Oetjen, Wilhelmine S, 1963, My 15,39:4
Oetjen, William P, 1940, N 23,17:2
Oetteking, Bruno, 1960, Ja 18,27:4
Oettel, Charles W, 1950, Ap 16,104:5
Oettinger, Estella (will), 1945, Je 21,20:3
Oettinger, Herbert C, 1950, Ja 30,17:5
Oettinger, Julius, 1957, F 26,29:1
Oettinger, Malcolm H, 1962, S 23,86:5
Oettler, William A, 1952, N 18,32:5
Of, George F, 1954, D 1,31:3
O'Fallon, Martin J Mrs, 1963, Ag 22,27:5
O'Farrell, George T, 1938, D 16,25:3
O'Farrell, Leo P, 1941, Ap 15,23:2
O'Farrell, Michael C Rev, 1918, Ja 4,11:5
O'Farrell, Patrick J, 1951, Ap 24,29:2
O'Farrell, Raymond A, 1962, O 31,37:3
O'Farrell, Robert M, 1966, Ja 19,41:5
O'Farrell, Teresa S, 1959, D 12,23:2
O'Farrell, V, 1934, O 8,17:3
O'Farrell, Valerian J Mrs, 1958, N 8,21:5
O'Farrell, William J Rev, 1906, D 2,7:5
O'Ferrall, Charles T, 1905, S 23,9:4
Off, Edward T, 1950, Ap 1,15:4
Off, Henry J, 1940, Ja 30,20:2
Off, Walter F, 1942, F 22,26:8
Offen, Roger L, 1964, My 28,37:2
Offenbach, Arthur, 1954, Ag 27,21:5
Offenbach, Jacques, 1880, O 6,5:3
Offenbach, Jules, 1880, O 12,3:1
Offenbacher, Wendel, 1951, My 23,35:1
Offenberg, Murray, 1958, O 15,39:2
Offenberg, Paul, 1955, S 12,25:2
Offenberg, Samuel F, 1959, F 7,19:1
Offenberg, Vladimir Mrs, 1944, Ag 26,11:6
Offeney, Clarence, 1941, Ja 28,19:1
Offenhauser, Christopher, 1947, My 24,15:5
Offer, George E, 1954, Ja 8,22:3
Offerman, George Mrs, 1945, Je 2,15:1
Offerman, Henry, 1968, S 9,47:3

Offerman, Henry C, 1959, Jl 27,25:4
Offerman, Henry F, 1953, My 22,27:5
Offerman, Theodore (por), 1937, Mr 18,25:3
Offerman, William C, 1943, N 15,19:3
Offermann, Ernst A, 1955, Jl 13,25:5
Offers, Martha, 1944, Ja 29,13:6
Offhouse, Douglas J, 1946, Ag 19,25:3
Officer, Harvey, 1947, My 24,15:5
Offield, Evelyn Mrs, 1939, Mr 1,21:1
Offineer, Beatrice M, 1950, O 29,93:1
Offinger, Henry, 1947, Ja 3,22:2
Offley, A M, 1945, O 27,15:5
Offley, Robert S, 1944, Je 27,19:3
Offley, W P Maj, 1871, My 8,1:7
Offner, Benjamin, 1917, S 21,9:5
Offner, Monrone, 1953, Mr 26,31:1
Offner, Mortimer, 1965, S 16,47:1
Offner, Mortimer Mrs, 1959, S 16,39:4
Offner, Richard, 1965, Ag 28,21:1
Offray, Claude V Sr, 1962, Mr 11,87:1
Offray, Claudius M, 1938, Jl 6,23:6
Offschanka, Gustave R, 1937, Mr 21,II,8:3
Offutt, Daniel E, 1943, Ag 22,36:7
O'Flaherty, Andrew J, 1945, Jl 28,11:5
O'Flaherty, Hugh, 1963, O 31,33:1
O'Flaherty, James (por),(will, My 9,25:8), 1939, Ap 21,23:1
O'Flaherty, John, 1950, Je 21,28:2
O'Flaherty, Mary F, 1957, Ap 18,29:3
O'Flaherty, William D Rev, 1949, Je 9,6:6
O'Flanangan, Michael (por), 1942, Ag 8,11:3
O'Flynn, Alden, 1939, N 14,23:1
O'Flynn, Charles J, 1964, Ap 26,88:8
O'Flynn, Jimmy, 1952, Ja 14,21:3
Ofner, Arthur, 1941, F 21,19:2
Ofstie, Ralph A, 1956, N 19,31:3
Oftedahl, Reider B, 1954, D 28,15:1
Oftedal, Christian S, 1955, Jl 12,25:1
Oftedal, Svan, 1948, Je 24,25:5
Oftedal, Sverre, 1948, F 6,26:6
Ofut, Frank, 1938, Ap 9,17:4
Ogan, Maude de Haven, 1922, Mr 26,27:2
Ogan, Morris L, 1958, My 5,29:2
O'Gara, Charles, 1942, N 23,23:1
O'Gara, Cuthbert M Bp, 1968, My 14,47:1
O'Gara, Harry K, 1967, O 11,47:3
O'Gara, John, 1945, Mr 12,19:2; 1945, S 6,25:4
Ogarte, Jesus C Col, 1937, S 20,23:2
Ogata, Taketora, 1956, Ja 29,92:3
O'Gatty, Packy (P Agati), 1966, O 11,47:1
Ogborn, Richard E, 1967, Je 3,31:4
Ogborne, A Roy, 1960, S 13,37:4
Ogborne, John, 1937, F 14,II,8:8
Ogburn, Charlton, 1962, F 24,27:4
Ogburn, William F, 1959, Ap 29,33:4
Ogden, Adele C Mrs, 1938, Jl 31,33:4
Ogden, Adeline M, 1944, N 4,15:4
Ogden, Annie H Mrs, 1950, Je 5,23:6
Ogden, Archibald Mrs, 1952, Je 3,29:2
Ogden, Arnold L, 1953, D 9,11:2
Ogden, Arnold Mrs, 1968, Ja 12,27:1
Ogden, C K, 1957, Mr 23,19:4
Ogden, Charles J, 1955, D 11,88:5
Ogden, Charles Smith, 1904, Ja 14,9:6
Ogden, Charles W, 1956, Ja 21,21:4
Ogden, Clara Foster, 1915, Jl 31,7:4
Ogden, Clement M, 1952, Mr 9,93:1
Ogden, Daniel L, 1961, Ag 2,29:5
Ogden, David, 1877, Jl 7,8:5
Ogden, David B, 1923, O 16,21:4
Ogden, Dunbar H, 1952, Ap 13,77:1
Ogden, Elmer S, 1959, S 26,23:3
Ogden, Ernest N, 1946, N 25,27:5
Ogden, Esther G, 1956, Ja 15,92:4
Ogden, Ferdinand E Jr, 1951, N 6,29:2
Ogden, Francis A, 1914, Je 11,11:5
Ogden, Frank, 1950, Ap 28,21:3
Ogden, Frank C, 1946, Ag 10,13:1
Ogden, Frank R, 1945, O 30,19:3
Ogden, Frederick J, 1941, D 8,23:3
Ogden, G D, 1936, O 5,21:1
Ogden, G M, 1884, Jl 21,2:6
Ogden, George B, 1938, D 27,17:2; 1952, S 9,31:4
Ogden, George S, 1946, D 11,31:4
Ogden, George W Sr, 1944, Ag 16,19:4
Ogden, Gordon A Mrs, 1961, Mr 30,29:3
Ogden, H Arthur Mrs, 1954, F 25,31:2
Ogden, H Bradley, 1951, My 16,35:3
Ogden, Harold C, 1957, Ap 15,29:2
Ogden, Harold P, 1949, Ap 30,13:5
Ogden, Henry N, 1947, S 30,25:2
Ogden, Henry N Mrs, 1948, F 9,17:2
Ogden, Herbert G Mrs, 1954, Ag 21,17:5
Ogden, Herschel C, 1943, F 1,15:2
Ogden, Howard N, 1915, Ja 28,9:4
Ogden, Hugh W, 1938, S 4,17:3
Ogden, I G, 1928, F 6,19:5
Ogden, J Herbert, 1939, F 22,21:3
Ogden, James W, 1950, Ag 22,27:3
Ogden, John E, 1950, Ja 22,77:1
Ogden, John Routh (funl, Ap 3,22:3), 1921, Ap 1,13:4
Ogden, John S, 1941, Je 16,15:4
Ogden, John W, 1964, O 17,29:6

Ogden, Joseph, 1896, Ag 5,5:2
Ogden, Joseph C Jr, 1964, N 25,37:1
Ogden, Joseph W, 1916, O 28,13:3; 1916, N 10,13:4
Ogden, Judge, 1865, F 27,8:5
Ogden, Kenneth C, 1949, F 25,23:4
Ogden, Lee, 1953, My 13,29:3
Ogden, Louis M, 1946, Jl 18,25:5
Ogden, Louis M Mrs, 1959, S 26,23:4
Ogden, M C, 1903, O 17,9:5
Ogden, M D, 1880, F 14,4:7
Ogden, Palmer H, 1959, Ap 18,23:1
Ogden, Palmer H Mrs, 1960, Je 20,31:5
Ogden, Phillip L, 1947, N 13,27:3
Ogden, Robert C (funl, Ag 8,7:6), 1913, Ag 7,7:3
Ogden, Robert C Mrs, 1909, D 4,11:1
Ogden, Robert M, 1939, N 12,49:3; 1959, Mr 5,31:4
Ogden, Rollo, 1937, F 23,1:4
Ogden, Russell L Sr, 1948, Je 13,68:4
Ogden, S G (see also S 12), 1877, S 14,8:6
Ogden, Suzie Eastman, 1949, Jl 19,29:3
Ogden, Tarrence F, 1962, Je 28,31:5
Ogden, Taylor R Mrs, 1943, Jl 16,17:2
Ogden, W B (funl) (see also Ag 4), 1877, Ag 7,5:4
Ogden, Wallace, 1912, N 6,15:4
Ogden, Walter, 1914, F 22,IV,5:5
Ogden, Wesley Sr, 1946, Ag 6,25:5
Ogden, William B, 1908, Jl 6,7:5; 1943, S 17,21:1; 1945, Ap 12,23:5
Ogden, William B Mrs, 1904, S 29,9:6
Ogden, William P, 1958, S 8,29:4
Ogdon, James W, 1949, Ag 30,27:4
Ogdon, James W Mrs, 1964, My 19,37:3
Ogelsby, William P, 1949, My 9,25:1
Oger, Bernard P, 1950, Jl 3,15:4
Ogg, Aikman, 1942, My 12,19:2
Ogg, David, 1965, Mr 31,39:3
Ogg, Emma Jessie, 1968, Mr 6,47:3
Ogg, Frederic A, 1951, O 25,29:4
Ogg, Frederick A Mrs, 1937, N 4,25:6
Ogg, William, 1903, S 22,7:5; 1959, D 26,13:6
Oggiano, Ralph, 1962, Ap 7,25:6
Oghooz, Ahmed D, 1965, Ag 2,29:1
Ogier, Walter W Jr, 1938, D 29,19:2
Ogilby, Charles, 1938, N 15,23:1
Ogilby, Elizabeth R, 1958, Jl 7,27:4
Ogilby, F D, 1877, Je 21,3:1
Ogilby, F D Maj, 1878, F 16,3:5
Ogilby, Frederick D, 1940, Ap 5,21:4
Ogilby, Henry B, 1949, D 24,15:4
Ogilby, John D, 1942, Ja 18,44:4
Ogilby, Remsen B Mrs, 1957, Ag 9,19:3
Ogilby, William S R, 1952, Mr 24,25:4
Ogilve, David, 1951, D 30,25:1
Ogilvie, Albert G (por), 1939, Je 12,17:4
Ogilvie, Alex Sr, 1948, My 7,23:4
Ogilvie, David M Rev, 1937, Mr 1,19:2
Ogilvie, Edward L, 1960, Ag 19,23:2
Ogilvie, Frank B, 1937, F 20,17:4
Ogilvie, Frederick, 1949, Je 11,17:4
Ogilvie, Frederick H, 1963, D 17,39:4
Ogilvie, Ida H, 1963, O 15,39:2
Ogilvie, James, 1950, Jl 13,25:2
Ogilvie, Jessica (por), 1943, O 25,15:3
Ogilvie, John, 1963, Mr 16,7:2
Ogilvie, John S, 1910, F 10,7:5
Ogilvie, John S Jr, 1938, D 22,21:4
Ogilvie, Mary G (por), 1942, Mr 5,23:6
Ogilvie, Thomas F, 1955, My 4,29:5
Ogilvie, Walter E, 1956, S 2,57:1
Ogilvie, Walter E Mrs, 1942, Ja 23,19:2
Ogilvie, William Ex-Gov, 1912, N 14,11:6
Ogilvie-Forbes, George, 1954, Jl 12,19:2
Ogilvie-McDonnell, John W, 1959, Je 30,31:4
Ogilvy, Charles (por), 1949, F 20,60:7
Ogilvy, David Lyulph Gore Wolseley (Earl of Airlie), 1968, D 29,52:3
Oginz, Phil, 1955, Ap 23,19:4
Ogle, Alfred M, 1944, My 9,19:6
Ogle, George B, 1949, O 11,31:2
Ogle, George H Jr, 1967, Mr 4,27:1
Ogle, H Lane, 1960, Ja 21,31:5
Ogle, Jack, 1916, D 1,4:5
Ogle, Nellie A, 1950, My 1,25:5
Ogle, Samuel E Mrs, 1950, Ag 3,23:2
Oglebay, Crispin, 1949, O 24,23:3
Oglee, Francis J, 1941, F 25,23:2
Oglesby, Albert Shipman, 1918, D 5,13:3
Oglesby, John G, 1938, My 27,17:2
Oglesby, Margaret, 1914, N 13,11:2
Oglesby, Nicholas E, 1957, Mr 10,89:2
Oglesby, William R, 1941, Mr 16,45:1
Oglesby, Woodson R, 1955, My 2,21:2
Ogley, Samuel A, 1951, Mr 10,13:5
Ogliby, F Rev (see also Mr 26), 1878, Mr 30,8:1
Ogloblin, Alex K, 1961, Ja 9,39:3
Ognibene, Bernard, 1966, My 21,31:2
Ognibene, Mary, 1965, My 28,33:1
Ognyeff, Nikolai, 1938, Je 24,19:6
Ogonowski, Casimir S, 1946, D 24,17:5
O'Gorman, Alice, 1965, Ag 14,23:2
O'Gorman, Edward J Rev, 1924, D 6,15:6
O'Gorman, Edward M, 1951, Mr 1,27:4
O'Gorman, Emma, 1942, Ja 10,15:5

O'Gorman, J Leo Prof, 1937, Mr 6,17:3
O'Gorman, James A (por), 1943, My 18,23:1
O'Gorman, James A Mrs, 1943, D 29,17:4
O'Gorman, James Bp, 1874, Jl 5,1:4
O'Gorman, Michael W, 1955, N 8,31:2
O'Gorman, Mr, 1867, N 22,5:2
O'Gorman, Patrick, 1952, Ja 18,27:2
O'Gorman, Patrick F, 1940, Mr 16,15:5
O'Gorman, Richard, 1895, Mr 2,9:5; 1940, My 25,17:5
O'Gorman, Robert, 1938, O 28,23:4
O'Gorman, Stephen V (will), 1940, Ag 10,7:8
O'Gorman, Terence J (por), 1943, S 20,21:1
O'Gorman, Thomas Bp, 1921, S 19,15:4
O'Gorman, William, 1903, Je 26,9:6
O'Gorman, William A, 1944, N 30,23:5
O'Gorman, William D, 1950, S 8,32:2
O'Gorman, William J, 1941, S 18,25:3
O'Grady, A Mrs, 1942, Mr 17,21:2
O'Grady, Augustine B Mrs, 1949, Jl 12,27:2
O'Grady, Benson J, 1944, F 12,13:3
O'Grady, Clara, 1951, O 18,29:4
O'Grady, Daniel C, 1956, My 9,33:4
O'Grady, Edward T, 1959, Mr 19,33:1
O'Grady, Ellen A Mrs, 1949, D 29,25:3
O'Grady, George W, 1938, O 29,19:4
O'Grady, Harry, 1942, N 11,25:3
O'Grady, Harry J Jr, 1968, Ap 27,39:5
O'Grady, James F, 1940, Mr 25,15:4; 1961, Mr 12,86:7
O'Grady, John, 1903, S 29,9:5; 1966, Ja 3,27:2
O'Grady, John A Msgr, 1919, Ja 16,13:3
O'Grady, John F, 1960, Je 11,44:8
O'Grady, John J, 1952, Ja 10,29:1
O'Grady, Joseph F, 1922, Ja 1,20:2
O'Grady, Robert C, 1960, Ap 29,31:4
O'Grady, S, 1928, My 22,27:5
O'Grady, Stanley G Mrs, 1949, Ja 13,23:4
O'Grady, Thomas, 1949, O 25,27:4
O'Grady, Thomas J, 1937, Mr 7,II,8:7
O'Grady, Tom (T A Atchinson), 1942, S 2,23:2
O'Grady, Valentine E, 1951, Ja 9,30:3
O'Grady, William E, 1962, O 29,29:3
O'Grady, William H, 1937, Ja 22,21:2
Ogsbury, James S, 1950, F 19,78:1
Ogsbury, John D, 1948, Ap 14,27:2
O'Guin, Sydney L, 1964, N 29,86:4
Ogur, Charles, 1949, Ap 9,17:6
Ogura, Masatsune, 1961, N 21,39:3
Oguri, Kanzo, 1950, O 25,35:1
Oguri, Kanzo Mrs, 1952, Jl 25,17:4
Ogurtsov, Nikolai, 1955, O 6,29:4
Ogush, Benjamin, 1941, D 1,19:5
Ogush, William B, 1956, Mr 5,23:5
Ogust, Max, 1968, D 23,39:2
O'Hagan, Ferdinand A, 1916, D 22,9:3
O'Hagan, Harry V, 1961, F 13,27:5
O'Hagan, Henry Mrs, 1903, D 15,9:5
O'Hagan, John, 1962, My 20,87:1
O'Hagan, T Baron, 1885, F 2,5:6
O'Hagan, Thomas, 1939, Mr 4,15:4
O'Hagan, Vincent, 1941, O 12,46:5
O'Hagan, William J, 1967, My 28,61:1
O'Hagen, Bessie R, 1956, My 29,27:5
O'Hair, Robert C, 1958, N 19,37:5
O'Haire, Joseph P, 1967, Ja 21,23:6
O'Hallaren, Bernard J, 1947, D 15,25:2
O'Halloran, Charles E, 1950, Je 14,31:4
O'Halloran, D W Mrs, 1904, My 14,5:4
O'Halloran, Paul V, 1939, Ja 17,22:2
O'Halloran, Stephen, 1951, S 14,18:3
O'Halloran, Thomas, 1940, Ap 10,25:2
O'Halloran, Thomas J, 1942, Je 12,21:3
O'Halloran, Thomas Mrs, 1963, D 22,34:4
O'Handly, Rodrick, 1944, D 21,22:2
O'Hanion, Thomas Rev Dr, 1912, O 1,13:6
O'Hanlan, Joseph F, 1938, Ap 17,II,6:6
O'Hanlon, Edward P, 1948, O 12,25:3
O'Hanlon, George V, 1962, Je 27,32:6
O'Hanlon, Harold F, 1962, Mr 27,37:3
O'Hanlon, J Ross Mrs, 1951, D 9,90:6
O'Hanlon, James Msgr, 1921, F 26,11:6
O'Hanlon, John M, 1939, S 2,17:5
O'Hanlon, Joseph, 1966, O 27,47:1
O'Hanlon, Patrick J, 1953, Ag 18,23:2
O'Hanlon, Phil F Dr, 1937, Je 11,23:6
O'Hanlon, Redmond L, 1964, Jl 4,13:4
Ohanna, Benyamin N, 1962, Mr 31,25:6
O'Hara, Abigail (Sister Mary Liquori), 1954, Je 14, 21:4
O'Hara, Bernard A, 1954, Je 22,27:3
O'Hara, Bernard S, 1965, S 1,37:3
O'Hara, Charles, 1950, N 5,93:1
O'Hara, Charles E, 1941, F 14,17:2
O'Hara, Charles E Mrs, 1948, Jl 4,27:1
O'Hara, Charles P, 1952, Ap 8,29:2
O'Hara, Christopher E Msgr, 1968, Ap 7,93:1
O'Hara, Edward H Mrs, 1940, O 6,48:1
O'Hara, Edward J, 1960, D 19,27:2
O'Hara, Edwin V, 1956, S 12,37:3
O'Hara, Emmett P, 1957, My 18,19:2
O'Hara, Fiske, 1945, Ag 3,17:2
O'Hara, Francis J, 1943, N 16,23:2; 1946, My 23,21:4; 1947, My 4,60:3; 1955, N 7,29:4
O'Hara, Francis W, 1938, Mr 6,II,8:7
O'Hara, Frank, 1938, Jl 31,33:3
O'Hara, Frank (funl, Jl 28,33:2; cor on obit, Ag 2,-18:3), 1966, Jl 26,35:4
O'Hara, Frank A, 1945, Ap 25,23:5
O'Hara, Fred H, 1955, O 3,27:6
O'Hara, Frederick S, 1950, O 2,23:3
O'Hara, Geoffrey (mem ser postponed, F 8,28:7), 1967, F 2,35:1
O'Hara, George, 1943, Ag 6,15:4
O'Hara, George E, 1961, Je 2,32:2
O'Hara, George V, 1941, S 14,51:4
O'Hara, George W, 1956, Ap 16,27:4
O'Hara, Gerald P (funl, Jl 20,19:6), 1963, Jl 17,31:1
O'Hara, Gordon H, 1942, S 21,15:5
O'Hara, Henry C (H Clive), 1960, D 16,33:1
O'Hara, Irving A, 1937, S 27,21:6
O'Hara, J F, 1926, D 19,26:2
O'Hara, James A, 1949, Je 21,25:4
O'Hara, James F, 1943, N 9,21:1; 1954, D 3,27:2
O'Hara, James J, 1923, Ap 17,21:4
O'Hara, James P, 1940, D 12,27:1
O'Hara, James W, 1945, O 30,19:1
O'Hara, John (funl plans, Ag 30,29:4; funl, S 6,35:2), 1960, Ag 29,1:4
O'Hara, John B, 1961, D 31,48:7
O'Hara, John E, 1960, S 12,29:5
O'Hara, John F Mrs, 1945, Ap 3,19:2
O'Hara, John F Rev (funl, Ap 20,13:4), 1916, Ap 18, 13:4
O'Hara, John J, 1924, Je 15,23:2; 1946, F 25,26:2; 1954, O 14,29:3
O'Hara, John Kenneth, 1968, Ja 16,39:1
O'Hara, John M, 1944, N 17,20:2
O'Hara, John Mrs, 1954, Ja 11,25:4
O'Hara, Joseph A, 1944, O 4,20:2
O'Hara, Joseph M, 1920, N 22,15:5; 1963, S 17,35:3
O'Hara, Joseph W, 1938, S 22,23:1
O'Hara, Joyce, 1953, Ja 10,17:5
O'Hara, Laura M, 1953, Ja 20,25:3
O'Hara, Louis J, 1947, O 29,27:1
O'Hara, Martin, 1951, O 28,85:2
O'Hara, Matthew J, 1943, O 28,23:4
O'Hara, Michael, 1944, Ja 24,17:4
O'Hara, Michael J, 1941, My 17,15:3; 1947, F 4,25:3
O'Hara, Michael Mrs, 1949, F 13,76:5
O'Hara, Neal Mrs, 1949, Ja 15,17:3
O'Hara, Norman, 1956, My 21,25:2
O'Hara, P J Mrs, 1943, Ja 7,19:6
O'Hara, Patrick H Mrs, 1962, My 14,29:5
O'Hara, Patrick J, 1943, My 10,19:4; 1950, My 16,31:5
O'Hara, Ralph L Mrs, 1955, N 17,35:5
O'Hara, Randall B, 1957, F 6,25:4
O'Hara, Rose G Mrs, 1948, Ja 11,56:1
O'Hara, Rose Mother, 1943, F 14,48:5
O'Hara, Sophia M R, 1954, Ap 28,31:5
O'Hara, Stephen F, 1946, D 2,25:2
O'Hara, Stephen F Mrs, 1948, D 12,92:3
O'Hara, Stephen J Mrs, 1955, Jl 7,27:2
O'Hara, Theodore Col, 1867, Je 16,5:3
O'Hara, Thomas A, 1960, Je 6,29:3
O'Hara, Thomas Ex-Justice, 1919, D 31,7:3
O'Hara, Thomas J, 1942, Ag 23,41:1
O'Hara, Thomas N, 1953, My 29,25:4
O'Hara, William, 1940, N 8,21:3
O'Hara, William F, 1948, Ag 8,56:6
O'Hara, William J, 1956, Jl 25,29:2; 1958, F 14,24:4; 1968, My 31,29:4
O'Hara, William J A, 1938, Ag 6,13:6
O'Hara, William L Rev Dr, 1916, F 24,13:5
O'Hare, Alex, 1964, D 3,45:5
O'Hare, Hugh A, 1941, N 8,19:4
O'Hare, John J, 1937, S 21,25:2; 1956, Ag 17,19:4
O'Hare, Joseph J, 1961, Ap 3,30:1
O'Hare, Margaret E, 1953, Jl 21,23:1
O'Hare, Patrick J, 1939, Jl 13,19:5
O'Hare, Thomas F (Sept 20), 1965, O 11,61:4
O'Hare, Thomas F Sr, 1948, My 11,25:4
O'Hare, Tom, 1960, S 2,23:2
O'Hare, William H, 1946, Je 7,19:3
O'Haren, William G, 1947, Jl 10,21:5
O'Harra, James J, 1947, O 29,27:3
O'Harra, M Glenn, 1955, F 7,21:3
O'Harra, Margaret T Mrs, 1942, N 22,52:7
O'Harrow, Dennis, 1967, Ag 31,33:4
Ohashi, Hydesaburo, 1918, O 2,13:2
Ohaus, Felix H, 1954, S 1,27:4
O'Hay, Irving P, 1944, O 20,20:2
Ohde, William F, 1947, Ap 14,27:2
Ohde, William F Mrs, 1950, O 3,31:2
Ohe, Adele Aus der, 1937, D 9,25:1
O'Hea, James F, 1938, Jl 9,13:3
O'Hea, Robert, 1952, Je 7,19:4
O'Hearn, Elizabeth Dr, 1938, N 12,30:5
O'Hearn, John A, 1956, S 1,15:6
O'Hearn, Margaret, 1953, Je 24,25:4
O'Hearn, Michael Mrs, 1943, D 27,19:1; 1952, Jl 19, 15:6
O'Hearn, Patrick, 1910, S 9,9:5; 1943, S 15,27:4
O'Hearn, Robert C, 1950, S 4,12:5
O'Hearn, William A, 1963, My 30,17:4
O'Hearne, John J, 1966, My 29,56:5
O'Hearne, Joseph Mrs, 1944, Ap 1,13:4
O'Herliky, Timothy, 1937, Jl 10,15:2
O'Hern, Charles Msgr, 1925, My 14,19:3
O'Hern, Daniel J, 1964, Ag 26,39:5
O'Hern, Edward P, 1945, N 17,17:3
O'Hern, Francis J, 1951, Ap 21,17:3
O'Hern, Joseph P, 1939, Ja 5,23:5
O'Hern, L J, 1930, D 13,19:3
O'Herron, Edward M, 1967, F 22,29:4
O'Higgins, H, 1929, Mr 1,25:3
O'Higgins, Thomas F, 1953, N 2,25:3
O'Higgins, William G Mrs, 1962, My 8,39:3
Ohira, Seisuke, 1950, O 17,31:2
Ohis, A Capt, 1907, D 8,11:6
Ohl, Eli R, 1947, My 7,27:2
Ohl, Emmy Mrs, 1950, D 30,13:7
Ohl, Fred, 1963, Ap 14,92:5
Ohl, Frederick A, 1946, Ja 17,23:1
Ohl, George A (will), 1947, Mr 5,23:5
Ohl, George Mrs, 1938, Ap 9,17:4
Ohl, Henry Jr, 1940, O 17,26:3
Ohl, Jeremiah F, 1941, Ja 22,21:5
Ohl, Josiah Kingsley, 1920, Je 28,15:3
Ohland, Henry Mrs, 1948, O 8,25:3
Ohland, Henry N Sr, 1960, Jl 7,28:7
Ohland, William E, 1950, N 17,28:3
Ohlbaum, Clarence J, 1952, Jl 13,61:2
Ohlberg, Ernest, 1953, Ag 26,27:2
Ohle, Ernest L, 1942, F 16,17:5
Ohlenbusch, John M, 1961, F 2,29:3
Ohlenslager, Jean C E, 1943, N 18,23:1
Ohler, Charles W Mrs, 1950, S 19,31:3
Ohlert, Gerard P, 1952, Ja 15,27:1
Ohley, H Maxwell, 1944, O 1,46:2
Ohliger, Frederick M, 1950, Mr 31,31:4
Ohlin, Hilda, 1954, F 13,13:4
Ohlinger, Carl T, 1943, Ja 28,20:2
Ohlman, Harry L, 1957, Ag 18,82:2
Ohlman, Maxwell, 1957, D 1,88:8
Ohlott, Joseph, 1948, Ap 30,23:4
Ohlott, Paul P, 1947, D 12,28:2
Ohlrich, Edward M, 1951, Ja 8,17:3
Ohlrich, Gustave W, 1954, F 10,29:5
Ohlrogge, Louis H, 1960, Ja 16,21:5
Ohls, Henry G, 1941, Mr 18,23:5
Ohlson, Gunnar E, 1944, Mr 21,19:1
Ohlson, John, 1956, Mr 4,88:1
Ohlson, John O, 1945, Ja 19,19:4
Ohlson, Olaf, 1946, F 26,26:2
Ohlweiler, Gustav, 1943, Je 15,21:3
Ohly, John H, 1956, D 15,25:2
Ohman, Phil, 1954, Ag 11,25:4
Ohman, Sven G, 1939, Ap 20,23:6
Ohmann, Burt C, 1945, Ja 26,21:3
Ohmeis, Hugo, 1920, O 11,16:1
Ohmeis, John, 1950, Ap 5,32:2
Ohmer, H Beckman, 1942, F 3,19:3
Ohmer, John F (por), 1938, N 5,19:2
Ohmer, John F, 1950, My 19,27:3
Ohmer, Raymond, 1937, Ja 21,23:5
Ohmes, Arthur K, 1937, F 13,13:4
Ohnan, Edward A, 1939, D 16,17:2
Ohnell, Ernst Jr, 1960, Mr 14,29:3
Ohnesorge, Johannes L von, 1952, F 1,21:3
Ohnesorge, Wilhelm, 1962, F 4,82:2
Ohnet, Georges, 1918, My 29,13:5
Ohnewald, George H, 1925, S 16,25:4
O'Hora, James T, 1949, N 11,25:4
Ohrbach, Henry W, 1937, Ap 1,23:2
Ohrbach, Louis E (por), 1944, F 22,24:3
Ohrbach, Morton J, 1960, O 14,33:3
Ohrenberger, William J, 1947, Ja 3,21:4
Ohriner, Jacob S Mrs, 1947, Ja 4,15:4
Ohringer, Irving, 1964, Ja 3,23:2
Ohringer, Isador, 1960, N 9,35:4
Ohrn, Arnold T, 1963, Ag 2,27:2
Ohrstrom, George L, 1955, N 11,25:1
Ohrt, Hans H, 1960, D 18,84:6
Ohrwalder, Father, 1913, Ag 9,7:6
Ohse, Albert, 1962, My 29,31:2
Ohsol, Johann G Dr, 1968, Jl 3,32:1
Ohswaldt, H F, 1946, O 23,27:4
Oishei, John R, 1968, Ja 28,76:8
Oislender, Naum Y, 1962, O 2,39:3
Ojeda, Emillio de Marquis, 1911, Je 6,9:5
Ojserkis, Sigmund, 1943, Mr 24,24:3
Oka, Ishonosuke Lt-Gen, 1916, Jl 20,11:6
Oka, Minoru, 1939, N 21,23:2
Okabe, Naosabure, 1946, D 1,79:5
Okada, Keisuke, 1952, O 18,19:3
Okada, Mokichi, 1955, F 13,86:6
Okakura, Kakuzo, 1913, S 5,9:5
Okamura, Yasuji, 1966, S 3,23:3
O'Kane, Adrian J, 1959, Ap 14,35:5
O'Kane, Bernard, 1939, Ja 8,42:5
O'Kane, Bernard F, 1950, N 10,27:1
O'Kane, Edward R, 1956, My 1,33:1
O'Kane, James, 1937, Ag 25,21:3
O'Kane, James J Sr, 1947, O 23,25:6
O'Kane, John F, 1944, Mr 11,13:4
O'Kane, John J, 1956, D 6,37:1
O'Kane, Michael A Rev, 1917, D 27,11:5
O'Kane, Richard A, 1960, Jl 6,33:3
Okane, T C Col, 1912, F 11,II,13:2
O'Kane, Thomas F Mrs, 1949, O 18,28:2

O'Kane, Thomas J, 1963, My 9,37:4
Okawa, Shumei, 1957, D 25,32:1
Okazaki, Katsuo, 1965, O 12,47:3
Okazawa, Gen, 1908, D 13,13:5
Oke, F G, 1937, My 1,19:5
Oke, Harris R, 1940, D 19,25:2
Oke, Mim K, 1955, F 1,29:4
O'Keefe, Arthur A, 1945, Ag 27,19:5
O'Keefe, Arthur B, 1964, My 13,47:3
O'Keefe, Arthur J, 1943, N 15,19:3
O'Keefe, Bernard E, 1952, My 15,31:4
O'Keefe, Charles C, 1957, F 11,29:3
O'Keefe, Chris J, 1939, Je 23,19:5
O'Keefe, Cornelius G, 1918, My 25,13:5
O'Keefe, Daniel J, 1966, My 2,37:2
O'Keefe, Daniel T, 1953, D 12,19:6
O'Keefe, Danny, 1948, D 5,92:3
O'Keefe, David H, 1925, Mr 3,23:5
O'Keefe, Dennis (funl, S 6,43:4), 1968, S 2,19:2
O'Keefe, Dennis J, 1952, O 10,25:3
O'Keefe, Dennis L, 1951, Ap 19,31:3
O'Keefe, Don P, 1939, D 19,26:4
O'Keefe, Edmund, 1965, O 13,47:2
O'Keefe, Edward J, 1954, My 24,27:4; 1959, Mr 1,86:8
O'Keefe, Francis, 1912, Ag 26,9:4
O'Keefe, Frank H, 1910, Ap 25,9:6
O'Keefe, G Merlyn, 1954, Ja 3,88:5
O'Keefe, Gerald P, 1949, Jl 28,23:1
O'Keefe, Gregory Mrs, 1950, S 10,92:4
O'Keefe, Gregory W, 1945, My 9,23:3
O'Keefe, Henry, 1940, Ag 21,19:4
O'Keefe, J G, 1939, Je 10,17:5
O'Keefe, Jack, 1948, O 27,27:5
O'Keefe, James C, 1942, Jl 27,15:5
O'Keefe, James M, 1942, O 20,21:5; 1965, S 11,27:5
O'Keefe, Jeremiah J, 1946, Mr 6,28:3
O'Keefe, John, 1912, N 22,13:3
O'Keefe, John E, 1944, Ja 22,13:6
O'Keefe, John F, 1967, O 16,45:3
O'Keefe, John J, 1938, Jl 11,17:3; 1955, Ja 23,85:2
O'Keefe, Joseph R, 1937, Jl 26,19:5
O'Keefe, Lawrence, 1942, My 14,19:5
O'Keefe, Lawrence E, 1941, Ja 21,21:2
O'Keefe, Martin R, 1941, Ag 3,35:1
O'Keefe, Michael, 1949, Mr 12,17:4
O'Keefe, Michael Capt, 1903, N 4,9:6
O'Keefe, Otto, 1952, D 18,29:1
O'Keefe, Padraigh, 1964, My 17,87:1
O'Keefe, Patrick A, 1943, D 23,19:3
O'Keefe, Patrick H, 1940, Ap 3,23:1
O'Keefe, Patrick J, 1951, D 8,11:5
O'Keefe, Patrick J Mrs, 1949, Ja 17,19:4
O'Keefe, Paul T Mrs, 1967, O 5,39:1
O'Keefe, Quincy M Mrs, 1958, F 18,27:2
O'Keefe, Raymond T, 1952, Ap 22,29:2
O'Keefe, Robert J, 1964, S 29,43:3
O'Keefe, T M, 1933, Ja 15,25:3
O'Keefe, Thomas H, 1921, My 10,17:5
O'Keefe, Walter F, 1965, Je 20,72:3
O'Keefe, William, 1951, Ja 24,27:2
O'Keefe, William J, 1937, Jl 2,21:1
O'Keeffe, Arthur, 1948, Jl 27,25:6
O'Keeffe, Arthur J, 1941, Ag 18,13:5
O'Keeffe, Dennis F, 1943, Ag 8,37:2
O'Keeffe, Eugene J, 1946, F 14,26:2
O'Keeffe, James E, 1943, Je 14,17:4
O'Keeffe, John A, 1941, Ap 29,19:2
O'Keeffe, John G (funl, Ag 20,26:5), 1922, Ag 18, 13:4
O'Keeffe, Thomas (por), 1940, Ag 20,19:4
O'Keeffe, William C, 1911, Ja 20,11:4
O'Keeffe, William D Mrs, 1947, Ap 7,23:3
O'Keeffe, William P, 1963, Ag 26,27:2
Okell, Charles C, 1939, F 10,23:4
Okell, Robert E, 1946, D 21,19:2
Okell, Stanley A, 1953, N 7,17:3
O'Kelley, Morris J Capt, 1910, Ja 20,11:4
O'Kelliher, Victor J, 1954, Ja 29,19:3
O'Kelly, James J, 1916, D 23,9:4
O'Kelly, Sean T, 1966, N 24,35:1
Okerblom, Andrew J, 1939, Mr 21,23:2
Okeson, Jane B, 1947, My 6,28:3
Okeson, Margaret A, 1952, Ap 4,33:7
Okeson, Walter R (por), 1943, N 5,19:1
Okey, George B, 1937, Je 12,15:5
Okey, Perry, 1963, My 19,86:5
Okie, Howard S, 1953, S 6,50:1
Okie, William B, 1952, Mr 28,23:1
O'Kieffe, Donald A, 1955, S 4,57:1
Okland, Nils J, 1952, N 3,27:2
Oklend, Tony (will, Mr 24,11:3), 1938, Mr 8,21:4
Oko, Adolph S, 1944, O 4,20:3
Oko, Adolph S Mrs, 1924, Ag 11,13:5
O'Kolski, Julius, 1949, O 27,27:4
Okongwu, Nnodu, 1947, Jl 5,11:5
Okrainetz, Clara, 1958, D 29,15:5
Okstel, Edmund H, 1953, Ap 9,27:1
Oksvik, Olav B, 1958, S 18,31:2
Oktavec, Martin M, 1957, Je 11,35:3
Oktay, Faruk, 1960, O 2,15:3
Oku, Y Count, 1930, Jl 20,II,8:3
Okuda, Gijin, 1917, Ag 25,7:6
Okulich, Frank, 1951, D 7,6:7
Okulicki, Leopold, 1955, O 20,6:4
Okuma, Marquis, 1922, Ja 10,19:3
Okuma, Shigenobu, 1922, Ja 7,13:5
Okun, Israel, 1941, O 23,23:1
Okun, Louis, 1952, F 28,27:5
Oladowski, H Col, 1878, Ag 25,9:4
Olaechea, Manuel A, 1946, My 4,15:5
Olafsson, Olaf J, 1957, F 18,27:1
Olam, Gustav A, 1949, Ap 9,17:7
Oland, Richard H, 1941, S 7,51:3
Oland, Warner, 1938, Ag 7,32:5
Olander, Milton M, 1961, D 31,48:7
Olander, Victor A, 1949, F 6,76:1
Olaneta, Jose R Col, 1882, My 2,2:4
Olanoff, Jacob A, 1945, Ag 11,13:6
O'Laughlin, Charles J, 1950, Ja 24,31:4
O'Laughlin, F D, 1934, Ap 19,25:5
O'Laughlin, John C (will, Mr 19,13:2), 1949, Mr 15, 28:2
O'Laughlin, John Mrs, 1947, D 25,21:2
Olaussen, Alfred, 1967, Mr 3,35:3
Olav, Hans, 1965, D 13,39:2
Olave, Kate R, 1943, Ag 26,17:7
Olaya Herrera, Enrique Dr, 1937, F 19,19:1
Olazabal, Francisco Rev, 1937, Je 12,15:4
Olberg, Charles, 1944, O 26,23:3
Olbon, Charles, 1906, Jl 29,9:5
Olbracht, Ivan, 1953, Ja 1,23:4
Olbricht, John S, 1948, Mr 19,23:4
Olcott, Alfred Van S, 1961, Jl 29,19:3
Olcott, Alfred Van S Mrs, 1966, Mr 30,45:3
Olcott, Anna W, 1946, My 12,44:5
Olcott, C, 1932, Mr 19,15:1
Olcott, C A Dr, 1905, Mr 31,9:6
Olcott, Charles A Mrs, 1923, S 2,22:3
Olcott, Charles T, 1966, Ag 3,37:4
Olcott, Chauncey Mrs, 1949, Je 13,19:1
Olcott, Dudley, 1919, D 29,9:2
Olcott, Dudley 2d, 1946, Je 28,22:2
Olcott, E E, 1929, Je 6,27:3
Olcott, E R Judge, 1869, S 17,2:3
Olcott, Ella C Mrs, 1942, Ja 28,19:5
Olcott, Emmett Robinson, 1908, Ja 13,7:4
Olcott, Frances J, 1963, Ap 4,47:3
Olcott, Frank Mrs, 1945, S 29,15:4
Olcott, Frederic P, 1909, Ap 16,9:1
Olcott, George C, 1942, Jl 19,30:6
Olcott, George Mann, 1917, S 15,11:5
Olcott, George N Dr, 1912, Mr 4,11:6
Olcott, George P Jr, 1958, Je 18,33:4
Olcott, Harley M, 1943, My 25,23:2
Olcott, Henry Steel Col, 1907, F 18,9:5
Olcott, J W, 1880, Mr 24,4:7
Olcott, Jackson P, 1959, Ag 30,83:2
Olcott, Jacob V, 1940, Je 2,44:6
Olcott, John N Mrs, 1909, Je 8,7:5
Olcott, Marvin, 1940, O 25,21:1
Olcott, Mary L B, 1962, My 24,35:4
Olcott, Neilson, 1914, Jl 12,5:4
Olcott, Richard Morgan, 1916, S 25,9:5
Olcott, Robert, 1947, My 11,60:6
Olcott, Sidney, 1949, D 18,88:5
Olcott, Thomas W, 1938, Jl 20,19:6
Olcott, W M K, 1933, My 11,17:1
Olcott, William M K Mrs, 1951, Jl 18,29:5
Olcott, William M K 2d, 1944, D 22,17:3
Old, Benjamin H, 1946, Ap 12,27:2
Old, Curtiss L, 1949, Ag 11,24:3
Old, Francis P, 1963, S 26,36:1
Oldach, Albert F, 1938, Ap 22,19:3
Oldaker, Wallace I, 1952, Mr 14,23:4
Oldberg, Charles R (por), 1938, Ap 5,21:5
Olde, Peter J, 1949, Je 21,25:2
Oldekop, Iwan, 1942, My 19,19:2
Olden, C S, 1875, O 4,4:5; 1876, Ap 8,2:2
Olden, Roosevelt W, 1947, O 20,23:4
Olden, Rudolf Mrs, 1959, F 10,33:4
Oldenburg, Andreas, 1939, S 11,19:4
Oldenburg, P von Prince, 1881, My 15,7:5
Oldenbuttel, Clarence F, 1953, D 29,23:1
Older, Andrew H, 1950, O 9,25:3
Older, Benjamin, 1950, Ap 21,23:1
Older, F, 1935, Mr 4,17:3
Older, Fremont Mrs, 1968, S 29,80:3
Older, Morris, 1946, D 24,17:2
Oldfather, Charles H, 1954, Ag 22,92:2
Oldfield, Barney, 1946, O 5,17:1
Oldfield, Barney Mrs, 1955, N 7,29:1
Oldfield, George A, 1960, Mr 24,33:3
Oldfield, Reuben B, 1954, Ap 2,28:3
Oldfield, Robert T, 1962, Ap 11,43:2
Oldfield, W A, 1928, N 20,31:1
Oldfield, William A Mrs, 1962, Ap 14,25:5
Oldham, F F Judge, 1912, Mr 20,13:5
Oldham, G Ashton, 1963, Ap 8,47:3
Oldham, Gilbert V, 1945, F 2,20:2
Oldham, J Bryan, 1954, O 6,25:4
Oldham, L P Mrs (will), 1939, F 18,17:4
Oldham, Mary Elizabeth Mrs, 1917, My 13,21:1
Oldham, Morris C (will), 1955, Ag 14,57:5
Oldham, Percy T, 1948, Ja 19,23:5
Oldham, U Grant, 1951, Ap 3,27:4
Oldham, William F Bp (por), 1937, Mr 30,23:3
Oldknow, Oscar S, 1951, D 28,21:2
Oldmeadow, Ernest J, 1949, S 13,29:4
Oldrin, J Merwin, 1903, Jl 26,7:6
Oldring, Henry Joseph, 1917, Ag 9,7:2
Oldring, Rube, 1961, S 11,27:4
Oldrini, Alexander, 1920, Je 18,11:4
Olds, Alfred W, 1943, My 7,19:1
Olds, C Burnell Mrs, 1939, Ap 23,III,6:8
Olds, Edwin G, 1961, O 11,47:3
Olds, Ernest A, 1947, Ag 4,17:4
Olds, F Perry, 1954, F 7,88:2
Olds, G D, 1931, My 12,25:1
Olds, George, 1956, Ag 12,85:1
Olds, H Kendall, 1956, Ag 2,8:8
Olds, Irving S (will, Mr 21,16:2), 1963, Mr 5,16:1
Olds, Irving S Mrs, 1957, Jl 27,17:7
Olds, John M Mrs, 1954, S 18,15:5
Olds, Leland, 1960, Ag 5,23:1
Olds, Nathaniel S, 1958, Mr 27,33:1
Olds, R E, 1932, N 25,15:3
Olds, Ransom E, 1950, Ag 27,89:1
Olds, Ransom E Mrs, 1950, S 3,38:4
Olds, Robert, 1943, Ap 29,21:1
Olds, W B, 1948, Ja 12,19:1
Oldt, Joel C, 1954, Jl 1,25:3
Oldus, Harold M, 1942, S 29,23:4
Olear, Andrew, 1950, N 7,27:4
Olearo, Victor J, 1945, S 20,23:3
O'Leary, Alice R, 1945, My 3,23:5
O'Leary, Arthur J, 1940, Jl 28,27:3; 1947, My 7,31:1
O'Leary, Arthur J A, 1959, Ag 2,81:1
O'Leary, Charles, 1952, N 1,21:4
O'Leary, Charles T, 1941, Ja 7,23:2
O'Leary, Conrad, 1947, S 26,23:5
O'Leary, Cornelius, 1947, N 21,27:1
O'Leary, Cornelius A, 1957, F 4,19:2
O'Leary, Cornelius J, 1942, My 22,21:3
O'Leary, Cornelius Jr, 1942, Ap 28,21:4
O'Leary, Cornelius N Dr, 1903, D 14,7:3
O'Leary, D, 1933, My 30,15:1
O'Leary, Daniel, 1949, Je 17,23:1
O'Leary, Daniel J, 1942, Ap 20,21:6
O'Leary, Daniel V, 1946, D 24,17:5
O'Leary, Daniel V Mrs, 1940, D 31,15:4
O'Leary, Denis, 1943, S 28,25:4
O'Leary, Dennis A, 1954, Ja 21,31:3
O'Leary, Dostaler, 1965, Ap 19,29:4
O'Leary, Edward J (funl), 1957, Jl 31,23:2
O'Leary, Edward J, 1964, S 20,82:6
O'Leary, Frank, 1952, F 4,17:5
O'Leary, Harold F, 1953, Ag 30,88:1
O'Leary, Henry J (por), 1938, Mr 7,17:3
O'Leary, Herbert, 1944, Jl 5,17:3
O'Leary, Humphrey F, 1953, O 17,15:6
O'Leary, Humphrey L, 1949, Ap 15,23:4
O'Leary, James A (por), 1944, Mr 17,17:1
O'Leary, James A Mrs, 1941, N 28,23:2
O'Leary, James C, 1948, Mr 19,23:1
O'Leary, James F Mrs, 1965, My 11,39:4
O'Leary, Jeremiah J Mrs, 1948, N 15,25:2
O'Leary, John, 1907, Mr 18,7:5
O'Leary, John D, 1939, F 22,21:5; 1953, My 15,23:2
O'Leary, John F, 1953, Ap 8,29:2
O'Leary, John J, 1942, Mr 29,45:2; 1947, O 28,25:1; 1957, O 19,21:2
O'Leary, John S (por), 1942, S 25,21:1
O'Leary, John S Mrs, 1944, My 16,21:3
O'Leary, John W, 1946, F 9,13:5
O'Leary, Joseph T, 1964, Ag 17,25:4
O'Leary, Joseph V, 1964, D 31,19:2
O'Leary, Kenneth W, 1963, Je 22,23:6
O'Leary, Lawrence J, 1948, D 27,21:2
O'Leary, Malachy T, 1945, Ap 8,36:2
O'Leary, Margaret Mrs, 1925, F 10,23:1
O'Leary, Margaret N, 1960, Ja 16,21:1
O'Leary, Margery C, 1955, Ja 19,27:5
O'Leary, Mary C, 1950, Ap 27,29:2
O'Leary, Mary J Mrs, 1938, Mr 18,21:1
O'Leary, Michael, 1956, Ag 10,17:5; 1961, Ag 3,23:5
O'Leary, Michael Mrs, 1948, Je 29,24:3
O'Leary, Patrick, 1946, Jl 25,21:2; 1959, N 10,47:2
O'Leary, Patrick B, 1955, F 8,27:3
O'Leary, Paul A, 1955, Jl 22,23:3
O'Leary, Ralph S, 1963, N 14,35:4
O'Leary, Richard F Sr, 1952, Jl 25,17:3
O'Leary, Thomas, 1925, Jl 27,13:4
O'Leary, Thomas A, 1950, Mr 16,31:1
O'Leary, Thomas M, 1949, O 11,31:4
O'Leary, Timothy F, 1958, Ja 3,23:2
O'Leary, Timothy J, 1925, D 12,15:5
O'Leary, Timothy Mrs, 1954, N 13,15:5
O'Leary, W L, 1903, My 10,7:6
O'Leary, Walter A, 1963, N 27,37:3
O'Leary, Walter A Mrs, 1962, Ag 23,29:2
O'Leary, Walter Cornelius, 1916, F 14,13:6
O'Leary, Walter E, 1951, Ja 15,17:6
O'Leary, Wesley A Dr, 1937, Ja 29,19:2
O'Leary, William D, 1955, F 2,27:3
O'Leary, William M, 1945, My 31,15:6
Oleinik, Zakhary, 1951, O 18,29:5
Oleksowicz, Stephen, 1952, Mr 8,13:2
Olen, Henry, 1959, S 3,27:4
Olena, Alfred D, 1949, D 31,15:6

Olena, Theophilus, 1920, S 21,11:6
Olendorf, C D, 1927, F 26,15:4
Olendorf, George F, 1941, S 6,15:5
Olenhausen, von Baroness, 1902, Ap 14,2:6
Olenin, Vassily M, 1956, Mr 29,27:5
Olensky, Morris, 1953, Ja 12,27:1
Olesen, H M Mrs, 1939, Ag 23,21:4
Olesen, Peter M Mrs, 1946, N 5,25:4
Olesen, Robert, 1945, Ag 19,40:2
Olesky, Leo, 1960, Jl 20,29:3
Olesky, Samuel, 1965, N 2,34:1
Oleson, John P, 1952, N 5,27:2
Olewine, Frank J, 1954, N 26,29:3
Olewine, George A, 1948, Ag 27,18:4
Olewine, Ted, 1946, Je 10,21:2
Oley, George F Rev, 1937, F 2,23:4
Oley, John H, 1953, Mr 14,15:6
Oleynick, Simeon A, 1944, Ja 18,20:3
Olf, Julius Mrs, 1949, N 12,15:4
Olf, Meyer L, 1959, Je 24,31:5
Olga, Dowager Queen of Greece, 1926, Je 20,26:5
Olga, Grand Duchess (cor, N 27,86:5; funl, D 1,35:2), 1960, N 26,21:2
Olga, Princess, 1880, N 2,1:5
Olgee, Edward J, 1951, Jl 17,27:1
Olgilvie, John L, 1950, S 8,32:4
Olgin, Moissaye J, 1939, N 23,27:2
Olgyay, Aladar, 1963, S 13,29:3
Oli, Joseph, 1953, Jl 2,23:6
Olian, Cyrus, 1948, Je 9,29:4
Olieslagers, Jan, 1942, Mr 26,23:2
Olim, Samuel, 1949, Mr 29,25:4
Olin, A B, 1879, Jl 8,5:4
Olin, Augusta Mrs, 1947, Ja 16,21:3
Olin, Bob, 1956, D 17,31:5
Olin, Emeline H Mrs (por),(will, Ag 18,17:4), 1938, Ag 14,33:4
Olin, Franklin W, 1951, My 22,31:2
Olin, Isaac, 1946, O 2,29:5
Olin, Jennie, 1911, O 20,13:4
Olin, Jessie, 1954, N 1,27:6
Olin, Lester C, 1952, O 23,31:1
Olin, Louis B, 1942, Jl 24,20:3
Olin, Milton, 1962, S 12,39:2
Olin, Raymond H, 1905, Ap 19,11:4
Olin, Richard N, 1938, O 5,23:5
Olin, Stephen Henry, 1925, Ag 7,15:6
Olin, William M Col, 1911, Ap 16,II,11:4
Olinger, Alphonse J Rev Dr, 1910, Ja 20,11:4
Olinger, Henri C, 1963, Ag 31,17:6
Olinger, Maurice, 1967, Je 22,39:3
O'Linn, J J, 1951, Ja 11,26:2
Olinsky, Ivan C, 1962, F 12,23:3
Oliphant, A Dayton, 1963, Je 27,33:1
Oliphant, A Dayton Mrs, 1951, O 13,17:6
Oliphant, Charles A, 1960, Mr 30,37:3
Oliphant, Charles W Sr, 1961, Jl 20,27:1
Oliphant, Claire Mrs, 1939, My 2,21:4
Oliphant, Duncan, 1950, Mr 5,92:4
Oliphant, Evelyn K Mrs, 1937, Mr 21,II,8:8
Oliphant, Herman, 1939, Ja 12,19:1
Oliphant, Lancelot, 1965, O 4,4:1
Oliphant, Margaret, 1897, Je 27,13:3
Oliphant, Robert T Mrs, 1953, Mr 24,42:2
Oliphant, S D Gen, 1904, O 24,9:5
Oliphant, Tom, 1922, My 25,19:4
Olis, Anthony, 1958, Je 4,33:3
Olis, Marcel, 1953, My 18,21:5
Olitsky, Peter K, 1964, Jl 22,33:4
Olitzka, Rosa, 1949, O 1,13:5
Olitzki, Walter, 1949, Ag 4,23:3
Olivares, Anthony, 1940, N 14,23:5
Olivares, Jose T, 1942, My 14,19:3
Olive, Lazar, 1956, D 10,31:4
Olive, Walter B Mrs, 1946, Jl 26,21:5
Oliveira, Alberto de, 1937, Ja 20,21:5
Oliveira, Javier C, 1954, Ap 13,31:2
Oliveira, Luis D A, 1950, N 4,17:5
Oliveira, Raul R de, 1942, Jl 10,17:3
Oliver, Adam H, 1948, N 23,29:3
Oliver, Alfred C Jr, 1952, Ja 29,25:4
Oliver, Allen H Dr, 1906, Mr 28,9:5
Oliver, Allen J, 1953, Jl 11,11:6
Oliver, Alwinn M, 1951, Ag 14,23:4
Oliver, Andrew, 1962, S 15,25:6
Oliver, Ann M Mrs, 1949, Mr 22,25:1
Oliver, Annie Mrs, 1940, Ap 24,23:6
Oliver, Augustus K, 1954, O 16,17:6
Oliver, Bertha, 1941, S 13,17:4
Oliver, Charles I, 1951, Ag 11,11:5
Oliver, Charles K, 1910, Ag 23,9:6
Oliver, Charles O, 1942, Jl 22,19:5
Oliver, Charles R, 1951, Ag 9,21:3
Oliver, Conrad D, 1947, F 17,19:4
Oliver, Curtis S, 1947, My 2,22:3
Oliver, Daniel, 1952, O 19,88:5
Oliver, David, 1945, Mr 31,19:3
Oliver, David H, 1938, My 3,23:6
Oliver, Ed (Porky), 1961, S 21,35:1
Oliver, Edna M (por), 1942, N 10,28:2
Oliver, Edna M (will), 1943, Ap 27,18:3
Oliver, Edwin, 1942, Je 11,23:2
Oliver, Edwin L, 1955, Ag 31,25:2
Oliver, Edwin W, 1956, Je 24,76:7
Oliver, Ellwood, 1944, Jl 10,15:5
Oliver, Elmer W, 1954, Je 27,69:3
Oliver, Elwood Mrs, 1948, N 13,15:5
Oliver, Ernest A, 1967, Mr 14,47:1
Oliver, Evelyn, 1947, D 2,29:4
Oliver, Frank, 1968, O 3,40:3
Oliver, Frank M, 1942, O 26,15:3
Oliver, Fred N, 1966, Jl 10,69:1
Oliver, Frederick L, 1963, Je 2,85:1
Oliver, Frederick W, 1937, N 20,17:2
Oliver, George (O Onions), 1961, Ap 10,31:5
Oliver, George E, 1941, S 27,17:5
Oliver, George F, 1952, Mr 21,24:3
Oliver, George H Dr, 1924, Je 6,17:5
Oliver, George S, 1963, Ag 4,81:1
Oliver, George T, 1919, Ja 23,13:3
Oliver, Harry C, 1949, S 7,29:2
Oliver, Henry F, 1965, O 18,35:1
Oliver, Henry Mrs, 1949, Jl 4,13:5
Oliver, Henry W, 1904, F 9,9:6
Oliver, Howard T Mrs, 1944, Jl 15,13:6
Oliver, Hudson J, 1955, S 21,33:2
Oliver, J, 1927, Ag 19,17:5
Oliver, J H, 1928, Ap 7,15:3
Oliver, J Jayden, 1960, Mr 26,21:4
Oliver, Jack, 1948, F 10,23:4
Oliver, James B Mrs, 1943, My 12,25:8
Oliver, James H, 1908, Mr 3,7:6; 1953, F 12,28:4
Oliver, James M, 1941, Jl 20,30:2
Oliver, James R, 1949, Ag 2,19:5
Oliver, James W (funl, S 22,11:6), 1911, S 19,13:3
Oliver, James 2d, 1944, My 22,19:6
Oliver, Jean N Mrs, 1946, Ap 3,25:6
Oliver, Jennie H Mrs, 1942, Je 4,19:3
Oliver, John G, 1939, Ap 15,19:4
Oliver, John M Maj-Gen, 1872, Mr 31,1:6
Oliver, John O, 1944, Ja 16,41:6
Oliver, John R (por), 1943, Ja 22,19:1
Oliver, John Sr, 1941, F 13,19:5
Oliver, John Wise, 1908, F 10,9:4
Oliver, Joseph, 1922, Ja 9,17:5
Oliver, Joseph Henry, 1919, Ja 17,13:5
Oliver, Josephine Mrs, 1955, My 13,25:2
Oliver, L Stauffer, 1966, Mr 5,27:5
Oliver, Leslie A, 1942, Ap 13,15:4
Oliver, Llewellen W, 1944, Je 14,19:4
Oliver, Mae, 1967, Je 11,87:2
Oliver, Mary A Mrs, 1938, O 1,17:3
Oliver, Neil, 1966, N 15,41:5
Oliver, Nelson S, 1942, Ja 30,20:2
Oliver, Nicholas, 1950, Ag 31,25:3
Oliver, Norman E (por),(cor, N 26,15:4), 1938, N 18,21:3
Oliver, Norman E Mrs, 1947, Mr 21,21:2
Oliver, Norris S, 1962, O 26,31:2
Oliver, Owen (por), 1944, Ja 28,17:2
Oliver, Paul A Gen, 1912, My 19,II,15:5
Oliver, Paul H, 1946, My 9,21:6
Oliver, Paul Q, 1939, D 1,23:4
Oliver, Peter, 1959, F 19,31:4
Oliver, R S, 1935, Mr 17,36:1
Oliver, Richard F, 1938, S 5,15:2
Oliver, Robert B, 1964, O 19,33:4
Oliver, Robert S Jr, 1937, S 26,II,8:7
Oliver, Robert T, 1948, F 21,13:3
Oliver, Robert T Col, 1937, Jl 12,17:3
Oliver, Robert W Mrs, 1950, N 14,31:3
Oliver, Roy G, 1941, D 3,26:2
Oliver, Royden C, 1944, N 2,19:4
Oliver, Samuel, 1943, Ag 10,19:4
Oliver, Samuel U, 1955, D 1,35:4
Oliver, Seabury Mrs, 1957, O 30,17:5
Oliver, Stephen, 1939, Ja 26,42:3
Oliver, Thomas, 1909, F 10,9:4; 1942, My 17,47:4
Oliver, Thomas E, 1946, S 15,9:7
Oliver, Vic, 1964, Ag 16,93:1
Oliver, Walter, 1946, F 15,25:4
Oliver, Walter E Mrs, 1951, Ag 17,17:4
Oliver, Webster J Mrs, 1963, S 15,87:1
Oliver, William Bentley (funl, N 13,11:4), 1910, N 11,9:5
Oliver, William C, 1947, Ap 8,27:3
Oliver, William L, 1946, My 28,21:4
Oliver, William P, 1943, Je 5,15:3
Oliver, William T, 1941, D 24,17:2
Oliver, William W, 1938, D 18,49:3
Oliver, Woodbury T, 1951, Jl 9,25:3
Oliveros, Inez F Mrs, 1946, Ag 19,25:1
Olivet, Alfred, 1942, My 6,19:2
Olivet, William E, 1947, S 17,25:2
Olivet, William E Mrs, 1947, S 17,25:2
Olivette, Marie (Mrs J R Ditmars), 1959, Mr 18,17:4
Olivetti, Adriano, 1960, F 29,27:4
Olivetti, James I, 1947, Ap 26,13:5
Olivier, Edith M, 1948, My 12,27:2
Olivier, Fernande, 1966, F 4,31:4
Olivier, Gerald K, 1939, Ap 2,III,6:7
Olivier, Lord, 1943, F 16,19:2
Olivier, Marcel (por), 1945, Ja 5,15:3
Olivier, Marcel Mrs, 1953, Ap 14,27:5
Olivier, Philippus, 1958, Mr 28,25:5
Oliviero, Lodovico, 1948, F 27,22:2
Olkhovsky, Victor G, 1945, Ag 14,21:4
Ollemans, Dominicus H, 1963, My 17,33:4
Ollemar, Anna E K, 1939, N 26,42:4
Ollemar, Nicholas, 1944, S 4,19:3
Ollendike, Byron H, 1951, Ap 12,33:3
Ollendorf, George, 1961, F 16,31:1
Ollendorf, William, 1918, Jl 20,9:4
Ollendorff, Herbert, 1962, Jl 15,61:1
Ollendorff, Morton Mrs, 1947, Mr 6,26:1
Ollendorff, Paula Mrs (por), 1938, O 17,15:6
Ollendorff, Walter, 1944, Mr 21,20:3
Ollenhauer, Erich, 1963, D 15,86:5
Oller, Richard H, 1946, Jl 31,27:3
Ollerenshaw, Benjamin, 1942, Ap 6,15:6
Ollerenshaw, Philip, 1943, D 2,27:5
Ollesheimer, Lawrence J, 1959, Mr 14,23:2
Ollesheimer, Sarah S Mrs, 1923, D 1,13:3
Olley, George, 1907, D 8,11:5
Ollier, Joseph O, 1949, Jl 12,27:5
Olliff, John, 1951, Je 30,15:4
Olliffe, Lewis W, 1966, My 8,82:2
Olliffe, W M, 1885, Mr 10,2:3
Ollivant, A Rev, 1882, D 17,2:6
Ollive, Thomas S, 1920, Je 12,13:4
Olliver, Father, 1910, S 21,9:4
Ollivett, William B, 1946, Ja 31,21:2
Ollivier, D, 1884, My 11,4:5
Ollivier, Daniel, 1941, O 7,23:1
Ollivier, Emile, 1913, Ag 21,9:5
Ollivier, Jessie, 1941, O 19,45:2
Ollman, Loyal F, 1966, Ap 10,76:5
Ollmore, Lewis F, 1940, O 2,23:5
Ollright, Joseph, 1937, Mr 30,23:3
Ollstein, Charles, 1967, Mr 27,33:1
Ollweiler, George F, 1958, My 6,35:3
Olly, Edward N Mrs, 1949, Mr 3,25:3
Olmos, Maria H de, 1949, S 17,17:5
Olmstead, A G Judge, 1914, S 20,15:4
Olmstead, Albert T, 1945, Ap 12,23:1
Olmstead, Asa, 1874, F 27,5:3
Olmstead, Charles I, 1945, S 11,23:4
Olmstead, Charles S, 1952, Ag 3,60:5
Olmstead, Charles Sanford Bp, 1918, O 22,13:2
Olmstead, Charles Tyler, 1924, Mr 27,19:6
Olmstead, Chauncey L, 1915, D 31,9:8
Olmstead, Clara H, 1940, Ap 2,25:4
Olmstead, Daniel P, 1960, D 23,19:4
Olmstead, Emily, 1954, Jl 13,23:2
Olmstead, Frederic W, 1959, D 12,23:3
Olmstead, G M, 1881, My 8,7:1
Olmstead, George H, 1950, Ja 27,23:3
Olmstead, John G, 1956, F 5,87:1
Olmstead, Leslie D, 1958, Mr 14,25:3
Olmstead, Marlin E, 1913, Jl 20,II,11:4
Olmstead, Paul D, 1947, Mr 9,60:6
Olmstead, U S, 1903, Ag 17,7:5
Olmstead, William Adams Brig-Gen, 1909, Mr 9,9
Olmstead, William H, 1921, Ja 5,13:6
Olmstead, William W Mrs, 1961, Ag 29,31:1
Olmsted, Allen S, 1942, N 24,26:2
Olmsted, Charles A, 1946, F 11,29:2
Olmsted, Denison Prof, 1859, My 14,4:6
Olmsted, Edward (por), 1941, Ag 22,15:1
Olmsted, Edward Mrs, 1953, Ja 29,28:7
Olmsted, Erastus R, 1948, Ja 18,60:3
Olmsted, Frank H, 1961, Jl 27,31:4
Olmsted, Fred Law, 1903, Ag 29,7:6
Olmsted, Frederick L, 1957, D 27,20:2
Olmsted, George, 1964, Mr 22,76:8
Olmsted, George W (por), 1940, Ja 17,21:3
Olmsted, Hawley, 1868, D 5,2:1
Olmsted, Herbert S, 1938, D 15,27:4
Olmsted, James M D, 1956, My 27,88:6
Olmsted, John, 1873, Ja 26,1:6; 1905, Ap 7,9:6
Olmsted, John A, 1953, O 23,23:3
Olmsted, John B Mrs, 1937, Ja 4,29:3
Olmsted, John C, 1920, F 26,11:4
Olmsted, John R, 1909, Jl 31,7:5
Olmsted, Julia C, 1944, My 14,46:5
Olmsted, La Verne N, 1947, D 21,52:4
Olmsted, Lucy, 1938, D 9,25:3
Olmsted, Mary A, 1939, S 14,23:5
Olmsted, Will H 2d, 1948, Ja 18,60:1
Olmsted, William B Jr (por), 1948, Ap 16,23:2
Olmsted, William L S, 1943, D 19,48:5
Olney, Benjamin, 1963, My 18,27:6
Olney, Bertha H H Mrs, 1949, F 8,29:6
Olney, Carl W, 1942, F 25,19:4
Olney, Channez, 1909, Mr 1,9:2
Olney, Clarence Crosby, 1908, Mr 8,7:6
Olney, George, 1950, Jl 28,21:3
Olney, George A, 1917, Jl 16,9:4
Olney, George Washington, 1916, Je 21,11:4
Olney, Jesse, 1872, Ag 17,3:1
Olney, Jesse W, 1954, Jl 24,13:3
Olney, La Fayette, 1905, Ja 8,2:5
Olney, Louis A, 1949, F 13,76:4
Olney, Peter B, 1968, S 24,47:3
Olney, Peter Butler, 1922, F 10,15:5
Olney, Richard, 1917, Ap 10,13:3
Olney, Richard F (por), 1939, Ja 16,15:3
Olney, Robert S, 1958, O 11,23:2
Olney, Sigourney B, 1956, Je 22,23:4

Olney, William B, 1949, Je 15,29:2
Olney, William R, 1965, Ap 8,39:4
Olofson, Leroy F, 1951, My 5,17:4
O'Loghlen, C Sir, 1877, Ag 12,5:3
O'Loghlen, Clement, 1941, My 3,15:2
O'Loughlen, James, 1960, D 6,41:1
O'Loughlin, Albert C, 1956, Ja 4,27:5
O'Loughlin, David L, 1955, Ja 11,25:2
O'Loughlin, Edward T, 1950, F 25,17:6
O'Loughlin, Edward T Mrs, 1958, O 4,21:2
O'Loughlin, Frank C Mrs, 1944, Je 26,15:4
O'Loughlin, Matthew J, 1937, N 30,23:4
O'Loughlin, Michael F Mrs, 1950, D 13,35:5
O'Loughlin, Thomas F, 1948, Ag 9,19:5
O'Loughlin, Walter F, 1960, D 9,31:1
Olozaga, Don Salustiana, 1873, S 27,4:7
Olp, Albert Carl, 1943, My 27,28:6
Olpp, Archibald E, 1949, Jl 27,23:2
Olrich, Ernest L, 1962, S 27,34:6
Olsan, Hiram, 1947, Mr 20,28:3
Olschki, Leo S, 1940, Je 22,15:7
Olschki, Leonardo, 1961, D 12,57:6
Olschwanger, Elias, 1952, S 23,33:3
Olsen, Arthur F Mrs, 1953, S 18,29:1
Olsen, Arthur J, 1939, F 22,21:6
Olsen, Arthur W, 1949, Ag 19,17:5
Olsen, Bernard A, 1947, Ja 30,14:6
Olsen, Charles D, 1954, F 7,88:2
Olsen, Charles K, 1915, D 12,9:3
Olsen, Chris F, 1965, Jl 1,28:5
Olsen, Edward, 1945, D 20,3:3
Olsen, Emerick W, 1963, Ap 3,47:1
Olsen, Everard F, 1956, Ap 18,31:3
Olsen, Frank, 1961, My 9,39:3
Olsen, Frederick O, 1954, Mr 24,27:5
Olsen, George F, 1954, F 11,29:4
Olsen, George W, 1954, Je 28,19:3
Olsen, Gershum L, 1942, D 7,27:3
Olsen, Gustave Mrs, 1958, Mr 25,33:4
Olsen, H P, 1949, F 9,28:2
Olsen, Harold G, 1953, O 31,17:4
Olsen, Harold M, 1960, Jl 11,29:3
Olsen, Harry M, 1962, Ag 30,29:2
Olsen, Herluf, 1966, S 14,43:5
Olsen, Herluf V Mrs, 1962, Ap 28,25:5
Olsen, Hjalmer, 1942, Ag 16,44:8
Olsen, Ivan C T, 1945, D 11,25:5
Olsen, James J, 1950, O 25,35:2
Olsen, John, 1954, F 11,29:2
Olsen, John A, 1937, D 12,39:2
Olsen, John C (por), 1948, Je 9,29:3
Olsen, John H, 1965, F 2,33:2
Olsen, John H Sr, 1947, Jl 7,17:3
Olsen, John J, 1951, Je 22,25:3
Olsen, Lawrence Mrs, 1953, F 19,23:4
Olsen, Martin, 1948, N 30,27:1
Olsen, Marvell A, 1959, Jl 8,29:2
Olsen, Moroni, 1954, N 23,35:1
Olsen, Neils, 1908, My 16,7:4
Olsen, Nils A (por), 1940, Jl 30,19:5
Olsen, Ole, 1943, O 8,19:5
Olsen, Ole (Jno S),(Jan 26), 1963, Ap 1,36:3
Olsen, Ole G, 1937, Ap 24,19:3
Olsen, Oscar E, 1956, Ap 26,33:3
Olsen, Oscar L, 1954, F 8,23:2
Olsen, P, 1942, Jl 6,9:7
Olsen, Peter C, 1950, O 16,27:5
Olsen, Peter F, 1947, My 9,22:3
Olsen, Rolf, 1939, My 26,23:5
Olsen, Rudolph, 1951, F 15,31:4
Olsen, Simon G, 1952, Mr 2,92:3
Olsen, Thomas S, 1956, D 13,37:1
Olsen, Thor, 1961, Mr 15,39:2
Olsen, Thorsten Y Mrs, 1954, Ap 12,29:6
Olsen, Victor A, 1959, Je 9,37:4
Olshan, Joseph, 1949, Mr 5,18:3
Olshevsky, Samuel, 1943, F 11,19:3
Olshin, Meyer D, 1956, Mr 23,28:2
Olsho, Sidney L, 1964, O 9,40:1
Olson, A Gustav Sr, 1945, N 9,20:2
Olson, Adolf, 1957, Je 8,19:6
Olson, Alfred E, 1941, Je 29,33:1
Olson, Alma L, 1964, Ap 29,41:3
Olson, Andrew, 1940, Mr 18,17:1
Olson, Andrew J Mrs, 1954, Ag 28,15:6
Olson, Andrew Mrs, 1951, S 20,31:4
Olson, Augustus C, 1939, Mr 2,21:4
Olson, C Howard Mrs, 1953, Je 17,27:4
Olson, C Walter, 1953, My 25,25:3
Olson, Carl T, 1960, Ap 3,86:2
Olson, Charles A, 1937, D 31,15:3; 1959, Mr 19,26:1
Olson, Charles O, 1954, F 9,27:4
Olson, Christina, 1968, Ja 29,31:2
Olson, Culbert L, 1962, Ag 14,25:5
Olson, Edward P, 1961, F 7,33:3
Olson, Edwin A, 1947, Je 28,13:5
Olson, Edwin G Dr, 1968, N 23,47:4
Olson, Edwin J, 1949, Jl 26,28:3
Olson, Egbert C, 1946, Ag 11,46:1
Olson, Enos, 1957, Ag 29,27:6
Olson, F B Gov, 1936, Ag 23,16:1
Olson, Frances B Mrs, 1954, My 9,89:2
Olson, Frank (late city ed), 1953, N 29,2:7
Olson, George S, 1942, Ja 19,17:3
Olson, Harold A Mrs, 1951, Ja 11,26:3
Olson, Harold M, 1939, My 23,23:2
Olson, Henry E, 1954, N 28,87:1
Olson, Hugo L, 1949, F 2,28:2
Olson, Ivan M (Ivy), 1965, S 4,21:5
Olson, J Arthur, 1964, Ja 8,34:8
Olson, James B E, 1957, O 5,17:2
Olson, John A, 1949, O 15,15:3
Olson, Julius E, 1944, F 27,38:1
Olson, Karl O Mrs, 1954, Ag 5,23:2
Olson, Kenneth E, 1967, Jl 15,25:5
Olson, Lyle H, 1944, Ja 15,13:5
Olson, Nels P, 1943, Jl 22,19:5
Olson, Olof, 1943, D 18,15:4
Olson, Oscar A, 1952, My 17,40:1
Olson, Oscar T, 1964, N 25,37:1
Olson, Sivert A, 1943, O 26,23:4
Olson, William B, 1958, Ap 23,33:5
Olson, William E, 1949, Ag 11,23:2
Olsson, Bengt, 1956, S 11,35:4
Olsson, Elis, 1959, My 25,29:2
Olsson, John V, 1955, Mr 31,27:1
Olsson, Nils W, 1954, Je 20,86:1
Olsson, Oscar, 1950, F 4,15:2
Olstein, Jacob B, 1967, F 28,34:2
Olsvanger, Immanuel, 1961, F 8,28:1
Olswang, Ralph R, 1965, Jl 12,27:2
Olswold, Leslie H, 1947, Je 2,25:4
Olszewski, Jerzy, 1964, F 15,23:2
Olt, George R, 1958, Je 29,69:2
Olt, Phil S, 1950, Ja 10,26:5
Oltarsh, David M (por), 1940, Jl 22,17:5
Oltman, Henry H, 1946, D 14,15:5
Oltmann, Adolph, 1937, Jl 18,II,7:2
Oltmanns, Herman J, 1952, N 3,27:5
Oltmans, Albert, 1939, Je 13,23:3
Olton, Percy Trafford Rev, 1953, F 20,19:1
Oluf, Johan, 1954, Jl 6,23:3
Olvany, George W, 1952, O 16,29:1
Olvany, George W Mrs, 1955, D 14,39:3
Olvany, Harriette E Mrs, 1938, Ag 13,13:7
Olvany, William J Sr, 1948, D 14,29:5
Olver, Paul S, 1953, O 18,87:1
Olvin, Laurence L, 1963, S 1,56:6
Olwell, Joseph E, 1963, Ag 25,82:6
Olwell, Lawrence A, 1939, Ja 23,13:3
Olwine, Richard E, 1954, F 2,27:3
Olwyler, John M, 1951, My 13,90:1
Olympio, Sylvanus Mrs, 1964, S 24,41:2
Olympius, Shirley, 1939, Je 24,17:6
Olyphant, D B, 1864, Jl 19,5:4
Olyphant, F Murray, 1924, Je 18,19:5
Olyphant, John Kensett, 1916, Je 23,11:7
Olyphant, Mary W Mrs, 1942, Mr 1,45:1
Olyphant, Murray, 1966, Jl 24,61:1
Olyphant, Robert M, 1918, My 4,15:5
Olyphant, Ruth, 1948, Je 22,25:3
Olyphant, Talbot, 1922, Ja 25,15:6
Olyphant, Talbot Gen, 1873, Ap 30,12:5
Om, Lady, 1911, Jl 21,9:4
O'Madigan, Isabel, 1951, Ja 25,25:2
O'Mahoney, Daniel J, 1951, Mr 3,13:6
O'Mahoney, Danno, 1950, N 4,20:5
O'Mahoney, Edward J, 1944, N 20,21:3
O'Mahoney, J J, 1881, Ag 27,5:4
O'Mahoney, John P, 1949, N 8,31:4; 1965, Jl 14,37:4
O'Mahoney, John R, 1941, N 20,27:1
O'Mahoney, Joseph C (funl, D 5,47:4), 1962, D 2, 88:4
O'Mahoney, Joseph C Mrs, 1963, N 23,17:1
O'Mahoney, Joseph M, 1959, F 5,31:2
O'Mahoney, Thomas F, 1946, Ag 22,27:5
O'Mahoney, Vincent P, 1959, D 12,23:6
O'Mahoney, William B, 1951, N 11,91:1
O'Mahony, J (funl, Mr 5,1:5) (see also O 8,12), 1877, O 14,5:6
O'Mahony, James Msgr, 1968, Jl 20,27:1
O'Mahony, John F, 1959, Ja 13,47:4
O'Mahony, Timothy J, 1950, Ag 26,13:6
O'Mailia, Miles J, 1952, Mr 15,13:4
O'Malia, Joseph R, 1949, S 12,21:4
O'Malley, A, 1932, F 26,19:5
O'Malley, Ann N, 1949, Ap 20,27:4
O'Malley, Anthony J, 1947, Mr 3,17:4
O'Malley, Austin, 1954, My 16,87:1
O'Malley, Charles A, 1940, Jl 22,17:2
O'Malley, Charles E, 1958, Ag 1,21:3
O'Malley, Charles J, 1955, O 11,39:4
O'Malley, Charles P, 1953, N 20,23:2
O'Malley, Dominick, 1943, Mr 8,15:5
O'Malley, Donagh Minister, 1968, Mr 11,37:1
O'Malley, Edward A, 1949, S 10,17:4
O'Malley, Edward F, 1952, N 25,29:3
O'Malley, Edward M, 1938, F 15,25:5
O'Malley, Edwin J, 1953, Ap 12,88:6
O'Malley, Edwin J Mrs, 1940, Je 4,24:3
O'Malley, Edwin J Sr, 1966, Ag 12,31:2
O'Malley, Ernie, 1957, Mr 27,31:3
O'Malley, Eugene F, 1954, Ag 3,19:3
O'Malley, F J, 1937, N 10,25:5
O'Malley, F W, 1932, O 20,21:3
O'Malley, Francis A, 1941, Je 3,21:2
O'Malley, Francis C, 1942, Ap 12,45:2
O'Malley, George P, 1941, S 7,51:3
O'Malley, James (por), 1947, D 26,15:1
O'Malley, John, 1940, S 17,23:2
O'Malley, John F, 1921, Ap 4,13:5; 1942, Ap 24,17:2
O'Malley, John J, 1944, F 5,15:3; 1960, Je 26,72:6
O'Malley, Joseph John Lt, 1918, Je 5,11:5
O'Malley, King, 1953, D 21,31:2
O'Malley, M V, 1931, My 27,27:1
O'Malley, Martin J, 1943, S 30,21:3
O'Malley, Mary, 1939, Ja 31,21:3
O'Malley, Mary F D Mrs, 1942, My 5,21:2
O'Malley, Michael J, 1943, O 14,21:2
O'Malley, Michael T, 1949, Ja 25,23:3
O'Malley, Warren J, 1955, N 23,48:4
O'Malley, William, 1939, S 13,25:2
O'Malley, William Capt, 1925, Ja 16,17:4
O'Malley, William H, 1945, Ap 5,23:2
O'Malley, William J, 1943, My 4,23:4; 1951, F 25,87:1
O'Malley, William P, 1944, Je 24,13:5; 1959, My 9, 21:6
Oman, A H, 1938, N 1,23:2
Oman, Carl, 1953, My 28,23:2
Oman, Charles (por), 1946, Je 25,21:5
Oman, Charles M (por), 1948, N 2,25:5
Oman, Charles M Mrs, 1966, Ap 8,28:8
Oman, John R, 1949, Ag 14,70:6
Oman, John 3d, 1960, Mr 21,13:1
Oman, Joseph W, 1941, Jl 3,19:5
Oman, Joseph W Mrs, 1954, F 27,13:3
Oman, Valadinar, 1945, F 20,19:1
Omansky, Jacob, 1938, D 12,19:4
O'Mara, Charles A, 1948, F 7,15:1
O'Mara, D A, 1934, F 7,19:3
O'Mara, Edward J (Feb 9), 1963, Ap 1,36:3
O'Mara, James, 1948, D 4,13:2
O'Mara, John, 1940, Ja 22,6:4
O'Mara, John A, 1943, Ja 21,21:2; 1959, Jl 30,27:5
O'Mara, John E, 1943, F 22,17:2
O'Mara, John T, 1947, F 4,26:2
O'Mara, Peter P, 1950, O 13,29:1
O'Mara, Roger, 1918, D 13,15:3
O'Mara, Roger Mrs, 1947, O 24,23:5
O'Mara, Thomas J, 1950, S 20,31:1
O'Marra, Patrick A, 1945, Ag 15,19:3
O'May, James, 1956, S 24,27:5
O'Mealey, J Warren Mrs (W de Campi), 1963, S 11, 43:1
O'Mealia, Harry F, 1944, N 5,54:4
O'Mealia, Leo E, 1960, My 8,88:3
O'Meara, A A Keith, 1956, O 31,33:2
O'Meara, Carroll G, 1962, F 21,45:2
O'Meara, David, 1947, Mr 21,21:2
O'Meara, Edward W, 1949, Jl 13,27:3
O'Meara, James J, 1938, Ag 18,20:6
O'Meara, John S, 1952, Ag 8,17:4
O'Meara, Joseph P, 1951, Jl 22,60:4
O'Meara, Leo B, 1940, Ap 19,21:2
O'Meara, Maurice, 1910, Ja 16,II,11:5
O'Meara, Michael J, 1940, D 13,23:1
O'Meara, Patrick, 1915, Mr 22,9:2
O'Meara, Patrick M, 1945, O 28,43:1
O'Meara, Patrick Mrs, 1915, Mr 22,9:2; 1948, Je 28, 19:3
O'Meara, Robert J, 1947, F 1,15:4
O'Meara, Stephen, 1918, D 15,22:4
O'Meara, William J, 1964, Ag 24,27:3
O'Mears, Ben, 1966, Ap 18,41:7
Omelczuk, Alex W, 1957, Mr 16,19:4
O'Melia, Pauline A, 1962, S 22,25:4
O'Melveny, Donald, 1942, Ag 29,15:3
O'Melveny, Henry W, 1941, Ap 15,23:3
Omenhiser, John T, 1963, Jl 24,31:4
Omer, Henry, 1946, Jl 13,15:4
Omer, Lewis, 1954, Ja 4,19:2
Omera, Mark Dr, 1937, F 7,II,8:5
Omholt, Andrew Mrs (Mother Bloor), 1951, Ag 11, 11:1
Omiker, William, 1944, S 13,19:2
Ommanney, Adm, 1904, D 22,9:4
Ommanney, Nelson, 1938, Ja 13,21:3
Omme, Henry C, 1937, Mr 19,24:1
Ommen, Alfred E Mrs, 1947, Mr 23,60:3
Omodeo, Adolfo, 1946, Ap 30,22:2
Omodeo, Angelo, 1941, Je 8,48:5
Omond, Henry, 1951, My 27,68:6
Omont, Henry A, 1940, D 17,26:2
Omori, Fusakichi, 1923, N 11,23:4
Omurtak, Salih, 1954, Je 25,21:3
Omwake, George I Dr (por), 1937, F 4,21:1
Omwake, Howard R, 1942, Jl 21,19:5
Omwake, John, 1939, Ap 24,17:2
Onaga, Yoshimatsu, 1955, O 10,27:2
Onasch, Charles F, 1959, S 16,39:4
Onatisia, J N, 1876, Jl 8,5:1
Onativia, Tomasieto Luis de, 1909, O 8,9:4
Oncken, Hermann, 1946, Ja 26,13:4
Oncken, William, 1961, S 19,35:2
Onda, Andrew R, 1959, S 21,31:4
Ondani, Julio, 1954, Jl 2,19:3
Ondek, John Sr, 1948, Ap 27,25:1
Onderdonk, Abraham F Prof, 1913, S 26,11:6
Onderdonk, Adelbert M, 1950, Ap 12,27:2

Onderdonk, Andrew, 1905, Je 22,9:6
Onderdonk, Andrew Joseph, 1925, My 25,17:6
Onderdonk, Chester D, 1960, D 22,23:2
Onderdonk, Frederick A, 1945, D 16,39:2
Onderdonk, Holmes, 1938, Ja 15,15:2
Onderdonk, J Clarke Jr, 1964, My 21,35:4
Onderdonk, John A, 1954, My 22,15:5
Onderdonk, W H, 1882, D 13,5:1
Onderdonk, William M, 1943, Mr 1,19:2
Ondrak, Ambrose L, 1961, F 24,36:3
Ondrey, John S, 1954, D 23,10:5
O'Neal, Charles T, 1950, Ap 17,23:2
O'Neal, Edward A, 1958, F 27,27:5
O'Neal, Emmet, 1967, Jl 20,37:3
Oneal, James Mrs, 1944, Je 17,13:6
O'Neal, John, 1948, S 1,24:3
O'Neal, John H, 1907, Jl 16,7:6
O'Neal, Samuel A, 1956, Je 18,25:2
O'Neal, Simie, 1937, Ap 9,21:1
O'Neal, William, 1953, O 13,29:1
O'Neal, William J, 1961, My 27,23:4
O'Neal, William W, 1955, Ag 10,25:1
O'Neale, James S Saunders Mrs, 1920, D 24,11:4
Onegin, Sigrid (por), 1943, Je 19,13:3
O'Neil, Alex J, 1963, S 30,29:3
O'Neil, Andrew S, 1947, Ag 15,17:3
O'Neil, Ann, 1951, N 3,17:2
O'Neil, Arthur, 1957, Jl 19,19:2
O'Neil, Augustine, 1918, Ja 6,18:6
O'Neil, Bryan H, 1954, O 25,27:2
O'Neil, Burke, 1960, O 16,88:6
O'Neil, C Rear Adm, 1927, Mr 1,27:3
O'Neil, Charles J Sr Mrs, 1951, D 1,13:4
O'Neil, Cosmo D, 1958, O 28,35:2
O'Neil, Cyril F Mrs, 1956, Ag 13,21:1
O'Neil, Edward A, 1964, O 10,29:3
O'Neil, Edward D, 1948, N 14,76:6
O'Neil, Edward J, 1925, N 14,15:6
O'Neil, Edwin H, 1944, F 23,19:3
O'Neil, Eugene J Jr, 1951, D 29,11:1
O'Neil, F Edward, 1952, O 2,29:6
O'Neil, Felix J, 1952, D 31,15:4
O'Neil, Felix J Rev, 1937, S 27,21:5
O'Neil, Francis J, 1954, D 1,31:5
O'Neil, Frank, 1951, S 27,31:5
O'Neil, Frank A, 1966, Je 14,47:3
O'Neil, Frank R, 1908, Ja 28,9:5
O'Neil, George (por), 1940, My 25,17:4
O'Neil, George F, 1921, Ja 31,9:4
O'Neil, George H Sr, 1942, Ag 7,17:6
O'Neil, George Michael, 1968, F 14,47:1
O'Neil, Harold G, 1940, Ap 8,3:1
O'Neil, Hugh L, 1937, D 5,II,9:1
O'Neil, J F, 1932, Ap 23,15:1
O'Neil, J Palmer, 1908, Ja 8,9:7
O'Neil, James (funl, Ag 13,9:1), 1920, Ag 11,9:1
O'Neil, James, 1944, D 2,13:3; 1946, Ja 22,27:1
Oneil, James H, 1911, O 12,9:4
O'Neil, James R, 1960, S 17,23:4
O'Neil, John, 1922, Ap 22,9:5
O'Neil, John E, 1956, O 27,21:4
O'Neil, John H, 1922, N 20,17:3
O'Neil, John J, 1944, My 17,19:4; 1945, Ag 6,15:4
O'Neil, John L, 1941, Mr 12,22:2
O'Neil, John Mrs, 1879, Ap 29,2:6
O'Neil, John S, 1951, D 12,37:5
O'Neil, John T, 1950, Mr 27,23:3
O'Neil, John W, 1952, Ag 17,77:2; 1953, O 20,29:3
O'Neil, Joseph B, 1947, N 3,23:3
O'Neil, Joseph E, 1940, Mr 23,13:6
O'Neil, Joseph P, 1938, Jl 28,19:6
O'Neil, Leo D, 1961, O 4,45:3
O'Neil, Leo M, 1958, N 15,23:5
O'Neil, Michael, 1914, Ja 23,11:5
O'Neil, Michael A, 1912, My 11,13:6
O'Neil, Michael J, 1945, Je 30,17:3
O'Neil, Nance, 1965, F 8,25:2
O'Neil, Owen A, 1951, Ja 1,17:3
O'Neil, Peggy, 1960, Ja 8,23:1
O'Neil, Ralph (por), 1940, My 26,34:2
O'Neil, Richard J, 1941, Ag 13,17:2
O'Neil, Richard V, 1961, Je 8,32:4
O'Neil, Rose, 1908, O 17,9:4
O'Neil, Ross, 1909, Jl 30,7:7
O'Neil, Thomas E, 1944, Ja 10,17:1
O'Neil, Thomas F, 1943, D 12,68:1
O'Neil, Thomas J, 1924, N 5,19:4; 1956, N 12,29:1
O'Neil, Thomas J W, 1964, F 11,39:2
O'Neil, Timothy, 1958, Je 5,31:4
O'Neil, W Jerold, 1942, D 21,23:5
O'Neil, W Jerold Mrs, 1951, N 23,30:2
O'Neil, Walter B, 1945, Mr 26,19:4
O'Neil, William B, 1948, Ap 20,27:5
O'Neil, William F, 1960, S 5,15:2
O'Neil, William H, 1945, F 13,23:2
O'Neil, William J, 1946, D 17,38:5
O'Neil, William J Mrs, 1961, Ap 24,29:1
O'Neil, William L, 1947, Mr 8,13:5; 1953, Ag 16,77:2
O'Neil, William T Sen, 1909, My 6,9:5
O'Neill, A Augustus, 1942, Ja 5,17:4
O'Neill, Addison D, 1940, Je 15,15:5
O'Neill, Albert R, 1947, Ag 14,23:3
O'Neill, Albert T, 1959, Ag 24,21:5
O'Neill, Alex R, 1955, Ap 25,23:4
O'Neill, Anna Mrs, 1925, My 29,17:5
O'Neill, Arthur C, 1960, F 21,92:8
O'Neill, Arthur I, 1937, My 28,21:2
O'Neill, Bernard, 1950, S 27,32:2
O'Neill, Bernard F, 1942, S 22,21:2
O'Neill, Bernard M, 1957, D 3,35:4
O'Neill, Bernard M Mrs, 1960, S 30,27:1
O'Neill, Charles (por), 1949, F 28,19:3
O'Neill, Charles, 1949, Mr 5,17:4; 1966, Mr 16,45:4
O'Neill, Charles A, 1951, Mr 10,13:1; 1965, Jl 26,23:3
O'Neill, Charles E, 1941, Ja 21,22:3
O'Neill, Charles J, 1956, D 26,27:1
O'Neill, Charles L, 1952, Ag 27,27:2
O'Neill, Charles Mrs, 1954, Ja 29,19:1
O'Neill, Charles T Mrs, 1947, Mr 14,24:3
O'Neill, Cornelius J Mrs, 1944, F 25,17:5
O'Neill, Donall, 1938, Ag 26,17:6
O'Neill, E Mark Dr, 1937, Je 14,38:4
O'Neill, Edmund J, 1947, O 22,29:2
O'Neill, Edward E, 1951, N 12,25:2
O'Neill, Edward F, 1940, Ja 23,21:1; 1957, Je 30,68:7
O'Neill, Edward F Mrs, 1960, My 25,39:4
O'Neill, Edward J, 1945, D 14,27:4; 1959, Jl 30,27:4; 1959, Ag 25,31:4
O'Neill, Edward L, 1948, D 13,23:4
O'Neill, Edward T, 1959, My 25,29:3
O'Neill, Elmer W, 1949, Jl 26,27:3
O'Neill, Emmett, 1948, Jl 15,23:6
O'Neill, Emmett Jr, 1940, Ap 16,23:5
O'Neill, Eugene, 1953, N 28,1:3; 1961, Ag 10,27:2
O'Neill, Eugene F Mrs, 1950, O 15,104:3
O'Neill, Eugene P, 1952, Ap 22,29:4
O'Neill, Eugene T, 1968, D 14,45:3
O'Neill, Father, 1902, N 5,9:6
O'Neill, Felix, 1949, S 7,29:4
O'Neill, Ferdinand J Mrs, 1961, D 31,48:3
O'Neill, Francis A, 1941, Jl 15,19:5; 1950, Ja 10,29:1; 1957, D 16,29:2
O'Neill, Francis Msgr, 1918, O 28,11:3
O'Neill, Frank, 1954, D 3,28:1
O'Neill, Frank (Buck), 1962, My 12,23:5
O'Neill, Frank J (Buck), 1958, Ap 22,33:5
O'Neill, Frank J, 1960, Mr 27,86:7
O'Neill, Frank Mrs, 1951, D 31,13:2
O'Neill, Frederick C, 1951, O 24,31:4; 1951, D 26,25:5
O'Neill, George, 1939, O 21,15:6
O'Neill, George F, 1947, Ja 6,23:6; 1954, Ap 30,23:3
O'Neill, Gerald, 1953, Ap 19,91:1
O'Neill, Gerald B, 1965, Mr 1,27:4
O'Neill, Gerard P, 1955, F 22,21:4
O'Neill, Gilbert L, 1950, S 19,31:2
O'Neill, Gordon A Sr, 1954, N 11,31:1
O'Neill, Gordon F, 1940, Je 15,15:2
O'Neill, Grace M Mrs, 1949, My 18,27:3
O'Neill, Harold, 1952, D 28,48:4
O'Neill, Harold E, 1942, My 24,24:5
O'Neill, Harry F, 1958, Ap 2,31:2
O'Neill, Harry J Sr, 1954, Jl 24,13:1
O'Neill, Harry P, 1953, Je 25,27:5
O'Neill, Harry S, 1954, D 28,23:2
O'Neill, Henry, 1918, F 26,13:4; 1961, My 22,31:4
O'Neill, Henry W, 1966, Jl 11,29:3
O'Neill, Herbert W, 1941, D 3,25:4
O'Neill, Howard F, 1954, Ja 9,15:3
O'Neill, Hubert J, 1961, Jl 22,21:4
O'Neill, Hugh, 1902, Mr 17,1:3; 1925, O 9,23:4; 1939, N 15,23:1
O'Neill, Isabel A, 1968, O 9,47:5
O'Neill, J E, 1931, Ag 25,21:3
O'Neill, J P, 1883, F 27,3:4
O'Neill, James, 1903, Je 10,9:6; 1923, N 9,17:5; 1944, N 29,23:1
O'Neill, James E, 1960, Ag 13,15:6
O'Neill, James F Mrs, 1943, Ja 15,18:2
O'Neill, James F X, 1955, Je 9,29:3
O'Neill, James J, 1925, Je 29,13:7; 1948, S 14,29:5
O'Neill, James L, 1939, Ja 16,15:4
O'Neill, James L (por), 1945, Ag 23,23:3
O'Neill, James L, 1950, Mr 13,21:4
O'Neill, James L Mrs, 1952, N 22,23:4
O'Neill, James M, 1941, Ja 6,15:4
O'Neill, James M Sr, 1953, Jl 25,11:4
O'Neill, James Mrs, 1922, Mr 2,21:4
O'Neill, James T (funl, S 25,21:6), 1925, S 22,25:5
O'Neill, James V, 1966, Ja 8,26:4
O'Neill, Jeremiah Mrs, 1951, D 8,11:3
O'Neill, Joan H, 1963, D 24,17:2
O'Neill, John, 1909, S 28,9:6; 1952, Ja 3,46:4
O'Neill, John A, 1941, Mr 15,17:3
O'Neill, John E, 1953, Ag 13,25:3
O'Neill, John F, 1953, My 16,19:5
O'Neill, John H, 1950, Mr 1,27:3
O'Neill, John I, 1955, O 8,19:4
O'Neill, John J (por), 1945, Je 7,19:4
O'Neill, John J, 1953, Ag 31,17:3; 1961, Ap 30,87:1
O'Neill, John J Jr, 1949, N 14,27:5; 1953, Je 2,29:3
O'Neill, John M, 1952, Mr 15,13:5
O'Neill, John Mrs, 1953, Je 13,15:4
O'Neill, John R, 1967, My 22,43:3
O'Neill, John R Mrs, 1963, N 10,87:2
O'Neill, John S, 1950, Ag 7,19:5
O'Neill, John T, 1958, N 13,33:5
O'Neill, John Vincent, 1968, Ja 25,40:1
O'Neill, Joseph A Mrs, 1952, N 1,21:6
O'Neill, Joseph C Sr, 1957, Ag 20,27:1
O'Neill, Joseph F, 1942, Ap 22,23:2
O'Neill, Joseph I, 1959, Ag 28,23:4
O'Neill, Joseph J, 1940, Ap 18,23:4
O'Neill, Joseph M, 1960, D 21,31:3
O'Neill, Joseph P Mrs, 1948, O 1,26:2
O'Neill, Lawrence, 1882, F 22,3:5
O'Neill, Lawrence V, 1955, Ja 9,87:2
O'Neill, Leo A, 1954, Jl 31,13:6
O'Neill, Lottie Mrs, 1967, F 18,29:5
O'Neill, Louis F, 1938, Ag 14,32:6
O'Neill, Maire, 1952, N 3,27:5
O'Neill, Mary Mrs, 1951, O 20,15:6
O'Neill, Michael C, 1943, Ap 14,23:2
O'Neill, Michael J, 1942, Je 27,13:5; 1949, O 17,23
1954, Ag 28,15:4; 1959, Ag 13,27:5
O'Neill, Norris J, 1937, N 17,23:4
O'Neill, Owen R Mrs (L E Nadelhoffer), 1964, Je
35:2
O'Neill, Patrick, 1937, Ag 8,II,6:5; 1947, Jl 20,44:1;
1958, Mr 27,33:1
O'Neill, Patrick F, 1942, Mr 5,23:3; 1943, F 1,17:2
O'Neill, Patrick J, 1942, O 8,27:3; 1954, Jl 18,57:1
O'Neill, Patrick Mrs, 1966, Je 2,43:4
O'Neill, Paul J, 1944, D 13,24:2
O'Neill, Paul M, 1965, Jl 21,37:6
O'Neill, Paul Sr Mrs, 1951, Ja 11,25:4
O'Neill, Peggy, 1947, F 8,17:4
O'Neill, Peter J, 1939, Ag 9,17:4
O'Neill, Peter L, 1958, F 26,27:2
O'Neill, Peter Mrs (M Delaney), 1961, Mr 28,35
O'Neill, Peter P, 1952, D 11,33:2
O'Neill, Raymond E, 1962, Jl 3,23:1
O'Neill, Richard J, 1947, Ag 31,36:7
O'Neill, Robert P, 1950, Ap 10,19:5
O'Neill, Rose, 1944, Ap 7,19:5
O'Neill, Sally (Mrs S S Battles), 1968, Je 20,45:4
O'Neill, Simon J Dr, 1913, N 14,11:6
O'Neill, Steve, 1962, Ja 27,21:4
O'Neill, Terence, 1956, F 12,88:8
O'Neill, Terence J, 1947, Ja 13,21:1
O'Neill, Terrence, 1940, F 29,19:2
O'Neill, Thomas E, 1949, Ag 21,68:3
O'Neill, Thomas H, 1954, Ap 15,29:2
O'Neill, Thomas J, 1942, Je 25,23:3; 1956, Jl 12,2
1964, F 14,33:4
O'Neill, Thomas L, 1951, Mr 31,15:5
O'Neill, Thomas Mrs, 1956, Ap 29,86:7
O'Neill, Timothy E, 1947, Mr 1,15:4
O'Neill, Timothy W, 1961, S 25,33:3
O'Neill, Vincent E, 1939, My 31,23:2
O'Neill, Vincent W P, 1966, Jl 17,68:5
O'Neill, W Paul, 1966, D 9,47:3
O'Neill, W Paul Mrs, 1949, Ag 26,19:4
O'Neill, Wilfrid N, 1950, My 29,17:5
O'Neill, William, 1950, S 6,29:1
O'Neill, William C Jr, 1952, Ap 15,27:1
O'Neill, William F, 1903, Jl 11,7:6; 1955, Ag 26,
O'Neill, William H, 1957, Ap 20,17:3
O'Neill, William J, 1957, O 16,35:3
O'Neill, William P, 1955, F 18,21:4
Onelli, Clementi, 1924, O 21,23:4
Ong, Eugene W, 1958, Je 7,19:4
Ong, Harry A, 1960, N 20,86:5
Ongley, Byron, 1915, O 24,17:6
O'Niel, James, 1872, Je 23,8:4
Onions, Charles T, 1965, Ja 12,37:4
Onions, Oliver (G Oliver), 1961, Ap 10,31:5
O'Nions, William E, 1950, N 20,25:4
Onkeles, Sydney, 1957, N 15,27:1
Onken, William H Jr, 1957, N 30,21:6
Onken, William H Jr Mrs, 1939, Ap 12,23:5
Onksen, Frederick, 1952, S 1,17:6
Onnou, Alphonse, 1940, N 21,29:4
Ono, Bamboku, 1964, My 29,29:4
Ono, Yoshio, 1956, O 15,25:5
Onofrio, Olimpia d' Mrs, 1946, Je 16,40:3
O'Nolan, Brian (F O'Brien), 1966, Ap 2,29:1
O'Nolan, Martin J, 1943, S 20,21:3
Onorato, Anthony, 1951, Jl 29,68:4
Onorato, Michael Mrs, 1964, Ja 31,27:2
Onorato, Rocco Sr, 1943, Ja 31,44:4
Onorato, Vito F, 1956, Je 26,29:5
Onorato, Vito N, 1950, Ag 5,15:6
Onoye, Kikugoro, 1949, Jl 11,17:4
Onozuka, Kiheiji, 1944, N 30,23:5
Onri, Archie O, 1944, D 8,21:5
Onslow, Earl of, 1945, Je 12,19:5
Onslow, Guilford, 1882, Ag 23,5:6
Onslow, John J (Jack), 1960, D 23,19:2
Onslow, William Hiller, 1911, O 24,13:6
Ontel, Edward, 1922, My 12,19:4
Ontra, Buddy, 1960, My 8,88:7
Onutt, B S, 1936, S 2,21:4
Onyx, Herbert P, 1949, N 18,29:3
Ooms, Casper W, 1961, F 20,27:3
Oostermeyer, Jan, 1967, Je 28,45:2
Oosting, Henry J Dr, 1968, N 2,37:3
Ootah, 1955, My 10,29:2
Oothout, Edward, 1903, S 2,7:6
Oothout, Marie J, 1938, N 5,19:2

Oothout, William Mrs, 1913, S 17,9:3
Opalinski, Wladyslaw, 1957, N 22,25:4
Opatoshu, Joseph, 1954, O 8,23:6
Opavsky, Frances V, 1958, Jl 31,9:3
Opdycke, E Gen, 1884, Ap 26,1:5
Opdycke, Henry G (por), 1938, D 31,15:4
Opdycke, John B, 1956, N 5,31:4
Opdycke, John B Mrs (T Helburn),(cor, Ag 20,25:4, 1959, Ag 19,29:3
Opdycke, Leonard E Mrs, 1946, Jl 2,25:6
Opdycke, William H, 1948, N 17,27:5
Opdyke, Charles P Dr, 1937, Ja 23,18:4
Opdyke, Charles W, 1907, Mr 10,9:6
Opdyke, George, 1880, Je 13,12:2
Opdyke, Henry, 1940, Ja 9,24:2
Opdyke, Leon A, 1961, O 16,29:1
Opdyke, Levings A, 1939, Jl 7,17:2
Opdyke, Mary B, 1937, N 18,23:2
Opdyke, Wilbur F, 1949, N 22,29:1
Opdyke, William Stryker, 1922, O 21,13:5
Opeka, Frank, 1944, D 31,25:1
Opel, Carlton A, 1955, D 13,39:3
Opel, Friedrich (por), 1938, Ag 31,15:5
Opel, Wilhelm von (por), 1948, My 3,21:1
Openchowski, Mieczyslaw, 1960, Ap 10,86:5
Openshaw, Henry C, 1959, My 19,33:3
Opfermann, John L, 1955, Mr 20,88:4
Ophuls, Max, 1957, Mr 27,31:3
Opie, Eugene L Mrs, 1965, D 7,47:1
Opie, Floyd R Mrs, 1949, N 9,27:1
Opie, Hierome L, 1943, F 27,13:6
Opie, John Walter, 1921, Ag 7,22:4
Opie, Thomas Dr, 1914, O 8,11:4
Opie, Thomas F, 1957, F 10,85:4
Opinsky, John E, 1949, Ap 1,25:4
Opitz, Albert M, 1945, F 4,38:8
Opjenski, Henry K, 1942, Ja 23,19:2
Opler, Arnold, 1949, D 22,23:1
Oplinger, Floyd F, 1949, My 11,29:6
Oporto, Duchess of, 1941, Ja 12,44:1
Opp, Frederick, 1940, N 17,49:2
Opp, Julie, 1921, Ap 9,11:6
Opp, Mary Mrs, 1938, O 30,41:3
Oppasser, John J, 1962, Ag 9,25:4
Oppe, John D, 1952, N 3,27:5
Oppegard, Ray, 1952, Je 7,19:2
Oppel, John J, 1953, Ja 22,23:4
Oppel, William P Jr, 1961, Je 22,31:1
Oppenheim, Albert D, 1914, D 9,13:4
Oppenheim, Ansel, 1916, D 10,21:2
Oppenheim, Ansel Mrs, 1915, S 7,13:6
Oppenheim, Austin N, 1962, D 5,47:3
Oppenheim, Ben J, 1968, F 10,34:1
Oppenheim, Burton E, 1943, Ag 28,11:3
Oppenheim, Charles, 1952, N 27,31:2
Oppenheim, Charles J Mrs, 1959, Ja 10,17:4
Oppenheim, Charles J Sr (por), 1941, My 30,15:1
Oppenheim, David, 1943, Je 9,21:1; 1967, Mr 22,47:1
Oppenheim, E Phillips (por), 1946, F 4,25:1
Oppenheim, E Phillips Mrs, 1946, N 26,29:2
Oppenheim, Eduard von, 1909, Ja 16,11:6
Oppenheim, Edward L, 1911, N 24,13:3
Oppenheim, Felix, 1951, Ag 10,15:4
Oppenheim, Hugo, 1940, S 1,20:8
Oppenheim, I E, 1954, F 21,68:1
Oppenheim, J, 1932, Ag 5,13:6
Oppenheim, Jack N, 1965, Mr 18,33:3
Oppenheim, Jacques Prof, 1924, O 14,23:3
Oppenheim, Jane D Mrs, 1947, Ja 30,25:3
Oppenheim, Laurent S Mrs, 1955, My 5,33:4
Oppenheim, Louis, 1951, S 9,90:1
Oppenheim, Maurice, 1949, O 28,23:3
Oppenheim, Nathan Dr (funl, Ap 8,15:4), 1916, Ap 6,13:7
Oppenheim, Richard W, 1948, D 22,24:2
Oppenheim, Robert Baron, 1918, Mr 2,13:5
Oppenheim, Robert Maj, 1917, O 2,13:6
Oppenheim, Waldemar von, 1952, D 16,31:2
Oppenheim, William, 1959, Jl 15,29:1
Oppenheim, William S, 1940, Ag 21,19:5
Oppenheimer, Adolph, 1946, N 28,27:6
Oppenheimer, Arthur, 1959, Ag 15,17:2
Oppenheimer, Arthur C, 1950, Mr 5,92:5
Oppenheimer, Arthur Mrs, 1955, Ap 22,25:3
Oppenheimer, Aug, 1937, F 6,17:4
Oppenheimer, Benjamin, 1909, Mr 28,13:5
Oppenheimer, Benton S, 1937, Mr 5,21:3
Oppenheimer, Bernard S, 1958, Je 11,35:1
Oppenheimer, Bernard S Mrs, 1966, Mr 19,29:4
Oppenheimer, Blanche, 1942, Jl 13,15:2
Oppenheimer, David, 1953, F 10,27:2
Oppenheimer, Donna, 1968, Jl 12,31:1
Oppenheimer, Edgar D (por), 1946, My 1,25:2
Oppenheimer, Edgar S, 1959, Ap 30,31:4
Oppenheimer, Edward S, 1941, My 28,25:3
Oppenheimer, Ernest (will, D 10,31:7), 1957, N 26, 33:1
Oppenheimer, Ernest F, 1939, Jl 14,19:2
Oppenheimer, Franz, 1943, O 1,19:6
Oppenheimer, Fred, 1942, D 20,45:1
Oppenheimer, Fritz E, 1968, F 6,43:2
Oppenheimer, Harry C, 1962, Mr 9,19:3
Oppenheimer, Harry D, 1953, N 1,86:5
Oppenheimer, Harry S, 1950, Jl 1,15:6
Oppenheimer, Henry, 1957, N 20,35:1; 1958, Jl 7,27:4
Oppenheimer, Henry S Dr, 1919, Jl 6,20:3
Oppenheimer, Herbert, 1955, Mr 7,27:4
Oppenheimer, Herbert D Mrs, 1945, Jl 28,11:4
Oppenheimer, Isaac, 1957, D 2,27:5
Oppenheimer, Isaac L, 1943, Jl 9,17:3
Oppenheimer, J Robert, 1967, F 19,1:6
Oppenheimer, Joseph, 1941, Je 14,17:5; 1948, O 27, 28:3
Oppenheimer, Joseph R, 1938, D 21,23:5
Oppenheimer, Julius, 1937, S 21,25:3
Oppenheimer, Julius S, 1948, Je 8,25:6
Oppenheimer, Leo H, 1944, Mr 1,19:5
Oppenheimer, Leon N, 1948, N 18,23:2
Oppenheimer, Leonard J, 1966, N 3,39:3
Oppenheimer, Leopold, 1938, Je 16,23:6
Oppenheimer, Louis, 1956, Ja 20,23:4
Oppenheimer, Louis E, 1939, Jl 7,17:5
Oppenheimer, Max, 1948, D 22,23:2; 1957, Ap 26,25:2
Oppenheimer, Max E, 1964, Je 4,37:2
Oppenheimer, Max Mrs, 1946, S 3,19:2
Oppenheimer, Maximilian, 1954, My 23,88:7
Oppenheimer, Moses J, 1907, Ap 22,9:5
Oppenheimer, Oscar F, 1949, Ja 23,68:5
Oppenheimer, Seymour, 1957, Ap 23,31:2
Oppenheimer, Seymour Mrs, 1957, Je 11,35:3
Oppenheimer, Siegfried, 1959, S 3,27:2
Oppenheimer, Sigmund, 1903, S 2,7:6
Oppenheimer, William T Jr, 1941, My 22,21:6
Oppenheimer, Wolf, 1943, Ap 27,23:1
Oppenheimer, Zach A, 1939, My 25,25:6
Oppenherimer, Kurt, 1945, Ja 22,17:5
Opper, Adolph, 1917, Je 25,11:5
Opper, Clarence V, 1964, Je 21,85:1
Opper, Emily M, 1937, O 6,25:4
Opper, Emma A, 1946, F 19,26:2
Opper, Frederick B (por), 1937, Ag 28,15:3
Opper, Frederick B (will), 1938, Mr 2,6:5
Opper, Frederick Mrs, 1947, Jl 5,11:6
Opper, Henry, 1955, D 3,17:4
Opper, Isadore, 1947, Ag 2,13:3
Opper, Laura, 1924, S 18,21:6
Opper, Victor M, 1940, Jl 29,13:4
Opperman, Adairn, 1908, Ap 29,9:6
Opperman, Eugene P, 1942, Jl 30,21:4
Opperman, Henry Jr, 1942, Mr 1,44:2
Opperman, Robert J, 1951, Ja 10,28:2
Oppersdorff, Jean G d' Count, 1948, Ap 10,13:4
Oppici, Francis, 1949, D 8,34:3
Oppikofer, Albert L Mrs, 1961, S 19,35:3
Oppikofer, Fred, 1941, F 23,40:1
Opportune, de Sainte Mrs, 1939, Mr 8,21:1
Oprey, Nicholas, 1953, Ap 5,76:3
Opsal, Tobias B, 1950, Ja 9,25:3
Optner, Saul, 1952, O 16,29:4
Oraff, Gustave, 1917, Jl 7,9:5
O'Rahilly, Patrick J, 1966, D 28,43:1
Oram, Charles E, 1951, Mr 31,15:3
Oram, E Jean, 1945, Ja 21,40:3
Oram, Elizabeth Mrs, 1865, My 11,5:4
Oram, George S, 1959, Ag 23,93:2
Oram, Henry Sir, 1939, My 7,III,7:2
Oram, Hugh P, 1945, F 28,23:5
Oram, John C Sr Mrs, 1955, D 19,27:1
Oram, Joseph H, 1957, Ag 26,23:3
Oram, Joseph V Mrs, 1961, N 1,43:4
Oram, Robert F, 1925, Ap 10,19:3
Oram, William F, 1940, Ja 7,50:1
Orama, Alejandro T, 1962, Ja 30,29:1
Orames, Benjamin Mrs, 1945, N 11,42:2
O'Ramey, G, 1928, Ap 3,32:2
Orange, Adolph, 1938, D 6,23:3
Orange, Adolph Mrs, 1946, Ja 22,27:4
Oranje, J, 1946, Ap 7,44:2
Oranovsky, Vladimir Col, 1918, O 3,13:3
Orans, David, 1964, O 3,29:5
Orans, Louis A, 1941, Jl 2,21:5
Oransky, Victor A, 1953, O 3,17:4
Oravetz, Paul P, 1950, S 4,17:7
Orayen, Elias, 1944, Ag 12,11:4
Orbach, Sigmund, 1943, D 17,27:4
Orbach, Wolf, 1959, My 11,27:4
Orbach, Wolf Mrs, 1958, O 14,37:3
Orban, Steven Mrs (Marianne), 1967, Je 28,45:1
Orbay, Rauf, 1964, Jl 17,27:1
Orbe, Lorenze F, 1949, S 8,29:4
Orbe, Lorenzo F Mrs, 1949, F 11,24:2
Orbeli, Leon A, 1958, D 13,2:4
Orbeliani, Irakli, 1954, Ap 2,28:3
Orbeliani, Roman, 1943, F 12,19:1
Orben, Charles S, 1958, Ja 30,23:4
Orbison, Douglas C, 1964, O 22,32:2
Orbison, John H Mrs, 1937, F 8,17:4
Orbison, Thomas J, 1938, Mr 27,II,6:1
Orbison, William D, 1952, F 16,6:3
Orborne, John F G Duke of Leeds, 1963, Jl 28,64:7
Orce, Victor J, 1951, Ag 1,23:5
Orchard, Charles R, 1944, My 5,19:3
Orchard, Edward F, 1948, Ag 16,19:3
Orchard, Edward Mrs, 1950, F 18,15:6
Orchard, Herman C, 1952, Je 23,19:4
Orchard, John E, 1962, Ja 30,33:7
Orchard, Roland M, 1941, S 28,48:4
Orchard, Walter J, 1960, My 15,86:2
Orchard, William I, 1953, Je 26,19:5
Orchard, William J, 1962, Jl 8,65:1
Orchard, William R, 1937, O 12,25:3
Orcutt, Albert C, 1942, F 13,21:2
Orcutt, Benjamin S Mrs, 1968, O 5,35:3
Orcutt, Calvin B, 1911, Ja 31,9:5
Orcutt, Charles C, 1960, N 15,39:4
Orcutt, Charles E, 1954, Ap 27,29:3
Orcutt, Daniel P, 1961, O 29,88:7
Orcutt, John C (por), 1942, Ap 10,17:2
Orcutt, Reginald, 1965, Je 13,85:2
Orcutt, William Cook, 1904, Ja 28,9:7
Orcutt, William W, 1942, Ap 29,21:2
Orcutt, William W (lr), 1942, My 13,18:6
Orczy, Baroness (por), 1947, N 13,27:4
Ord, E O C Gen, 1883, Jl 24,5:5
Ord, James, 1873, F 9,5:4
Ord, James G, 1960, Ap 17,92:3
Ord, Joseph P, 1913, Ja 10,11:2
Ord, Margaret J, 1949, F 21,23:5
Ord, Piacidus, 1876, Jl 16,7:2
Orde, Markham B, 1943, O 30,15:2
Orde, Markham B Mrs, 1942, Ap 14,21:4
Ordeman, C Lee, 1961, My 15,31:4
Ordeman, Herman W, 1948, Ja 1,23:1
Ordjonikdze, Gregory K, 1937, F 19,11:2
Ordonez, Castor, 1938, Je 29,19:6
Ordonez, Ezequiel, 1950, F 10,24:2
Ordonez Aguilera, Cayetano, 1961, O 1,87:2
Ordronaux, John Dr, 1908, Ja 21,7:6
Ordway, George T, 1948, D 4,13:4
Ordway, Lucius P, 1964, Mr 4,34:5
Ordway, Lucius P Mrs, 1945, D 1,23:4
Ordway, Lucius P Sr, 1948, Ja 13,25:5
Ordway, Paul B, 1951, Jl 27,19:2
Ordway, Stephen W, 1952, D 2,37:6
Ordway, Thomas, 1952, My 13,23:1
Ordway, William H, 1955, Ap 2,17:3
Ordway, William P, 1940, O 5,15:7
Ordwein, Louis E, 1962, F 10,23:4
Ordynski, Richard, 1953, Ag 16,77:1
Ore, Oystein Dr, 1968, Ag 15,37:4
O'Rear, John D, 1918, Jl 16,13:6
O'Reardon, Ignacio, 1949, Ap 13,29:3
O'Reardon, M, 1884, O 8,1:4
Orecchio, Joseph, 1953, Mr 23,23:1
Oreck, Abe R, 1961, Jl 12,31:5
Orefice, Antonio dell', 1959, Ja 13,47:2
O'Regan, Charles H Dr, 1968, Jl 13,27:6
O'Regan, Charles Mrs, 1960, My 29,56:4
O'Regan, Cornelius J, 1954, My 30,45:1
O'Regan, Daniel, 1948, D 2,29:3
O'Regan, Daniel T, 1954, Je 10,31:2
O'Regan, John, 1922, My 15,17:7
O'Regan, John A, 1948, O 7,30:2
O'Regan, Peter L, 1940, O 23,23:5
O'Regan, Stephen P, 1949, O 14,27:1
O'Regan, Thomas J, 1943, D 10,27:3
Oreglia, Cesare, 1939, D 19,26:2
Oreglia, Luigi Cardinal, 1913, D 7,19:2
O'Reilly, Andrew J, 1944, Jl 10,15:5
O'Reilly, Andrew Rev, 1909, S 10,9:6
O'Reilly, Bernard J, 1946, Ap 9,27:5
O'Reilly, Bernard Msgr, 1907, Ap 29,9:6
O'Reilly, C J Rev, 1884, D 22,5:2
O'Reilly, Catherine B Mrs, 1942, Ja 16,21:6
O'Reilly, Charles J, 1937, Ja 2,14:2
O'Reilly, Charles L, 1959, F 6,26:1
O'Reilly, Charles L Mrs, 1955, F 6,88:3
O'Reilly, Daniel, 1911, S 25,9:4; 1955, D 18,93:1
O'Reilly, Daniel J, 1913, N 7,9:3
O'Reilly, E J, 1880, S 10,5:4
O'Reilly, Edward F, 1956, S 5,27:5
O'Reilly, Edward J, 1957, Ap 27,19:2
O'Reilly, Edward P (por), 1941, D 6,17:2
O'Reilly, Edward S, 1946, D 9,25:1
O'Reilly, Elizabeth Boyle, 1922, S 13,21:5
O'Reilly, Francis J, 1938, D 12,19:5
O'Reilly, Francis M, 1964, N 5,45:4
O'Reilly, Frank A, 1949, Je 5,92:6
O'Reilly, Frank D, 1954, Ag 17,21:5
O'Reilly, Frank S, 1954, Ap 26,25:3
O'Reilly, Gerald A, 1938, O 16,44:5
O'Reilly, Gerald A Mrs, 1964, Jl 18,19:5
O'Reilly, Gordian, 1964, N 12,37:2
O'Reilly, Harry E, 1960, O 5,41:1
O'Reilly, Hugh J, 1948, Ag 26,21:2
O'Reilly, Hugh S, 1951, F 17,15:3
O'Reilly, J B, 1890, Ag 11,1:3
O'Reilly, J J, 1933, Ag 24,15:4; 1933, N 12,34:2
O'Reilly, James, 1924, Jl 15,9:3
O'Reilly, James B, 1960, Mr 19,21:1
O'Reilly, James J, 1941, Ap 5,17:4; 1947, Ag 21,23:3
O'Reilly, James T, 1947, Je 30,19:2
O'Reilly, James T Rev, 1925, N 13,19:5
O'Reilly, James V, 1945, N 12,22:2
O'Reilly, John B, 1944, Ag 9,17:6
O'Reilly, John C, 1955, My 4,29:6
O'Reilly, John D, 1957, Mr 10,89:2
O'Reilly, John F, 1943, N 23,25:2; 1956, N 24,19:4
O'Reilly, John J, 1942, S 1,20:2; 1950, D 27,27:2
O'Reilly, John T, 1950, D 10,104:3

O'Reilly, Joseph F, 1943, O 9,13:4; 1951, Ag 13,17:6
O'Reilly, Joseph P, 1948, Mr 23,25:2
O'Reilly, Joseph P Dr, 1937, Je 8,25:4
O'Reilly, Laurence J (funl, F 4,13:4), 1922, F 2,17:4
O'Reilly, Lennox A, 1949, Mr 18,25:2
O'Reilly, Luke, 1949, O 26,27:3
O'Reilly, Luke V, 1943, D 13,23:3
O'Reilly, Maitland Maj-Gen, 1912, N 4,11:5
O'Reilly, Martha M Mrs, 1937, O 14,25:3
O'Reilly, Mary, 1949, D 6,31:6; 1950, Jl 5,31:3
O'Reilly, Mary B, 1939, O 22,40:8
O'Reilly, Michael, 1942, Ag 3,15:6
O'Reilly, Michael J, 1948, F 2,19:1
O'Reilly, Miles Capt, 1920, D 9,13:3
O'Reilly, Myles, 1941, D 20,19:3
O'Reilly, Nan, 1937, Mr 1,19:5
O'Reilly, Patrick Mrs, 1945, F 2,19:2
O'Reilly, Peter S, 1948, Mr 24,25:4
O'Reilly, Richard, 1944, My 18,19:2
O'Reilly, Thomas, 1912, Ja 18,13:5; 1923, Jl 10,19:6; 1939, D 21,26:4
O'Reilly, Thomas B, 1940, Jl 12,15:4
O'Reilly, Thomas C, 1938, Mr 26,15:1
O'Reilly, Thomas C (Tom), 1962, Ap 6,35:3
O'Reilly, Thomas F, 1959, D 22,31:3
O'Reilly, Thomas J, 1939, F 27,15:3; 1949, Ja 19,27:4
O'Reilly, Thomas P Col, 1906, Ja 7,7:6
O'Reilly, Thomas S Msgr, 1918, F 5,13:8
O'Reilly, Thomas W, 1939, My 19,21:5
O'Reilly, William, 1938, F 11,23:3; 1940, Ja 20,15:6
O'Reilly, William E, 1943, Je 21,17:4
O'Reilly, William F, 1956, Ap 18,31:5
O'Reilly, William Very Rev, 1868, D 23,4:6
Orelie Intoire, King of Araucania and Patagonia, 1878, O 6,10:1
O'Rell, Max, 1903, My 25,1:2
Orellana, Pres of Guatemala, 1926, S 27,21:4
Orelup, John W, 1966, N 24,35:2
Orem, Belia B Mrs, 1938, N 13,45:1
Orem, Mary, 1881, Mr 6,10:6
Orem, Preston W, 1938, My 28,15:6
Oremieuix, Theophile de, 1881, Jl 5,3:2
Oremieulx, Laura Wolcott, 1908, D 2,9:5
Orenczak, John, 1949, F 17,23:3
Orendorf, Roy V, 1964, Mr 1,83:1
Orendorff, Ulysses G, 1944, Ja 2,38:7
Orens, Harold P, 1966, O 18,45:3
Orens, Martin H, 1961, S 15,30:6
Orens, Nathaniel, 1955, Ja 18,27:3
Orensey, Jose M, 1880, N 10,5:3
Orenstein, Abraham, 1939, Jl 14,19:3
Orenstein, Jacob, 1955, Ja 18,27:1
Orenstein, Leo, 1965, Ag 29,45:1
Orenstein, Samucl L, 1952, Ap 15,27:2
Oresman, Samuel R, 1959, N 25,29:1
Oretsky, Philip, 1966, F 23,39:2
Orford, George W, 1948, Jl 22,23:5
Organ, Frank A, 1948, F 13,21:2
Orgel, C J, 1946, Ja 20,42:2
Orgel, Isaac W, 1937, S 13,21:5
Orgel, Jacob, 1951, F 27,27:3
Orgel, William, 1953, D 23,26:3
Orgen, Martin, 1903, Ag 15,7:6
Orgo, Dominic, 1937, Jl 11,II,5:1
Orhard, Harry, 1954, Ap 14,20:4
Oriola, Adele Countess, 1903, S 20,4:5
Orione, Don L, 1940, Mr 14,23:4
O'Riordan, Conal H, 1948, Je 19,15:5
O'Riordan, Patrick J, 1949, F 6,76:4
Oritt, Harry, 1953, S 17,29:4
Oritt, Samuel, 1961, Je 26,31:2
Orkin, Abe, 1941, F 8,15:4
Orkin, Emanuel, 1937, My 9,II,10:1
Orkin, Otto, 1968, F 12,53:6
Orkin, Simpson M Mrs, 1955, Jl 19,27:4
Orkney, Countess of, 1946, My 10,19:5
Orkney, Earl of (E W Fitz-Maurice), 1951, Ag 22, 23:4
Orlandi, Alfred, 1950, Ag 29,27:3
Orlandini, Vitterio, 1939, O 5,23:6
Orlando, Anthony, 1952, Mr 28,23:1
Orlando, John, 1949, D 6,31:1
Orlando, Luigi, 1940, Ag 23,15:5
Orlando, Taddeo, 1950, S 3,38:4
Orlando, Vittorio E, 1952, D 2,31:1
Orlans, Abraham S, 1959, N 2,31:3
Orleans, Ilo, 1962, S 27,37:2
Orleans, Jacob S Mrs, 1948, Ap 26,23:3
Orleans, Robt-Phillippe-Louis-Eug of (Duke of Chartes), 1910, D 6,13:5
Orleans-Aosta, Duchess Elena of, 1951, Ja 21,78:2
Orleans e Braganza, Elizabeth de Princess, 1951, Je 12,29:3
Orlebar, Augustus H, 1943, Ag 5,15:1
Orlemanski, Stanislaus S, 1960, Mr 17,33:4
Orlian, Israel, 1965, My 21,35:1
Orlick, Abraham P, 1959, F 15,87:2
Orlick, James, 1946, S 21,15:3
Orlik, Alfred, 1957, My 9,31:4
Orloff, Maj-Gen, 1908, O 19,9:7
Orloff, Nicholas W, 1961, My 31,33:2
Orloff, Nicolai, 1964, Je 2,37:3
Orloff, Nikolai Prince, 1885, Mr 30,5:6
Orloff, Sergei, 1944, O 25,21:4
Orlov, George, 1955, Jl 30,17:5
Orlov, S V, 1958, Ja 16,29:2
Orlow, Abraham, 1950, My 1,25:5
Orlow, S Patriarch, 1944, N 22,19:2
Orlowski, Onufry I, 1944, S 27,21:6
Orly, Pierre, 1944, Ja 6,23:3
Ormandy, Rosalie Mrs, 1949, O 14,27:2
Ormathwaite, Lord (will, Ag 1,25:5), 1937, Mr 15, 24:1
Ormathwaite, Lord, 1943, O 28,23:4; 1944, F 14,17:3
Orme, Anne D Mrs, 1942, O 27,25:5
Orme, E B, 1937, N 30,23:2
Orme, George G, 1941, My 21,23:4
Orme, Harry W, 1958, N 24,29:5
Orme, James B L Mrs, 1963, Je 12,43:1
Orme, Margaret P Mrs, 1940, Mr 24,30:8
Ormella, Juan M, 1943, Ja 11,15:5
Ormerod, Henry V, 1951, Jl 4,17:3
Ormerod, William J Mrs, 1945, My 7,17:4
Ormiston, Frances I, 1954, My 1,15:1
Ormiston, Ken, 1951, S 3,13:4
Ormiston, Kenneth G, 1937, Ja 16,17:3
Ormiston, Lawrence R, 1954, Ap 26,25:3
Ormiston, Thomas W, 1914, Mr 30,9:4
Ormond, Alexander Thomas Dr, 1915, D 19,17:5
Ormond, Michael, 1949, F 24,23:3
Ormond, William J, 1949, Mr 14,19:6
Ormonde, Frederic, 1939, N 1,23:4
Ormonde, Marchioness of, 1948, My 19,27:1
Ormont, Dave, 1960, Ag 28,30:6
Ormont, James (J T Goldberg), 1962, Ag 30,29:5
Ormos, Laszlo E, 1948, Mr 21,61:1
Ormrod, William L, 1921, S 5,11:6
Ormsbee, Albert F Mrs, 1948, My 1,15:2
Ormsbee, Allen Ives, 1914, F 21,11:3
Ormsbee, Ebenezer J Gov, 1924, Ap 4,19:5
Ormsbee, Franklin S Mrs, 1947, My 5,23:2
Ormsbee, George F, 1943, Je 8,21:1
Ormsbee, Hamilton, 1923, N 2,17:3
Ormsbee, Hamilton Mrs, 1920, D 9,13:3
Ormsbee, Helen, 1957, S 8,83:3
Ormsbee, Herbert S Sr, 1953, Ap 8,29:4
Ormsbee, Ralph P, 1947, D 9,29:5
Ormsbee, Samuel G, 1962, Mr 31,25:4
Ormsbee, Willard A, 1951, Jl 4,17:5
Ormsby, Alex F, 1956, Je 20,31:3
Ormsby, Dorman L, 1945, S 8,15:1
Ormsby, Emmet (Red), 1962, O 12,31:4
Ormsby, George, 1952, Je 23,19:6; 1953, S 5,17:8
Ormsby, George Albert Bp, 1924, F 16,13:6
Ormsby, George V, 1950, Mr 6,21:2; 1950, Mr 25,13:4
Ormsby, Herbert F, 1957, Ag 25,86:5
Ormsby, James M, 1956, Ag 3,19:4
Ormsby, John A, 1949, Je 10,27:4
Ormsby, John D, 1941, Mr 5,22:3
Ormsby, John S, 1946, D 1,76:1
Ormsby, Joseph A, 1944, D 7,25:2
Ormsby, Lambert H Sir, 1923, D 22,13:3
Ormsby, Oliver S, 1954, Ap 11,86:3
Ormsby, R McK, 1881, F 22,4:7
Ormsby, W L Jr, 1908, Ap 30,9:5
Ormsby Gore, David Mrs (Lady Harlech),(funl, Je 3,31:3), 1967, My 31,49:1
Ormsby Gore, William G A (Lord Harlech), 1964, F 15,23:1
Ormsrod, E A Mrs, 1901, Jl 20,7:7
Ornburn, Ira M, 1949, D 18,88:7
Orndorf, Harry W, 1938, Jl 17,26:7
Orne, C Orville, 1956, Ja 20,23:3
Orne, Charles T Mrs, 1948, S 28,28:2
Orner, Arthur J, 1953, Je 6,17:1
Orner, I M, 1964, N 30,33:2
Ornes, Christian J Mrs, 1941, N 28,24:2
Ornitz, Samuel, 1957, Mr 12,33:3
Ornsteen, Albert Jr Mrs, 1951, My 18,27:3
Ornstein, Abraham, 1960, Mr 16,37:3
Ornstein, Charles L, 1966, S 9,45:1
Ornstein, David, 1945, Mr 29,23:4
Ornstein, Emanuel, 1955, D 14,39:2
Ornstein, George G, 1963, O 11,37:1
Ornstein, Max, 1944, F 19,14:8
Ornstein, Victor, 1958, Jl 26,15:7
O'Roark, L S, 1954, O 5,27:5
Orofino, Frank A, 1959, F 15,86:3
Orofino, Nicolino, 1941, Ja 10,19:4
Oromaner, Samuel, 1939, N 4,15:5
Oronhyatekha, Acland Dr, 1907, Jl 9,7:6
Oronhyatekha, Dr, 1907, Mr 4,9:6
O'Rorke, Andrew, 1947, Jl 19,13:3
O'Rorke, George M Sir, 1916, Ag 27,17:5
O'Rorke, James F, 1963, Je 26,39:3
O'Rorke, Jerimiah, 1949, O 22,12:3
O'Rourke, Andrew, 1945, D 14,28:3
O'Rourke, Annie E, 1925, D 17,23:4
O'Rourke, Anthony O, 1952, Ag 15,15:3
O'Rourke, Bart J, 1965, Mr 8,29:2
O'Rourke, Bernard F, 1952, F 10,93:2
O'Rourke, Bernard J, 1941, Je 14,17:6
O'Rourke, Bridget, 1879, S 29,5:2
O'Rourke, Bryan B, 1961, Ja 18,33:1
O'Rourke, C A, 1903, Ja 17,9:4
O'Rourke, Charles E, 1947, Ja 11,19:3
O'Rourke, Charlie, 1944, Jl 28,13:5
O'Rourke, Clement D, 1955, Ag 5,19:5
O'Rourke, Daniel (por), 1940, N 10,13:1
O'Rourke, Daniel J, 1942, S 24,27:2
O'Rourke, Edward E, 1940, Ja 3,22:3
O'Rourke, Eugene F, 1907, D 29,9:5
O'Rourke, George, 1961, Jl 8,19:6
O'Rourke, Innis Mrs, 1962, S 11,33:4
O'Rourke, J A, 1937, Je 19,15:6
O'Rourke, J F, 1934, Jl 30,13:6
O'Rourke, James A, 1948, Ja 17,17:4
O'Rourke, James E, 1954, Mr 8,27:4
O'Rourke, James F, 1947, N 13,27:3
O'Rourke, James J, 1938, Ja 22,15:5
O'Rourke, James P, 1943, D 29,17:2
O'Rourke, Jeremiah, 1915, Ap 24,11:6
O'Rourke, John A Rev, 1937, F 13,13:5
O'Rourke, John C, 1942, Mr 22,49:1
O'Rourke, John F, 1956, F 9,31:5
O'Rourke, John H, 1904, My 4,9:6
O'Rourke, John J, 1937, Mr 23,24:2; 1945, Ap 17,2 1951, Mr 15,29:4; 1952, D 4,35:6; 1958, Mr 28,25 1962, Ja 16,33:4; 1962, Ag 22,33:3
O'Rourke, John J (funl, D 12,86:4), 1965, D 8,47:
O'Rourke, John T (por), 1948, Je 4,23:2
O'Rourke, Joseph (Patsy), 1956, Ap 21,17:4
O'Rourke, Joseph J, 1958, F 4,29:4
O'Rourke, Katherine I Mrs, 1938, Jl 29,17:5
O'Rourke, Lorenzo, 1921, F 8,7:4
O'Rourke, Michael, 1941, N 8,19:5
O'Rourke, Michael F Dr, 1914, Jl 23,9:4
O'Rourke, Michael J, 1949, My 25,29:5; 1955, S 18 86:6
O'Rourke, Patrick I, 1948, Ap 4,60:5
O'Rourke, Patrick J, 1943, Mr 31,19:5
O'Rourke, Peter J, 1954, Mr 13,15:2
O'Rourke, Steve, 1944, S 23,13:6
O'Rourke, Tex, 1963, My 16,35:2
O'Rourke, Thomas F, 1963, Ag 15,29:2
O'Rourke, Thomas P, 1958, O 19,87:1
O'Rourke, Tim, 1938, Ap 23,15:1
O'Rourke, Vincent F, 1968, Ap 23,47:1
O'Rourke, Walter, 1963, S 29,86:6
O'Rourke, Walter A, 1965, Jl 22,31:4
O'Rourke, William, 1940, D 23,19:4; 1946, Jl 25,21
O'Rourke, William B, 1903, N 6,9:6
O'Rourke, William F, 1950, Ag 13,77:1
Orowicz, Stanley Mrs, 1952, Mr 6,31:4
Orozco, Aristeo C, 1943, My 30,26:3
Orozco, Jorge, 1941, O 1,21:4
Orozco, Jose C (por), 1949, S 8,29:4
Orpen, Abram M, 1937, S 23,27:5
Orpen, J Frederick, 1944, Jl 6,15:4
Orpen, W Sir, 1931, O 1,27:5
Orpet, Edward O, 1956, N 13,37:1
Orpheus, John J, 1938, Ap 8,19:4
Orr, Alexander Ector (trb, Je 5,11:4), 1914, Je 4,
Orr, Arthur D Mrs, 1941, Je 15,36:7
Orr, Carey, 1967, My 17,47:3
Orr, Charles B, 1952, Ag 18,17:3
Orr, Charles G, 1946, D 28,15:5
Orr, Charles L Sr, 1941, Jl 18,19:3
Orr, Charles P Judge, 1922, My 17,19:5
Orr, Chester A, 1950, O 15,105:1
Orr, Clifford, 1951, O 12,27:5
Orr, Clifford R, 1941, Mr 18,23:4
Orr, Cyrus P, 1937, Ja 27,21:3
Orr, Douglas W, 1966, Jl 31,73:1
Orr, Edwin W, 1961, Je 15,43:2
Orr, Frank, 1938, Ap 21,19:5
Orr, Frederick W, 1960, O 28,31:1
Orr, G A Bisler, 1956, Ja 15,47:5
Orr, G Frank, 1940, Ap 2,25:1
Orr, George, 1937, Ap 5,19:4
Orr, George E, 1945, D 25,23:1
Orr, George F, 1940, Jl 4,15:5
Orr, George P, 1962, Jl 7,17:2
Orr, George P Jr, 1939, F 26,39:3
Orr, Gilbert M, 1949, My 11,29:2
Orr, Hal N, 1946, O 8,24:2
Orr, Harold, 1952, D 27,9:3
Orr, Harold E, 1964, F 29,8:7
Orr, Harry Mrs, 1948, My 25,27:1
Orr, Hiram W (funl plans), 1956, O 25,33:4
Orr, Homer M, 1953, Jl 4,11:4
Orr, Hugh M, 1947, N 18,29:1
Orr, Isaac H, 1954, Ag 26,27:4
Orr, J Alvin, 1957, My 8,37:1
Orr, J Burton, 1960, My 3,39:2
Orr, James D, 1950, O 23,23:4
Orr, James F, 1947, O 7,27:5
Orr, James Prof, 1913, S 7,II,13:5
Orr, James S, 1952, Ap 19,15:2
Orr, John A J, 1949, My 12,31:4
Orr, John C, 1941, D 2,23:5
Orr, John Clifton Mrs, 1907, N 1,9:5
Orr, John Clinton, 1906, D 16,7:6
Orr, John J, 1952, My 11,92:4
Orr, John M, 1941, S 24,23:5
Orr, John Mrs, 1947, Ag 31,37:2
Orr, Joseph, 1960, Jl 12,35:4
Orr, Joseph C, 1946, O 26,17:3
Orr, Joseph G, 1942, N 9,23:4

Orr, Joseph K, 1938, S 19,19:2
Orr, Kenneth W, 1965, Mr 9,35:1
Orr, Louis, 1966, F 20,88:5
Orr, Louis H, 1916, Ag 7,9:6
Orr, Louis McD, 1961, My 24,41:1
Orr, Malcolm W, 1941, N 21,17:4
Orr, Manlius B, 1942, Ag 9,43:3
Orr, Margaret H, 1944, Ap 9,33:2
Orr, Marshall P, 1944, Jl 18,19:4
Orr, Mary E Mrs, 1938, My 8,II,7:2
Orr, Mary L, 1945, Ap 9,19:4
Orr, Millard R, 1943, D 28,17:1
Orr, Noah (Giant), 1882, Jl 5,8:2
Orr, Pauline V, 1955, N 22,35:4
Orr, Pence B, 1947, S 5,20:3
Orr, Robert, 1876, My 31,5:5
Orr, Robert E, 1939, Mr 11,17:2
Orr, Robert H Capt, 1937, O 7,27:1
Orr, Robert P (por), 1942, Mr 30,17:1
Orr, Robert T, 1950, S 7,31:5
Orr, Robert W, 1957, S 6,21:3
Orr, Sarah Mrs, 1924, O 22,21:4
Orr, Sutherland Mrs, 1948, N 28,92:3
Orr, Thomas, 1937, My 13,25:2; 1950, Jl 7,19:2
Orr, Thomas E, 1949, Jl 14,27:5; 1952, Ja 31,27:1
Orr, Thomas Mrs, 1956, N 7,31:4
Orr, Thomas P, 1957, F 2,19:4
Orr, W Wallace, 1962, Je 4,29:3
Orr, Walter C Mrs, 1951, O 13,17:3
Orr, Walter S, 1961, S 26,40:1
Orr, Walter S Mrs, 1946, F 21,21:4
Orr, Warren H, 1962, Ja 14,85:1
Orr, William, 1939, Jl 23,29:3
Orr, William A, 1950, Ap 19,29:1
Orr, William H, 1946, Je 17,21:4; 1954, S 17,27:3
Orr, William H Mrs, 1963, My 12,86:4
Orr, William M, 1940, O 11,21:6
Orr, William W, 1947, Ja 17,23:3
Orr-Ewing, Charles Lindsay, 1903, D 25,7:6
Orr-Ewing, Ian, 1958, Ap 28,23:1
Orraca, Cosme, 1946, D 14,15:6
Orrell, Edward P Jr, 1954, F 23,27:1
Orrell, Louis B, 1956, N 29,35:5
Orris, S Stanhope, 1905, D 18,9:4
Orris, William S, 1957, Mr 31,88:5
Orriss, Herbert F, 1954, Jl 18,57:2
Orrok, George A (por), 1944, Ap 7,19:3
Orry-Kelly, 1964, F 27,31:3
Orsatti, Frank, 1947, My 20,25:5
Orsatti, Pietro, 1961, D 2,23:1
Orsborn, Albert, 1952, My 9,23:3
Orsborne, George, 1957, D 24,15:4
Orsenigo, Cesare, 1946, Ap 2,27:4
Orser, William E, 1947, Jl 26,13:6
Orsini, Agnes R Mrs, 1953, Ag 25,21:2
Orsini, Domenico, 1947, Mr 22,13:6
Orsini, Henry, 1944, Ap 3,21:5
Orsini, Luigi, 1954, N 10,33:2
Orsino, Antonio, 1952, D 2,31:3
Orsor, Burdette C, 1939, Ag 1,19:3
Orszag, Ladislaus, 1950, Je 20,27:1
Ort, Lawrence, 1954, S 10,23:3
Orta, Manuel Mrs, 1963, S 30,29:3
Ortega, Frank G (J Hermida), 1967, N 2,47:4
Ortega y Gasset, Jose (funl, O 20,36:2), 1955, O 19, 33:1
Orteig, Evariste, 1957, Ja 31,27:4
Orteig, Jules P Jr, 1960, My 15,86:6
Orteig, Raymond (por), 1939, Je 8,25:1
Orteig, Raymond Mrs, 1954, Jl 23,17:5
Ortel, Otto, 1910, S 9,9:5
Ortel, William, 1939, My 28,III,6:6
Ortell, Frank J, 1960, S 30,27:1
Ortell, Frank Mrs, 1963, N 26,37:5
Ortes, Armand F, 1948, N 21,88:4
Ortgies, John, 1908, O 17,9:4
Ortgies, John Mrs, 1967, D 31,44:8
Ortgies, William S, 1956, Ag 29,29:5
Ortgies, William S Mrs, 1956, Mr 17,19:5
Orth, Albert, 1948, O 9,19:1
Orth, Arthur W, 1959, Mr 18,38:1
Orth, Charles D, 1949, Mr 24,28:3
Orth, Charles D Jr, 1959, Mr 5,31:5
Orth, Edgar A, 1948, Ja 2,23:1
Orth, Frank, 1962, Mr 19,29:1
Orth, Frank Mrs (A Codee), 1961, My 22,31:4
Orth, G S, 1882, D 17,2:6
Orth, John C B, 1947, My 12,21:3
Orth, John C B Mrs, 1945, My 9,23:2
Orth, Miles H, 1946, Mr 6,27:3
Orth, O Sidney, 1964, F 5,35:4
Orth, Phil Sr, 1937, N 16,23:4
Orth, Rudolph D, 1948, Mr 28,48:3
Orth, Samuel P Mrs, 1951, N 23,29:2
Orth, Samuel P Prof, 1922, F 27,13:6
Orthwein, Percy J, 1957, Jl 3,23:2
Orthwein, Percy Mrs, 1957, Ag 5,19:1
Orthwein, Ralph H, 1937, Je 14,23:5
Ortigaoburnay, Luis E, 1951, D 27,21:1
Ortiz, Andres, 1945, Ja 20,11:4
Ortiz, Carlos B, 1937, Ag 21,15:5
Ortiz, Pedro N, 1949, Ag 6,17:5
Ortiz, Roberto Mrs, 1940, Ap 4,23:3
Ortiz Rubio, Pascual, 1963, N 5,31:2
Ortleb, George E Sr, 1952, F 27,27:1
Ortleb, Mary M, 1951, My 25,27:3
Ortlieb, Frederick C, 1941, Ag 3,35:2
Ortlieb, William F, 1957, Ja 9,31:1
Ortlinghaus, Ernest Mrs, 1949, F 22,23:2
Ortlinghaus, Ernst, 1940, Ag 27,21:5
Ortlip, H Willard, 1964, O 16,39:4
Ortlip, Harry S, 1945, My 17,19:4
Ortman, Earl H, 1953, F 28,17:3
Ortman, Fred B, 1961, F 28,33:2
Ortman, Julius, 1948, D 13,23:5
Ortman, Julius Mrs, 1953, D 16,35:3
Ortman, Max J, 1957, Ag 27,29:4
Ortman, Otto G, 1956, Jl 8,64:3
Ortmann, Gustav A, 1948, Ag 12,21:5
Ortner, Hermann H, 1956, Ag 20,21:5
Ortolani, Giuseppe, 1958, Jl 14,21:3
Orton, Arthur (Tichborne Claimant), 1898, Ap 2,9:1
Orton, B Douglas, 1954, My 27,27:3
Orton, Douglas B, 1950, Ag 20,76:2
Orton, Ervin F, 1962, Ap 2,31:5
Orton, George H, 1947, Jl 4,13:3
Orton, George H Sr, 1950, Jl 6,27:5
Orton, George L, 1956, Ag 12,84:5
Orton, George L Mrs, 1950, S 13,27:4
Orton, George W, 1958, Je 27,25:4
Orton, Henry B, 1957, S 2,13:4
Orton, Homer Folks, 1968, F 28,47:4
Orton, James Prof, 1877, N 8,8:5
Orton, Jesse F, 1956, O 4,33:5
Orton, Jesse F Mrs, 1955, F 17,27:1
Orton, Joe (funl, Ag 19,17:3), 1967, Ag 10,47:1
Orton, Samuel T (por), 1948, N 19,27:3
Orton, W, 1878, Ap 24,8:4
Orton, Warren S, 1955, Je 25,15:4
Orton, William A, 1952, Ag 16,15:4
Orton, William C, 1953, F 2,21:1
Orton, William C Mrs, 1951, N 8,29:2
Orton, William Son of, 1874, My 4,5:4
Ortone, Ernest E Mrs, 1952, O 15,31:3
Orts, Peter, 1905, My 23,9:6
Ortseifen, George L, 1945, Ag 9,21:3
Ortstadt, Henry, 1949, My 5,27:3
Ortt, Charles H, 1947, N 21,27:3
Orttenburger, Charles G, 1944, Mr 29,21:2
Ortynsky, Lubomyr O, 1961, Jl 25,27:3
Ortynsky, Stephen Soter Bp, 1916, Mr 25,13:5
Orville, Howard T, 1960, My 26,33:3
Orvis, Arthur E, 1965, Jl 15,29:4
Orvis, Charles Eustis Col, 1915, Mr 9,9:6
Orvis, Edgar J, 1947, Ag 1,17:3
Orvis, Edwin W (will, Je 7,44:3), 1938, My 26,25:6
Orvis, Edwin W, 1939, Ap 30,44:6
Orvis, Edwin W Mrs (will), 1940, Je 25,26:2
Orvis, Fred B, 1951, My 16,35:3
Orvis, J M, 1883, Ap 1,2:4
Orvis, John Jay, 1920, Ap 9,13:3
Orvis, Julia S, 1949, Mr 18,25:3
Orvis, Paul Whitin, 1911, N 20,11:5
Orvis, Walter E, 1967, S 12,47:2
Orvis, Warner D, 1967, Je 29,43:1
Orwell, George, 1950, Ja 22,77:1
Orwig, Benton B, 1966, Ja 30,84:4
Orwig, Don C, 1958, Ag 6,25:3
Orwig, Harry M, 1953, O 30,23:4
O'Ryan, John F, 1961, Ja 31,29:1
O'Ryan, John F Mrs, 1958, O 15,39:4
O'Ryan, Patrick E, 1961, N 29,41:2
O'Ryan, Philip W, 1945, Ap 14,15:3
O'Ryan, William P, 1956, Ag 5,77:2
Orzack, Murray D Mrs, 1942, N 1,53:1
Orzechowski, John, 1962, O 15,29:5
Osada, Thadeus, 1950, O 11,33:4
Osadnik, John W, 1942, My 4,19:6
Osann, Frederick, 1948, S 9,27:3
Osann, Frederick Mrs, 1951, Mr 18,88:3
Osband, Helen, 1949, Ja 10,25:3
Osbon, A W Rev, 1882, Ag 8,4:7
Osbon, Bradley S, 1912, My 7,11:6
Osbon, Elias S Dr, 1925, S 27,7:3
Osbon, Elias Sillick Rev Dr, 1911, Ap 11,11:4
Osborn, A L, 1940, Ap 20,17:2
Osborn, A Perry, 1951, Mr 8,29:1
Osborn, Abigail Mrs, 1905, Mr 27,9:4
Osborn, Abraham Coles, 1916, Ja 18,11:5
Osborn, Albert, 1944, N 30,23:5
Osborn, Albert B, 1940, Je 24,15:6
Osborn, Albert S, 1946, D 16,23:5
Osborn, Albert W T, 1967, F 5,89:3
Osborn, Alex F, 1966, My 6,47:1
Osborn, Andrew R (por), 1949, Je 25,13:1
Osborn, Andrew R Mrs, 1948, Mr 28,48:8
Osborn, C A Mrs, 1954, F 21,69:1
Osborn, Charles A, 1960, D 10,23:3
Osborn, Charles J, 1910, Ap 19,9:5
Osborn, Chase R Mrs, 1948, F 5,23:2
Osborn, Chase S, 1949, Ap 12,29:1
Osborn, Clara A, 1950, Ap 30,102:3
Osborn, Clarence F, 1949, Ja 5,25:3
Osborn, Cuthbert, 1942, Ap 15,21:3
Osborn, Cyrus R, 1968, N 17,86:8
Osborn, David F, 1938, My 15,II,6:2
Osborn, Dudley P, 1945, Je 26,19:4
Osborn, E C, 1901, Je 16,7:7
Osborn, Edward Clark, 1925, Ag 1,11:5
Osborn, Edwin F Dr, 1937, Jl 30,19:3
Osborn, Emma, 1949, S 5,17:5
Osborn, Esther (Mrs E O Nelson), 1941, Ag 30,13:5
Osborn, Eugene T, 1957, Mr 20,37:2
Osborn, Ezra, 1944, Ag 16,19:1
Osborn, Francis A Gen, 1914, Mr 13,9:4
Osborn, Francis M, 1911, Jl 17,9:5
Osborn, Frank C, 1924, Ag 18,13:4
Osborn, Frederick G, 1950, Jl 11,31:5
Osborn, Frederick W Prof, 1919, D 2,13:2
Osborn, George A, 1941, S 24,23:3
Osborn, George A (por), 1947, My 2,21:1
Osborn, George H, 1942, Mr 27,23:1
Osborn, H F, 1935, N 7,23:1
Osborn, H Sanford, 1954, Je 21,23:4
Osborn, Henry B Dr, 1908, My 10,9:4
Osborn, Henry C, 1961, My 5,29:1
Osborn, Henry L, 1940, Ja 4,24:4
Osborn, Henry M, 1949, Je 22,31:4
Osborn, Herbert Mrs, 1915, Ja 19,9:5
Osborn, Hervey J, 1961, Ap 2,76:3
Osborn, Hiram, 1949, Jl 29,21:2
Osborn, Howard B, 1946, D 31,18:5
Osborn, Howard T, 1937, Ap 30,22:2
Osborn, James E, 1940, My 31,19:3
Osborn, James Marshall Mrs, 1968, D 24,20:8
Osborn, Jesse R, 1944, D 27,19:4
Osborn, John, 1882, Mr 26,9:3; 1916, Mr 10,9:6
Osborn, John C, 1951, S 20,31:4
Osborn, John T, 1949, Ag 1,17:5
Osborn, John W, 1925, S 14,19:5
Osborn, Josefa Neilson Mrs, 1908, N 12,9:5
Osborn, Kenneth G, 1956, My 5,19:6
Osborn, Kenneth H, 1949, Je 28,28:4
Osborn, L W, 1901, N 13,9:6
Osborn, Lincoln A, 1937, D 14,25:1
Osborn, Lyn, 1958, Ag 31,56:1
Osborn, Max, 1946, S 25,28:2
Osborn, Merritt J, 1960, Ja 17,86:6
Osborn, Minott A, 1959, Ja 16,27:1
Osborn, N, 1932, My 7,15:1
Osborn, Paul L, 1947, Mr 4,25:3
Osborn, Perry H, 1948, S 24,25:3
Osborn, Philip Mrs, 1945, Ap 23,19:5
Osborn, Phillips, 1942, O 9,22:2
Osborn, Richard, 1950, O 25,35:5
Osborn, Richard W Mrs, 1965, D 24,7:2
Osborn, Robert Mrs, 1950, Mr 27,23:5
Osborn, Salmon S, 1904, Mr 5,9:4
Osborn, Sherard Capt, 1875, My 8,4:7
Osborn, Sidney P, 1948, My 26,25:1
Osborn, Ulysses C, 1968, Ja 23,39:2
Osborn, W H, 1948, O 29,26:3
Osborn, Willard M, 1947, Ag 14,23:4
Osborn, William, 1908, My 11,7:4
Osborn, William B, 1963, O 23,41:4
Osborn, William C, 1951, Ja 4,29:1
Osborn, William C Mrs (por), 1946, Mr 31,46:2
Osborn, William Rev, 1922, F 16,15:3
Osborn, William U, 1947, S 2,21:4
Osborne, Abeel D, 1947, Mr 12,25:2
Osborne, Alice A, 1942, Jl 15,19:3
Osborne, Andrew, 1946, F 21,21:4
Osborne, Archie J, 1949, O 15,15:1
Osborne, Arthur Dimon, 1920, Ap 16,13:4
Osborne, Burnett M, 1943, Ja 10,48:4
Osborne, Carey S, 1952, D 6,21:2
Osborne, Charles, 1949, F 13,76:4
Osborne, Charles A, 1939, S 19,26:4
Osborne, Charles D, 1961, Je 2,31:1
Osborne, Charles F, 1957, O 26,21:2
Osborne, Charles T, 1944, N 6,19:2
Osborne, Consul W M, 1902, Ap 30,9:1
Osborne, David M, 1962, Jl 10,33:4
Osborne, David Munson Mrs, 1911, Jl 19,9:5
Osborne, Dean C (por), 1937, Ja 24,II,8:5
Osborne, Dorothy Mrs, 1950, Ja 3,25:2
Osborne, Duffield, 1917, N 22,13:4
Osborne, Edmund B, 1951, S 3,13:5
Osborne, Edward, 1946, N 5,25:2
Osborne, Edwin A, 1947, Mr 9,60:1
Osborne, Edwin D, 1939, Ag 29,21:3
Osborne, Ella U, 1953, N 24,29:5
Osborne, Elmer E, 1959, F 7,19:4
Osborne, Francis D'A G Duke of Leeds, 1964, Mr 21, 25:1
Osborne, Francis J, 1949, Je 26,60:4
Osborne, Frank J, 1949, Ag 6,17:2; 1965, Ja 24,80:7
Osborne, Frank W, 1941, Je 26,23:5
Osborne, George Jr, 1904, Ja 12,7:5
Osborne, George W Sr, 1937, Jl 3,15:1
Osborne, Grant W, 1949, Ap 11,25:2
Osborne, Harold A, 1941, S 8,15:2
Osborne, Harriet, 1944, My 17,19:5
Osborne, Harry E, 1954, Mr 3,27:4
Osborne, Harry L, 1925, S 15,25:3
Osborne, Harry V, 1952, Je 19,27:6
Osborne, Henry C, 1949, Ap 21,26:2
Osborne, Henry G, 1954, S 11,17:6
Osborne, Henry Z Capt, 1923, F 10,13:5

Osborne, Hubert B, 1958, N 22,21:5
Osborne, Irving H, 1954, S 28,29:6
Osborne, Isabelle, 1910, Ja 11,9:4
Osborne, J A Sr, 1948, Jl 26,17:4
Osborne, J K, 1903, O 24,9:6
Osborne, James, 1953, D 21,31:5
Osborne, James B, 1948, N 16,30:2
Osborne, James H, 1938, Mr 6,II,8:8
Osborne, James I, 1952, Ja 28,17:4
Osborne, James W (funl, S 9,17:2), 1919, S 8,13:4
Osborne, John E, 1943, Ap 25,34:6
Osborne, John F, 1953, Mr 12,27:3
Osborne, John L, 1956, Ag 13,19:6
Osborne, John R, 1949, F 3,23:4
Osborne, Joseph P, 1915, My 22,11:6
Osborne, Kenneth B, 1939, Jl 30,29:2
Osborne, L Allen Mrs, 1951, F 18,77:1
Osborne, Lawrence J, 1939, Ap 30,44:7
Osborne, Lawrence W, 1960, Mr 14,29:3
Osborne, Lewis K, 1950, Mr 22,27:4
Osborne, Lloyd, 1947, My 23,23:5
Osborne, Louis Shreve Rev Dr, 1912, Ja 28,II,13:5
Osborne, Loyall A (por), 1944, Ag 19,11:4
Osborne, Loyall A Mrs, 1950, Ja 18,31:4
Osborne, Maynard E, 1954, O 6,25:2
Osborne, Melville, 1915, S 24,11:5
Osborne, Naboth, 1940, Ap 19,21:5
Osborne, Nat, 1954, Mr 14,88:2
Osborne, Nelson C, 1967, S 30,33:3
Osborne, Nelson C Mrs, 1946, Mr 23,13:2
Osborne, Norris W, 1940, My 16,23:3
Osborne, Oliver T, 1940, N 12,23:5
Osborne, Percy S, 1951, S 29,17:2
Osborne, Peter, 1940, Mr 1,21:2
Osborne, Peter Mrs, 1948, O 18,23:2
Osborne, Phil, 1953, Ag 28,17:1
Osborne, Phil Mrs, 1940, S 29,44:2
Osborne, R B, 1882, Ja 5,5:5
Osborne, Ralph D, 1949, D 13,38:3
Osborne, Ralph H, 1959, N 9,31:4
Osborne, Raymond G, 1955, Ja 6,27:2
Osborne, Richard C, 1937, Mr 3,23:2
Osborne, Schuyler Mrs, 1960, Jl 6,33:1
Osborne, Sherrill B, 1949, Ja 26,25:3
Osborne, Sidney G, 1958, O 10,31:3
Osborne, St Lawrence, 1948, S 18,18:2
Osborne, Stafford L, 1952, O 26,88:5
Osborne, Susan M, 1918, S 5,11:6
Osborne, T M, 1926, O 21,15:1
Osborne, Thomas J, 1941, Mr 5,21:2
Osborne, Thomas W, 1937, My 6,25:2
Osborne, W E, 1879, Ja 15,8:6
Osborne, W S, 1880, D 5,7:4
Osborne, William, 1944, My 25,21:4
Osborne, William B, 1939, S 8,23:5
Osborne, William H, 1942, D 26,11:2
Osborne, William S, 1948, O 21,27:2
Osborne-Hill, Timothy Mrs, 1966, O 17,37:4
Osbornson, Edmund A Mrs, 1943, My 14,20:2
Osbourne, Henry H, 1951, My 24,35:2
Osbourne, John D, 1941, Je 28,15:2
Osbron, Charles F, 1939, O 31,23:6
Osbun, Clifford L, 1941, Ap 15,23:4
Osburn, Burl N, 1962, Ap 7,25:6
Osburn, Clarence De W Mrs, 1964, Ja 30,29:4
Osburn, Robert C, 1945, My 21,19:2
Oscar, King of Sweden, 1907, D 14,9:6
Oscar, William, 1940, My 5,53:2
Oscar Bernadotte, Prince of Sweden, 1953, O 4,86:1
Oscar I, King of Sweden, 1859, Jl 22,4:4
Oscar of the Waldorf (O Tschirky), 1950, N 8,29:1
Osceola, George, 1954, Ag 9,17:3
Osceola, Jimmy, 1947, S 10,27:5
Osceola, John, 1939, S 30,17:4
Oscher, Max, 1916, F 2,11:5
Oscherwitz, Sam H, 1950, D 9,15:6
Oschinsky, Lawrence, 1965, D 21,37:4
Oschwald, Gustave, 1962, F 18,92:6
Oschwald, John R, 1951, Mr 12,25:5
Oser, Marion E Mrs, 1965, Ap 17,19:2
Oser, Max (por), 1942, O 10,15:3
Oser, Max (will), 1943, Je 14,34:2
Oser, Max Mrs (will, My 29,2:3), 1947, My 19,21:5
Oser, Oscar, 1953, Je 13,15:6
Osetrov, Vladimir, 1952, D 1,23:5
Osgood, A M Rev (see also F 9), 1878, F 11,1:6
Osgood, Adelaide H, 1910, N 27,II,13:4
Osgood, Alfred T, 1959, Je 22,25:5
Osgood, C, 1881, Mr 19,2:7
Osgood, Charles (funl, My 28,22:3), 1922, My 27, 13:5
Osgood, Charles F Sr, 1959, Je 12,27:2
Osgood, Charles G, 1964, Jl 29,33:1
Osgood, Charles G Mrs, 1959, D 28,23:5
Osgood, Charles H, 1938, O 24,17:5
Osgood, Dana, 1951, My 26,17:5
Osgood, edw C, 1952, N 3,27:6
Osgood, Edward C Mrs, 1952, Je 29,59:4
Osgood, Edward H, 1952, O 6,25:4
Osgood, Edward Louis, 1911, Je 11,II,11:5
Osgood, Ellen L, 1958, Ag 15,21:3
Osgood, Erastus Dr, 1867, D 26,3:2
Osgood, Frank H Mrs, 1950, O 10,31:1
Osgood, Frank S, 1947, Ap 14,27:1
Osgood, G A, 1882, N 17,3:2
Osgood, G D Rev Dr, 1875, Jl 11,7:6
Osgood, George L Mrs, 1950, Jl 4,17:6
Osgood, H O, 1927, My 9,21:5
Osgood, Harold A, 1940, F 20,21:2
Osgood, Herbert Levi Prof, 1918, S 13,11:3
Osgood, Irene Mrs, 1922, D 13,21:5
Osgood, John, 1907, F 1,9:4; 1907, F 3,7:6
Osgood, John B, 1963, Je 30,56:1
Osgood, Joseph O, 1916, Je 29,11:6
Osgood, Luther J, 1948, O 7,89:1
Osgood, Phillips E, 1956, N 7,29:4
Osgood, Robert B, 1956, O 4,33:6
Osgood, Roy C, 1958, Jl 11,23:4
Osgood, Samuel (funl, Ap 20,8:3), 1880, Ap 15,5:4
Osgood, Theresa Mrs, 1938, Jl 3,13:2
Osgood, Wilfred H, 1947, Je 22,52:5
Osgood, William F, 1943, Jl 23,17:2
Osgood, William H, 1911, O 9,11:5; 1967, F 6,29:3
Osgood, William H Mrs, 1952, Je 18,27:4
Osgoodby, Daniel E, 1938, Ja 4,23:2
Osgoodby, George Melvin, 1908, Ag 19,7:5
Osgoodby, William W, 1916, Mr 16,13:4
Osgoode, H S Col, 1903, Ja 27,9:6
O'Shaughnessey, John H Mrs, 1958, My 2,27:1
O'Shaughnessey, Martin J, 1949, Ja 20,27:2
O'Shaughnessy, Edith C Mrs, 1939, F 19,39:2
O'Shaughnessy, Edward Joseph, 1923, Je 11,13:4
O'Shaughnessy, Elim, 1966, S 25,84:2
O'Shaughnessy, Hugh P, 1958, My 28,31:2
O'Shaughnessy, J Mrs, 1941, Mr 14,23:4
O'Shaughnessy, James, 1950, N 30,33:3
O'Shaughnessy, James Col, 1914, Mr 4,11:5
O'Shaughnessy, James J, 1945, Je 27,19:2
O'Shaughnessy, Louis B (funl, Mr 13,17:5), 1924, Mr 11,19:3
O'Shaughnessy, N, 1932, Jl 27,17:1
O'Shaughnessy, Thomas, 1937, Ap 4,II,10:8
O'Shaughnessy, Thomas A, 1956, F 13,27:2
O'Shaughnessy, Timothy J, 1948, N 1,23:2
O'Shaughnessy, William, 1943, Ap 4,40:2
O'Shaughnessy, William B, 1960, Ag 25,29:4
O'Shea, Alfred, 1954, Mr 21,89:1
O'Shea, Anna S Mrs, 1937, Mr 1,19:5
O'Shea, Arthur, 1950, S 10,92:4
O'Shea, Benjamin, 1952, My 3,21:4
O'Shea, Benjamin Mrs, 1966, O 12,43:1
O'Shea, Charles J, 1968, O 17,47:3
O'Shea, Daniel, 1959, Jl 7,33:4
O'Shea, Daniel B, 1943, My 12,25:2
O'Shea, Daniel J, 1948, Mr 2,23:2
O'Shea, Daniel J Mrs, 1960, N 3,39:2
O'Shea, Edmond I, 1949, Mr 21,23:5
O'Shea, Edward F, 1940, Jl 9,21:3
O'Shea, Edward K, 1958, F 25,27:2
O'Shea, Elizabeth Mrs, 1937, Jl 7,23:4
O'Shea, Florence F, 1948, Jl 19,19:1
O'Shea, Francis M, 1949, S 15,27:1
O'Shea, Frank R, 1945, Mr 1,21:1
O'Shea, George A, 1952, Ag 8,17:3
O'Shea, J vincent, 1957, F 20,33:5
O'Shea, James, 1949, D 30,19:2
O'Shea, James J, 1938, Ag 9,19:4
O'Shea, John, 1942, S 17,25:4
O'Shea, John A, 1939, S 18,19:3
O'Shea, John D, 1944, Ja 12,23:4
O'Shea, John J, 1920, Mr 3,11:4; 1949, Ap 11,25:2
O'Shea, John M Mrs, 1944, My 28,34:2
O'Shea, John Mrs, 1957, Jl 31,23:4
O'Shea, John P Jr, 1960, O 4,43:1
O'Shea, Kitty (Mrs Chas Stewart Parnell), 1921, F 6,22:3
O'Shea, Madalyn (Mrs J Gray), 1956, Je 2,19:3
O'Shea, Matt, 1964, Mr 31,35:2
O'Shea, Michael F, 1949, Ja 2,63:3
O'Shea, Michael P, 1959, Je 8,27:2
O'Shea, Michael V (por), 1948, F 6,33:4
O'Shea, Patrick, 1906, Mr 5,9:4
O'Shea, Patrick M, 1942, D 15,28:3
O'Shea, Thomas, 1954, My 10,23:3
O'Shea, Thomas E, 1939, O 23,19:5; 1949, Jl 17,58:2
O'Shea, Thomas J, 1962, S 23,86:5
O'Shea, Timothy J, 1948, Je 21,21:3; 1951, Ja 23,27:5
O'Shea, Vincent J, 1960, O 20,35:1
O'Shea, William F (por), 1945, F 28,24:2
O'Shea, William J (por), 1939, Ja 17,21:3
O'Shea, William J (trb, Ap 3,31:3; funl, Ap 5,25:1), 1957, Ap 2,31:3
O'Sheel, Blanche L Mrs, 1947, D 8,25:4
O'Sheel, Shaemas, 1954, Ap 4,87:1
Osher, Helen, 1953, F 1,88:4
Osherman, Jack A, 1960, Ag 24,29:1
Osherman, Samuel, 1942, Ja 4,48:1
Osherowitch, Mendel, 1965, Ap 17,19:3
Oshima, Kano, 1955, Mr 20,89:2
Oshins, Julie, 1956, My 10,31:3
Oshinsky, Ida Mrs, 1912, Ap 15,9:5
Oshkosh, Reuben E, 1954, My 15,15:4
Oshlag, Jacob, 1938, My 19,21:2
Oshlag, Jacob Mrs, 1962, F 18,92:7
Oshrin, Harry H, 1961, Ag 27,85:2
Osiecki, Walter, 1949, Mr 23,27:2
Osincup, Gilbert S, 1947, N 28,27:2
Osinoff, Hyman, 1963, Jl 3,25:2
Osinoff, Morris, 1957, N 20,35:3
Osiris, Daniel, 1907, F 5,9:6
Osius, George, 1941, S 24,23:2
Osk, Marcus L, 1956, O 3,33:3
Osk, Marcus L Mrs, 1954, My 6,33:2
Osk, Nat, 1960, Jl 16,19:2
Oskar, Prince of Prussia, 1958, Ja 28,27:2
Oskison, Hildegarde H Mrs, 1952, D 11,33:1
Oskison, John M (por), 1947, F 27,21:3
Osland, Birger, 1963, Ag 3,17:4
Osler, Britton, 1943, D 14,27:2
Osler, Chester A, 1947, Je 25,25:2
Osler, Clifford C, 1948, Ap 2,23:4
Osler, Edmund Boyd Sir, 1924, Ag 4,13:4
Osler, F Gordon, 1944, Jl 6,15:4
Osler, J Thompson Rev, 1907, O 10,9:4
Osler, William Sir, 1919, D 30,13:1
Osler-Toptani, Robert, 1953, Ap 19,90:5
Osley, William L, 1949, Ap 5,29:4
Osma, Pedro de, 1967, S 19,51:5
Osman, Digna, 1926, D 9,27:5
Osman, Frederic D, 1950, Ap 8,13:4
Osman, Harold C, 1953, Mr 20,23:3
Osman, Pasha, 1900, Ap 6,6:6
Osmanski, Frank E, 1945, Je 27,19:2
Osmena, Nicasio, 1963, Je 22,23:3
Osmena, Sergio (trb, O 20,33:4; funl plans, O 24,-37:2), 1961, O 19,35:1
Osment, William G, 1946, Ja 6,40:3
Osmer, Archibald R, 1953, N 17,31:5
Osmer, John L, 1949, Ag 30,27:5
Osmers, Frank C, 1949, Jl 12,27:4
Osmers, Frank C Mrs, 1941, Ap 7,17:5
Osmers, John, 1967, D 27,37:2
Osmers, Maria B Mrs, 1939, O 26,23:5
Osmond, Arthur E, 1939, Mr 11,17:5
Osmond, Charles S, 1940, Ja 14,43:1
Osmond, Martha E, 1942, O 17,15:4
Osmoy, Suzanne d' Vicomtesse, 1960, Jl 25,23:4
Osmun, A Vincent, 1954, Ja 11,25:2
Osmun, Dorinda E Mrs, 1942, Mr 15,42:5
Osmun, Luther, 1955, O 25,33:4
Osmun, Ralph M, 1966, Je 21,43:2
Osmun, Samuel D, 1955, Ja 4,21:1
Osnato, Charles, 1941, O 21,23:5
Osnato, John, 1945, N 26,21:1
Osnis, Benedict A, 1941, F 11,23:3
Osnis, Benedict A Mrs, 1939, Mr 9,21:2
Osnos, Sam, 1943, Mr 10,19:2
Osorio, Miguel A, 1942, Ja 15,19:5
Osowski, John T, 1945, F 7,21:2
Ossendorff, Kurt W, 1956, N 25,88:4
Osserman, Hyman A, 1963, Je 18,37:3
Osserman, Louis, 1959, Ap 27,27:4
Osserman, Simon E, 1966, N 2,45:1
Osserman, Stanley, 1963, My 9,37:3
Osserman, Stanley Mrs, 1967, F 8,31:1
Ossietzky, Carl von, 1938, My 5,23:1
Ossington, Lord, 1873, Mr 8,7:4
Ossip, Abraham, 1951, Jl 5,25:4
Ossman, Edwin K, 1958, S 3,33:5
Ossman, Frederick J, 1940, Ap 20,17:4
Ossman, John A, 1950, My 10,31:4
Osso, Bory Mrs, 1941, Mr 3,15:4
Ossorio, Miguel J, 1965, O 27,47:4
Ossorio Arana, Arturo, 1967, D 8,47:1
Ossorio y Gallardo, Angel, 1946, My 20,24:2
Osswalt, Robert L, 1943, F 16,19:5
Ostberg, J Harry, 1954, N 13,15:3
Ostberg, Ragnar, 1945, F 7,21:2
Ostby, Bryn, 1954, O 13,31:5
Osten, Frederick A Sr, 1942, D 23,19:2
Osten-Sacken, Nicolai D von der Count, 1912, M 13:6
Ostendorrf, Herman, 1942, N 1,53:1
Ostenso, Martha (Mrs D Durkin), 1963, N 26,3
Oster, Aaron J, 1967, Ap 15,31:3
Oster, Henry R, 1949, Ag 2,20:4
Oster, John, 1952, Ja 28,17:3
Oster, John Edward Dr, 1968, Je 10,45:3
Oster, Lewis A, 1948, S 16,29:3
Oster, Robert H, 1960, Ja 4,29:2
Osterberg, John S, 1951, D 6,33:3
Osterdahl, Borje Mrs, 1951, Je 6,31:5
Ostergaard, Povl, 1948, F 19,23:5
Ostergard, Martin P, 1952, Jl 30,24:8
Ostergren, Carl F, 1948, D 27,21:1
Ostergren, Erick Rev, 1909, F 16,9:3
Ostergren, Fred, 1945, Jl 5,13:6
Osterhaus, H, 1927, Je 12,25:4
Osterhaus, Peter J, 1917, Ja 6,13:5
Osterhoudt, Calvin, 1945, D 22,19:1
Osterhoudt, Charles E, 1947, Ag 29,17:3
Osterhoudt, Chester, 1922, D 31,4:2
Osterhoudt, Frank, 1947, Ap 8,27:1
Osterhoudt, Fred S, 1952, N 21,25:3
Osterhoudt, George W Mrs, 1947, O 7,27:6
Osterhoudt, Henry J, 1943, Mr 14,26:2
Osterhoudt, James S, 1945, Jl 1,18:2
Osterhoudt, Lewis E, 1945, S 19,25:5
Osterhoudt, Virgil, 1943, N 10,23:1

Osterhoudt, William, 1940, Jl 20,15:4
Osterhout, Albert V, 1957, Ap 4,33:1
Osterhout, Anna M Mrs, 1957, S 20,25:3
Osterhout, Burgess, 1966, N 1,41:3
Osterhout, Charles D, 1949, S 29,29:5
Osterhout, Elijah Mrs, 1950, Ap 16,104:4
Osterhout, George, 1940, My 30,17:4
Osterhout, Harold W, 1944, S 29,21:2
Osterhout, Leon B, 1948, Ap 7,25:4
Osterhout, Myron E, 1943, Ap 20,23:3
Osterhout, William B, 1940, Jl 19,19:5
Osterhout, Winthrop J, 1964, Ap 10,39:6
Osterhus, Francis O, 1966, Ja 17,47:4
Osterhus, Gustav K, 1952, Ag 19,23:2
Osterland, Alfred, 1945, N 24,19:2
Osterland, Samuel G, 1964, My 22,35:3
Osterle, George L, 1948, F 28,15:1
Osterloh, Albert F Sr, 1948, Ag 19,21:2
Osterlund, Otto W, 1951, Ap 21,17:2
Osterman, Albert H, 1956, Mr 23,27:1
Osterman, Emanuel, 1962, Ja 2,29:2
Osterman, Harry, 1949, My 30,13:4
Osterman, Jack (por), 1939, Je 9,21:3
Osterman, Jack Mrs, 1950, S 8,24:2
Osterman, John W, 1940, S 20,23:3
Osterman, Lester, 1939, My 10,23:2
Osterman, Lester Mrs, 1946, Je 6,21:4
Osterman, Michael Mrs, 1962, O 13,25:6
Osterman, Phil C Mrs, 1952, Je 6,23:4
Osterman, Phil J Mrs, 1949, Ap 8,26:3
Ostermann, Albert H, 1946, N 22,23:5
Ostermann, Charles H, 1952, F 20,29:2
Ostermann, Francis A, 1962, Ag 18,19:4
Ostermann, George E, 1955, Mr 25,23:4
Ostermann, Hubert, 1940, D 18,25:4
Ostermann, John Jr, 1944, Mr 10,15:4
Ostermayer, Martin N Mrs, 1949, F 3,23:4
Ostermueller, Frederick R (Fritz), 1957, D 18,35:2
Ostertag, Frances Mrs, 1953, Ja 28,27:5
Osterweil, Henry, 1948, Ja 10,15:4
Osterweil, Leon, 1941, O 19,44:2
Osterweis, Dayton Mrs, 1955, O 1,19:3
Osterweis, Gustav Mrs, 1947, N 27,31:3
Osterweis, Louis W, 1954, D 23,19:6
Osteyee, George, 1954, Mr 14,89:1
Ostgren, Gottfrid L, 1961, S 14,31:3
Ostheimer, Elizabeth G, 1960, F 17,35:3
Ostheimer, Maurice, 1953, O 30,23:3
Ostier, Oliver O, 1967, S 18,47:2
Ostmark, Harry E, 1947, Ap 27,60:2
Ostrand, James A, 1937, Ap 17,17:3
Ostrander, Albert A, 1964, S 30,43:1
Ostrander, Benjamin D, 1951, Je 10,93:1
Ostrander, Charles V, 1954, Ja 17,92:5
Ostrander, Egbert D, 1942, N 29,65:1
Ostrander, Elkana, 1951, Je 23,15:4
Ostrander, Elmer C, 1952, Je 12,34:4
Ostrander, Fannie E, 1921, My 5,17:3
Ostrander, Frank T Mrs, 1958, Ag 9,13:4
Ostrander, Fred D, 1955, Ap 20,33:5
Ostrander, George Augustus Dr, 1917, D 27,11:6
Ostrander, George N, 1944, Ja 20,19:4
Ostrander, Gideon, 1874, D 24,5:3
Ostrander, Gilbert G, 1953, Ag 22,15:6
Ostrander, J Kingsland, 1956, N 21,27:4
Ostrander, Jacob F, 1954, Mr 2,25:2
Ostrander, James H Dr, 1937, F 17,21:4
Ostrander, John E, 1938, O 20,23:1; 1957, Je 29,37:2
Ostrander, Lester S, 1965, My 24,31:4
Ostrander, Paul, 1956, Mr 17,19:6
Ostrander, Peter Wilson, 1918, Je 4,13:4
Ostrander, Robert H, 1949, Ap 23,13:3
Ostrander, Thomas E, 1903, O 11,20:2
Ostrander, William C Mrs, 1943, F 9,23:2
Ostreicher, Doris J S Mrs, 1955, Ag 26,40:2
Ostreicher, James P, 1963, Je 14,31:2
Ostreicher, Leonard M, 1967, Je 25,69:1
Ostrin, George H, 1954, Ja 8,21:1
Ostro, Marcus, 1948, My 13,25:1
Ostroff, Dora, 1953, S 23,31:4
Ostroff, Oscar Mrs (R Wallerstein), 1961, Ap 21,33:1
Ostroff, Samuel M, 1954, F 10,29:3
Ostrofsky, Abraham, 1947, F 12,25:3
Ostrolenk, Bernard, 1944, N 28,23:3
Ostrolenk, Samuel, 1968, D 2,47:3
Ostrom, Donald M, 1960, Jl 25,23:4
Ostrom, Frank T Mrs, 1946, Ag 8,21:4
Ostrom, Henry, 1941, D 22,17:1
Ostrom, Hiram R Mrs, 1959, My 4,29:4
Ostrom, Homer Irving Dr, 1925, Ap 6,19:5
Ostrom, Selden W Mrs, 1944, Ag 3,19:4
Ostrom, William L, 1940, Ja 13,15:4
Ostromislensky, Iwan I, 1939, Ja 19,19:3
Ostrorog, L Count, 1932, Ag 1,15:5
Ostrorog, Stanislaus, 1960, S 29,35:1
Ostrove, Max, 1963, Ag 26,27:2
Ostrovsky, Moser, 1947, Je 17,25:2
Ostrow, Albert A, 1961, My 8,35:3
Ostrow, August, 1960, Ap 29,31:1
Ostrow, Herman, 1954, Ag 9,17:6
Ostrow, Louis, 1950, S 7,31:4; 1956, Ap 21,17:6
Ostrow, Morris M, 1954, N 7,88:4
Ostrowski, Joseph S, 1961, Je 25,76:7
Ostrowski, Stanislaw K, 1947, My 15,25:5
Ostrup, Johannes, 1938, My 6,21:5
Ostrup, John C Maj, 1919, Mr 1,13:4
Ostuzhev, Alex A, 1953, Mr 4,27:4
Ostwald, Ernest, 1956, F 23,27:2
Ostwalt, Frederick E, 1960, My 25,39:4
O'Sullivan, Alice E Mrs, 1942, Je 28,33:2
O'Sullivan, Arthur J, 1952, D 28,50:7
O'Sullivan, Charles, 1939, D 9,15:6
O'Sullivan, Corinne, 1944, D 13,23:4
O'Sullivan, Cornelius, 1952, Ap 21,21:4
O'Sullivan, Daniel, 1951, S 14,25:3
O'Sullivan, Daniel E (por), 1946, Ap 14,46:3
O'Sullivan, Daniel F, 1945, N 27,23:3
O'Sullivan, Daniel J, 1947, Jl 17,19:3
O'Sullivan, Daniel M F, 1965, Ja 7,31:3
O'Sullivan, Daniel M Mrs, 1952, S 1,17:6
O'Sullivan, Denis, 1908, F 2,9:6
O'Sullivan, Denis H, 1949, Ag 19,17:2
O'Sullivan, Donald, 1944, F 4,15:3
O'Sullivan, Edna, 1950, Ag 31,25:1
O'Sullivan, Edward F Rev, 1915, O 24,17:6
O'Sullivan, Eugene D, 1968, F 9,27:3
O'Sullivan, Frank J, 1943, S 21,24:2
O'Sullivan, George J, 1963, D 21,23:5
O'Sullivan, George L, 1961, O 21,21:4
O'Sullivan, Honoria Mrs, 1938, My 3,23:4
O'Sullivan, Horace C, 1947, Je 17,25:5
O'Sullivan, J Francis, 1944, S 27,21:4
O'Sullivan, J Mortimer, 1961, F 19,86:2
O'Sullivan, James, 1939, Mr 21,24:2; 1949, F 16,25:3
O'Sullivan, James J, 1964, Ag 31,25:3
O'Sullivan, James P, 1949, D 16,31:1
O'Sullivan, Jeremiah A, 1951, F 12,23:2
O'Sullivan, John, 1946, N 16,19:4; 1950, S 6,31:7
O'Sullivan, John C A, 1942, My 27,23:2
O'Sullivan, John D, 1957, Je 15,17:6
O'Sullivan, John J, 1959, Jl 5,57:2
O'Sullivan, John M, 1948, F 11,27:1
O'Sullivan, Joseph M, 1966, Je 12,87:3
O'Sullivan, Martin R, 1951, My 14,25:5
O'Sullivan, Martin V, 1949, My 8,76:6
O'Sullivan, Mary (Sister Eamon),(funl, S 2,3:3), 1966, S 1,3:2
O'Sullivan, Mary E, 1950, Ag 9,29:2
O'Sullivan, Mary I, 1964, O 24,29:4
O'Sullivan, Patrick J, 1967, O 22,84:6
O'Sullivan, Percy B, 1946, Je 24,31:5
O'Sullivan, Raymond J, 1952, Mr 18,27:4
O'Sullivan, Richard P, 1950, My 1,25:4
O'Sullivan, Stephen, 1957, O 8,35:2
O'Sullivan, Sylvester J, 1911, N 27,11:6
O'Sullivan, Ted J, 1950, Ag 17,27:4
O'Sullivan, Thomas C, 1967, Mr 14,47:4
O'Sullivan, Thomas C Mrs, 1961, Jl 2,33:1
O'Sullivan, Thomas F, 1951, Mr 13,31:4
O'Sullivan, Thomas J (funl, Jl 31,7:6), 1913, Jl 30,7:6
O'Sullivan, Timothy, 1942, My 19,19:2
O'Sullivan, Walter, 1938, N 28,15:3
O'Sullivan, Walter R Sr, 1960, D 1,35:2
O'Sullivan, William J Dr, 1921, Ja 21,15:6
O'Sullivan, Woodrow S, 1957, Jl 8,46:6
O'Sullivan-Beare, Daniel Robert, 1921, Je 25,11:6
Osuna, Juan J, 1950, Je 20,27:5
Oswald, Arthur E, 1956, S 23,84:1
Oswald, Charles A, 1942, F 18,19:3
Oswald, David C, 1953, Ap 14,27:2
Oswald, Edwin H, 1951, Mr 7,33:5
Oswald, Emma K, 1918, Ja 30,9:5
Oswald, Ernest M, 1955, Je 4,15:3
Oswald, Francis L, 1940, S 29,44:2
Oswald, Henry C, 1944, Ap 27,23:2
Oswald, Henry P (por), 1940, Ap 10,25:4
Oswald, Hugo A, 1959, Ja 22,32:1
Oswald, John C, 1938, Je 23,21:3
Oswald, John P, 1950, My 1,25:2
Oswald, Otto T, 1958, Ag 30,15:5
Oswald, William (will), 1943, Ap 5,16:8
Oswald, William E Mrs, 1946, Ag 7,27:2
Oswalt, Walter L, 1951, Ag 21,27:2
Ota, Tadayuki, 1968, N 29,45:2
Ota, Tamekichi, 1956, D 2,87:1
Otani, Kikuzo Gen, 1923, N 29,21:4
Otani, Sonyu, 1939, Ag 3,19:4
Otapalik, Hugo, 1953, Jl 11,11:7
Otero, Caroline (La Belle), 1965, Ap 12,35:2
Otero, M S, 1904, F 3,9:5
Otero, Miguel A (por), 1944, Ag 8,17:3
Otero Vizcarrondo, Henrique, 1952, D 28,48:4
Otheman, Edward R (will, S 14,27:2), 1938, S 7,36:4
Otheman, Francis W, 1910, Mr 7,9:5
Otheman, Roswell C, 1964, Ap 4,28:3
Othenin, J (Comte d Haussonville), 1884, My 29,5:3
Othman, Frederick C, 1958, D 29,15:2
Othman, Sally Mrs, 1957, Ap 23,31:6
Otho I, Ex-King of Greece, 1867, Jl 28,5:2
Oths, Joseph A, 1941, Je 3,21:5
Otis, Alex (por), 1939, O 17,25:3
Otis, Alvah T, 1953, Ja 7,31:3
Otis, Arthur H, 1946, O 24,27:4
Otis, Arthur S, 1964, Ja 2,27:1
Otis, Caroline J, 1947, Ap 4,23:1
Otis, Charles, 1944, O 1,45:1
Otis, Charles A, 1953, D 10,47:3
Otis, Charles A Mrs, 1949, F 23,27:2
Otis, Charles A Sr, 1905, Je 29,9:6
Otis, Charles F, 1938, Je 14,21:4
Otis, Charles P, 1940, S 14,17:6
Otis, Charles W M Mrs, 1952, Ja 17,28:2
Otis, Clarence H, 1953, Mr 22,86:2
Otis, Dan H (por), 1941, N 22,19:2
Otis, Elisha G Mrs, 1903, Jl 7,7:6
Otis, Eliza Henderson Boardman Mrs, 1873, Ja 22,1:5
Otis, Elwell S Gen, 1909, O 23,11:1
Otis, Emma Mrs, 1941, F 13,19:5
Otis, Eunice P, 1943, Jl 5,15:6
Otis, F Burton, 1961, F 15,35:5
Otis, F G, 1878, Ag 11,7:4
Otis, Frank Alleyne, 1903, D 15,9:5
Otis, Frederick A, 1959, Ja 17,19:3
Otis, George S Mrs, 1945, Mr 17,13:2
Otis, H Frank, 1947, Ap 14,27:1
Otis, Harold, 1958, O 18,21:6
Otis, Harrison G, 1962, Ja 7,88:6
Otis, Harrison Gray Gen, 1917, Jl 31,9:3
Otis, James, 1869, S 4,5:5; 1875, N 2,4:7; 1942, Mr 31, 21:4
Otis, James F, 1867, F 10,6:2
Otis, James H, 1907, Jl 1,7:6
Otis, James Mrs, 1945, F 15,19:1
Otis, John F, 1949, N 16,29:3
Otis, John M, 1939, S 28,25:1
Otis, Joseph E Sr, 1959, N 26,38:1
Otis, L B, 1903, Ja 12,9:6
Otis, Louise, 1963, My 9,37:4
Otis, Merrill E, 1944, D 24,26:3
Otis, Michael E, 1946, Ap 15,27:2
Otis, Michael Mrs, 1951, Ja 15,17:4
Otis, Norton P, 1905, F 21,7:6
Otis, Norton P Mrs, 1945, O 8,15:5
Otis, Ralph C, 1950, S 15,25:1
Otis, Raymond, 1938, Jl 15,17:2
Otis, Raymond J, 1966, D 13,47:3
Otis, Samuel D, 1946, Je 13,27:3; 1961, N 25,24:4
Otis, Samuel D Mrs, 1964, Ja 25,23:6
Otis, Sidney, 1946, S 10,7:2
Otis, Stanley L, 1937, O 12,23:1
Otis, Waldemar, 1918, Jl 31,9:5
Otis, Waldemer Mrs, 1943, Jl 30,15:5
Otis, William A, 1944, Ap 1,13:1
Otis, William A Mrs, 1947, Jl 22,23:4; 1951, N 16,25:3
Otjen, C J, 1950, Jl 18,29:2
O'Toole, Arthur, 1949, F 13,77:1
O'Toole, Bartholomew, 1956, Ap 5,29:4
O'Toole, Bernard F Dr, 1925, Jl 3,13:7
O'Toole, Charles E, 1966, Jl 31,72:4
O'Toole, Clement B, 1944, D 17,38:2
O'Toole, Donald L, 1964, S 14,33:1
O'Toole, Edward, 1967, My 26,47:2
O'Toole, Edward J, 1958, My 10,21:5
O'Toole, George B (por), 1944, Mr 27,19:3
O'Toole, Gertrude (Sister Teresa), 1943, Ag 19,19:3
O'Toole, Henry J, 1959, D 15,39:3
O'Toole, James L, 1951, Ag 5,72:6
O'Toole, John, 1941, Ap 5,17:1; 1949, Ag 10,21:5
O'Toole, John A, 1942, D 1,25:3
O'Toole, John J, 1942, Ag 18,21:6; 1951, Jl 4,17:3
O'Toole, John L (por), 1945, S 10,19:3
O'Toole, John L Mrs, 1943, Je 15,21:3
O'Toole, Lawrence J, 1951, Ap 11,29:4
O'Toole, Luke E, 1960, F 16,37:3
O'Toole, Martin J, 1949, F 19,15:4
O'Toole, Thomas B, 1950, Jl 10,39:2
O'Toole, Thomas J Mrs, 1952, Je 10,27:6
O'Toole, Walter J, 1948, Mr 9,23:1
O'Toole, William J, 1944, My 5,19:2
O'Toole, William L, 1951, Jl 12,25:2
Ott, Adolph, 1953, Je 30,23:1
Ott, Albert V, 1952, Jl 9,27:3
Ott, Charles M, 1945, Je 14,19:3
Ott, Charles W, 1948, D 14,29:4
Ott, Dorothy Wilhelmina, 1937, N 19,23:5
Ott, Edgar F, 1954, O 16,17:6
Ott, Elbert C, 1947, N 25,32:3
Ott, Emil Jr, 1963, O 1,39:2
Ott, George, 1947, Ag 23,13:4
Ott, George J, 1941, Mr 30,48:8
Ott, Harry G, 1950, N 22,25:2
Ott, Henry Mrs, 1959, N 22,86:4
Ott, John, 1950, N 5,92:4
Ott, John N, 1942, Je 22,15:2
Ott, Joseph, 1943, Jl 2,19:3
Ott, Lambert Jr, 1955, Je 18,17:2
Ott, Leonard, 1948, Je 10,25:3
Ott, Leonard Mrs, 1949, Ag 19,17:3
Ott, Louis, 1947, N 25,29:3
Ott, Louis F, 1951, My 24,35:2
Ott, Ludwig F, 1963, D 27,25:1
Ott, Mel (funl, N 23,V,8:2), 1958, N 22,1:2
Ott, Roy H, 1958, Ap 30,33:5
Ott, Wallace F, 1962, Jl 21,19:6
Ott, William, 1945, F 8,19:4
Ott, William P, 1944, D 26,19:2
Ottarson, A D, 1876, D 5,5:6
Ottarson, F J, 1884, Ag 9,8:6
Ottaviano, Angelo E, 1954, D 15,31:1

Ottaviano, Francis, 1960, O 6,41:4
Ottaway, Lee L, 1961, Mr 11,21:4
Ottaway, Lee L Mrs, 1944, N 22,19:2
Otte, Fred W Mrs, 1946, Ap 3,25:3
Otte, Hugo E, 1942, Mr 11,19:4
Otte, William L, 1957, F 7,27:4
Ottemiller, John O, 1968, Jl 24,50:2
Otten, Anthony, 1946, D 4,31:4
Otten, Leonard F, 1946, Jl 10,23:5
Otten, Louis, 1944, Ja 19,19:3; 1946, N 19,17:4
Otten, Luke, 1921, Jl 27,15:5
Otten, William C Mrs, 1954, O 4,27:4
Otten, William J, 1914, Jl 20,7:2
Ottenberg, Bernard A, 1937, Mr 23,23:5
Ottenberg, Clarence, 1945, D 9,44:3
Ottenberg, Reuben, 1959, Ap 27,27:5
Ottendorfer, Oswald, 1900, D 16,7:4
Ottendorfer, Oswald Mrs, 1884, Ap 2,4:7
Ottendorfer, Peter G Mrs, 1940, O 4,23:3
Ottenheimer, Edward J, 1963, S 19,27:3
Ottenheimer, Samuel M, 1937, Ag 4,19:3
Otter, John M, 1909, Mr 4,9:5; 1965, Jl 21,37:5
Otter, Martin S Mrs, 1945, Ja 9,19:5
Otter, William D Lady, 1914, N 14,11:6
Otterback, Phil G, 1956, F 10,21:5
Otterbein, Henry, 1942, O 12,17:6
Otterbein, Henry C, 1952, Ap 13,77:1
Otterbein, William, 1941, Mr 10,17:1
Otterbourg, Albert M, 1963, N 7,37:2
Otterbourg, Edwin M, 1967, O 18,47:1
Otterman, Charles L, 1950, Ap 30,102:4
Otterson, John E, 1964, Ag 11,33:1
Otteson, Mary, 1959, N 15,86:5
Otteson, William Mrs, 1952, Ja 31,27:3
Ottiano, Rafaela (por), 1942, Ag 18,22:2
Ottinger, Albert, 1938, Ja 14,23:1
Ottinger, Benjamin H, 1953, My 1,21:2
Ottinger, Lawrence, 1954, D 20,29:1
Ottinger, Marx, 1923, My 9,19:4
Ottinger, Moses (funl, N 21,7:4), 1925, N 19,25:5
Ottinger, Nathan (por), 1940, N 18,19:6
Ottley, Gilbert, 1948, N 23,29:2
Ottley, James H Mrs, 1953, F 1,88:4
Ottley, James Henry, 1922, Mr 4,15:5
Ottley, John K Sr, 1945, N 2,19:2
Ottley, Roi, 1960, O 2,84:4
Ottman, Allen M, 1941, Je 21,17:2
Ottman, De Witt, 1905, Je 6,9:4
Ottman, F Leonard, 1950, Ap 17,23:1
Ottman, Frank, 1952, D 6,21:3
Ottman, Jacob, 1943, N 23,25:3
Ottman, Louis, 1925, Je 12,19:6
Ottman, William Mrs, 1944, D 8,21:5
Ottmann, William, 1954, Ap 22,29:3
Ottmann, William Jr, 1947, D 2,30:3
Ottmer, Henry H, 1956, F 27,23:3
Otto, Albert K Mrs, 1956, O 25,33:4
Otto, Albert T, 1944, Mr 6,19:5
Otto, Alexander F Mrs, 1946, Je 12,27:2
Otto, Alford G, 1954, Jl 26,17:4
Otto, Archduke, 1906, N 2,11:6
Otto, Benjamin, 1945, F 18,33:2
Otto, Caroline (Sister Mary Bernadine), 1956, Jl 12, 23:3
Otto, Elias, 1953, Ap 22,29:2
Otto, Erich A, 1966, D 15,47:1
Otto, Ernest, 1939, Ap 4,25:2; 1955, Ja 15,13:5; 1956, Ap 19,31:4
Otto, Frank B, 1957, O 6,84:6
Otto, Fritz, 1944, Mr 23,19:2
Otto, George, 1955, O 5,35:2
Otto, George G, 1944, Jl 6,15:2
Otto, George R, 1948, My 27,25:4
Otto, Gustav, 1904, Ja 5,9:5
Otto, Harold L, 1959, S 12,21:5
Otto, Helen M, 1945, Mr 15,23:1
Otto, Henry, 1952, Ag 5,19:3
Otto, Henry G, 1940, O 26,15:3
Otto, Henry S, 1962, Jl 29,61:3
Otto, Herbert, 1956, Mr 5,23:3
Otto, Hugo M, 1922, N 5,5:3
Otto, J Thomas, 1954, Jl 13,23:3
Otto, John M, 1923, My 12,15:6
Otto, K Konfried Mrs, 1962, Ap 10,43:4
Otto, King of Bavaria, 1916, O 13,11:3
Otto, Mahlon T, 1953, Jl 7,27:3
Otto, Paul A, 1949, N 8,31:3
Otto, Paul M, 1944, O 8,44:2
Otto, Richard H, 1940, Jl 12,15:2
Otto, Thomas N, 1949, My 2,25:3
Otto, Thomas N Mrs, 1950, Jl 28,21:4
Otto, Walter G C (por), 1943, Ag 26,17:3
Otto, Warren P S, 1942, My 2,13:4
Otto, Wayne K, 1946, Ap 5,25:4
Otto, William R, 1946, My 8,25:2
Otto, William Tod, 1905, N 9,9:3
Otto Rudolph, Friese, 1903, F 23,2:1
Ottolenghi, Mario L Mrs, 1967, Je 8,47:3
Ottolenghi, S, 1934, Jl 17,19:2
Ottolengui, Rodrigues Dr (por), 1937, Jl 13,19:4
Ottolini, Elsa A Mrs, 1946, S 20,31:3
Otty, Robert T, 1954, O 30,17:3
Otvos, A Dorian, 1945, Ag 29,23:3
Otway, Loftus, 1861, O 20,4:6
Otwell, Allie B, 1946, Je 12,27:1
Otwell, George H, 1942, O 14,25:2
Otz, Ernest, 1903, N 1,7:6
Otzmann, Henry Sr, 1959, D 25,21:4
Oualid, William, 1943, Mr 13,13:3
Ouchterloney, James D, 1963, D 24,17:2
Oudin, Folger Mrs, 1956, O 3,33:2
Oudin, G Folger, 1957, Ja 13,84:2
Oudin, Maurice A Mrs, 1956, Jl 8,65:2
Oudinot, Gen (Duke of Reggia), 1863, Jl 24,2:6
Ouellette, Francis J, 1951, Ja 4,29:4
Ouellette, John D, 1938, Ja 28,21:4
Ouerbacker, Emma A Y Mrs, 1963, D 13,36:2
Ougham, Harry R, 1942, S 12,13:7
Ougham, Marie, 1961, Je 5,9:3
Oughltree, Charles W, 1957, My 25,21:5
Oughton, John Sr, 1949, Jl 21,25:4
Ouimet, Francis D, 1967, S 3,52:6
Oulahan, R V, 1931, D 31,1:3
Oulahan, Richard, 1961, F 11,23:6
Oulahan, Richard V Mrs, 1916, Ap 13,13:5; 1964, N 22,85:5
Ould, R, 1882, D 16,4:7
Oulie, Marthe, 1941, Jl 22,20:2
Oulmann, Ludwig, 1940, S 17,23:4
Ouranis, Costas, 1953, Jl 15,25:4
Ouray, Ute Chief, 1880, Ag 29,1:6
Ourian, Adom K, 1951, O 30,29:3
Ouro Preto, Carlos C de, 1953, Ap 6,19:6
Oursler, Fulton, 1952, My 25,92:3
Oursler, Fulton Mrs, 1955, D 17,23:6
Oursler, John S, 1948, D 11,15:4
Ousley, Clarence, 1948, Ag 6,17:5
Ouspenskaya, Maria, 1949, D 4,108:6
Ouspensky, Nicholas, 1946, Ag 18,44:3
Ouspensky, P D Mrs, 1962, Ja 1,23:6
Ousterman, Elmer E, 1947, S 7,60:2
Ousterman, Peter, 1947, Je 17,25:4
Oustinoff, Platon M, 1951, D 31,13:4
Outcalt, Edmund R, 1946, F 27,25:6
Outcalt, Frederick G, 1965, My 18,39:3
Outcalt, Maybelle, 1937, S 3,38:3
Outcault, R F, 1928, S 26,27:5
Outen, Roland T, 1957, F 12,27:3
Outerbridge, E H, 1932, N 11,19:3
Outerbridge, Eugenius H Mrs, 1948, Ag 27,19:3
Outerbridge, George W, 1967, Ja 21,31:4
Outerbridge, Henry, 1953, F 26,25:4
Outerbridge, Joseph Mrs, 1943, Je 1,23:4
Outerbridge, Paul E, 1939, Je 17,15:3; 1958, O 26,88:8
Outerbridge, Samuel R, 1953, Je 29,21:2
Outerbridge, Samuel R Mrs, 1956, O 23,33:4
Outerbridge, T Hastings, 1940, F 21,19:4
Outerbridge, Thomas G, 1953, Je 24,25:3
Outerbridge, Thomas H, 1942, Mr 17,21:5
Outerbridge, Vivian L Col, 1937, D 5,II,9:1
Outerson, John W, 1941, D 25,25:5
Outhouse, Arthur J, 1944, O 11,21:4
Outhwaite, Joseph H, 1907, D 10,9:4
Outland, John H (por), 1947, Mr 25,25:4
Outland, Maurice, 1953, Jl 22,27:4
Outman, Robert E, 1955, Ag 9,25:4
Outram, James Sir, 1925, Mr 15,26:4
Outt, Walter J, 1945, F 24,11:2
Outterson, Frederick L, 1942, O 3,15:4
Outwater, Addison, 1964, N 15,86:6
Outwater, Barton J, 1938, Jl 24,29:5
Outwater, J Clifford, 1941, F 1,17:4
Outwater, John O, 1949, Jl 31,60:4
Outwater, William, 1952, Ap 16,27:3
Outwater, William W Mrs, 1949, My 23,23:1
Outwin, Edson L, 1966, My 27,43:1
Outz, James T, 1962, Jl 28,19:5
Ouvrier, P, 1881, Ap 11,8:5
Ouzelet, Charles A Mrs, 1948, N 28,92:6
Ouziel, Benzion M, 1953, S 6,50:1
Ouzounoff, Paul, 1942, O 28,23:5
Ouzounovitch, Nicholas T, 1954, S 23,33:5
Ovadia, Nessim J, 1942, Ag 31,17:5
Ovalo Castillo, Dario, 1949, S 5,17:4
Ovary, Francis, 1949, Mr 15,31:6
Ovens, Carrie H Mrs, 1949, My 24,28:2
Ovens, David, 1957, S 7,19:5
Ovens, Latham C, 1960, D 27,29:2
Ovens, Latham J, 1948, Je 29,23:3
Overaker, Charles B, 1940, Je 27,23:2
Overall, John H, 1967, O 1,84:5
Overall, Orval, 1947, Jl 16,23:6
Overbagh, Richard E, 1947, Ap 15,25:1
Overbagh, W Hoyt, 1939, O 1,53:3
Overbauh, Ralph H, 1946, N 20,31:3
Overbeck, Alice O Mrs, 1937, F 28,II,8:6
Overbeck, George A, 1948, Je 16,29:3
Overbeck, George H, 1945, Ja 22,17:5
Overbey, Andrew J, 1949, Jl 26,28:4
Overdeer, Frank N, 1947, F 17,19:5
Overend, Clarence, 1955, Mr 12,19:5
Overend, John F, 1959, F 24,29:3
Overfield, Charles W, 1948, My 26,25:1
Overfield, John S, 1947, Mr 13,27:4
Overfield, Lucy B Mrs, 1941, D 22,17:5
Overgaard, Anders R A, 1946, O 15,25:4
Overhamm, Francis B, 1948, Jl 6,23:2
Overholser, Charles E, 1962, Ap 5,33:1
Overholser, Earle L, 1949, Ap 19,25:4
Overholser, Winfred, 1964, O 7,47:4
Overholt, Earl, 1950, D 21,29:4
Overholt, George T, 1965, N 1,41:2
Overholt, Maria F Mrs, 1939, Ja 26,21:3
Overhysser, Gustave A, 1951, Mr 9,25:2
Overin, Sturtevant 3d, 1965, Ag 30,25:2
Overing, Henry Clinton, 1916, Ag 2,9:6
Overington, William Jr, 1950, O 20,28:3
Overland, Rolf G, 1952, Je 21,15:5
Overlander, Charles L, 1948, D 18,19:4
Overlock, Joseph L, 1946, Jl 23,25:1
Overlock, Russell F Mrs, 1947, Je 23,23:4
Overly, G Wylie, 1949, N 6,92:2
Overly, Sterling W, 1960, S 3,17:3
Overman, Donald G, 1959, Mr 13,26:6
Overman, Frank L, 1943, S 17,21:1
Overman, H J, 1884, Ap 3,4:7
Overman, John R, 1967, N 8,47:2
Overman, L S, 1930, D 12,25:1
Overman, Lynn Mrs, 1961, D 31,48:6
Overman, Lynne, 1943, F 20,13:1
Overman, Neill P, 1956, D 30,32:2
Overman, Ralph S, 1953, S 12,17:2
Overmann, Leon Sr Mrs, 1949, F 22,23:4
Overmyer, Chester P, 1953, Ja 5,16:1
Overn, Sarah J, 1946, S 26,25:2
Overocker, Edwin J, 1918, D 24,9:6
Overpeck, Elizabeth S, 1961, D 13,43:1
Overstreet, Charles L, 1950, O 23,23:3
Overstreet, Harry E, 1944, Ap 2,40:3
Overstreet, Harry M, 1948, F 13,21:3
Overstreet, Jesse, 1910, My 28,9:6
Overstreet, Joseph R, 1945, Ag 18,11:5
Overstreet, Roscoe C, 1952, Mr 15,13:3
Overton, Anthony, 1946, Jl 4,19:5
Overton, Bruce, 1955, Ag 4,25:5
Overton, Clough C, 1953, Jl 29,23:4
Overton, Clough C Mrs, 1942, N 9,23:2
Overton, Daniel H Rev Dr, 1920, Ag 24,9:3
Overton, David E, 1962, Ja 27,21:5
Overton, Edgar M, 1942, Mr 3,24:3
Overton, Edward Col, 1903, S 19,7:6
Overton, Elliott J, 1949, Ja 4,19:3
Overton, Evart E, 1949, Ja 29,13:4
Overton, Florence (por), 1948, My 9,68:5
Overton, Frank, 1953, O 12,27:5
Overton, Frank (mem ser set, Ap 27,45:3), 1967, Ap 25,43:3
Overton, Frank Mrs, 1953, N 23,27:4
Overton, George W, 1942, F 18,19:1
Overton, Grace S, 1963, S 4,39:4
Overton, James B, 1937, Mr 19,23:2
Overton, John H, 1948, My 15,15:5
Overton, John Jr Col, 1903, D 13,7:6
Overton, John S, 1910, Jl 26,7:6
Overton, Mary E, 1948, My 12,28:2
Overton, Mordecai H, 1951, Mr 29,27:4
Overton, Myron E, 1954, F 9,27:5
Overton, S Watkins, 1958, D 3,37:1
Overton, Walter G Sr, 1943, Ja 5,19:4
Overton, William, 1948, Ag 13,15:3
Overton, William A, 1947, Ja 7,27:1
Overton, William B Col, 1912, Mr 28,11:4
Overton, William S, 1943, My 19,25:4
Overton-Jones, Edward, 1963, Ag 1,27:5
Ovette, Joe, 1946, Ag 7,27:3
Ovey, Esmond, 1963, My 31,23:5
Oviatt, E Farnham, 1951, Jl 24,25:1
Oviatt, Edwin, 1955, Ja 25,25:4
Oviatt, Harry C, 1961, Mr 11,21:6
Oviatt, Percival, 1951, Jl 21,13:4
Oviatt, William H, 1939, D 2,17:5
Oviatti, Frank G, 1951, D 16,90:2
Ovington, E L, 1936, Jl 23,21:4
Ovington, Mary W, 1951, Jl 16,21:4
Ovington, Theodore T, 1909, My 20,9:4
Ovitt, Albert B, 1916, Ja 27,11:5
Ovitte, Winifred Mrs, 1953, Ag 4,21:2
Ovodow, Nicholas N, 1965, Ap 1,35:2
Ovsiew, Joseph, 1952, F 19,29:2
Ovsiew, Samuel, 1957, Jl 17,27:1
Ovson, Morris, 1961, S 7,35:2
Owen, A E, 1944, Mr 22,19:4
Owen, Abbie B Mrs, 1949, Ag 12,17:3
Owen, Alfred, 1921, Ap 11,11:3; 1942, F 26,19:5
Owen, Alfred Mrs, 1942, F 26,19:5
Owen, Alfred P, 1947, Mr 12,25:1
Owen, Allan F, 1951, Ap 6,25:3
Owen, Aloney R, 1951, Mr 17,15:3
Owen, Andrew H, 1960, Mr 12,21:1
Owen, Anna M Mrs, 1954, Jl 16,21:5
Owen, Benjamin F, 1948, F 28,27:1
Owen, Burt, 1964, Ag 29,18:2
Owen, Carl E, 1964, N 19,39:4
Owen, Carl M, 1954, Ap 13,31:1
Owen, Catherine D (Mrs H P Metzger), 1965, S 47:1
Owen, Cecil, 1954, O 6,25:2
Owen, Charles D Sr, 1937, My 25,28:1
Owen, Charles E, 1942, Mr 15,42:7

Owen, Charles H, 1950, Jl 9,68:7
Owen, Charles J, 1912, Ja 5,13:4
Owen, Charles S, 1946, F 2,13:2; 1950, F 8,28:2
Owen, Charlotte E, 1968, D 5,47:3
Owen, chas A, 1957, Jl 22,19:5
Owen, Chauncey E Mrs, 1957, Je 25,29:1
Owen, Clifford H, 1951, N 5,31:4
Owen, Daniel, 1939, F 23,23:2
Owen, Daniel L, 1942, Ap 2,21:3
Owen, Daniel M, 1939, Je 18,37:2
Owen, Daniel W, 1937, S 29,23:4
Owen, David, 1947, Jl 5,11:7; 1954, Jl 7,31:2
Owen, David B, 1943, Ja 9,13:4
Owen, David Edward Prof, 1968, F 14,47:3
Owen, David J, 1941, My 18,45:2
Owen, Derwyn T, 1947, Ap 10,25:5
Owen, E H, 1876, S 23,2:3; 1881, Ap 15,5:2
Owen, E Robert, 1957, F 2,19:4
Owen, Edmund Charles Mrs, 1917, Ja 31,11:5
Owen, Edward B, 1925, Ja 28,17:3
Owen, Elizabeth Mrs, 1939, Je 4,48:5
Owen, Emerson D, 1943, Ag 23,15:6
Owen, Emerson D Mrs, 1953, F 16,21:1
Owen, Emmett M, 1939, Je 22,23:5
Owen, Fay K Mrs, 1951, F 24,13:4
Owen, Ferd, 1955, O 9,87:2
Owen, Frank, 1907, N 26,9:4; 1968, O 15,47:2
Owen, Frank G Mrs, 1950, Ja 5,25:4
Owen, Frank P, 1953, Jl 8,27:4
Owen, Franklin S, 1945, D 27,19:2
Owen, Fred K, 1940, Mr 20,27:3
Owen, Frederick L, 1959, N 30,31:2
Owen, Frederick W, 1947, S 15,17:4
Owen, George, 1959, Ap 22,33:3; 1960, N 10,47:3
Owen, George D Mrs, 1949, Mr 22,25:1
Owen, George J, 1955, D 12,31:5
Owen, George T, 1950, Ap 22,19:4
Owen, George V Mrs, 1946, O 31,25:3
Owen, Griffith R, 1945, Je 29,15:3
Owen, Gwilym E, 1963, Je 23,85:1
Owen, Harry E, 1949, My 30,13:2
Owen, Harry O, 1944, Jl 7,15:4
Owen, Helen M, 1946, O 16,28:3
Owen, Herbert A, 1963, Ap 7,86:3
Owen, Horace T Mrs, 1957, My 1,37:3
Owen, Hubley R, 1955, O 9,86:4
Owen, Hugh, 1967, S 9,31:4
Owen, Irving L, 1961, O 26,35:5
Owen, Isabel Mrs, 1939, D 7,27:1
Owen, James, 1921, Jl 7,11:5
Owen, James E Mrs, 1951, Jl 24,25:3
Owen, James G Sir, 1939, Jl 9,30:8
Owen, James H, 1942, Jl 17,15:5
Owen, John B, 1951, Ap 8,93:1
Owen, John D Mrs, 1942, F 21,19:1
Owen, John J, 1947, Ap 23,25:1
Owen, John L, 1953, My 28,20:2
Owen, John P, 1954, Je 15,29:2
Owen, John R, 1949, My 12,31:5
Owen, John T, 1949, N 9,28:3
Owen, Judson L, 1945, Ag 9,21:6
Owen, June, 1964, My 17,87:2
Owen, Laurence, 1961, F 16,1:1
Owen, Leslie, 1947, Mr 3,21:2
Owen, Lewis R, 1951, Jl 14,13:4
Owen, Llewellyn S, 1944, Ja 13,21:4
Owen, Logan S, 1945, Jl 16,11:6
Owen, Maribel, 1961, F 16,1:1
Owen, Maribel V Mrs, 1961, F 16,1:1
Owen, Mary W Mrs, 1949, My 27,21:4
Owen, Narcissa Chisholm, 1911, Jl 17,9:5
Owen, Oliver Mrs, 1947, Ja 21,23:4
Owen, Ollie Mrs, 1954, D 3,27:1
Owen, Orville Dr, 1924, Ap 1,21:2
Owen, Paul D, 1941, Jl 27,30:8
Owen, Percy Sr, 1956, Je 1,23:2
Owen, Philip S, 1963, Jl 9,31:4
Owen, R D, 1877, Je 26,5:5
Owen, R Emmett, 1957, S 15,84:7
Owen, Raymond M, 1943, Ap 30,21:1
Owen, Raymond M Mrs, 1952, Ap 9,31:4
Owen, Reginald Mrs, 1956, O 20,21:1
Owen, Richard, 1942, Jl 5,29:2; 1959, F 16,29:3
Owen, Richard W, 1962, O 30,35:1
Owen, Robert, 1858, N 30,5:3
Owen, Robert B, 1949, D 31,15:2
Owen, Robert L, 1947, Jl 20,45:1
Owen, Russell, 1952, Ap 4,25:1
Owen, Russell E, 1955, Ap 29,23:2
Owen, S W Rev, 1916, Ap 17,11:4
Owen, Samuel K, 1940, N 30,17:4
Owen, Seena, 1966, Ag 19,33:4
Owen, Stephen S, 1943, Ja 24,42:2
Owen, Steve, 1964, My 18,29:1
Owen, Thomas M Jr, 1948, D 7,32:2
Owen, Thomas M Mrs, 1958, Mr 2,88:6
Owen, Thomas O, 1948, N 26,23:3
Owen, Toni, 1968, D 29,52:1
Owen, Trevor R, 1937, N 4,25:2
Owen, W David, 1942, Ja 19,17:4
Owen, Walter G Capt, 1937, Mr 12,24:1
Owen, Walter G Mrs, 1953, Ja 8,27:3
Owen, Wilfred C, 1951, Je 10,92:8
Owen, William, 1941, Mr 18,23:3
Owen, William A, 1904, D 5,7:3; 1956, D 11,36:8
Owen, William B, 1947, F 24,19:4; 1951, D 6,33:1
Owen, William B Prof, 1917, D 5,13:4
Owen, William B 3d, 1964, Mr 31,35:4
Owen, William F, 1906, My 5,9:6
Owen, William H, 1921, Mr 9,13:3; 1944, My 29,15:3
Owen, William H (will), 1944, Jl 1,13:1
Owen, William H, 1949, O 24,23:3
Owen, William H Mrs, 1943, N 20,13:4
Owen, William Mrs, 1943, F 28,49:2; 1945, N 8,19:2
Owen, William O, 1954, Ap 15,29:4
Owen, William R, 1938, Mr 31,23:5
Owen, William S, 1941, Mr 17,17:4
Owens, Albert A, 1956, Jl 26,25:5
Owens, Albert S Judge, 1937, Mr 31,24:3
Owens, Alfred V, 1950, F 3,23:2
Owens, Andrew E, 1952, O 5,88:8
Owens, Clarence (Brick),(por), 1949, N 12,15:1
Owens, Clarence J, 1941, F 8,15:1
Owens, Clifford A, 1937, Jl 29,19:4
Owens, Curtis A Sr, 1959, Ja 29,27:2
Owens, Donald H, 1959, S 4,21:4
Owens, Elizabeth A, 1946, Ap 21,21:4
Owens, Ellen M Mrs, 1941, Ja 8,19:3
Owens, Emma, 1962, Mr 31,25:1
Owens, Frank X, 1947, Ja 12,59:3
Owens, G Guy, 1960, Ja 21,31:4
Owens, George C, 1957, O 26,42:2
Owens, Gertrude A, 1950, S 18,23:3
Owens, Harry B, 1967, My 26,47:1
Owens, Henry R, 1950, Ag 23,29:5
Owens, Herbert H, 1957, Ag 16,19:4
Owens, Herbert H Mrs, 1951, S 21,23:2
Owens, Howard F, 1938, Ja 11,23:3
Owens, J, 1882, Ap 24,5:3
Owens, J E, 1886, D 8,2:6
Owens, J Hamilton, 1967, Ap 22,31:2
Owens, J J Brig-Gen, 1864, My 13,2:4
Owens, James B, 1946, D 29,35:4
Owens, James E, 1947, D 12,28:3
Owens, James Ex-Sen, 1911, Mr 8,11:4
Owens, James F, 1942, F 21,19:4; 1954, Je 22,27:3
Owens, James T, 1944, S 8,19:7
Owens, James T Mrs, 1953, S 10,25:4
Owens, Jane F, 1940, My 29,23:2
Owens, John E, 1963, O 29,36:7
Owens, John H, 1953, O 17,15:2
Owens, John J, 1949, Jl 27,23:4
Owens, John P, 1948, D 4,19:2
Owens, John R, 1947, S 1,19:5; 1950, My 26,23:2
Owens, John W, 1968, Ap 25,47:4
Owens, Joseph T, 1947, F 21,19:5
Owens, Louis C Jr, 1964, Ag 11,33:2
Owens, Louis J J, 1944, F 15,17:4
Owens, Martin S, 1960, Ag 2,29:5
Owens, Michael, 1949, S 27,27:1
Owens, Michael J, 1923, D 28,15:5; 1950, F 25,17:4
Owens, Michael J Mrs, 1948, Mr 19,23:3
Owens, Minnie E, 1951, Ja 17,27:3
Owens, O C, 1876, Mr 9,4:7
Owens, Patrick J, 1959, Ap 4,19:5
Owens, Ray L, 1948, Ag 17,21:3
Owens, Robert B, 1940, N 3,56:6
Owens, Robert F, 1944, Ag 11,15:5
Owens, S Logan, 1951, F 24,13:5
Owens, Sen (see also S 8,9,10), 1877, S 11,1:4
Owens, Thomas J, 1944, O 2,19:5
Owens, Thomas L, 1948, Je 8,25:5; 1952, Ag 22,21:2
Owens, Thomas Madison, 1910, D 9,11:4
Owens, Vilda S Mrs, 1950, Mr 6,21:4
Owens, W F, 1902, N 10,5:3
Owens, Walter A, 1948, O 12,25:5
Owens, Walter D, 1952, Je 24,29:1
Owens, Walter W, 1954, Ap 19,23:2
Owens, William G Mrs, 1948, Jl 10,15:2
Owens, William P, 1951, Jl 12,25:3
Owens, William W Mrs, 1944, O 10,23:3
Owensby, Newdigate M, 1952, Ag 11,15:5
Owings, Oliver O, 1948, O 26,31:5
Owl, Grey (por), 1938, Ap 14,23:2
Owlett, G Mason, 1957, Ja 25,21:1
Owlett, George Mrs, 1950, F 7,27:2
Own, Frank, 1947, F 21,19:2
Ownes, Thomas E, 1947, F 12,25:3
Ownley, Curtis A, 1939, Jl 24,16:7
Owre, Erling, 1961, F 1,35:3
Owsiak, Frank K, 1952, F 23,11:5
Owsley, Alvin C, 1938, Ap 28,23:1
Owsley, Alvin M, 1967, Ap 4,43:1
Owsley, Carl W, 1944, My 21,43:1
Owsley, Henry F, 1941, N 30,68:1
Owsley, John E, 1953, Jl 16,21:2
Owsley, John E Mrs, 1943, Ag 16,15:2
Owsley, Louis S, 1943, S 28,25:1
Owsley, Monroe (por), 1937, Je 9,25:5
Owsley, William ex-Gov, 1862, D 14,3:3
Owston, Charles W Capt, 1910, F 15,9:5
Oxanne, Henry, 1960, Je 6,29:4
Oxenberg, William, 1954, Ag 16,17:3
Oxenford, J, 1877, F 23,5:2
Oxenford, Leon P Sr, 1949, Ap 24,76:3
Oxenham, John, 1941, Ja 25,15:5
Oxenreiter, Sebastian, 1943, Ap 16,22:2
Oxer, George C, 1955, F 2,27:3
Oxford and Asquith, Countess of (por), 1945, Jl 29, 39:1
Oxford and Asquith, Earl of, 1928, F 15,1:5
Oxholm, Oscar O, 1949, Mr 27,76:2
Oxholm, Theodor S, 1940, Jl 2,21:6
Oxholm, Theodore S Mrs, 1953, F 24,25:3
Oxhorn, Sam, 1954, Ja 16,15:2
Oxley, Alexander J, 1944, Ja 20,19:3
Oxley, Charles J, 1951, Ag 7,25:6
Oxley, Freedrick, 1943, S 3,19:6
Oxley, John J, 1954, Ag 15,85:1
Oxley, Morton E, 1946, Ag 2,19:4
Oxley, Roland H, 1952, Je 28,19:2
Oxman, Frank, 1955, D 25,48:2
Oxman, Jacob, 1946, D 27,19:4
Oxman, Minnie Mrs, 1945, S 16,42:5
Oxmun, Edward Henry, 1910, D 10,11:4
Oxnam, G Bromley, 1963, Mr 14,16:2
Oxnard, Benjamin Alexander, 1924, Ag 20,13:4
Oxnard, James G (will), 1968, Jl 9,78:1
Oxnard, James Guerrero, 1919, Ap 20,22:2
Oxnard, Thomas, 1965, My 30,51:2
Oxner, Douglas, 1955, S 29,33:1
Oxx, Francis H, 1956, F 17,23:3
Oxx, Warren, 1947, Ja 9,23:3
Oyama, Iwao, 1916, D 11,9:3
Oyama, Princess, 1919, F 24,13:3
Oyandel Urrutia, Ab, 1954, Ja 30,17:1
Oye, Schimmelpennick Van der, 1943, My 3,17:4
Oyen, Adolph B, 1940, Mr 25,15:6
Oyer, Daniel J, 1947, Mr 18,27:4
Oyhanarte, Horacio, 1946, N 8,23:1
Oyler, Alma E, 1955, F 11,23:3
Oyler, Ralph H, 1947, Mr 5,25:2
Oyserman, Ben, 1967, Je 7,21:3
Oysher, Moishe, 1958, N 28,27:3
Oyster, George M, 1921, Ap 25,11:2
Ozab, Edward F, 1946, Ap 10,27:3
Ozai-Durrani, Ataullah K (will, Je 19,33:2), 1964, My 5,46:4
Ozaki, Yukio (funl, O 14,29:4), 1954, O 7,23:1
Ozamiz, Jesus, 1953, Ja 7,31:5
Ozenfant, Amedee, 1966, My 5,47:2
Ozer, Isadore Mrs, 1963, S 15,87:1
Ozgurel, Handi, 1955, Jl 19,27:5
Ozhegov, Sergei I, 1964, D 18,33:1
Ozier, Eugene C, 1947, N 30,76:5
Ozier, Mary D Mrs, 1953, Mr 26,31:2
Ozmus, Isaac D, 1946, D 10,31:4
Ozu, Yasujiro, 1963, D 13,36:4

P

Paalen, Bella, 1964, Ag 1,21:5
Paape, Walden W, 1949, Mr 22,25:5
Paaren, Sander, 1940, S 21,19:5
Paasch, William H, 1943, Mr 2,19:5
Paasche, Fredrik, 1943, S 3,19:2
Paasche, Hermann Dr, 1925, Ap 11,13:3
Paaschen, William H, 1954, D 6,27:5
Paashaus, Charles E, 1956, Ja 15,92:8
Paasikivi, Annikki, 1950, N 26,90:4
Paasikivi, Juho K (funl, D 24,13:1), 1956, D 15,25:1
Paasikivi, Juho K Mme, 1960, Jl 14,27:4
Paaswell, Benjamin, 1964, Je 11,33:4
Pabian, Joseph, 1962, N 19,31:2
Pabisch, F J, 1879, O 5,2:7
Pablos, Tomas M, 1948, Mr 16,27:4
Pabst, Fred, 1904, Ja 2,1:4; 1958, F 22,17:1
Pabst, G W, 1967, My 31,43:1
Pabst, Gustav Jr, 1960, Ja 15,31:2
Pabst, Gustave, 1943, My 30,27:1
Pabst, Gustave Mrs, 1951, Jl 10,27:1
Pabst, Henry Mrs, 1925, My 18,15:4
Pabst, Jean C, 1942, Ja 25,29:4
Pabst, John Sr, 1944, Ap 20,19:5
Pabst, Vivian E, 1950, Ap 13,29:1
Pacary, Lina, 1953, Ja 5,21:2
Pacaud, George W, 1937, Je 7,19:4
Pacaud, Lucien T, 1960, Mr 8,33:3
Paccard, Joseph, 1949, F 22,24:2
Paccione, Giovanni, 1947, Ja 23,23:1
Pace, Anderson, 1957, O 21,25:5
Pace, Anna, 1921, Ap 12,17:5
Pace, Charles A (por), 1940, D 13,23:1
Pace, Charles N, 1954, D 18,15:6
Pace, Charles R, 1957, Ag 1,25:4
Pace, Clement, 1949, D 22,23:3
Pace, Edward A (por), 1938, Ap 27,23:3
Pace, Frank Sr, 1949, S 23,23:2
Pace, Gerald F, 1966, O 29,29:4
Pace, Homer M, 1951, N 17,17:6
Pace, Homer S (por), 1942, My 23,13:5
Pace, Homer St C Mrs, 1966, O 20,43:5
Pace, James G, 1948, Ja 28,23:3
Pace, Leo L, 1963, S 27,29:1
Pace, Lorenzo, 1951, My 13,89:1
Pace, N Crittenden Mrs, 1952, Ag 12,19:6
Pace, Peter, 1949, O 14,27:2
Pace, Thaddeus P, 1952, My 9,23:2
Pace, Thomas J, 1949, Mr 12,17:2
Pace, Tommy, 1949, D 12,33:2
Pace, Walter W, 1955, Jl 11,23:5
Pace, William L, 1944, Jl 27,17:1
Pacelli, Eugenio (Pope Pius XII),(will; funl rites, O 11,1:6,8), 1958, O 9,1:8
Pacelli, William V, 1942, O 1,23:5
Pacello, Vincent J, 1951, My 19,15:4
Pacent, Louis G, 1952, Ap 9,31:1
Pacetta, Salvatore, 1963, Jl 2,26:6
Pacey, John W, 1966, Jl 13,43:1
Pach, Alex L, 1938, Mr 13,II,8:8
Pach, Alexander, 1968, Ap 23,47:2
Pach, Alfred, 1949, Jl 29,21:1
Pach, Gotthelf, 1925, Ap 18,15:6
Pach, Gustav W, 1904, O 11,9:4
Pach, Morris, 1914, Mr 30,9:4
Pach, Stewart L, 1955, Ag 28,85:3
Pach, Walter, 1958, N 28,30:3
Pach, Walter Mrs, 1950, N 11,15:4
Pachachi, Hamdi, 1948, Mr 28,48:7
Pacheco, Ramauldo Mrs, 1913, N 9,IV,7:5
Pachella, Dominick F, 1955, Ap 16,19:5
Pachella, Francesco Mrs, 1955, Je 25,15:5
Pachler, John A, 1945, S 22,17:5
Pachler, John E, 1951, My 20,88:8
Pachmann, V de, 1933, Ja 8,31:1
Pachnann, Adrien de, 1937, D 23,21:4
Pachner, Joseph, 1937, Jl 8,23:3
Pachon de la Torre, Alvaro, 1953, Mr 23,2:3
Pachtmann, Edward, 1958, Jl 29,23:4
Paci, Joseph, 1945, Mr 22,23:5
Paci, Joseph C, 1954, My 23,88:5
Paci, Mario, 1946, Ag 5,21:4
Paci, Vincencina Mrs, 1957, Ja 9,31:2
Pacini, Alfredo, 1967, D 24,49:1
Pacini, Jean Composer, 1867, D 13,1:1
Pack, Albert, 1941, N 16,56:2
Pack, Carl, 1945, Ag 9,23:3
Pack, Charles L (por),(will, Je 23,25:1), 1937, Je 15, 23:1
Pack, Mac, 1948, Mr 5,21:4
Pack, Mark, 1942, Ja 28,19:6
Pack, Matthew R, 1957, S 13,23:1
Pack, Randolph G, 1956, D 26,27:3
Pack, Robert W, 1965, Jl 5,17:4
Pack, Walter, 1960, O 1,19:4
Pack, William F, 1944, S 4,19:4
Packard, A S Prof, 1884, Jl 15,4:7
Packard, Alpheus A, 1948, Ag 8,56:6
Packard, Alpheus S Prof, 1905, F 15,1:2
Packard, Ansel A, 1957, Ag 27,29:4
Packard, Artemas, 1961, S 7,70:2
Packard, Artemas Mrs, 1961, S 7,70:2
Packard, Arthur W, 1953, Ja 27,25:1
Packard, C Herbert, 1937, O 5,25:5
Packard, Carlotta, 1940, D 4,27:5
Packard, Charles A, 1966, O 2,86:2
Packard, Charles S W (por), 1937, Jl 10,15:1
Packard, Daniel W, 1939, Mr 19,III,6:5
Packard, Edward N Dr, 1968, N 17,86:6
Packard, Edward N Rev, 1917, Ap 27,11:4
Packard, Edwin, 1921, Ap 28,13:4
Packard, Edwin A Mrs, 1951, Ag 21,27:4
Packard, Elizabeth H, 1947, Ja 25,17:6
Packard, Francis R, 1950, Ap 19,29:5
Packard, Frank E, 1961, F 10,24:2
Packard, Frank L, 1923, O 27,13:4
Packard, Frank L (por), 1942, F 18,19:1
Packard, Frederick A, 1867, N 12,5:1
Packard, George, 1949, O 2,81:1; 1956, My 28,27:3
Packard, George R, 1966, Ja 7,27:5
Packard, Harry O, 1940, My 25,17:3
Packard, Henry P, 1954, O 6,25:1
Packard, J Francis R, 1966, Mr 23,47:2
Packard, J W, 1928, Mr 21,27:3
Packard, James H, 1953, Jl 6,17:5
Packard, James W Mrs, 1960, Ja 20,31:4
Packard, John C, 1956, Jl 30,21:4
Packard, John H 3d, 1953, Ja 4,76:3
Packard, Joseph, 1923, N 25,23:2
Packard, Joseph S, 1944, Ja 10,17:2
Packard, Katherine B Mrs, 1940, F 12,17:3
Packard, L R Prof, 1884, O 27,5:6
Packard, Laurence B, 1955, Ja 15,13:4
Packard, Louis A Mrs, 1950, Ap 5,32:2
Packard, Nathan J Mrs, 1949, O 5,29:3
Packard, Ralph G Jr, 1944, Ap 24,19:5
Packard, Roscoe M, 1948, My 31,19:5
Packard, S S Mrs, 1903, Jl 25,7:6
Packard, Samuel W, 1937, Ja 28,25:3
Packard, Servia H Mrs, 1951, Ap 15,92:3
Packard, Walter E, 1966, N 2,45:3
Packard, William Alfred Dr, 1909, D 3,11:5
Packard, William D, 1923, N 12,17:5
Packard, Winthrop, 1943, Ap 3,15:5
Packer, Arthur H, 1953, My 16,19:5
Packer, Asa, 1879, My 18,2:5
Packer, Asa Mrs, 1882, N 18,5:2
Packer, August O, 1954, Ja 14,29:3
Packer, Bernard, 1954, Ja 26,27:1
Packer, Francis H, 1957, Jl 15,19:2
Packer, Fred L, 1956, D 9,89:1
Packer, H E Judge, 1884, F 2,5:4
Packer, Harold N, 1955, Ja 22,11:5
Packer, Herbert A, 1962, S 25,37:2
Packer, Herbert J Mrs, 1962, My 5,27:4
Packer, Horace B, 1940, Ap 15,17:2
Packer, Isadore, 1952, O 15,31:3
Packer, Jerry, 1964, Jl 23,27:3
Packer, John B, 1937, Ja 31,II,9:1
Packer, Launcelot, 1937, Mr 31,24:3
Packer, Mary Keys Mrs, 1918, Ap 9,13:4
Packer, Max, 1943, My 19,25:5
Packer, Melville K, 1941, Mr 28,23:4
Packer, Moses, 1948, N 19,27:4
Packer, P Hall, 1924, F 2,13:6
Packer, R A, 1883, F 22,5:4
Packer, Samuel H, 1944, S 25,19:5
Packer, Victor, 1958, Ja 29,28:1
Packer, William S, 1957, Ja 13,84:7
Packett, Harry, 1954, O 4,27:5
Pacy, Ernest H, 1943, Je 24,21:4
Padan, Wiley, 1947, F 15,15:2
Padden, Frank M, 1959, F 17,31:5
Padden, Michael C, 1925, Mr 18,21:5
Paddison, Walter J, 1965, Mr 5,33:2
Paddison, William R, 1951, F 5,23:1
Paddleford, Almon L, 1944, F 25,17:4
Paddleford, Clementine (will filed, D 6,31:2), 1967, N 14,47:2
Paddleford, Jesse F, 1949, Mr 24,28:2
Paddock, Alice, 1957, Je 12,35:5
Paddock, Andrew Billings, 1909, O 28,9:3
Paddock, Ben Rev, 1871, O 9,1:2
Paddock, Charles H Mrs, 1942, F 8,50:2
Paddock, Charles Henry, 1923, F 24,11:6
Paddock, Delmar, 1952, F 9,13:4
Paddock, E Ellsworth, 1948, S 10,23:2
Paddock, Edward H, 1952, Jl 11,17:4
Paddock, Ernest M, 1945, Jl 14,11:7
Paddock, Eugene H, 1912, D 10,15:4
Paddock, Eugene H Mrs, 1947, Ag 12,23:2
Paddock, Fan A Mrs, 1948, F 5,24:2
Paddock, Frank, 1959, My 28,31:4
Paddock, G, 1932, N 4,19:1
Paddock, George E, 1946, Je 2,44:4
Paddock, George F, 1955, Ag 17,27:2
Paddock, H Lester, 1948, Je 24,25:6
Paddock, Harry L, 1937, Ag 2,19:3
Paddock, Herbert H, 1952, Je 28,20:6
Paddock, James H, 1939, Jl 1,17:4
Paddock, James L Sr, 1962, O 10,51:5
Paddock, James N, 1912, Mr 21,11:5
Paddock, John A Mrs, 1956, Ja 20,23:5
Paddock, Josephine, 1964, F 22,21:5
Paddock, Leon A, 1954, Jl 28,23:5
Paddock, Paul D, 1952, F 24,85:1
Paddock, Ralph L, 1940, O 10,25:6
Paddock, Robert L (por),(will, Je 7,10:4), 1939, My 18,25:1
Paddock, Robert L Mrs (will, Mr 27,11:7), 1937, F 2,23:2
Paddock, W F Rev, 1903, Je 12,9:6
Paddock, Wendell Prof, 1953, F 21,13:4
Paddock, Willard D, 1956, N 26,27:4
Paddock, William A, 1962, Je 18,25:5
Paddock, William H, 1942, N 28,13:5
Paddock, Wirt A, 1949, S 25,92:7
Paddon, Granville, 1939, Je 9,21:4
Paddon, Harry L, 1939, D 26,19:5
Paddon, W Wallace Mrs (Mary), 1968, Je 9,84:5
Padel, Christian G (por), 1942, Mr 5,23:5
Padelford, Edward M, 1921, Je 26,22:3
Padelford, Edward M Mrs, 1911, D 26,9:5; 1963, Jl 29:3
Padelford, Frank W, 1944, F 21,15:4
Padelford, Frederick M, 1942, D 5,15:6
Padelford, K R Mrs, 1946, Je 20,23:4
Padelford, S, 1878, Ag 27,4:7
Paderewski, I J Mme, 1934, Ja 17,19:1
Paderewski, Ignace J, 1941, Je 30,1:2
Padersen, Frederick M, 1947, Ag 21,23:5
Padewski, Joseph, 1951, My 12,22:8
Padgett, B Lewis, 1951, My 12,21:3
Padgett, Emma G Mrs, 1949, F 4,23:2
Padgett, Ernest H (Red), 1957, Ap 17,31:2
Padgett, Eugene W, 1948, D 12,93:1
Padgett, Frederick W, 1966, Ja 18,34:2
Padgett, James T, 1947, Je 12,25:5
Padgett, Lemuel P, 1922, Ag 3,13:6
Padgham, Elizabeth Mrs, 1947, Je 13,23:2
Padgitt, Newton, 1959, Ag 30,82:8
Padilla Sanchez, Jose, 1960, O 26,39:2
Padilla Vega, Jose A, 1955, Ag 19,19:5
Padilla y Bell, Alejandro, 1954, Jl 23,17:4
Padin, Angel S, 1966, N 5,31:5
Padin, Manuel A, 1955, My 9,23:2
Padmore, George, 1959, S 25,29:1
Padovani, Gabriel, 1952, My 1,29:2
Padover, Saul K Mrs, 1952, My 12,25:4
Padow, Louis, 1962, F 22,25:3
Padres, Gustavo Jr, 1953, My 19,29:1
Paduano, Leonard, 1951, Ja 23,27:4
Padula, Andres A, 1950, My 3,29:4
Padula, Anthony Mrs, 1940, My 21,23:2
Padula, Matthew, 1964, Ag 18,31:1
Padula, Peter, 1954, O 5,27:2
Padusniak, Joseph Mrs, 1951, F 13,31:2
Padva, Harry J, 1967, N 11,33:3
Padve, Meyer, 1959, Ap 6,27:3
Padway, Joseph A, 1947, O 9,1:4
Padwe, Isadore, 1958, O 19,87:2
Pae, Herbert B, 1944, S 8,19:5
Paegelow, John A, 1944, N 24,23:4
Paepcke, Walter P, 1960, Ap 14,31:1
Paeschke, Charles W, 1938, O 20,23:1
Paetow, L J, 1928, D 23,19:2
Paets, Konstantin (reptdly died in '56), 1957, F 26
Paetzold, Edward J, 1952, F 26,27:4
Paez, Jose Antonia Gen, 1873, My 7,5:4
Pafe, J C, 1885, My 20,5:4
Paff, Harry L, 1959, N 18,41:4
Paff, Hugo Rev, 1914, Ja 10,9:5
Paff, James F Jr, 1952, S 3,29:2
Paff, Louis, 1968, My 2,47:3
Paff, Thomas A Mrs, 1946, My 19,42:2
Paffard, Frederic C, 1962, Ag 19,89:1
Paffrath, Hugo C Mrs, 1952, Ja 22,29:2
Paffrath, John, 1951, S 1,11:2
Paffrath, John J, 1949, Mr 18,25:2
Pagan, Bolivar, 1961, F 10,24:1
Pagan, C H F, 1924, Mr 6,17:4
Pagan, Clarence E, 1942, My 28,17:4
Pagan, Clarence Mrs, 1946, O 2,29:6
Pagan, John, 1944, Ag 7,15:4
Paganelli, T Richard, 1945, F 19,17:6
Pagani, Andre, 1951, N 7,29:6
Pagani, Ernesto, 1917, S 21,9:6
Paganini, August Mrs, 1947, F 1,15:4
Paganini, Bartholomew, 1960, Ap 17,92:8
Pagano, Bartolo, 1938, N 16,23:3
Pagano, Ernest S, 1953, My 1,21:5
Pagano, Joseph Sr, 1947, F 16,57:2
Pagano, Mario, 1954, My 9,88:5
Paganon, Joseph (por), 1937, N 3,23:3
Paganucci, Anthony, 1954, F 24,25:4
Paganucci, Anthony Mrs, 1959, Jl 26,69:1
Pagdin, William H, 1941, Ja 11,12:5
Page, A R, 1931, F 4,23:1

Page, Adele, 1882, F 26,4:5
Page, Albert L Mrs, 1950, Jl 20,25:5
Page, Albert W, 1954, Ap 18,89:2
Page, Albert W Mrs, 1959, S 27,86:4
Page, Albion L, 1949, Ap 17,77:1
Page, Alice W Mrs, 1942, F 8,50:2
Page, Alinson S, 1905, Ap 15,11:5
Page, Ambrose W, 1939, O 21,15:3
Page, Arch, 1949, Mr 8,25:1
Page, Arden E, 1946, Ap 5,25:5
Page, Arthur C, 1953, Ap 5,76:6
Page, Arthur D, 1922, O 30,15:5
Page, Arthur L Mrs, 1945, F 6,19:4
Page, Arthur W, 1960, S 7,41:3
Page, Arthur W Mrs, 1964, Je 10,45:1
Page, Augustus, 1883, S 18,4:6
Page, Benjamin Mrs, 1964, D 23,27:2
Page, Bertrand A, 1941, Jl 31,17:1
Page, Calvin G, 1951, F 26,23:4
Page, Calvin Judge, 1919, D 14,22:3
Page, Carroll S Sen, 1925, D 5,19:5
Page, Cecil Mrs, 1948, Je 25,23:2
Page, Charles B, 1912, Ag 15,9:2
Page, Charles C, 1945, O 7,45:1
Page, Charles H, 1912, Jl 23,9:5
Page, Charles L, 1950, Ja 6,21:4
Page, Charles T, 1958, Ja 9,36:2
Page, Clarence W, 1947, Ja 26,53:6
Page, Curtis H, 1946, D 13,23:2
Page, David, 1941, Ja 30,21:3
Page, David U, 1964, Ap 10,35:1
Page, De Witt (por),(will, Je 19,20:3), 1940, F 29, 20:3
Page, Dewitt, 1940, D 28,15:4
Page, DeWitt Mrs (will, O 10,13:2), 1959, O 6,39:4
Page, DeWitt Mrs (est inventory), 1960, F 2,22:7
Page, Donald, 1958, N 14,27:4
Page, Donald O, 1942, S 12,13:6
Page, Donald S, 1940, D 24,15:3
Page, Dudley L, 1942, N 22,52:5
Page, Earle C G, 1961, D 20,33:4
Page, Edward Day, 1918, D 26,11:4
Page, Edward G A, 1964, Je 24,37:3
Page, Edward J, 1965, N 4,47:6
Page, Ephraim J, 1950, Mr 2,27:1
Page, F LeMoyne, 1964, Ap 24,33:1
Page, Francis H, 1918, My 5,23:1
Page, Francis S, 1963, S 14,25:4
Page, Frank C, 1950, D 19,29:3
Page, Frank C B, 1938, D 26,23:2
Page, Frank C B Mrs, 1961, Jl 29,19:5
Page, Frank C Mrs, 1916, Ag 16,7:4
Page, Frank G, 1959, Mr 21,21:5
Page, Frank Rev Dr, 1918, Ap 19,13:6
Page, Fred B, 1939, O 31,23:5
Page, Frederick H, 1962, Ap 22,81:1
Page, George B, 1948, O 6,30:3
Page, George K, 1939, S 28,25:1
Page, George T (por), 1941, N 5,23:4
Page, George W, 1951, D 8,11:3
Page, Gertrude, 1922, Ap 2,29:3
Page, Grover, 1958, Ag 6,25:4
Page, Guy M, 1956, Jl 19,27:4
Page, H S, 1933, Jl 6,21:3
Page, Harold P (por), 1941, Je 21,17:5
Page, Harriet W Mrs, 1939, D 25,23:1
Page, Harry C Col, 1908, N 27,9:4
Page, Harry Sr, 1946, My 18,19:6
Page, Harvey, 1903, O 20,9:6
Page, Henry, 1957, Ag 30,19:4
Page, Henry Col, 1918, Ap 14,23:3
Page, Herman, 1942, Ap 22,24:3
Page, Horatio A C, 1957, Jl 14,73:1
Page, Howard E, 1949, Je 15,29:4
Page, Howard Mrs, 1937, Ap 28,23:3
Page, Howard W Mrs, 1955, F 20,88:8
Page, Irving H, 1924, Ag 7,15:6
Page, Izola F, 1944, Mr 7,17:3
Page, J Seaver, 1920, Mr 27,13:3
Page, J Seaver Mrs, 1916, Je 9,13:5
Page, J Stuart, 1940, Je 22,15:4
Page, James, 1944, S 12,19:2
Page, James E, 1953, N 11,31:4
Page, James E Mrs, 1953, N 11,31:4
Page, Jane A, 1957, Ap 21,89:1
Page, Jenny M, 1944, Je 7,19:4
Page, John, 1949, Ag 12,17:5
Page, John C, 1955, Mr 25,21:3
Page, John Ex-Gov, 1865, S 9,4:2
Page, John H Gen, 1916, O 10,11:6
Page, John L, 1957, S 6,21:2
Page, John R, 1960, Jl 30,17:6
Page, John W, 1948, My 21,23:3; 1950, My 7,108:2
Page, Joseph, 1947, Ap 5,19:2
Page, Joseph M W, 1938, D 7,23:3
Page, Junius R, 1938, My 13,19:5
Page, K F, 1885, Ap 23,5:6
Page, Kirby, 1957, D 18,35:1
Page, Klingmos B Dr, 1913, F 20,11:3
Page, L F, 1944, Ag 27,33:1
Page, L Rodman, 1949, Ja 10,25:3
Page, Lafayette Jr, 1955, S 17,15:5
Page, Laura L G, 1945, D 14,28:3
Page, Leigh, 1952, S 17,31:3
Page, Leigh Mrs, 1954, Ag 16,17:4
Page, Leslie M, 1959, N 18,41:3
Page, Lewis C, 1956, My 11,28:1
Page, Logan Waller, 1918, D 10,13:2
Page, M E, 1936, N 28,17:4
Page, Mann, 1961, Mr 18,23:3
Page, Marie D Mrs, 1940, Mr 5,23:3
Page, Mary H Mrs, 1940, F 11,48:5
Page, Maude Mrs, 1922, Ag 21,11:4
Page, Melville S Dr, 1937, O 13,23:3
Page, Milton E Jr, 1948, Ag 2,21:4
Page, Milton Jr, 1966, Mr 28,33:1
Page, N Clifford, 1956, My 16,35:2
Page, Norvell M, 1961, Ag 16,29:6
Page, Oran, 1954, N 7,88:4
Page, P W, 1918, Ja 12,11:4
Page, Parker W, 1937, Ja 23,18:4
Page, Percy R, 1944, N 9,27:3
Page, Philip, 1958, Je 28,17:6
Page, Pierson S, 1939, My 24,23:3
Page, R L Gen, 1901, Ag 10,7:6
Page, R N, 1933, O 4,23:3
Page, Ralph H, 1947, N 30,76:6
Page, Ralph H Mrs, 1949, Mr 16,27:2
Page, Ralph W, 1963, O 7,31:4
Page, Richard E, 1945, Mr 6,21:4
Page, Richard G, 1951, D 2,91:2
Page, Richard M, 1961, Je 6,37:5
Page, Richard R Mrs, 1950, Mr 10,27:2
Page, Rinaldo B, 1955, F 3,23:3
Page, Robert P Jr, 1949, Je 19,68:1
Page, Robert W, 1952, N 28,25:2
Page, Roger M, 1942, N 20,24:2
Page, Rolph Prof, 1910, Ag 10,11:5
Page, Rosewell, 1939, Ja 2,24:3
Page, Roy C Mrs, 1956, O 3,33:5
Page, S Davis Mrs, 1944, Je 25,30:2
Page, Stacy W (por), 1941, Ap 18,21:6
Page, Thomas N, 1922, N 3,17:4
Page, Thomas N Mrs (B Bostwick), 1959, Mr 2,27:1
Page, Thomas Nelson Mrs, 1921, Je 7,17:5
Page, Thomas W Dr (por), 1937, Ja 14,21:1
Page, Verna L, 1952, Jl 8,27:5
Page, Victor W, 1947, Ap 3,25:2
Page, Villa F, 1944, Ag 6,37:2
Page, W H, 1935, O 4,21:3
Page, Wallace W, 1919, My 2,13:6
Page, Walter, 1946, My 3,21:3; 1957, D 21,19:3
Page, Walter B, 1940, Ja 18,23:5
Page, Walter Hines, 1918, D 23,11:4
Page, William Curry, 1914, Jl 1,11:5
Page, William H, 1952, Jl 23,23:3
Page, William K Sr, 1953, O 30,23:5
Page, William R, 1923, Jl 19,15:4
Page, William Sr Mrs, 1944, Jl 30,36:1
Page, William T (por), 1942, O 21,21:5
Page, William Williamson Rev Dr, 1920, Je 15,11:4
Page-Wood, Gerald, 1939, Ag 22,19:4
Pagel, Edward, 1940, My 9,23:4
Pagels, Alice, 1913, Ag 14,9:3
Pagels, Frank, 1945, S 11,23:3
Pagenstecher, Albrecht Jr, 1964, Mr 5,33:2
Pagenstecher, Albrecht 3d, 1946, Ag 1,23:3
Pagenstecher, Felix (por), 1937, Mr 16,23:1
Pages, Eduardo, 1945, Jl 24,23:5
Pages, Jules, 1946, My 24,19:2
Paget, A, 1928, D 10,27:5
Paget, Alfred Adm, 1918, Je 19,11:7
Paget, Alfred Lady, 1914, My 4,9:5
Paget, Almeric Hugh Mrs, 1916, N 23,13:4
Paget, Bernard, 1961, F 18,19:1
Paget, Charles H A, 1947, F 22,13:3
Paget, Charles W, 1940, Ja 18,23:5
Paget, Dorothy W (est acctg; no will, Ap 7,4:4), 1960, F 10,38:1
Paget, Felisien Victor, 1903, D 24,9:5
Paget, Frank A, 1958, Ag 1,21:3
Paget, George T C, 1939, Ja 30,13:2
Paget, Gerald, 1913, O 28,11:6
Paget, Henry L Bp, 1937, Ap 28,23:4
Paget, John R, 1938, Ag 22,13:5
Paget, Louis G, 1943, S 13,19:6
Paget, Muriel (por), 1938, Je 17,21:3
Paget, Percy W, 1945, Mr 16,15:4
Paget, R H, 1926, Mr 18,23:5
Paget, Ralph Lady, 1915, Mr 26,13:2
Paget, Ralph S, 1940, My 14,23:6
Paget, Richard, 1955, O 24,27:2
Paget, Rosalind, 1948, Ag 21,15:3
Paget, Thomas G F, 1952, Mr 13,3:5
Paget, Victor, 1952, F 16,13:4
Pagliarini, Pietro, 1940, Jl 16,17:3
Pagliaro, Ignazio, 1938, Je 7,23:5
Paglin, Philip, 1960, Ag 31,29:2
Pagliuca, Charles E, 1951, Ap 25,29:1
Pagnucco, Achille, 1956, Je 15,25:3
Pagnucco, Flaminio, 1957, D 23,23:3
Pagnucco, Louis A Mrs, 1966, Ag 20,25:3
Pagursky, Samuel, 1947, Je 8,60:2
Pahlevi, Riza (por), 1944, Jl 27,17:5
Pahlson, Svante, 1959, S 4,21:2
Pahnke, Alfred, 1955, F 13,86:8
Pahuja, Mehr Chand, 1967, Ja 1,22:1
Pai Chung-hsi, 1966, D 9,47:1
Paiewonsky, Isaac, 1963, Jl 14,61:3
Paige, Alonzo C Mrs, 1867, Ap 7,5:3
Paige, Charles D, 1940, Ja 6,13:3
Paige, Clayton W, 1960, F 15,27:3
Paige, Clifford E, 1958, N 27,29:1
Paige, Douglas W, 1955, D 18,92:7
Paige, Ernest Linton, 1910, O 8,11:5
Paige, Eugene Walter, 1919, F 3,15:2
Paige, Fred Mrs, 1959, Je 21,92:8
Paige, Georgiana, 1867, Ap 7,5:4
Paige, H Worthington Mrs, 1953, Ja 27,25:1
Paige, James, 1940, F 5,22:2
Paige, James F, 1942, F 17,22:3
Paige, Jesse, 1949, D 22,23:5
Paige, Joseph W, 1940, Ja 11,23:5
Paige, Lincoln, 1963, Ag 17,19:4
Paige, Louis A, 1952, Ap 30,27:3
Paige, Lulu C Mrs, 1966, Ja 6,27:3
Paige, Mabel, 1954, F 10,29:2
Paige, Moses B, 1941, D 8,23:3
Paige, Nathaniel Fish, 1923, Je 23,11:6
Paige, Raymond, 1965, Ag 8,65:1
Paige, Sidney, 1968, F 5,35:4
Paige, Walter H, 1954, N 26,29:5
Paikea, Paraine K, 1943, Ap 7,26:3
Paikert, Aloysius de, 1948, O 20,29:2
Paikin, Harold, 1951, Je 8,27:4
Paikowski, Caesar J, 1947, N 1,15:4
Paillard, Mary C Mrs, 1939, Ap 17,17:5
Paille, Charles H, 1952, F 25,21:1
Pain, B, 1928, My 6,25:6
Pain, James C, 1923, O 14,6:2
Pain, O, 1885, Je 29,1:4
Paine, Albert B (por),(will, My 6,21:6), 1937, Ap 10, 19:1
Paine, Albert W, 1907, D 4,9:5
Paine, Augustus G, 1915, Mr 27,11:4; 1947, O 24,23:3
Paine, Byron H, 1953, Jl 1,29:4
Paine, Charles, 1906, Jl 6,7:4
Paine, Charles E, 1943, Ja 24,43:1
Paine, Charles Emery Dr, 1918, N 20,15:4
Paine, Charles J Gen, 1916, Ag 15,9:4
Paine, Charles L, 1963, S 16,35:1
Paine, Charles Maj, 1864, D 18,3:5
Paine, Charles S, 1952, D 6,21:5
Paine, Cordelia A, 1960, N 24,29:2
Paine, David, 1962, Je 18,25:4
Paine, Edward B, 1951, N 17,32:8
Paine, Edward S, 1943, F 12,19:4
Paine, Edward W, 1938, My 1,II,6:4
Paine, Frances F Mrs, 1962, O 23,37:3
Paine, Francis Brinley Hebard, 1917, S 14,9:3
Paine, Frank D, 1942, Jl 1,25:2
Paine, Frank H, 1961, S 8,32:1
Paine, Frederick H, 1938, D 14,25:3
Paine, George Clinton, 1912, Ag 27,9:4
Paine, George E, 1953, Mr 28,17:3
Paine, Gordon P, 1918, F 8,11:8
Paine, Gregory L, 1950, F 18,15:2
Paine, H G, 1929, My 31,21:2
Paine, Halbert E Gen, 1905, Ap 16,9:6
Paine, Harry B, 1945, Jl 6,11:7
Paine, Helen O C Mrs, 1937, D 4,17:5
Paine, Horatio M D, 1882, My 5,5:5
Paine, Howard E, 1949, Jl 7,25:5
Paine, Howard S, 1947, My 6,28:3; 1954, D 7,33:5
Paine, J K, 1906, Ap 26,11:6
Paine, James R, 1940, O 26,15:1
Paine, John, 1945, Jl 19,23:5
Paine, John B, 1951, Ag 3,21:3
Paine, John G, 1947, Ap 24,25:4
Paine, John H Mrs, 1964, O 24,29:1
Paine, John H Prof, 1912, Jl 25,9:6
Paine, John Hebard (por),(funl, O 4,13:2), 1920, O 3, 22:1
Paine, John S, 1903, Ap 21,9:5
Paine, L Frank, 1941, Ag 14,17:3
Paine, Lester J, 1941, O 8,23:4
Paine, M Dr (see also N 11), 1877, N 15,2:4
Paine, Marjorie, 1955, Mr 21,27:8
Paine, Martin S, 1942, Jl 15,19:3
Paine, Nathaniel E, 1948, D 1,29:3
Paine, Nathaniel E Jr, 1960, D 7,43:1
Paine, Overton, 1945, Ja 24,34:3
Paine, Paul F, 1948, Ja 5,19:1
Paine, Paul M, 1955, Jl 5,29:3; 1957, Ja 30,29:5
Paine, R T, 1885, Je 5,5:6
Paine, Ralph D, 1925, Ap 30,21:3
Paine, Robert C, 1958, S 17,37:1
Paine, Robert F, 1940, Ag 30,19:4
Paine, Robert F Jr, 1954, My 27,27:5
Paine, Robert Hitchcock Rev, 1908, Je 5,7:4
Paine, Robert Rev, 1882, N 21,4:7
Paine, Robert T, 1944, O 31,19:2; 1946, Ja 18,19:2; 1961, Ag 21,23:5
Paine, Robert T Mrs, 1916, Jl 18,9:6
Paine, Robert T 2d, 1943, N 14,57:2
Paine, Robert Treat, 1910, Ag 12,7:6
Paine, Samuel H, 1949, N 1,28:2
Paine, Samuel J, 1951, My 10,31:1
Paine, Silas H, 1921, Ap 12,17:4

Paine, Silas H Mrs, 1937, Ap 27,23:4
Paine, Stuart D L, 1961, Mr 16,38:1
Paine, Thomas B, 1940, Je 29,15:5
Paine, Tracy H, 1950, Je 25,68:6
Paine, W S, 1927, Ap 14,27:1
Paine, Walter S, 1947, Mr 9,60:7
Paine, Walter T, 1939, Mr 16,23:2
Paine, Washington Clark, 1924, O 24,19:5
Paine, William E (funl, My 26,21:5), 1925, My 25, 17:6
Paine, William H Mrs, 1949, Ja 23,68:6
Paine, William J Mrs, 1951, Jl 29,69:1
Paine, William N, 1956, F 25,19:6
Paine, William N Mrs, 1957, Jl 12,21:5
Painleve, P, 1933, O 30,17:3
Paino, Angelo, 1959, O 14,43:3
Paino, Anthony, 1954, Ja 2,11:3
Paino, Arcangelo, 1967, Jl 31,27:4
Painter, Augustus E W, 1903, Jl 5,7:5
Painter, Carl W Mrs, 1961, N 26,88:4
Painter, E O, 1913, My 23,13:4
Painter, Eleanor (por), 1947, N 5,27:3
Painter, George B, 1910, Mr 30,12:1
Painter, George E, 1942, Ap 10,17:4
Painter, Ira C, 1949, Je 26,60:5
Painter, J L, 1907, My 8,7:6
Painter, Jacob Jr, 1937, F 17,22:1
Painter, Jean H, 1966, N 19,33:3
Painter, John G Mrs, 1961, Ag 2,29:3
Painter, John S Mrs, 1963, My 16,35:1
Painter, Kenyon V, 1940, Mr 21,25:1
Painter, Robert J, 1965, F 26,29:3
Painter, Sidney, 1960, Ja 14,33:3
Painter, Stanley L, 1956, Ja 15,92:8
Painter, Wilfred I, 1949, Jl 11,1:2
Painter, William, 1906, Jl 16,7:7
Painter, William R Mrs, 1941, O 26,43:3
Painton, Frederick C, 1945, Ap 1,36:2
Painton, Henry M, 1953, O 8,29:5
Painton, Henry M Mrs, 1939, Mr 6,15:5
Pairo, Louis P, 1943, F 26,19:2
Pais, Antonio S, 1949, Je 29,27:1
Pais, Ettore, 1939, Mr 29,23:2
Pais de Souza, Mario, 1949, Ap 20,27:5
Paish, George, 1957, My 3,27:5
Paisley, Charles J, 1950, Ap 3,23:4
Paisley, James E, 1953, F 24,25:3
Paisley, James F Sr, 1950, Ap 18,32:3
Paisley, John O, 1945, O 12,23:3
Paisley, Robert J, 1952, Mr 11,27:5
Paisley, T Edwin, 1955, N 22,35:2
Paisley, W O, 1944, Je 14,19:5
Paisman, Aaron I, 1943, Jl 12,15:4
Paist, Frederic M, 1953, S 15,31:3
Paist, Henry M, 1952, Ag 26,25:2
Paist, Henry T, 1943, Je 11,19:1
Paitz, Theodore, 1904, Ja 21,2:4
Paiva, Nestor, 1966, S 11,86:7
Paivio, Carl, 1952, Ap 18,25:3
Paixao, Cearense Catulo da, 1946, My 12,44:5
Pajak, Antoni, 1965, D 1,47:5
Pajeau, Charles H, 1952, D 19,31:5
Pajol, Louis Gen, 1885, Ap 22,5:5
Pajtas, Bruce, 1950, D 15,31:4
Pakenham, Compton, 1957, Ag 18,82:4
Pakenham, Edward A H (Earl of Longford), 1961, F 5,80:4
Pakington, Herbert S (Lord Hampton), 1962, N 1, 31:5
Pakradooni, Haig H, 1937, F 18,21:4
Pakrul, Adolf, 1947, O 16,28:3
Pakulski, Vincent F, 1947, Mr 23,60:2
Pal, Radha B, 1967, Ja 12,39:4
Palache, Charles, 1954, D 6,27:5
Palache, Charles Mrs, 1949, O 29,15:3
Palache, Whitney, 1949, Mr 3,25:3
Palacio, Alfredo L, 1965, Ap 21,45:1
Palacio, Raimundo Andueza Dr, 1900, Ag 19,6:5
Palacios, Clara Mrs, 1951, S 20,31:6
Palacios, Miguel de, 1920, O 7,15:2
Palacky, Francis, 1876, My 18,1:5
Paladeau, N Louis Jr, 1953, F 20,19:5
Paladines, French Gen (White Feather), 1878, Ja 4, 2:1
Paladini, Riccardo, 1943, Mr 21,26:8
Paladino, Anthony C, 1944, Ag 12,11:5
Paladino, Don P, 1959, Mr 22,87:1
Palaeloogus, John Anthony Lascaris Prince, 1874, S 28,4:7
Palagi, Piero, 1947, Mr 20,27:3
Palairet, Michael, 1956, Ag 6,23:2
Palamara, Gerard A, 1961, O 12,29:4
Palamtier, Charles, 1938, O 20,23:4
Palanca, Carlos Gen, 1925, Je 20,13:6
Palander, Adolf Arnold, 1920, Ag 10,13:5
Palanske, John Sr, 1955, N 18,25:3
Palasti, Joseph, 1966, Je 14,47:4
Palavicini, Felix F, 1952, F 12,27:5
Palay, Lewis, 1953, Jl 17,17:4
Palazzi, Charles, 1950, O 4,31:4
Palazzi, Michael A Jr, 1962, D 4,41:4
Palazzo, Elia Mrs, 1949, Je 26,60:3
Palazzo, Vincent W, 1938, O 21,23:2
Palazzola, Stephen, 1951, Ap 29,88:3
Palazzolo, Antonio T, 1955, Ja 20,31:2
Palazzolo, Octavio, 1952, O 31,25:1
Palazzotto, Vincent Mrs, 1948, Ag 17,21:2
Palchek, James W, 1948, D 22,23:1
Paleck, Frank J, 1944, S 21,19:4
Palefski, Israel O, 1968, My 2,47:4
Palen, Elmer E, 1949, Ap 9,17:5
Palen, F P, 1933, D 4,19:4
Palen, Gilbert J, 1958, S 9,35:4
Palen, Gilbert R, 1953, Jl 8,27:3
Palen, J Albert Mrs, 1950, Ja 31,23:3
Palen, Louis E, 1948, My 17,19:5
Palen, Michael F, 1947, My 14,25:1
Palen, Neal B, 1951, Jl 8,60:1
Palen, William, 1904, O 8,9:6
Palen, William W, 1906, Ja 3,9:6
Palen-Klar, Adolphe J, 1948, Je 27,52:3
Palen-Klar, Adolphe J von der, 1944, O 26,23:3
Palencia, Angel G, 1949, O 31,4:6
Palencia, Julio, 1952, Mr 26,29:2
Palenik, Joseph, 1949, N 1,27:5
Palent, Joseph Mrs, 1949, Ja 13,24:2
Paleologue, Jean Prince, 1942, N 25,23:4
Paleologue, Maurice G, 1944, N 22,19:4
Palermi, Rail, 1948, F 4,23:3
Palermo, Anthony M, 1963, Ag 19,13:6
Palermo, Felix, 1937, F 1,9:3
Palermo, Italo, 1962, My 9,43:1
Palermo, Nicholas H, 1951, Jl 31,21:5
Pales Matos, Luis, 1959, F 24,29:4
Paleschuk, Maurice H, 1943, D 30,17:3
Palester, Charles Mrs, 1950, Je 15,31:2
Palethorp, William, 1952, Ag 25,17:2
Palethorp, William Mrs, 1944, Jl 8,11:6
Paley, Alex, 1962, Je 17,80:8
Paley, David, 1937, O 13,23:4
Paley, Herman, 1955, N 5,19:5
Paley, Jay, 1960, O 3,31:5
Paley, Jay Mrs, 1954, Ja 5,27:2
Paley, Joseph M, 1962, Ja 11,33:1
Paley, Louis N, 1937, D 17,25:2
Paley, Martin I, 1961, S 12,33:2
Paley, Meyer, 1956, Ja 2,21:5
Paley, Michael J, 1962, My 18,31:3
Paley, Samuel (will, Ap 25,30:1), 1963, Ap 1,27:3
Paley, Sol, 1941, F 14,17:4
Palffy, Aladar de, 1959, O 3,19:7
Palffy, Countess, 1952, O 5,88:2
Palfi, Janos, 1949, Mr 4,21:3
Palfrey, J G, 1881, Ap 27,5:4
Palfrey, John G, 1945, Jl 27,15:5
Paliano, Duke of (Prince Marc Antonio Colonna), 1912, Ja 30,9:5
Palin, Septer F (Sep), 1952, O 4,17:1
Palisa, Johann Dr, 1925, My 5,21:3
Palitz, Clarence Y, 1958, Ap 10,29:1
Palitz, Dave, 1940, N 19,23:4
Palitz, Laurence L Dr, 1968, S 23,35:2
Palitz, Samuel, 1948, N 8,21:2
Pall, Augustine F, 1956, Ja 30,27:2
Pall, David B Mrs, 1959, D 24,19:1
Pallace, John, 1943, Ja 31,46:3
Palladino, Daniel A Sr, 1947, O 2,27:5
Palladino, Eusapia, 1918, My 18,13:6
Pallain, Georges, 1923, My 14,15:5
Pallais, Emilio E, 1942, Ap 9,19:2
Pallais, Noel E, 1950, Ap 30,102:4
Pallas, John E, 1966, My 27,39:1
Pallas, John J, 1905, O 17,1:1
Pallas, Peter E, 1951, Jl 5,26:5
Pallat, Ludwig, 1946, N 29,25:3
Pallavacino, Marquis, 1878, Ag 22,3:7
Pallavicini, Emilio Gen, 1901, N 6,9:5
Pallavicini, Sandro, 1966, Je 15,47:3
Pallavincini, Marquis, 1921, S 23,15:6
Pallen, C B, 1929, My 27,25:3
Pallester, Paul, 1942, Jl 29,17:4
Pallette, Charles A, 1954, F 20,17:3
Pallette, Edward, 1944, N 17,19:3
Pallette, Eugene (will, S 9,36:8), 1954, S 4,11:3
Palliser, Melvin G, 1940, Jl 6,15:3
Palliser, W Sir, 1882, F 7,5:3
Pallister, Charles F, 1956, N 22,33:6
Pallister, Claude V, 1944, Ag 17,17:5
Pallman, A Oswald, 1941, D 12,25:2
Pallmeyer, Charles R, 1943, F 25,21:1
Pallmeyer, Paul H, 1955, Ag 16,23:2
Pallotti, Francis A, 1946, D 23,23:3
Palm, Axel O, 1939, F 1,21:3
Palm, Baron de (see also My 25,28), 1876, My 29, 1:4
Palm, Erik, 1952, Ap 14,19:4
Palm, Franklin B, 1952, O 5,89:2
Palm, Howard F, 1942, Ja 4,48:5
Palm, Joseph G, 1875, D 23,4:5
Palm, Robert, 1947, Jl 15,23:6
Palm, Tage, 1959, Jl 25,17:5
Palma, Baudilio, 1944, Je 22,19:4
Palma, J de Rev Dr, 1884, Jl 14,8:5
Palma, Jose J, 1952, Jl 22,25:4
Palma, Joseph A Jr, 1952, S 5,27:1
Palma, Joseph A Mrs, 1940, O 18,21:4
Palma, Rafael, 1939, My 25,25:3
Palma, Raffaele M Mrs, 1942, N 6,23:5
Palmade, Maurice, 1955, Ja 5,23:6
Palmarini, Umberto, 1943, Ja 2,11:4
Palmaro, Charles, 1962, Ap 17,35:4
Palmateer, Arthur C, 1956, Ap 28,17:4
Palmateer, George, 1939, Ap 13,23:2
Palmateer, John C, 1938, Ap 16,13:1
Palmateer, Richard A, 1949, N 17,29:2
Palmateer, Wilbur C, 1947, S 21,60:5
Palmatier, Arlyn, 1959, N 7,23:4
Palmatier, Katurah L Mrs, 1939, Je 3,15:6
Palmatier, William A C Mrs, 1957, Ag 25,86:2
Palmblad, Harry V E, 1940, Mr 18,18:2
Palme, Arthur, 1949, S 27,27:3
Palme, Josef F Mrs, 1948, Jl 31,15:3
Palmella, Duchess, 1909, S 4,7:5
Palmenberg, Theodore C, 1963, Jl 1,29:3
Palmenberg, William F, 1908, F 23,7:6
Palmer, A Emerson (funl, Ap 30,21:4), 1925, Ap 29 21:4
Palmer, A Kenny C, 1942, Ag 29,15:5
Palmer, A Kenny C Mrs, 1964, Mr 22,77:2
Palmer, A M, 1905, Mr 8,9:5; 1936, My 12,26:2
Palmer, A M Mrs, 1923, Mr 16,17:4
Palmer, A Mitchell Mrs, 1922, Ja 5,15:4
Palmer, A W, 1881, Ja 14,5:4; 1903, S 7,6:6
Palmer, Abraham J Dr, 1922, Ap 19,19:5
Palmer, Addison E, 1949, S 27,27:4
Palmer, Agnes P, 1940, Ap 28,37:2
Palmer, Alan M, 1957, Jl 18,25:2
Palmer, Albert D, 1940, Ja 14,43:2
Palmer, Albert D S, 1958, Jl 21,21:4
Palmer, Albert H Mrs, 1951, Ap 22,88:1
Palmer, Albert N, 1944, F 14,17:3
Palmer, Albert R (por), 1947, Ap 2,27:1
Palmer, Albert W, 1954, D 17,31:2
Palmer, Albert W Mrs, 1904, Ja 2,9:4
Palmer, Alice G, 1964, Ap 11,25:5
Palmer, Allen G, 1955, Ag 29,19:5
Palmer, Alonzo C, 1947, F 12,25:4
Palmer, Andrew H, 1942, D 27,34:3
Palmer, Appleton D, 1916, My 25,13:4
Palmer, Arthur, 1954, F 19,27:3
Palmer, Arthur C, 1922, Ja 11,21:6
Palmer, Arthur Hubbell Prof, 1918, N 8,15:3
Palmer, Arthur Sir Gen, 1904, F 29,5:4
Palmer, Arthur Wheatley, 1968, Ag 25,88:3
Palmer, Asher N, 1950, Ap 16,106:3
Palmer, Asher N Mrs, 1952, My 29,27:5
Palmer, Aug V, 1937, Mr 14,II,9:1
Palmer, Austin P, 1959, N 8,88:3
Palmer, B J Mrs, 1949, Ap 1,25:3
Palmer, Bartlett J, 1961, My 28,64:2
Palmer, Belle (Mrs Wheeler), 1874, Ap 24,2:3
Palmer, Benjamin F, 1940, Ap 9,23:2
Palmer, Benjamin P, 1916, F 22,11:5
Palmer, Bissell B, 1968, Ja 25,37:2
Palmer, Blanche S Mrs, 1940, Ja 16,23:1
Palmer, Brooks Mrs, 1963, O 1,39:4
Palmer, Burton E, 1947, Je 17,25:4
Palmer, C, 1888, Jl 24,5:6
Palmer, C Alanson Mrs, 1951, N 24,11:3
Palmer, C Clayton, 1960, N 14,31:2
Palmer, C G, 1940, Ag 14,19:2
Palmer, C H Capt, 1911, D 28,9:5
Palmer, C Ray, 1955, Ja 22,11:3
Palmer, Carl F, 1952, Mr 26,29:3
Palmer, Cecil, 1952, Ja 20,85:2
Palmer, Charles, 1964, Ag 29,21:5; 1966, My 28,27:
Palmer, Charles A, 1950, Je 5,23:1
Palmer, Charles B, 1962, Ja 20,21:3; 1968, Ja 22,47:
Palmer, Charles C, 1946, O 9,27:5
Palmer, Charles D, 1940, O 5,15:5
Palmer, Charles E, 1948, S 18,17:5
Palmer, Charles F, 1950, D 13,35:5
Palmer, Charles H, 1938, Je 30,23:2; 1939, Mr 26,II 6:8; 1953, Ja 21,31:5
Palmer, Charles J, 1944, Mr 30,21:4
Palmer, Charles L, 1947, D 17,29:4
Palmer, Charles Mark Sir, 1907, Je 4,7:6
Palmer, Charles R, 1947, My 1,25:2
Palmer, Charles Ray Rev Dr, 1914, Ap 23,13:6
Palmer, Charles S, 1939, D 2,17:6; 1946, Ja 21,23:1; 1954, Ag 19,23:6
Palmer, Charles V, 1968, D 1,86:6
Palmer, Charles W, 1956, My 13,86:6
Palmer, Chesley Robert, 1968, N 11,47:3
Palmer, Chester C, 1957, Ap 22,25:5
Palmer, Clara M K Mrs, 1938, Ja 7,19:4
Palmer, Clarence R, 1953, O 16,27:2
Palmer, Clarence W, 1941, F 4,21:3
Palmer, Claude I Mrs, 1954, O 9,17:5
Palmer, Clyde E, 1957, Jl 5,17:3
Palmer, Clyde N, 1918, S 21,9:5
Palmer, Connie, 1950, Mr 8,27:4
Palmer, Cordelia, 1941, Ja 8,19:5
Palmer, Corydon, 1940, Ap 14,45:1
Palmer, Courtland, 1874, My 12,1:3; 1951, F 12,23:
Palmer, Courtlandt, 1951, D 16,90:5
Palmer, Courtlandt (will), 1952, Ja 4,15:3
Palmer, Dana, 1954, N 14,88:8
Palmer, Daniel A, 1952, S 16,29:1

Palmer, Daniela, 1949, Ag 12,17:4
Palmer, David, 1879, My 22,5:3
Palmer, David P, 1961, Jl 21,23:5
Palmer, Dean, 1942, S 20,41:5; 1949, Mr 11,25:4
Palmer, Delancey Mrs, 1946, N 16,19:6
Palmer, Delos, 1960, My 5,35:3
Palmer, Donald F, 1951, O 9,29:6
Palmer, Douglass, 1954, My 20,31:3
Palmer, Dudley W, 1949, Ap 25,23:5
Palmer, E Russell, 1955, Jl 1,21:4
Palmer, Earl, 1946, N 25,27:2
Palmer, Earl C, 1966, Je 21,43:3
Palmer, Earle F, 1959, Ap 13,31:2
Palmer, Edgar (por),(will, Ja 21,16:5), 1943, Ja 9, 13:1
Palmer, Edgar S, 1945, F 21,19:5
Palmer, Edmond Janes Dr, 1917, My 30,9:4
Palmer, Edward A, 1955, Ap 25,43:2
Palmer, Edward Bishop Capt, 1922, Jl 4,13:6
Palmer, Edward H Mrs, 1943, N 30,27:1
Palmer, Edward Howard Mrs, 1923, Je 15,19:5
Palmer, Edward L, 1946, Ag 22,27:5
Palmer, Edward N, 1956, Ag 12,84:1
Palmer, Edward P (will, S 16,34:2), 1954, Jl 13,23:1
Palmer, Edward Vance, 1959, Jl 17,21:6
Palmer, Edwin R, 1963, O 15,39:4
Palmer, Effie (por), 1942, Ag 21,19:3
Palmer, Elbridge, 1948, Mr 13,15:5
Palmer, Elbridge W, 1953, N 19,31:1
Palmer, Elisha L, 1912, N 11,11:3
Palmer, Elizabeth Mrs, 1937, F 25,23:4
Palmer, Ella A, 1951, N 6,29:5
Palmer, Elwell Mrs, 1951, Ag 19,84:5
Palmer, Embury, 1955, Je 20,21:1
Palmer, Erastus Prof, 1937, D 10,26:2
Palmer, Eric H, 1952, Ap 1,30:3
Palmer, Ernest Dr, 1913, Ja 21,13:6
Palmer, Ernest G, 1949, My 25,29:3
Palmer, Ethel, 1951, Ag 18,11:4
Palmer, F A, 1902, N 2,7:4
Palmer, F Lewis, 1947, Jl 13,44:1
Palmer, Floyd P, 1945, Mr 29,23:3
Palmer, Francis E, 1950, My 31,29:5
Palmer, Francis Loomis, 1917, Jl 18,9:5
Palmer, Francis S, 1938, Ag 23,17:2
Palmer, Frank, 1940, Je 14,21:6
Palmer, Frank A Mrs, 1917, N 3,15:4
Palmer, Frank N, 1958, My 24,21:6
Palmer, Frank S, 1948, Mr 9,23:1
Palmer, Frank S Mrs, 1952, Je 19,27:5
Palmer, Franklin D, 1945, O 11,23:2
Palmer, Franklin W, 1949, Ap 30,13:2
Palmer, Fred L, 1948, Ap 4,60:2
Palmer, Frederic Jr, 1967, Ap 21,39:4
Palmer, Frederick, 1958, S 3,33:1
Palmer, Frederick A, 1965, Ag 5,29:2
Palmer, Frederick E, 1955, O 4,35:3
Palmer, Frederick O Mrs, 1956, Mr 15,31:5
Palmer, Frederick W, 1944, Ap 21,19:2
Palmer, G H Mrs, 1902, D 7,7:6
Palmer, G Russell, 1943, N 25,25:3
Palmer, G W Gen, 1887, Ja 3,1:6
Palmer, George, 1925, Ja 22,19:4; 1945, Je 20,23:1
Palmer, George A, 1944, S 13,19:4
Palmer, George E, 1951, My 31,27:3; 1957, Ap 30,29:2
Palmer, George F, 1957, Ja 13,84:2
Palmer, George F Sr, 1937, Ag 21,15:2
Palmer, George H Mrs, 1950, Ap 11,31:4; 1954, Ap 2, 27:2
Palmer, George L, 1956, F 12,88:5
Palmer, George Mrs, 1945, Ag 10,15:5
Palmer, George N, 1960, Je 14,37:2
Palmer, George S, 1924, Mr 24,15:4
Palmer, George W, 1903, N 19,9:7; 1912, D 19,15:3; 1945, Mr 9,19:1
Palmer, George Willaim, 1916, Mr 3,11:4
Palmer, Gideon, 1962, Ja 22,23:3
Palmer, Gordon, 1964, F 17,31:4
Palmer, Granville E, 1948, Ja 13,25:2
Palmer, Gretta, 1953, Ag 16,76:6
Palmer, Grove, 1939, Ap 27,25:5
Palmer, Guy H, 1962, F 12,23:5
Palmer, Gwendolyn Mrs, 1963, Jl 29,41:5
Palmer, H J, 1939, D 23,15:6
Palmer, H S, 1954, Mr 7,90:2; 1955, Ag 19,40:7
Palmer, Harlan G Sr, 1956, Jl 27,21:5
Palmer, Harold A, 1954, D 6,27:6
Palmer, Harold D, 1945, N 21,21:3
Palmer, Harold J, 1953, O 25,89:1
Palmer, Harry Butler, 1922, N 14,19:5
Palmer, Harry C, 1945, Ja 6,11:5
Palmer, Harry C Mrs, 1938, My 7,15:5
Palmer, Harry David, 1879, Jl 21,5:3
Palmer, Harry H, 1950, Ap 25,31:5
Palmer, Harry J, 1948, F 13,21:4
Palmer, Harry L, 1957, N 4,29:1
Palmer, Harry M Mrs, 1951, Ja 10,27:1
Palmer, Harry W, 1939, Je 25,37:2; 1949, F 7,19:1
Palmer, Helen (Mrs T S Geisel), 1967, O 24,47:3
Palmer, Helen M, 1952, Je 13,23:5
Palmer, Henry B, 1923, Je 23,11:5
Palmer, Henry Brewster Lt, 1917, N 16,11:5
Palmer, Henry O, 1948, Je 2,29:2
Palmer, Henry R, 1943, Mr 9,23:2; 1945, S 25,25:5
Palmer, Henry W, 1937, D 15,25:4
Palmer, Henry Wilbur, 1913, F 18,13:5
Palmer, Herbert, 1953, F 21,13:2; 1961, My 19,31:1
Palmer, Herbert S, 1943, Ag 13,17:5
Palmer, Honore, 1964, Mr 6,31:2
Palmer, Honore Jr, 1938, F 8,21:4
Palmer, Howard, 1944, O 25,21:5
Palmer, J C, 1883, Ap 25,5:5
Palmer, J Cuthbert Mrs, 1939, F 25,15:5
Palmer, J Edward Mrs, 1924, F 16,15:4
Palmer, J M, 1900, S 26,7:6
Palmer, James, 1903, D 24,9:5; 1943, S 30,21:1
Palmer, James C, 1947, S 1,19:5
Palmer, James H, 1945, Ap 19,27:3
Palmer, James L, 1941, Je 24,19:5; 1961, S 18,29:3
Palmer, James Mrs, 1946, Ja 6,40:2
Palmer, James R, 1907, My 12,9:5; 1947, O 4,17:2
Palmer, James S Adm, 1867, D 17,4:6
Palmer, John D, 1938, N 28,15:2
Palmer, John Gen, 1905, Ap 16,9:6
Palmer, John L, 1944, Ag 8,17:5; 1953, O 2,21:3
Palmer, John M, 1955, O 27,33:1; 1967, Ja 21,31:4
Palmer, John Mayo, 1903, Jl 12,7:6
Palmer, John S, 1952, Jl 14,17:5
Palmer, John W, 1944, S 30,13:3
Palmer, John William Dr, 1906, F 27,9:6
Palmer, Joseph, 1913, Ap 21,11:6
Palmer, Joseph B, 1956, Ja 27,23:2
Palmer, Joseph W Dr, 1871, Mr 4,5:3
Palmer, Josephine D Mrs, 1939, D 16,17:2
Palmer, Kyle D, 1962, Ap 4,43:3
Palmer, L Madge, 1938, Je 30,23:6
Palmer, Leigh C, 1955, F 27,86:1
Palmer, Leslie E, 1955, My 11,31:1
Palmer, Lester A, 1966, Jl 26,35:1
Palmer, Lew R (por), 1945, Mr 25,37:1
Palmer, Lewis R, 1949, S 21,32:2
Palmer, Lincoln B (por), 1945, Ja 14,39:1
Palmer, Lord, 1948, D 10,26:2
Palmer, Lord (E C Nottage), 1950, Je 7,29:4
Palmer, Lowell M, 1915, O 1,11:5; 1959, O 11,86:8
Palmer, M, 1936, My 22,23:3
Palmer, Margaretta, 1924, Ja 31,15:5
Palmer, Marion B, 1952, O 10,25:4
Palmer, Marion B Mrs, 1957, Mr 21,31:4
Palmer, Marsh M, 1952, My 22,27:1
Palmer, Martha A Mrs, 1937, F 16,23:5
Palmer, Martin F, 1965, Ag 15,83:1
Palmer, Marvin R Dr, 1914, Je 21,15:6
Palmer, Mary E S Mrs, 1941, F 17,15:2
Palmer, Mary W, 1943, Mr 8,15:2
Palmer, May S, 1941, D 29,15:3
Palmer, Mervyn W, 1966, D 28,43:3
Palmer, Miles W Dr, 1914, Ap 12,15:4
Palmer, Milton C, 1943, Ag 7,11:5
Palmer, Milton C Mrs, 1944, F 27,37:1
Palmer, N B, 1877, Je 23,5:4
Palmer, Nathaniel, 1951, Ag 10,15:3
Palmer, Nelson, 1939, D 14,27:5
Palmer, Nelson J, 1944, O 9,23:2
Palmer, Nicholas F, 1922, Ja 19,17:5
Palmer, Norah Mrs, 1937, O 28,25:4
Palmer, Noyes F, 1912, Ap 19,15:5
Palmer, O H Gen, 1884, F 4,2:4
Palmer, Oliver David, 1907, Jl 31,7:5
Palmer, Orson R, 1939, Je 6,23:5
Palmer, Otis A, 1957, Ap 16,33:5
Palmer, Paul, 1942, Je 22,15:4
Palmer, Paul A, 1948, Jl 24,15:4
Palmer, Pauline L, 1938, Ag 16,19:3
Palmer, Percival S, 1957, My 6,29:1
Palmer, Percy G, 1946, My 8,25:4
Palmer, Phebe A A Mrs, 1939, D 17,49:3
Palmer, Phil E, 1949, My 20,28:2
Palmer, Phil M, 1951, Je 6,31:5
Palmer, Philinese Mrs, 1937, F 28,II,8:5
Palmer, Phoebe, 1950, Ap 10,19:3
Palmer, Potter, 1902, My 5,9:1
Palmer, Potter Mrs, 1918, My 7,13:3
Palmer, Potter 2d (por),(will, O 14,19:3), 1943, S 5, 28:6
Palmer, Potter 2d Mrs, 1956, Jl 8,64:8
Palmer, Potter 3d, 1946, O 4,24:2
Palmer, R Gerald Sr, 1965, Ag 7,21:4
Palmer, Ralph D, 1944, O 14,13:4
Palmer, Ralph L, 1953, My 31,73:1
Palmer, Ralph R, 1954, Ag 19,23:4
Palmer, Ralph S, 1943, D 14,27:2
Palmer, Ray E, 1948, Ag 28,16:8; 1953, Ag 5,23:4
Palmer, Ray Jr, 1954, S 20,23:3
Palmer, Raymond G D, 1955, Ag 2,23:4
Palmer, Rhoda, 1919, Ag 12,9:6
Palmer, Richard, 1954, D 6,27:6; 1961, Je 25,76:3
Palmer, Robert H, 1948, My 20,29:5
Palmer, Robert K, 1940, N 19,23:5
Palmer, Robert K Mrs, 1954, S 1,27:2
Palmer, Robert N, 1967, S 5,43:4
Palmer, Robert W, 1952, D 3,33:5; 1960, Mr 12,21:2
Palmer, Robert W Mrs, 1948, F 12,23:3
Palmer, Roger S, 1968, O 16,47:4
Palmer, Roland S, 1952, F 25,21:4
Palmer, Rose A, 1961, Je 1,35:3
Palmer, Roswell C, 1951, N 3,17:1
Palmer, Roy H, 1945, D 25,23:4
Palmer, Rufus K, 1947, My 23,24:3
Palmer, Russell, 1940, Ag 9,15:2
Palmer, Samuel C, 1961, N 1,39:4
Palmer, Samuel D, 1951, D 20,31:4
Palmer, Sara A, 1923, My 12,15:4
Palmer, Sarah A, 1945, Ag 24,19:2
Palmer, Sidney Doane, 1909, Mr 13,7:5
Palmer, Sigmond, 1946, S 3,19:4
Palmer, Stephen S, 1913, Ja 31,11:5
Palmer, Sydney H, 1942, My 18,15:5
Palmer, Theodore A, 1941, O 19,45:2
Palmer, Theodore De Cue, 1921, My 12,17:4
Palmer, Theodore G, 1903, N 7,9:6
Palmer, Theodore W Sr, 1943, S 25,15:3
Palmer, Theresa Mrs, 1941, O 30,23:3
Palmer, Thomas, 1904, Ja 9,9:6; 1948, F 11,27:4
Palmer, Thomas (Pedlar), 1949, F 14,19:4
Palmer, Thomas D, 1948, Mr 13,15:2
Palmer, Thomas D (T C Buntin), 1966, O 5,47:3
Palmer, Thomas W Jr, 1957, Ja 13,85:1
Palmer, Thomas Waverly, 1968, My 31,29:3
Palmer, Thomas Witherell Ex-Sen, 1913, Je 2,7:3
Palmer, V Claude, 1943, S 17,22:3
Palmer, Victor F, 1953, D 5,2:8
Palmer, Virgil M, 1944, F 17,19:4
Palmer, W B, 1876, N 3,10:6
Palmer, W C Dr, 1883, Jl 22,5:3
Palmer, W Edwin, 1944, Ja 26,19:3
Palmer, W L, 1932, Ap 17,II,4:1
Palmer, W P, 1884, My 3,2:3
Palmer, Waldo E, 1951, Jl 16,21:2
Palmer, Walter, 1944, Ap 23,43:4; 1967, Jl 20,37:4
Palmer, Walter F, 1956, Mr 8,29:3
Palmer, Walter I Rev, 1937, F 13,13:2
Palmer, Walter L Mrs, 1939, F 3,15:2
Palmer, Walter W, 1950, O 29,92:6
Palmer, Warren B, 1916, Ja 8,9:6
Palmer, Warren R, 1941, Jl 3,19:5
Palmer, Washington, 1951, Ag 14,23:2
Palmer, Wilbur F, 1948, O 21,27:5
Palmer, Willard D, 1946, D 14,15:5
Palmer, Willard H, 1950, S 14,31:4
Palmer, William, 1879, Ap 13,2:3
Palmer, William B, 1951, My 26,17:5; 1951, Jl 24,25:4
Palmer, William F, 1942, S 5,13:3; 1960, Ag 22,25:5
Palmer, William G, 1964, Mr 20,33:2
Palmer, William H, 1909, S 30,9:4; 1942, Jl 13,16:4; 1947, Ap 5,19:3
Palmer, William J, 1956, S 1,15:4
Palmer, William J Gen, 1909, Mr 14,11:5
Palmer, William L, 1944, Ja 2,38:5
Palmer, William L Rev, 1912, Ap 19,15:5
Palmer, William Mrs, 1949, O 7,27:4
Palmer, William P Jr, 1948, O 19,27:5
Palmer, William R, 1959, Ag 12,29:4
Palmer, Worthington, 1940, Jl 4,15:4
Palmerone, Joseph, 1961, Je 29,33:2
Palmerston, Lord, 1865, N 1,1:2
Palmerton, Harley, 1938, Ap 8,19:5
Palmeter, Frank H, 1944, F 4,15:4
Palmieri, Charles C, 1948, My 19,27:3
Palmieri, Ferdinand, 1951, My 20,88:7
Palmieri, Gian G, 1961, Ag 18,21:1
Palmieri, John, 1937, N 6,17:4
Palmieri, Martin, 1953, O 27,27:3
Palmieri, Michele A, 1961, N 12,86:8
Palmieri, Pietro, 1964, Mr 6,9:1
Palmieri, Ralph, 1947, Mr 24,25:5
Palmieri, Vivian J, 1962, O 24,39:1
Palminteri, Peter J, 1966, Jl 10,69:2
Palmisano, Joe, 1952, Ag 26,25:1
Palmisano, Vincent L, 1953, Mr 6,18:3
Palmisano, William R, 1948, Je 20,60:3
Palmitier, Adele L, 1939, Je 14,23:6
Palmitier, Lewis L, 1955, My 28,15:4
Palmlund, David W, 1959, Ag 24,21:2
Palmo, F Senor, 1869, S 6,5:4
Palmore, William B, 1914, Jl 6,7:4
Palmquist, Elim A E, 1956, F 7,31:2
Palocce, Ernest E, 1965, F 22,21:2
Palombi, Alfonso, 1941, Mr 26,23:3
Palombo, David (Ag 13 death noted; mem ser plans), 1966, S 12,10:4
Pals, Frank, 1967, Ja 6,35:4
Pals, Roelof, 1955, S 16,23:4
Palsir, Jacob, 1952, Ja 29,25:2
Palsits, Victor H, 1952, O 5,89:1
Palsley, Fred D, 1951, My 8,31:5
Paltauf, Rudolf M, 1962, N 12,29:3
Palte, T O, 1948, F 5,24:3
Paltiel, Aaron D, 1961, F 15,35:1
Palting, Candido R, 1951, Ap 20,30:7
Paltridge, George L, 1948, O 6,29:1
Paltridge, Shane Min Sir, 1966, Ja 21,14:4
Paltridge, Willett, 1939, F 8,23:5
Paltrowitz, Myer, 1957, Ja 11,24:1
Paltsits, Victor H Mrs, 1944, Je 30,21:4
Paltz, Walter J, 1962, N 27,37:3
Paluch, John S, 1955, Je 7,33:5
Palumbo, Phyllis Mrs, 1956, Je 5,39:2
Palumbo, Vincent J (cor, S 21,89:1), 1952, S 20,15:4

Paluszek, Ludwik W, 1952, Ap 19,15:3
Pam, Albert, 1955, S 4,56:4
Pam, Edgar, 1945, D 22,19:4
Pam, H, 1930, My 30,19:3
Pam, Max, 1925, S 15,25:5
Pamaroni, Achille Mrs, 1952, Mr 14,23:3
Pambianco, Phil F, 1952, D 31,15:3
Pammoor, Lord, 1941, Jl 2,21:3
Pamphilon, Walter M, 1950, Ap 2,93:1
Pamplin, Jessie S Mrs, 1954, O 11,27:4
Panahi, Abolghassem, 1954, Jl 2,19:6
Panaro, Vincenzo, 1947, N 9,74:3
Panaroni, Alfred G, 1944, Ag 2,15:3
Panas, Basil P, 1942, Jl 2,21:5
Panasyuk, Mikhail P, 1956, Ja 17,33:1
Panati, Vincent G, 1958, Ap 23,33:4
Pancake, Carl, 1950, S 22,31:3
Pancake, Priscilla J Mrs, 1941, F 3,17:3
Panchak, John M, 1949, Ja 30,60:6
Panchard, Edouard, 1956, My 27,88:6
Panchard, Edouard Mrs, 1956, Ap 26,33:4
Panchen, Lama (por), 1937, D 4,17:4
Pancho, Kid (A Flores), 1951, O 16,31:2
Panciatichi, Francesco, 1953, Jl 29,23:4
Pancoast, Anna M Mrs, 1937, Ap 8,23:5
Pancoast, Chalmers L, 1966, Ja 1,17:3
Pancoast, Charles E 2d, 1956, N 25,88:3
Pancoast, Edgar T, 1952, N 23,88:1
Pancoast, Emma F Mrs, 1941, F 8,15:5
Pancoast, George E (por), 1939, Mr 16,23:3
Pancoast, George W, 1912, Ja 11,13:4
Pancoast, Henry K, 1939, My 22,17:4
Pancoast, Joseph, 1882, Mr 8,5:5
Pancoast, Linda H, 1941, My 27,23:4
Pancoast, Rebecca E Mrs, 1941, F 13,19:5
Pancoast, Samuel R, 1942, Ja 26,15:5
Pancoast, Thomas B, 1911, Mr 15,13:5
Pancoast, Thomas J, 1941, S 18,25:3
Pancoast, Wilbur H, 1945, S 22,17:6
Pancoast, William G, 1958, S 4,29:5
Pancoast, William H, 1943, O 9,13:4
Pancoast, William Mrs, 1947, Ap 22,27:1
Pancost, Ellsworth, 1954, Ap 17,13:5
Pancratia, Sister, 1938, Je 2,23:4
Pancrazi, Pietro, 1952, D 27,10:4
Pandaleon, George A, 1961, S 6,31:1
Pandit, R S, 1944, Ja 15,13:6
Pandolse, Joseph, 1924, Je 12,17:5
Pane, Michele, 1953, Ap 20,25:4
Pane-Gasser, John B, 1964, Je 9,35:4
Panella, Frank A, 1953, My 11,27:5
Panella, Louis J, 1940, Mr 15,23:4
Panero, Guy B, 1961, My 15,31:3
Panero, Hugh E, 1951, Mr 6,27:2
Panero, Mario B, 1945, My 1,23:2
Panero Torvado, Leopoldo, 1962, Ag 29,30:1
Panferov, Fedor, 1960, S 11,81:5
Pangal, Jean, 1950, O 9,25:5
Pangalos, Theodorus, 1952, F 28,27:1
Pangborn, Clyde (funl plans, Ap 2,31:5; funl, Ap 4,21:4), 1958, Mr 30,89:1
Pangborn, Earl L, 1964, Je 24,37:4
Pangborn, Franklin, 1958, Jl 21,21:2
Pangborn, H G, 1866, Ag 3,6:2
Pangborn, John W, 1907, Mr 16,9:6
Pangborn, Maj, 1902, N 2,7:5
Pangborn, Thomas W, 1967, My 21,87:1
Pangborn, Thomas W Mrs, 1947, My 27,25:1
Pangburn, Clifford H, 1949, D 18,88:6
Pangburn, Harry K, 1954, F 13,13:3
Pangburn, William D, 1941, Ag 20,19:3
Pangburn, William M Sr Mrs, 1943, My 21,19:5
Panger, Morris H, 1961, Je 5,31:4
Pangiris Bey, Mrs, 1912, Jl 2,11:3
Pangrac, Francis A, 1955, Je 26,77:1
Pani, Alberto J, 1955, Ag 26,19:1
Pani, Joseph, 1942, Mr 7,17:3
Paniagua, Raul, 1953, Ap 19,90:3
Panica, Mary Mrs, 1941, Je 26,23:4
Panico, Giovanni Cardinal, 1962, Jl 8,65:1
Panigel, Hal J, 1946, O 22,25:4
Panik, Stephen J, 1953, N 23,27:1
Panikkar, K M, 1963, D 11,47:3
Panin, Ivan Mrs, 1949, Ap 20,27:5
Panini, Carlos, 1951, N 22,50:3
Panitkin, D F, 1955, S 10,17:2
Panizzi, Antonio Sir, 1879, Ap 21,2:1
Pank, William C, 1962, S 20,34:1
Pankard, Harry I, 1948, N 23,29:3
Panke, William F, 1954, My 29,15:4
Panken, Abraham, 1953, S 21,25:3
Panken, Jacob, 1968, F 5,35:2
Panken, Jacob Mrs, 1918, Ja 29,15:3
Panken, Morris, 1952, Ja 23,27:2
Pankhurst, Charles H Mrs, 1921, My 29,22:3
Pankhurst, Christabel Dame, 1958, F 15,17:1
Pankhurst, E G Mrs, 1928, Je 15,25:5
Pankhurst, Estelle S (funl, S 29,35:3), 1960, S 28,39:2
Pankhurst, Frederick H Gov, 1921, F 1,11:2
Pankhurst, Howard E, 1916, Ag 24,9:2
Pankin, Aaron, 1958, Mr 9,70:5
Panko, Walter Jr, 1957, N 17,87:1
Pankonien, Oscar, 1952, Mr 2,92:3
Pankow, Rufus G Mrs, 1960, D 11,88:7
Pankratova, Anna M Mrs, 1957, My 27,31:4
Pankuch, John, 1952, Mr 1,15:3
Pankuch, Joseph Sr, 1948, N 17,27:5
Panky, Fred Mrs, 1966, Mr 4,33:2
Pann, Peter, 1948, D 31,16:2
Pannaci, A D, 1946, Mr 5,25:2
Pannaci, Edward, 1944, My 24,19:3
Pannash, Adolph T, 1952, Ja 25,22:5
Pannell, Charles F, 1938, Ja 4,23:3
Panner, Otto Dr, 1915, Jl 29,9:2
Pannes, John B Capt, 1909, Mr 10,9:4
Panneton, George E, 1940, Ag 2,15:2
Panneton, Philippe, 1960, D 31,17:4
Pannick, Frank, 1946, S 20,31:2
Pannill, Charles J, 1955, F 8,27:3
Pannill, F C, 1951, O 30,29:2
Panofsky, Erwin Dr, 1968, Mr 16,32:3
Panoini, Alfredo, 1939, Ap 12,23:4
Panoras, Steven E, 1949, D 25,26:5
Pansegrau, Gustav C, 1952, N 29,17:1
Pansiera, George W, 1951, S 23,86:6
Pansini, Louis, 1957, Jl 4,19:1
Pant, Govind B (funl, Mr 8,33:5), 1961, Mr 7,35:3
Pantages, Lois A Mrs, 1941, Jl 19,13:3
Pantaleo, Father, 1879, Ag 26,3:2
Pantaleoni, Guido, 1948, N 24,23:5
Pantaleoni, Matteo, 1924, O 30,19:5
Pantelides, Lazarus, 1950, Jl 13,25:3
Panter, Thomas A, 1939, Mr 13,17:5
Panthen, Karl A (por), 1947, Mr 31,23:1
Pantillo, Sylvia Mrs, 1952, Ja 1,27:5
Pantley, H Charles, 1950, Ag 15,29:4
Panton, Lawrence A C, 1954, N 23,35:3
Panton, Malcolm M, 1943, Ag 3,19:5
Pantz, Edward, 1940, S 1,21:2
Pantzer, Myron, 1966, Ja 24,35:2
Pantzer, Otto, 1924, Jl 13,22:2
Panuccio, Francesco, 1962, Mr 15,32:3
Panuch, Franz Mrs, 1946, O 22,25:6
Panunzio, Constantine M, 1964, Ag 11,33:1
Panunzio, Sergio, 1944, O 12,27:5
Panush, Simon A, 1968, O 5,35:3
Panuska, Frank, 1964, Jl 19,64:6
Panuska, Jaroslav, 1958, Ag 3,81:1
Panyity, Louis S, 1943, Ag 1,39:1
Panzer, Carl B, 1951, Jl 15,60:5
Panzer, Hugh R, 1950, Mr 1,27:4
Panzer, Paul, 1958, Ag 17,85:2
Pao Chu pu-Ju, Princess, 1952, F 21,27:1
Paoli, Antonio, 1946, Ag 27,27:5
Paoli, Xavier, 1923, Jl 9,13:5
Paolillo, Vincent A, 1950, Jl 23,58:2
Paolino, Lawrence A, 1953, S 10,25:4
Paolo, Cartaino S, 1955, D 21,29:4
Paolucci, Vincent, 1963, O 10,41:4
Paolucci di Val Maggiore, Raffaele, 1958, S 6,17:6
Paonessa, Angelo M, 1949, Jl 16,13:1
Pap, Arthur, 1959, S 8,35:4
Pap, Peter P, 1955, S 11,84:4
Papa, Anthony, 1953, Jl 7,21:1
Papa, Charles A, 1959, Je 19,25:6
Papadimitriou, John, 1963, Ap 13,19:2
Papagos, Alex, 1955, O 5,35:1
Papaleski, Nikolai, 1947, F 5,23:5
Papanastassiou, A, 1936, N 18,25:3
Papandreou, George (funl, N 4,1:2), 1968, N 1,47:1
Papanicolaou, George N, 1962, F 20,35:3
Paparoni, Humberto, 1959, O 3,3:7
Papas, Nick G, 1948, Ag 10,21:5
Papastephanou, Emmanuel, 1955, F 2,27:4
Papazian, George Mrs, 1955, My 14,1:1
Pape, Adolphus, 1918, Jl 28,19:3
Pape, Alexander, 1924, S 10,21:4
Pape, Charles F, 1953, Ap 14,27:1
Pape, Charles H, 1938, D 6,23:4
Pape, Charles Jr, 1957, Jl 18,25:4
Pape, Edward T, 1937, Mr 13,19:4
Pape, Eric, 1938, N 9,23:6; 1962, N 21,30:1
Pape, Garry, 1947, F 11,27:2
Pape, Henry (por), 1942, Jl 18,13:3
Pape, Henry H, 1952, D 29,19:1
Pape, Herman L, 1942, Mr 26,23:4
Pape, James C Mrs, 1950, Jl 29,13:5
Pape, John, 1947, D 30,24:2
Pape, Kilby, 1903, My 5,9:6
Pape, Lee J Mrs, 1947, Ap 22,27:3
Pape, Nina A, 1944, Mr 7,17:3
Pape, Thomas W, 1945, Jl 19,23:4
Pape, William J, 1943, N 14,57:2; 1961, Ja 30,23:1
Pape, William J Mrs, 1963, My 1,39:4
Papeno, Helene, 1948, D 31,16:4
Papert, Samuel W, 1951, Ap 15,92:2
Papetti, Luigi, 1940, Ag 13,19:3
Papez, James W, 1958, Ap 14,25:3
Papi, Gennaro (por), 1941, N 30,69:1
Papi, Margarita, 1925, Ap 16,21:5
Papier, Morris C, 1957, Ja 18,21:2
Papillaud, Henri, 1950, Jl 21,19:3
Papini, Giovanni, 1956, Jl 9,23:3
Papish, Aaron, 1948, D 21,29:6
Papish, Asher, 1947, S 4,25:6
Papp, Henry S, 1965, O 21,47:2
Papp, Joseph, 1950, My 16,31:3
Papp, Joseph Florian, 1968, Ag 2,33:3
Papp, Louis, 1950, Ag 19,13:2
Pappalardo, Victor, 1951, Ja 28,79:2
Pappalau, John J, 1944, My 13,19:3
Pappas, Charles W, 1962, Ag 6,25:5
Pappas, Clement D, 1966, Ja 6,27:1
Pappas, Gus, 1963, Ja 22,15:5
Pappas, James M, 1946, Je 13,27:3
Pappas, John, 1953, O 4,32:3
Pappas, John F, 1950, My 25,29:4
Pappaylion, Arthur T, 1954, Ja 23,13:6
Pappe, Theodore F, 1942, Ag 5,19:3
Pappenheim, Martin, 1943, N 23,26:2
Pappenheimer, Alwin M, 1955, F 22,21:3
Pappenheimer, Max, 1909, S 14,9:5
Papper, William C, 1924, Ja 6,23:1
Pappert, Aug V, 1938, S 17,17:3
Paprin, Philip, 1967, D 10,86:7
Paprocki, Frank J, 1941, Mr 21,21:1
Paprocki, John H, 1947, O 1,29:3
Papscoe, Joseph F, 1953, F 12,27:3
Papsdorf, Herman L, 1959, O 18,86:7
Papst, Eugen, 1956, Ja 5,34:1
Papworth, William A, 1943, Je 19,13:6
Paquet, Eugene, 1951, My 9,33:4
Paquette, Frederick Mrs, 1938, Ap 15,20:3
Paquette, Gabriel, 1939, D 16,17:4
Paquin, Albert J, 1967, Mr 14,47:2
Paquin, Charles H, 1949, O 8,13:5
Paquin, Elzear, 1947, Ja 19,52:1
Paquin, J Hector, 1950, Mr 23,29:3
Paquin, Samuel S, 1943, Ap 17,17:6
Paquin, 1907, D 22,9:4
Para, Fred, 1949, Je 28,52:3
Parada y Santin, Jose, 1923, Je 7,19:4
Paradies, Isidore, 1941, My 1,23:5
Paradies, Richard R, 1940, My 23,23:3
Paradine, John A (por), 1948, S 27,23:3
Paradine, Thomas E, 1962, Mr 19,29:1
Paradis, Adrian, 1940, S 14,17:4
Paradis, Adrian F, 1967, Mr 2,35:3
Paradis, Leo, 1955, O 6,29:4
Paradise, Bertrand, 1957, D 28,17:1
Paradise, N Burton, 1942, Ap 25,13:2
Paradise, Robert C, 1952, Jl 16,25:3
Paradise, Ruth, 1947, Ap 8,27:1
Paradise, Scott H, 1959, Ag 2,80:6
Paradise, Thomas F P, 1946, Jl 21,39:1
Paradiso, Donato A, 1955, S 16,23:3
Paraf, Chevalier Alfred, 1885, My 1,1:7
Paramananda, Swami, 1940, Je 22,15:2
Paramore, Edward E Jr, 1956, My 2,31:1
Paramore, Frederick Mrs, 1884, F 22,5:5
Parapiglia, Felix, 1942, Ap 8,19:3
Paraskevopoulos, J S, 1951, Mr 16,31:5
Parasol, Felix, 1950, N 27,25:2
Paratore, Giuseppe, 1967, F 27,29:2
Paravicini, Fritz, 1944, F 1,11:1
Parbury, Charles P, 1937, Mr 25,25:2
Parbury, Violet, 1952, S 10,29:3
Parcarella, Ermanno, 1946, Ja 30,25:5
Parcaut, Ralph, 1957, Je 26,31:3
Parce, Dwight A, 1951, O 21,93:1
Parcell, J Evans, 1959, Mr 10,35:1
Parcells, Frank H, 1946, F 10,40:8
Parcher, Samuel L, 1938, N 19,17:4
Parcorall, Pedro, 1946, Ja 21,25:3
Parde, Rudolph A, 1953, N 24,29:5
Pardee, Alfred D, 1942, Jl 28,17:5
Pardee, Allena G, 1947, D 17,30:2
Pardee, Ario, 1944, Ja 14,19:3
Pardee, Calvin, 1923, Mr 19,17:5
Pardee, Calvin 3d, 1947, O 4,17:6
Pardee, Charles L, 1949, Jl 24,52:5
Pardee, Charles M, 1947, D 2,29:2
Pardee, Clarke M, 1968, Ap 6,39:1
Pardee, Don Albert Judge, 1919, S 27,13:6
Pardee, Dwight W, 1920, F 22,20:4
Pardee, Elizabeth Van Steenberg Mrs, 1909, Je 2
Pardee, Emily, 1943, Ja 20,19:5
Pardee, Ensign B Dr, 1917, D 29,11:4
Pardee, Ensign B Mrs, 1951, F 10,13:1
Pardee, Frank, 1947, O 22,30:3
Pardee, George C, 1941, S 2,17:4
Pardee, Irving H, 1949, Ap 11,25:5
Pardee, Israel Mrs, 1944, O 24,23:2
Pardee, James T, 1944, Ja 4,17:5
Pardee, James T Mrs (will), 1944, O 13,25:3
Pardee, John E, 1948, F 14,13:3
Pardee, John H (por), 1938, Ap 22,19:1
Pardee, Joseph T, 1960, Mr 4,25:1
Pardee, L C Mrs, 1937, S 8,23:4
Pardee, Olive, 1952, Je 3,29:4
Pardee, Powell, 1947, Ag 10,53:1
Pardee, William D, 1944, Ag 21,15:5
Pardee, William E, 1946, N 22,23:4
Pardee, William O, 1944, Jl 6,15:5
Pardes, Jack, 1968, Ap 20,34:2
Pardessus, Ernest V, 1905, Mr 29,9:3
Pardi, Joseph A Sr, 1953, Je 14,85:1
Pardi, Justin A, 1951, F 12,23:3
Pardo, Jose, 1947, Ag 5,23:6

Pardo, Nestor M, 1956, Je 6,33:5
Pardo-Bazan, Emilia Countess, 1921, My 13,15:6
Pardoe, Jonathan B, 1944, Ap 13,19:2
Pardoe, William S, 1962, D 1,25:5
Pardow, Pauline Rev Mother, 1916, Jl 27,9:6
Pardow, R I Rev, 1884, My 10,5:3
Pardow, William O'Brien Rev, 1909, Ja 24,11:5
Pardridge, Albert J, 1947, F 19,26:3
Pardridge, Evelyn F, 1944, Jl 28,13:2
Parduba, John, 1946, N 28,27:3
Pardue, John J, 1944, S 18,19:4
Pardue, Lit J, 1944, Ag 3,19:5
Pardy, Augustus, 1909, Ja 27,9:6
Paredas, Enrique Sanchez Msgr, 1923, Mr 26,13:4
Paredes, Francisco A (por), 1946, Jl 31,27:5
Pareis, Claudius D, 1949, N 6,92:1
Pareis, Leigh, 1959, O 10,21:6
Parella, Angelo C, 1940, Jl 27,13:6
Parella, Peter, 1949, O 29,15:1
Parelli, Attilio, 1945, Ja 3,17:2
Parenago, Pavel, 1960, Ja 7,30:1
Parent, Charles E, 1938, S 17,17:2
Parent, Edward R, 1952, Ja 4,23:2
Parent, Elizabeth C, 1943, D 30,18:3
Parent, Frank D, 1960, Je 20,31:5
Parent, George, 1942, D 15,27:6
Parent, Homer J, 1949, Ja 1,13:2
Parent, John A Mrs, 1957, Ag 31,15:3
Parent, John F, 1954, Ag 7,13:6
Parent, Jules D, 1960, Ap 17,93:1
Parent, Levi W Mrs, 1964, Jl 20,25:4
Parent, W Earl, 1957, Je 18,29:2
Parente, Frank J, 1967, Mr 8,46:1
Parenzo, Anthony, 1954, N 18,33:2
Parepa-Rosa, Euphrosyne, 1874, Ja 23,4:7
Pares, Bernard (trb, My 4,28:6),(por), 1949, Ap 18, 25:3
Pares, Ramon, 1952, Mr 25,27:3
Paret, Benny (Kid),(funl plans, Ap 4,50:3; funl, Ap 8,V,7:8), 1962, Ap 3,1:1
Paret, Frank, 1919, Ap 5,15:3
Paret, Henry Wilbur, 1918, S 29,21:1
Paret, Merrill P, 1957, F 15,23:5
Paret, Theodore D Sr, 1949, Ja 26,25:1
Paret, William Bp, 1911, Ja 19,9:4
Paret, William Mrs, 1911, Ja 16,11:5
Pareto, Vilfredo, 1923, Ag 21,17:3
Paretti, Andrew, 1955, N 23,23:6
Paretti, Catherine Mrs, 1944, Ap 18,21:3
Parfenoff, Stephen, 1964, Ap 23,39:5
Parfitt, Charles D, 1951, N 21,25:2
Parfonry, Victor, 1946, Ag 19,25:5
Pargenstecher, Hugo, 1947, Ap 28,23:5
Parham, Richard P, 1938, S 21,25:3
Pariani, Alberto, 1955, Mr 3,27:2
Paribeni, Roberto, 1956, Jl 15,61:1
Paridon, John M, 1938, Jl 22,17:5
Paridy, Charles, 1941, Je 20,21:4
Parilli, Tony, 1964, Ja 2,41:5
Paris, A P, 1881, F 15,2:1
Paris, Allen E, 1951, Ap 27,47:2
Paris, Auguste J Jr, 1955, Mr 24,32:2
Paris, Charles Rogers Judge, 1920, Ja 6,15:1
Paris, Frances J Mrs (por), 1942, My 9,13:3
Paris, Frank Mrs, 1948, Jl 24,15:6
Paris, Gaston Prof, 1903, Mr 7,9:2
Paris, Irving, 1938, Ap 10,II,6:5
Paris, Jacques C, 1953, Jl 18,4:7
Paris, Jane, 1918, My 26,23:2
Paris, Leon K, 1963, Je 16,84:6
Paris, Rex L, 1952, F 14,27:2
Paris, Russel C, 1940, Je 18,23:6
Paris, Virginia, 1960, S 29,35:2
Paris, William E, 1955, N 3,31:4
Paris, William F, 1954, Je 8,27:4
Paris, William F Mrs, 1957, My 23,33:3
Paris, Zadok, 1942, D 25,17:2
Pariseau, Joseph A Mrs, 1960, N 27,86:5
Pariseau, Louis, 1958, Je 10,33:2
Pariseau, Wilfred F, 1952, N 10,25:1
Pariser, Milton, 1961, Ja 29,84:7
Parisette, Frederick W, 1943, Jl 8,19:3
Parish, Chester F, 1944, D 10,54:7
Parish, Daniel, 1914, D 18,13:6; 1967, Ja 18,43:4
Parish, Edward C, 1962, N 6,33:4
Parish, Edward J, 1955, Ja 21,23:1
Parish, Henry, 1917, S 19,13:6; 1942, Je 27,13:5
Parish, Henry Mrs (will, Jl 25,29:1), 1950, Jl 10,21:6
Parish, James H, 1925, Jl 31,15:5
Parish, John J, 1941, F 16,41:1
Parish, John J Mrs, 1947, Mr 6,25:2
Parish, John L, 1921, Mr 26,13:6
Parish, Lawrence A, 1937, Ap 15,23:2
Parish, Lawrence J, 1949, O 3,17:4
Parish, Margaret L Mrs, 1939, Ap 17,17:3
Parish, Mary A Mrs, 1951, Mr 22,31:5
Parish, Preston Mrs, 1951, Ja 9,29:4
Parish, Richard Laurence, 1968, Mr 12,43:1
Parish, Rufus J, 1954, F 2,27:2
Parish, Susan Delafield, 1916, F 16,11:4
Parish, Wainwright, 1941, O 2,25:5
Parish, Walter A, 1959, Ja 24,19:2
Parish, William F (por), 1939, Mr 8,21:4
Parish, Woodbine Sir, 1882, Ag 21,5:5
Parish-Watson, M, 1941, F 22,15:2
Parisi, Angela R (Mrs L Louison), 1961, Mr 21,37:1
Parisi, Anthony, 1941, D 20,19:6
Parisi, John C, 1957, Ja 24,29:4
Parisi, Joseph, 1956, S 19,37:4
Parisi, Paolo Mrs, 1951, Jl 4,17:7
Parisi, Pier L, 1953, Ag 5,23:5
Parisi, Savatore, 1959, D 27,61:1
Parisi, Vincent G, 1947, Ag 21,23:4
Parisot, Louis, 1945, F 3,11:3
Parissi, Louis, 1955, N 21,29:5
Parizeau, Telesphore, 1961, O 14,23:2
Parizot, Gustav F, 1912, Ap 29,11:5
Park, Alex, 1941, Ag 1,15:2
Park, Andrew T, 1943, O 13,23:1
Park, Anna E (good doctor), 1904, Je 1,9:5
Park, Archibald, 1944, Ja 7,18:3
Park, Archibald Spiers, 1912, N 11,11:5
Park, Charles D, 1937, Ja 24,II,8:1
Park, Charles F, 1944, S 27,21:7
Park, Charles F Jr (por), 1945, Je 30,17:5
Park, Clearfield Mrs, 1948, S 17,25:3
Park, Colin R, 1951, S 6,3:2
Park, D M Rev, 1912, Jl 16,9:6
Park, Daniel L, 1952, Je 7,19:3
Park, Darragh A, 1953, F 10,27:1
Park, David C, 1960, Ap 26,37:1
Park, Donald, 1958, Ag 12,29:3
Park, Edgar, 1938, N 10,27:3
Park, Eldon A, 1949, D 13,38:1
Park, Ernest S, 1951, N 20,31:5
Park, Frances F, 1953, Jl 24,13:6
Park, Frank C, 1948, D 19,76:4
Park, Frank L, 1939, D 26,19:4
Park, Franklin A, 1938, Je 18,15:3
Park, George B, 1964, D 16,43:2
Park, George C, 1909, N 23,9:4
Park, George Carpenter, 1916, Jl 7,11:5
Park, Hamilton G, 1965, D 4,31:5
Park, Harold H Mrs (Madeleine F), 1960, Ap 3,86:1
Park, Harry M, 1949, Jl 3,26:6
Park, Henry S, 1938, My 9,17:4
Park, Hobart J, 1948, Ja 7,25:5
Park, J Edgar, 1956, Mr 5,23:5
Park, J Edgar Mrs, 1962, N 19,31:2
Park, J Jr, 1883, Ap 22,8:7
Park, James, 1938, D 7,23:4; 1946, N 19,21:1
Park, James C, 1949, F 12,18:2
Park, James G, 1959, Ja 31,19:4
Park, James G Mrs, 1959, My 3,87:1
Park, James T, 1966, My 25,47:4
Park, James W, 1958, S 12,25:3
Park, John A, 1956, Mr 16,23:3
Park, Joseph, 1903, Ap 4,9:6; 1953, F 3,25:3
Park, Joseph A, 1952, Ap 21,21:3
Park, Joseph D Lt, 1913, My 10,11:1
Park, Joseph H Mrs, 1961, Ja 4,33:2
Park, Julian, 1965, Jl 18,68:7
Park, Kenneth G, 1959, O 10,21:1
Park, Lewis A, 1946, S 8,44:2
Park, Louis J Mrs, 1950, O 31,27:2
Park, Louis L, 1947, O 29,27:2
Park, M Amelia, 1947, Mr 10,21:4
Park, Maitland Hall Sir, 1921, Mr 16,9:4
Park, Marion E, 1960, My 7,23:3
Park, Mary F Mrs, 1939, O 29,40:5
Park, Matthew Jr, 1948, Mr 16,27:3
Park, Maud W Mrs, 1955, My 10,29:1
Park, Milton Col, 1914, My 10,IV,7:6
Park, Nathan B, 1948, Je 23,27:4
Park, Robert E, 1944, F 8,16:3
Park, Roswell Dr, 1914, F 16,7:4
Park, Rufus H, 1938, Ap 13,25:2
Park, Sam, 1937, My 7,25:3
Park, Samuel, 1955, Mr 31,27:4
Park, Samuel J, 1952, S 25,31:4; 1960, Ja 20,31:3
Park, Samuel R, 1949, Ap 21,26:2
Park, Sarah, 1957, Mr 10,1:4
Park, Stanley W, 1960, My 19,37:3
Park, Stephen F Mrs, 1952, Ag 1,18:4
Park, T W, 1882, D 21,2:1
Park, T W (funl), 1883, Ja 5,3:5
Park, Thomas C, 1949, F 12,17:4
Park, Thomas H, 1968, Je 13,47:3
Park, Trenor L, 1907, O 24,11:5
Park, William, 1937, Jl 1,27:6; 1940, N 21,29:3; 1961, Ap 19,39:4
Park, William E, 1949, D 18,90:4
Park, William G Mrs, 1949, O 14,27:2
Park, William H, 1939, Ap 7,21:1
Park, William H Mrs, 1949, Jl 9,13:2
Park, William M, 1948, F 1,60:3; 1965, Ap 9,33:3
Park-Lewis, Francis Mrs, 1944, Ag 26,11:5
Parkas, Peter, 1949, Jl 23,11:6
Parke, Francis N, 1955, Je 3,23:6
Parke, H S, 1879, My 14,5:3
Parke, Henry C, 1968, Ag 31,23:1
Parke, Henry H, 1957, My 27,31:3
Parke, Hervey C, 1951, My 7,25:5
Parke, Hervey C Mrs, 1967, Je 7,47:2
Parke, Hiram H Mrs, 1950, Ag 9,29:2
Parke, Jacob R, 1916, D 3,23:2
Parke, James J Mrs, 1959, O 12,19:5
Parke, John S (mem ser, Ag 19,23:4), 1954, Ag 14, 15:2
Parke, Margaret A, 1954, Ap 11,86:2
Parke, Nelson F, 1962, N 15,37:3
Parke, Richard A, 1950, Ag 24,27:4
Parke, Samuel, 1940, Mr 8,22:4
Parke, Samuel R, 1963, Ag 15,29:1
Parke, Sarah C, 1937, Ja 25,19:4
Parke, William, 1941, Jl 29,15:1
Parke, William E, 1944, Je 27,19:4
Parke, William Mrs, 1954, Je 7,23:5
Parker, A B Judge, 1926, My 11,1:2
Parker, A J, 1890, My 14,5:2
Parker, A Richmond, 1951, My 19,15:5
Parker, Abbie W Mrs (will), 1963, Mr 27,5:1
Parker, Abram X, 1909, Ag 11,7:5
Parker, Addison B, 1944, Mr 29,21:5
Parker, Addison B Mrs, 1951, Jl 10,27:4
Parker, Addison P, 1942, N 17,25:5
Parker, Albert G Jr, 1958, Mr 23,88:7
Parker, Albert J, 1940, S 8,49:1
Parker, Albert Mrs, 1937, Je 9,25:3
Parker, Alfred B, 1940, Jl 26,17:6
Parker, Alfred P, 1947, My 30,21:3
Parker, Alincia B Mrs, 1952, Mr 28,23:2
Parker, Allen E Mrs, 1941, Ap 30,19:4
Parker, Alton B Mrs, 1917, Ap 3,13:4; 1960, Ag 21, 84:6
Parker, Alton N (por), 1942, D 1,25:1
Parker, Amasa J, 1938, My 3,23:1
Parker, Andrew Mrs, 1943, N 13,13:5
Parker, Arthur, 1947, Jl 2,23:3
Parker, Arthur C, 1954, D 19,84:6; 1955, Ja 3,27:3
Parker, Arthur J Dr, 1937, Mr 21,II,9:3
Parker, Arthur L, 1945, Ja 3,17:3
Parker, Arthur T, 1938, Mr 8,19:5
Parker, Arthur V, 1955, N 26,19:1
Parker, Asa M, 1948, Ap 14,28:2
Parker, Ashton, 1938, Ap 13,25:2
Parker, Augustin H, 1951, Ap 3,27:5
Parker, Austin, 1938, Mr 21,15:2
Parker, Barnett, 1941, Ag 6,17:2
Parker, Bartol, 1944, D 30,11:6
Parker, Benjamin Capt, 1908, Ja 22,7:5
Parker, C Edward, 1963, My 30,17:2
Parker, C H, 1938, Ja 9,42:7
Parker, C Harrison, 1916, S 28,9:5
Parker, Charles, 1954, Je 1,27:2
Parker, Charles A, 1959, Ap 23,31:2
Parker, Charles A Mrs, 1954, N 13,15:5
Parker, Charles B, 1948, Ag 21,15:5
Parker, Charles D, 1925, D 29,23:5
Parker, Charles E Justice, 1909, Mr 3,9:5
Parker, Charles Henry, 1908, Ap 10,9:5
Parker, Charles J Mrs, 1949, F 20,60:4; 1953, Jl 30, 23:5
Parker, Charles L, 1938, S 21,25:3
Parker, Charles M, 1921, S 28,19:6; 1967, S 21,47:1
Parker, Charles Pomeroy Prof, 1916, D 3,23:1
Parker, Charles R, 1944, Ja 29,13:3; 1961, F 21,35:2
Parker, Charles S, 1941, Mr 29,15:3; 1953, D 26,13:5
Parker, Charles S Jr Mrs, 1964, Jl 16,31:4
Parker, Charles Thorndike Dr, 1912, S 1,II,9:4
Parker, Charles W, 1942, Jl 7,20:4; 1947, D 23,23:2; 1948, Ja 24,15:1
Parker, Charlie, 1955, Mr 15,17:5
Parker, Chauncey G, 1943, Jl 13,21:5; 1953, Ag 6,21:1
Parker, Chauncey G Sr Mrs, 1942, N 3,23:5
Parker, Clarence H Mrs, 1943, My 14,19:5
Parker, Clark W, 1944, Je 10,15:4
Parker, Clayton A, 1941, O 7,23:2
Parker, Clifford E Mrs, 1945, S 23,45:2
Parker, Cola G, 1962, Je 28,31:3
Parker, Cola G Mrs, 1959, N 7,23:5
Parker, Colin, 1951, Ja 20,15:3
Parker, Cortland, 1960, Ja 19,36:1
Parker, Cortlandt, 1907, Jl 31,7:5
Parker, Cortlandt (will), 1907, Ag 10,7:5
Parker, Cortlandt 2d, 1945, Ja 28,38:2
Parker, Courtlandt B, 1966, O 18,45:1
Parker, Crawford, 1947, O 22,29:3
Parker, Daingerfield Brig-Gen, 1925, F 26,21:4
Parker, Dale M, 1959, Mr 31,29:3
Parker, Dan, 1955, Ag 9,10:4
Parker, Dan Mrs, 1958, Jl 21,21:4
Parker, Daniel F (Dan), 1967, My 21,86:6
Parker, David N Mrs, 1948, Ag 12,21:5
Parker, De Witt H, 1949, Je 22,31:3
Parker, Donald C, 1955, Ap 8,21:5
Parker, Donald H, 1950, Je 22,27:4
Parker, Dorothy (funl, Je 10,33:1; will, Je 27,22:2), 1967, Je 8,1:2
Parker, Douglas G, 1960, My 23,29:6
Parker, E B, 1929, O 31,25:4
Parker, E S Gen, 1895, S 1,9:7
Parker, E T, 1881, Ap 15,5:2
Parker, Edmund L Sr, 1961, My 6,31:7
Parker, Edward A, 1943, N 30,27:1
Parker, Edward J, 1961, F 17,27:3
Parker, Edward J Mrs, 1959, F 11,39:4
Parker, Edward L, 1956, D 7,27:2; 1960, Je 3,31:1
Parker, Edward Melville Bp, 1925, O 23,23:5

Parker, Edward W Mrs, 1925, Je 11,19:4
Parker, Edwin G, 1945, Ja 1,21:2
Parker, Edwin Pond Rev, 1920, My 29,15:3
Parker, Elias G, 1937, Ja 9,17:5
Parker, Elizabeth D Mrs, 1942, Jl 3,17:4
Parker, Ella E, 1957, N 26,30:3
Parker, Ellis H Sr, 1940, F 5,6:1
Parker, Emma S Mrs, 1941, F 13,19:2
Parker, Emmett N, 1939, D 10,68:4
Parker, Erlon H, 1966, Ap 12,35:4
Parker, Ernest T, 1966, Ja 1,17:5
Parker, Ernest W, 1960, Ap 3,86:8
Parker, Ethlyn H Mrs, 1956, S 27,35:5
Parker, Eugene L, 1951, O 6,19:2
Parker, Evan J, 1964, Ja 28,31:1
Parker, Ezra Mrs, 1949, Ag 4,23:4
Parker, F A Commodore, 1879, Je 11,5:3
Parker, F J MRs, 1877, F 23,5:2
Parker, F Rev, 1882, Ap 8,5:4
Parker, F W Capt, 1871, My 27,1:7
Parker, Forrest H, 1918, Ap 25,13:4
Parker, Foster H, 1955, My 20,25:1
Parker, Frances Emily Jane, 1925, F 11,21:4
Parker, Frances R Mrs, 1939, Mr 15,24:2
Parker, Francis Jewett, 1909, Ja 22,7:6
Parker, Francis P, 1947, N 28,27:3
Parker, Frank, 1924, N 16,7:2; 1942, Ag 29,19:2; 1946, Mr 20,23:1
Parker, Frank (por), 1947, Mr 14,23:1
Parker, Frank, 1958, F 16,85:3
Parker, Frank C, 1952, O 22,27:3
Parker, Frank C Dr, 1952, Jl 4,13:3
Parker, Frank E, 1941, Ja 6,15:4
Parker, Frank Judson Dr, 1912, O 3,13:6
Parker, Frank Mrs, 1945, N 13,21:3
Parker, Frank S, 1954, Mr 4,25:4
Parker, Franklin D, 1949, S 2,17:2
Parker, Franklin E Jr, 1963, F 26,7:8
Parker, Franklin N, 1954, Mr 4,25:1
Parker, Fred B, 1944, Ja 7,17:6
Parker, Fred C, 1938, Ap 22,19:5
Parker, Fred H, 1949, Jl 6,30:2
Parker, Fred W Sr, 1949, O 31,25:5
Parker, Frederick, 1907, Ag 18,7:5
Parker, Frederick E, 1940, Jl 26,17:5
Parker, Frederick J, 1960, F 6,19:5
Parker, Frederick L, 1951, Mr 27,29:1
Parker, Frederick L Mrs, 1952, N 20,31:4
Parker, Frederick S, 1916, S 10,17:4
Parker, G F, 1928, Je 1,25:3
Parker, G Sir, 1932, S 7,19:1
Parker, George, 1876, F 12,2:4; 1949, D 14,31:4
Parker, George A, 1939, Jl 4,13:3; 1948, Mr 31,25:4
Parker, George B, 1948, D 31,16:2
Parker, George B Jr, 1960, My 20,31:3
Parker, George B Mrs, 1949, Je 19,68:5
Parker, George B Sr (will, O 20,31:6),(por), 1949, O 11,31:1
Parker, George H, 1952, Mr 7,23:1; 1955, Mr 28,27:2
Parker, George I, 1937, O 12,25:4
Parker, George J, 1950, O 18,33:3
Parker, George L Mrs, 1942, N 26,27:2
Parker, George M Maj-Gen, 1968, O 25,47:2
Parker, George Mrs, 1948, O 30,15:2
Parker, George P, 1961, Mr 3,27:1
Parker, George R, 1961, Ag 19,27:5
Parker, George S (por), 1937, Jl 20,23:1
Parker, George S, 1952, S 27,17:1
Parker, George S Col, 1937, D 15,25:1
Parker, George W, 1961, My 7,87:1
Parker, George W Jr, 1947, Je 14,15:5
Parker, George Waller, 1957, Ja 12,19:3
Parker, George William Sr, 1957, D 29,48:8
Parker, Gilbert Lady, 1925, S 13,5:1
Parker, Gladys, 1966, Ap 28,43:2
Parker, Glenn J Lt, 1924, Jl 20,20:4
Parker, Grenville, 1924, Jl 19,9:5
Parker, Grenville Mrs, 1950, Ja 7,17:2
Parker, Gurdon S, 1941, Je 4,23:6
Parker, H D, 1884, Je 1,2:5
Parker, H Griffith Jr, 1941, S 28,49:2
Parker, H T, 1934, Mr 31,11:1
Parker, Harold, 1955, My 13,25:2
Parker, Harold A Mrs, 1951, Jl 4,17:2
Parker, Harold E, 1950, Mr 28,31:2
Parker, Harold G, 1949, O 1,13:2
Parker, Harold L, 1958, Mr 9,86:3
Parker, Harold M, 1952, Ag 24,89:1
Parker, Harriet Stratton Mrs, 1914, S 20,15:4
Parker, Harrison E, 1953, My 2,15:5
Parker, Harry Doel, 1921, Ap 20,13:6
Parker, Harry E, 1942, Ja 1,25:1; 1949, Ag 11,23:1
Parker, Harry J, 1940, Je 15,15:3; 1965, Ag 8,64:6
Parker, Harry N, 1953, N 6,27:2
Parker, Harry W, 1938, Mr 29,21:5
Parker, Harvey, 1941, Mr 4,23:2
Parker, Henry C Jr, 1947, F 14,21:4
Parker, Henry E Mrs, 1943, Ap 15,25:4
Parker, Henry G, 1949, Mr 31,25:2; 1953, Je 22,21:2
Parker, Henry Lewis, 1916, D 21,11:5
Parker, Henry M, 1937, O 6,25:4
Parker, Henry S, 1954, My 23,89:1
Parker, Henry W, 1938, F 1,21:5; 1940, Ag 2,15:6
Parker, Herbert, 1939, F 12,44:6
Parker, Herbert H, 1961, D 6,47:5
Parker, Herbert J, 1948, Mr 22,23:3
Parker, Herman, 1965, Je 19,29:6
Parker, Hiram H, 1959, Ap 3,31:3
Parker, Homer C, 1946, Je 23,40:3
Parker, Homer M, 1949, O 24,23:2
Parker, Horace E, 1922, Ap 12,21:5
Parker, Horatio, 1949, S 2,17:3
Parker, Horatio William, 1919, D 19,15:3
Parker, Hosea W, 1922, Ag 22,17:5
Parker, Howard, 1950, My 14,106:7
Parker, Howard Mrs, 1951, F 3,15:4
Parker, Ira Mrs, 1939, Ap 20,23:5
Parker, Irving A, 1952, Je 4,27:2
Parker, Irving E, 1963, N 29,37:4
Parker, Isaac, 1872, Je 30,1:2
Parker, Isaiah Mrs, 1942, Ja 30,19:5
Parker, Issac Thomas Gen, 1911, Mr 6,7:5
Parker, J, 1883, Ap 3,4:7; 1934, Je 3,30:1
Parker, J B, 1884, My 20,5:3
Parker, J Brooks B, 1951, D 1,13:4
Parker, J Col, 1880, Mr 1,5:6
Parker, J H, 1884, F 1,5:6
Parker, J Heber, 1956, D 30,32:8
Parker, J Rev, 1879, Mr 16,10:5
Parker, J Roy, 1957, My 9,31:1
Parker, J S, 1933, D 20,21:1
Parker, J T, 1883, Je 11,5:1
Parker, James, 1868, Ap 5,5:5; 1924, Ap 20,22:1; 1940, O 28,17:4; 1942, Ja 19,17:3; 1956, Jl 23,24:2
Parker, James A, 1958, Ag 6,25:2
Parker, James Ex-Lt-Com, 1914, Mr 24,9:4
Parker, James F, 1925, My 7,19:5
Parker, James H Dr, 1915, Ja 28,9:5
Parker, James H Mrs, 1947, D 23,23:1
Parker, James P, 1948, N 15,25:2
Parker, James W, 1957, D 31,17:3
Parker, James 2d, 1953, F 11,29:5
Parker, Jennie S Mrs, 1937, Mr 14,II,8:5
Parker, Joel, 1888, Ja 2,1:4
Parker, Joel Prof (funl), 1875, Ag 21,1:6
Parker, John, 1952, N 19,29:2
Parker, John A, 1946, Ja 7,19:2
Parker, John A Lt-Col, 1906, Ja 9,9:4
Parker, John C, 1904, F 22,5:6; 1938, S 1,23:6; 1946, O 12,19:6; 1953, Mr 24,42:2
Parker, John E, 1951, My 23,35:1
Parker, John F Mrs, 1940, Je 17,15:6
Parker, John G, 1910, S 29,11:5; 1959, F 26,31:2
Parker, John H, 1942, O 14,25:1; 1944, F 19,13:4
Parker, John Henry Rev, 1925, Je 30,19:5
Parker, John J, 1949, Ja 5,25:3; 1958, Mr 18,29:1
Parker, John M, 1960, O 27,37:2
Parker, John M Jr, 1942, Jl 22,19:2
Parker, John M Judge, 1873, D 17,1:6
Parker, John M Sr, 1939, My 21,III,6:1
Parker, John N, 1907, F 24,7:6
Parker, John N Capt, 1911, D 13,11:4
Parker, John S Mrs, 1952, F 19,29:2
Parker, John T, 1944, O 30,19:5
Parker, John Van C, 1925, Mr 16,19:3
Parker, John W, 1945, Ap 20,19:4; 1948, Jl 31,15:6
Parker, Joseph B Rear-Adm, 1915, O 22,11:5
Parker, Joseph Dr, 1902, N 29,9:5
Parker, Joseph G, 1953, Je 22,12:2
Parker, Joseph L, 1959, Ag 12,29:1
Parker, Joseph M, 1938, Ja 31,19:5
Parker, Joseph P, 1958, My 24,21:5
Parker, Joshua W, 1942, Jl 22,19:6
Parker, Junius, 1944, Je 12,19:3
Parker, Kathrene C Mrs, 1954, Ag 28,15:5
Parker, Kenneth S Mrs, 1950, Je 2,24:3
Parker, L Capt, 1879, Ag 3,1:6
Parker, Laigh C, 1959, D 24,19:3
Parker, Lansing A, 1965, O 27,47:5
Parker, Lawton S, 1954, S 28,29:5
Parker, Leon L, 1958, Ja 4,15:6
Parker, Levi, 1940, Je 28,19:4
Parker, Lewis C, 1947, Je 30,19:4
Parker, Lewis R, 1957, F 17,92:2
Parker, Lewis W, 1906, My 18,9:5
Parker, Lewis Wardlaw, 1916, Ap 12,13:5
Parker, Lillian F Mrs, 1950, S 8,31:2
Parker, Lindsay R, 1958, Ja 3,21:5
Parker, Lindsay Rev, 1915, Jl 19,9:4
Parker, Linus Bishop, 1885, Mr 7,5:2
Parker, Lionel Montrose, 1916, Ja 3,13:3
Parker, Lottie B Mrs (will, Mr 10,6:4), 1937, Ja 6, 23:1
Parker, Louis N, 1944, S 22,19:4
Parker, Lucilia Mary Sister, 1919, My 6,15:6
Parker, Mary S Mrs, 1938, My 3,23:1
Parker, Maude (Mrs E W Pavenstedt), 1959, N 13, 29:2
Parker, Maurice Mrs, 1960, Ag 13,15:6
Parker, Melville B, 1944, D 27,19:1
Parker, Mercy A Mrs, 1948, My 2,76:6
Parker, Murray N, 1947, Je 10,27:3
Parker, Myron, 1959, Ag 8,17:5
Parker, N Freeman, 1948, F 23,25:5
Parker, Nathaniel B H, 1939, N 25,17:2
Parker, Norman C, 1949, Jl 17,56:7
Parker, Otto D, 1942, S 4,23:4
Parker, Painless, 1952, N 9,89:3
Parker, Percy A, 1940, S 27,23:3
Parker, Peter J, 1908, Je 16,9:6
Parker, Phil M Mrs, 1951, N 30,23:2
Parker, Philip, 1964, D 8,45:1
Parker, Quanah, 1911, F 24,9:4
Parker, R, 1879, Mr 16,10:5
Parker, R J, 1949, S 10,1:2
Parker, R U Mrs, 1937, N 12,22:1
Parker, R W, 1953, N 15,89:3
Parker, Ralph (funl, My 29,29:5), 1964, My 26,39:2
Parker, Ralph A, 1956, Ap 26,33:2
Parker, Ralph R (por), 1949, S 5,17:3
Parker, Ransom, 1903, N 27,9:5; 1940, My 4,17:6
Parker, Raymond A, 1941, Ag 5,19:1
Parker, Raymond M Jr (por), 1948, Ja 10,15:5
Parker, Richard S, 1960, Ag 10,31:2
Parker, Richard Wayne, 1923, N 29,21:4; 1923, D 14 21:5
Parker, Robert, 1945, S 10,19:5
Parker, Robert Ashton, 1918, My 7,13:2
Parker, Robert B, 1937, N 15,23:3; 1940, Ag 4,33:3; 1955, Ap 30,17:5
Parker, Robert B Sr, 1958, O 1,37:3
Parker, Robert C, 1952, Ja 13,88:3
Parker, Robert H Mrs, 1967, Je 26,33:2
Parker, Robert M, 1942, Jl 15,9:4
Parker, Robert M (por), 1945, Ja 24,21:2
Parker, Robert S, 1941, Mr 29,15:5
Parker, Roderick D, 1939, F 26,38:5
Parker, Ross W, 1964, O 19,33:6
Parker, Roy D Mrs, 1949, Ap 7,29:2
Parker, Roy T, 1939, Ap 8,23:8
Parker, Rupert, 1944, Jl 14,13:6
Parker, Russel, 1942, My 4,19:4
Parker, Ruth E, 1961, Jl 15,19:5
Parker, S, 1879, Mr 16,10:5
Parker, Sam F, 1945, F 8,19:4
Parker, Samuel A, 1872, F 6,1:6
Parker, Samuel C, 1945, Ap 29,37:1
Parker, Samuel C Prof, 1924, Jl 23,15:3
Parker, Samuel Col, 1920, Mr 25,11:5
Parker, Samuel D, 1953, O 23,23:3
Parker, Samuel Mortimer, 1910, N 12,9:5
Parker, Samuel Mrs, 1949, O 14,27:3
Parker, Sarah, 1958, Ap 20,84:6
Parker, Seth, 1907, F 19,9:6
Parker, Sheldon W Jr, 1943, F 7,48:3
Parker, Stanley Vincent Vice-Adm, 1968, Jl 17,43:2
Parker, Stephen C, 1961, Ap 15,21:3
Parker, Stephen H, 1925, My 19,21:4
Parker, Stewart, 1948, Ja 20,23:4
Parker, Stuart, 1950, Ja 17,28:2
Parker, Sumner A, 1946, My 20,24:2
Parker, Susan M, 1945, S 14,23:4
Parker, Sylvester C Mrs, 1943, Ag 2,15:6
Parker, T A, 1878, S 26,5:6
Parker, T L, 1881, Ag 1,8:4
Parker, T Mrs, 1881, Ap 11,1:4
Parker, Terry, 1956, Ja 18,31:1
Parker, Theodore B, 1944, Ap 28,19:1
Parker, Theodore E, 1938, Ja 11,23:6
Parker, Theodore R Mrs (M Hathway), 1955, N 88:3
Parker, Theodore Rev (funl, My 31,1:6), 1860, My 29,4:5
Parker, Theodore S, 1907, D 17,9:5
Parker, Thomas, 1874, Ja 3,4:7
Parker, Thomas C, 1967, Ja 23,43:1
Parker, Thomas J, 1946, N 19,31:3
Parker, Thomas L, 1952, S 16,29:1
Parker, Valeria H, 1959, O 26,29:3
Parker, W A Capt, 1882, O 25,2:2
Parker, W Dr, 1884, Ap 26,5:1
Parker, W H, 1935, N 8,23:4
Parker, W Leonard, 1949, Ap 3,79:3
Parker, Wadsworth A, 1938, Mr 20,II,9:2
Parker, Walter, 1924, O 26,7:1; 1938, Ap 3,II,7:2
Parker, Walter C, 1957, N 17,87:2
Parker, Ward F Mrs, 1963, S 25,20:7
Parker, Warren W, 1938, S 18,44:8
Parker, Wesby R, 1967, Ja 11,25:3
Parker, Willard Dr, 1907, Je 26,7:5
Parker, Willard Mrs (por), 1949, Ap 7,29:3
Parker, William, 1909, O 1,9:4; 1967, Ap 27,33:4
Parker, William A, 1943, Je 4,21:4
Parker, William C, 1917, O 24,15:5
Parker, William H, 1908, Je 27,9:4; 1937, Ap 24,1 1945, Je 2,15:3
Parker, William H (funl plans, Jl 18,27:3), 1966, Jl 17,68:2
Parker, William J, 1912, Ag 27,9:4; 1949, My 24,
Parker, William J Jr, 1938, Ja 14,23:6
Parker, William M, 1943, Ag 6,15:5; 1962, Ja 2,2
Parker, William N, 1959, S 6,72:3
Parker, William Riley Prof, 1968, O 29,47:4
Parker, William S, 1964, Jl 28,29:2
Parker, William T, 1944, Jl 10,15:4; 1949, Ap 26, 1952, F 23,11:3
Parker, Winthrop, 1937, My 3,19:5
Parker-Smith, A, 1939, O 10,23:3
Parkerson, Godfrey P, 1959, Ja 17,19:5

Parkes, Alanson W Jr, 1968, Je 1,27:2
Parkes, Alfred H, 1959, Ja 30,27:4
Parkes, Fred, 1962, Je 24,69:1
Parkes, Harry J Jr, 1938, Mr 22,21:4
Parkes, Harry Sir, 1885, Mr 23,5:4
Parkes, Henry B Mrs (R L Munroe), 1963, O 16,45:3
Parkes, Henry Sir, 1896, Ap 27,2:3
Parkes, Joseph, 1865, S 6,3:1
Parkes, Joseph M Mrs, 1951, Ja 26,23:3
Parkhill, Robert Mrs, 1951, Ag 9,21:4
Parkhirst, Douglass, 1964, My 21,35:2
Parkhurst, C H, 1933, S 9,13:1
Parkhurst, Charles W, 1947, Jl 18,17:4
Parkhurst, Christopher Francis, 1925, Jl 2,19:6
Parkhurst, Edward S Mrs, 1956, Je 27,31:5
Parkhurst, Edwin H, 1951, Je 23,15:5
Parkhurst, Eliot G, 1941, My 2,21:2
Parkhurst, Frank E, 1944, Ap 1,13:6
Parkhurst, Fred W, 1941, My 15,23:4
Parkhurst, George H, 1946, Ja 28,19:5
Parkhurst, George W, 1959, D 5,23:3
Parkhurst, Helen H (mem ser, My 20,19:4), 1959, Ap 15,33:3
Parkhurst, Ida L S Mrs, 1942, Mr 10,19:4
Parkhurst, J C Maj-Gen, 1906, My 8,9:6
Parkhurst, John J, 1954, My 21,27:4
Parkhurst, John Prof, 1925, Mr 3,23:5
Parkhurst, John W, 1937, D 24,17:6
Parkhurst, Laurence H, 1944, Jl 29,13:5
Parkhurst, Lewis, 1949, Mr 29,25:1
Parkhurst, Samuel C R, 1955, F 16,29:1
Parkhurst, Theresa L Mrs, 1942, D 17,29:2
Parkhurst, Walter S, 1949, F 9,27:3
Parkin, Charles, 1904, My 28,9:6
Parkin, Frank P, 1941, F 22,15:4
Parkin, George Robert Sir, 1922, Je 26,13:7
Parkin, Harry D Sr, 1946, My 15,12:5
Parkin, Margaret P Mrs, 1942, Ag 4,19:3
Parkin, Norman C, 1963, D 26,28:4
Parkin, Victor, 1958, Mr 21,21:3
Parkin, William, 1943, D 25,13:2
Parkin, William J, 1965, Jl 21,37:3
Parkin, Zorador Mrs, 1951, D 23,22:7
Parkins, Almon E, 1940, Ja 4,23:5
Parkins, George V, 1948, D 29,21:4
Parkinson, David I (will, S 8,17:3), 1941, Ag 28,19:4
Parkinson, Donald B, 1945, N 19,21:4
Parkinson, Edgar G, 1957, O 29,31:4
Parkinson, Elizabeth, 1922, Je 12,15:6
Parkinson, Emma C Mrs, 1940, Mr 28,24:3
Parkinson, Frank, 1946, Ja 29,25:4
Parkinson, Frank J, 1960, Jl 6,33:1
Parkinson, Frank P, 1954, Mr 26,21:2
Parkinson, Frank P Mrs, 1952, My 1,29:6
Parkinson, Frederick W, 1938, F 25,17:2
Parkinson, George R, 1953, D 2,2:7
Parkinson, Hargraves, 1950, My 25,29:2
Parkinson, Herman O, 1957, O 21,25:4
Parkinson, James C, 1941, Ja 26,36:2
Parkinson, James J, 1948, S 16,29:4
Parkinson, John, 1953, Ap 13,27:6
Parkinson, John A, 1941, D 8,23:2
Parkinson, LeRoy, 1940, Ag 15,19:6
Parkinson, Martin J, 1961, S 28,41:5
Parkinson, Ralph A, 1949, D 13,31:3
Parkinson, Richard F, 1946, Ja 5,13:4
Parkinson, Robert A, 1953, Mr 21,17:2
Parkinson, Stirling B, 1937, Ag 21,15:1
Parkinson, Thomas I, 1959, Je 18,31:2
Parkinson, William, 1905, N 21,10:4
Parkinson, William D, 1948, Ap 11,72:5
Parkinson, William H Mrs, 1946, F 23,13:3
Parkinson, William W Mrs, 1951, S 29,17:3
Parkman, F, 1893, N 10,5:1
Parkman, Harrison, 1951, Jl 18,29:3
Parkman, Henry, 1924, Je 25,23:5
Parkman, Henry Jr, 1958, My 28,31:4
Parkman, Mary P Mrs, 1942, Jl 15,19:1
Parkman, Samuel S, 1921, Mr 11,15:4
Parks, Allen E, 1954, F 12,12:3
Parks, Arthur A Mrs, 1950, Jl 15,13:1
Parks, Bernard R, 1950, D 12,33:4
Parks, C E Sr, 1958, Mr 22,17:3
Parks, Carroll, 1947, Jl 1,25:3
Parks, Charles H Rev, 1907, Ap 2,11:5; 1907, Ap 4,9:7
Parks, Charles J Rev, 1922, O 16,15:4
Parks, Charles L, 1939, My 8,17:4
Parks, Charles Sr Mrs, 1945, F 14,19:5
Parks, Charles W Sr, 1946, Mr 16,13:5
Parks, Edward, 1951, Mr 15,39:4
Parks, Edward F, 1952, Ap 6,89:1
Parks, Elton, 1943, D 22,23:5
Parks, Eva T Mrs, 1967, Ja 9,36:6
Parks, Floyd L, 1959, Mr 11,35:1
Parks, Francis R, 1939, Ag 22,19:5
Parks, Fred H, 1959, D 23,27:4
Parks, Frederick H, 1906, My 26,2:5
Parks, Frederick W, 1944, D 23,13:3
Parks, George H, 1917, Jl 2,9:5
Parks, J Lewis Mrs, 1938, Mr 30,21:3
Parks, J Lewis Rev Dr, 1912, F 19,9:5
Parks, James A, 1945, O 20,11:3
Parks, James J, 1939, D 22,19:2
Parks, John H, 1903, S 10,7:6; 1953, Jl 20,17:5
Parks, Joseph, 1948, S 29,29:5
Parks, Joseph Mrs, 1942, Ja 18,42:1
Parks, Leighton (por),(will, My 4,24:5), 1938, Mr 22, 21:1
Parks, Lyman L, 1964, Mr 10,34:4
Parks, Lyman L Mrs, 1948, N 28,94:6
Parks, Mark E Dr, 1968, S 15,84:4
Parks, Oscar E, 1942, D 30,23:3
Parks, Oscar E Mrs, 1940, Mr 30,15:2
Parks, Richard E, 1956, Mr 12,27:6
Parks, Robert E, 1944, F 8,16:3
Parks, Robert L M, 1959, F 21,21:2
Parks, Robert O, 1963, My 18,27:5
Parks, Robin E, 1946, Jl 12,17:4
Parks, Roscoe W, 1954, O 24,89:1
Parks, Roscoe W Mrs, 1958, Mr 17,29:4
Parks, Tilman B, 1950, F 13,21:2
Parks, Uriah, 1946, N 8,23:1
Parks, Warren S, 1962, Ag 25,19:1
Parks, William, 1950, Ag 5,15:5
Parks, William E Mrs, 1945, Ap 12,23:2
Parks, Wythe M, 1938, S 19,19:2
Parkton, George D, 1953, N 8,89:2
Parkyakarkus (H Einstein), 1958, N 25,67:1
Parkyn, Alfred I, 1942, D 4,25:5
Parlante, Frank, 1950, Ag 5,15:4
Parlante, James, 1963, My 4,25:2
Parlapiano, Libero, 1949, N 14,27:5
Parlby, George, 1944, My 5,19:5
Parlby, Irene Mrs, 1965, Jl 15,29:5
Parle, Hugh A Mrs, 1938, Je 14,21:3
Parlee, W K C, 1949, D 22,23:5
Parlett, H George, 1945, Jl 1,17:2
Parlett, Sydney, 1943, Mr 4,19:4
Parliment, Jacob F, 1953, My 21,31:4
Parlin, Albert C, 1950, Ja 30,17:3
Parlin, Charles C, 1942, O 16,19:4
Parlin, Daisy B Mrs, 1942, N 14,15:5
Parlin, W D Mrs, 1913, Jl 10,7:3
Parlini, Alex C, 1960, Je 5,86:6
Parloa, Maria, 1909, Ag 23,7:5
Parlow, George H, 1957, My 20,25:5
Parlow, Kathleen M, 1963, Ag 20,33:3
Parma, Duchess of, 1959, My 16,23:3
Parma, Edward B, 1954, Ap 6,29:3
Parmalee, Alice M Mrs, 1940, S 30,17:4
Parmalee, S Rev, 1882, F 12,2:6
Parmele, Charles R, 1938, Ap 22,19:2
Parmele, Charles R Jr, 1954, F 2,27:2
Parmele, George H, 1951, D 29,11:3
Parmele, H G W (Gil), 1958, Ag 6,25:5
Parmele, Henry M, 1940, D 19,25:4
Parmele, Joseph L Mrs, 1952, Ag 27,27:2
Parmelee, A E, 1948, My 16,68:4
Parmelee, Arthur L, 1937, Ag 6,17:5
Parmelee, Arthur L Mrs, 1945, S 2,32:2
Parmelee, Arthur N, 1950, Jl 24,17:5
Parmelee, Charles A, 1943, Jl 17,13:5
Parmelee, Cullen W (por), 1947, Ag 23,13:3
Parmelee, Elmer S Mrs, 1957, Ja 4,23:1
Parmelee, Frank, 1904, O 2,7:6
Parmelee, H S, 1902, S 28,2:3
Parmelee, Harry E, 1938, Ag 2,19:5
Parmelee, Horace J, 1957, O 8,35:4
Parmelee, Howard, 1919, F 16,20:3
Parmelee, Howard C, 1959, N 18,41:5
Parmelee, Howard C Mrs, 1946, O 3,27:4
Parmelee, John B, 1914, Je 13,9:4
Parmelee, Lena E, 1941, Jl 25,15:4
Parmelee, Lewis D, 1952, O 21,29:1
Parmelee, Samuel B, 1903, N 28,9:4
Parmelee, Theodore N, 1874, Jl 6,2:3
Parmeley, R M, 1902, D 2,9:4
Parmenter, Bert M, 1945, F 18,34:2
Parmenter, Charles L, 1959, Ja 2,25:2
Parmenter, Christine W Mrs, 1953, Mr 5,27:5
Parmenter, Clarence R, 1943, N 16,23:5
Parmenter, Elmer E, 1958, F 9,88:2
Parmenter, F J, 1883, D 10,1:4
Parmenter, Frank S, 1948, My 30,34:8
Parmenter, George E, 1938, N 12,15:4
Parmenter, George F, 1955, O 23,87:2
Parmenter, George L, 1949, Ag 14,70:6
Parmenter, Henry J, 1904, F 2,9:6
Parmenter, James P Judge, 1937, Ja 15,21:2
Parmenter, Reginald H, 1939, Jl 24,13:6
Parmenter, William H, 1947, O 12,76:4
Parmer, Charles B, 1958, N 9,88:3
Parmer, Perry H, 1937, S 20,23:4
Parmer, Raymond, 1954, Mr 15,25:4
Parmer, Wayne R, 1964, N 10,47:4
Parmerter, Almon L, 1946, S 18,31:1
Parmerton, John H, 1961, D 2,23:2
Parmiter, Daniel N, 1949, O 25,27:3
Parmley, Joe, 1940, D 14,17:5
Parmley, Johial, 1923, D 27,13:2
Parmly, Charles Howard Prof, 1917, S 9,23:2
Parmly, Dalton, 1938, Ja 18,23:3
Parmly, George, 1947, O 21,24:3
Parmly, Jay F, 1949, Ja 23,68:4
Parmly, Randolph, 1925, Ag 18,19:6
Parmly, S W, 1880, D 16,2:7
Parmoor, Lady, 1952, Jl 7,21:5
Parnall, Christopher G (por), 1943, Jl 17,13:1
Parnell, C S, 1891, O 8,1:5
Parnell, Charles Stewart Mrs (Kitty O'Shea), 1921, F 6,22:3
Parnell, Delia T S, 1898, Mr 27,7:2
Parnell, Fannie (funl, Jl 25,5:6), 1882, Jl 21,8:4
Parnell, John H Mrs, 1947, Ap 13,60:4
Parnell, John Howard, 1923, My 4,17:2
Parnell, Reg, 1964, Ja 9,31:5
Parnell, Thomas F (F Russell), 1957, O 15,30:2
Parnes, Harry Mrs, 1951, O 29,23:4
Parnes, Ira, 1967, Ja 28,27:4
Parnes, Louis, 1961, D 1,33:3
Parnes, Nathan, 1964, O 16,39:1
Parnham, James (Rube), 1963, N 26,37:4
Parnis, Jerry, 1965, Je 9,47:4
Parocchi, Card, 1903, Ja 16,9:7
Parodi, Flaviano E, 1939, Ag 24,19:3
Parodi, Giacomo Prof, 1923, F 1,11:4
Parodi, Humbert D, 1953, Je 18,29:1
Parolin, Angelo, 1953, F 21,13:4
Parolin, Gilda, 1923, Ja 21,6:2
Parounagian, Mihran B (por), 1946, Je 15,21:6
Parower, Abraham, 1962, F 9,29:5
Parpacen, Ramon Dr, 1937, O 16,19:2
Parpart, Arthur K (Sept 17), 1965, O 11,61:4
Parpart, Edward G, 1937, N 23,23:5
Parpart, Edward G Mrs, 1947, D 23,23:4
Parpart, Louis F, 1941, N 2,53:3
Parpart, Max, 1905, Je 8,9:6
Parquette, Clara Mrs, 1907, F 12,9:6
Parr, Charles H, 1941, Je 12,24:2
Parr, Dorothy Mrs, 1961, Je 11,54:6
Parr, George H, 1945, Ja 11,23:3
Parr, George W, 1941, O 17,23:1
Parr, Gershom Mrs, 1949, O 12,29:1
Parr, Harry L, 1964, Je 8,29:1
Parr, James, 1941, My 3,15:4
Parr, John D, 1954, Mr 11,31:2
Parr, John R, 1947, Ja 25,17:5
Parr, Joseph G, 1952, Ag 22,21:5
Parr, Linden L, 1917, N 4,3:6
Parr, Olive K (B Chase), 1955, Jl 5,29:3
Parr, Ral, 1939, O 11,27:4
Parr, Richard, 1921, O 29,13:6
Parr, Susan L Mrs, 1940, Mr 5,23:5
Parr, William J, 1942, Jl 4,17:5
Parr-Davies, Harry, 1955, O 15,15:2
Parrado, Augustin, 1946, O 9,27:2
Parran, Thomas Dr, 1968, F 17,1:1
Parran, Thomas Mrs, 1961, D 3,88:1
Parrat, Walter Sir, 1924, Mr 28,17:3
Parratt, Spencer D Mrs, 1950, Ja 1,45:3
Parravano, Nicola, 1938, Ag 11,17:4
Parreiras, Ary, 1945, Jl 11,11:8
Parrent, R H, 1925, Ag 7,15:6
Parrett, Arthur N, 1956, D 28,21:4
Parri, Huw M, 1950, D 23,15:6
Parrill, Flora M Mrs, 1958, Ap 12,19:2
Parrinello, Salvatore, 1954, F 18,32:7
Parrington, C Arthur, 1960, O 23,88:4
Parrini, Primo, 1961, Ag 23,33:6
Parrino, Nicholas J Mrs, 1962, Ja 1,23:2
Parriott, Foster B, 1957, F 7,27:4
Parriott, Tynan A, 1959, Jl 31,24:2
Parris, Edward L, 1921, N 19,13:5
Parris, Morris, 1952, My 15,31:3
Parris, Morris B, 1939, Ja 8,43:1
Parris, Samuel, 1956, N 1,39:5
Parris, Tisdale, 1954, Ap 30,23:1
Parrish, Anne (Mrs J Titzell), 1957, S 7,19:3
Parrish, Anne (will), 1958, F 5,1:1
Parrish, Anne (Mrs J C Titzell),(est acctg approved), 1960, Ja 29,50:7
Parrish, Bradford, 1955, Je 28,20:1
Parrish, Carl, 1965, N 28,88:6
Parrish, Charles J, 1945, Jl 27,15:4
Parrish, Clara Weaver Mrs, 1925, N 14,15:5
Parrish, Donald B, 1957, Jl 30,23:3
Parrish, Frank B, 1954, Je 24,27:2
Parrish, Frank M (por), 1938, N 4,23:5
Parrish, George, 1941, Ag 8,15:5
Parrish, Harcourt, 1955, My 22,88:2
Parrish, Helen (Mrs J Guedel), 1959, F 23,23:1
Parrish, Helen L, 1942, S 29,23:1
Parrish, Henry, 1916, F 3,9:4
Parrish, Herbert, 1941, Ag 9,15:2
Parrish, Isaac N, 1963, N 18,33:5
Parrish, J Mrs, 1880, N 8,5:6
Parrish, J Scott Mrs, 1942, Jl 28,17:2
Parrish, James W, 1940, F 12,17:4
Parrish, Jean C Mrs, 1941, F 8,15:4
Parrish, Lucian W, 1922, Mr 28,17:4
Parrish, Lucien W, 1922, Mr 21,19:6
Parrish, Margaret S, 1937, N 13,19:6
Parrish, Maxfield, 1966, Mr 31,39:1
Parrish, Maxfield Mrs, 1953, Mr 31,31:2
Parrish, Morris L, 1944, Jl 11,15:2
Parrish, Paul L, 1953, Ja 31,15:1
Parrish, Percival, 1955, Ag 21,93:1
Parrish, Phil H, 1956, O 15,25:4
Parrish, Randall, 1923, Ag 10,11:3

Parrish, Rebecca, 1952, Ag 24,89:1
Parrish, Robert, 1952, Ap 23,29:5
Parrish, Robert C, 1938, F 2,19:2
Parrish, Samuel L Mrs, 1962, F 26,27:4
Parrish, Shreve, 1956, Mr 13,27:5
Parrish, Stephen, 1938, My 16,17:5
Parrish, Wilfred, 1952, Ag 26,25:2
Parrish, William J, 1938, O 18,25:4
Parrish, William N Sr, 1949, Ja 16,68:5
Parrock, Richard A, 1938, Ja 10,17:4
Parrot, R H Capt, 1877, D 25,4:6
Parrot, Raymond T, 1962, S 9,84:8
Parrott, Alfred F, 1942, N 13,23:5
Parrott, Arthur F, 1957, Ja 8,31:4
Parrott, Dale K, 1938, Ag 7,32:8
Parrott, E A, 1931, S 21,17:3
Parrott, Edward M, 1944, Ag 12,11:6
Parrott, Harry, 1941, O 8,23:2
Parrott, Henry T, 1961, O 6,35:1
Parrott, J R, 1913, O 14,13:5
Parrott, Louis C, 1950, Mr 28,31:4
Parrott, Marcus J, 1925, Ap 22,23:4
Parrott, Percival J, 1953, Ag 11,27:1
Parrott, Rear-Adm, 1879, My 11,7:5
Parrott, Robert, 1904, Ag 27,7:6
Parrott, Roger S, 1950, N 13,27:6
Parrott, Roger S Mrs, 1950, Ap 13,29:4
Parrott, Samuel A Sr, 1941, Ap 2,23:4
Parrott, Sidney H, 1954, Ag 13,15:5
Parrott, Sidney H Mrs, 1954, N 29,25:4
Parrott, Thomas M, 1960, F 6,19:4
Parrott, Thomas M Mrs, 1957, Mr 18,27:5
Parrott, Walter C Mrs, 1953, Ap 7,29:2
Parry, A Solvay, 1953, O 4,88:5
Parry, Angenette, 1939, Mr 3,23:3
Parry, Benjamin A, 1952, F 13,29:3
Parry, Cecil R, 1956, Ja 4,27:1
Parry, Charles Hubert Hastings, 1918, O 10,11:3
Parry, Charles K, 1951, Jl 25,23:3
Parry, Corliss L, 1946, Jl 2,25:2
Parry, David McLean, 1915, My 13,15:5
Parry, David W, 1922, Ja 15,22:3
Parry, Edward C, 1939, Mr 25,15:6
Parry, Eleanor (will, Je 22,21:5), 1943, My 24,15:6
Parry, Ellwood C, 1962, Jl 25,33:6
Parry, Elton E, 1949, My 3,25:2
Parry, Elton E Mrs, 1940, N 27,23:5
Parry, Frederic J, 1950, Mr 11,15:4
Parry, Frederick S, 1941, My 24,15:2
Parry, George G, 1959, Ja 27,33:4
Parry, George G Jr, 1960, Mr 17,33:5
Parry, George G Mrs, 1941, Jl 26,15:5
Parry, J H, 1880, Ja 11,4:7
Parry, James R Mrs, 1944, S 6,19:4
Parry, James W, 1949, Ag 25,23:4
Parry, John, 1956, Ag 28,27:2; 1961, Ag 15,25:4
Parry, John C Jr, 1961, N 7,33:5
Parry, John C Jr Mrs, 1950, S 18,23:3
Parry, John F Sir Vice Adm, 1926, Ap 23,21:3
Parry, Joseph, 1903, F 18,9:6; 1911, Ag 8,9:4
Parry, Lewis H, 1943, S 26,49:1
Parry, Lewis H Mrs, 1944, Ag 6,37:3
Parry, May, 1957, O 26,21:6
Parry, Oliver R Mrs, 1938, Ja 22,18:3
Parry, R R, 1928, D 28,23:5
Parry, Ruth, 1959, O 13,39:4
Parry, Samuel, 1948, F 29,60:3
Parry, Samuel R, 1946, F 14,25:4
Parry, Sidney L, 1968, N 12,47:2
Parry, Theodore J, 1948, Ja 5,19:1
Parry, W M, 1879, D 8,3:5
Parry, Ward S, 1949, Jl 19,29:2
Parry, Will H, 1917, Ap 22,21:2
Parry, William, 1949, O 3,17:5
Parry, William E, 1952, N 27,31:6
Parry, William H, 1957, My 4,21:4
Parry-Jones, Richard, 1944, Ag 5,11:7
Parse, Myrtle, 1954, O 20,29:4
Parseghian, Michael, 1968, Ap 5,47:2
Parsell, Adell L U Mrs, 1942, N 3,23:3
Parsell, Edward B, 1962, My 7,31:1
Parsell, H R, 1901, My 30,7:5
Parsell, Increase A, 1938, Je 17,21:6
Parselle, John, 1885, F 18,5:6
Parsells, Al, 1954, Jl 7,31:3
Parsells, S J, 1903, Mr 25,9:6
Parser, Godfried, 1962, D 6,43:2
Parseval, Aug von (por), 1942, F 24,21:3
Parshall, Boyd C, 1939, Ja 1,24:8
Parshall, De Witt, 1956, Jl 8,64:4
Parshall, De Witt Mrs, 1958, Je 15,76:5
Parshall, Ernest V, 1949, F 18,23:3
Parshall, George G, 1952, D 25,29:3
Parshall, H M, 1950, D 1,25:3
Parshall, William A, 1937, Jl 19,15:4
Parshelsky, Moses L, 1955, Mr 14,23:4
Parshley, Edward J, 1941, Ap 6,48:7
Parshley, Howard M, 1953, My 20,29:3
Parsil, Clifford E, 1959, O 2,29:2
Parsil, Edward R Mrs, 1954, F 2,27:5
Parsley, William E, 1961, Ap 6,33:4
Parsly, E Griffith Mrs, 1966, Mr 23,47:1
Parson, Charles W, 1948, Ja 6,23:2
Parson, Donald, 1961, D 30,19:2
Parson, Elizabeth D, 1925, Je 10,23:5
Parson, Harry, 1949, O 2,82:4
Parson, Hubert T Mrs, 1956, Ap 29,87:1
Parson, John E Mrs, 1922, O 16,15:4
Parson, John T, 1951, Ap 30,21:5
Parson, Mary P Mrs, 1942, Ja 28,19:2
Parson, Walter R, 1945, Ja 6,11:1
Parsonett, Marion, 1960, D 9,31:1
Parsonnet, Aaron, 1950, Ag 21,19:5
Parsonnet, Victor Mrs, 1949, N 20,95:1
Parsons, A R, 1933, Je 15,17:5
Parsons, Albert W, 1949, Mr 28,23:4
Parsons, Alfred, 1920, Ja 22,17:2
Parsons, Alfred H, 1953, My 4,23:4
Parsons, Alice B Mrs, 1962, Ap 15,80:6
Parsons, Anna H, 1948, Mr 31,25:5
Parsons, Archibald L, 1953, S 26,17:5
Parsons, Archibald L Mrs, 1946, Ja 27,42:2
Parsons, Archie J, 1958, My 17,19:1
Parsons, Argyll R, 1961, Mr 20,29:3
Parsons, Arthur, 1948, O 1,26:2
Parsons, Arthur C, 1942, Ja 11,46:1
Parsons, Arthur H Jr, 1959, S 2,29:3
Parsons, Arthur L, 1951, Jl 1,51:2; 1957, Ja 8,31:1
Parsons, Arthur L Mrs, 1940, Jl 19,19:7
Parsons, Benjamin F, 1949, Ja 5,25:1
Parsons, Bertha R, 1946, Mr 13,29:3
Parsons, Birney C, 1947, D 15,25:1
Parsons, Burton B, 1941, Ja 23,21:3
Parsons, C A Sir, 1931, F 13,17:1
Parsons, C B Rev, 1871, D 15,5:1
Parsons, C L, 1942, Ag 28,19:2
Parsons, Carl B, 1956, D 23,30:6
Parsons, Charles, 1873, Mr 28,8:2; 1904, O 20,7:4; 1952, Je 11,29:1
Parsons, Charles B Capt, 1916, D 24,15:2
Parsons, Charles B Mrs, 1955, Ap 18,23:5
Parsons, Charles E, 1941, Ja 1,23:5
Parsons, Charles L, 1954, F 15,23:4
Parsons, Charles R Mrs, 1937, O 9,19:6
Parsons, Charles Rev, 1952, Ja 8,27:5
Parsons, Charles W, 1945, Ap 14,15:2
Parsons, Charles Wesley Rev Dr, 1907, D 23,9:5
Parsons, Clara L Mrs, 1940, Jl 9,21:3
Parsons, Clark H, 1943, F 21,32:7
Parsons, Claude V, 1941, My 25,36:7
Parsons, Clifford, 1943, N 26,23:1
Parsons, Delos E, 1955, Ja 12,27:3
Parsons, Don A, 1940, N 22,23:3
Parsons, Don H, 1948, O 11,23:3
Parsons, Dwight L, 1948, Ja 21,25:2
Parsons, E G, 1876, Jl 11,4:7
Parsons, Eben Burt Rev Dr, 1913, Ja 25,15:6
Parsons, Edgerton P Mrs, 1954, Jl 20,19:1
Parsons, Edith B S Mrs, 1956, S 27,35:5
Parsons, Edith F, 1959, Ap 6,27:1
Parsons, Edward L, 1960, Jl 20,29:3
Parsons, Edward S, 1943, Ap 23,17:6
Parsons, Edwin, 1921, F 15,9:5
Parsons, Edwin Charles, 1968, My 4,39:1
Parsons, Eli B, 1945, N 22,35:4
Parsons, Elias W, 1942, D 1,25:2
Parsons, Elizabeth I, 1957, S 12,31:5
Parsons, Elsie C, 1941, D 20,19:1
Parsons, Elsie C Mrs (will), 1942, Ja 10,18:3
Parsons, Elsie D Mrs, 1939, Jl 29,15:3
Parsons, Eugene W, 1951, Ja 19,25:5
Parsons, Fay C, 1946, Ag 5,21:4
Parsons, Ferdinand H, 1949, O 20,29:5
Parsons, Floyd W (por), 1941, Ag 9,15:3
Parsons, Francis, 1938, Ja 1,19:3
Parsons, Francis M, 1954, My 25,27:1
Parsons, Francis Mrs, 1950, Ap 24,25:5
Parsons, Frank B, 1949, Je 22,31:4
Parsons, Frank H, 1937, O 14,25:2
Parsons, Frank H Mrs, 1960, O 5,41:4
Parsons, Frank Prof, 1908, S 27,11:6
Parsons, Frank T, 1951, My 9,33:3
Parsons, Frank T Jr, 1957, Mr 23,19:3
Parsons, Fred O, 1946, D 19,29:5
Parsons, Frederick W, 1957, Jl 6,16:3
Parsons, Geoffrey Mrs, 1963, S 25,43:1
Parsons, Geoffrey Sr, 1956, D 9,88:2
Parsons, George, 1907, D 5,9:4
Parsons, George B, 1939, Je 30,19:6
Parsons, George B Mrs, 1950, F 10,23:1
Parsons, George C, 1958, F 14,23:4
Parsons, George C S A, 1903, F 1,7:5
Parsons, George G, 1937, F 9,23:1
Parsons, George H Sr, 1948, Ja 6,23:5
Parsons, George K, 1956, S 25,33:5; 1961, D 31,48:4
Parsons, George S, 1939, D 9,15:6
Parsons, George W, 1944, Ja 6,23:2
Parsons, Harold A, 1957, Mr 4,27:5
Parsons, Harold A Mrs, 1941, Ja 5,44:3
Parsons, Harold H, 1943, Ap 10,17:5
Parsons, Harold W, 1967, My 29,25:1
Parsons, Harriet L, 1960, O 27,37:4
Parsons, Harris C, 1952, F 13,29:5
Parsons, Harry A Mrs, 1946, My 23,21:5
Parsons, Hasmer Buckingham, 1908, Ap 16,9:4
Parsons, Henry, 1921, My 28,9:6
Parsons, Henry C, 1964, S 2,37:3
Parsons, Herbert (por),(funl, S U9,15:4), 1925, S 17, 23:3
Parsons, Herbert, 1941, Je 20,21:2; 1949, F 28,19:3; 1959, Jl 21,29:1
Parsons, Herbert C, 1941, My 24,15:4
Parsons, Hial K Mrs, 1952, S 25,31:6
Parsons, Hubert T, 1940, Jl 10,19:1
Parsons, Irving P, 1952, Ja 21,16:5
Parsons, Isabelle P Mrs, 1939, D 8,25:1
Parsons, J Lester, 1957, S 21,20:1
Parsons, J Lester Mrs, 1937, S 27,21:2
Parsons, Jabez Martin, 1912, Ap 15,9:6
Parsons, Jacob Cox, 1904, Ap 17,7:5
Parsons, James A, 1945, Mr 5,19:5
Parsons, James B Mrs, 1967, Jl 24,27:3
Parsons, James K, 1960, N 10,47:2
Parsons, James M, 1937, D 17,25:4
Parsons, James R Mrs, 1952, Je 11,29:2
Parsons, James Russell Jr, 1905, D 6,1:2
Parsons, John E (funl, Ja 19,9:6), 1915, Ja 17,3:5
Parsons, John F (Dunbar), 1942, Jl 20,13:4
Parsons, John J, 1955, Mr 13,87:1
Parsons, John R, 1947, S 5,19:1
Parsons, John S, 1940, My 5,52:2
Parsons, John S Mrs, 1955, Mr 16,33:5
Parsons, Joseph E, 1950, Mr 26,92:4
Parsons, Joseph H, 1958, N 21,29:2
Parsons, Joseph M, 1947, D 24,21:2
Parsons, Julia S, 1946, Mr 8,21:1
Parsons, L, 1926, Ap 24,17:5
Parsons, Lawrence (Earl of Rosse), 1908, Ag 31,7:
Parsons, Leon, 1941, F 22,15:3
Parsons, Lester W, 1941, Ja 10,19:4
Parsons, Lewis B, 1907, Mr 18,7:4
Parsons, Lewis H, 1945, O 25,21:2
Parsons, Llewellyn B Dr, 1968, Mr 1,37:1
Parsons, Lloyd H, 1968, F 15,43:2
Parsons, Loren J, 1946, My 30,21:4
Parsons, Louisa, 1916, N 23,13:4
Parsons, Luther, 1955, Je 28,27:2
Parsons, Luther M, 1949, F 25,23:3
Parsons, M Douglas, 1951, O 2,27:2
Parsons, Mabel, 1964, Ja 20,43:2
Parsons, Margaret, 1945, Mr 11,39:1
Parsons, Marselis C, 1941, S 27,17:3
Parsons, Mary (will, F 21,40:1), 1940, F 7,21:4
Parsons, Mathilda C Mrs, 1937, Ap 11,II,8:6
Parsons, May H Mrs, 1937, Mr 30,23:2
Parsons, Newell B, 1942, Jl 18,13:3
Parsons, P Allen, 1963, N 9,25:4
Parsons, P B, 1931, S 20,II,6:3
Parsons, Ralph Lyman Dr, 1914, F 27,11:3
Parsons, Raymond A, 1951, F 24,13:2
Parsons, Reginald H, 1955, Je 16,31:4
Parsons, Richard C, 1923, Ja 27,13:4
Parsons, Richard G, 1948, D 28,22:2
Parsons, Robert G, 1951, Ag 26,52:4
Parsons, Robert J, 1953, S 16,33:2
Parsons, Robert L, 1961, N 2,37:1
Parsons, Rolla C, 1965, D 11,33:4
Parsons, Russell D, 1948, Ap 15,25:2
Parsons, Russell D Mrs, 1950, N 2,31:3
Parsons, Samuel Brown Sr, 1906, Ja 5,11:3
Parsons, Sara E, 1949, O 26,27:1
Parsons, Schuyler L, 1967, N 23,33:3
Parsons, Schuyler Livingston, 1917, N 5,15:6
Parsons, Sheldon, 1943, S 26,49:2
Parsons, Sydney A, 1950, S 28,31:1
Parsons, T Brian, 1953, Jl 9,25:3
Parsons, Tatem, 1909, N 6,9:4
Parsons, Theophilus, 1882, Ja 27,5:4; 1952, My 15
Parsons, Theron E Col, 1912, Ja 3,13:4
Parsons, Thomas, 1873, F 11,1:6
Parsons, Thomas C, 1955, Ap 27,31:4
Parsons, Thomas W, 1944, D 22,17:3
Parsons, Truman N, 1942, N 14,15:6
Parsons, Usher Dr, 1868, D 20,5:4
Parsons, W B, 1932, My 10,21:3
Parsons, W D, 1865, N 15,5:2
Parsons, W Eugene Mrs, 1948, F 6,26:5
Parsons, W Everett Sr, 1940, N 1,25:3
Parsons, Walter B, 1950, My 3,29:2
Parsons, Walter B Mrs, 1957, F 5,23:2
Parsons, Wilfrid, 1958, O 29,35:4
Parsons, Willard Rev, 1907, S 29,9:4
Parsons, William, 1942, F 14,17:2
Parsons, William B, 1959, D 14,31:3
Parsons, William B Mrs, 1946, O 7,31:4; 1958, Ag 86:4
Parsons, William Barclay Mrs, 1922, N 5,5:2
Parsons, William E, 1939, D 18,23:2; 1952, D 13,
Parsons, William Edward (Earl of Rosse), 1918, Je 11,11:5
Parsons, William G, 1951, Jl 24,26:3
Parsons, William H, 1905, F 19,7:5; 1941, S 17,23 1943, O 24,44:3
Parsons, William S, 1953, D 6,2:8
Part, William Rev, 1925, Je 6,15:6
Partanen, John, 1942, Ag 14,17:2
Partch, Clarence E Mrs, 1947, Ja 21,23:3
Partelow, Alanson L, 1945, Ja 12,15:4
Partenheimer, Sarah C (will), 1956, N 18,19:1

Partgridge, Warren Jr, 1960, N 2,39:4
Parthasarathi, Gopalaswami Mrs, 1966, O 11,47:2
Parthynos, Andrew S, 1964, N 16,31:5
Partington, B!anche, 1951, Mr 16,31:3
Partington, John A, 1944, Ja 26,19:4
Partisano, Carl S, 1956, Mr 16,23:2
Partisch, Walter O, 1959, Mr 25,35:4
Partlan, Charles H, 1949, Mr 5,18:2
Partlan, Frank J, 1939, Je 18,37:3
Partlow, Ira J, 1952, Je 12,33:5
Partlow, Raymond A, 1956, S 3,13:2
Parton, A Taylor Mrs, 1955, Ap 24,86:4
Parton, Arthur, 1914, Mr 8,15:5
Parton, Charles H, 1966, O 12,43:4
Parton, Ethel, 1944, F 28,17:5
Parton, George F Sr, 1963, Ag 3,17:6
Parton, Hugo, 1955, Ag 9,25:1
Parton, J, 1891, O 18,5:4
Parton, James, 1941, My 10,15:4
Parton, James Mrs, 1962, S 30,87:2
Parton, Lemuel F (por), 1943, Ja 31,44:3
Parton, Mrs (Fanny Fern), 1872, O 13,5:3
Partrick, Walter A, 1961, D 23,23:2
Partridge, A H Rev, 1883, Ap 9,5:5
Partridge, Adam, 1915, My 25,15:5
Partridge, Albert G, 1952, Mr 14,20:6
Partridge, Arthur, 1953, F 11,29:4
Partridge, Bellamy, 1960, Jl 6,33:4
Partridge, Bernard (por), 1945, Ag 11,13:5
Partridge, Charles, 1885, Ja 25,7:5; 1955, O 21,27:5
Partridge, Charles Mrs, 1951, My 6,92:1
Partridge, Clark B, 1950, O 14,19:3
Partridge, Claude A, 1958, Ap 10,29:3
Partridge, Edmund R, 1949, N 23,29:2
Partridge, Edward L Dr, 1907, S 8,7:5
Partridge, Ernest C, 1955, My 7,17:4
Partridge, Frank C (por), 1943, Mr 3,23:4
Partridge, Frank E, 1952, Ja 6,93:1
Partridge, Fred F, 1947, D 2,29:1
Partridge, George F, 1940, Mr 17,48:6
Partridge, George S, 1875, My 25,6:7
Partridge, George T, 1949, Ag 29,17:3
Partridge, Harold R, 1961, O 31,31:2
Partridge, Harry C, 1949, Ag 29,17:4
Partridge, Harry T, 1948, Ap 25,70:3
Partridge, Harvey W, 1937, Ap 19,21:2
Partridge, Henry S, 1947, O 14,27:2
Partridge, Herman M (por), 1945, S 18,23:4
Partridge, John B Mrs, 1944, Ja 6,23:1
Partridge, John H, 1923, N 7,17:6
Partridge, John Nelson Col, 1920, Ap 9,13:4
Partridge, Lewis A, 1949, Mr 26,17:1
Partridge, Mary M, 1946, My 22,21:2
Partridge, N A, 1944, S 14,23:4
Partridge, Paul, 1956, Jl 15,60:5
Partridge, Prof, 1873, Ap 12,5:4
Partridge, Roland E, 1960, Ja 14,33:5
Partridge, Samuel S Sr, 1961, Ag 25,25:4
Partridge, Suzzanne Mrs, 1941, Ag 24,35:2
Partridge, W O, 1930, My 24,17:3
Partridge, Walter F, 1941, Je 20,21:5
Partridge, William Eugene, 1917, N 22,13:5
Partridge, William M, 1944, N 16,23:5
Partridge, William O Mrs, 1963, D 28,23:3
Partrige, Frank, 1941, O 2,25:6
Partyka, Arthur J, 1956, O 27,21:3
Parville, Pandefer de, 1909, Jl 12,7:7
Parvin, Emerson E, 1939, Ap 1,19:5
Parvin, Mary Ives, 1968, Mr 12,43:2
Parvin, T S, 1901, Je 29,5:3
Parvin, W Rodman, 1962, F 24,27:3
Parvin, Walter R, 1945, Jl 29,40:5
Parvis, Grover C, 1943, My 5,27:4
Parvis, J William, 1950, Ag 21,19:2
Parysko, Jacques, 1954, F 2,14:7
Paryz, Walter J Jr, 1957, My 17,25:4
Parziale, Alfonso, 1967, Mr 4,27:1
Parzini, Michael, 1946, D 5,31:3
Parzini, Michael Mrs, 1960, D 21,31:1
Pasachoff, Harry D, 1962, S 21,29:1
Pasbach, Oscar, 1938, Mr 23,23:4
Pasca, Alex Marie Adelaide, 1914, My 26,11:5
Pascal, Anthony A, 1956, My 25,23:2
Pascal, Emil Mrs, 1940, O 27,45:1
Pascal, Ernest Mrs, 1939, N 17,21:1
Pascal, F M, 1882, Ja 6,5:2
Pascal, Frank L, 1938, My 30,11:4
Pascal, Gabriel, 1954, Jl 7,31:1
Pascal, Joseph I, 1955, Ap 23,19:3
Pascal, Joseph L, 1966, F 11,33:1
Pascal, Katherine M, 1956, F 10,21:2
Pascal, Nathaniel, 1866, D 13,4:7
Pascale, Vincenzo, 1960, Je 2,33:2
Pascall, George C, 1956, My 20,86:7
Pascall, Geovanni, 1912, Ap 7,15:3
Pascall, Sydney W, 1949, Ag 7,61:1
Pascarella, Cesare, 1940, My 10,23:4
Pascarella, Theresa C Mrs, 1940, Je 8,15:5
Pascaud, Louis Sr, 1948, Jl 20,23:2
Paschal, Boykin, 1955, Ag 13,13:2
Paschall, Alfred, 1954, O 10,87:1
Paschall, John, 1953, My 9,19:3
Paschall, Nathaniel, 1937, Mr 11,23:1
Pasche, Charles W, 1939, N 16,23:4
Paschel, Phil P, 1949, O 5,29:3
Paschen, Christian P, 1954, D 31,13:3
Pascher, Samuel Mrs, 1965, F 6,25:5
Paschkes, Otto, 1955, O 26,31:4
Paschkis, Karl E, 1961, Ja 28,19:6
Paschkis, Rudolf, 1964, F 5,35:4
Pasco, Delbert E, 1948, N 11,27:4
Pasco, Franklin E, 1951, Ag 11,11:6
Pasco, George H, 1947, N 29,13:3
Pasco, Samuel, 1917, Mr 14,9:4
Pasco, Wyman D, 1959, Ap 4,19:4
Pascoe, Charles Edgar, 1912, N 24,II,17:4
Pascoe, Charles H, 1949, O 31,25:2
Pascoe, Fred W, 1949, Mr 12,17:2
Pascoe, George H Mrs, 1952, Je 19,27:2
Pascoe, Harry W, 1965, Ag 22,82:8
Pascoe, Herbert J, 1953, D 20,20:3
Pascoe, Herbert J Mrs, 1946, Mr 24,46:5
Pascoe, James B, 1939, Ap 18,23:4
Pascoe, Robert J Mrs, 1951, Ag 1,23:6
Pascoe, Robert L, 1951, O 18,29:5
Pascolini, Etelvoldo, 1956, Je 4,29:4
Pascover, Max, 1951, D 31,13:3
Pascu, Lazard, 1915, O 30,13:7
Pascual, William, 1944, S 27,21:7
Pascual Pinard, Carlos, 1955, My 12,29:2
Pascucci, Eugene A, 1954, D 1,31:3
Pascucci, Giovanni, 1952, Ag 24,88:3
Pasdeloup, Frank L, 1938, Ja 16,II,9:2
Pasdermadjian, Garo Dr, 1923, Mr 31,13:5
Paseltiner, Joseph P, 1945, Mr 16,15:3
Paseltiner, Solomon, 1959, O 11,86:7
Paseman, Gustave G, 1950, D 28,25:2
Pasetti, Frederick A, 1952, Ap 5,15:4
Pasetti, Leo, 1937, F 14,X,7:5
Pasha, Bucknam, 1915, My 30,13:5
Pasha, C K, 1948, Jl 14,23:4
Pasha, Djemil Mehemed, 1872, S 25,1:7
Pasha, Ibraham Fathy Gen, 1925, Ja 19,17:3
Pasha, Kiamil, 1913, N 16,IV,7:5
Pasha, Mustapha Kiritli, 1872, Ja 24,2:6
Pasha, Said, 1914, Mr 2,9:4
Pasha, Saleh Y, 1940, N 28,23:6
Pasha, Vehib, 1940, Je 15,15:6
Pasha, Z, 1927, Ag 24,23:5
Pasha Ali Kibrasli, Grand Vizier, 1871, S 7,1:4
Pashang, Adolph J, 1968, F 3,29:4
Pashayan, Nishan A, 1949, O 30,87:3
Pashby, Albert A, 1951, Ja 13,15:6
Pashcow, Leon, 1959, My 1,29:2
Pashek, Albert L, 1948, O 27,27:4
Pashitch, N P, 1926, D 11,17:1
Pashko, Josief, 1963, S 7,19:4
Pashley, George F Mrs, 1943, Ag 22,36:6
Pashley, George M, 1937, D 26,II,7:2
Pasholk, Anton, 1953, Ag 11,27:6
Pasinetti, Francesco, 1949, Ap 4,23:2
Pasini, Tina, 1944, Jl 24,15:5
Pasinsky, David, 1943, Mr 17,21:4
Pask, George T, 1940, N 7,25:3
Paskett, Harold R, 1942, Ja 23,19:1
Paskett, Robert D, 1942, Mr 22,48:5
Paskind, Harry A, 1942, Mr 26,23:4
Paskow, Larry J Mrs, 1963, N 10,86:4
Paskow, Samuel H, 1963, S 24,39:3
Paskus, Benjamin G, 1951, Ja 31,25:4
Paskus, Benjamin G Mrs, 1950, Mr 9,30:5
Paskus, Gasa, 1953, N 18,31:2
Pasley, Robert S, 1940, My 24,19:4
Pasley, Wynyard Mrs, 1956, S 5,27:5
Pasmantier, John L, 1955, Ja 24,23:2
Pasmore, Henry B, 1944, F 25,17:5
Pasner, Joseph M, 1945, Ja 11,23:4
Pasquale, Carmen H Mrs, 1954, Mr 25,29:4
Pasquall, Mario Lt, 1919, Mr 17,15:3
Pasquarelli, Blase, 1961, Je 15,43:1
Pasquarelli, Jerome E, 1953, S 2,25:3
Pasquel, Jorge, 1955, Mr 9,56:2
Pasquier, Charles, 1953, N 21,13:5
Pasquier, Paul, 1963, O 14,29:5
Pasquini, Guiseppe, 1923, Ag 17,13:3
Pasquini, Mario, 1966, S 19,43:2
Pass, Herman L, 1938, Ja 19,23:5
Pass, Joseph, 1950, N 6,27:5
Pass, Morris Mrs, 1962, O 13,25:4
Pass, Richard H, 1964, My 15,35:2
Passage, Albert J Mrs, 1950, Ja 7,17:4; 1953, F 21,13:5
Passalidis, Ioannis, 1968, Mr 16,31:2
Passanante, Anthony J, 1960, D 4,88:7
Passannante, Charles A, 1956, Mr 24,19:5
Passannante, Charles Mrs, 1955, Ap 19,31:3
Passano, Edward B, 1946, Je 15,21:2
Passano, L Magruder, 1943, F 1,15:1
Passant, Gerard J, 1957, N 5,31:4
Passavant, Henry E Mrs, 1944, My 25,21:4
Passerini, Angelo, 1940, Ja 11,23:4
Passet, Camillo, 1959, Ap 26,86:7
Passetti, David, 1957, S 1,56:8
Passeur, Steve, 1966, O 14,40:3
Passfield, Lord, 1947, O 14,27:1
Passino, Fred J, 1950, Mr 23,36:2
Passloff, Robert, 1952, Ja 28,17:4
Passmore, Deborah C, 1937, My 13,25:3
Passmore, Ellen F F Mrs, 1939, Mr 4,15:1
Passmore, Frank T Mrs, 1951, F 15,31:2
Passmore, George S, 1939, O 28,23:1
Passmore, Horace B, 1958, Ap 19,21:3
Passmore, John H, 1947, Ag 29,17:1
Passmore, L Alan, 1959, O 9,29:3
Passmore, Ray, 1959, N 21,23:5
Passmore, Roy H, 1964, Je 22,27:4
Passmore, Roy H Mrs, 1964, My 20,43:4
Passmore, Walter, 1946, Ag 30,17:2
Passos, Gabriel, 1962, Je 20,35:2
Passow, Frederick M Capt, 1918, Ag 2,11:6
Passow, L Arthur, 1947, F 6,23:2
Passweg, Ben, 1965, N 12,47:3
Passweg, Solomon Mrs, 1960, D 18,84:1
Passy, Frederic, 1912, Je 13,11:6
Passy, H P, 1880, Je 3,5:2
Passy, Louis Charles Paulin, 1913, Ag 1,7:6
Pastau, Carl, 1949, Je 10,27:4
Pasteelnick, Michael, 1961, Mr 26,92:8
Pasternack, Aaron B, 1951, Ap 5,29:4
Pasternack, Ida P, 1941, Ag 12,19:1
Pasternack, Josef A, 1940, Ap 30,21:1
Pasternak, Boris (funl plans, Je 1,16:4; funl, Je 3,10:5), 1960, My 31,1:7
Pasternak, Boris L Mrs, 1966, Je 29,47:2
Pasternak, Julian, 1952, My 15,31:3
Pasternak, Leonid, 1945, Je 6,21:3
Pasteur, Louis, 1895, S 29,1:7
Pastille, John J, 1949, Ag 25,23:4
Paston, Simon, 1953, Ja 24,15:5
Pastor, Antonio (funl, Ag 29,9:4), 1908, Ag 27,7:1
Pastor, Charles, 1867, O 7,1:4
Pastor, Charles J, 1943, D 18,15:5
Pastor, Luis, 1921, Ap 13,15:6
Pastor, Tony (est), 1910, O 7,11:4
Pastor, W (Billy) (see also O 24), 1877, O 26,8:4
Pastore, Arthur Mrs, 1965, O 17,87:1
Pastore, John B, 1951, Ag 20,19:3
Pastore, Umberto M, 1958, Mr 4,29:2
Pastorelle, Dominic J, 1967, O 24,47:3
Pastori, Onofrio, 1960, Mr 31,33:2
Pastorius, Daniel B Mrs, 1958, F 11,31:4
Pastorius, Francis D, 1962, Ap 12,35:3
Pastorius, James W, 1941, My 11,45:1
Pastre, Gaston, 1939, O 19,24:2
Pasvolsky, Leo, 1953, My 7,31:1
Paszthory, Arpad de, 1946, Ap 4,25:5
Pat, Jacob, 1966, Ap 27,47:2
Patai, Imre F, 1949, Ja 21,21:3
Patai, Joseph, 1953, F 25,27:2
Patane, Franco (cor, My 16,47:1), 1968, My 15,47:2
Patania, Giovana B G, 1871, Ap 20,5:6
Pataudi, Nawab of, 1952, Ja 6,94:2
Patch, Alexander M, 1946, F 13,23:3
Patch, Alexander M Jr, 1945, N 22,1:2
Patch, Bradford C, 1961, Mr 14,35:2
Patch, Clyde L, 1952, F 12,27:4
Patch, Don I, 1953, Je 6,17:5
Patch, Elias H Jr, 1960, My 6,31:3
Patch, George M Mrs, 1944, D 4,23:4
Patch, Helen E, 1959, Ja 19,27:4
Patch, Isaac P, 1938, Ap 18,15:5
Patch, Olive P, 1946, Mr 30,15:2
Patch, Ralph S, 1939, Jl 23,29:2
Patch, Richard H, 1954, N 15,27:2
Patch, Roland H, 1957, Ap 10,33:1
Patch, Walter E, 1950, Je 2,23:3
Patchen, Aaron D, 1864, Ag 1,8:5
Patchin, Frank G, 1925, Mr 24,23:4
Patchin, Lillian M, 1949, Ag 28,72:6
Patchin, Phil H, 1954, N 30,29:5
Patchin, Philip H Mrs, 1963, Ag 30,21:3
Patchin, Robert H, 1955, Jl 2,15:4
Patchin, Robert H Mrs, 1957, Jl 9,29:5
Pate, Carl R, 1953, S 15,31:4
Pate, Carlton O Sr, 1953, S 3,21:2
Pate, Charles L, 1942, D 20,44:5
Pate, Henry, 1942, S 26,15:6
Pate, Joe, 1948, D 27,21:4
Pate, Louis B, 1965, S 4,21:4
Pate, Maurice (funl, Ja 23,25:3), 1965, Ja 20,39:1
Pate, Randolph McC (funl, Ag 4,21:5), 1961, Ag 2, 29:4
Pate, Richard E Mrs, 1956, F 4,19:1
Pate, Vernon S, 1958, N 22,88:7
Pate, Walter L, 1946, Je 17,23:7
Pate, Walter L Mrs, 1940, My 5,53:2
Pate, Walter R, 1952, O 20,23:2
Pate, William S, 1939, Ap 29,17:4
Patel, Sadar V, 1950, D 15,31:1
Patel, V J, 1933, O 23,15:6
Patella, Louis, 1953, Jl 27,19:5
Patelski, Ray A, 1951, S 8,17:6
Pateman, Everett E, 1941, Je 25,21:6
Pateman, Robert, 1924, Je 9,17:6
Pateman, William A, 1962, Ja 3,33:4
Paten, Marion D, 1953, Ap 18,19:6
Patenaude, Esioff L Mrs, 1940, Je 25,23:3
Patenotre, Jules, 1925, D 28,15:2
Patenotre, Raymond, 1951, Je 20,27:2
Pater, B J, 1955, Mr 22,31:3

Pateracki, John, 1948, D 28,21:5
Paterno, Angelo, 1963, N 10,86:2
Paterno, Angelo L, 1955, O 1,19:4
Paterno, Angelo Mrs, 1963, N 10,86:2
Paterno, Anthony, 1959, D 21,27:3
Paterno, Anthony A Mrs, 1957, D 30,23:4
Paterno, Charles V, 1946, My 31,23:1
Paterno, Charles V Mrs, 1943, Mr 29,15:3
Paterno, Francis S Mrs, 1914, Je 28,15:4
Paterno, John Mrs, 1925, Ap 17,21:4
Paterno, Joseph (por), 1939, Je 14,23:1
Paterno, Michael E, 1946, Jl 15,25:4
Paterno, Vincent Mrs, 1952, F 25,21:5
Paterson, Albert B, 1952, Ag 7,21:5
Paterson, Albert E, 1944, N 26,58:3
Paterson, Albert G, 1952, F 14,27:3
Paterson, Alex H, 1941, F 5,19:4
Paterson, Alexander, 1947, Ap 15,25:2
Paterson, Alexander (por), 1947, N 9,72:3
Paterson, Alexander M, 1967, Je 10,33:2
Paterson, Andrew, 1950, Jl 27,25:5
Paterson, Banjo, 1941, F 6,21:5
Paterson, Cecelia J, 1942, Ap 15,21:3
Paterson, Charles D, 1943, O 21,27:5
Paterson, David A, 1965, D 13,39:2
Paterson, Douglas C, 1952, F 27,27:2
Paterson, George C, 1945, N 30,23:4
Paterson, Harrie C, 1944, N 10,19:1
Paterson, Isabel B, 1961, Ja 11,47:2
Paterson, James A, 1947, Mr 25,25:3
Paterson, Lester B, 1957, Jl 25,23:4
Paterson, Murray G, 1945, Jl 3,13:6
Paterson, R K, 1952, Mr 2,92:2
Paterson, Robert, 1948, Ap 1,25:1
Paterson, Robert W, 1957, O 31,31:2
Paterson, Robert Warden, 1917, O 24,15:5
Paterson, Stuart, 1952, Ag 30,13:6
Paterson, Thomas M, 1937, Ap 11,II,9:2
Paterson, William, 1914, Mr 19,9:6
Paterson, William Lt -Col, 1924, Mr 6,17:4
Paterson, Wilmot M, 1941, Jl 13,28:7
Paterson-Smyth, Charles, 1941, Ja 1,23:4
Pates, Frederick B, 1939, D 6,25:4
Patey, C J Adm, 1881, Mr 30,5:8
Patey, John J Rev, 1909, Ja 18,9:6
Pathe, Charles, 1957, D 27,19:1
Pathe, Emile, 1937, Ap 7,25:4
Patiala, Maharajah of (por), 1938, Mr 24,23:1
Patience Denis, Bro (por), 1948, Mr 20,13:6
Patigian, Haig, 1950, S 20,31:2
Patin, J G (see also F 20), 1876, Mr 11,1:5
Patin, Jacques, 1948, Ap 20,27:5
Patinggi, Datu, 1946, N 24,79:6
Patino, Jaime O Mrs, 1957, Jl 3,23:4
Patino, Simon I, 1947, Ap 21,27:3
Patino, Simon I Mrs, 1953, Mr 29,92:2
Patitz, Gerhardt J, 1954, Ag 10,19:4
Patitz, Gerhardt J Mrs, 1950, S 13,27:5
Patitz, J P M, 1937, Ja 4,7:6
Patitz, Martha, 1937, Ja 4,7:6
Patla, Abraham Rabbi, 1925, N 10,25:5
Patman, Bruce, 1958, Ap 21,23:5
Patman, Wright Mrs, 1967, Jl 3,17:5
Patmor, John B, 1953, Ap 16,29:3
Patmore, Amy F, 1956, Mr 19,31:2
Patmos, Krine, 1944, D 7,25:1
Paton, Alan Mrs, 1967, O 24,47:1
Paton, Charles, 1952, Jl 29,21:5
Paton, Daniel, 1947, F 24,37:2
Paton, E L, 1946, F 19,25:5
Paton, Eugene, 1953, Ag 14,19:5
Paton, Fred H, 1946, Ap 28,15:1
Paton, Hugh, 1941, Ja 29,17:2
Paton, James M, 1944, N 24,23:5
Paton, John G, 1939, D 7,27:2
Paton, John G Mrs, 1956, My 25,23:1
Paton, John H, 1967, Je 29,43:4
Paton, Lucy A, 1951, My 28,21:5
Paton, Margaret Mrs, 1937, O 17,II,9:2
Paton, Noel Sir, 1901, D 27,7:3
Paton, R W, 1940, D 2,23:4
Paton, Stewart, 1942, Ja 8,22:2
Paton, Stuart, 1944, D 18,19:1; 1961, Ap 1,17:3
Paton, T B, 1933, Mr 29,15:1
Paton, Thomas, 1874, Je 21,6:6
Paton, Thomas L, 1947, O 8,25:5
Paton, William, 1940, My 17,19:3; 1943, Ag 23,15:6; 1943, N 6,14:8
Paton, William Agnew, 1918, D 12,15:4
Paton, William F, 1948, Ap 5,21:5
Paton, William K, 1959, Ag 27,27:3
Paton, William T, 1946, Ap 17,25:5
Patorious, Henry C, 1951, Je 27,29:3
Patorzhinsky, Ivan, 1960, F 24,37:1
Patou, J, 1936, Mr 9,17:1
Patrey, Harry B, 1961, Ap 12,41:5
Patri, Angelo, 1965, S 14,39:1
Patri, Angelo Mrs, 1961, O 22,86:5
Patriarca, Joseph, 1950, Je 6,29:5
Patriarch of the East Indies, 1874, My 11,1:7
Patricia Mary, Sister, 1945, Ap 25,23:1
Patrick, Al, 1903, F 10,1:6
Patrick, Al (sister of), 1903, F 10,1:6
Patrick, Albert T, 1940, F 12,10:4
Patrick, Albert T Mrs, 1913, D 20,13:6
Patrick, Asa, 1955, O 11,39:5
Patrick, Benjamin H, 1945, Ja 2,19:2
Patrick, Bower R Mrs, 1948, S 30,27:5
Patrick, Bro, 1941, Ag 22,15:6
Patrick, Bro (Jos E Brown), 1953, F 27,6:6
Patrick, Bro (J Craven), 1955, O 16,86:1
Patrick, Casimir C, 1953, Ja 19,23:4
Patrick, Casimir C Mrs, 1941, O 30,23:3
Patrick, Charles F, 1947, Mr 26,25:2
Patrick, Dominick J, 1964, Ja 27,23:4
Patrick, Father, 1925, Mr 23,17:5
Patrick, Frank, 1960, Je 30,29:4
Patrick, Frank B, 1942, S 21,15:3
Patrick, Fred, 1965, Ap 3,29:6
Patrick, G W, 1882, N 25,2:7
Patrick, George H, 1950, Ag 11,19:2
Patrick, George N, 1954, My 30,45:1
Patrick, George N Mrs, 1960, Ag 8,21:3
Patrick, Herbert L, 1949, F 4,24:2
Patrick, Hugh T, 1939, Ja 6,22:2
Patrick, J Hill, 1940, My 30,17:4
Patrick, Jerome, 1923, S 28,7:3
Patrick, John, 1948, Ap 11,73:1
Patrick, John A, 1948, D 25,17:3
Patrick, John B, 1947, My 23,23:1
Patrick, John H Mrs, 1956, N 18,89:2
Patrick, John J, 1951, Ap 18,31:4; 1966, My 15,88:4
Patrick, John S, 1944, Je 1,19:6
Patrick, Joseph, 1941, Ja 30,21:5
Patrick, Joseph B, 1944, Ap 7,19:4
Patrick, Joseph C, 1965, Ap 8,39:5
Patrick, Joseph H, 1946, My 16,21:5
Patrick, Joseph Mrs, 1939, Mr 4,15:5
Patrick, Kenneth G Mrs, 1957, My 26,92:3
Patrick, Lester (will, O 2,V,7:1), 1960, Je 2,33:1
Patrick, Luther, 1957, My 27,31:1
Patrick, Mark, 1942, Ja 9,21:4
Patrick, Mary M (por), 1940, F 27,21:4
Patrick, Mason M (por), 1942, Ja 30,19:1
Patrick, Mason M Mrs, 1938, Ap 17,II,6:4
Patrick, Norman E, 1952, Ja 4,23:3
Patrick, Norman S, 1953, My 10,89:2
Patrick, Richard M Mrs, 1913, S 21,II,15:4
Patrick, Roy L, 1953, Ja 15,27:3
Patrick, Roy L Mrs (G Baker), 1957, D 18,35:1
Patrick, Samuel, 1956, N 6,35:5
Patrick, Ted (Edwin H), 1964, Mr 12,35:1
Patrick, Ted Mrs, 1963, O 4,35:4
Patrick, W Burton, 1945, S 3,23:5
Patrick, Ward H, 1947, D 2,22:8
Patrick, William, 1875, S 9,8:4; 1957, Je 25,29:3
Patrick, William Mrs, 1946, Je 26,25:4
Patrick, William Rev, 1911, S 29,9:4
Patricola, Isabelle (Mrs W A Morris), 1965, My 25, 41:4
Patricola, Tom, 1950, Ja 2,23:3
Patridge, John, 1965, Mr 17,45:4
Patrie, Harry, 1943, My 2,45:2
Patrie, Harry H, 1944, S 14,23:3
Patrie, Louis, 1958, O 21,33:2
Patrie, Robert G, 1943, S 8,23:6
Patrizi, Cardinal, 1876, D 18,5:1
Patrizi, Ettore, 1946, Je 5,23:5
Patrowich, Samuel B, 1951, O 17,31:2
Patsalos, Constantine, 1950, F 1,29:1
Patston, Doris, 1957, Je 13,32:1
Patsy, Thomas, 1947, N 3,23:2
Patt, Harry L, 1952, Jl 27,56:5
Pattangall, William R (por), 1942, O 22,21:1
Pattangall, William R Mrs, 1950, Mr 10,27:4
Pattani, Prabashanker, 1938, F 17,21:5
Patte, Harry C, 1943, My 19,25:4
Pattee, Alida F, 1942, Ap 4,13:4
Pattee, Ernest N, 1946, Ja 19,13:5
Pattee, Fred L, 1950, My 7,108:1
Patten, Bernard M Mrs, 1961, F 26,92:5
Patten, Dora J W Mrs, 1950, S 15,25:2
Patten, Florence M Mrs, 1942, Je 12,21:5
Patten, Frank A, 1949, O 27,27:4
Patten, Fred C, 1941, D 1,19:6
Patten, G W Col, 1882, Ap 29,5:1
Patten, George W, 1910, S 29,11:4
Patten, Gilbert Mrs, 1939, Ag 22,19:4
Patten, Harry R, 1962, My 22,37:1
Patten, Harry R Mrs, 1949, Je 23,27:3
Patten, Henry A (por), 1955, Ag 1,19:3
Patten, Henry J, 1938, F 25,17:4
Patten, Henry S, 1939, Ja 18,20:4
Patten, J, 1878, My 28,4:7
Patten, J A, 1928, D 9,31:4
Patten, James F, 1966, S 20,47:2
Patten, James H, 1941, N 16,57:4
Patten, John A, 1916, Ap 27,13:5
Patten, Katherine Mrs, 1923, N 10,13:4
Patten, Nathan R Sr, 1955, S 7,31:4
Patten, Raymond E, 1948, S 15,31:3
Patten, Roland T, 1951, F 20,25:4
Patten, Simon N Dr, 1922, Jl 25,11:6
Patten, Thomas F, 1955, D 17,23:6
Patten, Thomas G (por), 1939, F 24,19:1
Patten, Thomas G Mrs, 1954, S 28,29:3
Patten, Thomas R, 1939, Mr 13,17:2
Patten, W, 1932, O 28,19:5; 1936, Jl 29,19:3
Patten, Walter, 1947, Mr 10,21:4
Patten, Walter Mrs, 1956, Je 16,19:2
Patten, William D, 1947, Je 5,25:2
Patten, William Mrs, 1949, Jl 19,29:1
Patten, William S, 1873, D 28,1:2; 1916, Je 27,11:4; 1960, Mr 27,86:2
Patten, William W, 1944, Ap 28,19:3
Patten, Z C, 1925, Mr 21,13:4
Patten, Zeboim C (por), 1948, Je 8,25:1
Pattengell, James B, 1942, F 7,17:6
Pattengill, J W Judge, 1903, My 23,9:3
Patter, Julian, 1913, Ag 14,9:6
Patterg, Phil W, 1949, O 24,23:2
Patteri, Marquis of (Rudolph Ferdinand von Klenner-Dombrowski), 1914, Je 2,11:6
Pattermank, Joseph, 1947, Jl 30,21:5
Pattern, Merle, 1946, Je 11,23:2
Patterson, A Carl, 1968, Ap 18,47:5
Patterson, A Hamilton, 1907, D 8,11:5
Patterson, A M, 1930, Mr 7,23:5
Patterson, A Wellesley Jr Mrs, 1945, Je 12,19:5
Patterson, Adoniram J Rev, 1909, N 4,11:4
Patterson, Albert F Mrs, 1952, S 5,27:4
Patterson, Alex C, 1955, D 15,37:3
Patterson, Alex E (por), 1948, S 12,72:5
Patterson, Algernon E, 1952, Je 3,29:3
Patterson, Alice H Mrs, 1966, D 7,47:4
Patterson, Alicia (Mrs H Guggenheim),(funl plans, Jl 4,15:7), 1963, Jl 3,27:1
Patterson, Andrew Mrs, 1952, D 9,33:2
Patterson, Angelica S, 1952, Mr 14,20:6
Patterson, Anna H, 1955, D 11,88:8
Patterson, Anna M Mrs, 1941, Jl 27,30:1
Patterson, Arch W, 1940, My 9,23:4
Patterson, Archibald G, 1958, Je 14,21:4
Patterson, Arthur C, 1942, O 5,19:4; 1950, N 27,25:3
Patterson, Arthur C Mrs, 1955, My 30,13:3; 1959, F 15,86:2
Patterson, Arthur H, 1960, S 17,23:6
Patterson, Arthur J, 1948, Ag 25,25:1; 1955, Je 5,84:
Patterson, Arthur L, 1966, N 8,39:4
Patterson, Arthur R, 1951, Ja 10,27:3
Patterson, Arthur S, 1952, Ag 7,21:3
Patterson, Arthur W Jr, 1945, Mr 6,21:5
Patterson, Augusta R Mrs, 1940, Jl 28,26:6
Patterson, Austin M, 1956, F 27,23:4
Patterson, Benjamin, 1920, S 8,11:2
Patterson, Betty M, 1938, Ap 12,23:5
Patterson, Buell A, 1958, N 19,37:2
Patterson, C E, 1933, F 13,21:8
Patterson, C J, 1901, Je 6,9:6
Patterson, C R, 1946, N 19,31:6
Patterson, C Stuart, 1924, N 10,17:3
Patterson, C V, 1968, O 22,47:1
Patterson, Carl A, 1954, Jl 5,11:5
Patterson, Carl V S, 1965, Ap 18,80:7
Patterson, Caroline H, 1910, S 8,9:4
Patterson, Catherine E Mrs, 1941, F 20,20:2
Patterson, Charles, 1951, Ag 9,21:1
Patterson, Charles A, 1922, Jl 28,13:4; 1950, Ag 12, 13:1
Patterson, Charles Brodie Dr, 1917, Je 23,9:7
Patterson, Charles E, 1913, F 23,II,7:3
Patterson, Charles H, 1941, O 14,23:1
Patterson, Charles L (funl, O 17,39:3), 1962, O 14
Patterson, Charles L Mrs, 1946, D 30,22:8; 1963, N 88:3
Patterson, Charles R (trb lr, N 17,30:5), 1958, N 1 29:3
Patterson, Charles R Mrs, 1951, My 29,25:4
Patterson, Chester, 1954, Ja 8,21:5
Patterson, Chester A, 1937, My 3,19:5
Patterson, Clifford, 1948, Jl 28,23:3
Patterson, Daniel C, 1946, S 13,9:8
Patterson, David C, 1965, D 28,27:4
Patterson, David W T, 1967, O 5,39:5
Patterson, Dillon J, 1943, Ap 15,25:1
Patterson, Don D, 1949, My 19,30:4
Patterson, Donald, 1951, O 6,19:6
Patterson, Donald W, 1951, Ap 4,29:5
Patterson, Edgar H, 1950, S 26,31:4
Patterson, Edgar R, 1938, D 18,49:3
Patterson, Edward Justice, 1910, Ja 29,9:5
Patterson, Edward Justice (mem), 1910, Mr 24,9:
Patterson, Edward N Mrs, 1948, Je 13,69:1
Patterson, Edward W, 1940, Mr 9,15:2
Patterson, Edwin W, 1965, D 25,13:5
Patterson, Eleanor M Mrs, 1948, Jl 25,49:1
Patterson, Elizabeth, 1966, F 1,35:1
Patterson, Elizabeth Mrs, 1953, S 14,27:4
Patterson, Elizabeth P, 1941, O 27,17:5
Patterson, Elsa M Mrs, 1941, F 16,39:6
Patterson, Elwood H, 1945, My 8,19:2
Patterson, Esther Hoge, 1909, Ap 10,9:5
Patterson, Francis D, 1946, Je 3,21:3
Patterson, Frank A (por), 1944, Ag 5,11:3
Patterson, Frank A Mrs, 1957, My 26,93:1
Patterson, Frank D, 1950, Je 19,21:5
Patterson, Frank E, 1940, My 28,23:2; 1942, O 12,
Patterson, Frank L, 1925, N 7,15:4; 1950, F 12,84:
Patterson, Frank M (will, Ap 19,24:4), 1939, Ap 23:2

Patterson, Frank M Mrs, 1940, F 25,39:2
Patterson, Frank Newhall Dr, 1922, Ap 19,19:5
Patterson, Frank P, 1938, F 12,15:3; 1951, Je 17,84:4
Patterson, Frank W, 1950, S 26,31:5
Patterson, Frederick H, 1940, Je 24,15:5
Patterson, Frederick S, 1945, F 12,19:3
Patterson, G Dr, 1937, Jl 28,20:1
Patterson, Garnet L, 1967, Je 5,43:4
Patterson, Gaylard H, 1940, Je 6,25:5
Patterson, George E Mrs, 1952, Jl 24,27:2
Patterson, George F, 1950, Ag 31,25:5
Patterson, George J, 1964, My 28,37:3
Patterson, George Jr, 1951, D 30,24:4
Patterson, George L, 1942, D 8,25:3
Patterson, George R, 1906, Mr 22,9:3
Patterson, George S, 1943, My 9,40:3; 1951, D 10, 29:4; 1953, N 9,35:2
Patterson, George S Mrs, 1962, S 28,25:8
Patterson, George Sr Mrs, 1952, S 18,29:3
Patterson, George T, 1915, F 12,9:6
Patterson, George W, 1957, Ag 9,19:5
Patterson, George W Jr Mrs, 1966, Ag 27,29:5
Patterson, Gerald L, 1967, Je 15,47:3
Patterson, Gerard F, 1944, Mr 6,19:3
Patterson, Gerard F Mrs, 1962, N 27,37:1
Patterson, Gertrude R Mrs, 1941, Ag 10,37:2
Patterson, Gilbert Mrs, 1949, D 28,25:3
Patterson, Graham Mrs, 1954, O 20,30:2
Patterson, Grove (funl plans, Ag 9,25:1; funl, Ag 11,13:2), 1956, Ag 8,25:1
Patterson, H Arzo, 1942, N 25,23:4
Patterson, H R Capt, 1903, N 27,9:5
Patterson, Hamilton, 1945, N 26,21:5
Patterson, Hannah, 1937, Ag 22,II,6:3
Patterson, Harold, 1938, Je 14,21:2
Patterson, Harold C, 1960, N 30,37:2
Patterson, Harold H, 1965, F 1,23:5
Patterson, Harry E, 1957, O 18,23:3
Patterson, Harry F, 1945, N 8,19:3
Patterson, Harry J, 1948, S 14,29:5
Patterson, Harry K, 1941, N 13,27:2
Patterson, Harry V, 1945, F 17,13:4
Patterson, Henry C Mrs, 1947, D 6,15:4
Patterson, Henry H Mrs, 1964, Ja 3,24:2
Patterson, Henry Mrs, 1947, Ag 14,23:5
Patterson, Henry S, 1957, D 11,32:1
Patterson, Herbert M, 1949, My 25,29:4
Patterson, Herbert P Mrs, 1968, Ja 6,29:3
Patterson, Herbert W, 1952, Jl 30,23:2
Patterson, Heywood, 1952, Ag 26,14:4
Patterson, Horace H, 1949, N 15,25:3
Patterson, Howard Capt, 1916, N 2,13:6
Patterson, Howard S, 1958, D 30,35:2
Patterson, Isaac Matheson Rev, 1921, Jl 4,9:7
Patterson, J Curtis Mrs, 1950, D 2,13:4
Patterson, J Edward, 1954, D 24,13:1
Patterson, J M, 1883, Jl 8,7:5
Patterson, J Manley, 1956, My 25,23:2
Patterson, J Rea, 1950, O 21,17:6
Patterson, J W, 1881, Je 10,2:7
Patterson, James A, 1905, Ap 3,9:5; 1950, O 22,94:4
Patterson, James Albert Rev, 1923, Jl 21,9:7
Patterson, James C, 1945, F 19,17:6
Patterson, James C Mrs, 1951, Ap 28,15:6
Patterson, James H, 1949, Ap 13,29:2
Patterson, James L Dr, 1937, Je 1,23:5
Patterson, James M, 1912, My 17,13:5
Patterson, James Mrs, 1945, Ja 11,23:2
Patterson, James P Mrs, 1948, Mr 28,48:8
Patterson, James T, 1939, Ag 8,17:5
Patterson, James W, 1917, Ap 10,13:7; 1951, Je 30, 15:4
Patterson, Jane Mrs, 1910, S 12,9:3
Patterson, Jennie W Mrs, 1940, F 3,13:4
Patterson, Jesse P, 1951, Jl 31,22:2
Patterson, Jesse P Mrs, 1949, S 18,94:5
Patterson, Jessie Mrs, 1961, Jl 8,19:6
Patterson, Job N Gen, 1923, Jl 19,15:4
Patterson, John (por), 1943, Je 27,32:6
Patterson, John, 1950, D 27,34:1; 1956, F 24,25:2; 1967, My 29,25:3
Patterson, John A, 1954, Ja 24,84:4
Patterson, John D, 1937, O 4,21:6
Patterson, John F, 1942, F 24,21:4
Patterson, John Fulton Rev Dr, 1924, O 22,21:4
Patterson, John H, 1909, N 5,9:6; 1922, My 8,17:3; 1947, Je 20,20:2; 1951, Ag 17,17:4; 1954, Ap 14,29:5
Patterson, John Henry Brig-Gen, 1920, O 7,15:2
Patterson, John J, 1917, D 31,7:6; 1941, S 15,17:5
Patterson, John J ex-Sen, 1912, S 29,II,13:5
Patterson, John L Dr, 1937, F 28,II,9:1
Patterson, John N, 1948, D 22,23:4
Patterson, John T, 1954, Ap 1,31:5; 1960, D 6,41:2
Patterson, Joseph, 1882, Ja 9,8:5
Patterson, Joseph M, 1912, My 17,13:4; 1946, My 27, 1:2
Patterson, Joseph R, 1943, Ap 19,19:5
Patterson, Josiah Col, 1904, F 13,9:5
Patterson, Katrina L, 1950, S 6,29:3
Patterson, Kellogg M, 1949, Ap 5,30:7
Patterson, Kenneth A, 1956, Mr 31,15:6
Patterson, Kenneth L, 1961, Ag 1,31:5
Patterson, Laurence K, 1939, Je 15,23:4
Patterson, Lee, 1967, Jl 26,36:1
Patterson, Leon, 1954, N 22,23:5
Patterson, Leon B, 1957, N 25,31:4
Patterson, Leslie H, 1952, Ag 11,15:6
Patterson, Lester W, 1947, N 16,76:2
Patterson, Lillian B Mrs, 1954, S 10,23:3
Patterson, Louis H, 1941, Mr 5,21:4
Patterson, Louise, 1952, My 8,31:4
Patterson, Lovina Mrs, 1945, Ag 3,17:4
Patterson, Luke, 1920, Jl 15,7:3
Patterson, M Mrs, 1901, Jl 11,7:6
Patterson, Marion D, 1950, Ja 7,17:5
Patterson, Marjorie, 1948, Mr 12,23:4
Patterson, Mary B Mrs, 1951, D 10,29:3
Patterson, Mary L, 1940, Ap 20,17:2
Patterson, Mary P, 1950, D 26,23:4
Patterson, Matt G, 1948, F 18,27:2
Patterson, Max, 1957, O 13,86:7
Patterson, May, 1925, Mr 22,7:3
Patterson, May B Mrs, 1940, O 27,48:1
Patterson, Minna B Mrs (will), 1941, Ja 12,40:1
Patterson, Morehead, 1962, Ag 6,25:4
Patterson, Morehead Mrs (funl plans, S 24,19:5), 1955, S 19,25:5
Patterson, Mortimer B, 1957, D 7,21:4
Patterson, Mortimer B Mrs, 1951, S 15,15:5
Patterson, Myra D Mrs, 1957, My 5,88:4
Patterson, Owen G Jr, 1945, Jl 26,19:3
Patterson, Paul, 1952, Ap 22,29:1; 1954, N 13,15:2
Patterson, Paul L, 1956, F 1,31:3
Patterson, Peter C, 1943, Mr 5,18:2
Patterson, Phil, 1947, Ag 25,17:2
Patterson, Proctor, 1947, O 25,19:3
Patterson, R A Rev, 1904, Ap 26,9:5
Patterson, Ray H, 1942, Jl 9,21:4
Patterson, Raymond A (funl, N 16,9:5), 1909, N 14, 13:4
Patterson, Raymond L, 1960, F 29,27:3
Patterson, Richard C Jr (funl, O 5,47:3), 1966, O 1, 31:2
Patterson, Richard C Mrs, 1952, N 16,85:3
Patterson, Richard J, 1947, Mr 5,25:2
Patterson, Robert C, 1937, Mr 28,II,8:7; 1949, Ap 5, 29:4
Patterson, Robert E, 1943, N 6,13:5; 1945, F 12,19:1; 1953, Mr 16,19:4; 1959, D 2,43:3
Patterson, Robert F, 1944, D 3,57:1
Patterson, Robert Gen, 1881, Ag 8,5:6
Patterson, Robert J, 1955, Ap 14,36:1
Patterson, Robert L, 1939, F 7,20:2
Patterson, Robert L Jr, 1955, D 14,39:1
Patterson, Robert M, 1937, My 20,21:4
Patterson, Robert P, 1952, Ja 23,1:8
Patterson, Robert U, 1950, D 7,33:5
Patterson, Robert W, 1910, Ap 2,11:3; 1948, D 4,13:5
Patterson, Roscoe C, 1954, O 23,15:4
Patterson, Ross V, 1938, My 3,23:3
Patterson, Rowland, 1954, My 25,21:6
Patterson, Roy C, 1953, Ap 16,29:6
Patterson, Rufus L, 1943, Ap 12,23:5
Patterson, Rufus Lenoir Mrs, 1968, Ag 5,39:2
Patterson, Schuyler B, 1964, Ja 21,29:2
Patterson, Seely B, 1951, Je 13,29:2
Patterson, Shirley G, 1938, My 29,II,6:7
Patterson, Sidney F, 1944, D 19,21:5
Patterson, Simon T, 1937, Je 4,26:1
Patterson, Stewart Mrs, 1952, D 27,9:4
Patterson, Stuart H, 1954, Mr 26,21:1
Patterson, T C, 1907, S 22,9:5
Patterson, Thomas A, 1949, Ag 30,27:4
Patterson, Thomas J, 1952, Mr 12,27:1
Patterson, Thomas M, 1954, D 17,31:3
Patterson, Thomas MacDonald, 1916, Jl 24,9:7
Patterson, Thomas T Mrs, 1951, F 26,24:2
Patterson, Thomas V, 1920, D 4,13:6
Patterson, Trevonian H, 1945, D 24,15:3
Patterson, Tunis P, 1944, F 15,17:3
Patterson, Victor M, 1942, Ap 18,15:6
Patterson, W C, 1883, Je 21,4:7
Patterson, Walter G, 1940, Ag 11,31:2
Patterson, Walter H, 1951, Ag 23,23:6
Patterson, Ward S, 1951, My 22,31:3
Patterson, Warner F, 1949, F 8,25:4
Patterson, Wilfrid, 1954, D 17,31:6
Patterson, William, 1904, F 9,9:6; 1942, Mr 31,21:3; 1946, My 15,21:2
Patterson, William A, 1940, My 17,19:2
Patterson, William C, 1961, Ag 1,31:1
Patterson, William E, 1941, Je 2,17:5
Patterson, William E Mrs, 1954, F 1,23:5
Patterson, William H, 1918, S 12,11:2; 1944, N 17,19:3
Patterson, William J, 1953, N 17,31:1; 1955, N 26, 19:1; 1956, Jl 2,21:1
Patterson, William M, 1942, Ja 19,20:1; 1949, O 30, 84:3; 1950, Ag 7,19:6
Patterson, William Mrs, 1964, Ap 29,41:1
Patterson, William R Mrs, 1943, Je 3,21:5
Patterson, William W, 1954, Ja 8,22:3
Patterson, Wright A, 1954, My 20,31:4
Patterson, Zera D Mrs, 1952, Ja 17,27:2
Patteson, Henry Burr, 1907, O 27,9:6
Patteson, Robert A, 1941, Ag 4,13:4
Patti, Adelina, 1919, S 28,22:1
Patti, Carlo, 1873, Mr 18,1:7
Patti, Carlotta, 1889, Je 29,5:5
Pattillo, Frank A, 1963, Ap 1,27:6
Pattison, Ben J, 1948, Ja 24,15:1
Pattison, Charles V, 1954, Jl 8,23:1
Pattison, Edwin W, 1940, Jl 5,13:4
Pattison, Frank A (por), 1946, S 19,31:5
Pattison, Frank A Mrs, 1951, Je 29,21:3
Pattison, Gardner, 1946, Ag 10,13:4
Pattison, Gurney Crow Capt, 1874, F 25,10:2
Pattison, Harold, 1965, D 20,35:5
Pattison, Harry A, 1957, F 16,17:3
Pattison, Henry O Mrs, 1956, S 10,27:4
Pattison, Hubert A, 1960, O 11,45:1
Pattison, Hubert A Mrs, 1962, Je 14,33:3
Pattison, James William, 1915, My 30,13:4
Pattison, John M Gov (burial, Je 22,7:6), 1906, Je 19,9:1
Pattison, John M Mrs, 1959, Ap 18,23:3
Pattison, M Rev, 1884, Ag 1,5:3
Pattison, Melvin V, 1944, F 13,42:1
Pattison, Morgan M, 1961, Mr 15,39:4
Pattison, Nelson M, 1947, Ja 12,59:5
Pattison, Perry Mrs, 1959, Ag 15,17:2
Pattison, R, 1929, Ja 15,29:4
Pattison, R Maxine, 1956, My 16,35:4
Pattison, Rob E, 1904, Ag 2,7:6
Pattison, Robert J, 1903, S 15,9:6
Pattison, T Harwood Rev, 1904, F 14,7:6
Pattison, Theodore S, 1941, My 3,15:3
Pattison, Thomas Winfield, 1908, Je 22,7:4
Pattison, William J, 1939, D 28,21:6
Patton, Alfred, 1945, Ap 28,15:4
Patton, Andrew J, 1943, Mr 22,19:5
Patton, Anna C, 1904, Ap 12,9:6
Patton, Arch Mrs, 1967, O 18,47:2
Patton, Archdeacon, 1874, My 2,12:3
Patton, Ashley W, 1948, D 28,22:3
Patton, Charles E, 1937, D 16,27:5; 1939, O 12,25:4
Patton, Charles L, 1941, Je 5,23:4
Patton, Cornelius H, 1939, Ag 18,19:3
Patton, E E, 1961, Jl 27,31:3
Patton, E Paul, 1961, D 8,42:8
Patton, F L, 1932, N 27,34:1
Patton, Francis L Jr, 1949, D 29,25:3
Patton, Francis Theodore (funl, Mr 30,9:7), 1907, Mr 29,9:5
Patton, Fred, 1951, O 27,19:5
Patton, Frederic C, 1948, Ag 1,58:2
Patton, Frederic C Mrs, 1948, My 29,15:5
Patton, George S, 1937, Mr 26,21:4
Patton, George S Jr Mrs, 1953, O 1,30:3
Patton, George T, 1941, Ag 25,15:2
Patton, Guy, 1956, Je 16,19:5
Patton, Guy Mrs, 1942, O 4,53:1
Patton, H W Maj, 1922, My 26,19:6
Patton, Henry D, 1966, Mr 22,41:2
Patton, Henry J, 1952, My 24,19:6
Patton, J A, 1882, Ap 1,5:2
Patton, Jacob H, 1903, N 26,7:6
Patton, James M, 1959, Ap 25,21:2
Patton, James P, 1956, D 14,29:4
Patton, James R, 1961, O 17,39:2
Patton, Jeanette T (Mrs N Shalamon), 1963, Je 18, 37:3
Patton, John, 1956, D 25,22:2
Patton, John B, 1948, Je 4,23:2
Patton, John C Mrs, 1960, Ap 23,23:5
Patton, John Jr, 1907, My 25,9:4
Patton, John W Prof, 1921, Ap 26,15:4
Patton, Joseph C, 1937, S 11,17:6
Patton, Kenneth S, 1960, Jl 28,27:5
Patton, Kenneth S Mrs, 1960, F 8,29:4
Patton, Lee, 1950, Mr 8,25:2
Patton, Lincoln J, 1963, S 6,29:3
Patton, Lincoln J Mrs, 1947, Jl 25,17:3
Patton, Ludlow, 1906, S 7,9:6
Patton, Minnie, 1953, Je 9,27:2
Patton, Nat, 1957, Jl 29,19:3
Patton, Raymond S Rear-Adm (por), 1937, N 26,21:1
Patton, Robert H, 1939, Mr 13,17:5
Patton, Robert W, 1944, S 10,45:2
Patton, Rosa A Mrs, 1942, Ap 6,15:6
Patton, Thomas R (will), 1907, S 18,9:7
Patton, W A Maj, 1903, Je 19,9:5
Patton, Walter G, 1964, Mr 14,23:6
Patton, Walter L, 1959, Ja 30,27:1
Patton, William B, 1949, Jl 26,27:2
Patton, William F, 1956, Mr 25,74:1
Patton, William Gen, 1903, Je 6,7:6
Patton, William H 2d Mrs, 1966, Jl 3,35:1
Patton, William Rev, 1879, S 11,5:1
Patton, William W, 1959, My 10,87:1
Patton, William W Mrs, 1938, D 9,25:2
Pattou, Edith E Mrs, 1940, Jl 5,13:6
Pattullo, George, 1967, Jl 30,64:2
Pattwell, Michael P, 1957, Je 27,25:5
Patty, John C, 1948, My 24,19:2
Patuwai, Iripera Mrs, 1951, Ap 26,29:2
Paty, Raymond R, 1957, Ag 8,23:3
Patz, Ernest O, 1941, Mr 8,19:1
Patz, Gustav, 1953, Ja 11,91:3

Patzowsky, Fred R, 1947, N 26,23:3
Pau, P G, 1932, Ja 3,II,9:1
Pauer-Budahegy, Josephine Mrs, 1956, D 12,39:4
Pauer-Budahegy, Leo de, 1940, Je 26,23:1
Pauk, Paul, 1941, Ja 5,44:8
Pauker, Edmond, 1962, My 7,31:4
Pauker, George, 1964, My 23,23:5
Pauker, Harry, 1953, F 3,25:1
Pauker, Morris, 1954, Je 7,23:4
Paul, A J Drexel, 1958, Jl 9,27:2
Paul, A J Drexel Mrs, 1953, D 10,47:2
Paul, Abban, 1940, Mr 26,21:2
Paul, Abe, 1913, Ag 13,9:5
Paul, Ada W Mrs, 1941, D 31,17:1
Paul, Alex, 1957, O 30,29:4
Paul, Alexander, 1937, O 20,19:1
Paul, Alexander Mrs, 1965, F 11,39:3
Paul, Alfred, 1947, N 16,65:4
Paul, Andrew B, 1956, Je 20,31:2
Paul, Arthur D, 1945, Mr 17,13:2
Paul, Brenda D, 1959, Jl 27,25:6
Paul, Bro, 1943, Ap 5,19:2
Paul, Bro (Daniel O'Connell), 1943, My 28,21:4
Paul, Bro (P E Scanlan), 1950, Je 19,21:3
Paul, C K, 1902, Jl 21,7:3
Paul, C R Col, 1901, N 10,7:6
Paul, Capton M Mrs, 1962, Ag 7,29:4
Paul, Carl F, 1942, D 13,75:4
Paul, Charles E, 1957, D 9,35:3; 1961, My 4,37:5
Paul, Charles J Jr, 1955, S 17,15:2
Paul, Claude, 1943, N 5,19:2
Paul, Clinton, 1949, Ap 5,30:3
Paul, Clyde L, 1962, Jl 7,17:4
Paul, David Rev Dr, 1903, Ja 26,9:6
Paul, Duc de Noailles, 1885, My 31,9:3
Paul, E W, 1880, Jl 1,5:6
Paul, Edgar T, 1942, My 24,42:6
Paul, Edward A Mrs, 1945, Ag 5,37:2
Paul, Edward F, 1946, Mr 24,46:3
Paul, Edward J, 1940, My 10,23:4
Paul, Edward T Mrs, 1940, Jl 17,21:5
Paul, Elizabeth F, 1947, Ag 12,25:4
Paul, Elliot, 1958, Ap 8,29:1
Paul, Elsa M, 1965, O 18,35:1
Paul, Elthan E, 1938, Mr 2,19:2
Paul, Emanuel, 1957, Ap 16,33:5
Paul, Emma, 1951, Mr 19,27:1
Paul, Eugene, 1940, Mr 2,13:6
Paul, Eugene H, 1938, Ja 30,II,8:3
Paul, Francis, 1941, Jl 31,17:2
Paul, Frank R, 1963, Je 30,56:1
Paul, Frank W Capt, 1912, D 27,9:4
Paul, Frederick W, 1944, Ag 17,17:2
Paul, G R Gen, 1863, Jl 10,1:4
Paul, George P, 1962, Mr 26,31:5
Paul, Gerome A, 1958, Mr 28,25:2
Paul, Gus J, 1940, Ap 1,19:2
Paul, Gus J Mrs, 1952, D 24,17:6
Paul, H M, 1931, Mr 17,29:2
Paul, Harry G, 1945, S 28,21:5
Paul, Henry N, 1954, N 30,17:5
Paul, Herbert J, 1949, Ag 4,23:6
Paul, Herman, 1953, Jl 16,21:3
Paul, Howard Mrs, 1879, Je 10,5:4
Paul, Hugh C, 1964, My 25,33:2
Paul, Ignatius A, 1947, Jl 4,13:6
Paul, Isadore, 1949, S 11,94:5
Paul, J Archer, 1952, Je 20,23:3
Paul, J Rodman, 1941, Ja 28,19:3
Paul, Jacob M, 1955, S 13,31:5
Paul, James A, 1957, My 5,89:1
Paul, James W, 1908, S 26,7:3; 1945, Ap 17,23:5; 1967, Ap 18,41:4
Paul, Jessie L, 1959, O 17,23:4
Paul, John, 1964, F 15,23:4
Paul, John Davis, 1953, F 25,27:3
Paul, Jonathan S, 1950, Jl 12,29:5
Paul, Jose De Jesus Dr, 1919, Mr 5,11:3
Paul, Joseph, 1946, O 17,23:1
Paul, Joseph D, 1946, Ag 23,19:4
Paul, Josephine F, 1947, Ap 16,25:6
Paul, Justus, 1946, F 20,25:4
Paul, Lawrence K, 1955, S 19,25:2
Paul, Lester L, 1958, Ja 13,29:1
Paul, Luther G, 1954, O 7,23:5
Paul, M H B (Cholly Nickerbocker), 1942, Jl 18,13:5
Paul, Martin A, 1950, Ag 21,19:4
Paul, Morris, 1953, My 1,22:3
Paul, Murray, 1966, Mr 13,86:8
Paul, Norman M, 1958, Mr 19,31:4
Paul, Randolph E (mem ser plans, F 8,33:1), 1956, F 7,19:3
Paul, Ray S, 1957, Je 23,84:6
Paul, Richard F, 1952, N 5,27:4
Paul, robt J T, 1954, D 18,15:6
Paul, Sophie, 1951, F 8,33:1
Paul, Stephen, 1937, Jl 11,II,5:1
Paul, Thomas W, 1946, F 15,26:3
Paul, Wallace C, 1955, My 31,27:2
Paul, Willard S, 1966, Mr 22,42:1
Paul, William, 1951, O 26,23:4
Paul, William G, 1962, O 9,41:3
Paul, William J Mrs, 1959, Je 25,29:1
Paul, William M, 1925, My 19,21:3
Paul, Winston Mrs, 1961, S 5,35:5
Paul-Boncour, Jean Mrs, 1967, Jl 16,64:4
Paul-Dubois, Louis, 1938, D 28,21:5
Paul Edward, Bro (D F McGrath), 1943, S 25,15:4
Paul Frederic Emil Leopold, Prince of Leppe-Detmold, 1875, D 10,4:6
Paul I, King of Greece (funl, Mr 13,10:1), 1964, Mr 7,1:7
Paul Wilfred, Bro, 1945, O 20,11:5
Paula, Frank, 1955, Ag 14,81:3
Paulcke, Wilhelm, 1949, O 13,27:4
Paulding, Anne D (will, O 30,17:7), 1943, O 22,17:5
Paulding, C Gouverneur Mrs (V Peterson), 1966, D 27,32:1
Paulding, Charles C (por),(will, O 1,17:3), 1938, S 27,21:1
Paulding, Charles G Mrs, 1944, Jl 11,15:5
Paulding, Emma, 1941, F 23,39:6
Paulding, Emma G, 1952, Mr 28,23:1
Paulding, Fidelis, 1944, S 6,19:3
Paulding, Frederick Dr (por), 1937, S 8,23:5
Paulding, Gouverneur, 1913, D 18,9:6; 1965, Ag 11, 35:3
Paulding, Hiram Maj, 1901, S 19,7:6
Paulding, Hiram Rear-Adm, 1878, O 21,1:5
Paulding, James K, 1943, D 13,23:1
Paulding, James Kirke, 1860, Ap 6,4:5
Paulding, John L, 1942, Ja 3,19:5
Paulding, Pierre L, 1923, S 5,15:3; 1950, Mr 9,29:2
Paulding, Pierre L Mrs, 1952, Jl 30,23:1
Paulding, Roy C, 1954, Je 8,27:1
Paulding, Tatnall, 1907, Mr 6,9:5
Paulen, Ben S, 1961, Jl 12,31:1
Paulet, Henry W M Marquess of Winchester, 1962, Je 29,27:5
Pauletta, Giovanni, 1951, D 19,19:3
Pauley, Albert C, 1943, Ja 17,45:1
Pauley, Elbert L, 1950, Mr 30,29:2
Pauley, Elbert L Mrs, 1949, Jl 19,29:5
Pauley, Harold R, 1954, My 9,88:4
Pauley, Maurice J, 1952, S 15,25:3
Paulhan, Jean, 1968, O 11,47:3
Paulhus, Anthony J, 1958, O 13,29:6
Pauli, Erwin J, 1959, O 20,39:4
Pauli, Wolfgang, 1958, D 29,15:5
Paulin, L R E, 1952, Je 17,27:4
Paulin, Willard B, 1954, Ap 13,31:2
Pauline, George W, 1941, Ag 18,13:2
Pauline, Grand Duchess, 1904, My 18,2:6
Pauline, J Robert, 1942, N 12,25:2
Pauline, John M, 1945, S 20,23:4
Pauling, Edward G, 1945, Ag 1,19:4
Pauling, John W, 1945, Ja 19,19:5
Pauling, Walter Y, 1950, F 10,23:4
Pauling-Emrich, Marguerite L Mrs, 1942, Mr 13,19:2
Paulison, C McK, 1881, O 25,3:5
Paulison, J C, 1882, S 13,2:7
Paulison, William H, 1941, D 6,17:4
Paulissier, P C J, 1881, N 15,5:2
Paull, Frederick M, 1958, Ag 22,21:1
Paull, G Bertrand, 1952, F 25,21:4
Paull, G R, 1882, Je 7,5:4
Paull, Harry W, 1938, Ag 16,19:5
Paull, Irving S, 1937, Ja 15,22:2
Paull, Joseph R, 1941, F 1,18:2
Paull, Norman M, 1949, My 8,76:5
Paull, William, 1903, F 6,2:5
Paullin, Enos, 1940, My 11,19:4
Paullin, James E, 1951, Ag 15,27:3
Paullin, Norman Rev, 1968, My 28,47:1
Paulman, George P, 1946, O 15,25:4
Paulmenn, Frank H, 1952, Ja 31,27:2
Paulonis, Joseph F, 1961, Ag 1,31:4
Paulovna, Helene Grand Duchess, 1873, Ja 23,1:7
Paulsen, Albert S, 1948, Ap 29,23:3
Paulsen, Alice E, 1943, Mr 17,21:1
Paulsen, Axel, 1938, F 10,21:5
Paulsen, Christian P, 1944, My 28,33:2
Paulsen, Edward H, 1949, F 3,23:3
Paulsen, Emil, 1939, Ja 9,15:5
Paulsen, Friedrich Prof, 1908, Ag 16,7:6
Paulsen, Herbert, 1952, Je 30,25:6
Paulsen, Howard Mrs, 1945, N 29,23:2
Paulsen, Irwin G, 1940, My 13,17:3
Paulsen, Mabelle E, 1955, Mr 16,33:3
Paulsen, P Marinus, 1944, O 25,21:3
Paulsen, William, 1943, Ja 29,38:4
Paulson, Alfred C, 1953, Ag 29,17:3
Paulson, Charles W, 1960, Mr 8,33:1
Paulson, Frank A, 1913, O 28,11:6
Paulson, Frederick H, 1959, O 2,29:3
Paulson, Frederik E, 1947, Ag 14,23:6
Paulson, Friedrich (cremated, F 7,27:5), 1957, F 3, 77:1
Paulson, Henry W, 1949, Mr 24,28:2
Paulson, Holger D (Mar 24), 1963, Ag 1,36:4
Paulson, Howard C, 1957, Mr 23,19:2
Paulson, James A, 1940, Ap 22,17:5
Paulson, Stephen M, 1958, N 3,37:2
Paulson, Thomas Mrs, 1944, Jl 12,19:4
Paulson, William, 1950, Je 1,27:5
Paulton, Edward, 1939, Mr 21,23:3
Paulus, Edwin J, 1950, D 24,34:1
Paulus, Friedrich von Mrs, 1949, N 10,31:1
Paulus, W K, 1947, D 24,22:2
Paulus, Whilemina, 1957, Ja 21,25:4
Paulus, William, 1946, O 31,25:1
Pauly, Howard C, 1966, O 28,41:3
Paumgarten, Baroness von, 1948, N 3,27:1
Paumgarten, Harold, 1952, F 8,25:7
Pauncefote, Lord, 1902, My 25,9:4
Paura, Anthony F, 1945, My 6,38:3
Paus, Herbert, 1946, Je 2,44:4
Pausback, Nicholas J, 1953, My 14,29:5
Pausinger, Franz von, 1915, Ap 8,13:5
Paust, Gilbert Mrs, 1958, S 21,86:6
Paust, Max W, 1938, Ap 11,16:4
Paustovsky, Konstantin G (funl, Jl 18,33:4), 1968, Jl 15,31:3
Pautke, Johannes, 1955, N 29,29:4
Pauwels, Desire, 1942, F 19,19:3
Pauxtis, Simon F, 1961, Mr 15,39:4
Pavanelli, Livio, 1958, My 2,27:4
Pavarini, George F, 1957, N 1,27:1
Pavel, Henry J Sr, 1948, N 7,88:5
Pavelic, Ante, 1959, D 30,21:1
Pavelic, Ante (funl), 1960, Ja 1,19:4
Pavenick, Stanford Mrs, 1966, Ja 27,33:4
Pavenstedt, Adolph J, 1941, O 10,23:4
Pavenstedt, Adolph J Mrs, 1959, N 7,23:4
Pavenstedt, Edmund W Mrs (M Parker), 1959, N 13,29:2
Pavese, Generoso, 1947, Ja 16,25:5
Pavesich, Francis X, 1957, Ag 14,25:1
Paveskovich, Jacob M, 1948, O 8,25:4
Pavey, Frank D, 1946, Ap 16,25:6
Pavey, Max, 1957, S 5,29:3
Pavia, Paul P, 1962, Ja 20,21:5
Pavick, William, 1949, Ja 21,21:2
Pavie, E Harold, 1951, D 11,33:3
Paviour, Robert S, 1924, My 15,19:3
Pavis, Frank A, 1958, N 3,37:2
Pavis, Victor S, 1949, F 17,23:2
Pavitt, Frank S, 1949, N 27,104:6
Pavitt, William H, 1956, N 22,33:5
Pavlenko, Peter, 1951, Je 17,84:7
Pavlicek, Frederick, 1966, O 28,31:2
Pavlis, Andrew C, 1944, Ag 25,13:2
Pavloff, Edith Brooks Mrs, 1953, Ag 17,15:2
Pavloska, Irene, 1962, F 14,33:2
Pavlov, I, 1936, F 27,19:1
Pavlov, Mikhail A, 1958, Ja 13,29:1
Pavlovsky, Louis H, 1947, Je 10,27:3
Pavlovsky, Valentin, 1959, F 11,39:4
Pavlovsky, Yevgeny N, 1965, My 28,33:2
Pavlowa, A, 1931, Ja 23,1:4
Pavlychenko, Thomas K, 1958, Ag 7,25:4
Pavolini, Paolo E, 1942, S 17,25:4
Pavone, Giuseppe, 1944, My 8,19:4
Pavoni, Ferdinando, 1950, Ja 20,25:4
Pavourdjiev, Vassily, 1948, Ja 6,23:3
Pavuk, John J R, 1965, Je 14,33:4
Pavy, Benjamin H, 1943, Ap 20,23:5
Pawley, Clifton D, 1951, S 27,31:6
Pawley, Stephen E, 1943, S 23,21:5
Pawley, William, 1952, Je 18,27:2
Pawlin, Walter T Mrs, 1960, N 9,35:4
Pawling, George F, 1954, D 3,28:1
Pawlowski, Paul, 1966, N 13,89:2
Pawlowski, Witold P, 1953, Ja 29,28:3
Pawson, Charles T, 1948, F 11,28:2
Pawson, Frank E, 1937, Je 24,25:2
Pawson, John E, 1947, S 26,23:2
Pax, Paulette, 1942, Je 19,23:3
Paxson, Charles S, 1947, Je 18,25:5
Paxson, Edward M, 1905, O 13,9:5; 1952, Ja 10,30:
Paxson, Frederic J, 1939, Jl 1,17:3
Paxson, Frederic L, 1948, O 25,23:4
Paxson, H D, 1933, Ja 31,18:1
Paxson, Newlin F Mrs, 1940, O 8,25:1
Paxson, Oscar, 1937, D 14,25:3
Paxson, Ruth, 1949, O 3,17:6
Paxson, Thomas D Mrs, 1953, O 1,29:5
Paxton, Burton, 1948, S 5,40:5
Paxton, C Sherman, 1950, My 30,17:5
Paxton, Edward G, 1952, D 27,10:4
Paxton, Edwin J Sr, 1961, Jl 23,69:3
Paxton, Evelyn Norris Mrs, 1925, Ap 17,21:4
Paxton, George (por), 1948, Jl 31,15:4
Paxton, Henry C, 1946, D 19,29:5
Paxton, J F, 1939, Je 13,23:2
Paxton, J Hall, 1952, Je 25,29:1
Paxton, J R, 1883, Ja 15,5:3
Paxton, Jean G, 1939, D 26,19:3
Paxton, John Randolph Dr, 1923, Ap 12,19:4
Paxton, Joseph Sir, 1865, Je 21,1:1
Paxton, Margaretta, 1950, My 1,25:3
Paxton, Robert Mrs, 1946, N 29,25:1
Paxton, William C, 1953, Ag 2,72:5
Paxton, William M, 1941, My 14,21:6
Paxton, William M Rev, 1904, N 29,9:4
Paya, Princess, 1947, Je 7,13:5
Payan, Frank J, 1948, Ag 30,25:2
Payan, Luis A, 1950, Mr 25,13:4
Payard, Camille, 1946, O 13,59:3

Payen, Fernand, 1946, Ja 9,23:3
Payer, Harry F, 1952, O 14,31:4
Payer, Harry F Mrs, 1956, Ag 1,23:2
Payer, John Martin Com, 1922, My 14,30:2
Payerk, Julius, 1915, S 1,9:5
Paylys, Stanley, 1949, Ap 23,13:6
Payn, James, 1898, Mr 26,7:2
Payn, Louis F, 1923, Mr 20,21:3
Payne, Albert E Dr, 1937, Je 23,25:2
Payne, Albert J, 1949, D 30,19:3
Payne, Alfred W, 1942, D 30,23:2
Payne, Alvan T, 1908, N 11,9:6
Payne, Amos, 1938, S 28,25:5
Payne, Arthur C, 1952, N 14,23:2
Payne, Arthur F, 1939, My 22,17:2
Payne, Augustus H, 1959, D 14,31:1
Payne, B H, 1883, Je 8,2:4
Payne, Bruce R Dr, 1937, Ap 22,23:3
Payne, C Dr, 1881, Mr 16,5:4
Payne, Charles E, 1947, D 1,21:2; 1949, O 30,84:7
Payne, Charles E B, 1949, N 15,25:2
Payne, Charles L, 1959, D 17,37:5
Payne, Charles L Mrs, 1951, Ag 18,11:6
Payne, Christy, 1962, S 7,30:1
Payne, Christy Sr Mrs, 1954, Ag 13,15:4
Payne, Clinton F, 1948, O 16,15:3
Payne, Conrad Mrs (Helen Twelvetress), 1958, F 14,23:1
Payne, Cyrus Fay, 1921, Je 12,22:3
Payne, D J Capt, 1918, F 2,11:8
Payne, D L Capt, 1884, N 29,1:6
Payne, Daniel A, 1938, Ja 20,23:1
Payne, Daniel R, 1946, Ap 1,28:2
Payne, David, 1921, Mr 6,21:3
Payne, Donald Mrs, 1951, S 29,17:4
Payne, E George, 1953, Je 29,21:3
Payne, Earl D, 1951, F 8,34:4
Payne, Edgar A, 1947, Ap 9,25:3
Payne, Edith, 1940, Jl 28,27:2
Payne, Edmund, 1914, Jl 2,9:5
Payne, Edward F, 1955, Ja 9,87:2
Payne, Edward Mrs, 1944, Ja 11,19:4
Payne, Edwin F, 1941, N 11,24:2
Payne, Edwin Van R, 1962, Mr 7,35:3
Payne, Elmer E, 1938, F 3,23:6
Payne, Emeline M Mrs, 1941, D 5,23:5
Payne, Ernest C, 1952, N 1,21:3
Payne, Eugene B Brig-Gen, 1910, Ap 8,9:5
Payne, F Ursula, 1946, Ja 4,21:1
Payne, Fannie, 1909, F 13,9:4
Payne, Florence I, 1938, Ag 25,19:4
Payne, Francis F, 1949, O 10,23:3
Payne, Francis H, 1942, N 12,25:5
Payne, Frank C, 1949, My 21,13:4
Payne, Frank E, 1955, N 21,29:5
Payne, Fred, 1954, Ja 17,92:2
Payne, Frederick C, 1924, N 1,15:3
Payne, Frederick H, 1960, Mr 25,28:3
Payne, Frederick H Mrs, 1943, Ag 25,19:2
Payne, Frederick W, 1966, Ag 19,33:4
Payne, George, 1938, O 19,23:5
Payne, George F, 1908, Je 8,7:6
Payne, George Frederick Dr, 1923, Ap 20,17:4
Payne, George H, 1945, Mr 4,37:1
Payne, George M, 1940, Ap 23,23:1
Payne, George R, 1957, O 13,86:6
Payne, Gerald, 1950, Mr 7,27:5
Payne, Grattan, 1939, Jl 2,15:1
Payne, Guy, 1956, Jl 3,25:3
Payne, H Judd, 1966, O 27,47:1
Payne, Harold C, 1950, Mr 13,21:3
Payne, Harry M, 1950, D 9,15:2
Payne, Harry O, 1967, F 12,92:8
Payne, Henry A, 1940, Jl 6,15:5
Payne, Henry C, 1904, O 5,1:3
Payne, Henry E, 1938, N 20,38:8
Payne, Henry M, 1943, Ja 9,13:5
Payne, Herbert W, 1951, D 3,31:4
Payne, Horace, 1953, Ap 26,65:2
Payne, Howard M, 1961, S 14,31:3
Payne, Inman H, 1949, S 18,92:2
Payne, Ira G, 1953, Jl 20,17:3
Payne, J B, 1935, Ja 24,19:1
Payne, James E, 1949, N 16,29:2
Payne, James H M Mrs, 1942, My 15,19:3
Payne, James Henry Dr, 1909, My 16,9:5
Payne, Jetur R, 1940, O 4,23:4
Payne, John A, 1924, My 24,15:4
Payne, John A (por), 1947, Ap 19,15:5
Payne, John B, 1938, N 11,25:2; 1941, S 14,50:3
Payne, John C, 1954, My 12,25:3
Payne, John E, 1911, F 17,9:5
Payne, John F, 1950, N 1,35:3
Payne, John G, 1961, Je 29,33:5
Payne, John H, 1951, S 11,29:2
Payne, John L, 1951, Mr 13,31:3
Payne, John W, 1952, D 8,41:2
Payne, Joseph G Mrs, 1946, Ag 20,27:1
Payne, Kenneth W, 1962, O 20,25:4
Payne, Leon F, 1947, Je 23,23:5
Payne, Lewis A, 1941, N 26,23:4
Payne, Luther C Mrs, 1946, N 15,23:3
Payne, Martha, 1947, N 23,74:4
Payne, Mary D, 1961, My 27,23:4
Payne, Mary F Mrs, 1942, Jl 26,31:1
Payne, N P, 1885, My 12,5:4
Payne, Nathan B, 1952, Ap 29,27:3
Payne, Oliver H, 1961, Ap 14,18:2
Payne, Oliver Hazard Col (est, Jl 7,9:1), 1917, Je 28,11:4
Payne, Phil F, 1941, My 10,15:2
Payne, Phil M Mrs, 1953, My 17,88:6
Payne, Philip M, 1950, Jl 15,13:6
Payne, R T, 1882, N 14,5:3
Payne, Ray, 1950, D 14,35:5
Payne, Richard W, 1947, Je 11,27:3
Payne, Richmond Mrs, 1953, Ap 17,26:4
Payne, Robert, 1906, My 23,9:4
Payne, Robert F, 1951, D 29,11:4
Payne, Robert L, 1947, S 11,27:6
Payne, Robert R, 1944, Ap 17,23:3
Payne, Roger, 1955, F 24,18:4
Payne, Rolly, 1943, Je 24,21:3
Payne, Ronald J Mrs, 1955, Jl 29,17:5
Payne, Sereno E, 1914, D 12,15:4
Payne, Sereno E Mrs, 1911, Ap 24,9:5
Payne, Sheldon F, 1939, D 10,68:4
Payne, Stephen H Mrs, 1951, O 4,33:1
Payne, Theodore, 1963, My 8,39:5
Payne, Thomas B Jr, 1944, F 10,15:4
Payne, Thomas H, 1924, D 26,15:6
Payne, Thomas J, 1942, Ap 2,21:4
Payne, Vera D Mrs, 1943, Jl 11,34:6
Payne, W A, 1942, Mr 17,21:3
Payne, W H, 1879, Ja 13,2:7
Payne, W O, 1944, Mr 25,15:5
Payne, W T, 1928, O 12,25:5
Payne, W Wallace (por), 1955, Jl 6,27:3
Payne, Walter, 1949, N 1,27:6
Payne, Whitney, 1945, Ap 5,23:6
Payne, Will, 1954, My 21,28:3
Payne, William, 1925, Mr 13,19:3; 1951, Ja 24,27:5
Payne, William A, 1951, F 13,31:5
Payne, William E, 1949, Mr 19,15:3
Payne, William H, 1905, D 29,9:5; 1952, Mr 20,29:4
Payne, William H Gen, 1904, Mr 30,9:5
Payne, William L (Lou), 1953, Ag 18,23:1
Payne, William Morton, 1919, Jl 12,9:6
Payne, William S, 1939, Ag 2,19:6
Payne, William T, 1943, D 1,21:4
Payne, Winona W Mrs, 1949, Ja 9,72:7
Payne-Jennings, Victor, 1962, Je 19,35:2
Paynter, Harry L, 1948, My 30,34:3
Paynter, Harry S, 1952, F 12,27:3
Paynter, Henry M, 1960, O 31,31:5
Paynter, Richard K, 1940, Ag 10,13:3
Paynter, Roland G, 1944, D 17,37:2
Paynter, Russell, 1940, Jl 27,13:4
Paynter, Thomas E, 1949, F 6,76:4
Paynter, Thomas H Ex-Sen, 1921, Mr 9,13:4
Paynter, William C, 1942, S 22,21:4
Paynton, Harry, 1964, Jl 29,33:4
Payot, Jules, 1940, F 4,40:4
Payson, Caroline B, 1939, F 7,20:2
Payson, Edgar R, 1946, Jl 2,25:6
Payson, Eliot R, 1945, N 4,43:1
Payson, Eliot R Mrs, 1940, O 7,17:3
Payson, Francis, 1904, Ja 22,9:5
Payson, George H Mrs (por), 1941, O 21,23:3
Payson, George P (por), 1944, N 10,19:5
Payson, George Shipman Rev, 1923, F 21,15:5
Payson, Harold, 1951, My 29,25:5
Payson, Henry, 1962, O 9,41:3
Payson, Henry Mrs, 1948, Je 16,29:6
Payson, Herbert Jr, 1967, Ag 7,29:5
Payson, Horace E Mrs, 1945, My 4,19:4
Payson, James M, 1941, O 29,23:2
Payson, Lawrence G, 1962, D 22,8:1
Payson, Lewis E, 1909, O 7,9:4
Payson, Peter, 1961, N 28,37:3
Payson, Sarah L, 1944, F 15,17:5
Payson, William F, 1939, Ap 16,III,6:6
Payton, Barbara (Mrs J Rawley), 1967, My 11,47:2
Payton, C, 1934, F 24,13:4
Payton, Corse Mrs, 1915, O 12,11:4; 1958, N 29,21:5
Payton, Emily Mrs, 1954, D 23,19:5
Payton, Eugene J, 1941, Mr 16,45:2
Payton, Gwynne H (Jimmie), 1955, N 19,19:3
Payton, Harold B, 1950, Je 25,70:2
Payton, Terence, 1946, N 15,23:3
Payton, William M, 1961, F 15,35:2
Payton, William S, 1940, N 3,57:1
Paytosh, George, 1947, Ag 2,13:4
Paz, Ezequiel, 1953, Mr 25,31:1
Paz, Ezequiel P (Sra), 1956, Mr 19,31:3
Paz, Jesus H, 1955, Je 23,29:4
Paz, Leopoldo de Mrs, 1947, D 16,33:2
Paz, Marcelino, 1954, F 13,13:2
Paz Barona, Miguel Dr, 1937, N 13,19:4
Pazmino, Ismael P, 1944, N 3,21:4
Peabody, A Russell, 1908, S 24,9:4
Peabody, A Russell Mrs, 1946, D 8,77:3
Peabody, Alex M, 1942, Ag 11,19:2
Peabody, Alfred, 1954, Ag 14,15:3
Peabody, Alfred Mrs, 1948, Jl 17,16:3
Peabody, Archibald Russell, 1908, S 27,11:6
Peabody, Arthur, 1942, S 8,23:5
Peabody, Arthur J Mrs, 1910, N 5,7:4
Peabody, Benjamin B, 1965, My 3,33:4
Peabody, C A, 1931, Ap 27,21:1
Peabody, C A Judge, 1901, Jl 4,7:4
Peabody, Charles, 1939, Ag 19,15:5
Peabody, Charles A Mrs, 1910, D 27,9:4
Peabody, Charles Jones (funl, F 28,19:5), 1924, F 25, 15:3
Peabody, Charles M, 1942, Ja 6,23:5
Peabody, Charles M Mrs, 1954, Mr 19,23:5
Peabody, Charles M Sr, 1967, Ap 21,39:2
Peabody, Charles W, 1963, N 9,25:1
Peabody, Dean Jr, 1951, Ag 9,21:6
Peabody, Dudley H, 1962, Mr 3,8:5
Peabody, Dudley H Mrs, 1962, Mr 3,8:5
Peabody, Endicott, 1944, N 18,13:3
Peabody, Endicott Mrs, 1946, Mr 5,26:2
Peabody, Ernest H, 1965, Mr 8,29:3
Peabody, Ernest H Mrs, 1948, Je 21,21:4
Peabody, F G, 1936, D 30,22:1
Peabody, Francis, 1938, F 10,21:3; 1943, O 13,23:1
Peabody, Francis Col, 1910, Ap 30,9:6
Peabody, Francis H, 1905, S 23,9:4
Peabody, Francis Stuyvesant, 1922, Ag 28,11:7
Peabody, Frederick W, 1938, Ag 17,19:2
Peabody, George, 1869, N 5,1:4; 1958, Ag 24,87:2
Peabody, George F, 1909, S 13,9:5; 1938, Mr 5,17:1
Peabody, George Foster Mrs (Katrina Trask),(por), 1922, Ja 9,17:1
Peabody, George H, 1912, My 23,13:5
Peabody, George Lee, 1911, F 10,9:3
Peabody, George Livingston Dr, 1914, O 31,11:6
Peabody, George R, 1946, My 2,21:4
Peabody, Henry Clay Justice, 1911, Mr 30,11:6
Peabody, Henry G, 1951, Mr 28,29:5
Peabody, Henry Oliver, 1903, Je 30,7:5
Peabody, Herbert C, 1953, N 28,15:4
Peabody, J D, 1877, Je 8,5:2
Peabody, Jacob C R, 1949, Ja 10,25:2
Peabody, James E, 1954, Je 26,13:6
Peabody, James Hamilton Ex-Gov, 1917, N 24,13:5
Peabody, John D, 1944, Ag 28,11:6
Peabody, John E, 1921, Ag 19,13:4
Peabody, Joseph, 1905, Ap 7,9:6
Peabody, Joseph L, 1949, D 5,23:2
Peabody, Josiah Rev, 1873, Je 29,3:7
Peabody, Kemper Mrs, 1944, Ja 20,19:1
Peabody, May E, 1943, D 8,23:2
Peabody, Nelson J, 1966, My 19,47:2
Peabody, P G, 1934, F 26,17:1
Peabody, Rev Dr, 1880, N 26,3:6
Peabody, Richard, 1937, D 27,16:2
Peabody, Robert S, 1917, S 24,13:6
Peabody, Rogers C Mrs, 1950, N 7,27:4
Peabody, Roland E, 1950, F 1,29:3
Peabody, Royal Canfield, 1917, S 17,13:4
Peabody, Rushton, 1954, D 18,15:6
Peabody, S H Dr, 1903, My 27,9:3
Peabody, Stephen, 1945, Ja 8,17:3
Peabody, Stuart Mrs, 1956, Ag 28,27:1
Peabody, Stuyvesant Sr, 1946, Je 8,21:5
Peabody, William, 1941, Ja 13,15:3
Peabody, William F, 1939, Ag 5,15:6
Peabody, William J, 1955, Ja 26,3:3
Peabody, William W, 1959, Ap 13,31:5
Peabody, Winthrop, 1944, Je 19,19:5
Peace, Arthur W, 1959, Ja 19,27:5
Peace, Charles, 1958, My 16,25:2
Peace, Ernest J, 1948, Ag 3,25:5
Peace, George William, 1905, Mr 15,9:6
Peace, John D Sr, 1937, S 10,23:5
Peace, John E, 1956, Ja 14,19:5
Peace, Lillian M, 1967, S 13,47:2
Peace, Marshall C, 1961, Ja 9,39:4
Peace, William S, 1961, O 29,88:7
Peace, Willis G, 1941, F 13,19:5
Peach, R W, 1936, D 24,17:3
Peachey, John F Mrs, 1908, S 6,9:2
Peachman, Aug, 1953, F 1,89:1
Peacock, A R, 1928, Jl 13,17:5
Peacock, Arthur G, 1944, O 20,19:3
Peacock, Bertram, 1963, Ap 27,25:3
Peacock, Chauncey H Mrs, 1958, Jl 13,69:2
Peacock, D J Mrs, 1953, My 8,25:5
Peacock, Edgar H, 1953, Mr 23,23:2
Peacock, Edward R, 1962, N 20,35:1
Peacock, Edwin Mrs, 1948, Mr 18,27:3
Peacock, Elizabeth F Mrs, 1953, Jl 10,19:1
Peacock, Everett R, 1949, O 21,25:3
Peacock, Frank W, 1938, Ap 26,21:3
Peacock, Henry W, 1959, Jl 21,30:5
Peacock, Hugh, 1942, Je 13,15:5
Peacock, James, 1938, D 28,26:5
Peacock, James K, 1939, Mr 8,21:4
Peacock, John, 1953, Ap 21,27:3
Peacock, Joseph L, 1954, S 25,15:4
Peacock, Kenneth C, 1962, D 2,88:7
Peacock, Ray, 1943, Ag 9,13:5
Peacock, Robert, 1956, Jl 20,17:2
Peacock, Robert E, 1945, Jl 3,13:4
Peacock, Samuel M, 1946, D 13,23:4
Peacock, Sterling E Mrs, 1943, Mr 7,38:4

Peacock, Thomas P Mrs, 1947, Je 6,23:5
Peacock, Thomas R, 1937, N 12,21:5
Peacock, William H, 1967, O 16,45:3
Peacock, William T, 1967, N 11,33:3
Peacocke, Joseph Ferguson Archbishop, 1916, My 27, 11:6
Peacocke, Mary F Superioress, 1873, F 15,8:6
Peacocke, Vereker T, 1937, Ag 17,19:2
Peagnet, E, 1879, O 11,8:3
Peairs, Hervey B, 1940, S 3,17:6
Peairs, Leonard M, 1956, F 2,25:3
Peairs, Ralph P Mrs, 1940, Mr 13,23:4
Peak, George J, 1944, N 30,23:1
Peak, George J Mrs, 1938, S 27,21:5
Peak, John L, 1910, S 25,II,13:5
Peake, Alonzo W, 1958, Ag 29,23:1
Peake, Charles B, 1958, Ap 11,25:1
Peake, Chester A, 1961, Je 17,21:6
Peake, Harold J, 1946, S 24,29:2
Peake, Howard D, 1955, O 18,37:4
Peake, John G (connection, Ag 4,33:3), 1966, Ag 3, 37:5
Peake, Margaret I Mrs, 1941, Ag 28,19:5
Peake, Mervyn, 1968, N 19,40:1
Peake, W I, 1883, Ag 10,5:5
Peake, William W, 1951, N 13,29:3
Peakes, J G, 1901, N 7,9:6
Peal, E Joseph, 1952, F 10,93:3
Peale, Arthur L, 1947, Mr 4,26:2
Peale, C C Mrs, 1967, D 13,47:1
Peale, Charles C, 1955, S 22,31:4
Peale, Charles C Mrs, 1939, Jl 30,29:2
Peale, Charles W, 1940, Jl 24,21:4
Peale, Elizabeth K, 1924, Ap 30,19:2
Peale, Frank P, 1952, F 8,23:3
Peale, Franklin D, 1945, Je 9,13:4
Peale, Franklin V, 1952, Mr 13,23:1
Peale, John W, 1925, My 8,19:4
Peale, Joseph M, 1940, N 30,17:4
Peale, M L, 1947, My 15,25:1
Peale, Mary J, 1902, N 23,7:5
Pear, Samuel, 1944, Ag 7,15:4
Pear, William W, 1965, D 9,47:4
Pearburn, Alice, 1905, Ap 25,1:2
Pearce, Al, 1961, Je 3,23:1
Pearce, Alfred D, 1949, F 26,15:6
Pearce, Alice (Mrs P Davis), 1966, Mr 4,33:3
Pearce, Archibald Capt, 1914, Je 17,11:7
Pearce, Benjamin Mrs, 1949, Jl 2,15:1
Pearce, C E, 1902, Ja 31,9:5
Pearce, Charles L, 1947, O 30,25:3
Pearce, Charles S, 1965, Mr 17,45:5
Pearce, Cohen S, 1942, D 6,77:2
Pearce, E Freeman, 1962, D 8,27:1
Pearce, E L, 1940, Ag 3,15:2
Pearce, Earle D, 1941, D 27,19:4
Pearce, Edgar L, 1954, Mr 31,27:3
Pearce, Edith T, 1951, N 5,31:4
Pearce, Edward D Jr, 1960, F 16,37:4
Pearce, Edward E, 1922, O 31,15:4
Pearce, Edward R, 1953, Mr 19,29:3
Pearce, Elmer E, 1952, S 6,17:2
Pearce, Elston E, 1966, D 13,47:4
Pearce, Eugene F Dr, 1914, My 1,13:6
Pearce, Eugene S Mrs, 1948, Ja 21,25:4
Pearce, Frank B, 1914, My 21,11:4
Pearce, Frank T, 1942, S 4,23:5
Pearce, Fred W, 1959, Ag 16,82:2
Pearce, Frederick H, 1943, Mr 15,13:4
Pearce, Frederick Sr, 1953, Ja 13,27:4
Pearce, George, 1952, Je 25,29:2
Pearce, George C, 1940, Ag 14,19:6
Pearce, George G, 1950, N 8,29:4
Pearce, George T Mrs, 1943, Ap 21,25:3
Pearce, Harold W, 1948, F 7,15:2
Pearce, Harry, 1943, O 12,27:2
Pearce, Haywood J, 1943, My 2,44:6
Pearce, Henry A Mrs, 1949, Ja 22,13:1
Pearce, Henry M, 1920, Ja 20,7:2
Pearce, Howard A, 1952, O 28,31:4
Pearce, J Elmer, 1955, My 13,25:3
Pearce, John I, 1951, F 3,15:2
Pearce, John M, 1960, Mr 23,28:3
Pearce, Joseph A, 1946, O 28,27:5
Pearce, Louise, 1959, Ag 11,27:1
Pearce, Matthew C, 1966, Je 9,47:3
Pearce, McLeod M, 1948, N 23,29:4
Pearce, Myron C, 1961, Mr 25,25:4
Pearce, Owen C Mrs, 1958, F 26,27:4
Pearce, Patrick D, 1949, Jl 4,13:3
Pearce, Ralph E, 1967, N 19,85:2
Pearce, Ralph S, 1952, My 6,29:2
Pearce, Raymond S, 1943, Ja 11,15:2
Pearce, Reginald B, 1939, Ap 5,25:3
Pearce, S Bartley (por), 1938, Ja 30,II,8:6
Pearce, S Bartley Mrs, 1944, D 11,23:5
Pearce, Sadie E, 1951, Jl 14,13:3
Pearce, Samuel, 1951, My 1,29:5
Pearce, Stanley D, 1951, N 22,31:2
Pearce, Thomas B, 1947, Ap 16,25:6
Pearce, Thomas E, 1948, F 9,17:2
Pearce, Vera, 1966, Ja 21,47:4
Pearce, Walter C, 1949, Je 24,23:3
Pearce, Walter H, 1940, Ja 30,20:2
Pearce, Warren W, 1951, F 20,25:2
Pearce, Webster H, 1940, O 11,21:5
Pearce, William G, 1952, Jl 16,25:2
Pearce, William George Sir, 1907, N 4,9:4
Pearce, William H, 1964, S 12,25:2
Pearce, William P, 1947, S 3,25:2
Pearce, William S, 1953, Je 12,27:4
Peard, John E, 1958, Mr 9,86:3
Peare, Charles B, 1952, Je 7,19:5
Peare, Robert S, 1951, Mr 19,27:3
Pearl, Abraham, 1940, Mr 10,51:4
Pearl, Azariah Y, 1943, Ja 30,15:3
Pearl, Dyer, 1955, My 31,27:1
Pearl, E G, 1881, Ag 17,5:5
Pearl, Frank H, 1939, Mr 5,49:2
Pearl, George C, 1959, N 12,35:1
Pearl, Harry Mrs, 1952, Mr 22,13:3
Pearl, Manuel A, 1952, F 26,27:2
Pearl, Mary J, 1966, F 17,33:1
Pearl, Nellis C Mrs, 1937, O 13,24:1
Pearl, Philip, 1966, Jl 11,29:2
Pearl, Raymond, 1940, N 18,19:1
Pearl, Samuel, 1947, Ap 11,25:3
Pearl, William A, 1962, S 13,37:2
Pearl, William Ellery, 1906, Ja 16,11:5
Pearlmain, Alice U Mrs, 1946, Ag 30,17:6
Pearlman, Bernard Mrs, 1958, Mr 9,86:7
Pearlman, Joseph, 1963, Je 28,30:1
Pearlman, Joseph L, 1959, D 18,29:3
Pearlman, Meyer A, 1968, F 3,29:5
Pearlman, Morris, 1966, O 2,86:3
Pearlman, Morris L, 1943, Jl 22,19:3
Pearlman, Saul J, 1953, O 8,29:3
Pearlstein, A I Mrs, 1953, Jl 23,23:1
Pearlstein, Abraham, 1924, Je 6,17:5
Pearlstein, Benjamin, 1946, Ap 21,47:2
Pearlstein, Jacob, 1955, S 14,35:6
Pearlstein, Phil, 1955, O 6,29:2
Pearmain, Samuel B, 1941, My 3,15:3
Pearman, A J Capt, 1903, Ag 30,7:6
Pearman, Joseph B Mrs, 1959, D 30,21:2
Pearman, Mabel B Mrs, 1940, D 19,25:2
Pears, Andrew, 1909, F 11,7:4
Pears, Charles, 1958, Ja 30,23:2
Pears, Edwin Sir, 1919, D 9,17:4
Pears, Thomas C Jr, 1943, D 27,19:3
Pearsall, Alfred Everson, 1919, Ap 29,15:4
Pearsall, Arthur R Mrs, 1955, O 26,31:1
Pearsall, Charles H C, 1958, My 7,35:1
Pearsall, D, 1879, Ap 8,8:3
Pearsall, Denton, 1950, Ap 8,13:6
Pearsall, Denton Mrs, 1948, Je 19,15:5
Pearsall, Earle S, 1944, Mr 16,19:6
Pearsall, Edgar R Mrs, 1949, F 9,27:5
Pearsall, Eleanor J B Mrs, 1937, My 18,23:1
Pearsall, Elmer E, 1949, Ja 28,22:2
Pearsall, Everett H, 1955, F 21,21:2
Pearsall, Ferris R Mrs, 1955, Ja 29,15:3
Pearsall, Franklin Mrs, 1954, Jl 14,27:6
Pearsall, George H, 1954, Mr 9,27:4
Pearsall, George W, 1941, Jl 29,15:4
Pearsall, Gilbert B, 1958, Ja 1,25:5
Pearsall, Gilbert H, 1957, Ag 14,25:5
Pearsall, Gilbert H Mrs, 1952, Ag 21,19:6
Pearsall, Harold W, 1947, D 1,21:3
Pearsall, Harry, 1947, S 25,29:6
Pearsall, Harry E, 1940, Ja 16,23:3
Pearsall, Henry S, 1939, F 20,17:5
Pearsall, Howard E, 1945, Ja 7,38:3
Pearsall, James Buchanan Gen, 1916, Ja 21,9:3
Pearsall, James H, 1946, My 6,21:4
Pearsall, Jay H, 1951, Ag 12,76:8
Pearsall, John, 1874, Mr 31,4:7
Pearsall, John V, 1939, Ap 7,21:4
Pearsall, Leigh M, 1964, Ap 12,86:8
Pearsall, Lewis R, 1953, D 30,23:2
Pearsall, Lillian I Mrs, 1940, Je 2,45:1
Pearsall, Samuel (will, Ag 31,19:8), 1963, Ag 16,28:2
Pearsall, Thomas W, 1909, Ja 2,9:6
Pearsall, W V, 1944, Mr 13,15:2
Pearsall, William V, 1964, Ag 20,29:2
Pearse, Arthur S, 1956, D 13,37:1
Pearse, Carroll G, 1948, My 3,21:4
Pearse, Charles B, 1941, S 26,24:2
Pearse, Chester A Sr, 1955, Ap 14,36:2
Pearse, Frederic M P, 1953, N 15,89:3
Pearse, George S, 1950, Ap 28,21:2
Pearse, Howard S, 1951, Mr 6,27:2
Pearse, Langdon, 1956, Jl 21,15:2
Pearse, Nicholas Rev, 1909, My 21,9:6
Pearse, Paul, 1953, My 23,15:5
Pearse, Richard A Rev, 1924, My 17,15:5
Pearse, Robin, 1956, N 21,27:5
Pearse, W F, 1880, F 27,5:6
Pearson, A C, 1933, Ap 1,15:1
Pearson, A L Gen, 1903, Ja 7,9:6
Pearson, A Y, 1903, Ja 30,9:5
Pearson, Adam, 1937, Mr 10,23:3
Pearson, Al, 1943, S 25,17:8
Pearson, Albert F, 1946, Ap 26,21:1
Pearson, Alex W, 1903, D 17,9:4
Pearson, Alfred J, 1939, Ag 11,15:4
Pearson, Alvin J, 1947, F 20,25:5
Pearson, Andrew F, 1952, Ag 15,16:6
Pearson, Anita C, 1953, Ja 13,27:3
Pearson, Ardys Mrs, 1951, Ag 16,21:2
Pearson, Arthur Sir, 1921, D 10,13:3
Pearson, August S, 1960, My 29,57:2
Pearson, B F, 1912, F 1,13:4
Pearson, C Alfred, 1962, Ja 20,21:4
Pearson, Carl E, 1951, Ag 7,25:3
Pearson, Charles B, 1941, Mr 30,49:1; 1941, Jl 20,31:
Pearson, Charles E, 1950, S 17,104:4
Pearson, Charles H, 1958, O 9,37:1; 1968, N 16,37:4
Pearson, Charles Y, 1947, My 15,25:3
Pearson, Clifford C, 1903, S 12,9:6
Pearson, Dane A, 1958, Mr 5,31:3
Pearson, David, 1914, Ap 12,15:4
Pearson, Dennis, 1967, F 1,16:1
Pearson, E J, 1928, D 8,19:3
Pearson, E Pennington, 1944, Mr 21,19:2
Pearson, Earle, 1950, F 19,78:2
Pearson, Ebbert, 1955, Ap 22,25:3
Pearson, Edmund L, 1937, Ag 8,33:4
Pearson, Edna R W Mrs, 1942, Ap 16,21:3
Pearson, Edward, 1938, Ap 21,19:4
Pearson, Edward H, 1954, My 15,15:5
Pearson, Edward J Mrs, 1951, Je 3,92:5
Pearson, Edward M, 1904, Ap 14,6:4
Pearson, Edward Nathan, 1924, Ja 27,23:2
Pearson, Edward P Jr, 1959, D 3,37:5
Pearson, Elbert A, 1962, My 9,43:2
Pearson, Ellen Mrs, 1944, My 26,19:5
Pearson, Elmer R, 1955, Ja 1,13:5
Pearson, Enoch W, 1952, F 27,27:5
Pearson, Fisher H, 1940, Ag 6,19:4
Pearson, Fred C, 1947, Mr 14,23:3
Pearson, Frederick, 1955, Ag 10,25:4
Pearson, Frederick D, 1946, Ja 30,25:2
Pearson, Frederick F A, 1958, S 16,28:1
Pearson, Frederick S, 1960, Ja 18,27:2
Pearson, G Fred, 1938, S 22,23:5
Pearson, George F Rear-Adm, 1867, Jl 2,4:7
Pearson, H G, 1889, Ap 21,16:5
Pearson, Hans Mrs, 1952, Mr 11,27:4
Pearson, Harlan C, 1943, Ja 7,20:2
Pearson, Harold G Mrs, 1951, D 11,33:1
Pearson, Harry B, 1951, Ag 12,76:7
Pearson, Harry Capt, 1937, N 18,23:5
Pearson, Haydn S, 1967, Je 8,47:1
Pearson, Henry A, 1938, Mr 9,23:3
Pearson, Henry F, 1964, Ag 16,93:1
Pearson, Henry G, 1939, D 29,15:5
Pearson, Henry H, 1937, D 8,25:3
Pearson, Henry Havens, 1903, Ag 10,7:6
Pearson, Henry L Mrs, 1960, O 22,23:6
Pearson, Hesketh, 1964, Ap 10,35:2
Pearson, Hugh W, 1941, F 26,21:5
Pearson, Hyman (Bud), 1959, N 22,86:5
Pearson, Isaac Green, 1874, Je 2,4:7
Pearson, James B, 1917, My 31,11:6
Pearson, James H T, 1951, Ja 5,21:2
Pearson, Jay F W, 1965, Ag 9,25:2
Pearson, John A, 1948, Ag 8,56:5
Pearson, John L, 1956, D 7,27:5
Pearson, John M, 1952, N 17,25:4
Pearson, John W, 1948, Jl 21,23:6; 1954, Je 5,17:5
Pearson, Joseph Jr, 1951, F 24,13:3
Pearson, Joseph W, 1945, Ag 28,19:2
Pearson, Joshua A, 1950, D 5,31:1
Pearson, Keith N, 1955, Ag 25,23:4
Pearson, Kendrick, 1967, Mr 1,33:8
Pearson, Leon M, 1963, Ap 30,35:3
Pearson, Leopold L, 1941, S 5,21:4
Pearson, Lewis W, 1958, N 27,29:2
Pearson, Malcolm L, 1957, D 12,30:1
Pearson, Mary, 1954, N 20,17:2
Pearson, Maurice Mrs, 1962, Ap 24,37:1
Pearson, Molly (Mrs E Hales), 1959, Ja 30,27:4
Pearson, Nelson R, 1966, F 15,36:1
Pearson, Oliver W, 1946, Mr 19,27:3
Pearson, Oscar, 1963, Ag 13,31:4
Pearson, Oscar W, 1968, F 28,47:3
Pearson, Paul M (por), 1938, Mr 27,II,7:1
Pearson, Paul W, 1943, Jl 27,17:3
Pearson, Peter H, 1940, Jl 6,15:4
Pearson, Phil C, 1955, Ja 28,19:3
Pearson, R M, 1878, Ja 7,1:5
Pearson, Ralph M, 1958, My 1,31:2
Pearson, Raymond A (por), 1939, F 14,19:3
Pearson, Richard M, 1957, Mr 25,25:3
Pearson, Richmond, 1923, S 13,19:3
Pearson, Robert B, 1954, F 14,92:4
Pearson, Robert C, 1941, Je 24,19:2
Pearson, Robert H, 1950, Ja 13,23:3
Pearson, Robert L, 1952, D 1,23:4
Pearson, Robert N, 1903, O 7,9:8
Pearson, Samuel, 1943, O 16,13:4
Pearson, Samuel H, 1925, Ap 10,19:5
Pearson, Samuel K, 1957, N 20,35:2
Pearson, Stanley Sr, 1949, Ap 20,27:1
Pearson, Ted (T A Pehrson), 1961, O 8,87:1
Pearson, Thomas G (por), 1943, S 5,29:1
Pearson, Thomas G Mrs, 1962, F 19,31:3
Pearson, Thomas H, 1958, F 13,29:4

Pearson, Virginia, 1958, Je 10,33:3; 1964, Ja 16,26:1
Pearson, Virginia P, 1942, Je 2,23:5
Pearson, W C, 1933, N 20,15:3
Pearson, Walter B, 1941, My 26,19:5
Pearson, Walter F, 1958, F 24,19:4
Pearson, Wellington E, 1944, Ap 27,23:4
Pearson, William A, 1959, F 17,32:1
Pearson, William C, 1922, Ag 12,9:6; 1945, Ag 14,21:4
Pearson, William E, 1904, F 2,9:6; 1956, Ja 14,19:6
Pearson, William E Capt, 1916, Mr 23,11:5
Pearson, William G, 1949, Je 22,31:3
Pearson, William H, 1914, My 15,15:6; 1946, Jl 5,19:4
Pearson, William S, 1957, Ja 14,23:5
Pearsons, Forrest G Sr, 1952, Ap 11,23:2
Pearsons, Harry P, 1952, F 3,84:4
Peart, Alfred G, 1957, D 17,35:3
Peart, Hartley F, 1954, N 24,23:5
Peart, William (por), 1949, Ja 2,60:6
Peartree, Henry, 1938, O 23,40:8
Peary, Robert E Mrs (funl, D 28,23:1), 1955, D 20, 31:1
Pease, A H, 1882, Jl 16,7:2
Pease, Alan W (por), 1955, My 14,19:2
Pease, Albert W, 1946, S 29,61:1
Pease, Alfred E Sir, 1939, Ap 28,25:4
Pease, Anna G Prof (por), 1937, Jl 9,21:3
Pease, Arthur S, 1964, Ja 8,37:1
Pease, Charles G (por), 1941, O 9,23:1
Pease, Charles H Mrs, 1950, S 2,15:3
Pease, Charles Mrs, 1950, O 27,29:3
Pease, Charles W, 1964, Jl 10,29:4
Pease, D P Dr, 1902, D 8,9:5
Pease, Edward, 1955, Ja 7,21:2
Pease, Edward A, 1940, Je 22,15:7
Pease, F (Sister Frances), 1878, O 5,5:2
Pease, Frances, 1920, Jl 31,7:6; 1940, Ja 2,20:1
Pease, Francis G (por), 1938, F 8,21:3
Pease, Franklin W, 1944, Ja 27,19:2
Pease, Fred W, 1951, My 13,88:8
Pease, Frederick S, 1951, Ag 19,85:1
Pease, George W Jr, 1947, O 29,27:3
Pease, Harold C, 1945, My 8,34:5
Pease, Harry, 1945, N 9,19:4
Pease, Harry F, 1957, Ag 3,15:4
Pease, Henry H, 1937, Ag 17,19:3; 1945, Ja 4,19:5
Pease, Henry M (por), 1947, Mr 8,13:1
Pease, Herbert, 1940, My 1,23:5
Pease, Herbert D, 1950, F 16,23:2
Pease, Howard A, 1946, D 9,25:4
Pease, J Robert, 1963, My 30,17:4
Pease, James, 1967, Ap 27,45:3
Pease, John H, 1941, O 16,21:3
Pease, John W, 1946, O 29,25:5
Pease, Joseph W Sir, 1903, Je 24,9:6
Pease, Josiah C, 1948, S 1,23:3
Pease, Le Roy T Mrs, 1952, D 3,33:4
Pease, LeRoy B Col, 1916, Je 29,11:5
Pease, Lute (Lucius C), 1963, Ag 17,19:2
Pease, Lute Mrs, 1958, Ag 7,25:2
Pease, Luther M, 1952, Ja 16,25:4
Pease, Mary F, 1874, Ag 18,1:4
Pease, Murray, 1964, Ag 14,27:5
Pease, Nicholas Mrs, 1951, Jl 28,11:5
Pease, Peter L Mrs, 1952, My 26,23:3
Pease, Richard Mrs Lady, 1957, N 5,31:4
Pease, Robert N, 1964, Je 17,43:5
Pease, Sumner, 1938, Jl 24,29:4
Pease, Theodore C, 1948, Ag 12,21:3
Pease, W Albert Jr, 1940, N 27,23:3
Pease, W C Capt, 1866, Ja 8,1:7
Pease, Walter A, 1915, Mr 4,9:5
Pease, William E, 1943, Ap 1,23:2
Peaslee, Arthur N, 1956, Ag 10,17:3
Peaslee, E R Dr (see also Ja 22), 1878, Ja 25,8:6
Peaslee, Edward N Mrs, 1950, My 20,15:4
Peaslee, Horace W, 1959, My 19,33:2
Peaslee, Leon D, 1950, Ap 9,84:2
Peaslee, Robert J Mrs, 1952, N 13,31:4
Peasley, Frederick M, 1943, F 19,29:3
Peasley, James C, 1920, Jl 14,9:6
Peasley, John C, 1943, Jl 15,21:5
Peasley, Ralph E, 1948, D 14,29:2
Peat, Harold, 1960, Mr 31,33:1
Peat, Louisa W Mrs, 1953, Mr 26,31:3
Peat, Wilbur D, 1966, D 16,47:3
Peats, Alfred, 1908, Mr 15,9:4
Peattie, Donald C, 1964, N 17,41:1
Peattie, Edward C, 1963, S 1,56:4
Peattie, Margaret R, 1946, O 17,23:5
Peaty, Andrew A, 1949, Jl 26,27:2
Peaty, Francis H, 1960, Je 14,37:2
Peavey, Charles T, 1941, O 26,43:2
Peavey, Leroy D, 1937, Mr 26,22:1
Peay, A, 1927, O 3,23:3
Peay, George H L, 1946, F 3,40:2
Pebelier, Eugene, 1952, Mr 31,19:4
Pecci, Bro of the Pope, 1881, Mr 25,1:6
Pecci, Camillo Count, 1920, F 23,13:6
Pecci, Cardinal, 1890, F 7,4:6
Pecha, Anton F Sr, 1967, Ap 26,47:3
Pechenard, Msgr, 1920, My 28,13:4
Pecher, William F, 1904, F 23,5:5
Pecheux, Henry, 1948, Ag 13,15:4
Pechey, Archibald T, 1961, N 30,34:5
Pechin, John R, 1938, Ja 2,39:5
Pechiney, George A, 1943, Jl 15,21:3
Pechkoff, Zinovi, 1966, N 29,43:1
Pechner, Gerhard Mrs, 1966, Ja 15,27:6
Pechota, John, 1945, Mr 31,20:3
Pechstein, Max, 1955, Je 30,25:2
Pechter, David, 1968, Ag 17,27:4
Pechter, Harry, 1968, Ap 23,44:1
Pechter, William, 1961, Mr 26,93:1
Peck, A S, 1935, Jl 19,17:1
Peck, A W, 1884, Ja 5,2:6
Peck, Albert B, 1943, F 16,19:3
Peck, Albert M, 1937, F 22,17:3
Peck, Albert W, 1951, F 16,25:4
Peck, Alfred A, 1954, D 28,23:3
Peck, Alfred E, 1949, S 28,27:4
Peck, Alfred L (funl, O 6,13:6), 1911, S 19,13:2
Peck, Allen S, 1871, S 16,1:6
Peck, Alonzo R, 1922, S 23,15:4
Peck, Alonzo R Mrs, 1912, Ag 4,II,11:6
Peck, Andrew, 1918, Mr 22,13:5
Peck, Annetta W, 1958, Jl 15,25:2
Peck, Arthur, 1964, Jl 4,13:3
Peck, Arthur H, 1939, My 24,23:5
Peck, Arthur N, 1940, Ag 6,20:3
Peck, Augustus H, 1907, Mr 29,9:6
Peck, Barney, 1957, O 28,27:4
Peck, Bernard W, 1949, N 6,92:4
Peck, Brayton E Mrs, 1947, D 5,26:2
Peck, C H, 1927, Mr 30,25:5
Peck, C S Mrs, 1928, Ap 18,25:5
Peck, Carl E, 1940, D 7,17:5
Peck, Carl E Mrs, 1962, Je 23,23:4
Peck, Carson C (funl, My 1,13:5), 1915, Ap 30,13:4
Peck, Charles, 1957, Ag 23,19:4
Peck, Charles E, 1937, Jl 11,II,4:8
Peck, Charles E Jr, 1962, S 16,86:6
Peck, Charles Howard Jr, 1918, Mr 11,11:6
Peck, Charles M, 1920, O 15,13:3
Peck, Charles T, 1939, Ag 13,29:3
Peck, Chester G, 1948, My 24,19:1
Peck, Clair B, 1959, Ag 15,17:6
Peck, Clarence N, 1946, Jl 31,27:4
Peck, Clifton C, 1952, F 24,28:6
Peck, Cyrus, 1907, My 9,9:5
Peck, Cyrus W, 1956, S 28,27:1
Peck, Darius, 1944, D 7,25:2
Peck, David B, 1957, N 8,29:6
Peck, Dever J, 1940, Ja 29,15:3
Peck, Duncan W, 1923, F 17,13:4
Peck, E Adorno, 1943, Je 29,19:4
Peck, E Stanley, 1967, Jl 23,60:7
Peck, E Stuart, 1951, F 8,33:2
Peck, Ebenezer, 1881, My 26,5:4
Peck, Edgar W Mrs, 1939, Mr 16,23:2
Peck, Edith W, 1953, Ap 16,29:1
Peck, Edward G, 1940, F 3,13:5
Peck, Edwin D, 1962, Ja 15,27:2
Peck, Edwin O Dr, 1914, O 5,11:5
Peck, Elisha Capt, 1866, Jl 12,2:5
Peck, Eliza F Mrs, 1937, Je 20,II,5:5
Peck, Elliott W, 1956, O 2,35:5
Peck, Emma W Mrs, 1943, Mr 25,21:5
Peck, Epaphroditus, 1938, O 30,41:3
Peck, Erastus Judge, 1904, Ja 23,9:5
Peck, Eugene B, 1951, D 23,22:5
Peck, Eugene W, 1952, Jl 13,61:1
Peck, Everett J, 1957, F 3,76:1
Peck, Ferdinand W, 1960, Ja 19,35:3
Peck, Ferdinand W Mrs, 1944, Ap 22,15:5
Peck, Fletcher Clay, 1920, D 1,15:4
Peck, Florence S Mrs, 1940, Je 25,23:4
Peck, Flroence T Mrs, 1952, Ap 29,27:3
Peck, Fowler G, 1944, F 27,38:4
Peck, Frank W, 1944, My 24,19:2
Peck, Franklin G, 1941, My 23,21:2
Peck, Franklin H, 1965, Jl 14,37:4
Peck, Fred, 1942, O 2,25:5
Peck, Frederick B Dr, 1925, N 3,25:6
Peck, Frederick J, 1941, Je 8,49:1
Peck, Frederick J Capt, 1911, Mr 23,9:4
Peck, Frederick S (por), 1947, Ja 12,23:3
Peck, Frederick S Mrs, 1958, O 14,37:1
Peck, Fredinand W, 1924, N 5,19:4
Peck, George, 1937, Ap 6,23:4; 1961, S 18,24:5
Peck, George A, 1959, S 27,87:1
Peck, George H, 1937, F 28,II,9:2
Peck, George L, 1966, Je 27,35:3
Peck, George M, 1952, Ap 12,11:2
Peck, George R Col, 1923, F 23,13:5
Peck, George W, 1947, O 11,17:2; 1956, My 18,25:3
Peck, George Webster, 1915, My 30,13:4
Peck, Gideon H, 1923, S 4,17:2
Peck, Gideon H Mrs, 1950, Ja 16,26:2
Peck, Gordon C, 1949, D 24,15:5
Peck, Gordon C Mrs, 1948, N 15,25:5
Peck, Gordon H, 1921, F 19,11:3
Peck, Graham, 1968, Jl 23,39:2
Peck, Gregory P, 1962, Ag 26,82:6
Peck, Guy A, 1937, S 14,23:6
Peck, Guy D Jr, 1964, Mr 17,35:3
Peck, Guy Mrs, 1941, O 8,23:3
Peck, H G, 1867, Je 27,5:1
Peck, Harold B, 1950, Ja 27,23:2
Peck, Harrison W, 1966, N 22,45:3
Peck, Harry, 1949, Ja 29,13:6
Peck, Helen D Mrs (will), 1958, Ag 13,29:2
Peck, Henderson, 1918, N 27,13:2
Peck, Henry Allen, 1921, N 18,17:6
Peck, Herbert R, 1965, Jl 10,25:4
Peck, Herman Mrs, 1938, My 16,17:2
Peck, Hiram Harper, 1908, O 19,9:7
Peck, Howard C, 1952, Ag 16,15:5
Peck, Howard J, 1954, My 12,31:5
Peck, Howard M, 1948, O 10,76:6
Peck, Irving H, 1955, Mr 3,27:4
Peck, Isaac Rev, 1911, Jl 2,9:4
Peck, J J, 1878, Ap 22,1:6
Peck, J M, 1882, S 8,3:2
Peck, J Milton, 1945, N 29,23:4
Peck, J Raymond, 1956, O 2,35:1
Peck, J T Bp, 1883, My 19,5:3
Peck, James C, 1938, Ap 16,13:2
Peck, Jerome, 1962, Ap 28,25:5
Peck, Jerome A, 1938, N 4,23:3
Peck, Jesse C, 1955, F 1,29:3
Peck, John B, 1958, Jl 16,29:4
Peck, John C Mrs, 1962, F 22,25:5
Peck, John G, 1940, Mr 30,15:3
Peck, John Hudson, 1919, My 5,13:6
Peck, John M, 1944, O 7,13:2
Peck, John S, 1950, F 5,84:4
Peck, John S Prof, 1968, Ja 23,39:2
Peck, John W, 1937, Ag 11,24:2; 1948, Jl 31,15:2
Peck, Josiah H, 1940, My 29,23:2
Peck, Kelso, 1968, Je 27,43:4
Peck, Kenneth, 1946, D 27,19:3
Peck, L C, 1876, F 7,5:6
Peck, La Rue, 1942, Ja 12,21:4
Peck, Laderna, 1950, Ap 25,31:1
Peck, Laurence F, 1951, Jl 20,21:1
Peck, Laurence F Mrs, 1950, Ap 24,25:2
Peck, Leopold, 1904, Je 26,1:5
Peck, Levi M, 1940, Jl 18,19:5
Peck, Lillie M, 1957, F 22,21:1
Peck, Lizzie M, 1940, Ja 8,15:6
Peck, Lorraine T, 1956, N 17,21:4
Peck, Lorraine T Mrs, 1963, Ag 23,25:1
Peck, Louis E, 1942, D 3,25:5
Peck, Louis F, 1966, Je 23,39:4
Peck, Lucius B, 1866, D 29,1:7
Peck, Lydia R, 1949, Mr 31,25:3
Peck, Marcus R, 1951, O 27,19:5
Peck, Mary C, 1938, Ja 7,19:5
Peck, Mary G, 1957, Ja 13,84:4
Peck, Miles L, 1942, Ap 24,17:3
Peck, Milo B, 1941, Mr 30,48:7
Peck, Norman, 1955, N 4,29:2
Peck, Norman Mrs, 1947, S 27,15:4
Peck, Oscar T, 1943, Jl 14,19:5
Peck, Oscar T Mrs, 1951, O 3,33:4
Peck, P, 1879, Ja 17,8:1
Peck, Paul, 1949, N 3,3:1
Peck, Paul Frederick Prof, 1925, N 21,17:4
Peck, Paul Mrs, 1949, N 3,3:1
Peck, Percy S, 1950, Je 10,17:6
Peck, Peter G, 1872, Ap 1,7:5
Peck, Phil C, 1954, Jl 7,31:2
Peck, Raymond W, 1950, Mr 16,31:1
Peck, Richard, 1954, N 20,17:2
Peck, Richard H, 1952, S 13,17:4
Peck, Robert N, 1921, My 12,17:4
Peck, Robert W, 1963, Ap 30,35:4
Peck, Roscoe H, 1937, S 4,15:5
Peck, Roy A, 1954, O 29,23:4
Peck, Samuel, 1937, My 19,23:4
Peck, Samuel A, 1960, Ja 14,33:3
Peck, Sarah V, 1940, Je 27,23:6
Peck, Seymour Mrs, 1956, N 22,33:6
Peck, Solon, 1966, S 19,43:4
Peck, Staunton B, 1950, Jl 18,30:4
Peck, Stuart Grant, 1915, D 4,15:6
Peck, Thomas B, 1958, Ap 6,90:2
Peck, Thomas Bloodgood, 1912, My 16,11:4
Peck, Thomas L, 1944, Jl 1,15:6
Peck, Thomas L Mrs, 1941, F 14,17:1
Peck, Thomas M, 1913, D 19,11:4
Peck, Tracy, 1921, N 26,13:6
Peck, Vernon W, 1942, Jl 23,19:5
Peck, W B, 1880, Ag 1,2:4
Peck, W E, 1926, O 23,17:3
Peck, Walter A Mrs, 1957, Je 12,35:3
Peck, Walter C, 1952, Ap 30,27:3
Peck, Walter E, 1954, Ja 16,12:7
Peck, Walter J, 1909, Ap 17,9:5
Peck, Wilbur, 1952, Ap 8,29:3
Peck, William B, 1940, My 21,23:1; 1941, Ag 21,17:3; 1958, O 15,39:1
Peck, William C, 1951, Jl 27,19:3
Peck, William E Mrs, 1943, Ap 27,24:3
Peck, William H, 1949, N 27,104:7
Peck, William J, 1869, N 1,4:7; 1938, N 10,27:2; 1947, Je 2,25:2
Peck, William Jay Rev Dr, 1920, S 17,11:5
Peck, William L, 1965, My 17,35:5
Peck, William R, 1948, Ag 10,21:4

Peck, Willys B, 1952, S 3,29:2
Pecker, David S Dr, 1968, F 17,29:4
Pecker, Jonathan Eastman Col, 1915, Ag 13,9:6
Pecker, Joseph S, 1947, My 9,21:2
Pecker, Nota, 1950, Mr 30,29:2
Peckett, Robert P Jr, 1950, F 28,29:2
Peckett, Robert P Mrs, 1951, S 18,32:4
Peckham, Adelaide, 1944, My 16,21:4
Peckham, Alva L, 1943, S 16,21:3
Peckham, Alvah L Mrs, 1945, O 18,23:5
Peckham, Charles P, 1945, Mr 1,21:6
Peckham, Fenner H Dr, 1915, D 27,9:4
Peckham, Frances M Mrs, 1959, Je 9,37:2
Peckham, Frederick A, 1958, F 3,23:4
Peckham, G W, 1873, D 8,2:4
Peckham, George E, 1941, Mr 11,23:4
Peckham, George G, 1945, Ag 9,21:4
Peckham, Harold A, 1937, O 16,19:5
Peckham, Howard L Mrs, 1963, My 22,41:5
Peckham, Joseph R, 1947, Ja 7,28:2
Peckham, Julia A, 1938, D 20,25:4
Peckham, Phil H, 1955, Je 9,29:1
Peckham, Rufus W Judge, 1873, D 4,4:7
Peckham, Rufus W Mrs, 1917, Jl 26,11:6
Peckham, Stephen Farnum Prof, 1918, Jl 13,9:5
Peckham, W H, 1879, D 7,7:1
Peckham, Walton Cheseborough (est), 1913, Ag 29, 9:5
Peckham, Walton Milderberger, 1911, Jl 28,9:6
Peckham, Wheeler H, 1954, My 30,44:7
Peckham, Wheeler H Mrs, 1916, O 31,13:7; 1965, F 25,32:1
Peckham, Wheeler Hazard, 1905, S 28,1:1
Peckham, William Clark Prof, 1922, O 5,23:2
Peckham, William D, 1940, S 11,26:2
Peckham, William E Mrs, 1944, Ja 28,17:3
Peckham, William G, 1924, Ap 15,21:2
Peckham, William L, 1940, Mr 12,25:4
Peckinpaugh, Frank, 1946, S 1,35:1
Peckitt, Leonard, 1952, Jl 23,23:3
Pecklers, Arthur H Sr, 1952, D 17,33:5
Peckman, F Baring, 1903, D 8,9:5
Peckover, Alexander Lord, 1919, O 23,13:4
Peckworth, Charles H, 1965, Mr 11,33:2
Pecora, Louis Mrs, 1948, N 24,23:3
Pecora, Michael, 1962, Ja 24,33:2
Pecora, Nicholas, 1957, O 22,33:4
Pecoraro, Amadeo M, 1950, Jl 31,17:4
Pecord, Ollie, 1941, Jl 2,21:2
Pecori-Giraldo, G Count, 1941, F 16,41:2
Pecorini, Margaret Countess (Mrs Daniele Pecorini), 1963, N 6,41:1
Pecoy, James, 1903, Jl 26,7:6
Pedanyuk, Ivan M, 1965, N 1,37:7
Peddicord, Charles E, 1941, N 2,53:3
Peddicord, Stephen B, 1953, F 11,29:2
Peddie, John W, 1940, Ja 18,23:1
Peddle, Henry G, 1939, Jl 3,13:6
Peddrick, Charles H, 1940, Ap 6,17:6
Peddy, George E B, 1951, Je 14,27:4
Pedell, Hugo, 1962, Ag 3,23:2
Peden, Horatio H, 1941, Ag 21,17:6
Peden, James L, 1948, My 4,25:5
Peden, John B, 1946, Je 1,13:4
Peden, Robert W B, 1947, F 18,25:2
Pedersen, Albert H, 1951, Je 14,27:5
Pedersen, Bernt, 1947, Ag 24,56:3
Pedersen, Carl (C Brisson),(funl, S 30,31:5), 1958, S 26,27:3
Pedersen, Erick J, 1961, My 19,31:2
Pedersen, Halvor, 1952, Je 21,15:7
Pedersen, James, 1947, My 13,25:3
Pedersen, Olaf S, 1944, S 27,21:6
Pedersen, Paul, 1962, D 17,15:8
Pedersen, Peder A, 1951, S 7,29:4
Pedersen, Victor C, 1958, Ap 15,33:2
Pedersen, Victor E, 1951, S 13,31:2
Pedersen, Walter B, 1959, Mr 28,17:1
Pedersen, William S, 1945, O 14,42:7
Pederson, Andrew, 1942, Jl 4,17:7
Pederson, Fred, 1944, Je 28,23:5
Pederson, Jacob O, 1958, Ja 21,29:1
Pedisich, Michael, 1950, Ag 7,19:3
Pedivo, Walter R, 1942, Mr 10,19:2
Pedler, Harry W Sr, 1950, S 27,31:3
Pedler, James S, 1967, Mr 2,35:2
Pedler, Margaret Mrs, 1948, D 29,21:3
Pedley, Alice M, 1947, Ja 7,28:2
Pedley, John C, 1949, N 7,27:2
Pedlow, George W, 1947, Ja 3,21:3
Pedolski, Harry Mrs, 1952, S 1,17:5
Pedrazzini, Eduardo, 1948, D 21,31:1
Pedreira, Antonio S, 1939, O 24,23:5
Pedrell, Felipe, 1922, Ag 21,11:4
Pedrick, Bertrice H, 1961, Jl 12,32:1
Pedrick, Clarence S, 1951, S 28,31:3
Pedrick, Howard A, 1941, Mr 7,21:3
Pedrick, Lytle C Mrs, 1949, N 8,31:3
Pedrick, Margaret S Mrs, 1938, O 21,23:4
Pedrick, Norman O, 1942, D 11,23:5
Pedrick, Reuben J, 1939, Je 21,23:5
Pedrick, Rose A, 1951, D 19,31:3
Pedrick, William A, 1958, Ap 16,33:4
Pedrick, William J (por), 1949, My 5,27:1
Pedrick, William Jr, 1938, Ja 25,21:2
Pedrini, Armando, 1940, Ja 21,34:7
Pedro, ex-Emperor of Brazil, 1891, D 3,4:6
Pedro VII, King of the Congo, 1955, Ap 18,23:2
Pedrotti, Silvio, 1955, Ag 4,7:2
Pedrow, Oscar B, 1946, My 25,15:3
Peebles, Harry O, 1948, Ag 17,21:1
Peebles, Hubert J, 1941, O 2,25:6
Peebles, James C, 1954, F 19,34:2
Peebles, James Martin Dr, 1922, F 16,15:4
Peebles, John C, 1945, Je 21,19:5
Peebles, Leighton H, 1961, Ja 29,84:2
Peebles, Mary, 1915, Ap 26,9:6
Peebles, Peter P, 1938, O 10,19:4
Peebles, Richard E, 1953, Je 16,27:3
Peebles, Rose J, 1952, My 16,23:1
Peebles, Rufus W, 1968, Mr 9,29:3
Peebles, William B, 1957, Ja 16,31:5
Peecock, Lambert K, 1944, F 20,36:1
Peed, Garland P Sr, 1962, Ap 1,86:6
Peed, Roy, 1951, Ag 9,21:2
Peede, James G, 1938, S 3,13:4
Peeds, Thomas R, 1948, N 14,76:2
Peehl, Carl A Mrs, 1941, N 1,15:3
Peek, Andrew, 1945, Ag 5,38:4
Peek, Burton F, 1960, Je 16,33:4
Peek, Ernest D, 1950, Ap 24,25:4
Peek, George N, 1943, D 18,16:2
Peek, George W Ex-Gov, 1916, Ap 17,11:5
Peek, George W Jr, 1954, Mr 28,88:3
Peek, Robert L Jr, 1967, Jl 8,25:3
Peek, Robert L Jr Mrs, 1949, Ja 28,21:3
Peel, Albert, 1949, N 5,13:1
Peel, Arthur, 1952, O 10,25:2
Peel, Arthur Wellesley Viscount, 1912, O 25,13:3
Peel, Earl, 1937, S 30,23:1
Peel, Frank L, 1945, Mr 27,19:1
Peel, Fred, 1914, My 6,11:6
Peel, Frederick Sir, 1906, Je 7,7:2
Peel, Graham, 1937, O 18,17:4
Peel, Henry A, 1953, N 6,22:1
Peel, J, 1879, F 14,4:7
Peel, Lady, 1859, N 14,2:1
Peel, Lawrence Sir, 1884, Jl 24,5:3
Peel, Robert, 1950, Ap 23,92:5
Peel, Rose Mrs, 1940, Mr 7,23:5
Peel, Sidney, 1938, D 20,25:2
Peel, William George Rev, 1916, Ap 16,21:4
Peele, Robert (will, D 17,26:4), 1942, D 9,27:2
Peele, William W, 1959, Jl 3,17:5
Peeler, James A, 1951, S 4,27:3
Peeler, Robert L, 1949, F 3,23:2
Peelle, Robert S, 1943, O 6,23:3
Peelor, J Rodney, 1952, Ap 6,88:2
Peelor, Philip R, 1943, Jl 9,17:6
Peene, Edith A, 1951, N 23,29:1
Peene, Frank W, 1947, S 1,19:2
Peene, Frederick, 1944, Jl 27,17:4
Peene, George W, 1944, My 28,33:1
Peene, Joseph J Capt, 1918, D 22,17:4
Peene, Myra, 1956, Ag 2,25:4
Peene, Stephen J, 1944, O 24,23:5
Peeney, C Alfred, 1948, Mr 28,48:6
Peeples, Thomas Whinston, 1907, Ap 30,9:6
Peer, Alfred J, 1960, D 8,35:4
Peer, John, 1943, N 13,13:4; 1955, Jl 29,17:4
Peer, Oscar, 1949, N 1,27:3
Peer, Ralph S, 1960, Ja 21,31:3
Peer, Verner D, 1952, D 7,89:3
Peer, Walter, 1937, O 20,23:4
Peereboom, Pieter, 1941, Jl 6,27:2
Peers, Frank O, 1938, Je 29,19:5
Peery, Ben F, 1938, S 18,44:4
Peery, George C, 1952, O 15,31:5
Peery, William W, 1964, Ap 29,14:5
Peeso, Frank W, 1942, D 20,44:7
Peet, Alexander J, 1967, N 21,47:3
Peet, C B, 1902, D 11,9:5
Peet, Charles D, 1967, Ja 3,34:1
Peet, Clayton L, 1941, F 22,15:3
Peet, Edward B, 1961, Ag 27,85:2
Peet, Edward W, 1948, Ja 5,20:2
Peet, Edward W Mrs, 1946, Ja 24,21:4
Peet, Edwin B, 1947, Ap 5,19:4
Peet, Eric, 1938, Je 10,3:8
Peet, Frederick T, 1925, Ja 28,17:3
Peet, George Herbert, 1920, Ag 28,7:5
Peet, George O, 1923, F 22,15:4
Peet, Gerald D, 1963, My 1,39:2
Peet, Harold L, 1965, F 23,33:4
Peet, Harvey Prindle, 1873, Ja 2,5:2
Peet, Henry, 1938, Ag 21,32:5
Peet, Hubert W, 1951, Ja 11,26:2
Peet, J Carlisle, 1950, D 24,34:4
Peet, John K, 1944, F 4,15:2
Peet, John Northrup, 1913, Ja 2,11:4
Peet, Lewis R, 1958, Ap 4,21:2
Peet, Louis Harman, 1905, O 19,9:5
Peet, Mark H, 1961, O 1,86:3
Peet, Mark H Mrs, 1953, Jl 2,23:2
Peet, Max M (por), 1949, Mr 26,17:6
Peet, Robert E, 1940, Mr 22,19:5
Peet, Robert L, 1958, O 19,86:5
Peet, William, 1946, Jl 30,23:1
Peet, William C, 1937, N 28,II,9:3
Peet, William C Mrs, 1955, Mr 12,19:6
Peet, William W, 1942, S 10,27:4
Peete, Charles, 1956, N 28,1:3
Peets, Edward C, 1948, O 21,27:4
Peets, Edward C Mrs, 1952, Ag 29,23:1
Peets, Everett J, 1965, Ag 31,33:1
Peets, Orville Houghten, 1968, Ap 18,47:4
Peever, Alfred, 1950, Mr 31,32:3
Peever, Arthur E, 1949, N 18,29:2
Peff, Peter, 1952, N 22,23:1
Peffer, Crawford A, 1961, D 14,43:1
Peffer, Crawford A Mrs, 1945, Ja 21,39:1
Peffer, Henry I, 1952, Ap 2,33:3
Peffer, Nathaniel (trb lr, My 1,34:5), 1964, Ap 14, 37:3
Peffer, William Alfred Ex-Sen, 1912, O 8,13:6
Peffers, Harold W, 1960, Je 3,31:2
Peffers, John M Mrs, 1956, Ag 27,19:5
Pegana, Peter J, 1938, Ag 12,17:2
Pegau, Robert V, 1956, Ap 20,25:3
Pegg, George W, 1955, D 16,30:1
Pegg, Helen, 1949, Ag 21,68:8
Pegg, John W, 1955, F 25,21:2
Peggin, Andrew, 1903, F 13,3:2
Peggs, Harry M, 1957, Ap 24,33:1
Pegler, Arthur J, 1961, Mr 8,33:4
Pegler, Jack A Mrs, 1954, Ag 26,27:3
Pegler, Westbrook Mrs, 1955, N 10,35:2
Peglow, Emil W, 1950, F 10,23:2
Pegram, Edward S Jr, 1964, Ag 2,77:3
Pegram, Frank H (por), 1944, Mr 10,15:2
Pegram, Frederick, 1937, Ag 28,15:2
Pegram, George B (mem ser set, O 3,29:1), 1958, Ag 13,27:1
Pegram, George H (por), 1937, D 24,17:7
Pegram, Henry (por), 1937, Mr 28,II,9:1
Pegram, Robert B 3d, 1955, Jl 21,23:1
Pegues, Albert S, 1960, Ag 29,25:2
Pegues, John E, 1955, S 14,35:5
Peguillan, Raoul, 1967, O 14,27:4
Peguy, Pierre, 1941, O 15,21:4
Pehl, J Carl, 1959, F 10,33:3
Pehl, J Carl Mrs, 1958, My 12,29:4
Pehlert, William K, 1959, Ap 16,33:1
Pehm, Barbara Mme, 1960, F 6,19:5
Pehr, Otto, 1963, D 8,86:6
Pehrson, Theodore A (T Pearson), 1961, O 8,87:1
Pehrsson-Bramstorp, Axel, 1954, F 20,17:6
Peierls, Edgar S, 1962, My 6,88:3
Peifer, Louis F, 1945, Ja 15,19:5
Peifer, Raymond E, 1953, S 20,87:2
Peiffer, Henry B Mrs, 1942, O 23,21:2
Peiffer, Robert E, 1956, N 7,29:4
Peignan, Albert Lt, 1912, Je 20,11:5
Peiker, Albyn J, 1942, F 17,22:2
Peiker, Harry C, 1952, O 8,31:5
Peikin, Harry S, 1962, Ja 1,23:3
Peikin, Harry S Mrs, 1948, Ag 19,21:5
Peiler, Maximilian H, 1938, Mr 2,19:4
Peilly, Mary Frances, 1908, Ja 28,9:5
Peine, Charles A, 1953, N 19,31:4
Peins, Frederick B, 1937, Je 4,23:5
Peins, Frederick B Mrs, 1950, Jl 19,31:2
Peipler, Samuel Mrs, 1952, Ja 2,25:1
Peirce, Benjamin Osgood, 1914, Ja 15,9:5
Peirce, Benjamin Prof, 1880, O 7,2:2
Peirce, Cyrus, 1945, O 5,23:2
Peirce, Edward C, 1955, F 1,18:6
Peirce, Elizabeth Mrs, 1940, N 23,17:2
Peirce, Frederick, 1948, My 31,19:5
Peirce, George L Mrs, 1946, Mr 29,23:2
Peirce, George M, 1947, F 16,57:1
Peirce, Harry H, 1954, N 3,29:1
Peirce, Hayford, 1946, Mr 5,26:3
Peirce, Herbert B, 1955, N 22,35:1
Peirce, Herbert B Mrs (B Graeme), 1963, S 11,43
Peirce, Horatio J, 1948, D 16,29:4
Peirce, Isabelle T L Mrs, 1937, O 3,II,8:5
Peirce, James B, 1968, D 14,45:2
Peirce, John, 1960, Ap 21,31:4
Peirce, L Rev, 1879, N 11,5:4
Peirce, Leona M, 1954, S 29,31:4
Peirce, Mary B, 1960, F 23,32:1
Peirce, Paul S, 1951, Ap 1,93:2
Peirce, Thomas E, 1968, D 30,31:3
Peirce, Thomas M Jr, 1945, N 4,43:2
Peirce, Thomas 3d, 1949, Jl 3,10:4
Peirce, Vernon M, 1937, Ag 19,19:6
Peirce, William, 1918, Mr 8,11:5
Peirce, William F, 1967, Jl 18,38:1
Peirce, William H (por), 1944, My 27,15:4
Peirez, Louis A, 1968, S 11,51:3
Peirse, Richard H, 1940, Jl 11,19:6
Peirson, Henry W, 1946, Ap 24,25:2
Peirson, Joseph B, 1950, Je 11,92:3
Peirson, Joseph E, 1937, F 18,21:2
Peirson, Walter, 1938, S 27,21:4
Peirson, William R, 1947, Mr 3,21:5
Peiser, Eric, 1961, Je 10,23:5

Peiser, Solomon, 1951, D 6,33:1
Peissachowitz, Victor J, 1958, Mr 26,37:4
Peitz, Henry C, 1943, O 24,44:2
Peixetto, Ernest C Mrs, 1956, N 12,29:6
Peixotto, Ernest C, 1940, D 7,17:3
Peixotto, George, 1937, O 13,23:2
Peixotto, Jessica B, 1941, O 21,23:5
Peixotto, Percy, 1938, Jl 6,23:2
Peizer, Saul L, 1952, Ja 17,27:2
Pekar, Martin Mrs, 1954, O 16,17:2
Pekar, Stephen, 1959, F 14,21:4
Pekarek, John, 1949, Ap 30,13:5
Pekarsky, Herman M, 1963, S 18,39:3
Pekarsky, Maurice B, 1962, Jl 12,29:3
Pekary, Charlotte H, 1967, F 14,43:2
Pekelis, Miriam R Mrs, 1945, N 6,19:5
Peker, Recep, 1950, Ap 3,23:3
Pekins, Frank L, 1951, Je 17,86:1
Pekins, Roy S, 1944, D 4,23:2
Pekkala, Mauno, 1952, Jl 2,25:4
Peko, Joseph, 1952, Ag 26,25:4
Pekurin, Roman S, 1955, S 8,31:4
Pelade, Germaine J, 1965, D 18,29:2
Pelander, Carla, 1944, F 27,38:5
Pelantova, Ruzena Mrs, 1959, S 3,27:3
Pelby, Ellen, 1873, O 19,5:4
Pelczarski, Wojceich, 1948, My 10,21:5
Pelenyi, Harriet Mrs, 1941, Ag 29,17:2
Pelesh, Beacon B D, 1950, Ja 15,84:4
Pelet, Emile, 1961, Ja 5,31:4
Pelham, Arleigh, 1957, Ap 6,19:5
Pelham, Edith M, 1937, Je 15,23:4
Pelham, Eugene T, 1939, Mr 4,15:4
Pelham, George F, 1937, F 9,23:2
Pelham, George F 2d, 1967, Je 20,39:1
Pelham, Laura Dainty Mrs, 1924, Ja 23,17:4
Pelham, Meta, 1948, N 30,27:4
Pelham, Samuel D, 1942, N 24,25:5
Pelham, Walter, 1907, Mr 18,7:4
Pelham-Clinton-Hope, Henry F H, 1941, Ap 22,21:4
Peliken, Edward R, 1943, O 4,17:4
Pelin, Elin, 1949, D 4,108:3
Pelissier, Harry G, 1913, S 27,13:6
Pelissier, William J, 1959, Jl 16,27:6
Pelka, John A, 1940, Ap 21,42:3
Pelkey, William C, 1944, Ag 22,17:6
Pelkus, William R, 1951, Mr 11,93:1
Pell, Alfred Duane Rev, 1924, Mr 8,11:6
Pell, Arthur Cortlandt, 1914, D 26,7:4
Pell, Clarence C, 1964, N 4,39:3
Pell, Clarence Mrs, 1916, N 3,13:5
Pell, Cornelia L (will, S 13,27:4), 1938, Ag 18,20:4
Pell, Duncan A, 1874, O 22,8:2
Pell, Duncan Archibald Rev, 1916, Ja 18,11:5
Pell, Duncan C, 1874, Ja 17,5:3; 1964, Ja 10,43:1
Pell, Edward L, 1943, Je 13,45:1
Pell, Francis L, 1945, S 8,15:2
Pell, Francis L Mrs, 1954, Mr 11,31:1
Pell, Frederick Aycrigg, 1913, Ja 10,11:4
Pell, George Hamilton, 1913, Jl 7,5:4
Pell, H G, 1926, My 15,21:5
Pell, Hamilton, 1956, Ag 25,15:7
Pell, Hamilton Mrs, 1945, S 17,19:4
Pell, Herbert C, 1961, Jl 19,29:1.
Pell, Howland (por), 1937, Je 10,23:3
Pell, Howland H, 1949, Je 7,31:2
Pell, Isabel T, 1952, Je 6,46:1
Pell, J B Capt, 1882, D 17,7:2
Pell, James D, 1949, Jl 30,15:5
Pell, James D Mrs, 1947, My 20,25:3
Pell, James T Jr, 1948, D 7,31:1
Pell, John F, 1956, Je 13,37:2
Pell, John Howland Mrs, 1911, Ja 12,13:2
Pell, Katherine L K Mrs, 1948, S 2,23:3
Pell, R L, 1880, F 14,4:7
Pell, Robert P, 1941, F 9,48:2
Pell, Stephen H P, 1950, Je 23,25:4
Pell, Stephen H P Mrs (por), 1939, Ag 5,15:5
Pell, Stuyvesant M, 1943, Ag 31,17:4
Pell, Theodore R, 1967, Ag 19,25:4
Pell, W H Dannat Mrs, 1942, Ag 29,15:3
Pell, W W, 1884, Jl 26,4:7
Pell, Walden, 1956, Ja 12,27:2
Pell, Walter T, 1904, Ja 6,9:5
Pell, William F S, 1937, Ja 20,21:3
Pell, William H, 1957, My 22,33:1
Pell, William H D, 1962, Je 16,19:2
Pell, Williamson (por), 1949, Ag 23,23:1
Pell, Williamson Jr Mrs, 1965, Ag 21,21:5
Pella, Vespasian V, 1952, Ag 25,17:3
Pellas, Silvio F, 1952, Jl 24,27:2
Pellaton, Roger A, 1953, Ap 9,27:2
Pellatt, Henry Sir, 1939, Mr 9,21:3
Pelle, M C J Gen, 1924, Mr 17,15:5
Pellegrine, Michael, 1950, Ag 9,29:5
Pellegrinetti, Ermenegildo (por), 1943, Mr 30,21:3
Pellegrini, A S, 1885, Ap 19,3:3
Pellegrini, Frank, 1956, Ja 15,93:1
Pellegrini, George, 1952, S 22,23:2
Pellegrini, Irene, 1955, F 22,21:5
Pellegrini, Quirino Count, 1953, Jl 3,19:6
Pellegrino, Dominick, 1951, Ag 1,23:4
Pellegrino, Frank, 1954, Jl 11,73:3
Pellegrino, John, 1944, Ag 15,17:6
Pellegrino, William V, 1960, S 29,71:4
Peller, Frank, 1944, Ap 8,13:4
Peller, Joseph H Sr, 1955, Je 8,29:5
Peller, Sigismund Mrs, 1966, S 1,35:4
Peller, Sol, 1950, Ag 2,25:2
Pellerano Carvajal, Manuel, 1952, Ja 9,29:3
Pellerey, Elsa A, 1947, My 16,23:5
Pellet, Marcellin, 1942, D 12,17:2
Pellet, William W, 1965, D 9,47:3
Pelletau, P C, 1884, D 15,2:3
Pelleteri, Anthony, 1952, N 24,23:3
Pelleteri, Anthony Mrs, 1958, Je 11,36:1
Pelletier, A P Rev, 1879, Ja 30,5:4
Pelletier, Alphonse, 1955, Ja 25,25:4
Pelletier, Andrew N, 1951, Jl 29,69:1
Pelletier, Auguste, 1945, O 19,23:1
Pelletier, E Leroy, 1938, S 6,21:3
Pelletier, Elzear, 1944, D 9,15:3
Pelletier, George, 1947, Ja 21,23:1
Pelletier, J Arthur, 1954, Jl 28,23:4
Pelletier, Joseph, 1924, Mr 26,19:4; 1944, F 14,17:3
Pelletier, Leslie, 1910, Jl 28,7:2
Pelletier, Robert Mrs, 1944, N 9,14:7
Pelletieri, Isabelle, 1955, S 6,25:1
Pelletreau, Charles Rev Dr, 1903, Jl 22,7:6
Pelletreau, Helen E, 1915, Ag 5,11:6
Pelletreau, Jessie, 1944, O 7,13:2
Pelletreau, John R, 1960, Mr 6,84:4
Pelletreau, Robert S, 1943, Ap 8,23:1
Pelletreau, Robert S Mrs, 1947, S 21,60:4
Pelletreau, William Smith, 1918, Ja 8,15:2
Pellett, Frank C, 1951, Ap 30,21:5
Pellett, Jackson B, 1939, My 4,23:6
Pellett, Le Grand W, 1945, Ja 22,17:4
Pellettieri, Rocco J, 1950, Ja 7,17:5
Pelley, John J, 1946, N 13,28:2
Pelley, John J Mrs, 1948, N 12,23:4
Pelley, William D, 1965, Jl 2,27:1
Pellicone, Dominick, 1961, Jl 20,27:4
Pellicoro, Paul F, 1967, Ja 4,41:1
Pelligrini, Carlos Dr, 1906, Jl 18,4:2
Pelliot, Paul, 1945, O 30,19:5
Pellissier, Louis D, 1955, Jl 11,23:5
Pelloux, Luigi Gen, 1924, O 27,19:5
Pells, Albertina, 1937, Jl 22,19:4
Pells, William C, 1957, Mr 9,19:6
Pells, William C Mrs, 1942, Jl 19,30:5
Pelly, Farrell, 1963, Ap 24,35:1
Pelly, J Harold, 1956, Jl 25,29:5
Pelly, Raymond T, 1952, Jl 1,23:1
Pelo, William J, 1944, D 23,13:2
Pelonsky, Nathan A, 1954, S 19,89:2
Pelosi, A Victor, 1949, O 27,28:3
Pelosi, Francesco, 1948, Ag 3,25:2
Pelosi, Michael H Mrs, 1959, Mr 17,30:4
Peloubet, Francis N Rev Dr, 1920, Mr 30,11:4
Peloubet, William S, 1943, Ag 15,38:8
Pelouze, L H, 1878, Je 3,5:3
Pelouze, Percy S (por), 1947, Mr 14,23:3
Pelouze, William N, 1943, Je 22,20:3
Pelouze, William N Mrs, 1953, My 5,29:2
Pelovski, Pelo, 1957, Jl 30,23:1
Pelphrey, Will H, 1938, My 27,17:2
Pelstring, Herman J, 1956, My 22,42:5
Pelt, Harry V Jr, 1946, S 3,19:2
Pelt, Jean-Baptiste Msgr, 1937, S 10,23:3
Pelt, Lulu Van (Mrs L Shephard), 1877, F 7,8:2
Pelter, Paul J, 1952, Ag 6,21:4
Peltier, Frank D, 1961, D 17,83:1
Peltier, Frederic D Mrs, 1919, Ap 16,13:2
Peltier, Moses F, 1941, Ap 3,23:4
Pelton, A H Mrs, 1878, Je 23,2:3
Pelton, Avery, 1944, Je 2,15:2
Pelton, Avery Mrs, 1942, F 23,21:3
Pelton, Burt M, 1945, O 18,23:4
Pelton, Charles A, 1950, D 24,36:1
Pelton, De Witt L, 1940, O 20,50:1
Pelton, Edmund F, 1952, Jl 8,27:2
Pelton, Edward F, 1941, S 28,49:2
Pelton, Frank A, 1950, Mr 28,31:3
Pelton, Frank C, 1943, Je 8,21:4
Pelton, Fred, 1948, Jl 10,15:6
Pelton, Henry Varick, 1925, Jl 14,21:5
Pelton, Jessie, 1957, D 22,40:7
Pelton, L F, 1883, S 18,4:6
Pelton, W T (see also Jl 9), 1880, Jl 19,1:3
Pelts, Philip W, 1947, F 27,21:2
Pelty, Barney, 1939, My 25,25:2
Peltz, Alberta, 1952, N 23,89:2
Peltz, David, 1953, N 21,13:3
Peltz, Elizabeth M Mrs, 1960, Ap 16,17:2
Peltz, Emil A, 1960, F 7,84:6
Peltz, George M D, 1944, Ja 25,19:2
Peltz, H, 1932, Ag 26,17:4
Peltz, John D, 1957, Ja 5,17:6
Peluso, Felix V, 1960, O 14,33:3
Peluso, Pasquale, 1956, O 16,33:4
Pelver, John, 1960, Jl 31,68:5
Pelz, George V, 1951, Je 28,25:6
Pelz, Irma M, 1962, Je 24,69:1
Pelz, Paul R, 1938, N 12,15:2
Pelz, Phil, 1942, O 28,23:3
Pelz, Victor H, 1968, O 28,47:1
Pelzer, B Henry, 1958, N 3,37:4
Pelzer, Egbert M, 1945, My 31,15:5
Pelzer, Francis J, 1939, Ag 23,21:6
Pelzer, John J von, 1942, Ja 22,18:3
Pelzer, Louis, 1946, Je 30,38:7
Pelzer, William, 1955, Ap 25,23:6
Pelzman, Ivy A Mrs, 1968, F 22,32:8
Pember, Edward E, 1939, Ap 19,23:4
Pember, F Howard, 1940, Ap 26,21:4
Pember, Walter P R, 1953, D 15,39:3
Pember, William H, 1953, Ja 13,27:2
Pemberton, Albert G, 1941, Ja 9,21:5
Pemberton, Brock, 1950, Mr 12,1:2
Pemberton, Edward L, 1946, My 14,21:3
Pemberton, Ella M Mrs, 1937, Ja 31,II,8:4
Pemberton, Francis R Sr Mrs, 1957, Mr 24,86:2
Pemberton, Francis Rawle, 1923, F 15,19:4
Pemberton, Harry H Dr, 1914, N 13,11:6
Pemberton, J C Gen, 1881, Jl 14,5:5
Pemberton, James M, 1947, Mr 22,13:5
Pemberton, John, 1955, Jl 30,17:1
Pemberton, John C Mrs, 1907, Ag 15,7:6
Pemberton, John de J, 1967, My 20,35:2
Pemberton, John Lt-Com, 1903, S 29,9:4
Pemberton, Mattie Mrs, 1946, N 10,62:4
Pemberton, Max, 1950, F 23,27:3
Pemberton, Ralph, 1949, Je 18,13:1
Pemberton, Richard J, 1944, D 2,13:4
Pemberton, Ruth, 1948, F 12,23:2
Pemberton, T Edgar, 1905, S 29,9:1
Pemberton, Thomas H, 1941, My 21,23:3; 1955, N 30, 33:2
Pemberton-Billing, Noel, 1948, N 13,15:3
Pemboss, Lucinda Mrs, 1938, O 11,25:5
Pembridge, Stanley Mrs, 1961, F 22,25:2
Pembroke, Countess of, 1944, Mr 13,15:5
Pembroke, Earl of (Sidney Herbert), 1913, Ap 2,11:5
Pembroke, Earl of (R Herbert), 1960, Ja 14,33:2
Pembrooke, Theodore, 1917, S 23,23:1
Pemburn, Charles S, 1963, My 28,28:4
Pemsler, Samuel, 1954, Mr 25,29:5
Pena, Antonio, 1947, D 11,33:2
Pena, Carlos Maria de Dr (funl, My 2,13:8), 1918, My 1,13:5
Pena, Juan M Mrs, 1950, D 19,29:4
Pena, Julio, 1949, N 22,29:1
Pena, Pedro, 1943, Jl 30,15:4
Pena, Roque Saenz Dr, 1914, Ag 10,7:5
Penale, Evangeline G Mrs, 1962, O 17,39:2
Penard, Jean M Father, 1939, N 15,23:4
Pence, Arthur W, 1954, N 9,27:2
Pence, Charles E, 1941, Jl 23,19:4
Pence, George B, 1957, Ag 30,19:1
Pence, Homer L, 1941, N 7,23:3
Pence, Thomas J, 1916, Mr 28,13:5
Pence, William D, 1946, Je 18,25:5
Pence, William P Maj, 1915, Ap 8,13:5
Penchard, Charles W, 1957, F 6,25:2
Penck, Albrecht, 1945, Mr 10,17:2
Pencoast, Garfield, 1947, N 21,27:2
Pendell, George J, 1952, My 31,17:1
Pendell, Thomas G, 1947, F 1,15:2
Pender, David, 1950, S 24,104:3
Pender, Edward J, 1956, Jl 21,15:5
Pender, George, 1948, My 8,15:5
Pender, George Mrs, 1946, Ag 8,21:3
Pender, George W, 1949, N 18,29:1
Pender, Harold, 1959, S 7,15:4
Pender, Horace G, 1962, My 15,39:4
Pender, James J, 1948, D 31,15:2
Pender, James W Col, 1914, Jl 2,9:6
Pender, John L, 1940, D 14,17:3
Pender, John M, 1960, Ag 23,29:5
Pender, John Sir, 1896, Jl 8,9:3
Pender, Lord (J C Denison-Pender), 1949, D 5,23:1
Pender, Lord (Jno Denison-Pender), 1965, Ap 1,35:1
Pender, William F Mrs, 1954, N 5,15:1
Pender, William Mrs, 1943, Ja 17,18:5
Pendergast, Arthur E, 1950, Je 17,15:5
Pendergast, Edward S H, 1961, F 18,19:1
Pendergast, J Lynch, 1924, D 17,21:3
Pendergast, James, 1951, Ap 3,27:3
Pendergast, James J, 1952, Ap 27,91:1
Pendergast, James M (more details, Mr 30,45:1; funl, Ap 1,35:5), 1966, Mr 29,41:1
Pendergast, Joe, 1939, Je 29,23:6
Pendergast, John J, 1967, Mr 9,39:2
Pendergast, Michael Mrs, 1953, Ap 30,31:3
Pendergast, Norbert R, 1925, My 18,15:5
Pendergast, Raymond A, 1946, F 12,28:2
Pendergast, Stephen W, 1965, Jl 10,25:3
Pendergast, Thomas J, 1945, Ja 27,11:1
Pendergast, Tom J Mrs, 1951, Je 14,27:4
Pendexter, Hugh, 1940, Je 12,25:4
Pendexter, Sidney E, 1962, Je 7,35:4
Pendlebury, Jonas, 1943, Ag 23,15:3
Pendlebury, Severette Mrs, 1944, F 2,21:6
Pendleton, Alan Maj, 1937, Ja 13,23:4
Pendleton, Alex G, 1950, Mr 27,23:2
Pendleton, Alice L, 1952, My 9,23:2
Pendleton, Allan T, 1951, Ap 21,17:2
Pendleton, Andrew, 1938, Ja 27,21:4

Pendleton, Arthur T Mrs, 1946, Ja 19,13:1
Pendleton, C R Mrs, 1938, Mr 9,23:4
Pendleton, Charles Rittenhouse, 1914, Ja 17,9:4
Pendleton, Cyrus E, 1950, My 10,31:3
Pendleton, Dudley D, 1954, O 12,27:4
Pendleton, E F, 1936, Jl 27,15:3
Pendleton, Edgar H, 1946, Ag 12,21:4
Pendleton, Edmund, 1954, Mr 25,29:3
Pendleton, Edmund L Mrs, 1939, D 13,27:2
Pendleton, Edmund M Mrs, 1946, Ag 21,28:3
Pendleton, Edwin C Rear-Adm, 1919, S 28,22:3
Pendleton, Emily B Mrs, 1940, F 25,38:5
Pendleton, Emma A Mrs, 1937, Mr 1,20:1
Pendleton, Ernest N, 1947, Mr 16,60:4
Pendleton, Everett H, 1964, D 5,31:4
Pendleton, F K, 1930, Jl 27,II,8:1
Pendleton, Fields S, 1923, Ja 27,13:4
Pendleton, Frank E, 1960, Ja 22,27:1
Pendleton, Frank L, 1942, Ja 16,21:4
Pendleton, Frederick S, 1951, Ag 27,19:3
Pendleton, G H, 1889, N 26,5:1
Pendleton, George H, 1938, S 9,21:4
Pendleton, Henry M, 1941, D 16,27:2
Pendleton, Herbert H, 1938, Ag 4,17:5
Pendleton, James M, 1940, My 19,43:2
Pendleton, Joseph B, 1953, My 12,27:1
Pendleton, Joseph H (por), 1942, F 5,21:1
Pendleton, Joseph H Mrs, 1952, Je 26,29:6
Pendleton, Judson P, 1948, Ja 22,27:2
Pendleton, Laura S, 1958, S 9,35:1
Pendleton, Louis B, 1939, My 14,III,6:7
Pendleton, Mary L Y Mrs, 1939, Ja 2,24:3
Pendleton, Moses, 1950, Ap 24,25:1
Pendleton, Moses Mrs, 1949, D 11,91:2
Pendleton, Nat, 1967, O 13,39:4
Pendleton, Nathaniel D Bp (por), 1937, D 30,19:5
Pendleton, Ralph E, 1948, F 19,23:2
Pendleton, Ralph E Mrs, 1948, Ja 18,60:2
Pendleton, Raymond K Mrs, 1964, Je 23,33:2
Pendleton, W N, 1883, Ja 17,5:5
Pendleton, Walter, 1942, S 4,23:5
Pendleton, Walter A, 1941, Mr 5,21:2
Pendleton, William S, 1952, Je 11,29:2
Pendleton, William W, 1944, O 28,15:4
Pendleton, Winfield S Capt, 1911, O 23,11:5
Pendola, Anthony S, 1948, Ja 11,56:3
Pendorf, Angelo, 1947, O 8,25:3
Pendray, W J Mrs, 1958, N 24,29:2
Pendrick, Elias J, 1904, Ja 19,9:6
Pendry, Bryer H, 1951, Mr 17,15:2
Pendry, Harry E, 1953, Jl 11,11:5
Pendry, W R, 1942, My 3,54:1
Penelon, Jose F, 1954, O 26,27:2
Penfield, A W Mrs, 1932, F 27,17:3
Penfield, Charles E, 1953, S 22,31:1
Penfield, Clarence, 1951, N 7,29:5
Penfield, Edward, 1925, F 10,23:3
Penfield, Edward W, 1953, N 20,23:3
Penfield, Frederic Courtland Mrs, 1905, O 6,9:6
Penfield, Frederick Courtland (funl, Je 23,17:6), 1922, Je 20,19:5
Penfield, George W, 1962, O 18,39:3
Penfield, Harold W, 1955, Mr 22,31:3
Penfield, Norman Walker, 1924, F 21,17:6
Penfield, R C, 1932, Jl 12,17:3
Penfield, Raymond C Mrs, 1944, S 27,21:3
Penfield, Roderick C, 1921, Ap 9,11:5
Penfield, Smith N Dr, 1920, Ja 8,17:1
Penfield, Thornton B, 1958, F 6,27:2
Penfield, William L Ex-Judge, 1909, My 10,9:4
Penfold, Edmund, 1925, F 5,19:4
Penfold, John S (por), 1948, N 12,23:4
Penfold, Saxby V, 1958, Ap 10,29:4
Penford, William Hall, 1912, S 20,11:6
Penfrase, Edward L, 1951, N 12,25:4
Peng Tao, 1961, N 15,43:6
Penha, Julius L Jr, 1950, Mr 17,23:1
Penhale, Clayton A, 1950, S 28,31:3
Penhale, John H, 1956, S 28,27:2
Penhallow, David Pearce Prof, 1910, O 27,11:4
Penhallow, Walter G, 1940, Ap 13,17:4
Peni, Olga C de, 1951, Je 19,29:2
Peniakoff, Vladimir, 1951, My 17,31:3
Penick, Albert D (cor of N 10 obituary), 1967, N 11, 33:2
Penick, Charles Clinton Rev, 1914, Ap 14,11:5
Penick, Daniel A, 1964, N 10,47:4
Penick, Edwin A, 1959, Ap 7,33:3
Penick, John N, 1967, Jl 2,35:2
Penick, June M, 1940, Ag 9,15:3
Penick, S Barksdale Mrs, 1962, Mr 15,32:4
Penick, Sydnor B, 1953, My 26,29:3
Penick, William M, 1959, Ja 11,88:5
Penio, Lambertino, 1921, Ja 12,15:5
Peniston, Denman, 1961, S 3,60:4
Peniston, John F Jr, 1941, Ap 1,23:5
Penley, Clarence M, 1947, S 22,15:3
Penley, William Sydney, 1912, N 12,13:5
Penlington, Zoe K, 1944, Mr 29,21:2
Penlon, Rox, 1951, My 21,21:1
Penman, E, 1929, Ja 16,25:3
Penman, Robert, 1946, Ap 25,21:3
Penman, Roy F, 1966, S 1,35:4

Penn, Al T, 1949, Jl 13,27:4
Penn, Albert M, 1947, S 23,25:5
Penn, Arthur, 1960, D 31,17:4
Penn, Arthur A, 1941, F 7,19:2
Penn, Barnes R, 1939, Ag 23,21:6
Penn, C A, 1931, O 23,23:1
Penn, Charles A Jr, 1950, Ja 6,21:3
Penn, David E, 1951, O 5,27:2
Penn, David V (por), 1937, N 27,17:1
Penn, Hamilton O (por), 1946, F 2,13:4
Penn, Henry Mrs, 1948, Ag 9,19:5
Penn, J, 1878, S 26,5:6
Penn, J Pemberton, 1947, O 19,66:6
Penn, John C, 1952, Jl 21,19:6
Penn, John N Jr Mrs, 1965, Ag 3,31:2
Penn, Lemuel A Mrs, 1965, Jl 22,31:6
Penn, Leo G, 1948, Mr 24,25:5
Penn, Marion (por), 1942, Mr 30,17:4
Penn, Moise, 1956, Ja 13,23:2
Penn, T J, 1869, S 19,1:2
Penn, Thomas J Mrs, 1965, F 22,21:2
Penn, W Frank, 1958, O 9,37:3
Penn, William, 1948, Mr 13,15:1
Penna, Alfonso A Moreira Dr, 1909, Je 15,7:5
Penna, Felix J, 1962, Jl 18,29:6
Penna, Jose Dr, 1919, Mr 31,13:4
Penna, Phil H, 1939, Ja 7,15:2
Penna, S Thomas, 1950, O 28,17:6
Pennamacoor, Emanuel G, 1946, Je 22,19:4
Pennamacoor, Isaac Mrs, 1944, O 11,21:4
Penndorf, Alfred W, 1955, S 27,35:4
Penndorf, Max Mrs, 1948, Ja 23,23:2
Penndorf, Richard H, 1959, My 11,27:5
Pennebaker, Sarah, 1916, N 19,21:2
Pennell, Amos G, 1957, D 20,24:4
Pennell, Arthur J, 1957, Mr 9,19:2
Pennell, Charles T, 1937, N 12,21:4
Pennell, E R Mrs, 1936, F 8,15:1
Pennell, Ella L, 1958, My 22,29:2
Pennell, Eugene D, 1940, Je 6,25:5
Pennell, Francis W, 1952, F 5,29:3
Pennell, H Barrett, 1955, Ja 5,23:2
Pennell, Harry L L Com, 1916, Jl 20,11:6
Pennell, Henry B, 1967, My 17,47:1
Pennell, Howard Y, 1952, Ap 1,29:5
Pennell, Joseph, 1926, Ap 24,1:2
Pennell, Joseph B, 1949, Je 19,68:3
Pennell, Samuel, 1959, Ja 2,25:2
Pennell, Thomas, 1959, Mr 1,86:8
Pennels, Waldo W Mrs, 1958, Mr 28,25:3
Penner, Barbara Mrs, 1937, O 7,27:4
Penner, Joe (por),(will, F 5,17:3), 1941, Ja 11,12:4
Penner, Ken, 1959, My 30,17:2
Penner, Mark E Dr, 1937, Ag 13,17:3
Pennes, Harry H, 1963, N 14,35:2
Pennes, Sholem, 1956, S 24,27:5
Pennes, Sholem Mrs, 1954, Jl 27,21:3
Penney, Albert W, 1946, S 20,31:1
Penney, Arthur H, 1952, N 24,23:2
Penney, Edgar R Mrs, 1943, N 3,25:6
Penney, Fred J H, 1950, Je 2,23:5
Penney, Fred M, 1941, D 7,77:1; 1950, F 9,29:2
Penney, Frederick C Mrs, 1941, O 7,23:5
Penney, George S, 1950, Je 15,31:2
Penney, Harold D, 1941, F 4,21:5
Penney, Herbert R, 1966, Mr 3,33:4
Penney, J C Jr, 1938, Je 8,23:2
Penney, James, 1951, My 17,31:5
Penney, Samuel R, 1946, F 6,23:5
Penney, Theodore W, 1944, N 30,23:2
Penney, Thomas Mrs, 1951, Mr 4,93:1
Penney, William A (por), 1949, O 8,13:2
Pennick, Jack (Ronald), 1964, Ag 19,37:4
Pennicke, Harold C, 1954, Mr 1,25:4
Pennie, John C, 1921, D 24,11:6
Penniman, Harry A, 1952, N 2,89:2
Penniman, Henry G, 1941, Mr 30,49:2
Penniman, J F, 1876, Ja 8,5:2
Penniman, J H, 1931, Ap 7,27:3
Penniman, Josiah H Dr (por), 1941, Ap 11,21:1
Penniman, S J, 1876, Ag 8,3:3
Penniman, William B D, 1938, D 18,48:6
Penniman, William M, 1903, Ag 14,7:7
Penniman, William T, 1942, D 10,30:2
Pennington, A S, 1947, Ja 6,23:3
Pennington, Alexander Cummings McM Brig-Gen, 1917, D 1,13:5
Pennington, Ann B Mrs, 1940, Ap 12,23:5
Pennington, C Gordon, 1943, S 19,49:1
Pennington, Caroline Burnet, 1872, My 4,8:4
Pennington, Charles T, 1938, Ap 22,19:3
Pennington, Edgar L, 1951, D 11,33:4
Pennington, Frank H, 1945, N 3,15:4
Pennington, George L, 1953, My 6,31:2
Pennington, Hall P, 1942, Ap 3,21:4
Pennington, Harold, 1945, Ja 4,19:5
Pennington, Harvey G Mrs, 1940, Ag 30,19:1
Pennington, J Wilson, 1956, Ag 16,25:2
Pennington, Jefferson C, 1947, D 14,80:5
Pennington, Louis W Capt, 1916, O 1,23:5
Pennington, Mary E, 1952, D 28,48:5
Pennington, Mary V Mrs (will), 1951, Ap 17,26:4
Pennington, W Harry Sr, 1968, Mr 11,37:1

Pennington, Warren L Mrs, 1945, Mr 3,13:3
Pennington, William, 1862, F 18,1:5
Pennington, William B, 1945, Ja 9,19:4
Pennington, William H Mrs, 1951, My 9,33:5
Pennington, William R, 1941, O 14,23:5; 1951, Jl 15 60:4
Pennington-Bickford, W, 1941, Je 14,17:5
Pennisi, Vincenzo, 1965, Ag 5,29:4
Pennock, A M (see also S 21), 1876, S 27,2:3
Pennock, Erastus W, 1960, N 2,39:1
Pennock, Frederick, 1940, F 14,21:1
Pennock, George L, 1937, D 31,15:2
Pennock, Henrietta P Mrs, 1942, F 12,23:6
Pennock, Herb (por), 1948, Ja 31,19:1
Pennock, John D, 1921, Mr 12,11:5
Pennock, John D Mrs, 1950, O 7,17:2
Pennock, John S, 1951, N 16,25:4
Pennock, Joseph E, 1941, Je 7,17:1
Pennock, Joseph W, 1962, Je 16,19:5
Pennock, Norton I, 1949, N 6,92:3
Pennock, Samuel S, 1941, Ap 13,39:1
Pennoyer, A Sheldon, 1957, Ag 19,19:3
Pennoyer, Albert A Mrs, 1948, Je 22,26:3
Pennoyer, Blanche Mrs, 1951, F 2,23:2
Pennoyer, Clarence (Pete), 1950, N 29,34:2
Pennoyer, Frederick Mrs, 1945, My 8,19:2
Pennoyer, Frederick W, 1942, F 13,21:2
Pennoyer, Grant P, 1950, Ap 12,28:2
Pennoyer, Richard Edmunds, 1968, N 19,40:2
Pennoyer, Syl ex-Gov, 1902, My 31,9:5
Pennoyer, William A Capt, 1904, F 3,9:6
Penny, Arthur N Mrs, 1968, Ja 13,31:2
Penny, Charles Leon, 1915, Mr 30,11:4
Penny, David H G, 1968, F 14,47:4
Penny, Emma J Mrs, 1954, D 16,37:1
Penny, Enos E, 1956, S 2,57:1
Penny, Fred C, 1942, N 5,26:2
Penny, Frederick G (Lord Marchwood), 1955, Ja 27:2
Penny, Frederick W, 1940, D 14,17:2
Penny, George F Mrs, 1948, N 23,30:2
Penny, George L 3d Mrs, 1944, Ag 2,15:3
Penny, James P, 1963, My 9,37:2
Penny, John Capt, 1937, Mr 11,23:4
Penny, Merritt C Mrs, 1947, Ja 13,21:2
Penny, Norman F, 1962, F 14,35:2
Penny, Prudence, 1948, My 27,25:4
Penny, Prudence (Mrs L A Malek), 1951, Mr 22,
Penny, Vernon H, 1921, Ap 8,13:5
Penny, Warwick W Mrs, 1952, F 8,23:4
Penny, William L Msgr, 1920, D 2,11:4
Pennybacker, James E (por), 1941, F 26,22:2
Pennybacker, Percy V Mrs, 1938, F 5,15:1
Pennypacker, Anna M W, 1952, F 24,84:1
Pennypacker, Bevan A, 1954, Jl 29,23:6
Pennypacker, Charlotte W Mrs, 1937, O 29,21:2
Pennypacker, Galusha Gen, 1916, O 2,11:6
Pennypacker, H, 1933, N 20,15:6
Pennypacker, Isaac A, 1950, Jl 29,13:2
Pennypacker, Julia E, 1953, F 3,25:4
Pennypacker, Morton, 1956, S 10,27:2
Pennypacker, Samuel W Ex-Gov, 1916, S 3,19:5
Penrhyn, Baron (H N Douglas-Penant), 1949, Je 27:4
Penrhyn, Lord, 1907, Mr 12,9:6
Penrhyn, Lord (F Douglas-Pennant), 1967, F 5,88
Penrose, Beatrice Mrs, 1943, Jl 5,15:3
Penrose, Boles Sen (funl, Ja 6,17:4), 1922, Ja 2,17
Penrose, Charles, 1958, My 17,19:5
Penrose, Charles Bingham, 1925, F 28,13:5
Penrose, Charles William, 1925, My 18,15:5
Penrose, Clement A Dr, 1919, Jl 5,17:6
Penrose, Emerson B, 1942, Ja 28,19:3
Penrose, Emily L, 1938, Ja 17,19:3
Penrose, George H, 1938, Ja 8,15:4
Penrose, Oliver J, 1939, Ja 25,22:1
Penrose, R A F, 1931, Ag 1,13:1
Penrose, Richard A F Dr, 1908, D 27,9:7
Penrose, Spencer (will, D 19,21:2), 1939, D 7,27:
Penrose, Spencer Mrs, 1956, Ja 25,31:5
Penrose, Stephen B L, 1947, Ap 30,26:2
Penrose, Stephen B L Jr (funl, D 11,13:1), 1954, D 10,27:1
Penrose, William H Gen, 1903, Ag 30,2:6
Penrose, William R, 1953, Mr 24,31:5
Penry, Melborn E, 1952, F 29,23:2
Pensberger, Anton, 1966, F 6,V,1:2
Pense, Fred Booth, 1955, Ag 16,49:2
Penson, Isaac Mrs, 1960, Ap 17,92:6
Pensyl, D Sylvester, 1946, F 22,25:1
Pensyl, John, 1903, D 15,2:3
Pentecost, Arthur, 1961, Ap 12,41:5
Pentecost, Clement B, 1937, D 18,21:2
Pentecost, Ernest H, 1943, S 19,48:6
Pentecost, George Frederick Rev (funl, Ag 12,9:2), 1920, Ag 9,9:6
Pentermans, Mrs, 1871, Je 10,4:2
Penterson, George F Mrs, 1945, My 15,19:4
Penthievre, Duke of, 1919, Jl 19,9:7
Pentlarge, Frank Mrs, 1957, O 6,85:1
Pentlarge, Frank R, 1948, N 5,25:2
Penton, Brian C, 1951, Ag 25,11:3
Penton, John A, 1940, S 10,23:4

Penton, Leonard R, 1956, F 23,27:4
Pentuff, James R, 1942, D 2,25:5
Pentz, Archibald Maclay, 1914, Ap 25,15:6
Pentz, Robert H, 1941, Je 13,19:3
Pentz, Thomas D, 1966, Mr 31,39:2
Pentzien, Louis I, 1968, Jl 12,31:3
Penwarden, Charles S, 1942, My 15,19:4
Penwarden, Charles S Mrs, 1938, Jl 22,17:3
Penwell, Leroy V, 1949, Ag 10,21:2
Penza, Alfred A Jr, 1968, Ag 8,33:4
Penza, Andrew, 1937, My 8,19:6
Penza, John G, 1946, Jl 21,40:4
Penza, Saverio, 1964, Je 17,43:4
Penza, Thomas, 1948, O 22,26:3
Penzato, Joseph, 1948, Je 3,25:1
Penzik, Abraham, 1945, D 17,21:5
Penzotti, Francis G Rev, 1925, Ag 9,5:3
Peo, Ralph F, 1966, N 30,47:1
Peoble, Charles W, 1948, Ag 21,15:2
Peoples, Alfred D, 1939, Je 3,15:5
Peoples, Christian J (por), 1941, F 4,21:1
Peoples, Robert E, 1955, S 20,31:1
Peoples, Walter, 1947, N 25,29:4
Peotter, R S, 1937, O 25,20:1
Pepe, Angelo, 1950, Mr 10,27:4
Pepe, Anthony, 1965, D 21,37:1
Pepe, Frank, 1944, My 21,44:1
Pepe, Raymond V, 1964, Ag 17,25:3
Peper, Frederick J, 1937, Je 30,23:5
Peper, Loring, 1960, S 29,35:3
Peper, Walter S, 1951, N 24,11:1
Pepere, Alberto, 1940, Jl 20,15:4
Pepersack, John J, 1947, O 19,66:5
Pepis, Betty, 1968, D 29,53:2
Peple, Edward H, 1924, Jl 29,15:6
Peploe, Fitzgerald Cornwall, 1906, F 5,9:5
Pepoon, Clarence G, 1948, Mr 8,23:5
Peppard, Frank, 1903, My 30,7:5
Peppard, George J, 1952, Ja 8,27:4
Peppard, George W, 1941, Jl 26,15:1
Peppard, Irving A, 1946, D 31,17:1
Peppard, S Harcourt, 1957, N 17,86:4
Peppard, Sherman H, 1951, Jl 9,25:4
Peppe, James V, 1957, D 27,19:1
Pepper, Albert, 1949, Je 14,31:4
Pepper, Albert H, 1954, Ag 22,92:1
Pepper, Allan H, 1962, Je 29,27:3
Pepper, Benjamin F, 1953, Mr 1,92:5
Pepper, Benjamin F Mrs, 1955, F 6,89:2
Pepper, C M, 1930, N 5,21:5
Pepper, Charles H, 1950, Ag 26,13:7
Pepper, Christian, 1903, S 27,7:6
Pepper, David, 1937, F 15,17:2
Pepper, Ellis H, 1915, S 10,11:7
Pepper, George Hubbard, 1924, My 14,19:5
Pepper, George W, 1961, My 25,37:2
Pepper, George W Jr, 1949, D 16,31:5
Pepper, George W Mrs, 1951, Mr 23,21:2
Pepper, Harry C, 1965, Ap 9,33:3
Pepper, Irvin S, 1913, D 23,9:6
Pepper, J E Col, 1906, D 25,1:3
Pepper, J W Mrs, 1961, Je 9,33:2
Pepper, James H, 1941, S 20,17:4
Pepper, John Worrell Mrs, 1908, Ag 7,5:4
Pepper, Joseph W, 1945, Jl 9,11:7
Pepper, Mabel G, 1947, Mr 28,23:1
Pepper, O H Perry, 1962, Ja 30,29:1
Pepper, P H, 1884, Ja 5,1:7
Pepper, Richard Mrs, 1951, Ap 23,27:7
Pepper, Robert H Lt-Gen, 1968, Je 2,89:2
Pepper, W M Sr Mrs, 1958, Ag 19,27:1
Pepper, William M Sr, 1941, F 24,15:6
Pepper, William Mrs, 1944, F 1,19:5
Pepper, William Platt, 1907, Ap 28,9:5
Pepperday, Thomas M, 1956, My 17,31:2
Pepperdine, George, 1962, Ag 1,31:1
Pepperman, Bozeman, 1951, Ag 9,21:3
Peppers, Thomas H, 1953, N 16,25:5
Peppler, Charles W, 1953, My 13,29:5
Peppler, Thomas, 1937, N 6,17:5
Pepys, Keneim Charles Edward (Earl of Cottenham), 1919, Ap 23,17:2
Pequigney, Francis F, 1947, N 28,27:2
Pequignot, Frank C, 1937, F 1,19:4
Pequignot, Joseph V, 1952, My 31,14:7
Perabo, Fred W, 1968, N 23,47:3
Perak, Sulton of, 1938, O 15,17:3
Perales, Alonso S, 1960, My 10,37:3
Perali, Pericle, 1949, D 31,15:5
Peralta, Angela, 1883, S 9,7:3
Peralta, F, 1933, D 23,15:3
Peralta-Ramos, Arturo de Mrs, 1953, My 22,27:1
Perard, Victor, 1957, Jl 10,27:4
Perard, Victor Mrs, 1962, Ja 5,29:1
Perazzo, David R Jr, 1958, Ag 17,85:2
Perazzo, Gianbatista, 1950, S 14,31:3
Percas, Nicolas, 1965, Ag 9,25:3
Perce, Elbert, 1869, Ja 21,4:7
Perce, Hyde W, 1947, Mr 15,13:2
Perce, Legrand W Col, 1911, Mr 18,13:6
Perce, William T, 1943, D 28,17:1
Perceval, Augustus Arthur (Earl of Egmont), 1910, Ag 12,7:6
Perceval, Charles Alexander Spencer, 1916, Ap 3,13:5
Perch, Dennis D, 1954, Je 12,15:3
Perche, Archbishop, 1883, D 26,1:6
Percin, F Petregille de, 1945, O 10,36:2
Percival, Arthur E, 1966, F 2,35:3
Percival, Arthur W, 1966, O 13,45:4
Percival, Charles G, 1940, Mr 1,21:3
Percival, David C, 1956, O 3,33:2
Percival, Edwin, 1941, Mr 5,21:3
Percival, George Mrs, 1961, Ja 30,23:1
Percival, Gordon P, 1965, D 3,39:1
Percival, Henry R Rev, 1903, S 24,9:6
Percival, James M Mrs, 1947, Je 20,20:2
Percival, John C, 1950, Ja 25,27:4
Percival, Mary, 1949, Ag 30,27:2
Percival, Milton F, 1962, Ja 19,31:4
Percival, Robert Albert, 1920, Jl 6,15:1
Percival, Robert T, 1964, S 15,37:3
Percival, S Thomas Jr, 1961, S 29,35:2
Percival, Thomas G, 1945, My 25,19:2
Percival, Walter, 1937, N 8,23:2
Percival, Walter S Mrs, 1957, Je 18,33:2
Percival, William A Sr, 1945, O 30,19:4
Percival, William J, 1963, Ag 29,29:4
Percoco, Michael, 1959, Jl 28,27:2
Percy, Allan L, 1959, N 4,35:1
Percy, Carl, 1951, Ap 5,29:5
Percy, Charles Alexander, 1923, Je 14,19:5
Percy, Esme (trb lr, Jl 6,14:7), 1957, Je 18,33:1
Percy, Eustace, 1958, Ap 4,21:3
Percy, Frank E Sr, 1944, D 9,15:3
Percy, George W Mrs, 1948, Ag 6,17:6
Percy, Grace M, 1945, Mr 28,23:3
Percy, Harry L, 1942, Ap 20,21:5
Percy, Harry P, 1940, Ap 23,23:3
Percy, Henry George (Duke of Northumberland), 1918, My 16,13:6
Percy, James F, 1946, Ap 29,21:4
Percy, Julia Mrs, 1954, My 14,23:1
Percy, Nelson M, 1958, O 11,23:2
Percy, Paul, 1950, S 10,92:3
Percy, Welton Mrs, 1943, Jl 6,21:4
Percy, William A (por), 1942, Ja 22,17:3
Perdew, W E Mrs, 1948, Ap 28,28:2
Perdicaris, G A, 1883, Ap 27,5:4
Perdicaris, Ion, 1925, Je 1,15:3
Perdoma, Ismael B, 1950, Je 4,92:2
Perdue, Eugene H, 1925, Mr 11,21:4
Perdue, J Randolph, 1952, Mr 28,23:3
Perdue, Robert E, 1945, S 18,23:5
Perdue, Virginia Mrs, 1945, F 25,38:1
Pere Enfantin, 1864, O 2,3:5
Peredery, Grigory, 1953, D 18,29:3
Peregoy, Lamar S, 1942, Ja 4,48:3
Pereira, Charles A, 1944, Jl 8,11:3
Pereira, Daniel J, 1962, Je 13,41:3
Pereira, Domingos L, 1956, O 29,29:3
Pereira, F L C, 1958, Ag 30,15:5
Pereira, Javier, 1958, Ap 1,31:4
Pereira, Rev (Archbishop of Daman), 1925, Ag 25, 17:5
Pereira Carneiro, Ernesto, 1954, F 23,27:5
Pereira da Costa, Canrobert (funl, N 2,35:5), 1955, N 1,31:4
Pereira de Souza, Washington L, 1957, Ag 6,27:3
Pereire, J, 1880, Jl 13,5:4
Pereles, Maurice, 1959, Ag 28,23:2
Perell, Morris, 1952, Ap 16,27:3
Perello y Pou, Juan, 1955, Jl 29,17:3
Perelman, Jules S, 1958, Jl 15,25:4
Perelman, Luis Mrs, 1959, N 17,35:1
Perelmuth, Louis, 1962, Je 6,41:4
Peremi, Edmund, 1953, S 19,15:3
Perenyi, Ladislaus, 1947, Ja 20,25:3
Perera, Guido, 1953, Ja 18,93:2
Perera, Lionel C, 1964, Ja 31,27:2
Perera, Lionello, 1942, Ap 27,15:3
Perera, Lionello Mrs, 1966, S 25,84:8
Perera, Mario, 1946, D 21,19:4
Perera, Silvio, 1960, Ag 14,92:8
Peres-Jalin (Jules Gil Peres), 1882, F 26,4:5
Peress, Henry M, 1965, F 27,25:4
Peret, Raoul, 1942, Jl 23,19:1
Peretz, Haym, 1956, D 6,37:1
Peretz, Isaac Loeb, 1915, Ap 5,11:4
Pereyra, Carlos, 1942, Jl 1,25:5
Pereyra Rosas, Carlos, 1949, F 27,69:1
Perez, Anita B, 1951, Ag 27,19:3
Perez, Charles G, 1953, Mr 24,42:3
Perez, Ernetina, 1953, Je 10,29:1
Perez, Filemon, 1943, My 22,13:5
Perez, Florencia M, 1941, Je 24,19:1
Perez, Gilbert S, 1959, N 24,34:1
Perez, Henry L Mrs, 1961, Jl 13,29:1
Perez, Isidro, 1952, F 21,27:2
Perez, Lopez Abraham, 1941, S 6,15:6
Perez, Marcelino, 1920, S 17,11:5
Perez, Ramon, 1952, Ja 7,19:5
Perez, Rogelio, 1947, D 16,33:1
Perez Alfonseca, Ricardo, 1950, D 31,43:1
Perez Casas, Bartolome, 1956, Ja 16,21:4
Perez Cisneros, Guy, 1953, S 4,34:2
Perez de Arce, Guillermo, 1958, Ja 3,21:5
Perez de Ayala, Ramon, 1962, Ag 6,25:6
Perez-Gacitua, Lindor Vice-Adm, 1916, Ap 11,13:5
Perez Martinez, Hector, 1948, F 13,15:5
Perez Munos, Adolfo, 1945, D 22,19:5
Perez Ordega, Ignacio (por), 1948, Ja 13,25:3
Perez Ortiz, Quirino, 1951, D 9,91:1
Perez Sarmiento, Jose M, 1948, My 8,15:5
Perez Serantes, Enrique Archbishop, 1968, Ap 20,33:3
Perez Vega, Modesto, 1947, My 30,21:1
Perfect, Otis L Mrs, 1950, Je 20,27:1
Pergament, Ossip Y, 1909, My 30,9:6
Pergler, Charles, 1954, Ag 15,84:3
Perhach, Michael J, 1953, Ag 30,88:5
Perham, Charles B, 1918, Je 18,13:8
Perham, Charles B Mrs, 1918, Je 18,13:8
Perham, F E, 1905, Mr 21,11:6
Perier, Gilbert, 1968, Mr 15,39:3
Perignat, Jose de, 1903, Mr 27,9:6
Perigney, Countess de (will), 1942, Ap 9,21:1
Perigny, Countess de (will), 1942, Ja 16,22:3
Perigny, Roger M F S de, 1945, N 8,19:3
Perigoe-Hayter, Stanley H Mrs, 1943, Ap 3,15:6
Perigord, Paul, 1959, N 6,30:3
Perillo, Daniel R, 1946, Ap 18,27:2
Perillo, Joseph A, 1954, My 6,33:3
Perillo, Joseph M Mrs, 1966, Ap 24,86:3
Perillo, Michael, 1952, S 16,29:2
Perin, Charles P Dr (por), 1937, F 17,21:5
Perin, Charles P Mrs, 1914, Mr 8,15:5
Perin, Charles T, 1937, Ja 2,14:1
Perin, Frank L, 1947, O 16,27:5
Perin, George Landor Dr, 1921, D 23,13:6
Perin, Glover F, 1946, My 30,21:4
Perin, Nelson, 1904, My 13,9:6
Perin, O, 1880, N 30,5:3
Perin, William M, 1947, D 5,25:1
Perinchief, Morris K, 1945, Je 20,23:4
Perine, Carleton C Mrs, 1954, Jl 28,23:2
Perine, Clara N, 1952, Jl 18,19:5
Perine, David M, 1919, Ap 23,17:2
Perine, Edward T, 1941, Ja 18,15:2
Perine, Everett G, 1949, S 3,13:4
Perine, Harvey G, 1956, Mr 17,19:5
Perine, Jacob H, 1942, Ag 11,19:5
Perine, Mary E Mrs, 1938, Je 18,15:3
Perini, Carlo, 1952, Mr 5,29:2
Perini, Charles, 1961, Ap 8,19:5
Periolat, George, 1940, F 21,12:5
Perisi, Anna Mrs, 1916, D 26,11:4
Perit, Pelatiah, 1864, Mr 10,5:1
Peritz, Harry Mrs, 1965, O 12,47:3
Periwinkle, Madame (Mrs Susanne Martin), 1910, F 12,9:4
Perkal, Reuben W, 1950, Je 29,29:5
Perkell, Murray E, 1961, Je 13,35:4
Perkerson, William T, 1943, O 19,19:2
Perkin, Arthur G, 1937, My 31,15:2
Perkin, Charles A Mrs, 1921, Ja 30,22:4
Perkin, Frank B, 1955, Jl 24,65:2
Perkin, William Sir, 1907, Jl 15,7:6
Perkins, A E (Cy), 1951, N 22,31:4
Perkins, Adah R, 1946, S 2,17:4
Perkins, Agar L, 1948, S 1,23:3
Perkins, Agnes F, 1959, D 28,23:4
Perkins, Albert, 1958, Ja 11,17:4
Perkins, Albert J, 1910, S 25,II,13:5
Perkins, Albert W, 1947, Ap 28,23:3
Perkins, Alice J G, 1948, F 16,21:3
Perkins, Alice P, 1958, Ja 7,47:4
Perkins, Alvin S, 1938, Ap 16,13:4
Perkins, Arthur C, 1942, F 17,21:3
Perkins, Arthur L, 1953, Mr 10,29:1
Perkins, Azubah E Mrs, 1944, Jl 6,15:5
Perkins, Benjamin, 1904, O 11,9:4
Perkins, Bernard J, 1950, Jl 12,29:5
Perkins, Bertram J, 1964, N 6,38:1
Perkins, Bishop, 1866, N 25,1:7
Perkins, C A, 1930, Ja 17,23:4
Perkins, C Eugene, 1957, N 17,86:7
Perkins, Carroll E, 1968, Ag 6,37:4
Perkins, Charles, 1950, My 22,21:3
Perkins, Charles A, 1945, N 28,27:2
Perkins, Charles A Mrs, 1945, N 1,23:2
Perkins, Charles B Mrs (cor, S 5,51:2), 1954, S 1,27:5
Perkins, Charles C Mrs, 1909, Mr 22,7:5
Perkins, Charles E, 1907, N 9,9:4; 1943, Je 20,35:2; 1948, My 13,26:3
Perkins, Charles E Rev, 1937, F 28,II,8:7
Perkins, Charles Edwin Dr, 1924, O 24,19:5
Perkins, Charles Elwelt, 1923, S 11,15:3
Perkins, Charles H, 1953, Ap 8,29:2; 1963, Mr 7,7:2
Perkins, Charles Lawrence, 1919, D 11,13:3
Perkins, Charles P Commodore, 1913, O 9,13:5
Perkins, Charles T, 1946, S 6,21:4
Perkins, Charles W, 1954, O 8,23:3
Perkins, Cy (Ralph), 1963, O 3,35:5
Perkins, Donald G, 1964, F 10,27:5
Perkins, Dudley C, 1941, Ap 5,17:2
Perkins, Dwight H, 1941, N 4,26:5
Perkins, Dwight H Mrs, 1937, Mr 19,23:3
Perkins, E C, 1902, N 1,9:5
Perkins, E Stanley, 1938, My 4,23:3
Perkins, Edmond, 1865, Ag 7,5:1

Perkins, Edmund A, 1961, My 17,37:1
Perkins, Edward E, 1952, Jl 25,17:3
Perkins, Edward R, 1942, N 2,21:5; 1952, Ap 19,15:4
Perkins, Edward Richard, 1912, Ja 19,11:5
Perkins, Edward W, 1949, Mr 28,21:4
Perkins, Eli, 1910, D 17,13:5
Perkins, Elizabeth A Mrs, 1947, Mr 19,25:6
Perkins, Elizabeth B, 1952, Ap 12,11:5
Perkins, Ella S Mrs, 1937, F 21,II,10:6
Perkins, Emaline Mrs, 1941, N 17,19:1
Perkins, Emily S, 1941, Je 28,15:3
Perkins, Enoch, 1966, My 9,39:2
Perkins, Erickson Sr, 1941, S 24,23:6
Perkins, Estelle K, 1945, Mr 27,19:2
Perkins, F C Mrs, 1948, O 13,25:6
Perkins, F G Com, 1924, D 24,15:2
Perkins, F Nathaniel, 1937, Ag 11,23:5
Perkins, Ferdinand, 1925, F 3,13:4
Perkins, Ferdinand Mrs, 1925, F 3,13:4
Perkins, Frances (funl plans; trb, My 16,88:6; funl, My 18,39:5), 1965, My 15,1:6
Perkins, Frank, 1967, O 16,45:3
Perkins, Frank K Dr, 1925, Je 25,21:7
Perkins, Frank W, 1924, Ap 21,17:5; 1957, My 23,33:2
Perkins, Franklin Mrs, 1951, O 16,31:1
Perkins, Fred, 1951, Je 3,93:1
Perkins, Frederic W, 1943, Jl 9,17:5
Perkins, Frederick, 1938, D 16,25:1; 1940, Ap 28,36:4
Perkins, Frederick Capt, 1912, Ja 25,11:5
Perkins, Frederick E Mrs, 1951, Je 14,27:3
Perkins, Frederick P, 1941, F 7,19:4
Perkins, G Laurence, 1941, Mr 31,15:5
Perkins, G W, 1882, D 28,5:5
Perkins, George C, 1945, S 9,45:1
Perkins, George Clement Ex-Sen, 1923, F 27,19:3
Perkins, George F, 1940, F 22,23:6
Perkins, George H, 1949, Ja 1,13:6
Perkins, George R, 1947, Ag 27,23:5
Perkins, George S, 1961, Ap 8,19:3
Perkins, George W, 1920, Je 19,13:1; 1947, Ap 29, 27:3; 1949, F 3,23:5
Perkins, George W (trb lr, Ja 15,30:6), 1960, Ja 12, 47:1
Perkins, George W Mrs, 1909, Mr 28,13:5; 1912, S 24, 13:6
Perkins, George W Sr Mrs, 1960, Mr 16,37:4
Perkins, Grafton B, 1951, D 8,11:4
Perkins, H Norman, 1939, N 30,21:3
Perkins, H Norman Mrs, 1967, N 9,61:7
Perkins, Harold E, 1952, Ap 29,27:2
Perkins, Harold G, 1947, Ap 1,27:3
Perkins, Harry H, 1943, O 25,15:3
Perkins, Helen D, 1938, S 10,17:4
Perkins, Henry A (est appr, N 7,23:1), 1959, Jl 16, 27:2
Perkins, Henry C, 1903, O 15,9:7; 1947, Ag 5,23:6
Perkins, Henry D, 1955, Ja 26,25:5
Perkins, Holton B Col, 1937, F 7,II,9:2
Perkins, Horace O, 1948, Je 3,25:5
Perkins, Hosea B, 1902, Jl 30,9:5
Perkins, J B, 1903, Ap 26,3:3
Perkins, J L Sr Mrs, 1949, F 15,23:2
Perkins, J Newton Rev, 1915, Ap 8,13:6
Perkins, Jacob R, 1958, Ja 21,31:5
Perkins, James A, 1940, N 28,23:2
Perkins, James B, 1948, Ja 15,23:3
Perkins, James Dudley, 1911, Mr 28,13:5
Perkins, James G, 1949, F 18,23:4
Perkins, James H (por), 1940, Jl 13,13:1
Perkins, James L Mrs, 1956, Mr 16,23:2
Perkins, James M, 1938, Mr 27,II,7:4
Perkins, Jay, 1947, O 19,64:4
Perkins, Jay S, 1945, Ap 3,19:4
Perkins, John C, 1950, D 25,19:6
Perkins, John F, 1966, Ag 10,41:2
Perkins, John H, 1944, O 17,23:4
Perkins, John N, 1946, D 26,25:3
Perkins, John Richard Dr, 1918, O 11,11:3
Perkins, John W, 1911, N 2,11:5
Perkins, Joseph G Brig-Gen, 1925, Je 30,19:5
Perkins, Joseph H, 1954, O 8,23:2
Perkins, Joseph Mrs, 1903, My 25,9:6
Perkins, Julian L, 1950, Ap 5,31:1
Perkins, Kenneth, 1951, Je 21,27:3
Perkins, Leroy S, 1955, N 28,31:4
Perkins, Lionel N, 1958, S 18,31:4
Perkins, Louis E, 1964, F 3,27:3
Perkins, Lucy J Mrs, 1937, Mr 21,II,8:1
Perkins, M B Prof, 1901, Je 19,7:6
Perkins, Mahlon F (funl;death ruled suicide), 1962, Jl 7,5:7
Perkins, Margaret V Mrs, 1942, Jl 23,19:5
Perkins, Marie S Mrs, 1939, Jl 21,19:3
Perkins, Marion, 1961, D 21,27:3
Perkins, Marion E Mrs, 1949, F 10,27:5
Perkins, Mary L Mrs, 1923, Mr 16,17:5; 1941, O 10, 23:5
Perkins, Mary M Mrs, 1941, F 28,19:1
Perkins, Maurice, 1959, Je 20,21:1
Perkins, Maxwell E, 1947, Je 18,25:3
Perkins, Merritt G, 1942, Mr 25,21:3
Perkins, Milicent, 1968, S 25,47:1
Perkins, Norton, 1925, Jl 16,19:6
Perkins, Oliver P, 1937, O 5,25:2
Perkins, Ora W Mrs, 1942, Jl 5,29:3
Perkins, Orman C, 1958, Ag 21,25:2
Perkins, Oscar J, 1951, S 4,27:4
Perkins, Osgood, 1937, S 22,27:1
Perkins, Percy P, 1958, Je 25,29:4
Perkins, Phil S, 1948, Ap 23,23:3
Perkins, R, 1936, My 26,23:1
Perkins, Raymond G, 1952, S 20,15:4
Perkins, Richard A, 1965, Ja 30,24:4
Perkins, Richard C, 1907, Mr 1,9:5
Perkins, Robert, 1875, S 22,4:7
Perkins, Robert A, 1956, Jl 2,21:1
Perkins, Robert F, 1938, F 21,19:4
Perkins, Robert M, 1959, N 7,23:2
Perkins, Robert R, 1923, F 13,21:5
Perkins, Robert S, 1943, Je 5,15:2
Perkins, Robert W, 1937, F 24,23:3
Perkins, Samuel F, 1924, Ap 10,23:4
Perkins, Sanford B, 1945, S 18,23:6
Perkins, Seymour Mrs, 1957, S 29,86:2
Perkins, Sidney A (Sam), 1955, N 1,31:3
Perkins, Silas H, 1952, Je 3,29:2
Perkins, Thomas A, 1909, Ja 2,9:6
Perkins, Thomas J, 1952, F 3,84:4
Perkins, Thomas N (por), 1937, O 8,23:1
Perkins, True, 1951, S 10,21:4
Perkins, Valentine, 1865, Ap 9,3:1
Perkins, W W, 1878, N 13,8:5
Perkins, Walter E, 1925, Je 5,17:5
Perkins, Walter H, 1953, N 10,31:3
Perkins, Walter P, 1942, Je 27,13:6
Perkins, William C, 1943, O 29,19:3
Perkins, William E, 1944, My 5,19:2; 1952, Ja 3,27:5
Perkins, William H (will, Mr 12,23:2), 1940, F 20, 21:3
Perkins, William R, 1945, Je 16,13:5
Perkins, William Tecumseh, 1909, O 6,9:2
Perkins, Willis D Sr, 1954, Jl 27,21:5
Perkins, Worcester, 1952, Jl 13,61:1
Perkinson, H Ellery Mrs, 1963, O 23,41:3
Perkinson, Howard, 1957, Jl 23,25:2
Perkinson, J E, 1937, S 3,17:3
Perkinson, Marion A, 1951, F 7,29:3
Perkinson, Preston W, 1941, F 14,17:3
Perkinson, Stewart, 1941, Ap 29,19:6
Perks, John, 1948, Ag 17,22:2
Perkul, Roman, 1960, Je 9,33:5
Perky, Henry D, 1906, Je 30,7:6
Perky, Kirtland I, 1939, Ja 10,19:5
Perl, Emanuel M, 1955, F 13,86:5
Perl, Emil A, 1942, O 30,19:3
Perl, Louis F, 1950, F 19,78:2
Perl, Samuel, 1949, O 2,81:1
Perla, David, 1940, Je 15,15:3
Perla, Jozue, 1941, Mr 23,45:2
Perlberg, Jonas D, 1958, Ja 29,27:4
Perlbinder, Joseph, 1946, F 9,13:4
Perlee, Clarence H Rev, 1915, Jl 17,7:6
Perlemoyer, Sylvester, 1918, N 15,13:1
Perles, Abraham Mrs, 1953, F 22,61:1
Perles, Jules B, 1966, F 7,29:3
Perles, Max A, 1947, F 4,26:3
Perlet, Herman, 1916, Ja 12,13:4
Perley, Frank E, 1947, Ap 14,27:4
Perley, Frank E Mrs, 1949, Ap 8,25:1
Perley, Frank G, 1966, O 13,45:1
Perley, Frank L, 1952, Mr 18,27:5
Perley, George A, 1962, O 16,39:2
Perley, George F, 1944, F 24,15:3
Perley, George H (por), 1938, Ja 5,21:1
Perley, Henry C, 1947, Ja 17,24:2
Perley, Henry C Col, 1920, F 14,11:2
Perley, Ira Chief-Justice, 1874, F 27,5:3
Perley, J Marshall, 1946, Mr 15,22:2
Perley, J Marshall Mrs, 1943, Je 22,20:2
Perley, Myron C, 1939, D 13,27:1
Perley, Ward B, 1951, Jl 10,27:3
Perling, Joseph J, 1967, F 17,37:2
Perlish, Henry, 1949, Je 21,25:5
Perlitt, William A, 1943, N 6,13:3
Perlitz, Charles A Jr, 1964, Ag 2,77:2
Perlman, Abram M, 1962, Mr 16,31:4
Perlman, David K, 1962, Ag 12,81:2
Perlman, Elias R, 1954, Mr 26,21:1
Perlman, Harry W, 1966, Ap 2,29:5
Perlman, Jacob Dr, 1968, Ap 10,43:4
Perlman, Janet D, 1950, N 18,15:4
Perlman, Jesse B, 1957, Ap 13,19:2
Perlman, Louis, 1940, My 19,42:4
Perlman, Maris L, 1960, My 11,39:5
Perlman, Max, 1956, Mr 6,31:4; 1961, My 15,31:4
Perlman, Max Mrs, 1966, Ap 25,31:4
Perlman, Morris B, 1958, My 16,25:3
Perlman, Nathan D, 1952, Je 30,19:1
Perlman, Philip B (funl, Ag 5,23:2), 1960, Ag 1,23:2
Perlman, Samuel, 1938, O 4,25:2; 1961, N 26,88:6
Perlman, Samuel (S Price), 1963, O 20,88:8
Perlman, Samuel A, 1963, O 31,33:2
Perlman, Selig (trb, Ag 18,31:7), 1959, Ag 15,17:1
Perlman, William J, 1954, N 20,17:6
Perlman, William S (por), 1949, Mr 17,25:5
Perlmutter, Aaron, 1968, Ag 10,27:2
Perlmutter, Albert A Mrs, 1958, O 14,37:5
Perlmutter, Arthur, 1961, D 3,88:2
Perlmutter, David, 1947, O 9,25:5
Perlmutter, Emanuel Mrs, 1938, S 9,21:3
Perlmutter, Fred, 1954, D 28,23:4
Perlmutter, Herbert M, 1966, N 28,39:4
Perlmutter, Joseph, 1938, Ag 25,19:6
Perlmutter, Nathan, 1943, Mr 2,19:5
Perlmutter, Samuel, 1951, Ja 5,21:5
Perlmutter, Sholom, 1954, O 20,29:1
Perlmutter, William, 1952, Ap 12,11:5
Perlo, Felix L, 1954, Ja 30,17:2
Perlow, Abraham L, 1968, Ap 11,45:3
Perls, Kate K, 1945, Ag 24,19:1
Perlstein, Harris Mrs, 1956, S 2,57:2
Perlstein, Harry, 1958, Ag 20,27:5
Perlstein, Moses A, 1943, N 14,57:1
Perlzweig, William A, 1949, D 12,33:4
Permeke, Constant, 1952, Ja 6,95:5
Permut, Theodore J, 1960, Ag 8,21:2
Perna, Amadeo, 1948, O 17,76:2
Perna, Carmine J, 1947, Ag 6,23:4
Perna, Marianna Mrs, 1915, Ag 6,9:6
Pernar, Ivan, 1967, Ap 3,33:4
Pernas, Francis, 1955, Ag 15,15:2
Perne, Henry, 1944, F 7,17:6
Pernice, Salvatore Mrs, 1955, Ja 20,31:2
Pernicone, Carl J, 1961, S 11,27:5
Pernicone, Petronilla Mrs, 1957, Ag 22,27:3
Pernicone, Salvatore, 1961, My 29,19:4
Pernod, Peter J, 1941, N 17,19:5
Pernot, Hubert, 1946, Je 30,38:6
Pernoud, Flavius G Sr, 1952, Je 10,27:2
Pero, George H, 1937, D 9,25:1
Pero, Giuseppe, 1963, N 15,35:3
Peron, Juan D Senora, 1952, Jl 27,1:3
Peron, Juana S de Mrs, 1953, My 31,74:2
Peron, Mario, 1955, Ja 14,19:6
Perona, John, 1961, Je 11,87:1
Peroni, Carlo (por), 1944, Mr 13,15:1
Perosi, C, 1930, F 23,30:3
Perosi, Joseph J, 1954, O 14,29:4
Perosi, Lorenzo, 1956, O 13,19:4
Perosky, Fred, 1948, D 23,19:3
Perot, Carolin B G Mrs, 1940, F 12,17:5
Perot, Edward S, 1963, Je 27,33:3
Perot, Elizabeth L Mrs, 1937, O 1,21:2
Perot, John, 1940, Je 7,23:2
Perot, L Knowles Mrs, 1957, My 14,35:2
Perot, Mary B Mrs, 1944, Je 5,19:3
Perot, Robeson L, 1944, Jl 29,13:4
Perot, T M, 1902, N 16,7:6
Perot, T Morris Jr, 1945, D 1,23:6
Perot, W H, 1903, Je 10,9:6
Perotti, J, 1933, S 15,19:3
Perowne, John V T, 1951, Ja 9,30:4
Perpetua, Sister, 1946, Jl 27,17:4; 1947, D 30,24:3
Perpetuo, Antonio H, 1943, F 9,23:2
Perpignan, Alfred, 1961, My 10,45:5
Perrapato, Nicholas L, 1958, Ap 26,19:2
Perrault, Antonio, 1955, Ja 21,23:1
Perrault, Joseph E, 1948, Je 15,27:2
Perrault, Leo T, 1939, Ag 27,35:2
Perreau, Paul, 1942, S 11,21:6
Perreault, Paul J, 1955, Ag 4,25:3
Perreault, Wilfrid, 1940, My 24,19:5
Perregaux, Alfred L, 1953, D 24,15:3
Perrell, Thomas O, 1966, Mr 26,29:3
Perrelli, Frank V, 1952, S 20,15:6
Perret, Frank A (por), 1943, Ja 13,23:1
Perret, Jean M, 1958, Jl 4,19:1
Perret, Paul, 1948, D 29,21:4
Perret, Robert, 1965, Ap 5,31:5
Perret, Victor, 1941, Ag 8,15:4
Perrett, Charles W, 1954, My 28,23:1
Perrett, Galen J, 1949, Ag 14,70:7
Perrett, Galen J Mrs, 1952, My 1,29:5
Perretta, John C, 1938, N 6,49:3
Perretta, Louis, 1966, N 21,45:3
Perretta, Rocco, 1947, Je 25,25:2
Perri, Joseph M, 1939, D 31,18:5
Perri, Michael S Jr, 1959, F 3,31:3
Perricone, Giuseppe, 1947, Jl 19,13:6
Perrie, Alice J Mrs, 1938, My 20,19:3
Perrie, David, 1968, D 18,47:3
Perrier, Carlo, 1948, My 24,19:4
Perrier, Edmond, 1921, Ag 2,9:4
Perrier, Hector, 1964, My 12,37:6
Perrier, Joseph L, 1956, My 5,19:7
Perrier, L Omer, 1958, Je 8,88:6
Perrier, Leon, 1948, D 25,17:2
Perrigo, Cyrus, 1946, D 11,31:4
Perrigo, Harlan S, 1950, N 26,91:1
Perrill, Fred M, 1948, Je 16,29:4
Perrin, Alfred R, 1946, N 9,17:5
Perrin, Charles C, 1968, D 14,45:2
Perrin, Charles L, 1939, N 2,23:5
Perrin, Dwight S, 1952, O 21,29:3
Perrin, Edwin O, 1947, O 31,23:2
Perrin, Edwin O Mrs, 1921, D 4,22:3
Perrin, Emile, 1885, O 9,5:3
Perrin, Ernest, 1937, N 22,19:4
Perrin, Ethel, 1962, My 16,41:5

Perrin, Howell C, 1942, O 27,26:2
Perrin, James J, 1903, Jl 28,7:6
Perrin, Jean (por), 1942, Ap 18,15:5
Perrin, John N, 1940, Ja 22,15:3
Perrin, Lee J, 1946, S 15,9:6
Perrin, Lee J Mrs, 1966, N 1,28:2
Perrin, Louis, 1945, Je 22,15:2
Perrin, Marie R, 1957, D 12,30:1
Perrin, Porter G, 1962, S 10,29:1
Perrin, Raymond S, 1915, Ag 31,9:5
Perrin, Rene, 1966, Ja 22,29:5
Perrin, Susan L Mrs, 1938, S 11,II,11:2
Perrin, Sydney T, 1940, Ja 29,15:5
Perrin, William A, 1958, Mr 9,86:2
Perrin, William J, 1945, N 27,23:4
Perrin, William N, 1946, Ag 8,21:5
Perrin, William R, 1945, Ag 24,19:4
Perrine, Albert M, 1961, Je 12,29:2
Perrine, An Carson, 1919, Mr 15,15:2
Perrine, Annie E Mrs, 1940, D 16,23:6
Perrine, Augustus W, 1955, Ja 31,19:5
Perrine, Augustus W Mrs, 1957, N 27,31:3
Perrine, Cornelius C, 1956, Je 23,17:5
Perrine, Daisy E, 1939, Je 26,15:5
Perrine, David V, 1939, D 29,15:3
Perrine, Edward W, 1916, Jl 17,11:7
Perrine, Emma Folsom Mrs, 1915, D 28,11:4
Perrine, Franklin Pierce, 1925, Jl 7,19:5
Perrine, Frederic A C Dr, 1908, O 21,9:5
Perrine, George, 1949, Ja 21,21:3
Perrine, Harry C, 1956, O 19,27:2
Perrine, Henry P Mrs, 1947, F 8,17:2
Perrine, Howland D, 1937, My 3,19:2
Perrine, J Franklin Sr, 1961, D 17,82:4
Perrine, Joseph M, 1947, Ja 11,19:4
Perrine, Joseph M Mrs, 1947, Ja 3,22:2
Perrine, Lewis, 1877, My 29,4:7
Perrine, Margaret J Mrs, 1938, My 18,21:3
Perrine, Martha G (will), 1951, Mr 9,27:8
Perrine, Orlando, 1943, O 26,23:1
Perrine, Russell J, 1955, D 6,37:4
Perrine, Stanley M, 1938, Mr 28,15:2
Perrine, Van D, 1955, D 11,88:5
Perrine, William, 1921, Mr 26,13:5
Perrine, William A, 1945, D 12,27:5
Perring, Allen J, 1952, N 15,17:1
Perrins, Harlan B, 1950, N 11,15:2
Perrins, John, 1954, Je 16,31:5
Perrins, Neil, 1965, My 29,27:6
Perritt, William D, 1947, O 17,22:5
Perrochei, Count de, 1881, D 11,2:6
Perron, Louis R, 1950, Ag 9,29:5
Perrone, Charles, 1951, Mr 20,29:3
Perrone, Pio, 1952, Ja 18,27:5
Perrot, Emile G Sr, 1954, F 8,23:5
Perrott, Emanuel, 1941, My 15,23:3
Perrott, John J, 1942, F 28,17:5
Perrott, Ward S, 1955, Ja 15,13:2
Perrott, William, 1966, N 15,47:2
Perrow, Arthur, 1953, Ja 1,23:6
Perrow, Claiborne C Mrs, 1939, Ja 3,18:2
Perruchot, Henri, 1967, F 18,29:3
Perrusi, Paschal J, 1968, D 23,39:1
Perry, A B F, 1956, F 16,29:4
Perry, A E, 1939, Jl 30,29:4
Perry, Albert L, 1914, D 26,7:4
Perry, Alexander, 1943, N 17,25:5
Perry, Alfred H Mrs, 1961, Mr 1,33:1
Perry, Alfred M, 1954, Ja 16,15:4
Perry, Alfred Rev Dr, 1912, O 19,11:5
Perry, Alfred T Mrs, 1947, Jl 8,24:3
Perry, Allen E, 1947, Ja 2,27:2
Perry, Andrew J, 1907, Je 30,7:7
Perry, Antoinette (por), 1946, Je 29,19:3
Perry, Arthur C, 1961, Jl 31,19:3
Perry, Arthur C Mrs, 1957, F 3,77:3
Perry, Arthur F, 1941, D 22,17:1; 1965, Ja 14,35:1
Perry, Arthur I, 1959, N 16,31:6
Perry, Arthur J Mrs, 1947, Ja 23,23:4
Perry, August J, 1950, My 13,17:6
Perry, Ben Edwin Dr, 1968, N 3,89:1
Perry, Benjamin F 3d, 1964, D 2,50:8
Perry, Bertrand Mrs, 1950, My 27,17:4
Perry, Bliss (cor, F 16,25:2), 1954, F 15,23:3
Perry, Calbraith Rev, 1914, D 7,11:6
Perry, Charles A, 1944, D 25,19:3
Perry, Charles B, 1940, D 18,25:5
Perry, Charles C, 1948, Ag 5,21:2
Perry, Charles D, 1964, S 20,88:5
Perry, Charles E Mrs, 1903, N 30,7:6
Perry, Charles F, 1943, Ap 13,26:3; 1948, D 19,76:2
Perry, Charles H, 1944, Mr 28,19:2
Perry, Charles J Dr, 1913, Jl 14,7:7
Perry, Charles L Rev, 1908, Jl 27,7:6
Perry, Charles Mrs, 1950, My 5,22:3
Perry, Charles O, 1940, S 11,25:4
Perry, Charles S Mrs, 1954, D 1,31:4
Perry, Chauncy, 1912, O 11,11:3
Perry, Chesley R, 1960, F 24,37:3
Perry, Clair W, 1961, N 20,31:3
Perry, Clara F Mrs, 1941, S 30,23:2
Perry, Clarence A (por), 1944, S 7,23:5
Perry, Clarence A, 1951, Je 6,31:4
Perry, Clay Mrs, 1947, Je 17,25:4
Perry, Clell, 1951, S 1,11:4
Perry, Cooper, 1938, D 18,49:2
Perry, Cutler D, 1952, Ap 11,23:2
Perry, Cyrus C, 1955, D 28,24:5
Perry, Daniel, 1953, My 10,88:2
Perry, David A, 1954, O 14,29:5
Perry, David B, 1950, Je 16,25:4
Perry, David Brig-Gen, 1908, My 20,7:5
Perry, David M, 1938, F 19,15:4
Perry, Dean N Mrs, 1952, D 10,35:4
Perry, Delbert K, 1954, Je 20,84:5
Perry, Dominick Bro, 1939, Ag 26,15:6
Perry, Donald P, 1957, My 1,37:2
Perry, Donald R, 1953, Mr 3,27:3
Perry, Dwight J, 1950, Mr 29,29:3
Perry, E, 1878, N 3,1:2
Perry, E Lt-Col, 1864, Je 10,2:2
Perry, E W, 1904, Je 6,9:6
Perry, Earl B, 1959, S 10,35:3
Perry, Edmund R Mrs, 1963, Je 30,56:3
Perry, Edward Allen, 1911, Ja 10,11:5
Perry, Edward Baxter, 1924, Je 15,23:2
Perry, Edward C, 1947, Jl 2,23:4
Perry, Edward D, 1938, Mr 29,21:1
Perry, Edward L, 1938, Jl 29,17:3
Perry, Edward O, 1951, F 22,31:4
Perry, Edward R Mrs, 1946, Ag 13,27:3
Perry, Edward S, 1941, Mr 1,15:5
Perry, Edward T, 1958, Ap 27,1:3
Perry, Eli, 1881, My 18,2:7
Perry, Elizabeth, 1939, Ag 10,19:3
Perry, Eugene A, 1944, My 27,15:6
Perry, Foster, 1952, S 6,17:5
Perry, Frances M Mrs, 1945, Ap 19,27:4
Perry, Francis W, 1947, My 24,15:3
Perry, Frank, 1950, Ap 12,27:4
Perry, Frank J, 1948, O 14,30:3
Perry, Frank J Mrs, 1965, Mr 13,25:4
Perry, Frank L, 1947, D 2,29:2
Perry, Fred, 1945, My 21,19:4
Perry, Fred W, 1952, Mr 23,94:4
Perry, Frederic Wiley, 1918, Ag 17,7:8
Perry, Gardner B, 1964, Ag 19,37:4
Perry, Gardner Blanchard, 1910, D 12,9:4
Perry, George, 1952, Jl 4,13:3
Perry, George A, 1941, N 18,25:4
Perry, George F, 1945, D 27,19:1
Perry, George H, 1945, Ag 16,19:6
Perry, George W, 1947, S 24,23:5
Perry, Grace, 1937, D 30,19:3
Perry, Grace A, 1948, Ja 26,19:5
Perry, Graham T, 1960, S 12,29:4
Perry, H T, 1930, Mr 30,II,8:1
Perry, Harold G, 1959, Mr 18,38:1
Perry, Harold J, 1952, Mr 14,23:3
Perry, Harold M, 1940, O 11,21:5
Perry, Harold Mrs (Josephine Bartlett), 1910, O 16, II,13:4
Perry, Harry C (por), 1941, Jl 21,15:3
Perry, Harry E, 1945, My 12,13:4
Perry, Harry H, 1965, Jl 22,31:5
Perry, Helene H Mrs, 1944, O 22,46:6
Perry, Henry E, 1950, Mr 16,21:4
Perry, Henry H Mrs, 1954, F 12,25:1
Perry, Henry P Mrs (por), 1948, N 17,28:2
Perry, Henry W Mrs, 1954, D 27,17:4
Perry, Herbert W, 1945, Ap 25,23:3
Perry, Herman L, 1954, Je 12,15:5
Perry, Howard R, 1945, Ap 25,23:2
Perry, Hoyt O, 1966, F 10,34:2
Perry, Hugh, 1938, O 31,15:6
Perry, I Newton, 1942, Jl 13,15:5
Perry, Ira W Dr, 1937, Mr 28,II,8:7
Perry, J A, 1881, Ag 27,5:4
Perry, J C, 1884, Ap 15,2:2; 1936, O 21,27:3
Perry, J De W, 1927, Ap 12,27:3
Perry, J Douglas Mrs, 1958, N 1,19:4
Perry, J Franklin, 1946, Ja 18,19:1; 1957, My 14,35:4
Perry, J H, 1928, S 4,23:3
Perry, J J Gen, 1885, Ap 25,5:3
Perry, J O, 1928, N 21,29:3
Perry, James Capt, 1914, Jl 11,7:6
Perry, James D (por), 1947, Mr 21,21:1
Perry, James D Mrs, 1955, F 25,21:4
Perry, Jerome, 1961, O 1,86:4
Perry, John, 1879, F 22,2:3
Perry, John A, 1937, N 22,19:3; 1957, Ag 11,80:7
Perry, John F, 1965, S 6,15:3
Perry, John H, 1953, D 14,31:2; 1960, O 25,35:3
Perry, John H Sr, 1952, D 5,27:4
Perry, John L, 1952, My 28,29:1
Perry, John L Dr, 1915, Ap 14,13:3
Perry, John M, 1951, Mr 2,25:1; 1964, Ja 18,23:5
Perry, John P H, 1956, Ap 15,89:1
Perry, John R, 1955, S 27,35:1; 1956, O 26,29:2
Perry, John W, 1952, N 14,23:3
Perry, John W Mrs, 1955, Mr 11,25:1
Perry, Joseph A, 1948, Je 23,27:2
Perry, Joseph E, 1942, S 11,21:2
Perry, Josephine, 1943, My 18,23:2
Perry, Josiah Q, 1945, O 5,23:5
Perry, K M, 1949, My 4,29:4
Perry, Kenneth, 1964, D 24,19:4
Perry, Lafayette, 1948, Ap 10,13:1
Perry, Lawrence (trb lr, S 19,II,3:8), 1954, S 7,25:3
Perry, Lawrence Mrs, 1957, Ap 23,31:6
Perry, Len, 1949, Mr 25,23:3
Perry, Leroy C, 1960, Je 27,25:2
Perry, Lewis E, 1963, Je 9,87:1
Perry, Lewis H, 1945, Mr 14,19:2
Perry, Lillian G, 1940, Ap 12,23:4
Perry, Lillian M, 1946, Ap 27,17:4
Perry, Lycus D, 1948, Ja 19,23:5
Perry, M W, 1951, F 20,25:3
Perry, Mabelle J, 1950, My 18,29:3
Perry, Marian L Mrs, 1938, Je 14,21:4
Perry, Martin N, 1967, Ja 14,31:2
Perry, Marvin B Mrs, 1951, Ag 27,19:4
Perry, Mary P, 1957, Mr 11,25:4
Perry, Matthew C Capt, 1873, N 18,5:7
Perry, Miles Mrs, 1951, Mr 19,27:3
Perry, N A Sr, 1960, Ag 21,84:8
Perry, Nathan Benjamin, 1903, Ag 3,7:7
Perry, Nehemiah, 1881, N 2,5:2
Perry, Nehemiah Mrs, 1881, N 2,5:2
Perry, Nellie A, 1952, F 14,27:2
Perry, Nelson P, 1964, S 18,35:2
Perry, Norm, 1957, N 19,30:1
Perry, Norman Leslie, 1921, Mr 2,9:4
Perry, O H, 1933, Ja 23,13:4
Perry, Oliver H, 1949, D 14,31:5; 1965, Jl 25,69:1
Perry, Oliver Hazard, 1908, O 17,9:5; 1913, Ap 12, 11:4
Perry, Oliver M, 1941, O 26,42:3
Perry, Oscar H, 1948, Ap 26,23:4
Perry, Percival L D Lord, 1956, Je 20,31:2
Perry, Pettis, 1965, Jl 28,35:3
Perry, R C, 1884, O 3,5:3
Perry, Ralph B, 1957, Ja 23,29:1
Perry, Ralph H Mrs, 1959, N 22,87:1
Perry, Ralph I Mrs, 1944, F 22,23:3
Perry, Raymond, 1960, N 17,37:2
Perry, Raymond Mrs, 1945, Ja 27,11:4
Perry, Raymond S B, 1943, My 15,15:6
Perry, Raymond W, 1948, O 29,26:2
Perry, Robert D, 1946, Mr 26,29:3
Perry, Robert E, 1937, D 4,17:4
Perry, Robert S Jr, 1948, Ag 30,17:3
Perry, Roland H (por), 1941, O 29,23:1
Perry, Ruben Mrs, 1946, O 19,21:2
Perry, Ruth D, 1954, Ja 4,19:4
Perry, Samuel, 1954, O 20,29:3
Perry, Samuel J, 1943, Mr 30,26:4
Perry, Sara (Mrs S Stainach), 1959, Ja 23,25:3
Perry, Silent Bill, 1939, My 25,25:5
Perry, Stuart H, 1957, F 16,17:2
Perry, T S, 1928, My 8,27:4
Perry, Thomas C, 1941, Ag 12,19:5
Perry, Thomas D, 1958, Mr 12,31:2
Perry, Thornton T, 1954, O 7,23:1
Perry, W C, 1907, My 27,7:6
Perry, Walter, 1946, N 2,15:5
Perry, Walter Mrs, 1952, Ag 31,45:1
Perry, Wesley V, 1955, S 21,33:4
Perry, William, 1948, My 2,76:6
Perry, William A (por), 1938, Jl 6,23:5
Perry, William A, 1962, Je 22,25:3
Perry, William Alfred, 1916, F 18,11:6
Perry, William C, 1938, My 6,6:3; 1949, N 9,27:4
Perry, William E, 1937, Ja 21,23:3; 1943, Ja 12,23:2
Perry, William H, 1953, Ja 29,27:1
Perry, William R, 1946, Jl 6,15:2
Perry, William S, 1958, Mr 25,33:2
Perryman, E W, 1940, N 3,57:1
Perryman, Francis S, 1959, D 2,43:3
Perryman, Francis S Mrs, 1952, Ap 16,27:3
Perryman, George A, 1940, Je 11,25:3
Persall, Arthur M, 1938, N 24,18:4
Persano, Charles Comte Pelion de, 1883, Jl 30,5:6
Persans, Ferdinand F, 1952, S 3,29:4
Persaud, Ajudhya, 1943, S 27,19:3
Persch, Sarah Mrs, 1924, F 12,17:3
Persee, Henry S, 1960, S 6,35:3
Perselay, Arthur Mrs, 1952, My 5,23:4
Persell, Charles B Mrs, 1968, S 16,47:3
Pershall, Sam F, 1953, O 30,23:1
Pershing, Anna M, 1955, Ag 4,25:5
Pershing, Benjamin H, 1966, Ag 6,23:1
Pershing, Cyrus L Judge, 1903, Je 30,7:5
Pershing, David Mrs, 1939, N 6,23:3
Pershing, Edward H (died Nov 12; funl set), 1955, N 29,29:4
Pershing, Gale C, 1965, My 31,17:2
Pershing, Helen R, 1949, Ag 31,23:3
Pershing, J F, 1933, F 10,17:1
Pershing, John C, 1918, Mr 1,11:4
Pershing, John J Gen, 1948, Jl 1[illegible]
Pershing, Richard Warren [illegible] F 20,5:3
Pershing, Thompson F Rev, [illegible]
Pershing, Ward P Mrs, 1944 [illegible]
Persian Shah Assassinated, 1[illegible]
Persiani, Luigi, 1958, My 23,[illegible]
Persiani, Mme, 1867, My 19,[illegible]
Persin, Max, 1953, D 17,37:5

Persina, C David, 1958, Ap 15,33:4
Persing, Harry M Sr, 1950, Ag 7,19:5
Persinger, Louis, 1967, Ja 1,53:1
Persion, Achille P, 1950, O 1,105:1
Persius, Lothar, 1944, N 5,53:1
Perskie, Jacob H, 1941, Jl 29,15:5
Perskie, Joseph B, 1957, My 30,19:2
Perskin, Israel H, 1942, O 19,19:5
Persky, Daniel, 1962, Mr 16,31:3
Person, Carl E, 1950, My 8,23:3
Person, Charles H, 1953, Mr 11,27:5
Person, E Cooper Jr, 1952, S 6,17:5
Person, Edgar, 1951, Ja 28,76:5
Person, Harlow S, 1955, N 8,31:3
Person, John L Brig-Gen, 1968, O 5,35:5
Person, Norman, 1940, Je 23,31:2
Person, Otto, 1948, O 7,29:4
Personius, Ely, 1944, D 13,23:1
Persons, Alex M, 1951, Ap 16,25:4
Persons, Clarence P, 1950, Ja 26,28:5
Persons, E Gray, 1961, N 23,31:2
Persons, Gordon (further details, My 31,17:2), 1965, My 30,51:2
Persons, Henry Z Mrs, 1961, Je 1,35:4
Persons, James O, 1952, Ja 23,27:4
Persons, Millard F, 1944, S 6,19:6
Persons, W Frank, 1955, My 29,45:1
Persons, Warren M, 1937, O 14,25:2
Persons, Wilbur F, 1944, Mr 31,21:4
Persons, William O, 1938, My 13,20:3
Persons, William O Mrs, 1962, Ap 5,33:4
Persse, Dudley, 1864, F 7,8:5
Persse, Fred B, 1939, Je 2,23:3
Persson, Edward, 1957, S 26,25:3
Persson, Edwin, 1951, O 5,27:2
Persson, Frederic J, 1966, S 19,43:4
Persson, John, 1951, Ap 14,15:4
Persson, Per G, 1952, Ap 3,35:1
Pert, D W Mrs, 1944, Jl 23,36:1
Pertain, Nicholas Maj, 1912, Mr 18,11:6
Perter, Charles Dr, 1914, D 14,11:5
Perth, Earl of, 1902, Mr 1,9:1; 1937, Ag 21,15:3
Perth, Earl of (E Drummond), 1951, D 17,31:3
Pertile, Aureliano, 1952, Ja 13,88:5
Pertrand, Andre, 1946, O 11,23:2
Pertsch, Arthur J, 1959, Ag 1,17:5
Pertsch, C Frederick, 1963, My 18,27:4
Pertsch, Jacob, 1944, Mr 21,19:1
Pertwee, Roland, 1963, Ap 28,88:4
Peruggi, Ernesto, 1957, Je 15,17:6
Perugi, Giulio, 1949, F 25,24:3
Perugini, Angelo, 1960, S 18,86:5
Perugini, Signor (Jno Chatterton), 1914, D 5,13:6
Perutz, Leo, 1957, Ag 28,27:3
Perutz, Paul D, 1956, Jl 6,21:3
Perutz, Witold S, 1959, Je 12,27:1
Peruzzi, Mario Sr, 1955, D 11,88:4
Perwein, Alex, 1951, Mr 20,29:2
Perz, G N, 1876, O 11,4:6
Perzel, William, 1907, Mr 26,9:4
Pesaro, Lino, 1938, Jl 6,11:6
Pesata, Rudolph G, 1964, D 13,86:5
Pesatauro, Michele, 1948, Ap 29,23:2
Pesaturo, Constance, 1960, Jl 24,65:1
Pesavento, Frederick, 1952, Jl 31,23:2
Pescia, Astolfo, 1961, O 13,35:1
Pescosta, Frank J, 1945, Ja 10,23:5
Pescovitz, Harold Mrs, 1956, O 1,27:2
Peshall, Charles J, 1907, Ap 18,11:6
Pesick, John, 1951, My 17,31:6
Pesin, Samuel, 1949, My 6,25:2
Peske, Gertrude, 1950, Ag 2,25:3
Peskin, Samuel, 1939, My 24,23:5
Peskoe, Benjamin, 1966, Je 10,45:2
Peskoe, Bernard, 1966, O 28,31:3
Pesky, Phil, 1957, S 17,35:3
Pesky, Wilfred P, 1966, S 26,41:1
Pesotta, Rose, 1965, D 8,43:3
Pesqueira, Ignacio, 1940, O 21,17:6
Pesquidoux, Joseph de, 1946, Mr 19,28:2
Pessin, Morris J, 1960, O 4,43:4
Pessl, Helene Mrs, 1954, S 1,27:2
Pessl, Sigmund, 1955, My 25,33:3
Pessman, George J, 1953, Ap 4,13:2
Pessoa, Epitacio (por), 1942, F 14,15:1
Pessou, Alphonse O, 1938, O 4,25:3
Pessou, Alphonse O Mrs, 1948, Ja 15,23:1
Pestana, Angel, 1937, D 12,II,8:8
Pestarini, Joseph M, 1957, Jl 20,15:6
Pestelli, Gino, 1965, S 8,47:1
Pester, Harry, 1945, Je 3,32:1
Pester, Isaac, 1958, Mr 27,33:5
Pester, William, 1950, My 2,29:4
Pestronk, Max, 1956, D 29,15:3
Petacci, Gillseppe Dr, 1912, O 2,13:6
Petailliau, Edmund, 1961, S 30,25:5
Petain, Antoine, 1948, Jl 2,21:1
Petain, Henri-Philippe (Marshal), 1951, Jl 24,1:2
Petain, Henri-Philippe Mrs, 1962, Ja 31,31:1
etch, John P F, 1958, D 9,41:1
chek, Ernest F, 1956, F 7,31:1
hers, Nachum Mrs, 1960, O 4,43:1
rs, Solomon N, 1966, Ja 29,27:1

Petching, Paul R, 1950, My 21,106:4
Petchtle, Claude B, 1951, D 30,25:1
Petcoff, Boni E, 1965, Ag 7,21:1
Petegorsky, David W (funl plans, Jl 17,23:4; funl, Jl 18,27:3), 1956, Jl 16,21:5
Peteler, Alois, 1950, D 25,19:2
Peteler, Frank A, 1925, S 23,25:3
Peteler, Margaret M Mrs, 1939, Ap 20,23:4
Peter, Alfred, 1952, Ap 18,25:1
Peter, Bro, 1948, S 27,23:2
Peter, Frances Paca Mrs, 1907, Mr 5,9:5
Peter, Herbert L, 1949, Jl 2,15:7
Peter, King of Serbia (por), 1921, Ag 17,11:3
Peter, Kyr, 1964, My 19,37:1
Peter, Luther C, 1942, N 14,15:6
Peter, Marc Mrs, 1966, F 12,25:3
Peter, Sarah, 1877, F 7,4:7
Peter, Theodore, 1941, Ap 7,17:1
Peter, Wilbur H, 1957, F 15,23:5
Peter, William Sr, 1951, S 18,31:4
Peter, William 2d, 1937, Ja 7,22:1
Peter Claver, Mother (M L Bilodeau), 1953, S 13, 84:8
Peterken, William H, 1944, D 4,23:3
Peterkin, Clinton R, 1944, Mr 4,13:3
Peterkin, Daniel Sr, 1941, Mr 11,23:2
Peterkin, De Witt Jr Mrs, 1947, My 26,21:4
Peterkin, De Witt Mrs, 1952, S 29,23:6
Peterkin, DeWitt, 1954, Ag 22,93:3
Peterkin, Norman, 1959, My 18,27:4
Peterkin, Walter G, 1948, Ag 29,56:5
Peterkin, William G, 1938, N 25,23:3
Peterking, William Mrs (Julia M), 1961, Ag 11,23:3
Peterman, Albert E, 1944, O 16,19:5
Peterman, Harry G, 1953, Jl 19,57:2
Peterman, Robert J, 1951, Je 11,25:3
Petermann, A H, 1876, Je 16,4:7; 1878, S 28,5:4
Peters, A W, 1898, D 30,12:1
Peters, Albert R Rev, 1922, Ja 6,17:5
Peters, Albert T, 1938, S 13,23:2
Peters, Alex, 1951, Je 13,29:5
Peters, Alfred, 1908, Jl 20,9:4
Peters, Allen B, 1956, Ja 9,25:4
Peters, Alonzo G, 1945, F 24,11:5
Peters, Andrew J (por), 1938, Je 27,17:3
Peters, Andrew J Mrs, 1960, D 10,23:5
Peters, Arthur E, 1950, Jl 11,31:5
Peters, August B Mrs, 1944, Ja 15,13:2
Peters, Brandon, 1956, F 28,31:3
Peters, C A F, 1880, My 21,2:2
Peters, Carl B, 1954, N 21,87:1
Peters, Carl W H, 1939, Ja 22,34:5
Peters, Charles, 1943, Ap 4,40:7
Peters, Charles F, 1948, Je 22,25:2
Peters, Charles G, 1947, Ag 16,13:4
Peters, Charles M, 1941, D 27,19:6
Peters, Charles R, 1967, Ja 22,76:6
Peters, Charles V, 1948, Ag 31,26:2
Peters, Clarence A, 1939, My 5,23:4
Peters, Claude W, 1945, Ag 4,11:4
Peters, Clayton A, 1946, N 7,31:6
Peters, Clifton, 1944, D 30,11:3
Peters, Clinton, 1948, My 13,25:4
Peters, Cortez W, 1964, D 8,45:4
Peters, David, 1942, Mr 4,20:3
Peters, David Mrs, 1955, Je 8,29:6
Peters, David W, 1951, Ag 3,21:4
Peters, De Witt C, 1966, Jl 24,61:3
Peters, Edith Theresa Haynes Mrs, 1968, F 1,37:1
Peters, Edward Dyer Prof, 1917, F 18,17:3
Peters, Edward McClure Capt, 1924, Ag 12,11:3
Peters, Edward V, 1962, N 12,29:1
Peters, Emil S, 1937, Ap 11,II,9:3
Peters, Frances, 1924, O 24,19:5
Peters, Francis C, 1951, F 27,27:2
Peters, Frank M, 1922, Jl 1,13:6
Peters, Frank M Mrs (will), 1963, S 5,10:6
Peters, Fred, 1952, F 3,85:2
Peters, Fred B, 1945, D 23,3:4
Peters, Fred H V, 1952, S 25,31:6
Peters, Fred J, 1949, S 15,27:5
Peters, Frederic J, 1946, Ja 22,27:4
Peters, Frederick, 1907, Ag 17,7:6
Peters, Frederick A, 1948, My 1,15:6
Peters, Frederick E, 1959, Jl 30,19:1
Peters, Frederick M Mrs, 1941, N 11,23:3
Peters, Frederick W, 1940, Ap 13,17:5
Peters, George, 1939, Ap 5,25:4
Peters, George D, 1956, Ag 21,29:5
Peters, George H, 1952, Ap 6,88:4; 1956, Jl 13,19:4
Peters, George L, 1952, Ja 1,25:5
Peters, Gordon L Sr, 1951, O 8,21:5
Peters, H Elmer, 1941, N 17,19:3
Peters, H LeBaron, 1940, Ag 3,15:3
Peters, H N, 1878, D 8,5:6
Peters, Harold, 1943, F 2,20:2
Peters, Harry, 1940, O 29,25:5
Peters, Harry A Jr, 1959, Jl 12,72:7
Peters, Harry L, 1939, N 26,43:2
Peters, Harry T, 1948, Je 2,29:1
Peters, Heber C, 1953, Ap 8,29:5
Peters, Heber C Mrs, 1952, Jl 9,27:5
Peters, Henry P, 1952, Je 14,15:3

Peters, Hugh, 1948, Je 10,25:2
Peters, Isaac, 1919, Ag 16,7:5
Peters, Isabel M, 1965, Ap 20,39:1
Peters, J Dodge, 1946, O 22,25:6
Peters, J L, 1942, My 4,19:2
Peters, J M, 1903, D 26,7:7
Peters, J Theodore Mrs, 1953, Mr 27,23:2
Peters, J Wilton, 1950, My 28,45:1
Peters, James L, 1952, Ap 21,21:4
Peters, John A, 1953, Ag 23,89:1
Peters, John E, 1942, Jl 14,19:3
Peters, John H, 1954, O 29,23:5
Peters, John J, 1954, F 24,25:1
Peters, John L (por), 1945, My 20,32:1
Peters, John M, 1946, Ja 28,19:3
Peters, John P, 1955, D 30,19:1
Peters, John P Mrs, 1963, N 27,37:4
Peters, John Punnett Rev Dr (funl, N 13,22:3), 192 N 11,13:5
Peters, John S, 1956, My 21,25:2
Peters, Joseph D, 1939, Ap 11,24:4
Peters, Joseph R, 1946, Mr 28,25:3
Peters, Justin, 1938, My 17,23:3
Peters, Kenneth Mrs, 1940, N 4,19:3
Peters, L Franklin Mrs, 1951, My 2,31:4
Peters, Le Roy, 1941, D 18,27:4
Peters, Leonard A, 1949, D 1,31:2
Peters, Lewis C, 1949, Je 28,27:1
Peters, Lisa, 1954, D 4,17:3
Peters, Louis W, 1924, D 11,23:4
Peters, Louise, 1903, S 4,7:7
Peters, Madison C, 1918, O 13,23:1
Peters, Madison Clinton Rev Dr, 1918, O 13,23:1
Peters, Margaret E, 1967, Ja 18,43:2
Peters, Mason S, 1965, Mr 22,33:3
Peters, Matthew V Msgr, 1968, N 2,37:2
Peters, Maurice C, 1962, Ap 3,39:4
Peters, Morgan A, 1945, Ag 30,21:2
Peters, Nicholas, 1903, Ag 17,7:5
Peters, Nicholas D, 1940, Mr 19,25:5
Peters, Norman A, 1951, Ja 24,27:1
Peters, Phil P Sr, 1956, S 13,35:5
Peters, Phineas, 1951, F 22,31:2
Peters, R C, 1876, My 8,5:4
Peters, R Earl, 1952, F 20,29:5
Peters, R W Mrs, 1875, N 2,4:7
Peters, Ralph (funl, O 11,21:4), 1923, O 10,21:1
Peters, Ralph A, 1950, Jl 9,69:3
Peters, Ralph Jr, 1957, Mr 1,23:2
Peters, Ralph L, 1944, S 1,13:4
Peters, Ralph Mrs, 1949, Ap 26,25:1
Peters, Reaves, 1966, Ja 31,39:2
Peters, Reinold, 1944, Mr 30,21:6
Peters, Richard, 1921, My 27,17:6
Peters, Richard F, 1965, D 10,42:3
Peters, Richard Jr, 1941, F 16,40:2
Peters, Richard W, 1939, Ap 18,23:2
Peters, Robert D, 1955, Ap 27,31:5
Peters, Robert L, 1956, My 28,27:3
Peters, Rose Mrs, 1944, Jl 11,15:6
Peters, Ruth M, 1961, My 13,19:3
Peters, Samuel L, 1937, Je 25,21:5
Peters, Samuel T, 1921, O 22,13:7
Peters, Samuel T Mrs, 1943, Mr 12,17:4
Peters, Stanley Jr, 1950, My 3,29:1
Peters, Stephen S, 1948, D 24,17:4
Peters, Susan (will, D 10,23:3), 1952, O 25,17:1
Peters, Theodore, 1940, O 28,17:5
Peters, Thomas W, 1946, S 7,15:4
Peters, Thomas Willing Gen, 1917, Ja 3,11:4
Peters, Walter H, 1960, Mr 13,85:3
Peters, William A, 1916, Je 18,18:4
Peters, William F, 1938, D 2,24:2
Peters, William L, 1916, Ja 23,17:4
Peters, William Mrs, 1951, My 10,31:2
Peters, William R, 1944, F 20,36:3
Petersen, Aage G, 1961, D 9,27:3
Petersen, Albert Mrs (V R Southard), 1964, S 2
Petersen, Andrew M, 1951, Mr 31,15:3
Petersen, Andrew N, 1953, S 30,31:4
Petersen, Anna C Mrs, 1955, D 26,19:5
Petersen, Anthony N (por), 1940, D 14,17:4
Petersen, Axel, 1955, Mr 18,27:4
Petersen, Berthe C Mrs, 1941, F 16,40:1
Petersen, C, 1880, Je 30,5:2
Petersen, Carl, 1941, N 15,17:1
Petersen, Carl E, 1944, Jl 25,19:3
Petersen, Carol O (por), 1941, N 12,23:3
Petersen, Charles, 1945, O 7,44:3
Petersen, D Detmar Mrs, 1952, F 26,27:4
Petersen, D Detmer, 1953, Jl 22,27:4
Petersen, Eric, 1951, Ag 19,85:2
Petersen, Francis Sr, 1966, Jl 12,22:7
Petersen, Franklin G, 1939, Ja 15,38:5
Petersen, Frederick M, 1968, Jl 12,31:4
Petersen, George A, 1958, S 6,17:5
Petersen, George H E, 1942, Ap 10,17:4
Petersen, Gerhard, 1938, S 29,25:4
Petersen, Hans, 1941, My 6,21:1; 1947, F 7,23:2
Petersen, Hans C, 1945, Ja 25,19:4
Petersen, Hans L, 1947, Ap 4,23:2
Petersen, Hans Mrs, 1947, Ja 22,23:4
Petersen, Henry F, 1946, Ap 24,25:4

Petersen, Herman H, 1962, Je 7,35:4
Petersen, Hertha Mrs, 1952, Mr 16,90:2
Petersen, Hjalmar Ex-Gov, 1968, Mr 30,33:3
Petersen, Iver U, 1947, N 23,72:4
Petersen, John A, 1952, F 9,13:5
Petersen, Joseph E, 1951, Mr 5,21:1
Petersen, Julius, 1949, Ja 23,68:7
Petersen, Julius C Capt, 1916, Mr 18,11:7
Petersen, Leo S Dr, 1918, O 23,13:2
Petersen, Leonard, 1962, O 14,85:4
Petersen, Louis P, 1958, Je 14,21:4
Petersen, Martin, 1956, N 22,33:2
Petersen, N Peter, 1951, Je 8,27:4
Petersen, Nicholas, 1940, Ap 27,15:3
Petersen, Otto L, 1912, Mr 2,13:5
Petersen, Theodore C, 1966, Mr 15,39:2
Petersen, Theodore S, 1966, S 17,29:1
Petersen, Thorwald W, 1954, Je 5,17:6
Petersen, V I G, 1961, D 20,33:5
Petersen, Walter, 1939, O 4,25:3
Petersen, William, 1949, D 30,19:4
Petersen, William F, 1950, Ag 21,19:4
Petersen, William Sir, 1925, Je 13,15:5
Petersham, Miska, 1960, My 16,31:2
Petersheim, John P, 1947, N 14,23:4
Petersilea, Charles Prof, 1903, Je 14,8:6
Petersime, Ira, 1958, Ja 26,88:3
Peterson, A Everett, 1943, Mr 28,24:3
Peterson, Albert E, 1940, Je 11,25:4; 1959, D 31,21:5
Peterson, Albert N, 1947, N 29,13:2
Peterson, Albert P, 1944, N 7,27:5
Peterson, Alfred D, 1937, F 21,II,11:1
Peterson, Alfred E, 1956, F 25,19:6
Peterson, Alice F Mrs, 1941, S 17,23:4
Peterson, Andrew, 1950, O 5,32:2
Peterson, Andrew A, 1951, S 9,90:4
Peterson, Andrew H, 1957, N 10,85:2
Peterson, Anna A, 1949, N 4,27:3
Peterson, Anna J Mrs, 1952, Jl 20,52:3
Peterson, Anna W, 1946, D 15,76:1
Peterson, Arthur D, 1946, F 17,42:4
Peterson, Arthur H, 1966, Je 30,39:5
Peterson, Arthur J, 1948, Je 27,52:3
Peterson, Arthur L, 1955, S 23,26:4
Peterson, Arthur T, 1962, Jl 31,27:1
Peterson, Arvid, 1946, D 20,23:1
Peterson, Axel G L, 1954, Mr 15,25:3
Peterson, Bertha B Mrs, 1946, Je 15,21:5
Peterson, C E, 1941, N 20,27:2
Peterson, Carl, 1949, My 13,23:4; 1953, O 20,29:5; 1955, S 28,35:1
Peterson, Carl A, 1949, D 23,22:3; 1951, O 29,23:4
Peterson, Carl F, 1950, S 16,19:4; 1956, S 17,27:4
Peterson, Charles, 1940, N 1,25:4
Peterson, Charles A, 1951, F 21,27:4; 1963, S 8,86:3
Peterson, Charles C, 1962, Je 26,28:6
Peterson, Charles F, 1943, N 11,23:2
Peterson, Charles Mrs, 1961, S 22,33:4
Peterson, Charles P, 1938, Ap 29,21:1
Peterson, Charles S, 1943, S 9,26:4
Peterson, Charles S Mrs, 1946, Ap 2,27:3
Peterson, Charles W, 1949, S 20,29:1
Peterson, Christian George, 1903, D 4,9:6
Peterson, Clara G Mrs, 1910, Jl 26,7:6
Peterson, Clarence O, 1951, O 5,27:3
Peterson, Clifford E, 1953, F 11,29:4
Peterson, Curt Mrs (por), 1946, Je 12,27:4
Peterson, Donald Mrs (M Kavasz), 1960, Ag 28,83:2
Peterson, Dutton S, 1964, O 21,43:4
Peterson, Edmund N, 1968, F 20,47:1
Peterson, Edward E, 1965, Ja 19,33:1
Peterson, Edward M, 1961, Je 7,38:5
Peterson, Edward S (por), 1955, S 6,25:3
Peterson, Edward W, 1960, O 4,43:2
Peterson, Edward W Mrs, 1966, N 9,39:4
Peterson, Emily L, 1938, Mr 17,21:4
Peterson, Emma L Mrs, 1942, Ap 7,22:4
Peterson, Eric, 1961, Mr 5,86:7
Peterson, Eric E, 1948, Ag 28,15:2
Peterson, Erwin A, 1947, S 7,60:4
Peterson, Frank D, 1944, D 28,19:4
Peterson, Frank R, 1938, D 28,26:6
Peterson, Fred B, 1943, Je 15,21:4
Peterson, Frederick (por),(cor, Jl 26,3:5), 1938, Jl 11, 17:3
Peterson, Frederick A, 1948, My 28,23:2
Peterson, Frederick Mrs, 1959, My 21,31:4
Peterson, Frederick W, 1953, Ap 26,85:4
Peterson, George C, 1905, Mr 1,9:5
Peterson, George E, 1951, D 27,21:3
Peterson, George J, 1959, F 1,84:5
Peterson, George W, 1946, Ap 28,44:4
Peterson, Gust C, 1940, My 31,19:4
Peterson, Gustaf Mrs, 1943, N 21,57:1
Peterson, Gustav Mrs, 1949, F 11,23:1
Peterson, Guy C, 1949, S 19,23:5
Peterson, Guy M, 1944, F 3,19:5
Peterson, Harold A, 1959, O 4,86:3
Peterson, Harry O Mrs, 1948, S 14,30:2
Peterson, Henry P, 1953, O 24,15:4
Peterson, Herman, 1950, Je 14,31:5
Peterson, Herman G, 1943, O 28,23:5
Peterson, Hermod, 1938, D 29,19:1

Peterson, Hulda C Mrs, 1942, Je 25,23:6
Peterson, Irvine E, 1951, Ja 8,11:5
Peterson, J C Rev, 1903, Jl 24,7:7
Peterson, J Earl, 1948, N 20,13:6
Peterson, Jack, 1940, My 5,52:2
Peterson, James B, 1912, Ja 10,17:4
Peterson, James N, 1967, Ap 27,45:4
Peterson, Jerome B, 1943, F 22,17:3
Peterson, Jesse D, 1950, Ap 11,31:2
Peterson, Jesse D Mrs, 1954, O 28,35:5
Peterson, Jesse Dudley Mrs (Edith), 1968, Je 22,33:4
Peterson, Joel B, 1953, Ap 1,29:2
Peterson, John, 1939, Jl 13,19:2
Peterson, John B, 1944, Mr 16,19:6
Peterson, John Capt, 1908, N 8,11:4
Peterson, John H, 1944, S 23,13:4
Peterson, John L, 1942, Je 7,43:1
Peterson, John M, 1948, My 3,21:3; 1962, N 2,31:5
Peterson, John M Mrs, 1966, My 28,27:2
Peterson, John N, 1943, Jl 4,21:1
Peterson, John Sr Mrs, 1948, Jl 20,23:5
Peterson, Jon P, 1948, Ja 25,56:6
Peterson, Jonathan W, 1959, O 7,43:4
Peterson, Jorgen Mrs, 1962, Ap 7,25:4
Peterson, K Dorph Prof, 1937, S 27,21:3
Peterson, Karen, 1940, F 19,17:5
Peterson, Lars O, 1956, My 23,31:3
Peterson, Lawrence, 1915, N 26,13:5
Peterson, Lawrence E, 1963, Ap 4,47:2
Peterson, Liss C, 1952, Ja 30,26:2
Peterson, M E, 1940, O 28,17:4
Peterson, Mary Mrs, 1953, N 4,33:1
Peterson, Maurice D, 1952, Mr 16,90:3
Peterson, May (Mrs E Thompson), 1952, O 9,31:3
Peterson, N Vern, 1959, Ja 17,19:6
Peterson, Neilse G, 1952, F 19,29:4
Peterson, Nels N, 1949, My 12,31:5
Peterson, Nelson S, 1965, D 7,47:1
Peterson, Nicholas E Mrs, 1948, My 17,19:5
Peterson, Norman E, 1939, Je 20,21:1
Peterson, Oscar, 1954, F 26,20:3
Peterson, Oscar W, 1954, S 21,27:4
Peterson, Otto P, 1946, Mr 1,21:4
Peterson, P B, 1938, Ag 9,19:3
Peterson, P O, 1941, Ja 27,15:2; 1947, Jl 24,21:1
Peterson, Perry, 1958, N 30,87:1
Peterson, Peter, 1940, Ja 4,24:2; 1960, O 29,23:6
Peterson, Peter A, 1948, O 21,27:3
Peterson, Peter Mrs, 1961, N 10,35:1
Peterson, Ragnar G, 1963, My 5,86:7
Peterson, Ralph, 1949, Mr 23,27:3
Peterson, Reuben, 1942, N 26,28:2
Peterson, Richard B Mrs, 1944, Mr 4,13:5
Peterson, Robert, 1939, O 19,23:3
Peterson, Robert S, 1925, Jl 16,19:5
Peterson, Roger, 1959, F 4,66:3
Peterson, Ronald B Comr, 1968, O 12,37:4
Peterson, Ruben O, 1958, D 30,32:2
Peterson, Sara J Mrs, 1948, S 15,31:4
Peterson, Taft M, 1968, D 16,47:1
Peterson, Theodore O, 1950, Ja 16,26:3
Peterson, Thomas F, 1962, Ag 27,23:6
Peterson, Thorsten E, 1960, Ap 30,23:3
Peterson, Vernon A, 1956, My 28,51:5
Peterson, Victor N, 1946, Ap 9,27:4
Peterson, Virgil L, 1956, F 16,29:3
Peterson, Virgilia (Mrs C G Paulding), 1966, D 27, 32:1
Peterson, Walfred A, 1944, F 9,19:4
Peterson, Walter A, 1939, Ja 3,17:2; 1958, Ja 10,23:3
Peterson, Walter C, 1945, Mr 20,19:2
Peterson, Walter M, 1962, O 6,25:6
Peterson, William, 1938, D 3,19:5
Peterson, William A, 1949, O 11,34:1; 1951, Je 9,19:6
Peterson, William E, 1951, S 12,31:3
Peterson, William F, 1959, Ja 29,27:4
Peterson, William G, 1942, Jl 28,17:3
Peterson, William H, 1960, Jl 2,17:2
Peterson, William M, 1954, O 30,17:3
Peterson, William Sir, 1921, Ja 5,13:5
Peterson, Winfield A, 1965, N 5,37:3
Petery, Jozsef, 1967, N 28,47:1
Pethard, George, 1951, N 19,23:6
Petherbridge, Elizabeth, 1965, Ag 26,33:4
Pethick, Ford C Mrs, 1964, D 1,41:1
Pethick, Harry H, 1966, Ap 1,35:3
Pethick, Lea O, 1949, F 15,23:5
Pethick, W N, 1901, D 21,1:6
Pethick-Lawrence, Frederick W, 1961, S 12,33:2
Pethick-Lawrence, Lady, 1954, Mr 12,21:1
Pethybridge, John F, 1951, My 25,27:6
Petich, Chevalier Luigi, 1903, N 16,1:5
Peticolas, Ben C, 1960, D 10,23:6
Petigrue, Winfred K, 1963, O 9,43:1
Petillo, Diomede, 1958, Mr 26,37:3
Petillo, Giovanni Mrs, 1949, S 16,29:1
Petina, Joseph, 1947, S 1,19:5
Petina, Stephen I, 1947, Ap 14,27:1
Petiot, Henri J C (H Daniel-Rops), 1965, Jl 28,35:1
Petit, Adelor J, 1951, F 14,29:2
Petit, Douglas E, 1925, D 22,21:4
Petit, Lucienne, 1941, S 23,23:5
Petit, Robert Mrs, 1968, Mr 22,44:5

Petitjean, Gaston Francois Dr, 1909, N 27,9:5
Petitjean, Marie de la, 1947, Ap 5,19:2
Petito, Amadio, 1949, Je 30,23:5
Petito, Anthony, 1940, Mr 24,31:1
Petitpas, Marie, 1947, Mr 2,60:1
Petitt, George E, 1956, Je 10,88:3
Petluck, Joseph, 1950, F 19,78:3
Petluck, Joseph Mrs, 1953, D 11,31:2
Peto, John F Mrs, 1944, Jl 2,19:2
Petr, Alois, 1951, D 15,13:4
Petracca, Joseph R, 1963, O 2,41:2
Petraitis, Joseph, 1939, Je 25,36:6
Petraitis, Michael D, 1955, Mr 8,27:4
Petrakis, Mark E, 1951, My 31,27:4
Petralia, Andrew E, 1954, S 16,21:5
Petralia, Vincent, 1950, My 3,29:2
Petran, Michael, 1952, Ja 1,25:5
Petranek, Augustine, 1960, My 7,23:5
Petrascu, Gheorghe, 1949, My 3,25:3
Petraske, Herman Mrs, 1956, My 15,31:2
Petre, Charles, 1964, O 22,35:1
Petre, Edmond J, 1951, F 22,31:3
Petree, John W, 1955, Je 14,29:3
Petree, Robert F, 1953, Je 1,23:2
Petregille de Percin, M Mrs, 1940, D 15,60:2
Petrelis, George P, 1964, O 26,31:4
Petrella, H, 1877, Ap 9,5:4
Petrelli, Eleonora, 1904, F 24,9:6
Petrequin, Edouard A, 1949, Ag 25,23:1
Petrescu-Comnen, Nicolas, 1958, D 14,2:5
Petrewitz, Peter Mrs, 1947, O 29,28:2
Petri, Angelo, 1961, O 5,37:4
Petri, Charles F, 1950, F 3,23:5
Petri, Egon, 1962, My 28,29:1
Petri, Herman, 1942, O 16,19:2
Petri, John A, 1950, Mr 8,27:2
Petri, Maitland, 1919, Ja 27,13:4
Petricek, Gustav J, 1955, Jl 22,23:1
Petrick, Alex W, 1952, Ag 27,27:5
Petrick, Joseph Mrs, 1950, Ap 4,29:4
Petrides, George G, 1942, Ap 10,17:2
Petrie, Alex R, 1966, N 22,41:3
Petrie, Charles B, 1956, F 7,31:4
Petrie, David H, 1948, Jl 31,15:3
Petrie, Edward C, 1954, Ap 26,25:2
Petrie, Flora R, 1945, Mr 24,17:3
Petrie, Francis J, 1966, Jl 18,27:2
Petrie, Frank B, 1953, F 4,27:4
Petrie, George, 1947, S 7,60:6
Petrie, Harry, 1948, Ja 15,23:3
Petrie, Howard A, 1968, Mr 26,46:1
Petrie, J L, 1879, Ja 3,2:1
Petrie, John, 1953, D 20,76:3
Petrie, John A, 1954, F 4,25:3
Petrie, John F, 1944, F 17,19:4
Petrie, Jonathan, 1879, D 2,4:7
Petrie, Kerr N, 1961, My 27,23:6
Petrie, Laverne V, 1951, D 15,13:6
Petrie, M Josephine, 1940, My 25,17:4
Petrie, Peter C Capt, 1909, N 14,13:4
Petrie, Robert I, 1942, My 9,13:5
Petrie, William M F (por), 1942, Jl 30,21:1
Petrillo, Anthony T, 1954, Ag 24,21:5
Petrillo, Caesar J, 1963, N 23,29:4
Petrillo, Carlo Jr, 1948, S 28,27:2
Petrillo, Carlo Mrs, 1957, Mr 19,37:4
Petrillo, James C Mrs, 1962, O 22,29:2
Petrillo, James V, 1952, Je 12,33:5
Petrillo, Louis, 1962, Je 9,25:4
Petrinovic, Francisco, 1951, My 20,89:2
Petroccitto, Gaetano, 1954, Jl 17,13:3
Petrocine, Anthony Mrs, 1952, D 9,33:3
Petroff, Boris P, 1966, S 21,47:1
Petroff, Gen, 1942, Ja 24,17:2
Petroff, George, 1949, Ap 26,25:1
Petroff, Ivan, 1963, S 22,86:6
Petroff, Peter A, 1957, Ja 20,93:1
Petroff, S A, 1948, N 27,17:1
Petroff, Vassily, 1957, Jl 11,25:4
Petrokubi, Stephen J, 1962, Je 23,23:1
Petrone, Charles C, 1959, Ap 7,33:1
Petrone, Patrick P, 1959, Je 18,31:5
Petrone, Susan, 1963, Ag 28,66:7
Petronella, Albert, 1951, Je 1,23:3
Petronio, Francesco A, 1937, Ap 6,23:5
Petronio, Romeo F, 1960, F 16,37:4
Petronzi, Henry, 1907, Ja 10,9:6
Petronzio, Carmella Mrs, 1957, N 8,29:4
Petrose, Samuel, 1952, F 6,29:4
Petroskey, Walter J, 1950, S 30,17:5
Petroski, Andrew S, 1940, Ag 18,37:3
Petroski, Frank P, 1950, Ap 12,27:3
Petrov, Ivan A, 1954, F 13,13:6
Petrov, Ivan E, 1958, Ap 11,26:1
Petrov, Nikolai N, 1964, Mr 4,34:5
Petrov, Vladimir M, 1966, Ja 9,
Petrova, Maria, 1948, My 20,29
Petrovic, Mihajlo, 1949, Je 23,2
Petrovitch, Ivan Pavloff, 1916, F
Petrovsky, Grigory I, 1958, Ja 11
Petrovsky, Joseph G, 1954, Ja 2,
Petrovsky, Vladimir, 1950, N 3,2
Petruccelli, Dominick, 1947, Je 2

Petrullo, Anthony, 1964, Ap 24,33:1
Petrunkevitch, Alex, 1964, Mr 10,37:1
Petruzzi, Alfred, 1950, N 2,31:2
Petruzzi, Joseph A, 1956, Ap 21,17:2
Petry, Ambrose F, 1937, O 7,27:4
Petry, David W, 1938, D 28,26:2
Petry, Francis J W, 1955, Ap 8,21:1
Petry, George A, 1941, O 10,23:6
Petry, Louis M, 1939, Je 1,25:5
Petry, Martin, 1941, Ap 3,23:5
Petry, Peter H, 1941, D 12,26:2
Petry, Victor J, 1924, Jl 13,22:4
Petry, William, 1961, D 30,19:1
Petry, William M, 1950, S 28,31:1
Petryszyn, Peter, 1952, N 4,29:2
Petsarath, Prince of Laos, 1959, O 15,39:2
Petsche, B William, 1959, Je 9,37:3
Petsche, Henrietta, 1949, My 11,30:5
Petsche, Maurice, 1951, S 17,21:3
Petscheck, George, 1947, S 8,21:5
Petschek, Frank C, 1963, Je 27,33:4
Petschek, Hans, 1968, Ja 7,84:4
Petschek, Ignaz Mrs, 1951, Ja 4,29:2
Petschek, Paul, 1946, Ag 24,11:5
Petschow, Johannes K, 1957, Mr 20,37:2
Pett, Charles E, 1961, Ag 12,17:5
Pette, Michael, 1952, My 18,92:3
Pette, Nicholas M Mrs, 1943, Mr 6,13:2
Pettebone, Harry O Mrs, 1941, O 5,49:1
Pettee, Charles H, 1938, Mr 24,23:2
Pettee, George M, 1949, Jl 5,23:2
Pettee, James H Rev, 1920, F 18,11:2
Pettee, John Tyler Rev, 1907, F 18,9:6
Pettee, Julia, 1967, My 31,49:3
Pettee, William Henry Prof, 1904, My 27,9:2
Pettengill, A A, 1882, Ja 18,5:1
Pettengill, Charles W Mrs, 1945, My 26,15:5
Pettengill, Emma F Mrs, 1912, S 4,11:3
Pettengill, Ernest E, 1951, My 29,25:2
Pettengill, George T, 1959, Ja 12,39:3
Pettengill, Samuel B Mrs, 1948, Je 29,24:3
Petter, Ernest W Sir, 1954, Jl 19,19:3
Petter, John M, 1938, Jl 21,21:5
Pettersen, Roy H, 1942, Ja 10,15:4
Petterson, Carl L, 1939, S 14,23:4
Petterson, Charles Capt, 1937, D 16,25:1
Petterson, George, 1950, F 19,78:1
Petterson, Victor M, 1949, O 21,25:4
Pettes, Benjamin H, 1942, My 7,19:1
Pettet, John D, 1959, Ja 8,29:1
Petteys, Jesse C, 1949, O 19,29:4
Pettibone, C Eugene, 1948, O 11,23:3
Pettibone, Charles L, 1966, O 7,43:5
Pettibone, Ralph D, 1956, Jl 4,19:2
Pettibone, William H, 1943, D 9,27:4
Pettiford, Oscar, 1960, S 9,30:1
Pettigrew, B L, 1947, F 27,21:5
Pettigrew, Edward S, 1951, Jl 15,60:4
Pettigrew, Edward S Mrs, 1945, Ag 6,15:6
Pettigrew, James, 1945, D 20,23:2
Pettigrew, John Allgood, 1912, Jl 3,11:6
Pettigrew, Ned, 1952, Ag 21,19:6
Pettigrew, Thomas, 1941, Ag 29,19:4
Pettigrew, Todd M, 1951, D 15,13:5
Pettigrew, Walter E, 1948, N 30,27:3
Pettigru, James L, 1863, My 10,3:5
Pettijohn, Charles C, 1948, My 20,29:1
Pettijohn, Charles C Mrs, 1960, Je 18,23:4
Pettine, Giuseppe, 1966, Je 18,31:4
Pettinell, Armida P, 1949, Ja 13,23:4
Pettingdale, William M, 1944, Mr 9,17:4
Pettingell, Charles I, 1948, N 17,27:2
Pettingell, George H, 1944, Ag 11,15:6
Pettingell, Harold L, 1957, S 4,33:4
Pettingell, Ralph D, 1950, Mr 27,23:4
Pettinger, Herbert, 1959, Mr 17,33:4
Pettingill, Raymond A, 1956, Mr 22,35:4
Pettingill, William L, 1950, S 16,19:5
Pettinos, Charles E, 1951, N 16,25:2
Pettinos, George F, 1958, F 25,27:5
Pettinos, George F Mrs, 1941, Ja 27,15:2
Pettis, F S Mrs, 1878, D 27,8:1
Pettis, H E, 1944, N 7,27:2
Pettis, John H, 1940, Ja 31,19:1
Pettis, Willard A, 1925, Jl 9,19:3
Pettit, Albert E, 1944, N 25,13:1
Pettit, Albert S Mrs, 1943, Jl 9,17:6
Pettit, Clarence M, 1962, My 2,37:1
Pettit, Donald, 1957, Mr 15,25:3
Pettit, Ford M, 1952, Mr 11,27:3
Pettit, Franklin, 1943, Ja 20,19:2
Pettit, Gaylor Joel Dr, 1922, Jl 8,11:7
Pettit, George A, 1961, Ap 1,17:2
Pettit, George A Rev, 1917, Mr 1,13:4
Pettit, George Henry, 1919, S 25,15:5
Pettit, Glenford, 1956, Ag 28,27:4
Pettit, Henry H, 1945, Ja 13,11:2
Pettit, J Erwin Sr, 1955, Mr 19,15:2
Pettit, J U, 1881, Mr 23,5:3
Pettit, John, 1877, Je 18,5:5
ttit, John M, 1955, My 24,31:2
it, Leicester S, 1947, S 11,27:2
Lowell E, 1964, Jl 7,35:2

Pettit, Lyman C, 1950, Mr 9,29:1
Pettit, Mortlock S, 1962, Ag 1,31:2
Pettit, Richard Tone, 1919, S 8,13:2
Pettit, Roland J, 1954, Jl 28,23:2
Pettit, Samuel B, 1955, D 19,27:1
Pettit, Stanley C, 1964, Jl 3,21:2
Pettit, Stephen C Dr, 1914, D 4,11:6
Pettit, Stephen P (funl, S 4,23:6), 1925, S 10,25:6
Pettit, Susan Seaman Mrs, 1916, F 4,9:6
Pettit, Walter R, 1938, N 12,15:4
Pettit, Walter W, 1960, D 24,15:1
Pettit, Warren, 1921, Jl 12,13:4
Pettit, William S, 1948, My 23,70:2
Pettitt, Edward G, 1967, S 21,47:1
Pettitt, H, 1893, D 23,1:4
Pettitt, Thomas, 1946, O 18,23:3
Petton, Franklin Dwight, 1913, Ja 9,9:5
Pettus, Edmund Winston Ex-Sen, 1907, Jl 28,7:5
Pettus, Florence, 1950, Ap 4,34:1
Pettus, Joseph Capt, 1925, Ag 12,21:4
Pettus, William B, 1959, D 9,42:2
Pettus, William J, 1947, D 31,15:4
Petty, A R, 1932, O 28,19:3
Petty, A Smith, 1958, Mr 9,86:2
Petty, Alfred C, 1962, F 7,37:3
Petty, Carl W Mrs, 1951, D 6,33:3
Petty, David M, 1960, My 29,57:1
Petty, Everett C, 1943, D 1,21:3
Petty, George J, 1945, F 6,19:4
Petty, Harry F, 1948, D 9,33:2
Petty, Irving D, 1939, D 10,69:2
Petty, James T (funl, Ap 21,11:6), 1923, Ap 20,17:4
Petty, James Taylor, 1923, Ap 19,19:5
Petty, James W, 1965, S 11,27:2
Petty, Jesse Mrs, 1944, F 23,19:4
Petty, John, 1947, D 30,23:2
Petty, John P, 1944, Ja 7,17:2
Petty, Joseph D, 1956, Ja 12,27:5
Petty, Julius, 1956, D 22,11:5
Petty, Nathan O, 1944, Ag 27,33:3
Petty, Nelson S, 1945, S 18,23:3
Petty, Orville A, 1942, Ag 14,17:1
Petty, Peyton D, 1956, F 3,23:3
Petty, R D, 1932, Je 4,15:1
Petty, Raiman Dr, 1937, Ap 14,25:5
Petty, Robert M, 1916, My 16,13:5
Petty, Spencer W Sr, 1962, Ja 17,33:4
Petty, Stanley W, 1946, Ag 27,27:3
Petty, William E, 1945, F 14,20:2
Petukhov, Alex, 1950, Ap 4,29:1
Petulengro, 1957, Je 17,23:2
Petz, Adam E, 1966, Ja 16,83:1
Petz, Henry H, 1952, My 15,31:4
Petz, Peter, 1947, D 3,29:3
Petz, Thomas Jr, 1948, S 21,27:3
Petze, Charles L, 1939, N 8,23:4
Petzhold, Cornelius J, 1952, Jl 18,19:2
Petznek, Leopold Mrs (Elisabeth Marie), 1963, Mr 22,9:5
Petzold, Herman G, 1955, D 14,39:5
Petzoldt, Edward F, 1951, Ap 24,29:2
Peugeot, Charles A, 1957, F 15,23:3
Peugeot, Jean-Pierre, 1966, O 19,38:7
Peugnet, Ramsay, 1944, O 23,19:3
Peugnet, Ramsay Mrs, 1960, N 16,41:3
Peurifoy, Daniel B (body cremated, Ag 15,15:5; funl, O 7,25:3), 1955, Ag 13,1:4
Peurifoy, John E (body cremated, Ag 15,15:5; funl, O 7,25:3), 1955, Ag 13,1:4
Pevear, Barton T, 1954, D 16,37:4
Pevear, Henry A, 1914, My 15,15:6
Pevear, Jesse H, 1941, Mr 7,21:5
Peverelly, Theodore L, 1904, F 5,9:4
Pevsner, Antoine, 1962, Ap 14,25:1
Pew, Arthur E Jr, 1965, Ja 20,39:5
Pew, Arthur E Mrs, 1944, Je 4,41:1
Pew, J Edgar (por), 1946, N 23,15:3
Pew, J Howard Mrs, 1963, D 31,19:5
Pew, J Howard Mrs (est acctg), 1965, Ja 2,12:4
Pew, James E, 1955, Je 21,31:2
Pew, John G, 1954, Jl 2,19:4; 1964, S 22,39:2
Pew, John G Mrs, 1958, Ja 10,23:3
Pew, Joseph N Jr (funl, Ap 12,27:2; will, Ap 17,37:3), 1963, Ap 10,39:1
Pew, M E, 1936, O 16,25:1
Pew, Paul B, 1958, O 10,31:1
Pew, Robert C Mrs, 1947, Jl 16,23:2
Pew, Samuel H, 1956, My 11,27:2
Pew, Thomas W, 1954, Ja 6,31:2
Pew, William A, 1912, Ag 25,II,11:5
Pexton, Lorenzo R (will), 1941, N 25,29:7
Peycelor, Gilbert, 1940, Jl 26,17:6
Peyer, Charles, 1956, O 27,21:3
Peyer, Charles Mrs, 1968, N 12,47:1
Peynado, Jacinto B, 1940, Mr 8,21:3
Peyraud, Frank C, 1948, Je 1,23:2
Peyre, Gabriel, 1956, Ag 28,27:4
Peyre, Joseph, 1968, D 28,27:2
Peyron, Albin, 1944, Ap 12,21:4
Peyser, Ethel R, 1961, S 14,31:2
Peyser, Harry M Mrs, 1940, D 27,19:2
Peyser, Harry W, 1960, O 15,23:6
Peyser, Henry, 1941, N 17,19:1

Peyser, Henry M, 1910, Ja 18,11:4
Peyser, Herbert F, 1953, O 20,29:3
Peyser, Joel L, 1955, Je 8,29:1
Peyser, Joseph, 1938, Ap 5,21:3
Peyser, Lincoln G, 1961, Ap 19,39:3
Peyser, Melvin W, 1963, S 25,31:8
Peyser, Michael, 1950, My 4,106:8
Peyser, N, 1936, F 10,17:1
Peyser, Nathan J, 1956, Ag 8,25:5
Peyser, Percy A, 1959, Mr 30,31:4
Peyser, Seymour M, 1942, Ag 5,19:4
Peyser, Simon L, 1924, S 1,13:4
Peyser, Sol D Mrs, 1957, Ag 29,27:2
Peyser, Theodore A, 1937, Ag 9,19:1
Peyser, William, 1937, D 11,19:2
Peyster, Frederic A, 1951, My 6,92:2
Peyster, James F, 1874, Je 20,2:2
Peyton, Baillie, 1878, Ag 20,5:2
Peyton, Bernard Sr Mrs, 1953, My 20,18:2
Peyton, Edward X, 1965, Je 21,29:3
Peyton, Ephraim G, 1950, Ja 2,23:4
Peyton, Gordon P, 1956, D 28,21:5
Peyton, Harlan I, 1958, My 25,87:1
Peyton, Phil B (por), 1949, Je 25,13:6
Peyton, Thomas Roy Dr, 1968, Ag 8,33:1
Peyton, W E, 1931, N 15,30:3
Peyton, William C Mrs, 1944, O 8,44:2
Peyton-Griffin, R T, 1950, D 31,42:6
Peytral, Paul Louis Sen, 1919, D 2,13:2
Pezet, Jose, 1963, N 17,87:1
Pezzolo, Francis S (P Bodie), 1961, D 19,29:3
Pfaff, Albert, 1903, F 17,3:1
Pfaff, Arthur W, 1948, Ag 17,21:3
Pfaff, Charles W, 1937, Ag 25,21:2
Pfaff, Edward H, 1952, My 9,23:2
Pfaff, Frank J, 1958, Ag 8,19:2
Pfaff, Frank J Mrs, 1967, Ap 3,33:3
Pfaff, Frederick W, 1958, S 25,33:4
Pfaff, George H, 1954, F 10,29:4
Pfaff, Henry C, 1943, Mr 31,19:5
Pfaff, Henry C Mrs, 1968, Ja 12,27:2
Pfaff, Isabelle, 1949, Ag 27,13:6
Pfaff, Oswald F, 1940, Ag 31,13:5
Pfaff, Otto Dr, 1948, F 20,27:3
Pfaff, William, 1940, Ja 29,15:4
Pfaffinger, Frank X, 1940, F 5,17:4
Pfahl, Dan S, 1948, Ap 26,23:4
Pfahl, Edward C, 1955, Ap 20,33:4
Pfahl, Edward G, 1943, Mr 14,25:2
Pfahler, George E, 1957, Ja 30,29:1
Pfaltz, Ferdinand H, 1941, Mr 31,15:3
Pfaltz, Harry E, 1955, Ja 26,25:1
Pfalz, Henry G Prof, 1914, Ap 23,13:4
Pfalzgraf, Henry W, 1962, F 8,31:4
Pfankuchen, Otto P, 1942, Mr 7,17:5
Pfannkuch, George, 1916, Jl 10,11:4
Pfannmuller, Henry C, 1954, Ja 22,28:5
Pfannmuller, Julius F, 1961, Jl 5,33:2
Pfanstiehl, Carl, 1942, Mr 2,19:3
Pfanstiel, William F, 1949, F 28,19:5
Pfantz, Alice Mrs, 1962, F 12,46:7
Pfarr, Thomas L, 1946, Ap 18,27:3
Pfarr, William, 1945, Je 16,13:3
Pfarrer, Herman A, 1947, Jl 15,23:2
Pfarrer, Theodore, 1953, D 12,19:6
Pfarrer, Theodore C, 1937, My 1,19:4
Pfarrer, William, 1950, Ap 19,29:2
Pfatteicher, Carl, 1957, O 1,33:3
Pfatteicher, E P (comment, Ja 14,18:1), 1943, Ja 48:3
Pfau, Julius W Mrs, 1958, Ag 29,23:3
Pfau, Matthias, 1943, F 12,19:5
Pfau, Ralph S, 1967, F 20,37:3
Pfaudler, John M, 1941, Mr 14,21:2
Pfautz, Christian E, 1957, Jl 3,23:3
Pfeferstein, Jacob, 1959, O 8,39:2
Pfeferstein, Sarah Mrs, 1945, Jl 3,13:6
Pfeffer, Clarence A, 1950, S 4,17:5
Pfeffer, Edward C, 1954, N 27,13:6
Pfeffer, Elizabeth L, 1940, O 20,49:1
Pfeffer, Felix, 1957, O 10,33:1
Pfeffer, Kay (Mrs G Kaman), 1966, Ja 9,56:4
Pfeffer, Raymond, 1947, Je 27,21:5
Pfeffer, Richard G, 1948, O 19,27:1
Pfeifer, Charles, 1939, My 5,23:3
Pfeifer, Frederick (por), 1944, O 13,19:4
Pfeifer, Henry M, 1949, O 26,27:3
Pfeifer, Phil E Mrs, 1938, Ag 9,19:5
Pfeifer, Philip E (por), 1946, Jl 13,15:4
Pfeifer, Walter B, 1959, Jl 7,33:4
Pfeiffenberger, Otto E, 1950, Ap 13,29:1
Pfeiffer, Alex, 1963, Ap 28,87:3
Pfeiffer, Alfred, 1967, F 22,29:3
Pfeiffer, Bernard V, 1950, My 14,106:6
Pfeiffer, Carl, 1951, Ap 13,16:7
Pfeiffer, Charles C, 1961, Jl 8,19:6
Pfeiffer, Curt G, 1950, Mr 16,31:4
Pfeiffer, Edward B, 1951, Jl 22,61:2
Pfeiffer, Ehrenfried E, 1961, D 1,33:4
Pfeiffer, Elmer C, 1957, O 7,27:1
Pfeiffer, Ernest H, 1960, Ag 28,83:1
Pfeiffer, Ernst E, 1956, My 16,35:3
Pfeiffer, Frank H, 1941, Ap 29,19:3

Pfeiffer, Frederick F, 1965, N 24,39:1
Pfeiffer, G S Dr, 1883, D 1,5:4
Pfeiffer, George A, 1943, D 30,17:4
Pfeiffer, Gustavus (est tax appr), 1956, Ag 1,23:2
Pfeiffer, Gustavus A (will, S 10,30:6), 1953, Ag 23, 88:3
Pfeiffer, Gustavus A Mrs, 1948, O 7,29:5
Pfeiffer, Harry E, 1956, O 6,21:4
Pfeiffer, Harry F, 1960, Ja 17,86:3
Pfeiffer, Henry (por),(will, My 6,20:3), 1939, Ap 14, 23:5
Pfeiffer, Henry (will), 1942, Mr 5,15:4
Pfeiffer, Henry, 1944, Ag 20,33:2
Pfeiffer, Henry C, 1954, O 26,27:4
Pfeiffer, Henry Mrs (por),(will, Ja 23,28:3), 1946, Ja 9,24:3
Pfeiffer, Ida, 1858, N 16,4:5
Pfeiffer, Irving E, 1950, Ap 4,29:5
Pfeiffer, J P, 1947, N 20,29:2
Pfeiffer, Jacob, 1937, D 4,17:3
Pfeiffer, Joseph Sr, 1957, Mr 3,84:8
Pfeiffer, Max, 1950, Ja 4,35:2
Pfeiffer, Noah R, 1941, N 1,15:5
Pfeiffer, Pancratius, 1945, My 14,17:6
Pfeiffer, Philip, 1925, Jl 6,11:6
Pfeiffer, Richard O, 1950, D 30,13:3
Pfeiffer, Robert H, 1958, Mr 17,29:2
Pfeiffer, Timothy N Mrs, 1968, O 2,39:2
Pfeiffer, Walter P, 1949, My 27,21:2
Pfeiffer, Weyland, 1960, Jl 4,15:5
Pfeiffer, William J, 1961, Ja 2,25:3
Pfeifle, Louis C, 1940, Ja 28,33:1
Pfeil, Aloysius Rev, 1937, Ap 5,19:6
Pfeil, C William, 1937, Jl 31,15:7
Pfeil, Henry H, 1951, Ap 5,29:2
Pfeil, Ralph T, 1965, Je 13,84:8
Pfeil, William H, 1941, S 14,48:2
Pfeil, William Sr Mrs, 1952, F 6,29:3
Pfeltz, Albert R, 1949, Ja 5,25:4
Pfennig, Richard E (por), 1946, D 19,29:5
Pfenninger, Charles, 1940, Ap 8,20:4
Pferdmenges, Robert (funl plans, O 3,18:5), 1962, S 30,87:1
Pfieffer, A, 1935, S 25,23:4
Pfieffer, Karl G, 1964, Mr 26,35:3
Pfieger, Paul, 1946, Ja 22,27:2
Pfiester, Frederick, 1947, Ap 1,27:1
Pfiester, Jack, 1953, S 5,15:6
Pfiffer, N A, 1872, O 29,1:2
Pfingst, George B, 1950, Mr 17,23:1
Pfirman, Charles H, 1937, My 17,19:3
Pfirmann, Edward, 1956, Je 16,19:5
Pfister, Alfred, 1964, Ap 7,32:3
Pfister, Carl E, 1958, N 10,29:5
Pfister, Charles, 1955, Jl 15,21:2
Pfister, Christian A, 1955, Mr 23,31:4
Pfister, Fay B, 1952, My 21,27:3
Pfister, Franz, 1942, Mr 3,24:3
Pfister, George, 1951, Ap 3,27:4
Pfister, George F, 1945, Ja 4,19:3
Pfister, Jacob, 1956, Ag 14,25:3
Pfister, Jacob Mrs, 1949, My 17,25:1
Pfister, Jean J, 1949, Je 9,31:3
Pfister, Joseph, 1952, Ag 18,17:4
Pfister, Joseph C, 1948, Ag 23,17:1
Pfister, William Jr, 1945, Jl 6,11:6
Pfisterer, Raphael, 1942, F 6,19:3
Pfitzenmayer, Jacob E, 1944, My 19,19:4
Pfitzner, Hans, 1949, My 23,23:4
Pfizenmayer, Walter J, 1960, D 19,27:3
Pfizer, Charles Sr, 1906, O 21,9:6
Pfizer, Emile (will, Ag 1,34:3), 1941, Jl 20,30:1
Pfizer, William R, 1958, Ja 10,23:1
Pflanz, Arthur E, 1957, Ag 3,15:4
Pflaster, Nathan, 1960, Ag 25,29:5
Pflaum, George A, 1963, N 20,40:4
Pflaum, Max, 1964, S 9,43:2
Pflaum, Samuel Mrs, 1959, My 13,37:5
Pflaumer, Eugene G Mrs, 1958, My 17,19:2
Pfleger, Frederick P, 1942, Ja 23,19:1
Pfleger, George F Mrs, 1951, O 6,19:7
Pfleger, Kenneth W, 1965, Ap 16,29:1
Pfleiderer, Karl G, 1957, O 10,33:4
Pfleiderer, Otto, 1908, Jl 21,7:6
Pfletschinger, Frederic, 1951, Mr 20,29:2
Pflieger, Robert, 1955, Je 19,93:2
Pflomm, Elliott R, 1951, F 19,23:2
Pflomm, Frederick, 1942, S 4,24:3
Pfloom, George, 1941, My 21,23:1
Pflueger, Albert, 1962, N 29,30:3
Pflueger, Charles T, 1950, O 22,92:2
Pflueger, J, 1929, Ja 12,17:3
Pflueger, Timothy L, 1946, N 22,23:4
Pflueger, Wellington C, 1948, My 1,15:5
Pfluegl, Emeric de, 1956, F 17,21:3
Pflug, Charles J, 1947, Mr 23,60:1
Pflug, Fritz, 1952, Ap 1,30:3
Pflug, Harold A, 1964, Mr 11,39:3
Pflug, Henry, 1961, O 21,21:2
Pflug, Louis H, 1942, Ja 10,15:6
Pflugbeil, William F, 1949, Je 24,23:1
Pflugheber, George J, 1948, My 21,23:2
Pflum, Raymond J, 1965, D 13,39:3

Pflum, Walter J, 1949, N 25,31:3
Pfohl, Catherine S Mrs, 1947, Ap 1,27:4
Pfohl, Edson P, 1944, Ap 2,40:2
Pfohl, J Kenneth, 1967, N 29,40:6
Pforzheimer, Arthur, 1949, Ap 24,76:2
Pforzheimer, Carl H, 1957, Ap 6,19:1
Pforzheimer, Carl H Mrs, 1956, Ag 1,23:6
Pforzheimer, Walter, 1955, Mr 7,27:5
Pforzheimer, Walter Mrs, 1958, O 22,35:1
Pfost, August D Rev, 1937, S 29,23:4
Pfost, Carl A, 1961, O 11,47:3
Pfost, Charles J Mrs, 1962, D 2,88:7
Pfost, Gracie B Mrs, 1965, Ag 12,27:4
Pfotenhauer, Frederick, 1939, O 10,23:6
Pfotenhauer, Frederick Mrs, 1939, F 11,15:4
Pfouts, Earl Mrs, 1944, D 9,15:6
Pfouts, William C, 1943, F 14,48:6
Pfraengle, Abbott Hilary Rev, 1909, D 22,11:5
Pfreundschuh, George C, 1960, Je 30,29:4
Pfrommer, Howard G, 1953, Ja 27,25:3
Pfund, A Herman, 1949, Ja 6,23:5
Pfundstein, Adam, 1942, S 17,25:1
Pfyffer Daltishofen, Heinrich de, 1957, Mr 24,86:5
Phaff, Harris, 1953, O 22,29:2
Phair, Charles, 1943, Jl 3,13:6
Phair, James H Mrs, 1944, Ag 1,15:2
Phair, Joseph Mrs, 1967, Jl 26,36:1
Phair, Joseph W, 1957, N 15,27:2
Phair, Philip D, 1965, Jl 7,37:2
Phalen, Clotilde E, 1941, D 27,20:2
Phalen, Harold R, 1955, My 31,27:1
Phalen, James R, 1947, S 28,60:3
Phalen, Matilda T, 1944, Ap 27,23:4
Phalon, Joseph E, 1940, Ag 20,19:3
Phan Van Giao, 1965, N 14,88:4
Phaneuf, Louis E, 1953, S 21,25:4
Phanit, Monthien, 1952, Ag 13,2:6
Phannemiller, George M, 1960, Je 25,21:4
Phao Sriyanond, 1960, N 23,29:1
Phares, Burl W, 1956, D 17,31:6
Phares, Carl, 1948, Je 17,25:2
Phares, Elwood W, 1941, Ag 20,19:5
Phares, Jesse L, 1953, Je 18,29:2
Phares, Stanley U Mrs, 1953, D 9,11:6
Pharis, Charles S, 1960, Mr 5,19:4
Pharis, W E, 1938, D 2,23:1
Pharmakides, Theocletus Prof, 1860, Je 16,2:4
Pharo, Arthur H, 1965, N 27,31:2
Pharo, Eugene M, 1945, Mr 6,21:2
Phayre, Arthur, 1940, D 14,17:3
Pheasant, Frederick H, 1944, Mr 4,13:3
Pheffer, Phil, 1958, Je 27,25:5
Pheiffer, Harry E, 1951, Mr 27,29:2
Pheiffer, William Mrs, 1941, O 14,23:3
Phelan, Albert B, 1947, Ap 1,27:2
Phelan, Albert Rev, 1925, Ag 3,15:6
Phelan, Andrew, 1903, Je 1,7:7
Phelan, Arthur, 1962, Ap 24,37:1
Phelan, Carrie H Mrs, 1951, N 2,23:2
Phelan, Charles A, 1937, N 13,19:4
Phelan, Charles J, 1958, F 5,27:2
Phelan, Christopher S, 1956, Jl 18,27:5
Phelan, D Halsey, 1961, Je 4,86:5
Phelan, Daniel Dr, 1937, My 3,19:2
Phelan, David S Rev, 1915, S 22,11:6
Phelan, Edmund J, 1937, Ap 23,21:5
Phelan, Edward A Sr, 1950, Ap 6,29:4
Phelan, Edward J, 1967, S 16,33:2
Phelan, Eugene, 1948, O 17,76:6
Phelan, Finton J, 1951, N 12,25:4
Phelan, Frank W, 1956, My 16,35:1
Phelan, Gerald B, 1965, Je 1,39:4
Phelan, Harold V, 1946, S 4,24:2
Phelan, Henry C Rev Dr, 1924, Ag 24,24:4
Phelan, J D, 1930, Ag 8,17:1
Phelan, James A, 1948, Ja 4,52:1
Phelan, James J, 1908, Ag 4,7:5; 1908, Ag 7,5:4
Phelan, James J Mrs, 1949, Mr 18,26:3
Phelan, James J Sr, 1946, My 7,21:2
Phelan, James P, 1943, Ag 27,17:4
Phelan, John, 1952, Ag 19,23:4
Phelan, John C, 1952, Jl 12,13:4
Phelan, John E, 1938, O 29,19:3; 1960, My 28,21:6
Phelan, John H, 1957, My 20,25:5
Phelan, John J, 1946, Ja 24,21:3
Phelan, John J Mrs, 1964, Ap 15,39:3
Phelan, John J Sr, 1966, Je 14,47:2
Phelan, John M, 1952, Je 17,27:5
Phelan, John V, 1946, Ap 15,27:2; 1955, Ag 10,25:4
Phelan, Joseph C, 1948, F 3,25:2; 1952, F 14,27:2
Phelan, Joseph F Sr, 1951, F 16,25:3
Phelan, Joseph P, 1949, S 8,29:3; 1957, Je 19,33:4
Phelan, Marie G (Mother Gerard),(funl, Mr 26,21:3), 1960, Mr 23,37:1
Phelan, Matthew, 1944, N 11,13:3
Phelan, Michael, 1871, O 9,5:3
Phelan, Michael F, 1941, O 13,17:3
Phelan, Michael J, 1913, Ja 10,11:4
Phelan, Michael J Msgr (funl, My 26,19:5), 1922, My 25,19:5
Phelan, Paul J, 1965, Ja 18,35:5
Phelan, Paul L, 1949, Ja 14,23:4
Phelan, Richard Bp, 1904, D 21,9:6

Phelan, Robert E, 1948, F 22,48:5
Phelan, Robert K, 1955, N 19,19:5
Phelan, Robert P Mrs, 1954, S 17,27:3
Phelan, Sidney M Jr, 1950, N 9,33:3
Phelan, Thomas A, 1914, Je 15,9:6
Phelan, Thomas Capt, 1909, S 15,9:5
Phelan, Thomas F, 1954, Je 16,31:4
Phelan, Thomas J, 1958, Ja 13,29:1
Phelan, Walter F, 1954, D 26,61:3
Phelan, Walter F Mrs, 1937, Je 17,23:5
Phelan, William A, 1946, D 4,31:4
Phelan Rulfo, Edmundo J, 1955, Je 5,84:6
Pheland, Thomas A, 1950, Je 10,17:3
Phelen, John A, 1905, Ap 28,9:4
Phelos, Charles E, 1940, Ap 10,25:1
Phelps, A M Dr, 1902, O 7,9:5
Phelps, Abel M Mrs, 1959, D 25,21:1
Phelps, Albert C, 1937, Jl 7,23:3
Phelps, Almira H L, 1884, Jl 16,5:1
Phelps, Andrew H, 1962, Jl 26,27:3
Phelps, Anna R, 1938, Jl 15,17:4
Phelps, Ansel, 1950, F 25,17:3
Phelps, Ansel Mrs, 1961, Ja 1,49:2
Phelps, Anson G, 1944, Je 3,13:5
Phelps, Arthur C, 1944, Ja 22,13:3
Phelps, B K, 1880, D 31,5:5
Phelps, B K (funl), 1881, Ja 3,5:6
Phelps, B K Mrs, 1880, D 25,8:3
Phelps, C H, 1881, Ja 12,4:7
Phelps, Carl W Mrs, 1949, S 9,25:3
Phelps, Carrington A, 1959, My 21,31:4
Phelps, Charles, 1940, F 4,41:2
Phelps, Charles C, 1952, Je 21,15:6
Phelps, Charles Dr, 1913, D 31,9:5
Phelps, Charles E, 1961, Je 4,86:5
Phelps, Charles Egbert, 1918, S 16,11:8
Phelps, Charles H, 1944, F 23,19:6; 1960, My 13,31:2
Phelps, Charles H Mrs, 1937, D 27,15:2
Phelps, Charles P, 1912, Ja 14,II,16:2
Phelps, Charles S, 1946, Ja 4,11:2
Phelps, Clancy C, 1952, Jl 4,13:4
Phelps, D Winthrop Mrs, 1946, Je 30,38:5
Phelps, Delos P, 1914, Je 29,9:6
Phelps, Deputy Controller, 1876, Jl 14,2:4
Phelps, Duane F, 1945, Jl 17,13:5
Phelps, Dudley, 1952, Jl 1,23:3
Phelps, Dudley F, 1908, Je 24,7:4
Phelps, Dudley Mrs, 1952, Ap 11,23:2
Phelps, E W, 1953, Ap 4,13:1
Phelps, Earle B, 1953, My 30,15:5
Phelps, Edgar M, 1953, F 6,19:1
Phelps, Edgar M Mrs, 1959, D 9,45:3
Phelps, Edward, 1942, F 1,43:2
Phelps, Edward Bunnell, 1915, Jl 25,15:4
Phelps, Edward J, 1900, Mr 10,9:5
Phelps, Edward J Mrs, 1909, Mr 7,11:7
Phelps, Edwin F, 1903, Jl 14,14:6
Phelps, Ellsworth C Prof, 1913, D 1,9:4
Phelps, Esmond J, 1950, O 20,27:4
Phelps, Fanny R, 1940, F 22,23:2
Phelps, Francis R, 1938, Je 28,19:5
Phelps, Frank, 1937, S 30,23:4
Phelps, Frank N, 1953, Je 16,27:2
Phelps, Frank W, 1949, O 9,43:2
Phelps, Fred M, 1939, My 16,23:4
Phelps, Frederick A, 1948, Ap 1,25:4
Phelps, Frederick G, 1954, Ja 5,27:2
Phelps, G D Jr, 1883, Je 23,8:3
Phelps, G Sidney, 1961, S 20,29:4
Phelps, Gaylord, 1949, D 3,15:3
Phelps, George A, 1963, Je 4,39:2
Phelps, George A Mrs, 1958, My 31,15:4
Phelps, George B Mrs, 1907, My 10,7:5
Phelps, George C Mrs, 1948, Jl 8,23:2
Phelps, George D, 1948, S 22,31:3
Phelps, George E, 1948, D 3,25:5
Phelps, George H, 1945, S 17,19:5
Phelps, George W, 1947, S 19,23:1
Phelps, Gouverneur M, 1954, O 19,27:5
Phelps, Gouverneur M Mrs, 1952, S 25,31:3
Phelps, Guy M, 1946, S 29,62:1
Phelps, Guy R Dr, 1869, Mr 19,1:3
Phelps, H Frank Mrs, 1957, F 15,23:4
Phelps, H Perry, 1947, N 6,27:4
Phelps, Harry E, 1947, F 6,23:5
Phelps, Helen W, 1944, F 7,15:3
Phelps, Henry Delafield, 1910, Jl 4,7:6
Phelps, Henry W, 1944, Jl 8,11:7
Phelps, Henry W Mrs, 1946, Ap 11,25:5
Phelps, Howard M, 1967, My 4,39:2
Phelps, Hubbard Mrs, 1941, N 30,69:4
Phelps, J I Gov Mrs, 1878, Ja 26,2:4
Phelps, J T (Bossy),(por), 1942, Ja 14,21:3
Phelps, J W Gen, 1885, F 3,2:3
Phelps, John, 1955, D 17,23:5
Phelps, John J (por), 1948, Jl 5,15:1
Phelps, John Mrs, 1955, Ag 21,93:2
Phelps, John P, 1952, Ja 18,27:2
Phelps, Julia Mrs, 1912, Jl 6,7:4
Phelps, Kenneth P, 1968, S 5,57:5
Phelps, L, 1878, N 7,5:5
Phelps, Lancelot, 1950, O 10,31:3
Phelps, Lawrence H, 1955, Je 21,31:4

Phelps, Lee, 1953, Mr 21,17:5
Phelps, Lee F, 1937, My 26,25:5
Phelps, Lee F Mrs, 1950, Ag 9,29:6
Phelps, Leighton L, 1966, My 24,47:1
Phelps, Leroy G, 1964, F 18,35:4
Phelps, Lewis M, 1921, My 14,9:4
Phelps, Lillian G, 1939, S 28,25:4
Phelps, Marshall L, 1961, Ja 14,23:1
Phelps, Mary C Mrs (will), 1942, Ja 10,18:3
Phelps, Newton B, 1941, F 9,49:3
Phelps, R Gorman Sr, 1953, Je 19,21:4
Phelps, Ransom, 1912, Jl 23,9:5
Phelps, Raymond W, 1960, O 19,45:2
Phelps, Raymond W Mrs, 1958, Mr 6,27:1
Phelps, Robert A, 1944, Ja 10,17:3
Phelps, Roy A, 1947, Jl 21,17:5
Phelps, Royal, 1884, Jl 31,4:6
Phelps, S D, 1878, N 14,1:4
Phelps, S L, 1885, Je 25,5:3
Phelps, Samuel M, 1960, My 13,31:1
Phelps, Sheffield Col, 1902, D 10,9:4
Phelps, Shelton J, 1948, Ap 10,13:2
Phelps, Stowe, 1952, N 15,17:2
Phelps, T S Rear Adm, 1901, Ja 11,9:5
Phelps, Thomas S Rear-Adm, 1915, N 4,11:4
Phelps, W W, 1894, Je 17,1:5
Phelps, Walter K Mrs, 1962, My 18,31:2
Phelps, Warren A, 1939, Ap 10,17:3
Phelps, William, 1879, Jl 25,1:6
Phelps, William A, 1947, O 3,26:3
Phelps, William C, 1959, O 10,21:5
Phelps, William D, 1962, Ja 24,33:5
Phelps, William H, 1939, Je 24,17:5; 1940, Ap 11,25:2
Phelps, William L, 1943, Ag 22,37:1
Phelps, William L Mrs (por), 1939, Mr 23,23:3
Phelps, William M, 1949, My 30,13:6
Phelps, William R, 1939, My 9,24:4
Phelps, William W (por), 1938, My 12,23:3
Phelps, Winthrop E, 1937, Mr 9,23:4
Phelps, Zack, 1945, Jl 16,11:7
Phemister, Dallas B, 1951, D 29,11:1
Phemister, Walter R, 1943, My 24,15:6
Phenis, Albert, 1924, Ja 27,23:2
Phibbs, Thomas, 1952, D 28,48:3
Phieme, Carl O, 1946, D 30,22:3
Phifer, Charles H, 1957, Mr 29,21:1
Phifer, William E, 1948, Ap 9,23:2
Phifer, William E Mrs, 1965, Ap 22,33:1
Philarete, Charles, 1873, Ag 3,1:6
Philbin, Arthur J, 1943, Ja 13,23:2
Philbin, Eugene A Justice (funl, Mr 17,11:4), 1920, Mr 15,15:5
Philbin, Eugene A Mrs, 1946, Ag 4,45:1
Philbin, Ewing R, 1957, S 6,21:2
Philbin, Patrick S, 1944, S 12,19:7
Philbin, Stephen H Mrs, 1957, Ag 28,27:3
Philbin, Thomas G, 1957, Ag 24,15:5
Philbrick, Allen E, 1964, N 15,86:7
Philbrick, Eliphalet F, 1942, F 7,17:4
Philbrick, Frank S Mrs, 1949, O 3,17:4
Philbrick, Guy E, 1952, D 6,21:4
Philbrick, Halsey R, 1948, Mr 27,13:2
Philbrick, Harry C, 1954, Mr 13,15:3
Philbrick, Howard R, 1951, O 12,27:2
Philbrick, John A, 1939, My 9,24:3
Philbrick, Joseph M, 1955, S 17,15:4
Philbrick, Margaret L Mrs, 1940, F 21,19:5
Philbrick, Samuel W, 1940, Ag 16,15:3
Philbrook, Barnabas F, 1941, N 18,25:4
Philbrook, Charles F, 1947, D 3,29:3
Philbrook, Mary, 1958, S 3,33:2
Philbrook, Ralph A, 1963, Ap 13,19:6
Philbrook, Rowland F, 1946, S 30,25:3
Philburn, R Joseph, 1959, Ag 14,21:2
Philby, Harold A R Mrs (Eleanor Carolyn Kearns Philby), 1968, N 15,47:3
Philby, Harry St J, 1960, O 2,85:1
Philes, George Philip, 1913, S 13,11:5
Philhower, Benyew D, 1952, Ag 5,19:3
Philhower, Charles A, 1962, Ja 4,33:2
Philhower, Charles A Mrs, 1959, Ap 27,27:4
Philhower, Harold W, 1960, Ag 15,23:5
Philhower, Isaac M, 1955, F 22,21:5
Philibert, Louis C, 1914, Je 17,11:7
Philip, Abban, 1950, N 27,25:4
Philip, Albert, 1954, Ja 26,27:3
Philip, Albert B Mrs, 1967, Je 1,43:1
Philip, Bro (P Waloszec), 1953, Ap 11,17:6
Philip, George, 1937, D 9,25:4
Philip, Hoffman, 1951, N 1,29:3
Philip, J Van Ness, 1949, D 30,19:4
Philip, John, 1963, Ag 11,85:2
Philip, John W Adm, 1900, Jl 1,6:3
Philip, Maximilian, 1949, Ja 18,23:4
Philip, Olga Mrs, 1947, My 8,25:3
Philip, Percy J (funl, N 13,37:1), 1956, N 10,19:1
Philip, Percy J Mrs, 1956, D 30,33:1
Philip, Rev Bro, 1939, My 19,21:4
Philip, Robert W, 1939, Ja 27,19:4
Philip, Sarah L P Mrs, 1940, Mr 27,21:2
Philip, Terence, 1950, Jl 29,13:5
Philip, William G, 1938, S 16,22:2
Philip Joseph, Bro (P Bassett), 1951, Jl 8,61:2

Philipe, Gerard, 1959, N 26,37:4
Philipovsky, Adam, 1956, My 2,31:4
Philipp, A, 1936, Jl 31,19:4
Philipp, Emanuel L Ex-Gov, 1925, Je 16,21:6
Philipp, Felix, 1921, N 25,15:5
Philipp, Herbert C, 1937, Ja 3,II,8:5
Philipp, Isidor, 1958, F 21,24:2
Philipp, Leopold, 1965, N 8,35:3
Philipp, Oscar, 1937, Je 22,23:3
Philipp, Paul, 1923, My 23,21:4
Philipp, Phil B (por), 1941, Jl 12,13:4
Philipp, William P, 1951, N 22,31:3
Philippe, Joseph, 1956, O 22,29:6
Philippe, Louis, 1959, Jl 9,27:2
Philippe VII (Comte de Paris), 1894, S 9,5:3
Philippi, Carl L, 1961, Ja 25,33:3
Philippi, E Martin, 1946, Jl 4,19:3
Philippi, Rudolph A Dr, 1904, Jl 26,7:5
Philippoff, Georges, 1946, Ap 17,25:1
Philippoteaux, F E H, 1884, N 10,1:5
Philippoussis, John, 1959, N 11,35:4
Philipps, Josie Mrs, 1938, D 24,15:6
Philipps, Robert H Jr, 1957, My 16,31:5
Philippsohn, Max L, 1949, O 13,27:2
Philips, Anna M H Mrs, 1942, Ja 15,19:3
Philips, Anton F, 1951, O 8,21:3
Philips, August, 1954, D 23,19:4
Philips, Benjamin, 1961, S 3,61:1
Philips, Carlin Mrs, 1942, N 30,23:4
Philips, Euclid Mrs, 1944, F 6,42:5
Philips, F C, 1921, Ap 22,13:6
Philips, G A, 1885, F 27,5:3
Philips, Gerard L F, 1942, Ja 27,21:3
Philips, Herman Mrs, 1958, N 27,29:5
Philips, Horace G, 1949, S 22,31:4
Philips, Horace G Mrs, 1949, F 16,25:3
Philips, Ivor (por), 1940, Ag 16,15:4
Philips, James H, 1959, Jl 23,27:2
Philips, James H Mrs, 1961, My 4,37:2
Philips, Jesse E, 1945, My 14,17:4
Philips, Samuel K, 1940, Ap 14,44:7
Philips, Walter L, 1954, F 3,23:5
Philips, William Edwin, 1916, Jl 23,17:5
Philips, William Mrs, 1956, Mr 24,19:2
Philips, William P, 1950, D 19,29:1
Philips, William P (will), 1951, Ja 17,24:8
Philipson, Barnett, 1923, Ap 5,19:5
Philipson, David, 1949, Je 30,23:1
Philipson, Hilton Mrs, 1951, Ja 10,27:3
Philler, Richard M, 1951, Ag 27,19:5
Philler, William R, 1944, Mr 11,13:3
Phillhardt, George W, 1945, Ja 25,19:5
Phillimore, Lord, 1929, Mr 14,27:3
Phillimore, Lord (por), 1947, D 2,29:3
Phillip, John F, 1943, F 5,21:4
Phillipp, Theodore, 1920, Je 1,15:1
Phillippe, Charles L, 1952, Ap 1,29:2
Phillippe, Gerald L, 1968, O 18,47:1
Phillippe, Marshall K, 1941, S 4,21:5
Phillippi, Alfred, 1906, F 7,9:5
Phillippi, Joseph F, 1940, Ap 10,25:1
Phillipps, Adelaide, 1882, O 5,5:4
Phillips, A P, 1952, D 31,15:2
Phillips, Abraham B, 1950, Jl 20,25:5
Phillips, Abraham D, 1939, D 1,23:3
Phillips, Albanus (por), 1949, Ja 18,23:3
Phillips, Albert, 1925, Je 15,15:6; 1940, F 26,15:2
Phillips, Albert C (funl, F 9,11:5), 1916, F 8,11:2
Phillips, Albert E, 1959, O 15,39:5
Phillips, Albert H F, 1939, Ap 14,23:4
Phillips, Albert Mrs, 1940, Jl 18,19:3
Phillips, Albert T, 1951, Ag 29,25:5
Phillips, Alex, 1950, Ag 10,25:1
Phillips, Alex H Prof, 1937, Ja 21,23:5
Phillips, Alex R Mrs, 1956, Jl 22,61:1
Phillips, Alexander R, 1945, N 9,19:2
Phillips, Alfred, 1913, Ag 21,9:2; 1958, S 15,21:5
Phillips, Alfred H, 1958, O 12,86:8
Phillips, Alfred J, 1963, D 12,39:4
Phillips, Alfred N, 1944, Ag 2,15:2
Phillips, Almarin, 1948, Mr 17,25:4
Phillips, Andrew, 1911, F 1,11:5
Phillips, Andrew Wheeler Prof, 1915, Ja 21,9:4
Phillips, Arthur, 1903, Je 1,7:7; 1946, Ja 29,25:4; 1947, Ap 12,17:4
Phillips, Arthur B, 1948, S 21,27:3
Phillips, Arthur J, 1950, F 28,29:3
Phillips, Arthur Jr Mrs, 1962, My 10,37:5
Phillips, Arthur L (por), 1937, Mr 23,23:3
Phillips, Arthur M, 1942, D 18,27:2
Phillips, Arthur R, 1944, Mr 14,19:3
Phillips, Arthur S, 1941, Mr 19,21:2
Phillips, Arthur Spencer, 1925, Jl 3,13:5
Phillips, Asa E Mrs, 1951, Mr 3,13:4
Phillips, Barnet, 1942, Ag 2,39:3
Phillips, Barnett, 1905, Ap 9,9:5
Phillips, Benjamin M (por), 1940, Ja 20,15:5
Phillips, Bessie, 1954, O 29,23:3
Phillips, Boris Mrs, 1959, Ap 1,37:3
Phillips, Brewer D, 1941, Ja 31,19:3
Phillips, C, 1933, D 30,13:3
Phillips, C Alan, 1962, Ag 16,27:2
Phillips, C C, 1927, Je 14,27:3

Phillips, C Gager, 1952, Jl 10,31:3
Phillips, Caleb N Mrs, 1955, N 21,29:4
Phillips, Camilla H Mrs, 1947, Mr 14,23:1
Phillips, Charles, 1859, F 24,2:2; 1960, O 7,35:3; 196 Ag 5,17:5
Phillips, Charles A, 1945, Je 3,32:4; 1946, My 4,15:2
Phillips, Charles A Mrs, 1955, S 30,25:4
Phillips, Charles C, 1946, My 5,44:5
Phillips, Charles E, 1955, Jl 7,27:4
Phillips, Charles F, 1950, S 27,31:4
Phillips, Charles G, 1948, Ag 21,15:3
Phillips, Charles H, 1943, Jl 7,19:4; 1951, Ap 13,23:2
Phillips, Charles H Mrs, 1948, My 8,15:6; 1948, Je 2 23:3
Phillips, Charles J, 1940, Je 3,15:3
Phillips, Charles L Brig-Gen, 1937, Mr 16,23:2
Phillips, Charles L Mrs, 1960, F 18,33:2
Phillips, Charles M, 1961, Ap 22,25:5
Phillips, Charles P, 1940, Ap 1,19:4
Phillips, Charles R, 1947, Ap 15,25:4
Phillips, Charles S, 1941, F 12,25:5
Phillips, Charles Stuart, 1910, D 10,11:4
Phillips, Chester H, 1950, F 21,25:2
Phillips, Christian S, 1959, N 2,31:4
Phillips, Clara A Mrs, 1952, Ap 3,35:2
Phillips, Clarence E Sr, 1950, D 30,13:5
Phillips, Claude B, 1953, S 3,22:4
Phillips, Clovis H, 1958, Je 1,87:1
Phillips, Coles, 1959, F 20,25:4
Phillips, Crandall F, 1951, O 17,31:2
Phillips, Dan T, 1905, Ja 4,9:3
Phillips, Daniel Mrs, 1949, Mr 16,28:2
Phillips, David, 1963, Ap 29,31:3
Phillips, David D, 1947, Mr 20,27:2
Phillips, David Graham (funl), 1911, Ja 28,11:4
Phillips, David K, 1905, Ap 7,1:2
Phillips, David L, 1921, Mr 24,17:6
Phillips, Dean K, 1960, Je 7,35:5
Phillips, Donald K Mrs, 1950, My 10,31:1
Phillips, Duncan, 1966, My 12,1:5
Phillips, E Franklin, 1951, Ag 22,23:6
Phillips, E J Mrs, 1904, Ag 10,7:7
Phillips, Edgar, 1951, Jl 21,13:6
Phillips, Edna, 1952, F 27,27:5
Phillips, Edward C, 1952, My 10,21:2
Phillips, Edward H, 1962, My 1,37:1; 1965, Mr 22,
Phillips, Edward J, 1947, Jl 10,21:2
Phillips, Edward Lindon, 1905, Ja 16,9:5
Phillips, Eliza Mrs, 1938, Je 7,23:3
Phillips, Elizabeth L, 1954, D 7,33:4
Phillips, Ella F Mrs (will, Ag 7,13:2), 1937, Jl 27,
Phillips, Ellen A G, 1961, Ap 20,33:4
Phillips, Elliot S, 1966, Mr 17,39:3
Phillips, Ellis L, 1959, Ja 30,27:1
Phillips, Emma L, 1949, Ja 13,23:2
Phillips, Esther B, 1945, Ap 1,36:1
Phillips, Esther M, 1945, Ja 10,23:1
Phillips, Ethel C, 1947, F 7,24:3
Phillips, Ethel Q, 1959, Ag 15,17:4
Phillips, Eugene J, 1939, Ja 28,15:4
Phillips, Eugene R (will, F 1,55:3), 1955, Ja 15,1
Phillips, Everett A, 1958, S 22,31:2
Phillips, F Stanhope Mrs, 1943, Ag 28,11:2
Phillips, Farndale, 1961, F 27,27:4
Phillips, Forbes Alexander Rev, 1917, My 30,9:5
Phillips, Francis, 1957, S 4,33:2
Phillips, Francis C Dr, 1920, F 17,9:4
Phillips, Francis M, 1944, Jl 6,15:3
Phillips, Francis T, 1943, Mr 30,26:4
Phillips, Francis W Mrs, 1955, Mr 13,86:1
Phillips, Frank, 1949, D 10,18:2; 1950, Ag 24,27:1
Phillips, Frank G, 1951, Ap 23,25:4
Phillips, Frank H, 1951, Ap 13,23:3
Phillips, Frank Mrs, 1948, Ag 2,21:5
Phillips, Frank R, 1942, O 24,15:1
Phillips, Franklin, 1943, D 16,27:4
Phillips, Fred, 1956, O 14,87:1
Phillips, Frederic A, 1961, O 1,87:1
Phillips, Frederick (por), 1943, Ag 17,17:2
Phillips, Frederick, 1952, My 1,29:5
Phillips, Frederick N, 1947, Je 2,25:2
Phillips, Frederick R, 1940, O 28,17:3
Phillips, Frederick W, 1941, Ja 14,21:5
Phillips, G Clarence, 1942, D 4,25:4
Phillips, G S, 1949, My 10,25:4
Phillips, Genevieve U, 1958, O 20,29:5
Phillips, George A, 1942, O 11,56:3
Phillips, George D Mrs (will), 1960, Ja 23,43:5
Phillips, George E, 1943, Jl 31,13:6
Phillips, George F, 1904, Je 6,2:3; 1943, O 28,23: 1956, F 18,19:3
Phillips, George H, 1916, Ap 18,13:4; 1955, Ap
Phillips, George M, 1938, Mr 13,II,9:2
Phillips, George R, 1950, Jl 5,31:3
Phillips, George W, 1955, Jl 20,27:2
Phillips, George W M, 1955, Ap 27,31:3
Phillips, Gilbert A, 1908, N 26,9:6
Phillips, Godfrey Mrs, 1949, Ag 5,19:5
Phillips, Gordon G, 1953, N 1,86:4
Phillips, Guy B Dr, 1968, F 13,43:3
Phillips, H Albert, 1955, S 21,33:3
Phillips, H C, 1879, Ja 6,2:6; 1951, Ja 3,27:2
Phillips, H Godfrey, 1941, Ja 1,23:5

Phillips, H H S Jr Mrs, 1952, F 23,11:6
Phillips, H I (Harry I), 1965, Mr 16,39:1
Phillips, H I Mrs, 1938, Mr 6,II,8:2; 1962, My 4,33:4
Phillips, H L, 1903, My 7,9:6
Phillips, H M, 1884, Ag 29,5:3
Phillips, H Russell, 1945, Ja 18,19:6
Phillips, H Webster, 1958, Mr 26,34:2
Phillips, Harold M (funl plans, Ja 9,39:1), 1967, Ja 8,89:2
Phillips, Harriet, 1945, F 18,33:1
Phillips, Harrison B, 1940, Je 25,23:1
Phillips, Harry D, 1947, O 13,24:2
Phillips, Harry E, 1937, S 23,27:5
Phillips, Harry H S, 1952, Mr 15,13:3
Phillips, Harry Hungerford Spooner Jr, 1968, Ag 22, 37:3
Phillips, Harry J, 1940, Ja 31,19:1
Phillips, Harry L, 1947, My 29,21:3
Phillips, Harry S, 1959, D 10,39:5
Phillips, Harry W, 1952, Ja 26,13:5
Phillips, Henry, 1948, S 30,27:1
Phillips, Henry A, 1950, Ja 16,26:2; 1951, Ja 29,19:3
Phillips, Henry B, 1950, Mr 20,22:2
Phillips, Henry D, 1955, Jl 1,21:4
Phillips, Henry M, 1948, N 5,25:2; 1948, D 18,19:3; 1954, D 24,13:3
Phillips, Henry M Mrs, 1948, Ap 14,27:4
Phillips, Herman A, 1921, Mr 16,9:4
Phillips, Howard, 1941, Ag 21,17:7
Phillips, Howard C, 1943, N 16,23:5
Phillips, Howard E, 1968, O 2,19:3
Phillips, Howard V, 1956, N 1,39:2
Phillips, Hugh J, 1943, Mr 18,19:2
Phillips, Hugh J Jr, 1958, Jl 5,17:6
Phillips, Irving, 1955, N 5,19:6
Phillips, Isaac L, 1923, N 24,13:3
Phillips, Isabelle M, 1948, Ja 30,23:2
Phillips, J Campbell (por), 1948, S 25,17:3
Phillips, J D, 1880, F 6,2:5
Phillips, J Dudley, 1959, Je 10,37:3
Phillips, J F, 1880, Je 27,2:1
Phillips, J Foster, 1967, F 26,84:7
Phillips, J G Mrs, 1911, Je 23,11:4
Phillips, J M, 1928, Jl 4,1:1
Phillips, Jacob L, 1910, My 24,9:5; 1924, F 18,13:1
Phillips, James, 1941, My 28,25:4
Phillips, James A, 1949, D 6,31:3
Phillips, James D, 1949, N 13,13:1; 1954, O 20,29:4
Phillips, James E, 1940, O 28,17:5
Phillips, James Laughlin, 1918, N 12,13:6
Phillips, James Professor, 1867, Mr 17,4:6
Phillips, Jessamine O, 1968, D 6,47:2
Phillips, Jesse S, 1954, N 7,88:1
Phillips, Jesse S Mrs, 1939, D 20,28:2
Phillips, Joe T, 1944, D 11,23:5
Phillips, John B Mrs, 1952, Ja 1,25:4
Phillips, John C, 1938, N 15,23:3
Phillips, John C (por), 1943, Je 26,13:3
Phillips, John D, 1955, Ag 14,3:3
Phillips, John F, 1937, Ja 10,II,10:8
Phillips, John G, 1964, Ap 6,31:1
Phillips, John J H Mrs, 1939, Ja 2,23:1
Phillips, John L, 1948, My 17,19:4
Phillips, John M, 1953, S 9,29:1
Phillips, John Marshall, 1953, My 9,19:4
Phillips, John Mrs, 1950, Mr 30,29:2
Phillips, John Prof, 1874, Ap 25,6:7
Phillips, John R, 1942, D 30,23:1; 1944, D 28,19:6
Phillips, John R Mrs, 1950, Ja 23,23:5
Phillips, John S (por), 1949, Mr 2,25:1
Phillips, John Sr, 1948, Mr 4,25:4
Phillips, John W, 1938, S 3,13:4; 1948, F 28,15:5; 1949, O 3,17:5; 1959, Ap 7,33:4
Phillips, Jonas B, 1867, My 16,2:6
Phillips, Joseph, 1907, N 26,9:6
Phillips, Joseph A, 1963, D 27,25:3
Phillips, Joseph B Mrs, 1965, Mr 27,27:2
Phillips, Joseph C, 1950, S 13,27:1
Phillips, Joseph D, 1946, F 27,25:5
Phillips, Joseph D Mrs, 1958, Ja 29,27:4
Phillips, Joseph Maxwell, 1922, Jl 20,17:3
Phillips, Joseph W, 1945, S 19,25:3
Phillips, L C, 1948, N 6,13:2
Phillips, Laurence M, 1954, O 29,21:1
Phillips, Lavinia, 1949, Ja 14,24:3
Phillips, Lawrence, 1954, O 9,17:2
Phillips, Lee A, 1938, Ja 9,43:3
Phillips, Lee E, 1944, Ap 17,23:6
Phillips, Lena M (funl, My 24,31:1), 1955, My 22, 88:4
Phillips, Leo J, 1955, Jl 1,21:1
Phillips, Leon C, 1958, Mr 28,25:4
Phillips, Levi, 1911, F 19,II,11:4
Phillips, Levi B, 1945, Ap 9,19:2
Phillips, Lewis, 1940, Ag 16,15:6
Phillips, Lionel F, 1956, O 3,33:2
Phillips, Lloyd J, 1964, Mr 15,86:6
Phillips, Lorenzo B, 1947, Ap 1,27:2
Phillips, Lottie C Mrs, 1940, Jl 29,13:3
Phillips, Louis, 1959, Ag 30,82:6
Phillips, Louis A, 1938, Ag 2,19:3; 1945, Ja 13,11:4
Phillips, Maj, 1915, My 2,20:4
Phillips, Margaret I C, 1952, F 13,29:1
Phillips, Marie T (Mrs C J Yaegle), 1962, Je 6,41:5
Phillips, Mary A, 1922, D 3,5:3
Phillips, Mary F, 1958, Jl 20,65:2
Phillips, Mary M, 1937, Ap 19,21:2
Phillips, Matthew J, 1944, Je 4,41:2
Phillips, Maud G, 1951, Jl 31,22:5
Phillips, Maurice A, 1960, Je 30,29:2
Phillips, Maurice J (Oct 7), 1965, O 11,61:4
Phillips, Max, 1943, Ja 15,17:3
Phillips, Mazie Queen of the Bowery (funl, Je 12,-35:4), 1964, Je 11,33:1
Phillips, Merrick C, 1946, Ap 13,17:4
Phillips, Merton O, 1958, Mr 26,37:2
Phillips, Michael J C, 1925, Ja 19,17:3
Phillips, Milton H, 1951, Ja 25,25:4
Phillips, Milton H Mrs, 1953, Ja 15,27:4
Phillips, Morgan W, 1963, Ja 16,16:1
Phillips, Morris, 1904, Ag 31,7:6
Phillips, Moss Mrs, 1941, My 28,25:2
Phillips, Murray, 1942, My 2,13:6
Phillips, N Taylor, 1955, My 1,88:8
Phillips, N Taylor Mrs (por), 1946, F 7,23:3
Phillips, Nadine A, 1947, F 26,25:2
Phillips, Neill Mrs (Grace), 1966, My 25,47:4
Phillips, Nelson, 1939, Ap 1,19:4
Phillips, Nelson L, 1940, Mr 5,23:5
Phillips, Norman, 1965, O 19,43:2
Phillips, O, 1934, Ag 23,17:1
Phillips, Oscar L, 1947, Ap 6,60:7
Phillips, P Elias, 1953, S 17,29:3
Phillips, P Kendrick, 1941, O 21,23:4
Phillips, Patricia, 1946, N 19,31:4
Phillips, Patrick, 1939, Ap 22,17:5
Phillips, Patrick F, 1948, D 8,31:2
Phillips, Paul, 1950, Ag 8,29:2
Phillips, Paul A, 1952, Jl 9,27:2
Phillips, Paul C, 1942, Ja 5,17:3; 1956, D 24,13:4
Phillips, Percival Sir, 1937, Ja 30,17:1
Phillips, Percy F, 1944, Ja 5,18:3
Phillips, Perry W, 1943, O 8,19:4
Phillips, Perry W Mrs, 1942, Jl 12,36:3
Phillips, Peter P Sr, 1958, F 15,17:3
Phillips, Philip, 1884, Ja 15,5:4; 1960, Ag 17,31:3
Phillips, Philip G, 1944, O 18,21:2
Phillips, R LeClerc, 1939, Ap 25,23:3
Phillips, Rae, 1946, Mr 10,47:1
Phillips, Ralph G, 1950, Ja 19,27:3
Phillips, Ralph P Mrs, 1960, O 6,41:5
Phillips, Ray E, 1967, Mr 10,39:2
Phillips, Raymond G, 1941, D 5,23:6
Phillips, Richard E B, 1949, D 19,27:3
Phillips, Richard H, 1952, S 23,33:2
Phillips, Richard I Mrs, 1964, Jl 25,19:5
Phillips, Richard O, 1951, Ag 23,23:2
Phillips, Richard O Dr, 1923, S 28,7:3
Phillips, Robert, 1944, O 29,43:1; 1948, D 12,92:8; 1949, Je 27,27:4
Phillips, Robert H, 1940, O 27,45:2
Phillips, Robert H Sr, 1941, Ja 4,13:2
Phillips, Robert W (por), 1943, N 16,23:3
Phillips, Robert W, 1944, S 29,21:4
Phillips, Rolland W, 1959, O 14,43:5
Phillips, Rosamond B Mrs, 1941, Ja 29,17:2
Phillips, Rose B, 1938, My 16,17:2
Phillips, Ross M C, 1939, Jl 27,19:5
Phillips, Roy C, 1947, F 26,25:5
Phillips, Rufus C Jr, 1963, O 12,23:4
Phillips, Samuel, 1949, O 18,27:4
Phillips, Samuel C, 1950, Jl 29,13:3
Phillips, Samuel F, 1942, Mr 31,21:1
Phillips, Samuel F Judge, 1903, N 19,9:7
Phillips, Samuel H Mrs, 1949, F 22,23:5
Phillips, Samuel J, 1942, Ag 5,19:6
Phillips, Samuel K, 1925, Ap 6,19:5
Phillips, Samuel M, 1958, Mr 31,27:4
Phillips, Samuel V, 1952, S 20,15:4
Phillips, Samuel V Mrs, 1948, Jl 12,19:4
Phillips, Schuyler, 1955, Mr 13,86:3
Phillips, Sidney G Mrs, 1953, Ag 7,19:1
Phillips, Sidney H, 1949, Je 6,19:5
Phillips, Stephen, 1915, D 10,13:5; 1938, O 13,23:5
Phillips, Stephen W Mrs, 1938, N 1,23:3
Phillips, Steve, 1961, O 8,87:1
Phillips, Steven W, 1955, Jl 8,23:4
Phillips, Sydney A, 1937, S 20,23:4
Phillips, Sylvan B, 1944, O 15,44:5
Phillips, Taylor R, 1952, F 24,85:1
Phillips, Theodore A Mrs, 1968, Je 1,27:5
Phillips, Theodore R, 1942, My 14,19:5
Phillips, Thomas R, 1945, D 25,23:5; 1965, Jl 29,27:3
Phillips, Thomas W Jr, 1956, Ja 3,31:2
Phillips, U B, 1934, Ja 22,15:1
Phillips, Ulric B, 1957, Ag 1,25:3
Phillips, Ulrich B Mrs, 1961, Ag 25,25:1
Phillips, Vernon, 1951, Je 20,27:2
Phillips, Vernon Mrs, 1948, Jl 15,23:1
Phillips, Victor, 1941, Ag 10,37:2
Phillips, Vivian Capt, 1937, N 25,31:2
Phillips, W A Mrs, 1954, My 6,33:1
Phillips, W Henry, 1915, O 5,11:6
Phillips, W Stanwood, 1948, O 27,28:2
Phillips, W W Rev, 1865, My 1,2:3
Phillips, W Wurt Rev Dr, 1865, Mr 22,5:3
Phillips, Waite, 1964, Ja 29,33:5
Phillips, Wallace B, 1952, Ap 15,27:1; 1961, Je 21,37:3
Phillips, Walter, 1967, Ja 30,29:4
Phillips, Walter G, 1952, My 2,25:3
Phillips, Walter G Mrs, 1949, My 31,23:4
Phillips, Walter Mrs, 1952, Mr 9,92:3
Phillips, Walter P, 1920, F 1,22:3
Phillips, Walter P Mrs, 1914, N 30,9:6
Phillips, Walter S, 1940, S 3,17:4
Phillips, Warren C, 1951, Mr 13,31:1
Phillips, Watson L, 1944, D 31,26:2
Phillips, Watts, 1874, D 18,4:7
Phillips, Wayne Mrs, 1955, Ap 8,21:4
Phillips, Wendel C, 1944, N 26,58:3
Phillips, Wendell, 1884, F 3,1:3
Phillips, Wendell C Mrs, 1943, O 2,13:3
Phillips, Wendell E, 1959, My 29,23:1
Phillips, Wilbur C Mrs, 1961, Ap 12,41:2
Phillips, Willard A, 1950, F 11,15:5
Phillips, William (por), 1943, Mr 11,21:1
Phillips, William, 1957, Mr 30,19:6
Phillips, William B, 1949, N 19,17:4
Phillips, William C, 1941, O 27,17:5; 1947, F 7,24:2; 1951, S 11,18:7; 1953, O 1,29:5
Phillips, William Col, 1874, Ap 15,4:7
Phillips, William E, 1921, Ap 28,13:4; 1952, Mr 28, 23:3; 1964, D 27,64:2
Phillips, William Ex-Amb, 1968, F 24,27:1
Phillips, William F, 1943, F 19,19:3
Phillips, William H, 1916, Ag 29,9:2; 1949, Ag 11, 23:3; 1957, Ap 18,29:3
Phillips, William L, 1956, Je 22,23:4; 1967, O 11,27:3
Phillips, William Mrs, 1950, My 15,21:4; 1965, Ja 9, 25:2
Phillips, William R, 1942, Jl 7,19:6; 1946, Je 10,21:3; 1952, Ag 23,13:2
Phillips, William S, 1954, F 8,23:5
Phillips, William T, 1948, Je 6,72:4; 1964, My 22,35:2
Phillips, William Wirt, 1917, Jl 10,13:5
Phillips, Wolfe, 1916, Ja 29,9:6
Phillipse, Alphonse D, 1940, My 19,43:1
Phillipson, Irving J, 1955, Ap 6,29:1
Phillipson, Samuel W, 1956, N 16,27:2
Phillipson, William, 1959, Ja 3,17:4
Phillipy, William T, 1939, My 10,23:2
Phillmore, Rich, 1940, N 12,23:3
Phillpotts, Eden, 1960, D 30,19:1
Philo, E E, 1948, Jl 19,19:4
Philo, George E, 1937, Jl 26,19:6
Philo, Solomon Rev, 1923, Ag 20,11:4
Philomena, Sister (Religious of the Cenacle), 1951, F 16,25:2
Philomena, Sister (K Conway), 1952, My 24,16:8
Philp, Alfred E, 1939, Je 28,21:5
Philp, Harold A, 1946, Je 2,44:5
Philp, William, 1914, Je 1,11:5
Philpot, Ellen T, 1950, Mr 23,29:2
Philpot, George J, 1939, Mr 15,23:1
Philpot, Glyn W, 1937, D 18,21:4
Philpot, Herman Mrs, 1912, Ja 6,13:5
Philpot, Herman Rev, 1909, S 24,11:6
Philpot, Romaine A, 1937, D 29,21:4
Philpot, Sheppard B, 1953, Ap 13,27:3
Philpot, William C C Dr, 1937, Mr 23,24:1
Philpott, Anthony J, 1952, Mr 1,15:6
Philpott, Benjamin C Sr, 1955, Ap 12,29:1
Philpott, H Cloyd, 1961, Ag 20,86:5
Philson, Horace B, 1939, D 23,15:4
Phin, John F, 1942, Mr 15,42:7
Phin, John Prof, 1913, D 30,9:5
Phinizy, Ferdinand, 1950, Mr 30,30:3
Phinizy, Hamilton, 1938, Ap 17,II,6:6
Phinney, Elmer G, 1953, My 13,29:1
Phinney, Frederick, 1938, F 19,15:3
Phinney, H F, 1875, N 1,5:3
Phinney, Harold T, 1956, Ag 5,77:1
Phinney, Herman K, 1939, Ap 12,23:1
Phinney, Horatio A, 1938, Ja 5,21:4
Phinney, Lola, 1949, D 16,31:2
Phinney, Lorenzo N Dr, 1915, Ap 23,13:4
Phinney, Marshall M, 1949, Ja 7,21:1
Phinney, Priscilla C M Mrs, 1938, S 21,25:3
Phinney, S H, 1932, My 10,24:2
Phinney, Warren, 1949, Mr 17,25:5
Phinney, William, 1940, Jl 25,17:3
Phipard, Willard, 1942, O 7,25:4
Phippen, William S, 1945, S 30,46:5
Phippin, William G, 1944, O 13,19:5
Phipps, A S Mrs, 1934, O 25,23:4
Phipps, A W Maj, 1911, Ag 3,7:6
Phipps, Anita E, 1953, Jl 19,56:6
Phipps, Anne H Mrs (will), 1938, Ja 20,13:4
Phipps, Cadis, 1949, D 6,31:5
Phipps, Charles A, 1947, Mr 25,25:3
Phipps, D Goffe, 1903, S 11,7:7
Phipps, Dean H, 1957, Je 7,23:1
Phipps, Edward L, 1947, D 13,15:1
Phipps, Eric (por), 1945, Ag 14,21:3
Phipps, Francis H, 1961, Ja 17,37:5
Phipps, Frank H, 1925, Mr 29,7:1; 1948, Jl 10,15:4
Phipps, George S, 1955, F 17,27:1
Phipps, H, 1930, S 23,25:1
Phipps, Henry C, 1953, Mr 23,23:1

Phipps, Henry O, 1962, Ag 12,22:3
Phipps, Howard M, 1956, Ja 17,33:2
Phipps, John E, 1944, F 28,17:4
Phipps, John H, 1950, My 27,17:3
Phipps, John M, 1916, D 12,11:4
Phipps, John S, 1958, Ap 28,23:1
Phipps, John S Mrs, 1957, D 3,35:3
Phipps, Kenneth M, 1968, F 6,43:4
Phipps, Lawrence C, 1958, Mr 3,27:1
Phipps, Louis E, 1952, Ap 6,88:2
Phipps, Mack E, 1957, Jl 22,19:4
Phipps, Michael Grace Mrs, 1968, Jl 11,37:4
Phipps, Ross T, 1956, D 29,15:3
Phipps, William A P, 1947, O 27,21:6
Phipps, William G, 1947, N 3,23:2
Phipps, William Wilton, 1911, F 22,9:4
Phister, Charles, 1903, S 14,7:5
Phister, Montgomery, 1917, Jl 10,13:7
Phister, Nat P Lt-Col, 1911, My 11,11:6
Phister, Thomas R Mrs, 1943, My 1,15:5
Phisterer, Frederick Gen, 1909, Jl 14,7:5
Phisterer, Frederick W, 1938, F 20,II,8:7
Phoebus, G A Rev, 1903, My 29,9:6
Phoebus, Harry T, 1964, D 1,41:4
Phoebus, Jesse W, 1938, S 24,17:6
Phoenix, Clifford D, 1957, S 22,86:8
Phoenix, Edward A, 1955, O 17,3:8
Phoenix, Edward A Mrs, 1955, O 17,3:8
Phoenix, Harry D, 1956, Jl 22,61:3
Phoenix, Joseph N, 1937, My 25,16:3
Phoenix, Phillips, 1921, Ap 12,17:5
Phoenix, S W, 1881, N 4,5:3
Pholien, Joseph, 1968, Ja 5,35:2
Photios II, 1935, D 30,19:1
Phraner, Francis S, 1922, Je 22,15:6
Phraner, Stanley L, 1968, Jl 2,41:1
Phurman, William J, 1944, My 23,23:5
Phya Phanon Pholphayuma Sena, 1947, F 15,15:4
Phyfe, Benjamin P, 1958, F 13,29:4
Phyfe, Hal, 1968, S 14,28:1
Phyfe, J M, 1881, O 26,3:1
Phyfe, James D, 1948, Ap 25,68:4
Phyfe, Lloyd I, 1950, Ja 28,13:6
Phyfe, William Henry Pinkney, 1915, Mr 8,9:5
Phyffe, Duncan Mrs, 1945, N 7,23:3
Phyle, William J, 1953, Ag 8,11:5
Physick, Emlen Dr, 1916, Mr 22,13:7
Physioc, Joseph A, 1951, Ag 5,73:3
Physioc, Joseph A Mrs, 1948, N 8,21:2
Pi-Suner, Augusto, 1965, Ja 16,27:1
Pia, Maria Princess, 1915, F 3,11:7
Piaf, Edith (funl, O 15,39:3), 1963, O 12,1:5
Piaget, H F, 1883, Jl 3,4:7
Piaget, William E, 1944, D 29,15:2
Piaget, William E Jr, 1943, D 30,17:3
Piaget, William E Mrs, 1942, Mr 30,17:4
Pialoglou, John, 1959, O 21,43:1
Piana, William B, 1954, Jl 11,73:2
Piani, Guillermo, 1956, S 28,27:3
Piantadosi, Al, 1955, Ap 10,88:7
Piantadosi, George Mrs, 1944, Ja 18,19:3
Piantadosi, George R Mrs, 1958, O 25,21:3
Piantadosi, George W, 1943, Je 17,21:2
Piantanida, Nicholas, 1966, Ag 30,41:1
Piantoni, Adele, 1945, Je 3,32:1
Piasecki, Bodham, 1958, D 10,16:4
Piasecki, Edmund J, 1965, Mr 9,35:2
Piasecki, Joseph L, 1957, N 9,27:5
Piasecki, Nikodem, 1950, N 7,27:4
Piaskowsky, Meyer, 1967, Ag 6,76:1
Piatkowski, Romauld G, 1939, D 2,17:2
Piatt, Arthur Donn, 1914, Ap 13,11:4
Piatt, Cecil, 1949, D 19,28:2
Piatt, Don, 1891, N 13,1:6
Piatt, Louise Kirby Mrs, 1864, O 7,2:3
Piatt, Thomas D, 1965, D 3,39:2
Piatta, Ernesto B, 1939, D 21,23:6
Piatti, Alfred, 1901, Jl 20,7:6
Piaz, Tito, 1948, Ag 8,58:3
Piazza, Adeodato G, 1957, D 1,88:1
Piazza, Ferdinand Dr, 1968, Ap 23,44:1
Piazza, Frank P Sr, 1966, My 1,87:3
Piazza Breland, Micaela Mrs, 1958, F 9,88:3
Piazzoni, Gottardo, 1945, Ag 2,19:4
Pibul Songgram (details, Je 13,23:5), 1964, Je 12,35:1
Picabia, Francis, 1953, D 12,19:3
Picado, Teodoro (cor, Je 7,35:2), 1960, Je 2,33:2
Picani, Dominick, 1951, Ag 21,27:5
Picard, Alcide, 1914, F 13,9:6
Picard, Alfred Maurice, 1913, Mr 9,IV,7:4
Picard, Amedee, 1918, Ag 13,9:2
Picard, Andre L, 1948, Ag 6,17:3
Picard, Arthur J, 1942, Ap 28,21:5
Picard, Augustin C, 1962, Mr 24,25:2
Picard, Cornelius J, 1949, Ag 18,21:4
Picard, E (see also My 14), 1877, My 27,6:6
Picard, Emil, 1941, D 13,21:2
Picard, Frederick W (will), 1952, Mr 19,60:3
Picard, George A, 1952, Ap 4,33:6
Picard, Irving, 1966, My 22,86:4
Picard, J Milton, 1940, N 7,25:2
Picard, Louis-Alphonse, 1943, Ag 14,11:7
Picard, Louis-Philippe, 1959, My 23,25:4
Picard, Paul, 1871, Ag 21,4:1
Picard, William H, 1959, Ap 8,30:6
Picard, William J, 1951, Jl 10,27:2
Picaroni, John S, 1954, Mr 23,27:2
Piccard, Auguste, 1962, Mr 26,1:7
Piccard, Jean F, 1963, Ja 29,7:4
Piccaver, Alfred, 1958, S 24,27:5
Picchi, Italo, 1937, Ja 4,29:2
Piccinini, Giovanni, 1945, F 25,38:1
Piccirill, Horatio, 1954, Je 29,27:5
Piccirilli, Attilio (por), 1945, O 9,21:1
Piccirillo, Joseph P (funl, N 2,27:5), 1954, O 28,35:5
Piccirillo, Salvatore, 1953, Ag 25,21:3
Picco, Peter B, 1962, Jl 1,56:2
Pice, Morton M, 1952, S 12,21:3
Picenardi, Marchesa S, 1950, O 11,33:5
Picha, Moric, 1956, N 14,35:2
Pichardo Moya, Gabriel, 1956, Jl 28,17:6
Pichardo Moya, Serafin, 1956, O 2,3:5
Piche, Emilie S Mrs, 1948, S 7,25:2
Pichel, Irving, 1954, Jl 14,27:3
Pichel, Isaac, 1954, F 7,88:5
Pichel, Isaac Mrs, 1953, Je 16,27:2
Pichel, James F, 1963, Ag 1,27:3
Picher, Emily S Mrs, 1941, Ag 11,13:7
Pichetto, Stephen (por), 1949, Ja 22,13:5
Pichon, S, 1933, S 19,21:1
Pichon, Walter, 1967, F 27,29:2
Picinich, Albert D, 1957, O 14,27:4
Picinich, Mary J Mrs, 1937, My 21,21:2
Picinich, Val, 1942, D 6,76:5
Pick, Albert Sr, 1955, Jl 10,72:4
Pick, Alfred R, 1924, My 13,21:5
Pick, Arthur, 1961, Mr 29,33:1
Pick, Behrendt, 1940, My 30,17:5
Pick, Charles J, 1938, Ap 23,15:4
Pick, Charlie, 1954, Je 28,19:3
Pick, Ernest P, 1960, Ja 16,21:1
Pick, Frank, 1941, N 8,19:5
Pick, George, 1937, Ag 3,23:6; 1941, Ja 7,17:1
Pick, Gustav, 1939, F 5,40:6
Pick, Hugo, 1954, Ag 6,17:4
Pick, Joseph Prof, 1968, N 11,47:1
Pick, Lewis A (funl, D 8,19:4), 1956, D 3,29:1
Pick, Marguerite, 1951, Mr 20,29:4
Pick, Martin, 1954, F 15,23:4
Pick, Mary K Mrs, 1941, D 16,27:3
Pick, Max, 1940, Ag 21,19:5
Pick, Morris, 1953, Ja 8,30:1
Pick, Richard, 1938, Ja 6,19:5
Pickands, Jeanne Mrs, 1942, F 24,21:1
Pickard, Alfred A, 1958, My 11,87:2
Pickard, Arthur, 1949, O 20,29:4
Pickard, Benjamin F, 1957, O 16,32:7
Pickard, Benjamin M P, 1904, F 4,9:5
Pickard, Byron O, 1946, Mr 8,21:2
Pickard, Charles, 1957, My 15,35:2
Pickard, Darwin F, 1950, Je 17,15:7
Pickard, Edward T, 1958, S 29,27:5
Pickard, Frank A, 1963, Mr 1,4:6
Pickard, Frederick W, 1952, Mr 8,13:5
Pickard, George E Rev, 1925, O 26,19:4
Pickard, George Mrs, 1948, Jl 18,54:3
Pickard, Greenleaf W, 1956, Ja 9,25:2
Pickard, Helena (coroner rept, O 8,34:4), 1959, S 28, 31:4
Pickard, Nathan, 1963, Ag 23,25:4
Pickard, Robert, 1949, O 20,29:4
Pickard, W B, 1950, Jl 23,56:2
Pickard, Ward W, 1943, Ag 24,19:5
Pickard, Ward W Mrs, 1967, Ja 22,76:5
Pickard, Wilder A, 1939, My 28,III,6:7
Pickel, Charles O, 1938, Ja 3,22:1
Pickel, George S A, 1941, Je 15,36:6
Pickel, John C, 1956, O 16,33:1
Pickel, Margaret B, 1955, Ja 8,13:4
Pickel, Peter J, 1937, Je 5,17:4
Pickell, F G, 1936, N 28,17:1
Pickell, J Ralph, 1939, O 27,23:3
Pickell, Nelson, 1954, My 11,29:4
Picken, John, 1949, Mr 15,27:6
Picken, John Mrs, 1966, My 12,45:1
Picken, Thomas H, 1947, N 4,25:3
Picken, William H Jr, 1947, Jl 25,17:4
Pickenbach, Harry E, 1967, N 16,47:4
Pickens, Andrew C, 1944, D 1,23:5
Pickens, F W Ex-Gov, 1869, Ja 28,4:7
Pickens, Monte, 1954, My 14,23:5
Pickens, Patti Mrs, 1947, Ja 21,23:1
Pickens, Samuel O, 1944, F 10,15:1
Pickens, William, 1954, Ap 7,31:2
Pickens, William Mrs, 1955, Ja 11,25:5
Picker, Isaac, 1961, Ap 19,39:2
Picker, Isaac Mrs, 1945, Ja 16,20:2
Picker, James, 1963, My 30,17:4
Picker, James Mrs, 1968, Ja 18,39:2
Picker, Leonard S, 1961, N 25,23:5
Picker, Myram, 1950, Ag 12,13:5
Picker, Myrtle (Mrs L Kolker), 1958, N 7,27:1
Pickerill, Elmo N, 1968, Ja 15,47:2
Pickering, Adeline, 1874, Ap 1,5:3
Pickering, Albert W, 1957, D 27,19:2
Pickering, Alphonse, 1944, S 21,19:4
Pickering, David B, 1946, Je 15,21:3
Pickering, Edward Charles Prof, 1919, F 4,11:1
Pickering, Frank L, 1942, Je 11,23:2
Pickering, Frederick, 1944, Ap 20,19:6
Pickering, H Russell (est inventory), 1956, Ja 29,22:
Pickering, Herbert E, 1957, N 6,35:1
Pickering, James A, 1948, Jl 26,17:5
Pickering, James R, 1943, My 15,15:1
Pickering, John, 1945, Ap 11,23:2
Pickering, John C, 1956, O 12,29:5
Pickering, John E, 1962, Je 8,31:2
Pickering, John E Mrs, 1950, S 6,29:4
Pickering, Joseph, 1949, Mr 27,76:4
Pickering, Langdon D, 1958, My 20,34:3
Pickering, Leon D, 1940, My 31,19:4
Pickering, Loring, 1959, Mr 13,29:1
Pickering, Marshall V, 1947, Mr 13,28:3
Pickering, Maylin J, 1954, Ag 25,27:1
Pickering, Minnie Mrs, 1938, S 29,23:3
Pickering, Myles, 1937, Mr 16,23:4
Pickering, Myles Mrs, 1939, Ap 13,23:5
Pickering, Oliver D, 1952, Ja 23,27:3
Pickering, Richard, 1903, Ag 24,7:6
Pickering, Russell, 1947, Ap 17,27:5
Pickering, Samuel A, 1942, Je 21,36:8
Pickering, W C Mrs, 1939, Ag 1,19:4
Pickering, Walter, 1958, D 7,88:8
Pickering, William H (por), 1938, Ja 22,15:1
Pickersgill, Harold E, 1942, My 29,17:1
Pickert, Elizabeth W Mrs, 1937, Mr 17,25:3
Pickert, Heinrich A (por), 1949, Je 5,94:1
Pickert, Walter, 1951, F 6,27:5
Picket, David, 1962, My 4,33:3
Picket, Fermen L, 1940, Je 28,19:3
Picket, John R, 1945, O 18,23:4
Picket, Nathan, 1944, D 6,23:4
Pickett, A B, 1904, F 2,9:6
Pickett, Arthur D, 1967, Mr 25,3:4
Pickett, Arthur W, 1950, Je 15,31:3
Pickett, Charles J, 1941, My 8,23:2
Pickett, Clarence E, 1965, Mr 19,35:1
Pickett, Earle R, 1943, N 9,21:4
Pickett, Edward M, 1964, Ja 23,31:4
Pickett, Edwin S, 1948, Jl 12,19:4
Pickett, Elizabeth L, 1951, Ap 16,25:5
Pickett, Frank S, 1903, N 8,12:2
Pickett, G E Gen (funl), 1875, O 25,1:6
Pickett, George E Gen, 1875, Jl 31,4:5
Pickett, George E Maj, 1911, Ap 22,13:6
Pickett, George E 3d, 1959, Je 9,37:4
Pickett, Harry H, 1938, N 10,27:1
Pickett, James, 1951, Jl 5,8:5
Pickett, John A, 1955, Ag 14,80:4
Pickett, John E, 1952, D 27,9:3
Pickett, John F, 1958, N 8,21:6
Pickett, Joseph A, 1957, O 9,35:3
Pickett, Josiah Gen, 1908, Ja 15,9:4
Pickett, L L Mrs, 1953, Mr 3,27:4
Pickett, La Salle C Mrs, 1931, Mr 23,21:3
Pickett, Patrick Henry, 1915, O 30,13:6
Pickett, Sallie V H, 1939, Jl 26,19:2
Pickett, Walter F, 1943, O 15,19:2
Pickett, Warren W, 1952, Ap 21,21:5
Pickett, William C Prof, 1907, F 7,9:6
Pickett, William J, 1938, Ag 14,33:4
Pickford, Albert W, 1938, D 13,25:2
Pickford, Alfred D, 1947, O 8,25:3
Pickford, Charles C, 1953, N 24,29:4
Pickford, Charles C Mrs, 1954, S 7,25:1
Pickford, J, 1933, Ja 4,17:1
Pickford, W, 1938, N 7,19:4
Pickhardt, Carl (por), 1939, Ap 17,17:3
Pickhardt, Carl Mrs, 1944, F 15,17:3
Pickhardt, William P (por), 1941, Ja 23,21:4
Picking, Harry H, 1952, Ap 11,23:2
Pickle, Charles E, 1937, N 27,17:6
Pickman, Dudley L, 1938, Je 10,21:5
Pickman, Dudley L Mrs (Oct 5), 1965, O 11,61:4
Pickman, Harry A, 1959, D 12,23:4
Picknell, George W, 1943, Ap 3,15:3
Pickrell, James McCaw Lt, 1909, S 19,11:4
Pickslay, Henry G, 1937, Ap 19,21:5
Pickslay, William M, 1938, N 17,25:2
Pickup, Archie M, 1937, F 12,23:4
Pickwick, Lambert B, 1937, My 18,23:4
Pickworth, John W, 1964, Ap 3,33:3
Pico, Octavio S, 1943, Je 14,17:4
Picoli, Charles, 1941, My 9,21:4
Picon, Clara O Mrs, 1953, O 12,27:6
Picone, Joseph, 1944, D 6,23:2
Picot, Georges, 1909, Ag 18,9:6
Picot, Louis J Dr, 1924, Ag 16,11:7
Picot, Yves, 1938, Ap 20,23:1
Picou, Alphonse (funl, F 10,21:4), 1961, F 5,80:7
Picquet, Charles, 1907, Je 1,9:6
Picton, John M, 1950, My 21,104:4
Picton-Turbevill, Edith, 1960, S 3,17:2
Picutti, Romano, 1956, O 27,21:3
Piddian, Joseph A, 1965, Ag 29,85:1
Piderit, Fred W, 1961, Je 20,33:3
Pidgeon, Ashley E, 1964, Mr 26,35:2
Pidgeon, David B, 1953, Ja 31,15:6
Pidgeon, Edward E, 1941, S 1,15:3

Pidgeon, Francis, 1884, Je 13,5:4
Pidgeon, Frank K, 1963, O 3,35:4
Pidgeon, Frank K Mrs, 1953, Jl 14,27:4
Pidgeon, George J, 1955, Je 17,23:4
Pidgeon, Howard A, 1943, F 8,19:5
Pidgeon, James H, 1940, S 1,21:1
Pidgeon, Jeannette S F, 1960, Ap 26,37:4
Pidgin, Charles F, 1923, Je 5,21:5
Pidhorecky, Nicholas, 1949, Ja 29,14:2
Pidnell, Eliza S Mrs, 1937, Mr 12,23:2
Pie, Cardinal, 1880, My 19,5:2
Piechocinski, Anthony J, 1964, S 19,27:3
Piechocki, Paul W, 1953, D 11,34:2
Pieck, Margarette, 1952, O 15,31:3
Pieck, Phil, 1956, Je 12,35:2
Pieck, Wilhelm (trb, S 10,21:1; funl, S 11,81:4), 1960, S 8,35:4
Pieczenik, Srul, 1967, S 2,22:8
Piedl, Julius, 1943, Ja 27,21:5
Piedra, Leandro C, 1943, S 7,23:3
Piedra, Ramon, 1962, S 8,19:2
Pieh, E John, 1945, S 15,15:6
Piehl, Christian F, 1952, Ja 23,27:4
Piehler, Maurice W, 1957, Ap 6,19:4
Piek, Stefaan, 1939, D 14,27:2
Piekarski, Alex, 1953, S 9,29:3
Piekarski, Frank A, 1951, Ag 15,27:5
Piekarski, Maximilian, 1946, Ja 11,21:2
Piel, Michael, 1915, Je 14,9:4
Piel, Robert, 1952, Je 27,23:4
Piel, Rudolf A Mrs, 1958, Ap 9,33:5
Piel, Rudolph A, 1961, Ag 20,86:2
Piel, Samuel B, 1964, S 13,58:8
Piel, William F J, 1953, Ap 7,29:1
Piel, William F J Mrs, 1948, O 28,29:2
Pielstick, Don F, 1955, Je 28,27:2
Piemonte, Giuseppe E, 1960, F 18,33:1
Piemonte, Pasquale, 1962, S 11,33:3
Pienkovsky, Stefan, 1953, N 22,88:4
Piens, Arthur A, 1942, O 3,15:3
Piepenburg, Fritz, 1950, Ag 17,28:5
Pieper, Arnold C, 1955, Ap 21,29:2
Pieper, August, 1946, D 24,17:3
Pieper, Eric O, 1965, Mr 25,37:5
Pieper, Fred H, 1939, Ap 19,23:3
Pieper, John J, 1939, N 27,17:4
Pieper, Louis E, 1957, Mr 23,19:5
Pieper, Oscar H, 1943, Ja 28,19:3
Piepgras, Henry, 1910, F 22,9:4
Pier, Arthur S, 1966, Ag 17,39:1
Pier, Garrett C, 1943, D 31,15:5
Pier, Timothy, 1954, Je 17,29:5
Pieraccini, Gaetano, 1957, Ap 15,29:4
Pierantoni, Alceo, 1945, Je 7,19:3
Pierantoni, Umberto, 1959, N 18,41:5
Pierard, Louis, 1951, N 4,86:8
Pierce, Adin, 1944, Jl 27,17:2
Pierce, Albert F Rev, 1937, Ag 23,19:5
Pierce, Albert G, 1959, Mr 25,35:1
Pierce, Albert R, 1948, D 10,25:4
Pierce, Amasa D, 1954, D 4,17:4
Pierce, Andrew G, 1903, S 12,9:6; 1950, N 20,25:3
Pierce, Anna F, 1961, Ap 18,37:1
Pierce, Arthur C, 1945, Ja 31,21:4; 1950, S 16,19:6
Pierce, Arthur D, 1967, D 20,49:3
Pierce, Arthur Henry Prof, 1914, F 21,11:3
Pierce, Arthur L, 1956, My 31,27:5
Pierce, Arthur W Mrs, 1950, O 18,33:2
Pierce, Bion C, 1947, Jl 25,17:4
Pierce, Burt N, 1956, Ag 25,15:6
Pierce, Burt N Mrs, 1959, My 30,17:6
Pierce, Burton Mrs (funl plans, O 13,45:3), 1966, O 10,47:3
Pierce, Caleb C, 1938, F 18,19:4
Pierce, Carleton C, 1958, N 6,37:5
Pierce, Carroll, 1937, Mr 9,23:2
Pierce, Charles, 1943, Mr 20,15:5; 1965, Jl 10,25:3
Pierce, Charles B Sr Mrs, 1957, S 14,19:2
Pierce, Charles C Lt-Col, 1921, My 17,17:5
Pierce, Charles E, 1949, Jl 28,24:2; 1950, Ap 1,15:2
Pierce, Charles F, 1957, Mr 26,33:5
Pierce, Charles H, 1921, F 25,11:7
Pierce, Charles S, 1949, Mr 27,76:2
Pierce, Charles Santiago Sanders, 1914, Ap 22,15:6
Pierce, Charlotte, 1950, Jl 26,25:3
Pierce, Clinton H, 1944, Je 9,15:5
Pierce, Cornelius, 1942, Jl 13,15:5
Pierce, Curtis W, 1951, N 16,25:6
Pierce, Daniel, 1944, Ag 30,17:2
Pierce, Daniel T, 1952, F 17,84:7
Pierce, Dante M, 1955, Jl 29,17:5
Pierce, David E, 1958, Ja 23,27:2
Pierce, David H, 1949, S 22,31:4
Pierce, Douglas, 1954, Je 1,27:5
Pierce, Dwight S, 1946, D 9,25:3
Pierce, E B, 1879, Jl 18,4:3
Pierce, E Wallace, 1941, F 11,23:5
Pierce, Earl W, 1945, Je 15,19:3
Pierce, Edward F, 1937, S 27,21:4
Pierce, Edward L, 1954, D 2,31:2
Pierce, Edward L Mrs, 1961, Ja 5,31:2
Pierce, Edward P, 1938, Je 23,21:2; 1953, O 20,29:2
Pierce, Edward T, 1937, S 12,II,6:4; 1938, N 9,23:5; 1967, My 15,43:3
Pierce, Edward T Mrs, 1943, Jl 20,19:1
Pierce, Edwin E, 1952, Jl 1,23:4
Pierce, Edwin L, 1960, Ja 11,45:3
Pierce, Edwin S Col, 1912, S 1,II,9:4
Pierce, Eldridge W, 1947, Ap 5,19:4
Pierce, Ernest E Mrs, 1954, Jl 22,23:3
Pierce, Evelyn, 1937, Ja 25,19:3
Pierce, Flora M Mrs, 1937, Mr 25,25:3
Pierce, Florence B Mrs, 1958, Jl 9,27:6
Pierce, Frank A, 1960, My 22,86:1
Pierce, Frank A Mrs, 1947, O 4,17:3
Pierce, Frank C, 1951, O 15,25:2
Pierce, Frank D, 1952, Je 13,23:4
Pierce, Frank W, 1964, F 18,35:2
Pierce, Frank W Mrs, 1951, Ap 28,15:5
Pierce, Franklin E, 1938, D 27,17:2
Pierce, Franklin Ex-President, 1869, O 9,3:6
Pierce, Fred, 1923, Ap 23,15:6
Pierce, Fred W, 1943, S 20,21:3
Pierce, Frederick E, 1953, S 16,33:2
Pierce, Frederick K, 1958, Ja 1,25:1
Pierce, G E, 1934, Mr 17,15:5
Pierce, G F, 1884, S 4,4:6
Pierce, George, 1944, My 5,19:2; 1945, Ag 29,23:5
Pierce, George E, 1951, O 8,21:2
Pierce, George F, 1942, F 10,15:5
Pierce, George H, 1967, O 23,45:2
Pierce, George H Capt, 1913, S 11,11:6
Pierce, George L, 1941, F 16,41:2
Pierce, George W, 1965, O 8,6:1
Pierce, Gerald, 1952, F 22,21:1
Pierce, Gilbert Mrs, 1957, S 30,31:5
Pierce, Gordon D, 1964, O 19,33:5
Pierce, Guy C, 1956, F 25,19:5
Pierce, H Gordon, 1959, N 29,86:7
Pierce, H H, 1883, Jl 29,7:1
Pierce, Harlow W, 1948, Mr 14,72:3
Pierce, Harold C, 1950, N 30,33:2
Pierce, Harold M, 1961, Ja 29,85:1
Pierce, Harold W, 1958, D 2,37:5
Pierce, Harry M, 1943, N 24,21:4
Pierce, Henry B, 1905, Ja 18,9:4
Pierce, Henry C, 1927, Je 28,25:4
Pierce, Henry H (will, Ap 12,20:7), 1940, Mr 19,25:6
Pierce, Henry H, 1943, N 28,68:7
Pierce, Henry J, 1947, Ag 10,53:1
Pierce, Henry J Mrs, 1965, D 30,23:2
Pierce, Henry M, 1945, F 17,13:4
Pierce, Herbert A (Bert), 1958, Ap 3,31:1
Pierce, Herbert R, 1949, Ag 6,17:4
Pierce, Howard C Mrs, 1955, Je 2,29:3
Pierce, Howard G, 1953, Ap 11,17:2
Pierce, Hugh C, 1947, F 7,23:3
Pierce, Hugh M Sr, 1962, N 13,37:3
Pierce, J D, 1882, Ap 6,2:5
Pierce, James, 1953, Jl 20,17:2
Pierce, James F, 1960, O 28,31:4
Pierce, James H, 1943, N 21,56:3
Pierce, James M Mrs, 1953, D 17,37:5
Pierce, James Mill Prof, 1906, Mr 22,9:2
Pierce, James W, 1911, N 17,13:5; 1953, Ag 18,23:5
Pierce, Jason N (por), 1948, Mr 17,25:1
Pierce, John J, 1944, Ap 17,23:1
Pierce, John J Mrs, 1938, Jl 8,17:5; 1948, Ag 25,25:4
Pierce, John M, 1954, Ja 11,25:3
Pierce, Jonathan C, 1941, D 4,25:4
Pierce, Jonathan D, 1937, N 8,23:5
Pierce, Joshua W Col, 1874, Ap 12,1:4
Pierce, Julia, 1943, Mr 11,21:2
Pierce, Julia E, 1942, N 3,24:4
Pierce, Julia G, 1964, Ap 3,33:2
Pierce, Kenneth W, 1941, Ap 1,23:5
Pierce, L W Rev, 1922, Ag 22,17:6
Pierce, Lee R, 1963, Ap 4,47:1
Pierce, Lena C Mrs, 1951, Ag 24,15:3
Pierce, Leo T, 1950, Je 26,27:1
Pierce, Leslie D, 1947, O 30,25:2
Pierce, Leslie D Jr Mrs, 1953, F 9,27:4
Pierce, Leslie M Mrs, 1958, Ja 25,19:5
Pierce, Lewis Leland, 1921, Ja 11,11:3
Pierce, Lorne, 1961, N 28,37:4
Pierce, Louis L, 1940, My 5,52:2
Pierce, Louise F Mrs, 1953, Ag 24,23:5
Pierce, Lyman L, 1940, Jl 21,28:6
Pierce, Mabel L, 1942, N 18,25:5
Pierce, Margaret W (will), 1950, S 23,1:2
Pierce, Marion B, 1953, Je 10,29:2
Pierce, Mary E Mrs, 1939, O 4,25:3
Pierce, Maurice R Rear-Adm, 1968, Jl 24,50:3
Pierce, Newton L, 1950, Ag 10,25:6
Pierce, Norval H, 1946, O 29,25:2
Pierce, Orrin S, 1948, F 25,23:5
Pierce, Palmer E (por), 1940, Ja 18,23:3
Pierce, Palmer E Mrs (will), 1961, Ap 6,36:6
Pierce, Pauline Robinson Mrs, 1949, S 24,1:2
Pierce, Percy, 1940, Ag 30,19:1; 1962, Ag 2,25:1
Pierce, Perry, 1945, S 20,23:2
Pierce, Phoebe Mrs, 1953, S 22,31:2
Pierce, R A, 1936, Je 13,17:4
Pierce, R F Y, 1934, D 6,23:4
Pierce, Reginald F, 1958, Ja 12,86:3
Pierce, Robert L, 1968, F 24,29:4
Pierce, Roy Ensworth, 1925, My 19,21:5
Pierce, Ruby E, 1960, D 27,29:4
Pierce, S W, 1903, Mr 25,9:6
Pierce, Sam, 1943, N 23,26:2
Pierce, Samuel J, 1943, Jl 13,22:2
Pierce, Samuel Mrs, 1950, F 12,84:2
Pierce, Shelly, 1956, Ap 18,31:1
Pierce, Stephen F, 1957, N 25,31:1
Pierce, Stephen G, 1945, F 4,38:7
Pierce, Susan, 1924, Jl 30,13:4
Pierce, Susan L, 1945, Ja 23,19:1
Pierce, T Raymond, 1958, Ag 23,15:5
Pierce, Thomas L, 1955, F 18,22:2
Pierce, Ulysses G (por), 1943, O 12,27:5
Pierce, V Mott, 1942, My 28,17:5
Pierce, Victor L, 1961, Ja 17,37:2
Pierce, W B Dr Mrs, 1879, F 20,5:5
Pierce, W S Brig-Gen, 1923, Jl 12,17:4
Pierce, Wallace E (por), 1940, Ja 4,23:1
Pierce, Walter H, 1954, Je 3,27:4
Pierce, Walter L S, 1950, O 24,29:1
Pierce, Walter L S Mrs, 1950, S 3,38:5
Pierce, Walter M, 1954, Mr 28,88:5
Pierce, Walter M Mrs, 1957, F 14,27:5
Pierce, Walworth, 1965, Jl 26,23:5
Pierce, Walworth Mrs, 1961, D 31,48:4
Pierce, Watson O, 1963, Jl 6,15:3
Pierce, William A, 1951, Ja 16,29:4
Pierce, William H, 1925, O 27,23:4; 1950, Ja 2,23:6
Pierce, William L Jr, 1944, N 24,23:3
Pierce, William W, 1939, My 3,24:2
Pierce, Winslow S, 1938, Jl 24,28:8
Pierce, Winslow S Jr, 1950, O 6,27:5
Piercey, Gabriel, 1904, Je 4,2:4
Piercy, A I, 1884, Mr 18,5:4
Piercy, George H, 1919, F 13,15:4
Piercy, Joseph W, 1943, N 24,21:5
Piercy, S W, 1882, Ja 10,5:4
Piercy, Samuel K, 1949, F 22,23:4
Piercy, William Benton (Bill), 1951, Ag 30,23:4
Piergrossi, Biagio, 1949, N 24,31:2
Pieri, Lou, 1967, Je 17,31:2
Pierie, George G Jr, 1955, Jl 1,21:2
Pierini, Vincent, 1964, S 5,19:3
Pierkowski, Arthur E Lt-Col, 1918, D 4,15:2
Pierlot, Francis, 1955, My 13,25:4
Pierlot, Hubert, 1963, D 14,27:1
Pierman, John W, 1951, Je 11,25:3
Pierman, Phil G, 1948, N 13,15:6
Piermont, Sidney H, 1968, F 24,29:5
Pierne, Gabriel, 1937, Jl 18,II,7:3
Pierneef, Hendrix, 1957, O 5,17:6
Pierola, Nicholas, 1913, Je 25,9:6
Pierot, Felix R, 1952, F 24,84:6
Pierot, Jacques Jr, 1953, Ag 9,76:4
Pierpont, Affa M Mrs, 1950, O 29,95:1
Pierpont, Clarence S, 1948, N 17,28:2
Pierpont, George H, 1955, Ag 25,23:3
Pierpont, George W, 1950, S 17,104:4
Pierpont, Henry E, 1947, Ja 15,26:3
Pierpont, James, 1938, D 11,60:6
Pierpont, John Rev, 1866, Ag 30,3:2
Pierpont, Robert G, 1957, My 9,31:3
Pierpont, Walter L, 1948, Ag 12,21:5
Pierre, C, 1934, O 9,19:1
Pierre, C Grand, 1940, Mr 18,19:2
Pierre, Charles H, 1937, My 11,25:1
Pierre, Charles Mrs (will), 1958, Ja 24,10:8
Pierre, Eugene, 1925, Jl 8,17:6
Pierre, Jean Henri Rev Dr, 1874, Jl 29,5:2
Pierre, Prince of Monaco, 1964, N 11,43:1
Pierrepoint, Thomas W, 1954, F 12,5:8
Pierrepont, Anna J, 1940, N 19,23:3
Pierrepont, E, 1892, Mr 7,1:7
Pierrepont, Edward, 1885, Ap 17,5:4
Pierrepont, Evelyn R (Earl of Manvers), 1940, Ap 8, 19:1
Pierrepont, Henry E, 1911, N 5,II,15:5
Pierrepont, John, 1882, Ja 8,7:2
Pierrepont, John J, 1950, O 16,27:3
Pierrepont, John Jay, 1923, S 27,7:3
Pierrepont, Julia J (will, Ap 8,12:6), 1937, F 9,23:2
Pierrepont, R Stuyvesant, 1950, D 16,17:2
Pierrepont, Robert L, 1945, Ja 19,19:5
Pierrepont, Robert L Mrs, 1960, Ap 9,23:2
Pierrepont, Seth L (will, My 19,10:7), 1956, Ap 1,88:6
Pierrepont, Seth L Mrs, 1960, Mr 2,37:4
Pierrepont, W A Dr, 1902, Ja 7,7:5
Pierret, Antonio P, 1937, Ja 17,II,8:7
Pierron, Armand A, 1942, F 5,21:4
Pierron, Joseph, 1949, Ap 27,27:2
Piers, Harry, 1940, Ja 25,21:1
Piersall, John W, 1961, S 6,31:4
Piersig, Caroline, 1951, Mr 29,27:5
Piersol, George A Mrs, 1951, N 14,31:5
Piersol, George Arthur Dr, 1924, Ag 8,13:6
Piersol, George M, 1966, Ag 20,25:1
Piersol, James V, 1962, Ag 21,33:3
Pierson, A Lawrence, 1944, D 28,19:3
Pierson, A R, 1929, Ap 3,2:6
Pierson, Adrian A, 1944, Ja 4,18:2
Pierson, Alden, 1921, My 4,10:5
Pierson, Aldus H, 1943, Je 20,34:7

Pierson, Allard, 1955, Ag 11,21:3
Pierson, Andrew N, 1925, O 30,21:5
Pierson, Arthur N, 1957, Mr 9,19:6
Pierson, Arthur N Mrs, 1949, S 6,27:3; 1958, Ap 8,30:5
Pierson, Arthur T Rev, 1911, Je 4,II,11:5
Pierson, Augustus B, 1949, Jl 21,26:2
Pierson, Aylin, 1955, Jl 27,23:4
Pierson, Bowen W Mrs, 1946, My 28,21:5
Pierson, C Albert, 1954, N 28,87:2
Pierson, C W, 1934, My 5,17:6
Pierson, Charles E, 1967, Ja 14,31:5
Pierson, Charles J, 1950, Mr 2,27:5
Pierson, David, 1911, Ap 7,13:4
Pierson, David H, 1940, Ap 16,23:6
Pierson, David L (por), 1938, Jl 12,19:3
Pierson, Delavan L, 1952, N 6,29:6
Pierson, Delavan L Mrs, 1937, Je 19,17:4
Pierson, E M Mrs, 1948, F 21,13:5
Pierson, Earle B Jr, 1967, Mr 31,37:3
Pierson, Edgar H, 1947, My 11,60:5
Pierson, Edward Franklin, 1916, F 24,13:5
Pierson, Edward J, 1949, N 15,25:4
Pierson, Elizabeth, 1937, Jl 1,27:5
Pierson, Ellen C, 1946, Jl 9,21:5
Pierson, Ernest A, 1944, Jl 4,19:5
Pierson, Eugene C, 1943, Ap 21,25:5
Pierson, Eugene C Mrs, 1956, F 12,88:8
Pierson, Francis H, 1920, D 4,13:6
Pierson, George E, 1952, F 6,29:5
Pierson, George M, 1948, S 25,17:5
Pierson, George P, 1939, Ag 2,19:5
Pierson, George S, 1952, Ja 1,25:2
Pierson, George W, 1947, S 13,11:4
Pierson, Grace P Mrs, 1950, Ag 29,27:2
Pierson, H Frank, 1938, F 14,17:5
Pierson, Harold A, 1966, S 14,47:2
Pierson, Harry E, 1950, Ja 24,31:3
Pierson, Helen P, 1963, Jl 9,31:2
Pierson, Henry B, 1951, D 10,29:5
Pierson, Henry Louis, 1916, Je 3,13:7
Pierson, Herbert S, 1951, O 7,86:5
Pierson, Homer C, 1951, F 17,15:5
Pierson, Howard O Mrs, 1944, Mr 21,19:4
Pierson, Hubert L, 1908, Je 1,7:4; 1958, My 27,29:1
Pierson, Ida G Mrs, 1937, Mr 13,19:1
Pierson, J Fred Mrs, 1955, Ja 12,27:2
Pierson, James R, 1959, My 4,29:4
Pierson, John A Mrs, 1959, Ja 22,31:4
Pierson, John D Sr, 1943, O 8,19:3
Pierson, John F, 1951, Je 11,25:3
Pierson, John J Mrs, 1958, O 29,35:2
Pierson, John S, 1948, F 11,28:2
Pierson, Leslie C, 1916, Jl 15,9:7
Pierson, Lewis E (will, D 17,22:5), 1954, N 11,31:3
Pierson, Lewis E Mrs, 1955, N 12,19:5
Pierson, Lewis H, 1944, S 28,19:6
Pierson, Louise B, 1903, N 7,9:6
Pierson, Louise R (will, My 17,35:2), 1942, My 5, 21:3
Pierson, Mabel E, 1939, Ag 24,19:3
Pierson, Malcolm H, 1947, O 17,22:2
Pierson, Neil, 1948, Mr 12,23:4
Pierson, Norris E, 1962, Jl 14,21:4
Pierson, Orrin T, 1944, O 5,23:1
Pierson, Patrick F, 1949, My 27,21:1
Pierson, Paul R B, 1966, S 19,43:3
Pierson, Philander B, 1939, My 29,15:2
Pierson, Philip H, 1946, Ja 18,19:4
Pierson, Raymond J, 1959, F 24,29:2
Pierson, Reginald K, 1948, Ja 11,56:5
Pierson, Robert A, 1941, Ja 7,23:2
Pierson, Robert H, 1945, Je 3,32:1
Pierson, Roger F, 1949, My 24,27:2
Pierson, Russell D, 1948, Ja 4,52:8
Pierson, Russell E, 1947, N 8,17:2
Pierson, Ruth O, 1943, S 14,23:2
Pierson, Samuel Dr, 1937, Ap 23,21:3
Pierson, Samuel N, 1946, O 18,23:4
Pierson, Sarah, 1940, Ag 27,21:6
Pierson, Sterling (por), 1949, Je 2,27:1
Pierson, Thomas H, 1942, D 14,28:1
Pierson, W S, 1879, Ap 19,5:2
Pierson, W W, 1883, Ap 6,4:7
Pierson, Wallace R, 1946, N 6,23:6
Pierson, Walter C, 1950, Mr 23,29:3
Pierson, Walter H, 1938, F 11,23:1
Pierson, Wilbur H, 1951, Ap 6,25:2
Pierson, William, 1882, O 2,5:4
Pierson, William H, 1940, D 6,23:2
Pierson, William M, 1946, Ag 10,13:5
Piersons, A M Dr, 1903, Ag 30,7:6
Piersons, Harold C, 1948, D 12,92:3
Piesen, Hugo H, 1942, Je 24,19:1
Piesen, Hugo H Mrs, 1959, My 5,33:1
Piesen, Margery Korman (Mrs M Piesen), 1968, N 16,37:3
Piester, Harry C, 1949, My 12,31:5
Pieters, A J, 1940, Ap 27,15:3
Pieters, Alex A, 1958, Jl 1,31:2
Pietrangeli, Antonio, 1968, Jl 13,27:2
Pietri, Francois (more details, Ag 20,25:2), 1966, Ag 19,33:1
Pietro, Angelo di Cardinal, 1914, D 6,19:5
Pietrzak, John, 1950, O 29,93:2
Pietsch, Charles F, 1955, N 1,31:4
Pietsch, Ernest L, 1937, Ag 3,23:4
Pietsch, James A, 1940, D 17,25:3
Pietsch, Reinhold Jr, 1946, Ja 27,42:4
Pietsch, Walter G, 1938, D 15,27:3
Pietschker, Arthur, 1953, N 26,31:3
Piette, Eugene C, 1946, D 6,24:2
Piette, Maximin C, 1948, N 9,27:4
Piez, C, 1933, O 3,23:1
Piez, Richard K, 1946, Je 9,40:4
Piffard, Henry Grainger Dr, 1910, Je 9,7:5
Pifferi, Guglielmo Msgr, 1910, Ap 30,9:6
Piga, Stephen P, 1953, Je 17,27:4
Pigeon, Fred L, 1950, My 10,31:5
Pigeon, Helen D, 1945, O 1,19:4
Pigeon, Marguerite, 1938, Mr 15,23:1
Pigeon, Stanley, 1941, N 14,23:2
Pigford, Clarence E, 1945, Ja 9,19:2
Piggott, Stuart, 1919, My 8,17:3
Piggott, Theodore C, 1944, Jl 5,17:5
Pigman, Augustus Mrs, 1945, Jl 20,19:6
Pigna, Salvatore, 1955, Mr 3,27:4
Pignatelli, Ettore Prince, 1925, Je 26,17:6
Pignatelli, Guido Princess (will, N 19,16:5), 1948, Je 4,23:6
Pignatelli, Valerio Prince, 1965, F 8,25:1
Pignatelli de Aragon, Ludovica Princess, 1952, Ag 27, 27:3
Pignatelli di Belmonte, Gennaro G, 1948, F 17,25:1
Pignona, Ernest E, 1949, Mr 17,26:2
Pigot, Eliza H, 1946, My 13,21:2
Pigot, Joseph Beadel, 1903, D 10,9:5
Pigott, Baron, 1875, My 26,10:4
Pigott, George F Jr, 1954, Ap 30,23:3
Pigott, Gillery Sir, 1873, D 23,4:7
Pigott, Mary A, 1947, F 20,25:2
Pigott, Pat, 1962, O 15,41:1
Pigott, Paul, 1961, Ja 25,33:4
Pigott, Richard J, 1963, N 18,33:4
Pigott, Stephen, 1955, Mr 1,25:2
Pigott, Tydingham V, 1937, F 16,23:5
Pigozzi, Henri T, 1964, N 20,37:1
Pigueron, George H, 1955, F 26,15:6
Pigueron, George H Mrs, 1957, Ap 19,21:3
Pigueron, William Mrs, 1966, F 13,84:7
Pihlblad, Ernest F, 1943, D 10,27:3
Pihlfeldt, Thomas, 1941, Ja 24,17:4
Pijade, Moshe (funl plans, Mr 18,27:1; funl, Mr 19,-2:5), 1957, Mr 16,19:1
Pijoan, Jose, 1963, Je 18,37:4
Pijper, Adrianus, 1964, Ja 14,31:2
Pijper, Willem, 1947, Mr 20,27:4
Pike, A F, 1886, O 9,1:4
Pike, Adelaide D Mrs (will), 1942, Jl 22,16:6
Pike, Albert H, 1957, Ja 12,19:5
Pike, Alfred J W, 1957, Je 29,17:6
Pike, Archie E, 1948, S 8,29:3
Pike, Benneville F, 1946, F 26,25:3
Pike, Charles B, 1941, Ap 27,38:1
Pike, Chauncey T, 1949, Mr 6,72:1
Pike, Clayton W, 1939, Ja 1,25:2
Pike, Eugene R, 1946, Ja 5,13:5
Pike, Eugene W, 1944, N 19,49:1
Pike, Forrest F Mrs, 1943, S 6,17:6
Pike, Francis W, 1943, S 30,21:5
Pike, Frank H, 1953, N 15,88:3
Pike, Frank W, 1949, Ag 10,21:2
Pike, Frederick, 1949, Mr 18,25:2
Pike, Frederick Owen Vice-Adm, 1921, Ap 8,13:5
Pike, George H, 1956, O 12,29:5
Pike, Gordon P, 1925, Mr 8,5:2
Pike, Harry W, 1951, Ag 4,15:6
Pike, Henry H, 1944, F 1,19:4
Pike, Howard E, 1959, F 19,31:4
Pike, J S, 1882, N 30,2:7
Pike, Jacob S Mrs, 1948, Mr 29,21:3
Pike, James, 1942, Mr 5,23:2
Pike, Katherine R, 1947, My 3,17:5
Pike, Kenneth W, 1957, My 31,19:2
Pike, Laura A, 1941, Ja 27,15:5
Pike, Lawrence, 1906, Mr 19,9:6
Pike, Lemuel G, 1955, Ja 20,31:5
Pike, Marion J, 1940, F 6,21:4
Pike, Mary R Mrs, 1922, My 17,19:5
Pike, Mildred L, 1967, Ja 29,76:8
Pike, Nathan R, 1965, Ja 29,34:1
Pike, Nicholas Col, 1905, Ap 13,11:5
Pike, Otis W, 1950, O 10,31:3
Pike, Peter P, 1949, S 5,17:2
Pike, Robert D, 1955, Ap 14,29:4
Pike, Roy B, 1955, Ja 28,19:2
Pike, S Sidney, 1968, F 25,76:6
Pike, Samuel N, 1872, D 8,8:2
Pike, Sidney J Jr Mrs, 1959, S 20,87:1
Pike, Theodore F, 1953, My 26,29:3
Pike, Wilbert V Sr, 1950, Jl 14,21:2
Pike, Wilfred E, 1940, F 18,41:1
Pike, William, 1941, Jl 1,23:3
Pike, William J, 1923, Ap 25,21:5; 1950, Jl 4,17:4
Pikul, Stanislaw, 1953, Ja 26,19:2
Pilar, John O, 1954, Ag 2,17:3
Pilar, Maria del (Spanish Infanta), 1879, Ag 6,1:2
Pilar, Maria del Princess, 1918, My 9,13:5
Pilat, Ignatz A, 1870, S 20,4:7
Pilat, Konstantin, 1952, S 20,15:5
Pilat, Oliver I, 1958, Ja 9,36:2
Pilates, Joseph H, 1967, O 10,47:2
Pilatsky, Charles, 1943, D 18,15:5
Pilavin, Albert, 1964, Ja 28,31:1
Pilcer, Edward, 1953, Ag 28,17:3
Pilcer, Harry, 1961, Ja 16,27:5
Pilcer, Joseph, 1953, Ja 20,25:4
Pilch, Frederic R, 1960, F 6,19:5
Pilch, Henry G, 1944, Mr 1,19:6
Pilcher, Campbell, 1961, My 18,35:3
Pilcher, Cobb, 1949, S 23,23:2
Pilcher, James D, 1954, My 6,33:4
Pilcher, James Evelyn Gen, 1911, Ap 10,13:4
Pilcher, James T, 1947, Ap 8,27:4
Pilcher, Lewis F, 1941, Je 16,15:3
Pilcher, Margaret Mrs, 1947, Mr 5,25:2
Pilcher, Paul M Dr, 1917, Ja 5,9:3
Pile, Fred M, 1948, Mr 20,13:5
Pile, Joseph A, 1949, Ja 30,II,61:1
Pile, R C, 1948, My 18,23:1
Pile, Sterling, 1957, O 17,33:1
Pileggi, Vincent R, 1958, Ja 29,27:2
Piles, Mattie E Mrs, 1943, Je 30,21:4
Piles, Samuel H, 1940, Mr 12,23:4
Pilet-Golaz, Marcel, 1958, Ap 12,19:5
Pilger, Charles Jr, 1951, S 13,34:2
Pilgrim, James, 1879, Mr 16,7:5
Pilgrim, John, 1951, Ag 28,48:1
Pilgrim, Maurice F, 1903, O 20,9:6
Pilgrim, Paul H, 1958, Ja 8,47:2
Pilgrim, S V Dr, 1885, Je 2,5:6
Piliere, Frank, 1958, Ap 3,31:1
Pilkington, George Edward, 1925, F 10,23:3
Pilkington, George L, 1946, N 13,27:2
Pilkington, H Gordon, 1954, My 15,15:4
Pilkington, Henry J, 1945, F 14,19:3
Pilkington, J, 1929, Ap 26,25:5
Pilkington, Kate L Mrs, 1940, Ag 1,21:2
Pilkinton, Philip L, 1965, Ja 17,88:4
Pill, Rose B Mrs, 1941, Ja 22,21:3
Pillans, James Forrest, 1922, Mr 14,15:4
Pillatt, Frank D Mrs, 1952, Je 7,19:5
Pillatt, Harold B, 1964, S 5,19:4
Pillen, Harry, 1945, My 19,19:2
Pillers, J M (Dale), 1950, Ja 17,27:3
Pilley, Frank, 1949, F 7,19:1
Pillicono, Phillip, 1922, Jl 31,11:7
Pilling, Charles J, 1944, F 2,21:5
Pilling, George P, 1943, O 22,17:2
Pilling, Percy J, 1964, F 22,21:1
Pilling, Robert W S, 1941, F 24,15:1
Pilling, William S, 1945, Ap 24,19:5
Pilliod, James J Mrs, 1953, Je 7,84:4
Pillion, Joseph C, 1965, Ap 3,29:6
Pillion, Lester H, 1949, My 6,25:4
Pillot, A P, 1880, Jl 13,5:4
Pillot, Andre P, 1963, Jl 16,21:4
Pillot, Camille G, 1953, O 23,23:3
Pillot, F L, 1884, Jl 8,2:2
Pillow, G J Gen, 1878, O 10,5:6
Pillsbury, A E, 1930, D 24,15:1
Pillsbury, Alfred F, 1950, Mr 13,21:1
Pillsbury, Alfred F Mrs, 1946, N 3,63:4
Pillsbury, Alice T Mrs, 1940, O 25,21:3
Pillsbury, Amos Gen, 1873, Jl 15,4:7
Pillsbury, Anna S, 1879, Jl 18,3:6
Pillsbury, Charles A, 1899, S 18,7:6
Pillsbury, Charles S, 1939, My 22,17:5
Pillsbury, Charles S Mrs, 1957, D 8,88:8
Pillsbury, Edward, 1882, Ag 11,5:2
Pillsbury, Edwin S, 1955, S 30,25:4
Pillsbury, Edwin S Mrs, 1956, D 6,37:1
Pillsbury, Franklin C, 1937, My 17,19:4
Pillsbury, Franklin H, 1958, Ag 18,19:3
Pillsbury, Henry C, 1955, Jl 19,27:5
Pillsbury, Henry Nelson, 1906, Je 18,7:5
Pillsbury, Horace D, 1940, Ja 19,19:4
Pillsbury, J S ex-Gov, 1901, O 19,9:6
Pillsbury, John E Rear-Adm, 1919, D 31,7:4
Pillsbury, John Sargent, 1968, F 2,35:2
Pillsbury, Samuel H, 1938, My 20,19:5
Pillsbury, William H, 1953, Ap 13,27:4
Pilot, James C, 1949, F 15,23:4
Pilpel, Cecile M Mrs, 1956, Mr 10,17:6
Pilsbry, Henry A, 1957, O 27,85:3
Pilson, Frank K, 1948, Ja 22,27:1
Pilson, George, 1916, Ap 24,13:7
Pilsudski, J, 1935, My 13,1:4
Pilsworth, Elizabeth Mrs, 1942, Ja 13,15:5
Piluso, Michael J, 1945, O 27,15:5
Pilzer, Leopold, 1961, Jl 20,27:4
Pilzer, Maximilian (death laid to heart ailment, Je 1,86:5), 1958, My 31,17:7
Pim, G F (see also Ap 16), 1878, Ap 18,8:4
Pim, William P, 1950, Jl 27,25:3
Pimley, David H Mrs, 1945, Ag 9,21:5
Pimsleur, Solomon, 1962, Ag 23,29:2
Pina-Chevalier, Plinio, 1956, O 19,27:1
Pinanski, Abraham E, 1949, O 6,31:5
Pinansky, Max L, 1951, Ap 12,33:2

Pinard, J B, 1883, O 17,5:2
Pinard, Pierre Ernest, 1909, S 15,9:5
Pinard, Theodore W, 1960, Ja 28,31:4
Pinault, Louis G, 1940, Ja 9,24:3
Pinchard, Raymond, 1961, Ag 23,33:3
Pinchbeck, Frank, 1965, Ap 3,29:3
Pinchbeck, Hattie A Mrs, 1938, Ag 24,21:4
Pinchbeck, Raymond B, 1957, F 6,25:6
Pincherle, Maurizio, 1949, S 14,31:5
Pinchot, Amedee, 1877, F 14,5:3
Pinchot, Amos R E, 1944, F 19,13:1
Pinchot, Amos R E Mrs (por),(will, Jl 8,32:3), 1939, My 17,23:4
Pinchot, Gifford, 1946, O 6,56:2
Pinchot, Gifford Mrs, 1960, S 10,21:5
Pinchot, James W, 1908, F 7,7:6
Pinchot, Mary Mrs, 1914, Ag 26,9:6
Pinciurek, Anthony, 1943, N 19,19:4
Pinck, Guy W, 1951, Mr 14,33:5
Pinckard, George H, 1950, S 10,92:3
Pinckard, William H, 1957, O 21,25:2
Pinckney, B F, 1865, F 25,8:4
Pinckney, C Cotesworth, 1946, F 21,21:4
Pinckney, Charles A, 1954, Ja 1,23:2
Pinckney, Frank H, 1963, N 28,39:2
Pinckney, J C, 1881, Mr 12,8:2
Pinckney, J Stewart, 1940, D 14,17:4
Pinckney, John I, 1948, O 17,76:5
Pinckney, Josephine, 1957, O 6,84:2
Pinckney, Orient C, 1940, S 22,49:3
Pinckney, Stephen L, 1949, F 23,27:6
Pinckney, Thomas, 1903, N 12,9:5
Pinckney, William T, 1865, My 24,8:4
Pinco, Robert A, 1966, S 17,31:1
Pincoffs, Adolph L, 1919, N 26,13:1
Pincoffs, Peter Adrian, 1914, D 22,13:4
Pincon, M, 1872, N 16,1:1
Pincus, Abraham (A P Mollison), 1956, S 22,17:6
Pincus, Felix, 1944, S 16,13:3
Pincus, Gregory G, 1967, Ag 23,45:1
Pincus, Harry, 1950, Jl 4,17:2; 1952, S 9,31:2
Pincus, Harry Jr, 1962, Je 19,35:1
Pincus, Henry, 1949, N 24,31:2
Pincus, Jacob M, 1956, Ap 11,33:6
Pincus, Joel J, 1949, Ag 3,23:2
Pincus, Joseph W, 1951, Ja 15,17:5
Pincus, Joseph W Mrs, 1946, Ap 7,46:1
Pincus, Julius, 1957, Jl 28,61:1
Pincus, Leah, 1963, Ag 21,33:1
Pincus, Lillie R, 1952, F 17,86:5
Pincus, Louis Mrs, 1950, My 9,29:3
Pincus, Max, 1947, S 27,15:1
Pincus, Nathan, 1960, Ap 6,41:4
Pincus, Samuel, 1951, Ag 7,16:6
Pincus, Sidney, 1954, Ap 14,29:2
Pincus, Victor A, 1956, My 21,25:3
Pindar, David B, 1940, My 7,25:2
Pindar, George N, 1959, O 24,21:4
Pindar, Helen (Sister M De Lourdes), 1959, S 16,39:3
Pindar, Henry F, 1964, Ag 21,29:3
Pindar, P F, 1938, Ja 29,15:5
Pindar, William A, 1947, N 13,28:3
Pindel, Thomas H, 1944, N 11,13:4
Pindell, Henry M, 1924, Ag 9,11:4
Pindell, Howard M Mrs, 1941, Mr 18,23:2
Pindell, Thomas H Mrs, 1959, Ag 4,27:5
Pinder, Ernest L, 1944, Ap 11,20:2
Pinder, John S, 1907, Jl 2,9:6
Pindyck, Sylvester, 1968, N 5,47:2
Pine, Alice, 1940, F 8,23:2
Pine, Ben, 1953, F 24,25:5
Pine, Charles H, 1915, Mr 15,11:5
Pine, Cornelia B, 1942, Ja 12,15:2
Pine, E Frank Sr, 1954, Ja 7,31:4
Pine, Frederick, 1952, S 30,31:3
Pine, James, 1953, F 22,63:5
Pine, John B, 1922, O 29,30:2; 1922, N 1,19:5
Pine, Kurt, 1962, My 21,33:4
Pine, M, 1928, Mr 3,17:5
Pine, Samuel H, 1904, Je 5,7:6; 1961, Ap 10,31:5
Pine, Vanderlyn T, 1952, D 10,35:5
Pine, William B, 1942, Ag 26,19:6
Pine, William E, 1944, Ag 22,17:4
Pine, William H, 1955, Ap 30,17:3
Pineault, Victoria (Sister Mary Theodore), 1951, D 4,33:3
Pinedo, M, 1945, S 29,15:2
Pinel, Fernand, 1962, N 9,35:1
Pinelli, Ermida Mrs, 1955, Mr 17,45:1
Pinelli, Sergio, 1942, Ja 1,25:2
Pinero, A W, 1934, N 24,15:1
Pinero, Jesus T, 1952, N 20,31:1
Pinero, Jose L, 1951, My 18,28:3
Pines, Bernard, 1960, D 22,26:2
Pines, Charles, 1948, Ag 23,17:1
Pines, George, 1964, F 19,39:2
Pines, Julius L, 1945, My 12,13:6
Pines, Louis, 1953, Ag 25,21:5
Pines, Robert A, 1949, Ag 10,21:2
Pines, Samuel, 1956, S 25,33:4
Pines, Samuel S, 1962, Ja 10,47:4
Pines, Samuel S Mrs, 1956, Mr 9,23:3
Piness, William L, 1957, Ap 21,89:1
Pingel, Oscar D W, 1964, Jl 4,13:1
Pingel, Oscar D W Mrs, 1956, Je 19,29:1
Pingitore, Anthony J, 1948, Ag 15,60:5
Pingitore, Michael, 1952, N 2,88:1
Pingree, Samuel E Ex-Gov, 1922, Je 2,17:6
Pingree, Sumner, 1965, F 20,25:3
Pingry, John F, 1938, S 14,23:2
Pings, George H, 1942, D 3,25:1
Pini, Giovanni, 1959, Ag 25,31:5
Pininfarina, Battista, 1966, Ap 4,31:4
Pink, Andrew, 1946, Mr 25,25:3
Pink, Benjamin P, 1948, Ag 5,21:4
Pink, Berry, 1962, Je 25,29:3
Pink, Edward F, 1937, Ag 24,21:2
Pink, Elvin Mrs, 1949, Ja 9,73:2
Pink, Harold A, 1944, Ag 18,13:5
Pink, Harry, 1951, N 14,31:4
Pink, Ira M, 1961, D 8,37:1
Pink, Louis H, 1955, My 19,29:5
Pink, Louis H Mrs, 1967, N 17,47:1
Pink, William F, 1951, D 20,31:3
Pinkard, Maceo, 1962, Jl 20,25:4
Pinkas, David Z, 1952, Ag 15,15:2
Pinkava, Charles, 1952, S 8,21:4
Pinker, George W, 1950, Ag 6,72:7
Pinker, James B, 1922, F 10,15:4
Pinkerton, Alfred S, 1922, N 28,21:5
Pinkerton, Allan, 1884, Jl 2,1:5
Pinkerton, Allan Mrs, 1945, Ag 14,21:2
Pinkerton, Charles Mrs, 1915, S 7,13:6
Pinkerton, Howard, 1938, S 13,23:5
Pinkerton, Hugh W, 1949, N 23,29:2
Pinkerton, J Clarence, 1949, Ja 13,23:2
Pinkerton, Kathrene (Mrs Robt Pinkerton), 1967, S 7,45:4
Pinkerton, Lowell C, 1959, F 21,21:3
Pinkerton, Robert A (por),(funl, S 3,9:5), 1907, Ag 18,7:6
Pinkerton, Robert A, 1967, O 12,45:4
Pinkerton, Robert D, 1958, Ja 27,27:4
Pinkerton, Roy Mrs, 1966, Je 28,42:3
Pinkerton, William, 1948, Ap 5,21:5
Pinkerton, William A, 1923, D 17,17:4
Pinkerton, William W, 1940, Ap 4,23:6
Pinkett, Daniel, 1946, O 2,29:4
Pinkham, Arthur D, 1959, F 14,21:5
Pinkham, Arthur W, 1961, Ja 1,48:3
Pinkham, C H, 1902, D 9,9:5
Pinkham, Charles, 1938, Mr 8,19:4
Pinkham, Charles A, 1937, Ap 23,21:3
Pinkham, Charles B, 1944, Jl 15,13:6
Pinkham, Charles H Capt, 1920, N 7,22:5
Pinkham, Dora B Mrs, 1941, N 20,37:3
Pinkham, Edward W, 1960, Ag 31,29:2
Pinkham, Edwin G, 1948, S 13,21:1
Pinkham, Francis C Mrs, 1948, D 18,19:4
Pinkham, Herbert, 1944, Mr 28,19:4
Pinkham, Herbert N Jr, 1944, My 12,19:4
Pinkham, Lucius E, 1922, N 3,17:5
Pinkham, Lydia, 1883, My 19,5:2
Pinkley, Frank, 1940, F 15,19:3
Pinkley, Virgil M Sr, 1957, F 14,27:4
Pinkley, Virgil Mrs, 1964, F 2,89:2
Pinkney, Albert U, 1957, F 25,25:3
Pinkney, Alex T, 1948, N 30,27:5
Pinkney, Bruno Mrs, 1951, D 5,35:1
Pinkney, C W Judge, 1903, Je 29,7:6
Pinkney, Cornelius S, 1921, Ja 21,15:5
Pinkney, E W R, 1940, O 23,23:5
Pinkney, J H, 1880, D 3,2:5
Pinkney, James E, 1937, Ag 14,13:5
Pinkney, Louis M, 1940, Je 18,23:3
Pinkney, N Dr, 1877, D 17,4:6
Pinkney, R R, 1942, Je 9,24:5
Pinkney, Thomas, 1952, N 14,23:4
Pinkney, William Bp, 1883, Jl 5,5:5
Pinkofsky, Abraham, 1943, Ag 16,15:4
Pinkofsky, Samuel, 1963, Je 9,87:1
Pinks, James L, 1947, S 19,23:4
Pinkston, Clarence E, 1961, N 19,89:2
Pinkston, Eliza, 1883, Ap 26,1:4
Pinkus, George, 1943, My 22,13:3
Pinkus, Jacob B Mrs, 1940, D 17,25:5
Pinkus, Walter D, 1948, Ag 3,26:2
Pinkussohn, Lewis A, 1956, N 15,35:3
Pinkussohn, Lewis A Mrs, 1956, O 27,21:6
Pinles, Ely, 1956, D 5,39:3
Pinn, Paul C, 1940, Mr 1,21:3
Pinna, John A, 1947, D 7,76:4
Pinna, Joseph, 1962, Ja 5,29:3
Pinned, Dorothy A, 1948, My 6,25:4
Pinnell, Charles, 1955, F 7,21:1
Pinneo, Alfred, 1949, O 15,15:3
Pinneo, Catherine Curtis Mrs, 1905, Mr 31,9:6
Pinneo, Clarence C, 1937, Ja 4,29:2
Pinneo, Edgar H, 1954, Je 6,86:2
Pinneo, Frank W Dr, 1937, N 19,23:3
Pinneo, George W, 1943, Ap 17,17:4
Pinner, Guy, 1939, Je 27,23:5
Pinner, Max (por), 1948, Ja 9,22:2
Pinner, Warren E, 1942, O 24,15:4
Pinnera, Gina, 1951, N 21,25:3
Pinney, Charles B, 1961, N 17,35:1
Pinney, E S, 1876, N 4,5:2
Pinney, Edward J, 1945, Jl 30,19:1
Pinney, Frank L, 1945, D 7,21:2
Pinney, George M, 1921, Jl 19,15:5
Pinney, Harry H, 1958, D 5,32:3
Pinney, Harvey F, 1945, N 25,48:4
Pinney, Thomas H, 1958, N 30,86:5
Pinnola, James J, 1964, Mr 2,27:3
Pino, Alessandro, 1941, My 2,21:5
Pino, Salvatore M Sr, 1962, S 29,23:3
Pinoteau, Claude L Mrs, 1959, Ag 28,23:3
Pinover, Irving E, 1941, S 8,15:2
Pinover, Maurice A, 1965, S 11,27:5
Pinover, Samuel, 1938, Jl 19,22:7
Pinsard, Amand, 1953, My 12,27:5
Pinsker, Dewey, 1959, My 6,39:2
Pinsker, Samuel D, 1950, F 19,78:5
Pinski, David, 1959, Ag 13,27:6
Pinsky, Jacob S, 1944, Ag 22,17:3
Pinsky, Morris Mrs, 1943, Je 19,13:5
Pinson, Jacob D, 1957, Jl 6,15:1
Pinson, Koppel S, 1961, F 6,23:1
Pinson, R A Col, 1873, My 18,1:7
Pintard, William A, 1951, F 8,23:7
Pintcher, Nicholas C, 1949, O 12,30:4
Pinten, Joseph G, 1945, N 7,23:4
Pinter, Bruce E, 1944, D 5,23:6
Pinter, William S, 1950, O 10,31:4
Pintler, H E, 1946, Ap 27,17:2
Pintner, Rudolf, 1942, N 8,51:3
Pintner, Rudolph Mrs, 1967, My 28,60:8
Pinto, A S, 1944, D 8,21:2
Pinto, Benjamin, 1941, D 9,31:4
Pinto, Francisco J, 1942, My 9,13:5
Pinto, John C, 1956, S 26,33:4
Pinto, Joseph F, 1958, Ag 21,25:5
Pinto, Joshua A, 1960, Mr 18,26:5
Pinto, Liberato, 1949, S 6,27:5
Pinto, Mary A Mrs, 1943, My 20,21:4
Pinto, Michael F, 1965, Mr 24,43:4
Pinto, Octavio, 1950, N 16,31:1
Pinto, Oreste, 1961, S 20,29:1
Pinto, Salvatore, 1966, O 8,31:5
Pinto, William A Mrs, 1951, S 4,27:4
Pintt, J B, 1937, F 26,21:2
Pinza, Ezio (funl plans, My 10,27:5; funl, My 12,-86:3), 1957, My 9,1:1
Pinzino, Russell F (T Speno), 1959, Je 24,31:3
Pio, Padre (Francesco Forgione), 1968, S 24,47:2
Pioch, Otto M, 1944, My 13,19:1
Piollon, Harry C, 1949, N 26,15:2
Pione, Joseph M, 1948, N 11,27:5
Piontkowski, Adalbert J, 1958, Ja 3,23:2
Piossek, Alois, 1953, Ag 29,17:4
Piot, Jean, 1948, Je 6,72:4
Piotrowski, Maj, 1871, My 20,2:4
Pipal, Joseph A, 1955, Ag 12,19:2
Pipala, Ino, 1953, S 23,14:6
Pipe, Charles R, 1960, O 14,33:4
Pipe, Edward F, 1948, S 22,31:4
Piper, Alex R, 1952, N 22,23:4
Piper, Alexander Mrs, 1944, Je 13,19:5
Piper, Augustus A, 1941, O 16,21:6
Piper, Augustus B, 1937, F 20,17:5
Piper, Barton L, 1937, O 15,23:3
Piper, Charles M, 1946, Ap 24,25:1
Piper, Charles R, 1961, Ja 13,29:3
Piper, Clayton L, 1958, N 14,27:2
Piper, Dan, 1961, My 30,33:1
Piper, Edwin, 1951, O 19,27:1
Piper, Edwin F, 1939, My 19,21:5
Piper, Frederick P, 1937, Ag 29,II,6:5
Piper, G W, 1880, Mr 28,7:3
Piper, Giles S, 1939, F 23,23:3
Piper, Harold Mrs, 1950, Mr 23,36:3
Piper, Henry, 1951, Ag 21,27:1
Piper, Henry A, 1941, Ja 8,19:3
Piper, Henry H, 1942, Ap 10,17:2
Piper, Homer A, 1968, N 19,40:7
Piper, James Sr, 1965, My 20,43:3
Piper, John S, 1952, D 31,15:4
Piper, Lawrence F, 1945, Ap 13,17:4
Piper, R Foster, 1955, Ag 19,19:3
Piper, Ralph E Sr, 1950, Je 30,23:2
Piper, Ralph R, 1962, F 17,19:2
Piper, Rulett V, 1952, Ag 18,17:1
Piper, Thomas Mrs, 1948, F 8,60:1
Piper, Thomas O, 1919, F 3,15:4
Piper, William R, 1910, D 26,7:5
Piper, William R Mrs, 1953, S 1,23:4
Piperoux, Rene P, 1964, S 29,43:2
Pipes, Walter L Mrs, 1945, N 30,23:2
Pipes, Warner L, 1942, Ja 22,17:2
Pipi, Michael G, 1944, Mr 14,19:2
Pipitone, Ruth P Mrs, 1938, Jl 18,13:4
Pipkin, Charles W, 1941, Ag 5,20:3
Pipkin, James J Mrs, 1954, Jl 15,27:5
Pipkin, Marvin Mrs, 1957, Ja 29,20:6
Piplani, Bal Mokand, 1954, Ja 21,31:3
Pipp, Walter C, 1965, Ja 12,37:3
Pippen, Rodger H, 1959, Je 9,37:5
Pipper, Arnold L, 1950, S 26,32:3
Pippin, Horace, 1946, Jl 7,36:3

Pippinger, Daniel W, 1952, Ap 6,88:1
Piquet, Charles J, 1943, Jl 11,35:2
Piquet, Charles J Mrs, 1943, Jl 26,19:4
Piquet, Samuel D, 1961, Ap 27,21:3
Piquett, louis, 1951, D 13,33:3
Pirandello, L, 1936, D 10,27:1
Pirandello, Luigi (Sra), 1959, D 19,27:2
Pirard, Charles Prof, 1916, Mr 6,13:5
Pirbright, H de Worms Baron, 1903, Ja 10,9:7
Pirelli, Piero, 1956, Ag 9,25:4
Pirie, Allan H, 1958, N 19,37:4
Pirie, Charles C, 1940, S 17,23:2
Pirie, Frederick W, 1956, O 4,33:4
Pirie, Gordon L, 1944, F 17,19:4
Pirie, Jack, 1955, Ja 21,23:3
Pirie, John H, 1944, Jl 5,17:6
Pirie, John T (funl), 1913, Ap 28,11:1
Pirie, John T, 1940, F 26,15:3
Pirie, John T 2d, 1951, D 13,33:2
Pirie, Lockwood M, 1965, My 6,39:3
Pirie, Margaret C, 1942, D 7,27:4
Pirie, Samuel C, 1938, Ag 12,17:3
Pirie, Samuel C Jr, 1963, Je 30,56:3
Pirie, Sarah L, 1944, F 15,17:4
Piriz Coelho, Ramon, 1960, My 30,17:2
Pirka, Joseph, 1942, S 8,23:3
Pirkner, Ernest H, 1957, My 23,33:5
Pirnce, John H Mrs, 1958, My 29,27:5
Pirnie, George, 1925, O 24,15:6
Pirnie, James, 1918, Je 7,13:6
Pirnie, Malcolm, 1967, F 25,27:3
Pirnie, Malcolm Mrs, 1964, Je 24,37:4
Pirnie, Nelson R, 1953, Je 29,21:2
Piro, Guido, 1960, Ap 24,88:5
Piron, Emil H, 1950, O 6,27:4
Pirone, A M Matthew Mrs, 1951, O 22,23:4
Pirone, Domenico, 1961, D 5,43:1
Pironneau, Andre, 1948, D 2,29:3
Pironneau, Emmanuel, 1949, My 17,26:3
Pirou, Gaetan, 1946, Mr 13,30:2
Pirow, Oswald, 1959, O 12,19:5
Pirretti, John N, 1963, D 22,34:3
Pirro, Vincent H, 1967, S 11,45:2
Pirrone, Frank, 1958, F 1,19:6
Pirrong, John F M, 1947, D 19,25:2
Pirsch, Peter T, 1954, Jl 16,21:3
Pirsson, Henry A, 1952, Mr 11,27:5
Pirsson, John W, 1903, S 8,7:6
Pirsson, Louis Valentine Prof, 1919, D 9,17:4
Pirtle, James S, 1966, Je 21,43:4
Pisa, Vito, 1966, Ag 12,31:2
Pisacano, Albert C, 1943, Ap 4,40:2
Pisacano, Salvatore Sr, 1948, Ja 1,23:1
Pisani, Adolfo, 1959, F 17,31:3
Pisani, Antonio, 1954, O 15,23:3
Pisani, J Alfredo, 1958, D 4,39:1
Pisani, Lorenzo M, 1955, F 24,27:4
Pisani, Victor, 1941, Ap 18,21:3
Pisar, Charles J, 1955, O 18,37:4
Pisarra, Vincent N, 1942, Ag 5,19:2
Pisarra, Vincent T, 1939, Je 11,44:4
Pisarra, Vincent T Mrs, 1956, Mr 28,31:5
Pisart, Fernand, 1942, Ja 21,17:3
Piscator, Erwin, 1966, Mr 31,39:5
Pischkittel, Louis, 1948, D 14,29:2
Pisciotta, Gaspare, 1954, F 10,3:6
Pisciotta, Vita Mrs, 1939, F 5,40:3
Pisculli, Joseph M, 1948, O 25,23:3
Pise, Charles C Rev, 1866, My 28,4:2
Pisek, Godfrey R Dr, 1921, Ja 20,9:4
Piselli, John H, 1964, Je 5,31:5
Piser, Alfred O, 1948, N 19,27:3
Pisis, Filippo de, 1956, Ap 3,29:5
Pisko, Ernest S, 1966, O 15,29:4
Pisko, Seraphine E Mrs, 1942, Jl 31,15:4
Piskorski, Abdon V, 1949, S 30,24:3
Pissarro, Lucien, 1944, Jl 13,17:4
Pissoort, Elizabeth P, 1958, D 5,32:1
Pistarini, Juan, 1956, My 31,27:5
Pistell, John N, 1951, Je 30,15:5
Pister, Jacob Rev Dr, 1914, O 9,9:4
Pistor, Ferdinand, 1949, N 30,27:4
Pistor, George E J, 1958, Mr 25,31:1
Pistorius, Ernest, 1939, D 16,17:5
Pita, Frank, 1944, Ag 25,13:6
Pitass, Alexander, 1944, Jl 31,13:6
Pitassy, Julius F, 1951, Ja 15,17:2
Pitbladdo, Guthrie, 1939, Ag 10,19:2
Pitcairn, Edward, 1937, Ja 31,II,8:7
Pitcairn, John, 1916, Jl 23,17:5
Pitcairn, Norman B (por), 1948, F 17,26:3
Pitcairn, Raymond, 1966, Jl 13,43:2
Pitcairn, Raymond (est acctg filed), 1967, O 13,41:8
Pitcairn, Robert, 1909, Jl 26,7:5
Pitcher, Carl C, 1950, O 25,35:4
Pitcher, Charles R Jr, 1950, Jl 26,25:6
Pitcher, Conrad N, 1951, Ag 5,72:3
Pitcher, Flora Mrs, 1948, O 30,15:1
Pitcher, Fred A, 1944, My 1,15:3
Pitcher, Ira D, 1941, Jl 25,15:4
Pitcher, John B, 1946, Ja 24,22:3
Pitcher, John D, 1949, N 19,17:5
Pitcher, Perley A, 1939, F 21,1:5
Pitcher, Perley A (will), 1940, F 15,40:3
Pitcher, Perley A Mrs, 1947, N 16,76:2
Pitcher, Ralph M, 1967, F 9,35:4
Pitcher, W L, 1954, F 14,94:2
Pitcher, William H Dr, 1872, Je 2,1:6
Pitcherelli, Frank P, 1952, S 3,29:4
Pite, William A, 1949, Ag 18,22:2
Pitfield, Robert L, 1942, O 4,52:4
Pitfield, Robert L Mrs, 1951, N 11,90:4
Pitfield, Ward C, 1939, Ja 12,19:5
Pitigliani, Fausto Mrs, 1948, Ja 10,15:5
Pitkin, Albert H, 1917, O 16,19:7
Pitkin, Albert J, 1905, N 17,9:5
Pitkin, Albert J Mrs, 1938, Ap 24,II,7:3
Pitkin, Charles L, 1939, D 19,26:2
Pitkin, Dwight L, 1968, O 22,47:2
Pitkin, E Winifred, 1960, Ja 4,29:1
Pitkin, Edgar S, 1921, Ap 22,13:6
Pitkin, Elliott W, 1942, D 21,23:1
Pitkin, Frederick E, 1910, Ja 10,9:2
Pitkin, George D, 1954, Ag 30,17:5
Pitkin, George P, 1943, S 4,15:5
Pitkin, H Le Roy, 1946, F 26,25:2
Pitkin, Harry S, 1942, O 28,23:4
Pitkin, James M, 1942, D 22,25:6
Pitkin, James S, 1950, Ag 17,27:2
Pitkin, John H, 1938, D 17,15:5
Pitkin, LeRoy Brinckerhoff, 1968, Ap 15,43:2
Pitkin, Walter B, 1953, Ja 26,19:1
Pitkin, Walter B Mrs, 1943, O 15,19:1
Pitkin, Ward C, 1940, My 4,17:5
Pitkin, William Mrs, 1903, Jl 3,9:6
Pitkin, William R, 1938, Ap 7,23:4
Pitkin, Wolcott H, 1952, Ag 19,23:1
Pitkow, Harry M, 1959, O 24,21:5
Pitkow, Jerome D, 1968, Jl 9,35:3
Pitkowsky, Moses, 1954, Ja 1,23:5
Pitler, Harry (J Ray), 1961, Jl 17,21:2
Pitler, Jake (Jacob A Pitler), 1968, F 4,81:1
Pitman, Benn, 1910, D 29,9:5
Pitman, Clarence A, 1942, Ja 26,15:4
Pitman, Frank W, 1949, Ap 13,29:4
Pitman, George D, 1946, F 28,23:5
Pitman, I Sir, 1897, Ja 23,7:4
Pitman, J R, 1933, Ag 30,19:4
Pitman, J S, 1883, S 17,5:5
Pitman, James H, 1958, O 3,29:4
Pitman, James J, 1961, F 11,23:5
Pitman, John H, 1952, S 25,31:4
Pitman, John P, 1957, Jl 12,21:1
Pitman, John R, 1950, Je 18,76:2
Pitman, John R Mrs, 1945, N 28,27:5
Pitman, Joseph A, 1952, Ag 31,45:2
Pitman, Lord, 1941, F 12,21:4
Pitman, Mark, 1905, D 4,9:6
Pitman, Richard, 1941, N 14,23:3
Pitman, Richard Mrs, 1937, S 28,23:2
Pitman, William R, 1914, O 5,11:5
Pitney, Elizabeth V Mrs, 1941, O 3,23:3
Pitney, Freeman S, 1955, Ag 12,19:5
Pitney, Henry C, 1911, Ja 11,13:5
Pitney, John M, 1950, Ap 3,23:4
Pitney, John O H Mrs, 1943, D 18,15:1
Pitney, Mahlon (funl, D 11,23:4), 1924, D 10,23:3
Pitney, Mary B, 1944, N 10,19:3
Pitney, Robert H, 1944, Je 3,13:1
Pitney, Shelton, 1946, Ja 14,19:3
Pitoeff, Georges, 1939, S 19,26:3
Pitoeff, Ludmilla, 1951, S 16,84:5
Piton, Eugene, 1912, Je 6,11:4
Pitou, Augustus, 1915, D 5,3:6; 1957, N 19,33:5
Pitou, Augustus Mrs, 1952, S 13,17:6
Pitou, Eugene, 1956, D 22,19:3
Pitou, George Washington, 1912, N 5,13:5
Pitou, Maurice I, 1946, O 4,23:4
Pitou, Spire Sr, 1946, O 28,27:4
Pitsonis, Joseph, 1944, N 22,19:2
Pitt, Addison, 1968, F 4,80:7
Pitt, Alfred Scott, 1918, O 2,13:4
Pitt, Archie, 1940, N 13,23:6
Pitt, Arthur I, 1966, D 8,47:4
Pitt, David A, 1949, N 8,31:5
Pitt, Edith, 1966, Ja 28,47:5
Pitt, Fanny A Mrs, 1937, Ja 10,II,9:2
Pitt, George I, 1948, Mr 13,15:6
Pitt, Gilbert, 1947, My 13,27:6
Pitt, Gracie, 1948, Ja 6,25:3
Pitt, Harry A, 1955, Ag 4,25:1
Pitt, Jimmy, 1965, N 22,37:2
Pitt, Louis W, 1959, Ap 3,27:1
Pitt, Margaret B, 1947, Ja 10,21:3
Pitt, Melvin, 1952, Ja 4,23:5
Pitt, Robert H Rev Dr, 1937, F 16,23:5
Pitt, W Raymond, 1949, Ag 14,69:1
Pitt, William E, 1952, Mr 24,25:5
Pitt, William H, 1945, My 7,17:1
Pitt, William P, 1950, Je 1,27:3
Pitt-Taylor, Walter, 1950, N 23,35:4
Pitta, John C S Dr, 1937, D 12,II,8:7
Pittard, Boley, 1967, Je 11,V,24:3
Pittarelli, Emilio, 1949, D 2,29:4
Pittaro, Vito M Dr, 1942, D 23,10:2
Pittenger, Howard L, 1950, Ag 15,29:2
Pittenger, James E, 1950, Ag 29,27:1
Pittenger, Lemuel A, 1953, Jl 14,27:4
Pittenger, Ralph R, 1954, Ap 30,23:2
Pittenger, William A, 1951, N 27,31:2
Pittinger, Harry H, 1938, N 19,17:6
Pittini, Ricardo, 1961, D 11,31:3
Pittman, Annette R, 1941, S 9,23:4
Pittman, Charles, 1942, O 25,46:2
Pittman, Charles R, 1953, O 6,29:6
Pittman, Eli, 1946, O 24,28:2
Pittman, Henry H, 1944, Ja 3,21:1
Pittman, Henry H Mrs, 1940, N 5,25:1
Pittman, John H Mrs, 1950, O 6,27:4
Pittman, Joseph T, 1946, Mr 24,46:6
Pittman, Key, 1940, N 11,1:3
Pittman, Key Mrs, 1952, N 15,17:4
Pittman, Marvin S, 1954, F 28,92:5
Pittman, Milan L Sr, 1957, S 15,84:8
Pittman, Ora Story Mrs, 1949, Jl 19,29:3
Pittman, Raymond E Mrs, 1945, Mr 24,17:2
Pittman, Raymond L Jr, 1952, Ap 17,29:5
Pittman, Thomas W, 1916, Mr 24,11:7
Pittman, Vail M, 1964, Ja 30,29:2
Pittman, William H, 1941, S 8,15:2
Pittner, Jacob, 1951, N 7,29:5
Pittock, Henry L, 1919, Ja 30,13:3
Pittoni, Angelo, 1960, My 16,31:5
Pitts, Charles E, 1955, Ap 16,19:2
Pitts, Clarence V R Mrs, 1947, Ag 21,23:4
Pitts, Frank B, 1945, N 9,19:1
Pitts, Friend, 1906, Je 17,9:6
Pitts, Harry F, 1953, Mr 6,23:3
Pitts, Herman C, 1960, Ag 7,61:5
Pitts, Llewellyn W, 1967, Je 25,69:1
Pitts, R, 1878, N 24,1:7
Pitts, ZaSu (Mrs Jno E Woodall), 1963, Je 8,25:2
Pittsford, Marion J, 1949, Ag 8,15:1
Pittuck, A A, 1904, Ja 4,9:6
Pitz, John F, 1943, O 18,15:2
Pitzele, Joseph M, 1958, Ap 29,29:5
Pitzer, Melville W, 1955, F 17,27:1
Pitzipio, G D, 1884, Ap 12,5:3
Piucci, Virginio Mrs, 1945, Mr 10,17:3
Pius, E, 1948, F 6,23:4
Pius, William B, 1963, N 4,35:2
Pius Patrick, Bro (P Dunne), 1956, D 3,29:3
Pius X, Pope (funl, Ag 29,9:3), 1914, Ag 23,13:1
Pius XI, 1939, F 10,1:8
Pius XII, Pope (Eugenio Pacelli),(funl rites; will, O 11,1:6,8), 1958, O 9,1:8
Pivarnick, Louis, 1922, Je 8,19:5
Pivarnik, Joseph A, 1951, Mr 20,29:2
Pivirotto, Carlo A, 1958, Ja 11,17:3
Pivnick, Barney R, 1962, N 7,39:5
Piwonka, Charles, 1943, My 31,17:3
Pixley, Albert J, 1954, Jl 21,16:3
Pixley, Emery C, 1945, Ap 20,19:5
Pixley, Frank, 1920, Ja 1,15:2
Pixley, Henry D, 1960, D 12,29:4
Pixley, Lloyd A, 1954, Ag 1,84:6
Pixton, Marvin F, 1957, My 16,31:2
Piza, Alvin Mrs, 1957, O 3,29:2
Piza, Samuel E, 1961, D 26,25:3
Pizarro, Fernando Mrs, 1940, Ja 10,12:5
Pizarro, Miguel, 1956, Ja 12,27:4
Pizitz, Louis, 1959, Je 23,33:4
Pizza, Santo, 1950, F 13,21:5
Pizzella, John Mrs, 1924, N 15,13:5
Pizzetti, Ildebrando, 1968, F 14,47:3
Pizzi, Emilio, 1940, N 29,21:4
Pizzi, Frederick A, 1959, N 22,86:8
Pizzini, Andrew J, 1962, My 31,27:3
Pizzini, B Winthrop Sr, 1967, S 11,45:4
Pizzirulli, Fred Mrs, 1948, Ja 23,23:2
Pizzo, John F, 1952, My 11,93:1
Pizzoni, Alfredo, 1958, Ja 5,86:4
Pizzuti, Michele, 1938, My 31,19:3
Pkhaladze, Mikhail (Melkhisedek III), 1960, Ja 17, 86:5
Pla y Deniel, Enrique Cardinal, 1968, Jl 6,21:4
Pla y Martin, Francisco, 1944, Ag 19,11:4
Placa, James A, 1953, O 26,21:1
Place, Charles A, 1940, N 19,24:2
Place, Charles A Capt, 1919, My 3,15:6
Place, Charles E S, 1957, My 12,87:1
Place, Charles H, 1954, S 12,85:2
Place, Charles W, 1919, My 1,17:6
Place, Clyde R (por), 1946, Mr 29,23:1
Place, E Eugene, 1952, D 7,88:5
Place, Frank, 1959, S 9,41:1
Place, Fred C, 1949, My 26,29:2
Place, Frederick E, 1941, Jl 14,13:5
Place, Frederick R Mrs, 1948, Ap 2,23:2
Place, George, 1955, D 23,18:2
Place, George Morris, 1921, Ap 27,17:4
Place, Homer D, 1950, Mr 19,95:3
Place, I A, 1928, Ja 25,1:4
Place, John S, 1948, D 5,92:4
Place, Joseph V, 1950, O 17,31:1
Place, Josiah W, 1952, Ap 19,15:6
Place, Louis V Jr (por), 1947, S 9,32:2
Place, N, 1878, Ja 29,5:2
Place, Nelson Jr, 1881, Jl 9,5:3
Place, Perley O, 1946, F 11,29:4

Place, Willard F, 1961, Ag 20,86:2
Place, William D, 1945, My 17,19:4
Place, William H Jr, 1959, N 12,35:3
Place, William T, 1945, Je 8,19:2
Plachy, Joseph (est appr), 1965, My 1,62:7
Placide, Henry, 1870, Ja 24,5:5
Placide, T, 1877, Jl 22,8:4
Plack, William L, 1944, Ag 29,17:2
Placzek, Siegfried (por), 1946, Mr 9,14:2
Plage, Frederick, 1946, Ag 23,19:4
Plage, Martin F, 1944, My 23,23:4
Plage, William H, 1941, S 24,23:4
Plager, Heyman, 1952, D 4,35:4
Plager, Max Z, 1963, Ap 18,35:5
Plagwit, Eric, 1952, Ap 15,56:4
Plaisted, Frederick A (por), 1946, My 2,21:1
Plaisted, Frederick W, 1943, Mr 5,17:1
Plaisted, Howard H, 1957, O 5,17:1
Plaisted, Ralph P Judge, 1914, Je 24,11:2
Plakhin, Andre I, 1957, Je 9,88:8
Plamer, G H, 1933, My 8,15:4
Plamondon, Alfred D, 1941, My 5,17:2
Plamondon, Alfred D Jr, 1965, O 29,43:2
Plamondon, Charles A, 1958, O 8,35:3
Planas, Bernabe Gen, 1913, N 13,11:5
Planche, J R, 1880, My 31,5:4
Planches, Edmondo Mayor des Baron, 1920, D 28,11:5
Planck, Max, 1947, O 5,68:1
Planco, Gussie P Mrs, 1943, Jl 1,19:5
Plancon, Pol Henri, 1914, Ag 13,9:6
Plane, William F Mrs, 1925, Ap 25,15:4
Planel, Henry, 1872, F 16,2:7
Planer, Charles P, 1952, Ag 24,88:2
Planer, Joseph J, 1955, Mr 10,27:4
Planer, Louis M, 1968, My 18,33:2
Planer, Max, 1958, N 12,27:3
Planer, Paul, 1954, D 22,23:3
Planeta, Paul H, 1955, Ap 16,19:5
Planiol, Andre P E, 1955, Jl 1,21:1
Planitz, Horst A Von Der, 1941, Je 14,17:2
Plank, Earl A, 1952, O 2,29:3
Plank, Edward R Dr, 1937, Mr 14,II,9:2
Plank, Ethel Mrs, 1966, Je 19,71:3
Plank, Howard J, 1949, Ag 16,23:2
Plank, Howard Mrs, 1963, My 23,37:5
Plank, Ira D, 1951, S 15,15:3
Plank, William B, 1956, Je 21,31:5
Plankey, Harold J, 1940, Jl 13,13:6
Plankington, William, 1905, Ap 30,7:6
Plankinton, Walter K, 1948, N 17,27:4
Planquette, Robert, 1903, Ja 29,9:6
Plansoen, Hector, 1954, My 15,15:4
Plant, Arthur A Mrs, 1944, Mr 17,17:4
Plant, Edward J, 1940, Mr 1,21:4
Plant, Edward J Mrs, 1939, My 28,III,7:2
Plant, Francis G, 1940, Mr 30,15:4
Plant, George Mrs, 1965, Jl 5,17:6
Plant, George R, 1951, Ag 12,76:5
Plant, Henry B (funl), 1899, Je 24,1:5
Plant, Henry B, 1938, F 22,21:6
Plant, James S, 1947, S 8,21:3
Plant, John D, 1954, F 21,68:4
Plant, Mildred E, 1956, N 21,27:6
Plant, Morton F Com (funl, N 6,17:3), 1918, N 5,13:2
Plant, Morton F Mrs, 1913, Ag 8,7:7
Plant, Oscar H, 1939, O 2,17:4
Plant, Phil M, 1941, Je 19,21:1
Plant, Philip M (will), 1945, Mr 21,16:2
Plant, Robert W, 1940, O 14,19:2
Plant, Thomas C, 1941, Jl 26,16:6
Plant, Thomas G Mrs, 1947, Je 5,25:2
Plant, Woodford H, 1950, Mr 25,13:4
Plantamour, Emile, 1882, S 15,2:7
Plante, C Bertram, 1959, N 27,26:6; 1968, Ap 9,47:1
Plante, John T, 1960, F 26,9:1
Plante, Stuart B, 1952, Ja 2,25:2
Planteau, Emile, 1917, Mr 15,11:4
Planten, John R, 1912, D 9,11:4
Planten, W Ruters J, 1945, Mr 24,17:4
Plantenga, Jan H, 1942, N 26,27:5
Planteroth, Daniel G, 1948, Ag 6,17:4
Plantz, Laura M Dr, 1923, My 25,21:5
Plantz, Samuel Dr, 1924, N 15,13:5
Plaschke, Paul A, 1954, F 14,92:1
Plaskett, John S (por), 1941, O 18,19:1
Plaskow, Maude, 1955, Mr 24,32:1
Plass, Dudley, 1942, O 27,25:3
Plass, Frank L, 1948, S 2,23:4
Plass, George F, 1961, F 15,35:5
Plass, Harold, 1950, Ap 29,15:3
Plass, J Loring, 1945, F 20,19:3
Plass, John W Mrs, 1943, Je 13,45:1
Plass, Ludwig A, 1952, Ap 10,29:3
Plass, Van Ness, 1946, Jl 5,19:4
Plass, Webster, 1952, Ag 18,17:2
Plasschaert, Henry F, 1940, D 14,17:1
Plasse, Henry, 1941, F 9,48:1
Plassmann, Thomas, 1959, F 14,21:2
Plastino, Frank, 1948, Ag 8,56:6
Plastiras, Nicholas, 1953, Jl 27,19:3
Platak, Joe, 1954, N 9,27:5
Plate, A S Mrs, 1882, Jl 15,3:4
Plate, George, 1914, F 5,9:5
Plate, H Robinson, 1941, Ja 6,15:5
Plate, Harold F Mrs, 1946, S 8,44:7
Plate, Louis, 1939, S 30,17:4
Plate, Peter, 1938, Je 7,23:4
Plate, William, 1937, F 7,II,8:7
Platen-Hallermund, Count, 1943, Jl 28,15:5
Plater, Richard Jr Mrs, 1937, Ag 11,24:3
Plater-Syberg, Casimir de, 1963, D 18,37:7
Plath, William, 1952, Ag 15,15:4
Plati, Joseph, 1947, O 9,25:4
Platky, Ira Mrs, 1942, S 4,23:4
Platner, C H, 1927, Je 7,29:3
Platner, Harold, 1946, D 26,25:4
Platner, John Winthrop Dr, 1921, Mr 19,11:6
Platner, Leon W, 1942, D 3,25:2
Platner, Samuel Ball Dr, 1921, Ag 23,15:6
Platnick, Samuel, 1957, Mr 28,31:6
Platoff, John N, 1954, Ag 10,19:2
Platon, Archbishop, 1934, Ap 21,15:3
Platova-Jaffe, Helene Mme, 1958, Ja 26,88:5
Platowsky, Harry C, 1946, F 9,13:3
Platt, Albert E, 1948, Ap 10,13:3
Platt, Arthur S, 1963, D 4,47:1
Platt, Bertha, 1952, Ja 1,25:5
Platt, C A, 1933, S 14,23:5
Platt, C E (Jack), 1950, D 11,25:4
Platt, C H Rev, 1869, F 26,5:2
Platt, Charles A Mrs, 1953, N 27,27:3
Platt, Charles B, 1962, Jl 25,33:4
Platt, Charles C, 1967, D 7,52:1
Platt, Charles F, 1951, O 24,31:2
Platt, Charles Howard, 1921, F 12,13:5
Platt, Chester C Jr, 1944, Jl 2,20:1
Platt, Dan F, 1938, My 7,15:3
Platt, David, 1948, Jl 28,23:2
Platt, E Cuthbert Lt, 1917, N 16,11:4
Platt, E R Col, 1884, Je 18,4:7
Platt, Edgar K Sr, 1952, D 28,49:1
Platt, Edith H, 1902, D 7,8:2
Platt, Edmund, 1939, Ag 28,19:3
Platt, Edward C, 1924, S 16,23:5
Platt, Edward L, 1966, N 8,39:3
Platt, Edward Truex, 1918, F 28,9:4
Platt, Elizabeth F, 1948, F 7,15:3
Platt, Elizabeth T, 1943, My 23,42:6
Platt, Ellen Barstow, 1907, F 18,9:6
Platt, Elroy S, 1903, N 7,3:2
Platt, Emilie L, 1960, S 15,37:2
Platt, Estelle, 1950, D 1,25:2
Platt, Ethel S Mrs, 1953, Ja 20,25:1
Platt, Eugene, 1960, F 16,37:2
Platt, Frank, 1955, Jl 10,72:8
Platt, Frank E Mrs, 1949, Mr 16,27:2
Platt, Frank H Mrs, 1964, Mr 3,35:3
Platt, Frank Henry, 1925, Ap 29,21:6
Platt, Frank Hinchman, 1920, Mr 31,11:5
Platt, Frederick, 1918, Ja 17,13:3
Platt, Frederick G Mrs, 1954, Ja 24,85:2
Platt, Frederick J Mrs, 1951, N 15,29:1
Platt, Frederick P (cor, Mr 29,29:1), 1955, Mr 28,27:5
Platt, G W, 1881, Ap 4,5:3
Platt, Gardiner Mrs, 1960, Jl 23,19:4
Platt, George F Jr, 1951, N 11,91:1
Platt, George G Dr, 1937, Ja 9,17:5
Platt, George W, 1951, D 22,15:5; 1961, Mr 18,23:3
Platt, Harold B, 1951, Mr 1,27:2
Platt, Harry A, 1943, Mr 11,21:4
Platt, Harry H, 1947, D 24,21:3
Platt, Henry B, 1938, O 21,23:5
Platt, Henry B Mrs, 1907, Jl 15,7:7
Platt, Henry Clay, 1904, D 18,7:7
Platt, Henry L, 1956, N 22,33:2
Platt, Henry W, 1955, N 23,23:5
Platt, Howard V, 1945, F 28,24:2
Platt, Ida R Mrs, 1938, Mr 11,19:3
Platt, Isaac, 1956, D 11,39:5
Platt, Isaac Hull Dr, 1912, Ag 16,9:6
Platt, Isaac S, 1904, N 16,9:3
Platt, J A, 1925, Mr 17,21:5
Platt, J Curtis, 1950, Mr 20,21:1
Platt, J Curtis Mrs, 1944, S 16,13:5
Platt, J H, 1931, Jl 31,17:3
Platt, J Wood, 1959, D 10,39:4
Platt, James B, 1909, Ap 16,9:3
Platt, James B Judge, 1913, Ja 27,9:4
Platt, Jesse, 1914, Jl 25,7:5
Platt, John, 1942, Ap 28,21:6; 1946, Ja 25,23:1
Platt, John I, 1907, My 7,9:5
Platt, John James, 1917, F 17,11:6
Platt, John N, 1953, My 7,31:3
Platt, John O, 1947, Jl 12,13:6
Platt, Joseph, 1962, Je 8,31:5
Platt, Joseph B, 1968, F 8,49:3
Platt, Lewis C, 1913, F 23,II,7:2
Platt, Livingston, 1968, N 11,47:3
Platt, Mark C, 1958, Ag 11,21:4
Platt, Milton J, 1914, F 13,9:6
Platt, Nathaniel, 1951, My 25,27:3
Platt, Norman H, 1940, S 12,25:4
Platt, Orville H, 1905, Ap 22,1:3
Platt, Percy E, 1944, Ap 9,34:2
Platt, Randall M, 1951, D 19,31:1
Platt, Reuben B, 1948, N 24,24:2
Platt, Richard B, 1952, O 15,31:1
Platt, Robert Com, 1910, D 8,13:3
Platt, Robert S, 1964, Mr 2,27:3
Platt, Roger, 1948, Jl 19,19:2
Platt, Roger Mrs, 1960, My 23,29:3
Platt, S R, 1884, D 3,2:3
Platt, Samuel C Capt, 1913, Ap 5,15:4
Platt, Sanford L, 1967, Ag 10,37:4
Platt, Theodora, 1948, S 13,21:5
Platt, Thomas C Ex-Sen, 1910, Mr 10,9:3
Platt, W P Justice, 1926, N 3,23:3
Platt, Walter F, 1953, S 28,25:5
Platt, William L, 1946, F 15,25:2
Platt, William W, 1952, Ja 6,93:1
Platt, William Woodbury Rev Dr, 1916, F 11,11:6
Platte, Frederick A, 1953, N 15,89:2
Platte, Harry J, 1947, Jl 21,17:4
Platte, Henry, 1937, N 12,21:3
Platten, John W, 1954, N 6,17:6
Platten, John W Mrs, 1960, Je 19,88:3
Platter, Richard C Mrs, 1961, Jl 5,33:4
Platz, Theodore A, 1964, Jl 13,29:6
Platzek, M W, 1932, Jl 22,15:1
Platzer, Frank Mrs, 1947, Ag 6,23:6
Platzer, Otto, 1944, O 23,19:5
Platzer, Samuel Mrs, 1967, Ap 29,35:3
Platzker, Joseph, 1968, Ag 18,89:1
Platzker, Philip H, 1967, Ja 8,88:7
Plaunt, Alan B, 1941, S 13,17:2
Plaut, Albert, 1915, Je 19,9:6
Plaut, Alfred, 1962, O 1,31:1
Plaut, Carl S, 1944, Ap 28,19:3
Plaut, Harry J D, 1937, F 14,II,8:5
Plaut, Irving E, 1963, My 30,17:1
Plaut, Joseph, 1949, Ap 9,17:2
Plaut, Leo M, 1950, N 4,17:6
Plaut, Leopold, 1947, D 22,21:4
Plaut, Leopold Mrs, 1954, Je 3,27:1
Plaut, Leopold S Mrs, 1955, Ag 10,25:1
Plaut, Moses, 1950, Je 3,15:3
Plaut, Samuel, 1951, Mr 13,31:2
Plaut, Seymour, 1947, Je 14,15:5
Plaut, Theodore Mrs, 1941, Ag 8,15:3
Plaut, Walter H, 1964, Ja 4,23:3
Plaxton, Iola M R, 1948, Ja 16,21:4
Player, John D, 1950, Ap 7,25:1
Player, William O Jr, 1951, Mr 31,15:3
Playfair, Arthur, 1918, Ag 29,7:3
Playfair, C H, 1947, Ag 14,23:2
Playfair, James, 1937, My 26,25:2
Playfair, Lady, 1948, Je 10,25:5
Playfair, Lord, 1939, D 27,21:5
Playfair, N, 1934, Ag 20,13:4
Playfair, Robert S, 1948, Ag 15,60:3
Playfair, W E (Bill), 1953, S 10,25:3
Playfair, W S Dr, 1903, Ag 14,7:2
Plaza, Billy, 1959, O 24,21:7
Pleadwell, Theodosia Mrs, 1938, Jl 5,17:2
Pleasant, John J, 1952, Ap 11,23:1
Pleasant, John L, 1958, My 30,21:2
Pleasant, R B, 1937, F 13,13:2
Pleasant, Richard, 1961, Jl 6,29:3
Pleasant, Ruffin G, 1937, S 13,21:6
Pleasanton, A Gen, 1897, F 18,7:5
Pleasants, Cameron E, 1949, Jl 15,19:4
Pleasants, Frederick, 1939, O 20,23:2
Pleasants, Frederick Mrs, 1953, S 13,85:2
Pleasants, James J, 1950, Je 4,47:1
Pleasants, Mary E F Mrs, 1941, Jl 29,15:1
Pleasants, William H, 1919, Mr 19,11:3
Pleasure, Max A, 1965, D 7,47:2
Pleck, Joseph H, 1962, My 9,43:5
Pleck, von Gen, 1921, F 20,22:1
Pledger, Ben, 1948, D 17,27:4
Pledger, Dennis J, 1954, S 11,17:5
Plehn, Frank W, 1952, Ag 26,25:3
Plehn, Henry M, 1963, O 14,29:2
Plein, Leo N, 1964, Je 3,43:4
Pleiss, Paul, 1947, O 19,64:7
Pleister, Henry W, 1951, Ap 18,31:1
Plender, Lord, 1946, Ja 21,23:3
Plensler, Alex W, 1949, D 1,31:3
Plenti, Albert A Dr, 1968, Ja 12,27:1
Plenty, Charles L (Sept 21), 1965, O 11,61:4
Plenty, Coos, 1932, Mr 5,10:1
Plenty, Josephus, 1904, F 22,5:7
Plesch, Johann O, 1957, Mr 2,21:6
Pleschinger, Martin J, 1943, Mr 25,21:4
Pleshko, Nicholas, 1959, D 15,39:2
Pleshkoff, Michael, 1956, N 13,37:2
Plesman, Albert, 1954, Ja 1,23:1
Plesner, Levi J, 1944, My 17,21:2
Pless, Jean Henry Duke, 1907, Ag 15,7:6
Pless, Mary T O, 1943, Jl 3,13:1
Plessen, Leopold Mrs, 1949, S 4,40:8
Plessis, Wentzel D, 1957, Ap 1,25:5
Plessner, Theodore, 1946, S 7,15:3
Pletinckx, John L, 1955, Jl 20,27:2
Plettenberg, Karl von, 1938, F 13,II,7:1
Pletterer, Joseph, 1951, Jl 10,27:1
Pleus, Albert, 1954, Ja 24,84:4
Pleuthner, Walter K Mrs, 1957, Ja 15,17:5
Pleuthner, Willard A (Mar 13), 1963, Ap 1,36:4

Plevitskaia, La (N Skobline), 1940, O 5,15:4
Plew, Fred B Mrs, 1949, Ap 16,15:6
Plewacka, Catherine Mrs, 1942, N 26,27:1
Plewman, William R, 1963, S 25,43:1
Plews, William J, 1950, O 12,31:5
Pleydell-Bouverie, Alice Mrs (will, N 6,32:6), 1956, Jl 20,17:4
Pleydell-Bouverie, Audrey Evelyn Mrs, 1968, F 17, 29:5
Plievier, Theodor, 1955, Mr 14,23:2
Plimer, Walter J Sr, 1944, S 2,11:6
Plimley, William Maj, 1913, O 3,11:5
Plimmer, Harry, 1947, N 11,28:3
Plimmer, Walter J Rev, 1968, S 19,47:3
Plimpton, Albert, 1946, O 25,23:4
Plimpton, Bentley A, 1942, Ja 6,23:5
Plimpton, Fred J, 1959, Ja 6,33:2
Plimpton, G A, 1936, Jl 2,21:1
Plimpton, George A Mrs, 1950, Ag 2,25:4
Plimpton, George F, 1963, Ag 8,27:4
Plimpton, Helen S Mrs, 1937, Mr 14,II,8:6
Plimpton, John C, 1937, Mr 7,II,9:2
Plimpton, Lireus B, 1904, F 17,9:7
Plimpton, Samuel J, 1948, D 30,19:3
Plimsoll, Samuel, 1898, Je 4,7:1
Pliska, Joseph S, 1940, Ag 26,15:5
Pliskin, Jacob, 1959, O 16,31:2
Plisnier, Charles, 1952, Jl 20,52:3
Plitnick, Frank, 1951, Ja 3,25:1
Plitnik, Frank Mrs, 1950, N 13,27:5
Plitt, E Alfred, 1946, Jl 6,15:3
Plitt, J Russell, 1946, O 15,25:1
Plitt, Norman Sr, 1954, F 2,27:4
Ploch, Charles J, 1958, Ag 25,21:3
Plocharski, Aug, 1942, F 15,44:4
Ploda, Jean Baptiste, 1914, D 2,13:5
Ploeser, Joseph, 1916, Je 3,13:4
Plofsky, Milton, 1940, Jl 23,19:4
Plog, William A, 1952, Ap 17,29:3
Plohn, Edmund, 1959, Je 9,37:4
Ploneis, Yves L, 1966, My 19,47:5
Plonk, J C, 1939, N 30,21:4
Plonley, Irving S Mrs, 1946, F 16,13:4
Plontier, Claude H A Bp, 1875, My 26,1:5
Plost, A Walter, 1959, D 17,37:5
Plotkin, A Louis, 1942, Je 11,23:4
Plotkin, Charles, 1963, Ag 31,17:5
Plotkin, David George (David Geo Kin), 1968, Ap 1,45:1
Plotkin, Ely, 1951, Mr 30,23:4
Plotkin, George, 1963, S 19,27:5
Plotkin, Harry, 1955, D 24,13:4
Plotkin, Hyman, 1961, Ag 27,85:1
Plotkin, Louis A Mrs, 1941, Jl 22,19:3
Plotkin, Oscar H, 1950, Mr 3,25:4
Plotle, Benjamin, 1949, My 5,27:5
Plotner, Chester A Mrs, 1950, Mr 22,27:3
Plotnick, Samuel, 1950, Ag 11,19:3
Plotnikoff, Eugene, 1951, S 29,17:4
Plotz, Harry, 1947, Ja 7,27:3
Plotz, Harry Dr, 1922, Ap 14,17:6
Plotz, Milton B, 1962, O 3,41:3
Plough, David H, 1960, Mr 5,19:1
Plough, Kenneth A, 1947, Ag 2,13:1
Plough, S Harly, 1942, Mr 14,15:5
Plowden, Roger S, 1960, S 27,37:1
Plowe, Robert, 1947, Ag 23,13:6
Plowitz, Paul, 1953, Mr 9,29:1
Plowman, Beulah W Mrs, 1937, Ja 11,20:3
Plowman, Gilbert, 1908, Ja 10,7:2
Plowman, Paul, 1959, N 10,47:4
Plowright, Joseph L, 1957, S 20,25:2
Pluchos, George, 1949, N 6,94:3
Plude, Grace R, 1949, F 26,15:3
Pluenacher, Charles F, 1923, Ag 14,15:4
Pluff, Louis E Mrs, 1953, Je 17,27:2
Plugge, Charles H Prof, 1915, Ap 16,13:4
Plugge, Ildephonse, 1949, O 26,27:1
Plum, David B Mrs, 1940, Jl 1,19:3
Plum, George H, 1939, Ap 25,23:5
Plum, George Willard, 1923, Mr 9,15:4
Plum, James R, 1909, D 11,11:3
Plum, Matthias, 1916, F 15,11:6
Plum, Stephen H 2d, 1954, F 18,31:1
Plum, T M Col, 1876, Ja 9,6:6
Plum, William T Mrs, 1961, S 27,41:3
Plumacher, Eugene H Col, 1910, S 27,13:5
Plumb, Charles S, 1939, Mr 5,49:1
Plumb, Eleanora D, 1950, D 29,19:4
Plumb, Fayette R, 1905, Ja 9,1:6; 1966, S 3,23:2
Plumb, Frank H, 1948, Ap 6,23:4
Plumb, George H Mrs, 1949, F 8,25:5
Plumb, Glen E, 1922, Ag 2,17:6
Plumb, Harold A, 1959, My 24,88:6
Plumb, Henry B, 1940, My 4,17:1
Plumb, John F, 1949, Ag 12,18:2
Plumb, Joseph H Sr, 1951, S 7,29:3
Plumb, Louis J, 1942, N 8,53:1
Plumb, Lucius H, 1966, D 15,47:1
Plumb, Lucius H Mrs, 1940, N 7,25:5
Plumb, P B Sen, 1891, D 21,1:7
Plumb, Ralph H, 1905, Je 12,9:5
Plumb, Robert H, 1961, Ja 5,31:5
Plumb, Ronald A, 1952, My 28,29:3
Plumb, T S, 1885, My 30,5:6
Plumb, W D, 1936, N 21,20:1
Plumb, William D, 1944, Mr 24,19:4
Plume, Alan C, 1958, S 13,19:2
Plume, Charles J, 1955, Ap 21,29:1
Plume, Hannah F, 1923, Ap 5,19:5
Plume, Joseph W Gen, 1918, Ja 13,21:1
Plume, William F, 1949, Ag 2,19:4
Plumer, Arnold, 1869, My 3,2:5
Plumer, Edward A, 1955, N 1,31:4
Plumer, Elizabeth, 1939, Mr 22,17:4
Plumer, George, 1872, Je 5,1:6
Plumer, Richard C, 1954, My 30,45:1
Plumer, Samuel, 1952, My 15,31:4
Plumer, Viscount, 1932, Jl 17,20:1; 1944, F 25,17:6
Plumeri, Joseph, 1950, My 14,106:7
Plumley, Audy, 1943, Mr 27,13:6
Plumley, Charles A, 1964, N 1,88:7
Plumley, Charles B, 1954, S 1,27:4
Plumley, Emily L, 1950, Mr 3,25:5
Plumley, Fletcher, 1965, Jl 6,33:3
Plumley, Frank, 1924, My 2,19:5
Plumly, Lindsay, 1950, Je 13,28:2
Plummer, Charles A, 1961, S 4,15:2
Plummer, Charles C, 1947, Ap 24,25:5
Plummer, Charles H, 1939, D 17,48:8
Plummer, Charles Warren Mrs, 1925, S 28,19:5
Plummer, Clyde I, 1947, S 17,25:4
Plummer, Daniel C, 1956, Jl 1,57:2
Plummer, E C, 1932, Mr 21,15:3
Plummer, Edmund, 1925, F 8,7:1
Plummer, Enfield Mrs, 1957, N 24,87:1
Plummer, Everett H, 1955, Jl 15,21:2
Plummer, Frank Myrell Dr, 1916, Ag 20,15:5
Plummer, Franklin A, 1945, O 31,23:5
Plummer, Georgia V Mrs, 1937, O 3,II,9:2
Plummer, Georgios W, 1944, Ja 25,19:4
Plummer, H C, 1946, O 2,29:3
Plummer, Henry S Dr, 1937, Ja 2,14:2
Plummer, Herbert C, 1955, My 8,88:6
Plummer, Howard A, 1960, Ap 20,39:2
Plummer, J Len, 1948, D 26,52:6
Plummer, John F, 1906, D 11,9:5; 1954, My 19,32:5
Plummer, John S, 1950, N 5,93:1
Plummer, L Flora Mrs, 1945, Ap 9,19:5
Plummer, Leslie A, 1963, Ap 17,41:3
Plummer, Lillian F Mrs, 1939, Jl 16,30:7
Plummer, Lucinda Jones Mrs, 1918, Mr 20,13:4
Plummer, Mary, 1916, S 22,7:4
Plummer, Morgan H, 1949, O 17,23:3
Plummer, Morgan Mrs, 1949, Je 28,27:4
Plummer, Ralph W, 1950, Ag 29,27:5
Plummer, Robert S, 1955, F 27,87:2
Plummer, S C, 1881, N 15,5:2
Plummer, Samuel V, 1952, N 22,23:3
Plummer, Seney, 1922, S 15,19:6
Plummer, Stanley D, 1957, F 13,35:5
Plummer, W G, 1880, O 23,2:7
Plummer, W P Mrs, 1941, Je 18,21:4
Plummer, William, 1942, My 30,15:2
Plummer, William A Justice, 1925, N 30,19:5
Plummer, William E, 1940, S 10,23:4
Plummer, William H, 1948, Ja 1,23:3
Plummer, William R Rev, 1923, Mr 1,15:3
Plummer, William T, 1945, Je 13,23:3
Plummer, William W, 1959, Ap 11,21:6
Plummer, William Ward, 1953, F 18,31:2
Plump, Eric M, 1953, N 8,89:3
Plumpton, Alfred, 1944, Jl 1,15:5
Plumridge, Charles E, 1954, F 6,19:2
Plumridge, Theodore E Jr, 1962, O 9,41:4
Plungian, Mikhail B, 1953, Ja 30,21:4
Plunket, Benjamin J, 1947, Ja 28,23:4
Plunket, Owen T, 1947, Ap 19,15:2
Plunkett, Albert W, 1957, Ap 21,88:3
Plunkett, Andrew J, 1939, Ap 16,III,7:3; 1941, Je 24, 19:5
Plunkett, Bernard F, 1942, Ja 26,15:6
Plunkett, C P, 1931, Mr 25,28:2
Plunkett, Charles T Jr, 1942, Ja 28,19:4
Plunkett, Charles T Mrs, 1941, Ag 21,17:2
Plunkett, Chris F, 1938, My 30,11:3
Plunkett, Chris J, 1938, S 8,23:2; 1939, Ag 18,19:5
Plunkett, Count, 1948, Mr 13,15:1
Plunkett, Edmund R, 1955, My 5,33:2
Plunkett, Edward J M D (Lord Dunsany), 1957, O 27,86:1
Plunkett, Edward M, 1948, Mr 14,73:2
Plunkett, F Scott, 1956, O 24,37:5
Plunkett, Flavius O, 1946, D 20,24:3
Plunkett, Francis, 1907, Mr 2,9:7
Plunkett, George J, 1937, Ag 27,19:4
Plunkett, Guy D, 1963, D 12,39:4
Plunkett, H Sir, 1932, Mr 27,II,5:3
Plunkett, Harold J, 1955, Jl 29,17:2
Plunkett, J L, 1875, O 7,4:6
Plunkett, James H, 1949, Ja 4,19:2
Plunkett, John, 1960, Ag 28,82:7
Plunkett, John E, 1953, Ja 13,27:3
Plunkett, John F, 1957, Mr 24,86:1
Plunkett, John F Mrs, 1954, Je 27,68:4
Plunkett, John J, 1942, D 23,19:3; 1948, Ja 23,24:3
Plunkett, John L, 1950, Je 3,15:5
Plunkett, Martin F, 1954, D 28,23:4
Plunkett, Mary J, 1951, O 31,29:1
Plunkett, Michael, 1939, D 10,52:7
Plunkett, Morley B, 1953, Ap 1,29:2
Plunkett, Richard M Col, 1919, O 30,13:2
Plunkett, Richard Mrs, 1947, N 19,27:1
Plunkett, Robert Andrew, 1922, D 21,15:3
Plunkett, Robert E, 1967, Jl 13,37:3
Plunkett, T (funl), 1885, Mr 11,1:6
Plunkett, T F, 1875, N 1,5:3
Plunkett, Theodore R, 1946, Ap 15,27:5
Plunkett, Thomas F, 1941, Jl 22,19:5
Plunkett, Thomas J, 1943, O 24,44:5
Plunkett, W R, 1903, D 9,9:5
Plunkett, William B, 1917, O 26,15:5
Plunkett, William C, 1940, Je 6,25:1; 1963, D 28,2
Plunkett-Ernie-Erle-Drax, Reginald, 1967, O 18,47
Plunkitt, George W, 1924, N 23,7:2
Pluta, Joseph Mrs, 1949, Je 4,13:3
Plutano (Wild man of Borneo), 1912, Je 1,11:4
Plutzik, Hyam, 1962, Ja 10,47:5
Plutzik, Samuel, 1956, Jl 29,65:2
Pluymert, Nicolaas J, 1955, O 11,39:5
Plyer, Arthur M, 1951, Jl 9,25:4
Plyer, William, 1938, Je 8,23:5
Plym, F J, 1940, Ja 13,16:8
Plymouth, Earl of (por), 1943, O 3,49:1
Plympton, Frank B, 1948, D 22,24:2
Plympton, George W Prof, 1907, S 13,7:6
Plympton, Gilbert M Mrs, 1904, F 12,9:6
Po-Li, Chiang, 1938, N 8,23:4
Poage, M Annie, 1938, Je 24,19:4
Poarch, Myron F, 1959, Ap 21,35:3
Pobe, George O, 1940, D 5,25:1
Pocaterra, Jose R, 1955, Ap 20,33:4
Poch, Jacob Mrs, 1946, S 6,21:4
Pochat, Louis G, 1953, S 17,29:6
Pochkhanawala, Sorabji Sir, 1937, Jl 5,17:5
Pochon, Alfred, 1959, F 28,19:6
Pochon-Jent, Frederic, 1950, O 9,25:2
Poci, Joseph Mrs, 1954, S 24,24:1
Pocker, Victor L, 1950, D 5,31:2
Pockmann, Philetus Theodore Dr, 1919, N 18,13:2
Pocock, Cyrene (C Van Gordon), 1964, Ap 6,31:
Pocock, James J, 1952, Ag 28,23:2
Pocock, Roger, 1941, N 14,23:2
Pocock, William M Mrs, 1953, Jl 19,56:4
Poda, Emil, 1949, S 10,17:5
Poda, Frank, 1944, Ap 27,23:3
Poda, Frank A Mrs, 1942, Ag 18,21:4
Podbielski, Viktor von Gen, 1916, Ja 26,11:2
Poddubny, Ivan M, 1949, Ag 11,24:6
Podell, David L (por), 1947, F 2,57:3
Podell, Maurice, 1967, Ag 6,76:7
Podell, Morris, 1967, Ag 4,29:1
Podesta, Frank, 1955, Mr 26,15:2
Podesta, Italo, 1964, Ag 17,25:3
Podesta, Lawrence Sr, 1947, My 6,28:2
Podeswa, Albert, 1951, N 10,17:5
Podeyn, George J, 1955, Mr 9,27:1
Podgorski, Ignacy, 1957, N 8,29:2
Podmajersky, John E, 1967, My 6,31:2
Podmore, Frank, 1910, Ag 20,7:4
Podmore, Thomas, 1948, Ag 15,60:3
Podolak, Walter, 1964, O 12,29:1
Podoll, Arthur C, 1962, My 3,33:2
Podolsky, David, 1945, D 23,18:2
Podolsky, Michael M, 1955, Jl 8,23:3
Podolsky, Nathan, 1950, Ag 22,23:8
Podowski, Victor, 1960, Ag 2,29:4
Podrasnik, Alois, 1937, S 1,19:4
Podrecca, Vittorio de, 1959, Jl 8,29:5
Podskoc, Joseph, 1949, Ag 9,25:4
Poduska, Frank Sr, 1953, Mr 24,31:2
Podway, Abraham, 1964, My 28,37:1
Podzelni, Richard S, 1959, S 28,31:5
Poe, Arthur, 1951, Ap 16,25:1
Poe, Clarence, 1964, O 9,39:1
Poe, E Holley, 1951, Mr 11,94:3
Poe, Edgar A, 1961, D 1,33:2
Poe, Elizabeth E, 1947, S 30,25:2
Poe, George Prof, 1914, F 4,9:6
Poe, Grace O, 1958, D 9,41:3
Poe, Gresham H, 1956, Ap 27,27:2
Poe, Harmon, 1966, Ja 22,29:2
Poe, J B, 1937, F 26,21:2
Poe, John P, 1909, O 15,11:5; 1968, Jl 5,25:2
Poe, Louis L, 1961, Je 5,31:2
Poe, Neilson, 1884, Ja 4,5:2
Poe, Net (Neilson Poe), 1963, S 23,29:3
Poe, O M Gen, 1895, O 3,8:4
Poe, Pascal, 1963, S 13,30:1
Poe, Reginald W, 1937, N 2,25:5
Poe, S J, 1933, Ap 12,19:4
Poe, Virgil C, 1956, Ap 22,85:5
Poe, William D, 1958, Ap 3,31:4
Poe-Eng Yu, 1958, Jl 29,23:5
Poebel, Arno, 1958, Mr 4,29:4
Poehler, Franklin, 1940, N 8,21:5
Poehlmann, Johanna, 1909, My 4,9:4
Poeller, Albert G, 1957, My 8,37:4
Poels, Henricus A, 1948, S 8,29:1

Poensgen, Carl E Rev, 1937, O 15,23:5
Poet, William E, 1953, Jl 9,25:5
Poeter, Ernest E, 1953, Ja 5,21:2
Poeterfield, William M Jr, 1966, Mr 27,86:4
Poethke, Charles, 1940, Ap 23,23:4
Poetker, Albert H, 1960, My 7,23:5
Poetsch, Leopold, 1942, O 18,53:2
Poetzl, Otto, 1962, Ap 4,43:2
Poffenbarger, Livia N Mrs, 1937, O 29,21:4
Poffenberger, Albert T Mrs, 1943, N 5,19:3
Poffenberger, Alvin C, 1957, N 30,21:2
Poffenberger, James C, 1954, Je 9,31:5
Pogany, Willy, 1955, Jl 31,69:1
Poggenburg, Emily Mrs, 1947, Jl 15,23:3
Poggenburg, George Mrs, 1966, My 25,47:1
Poggenburg, Paul, 1950, Je 22,27:4
Poggi, C Godfrey Mrs, 1942, Je 2,23:2
Poggi, C Godrey, 1957, F 16,17:6
Poggi, Edmund H, 1952, N 26,23:5
Poggi, Felice, 1941, N 5,23:5
Poggi, Giovanni, 1961, Mr 29,33:4
Poggiani, Joseph, 1939, Ap 18,23:6
Poggio, Joseph J, 1947, D 29,17:5
Poggioli, Renato, 1963, My 4,25:6
Pogia, Bp of (Mgr Racicot), 1915, S 15,9:5
Pognon, L L, 1914, S 10,9:6
Pogodin, Nikolai F (trb, S 30,II,1:1), 1962, S 20,33:1
Pogoneanu, Titus R, 1952, N 26,23:2
Pogson, Henry B, 1955, Mr 1,25:2
Pogson, Matthew Henry Rev Dr, 1918, My 25,13:4
Pogson, Percy W, 1956, Ag 4,15:3
Pogue, Cooper, 1938, Je 14,21:4
Pogue, Davenport, 1937, S 19,II,6:5
Pogue, Robert B, 1956, S 27,35:3
Pogue, Robert W, 1937, Ap 17,17:4
Pogue, Russell L, 1955, Jl 19,27:2
Pogue, Thomas L, 1947, O 28,25:3
Pogue, V Richard, 1945, Ag 3,17:2
Poh, Adam Jr, 1937, Ja 14,22:1
Pohl, Archibald W J, 1960, O 20,35:4
Pohl, Carl M, 1938, Je 4,15:2
Pohl, Elizabeth, 1938, Ap 6,23:4
Pohl, Frederick J, 1939, Je 4,49:2
Pohl, Hero J, 1951, Mr 27,29:4
Pohl, Hugo von Vice-Adm, 1916, F 25,11:7
Pohl, John C, 1951, N 1,29:3
Pohl, John G A, 1956, Ag 11,13:4
Pohl, Lydia D, 1946, Ap 28,42:4
Pohl, Samuel H, 1962, O 31,37:2
Pohl, William A, 1952, D 13,21:2
Pohle, Francis W, 1941, F 2,44:2
Pohle, Herman R, 1960, Ja 15,31:1
Pohle, Theodore T Mrs, 1954, D 17,31:2
Pohlers, Camillo A, 1950, Ag 17,23:2
Pohlers, Richard C, 1959, Ap 23,31:2
Pohlhaus, John M, 1947, My 9,22:2
Pohlig, Charles, 1937, Ja 3,II,8:4
Pohlman, Albert M, 1942, Ag 8,11:5
Pohlman, Arthur W, 1952, Ja 2,25:3
Pohlman, Aug, 1938, O 11,25:2
Pohlman, Augustus G, 1950, Ap 2,95:3
Pohlman, Fred C, 1949, Jl 20,25:4
Pohlman, Kenneth H, 1951, Jl 20,21:5
Pohlmann, Ernst, 1949, My 19,29:3
Pohlmann, Fredericka S Mrs, 1941, My 20,23:4
Pohlmann, Frieda, 1954, Ag 10,9:3
Pohlmann, George, 1946, My 9,21:6
Pohly, Albert, 1955, Ag 11,21:5
Pohn, Jacob S, 1945, Ag 12,39:2
Pohn, William L, 1955, Jl 6,27:2
Pohndorf, Henry, 1922, My 15,17:3
Pohndorff, Federico G, 1957, Mr 25,25:2
Pohs, Herbert J, 1967, My 22,43:2
Poillion, C C, 1881, Jl 13,5:4
Poillon, Arthur, 1948, F 6,26:7
Poillon, Arthur Mrs, 1962, Ja 28,76:2
Poillon, Charles F Jr, 1939, O 6,25:5
Poillon, Howard A, 1954, Ja 21,31:5
Poillon, K, 1935, S 20,23:6
Poillon, Richard H, 1925, Ag 2,5:5
Poillon, William, 1918, Ap 13,13:5
Poillon, William C, 1947, My 13,25:4
Poincare, Henri Jules (trb, Jl 19,9:6), 1912, Jl 18,9:4
Poincare, Lucien, 1920, Mr 10,11:4
Poincare, Mrs, 1913, Ap 12,11:4
Poincare, R, 1934, O 15,1:4
Poincare, Raymond Mrs, 1943, My 20,21:4
Poincenot, Jacques, 1952, Ja 3,2:7
Poindexter, Edwin L, 1954, D 23,19:2
Poindexter, Joseph B, 1951, D 4,33:3
Poindexter, Miles, 1946, S 22,63:3
Poinier, J Woods, 1914, Ja 28,9:5
Poinier, Phil C, 1949, O 31,25:3
Point, Fernand, 1955, Mr 6,88:4
Pointer, James D Mrs, 1941, Jl 2,21:2
Pointer, Robert R, 1937, F 12,23:2
Points, Frank W, 1947, D 31,15:2
Poire, Emmanuel (Caran d'Ache), 1909, F 27,9:4
Poiret, Paul (por), 1944, My 3,19:1
Poirier, Charles J, 1947, Je 13,24:3
Poirier, Hector, 1938, Ag 17,19:5
Poirier, J E, 1940, My 27,19:3
Poirier, Julien, 1939, Jl 25,9:4
Poisal, John, 1882, Je 26,1:6
Poitras, Nancy Mrs, 1939, O 5,23:2
Pokart, S Walter, 1952, N 13,31:1
Pokorny, Amos, 1949, Ag 20,11:5
Pokorny, Charles A, 1952, Jl 29,21:3
Pokorny, Jaroslav, 1958, S 2,25:4
Pokorny, Victor J, 1949, Je 18,13:6
Pokotiloff, M D, 1908, Mr 8,7:6
Pokras, Lewis, 1959, D 26,13:3
Pokrass, Louis I Mrs, 1960, Ag 1,23:6
Pokrass, Samuel, 1939, Je 16,23:4
Pokroisky, Louis, 1939, N 23,27:5
Pol, Henri, 1918, Je 19,11:5
Pol, Vincent, 1872, D 30,5:3
Pola, Angel, 1948, Ja 26,19:3
Polacco, Giorgio, 1960, My 2,29:1
Polachek, John, 1955, Ap 18,23:4
Polachek, Max Mrs, 1946, S 24,30:2
Polachek, Victor H, 1940, Je 12,25:3
Polack, Irving J, 1949, Jl 16,13:3
Polack, Isaac, 1952, Je 12,33:3
Polack, William G, 1950, Je 6,29:3
Polah, Andre, 1949, My 20,27:2
Polaire, Mlle, 1939, O 15,49:3
Polak, Archibald L, 1968, Jl 14,65:1
Polak, Edward, 1937, S 10,23:2
Polak, Henry, 1943, Mr 13,13:5
Polak, Henry B, 1953, Ja 14,31:1
Polak, Henry E Mrs, 1961, O 24,37:1
Polak, J O, 1931, Je 30,25:3
Polak, Michel, 1954, Mr 27,17:6
Polak, Nahum, 1958, D 3,37:4
Polakoff, Max, 1939, S 1,17:5
Polakoff, Murray Mrs, 1968, Mr 28,47:3
Polanco, Mario, 1950, N 12,93:1
Poland, Addison B Dr, 1917, S 16,18:7
Poland, Addison B Jr, 1967, My 25,42:7
Poland, Albert H, 1951, D 9,90:6
Poland, Bernard Mrs, 1958, O 26,88:6
Poland, Bernard V, 1955, My 16,23:4
Poland, Carter D Sr, 1961, My 18,35:5
Poland, Charles H, 1950, F 22,29:2
Poland, Charles J, 1962, N 25,86:8
Poland, Fred W Rev, 1937, Ap 16,23:1
Poland, George H, 1954, Jl 3,11:5
Poland, H Sir, 1928, Mr 4,26:6
Poland, John N, 1907, Mr 5,9:6
Poland, John R, 1952, D 18,29:4
Poland, Naph, 1962, Ap 28,25:5
Poland, William B, 1950, Je 28,27:2
Polaner, George, 1962, Mr 1,31:4
Polangin, Frederick N, 1956, Ja 4,27:4
Polansky, Mahlon, 1946, O 13,59:4
Polanyi, Karl, 1964, Ap 25,29:1
Polasek, Albin, 1965, My 20,43:1
Polatschek, Victor, 1948, Jl 28,23:6
Polayes, Silik H, 1962, Ag 26,83:1
Polcha, Stephen, 1953, D 29,25:5
Polcini, Ralph L, 1954, My 25,27:2
Poldervaart, Arie, 1964, O 29,35:4
Pole, Henry S 2d, 1953, S 12,17:4
Pole, Henry Stier Dr, 1913, D 30,9:5
Pole, John W, 1958, My 3,19:6
Pole, Vera, 1915, Mr 9,9:4
Polehemus, Peres B Mrs, 1944, S 19,21:3
Poleman, Horace I, 1965, N 8,35:5
Polenz, Wilhelm von, 1903, N 14,9:6
Poler, Amnon B, 1943, Ap 29,21:5
Poler, F Marion Mrs, 1948, S 14,29:3
Poleri, David S, 1967, D 14,47:1
Poleri, David S Mrs, 1967, D 14,47:1
Poletis, Gregory J, 1946, S 11,7:5
Polev, N P, 1955, Jl 21,23:5
Polevitzky, Boris A, 1950, D 7,33:3
Polewski, Joseph S, 1948, O 24,76:2
Poley, Morris, 1965, Ap 30,35:4
Poley, Phil, 1948, Je 11,23:2
Poleyeff, Moses A, 1966, N 16,47:2
Polgar, Alfred, 1955, Ap 25,23:2
Polglase, William, 1960, My 18,41:4
Polglase, William Austin Dr, 1915, My 8,15:5
Polgreen, Henry W, 1944, Je 23,19:5
Polhemus, Anna V Mrs, 1940, F 11,48:2
Polhemus, Caroline H Mrs (will), 1906, N 8,10:4
Polhemus, David A Mrs, 1953, Ap 13,27:2
Polhemus, Frederick S, 1963, Je 19,37:1
Polhemus, George E, 1949, O 27,28:2
Polhemus, George W, 1945, Jl 7,13:7
Polhemus, Halsey D, 1952, F 11,25:5
Polhemus, Henry W, 1917, O 14,23:4
Polhemus, James S Mrs, 1946, O 28,27:6
Polhemus, P Garretson, 1968, Je 27,43:5
Polhemus, Peter G, 1908, D 20,11:5
Polhemus, Piers G Mrs, 1944, My 7,45:2
Polhemus, William A, 1965, Ap 17,19:5
Polhenus, Eugene E, 1943, Ag 14,11:4
Polheumus, G Warren Mrs, 1951, N 5,31:2
Polhill, Cecil H, 1938, Mr 11,19:1
Polhill, Milton E, 1952, Ja 5,11:5
Poli, George, 1955, Mr 15,29:2
Poli, Joseph H Mrs, 1962, Ja 21,88:6
Poli, Oreste, 1940, S 13,23:4
Poli, Sylvester Z (will, Je 13,13:1), 1937, Je 1,23:3
Poli, Sylvester Z Mrs, 1960, Ja 6,35:4
Poliakoff, Alexander, 1942, O 4,41:2
Poliakoff, Vladimir (Augur), 1956, Je 6,33:3
Poliakoff-Litovtzeff, S, 1945, N 3,15:4
Poliakova, Nastia, 1947, O 21,23:3
Polich, Alexander, 1967, S 21,47:2
Polidoro, William Mrs, 1951, Ja 12,27:1
Polifeme, Augusta W Mrs, 1946, Ja 8,23:4
Polignac, Camille de Prince, 1913, N 16,IV,7:5
Polignac, Edmond de Princess, 1943, N 27,13:3
Polignac, Melchoir de, 1950, D 21,29:3
Polikarpoff, Nikolai N, 1944, Ag 1,15:3
Polin, Morris, 1943, Ag 21,11:6
Poling, Charles C, 1947, Je 16,21:4
Poling, Daniel A Mrs, 1967, Ja 24,28:4
Poling, Daniel A Rev Dr (funl, F 12,39:4), **1968, F 8, 1:8**
Poling, Forrest B, 1940, Mr 5,23:2
Poling, William H, 1940, D 6,27:3
Poling, William H Mrs, 1940, D 6,27:3
Poling, William J, 1958, Ap 6,88:2
Polinsky, David, 1959, F 3,27:8
Polis, Albert, 1915, Mr 12,11:6
Polis, Albert Capt, 1915, F 27,11:5
Polisar, Eric, 1968, Ag 2,33:2
Polishuck, Isidore, 1964, S 20,88:2
Polisky, Max, 1951, Ag 10,15:3
Polisky, Max Mrs, 1950, Jl 19,31:4
Polite, William B Jr, 1949, My 10,25:4
Polites, Adam A, 1967, Je 29,43:3
Politis, Athanase G, 1968, Ap 6,39:3
Politis, John, 1959, Je 4,31:5
Politis, Michael J, 1948, Je 23,27:3
Politis, Nicholas S, 1942, Mr 5,23:3
Politis, Nicholas S Mrs, 1948, Ap 17,15:4
Politis, Panos (will), 1955, Jl 20,17:3
Polito, Saverio, 1959, My 13,37:4
Politz, Joseph B, 1941, Ja 4,13:3
Politzer, Abame Prof, 1920, Ag 13,9:3
Politziner, Morris H, 1916, N 22,13:4
Polivka, Jaroslav J, 1960, F 11,35:2
Polivnick, Isidor, 1957, Mr 16,19:5
Polivnick, Isidore Mrs, 1948, Ag 2,21:1
Polivy, Charles, 1958, Jl 6,56:4
Polk, David D, 1955, Ap 29,23:3
Polk, Frank L (por), 1943, F 8,19:1
Polk, Frank L, 1952, S 21,88:3
Polk, Frank L Mrs, 1960, O 27,37:2
Polk, Gordon, 1960, Je 12,86:5
Polk, Harry H, 1949, Ag 29,17:3
Polk, J B, 1902, Ja 6,7:4
Polk, J K Mrs, 1891, Ag 14,1:4
Polk, James G, 1953, My 25,25:4
Polk, James T Mrs, 1910, Ja 21,11:4
Polk, John M, 1948, Ja 14,25:4
Polk, Latham Lt, 1918, My 27,13:5
Polk, Leonidas Rebel Gen, 1864, Je 17,2:6
Polk, Lucy E Mrs, 1906, Ja 13,9:5
Polk, M T, 1884, Mr 1,4:7
Polk, Marie D Mrs, 1941, F 9,49:2
Polk, Newton N, 1940, My 17,19:2
Polk, Oscar L, 1957, Ja 24,92:3
Polk, Prudence, 1952, D 17,33:1
Polk, R H, 1939, Ja 6,21:5
Polk, Ralph L Sr, 1949, Ag 6,17:3
Polk, Robert S, 1924, Mr 25,21:4
Polk, Rudolph, 1957, Je 17,23:2
Polk, Trusten, 1876, Ap 17,1:2
Polk, William A, 1949, Ja 17,19:5
Polk, William H Mrs, 1906, Ja 13,9:5
Polk, William M (funl), 1918, Je 27,11:6
Polk, William Mecklenbeug Dr, 1918, Je 25,13:3
Polk, William T, 1955, O 17,27:2
Polk, Willis, 1924, S 13,13:5
Poll, Daniel, 1952, D 25,29:3
Poll, Max Dr, 1937, Ap 16,23:2
Polla, Pauline M Mrs, 1940, Ap 10,25:2
Pollack, Abraham B, 1954, D 21,27:4
Pollack, Albert H, 1947, Ap 30,25:2
Pollack, Emil J (est acctg), 1957, N 26,53:4
Pollack, H William, 1945, Jl 29,40:5
Pollack, Harold, 1958, F 20,25:4
Pollack, Henry, 1952, S 12,21:4
Pollack, Herman G, 1961, Ja 17,37:1
Pollack, Jacques, 1962, N 7,39:5
Pollack, James K, 1968, O 6,84:5
Pollack, Josef, 1958, S 24,27:4
Pollack, Leo, 1947, Mr 2,60:6
Pollack, Lew (por), 1946, Ja 19,13:3
Pollack, Louis B, 1959, Ag 28,23:3
Pollack, Milton Mrs, 1967, Jl 28,31:1
Pollack, Morris, 1950, S 2,15:3
Pollack, Philip, 1962, F 11,87:2
Pollack, Sam, 1941, My 11,45:1
Pollack, Samuel L Mrs, 1961, F 22,25:1
Pollack, Simon Dr, 1903, N 2,7:5
Pollack, William E, 1968, Mr 19,47:3
Pollain, Rene (por), 1940, N 13,23:5
Pollak, Bernard E, 1948, S 6,13:4
Pollak, Berthold S (por), 1948, Je 28,19:1
Pollak, Berthold S Mrs, 1937, My 29,17:3
Pollak, Carl, 1908, My 6,7:5
Pollak, Eduard, 1937, O 22,23:1

Pollak, Edward J, 1946, F 23,13:4
Pollak, Elmer L, 1958, D 6,23:5
Pollak, Emil Mrs, 1952, N 16,89:1
Pollak, Ernst, 1938, O 7,23:5
Pollak, Francis D Mrs, 1956, F 25,19:6
Pollak, Francis Deak, 1916, O 6,11:4
Pollak, Henry, 1941, Je 7,17:4
Pollak, Joseph, 1945, S 13,23:4
Pollak, Julian A, 1961, Ap 2,77:1
Pollak, Leo Mrs, 1967, F 1,40:1
Pollak, Leopold B Mrs, 1959, Ag 12,29:4
Pollak, Louis, 1959, F 6,25:1
Pollak, Phil, 1949, F 17,23:1
Pollak, Robert M, 1952, Je 13,23:3
Pollak, Rudolf (por), 1949, N 7,27:1
Pollak, Walter H (por), 1940, O 3,25:1
Pollak, William, 1953, Ag 31,7:2
Pollan, Arthur A, 1958, Je 11,36:1
Pollard, Albert, 1948, Ag 5,21:2
Pollard, Amanda Mrs, 1937, O 5,25:3
Pollard, Bartlett, 1947, D 29,17:4
Pollard, Bud, 1952, D 18,29:3
Pollard, C B, 1959, Je 2,35:2
Pollard, Charles, 1938, D 18,49:1
Pollard, Charles W, 1946, Mr 20,23:2
Pollard, David H, 1953, Ap 30,31:6
Pollard, E B, 1927, Jl 14,23:3
Pollard, Ed A, 1872, D 18,1:6
Pollard, Ernest M, 1939, S 25,20:2
Pollard, Fred R E, 1937, Ap 6,23:4
Pollard, Frederick E, 1938, D 3,19:3
Pollard, George M, 1954, Jl 28,23:2
Pollard, George P, 1955, Ja 18,27:1
Pollard, George S Mrs, 1949, F 25,24:3
Pollard, Glenn E, 1940, Ag 8,19:6
Pollard, H S, 1905, Mr 13,8:4
Pollard, Harold S, 1953, S 22,31:1
Pollard, Harry (Snub), 1962, Ja 21,88:1
Pollard, Harry E, 1937, Ja 27,21:2
Pollard, Harry G, 1948, Jl 20,23:4
Pollard, Harry W, 1943, O 21,27:4
Pollard, Hencewood M, 1948, My 23,68:5
Pollard, Henry D, 1942, Ja 8,22:3
Pollard, Howard L, 1948, My 2,76:6
Pollard, I B Mrs, 1954, O 30,17:4
Pollard, I Benjamin, 1968, D 10,77:2
Pollard, J Devillo, 1956, My 6,87:1
Pollard, John A Dr, 1968, Mr 28,47:1
Pollard, John G (por), 1937, Ap 29,21:3
Pollard, John H Rev, 1873, S 29,8:5
Pollard, Julian A Mrs, 1940, My 30,17:5
Pollard, Nelson L Mrs, 1947, Je 8,60:4
Pollard, Percival, 1911, D 18,11:4
Pollard, Robert N, 1954, My 25,27:4
Pollard, Robert S Mrs, 1947, Je 3,25:3
Pollard, Robert T, 1939, Ap 13,23:5
Pollard, Walter H, 1959, My 13,32:3
Pollard, William B, 1957, Jl 13,17:3
Pollard, William J Judge, 1913, D 13,13:6
Pollard, William M, 1938, D 7,23:2
Pollare, Frank, 1943, N 6,15:8
Pollatchek, Morris, 1922, N 26,6:3
Pollatschek, Sigmund, 1946, My 2,21:1
Pollen, Arthur J H, 1937, Ja 29,19:1
Pollet, Max J, 1942, Ap 24,17:4
Polleys, Graham, 1903, Mr 13,9:4
Polleys, Louise A Mrs, 1941, O 24,23:6
Polleys, Thomas A, 1924, F 25,15:3
Pollia, Joseph P, 1954, D 14,33:4
Polliak, Herman, 1949, Mr 15,27:5
Pollinger, Jules Mrs, 1964, S 9,43:3
Pollinger, Samuel, 1943, Mr 23,20:3
Pollio, Raphael L, 1941, Mr 9,40:6
Pollison, Robert, 1954, Je 20,85:1
Pollister, Edward B, 1954, Jl 30,17:5
Pollitt, Alfred O, 1958, O 11,23:2
Pollitt, Harry (funl, Jl 10,72:2), 1960, Je 28,31:2
Pollitz, Edward A, 1968, Ag 18,88:5
Pollitz, George S, 1952, F 12,27:1
Pollitz, George S Sr Mrs, 1959, Mr 21,21:6
Pollitzer, Sigmund Dr (por), 1937, N 2,25:1
Pollman, Arnold, 1944, Ag 14,24:2
Pollock, Albert V, 1940, Jl 24,21:6
Pollock, Alexander C, 1945, Jl 1,18:1
Pollock, Alice L Mrs, 1957, S 8,84:8
Pollock, Allan, 1942, Mr 1,44:5
Pollock, Beatrice Mrs, 1942, D 3,25:2
Pollock, Benjamin, 1937, Ag 7,15:6
Pollock, Benjamin R, 1949, Mr 6,72:3
Pollock, Carl B, 1959, N 2,31:2
Pollock, Channing, 1946, Ag 18,47:3
Pollock, Channing Mrs, 1946, Ap 1,27:4
Pollock, Charles A, 1938, Ag 9,19:5; 1944, Ag 15,17:4
Pollock, David S Mrs, 1910, F 2,9:4
Pollock, Edward M, 1943, Je 9,21:3
Pollock, Edward Mrs, 1947, D 1,21:4
Pollock, Emma, 1945, My 26,15:2
Pollock, Frederick Sir, 1870, Ag 24,4:7; 1937, Ja 19, 23:1
Pollock, George E, 1918, Ag 3,9:3; 1905, Mr 18,11:5
Pollock, George Sir, 1872, O 21,8:4
Pollock, Gordon W (funl plans), 1956, Ag 2,25:5
Pollock, Harry, 1955, F 6,88:6
Pollock, Harry C, 1943, S 26,49:1
Pollock, Harry Mrs (Esther Mullin), 1953, F 21,13:2
Pollock, Henry M, 1954, Mr 19,23:2
Pollock, Henry W, 1954, D 10,27:4
Pollock, Horatio M, 1950, My 9,29:5
Pollock, Horatio M Mrs, 1937, F 8,17:5
Pollock, Hugh M (por), 1937, Ap 16,23:2
Pollock, Israel, 1945, Jl 25,23:6
Pollock, Jackson, 1956, Ag 12,1:3
Pollock, James, 1869, O 9,4:6
Pollock, James A, 1949, Mr 6,16:6; 1951, S 26,31:4
Pollock, John, 1945, Jl 30,19:6; 1946, O 31,25:1
Pollock, John C Judge, 1937, Ja 24,35:1
Pollock, John J, 1943, Jl 27,17:2
Pollock, Joseph K, 1943, Je 16,21:3
Pollock, Louis, 1964, Ag 24,27:1
Pollock, Marcella F Mrs, 1961, Mr 13,29:3
Pollock, Max E, 1966, Mr 12,27:3
Pollock, Morris, 1945, Je 1,15:3
Pollock, Robert G, 1964, My 25,33:3
Pollock, Roland D, 1948, Je 19,15:6
Pollock, Royal J Sr, 1952, Jl 13,61:2
Pollock, Sheldon L, 1956, Jl 30,21:1
Pollock, Thomas C, 1948, Mr 9,23:2
Pollock, Walter B, 1948, Ja 15,23:4
Pollock, Walter R, 1940, My 29,24:2
Pollock, Walter W, 1953, Ag 24,23:6
Pollock, William, 1916, N 2,13:6
Pollock, William B, 1939, N 20,19:5
Pollock, William C Jr, 1951, S 15,15:3
Pollock, William R, 1941, N 15,17:3
Pollock, Wilma, 1948, Je 30,25:4
Polly, Peter Mrs, 1950, Ja 18,31:2
Polo, Andrea, 1958, My 23,23:1
Polo, Eddie, 1961, Je 15,43:3
Polo, S, 1934, S 5,22:1
Polock, Moses, 1903, Ag 17,7:5
Polon, Albert Mrs, 1953, Ag 26,27:4
Poloquin, Edward, 1958, O 13,29:2
Polowe, David, 1952, Ap 5,15:3
Pols, Margaretha Mrs, 1940, Jl 13,13:5
Polsenski, Joseph, 1942, Jl 13,15:3; 1944, Ja 1,13:4
Polsenski, William Mrs, 1946, Je 14,21:4
Polsinelli, Vincent Mrs, 1961, F 28,33:3
Polsky, Solomon, 1945, My 18,19:4
Polson, Henry G Mrs, 1953, Mr 10,29:2
Polson, James A, 1950, N 5,92:7
Polson, Thomas A, 1946, Ag 23,19:4
Polstein, Joseph, 1938, F 19,15:4
Poltchaninoff, Nicholas J, 1950, Je 23,25:2
Polten, Jacob, 1949, Ap 21,26:2
Poltere, Louis, 1939, My 17,23:4
Poltronieri, Edmund, 1966, Ja 17,47:2
Poltronieri, Hugo E, 1945, D 25,23:1
Polushkin, Eugene P, 1964, My 1,35:4
Polyacheck, S Rabbi, 1928, Jl 10,23:3
Polyak, Stephen L, 1955, Mr 11,25:2
Polyakov, Leonid M, 1965, Je 23,41:2
Polycarpa, Mother, 1947, Mr 15,13:5
Polychrone, Nick, 1954, S 13,23:4
Polzer, Conrad, 1959, My 22,27:2
Polzer, Fridolin, 1962, Je 4,29:4
Polzikoff, Michael, 1938, Je 14,21:2
Pomar, Gregorio, 1954, My 22,15:3
Pomare, Queen of the Society Islands, 1877, O 25,1:3
Pomares, Ferdinand R, 1941, N 22,19:4
Pomarlen, Joseph M Mrs, 1967, F 14,43:3
Pombo, Alejandro C, 1950, F 10,24:4
Pome, Luigi, 1945, Ja 13,11:4
Pomerance, Abraham, 1964, Ap 13,29:4
Pomerance, Max, 1962, Mr 28,39:4
Pomerance, Samuel H, 1955, O 2,86:7
Pomeranchuk, Isaak Y, 1966, D 16,47:6
Pomerantz, A, 1942, Ja 11,44:1
Pomerantz, Alexander, 1965, Ja 11,45:2
Pomerantz, Arnold, 1940, Ag 2,15:2
Pomerantz, Harris, 1956, F 28,31:4
Pomerantz, Jacob S, 1962, Ag 17,23:4
Pomerantz, Julius Dr, 1968, Ag 26,39:3
Pomerantz, Louis, 1955, Ap 30,17:5
Pomerantz, Michael, 1964, Ap 14,37:2
Pomerantz, Solomon, 1956, D 23,30:5
Pomeranz, Herman, 1956, O 29,29:5
Pomeranz, Raphael, 1951, Ag 21,27:3
Pomerene, Atlee (por),(will, N 23,21:7), 1937, N 13, 19:1
Pomerene, James A (will), 1940, Ap 16,19:4
Pomeroy, Annie L, 1959, Ap 19,86:1
Pomeroy, Arthur C, 1956, D 31,13:4
Pomeroy, Brenton C, 1941, Ap 4,21:4
Pomeroy, Brenton C Mrs, 1952, My 20,25:5
Pomeroy, Cashel S, 1943, D 18,15:2
Pomeroy, Daniel E, 1965, Mr 26,35:4
Pomeroy, E Sterling Dr, 1917, Ap 22,21:2
Pomeroy, Ethel M, 1966, Je 21,43:4
Pomeroy, Eugene C, 1962, F 11,87:2
Pomeroy, F W, 1924, My 27,21:4
Pomeroy, Fannie L, 1945, Je 1,15:4
Pomeroy, George S Sr, 1925, S 14,19:5
Pomeroy, Harry, 1949, Ja 11,31:4
Pomeroy, Horace B, 1957, Ja 25,21:4
Pomeroy, Hugh R, 1961, Jl 2,33:1
Pomeroy, J H, 1932, O 1,34:4
Pomeroy, J Nevin Sr, 1961, Jl 12,31:1
Pomeroy, Jay, 1955, Je 3,23:4
Pomeroy, John, 1950, Ag 22,27:2
Pomeroy, John L, 1941, Mr 26,23:2
Pomeroy, John M, 1961, Ja 29,84:3
Pomeroy, John Norton, 1924, Je 2,17:6
Pomeroy, Lendall W, 1948, My 2,76:3
Pomeroy, Lillie C K Mrs, 1942, S 20,40:2
Pomeroy, Louis R, 1917, My 8,11:6
Pomeroy, M M (Brick), 1896, My 31,16:1
Pomeroy, Mary E, 1874, Ag 19,8:6
Pomeroy, Owen, 1938, My 26,25:4
Pomeroy, Paul P, 1942, Ag 22,13:3
Pomeroy, Ralph H Dr, 1925, Ag 23,7:3
Pomeroy, Reynolds, 1958, Mr 3,27:2
Pomeroy, Robert W Sr Mrs, 1958, Ap 19,21:2
Pomeroy, Sanford B, 1937, Ap 6,23:5
Pomeroy, T, 1927, D 5,23:5
Pomeroy, Theodore L Mrs, 1913, D 27,9:5
Pomeroy, Theodore M, 1905, Mr 24,9:6
Pomeroy, Theodore Mrs, 1940, My 15,25:4
Pomeroy, Vivian T, 1961, N 9,35:3
Pomeroy, Walter H Mrs, 1911, Ag 25,7:5
Pomeroy, William M, 1961, F 26,92:6
Pommayrac, P P de, 1880, Jl 13,5:5
Pommer, Eric, 1966, My 13,38:5
Pommerenck, Henry Mrs, 1947, Mr 29,15:5
Pommerer, Robert W, 1956, My 29,27:2
Pomper, Irving, 1958, Jl 24,25:3
Pompilj, B, 1931, My 5,27:2
Pomroy, Frederic H, 1917, Mr 7,11:6
Pomroy, Henry Keney (por), 1925, D 24,13:5
Pomykalo, Stephen A, 1950, D 12,33:3
Ponce, Francisco, 1949, D 14,31:2
Ponce, Francisco E, 1947, My 27,25:3
Ponce, Manuel M, 1948, Ap 26,23:5
Ponce, Philip L, 1945, Ag 23,23:3
Poncelet, Eugene, 1923, D 16,23:2
Ponchardier, Pierre, 1961, Ja 28,4:6
Ponchon, Raoul, 1937, D 3,23:2
Pond, Anson Phelps, 1920, Ja 22,17:2
Pond, Bert C, 1955, My 10,29:1
Pond, Bert C Mrs, 1945, Ja 10,23:3
Pond, Bremer W, 1959, S 5,15:4
Pond, Caroline F Mrs, 1938, Ja 18,23:2
Pond, Charles H, 1945, F 18,33:2
Pond, Charles H Mrs, 1939, Mr 24,21:3
Pond, Chester H, 1912, Je 12,13:6
Pond, Clarke P, 1964, F 1,23:4
Pond, De Witt C, 1953, S 7,19:6
Pond, Donald M Mrs (L Strong), 1966, F 3,31:1
Pond, Edgar L, 1941, Ja 26,36:1
Pond, Enoch, 1882, Ja 23,5:4
Pond, Florence L, 1955, Jl 20,27:4
Pond, Francis J, 1943, F 20,13:4
Pond, Frank N, 1948, N 17,27:4
Pond, Frank N Mrs, 1967, Ja 23,43:4
Pond, Frederick Eugene (Will Wildwood), 1925, 23:5
Pond, Frederick H, 1953, My 1,21:5
Pond, Frederick L, 1954, Je 23,26:5
Pond, George E Brig-Gen, 1907, N 22,9:5
Pond, Harold W Mrs, 1951, S 23,86:4
Pond, Harry B, 1950, My 24,30:3
Pond, Harry H, 1955, F 11,23:3
Pond, Horace B, 1960, Ap 21,31:1
Pond, Horace P, 1945, Ag 12,39:2
Pond, Irving K (por), 1939, S 30,17:3
Pond, J O, 1881, F 2,5:1
Pond, James B, 1961, Mr 6,25:6
Pond, John E, 1941, N 26,23:5
Pond, Joseph A, 1867, N 1,1:3
Pond, Julia Mrs, 1941, S 18,25:4
Pond, Lyman B, 1950, S 3,38:3
Pond, Melbourne J, 1957, D 26,19:1
Pond, Nathan P Col, 1921, Ja 17,11:4
Pond, Philip, 1946, D 22,41:2
Pond, Samuel N, 1942, Ja 20,19:4
Pond, Shepard, 1945, My 30,19:3
Pond, Susan M Mrs, 1942, D 8,25:2
Pond, Thomas T, 1961, Ap 24,29:1
Pond, Van R, 1941, S 22,15:3
Pond, Wallace L, 1956, Ap 28,17:3
Ponder, James W, 1942, F 10,19:2
Ponder, W T (por), 1947, F 28,23:1
Ponemon, Louis A, 1943, F 25,21:2
Ponemone, Jacob, 1959, Mr 14,23:5
Ponger, William H, 1959, Ag 25,31:3
Poniatowski, Andre Prince, 1954, Mr 18,31:2
Poniatowski, Andre Princess, 1911, Ag 7,7:6
Poniatowski, Charles Prince, 1906, My 6,1:6
Poniatowski, Joseph Count, 1873, Jl 5,1:5
Ponis, Elizabeth, 1899, F 22,9:5
Ponjoulat, J J, 1880, Ja 8,5:2
Ponomareff, Alex I, 1962, S 29,23:6
Pons, Adolphe A, 1951, D 27,21:2
Pons, Alfred, 1949, My 23,8:3
Pons, August Mrs, 1963, Je 11,37:3
Pons, Edwin Mrs, 1950, Ja 4,35:4
Pons, George C, 1959, Ja 30,27:3
Pons, Juan M, 1941, Mr 12,22:3
Ponsard, Francis, 1867, Jl 10,4:6

Ponselle, Robert A D, 1963, S 15,86:3
Ponsonby, Arthur Mrs, 1952, S 14,86:1
Ponsonby, Lord, 1946, Mr 25,26:2
Ponsonby, Vere B (Earl of Bessborough), 1956, Mr 11,88:1
Pontani, Corrado, 1958, My 18,4:3
Pontaro, Philip, 1924, Ap 21,17:4
Ponte Rodriguez, Manuel, 1964, Jl 26,57:1
Ponte y Jimenez, Francisco, 1958, F 16,86:6
Ponter, George C, 1954, Je 25,21:4
Pontes, Jose, 1961, S 26,39:4
Pontez, C W, 1879, F 8,3:2
Ponti, Giovanni, 1961, D 29,23:2
Pontillo, Sam, 1944, Ag 24,19:2
Pontin, Elmer, 1956, Jl 7,13:6
Pontin, Frederick K, 1941, D 11,27:3
Pontin, William S, 1939, Ag 13,29:4
Ponting, Harry C, 1950, Ag 17,28:3
Pontius, Albert W, 1923, F 26,13:4; 1923, F 28,17:3
Pontius, David W, 1955, S 4,56:3
Pontius, David W Mrs, 1945, Ap 25,23:5
Pontius, George W, 1943, Jl 21,15:5
Pontius, Miller H, 1960, N 6,89:1
Pontius, Paul J, 1938, F 17,21:5
Ponto, John A, 1949, Mr 25,23:3
Ponton, Georges L, 1944, Ag 3,19:6
Ponton, John, 1925, N 10,25:5
Ponton, Thomas R, 1948, Ap 3,15:5
Pontone, Enrico, 1950, Ja 28,13:6
Pontoppidan, Henrik, 1943, Ag 22,36:3
Pontus, Raoul, 1947, Mr 14,23:1
Ponty, Frederick H, 1941, Je 20,21:5
Ponvert, Antonio (Sept 20), 1965, O 11,61:4
Ponvert, Antonio Mrs, 1962, Ag 22,33:3
Ponvert, Elias, 1882, Ag 9,5:2
Ponzi, Andrew, 1950, Ap 12,28:4
Ponzi, Charles (por), 1949, Ja 19,56:3
Ponzio, Mario, 1956, S 9,85:1
Poock, Louis Mrs, 1948, Ap 14,27:5
Poodry, Aaron H, 1945, F 9,15:1
Pook, S M, 1878, D 1,5:3
Pool, Edgar, 1903, N 8,3:1
Pool, Eleazar, 1938, Jl 28,19:4
Pool, Eleazar Mrs, 1939, S 23,17:4
Pool, Ernest Mrs, 1968, My 13,43:3
Pool, Eugene H (por), 1949, Ap 11,25:3
Pool, G H, 1881, F 16,8:2
Pool, Harwood-Redington, 1903, D 31,9:5
Pool, J, 1884, Ag 17,6:7
Pool, Joe R, 1968, Jl 15,31:1
Pool, W F, 1883, Ag 29,5:6
Pool, W Henry, 1967, Ja 2,19:3
Pool, William P, 1941, S 3,23:2
Poole, Abram, 1961, My 25,37:4
Poole, Alice M Mrs, 1956, Jl 7,13:4
Poole, Amos R, 1960, D 19,27:3
Poole, Anthony C, 1944, Ap 19,23:1
Poole, Arthur B Jr, 1954, Ag 4,21:1
Poole, Ava W, 1941, Mr 15,17:2
Poole, Clesson O, 1961, F 12,86:2
Poole, Dewitt C, 1952, S 4,27:1
Poole, Edward G, 1937, Ja 17,II,8:5
Poole, Elmer E, 1939, D 29,15:2
Poole, Ernest, 1950, Ja 11,23:1
Poole, Ernest J, 1937, N 17,23:2; 1945, F 20,19:3
Poole, Fenn E, 1952, S 22,20:1
Poole, Frank A, 1942, D 22,25:3
Poole, Frank B Mrs, 1968, Ag 26,39:2
Poole, Franklin O (por), 1943, F 8,19:3
Poole, Frederic Mrs, 1956, Jl 28,17:5
Poole, Frederick A, 1942, N 8,52:7
Poole, Frederick A Mrs, 1950, Ja 2,23:5
Poole, Gardner, 1940, Jl 7,25:4
Poole, George W, 1941, F 6,21:2
Poole, Harold S, 1945, Mr 3,13:3
Poole, Ira, 1951, N 13,30:7
Poole, J Edward, 1942, Ja 24,17:1
Poole, J Elmer Mrs, 1941, Je 11,21:6
Poole, Jennie L, 1940, My 8,23:4
Poole, John H, 1907, Ja 29,9:6
Poole, John M 3d, 1942, Ag 11,19:6
Poole, Joseph E, 1942, F 18,19:5
Poole, Lyman C, 1957, Jl 28,61:3
Poole, Monroe Van Brackle, 1968, D 8,86:5
Poole, Murray E, 1925, Ap 11,13:4
Poole, Ralph H, 1961, Ja 12,29:1
Poole, Reginald, 1941, Ag 12,19:6
Poole, Reginald L, 1939, O 30,17:2
Poole, Robert, 1903, Ja 16,9:7
Poole, Robert F, 1958, Je 8,89:1
Poole, Rufus G, 1968, N 24,87:1
Poole, Sidman P, 1955, O 30,88:5
Poole, Thomas Henry, 1919, Ag 2,7:6
Poole, W F Dr, 1894, Mr 2,8:3
Poole, Walter A, 1953, O 20,29:2
Poole, William C Rev, 1915, Ap 11,11:5
Poole, William E M, 1948, Mr 15,23:5
Poole, William F, 1947, Mr 7,25:4
Poole, William H, 1938, S 17,17:6
Pooler, H Wheelock, 1951, F 13,31:4
Pooley, C A, 1932, N 19,15:1
Pooley, C E, 1912, Mr 30,13:5
Pooley, Claude N A, 1943, Mr 28,24:5
Pooley, Frederick A, 1959, N 13,29:3
Pooley, Richard P, 1950, D 4,29:2
Pooley, Samuel N Maj, 1924, Ap 10,23:4
Pooley, William R, 1951, D 7,27:3
Poons, Edward M, 1938, Mr 25,20:4
Poor, Artemas, 1943, S 5,29:2
Poor, C H Rear-Adm, 1882, N 6,5:4
Poor, Charles L, 1951, S 28,31:5
Poor, Charles L Mrs, 1957, My 9,31:5
Poor, Clarence H, 1946, Ap 27,17:2
Poor, Daniel S, 1968, My 27,47:3
Poor, Edmund W, 1966, Ja 18,37:3
Poor, Edward E, 1951, O 7,86:6; 1957, Je 9,88:5
Poor, Edward W 3d Mrs, 1968, Ap 19,47:4
Poor, Elwyn W, 1924, O 21,23:4
Poor, Frank A, 1956, Je 18,25:4
Poor, Fred A, 1953, Ag 27,25:5
Poor, Fred A Mrs, 1938, Je 4,15:4
Poor, Frederick E, 1941, Ag 6,17:5
Poor, Henry V, 1905, Ja 6,9:3
Poor, Henry W, 1915, Ap 14,13:5
Poor, Horace F, 1947, N 3,23:3
Poor, James Harper, 1919, Ag 24,22:4
Poor, John A, 1871, S 8,2:7
Poor, John R, 1903, D 20,7:6
Poor, Joseph F, 1960, Ag 16,29:3
Poor, Lucy T, 1946, D 27,19:5
Poor, Robert T Mrs, 1962, Ap 7,25:3
Poor, Roger M, 1923, O 27,13:4
Poor, Ruel A Mrs, 1953, O 10,17:4
Poor, Ruel W, 1941, Ag 9,15:6
Poor, Walter E, 1950, Ap 5,31:1
Poor, Walter F, 1941, Ja 13,15:5
Poor, Walter S, 1906, Je 22,7:6; 1945, Ag 25,11:5
Poore, Alan C, 1951, D 4,33:2
Poore, Ben Perley Maj, 1887, My 29,3:4
Poore, Benjamin A (por), 1940, Ag 28,19:1
Poore, Charles, 1908, Jl 22,5:4
Poore, Charles G Jr, 1959, D 13,86:3
Poore, Gilman W, 1951, D 19,31:2
Poore, Henry R (por), 1940, Ag 16,15:1
Poore, John B, 1951, Mr 22,31:2
Poore, John G, 1952, Jl 20,53:1
Poore, William E Sr, 1955, Ja 20,31:1
Poorman, Amanda E Mrs, 1920, Jl 22,11:5
Poorman, Archie E, 1954, S 8,31:5
Poorman, Wallace, 1938, N 14,19:4
Pooton, James, 1914, F 25,9:5
Poots, Ellsworth E, 1952, Jl 19,15:4
Popaca, John J, 1954, D 28,23:2
Popcke, William, 1945, S 13,23:6
Pope, Albert A, 1948, D 8,32:2
Pope, Albert A Col, 1909, Ag 11,7:5
Pope, Albert L, 1955, Ag 12,19:2
Pope, Alfred A, 1913, Ag 6,7:4
Pope, Alfred M Mrs, 1967, Ag 1,33:2
Pope, Allan M Mrs, 1960, O 25,35:4
Pope, Alvin E, 1940, Mr 5,23:3
Pope, Arthur W Mrs, 1948, O 26,31:3
Pope, Asa P, 1945, Ag 29,23:6
Pope, Bayard F, 1968, N 12,47:1
Pope, Benjamin, 1955, Jl 27,23:5
Pope, Bentley H Mrs, 1952, Ag 20,25:4
Pope, Cecily J, 1938, Je 7,23:4
Pope, Charles, 1922, Mr 26,27:2
Pope, Charles A, 1963, My 19,86:7
Pope, Charles C Mrs, 1922, D 20,19:5
Pope, Charles F (will), 1939, Ja 31,19:1
Pope, Charles Hudson, 1904, F 10,9:6
Pope, Charles M, 1945, F 26,19:2
Pope, Chester H, 1956, Mr 7,33:3
Pope, Christopher H Mrs, 1944, N 28,23:1
Pope, Clara E Mrs, 1950, Mr 8,27:3
Pope, Clarence J, 1955, Ja 15,13:2
Pope, Clem, 1947, F 2,57:1
Pope, Clyde W, 1950, O 15,104:4
Pope, Coleman Mrs, 1880, Mr 17,1:6
Pope, D Maj, 1880, F 11,5:5
Pope, Donald S, 1968, Ag 13,45:2
Pope, Edward S, 1942, Ja 24,17:6
Pope, Frank, 1942, O 6,24:2
Pope, Frank J, 1943, F 11,20:3
Pope, Frank T, 1954, N 12,15:1
Pope, Franklin, 1916, Ag 9,11:4
Pope, Frederic S, 1949, Mr 30,25:5
Pope, Frederick, 1961, Ag 13,88:4
Pope, Frederick A, 1952, Je 23,19:2; 1958, F 1,19:6
Pope, Frederick Mrs, 1957, My 25,21:3
Pope, Generoso, 1950, Ap 29,15:1
Pope, George A, 1942, O 18,55:4
Pope, George Col, 1918, Ap 20,13:5
Pope, George H, 1952, Ag 28,23:4
Pope, George P, 1917, N 27,13:4
Pope, Gustavus D, 1952, Mr 6,32:3
Pope, Gustavus D Mrs, 1940, Ag 10,13:4
Pope, H Montague Mrs, 1956, F 26,89:2
Pope, Harold L Sr, 1962, Ap 6,35:2
Pope, Harry M, 1950, O 13,29:3
Pope, Helen M, 1945, Je 1,15:3
Pope, Henry F, 1950, Jl 30,60:3
Pope, Henry J, 1941, S 9,23:1
Pope, Henry Sr (por), 1947, Ja 9,23:3
Pope, Henry W, 1916, Mr 1,11:6
Pope, Henry Washington, 1953, F 10,27:3
Pope, Herbert, 1958, Jl 24,25:3
Pope, Ira S, 1961, Ag 25,25:3
Pope, J J, 1942, Ja 14,21:1
Pope, J W, 1931, N 22,31:1
Pope, James E, 1943, Ap 22,23:2; 1951, Mr 22,31:4
Pope, James G, 1960, Ja 11,45:1
Pope, James L Sr, 1943, Je 7,13:5
Pope, James P, 1966, Ja 24,35:4
Pope, James P Mrs, 1957, Ja 22,29:6
Pope, James Warden Gen, 1919, Ag 25,11:4
Pope, John, 1880, D 31,8:4
Pope, John C, 1955, Ag 13,13:6
Pope, John Commodore, 1876, Ja 18,4:7
Pope, John H, 1941, Jl 29,15:3
Pope, John R, 1937, Ag 28,15:1
Pope, Joseph A, 1961, S 20,29:3
Pope, Joseph Daniel Dr, 1908, Mr 22,9:5
Pope, Joseph T, 1942, O 24,15:4
Pope, Katherine R, 1940, Je 29,15:3
Pope, Lester B, 1938, N 29,24:1
Pope, Lewis C, 1942, D 11,24:2
Pope, Paul M, 1958, O 24,33:4
Pope, Paul M Mrs, 1958, Je 3,31:3
Pope, Paul R, 1950, Ja 13,23:3
Pope, Peter Paul, 1908, Mr 27,9:6
Pope, Quentin, 1961, Mr 10,27:2
Pope, Richard D, 1947, D 10,38:4
Pope, Ruel P, 1941, Ag 29,17:4
Pope, Samuel K C, 1901, Jl 28,3:2
Pope, Samuel Mrs, 1910, Je 24,9:5
Pope, Sidney E, 1944, Jl 16,31:3
Pope, Thomas, 1943, F 18,23:2
Pope, Thomas B, 1957, Ap 24,33:4
Pope, Verle A Mrs (Edith), 1961, F 1,35:1
Pope, Willard, 1949, Je 3,25:5
Pope, William, 1916, Ja 22,9:3
Pope, William C Mrs, 1948, Je 23,27:4
Pope, William Hayes Judge, 1916, S 14,7:7
Pope, William J Sir, 1939, O 18,26:2
Pope, William K, 1951, O 12,28:3
Pope, William S, 1941, Ja 26,36:1
Pope, William W, 1903, Jl 31,7:6
Pope, Young John Justice, 1911, Mr 30,11:5
Pope-Hennessy, Ladislaus H R, 1942, Mr 4,19:2
Pope-Hennessy, Una, 1949, Ag 18,21:4
Pope Pius IX, Brother of, 1872, O 7,8:1
Pope Pius IX, 1878, F 8,1:7
Popeney, Harry V, 1958, Je 1,86:6
Popescu, Stelian, 1954, Mr 10,8:4
Popham, Charles W, 1958, Je 20,23:2
Popham, Henry B, 1947, Ap 17,27:4
Popham, Henry M, 1955, Ag 14,81:2
Popham, James L, 1941, Ja 12,44:3
Popham, John B, 1963, My 7,43:3
Popham, John N, 1941, O 1,21:6
Popham, Richard Morris, 1919, O 4,11:3
Popham, W H, 1880, Je 29,5:6
Popham, W S, 1885, Je 19,2:6
Popick, Joseph, 1949, Ja 18,23:2
Popick, Nat, 1947, S 18,25:3
Popiel, Walter, 1955, Mr 24,31:3
Popilow, Hyman L, 1956, N 4,87:2
Popjoy, Walter J, 1961, Ag 24,29:3
Popke, Emil H, 1952, F 28,27:2
Popke, John, 1949, Jl 2,15:3
Popkin, Jacob Mordecai, 1917, Ja 18,11:2
Popkin, Louis, 1943, Ja 12,23:4
Popkin, Martin E, 1940, Ja 30,19:4
Popkin, William E, 1959, Ja 7,33:4
Popky, Charles, 1953, O 30,23:2
Pople, George, 1913, N 20,11:5
Pople, George W, 1939, My 9,23:6
Popma, Gerrit J, 1967, My 21,87:1
Popoff, Constantine, 1942, My 31,38:2
Popoff, George S, 1953, Mr 2,23:3
Popon, Louise, 1952, Ja 15,30:8
Popot, James A, 1943, Ag 11,19:5
Popov, Dimitry M, 1952, Ja 9,29:2
Popov, Vasily F, 1964, D 5,31:4
Popover, Morris, 1961, Ap 16,86:6
Popovich, Matthew, 1943, Jl 21,15:6
Popovici, Andrei, 1965, My 26,47:2
Popp, Andrew, 1941, Ap 11,21:1
Popp, Bert, 1944, Ag 5,11:2
Popp, Carl A J, 1944, Jl 28,13:4
Popp, Harold M, 1954, Jl 8,23:1
Popp, Joseph A, 1940, Mr 5,24:3
Popp, Walter C, 1949, Je 6,19:5
Poppen, Emmanuel, 1961, F 15,35:4
Poppenberg, Felix, 1915, S 2,9:6
Poppenberg, Jerome, 1959, My 21,31:1
Poppenga, Adolph U, 1950, Mr 19,92:3
Poppenhusen, A C, 1882, F 28,3:4
Poppenhusen, Conrad H, 1949, Mr 21,23:5
Popper, Alice I Mrs, 1946, My 19,42:3
Popper, Arthur W, 1959, F 27,25:2
Popper, Benjamin, 1947, Ap 12,17:5
Popper, Edwin S Mrs, 1939, Jl 27,19:3
Popper, Emanuel J, 1964, F 2,89:2
Popper, Emil L, 1959, S 5,15:5
Popper, Hermine L, 1968, N 19,40:4
Popper, Howard I, 1953, Jl 27,19:1

Popper, Isaac C, 1940, Mr 2,13:6
Popper, John E (will), 1941, Ag 21,10:2
Popper, Leopold, 1905, Ap 11,9:2
Popper, Ludwig E, 1954, Je 14,21:2
Popper, Richard, 1948, Ja 8,25:2
Popper, William J, 1962, Mr 29,33:3
Poppy, Frederick W, 1960, Ap 27,37:5
Poptomov, Vladimir, 1952, My 3,21:5
Porath, Julius, 1941, O 3,23:5
Porazzi, Carlo, 1946, Ag 9,17:5
Porazzi, Mario A, 1967, My 5,39:3
Porcajlowicz, Antoni S, 1949, Jl 16,13:2
Porcella, John, 1954, Ag 19,23:6
Porcello, James V, 1950, Ap 18,31:3
Porch, Montagu, 1964, N 10,47:3
Porche, Francois, 1944, My 2,19:5
Porcher, Christopher G, 1958, D 29,15:5
Porcher, Samuel, 1944, Ap 5,19:6
Porcile, Eugene Henry Rev, 1912, Ja 4,13:5
Porel, Paul, 1917, Ag 6,9:4
Porello, John M, 1946, Je 27,21:2
Porensky, George, 1962, Ja 25,31:1
Pores, Charles, 1951, My 25,27:5
Porges, Barbara Mrs, 1938, N 15,23:1
Porges, Edmond, 1941, Mr 20,21:2
Porges, Edwin, 1951, N 22,31:3
Porges, George M, 1968, Ja 8,35:1
Porges, Gustave Mrs, 1959, Mr 11,35:3
Porges, John C, 1967, Ap 13,43:4
Porges, Max, 1947, Ja 9,23:4
Porges, Max J, 1923, Ja 5,11:6
Porges, Milton A, 1950, F 1,29:4
Porgie, Leo A, 1950, F 7,27:4
Porille, Chaim Rabbi, 1968, S 10,44:6
Porjes, Gustave (por), 1940, My 14,23:4
Poronto, Halsey E, 1943, Ag 25,19:1
Porosky, Mathew J, 1957, Mr 4,27:4
Porosky, Mathew J Mrs, 1957, Mr 4,27:4
Porper, Robert B, 1941, O 14,24:4
Porphy, Albert R, 1952, D 2,31:6
Porras, Belisario (por), 1942, Ag 30,42:8
Porras, Meliton F, 1944, Ap 7,19:1
Porres, Julius E, 1920, Je 11,13:3
Porro, Carlo, 1939, Ap 20,23:2
Porry, Joseph de Mrs, 1943, Je 20,34:6
Porsche, Ferdinand, 1951, Ja 31,25:5
Porson, Benjamin H, 1946, D 5,31:5
Porst, Charles R, 1950, My 16,31:4
Port, Arthur C, 1940, N 22,23:3
Port, Jacob G Mrs, 1947, Jl 2,23:5
Port, Meyer, 1968, D 5,47:4
Porta, A J, 1967, O 14,27:3
Porta, Mario, 1947, S 7,60:4
Portago, Marquis de (funl, My 16,62:6), 1957, My 13,1:5
Portago, Marquis of, 1942, My 7,19:2
Portal, De Witt A, 1953, S 28,25:4
Portal, Lord (will, Jl 29,6:4),(por), 1949, My 7,13:3
Porte, John Cyril Lt-Col, 1919, O 28,13:3
Portela Moeller, Guillermo, 1958, Mr 4,29:5
Portela Valladares, Manuel, 1952, My 3,21:5
Portella, Epifanio Dr, 1916, Ap 12,13:4
Portelli, Dominick Mrs, 1958, Mr 20,29:3
Porten, Henny, 1960, O 17,29:4
Porten, Max von der, 1943, S 7,23:3
Porteous, Arthur T, 1939, Ap 26,23:5
Porteous, Carlyle A, 1949, Mr 15,27:3
Porteous, Douglas C, 1953, Ja 25,86:4
Porteous, G B Rev Dr (see also S 30), 1875, O 1,5:3
Porteous, J L Mrs, 1957, Ag 15,21:4
Porteous, John, 1939, My 23,23:2
Porter, A A, 1946, F 4,25:5
Porter, A D Col, 1926, N 8,19:4
Porter, A Kingsley Mrs (will, N 7,79:3), 1962, S 21, 30:2
Porter, A S, 1872, S 19,1:6
Porter, A W, 1877, Mr 17,5:2
Porter, Aaron M, 1951, S 1,11:5
Porter, Alan, 1942, D 3,25:1; 1944, My 4,19:5
Porter, Albert L, 1956, O 18,33:2
Porter, Alfred J, 1954, Ag 13,15:6
Porter, Alfred W, 1939, Ja 14,17:1
Porter, Alice D, 1947, N 21,27:5
Porter, Andrew Gen, 1872, Ja 6,5:3
Porter, Andrew J, 1946, N 18,23:2
Porter, Andrew R, 1947, Je 10,27:5
Porter, Andrew T Mrs, 1953, O 9,27:1
Porter, Arlington W, 1948, S 9,27:2
Porter, Arthur F, 1942, F 9,15:2; 1950, Jl 18,30:4
Porter, Augustus G, 1950, Ag 5,15:7
Porter, B C, 1879, Mr 22,5:2
Porter, B Grace, 1948, Ag 14,13:2
Porter, Bela J, 1940, My 8,23:5
Porter, Benjamin C, 1908, Ap 3,9:6
Porter, Benton, 1947, Ap 8,27:3
Porter, Byron B, 1960, D 31,17:2
Porter, C Scott, 1966, Ja 14,39:1
Porter, Carlile P, 1949, O 31,25:5
Porter, Carlisle Patterson Lt-Col, 1914, My 22,13:6
Porter, Catherine, 1962, O 12,32:4
Porter, Charles, 1950, F 12,86:5
Porter, Charles A, 1907, D 30,7:6
Porter, Charles B, 1938, Ag 5,17:4
Porter, Charles C, 1939, S 29,23:4
Porter, Charles F, 1951, Jl 18,29:4
Porter, Charles F Mrs, 1938, F 16,21:5
Porter, Charles H, 1957, Mr 2,21:5
Porter, Charles P, 1965, F 23,33:5
Porter, Charles T, 1910, Ag 30,7:5; 1945, Ap 20,19:3
Porter, Charles W, 1939, Mr 10,23:5
Porter, Charlotte E, 1942, Ja 19,17:5
Porter, Clara F, 1956, Je 27,31:3
Porter, Clarence, 1917, Mr 2,11:6
Porter, Clarence H, 1947, Ap 15,25:2
Porter, Clarence L, 1950, Ja 13,24:3
Porter, Claude R, 1946, Ag 18,46:3
Porter, Clifford J, 1949, N 14,27:4
Porter, Cole (trb, O 25,II,3:7), 1964, O 16,1:1
Porter, Cole Mrs, 1954, My 21,28:3
Porter, Cole Mrs (est appr), 1956, Jl 11,19:3
Porter, D D Adm, 1891, F 14,8:1
Porter, David, 1958, D 29,15:6
Porter, David D, 1944, F 26,13:4
Porter, David D Mrs, 1945, N 3,15:6; 1949, N 12,15:2
Porter, David R Mrs, 1872, My 3,5:2; 1949, D 3,15:1
Porter, Donald W, 1939, S 9,17:4
Porter, Dorothy E, 1955, Jl 8,23:1
Porter, Dudley, 1905, Mr 27,9:2
Porter, Edmund H, 1940, Mr 12,23:3
Porter, Edna, 1946, D 18,30:3
Porter, Edward, 1963, My 22,41:4
Porter, Edward F, 1953, Ap 4,13:3
Porter, Edward G, 1944, My 6,15:3
Porter, Edwin L, 1948, D 15,33:1
Porter, Edwin S, 1941, My 1,23:5
Porter, Emery M, 1957, N 5,31:1
Porter, Emma F F Mrs, 1937, Mr 18,25:4
Porter, Esten W, 1941, N 9,53:2
Porter, Eugene H Mrs, 1940, F 29,19:3
Porter, Eva E, 1948, O 7,30:3
Porter, F Addison, 1941, Ja 5,45:2
Porter, F J Gen, 1901, My 22,9:1
Porter, Finley R, 1964, F 10,27:4
Porter, Fitz John, 1946, Ap 3,25:2
Porter, Fitz John Gen, 1924, D 3,11:3
Porter, Francina E, 1939, Mr 25,15:5
Porter, Frank, 1882, Jl 11,8:4
Porter, Frank C, 1946, Ja 25,23:4
Porter, Frank G, 1942, D 17,37:3
Porter, Frank H, 1952, Mr 26,29:3
Porter, Frank L Mrs, 1943, Je 1,23:2
Porter, Frank L Mrs (will), 1955, Mr 27,46:6
Porter, Frank M, 1949, Jl 1,19:1; 1962, D 1,25:5
Porter, Fred E, 1941, O 28,19:2
Porter, Fred L, 1938, S 6,21:2
Porter, Garrett, 1954, O 27,29:3
Porter, George, 1941, Mr 30,49:2
Porter, George A, 1949, Ap 9,17:3
Porter, George D, 1946, Ag 3,15:2
Porter, George E, 1938, Ap 13,25:4; 1948, F 20,27:1
Porter, George F, 1907, N 30,7:5; 1949, Jl 26,27:1
Porter, George H, 1950, N 14,31:2
Porter, George J Mrs, 1948, Je 14,23:2
Porter, George M, 1944, Jl 19,19:5
Porter, George S, 1960, D 12,29:3
Porter, George W, 1923, Je 7,19:4; 1952, D 13,21:6
Porter, George W Mrs, 1948, Je 26,17:3
Porter, Gilbert E, 1942, Mr 5,24:2
Porter, Gilbert E 3d, 1939, Ap 11,23:1
Porter, Giles Maj, 1878, Je 2,7:5
Porter, H Fitz John, 1933, Ja 26,17:4
Porter, H Hobart (por), 1947, F 10,29:1
Porter, H Hobart Mrs, 1945, My 5,15:2
Porter, Harold G, 1940, D 31,15:4
Porter, Harold V, 1955, D 26,19:2
Porter, Harry F, 1963, O 10,41:2
Porter, Harry L, 1958, My 7,35:4
Porter, Harry O Lt, 1872, Je 1,4:7
Porter, Harry W, 1955, Jl 16,15:4
Porter, Henry A, 1946, N 18,23:3
Porter, Henry G, 1957, Mr 7,29:4
Porter, Henry Hobart, 1904, Ap 16,9:6
Porter, Henry Kirke, 1921, Ap 12,17:5
Porter, Herbert, 1939, My 12,21:5
Porter, Horace C, 1944, Je 16,19:5
Porter, Horace Gen, 1921, My 27,17:6
Porter, Horace Gen (por), 1921, My 30,9:1
Porter, Horace Gen, 1921, S 10,11:4
Porter, Horace Mrs, 1903, Ap 7,9:6
Porter, Hubert E V, 1946, Mr 26,29:2
Porter, Hugh, 1960, S 23,29:1
Porter, Hugh C, 1964, Mr 13,33:4
Porter, Irving W, 1951, S 3,13:5
Porter, Irving W Mrs, 1952, N 22,24:5
Porter, J Elmer, 1961, S 9,19:6
Porter, J Robert, 1965, N 6,29:5
Porter, J Y, 1927, Mr 17,23:3
Porter, James D Ex-Gov, 1912, My 19,II,15:5
Porter, James E, 1954, O 31,89:2
Porter, James F, 1939, Jl 31,13:4
Porter, James J, 1918, N 14,13:1
Porter, James O, 1942, O 8,27:3
Porter, James O Mrs, 1942, N 27,23:3
Porter, James P, 1956, S 16,84:6
Porter, James W, 1948, Ap 8,25:2; 1951, D 29,11:5
Porter, Jessie, 1940, Ap 16,23:4
Porter, John, 1913, N 22,15:4; 1946, S 12,9:6
Porter, John A, 1866, Ag 29,3:1
Porter, John B, 1937, S 12,II,7:1; 1944, Ap 18,21:5
Porter, John B Lt-Col, 1915, Je 22,15:6
Porter, John C, 1959, My 29,23:2
Porter, John E, 1942, Je 29,15:4
Porter, John H, 1945, F 3,11:3; 1947, S 30,25:2
Porter, John Lyman Mrs (Eleanor Hodgman Porter) 1920, My 23,22:4
Porter, John W Dr, 1937, S 9,23:2
Porter, Joseph A, 1955, My 20,25:2
Porter, Joseph D, 1953, Ag 29,17:3
Porter, Joseph F, 1942, N 8,51:1
Porter, Joseph L (will, Ja 10,18:3), 1942, Ja 7,20:3
Porter, Joseph S, 1948, Ap 25,69:1
Porter, Josiah Gen, 1894, D 15,1:5
Porter, Kate Mrs, 1952, Ag 4,15:4
Porter, Kenneth, 1943, Mr 9,23:4
Porter, King A, 1940, Mr 9,15:3
Porter, Leon A, 1961, Jl 12,32:4
Porter, Leroy V, 1944, D 23,13:2
Porter, Lester W, 1960, F 7,84:8
Porter, Lew (L J Tableporter), 1956, Ja 30,27:2
Porter, Linn Boyd, 1916, Je 30,11:5
Porter, Livingston, 1955, Mr 22,31:4
Porter, Logan W, 1937, Ag 18,19:1
Porter, Louis H (por), 1946, Ja 20,42:4
Porter, Louis H Mrs, 1946, Jl 1,31:2
Porter, Louis M, 1920, Je 12,13:4; 1942, Je 5,17:2
Porter, Lucius C, 1958, S 9,35:5
Porter, Lucy K W Mrs, 1940, D 7,17:5
Porter, Luther A, 1943, O 23,13:5
Porter, M Adeline, 1947, D 18,29:3
Porter, M Burr Col, 1871, Mr 19,1:6
Porter, M Gibson, 1947, O 27,21:5
Porter, M J Mrs, 1949, N 27,104:4
Porter, Maria Morgan, 1913, N 27,13:6
Porter, Marion A Mrs, 1941, My 25,36:6
Porter, Mark L, 1955, My 5,33:2
Porter, Martha Day, 1922, N 7,17:4
Porter, Martha S, 1960, Ja 5,31:1
Porter, Martin J, 1954, Mr 28,88:6
Porter, Martin R, 1951, My 29,25:5
Porter, Matthew, 1951, D 21,27:5
Porter, Matthew B, 1952, My 8,31:4
Porter, Mildred J Mrs, 1954, N 6,17:1
Porter, Nathan Jr Mrs, 1945, D 25,23:5
Porter, Nathan T, 1914, Ap 20,9:3; 1953, O 23,23:
Porter, Nathan T Jr, 1947, F 21,20:2
Porter, Newton H, 1945, My 17,19:3
Porter, Noah, 1892, Mr 5,4:6
Porter, Oliver M, 1959, D 1,39:2
Porter, Omer J, 1967, D 20,45:1
Porter, P S, 1884, Jl 26,5:4
Porter, Paul, 1957, O 19,21:1
Porter, Peter A, 1864, Je 5,4:5; 1925, D 16,25:5
Porter, Peter A Col, 1871, Je 26,2:6
Porter, Pleasant Gen, 1907, S 4,7:5
Porter, Quincy, 1966, N 13,89:1
Porter, R L (Oct 5), 1965, O 11,61:4
Porter, R Marion, 1949, F 14,19:4
Porter, Ralph C Mrs, 1955, My 29,45:1
Porter, Ralph C Sr, 1950, Ap 18,31:2
Porter, Ray W, 1956, Jl 11,29:5
Porter, Raymond A, 1949, Ap 3,76:2
Porter, Raymond E, 1954, Mr 19,23:4
Porter, Raymond W, 1950, D 12,33:4
Porter, Richard A, 1925, S 18,23:5
Porter, Richard A Mrs, 1937, N 11,25:1
Porter, Robert E Mrs, 1937, Ja 14,21:2
Porter, Robert P, 1917, Mr 17,13:4
Porter, Robert Percival, 1917, Mr 1,13:5
Porter, Robert W, 1948, O 28,29:4
Porter, Roland G, 1953, S 4,15:2
Porter, Roy P, 1947, D 27,14:2
Porter, Roy W, 1946, S 2,17:4
Porter, Russell B (funl plans, Ap 18,39:1; funl, Ap 20,27:1), 1962, Ap 17,42:2
Porter, Russell W, 1949, F 24,24:2
Porter, S G, 1930, Je 28,15:6
Porter, S L, 1946, O 28,27:3
Porter, Samuel Prof, 1901, S 4,2:2
Porter, Samuel Q, 1907, F 23,9:6
Porter, Seth Grosvenor Capt, 1910, O 28,9:6
Porter, Seton, 1953, F 7,15:1
Porter, Seton Mrs, 1954, Je 14,21:3
Porter, Silas W, 1937, My 18,23:6
Porter, Stanley P, 1946, Je 18,25:3
Porter, T D, 1880, D 13,1:4
Porter, Thomas Wyman, 1924, Ag 14,15:5
Porter, W C, 1958, Ap 22,33:4
Porter, W D Commodore, 1864, My 2,1:4
Porter, W H, 1926, D 1,1:5
Porter, Walter B, 1953, O 13,29:2
Porter, Walter R, 1941, Jl 20,30:2
Porter, Wilfred W, 1949, O 22,17:3
Porter, Willard B, 1941, My 13,23:4
Porter, William A, 1873, N 1,8:2
Porter, William B (por), 1947, Je 24,23:4
Porter, William E, 1948, Mr 25,27:2; 1951, N 17
Porter, William Evelyn Dr, 1925, Mr 27,19:6
Porter, William H, 1944, My 7,45:1; 1953, D 10
1954, S 11,17:6; 1962, My 8,39:2

Porter, William H Jr Commander, 1937, Ja 22,21:5
Porter, William M, 1937, Jl 22,19:5
Porter, William O, 1938, Jl 15,17:5
Porter, William S, 1943, Mr 9,24:3
Porter, William S Mrs, 1959, Ag 15,17:2
Porter, William Sterling, 1915, Ag 11,9:6
Porter, Willis D, 1945, N 21,21:3
Porterfield, Allen W, 1952, Ap 22,29:2
Porterfield, Austin R, 1961, D 18,35:4
Porterfield, E L, 1926, N 10,27:3
Porterfield, John F, 1944, O 7,13:5
Porterfield, Thomas B, 1947, Je 8,60:4
Porterfield, William H, 1958, N 18,37:4
Porteus, Luke C, 1949, N 4,28:6
Portfolio, Almerindo, 1966, Ja 26,37:1
Portfolio, Almerindo Mrs, 1948, My 1,15:2
Portfolio, Pasquale, 1946, Je 10,21:3
porth, Charles A, 1952, Mr 17,21:2
Porth, Henry W, 1938, Ag 11,17:5
Porth, Mathias, 1952, Mr 4,27:3
Portinari, Candido, 1962, F 8,31:4
Portis, Jack Mrs, 1958, My 4,89:1
Portland, Dowager Duchess of, 1954, Jl 31,13:3
Portland, Duke, 1879, D 7,7:1
Portland, duke of (por), 1943, Ap 27,23:3
Portlock, Miles F, 1937, D 1,23:2
Portman, Gerald B, 1948, S 4,15:6
Portman, Gerald W B Viscount, 1967, N 4,33:2
Portman, Henry Berkeley Viscount, 1923, Ja 19,17:6
Portman, John N, 1951, Ap 29,88:8
Portman, Lord, 1946, N 5,25:2
Portman, Viscount, 1942, Jl 15,19:5
Portmann, Ursus V, 1966, My 23,41:3
Portner, William, 1948, Ag 6,17:5
Portney, Jan K, 1941, S 30,23:6
Portnof, Hyman, 1952, Jl 1,23:4
Portnof, Hyman Mrs, 1939, My 6,17:5
Portnoff, Alex, 1949, D 21,29:2
Portnow, Andrew, 1956, My 5,19:4
Portong, Henry A, 1963, N 19,41:1
Portong, Ludolf, 1939, My 27,15:5
Portou, Ralph, 1948, Jl 11,53:1
Portrafke, Aug R, 1941, Jl 23,19:6
Ports, Earl G, 1952, D 5,27:4
Portsea, Lord, 1948, N 2,25:4
Portsmouth, Countess of, 1938, My 10,21:2
Portugal, Jose, 1948, Je 1,23:3
Portugal, Joseph H, 1940, S 22,49:2
Portuondo, Rafael Gen, 1908, Jl 17,7:6
Porvers, Patrick T (funl, S 1,21:6), 1925, Ag 29,11:5
Pos, Julius, 1964, Ap 28,37:1
Posadas, Juan, 1940, Ja 4,23:3
Posansky, Edmond, 1913, Ap 28,11:4
Poschinger, Ludwig von Mrs, 1951, S 8,17:6
Posegate, Charles S Mrs, 1950, Ap 29,15:5
Posella, Anthony, 1955, My 19,29:1
Posella, Dante L, 1957, Mr 18,10:7
Posen, Alvah (Al), 1960, Je 12,86:5
Posener, Phil, 1955, F 18,21:2
Posener, Salomon, 1946, O 25,23:1
Poser, Max H, 1946, Ja 5,14:2
Posey, Cumberland W, 1946, Mr 29,24:3
Posey, John B, 1956, F 5,86:2
Posey, Louis C, 1949, My 2,25:4
Posey, William T, 1947, Ag 19,23:6
Poskay, Joseph A Sr, 1955, Ja 23,85:2
Poskitt, George A, 1941, N 12,23:1
Poskitt, Henry J, 1950, F 20,25:2
Posnanaski, Jan Mrs (P Frijsh), 1960, Jl 11,29:1
Posnansky, Arturo, 1946, Jl 29,21:4
Posnansky, Israel, 1968, Jl 4,19:1
Posner, Abraham Mrs, 1943, D 20,23:4
Posner, Alex Mrs, 1952, D 11,33:5
Posner, Arnold J, 1967, Ja 9,36:7
Posner, Benjamin, 1960, Ag 8,21:5
Posner, Emil R, 1951, S 14,25:2
Posner, Harry, 1960, Je 19,88:2; 1962, Ag 7,29:2
Posner, Jacob D Mrs, 1962, My 21,33:3
Posner, John J, 1965, F 21,76:6
Posner, Joseph, 1962, Ag 8,31:4
Posner, Louis, 1947, Jl 6,40:4; 1949, Ap 1,25:1
Posner, Louis D, 1953, Jl 14,27:1
Posner, Louis S Mrs, 1963, D 20,26:7
Posner, Morris, 1949, Ag 26,19:1; 1957, D 16,29:2
Posner, Nathan E, 1962, Je 2,19:4
Posner, Ralph, 1968, F 15,43:4
Posner, Reuben A, 1966, Ap 17,87:2
Posner, Samuel, 1940, F 24,13:1
Posner, William, 1961, Ap 18,37:3
Posnjak, Eugene W, 1949, Ag 6,17:4
Pospesel, Howard I, 1948, Ap 25,68:3
Pospeshil, Joseph B, 1950, F 24,23:4
Pospichal, Hubert M Rev, 1968, Mr 29,45:3
Pospisil, Vilem, 1942, D 2,25:5
Pospisil, William Mrs, 1937, O 24,II,8:5
Poss, George W, 1947, D 4,31:2
Poss, Louis, 1959, Jl 20,25:5
Possehl, John, 1940, S 16,10:3
Posselt, Frederick G, 1950, S 12,27:2
Posser, Carlo, 1949, Ap 13,29:1
Posser, Paul B, 1956, Mr 4,89:1
Possony, Ernst, 1957, Ap 10,33:3
Post, A H S, 1961, Je 6,37:3
Post, A K, 1872, Jl 9,4:7
Post, A Seton (por), 1942, Ja 16,22:4
Post, A Van Zo, 1938, Ja 24,23:4
Post, Adrian, 1903, Ag 18,7:6; 1946, Mr 2,13:5
Post, Adrian T, 1948, S 1,24:2
Post, Albert M Mrs, 1941, Mr 14,21:6
Post, Albert W, 1950, Ap 21,23:2
Post, Alfred H, 1940, My 8,23:2
Post, Alfred P, 1940, Ja 7,48:7
Post, Alfred Seton, 1914, Ap 7,9:6; 1922, Ap 15,15:4
Post, Allen T, 1949, Ja 7,21:4
Post, Allison W, 1944, N 22,19:5
Post, Allison W Mrs, 1961, Mr 12,86:8
Post, Andrew J Mrs, 1945, D 6,27:5
Post, Andrew Jackson, 1968, D 19,47:1
Post, Arlington G, 1950, N 23,35:1
Post, Arthur E, 1952, O 9,31:1
Post, Arthur E Mrs, 1949, Mr 13,76:4
Post, Arthur F, 1940, N 12,23:2
Post, Arthur W, 1947, S 19,23:2; 1967, S 26,47:1
Post, Augustus, 1952, O 5,88:1
Post, B P, 1927, F 26,15:5
Post, C L Mrs, 1948, Ja 5,19:4
Post, Carroll L (will, My 14,9:7), 1948, Ap 27,25:5
Post, Chandler R, 1959, N 4,35:2
Post, Charles A, 1943, My 4,23:3
Post, Charles Alfred, 1921, Ap 27,17:4
Post, Charles F, 1948, My 18,23:4; 1963, Jl 11,29:5
Post, Charles H, 1925, Ja 17,15:4
Post, Charles I, 1954, O 12,27:5
Post, Charles J, 1956, S 26,33:2
Post, Charles J Mrs, 1965, Je 7,37:2
Post, Charles M Jr, 1958, F 5,27:2
Post, Charles Mrs, 1951, Je 22,25:3
Post, Charles T, 1951, F 1,25:5
Post, Chester L, 1950, Ag 22,27:4
Post, D J, 1933, Je 26,15:4
Post, David E Mrs, 1943, N 5,19:1
Post, Edward C (funl, Jl 8,13:7), 1915, Jl 6,9:6
Post, Edward C Mrs, 1948, Mr 22,23:3
Post, Edward M, 1946, Je 10,21:3
Post, Edward S, 1923, N 17,13:4
Post, Edwin A, 1912, Ja 23,11:4
Post, Edwin Frederick, 1914, Jl 24,9:6
Post, Elias G, 1943, N 18,23:3
Post, Emily Mrs (funl, S 30,27:2), 1960, S 27,1:4
Post, Erastus F (por), 1937, Mr 31,23:4
Post, Erastus L, 1948, Je 30,25:3
Post, Frank A, 1943, S 28,25:3; 1956, Ag 18,17:6
Post, Frank C Mrs, 1940, Ag 14,19:3
Post, Frank T, 1941, Mr 6,21:4
Post, Frederick A, 1950, Ap 1,15:5
Post, Frederick A Mrs, 1950, Ap 1,15:5
Post, Frederick R, 1945, Je 18,19:1
Post, Frederick W Mrs, 1964, D 17,41:2
Post, George A, 1950, Mr 28,32:2
Post, George A Mrs, 1946, O 3,27:4
Post, George Adams (funl, N 4,23:3), 1925, N 2,23:3
Post, George B, 1937, My 26,25:2; 1952, D 20,17:2; 1960, Mr 5,19:4
Post, George B Mrs, 1957, O 26,21:5
Post, George Browne (funl, D 2,11:6), 1913, N 29, 13:4
Post, George Edward Dr, 1909, O 1,9:4
Post, George W 3d, 1944, Mr 4,13:5
Post, Gerardus, 1864, D 8,4:5
Post, Grace F Mrs, 1937, My 25,28:1
Post, Guy Bates, 1968, Ja 18,39:4
Post, H B, 1937, Jl 2,21:6
Post, Harold J, 1950, O 5,31:2
Post, Harold W, 1923, Ag 16,15:3
Post, Harry, 1954, Jl 16,21:2
Post, Harry G, 1954, Jl 22,23:5
Post, Henry A B Col, 1914, Ja 27,9:6
Post, Henry K, 1945, O 16,23:5
Post, Henry M, 1948, N 4,29:3
Post, Henry M Mrs, 1955, N 17,35:3
Post, Herbert W, 1951, F 19,23:2
Post, Herman Casper von, 1913, O 11,15:4
Post, Hiram F, 1948, N 25,31:2
Post, Howard G, 1955, Mr 27,86:8
Post, Hoyt G, 1958, My 17,19:6
Post, Irving B, 1947, S 25,29:4
Post, Jacob Gould, 1904, F 13,9:5
Post, Jacob Mrs, 1938, D 23,19:1
Post, James H (por), 1938, Mr 6,II,9:1
Post, James H Mrs, 1944, Mr 6,19:5
Post, James O, 1951, Ap 22,89:1
Post, James O Mrs, 1964, Jl 28,29:2
Post, John D, 1952, Mr 4,27:3
Post, John F, 1947, F 18,25:4
Post, John H, 1907, Ap 7,9:5
Post, John J, 1945, Je 5,19:5
Post, John R, 1955, O 10,27:4
Post, Judson K, 1940, Je 23,30:6
Post, Kenneth, 1955, O 26,31:2
Post, L D, 1933, D 2,13:3
Post, L F, 1928, Ja 11,29:1
Post, Lawrence T, 1958, My 15,29:3
Post, Leonard E, 1955, Je 27,21:6
Post, Lewis E, 1949, Ja 21,21:2
Post, Louis J, 1944, Je 13,19:6
Post, Louise F Mrs, 1947, F 6,23:4
Post, M D, 1930, Je 24,25:3
Post, Mabel L, 1943, Ap 2,21:5
Post, Marilla Mrs, 1921, F 24,13:6
Post, Mary W H Mrs, 1942, O 16,19:6
Post, May Mrs, 1959, Ap 13,31:1
Post, Minturn Dr, 1869, Ag 28,7:3
Post, Morris, 1956, N 28,35:4
Post, Nathan E, 1953, Jl 8,27:4
Post, Peter, 1948, D 26,52:3
Post, Philip Sidney, 1920, Je 28,15:4
Post, Rawson J Capt, 1908, F 3,9:5
Post, Regis H, 1944, O 6,23:1
Post, Richard Sr, 1943, F 28,47:5
Post, Robert C, 1945, My 3,23:1
Post, Robert F, 1950, D 3,89:1
Post, Russell L, 1948, Ap 2,23:5
Post, S A L, 1873, Ja 11,1:6
Post, Samuel, 1937, O 20,10:6
Post, Susan P Mrs, 1937, S 6,17:5
Post, W, 1935, Ag 17,1:8
Post, W F, 1946, F 4,25:5
Post, Waldron, 1946, Ja 24,22:2
Post, Waldron K, 1955, F 7,21:4
Post, Waldron K Mrs (will, S 3,5:1), 1939, Ag 14,15:5
Post, Waldron Mrs, 1960, O 19,45:2
Post, Walter A, 1912, F 13,11:4
Post, Walter L, 1963, D 1,84:4
Post, Wilfred M, 1966, Ja 20,30:2
Post, Wilfred M Mrs, 1925, S 10,25:5
Post, Willard Mrs, 1947, Jl 16,23:4
Post, William, 1945, Ag 2,19:6; 1965, Ag 24,36:1
Post, William D, 1943, Ag 11,19:6
Post, William G, 1964, My 11,31:2
Post, William S, 1940, Jl 9,21:4
Post, William S Mrs, 1956, O 13,19:3
Post, Woodruff L, 1951, O 12,28:2
Post, Wright E, 1907, S 2,7:6
Postance, William C, 1953, Ap 15,31:1
Postel, August C, 1955, Mr 26,15:2
Postel, Harry Sr, 1946, O 16,27:3
Postelwaite, Edward T, 1917, N 16,11:4
Posten, Herbert W, 1962, Ag 26,82:6
Postgate, George W, 1942, D 6,76:2
Postgate, J P Dr, 1926, Jl 16,15:4
Postgate, John William, 1921, My 4,10:5
Postgate, Margaret J, 1953, O 1,29:2
Posthauer, Charles W, 1937, My 22,15:3
Postlethwaite, Clarence E, 1943, Ap 16,21:4
Postlethwaite, Clarence E Mrs, 1948, O 26,31:4
Postlethwaite, Muriel, 1952, Ja 20,85:1
Postley, Clarence Ashley Col, 1908, My 29,7:3
Postley, Evelyn T Mrs, 1956, Jl 2,21:1
Postley, John E, 1966, S 23,37:1
Postoll, Harry H, 1948, Ap 6,23:5
Poston, Grace, 1952, D 17,25:3
Poston, Ulysses S, 1955, My 16,23:6
Poston, Wade H Sr, 1951, Jl 28,11:3
Potanos, John N, 1963, Je 6,35:4
Potanovic, John F, 1950, N 23,35:3
Poteat, E McNeill Rev, 1937, Je 27,II,6:7
Poteat, Edwin M, 1955, D 18,92:4
Poteat, James D, 1950, Mr 18,14:2
Poteat, W L, 1938, Mr 13,II,8:7
Poteet, Fred H, 1941, Jl 30,17:6
Potel, Victor, 1947, Mr 10,21:5
Potemkin, Vladimir P (por), 1946, F 24,44:1
Poten, Frederick W, 1950, N 18,15:7
Potente, Nicholas J, 1942, S 26,15:2
Poterfield, Lewis B, 1942, Ap 6,15:4
Potestad, R E L de Marquis, 1917, F 19,11:5
Poth, George Mrs, 1949, S 24,13:3
Poth, John, 1924, N 9,7:1
Poth, William, 1963, Je 23,85:1
Pothier, A J, 1928, F 5,29:6
Pothier, Aram J Mrs, 1947, Mr 1,15:6
Pothier, Joseph C, 1943, D 2,27:3
Pothier, William A, 1937, Ja 3,II,8:1
Pothin, Alfred J Mrs, 1950, N 4,17:5
Potie, Auguste, 1939, O 18,25:5
Potin, 1871, Ag 8,1:5
Potnofsky, Benjamin Mrs, 1949, Je 2,27:4
Potocki, Jerzy, 1961, S 22,34:1
Potofsky, Jacob S Mrs, 1946, My 17,22:3
Potoker, Benjamin, 1954, O 28,35:5
Potookian, Alan, 1959, Ap 8,37:3
Pototzky, Carl, 1948, S 22,31:3
Potozky, Henry, 1955, O 24,27:4
Potsdamer, Joseph B, 1947, F 17,19:3
Potskowski, Edward, 1942, F 19,38:7
Pott, Francis L H, 1947, Mr 8,13:6
Pott, Henry R, 1944, Je 15,19:3
Pott, Herbert, 1945, Ag 6,15:5
Pott, James, 1905, F 9,9:4
Pott, John, 1905, Ap 4,20:1
Pott, Richard M (por), 1948, D 16,29:6
Pott, Richard M Mrs, 1953, Ag 19,29:5
Pott, William H, 1941, D 23,22:2
Pott, William S, 1967, N 8,47:2
Pottberg, Charles, 1938, Ja 11,23:5
Pottberg, Henry R, 1950, Je 30,23:5
Pottberg, Henry R Mrs, 1951, Ja 24,27:3
Pottenger, Francis M, 1961, Je 11,86:2
Pottenger, James L, 1950, Je 16,25:5

Potter, A Cuthbert, 1956, Ap 12,23:5
Potter, Aaron A, 1949, N 17,29:4
Potter, Adrian M, 1960, S 28,39:5
Potter, Albert E, 1949, Je 29,27:5
Potter, Albert K, 1948, N 18,27:5
Potter, Alex (por), 1940, Je 21,21:5
Potter, Alexander B, 1945, Je 22,15:5
Potter, Alfred C, 1940, N 2,15:6
Potter, Allen, 1958, S 28,88:5
Potter, Alonzo, 1957, S 1,56:4
Potter, Alonzo Mrs, 1909, O 29,9:6; 1956, Ap 8,84:3
Potter, Andrew B, 1903, O 2,7:6
Potter, Anna M, 1945, D 25,23:4
Potter, Arthur D Mrs, 1953, My 20,29:1
Potter, Asa P, 1967, S 6,44:6
Potter, Ashton Capt, 1914, Ag 6,11:7
Potter, Beatrix (will), 1944, Mr 8,12:3
Potter, Benjamin C, 1963, My 7,43:1
Potter, Beverly R, 1950, F 23,27:3
Potter, Bishop, 1865, Jl 21,5:3
Potter, Blanche, 1942, O 6,23:2
Potter, Bp Mrs, 1874, D 29,8:1
Potter, C Col, 1881, F 2,5:3
Potter, C H Col, 1901, D 11,9:4
Potter, C L, 1928, Ag 7,21:1
Potter, C N, 1882, Ja 22,2:2
Potter, Carl H, 1946, My 19,42:4
Potter, Carl S, 1942, Ap 11,13:1
Potter, Carlton, 1962, Je 4,29:5
Potter, Charles, 1925, N 2,23:4
Potter, Charles A Jr, 1958, Ag 7,25:5
Potter, Charles E, 1947, S 22,23:3
Potter, Charles F, 1962, O 5,33:1
Potter, Charles G, 1956, J. 9,23:4
Potter, Charles H, 1943, F 21,32:8
Potter, Chester, 1956, O 18,33:4
Potter, Clarence A, 1948, N 19,28:3
Potter, Clarence H, 1958, Ja 12,86:2
Potter, Clarkson, 1953, O 6,29:2
Potter, Clarkson A, 1944, F 22,23:1
Potter, Claude J, 1951, Jl 20,21:1
Potter, Courtland N, 1950, Ja 24,32:4
Potter, Dean, 1939, N 22,21:2
Potter, E Clifford, 1937, D 12,II,9:1
Potter, E E Com, 1902, Ja 9,9:6
Potter, E K, 1882, Ap 11,5:3
Potter, E L, 1880, Ap 22,4:7
Potter, E P, 1925, N 6,23:6
Potter, E S, 1936, My 27,23:3
Potter, Edmund, 1883, N 18,4:7
Potter, Edward C, 1923, Je 23,11:6; 1951, Mr 14,33:3
Potter, Edward C Mrs, 1938, My 31,19:4
Potter, Edward H, 1967, Je 4,86:4
Potter, Edward Jr Mrs, 1949, Ag 16,23:1
Potter, Edward T, 1904, D 22,9:4
Potter, Edward W, 1912, Jl 13,9:4
Potter, Edwin A, 1940, Ag 22,19:4
Potter, Elizabeth S Mrs, 1942, My 15,20:2
Potter, Ellen C, 1958, F 10,23:4
Potter, Elmer C Mrs, 1948, F 3,25:1
Potter, Emory E, 1945, D 25,23:4
Potter, Erastus E, 1906, D 7,11:5
Potter, Flora M Mrs, 1937, Ap 29,21:2
Potter, Floyd A, 1949, Je 6,19:4
Potter, Frances Boardman Squire Mrs, 1914, Mr 26, 11:5
Potter, Frances G Mrs, 1940, D 17,26:3
Potter, Francis D, 1941, F 20,19:2
Potter, Francis H Mrs, 1924, D 19,21:3
Potter, Francis M, 1946, N 13,27:4; 1952, Ag 18,17:3
Potter, Frank A, 1950, D 20,31:2
Potter, Frank A Mrs, 1947, Ap 7,23:5
Potter, Frank E, 1945, My 24,19:2
Potter, Frank M, 1950, Mr 19,93:1
Potter, Frank R, 1941, Ag 11,13:2
Potter, Franklin E, 1954, Mr 9,27:5
Potter, Fred W, 1947, N 11,27:1
Potter, Frederick, 1923, Mr 24,13:5
Potter, Frederick D (por), 1946, N 18,23:6
Potter, G, 1883, Mr 20,5:1
Potter, George, 1954, Ap 14,29:4
Potter, George F, 1952, F 3,84:2
Potter, George H, 1953, Ja 16,23:2
Potter, George H Mrs, 1951, Ja 27,13:5
Potter, George W, 1940, Mr 23,13:2; 1959, Ag 11,27:4
Potter, Grace, 1943, Jl 31,13:6
Potter, Grace (cor, F 16,25:2), 1951, F 15,31:3
Potter, Guy D, 1953, Jl 1,29:4
Potter, H C Bishop Mrs, 1901, Je 30,1:2
Potter, Harriet B Mrs, 1937, My 5,25:5
Potter, Harriet J Mrs, 1937, F 19,19:3
Potter, Harry, 1940, F 6,22:3
Potter, Harry Mrs, 1948, N 13,15:4
Potter, Helen F Mrs, 1937, Mr 12,23:2
Potter, Henry Albert Col, 1917, Ap 12,11:6
Potter, Henry B, 1940, N 23,17:5
Potter, Henry C Bp, 1909, Mr 5,9:3
Potter, Henry C Mrs, 1909, Mr 15,9:4
Potter, Henry Clay, 1912, Ja 2,11:5
Potter, Henry Langdon Col, 1907, Mr 31,9:7
Potter, Henry R, 1946, Ja 24,21:5
Potter, Horace E, 1948, F 21,13:3
Potter, Horatio Lt, 1874, Jl 28,4:6
Potter, Horatio Rev, 1887, Ja 3,1:5
Potter, Howard E, 1961, Je 30,27:2
Potter, Howard L, 1952, O 6,25:3
Potter, Howard N, 1937, Ag 1,II,6:1
Potter, Irving W, 1956, S 18,35:1
Potter, J B, 1938, Je 5,45:1
Potter, J Forbes, 1937, N 26,21:4
Potter, J H, 1903, Je 3,9:6
Potter, J Robert, 1968, S 23,35:4
Potter, J S, 1904, S 14,1:6
Potter, J W Fuller, 1945, Jl 17,13:4
Potter, Jacob F, 1941, Jl 5,11:2
Potter, James Boyd, 1918, F 6,9:5
Potter, James Brown (funl, F 25,13:5), 1922, F 23, 15:3
Potter, James S, 1948, S 15,31:1
Potter, James T, 1946, N 19,31:4
Potter, Jennie E, 1945, Je 22,15:3
Potter, Jennie S Mrs, 1939, Ja 21,15:1
Potter, Jesse, 1959, Ap 12,86:4
Potter, John C Mrs, 1944, Ja 14,19:3
Potter, John D Sr Mrs, 1954, Ag 8,85:2
Potter, John E, 1947, D 23,23:2
Potter, John E Mrs, 1949, Ag 28,72:1
Potter, John H, 1966, Je 27,35:5
Potter, John H N, 1961, Ag 6,85:2
Potter, John J, 1945, D 8,17:2
Potter, John M (por), 1947, Ja 10,21:1
Potter, John S, 1942, Ag 27,19:5
Potter, John W, 1942, Je 4,19:4; 1947, My 18,60:5
Potter, Joseph C, 1964, O 27,39:4
Potter, Joseph Judge, 1902, Mr 31,9:6
Potter, Justin, 1961, D 10,88:7
Potter, Lloyd G, 1961, Ja 17,27:4
Potter, M Henry, 1942, Je 11,23:5
Potter, Marion C, 1943, Mr 24,23:1
Potter, Marion E, 1953, Je 4,29:4
Potter, Mark W (por), 1942, Ag 13,19:5
Potter, Mark W Mrs, 1962, Ja 5,29:3
Potter, Mary D Mrs, 1937, S 1,19:2
Potter, Mary G, 1943, Ja 14,21:4
Potter, Mildred, 1915, S 26,15:4
Potter, Morey J, 1950, Ap 11,31:2
Potter, Murray Anthony Prof, 1915, My 18,13:6
Potter, Nathaniel Bowditch Dr, 1919, Jl 6,20:3
Potter, O B, 1894, Ja 3,1:5
Potter, Olin C Mrs, 1965, Mr 13,25:4
Potter, Ormsby F, 1948, S 22,31:5
Potter, Orrin W, 1907, My 18,7:6
Potter, Osler F, 1938, Ag 13,13:6
Potter, Oswald W, 1951, F 24,13:1
Potter, Page F, 1953, Je 25,27:4
Potter, Paul Meredith, 1921, Mr 8,11:4
Potter, Philip C, 1960, N 8,29:3
Potter, Philip S Sr, 1963, Ap 20,27:4
Potter, Phineas T, 1946, D 10,31:4
Potter, Phyllis, 1950, Je 16,25:4
Potter, Pittman B Mrs, 1940, Ja 10,21:4
Potter, R B Mrs, 1954, O 8,23:1
Potter, Ralph F, 1944, S 4,19:2
Potter, Raymond B, 1947, S 11,27:2
Potter, Raymond G, 1947, Ap 5,19:5
Potter, Raymond T Dr, 1968, Ag 14,39:3
Potter, Robert B Gen (est), 1914, My 2,9:7
Potter, Robert B Mrs, 1939, Mr 18,17:2
Potter, Robert Bruce, 1913, S 21,II,15:4
Potter, Robert S, 1947, Ap 13,61:1
Potter, Rockwell H, 1967, My 17,47:2
Potter, Roderick, 1959, Mr 6,25:4
Potter, Russell F, 1957, O 31,31:4
Potter, Russell Mrs, 1968, Ag 18,88:5
Potter, Samuel, 1937, F 12,23:5
Potter, Samuel E, 1948, Ja 7,25:3
Potter, Samuel E Mrs, 1950, F 9,29:5
Potter, Samuel H, 1963, O 15,39:4
Potter, Samuel L, 1937, Mr 27,15:4
Potter, Stephen J, 1951, Jl 28,11:6
Potter, Steven S, 1937, Ja 31,II,8:7
Potter, T Irving, 1963, D 18,37:7
Potter, Thomas, 1955, S 23,26:4
Potter, Thomas A (por), 1949, Ja 26,25:5
Potter, Thomas Col, 1910, D 3,11:4
Potter, Thomas Jr Mrs, 1954, Ja 3,88:6
Potter, Vincent G, 1963, Ag 3,17:4
Potter, Virginia (por), 1937, O 28,25:3
Potter, W, 1926, Ap 30,19:4
Potter, W F, 1905, Ap 3,1:1
Potter, Walter N, 1955, Mr 26,15:2
Potter, Wellington, 1946, My 2,21:2
Potter, Wilfrid C, 1947, Je 14,15:6
Potter, William, 1968, Ja 24,42:1
Potter, William Appleton, 1909, F 22,9:6
Potter, William Bleeker, 1914, Jl 15,9:6
Potter, William C, 1957, Ja 3,33:3
Potter, William C Mrs, 1946, N 30,15:6
Potter, William Clarkson, 1919, F 22,9:4
Potter, William F, 1941, Je 23,17:5
Potter, William H, 1940, Ja 11,23:2
Potter, William J, 1964, Jl 11,25:3; 1965, My 24,31:5
Potter, William P Justice, 1918, Ap 15,15:6
Potter, William P Rear-Adm, 1917, Je 22,13:4
Potter, William S, 1964, Jl 9,33:3
Potter, William W Jr, 1937, Ja 25,19:2
Potter, Wilson, 1937, Ja 1,23:3; 1946, Je 13,27:4
Potter, Winfield Scott, 1919, Ja 5,22:4
Potter, Zenas L, 1958, Jl 10,27:5
Potters, Barney, 1941, Mr 22,15:4
Potters, Henry A, 1946, Jl 19,19:5
Potterton, Alfred B, 1940, N 8,21:5
Potterton, Arthur, 1958, Mr 24,27:4
Potterton, Frederick, 1940, F 19,17:5
Potterton, James E Sr, 1941, Je 27,17:5
Potterton, T E, 1933, D 10,II,8:7
Pottinger, David T, 1958, D 2,37:5
Pottle, Frank B, 1943, N 20,13:5
Pottle, Juliet W T Mrs, 1956, Ja 30,27:2
Potts, Abraham G, 1952, Je 3,29:4
Potts, Ada M, 1942, Ag 11,19:2
Potts, Albert C, 1952, My 20,25:3
Potts, Allan, 1952, N 7,23:1
Potts, Amos H, 1941, Ag 29,17:4
Potts, Anne M, 1956, Mr 3,19:5
Potts, Catherine (Sister M Dolorosa), 1952, Jl 27, 57:2
Potts, Charles E, 1956, Ag 30,35:2
Potts, Charles H, 1941, Ja 2,23:4
Potts, Charles P Mrs, 1941, N 25,26:2
Potts, Claude W Sir, 1953, Ag 13,25:6
Potts, Clyde, 1950, My 20,15:4
Potts, Douglas, 1940, Mr 25,15:2
Potts, Dwight W, 1952, Ag 23,13:4
Potts, Edith M, 1959, Ap 12,86:5
Potts, Edward E, 1946, My 16,21:5
Potts, Franklin M, 1943, Ja 22,20:3
Potts, Fred A, 1956, Je 9,17:6
Potts, George H, 1911, N 2,11:5
Potts, Gilbert R, 1962, N 27,37:1
Potts, Godfrey, 1952, My 27,27:3
Potts, Harlan L, 1950, My 22,21:3
Potts, Herbert, 1942, O 8,27:2
Potts, Heston Nelson, 1968, Mr 6,47:3
Potts, Horace M, 1961, F 8,28:1
Potts, Hugh E Mrs, 1940, My 29,23:3
Potts, J E (see also D 13), 1877, D 14,8:4
Potts, J Herbert, 1907, Ap 3,9:7
Potts, James A, 1943, N 16,23:1
Potts, James D, 1958, S 7,87:2
Potts, Jimmy, 1949, Ja 4,24:1
Potts, John, 1872, Jl 25,8:6; 1938, Ap 29,21:1; 1942, Je 4,19:4
Potts, John C, 1955, O 29,19:2
Potts, John H, 1949, Mr 18,26:3
Potts, John H Sr, 1950, Je 24,13:3
Potts, John J, 1946, Jl 6,15:4
Potts, Joseph, 1953, Je 20,17:4
Potts, Joseph H, 1943, N 26,23:4
Potts, Joshua R H, 1957, Ag 7,27:4
Potts, Louis J, 1938, Ag 18,20:2
Potts, Mary A, 1947, S 19,23:5
Potts, Peter T, 1946, O 26,17:2
Potts, Richard T, 1940, Ja 10,21:2
Potts, Robert F, 1937, Ap 11,II,9:2
Potts, Robert M, 1957, Ap 7,88:1
Potts, Robert Mrs, 1909, Ag 24,9:5
Potts, Robert Rear-Adm, 1913, Je 25,9:5
Potts, Rockhill B Mrs, 1953, O 23,23:4
Potts, Samuel T, 1938, Ap 9,17:1
Potts, Susan, 1956, N 22,33:5
Potts, Thomas, 1916, Ja 3,13:2
Potts, Thomas C, 1955, Je 15,31:1
Potts, Thomas D, 1952, S 26,21:3
Potts, W G, 1937, S 4,15:1
Potts, William, 1908, Jl 31,5:4
Potts, William A, 1939, Jl 25,19:2
Potts, William B, 1960, Ap 7,35:2
Potts, William M, 1943, Je 2,25:4
Potts, William Mrs, 1942, D 19,19:2
Potts, William R, 1949, Ap 19,26:5
Potts, William Rockhill, 1922, F 19,22:2
Potts, Willis J, 1968, My 8,44:5
Potvin, Albert J, 1950, S 16,19:6
Potvin, Alfred, 1949, Ap 30,13:2
Potwin, Charles C, 1941, S 26,23:4
Potwin, Stephen G, 1952, Je 26,29:2
Potzger, John E, 1955, S 20,31:5
Pou, E W, 1934, Ap 2,17:1
Pouch, Alfred T, 1966, D 12,47:3
Pouch, Alonzo B, 1923, Je 18,13:7
Pouch, Alonzo B Mrs, 1947, Ap 17,27:4
Pouch, Frederick H Y, 1943, Ag 24,19:5
Pouch, Harriet E Mrs, 1905, Mr 9,7:6
Pouch, Kenneth A, 1955, Je 23,29:4
Pouch, O G, 1949, D 9,32:2
Pouch, William H, 1959, F 17,31:3
Pouch, William H Mrs (H Hellwig), 1960, N 27,8
Poucher, Barent G, 1952, Mr 20,29:1
Poucher, Charlotte B Mrs, 1913, S 19,9:4
Poucher, Franklyn J, 1950, D 22,23:2
Poucher, Henry, 1949, Ja 28,21:4
Poucher, Isaac B, 1920, My 13,11:3
Poucher, John W, 1948, F 18,28:2
Poucher, Morris R Mrs, 1950, S 12,27:3
Poucher, Refine B Mrs, 1943, Ag 15,39:3
Poucher, Timothy D Mrs, 1962, N 17,25:5
Pouelsen, John, 1967, S 7,33:5
Poughkeepsie Seer (Dr Andrew J Davis), 1910, Ja 14,9:4

Pougny, Jean, 1956, D 30,32:3
Pougy, Liane de, 1950, D 29,19:2
Pouilot, Leonidas Jr, 1939, O 21,15:4
Pouishnoff, Leff N, 1959, My 29,23:2
Poulbot, Francisque, 1946, S 17,7:3
Poulenc, Francis, 1963, Ja 31,7:2
Poulin, Mary C, 1948, Je 14,24:2
Poulin, Philippe P, 1958, O 13,29:4
Pouliot, Jean P, 1945, Ja 7,38:4
Poullet, Viscount, 1937, D 4,17:2
Poulsen, Valdemar, 1942, Ag 7,17:7
Poulson, Andrew T, 1946, N 24,79:7
Poulson, Ann A, 1951, Ap 27,23:4
Poulson, Edward, 1949, D 13,38:2
Poulson, Francis W, 1950, Mr 30,29:3
Poulson, G Lester, 1950, Ag 3,23:4
Poulson, Niels (funl, My 7,11:4), 1911, My 4,11:4
Poulsson, Anne E, 1939, Mr 20,17:5
Poulter, S Thomas, 1949, My 7,13:5
Poulterer, William T, 1954, Jl 28,23:3
Poultney, Charles, 1943, O 6,23:5
Poultney, Evan, 1940, Ap 7,45:2
Poulton, Edward, 1943, N 22,19:4
Poulton, Edward L, 1937, N 20,17:3
Pound, Arthur, 1966, Ja 15,27:1
Pound, C W, 1935, F 4,15:1
Pound, Dudley Mrs, 1943, Jl 22,19:2
Pound, George W, 1925, D 3,25:4
Pound, Jerome B, 1952, F 18,19:3
Pound, John F, 1946, F 9,13:1
Pound, John F Mrs, 1959, D 3,37:5
Pound, Louise, 1958, Je 29,69:1
Pound, Presley L, 1940, Ap 4,23:2
Pound, Root E, 1949, F 8,26:3
Pound, Roscoe (mem ser, Jl 8,35:5; trb lr, Jl 12,-IV,10:5), 1964, Jl 2,1:5
Pound, Roscoe Mrs, 1959, Ja 23,26:1
Pound, Sidney C Mrs, 1959, F 28,19:4
Pound, William H, 1959, S 16,39:5
Pound, William H Mrs, 1940, Ag 21,19:4
Pound, William R Jr, 1967, Jl 19,39:2
Pounds, C, 1927, D 22,23:5
Pounds, Harry M, 1940, Ap 12,23:2
Pounds, Lewis C, 1947, Ja 24,21:2
Pounds, Lewis H, 1947, D 17,29:1
Pounds, Lewis H Mrs, 1940, Je 23,30:8
Pounds, William S, 1950, Mr 17,23:1
Pounsford, Harry G, 1963, Jl 12,25:4
Pountain, George H, 1947, Ag 16,13:3
Poupko, Abraham L, 1964, S 5,19:5
Poupko, Eliezer, 1961, S 24,86:3
Poupko, Reuben, 1949, Jl 21,25:1
Pourchet, Philippe, 1941, Mr 11,24:3
Pouria, Deric Sr Mrs, 1949, Jl 4,13:3
Pouria, Samuel L, 1950, Jl 16,69:2
Pourie, Robert, 1922, D 14,21:4
Pouroukoundou, Eleni, 1953, Jl 17,17:2
Pourtales, Count de, 1880, Jl 21,5:6
Pourtales, Edmond de Countess, 1914, My 7,11:6
Pourtales, Guy de (por), 1941, Je 13,19:5
Pousette-Dart, Nathaniel, 1965, O 18,35:4
Poust, Herbert M, 1949, F 9,27:4
Poutiatin, Alex Prince, 1954, F 27,13:3
Poutiatine, Serge M Prince, 1966, F 27,84:3
Poutney, Charles S, 1952, S 5,27:3
Pouzargues, Armand de, 1962, My 20,86:6
Povall, William, 1940, D 29,24:5
Povdin, Edward C, 1944, S 29,21:4
Poveruomo, Amelto, 1953, Je 22,3:8
Povitzky, Olga R, 1948, My 23,68:4
Pow, Samuel, 1939, S 11,19:3
Powderly, Robert J, 1950, O 28,17:6
Powderly, Terence, 1924, Je 25,23:4
Powdermaker, Eugene, 1955, Ja 14,21:2
Powdermaker, Florence B, 1966, Ja 13,25:2
Powdrell, Fred A, 1945, Mr 21,24:2
Powdrell, Fred A Mrs, 1949, D 2,29:1
Powdrell, Joseph W, 1955, Ag 28,85:1
Powel, Elizabeth C Mrs, 1941, S 7,49:1
Powel, Marion H Mrs, 1938, N 9,23:2
Powel, Robert J, 1959, Ja 22,31:4
Powel, Thomas I H, 1939, Ag 18,19:1
Powel, William M Sr, 1942, Ag 21,19:2
Powell, A Clayton Sr Mrs, 1945, Ap 23,19:2
Powell, Abner, 1953, Ag 8,11:4
Powell, Abraham, 1944, Ap 10,19:3
Powell, Abraham M, 1958, My 30,21:4
Powell, Adam C Sr, 1953, Je 13,15:3
Powell, Adam C Sr Mrs, 1961, S 2,15:6
Powell, Albert, 1947, Ag 13,23:3
Powell, Albert C, 1949, My 24,27:5
Powell, Albert E, 1950, Je 21,27:5
Powell, Albert H, 1955, My 19,29:4
Powell, Alfred L, 1960, N 6,88:3
Powell, Alfred W, 1954, F 2,27:3
Powell, Allan (por), 1948, Ja 25,56:5
Powell, Allan L, 1940, Ap 8,19:6
Powell, Alvin L, 1940, Ag 22,19:3
Powell, Alvin M, 1955, Mr 22,31:4
Powell, Arthur B, 1910, Jl 2,7:5
Powell, Arthur C, 1944, F 7,15:3
Powell, Arthur E, 1948, S 14,29:2
Powell, Arthur J E, 1956, Jl 16,21:6
Powell, Arthur Mrs, 1949, My 20,28:3
Powell, Avery, 1939, Ja 25,22:1
Powell, Baden Prof, 1860, Jl 4,4:6
Powell, Bonney M, 1953, Je 26,19:3
Powell, Bradford, 1943, Ja 17,44:4
Powell, Bud (Earl),(funl plans, Ag 4,33:4; funl, Ag 9,27:3), 1966, Ag 2,31:1
Powell, Byron S, 1958, O 14,37:2
Powell, C A (see also My 31), 1877, Je 5,5:2
Powell, Carroll H, 1948, Je 22,25:4
Powell, Charles, 1909, S 1,9:7
Powell, Charles A, 1950, D 30,13:3; 1952, My 20,25:3
Powell, Charles A Sr, 1952, Je 15,84:4
Powell, Charles B, 1938, F 9,19:3
Powell, Charles F Brig-Gen, 1907, Jl 31,7:5
Powell, Charles H, 1938, F 17,21:3
Powell, Charles J, 1953, Jl 11,11:3
Powell, Charles U, 1956, Mr 27,35:2
Powell, Clarence E, 1939, Jl 25,19:6
Powell, D A, 1948, D 20,25:5
Powell, D Frank Dr, 1906, My 9,9:5
Powell, D K Mrs, 1904, D 1,9:3
Powell, David B, 1904, S 18,7:7
Powell, Dawn (Mrs J R Gousha), 1965, N 16,47:1
Powell, Dick (Richd E),(mem ser, Ja 5,8:5; will, Ja 11,5:2), 1963, Ja 4,1:4
Powell, Doane, 1951, Ag 28,24:2
Powell, Donald A, 1952, O 14,31:3
Powell, E Ainger, 1948, S 17,26:2
Powell, E Alex, 1957, N 14,34:1
Powell, E Henry, 1961, Mr 28,35:4
Powell, E L, 1938, O 20,23:5
Powell, Edgar W, 1956, Ja 26,29:2
Powell, Edmund G, 1949, Ja 16,68:8
Powell, Edward (will, My 2,11:3), 1941, Ap 23,21:5
Powell, Edward A, 1925, N 20,21:4
Powell, Edward E, 1939, My 5,23:2
Powell, Edward Payson, 1915, My 15,13:6
Powell, Elizabeth B Mrs, 1962, My 2,37:2
Powell, Elmer E, 1947, Jl 8,23:1
Powell, Elmer Mrs, 1949, Je 15,29:2
Powell, Ewing, 1945, Ag 25,11:1
Powell, Eyre, 1949, Ja 16,69:1
Powell, Francis E (por), 1938, Je 3,21:4
Powell, Francis E, 1964, D 23,27:1
Powell, Francis E Mrs, 1948, Ja 4,52:7; 1965, Ag 15, 83:3
Powell, Frank H, 1949, Jl 7,25:6
Powell, Frederick C, 1938, Ja 14,23:2
Powell, Frederick E, 1938, F 28,15:2
Powell, G Thomas, 1959, F 3,31:3; 1963, D 8,87:1
Powell, Garfield, 1943, Ap 6,21:2
Powell, Garland W, 1959, Ag 31,21:4
Powell, George, 1953, Je 20,17:6
Powell, George H, 1951, D 4,33:1
Powell, George J, 1941, Ag 1,15:5
Powell, George K Mrs, 1965, F 16,28:5
Powell, George M, 1939, Mr 25,15:6
Powell, George M Jr, 1961, D 24,36:4
Powell, Gideon, 1914, N 26,13:4
Powell, Ginnie (Mrs B Raeburn), 1959, Jl 30,27:2
Powell, H Dr, 1885, Ja 24,5:4
Powell, Harford, 1956, Ag 18,17:5
Powell, Harry F, 1941, Mr 26,23:3
Powell, Harry H, 1943, F 13,11:6
Powell, Harry H Mrs, 1940, O 14,19:5
Powell, Helen C, 1948, F 16,21:4
Powell, Henrietta K T Mrs, 1938, Ag 23,17:3
Powell, Henry A, 1910, N 29,11:4
Powell, Henry M, 1953, My 11,27:3
Powell, Henry R, 1958, Mr 7,23:4
Powell, Henry W Mrs, 1950, Je 29,29:5
Powell, Herbert N, 1948, Ap 3,15:3
Powell, Hickman, 1966, D 23,25:3
Powell, Horatio W, 1941, Ja 18,15:6
Powell, Howard L, 1938, My 3,23:4
Powell, Howard Willis, 1912, D 3,15:5
Powell, Isaac A, 1953, Jl 14,27:2
Powell, J W Maj, 1902, S 24,9:3
Powell, James, 1949, N 25,31:3
Powell, James A, 1948, Je 10,25:2
Powell, James B Mrs, 1966, Ag 15,27:2
Powell, James C, 1941, N 15,17:4
Powell, James E, 1957, F 10,86:4
Powell, James W Dr, 1872, Ap 15,5:6
Powell, Jeanette M, 1944, Mr 9,17:1
Powell, John, 1944, O 19,23:5; 1963, Ag 16,27:3; 1966, F 19,27:4
Powell, John B, 1947, Mr 1,6:6; 1952, D 6,21:4
Powell, John B Mrs, 1967, N 18,37:5
Powell, John G, 1956, O 6,21:5
Powell, John Hare Col, 1908, Ja 3,9:4
Powell, John J, 1943, My 13,21:2; 1945, Ja 14,40:2
Powell, Joseph, 1873, Mr 22,12:5; 1920, Jl 2,11:5
Powell, Joseph A Mrs, 1938, Ja 4,23:4
Powell, Joseph Mrs, 1949, Je 29,27:5
Powell, Joseph N, 1939, Mr 27,15:4
Powell, Joseph W, 1954, Ja 28,27:1
Powell, Junius L, 1966, My 1,88:8
Powell, Junius L Mrs, 1965, Je 2,45:4
Powell, Kenneth S, 1960, Ag 16,29:3
Powell, Kenneth T, 1953, Ap 10,21:3
Powell, L M Rear-Adm, 1885, Ja 17,2:3
Powell, L W Ex-Gov, 1867, Jl 7,5:6
Powell, Lillie L, 1960, D 6,37:1
Powell, Louis J, 1940, Ag 31,13:6
Powell, Lula E L Mrs, 1953, N 15,88:7
Powell, Lyman P (por), 1946, F 11,29:3
Powell, Maud, 1920, Ja 9,17:1
Powell, Minna K Mrs, 1938, Mr 9,23:3
Powell, Netti M Mrs, 1959, My 29,23:2
Powell, Noble C Rev, 1968, N 30,39:2
Powell, Oliver, 1952, F 5,29:4
Powell, Page, 1953, D 30,23:2
Powell, Paul M, 1944, Jl 5,17:3
Powell, Paulus P, 1963, Ag 1,27:1
Powell, Percy A, 1942, Jl 16,19:5
Powell, Perry E, 1955, Je 7,33:2
Powell, R Bruce, 1955, Ag 9,25:2
Powell, Rachel H, 1953, Jl 30,23:6
Powell, Raymond E, 1954, D 12,89:2
Powell, Raymond K, 1953, N 20,23:3
Powell, Richard, 1958, Mr 2,88:5
Powell, Richard C, 1946, Jl 20,13:6
Powell, Richard Douglas, 1925, D 16,25:4
Powell, Richard R B Mrs, 1939, S 8,23:5
Powell, Robert, 1942, Jl 12,III,7:4; 1965, Ag 22,82:8
Powell, Robert I, 1963, N 26,37:1
Powell, Roger G, 1957, Ja 4,14:2
Powell, Roger S Mrs, 1944, Ja 21,17:4
Powell, S Robert, 1967, O 3,47:2
Powell, S S, 1879, F 7,5:2
Powell, Sally R Mrs, 1940, Jl 4,15:5
Powell, Scott Mrs, 1947, Je 24,23:5
Powell, Seneca D Mrs, 1948, N 27,17:4
Powell, Solomon C, 1952, D 14,90:5
Powell, Spencer H, 1949, Ag 9,17:6
Powell, Stanley Mrs, 1951, S 30,74:5
Powell, Stephen D, 1938, D 27,17:4
Powell, Sylvester S, 1947, Ag 1,17:5
Powell, T H, 1950, S 7,31:3
Powell, Talcott W (por), 1937, Ap 5,19:4
Powell, Thomas C, 1945, F 10,11:2
Powell, Thomas D, 1946, Ja 27,42:3; 1952, Ja 31,27:2
Powell, Thomas F, 1949, Ja 20,27:4
Powell, Thomas F J, 1937, Jl 24,15:2
Powell, Thomas R, 1955, Ag 17,27:3
Powell, Tod, 1954, Je 23,25:1
Powell, W Bleddyn, 1910, Ap 27,9:4
Powell, W Edgar, 1956, Ap 18,31:2
Powell, W H, 1879, O 7,2:4
Powell, W H Col, 1901, N 17,7:6
Powell, W Hunter Sr, 1961, Ja 2,25:1
Powell, W M, 1935, Ag 19,15:3
Powell, Walter A, 1948, F 7,15:3
Powell, Walter D, 1948, N 7,88:4
Powell, Warren T, 1946, D 30,19:6
Powell, Weldon (mem ser, O 29,43:3), 1965, O 24, 83:6
Powell, Weldon Mrs (mem ser, O 29,43:3), 1965, O 24,83:6
Powell, Wilfred, 1942, F 8,48:2
Powell, William, 1880, N 21,7:2; 1903, F 8,1:5; 1910, Ag 11,7:6; 1949, Ag 26,19:3; 1954, Ag 28,16:5
Powell, William B, 1940, Mr 3,44:6; 1954, Je 22,27:5; 1962, O 20,25:5
Powell, William Bramwell Mrs, 1925, F 7,15:5
Powell, William D, 1943, O 9,13:3
Powell, William F, 1959, Je 7,85:1
Powell, William H, 1939, Mr 9,21:5; 1950, F 22,29:6; 1963, Ag 21,33:4
Powell, William I, 1946, Mr 9,13:3
Powell, William J, 1966, My 10,45:1
Powell, William J Jr, 1967, Je 7,47:3
Powell, William M, 1951, My 15,31:5
Powell, William P, 1948, Mr 29,21:4
Powell, William S, 1940, Mr 3,44:7
Powell, William S S Mrs, 1940, F 28,21:5
Powell, Wilson M Mrs, 1961, Mr 1,33:2
Powelson, Jessey A, 1940, Je 25,23:3
Powelson, Milton E, 1950, F 28,29:3
Powelson, Wilfrid Van N, 1960, My 22,86:5
Power, A Charles, 1941, My 29,19:4
Power, Albert, 1945, Jl 11,11:7
Power, Antonio, 1940, F 7,21:1
Power, Arthur, 1960, Ja 29,25:3
Power, Cecilia K, 1948, N 20,13:5
Power, Charles Gavan Sen, 1968, My 31,29:2
Power, Charles W Mrs, 1950, Ap 24,25:5
Power, Clarence E, 1939, Je 2,23:5
Power, D F, 1882, O 10,5:3
Power, D'Arcy, 1941, My 19,17:2
Power, Daniel D Mrs, 1939, Jl 1,17:5
Power, Earl D, 1952, Ap 15,27:2
Power, Edmund A, 1956, D 17,31:2
Power, Emelie Mrs, 1949, My 10,25:4
Power, Eustace B, 1939, Ag 14,15:6
Power, Francis W (por), 1944, D 17,38:4
Power, Frank S, 1951, N 15,29:1
Power, George F, 1955, Ja 9,87:2
Power, George T, 1940, D 24,15:3
Power, George T Mrs, 1943, Je 7,13:5
Power, H Josephine Mrs, 1937, Mr 3,23:2
Power, Hartley, 1966, Ja 31,39:4
Power, Henry E, 1938, O 25,23:2

Power, J W Msgr, 1926, F 22,17:4
Power, James E, 1955, D 18,93:1
Power, James J, 1939, S 24,44:4
Power, James M, 1957, D 14,21:5
Power, James W, 1940, Jl 10,19:3
Power, John, 1954, N 4,31:2
Power, John D, 1941, Ja 9,21:4
Power, John M Mrs, 1949, My 6,25:1
Power, John Rev, 1937, O 27,31:2
Power, Joseph T, 1948, My 24,19:3
Power, Kate Sarjeantson (Kate Sarjeantson), 1918, F 18,11:6
Power, M J, 1902, S 9,9:5
Power, Mary C, 1951, F 10,13:3
Power, Maurice F, 1943, My 1,15:2
Power, Maurice J, 1950, Mr 2,27:4
Power, Maxwell, 1954, Mr 7,24:3
Power, Michael J, 1949, Ap 23,13:2
Power, Michael J Mrs, 1957, Mr 4,27:3
Power, Millard R, 1939, Mr 2,21:2
Power, Myrtle B Mrs, 1968, N 9,33:3
Power, Neal, 1940, F 26,15:5
Power, Nicholas, 1921, F 11,11:3; 1938, O 3,15:1
Power, Patia Mrs, 1959, S 30,37:3
Power, Paul E, 1950, S 7,31:5
Power, Richard H, 1940, Ap 27,15:3
Power, Richard J, 1961, D 25,23:3
Power, Stanley L, 1945, D 22,19:2
Power, T, 1931, D 31,19:1
Power, Thomas A, 1952, Ag 30,13:6
Power, Thomas C, 1960, Ap 13,39:2
Power, Thomas F Mrs, 1955, S 3,15:4
Power, Tyrone (funl plans, N 20,35:4; funl, N 22,21:3), 1958, N 16,1:4
Power, Tyrone Mrs (Edith Crane), 1912, Ja 4,13:6
Power, Walter J, 1948, Ap 3,15:5
Power, Walter J Rev, 1914, F 9,7:6
Power, William A, 1949, My 3,25:1; 1960, D 4,88:5
Power, William E, 1940, Jl 22,17:6
Power, William G, 1960, Ja 24,88:4
Power, William H, 1937, Ag 15,II,6:7
Power, William M, 1941, Ag 21,17:2
Power, William M A, 1965, D 8,43:5
Power, Wyse, 1950, Je 17,15:1
Power-Waters, Pierce, 1942, D 17,37:4
Powers, Ada L Mrs, 1942, Ap 30,19:5
Powers, Albert E, 1952, O 18,19:4
Powers, Albert H, 1951, Ag 19,84:6
Powers, Albert W Mrs, 1951, N 30,23:2
Powers, Augustin J, 1956, Ja 18,31:3
Powers, Augustin J Mrs, 1961, Mr 15,39:5
Powers, Augustine J, 1953, Mr 9,29:1
Powers, Bentley S, 1937, My 7,25:3
Powers, Bernard, 1962, My 24,35:4
Powers, Bertram A, 1943, My 30,26:2
Powers, Bradford C, 1949, O 31,25:4
Powers, C, 1932, Jl 27,17:5
Powers, C J, 1882, Ag 28,1:2
Powers, C S Ex-Gov, 1912, N 13,15:5
Powers, Carol H Mrs, 1940, Je 9,44:3
Powers, Catherine Mrs, 1909, Mr 13,9:4
Powers, Charles Andrew Dr, 1922, D 24,20:4
Powers, Charles Sir, 1939, Ap 26,23:5
Powers, Clifford S, 1951, Ap 10,27:5
Powers, Clinton R, 1951, D 4,33:2
Powers, Cornelius R Sr, 1948, F 2,19:2
Powers, Dan W Mrs, 1904, S 28,9:5
Powers, Daniel M, 1947, Je 14,15:4
Powers, David C, 1967, Ja 18,43:1
Powers, David E Mrs, 1952, Je 23,19:2
Powers, David G, 1967, D 16,41:3
Powers, Denis J, 1946, Ap 30,21:5
Powers, Donald H Dr, 1968, Ja 18,40:1
Powers, Donald J, 1956, Je 20,31:1
Powers, E, 1935, Ja 9,19:3
Powers, Earl L, 1949, O 31,25:3
Powers, Edmonds J, 1943, Ap 18,48:4
Powers, Edward, 1943, Ja 18,15:5
Powers, Edward A, 1950, O 10,31:4
Powers, Edward B, 1943, F 27,14:8
Powers, Edward E, 1952, Ja 11,21:4
Powers, Edward J, 1948, S 9,27:1
Powers, Edward J Mrs, 1944, D 5,23:4
Powers, Edward W, 1948, S 11,15:5
Powers, Edwin B, 1949, Ag 27,13:5
Powers, Elizabeth M, 1954, O 31,89:1
Powers, Elmer W Mrs, 1944, S 4,19:5
Powers, Eugene P Dr, 1968, Jl 21,57:1
Powers, Florence Powers Mrs, 1966, Jl 14,35:4
Powers, Francis, 1940, My 12,48:8
Powers, Francis J, 1959, D 22,31:3
Powers, Frank E, 1943, O 2,13:4
Powers, Frank T (por), 1948, Ja 13,25:5
Powers, Frederick A, 1923, F 15,19:4
Powers, Frederick D, 1955, Ja 18,27:2
Powers, George, 1942, D 16,25:6
Powers, George A, 1943, Ag 4,17:4; 1955, Ag 1,19:5
Powers, George B, 1955, My 27,23:2
Powers, George F, 1958, O 16,37:1
Powers, George H, 1941, O 6,17:5
Powers, George M, 1938, Je 25,15:6
Powers, Grover F Mrs, 1967, S 6,47:2
Powers, Grover Francis Dr, 1968, Ap 20,34:2
Powers, H Henry, 1913, D 9,11:4
Powers, Harry J, 1941, F 22,15:4
Powers, Harry L, 1939, O 26,23:2; 1942, D 26,9:1
Powers, Henry J, 1952, O 4,29:3
Powers, Henry J Mrs, 1951, My 27,68:6
Powers, Henry P, 1937, F 20,17:6
Powers, Herbert T, 1961, O 28,21:6
Powers, Hiram, 1873, Je 28,7:3
Powers, J Fred, 1946, S 9,9:5
Powers, James B, 1950, Ag 24,27:4
Powers, James C Mrs, 1957, Jl 27,17:6
Powers, James E, 1967, S 8,39:1
Powers, James F, 1949, Ag 22,21:6
Powers, James J, 1944, Je 25,29:2; 1945, My 10,23:2; 1965, N 4,47:5
Powers, James J Sr, 1948, Ja 4,52:5
Powers, James M, 1949, Ja 31,19:5
Powers, James P Sr, 1948, Ap 17,15:2
Powers, James T (por), 1943, F 11,19:1
Powers, James T, 1944, Mr 29,21:5; 1952, F 9,13:6
Powers, James T Mrs, 1955, Jl 24,65:2
Powers, John, 1949, F 3,24:2
Powers, John C, 1944, F 22,24:3; 1946, Ap 16,25:2
Powers, John E, 1919, Ap 22,17:3; 1939, D 14,27:3
Powers, John F, 1937, Ap 14,25:6; 1961, My 13,19:5
Powers, John I, 1939, D 7,17:2
Powers, John J, 1943, Jl 29,19:2; 1945, S 25,26:2; 1949, Ag 1,17:4; 1960, Ap 18,29:3
Powers, John J Jr, 1951, D 3,31:1
Powers, John J Sr, 1960, O 11,45:2; 1967, Mr 26,68:5
Powers, John M, 1950, O 7,17:1; 1966, F 8,39:2
Powers, John Mrs, 1943, Jl 27,17:2
Powers, John O, 1937, Jl 19,15:4
Powers, John O Mrs, 1947, O 8,25:3
Powers, John P, 1924, Jl 17,15:5; 1959, N 24,37:4
Powers, John P Mrs, 1950, Ja 21,18:2
Powers, John T, 1937, Mr 13,19:3
Powers, Joseph, 1946, F 10,40:6
Powers, Joseph D, 1954, Jl 19,19:4
Powers, Joseph L, 1955, D 4,89:2
Powers, Joseph P, 1965, O 21,47:2
Powers, Katherine, 1940, Ja 24,23:3
Powers, Lawrence E, 1950, Mr 30,29:1
Powers, Leo F, 1948, F 12,23:1
Powers, Lewis J, 1915, S 16,11:4
Powers, Lillian D, 1953, Ja 13,32:3
Powers, Louis, 1937, Ap 29,21:5
Powers, M Ray, 1942, Ag 16,44:7
Powers, Margaret (will), 1940, Ap 21,9:5
Powers, Marsh K, 1945, S 14,23:2
Powers, Martin F, 1946, F 26,25:2
Powers, Martin T, 1940, Je 15,15:6
Powers, Mary B, 1948, Jl 22,18:1
Powers, Mary C, 1956, Ja 28,17:4
Powers, Mary W Mrs, 1942, My 2,13:6
Powers, Michael F, 1957, D 12,29:1
Powers, Michael Mrs, 1943, Ap 15,25:2
Powers, Millard M, 1957, Ja 10,29:4
Powers, Millard R Mrs, 1938, D 5,23:2
Powers, Orlando Woodworth, 1914, Ja 3,11:5
Powers, Orville M, 1937, Jl 11,II,4:5
Powers, Patrick, 1911, My 30,11:5
Powers, Patrick A, 1948, Ag 1,57:2
Powers, Patrick J, 1948, Jl 30,17:4
Powers, Phil C, 1954, Ja 9,15:1
Powers, Philip E, 1943, Jl 7,19:5
Powers, Phillip M, 1921, Ap 19,17:6
Powers, Pliny H, 1966, D 9,47:4
Powers, R J, 1927, F 18,21:5
Powers, Rhea, 1951, Ja 6,15:2
Powers, Richard J Jr, 1956, Mr 24,19:1
Powers, Robert E, 1943, Ag 31,17:5; 1952, Mr 31,19:4
Powers, Robert H Sr, 1950, My 14,108:1
Powers, Roland C, 1956, Ap 22,85:3
Powers, Russell A Mrs, 1947, Jl 10,22:2
Powers, Seaman W, 1944, Mr 21,19:5
Powers, Stephen J, 1959, Ap 22,33:4
Powers, T H, 1878, N 26,1:6
Powers, Thomas, 1941, Ja 18,15:2
Powers, Thomas C, 1941, Jl 25,15:2; 1962, Jl 28,19:3
Powers, Thomas E (por), 1939, Ag 15,19:3
Powers, Thomas F, 1949, O 4,27:2
Powers, Thomas H, 1962, N 19,31:2
Powers, Thomas J Jr, 1949, Mr 10,27:5
Powers, Tom, 1955, N 10,35:1
Powers, W J Sweasey, 1938, D 13,25:5
Powers, W Stuart, 1968, S 19,47:1
Powers, Wallace M, 1968, Ap 11,45:4
Powers, Wallace Mrs, 1953, N 14,17:5
Powers, Walter A Mrs, 1946, N 5,25:4
Powers, Walter F, 1955, N 26,19:1
Powers, Walter H, 1967, O 23,45:3
Powers, William, 1920, S 25,13:5; 1961, S 23,19:6
Powers, William A, 1957, Ap 12,25:1
Powers, William B, 1943, Ja 18,15:4
Powers, William C, 1947, O 2,27:3
Powers, William E, 1952, Ag 2,15:4
Powers, William F Mrs, 1959, N 14,21:5
Powers, William H, 1944, D 31,26:8; 1964, S 1,35:1
Powers, William J, 1944, F 7,15:4; 1948, My 24,19:6
Powers, William J Sr, 1954, Ap 16,21:2
Powers, William L, 1943, Ap 19,19:3; 1967, Je 9,37:3
Powers, William O, 1945, S 26,23:4
Powers, William P, 1942, Ag 29,15:4
Powers, William T, 1950, Ag 29,27:5; 1950, S 2,15:7
Powers, William T Mrs, 1959, Ag 7,23:2
Powers, William W, 1938, Jl 15,17:2
Powers (Sister Mary Pauline), 1962, S 18,39:1
Powerscourt, Lord, 1904, Je 6,9:6
Powerscourt, Viscount, 1947, Mr 22,13:4
Powicke, Maurice, 1963, My 21,37:4
Powis, Alfred, 1959, Ag 10,27:5
Powis, Earl of (G C Herbert), 1952, N 10,25:3
Powler, Susan, 1911, My 2,11:4
Powles, George H, 1943, Ag 21,11:5
Powlesland, Walter W, 1948, D 21,31:3
Powley, Edward H, 1957, Ap 25,31:5
Powley, Ned R, 1956, D 20,29:5
Powlison, Charles F, 1942, Jl 2,21:3
Powlison, Ernest K, 1959, Ap 16,33:5
Pownall, George H, 1916, D 17,19:2
Pownall, Henry R, 1961, Je 10,23:2
Pownall, Levi W, 1939, D 3,61:2
Powrie, Lillis, 1945, F 5,17:6
Powyer, L L Mrs, 1938, Je 24,19:5
Powys, John C, 1963, Je 19,37:1
Powys, Llewelyn Mrs (A Gregory), 1967, Ag 31,3
Powys, Llewlyn, 1939, D 5,28:2
Powys, Theodore F, 1953, N 28,15:6
Poyer, Frank P, 1943, Ap 18,49:1
Poyer, Nellie E Mrs, 1947, Ap 3,25:4
Poylo, Michael C Mrs, 1947, Ap 29,27:1
Poynter, Ambrose M Sir, 1923, Je 1,19:6
Poynter, Edward John Sir, 1919, Jl 27,22:3
Poynter, Horace M, 1953, Mr 5,27:3
Poynter, Matchett Y, 1967, Ag 1,33:2
Poynter, Nelson P Mrs (Henrietta), 1968, Ja 26,47
Poynter, Paul, 1950, N 22,25:5
Poynter, Ralph D, 1949, S 8,29:2
Poynter, Rebecca C, 1953, Ag 13,25:4
Poynter, William A Ex-Gov, 1909, Ap 6,9:5
Poynting, John Henry Prof, 1914, Ap 1,13:6
Poynton, J A, 1934, O 24,23:1
Poyourow, Julian, 1960, F 16,37:2
Poysher, Jonah P, 1941, S 18,25:2
Poysti, Nicolai J, 1947, N 21,27:3
Poyzer, Glenn W, 1944, N 18,13:4
Poz, William M, 1941, Ag 5,19:4
Pozdena, Otto R, 1953, Ap 21,27:4
Pozdyunin, Valentin, 1948, My 26,25:3
Pozen, Morris S, 1942, S 30,23:5
Pozier, Pierre, 1952, Ap 10,29:5
Pozniak, Bronislav von, 1953, Ap 26,86:7
Pozo, Carlos del, 1943, O 30,15:6
Pozzi, Angelo, 1949, Jl 7,25:5
Pozzoli, Amilcare, 1948, Jl 9,19:1
Prabasco, Samuel K Mrs, 1947, Ja 26,53:3
Prabel, Madame, 1950, Ja 4,35:3
Pracht, Clark, 1949, Je 9,31:3
Pracht, Frederick, 1950, D 23,15:5
Prack, Carl A Sr, 1944, Ap 20,19:6
Pracuta, John, 1947, Mr 15,6:4
Prada, Joachim de, 1958, Ap 28,23:3
Pradap Sekhar Deo, Bir Mitra Rajah, 1938, Je 27,1
Pradilla, Francisco, 1921, N 2,17:5
Pradillo, August E, 1957, Jl 27,17:3
Prado, Manuel I (mem ser plans, N 28,47:1), 1967, N 11,33:4
Prado, Mariano I Mrs, 1950, My 4,27:2
Prado, Saturno C, 1957, D 3,35:3
Prado, Xavier Dr, 1921, Je 26,22:3
Prado Ugarteche, Manuel, 1967, Ag 15,39:2
Pradrick, Charles A Rev Dr, 1937, D 12,II,9:2
Pradt, Alan E, 1953, Ja 24,15:2
Praeg, Harry C, 1950, D 20,31:3
Praeger, John Francis, 1916, D 2,11:5
Praeger, Leo F, 1938, Je 16,23:4
Praeger, Louis J, 1953, N 15,89:3
Praeger, Otto, 1948, F 6,23:3
Praeger, Otto Mrs, 1951, F 26,23:2
Praeger, Robert L, 1953, My 7,31:4
Praeger, Rosamund, 1954, Ap 18,89:3
Praet, Henry A, 1903, O 16,7:6
Praetz, Joseph H, 1943, My 30,27:1
Praga, Alfred, 1949, F 27,68:8
Prager, Clem, 1939, Ap 11,23:4
Prager, Harry P, 1952, Ag 16,15:5
Prager, Jacob, 1951, Mr 9,25:2
Prager, Morris, 1902, N 29,9:7
Prager, Nathan, 1963, My 3,32:1
Prager, Richard, 1945, Jl 22,38:2
Prager, Theodor, 1961, My 19,32:8
Prager, William, 1938, Ja 9,42:3
Prager, William (will), 1940, Mr 1,41:1
Prager, William L, 1966, Mr 14,31:2
Pragnell, George Sir, 1916, F 15,11:7
Prahar, Renee, 1962, Ag 19,88:2
Prahl, Frederick A (por), 1944, F 11,19:6
Prahl, Victor, 1953, Ag 29,17:2
Prain, David, 1944, Mr 18,13:6
Prairie, Charles F, 1948, Jl 1,23:5
Praissman, Charles, 1951, Jl 12,25:4
Prajadhipok, Former King of Siam, 1941, My 31,2
Prakasam, Thanguthuri, 1957, My 22,33:4
Prall, Anning M, 1949, O 19,29:2
Prall, Anning S (por), 1937, Jl 24,15:1

Prall, Anning S Mrs, 1950, Ja 29,68:5
Prall, David W, 1940, O 22,23:4
Prall, Frederick M, 1946, O 13,58:6
Prall, Horace G, 1951, Ap 24,29:4
Prall, John C, 1940, Ag 6,20:2
Prall, Josephine R Mrs, 1921, My 26,13:4
Prall, Margaret C, 1955, Ja 27,23:1
Prall, W, 1933, Mr 24,17:5
Prall, William Mrs, 1949, Je 3,25:5
Prall, William R, 1937, S 8,23:5
Prance, Joseph G, 1939, F 22,21:3
Prandtl, Ludwig, 1953, Ag 20,27:6
Prang, Louis, 1909, Je 16,7:5
Prange, Charles J, 1967, My 10,44:6
Prange, Edward E, 1952, Ag 6,21:5
Prangen, Richard M, 1942, D 7,27:5
Prankard, Charles W, 1909, Ap 19,9:5
Prankard, George W, 1943, Ja 10,50:5
Prankard, Harry I 2d, 1964, Jl 20,25:4
Pransketis, Anthony, 1951, Je 26,29:4
Pransky, David L, 1963, Jl 17,31:5
Praporgescu, Dumitru, 1961, Ap 29,23:2
Prarie, Francis J, 1945, F 20,19:6
Prarie, Milton L, 1948, Ag 21,15:6
Prasad, Rajendra, 1963, Mr 1,4:5
Prasch, John, 1942, Je 2,23:3
Prashker, Louis, 1959, Ja 23,25:3
Prasolov, Leonid, 1954, Ja 18,23:3
Prasse, Carl S, 1945, F 3,11:5
Prasse, John C, 1941, S 11,23:5
Prat, Jean, 1940, Ja 4,23:3
Prater, J William, 1944, S 23,13:7
Pratesi, Honore, 1952, N 7,31:2
Prather, A Lyle, 1950, N 20,25:4
Prather, Ed Mrs, 1951, Ag 24,15:6
Prather, John, 1965, F 13,21:2
Prather, Ralph C, 1953, Ap 8,29:1
Prather, Victor A, 1961, My 5,1:2
Prati, Giovanni, 1884, My 11,9:3
Pratley, Phil L, 1958, Ag 2,17:6
Prato, David, 1951, Mr 8,29:6
Prato, Gino, 1966, Ja 21,47:1
Pratt, A G, 1937, N 23,23:6
Pratt, A Stuart, 1952, D 6,21:5
Pratt, Addison S Mrs, 1954, Ag 27,21:3
Pratt, Adelaide Booth Mrs, 1951, O 4,33:3
Pratt, Alex, 1955, S 7,31:2
Pratt, Alexander D B (cor, Mr 2,60:1), 1947, Mr 1, 15:5
Pratt, Alfred A Com, 1911, Jl 6,9:4
Pratt, Alfred M, 1939, My 29,15:4
Pratt, Alice M, 1962, S 2,56:7
Pratt, Ambrose E, 1942, Je 22,15:5
Pratt, Arthur H, 1942, F 2,15:5
Pratt, B H, 1941, N 13,27:5
Pratt, Bela L, 1917, My 19,13:5
Pratt, Best, 1952, Mr 31,19:4
Pratt, Boris, 1940, D 9,19:5
Pratt, C C Col, 1916, Ja 28,9:5
Pratt, C M, 1935, N 27,21:5
Pratt, Caroline (trb lr, Je 12,14:6), 1954, Je 7,23:3
Pratt, Carroll H, 1958, Ag 20,27:1
Pratt, Catherine Trout Mrs, 1951, Mr 22,31:5
Pratt, Charles, 1891, My 5,1:7; 1904, N 8,5:2
Pratt, Charles (funl, Ja 11,29:1), 1956, Ja 8,86:5
Pratt, Charles A, 1911, Ag 6,II,9:6; 1951, Ap 4,29:4
Pratt, Charles H, 1953, S 10,25:4
Pratt, Charles M Mrs (will, N 4,52:5), 1947, O 25, 19:2
Pratt, Charles Mrs, 1907, Ja 21,9:2
Pratt, Charles R Mrs, 1955, D 30,19:3
Pratt, Chester M, 1944, O 10,23:4
Pratt, Cornelia C, 1963, Je 5,41:2
Pratt, Curtis G, 1955, Jl 27,23:3
Pratt, D D, 1877, Je 18,5:5
Pratt, Dallas B Mrs, 1948, D 19,76:4
Pratt, Daniel, 1884, Jl 24,5:3
Pratt, David D, 1940, Ja 31,19:5
Pratt, David W, 1964, My 4,29:2
Pratt, Donald L, 1965, F 19,36:4
Pratt, Donald R, 1968, S 26,47:1
Pratt, E H, 1883, Jl 6,2:1
Pratt, Edgar G, 1940, Je 6,25:5
Pratt, Edmund A, 1961, Jl 15,19:1
Pratt, Edward I Sr, 1952, Mr 7,24:3
Pratt, Edward J, 1937, D 22,25:6
Pratt, Edward L, 1940, Ja 20,15:3
Pratt, Edward S, 1963, Je 5,41:4
Pratt, Edwin A, 1904, Ja 20,9:7
Pratt, Edwin J, 1954, O 21,27:5; 1964, Ap 27,31:4
Pratt, Elgin C, 1943, D 30,17:2
Pratt, Elizabeth (Mrs R W), 1964, Ja 22,37:3
Pratt, Elmer C, 1949, D 2,29:3
Pratt, Elon G, 1964, F 25,31:2
Pratt, Elsa W Mrs, 1940, Je 5,25:6
Pratt, Emory B, 1941, F 7,19:2
Pratt, Ernest L, 1954, N 27,13:5
Pratt, Ex-Gov, 1869, N 11,5:4
Pratt, F A, 1902, F 11,9:5
Pratt, F L, 1947, My 2,22:3
Pratt, Fabian L, 1944, D 20,23:5
Pratt, Fletcher, 1956, Je 11,31:1
Pratt, Fletcher S, 1941, Je 10,23:4
Pratt, Frances J, 1965, O 15,45:2
Pratt, Francis C Mrs, 1961, D 3,88:1
Pratt, Francis O 3d, 1951, My 31,27:5
Pratt, Frank R, 1954, F 26,20:6
Pratt, Frederic B (por), 1945, My 4,19:1
Pratt, Frederic B Mrs, 1946, Je 13,28:2
Pratt, Frederic R, 1966, Ap 20,47:2
Pratt, Frederick Sanford, 1968, Je 1,27:4
Pratt, G D, 1935, Ja 21,15:1
Pratt, G Herbert, 1949, Ja 29,13:1
Pratt, George, 1949, Jl 9,13:5
Pratt, George B, 1937, Jl 30,19:4
Pratt, George Dupont Mrs (funl, Ja 8,17:6), 1923, Ja 6,13:5
Pratt, George K, 1957, D 12,29:1
Pratt, George Starkweather Rev, 1920, Jl 29,9:4
Pratt, George W, 1953, Ja 23,19:3
Pratt, Gilbert F, 1952, D 14,90:4
Pratt, Guy W, 1948, O 5,25:5
Pratt, H Ruthven, 1924, Ja 18,17:5
Pratt, H Z Mrs, 1908, O 25,13:3
Pratt, Harlan A, 1953, Je 3,31:3
Pratt, Harold, 1953, Mr 19,29:3
Pratt, Harold I, 1939, My 22,17:1
Pratt, Harold J, 1965, Ag 11,35:2
Pratt, Harrison M Mrs, 1962, Jl 17,25:4
Pratt, Harry, 1951, O 10,23:6
Pratt, Harry E, 1956, F 13,27:1; 1957, D 16,29:4
Pratt, Harry R, 1956, My 7,27:4
Pratt, Harry W, 1957, D 9,35:4
Pratt, Helen Marshall, 1924, My 23,19:5
Pratt, Henry B, 1943, D 22,23:1
Pratt, Henry B Rev, 1912, D 12,13:3
Pratt, Henry C, 1966, Ap 7,36:1
Pratt, Henry F, 1944, Ap 12,21:3
Pratt, Henry S, 1946, O 8,24:2
Pratt, Henry S Mrs, 1937, N 27,17:6
Pratt, Henry Z, 1961, Jl 26,31:3
Pratt, Henry Z Jr, 1955, Ag 12,19:2
Pratt, Herbert H, 1948, D 18,19:2
Pratt, Herbert L (por),(will, F 14,21:4), 1945, F 4, 37:1
Pratt, Howard A, 1963, My 31,25:1
Pratt, Isabelle L, 1947, Jl 1,25:3
Pratt, J Stanley, 1944, D 16,15:2
Pratt, J T, 1927, Je 18,17:3
Pratt, James B, 1944, Ja 16,42:5
Pratt, James E, 1946, Jl 18,10:3
Pratt, James L, 1938, N 1,23:5
Pratt, James Leroy, 1907, D 8,11:5
Pratt, James Lt, 1881, Ag 14,7:6
Pratt, James T Sr, 1952, My 13,23:1
Pratt, Jenny L Mrs, 1939, Ja 27,19:2
Pratt, John, 1954, Je 16,31:3
Pratt, John B (por), 1943, O 2,13:3
Pratt, John B Mrs, 1918, Je 6,13:6; 1939, O 3,23:4
Pratt, John H, 1949, Je 15,29:4
Pratt, John Lowell, 1968, D 26,37:1
Pratt, John T Mrs (Ruth B),(will filed, Ag 31,33:2), 1965, Ag 24,36:1
Pratt, Joseph H, 1942, Je 3,23:2; 1956, Mr 5,23:2
Pratt, Joseph M, 1946, Jl 20,13:5
Pratt, Julius Howard, 1909, O 15,11:4
Pratt, Julius R, 1947, S 28,61:1
Pratt, L Raymond, 1953, Ja 17,15:6
Pratt, L W S Col, 1903, O 5,6:7
Pratt, Le Gage, 1911, Mr 10,9:4
Pratt, Leo E, 1948, Mr 29,21:3
Pratt, Lewellyn, 1913, Je 16,9:2
Pratt, Loring, 1953, Jl 28,19:6
Pratt, Louis M, 1944, Mr 13,15:1
Pratt, M Walter Mrs, 1948, Je 9,29:2
Pratt, Margaret S J Mrs, 1940, Ap 14,45:3
Pratt, Marion, 1964, S 29,43:4
Pratt, Mary H Mrs, 1940, N 13,23:4
Pratt, Mirriam Choate Mrs, 1906, D 11,9:5
Pratt, Nathaniel P, 1942, N 16,19:5
Pratt, Oliver G, 1963, Ap 6,19:1
Pratt, Orson, 1881, O 8,5:5
Pratt, Percy R, 1956, Ap 5,29:2
Pratt, R M, 1880, S 1,4:7
Pratt, Ray G, 1941, My 11,44:6
Pratt, Richard Henry Brig-Gen, 1924, Mr 16,23:2
Pratt, Richard Mrs (Dorothea), 1962, S 28,33:4
Pratt, Richardson, 1959, Ag 17,23:1
Pratt, Robert E, 1957, O 9,35:4
Pratt, Robert W, 1946, D 22,42:4
Pratt, Samuel, 1922, F 24,12:6
Pratt, Sarah A, 1954, Ag 15,84:5
Pratt, Sereno S (funl, S 18,9:6), 1915, S 15,9:5
Pratt, Sherman, 1964, S 16,31:3
Pratt, Silas Gamaliel, 1916, N 1,11:4
Pratt, Stewart C, 1951, Je 15,23:3
Pratt, Susanna K Mrs (will), 1938, Ap 16,16:6
Pratt, T B, 1878, O 13,1:6
Pratt, Thomas A Mrs, 1945, Je 19,19:3
Pratt, Thomas B Mrs, 1958, D 8,31:5
Pratt, Thomas H, 1944, Mr 4,13:4
Pratt, W H, 1883, Mr 4,9:5
Pratt, Waldo S, 1939, Jl 30,29:3
Pratt, Wallace E Mrs (Iris C), 1966, Mr 8,30:1
Pratt, Ward E, 1954, O 7,23:5
Pratt, William A, 1945, N 7,23:4
Pratt, William B, 1948, Mr 6,13:1
Pratt, William F, 1944, Ap 20,19:3
Pratt, William H B Dr, 1916, Ag 28,9:5
Pratt, William H Gen, 1911, N 7,13:4
Pratt, William Orrin, 1925, My 21,23:4
Pratt, William P, 1948, Ag 16,19:3
Pratt, William V, 1957, N 26,33:2
Pratt, Willis C, 1962, Ja 10,47:5
Pratt, Willis Mrs, 1949, O 26,27:4
Pratt, Winthrop Mrs, 1955, Jl 22,23:4
Pratt, Zadoc Col (funl), 1871, Ap 9,8:3
Praul, John H, 1959, O 10,21:4
Prawin, Jakub, 1957, Jl 9,11:4
Praxy, Raoul (cor, Ag 12,25:5), 1967, Jl 29,25:5
Pray, A Brooks, 1952, O 1,34:4
Pray, Charles F, 1953, F 26,25:5
Pray, Charles N, 1963, S 14,25:4
Pray, E H, 1876, Mr 19,7:1
Pray, F Civille, 1956, S 21,25:1
Pray, F Civille Mrs, 1956, F 19,92:1
Pray, J Parker Mrs, 1946, N 23,15:1
Pray, Kenneth L M, 1948, Mr 3,24:2
Pray, Maria (Mrs Barney Williams), 1911, My 7,II, 11:4
Pray, Mis, 1878, Je 18,2:1
Pray, Perry S, 1937, S 1,19:2
Pray, Samuel B, 1938, S 9,22:6
Pray, Stephen E, 1961, My 27,23:3
Pray, Susan R Dr, 1903, Ja 15,9:6
Pray, Wilbur F, 1950, Ap 18,31:2
Pray, Wilder P, 1944, Ja 5,17:2
Prchala, Lev, 1963, Je 13,33:3
Preas, James H, 1949, S 8,29:3
Preault, A A, 1879, Ja 13,2:2
Preaux, R J, 1867, Ap 7,5:4
Prebensen, Preben, 1961, O 22,86:3
Preble, Edgar W, 1943, N 9,21:3
Preble, G H Adm, 1885, Mr 2,2:3
Preble, Harold C, 1952, O 26,88:3
Preble, J Q, 1909, Je 24,7:4
Preble, John K, 1950, Ja 20,25:1
Preble, Robert B, 1948, Jl 27,25:5
Preble, Theodore Lunt, 1968, Ag 3,25:5
Preble, Thomas M Rev, 1907, D 14,9:4
Prebula, Hyman, 1937, Ap 18,II,8:2
Precan, Leopold, 1947, Mr 3,21:3
Precheur, John V, 1937, N 2,28:2
Precht, Edward, 1953, F 1,88:2
Precht, Harry A, 1949, N 13,92:4
Preciado, Rogelio, 1955, D 22,23:4
Precobb, William G Mrs, 1951, N 15,29:4
Predale, John O, 1967, Mr 31,37:3
Predergast, Richard Q, 1941, Jl 24,17:2
Predmesky, Eliezer Rabbi, 1968, D 9,47:2
Predmore, Mary A, 1967, Ja 21,31:5
Predmore, Royal L, 1944, Ag 15,17:2
Preece, Godfrey, 1944, Ja 16,41:6
Preece, Thomas R, 1940, Jl 23,19:3
Preece, William H Sir, 1913, N 7,9:3
Preetorius, Emil Dr, 1905, N 20,9:6
Prefontaine, Charles E, 1956, F 12,88:5
Prehm, Herman L, 1950, N 7,27:5
Prehn, George M, 1939, Ja 3,17:1
Preis, Arthur L, 1964, D 27,64:4
Preis, Carl G, 1959, Mr 11,35:3
Preise, Henry, 1912, D 11,13:4
Preisendanz, Charles W, 1941, S 7,49:2
Preisinger, Charles V, 1956, D 5,39:4
Preiskel, Abraham, 1967, Je 17,31:2
Preiss, Elias, 1938, My 29,II,6:5
Preiss, Emil, 1947, S 3,25:6
Preiss, Jacob, 1950, S 2,15:6
Preiss, Lily Mrs, 1942, S 20,41:7
Preisser, Victorine Mrs, 1941, My 6,21:1
Prell, Cyrus D, 1921, Mr 1,13:4
Preller, Friedrich, 1901, O 24,9:1
Prellwitz, Henry, 1940, Mr 14,23:2
Prellwitz, Henry Mrs, 1944, Ag 20,34:5
Premer, Oren A, 1944, O 12,27:3
Premesnil, Charles Regnault de Vice-Adm, 1908, Je 27,9:6
Premo, Alfred N, 1964, Ap 28,37:2
Premrose, Catherine, 1910, O 7,11:1
Premus, Augustus F Mrs, 1950, Mr 3,25:2
Premyslav, Leopold, 1952, Mr 17,21:5
Prendergast, Anthony J, 1947, My 16,23:1
Prendergast, Charles, 1948, Ag 22,60:3
Prendergast, Edmond Francis Archbishop (funl, Mr 6,9:4), 1918, F 27,11:3
Prendergast, Edmund J, 1945, Je 4,19:4
Prendergast, Francis A, 1953, Mr 29,93:1
Prendergast, Frank L, 1957, O 8,35:2
Prendergast, George M, 1937, Ag 28,15:4
Prendergast, J J Msgr, 1914, Ja 20,9:6
Prendergast, James F, 1939, Mr 11,17:4
Prendergast, James M, 1920, D 1,15:4
Prendergast, James Mrs, 1959, D 16,41:3
Prendergast, James W, 1938, Ja 27,21:3
Prendergast, John, 1938, Ap 18,15:5
Prendergast, John (E Shevlin), 1959, F 8,86:8
Prendergast, John C, 1949, O 26,27:3; 1958, Ja 17,25:2
Prendergast, John E, 1962, S 26,39:2
Prendergast, John J, 1956, F 13,27:4

Prendergast, Joseph F, 1914, Je 19,13:5
Prendergast, Joseph J Rev, 1924, D 8,19:4
Prendergast, Margaret A, 1952, Ag 15,15:5
Prendergast, Marian E, 1941, Ag 15,17:1
Prendergast, Mary Mrs, 1925, O 24,15:6
Prendergast, Moret y, 1913, Ja 29,11:5
Prendergast, Thomas F, 1955, Jl 4,11:5
Prendergast, Thomas H, 1963, N 15,35:3
Prendergast, W C, 1931, D 1,14:3
Prendergast, William A (trb lr, Je 30,26:5), 1954, Je 22,27:1
Prendergast, William A Mrs, 1963, Ja 10,15:8
Prendergast, William R Mrs, 1967, Je 12,53:1
Prendergrast, Raymond A, 1958, O 24,33:1
Prendible, William M, 1960, Ag 6,19:5
Prenosil, Stanley W, 1967, Ap 13,43:4
Prensky, Phil, 1941, My 24,15:1
Prenter, W B, 1927, D 8,9:4
Prentice, A, 1942, Mr 5,23:1
Prentice, Alfred C, 1949, Ja 15,17:4
Prentice, Andrew L, 1940, Ag 26,15:1
Prentice, Augustus Browning, 1907, D 11,11:3
Prentice, Bernon S (por), 1948, Je 14,23:1
Prentice, Bernon S Mrs, 1952, F 17,85:2
Prentice, Daisy, 1949, O 6,31:3
Prentice, E Parmalee Mrs (will, Je 28,28:7), 1962, Je 22,25:4
Prentice, Edward H, 1944, My 7,45:3
Prentice, Eugene M (por), 1938, O 9,44:6
Prentice, Ezra P, 1955, D 17,23:3; 1966, Jl 20,41:4
Prentice, Frank E Mrs, 1963, My 19,86:5
Prentice, George Bassett Dr, 1907, Je 22,7:4
Prentice, George D, 1870, Ja 23,1:5
Prentice, George E, 1943, N 9,21:2
Prentice, George G, 1941, D 6,17:1
Prentice, George S, 1945, Ja 1,21:4
Prentice, Harry W, 1955, My 6,23:2
Prentice, J H, 1881, Mr 15,5:3
Prentice, James Douglas, 1911, O 27,13:6
Prentice, John, 1940, Jl 1,19:5
Prentice, John Hill, 1925, O 2,23:6
Prentice, Kate H Mrs, 1941, D 30,19:2
Prentice, Oscar Ex-Justice, 1924, N 3,17:4
Prentice, Robert K, 1958, Ap 7,21:4
Prentice, Samuel B, 1948, Ag 28,15:3
Prentice, Samuel O Mrs, 1924, Jl 2,19:5
Prentice, Sartell Mrs, 1956, N 11,86:4
Prentice, Sartell Rev Dr (por), 1937, O 28,25:1
Prentice, Spelman Mrs, 1967, Je 29,43:5
Prentice, Sydney, 1943, S 16,21:5
Prentice, Thomas, 1949, F 8,25:1
Prentice, William K, 1964, D 15,43:5
Prentice, William Packer Mrs, 1924, O 2,23:3
Prentice, William S P, 1923, N 15,19:3
Prentis, Edmund A, 1967, Mr 13,37:1
Prentis, Edward, 1938, Je 3,21:4
Prentis, Edward Jr, 1941, Ja 19,41:1
Prentis, Henning W Jr, 1959, O 29,33:3
Prentis, Mary F Mrs, 1941, O 2,25:5
Prentiss, Adam (Whaler), 1878, Jl 28,8:6
Prentiss, Albert N, 1957, Ap 19,21:2
Prentiss, Albert N Mrs, 1957, F 12,27:5
Prentiss, Caroline E Mrs, 1940, Mr 28,24:3
Prentiss, Elizabeth S Mrs (will, Ja 10,11:4), 1944, Ja 5,17:5
Prentiss, F F Delight Mrs, 1903, Jl 15,5:2
Prentiss, Francis F, 1937, Ap 2,23:2
Prentiss, Frederick L, 1952, Jl 13,60:2
Prentiss, G L Rev, 1903, Mr 19,9:6
Prentiss, Guernsey D, 1955, Ja 18,27:2
Prentiss, Henrietta, 1940, My 15,25:4
Prentiss, Henry S, 1907, My 6,9:3
Prentiss, Horace D, 1953, Mr 26,31:1
Prentiss, John, 1873, Je 7,5:4
Prentiss, John W, 1938, Mr 19,15:1; 1953, O 11,89:2
Prentiss, John W Mrs, 1949, D 3,15:3
Prentiss, Lydia F, 1955, F 28,19:5
Prentiss, Mark O, 1948, Mr 23,25:4
Prentiss, May E, 1950, My 2,29:5
Prentiss, Robert W Prof, 1913, Ap 6,IV,7:4
Prentiss, Russell E, 1953, Ap 28,27:5
Prentiss, William A, 1954, Ag 24,21:5
Prentys, Roland F, 1947, D 28,40:1
Preo, John L, 1953, S 19,15:4
Preoteasa, Grigore, 1957, N 6,2:3
Prepiak, William C, 1955, My 4,29:2
Prerau, Sydney, 1968, Ja 13,31:1
Presbrey, Charles, 1958, My 10,21:2
Presbrey, Clifton H, 1964, Mr 5,33:1
Presbrey, Clinton H Mrs, 1955, S 6,25:1
Presbrey, F, 1936, O 11,II,11:1
Presbrey, F Carleton Mrs, 1954, D 6,27:3
Presbrey, Frank Mrs, 1951, Ja 18,27:2
Presbrey, Fred C, 1957, My 31,19:3
Presbrey, Marguerite C, 1959, N 17,35:4
Presbrey, Oliver H, 1941, O 21,23:4
Presbury, G G, 1883, Je 9,2:3
Presby, Frank N, 1924, N 10,17:2
Preschel, Louis, 1943, D 17,27:3
Preschepa, Efiem, 1951, Ag 2,21:3
Prescher, George H, 1948, N 16,29:1
Prescott, Albert B Dr, 1905, F 26,7:6
Prescott, Annie L, 1937, Ap 26,19:3
Prescott, Arthur T, 1959, Mr 27,24:8
Prescott, Blake D, 1957, F 23,17:5
Prescott, Charles (cor, D 4,35:4), 1952, D 3,33:6
Prescott, Charles A, 1941, Ap 3,23:2
Prescott, Edward, 1960, S 16,28:6
Prescott, Francis, 1944, O 13,19:2
Prescott, Frederick C, 1957, Jl 28,61:3
Prescott, George L, 1941, Je 4,23:2
Prescott, George Washington, 1908, S 10,9:7
Prescott, Harold M (por), 1944, D 27,19:3
Prescott, Harriet B, 1958, Ag 21,25:3
Prescott, Harry L, 1948, Ap 15,25:4
Prescott, Herbert F, 1948, N 5,25:1
Prescott, Herbert S, 1939, O 11,27:2
Prescott, John, 1879, O 7,3:3
Prescott, John A, 1953, O 26,21:3
Prescott, John H Rev, 1923, Ja 15,15:5
Prescott, John P, 1957, Jl 23,27:4
Prescott, John S (por), 1949, My 20,27:3
Prescott, John T, 1959, N 19,39:5
Prescott, Josie F, 1949, Ja 8,15:3
Prescott, Marguerite C, 1949, N 26,15:5
Prescott, Mary, 1961, Ja 8,86:8
Prescott, Oliver, 1938, D 10,17:4
Prescott, Orville W Mrs, 1953, S 24,33:2
Prescott, Patrick B, 1945, D 15,17:6
Prescott, Peter, 1965, N 16,23:1
Prescott, Ralph P, 1957, Je 1,17:5
Prescott, Ralph P Mrs, 1957, Je 1,17:5
Prescott, Ray B, 1960, N 14,31:2
Prescott, Roger B, 1958, O 12,86:7
Prescott, Samuel C, 1962, Mr 21,39:2
Prescott, Sherburne, 1967, Jl 19,39:3
Prescott, Standish, 1954, O 14,29:3
Prescott, Thomas E Mrs, 1957, Jl 23,27:3
Prescott, W B, 1916, Ja 26,11:2
Prescott, William, 1937, N 17,23:3
Prescott, William H, 1945, Je 16,13:2
Prescott, William H Dr, 1937, My 7,25:3
Prescott, William Hickling (funl, F 1,1:5), 1859, Ja 31,1:4
Present, Amos M, 1949, F 25,24:2
Present, Emanuel, 1944, N 6,19:2
Presley, Earl Warren Dr, 1925, S 16,25:4
Presley, Fred Y, 1963, D 11,47:2
Presley, Hannah M Mrs, 1937, Ap 14,25:3
Preslie, Benjamin K, 1949, My 26,29:1
Presnell, James F, 1952, Mr 3,21:5
Presno, Jose A, 1953, S 14,27:5
Presper, E John, 1943, D 4,13:6
Press, Benjamin Mrs, 1947, Jl 10,21:4
Press, Eliza J S Mrs, 1940, N 14,23:3
Press, John H, 1953, Je 15,29:5
Press, Joseph, 1924, O 6,19:5
Press, Max, 1956, Mr 15,31:4
Press, Michael (por), 1938, D 24,15:3
Press, Paul, 1950, N 18,15:5
Press, Samuel, 1950, S 20,31:5
Press, Solomon, 1962, Ag 5,33:4
Press, Solomon Mrs, 1961, Je 29,33:3
Pressburger, Arnold, 1951, F 19,23:5
Pressel, Charles, 1953, Je 23,29:2
Pressell, George W, 1950, Je 6,29:1
Pressense, Francis de, 1914, Ja 21,9:4
Presser, Joseph, 1967, Ap 22,31:3
Presser, Karl, 1958, My 28,31:1
Presser, Theodore, 1925, O 29,25:5
Pressey, Conrad C, 1949, F 12,17:1
Pressey, Edwin P, 1950, Jl 22,15:1
Pressey, George W, 1966, Ap 23,31:1
Pressey, R P, 1946, N 9,17:6
Pressey, William, 1947, Ag 29,17:1
Pressinger, Arnott M, 1938, D 30,15:2
Pressinger, Whitfield Mrs, 1949, S 25,92:4
Pressinger, Whitfield Price, 1920, Je 12,13:4
Pressler, Frank, 1952, N 26,23:5
Pressley, Charles E, 1953, Jl 15,25:2
Pressley, Charles P, 1945, O 3,19:4
Pressley, Louis (Babe),(Sept 15), 1965, O 11,61:4
Pressly, William L, 1954, S 28,29:2
Pressman, Albert, 1955, Jl 31,69:3
Pressman, Aron Mrs, 1956, Je 24,77:1
Pressman, Donald J, 1964, D 5,31:1
Pressman, Jack, 1959, Ap 7,33:1
Pressman, Joel J Dr, 1968, F 27,43:1
Pressman, Louis, 1951, O 24,31:3
Pressman, Michael, 1951, Mr 22,31:4
Pressner, Morris, 1960, Mr 5,19:6
Presson, George M, 1951, Ap 18,31:1
Presson, Harold W, 1939, Ap 1,19:4
Pressprich, Marie L Mrs, 1940, S 20,23:5
Pressprich, Reginald W (por), 1955, D 16,29:4
Pressprich, Reginald W, 1966, Ag 18,32:4
Pressprich, Reginald W Mrs, 1948, Mr 11,27:3
Pressy, Warren F, 1942, Ja 6,23:4
Prest, C C Rev, 1875, S 14,4:7
Prest, Charles S, 1954, N 12,21:3
Prest, Charles S Mrs, 1958, Mr 23,88:7
Prest, Edward J, 1941, Mr 1,15:2
Prest, George B, 1938, Jl 30,13:6
Prest, Jessie H, 1944, D 17,37:2
Prest, John B, 1961, D 20,33:2
Prest, John B Mrs, 1956, D 12,39:2
Prest, William M, 1945, S 16,44:3
Prestage, Albert M, 1947, O 9,25:4
Prestes, Julio (por), 1946, F 10,42:1
Prestgaard, Kristian, 1946, Ja 26,13:3
Presti, Ida, 1967, Ap 26,47:3
Prestia, Charles J, 1953, Ja 5,21:5
Prestidge, John Newton Rev, 1913, O 30,9:3
Prestige, George L, 1955, Ja 20,31:3
Prestin, Charles, 1958, Ag 2,17:5
Preston, Alfred I Jr, 1960, Ap 20,39:3
Preston, Alice, 1955, N 18,25:3
Preston, Andrew W, 1924, S 27,16:5
Preston, Anne Dr, 1872, Ap 19,1:5
Preston, Arthur, 1948, Ap 13,27:3
Preston, Arthur P, 1957, Je 15,17:5
Preston, Belle, 1951, D 5,35:6
Preston, Charles L, 1937, F 20,17:5
Preston, Charles M, 1909, Ap 17,9:5
Preston, Clifford H, 1954, Ap 16,22:4
Preston, Columbia L R Mrs, 1949, D 3,7:8
Preston, Duncan C, 1922, Je 10,11:5
Preston, Edna (Mrs J Coots), 1960, Ag 20,19:3
Preston, Edward S, 1947, My 3,17:5
Preston, Edwin W, 1941, D 21,40:8
Preston, Elwyn G, 1951, D 19,31:2
Preston, Ernest R, 1946, S 28,17:2
Preston, Frances A, 1951, O 7,85:6
Preston, Frances Eaton, 1968, Jl 27,27:1
Preston, Frederic, 1910, D 20,13:3
Preston, Frederick A, 1947, Je 9,21:5
Preston, Frederick D, 1940, Jl 4,15:5; 1952, F 9,13:4
Preston, Frederick P, 1949, Jl 20,25:5
Preston, G Davies, 1950, N 4,17:5
Preston, George, 1948, F 27,21:3
Preston, George B, 1938, N 28,15:4
Preston, George B Mrs, 1947, N 3,23:2
Preston, George L, 1947, Ag 5,23:2
Preston, George R, 1943, Mr 27,14:7
Preston, George R Mrs, 1905, N 13,9:5
Preston, Guy H, 1952, D 13,21:1
Preston, H, 1936, Ag 14,17:4
Preston, H Raymond, 1944, Ap 18,21:6
Preston, Hamilton G, 1942, Jl 10,17:6
Preston, Harold, 1938, Ja 2,40:3
Preston, Harold A, 1939, S 30,17:3
Preston, Harold P, 1953, N 3,31:3
Preston, Henry G Dr, 1917, Je 23,9:6
Preston, Henry H, 1949, Jl 18,17:5
Preston, Herbert R, 1937, O 16,19:4
Preston, J S, 1881, My 3,5:3
Preston, James D, 1959, Ja 31,19:5
Preston, James F Mrs, 1947, D 13,15:5
Preston, James H, 1938, Jl 15,17:3
Preston, James M, 1962, Ja 17,33:2
Preston, Jenico William Joseph (Viscount Gormanston), 1907, O 30,9:5
Preston, Jewel J Mrs, 1937, Jl 11,II,4:7
Preston, John, 1945, D 8,17:4
Preston, John A, 1938, My 15,II,6:6
Preston, John C, 1938, Ap 13,25:3
Preston, John E, 1943, O 24,44:3
Preston, John J, 1938, Mr 13,II,8:6
Preston, Joseph A, 1950, Mr 15,29:5
Preston, L S W, 1865, F 2,4:5
Preston, Lawrence G, 1947, D 12,28:2
Preston, Leonard J, 1937, Jl 13,19:2
Preston, Lewis Butler, 1922, Ap 15,15:6
Preston, Lewis T, 1937, F 11,23:5
Preston, Lillie D Mrs, 1939, Jl 31,13:6
Preston, Mary, 1948, Je 5,15:5
Preston, Mary H Mrs, 1941, Mr 3,15:1
Preston, May, 1923, N 7,17:6
Preston, May W Mrs, 1949, My 19,29:4
Preston, Ord, 1949, F 5,15:4
Preston, Ord Mrs, 1941, My 2,21:2
Preston, Prince H, 1961, F 9,31:3
Preston, Ralph A D, 1954, My 17,23:3
Preston, Ralph J, 1919, O 26,22:3
Preston, Ralph W, 1950, My 26,23:2
Preston, Richard W Sr, 1957, Ap 20,17:4
Preston, Robert, 1949, Ag 27,13:3
Preston, Robert H, 1953, S 2,25:1
Preston, Robert M, 1955, D 8,37:2
Preston, Samuel I, 1957, Ag 18,82:2
Preston, Sherwood C, 1944, My 20,15:3
Preston, Stella J Mrs, 1937, F 20,17:3
Preston, T S Msgr, 1891, N 4,4:7
Preston, Thomas J Jr, 1955, D 26,19:4
Preston, Thomas J Jr Mrs, 1947, O 30,25:1
Preston, Thomas L, 1957, My 22,33:1
Preston, Thomas R, 1949, Ag 15,17:5; 1953, O 31,1
Preston, Thomas W, 1940, Ja 6,13:4; 1943, S 22,23:
Preston, Toni, 1953, My 17,89:1
Preston, Walter C, 1950, Je 14,31:6
Preston, Wheeler B, 1953, My 18,21:5
Preston, Wilbur F, 1958, S 16,28:2
Preston, William B, 1956, Jl 16,21:2
Preston, William D, 1948, Ja 26,19:4
Preston, William G, 1956, Ja 5,33:4
Preston, William T Mrs, 1941, D 17,27:5; 1950, My 28,44:6
Preston, William T R, 1942, N 4,23:4
Prestopnik, Irving, 1949, Mr 21,23:4

Prestwich, Thomas W, 1953, N 16,25:2
Presutti, Enrico, 1949, Jl 27,23:3
Pretie, Paul G, 1949, Ja 12,27:4
Preto, Ouro Viscount, 1912, F 23,11:4
Pretorius, Philip J, 1945, N 25,48:6
Pretot, Fanny Mrs, 1954, Ap 20,29:4
Pretto, Jose R, 1949, Ja 8,15:2
Pretty, Harry E, 1941, Ja 24,17:2
Pretty, Royden K, 1942, Jl 13,15:4
Prettyman, Albert B, 1938, Ja 17,19:4
Prettyman, Albert I, 1963, My 25,25:4
Prettyman, Arthur S (trb, F 6,25:1), 1957, F 5,23:1
Prettyman, C William, 1946, Ag 10,13:5
Prettyman, Charles B Jr, 1955, Ja 16,92:1
Prettyman, Forrest J (por), 1945, O 13,15:6
Prettyman, Hugh W, 1949, Ag 1,17:5
Prettyman, John B, 1947, Je 16,21:3
Prettyman, Virgil, 1957, O 14,27:3
Pretzel, Frank E, 1965, Ag 17,19:2
Pretzell, Carl E, 1952, Ap 4,25:3
Pretzfeld, Eugene W, 1948, Ja 9,21:3
Pretzfeld, George E, 1959, Ap 6,27:4
Pretzfelder, Albert, 1958, Je 14,21:6
Preus, Jacob A O, 1961, My 26,33:1
Preus, O J H, 1951, F 15,31:4
Preuss, George U Rev, 1937, F 24,23:5
Preuss, Hugo Dr, 1925, O 10,15:5
Preuss, Jacob A, 1937, D 18,21:3
Preuss, Joseph G, 1958, Mr 31,27:4
Preuss, Lawrence, 1956, Jl 8,64:8
Preusser, August, 1944, Ja 2,39:1
Preusser, Helen E, 1957, Mr 28,31:5
Preusser, Minnie E, 1962, O 12,31:2
Preussner, Otto, 1946, My 8,25:5
Preve, Cesare, 1940, Ap 5,22:3
Prevette, Earl, 1960, Ag 30,29:2
Previtali, Mario, 1953, F 5,23:5
Previte-Orton, Charles W, 1947, Mr 13,27:3
Prevost, Edouard, 1943, O 14,21:5
Prevost, Emily L, 1941, Jl 15,19:4
Prevost, Henri, 1940, F 27,21:3
Prevost, Jean A Msgr, 1925, S 17,23:4
Prevost, Mabel R, 1961, S 9,19:4
Prevost, Marcel, 1941, Ap 10,24:3
Prevost, Marie (por),(will, F 20,8:4), 1937, Ja 24,25:1
Prevost, Marie L, 1961, S 27,42:1
Prevost, Sterett R, 1943, Ja 17,44:5
Prevost, Sutherland M, 1905, O 1,9:6
Prew, Robert J, 1952, F 18,19:4
Prewitt, Perkins J, 1953, F 12,27:3
Prey, Elting A, 1950, S 27,31:2
Preyer, Allan T, 1965, N 2,34:1
Preyer, David C, 1913, Ag 13,9:3
Preyora, Charles, 1922, Mr 27,15:6
Preysing, Konrad von, 1950, D 22,23:3
Preza, Velino M, 1944, D 18,19:1
Prezan, Constantin, 1943, Ag 28,11:6
Prezant, Simon, 1956, S 13,35:1
Preziosi, Andrew, 1947, My 2,22:2
Prezzano, Edward P, 1963, Je 18,41:1
Prezzano, Edward P Mrs, 1968, Jl 8,39:2
Prial, Edward B, 1939, F 1,21:2
Prial, Frank J, 1948, F 25,23:3
Priaulx, Joseph M, 1956, Jl 15,61:2
Priaulx, Nicholas, 1966, Ag 9,37:3
Priboj, Julia Mrs, 1953, S 19,15:5
Price, A Leslie, 1961, N 6,37:2
Price, Abel Fitzwater Dr, 1919, Mr 23,20:4
Price, Alan W, 1953, Ap 26,85:2
Price, Albert, 1950, D 22,23:3
Price, Alexander Hamilton Capt, 1915, S 27,9:4
Price, Allan M, 1943, F 17,21:2
Price, Anna W Mrs, 1946, S 10,7:3
Price, Arthur M, 1954, My 19,31:2
Price, Benjamin, 1939, Ag 10,19:3; 1966, Ap 14,39:3
Price, Benjamin M, 1945, Mr 9,19:3; 1965, O 23,31:4
Price, Bernard S, 1956, O 21,86:2
Price, Bruce, 1903, My 31,7:5
Price, Burr, 1952, Mr 19,29:4
Price, Burroughs M, 1944, D 5,23:6
Price, C Matlack, 1962, Ap 30,27:4
Price, C W, 1934, My 12,16:3
Price, Carl F, 1919, S 1,7:4; 1948, Ap 14,27:3
Price, Caroline M Mrs, 1944, Ja 14,19:5
Price, Chalkley M, 1946, Ag 4,46:1
Price, Charles A, 1959, Je 21,93:1
Price, Charles F, 1941, Jl 28,13:6
Price, Charles F Mrs, 1940, D 8,68:2
Price, Charles H, 1942, Ap 6,15:1; 1955, F 9,25:2
Price, Charles R, 1944, Ap 12,21:4
Price, Charles W, 1957, Ag 3,15:5
Price, Chester B, 1962, Jl 4,21:1
Price, Cicero Mrs, 1910, O 26,9:4
Price, Clara B, 1941, F 3,17:2
Price, Clara B Mrs, 1940, Mr 18,17:2
Price, Clarence L, 1954, S 14,27:4
Price, Clarence M, 1949, D 14,31:4
Price, Clarence Mrs, 1948, Ja 28,23:2
Price, Clinton F, 1943, N 18,23:6
Price, Clinton Sr, 1952, Ag 28,23:4
Price, Daniel, 1950, Ja 30,17:3
Price, Daniel B Mrs, 1942, Ja 14,21:1
Price, Daniel T, 1938, Jl 7,19:2
Price, David, 1957, Je 30,69:3
Price, David D, 1941, Ag 26,19:5
Price, David J, 1923, Ap 6,17:4; 1951, My 30,21:2
Price, David S, 1903, D 18,9:6
Price, Denis W, 1966, Mr 24,39:2
Price, Donald O, 1957, O 25,27:2
Price, E Melville, 1953, Ag 29,17:3
Price, Earl A Mrs, 1949, Je 18,13:6
Price, Earl P, 1946, F 18,21:2
Price, Edgar F Mrs, 1946, Mr 2,13:2
Price, Edgar K, 1955, D 27,23:2
Price, Edmund B, 1947, My 13,25:2
Price, Edward, 1907, D 22,9:4; 1951, N 26,45:5
Price, Edward A, 1906, N 23,9:5
Price, Ellen, 1968, Mr 8,39:5
Price, Enoch J, 1945, F 26,19:3
Price, Evan L, 1968, F 16,37:2
Price, Florence A, 1957, Ap 15,29:4
Price, Florence E, 1949, Ap 1,25:2
Price, Frank E, 1947, D 1,21:3
Price, Frank J, 1939, O 7,17:5; 1950, Mr 6,22:2
Price, Frank L, 1937, Mr 16,II,8:5
Price, Frank O Mrs, 1962, N 29,38:7
Price, Franklin H, 1958, Ja 10,26:1
Price, Fraser P, 1941, Ag 29,17:4
Price, Frederic N, 1963, My 28,28:7
Price, Frederick J, 1965, O 27,47:4
Price, Frederick V Jr, 1938, Je 18,15:3
Price, Freeman Mrs, 1964, My 2,27:1
Price, G Ward, 1961, Ag 23,33:1
Price, George A, 1953, Je 7,83:1
Price, George Allen Col, 1924, Ja 18,17:5
Price, George J, 1941, Ja 28,19:1
Price, George M (por), 1942, Jl 31,15:3
Price, George S, 1947, Ja 20,25:2
Price, Georgie (Geo E), 1964, My 11,31:1
Price, Guernsey, 1952, Ja 9,29:2
Price, Harley C, 1964, O 6,39:1
Price, Harold C, 1962, Ja 29,25:4
Price, Harriet Ann, 1925, My 20,23:4
Price, Harriet L, 1948, Je 21,21:5
Price, Harriet O, 1942, N 13,23:2
Price, Harrison B, 1942, O 22,21:1
Price, Harrison J, 1945, S 18,24:2
Price, Harry (por), 1948, Mr 30,23:1
Price, Harry, 1960, Ag 16,29:1
Price, Harry C, 1948, Ap 16,23:1; 1951, S 12,31:4
Price, Harry E, 1959, Je 6,21:6
Price, Harvey L, 1951, F 20,25:2
Price, Health Mrs, 1947, Je 12,25:3
Price, Henry, 1958, Mr 7,23:4
Price, Henry F Mrs, 1947, My 16,23:2
Price, Henry M Mrs, 1957, Ap 9,33:1
Price, Herman, 1968, D 17,50:1
Price, Hickman, 1939, D 15,25:1
Price, Hickman 3d, 1963, S 11,88:1
Price, Homer C, 1943, Mr 26,19:4
Price, Howard E, 1939, Mr 12,III,6:7
Price, Hugh H, 1940, Ag 27,21:2
Price, Humphrey J, 1949, Ag 13,12:2
Price, Ira M, 1939, S 19,26:3
Price, Irving, 1948, F 12,24:3
Price, Isaac, 1903, D 12,1:3; 1946, Jl 6,16:6
Price, Isaac N, 1937, N 7,II,9:2
Price, J E, 1935, S 22,II,11:3
Price, J Howell Mrs, 1951, Mr 9,25:5
Price, Jacob A, 1942, N 15,59:2
Price, Jacob C Dr (funl, My 19,21:3), 1925, My 18, 15:5
Price, James Capt, 1902, Ap 19,9:2
Price, James H, 1943, N 23,25:1
Price, James K (funl, Jl 15,7:6), 1913, Jl 12,7:5
Price, James L Justice, 1912, Mr 12,13:4
Price, James M, 1958, Ap 14,25:4
Price, James W, 1951, F 26,23:4
Price, Jean C Mrs, 1955, Ap 13,29:1
Price, Jerome Mrs, 1961, N 12,86:5
Price, Jerry, 1947, Ja 17,23:2
Price, Jerry P Mrs, 1964, Jl 15,35:5
Price, Jesse D, 1939, My 16,23:3
Price, John A, 1950, Ag 12,13:1
Price, John B, 1950, Ja 17,27:5; 1952, My 13,23:3
Price, John C, 1940, Ag 29,21:6
Price, John D, 1939, N 11,15:2; 1957, D 19,31:2
Price, John E, 1910, N 25,11:6
Price, John E Mrs, 1937, N 11,25:1
Price, John H, 1945, Ap 17,23:4; 1950, F 28,19:3
Price, John H Sr, 1949, S 22,31:3
Price, John J, 1940, F 6,21:5; 1942, O 29,23:5
Price, John L Mrs, 1943, N 26,23:2
Price, John M, 1961, Ag 2,29:3; 1963, Mr 5,16:1
Price, John S Jr, 1948, Je 19,15:2
Price, John T, 1955, Ap 19,31:4
Price, John T Mrs, 1944, Ja 10,17:4
Price, John W, 1939, S 14,23:5; 1959, Je 10,37:2
Price, Jorge W, 1953, O 10,17:5
Price, Joseph, 1947, Jl 9,23:5; 1956, My 15,32:7
Price, Joseph D, 1959, Mr 27,23:2
Price, Joseph F, 1941, Ag 15,17:6
Price, Joseph L, 1947, N 15,17:6
Price, Joseph M (lr, My 20,26:6),(por), 1949, My 14, 13:3
Price, Joseph M Mrs, 1957, Mr 4,27:3
Price, Kate, 1943, Ja 6,25:5
Price, Kathryn W, 1942, S 17,25:2
Price, Kirk, 1967, Mr 15,47:4
Price, Lawrence W Mrs, 1953, Mr 20,23:3
Price, Lee Jr, 1962, F 8,31:3
Price, Leo A, 1949, F 10,27:5
Price, Lester I, 1951, Ja 12,27:2
Price, Levi, 1966, D 1,47:3
Price, Levi A, 1951, N 29,33:2
Price, Llewellyn Sr, 1941, Mr 9,41:2
Price, Louis R, 1963, Jl 20,19:4
Price, Louis V, 1956, Ja 7,17:5
Price, Louise, 1964, Mr 2,27:3
Price, Lucien B Mrs, 1951, N 24,11:6
Price, Luther E, 1941, D 20,19:3
Price, Luther E A Mrs, 1943, Ja 10,50:2
Price, Margaret (Mrs Hickman Price Jr),(funl, Jl 27,27:4), 1968, Jl 24,41:3
Price, Marguerite W Mrs, 1946, O 14,29:1
Price, Mark, 1917, Ap 1,19:2
Price, Marshall L Dr, 1915, Ap 19,9:5
Price, Mary E, 1958, S 11,33:3
Price, Mathias J, 1946, N 11,27:5
Price, Maurice T, 1964, Mr 3,35:1
Price, Maurice W, 1952, S 11,31:4
Price, Miles O, 1968, Ag 22,37:5
Price, Miles R, 1956, N 22,33:6
Price, Milton W, 1942, Ap 4,13:2
Price, Mordecai M, 1948, F 14,13:5
Price, Morris, 1963, S 16,35:4
Price, Nathan, 1963, S 20,33:3
Price, Nellie B, 1954, Mr 6,15:6
Price, Newman S, 1951, Ja 19,25:2
Price, Norman H, 1944, N 30,23:2
Price, Norman M, 1951, Ag 4,15:6
Price, Oliver J, 1956, Ja 7,17:5
Price, Orlo J, 1943, F 14,49:1
Price, P Frank, 1954, My 12,31:3
Price, P Frank Mrs, 1950, My 20,15:1
Price, Paul H, 1955, Jl 25,19:2
Price, Paul L, 1966, S 25,84:5
Price, Paul W, 1945, Ag 6,21:2
Price, R C Prof, 1937, Ag 26,21:4
Price, Ralph, 1959, Mr 28,17:5
Price, Ralph G, 1957, D 15,86:6
Price, Rebecca, 1925, Mr 25,21:4
Price, Robert, 1904, S 14,3:7; 1957, Ap 14,87:1
Price, Robert C, 1952, N 15,17:5
Price, Robert C L, 1949, Je 1,31:4
Price, Robert G, 1939, O 21,15:3; 1954, O 30,17:6
Price, Rodman M, 1953, Ja 18,92:6
Price, Rupert H, 1953, Ja 27,25:1
Price, Sabina L Mrs, 1940, Je 12,25:5
Price, Sammy (S Perlman), 1963, O 20,88:8
Price, Samuel, 1945, My 11,19:3
Price, Samuel E, 1914, Ja 9,11:5
Price, Samuel F, 1961, Ja 12,29:1
Price, Samuel Mrs, 1954, Jl 1,25:4
Price, Sidney, 1903, Ap 29,9:6
Price, Stanley L, 1955, Jl 15,21:3
Price, Starling W, 1946, Ag 17,13:3
Price, Sterling, 1865, Ja 7,1:4
Price, Sterling Gen (funl), 1867, O 1,5:2
Price, T Duane, 1966, Je 2,43:3
Price, T Fraser, 1960, F 9,31:4
Price, T H, 1935, My 5,II,7:1
Price, T N, 1928, Ag 6,19:5
Price, T R Prof, 1903, My 9,9:5
Price, Theodore, 1951, O 15,25:5
Price, Theodore H Mrs, 1950, D 5,31:2
Price, Theopolus, 1938, Ap 6,23:5
Price, Thomas, 1903, Je 24,9:6
Price, Thomas C Sr, 1959, N 12,35:1
Price, Thomas F Rev, 1919, S 24,17:6
Price, Thomas Grenville, 1924, Jl 16,11:5
Price, Thomas I, 1953, Mr 6,20:6
Price, Thomas J, 1947, S 13,11:6
Price, Thomas M, 1962, S 13,37:5
Price, Thomas R, 1938, Ja 18,23:3
Price, Towson Mrs, 1963, S 5,31:3
Price, U Seymour, 1940, Jl 13,13:5
Price, Victor, 1965, My 22,31:5
Price, Vincent C Dr, 1914, Jl 15,9:5
Price, Virgil M, 1962, Ja 16,33:3
Price, W A, 1903, O 10,9:6; 1940, F 23,15:4
Price, W C, 1901, Ag 7,7:6
Price, W H, 1882, Ag 15,5:1
Price, W H C, 1881, S 26,5:3
Price, W R, 1881, D 31,5:3
Price, Walter, 1959, Ap 25,21:1
Price, Walter L, 1962, My 15,39:2
Price, Walter S, 1953, Je 18,29:3
Price, Walter W, 1943, N 20,13:3
Price, Walter W Mrs, 1954, Ap 21,29:2
Price, Warner W, 1938, F 13,II,6:8
Price, Warren G, 1957, S 25,29:4
Price, Weston A, 1948, Ja 24,15:3
Price, Whitely K, 1950, D 22,23:3
Price, Will, 1962, Jl 6,25:4
Price, William, 1938, Ap 18,15:5; 1945, O 2,23:4; 1965, My 14,37:2
Price, William B, 1950, F 8,28:2
Price, William C, 1937, N 22,19:5

Price, William D, 1939, Je 18,37:1
Price, William E, 1943, F 4,23:4; 1954, D 10,27:2
Price, William G F, 1914, Ap 5,15:2
Price, William G Jr, 1960, F 25,29:2
Price, William H, 1941, N 1,15:3; 1957, Jl 21,61:3
Price, William J, 1952, My 22,27:6
Price, William L, 1950, Ap 19,30:3
Price, William N, 1949, D 18,88:4
Price, William S, 1912, D 18,15:4; 1949, My 15,90:2
Price, William Thompson, 1920, My 4,11:1
Price, William W, 1961, Ag 25,35:1
Price, Wilson C, 1937, Jl 5,17:5
Price, Winfield S, 1956, O 2,35:5
Price, Yearsley A, 1963, N 17,87:1
Price, Yolande, 1945, Je 27,19:5
Pricer, John S, 1950, N 14,64:4
Prichard, Harold A, 1944, My 8,19:4
Prichard, Hubert J, 1963, S 29,86:3
Prichard, Karl C, 1940, Ja 7,48:6
Pricher, Lawrence S, 1947, S 17,25:3
Prichett, Wilson, 1956, Ag 7,27:3
Prickett, Charles F, 1954, Jl 26,17:2
Prickett, Clifford, 1949, D 30,20:5
Prickett, Henry M Mrs, 1945, Ap 26,23:4
Prickett, Irvin, 1953, Ap 20,25:1
Prickett, McIver, 1959, Jl 16,27:3
Prickett, Wesley, 1937, My 9,II,10:1
Priddey, Edward J, 1954, Jl 14,28:5
Priddie, Tazewell, 1947, Jl 22,23:5
Priddie, William A, 1940, N 9,17:3
Priddy, Benjamin E Mrs, 1952, Ag 29,23:2
Priddy, Julia H Mrs, 1946, D 28,16:3
Priddy, Lawrence, 1944, S 4,19:4
Pride, Andrew Hamilton, 1903, N 27,9:5
Pride, Edward F, 1958, Ja 2,29:1
Pride, Fred, 1940, Mr 31,45:1
Pride, Nathaniel H, 1920, D 12,22:2
Pride, Robert E, 1954, S 19,89:1
Prideaux, J Raymond, 1952, D 6,21:5
Pridham-Wippell, Henry, 1952, Ap 3,35:5
Pridmore, John E O, 1940, F 4,40:2
Pridvoroff, Efin A, 1945, My 26,15:4
Prie, Harry J, 1949, Ap 4,23:3
Priebe, William L, 1925, Jl 28,13:5
Prien, John C, 1939, Je 11,45:1
Pries, August M Sr, 1937, S 10,23:4
Pries, George H Mrs, 1945, Jl 21,11:2
Pries, John C, 1945, F 20,19:1
Pries, Theodore, 1952, Ap 19,15:5
Priess, Adele D Mrs, 1952, Ap 24,31:1
Priess, George H, 1954, Mr 27,17:2
Priess, William, 1952, Mr 6,31:2
Priest, Arthur Mrs, 1951, My 8,31:2
Priest, Benjamin H Mrs, 1952, Ja 31,27:3
Priest, Carlton, 1939, Jl 7,17:3
Priest, Charles, 1942, My 26,21:2
Priest, Daniel B, 1949, F 27,68:4
Priest, Daniel S, 1948, O 25,23:4
Priest, Ella J Mrs, 1915, Ap 5,11:4
Priest, George E, 1921, Ja 9,23:2
Priest, George M, 1947, F 19,25:3
Priest, Harry L, 1945, Ap 30,21:3
Priest, Henry Prof, 1912, S 28,13:6
Priest, J Percy, 1956, O 13,19:3
Priest, James H, 1952, Mr 1,15:3
Priest, Louis, 1946, F 17,42:6
Priest, Louis Mrs, 1944, D 14,23:4
Priest, Roy F, 1959, Je 12,27:1
Priest, Samuel Mrs, 1944, O 15,44:3
Priest, W Edwin, 1953, O 11,89:1
Priest, Ward C, 1945, D 22,19:4
Priest, Wells B, 1951, S 21,23:1
Priester, Andre A, 1955, N 29,29:4
Priester, Owen, 1908, Mr 8,7:5
Priestes, John Dr, 1937, Ja 12,23:2
Priestley, Alfred, 1958, N 4,27:5
Priestley, Craykee Dr, 1904, My 14,1:4
Priestley, Herbert I, 1944, F 11,19:4
Priestley, J E, 1948, Jl 17,15:3
Priestley, John A, 1949, Ap 15,23:4
Priestley, Kenneth, 1949, Mr 18,25:3
Priestley, Louis A, 1965, Ja 25,37:3
Priestley, William J, 1968, S 5,57:3
Priestley, William Sr, 1961, Je 17,21:1
Priestly, George C, 1938, Ap 6,23:5
Priestly, James Taggart Dr, 1925, D 12,15:5
Priestman, Gerald, 1953, Jl 25,11:6
Priestman, Glyndon, 1964, Mr 3,35:1
Priestman, John Sir, 1941, Ag 7,17:4
Priestnall, William Rev, 1937, Je 21,19:3
Prieth, B, 1879, O 30,5:2
Prieto, Genaro, 1946, Mr 5,27:5
Prieto, Indalecio, 1962, F 13,35:1
Prieto, Manuel G, 1956, O 2,35:5
Prigge, Charles L Mrs, 1951, Ap 6,25:3
Prigge, John Mrs, 1953, Ap 20,25:3
Prigge, John S, 1952, Jl 26,13:4
Prigge, William, 1953, My 12,27:2
Prignano, Daniel, 1941, Jl 8,19:6
Prigot, Aaron Dr, 1968, Jl 20,27:2
Prihoda, Vasa, 1960, Jl 29,25:3
Prikhidko, Nikolai Y, 1957, D 25,5:1
Prim, Gen, 1871, Ja 2,1:4
Prim, Polly, 1920, My 6,11:3
Prime, Alanson J, 1913, Ja 1,17:4
Prime, Cornelia, 1923, F 17,13:4
Prime, Edward, 1915, N 6,11:6
Prime, Frederick, 1952, O 14,34:3
Prime, Frederick Prof, 1915, Jl 16,9:5
Prime, Hubert William, 1968, Jl 27,27:4
Prime, Nina T Mrs, 1939, D 11,23:4
Prime, Ralph E, 1920, S 28,13:1
Prime, Ralph E Jr, 1942, My 23,13:5
Prime, Ralph E Mrs, 1956, Ag 24,19:6
Prime, S I Rev, 1885, Jl 19,7:4
Prime, S T K, 1907, Ap 28,9:5
Prime, Sarah, 1923, Ap 23,15:6
Prime, Temple, 1903, F 26,9:5
Prime, Wendell Rev Dr, 1907, D 1,11:5
Prime, William C, 1960, Ja 31,94:3
Prime, William Cowper, 1905, F 14,9:3
Prime-Stevenson, Edward, 1942, Ag 1,11:4
Primerano, Eugene S, 1957, F 12,27:4
Primiano, Nicholas J, 1966, My 18,47:1
Primo de Rivera, Miguel, 1964, My 9,27:2
Primrose, Alexander, 1944, F 9,19:2
Primrose, Durward H, 1961, Ap 30,86:8
Primrose, Fannie B Mrs, 1938, My 17,23:2
Primrose, George F Mrs, 1903, Jl 30,7:6
Primrose, George H, 1919, Jl 24,9:2
Primrose, John (por), 1955, Ag 11,21:4
Primrose, Phil C H Col, 1937, Mr 18,25:4
Primrose, William Mrs, 1951, D 15,13:4
Primus, Edward G O R, 1953, D 22,31:3
Prin, Alice (Kiki), 1953, Mr 24,31:2
Prince, Adolf Mrs, 1943, F 9,23:1
Prince, Albert I, 1956, Mr 4,89:1
Prince, Alex L, 1938, My 26,25:5
Prince, Arthur, 1948, Ap 16,23:4
Prince, Arthur C, 1951, S 24,27:4
Prince, Arthur D, 1925, Ja 22,19:5; 1950, O 14,19:4
Prince, Benjamin Mrs, 1954, Ag 18,29:3
Prince, Carie S Mrs, 1948, Ja 22,27:3
Prince, Charles A, 1937, O 11,21:4
Prince, Clara B Mrs, 1941, S 14,49:2
Prince, Cornelia K Mrs, 1942, F 26,19:2
Prince, Duffield, 1954, N 12,21:2
Prince, Edgar G, 1946, Ag 17,13:7
Prince, Ernest F, 1938, Mr 22,21:2
Prince, F C Capt, 1909, Ja 17,11:6
Prince, Frederick D Mrs, 1949, Mr 1,25:6
Prince, Frederick H (will, F 20,21:4), 1953, F 3,25:1
Prince, Frederick H Jr, 1962, O 6,25:3
Prince, Frederick H Mrs, 1949, F 27,68:7
Prince, Frederick W Col, 1907, Ap 6,7:7
Prince, George S Mrs, 1954, Ag 21,17:6
Prince, George W, 1939, S 28,25:2
Prince, Gerald, 1963, N 14,35:3
Prince, Harry J, 1950, D 28,25:1
Prince, Herbert W Mrs, 1948, Mr 28,48:4
Prince, Howard L, 1948, N 19,27:2
Prince, Irving, 1958, S 16,27:1
Prince, J D, 1883, N 22,2:5
Prince, James F, 1964, Ja 13,35:3
Prince, John D (por), 1945, O 12,23:1
Prince, John D Mrs (por), 1944, My 24,19:2
Prince, John D Mrs, 1950, Ja 4,27:5
Prince, John T, 1916, Ag 6,17:6
Prince, Joseph, 1944, D 5,23:1; 1949, D 29,25:3
Prince, L B Mrs, 1880, F 28,8:4
Prince, L Ward, 1960, N 25,27:5
Prince, Le Baron Bradford, 1922, D 10,6:3
Prince, LeBaron Bradford, 1925, D 29,23:4
Prince, Leila W Mrs, 1954, Je 26,13:4
Prince, Leon C Dr, 1937, F 1,19:3
Prince, Leopold (trb, Ag 20,16:6), 1951, Ag 18,11:3
Prince, Linnaeus, 1939, Jl 12,19:4
Prince, Lionel D, 1942, Mr 7,17:2
Prince, Lucien B, 1958, Jl 26,15:5
Prince, M, 1929, S 1,II,5:1
Prince, Matthew A, 1950, O 2,23:4
Prince, Milton A, 1968, Ap 14,76:7
Prince, Nathan D, 1942, S 4,23:1
Prince, Noy A, 1948, Mr 1,23:4
Prince, Samuel, 1914, Ag 12,9:5
Prince, Samuel H, 1960, O 21,33:1
Prince, Theodore, 1953, F 18,31:3
Prince, Walter G, 1952, D 12,29:2
Prince, William, 1958, Ja 30,24:1
Prince, William A, 1952, F 19,29:2
Prince, William B, 1955, Ap 26,29:4
Prince, William Capt, 1880, D 21,2:6
Prince, William S, 1953, Ja 22,23:4
Prince Adalbert of Prussia, 1873, Je 7,5:4
Prince Alexander John Couza of Moldavia, 1873, My 2,3:7
Prince Esterhazy De Galantha, 1873, S 13,4:6
Prince Frederick Henry Albert of Germany, 1872, O 16,1:7
Prince George Galitzen, 1872, O 12,1:6
Prince Jno Anthony Lascaris Palaeloogus, 1874, S 28, 4:7
Prince of Conde, the, 1866, Jl 15,3:3
Prince of Crony-Chanel, 1873, S 29,2:2
Princess, D'Oubril, 1874, Je 30,1:6
Princess Augusta De Liegnitz, 1873, Je 7,5:4
Princess of Hohenlohe, 1872, S 26,1:1
Princi, Frank, 1963, S 20,33:3
Principe, Francis J Mrs, 1947, Ag 10,53:1
Principe, Louis, 1944, My 19,19:6
Prindeville, Charles H, 1947, Je 17,28:5
Prindiville, Thomas J, 1955, My 10,29:2
Prindle, Almira Mrs, 1914, O 20,13:6
Prindle, E B, 1903, Ag 21,9:6
Prindle, E Brewster, 1957, N 19,33:1
Prindle, Edwin J, 1942, D 19,20:2
Prindle, Edwin J Mrs, 1946, S 15,10:1
Prindle, Franklin C, 1923, Mr 8,17:3
Prindle, Frederick J, 1943, O 21,27:4
Prindle, John G, 1951, Ja 13,15:5
Prindle, Lester M, 1949, F 15,23:6
Prindle, Roscoe S, 1944, Mr 6,19:1
Prinetti, Giullo, 1908, Je 10,7:5
Pringle, Arthur W, 1940, O 4,23:1
Pringle, Aubrey C, 1942, Jl 23,19:6
Pringle, Edward O, 1949, Jl 25,15:3
Pringle, F Harold, 1954, D 31,13:6
Pringle, George O, 1949, S 9,26:7
Pringle, Harry Mrs, 1943, Ag 4,17:5
Pringle, Henry F, 1958, Ap 9,33:1
Pringle, J F, 1949, F 9,27:1
Pringle, J R P, 1932, S 26,15:1
Pringle, J R P Mrs, 1954, Ag 28,15:6
Pringle, James N, 1946, Jl 24,27:3
Pringle, James S, 1951, F 28,28:3
Pringle, James W, 1905, Ap 19,11:4
Pringle, John C, 1938, Ap 13,25:2
Pringle, John Dunbar, 1922, Ja 30,11:4
Pringle, Margaret E, 1939, S 15,23:5
Pringle, Marie, 1940, F 8,23:3
Pringle, Marie Mrs, 1937, Ja 23,17:4
Pringle, Peter C, 1951, S 18,31:3
Pringle, Robert, 1919, F 12,13:4
Pringle, Rose, 1947, My 10,13:6
Pringle, Stewart H, 1954, Ja 17,93:2
Pringle, Walter H, 1965, F 13,21:4
Pringle, William, 1965, My 29,27:6
Pringle, William J, 1938, Je 12,38:8; 1940, S 19,23:3
Prink, John H, 1940, O 27,44:2
Prink, Lester, 1959, D 17,37:1
Prins, David J B, 1962, Je 1,27:2
Prins, Huibert, 1939, My 31,23:5
Prinsep, V C, 1904, N 13,7:6
Printiss, Horace Mrs, 1907, N 18,7:6
Printon, Thomas A, 1965, Ap 19,29:4
Printz, Aaron A, 1948, S 17,26:2
Printz, Alexander (por), 1947, N 19,27:5
Printz, Carl J, 1960, Ag 21,84:3
Printz, Harold Mrs, 1961, Mr 29,33:1
Printz, Simon, 1968, S 1,53:3
Printzlien, Conrad P, 1962, S 7,30:1
Prinz, Hermann, 1957, N 26,33:5
Prinz, Milton, 1957, Ja 17,29:4
Prinz, Phil F, 1942, Jl 30,21:3
Prinzing, John F, 1944, Mr 12,38:3
Priolo, Frank C, 1952, Je 27,23:2
Prior, Daniel H, 1953, My 3,89:2
Prior, Elroy, 1944, Je 23,19:4
Prior, J Douglas, 1967, O 31,45:2
Prior, J J, 1875, My 2,7:3
Prior, J J Mrs, 1883, O 10,5:2
Prior, James V, 1940, Mr 11,15:1
Prior, Joseph A, 1950, My 22,21:2
Prior, Melton, 1910, N 3,9:5
Prior, Perley A Mrs, 1947, Mr 10,22:2
Prior, Peter J, 1937, Je 4,23:1
Prior, Roscoe N, 1952, Ag 18,17:3
Prior, Russell D, 1951, Jl 6,11:5
Prior, Stanley M, 1946, O 23,27:3
Prior, Walter R (funl), 1871, Jl 21,8:2
Prior, Walter Sr, 1943, My 25,23:5
Priore, Joseph C, 1954, S 7,25:3
Priory, Michael, 1940, Jl 21,29:2
Priory, Teresa M Mrs, 1941, Jl 19,13:1
Priory, William, 1951, Jl 21,13:3
Pripstein, Samuel, 1953, Ja 16,23:3
Prisament, Paul, 1941, N 8,19:2
Prisament, Theodore J, 1947, S 13,11:2
Prisbrey, Edward A, 1907, O 8,11:6
Priscilla, Louis, 1956, D 8,19:5
Prisco, Guiseppe Cardinal, 1923, F 6,19:4
Prishvin, Mikhail, 1954, Ja 18,23:4
Prising, Frederic W Mrs, 1963, Je 9,87:1
Prisk, Charles H, 1940, Mr 5,23:2
Prisk, Joseph H, 1923, Ag 9,13:5
Prisk, Laura B Mrs, 1950, My 31,29:5
Pristash, Andrew, 1951, F 19,23:1
Pritchaird, J Ambrose, 1905, F 7,9:5
Pritchard, Arthur J Adm, 1916, S 6,9:5
Pritchard, Charles A, 1951, D 30,24:2
Pritchard, Charles B, 1947, D 2,29:2
Pritchard, Dave, 1945, Ag 4,11:4
Pritchard, David R, 1948, Ja 29,23:4
Pritchard, Edward J, 1944, S 24,45:2
Pritchard, F J, 1931, Ja 15,23:5
Pritchard, Griffith B, 1941, Ag 20,19:6
Pritchard, Helen V, 1941, O 2,25:2
Pritchard, Hugh J D, 1937, My 5,25:4
Pritchard, Hugh Rev, 1917, D 28,11:5

Pritchard, James C, 1952, Ag 16,15:4
Pritchard, James F, 1940, S 24,23:5
Pritchard, James H, 1948, O 12,25:4
Pritchard, Jeter Conley Judge, 1921, Ap 11,11:3
Pritchard, John A, 1952, Mr 10,21:5; 1967, My 13,33:3
Pritchard, John Capt, 1922, Ja 31,12:4
Pritchard, Lester A, 1946, F 10,42:8
Pritchard, Miriam C, 1950, D 10,104:7
Pritchard, Paul W, 1953, F 28,17:6
Pritchard, Ralph L, 1945, My 6,37:1
Pritchard, Richard E, 1961, F 20,27:4
Pritchard, Robert H, 1950, Ag 16,29:2
Pritchard, Robert H Mrs, 1942, My 13,19:4
Pritchard, Stuart, 1940, Ag 5,13:4
Pritchard, Trevor, 1939, My 17,47:3
Pritchard, W B, 1932, Je 8,19:1
Pritchard, William C, 1953, Ag 5,23:7; 1962, O 22,29:3
Pritchard, William S, 1955, My 13,25:4
Pritchett, Carr W Rev, 1910, Mr 19,9:4
Pritchett, Charles M, 1953, F 9,27:5
Pritchett, Charles W, 1950, Ja 27,23:3
Pritchett, Clayton Mrs, 1947, Ja 20,25:3
Pritchett, Florence (Mrs E E T Smith), 1965, N 11, 47:1
Pritchett, Henry S (por), 1939, Ag 29,21:1
Pritchett, Jesse C, 1941, S 4,21:2
Pritchett, Norton G, 1951, Jl 18,29:6
Pritham, Carroll F, 1951, S 13,31:5
Pritting, Charles, 1941, N 19,23:2
Prittwitz, Max von Gen, 1917, Ap 2,13:4
Prittwitz und Gaffron, Friedrich W, 1955, S 3,15:3
Pritz, Carl E, 1948, O 12,25:2
Pritzker, Charles M, 1966, Mr 29,41:3
Pritzker, Louis J Dr, 1937, N 6,17:5
Prizer, Edward L, 1938, S 8,23:1
Prizer, John C, 1961, Ag 9,33:2
Prizer, Mary C, 1952, F 7,27:4
Prizer, William M, 1949, Mr 9,25:3
Proal, Arthur Breese, 1914, F 4,9:6
Probasco, Henry, 1902, O 30,9:5
Probasco, John B Dr, 1908, F 26,7:6
Probasco, John T Mrs, 1948, Jl 12,19:5
Probasco, Norman H Dr, 1925, Ap 7,19:5
Probasco, Samuel Kingsley, 1922, Ag 15,11:5
Probasco, Samuel R, 1910, Ja 21,11:4
Probasco, Scott L, 1962, Je 26,28:6
Probeck, Robert, 1952, Jl 13,60:2
Probert, Frank H, 1940, My 9,23:4
Probert, George L, 1957, Jl 14,73:3
Probert, L C (will, F 13,27:6), 1937, F 3,23:4
Probert, Mary Mrs, 1949, Mr 29,25:5
Probest, George E Jr, 1944, N 19,50:4
Probolsky, Michael Mrs, 1958, Ap 30,33:2
Probst, Agnes T Mrs, 1937, Mr 4,23:5
Probst, Arthur Oxley, 1920, Je 2,11:2
Probst, August, 1948, Mr 6,13:1
Probst, Edward, 1942, Ja 10,18:2
Probst, Eva-Maria Mrs, 1967, My 2,47:2
Probst, F, 1880, My 2,5:4
Probst, Frank, 1948, Ap 23,23:2
Probst, Frank B, 1945, Je 10,32:4
Probst, John F, 1954, D 5,89:2
Probst, John J Sr, 1960, D 8,35:2
Probst, Karl K, 1963, Ag 27,31:4
Probst, Louise, 1951, Ja 3,27:4
Probst, Nathan, 1967, Ja 2,19:3
Probst, Thorwald, 1948, D 26,52:3
Probyn, Dighton Sir, 1924, Je 21,13:6
Probyn, Leslie, 1938, D 19,23:2
Prochaska, Ernst A Mrs (E Zweybrueck), 1956, Je 5,35:2
Prochazka, George A Mrs, 1956, Ap 10,31:4
Prochazka, Helena K, 1967, My 10,47:1
Prochazka, Jan, 1948, D 19,76:4
Prochazka, Joseph O Von, 1943, O 10,48:7
Prochet, Matteo Rev Dr, 1907, Mr 12,9:6
Prochet, Ottavio Mrs, 1965, O 15,45:2
Prochnik, Edgar L, 1964, Ap 13,29:3
Procope, Hjalmar J, 1954, Mr 9,27:1
Procopio, Vito V, 1943, F 12,19:4
Procter, E B, 1943, Ja 3,42:7
Procter, Harley T, 1920, My 16,22:4
Procter, Jewell B, 1957, Mr 18,27:4
Procter, John R, 1903, D 12,7:5
Procter, Rodney, 1957, Ag 5,21:5
Procter, Thomas Sr, 1943, D 25,13:4
Procter, W C, 1934, My 3,19:4
Proctor, Addison G, 1925, F 17,23:4
Proctor, Alex P, 1950, S 6,29:3
Proctor, Andre M, 1938, Mr 26,15:2
Proctor, Arthur B, 1949, Je 23,27:4
Proctor, Arthur M, 1955, Ag 28,85:2
Proctor, Arthur W, 1961, D 1,33:3
Proctor, Benjamin, 1939, D 17,48:6
Proctor, Bernard E, 1959, S 25,24:1
Proctor, Byron Walter (Barry Cornwall), 1874, O 6, 5:6
Proctor, Charles A, 1961, Ap 15,21:3
Proctor, Charles E, 1950, N 28,32:3
Proctor, Clayton B, 1957, D 24,15:1
Proctor, David G, 1958, Ja 21,29:1
Proctor, David Redfield, 1907, O 17,9:6
Proctor, Daysie, 1956, Mr 7,33:3
Proctor, Edgar C, 1937, N 12,22:1
Proctor, Edna Dean, 1923, D 19,19:4
Proctor, Edward A, 1942, Mr 5,24:3
Proctor, Edward E, 1951, Mr 21,33:2
Proctor, Elizabeth S Mrs, 1937, My 23,II,11:2
Proctor, Emily D, 1948, D 18,19:2
Proctor, Ernest R, 1942, O 8,27:2
Proctor, F F, 1929, S 5,29:3
Proctor, Fletcher Dutton, 1911, S 28,9:6
Proctor, Francis R, 1945, N 20,21:3
Proctor, Fred W, 1949, N 29,29:3
Proctor, Frederic W, 1947, F 19,25:3
Proctor, Frederick T Mrs, 1937, D 25,15:5
Proctor, George, 1951, F 27,27:5
Proctor, George N, 1952, F 27,27:1
Proctor, Harold B, 1952, Ja 19,15:5
Proctor, Harry G, 1946, Jl 21,40:1
Proctor, Herbert L, 1946, My 16,21:2
Proctor, J C, 1879, O 28,4:7
Proctor, James H, 1946, S 9,9:4
Proctor, James M, 1953, S 18,29:2
Proctor, James W, 1949, Ag 27,13:6
Proctor, James W Mrs, 1951, Mr 24,13:2
Proctor, John, 1922, S 19,19:4
Proctor, John A Mrs, 1952, D 11,33:4
Proctor, John C, 1950, D 22,23:2
Proctor, John M, 1911, Mr 26,II,15:4
Proctor, Joseph Mrs, 1948, Ap 29,23:4
Proctor, Joseph W, 1961, My 3,37:3
Proctor, Milton D Mrs, 1958, Je 6,23:5
Proctor, Mortimer R, 1968, My 1,47:3
Proctor, Peter J, 1949, Jl 14,27:1
Proctor, R A Prof, 1888, S 13,1:1
Proctor, Ralph F, 1940, My 31,19:4
Proctor, Reafield Sen, 1908, Mr 6,7:4
Proctor, Redfield, 1957, F 7,27:2
Proctor, Robert A, 1941, D 6,17:4
Proctor, Robert E, 1951, Je 22,25:2
Proctor, Rodney Mrs, 1962, Je 20,35:4
Proctor, Thomas J, 1963, Jl 11,29:1
Proctor, William (will, Ag 5,63:2), 1951, Ap 21,17:6
Proctor, William C, 1937, F 19,19:3
Proctor, William C Mrs, 1953, Mr 19,29:6
Proctor, William F Mrs, 1913, D 16,11:6
Proctor, William M, 1937, O 29,21:4
Proctor, William Mrs, 1949, S 26,25:3
Prodger, Clift, 1920, Ag 23,11:4
Prodhon, Jean, 1966, O 17,37:4
Prodoehl, Jerome H, 1965, Ap 29,35:3
Prodromidis, Peter, 1967, Je 13,47:1
Proebstel, Jacob Mrs (Alice Gentle), 1958, Mr 2,88:5
Proefke, Otto, 1949, D 25,26:3
Proehl, Henry B, 1949, Mr 20,76:6
Proehl, Henry E, 1964, D 22,29:4
Proenza, Justo A, 1954, F 2,27:2
Proescholdt, Frederick, 1937, O 8,23:4
Proescholdt, William A Mrs, 1940, Ja 27,13:6
Proetz, Arthur Mrs, 1944, Ag 8,17:5
Proetz, Victor H, 1966, Ag 23,39:5
Profaci, Joseph, 1962, Je 8,32:3
Profeta, William S, 1960, Ap 15,23:1
Proffitt, Charles C Mrs, 1947, My 18,60:5
Proffitt, Charles C Rev, 1937, N 12,22:1
Proffitt, Frank, 1965, N 28,88:7
Profumo, Albert Baron, 1940, Mr 28,23:3
Progel, Edward, 1938, Ja 17,19:4
Prohme, R, 1927, N 22,4:5
Prokesch-Osten, Baron Von, 1876, O 27,4:7
Prokhorov, Pavel M, 1954, Jl 31,13:3
Prokofieff, Sergei, 1953, Mr 9,1:6
Prokofiev, Andrei, 1949, O 22,17:5
Prokop, Eddie, 1955, My 31,27:4
Prokop, Joseph W, 1954, Jl 2,19:6
Prokop, Nicholas Mrs, 1946, Ag 22,27:3
Prokopchak, William D, 1942, Mr 1,44:2
Prokopchuk, Vsevolod I, 1957, S 29,86:4
Prokopovich, Sergei N, 1955, Ap 6,29:4
Prokopy, Otto, 1955, Je 11,15:3
Proksch, William, 1965, Ja 21,31:3
Promin, David, 1956, My 27,89:1
Proner, William, 1968, Je 6,47:4
Pronin, Mikhail M, 1967, D 20,26:6
Pronin, Nikolai, 1952, F 27,27:2
Pronk, Devin N Mrs, 1948, My 25,27:2
Pronk, Frank S, 1953, Mr 15,92:1
Prooyen, D J Van, 1942, Mr 19,21:6
Proper, Clyde H, 1941, Mr 12,22:2
Proper, Datus De Witt Rev Dr, 1922, Mr 3,13:5
Proper, Jacob S, 1947, O 1,29:1
Propert, Frank C, 1955, D 29,23:4
Propert, Henry J, 1964, Ja 11,23:4
Propert, P S G, 1940, F 20,21:1
Prophet, Edwar W, 1943, Je 26,13:2
Prophet, Lachlan B, 1941, D 2,23:3
Propheta, Demetri, 1957, O 9,35:2
Propheta, Demetri Mrs, 1957, O 9,35:2
Prophett, Henry G Mrs, 1957, My 16,31:3
Prophett, Knight, 1954, D 17,31:2
Propp, Isaac L, 1955, Ja 15,13:1
Propp, Louis A, 1941, D 8,23:3
Propp, Samuel, 1944, D 19,21:1
Propper, Henry, 1967, Ag 19,25:4
Propper, Julius, 1942, Je 29,15:4
Propper, Karl, 1965, N 1,41:4
Propper, Leo, 1962, F 4,82:3
Propper, Leo Mrs, 1963, D 11,47:3
Propper, Leonard M, 1957, F 6,25:2
Propping, Louise Mrs, 1913, Je 13,9:5
Propping, Maurice F, 1913, Je 13,9:5
Propst, Charles F, 1947, Ag 1,17:2
Propst, Kenneth E, 1955, My 7,17:1
Prosch, Carl F, 1937, Je 27,II,6:7
Prosch, Frederick, 1947, D 20,17:2
Proschowski, Frantz J E, 1957, Ag 8,23:5
Proshek, James V, 1953, Jl 22,27:2
Proskauer, J, 1936, O 30,23:3
Proskauer, Joseph M Mrs, 1959, Mr 19,33:5
Proskauer, Julien J, 1958, D 20,2:5
Proskauer, Richman, 1967, N 7,43:3
Prosnitz, Ludwig B, 1965, Mr 1,27:4
Prosper, Bro (Redel), 1960, Mr 29,37:2
Prosperi, Muarizio, 1955, Mr 22,31:5
Prospero, Colonna Prince, 1937, S 17,25:2
Pross, Albert W, 1950, D 28,25:5
Pross, Benjamin F, 1950, Mr 3,25:4
Pross, Carr F, 1954, Je 11,23:5
Pross, Charles A, 1948, Ag 6,17:1
Pross, William H, 1941, Ag 16,15:5
Pross, William L, 1945, D 13,29:3
Prosseda, John B, 1938, Jl 28,19:6
Prosser, Alvin V, 1948, O 10,76:5
Prosser, Catherine D, 1955, My 9,23:2
Prosser, Charles A, 1952, N 28,26:3
Prosser, Charles R, 1951, Je 20,27:4
Prosser, Charles S, 1916, S 13,9:5
Prosser, David L, 1950, Mr 1,27:5
Prosser, Edgar A, 1940, N 20,21:3
Prosser, Guy W, 1960, Ap 23,23:5
Prosser, Harriet R, 1955, S 24,19:3
Prosser, Herman A, 1958, N 24,29:4
Prosser, J Roy, 1962, O 21,88:7
Prosser, Judson C Mrs, 1959, Mr 29,80:3
Prosser, Reese W, 1945, Mr 11,40:3
Prosser, Reynolds, 1941, O 12,53:2
Prosser, Richard, 1937, Jl 13,20:3
Prosser, Robert Mrs (B Willoughby), 1959, Jl 31,24:4
Prosser, Seward (por), 1942, O 3,15:1
Prosser, Seward Mrs, 1948, Jl 14,23:2
Prosswimmer, Rudolph A, 1966, S 4,64:7
Prost, Andre (mem mass set), 1964, O 7,47:4
Prost, J J, 1939, Ag 22,3:5
Protas, Barnet, 1960, Ag 15,23:4
Protay, Marc, 1950, D 6,33:4
Prote, Joseph C Sr, 1953, S 5,15:4
Prothero, George Sir, 1922, Jl 12,11:2
Prothero, Rowland (Ernle Baron), 1937, Jl 3,15:3
Protheroe, D, 1934, F 26,17:3
Protheroe-Smith, Hugh B, 1961, N 29,41:3
Protitch, Mihailo Mrs, 1949, N 2,27:5
Prott, George Mrs, 1950, Jl 14,21:3
Protter, Franz von Prof, 1903, S 20,4:5
Protto, Cesare, 1943, Ja 23,13:4
Protz, Albert G O, 1946, Ap 27,17:4
Protzmann, Henry Mrs, 1953, Ag 20,27:3
Proud, Benjamin F, 1951, O 18,29:5
Proud, George B Sr, 1955, O 6,29:4
Proudfit, A M, 1882, My 1,5:1
Proudfit, Alex C, 1942, Mr 4,19:5
Proudfit, Alex C Mrs, 1953, F 2,21:2
Proudfit, Edwin H, 1953, S 29,29:1
Proudfoot, Andrea H Mrs, 1949, O 15,15:5
Proudfoot, Arnold S, 1952, S 12,21:3
Proudfoot, David M, 1962, Ja 6,19:5
Proudfoot, E N (see also Ap 21), 1877, Ap 23,8:3
Proudfoot, Lida D Mrs, 1942, Mr 2,19:1
Proudfoot, Malcolm, 1955, N 23,23:4
Proudfoot, Perry A, 1966, Jl 13,43:5
Proudfoot, William A, 1939, Je 12,17:5
Proudfoot, William A Mrs, 1955, D 31,13:6
Proudfoot, William F, 1943, Je 13,45:1
Proudhon, Pierre Joseph, 1865, F 5,3:5
Proudman, Edward H, 1951, N 23,29:1
Proul, Albert B Mrs, 1942, Mr 11,20:2
Proulx, Leo, 1952, Ja 6,95:6
Proulx, Roy J, 1964, Jl 15,35:3
Proulx, Willie, 1958, My 21,33:2
Prouse, Clarence M, 1956, O 5,25:2
Prouse, Howard H, 1947, Je 21,17:3
Proust, Antonin, 1905, Mr 23,5:5
Prout, Alice, 1909, My 31,7:4
Prout, Charles D, 1958, My 5,29:4
Prout, Everett R, 1952, Mr 11,27:3
Prout, Frank J, 1967, Mr 30,45:4
Prout, George R, 1953, Mr 9,29:1
Prout, Gordon E, 1940, D 28,15:1
Prout, James H, 1957, Je 4,35:1
Prout, Ray H, 1953, Mr 19,29:4
Prout, Thomas P, 1946, Ap 28,44:6
Prout, William C, 1938, S 8,24:4
Prouty, Almond E, 1959, F 5,31:2
Prouty, Carll R, 1954, Ap 1,31:3
Prouty, Charles A, 1921, Jl 9,9:6
Prouty, G Edward, 1943, S 9,26:3
Prouty, G H Ex-Gov, 1918, Ag 20,9:4
Prouty, Harley H, 1916, S 13,9:6
Prouty, Isaac Lothrop, 1904, F 7,7:6

Prouty, J Cecil, 1957, S 22,86:3
Prouty, James L Mrs, 1945, Ap 18,23:4
Prouty, Nelson H, 1940, F 4,40:5
Prouty, Willard, 1952, F 9,13:3
Prouty, William F, 1949, Je 29,27:4
Prouty, Winston L Mrs, 1960, D 4,88:8
Provan, David B, 1937, Je 28,19:4
Proven, David D, 1952, Ap 6,90:4
Provenzano, Peter J, 1946, Je 2,44:3
Provin, Harry H, 1959, Je 18,31:4
Provine, J W, 1949, N 4,28:5
Provine, Robert C Mrs, 1966, O 26,47:2
Provine, Walter M, 1955, Ja 27,23:1
Provinse, John H, 1965, Ja 23,25:5
Provis, F L, 1938, My 3,23:2
Provisero, Samuel J, 1946, Ag 29,27:4
Provost, Andrew J, 1925, Ap 23,21:1
Provost, Anthony, 1938, D 31,15:4
Provost, Charles B, 1950, Ag 12,13:2
Provost, Cornelius W, 1954, N 3,29:1
Provost, Donald L, 1963, Jl 29,19:3
Provost, Federico G, 1952, S 29,23:6
Provost, Frederick, 1940, S 11,25:1
Provost, Harriet A, 1939, Ap 13,23:5
Provost, Henry G, 1950, Ag 10,25:5
Provost, Howard G, 1941, Je 5,24:3
Provost, Katherine, 1948, Mr 21,60:8
Provost, Louis S, 1945, N 19,21:3
Provost, Miriam A, 1949, Ja 22,13:2
Provost, Reginald M, 1948, Mr 12,23:3
Provosty, Oliver O Ex-Justice, 1924, Ag 4,13:5
Provot, F Adolph, 1943, Mr 7,38:5
Prowell, Jack, 1955, Mr 18,28:4
Prowse, James, 1948, F 21,13:3
Prowse, Montague W, 1954, N 25,29:3
Prowse, W B Lt-Col, 1937, Ja 17,II,8:4
Proxmire, Theodore S, 1959, D 17,37:4
Pruce, L H Mrs, 1940, Ap 13,17:4
Prucha, Anthony, 1940, Jl 5,13:3
Prudden, Burritt F (will), 1951, S 29,1:8
Prudden, Geneva, 1941, Ja 28,19:5
Prudden, Halsey G, 1952, Mr 1,15:6
Prudden, Lillian E, 1937, My 24,19:4
Prudden, Theophile Mitchell Dr, 1924, Ap 11,21:6
Pruden, Arthur G, 1949, S 16,28:2
Pruden, Edward A, 1946, My 11,27:4
Pruden, Harold O, 1952, Mr 27,29:4
Pruden, O L Maj, 1902, Ap 20,7:7
Pruden, Russell G (will, F 2,34:7), 1949, Ja 27,24:3
Pruden, Walter R, 1954, N 18,33:2
Pruden, Warren E, 1953, Ag 29,17:1
Pruden, William H, 1957, Ja 8,31:5
Prudhomme, Andre (por), 1949, Ja 16,68:3
Prud'homme, Cameron, 1967, N 29,40:1
Prudhomme, J (H Monnier), 1877, F 3,5:1
Prud'homme, Louis A, 1941, Mr 3,15:2
Prudhomme, Lucien F Capt, 1912, Mr 17,15:3
Prudon, Francisque, 1925, My 1,19:5
Pruette, William, 1918, Jl 16,13:6
Pruetzel, Henry J, 1955, Ja 7,21:4
Pruever, Julius (por), 1943, Jl 9,17:2
Prugar-Ketling, Bronislaw, 1948, F 19,23:2
Prugh, Byron E P, 1941, Ap 29,19:5
Prugh, Esther E Mrs, 1947, Ja 19,53:2
Prugh, John H Rev Dr, 1915, D 23,13:5
Prugh, Phil L, 1957, D 6,29:1
Pruiett, Moman, 1945, D 18,27:3
Pruitt, Andrew, 1949, Je 16,29:3
Pruitt, C W Mrs, 1948, Je 21,21:3
Pruitt, Cicero W, 1946, N 28,27:3
Pruitt, Forrest A, 1953, Je 6,17:6
Pruitt, Raymond S, 1957, S 2,13:1
Prumm, Hans, 1937, My 26,25:4
Pruna, Luciano Mrs, 1960, Mr 9,33:4
Prunas, Renato, 1951, D 26,25:2
Pruneda, Alfonso, 1957, Je 9,89:1
Pruner, A William, 1958, Ag 12,29:4
Prunier, David, 1951, Je 21,27:5
Prunier, David Mrs, 1959, D 2,43:3
Prunty, Francis J, 1939, N 25,17:1
Prunty, Peter P, 1945, Ap 24,19:2
Prunty, Peter S, 1961, Je 22,31:5
Prunty, William S, 1951, N 8,29:2
Pruser, Herman H Sr, 1946, Mr 16,13:5
Prushanski, Harry H, 1952, N 27,31:2
Prusinski, Anthony J, 1950, Ja 3,25:1
Prusoff, Henry, 1943, My 5,27:2
Pruss, Max, 1960, N 30,37:3
Prussia, Charles W, 1945, Mr 16,15:1
Prussin, George, 1953, D 9,11:3
Prussing, Harold, 1951, F 23,27:2
Prutting, Robert H, 1945, S 7,23:4
Pruyn, Anna W Mrs, 1939, Ja 16,15:5
Pruyn, Carmello M, 1955, O 18,37:2
Pruyn, Charles L, 1906, Jl 8,9:6
Pruyn, Claude L, 1950, Jl 31,17:4
Pruyn, Edward L, 1950, Ap 22,19:4
Pruyn, Francis L, 1965, F 10,41:3
Pruyn, Frederic, 1938, N 20,39:3
Pruyn, J V L, 1877, N 22,4:6
Pruyn, John B, 1949, F 9,27:4
Pruyn, John I Mrs, 1947, Je 15,60:6
Pruyn, John V L, 1904, S 23,9:7
Pruyn, John W Mrs, 1954, Jl 30,17:4
Pruyn, Mary, 1885, F 12,2:4
Pruyn, Mary L, 1943, D 22,23:4
Pruyn, R C, 1934, O 30,19:3
Pruyn, R H, 1882, F 27,1:5
Pruyn, Robert D, 1955, D 19,27:2
Pruyn, Robert D Mrs, 1943, O 16,13:1
Pruyn, Robert S, 1951, D 18,32:3
Pruzan, Alex Mrs, 1947, Je 1,62:4
Pryakhin, Tikhon S, 1967, Mr 25,23:4
Pryanishnikov, Dmitri, 1948, My 4,25:4
Pryce, John R, 1953, D 28,22:3
Pryde, David J, 1959, Ag 3,25:5
Pryde, Robert D, 1951, Mr 30,23:3
Pryer, Charles, 1916, Je 9,13:5
Pryer, Harry C, 1957, Ap 26,25:3
Pryer, Harry C Mrs, 1943, D 24,13:3
Pryer, Jasper Mrs, 1946, Ag 2,19:4
Pryibil, Paul, 1947, D 30,23:4
Pryke, W Sir, 1932, Mr 31,21:5
Pryor, Ainslie, 1958, My 29,27:4
Pryor, Arthur (por), 1942, Je 19,23:1
Pryor, Arthur Jr, 1954, My 26,29:1
Pryor, Daniel H, 1946, Je 24,31:3
Pryor, Frederick L, 1961, My 11,37:3
Pryor, Frederick M, 1938, O 10,19:4
Pryor, George H, 1938, D 28,26:4; 1955, Mr 15,29:3
Pryor, Ike T Col, 1937, S 25,17:4
Pryor, J Donald Mrs, 1941, Ja 15,23:1
Pryor, Jacques F, 1953, N 28,15:5
Pryor, James A, 1963, Ag 28,33:4
Pryor, James C, 1947, S 9,31:5
Pryor, James Mrs, 1943, My 16,42:8
Pryor, James W, 1924, Ap 11,21:5
Pryor, John H Dr, 1923, Jl 22,24:5
Pryor, Joseph A Sr, 1952, Ja 9,29:4
Pryor, Joseph E, 1941, F 15,15:5
Pryor, P Lucius, 1947, O 24,23:2
Pryor, Patrick, 1955, D 30,19:1
Pryor, Patrick (funl), 1956, Ja 1,51:1
Pryor, Robert L, 1964, Mr 11,39:4
Pryor, Roger A Gen, 1919, Mr 15,15:3
Pryor, Roger A Mrs, 1912, F 16,9:4
Pryor, Ruth, 1946, Ag 5,21:5
Pryor, S W Mrs, 1965, Ap 21,45:1
Pryor, Samuel F Mrs, 1953, Jl 2,23:3
Pryor, Samuel J, 1924, Mr 26,19:4
Pryor, Samuel O, 1943, F 11,19:4
Pryor, Thomas F Jr, 1945, N 30,23:4
Pryor, Thomas L, 1938, D 6,23:2
Pryor, W S Justice, 1914, N 17,13:4
Pryor, William A Dr, 1904, Ag 26,1:6
Pryor, William C, 1949, Ap 1,25:1
Pryor, William M, 1948, Je 26,17:5
Pryor, William W, 1947, D 31,15:3
Pryse, William M, 1944, Ap 27,23:1
Pryseski, Michael Mrs, 1964, N 5,45:4
Prytherch, Thomas M, 1966, Mr 15,39:4
Przebel, John, 1951, Jl 26,21:2
Przedpelski, Wiktor, 1941, Ag 8,15:5
Przeseink, Steven, 1938, Ap 11,32:1
Przeworska, Jerzy Mrs, 1965, Jl 11,69:3
Przeworski, Roman A, 1953, F 12,27:2
Przezwicki, Vicktoria Mrs, 1949, F 22,24:2
Przybylinski, Walter J, 1939, Je 22,23:5
Psaki, Nicholas G, 1938, Ap 13,25:4
Psaty, Charles I, 1963, O 12,19:8
Psaty, Leon, 1958, Je 3,31:3
Psaty, Max, 1944, S 20,23:5
Pschorr, Frederick G, 1959, Ag 15,17:1
Psenka, Jaromir R, 1939, N 30,21:4
Psota, Joseph Sr, 1950, Mr 2,28:4
Ptaszynski, John A, 1954, D 22,23:1
Pu Hsin-yu, 1963, N 19,41:3
Pu Yi, Henry, 1967, O 19,47:1
Puar, Tukoji R Sir, 1937, D 23,22:2
Publicker, Harry, 1951, Mr 17,15:5
Publicker, Harry Mrs, 1955, My 21,17:4
Publicker, Harry Mrs (will), 1956, Jl 4,21:1
Publicker, Philip, 1964, N 29,87:1
Publow, William Angus, 1922, O 7,15:7
Pucci, Enrico, 1952, S 6,17:3
Pucci, Ercolano, 1944, Ap 23,43:6
Pucci, Lawrence R, 1965, O 17,87:1
Puccini, Angelica, 1922, O 8,30:4
Puccini, Giacomo (funl), 1924, D 2,25:1
Puchall, Murray (cor, N 17,48:1), 1965, N 15,37:1
Pucher, George W, 1947, N 21,27:3
Puchez, Mario, 1954, Jl 7,4:7
Puchkoff, Pincus, 1951, Mr 1,27:2
Pucholski, Leon F Jr, 1953, Ja 14,31:2
Puchta, George, 1937, Ap 19,21:2
Puck, Harry, 1964, Ja 29,33:4
Puckett, Claude E, 1949, Je 19,68:1
Puckett, E N, 1954, My 8,17:2
Puckett, Fred, 1943, Jl 9,17:3
Puckett, Roswell C, 1939, S 12,25:3
Puckette, Charles M (trb lr, Ja 19,14:7), 1957, Ja 16, 31:2
Puder, Abraham A, 1962, My 7,31:3
Puder, Harry H Mrs, 1958, Jl 20,65:2
Puder, Moe, 1950, Ja 2,23:3
Pudester, John C, 1947, Ap 24,25:3
Pudovkin, Vsevolod, 1953, Jl 2,23:4
Puech, Denys, 1942, D 13,74:2
Puello, Gen, 1871, D 16,1:7
Puenkoesti, Elisabeth de, 1948, O 16,15:5
Puente, Felipe, 1945, Mr 24,17:1
Puente, Ricardo de la, 1952, Mr 19,29:1
Pueyrredon, Honorio, 1945, S 24,19:3
Puff, Charles F Jr, 1965, Mr 25,37:4
Puff, Charles V, 1941, Ap 7,17:3
Puff, Charles Z, 1952, Jl 10,31:2
Puff, Myron, 1944, Ap 20,19:5
Puffer, Alfred F Capt, 1875, Jl 15,8:2
Puffer, Floyd A, 1947, N 18,29:3
Puffer, Louis B, 1951, O 12,27:1
Pugh, Achilles H, 1954, Mr 26,21:1
Pugh, Alexander L, 1945, D 29,13:1
Pugh, Arthur, 1955, Ag 3,23:4
Pugh, C Ezra, 1942, Ap 9,20:2
Pugh, Charles E, 1913, Ap 9,9:4
Pugh, David B Mrs, 1907, F 16,9:6
Pugh, David E, 1944, Je 24,13:3
Pugh, Douglas, 1962, S 4,31:6
Pugh, Florence K Mrs, 1942, My 10,43:2
Pugh, Fred W, 1946, Mr 25,25:4
Pugh, G E, 1876, Jl 20,5:5
Pugh, Harry C, 1951, S 1,11:3
Pugh, Harry J, 1965, Ag 12,27:5
Pugh, Harry J Mrs, 1954, S 11,17:5
Pugh, Harry W, 1953, F 14,17:4
Pugh, Henry Mrs, 1954, S 16,29:3
Pugh, Howard R, 1968, O 19,37:3
Pugh, James A, 1925, Je 24,17:4
Pugh, James L, 1938, Jl 10,29:2
Pugh, James Lawrence, 1907, Mr 10,9:6
Pugh, James R, 1941, O 9,23:3
Pugh, Joseph M, 1952, My 31,14:7
Pugh, Louis H Sr, 1942, Ap 30,19:1
Pugh, Lucile, 1960, My 13,31:3
Pugh, Sterling B Mrs, 1952, My 20,25:3
Pugh, T K, 1881, Jl 12,5:3
Pugh, Walter C, 1946, Je 9,40:3
Pugh, William B, 1950, S 15,26:2
Pughe, Earl W Mrs, 1956, Ag 13,19:5
Pugielli, Peter, 1950, F 23,27:3
Pugile, John Mrs, 1955, Je 21,31:5
Pugin, E Welby, 1875, Je 8,1:7
Puglia, William G, 1949, Ja 3,23:3
Pugliese, Anthony, 1953, D 25,17:5
Pugliese, Anthony J, 1937, F 17,21:4
Pugliese, Frank M, 1953, Ag 14,19:4
Pugmire, Ernest I, 1953, Je 25,27:1
Pugmire, Joseph, 1942, F 6,19:2
Pugsley, Aaron H, 1937, My 19,23:6
Pugsley, C A, 1936, S 11,25:3
Pugsley, Charles E, 1951, Ja 3,27:5
Pugsley, Charles W, 1940, D 18,25:5
Pugsley, Frederick I, 1952, O 14,31:4
Pugsley, J W, 1939, F 8,23:3
Pugsley, James H Mrs, 1946, O 12,19:5
Pugsley, John E, 1947, Ja 11,19:5
Pugsley, Luther C, 1947, My 26,21:4
Pugsley, R M Capt, 1918, Mr 24,13:1
Pugsley, Robert T, 1944, Je 10,15:6
Pugsley, Wilson A, 1921, Ag 17,11:6
Pugsley, Winfield B, 1948, D 27,21:4
Puhl, Arthur J, 1949, Ag 21,68:4
Puhl, Carl Mrs, 1937, Ap 30,22:2
Puhl, Paul W, 1955, Ja 24,23:2
Puig, Ignacio, 1961, O 17,39:5
Puig, Pedro, 1925, F 15,7:3
Puig Casauranc, Jose M, 1939, My 10,23:5
Puiseaux, V A, 1883, S 18,4:6
Puitz, Theodore H, 1938, Je 11,15:2
Pujo, Arsene P, 1940, Ja 1,23:5
Pujo, Maurice, 1955, S 7,31:3
Pujol, Carlos, 1950, F 20,25:1
Pukhov, Nikolai P, 1958, Mr 31,27:5
Pulas, Arthur Mrs, 1937, Jl 30,19:2
Pulaski, Alexis E, 1968, Jl 11,37:5
Pulaski, Francois, 1956, My 19,19:5
Pulaski, Jack (por), 1948, Jl 17,15:1
Pulbrook, Eustace, 1953, Ja 21,31:4
Puleston, John Henry Sir, 1908, O 20,9:5
Pulford, Harvey, 1940, N 1,25:3
Pulford, William J, 1942, Ap 23,24:4
Pulfrey, Arthur L (por), 1947, O 31,23:4
Pulham, C H, 1879, My 14,5:3
Puliam, George S, 1956, Jl 3,25:5
Pulido, Manuel A, 1965, My 13,37:3
Pulis, Charles H, 1952, Je 5,31:2
Pulis, Charles H Mrs, 1948, Mr 24,25:2
Pulis, Earl B, 1938, N 8,23:4
Pulis, J Everett Mrs, 1953, D 11,31:1
Pulis, Lester W, 1942, F 22,26:2
Pulis, William V, 1949, Ap 24,78:1
Puliti, Oreste, 1958, F 8,19:2
Pulitzer, Herbert (funl plans, S 6,21:3), 1957, S
Pulitzer, Herbert Mrs (will, Jl 26,17:6), 1938, Jl 19:5
Pulitzer, Herbert Mrs (will), 1939, My 24,23:2
Pulitzer, J Mrs, 1927, Jl 30,15:3
Pulitzer, Joseph (funl), 1911, N 2,11:5

Pulitzer, Joseph (funl, Ap 3,86:4; will, Ap 7,22:3), 1955, Ap 1,27:1
Pulitzer, Joseph (est acctg), 1958, Mr 28,23:5
Pulitzer, Joseph Jr Mrs, 1968, D 22,52:8
Pulitzer, Joseph Mrs, 1925, Mr 17,21:5
Pulitzer, Ralph, 1939, Je 15,23:1
Pulitzer, Ralph Jr, 1965, S 16,47:2
Pulitzer, Walter Mrs, 1951, F 2,24:2
Pullen, Clifford L, 1913, S 6,7:3
Pullen, Eddie, 1940, O 7,17:1
Pullen, Gregson T, 1966, Je 26,57:3
Pullen, Guy F, 1957, Ap 3,31:1
Pullen, Hester Mrs, 1915, Mr 25,11:5
Pullen, Hezekiah T, 1949, Je 29,27:5
Pullen, Roscoe L, 1960, Mr 9,33:2
Pullen, Stanley T, 1910, F 16,9:4
Pullen, Welles B, 1939, Ag 8,17:4
Pullen, William H, 1939, F 2,19:5
Puller, George, 1963, Jl 13,17:5
Puller, Ordway, 1938, Je 21,19:5
Pulley, William J (por), 1945, N 17,17:3
Pulleyn, John J (por), 1947, Ap 4,23:1
Pulliam, Dick D, 1953, Mr 7,15:2
Pulliam, Henry A, 1952, D 19,31:1
Pulliam, Irvin B, 1946, S 18,31:6
Pulliam, Robert C, 1953, F 1,88:1
Pulliam, Roscoe, 1944, Mr 28,19:6
Pulliam, William E, 1949, Ag 10,22:3
Pulling, Arthur C, 1963, S 30,29:1
Pulling, Howard E (mem ser set), 1956, My 2,31:2
Pulling, John T Jr, 1963, Ap 11,33:3
Pulling, Leo R, 1962, Jl 18,29:4
Pulling, Thomas J, 1941, Ap 4,21:4
Pulling, William J, 1938, Ja 19,23:3
Pullinger, Bertram W, 1950, Mr 9,29:1
Pullinger, Herbt, 1961, Je 15,43:4
Pullman, F W, 1879, Mr 25,3:2
Pullman, G M, 1897, O 20,4:1; 1901, N 29,7:5
Pullman, George M Mrs, 1921, Mr 29,15:5
Pullman, J M Rev, 1903, N 23,7:3
Pullman, James C, 1925, S 10,25:6
Pullman, John S, 1943, Ap 1,23:3
Pullman, Joseph Rev, 1902, Ja 5,5:6
Pullman, Katie, 1950, Ja 28,13:1
Pullman, Morris Mrs, 1957, Mr 30,19:2
Pullman, Raymond Maj, 1920, F 23,13:6
Pullman, Samuel Cooper, 1903, O 29,9:4
Pullman, William T, 1937, D 5,II,9:2
Pullum, Howard J, 1924, N 22,15:5
Puls, Alfred E, 1953, Mr 19,29:3
Pulsifer, David Tenny, 1910, N 16,11:4
Pulsifer, George H (son), 1937, Ap 27,20:6
Pulsifer, Hale, 1957, D 15,86:3
Pulsifer, Harold T, 1948, Ap 9,23:3
Pulsifer, Harry B, 1946, S 4,23:6
Pulsifer, John C, 1947, Ag 27,23:2
Pulsifer, L Valentine, 1957, Jl 25,23:2
Pulsifer, Lawson Mrs, 1945, Ag 3,17:4
Pulteney, William, 1941, My 16,23:6
Pultz, Cora I, 1952, Je 6,23:5
Pultz, Jennie, 1950, O 25,35:4
Pultz, John E, 1949, O 20,29:2
Pultz, John L, 1939, Je 18,37:4
Pultz, John T, 1916, Ap 10,11:4
Pultz, Mary, 1946, Ap 10,27:2
Pultz, William L, 1938, O 24,17:5; 1951, Jl 19,23:7
Pulver, Arthur L, 1939, F 25,15:3
Pulver, Frank F, 1955, O 7,25:4
Pulver, Fred S Mrs, 1944, Je 9,15:6
Pulver, Harriette C, 1951, Jl 23,17:6
Pulver, Henry J, 1947, Je 30,19:4
Pulver, Hugo, 1951, D 26,25:3
Pulver, Jean A, 1961, Ap 18,37:4
Pulver, John D, 1947, O 11,17:2
Pulvermacher, Joseph, 1962, Mr 10,21:4
Pulvermacher, Louis Dr, 1925, My 5,21:4
Pulvermacher, William D, 1948, Ja 29,23:6
Puma, Fernando, 1955, D 9,27:1
Puma, Vincent la, 1943, N 5,19:2
Pumpelly, Josiah Collins, 1920, Ja 6,15:1
Pumpelly, Laurence, 1954, Mr 16,29:2
Pumpelly, Raphael, 1923, Ag 11,9:6
Pumpelly, Raphael W, 1949, O 17,23:5
Pumphery, Clarence, 1945, D 31,17:2
Pumphrey, Edward A, 1964, N 7,27:1
Pumphrey, Morris E, 1945, Je 2,15:1
Punchard, G Rev, 1880, Ap 3,5:2
Punderford, James C, 1939, D 24,14:7
Punderson, Henry F, 1940, O 5,15:5
Pungs, William A, 1941, Jl 26,15:5
Punnett, Jack, 1955, F 27,87:2
Punshon, W M, 1881, Ap 15,5:2
Pupchyk, Aftan, 1951, N 6,29:2
Pupin, M I, 1935, Mr 13,19:1
Pupo, Delfin A, 1953, N 17,31:4
Purcel, Dick, 1944, Ap 12,19:2
Purcell, Alban W, 1913, D 21,IV,5:5
Purcell, Alex Mrs, 1951, Ag 9,21:2
Purcell, Alexander H, 1943, D 10,27:3
Purcell, Alfred C, 1944, Je 5,19:1
Purcell, Archbishop, 1883, Jl 6,1:7
Purcell, Carl, 1964, N 23,37:2
Purcell, Carl M, 1955, F 27,86:3
Purcell, Charles, 1951, S 9,89:2; 1962, Mr 22,35:2
Purcell, Charles S, 1950, Ja 19,27:1
Purcell, E Father, 1881, Ja 23,1:6
Purcell, Edward A, 1956, D 10,31:3
Purcell, Edward W, 1952, S 2,23:3
Purcell, Ganson, 1967, N 23,33:4
Purcell, George W, 1952, O 27,27:4
Purcell, Gillis Mrs, 1968, My 14,47:3
Purcell, Harold, 1952, O 23,31:3
Purcell, Herbert W, 1954, F 19,27:1
Purcell, J J Mrs, 1941, S 1,15:6
Purcell, James, 1937, My 3,19:5
Purcell, James B, 1953, My 14,29:6
Purcell, James C, 1938, S 23,34:2
Purcell, James J, 1952, D 5,27:3
Purcell, James N, 1962, Ag 12,80:2
Purcell, Jefferson D, 1943, Je 28,21:1
Purcell, John A, 1939, Ja 17,22:4
Purcell, John F, 1952, Mr 13,30:4
Purcell, John J, 1938, O 22,17:6; 1966, Mr 13,86:2
Purcell, Joseph F Mrs, 1950, Mr 19,94:4
Purcell, Joseph Mrs, 1948, S 11,15:4
Purcell, Mark, 1953, N 18,31:1
Purcell, Martin J, 1949, S 4,40:6
Purcell, Michael W, 1957, Ag 10,15:5
Purcell, Murat G Mrs, 1942, Ag 4,19:4
Purcell, Peter, 1944, N 10,19:3
Purcell, Peter P, 1956, S 13,35:1
Purcell, Phil, 1939, F 8,23:2
Purcell, Raymond C, 1940, N 28,23:1
Purcell, Richard, 1950, Ja 4,35:2; 1956, My 25,23:1
Purcell, Richard J, 1912, Ap 10,13:4
Purcell, Richard Mrs, 1956, My 25,23:1
Purcell, Steuart, 1946, Ap 19,29:4
Purcell, Thomas, 1942, My 7,19:5
Purcell, Thomas E, 1942, Ap 2,21:6
Purcell, Thomas F, 1951, Ap 13,23:3
Purcell, Thomas V, 1944, My 23,23:4
Purcell, Thomas W, 1940, Jl 9,21:1
Purcell, W H, 1944, My 30,21:3
Purcell, Walter A Rev, 1912, Jl 31,9:5
Purcell, Walter F, 1967, Je 3,31:5
Purcell, William, 1909, F 6,9:3; 1913, Ag 15,7:5
Purcell, William P, 1958, Mr 9,86:5
Purcell, William T, 1945, S 13,23:3
Purcell, William V, 1964, Je 2,37:2
Purcella, William R, 1954, Ja 11,25:3
Purchas, Albert E Mrs, 1953, Ja 23,19:1
Purchas, Fred A (will, O 6,6:3), 1951, Ag 6,21:5
Purchas, Frederick A Mrs, 1958, N 28,30:4
Purchase, William B, 1961, S 28,22:2
Purdell, Reginald, 1953, Ap 23,29:4
Purdin, Charles L, 1951, D 22,15:3
Purdin, Martha L, 1953, O 27,27:5
Purdon, Henry Mrs, 1938, Ja 15,15:3
Purdon, Rupert L Mrs, 1937, Je 4,24:2
Purdon, William D, 1949, D 3,15:1
Purdue, J, 1876, S 13,5:6
Purdue, Margaret J, 1952, Mr 6,31:3
Purdue, William T, 1921, O 12,15:5
Purdum, Smith W, 1945, O 5,23:3
Purdy, Algernon J, 1961, F 10,24:2
Purdy, Ambrose H, 1919, Ag 13,11:4
Purdy, Arthur R, 1954, N 4,31:5
Purdy, Arthur R Mrs, 1952, Ap 18,25:2
Purdy, Augustus, 1865, Ja 9,2:4
Purdy, Aurelia W Mrs, 1951, Mr 8,29:5
Purdy, Charles E, 1942, S 30,23:5
Purdy, Charles H, 1953, Jl 2,23:5
Purdy, Charles I, 1950, S 2,15:4
Purdy, Charles I Mrs, 1945, D 21,21:2
Purdy, Charles K, 1948, F 1,60:6
Purdy, Clarence M, 1950, O 26,31:2
Purdy, Corydon T, 1944, D 28,19:2
Purdy, Donald A, 1962, Je 12,37:3
Purdy, E H, 1903, Ag 14,7:7
Purdy, E S Col, 1881, O 14,2:7
Purdy, Edgar A, 1871, Mr 6,8:4
Purdy, Edward L, 1953, Mr 3,27:3
Purdy, Edward L Mrs, 1944, Jl 1,15:6
Purdy, Elbert C, 1962, Ag 10,19:2
Purdy, Elijah F, 1866, Ja 9,5:1
Purdy, Elizabeth Hagadorn, 1908, F 2,9:6
Purdy, Emery J, 1944, Mr 2,17:5
Purdy, Frank, 1943, Mr 21,26:7
Purdy, Frank L, 1948, Je 29,24:3
Purdy, Frederick H, 1967, Ag 27,89:1
Purdy, George D Capt, 1925, Jl 20,15:7
Purdy, Guy H, 1941, O 19,46:3
Purdy, Harriet S Mrs, 1940, Jl 9,21:4
Purdy, Heman M, 1946, Ja 5,13:1
Purdy, Henry T, 1940, F 2,17:4
Purdy, Herbert M, 1957, Ap 3,31:2
Purdy, Ikua, 1945, Jl 8,11:6
Purdy, Isaac H, 1956, My 14,25:5
Purdy, J H, 1903, Je 17,9:7; 1926, F 17,19:3
Purdy, James E, 1955, Ja 10,23:3
Purdy, James G Mrs, 1949, O 4,27:2
Purdy, Jane C, 1942, Jl 16,19:3
Purdy, Jay V, 1951, Je 24,73:1
Purdy, John E, 1941, Ap 1,23:2
Purdy, John M, 1942, My 24,42:2
Purdy, John W, 1947, O 20,23:1
Purdy, K Herschel, 1953, N 15,89:2
Purdy, Lawson, 1959, S 1,29:3
Purdy, Leander C, 1939, Ap 13,23:5
Purdy, Lovell, 1873, Ag 6,5:7
Purdy, Lovell Maj, 1912, Ja 2,11:6
Purdy, Mathilda Mrs, 1942, Ap 15,21:2
Purdy, Milton D, 1937, F 14,II,9:3
Purdy, Orville W, 1946, Mr 25,25:4
Purdy, Ray F, 1965, N 1,41:1
Purdy, Richard E, 1946, My 24,19:4
Purdy, Robert W, 1944, Ap 15,11:7
Purdy, Ross C, 1949, Ja 7,21:3
Purdy, Stephen L, 1952, O 12,88:1
Purdy, Strother B, 1952, Ja 16,25:2
Purdy, Sylvanus, 1943, Mr 3,24:2
Purdy, Thomas L Mrs, 1956, O 12,29:5
Purdy, W E Mrs, 1937, O 27,31:3
Purdy, W Frank, 1943, D 25,13:5
Purdy, Warren G, 1910, O 14,11:5
Purdy, William A, 1943, Mr 21,26:6
Purdy, William C, 1954, O 7,23:2
Purdy, William E, 1955, Mr 29,30:4
Purdy, William F Mrs, 1943, Ag 22,36:3
Purdy, William H, 1938, Ap 27,23:6
Purdy, William H Dr, 1925, D 17,23:5
Purdy, William L, 1943, D 9,27:1
Purdy, William Mrs, 1948, Mr 20,13:2
Purdy, William T, 1914, D 24,9:4
Purdy, Willis I, 1938, Je 8,23:5
Puretz, Julius, 1949, Jl 14,27:2
Purey-Cust, Herbert, 1938, N 12,15:1
Purick, James R, 1948, D 8,31:4
Purim, Esther P Mrs, 1963, Ap 24,35:3
Purin, Charles M, 1957, S 20,25:1
Purinton, Arthur J, 1945, Mr 6,21:2
Purkayev, M A, 1953, Ja 4,76:5
Purkis, Thornton, 1956, Je 10,89:1
Purkiss, Albert C, 1967, Jl 2,35:1
Purlington, Florence, 1950, My 23,29:3
Purlington, Paul Mrs, 1937, Je 22,23:4
Purman, W J, 1928, Ag 15,21:1
Purmont, Katherine Mrs, 1950, Ja 10,29:3
Purnell, Caroline Dr, 1923, F 5,15:6
Purnell, Edward, 1939, Ap 15,19:1
Purnell, Frank, 1953, Ap 19,90:1
Purnell, Fred S, 1939, O 22,40:4
Purnell, Harold W T, 1965, F 7,92:3
Purnell, Jim, 1950, D 5,31:1
Purnell, Keg, 1965, Je 29,35:4
Purnell, Mary Mrs, 1953, Ag 22,15:2
Purnell, Maude, 1947, My 26,21:5
Purnell, William R, 1955, Mr 7,27:4
Purney, John, 1941, Jl 19,13:5
Puron, Juan Garcia Dr, 1912, Je 27,13:5
Puron, Juan Garcia Mrs, 1922, Jl 15,9:6
Purple, N H Judge, 1863, Ag 13,5:3
Purpura, Leopold, 1951, O 6,19:4
Purrington, Ralph F, 1950, Mr 21,29:1
Purrington, W A, 1926, O 27,27:5
Purroy, Charles D, 1938, My 23,17:2
Purroy, Josephine M, 1925, Ap 27,17:6
Pursche, Anna, 1953, Mr 14,15:2
Purse, Benjamin S, 1941, Ap 20,43:1
Purse, Clifford B, 1953, Ag 30,89:1
Purse, James A Jr, 1952, O 4,17:5
Pursel, Stewart H, 1953, N 14,17:3
Pursell, James P, 1947, Ag 16,13:5
Pursglove, Joseph, 1951, Ap 26,29:4
Pursglove, Samuel, 1947, Je 12,25:3
Pursley, James M, 1938, My 18,9:2
Pursley, Robert M, 1967, Jl 4,19:4
Purtell, J R, 1903, Jl 4,7:6
Purtell, Louis, 1918, Ag 2,11:5
Purtell, Michael A, 1945, My 27,26:3
Purtell, Regina, 1950, O 25,35:1
Purtill, Agatho, 1941, Ja 16,21:4
Purvere, Lester H, 1959, F 11,39:3
Purves, Alexander Mrs, 1946, Ja 7,19:2
Purves, Arthur S, 1939, S 27,25:5
Purves, Austin Montgomery, 1915, O 14,11:6
Purves, Dale, 1966, My 15,88:8
Purves, Edmund R, 1964, Ap 9,31:1
Purves, Elinor K, 1952, Jl 7,21:5
Purves, George T, 1951, D 3,31:5
Purves, Rev Dr (funl, S 29,7:6), 1901, S 25,1:6
Purves, T D A, 1945, Jl 29,40:3
Purves, William M, 1938, My 9,17:6
Purves-Stewart, James, 1949, Je 16,30:6
Purviance, Edna (Mrs J P Squire), 1958, Ja 16,29:1
Purviance, H Y Commodore, 1882, O 22,2:6
Purviance, Nancy (Mrs D L Sayenni), 1960, D 24, 15:4
Purviance, S A, 1882, F 15,5:1
Purvin, Moses L, 1942, Ag 4,19:5
Purvin, Myles, 1951, Jl 28,11:1
Purvis, Albert D, 1958, O 29,35:3
Purvis, Alexander, 1905, Mr 31,3:1
Purvis, Ernest R, 1965, Ja 1,19:1
Purvis, Harry Hale, 1968, Mr 9,29:5
Purvis, John G, 1965, N 2,33:4
Purvis, John M, 1937, S 6,17:4
Purvis, Melvin H Sr, 1938, Ja 17,19:4
Purvis, Samuel W, 1941, N 24,17:5

Purvis, Stewart P, 1962, N 9,26:1
Purvis, Walter S Mrs, 1952, S 30,31:2
Purvlance, Wynne, 1923, Je 19,19:2
Pury, Arthur de, 1947, N 19,27:3
Puryear, R C, 1867, Ag 10,3:1
Puryear, Thomas L, 1958, S 30,31:4
Pusack, George F, 1957, My 25,21:2
Pusch, Harry, 1947, N 5,27:6
Pusch, Reinhold T, 1955, D 17,23:5
Puschel (Sister Mary Edilburga), 1965, My 22,31:1
Puschman, Harry R, 1945, Mr 21,24:3
Pusey, E B Dr, 1882, S 17,14:4
Pusey, J Carver, 1953, Jl 18,13:5
Pusey, Joseph M, 1946, Je 22,19:2
Pusey, Walter, 1947, D 24,21:3
Pusey, William A, 1940, Ag 31,13:3
Pushkin, Georgi M, 1963, Ap 3,47:4
Pushman, Hovsep, 1966, F 13,84:4
Pushman, Hovsep Mrs, 1966, My 23,41:2
Pusterla, Attilio, 1941, My 2,21:2
Puth, Leonard G, 1945, Je 24,22:3
Puth, Otto L, 1953, Mr 11,29:2
Putlitz, Lois (Mrs G Braverman), 1962, S 14,31:4
Putman, G Rev, 1878, Ap 12,5:6
Putman, J P, 1882, Ja 6,5:2
Putman, James W, 1938, Mr 24,23:2
Putman, Patrick T L Mrs, 1967, Ja 30,29:2
Putnam, A B Maj, 1915, Je 10,11:5
Putnam, Albert W, 1955, Ap 1,27:3
Putnam, Albert W Mrs, 1960, Je 14,34:3
Putnam, Alice, 1957, Ja 28,23:6
Putnam, Amelia T, 1944, Ja 2,38:6
Putnam, Anna G Mrs, 1946, Jl 27,17:5
Putnam, Arthur J, 1966, F 6,92:4
Putnam, Augustus L, 1947, Jl 10,21:6
Putnam, Bertha H, 1960, F 27,19:6
Putnam, Boyd, 1908, My 25,7:2
Putnam, Carolyn R R H Mrs, 1941, Ja 1,23:2
Putnam, Charles C, 1943, Ja 29,19:2
Putnam, Charles R, 1941, Mr 16,45:2
Putnam, Charles R L Mrs, 1940, Ja 14,43:1
Putnam, Charles S, 1942, Jl 28,17:4
Putnam, chas R L, 1962, Ap 20,28:1
Putnam, Clarence F Mrs, 1953, S 19,15:2
Putnam, Claude G Sr, 1955, Jl 20,27:4
Putnam, E, 1933, Ja 23,13:1
Putnam, E Rear Adm, 1926, Ja 1,23:4
Putnam, Earl B, 1943, Ja 23,13:5
Putnam, Earl B Mrs, 1943, Ag 18,19:5
Putnam, Edmund W, 1940, D 30,17:6
Putnam, Edward W Mrs, 1949, Mr 6,72:4
Putnam, Elizabeth Cabot, 1922, O 11,19:5
Putnam, Erastus Gaylord, 1915, O 2,11:2
Putnam, Ethel, 1955, Ag 6,15:4
Putnam, F Delano, 1943, Ja 9,13:3
Putnam, Francis J, 1967, Ja 26,33:2
Putnam, Frank A, 1949, D 7,31:3
Putnam, Frederick A, 1911, S 4,7:6
Putnam, Frederick Ward, 1915, Ag 15,13:6
Putnam, G H, 1930, F 28,23:1
Putnam, Genevieve W, 1941, Jl 1,23:3
Putnam, George, 1937, S 8,23:2; 1960, Ja 25,27:5; 1961, Ag 19,39:1
Putnam, George E, 1939, Je 25,36:5; 1952, Mr 3,21:1
Putnam, George H Mrs, 1944, S 9,15:5
Putnam, George I, 1937, My 6,25:5
Putnam, George J, 1945, Ja 14,40:6
Putnam, George K, 1940, Ag 4,33:2
Putnam, George M, 1951, F 10,13:2
Putnam, George P, 1873, Ja 11,8:4; 1950, Ja 5,25:1
Putnam, George Palmer, 1872, D 21,6:7
Putnam, George R, 1953, Jl 3,19:3
Putnam, H V (por), 1946, Ja 18,19:3
Putnam, Harold A, 1944. Je 30,21:3
Putnam, Harrington (por), 1937, Ap 8,23:1
Putnam, Harry B, 1952, Ag 29,23:4
Putnam, Hattie Mrs (will), 1938, D 3,30:2
Putnam, Helen C, 1951, F 5,23:2
Putnam, Henry St Clair, 1924, Ja 31,15:5
Putnam, Henry W (will, Ap 8,3:8), 1938, Ap 4,17:5
Putnam, Herbert, 1955, Ag 16,23:1
Putnam, J H S Mrs, 1958, Mr 6,27:4
Putnam, J O, 1903, Ap 25,9:4
Putnam, James C, 1956, O 14,87:1
Putnam, James W, 1940, Ja 24,21:4
Putnam, Jesse H Mrs, 1958, Ap 30,33:3
Putnam, John B, 1915, O 9,9:3; 1951, My 24,35:3
Putnam, John H S, 1948, S 27,23:2
Putnam, John R, 1949, Ap 8,25:4
Putnam, Joseph W, 1946, Ja 23,27:2
Putnam, Joseph W Rev Dr, 1917, Je 10,23:3
Putnam, Le Roy E Sr, 1949, Ja 11,31:3
Putnam, M Howard, 1944, Ap 29,15:5
Putnam, Mary J Mrs, 1943, Je 22,20:3
Putnam, Mary Nicoll Mrs, 1923, N 7,17:6
Putnam, N Devereaux, 1923, Ap 10,21:4
Putnam, Nina W Mrs, 1962, Mr 9,29:1
Putnam, Oliver O, 1959, O 27,37:2
Putnam, Patrick T, 1953, D 29,23:4
Putnam, Richard Mrs (Nancy), 1968, My 19,86:6
Putnam, Robert Faulkner, 1918, O 24,13:1
Putnam, Ruth, 1964, Je 3,24:1
Putnam, Samuel, 1949, Ja 4,40:3; 1950, Ja 18,31:3
Putnam, Samuel R, 1953, Ja 14,31:5
Putnam, Sarah J, 1942, Ap 5,42:1
Putnam, Sidney H, 1938, Je 8,23:1
Putnam, Stuart T, 1958, D 9,41:3
Putnam, Sumner, 1967, F 11,29:2
Putnam, Terry, 1949, N 27,72:4
Putnam, Thad L, 1956, Je 8,25:3
Putnam, Thomas M, 1942, S 23,25:5
Putnam, William H, 1952, F 16,13:3; 1958, Mr 11,29:3
Putnam, William Le Baron Judge, 1918, F 6,9:5
Putnam, William Lowell, 1924, Jl 27,23:4
Putnam, William R, 1957, N 14,33:5
Putney, A H, 1928, O 23,29:3
Putney, Aaron S, 1941, N 14,23:3
Putney, Elmore M, 1951, O 3,36:3
Putney, Frances K Mrs, 1937, Ag 24,21:1
Putney, Frank O Mrs, 1951, N 22,31:4
Putney, George E, 1938, Je 3,21:5
Putney, Nellie L, 1937, Ap 2,23:3
Putney, Oscar, 1944, Ap 13,19:4
Putney, Rufus Stanley Rev, 1920, F 25,11:4
Putney, William B, 1904, S 11,7:6
Putnik, Radomir, 1917, My 18,13:7
Putt, Earl B, 1955, Ag 1,19:5
Putterman, Benjamin, 1958, My 13,29:4
Putterman, David Mrs, 1955, My 23,23:1
Putti, L de, 1931, N 27,21:1
Putti, Vittorio, 1940, N 2,15:1
Puttkamer, Jesko von Baron, 1917, Ja 27,9:2
Putts, Anna M W Mrs, 1940, Je 4,23:4
Putts, B Swayne, 1952, F 1,21:3
Putz, Alfred, 1966, My 14,31:4
Putz, Benedict P, 1940, Jl 1,19:3
Putz, Thomas J, 1962, Ag 31,21:1
Putzel, Howard J, 1945, Ag 7,23:6
Putzer, Irving, 1963, Ag 15,29:5
Putziger, Anna S Mrs, 1953, S 1,23:2
Puy, Jean, 1960, Mr 8,33:4
Puyans, B Emilio, 1956, D 22,19:4
Puzak, Kazimierz, 1950, Ag 12,2:6
Puzinas, Paul P, 1967, O 27,45:3
Puzio, Casper, 1944, My 17,19:3
Puzio, John, 1951, O 24,31:1
Puzzella, Antonio, 1956, Ja 29,93:2
Pwters, George H Com, 1916, Je 16,13:4
Pyburn, John, 1908, N 10,9:4
Pybus, Henry, 1938, Jl 7,19:5
Pye, Col, 1864, Je 26,5:4
Pye, David W, 1951, S 9,89:1
Pye, Hugh, 1942, Ag 25,23:6
Pye, Mary Mrs, 1945, F 8,19:3
Pye, Robert C, 1950, F 26,78:2
Pyeatt, John S (por), 1946, O 22,25:3
Pyers, Albert Mrs, 1946, N 5,25:3
Pyk, Alex, 1938, Ja 7,19:3
Pyke, Bernice S Mrs, 1964, My 13,47:3
Pyke, Richard, 1938, Mr 5,17:4
Pyke, Robert W, 1949, F 2,28:2
Pykett, Daniel J, 1954, Mr 31,27:5
Pyl, Nicholas van der, 1943, S 2,19:5
Pyle, Adelaide M Mrs, 1937, S 23,27:4
Pyle, Byron H, 1966, Mr 16,45:4
Pyle, C C (por), 1939, F 4,15:4
Pyle, Charles G, 1954, Jl 17,13:3
Pyle, Clarence E, 1964, My 12,37:5
Pyle, Clifford H (por), 1944, Mr 8,19:2
Pyle, David G Rev, 1937, F 23,27:3
Pyle, David H M, 1944, N 6,19:3
Pyle, Edwin, 1961, F 27,27:4
Pyle, Elizabeth, 1937, Ja 7,22:1
Pyle, Enos A, 1938, F 24,3:1
Pyle, Ernie Mrs, 1945, N 24,19:4
Pyle, F Winthrop, 1938, My 21,15:6
Pyle, Francis C, 1947, My 23,24:2
Pyle, George W, 1957, Jl 19,19:5
Pyle, H T, 1942, Mr 18,23:5
Pyle, Harry Calhoun, 1922, N 7,17:5
Pyle, Horace A, 1950, Mr 15,29:1
Pyle, Howard, 1911, N 10,11:4
Pyle, Howard L, 1947, O 19,66:5
Pyle, Howard Mrs, 1939, Mr 15,23:5
Pyle, Immanuel, 1940, D 31,15:2
Pyle, Ira L, 1944, My 2,19:4
Pyle, J C, 1941, My 5,17:2
Pyle, James, 1912, F 9,9:5
Pyle, James E Mrs, 1943, Ap 20,23:2
Pyle, John, 1903, N 6,9:6
Pyle, Louis A, 1964, Je 14,84:6
Pyle, Maria Adelia McAlpin, 1968, Ap 30,53:4
Pyle, Milton C, 1950, F 18,15:6
Pyle, Robert, 1951, S 29,17:6
Pyle, Robert Mrs, 1952, Mr 18,27:3
Pyle, Theodore, 1952, Ja 2,25:2
Pyle, Vallie H, 1938, F 14,17:3
Pyle, Victor R, 1948, Ag 15,61:2
Pyle, W Scott, 1938, F 17,21:6
Pyle, Wallace, 1948, Je 12,15:6
Pyle, Wallace Mrs, 1956, Je 4,29:4
Pyle, Willard R, 1941, Mr 20,21:3
Pyle, Willard R Mrs, 1945, Mr 20,19:2
Pyle, William C, 1951, Jl 26,21:2
Pyle, William F, 1941, F 9,49:2
Pyle, William S, 1942, Ap 24,17:4
Pyle, William S Mrs, 1946, Ag 13,27:4; 1954, Ja 11 25:2
Pyles, Franklin P, 1952, N 19,29:1
Pyles, Virgil E, 1965, Ap 29,35:3
Pyles, Will L (por), 1945, Mr 14,19:4
Pyles, Will L Mrs, 1952, Ag 17,77:1
Pym, Leslie R, 1945, Jl 19,23:5
Pym, Percy, 1945, O 17,19:4
Pym, Percy A Mrs, 1939, Mr 12,III,7:2
Pym, Thomas W, 1945, Jl 22,37:1
Pynchon, George M (por), 1940, Mr 10,49:1
Pynchon, Mary H, 1938, Ja 30,II,8:3
Pyne, Charles C, 1962, Je 12,37:1
Pyne, Francis R, 1955, D 29,23:5
Pyne, Frederick G, 1962, Ap 16,29:3
Pyne, Frederick G Mrs, 1954, N 25,29:6
Pyne, Grafton H Mrs, 1957, Ag 15,21:2
Pyne, H Rivington, 1952, Mr 25,27:5
Pyne, Henry R, 1953, Ja 24,15:5
Pyne, J, 1881, Ja 5,5:3
Pyne, James K, 1938, S 4,16:6
Pyne, John X Rev (por), 1937, My 4,25:1
Pyne, M Taylor Jr, 1923, N 18,23:3
Pyne, Margaretta S Mrs, 1939, Ap 23,III,6:7
Pyne, Milton, 1905, Ap 21,9:5
Pyne, Moses Taylor (funl, Ap 24,22:4), 1921, Ap 11:5
Pyne, P R, 1929, Ag 23,21:1
Pyne, Percy R Jr, 1941, D 10,25:5
Pyne, Percy R Mrs, 1952, My 2,25:1
Pyne, Percy R 2d, 1950, Ag 17,27:3
Pyne, Robert, 1913, My 20,11:6
Pyne, Smith Rev Dr, 1875, D 9,4:7
Pyne, Susan L Mrs, 1937, S 18,19:1
Pyne, Thomas, 1949, Je 12,78:5
Pyne, Thomas Sr, 1948, Je 2,29:4
Pyre, Walton H, 1956, Ag 5,76:7
Pyrke, Allen W, 1961, Mr 14,35:3
Pyrke, Berne Ag, 1953, Ap 8,29:3
Pyron, Walter B, 1951, Ja 9,30:3
Pyterman, T Arthur, 1950, F 3,23:5
Pythian, Robert Lees Com, 1917, Ja 21,17:1
Pyzel, Frederic M, 1964, S 30,43:1

Q

Quaas, Joseph A, 1949, Je 20,19:5
Quackenbos, G P, 1881, Jl 26,5:4
Quackenbos, George P, 1947, N 16,76:2
Quackenbos, J D Dr, 1926, Ag 2,17:5
Quackenbos, Nicholas I, 1939, Ja 25,21:4
Quackenboss, Alex W, 1951, Jl 13,21:2
Quackenbuch, Edgar, 1939, Ja 15,38:5
Quackenbusch, Leonard C, 1959, O 2,29:2
Quackenbush, A, 1877, Mr 13,4:6
Quackenbush, Anna T Mrs, 1942, Ag 26,19:5
Quackenbush, Charles A, 1940, Mr 28,23:5
Quackenbush, Clarence Mrs, 1944, Mr 10,15:2
Quackenbush, Curtis Mrs, 1949, N 9,27:2
Quackenbush, Earl R, 1946, Ap 11,25:6
Quackenbush, Frank, 1938, Ag 4,17:4
Quackenbush, Frank Mrs, 1964, Mr 17,35:2
Quackenbush, George, 1920, S 23,13:4; 1944, O 17, 23:2
Quackenbush, Harold S, 1949, O 16,88:4
Quackenbush, Harriet F Mrs, 1940, F 16,19:3
Quackenbush, Howard, 1937, F 22,17:4
Quackenbush, J V, 1903, Je 6,7:6
Quackenbush, James L, 1956, Je 1,23:4
Quackenbush, James L Jr, 1958, Ap 17,31:2
Quackenbush, Jeremiah H, 1925, O 2,23:6
Quackenbush, John R, 1938, Je 12,39:2
Quackenbush, Lambert Suydam, 1915, F 18,11:6
Quackenbush, Mahlon W, 1952, Ja 11,22:2
Quackenbush, Paul H, 1946, O 20,60:5
Quackenbush, Percy J, 1946, F 12,28:2
Quackenbush, Samuel A, 1953, N 1,87:2
Quackenbush, Timothy A, 1951, Mr 20,29:1
Quackenbush, Walter G, 1941, Jl 15,19:4
Quad, Louis J, 1957, Mr 15,26:1
Quad, M, 1924, Ag 23,9:3
Quade, Maurice N (mem ser set, Je 17,45:3), 1966, Je 14,47:2
Quadland, John H, 1955, My 14,19:3
Quadra, Vicente, 1943, My 23,43:2
Quaglia, Angelo Cardinal, 1872, Ag 29,1:7
Quaid, Michael S, 1949, Ag 18,21:3
Quaid, William, 1956, Ap 15,89:1
Quaife, Milo M, 1959, S 4,6:4
Quail, J N, 1933, Ja 25,17:5
Quaile, Emerson B, 1942, Mr 3,24:3
Quain, Helen P, 1949, My 14,13:1
Quain, John M, 1945, F 16,24:2
Quain, William T, 1945, Jl 27,15:5
Quaine, William J, 1944, Jl 25,19:1
Quaintance, Grace L Mrs, 1938, Ja 30,II,8:4
Quainton, C S, 1938, F 24,19:3
Qualben, Lars P, 1956, F 21,33:2
Qualey, James J, 1942, N 5,26:4
Qualey, James J Mrs, 1949, O 22,17:5
Qualfe, Stephen, 1903, Jl 3,9:6
Qualles, Thomas H Jr, 1942, Ap 2,21:4
Qualtere, Thomas, 1946, S 16,5:4
Qualters, James E Mrs, 1950, N 20,25:4
Qualters, Thomas, 1968, Jl 26,33:3
Quam, James P, 1956, D 17,31:5
Quan, James E, 1938, Ja 5,21:4
Quan Yick Nam, 1954, Ap 25,86:1
Quander, Charles C, 1957, S 30,31:2
Quandt, Guenther, 1955, Ja 3,27:1
Quann, Simeon T, 1942, Je 24,19:5
Quantmeyer, August, 1950, My 5,22:3
Quantrell, Charles F, 1948, Mr 27,13:2
Quantrell, Ernest E, 1962, N 18,86:4
Quantrell, Guerrilla, 1871, Ag 5,1:4
Quaranta, John V, 1958, Mr 26,34:4
Quaremba, John, 1951, F 28,27:2
Quarenghi, Frank, 1967, Ag 13,80:7
Quarenghi, Frank Mrs, 1948, My 4,25:1
Quaritch, Bernard, 1899, D 19,4:6
Quarles, Carolyn W Mrs, 1965, Ag 5,29:2
Quarles, Donald A (funl, My 13,37:5), 1959, My 9, 1:2
Quarles, Emmet A, 1960, Jl 8,21:4
Quarles, Francis F, 1938, S 9,21:3
Quarles, Frank, 1961, N 20,31:5
Quarles, J F, 1885, Ja 29,4:7
Quarles, James, 1950, S 10,92:5
Quarles, Joseph V, 1946, My 31,23:4
Quarles, Joseph V Ex-Sen, 1911, O 8,II,13:5
Quarles, Sherrod H, 1944, Ap 25,23:1
Quarles, William C, 1939, Ap 18,23:1
Quarles, William W, 1955, Ag 20,17:4
Quarrie, Bertram D, 1953, F 16,21:2
Quarrie, William F, 1956, N 17,21:4
Quarrier, Archie B (cor, F 29,31:2), 1956, F 28,31:5
Quarrier, Sidney S, 1953, Mr 27,23:4
Quarrington, Nelson, 1957, F 26,29:1
Quarrington, Walter, 1949, Ap 18,25:5
Quartararo, Katherine Mrs, 1948, N 10,29:3
Quartermaine, Leon, 1967, Je 28,45:5
Quarterman, Frederick G, 1948, My 10,21:3
Quartitch, Bernard, 1913, Ag 28,9:3
Quarton, W B, 1941, D 15,19:4
Quartullo, Alfred, 1954, O 28,35:1

Quashie-Idun, Samuel O, 1966, Mr 15,39:4
Quasimodo, Salvatore, 1968, Je 15,35:1
Quasman, Alfred, 1960, Jl 27,29:4
Quast, Fredinand von, 1939, Mr 29,23:4
Quattlander, Albert T Mrs, 1949, Ja 6,23:5
Quattrini, Enrico, 1950, Ap 27,29:2
Quattrocchi, Jerome, 1950, Jl 24,17:3
Quattrone, Francesco (por), 1943, My 17,15:5
Quay, Arthur H, 1951, S 27,31:3
Quay, Jerome A, 1910, S 25,II,13:5
Quay, M S Sen, 1904, My 29,3:3
Quayle, Edward A Jr, 1951, Ja 6,15:5
Quayle, Frank J, 1943, S 7,23:4
Quayle, Frank J Mrs, 1948, Mr 6,13:4
Quayle, Harry, 1952, Ag 2,15:5
Quayle, J F, 1930, N 28,19:4
Quayle, John F Mrs, 1952, N 13,31:3
Quayle, John H, 1944, Ap 26,19:3
Quayle, John H Jr, 1966, Je 25,31:4
Quayle, Oliver A, 1956, Jl 5,25:3
Quayle, Robert K Sr, 1940, Ag 7,19:2
Quayle, William A Bp, 1925, Mr 10,21:3
Quayle, William H Mrs, 1956, Mr 4,88:7
Queal, William N, 1960, Jl 10,72:4
Queally, Thomas F, 1959, S 5,15:5
Quealy, Horace A, 1948, N 15,25:4
Quealy, Matthew L, 1953, Ap 13,27:5
Quealy, Peter, 1959, Ja 21,31:4
Quealy, William I, 1940, F 14,21:2
Quebedo, John, 1950, S 4,17:4
Queen, Charles W, 1949, Mr 17,25:4
Queen, Frank, 1882, O 19,2:7; 1942, O 7,25:6
Queen, Hyman L, 1942, O 1,23:4
Queen, Hyman Mrs, 1941, D 13,21:5
Queen, J, 1884, F 12,8:4
Queen, Jack R, 1961, O 9,35:2
Queen, James S, 1905, Mr 24,9:6
Queen, John, 1946, Jl 15,25:3
Queen, Robert, 1960, S 3,17:4
Queen, Walter K, 1960, Je 15,41:2
Queen Victoria, Sister of, 1872, O 19,1:3
Queeney, Joseph A, 1950, O 1,104:2
Queens, J Ferril, 1945, F 24,11:2
Queensberry, Marquess of (F A K Douglas), 1954, Ap 28,31:1
Queensberry, Marquis of, 1900, F 1,1:5
Queensborough, Lord (A H Paget), 1949, S 23,23:5
Queeny, Edgar Monsanto, 1968, Jl 8,39:1
Queipo de Llano, Gonzalo, 1951, Mr 10,13:3
Queiroz Filho, Antonio de, 1963, O 12,23:5
Queiroz Veloso, Jose M de, 1952, N 1,21:2
Queisser, Richard H, 1937, Mr 28,II,8:8
Queitzsch, Albert E, 1954, Mr 24,27:3
Quel, Seymour R Judge, 1968, F 3,29:5
Quelch, Ralph M, 1942, Mr 11,19:3
Quell, Henry, 1939, Je 16,23:3
Quelly, Louis, 1947, N 14,23:4
Quennell, Ada M, 1943, Mr 14,26:3
Quennell, John Cooper Dr, 1909, Mr 13,7:7
Quensell, George, 1956, Ap 2,23:5
Quentin, Emile Rene, 1914, Mr 17,11:5
Queralta, C L de Col, 1903, Mr 16,9:5
Querbes, Justin R Sr, 1954, Ja 11,5:3
Querbes, Randolph, 1954, Ja 11,5:3
Quereaux, Catharine S Mrs, 1952, Ja 21,15:5
Querel, Ernest, 1907, Mr 18,7:2
Querel, Ernest Mrs, 1907, Mr 18,7:2
Quermann, Walter, 1956, Mr 4,88:6
Querol, Augustin, 1909, D 15,11:3
Querrie, Charles, 1950, Ap 6,29:2
Query, Leander, 1967, O 3,47:3
Querze, Adolpho, 1950, My 29,17:1
Querze, Angelo, 1922, F 28,19:1
Quesada, Jose, 1961, Ja 23,23:4
Quesada, Miguel M, 1948, Ap 11,72:5
Quesenberry, Isaac J, 1964, Jl 4,13:1
Quesenberry, Preston B, 1964, Jl 4,13:1
Quesnel, Edgar G, 1964, Jl 12,68:4
Questa, E J, 1962, F 12,20:6
Quetelet, M, 1874, Mr 4,3:3
Quevado, Samuel Latone, 1920, Je 20,18:4
Quevedo, Miguel A de, 1946, Jl 16,23:5
Queyrel, Gaston Mrs, 1955, Ap 29,23:5
Quezon, Manuel Mrs, 1949, Ap 29,1:5
Quibell, David J K, 1962, Ap 17,35:3
Quibysheff, V V, 1935, Ja 26,17:1
Quicherat, Jules E J, 1882, Ap 11,5:3
Quick, Alfred M, 1944, Ap 2,39:3
Quick, Arthur C, 1946, My 7,21:5
Quick, Arthur F, 1943, N 1,18:2
Quick, Arthur F Mrs, 1954, Ag 30,17:3
Quick, Audley V, 1954, F 15,23:5
Quick, Augustus M, 1947, Ag 17,53:1
Quick, Carol Mrs, 1948, Je 3,25:4
Quick, Clifford D, 1963, Ag 27,31:2
Quick, Dorothy (Mrs J A Mayer), 1962, Mr 16,31:5
Quick, Douglas, 1966, F 3,32:1
Quick, Douglas Mrs, 1963, S 30,29:4
Quick, Edwin A, 1913, O 20,7:4

Quick, Ernest E, 1943, Ag 25,19:3
Quick, G C, 1869, Ja 21,4:7
Quick, George H, 1940, Ag 16,15:5
Quick, Grose, 1943, Jl 28,15:4
Quick, Guernsey, 1947, Jl 11,15:2
Quick, H H Lt-Col, 1903, My 20,9:4
Quick, H Lansing, 1945, Ag 20,19:5
Quick, H Lansing Mrs, 1942, Mr 2,19:6
Quick, Henry Ludlow, 1916, O 20,9:4
Quick, Herbert, 1925, My 11,17:5
Quick, Howard P, 1951, Ap 10,27:4
Quick, John W, 1948, D 24,18:3
Quick, Joseph F, 1964, Ag 28,29:2
Quick, Lawrence B, 1948, Jl 13,27:5
Quick, Martin, 1946, Ja 3,20:2
Quick, Myron, 1943, Ag 1,39:3
Quick, Newton, 1939, D 17,49:2
Quick, O DeWitt Mrs, 1952, Jl 16,25:2
Quick, Oliver, 1944, Ja 24,17:6
Quick, Oscar, 1950, N 1,35:5
Quick, Richard, 1947, N 18,29:2
Quick, Robert L, 1941, N 16,56:4
Quick, S Francis, 1914, Ap 14,11:6
Quick, Sydney C, 1962, S 26,39:1
Quick, Sydney F, 1965, Ag 25,39:4
Quick, Walter L Mrs, 1955, Ja 19,27:3
Quick, Walter R, 1925, Ja 10,13:5
Quick, William D, 1949, Mr 24,28:3
Quicke, Charles E G, 1954, Mr 9,27:1
Quicke, Rose G Mrs, 1945, F 15,19:3
Quicke, W T S, 1967, Ag 18,30:5
Quickenbush, Fred S, 1944, S 23,13:5
Quicksall, William Francis Mrs, 1923, F 21,15:5
Quickswood, Lord (H R H Cecil), 1956, D 11,39:2
Quidde, Ludwig Q, 1941, Mr 8,19:4
Quidor, jno, 1881, D 15,8:2
Quien, Louis Jr, 1942, Je 16,23:6
Quien, Louis Jr Mrs, 1956, F 19,92:4
Quien, Louis 3d, 1945, Jl 1,17:2
Quier, Edwin A, 1939, Ag 31,19:6
Quigan, Frank J, 1952, Jl 9,27:6
Quigg, Daniel H, 1964, F 9,88:5
Quigg, E K, 1950, Ap 1,15:2
Quigg, James F, 1960, Mr 26,21:3
Quigg, John H, 1943, Ap 22,23:2
Quigg, Joseph H, 1941, N 7,24:2
Quigg, Lemuel Ely, 1919, Jl 3,13:4
Quigg, Mary B, 1957, Mr 8,25:2
Quigg, Murray T, 1956, Mr 1,33:5
Quiggle, Joseph R, 1963, Ag 31,17:5
Quigley, Albert M, 1938, Mr 30,21:5
Quigley, Amadeus, 1947, N 10,29:3
Quigley, Charles C, 1953, D 20,77:2
Quigley, D E Msgr, 1903, N 28,9:4
Quigley, Edward V, 1873, N 18,3:7
Quigley, Elizabeth C, 1950, N 29,33:2
Quigley, Ernest C, 1960, D 11,88:4
Quigley, Eugene, 1938, Ap 7,23:2
Quigley, Francis E, 1950, Ja 1,42:6
Quigley, Francis J, 1950, Ja 30,17:5
Quigley, Frederic J, 1955, D 25,48:8
Quigley, George A, 1953, Ag 3,17:4
Quigley, George D, 1942, Je 19,23:2
Quigley, George E, 1942, Je 16,23:5
Quigley, George W, 1949, D 27,23:4
Quigley, Harold Scott, 1968, Jl 22,35:4
Quigley, Henry C, 1939, S 21,23:2
Quigley, Ithamar Mrs, 1953, F 6,19:2
Quigley, James C, 1960, Jl 31,69:2
Quigley, James Edward Archbishop (funl, Jl 13,11:7), 1915, Jl 11,15:3
Quigley, James J, 1946, O 31,25:5; 1954, Ap 25,87:3
Quigley, James K, 1964, N 11,43:4
Quigley, James M, 1907, Jl 10,7:5
Quigley, James P, 1950, F 2,27:2
Quigley, John (por), 1943, Jl 21,15:1
Quigley, John Francis, 1915, My 7,13:6
Quigley, John H J, 1956, My 13,86:4
Quigley, John J Dr (funl, Ja 12,9:5), 1909, Ja 9,9:5
Quigley, John Mrs, 1948, F 28,15:3
Quigley, John T, 1941, Ja 21,21:2
Quigley, Joseph J, 1968, Jl 11,37:4
Quigley, Lawrence F, 1948, D 21,25:2
Quigley, M, 1883, N 3,5:2
Quigley, Margery C, 1968, Ap 18,47:4
Quigley, Martin, 1964, My 5,43:3
Quigley, Martin J, 1948, Ag 1,59:1
Quigley, Mary Mrs, 1948, F 28,15:5
Quigley, Michael J, 1945, Mr 31,19:3
Quigley, Owen F, 1946, Ag 20,28:2
Quigley, Robert P, 1951, Ap 26,29:3
Quigley, Samuel, 1946, N 15,24:2
Quigley, Sarah B G Mrs, 1940, S 14,17:5
Quigley, Silverius J, 1960, Jl 30,17:3
Quigley, Thomas, 1951, My 24,35:2
Quigley, Thomas Capt, 1913, S 15,9:4
Quigley, Thomas F Mrs, 1959, My 29,23:4
Quigley, Thomas H, 1954, Je 24,27:6
Quigley, Thomas J, 1960, D 28,27:4

Quigley, Thomas M, 1946, O 17,23:1
Quigley, William A, 1942, Mr 25,21:2
Quigley, William F (por), 1939, Ag 26,15:5
Quigley, William J Jr, 1959, Mr 15,89:1
Quigley, William M, 1957, Ap 23,31:6
Quigley, Wirt S, 1944, Jl 17,15:6
Quigly, William J, 1939, Jl 26,19:4
Quigney, James, 1968, O 16,47:1
Quigno, Joseph, 1951, N 22,31:1
Quijano, Jazmin H, 1952, Ap 4,5:3
Quijano, Manuel D, 1950, Ap 20,29:3
Quill, James J, 1951, Ag 10,15:4
Quill, John A, 1941, Mr 26,23:6
Quill, John H, 1947, N 12,28:2
Quill, John J, 1958, My 27,31:4
Quill, Michael J (funl plans, F 1,16:1), 1966, Ja 29, 1:2
Quill, Michael J Mrs, 1959, Ag 18,29:2
Quill, Patrick, 1964, Ag 31,25:1
Quill, William J, 1953, O 10,17:5; 1967, S 12,47:1
Quille, C J, 1942, Mr 11,20:2
Quille, Timothy D, 1945, D 24,15:3
Quillen, Emma R, 1944, Ap 8,13:2
Quillen, Joseph H, 1942, Ap 9,20:2
Quillen, Joseph H Mrs, 1948, D 4,19:1
Quillen, Robert, 1948, D 10,25:3
Quiller-Couch, Arthur T (por), 1944, My 13,19:1
Quillet, Aristide, 1955, My 2,21:5
Quilliams, Frederick F, 1939, Mr 11,17:3
Quillian, William F, 1960, O 27,37:4
Quillin, Frank U, 1962, Mr 31,25:2
Quillinan, Timothy J, 1937, My 23,II,10:6
Quilter, Roger, 1953, S 22,31:4
Quilty, Daniel C, 1950, N 6,27:5
Quilty, John J, 1955, F 24,27:5
Quilty, Joseph P, 1943, Ag 12,19:6
Quilty, Patrick, 1955, Mr 14,23:3
Quilty, Theresa A, 1938, F 11,23:1
Quilty, Thomas J, 1956, S 28,27:2
Quilty, Thomas P, 1967, F 20,37:3
Quimby, A Judson, 1958, Ag 26,29:2
Quimby, Alfred C P, 1942, N 22,53:1
Quimby, Alfred R, 1939, F 28,19:3
Quimby, Arthur C, 1947, Jl 19,13:6
Quimby, Brooks Ex-Prof, 1968, D 14,45:4
Quimby, Charles Elihu Dr, 1921, N 7,15:4
Quimby, Charles S, 1951, F 1,25:3
Quimby, Cora A, 1941, Ja 4,13:5
Quimby, E E, 1902, F 19,9:5
Quimby, Edward C, 1950, Ag 7,19:4
Quimby, Edward N, 1909, Jl 5,7:5
Quimby, Eugene A, 1949, S 11,92:1
Quimby, Fred L, 1949, Jl 12,27:5
Quimby, H B, 1883, F 21,2:4
Quimby, Harriet (mem, Jl 5,13:6), 1912, Jl 4,7:5
Quimby, Howard E, 1955, D 27,23:2
Quimby, James M, 1874, Jl 22,4:7
Quimby, Joseph H, 1953, N 26,31:4
Quimby, Karl K Mrs, 1964, Ja 29,30:2
Quimby, Louis S, 1940, Jl 19,19:6
Quimby, Milton C, 1941, F 6,22:2
Quimby, Richard K, 1952, F 8,23:4
Quin, Aloysius, 1945, Jl 1,18:1
Quin, Barbara S, 1945, Je 8,19:1
Quin, Clinton S, 1956, N 30,23:3
Quin, Edwin S Sr, 1955, Je 20,21:5
Quin, Huston, 1938, Ag 16,19:4
Quin, James M Dr, 1868, Ap 5,5:5
Quin, John A Mrs, 1948, Jl 3,15:5
Quin, John M, 1952, Ja 12,13:2
Quin, Mike, 1947, Ag 16,13:2
Quin, P E, 1932, F 5,6:1
Quin, Walter V, 1954, D 5,88:1
Quin, Walter V Mrs, 1946, F 22,25:4
Quin, William F, 1904, Ja 14,9:7
Quinan, Edward P, 1960, N 16,41:2
Quinan, Henry B, 1948, My 22,15:2
Quinby, F H, 1932, Ag 11,15:3
Quinby, Frank E, 1960, D 30,19:1
Quinby, George A Dr, 1916, My 4,11:5
Quinby, George E Mrs, 1944, Mr 24,19:5
Quinby, Harold W, 1954, Ag 6,17:6
Quinby, Henry Brewer Ex-Gov, 1924, F 9,13:6
Quinby, Henry C Mrs, 1962, Mr 25,88:8
Quinby, Henry Cole, 1922, O 24,17:4
Quinby, Henry D, 1949, D 19,27:5
Quinby, J Sidney, 1940, N 2,15:2
Quinby, Jane, 1965, F 2,33:5
Quinby, John G, 1939, D 1,23:6
Quinby, Maria Antoinette, 1909, Mr 9,9:5
Quinby, William C, 1953, Ja 3,15:6
Quinby, William Emory, 1908, Je 8,7:6
Quinby, William O, 1941, Mr 25,26:1
Quinby, Wilmont, 1946, F 5,23:4
Quincannon, Thomas H, 1948, F 22,48:6
Quince, Louis V, 1954, S 26,86:8
Quincey, Charles E, 1924, N 16,7:3
Quinche, Othon, 1964, O 5,33:4
Quincy, Charles F Mrs, 1950, O 7,19:2
Quincy, J W, 1883, Ja 22,5:4
Quincy, Josiah, 1864, Jl 4,4:6; 1919, S 9,17:6
Quincy, Josiah Mrs, 1874, Ag 16,3:7
Quincy, Josiah Sr, 1882, N 3,5:5
Quincy, Mary H Mrs, 1941, D 5,23:5
Quine, Herbert, 1944, N 26,56:4
Quine, L M Mrs, 1903, Je 15,7:6
Quine, William E Dr, 1922, D 8,17:4
Quinette, George T, 1940, S 11,25:6
Quiney, James J Dr, 1937, Ap 2,23:5
Quinlan, Agnes C, 1949, My 23,23:2
Quinlan, Aloysius S, 1955, Ag 17,27:2
Quinlan, Anna V, 1941, Mr 12,21:2
Quinlan, Daniel B, 1938, N 6,48:8
Quinlan, Daniel J, 1940, Jl 13,13:2; 1950, Ap 15,15:1
Quinlan, David W, 1955, F 23,27:2
Quinlan, Edward, 1946, Ap 9,27:1
Quinlan, Elizabeth A M Mrs, 1941, Ja 19,41:2
Quinlan, Elizabeth C, 1947, S 18,25:4
Quinlan, Frances N Mrs, 1941, S 23,23:4
Quinlan, Gertrude, 1963, D 1,84:6
Quinlan, Isaac D, 1938, My 5,23:3
Quinlan, J Bp, 1883, Mr 10,2:6
Quinlan, J C, 1881, Ag 6,5:4
Quinlan, James L, 1941, Ag 27,19:1
Quinlan, James Mrs, 1943, O 30,15:1
Quinlan, Jeremiah P, 1954, N 5,21:4
Quinlan, John A, 1950, Ag 10,25:6
Quinlan, John C, 1954, D 3,27:3
Quinlan, John D, 1949, Je 28,27:4
Quinlan, John F, 1955, Ja 11,25:2
Quinlan, John H, 1948, Jl 22,23:5
Quinlan, John Henry, 1924, My 21,19:2
Quinlan, John J, 1914, D 17,13:6; 1937, Jl 29,19:6
Quinlan, John W, 1946, Je 7,20:2
Quinlan, Joseph A, 1959, Ja 18,88:5
Quinlan, Joseph A Mrs, 1954, Ja 2,11:3
Quinlan, Joseph J, 1941, Ja 26,36:8
Quinlan, Joseph N, 1954, S 20,23:2
Quinlan, Lawrence L, 1945, Ap 14,15:4
Quinlan, Margaret, 1940, My 31,13:3
Quinlan, Maurice P, 1915, Jl 8,13:7
Quinlan, Paul F, 1948, Jl 10,15:1
Quinlan, Peter, 1903, Jl 9,7:6
Quinlan, Robert Mrs, 1943, S 17,21:4
Quinlan, Walter J, 1943, Ap 17,17:6
Quinlan, William, 1939, Ja 4,21:3; 1949, Jl 15,19:4
Quinlan, William H, 1957, Ja 22,29:5
Quinland, Charles E, 1918, S 16,11:6
Quinn, Andrew, 1919, My 11,22:4
Quinn, Anna M, 1949, My 8,76:7
Quinn, Arthur A, 1957, F 3,76:3
Quinn, Arthur A Mrs, 1957, S 21,19:1
Quinn, Arthur H, 1960, O 17,29:1
Quinn, Arthur J, 1959, Ap 21,38:1
Quinn, Bernard J (por), 1940, Ap 8,19:1
Quinn, Bernard W, 1938, O 20,23:5
Quinn, Charles, 1952, Ag 30,13:6
Quinn, Charles C, 1940, Mr 28,15:4
Quinn, Charles J, 1940, O 20,49:2; 1957, Je 22,15:5
Quinn, Charles J 2d, 1956, Ap 28,17:6
Quinn, Charles M Mrs, 1955, N 10,35:5
Quinn, Clarence R Mrs, 1962, Ap 26,33:3
Quinn, Conrad, 1955, N 8,29:4
Quinn, Dan W, 1938, N 8,23:1
Quinn, Daniel, 1906, F 25,9:6
Quinn, Daniel I, 1954, F 22,19:3
Quinn, Daniel J (por), 1940, Mr 10,51:3
Quinn, Daniel P, 1953, S 1,24:3
Quinn, Denis, 1952, N 29,27:4
Quinn, Denis C, 1958, My 29,27:1
Quinn, Don, 1967, D 31,44:4
Quinn, Edmond J, 1967, F 13,33:2
Quinn, Edward F, 1947, D 31,15:4
Quinn, Edward J, 1940, Je 25,23:6; 1953, O 8,29:2
Quinn, Eleanor, 1950, O 23,23:3
Quinn, Elmer F, 1952, S 3,29:1
Quinn, Elwood T, 1953, Jl 31,19:3
Quinn, Eugene P, 1948, Jl 23,19:5
Quinn, Francis M, 1944, Ja 9,43:2
Quinn, Francis W, 1950, Jl 27,25:2
Quinn, Francis X, 1950, Ja 20,25:3
Quinn, Frank J, 1952, N 18,31:1
Quinn, Frank W, 1949, Je 3,25:1
Quinn, Franklin E, 1945, Ag 25,11:4
Quinn, George, 1949, N 30,27:2
Quinn, Harry A, 1954, Mr 9,27:4
Quinn, Harry L, 1962, Je 2,19:5
Quinn, Henry, 1953, N 10,31:2
Quinn, Henry T, 1958, N 22,21:4
Quinn, Hugh, 1956, Ap 28,17:4
Quinn, Hugh F, 1940, O 23,23:3; 1946, D 5,31:2
Quinn, Ignatius A, 1953, Jl 30,23:3
Quinn, J A Robert (Bob), 1954, Mr 13,15:4
Quinn, J Edward, 1960, Je 21,33:4
Quinn, J J (see also Mr 14), 1878, Mr 15,8:4
Quinn, J J, 1903, Ja 4,2:4
Quinn, Jack (por), 1946, Ap 19,30:2
Quinn, James, 1940, Ag 23,15:6; 1948, Ag 22,60:6; 1952, My 7,27:5
Quinn, James A, 1950, Ag 3,23:2
Quinn, James B Col, 1915, F 27,11:5
Quinn, James B Sr, 1950, Ja 28,13:3
Quinn, James C, 1905, My 5,9:4
Quinn, James F, 1947, F 2,57:8
Quinn, James H, 1956, Mr 9,23:2
Quinn, James J, 1948, Mr 16,27:3
Quinn, James L, 1960, N 14,31:3
Quinn, James L Jr, 1967, Ap 20,43:4
Quinn, James L Sr, 1955, O 27,33:4
Quinn, James M, 1950, Je 1,27:3
Quinn, James M Mrs, 1947, Ja 6,23:5
Quinn, James W, 1945, Ag 24,19:3
Quinn, Jay H, 1958, Ap 3,31:2
Quinn, John, 1874, N 18,6:3; 1924, Jl 29,15:3; 1942, Ag 14,17:1; 1958, My 3,19:2; 1961, S 13,17:2; 196 Mr 1,37:2
Quinn, John A, 1946, Ag 9,17:5
Quinn, John B, 1945, O 8,15:4; 1952, S 27,17:2
Quinn, John E, 1944, D 1,23:5
Quinn, John E Mrs, 1939, Ag 30,17:5
Quinn, John F, 1941, My 22,21:6
Quinn, John G, 1955, Mr 9,27:2
Quinn, John H, 1945, S 26,23:4; 1945, N 10,15:2; 1 Ja 13,21:4
Quinn, John J, 1937, Ag 31,23:2
Quinn, John J (por), 1947, My 6,27:5
Quinn, John J, 1950, Jl 17,21:3; 1952, S 23,33:3; 19 Ja 3,15:2; 1953, Je 23,29:4; 1957, Ap 22,25:2
Quinn, John J Jr (por), 1939, Jl 14,19:1
Quinn, John J Mrs, 1946, Ag 28,27:4; 1947, Mr 25
Quinn, John M, 1943, O 13,23:4; 1954, My 25,27:
Quinn, John M J, 1955, Ag 30,27:2
Quinn, John P, 1916, Ap 19,13:4; 1942, S 17,25:2; 1946, Mr 26,29:1; 1954, Jl 9,17:4
Quinn, John S, 1955, Ja 4,21:5; 1960, Mr 5,19:2
Quinn, Joseph A, 1918, Ap 2,13:4
Quinn, Joseph A Sr, 1956, Mr 8,29:5
Quinn, Joseph C, 1967, Ja 5,37:2
Quinn, Joseph G, 1965, N 3,35:5
Quinn, Joseph J, 1940, N 13,23:3; 1942, Mr 20,19
Quinn, Joseph J Mrs, 1947, Mr 12,25:1
Quinn, Joseph L, 1946, D 1,76:2
Quinn, Joseph M, 1950, N 1,35:4
Quinn, Joseph T, 1941, O 19,46:1
Quinn, Katherine J, 1948, F 25,23:4
Quinn, Lawrence R, 1948, N 27,17:1
Quinn, Leo C, 1964, Ja 21,29:4
Quinn, Louis, 1962, N 7,39:5
Quinn, M Seraphine, 1944, Ag 27,33:2
Quinn, Margaret R, 1952, My 13,30:2
Quinn, Martin, 1942, D 17,37:6
Quinn, Martin F Mrs, 1950, Je 9,23:6
Quinn, Martin J, 1952, N 18,31:5
Quinn, Mary, 1941, Ap 21,19:5
Quinn, Mary D Mrs, 1941, Jl 27,30:1
Quinn, Mary T, 1957, Je 22,15:5
Quinn, Matthew C, 1946, Ag 2,19:3
Quinn, Matthew F, 1952, O 4,17:6
Quinn, Matthew W, 1947, N 24,23:3
Quinn, Maurice A, 1951, N 28,31:4
Quinn, Michael, 1921, O 22,13:6
Quinn, Michael J, 1937, O 6,25:5; 1947, Je 26,23 1960, Jl 6,33:1
Quinn, Michael J Mrs, 1948, Ja 20,23:4
Quinn, Mr, 1951, Jl 22,46:4
Quinn, Murtha P, 1940, Je 9,44:2; 1950, Ap 17,2
Quinn, P, 1936, Je 10,23:1
Quinn, P Leo, 1950, Ja 23,23:3
Quinn, Patrick F, 1941, O 12,52:3
Quinn, Patrick H, 1956, Mr 6,31:5
Quinn, Patrick H Mrs, 1950, Mr 26,96:2
Quinn, Patrick J, 1962, Jl 14,21:2
Quinn, Peter, 1922, Je 8,19:4
Quinn, Philip A, 1945, N 14,19:5
Quinn, R Frank, 1942, Ag 26,19:4
Quinn, Ralph H, 1940, My 3,21:2
Quinn, Raphael V, 1943, Mr 26,19:2
Quinn, Robert, 1952, Ja 29,25:3
Quinn, Robert E, 1949, Ap 6,29:4
Quinn, Robert J, 1955, Mr 10,27:3
Quinn, Robert W, 1959, My 7,17:1
Quinn, Scholastica Mother, 1956, F 29,28:6
Quinn, Stanley J, 1958, F 6,27:5
Quinn, T J, 1878, Je 19,5:2
Quinn, T Stephen, 1938, S 19,19:4
Quinn, Theodore K, 1961, Ag 29,31:4
Quinn, Thomas, 1953, O 6,29:2
Quinn, Thomas C Mrs, 1962, N 26,29:2
Quinn, Thomas E, 1946, N 27,25:3
Quinn, Thomas F, 1942, Je 10,21:3; 1950, F 24,
Quinn, Thomas F Sr, 1952, Ag 15,15:4
Quinn, Thomas H, 1939, O 5,23:5
Quinn, Thomas J, 1949, Mr 16,28:2; 1953, My
Quinn, Thomas J Mrs, 1956, N 11,87:1
Quinn, Thomas Mrs, 1955, Je 9,29:4
Quinn, Thomas S, 1955, Jl 12,25:5; 1955, D 7,3
Quinn, Thomas Sydney, 1955, F 21,21:4
Quinn, Tony, 1967, Je 3,31:1
Quinn, Vernon (Eliz V), 1962, Mr 22,35:3
Quinn, W Johnson, 1944, F 27,37:1
Quinn, Wellington H, 1954, S 2,21:3
Quinn, William (por), 1938, Ap 24,II,7:1
Quinn, William A, 1950, N 28,31:5
Quinn, William C, 1960, Mr 14,30:1
Quinn, William F, 1966, S 24,23:5; 1968, F 2,3
Quinn, William H, 1940, My 7,25:3
Quinn, William H Capt, 1918, N 14,13:2
Quinn, William J, 1939, S 17,51:4; 1960, Jl 14,
Quinn, William J Mrs (E Varden),(cor, Jl 14,21 1958, Jl 13,68:6

Quinn, William Mrs, 1945, Ag 23,23:2
Quinn, William P, 1957, Ja 3,31:3
Quinn, William T, 1946, F 10,42:2
Quinn, William T Mrs, 1950, N 17,27:3
Quinn, William V, 1952, D 18,29:1
Quinn (Sister Maria Ignatia), 1962, Jl 21,19:4
Quinones, Ascension Mrs, 1946, Mr 11,25:1
Quinones, Francisco Mariano, 1908, S 15,9:6
Quinones, Francisco P, 1925, D 9,27:2
Quinones, Jose Severo Justice, 1909, Mr 13,7:7
Quinones y Molina, Alfonso, 1950, My 24,30:4
Quinson, Gustave, 1943, Ag 3,19:5
Quint, Theodore I, 1964, Ja 20,43:4
Quintal, Edward, 1951, F 7,29:5
Quintal, Theodore G, 1950, N 10,28:4
Quintana, Federico M, 1941, Ag 31,22:7
Quintana, Leonardo (funl), 1966, O 12,10:6
Quintana, Manuel Pres, 1906, Mr 12,2:5
Quintano, Anthony J, 1966, F 27,85:1
Quintano, Giacomo Countess, 1952, O 23,31:3
Quintard, Charles A, 1909, D 27,7:4
Quintard, George W, 1919, Ap 11,11:3
Quintard, George William, 1913, Ap 3,9:5
Quintard, John A, 1905, O 24,9:5
Quintard, Orestes, 1885, Mr 3,2:3
Quintard, William, 1909, D 27,7:4
Quintero, Angel A, 1943, O 5,25:6
Quintero, Joaquin A (por), 1944, Je 15,19:4
Quintero, Serafin, 1938, Ap 14,23:3
Quintero Canizares, Emiro, 1954, Ja 5,27:3
Quinterro, Frederick S, 1951, Ag 25,11:2
Quintin, John R, 1954, Jl 23,17:5
Quintinian, Bro, 1914, N 21,13:6
Quinton, Cecil E Mrs, 1945, Ag 10,15:4
Quinton, Herman W, 1952, Ap 3,35:3
Quinton, John R, 1939, My 11,25:3
Quinton, William W, 1941, D 6,17:5
Quintus, Charles, 1939, S 30,17:5
Quinzel, Charles S Mrs, 1960, Jl 11,29:4
Quipp, Frank W, 1954, N 5,21:3
Quirino, Elpidio, 1956, Mr 1,33:1
Quirino, Ernesto, 1952, N 11,29:4
Quirk, Allen H, 1951, D 5,35:3
Quirk, Barton B, 1947, D 31,15:3
Quirk, Daniel L, 1955, O 16,86:3
Quirk, Edward J (por), 1940, O 29,25:5
Quirk, Edward J Jr, 1943, F 24,21:2
Quirk, Frank T, 1962, N 2,31:2
Quirk, George C, 1968, S 15,84:1
Quirk, J R, 1932, Ag 2,17:1
Quirk, James E, 1952, Je 6,23:3
Quirk, John P, 1937, F 17,22:1
Quirk, Joseph, 1940, Ja 15,15:5
Quirk, Joseph C Mrs, 1956, F 21,33:4
Quirk, Michael H, 1939, Mr 5,48:7
Quirk, Stephen F Mrs, 1950, D 21,29:2
Quirk, Thomas A Msgr, 1937, S 13,21:4
Quirk, Thomas K, 1954, F 22,19:3
Quirk, W T, 1945, Je 7,19:1
Quirke, William, 1955, Mr 6,88:1
Quiroga, Abraham, 1939, F 13,15:4
Quiroga, Ulises, 1938, O 24,17:5
Quis, Harold J, 1956, Ag 31,17:3
Quis, Harold J Mrs, 1959, My 2,23:4
Quisenberry, George E, 1956, N 23,27:4
Quisenberry, Joel T, 1956, Mr 7,33:2
Quisenberry, Thomas E, 1964, Mr 14,23:2
Quisling, Gunnar D, 1951, Mr 19,27:2
Quist, Alarik W, 1944, Jl 17,15:4
Quist, Albert J Mrs, 1956, D 21,23:4
Quist, Emmanuel C, 1959, Mr 2,27:3
Quist, Hugo, 1941, F 15,15:3
Quist, Reinee M, 1946, O 24,27:5
Quitman, Albert H, 1955, N 7,29:2
Quitman, Harry W, 1949, S 8,29:5
Quittmeyer, Ernest M, 1952, Mr 15,13:5
Quittner, Carl Mrs, 1947, Ap 29,27:5
Quittner, Frederick, 1953, My 7,31:3
Quivedo, John, 1905, F 5,2:6
Quivey, O Kenneth, 1949, Jl 22,19:4
Quku, Faik, 1963, Jl 20,19:4
Quo Tai-chi, 1952, Mr 1,15:4
Quortrup, August, 1912, N 6,15:4
Quortrup, Richmond C, 1956, My 26,17:6
Qvigstad, Knud, 1957, Mr 17,86:8

R

Raab, Edward R (por), 1946, D 13,23:4
Raab, George, 1943, Ja 24,42:2; 1943, S 26,48:2
Raab, Harold S, 1961, Ap 25,35:1
Raab, Henry F, 1957, Jl 22,19:2
Raab, Henry G, 1965, Ja 12,37:4
Raab, Julius, 1945, F 9,16:2
Raab, Julius (funl), 1964, Ja 9,31:2
Raab, Julius C, 1960, Mr 18,26:3
Raab, Michael, 1944, O 4,19:1
Raab, William H, 1938, F 16,21:2
Raab, William J, 1905, Mr 16,9:6
Raab, William R, 1953, Ja 30,23:2
Raabe, Arthur E, 1965, Jl 6,33:4
Raabe, Hedwig Niemann, 1905, Ap 23,9:6
Raaby, Torstein, 1964, Mr 24,8:5
Raap, Robert R Sr, 1950, N 9,33:4
Raare, Henryk, 1951, F 1,25:4
Raas, Rene, 1966, Mr 3,33:5
Raasch, Emil E E, 1948, F 22,48:4
Raasch, Herman, 1942, D 10,25:4
Rab, Edward A, 1955, My 26,31:1
Raba, Joseph, 1959, D 24,20:1
Rabaud, Henri (por), 1949, S 13,29:5
Rabbage, Lewis J, 1941, My 30,15:3
Rabbe, Frederick, 1968, Ja 15,47:1
Rabbie, Jacob S, 1957, F 2,19:5
Rabbino, B, 1933, N 25,15:3
Rabbino, Herman, 1941, S 8,15:5
Rabbino, Herman Mrs, 1954, O 16,17:2
Rabbino, Lester, 1967, N 7,39:5
Rabbitt, John C, 1957, Je 12,35:6
Rabbitt, Wade H, 1943, Mr 8,15:1
Rabe, Robert H, 1954, Je 12,15:4
Rabell, Burlock E, 1954, S 2,21:6
Rabell, Burlock E Mrs, 1961, S 1,17:1
Rabell, Lida Valentine, 1918, Je 12,13:5
Rabello, Manoel, 1945, N 9,19:1
Raben Levetzau, Countess, 1946, Mr 10,46:3
Rabenou, Khlalil, 1961, My 25,37:5
Raber, Cora M Mrs, 1941, O 6,17:5
Raber, Edward N, 1943, Je 25,17:4
Raber, Edwin J, 1947, Ap 2,27:1
Raber, Oran L, 1940, Mr 1,21:2
Raber, William F, 1945, Je 19,19:1
Rabey, Daniel F, 1945, N 3,15:2
Rabig, George J, 1951, My 21,27:4
Rabig, George J Mrs, 1950, S 26,31:4
Rabig, George Mrs, 1950, N 15,31:3
Rabig, John L, 1940, Ja 7,48:8
Rabig, Joseph F, 1952, D 31,15:4
Rabild, Helmer, 1948, Ja 2,23:1
Rabin, Ben, 1961, Ag 30,33:1
Rabin, Charles, 1954, My 9,88:5; 1964, Jl 4,13:3
Rabin, Ely, 1964, Ag 8,19:5
Rabin, Harry Mrs, 1962, Jl 10,33:3
Rabin, I George, 1966, Mr 22,42:1
Rabin, Rose D Mrs, 1962, Ap 20,27:2
Rabin, Sarah I Mrs, 1937, Ja 23,18:6
Rabin, Zell, 1966, N 15,47:2
Rabinavicius, Henrika, 1962, S 1,19:4
Rabiner, Ella F (Mrs Abr M), 1960, Je 17,31:2
Rabing, Herman, 1950, Ap 21,24:2
Rabinoff, Adolph Mrs, 1968, Ap 13,25:4
Rabinoff, Anastasia, 1951, Je 23,15:5
Rabinoff, Max, 1966, Ap 20,48:1
Rabinoff, Sophie, 1957, O 3,29:2
Rabinovich, Frank, 1944, Ap 11,19:4
Rabinovitch, Leon, 1962, Mr 11,86:1
Rabinovitch, Ljuba, 1944, Jl 19,19:1
Rabinovitch, S, 1936, Ja 24,19:2
Rabinovitz, Bernard, 1957, F 15,23:4
Rabinovitz, Jacob Mrs, 1947, Ag 31,36:6
Rabinovitz, Joseph, 1967, D 25,21:4
Rabinovitz, Joseph Mrs, 1958, D 9,41:1
Rabinowitz, Abraham, 1942, O 17,15:3
Rabinowitz, Benjamin (por), 1948, Ap 29,23:3
Rabinowitz, Benjamin, 1951, F 12,23:2
Rabinowitz, David S, 1967, D 21,37:4
Rabinowitz, Eleizer, 1958, S 1,13:4
Rabinowitz, Elias, 1952, Ap 25,23:4
Rabinowitz, Elias N, 1960, F 10,38:1
Rabinowitz, Harold M, 1958, Mr 10,23:5
Rabinowitz, Harry A, 1952, Ag 12,19:6
Rabinowitz, Isaac, 1948, Jl 8,23:1
Rabinowitz, Isaac Mrs, 1944, Mr 20,17:2
Rabinowitz, Isadore, 1956, F 25,19:3
Rabinowitz, Jacob, 1939, D 10,69:3
Rabinowitz, Jacob J, 1960, Ja 13,48:2
Rabinowitz, Joseph E, 1947, S 17,25:2
Rabinowitz, Julius, 1955, My 13,25:3
Rabinowitz, Louis, 1949, Ag 25,23:1
Rabinowitz, Louis M, 1957, Ap 28,86:3
Rabinowitz, Louis M Mrs, 1968, Ag 18,89:2
Rabinowitz, Louis Mrs, 1954, Je 11,23:1
Rabinowitz, Mordecai, 1957, Ag 29,27:3
Rabinowitz, Morris, 1942, Ap 7,21:4
Rabinowitz, Olga L Mrs, 1942, D 3,25:4
Rabinowitz, Osheah Rabbi, 1938, Ap 28,23:4
Rabinowitz, Phil, 1948, Ja 11,56:1
Rabinowitz, Rubin Mrs, 1966, Jl 5,27:2
Rabinowitz, S A, 1948, N 15,25:3
Rabinowitz, Samuel, 1946, D 13,23:5
Rabinsohn, Zvi, 1951, Mr 31,15:2
Rabishaw, David N, 1958, F 25,27:4
Rabitor, Eugene J, 1947, My 27,25:4
Rabke, Carl Y, 1957, D 24,15:3
Rabkin, William, 1956, N 14,26:4
Raboch, Wenzel A, 1942, Jl 20,13:6
Rabona, Philip Mrs, 1962, Je 4,29:4
Raborg, H Mason, 1913, D 12,11:6
Rabout, Louis C, 1961, N 13,31:3
Raboy, Mac, 1967, D 24,49:1
Rabsey, Carl Mrs, 1966, My 21,31:1
Rabshaw, Gideon A, 1952, Ap 2,33:2
Rabuck, Donald, 1950, O 26,41:4
Raby, George, 1925, N 12,25:4
Raby, Mahlon R, 1954, F 2,27:4
Raby, Noah, 1904, Mr 2,9:7
Raby, Peter, 1948, Ag 11,21:2
Rac, Adolf P Sr, 1950, Mr 22,27:1
Rac, Joseph F, 1948, N 17,28:3
Racah, Giulio, 1965, Ag 30,25:3
Race, C Bertrand, 1937, O 29,21:2
Race, John H, 1954, O 16,17:3
Race, Walter L, 1953, Mr 27,23:1
Racey, Arthur G, 1941, D 22,17:2
Racey, Russell S, 1942, Je 3,23:6
Rach, Carl, 1940, Je 30,32:6
Rachbauer, Frederick, 1952, Ja 13,89:2
Rache, Leo E, 1951, Mr 8,29:3
Rachek, John, 1964, Ap 16,37:3
Rachels, J Joseph, 1966, F 28,27:3
Rachford, Benjamin K Mrs, 1956, Ja 15,92:8
Rachilde (Mrs A Vallette), 1953, Ap 6,19:4
Rachin, William, 1954, Jl 22,23:1
Rachkoffsky, M, 1910, N 2,11:4
Rachlin, Abraham H, 1967, Mr 7,38:5
Rachlin, Abraham H Mrs, 1963, Ag 6,31:3
Rachlin, Alred D, 1943, Ja 1,23:3
Rachlin, Fannie Mrs, 1949, Je 19,68:1
Rachlin, Harold H, 1944, Mr 3,15:5
Rachlin, Israel J, 1949, D 6,32:3
Rachlin, William Mrs, 1947, F 9,61:3
Rachlis, Burech, 1961, Ja 1,49:1
Rachman, Jake, 1952, S 6,17:4
Rachmaninoff, Sergei, 1943, Mr 29,1:2
Rachmaninoff, Sergei Mrs, 1951, Ja 18,27:5
Racht, Leon, 1957, F 13,35:6
Rachunow, Jacob C, 1963, N 24,22:3
Racicot, Joseph E, 1949, Jl 25,15:2
Racicot, Louis, 1946, Je 22,19:5
Racicot, Msgr (Bp of Pogia), 1915, S 15,9:5
Racicot, William, 1946, Ag 23,19:4
Racine, Anthony, 1953, D 19,15:4
Racine, Charles W, 1944, N 21,25:5
Racine, Francois M J A, 1951, F 5,23:1
Racine, Hector, 1956, Mr 13,27:3
Racine, Pierre H, 1954, Ja 1,23:1
Racite, John, 1943, S 15,27:5
Raciti, Rosaria, 1946, O 25,24:2
Rack, Sebastian Mrs, 1960, S 22,27:5
Rackham, Arthur, 1939, S 8,23:5
Rackham, Horace H Mrs, 1947, Jl 24,21:3
Rackliffe, Alfred E, 1944, Ja 14,19:4
Rackliffe, Benjamin D Mrs, 1951, N 12,25:1
Rackliffe, Charles W, 1939, O 12,25:4
Rackoff, Leo, 1959, O 28,37:4
Rackow, Franz, 1907, Mr 14,7:6
Rackway, John S, 1955, Je 6,27:4
Racolin, Mendel, 1950, Mr 31,31:5
Racon, Albert, 1949, Ap 17,76:7
Racoosin, Abram W, 1953, O 4,88:5
Racusin, M Jay, 1962, N 29,37:4
Raczkiewicz, Wladyslaw, 1947, Je 7,13:1
Raczowski, Ignatius W, 1941, N 18,25:2
Raczynski, Roger, 1945, N 15,19:2
Rada, Karel E, 1949, Je 15,29:5
Radabaugh, R C, 1950, N 25,13:1
Radabaugh, Roy (R Cromwell), 1960, O 13,37:4
Radaceanu, Lotar, 1955, Ag 27,15:4
Radaelli, Giuseppi, 1939, F 2,19:4
Radam, William, 1902, F 4,9:5
Radan, Vlado, 1959, Jl 28,27:4
Radasch, H E, 1942, D 2,25:4
Radbill, Samuel, 1956, N 29,35:3
Radbord, Julius, 1947, Ag 5,23:4
Radcliff, Anna S Mrs, 1940, Je 19,23:5
Radcliff, Jane, 1943, My 4,23:5
Radcliff, John P Jr, 1940, Jl 25,17:6
Radcliff, Lillie B Jr Mrs, 1942, D 27,34:4
Radcliff, Raymond A (Rip), 1962, My 25,33:4
Radcliff, Sue Dr, 1924, Ap 16,23:4
Radcliffe, Albert V, 1959, O 4,86:4
Radcliffe, Amos H, 1950, D 30,13:2
Radcliffe, Amos H Mrs, 1945, Je 5,19:1
Radcliffe, Arthur, 1942, Jl 28,17:1
Radcliffe, Evan, 1940, Mr 3,45:2
Radcliffe, Fred T, 1951, D 3,31:5
Radcliffe, Harry S, 1968, Ja 2,41:5
Radcliffe, James E Mrs, 1945, My 16,19:2
Radcliffe, John A, 1944, My 5,19:3
Radcliffe, Lewis Mrs, 1949, Ap 8,25:2
Radcliffe, Lloyd S, 1960, Je 4,23:5
Radcliffe, M, 1936, F 29,15:6
Radcliffe, Mortimer Mrs, 1944, Ja 11,19:5
Radcliffe, Percy L, 1947, S 5,19:2
Radcliffe, Phinley Walter, 1925, Ap 5,5:1
Radcliffe, W, 1930, Je 9,19:5
Radcliffe, William, 1938, My 11,19:5
Radcliffe, William G, 1951, N 24,11:5
Radcliffe, William H, 1947, D 17,29:4; 1952, N 30,89
Raddatz, Richard C, 1937, F 24,23:2
Radde, W, 1884, My 20,5:3
Radding, Bernhard, 1958, O 23,31:1
Raddock, David Mrs, 1957, F 7,27:1
Radeau, Richard, 1950, Je 29,29:2
Radecki, Waclaw, 1953, Mr 27,23:2
Radeke, Aug C, 1942, F 3,19:3
Radeker, Junius, 1957, S 20,25:1
Radel, Andrew, 1915, O 16,11:6
Radel, Frederick M, 1943, Ja 22,19:1
Rademacher, John, 1947, Jl 22,23:2
Rademaker, L A, 1954, S 9,31:3
Radenhausen, Paul, 1966, My 19,47:4
Rader, Allen F, 1947, S 23,25:6
Rader, Arch F, 1939, O 9,19:5
Rader, Archibald Mrs, 1954, D 14,33:2
Rader, August C, 1946, N 13,27:5
Rader, Bud H, 1943, N 8,19:4
Rader, Jacob C, 1952, Je 22,70:5
Rader, Jennie E Mrs, 1946, Je 22,19:3
Rader, L B, 1881, Mr 11,3:4
Rader, Lucile, 1967, Ja 21,31:4
Rader, Lyell M Dr, 1937, N 3,24:4
Rader, Paul (por), 1938, Jl 20,19:1
Rader, Phil, 1940, My 5,52:1
Rader, William, 1964, D 10,47:3
Raderschatt, Peter, 1910, Ag 4,7:4
Radescu, Micolae, 1953, My 19,29:1
Radest, Franklin P, 1966, S 24,23:4
Radetzky, Abraham, 1945, D 5,25:2
Radev, John, 1940, D 9,19:4
Radford, Basil, 1952, O 21,29:6
Radford, C Montgomery Mrs, 1956, Ap 17,31:1
Radford, Cyrus S, 1951, Ja 21,76:5
Radford, E A, 1944, My 28,34:1
Radford, John, 1921, D 26,13:3
Radford, Ovis C, 1946, My 12,20:2
Radford, Paul R, 1945, F 24,11:1
Radford, Percy E, 1956, Je 6,33:3
Radford, Robert, 1944, D 19,21:2
Radford, Robert A, 1948, O 8,25:2
Radford, Walter A, 1955, Mr 31,27:4
Radford, William, 1922, D 17,6:4
Radford, William H, 1966, My 10,39:5
Radhakrishnan, Sarrepalli Mrs (Sivakamu Amma), 1956, N 27,37:2
Radican, Martin J, 1947, O 23,25:4
Radick, Aaron D, 1943, Ja 10,49:1
Radigan, Bernard J Mrs, 1949, F 4,23:3
Radigan, Frank J, 1959, D 9,45:3
Radigan, John F, 1947, N 27,45:3
Radigan, John J, 1949, D 22,23:1
Radigan, William H, 1953, Ja 24,15:2
Radiker, James S, 1943, Ap 10,17:1
Radikin, Earle E, 1947, Mr 15,13:3
Radiman, Otto, 1945, O 7,44:6
Radin, Abraham, 1968, Ja 10,43:3
Radin, Edward D, 1966, Mr 29,41:4
Radin, Harry R, 1956, F 2,25:3
Radin, Jacob, 1962, Ap 12,35:2
Radin, James J, 1943, My 19,25:4
Radin, Louis, 1945, Ja 18,19:3
Radin, Max Mrs, 1948, O 16,15:2
Radin, Oscar, 1957, F 15,23:4
Radin, Paul, 1959, F 22,88:3
Radington, Thomas G, 1944, Ap 10,19:4
Radinsky, Benjamin, 1947, Jl 11,15:5
Radis, Frank G, 1964, Ag 3,25:2
Raditch, S, 1928, Ag 9,10:2
Raditz, Mark, 1954, S 16,29:5
Radivojevic, Lazar, 1958, N 26,29:5
Radix, Harry E (will, Ag 24,63:3), 1965, Ag 20,2
Radke, Louis C, 1947, My 22,27:2
Radlein, Jacob, 1948, My 21,23:1
Radlein, William, 1950, Ap 25,31:5
Radlein, William H, 1954, S 9,31:2
Radler, Milton C, 1955, N 25,27:3
Radler, Robert C Mrs, 1950, Je 7,29:1
Radley, Francis H J, 1940, N 6,23:4
Radley, Guy R, 1962, Ap 5,33:1
Radley, Ignatius, 1908, Ap 7,9:4
Radley, Ja H, 1954, S 11,17:6
Radley, John J Jr, 1956, My 6,86:6
Radley, John J Mrs, 1944, O 5,23:1
Radley, Thomas, 1943, Ja 27,21:1
Radman, Calvin J, 1952, Ag 23,13:1

Radnai, Josef, 1942, Ap 19,43:1
Radnai, Morton, 1950, Jl 26,25:5
Radner, William, 1951, O 23,29:1
Radnitz, Samuel, 1944, My 22,19:4
Radnitz, Samuel E Jr, 1963, Ap 9,32:1
Radnor-Lewis, Herbert Mrs, 1940, Mr 8,21:5
Rado, Henry R, 1962, My 16,41:2
Rado, Sandor Mrs, 1961, Ja 12,29:1
Rado, Tibor, 1965, D 31,21:1
Rado, William, 1940, Ja 1,23:4
Radolin, Prince von, 1917, Jl 24,11:8
Radom, Elizabeth L Dr, 1921, D 4,22:3
Radon, Clarence C, 1951, N 28,31:3
Radon, Ernest O, 1945, Ja 22,17:3
Radon, Johann, 1956, My 28,27:2
Radon, William F, 1940, S 8,49:2
Rados, Andrew, 1949, S 21,31:3
Radosavljevich, Paul R (cor, Ap 19,21:3), 1958, Ap 9,33:5
Radoslavoff, V, 1929, O 22,29:5
Radosta, Philip, 1947, Je 14,15:5
Radovitz, Joseph M von Baron, 1912, Ja 17,13:4
Radowitz, Joseph M von, 1956, Je 2,19:2
Radsch, Robert H, 1961, Mr 6,25:2
Radspinner, Fred, 1957, S 16,28:8
Radtke, John H, 1942, S 20,39:2
Radut, Harold V, 1959, F 4,33:1
Radven, Chester J Sr, 1956, F 12,88:6
Radwan, Edmund P, 1959, S 8,35:2
Radway, Edward Mailler, 1922, D 16,15:5
Radway, Ignatius L Mrs, 1941, F 5,20:3
Radway, John S, 1967, N 27,47:3
Radzinsky, Charles F Mrs, 1945, Jl 15,15:4
Radzinsky, Emanuel (est), 1968, Jl 11,16:8
Radzio, Carl, 1954, N 23,35:2
Radziwill, Anton Prince, 1904, D 17,9:5
Radziwill, Constantin Prince, 1920, S 10,11:3
Radziwill, Helen Princes, 1924, S 16,23:4
Radziwill, Janusz Prince (funl, O 8,87:1), 1967, O 7, 29:4
Radziwill, Leon Princess, 1947, Ag 23,13:5
Radziwill, Marie Princess, 1915, Jl 13,11:5; 1941, Ag 9,15:6
Rae, Albert C, 1951, Ap 7,15:3
Rae, Alexander C, 1947, Ap 5,19:3
Rae, Arne G, 1953, S 4,24:1
Rae, Arthur L, 1940, Ap 15,17:6
Rae, Bruce (trb lr, Mr 17,24:6), 1962, Mr 13,35:1
Rae, Charles Whiteside Rear-Adm, 1908, My 15,9:6
Rae, Fred, 1951, My 16,35:4
Rae, Henry R, 1919, D 20,11:4
Rae, James S, 1956, O 7,86:8
Rae, Jimmy, 1940, My 7,25:4
Rae, John, 1962, F 6,32:6; 1963, O 18,28:3
Rae, John B, 1941, N 21,17:5
Rae, John M, 1938, N 1,23:3
Rae, Margaret P, 1938, S 20,23:6
Rae, Thomas F, 1943, S 2,19:5
Rae, Tommy, 1961, Ja 17,37:2
Rae, William E, 1961, Ja 25,33:4
Rae, William F, 1950, Ja 19,28:3
Rae, William J G, 1938, Ja 18,23:5
Rae, William L, 1953, Ap 27,23:5
Raeburn, Abner A, 1966, Ap 20,47:4
Raeburn, Andrew Mrs, 1951, N 15,29:2
Raeburn, Boyd, 1966, Ag 4,33:4
Raeburn, Boyd Mrs (G Powell), 1959, Jl 30,27:2
Raeburn, Ernest Sir, 1922, Je 2,17:6
Raeburn, George F, 1939, My 17,23:5
Raecke, Walter R, 1960, Ap 11,31:4
Raedecker, John, 1956, Ja 14,19:6
Raeder, Emil G Sr, 1956, D 30,33:1
Raeder, Erich (funl, N 12,21:6), 1960, N 7,35:2
Raeder, Waldemer C, 1947, Jl 21,17:6
Raegner, L C, 1928, Jl 7,13:4
Raeicchi, Peter, 1952, Ag 24,66:4
Raemaekers, Louis, 1956, Jl 27,21:4
Raemisch, Waldemar, 1955, Ap 16,19:6
Raestad, Arnold, 1945, S 20,23:1
Raetz, William F, 1951, Mr 27,29:4
Raetzer, Otto, 1957, Ap 21,89:1
Rafael, Bro (R Sanchez Guerra), 1964, Ap 3,33:2
Rafael, Mac C Dr, 1904, F 14,9:7
Rafaj, Paul, 1962, Mr 17,25:5
Rafalsky, Henry, 1945, N 13,22:3
Rafalsky, Mark (por), 1943, O 29,19:3
Rafalsky, Richard L, 1964, Ja 14,31:4
Rafel, Samuel, 1967, My 24,32:5
Rafel, Will, 1953, N 6,27:1
Rafeld, Herman, 1955, Ap 24,86:4
Raff, Alex B, 1938, F 13,II,7:2
Raff, Joachim, 1882, Je 27,5:5
Raff, Nathan, 1953, Ja 1,23:2
Raff, Raymond, 1947, D 11,33:5
Raffaelli, Jean Francois, 1924, F 12,17:3
Raffalovich, George Sr, 1958, My 22,29:5
Raffe, Genevieve M, 1947, Ap 9,25:4
Raffel, Harry L, 1958, Ja 1,25:3
Raffel, Isaac, 1920, Mr 2,11:4
Raffel, Jacob M, 1918, D 13,15:3
Raffen, Peter W, 1940, Jl 1,16:4
Rafferty, Charles D, 1949, O 29,15:1
Rafferty, Col, 1872, Jl 25,8:5
Rafferty, Frank J, 1942, F 8,50:1
Rafferty, George J, 1946, Ap 17,25:3
Rafferty, James A, 1951, D 21,27:1; 1965, Ja 28,29:4
Rafferty, James A Mrs, 1961, F 8,31:2
Rafferty, James J Mrs, 1965, Mr 15,31:2
Rafferty, John H, 1940, N 30,17:4
Rafferty, John J, 1954, Ja 14,29:2; 1968, N 9,33:2
Rafferty, John W, 1945, F 26,19:5; 1947, Ag 15,17:4
Rafferty, Joseph A, 1967, F 15,41:2
Rafferty, Malcolm A Capt, 1903, Ag 19,9:6
Rafferty, Martin X, 1948, My 6,25:5
Rafferty, Oliver, 1922, Jl 19,13:6
Rafferty, Patrick, 1957, Ja 14,23:5
Rafferty, Peter F Capt, 1910, My 5,11:4
Rafferty, Peter F Mrs, 1945, S 7,23:3
Rafferty, Peter P Dr, 1924, Jl 21,11:5
Rafferty, Robert D Mrs, 1951, Jl 25,24:2
Rafferty, William A, 1944, Ag 29,17:5
Rafferty, William B, 1939, Ja 5,23:1
Rafferty, William C, 1941, My 23,21:5
Rafferty, William F, 1956, N 4,86:4
Rafferty, William M, 1954, D 22,23:2
Raffetto, Joseph L, 1942, O 15,23:1
Raffin, Frank E, 1949, Mr 29,26:2
Raffin, Isidor D, 1948, N 9,27:2
Raffman, Louis Mrs, 1958, Ap 19,21:4
Raffo, Adele, 1953, Mr 21,17:5
Raffo, Juan, 1964, My 2,27:4
Raffo, Peter J, 1951, Ja 1,17:5
Raffo, Peter J Mrs, 1951, Ja 1,17:5
Raffo, Victor A, 1957, F 23,17:6
Rafkin, Maurice M, 1962, Ja 19,31:4
Rafle, Philip J, 1959, O 14,43:2
Rafsky, Henry A, 1954, Ag 1,85:1
Rafstky, Abraham, 1945, S 13,23:5
Raft, Eva Mrs, 1937, Jl 2,21:3
Rafter, Adele, 1911, Ja 31,9:4
Rafter, Augustine L, 1938, D 31,15:3
Rafter, David A, 1905, Je 7,9:5
Rafter, Edward Father, 1912, Ja 23,11:4
Rafter, James A, 1940, D 27,19:3
Rafter, James J, 1915, Mr 2,9:4
Rafter, William J (por), 1946, O 30,27:4
Rafter, William L, 1942, F 8,50:1
Raftery, Clarence A, 1950, Ja 1,42:5
Raftery, Edward C, 1967, My 17,47:1
Raftery, Edward C Mrs, 1944, S 26,23:5
Raftery, John H, 1944, Ag 1,15:4
Raftery, John J, 1959, F 13,27:1
Raftery, Matthew A, 1961, D 10,88:5
Raftery, Timothy E, 1956, Ap 19,31:1
Raftes, Panos A, 1959, My 1,29:4
Raftis, James T, 1946, My 11,27:5
Rafuse, Robert W, 1957, O 11,27:4
Ragan, Carroll, 1944, Ap 11,19:5
Ragan, Carroll Mrs, 1952, Mr 6,31:3
Ragan, Charles A Mrs, 1943, Mr 17,21:5
Ragan, Claude E, 1953, Ja 1,23:2
Ragan, Robert R, 1955, D 23,17:5
Ragan, William F, 1946, My 7,21:3
Ragar, Sam, 1949, Jl 24,52:4
Ragaway, Sheila, 1951, Mr 19,27:4
Ragel, William A, 1944, Ja 6,23:3
Ragg, Clara Mrs, 1939, Ja 7,15:1
Ragg, Lonsdale, 1945, Ag 3,17:3
Raggatt, Harold Sir, 1968, N 4,47:3
Raggi, Gonippo, 1959, O 23,29:2
Raggio, Andrew Paul Prof, 1917, D 22,11:5
Raggio, Dante A, 1945, N 7,23:5
Ragins, Oscar B, 1955, N 20,88:6
Ragionieri, Giovanna, 1962, Mr 17,21:8
Ragir, Benjamin A, 1958, Jl 31,23:5
Raglan, Baroness, 1940, Je 25,23:2
Raglan, Lord (F R Somerset), 1964, S 15,37:1
Ragland, Esther C, 1939, Jl 10,19:4
Ragland, Herbert S Mrs, 1944, Ja 13,21:6
Ragland, Howard N, 1952, Ja 2,25:3
Ragland, Rags, 1946, Ag 21,27:4
Ragland, Wilhelmina A, 1952, Je 28,19:3
Ragle, B Harrison, 1956, My 2,31:2
Ragner, Bernard, 1947, Jl 13,44:8
Ragni, Ottorino, 1940, My 10,23:4
Ragniny, Michael M, 1940, Mr 18,18:2
Ragon, Heartsill (por), 1940, S 16,19:5
Ragona, Mario, 1968, Mr 14,43:1
Ragona, Mario Mrs, 1958, Ag 26,29:1
Ragonesi, F, 1931, S 15,25:5
Ragonnet, Eugene L, 1940, D 24,15:4
Ragovin, David, 1957, Ja 1,23:2
Ragovin, Harry, 1958, Ag 27,29:4
Ragovin, Harry Mrs, 1958, D 10,39:1
Ragovin, Samuel S, 1960, S 7,41:2
Ragozin, Vyacheslav, 1962, Mr 13,35:3
Ragsdale, Earl J W, 1946, F 25,25:5
Ragsdale, Edmund M, 1966, Ag 4,33:5
Ragsdale, George T Prof, 1937, F 8,2:4
Ragsdale, Isaac N, 1937, N 28,II,8:7
Ragsdale, J K P Lt, 1874, My 24,2:4
Ragsdale, J W, 1919, Jl 24,9:1
Ragsdale, Jean M, 1941, Mr 4,23:4
Ragsdale, John P, 1938, D 10,17:4
Ragsdale, Joseph, 1938, F 3,23:6
Ragsdale, William A, 1958, Mr 3,27:1
Ragsdale, William H, 1957, Ja 18,21:2
Rague, Charles J, 1942, Ja 29,19:3
Rague, William J, 1940, D 24,15:2; 1949, F 8,26:3
Ragula, Bazyli, 1955, Je 19,93:1
Ragusa, Vincent, 1946, S 14,7:5
Rahauser, Amelia, 1945, Ap 21,13:2
Rahb, C Henry, 1945, O 16,23:5
Rahde, J W, 1968, Jl 14,65:1
Rahe, Paul G Mrs, 1937, S 11,17:5
Rahel, Walter E, 1962, Mr 1,31:1
Rahill, William J, 1944, Jl 13,17:3
Rahilly, Margaret C Mrs, 1940, N 9,17:2
Rahim, Kamil A, 1966, F 17,33:3
Rahin, Abdur, 1952, Ag 16,15:3
Rahman, Abdel, 1959, Mr 25,35:2
Rahman, Abdu (Emir), 1966, F 24,37:4
Rahman, Abdul (trb, Ap 2,23:4; funl plans, Ap 4,29:4), 1960, Ap 1,33:3
Rahman, Lincoln, 1956, Ag 12,29:4
Rahmann, Arthur H, 1958, N 2,88:4
Rahmeyer, Johannes, 1960, Jl 5,31:5
Rahn, Andrew A A D, 1948, N 27,18:2
Rahn, Bruno, 1948, S 7,25:3
Rahn, Charles S, 1950, Mr 6,21:2
Rahn, Melvin T, 1951, Ja 27,13:5
Rahn, Muriel, 1961, Ag 9,33:2
Rahn, Otto, 1957, S 28,17:4
Rahn, Theodore H, 1941, S 27,17:1
Rahn, Virgil, 1959, Ja 18,88:1
Rahner, Balbina Mrs, 1938, Ja 4,24:3
Rahnn, William A, 1955, Mr 5,17:2
Raho, Edward, 1953, Ja 10,17:4
Rahr, Chester E, 1948, My 17,19:2
Rahr, Harry F, 1948, Je 1,23:4
Rahtjen, Philip Dr, 1924, D 25,17:4
Raia, Joseph G, 1952, Ag 3,61:2
Raia, Vito L, 1938, N 22,23:4
Raible, John R, 1948, Mr 4,25:2
Raibourn, W A Capt, 1905, My 1,1:4
Raich, Paul A, 1960, D 2,29:3
Raiche, Edward, 1941, Ja 21,22:2
Raiche, James T Mrs, 1951, N 13,29:3
Raichle, Herman C, 1966, D 6,47:2
Raidiger, Bob, 1949, My 23,19:2
Raidy, Arthur F, 1951, D 16,91:2
Raidy, Arthur F Mrs, 1952, Je 20,23:5
Raiff, Isadore, 1940, Mr 8,22:3
Raifman, Herman, 1951, O 11,37:5
Raiford, F T Mrs, 1959, Jl 12,72:5
Raiford, Frazier T, 1937, Ap 20,26:1
Raihl, Peter R, 1946, F 24,44:1
Raikes, John H, 1967, My 11,54:5
Raikes, Robert, 1953, My 27,31:4
Raile, J Rev, 1949, S 7,31:7
Railett, Charles E Capt, 1917, My 5,13:6
Railey, Thomas T, 1956, D 5,39:3
Railing, Curtis B Mrs, 1952, My 8,31:5
Raill, Theodore P, 1906, Ja 4,11:4
Railsback, Walter S, 1941, F 9,47:6
Raimo, Joseph, 1961, Je 17,21:4
Raimu, Jules, 1946, S 21,15:5
Rain, Frank L, 1941, D 25,25:5
Rain, Louis C, 1957, Ag 11,81:2
Rainault, Homer C, 1944, D 15,19:3
Rainbeaux, Firmin, 1916, Jl 14,11:5
Rainbow, John R, 1950, Ja 5,26:6
Raine, Charles Daniels Dr, 1919, O 19,22:3
Raine, David L, 1958, O 28,35:3
Raine, Edward, 1911, Ap 24,9:5
Raine, Grace C Mrs, 1956, O 10,39:4
Raine, Hunter, 1922, Jl 22,7:5
Raine, Julia Mrs, 1937, S 15,23:6
Raine, Wendell P, 1952, S 14,86:2
Raine, William MacLeod, 1954, Jl 26,17:4
Rainer, Alfred, 1956, S 13,35:4
Rainer, Charles L, 1938, Ap 29,21:4
Rainer, Ferdinand Archduke, 1913, Ja 28,11:5
Raines, Arnold J, 1944, Mr 8,19:2
Raines, Attilius H (por), 1947, Ja 23,23:2
Raines, Ernest, 1951, Ja 1,17:3
Raines, George, 1908, N 28,9:5
Raines, George N, 1959, S 17,39:4
Raines, Helen B Mrs, 1949, Je 10,20:4
Raines, Ivy, 1945, Jl 18,27:2
Raines, John, 1946, D 4,31:1
Raines, Julia M, 1939, My 24,23:5
Raines, Leonora Mrs, 1952, Je 27,23:1
Raines, Thomas, 1924, Ag 12,11:3
Raines, Whitney, 1953, Jl 5,49:1
Raines, William G, 1925, Ja 8,25:5
Rainess, Clarence, 1964, Je 22,27:3
Rainey, Ernest A, 1963, Je 2,84:5
Rainey, Eugene T, 1951, Mr 5,21:1
Rainey, H T, 1934, Ag 20,1:1
Rainey, Henry T Mrs, 1945, S 29,15:5
Rainey, John M, 1947, S 15,17:4
Rainey, John W, 1923, My 9,19:4
Rainey, Julian D, 1961, Ap 1,17:4
Rainey, L Hamilton, 1937, S 10,24:1
Rainey, Morton J Mrs, 1947, S 19,23:4
Rainey, Norman (W Morison), 1960, S 13,37:1
Rainey, Paul J, 1923, S 20,4:7
Rainey, Roy A Jr, 1938, Je 10,21:2

Rainey, Samuel, 1903, N 26,7:6
Rainey, Thomas A, 1947, Ja 14,25:2
Rainey, Thomas Dr, 1910, Mr 30,12:3
Rainey, William S, 1964, S 14,37:4
Rainey, William T, 1954, O 5,27:5
Rainier, George S, 1944, My 21,44:2
Rainier, Jack A, 1965, O 12,47:1
Rainier, John T, 1940, Mr 30,15:4
Rainone, Canio Mrs, 1948, Ja 20,23:4
Rainone, G Thomas Mrs, 1967, Ag 20,88:2
Rains, Claude, 1967, My 31,43:2
Rains, Claude Mrs, 1965, Ja 1,19:5
Rains, Edward T, 1949, S 27,27:4
Rains, Fred, 1945, D 4,29:2
Rains, J S, 1880, My 25,2:7
Rains, Leon, 1954, Je 13,88:5
Rains, Leon A, 1949, Jl 21,25:2
Rains, Leon L, 1954, Jl 7,31:2
Rains, Solomon B, 1957, My 13,31:2
Rains, Solomon E, 1946, Je 17,21:5
Rainsford, G S, 1880, Je 9,3:3
Rainsford, Laurence F, 1957, Jl 6,15:2
Rainsford, Laurence Frederick Mrs, 1968, Jl 12,31:2
Rainsford, Ralph S, 1950, Ja 23,23:4
Rainsford, W S, 1933, D 18,19:1
Rainsford, William S Rev, 1923, Mr 31,13:4
Rainville, Henri B, 1937, Ag 7,15:5
Raiquel, George E, 1958, Ap 1,31:1
Rairdon, Charles B, 1961, O 16,29:4
Rais, Albert, 1939, Ap 29,17:5
Raisa, Rosa (Mrs G Rimini), 1963, O 3,35:1
Raisbeck, E A, 1933, Jl 15,11:4
Raisbeck, John E, 1937, Jl 16,19:1
Raiser, Frederick, 1951, My 12,21:5
Raiser, Victor N, 1957, My 21,35:1
Raisin, Jacob S, 1946, Ja 12,15:4
Raisin, Max, 1957, Mr 10,88:6
Raisler, Abraham, 1958, Ap 6,88:8
Raiss, Carl, 1939, Jl 20,19:1
Raiss, John, 1960, F 2,35:3
Raissman, Lazar, 1938, F 20,II,8:6
Raisz, Erwin J Dr, 1968, D 5,47:4
Rait, R, 1936, My 26,23:4
Rait, Robert, 1870, F 9,2:2
Raithel, A Christ, 1937, Je 9,25:4
Raitt, Francis J Mrs, 1949, Jl 22,19:4
Raizen, Charles S, 1967, My 15,43:3
Raiziss, George W, 1945, Jl 17,13:5
Raja, A S Thumbia, 1951, O 31,29:4
Rajadhyaksha, Ganpat S, 1955, F 10,31:5
Rajagopalan, Srinivasa, 1958, S 18,13:1
Rajawangsan, Phya, 1940, F 24,13:1
Rajchman, Henryk F, 1951, Mr 27,29:5
Rajchman, Ludwik J, 1965, Jl 25,69:1
Rajendrasinhji, Shri, 1964, Ja 2,27:1
Rajpipla, Maharajah of, 1951, Ap 30,21:3
Rakauskas, Stanley J, 1950, D 14,35:3
Rake, Frank P Jr, 1954, Jl 23,17:3
Rake, Fred, 1952, S 19,23:2
Rake, Geoffrey W, 1958, Ap 22,33:1
Rake, Margaret S Mrs, 1950, Ap 21,24:2
Raker, John H, 1941, My 9,21:4
Raker, Lewis J Mrs, 1946, Jl 24,27:2
Rakestraw, Frederick A, 1937, Ag 14,13:3
Rakestraw, Linn M, 1952, Mr 25,27:2
Rakestraw, Robert R, 1953, F 13,21:2
Rakhit, Hemendra K, 1963, D 20,26:8
Rakita, Sidney M, 1968, Ap 17,47:1
Raklios, John, 1957, N 20,35:4
Rakoczy, Adolf, 1942, Je 9,23:3
Rakosi, Matyas, 1963, Ag 14,4:3
Rakotomalala, Louis (Amb), 1968, Jl 2,26:1
Rakov, Michael D, 1955, D 11,88:6
Rakowitz, Samuel, 1950, D 29,20:3
Rakowski, Bronislaw, 1950, D 31,42:3
Raland, G A Fredrik, 1938, O 13,23:2
Ralbag, Aryeh L, 1943, Ap 13,25:4
Rale, Michael W, 1940, Jl 9,21:4
Ralea, Mihail, 1964, Ag 18,31:2
Raleigh, Cecil, 1914, N 11,13:6
Raleigh, Charles J, 1939, Ap 15,19:5
Raleigh, Gordon W, 1955, Ap 14,36:2
Raleigh, Lord (Jno Wm Strutt), 1919, Jl 2,13:3
Raleigh, Walter Sir, 1922, My 14,30:2
Raleigh, William A, 1954, Mr 1,25:5
Ralf, Torsten, 1954, Ap 28,31:4
Rall, John J, 1937, Mr 23,23:2
Ralli, Anthony P Mrs, 1953, O 12,27:6
Ralli, Constantine P, 1952, O 15,31:3
Ralli, Elaine Pandia Dr, 1968, O 8,44:1
Ralli, Pandia A, 1945, Je 8,19:4
Ralli, Paul, 1953, S 7,19:6
Rallo, Bartolo, 1965, Ja 26,37:3
Rally, Edward Bayard, 1907, D 13,11:4
Rally, Gen (Tiger of Alica), 1871, Jl 19,1:1
Ralph, Addington D Mrs, 1947, Je 20,19:1
Ralph, Albert H, 1951, Jl 29,69:1
Ralph, Arthur E, 1959, Ap 4,19:3
Ralph, Edward, 1904, F 7,7:6
Ralph, Georgia C Mrs, 1949, S 22,31:3
Ralph, Georgia G, 1956, F 6,23:5
Ralph, Guy H, 1954, Mr 24,27:4
Ralph, Guy H Mrs, 1943, Jl 30,15:2
Ralph, Henry W, 1948, F 4,23:1
Ralph, Isabel M, 1964, S 27,86:6
Ralph, Jessie (por), 1944, My 31,19:3
Ralph, Joseph E, 1922, D 31,4:2
Ralph, Julian, 1903, Ja 21,2:5
Ralph, Julian Mrs, 1912, O 8,13:5
Ralph, Katherine L, 1948, N 15,25:4
Ralph, Martin Mrs, 1945, O 21,45:1
Ralph, Matthew, 1947, Je 15,60:5
Ralph, Merle W, 1954, Mr 19,24:4
Ralph, Richard F, 1949, O 4,27:4
Ralph, Stuart H, 1956, S 8,17:4
Ralph, William E Le Grange, 1907, Jl 10,7:5
Ralph (Sister Mary Vincent), 1968, Jl 21,56:7
Ralphs, John T, 1940, Ap 18,23:2
Ralphs, Walter B, 1954, My 21,27:2
Ralston, A E, 1945, Mr 12,19:5
Ralston, Albert L, 1941, Ap 5,17:2
Ralston, Anderson W, 1948, D 6,25:5
Ralston, Arch, 1942, Jl 4,17:6
Ralston, B W Mrs, 1942, Ag 10,19:5
Ralston, Francis W Lt-Col, 1920, O 10,22:3
Ralston, Fred H, 1942, My 25,15:6
Ralston, Glenn B, 1942, O 22,21:5
Ralston, J Craig, 1954, Ag 22,93:3
Ralston, Jackson H, 1945, O 14,43:1
Ralston, James L (por), 1948, My 23,68:3
Ralston, Jobyna, 1967, Ja 23,43:3
Ralston, Lillie M, 1958, F 7,21:1
Ralston, Mary F Mrs, 1956, My 15,31:4
Ralston, Oliver C, 1965, Je 25,33:1
Ralston, Robert Judge, 1916, Ja 23,17:4
Ralston, Robert R Mrs, 1957, S 4,33:2
Ralston, Ruth A, 1946, N 6,23:2
Ralston, Samuel M Mrs, 1954, Je 26,13:6
Ralston, Samuel M Sen, 1925, O 15,23:3
Ralston, Thomas M, 1949, Ag 1,17:2
Ralston, William E, 1942, Ap 4,13:3
Ralston, William J, 1945, S 11,23:1
Ralton, Harry, 1953, Ap 4,13:6
Ralyea, John R, 1958, Ja 30,24:1
Ram, Granville, 1952, D 28,48:4
Ram, V S, 1951, Ja 14,84:6
Ramadier, Paul, 1961, O 15,88:2
Ramage, James B, 1952, N 10,25:3
Ramage, John A, 1947, D 23,24:3
Ramage, John L, 1909, F 21,7:7
Ramage, Lawrence A, 1941, N 8,19:1
Ramage, Samuel Y, 1940, Ap 16,23:5
Ramage, William, 1952, O 3,23:1
Ramagosa, Sebastian B, 1953, N 10,31:5
Ramaker, Albert J, 1946, F 14,25:3
Ramaker, Albert J Mrs, 1950, Je 28,27:3
Raman, Tirungari A, 1961, My 6,31:6
Ramazzotti, Ezio Dr, 1968, Jl 15,31:1
Rambaud, George Gibier Mrs (Jeanne Gerville-Reache), 1915, Ja 6,13:5
Rambaut, Daniel F Dr, 1937, D 1,23:2
Rambo, Charles N, 1941, F 11,24:3
Rambo, Charles N Mrs, 1948, N 6,13:5
Rambo, Eleanor F, 1955, Ap 2,17:4
Rambo, Harold S, 1955, N 3,31:5
Rambo, Katherine R, 1955, Mr 25,23:3
Rambo, Nathan R, 1952, Mr 27,29:3
Rambo, Ormond Jr, 1949, S 18,94:3
Rambo, William S, 1955, Ap 19,31:2
Rambone, Elizabeth Mrs, 1940, N 6,5:4
Rambonnet, Jean J, 1943, Ag 5,15:4
Rambova, Natacha (W Shaunessy) (will, Ag 6,15:8), 1966, Je 8,47:1
Rambusch, Frode C W, 1924, O 21,23:4
Rambusch, Frode Mrs, 1937, F 24,24:2
Ramcke, Bernhard, 1968, Jl 6,19:1
Ramdohr, Caesar A Dr, 1912, N 20,15:6
Rameau, Jean, 1942, F 25,19:2
Rameau, Themagne, 1870, N 24,5:3
Ramee, Louis C Mrs, 1947, Ag 22,15:2
Ramee, Louise de la (Ouida), 1908, Ja 26,9:3
Ramel, Emile C, 1948, Je 20,60:3
Ramel, Emile C Mrs, 1961, Ag 3,23:4
Ramelkamp, Edward W, 1961, Jl 6,29:3
Ramer, George R, 1938, Ja 16,II,9:3
Ramer, Ralph J Maj, 1937, N 29,23:5
Ramer, Walter W Sr, 1937, Ja 31,II,9:2
Ramey, Homer A, 1960, Ap 15,23:4
Ramey, John W, 1958, Mr 6,27:2
Ramig, Frederick A, 1950, O 1,104:1
Ramirez, Alfredo E, 1949, F 24,23:5
Ramirez, Clara, 1938, N 25,23:2
Ramirez, Felix G, 1956, S 17,27:3
Ramirez, Guadalupe, 1948, O 9,19:4
Ramirez, Irinarco, 1944, Mr 22,19:1
Ramirez, Jose Santos Col, 1912, Je 26,13:4
Ramirez, Joseph L Mrs, 1950, F 6,25:3
Ramirez, Juan A, 1963, Ja 7,15:1
Ramirez, Mario G, 1955, D 17,3:6
Ramirez, Maximilian A (por), 1946, Mr 5,25:3
Ramirez, Pablo, 1949, Jl 12,27:2
Ramirez, Pedro P, 1962, Je 12,37:5
Ramirez, Salvador C, 1941, D 28,28:8
Ramirez Pinto, Arturo, 1960, Mr 12,21:6
Ramish, Adolph, 1944, N 25,13:6
Ramm, Fredrik, 1943, N 17,25:1
Ramm, Henry, 1952, Ja 24,27:1
Rammens, Adolph, 1874, Mr 11,4:7
Ramon, Gaston, 1963, Je 11,37:4
Ramondou, Henri, 1912, Jl 28,II,11:5
Ramos, Angel, 1960, S 3,17:3
Ramos, Aristides, 1962, Je 23,23:1
Ramos, Arthur, 1949, N 1,27:2
Ramos, Evangelist, 1949, Je 9,32:7
Ramos, Maria V, 1954, Jl 6,23:4
Ramos Antonini, Ernesto, 1963, Ja 11,5:4
Ramos y Casellas, Ramon, 1944, Ag 4,13:4
Ramoska, Andrew, 1948, S 20,25:1
Rampe, Charles W, 1952, F 16,13:2
Rampolla del Tindaro, Mariano, 1945, O 23,17:5
Ramsay, A Milne, 1947, O 29,27:2
Ramsay, Andrew C, 1937, Ap 27,23:3
Ramsay, Andrew Mrs, 1943, D 30,17:3
Ramsay, Archibald H M, 1955, Mr 12,19:6
Ramsay, August, 1943, Ag 7,11:5
Ramsay, Austin J G, 1940, F 7,21:5
Ramsay, Beattie, 1952, O 1,33:2
Ramsay, Berlin, 1907, Je 24,7:6
Ramsay, C R Lt, 1901, Jl 14,4:6
Ramsay, Charles C, 1942, Jl 22,19:4
Ramsay, Charles S Mrs (Gertrude F), 1965, Ag 25 39:4
Ramsay, Dean, 1872, D 29,5:5
Ramsay, Douglas M Mrs, 1954, Ag 11,25:3
Ramsay, Dwight M Mrs, 1965, Jl 7,37:3
Ramsay, F P Rev, 1926, O 1,23:2
Ramsay, Francis Munroe Rear-Adm, 1914, Jl 21,9:5
Ramsay, Franklin P Jr, 1943, D 26,32:2
Ramsay, G D, 1882, My 25,5:3
Ramsay, Henrik, 1951, Jl 26,21:6
Ramsay, Herbert H (por), 1939, Ja 28,15:5
Ramsay, Ivor E S, 1956, Ja 23,9:5
Ramsay, James A, 1956, Jl 31,23:3
Ramsay, James M, 1953, Je 29,21:3
Ramsay, James Sir, 1925, F 19,19:5
Ramsay, Janet, 1940, Ja 28,26:5
Ramsay, John B, 1921, S 8,13:4
Ramsay, John L, 1946, My 18,19:5
Ramsay, John P, 1959, D 1,39:2
Ramsay, Martin M Mrs, 1957, N 24,87:3
Ramsay, Oliver W Mrs, 1950, Ag 14,17:6
Ramsay, Otto Gustaf Dr, 1914, Je 13,9:4
Ramsay, Paul H, 1960, Ja 2,13:2
Ramsay, Ted Mrs, 1946, My 30,21:3
Ramsay, Walter W, 1960, S 21,37:2
Ramsay, Werdebaugh, 1941, Ap 21,19:4
Ramsay, Wilbur H, 1871, D 11,1:2
Ramsay, William A Mrs, 1943, O 9,13:6
Ramsay, William B, 1939, F 11,15:4
Ramsay, William G Maj, 1916, S 29,13:5
Ramsay, William M, 1945, Mr 17,13:3
Ramsay, William R, 1941, Je 27,17:5
Ramsay, William Sir, 1916, Jl 24,9:6; 1939, Ap 22,
Ramsay, William Wilson, 1925, Mr 7,13:7
Ramsaye, Terry, 1954, Ag 20,19:3
Ramsbell, Edgar L, 1951, My 17,31:1
Ramsberger, Jack F, 1967, My 26,47:3
Ramsbottom, George R Mrs, 1950, My 4,27:5
Ramsburg, Charles J, 1954, Ja 18,23:2
Ramsburgh, W Dorsey, 1960, Mr 2,37:5
Ramsdale, Charles C, 1951, Ag 21,27:5
Ramsdale, Fred, 1956, Jl 3,25:4
Ramsdell, C P, 1882, S 17,9:5
Ramsdell, Charles F Mrs, 1950, N 15,31:5
Ramsdell, Clifford R, 1911, D 31,II,11:4
Ramsdell, E Benjamin, 1938, Ja 20,23:5
Ramsdell, Edwin G, 1960, Ap 14,37:3
Ramsdell, Edwin G Mrs, 1964, F 5,35:5
Ramsdell, Fred H, 1941, Ap 2,23:1
Ramsdell, Henry P Mrs, 1947, N 5,27:3
Ramsdell, Irving (Kirby), 1965, Jl 5,17:4
Ramsdell, Lon, 1950, Ag 11,19:4
Ramsdell, R L, 1927, N 4,21:5
Ramsdell, Roger G, 1968, Ap 1,45:4
Ramsdell, Sayre M, 1943, O 5,25:3
Ramsdell, Willett F, 1951, O 2,27:2
Ramsdell, William M, 1948, Ja 2,23:3
Ramsdell, William M Mrs, 1951, Mr 26,23:4
Ramsden, Eugene J S Lord, 1955, Ag 10,25:1
Ramsden, George E, 1950, Jl 18,29:5
Ramsden, Omar, 1939, Ag 15,19:5
Ramsden, Walter, 1947, Mr 27,28:3
Ramsey, Alex Ex-Gov, 1903, Ap 23,9:5
Ramsey, Andrew M, 1951, S 14,26:3
Ramsey, Charles Cyrus, 1917, Ja 12,13:3
Ramsey, Charles F, 1951, My 24,35:6
Ramsey, Charles G, 1963, D 11,47:1; 1966, D 20
Ramsey, Daniel L, 1949, Ag 23,23:1
Ramsey, David, 1954, N 19,28:7
Ramsey, David H, 1938, Jl 15,17:3
Ramsey, David J, 1963, S 11,43:1
Ramsey, Davis W C, 1939, S 3,19:2
Ramsey, DeWitt C (funl, S 10,86:3), 1961, S 8,
Ramsey, Donald J Rear-Adm, 1968, Mr 1,37:1
Ramsey, Frank De Witt Capt, 1906, Ja 20,6:3
Ramsey, Frank DeW Mrs, 1962, My 1,38:1
Ramsey, Fred F, 1952, My 18,93:1
Ramsey, George, 1939, My 20,15:6; 1950, F 12,
Ramsey, George B, 1938, Jl 5,17:5

Ramsey, George E, 1940, D 15,61:1
Ramsey, George H, 1948, D 1,30:2
Ramsey, George Mrs, 1956, Mr 7,33:3
Ramsey, George T, 1945, D 11,25:4
Ramsey, Gilbert M, 1945, O 4,23:4
Ramsey, J Bradford Jr, 1948, Ja 23,23:1
Ramsey, J Nelson, 1959, Ap 30,31:4
Ramsey, James N, 1938, Ja 18,23:2
Ramsey, James P Mrs, 1946, Jl 16,23:3
Ramsey, John E, 1939, Ap 19,23:3
Ramsey, Joseph H, 1949, F 20,60:2
Ramsey, Joseph Jr, 1916, Jl 8,9:5
Ramsey, Joseph W, 1968, Ag 25,88:7
Ramsey, Justus, 1881, Ja 27,5:4
Ramsey, Kirby, 1949, Je 23,27:5
Ramsey, L W, 1947, Ja 3,22:2
Ramsey, Maria C Mrs, 1941, F 25,23:3
Ramsey, McKinney H, 1956, Mr 3,19:1
Ramsey, Murray E, 1940, My 10,23:2
Ramsey, Murray E Mrs, 1947, Mr 21,22:3
Ramsey, Norman F, 1963, Ap 12,27:2
Ramsey, Oswald T, 1961, N 24,28:5
Ramsey, Patrick A, 1943, D 25,13:2
Ramsey, Raymond R, 1960, O 5,41:1
Ramsey, Rolla R, 1955, Je 13,23:3
Ramsey, Russell, 1942, D 28,19:4
Ramsey, Samuel D, 1940, Ag 3,15:7; 1954, Jl 2,19:4
Ramsey, Thomas Mrs, 1946, N 13,27:5
Ramsey, Thomas W, 1951, Ja 31,25:1
Ramsey, W F Mrs, 1961, O 17,39:4
Ramsey, William C, 1938, My 21,15:4
Ramsey, William T, 1937, D 13,27:5
Ramseyer, C William, 1943, N 2,25:6
Ramsin, chas L, 1951, Jl 13,21:4
Ramson, Archdeacon, 1944, My 6,15:3
Ramson, Erskine, 1953, Ag 17,15:3
Ramson, Francis Mrs, 1953, Mr 16,19:3
Ramson, Mary Mrs (will), 1952, My 29,18:5
Ramsperger, Herman G, 1940, N 19,23:3
Ramus, Ira, 1951, D 13,33:3
Ramus, Ira Mrs, 1955, O 2,87:2
Ramuz, Charles F, 1947, My 25,60:2
Ramzi, Abdelmeguid, 1944, My 4,13:3
Ramzin, Leonid K, 1948, Jl 1,23:6
Rana, Bijaya Shumshere Jung Bahadur (cor, Ja 1,2:3), 1953, D 30,4:4
Rana, Shumshere Jung Bahadur, 1961, Ap 12,41:4
Ranallo, William J, 1961, S 19,14:2
Ranavalona, Queen, 1917, My 25,11:6
Ranavalona II, Queen of Madagascar, 1883, Ag 28, 5:5
Ranc, Arthur, 1908, Ag 12,5:5
Rance, Charles A, 1967, My 3,42:5
Ranck, Dayton L, 1960, Mr 12,21:6
Ranck, Henry H, 1948, Ag 21,15:6
Ranck, Joseph A, 1951, Ja 12,27:5
Ranck, Paul S Mrs (will), 1965, My 1,24:1
Rand, Alfred Mrs (Gail), 1962, S 1,19:4
Rand, Alonzo T, 1925, N 2,23:4
Rand, Augustus S, 1948, Ag 9,19:1
Rand, B H Dr, 1883, F 16,2:5
Rand, Benjamin L, 1952, F 28,27:6
Rand, C F, 1927, Je 22,27:3
Rand, Carleton B, 1951, My 13,31:1
Rand, Charles E Mrs, 1947, N 25,32:2
Rand, Charles Franklin Dr, 1908, O 14,9:5
Rand, Charles L, 1940, Mr 13,23:5
Rand, Christopher Temple Emmet, 1968, S 27,47:1
Rand, Clifford A Sr, 1967, F 7,39:1
Rand, E D Mrs (will), 1905, O 11,1:2
Rand, Edgar E, 1907, Ap 29,9:6; 1955, O 27,68:1
Rand, Edson R, 1959, Jl 10,25:5
Rand, Edward A Rev, 1903, O 7,2:4
Rand, Edward K, 1945, O 29,19:2
Rand, Edward S, 1954, Jl 26,17:3
Rand, Egbert, 1925, Ag 21,13:6
Rand, Ellen E Mrs, 1941, D 19,25:1
Rand, Ellsworth Mrs, 1966, Je 18,31:4
Rand, Frank C (will, D 31,16:7), 1949, D 4,108:5
Rand, Frederick E, 1942, O 7,25:5
Rand, George Curtis, 1907, My 14,11:4
Rand, George F (por), 1942, N 20,23:1
Rand, George W Maj, 1904, Ja 20,9:5
Rand, Henry H, 1948, Je 16,29:3; 1962, Ja 19,31:1
Rand, Herman, 1968, Ap 16,44:2
Rand, Jacob H, 1962, Je 1,27:1
Rand, James H Sr (por), 1944, S 17,41:1
Rand, James Henry, 1968, Je 4,47:1
Rand, Jasper, 1909, Ap 1,9:5
Rand, John Gough, 1873, Ja 25,8:5
Rand, John H Mrs, 1960, Ja 12,47:2
Rand, John L, 1942, N 20,23:4
Rand, Lionel (L Van Clouser), 1942, O 16,19:5
Rand, Mary M Mrs, 1941, D 3,25:1
Rand, Nelson R Rev, 1937, D 18,21:6
Rand, Richard F, 1960, Ja 20,31:4
Rand, Robert C, 1949, Jl 21,25:2
Rand, Robert C Mrs, 1964, Ap 4,28:6
Rand, Rosalie C Mrs, 1937, N 11,25:3
Rand, Rufus R, 1921, Ap 16,11:5
Rand, Samuel, 1950, Je 24,13:3
Rand, Stephen Rear-Adm, 1915, Jl 13,11:5
Rand, W, 1931, F 11,25:1
Rand, W H Dr, 1925, Je 24,17:4
Rand, Wilberforce J, 1956, O 28,89:1
Rand, William, 1947, Je 13,24:2; 1965, My 4,43:2
Rand, William B, 1956, Jl 11,29:6
Rand, William H, 1915, Je 22,15:5
Rand, William Wilberforce Rev Dr, 1909, Mr 4,9:5
Randa, Charles A, 1952, Je 4,27:4
Randak, Arthur S, 1959, My 6,39:2
Randall, A W, 1872, Jl 26,5:6
Randall, Albert B (por), 1945, D 4,29:1
Randall, Albert E, 1944, O 28,15:4
Randall, Alex, 1951, N 19,23:1
Randall, Alexander, 1881, N 22,5:2
Randall, Alfred G, 1939, Ap 11,24:2
Randall, Alice M, 1943, Mr 31,19:4
Randall, Allan B, 1958, O 4,21:2
Randall, Annie Mrs, 1961, Ag 22,29:1
Randall, Arthur G, 1953, N 9,35:5
Randall, Bishop (funl, O 8,5:4), 1873, S 29,5:2
Randall, Blanchard, 1942, Ag 25,23:5
Randall, Blanchard Mrs, 1937, F 28,II,8:6
Randall, Caroline P H Mrs, 1942, Jl 15,19:4
Randall, Charles, 1923, Ag 11,9:3
Randall, Charles P (will, Je 9,23:2), 1939, My 31, 23:5
Randall, Clarence B (trb, Ag 7,28:2), 1967, Ag 6,1:2
Randall, Clyde S, 1942, S 9,23:5
Randall, Cynthia Mrs, 1948, Ag 22,63:4
Randall, David J, 1945, F 7,21:1; 1957, N 15,8:5
Randall, E W, 1940, Ag 21,19:5
Randall, Edmund B, 1962, My 8,39:3
Randall, Edwin J, 1962, Je 14,33:3
Randall, Edwin M, 1939, Je 29,23:3
Randall, Ernest R, 1956, D 23,31:1
Randall, Frank A Mrs, 1955, Mr 4,23:3
Randall, Frank E, 1915, S 16,11:4; 1941, Ja 12,45:2
Randall, Frank L, 1921, Ag 7,22:5
Randall, Franklin C, 1955, O 25,33:3
Randall, Fred C, 1954, Ag 29,89:1
Randall, Fred G (por), 1939, D 27,21:1
Randall, Frederick W, 1943, Mr 24,23:4
Randall, G Ward Sr, 1955, Ap 23,19:3
Randall, George, 1960, Ap 18,29:1
Randall, George M Gen, 1918, Je 15,11:5
Randall, George P, 1962, Je 3,88:3
Randall, Harry D, 1944, D 30,11:4
Randall, Henry Capt, 1874, Jl 9,4:7
Randall, Henry L, 1947, F 20,25:4
Randall, Herbert D, 1951, My 27,68:5
Randall, I Newton, 1950, N 11,15:1
Randall, Ira S, 1951, O 8,21:2
Randall, James B, 1942, Jl 26,31:1
Randall, James C, 1941, Ag 20,19:6
Randall, James Garfield Prof, 1953, F 22,61:1
Randall, James Ryder, 1908, Ja 15,9:6
Randall, Jay M, 1948, S 26,77:1
Randall, John B, 1955, Ap 23,19:3
Randall, John H, 1946, My 17,21:2; 1957, Je 17,23:4
Randall, John J, 1943, My 1,15:4
Randall, John T, 1944, F 21,15:2
Randall, Josiah, 1866, S 11,5:2
Randall, Josiah Mrs, 1880, My 28,3:6
Randall, Karl C, 1944, D 5,23:4
Randall, Ken, 1947, Je 18,25:1
Randall, Kennedy Sr, 1947, F 4,26:2
Randall, Leo, 1952, N 1,21:5
Randall, Leon B, 1953, Jl 6,17:4
Randall, Mable, 1939, Jl 23,29:2
Randall, Martha, 1918, Je 22,11:6
Randall, Mary B, 1939, O 16,19:4
Randall, Mary E, 1949, N 24,31:3
Randall, Maurice W, 1947, Ap 19,15:2
Randall, Merle, 1950, Mr 18,13:4
Randall, Murray W, 1964, S 11,33:2
Randall, Neal D, 1947, Jl 20,45:2
Randall, Otis E, 1946, Ag 12,21:4
Randall, Paul K, 1959, F 3,31:2
Randall, Phineas B, 1941, My 23,21:2
Randall, Raymond, 1951, Ap 9,25:4
Randall, Raymond Col, 1968, Mr 24,92:7
Randall, Richard, 1913, O 18,13:4
Randall, Robert H, 1966, S 2,31:4
Randall, Rosewell Gen, 1871, Ag 21,4:1
Randall, Rowena Mrs, 1938, F 6,II,9:2
Randall, S J, 1890, Ap 14,1:7
Randall, S S, 1881, Je 4,5:1
Randall, Stephen M, 1909, My 4,9:4
Randall, W P Comr, 1904, F 22,5:6
Randall, Wayne L, 1967, Mr 3,35:4
Randall, William, 1937, Jl 19,15:3; 1939, Ap 23,III,7:1
Randall, William B, 1940, Mr 17,51:1
Randall, William B Mrs, 1956, Je 20,31:2
Randall, William J, 1925, N 17,25:3
Randall, William S, 1949, Ag 15,17:5
Randall, Wilmot, 1947, S 21,60:5
Randall-MacIver, David (por), 1945, My 1,23:1
Randall-MacIver, David Mrs, 1961, My 17,37:2
Randall-Mills, Horace A W, 1958, Mr 2,88:8
Randau, Clem J, 1954, S 22,29:3
Randazzo, Joseph, 1944, Ag 28,11:5
Randazzo, Joseph A, 1943, Jl 25,30:8
Randebrock, Ernest Mrs, 1952, N 30,88:5
Randegger, Alberto, 1911, D 18,11:4
Randegger, Guiseppe, 1946, D 1,78:2
Randel, Andreas, 1952, Je 22,68:8
Randel, Frank H Mrs, 1947, O 7,27:2
Randel, Samuel, 1955, Mr 24,31:4
Randell, James W Mrs, 1906, D 6,9:4
Randell, Rufus, 1925, Je 16,21:3
Randle, C Wilson, 1964, S 29,43:4
Randle, Harry T, 1967, D 23,23:3
Randle, John W Mrs, 1960, S 17,23:6
Randle, Thomas P, 1950, Je 7,29:5
Randle, Thurman, 1957, F 4,19:2
Randles, Arthur Mrs, 1954, Mr 30,27:3
Randles, Earl C, 1948, Je 6,72:6
Randles, Patricia A, 1958, My 15,19:1
Randles, Patrick J, 1944, S 26,23:4
Randlett, Clarence W, 1945, F 20,19:3
Randlett, Oran J, 1938, F 9,19:2
Randol, James Butterworth, 1903, D 24,9:5
Randolph, A Phillip Mrs, 1963, Ap 15,29:4
Randolph, Alan F Mrs, 1942, O 9,21:4
Randolph, Amanda, 1967, Ag 25,35:4
Randolph, Anne P, 1949, My 4,29:3
Randolph, Anthony J, 1965, O 25,37:2
Randolph, Archibald C, 1960, N 29,37:1
Randolph, Bessie C, 1966, Jl 3,35:2
Randolph, Briant W F, 1939, N 29,23:1
Randolph, Carman Fitz, 1920, O 14,13:1
Randolph, Carolina R, 1958, Mr 2,88:5
Randolph, Catherine F, 1913, O 10,11:4
Randolph, Charles C, 1937, N 8,23:3
Randolph, Charles P Jr, 1937, D 2,25:5
Randolph, Daniel F, 1942, My 29,17:2
Randolph, Edmund, 1922, F 19,22:3
Randolph, Edmund Dutilh, 1919, D 22,15:3
Randolph, Edward, 1918, O 12,13:3
Randolph, Edward F, 1955, My 27,23:3
Randolph, Edward S F, 1951, D 22,15:3
Randolph, Edward T, 1955, Mr 8,27:4
Randolph, Elwood H, 1950, D 28,25:2
Randolph, Epes, 1921, Ag 24,11:4
Randolph, George W, 1867, Ap 5,5:2
Randolph, H, 1927, Jl 7,25:5
Randolph, Hanna F, 1913, O 10,11:4
Randolph, Harry F, 1957, D 5,35:2
Randolph, Henry W, 1942, S 29,23:5
Randolph, Herbert Jr Mrs, 1947, Ja 31,23:3
Randolph, Hollins N, 1938, My 1,II,7:3
Randolph, Howard S F, 1956, Ap 30,23:5
Randolph, Isham, 1920, Ag 4,11:3
Randolph, J, 1877, Je 3,12:2
Randolph, J F Mrs (sister of), 1903, Mr 20,9:7
Randolph, J F Mrs, 1903, Mr 20,9:7
Randolph, John, 1939, N 5,49:3; 1949, Ag 8,15:2; 1954, N 18,33:3
Randolph, John G, 1962, Jl 4,21:4
Randolph, John Joseph Fitz, 1911, D 11,11:3
Randolph, John R, 1967, Ja 27,45:3
Randolph, John W (mem ser set, Je 23,25:4; held, Je 24,21:3), 1961, Je 22,31:4
Randolph, Larned D Mrs, 1937, D 7,25:4
Randolph, Lewis Van Syckle, 1921, Ja 3,15:6
Randolph, Lothrop, 1923, Ja 26,17:4
Randolph, M J, 1876, Ap 4,8:4
Randolph, Milton, 1954, D 5,89:1
Randolph, Mortimer Fitz Mrs, 1919, D 27,9:5
Randolph, Nelson C N Dr, 1907, Ap 27,9:6
Randolph, Norman, 1953, My 17,89:2
Randolph, Oliver, 1951, S 3,13:5
Randolph, Oliver W, 1956, F 4,19:2
Randolph, Orville F, 1942, N 9,23:6
Randolph, Otto C F, 1938, My 10,21:3
Randolph, Phil S P Sr (will, Je 20,14:5), 1940, Ja 7, 49:2
Randolph, Philip S P, 1962, Jl 11,36:1
Randolph, R F, 1883, N 11,1:6
Randolph, R J, 1877, Ap 18,2:4
Randolph, Ralph C, 1946, O 28,27:4
Randolph, Richard W, 1939, Je 29,23:6
Randolph, Robert C, 1966, Ja 8,25:2
Randolph, Robert I, 1951, O 25,29:3
Randolph, Robert J Mrs, 1948, Ja 6,23:6
Randolph, Robert L, 1944, O 27,24:2; 1952, N 30,88:7
Randolph, Robert Lee Dr, 1919, D 13,13:3
Randolph, Robert M, 1956, Je 2,19:4
Randolph, T E F, 1905, Ja 29,7:6
Randolph, T F, 1883, N 8,2:5
Randolph, Thomas H, 1968, My 22,47:4
Randolph, Thomas Jefferson Maj, 1872, Ag 10,1:6
Randolph, Verne C, 1937, D 18,21:3
Randolph, Virgil P, 1942, Ja 16,21:5
Randolph, Virginia E, 1958, Mr 18,29:2
Randolph, Walter B, 1950, N 28,31:4
Randolph, William Fitzhugh, 1914, Ag 1,9:6
Randolph, William H, 1951, O 21,93:2
Randolph, William H Mrs, 1941, Ja 29,17:5
Randolph, William M Mrs, 1958, Mr 18,29:1
Randolph, Wilson F, 1968, Ja 24,42:3
Randolph, Woodruff, 1966, O 26,47:4
Randolph, Woodruff Mrs, 1947, Jl 25,17:2
Ranen, Ellis (por), 1946, Mr 29,23:3
Raney, Bates O, 1968, Ag 31,23:5
Raney, Glenn, 1965, Ag 14,8:3
Raney, Jackson A, 1963, Ap 3,47:3

Raney, James R, 1951, My 11,27:2
Raney, Murray, 1966, Mr 5,27:5
Raney, Rupert B, 1959, N 30,31:4
Raney, Thomas J, 1949, F 2,27:5
Raney, Thomas J Jr, 1965, Ag 14,8:3
Raney, Thomas J Jr Mrs, 1965, Ag 14,8:3
Ranft, Earl F, 1966, S 25,76:4
Ranft, Joseph L, 1937, Je 24,25:2
Ranfurly-Challice, Miriam, 1937, N 6,17:4
Rangecroft, Benjamin, 1950, D 4,29:5
Rangeler, W F, 1949, Jl 1,19:5
Ranger, Henry Ward, 1916, N 8,13:5
Ranger, Richard H, 1962, Ja 12,23:4
Ranger, Walter E, 1941, N 5,23:4
Ranghet, Iosif, 1952, S 3,29:3
Ranglack, Clarence J, 1952, S 27,17:3
Rango, Patrick Mrs, 1958, Mr 25,33:4
Rangsit, Prince of Chainat, 1951, Mr 8,29:4
Rangstroem, Ture, 1947, My 13,26:3
Ranjitsinhji, Shree, 1949, S 10,17:5
Rank, Arthur I Sr, 1963, N 3,88:3
Rank, Beata H Mrs, 1967, Ap 14,39:4
Rank, Ira M, 1940, O 17,26:3
Rank, James V, 1952, Ja 4,40:3
Rank, Joseph (por), 1943, N 15,19:5
Rank, Levin, 1951, Ap 3,27:5
Rank, Otto (por), 1939, N 1,23:1
Rank, Patricia Mrs (will), 1955, Ja 7,9:3
Ranke, L von, 1886, My 24,5:2
Rankeillour, Lady, 1938, Ap 26,21:5
Rankeillour, Lord (J F Hope), 1949, F 15,23:4
Rankeillour, Lord (A O J Hope), 1958, My 27,31:3
Ranken, David Jr, 1910, Ag 19,9:5
Ranken, Harold R, 1954, S 15,33:5
Ranken, John M, 1907, O 16,9:5
Ranker, Bernard, 1942, Ja 13,19:2
Rankin, Alex, 1937, S 9,23:4; 1951, N 1,29:4
Rankin, Arthur, 1947, Mr 24,25:5
Rankin, C W, 1936, F 7,19:1
Rankin, Capt, 1871, Je 15,1:3
Rankin, Charles, 1951, My 26,17:5
Rankin, Charles W Mrs, 1945, F 2,19:2
Rankin, Edward E, 1949, Ag 8,15:5
Rankin, Edward P Rev, 1937, Ap 13,25:4
Rankin, Edward S, 1945, Mr 9,19:5
Rankin, Egbert Guernsey Dr, 1922, N 27,15:3
Rankin, Emmett W, 1954, S 5,50:6
Rankin, Evelyn W Mrs, 1944, My 2,19:6
Rankin, Fred E, 1946, S 4,24:2
Rankin, Fred J, 1940, My 21,23:5
Rankin, Fred W, 1954, Mr 23,89:1
Rankin, Frederic, 1905, O 20,9:6
Rankin, George, 1946, Ap 9,27:3
Rankin, George D, 1953, Je 25,27:2; 1955, F 11,23:4
Rankin, George D Mrs, 1947, Mr 4,25:3
Rankin, George Jr, 1949, My 8,76:6
Rankin, Helena Mrs (cor, Ja 15,8:5), 1955, Ja 8,30:2
Rankin, Henry W, 1947, Mr 16,60:1
Rankin, Herman Mrs, 1955, O 21,27:2
Rankin, Hilda M, 1954, Jl 15,27:6
Rankin, Hugh, 1938, Je 20,15:5
Rankin, J C, 1903, Mr 21,9:5
Rankin, J Douglas, 1951, S 7,29:4
Rankin, J Duncan Mrs, 1938, My 10,21:5; 1954, N 2, 27:6
Rankin, James B, 1946, Je 28,21:2
Rankin, James R Mrs, 1958, S 7,86:3
Rankin, James W, 1951, Ag 31,15:2
Rankin, John Dr, 1921, D 23,13:6
Rankin, John E (funl plans, N 28,31:2), 1960, N 27, 86:1
Rankin, John H, 1952, Je 22,68:3
Rankin, John Hall Lt, 1916, Mr 20,11:5
Rankin, John K Col, 1913, O 30,9:3
Rankin, John M, 1947, Je 21,17:4
Rankin, Leonard S, 1949, F 20,60:5
Rankin, Louise S Mrs, 1951, N 22,31:1
Rankin, M Theron, 1953, Je 28,61:2
Rankin, McKee (funl, Ap 23,13:6), 1914, Ap 18,11:5
Rankin, McKee Mrs (Kitty Blanchard),(funl, D 17,-13:4), 1911, D 15,13:5
Rankin, Percy Mrs, 1953, Jl 17,17:6
Rankin, R G, 1878, Ag 30,5:5
Rankin, R Rush, 1949, Ag 21,69:3
Rankin, Rebecca B, 1965, Mr 3,41:1
Rankin, Renville S, 1960, Je 8,39:4
Rankin, Richard H, 1948, O 15,23:3
Rankin, Robert G, 1966, N 30,47:2
Rankin, Russell G, 1967, Jl 1,23:3
Rankin, Samuel M, 1938, Ag 9,19:3
Rankin, Walker Mrs, 1948, F 14,13:5
Rankin, Walter M, 1947, My 26,21:1
Rankin, Wellington D, 1966, Je 6,41:4
Rankin, William, 1912, O 21,11:6
Rankin, William A J, 1942, D 20,45:1
Rankin, William B, 1940, Ag 14,19:4
Rankin, William H, 1919, D 18,13:2; 1939, Je 4,49:2; 1957, Ap 1,25:2
Rankin, William J, 1945, S 17,19:3
Rankine, Alex O, 1956, Ja 21,21:3
Rankine, Isabella Mathewson Dr, 1921, S 28,19:5
Rankine, Jennie W Mrs, 1942, Mr 10,19:4
Rankine, William Birch, 1905, O 1,9:6

Rankins, M, 1877, Je 28,5:1
Ranlett, David L, 1944, Ja 26,19:4
Rannells, Benjamin U, 1950, O 27,29:1
Rannels, Elizabeth D, 1955, D 21,29:3
Rannenberg, W, 1932, Ja 29,17:5
Ranney, A Elliott, 1938, Je 22,23:3
Ranney, A H Mrs, 1946, My 16,21:3
Ranney, Ambrose L, 1905, D 2,9:5
Ranney, Archie H, 1948, F 22,48:3
Ranney, Arthur E Mrs, 1951, N 6,29:6
Ranney, Edward C, 1946, Ap 2,27:3
Ranney, Elizabeth B Mrs, 1940, Ap 1,19:3
Ranney, George A (por), 1947, Ag 17,52:5
Ranney, H D Dr, 1879, Ja 13,5:4
Ranney, Harr F, 1955, Jl 1,21:5
Ranney, John C, 1950, Ja 7,17:4
Ranney, Joseph P, 1941, Ja 2,23:2
Ranney, Lafayette, 1883, F 16,2:5
Ranney, Leo, 1950, S 19,31:1
Ranney, Willet B, 1949, F 11,23:4
Ranney, Winthrop R, 1951, S 21,24:4
Ranno, Mariano, 1965, Ap 1,35:4
Rannus, Waldemar A, 1944, N 29,23:5
Ranous, Rodney, 1940, Ap 25,23:1
Ransahoff, Nicholas B Mrs, 1941, Ag 20,19:2
Ransbottom, Frank M, 1937, Mr 1,19:3
Ranscht, Frederick Mrs, 1951, Ag 3,21:6
Ranscht, Theodore C, 1960, Jl 7,31:5
Ransdell, Daniel Moore Col, 1912, N 29,15:5
Ransdell, Joseph E, 1954, Jl 28,23:3
Ransdorf, William, 1957, N 19,33:1
Ransford, Carroll F, 1955, Mr 16,33:4
Ranshofen-Wertheimer, Egon F, 1957, D 28,17:6
Ransiear, Almond, 1948, Ap 28,27:4
Ransier, Julian, 1948, N 9,27:2
Ransier, Julian Mrs, 1948, N 12,23:2
Ransley, David W, 1955, F 21,21:2
Ransley, Harry C, 1941, N 7,24:4
Ransohoff, Fred, 1942, S 6,30:6
Ransohoff, Fred Mrs, 1949, Jl 19,29:5
Ransohoff, J Louis, 1958, Je 18,33:6
Ransohoff, James B Sr, 1951, My 26,17:4
Ransohoff, Joseph Dr, 1921, Mr 11,15:5
Ransohoff, Nathan, 1956, S 26,33:4
Ransohoff, Nicholas S, 1951, Ap 26,29:1
Ransom, Alfred L, 1946, Ap 25,21:1
Ransom, Brayton H Dr, 1925, S 19,15:5
Ransom, Charles C Dr, 1910, S 14,9:6
Ransom, E G, 1903, Ag 21,9:6
Ransom, Elmer I, 1942, O 29,23:5
Ransom, Elmer P, 1942, F 3,19:4
Ransom, Elmer P Mrs, 1959, Mr 6,25:4
Ransom, Frank M Mrs, 1954, Ag 25,27:5
Ransom, Frank McN, 1965, Ja 1,17:2
Ransom, Gen, 1864, N 1,5:6
Ransom, George C, 1941, Ag 20,19:1
Ransom, H L, 1940, Jl 23,19:2
Ransom, Harriet Mrs, 1925, O 18,5:1
Ransom, Harry E, 1942, N 3,23:1
Ransom, Henry N, 1951, D 26,25:4
Ransom, J Clinton, 1938, D 4,60:7
Ransom, James, 1941, D 31,17:2
Ransom, James H, 1940, My 31,19:6
Ransom, Julius C, 1953, D 9,11:4
Ransom, Julius E Dr, 1923, Mr 16,17:5
Ransom, Lewis E, 1923, Mr 21,19:5
Ransom, Manley, 1940, F 5,18:2
Ransom, Mary H, 1939, Mr 22,23:5
Ransom, Matt W, 1904, O 9,9:5
Ransom, Neale, 1955, Mr 1,25:1
Ransom, Nelson Mrs, 1951, O 20,15:3
Ransom, Orlando B, 1950, Ja 8,77:2
Ransom, Rastus Seneca, 1914, D 21,9:4
Ransom, Rebecca Aldrich Mrs, 1922, Ja 18,17:3
Ransom, S, 1881, Ap 11,5:6
Ransom, Samuel R, 1941, Je 25,21:2
Ransom, Stephen B Mrs, 1950, Ap 27,29:1
Ransom, Susan D Mrs, 1941, Mr 15,17:4
Ransom, Thomas W, 1947, Jl 15,23:3
Ransom, William A, 1941, Mr 4,23:5
Ransom, William A Mrs, 1948, My 25,27:5
Ransom, William E, 1950, Mr 31,32:2
Ransom, William L (por), 1949, F 20,60:1
Ransom, William L Mrs, 1941, Ap 3,23:5
Ransome, Amy C Mrs, 1942, Ag 16,45:4
Ransome, Arthur, 1967, Je 6,44:3
Ransome, Violet J, 1963, N 5,31:1
Ranson, Ambrose Gen, 1872, D 22,1:1
Ranson, George B Rear-Adm, 1924, F 26,17:3
Ranson, Harriott W Mrs, 1942, Mr 30,17:1
Ranson, Jo, 1965, Jl 28,35:1
Ranson, John, 1952, O 18,19:6
Ranson, Louis Mrs, 1964, N 18,47:3
Ranson, Ronald, 1947, D 3,29:4
Ranson, Stephen W, 1942, Ag 31,17:4
Ranson, William I, 1954, Ap 4,43:2
Rantoul, Edward L, 1944, S 2,11:6
Rantoul, Neal Mrs, 1947, N 8,17:4
Rantoul, William G, 1949, Je 11,17:4
Ranung, Christen, 1950, Ja 16,26:2
Ranzato, Virgilio, 1937, Ap 20,25:3
Ranzow, Maria, 1953, N 6,27:3
Rao, Anthony, 1954, Jl 11,72:4

Rao, Dominick, 1956, Je 19,29:3
Rao, E Raghavenddra, 1942, Je 16,23:4
Rao, Joseph (Joey), 1962, My 11,18:1
Rao, Vincent, 1937, S 10,23:3
Raoul, William P, 1954, Jl 28,23:1
Rapacz, Max P, 1964, Ag 14,27:4
Rapalee, Hettie H Mrs, 1952, Mr 9,93:1
Rapalee, Weldon, 1946, Ap 22,21:5
Rapalje, De Witt, 1950, Je 25,68:3
Rapallo, C A Judge, 1887, D 29,5:3
Rapallo, Edna, 1942, Jl 30,21:2
Rapallo, Edward S, 1937, Ag 13,17:6
Rapaport, Barney, 1961, Ja 17,37:3
Rapaport, David, 1960, D 16,38:3
Rapaport, Jacob, 1943, Jl 28,15:2
Rapaport, Joseph, 1955, F 26,15:3
Rapaport, Max, 1955, N 9,33:5
Rapaport, Meyer Mrs, 1964, D 28,29:2
Rapee, Erno (por), 1945, Je 27,19:3
Rapelje, John Malcolm, 1925, Ja 21,21:5
Rapelje, Walter S, 1956, Ag 17,19:4
Rapell, Bruno Mrs, 1955, F 24,27:4
Rapelye, Elijah P, 1938, Jl 11,17:5
Rapelye, George L, 1957, O 26,21:6
Rapelye, Gertrude V Mrs, 1939, Ap 28,25:3
Rapelye, John A, 1944, Mr 27,19:5
Rapelye, Martin S Mrs, 1940, Ja 25,21:3
Raper, Charles L, 1957, D 29,48:5
Raper, Henry S, 1951, D 14,31:5
Raper, James A, 1948, Je 25,23:2
Raper, John W, 1950, D 13,35:5
Rapf, Arthur M, 1964, F 18,35:1
Rapf, Eliza Mrs, 1945, D 4,29:4
Rapf, Harry (por), 1949, F 7,19:1
Rapf, Joe, 1939, Ja 31,21:1
Rapfogel, Abran B Mrs, 1946, Jl 14,38:1
Raphael, Albert A, 1960, Ap 5,37:4
Raphael, Angus M, 1963, Ag 7,33:4
Raphael, Arthur M, 1952, Je 8,86:4
Raphael, B I, 1880, Mr 19,3:5
Raphael, Enid (Mrs S Katz), 1964, Mr 7,23:4
Raphael, Louis R, 1955, My 29,44:3
Raphael, Otto (por), 1937, S 1,17:3
Raphael, Ralph L, 1938, S 16,22:4
Raphael, Ralphael, 1942, N 24,25:2
Raphael, Sidney O Mrs, 1957, Ap 15,29:5
Raphael, Sol, 1943, F 25,21:3
Raphael, William M, 1947, D 28,40:4
Raphaelian, Harry M, 1966, My 3,47:2
Raphall, Alfred M, 1903, Je 21,7:6
Raphel, Henry J, 1948, D 22,23:4
Raphelson, Harry A, 1940, Je 25,12:4
Raphold, Amelia, 1921, Mr 29,15:3
Rapier, John L Col, 1905, My 8,9:5
Rapier, Stephen A, 1964, F 17,31:3
Rapion, Bernard, 1952, S 9,31:2
Rapisardi, Fernanda, 1960, Ja 12,47:2
Rapisardi, Mario, 1912, Ja 5,13:3
Rapley, Edward E, 1946, Jl 31,27:4
Rapnel, William, 1945, Ag 28,19:1
Rapoli, Elizabeth M, 1950, Ag 15,29:2
Rapoport, Boris, 1948, My 5,25:2
Rapoport, Boris Mrs (Eda), 1968, My 12,85:1
Rapoport, Gerson G, 1966, F 28,27:5
Rapoport, Harry, 1960, My 31,31:3; 1967, My 30,
Rapoport, Jack, 1963, D 12,39:4
Rapoport, Joseph, 1951, Ap 1,92:6
Rapoport, Maurice, 1952, Jl 1,23:3
Rapoport, Milton, 1963, My 4,25:4
Rapoport, Yakov D, 1962, Jl 4,21:3
Raport, Frederick J, 1948, Jl 28,23:3
Raposo, Bettencourt Dr, 1937, Jl 4,II,6:7
Rapoza, Simoes, 1948, Jl 9,19:5
Rapp, Arthur (Father Dominic), 1960, Ja 31,92:
Rapp, Bernard, 1966, Jl 1,35:3
Rapp, David J, 1957, N 21,30:3
Rapp, Frederic E, 1959, Ag 11,27:4
Rapp, Helen N Mrs, 1937, Mr 25,25:2
Rapp, Henry, 1947, S 1,19:5
Rapp, Herbert A, 1964, Jl 28,29:5
Rapp, John W, 1922, Ag 18,13:4
Rapp, Reuben B, 1968, Jl 6,21:4
Rapp, Roy I, 1942, My 2,13:4
Rapp, Rudolph, 1955, F 1,29:4
Rapp, Ryan, 1950, F 1,29:3
Rapp, Theresa Mrs, 1937, Mr 12,23:2
Rapp, William C, 1949, My 9,25:4
Rapp, William J, 1942, Ag 13,19:3; 1965, D 21,3
Rapp, William M Mrs, 1939, Ja 1,25:2
Rappaport, Aaron B, 1964, S 2,37:4
Rappaport, Arthur, 1952, Ja 25,21:1
Rappaport, Charles, 1941, N 22,19:2
Rappaport, Harry, 1955, Je 16,35:5
Rappaport, Julius Dr, 1937, Ap 22,23:4
Rappaport, Melville L, 1954, Ja 16,15:5
Rappaport, S, 1920, N 11,13:5
Rappard, Anthon G A van, 1946, Je 1,13:6
Rappard, William E, 1958, Ap 30,33:1
Rappart, Hugo, 1966, Mr 8,39:4
Rappe, Amedius Bp (see also S 10,12), 1877, S
Rappe, Harold T, 1963, Jl 19,25:1
Rappeport, Hyman, 1940, Ap 18,23:5
Rappleyea, Guy, 1943, S 26,48:1

Rappold, Julius Caesar Dr, 1924, S 7,31:3
Rappold, Marie, 1957, My 14,35:3
Rappold, Regina Mrs, 1939, Jl 30,26:6
Rappoport, Angelo S, 1950, Je 4,92:3
Rappoport, Nathan H, 1943, Je 26,13:3
Rapport, Adolph M, 1940, D 18,25:5
Rapport, Ann, 1960, Je 7,35:4
Rapport, David M, 1953, Ap 17,25:2
Rapport, Helena, 1954, D 10,27:2
Rapport, Samuel, 1938, Ja 7,19:1
Rapps, Hyman D, 1950, Mr 5,92:6
Rapps, Max Mrs, 1947, Jl 11,15:4
Rappuhn, Albert, 1953, S 20,86:5
Raprager, James H, 1962, Ap 20,27:1
Raps, Henry G, 1967, Ja 25,43:3
Rapsher, William H, 1949, F 11,23:2
Rapson, Edward J, 1937, O 4,21:5
Rarcher, Nellie Mrs, 1924, Je 23,19:3
Rardin, Claude S, 1956, Ag 3,19:2
Rareshide, Lizzie W Mrs, 1937, Ja 3,II,8:2
Rareshide, Shepard (por), 1938, D 19,23:4
Rarey, C Donald, 1939, Je 17,15:4
Rarey, John S, 1866, O 8,5:2
Rarick, Alfred, 1956, D 20,29:2
Rarick, Clarence E, 1941, Ag 2,15:6
Rarick, Donald C, 1968, S 18,47:3
Ras Alula, Abyssinian Chief, 1897, F 27,9:1
Rasbach, James C, 1947, O 28,25:2
Rasbury, Ed L, 1951, F 5,23:4
Rascey, Charles A, 1950, D 4,29:5
Rasch, Albertina (Mrs D Tiomkin), 1967, O 6,39:1
Rasch, Frederick J, 1937, Je 29,21:2
Rasch, Simon (por), 1941, My 19,17:6
Raschdau, Ludwig, 1943, Ag 26,17:4
Rasche, William H, 1951, My 10,31:5
Raschkover, David, 1958, N 5,35:1
Rasco, David, 1955, Ap 29,23:2
Rasco, Manuel Jr, 1963, N 20,43:5
Rascoe, Burton, 1957, Mr 20,37:3
Rascoe, David, 1951, S 2,48:8
Rascoe, James B, 1943, D 23,19:2
Rascoff, Henry, 1957, O 7,27:3
Rascovar, Abraham S, 1914, Jl 2,9:6
Rascovar, Edward, 1924, Jl 2,19:5
Rascovar, H, 1927, O 30,17:1
Rascovar, James, 1916, S 27,11:6
Rascovar, Louis (will), 1954, My 15,17:7
Rascovich, Mark B, 1939, My 9,23:2
Raseley, Charles W Sr, 1953, Ag 27,25:2
Rasely, George E, 1965, Ja 5,33:5
Rasely, Homer H, 1950, D 31,43:1
Raser, Albert A, 1946, Je 19,21:2
Raser, John B, 1939, F 15,23:1
Raser, Thomas J Sr, 1953, Ag 30,88:8
Rasera, Dioniesio Mrs, 1951, D 20,31:2
Rash, Frank D, 1946, Ap 20,13:5
Rash, John B, 1949, N 29,29:4
Rash, Louis B Sr, 1951, Ap 6,25:3
Rash, Wilbur J, 1941, Jl 2,21:4
Rashdall, Hastings Rev, 1924, F 10,23:1
Rashkis, Lillian L Mrs, 1959, N 27,29:1
Rashkis, Teresa W, 1951, Ag 15,27:2
Rashkoff, Ben, 1954, Mr 15,25:4
Rashmajian, Hamayag Mrs, 1947, Jl 6,40:7
Rasi, Accursio, 1950, F 22,29:4
Rasi, Hazimeh S, 1956, S 6,25:4
Rasin, I Freeman, 1907, Mr 10,9:7
Rasin, Thomas M, 1910, Ap 15,9:4
Rasin, William, 1957, N 9,27:3
Raska, Francis J, 1955, O 12,31:4
Raskin, Abraham, 1964, Ap 16,37:1
Raskin, Emanuel, 1960, S 21,32:3
Raskin, Harry A, 1962, N 4,88:4
Raskin, Harry Mrs, 1947, O 29,27:2
Raskin, Henry, 1947, Ap 28,23:5
Raskin, Henry Mrs, 1955, Je 10,25:3
Raskin, Joseph, 1953, Ag 9,77:1
Raskin, Max, 1952, O 21,29:4
Raskin, Philip M (por), 1944, F 8,15:4
Raskin, Philip M Mrs, 1961, D 13,43:5
Raskin, Saul, 1966, S 23,37:3
Raskind, David M Mrs (S M Baron), 1961, Ag 14, 25:3
Rasko, Maximilian A R, 1961, Ap 24,29:4
Raskob, John, 1950, O 16,27:1
Raskolnikov, Fedor, 1939, S 23,35:5
Rasmus, Alfred Mrs, 1945, Jl 27,15:3
Rasmus, Antonio T Mrs, 1959, Mr 24,39:4
Rasmuson, Edward A, 1949, Ja 30,60:3
Rasmuson, Elmer E Mrs, 1960, My 1,87:1
Rasmussen, Andrew, 1948, Ap 3,15:4
Rasmussen, Arne, 1962, My 21,33:4
Rasmussen, Carl C, 1940, F 17,13:6
Rasmussen, Christian, 1922, Ap 24,15:4
Rasmussen, Clarence L, 1956, My 19,19:4
Rasmussen, Gustav, 1953, S 14,27:1
Rasmussen, Harry, 1958, Ap 29,29:4
Rasmussen, Howard A, 1951, S 27,63:8
Rasmussen, Howard A Mrs, 1951, S 27,63:8
Rasmussen, K, 1933, D 22,21:1
Rasmussen, Knud Mrs, 1965, Ap 24,29:4
Rasmussen, Niels Mrs (L Larsen), 1959, Mr 11,35:3
Rasmussen, Robert P, 1940, F 4,40:3
Rasmussen, Robert T, 1940, O 26,15:5
Rasmussen, Rolf Mrs, 1959, N 11,35:4
Rasmussen, Theobald T, 1937, S 24,21:1
Rasmussen, Thomas E Sr, 1954, Ja 11,25:5
Rasmussen, Thomas Mrs, 1949, Mr 3,25:5
Rasmussen, Thorvald, 1951, Je 20,27:1
Rasmussen, William F, 1951, S 27,63:8
Rasmusson, Halvor, 1961, N 7,33:4
Rasnick, Nathan N, 1961, Je 17,21:5
Rason, Paul E, 1944, O 17,23:2
Rasor, Charles A, 1962, Ja 1,23:4
Rasor, Paul Edwin Mrs, 1924, Ja 12,13:3
Rasp, Edward J, 1946, D 20,23:1
Raspail, F N, 1878, Ja 22,5:5
Raspail, M, 1870, Ja 19,5:4
Rasper, Ned, 1944, Mr 7,17:1
Raspet, August W, 1960, Ap 28,10:7
Raspetti, J, 1936, Je 23,23:3
Raspigliosi, Francesca Princess, 1920, Je 11,13:5
Rasquin, Almon G (por), 1940, N 5,25:3
Rasquin, H S, 1931, D 29,21:1
Rassadin, Grigori I, 1960, Ap 11,31:5
Rassam, Hormuzd, 1910, S 18,II,13:5
Rasser, Fred H, 1952, Ap 1,29:2
Rasskopf, Elizabeth, 1938, Ja 17,19:5
Rassow, George R, 1937, Ag 11,23:6
Rast, John A, 1957, D 20,24:6
Rastall, Benjamin M, 1956, My 8,33:3
Rastede, Hans G, 1955, Je 7,33:1
Raster, Walter B, 1944, Ja 15,13:2
Rasumny, Mikhail, 1956, F 19,93:1
Ratajack, Joseph, 1939, Je 3,15:6
Ratchford, Frank J, 1957, N 24,87:2
Ratchford, James E, 1925, My 2,15:5
Ratchford, M D, 1927, D 13,29:5
Ratchford, Stephen P, 1947, My 28,25:5
Ratckiffe, Samuel K, 1958, S 2,25:3
Ratckiffe, Sidney J, 1942, S 14,15:5
Ratcliff, Dillwyn F, 1961, O 20,33:2
Ratcliff, John M Dr, 1953, F 24,25:2
Ratcliff, Joseph, 1940, Mr 15,23:4
Ratcliffe, Charles F, 1940, N 5,34:1
Ratcliffe, George W, 1941, Mr 21,21:5
Ratcliffe, John C, 1956, Ja 25,31:1
Ratcliffe, W A, 1942, Jl 25,13:4
Ratell, Leon G, 1940, Mr 17,48:7
Rath, August, 1943, O 3,49:1
Rath, Charles K Sr Mrs, 1950, S 27,32:2
Rath, Frederick Sr, 1955, Ja 29,15:1
Rath, Henry A, 1940, Ap 2,26:2; 1951, Ja 16,29:4
Rath, Henry F, 1956, N 19,31:2
Rath, John F, 1960, D 12,29:4
Rath, John W, 1951, D 23,22:6
Rath, Otto A, 1951, Mr 11,96:2
Rath, Virginia Mrs, 1950, O 28,17:5
Rath, Walter F, 1960, Mr 16,37:1
Rath, William H, 1959, Ja 15,33:1
Rathaus, Karol, 1954, N 22,23:1
Rathaus, Rudolf, 1968, Ja 13,31:4
Rathaus, Rudolf Mrs, 1959, Ja 14,27:4
Rathbert, Frederic H, 1949, N 7,27:4
Rathbone, Albert (por), 1943, Ag 21,11:3
Rathbone, Alfred D 4th, 1949, N 12,15:3
Rathbone, Basil (funl, Jl 26,39:4; will, Ag 19,22:3), 1967, Jl 22,1:1
Rathbone, Charles A, 1943, O 11,19:5
Rathbone, Charles H, 1937, O 8,23:2
Rathbone, Eleanor, 1946, Ja 3,20:3
Rathbone, Floyd L Mrs, 1946, O 6,59:4
Rathbone, H R, 1928, Jl 16,19:5
Rathbone, Henry B (por), 1945, Je 14,19:3
Rathbone, Henry Reed Maj, 1911, Ag 16,7:6
Rathbone, Howard B Mrs, 1960, Mr 16,37:4
Rathbone, J Arnot Mrs, 1950, O 26,31:3
Rathbone, J Henry Mrs, 1923, F 24,11:6
Rathbone, James B, 1919, N 24,15:2
Rathbone, Jared L Maj, 1907, My 3,7:4
Rathbone, Joel, 1938, Jl 2,13:7; 1953, N 21,13:6
Rathbone, John A, 1957, O 25,27:3
Rathbone, John S, 1925, Je 26,17:6
Rathbone, John S Mrs, 1925, Je 26,17:6
Rathbone, Josephine A (por), 1941, My 19,17:4
Rathbone, R Bleecker (will, Je 16,21:5), 1937, Ap 24,19:3
Rathbone, Richard A, 1960, N 1,39:4
Rathbone, Robert C, 1915, F 11,9:5; 1966, N 8,39:5
Rathbone, Robert C Mrs, 1938, N 20,38:8
Rathborne, Joseph C, 1954, Jl 23,17:4
Rathborne, Paul L, 1948, Ja 10,15:2
Rathborne, St George H, 1938, D 18,48:7
Rathbun, Burpee, 1959, Je 2,35:2
Rathbun, Charles F, 1955, N 29,29:3
Rathbun, Don S, 1943, S 20,21:4
Rathbun, E W, 1903, N 25,9:5
Rathbun, Edward H, 1948, N 14,76:7
Rathbun, Edward H Mrs, 1950, Ja 29,68:4
Rathbun, Elmer, 1952, D 23,23:3
Rathbun, Frank B, 1944, My 9,19:5
Rathbun, George J, 1950, Je 21,27:5
Rathbun, Henry H (por), 1948, O 1,25:3
Rathbun, John C, 1958, N 14,27:3
Rathbun, Ken, 1961, Jl 11,31:2
Rathbun, Nathl P, 1949, F 27,68:5
Rathbun, Robert, 1940, N 6,5:4
Rathbun, W S, 1926, Jl 29,19:4
Rathbun, Walter L, 1949, Ap 29,23:4
Rathbun, William S, 1959, My 21,31:1
Rathe, Harold F, 1967, Ja 5,37:1
Rathell, Geron E, 1946, Jl 21,39:1
Rathenau, Emil, 1915, Je 21,9:4
Rathfelder, C, 1926, Jl 24,11:3
Rathfelder, Charles Mrs, 1925, Jl 27,13:4
Rathgeb, Albert E, 1958, My 28,31:2
Rathgeb, Clarence W, 1942, N 18,26:3
Rathgeber, Charles F, 1962, My 22,37:2
Rathgeber, John A, 1944, Ap 22,15:6
Rathje, Merritt W Mrs, 1949, Ag 1,17:5
Rathjen, Henry F, 1953, N 24,29:4
Rathjen, John, 1942, Mr 11,19:2
Rathjen, John Mrs, 1942, Mr 11,19:2
Rathkamp, Laura L, 1939, Ap 9,III,7:2
Rathke, Fred A Sr, 1964, Mr 5,30:4
Rathkopf, Charles A, 1957, Ap 27,11:5
Rathkopf, Charles A Mrs, 1957, Ap 27,11:5
Rathman, Gilbert, 1957, N 12,37:1
Rathom, John Revelstoke (por), 1923, D 12,21:1
Rathvon, N Peter Mrs, 1964, D 6,89:1
Rathvon, William R, 1939, Mr 3,24:2
Rathwell, Frank S, 1951, N 18,90:4
Ratigan, Francis A, 1941, Je 16,15:2
Ratigan, John B Justice, 1915, F 1,9:4
Ratislar-Andrejewitch, Gen, 1884, Ja 13,2:1
Ratledge, Clarence H, 1946, Ap 23,21:3
Ratledge, Ernest S, 1956, Ap 8,84:3
Ratledge, Moses, 1948, F 17,26:3
Ratliff, Hallie M, 1941, S 30,23:2
Ratliff, J M Dr, 1921, N 7,15:4
Ratliff, Joseph M, 1944, Mr 28,19:4
Ratliff, Paul Mrs (Mrs B Amidon), 1958, S 25,33:2
Ratliffe, Thomas A, 1937, My 18,23:5
Ratner, Abraham Mrs (cor, Ja 11,17:1), 1958, Ja 10, 23:1
Ratner, Bret, 1957, O 12,19:3
Ratner, George P, 1959, S 5,15:6
Ratner, Hyman, 1960, My 19,37:4
Ratner, Jacob, 1956, Jl 31,23:4
Ratner, Robert J, 1955, N 22,35:1
Ratner, Samuel J, 1957, Jl 30,23:1
Ratner, Semion Mrs, 1967, Mr 21,43:2
Ratnoff, Hyman L, 1944, Je 27,19:4
Ratnoff, Nathan (por), 1947, D 24,21:5
Ratoff, Gregory (funl plans, D 15,43:2), 1960, D 14, 39:1
Ratoff, Herman, 1960, Je 22,35:5
Ratsey, George E, 1942, D 26,11:5
Ratshesky, Abraham C (por), 1943, Mr 17,21:2
Rattazzi, Urhaus, 1873, Je 6,5:4
Rattenberger, Placidus M, 1948, O 31,88:4
Rattenni, Nicholas A Jr Mrs, 1954, Jl 3,11:5
Ratterman, Lee F, 1955, F 1,24:2
Rattermann, Edwin F, 1950, D 13,35:2
Rattermann, Henry A, 1923, Ja 7,7:3
Ratti, Donna C, 1946, S 17,7:4
Ratti, Franco, 1953, Ja 29,28:7
Ratti, Joseph, 1955, Ap 2,38:1
Ratti, Marion R Mrs, 1951, Je 17,86:2
Rattigan, Charles F, 1956, S 11,35:2
Rattleman, William A, 1956, Jl 5,25:3
Rattner, David, 1958, My 7,35:1
Rattner, Herbert, 1962, Ap 5,33:5
Rattner, Joseph Mrs, 1952, Ag 24,89:3
Rattray, Arnold E, 1954, Jl 12,19:5
Rattray, George Mrs, 1951, Mr 16,31:4
Rattray, James, 1940, N 6,23:3
Raty, Jean, 1958, Je 21,19:1
Ratz, Albert F, 1952, F 6,29:5
Ratzan, Martyn C, 1963, D 17,39:1
Ratzan, Michael N, 1949, Ja 22,13:2
Ratzenhofer, Field Marshall, 1904, O 11,9:5
Ratzlaff, Carl J, 1951, Mr 25,74:6
Rau, Alfred M, 1945, F 21,19:3
Rau, Andrew, 1946, Ag 18,47:2
Rau, Benegal N, 1953, N 30,1:4
Rau, C Fred Mrs, 1959, Jl 8,29:4
Rau, Charles W, 1942, Je 22,15:1
Rau, Eugene, 1945, Ja 20,11:5
Rau, George, 1948, Jl 15,23:6; 1951, F 22,31:2; 1953, D 17,37:2
Rau, Gustav, 1954, D 6,27:5
Rau, Heinrich (funl, Mr 27,31:1), 1961, Mr 24,31:3
Rau, Leonard S, 1946, N 1,23:5
Rau, Louis V, 1953, Je 9,27:1
Rau, Oscar Sr, 1953, Ag 3,17:6
Rau, Raymond M, 1950, Ja 11,23:6
Rau, Roscoe B, 1965, My 22,31:2
Rau, T Arnold, 1956, D 27,25:2
Rau, William, 1956, Ap 25,35:4
Rau, William L, 1944, Ja 20,19:3
Raub, Charles H, 1950, F 2,27:1
Raub, Edward B, 1955, Jl 31,69:2
Raub, Eve I Mrs, 1941, N 30,68:2
Raub, F Elwood, 1943, S 17,22:2
Raub, Frank Mrs (will), 1946, S 21,12:1
Raub, George A, 1949, D 14,31:2
Raub, Herman, 1915, Ag 7,7:6
Raub, Jacob S, 1952, N 14,23:1

Raub, Josephine, 1948, N 30,27:2
Raub, Reuben S, 1943, My 30,26:2
Raub, Thomas, 1949, F 16,25:5
Raube, Stephen E Mrs, 1940, Mr 17,49:2
Raubenheimer, Otto, 1946, Je 11,23:1
Rauber, Alice, 1957, Ag 25,86:7
Rauber, Charles S Mrs, 1944, S 12,19:3
Rauber, Frederick S, 1953, Mr 21,17:5
Rauber, L J, 1949, F 1,18:8
Raubicheck, Frank, 1952, S 20,15:3
Raubitschek, Walter, 1960, S 24,23:4
Raubs, William, 1921, Ja 20,9:4
Rauch, Aron, 1953, F 5,23:4
Rauch, Aron Mrs, 1959, O 4,86:1
Rauch, Ben D Mrs, 1940, Jl 2,21:5
Rauch, Benjamin D, 1941, Ag 12,19:5
Rauch, Celia, 1947, D 3,29:5
Rauch, E H, 1902, S 21,32:5
Rauch, Edward C, 1938, Ap 13,25:4
Rauch, Frank C Jr, 1941, Ap 17,23:4
Rauch, Frederick C Mrs, 1940, D 17,26:2
Rauch, George W, 1940, N 5,25:3
Rauch, Harry, 1942, F 6,19:2
Rauch, Harry E, 1948, F 26,23:3
Rauch, Henry, 1949, F 3,23:4
Rauch, Isaac, 1946, N 21,31:1
Rauch, Joseph, 1957, F 19,31:5
Rauch, Milton A, 1938, Ja 22,15:4
Rauch, Peter, 1951, Mr 19,27:1
Rauch, Peter Mrs, 1946, My 13,21:5
Rauch, Richard, 1948, S 16,29:1
Rauch, Wendelin, 1954, Ap 29,31:3
Rauch, William J, 1940, Je 18,23:3
Rauchenbach, Walter, 1909, Ag 4,7:3
Rauchfuss, William H, 1945, My 25,19:3
Raud, Gans P, 1953, O 6,29:4
Raudenbush, George K, 1956, My 28,27:4
Raudenbush, Ralph H, 1953, Ap 5,77:1
Rauer, Alex, 1948, Je 5,15:5
Rauf, Arthur A, 1948, Mr 17,25:4
Raufeisen, Charles, 1951, D 11,33:3
Rauh, Andrew Mrs, 1951, My 16,35:1
Rauh, Bernard L, 1952, F 14,27:5
Rauh, Charles S, 1956, Ag 3,20:2
Rauh, Edgar M, 1948, F 12,23:4
Rauh, Frank J, 1951, F 17,15:4
Rauh, Henry, 1951, Mr 10,13:3
Rauh, Julius J, 1948, Ja 29,24:2
Rauh, Marcus, 1940, O 18,21:6
Rauh, Matthew A, 1966, D 4,88:8
Rauh, Stanley F, 1953, D 25,17:2
Rauh, William A, 1949, S 2,17:1
Rauhoff, Millard A, 1950, S 19,29:1
Raul, Leo, 1947, My 20,25:2
Raulston, John T (funl plans, Jl 13,19:3), 1956, Jl 12, 23:1
Raum, Green Berry Gen, 1909, D 19,11:7
Raupp, William A, 1946, My 6,21:4
Rausch, Arthur F, 1956, O 11,39:5
Rausch, Carl, 1949, Je 10,28:5
Rausch, Clarence C, 1952, Ap 30,27:1
Rausch, Emil H, 1938, Ag 21,32:6
Rausch, Emily M, 1940, Jl 26,17:3
Rausch, Emma, 1903, Mr 2,1:6
Rausch, Franz, 1939, F 16,11:2
Rausch, Frederick W, 1961, Je 13,35:1
Rausch, George J, 1954, Ag 20,19:5
Rausch, Henry, 1945, Ja 15,19:2
Rausch, John H, 1939, Jl 22,15:4
Rausch, Michael, 1959, Je 30,31:4
Rausch, Peter E, 1945, Je 5,19:1
Rausch, Peter G, 1962, My 20,87:1
Rausch, Stella J Mrs, 1952, F 11,25:5
Rauschelbach, Paul F, 1961, S 24,87:1
Rauschenbach, Paul E, 1943, F 25,21:4
Rauschenbusch, Walter Mrs, 1949, N 17,29:5
Rauschenbusch, Walter Prof, 1918, Jl 26,11:5
Rauscher, August J, 1968, Je 27,43:5
Rauscher, Charles F, 1946, Ag 11,46:4
Rauscher, John C, 1959, O 26,29:4
Rauscher, Joseph Othmaroon Cardinal, 1875, N 25,4:6
Rauscher, Martin J, 1923, O 8,17:4
Rauscher, Walter C, 1946, Ja 19,13:3
Rauseo, Angelina Mrs, 1954, N 20,17:3
Rauseo, Marian Mrs, 1945, O 1,19:2
Rausnitz, Julius Mrs, 1959, S 10,35:5
Rauso, Antimo, 1950, Ap 29,15:3
Rautenburg, Robert, 1940, F 22,23:3
Rautenstrauch, Walter, 1951, Ja 5,21:1
Rauter, Christine A, 1956, D 16,86:3
Rauth, Charles R, 1939, My 18,25:6
Rauth, John E, 1945, Mr 7,22:2
Rautu, Mihai, 1959, Mr 31,29:4
Rava, Luigi, 1938, My 13,19:5
Rava, Maurizio, 1941, Ja 24,17:3
Ravage, Marcus E, 1965, O 12,47:2
Ravagli, Angelino Mrs, 1956, Ag 12,84:3
Ravasz, Ladislaus Mrs, 1947, Je 17,25:4
Ravazza, Edorado Gen, 1925, O 6,27:5
Rave, Adolph G, 1941, Mr 28,23:2
Ravekes, Gertrude A, 1946, Ag 18,47:2
Ravekes, William P, 1952, Je 4,27:4
Ravel, Gaston, 1958, F 24,19:4
Ravel, Maurice, 1937, D 29,21:1
Ravel, Sandra, 1954, Ag 15,85:1
Raven, Albert L, 1951, Jl 13,21:2
Raven, Anton A, 1919, Ja 16,13:2; 1955, Mr 9,27:3
Raven, Charles E, 1964, Jl 10,29:4
Raven, Charles E Mrs (will, Ap 27,7:1), 1954, Ap 7, 31:5
Raven, Henry C (por), 1944, Ap 6,23:1
Raven, John H, 1949, F 27,68:6
Raven, John H Mrs, 1956, Je 24,76:7
Raven, Mary S Mrs, 1939, O 18,26:2
Raven, Richard M, 1905, Je 17,9:5
Raven, Wilbur, 1946, D 4,31:3
Raven-Hill, Leonard, 1942, Ap 1,21:4
Ravenall, William D Jr Lt, 1918, Jl 1,11:2
Ravenel, Gaillard F, 1956, My 6,87:1
Ravenel, Mazyck P, 1946, Ja 15,23:4
Ravenel, S Prioleau, 1940, Ag 22,20:3
Ravenel, St Julien Mrs, 1956, Je 9,17:3
Ravenell, William S, 1966, Je 14,47:4
Ravener, Joseph F, 1964, Ja 30,30:1
Ravenhall, Richard Sr, 1946, F 16,13:2
Ravenscroft, Hubert F, 1947, Ja 14,25:5
Ravenscroft, Jonas, 1943, D 28,17:3
Ravensdale of Kedleston, Baroness (Mary I Curzon), 1966, F 10,37:1
Ravensworth, Baron (R A Liddell), 1950, Ag 5,15:6
Ravensworth, Countess of, 1939, F 2,19:2
Ravensworth, Earl of, 1903, Jl 24,7:3
Ravey, Charles, 1947, Ag 29,17:5
Ravich, Max, 1940, S 18,23:2
Ravid, Jacob M, 1967, F 28,34:1
Ravignani, Emilio, 1954, Mr 10,25:3
Ravin, James A, 1960, F 28,82:5
Ravine, William, 1950, Ap 13,29:4
Ravis, Phil, 1940, S 6,21:1
Ravitch, Bernard, 1950, Ap 10,19:3
Ravitch, Boris, 1958, Jl 23,27:2
Ravitch, Joseph, 1950, N 11,15:3
Ravitch, Saul, 1952, Mr 4,27:4
Ravn, Clara I von Baroness, 1942, Ag 8,11:6
Ravn, Frederick Kolpin Dr, 1920, My 27,11:3
Ravndal, G Bie, 1950, Mr 24,25:4
Rawak, Samuel J, 1937, Je 20,II,5:4
Rawidowicz, Simon, 1957, Jl 22,19:1
Rawiston, Zelma, 1915, O 31,17:4
Rawitser, Herman, 1924, Ag 3,24:4; 1924, S 14,31:2
Rawitz, Sidney B, 1954, Mr 27,17:2
Rawl, Bernard H, 1924, S 25,23:5
Rawle, Henry Mrs, 1966, S 9,45:1
Rawle, James, 1912, My 3,11:5
Rawle, Joseph N B, 1938, O 2,49:1
Rawle, William Brooke, 1915, D 2,11:6
Rawleigh, W T, 1951, Ja 24,27:5
Rawles, James 2d, 1967, My 8,41:4
Rawley, Jesse Mrs (B Payton), 1967, My 11,47:2
Rawling, Sylvester (funl, F 18,11:4), 1921, F 17,11:6
Rawlings, Anna M, 1941, S 12,21:4
Rawlings, Anne C Mrs, 1942, O 13,24:3
Rawlings, Arthur L, 1959, N 18,22:3
Rawlings, Bruce E, 1957, My 4,21:6
Rawlings, Carroll C, 1918, Ap 5,15:5
Rawlings, Edward, 1911, D 13,11:4
Rawlings, Ella Mrs, 1955, Je 27,21:4
Rawlings, George B, 1948, S 3,19:4
Rawlings, Gertrude B, 1939, Mr 14,21:3
Rawlings, Henry B, 1962, O 2,39:2
Rawlings, Henry E, 1949, O 23,86:4
Rawlings, John T, 1959, D 16,41:2
Rawlings, Joseph A Mrs, 1948, N 16,29:4
Rawlings, Marjorie K, 1953, D 16,35:1
Rawlings, Marjorie K (will), 1954, Ja 28,22:4
Rawlings, Percy C, 1949, Ag 16,23:4
Rawlings, Richard H, 1965, S 7,39:4
Rawlings, Russell H, 1949, Ja 1,13:4
Rawlings, William D, 1961, D 22,23:2
Rawlings, William L, 1950, Jl 25,27:1
Rawlins, Gen Mrs, 1874, N 7,1:4
Rawlins, H Charles, 1951, F 21,27:1
Rawlins, Herbert N Jr, 1956, Mr 20,23:2
Rawlins, John A Gen (funl, S 10,1:1), 1869, S 7,1:1
Rawlins, Stuart B, 1955, Ap 3,86:5
Rawlinson, Canon, 1902, O 7,9:5
Rawlinson, Edmund A, 1948, D 19,76:2
Rawlinson, Frank J Mrs, 1961, D 2,23:4
Rawlinson, Henry C Sir, 1895, Mr 6,5:2
Rawlinson, Henry Seymour Gen, 1925, Mr 28,15:5
Rawlinson, Herbert, 1953, Jl 14,27:1
Rawlinson, Joseph F, 1953, Ap 14,35:2
Rawlinson, Robert, 1915, O 27,11:4
Rawlls, Herbert F, 1947, Ja 14,25:2
Rawls, Edward H Jr, 1957, D 26,19:2
Rawls, Huston, 1962, O 20,25:6
Rawls, James M, 1961, O 25,37:5
Rawls, Junius F, 1945, O 22,17:5
Rawls, Reginald M Dr (por), 1937, Ja 1,23:2
Rawls, William L, 1946, Jl 27,17:5
Rawolle, Frederick C, 1954, D 23,19:4
Raws, William L, 1958, Ap 21,23:4
Rawson, Adriel A, 1937, My 8,19:5
Rawson, Arturo, 1951, D 9,26:3; 1952, O 9,31:2
Rawson, David F, 1948, Jl 20,23:3
Rawson, E G Dr, 1882, O 28,5:2
Rawson, Edmund G Mrs, 1957, My 11,21:4
Rawson, Edward B, 1947, Ap 11,25:2
Rawson, Edward L, 1948, Ag 20,17:5
Rawson, Frank L, 1956, N 2,27:5
Rawson, Frederick H, 1937, F 6,17:5
Rawson, G A, 1877, D 14,5:5
Rawson, Harry Holdsworth Adm, 1910, N 4,9:4
Rawson, Hobart, 1958, F 17,23:2
Rawson, Jonathan A Mrs, 1956, D 7,27:2
Rawson, Lucy R Mrs, 1938, Ap 2,15:1
Rawson, Mitchell, 1961, O 23,29:2
Rawson, Thomas R Sr, 1947, Jl 8,23:1
Rawson-Rawson, Roland, 1952, Ap 1,29:2
Ray, Andrew W, 1948, Ja 27,26:2
Ray, Anna C, 1945, D 14,27:5
Ray, Arthur B, 1951, D 26,25:3
Ray, B Dwight, 1950, Jl 14,42:3
Ray, Beecher B Col, 1920, Ag 25,9:3
Ray, Bertha, 1947, Mr 13,27:5
Ray, Bob, 1941, S 9,23:5
Ray, Carl, 1949, Jl 23,11:4
Ray, Charles, 1943, N 24,21:3
Ray, Christian M, 1948, Je 6,72:3
Ray, Daniel G, 1958, My 13,22:5
Ray, David B Rev Dr, 1913, N 1,11:4
Ray, David E, 1946, Je 9,42:3
Ray, David H Mrs, 1943, Ap 17,17:4
Ray, E Lansing (funl, S 4,56:1; est inventory filed, D 31,18:5), 1955, Ag 31,25:1
Ray, E Lansing (est tax appr), 1957, Ap 6,22:8
Ray, E Lansing Jr (por), 1946, Je 8,21:3
Ray, E Lansing Mrs, 1946, Mr 17,44:3
Ray, Edgar T, 1943, Ag 28,11:5
Ray, Edward, 1908, D 30,9:6
Ray, Edward A, 1907, O 6,11:6
Ray, Francis A, 1874, Mr 27,3:1
Ray, Francis E, 1966, D 2,39:5
Ray, Frank H Col, 1925, Ap 13,19:5; 1925, Ap 14,2
Ray, Frank R, 1937, O 6,25:4
Ray, Frederick A, 1937, F 20,17:3
Ray, Frederick R (por), 1941, My 29,19:4
Ray, George B (por), 1945, Jl 7,13:5
Ray, George B Mrs, 1958, F 1,19:6
Ray, George J, 1962, Mr 7,35:1
Ray, George J Mrs, 1942, Ja 25,41:2
Ray, George P, 1941, My 23,21:3
Ray, George W Judge, 1925, Ja 10,13:5
Ray, Guy W, 1950, S 25,23:5
Ray, Hal S, 1937, Ag 24,21:4
Ray, J (Sam Johnson) (see also N 4), 1876, N 5,9:
Ray, J Chester, 1964, Ag 20,29:1
Ray, James A, 1951, S 7,29:2
Ray, James A Mrs, 1942, Je 5,17:5
Ray, James E, 1940, Ap 17,23:3
Ray, James G, 1966, My 16,37:1
Ray, James R, 1955, S 12,25:4
Ray, John, 1943, D 19,49:1
Ray, John C, 1963, D 30,21:2
Ray, John H, 1953, O 23,23:2
Ray, John J, 1952, My 8,31:1
Ray, Johnny (H Pitler), 1961, Jl 17,21:2
Ray, Joseph J, 1958, Jl 16,29:3
Ray, Joseph L, 1966, Ap 15,39:4
Ray, Joseph R Sr, 1959, D 1,39:4
Ray, Louis D, 1937, F 18,21:4
Ray, Louis D Mrs, 1954, Mr 18,31:4
Ray, Mable, 1967, My 21,86:8
Ray, Medora L Mrs, 1937, O 8,23:4
Ray, Melville B, 1938, Ja 7,19:5
Ray, Milton S, 1946, My 7,21:6
Ray, N Norton Mrs, 1949, Mr 18,25:4
Ray, Nathaniel D, 1953, Mr 4,27:1
Ray, Olaf E, 1943, O 30,15:2
Ray, Patrick Henry Brig-Gen, 1911, O 31,9:3
Ray, Peter P, 1946, D 29,35:5
Ray, R N Mrs, 1951, N 5,31:3
Ray, Ralph D, 1963, S 9,27:3
Ray, Randolph (funl, Je 4,39:2), 1963, Je 2,84:2
Ray, Randolph Mrs, 1938, O 27,23:5
Ray, Raymond Mrs, 1952, N 29,17:4
Ray, Reginald P, 1960, Ap 28,35:5
Ray, Reginald P Mrs, 1948, Je 11,23:2; 1951, My 15:2
Ray, Robert, 1879, Mr 8,8:3
Ray, Robert E, 1949, Ap 7,29:3
Ray, Robert R, 1941, D 12,26:2
Ray, Sandy F Mrs, 1966, Ja 4,31:4
Ray, Sydney H, 1939, Ja 4,21:3
Ray, Ted (por), 1943, Ag 29,39:1
Ray, Thomas, 1945, My 21,19:4
Ray, Thomas E, 1950, N 4,17:4
Ray, W A, 1954, Ja 28,27:5
Ray, W H, 1881, Ja 26,5:4
Ray, W L, 1938, Ja 22,15:3
Ray, Wayne B, 1952, My 29,27:5
Ray, Whitaker, 1938, Ja 15,15:5
Ray, William E, 1953, My 30,15:3
Ray, William F, 1913, S 27,13:5
Ray, William Porter Dr, 1864, Mr 5,3:2
Ray, William Sir, 1937, O 1,21:5
Ray, Wyeth E, 1944, O 26,23:6
Raybert, Sarah E, 1942, D 20,45:1
Raybet, Ferdinand, 1920, Ap 12,15:3

Raybold, Walter, 1938, Ap 22,19:5
Rayburn, Charles, 1956, Mr 19,31:1
Rayburn, James, 1950, My 7,108:4
Rayburn, James L Mrs, 1956, Mr 19,31:1
Rayburn, Lucinda, 1956, My 27,88:8
Rayburn, Merle Mrs, 1943, Ag 22,36:5
Rayburn, Richard A, 1962, Ja 31,31:1
Rayburn, Sam (funl plans, N 18,23:4), 1961, N 17,1:1
Rayburn, Stanley, 1961, Je 15,43:2
Rayburn, Tom, 1960, Mr 3,29:3
Rayburn, Will, 1943, Mr 20,15:3
Raycroft, Alice, 1956, Ag 31,17:3
Raycroft, John F, 1963, S 18,39:3
Raycroft, Joseph E, 1955, O 2,87:1
Raycroft, Thomas, 1925, Mr 23,17:4
Rayel, William E, 1951, S 14,25:4
Rayens, E F, 1934, Mr 22,21:3
Rayens, Michael W (por), 1948, Ap 2,23:3
Rayfiel, Hyman, 1950, Ap 7,25:5
Rayfield, Wallace W, 1954, S 24,24:2
Raygada, Carlos, 1953, F 9,27:3
Raygosa de Diaz, Maria L, 1939, N 7,25:2
Rayher, Edward R, 1958, My 13,29:2
Rayleigh, Baron, 1947, D 14,76:5
Raymaker, Herman, 1944, Mr 9,17:1
Rayman, Elias A, 1957, Ag 8,23:1
Raymaster, Joseph R Mrs, 1945, D 10,21:1
Raymen, Meyer, 1955, Mr 30,29:3
Raymend, William A, 1947, Mr 25,25:2
Raymenton, W H Dr, 1937, S 12,II,6:8
Raymer, Frances H Mrs, 1941, Ja 30,21:4
Raymer, Jacob, 1951, O 27,19:2
Raymer, Max, 1949, Ja 11,31:3
Raymer, Paul H, 1966, N 21,45:1
Raymond, Adelard, 1962, F 24,27:1
Raymond, Albert W, 1953, Je 20,17:4
Raymond, Alex, 1956, S 7,24:6
Raymond, Alexander G Mrs, 1945, F 21,19:4
Raymond, Allen, 1957, Je 9,89:1
Raymond, Allen A, 1950, S 1,21:4
Raymond, Alphonse, 1958, Je 8,88:3
Raymond, Andrew Van Franken Dr, 1918, Ap 6,15:4
Raymond, Andrew Van Vranken Mrs, 1907, Je 12,9:5
Raymond, Bradford Paul Dr, 1916, F 28,9:6
Raymond, C Nelson, 1938, O 7,23:6
Raymond, Carlton S, 1949, Jl 7,25:4
Raymond, Charles, 1948, Mr 22,23:2
Raymond, Charles A, 1949, S 14,31:4
Raymond, Charles B, 1945, Ag 1,19:5
Raymond, Charles G Mrs, 1951, O 28,84:6
Raymond, Charles H, 1939, Mr 15,24:2; 1944, D 25, 19:5
Raymond, Charles H Col, 1916, S 30,11:4
Raymond, Charles H Mrs, 1946, O 17,23:3; 1965, Je 3,35:4
Raymond, Charlotte, 1967, D 4,61:1
Raymond, Cleophas H, 1946, D 15,77:4
Raymond, Clifford S, 1950, O 22,92:1
Raymond, Cornelia, 1952, N 1,21:7
Raymond, D D, 1875, Jl 11,7:6
Raymond, Donat, 1963, Je 7,31:4
Raymond, Dora N Mrs, 1961, D 4,37:2
Raymond, Edgar L, 1961, Ag 18,21:5
Raymond, Edith M Mrs, 1941, Ag 29,17:6
Raymond, Edward Abiel, 1925, N 10,25:4
Raymond, Edward H, 1939, Mr 26,III,7:1; 1958, S 10, 33:2
Raymond, Edward H Mrs, 1960, S 4,69:1
Raymond, Edward W Rev, 1914, S 11,9:6
Raymond, Elmer G, 1956, O 20,21:1
Raymond, Emil, 1946, Ja 19,13:3
Raymond, Emma Marcy Mrs, 1913, N 8,13:6
Raymond, Eugene L, 1966, Je 13,39:1
Raymond, Floyd C, 1947, My 6,28:3
Raymond, Frances S, 1958, Mr 18,29:3
Raymond, Frank, 1909, N 14,13:4
Raymond, Frank F, 1952, F 10,92:3
Raymond, Frank G, 1948, O 28,29:4
Raymond, Frank T, 1949, Jl 9,13:2
Raymond, Frankie (Mrs D Henderson), 1961, Je 22, 31:3
Raymond, G D Mrs, 1940, Ag 13,19:5
Raymond, Gene Mrs (J A MacDonald),(funl plans, Ja 16,27:1), 1965, Ja 15,1:2
Raymond, George B, 1916, Ja 17,11:4
Raymond, George E, 1944, S 28,19:5
Raymond, George E Mrs, 1938, Mr 15,23:1
Raymond, George G, 1938, D 16,25:5
Raymond, George G (por), 1944, My 6,15:3
Raymond, George Mrs, 1949, O 20,29:5
Raymond, Gus F, 1967, Je 3,31:3
Raymond, H E, 1928, O 9,31:2
Raymond, H H, 1935, D 28,15:1
Raymond, Harold, 1903, S 25,7:4; 1957, D 13,27:4
Raymond, Harriet M, 1948, My 26,25:2
Raymond, Harry, 1961, Mr 26,93:1
Raymond, Harry D, 1940, S 28,17:6
Raymond, Helen, 1965, N 29,35:2
Raymond, Henry Gen, 1878, S 21,5:3
Raymond, Henry J, 1869, Je 19,4:2
Raymond, Henry J Mrs, 1914, O 14,11:6
Raymond, Henry V, 1945, Mr 17,13:6
Raymond, Henry W, 1925, F 19,19:5
Raymond, Herman B, 1948, My 30,34:7
Raymond, Howard M, 1943, Ja 26,19:1
Raymond, Howard W, 1945, Mr 8,23:5
Raymond, Irving F, 1962, Jl 21,19:6
Raymond, Irving O, 1944, F 19,13:2
Raymond, Irving W, 1964, Ag 12,35:3
Raymond, J, 1881, Je 7,5:1
Raymond, J C Capt, 1909, Jl 2,7:4
Raymond, J H (see also Ag 15), 1878, Ag 16,8:2
Raymond, J T, 1887, Ap 11,1:5
Raymond, Jack, 1953, Mr 21,17:4
Raymond, James G, 1963, Ap 16,35:1
Raymond, James Howard Dr, 1915, Mr 8,9:4
Raymond, James I, 1905, Ap 19,11:4
Raymond, James I (will), 1906, F 11,7:3
Raymond, James Mrs, 1909, N 29,9:1; 1947, D 28,40:5
Raymond, Jarvis, 1868, S 8,4:7
Raymond, John T, 1941, D 17,27:5
Raymond, John W, 1941, F 4,22:3
Raymond, Jonathan S, 1963, Ap 16,35:2
Raymond, Joseph S, 1916, F 29,11:4; 1942, S 9,23:2
Raymond, Katherine Platt Dr, 1925, Ap 4,17:6
Raymond, Lew (L Malitz), 1953, Ap 19,90:4
Raymond, Lillian, 1911, Jl 17,9:5
Raymond, Manley A, 1941, Ja 9,21:5
Raymond, Maria, 1881, Ap 17,5:6
Raymond, Mary Sister, 1924, Ja 10,21:4
Raymond, Maurice F (por), 1948, Ja 29,23:4
Raymond, Myron A Mrs, 1962, Jl 6,25:1
Raymond, Oscar A Mrs, 1946, Mr 31,46:4
Raymond, Oscar K, 1950, Ap 23,93:1
Raymond, Percy E, 1952, My 20,25:4
Raymond, Robert B, 1948, Ja 14,26:2
Raymond, Robert B Mrs, 1956, F 2,25:3
Raymond, Robert P, 1958, N 22,21:4
Raymond, Robert R, 1944, Ja 20,19:2
Raymond, Robert R Jr, 1953, Je 19,21:2
Raymond, Ross, 1909, D 15,11:3
Raymond, Rossiter Worthingham Dr, 1919, Ja 2,9:3
Raymond, Russell, 1911, Ag 1,9:6
Raymond, Sadie U Mrs, 1937, O 18,17:5
Raymond, Samuel M, 1949, Ag 2,19:4
Raymond, Sidney R Mrs, 1959, Ap 3,27:4
Raymond, Sidney W, 1946, Ja 16,23:2
Raymond, Sister (E Palmer), 1951, Jl 25,23:1
Raymond, T L, 1928, O 7,30:4
Raymond, Thomas U, 1925, D 25,17:5
Raymond, Valentine K Mrs, 1956, N 27,38:5
Raymond, W L, 1941, N 14,23:1
Raymond, Walter L, 1958, Ap 16,33:1
Raymond, Wayte, 1956, S 24,27:3
Raymond, William, 1944, D 8,21:2
Raymond, William C Prof, 1937, Ag 17,19:4
Raymond, William H, 1952, Ag 21,19:4
Raymond, William L, 1942, Mr 20,19:5; 1946, N 13, 27:2
Raymond, William Lewis, 1913, Ja 20,11:6
Raymond, William M, 1960, N 1,39:4
Raymond, William W, 1940, Ap 4,23:2
Raynal, Sylvain, 1939, Ja 14,17:6
Raynaldy, Eugene (por), 1938, Je 16,23:5
Rayne, J Edward, 1940, Je 30,33:2
Rayne, J Edward Mrs, 1947, F 19,25:4
Rayner, Archibald Mrs, 1963, N 2,25:1
Rayner, Charles E, 1961, Mr 12,86:8
Rayner, Earl C, 1952, Ag 19,23:3
Rayner, Edward W, 1940, S 25,27:5; 1954, Ag 5,23:4
Rayner, Frank, 1937, O 30,19:3
Rayner, George, 1924, Je 27,19:5; 1937, Mr 19,23:4
Rayner, George R, 1938, Ag 17,19:1
Rayner, Harold M, 1954, D 9,33:2
Rayner, Henry W Mrs, 1961, Je 7,41:3
Rayner, K, 1884, Mr 6,5:6
Rayner, Leonard M, 1956, My 26,17:6
Rayner, Mabel M C, 1948, D 22,23:5
Rayner, Minnie, 1941, D 14,69:2
Rayner, Thomas Crossley Justice, 1914, My 23,11:6
Rayner, William S, 1941, S 12,21:2
Raynes, Herbert A Mrs, 1949, Ag 26,19:3
Raynes, Nathan Mrs, 1955, My 9,23:3
Rayniak, Joseph G, 1964, D 20,69:1
Raynolds, Arthur H Mrs, 1944, F 10,15:3
Raynolds, Edward H, 1940, Mr 15,23:6
Raynolds, Harold Mrs, 1938, Je 21,19:4
Raynolds, J Albert, 1955, O 26,31:3
Raynolds, Robert, 1965, O 26,45:3
Raynolds, William W, 1958, Ag 11,21:5
Raynor, Albertus D, 1953, Ap 29,29:4
Raynor, Celia E S Mrs, 1941, Je 21,17:5
Raynor, Charles G, 1949, O 2,81:2
Raynor, Charles W, 1943, D 19,48:5
Raynor, Cordelia L Mrs, 1940, Jl 19,19:2
Raynor, D Stanley, 1940, S 17,23:2
Raynor, Edward S, 1949, S 22,31:2
Raynor, Elmer I, 1955, Ja 5,23:3
Raynor, Eugenia, 1955, My 2,21:5
Raynor, Forrest, 1946, Mr 13,29:3
Raynor, Fred E, 1903, Ap 23,9:5
Raynor, George C, 1950, O 6,27:2
Raynor, George C Mrs, 1947, D 21,54:2
Raynor, George E, 1956, Mr 27,35:5
Raynor, George F, 1939, N 3,21:4
Raynor, George H, 1963, O 8,43:4
Raynor, Hiram Martling, 1916, Ag 13,15:6
Raynor, Horace W, 1912, S 2,9:5
Raynor, J A, 1885, Ja 22,5:3
Raynor, Joseph J, 1944, Ja 8,13:5
Raynor, Lucian B, 1948, My 3,21:2
Raynor, M W, 1935, O 6,II,11:3
Raynor, Mary, 1941, Ap 25,19:4
Raynor, Nina F (est tax appr), 1958, Ap 25,25:1
Raynor, Russell, 1940, Jl 11,19:5
Raynor, Stewart, 1941, Je 28,15:3
Raynor, William A, 1949, F 24,23:2
Raynor, William B, 1959, Ag 25,31:4
Raynor, William C, 1943, F 23,21:1
Raynor, William H, 1874, N 5,8:4
Raynor, William H Gen, 1912, D 21,13:4
Rayport, Gregory A, 1950, N 9,33:2
Rayson, Catherine E Mrs, 1967, Ja 12,39:1
Rayton, Wilbur A, 1946, N 1,23:5
Rayton, Willis M, 1957, S 22,86:3
Rayvid, Louis, 1956, My 10,31:4
Rayworth, Mary A, 1954, Ag 3,19:5
Razee, Rush, 1945, Ap 22,36:1
Razek, Joseph, 1950, F 23,27:1
Razinsky, Louis, 1951, Mr 11,94:5
Razon, Jose, 1961, F 14,37:4
Razook, Frank R, 1963, Ag 15,29:3
Razzack, H H A, 1961, D 9,27:4
Razzi, L, 1935, Ag 9,1:3
Re, John Mrs, 1965, Ap 1,35:4
Rea, Al, 1954, O 25,27:2
Rea, Alexander, 1944, F 12,28:2
Rea, Angelo R, 1958, Mr 10,23:4
Rea, Charles Mrs, 1945, My 29,15:5
Rea, Daniel R Mrs, 1948, Ja 1,23:6
Rea, Emma E C (Sister Josephine Rosaire), 1960, F 11,35:4
Rea, Gardiner, 1966, D 29,31:1
Rea, George, 1952, Ja 20,85:2; 1959, Ja 16,27:2
Rea, James, 1942, Ag 3,15:5
Rea, James C Mrs, 1965, My 31,17:5
Rea, James Mrs, 1958, Jl 22,27:3
Rea, James W, 1938, F 2,19:3
Rea, Jane, 1941, Ap 30,19:2
Rea, John A, 1941, F 21,19:2
Rea, John G, 1945, Mr 13,23:4
Rea, John H, 1944, S 29,21:5
Rea, Kennedy F, 1938, N 29,24:1
Rea, Lord, 1948, My 27,25:3
Rea, Marion H, 1946, N 2,15:5
Rea, Paul M, 1948, Ja 17,18:2
Rea, Phil V, 1956, Je 12,35:2
Rea, Richard B, 1951, F 22,31:2
Rea, Robert, 1957, Ap 9,33:3
Rea, Russell, 1916, F 6,15:6
Rea, S, 1929, Mr 25,1:5
Rea, Samuel G, 1938, N 17,25:4
Rea, Thomas B, 1925, D 17,23:4
Rea, W George, 1944, Ap 8,13:4
Rea, William C, 1954, My 28,23:4
Rea, Wilton T, 1966, Je 4,12:3
Reaber, Karl, 1953, Je 27,15:5
Reach, A J, 1928, Ja 15,29:1
Reach, Charles H, 1954, Ja 2,11:6
Reach, Eric, 1949, Jl 20,25:1
Reach, George A, 1954, D 8,35:4
Reach, George A (est acctg), 1956, Ja 25,35:1
Reach, James, 1939, Je 24,17:1
Reach, Milton B, 1961, Mr 16,38:1
Reach, Robert, 1922, My 20,15:6
Read, Agnes M Mrs, 1937, Ap 29,21:2
Read, Albert C, 1967, O 12,50:2
Read, Allanro Dr, 1901, D 31,7:5
Read, Alton E, 1950, D 3,88:6
Read, Barclay K, 1968, O 17,47:4
Read, Bernard E, 1949, Je 16,30:2
Read, Caroline M Mrs, 1939, N 24,23:5
Read, Charles, 1957, Ag 22,27:4
Read, Charles C, 1954, Mr 28,87:4
Read, Charles F, 1937, Ag 6,17:2
Read, Charles F (por), 1946, Mr 12,25:4
Read, Charles L, 1967, D 12,47:4
Read, Charles L Mrs, 1952, N 26,23:5
Read, Conyers, 1959, D 25,21:1
Read, D Knowlton, 1955, S 22,31:3
Read, David H, 1947, Ap 13,60:3
Read, E G, 1933, S 29,19:1
Read, Edgar N, 1946, Ag 21,27:3
Read, Edgar T, 1947, My 24,15:6
Read, Edith M, 1963, Ap 17,41:1
Read, Edward C, 1913, N 28,15:6
Read, Edward Mrs, 1952, D 25,29:3
Read, Edwim Oliver, 1909, Ag 22,9:6
Read, Eldon H Jr, 1959, S 25,29:2
Read, Elizabeth F, 1943, D 14,28:3
Read, Emery C, 1937, Ja 11,20:2
Read, Emma T, 1955, Ja 10,23:3
Read, Emma Van H Mrs, 1941, Ap 26,15:5
Read, Francis A, 1942, Ag 15,11:6
Read, Frank, 1938, F 18,19:2
Read, Frank Mrs, 1957, Mr 28,31:3
Read, Franklin C, 1938, Ap 7,23:4
Read, G Bleecker, 1924, Ap 19,13:5
Read, G W, 1934, N 7,21:1

Read, George, 1907, F 13,9:2
Read, George A, 1952, F 19,29:4
Read, George E, 1946, S 24,29:3; 1959, Je 24,31:4
Read, George J, 1958, D 11,13:3
Read, Grantly Dick-, 1959, Je 12,27:4
Read, Granville M, 1962, D 2,89:1
Read, Harmon Pumpelly Maj, 1925, D 23,19:4
Read, Harold D, 1945, O 10,21:4
Read, Harry C, 1957, O 23,33:1
Read, Henry Nash Dr, 1917, S 4,11:5
Read, Herbert E, 1954, Ja 23,13:3
Read, Herbert H Jr, 1947, Jl 18,17:1
Read, Herbert Sir, 1968, Je 13,47:1
Read, Howard M, 1942, Jl 22,19:1
Read, Howard W, 1953, Ja 1,23:4
Read, Isaac, 1907, Ja 3,9:5
Read, J M, 1896, D 28,5:2; 1901, N 7,16:4
Read, Jacob, 1945, Ag 25,11:2
Read, Jacob Y, 1938, Ap 13,25:5
Read, James C, 1948, O 25,23:2
Read, James P, 1958, N 2,89:1
Read, Jeanette M Mrs, 1959, Mr 27,23:4
Read, John, 1946, Ag 22,27:6
Read, John A Mrs, 1951, Ag 7,25:3
Read, John H, 1938, Ap 19,21:3
Read, John J Rear-Adm, 1910, O 25,11:5
Read, John M Ex-Judge, 1874, N 30,5:2
Read, John S, 1967, Ja 28,27:4
Read, Josiah C (por), 1939, My 24,23:4
Read, Knowlton D Jr, 1955, Ap 20,33:3
Read, Louise A, 1951, F 17,15:1
Read, Margaret, 1925, Ja 29,19:3
Read, Nathan, 1941, N 14,13:3
Read, Newbury F, 1950, F 8,27:5
Read, Norman Mrs, 1941, O 3,23:5
Read, Opie, 1939, N 3,21:3
Read, Patrick J, 1947, N 17,21:4
Read, Peggy (Mrs W Fischer Williams), 1968, Jl 3, 32:1
Read, Randall, 1962, O 25,39:1
Read, Raymond L, 1949, My 11,29:6
Read, Raymond P, 1939, F 13,15:2
Read, Rhoda M, 1938, Ap 7,23:5
Read, Richard G, 1952, F 21,27:1
Read, Richard R, 1967, Ap 24,33:2
Read, Robert, 1937, Ja 14,21:4
Read, Robert J, 1955, Ag 25,23:5
Read, Robert Mrs, 1944, O 24,23:1
Read, Roy A, 1957, D 15,86:8
Read, Samuel R Mrs, 1952, My 18,92:6
Read, Semmes Lt-Com, 1920, Mr 25,11:6
Read, Sheridan Pitt, 1912, N 1,13:4
Read, Thomas, 1962, Ap 8,87:2
Read, Thomas Buchanan, 1872, My 12,1:3
Read, Thomas T (por), 1947, My 30,21:1
Read, W H A, 1938, Jl 16,13:3
Read, Walter A, 1943, My 2,44:5
Read, Walter V H, 1961, S 14,31:2
Read, Warren K Jr, 1946, Je 10,21:4
Read, Warren W Mrs, 1937, D 12,II,9:2
Read, William A, 1916, Ap 8,15:4
Read, William B, 1869, Ja 12,5:2; 1947, D 17,29:3
Read, William T Sr, 1954, Ag 8,85:2
Read, William W Mrs, 1951, Je 4,27:5
Reade, A Lee, 1955, S 15,33:2
Reade, Aaron W, 1968, Mr 5,41:2
Reade, Catherine, 1915, D 6,9:4
Reade, Charles, 1884, Ap 27,6:4
Reade, Charles L, 1948, S 15,31:1
Reade, Harry Capt, 1907, Ap 2,11:5
Reade, Harry W, 1948, F 16,21:1
Reade, Irving P, 1941, Ag 2,15:6
Reade, John M Dr, 1937, My 10,19:3
Reade, Joseph J, 1940, Ag 6,20:2
Reade, Joseph W, 1941, O 15,21:3
Reade, Philip Gen, 1919, O 22,17:2
Reade, Richard S Mrs, 1952, N 1,21:3
Reade, Walter, 1952, F 5,29:1
Reader, Charles D, 1965, My 20,43:2
Reader, Houston P, 1957, N 1,23:1
Reader, William H, 1954, My 2,88:5
Readey, Maurice, 1966, Jl 6,45:1
Reading, Alfred A, 1958, Ja 17,25:4
Reading, Alfred S, 1947, Jl 13,44:2
Reading, Arthur K, 1942, Jl 10,17:5
Reading, Bart S, 1945, Mr 8,23:2
Reading, Charles N, 1915, Je 17,11:5
Reading, Henry G, 1948, Je 15,27:5
Reading, John H Jr Mrs, 1955, My 19,29:3
Reading, L Willard, 1954, Je 22,27:3
Reading, Lady, 1930, Ja 31,21:5
Reading, Lord, 1935, D 31,1:2
Reading, Marquess of (G R Isaacs), 1960, S 21,37:2
Reading, Richard W, 1952, D 10,43:4
Reading, William C, 1942, Jl 31,15:5
Readingell, Charles J Rear-Adm, 1909, F 18,7:5
Readinger, Milton G, 1951, Je 15,23:5
Ready, Felix, 1940, Ap 8,19:2
Ready, Frank A, 1961, N 7,33:1
Ready, Hartnett H, 1961, Je 9,33:3
Ready, John, 1911, S 5,7:5
Ready, Joseph A, 1964, Mr 17,35:2
Ready, Joseph L, 1955, F 16,29:5
Ready, Michael J (funl, My 9,31:1), 1957, My 3,28:1
Ready, Nancy, 1960, O 24,29:5
Ready, Robert M Mrs, 1954, N 14,85:6
Ready, William H, 1949, D 11,92:7
Reagan, Allen L Lt-Col, 1937, Jl 11,II,4:6
Reagan, C R, 1948, Ag 4,21:3
Reagan, Catherine Mrs, 1938, D 9,25:4
Reagan, Cornelius B, 1941, F 21,19:2
Reagan, Daniel E, 1937, My 12,23:4
Reagan, Frank H, 1944, S 11,17:5
Reagan, James, 1944, D 14,23:1
Reagan, James A, 1937, F 25,23:2
Reagan, John B, 1958, Ja 13,29:4
Reagan, John E, 1941, My 19,17:4
Reagan, John H Judge, 1905, Mr 7,9:5
Reagan, Joseph F, 1944, N 23,31:4
Reagan, Mary B Mrs, 1939, D 5,27:2
Reagan, Michael J, 1938, Mr 5,17:4
Reagan, Michael Mrs, 1950, Mr 15,29:4
Reagan, Michael V Mrs, 1958, My 17,19:4
Reagan, Oliver, 1958, Je 4,33:3
Reagan, Patrick L, 1946, Ag 5,21:5
Reagan, William J, 1937, Je 11,23:4
Reager, Richard C, 1956, F 17,21:1
Reaghan, James R, 1949, My 16,21:4
Reagle, Charles H, 1942, Ag 27,19:4
Reagle, Fred P, 1953, Jl 11,11:7
Reakirt, Llewellyn, 1948, D 24,18:4
Reakirt, Robert H Mrs, 1921, D 12,15:3
Real, Cristobal, 1966, Ap 23,31:2
Real, E, 1877, My 11,5:6
Real, Romualdo, 1959, S 6,72:4
Real del Sarte, Maxime, 1954, F 17,31:3
Reale, Vito, 1953, Ap 29,29:4
Realey, Henry C, 1951, Jl 29,68:5
Reals, Grace, 1925, S 2,23:4
Ream, Charles W, 1939, Ag 11,15:2
Ream, Norman B, 1915, F 10,11:3
Ream, Norman B Mrs, 1924, D 13,15:3
Ream, Robert C, 1957, Je 3,27:4
Ream, Robert C Mrs, 1964, O 31,29:2
Reamer, Abraham, 1951, Ap 9,25:6
Reamer, Ernest D Jr, 1965, Jl 15,29:3
Reamer, Robert C, 1938, Ja 8,15:4
Reamey, Lazarus Com, 1914, My 26,11:5
Reamy, Thaddeus Asbury, 1909, Mr 12,7:6
Reaney, George, 1967, D 4,47:2
Reaney, George H, 1947, Jl 13,44:4
Reaney, Joseph H, 1947, Ap 1,27:3
Reaney, William Henry Ironsides Rev Father, 1915, N 21,19:5
Reantillo, Theodore P, 1953, Je 2,29:3
Reap, Edward J Sr, 1949, D 3,15:4
Reap, Leo, 1943, Mr 7,38:7
Rear, George W, 1942, F 12,23:1
Rearden, John B, 1962, N 14,39:1
Reardon, Bernard E, 1940, N 23,17:4
Reardon, Bernard E Mrs, 1962, Mr 29,33:4
Reardon, Casper, 1941, Mr 10,17:3
Reardon, Charles J, 1961, My 13,19:4
Reardon, Cornelius A, 1948, Ag 28,16:3
Reardon, Cornelius B, 1942, My 20,20:3
Reardon, Cornelius E, 1953, Je 11,29:4
Reardon, Cornelius L, 1949, My 23,23:3
Reardon, Daniel L, 1946, Jl 14,38:6
Reardon, Edmund, 1939, O 25,23:3
Reardon, Edward E, 1956, My 26,17:5
Reardon, Edward J, 1913, D 27,9:5; 1956, Ja 12,27:4; 1966, Je 24,37:2
Reardon, Elizabeth, 1924, Je 17,19:4
Reardon, Francis X (Foxo), 1955, D 1,35:2
Reardon, Frank J, 1942, Ap 14,22:3
Reardon, George C, 1952, N 17,25:4
Reardon, George J, 1940, Ag 15,17:5
Reardon, Henry Jr Mrs, 1950, Ap 24,25:2
Reardon, J Tiers, 1947, F 26,25:3
Reardon, Ja Sgt, 1904, F 11,9:5
Reardon, James S, 1952, D 8,41:5
Reardon, James S Mrs, 1949, S 6,27:4
Reardon, James T, 1949, Ap 4,23:1
Reardon, James W, 1940, My 31,19:2
Reardon, John, 1956, O 9,9:4
Reardon, John B, 1937, S 30,38:2
Reardon, John E, 1905, Mr 17,9:4
Reardon, John J, 1922, S 30,13:6
Reardon, John M, 1949, Ja 17,19:4
Reardon, John S, 1959, Ap 12,87:1
Reardon, Joseph M, 1959, Ja 25,92:7
Reardon, Laura Mrs, 1938, F 19,15:5
Reardon, Leo F, 1965, Ag 27,29:3
Reardon, Margaret Mrs, 1922, F 27,13:6
Reardon, Owen, 1950, Ag 3,23:5
Reardon, Raymond C, 1951, Ag 17,17:2
Reardon, Robert E, 1966, Ja 25,41:3
Reardon, Theodore J Sr, 1953, My 28,23:3
Reardon, Timothy J, 1938, F 18,19:1; 1946, F 15,25:1
Reardon, Timothy Mrs, 1940, N 20,21:1
Reardon, William F, 1957, Ap 1,25:2
Reardon, William G, 1956, Mr 26,29:5
Reardon, William I, 1953, Ja 17,15:2
Reardon, William I Mrs, 1957, My 22,33:5
Reardon, William J, 1941, D 25,25:5
Reardon, William Mrs, 1961, Ja 23,23:1
Reardon-Smith, Willie, 1950, N 25,13:3
Rearick, Allan C, 1940, Je 4,23:5
Rearick, Allan C Jr, 1963, O 7,31:4
Rearick, Daniel, 1951, D 29,11:2
Rearick, Walter S, 1949, N 14,27:1
Rearwin, Harry T, 1951, Mr 10,13:3
Reaser, Budd J, 1949, Ag 9,25:2
Reaser, Matthew, 1948, F 19,23:3
Reaser, Willbur A, 1942, D 11,24:3
Reasner, William F, 1949, O 4,27:4
Reasoner, Andrew Mrs, 1908, S 15,9:6
Reass, Benjamin, 1946, Ag 27,29:2
Reath, Theodore W, 1948, F 1,60:4
Reaume, Adelaide Mrs, 1944, Ag 7,15:6
Reaveley, Thomas T, 1951, Ja 12,27:5
Reavey, Edward P, 1953, My 26,29:3
Reavill, Fred A, 1939, Ap 28,25:5
Reavis, C F, 1932, My 27,21:5
Reavis, James O, 1959, Ag 24,21:4
Reavis, Logan U, 1958, Je 3,31:5
Reavis, Smith F, 1940, F 25,38:8
Reavis, William C, 1955, Je 3,23:5
Reavy, Grace, 1959, F 21,21:6
Reay, Elmer S, 1946, S 27,23:4
Reay, Lord (Donald Jas Mackay), 1921, Ag 2,9:4
Reay, Lord (A A Mackay), 1963, Mr 12,7:5
Reay, Thomas M Sr, 1952, F 7,27:2
Reay, William M, 1942, Ag 8,11:3
Reazor, Frank B Rev Dr, 1937, F 19,19:3
Reb, John H, 1946, F 12,25:3
Rebay, Hilla, 1967, S 29,47:1
Rebbeck, Frank, 1941, Je 5,24:3
Rebbeck, Frederick E, 1964, Je 28,56:7
Rebecca, Sister, 1937, Ap 18,II,8:7
Reben, Max L, 1939, My 12,21:3
Reber, Charles E, 1943, Jl 27,17:2
Reber, Charles J, 1952, F 25,21:3
Reber, Charles S, 1950, Je 2,23:4
Reber, J, 1883, Ag 28,5:5
Reber, J Howard, 1949, Ap 6,29:5
Reber, John (por), 1944, My 18,19:5
Reber, John, 1960, O 17,29:3
Reber, John U, 1955, Jl 4,11:4
Reber, Louis E, 1948, My 13,25:5
Reber, Neil E, 1951, Je 25,19:5
Reber, S, 1933, Ap 18,15:1
Reber, Samuel Mrs, 1952, S 11,32:4
Rebert, Charles, 1951, S 20,31:2
Rebert, Gordon N, 1948, My 5,25:2
Rebesher, Conrad F, 1938, Je 26,27:4
Rebholz, Joseph G, 1951, Je 13,29:4
Rebhuhn, Ben, 1965, Jl 21,37:5
Rebin, Edgar, 1951, My 5,17:1
Rebman, Conrad Jr, 1948, N 14,76:6
Rebman, Walter H, 1965, N 13,29:3
Rebmann, Frederick, 1943, D 18,16:3
Rebmann, Godfrey R, 1947, My 2,21:4
Rebner, Arthur, 1949, D 13,38:1
Rebolledo, Alvaro, 1946, Mr 5,25:3
Rebori, Andrew N, 1966, Je 1,44:1
Rebori, Andrew P, 1952, S 16,29:2
Reboul, Jean B, 1968, D 28,27:5
Reboul, Marius, 1952, Ja 26,13:4
Rebre, Charles, 1939, Ap 12,24:3
Rebsamen, Paul M, 1947, Mr 14,24:3
Rebsch, Charles, 1951, Mr 18,88:4
Rebull, Reinaldo F, 1956, N 3,23:6
Recat, Emile de, 1949, Jl 29,21:5
Recavarren, Paul, 1950, Mr 15,38:4
Recca, Blaise D, 1961, O 23,30:1
Recco, Ernest, 1937, D 5,II,8:6
Rech, Henry, 1949, Ap 12,30:3
Rechberg, Arnold, 1947, Mr 2,60:2
Rechenberg, Hans A von, 1953, Ja 20,25:4
Rechert, Henry K, 1921, My 10,17:3
Rechholtz, August B, 1960, D 18,84:7
Rechlin, Edward, 1961, D 23,23:4
Recht, Charles, 1965, Jl 17,25:1
Recht, Rudolph, 1944, Ap 10,19:4
Rechtin, Eberhardt C, 1957, N 10,85:4
Recinos, Adrian, 1962, Mr 13,32:1
Recio y Forns, Alberto, 1956, Ja 30,27:5
Reck, Arthur R Mrs, 1953, Ap 5,76:6
Reck, Louis, 1951, Jl 20,21:3
Reck, William M, 1956, F 20,23:4
Reckefus, Charles H Jr, 1955, S 14,35:2
Reckenbacker, Ralph, 1941, F 3,17:4
Reckert, Bernard Bro, 1950, S 20,31:6
Reckford, John K, 1941, F 21,19:4
Reckford, Joseph S, 1949, Ag 12,17:5
Reckford, Louise K Mrs, 1937, S 3,17:2
Reckford, Sam J, 1949, Je 17,23:2
Reckitt, Albert L, 1947, Je 6,23:2
Reckitt, Ernest, 1955, My 23,23:1
Recknagel, Arthur B, 1962, Ag 10,19:4
Recknagel, Arthur B Mrs, 1945, S 24,19:3
Recknagel, Harold S, 1943, N 9,21:6
Reckord, Lydia A Mrs, 1945, My 9,23:3
Reckord, Mabbett K (por), 1946, D 26,25:5
Reckseit, Bernard, 1964, Ag 11,33:1
Reclam, Hans E, 1943, Ap 21,25:2
Reclus, Elie, 1904, Mr 6,4:4
Reclus, Paul Prof, 1914, Jl 30,9:5

Recor, H H, 1903, Mr 25,9:6
Recor, Karl, 1949, Jl 23,11:4
Record, Edgar W, 1943, F 20,13:2
Record, Fred A Mrs, 1952, Ag 8,17:4
Record, G L, 1933, S 28,24:4
Record, James L, 1944, Mr 3,16:2
Record, Samuel J (por), 1945, F 4,38:1
Record, Walter, 1948, F 20,27:4
Records, Francis B, 1949, My 18,27:4
Recouly, Raymond, 1950, S 13,27:1
Recoura, Alfred, 1940, D 23,19:4
Recto, Claro M, 1960, O 3,31:6
Rector, Albert E, 1947, Ja 14,25:2
Rector, Charles E, 1914, S 23,9:5
Rector, Charles Mrs, 1946, Ja 1,27:1
Rector, Dimont M, 1954, O 15,24:2
Rector, Enoch, 1957, Ja 27,85:2
Rector, Enoch Mrs, 1956, Je 19,29:5
Rector, George, 1947, N 27,31:1
Rector, George Mrs, 1948, Ja 13,52:1
Rector, James A, 1950, Mr 11,15:4
Rector, Joseph M, 1939, Ja 11,19:4
Rector, Lizzie, 1955, Ja 7,21:2
Rector, Orville Mrs, 1944, Mr 10,15:3
Rector, Thomas M, 1950, Ap 1,15:7
Rector, Van B Mrs, 1937, S 11,17:5
Rector, Walter W, 1953, My 18,21:5
Recum, Marie E von Baroness, 1954, Ja 23,13:5
Recum, Otton von, 1964, Jl 31,23:4
Red, Charles H, 1937, Ja 16,17:3
Red Cloud, 1909, D 11,11:4
Redaelli, Francesco, 1939, Ag 4,13:1
Redcliffe, Stratford de Lady, 1882, N 27,5:3
Redcross, Arnold J, 1964, My 9,27:3
Reddan, John A (por), 1937, Mr 2,21:1
Reddan, William J, 1944, Jl 3,12:6
Reddaway, William F, 1949, F 1,25:2
Redden, Charles F, 1942, Mr 12,19:2
Redden, Charles F Mrs, 1959, Ag 7,23:4
Redden, Charles Mrs, 1964, S 5,19:3
Redden, Harral A, 1959, O 29,33:2
Redden, John D, 1959, Je 12,27:2
Redden, Joseph E, 1964, Mr 12,35:3
Redden, Maurice J, 1952, Mr 24,25:5
Redden, William R, 1952, Ag 11,15:4
Reddick, Cummins C, 1937, N 25,31:4
Reddick, David W Mrs, 1948, Je 1,23:4
Reddick, Harry W, 1962, Ag 12,81:1
Reddick, William, 1965, My 20,43:2
Reddicks, James A, 1960, O 9,86:7
Reddig, David M, 1961, Ja 4,33:4
Reddig, James B, 1944, F 19,13:1
Reddin, John H, 1940, D 31,15:4
Reddin, John P, 1950, Ja 11,23:2
Reddin, William, 1925, Ag 2,5:3
Redding, A Merrill, 1955, Ja 21,23:1
Redding, Alfred H, 1961, F 15,35:5
Redding, B B, 1882, Ag 22,5:1
Redding, Charles S, 1959, Ja 3,17:5
Redding, Cyrus, 1870, Je 2,1:5
Redding, D George, 1946, Ap 30,21:3
Redding, George H, 1956, N 25,89:1; 1961, Ag 30,33:2
Redding, Henry G, 1955, Ap 2,17:5
Redding, Jerome, 1939, N 25,17:6
Redding, John H, 1951, Jl 18,29:1
Redding, John M, 1965, Ap 3,29:2
Redding, Josephine, 1915, O 8,11:3
Redding, Matthew, 1966, Ap 5,39:4
Redding, Robert J, 1914, Je 6,9:4
Redding, W A, 1931, O 31,17:1
Redding, Walter C, 1954, O 14,29:1
Redding, William F, 1950, Je 27,29:4
Redding, William H, 1911, D 30,11:5
Redding, William M, 1968, Je 10,45:3
Redding, William P (por), 1947, F 18,25:3
Reddinger, Newton, 1907, N 2,9:2
Reddington, Bernard M, 1965, Ag 10,29:1
Reddington, E J, 1903, My 14,9:6
Reddington, Frank J, 1961, O 21,21:5
Reddington, Martin F, 1959, D 13,86:5
Reddington, Thomas, 1940, Ap 16,23:1
Reddington, William F, 1946, O 7,31:3
Reddish, George F, 1962, Ap 17,35:3
Reddy, Albert W, 1953, Mr 13,27:2
Reddy, Eugene J, 1950, Je 14,31:3
Reddy, George, 1914, D 30,11:5
Reddy, George O, 1968, Mr 15,39:2
Reddy, John J, 1954, F 11,29:5
Reddy, Joseph E, 1952, O 14,31:1
Reddy, Leo Mrs (Agnes), 1968, D 22,52:7
Reddy, Martin F, 1949, Je 3,26:3
Reddy, Michael J Mrs, 1947, My 8,25:1
Reddy, Patrick J, 1941, Je 22,32:2
Reddy, Thomas, 1961, Ag 14,45:5
Reddy, William E, 1947, Je 2,25:3
Rede, Carol W, 1964, S 17,43:5
Rede, Wyllys, 1938, S 25,39:1
Rede, Wyllys Mrs, 1951, Mr 6,27:2
Redeke, Ernest W, 1962, Mr 20,37:1
Redeke, Henry Mrs, 1955, F 25,21:3
Redeker, Allen, 1958, S 18,31:2
Redel (Bro Prosper), 1960, Mr 29,37:2
Redelheim, Abraham A, 1965, Jl 28,35:2
Redell, Emma (por), 1940, F 3,13:4
Redell, Walter S, 1949, Ap 24,76:2
Redelsheimer, Jonas C, 1951, S 5,22:6
Redemann, Helmuth C, 1966, Jl 28,33:2
Reden, Herbert A, 1943, Ag 24,19:4
Redenburg, Adam J, 1952, My 29,27:2
Reder, Bernard, 1963, S 9,27:4
Reder, E Louis, 1965, N 21,87:2
Redesdale, Baron (Algernon Bertram Freeman-Mitford), 1916, Ag 18,9:4
Redesdale, Lord (D B Freeman-Mitford), 1958, Mr 18,29:4
Redesdale, Sydney Lady, 1963, My 27,29:3
Redfern, Albert, 1946, Ag 7,27:5
Redfern, Arthur, 1917, My 9,11:4
Redfern, Forrest, 1947, Je 27,21:3
Redfern, Frederick S, 1941, N 8,19:3
Redfern, Merrill F, 1952, Je 25,29:5
Redfern, Ralph B, 1942, Ag 18,21:3
Redfield, Allen W, 1941, D 2,23:3
Redfield, Charles M, 1941, N 12,24:2
Redfield, Edgar G Mrs, 1951, S 15,15:2
Redfield, Edgar P, 1942, Ja 23,19:6
Redfield, Edward W, 1965, O 20,47:1
Redfield, Edward W Mrs, 1947, Mr 5,25:2
Redfield, Edwin E, 1946, Ag 22,27:5
Redfield, Eleanor B Mrs, 1937, Mr 25,25:5
Redfield, Elise M F Mrs, 1941, Mr 14,21:4
Redfield, Florence L Mrs, 1941, S 3,23:5
Redfield, H, 1883, S 12,4:7
Redfield, H V, 1881, N 18,1:2
Redfield, Heman J, 1947, Ag 9,13:5
Redfield, Henry L, 1956, Je 28,29:4
Redfield, Henry W Mrs, 1943, My 9,40:5
Redfield, Herman J Mrs, 1959, Je 29,29:4
Redfield, Horace, 1948, F 1,60:4
Redfield, Humphrey F, 1960, S 9,29:4
Redfield, Isabella T, 1939, D 31,18:7
Redfield, J Bayard Rear-Adm, 1907, Ap 21,9:3
Redfield, J Mansfield, 1924, Ap 26,15:3
Redfield, James A S, 1940, Ap 6,17:5
Redfield, James Col, 1864, O 26,5:1
Redfield, John A, 1939, F 28,19:4
Redfield, John J, 1968, Ja 29,31:1
Redfield, John J Mrs, 1964, S 12,25:5
Redfield, John R, 1908, Mr 15,9:5
Redfield, L, 1878, S 11,2:4
Redfield, L H, 1882, Jl 15,5:2
Redfield, Leonard D, 1944, Jl 17,15:5
Redfield, Margaret, 1941, Ap 28,15:4
Redfield, Mary A Mrs, 1913, Ag 20,9:6
Redfield, Melissa J Mrs, 1942, Mr 10,19:5
Redfield, Oliver S, 1956, O 16,34:2
Redfield, Orrin L, 1942, F 21,19:2
Redfield, Raymond S, 1957, F 13,35:5
Redfield, Robert, 1958, O 17,29:1
Redfield, Scott E Mrs, 1954, O 25,27:4
Redfield, Victor A, 1938, D 7,23:6
Redfield, W C, 1932, Je 14,21:1
Redfield, William G, 1941, S 19,23:2
Redfield, William H, 1944, Ja 5,18:2
Redfield, William M, 1938, My 29,II,6:6
Redford, John B Mrs, 1951, O 22,23:3
Redford, Lewis I, 1949, Je 1,32:6
Redgate, B Henry, 1951, My 7,25:5
Redgate, O K, 1954, O 23,15:1
Redgrave, Arnold I, 1956, Ap 23,27:5
Redhead, Edward Richard, 1924, My 31,15:4
Redhill, Charles S, 1952, N 12,27:3
Redholz, Anthony F, 1946, Ag 18,44:6
Redican, Packey, 1952, D 27,21:1
Redick, Emma C, 1959, S 6,72:5
Redigan, John J, 1964, O 25,88:8
Redigan, Mary (Mother Gabriel), 1916, Ap 1,13:4
Rediker, George H, 1956, Je 30,17:2
Rediman, Walter V, 1959, Ag 3,25:4
Redington, Alfred Gen, 1875, Je 2,4:5
Redington, Frances Mrs, 1947, O 7,27:2
Redington, George O, 1958, Ap 19,21:5
Redington, John C, 1946, Jl 27,17:6
Redington, Laurence Col, 1937, N 13,19:4
Redington, Lucius K, 1959, Ag 10,27:5
Redington, Lyman W Ex-Judge, 1925, O 19,21:4
Redington, Paul G, 1942, Ja 13,19:3
Redish, Jules, 1952, Ja 19,15:6
Redish, Milton H, 1952, Ag 30,13:3
Redler, Joseph, 1905, Ap 27,6:2
Redlich, J, 1936, N 12,27:5
Redlich, Nathan Jr, 1955, D 4,89:2
Redlich, Oswald, 1944, F 16,17:2
Redlich, Rosa O Mrs, 1938, O 7,23:5
Redlich, Samuel Mrs, 1947, Jl 7,17:3
Redling, Conrad, 1960, Mr 27,86:5
Redman, Augustus A, 1949, Jl 21,26:3
Redman, Benjamin F, 1945, Ja 13,11:2
Redman, Frank E, 1940, Jl 25,17:2
Redman, Herbert L, 1951, Ap 22,88:3
Redman, John R Mrs, 1955, O 16,86:3
Redman, Joseph Hodgson, 1914, D 16,15:6
Redman, Kathryn B, 1948, D 1,29:5
Redman, L V, 1946, N 26,29:1
Redman, Lyman, 1904, O 7,1:4
Redman, Mark H Mrs, 1955, Ag 28,85:2
Redman, Michael J, 1938, F 12,15:4
Redman, Robert B, 1960, Je 10,31:1
Redman, Rufus S, 1937, Ja 1,23:4
Redman, Walter H, 1953, Ja 23,19:1
Redman, Walter H Mrs, 1951, Ap 8,92:3
Redmon, Preston F Jr, 1946, Ag 3,17:2
Redmon, Richard L, 1964, S 26,23:5
Redmond, Abram K, 1957, My 2,31:2
Redmond, Andrew J, 1948, F 3,25:4
Redmond, Charles J, 1942, D 25,18:3
Redmond, D W, 1934, N 14,19:1
Redmond, Daniel G, 1955, F 23,27:2
Redmond, Daniel H Mrs, 1941, Ap 3,23:3
Redmond, Dennis, 1914, Ja 22,11:5
Redmond, Edward J, 1940, Je 17,15:6
Redmond, Forrest H, 1953, Ja 27,25:2
Redmond, Frank E, 1949, Je 1,31:3
Redmond, Geraldyn, 1916, Je 18,18:4
Redmond, Harry A, 1938, S 28,25:2
Redmond, Henry, 1914, Ag 14,11:6
Redmond, Henry S, 1910, F 26,7:4
Redmond, Henry S Mrs, 1959, D 9,45:2
Redmond, Hugh F, 1962, O 31,37:2
Redmond, Hugh F Sr, 1959, My 30,17:2
Redmond, James A, 1949, Ap 17,76:4
Redmond, James C, 1943, F 8,19:4
Redmond, James F, 1955, S 4,58:1
Redmond, James J Mrs, 1952, Ja 22,29:2
Redmond, Jasper, 1949, Ja 17,19:5
Redmond, John (trb, Mr 8,11:4), 1918, Mr 7,11:1
Redmond, John, 1953, S 7,19:3
Redmond, John A, 1958, D 4,39:5
Redmond, John C Mrs, 1955, Ja 1,13:3
Redmond, John Francis, 1923, Jl 3,13:5
Redmond, John L, 1944, My 28,33:3
Redmond, John P, 1957, D 12,29:3
Redmond, John V Capt, 1968, Ja 26,47:2
Redmond, John W, 1942, Ap 29,21:4
Redmond, Lawrence B, 1961, Ag 17,27:6
Redmond, Lydia, 1924, Jl 23,15:3
Redmond, Mark, 1937, S 14,23:2
Redmond, Olney, 1947, D 2,30:2
Redmond, Paul A, 1955, Ag 4,25:2
Redmond, S D, 1948, F 13,21:3
Redmond, T Fergus, 1963, Je 18,41:3
Redmond, Thomas F Mrs, 1958, Ag 25,21:4
Redmond, William, 1913, F 24,11:5
Redmore, Morrell, 1953, Ag 7,19:1
Redmund, William, 1915, O 19,11:4
Rednor, Daniel Mrs, 1966, My 23,41:3
Redpath, Frederick L Mrs, 1947, D 28,40:6
Redpath, George O, 1940, S 14,17:3
Redpath, James, 1891, F 11,8:2
Redpath, John M, 1947, Ag 13,23:6
Redpath, Mary C Mrs, 1914, Ag 22,7:6
Redpath, Robert U Mrs, 1959, O 13,39:5
Redpath, William, 1949, Ag 11,23:4
Redpath, William J Mrs, 1943, My 13,21:2
Redsinak, Stephen, 1968, F 3,29:4
Redstrom, John, 1951, Je 26,29:2
Redway, Albert J, 1966, S 28,47:4
Redway, Jacques W (por), 1942, N 7,15:3
Redway, Jacques W Mrs, 1947, D 12,28:3
Redway, Laurance D, 1960, N 19,21:4
Redwood, Francis T, 1906, N 30,1:7
Redwood, Frank H, 1949, My 28,15:5
Redwood, John E, 1941, Ag 1,15:5
Redwood, John P, 1958, S 24,27:5
Redwood, Lizzie Mrs, 1943, My 27,25:5
Redy, Patrick H, 1949, Mr 3,25:2
Ree, Max, 1953, Mr 8,89:5
Ree, Virginia Mrs, 1925, My 5,21:3
Reeb, C W, 1937, S 27,5:4
Reebeck, Joseph, 1965, Ag 25,39:5
Reeberg, Lucien, 1964, F 1,23:5
Reece, B Carroll, 1961, Mr 20,29:1
Reece, Byron H, 1958, Je 5,28:6
Reece, Franklin A, 1961, Jl 14,23:2
Reece, John, 1944, My 3,19:3
Reece, Nate E Sr, 1954, S 26,87:2
Reece, Raleigh V, 1946, Jl 20,13:3
Reece, Tom, 1953, O 17,15:4
Reece, Wade W, 1951, Ag 1,23:5
Reed, A Stuart, 1943, Ja 20,20:2
Reed, Agnes C, 1952, Mr 16,90:3
Reed, Agnes S Mrs, 1940, Ag 18,37:2
Reed, Albert A, 1947, N 30,76:5
Reed, Albert J, 1954, Jl 25,69:3
Reed, Albert V, 1946, O 3,27:2
Reed, Alfred, 1924, O 31,19:5
Reed, Alfred C, 1951, Je 21,27:1
Reed, Alfred Ex-Justice, 1918, D 7,15:5
Reed, Alfred F, 1953, F 7,15:5
Reed, Alfred H, 1953, Ag 3,17:5
Reed, Alfred S, 1958, O 12,86:3
Reed, Alfred Z, 1949, Mr 12,17:3
Reed, Allan M, 1946, S 28,17:5
Reed, Allen V Rear-Adm, 1917, Ja 16,9:3
Reed, Alma M Mrs, 1966, N 21,45:1
Reed, Alter S Dr, 1937, Mr 1,19:4
Reed, Amy L, 1949, Ja 26,25:3
Reed, Annie Allen Mrs, 1925, Mr 3,23:4
Reed, Annie M, 1953, Ja 23,20:3

Reed, Arthur J, 1945, Ap 11,23:6
Reed, Arthur L, 1942, Mr 19,21:5
Reed, Arthur M, 1948, My 27,25:1
Reed, Augusta Dr (Mrs Chas B Reed), 1911, F 11, 11:6
Reed, Austin, 1954, My 6,33:3
Reed, Axel H, 1954, Jl 22,23:5
Reed, B, 1905, S 19,9:6
Reed, Bernard W, 1962, N 15,37:4
Reed, Blossom Mrs, 1964, Ag 23,87:2
Reed, C A L, 1928, Ag 29,21:4
Reed, C Lawson, 1923, D 18,19:3
Reed, C Sir, 1881, Mr 26,5:3
Reed, Calvin E, 1905, Mr 1,9:5
Reed, Carl A, 1958, N 9,88:1
Reed, Carl A Mrs, 1939, My 5,23:3
Reed, Carl D, 1962, Jl 12,29:5
Reed, Carrie Mrs, 1942, Ja 15,19:1
Reed, Carroll R, 1960, Ja 9,21:5
Reed, Charles, 1941, Ja 8,19:3
Reed, Charles A, 1911, N 14,13:6; 1940, D 18,25:5; 1947, F 1,15:6; 1950, Ag 20,77:1
Reed, Charles A Mrs, 1955, My 17,29:3
Reed, Charles B, 1911, Mr 27,11:4; 1940, S 6,21:3; 1941, Je 26,23:2
Reed, Charles B Mrs (Dr Augusta Reed), 1911, F 11,11:6
Reed, Charles F, 1939, My 19,21:5
Reed, Charles H, 1963, Ag 9,23:5
Reed, Charles L, 1944, D 18,19:3
Reed, Charles M, 1958, Ap 13,83:4
Reed, Charles P, 1944, Ag 29,17:1
Reed, Charles S, 1947, N 27,31:5
Reed, Charles W, 1937, Ap 21,23:2; 1953, Ap 25,15:6
Reed, Chauncey W, 1956, F 10,21:1
Reed, Chester A Mrs, 1941, Je 2,17:3
Reed, Chester I, 1873, S 3,5:5
Reed, Clarence, 1953, Ja 14,41:3
Reed, Clinton H Mrs, 1963, N 9,25:4
Reed, Clyde M, 1949, N 9,1:8
Reed, Clyde M Mrs, 1952, Mr 14,20:6
Reed, Daniel A (funl plans, F 21,21:6; funl, F 22,88:2), 1959, F 20,25:1
Reed, Dave, 1946, Ap 12,27:4
Reed, David, 1912, F 3,11:4
Reed, David A Mrs, 1948, Je 10,25:5
Reed, David Aiken, 1953, F 11,29:1
Reed, David H, 1941, Ap 13,39:3
Reed, DeWitt C Mrs, 1957, O 8,35:4
Reed, Dian Mrs, 1952, O 16,32:2
Reed, Donald W Sr, 1950, N 18,15:4
Reed, Dudley B, 1955, Je 30,25:2
Reed, E Grant Mrs, 1949, D 3,15:2
Reed, Edgar S, 1963, N 6,36:3
Reed, Edgar T, 1945, N 26,21:2
Reed, Edward B, 1940, F 17,13:3
Reed, Edward C Capt, 1912, O 27,II,17:5
Reed, Edward E, 1941, Ag 25,15:4
Reed, Edward E Mrs, 1938, Ag 7,32:7
Reed, Edward P, 1942, Ag 4,10:3
Reed, Edward Townsend, 1921, O 24,15:4
Reed, Edwin, 1908, O 17,9:5
Reed, Edwin W, 1937, F 14,II,9:1
Reed, Elias A, 1951, D 30,25:1
Reed, Eliott W, 1964, Ap 25,29:5
Reed, Elizabeth Armstrong Mrs, 1915, Je 19,9:7
Reed, Elizabeth F, 1953, F 1,89:2
Reed, Emma Du P Mrs, 1962, Ag 27,23:2
Reed, Ernest A, 1949, My 3,25:3
Reed, Ernest B, 1950, Ja 25,25:1
Reed, Eugene C, 1953, N 21,13:2
Reed, Eugene E, 1940, D 16,23:3
Reed, Ezekil, 1947, My 20,25:5
Reed, F Dana, 1910, O 23,II,13:3
Reed, Florence, 1916, S 6,9:5; 1967, N 22,47:1
Reed, Floyd O, 1957, F 17,92:7
Reed, Francis H, 1942, Ja 25,31:2
Reed, Frank, 1941, My 26,19:4
Reed, Frank A, 1947, S 30,25:2
Reed, Frank A Sr, 1954, O 29,23:4
Reed, Frank C, 1953, S 18,23:4
Reed, Frank C Mrs, 1953, Ag 18,23:4
Reed, Frank D, 1939, Ap 25,23:2
Reed, Frank L, 1943, F 1,15:5
Reed, Frank Mrs, 1951, Ag 10,15:5
Reed, Franklin C Mrs, 1948, O 16,15:1
Reed, Franklin L Mrs, 1962, Ap 7,25:2
Reed, Freda H Mrs, 1946, S 2,17:5
Reed, Frederic Holly, 1916, D 10,21:2
Reed, Frederick D, 1937, D 20,27:5
Reed, G B, 1955, F 22,21:4
Reed, George, 1943, My 30,26:3
Reed, George E, 1952, Je 14,15:5
Reed, George H, 1939, Ja 23,13:2; 1947, Ja 23,23:3; 1952, Je 23,19:4
Reed, George M, 1947, My 14,25:2
Reed, George Rev, 1908, S 25,7:5
Reed, George Sir, 1918, S 13,11:1
Reed, George W, 1947, S 7,60:2; 1949, N 12,15:5
Reed, Gordon W Mrs, 1967, My 7,87:1
Reed, Grace H Mrs, 1937, Mr 1,19:5
Reed, Graham, 1952, O 18,19:2
Reed, Guy E, 1959, Ja 4,88:4
Reed, H A, 1930, N 23,30:1
Reed, H E, 1876, Ag 10,2:3
Reed, Harrie P Capt, 1914, Ag 11,9:4
Reed, Harry A, 1946, Mr 4,23:3
Reed, Harry E, 1941, O 16,21:1
Reed, Harry J, 1960, N 6,88:3
Reed, Harry L, 1964, My 24,93:1
Reed, Harry W, 1941, Jl 19,13:7
Reed, Henry A, 1919, Ag 24,22:4
Reed, Henry Charles, 1948, Je 8,25:2
Reed, Henry D, 1943, Ap 28,23:2
Reed, Henry G, 1954, Ja 28,27:5
Reed, Henry H, 1963, Ag 6,31:4
Reed, Henry M (por), 1947, Ag 13,23:1
Reed, Henry Mrs, 1945, Ja 14,40:1
Reed, Henry R, 1905, Mr 15,16:2
Reed, Herbert, 1944, N 3,21:4
Reed, Herbert C, 1940, Jl 26,17:3
Reed, Herbert E, 1959, F 7,19:3
Reed, Herbert T, 1945, Ap 28,15:6
Reed, Horace, 1960, Ja 22,27:2
Reed, Horace G, 1967, My 24,47:1
Reed, Horatio R, 1953, S 19,15:2
Reed, Howard S, 1950, My 13,17:4
Reed, Howard S Mrs, 1952, My 20,25:2
Reed, Hudson W, 1955, Mr 14,23:4
Reed, Hugh B 2d, 1959, Ap 19,86:3
Reed, Hugh D Prof, 1937, Ag 24,21:1
Reed, I G, 1903, Ja 25,8:2
Reed, Ira S, 1954, O 22,27:1
Reed, J Duff, 1966, Jl 12,43:1
Reed, J G, 1878, Jl 4,5:4
Reed, J Homer, 1937, N 20,17:5
Reed, J Warren, 1912, S 10,9:5
Reed, Jack, 1937, O 15,23:3
Reed, James, 1868, F 9,8:5; 1946, O 22,25:3; 1960, Ag 19,23:4
Reed, James H, 1950, O 3,31:2
Reed, James H Mrs, 1945, My 3,23:4
Reed, James Rev, 1872, N 10,5:3
Reed, James S, 1958, N 25,33:2
Reed, James Sr, 1941, Jl 24,17:3
Reed, Jared, 1962, S 12,39:2
Reed, Jay T, 1959, F 25,31:3
Reed, Jesse D, 1872, D 17,1:6
Reed, Jessie, 1940, S 19,23:1
Reed, Joanna A, 1944, Jl 8,11:4
Reed, Joel H, 1924, O 4,13:4
Reed, John, 1920, O 19,11:5
Reed, John Addison, 1905, Mr 26,9:4
Reed, John C, 1938, Ag 6,13:6; 1952, Je 15,84:1
Reed, John C Judge, 1910, Ja 13,9:4
Reed, John H, 1940, Mr 13,23:6; 1941, Je 20,21:2; 1967, Ag 25,35:4
Reed, John J, 1938, N 14,19:1; 1948, My 25,27:3
Reed, John Joseph Rev, 1911, O 24,13:4
Reed, John O Dr, 1916, Ja 24,11:2
Reed, John O H, 1946, S 14,7:5
Reed, John T S, 1950, My 4,27:2
Reed, John W, 1950, Ap 5,31:2
Reed, Joseph, 1942, Mr 4,19:6
Reed, Joseph J, 1873, Mr 9,5:3
Reed, Joseph P, 1940, D 20,25:1
Reed, Joseph Rea Ex-Justice, 1925, Ap 4,17:5
Reed, Julius H, 1938, F 1,21:2
Reed, Kenneth M, 1944, Ag 7,15:1
Reed, Kenneth T, 1945, F 21,19:2
Reed, Lansing P (por), 1937, D 3,23:1
Reed, Latham G (por), 1945, N 30,23:3
Reed, Latham G Mrs, 1943, N 27,13:2
Reed, Latham R, 1946, O 7,31:6
Reed, Lawrence A, 1958, Mr 9,86:4
Reed, Leslie H, 1950, N 17,27:3
Reed, Lewis B, 1941, Ap 25,19:4
Reed, Lewis Benedict, 1924, Jl 24,13:4
Reed, Lewis G, 1907, D 7,9:6; 1955, N 12,19:1
Reed, Lewis T, 1953, S 5,15:4
Reed, Lewis T Mrs, 1937, O 24,II,9:1
Reed, Linn V, 1940, D 23,19:4
Reed, Lorde S, 1951, D 24,13:4
Reed, Lorin H, 1941, Mr 5,21:5
Reed, Louis C M, 1951, Mr 27,29:3
Reed, Louis F, 1951, Ja 8,17:2; 1958, N 6,37:4
Reed, Louis Mrs, 1939, O 12,25:5
Reed, Lowell J, 1966, Ap 30,31:3
Reed, Luther A, 1961, N 17,35:1
Reed, Luther D Mrs, 1942, Jl 30,21:5
Reed, Margaret A, 1949, F 19,15:5
Reed, Margaret Mrs, 1941, Mr 19,21:3
Reed, Margaretta Mrs, 1957, Ja 8,31:1
Reed, Martin M, 1963, Jl 30,29:2
Reed, Mary, 1943, My 21,19:5; 1960, N 30,37:2
Reed, Merril V, 1954, D 24,13:2
Reed, Merriman M, 1957, N 14,33:3
Reed, Morton W, 1943, Jl 2,19:4
Reed, Nathl (Texas Jack), 1950, Ja 9,25:3
Reed, Newton C, 1959, Ja 25,94:1
Reed, Oren, 1953, O 30,23:1
Reed, Paul C, 1964, O 5,33:4
Reed, Paul E Mrs, 1951, Ap 21,17:2
Reed, Phil S Mrs, 1939, Mr 30,23:5
Reed, Philip L, 1964, Jl 28,29:5
Reed, Philip L Mrs, 1964, Ap 13,29:4
Reed, Philip S, 1966, Ap 15,39:2
Reed, Phillip C, 1956, S 6,25:3
Reed, Pleasant L, 1951, Ap 15,92:6
Reed, Prentiss B, 1953, Je 28,60:7
Reed, R Ralston, 1951, Mr 13,31:1
Reed, Ralph, 1958, My 12,18:8
Reed, Ralph D, 1940, Ja 31,19:4
Reed, Ralph Sir, 1958, My 30,21:1
Reed, Ralph T, 1968, Ja 23,43:6
Reed, Raymond C, 1940, O 13,48:6
Reed, Raymond S, 1965, Ja 26,37:1
Reed, Richard Capt, 1923, Ja 2,13:2
Reed, Richard Clark Dr, 1925, Jl 10,17:6
Reed, Richard J Dr, 1909, O 13,11:5
Reed, Robert, 1950, My 13,17:6
Reed, Robert B, 1944, N 16,23:6
Reed, Robert B Mrs, 1942, N 18,25:6
Reed, Robert H, 1950, Je 13,27:2
Reed, Robert L, 1965, My 22,31:1
Reed, Robert R, 1945, Je 17,26:5
Reed, Robert R Mrs, 1953, N 23,27:3
Reed, Robert W, 1949, D 9,31:2
Reed, Rodman S Jr, 1961, N 22,21:1
Reed, Roy E, 1943, Ag 22,36:4; 1957, N 21,33:4
Reed, S A, 1935, O 2,23:1
Reed, S G, 1948, Mr 23,25:3
Reed, Sam, 1924, Ap 12,15:3
Reed, Samuel C, 1923, Ja 23,21:4; 1943, N 1,17:2
Reed, Samuel J, 1905, My 24,9:6
Reed, Spencer A, 1953, Ag 19,29:5
Reed, Stephen K, 1923, Ap 27,17:5
Reed, Stephen W, 1966, Ap 10,79:4
Reed, Stuart H Dr, 1904, Ja 7,9:5
Reed, Stuart R, 1960, O 1,19:2
Reed, Sylvanus Gallup Mrs, 1914, N 18,11:5
Reed, Theodore B, 1958, Jl 3,26:1
Reed, Thomas E, 1941, Jl 18,19:6
Reed, Thomas J, 1959, My 24,88:6
Reed, Verner Z, 1919, Ap 22,17:4
Reed, Verner Z Jr Mrs, 1966, F 10,37:4
Reed, Verner Z Mrs, 1945, My 28,19:5
Reed, W B, 1876, F 21,8:4
Reed, W Boardman Mrs, 1946, S 20,31:2
Reed, W N P, 1949, S 11,94:4
Reed, W P, 1903, Ap 18,9:6
Reed, Walter A, 1918, D 15,22:3
Reed, Walter J, 1961, Ap 23,86:4
Reed, Walter Maj, 1902, N 24,9:5
Reed, Walter O, 1937, S 4,15:2
Reed, Walter P, 1960, Je 25,21:4
Reed, Walter R, 1940, Ja 17,21:2
Reed, Walter S, 1958, My 12,29:5
Reed, Ward L, 1959, N 6,30:8
Reed, Wellford C, 1907, D 8,11:5
Reed, Wilbur L, 1955, Je 14,29:5
Reed, Willard J, 1944, S 7,23:4
Reed, William A, 1952, My 13,30:3
Reed, William C, 1953, My 24,88:5
Reed, William D, 1940, My 25,17:6; 1952, Je 15,84
Reed, William D Mrs, 1951, Ag 10,15:3
Reed, William E, 1947, Ja 26,53:2; 1953, S 9,29:2
Reed, William F Jr, 1956, D 26,27:2
Reed, William G, 1944, D 30,11:6; 1946, O 14,29:5 1961, Ag 27,85:2
Reed, William Gordon, 1920, O 9,15:1
Reed, William H, 1949, S 10,17:6; 1950, O 7,19:5; 1952, My 8,31:5; 1960, S 6,35:1
Reed, William I, 1947, S 16,24:2
Reed, William L, 1941, Je 12,23:2; 1943, F 6,13:2
Reed, William R Mrs, 1954, N 1,27:5
Reed, William T Mrs, 1955, Je 22,29:4
Reed, William W Mrs, 1951, N 17,17:6
Reed, Wilson Jr, 1941, Mr 27,23:4
Reed, Winder E, 1952, Ap 29,27:5
Reed, Witmel H, 1937, D 2,25:5
Reed (Mother Mary Cecilia), 1961, F 15,35:3
Reeder, A H Gov, 1864, Jl 8,4:6
Reeder, Arthur L, 1937, My 25,28:2
Reeder, Earl E, 1951, Je 12,29:5
Reeder, Frank Gen, 1912, D 8,17:4
Reeder, Gilbert T, 1955, Ag 19,19:5
Reeder, Howard E, 1950, Ag 16,29:3
Reeder, J Knight, 1957, Jl 8,23:4
Reeder, John F, 1960, Je 16,33:3
Reeder, Leland P, 1955, Jl 13,25:4
Reeder, Nathaniel S, 1957, Ja 22,29:2
Reeder, R R, 1934, O 14,32:3
Reeder, Robert P, 1956, Jl 18,27:2
Reeder, Rudolph R Mrs, 1950, Jl 6,27:1
Reeder, Russell P, 1942, N 8,51:4
Reeder, Sherwood, 1955, D 21,29:2
Reeder, William C, 1958, N 29,21:1
Reedmoyer, Milton H, 1942, My 18,15:5
Reedy, George E Sr, 1953, Je 10,29:4
Reedy, George L, 1961, Ap 19,39:4
Reedy, John H, 1950, F 22,29:6
Reedy, Joseph, 1951, Jl 13,21:5
Reedy, Thomas J, 1944, Ap 7,19:3; 1961, Ap 30,8
Reedy, William M Mrs, 1949, D 28,32:3
Reedy, William Marion, 1920, Jl 29,9:1
Reedy, William T, 1958, S 23,33:1
Reehm, Harold M, 1953, D 18,29:1
Reeke, George C, 1944, My 13,19:5

Reekie, William M, 1948, Ag 16,19:6
Reel, Gordon, 1951, Ag 19,85:1
Reel, Henry J, 1942, O 19,19:6
Reel, Henry J Mrs, 1952, Ag 22,21:4
Reel, Ida V, 1948, Ap 30,23:1
Reel, William D Jr, 1949, O 11,31:2
Reel, William J, 1952, My 29,27:1
Reeman, Edmund H, 1950, Ja 10,29:5
Reemelin, Clarence B, 1951, D 12,37:1
Reemtsma, Philipp F, 1959, D 12,23:4
Reene, Clifford C, 1908, F 17,7:4
Reens, Louis Mrs (Renee), 1968, My 8,44:5
Reens, Richard, 1954, S 12,84:5
Reep, Charles W, 1948, F 26,23:1
Rees, Alfred C, 1941, Jl 27,30:4
Rees, Arthur D, 1961, D 30,6:6
Rees, Arthur L, 1942, N 15,56:3
Rees, Bird Mrs, 1948, My 22,15:5
Rees, Caradoc, 1943, Ja 6,27:1
Rees, Charles P, 1938, Ja 20,23:1
Rees, Charles Sumner, 1921, Jl 18,11:7
Rees, Charles W, 1966, O 11,47:2
Rees, Corwin P, 1924, S 15,21:2
Rees, E Philip, 1964, N 29,87:2
Rees, Edwin, 1940, Jl 6,15:6
Rees, Fred, 1951, Ag 15,27:5
Rees, Fred H, 1952, O 15,31:2
Rees, Gomer C, 1949, My 14,13:5
Rees, Gordon B, 1952, Je 20,23:5
Rees, Harry F, 1946, Je 11,23:1
Rees, Henry J, 1940, Je 23,30:8
Rees, Hubert L, 1948, S 17,25:3
Rees, James, 1885, Ap 30,2:4
Rees, Janet E Ruutz Mrs, 1924, Ap 16,23:5
Rees, John H, 1952, D 14,91:1
Rees, John K Prof, 1907, Mr 11,7:6
Rees, Joseph, 1952, Mr 5,29:4
Rees, Julie M Mrs, 1940, Ja 26,17:3
Rees, Kelley, 1954, Je 19,15:6
Rees, Lionel W B, 1955, S 29,33:2
Rees, Mary G Mrs, 1950, Ap 30,102:3
Rees, Norman I, 1910, Ag 4,7:6
Rees, R I, 1936, N 24,27:1
Rees, Ramsey, 1955, O 24,27:2
Rees, Robert, 1965, Jl 4,25:1
Rees, Robert J, 1939, F 10,23:4
Rees, Stanley M, 1937, Ag 30,21:5
Rees, Thomas H, 1942, S 22,21:1
Rees, Thomas W, 1959, O 17,23:1
Rees, Walter E, 1949, Je 7,31:2
Rees, William A Mrs, 1945, O 9,21:2
Rees, William E, 1955, Jl 13,25:2
Reese, Al, 1956, Mr 24,19:2
Reese, Arthur A, 1943, D 29,17:2
Reese, Ben H Mrs, 1958, Ag 30,15:4
Reese, C Herbert, 1945, Ag 24,19:2
Reese, Charles L (por), 1940, Ap 13,17:5
Reese, Charles L Mrs, 1959, D 12,23:4
Reese, Chauncey A, 1948, F 1,60:6
Reese, Dave Mrs, 1949, Ag 5,19:2
Reese, David R, 1945, O 22,17:5
Reese, Donald T, 1950, Mr 11,15:2
Reese, Edan A, 1938, Ja 26,23:3
Reese, Everett (Dixie), 1955, My 1,3:1
Reese, F F, 1936, D 23,21:4
Reese, Fred S, 1947, My 31,13:2
Reese, Gilbert A, 1943, O 31,49:1
Reese, Harry, 1964, Je 14,84:6
Reese, Harry Mrs, 1965, F 4,31:4
Reese, Harry W, 1956, O 29,29:3
Reese, J D, 1931, N 30,19:3
Reese, J Ramsey Mrs, 1939, Ja 17,21:6
Reese, Jacob, 1907, Mr 27,9:7
Reese, Jacob Reese, 1920, Ap 5,15:4
Reese, James Lt, 1919, My 14,17:6
Reese, John A, 1947, D 11,34:3
Reese, John D, 1940, Ja 28,32:2; 1958, O 8,35:4
Reese, John Mrs, 1947, Ap 19,16:2
Reese, Leal W, 1954, Ja 30,17:4
Reese, Lew P, 1952, Je 7,19:6
Reese, Ludwig L, 1944, Je 8,21:4
Reese, M, 1878, Ag 4,7:5
Reese, Margaret M, 1961, S 24,87:2
Reese, Melvin H, 1957, F 23,17:2
Reese, R G Dr, 1926, O 19,29:4
Reese, Ramsay, 1951, Ja 22,17:4
Reese, Raymond P, 1955, Ja 18,27:3
Reese, Raymond T, 1949, Je 15,29:1
Reese, Reese R, 1944, Ja 21,17:2
Reese, Rex, 1941, Ja 8,19:3
Reese, Richard G, 1964, My 13,47:4
Reese, Richmond J, 1953, N 23,27:2
Reese, Samuel R, 1963, D 26,27:1
Reese, Sherman W, 1953, Je 2,29:3
Reese, T M, 1875, D 8,6:6
Reese, Thomas J, 1948, F 17,25:4
Reese, Thomas L, 1961, My 21,87:2
Reese, W A Mrs, 1948, Ja 17,17:2
Reese, W James, 1960, F 19,27:3
Reese, William R, 1952, S 18,29:2
Reese, William W, 1942, Mr 30,17:6
Reeser, Edward F, 1950, Ja 10,29:4
Reeser, Edwin B, 1953, S 16,33:2
Reeser, Elmer A, 1940, Ag 16,15:5
Reeser, Myron D, 1966, D 7,47:3
Reeside, John E, 1906, N 30,9:6
Reesman, Clay W, 1949, Ja 4,19:4
Reet, Peter, 1959, O 3,19:4
Reethof, Oscar, 1948, Ja 3,13:2
Reeve, A B, 1936, Ag 10,19:5
Reeve, Ada, 1966, S 26,41:1
Reeve, Alan, 1962, S 1,19:4
Reeve, Archie F, 1959, D 29,25:4
Reeve, Archie F Mrs, 1961, My 7,86:6
Reeve, Arthur, 1943, Mr 23,19:3
Reeve, Augustus H, 1945, N 2,19:2
Reeve, Augustus H Mrs, 1954, D 26,61:2
Reeve, Charles H, 1962, Mr 26,31:4
Reeve, Charles M, 1947, Je 25,26:3
Reeve, Charles R, 1940, Je 7,23:5
Reeve, David B, 1907, S 14,9:6
Reeve, Elizabeth L, 1957, Je 12,35:4
Reeve, Francis F, 1956, My 23,31:5
Reeve, Fred E, 1940, Je 23,30:5
Reeve, Frederic E, 1944, Mr 15,19:4
Reeve, George A, 1943, D 30,17:4
Reeve, George T Jr, 1944, Ja 16,41:7
Reeve, George T Mrs, 1938, Ja 25,21:2
Reeve, Guy C, 1950, Ag 28,17:4
Reeve, Harry H, 1949, O 25,27:3
Reeve, Henry L Mrs, 1952, D 20,17:4
Reeve, Herman F, 1946, F 18,21:2
Reeve, J Stanley, 1960, D 18,84:1
Reeve, James B, 1944, Je 29,23:5
Reeve, James B Mrs, 1954, Ja 25,19:4
Reeve, Jay F, 1956, Jl 25,29:3
Reeve, John G, 1951, D 2,90:3
Reeve, Mark A, 1941, Ap 5,17:5
Reeve, Marshall S, 1949, Ja 7,21:3
Reeve, Maurice E, 1954, Ap 6,30:6
Reeve, Percival J, 1957, N 9,27:4
Reeve, Ralph W, 1949, O 15,15:3
Reeve, Robert Mrs, 1940, D 3,25:3
Reeve, Sidney A, 1941, Je 13,19:3
Reeve, Theodore E, 1943, D 28,18:3
Reeve, W D Bp, 1925, My 13,21:3
Reeve, Walter J, 1958, Je 11,35:3
Reeve, Warren S, 1961, Ap 22,25:4
Reeve, William B, 1946, S 12,7:1
Reeve, William D, 1961, F 17,28:1
Reeve, William E, 1963, O 27,89:1
Reeves, A C, 1936, F 16,II,11:1
Reeves, A G, 1927, Ja 11,31:3
Reeves, Al, 1940, F 28,21:3
Reeves, Alfred (por), 1946, Ap 8,27:3
Reeves, Alfred, 1962, Mr 9,19:4
Reeves, Alfred P Mrs, 1961, Jl 8,19:6
Reeves, Billy, 1943, D 30,17:4
Reeves, Charles F, 1954, S 9,31:3
Reeves, Claude L, 1956, O 23,33:4
Reeves, Clifton, 1938, S 22,23:5
Reeves, Conrad Sir, 1902, Mr 30,8:5
Reeves, D Le Roy, 1949, Ag 13,11:2
Reeves, Earl C Sr, 1962, Ja 25,31:4
Reeves, Edward, 1943, N 4,23:3
Reeves, Edward J, 1943, Ja 27,21:4
Reeves, Embery Sanford, 1968, S 14,31:4
Reeves, Firman M, 1962, Je 25,29:2
Reeves, Floyd D, 1946, Mr 16,13:2
Reeves, Floyd E, 1950, N 21,31:4
Reeves, Frank J, 1948, My 11,25:3
Reeves, Frank J Mrs, 1948, D 15,33:5
Reeves, Frank Mrs, 1948, Ja 4,52:3
Reeves, Frederick L, 1948, S 10,23:3
Reeves, Furman W, 1966, D 6,47:2
Reeves, G L, 1947, O 22,29:3
Reeves, George (see also Ag 8), 1876, Ag 14,1:6
Reeves, George H, 1954, Ag 31,21:6
Reeves, George I, 1946, D 11,32:3
Reeves, George O, 1947, Jl 23,23:5
Reeves, George S, 1941, Mr 25,23:3
Reeves, George W, 1914, Ag 25,9:4
Reeves, Grover C, 1952, Ag 31,45:1
Reeves, Harrison S, 1945, Ja 6,11:6
Reeves, Harry O, 1950, Ag 22,27:2
Reeves, Herbert, 1947, N 16,76:7
Reeves, Ira L, 1939, O 26,23:1
Reeves, Isaac S K, 1949, D 21,30:2
Reeves, J Franklin, 1946, S 20,31:2
Reeves, James, 1920, N 8,15:6; 1957, O 12,19:5
Reeves, James A W, 1947, Mr 8,13:4
Reeves, Jesse S (por), 1942, Jl 8,23:3
Reeves, Jim, 1964, Ag 3,44:6
Reeves, John D Jr, 1964, Mr 7,23:3
Reeves, John J Mrs, 1943, O 23,13:4
Reeves, John L, 1947, Ja 9,23:5
Reeves, Joseph M, 1948, Mr 26,21:1
Reeves, Joseph M Mrs, 1947, N 29,13:2
Reeves, Joseph Sr, 1947, Mr 19,26:3
Reeves, Marb B, 1939, Ag 16,23:6
Reeves, Margaret Mrs, 1951, My 19,17:8
Reeves, Micajah R (will, S 26,4:2), 1942, S 8,23:4
Reeves, Nathaniel S, 1965, S 13,35:3
Reeves, Nathaniel S Mrs, 1958, Ag 5,27:1
Reeves, Noah C, 1953, My 4,23:4
Reeves, P Kennedy, 1942, D 20,44:8
Reeves, Peter, 1958, Ag 2,17:4
Reeves, Robert J Dr, 1968, F 26,37:2
Reeves, Robert R, 1950, S 7,31:2
Reeves, Robert S, 1959, Ag 22,17:5
Reeves, Ruth, 1966, D 24,19:5
Reeves, Samuel A (por) ,(cor, Ap 9,24:3), 1940, Ap 7,44:5
Reeves, Silas, 1880, Mr 1,2:6
Reeves, Solomon M, 1952, O 26,88:2
Reeves, Stacy, 1957, Je 26,31:2
Reeves, Theodore W, 1942, Ag 22,13:3
Reeves, Timothy, 1940, S 18,23:4
Reeves, Walter J, 1945, My 22,19:5
Reeves, William H, 1962, My 26,25:4
Reeves, William J, 1951, Ja 30,25:1
Reeves, William P, 1945, Ja 31,21:3
Reeves, Willis L, 1944, O 30,19:5
Reeves-Smith, George (por), 1941, My 30,15:4
Reeves-Smith, H (por), 1938, Ja 30,II,9:1
Refet Pasha (Refet Bele), 1963, O 7,31:2
Reffell, Edward, 1954, O 2,17:6
Refice, Licinio, 1954, S 13,23:5
Refo, Miles Jr, 1947, Je 10,27:3
Reford, Robert W, 1951, D 17,31:2
Refoule, Paul R, 1948, F 14,11:2
Regal, Francis E, 1942, Ap 11,13:3
Regal, Howard K Mrs, 1956, Je 27,31:5
Regalado, Francisco, 1959, Ja 1,31:3
Regalado, Paul, 1947, Ja 30,12:3
Regalbuto, Samuel B, 1958, My 5,29:3
Regamey, Felix, 1907, My 6,9:3
Regan, Alice E, 1957, Ag 10,15:6
Regan, Anthony Jr, 1950, Je 16,25:3
Regan, Charles F, 1950, Jl 20,25:4
Regan, Cornelius H Mrs, 1963, O 1,39:3
Regan, Dennis S Mrs, 1955, N 2,35:4
Regan, Edward C, 1950, F 28,29:4
Regan, Edward E, 1940, My 6,17:6
Regan, Edward F, 1962, O 1,31:4
Regan, Edward J, 1955, O 25,33:2
Regan, Eileen M Mrs, 1951, Ag 3,21:4
Regan, Frank, 1940, Je 9,44:2
Regan, Frank J Col, 1919, O 11,9:2
Regan, Frank W, 1967, Mr 4,27:5
Regan, George W, 1940, F 1,21:2; 1944, Ap 13,19:5
Regan, Harry G Mrs, 1949, D 12,33:3
Regan, Harry T, 1951, Ap 12,33:5
Regan, Henry T Rev, 1937, Jl 17,15:4
Regan, J B, 1932, F 15,17:1
Regan, James D, 1960, Je 11,21:6
Regan, James J, 1945, S 30,45:1; 1955, Je 18,17:6
Regan, James S, 1913, N 7,9:3; 1951, F 18,78:4; 1955, Ag 11,21:2
Regan, James W, 1954, Jl 27,21:6; 1958, Je 4,33:2
Regan, Jeremiah T, 1945, Mr 26,19:5
Regan, John, 1950, Je 20,27:1
Regan, John A, 1949, D 11,92:5
Regan, John E, 1946, Mr 9,13:4
Regan, John F, 1925, N 25,21:4
Regan, John F Mrs, 1954, Ag 19,23:4
Regan, John H (por), 1937, Je 29,22:2
Regan, John J, 1948, My 1,15:5; 1949, Je 6,19:5; 1954, N 23,33:1
Regan, John J Mrs, 1954, Mr 18,31:5
Regan, John T, 1941, My 10,15:5
Regan, John V, 1959, F 8,86:2
Regan, John W, 1945, F 12,19:1
Regan, Joseph C, 1948, N 19,27:3
Regan, Joseph C G, 1945, Ag 16,19:5
Regan, Joseph F Sr, 1950, D 28,26:4
Regan, Joseph M Mrs, 1967, S 19,51:6
Regan, Julia B, 1950, Ja 17,27:2
Regan, Kenneth M, 1959, Ag 16,82:7
Regan, L A, 1936, Ap 17,21:3
Regan, Lawrence V, 1942, F 1,43:2
Regan, Madge Mrs, 1939, Je 20,21:4
Regan, Margaret, 1951, Ap 10,28:2
Regan, Martin J, 1946, F 1,23:2
Regan, Mary E, 1952, S 7,85:1
Regan, Michael, 1925, N 18,23:4
Regan, Michael J Mrs, 1967, Ap 15,31:4
Regan, Patrick, 1923, Je 12,19:3
Regan, Patrick J, 1943, N 1,17:4
Regan, Peter Mrs, 1952, Mr 6,31:1
Regan, Raymond R, 1958, D 6,23:4
Regan, Richard E, 1952, O 31,25:2
Regan, Richard H, 1938, Ap 30,15:4
Regan, Robert J, 1942, S 5,13:4
Regan, Stephen P, 1942, Ag 23,43:4
Regan, Thomas E, 1959, S 1,29:3
Regan, Thomas F, 1951, Mr 30,23:4
Regan, Thomas J, 1959, Ja 18,88:3
Regan, Thomas J Mrs, 1940, Jl 21,28:7
Regan, Thomas M J, 1937, D 22,25:1
Regan, Thomas P, 1956, My 9,33:2
Regan, Timothy W, 1953, Mr 21,17:4
Regan, W Martin, 1965, Je 17,33:3
Regan, William F, 1948, Ag 25,25:3
Regan, William J, 1939, N 10,23:5; 1950, N 22,25:4
Regan, William P, 1952, Ag 29,23:1
Regan, William T, 1963, Ap 1,27:6
Reganthal, Frank, 1950, Ap 11,32:3
Regar, G Betram, 1946, N 29,25:3

Regar, H K, 1940, D 14,17:3
Regas, George, 1940, D 14,17:5
Regensburg, Alvin, 1961, My 2,37:4
Regensburg, Bellette, 1944, F 19,14:8
Regensburg, Irvin A, 1940, Jl 4,15:4
Regensburg, Isaac, 1943, D 2,27:4
Regensburg, Jerome, 1941, O 28,23:1
Regensburg, Melville E (por), 1949, Je 10,27:3
Regensburg, Mortimer, 1952, Ap 12,11:2
Regenstein, Harold L, 1962, Jl 25,33:6
Regenstein, Julius Mrs, 1949, Mr 30,25:3
Regensteiner, Theodore, 1952, Jl 16,25:1
Regenthal, Alan K, 1955, S 7,31:4
Regenthal, Ernest Sr, 1950, My 25,29:5
Regenthal, Henry, 1946, Je 14,21:4
Regenthal, Henry J, 1945, Jl 29,19:4
Regenthal, William, 1951, F 3,15:3
Reger, Boniface, 1946, My 5,44:2
Reger, Erik, 1954, My 11,29:2
Reger, John F, 1956, S 18,35:4
Reger, Lyman C, 1946, Ag 8,21:3
Reger, Max Dr, 1916, My 13,9:4
Reger, William A, 1954, S 17,27:1
Reger, William H, 1942, Mr 1,44:3
Regestein, Ernest E Mrs, 1957, Ja 26,19:1
Regester, Maude Mrs, 1952, F 8,23:2
Regg, Edward Sr, 1953, Mr 1,93:2
Reggio, A Nicholas, 1939, Ap 14,23:3
Reggio, Steven A, 1941, S 20,17:5
Regina Cecilia, Sister (H MaGuire), 1953, My 12, 27:3
Reginelli, Marco, 1956, My 26,12:1
Register, Edward C Lt-Col, 1920, Ja 15,11:3
Register, Samuel C, 1951, My 28,21:5
Regit, Stephen J, 1942, N 21,13:2
Regler, Gustav, 1963, Ja 18,9:3
Regnault, Charles H, 1938, Mr 2,19:4
Regneas, Joseph Mrs, 1943, D 23,20:2
Regnery, William F, 1959, F 8,86:1
Regnier, Adrian E, 1956, Mr 4,88:1
Regnier, Eugene A, 1956, D 11,36:2
Regnier, F J, 1885, Ap 28,5:5
Regnier, H de, 1936, My 24,II,9:1
Regnier, J A A, 1884, O 23,5:6
Rego, Leotte Adm, 1923, Je 27,19:4
Regout, Robert, 1943, F 3,19:2
Reh, Alex, 1949, Je 1,32:3
Reh, Bertram, 1952, Ag 1,17:4
Reh, Frank, 1954, Je 13,89:2
Rehage, Maudella Mrs, 1919, Ap 5,15:4
Rehan, Ada (por),(funl, Ja 11,11:5), 1916, Ja 9,17:1
Rehan, Mary, 1963, Ag 30,21:1
Rehauser, John W (por), 1947, N 28,27:3
Rehberg, Albert G, 1957, N 19,33:2
Rehberg, Richard A, 1956, My 19,19:5
Rehder, Alfred, 1949, Jl 23,11:6
Rehder, Ernest P C, 1945, Ag 5,37:1
Rehder, Henry A, 1955, S 12,25:5
Reheis, Barbara, 1949, My 26,29:2
Reheis, Daniel H, 1967, Jl 26,39:2
Rehermann, John F, 1954, N 25,29:6
Rehfuss, Martin E, 1964, Jl 30,27:3
Rehfuss, Martin O, 1940, F 10,15:3
Rehfuss, Wallace N, 1939, N 6,23:6
Rehill, Catherine, 1941, Jl 13,28:4
Rehill, Claudine L, 1951, Mr 27,29:1
Rehill, Corinne A, 1952, Je 26,29:5
Rehill, Elizabeth, 1944, Ja 19,19:3
Rehill, Hugh F, 1940, N 28,23:4
Rehill, John C Mrs, 1952, Ap 13,77:2
Rehill, Mary R, 1945, Ja 31,21:2
Rehill, Thomas F, 1960, My 3,39:4
Rehkopf, Karl, 1944, F 12,28:2
Rehkopf, Ned B, 1950, Ja 13,23:2
Rehling, William Mrs, 1951, F 15,31:2
Rehm, Charles J, 1941, O 8,23:1
Rehm, Chris D, 1939, My 23,23:2
Rehm, Conrad C, 1945, D 2,46:5
Rehm, Edward L, 1952, Ag 25,17:5
Rehm, Frank E, 1955, N 29,29:4
Rehm, John C, 1948, D 13,23:4
Rehm, Joseph M, 1944, Jl 1,15:4
Rehm, Madison P, 1965, N 4,47:2
Rehm, W Wallace, 1951, Jl 22,61:2
Rehm, William, 1938, N 28,15:4
Rehmann, Albert J Sr, 1947, Ap 1,27:4
Rehn, Frank K Jr, 1956, Mr 5,23:4
Rehn, Frank K M Mrs, 1941, My 27,23:2
Rehn, Frank Knox Morton, 1914, Jl 8,9:4
Rehn, Frederick J, 1951, Mr 23,21:1
Rehn, James A G, 1965, Ja 29,34:3
Rehn, John J, 1951, N 6,29:3
Rehrey, Harold J, 1950, N 9,33:5
Rehrig, B Franklin Mrs, 1946, Je 28,21:3
Rehthaler, Louis M, 1941, Jl 6,26:8
Rei, August, 1963, Ap 2,48:1
Reibel, Harry B, 1952, Je 28,19:4
Reibel, Julius Mrs, 1951, My 6,92:3
Reibel, Samuel, 1954, Mr 19,23:1
Reibel, William E, 1967, My 2,47:3
Reiber, Albert H, 1943, F 3,19:5
Reiber, Albert S, 1941, Jl 18,19:4
Reiber, John M, 1955, D 27,23:1
Reiber, Joseph N (will), 1939, Ag 31,21:4
Reiberl, Noah, 1956, Ja 29,93:2
Reibis, August F, 1958, My 8,29:1
Reibling, Albert L, 1943, F 19,19:1
Reibola, Leonard Edward, 1914, N 27,11:6
Reibstein, Harry B, 1956, Ja 12,27:4
Reich, Adolf, 1965, D 15,48:1
Reich, Adolph, 1943, Ap 28,23:1
Reich, Al (Alf J), 1963, Jl 30,29:2
Reich, Andrew, 1914, Ag 14,11:7
Reich, Arthur S, 1951, Ja 1,17:1
Reich, Benjamin, 1947, Mr 30,56:8; 1957, Mr 26,33:1
Reich, E Wilbur, 1950, S 11,23:5
Reich, Emil Dr, 1910, D 13,13:5
Reich, Emma S Mrs, 1948, Jl 27,25:5
Reich, George Sr Mrs, 1943, S 29,21:1
Reich, Gustave T, 1958, Ag 20,27:5
Reich, Ignaz, 1941, Je 9,19:5
Reich, Jacques, 1923, Jl 10,19:6
Reich, Joseph Mrs, 1962, Mr 24,25:5
Reich, Julius, 1948, Ag 30,25:1
Reich, L, 1931, My 3,II,6:6
Reich, Leonard, 1941, Mr 21,21:3
Reich, Lorenz Mrs, 1959, Ag 29,17:6
Reich, Max I, 1945, Ag 13,19:6
Reich, N Sidney (por), 1947, My 11,62:4
Reich, Nathan, 1955, Je 8,29:5
Reich, Nathaniel J, 1943, O 6,23:6
Reich, Ralph W, 1957, Ag 2,19:5
Reich, Sam, 1961, D 29,23:1
Reich, Samuel, 1950, Jl 8,13:6
Reich, Samuel D, 1941, Je 12,23:5
Reich, Wilhelm (trb lr, D 7,20:6), 1957, N 5,31:4
Reichard, George H, 1957, Je 7,23:2
Reichard, Gladys A, 1955, Jl 26,25:5
Reichard, Harry H, 1956, Ag 28,27:1
Reichard, Paul, 1938, S 18,44:7
Reichardt, D Harper, 1946, Je 12,27:1
Reichardt, G, 1884, N 5,4:7
Reichardt, Horace E, 1953, Mr 26,31:4
Reichardt, Joseph L, 1948, N 2,25:6
Reichart, James H, 1950, My 6,15:5
Reichart, Otto, 1941, Je 25,21:3
Reichbach, Samuel, 1954, O 3,86:6
Reichbaum, Theodore, 1952, Ap 17,29:2
Reiche, Karl A, 1955, Ap 5,29:1
Reichel, Charles, 1879, Mr 12,2:7
Reichel, Frank H, 1964, N 30,33:3
Reichel, John Sr, 1957, Ag 18,82:6
Reichel, Leo M, 1953, D 24,15:5
Reichel, Max, 1943, Je 12,13:2
Reichel, Wladimir A, 1964, D 4,39:1
Reichelderfer, Luther H, 1945, Je 21,19:5
Reichelt, Helen, 1946, F 1,24:3
Reichelt, Victor H, 1951, Ap 2,25:4
Reichenau, W von Gen Field Marshal, 1942, Ja 18,1:5
Reichenbach, Charles E, 1947, F 25,25:3
Reichenbach, H L, 1931, Jl 4,13:3
Reichenbach, Hans, 1953, Ap 11,17:6
Reichenbach, Henri, 1942, N 7,15:3
Reichenbach, Max, 1956, O 10,39:6
Reichenbach, Robert, 1945, Je 12,19:4
Reichenberg, Suzanne, 1924, Mr 12,19:5
Reichenberger, Alfred E Mrs, 1963, S 19,27:5
Reichenstein, Herman H, 1950, F 21,25:2
Reichenstein, Jacob M, 1950, D 3,89:1
Reichenstein, Samuel, 1943, D 29,17:4
Reicher, Emanuel, 1924, My 17,15:5
Reicher, Frank, 1965, Ja 23,25:2
Reichers, Louis T, 1962, Mr 3,21:1
Reichert, E T, 1931, D 26,11:5
Reichert, Eugene Mrs, 1957, Ja 1,23:4
Reichert, Irving F Mrs, 1960, Je 7,35:2
Reichert, Isidor Mrs, 1944, F 2,21:3
Reichert, Jacob, 1947, My 15,26:2
Reichert, John, 1940, Ja 29,15:5
Reichert, Leo T, 1954, Ap 8,27:2
Reichert, Louis, 1965, Jl 5,17:1
Reichert, William G, 1968, Mr 30,33:2
Reichgott, Henry, 1957, Ap 27,19:2
Reichhelm, Caroline Mrs, 1939, O 15,49:3
Reichhelm, Paul F, 1941, O 4,15:7
Reichle, William G, 1943, O 13,23:2
Reichler, Max, 1957, Ag 24,15:2
Reichler, Max Mrs, 1944, N 17,19:1
Reichlin, Solomon, 1939, N 26,42:5
Reichman, Arthur J, 1958, Ag 1,21:5
Reichman, Lee, 1943, O 31,48:3
Reichmann, Albert F, 1947, Mr 5,25:1
Reichmann, Charles Sir, 1903, Ag 20,9:6
Reichmann, Theodor, 1903, My 23,9:2
Reichner, Louis I, 1942, N 18,26:2
Reichow, Oscar, 1950, Jl 9,69:3
Reichstein, Ethel Mrs, 1925, Je 13,15:5
Reichwald, William P, 1949, O 13,27:1
Reick, William C (por), 1924, D 8,19:3
Reid, A Duncan, 1944, S 28,19:2
Reid, A Gordon, 1948, Ap 11,72:2
Reid, A Lionel, 1967, O 16,45:2
Reid, Aaron Bertrand Mrs, 1903, Ag 23,7:5
Reid, Adam, 1954, N 26,29:3
Reid, Addison Y, 1937, F 2,23:1
Reid, Adelia, 1951, Jl 30,17:6
Reid, Albert, 1943, O 31,49:1
Reid, Albert L, 1942, Je 2,23:5
Reid, Albert T, 1955, N 28,31:2
Reid, Alex H, 1938, Mr 27,II,7:3
Reid, Alex Sr, 1950, Mr 27,23:1
Reid, Alexander F, 1915, Je 1,15:7
Reid, Alfred E, 1955, O 9,87:1
Reid, Andrew G, 1941, Jl 27,31:2
Reid, Andrew M Mrs, 1937, My 12,23:5
Reid, Anne H Mrs (Heywood), 1961, Ja 23,23:3
Reid, Arch E, 1942, Jl 28,17:2
Reid, Arch E Mrs, 1939, Ap 14,23:3
Reid, Archibald M, 1967, N 25,39:4
Reid, Arthur P, 1950, Jl 19,32:2
Reid, Bertha W Mrs, 1939, Jl 29,15:6
Reid, Calvin P, 1940, My 17,19:4
Reid, Charles A Sr, 1958, Ja 11,17:5
Reid, Charles B, 1952, Ja 18,27:3
Reid, Charles E (por), 1939, F 20,17:1
Reid, Charles F, 1944, O 1,45:2
Reid, Charles L Jr Mrs, 1953, Ja 13,27:3
Reid, Charles M, 1962, My 23,45:2
Reid, Charles W Mrs, 1939, Ap 30,45:2
Reid, Christopher, 1938, N 2,24:2
Reid, Clarence L, 1907, Ag 8,7:6
Reid, Cliff, 1959, Ag 25,31:2
Reid, Clive M, 1954, O 7,23:3
Reid, Dana B, 1945, Ag 2,19:4
Reid, Daniel G, 1925, Ja 20,21:3
Reid, Daniel G Mrs, 1904, N 30,9:4
Reid, David C, 1943, My 22,13:5
Reid, David D Sir, 1939, Mr 24,21:2
Reid, David W, 1941, N 27,23:2
Reid, Douglas A, 1937, F 13,13:5
Reid, Edward O, 1959, D 11,65:6
Reid, Edward W, 1941, S 25,25:6
Reid, Edwin S, 1941, N 25,25:3
Reid, Ernest M, 1945, D 22,19:3
Reid, Ernest W, 1966, Jl 16,25:2
Reid, Eugene, 1946, Ag 13,27:4
Reid, Fergus, 1941, D 1,19:4
Reid, Fergus Mrs, 1947, O 4,17:5
Reid, Forrest, 1947, Ja 6,23:4
Reid, Frank L, 1950, Mr 1,27:5
Reid, Frank R Sr, 1945, Ja 26,21:1
Reid, Fred T, 1941, F 11,23:3
Reid, Frederic S, 1949, F 21,23:4
Reid, Frederick L, 1940, Ja 12,17:2
Reid, G, 1927, O 1,19:5
Reid, George, 1954, N 15,13:2
Reid, George A, 1941, Jl 11,15:5; 1947, Ag 26,23:4
Reid, George C (cor, Jl 7,7:5), 1910, Jl 5,13:6
Reid, George E, 1938, Ja 18,23:1
Reid, George F, 1946, S 23,23:4; 1965, N 24,39:5
Reid, George Mrs, 1951, Mr 25,72:4
Reid, George Sir, 1913, F 13,15:4
Reid, George W, 1954, N 19,23:2
Reid, H A, 1953, O 22,29:5
Reid, Harriet M, 1954, My 8,17:3
Reid, Harry B, 1954, S 16,29:3
Reid, Harry C, 1952, Ag 25,17:1
Reid, Harry F, 1944, Je 19,19:4
Reid, Helen, 1941, Je 9,19:4
Reid, Helen D, 1965, Ag 8,27:3
Reid, Helen Grace Mrs (Helen Grace Carlisle), 1968, Ap 4,47:2
Reid, Henry J E Dr, 1968, Ag 1,31:3
Reid, Herbert L, 1946, F 18,21:5
Reid, Howard C, 1948, F 13,21:2
Reid, Howard C Mrs, 1940, N 8,23:3
Reid, Howard E, 1962, Mr 4,33:4
Reid, Hugh, 1958, S 19,27:1
Reid, Hugh W, 1951, F 27,27:2
Reid, Hugo, 1941, N 17,19:1
Reid, Ira D Mrs, 1956, Je 18,25:4
Reid, Ira De Augustine Dr, 1968, Ag 17,27:1
Reid, J B, 1877, Je 2,5:5
Reid, J C, 1897, Ja 26,7:5
Reid, J Herbert, 1960, Ap 16,17:4
Reid, J R Judge, 1902, My 11,9:6
Reid, J W, 1902, Ja 3,7:5
Reid, James, 1937, Ag 6,17:5; 1945, My 20,32:4; 1950 Ja 22,76:7
Reid, James John (Lord Loreburn), 1923, D 1,13:4
Reid, James Mrs, 1948, N 11,27:4
Reid, James R, 1953, Ja 13,27:1
Reid, James W, 1943, S 24,23:1; 1965, Je 1,39:4
Reid, James W Mrs, 1948, Ap 1,25:2
Reid, Jean A, 1955, O 16,87:2
Reid, John, 1904, Ja 6,9:5; 1948, Ja 27,25:3; 1948, Ag 29,56:6; 1958, O 28,35:4
Reid, John A, 1951, O 11,37:6; 1953, Je 10,29:4
Reid, John Gordon, 1905, My 24,9:6
Reid, John J Jr, 1953, My 22,27:3
Reid, John Jr, 1925, Je 29,13:6
Reid, John M, 1914, Mr 17,11:4
Reid, John Mrs, 1925, D 7,21:4
Reid, John Rev, 1904, D 19,1:5
Reid, John S, 1948, O 22,25:3
Reid, John W, 1961, Ag 17,27:4
Reid, Josiah E, 1942, F 11,22:2
Reid, Kenneth, 1882, Ja 23,5:4; 1960, Mr 17,33:4
Reid, Lee A, 1948, S 11,15:2

Reid, Leon H, 1939, D 22,19:2
Reid, Leonard G, 1939, O 16,19:6
Reid, Leonard J (por), 1938, O 27,23:4
Reid, Lewis S, 1959, Jl 17,21:2
Reid, Louis R, 1965, S 2,31:2
Reid, M Frank Jr, 1953, Ap 29,18:4
Reid, M Hunter, 1939, O 2,17:4
Reid, Mary, 1953, D 28,21:2
Reid, Mayne, 1883, O 23,5:3
Reid, Michael, 1918, D 11,15:4
Reid, Mont R, 1943, My 12,25:4
Reid, Ogden M, 1947, Ja 4,1:3
Reid, Patrick (Bro Basil), 1953, O 14,29:2
Reid, Peter, 1912, D 8,17:5
Reid, Phil, 1941, Je 10,23:5
Reid, R Kearny, 1941, Je 9,19:4
Reid, R William, 1952, Ap 29,27:4
Reid, Ralston B Mrs, 1967, My 27,31:3
Reid, Raymond, 1954, Ja 28,27:5
Reid, Richard, 1961, Ja 25,33:1
Reid, Robert, 1909, Ag 23,7:4; 1943, N 1,17:4; 1957, D 27,19:1
Reid, Robert B, 1965, Je 4,35:2
Reid, Robert E, 1954, My 18,29:3
Reid, Robert G Sir, 1908, Je 4,7:6
Reid, Robert H, 1960, N 24,29:4
Reid, Robert W, 1939, Jl 29,15:5
Reid, Roland T, 1958, Je 11,36:1
Reid, Rollin H, 1939, F 23,23:6
Reid, S Malcolm Mrs, 1938, Ap 21,19:1
Reid, Samuel J, 1954, S 10,23:2
Reid, Thomas B, 1925, Ja 3,13:4
Reid, Thorburn Mrs, 1954, Jl 1,25:6
Reid, W B Mrs, 1961, O 28,21:3
Reid, W Mrs, 1931, Ap 30,23:1
Reid, W Rowley, 1942, Ap 25,13:3
Reid, Wallace, 1923, Ja 19,17:5; 1957, Jl 24,26:5
Reid, Walter E, 1955, My 31,27:2
Reid, Walter W, 1950, N 26,90:5
Reid, Walter W Jr, 1960, Mr 3,29:5
Reid, Walter W Jr Mrs, 1961, Ag 26,17:6
Reid, Wemyss Sir, 1905, F 27,7:5
Reid, Wilbur, 1944, D 24,26:4
Reid, Wilbur A, 1954, Je 5,17:5
Reid, Will J, 1956, Ap 9,27:4
Reid, Willard, 1925, O 14,25:2
Reid, Willard MacC, 1959, Je 25,29:5
Reid, William, 1949, D 31,15:5; 1965, Mr 8,29:4
Reid, William A, 1922, Ag 31,15:4; 1940, Je 27,23:6; 1947, Ja 19,53:1; 1947, N 23,74:3; 1955, O 31,25:5
Reid, William B, 1939, N 11,15:5; 1951, D 2,91:3
Reid, William C, 1941, D 2,23:3; 1944, D 25,19:6
Reid, William C Mrs, 1956, Je 29,21:5
Reid, William D, 1949, S 30,24:3
Reid, William E, 1948, Ja 24,15:4
Reid, William G, 1939, Ja 6,21:2
Reid, William H Mrs, 1952, Ja 5,11:5
Reid, William H Sr, 1948, Je 8,25:5
Reid, William L, 1941, My 9,21:2
Reid, William M, 1954, F 9,27:2
Reid, William Maxwell, 1911, N 28,13:5
Reid, William Mrs, 1957, Je 15,17:3
Reid, William O Lt-Col, 1922, O 16,15:4
Reid, William Sir, 1858, N 23,8:1
Reid, William Sr, 1955, Ja 13,27:3
Reid-Rogers, Elisabeth (Princess Christian of Hesse), 1957, F 3,46:1
Reidel, Albert, 1937, O 13,6:2
Reidelbach, John G, 1938, N 2,23:1
Reidemeister, Friedrich, 1955, S 7,31:2
Reidenhardy, H Victor, 1908, S 12,7:6
Reider, Edward E, 1961, Je 8,35:5
Reider, Joseph, 1960, D 1,35:3
Reider, W A Herbert, 1945, N 16,19:4
Reidy, Anne, 1943, Je 11,19:1
Reidy, David B, 1949, My 24,27:2
Reidy, Edward J, 1946, My 24,19:2
Reidy, Ellen A B Mrs, 1937, Jl 6,19:5
Reidy, James, 1953, My 16,19:3
Reidy, John, 1903, Jl 28,7:6
Reidy, John F Mrs, 1939, Je 24,17:4
Reidy, John P, 1962, Jl 31,27:2
Reidy, Maurice J, 1947, F 8,17:4
Reidy, Maurice P, 1944, F 21,15:5
Reidy, Maurice P Mrs, 1958, O 12,86:3
Reidy, Michael J, 1938, Je 17,21:5; 1940, S 13,23:4; 1954, Jl 23,17:6
Reidy, Nona I, 1954, Je 3,27:4
Reidy, Peter J Mrs, 1942, D 3,25:3
Reidy, R F, 1956, Je 15,25:4
Reidy, Thomas J, 1948, O 19,28:3
Reidy, William N, 1952, My 31,17:2
Reierson, Charles L, 1937, Mr 3,23:2
Reif, Charles F, 1942, My 7,19:5; 1943, Je 20,35:1
Reif, Edward C, 1961, S 3,60:3
Reif, Leo, 1964, Mr 15,86:1
Reif, Murray, 1959, F 3,27:6
Reife, Harris, 1947, Ja 26,53:4
Reifeiss, William, 1943, Mr 18,19:4
Reifenberger, George J, 1948, D 3,25:1
Reiff, Anthony, 1916, O 7,11:4
Reiff, George W, 1940, Ap 10,25:3; 1950, Jl 9,69:1
Reiff, Harry, 1948, Ap 29,23:4
Reiff, Herman, 1950, N 14,31:1
Reiff, Jacob, 1949, Ag 14,25:1
Reiff, Josiah Col, 1911, Mr 2,9:5
Reiff, Stanley T, 1954, F 8,23:3
Reiff, William S Mrs, 1949, O 11,31:2
Reiffarth, Jennie Mrs, 1913, F 16,II,7:4
Reiffel, Isadore, 1964, F 28,29:2
Reiffert, Edith A, 1924, Jl 31,13:6
Reifschneider, Felix, 1924, S 18,21:5
Reifschneider, Felix E, 1905, Ap 4,11:6
Reifsnider, Lawrence F, 1956, My 16,35:5
Reifsnyder, Henry G, 1967, Ap 9,92:6
Reifsnyder, James D, 1961, Ag 25,25:2
Reifsnyder, T Bancroft, 1957, Je 26,31:3
Reifsteck, Edward J, 1952, O 14,31:2
Reig, Ben, 1968, O 18,47:2
Reigart, John F, 1946, Ap 24,26:2
Reigart, John F Mrs, 1953, D 24,15:4
Reigel, William E, 1946, S 4,23:3
Reigeluth, Ray J, 1963, N 27,37:2
Reiger, Michael Rev, 1917, My 14,11:1
Reighard, Jacob E, 1942, F 15,44:5
Reighley, Henry Whitehouse, 1918, F 1,9:5
Reighley, Lyster C, 1956, N 12,29:5
Reigi, Charles L, 1963, Jl 27,17:6
Reigi, Emil J Sr, 1956, Ag 21,29:1
Reigner, Jacob H, 1947, Mr 28,23:3
Reigrod, Solomon, 1951, Ag 7,25:3
Reihart, Chauncey R, 1944, D 14,23:3
Reihl, Charles W, 1948, Ja 31,19:5
Reihl, J George, 1950, Ja 1,42:4
Reik, Henry O, 1938, Je 3,21:2
Reik, Raymond C, 1963, O 26,27:4
Reiker, Emanuel H, 1942, Mr 30,17:1
Reil, David, 1954, My 15,15:4
Reil, Frank T, 1951, Je 18,23:2
Reiland, Karl, 1964, S 13,86:1
Reiland, Karl Mrs, 1958, D 30,32:2
Reiley, A C, 1947, F 4,25:6
Reiley, Alan C Jr, 1956, N 28,35:2
Reiley, Anna C, 1937, D 21,23:3
Reiley, Austin D, 1961, My 25,37:3
Reiley, Blair, 1966, Ap 15,39:2
Reiley, De Witt V, 1940, F 13,23:3
Reiley, Henry B Mrs, 1960, My 16,31:3
Reiley, Robert E, 1938, Ag 2,19:5
Reiley, Robert J, 1961, Je 9,33:5
Reiley, Thomas, 1941, Ja 12,44:4
Reiling, Joseph L Mrs, 1941, Je 18,21:5
Reill, William, 1874, Jl 17,8:2
Reilley, Charles S Jr, 1952, Mr 3,23:8
Reilley, Sibbie Mrs, 1904, F 9,9:5
Reilley, Thomas T, 1940, Ja 28,33:1
Reilly, Agnes F Mrs, 1939, D 14,27:5
Reilly, Albert, 1947, O 24,23:1
Reilly, Albert A, 1954, Ap 18,89:2
Reilly, Alice D Mrs, 1937, Ag 20,17:4
Reilly, Anastasia (Mrs T De L Buhl), 1961, D 29, 23:2
Reilly, Ann M, 1944, N 2,19:3
Reilly, Bernard J, 1943, N 19,19:4; 1945, Mr 30,15:2
Reilly, Bernard J Sr, 1952, D 29,19:1
Reilly, C Cecil, 1951, D 27,21:1
Reilly, Charles E, 1967, Mr 10,39:4
Reilly, Charles F, 1948, Jl 22,23:6
Reilly, Charles H, 1948, F 3,25:4
Reilly, Dan Sr, 1953, My 12,27:3
Reilly, Daniel J, 1937, Je 9,25:6
Reilly, Daniel J Mrs, 1950, Jl 25,27:5
Reilly, David F Mrs, 1953, N 6,27:3
Reilly, Declan, 1942, S 29,23:3
Reilly, Declan Mrs, 1944, N 30,23:3
Reilly, Edmund J (funl, N 8,21:2), 1958, N 5,35:1
Reilly, Edward, 1903, Jl 6,7:6; 1921, O 9,22:4
Reilly, Edward A, 1944, N 15,27:5; 1951, S 15,15:4
Reilly, Edward F, 1943, S 23,21:3
Reilly, Edward J, 1946, D 27,19:1; 1952, O 29,29:4; 1960, F 6,19:1
Reilly, Edward Mrs, 1944, Mr 12,38:3
Reilly, Eugene, 1937, Jl 29,19:4
Reilly, Fairfax A, 1968, Je 25,41:5
Reilly, Francis H, 1942, Ap 1,21:3
Reilly, Frank, 1914, Mr 26,11:6; 1949, Ap 6,29:1
Reilly, Frank C (por), 1947, Ap 11,25:3
Reilly, Frank D, 1937, Jl 30,19:5
Reilly, Frank J, 1952, Ja 15,27:2; 1953, Je 12,27:1; 1957, O 4,23:4; 1967, Ja 16,41:3
Reilly, Frank P, 1948, Mr 6,13:3
Reilly, Frank R Mrs, 1949, Je 13,19:4
Reilly, George A, 1939, N 29,23:3
Reilly, George F A, 1941, Ap 16,23:3
Reilly, George J, 1953, S 27,87:2
Reilly, George W, 1943, S 30,21:3
Reilly, Harold Mrs, 1958, My 20,33:2
Reilly, Harry S Mrs, 1950, Jl 13,25:4
Reilly, Henry J, 1949, O 13,27:2; 1963, D 14,27:4
Reilly, Hugh, 1903, Ap 17,9:6
Reilly, J Edward, 1943, Mr 19,19:1
Reilly, J Norman, 1962, Ag 17,23:2
Reilly, J Ridgway, 1938, Je 9,23:5
Reilly, J William, 1966, Je 13,39:2
Reilly, James, 1937, D 24,17:4; 1939, O 4,25:5; 1958, Ag 8,17:6
Reilly, James A, 1953, Jl 25,11:3
Reilly, James A Lt-Col, 1953, N 13,28:3
Reilly, James A Mrs, 1961, Ap 21,33:2
Reilly, James B, 1939, Jl 23,29:3
Reilly, James D, 1943, Ja 23,13:5; 1945, F 17,13:5
Reilly, James F, 1939, Ja 9,15:3; 1954, D 17,31:2; 1967, Ag 6,77:1
Reilly, James H, 1941, Ja 25,15:3; 1957, Ag 16,19:3
Reilly, James H Mrs, 1942, D 15,28:2
Reilly, James H P, 1940, N 7,25:6
Reilly, James H Sr, 1962, Mr 5,23:3
Reilly, James J, 1941, O 16,21:4; 1948, Ja 8,25:5; 1949, Mr 28,21:3
Reilly, James Mrs, 1946, Ja 1,28:2
Reilly, James N, 1947, My 12,21:6
Reilly, James P, 1940, Ja 2,19:5; 1948, My 21,23:4
Reilly, James P Dr, 1925, Ag 16,5:1
Reilly, James P Mrs, 1948, Ag 10,21:3; 1952, Ag 1, 18:5
Reilly, James Thomas, 1915, D 30,13:3
Reilly, Jeremiah J, 1966, My 6,47:3
Reilly, Jeremiah P, 1950, Jl 15,13:4
Reilly, John, 1872, O 17,5:3; 1903, F 26,2:4; 1937, Je 2,23:6
Reilly, John B Rev, 1919, D 14,22:4
Reilly, John C, 1907, Mr 21,9:6
Reilly, John E, 1941, D 9,31:1; 1949, S 12,21:4
Reilly, John E (funl, Ap 29,86:6), 1956, Ap 25,35:4
Reilly, John E, 1958, N 1,19:3
Reilly, John F, 1939, My 12,21:2; 1959, Ja 19,27:2
Reilly, John F Sr, 1953, Je 17,27:4
Reilly, John Francis, 1919, D 7,22:2
Reilly, John H Jr, 1941, Ja 14,21:2
Reilly, John J, 1939, Ag 8,17:5; 1940, N 29,21:5; 1942, S 12,13:1; 1943, Ag 12,19:3; 1947, O 21,24:2; 1950, N 14,31:3; 1950, D 30,13:2; 1952, Ja 1,25:3; 1953, Je 23,29:2; 1956, Ag 18,17:2; 1957, Ja 6,89:1; 1961, N 24,31:1; 1966, My 27,43:2
Reilly, John J Mrs, 1955, O 30,88:8
Reilly, John L, 1945, Ap 27,19:4; 1956, Je 24,77:1
Reilly, John M, 1952, O 11,19:5
Reilly, John R, 1956, N 27,37:4
Reilly, John W, 1938, Mr 8,20:8
Reilly, Joseph, 1958, N 1,19:4
Reilly, Joseph A, 1937, S 16,25:6; 1939, Ag 17,21:2; 1951, N 12,25:3
Reilly, Joseph F, 1946, Je 27,21:3
Reilly, Joseph F Mrs, 1948, Ja 30,24:3
Reilly, Joseph F Sr, 1945, O 20,11:6
Reilly, Joseph H, 1939, Jl 15,15:3
Reilly, Joseph J, 1950, Mr 3,25:2; 1951, Ja 25,25:5
Reilly, Joseph M, 1947, My 10,13:4
Reilly, Joseph Mrs, 1957, Mr 3,85:1
Reilly, Joseph P, 1962, Mr 13,35:4
Reilly, Joseph R, 1959, Ag 12,29:2
Reilly, Katherine Mrs, 1937, S 1,19:3
Reilly, Laurence A, 1956, D 12,39:4
Reilly, Lawrence C Mrs, 1948, F 25,23:2
Reilly, Leigh, 1954, Ap 8,27:4
Reilly, Leo J, 1961, My 21,87:2
Reilly, Louis I, 1958, Ap 12,19:4
Reilly, Louis J, 1938, Mr 6,II,8:5
Reilly, Martin A, 1950, Je 5,23:3
Reilly, Matthew A, 1950, F 7,27:2
Reilly, Matthew F, 1958, Ag 13,27:4
Reilly, Maurice T, 1962, Je 21,31:3
Reilly, Michael A (por), 1947, Mr 12,25:3
Reilly, Michael F, 1921, Je 27,13:5
Reilly, Michael H, 1948, Mr 26,21:2
Reilly, Michael K, 1944, O 16,19:5
Reilly, Myles F, 1954, My 14,23:2
Reilly, Nellie N Mrs, 1939, Jl 10,19:4
Reilly, Owen, 1944, O 10,23:1
Reilly, Patrick, 1950, N 1,35:1
Reilly, Patrick J, 1943, Je 3,21:4; 1947, My 3,17:2; 1955, Ag 15,15:4
Reilly, Patrick P, 1951, My 26,17:4
Reilly, Paul H, 1944, My 15,19:5
Reilly, Paul Mrs (Helen), 1962, Ja 12,23:3
Reilly, Pete, 1951, F 28,27:3
Reilly, Peter, 1945, Je 28,19:1
Reilly, Peter C, 1952, Ja 6,92:3
Reilly, Peter M, 1904, Ja 12,7:5
Reilly, Peter W Jr Mrs, 1958, Jl 9,27:2
Reilly, Phil, 1942, Ja 10,15:6
Reilly, Philip, 1903, My 30,7:5; 1943, Ap 24,13:2
Reilly, Philip J, 1945, Je 7,19:5
Reilly, Philip J (Bro Columba), 1961, Ag 15,29:2
Reilly, Phillip W, 1946, O 27,60:7
Reilly, Richard, 1966, S 29,47:3
Reilly, Robert A, 1946, Jl 20,13:4
Reilly, Robert M, 1944, N 17,19:2
Reilly, Ronan F, 1956, Ap 15,89:2
Reilly, Sarah C Mrs, 1941, Ja 9,21:3
Reilly, Susan A, 1938, Mr 18,19:3
Reilly, Terrence, 1958, Je 4,31:1
Reilly, Thomas, 1949, Je 21,25:1
Reilly, Thomas Alexander, 1907, F 10,7:6
Reilly, Thomas D, 1904, F 24,9:6
Reilly, Thomas F, 1937, F 12,23:1; 1938, Ap 30,15:6; 1948, Ag 7,15:2; 1950, Mr 17,23:4; 1952, Ap 23,29:3
Reilly, Thomas H, 1965, Je 11,31:1
Reilly, Thomas J, 1941, Jl 29,15:3; 1951, Je 20,27:4; 1955, Mr 27,86:7

Reilly, Thomas L, 1924, Jl 7,15:4
Reilly, Thomas P, 1939, My 16,23:4
Reilly, Thomas S, 1948, My 5,25:3; 1949, Mr 6,72:3
Reilly, Thomas U, 1953, S 27,86:2
Reilly, Thomas W, 1946, My 19,40:5
Reilly, Vincent J, 1960, Ap 30,23:6
Reilly, Walter P, 1957, Ag 22,27:5
Reilly, Wendell S, 1950, O 8,104:2
Reilly, William, 1966, N 13,88:7
Reilly, William A R Mrs, 1941, Mr 6,21:5
Reilly, William B, 1946, My 24,19:2; 1950, Ap 19, 29:4; 1955, O 2,86:7
Reilly, William B Mrs, 1941, O 30,23:5
Reilly, William C, 1944, Je 21,19:3
Reilly, William D, 1941, Ja 26,37:1; 1964, Ap 6,31:1
Reilly, William E, 1955, N 25,27:4
Reilly, William F, 1941, Je 5,23:4; 1951, O 15,25:4
Reilly, William G Mrs, 1944, My 31,19:1
Reilly, William J, 1958, Ja 15,29:2
Reilly, William J Mrs, 1938, O 18,26:5
Reilly, William N, 1957, N 11,29:5
Reilly, William P, 1949, F 26,15:2
Reilly, William P H, 1959, My 28,31:3
Reilly, William T, 1955, Ap 13,29:1
Reilly, William W, 1947, Ag 27,23:2; 1968, O 10,47:3
Reilly (Sister Mary Agnita), 1963, Jl 20,19:3
Reily, E Mont, 1954, N 1,27:4
Reily, George W, 1954, Je 6,86:2
Reily, Michael M, 1964, Jl 28,29:2
Reim, Frank H Jr, 1938, Je 7,8:5
Reimann, Lewis C, 1961, Ag 22,29:2
Reimann, Stanley Philip Dr, 1968, F 23,33:2
Reimel, Clara, 1953, Jl 2,23:5
Reimer, Arthur A, 1941, Jl 9,21:6
Reimer, August C, 1958, Ja 4,15:5
Reimer, Benjamin, 1949, D 9,32:2
Reimer, Bernhard W, 1941, S 9,23:1
Reimer, Henry Clay, 1918, Ag 26,11:4
Reimer, John A, 1949, Jl 30,15:4
Reimer, John B, 1945, N 17,17:6
Reimer, Margareth B, 1952, Ja 31,28:2
Reimer, Marie, 1962, My 1,37:1
Reimer, Otto Berend Mrs, 1968, Mr 14,43:2
Reimer, Otto E, 1955, My 7,17:3
Reimer, Otto E Mrs, 1955, O 2,86:6
Reimer, Peter W, 1948, N 8,21:1
Reimer, Rudolph (por), 1948, Jl 29,21:1
Reimer, William, 1923, D 13,21:5
Reimer, William A, 1951, F 20,25:2
Reimers, Adolph H, 1943, Je 13,44:6
Reimers, Edward G, 1937, F 11,23:4
Reimers, Fred G, 1945, Mr 29,23:4
Reimers, Irving J, 1960, F 18,33:2
Reimers, Paul H, 1942, Ap 15,21:2
Reimers, William, 1949, Jl 8,19:1
Reimers, William E, 1921, O 21,15:5
Reimherr, Frederick W, 1944, F 6,42:3
Reimherr, Otto, 1941, S 4,21:4
Reimold, Abraham G H, 1962, F 23,30:1
Reimold, Abraham G Mrs, 1948, Mr 24,25:5
Reimold, Orlando S, 1962, Ap 14,25:2
Rein, Charles R, 1957, My 16,31:5
Rein, Fred, 1947, O 9,27:6
Rein, John, 1961, N 15,43:5
Rein, John H Mrs, 1952, Ja 1,25:3
Rein, Otto W, 1952, S 4,27:3
Rein, Prof, 1942, D 8,25:4
Rein, Robert Rev, 1923, D 19,19:4
Reina, Carmen C, 1942, Ap 19,43:3
Reina, Henry J, 1947, F 21,19:4
Reina, Joseph, 1945, Ap 24,19:5
Reinach, Joseph, 1921, Ap 19,17:6
Reinach, S, 1932, N 5,15:3
Reinach, Udo M, 1960, Ja 24,88:6
Reinach, Udo M Mrs, 1948, Ja 29,23:5
Reinan, Frank, 1908, D 31,9:6
Reinartz, John L, 1964, O 7,47:3
Reinau, Francis D, 1909, Ja 4,9:6
Reinberger, Max, 1925, N 22,9:1
Reinboth, William A, 1950, Ag 1,23:5
Reinbott, Frederick, 1965, Jl 18,68:7
Reinburg, Leroy, 1956, S 28,27:5
Reindel, George S, 1945, Mr 31,19:2
Reindel, Robert, 1947, Ag 29,17:4
Reindel, William G, 1948, D 18,19:3
Reindfusz, Ralph E, 1947, Ap 11,25:4
Reindollar, Robert M, 1956, N 21,27:4
Reinecke, Carl, 1910, Mr 18,11:5
Reinecke, George W Mrs, 1958, Mr 9,86:3
Reinecke, H George, 1938, Je 26,27:2
Reinecke, Julius, 1953, D 11,34:3
Reineke, P, 1948, F 20,27:2
Reinemann, Paul, 1944, Ag 19,11:5
Reiner, Bella Mrs, 1942, F 13,21:2
Reiner, Charles, 1919, Jl 19,9:7
Reiner, Fritz (funl, N 19,41:1), 1963, N 16,27:2
Reiner, Henry, 1953, D 23,25:1
Reiner, Ignatz, 1952, D 2,36:6
Reiner, Irving, 1965, O 16,27:4
Reiner, Jacob, 1948, My 10,21:5; 1956, Ap 12,31:1
Reiner, John, 1960, F 26,16:3
Reiner, Jonas, 1956, S 10,27:2
Reiner, Laszlo, 1955, N 28,31:4
Reiner, Maxmillian Dr, 1937, F 24,23:5
Reiner, Otto, 1950, Je 9,23:3
Reiner, Robert, 1960, Ag 26,26:3
Reiner, Thomas, 1919, Jl 19,9:7
Reiner, Wilhelmine M Mrs, 1937, Jl 8,23:3
Reiners, Dorothea W, 1952, Mr 3,21:4
Reiners, Walter A, 1960, Ag 15,23:2
Reinert, Egon, 1959, Ap 24,3:7
Reinert, F J Mrs, 1952, D 30,19:2
Reinert, Peter, 1950, D 26,23:4
Reines, Morris, 1953, F 3,25:5
Reines, Phil, 1948, O 10,76:4
Reinfeld, Fred, 1964, My 30,17:4
Reinfelder, Edward C, 1947, Je 11,27:4
Reingold, Harold I, 1957, S 24,35:1
Reingold, Isaac, 1903, O 22,9:6
Reingold, Louis, 1944, Ag 28,11:6
Reinhard, Edward W, 1965, My 10,33:1
Reinhard, Frank A, 1946, O 21,31:4
Reinhard, H Laurence, 1953, My 26,29:5
Reinhard, Henry S, 1908, N 4,11:6
Reinhard, John F Mrs, 1956, F 9,32:2
Reinhard, Joseph B, 1953, D 28,21:2
Reinhard, L Andrew, 1964, Ag 3,25:5
Reinhard, Wilhelm, 1955, Ja 19,27:2
Reinhardsen, G A, 1928, Jl 4,15:5
Reinhardt, Abraham, 1957, Mr 18,27:4
Reinhardt, Ad, 1967, S 1,31:1
Reinhardt, Anthony F, 1949, O 12,30:2
Reinhardt, Arthur E, 1956, F 27,23:4
Reinhardt, Aurelia H (por), 1948, Ja 29,23:3
Reinhardt, Charles, 1954, My 11,29:3
Reinhardt, Charles F, 1940, D 22,30:8
Reinhardt, Charles G, 1946, Jl 2,25:4
Reinhardt, Django, 1953, My 18,21:6
Reinhardt, Frank A, 1944, O 17,23:5
Reinhardt, Franz C, 1943, N 13,13:4
Reinhardt, Frederick, 1913, Jl 18,9:6
Reinhardt, Guenther, 1968, D 3,47:1
Reinhardt, Harry, 1965, N 16,43:5
Reinhardt, Henry, 1921, Ja 14,11:3
Reinhardt, Henry B, 1948, S 9,27:2
Reinhardt, Herman F, 1964, Ap 8,43:1
Reinhardt, James H, 1947, Ap 30,25:3
Reinhardt, James W, 1946, My 21,24:2
Reinhardt, John, 1946, My 2,21:2; 1953, Ag 12,31:4
Reinhardt, John B, 1946, S 26,25:2
Reinhardt, Julia, 1924, S 3,17:2
Reinhardt, Leon A, 1944, Ja 25,19:2
Reinhardt, Max, 1943, N 1,17:1
Reinhardt, Paul, 1945, Ja 15,19:2
Reinhardt, Paul R, 1951, My 13,89:1
Reinhardt, Phil, 1938, My 21,15:3
Reinhardt, R S Col, 1925, S 12,15:6
Reinhardt, Robert L, 1944, Mr 3,15:4
Reinhardt, Theodore, 1950, Ja 13,24:2
Reinhardt, William A Mrs, 1964, Ja 30,29:1
Reinhardt, William H, 1952, Ja 8,27:3
Reinhardt, Willis F, 1945, Ap 15,14:6
Reinhart, Alfred C, 1949, My 1,88:3
Reinhart, Art, 1946, N 12,41:4
Reinhart, Charles S, 1959, Ag 6,27:5
Reinhart, Earl F, 1949, O 22,17:6
Reinhart, Edgar, 1954, Ap 30,23:4
Reinhart, Fred A, 1961, My 25,37:4
Reinhart, Martin, 1946, F 14,27:2
Reinhart, Nicholas, 1955, D 4,88:7
Reinhart, P D Mrs, 1954, My 7,23:4
Reinhart, Roger W Mrs, 1963, N 6,41:2
Reinhart, Rudolf Mrs, 1953, Ja 28,27:2
Reinhart, Willard O, 1940, My 8,23:4
Reinhart, William Alvin, 1923, D 10,17:4
Reinheimer, Bartel H (por), 1949, N 13,92:3
Reinheimer, Henry E, 1954, S 22,29:2
Reinheimer, Henry E Mrs, 1957, D 20,24:4
Reinhert, Isabella C Mrs, 1951, Ap 17,29:2
Reinhold, Charles F, 1950, Jl 7,19:2
Reinhold, Edward E Mrs, 1953, Ap 10,21:2
Reinhold, James P, 1961, Jl 16,69:2
Reinhold, Louis, 1950, Jl 1,15:1
Reinhold, Milton D, 1948, S 2,23:5
Reinhold, Otto F, 1952, N 20,31:4
Reinhold, Ralph W, 1967, Ja 25,43:3
Reinicke, John A, 1941, D 19,25:4
Reinicker, Norman G, 1946, Ja 15,23:5
Reininger, Frederick A, 1948, Jl 1,23:4
Reininger, Rose J, 1957, Jl 19,19:5
Reinisch, Harry E, 1949, Je 28,28:3
Reinisch, Max, 1950, S 5,27:2
Reinisch, Paul, 1956, O 9,35:3
Reinitz, Bertram, 1960, Je 14,37:1
Reinke, Alfred E, 1943, Ja 25,13:2
Reinke, Edward E, 1945, Ja 27,11:6
Reinker, Martin F, 1951, Mr 8,29:2
Reinl, Minnie (will), 1945, Ag 23,25:4
Reinlieb, Samuel Mrs, 1954, Ap 21,29:3
Reinman, Alfred E, 1951, My 22,31:5
Reinoehl, Charles M, 1957, Mr 6,31:1
Reinoehl, John K, 1954, My 14,23:1
Reinold, Bernard A, 1940, Mr 20,34:6
Reinold, Bernard A Mrs, 1939, Mr 14,21:4
Reinsch, Paul S Dr, 1923, Ja 26,17:4
Reinschmidt, Harry G, 1955, O 8,19:2
Reinsholm, Emma, 1938, F 5,15:5
Reinstein, Harry, 1956, Je 16,19:3
Reinthal, Albert E Mrs, 1958, Jl 22,27:1
Reinus, Bernard, 1951, Je 25,19:3
Reinwald, Charles A, 1955, Ja 2,77:2
Reis, Amphiloquio, 1941, S 8,15:4
Reis, Anna B, 1947, D 6,15:6
Reis, Arthur M (por), 1947, D 24,21:3
Reis, Arthur V A, 1955, Jl 11,8:4
Reis, Augustin, 1949, My 2,25:4
Reis, Benedict (por), 1939, D 26,19:4
Reis, Charles H Sr, 1962, S 20,33:2
Reis, Christopher J, 1945, D 21,22:2
Reis, George C, 1962, O 17,39:4
Reis, Gordon, 1948, Ap 21,27:1
Reis, Harry S, 1960, Ja 9,21:1
Reis, Henry J, 1961, Ja 2,25:5
Reis, Henry W Jr, 1959, O 5,31:1
Reis, Herman L, 1967, O 16,45:1
Reis, Irving, 1953, Jl 4,11:3
Reis, Jacob A, 1946, Ja 12,15:4
Reis, Luis da C, 1961, O 29,89:1
Reis, Moses, 1937, O 25,22:2
Reis, Nannie A Mrs, 1940, O 15,23:5
Reis, Robert, 1918, Je 22,11:6
Reisberg, Elias (por), 1943, Ag 19,19:1
Reisch, Richard, 1938, D 17,15:3
Reischmann, George M, 1956, O 21,87:2
Reischmann, George Michael, 1922, F 8,17:5
Reischmann, Henry R, 1946, My 28,21:1
Reischmann, Theodore, 1963, Jl 22,23:4
Reiselt, Emil, 1905, Je 26,1:4
Reisen, Abraham, 1953, Ap 2,27:3
Reisen, C Joseph, 1949, D 21,29:5
Reisen, William F, 1951, Mr 28,29:2
Reisenberger, Edwin A, 1948, S 26,76:2
Reisenberger, John, 1904, Mr 20,20:6
Reisenweber, J, 1931, Ag 10,15:1
Reiser, Alden M, 1961, O 8,87:3
Reiser, Benjamin, 1951, F 15,31:4
Reiser, Fidelis, 1940, O 3,25:5
Reiser, Paul Dr, 1968, Mr 29,41:2
Reisig, Anna, 1937, My 25,28:2
Reisig, Charles H, 1941, D 11,27:5
Reisig, Mary E S Mrs, 1941, D 13,21:5
Reising, Eugene G, 1967, F 22,29:4
Reisinger, Curt H, 1964, D 19,29:3
Reisinger, Harold C, 1945, Ja 31,21:3
Reisinger, Hugo, 1914, S 29,11:5
Reisinger, Hugo (est, O 30,9:5), 1914, O 29,11:4
Reisinger, Jacob A, 1947, Ap 30,25:5
Reisinger, Paul, 1941, O 13,17:5
Reisinger, Walter B (por), 1948, Je 5,15:4
Reisinger, Walter B Mrs, 1941, Mr 13,21:1; 1953, Jl 11,11:5
Reisler, Edward, 1937, N 24,23:2
Reisler, Frank O, 1944, O 19,23:4
Reisler, Leo J, 1958, F 3,23:4
Reisling, Frank C, 1955, Mr 6,89:2
Reisman, Henry A, 1956, Mr 31,15:3
Reisman, Leon, 1961, D 19,33:1
Reisman, Leonard (funl, D 9,47:2), 1967, D 8,42:6
Reisman, Morris, 1966, Je 18,31:3
Reisman, Sidney Mrs, 1965, My 24,31:3
Reisner, Christian F, 1940, Jl 18,19:1
Reisner, Christian F Mrs, 1961, F 18,19:2
Reisner, David Mrs (E Freund-Reisner), 1958, N 31:5
Reisner, Edward H, 1958, My 31,15:3
Reisner, Edward H Mrs, 1951, Mr 14,33:6
Reisner, Elis Mrs, 1952, D 10,35:2
Reisner, Elis W, 1948, Mr 16,27:2
Reisner, Francis, 1949, Jl 8,19:3
Reisner, George A, 1942, Je 8,15:4
Reisner, George A (will), 1942, N 4,20:4
Reisner, George A Mrs, 1950, Ap 20,29:2
Reisner, Herbert E Mrs, 1952, Ja 31,27:2
Reisner, Herbert W, 1963, N 2,25:4
Reisner, John H, 1965, Ap 27,37:3
Reisner, Leon Sr, 1957, F 23,17:3
Reisner, Lewis E, 1949, Ja 11,27:2
Reison, Isidor, 1961, S 12,33:4
Reiss, Adolph, 1946, N 20,31:4
Reiss, Bernard, 1948, Ja 18,60:3
Reiss, Charles, 1959, Jl 6,27:3
Reiss, Elias, 1958, Jl 19,15:4
Reiss, Erich, 1951, My 9,33:2
Reiss, George A Mrs, 1965, Mr 25,37:4
Reiss, George G, 1962, F 9,26:8
Reiss, George J, 1951, F 26,23:4
Reiss, George S, 1951, Mr 3,13:5
Reiss, Harold E, 1948, Ag 25,25:2
Reiss, Harry A, 1938, My 14,15:5
Reiss, Henry (will), 1961, O 22,59:1
Reiss, Henry G, 1944, F 27,37:1
Reiss, Herman L, 1951, O 31,29:1
Reiss, Honora R Mrs, 1941, Ap 2,23:2
Reiss, I, 1948, Ja 7,25:1
Reiss, Isaac, 1943, Je 10,21:3
Reiss, Jack, 1966, D 22,33:4
Reiss, Jacob C, 1949, Mr 24,28:5
Reiss, Jacob L, 1955, Ja 13,27:6

Reiss, Jacob Mrs, 1937, D 6,27:3
Reiss, John E, 1942, My 2,13:5
Reiss, Joseph, 1960, Jl 24,64:4
Reiss, Julian J, 1959, D 14,31:5
Reiss, Leo J, 1954, Ja 12,23:4
Reiss, Leopold Mrs, 1949, Jl 9,13:6
Reiss, Pincus, 1946, Ja 16,23:3
Reiss, Richard A Dr, 1949, Je 29,56:6
Reiss, Samuel, 1964, Jl 20,25:5
Reiss, Sydnor, 1962, S 1,19:1
Reiss, Walter F, 1958, Je 27,25:3
Reiss, William A, 1959, O 26,29:4
Reiss, Winold, 1953, Ag 31,18:5
Reist, Henry G, 1942, Jl 6,15:2
Reistad, Ole, 1949, D 23,22:4
Reitano, James P, 1949, O 26,27:2
Reitano, Joseph R, 1964, Jl 2,31:3
Reitchmyre, James, 1939, F 6,13:6
Reitemeyer, Albert F, 1949, Je 18,13:3
Reitemeyer, John R, 1945, O 2,23:1
Reiter, Arthur P, 1950, Je 24,13:1
Reiter, Bela Z, 1957, Je 5,35:5
Reiter, Bernard L, 1968, Ap 24,47:3
Reiter, Edward, 1955, F 6,88:8
Reiter, Henry, 1947, Ap 25,22:3
Reiter, Howard R, 1957, N 12,34:2
Reiter, J Harkey, 1961, D 13,43:3
Reiter, Lues, 1947, F 4,25:5
Reiter, Max A, 1950, Ap 8,13:2
Reiter, Naftalie Rabbi, 1911, Mr 17,9:4
Reiter, Phil, 1948, F 3,25:2
Reiter, Victor, 1944, My 25,21:5
Reiter, Xavier, 1938, My 13,19:2
Reith, George, 1939, S 15,23:4
Reith, Henry L, 1962, S 16,86:5
Reith, Joseph P, 1959, N 3,31:1
Reith, William R, 1943, O 11,19:5
Reith, William R Mrs, 1944, Mr 24,19:6
Reithe, Aloise D, 1943, S 7,23:5
Reithebuch, Reinhard, 1951, O 16,31:1
Reithmeier, Bonaventure A, 1950, F 21,25:3
Reithoffer, Georg M, 1959, Ap 25,21:5
Reitinger, John H, 1950, F 21,25:3
Reitinger, T Phil, 1957, Jl 27,17:3
Reitler, Joseph (por), 1948, Mr 13,15:5
Reitman, Ben, 1942, N 17,26:3
Reitman, Jacob, 1943, D 11,15:1
Reitman, Louis B, 1941, Jl 4,13:5
Reitman, Martin, 1958, Ja 18,15:3
Reitmeier, William Mrs, 1946, O 25,30:6
Reitmeyer, Frank J, 1944, Ap 18,21:4
Reitter, George S, 1947, Mr 6,25:3
Reitwiesner, Andrew A, 1962, N 21,30:1
Reitwiesner, George C, 1949, D 3,15:4
Reitz, Deneys, 1944, O 20,19:2
Reitz, George B, 1952, F 25,21:4
Reitz, John A, 1950, Mr 12,92:5
Reitz, John A Mrs, 1950, Mr 12,92:5
Reitz, Ralph M, 1958, S 2,25:1
Reitz, S C Bosch, 1938, Ap 10,II,6:6
Reitz, Walter R, 1957, My 27,31:5
Reitze, William B J, 1964, My 13,47:4
Reitzel, Albert E, 1960, Jl 2,17:7
Reitzel, Frank S, 1943, D 26,32:5
Reitzell, Franklin A, 1942, S 20,41:2
Reitzfeld, Isaac (por), 1945, Ap 10,19:5
Reiwitch, Herman L, 1944, D 24,26:5
Reizenstein, Franz, 1968, O 17,47:2
Reizenstein, Harry S, 1958, F 15,17:4
Reizenstein, Louis, 1947, Jl 7,17:5
Rejebian, Hagop H Dr, 1937, Ap 4,II,11:2
Rekemeier, Emma, 1945, My 3,23:5
Rekemeier, Henry G, 1961, Jl 23,69:2
Relander, Lauri K, 1942, F 10,19:5
Relf, Albert E, 1937, Mr 28,25:1
Relf, Richard, 1956, O 14,86:6
Relihan, Christian J, 1944, Ag 17,17:7
Relihan, John J, 1957, Ag 1,25:6
Relin, Morris, 1954, Ja 17,92:4
Relin, Morris Mrs, 1959, My 20,35:4
Relkin, Edwin A, 1952, O 12,88:1
Relkin, Maurice L, 1964, F 9,88:6
Reller, Charles J, 1961, Ja 30,23:3
Reller, Henry Rev, 1925, N 2,23:6
Relles, Emanuel, 1958, Ap 3,31:4
Rellihan, Patrick Thomas, 1922, Ag 22,17:5
Rellis, Morris, 1923, F 28,17:3
Rellstab, Herman J, 1948, Mr 2,23:1
Rellstab, Theodore J, 1949, Je 30,23:3
Relph, George, 1960, Ap 25,29:2
Relter, Max, 1950, D 14,35:2
Relyea, Eugene Mrs, 1945, O 18,23:3
Relyea, Floyd P, 1946, O 2,29:3
Relyea, Frank, 1951, O 20,15:3
Relyea, George E Mrs, 1951, Ag 3,21:3
Relyea, Harry A, 1947, My 13,25:2
Relyea, Hiram Mrs, 1952, O 11,19:3
Relyea, Le Roy, 1960, F 1,27:4
Relyea, Marjorie, 1946, Mr 13,29:3
Relyea, Rudolph, 1952, Je 30,19:1
Remack, Edmund, 1868, N 8,5:3
Remacle, Augusta, 1946, S 29,61:1
Rembao, Alberto, 1962, N 13,37:4
Rembar, Louis Mrs, 1957, S 28,17:2
Rembaugh, Bertha, 1950, F 1,30:2
Rembert, Ernest W, 1956, O 22,29:4
Rembert, Gilliard, 1940, Jl 1,19:2
Remele, Charles W, 1955, Je 1,33:4
Remels, Christian F Capt, 1923, D 15,13:3
Remensnyder, Edward H, 1944, Ag 25,13:4
Remensnyder, J B, 1927, Ja 3,19:1
Remenyi, E, 1898, My 16,7:1
Remenyi, Joseph, 1956, S 26,33:5
Remer, Daniel F, 1946, S 7,15:4
Remer, John, 1949, S 30,23:3
Remer, John W, 1944, Mr 16,19:2
Remer, Kate, 1925, Jl 12,7:3
Remey, G C, 1928, F 12,30:1
Remey, George C Mrs, 1938, Mr 3,21:5
Remey, John T, 1960, N 10,47:4
Remez, David, 1951, My 20,89:1
Remi, Bro (Christian Bros), 1956, Je 30,17:2
Remick, Albert, 1906, F 3,9:4
Remick, Arthur T, 1939, O 1,53:1
Remick, J Gould, 1962, Jl 21,19:4
Remick, James W, 1943, F 11,19:2
Remick, Raymond M, 1948, O 14,29:4
Remick, William H, 1922, Mr 10,15:5
Remiddi, Enrico, 1944, Jl 27,17:5
Remie, Jean, 1950, Je 27,33:6
Remig, John H, 1954, S 18,15:2
Reming, Joseph Prince Dr, 1918, Ja 2,11:6
Remington, A D, 1909, Mr 10,9:3
Remington, Berthold M, 1951, N 23,29:2
Remington, Carl, 1919, Je 7,13:6
Remington, Charles C, 1949, Ja 4,19:3
Remington, Charles H, 1938, Mr 23,23:3
Remington, Charles H Mrs, 1943, Je 1,23:3; 1948, My 20,29:3
Remington, Clement, 1940, Mr 2,13:5
Remington, Cray R, 1949, O 11,31:4
Remington, Daniel H, 1941, N 6,23:2
Remington, Eliphalet, 1924, Ap 3,21:6; 1938, N 16,23:5
Remington, Franklin, 1955, O 21,27:1
Remington, Franklin Mrs, 1947, N 18,29:2
Remington, Frederic, 1909, D 28,9:5; 1965, D 15,47:4
Remington, Frederick C, 1956, S 12,37:5
Remington, George W, 1940, N 11,20:2
Remington, Harold, 1937, D 16,27:3
Remington, Harold G, 1946, Jl 19,19:6
Remington, Harold K, 1956, Ag 14,17:6
Remington, Harvey F, 1949, Mr 19,15:4
Remington, Herbert M, 1941, Mr 25,23:4
Remington, Horace W, 1968, My 1,47:3
Remington, John C Jr, 1951, Mr 8,29:3
Remington, Mortimer Mrs, 1963, Ap 4,47:1
Remington, Rob R, 1950, My 24,29:2
Remington, Samuel, 1882, D 2,5:1
Remington, Thomas F, 1941, N 11,23:5
Remington, Walter H B, 1945, Je 26,19:3
Remington, William B, 1947, D 7,76:2
Remington, William M, 1940, Ja 13,15:2
Remington, William P, 1963, D 21,23:4
Remington, Woobern E, 1949, Ja 20,27:3
Remizov, Alexey M, 1957, N 28,31:5
Remke, Ignatius B, 1944, Ag 7,15:5
Remlein, Stanley L, 1958, S 29,27:5
Remley, Charles E, 1942, My 30,15:4
Remley, Frank, 1967, Ja 31,31:5
Remley, Ralph M, 1939, My 28,III,6:5
Remley, Roland E Sr, 1950, Jl 30,61:1
Remly, Samuel, 1950, Jl 30,46:4
Remmbers, Lucas, 1938, D 27,17:4
Remmel, Frank, 1949, Ag 9,25:3
Remmel, H L Col, 1927, O 15,19:5
Remmele, Louis P, 1939, D 6,25:6
Remmele, Teresa B Mrs, 1940, O 26,15:3
Remmelman, Egmont G, 1944, My 18,19:5
Remmer, Robert, 1950, F 25,30:3
Remmers, Walter E Mrs, 1952, D 20,17:3
Remmert, Caryl Mrs, 1939, Ap 19,23:2
Remmert, Edward H, 1959, Je 24,31:2
Remmert, Karl, 1956, Ap 21,13:2
Remmey, D P Col (see also D 26), 1877, D 28,3:4
Remmy, John, 1951, Jl 30,19:3
Remond, Charles F, 1951, N 11,90:7
Remond, Charles Lenox, 1873, D 26,1:6
Remond, John C, 1946, Mr 28,25:1
Remont, Ralph W (por), 1944, D 2,13:1
Remont, Ralph W Mrs, 1950, D 14,35:2
Remos, Paul, 1953, Mr 14,15:3
Rempel, Charles A, 1939, D 27,21:1
Rempel, Milton, 1964, Ag 23,87:1
Rempes, Clifford E, 1951, N 20,31:1
Remsberg, E E Mrs, 1951, N 4,86:7
Remsburg, John Eleaser, 1919, S 25,15:5
Remsen, Charles A, 1951, Ja 10,27:2
Remsen, Charles C (cor, N 28,35:3), 1956, N 27,37:3
Remsen, Charles Mrs, 1952, My 12,25:5
Remsen, Ethel F W Mrs, 1938, F 2,19:6
Remsen, Frank W, 1959, My 9,21:5
Remsen, Garret S K, 1960, D 29,25:3
Remsen, Garret S K Mrs, 1942, S 24,27:6
Remsen, Garrett Mrs, 1904, Mr 20,7:7
Remsen, George F, 1911, Mr 16,9:5
Remsen, Henry Rutgers, 1874, Ap 8,5:6
Remsen, I, 1927, Mr 6,II,11:1
Remsen, Jacob, 1943, F 24,21:4
Remsen, John Schenck Suydam, 1911, O 4,13:5
Remsen, John W, 1949, F 10,27:4
Remsen, Joseph Mrs, 1946, Ag 24,11:5
Remsen, Lester C, 1959, Jl 23,27:4
Remsen, Richard, 1914, Ap 6,9:4
Remsen, Thomas R, 1958, N 7,27:4
Remsen, William, 1956, D 25,25:4
Remsen, William A, 1937, S 25,17:5
Remsen, William C S, 1953, Ja 11,91:1
Remsen, William Mrs, 1945, N 23,23:4
Remsen, Winfred H, 1953, S 6,50:2
Remson, John, 1906, Jl 15,9:5
Remus, George, 1952, Ja 21,10:2
Remy, Alfred, 1937, Mr 1,19:5
Remy, Arthur F J, 1954, O 26,27:2
Remy, Frank, 1903, Ag 3,7:6
Remy, Frank F Sr, 1954, D 8,35:4
Renaldi, Anthony Sr, 1953, Ap 17,25:6
Renan, Ernest, 1892, O 3,1:7
Renander, Arthur W, 1964, Jl 5,43:2
Renard, Andre, 1962, Jl 21,19:2
Renard, Col, 1905, Ap 14,9:6
Renard, Fred O, 1950, Jl 3,15:2
Renard, George A, 1968, D 6,47:1
Renard, Henry R, 1944, Ap 17,23:3
Renard, Jacques F, 1960, F 1,27:3
Renard, Marius, 1948, Jl 21,23:5
Renard, Rosita (por), 1949, My 26,29:5
Renard, Suzanne G, 1959, Ag 10,27:5
Renardy, Ossy, 1953, D 9,11:2
Renau, Edward, 1909, My 18,9:4
Renaud, Damase F, 1956, Mr 14,33:3
Renaud, George L, 1949, Jl 10,56:7
Renaud, Jean J, 1953, D 9,11:5
Renaud, Joseph M, 1941, Ag 3,34:7
Renaud, M, 1933, O 18,21:4
Renaud, Maurice, 1939, N 21,23:3
Renaud, Ralph E, 1948, Ag 11,21:1
Renaud, Ralph E Mrs, 1947, N 29,13:5
Renaud, Robert, 1941, D 17,27:2
Renaud, Ted, 1952, Ja 22,29:4
Renaudel, P, 1935, Ap 3,23:3
Renauld, August, 1950, Ap 5,32:2
Renauld, John B, 1921, Je 14,15:3
Renault, Albert B, 1942, Ap 7,22:3
Renault, Fernand, 1909, Mr 24,9:4
Renault, Francis, 1955, My 22,88:5
Renault, Henri R, 1952, Mr 24,25:1
Renault, J Paul, 1967, F 6,29:4
Renault, Louis, 1944, O 25,21:3
Renault, Marcel, 1903, My 28,1:3
Renaut, William C (por), 1949, F 3,23:3
Rench, G W, 1949, Je 21,25:4
Rencken, John M, 1945, Jl 1,17:2
Rencurel, Regis Mrs, 1909, S 12,9:2
Renda, Carmela Mrs, 1947, My 27,25:2
Rendall, Gerald H, 1945, F 20,19:1
Rendall, Guy A, 1949, S 28,27:3
Rendall, Guy A Mrs, 1937, Mr 22,23:4
Rendall, Isaac Norton Dr, 1912, N 19,15:4
Rendall, James W, 1957, Ap 4,33:4
Rendall, John B, 1924, S 5,17:3
Rendall, Montague J, 1950, O 6,27:2
Rendall, Raymond E, 1949, D 26,29:4
Rendall, Robert J, 1950, Ag 19,13:6
Rende, Raffaele, 1953, O 16,27:1
Rendel, John Mrs, 1939, Je 24,17:3
Rendel, Lord, 1913, Je 5,11:5
Rendell, Godfrey Mrs, 1959, D 17,37:4
Rendell, Harry, 1943, F 17,21:5
Rendell, Harry M Mrs, 1937, Mr 16,23:1
Rendell, William O, 1951, Jl 26,21:4
Rendi, Renzo, 1945, D 13,29:3
Rendich, Richard A, 1956, O 13,19:4
Rendle, Alfred B, 1938, Ja 13,21:1
Rendlesham, Lord, 1943, D 14,27:3
Rendt, David S (por), 1944, Jl 16,31:1
Rendt, David S Mrs, 1941, O 1,21:4
Rendt, Louis, 1904, F 20,9:5
Rendtorff, Edmund J, 1946, D 7,21:1
Rendueles, Manuel, 1951, D 12,37:4
Rendy, Charles A, 1939, Ap 17,17:3
Renee, Ruth (Mrs D Shafran), 1967, My 12,47:3
Renevier, Eugene Prof, 1906, My 6,4:1
Renfield, Joseph H, 1958, D 30,35:3
Renforth, James, 1871, Ag 24,1:5
Renforth, James (funl), 1871, S 11,1:7
Renfrew, F Ward, 1948, Ap 30,23:1
Renfrew, Leonard W, 1948, N 8,21:1
Rengifo, Inacio Gen, 1937, Ja 29,19:5
Renick, John F, 1945, S 15,15:1
Renick, Ralph A, 1945, F 7,21:4
Renick, Robert A, 1944, Ap 21,19:5
Renicks, Elizabeth M Mrs, 1941, Je 24,19:3
Renie, Stewart S, 1942, Ja 6,23:1
Renier, C A L, 1885, Je 13,5:3
Renier, Henri, 1948, Ja 8,25:5
Renier, Joseph E, 1966, O 9,86:2
Reninger, Henry A, 1949, D 10,18:3
Renison, Patrick M, 1965, N 12,47:3
Renison, Robert J, 1957, O 8,35:2

Renkel, George W, 1948, Ap 1,25:3
Renker, Henry G, 1947, Jl 13,44:7
Renker, William L, 1948, Ap 25,68:4
Renkin, J Dr, 1934, Jl 16,15:4
Renkin, W O, 1943, Ap 18,48:4
Rennard, John C, 1945, Mr 7,21:4
Rennard, John C Mrs, 1946, F 16,13:5
Renne, James E, 1968, O 6,84:6
Rennebohm, Oscar, 1968, O 16,47:2
Renneker, Alvin, 1945, Ja 6,11:5
Rennell, Christian, 1878, Jl 26,5:4
Rennell, Henry H Mrs, 1952, Jl 27,57:2; 1954, S 25, 15:6
Rennell, Lord, 1941, Jl 28,13:3
Rennell, Thornton B, 1944, O 10,21:3
Rennen, Elizabeth Mrs, 1939, Ja 28,13:7
Renner, Albert E, 1941, My 13,23:2
Renner, Alois Mrs, 1952, Mr 28,23:4
Renner, Charles L, 1942, N 20,23:1
Renner, Dan S Dr, 1937, D 14,25:4
Renner, Edward P Mrs, 1965, D 9,47:2
Renner, Frederick C, 1945, Je 27,19:2
Renner, George T, 1955, O 15,15:1
Renner, Harry Jr, 1952, Je 8,87:1
Renner, Heinz, 1964, Ja 13,35:2
Renner, John F, 1954, Je 5,17:4
Renner, Karl Pres, 1950, D 31,1:6
Renner, Louis, 1949, D 22,23:3
Rennert, Charlotte A, 1941, D 27,19:2
Rennert, Edward, 1944, F 12,13:5
Rennert, Elizabeth, 1941, Ag 12,15:1
Rennert, Hugo A Mrs, 1944, N 11,13:3
Rennette, Ferdinand C J B de, 1947, O 30,25:2
Rennick, Henry L, 1940, Je 30,32:5
Rennick, Percival G, 1938, Je 24,19:3
Rennie, Hugh, 1965, F 13,2:3
Rennie, James, 1965, Ag 1,77:2
Rennie, James M, 1964, Ag 20,29:2
Rennie, John, 1946, Ja 9,23:3
Rennie, John O D, 1952, Ag 21,19:6
Rennie, John O Mrs, 1964, O 3,29:5
Rennie, Joseph, 1943, O 1,19:2
Rennie, Norman L, 1940, Ja 19,19:5
Rennie, Ralph W, 1953, Mr 8,90:5
Rennie, Rutherford (Rud), 1956, O 7,86:4
Rennie, Thomas A C, 1956, My 22,33:5
Rennie, William L, 1942, Ag 23,43:1
Rennieburgh, Henry J, 1961, My 7,86:5
Renninger, Christian, 1945, Mr 18,42:1
Rennison, Clarence H, 1948, S 15,31:2
Rennison, Edwin H, 1954, D 3,27:2
Rennon, Joel E, 1945, Ap 28,15:6
Rennyson, Gertrude, 1953, Ja 5,21:4
Reno, Charles S, 1940, N 16,17:5
Reno, Claude T, 1961, Je 13,35:2
Reno, Edward M, 1949, Ap 3,76:2
Reno, Harold P, 1951, Ja 8,17:4
Reno, Jesse W, 1947, Je 3,25:1
Reno, Joseph F, 1943, Jl 25,30:8
Reno, Leonard M, 1944, D 27,19:3
Reno, M, 1936, My 6,23:1
Reno, Morris, 1917, Je 12,13:5
Reno, Morris Mrs, 1915, N 14,19:5
Reno, Samuel J Jr, 1943, My 15,15:1
Renoe, John R, 1965, D 2,41:4
Renoir, Edmond, 1944, Mr 26,42:1
Renoir, Pierre, 1952, Mr 12,27:2
Renouard, Charles A, 1953, Je 12,27:4
Renouf, Edward M, 1941, Ap 21,19:6
Renoult, Father, 1940, D 6,23:3
Renoult, Rene, 1946, Ap 28,44:3
Rensburg, Jan J van, 1938, Je 15,23:6
Renshaw, Alfred, 1953, Ap 10,21:4
Renshaw, Alfred H, 1939, Je 18,38:1; 1961, Jl 20,10:7
Renshaw, Charles C, 1967, Ja 31,31:2
Renshaw, Donald, 1961, My 4,37:3
Renshaw, Elbert N, 1939, My 17,23:4
Renshaw, Elbert N Mrs, 1956, Mr 31,15:7
Renshaw, Fred M, 1944, D 30,11:4
Renshaw, Frederick William, 1920, F 2,13:3
Renshaw, George Y Jr, 1939, Ja 21,15:4
Renshaw, Lloyd, 1942, Je 16,23:5
Renshaw, Wallace W, 1961, O 30,29:5
Rensin, Joseph, 1959, S 11,14:3
Rensing, Ignatz, 1937, F 26,21:4
Renskorf, Millie H Mrs (will), 1938, D 25,III,10:4
Rensley, Alvoid Z Mrs, 1948, D 25,17:1
Rensselaer, Cornelius G, 1944, O 20,19:1
Rente, Henry J, 1950, S 15,25:3
Rentis, Constantine, 1958, O 19,37:1
Rentner, Maurice, 1958, Jl 8,27:2
Renton, David C Sr, 1964, D 28,29:3
Renton, Edward, 1941, Je 21,17:3
Renton, Edward A, 1960, Ag 25,29:5
Renton, Herbert S, 1939, Mr 24,21:1
Renton, Homer C, 1943, F 25,21:3
Renton, Joseph R, 1947, My 1,25:4
Rentschler, Frederick B, 1956, Ap 26,33:1
Rentschler, Frederick B Mrs, 1953, Mr 8,91:2
Rentschler, Frederick G, 1959, Je 18,31:4
Rentschler, Gordon S, 1948, Mr 5,21:1
Rentschler, Harvey C (por), 1949, Mr 24,27:1
Rentschler, Henry A, 1941, Ag 6,17:4
Rentschler, J Fred, 1940, F 16,19:3
Rentschler, Mahlon J, 1948, O 27,27:5
Rentz, Frank R, 1939, Ag 13,29:4
Rentz, George Mrs, 1952, D 29,35:8
Rentz, Jacob F Sr, 1954, Jl 8,23:1
Renvers, Rudolf von, 1909, Mr 23,9:5
Renville, George H, 1912, Ag 14,9:4
Renville, Herbert, 1940, My 6,17:4
Renwick, Allyn K, 1947, N 18,29:5
Renwick, Edward A, 1941, Ja 11,17:5
Renwick, Edward Sabine, 1912, Mr 21,11:5
Renwick, Harold C, 1955, S 27,35:2
Renwick, Harry L, 1958, S 17,32:4
Renwick, Harry L Mrs, 1958, Ap 17,31:4
Renwick, Henry Brevoort, 1922, O 19,21:6
Renwick, Henry Brevoort Mrs, 1907, S 30,7:6
Renwick, James, 1895, Je 25,9:5
Renwick, James A, 1937, Ag 17,19:5
Renwick, James A Mrs, 1945, Ag 9,21:4
Renwick, John B, 1937, Jl 11,II,4:3
Renwick, John S, 1967, F 20,45:1
Renwick, W R, 1883, My 15,5:6
Renwick, W W, 1933, Mr 16,20:2
Renwick, William W, 1950, Mr 28,31:1
Reny, Edward A, 1953, Jl 3,19:3
Renyi, George S de, 1945, Ag 26,43:1
Renz, Adrian N, 1950, Mr 7,27:3
Renz, Carl Julius Rev, 1921, F 12,13:3
Renz, E Justin Mrs, 1949, O 25,28:5
Renz, Franz, 1901, Jl 8,7:1
Renz, Frederick, 1939, Je 1,25:1
Renz, L Everett, 1962, S 1,19:3
Renz, Lorenzo F Mrs, 1944, N 23,31:5
Renza, Antonio S, 1945, D 6,27:3
Renzi, Paolo, 1963, My 28,37:2
Renzi, Remigio, 1938, N 22,23:4
Renziehausen, Emelie, 1947, S 18,25:4
Renzo, Frank Di, 1940, Mr 2,13:4
Reock, Ernest C, 1957, My 12,86:5
Reohr, Charles D, 1940, Je 9,44:2
Reohr, Frederick W, 1937, Ag 15,II,7:3
Reordan, Charles E, 1947, Mr 24,25:3
Reoux, Harry A, 1968, Mr 3,89:2
Reoux, Louis E, 1938, S 12,17:6
Repa, John, 1957, S 4,33:4
Repass, William C, 1945, Mr 12,19:3
Repcka, Charles W, 1954, D 22,23:3
Repcka, William C, 1951, F 20,25:4
Repella, Anthony, 1957, Je 17,23:4
Repetta, Stanley T Jr, 1965, My 27,37:3
Repetti, George W, 1956, Jl 1,57:2
Repetto, Andrew M, 1953, Ap 12,89:1
Repetto, Charles E, 1949, N 14,27:3
Repetto, Frances Mrs, 1948, F 13,21:4
Repetto, Nicholas, 1965, D 1,47:1
Repetto, Roberto, 1950, Je 22,27:4
Repholz, Frank, 1950, Jl 25,27:4
Repicky, Paul, 1945, S 24,19:4
Repington, C A Lt-Col, 1925, My 27,23:2
Repke, George, 1956, My 27,88:8
Repkie, Charles A, 1949, N 18,29:2
Repkie, Fred C, 1943, O 15,19:5
Repkie, John R, 1954, Jl 23,17:3
Replogle, Arnold M Mrs, 1943, Je 13,44:7
Replogle, Harry H, 1955, Mr 9,27:3
Replogle, Harry H Mrs, 1938, D 2,23:3
Replogle, Herbert R, 1954, Mr 12,21:3
Replogle, J Leonard (por), 1948, N 26,23:1
Replogle, J Leonard Mrs, 1948, S 7,25:1
Repole, Patsy, 1948, F 9,17:5
Repole, Rosario, 1950, F 9,29:6
Repoulis, Emanuel, 1924, My 15,19:3
Repp, Harry L, 1951, F 23,27:2
Repp, Herbert J, 1948, O 26,31:4
Repp, Herbert N Mrs, 1957, Jl 9,29:4
Repp, John H, 1938, Ag 26,17:3
Repp, John J, 1952, My 1,29:5
Repp, William F (por), 1943, My 27,25:3
Repp, William H G, 1948, Ja 17,17:2
Reppa, Charles, 1939, Je 30,19:6
Repper, Frederick D, 1945, Jl 29,40:3
Reppert, Adolph, 1942, Je 24,19:3
Reppert, Norman S, 1938, N 24,27:3
Reppetti, Charles E, 1944, N 25,13:1
Repplier, James M, 1940, Ag 12,15:4
Repplier, Mary, 1946, Je 28,22:2
Reppy, Alison, 1958, Ag 21,25:1
Requa, Arthur, 1944, S 23,13:6
Requa, Charles H, 1938, D 22,21:3
Requa, Edwin B, 1966, O 27,47:2
Requa, H Merrill Mrs, 1949, Ap 23,13:5
Requa, Isaac L, 1905, Mr 30,9:6
Requa, James M, 1912, O 19,11:5
Requa, Kate, 1903, D 20,7:6
Requa, Mark L (por), 1937, Mr 7,II,8:6
Requa, Mark L Mrs, 1955, F 24,27:2
Requa, Sam Capt, 1903, Ap 19,7:4
Reque, John L, 1951, S 5,31:4
Reque, Lars Mrs, 1957, My 30,19:4
Requena, Rafael, 1946, Ap 21,46:2
Requin, Edouard Jean Gen, 1953, F 3,25:3
Rerberg, Dimitri Mrs, 1957, S 10,33:2
Resa Garbayo, Ramon, 1958, Ag 3,80:7
Resch, Henry U Mrs, 1957, N 14,33:2
Resch, Joseph, 1941, Ja 26,35:6
Resch, Oliver B, 1953, My 29,25:4
Resch, Robert P Mrs, 1950, F 6,25:3
Reser, E Newton, 1938, N 29,23:4
Reser, Harry, 1965, S 29,3:8
Reser, Stanley H, 1959, Ja 27,33:2
Reshkin, Louis, 1956, Mr 12,27:1
Resko, Michael, 1958, S 10,33:1
Resnati, Antonio Sylvia Capt, 1919, Ag 17,22:4
Resnatti, Antonio Silvia Capt, 1918, My 22,13:3
Resnick, David, 1961, S 25,33:6
Resnick, George J, 1959, D 20,60:3
Resnick, Harris Mrs, 1951, Ja 6,29:3
Resnick, Hyman M, 1958, S 1,13:3
Resnick, Joseph S Mrs, 1968, Je 23,73:1
Resnick, Louis (por), 1941, Mr 19,21:5
Resnick, Louis, 1951, Je 16,15:6
Resnick, Max, 1945, O 19,23:3
Resnick, Paul, 1966, Je 18,31:4
Resnick, Samuel, 1952, F 19,29:4
Resnik, Ernest D, 1955, Je 21,31:3
Resnikoff, Carl, 1967, Ag 12,25:5
Resnikoff, Hyman Mrs, 1965, Ap 30,35:4
Resnikoff, Vladimir, 1920, F 8,22:2
Resor, Reuben P, 1954, N 11,31:4
Resor, Stanley B, 1962, O 30,35:1
Resor, Stanley B Mrs, 1964, Ja 3,24:1
Respess, Jerome B, 1939, Jl 26,19:1
Respess, Roland B, 1950, Ap 29,15:4
Respighi, Carlo, 1947, Je 7,13:5
Respighi, O, 1936, Ap 18,15:1
Respighi, Peter Cardinal, 1913, Mr 23,IV,7:5
Ress, Charles, 1957, Mr 21,31:5
Ress, Emanuel, 1967, Jl 26,39:2
Resseger, L E, 1940, Ja 5,19:3
Resser, Charles E, 1943, S 19,48:3
Ressler, Hubert B, 1955, My 5,33:5
Ressmeyer, Rudolph S, 1961, Mr 30,29:3
Ressner, Joseph Mrs, 1956, F 23,27:3
Rest-Blanchet, Paul du, 1914, Mr 31,11:1
Resta, Francis E Col, 1968, Ag 17,27:2
Restaino, Felix G, 1967, S 26,19:3
Restarick, Charles W, 1944, Ap 18,21:4
Restin, Erich H, 1952, S 14,86:8
Reston, James, 1960, My 31,31:4
Restrapo, Carlos E, 1937, Jl 7,23:5
Restrepo, A Gomez, 1947, N 8,17:2
Restrepo, Fabio, 1949, S 20,29:5
Restrepo, Ganzolo, 1952, Je 24,29:3
Restrepo, Juan M, 1944, O 30,19:6
Restrepo, Roberto L, 1953, S 26,17:1
Reswick, William, 1954, Je 3,27:5
Reszka Moreaux, Pedro, 1960, Mr 7,29:3
Reszke, Edouard de, 1917, My 31,11:4
Reth, J Harry, 1937, Mr 20,19:5
Rethy, Wolf A, 1967, F 22,29:3
Reti, Rudolph, 1957, F 9,19:6
Reti, Rudolph R Mrs, 1942, S 10,27:2
Reticker, Edward, 1952, Ja 21,15:1
Retinger, Joseph H, 1960, Je 24,27:4
Retivov, George, 1957, S 3,27:4
Retta, Francis, 1948, My 5,25:2
Retteg, Anna Mrs, 1956, My 4,51:5
Rettew, Thomas M, 1953, N 19,31:4
Rettger, E W, 1938, O 10,19:4
Rettger, Louis J, 1943, D 2,27:4
Rettie, Charles S, 1945, S 24,19:4
Rettig, Martin, 1956, Ja 26,29:1
Rettinger, Rosa Mrs, 1940, D 4,27:3
Rettino, Ernest V, 1954, Ja 28,27:2
Rettino, Solvi V, 1964, N 30,33:3
Rettker, Walter F, 1961, F 22,25:3
Retz, Charles, 1960, Ag 17,31:4
Retz, Frederick, 1946, My 26,32:6
Retz, George W, 1953, O 23,23:1
Retz, Louis D, 1941, O 24,23:4
Reu, Johann M (por), 1943, O 16,13:6
Reubel, Henry, 1941, Ja 28,19:3
Reuben, Ben W, 1949, Ap 21,26:4
Reuben, Carmen, 1944, Jl 28,13:4
Reuben, Herbert F, 1965, Ap 27,37:2
Reuben, Mark S, 1947, Ja 19,53:2
Reuben, Robert E, 1964, Ap 23,39:4
Reubens, Charles M, 1916, O 11,11:3
Reuche, Marie L, 1951, O 6,19:1
Reukauff, Henry J, 1939, O 4,25:4
Reul, Alexander, 1947, Ja 21,23:3
Reul, George P J, 1953, My 1,22:3
Reul (Bro Jno William), 1966, Mr 19,29:3
Reulbach, Ed, 1961, Jl 19,29:3
Reule, John J, 1947, Ag 27,23:5
Reuling, August, 1966, D 10,37:4
Reuling, George Dr, 1915, N 26,13:6
Reuling, Phil, 1957, S 19,29:2
Reuman, Theodore H, 1954, Ag 6,17:3
Reuning, Wilhelm, 1950, F 16,24:2
Reurs, Jan H, 1961, Ap 5,37:2
Reusch, Alfred Mrs, 1957, Je 27,25:4
Reusch, Harry E, 1949, F 22,23:1
Reusch, Howard E, 1955, N 9,33:1
Reusche, E Fred, 1966, Je 3,40:1
Reusche, Frank L, 1940, N 12,23:5

Reuss, Edward H Jr, 1959, My 7,33:4
Reuss, Francis G, 1955, D 22,23:2
Reuss, Gustav A, 1946, O 26,17:5
Reuss, Russell E, 1959, Ap 30,31:1
Reuss-Graitz, Henry XXII, 1902, Ap 20,7:6
Reussille, Leon Jr Mrs, 1951, F 17,15:2
Reussner, Ella (will), 1938, Ag 2,9:3
Reuter, Albert A, 1955, N 22,35:5
Reuter, Antonie M, 1948, N 24,24:2
Reuter, Edward B, 1946, My 29,24:3
Reuter, Edward F, 1937, D 25,15:4
Reuter, Ernst, 1953, S 30,1:2
Reuter, Fritz, 1874, Jl 14,4:7
Reuter, Gebriele, 1941, N 16,56:6
Reuter, George, 1924, Ap 16,23:5
Reuter, George F, 1967, Ag 3,33:3
Reuter, George J, 1946, N 15,24:2
Reuter, Henry, 1939, O 4,25:4
Reuter, Jacob, 1941, O 2,25:2
Reuter, John, 1953, Ag 1,11:6
Reuter, John M, 1949, O 25,27:2
Reuter, Ludwig von, 1943, D 22,24:2
Reuter, Max, 1947, S 9,31:3
Reuter, Paul J Baron, 1899, F 26,7:3
Reuterdahl, Henry Lt-Com, 1925, D 24,13:6
Reutershan, Josef W Jr, 1951, D 26,25:4
Reutershan, Paul V, 1941, Mr 30,49:1
Reuterskioeld, Carl-Axel, 1944, Ap 13,19:4
Reuterwall, Bengt E, 1944, O 11,21:5
Reuther, Charles M, 1945, F 15,20:2
Reuther, Edward A, 1962, Ap 3,39:5
Reuther, Ernest F, 1950, My 13,17:5
Reuther, Frank A, 1940, Ja 16,23:4
Reuther, George W, 1947, Ja 13,21:4
Reuther, John, 1950, Ag 20,77:1
Reuther, John K Jr, 1945, Je 7,19:3
Reuther, Roy, 1968, Ja 11,37:3
Reuther, Valentine, 1967, N 18,37:1
Reutlinger, Emil, 1947, Ag 24,58:1
Reutlinger, Harry F, 1962, N 21,33:2
Rev, George S, 1961, N 10,35:2
Revai, Josef, 1959, Ag 5,27:1
Reveille, Alex (will), 1952, Ag 20,19:5
Revel, Bernard, 1940, D 2,23:4
Revel, Harry, 1958, N 4,27:3
Revel, Paola T di, 1948, Mr 25,27:4
Revell, Dorothy, 1908, Jl 8,7:4
Revell, F H, 1931, O 12,21:5
Revell, Nellie (Mrs Arth J Kellar), 1958, Ag 14,29:3
Revelle, Hamilton, 1958, My 28,31:5
Revelle, Orville, 1962, Ag 15,31:1
Revelle, Thomas P, 1937, Jl 6,19:6
Revels, Frederick W Prof, 1937, O 16,19:2
Revenaugh, Lynn, 1954, S 14,27:4
Revenel, Beatrice W Mrs, 1956, Mr 17,19:6
Reventlow, Eduard Count, 1963, Jl 28,64:5
Reventlow, Ernst zu, 1943, N 22,19:3
Revercomb, George A, 1937, Ja 11,20:3
Revere, Clinton T, 1949, My 9,25:6
Revere, Clinton T Mrs, 1964, Ag 25,33:1
Revere, Edward H R, 1957, My 5,89:1
Revere, George Otis, 1925, N 23,21:4
Revere, Paul, 1950, Jl 6,27:4
Revere, Thomas H, 1951, Ja 26,23:5
Reverman, Theodore H, 1941, Jl 19,13:6
Reveron, Armando, 1954, S 20,23:1
Reverter, Navarro, 1924, Ap 3,21:6
Revill, Milton K, 1955, F 10,31:2
Reville, Patrick J, 1943, My 7,19:2
Reville-Terry, William W, 1948, O 9,19:1
Revilliod, Henri J, 1956, Mr 8,29:3
Revillion, Theodore, 1924, Ja 12,13:1
Revillon, Anatole, 1916, Ja 23,17:3
Revillon, Jacques, 1945, F 16,23:4
Revillon, Leon, 1915, F 3,11:7
Revillon, Rene, 1937, F 25,23:2
Revillon, Theodore L, 1949, D 10,17:5
Revillon, Tony, 1957, Ja 12,19:4
Revillon, Victor, 1950, F 14,25:5
Reviol, Charles, 1937, D 5,II,9:3
Revman, Harry H, 1941, O 6,17:4
Revoil, Paul, 1914, Ap 29,11:6
Revoir, Charles, 1966, Je 29,47:3
Revoir, Lester C, 1954, Jl 28,23:2
Revson, Douglas, 1967, Jl 31,34:8
Revueltas, S, 1940, D 22,IX,7:4
Revusky, Abraham, 1946, F 9,13:5
Rew, Kenneth S, 1956, Mr 7,33:4
Rewalt, Jay W, 1959, Mr 31,29:3
Rewell, Viljo, 1964, N 9,33:4
Rewey, E Munn, 1916, Ja 15,9:5
Rex, Albert E, 1944, My 14,45:2
Rex, Clarence H, 1949, Ap 6,29:3
Rex, Frederick, 1961, Ap 15,21:3
Rex, George M, 1948, Je 26,17:2
Rex, John B S, 1942, Ja 26,15:3
Rex, Oliver P Dr, 1910, My 18,11:4
Rex, Walter A, 1953, My 23,15:4
Rexford, Chester P, 1954, O 9,17:2
Rexford, Eben Eugene, 1916, O 19,9:3
Rexford, Elliott P, 1948, O 18,23:3
Rexford, Frank A (por), 1941, Ja 5,44:6
Rexford, Irving P, 1955, Mr 6,89:1

Rexicker, Minerva Mrs, 1946, F 4,25:3
Rexroth, Andrew J, 1957, Ja 14,23:4
Rexroth, Frieda, 1939, Ag 16,23:3
Rextrew, Harry W, 1938, Je 18,15:5
Rey, Jean, 1950, N 14,14:5
Rey, Louis Etienne Ernest, 1909, Ja 16,11:6
Rey, Pierre, 1968, Mr 5,41:3
Rey, Victor M, 1937, Ag 30,21:6
Rey, Vincent B, 1961, My 5,29:5
Reyam, David H, 1943, Ap 21,25:5
Reybert, J Jarvis Capt, 1937, Ag 11,II,8:8
Reybold, Eugene, 1961, N 22,33:1
Reybolds, William, 1906, N 1,9:5
Reyburn, John Edgar, 1914, Ja 5,9:6
Reyburn, John R Mrs, 1950, Je 24,13:3
Reyburn, Margaretta C Mrs, 1941, O 2,25:4
Reyburn, Robert Dr, 1909, Mr 27,9:4
Reyburn, Samuel W, 1962, Je 8,31:1
Reyburn, William S, 1946, Jl 26,21:2
Reychkof, John, 1952, My 23,21:2
Reycraft, James L Mrs, 1947, My 18,60:2
Reycraft, John J Sr, 1944, N 19,50:5
Reycraft, John W, 1940, D 29,24:7
Reycraft, Joseph Bass, 1925, Ag 5,17:6
Reydel, Joseph, 1955, Jl 1,21:4
Reyelt, Gustav, 1960, Ag 29,25:1
Reyes, Alberto, 1947, Mr 19,25:3
Reyes, Alfonso, 1959, D 28,23:1
Reyes, Antonio, 1939, Mr 2,21:1
Reyes, Benn F, 1968, D 10,77:3
Reyes, Francisco D, 1937, Je 12,15:3
Reyes, Gabriel M, 1952, O 11,19:2
Reyes, Juan, 1941, Ja 23,6:1
Reyes, Manuel C, 1944, Ja 13,21:1
Reyes, Maria Mrs, 1941, S 20,6:2
Reyes, Rafael Gen, 1921, F 21,11:6
Reyes, Victor Calderon Gen, 1909, My 16,9:6
Reyes, Victor M, 1937, N 4,25:2
Reyes Ocho, Rodolfo, 1954, Je 5,17:6
Reyher, Max, 1944, D 8,21:1
Reyles, Carlos, 1938, Jl 25,15:7
Reymann, John H, 1941, Mr 6,21:5
Reymer, Jacob (will), 1905, Jl 15,1:6
Reymert, Martin L, 1953, Je 4,29:5
Reymond, Martin H, 1947, N 16,76:4
Reymont, Wladislaw Stanislaw, 1925, D 6,13:2
Reyna, Rafael H, 1950, D 20,31:1
Reyna Andrade, Jose M, 1947, Ag 28,23:5
Reynal, Adele F Mrs, 1940, F 18,43:5
Reynal, Eugene, 1968, Mr 21,53:4
Reynal, Eugene S, 1940, Ja 1,23:4
Reynal, Louis, 1960, F 22,17:2
Reynal, Nathaniel C Mrs, 1947, Ja 5,53:2
Reynal, Victor M, 1959, Ja 20,35:5
Reynard, Elizabeth, 1962, Ja 10,47:1
Reynard, Grant Tyson, 1968, Ag 14,39:2
Reynaud, Paul (funl, S 25,84:6), 1966, S 22,1:1
Reynders, Caroline Mrs, 1940, F 14,21:3
Reynders, Harry W, 1950, Mr 20,21:3
Reynders, John V, 1944, Jl 11,15:3
Reyneau, Betsy G Mrs, 1964, O 21,43:1
Reyneau, Paul O, 1952, D 4,35:3
Reynell, Carleton, 1953, S 9,29:1
Reynes, Jaime, 1913, D 19,11:4
Reynes, John Francis, 1925, S 2,23:5
Reynes, Joseph A Jr Mrs, 1951, D 4,33:4
Reyniers, James A, 1967, N 5,86:1
Reynolds, A Craig, 1948, Mr 29,21:4
Reynolds, A D Maj, 1925, S 24,25:3
Reynolds, A H Gen, 1884, Jl 23,5:1
Reynolds, A W, 1876, Jl 2,5:3
Reynolds, A Westcott, 1941, Je 3,21:2
Reynolds, Abraham Bp, 1907, D 30,7:6
Reynolds, Alice E, 1954, Mr 28,88:6
Reynolds, Allen S, 1939, My 5,23:2
Reynolds, Ann T, 1948, Ap 7,25:1
Reynolds, Arch C, 1948, Je 8,25:2
Reynolds, Archie C, 1938, Ja 12,21:2
Reynolds, Arthur, 1943, Ja 3,42:5
Reynolds, Asa P, 1946, My 22,21:1
Reynolds, Augustus R, 1945, Mr 26,19:5
Reynolds, Barney, 1909, Ja 5,9:5
Reynolds, Baxter, 1949, D 8,33:1
Reynolds, Belle Dr, 1937, Jl 30,19:5
Reynolds, Benjamin Mrs, 1967, F 11,29:3
Reynolds, Blythe M, 1961, Je 26,31:1
Reynolds, Boyd E, 1947, My 13,25:3
Reynolds, Brice S, 1946, Ja 27,42:5
Reynolds, Bruce, 1948, S 2,23:5
Reynolds, Bruce D, 1957, Ap 28,86:7
Reynolds, C Hal, 1958, D 9,41:4
Reynolds, C Leslie, 1913, Ag 14,9:6
Reynolds, C O, 1880, Jl 5,5:2
Reynolds, Charles B, 1940, N 11,19:4; 1942, Mr 2,19:2
Reynolds, Charles B Mrs, 1940, Mr 28,23:3
Reynolds, Charles F, 1938, D 3,19:5
Reynolds, Charles G, 1955, N 24,29:5
Reynolds, Charles H, 1940, S 1,20:7
Reynolds, Charles J, 1937, D 5,II,8:8; 1947, Ja 31,23:4
Reynolds, Charles L, 1938, Jl 6,23:2; 1959, N 1,85:1
Reynolds, Charles L Mrs, 1938, Ag 14,33:4
Reynolds, Charles N, 1953, Ap 10,21:4
Reynolds, Charles R, 1961, D 3,88:2

Reynolds, Charles T, 1945, Ag 24,20:3
Reynolds, Charles W P, 1951, D 27,21:4
Reynolds, Clarence, 1949, S 19,23:4
Reynolds, Clarence K Jr Mrs, 1965, D 13,39:4
Reynolds, Clifford T, 1951, My 15,31:2
Reynolds, Craig, 1949, O 23,84:5
Reynolds, Cuyler Mrs, 1943, S 1,19:4
Reynolds, David B, 1938, Ap 10,II,6:7
Reynolds, De Witt C, 1951, S 27,31:3
Reynolds, Delmar F, 1938, D 28,26:7
Reynolds, Dexter, 1906, Ag 21,7:6
Reynolds, Donald L, 1957, Jl 26,19:4
Reynolds, Donald W, 1953, D 14,31:4
Reynolds, E Ten Eyck, 1905, F 6,7:6
Reynolds, Earl, 1954, O 2,17:2
Reynolds, Edgar C, 1951, Je 23,15:2
Reynolds, Edgar P, 1945, Jl 21,11:4
Reynolds, Edith L (will), 1964, Ap 17,32:6
Reynolds, Edward B, 1939, N 8,23:4
Reynolds, Edward F, 1943, D 3,23:5
Reynolds, Edward G, 1944, F 6,41:1
Reynolds, Edward W, 1938, Je 28,19:3
Reynolds, Edwin L Mrs, 1955, My 6,23:2
Reynolds, Edwin M, 1953, Ag 5,23:3
Reynolds, Edwin S Mrs, 1957, Mr 13,31:6
Reynolds, Edwin T, 1940, F 6,22:2
Reynolds, Elizabeth L Mrs, 1937, Ag 5,23:5
Reynolds, Elizabeth M D Mrs (est acctg, D 20,5:4), 1961, D 11,31:2
Reynolds, Elmer L, 1964, Ap 1,39:3
Reynolds, Elmer L Mrs, 1966, S 12,45:3
Reynolds, Elmer R Dr, 1907, S 20,9:6
Reynolds, Elsbery W, 1943, Ja 16,13:2
Reynolds, Eugene S, 1957, Ag 15,21:6
Reynolds, F B Capt, 1905, My 27,9:4
Reynolds, Fletcher A, 1957, D 14,21:2
Reynolds, Florence M Mrs, 1941, S 19,23:8
Reynolds, Floyd G, 1951, Ag 18,11:2
Reynolds, Forman J, 1915, Ja 7,13:4
Reynolds, Francis B (por), 1944, Jl 22,15:4
Reynolds, Francis B Dr, 1944, Ag 28,11:5
Reynolds, Francis H, 1943, Je 6,44:6
Reynolds, Francis J, 1937, N 29,23:4
Reynolds, Francis X, 1954, Ag 14,15:5
Reynolds, Frank, 1909, N 12,11:4
Reynolds, Frank A, 1953, Ap 2,27:3
Reynolds, Frank C, 1942, S 1,19:2
Reynolds, Frank J, 1946, Jl 16,23:4; 1958, F 16,87:1; 1963, Je 3,29:4
Reynolds, Frank Mrs (Adeline D), 1961, Ag 17,27:4
Reynolds, Frank N, 1952, D 25,29:6
Reynolds, Frank V, 1937, O 30,19:6
Reynolds, Frank W, 1951, My 28,21:2
Reynolds, Fred C, 1961, Jl 9,77:2
Reynolds, Fred Mrs, 1957, N 7,35:5
Reynolds, Fred N, 1951, Ap 26,29:4
Reynolds, Frederic C, 1949, N 16,29:2
Reynolds, Frederick, 1959, O 28,37:1
Reynolds, Frederick G, 1944, Je 10,15:5
Reynolds, Frederick J, 1937, My 28,21:2
Reynolds, Frederick N, 1951, O 27,19:2
Reynolds, Frederick P, 1956, My 20,87:1
Reynolds, G W M, 1879, Je 25,4:7
Reynolds, Garry W, 1952, O 25,17:5
Reynolds, George C Mrs, 1915, S 2,9:4
Reynolds, George E, 1946, D 21,19:4
Reynolds, George G, 1958, F 16,86:8
Reynolds, George Greenwood, 1913, Ja 24,11:4
Reynolds, George H, 1945, F 6,19:5; 1946, O 21,31:5; 1951, N 3,17:1
Reynolds, George M (por), 1940, F 27,21:1
Reynolds, George O, 1956, Je 4,29:4
Reynolds, George P, 1939, Je 8,25:2
Reynolds, George W, 1944, Je 14,19:2
Reynolds, Gerard A, 1964, Je 7,87:1
Reynolds, Grace Mrs, 1963, Ag 2,11:2
Reynolds, Gregorio, 1948, Je 15,28:2
Reynolds, Guy M, 1959, Ja 19,27:3
Reynolds, Hallock Mrs, 1952, O 7,29:2
Reynolds, Hardin W, 1944, F 6,42:6
Reynolds, Harold R Mrs, 1947, S 13,11:3
Reynolds, Harrah B, 1941, Je 26,23:3
Reynolds, Harris Mrs, 1957, Mr 24,86:1
Reynolds, Harrison G, 1958, Ap 28,23:6
Reynolds, Harry A, 1938, S 8,23:2
Reynolds, Harry B, 1963, Ap 20,27:5
Reynolds, Harry C, 1942, N 22,52:6
Reynolds, Harry D, 1943, Ja 14,21:3; 1964, Je 9,35:3
Reynolds, Harry G, 1947, Jl 12,13:6
Reynolds, Harry K, 1942, D 30,23:1
Reynolds, Helen W, 1943, Ja 5,20:3
Reynolds, Herbert E, 1957, Ap 9,33:1
Reynolds, Herbert J, 1937, Ap 13,25:6
Reynolds, Hiram F, 1938, Jl 14,21:5
Reynolds, Howard A, 1954, Je 17,29:3
Reynolds, Howard C, 1942, Jl 8,23:6
Reynolds, Irving, 1957, My 31,19:2
Reynolds, Irving C, 1968, S 19,47:3
Reynolds, Isaac W, 1950, Ja 10,29:4
Reynolds, J B Dr, 1882, Ag 21,5:5
Reynolds, J Edward, 1956, S 19,37:3
Reynolds, J F Maj-Gen, 1863, Jl 8,3:2
Reynolds, J Frank, 1951, D 9,91:2

Reynolds, J H, 1875, S 25,4:5; 1949, N 24,31:2
Reynolds, J Howard, 1953, Jl 3,19:3
Reynolds, J Lacey, 1963, Jl 18,27:2
Reynolds, Jack, 1945, Ja 10,23:6
Reynolds, Jackson E, 1958, Ag 19,27:1
Reynolds, Jackson E Mrs, 1950, S 6,29:2
Reynolds, James, 1957, Jl 24,25:3
Reynolds, James A, 1937, D 24,19:2; 1940, Ap 7,45:3; 1951, Ap 17,29:3
Reynolds, James A Rev, 1914, My 26,11:5
Reynolds, James B (por), 1948, F 8,60:4
Reynolds, James B Mrs, 1943, Ja 15,17:4
Reynolds, James Bronson, 1924, Ja 2,17:4
Reynolds, James D, 1961, Ag 19,18:1
Reynolds, James D H, 1951, D 24,13:2
Reynolds, James F, 1938, Ap 1,23:5; 1954, D 24,13:4
Reynolds, James H, 1941, F 24,15:1
Reynolds, James J (por), 1945, My 27,25:1
Reynolds, James J, 1945, O 3,19:2
Reynolds, James J Mrs, 1939, N 22,21:2; 1961, My 31,33:5
Reynolds, James T, 1960, Je 29,33:6
Reynolds, Jennie, 1946, My 17,22:2
Reynolds, John, 1939, D 14,27:2; 1946, Ag 20,27:2; 1966, Mr 14,31:2
Reynolds, John A, 1941, Ap 9,25:5; 1945, D 4,29:3
Reynolds, John B, 1946, Je 22,19:5
Reynolds, John C, 1957, N 30,21:1
Reynolds, John D, 1949, S 1,21:4
Reynolds, John E, 1947, My 5,23:5; 1954, Ja 25,19:3
Reynolds, John F, 1949, Mr 8,25:1
Reynolds, John H, 1938, Ap 8,19:3; 1949, My 4,29:4; 1951, Ja 9,29:3; 1968, Ag 30,33:2
Reynolds, John H Maj, 1916, Je 27,11:7
Reynolds, John J, 1943, Ag 6,15:5; 1944, Ap 27,23:2; 1944, N 9,27:5; 1949, Je 8,29:1; 1951, My 4,27:3
Reynolds, John J Mrs, 1948, Ag 23,17:5
Reynolds, John L, 1961, O 15,88:8
Reynolds, John W, 1915, F 15,7:3
Reynolds, John W Mrs, 1967, D 22,31:1
Reynolds, Joseph, 1959, O 11,86:7
Reynolds, Joseph A, 1957, My 16,31:6
Reynolds, Joseph B, 1937, F 24,24:2
Reynolds, Kenneth G, 1955, Jl 2,15:5
Reynolds, Kiah M, 1939, D 17,49:2
Reynolds, L H, 1929, My 23,29:1
Reynolds, L W, 1903, Ag 1,7:6
Reynolds, Lafayette C, 1944, S 18,19:5
Reynolds, Lawrence, 1961, Ag 19,17:5
Reynolds, Leland F, 1948, Ja 21,25:3
Reynolds, Letitia Mrs, 1946, Ap 27,17:2
Reynolds, Lewis B, 1965, Ap 6,39:3
Reynolds, Lewis G, 1960, Jl 23,19:4
Reynolds, Lillian M Mrs, 1947, Je 22,52:2
Reynolds, Lloyd G, 1947, S 26,23:3
Reynolds, Lorraine Mrs, 1950, My 30,32:5
Reynolds, Luther, 1954, Je 16,31:2
Reynolds, M K, 1952, N 4,29:3
Reynolds, Marcus T, 1864, Jl 16,1:3; 1937, Mr 19,24:3
Reynolds, Marie, 1941, F 14,19:4
Reynolds, Martha E S Mrs, 1939, F 7,19:4
Reynolds, Martin M, 1914, Je 18,11:6
Reynolds, Mary B Mrs, 1951, Jl 6,23:3
Reynolds, Mary E, 1956, Ag 7,27:3
Reynolds, Mary L Mrs, 1941, Ag 12,19:2
Reynolds, May L, 1953, S 2,25:2
Reynolds, Mercer Sr, 1954, Ja 14,29:4
Reynolds, Merrick, 1949, N 24,31:4
Reynolds, Michael T, 1943, F 28,49:2
Reynolds, Milton Mrs, 1958, Ap 28,23:4
Reynolds, Muriel, 1949, N 24,31:4
Reynolds, N Burr, 1947, F 5,23:3
Reynolds, Noah, 1948, S 22,31:2
Reynolds, Patrick J, 1956, O 17,35:2
Reynolds, Paul E, 1952, F 25,21:2
Reynolds, Paul R, 1944, Ag 20,34:5
Reynolds, Paul R Mrs, 1949, D 20,31:2
Reynolds, Percy J, 1949, Mr 1,25:5
Reynolds, Percy L, 1944, Ag 7,15:2; 1957, Ja 2,27:2
Reynolds, Percy L Mrs, 1938, F 5,15:4
Reynolds, Philip, 1867, Ap 7,5:3
Reynolds, Philip D, 1960, Ag 16,29:2
Reynolds, Philip E, 1960, N 14,31:5
Reynolds, Powell B Rev Dr, 1914, D 30,11:5
Reynolds, Quentin (funl, Mr 20,27:3; will, Mr 27,-30:8), 1965, Mr 18,33:1
Reynolds, R C, 1954, D 1,31:4
Reynolds, R Foster, 1955, N 13,89:1
Reynolds, R J, 1918, Jl 30,11:6
Reynolds, Ralph A, 1956, Je 26,29:3
Reynolds, Ralph E, 1964, Je 19,31:4
Reynolds, Ralph K, 1955, Ap 3,23:4
Reynolds, Ralph W, 1947, S 21,60:4
Reynolds, Rex B, 1947, Mr 14,23:2
Reynolds, Rex S, 1951, S 23,87:1
Reynolds, Richard J Jr (funl, D 18,33:1), 1964, D 16, 43:1
Reynolds, Richard J Mrs, 1957, D 23,23:1
Reynolds, Richard R, 1966, O 13,45:2
Reynolds, Richard S Sr (will, Ag 4,44:3), 1955, Jl 30, 17:3
Reynolds, Robert A, 1941, O 19,45:2; 1942, Je 7,41:1
Reynolds, Robert D, 1952, F 17,85:1
Reynolds, Robert E Mrs, 1949, My 26,29:2
Reynolds, Robert G, 1958, O 20,29:3
Reynolds, Robert J, 1943, Ag 16,15:3
Reynolds, Robert John, 1909, Je 11,9:6
Reynolds, Robert L, 1960, F 12,28:1
Reynolds, Robert R, 1963, F 15,9:8; 1967, N 19,85:1
Reynolds, Robert S, 1952, Ap 25,23:2
Reynolds, Rollin Mrs, 1952, Jl 1,23:3
Reynolds, Roseanne F, 1952, F 20,29:2
Reynolds, Roy A, 1940, D 26,19:5
Reynolds, Russell R, 1952, Je 26,29:5
Reynolds, Sidney H, 1949, Ag 24,25:5
Reynolds, Simon H, 1940, Mr 19,25:5
Reynolds, Stafford C, 1953, My 2,15:2
Reynolds, Stephen, 1947, N 15,17:5
Reynolds, Stephen C, 1947, Ja 12,59:2
Reynolds, Stephen Capt, 1864, Ag 11,5:3
Reynolds, Stephen E, 1948, Je 26,17:5
Reynolds, Stephen J Mrs, 1960, My 20,29:1
Reynolds, Sumner C, 1944, Mr 6,19:3
Reynolds, Sylvia C Mrs, 1949, Mr 8,26:2
Reynolds, Theodore B, 1944, My 13,19:7
Reynolds, Thomas, 1941, N 4,23:4
Reynolds, Thomas F, 1952, F 20,30:2
Reynolds, Thomas H Sr, 1963, Ap 15,29:3
Reynolds, Thomas J, 1916, N 23,13:4; 1950, Mr 24, 25:2; 1955, Je 20,21:5; 1959, D 18,59:2
Reynolds, Thomas Mrs, 1948, N 18,27:2
Reynolds, Thomas P, 1937, Jl 11,II,4:5
Reynolds, Thomas S, 1947, Jl 6,41:2
Reynolds, Tom, 1947, Ja 27,23:2
Reynolds, Verne L, 1959, S 19,23:4
Reynolds, W Engelbert, 1966, N 1,41:2
Reynolds, W Frederick Jr, 1953, O 28,29:2
Reynolds, W H, 1931, O 14,23:1
Reynolds, W Rear-Adm, 1879, N 6,4:7
Reynolds, Walter, 1941, Mr 21,21:2; 1962, Ag 4,19:6
Reynolds, Walter A, 1964, Ag 6,29:3
Reynolds, Walter B, 1949, Mr 15,27:3
Reynolds, Walter Dr, 1937, Ap 19,21:5
Reynolds, Walter H, 1949, S 13,29:3
Reynolds, Walter M, 1964, Jl 21,33:5
Reynolds, Walter V, 1947, Ja 8,23:5
Reynolds, Ward B, 1961, S 9,19:4
Reynolds, Wiley R, 1948, D 8,31:1
Reynolds, William, 1863, Ag 1,3:3; 1944, Ja 26,19:5
Reynolds, William D, 1951, Ap 3,27:6
Reynolds, William E, 1939, Ap 2,III,7:1
Reynolds, William F, 1941, D 30,19:5
Reynolds, William G, 1950, Ag 1,23:5
Reynolds, William H, 1943, O 22,17:2
Reynolds, William J, 1940, F 18,41:2; 1948, Mr 21, 60:5; 1954, D 10,27:3
Reynolds, William M, 1950, N 22,25:5
Reynolds, William N, 1951, S 11,29:1
Reynolds, William S, 1949, Mr 2,25:1; 1950, D 6,33:4
Reynolds, William W, 1955, N 6,86:8; 1958, Ja 20,23:1
Reynolds, Wilson, 1938, Ap 12,23:3
Reynolds, Winfred E, 1961, Mr 9,30:1
Reynolds-Stephens, William, 1943, F 27,13:4
Reyntjes, Gerrit V, 1939, Ap 19,45:7
Reznicek, Emil N von, 1945, Ag 6,15:5
Reznicek, William, 1965, My 2,88:2
Reznick, Samuel, 1965, D 23,27:3
Reznikoff, Elias J, 1941, Ja 16,21:2
Rezzemini, Louis J, 1947, F 21,19:3
Rezzonico, Nicolo C P, 1959, O 20,44:1
Rhallis, G A, 1883, S 26,4:6
Rhallis, John, 1946, O 27,33:5
Rhallis, Pericles, 1945, Ag 23,23:3
Rhallis, Petros, 1945, Ag 23,23:3
Rhallys, Demetrios, 1921, Ag 20,7:7
Rham, Charles de, 1909, F 24,9:5
Rhame, Charles C, 1961, Jl 8,19:6
Rhatigan, Edward J, 1941, O 9,23:2
Rhatigan, Edward R, 1967, Je 14,47:4
Rhatigan, Frank M, 1966, Mr 18,39:3
Rhayader, Baron, 1939, S 27,25:6
Rhea, Edwin M, 1962, Ja 15,27:5
Rhea, J C, 1927, Ag 4,21:5
Rhea, John Mrs, 1948, My 23,68:3
Rhea, Joseph C Mrs, 1951, My 19,15:5
Rhea, Lawrence J, 1944, Jl 5,17:5
Rhea, Mlle, 1899, My 23,7:6
Rhea, R M Dr, 1903, Ag 12,9:6
Rhea, Robert, 1939, N 7,25:4
Rhea, Thomas S, 1946, Ap 17,25:4
Rhea, William E, 1946, Je 1,13:2
Rhead, Frederick H, 1942, N 4,23:2
Rhead, L, 1926, Jl 30,17:3
Rhears, James V, 1941, Ap 26,15:4
Rhee, Syngman (funl plans, Jl 22,31:5; funl, Jl 28,-35:2), 1965, Jl 20,1:5
Rheel, Harry R Mrs, 1950, Jl 31,17:4
Rheem, Nancy, 1950, N 11,15:6
Rhees, Benjamin R, 1950, Je 30,23:3
Rhees, Morgan J, 1941, Ag 26,19:4
Rhees, Rush, 1939, Ja 5,23:2
Rhees, Rush Mrs, 1949, Ap 4,23:6
Rhees, W J, 1907, Mr 19,9:6
Rheiff, Edward Capt, 1871, Ag 4,3:1
Rhein, M L, 1928, Jl 18,21:5
Rhein, Walter E, 1945, Jl 12,11:6
Rheiner, R H, 1939, Jl 20,19:6
Rheinfrank, Eugene, 1954, Je 25,21:2
Rheinfrank, Frederick W, 1957, Mr 27,31:5
Rheinfrank, John Mrs, 1948, Jl 15,23:2
Rheinhart, Milton W, 1957, Ap 13,19:1
Rheinhart, William E, 1956, Ja 18,31:2
Rheinstein, Sidney, 1968, My 8,44:1
Rheinstrom, Albert, 1956, D 5,39:2
Rheinstrom, Robert I, 1959, Je 20,21:1
Rheinstrom, Sigmund, 1925, Mr 8,5:3
Rhett, B S, 1866, Jl 7,1:2
Rhett, Edward Lowndes, 1913, D 14,III,15:5
Rhett, Florence, 1921, N 1,19:6
Rhett, Henry J Dr, 1912, O 8,13:6
Rhett, R B, 1876, S 15,2:6
Rhett, R Goodwyn, 1939, Ap 17,17:4
Rhett, T G Gen, 1878, Jl 31,3:2
Rheuby, Gould G, 1943, Jl 29,19:5
Rheuby, William P, 1965, Mr 24,43:4
Rhiel, William J, 1946, Ag 18,47:1
Rhind, John E, 1942, Jl 6,15:5
Rhine, Abraham B, 1941, Ag 9,15:6
Rhine, Edward, 1942, F 17,22:3
Rhinehart, Benjamin M, 1941, S 10,23:6
Rhinehart, Edward, 1951, N 6,29:3
Rhinehart, Frank, 1943, O 15,19:1
Rhinehart, Vivian Mrs, 1966, My 12,14:1
Rhinehart, William, 1874, D 1,8:3
Rhinehart, William C, 1949, N 6,92:2
Rhinelander, Alice K, 1942, Ag 25,23:4
Rhinelander, Charles E, 1915, D 8,15:3
Rhinelander, Charles E Mrs, 1912, Ja 13,13:3
Rhinelander, Fred W, 1904, S 26,9:6
Rhinelander, Frederic W, 1942, Ja 10,15:2
Rhinelander, Frederic W Mrs, 1948, Mr 25,27:4
Rhinelander, Hortense Le Brun Parsons Mrs, 1968, My 29,36:3
Rhinelander, Laura Virginia, 1914, D 11,13:5
Rhinelander, Olive F, 1942, Je 13,15:5
Rhinelander, Phil (will, Mr 27,13:2), 1940, Mr 19, 25:1
Rhinelander, Phil K, 1939, My 22,17:5
Rhinelander, Phil M (por), 1939, S 22,23:3
Rhinelander, Philip K (will), 1943, Ap 13,36:6
Rhinelander, Serena (funl, Je 15,9:6), 1914, Je 12,
Rhinelander, T J Oakley Mrs, 1923, Ag 6,11:2
Rhinelander, Thomas J O (por), 1946, Jl 26,21:1
Rhinelander, W C (see also Je 21), 1878, Je 24,8:2
Rhinelander, William, 1908, Ja 4,9:4
Rhinelander, William Mrs, 1914, F 14,11:5
Rhines, George V, 1938, Jl 1,19:3
Rhines, Isaac Olcott, 1922, Ap 5,17:5
Rhines, Olcott Mrs, 1908, O 5,7:7
Rhinesmith, Noble, 1964, Je 16,39:5
Rhinow, Arthur B, 1945, D 10,21:2
Rhoad, George W Sr, 1960, Ag 21,84:5
Rhoades, Albert B, 1948, Jl 19,19:5
Rhoades, Albert C, 1945, Mr 4,38:4
Rhoades, Amanda Mrs, 1937, S 22,27:4
Rhoades, Arthur W, 1953, Mr 6,23:3
Rhoades, Cornelia H, 1940, N 29,21:2
Rhoades, David Peck, 1907, F 4,9:5
Rhoades, Edward Henry Jr, 1949, Jl 19,30:2
Rhoades, Howard P, 1941, Je 28,15:1
Rhoades, James Dr, 1923, Mr 17,13:3
Rhoades, John H (por), 1943, Ja 16,13:1
Rhoades, John H Mrs, 1954, Ag 31,21:5; 1968, Mr 47:2
Rhoades, John Harsen (funl, D 9,13:2), 1906, D 7 11:3
Rhoades, John Washington, 1907, Ap 1,9:7
Rhoades, Lewis A Mrs, 1943, My 12,25:2
Rhoades, Lewis T, 1939, D 21,26:2
Rhoades, Lyman, 1907, Mr 7,9:6; 1960, Ap 25,29:5
Rhoades, Mary J R Mrs, 1941, Mr 14,21:5
Rhoades, O, 1961, Jl 21,23:3
Rhoades, R E, 1950, Mr 22,28:3
Rhoades, R W, 1967, Jl 5,41:1
Rhoades, Richard W (por),(will, D 27,17:2), 1940 Je 30,32:6
Rhoades, Robert Sr, 1956, Ja 22,89:2
Rhoades, Theodore E, 1949, Ap 3,77:1
Rhoades, William A, 1942, My 3,54:2
Rhoads, Benjamin T, 1909, Je 13,9:5
Rhoads, Charles J, 1956, Ja 4,27:3
Rhoads, Cornelius P (mem ser set, S 21,31:3; ser, S 23,35:2), 1959, Ag 14,21:1
Rhoads, E Clinton, 1939, Ja 11,19:4
Rhoads, George A, 1937, My 10,19:1
Rhoads, Harriet Mrs, 1951, D 11,33:4
Rhoads, Horace E, 1941, N 3,19:6
Rhoads, Howard F, 1950, Ap 15,15:5
Rhoads, J N, 1928, Ja 30,21:5
Rhoads, John G, 1948, S 29,29:3
Rhoads, Joseph J, 1938, Ag 12,17:5
Rhoads, Katherine, 1938, Jl 26,19:1
Rhoads, Samuel N, 1952, D 31,15:6
Rhoads, Thomas L, 1940, Ag 21,19:1
Rhoads, Wayland Mrs, 1941, Jl 17,19:5
Rhoads, Webster S Jr, 1941, Ag 26,19:2; 1967, D 34:6
Rhoads, William A Mrs, 1946, D 21,19:5
Rhodbeck, Richard, 1965, N 9,43:1

Rhode, Harold C, 1961, S 7,35:3
Rhode, Henry, 1945, N 12,21:2
Rhode, Homer J, 1949, Je 5,92:3
Rhode, Paul P, 1945, Mr 4,38:5
Rhode, William, 1946, N 28,27:1
Rhoden, Dolly Mrs, 1958, Ag 23,7:3
Rhoden, Elmer C Jr, 1959, Jl 7,33:6
Rhodes, Albert, 1948, Ja 29,23:5; 1963, Ap 4,47:4
Rhodes, Annie, 1914, O 7,9:5
Rhodes, Benjamin Mrs, 1944, Je 19,19:4
Rhodes, Bernard, 1968, D 1,86:4
Rhodes, Bradford, 1920, Ja 6,15:3; 1924, Ap 16,23:5
Rhodes, Campbell, 1941, F 8,15:2
Rhodes, Cecil, 1902, Mr 27,9:1
Rhodes, Charles C, 1952, Ja 28,17:2
Rhodes, Charles E, 1950, S 26,31:3; 1966, Jl 6,42:5
Rhodes, Charles H, 1946, D 20,24:3
Rhodes, Charles K, 1942, S 12,13:6
Rhodes, Clayton D, 1952, O 20,23:2
Rhodes, Daniel P, 1949, My 9,25:3
Rhodes, Diana Lady, 1937, D 14,25:2
Rhodes, Dorothy V, 1966, Jl 18,27:2
Rhodes, Dudley W Rev, 1925, Ag 5,17:5
Rhodes, Edgar N (por), 1942, Mr 16,15:5
Rhodes, Edward E, 1959, Ja 20,35:5
Rhodes, Edward E Mrs, 1946, D 10,31:4
Rhodes, Edwin T Sr Mrs, 1946, O 8,23:2
Rhodes, Eugene M Mrs, 1957, Mr 21,31:4
Rhodes, F L, 1933, Mr 19,33:5
Rhodes, Francis William, 1905, S 22,9:6
Rhodes, Frank B, 1939, Ja 19,19:3
Rhodes, Frank B Jr, 1950, D 13,35:4
Rhodes, Frank C, 1916, My 26,11:6
Rhodes, Frank S, 1948, Ag 10,21:4
Rhodes, Frederic H, 1942, N 1,52:7
Rhodes, George, 1950, S 9,17:4
Rhodes, George A, 1942, Mr 20,19:5
Rhodes, George C, 1944, My 30,21:2
Rhodes, George H, 1925, Ja 11,5:2
Rhodes, George P Jr, 1940, D 13,26:7
Rhodes, George S, 1949, Je 4,13:5
Rhodes, Gerald, 1938, D 10,17:3
Rhodes, Gilbert L, 1968, Ag 10,27:4
Rhodes, H Douglass, 1953, F 1,89:1
Rhodes, Harry J, 1945, N 16,19:3
Rhodes, Henry H Mrs, 1955, N 11,25:4
Rhodes, Ivan B, 1952, Je 10,27:4
Rhodes, J F, 1927, Ja 23,II,8:8
Rhodes, James D, 1943, O 23,13:4
Rhodes, James Mauran, 1925, Ap 6,19:5
Rhodes, James O, 1952, Ja 6,92:3
Rhodes, James R, 1944, Ja 10,17:3
Rhodes, Jeremiah, 1938, Ja 7,20:1
Rhodes, John, 1951, My 26,17:3
Rhodes, John B, 1947, Ja 30,25:5
Rhodes, John E Dr, 1925, S 3,25:5
Rhodes, John Edgar, 1923, Je 3,8:1
Rhodes, John J, 1945, N 19,21:1
Rhodes, John Q Jr, 1959, My 19,34:1
Rhodes, Joshua, 1909, Ja 6,11:5
Rhodes, Julian H Jr, 1956, My 29,27:1
Rhodes, Lawrence I, 1961, Mr 30,29:2
Rhodes, Leland C, 1955, F 10,31:3
Rhodes, Leland C Mrs, 1946, My 8,25:5
Rhodes, Leland S, 1958, Ja 13,29:5
Rhodes, Lena M, 1953, Jl 7,27:1
Rhodes, Leo D, 1968, My 10,44:5
Rhodes, Leon C, 1939, Ap 27,25:3
Rhodes, Leonard H, 1940, Ja 14,43:2
Rhodes, Lewis, 1951, Mr 14,33:3
Rhodes, Martin L, 1940, N 19,24:2
Rhodes, Oliver W, 1942, S 30,23:6
Rhodes, Ralph A, 1958, Ja 12,86:1
Rhodes, Robert, 1956, Ag 2,25:3
Rhodes, Roy V, 1948, Ja 12,19:1
Rhodes, Rufus Napoleon, 1910, Ja 13,9:5
Rhodes, Sara L, 1963, Ap 30,35:4
Rhodes, Sheppard F, 1948, Jl 16,19:3
Rhodes, Stanley, 1911, Ag 17,7:6
Rhodes, Stephen Holbrook, 1909, Je 13,9:5
Rhodes, Susan H Mrs, 1950, N 24,36:4
Rhodes, Thomas D, 1937, Mr 30,23:2
Rhodes, Thomas L, 1953, Ja 29,28:6
Rhodes, Thomas W, 1948, Ag 12,21:4
Rhodes, Thomas W Mrs, 1953, F 11,29:4
Rhodes, Urias, 1942, Ap 18,15:7
Rhodes, Vincent A, 1948, Ap 10,13:1
Rhodes, W C, 1877, Ap 10,4:7
Rhodes, W Carson, 1955, S 28,35:4
Rhodes, Walter, 1938, O 11,25:5
Rhodes, Walter K, 1945, D 13,29:3
Rhodes, William Caldwell Rev Dr, 1923, N 6,19:4
Rhodes, William K, 1951, Je 19,29:4
Rhodes, William S Mrs, 1942, N 3,23:5
Rhodes, Yorke E, 1953, S 12,17:5
Rhodius, Sen, 1938, D 29,6:6
Rhody, James B, 1953, Ap 29,29:3
Rhody, Richard B, 1957, Ag 15,21:3
Rhome, Lily B P Mrs, 1943, Ap 2,21:2
Rhondda, Viscountess, 1958, Jl 21,21:6
Rhonddd, Viscount (David Alf Thomas), 1918, Jl 4, 13:3
Rhone, Blanche Mrs, 1943, Jl 4,21:2
Rhone, David S, 1967, Ja 12,39:5
Rhone, Mary E W Mrs, 1940, D 14,17:5
Rhoney, Richard D, 1955, Ja 6,27:4
Rhoton, Alvis L, 1938, D 2,23:1
Rhymer, Paul, 1964, O 28,45:3
Rhynas, Margaret Mrs, 1953, My 27,31:5
Rhyne, Clarence E, 1951, F 17,15:3
Rhyne, Hugh J, 1942, N 15,59:3
Rhys, Cyril O, 1960, My 12,35:4
Rhys, Ernest, 1946, My 26,32:4
Rhys, John Sir, 1915, D 19,17:5
Rhys, Samuel H, 1945, N 25,48:6
Riaboff, Peter J, 1958, Mr 1,17:5
Riaboyshinsky, Paul, 1964, Je 25,33:4
Riach, May T, 1946, D 9,25:4
Riach, Nancy, 1947, S 16,23:4
Rial, James, 1903, D 22,9:5
Rial, Jay, 1920, O 20,13:5
Rial, Louise, 1940, Ag 11,31:2
Rial, Vira, 1950, D 19,29:2
Rial, William S, 1941, Jl 20,31:4
Riall, Thomas R, 1949, Mr 4,29:3
Rialp, Frank de, 1911, S 6,9:5
Rianhard, Henry W, 1947, S 15,17:5
Rianhard, Henry W Mrs, 1949, O 31,25:4
Rianhard, Thomas M (por), 1939, Jl 24,13:5
Rianhard, Thomas M Mrs, 1948, Je 26,18:2
Rianhard, William L, 1942, Jl 25,13:4
Riano, Irene Mrs, 1940, Mr 22,20:2
Riano y Gayangos, Juan (will, N 26,34:5), 1939, N 19,39:1
Rianzores, Duke of, 1873, S 29,5:3
Riart, Luis A, 1953, O 3,17:6
Ribadu, Muhammadu, 1965, My 2,89:1
Ribakoff, Charles K, 1946, Ja 25,24:3
Ribalow, Menachem, 1953, S 18,23:3
Ribar, Ivan Dr, 1968, F 3,29:3
Ribarich, Anthony, 1959, Mr 25,35:2
Ribaudo, Nicola, 1958, N 8,21:4
Ribbans, Robert C, 1956, N 13,37:4
Ribbentrop, Henry A, 1940, Ap 28,37:3
Ribbentrop, Richard von, 1941, Ja 3,19:5
Ribble, Benjamin H, 1956, D 7,31:4
Ribble, George, 1952, N 26,23:2
Ribblesdale, Lady (Mrs Ava W),(will, Je 14,8:4), 1958, Je 11,35:3
Ribblesdale, Lord (Thos Lister), 1925, O 22,25:4
Ribby, Eugene G, 1948, Ap 24,15:2
Ribeiro, Aquilino, 1963, My 28,28:5
Ribeiro, J Gomes, 1947, D 27,13:4
Ribeiro, Manuel, 1941, N 29,17:3
Ribeiro, Militao B, 1950, Ja 6,21:3
Ribeiro de Barros, Joao, 1947, Jl 22,23:3
Riber, Lornezo, 1958, O 12,86:5
Riber, Samuel J, 1948, My 16,70:2
Ribera, Charles I, 1954, S 24,23:2
Ribert, Antonio, 1967, D 17,92:6
Ribeth, William C, 1956, Ja 27,23:3
Ribicoff, Samuel Mrs, 1959, My 3,86:1
Ribino, Michele Mrs, 1953, Ja 20,25:4
Riblet, Mary V, 1947, My 12,21:3
Riblet, Walter V G, 1943, F 3,19:4
Ribley, Frank C, 1957, Jl 27,17:2
Ribman, Benjamin C (por), 1949, Jl 2,15:1
Ribner, Maurice E, 1952, O 23,31:4
Ribner, Maurice E Mrs, 1955, Je 20,21:1
Ribner, Samuel, 1960, Ja 9,21:5
Ribnik, Joseph, 1948, Mr 2,23:2
Ribnik, Rupert, 1951, My 8,31:3
Ribnikar, Vladislav, 1955, D 2,27:2
Ribot, Alexandre, 1923, Ja 15,15:6; 1925, Ag 20,19:7
Ribot, Theodule Armand Prof, 1916, D 10,21:1
Ricaldone, Pietro, 1951, N 26,25:2
Ricard, A (see also My 27), 1876, My 28,1:7
Ricard, George, 1881, Ja 8,2:4
Ricard, Gustave, 1873, F 14,6:7
Ricard, J S, 1930, D 9,24:6
Ricard, Pierre, 1956, Ap 6,26:2
Ricardel, Molly (Mrs Wm Boehnel), 1963, Ap 3,47:3
Ricardo, George, 1914, Ag 3,11:5
Ricardo, Gracia, 1955, O 22,19:5
Ricardo, Wilfrid Mrs, 1944, Jl 6,15:6
Ricardo (F McKeever), 1883, N 2,8:2
Ricasoli, Bettino, 1880, O 25,5:2
Ricaurte, Gustavo W, 1953, Mr 23,2:3
Ricca, Hugo F, 1951, My 5,17:3
Ricca, Joseph F, 1939, Ap 23,III,7:1
Ricca, Paul L, 1956, D 20,29:4
Riccadonna, Angelo, 1909, Jl 24,7:2
Riccamboni, Richard L, 1948, N 4,30:2
Riccardi, A Rex, 1953, N 13,27:3
Ricci, Bernard, 1950, Mr 2,27:1
Ricci, Borea, 1942, F 11,22:2
Ricci, C, 1934, Je 6,21:3
Ricci, Elisio V, 1955, S 24,19:5
Ricci, Federico, 1963, N 17,87:1
Ricci, Giulio, 1950, Mr 6,2:4
Ricci, James V (por), 1955, My 13,25:3
Ricci, John E Mrs, 1954, S 23,33:5
Ricci, Peter Mrs, 1961, Mr 24,27:8
Ricci, Renato, 1956, Ja 24,31:3
Ricci, Ulysses A, 1960, Je 27,25:1
Ricciardi, Vitale F, 1954, Mr 18,31:4
Ricciardulli, Domenico A Sr, 1958, N 2,89:2
Riccio, Beniamino, 1951, Ap 5,29:3
Riccio, Domenico, 1941, S 13,17:5
Ricciotti, Giuseppe, 1964, Ja 24,24:4
Riccius, Saidee F, 1959, F 5,31:5
Riccobono, Frederick W, 1946, My 3,22:2
Riccobono, Ottillie L, 1946, S 10,7:3
Riccobono, Salvator, 1958, Ap 7,21:4
Riccochi, James, 1921, Jl 25,13:2
Rice, A E Dr, 1903, My 9,9:6
Rice, A H, 1895, Jl 23,9:5
Rice, A T, 1889, My 17,5:1
Rice, Abraham, 1940, Je 21,25:6
Rice, Alex, 1959, Ap 11,21:5
Rice, Alex H, 1956, Jl 24,25:5
Rice, Alex H Mrs, 1937, Jl 14,21:1
Rice, Alfred R Mrs, 1947, Ap 7,23:4
Rice, Alfred W, 1958, N 13,33:5
Rice, Alice H Mrs (por), 1942, F 11,21:1
Rice, Alice M, 1951, N 23,30:3
Rice, Alonzo L, 1946, D 18,29:4
Rice, Arthur, 1945, Jl 18,27:4
Rice, Arthur F, 1922, Ap 22,9:5
Rice, Arthur H, 1951, Jl 20,21:1
Rice, Arthur Hamilton, 1922, Jl 6,19:5
Rice, Arthur Mrs, 1944, Mr 4,13:2
Rice, Arthur W, 1938, Mr 26,15:5
Rice, Aubrey Mrs, 1945, F 23,18:2
Rice, Austin M, 1955, O 20,35:4
Rice, Barbara E, 1944, S 6,19:3
Rice, Bernard L, 1949, D 26,29:5
Rice, Beulah Mrs, 1941, Ag 23,13:4
Rice, Billy, 1902, Mr 2,9:2
Rice, Billy (F Greffly), 1965, F 14,89:1
Rice, Bruce L Mrs, 1920, S 11,13:5
Rice, Bryan A A, 1952, Mr 14,20:5
Rice, Budd G, 1943, S 30,21:3
Rice, C C, 1935, Jl 10,21:3
Rice, C E, 1934, O 3,21:3
Rice, C Herbert Mrs, 1961, Je 29,33:1
Rice, C Hilton Dr, 1937, My 28,21:2
Rice, C Kent, 1953, Ag 4,21:5
Rice, C Willard, 1949, O 2,80:7
Rice, Charles A, 1913, Ja 10,11:4; 1937, S 16,25:2; 1948, Ja 31,19:3; 1959, Mr 30,31:4
Rice, Charles D, 1939, S 11,19:4
Rice, Charles E Judge, 1919, Ap 17,13:5
Rice, Charles G, 1943, Jl 30,15:2
Rice, Charles H, 1903, Je 22,7:7
Rice, Charles L, 1950, My 17,29:3; 1953, D 9,11:2
Rice, Charles M, 1950, Je 20,27:4
Rice, Charles P, 1946, Ja 11,22:2
Rice, Charles R, 1960, Jl 15,23:2
Rice, Charles S Mrs, 1937, O 18,17:3
Rice, Chester P, 1957, F 21,27:1
Rice, Chester W, 1951, Mr 10,13:1
Rice, Clarence B, 1951, My 13,89:1
Rice, Clifford H, 1939, Mr 31,21:4
Rice, Corinne, 1944, O 16,19:5
Rice, Craig, 1957, Ag 29,25:1
Rice, Daniel J, 1940, Je 2,44:7; 1947, Ag 16,13:4
Rice, David, 1945, S 19,25:2
Rice, David E Mrs, 1954, O 30,17:3
Rice, Deborah L Mrs, 1942, Mr 1,44:2
Rice, Diana M Mrs, 1964, My 28,37:4
Rice, Don M, 1944, D 22,17:5
Rice, Durant, 1950, S 27,31:5
Rice, Edmund Brig-Gen, 1906, Jl 21,7:4
Rice, Edward, 1955, Ag 8,21:5; 1966, My 21,31:4
Rice, Edward C, 1914, Je 27,7:6
Rice, Edward E (funl, N 20,23:3), 1924, N 17,19:5
Rice, Edward E Mrs, 1950, O 28,17:3
Rice, Edward J, 1941, My 7,25:2; 1951, F 19,23:3; 1958, Jl 24,25:2
Rice, Edward L, 1945, S 16,44:2
Rice, Edward L Jr, 1939, F 9,21:4
Rice, Edward Mrs, 1963, My 2,35:3
Rice, Edward R, 1937, N 8,24:1
Rice, Edward T, 1957, Je 12,35:3
Rice, Edwin T (por), 1940, F 3,13:1
Rice, Edwin T, 1959, N 2,31:1
Rice, Elbridge W, 1941, My 26,19:4
Rice, Elmer (funl plans, My 11,47:4), 1967, My 9,1:7
Rice, Elsie G F Mrs, 1938, D 14,25:5
Rice, Frank H, 1905, Mr 29,9:3
Rice, Frank J Mayor, 1917, Ja 19,7:2
Rice, Frank R, 1957, Ja 23,29:2
Rice, Frank V, 1961, Je 1,35:2
Rice, Fred A, 1944, D 24,26:3
Rice, Frederick A, 1959, Je 9,37:3
Rice, Frederick D, 1939, N 12,49:3
Rice, Frederick W (por), 1948, Mr 31,25:1
Rice, Frederick W Dr, 1937, S 1,19:2
Rice, G S Mrs, 1926, Mr 25,23:3
Rice, George, 1905, Mr 1,5:2
Rice, George (will), 1941, Je 26,26:4
Rice, George B, 1943, Mr 30,26:4
Rice, George B (por), 1948, F 3,26:2
Rice, George B, 1951, Ja 4,30:2
Rice, George C, 1938, O 2,49:2
Rice, George E (por), 1938, O 10,19:2
Rice, George E Mrs, 1938, Je 14,21:5
Rice, George K, 1963, Jl 8,29:2

Rice, George P Mrs, 1947, My 21,25:3
Rice, George S, 1950, Ja 5,25:2
Rice, George Staples, 1920, D 8,17:4
Rice, Gitz, 1947, O 17,22:2
Rice, Glen Mrs, 1908, O 22,9:5
Rice, Grantland (A Daley trb, Jl 15,30:7; funl, Jl 17,13:4), 1954, Jl 14,27:1
Rice, Grantland Mrs, 1966, S 23,37:3
Rice, Greek L, 1950, F 22,29:2
Rice, Harold A, 1961, My 27,23:6
Rice, Harry C, 1960, N 18,31:2
Rice, Harry E, 1940, Mr 30,15:4; 1950, Ja 19,27:2
Rice, Harry L, 1940, Mr 6,23:1
Rice, Harry M, 1958, Ap 6,88:8
Rice, Harry M Mrs, 1963, Je 14,29:3
Rice, Heber H, 1958, F 10,23:3
Rice, Henry, 1914, Je 8,7:5
Rice, Henry A, 1945, N 17,17:4
Rice, Henry G, 1903, S 11,7:7
Rice, Henry H, 1906, N 24,11:4
Rice, Henry R, 1940, S 4,23:5
Rice, Herbert H, 1938, N 16,2:7
Rice, Herbert R, 1953, S 9,29:4
Rice, Herbert W, 1941, Ja 18,15:3
Rice, Herman, 1952, D 30,19:5
Rice, Homer M, 1960, O 21,33:5
Rice, Hugh, 1942, Ag 7,17:4
Rice, Hugh S, 1962, N 15,37:4
Rice, Isaac L, 1915, N 3,13:5
Rice, Isaac L 3d (Tom), 1956, Ja 7,17:4
Rice, J Kearny Ex-Judge, 1920, Ja 15,11:3
Rice, J Lee, 1951, Je 23,15:2
Rice, J M, 1934, Je 25,15:3
Rice, Jack E Jr, 1968, D 1,86:6
Rice, James, 1882, My 9,4:7
Rice, James C, 1953, Mr 17,29:3
Rice, James C Brig-Gen , 1864, My 13,2:4
Rice, James C Jr, 1958, Ap 3,31:5
Rice, James E, 1953, O 27,27:3
Rice, James Edward, 1913, N 21,9:6
Rice, James G, 1924, D 26,15:5
Rice, James K Jr, 1957, Jl 26,19:3
Rice, James P, 1953, Mr 14,15:5
Rice, James R, 1946, My 2,21:3
Rice, Jay V, 1948, S 3,19:2
Rice, Jenny L, 1945, Jl 10,11:7
Rice, Jerome, 1939, My 12,21:2
Rice, Jerome B Jr, 1949, N 7,27:4
Rice, Jerome Mrs, 1940, Mr 22,19:2
Rice, Jessie P, 1949, S 13,29:3
Rice, John, 1952, My 23,21:5
Rice, John Andrew, 1968, N 28,37:2
Rice, John B, 1874, D 19,2:6
Rice, John C, 1915, Je 6,17:6; 1937, N 8,23:5; 1949, Ja 28,21:2
Rice, John D, 1952, Mr 18,27:4; 1956, F 6,23:3
Rice, John Foster, 1924, Je 4,23:5
Rice, John H, 1940, Ja 9,24:2
Rice, John H Mrs, 1925, S 23,25:4; 1944, O 24,23:4
Rice, John J, 1949, F 6,76:1
Rice, John Jay Dr, 1920, D 16,17:4
Rice, John M, 1907, Je 27,7:6
Rice, John P, 1941, D 25,25:5
Rice, John S, 1953, F 3,25:4
Rice, John V Jr, 1962, F 1,31:2
Rice, John W, 1941, S 30,23:3; 1954, D 2,31:3
Rice, Jonathan, 1903, N 24,9:5
Rice, Joseph, 1946, Jl 29,21:4; 1947, D 21,52:4; 1950, Jl 23,56:3
Rice, Joseph J, 1938, Ap 2,15:3; 1949, F 9,27:3
Rice, Joseph T, 1956, Mr 8,29:1
Rice, Karl A, 1964, My 4,29:2
Rice, Kenneth I, 1943, F 17,21:5
Rice, Kingsley L, 1960, Ag 17,31:4
Rice, Laurence J, 1946, F 12,25:3
Rice, Leo, 1963, N 10,86:1
Rice, Leonard A, 1957, O 3,29:5
Rice, Lewis C, 1939, O 22,40:6
Rice, Lillian E Mrs (L Eddy), 1966, Ag 27,30:3
Rice, Lloyd P, 1958, My 11,86:4
Rice, Louis S, 1957, N 13,32:3
Rice, Louis S Mrs, 1951, D 12,37:3
Rice, Lucius C, 1953, Jl 22,27:5
Rice, M Wilfred, 1968, Mr 7,43:4
Rice, Mabel E, 1944, Jl 14,13:4
Rice, Marie D Mrs, 1946, O 29,25:1
Rice, Martin P, 1950, D 20,31:3
Rice, Mary G, 1948, Ja 29,23:4
Rice, Mary N Mrs, 1937, My 29,17:4
Rice, Matthew G, 1952, O 14,34:6
Rice, Maurice, 1952, Ap 22,29:2
Rice, Max, 1950, Je 8,31:1
Rice, Maxwell J (por), 1943, D 2,27:3
Rice, May Cushman Dr, 1920, F 5,9:4
Rice, Melvin A, 1925, Ja 3,13:4
Rice, Merton S, 1943, Mr 18,19:4
Rice, Michael G, 1966, Je 25,31:4
Rice, Myron B, 1917, D 23,15:4
Rice, Nanette W Mrs, 1949, Ag 7,61:1
Rice, Nathan E, 1941, My 22,21:6
Rice, Nell A Mrs, 1960, Mr 18,25:3
Rice, Oscar H, 1959, Ja 24,19:2
Rice, Oscar S, 1947, D 28,40:3
Rice, Oswald D, 1939, My 24,23:6
Rice, Otis R, 1960, Jl 9,19:5
Rice, Pat H Jr, 1966, Je 24,37:3
Rice, Patrick, 1949, F 8,25:3
Rice, Patrick J Mrs, 1947, S 2,21:5
Rice, Paul B, 1950, N 30,33:4
Rice, Paul H, 1958, Mr 25,33:4
Rice, Paul K, 1948, My 8,15:4
Rice, Paul N, 1967, Ap 18,41:2
Rice, Peter, 1881, Jl 16,5:2
Rice, Phil E, 1948, Ap 30,23:2
Rice, Phil F, 1956, Ag 30,25:5
Rice, Philip R, 1915, Ap 28,13:5
Rice, R K G, 1945, Ag 3,17:2
Rice, R M Mrs, 1927, S 6,52:2
Rice, Ray, 1950, Ag 19,13:5
Rice, Richard A, 1955, Ag 8,21:3
Rice, Richard J, 1938, Ap 12,23:3
Rice, Robert L Sr, 1949, O 19,29:5
Rice, Robert W, 1948, N 24,23:6
Rice, Rolland R, 1941, Jl 2,21:1
Rice, Rufus C Mrs, 1946, Je 5,23:4
Rice, S H, 1944, O 12,27:4
Rice, S Neilson, 1960, Ja 16,21:3
Rice, Samuel W, 1953, Ag 27,25:4
Rice, Sophie D Mrs, 1941, Ja 9,21:3
Rice, Stephen, 1956, Ap 8,84:6
Rice, Stephen E, 1958, F 11,31:3
Rice, Stephen Mrs, 1944, Je 25,29:2
Rice, Susan T, 1937, Ag 24,21:3
Rice, Thomas N, 1907, Ag 1,7:6
Rice, Thomas S, 1942, F 15,44:7
Rice, Thurman B, 1952, D 28,48:3
Rice, Vernon, 1954, My 7,23:5
Rice, Victor M, 1869, O 20,5:5
Rice, Vincent F, 1956, Ap 14,17:5
Rice, W N, 1939, Ag 11,15:3
Rice, Wallace, 1939, D 16,17:3
Rice, Wallace E, 1959, Je 2,35:4
Rice, Wallace G, 1947, Ag 25,17:5
Rice, Walter, 1924, Mr 18,21:5
Rice, Walter D, 1946, Ag 7,27:4
Rice, Wendell P, 1912, Jl 6,7:6
Rice, Willard E, 1965, Ag 28,21:2
Rice, Willard M, 1945, F 26,19:2
Rice, William A (por), 1946, Mr 2,13:3
Rice, William A, 1946, Ap 16,25:5
Rice, William A (por), 1947, Je 23,23:6
Rice, William A Mrs, 1937, Mr 5,21:3
Rice, William B Dr, 1915, My 3,11:2
Rice, William C Mrs, 1961, Mr 6,25:5
Rice, William G, 1937, Ap 4,II,10:6; 1941, S 5,21:5; 1945, S 12,25:2
Rice, William G Mrs, 1939, Jl 4,13:6
Rice, William H, 1948, S 5,40:6
Rice, William Henry, 1907, D 22,9:4
Rice, William J, 1946, Mr 18,21:6
Rice, William J B, 1962, S 2,57:2
Rice, William M (final est appr), 1905, O 15,15:2
Rice, William R, 1953, D 19,15:1
Rice, William W, 1942, F 12,23:2; 1957, Jl 10,27:5
Rice, Winthrop M, 1957, Mr 27,31:3
Riceman, John J, 1911, Mr 13,9:5
Rich, Adolph M, 1948, D 3,25:5
Rich, Arnold H, 1955, S 20,31:2
Rich, Arnold Rice Dr, 1968, Ap 19,47:5
Rich, Benjamin E, 1913, S 14,15:7
Rich, Burdett A, 1925, S 23,25:4
Rich, Burt L, 1941, Ap 3,23:5
Rich, Charles, 1953, Ja 24,15:6; 1961, F 15,35:3
Rich, Charles A, 1943, D 5,66:5
Rich, Charles E, 1921, Mr 24,17:6
Rich, Charles F, 1942, Ap 12,45:2
Rich, Charles H, 1956, Ap 26,33:2
Rich, Charles J, 1921, My 18,17:4
Rich, Charles L, 1960, O 31,31:1
Rich, Charles T, 1940, Je 24,15:5; 1947, N 18,29:4
Rich, Charles V, 1951, Ja 5,21:3
Rich, D Homer, 1959, Je 24,31:3
Rich, Daniel F, 1959, N 12,35:2
Rich, Daniel L, 1951, F 16,25:5
Rich, Dominic W, 1965, F 21,77:1
Rich, E H, 1940, O 30,23:5
Rich, Eddie, 1968, Jl 21,56:5
Rich, Edgar J (will, Jl 27,4:5), 1948, Jl 19,19:4
Rich, Edward, 1943, My 11,21:3
Rich, Edward N Mrs, 1937, F 25,23:5
Rich, Ella D Mrs, 1942, N 16,20:3
Rich, Elmer, 1967, Ap 9,92:5
Rich, Elmer A Jr, 1955, My 13,25:3
Rich, Endicott G, 1939, S 7,25:3
Rich, Ernest E, 1951, Je 4,27:3
Rich, Eugene C C, 1957, N 9,27:4
Rich, Floyd, 1941, F 8,15:1
Rich, Floyd J Mrs, 1955, My 22,89:1
Rich, Frank, 1951, F 21,27:5
Rich, Franklin, 1910, D 9,11:4
Rich, Freddie, 1956, S 9,84:7
Rich, G Barrett, 1961, Ag 20,86:4
Rich, George A, 1957, Ag 14,25:2
Rich, George R, 1951, N 26,25:3
Rich, Gertrude V B, 1953, Jl 8,27:5
Rich, Giles W (por), 1949, F 8,25:4
Rich, Giles W Mrs, 1959, F 20,25:4
Rich, Grace E, 1959, N 5,35:1
Rich, Helen, 1963, Ag 30,21:4
Rich, Henry W, 1922, Mr 28,17:4
Rich, Irving W, 1963, My 24,32:1
Rich, Isaac (will), 1872, Je 28,1:4
Rich, Isaac B, 1908, Je 11,7:4
Rich, Jacob A, 1938, D 25,3:5
Rich, Jacob L Mrs, 1946, O 22,25:4
Rich, James P, 1965, N 8,35:4
Rich, John B Dr, 1910, Ag 14,II,9:5
Rich, John H, 1924, My 21,19:2; 1954, Mr 31,27:1
Rich, Joseph, 1956, Ag 8,25:4
Rich, Joseph B, 1961, Jl 13,29:4
Rich, Lawson C, 1942, Mr 5,24:4
Rich, Leo H, 1966, Ap 25,31:5
Rich, Louis, 1943, Jl 31,13:5; 1953, Ja 6,29:2; 1958, S 20,19:6
Rich, M B, 1930, Ag 10,II,8:1
Rich, M John, 1966, D 29,28:7
Rich, Margaret E, 1956, My 7,27:5
Rich, Martin F, 1937, O 17,II,8:7
Rich, Matthew, 1955, F 25,21:4
Rich, Maurice H, 1963, Jl 9,31:3
Rich, Milton, 1960, Mr 27,87:1
Rich, Nathan H, 1958, S 28,88:7
Rich, Paul J, 1953, My 24,88:6
Rich, Phineas Mrs, 1913, My 19,9:4
Rich, Ralph E, 1944, D 21,21:6
Rich, Raymond T, 1959, Jl 16,27:3
Rich, Richard H Mrs, 1957, Ja 9,31:2
Rich, Robert F, 1968, Ap 30,53:2
Rich, S Heath, 1947, Je 9,21:4
Rich, Samuel Mrs, 1943, D 15,27:1
Rich, Sol, 1947, Ap 11,25:5
Rich, Stephen G, 1958, Ag 11,21:2
Rich, Stephen Sherman, 1925, S 11,23:5
Rich, Tom, 1944, Ag 2,15:4
Rich, Walter H, 1947, N 4,25:4; 1948, O 20,29:4
Rich, Walter J, 1942, Ap 22,24:5
Rich, Wesley E Prof, 1918, S 28,13:4
Rich, Wilder M, 1945, S 25,25:4
Rich, William, 1937, Ap 27,23:3
Rich, William F, 1943, Mr 9,23:4
Rich, William G, 1940, Ag 16,15:2; 1952, Mr 22,13:2
Rich, William J, 1950, F 10,23:3
Rich, William T, 1942, Jl 7,19:4
Rich, Willis D, 1937, Mr 23,24:2
Richard, Albert E, 1937, D 3,23:4
Richard, Ann B Mrs, 1949, F 16,25:1
Richard, Arthur W, 1948, N 3,27:4
Richard, Aubert (por), 1947, F 23,53:5
Richard, Auguste, 1908, Ja 21,7:6
Richard, Auguste Mrs, 1961, D 12,57:3
Richard, Burt R, 1961, S 24,86:5
Richard, C B, 1881, F 21,8:2
Richard, Charles, 1940, Ap 21,43:2
Richard, Charles D, 1965, Mr 22,33:2
Richard, Edmund M, 1946, Jl 24,27:1
Richard, Edwin A, 1939, Ja 21,15:4
Richard, Edwin H Mrs, 1963, N 27,27:2
Richard, Elvine, 1940, Mr 24,31:2
Richard, Ernest D Dr, 1914, N 21,13:3
Richard, Frances G Mrs, 1952, Ap 3,35:1
Richard, Francois Marie Benjamin Archbishop, 1908, Ja 29,7:5
Richard, Frederick, 1912, F 1,13:4
Richard, Freida Mrs, 1946, S 14,7:6
Richard, George C 2d, 1963, D 25,33:3
Richard, George N Mrs (H Menken),(mem ser set, A 7,36:6), 1966, Mr 28,33:2
Richard, Greville, 1956, My 4,25:4
Richard, Harold C, 1958, Jl 29,23:1
Richard, Howard M, 1947, N 13,28:3
Richard, Jean, 1938, Ag 15,15:6
Richard, John A Mrs, 1947, F 11,27:5
Richard, Joseph R, 1954, Je 13,88:4
Richard, Jules, 1945, Ja 25,19:4
Richard, Julia L Mrs, 1941, Jl 10,19:5
Richard, Leo P, 1947, Ag 12,23:5
Richard, Leyton, 1948, Ag 25,25:4
Richard, Louis, 1940, Jl 13,13:6; 1955, My 14,19:2
Richard, Marion G, 1945, Jl 26,19:5
Richard, Mary L Mrs, 1947, Ag 12,23:5
Richard, Oscar L (por), 1948, Mr 6,13:1
Richard, Paul Cardinal, 1968, F 6,43:2
Richard, Pierre Mrs, 1948, O 23,15:6
Richard, Roy R, 1958, Je 10,33:4
Richard, Ruth H, 1965, S 6,15:5
Richard, Walter E, 1964, N 11,43:2
Richard, William Armstrong Rev, 1922, Ap 15,15:5
Richards, A K, 1881, Mr 21,5:3
Richards, Addison, 1964, Mr 27,27:5
Richards, Albert A Mrs, 1943, Ja 6,25:3
Richards, Albert P, 1963, S 19,27:4
Richards, Alfred E, 1946, S 26,25:2
Richards, Alfred H, 1951, S 5,31:3
Richards, Alfred N, 1966, Mr 25,41:1
Richards, Allen P, 1954, Ag 22,33:1
Richards, Alma W, 1963, Ap 5,47:4
Richards, Alston M Mrs, 1953, Je 24,25:4
Richards, Alton W, 1957, Ap 30,29:4
Richards, Anna E, 1952, N 9,90:1

Richards, Anna Mrs, 1938, Ja 18,23:3
Richards, Anna S Mrs, 1940, Ja 4,24:3
Richards, Arthur, 1963, S 28,19:1
Richards, Arthur M, 1955, Mr 17,45:1
Richards, Arthur S, 1947, Ag 6,23:3
Richards, Arthur W, 1948, Jl 25,48:4
Richards, Ashley, 1947, Ja 28,23:1
Richards, Augustus L, 1951, Ja 9,29:2
Richards, Bartlett, 1911, S 5,7:5
Richards, Bernard G Mrs, 1965, F 23,33:1
Richards, Brinley, 1885, My 5,5:3
Richards, C D (funl), 1956, S 20,33:3
Richards, C L, 1877, Jl 7,5:5
Richards, C M, 1941, S 13,17:2
Richards, C R, 1936, F 22,15:1
Richards, Charles, 1961, F 20,27:3
Richards, Charles A, 1942, Ap 1,21:1
Richards, Charles A Jr, 1949, Ap 26,28:2
Richards, Charles Brinckerhoff, 1919, Ap 21,15:3
Richards, Charles E, 1942, O 9,21:1
Richards, Charles F, 1962, Je 13,41:4
Richards, Charles H, 1959, F 24,29:4
Richards, Charles H Rev Dr, 1925, F 17,23:3
Richards, Charles R, 1941, Ap 18,21:4
Richards, Charles R Mrs, 1948, F 22,48:4
Richards, Charles Walter, 1903, S 8,7:6
Richards, Clarence E, 1948, Je 12,15:6
Richards, Clarence Mrs, 1940, Ap 29,15:3
Richards, Cortland O, 1949, O 8,13:2
Richards, Cyril F, 1954, S 9,32:1
Richards, David D, 1950, D 31,42:7
Richards, De Forest Gov, 1903, Ap 29,9:6
Richards, Dickinson C, 1951, D 3,31:3
Richards, Dickinson W Mrs, 1949, Jl 4,13:4
Richards, E Gilmore, 1948, Je 23,27:5
Richards, E O, 1928, My 2,25:3
Richards, E U, 1943, Ap 21,25:4
Richards, E Wayne, 1912, F 10,11:4
Richards, Eben, 1942, O 10,15:4
Richards, Eddie, 1947, My 14,25:1
Richards, Edgar Windsor, 1924, Ag 12,11:3
Richards, Edward A, 1947, Jl 25,17:5; 1956, O 16,34:1
Richards, Edward J, 1912, Ap 15,9:5
Richards, Elijah J, 1944, My 21,44:2
Richards, Ellen H Mrs (Mrs Robt H Richards), 1911, Mr 31,11:4
Richards, Emerson L, 1963, O 22,37:2
Richards, Emily Mrs, 1948, My 30,34:5
Richards, Eugene L Mrs, 1943, D 3,23:5
Richards, Eugene L 3d, 1943, S 1,19:2
Richards, Eugene Lamb Prof, 1912, Ag 6,9:6
Richards, Ferdinand B, 1937, My 18,23:3
Richards, Frances E Mrs, 1940, O 13,49:2
Richards, Frank A, 1950, Mr 24,25:2
Richards, Frank B, 1913, My 22,11:4
Richards, Frank J, 1958, O 9,37:2
Richards, Frank M, 1961, F 3,23:2
Richards, Franklin B, 1940, D 31,15:3
Richards, Fred L, 1949, My 20,27:2
Richards, Frederick B, 1958, F 25,27:2
Richards, Frederick D, 1950, O 17,31:2
Richards, Frederick H, 1943, F 7,49:2
Richards, Frederick T, 1921, Jl 9,9:6
Richards, G Darlington, 1963, My 29,33:2
Richards, G Sherman, 1944, My 30,21:2
Richards, George, 1916, My 3,13:6; 1943, My 19,25:3; 1948, Ja 10,15:2
Richards, George A, 1951, My 28,21:2
Richards, George D, 1942, O 6,23:3
Richards, George E, 1945, F 17,13:4
Richards, George F, 1950, Ag 10,25:1
Richards, George H, 1958, O 27,27:2
Richards, George H Dr, 1919, S 10,11:1
Richards, George Henry Maj, 1923, Ag 13,13:4
Richards, George W, 1955, Je 13,23:5
Richards, Gordon, 1964, Ja 17,40:1
Richards, Gordon E, 1949, Ja 14,23:3
Richards, Greenough T, 1953, N 26,31:2
Richards, Guy, 1952, Je 7,19:4
Richards, Guy Mrs, 1955, Ja 13,27:1
Richards, H Alice Mrs, 1903, O 28,9:5
Richards, Harold D, 1956, Mr 4,88:1
Richards, Harriet E, 1945, S 2,32:1
Richards, Harry Ames Mrs, 1968, My 30,25:2
Richards, Harry E Dr, 1923, S 16,8:3
Richards, Helen G M, 1952, My 27,27:2
Richards, Helen Hughes Dulany (Mrs A Richards), 1968, N 20,47:2
Richards, Henry, 1949, Ja 27,23:3
Richards, Henry C, 1905, Je 2,9:5
Richards, Henry Howe, 1968, N 19,40:5
Richards, Henry M, 1957, D 10,35:1
Richards, Henry Mrs (por), 1943, Ja 15,17:1
Richards, Henry S, 1953, Ja 15,27:6; 1961, Mr 11,21:6
Richards, Herbert M Mrs, 1956, O 29,29:2
Richards, Herbert Paul, 1916, F 19,11:4
Richards, Horace C, 1945, My 21,19:3
Richards, Houston, 1965, Ag 24,31:1
Richards, Howard S, 1937, Mr 7,II,9:2
Richards, Ira, 1961, Ap 16,86:8
Richards, Irene E D, 1951, S 8,17:4
Richards, J De Forest, 1949, S 7,29:4
Richards, J De Forest Mrs, 1955, Je 10,25:4
Richards, J Harvey, 1963, My 15,39:3
Richards, J Harvey Jr Mrs, 1959, N 18,41:5
Richards, J Permar, 1943, F 4,23:5
Richards, J Wesley Mrs, 1952, Jl 26,13:5
Richards, James, 1923, Ja 2,13:2; 1958, N 14,27:3
Richards, James B Mrs, 1944, Ap 16,41:2
Richards, James H, 1941, Ja 17,17:1
Richards, James L, 1955, Ja 4,21:5; 1956, Ap 4,29:2
Richards, Janet E, 1948, Ap 5,21:6
Richards, Jean M, 1953, N 21,13:3
Richards, John F, 1958, Ja 6,39:5
Richards, John G (por), 1941, O 10,23:6
Richards, John H, 1940, F 14,21:2
Richards, John H, 1958, O 28,35:1
Richards, John K, 1959, Jl 27,25:2
Richards, John Lt-Col, 1937, My 29,17:2
Richards, John M, 1963, O 27,88:4
Richards, John Morgan, 1918, Ag 12,9:7
Richards, John Morgan Mrs, 1914, Ag 13,9:6
Richards, John N, 1962, Ag 16,27:2
Richards, John R, 1937, O 31,II,10:3; 1947, Ag 2,13:3; 1947, O 29,27:4
Richards, John R (will), 1947, N 21,22:6
Richards, John S, 1943, D 24,13:2
Richards, John W, 1944, Ap 11,19:4; 1957, F 28,27:4
Richards, John W Mrs, 1959, Je 24,31:3
Richards, Johnny (John Cascales), 1968, O 9,47:2
Richards, Joseph E, 1958, Jl 8,27:2
Richards, Joseph H, 1942, D 21,23:4
Richards, Joseph Haven Cowles Rev, 1923, Je 10,6:3
Richards, Joseph R, 1952, Mr 31,19:3
Richards, Joseph W Dr, 1921, O 13,15:4
Richards, Julia Mrs, 1938, Mr 2,19:2
Richards, Junius A Sr, 1964, Mr 6,31:3
Richards, Keene, 1953, Jl 7,27:3
Richards, Leonard, 1946, D 27,20:2
Richards, Lewis, 1940, F 16,19:2
Richards, Llewellyn R, 1939, Jl 8,15:5
Richards, Louis J, 1966, S 2,31:4
Richards, Lowell L, 1946, Jl 8,29:3
Richards, M, 1879, Ja 10,8:2
Richards, Margaret Mrs, 1944, Ja 12,4:4
Richards, Marian, 1923, F 6,19:4
Richards, Mark V, 1952, N 24,23:3
Richards, Mary F Mrs, 1957, S 24,35:3
Richards, Mary H, 1946, Ap 21,45:1
Richards, Mentina Mrs, 1938, F 19,15:2
Richards, Morris, 1957, Ag 28,27:5
Richards, Nathaniel A, 1943, Ja 20,19:2
Richards, O H, 1942, Ag 23,41:1
Richards, Oscar L Mrs, 1923, My 16,19:4
Richards, Owen L, 1961, F 3,23:3
Richards, Pat, 1944, My 13,19:1
Richards, Patrick C, 1959, D 2,43:2
Richards, Perry R, 1947, My 22,27:3
Richards, Ralph C, 1925, Ja 4,7:1
Richards, Ralph R, 1943, Je 11,19:5
Richards, Ralph S, 1945, F 22,27:2
Richards, Raymond M, 1946, N 20,31:4
Richards, Richard, 1949, O 2,80:8
Richards, Richard R, 1925, F 1,7:3; 1960, Mr 18,25:1
Richards, Robert, 1954, D 23,19:3
Richards, Robert H, 1945, Mr 28,23:3; 1951, Ag 28, 24:2
Richards, Robert H Mrs (Mrs Ellen H Richards), 1911, Mr 31,11:4
Richards, Robert J, 1949, Je 3,31:1
Richards, Robert R Mrs, 1948, Mr 17,25:3
Richards, Robert W, 1963, F 13,9:2
Richards, Rowland, 1951, Ag 22,23:6
Richards, S N, 1927, Je 21,25:3
Richards, S S, 1883, My 8,4:7
Richards, S T Rev, 1881, Ja 25,8:3
Richards, S Wilson, 1944, D 22,17:1
Richards, Sarah Mrs, 1951, Ag 25,11:3
Richards, Selden S Mrs, 1915, Ja 5,15:4
Richards, Stephen L, 1959, My 20,35:2
Richards, T P, 1880, Ja 10,5:6
Richards, T T, 1942, Jl 24,20:3
Richards, T W, 1928, Ap 3,29:3
Richards, Theodore, 1948, Ap 3,15:3
Richards, Theodore N, 1948, O 30,15:5
Richards, Theophilus P, 1948, S 9,27:5
Richards, Thomas D, 1938, O 21,23:2
Richards, Thomas M, 1908, S 6,9:6
Richards, Thomas O, 1953, My 19,29:3
Richards, Thomas P, 1954, Je 22,27:2
Richards, V H, 1939, Jl 17,19:5
Richards, Vere Mrs, 1956, My 24,31:2
Richards, Vernon, 1937, D 31,15:4
Richards, Vernon C, 1968, S 28,33:2
Richards, Vincent (funl plans, S 30,37:2), 1959, S 29, 39:3
Richards, Vincent R Mrs, 1950, D 17,71:6
Richards, W G Dr, 1912, Jl 1,11:6
Richards, W V Lt Col, 1901, D 10,9:4
Richards, Wallace, 1959, Ja 26,29:5
Richards, Walter B, 1943, O 21,27:5
Richards, Wayland, 1946, Ag 7,27:1
Richards, Wesley, 1875, D 4,1:3
Richards, William, 1907, F 15,11:4; 1937, F 11,23:2
Richards, William, 1940, Ag 1,21:2
Richards, William Alford Ex-Gov, 1912, Jl 27,7:6
Richards, William C, 1956, N 30,23:5
Richards, William E, 1950, F 23,27:3
Richards, William J, 1949, Ag 18,21:2
Richards, William J Maj, 1918, Mr 25,11:4
Richards, William L, 1951, F 9,25:3; 1953, N 28,15:4
Richards, William M, 1939, S 12,25:5
Richards, William R Mrs, 1948, S 5,40:6
Richards, William Rogers Rev Dr (funl, Ja 11,9:4), 1910, Ja 8,9:3
Richards, William W, 1942, Ja 24,17:4
Richards, William Whiting, 1924, Jl 26,9:6
Richards, Willis B Sr, 1938, Ag 10,19:4
Richardson, A Frank, 1925, O 28,25:5
Richardson, A Madeley, 1949, Jl 24,53:1
Richardson, A N Mrs, 1942, Je 9,24:3
Richardson, Adoniram J, 1951, N 14,31:2
Richardson, Albert, 1964, F 4,33:3
Richardson, Albert D, 1869, D 3,2:6
Richardson, Albert E, 1939, D 10,69:2
Richardson, Alden B Mrs, 1956, F 26,88:4
Richardson, Alfred W Sr Mrs, 1959, Mr 21,31:2
Richardson, Alice Mrs, 1938, Ag 24,21:3
Richardson, Allan H, 1955, N 28,31:2
Richardson, Alphyon P, 1949, Ja 9,72:3
Richardson, Anna G, 1941, F 4,21:2
Richardson, Anna M, 1953, S 11,21:4
Richardson, Anna S Mrs (por), 1949, My 11,29:3
Richardson, Anne P, 1943, Ja 19,19:1
Richardson, Anne S, 1965, Ag 8,64:6
Richardson, Arthur A, 1945, Jl 22,38:1
Richardson, Arthur H, 1958, Jl 24,25:4
Richardson, Basil, 1937, Ja 26,21:3
Richardson, Belle, 1940, O 13,49:1
Richardson, Benjamin H, 1908, Je 20,9:6
Richardson, Benjamin R, 1947, D 28,40:2
Richardson, Bonnie A Mrs, 1960, Mr 17,33:2
Richardson, Briton Havelock Dr, 1923, My 3,19:3
Richardson, Byron, 1938, D 17,15:5
Richardson, C Tiffany, 1967, Ag 2,37:2
Richardson, C Tiffany Mrs, 1944, Ag 2,15:4
Richardson, Carleton, 1943, Ja 10,50:2
Richardson, Carleton W, 1957, F 14,27:2
Richardson, Carrie L, 1948, S 24,25:1
Richardson, Carrie S Mrs, 1941, Ja 31,19:6
Richardson, Channing A, 1950, Ap 15,15:6
Richardson, Charles A, 1957, D 9,35:3
Richardson, Charles E (will), 1941, Mr 30,46:3
Richardson, Charles E, 1951, Jl 6,23:3
Richardson, Charles E Mrs, 1939, Je 13,23:5
Richardson, Charles F, 1939, Jl 18,19:4
Richardson, Charles F Prof, 1913, O 9,13:5
Richardson, Charles G, 1955, N 25,27:2
Richardson, Charles H, 1946, Mr 28,25:3
Richardson, Charles H Dr, 1916, Ap 6,13:6
Richardson, Charles H Mrs, 1954, Je 2,31:2
Richardson, Charles O Sr, 1963, My 5,86:5
Richardson, Charles S, 1948, O 27,27:2
Richardson, Charles W, 1943, Ja 29,19:5
Richardson, Charlotte L Mrs, 1938, Mr 12,17:4
Richardson, Clarence B, 1962, Jl 13,23:2
Richardson, Clarence H, 1955, Mr 14,23:3
Richardson, Craig, 1962, S 9,84:5
Richardson, D Rait, 1939, My 9,24:3
Richardson, D Rait Mrs, 1960, F 12,27:1
Richardson, Dan C, 1947, F 1,15:5
Richardson, Davis, 1909, Ap 7,11:5
Richardson, Dennett L, 1946, S 8,46:2
Richardson, Donald E, 1916, Jl 12,11:4
Richardson, Dorothy, 1955, Mr 29,29:2
Richardson, Dorothy M, 1957, Je 18,33:2
Richardson, Duncan D, 1965, Ja 19,33:2
Richardson, E J Mrs, 1944, My 12,19:5
Richardson, Edward D, 1942, D 19,19:2; 1946, F 5, 23:4
Richardson, Edward M, 1941, N 17,19:2
Richardson, Edward P, 1944, Ja 28,18:3
Richardson, Edward R Mrs, 1940, O 24,25:5
Richardson, Emmet Mrs, 1952, O 30,31:1
Richardson, Ernest C, 1939, Je 4,49:3
Richardson, Ernest G, 1947, S 6,17:4
Richardson, Ernest G Mrs, 1956, F 16,29:4
Richardson, Ernest Gladstone Rev Dr, 1920, My 18, 11:4
Richardson, Eugene S Mrs, 1956, Ap 8,84:2
Richardson, Even F, 1951, My 1,29:3
Richardson, F N, 1903, F 23,1:2
Richardson, Ferdinand A, 1946, Ja 15,23:5
Richardson, Forrest E, 1968, Je 14,47:1
Richardson, Frank, 1917, Ag 2,9:4; 1942, D 24,15:1
Richardson, Frank Chase Dr, 1918, Je 21,13:4
Richardson, Frank D, 1949, D 22,23:4
Richardson, Frank H, 1907, Ja 18,7:3
Richardson, Frank H Mrs, 1958, S 4,29:3
Richardson, Frank T, 1938, D 11,60:6
Richardson, Frank W, 1917, O 27,17:4; 1937, D 5,II, 8:7; 1952, S 24,33:2
Richardson, Frankie J, 1962, F 1,31:3
Richardson, Franklin S, 1964, Ja 22,37:1
Richardson, Fred, 1951, Ag 18,11:3
Richardson, Fred A, 1951, Ja 11,25:4
Richardson, Frederick, 1937, Ja 16,15:1; 1955, Jl 24, 65:2
Richardson, Frederick B, 1937, My 27,23:1

Richardson, Frederick E, 1941, F 23,39:6
Richardson, Frederick F Mrs, 1944, Ap 1,13:5
Richardson, Frederick H, 1944, N 8,17:2
Richardson, Friend W, 1943, S 6,17:6
Richardson, G H, 1950, Ag 13,76:4
Richardson, Garwood C, 1953, Mr 5,27:5
Richardson, George, 1946, My 29,23:4; 1949, Jl 24, 52:5
Richardson, George A, 1939, D 17,49:1
Richardson, George B, 1949, Mr 20,76:7
Richardson, George D, 1947, Jl 25,17:4
Richardson, George M, 1948, Ag 15,61:3
Richardson, George Mrs, 1948, S 4,15:2; 1964, Jl 14, 33:4
Richardson, George P, 1964, O 30,37:3
Richardson, George P Mrs, 1957, My 1,37:6
Richardson, George R, 1937, F 19,19:6; 1951, Jl 10, 27:2
Richardson, George S, 1938, Je 13,19:5
Richardson, George T, 1938, S 12,17:4
Richardson, George V, 1953, Ja 9,21:4
Richardson, George W Dr, 1922, Ap 22,9:5
Richardson, George W Mrs, 1922, Ap 22,9:5
Richardson, Gerald (cor, Jl 6,49:1), 1952, Jl 5,15:5
Richardson, Guy A, 1960, O 5,41:5
Richardson, H A, 1928, Je 17,23:5
Richardson, H Edward, 1942, N 28,13:3
Richardson, H Smith Mrs, 1962, F 8,31:3
Richardson, Hadwin H, 1946, D 25,29:3
Richardson, Harold J, 1942, N 2,19:2
Richardson, Harold W, 1954, My 13,29:3
Richardson, Harry Leon, 1919, Ja 25,11:4
Richardson, Henry B, 1963, N 20,43:2
Richardson, Henry H, 1946, Mr 21,25:5
Richardson, Henry S, 1957, Mr 4,27:5
Richardson, Herbert S, 1954, F 25,31:1
Richardson, Hilary G, 1951, Ap 22,88:4
Richardson, Hilery G Mrs, 1945, Je 15,19:4
Richardson, Hiram K, 1948, Jl 17,15:5
Richardson, Holden C, 1960, S 3,17:5
Richardson, Howard E, 1956, My 17,31:4
Richardson, Howard S, 1950, Ag 3,23:5
Richardson, Ida B, 1943, D 20,23:3
Richardson, J F, 1903, O 12,7:7
Richardson, J Guy, 1949, Ja 12,27:5
Richardson, J Hall, 1945, Mr 22,23:2
Richardson, J Herbert, 1963, O 10,41:2
Richardson, J P (Big Bopper), 1959, F 4,66:3
Richardson, J W Moore, 1960, D 7,43:1
Richardson, J Wilbor, 1940, Ap 5,21:2
Richardson, James A, 1939, Je 27,23:3
Richardson, James A Mrs, 1940, F 25,38:3
Richardson, James B Judge, 1911, Ag 31,7:6
Richardson, James B Maj, 1917, F 12,9:6
Richardson, James D (funl, Jl 26,5:5), 1914, Jl 25,7:6
Richardson, James D, 1950, Mr 19,95:5
Richardson, James F Mrs, 1951, F 13,31:4
Richardson, James H, 1963, O 2,41:2
Richardson, James M Lt, 1937, Ap 29,21:4
Richardson, James Mrs, 1946, O 7,31:5; 1948, D 22, 23:1
Richardson, James P (por), 1947, Mr 25,25:1
Richardson, John, 1954, Jl 23,17:2
Richardson, John A, 1938, O 8,17:5
Richardson, John B, 1954, Mr 30,27:4
Richardson, John D Mrs, 1949, Mr 2,25:4
Richardson, John H, 1940, Je 4,23:3
Richardson, John Jr, 1939, Je 24,17:5
Richardson, John M, 1954, My 24,27:2
Richardson, John S, 1940, F 8,23:3
Richardson, Joseph A, 1947, Mr 26,25:3
Richardson, Joseph F, 1951, N 6,29:1
Richardson, Joseph L, 1953, My 14,29:3
Richardson, L Lee, 1967, Mr 8,46:1
Richardson, Laura A Mrs, 1941, F 20,19:2
Richardson, Laura M Mrs, 1942, Mr 2,19:2
Richardson, Leander (funl, F 4,9:6), 1918, F 3,15:2
Richardson, Lee, 1944, D 12,23:3
Richardson, Lee Mrs, 1944, Mr 24,19:1
Richardson, Leon B, 1951, O 26,24:2
Richardson, Lillian, 1956, Mr 30,19:3
Richardson, Lindsay R Capt, 1873, Je 5,2:1
Richardson, Lunsford (will, S 2,21:7), 1953, Ag 11, 27:5
Richardson, Luther L, 1956, S 9,84:6
Richardson, Margaret H Mrs, 1948, Mr 16,28:3
Richardson, Margaret M Mrs (will), 1949, D 2,36:1
Richardson, Marion, 1952, D 13,21:6
Richardson, Martha H Mrs, 1939, Ap 8,15:5
Richardson, Martin M, 1950, Mr 19,92:3
Richardson, Marvin, 1876, Je 16,4:7
Richardson, Matthew D, 1940, Jl 28,27:2
Richardson, Maurice E Dr, 1912, Ag 1,11:5
Richardson, Maxwell B, 1903, Jl 3,9:6
Richardson, Millard R, 1958, S 1,13:4
Richardson, Morris N, 1946, Je 14,21:3
Richardson, Moses Prof, 1968, D 10,77:3
Richardson, N S, 1883, Ag 8,5:3
Richardson, Nolen, 1951, S 26,31:4
Richardson, Norman E, 1945, O 29,19:2
Richardson, Norval, 1940, O 23,23:4
Richardson, Olin M, 1952, N 27,31:2
Richardson, Oliver S, 1939, N 23,27:4
Richardson, Oren Mrs, 1960, O 31,31:2
Richardson, Owen W, 1959, F 16,29:3
Richardson, Phil K A, 1948, S 24,25:1
Richardson, Phil W, 1953, N 25,23:5
Richardson, Ralph G, 1946, O 18,23:4; 1961, Ja 7,19:5
Richardson, Ralph R, 1964, O 2,37:4
Richardson, Ralph R Mrs, 1955, F 23,27:2
Richardson, Raymond J, 1939, F 16,21:4
Richardson, Robert, 1952, Ag 10,61:2
Richardson, Robert C, 1963, Je 18,37:3
Richardson, Robert C Jr (funl plans, Mr 15,25:3), 1954, Mr 3,27:1
Richardson, Robert C Mrs, 1951, Jl 29,69:2
Richardson, Robert E, 1944, O 13,19:6
Richardson, Robert W, 1951, Ag 13,17:4
Richardson, Roderick D, 1939, Mr 25,15:3
Richardson, Rodman, 1950, My 21,104:6
Richardson, Roland G D, 1949, Jl 20,25:3
Richardson, Roy R, 1951, F 13,31:4
Richardson, Rufus B Mrs, 1948, Mr 24,25:5
Richardson, Rufus Byam Prof, 1914, Mr 11,11:5
Richardson, Russell R, 1950, Jl 30,61:1
Richardson, Sandford, 1874, D 1,8:3
Richardson, Seth W, 1953, Mr 18,31:1
Richardson, Sid W (funl, O 3,19:5; will, O 7,68:6), 1959, O 1,35:1
Richardson, Sinclair, 1961, Ap 10,31:4
Richardson, Sophie F, 1916, F 3,9:4
Richardson, Spencer, 1925, N 9,19:4
Richardson, Stephen J, 1922, Jl 29,7:6
Richardson, T C, 1884, Ja 16,4:6
Richardson, T Chesley, 1924, S 6,11:7
Richardson, T Chesley Mrs, 1919, Jl 27,22:6
Richardson, Thomas, 1963, Ag 28,33:2
Richardson, Thomas C, 1956, N 22,33:4
Richardson, Thomas F, 1915, D 28,11:5
Richardson, Tolbert N, 1940, S 25,27:4
Richardson, Tracy, 1949, Ap 23,13:4
Richardson, W A, 1875, D 28,4:7
Richardson, W M, 1877, F 15,8:4
Richardson, Wallace A Mrs, 1939, My 4,23:3
Richardson, Wallace C, 1939, N 18,17:4
Richardson, Walter C (por), 1940, Je 10,17:5
Richardson, Walter H, 1940, My 10,23:4
Richardson, Wilfred L, 1957, Mr 13,31:3
Richardson, Willard, 1875, Jl 27,4:7
Richardson, Willard S, 1952, N 23,88:1
Richardson, William, 1914, Ap 1,13:4; 1945, Ag 14, 21:3
Richardson, William Arthur, 1968, O 1,47:1
Richardson, William B, 1944, N 11,13:6
Richardson, William D, 1947, Ag 9,13:4
Richardson, William E, 1945, Je 18,19:1; 1948, N 5, 25:2
Richardson, William G, 1938, Mr 11,19:4
Richardson, William H, 1906, Mr 9,1:2; 1937, Ap 26, 19:3; 1948, Ja 18,60:2
Richardson, William K, 1951, Ja 29,19:3
Richardson, William M, 1942, Je 12,21:5; 1951, S 9, 90:1
Richardson, William Mrs, 1941, Ap 13,39:2; 1951, O 30,29:3
Richardson, William O Brig-Gen, 1925, Ag 13,19:4
Richardson, William P, 1945, Ag 30,21:2
Richardson, William P Mrs, 1939, My 27,15:4; 1946, Ag 24,11:4
Richardson, William S, 1948, Ap 16,23:2; 1962, O 11, 39:4
Richardson, William T, 1953, Je 6,17:5
Richardson, William V Mrs, 1946, Ag 19,25:4
Richardson, Willoughby F, 1954, Ag 29,89:2
Richardt, Joseph W Mrs, 1958, N 23,89:1
Richart, D G, 1950, Ja 12,28:2
Richart, F Donald, 1961, Ap 26,39:5
Richart, Frank E, 1948, My 16,68:5; 1951, Jl 17,27:3
Richart, Theodore F Mrs, 1962, O 4,39:4
Richart, William Sr, 1948, Je 16,29:1
Richberg, Aleda B, 1939, Ag 26,15:3
Richberg, Donald R, 1960, N 28,31:1
Riche, Paul J, 1950, O 20,27:2
Richebourg, of Paris, 1858, N 17,2:6
Richeimer, Nellie Mrs, 1946, Ag 5,21:5
Richelmi, Enrico, 1959, D 19,8:8
Richelmy, Augustin Cardinal, 1923, Ag 11,9:5
Richens, Frederick, 1951, Ja 3,27:5
Richepin, J, 1926, D 13,21:3
Richepin, Jacques, 1946, S 3,19:3
Richer, Delbert E, 1942, F 27,17:5
Richer, Guy Mrs (M Casadesus), 1965, Ag 31,33:3
Richer, Mary, 1906, N 19,9:4
Richert, John A, 1955, Je 11,15:6
Richetti, Peter W, 1952, S 25,31:6
Richey, A, 1934, Je 29,21:6
Richey, Albert S, 1941, F 24,15:4
Richey, David, 1954, Jl 28,23:4
Richey, Francis H, 1959, Ap 22,33:3
Richey, Francis H Mrs, 1957, O 25,27:4
Richey, Frederick D, 1955, S 13,31:3
Richey, Henderson M, 1953, O 27,27:2
Richey, Irving G, 1941, Jl 10,19:4
Richey, J Rev, 1877, S 22,1:6
Richey, John B, 1947, N 20,29:1
Richey, Katherine E, 1965, S 11,27:4
Richey, Lawrence, 1959, D 28,23:4
Richey, S Hunter, 1949, Ja 17,19:4
Richey, Thomas B (por), 1949, Mr 31,25:1
Richey, Thomas B Mrs (por), 1949, O 15,15:4
Richey, Thomas Dr, 1905, Je 7,9:4
Richheimer, Isaac D, 1949, Ja 17,19:2
Richie, Donald W Mrs, 1942, Ap 11,13:2
Richie, Joseph, 1945, Ap 19,27:2
Richie, R L, 1949, D 27,23:1
Richier, Germaine, 1959, Ag 1,17:4
Richins, Leonard, 1947, Ja 14,25:1
Richlan, Frank, 1949, O 21,25:4
Richland, Arthur H, 1956, F 13,27:6
Richland, Herbert S, 1945, Ja 1,22:2
Richling, Jose (cor, F 24,23:1), 1950, F 23,27:4
Richman, Aaron L, 1958, O 14,37:3
Richman, Arthur (por), 1944, S 11,17:3
Richman, Charles (por), 1940, D 2,23:3
Richman, Clayton S, 1903, O 25,7:6
Richman, Edwin Jr, 1962, D 4,41:4
Richman, Frank N, 1956, My 1,33:5
Richman, Grover C Sr, 1963, O 31,33:2
Richman, H C, 1934, F 17,15:3
Richman, Harry H, 1956, N 11,87:1
Richman, Henry Mrs, 1952, Mr 20,29:4; 1954, Je 17 29:5
Richman, Irving B, 1938, D 7,23:5
Richman, Isaac, 1965, D 4,25:6
Richman, John F Sr, 1948, D 22,24:2
Richman, Julia, 1912, Je 26,13:5
Richman, Leon, 1955, D 8,37:2
Richman, Louis, 1950, N 23,35:4; 1956, D 16,86:4
Richman, Morris, 1940, D 23,19:5
Richman, Morris P, 1956, Ja 26,25:4
Richman, Nathan G, 1941, F 18,23:2
Richman, Paul, 1955, Ag 1,19:5
Richman, Paul Mrs, 1948, My 10,21:4
Richman, Walter C, 1953, S 22,31:3
Richman, William, 1954, Jl 13,23:5
Richman, William H, 1945, D 31,17:3
Richmond, A E, 1924, S 7,31:3
Richmond, Aaron, 1965, Ap 23,35:5
Richmond, Adam, 1959, D 3,37:6
Richmond, Afton W, 1943, Mr 19,19:4
Richmond, Allen P, 1948, Mr 18,27:4
Richmond, Arthur, 1956, Ja 7,17:1
Richmond, Beatrice M, 1953, Mr 9,29:1
Richmond, Charles A (por), 1940, Jl 13,13:4
Richmond, Charles A Mrs, 1950, Ag 6,72:6
Richmond, Dean, 1866, Ag 28,4:7; 1885, F 3,2:3
Richmond, Delia Mrs (will), 1939, Ja 26,42:3
Richmond, Dowager Duchess of, 1874, Mr 15,5:5; 1874, Mr 29,1:1
Richmond, Edward Gould, 1903, N 30,7:6
Richmond, Edwin B, 1939, My 17,23:1
Richmond, Frank, 1938, Ag 30,17:4
Richmond, Frank E, 1951, D 16,89:1
Richmond, Frank L, 1958, Je 17,29:5
Richmond, Frederick A, 1942, Mr 1,45:2
Richmond, George C, 1938, Ja 16,II,8:6
Richmond, George E, 1954, D 18,15:2
Richmond, George F, 1937, S 29,23:3
Richmond, George H, 1904, N 18,9:4
Richmond, Harry B, 1943, Ag 12,19:4
Richmond, Herbert, 1946, D 17,31:5
Richmond, Herbert W, 1948, Ap 23,23:4
Richmond, Hyman Mrs, 1950, Mr 24,25:1
Richmond, Isabel D, 1954, N 17,31:4
Richmond, J Henry, 1962, My 8,39:4
Richmond, James A, 1909, Je 9,7:4
Richmond, James H, 1945, Jl 25,23:4
Richmond, John F, 1961, S 10,86:5
Richmond, Julian, 1947, Ap 14,27:5
Richmond, Julian Mrs, 1961, F 9,31:2
Richmond, June, 1962, Ag 15,31:4
Richmond, Katherine C, 1966, N 15,47:2
Richmond, Kenneth L, 1950, Ap 3,23:2
Richmond, L Martin, 1959, D 14,31:2
Richmond, L Martin Mrs, 1965, F 9,37:2
Richmond, Lillian R (est appr), 1960, F 13,5:1
Richmond, M E, 1928, S 14,27:3
Richmond, Mariana N, 1954, Je 17,29:3
Richmond, Maurice, 1965, Je 9,47:2
Richmond, Nathan, 1968, My 3,54:8
Richmond, Neal W, 1939, N 21,23:4
Richmond, Nelson G Mrs, 1959, N 28,21:4
Richmond, Philip D, 1963, Jl 10,35:5
Richmond, Ralph S, 1959, Mr 12,31:6
Richmond, Robert G, 1939, Ag 8,17:2
Richmond, Robert L, 1951, Ap 16,25:5
Richmond, Stacy Courtis, 1918, D 17,13:4
Richmond, Van R, 1883, N 22,2:5
Richmond, Vance L, 1949, My 2,25:5
Richmond, Watts L, 1940, S 2,15:4
Richmond, William, 1945, F 7,21:5; 1967, F 22,29:
Richmond, William A, 1948, Ag 23,17:2
Richmond, William E, 1873, Mr 10,8:4
Richmond, William Mrs, 1953, D 24,15:3
Richmond, Winifred V, 1945, Jl 7,13:6
Richmond and Gordon, Duke of, 1903, S 28,7:5
Richner, George R, 1961, Mr 8,33:4
Richter, August, 1947, Ap 12,15:6
Richter, Bernard, 1942, Ja 24,17:4

Richter, Bruno, 1941, Mr 23,44:2
Richter, C Raymond, 1944, N 21,25:6
Richter, Carl A Mrs, 1953, D 23,25:1
Richter, Carl Guido Frederick, 1913, Mr 31,13:5
Richter, Charles, 1964, O 17,29:5
Richter, Edward, 1955, F 1,29:2
Richter, Edward L, 1968, N 6,39:3
Richter, Elizabeth Mrs, 1907, Ja 2,7:4
Richter, Erich, 1947, Ja 22,23:4
Richter, Eugen, 1906, Mr 11,9:6
Richter, Eugene, 1913, N 6,11:5
Richter, Frances Mrs, 1950, Mr 27,1:2
Richter, Frank J Sr, 1948, O 29,25:2
Richter, Franz R, 1960, O 18,40:1
Richter, Frederick, 1939, D 24,14:5
Richter, Frederick J P, 1963, Ag 28,33:1
Richter, Frederick Mrs, 1949, O 11,31:1
Richter, Frederick W, 1947, O 21,23:4
Richter, G, 1884, Ap 5,5:3
Richter, G Herbert, 1955, Jl 9,15:2
Richter, George A, 1945, O 24,21:5
Richter, George E, 1965, F 13,21:4
Richter, George M, 1942, Je 11,23:3
Richter, George P, 1937, Mr 6,17:5
Richter, Gerald E, 1958, F 18,28:1
Richter, Gustave, 1881, S 3,5:5
Richter, Hans, 1916, D 7,13:3
Richter, Harry, 1950, O 14,19:6
Richter, Henry, 1948, S 28,27:2
Richter, Henry J Bp, 1916, D 26,11:2
Richter, Herman C, 1953, My 22,27:3
Richter, Hermann E, 1950, Mr 19,95:4
Richter, Hermann E Mrs, 1950, Mr 19,95:4
Richter, Horace W, 1961, S 6,31:7
Richter, Hubert, 1962, Ap 12,35:4
Richter, Ignatz, 1948, S 23,29:5
Richter, Julius, 1965, N 11,47:1
Richter, Ludwig, 1884, Je 26,5:1
Richter, Max Dr, 1921, My 15,22:3
Richter, Maximilian Mrs, 1963, Ap 29,31:3
Richter, Moritz Mrs, 1943, N 6,13:1
Richter, Morris, 1960, D 26,23:4
Richter, Otto C, 1962, F 18,92:3
Richter, Otto G (will), 1960, Ag 17,33:2
Richter, Paul C, 1947, Jl 6,41:2
Richter, Paul E, 1949, My 16,21:4
Richter, Phil J, 1955, Mr 20,88:4
Richter, Samuel H, 1948, Ja 2,23:2
Richter, Stanley L, 1967, D 10,87:2
Richter, Theodore J, 1950, Ap 21,24:3
Richter, Thomas D, 1960, Mr 9,33:5
Richter, Wallace C, 1952, Ap 26,23:4
Richter, Walter H, 1960, O 15,23:5
Richter, Werner, 1960, S 21,37:2
Richter, William, 1949, Mr 22,25:1
Richter, Wolfgang D, 1942, O 24,15:1
Richters, Percy W, 1949, O 20,29:5
Richters, William, 1947, N 5,27:6
Richthofen, Ferdinand von (Prof Baron), 1905, O 8, 9:6
Richthofen, Hartmann F von, 1953, Mr 28,17:5
Richthofen, Oswald von Baron, 1906, Ja 18,9:3
Richtmann, William O, 1947, Mr 2,60:2
Richtmyer, Floyd K, 1939, N 8,23:3
Richwalski, Sophie Mrs, 1947, Mr 27,28:2
Richwine, Jesse, 1937, My 22,18:1
Richwine, William A, 1954, Mr 26,21:5
Richy, Henry A Dr, 1914, Jl 19,5:5
Rick, Edward, 1945, O 1,19:4
Rick, Jesse J (por), 1944, F 21,15:3
Rickaby, Fred, 1941, D 22,17:5
Rickaby, Hamilton C, 1956, F 16,29:2
Rickarby, Gustav C, 1953, F 21,13:6
Rickard, Chauncey, 1938, Ja 15,15:2
Rickard, Christopher E, 1949, Ap 16,15:5
Rickard, Edgar, 1951, Ja 22,17:1
Rickard, Edgar Mrs, 1938, F 10,21:4
Rickard, Elsmere R, 1951, Ja 18,27:1
Rickard, George L Mrs, 1925, O 31,17:3
Rickard, Horace D, 1939, Je 12,17:5
Rickard, James B, 1942, Ag 30,42:4
Rickard, James E Sr, 1956, S 20,33:3
Rickard, John, 1944, Ap 10,19:2
Rickard, Leo, 1945, My 3,23:3
Rickard, Peter L, 1950, F 4,15:1
Rickard, Richard D (por), 1946, N 13,27:5
Rickard, William L (por), 1937, O 6,25:5
Rickards, Caroline F J, 1954, Ap 24,17:5
Rickards, G G, 1933, Ja 16,12:2
Rickards, Louis A, 1945, Mr 10,17:2
Rickards, Robert P, 1945, S 19,25:5
Rickart, Lloyd H, 1943, Ag 1,39:3
Rickatson-Hatt, Bernard, 1966, Ag 9,37:1
Rickels, Edward H, 1956, Ja 12,27:2
Rickeman, George, 1940, N 19,23:2
Rickenbacker, Elizabeth Mrs, 1946, Ap 1,27:6
Rickenbaugh, Calvin R, 1944, D 30,11:4
Rickenbrode, Charles L, 1939, N 11,15:6
Ricker, Benjamin J, 1950, Ag 6,72:6
Ricker, Chester S, 1951, D 6,33:5
Ricker, Clarence B, 1941, My 25,36:5
Ricker, G A J, 1933, N 4,15:6
Ricker, George A, 1949, F 9,27:1
Ricker, Hiram Jr, 1937, Mr 31,24:3
Ricker, J S, 1877, O 8,8:1
Ricker, James H, 1949, My 18,27:2
Ricker, Jeanette M, 1944, Ja 15,13:5
Ricker, Marilla M Mrs, 1920, N 13,11:6
Ricker, Maurice G, 1952, S 12,21:1
Ricker, Rupert P, 1965, Mr 27,27:3
Ricker, S A, 1882, Ag 29,5:6
Ricker, Sara F Mrs, 1948, Je 17,25:4
Rickerich, Margaret F Mrs, 1954, Jl 16,21:4
Rickershauser, Charles, 1950, F 17,23:4
Rickerson, Charles E, 1958, Ja 1,25:5
Rickert, Alphonse M, 1940, My 30,17:2
Rickert, Charles H, 1939, Ja 31,21:4
Rickert, Christopher J, 1954, N 30,29:1
Rickert, Ernest, 1947, Ag 24,56:1
Rickert, Harold J, 1950, My 30,17:1
Rickert, Joseph W, 1941, D 17,27:2
Rickert, Julius F, 1946, F 6,23:4
Rickert, Louis A, 1939, S 28,25:2
Rickert, Martha E, 1938, My 24,17:2
Rickert, Thomas A (por), 1941, Jl 30,18:2
Rickert, Ura G, 1938, O 23,40:8
Rickert, Van Dusen, 1950, Ap 4,29:3
Ricketson, Anna C, 1949, Je 17,24:3
Ricketson, Frank B, 1944, N 23,31:3
Ricketson, James H, 1907, Ap 9,9:6
Ricketson, Oliver G, 1952, O 19,87:1
Rickett, Edmond W, 1957, Mr 16,19:3
Rickett, Louis D, 1940, Mr 5,23:5
Ricketts, C L, 1941, F 21,19:3
Ricketts, Edward F, 1948, My 12,27:3
Ricketts, Edwin B, 1956, Ja 10,34:1
Ricketts, Emily Mrs, 1918, My 24,13:3
Ricketts, George F, 1948, D 29,21:4
Ricketts, H P, 1903, Ag 23,7:5
Ricketts, Howard T Mrs, 1953, Ja 13,27:4
Ricketts, Howard T Prof, 1910, My 4,11:4
Ricketts, John E Sr, 1951, Je 27,29:4
Ricketts, Joseph W, 1943, S 17,21:3
Ricketts, Maude, 1944, Jl 28,13:2
Ricketts, Palmer C Mrs, 1937, Ap 2,23:2
Ricketts, Phil B, 1949, N 30,27:1
Ricketts, Pierre de Peyster Prof, 1918, N 21,15:3
Ricketts, Robb R, 1937, Ag 12,19:2
Ricketts, Robert Bruce Col, 1918, N 14,13:2
Ricketts, Thomas V, 1939, Ja 21,15:3
Ricketts, William D, 1941, Jl 6,26:6
Ricketts, William H Capt, 1909, S 24,11:6
Rickey, Branch (trb, D 11,39:1), 1965, D 10,1:1
Rickey, Branch Jr, 1961, Ap 11,37:3
Rickey, Clarence H, 1945, My 20,32:2
Rickey, Frank, 1953, O 27,27:3
Rickey, Fred, 1955, Je 25,15:6
Rickey, Harry N (por), 1948, Ag 28,15:1
Rickey, Harry N Mrs, 1938, O 1,17:5
Rickey, J Frank, 1939, D 13,27:3
Rickey, J H Col, 1903, Ap 24,1:6
Rickey, James W (por), 1943, Ap 22,23:1
Rickey, John M, 1951, Je 17,84:3
Rickey, Orla E, 1944, Ap 29,15:2
Rickfort, William O, 1944, D 15,19:5
Ricklin, Abraham, 1961, Jl 29,19:6
Ricklin, Joseph, 1962, N 9,26:3
Rickover, Abraham, 1960, N 10,47:2
Ricks, Augustus J, 1906, D 24,3:4
Ricks, Earl T, 1954, Ja 5,27:4
Ricks, George H, 1953, N 8,89:1
Ricks, James B, 1959, Ag 16,82:5
Ricks, James H, 1958, Mr 9,86:4
Ricks, Pammie L Mrs, 1937, D 15,25:6
Ricksen, Lucille, 1925, Mr 15,26:5
Rickus, George M, 1967, Jl 2,35:1
Rico y Fraga, Frederico, 1939, O 5,23:3
Ricord, William C, 1947, S 24,23:2
Ricordi, Guilio T, 1912, Je 7,13:5
Ricqles, Alphonse E, 1943, D 14,27:3
Ridabock, Henry G, 1923, F 21,15:5
Riddell, Edgar Mrs, 1957, D 17,35:4
Riddell, George H Mrs, 1955, Ap 19,31:1
Riddell, Guy C, 1959, Jl 21,30:4
Riddell, Herman E, 1966, Jl 16,25:3
Riddell, Herman E Mrs, 1958, Ja 10,26:3
Riddell, J H, 1941, Ja 27,15:4
Riddell, J L Dr, 1865, O 22,5:3
Riddell, John H, 1952, N 10,25:3
Riddell, John T, 1945, Jl 3,13:2
Riddell, Lady, 1946, O 4,24:2
Riddell, Louis D, 1947, Jl 25,17:3
Riddell, Matthew R, 1950, N 5,93:1
Riddell, Wallace D, 1948, Jl 8,23:3
Riddell, Walter A, 1963, Jl 29,19:4
Riddell, William A, 1954, D 24,13:2
Riddell, William R (por), 1945, F 19,17:4
Ridder, Charles H, 1964, O 11,89:1
Ridder, Charles H Mrs, 1941, Ap 19,15:5
Ridder, Herman (por),(funl, N 3,13:5; trb, N 4,11:2), 1915, N 2,11:5
Ridder, Herman Mrs, 1907, N 8,9:5
Ridder, Joseph E, 1966, Ap 21,39:1
Ridder, Joseph E Mrs, 1960, Ap 4,29:6
Ridder, Victor F, 1963, Je 15,23:2
Riddett, Albert Mrs, 1952, My 2,25:1
Riddett, Alex Sr, 1951, D 22,15:5
Riddett, Alexander Mrs, 1945, Ag 16,19:3
Riddett, Ernest G, 1946, O 20,60:4
Riddick, Augustus Mrs, 1953, D 15,39:2
Riddick, James Edward, 1907, O 10,9:4
Riddick, James Mrs, 1945, O 9,22:2
Riddick, Reginald Mrs (Ethel), 1967, F 17,37:1
Riddick, Vernon C, 1958, Ja 8,45:1
Riddick, Walter G, 1953, Ag 2,72:4
Riddle, Arthur J, 1947, F 9,61:3
Riddle, B V, 1951, Ja 7,76:3
Riddle, Baxter C, 1946, Ag 4,45:1
Riddle, C Kenneth, 1952, Jl 7,21:5
Riddle, C M Mrs, 1942, O 27,25:3
Riddle, Ernest, 1939, Mr 1,21:1
Riddle, George, 1910, N 27,II,13:4
Riddle, George R, 1867, Mr 31,1:7
Riddle, Griffith H, 1949, N 29,29:5
Riddle, Harry M, 1937, S 30,23:4
Riddle, Henry S, 1942, O 22,21:2
Riddle, Jack, 1952, D 9,33:1
Riddle, James R, 1958, Jl 30,29:5
Riddle, James Rev, 1873, Ag 23,1:7
Riddle, John W, 1941, D 9,32:2
Riddle, John W Mrs, 1946, Ag 21,15:3
Riddle, Joseph G, 1939, F 18,15:2
Riddle, Lawrence E, 1951, Ag 9,21:4
Riddle, Leander W, 1938, Ag 20,15:4
Riddle, Leland W Mrs, 1948, Mr 9,23:4
Riddle, Lt-Col, 1867, Je 4,5:5
Riddle, Oscar Dr, 1968, D 1,86:7
Riddle, Robert J, 1958, O 21,33:2
Riddle, Samuel D, 1951, Ja 9,29:3
Riddle, Samuel D Mrs (will, O 6,61:4), 1942, N 23, 23:6
Riddle, Thomas E, 1954, Ap 3,15:6
Riddle, William B, 1943, D 27,20:2
Riddle, William K, 1965, Ag 4,35:4
Riddle, William T, 1945, Ag 13,19:5
Riddleberger, H H, 1890, Ja 25,5:3
Riddleberger, Harrison H, 1941, S 9,23:3
Riddleberger, Ralph H (por), 1949, Je 6,19:1
Riddlestorffer, Sidney, 1948, Ap 13,27:4
Ridebout, Fred W, 1950, Jl 5,31:2
Rideing, William H, 1918, Ag 24,7:6
Ridenour, Charles F, 1953, D 20,77:2
Ridenour, Elijah C, 1951, My 3,29:2
Ridenour, J Frank, 1951, N 15,29:1
Ridenour, J H, 1928, Ja 8,31:1
Ridenour, Louis N Jr, 1959, My 22,27:1
Ridenour, William E, 1951, O 18,29:6
Rideout, A H, 1945, S 26,23:2
Rideout, H M, 1927, S 18,27:1
Rideout, John G, 1951, My 24,35:4
Rider, Albert C, 1949, Ap 30,13:2
Rider, Albert E, 1949, Ag 12,17:4
Rider, Alfred R, 1946, Mr 4,23:3
Rider, Archibald W, 1946, Ag 29,27:3
Rider, Dean L, 1940, N 16,17:2
Rider, Fremont A, 1962, O 28,88:4
Rider, Fremont Mrs, 1950, Je 6,29:4
Rider, Harry A, 1953, Je 24,25:5
Rider, Henry O, 1943, Ag 3,19:1
Rider, Ira E, 1906, My 28,6:3
Rider, James, 1876, My 1,4:6
Rider, Josiah C Mrs, 1951, Ja 19,25:3
Rider, Lloyd A, 1958, Mr 20,29:2
Rider, R E Mrs, 1903, My 15,9:6
Rider, Theodore H Sr, 1955, F 2,27:1
Rider, W W Col, 1908, O 25,13:5
Rider, William B, 1958, F 3,23:3
Rider-Reed, Corinne Mrs, 1947, Jl 11,15:3
Ridge, Albert A, 1967, Mr 3,35:4
Ridge, Herman D, 1950, S 20,31:5
Ridge, Lola, 1941, My 21,23:3
Ridge, Stanley C, 1951, Ap 23,25:2
Ridge, William N, 1942, Ap 15,21:4
Ridgeley, Randolph Jr, 1951, Je 15,23:5
Ridgely, Benjamin H, 1908, O 11,11:6
Ridgely, Clifford E Mrs, 1937, O 17,II,9:2
Ridgely, Henry, 1940, Jl 14,30:8
Ridgely, Henry Dr, 1904, S 18,12:2
Ridgely, Henry Mrs, 1962, Ja 13,21:5
Ridgely, J S, 1881, N 17,5:2
Ridgely, John, 1938, Ap 5,21:5
Ridgely, John T, 1957, Ap 3,31:4
Ridgely, Richard, 1949, D 2,29:2
Ridgely, William Barret, 1920, My 2,22:3
Ridgeway, Embert H, 1950, S 3,38:4
Ridgeway, George Loveland, 1968, My 13,43:1
Ridgeway, James J, 1941, N 29,17:6
Ridgeway, Peter, 1938, N 24,27:2
Ridgeway, Phil, 1954, O 28,35:2
Ridgeway, W Sir, 1926, Ag 13,17:5
Ridgeway, Willis E Mrs, 1954, F 9,27:2
Ridgley, John N, 1940, O 18,21:6
Ridgley, W B Mrs, 1902, Je 22,9:6
Ridgley, William (Bebe), 1961, Je 2,31:3
Ridgway, Amos C, 1945, Ag 11,13:4
Ridgway, Brandt, 1958, Mr 26,37:1
Ridgway, Charles A Mrs, 1949, F 5,15:6
Ridgway, Charles D, 1948, Je 16,29:5
Ridgway, Charles W, 1915, My 16,16:4

Ridgway, Ellis, 1953, Ag 15,15:1
Ridgway, Erman J (por), 1943, Je 18,21:1
Ridgway, Erman J Mrs, 1940, S 10,23:6
Ridgway, Frank, 1908, Ja 1,9:5
Ridgway, Frederic H Mrs, 1948, Ap 4,60:3
Ridgway, Frederick W, 1947, Ap 12,17:6
Ridgway, George Arthur, 1921, O 2,22:4
Ridgway, Hamlet C, 1955, O 8,19:6
Ridgway, Henry, 1913, Jl 6,II,11:3
Ridgway, James L, 1942, N 1,52:6
Ridgway, John J, 1924, Ag 22,13:7
Ridgway, John R, 1938, Je 4,15:6
Ridgway, John W, 1950, Ja 24,31:4
Ridgway, Robert (por), 1938, D 20,25:1
Ridgway, Thayer (por), 1955, Je 25,15:3
Ridgway, Thomas, 1939, My 6,17:2; 1943, D 8,23:4
Ridgway, Thomas C, 1938, Ag 12,17:6
Ridgway, William G, 1942, F 13,21:4
Ridgway, William H, 1945, F 21,19:1
Ridgwell, Audrey, 1968, O 30,47:3
Ridila, John J Sr, 1952, S 11,31:1
Ridings, Alfred, 1953, D 17,37:5
Ridings, Floyd D, 1948, Ag 17,21:3
Ridings, Gordon H, 1958, N 17,31:6
Ridings, J Willard, 1948, Mr 10,27:1
Ridings, William H, 1957, F 22,21:5
Ridington, Lawrence C K Mrs, 1955, F 4,19:4
Ridley, Edward, 1883, Ag 1,5:4
Ridley, Frederick A, 1963, D 10,43:4
Ridley, George, 1944, Ja 5,17:3
Ridley, Henry N, 1956, O 25,33:3
Ridley, Horace S, 1952, Ja 1,25:3
Ridley, Isabelle, 1947, Mr 1,15:2
Ridley, Jasper, 1951, O 2,27:4
Ridley, John L, 1943, Ja 20,20:3
Ridley, Oscar T, 1944, O 29,43:2
Ridley, Robert, 1903, Ap 23,1:3
Ridlon, J, 1936, Ap 28,21:3
Ridolfi, Americo V, 1960, O 17,29:4
Ridout, Dudley H, 1941, My 1,23:6
Ridout, George W, 1954, Mr 20,15:5
Ridout, Hugh, 1947, My 16,23:3
Ridpath, Robert F, 1950, Ag 11,19:1
Ridpath, Samuel J, 1950, D 19,29:4
Ridpath, William M, 1942, Ap 1,21:5
Ridsdale, Percival S, 1953, D 24,15:5
Ridsdale, William, 1957, N 26,33:3
Ridzik, Daniel, 1945, Je 22,15:2
Ridzik, Harry, 1947, D 16,33:4
Rie, Claude L, 1968, N 18,47:2
Rieb, Herman, 1943, Mr 25,21:5
Rieb, Walter, 1944, D 6,23:3
Riebel, Annie, 1948, Jl 14,24:2
Riebel, Ernest C Dr, 1937, Mr 29,19:3
Riebel, Frederick Jr (por), 1948, Je 27,52:5
Riebel, Julius, 1944, Jl 2,19:2
Riebel, William, 1947, D 24,21:2
Riebell, Charles, 1924, S 4,19:5
Rieben, Edward I, 1957, D 5,35:3
Riebenack, Max, 1910, My 15,II,11:4
Rieber, Charles H, 1948, Mr 1,23:6
Rieber, Frank, 1948, Jl 2,21:3
Rieber, Philip J, 1966, Ap 30,31:2
Rieber, Torkild, 1968, Ag 11,72:7
Riebesell, John F K, 1950, F 18,15:6
Riebs, John M Jr, 1937, Jl 31,15:5
Riechman, John T, 1963, My 7,43:4
Rieck, Emil W, 1953, O 17,15:3
Rieck, Waldemar Mrs, 1958, O 27,27:4
Riecken, Henry W, 1960, My 1,87:2
Riecks, Charles William, 1921, S 8,13:4
Ried, Robert C, 1953, Mr 31,31:1
Riedel, A, 1883, Ag 28,5:5
Riedel, Alfred, 1941, Ja 16,6:3
Riedel, George D, 1962, My 6,32:4
Riedel, Henry Dr, 1922, Ja 19,17:6
Riedel, John C, 1957, Jl 3,23:1
Riedel, Paul H, 1956, D 23,30:6
Riedel, Richard, 1960, Mr 19,13:5
Riedel, Walter A, 1939, D 23,15:4
Riedell, Albert C, 1958, Je 22,76:5
Riedell, Charles M, 1944, F 24,15:1
Riedell, John W, 1953, N 11,31:3
Riedell, William F, 1952, N 30,88:7
Riedemann, Heinrich von (will), 1959, O 4,86:4
Rieder, Charles A W, 1953, O 27,27:4
Rieder, Charles Jr, 1950, F 1,29:4
Rieder, Edmond A, 1968, Ag 5,39:2
Rieder, Joseph J, 1943, N 18,23:5
Rieder, Mathias, 1951, Mr 14,33:4
Rieder (Sister Mary Rudolpha), 1961, Jl 26,31:4
Riederer, Herman S, 1955, Ap 9,13:1
Riediger, Herman Mrs, 1951, Ag 15,27:5
Riedinger, August T Mrs (Margt Gaule), 1910, Je 10,9:4
Riedinger, George E, 1940, My 19,43:1
Riedinger, Theodore J G, 1955, Ag 13,13:1
Riedl, Hugo H, 1953, F 14,17:6
Riedlinger, John Mrs, 1945, O 7,44:5
Rieffel, Aristide, 1941, O 10,23:5
Rieffel, Jeanne A C D Mrs (J A Dauban), 1942, Je 27,13:4
Riefstahl, Rudolf M Dr, 1937, Ja 1,23:5
Rieg, Otto, 1954, F 26,20:4
Riegel, Adolph G, 1943, D 2,27:2
Riegel, Aug H, 1942, Jl 18,13:6
Riegel, Benjamin D, 1941, N 7,24:3
Riegel, Clarence L, 1964, N 30,33:2
Riegel, Ella (cor, F 6,11:4), 1937, Ja 22,21:5
Riegel, George E Mrs, 1967, Ap 9,92:6
Riegel, George F Sr, 1957, S 14,19:4
Riegel, Guy H Mrs, 1939, Mr 10,23:5
Riegel, Howard (will), 1939, Ja 6,19:5
Riegel, Philip H, 1959, D 2,43:1
Riegel, Reuben A, 1952, O 18,19:6
Riegelman, Charles A, 1950, Jl 22,15:5
Riegelman, Charles A Mrs, 1953, S 15,31:3
Riegelman, Herbert, 1961, Mr 12,87:1
Riegelman, John, 1942, Mr 5,23:4
Riegelman, Otto A, 1958, F 9,88:5
Riegelmann, Edward (por), 1941, Ja 16,21:1
Riegelmann, Fred G, 1921, Ag 3,13:5
Rieger, Bernard, 1951, D 18,31:2
Rieger, Charles L W, 1942, O 31,15:4
Rieger, Christian, 1947, Je 28,14:3
Rieger, Francis, 1958, My 12,29:4
Rieger, Frank M, 1943, F 6,13:2
Rieger, Frederick E, 1963, N 16,27:3
Rieger, George, 1941, Ja 9,21:4
Rieger, George W Jr, 1955, F 15,27:4
Rieger, Harry G, 1959, S 6,73:1
Rieger, Harry W, 1955, Ja 28,19:3
Rieger, Raymond Mrs, 1959, Je 24,31:3
Rieger, William H, 1942, S 24,27:4
Riegg, Richard H, 1950, N 25,13:4
Riegg, Richard H Mrs, 1950, N 18,15:6
Riegger, Wallingford (funl plans, Ap 3,30:2; funl, Ap 5,37:3), 1961, Ap 2,1:1
Riegler, Charles R, 1963, D 15,86:1
Riegler, Louis Jr, 1948, O 8,27:7
Riehl, Charles R, 1940, N 14,23:4
Riehl, Herman G Mrs, 1967, O 24,47:1
Riehle, Edwin A, 1966, S 20,47:3
Riehle, Theodore M, 1949, N 2,12:1
Riehlman, Grant L, 1955, My 6,23:3
Rieke, August, 1946, Ag 12,21:3
Rieke, Fred Mrs, 1959, Mr 22,87:1
Rieke, Frederick A, 1953, S 6,50:2
Rieke, Marcus C, 1962, My 20,86:6
Rieker, Carl L, 1947, Ag 15,17:5
Rieker, Frederick C, 1952, Ap 5,15:6
Riekers, Henry G, 1950, My 11,29:3
Riekert, Edward G, 1959, Mr 31,30:2
Rieley, Edward Mrs, 1940, Ap 12,23:5
Rielley, John F, 1946, Mr 17,44:4
Rielliet, J, 1880, Ag 25,5:6
Rielly, Joseph A, 1960, Ap 23,23:3
Rielly, William J, 1948, N 16,29:4
Riely, Compton, 1948, Jl 28,23:6
Riely, David H, 1965, Mr 8,29:4
Riely, Henry F (por), 1938, Jl 5,17:4
Rieman, Aloysius P, 1967, Ja 31,31:3
Riemann, Frederick A, 1960, Ag 1,23:5
Riemann, Paul E, 1953, F 6,20:4
Riemenschneider, Albert, 1950, Jl 21,19:2
Riemenschneider, Carl H, 1957, Mr 23,19:6
Riemer, Benjamin, 1943, S 8,23:4
Riemer, Guido C L, 1953, Mr 15,93:1
Riemer, Hugo B C, 1954, Jl 12,19:2
Riemuller, B Charles, 1945, Ja 30,20:3
Rienecke, William, 1937, F 17,21:1
Rienecker, Carl X, 1937, Je 30,23:6
Rienecker, George W, 1954, Ap 5,25:2
Rienhoff, William F Dr, 1937, Ag 31,23:3
Riepe, Ignatz A, 1938, Je 1,23:3
Riepert, Elsa A J, 1961, Je 17,21:2
Rierdon, James A, 1911, Jl 24,7:6
Ries, Anton, 1951, Ja 31,19:3
Ries, Elias E Mrs, 1959, Jl 30,27:2
Ries, Elmer C, 1957, D 4,39:4
Ries, Emil, 1939, N 15,23:2
Ries, H Theodore, 1960, Ag 27,19:6
Ries, Harry J, 1950, Ja 7,17:5
Ries, Heinrich, 1951, Ap 12,33:3
Ries, Henry R, 1947, O 27,21:5
Ries, John H Mrs, 1949, Mr 9,26:2
Ries, Leopold A, 1962, Jl 11,35:3
Ries, William F, 1944, Ja 31,17:6
Ries-Schaap, Rosette Mrs, 1949, D 21,29:4
Riesberg, Frederick W, 1950, Mr 15,29:2
Riesco, Jermain, 1916, D 9,11:5
Riesdorph, Frederick, 1944, Ap 10,19:6
Riese, Albert H, 1941, D 14,69:2
Riese, Henry G, 1943, Je 15,21:2
Riese, Samuel Mrs, 1962, O 22,29:1
Riesel, Sophie Mrs, 1966, My 31,43:1
Riesenberg, Adolph, 1939, N 30,21:2
Riesenberg, Felix, 1939, N 19,38:5
Riesenberger, Martin, 1965, Ap 16,29:5
Riesenfeld, Edwin A (por), 1948, N 9,27:6
Riesenfeld, Hugo, 1939, S 11,19:3
Riesenfeld, Norman S, 1955, Ja 21,23:1
Riesenkonig, Hans Mrs, 1948, O 20,29:5
Rieser, Frank Mrs, 1950, Ag 27,89:2
Rieser, Frank W, 1951, Ag 18,11:2
Rieser, Malcolm A, 1953, My 11,27:4
Rieser, Norbert, 1939, My 4,3:6
Rieser, Robert R, 1950, F 19,79:3
Rieser, Sidney L, 1951, Ap 13,23:6
Rieser, William H Mrs, 1945, Ap 26,23:4
Rieser, Willy, 1957, Ap 4,33:2
Rieske, Frederick W Mrs, 1942, O 31,15:3
Riesman, David, 1940, Je 4,23:1
Riesner, Benjamin, 1947, N 29,13:1
Riesner, Charles F, 1962, S 26,39:3
Riesner, Charles Mrs, 1947, Mr 3,21:3
Riesner, Edward, 1964, D 30,25:3
Riesner, Julius M, 1907, O 8,11:6
Riesner, S Herbert Mrs, 1962, My 31,27:1
Riess, Benjamin, 1946, Ja 6,40:4
Riess, Ernst (por), 1947, Je 13,23:3
Riester, John H, 1949, Ap 6,29:5
Rietzel, H A (funl), 1882, Je 11,10:5
Riezler, Kurt, 1955, S 8,31:3
Rifai, Samir el-, 1965, O 13,47:3
Rife, Lee E, 1938, O 19,23:3
Rife, Raleigh S, 1944, Mr 1,19:5
Rifenbary, Arthur M, 1952, Mr 8,13:4
Rifenbary, Jay W, 1953, Je 7,83:1
Riffe, James C, 1949, D 24,15:1
Riffe, John V (funl, Ja 11,17:5), 1958, Ja 8,45:1
Riffel, John, 1957, Je 6,31:3
Riffenburgh, Harry B, 1948, Ja 6,23:4
Rifflard, Ermand J, 1945, S 14,23:4
Riffmeyer, Walter, 1945, Je 22,15:1
Rifici, Vincent, 1967, Jl 20,37:3
Rifkin, Albert, 1961, My 15,31:3
Rifkin, Bernard, 1955, My 11,31:2
Rifkin, Bernard Mrs, 1957, N 9,27:3
Rifkin, Harris, 1953, Ag 31,17:3
Rifkin, Herman, 1966, Ja 15,27:5
Rifkin, Hyman, 1957, F 12,27:1
Rifkin, Saul, 1962, Ap 18,39:3
Rifkind, Jacob, 1955, Ja 29,15:2
Rigbie, Maria L Mrs, 1910, Ag 6,7:5
Rigby, Edmund, 1964, Je 22,27:2
Rigby, Edward, 1951, Ap 6,25:3
Rigby, Harold, 1907, F 16,9:5
Rigby, Harry J, 1943, My 12,25:6
Rigby, Hugh M, 1944, Jl 20,19:4
Rigby, J Lord, 1959, O 17,23:4
Rigby, John Sir Lord Justice, 1903, Jl 27,7:6
Rigby, Lee S, 1961, N 4,19:4
Rigby, Lee S Mrs, 1949, S 20,29:3
Rigby, R G, 1907, F 9,9:6
Rigby, Wallace J, 1959, Ja 24,19:4
Rigby, William C, 1945, Ap 18,23:2
Rigdon, Edna M, 1943, Ap 28,23:4
Rigelhaupt, William, 1950, Ap 11,31:1
Rigeon, Sidney, 1876, Jl 24,2:6
Rigg, Arthur, 1957, Ap 19,21:1
Rigg, Charles C, 1957, Mr 6,31:4
Rigg, Earl W, 1949, Jl 20,25:5
Rigg, Edgar T Mrs, 1953, F 7,15:2
Rigg, Ephraim, 1960, S 19,31:1
Rigg, Ernest H, 1956, O 17,35:4
Rigg, Harry Mrs, 1948, Je 13,69:2
Rigg, James Harrison Rev Dr, 1909, Ap 19,9:5
Rigg, Walter A, 1960, Ag 6,19:6
Riggin, Benjamin F Mrs, 1944, S 5,19:6
Riggins, Edwin N, 1961, N 18,23:4
Riggins, Francis G Mrs, 1955, My 26,31:1
Riggins, John A, 1949, S 1,21:3
Riggins, John C Dr, 1937, F 7,II,9:2
Riggins, Walter, 1954, Jl 20,19:2
Riggio, Amadeo M D, 1948, D 9,33:2
Riggio, Nicholas, 1956, Ja 30,27:2
Riggio, Vincent, 1960, S 7,41:1
Riggleman, James H, 1951, Jl 20,21:1
Riggles, Thomas A, 1960, Ja 23,21:5
Riggs, Alfred R, 1945, Jl 22,38:1
Riggs, Anne, 1951, Je 20,27:2
Riggs, Arthur F, 1948, N 2,25:1
Riggs, Arthur S, 1952, N 9,90:1
Riggs, Austen F, 1940, Mr 6,23:1
Riggs, Charles H, 1953, Mr 15,92:5
Riggs, Charles Mrs, 1950, S 6,29:5
Riggs, Charles T, 1953, F 15,93:1
Riggs, Clinton L, 1938, S 13,23:1
Riggs, Edward Gridley, 1924, Ja 18,17:3
Riggs, Elisha, 1881, Jl 9,5:3
Riggs, Ernest W, 1952, Mr 26,29:5
Riggs, Francis B, 1921, Jl 14,15:4; 1956, N 4,86:3
Riggs, Francis Behn Jr Dr, 1968, Ag 3,25:4
Riggs, Fred C, 1942, My 29,17:4
Riggs, G W, 1881, Ag 25,5:1
Riggs, Gardiner G, 1947, Mr 5,25:2
Riggs, Garry Mrs, 1951, Ja 15,17:4
Riggs, George, 1965, O 22,43:2
Riggs, George C, 1925, Jl 2,19:6
Riggs, H Clarence, 1943, D 12,68:6
Riggs, Harry, 1950, Mr 27,23:2
Riggs, Harry O, 1937, S 9,23:2
Riggs, Henry E, 1949, Jl 6,30:3
Riggs, Henry G, 1944, Ja 11,19:4
Riggs, Henry H, 1943, Ag 20,15:2
Riggs, Henry H Mrs, 1949, Je 4,13:3
Riggs, Homer, 1955, Mr 17,45:4
Riggs, Ida J W Mrs, 1937, Ja 18,17:1

Riggs, James F Rev Dr, 1918, Ja 25,11:8
Riggs, James Willoughby, 1909, Jl 14,7:6
Riggs, L C, 1903, D 12,9:6
Riggs, Lawrason, 1940, N 22,23:1
Riggs, Lois R Mrs, 1941, S 16,23:4
Riggs, Lynn, 1954, Jl 1,25:3
Riggs, Norman C, 1942, Jl 20,13:3
Riggs, Pliny S, 1949, O 31,25:4
Riggs, Ralph, 1951, S 17,21:6
Riggs, Ralph Mrs, 1967, Ap 21,39:4
Riggs, Rebecca F Mrs, 1937, Jl 23,19:4
Riggs, Richard A, 1962, My 10,37:4
Riggs, Royal E T, 1945, F 5,15:4
Riggs, T Lawrason, 1943, Ap 27,24:3
Riggs, Thomas, 1945, Ja 17,21:4
Riggs, Thomas J, 1953, S 18,23:2
Riggs, Thomas Jr, 1953, Jl 6,19:3
Riggs, Tommy, 1967, My 23,47:2
Riggs, Vincent J, 1961, Jl 6,29:2
Riggs, W H, 1881, F 24,5:6
Riggs, William D, 1953, D 13,86:8; 1965, Ja 23,25:2
Riggs, William Henry, 1924, S 2,19:3
Riggs, William K, 1944, D 12,23:1
Riggs-Miller, Thomas H, 1939, D 28,21:3
Riggs-Stead, Franklin Mrs, 1946, Ja 26,13:5
Riggsby, Jim, 1952, S 1,11:8
Righelli, Gennaro, 1949, Ja 7,21:2
Righi, Arrigo Mrs, 1938, Je 5,45:1; 1945, Je 7,19:4
Righter, Addison A, 1940, O 29,25:3
Righter, Clara, 1937, Ag 17,19:6
Righter, Frank P Mrs, 1956, D 17,27:5
Righter, Jane, 1940, S 29,44:4
Righter, Jessie H, 1961, Ap 26,39:1
Righter, Katherine A, 1967, Je 7,47:3
Righter, Mary, 1946, O 29,25:4
Righter, Stephen W, 1942, N 29,64:7
Righter, Walter L, 1939, Je 10,17:5
Righter, Walter L Mrs, 1946, Ja 10,23:3
Rightmeyer, Emma M Mrs, 1951, Ag 11,11:7
Rightmire, Estel D, 1946, N 26,29:5
Rightmire, George W, 1952, D 24,17:4
Rightmire, Oliver S Dr, 1937, F 22,17:2
Rightmyer, Lewis, 1949, Ap 25,23:2
Rightmyer, Sherman, 1947, N 29,13:5
Rights, Douglas L, 1956, D 2,87:1
Rights, Lewis D, 1951, O 31,29:5
Rights, Lewis D Mrs, 1949, S 11,92:1
Rigio, Frank W, 1949, F 24,23:2
Rigling, Alfred, 1940, D 10,25:3
Rigling, Walter, 1948, S 2,23:3
Rigney, Francis J, 1962, Ap 21,19:1
Rigney, Fred L, 1958, F 18,28:5
Rigney, Howard C, 1948, N 26,23:3
Rigney, Hugh M, 1950, O 13,29:3
Rigney, John J, 1944, Ja 23,38:1
Rigney, Michael S, 1942, Jl 18,13:4
Rigney, P S Rev, 1885, F 13,2:3
Rigney, Thomas F, 1941, F 4,21:5
Rigney, William D, 1937, Ja 27,21:2
Rignold, Stanley, 1943, Mr 23,19:3
Rignot, Georges, 1945, Je 12,19:3
Rigny, Alfred, 1912, F 5,9:6
Rigo, J, 1927, F 4,19:5
Rigo, John A, 1967, N 27,47:2
Rigo, Lajos, 1944, Je 16,19:5
Rigor, D Miles, 1941, D 11,27:5
Rigores, Jose, 1961, Je 4,V,1:4
Rigoulot, Charles F, 1914, N 23,11:6
Rigueur, Victor Prof, 1914, Ja 28,9:5
Riha, William W, 1946, Jl 1,31:3
Rihani, Neguib, 1949, Je 9,31:5
Rihas, Florencio, 1873, Ap 17,4:7
Rihbany, Abraham M, 1944, Jl 6,15:5
Rihm, Alex, 1952, Ja 25,22:2
Riippa, Antero, 1949, Je 25,13:4
Riis, Erling, 1965, Ap 21,45:4
Riis, Jacob A (funl, My 29,11:5), 1914, My 27,11:3
Riis, Jacob Mrs (mem ser set, Ag 6,76:4), 1967, Ag 5,23:1
Riis, John, 1946, S 30,25:6
Riis, Roger W, 1953, Ja 24,15:4
Riis, Rudolf G, 1947, S 8,21:6
Riiser-Larsen, Hjalmar, 1965, Je 5,31:5
Rikard, Wilbur L, 1939, F 17,19:3
Rike, Frederick H, 1947, N 21,27:4
Rike, Ronald V, 1961, N 18,23:5
Rikel, Clarence R, 1942, Mr 26,23:1
Rikel, James Mrs, 1951, O 25,29:4
Rikeman, Ambrose P, 1952, Ja 30,26:5
Riker, A L, 1930, Je 2,21:5
Riker, Alpheus P, 1940, Mr 3,44:2
Riker, Carleton B, 1952, S 16,29:3
Riker, Chandler W, 1919, Jl 6,20:4
Riker, Clarence B, 1947, Ja 3,22:2
Riker, Clarence V, 1957, N 19,30:3
Riker, Cortlandt, 1916, Ap 18,13:5
Riker, Donald B, 1959, F 27,52:8
Riker, Doris, 1962, N 6,33:1
Riker, Franklin W, 1958, Jl 17,27:4
Riker, George E, 1951, My 29,25:4
Riker, George W, 1937, Mr 17,25:4; 1948, Je 24,26:3
Riker, Harry J, 1965, F 2,33:2
Riker, Herbert Lawrence, 1922, N 18,15:5
Riker, Ira E, 1944, Je 10,15:2
Riker, J J, 1932, Ag 5,13:4
Riker, J Raymond, 1937, F 5,6:3
Riker, Ja B, 1904, F 9,9:6
Riker, James A, 1939, Jl 17,19:4
Riker, Jane Shaw Mrs, 1921, Jl 5,15:2
Riker, John J, 1951, F 27,27:3
Riker, John L Mrs, 1909, Ja 4,9:6
Riker, John Lawrence, 1909, Jl 7,9:4
Riker, John Lawrence 2d, 1909, Mr 26,9:4
Riker, Joseph, 1947, Ag 9,13:6
Riker, Joseph Lopez Diaz, 1916, Je 24,11:6
Riker, Richard L, 1941, N 16,57:2
Riker, Samuel Mrs, 1954, Ap 22,30:3
Riker, Sarah M Mrs, 1905, Je 20,9:4
Riker, Vincent J, 1941, D 17,27:6
Riker, Walter F, 1957, Je 10,27:2
Riker, William B, 1906, F 23,9:6
Riker, William H, 1944, Mr 23,19:4
Rikert, Ellen C Mrs, 1941, Ap 27,88:7
Rikhter, Andrei, 1947, Ap 4,23:1
Rile, John L, 1961, Jl 14,23:2
Rile, Joseph C, 1965, D 4,31:4
Rile, Lovett, 1943, Ja 20,19:1
Rile, Lovett Mrs, 1949, My 24,27:4
Riley, A Morton, 1960, Je 16,33:4
Riley, Adrian, 1947, F 5,23:2
Riley, Alfred A, 1966, Je 28,45:3
Riley, Alfred J, 1950, F 15,27:1
Riley, Almon C, 1960, F 20,23:3
Riley, Arch R, 1937, Jl 17,15:4
Riley, Armin W, 1954, F 12,25:5
Riley, Arthur B, 1937, N 13,19:3
Riley, Barney, 1939, F 5,40:2
Riley, Bart A Mrs, 1945, Jl 29,40:3
Riley, Ben, 1946, Ja 7,19:4
Riley, Benjamin B, 1956, My 8,33:3
Riley, Benjamin B Mrs, 1952, O 5,88:6
Riley, Bernard J, 1938, Jl 13,21:5; 1942, Ap 18,15:6
Riley, Champlain L, 1937, Ap 19,21:3
Riley, Charles E, 1937, Je 6,II,8:7
Riley, Charles S, 1938, N 1,23:3
Riley, Curtis C Mrs, 1939, O 7,17:6
Riley, Donald, 1946, Ap 8,27:3
Riley, E T, 1878, My 6,8:4
Riley, Edward, 1962, Ja 8,39:3
Riley, Edward F, 1938, My 23,17:1; 1957, Jl 25,23:4
Riley, Edward J Sr, 1953, Ag 29,17:5
Riley, Edward Johns Col, 1918, F 22,11:5
Riley, Edward Mrs, 1954, O 9,4:6
Riley, Edward P, 1958, Je 24,31:1
Riley, Edward P Mrs, 1962, My 5,27:3
Riley, Elizabeth R Mrs, 1948, Jl 20,23:4
Riley, Emily Mrs, 1939, D 13,27:6
Riley, Ernest H, 1943, Mr 31,20:3
Riley, Eugene B, 1951, F 20,25:5
Riley, Francis G Dr, 1968, Ag 5,39:3
Riley, Francis J, 1955, Ja 24,23:5
Riley, Frank, 1946, N 2,15:5
Riley, Frank E, 1950, O 31,27:2; 1953, Je 26,19:2
Riley, Frank J, 1942, S 17,25:6; 1961, Jl 24,23:5
Riley, Frank P, 1951, Ja 15,17:2
Riley, Franklin Studebaker, 1968, S 19,47:3
Riley, Frederick J, 1949, Ag 8,15:5
Riley, Frederick Mrs, 1948, Ja 28,23:4
Riley, George H, 1943, D 13,23:4
Riley, George H Mrs, 1959, Je 18,31:6
Riley, George W, 1954, S 27,21:3; 1967, Mr 3,35:3
Riley, George W Mrs, 1966, Je 25,31:5
Riley, Gordon E, 1947, Ja 6,23:3
Riley, Gus J, 1959, Mr 24,39:2
Riley, Halbert F, 1939, Ja 24,19:3
Riley, Harrison B, 1944, Je 16,19:3
Riley, Harrison B Mrs, 1955, Ag 11,21:2
Riley, Harry W (cor, Ja 25,19:5), 1958, Ja 24,23:2
Riley, Harry Z, 1959, N 25,29:4
Riley, Henry A, 1946, D 30,19:5; 1966, N 2,30:3
Riley, Henry B Sr, 1962, F 2,29:1
Riley, Henry W, 1959, S 17,39:1
Riley, Herbert N, 1966, Ag 18,35:3
Riley, Herbert W E, 1966, D 28,43:2
Riley, Howard C, 1940, My 24,19:1
Riley, Howard Mrs, 1955, Jl 27,23:6
Riley, J Stewart, 1965, Je 7,37:4
Riley, Jacob Rich, 1916, S 30,11:6
Riley, James A, 1952, Jl 22,25:3
Riley, James B, 1958, Je 30,19:4
Riley, James H, 1958, S 8,29:3
Riley, James W, 1962, N 1,31:3
Riley, John, 1884, Jl 20,2:5; 1939, Ja 12,19:2; 1939, N 19,39:2; 1943, My 9,40:8; 1945, Mr 5,19:4
Riley, John A, 1946, Ap 27,17:5
Riley, John B, 1916, N 18,11:4
Riley, John C, 1964, Mr 29,60:6
Riley, John H, 1948, Ja 12,19:4
Riley, John H Jr, 1947, N 18,29:4
Riley, John H T, 1948, S 24,25:4
Riley, John J, 1962, Ja 3,33:4
Riley, John Joseph, 1907, Ap 5,9:7
Riley, John P, 1942, Ja 4,48:3
Riley, John R Sr, 1958, My 3,19:5
Riley, John W, 1941, N 15,17:3
Riley, John Whitcomb (funl), 1916, Jl 25,9:6
Riley, Joseph C, 1950, Je 12,27:5
Riley, Joseph M, 1956, My 3,31:1
Riley, Laura A C Mrs, 1965, S 16,47:4
Riley, Leo M, 1967, Mr 4,27:5
Riley, Lester L, 1942, Jl 12,36:1
Riley, Lewis Adams, 1925, Ap 24,19:4
Riley, Louis E, 1947, Ja 31,23:5
Riley, Louise, 1957, Ag 10,15:5
Riley, Luke A, 1956, Jl 22,61:4
Riley, Mary L, 1960, O 12,39:3
Riley, Mathew I, 1943, S 26,48:1
Riley, Mickey (M Galitzen), 1959, Je 12,27:2
Riley, Minnie E V Mrs, 1939, D 1,23:1
Riley, Nelson S, 1962, Mr 5,23:1
Riley, Nicholas F, 1944, My 3,19:6
Riley, Paul J, 1952, Mr 21,23:2
Riley, Phil A, 1939, F 20,17:4
Riley, Philetus H, 1958, D 30,32:2
Riley, R L, 1953, My 21,31:5
Riley, R T, 1944, Jl 30,35:4
Riley, Raymond G, 1962, Jl 18,29:5
Riley, Robert, 1916, N 10,13:5
Riley, Robert H, 1961, D 16,25:5
Riley, Robert M, 1954, Ag 12,25:5
Riley, Ronald T, 1959, Je 25,29:2
Riley, Russell A, 1966, Jl 12,43:4
Riley, Samuel L, 1948, F 26,23:3
Riley, Sidney, 1953, F 26,25:3
Riley, T J, 1931, O 11,II,8:1
Riley, T M, 1883, Ja 21,7:4
Riley, Thomas A, 1955, Ja 25,25:4
Riley, Thomas F, 1913, S 19,9:5
Riley, Thomas H, 1950, D 23,16:4
Riley, Thomas H Jr, 1945, Je 23,13:4
Riley, Thomas W Mrs (funl), 1909, Jl 28,9:4
Riley, Thurman C, 1940, Mr 24,31:2
Riley, W B Mrs, 1943, Je 15,21:4
Riley, Walter A, 1944, Jl 31,13:5
Riley, Walter B, 1947, F 14,21:3
Riley, Walter H, 1960, Je 22,35:3
Riley, Wells L, 1960, My 25,39:4
Riley, Wilbur C, 1954, My 1,15:5
Riley, William, 1913, Ag 1,7:6
Riley, William A, 1938, Ja 21,19:4
Riley, William D, 1946, Jl 21,39:1
Riley, William E, 1949, Ja 7,22:3
Riley, William E Mrs, 1960, My 18,41:1
Riley, William F, 1956, D 31,13:5
Riley, William H, 1941, Ag 26,19:5; 1950, F 11,28:5
Riley, William H Mrs, 1953, N 10,31:3
Riley, William M, 1905, Je 8,4:1
Riley, William Mrs, 1960, D 12,29:3
Riley, William T, 1950, Ag 10,25:2
Riling, Raymond Mrs, 1962, Ja 18,29:2
Rille, John Jr, 1937, F 8,18:2
Rilley, Anthony G, 1955, Ag 30,27:4
Rilley, James R Sr, 1950, D 19,29:2
Rimailhi, Emile, 1954, S 30,31:3
Rimbault, Emile L, 1939, D 24,14:6
Rimbey, Samuel N, 1952, My 30,15:4
Rimbey, Stephen D, 1950, F 16,24:2
Rimelspacher, Charles, 1965, My 20,43:2
Rimer, Edward S, 1955, D 20,31:2
Rimes, Charles H, 1939, My 2,24:4
Rimington, Geoffrey B, 1952, My 16,23:4
Rimini, Giacomo, 1952, Mr 7,23:3
Rimini, Giacomo Mrs (R Raisa), 1963, O 3,35:1
Rimmer, Peter G, 1944, Jl 16,31:2
Rimoli, Nicholas A, 1943, Jl 24,13:2
Rimsky, Lev A (Feb 8), 1963, Ap 1,36:4
Rimsky, Louis, 1949, Ag 8,15:4
Rimsky-Korsakoff, Andrei N, 1940, Ag 11,IX,6:2
Rimsky-Korsakoff, Mikhail N, 1951, Mr 19,28:4
Rimsky-Korsakoff, Natalia L Mme, 1956, Ap 29,86:4
Rimsky-Korsakoff, Prof, 1908, Je 23,7:4
Rinaldi, Caesar M, 1963, My 14,39:4
Rinaldi, Filippo, 1955, O 20,36:2
Rinaldi, Joseph R, 1963, S 25,43:3
Rinaldi, Louis, 1956, Jl 23,23:6
Rinaldi, Mariano J, 1964, Jl 11,25:2
Rinaldis, Aldo de, 1948, Jl 28,23:4
Rinard, Mattie Mrs, 1950, D 16,7:2
Rinaud, Edward J, 1967, Je 26,33:2
Rinck, Edward A, 1948, O 23,15:5
Rinck, William J, 1945, Ap 10,19:3
Rincker, Leroy C, 1953, Ja 29,27:3
Rinckhoff, William, 1947, D 12,27:3
Rincon Galzalez, Felipe, 1946, My 14,21:4
Rincones, R, 1927, Ja 9,II,13:2
Rincones, Rafael A, 1918, Ja 22,11:5
Rinderman, Charles W, 1963, Ag 15,29:2
Rinderman, Henry V, 1950, Ap 9,84:2
Rindfusz, Ralph E Mrs, 1950, O 15,104:3
Rindge, Fulton Sr, 1968, Ag 20,41:1
Rindge, May K Mrs, 1941, F 9,48:1
Rindge, Milo P, 1954, Ja 20,27:2
Rindl, Robert, 1961, Mr 13,29:3
Rindsberg, Harry D Mrs, 1952, Ag 21,19:5
Rindskopf, Isaac, 1944, D 26,19:5
Rindskopf, Max Mrs, 1944, Ja 19,19:5
Rindt, Harold J, 1952, Je 17,8:5
Rine, Edwin M Mrs, 1938, Ap 25,15:3
Rinehart, Bentley L, 1941, Ap 3,23:5

Rinehart, Charles, 1953, Je 4,29:3
Rinehart, George F, 1950, Jl 23,56:2
Rinehart, Gratia B H Mrs, 1939, My 27,15:6
Rinehart, Harry P Jr, 1953, Ja 30,21:4
Rinehart, Hollis, 1943, Jl 14,19:4
Rinehart, James F, 1955, D 1,35:5
Rinehart, John B G, 1952, S 20,15:1
Rinehart, L D, 1941, F 5,19:4
Rinehart, Mary R (Mrs Stanley M),(funl plans, S 24,27:5), 1958, S 23,1:6
Rinehart, Roy J, 1957, Mr 24,86:4
Rinehart, Stanley M Mrs (Mary R),(est tax appr), 1961, Ja 25,14:3
Rinella, Ignazio, 1958, O 22,35:4
Riner, John A, 1940, Jl 24,21:3
Riner, Walter Mrs, 1948, O 23,15:6
Riner, William A, 1955, N 21,29:4
Rines, George E, 1951, D 1,13:5
Rinetti, Oreste, 1960, D 29,25:4
Rinfert, Fernand (por), 1939, Jl 14,19:5
Rinfret, Thibeaudeau, 1962, Jl 26,27:2
Ring, Allen G, 1952, Ja 12,13:2
Ring, Barbara T, 1941, S 1,15:4
Ring, Blanche, 1961, Ja 15,86:1
Ring, Emma Louise Mrs, 1916, Mr 24,11:6
Ring, George, 1950, Jl 31,17:4
Ring, George B Mrs, 1946, Ap 18,27:5
Ring, George W, 1957, Ag 13,27:5
Ring, Henry W, 1938, Ap 4,17:6
Ring, Herman B, 1964, N 2,39:2
Ring, Herman B Mrs, 1965, S 6,15:4
Ring, J H, 1882, Je 20,5:1
Ring, Jimmy, 1965, Jl 7,37:2
Ring, Morris A, 1941, My 1,23:3
Ring, Naomi Duncombe (Mrs Patk J Ring), 1911, D 21,11:5
Ring, Nathan, 1944, N 21,25:6
Ring, Patrick J Mrs (Naomi Duncombe Ring), 1911, D 21,11:5
Ring, Raymond H, 1949, N 1,27:5
Ring, Richard W, 1958, Je 9,48:6
Ring, Robert C, 1957, S 8,85:1
Ring, Rose P, 1964, Ja 11,23:1
Ring, Samuel, 1958, Je 2,27:2
Ring, Walt F Sr, 1951, N 15,31:6
Ring, Walter J, 1950, Ag 21,19:4
Ringe, H Ralph, 1959, F 11,39:2
Ringe, Herman (por), 1948, D 15,33:1
Ringe, Herman Jr, 1946, My 29,23:6
Ringe, Lester C, 1966, N 29,43:3
Ringe, Thomas B K, 1957, Ja 23,29:2
Ringel, Anna D, 1958, Ap 23,33:5
Ringel, George L, 1944, O 5,23:3
Ringel, Irving, 1962, My 26,25:2
Ringel, Max, 1961, Mr 23,33:3
Ringen, John, 1903, Ja 5,9:7
Ringenbach, Paul, 1960, S 15,37:1
Ringer, Carl F Sr, 1939, Ap 28,25:4
Ringer, Charles, 1947, Mr 4,26:2
Ringer, Fred C, 1950, Ja 28,13:4
Ringer, Kenneth C, 1941, My 8,23:5
Ringer, Paul H, 1952, My 10,21:3
Ringer, Severin, 1906, Ja 25,9:6
Ringer, Wilfred H, 1952, O 25,17:2
Ringgold, Rear-Adm, 1867, My 2,2:5
Ringham, Marian G Mrs, 1949, My 26,29:4
Ringius, Carl S, 1950, F 18,15:4
Ringland, Joseph, 1957, N 10,86:4
Ringle, Dave, 1965, Je 22,21:1
Ringle, Joshua, 1960, Je 8,39:3
Ringleb, Friedrich O, 1966, N 21,45:2
Ringler, Guido U, 1951, Ja 10,27:5
Ringler, Walter A, 1951, F 10,13:1
Ringley, James P, 1965, F 15,27:1
Ringling, Albert C Mrs, 1941, O 15,21:7
Ringling, Alfred T, 1919, O 22,17:2
Ringling, Alfred T Mrs, 1948, Ap 17,15:4
Ringling, Augustus, 1907, D 19,9:3
Ringling, C, 1926, D 4,17:3
Ringling, Charles Mrs, 1953, S 24,33:1
Ringling, Henry, 1918, O 12,13:3
Ringling, Henry E, 1955, D 10,21:4
Ringling, Henry Jr, 1962, Jl 29,25:2
Ringling, Henry Mrs, 1966, Ap 13,40:2
Ringling, J, 1936, D 2,27:1
Ringling, Otto, 1911, Ap 1,13:6
Ringling, Robert E, 1950, Ja 3,25:5
Ringling, Robert Mrs, 1939, S 6,23:4
Ringo, Jerry, 1963, Jl 29,19:3
Ringo, W D, 1884, Ja 23,1:7
Ringrose, Foster F, 1951, D 25,31:4
Ringrose, Hyacinthe, 1946, Je 20,23:2
Ringrose, Hyacinthe Mrs, 1945, F 21,19:4
Ringrose, William B, 1956, Je 23,17:6
Ringrose, William B Mrs, 1941, Je 1,41:1
Ringsdorf, Peter Mrs, 1912, Mr 2,13:4
Ringueberg, Eugene Dr, 1937, Mr 22,23:3
Ringueberg, Fred A, 1951, D 27,21:4
Ringvall, Nils W, 1949, O 18,27:1
Ringwald, Frederick E, 1959, Mr 6,25:3
Ringwall, Knut A, 1949, O 6,31:5
Ringwalt, Ralph C, 1946, Mr 10,47:1
Ringwood, Katherine R Mrs, 1938, Ap 3,II,7:2
Ringwood, W M, 1878, Je 10,8:4
Rini, Charles Mrs, 1952, F 27,27:3
Rini, Vincent, 1957, Ap 2,31:4
Rininsland, Charles R, 1968, Mr 2,29:4
Rink, John C, 1950, N 1,35:3
Rink, Joseph W, 1938, Je 29,25:6
Rink, William E, 1945, S 27,21:5
Rinke, Arthur W, 1949, Ag 1,17:5
Rinkel, Herbert, 1963, Je 22,23:4
Rinkel, Max, 1966, Je 10,45:2
Rinkenbach, Robert R, 1950, Ag 11,19:5
Rinker, Charles W, 1953, Jl 12,65:2
Rinker, Mildred (M Bailey), 1951, D 13,33:4
Rinker, Richard A, 1950, Mr 28,31:5
Rinn, Walter J, 1947, Jl 11,15:3
Rinsberg, Max, 1947, Ag 23,13:5
Rinsche, Eric, 1953, F 3,25:3
Rinschler, Wendelin, 1948, N 25,31:3
Rintelen, Anton (por), 1946, Ja 30,25:1
Rintelen, Franz von (por), 1949, My 31,23:3
Rintoul, Nancy A, 1954, O 24,89:1
Rintoul, Stephen R Sr, 1959, Jl 3,17:4
Rinyak, John, 1951, Ap 22,89:1
Rinzler, Irving, 1963, Ag 8,27:4
Rio, A Mrs (ed), 1938, Ja 22,14:4
Rio, John, 1967, My 17,95:4
Rio Branco, Baron do, 1912, F 11,II,13:3
Rion, Hanna, 1924, My 6,21:5
Rionda, Leandro J, 1952, D 14,91:2
Rionda, Manuel, 1943, S 3,19:5
Rionda, Manuel E, 1950, F 10,23:1
Riopel, Hop (Alb D), 1966, S 5,15:4
Riorda, Joseph I, 1949, O 30,86:2
Riordan, Arthur D, 1959, S 12,21:5
Riordan, Arthur H, 1953, F 14,17:5
Riordan, Charles F, 1942, Je 28,32:6
Riordan, Daniel C, 1947, Je 5,25:4
Riordan, Daniel J (funl, Ap 30,15:5), 1923, Ap 28, 13:4
Riordan, Daniel J, 1939, Ap 7,21:2
Riordan, Dennis A, 1960, F 13,19:5
Riordan, Dennis J, 1946, N 26,29:4
Riordan, Donovan H, 1959, Ap 7,33:1
Riordan, Edward, 1948, O 17,76:5
Riordan, Edward J, 1960, F 8,29:2; 1964, Ag 31,25:4
Riordan, Edwin, 1947, F 19,25:4
Riordan, Eugene A, 1952, F 16,13:2
Riordan, Eugene F, 1958, Jl 13,68:7
Riordan, George J, 1940, Ap 14,44:8
Riordan, James J, 1959, Ja 10,17:3
Riordan, Jeremiah, 1952, My 15,31:5
Riordan, John A, 1955, N 30,33:4
Riordan, John J, 1960, Ag 6,19:6; 1964, Ja 5,92:7
Riordan, Joseph A, 1957, Mr 13,31:3
Riordan, Joseph Rev, 1937, Ja 25,19:2
Riordan, Julia M, 1955, Ap 13,29:5
Riordan, Marion, 1952, N 14,44:2
Riordan, Martin J, 1945, F 6,19:3
Riordan, Mary J Mrs, 1941, Mr 20,21:4
Riordan, Patrick William Archbishop, 1914, D 28,9:5
Riordan, Raymond, 1940, Ap 22,17:3
Riordan, Robert B, 1946, D 5,31:5
Riordan, S John, 1941, Ag 24,34:2
Riordan, Thomas J, 1957, My 11,21:6
Riordan, Timothy J, 1957, S 19,29:4
Riordan, Timothy M, 1958, Ap 25,27:2
Riordan, William A, 1953, F 6,19:3; 1960, D 18,84:5
Riordan, William H, 1951, N 9,27:3
Riordan, William L, 1909, Jl 23,7:6
Riordan, William O, 1950, D 9,15:1
Riordan, William R, 1942, Mr 10,19:2
Riordon, Carl, 1958, Je 16,23:1
Riordon, Elizabeth, 1965, F 7,92:4
Riordon, Eric, 1948, D 28,21:4
Riordon, William L Mrs, 1951, O 8,21:5
Rios, Juan A, 1946, Je 28,21:1
Rios, Lucinda M de Mrs, 1942, Ag 11,19:4
Rios, Rafael, 1949, O 30,84:3
Rios Capape, Joaquin, 1963, Je 23,84:7
Riotte, Charles T, 1953, Jl 29,23:6
Ripka, Hubert, 1958, Ja 8,47:2
Ripley, Alfred J, 1938, Ap 7,23:4
Ripley, Alfred L, 1943, O 14,21:1
Ripley, Arthur D, 1961, F 15,35:4
Ripley, Arthur P, 1937, O 29,21:2
Ripley, Benjamin P Rev, 1916, Ja 5,13:5
Ripley, Charles D, 1941, D 26,13:2
Ripley, Clements Mrs, 1955, Jl 25,19:2
Ripley, Douglas E, 1957, Je 6,31:1
Ripley, Dwight, 1907, D 19,9:5
Ripley, Edward H Gen, 1915, S 15,9:4
Ripley, Edward Payson, 1920, F 5,9:5
Ripley, Edwin F, 1937, D 30,19:5
Ripley, Elmer E, 1952, Je 22,68:8
Ripley, Frank L, 1925, My 7,19:4
Ripley, George, 1880, Jl 5,5:2; 1907, O 25,11:5
Ripley, George H, 1952, My 7,27:3
Ripley, Gladys, 1955, D 22,23:5
Ripley, Grace W, 1945, Ap 10,19:3
Ripley, Harry H, 1960, Ap 14,31:2
Ripley, Henry B H, 1959, Ap 21,35:4
Ripley, Henry Dillon, 1913, F 10,11:4
Ripley, Herbert L, 1944, D 3,57:2
Ripley, Ira S, 1950, Ja 28,13:2
Ripley, John W, 1943, N 12,21:1
Ripley, Joseph, 1940, S 29,43:1
Ripley, Lewis W, 1939, Ap 14,23:2
Ripley, Louis A Mrs, 1961, Jl 24,23:3
Ripley, Lucy P Mrs, 1949, S 8,29:2
Ripley, Martha B Mrs, 1944, Je 25,30:2
Ripley, Paul M, 1967, N 21,47:3
Ripley, Read, 1951, Ap 7,15:5
Ripley, Robert H, 1954, My 31,13:2
Ripley, Robert L, 1949, My 28,15:1
Ripley, Sidney Dillon, 1905, F 25,9:3
Ripley, Stephen, 1965, Ap 5,31:2
Ripley, Warren, 1949, O 15,15:1
Ripley, William, 1944, N 19,50:1
Ripley, William Augustus, 1903, D 6,7:6
Ripley, William C, 1950, Ap 22,19:5
Ripley, William D, 1948, N 1,23:3
Ripley, William Z (por), 1941, Ag 17,39:1
Ripner, Jacob J, 1943, N 8,19:5
Ripon, Marquis of (Fredk Oliver Robinson), 1923, S 23,7:5
Riportella, Anthony Mrs, 1955, Ag 8,21:5
Ripp, Chris, 1942, Je 1,13:5
Rippard, Harry C, 1950, S 12,27:2
Rippe, Arnold, 1939, D 29,15:3
Rippe, John A, 1956, N 26,27:1
Rippel, Albert F Mrs, 1939, F 5,40:5
Rippel, Henry O, 1945, Mr 7,21:4
Rippel, Julius S, 1950, D 10,104:5
Rippel, Julius S (est acctg), 1954, S 23,25:8
Rippel, Julius S Mrs, 1943, F 6,13:5
Ripper, Henry, 1907, D 26,7:5
Ripper, Rudolf von, 1960, Jl 14,27:3
Rippere, John Rev, 1920, N 27,13:5
Rippere, Robert H, 1960, My 9,29:3
Ripperger, Albert A, 1947, My 23,24:3
Ripperger, C Wesley Lt, 1919, Mr 23,20:4
Ripperger, Charles Wesley Lt, 1920, S 15,9:1
Ripperger, George, 1938, Je 2,23:3
Ripperger, George Mrs, 1950, Jl 30,61:2
Ripperger, Mary E H, 1946, Jl 7,35:1
Ripperger, Maurice, 1958, Je 5,31:5
Ripperger, Walter F, 1944, Ag 2,15:5
Rippetoe, John R, 1958, Ag 23,15:6
Rippey, Harlan W (por), 1946, Mr 13,29:1
Rippey, James L Jr, 1952, D 29,19:2
Rippey, Tresher A, 1956, Je 19,29:3
Rippin, James Y Mrs, 1953, Je 3,31:1
Rippingille, Edward V Sr, 1964, Mr 26,35:1
Rippl, Charles H, 1947, N 1,15:2
Ripple, Frank Sr, 1946, Ag 27,27:5
Ripple, Jimmy, 1959, Jl 17,21:2
Ripple, Michael J, 1938, N 30,23:2
Ripple, Pacie, 1941, Ap 17,23:2
Ripps, Abraham V, 1955, Ag 25,23:6
Ripps, Isador, 1957, Ja 18,21:4
Ripps, Maurice L, 1942, O 29,23:4
Rips, Jacob, 1958, F 1,19:5
Rips, Jacob Mrs, 1957, Jl 2,27:1
Ripsom, Theodore N, 1946, F 7,23:4
Ripton, James R, 1952, Ja 29,25:2
Ris, Albert, 1962, My 27,92:6
Ris, Charles H, 1954, Je 21,23:2
Ris, Lester I, 1950, O 17,31:1
Ris, Lester Mrs, 1948, N 8,21:4
Risch, Otto C, 1956, N 13,37:4
Risch, Rene, 1968, F 20,47:1
Rischin, Meer, 1952, Jl 31,23:4
Risdon, Elizabeth, 1958, D 23,2:6
Risedorph, W Garrick, 1939, Mr 25,15:5
Riseley, Helen M, 1954, Je 13,88:4
Riseley, Minnie E, 1942, Ag 21,19:4
Rishel, Daniel W, 1949, Mr 27,76:2
Risi, Nicholas Mrs, 1954, O 13,31:1
Rising, Albert E, 1925, Ag 13,19:6
Rising, Albert S, 1953, O 17,15:4
Rising, B D, 1903, Ag 18,7:6
Rising, Edward H, 1917, O 5,11:6
Rising, Henry, 1939, Mr 6,15:2
Rising, Henry W, 1912, F 5,9:4
Rising, Joseph M, 1938, My 14,15:3
Rising, Loretta L Mrs, 1958, S 7,86:3
Rising, Richard B, 1937, S 6,17:2
Risk, Charles F, 1943, D 27,19:2
Risk, Frederick J, 1943, Ag 19,19:5
Risk, J Boyd Mrs, 1956, My 18,25:2
Risk, James, 1924, Ja 5,13:5
Risken, Law, 1961, Je 15,43:5
Riskin, Nochem, 1941, Mr 28,23:1
Riskin, Robert, 1955, S 22,31:2
Risko, Henry (Babe), 1957, Mr 8,25:2
Risko, Johnny, 1953, Ja 14,32:3
Riskus, Jacob, 1946, Ag 3,15:5
Risler, Charles F, 1944, Ja 16,43:1
Risler, Willis, 1946, S 6,21:3
Risley, Adna W, 1943, N 22,19:2
Risley, Albert Mrs, 1949, F 25,23:4
Risley, Charles E, 1938, S 29,25:5
Risley, Cora S Mrs, 1941, N 25,25:2
Risley, Elliott C, 1942, Ag 25,23:5
Risley, Everett E, 1947, N 28,27:1
Risley, Everett E Mrs (por), 1947, Mr 11,27:1

Risley, Fred M, 1949, Ag 14,69:1
Risley, Frederick S, 1941, Je 7,17:2
Risley, H W, 1882, Ag 31,5:5
Risley, Henry H, 1950, O 29,93:1
Risley, John, 1937, Ap 19,21:4
Risley, John P, 1938, Mr 28,15:1
Risley, Katherine, 1960, Ag 25,29:2
Risley, Marie T, 1944, N 29,23:3
Risley, Mary A C Mrs, 1939, My 16,23:5
Risley, Prof, 1874, My 27,1:4
Risley, Ralph G, 1962, Je 20,32:6
Risley, Roy W Mrs, 1945, Ap 10,19:5
Risner, Henry C, 1948, My 7,23:5
Riso, John G Rev, 1955, Jl 19,27:2
Rison, John R, 1954, D 31,13:4
Risse, Louis A, 1925, Mr 11,21:4
Risse, Marion Mrs, 1942, Jl 20,13:4
Rissel, John A, 1951, F 20,25:5
Rissinger, Robert H, 1958, O 8,35:3
Rissland, Rudolph, 1960, S 21,32:4
Rissler, Robert C, 1947, N 21,27:2
Rissman, Henry L, 1946, Ap 8,27:5
Rissman, John, 1939, O 6,25:3
Rissman, Sidney, 1951, Jl 27,19:5
Risso, Attilio, 1967, O 16,45:3
Rist, Charles, 1955, Ja 12,27:4
Rist, Edouard, 1956, Ap 15,88:8
Ristine, Charles S Mrs, 1964, Ap 9,32:1
Ristine, Edwin R, 1940, Jl 29,13:3
Ristine, Frank H, 1958, Jl 29,23:1
Ristine, Frederick P, 1959, Ag 7,23:4
Ristori, Adelaide (Marchesa de Grilio), 1906, O 10, 9:3
Rita, Frederick G, 1959, S 19,23:4
Rita Agnes, sister (D Casey), 1960, Mr 23,37:1
Rita Alma, Sister (Sisters of St Joseph), 1954, Je 11, 23:2
Rita Catherine, Sister (Franciscan Sisters), 1960, N 20,86:4
Rita Winnifred, Sister, 1947, F 19,25:2
Ritch, Amos M Dr, 1922, Ag 15,11:5
Ritch, Ella Mrs, 1937, N 29,2:5
Ritch, H L, 1875, O 5,6:7
Ritch, Justus B, 1938, My 2,17:3
Ritch, Orando S (por), 1938, Ap 13,25:1
Ritch, Richard B, 1940, N 5,25:3
Ritch, Thomas G, 1907, O 17,9:5
Ritch, William S, 1945, Ja 7,38:1
Ritchard, Cyril Mrs (M Elliott), 1955, Ag 9,26:5
Ritchey, B F Mrs, 1945, O 8,15:6
Ritchey, Claude, 1951, N 9,27:2
Ritchey, Daniel P, 1925, N 7,15:5
Ritchey, James V, 1941, Jl 28,13:2
Ritchey, William F, 1956, S 26,33:2
Ritchey, William M, 1937, Ja 16,17:4
Ritchie, A C, 1936, F 24,1:4
Ritchie, Agnes I, 1949, Ap 5,30:4
Ritchie, Albert, 1958, Je 20,23:4
Ritchie, Albert Judge, 1903, S 15,9:6
Ritchie, Albert S, 1937, Ja 1,23:4
Ritchie, Allan V, 1945, Je 20,23:2
Ritchie, Alva B Mrs, 1948, My 9,68:6
Ritchie, Arthur Rev, 1921, Jl 10,22:4
Ritchie, Bertha, 1960, F 15,27:4
Ritchie, C Lothrop, 1962, Ap 12,35:4
Ritchie, Charles A, 1940, F 3,13:6
Ritchie, Charles E, 1941, Mr 15,17:1
Ritchie, Charles T, 1906, Ja 10,9:7
Ritchie, David, 1867, Ja 28,8:2; 1956, Mr 13,27:4
Ritchie, David L, 1951, D 15,13:6
Ritchie, Douglas, 1967, D 16,41:1
Ritchie, Edmund J, 1951, N 14,31:4
Ritchie, Edwin C, 1955, Ja 8,13:5
Ritchie, Ella C, 1941, Ap 29,19:3
Ritchie, Fenwick W, 1951, N 26,25:4
Ritchie, Fenwick W Mrs, 1943, Mr 3,23:4
Ritchie, Frank (por), 1940, S 7,15:4
Ritchie, Frank W Mrs, 1962, S 22,25:2
Ritchie, Franklin, 1918, Ja 27,17:2
Ritchie, Frederick G, 1939, Mr 16,23:2
Ritchie, George, 1948, S 20,25:4
Ritchie, George A, 1949, O 5,29:2
Ritchie, George D, 1950, Mr 7,28:4
Ritchie, H F, 1933, F 23,25:4
Ritchie, Harry P, 1942, S 5,13:6
Ritchie, Henry A, 1945, S 18,23:5
Ritchie, J Wadsworth Mrs, 1903, Je 30,7:5
Ritchie, James F, 1951, Mr 28,29:1
Ritchie, James Wadsworth Mrs, 1903, Jl 5,7:5
Ritchie, John, 1939, Jl 23,29:4
Ritchie, John A, 1950, Mr 17,23:1; 1952, Ag 6,21:4
Ritchie, John A Mrs, 1961, D 25,23:5
Ritchie, John Mrs, 1951, F 13,31:2
Ritchie, John W, 1943, Je 3,21:4; 1962, Ap 23,29:2
Ritchie, L Carbery Mrs, 1957, Ja 7,25:2
Ritchie, Lawrence L, 1954, Jl 8,23:1
Ritchie, Lord, 1948, Jl 20,23:4
Ritchie, Louis C, 1954, S 7,25:1
Ritchie, M Adelaide E Mrs, 1937, Jl 26,19:6
Ritchie, Mabel Mrs (will), 1954, S 30,19:2
Ritchie, Mary H, 1905, F 2,1:6
Ritchie, Oscar, 1957, Ja 19,15:2
Ritchie, Oscar Mrs, 1960, Ap 16,17:6
Ritchie, Ralph J, 1944, Mr 21,20:2
Ritchie, Raymond D, 1967, Je 16,43:1
Ritchie, Richmond Sir, 1912, O 13,17:5
Ritchie, Robert Commodore, 1870, Jl 9,8:1
Ritchie, Robert H, 1942, Ag 1,11:6
Ritchie, Robert Rev Dr, 1907, Ja 8,9:2
Ritchie, Robert W, 1942, Ag 3,15:5
Ritchie, Ryerson, 1941, My 7,25:1
Ritchie, W, 1877, N 26,5:6
Ritchie, William, 1939, O 7,17:4; 1942, F 21,20:2; 1956, Mr 1,33:3
Ritchie, William E, 1943, My 13,21:5
Ritchie, William J, 1959, N 7,23:5
Ritchie, William Mrs, 1948, My 23,70:2
Ritchie, William Nelson Rev Dr, 1921, Ja 11,11:4
Ritenour, George, 1966, My 15,88:6
Ritenour, Joseph P, 1952, D 17,33:2
Riter, chas J, 1937, Ja 24,II,8:7
Riter, Henry G 3d, 1958, Jl 1,31:1
Riter, Henry G 3d Mrs, 1962, Ja 1,23:3
Riter, Michael M 4th, 1945, My 3,23:4
Riter, Thomas B, 1907, Ap 24,9:5
Ritey, Hector J Dr, 1968, O 16,47:3
Ritiman, Louis A (Bro Athanase-Emile), 1952, S 11, 31:2
Ritko, John, 1951, Je 12,29:5
Ritner, Fred V Mrs, 1959, Mr 12,31:5
Ritner, Thomas H, 1939, S 12,25:5
Ritschel, William, 1949, Mr 13,76:2
Ritscher, Charles H, 1950, Mr 17,24:3
Ritscher, William A Jr, 1955, Jl 7,27:2
Ritson, Douglas D, 1937, D 22,25:2
Ritson, Gerald F, 1947, Mr 19,26:3
Ritt, Adolph, 1949, O 23,84:2
Ritt, Joseph F, 1951, Ja 7,76:5
Ritt, Robert, 1961, D 12,43:1
Rittaker, Chris, 1903, O 1,3:2
Rittenberg, Ida K Mrs, 1943, Ja 10,50:1
Rittenberg, Isaac E, 1951, Mr 19,27:4
Rittenberg, Isaac Mrs, 1959, S 29,39:1
Rittenberg, Joseph M, 1948, Mr 23,25:5
Rittenberg, Joseph M Mrs, 1953, F 2,21:5
Rittenberg, Leonard, 1965, Je 1,39:4
Rittenberg, Louis, 1962, Jl 8,64:6
Rittenberg, Paul, 1955, O 25,33:3
Rittenberg, William C, 1951, My 26,17:4
Rittenhouse, Albert H, 1937, F 3,23:3
Rittenhouse, Charles A 3d, 1965, D 22,31:4
Rittenhouse, Charles F Mrs, 1948, Ag 30,17:3
Rittenhouse, Charles Sr, 1955, Je 3,23:3
Rittenhouse, chas, 1958, N 9,88:5
Rittenhouse, Cyrus E, 1950, F 25,17:2
Rittenhouse, Daniel, 1943, Jl 19,15:4
Rittenhouse, David, 1956, F 3,23:5
Rittenhouse, Elmer E, 1920, Ja 3,11:2
Rittenhouse, G Clifford, 1957, N 27,31:1
Rittenhouse, George B, 1954, Ja 29,19:3
Rittenhouse, George Rev, 1937, Ja 26,21:1
Rittenhouse, Harvey E, 1951, Ag 19,84:5
Rittenhouse, Jacob B, 1948, Ag 15,60:8
Rittenhouse, John P, 1951, D 25,31:4
Rittenhouse, Margaret L, 1939, D 13,27:5
Rittenhouse, Martin H Sr, 1949, Jl 22,19:4
Rittenhouse, Virgil, 1943, Mr 11,21:2
Rittenhouse, William A, 1949, N 22,29:3
Rittenhouse, William Mrs, 1949, My 20,27:4; 1952, Jl 26,13:5
Rittenhouse, William S, 1942, N 20,23:3
Ritter, Alex, 1941, S 5,21:5
Ritter, Alfred M, 1938, Jl 19,22:6
Ritter, Anne M (Mar 24), 1963, Ap 1,36:4
Ritter, Arthur, 1938, My 19,21:1
Ritter, Arthur J, 1941, Ap 7,17:4
Ritter, Augustus N, 1950, Jl 27,25:6
Ritter, C Lloyd, 1945, D 23,18:2
Ritter, Carl, 1953, Ag 26,27:2
Ritter, Carl J, 1960, D 20,33:1
Ritter, Charles A, 1960, D 28,27:2
Ritter, Christian E, 1953, F 19,23:4
Ritter, Daniel E, 1937, Je 15,23:3
Ritter, Edward P V, 1938, O 3,15:2
Ritter, Emma L Mrs, 1942, Ag 26,19:3
Ritter, Frank H, 1940, S 20,23:4
Ritter, Fred, 1949, Mr 2,26:3
Ritter, Frederick, 1951, Ja 4,29:4
Ritter, Frederick M Mrs, 1944, Je 30,21:5
Ritter, Frederick W, 1948, Jl 23,20:2
Ritter, George, 1954, Jl 2,19:3
Ritter, Henry H Mrs, 1956, Ja 7,17:3
Ritter, Horace S, 1961, My 19,32:7
Ritter, Howard L, 1967, N 23,33:5
Ritter, Irving, 1962, Mr 21,39:4
Ritter, Isidor L, 1964, Ag 22,21:6
Ritter, Jacob, 1951, N 2,24:4
Ritter, John, 1959, Ap 14,35:6
Ritter, John G Mrs, 1947, N 27,32:3
Ritter, John P, 1920, Ag 5,7:4
Ritter, Joseph E Cardinal, 1967, Je 11,1:5
Ritter, Leo, 1946, My 14,21:4
Ritter, Leo J Jr, 1968, Ag 28,47:3
Ritter, Louis, 1958, Jl 22,28:1
Ritter, Louis E, 1952, My 29,27:2
Ritter, Louis R, 1958, Jl 24,25:3
Ritter, Martin M, 1945, Je 14,19:3
Ritter, Monroe H, 1952, Jl 23,23:3
Ritter, Mortimer C, 1953, O 16,27:2
Ritter, Norman Y, 1954, Mr 16,29:2
Ritter, Phil Jr, 1948, F 1,60:3
Ritter, Phil Mrs, 1957, Mr 2,21:6
Ritter, Phil Sr, 1953, Ap 23,29:3
Ritter, R W, 1945, Ap 1,36:1
Ritter, Ralph, 1946, F 3,40:2
Ritter, Samuel, 1955, Ap 15,24:4
Ritter, Samuel P, 1960, Ag 31,29:1
Ritter, Saul I, 1964, O 21,47:4
Ritter, Verus T, 1942, O 7,25:6
Ritter, W M, 1952, My 22,27:1
Ritter, William C Sr, 1955, My 23,23:4
Ritter, William E, 1944, Ja 11,19:3
Ritter, William H, 1939, D 8,25:1; 1942, Mr 29,44:3
Ritter, William H Jr, 1960, Je 4,23:3
Ritter, William J, 1958, Je 24,31:1; 1965, O 20,47:4
Ritter, William J Mrs, 1951, Ja 23,27:4
Ritter, William M 2d, 1963, Ja 10,15:7
Ritterbush, Albert F, 1952, N 4,29:4
Ritterbush, Leonard C, 1949, Ja 22,14:2
Ritterhoff, Amalie, 1903, My 19,9:6
Ritterman, Henry A, 1961, F 20,27:4
Rittig, John, 1885, Je 19,1:1
Rittinghausen, Charles, 1956, Je 17,92:7
Rittman, Walter F, 1954, S 27,21:5
Rittner, Otto, 1949, Ap 8,25:2
Ritz, Al, 1965, D 23,28:1
Ritz, Anthony C, 1945, D 21,21:1
Ritz, Austin L, 1940, Mr 14,23:3
Ritz, Caesar, 1918, N 6,17:3
Ritz, Cesar Mme, 1961, Ja 14,23:6
Ritz, Frederick W, 1951, N 14,31:1
Ritz, Harold A, 1948, Ap 11,73:1
Ritz, Louis L Mrs, 1952, D 26,15:4
Ritz, Stuart L, 1958, O 7,35:3
Ritz, Stuart L Mrs, 1949, N 13,94:4
Ritz, Walter E, 1954, Ag 16,17:3
Ritz, William F, 1960, N 16,41:4
Ritzau, Erik, 1903, D 24,9:5
Ritzheimer, Phil, 1939, Ja 29,33:1
Ritzman, Ernest G, 1955, My 16,23:3
Ritzman, Walter H, 1951, S 11,29:4
Ritzmann, Otto A Jr, 1966, My 14,31:1
RitzRoy, Mary C B Mrs, 1940, Ja 10,21:5
Riva, Miguel A, 1948, N 18,27:5
Riva de Neira, Miguel, 1920, Mr 28,22:3
Rivalta, Augusto, 1925, Ap 16,21:5
Rivard, W Henry, 1957, F 7,27:1
Rivarde, Achille, 1940, Ap 2,26:3
Rivas, George C, 1953, Mr 21,17:5
Rivas, Gumersindo, 1914, Mr 10,9:5
Rivas, Raimundo, 1946, F 26,25:4
Rivas, Roman, 1945, Jl 1,18:3
Rivas, Victor M, 1965, Ja 21,37:4
Rivas Novoa, Gonzalo, 1958, N 30,86:4
Rivas Sanson, Gabriel, 1947, Jl 4,13:5
Rive, Caroline, 1882, N 1,4:7
Rive-King, Julie Mrs, 1937, Jl 25,II,7:2
Rivel, Andrew L, 1940, Ap 4,23:5
Rivel, Thomas M, 1947, Je 11,27:3
Rivenburg, Narola, 1942, O 15,23:3
Rivenburg, Romeyn H, 1961, Je 2,31:1
Rivenburgh, Charles H, 1947, S 3,25:4
Rivera, Antonio C, 1939, Mr 28,23:1
Rivera, Benito, 1939, Ap 20,7:3
Rivera, Diego (trb, N 26,30:2; funl, N 27,31:5), 1957, N 25,1:1
Rivera, Diego Mrs (F Kahlo), 1954, Jl 14,27:4
Rivera, Joseph Hosmer de, 1916, My 19,11:7
Rivera, Luis Munroz, 1916, N 17,9:3
Rivera, M P de, 1930, Mr 17,1:3
Rivera, Manuel P, 1961, Ap 25,35:5
Rivera Casares, Pascual D de, 1952, My 1,29:2
Rivera Otero, Rafael, 1958, Ja 27,27:4
Rivera Zayas, Rafael, 1958, Je 3,31:4
Riverdale, Lord (A Balfour), 1957, Jl 8,23:4
Riverin, Renato, 1942, Je 6,13:2
Riverkamp, Edward J Sr, 1945, N 8,19:4
Rivero y Alonso, Nicolas, 1946, Ap 20,13:4
Riveros, Bernabe, 1947, N 15,17:3
Riveros, Mariano, 1946, S 4,23:3
Riveros, Roberto, 1942, D 12,17:5
Rivers, Albert F, 1943, Ap 5,19:5
Rivers, Albert Mrs, 1954, Ja 10,86:5
Rivers, Alonzo A, 1941, Ja 7,23:4
Rivers, Andrew B, 1948, O 5,26:2
Rivers, Anthony J, 1944, Mr 17,17:5
Rivers, Carlos A, 1955, Ja 28,20:2
Rivers, Claude M, 1961, N 10,36:1
Rivers, Cliff, 1955, Ja 21,44:8
Rivers, Enrith D, 1967, Je 12,53:4
Rivers, Harry A, 1940, Mr 17,48:6
Rivers, Herbert, 1950, D 7,33:3
Rivers, Joe, 1957, Je 26,31:4
Rivers, Joseph Francis, 1968, O 16,47:4
Rivers, Marcy, 1950, Je 4,23:6
Rivers, Oscar J, 1937, Je 9,25:2
Rivers, Thomas M, 1962, My 13,88:6
Rivers, Tyree R Col, 1923, F 1,11:4
Rivers, William C, 1943, Jl 11,35:2

Rivers, William F, 1960, S 3,17:4
Riversmith, Everard S, 1941, Je 2,17:2
Rives, Alfred Landon Col, 1909, O 8,9:3
Rives, Amelie, 1945, Je 17,26:3
Rives, George B Mrs, 1953, S 4,15:3
Rives, George L Mrs, 1924, My 30,15:5
Rives, George Lockhart (funl, Ag 23,9:2), 1917, Ag 19,15:1
Rives, John C, 1864, Ap 11,5:1; 1864, Ap 13,9:4
Rives, Reginald B (will, Jl 6,13:4), 1957, Jl 1,24:1
Rives, Reginald W, 1948, F 19,23:5
Rives, W C, 1868, Ap 27,1:2
Rives, William C, 1938, D 19,23:6
Rivet, Paul, 1958, Mr 25,33:3
Rivett, David, 1961, Ap 4,37:1
Rivetta, Pietro S Count (Toddi), 1952, Jl 2,25:6
Riviere, A Joseph, 1946, Mr 24,44:6
Riviere, Albert, 1953, Je 29,21:2
Riviere, Briton, 1920, Ap 21,9:4
Riviere, Horace, 1942, Ap 29,21:5
Riviere, Louis A T, 1912, N 10,17:5
Riviere, Octave La, 1915, S 9,11:5
Rivinus, Edward F, 1945, O 10,21:2
Rivinus, Francis M, 1951, Ag 31,15:3
Rivise, Charles W, 1951, Ap 26,32:3
Rivitz, Hiram Mrs, 1948, Ap 13,27:4
Rivitz, Hiram S, 1951, Je 6,31:1
Rivkin, Arnold, 1968, S 21,33:3
Rivkin, Herman Mrs, 1960, My 27,31:4
Rivkin, Irving, 1965, O 25,37:3
Rivkin, Irving Mrs, 1954, D 6,27:3
Rivkin, Vivian, 1968, F 1,37:1
Rivkin, William R, 1967, Mr 20,31:4
Rivkind, Isaac Dr, 1968, F 20,47:1
Rivkins, Gregory S, 1961, O 27,30:8
Rivlin, Alte Mrs, 1951, My 30,21:4
Rivlin, Phillip S, 1943, Mr 21,26:8
Rivlin, Solomon, 1952, Ag 17,77:3
Rix, Arthur F, 1945, O 23,17:3
Rix, Carl B, 1963, O 2,41:3
Rix, Charles H, 1947, Ja 18,15:3
Rix, Charles P, 1952, O 29,29:4
Rix, Florence R, 1939, N 18,17:5
Rix, Frank Reader Dr, 1919, Mr 17,15:4
Rix, George A, 1945, Ap 3,19:1
Rix, Henry M, 1942, My 23,13:2
Rix, John C, 1955, S 9,23:3
Rix, Julian, 1903, N 25,9:5
Rix, Robert R Mrs, 1949, D 6,32:3
Rixen, Carl J, 1941, My 11,44:8
Rixey, Jeptha (Eppa), 1963, Mr 2,7:4
Rixey, John Franklin, 1907, F 10,7:6
Rixford, Emmet Dr, 1938, Ja 3,22:1
Rixley, Henry D, 1921, Ap 5,19:5
Rixon, Hans A, 1947, N 25,29:4
Rizenburgh, Edna Mrs, 1944, F 14,17:1
Rizow, Dimiter, 1918, My 22,13:6
Rizsak, Nicholas, 1960, F 24,37:2
Rizzi, Anthony, 1944, Ap 1,13:3
Rizzo, Andrew W, 1951, Ag 19,86:1
Rizzo, Angelo F, 1950, Ja 7,17:6
Rizzo, Angelo M, 1924, Ap 7,17:5
Rizzo, Anthony D, 1959, Ja 8,29:4
Rizzo, Dante O, 1957, O 8,35:1
Rizzo, Louis, 1942, Mr 3,23:4
Rizzo, Luigi, 1951, Je 29,21:5
Rizzo, Patrick C, 1952, Ja 16,25:3
Rizzo, Thomas V, 1945, Je 8,19:1
Rizzo, Vincent J, 1955, Ap 12,29:4
Rizzotte, Gaetano, 1941, D 24,17:4
Rizzotte, John C, 1947, Ap 18,21:1
Rizzuto, Dominick, 1954, Ja 17,93:2
Rizzuto, Joseph 3d, 1948, Ap 2,25:6
Rizzuto, Philip F Sr, 1966, Jl 8,35:1
Rizzuto, Philip J, 1962, S 20,34:1
Ro, G de, 1947, Je 14,15:6
Roach, Arno L, 1949, Je 11,17:2
Roach, Arthur T, 1946, N 29,25:3
Roach, Arvid E, 1955, Jl 30,17:1
Roach, Beatrice A, 1947, My 6,27:2
Roach, Belden (will), 1942, Ag 5,36:3
Roach, D A, 1953, Mr 5,27:2
Roach, David, 1923, My 24,19:6
Roach, David J, 1953, O 24,15:5
Roach, E C, 1946, S 6,18:1
Roach, Edward J, 1955, Jl 11,23:4
Roach, Edwin H, 1964, F 24,25:3
Roach, Ellen A Mrs, 1944, F 23,19:3
Roach, Eugene B, 1939, Je 18,37:1
Roach, George, 1949, Jl 4,13:5
Roach, George S, 1940, Je 22,10:8
Roach, George W, 1963, Jl 30,29:1
Roach, Hal Mrs, 1941, Mr 18,23:5
Roach, J Tatian, 1960, Ja 23,21:4
Roach, James A, 1947, S 23,25:4
Roach, James E, 1942, My 8,21:5
Roach, James H, 1961, Ap 22,25:6
Roach, James L, 1965, Jl 17,25:6
Roach, James P, 1957, S 14,19:6
Roach, John, 1887, Ja 11,2:1; 1907, Ag 12,7:6; 1938, N 11,25:3
Roach, John Baker, 1908, Je 17,9:5
Roach, John D (por), 1946, Ap 14,46:1
Roach, John Jr, 1961, N 27,29:1
Roach, John L, 1951, Ag 8,25:2
Roach, John L Mrs, 1945, Ja 9,19:1
Roach, Lavern, 1950, F 24,29:1
Roach, Lawrence G, 1950, S 6,29:5
Roach, M C, 1915, Ap 14,13:4
Roach, M J Mrs, 1929, Ja 14,23:4
Roach, Marjorie (Mrs W R Gilmour), 1966, Ja 24, 35:6
Roach, Max E Mrs, 1938, F 23,23:3
Roach, Milton Courtright, 1913, N 2,IV,7:6
Roach, Patrick J, 1908, S 12,7:6
Roach, S Frank, 1943, S 25,15:4
Roach, Verona E Mrs, 1938, Jl 20,19:5
Roach, Walter A Sr, 1956, Ap 8,84:3
Roach, Walter Mrs, 1955, Jl 24,64:5
Roach, Walter T, 1953, Ap 23,29:3
Roach, Wilbur C, 1947, D 27,13:1
Roach, William, 1907, Jl 8,7:2
Roach, William A, 1941, O 24,24:2
Roach, William J, 1937, Ap 14,25:4; 1958, D 9,41:5; 1959, N 9,31:3
Roach, William L, 1951, My 13,88:5
Roach, William R, 1937, S 7,21:5
Roache, J A Dr, 1903, My 5,9:6
Roache, Viola, 1961, My 19,31:1
Roachford, Samuel B, 1963, Je 26,39:5
Roadruck, Roy K, 1944, Ja 18,19:1
Roads, Charles Rev, 1937, Ag 2,19:3
Roahr, George, 1881, Ja 11,2:2
Roake, Angelo Mrs, 1944, Ag 15,17:4
Roake, William, 1949, N 17,29:4
Roake, William J, 1938, Ja 26,23:1
Roaman, Harry Mrs, 1960, F 4,31:1
Roaman, Mortimer Mrs, 1949, Mr 29,25:4
Roan, Frank J, 1942, Je 18,21:3
Roan, Leonard S, 1963, Je 12,43:1
Roan, Leonard S Judge, 1915, Mr 24,11:5
Roane, J S Ex-Gov, 1867, Ap 22,1:7
Roane, Sexton C, 1961, Mr 8,33:3
Roane, Thomas Sexton, 1953, F 7,15:2
Roantree, James E, 1957, S 9,25:6
Roantree, R Bertrand Mrs, 1949, O 22,17:5
Roarke, Alfred M, 1950, F 14,25:1
Roarty, Mae E, 1918, Je 25,13:7
Roat, Charles O, 1955, Ja 27,23:1
Roatta, Mario Gen, 1968, Ja 8,39:1
Robacher, Harl J, 1953, Je 23,29:3
Robaczewski, Theodore S, 1941, Mr 23,45:3
Robard, George, 1949, D 2,29:2
Robards, Jason Sr, 1963, Ap 6,19:1
Robart, Ralph W, 1949, Je 26,60:1
Robarts, Heber Dr, 1922, My 3,21:6
Robaskiewicz, Charles, 1945, N 27,23:5
Robb, Alex S, 1947, N 7,23:3
Robb, Alexander, 1919, O 12,22:3
Robb, Andrew W, 1957, N 10,86:7
Robb, Arthur T Mrs, 1962, Ap 11,43:1
Robb, Charles, 1949, O 28,23:2
Robb, Charles H, 1939, Je 11,44:6
Robb, Charles H Mrs, 1949, Ag 12,17:4
Robb, Charles W, 1947, Ap 15,25:2
Robb, Cloyd P, 1944, N 4,15:5
Robb, D W, 1938, F 23,23:3
Robb, David A, 1937, Ap 29,21:4
Robb, David S, 1944, Ap 20,19:3
Robb, David S Mrs, 1942, Ap 22,24:2
Robb, E Donald, 1942, Jl 10,17:5
Robb, Floyd N, 1957, Ja 23,29:4
Robb, Francis J M, 1964, F 22,21:4
Robb, Henderson Mrs, 1957, Ap 21,88:4
Robb, Hunter, 1940, My 16,23:5
Robb, J Addison, 1941, Ag 7,17:6
Robb, J H, 1929, N 12,31:3
Robb, J Hampden Ex-Sen, 1911, Ja 22,II,11:5
Robb, J Hampden Mrs, 1903, Jl 20,7:6
Robb, J Irvin, 1938, Jl 3,13:2
Robb, J Leslie, 1954, Jl 19,19:3
Robb, J Leslie Mrs, 1941, My 24,15:5
Robb, J M, 1942, D 12,17:3
Robb, J N, 1881, Ag 2,3:3
Robb, James Air Chief Marshal Sir, 1968, D 19,47:3
Robb, James Brig-Gen (por), 1937, F 16,23:1
Robb, Janet H (funl plans, S 17,29:1), 1966, S 16,37:4
Robb, John H, 1959, Ag 10,27:5
Robb, John H Jr, 1947, F 28,23:1
Robb, John W (por), 1944, Je 6,17:5
Robb, Louis A, 1962, Mr 18,87:1
Robb, Marshall V, 1958, Mr 6,27:1
Robb, Russell, 1957, Je 4,35:4
Robb, Theodore D, 1967, My 25,42:5
Robb, W L, 1933, Ja 27,22:2
Robb, W L (Wally), 1950, Mr 28,31:4
Robb, Walter E, 1941, D 1,19:3
Robb, William B, 1957, N 28,31:1
Robb, William D, 1947, Je 24,23:4
Robbe, Louis E, 1950, Ja 12,28:3
Robbers, Herman, 1937, S 16,25:6
Robbert, Frederick W, 1939, N 19,38:7
Robbie, Alex, 1964, O 1,35:3
Robbie, Archibald, 1913, Mr 13,11:3
Robbie, Kenneth, 1956, Ap 8,84:7
Robbie, Kenneth Mrs, 1946, S 7,15:2
Robbie, Reuben, 1872, Ja 22,4:7
Robbin, John P, 1874, N 13,4:7
Robbins, A F, 1882, O 11,2:6
Robbins, Aaron S, 1904, Jl 6,9:7
Robbins, Abel, 1951, Jl 26,21:4
Robbins, Abraham, 1948, O 2,15:4
Robbins, Adam O, 1942, Je 10,21:2
Robbins, Albert, 1938, N 12,45:2
Robbins, Albert I, 1948, Ap 15,25:6
Robbins, Alfred Augustus, 1919, Ap 12,15:2
Robbins, Alfred G, 1944, O 20,19:3
Robbins, Alfred H, 1945, Je 29,15:4
Robbins, Alice B A Mrs, 1951, O 24,32:3
Robbins, Allan A, 1947, F 18,25:3
Robbins, Anatole, 1955, Ja 26,25:4
Robbins, Arden M, 1942, O 10,15:5
Robbins, Benjamin B, 1948, Ja 12,19:4
Robbins, Bennett A, 1957, D 28,17:2
Robbins, Bernard, 1952, Ag 29,23:4
Robbins, Bernard S, 1959, D 17,37:2
Robbins, Bob, 1946, My 6,21:5
Robbins, Burnett W, 1952, Ap 12,11:4
Robbins, Burr, 1908, Ja 31,7:5
Robbins, Calvin B, 1948, D 10,25:4
Robbins, Carroll, 1907, S 2,7:6
Robbins, Chandler, 1882, S 12,2:6
Robbins, Chandler 2d, 1955, Je 3,23:5
Robbins, Charles B, 1943, Jl 6,21:3
Robbins, Charles C, 1960, O 4,43:2
Robbins, Charles E, 1949, My 24,28:4
Robbins, Charles F, 1943, D 24,14:6; 1957, S 10,33:
Robbins, Charles F Sr Mrs, 1943, Ag 27,17:3
Robbins, Charles H D, 1952, Ap 6,88:5
Robbins, Charles M, 1951, Ap 5,29:2
Robbins, Charles T, 1909, F 9,7:5
Robbins, Clarence A, 1949, My 13,23:2
Robbins, Daniel W, 1944, Ja 12,23:2
Robbins, David H, 1952, Ja 19,15:5
Robbins, Dwight, 1941, Ja 8,19:1
Robbins, E A, 1942, Je 29,15:1
Robbins, Edmund J, 1940, Mr 26,21:4
Robbins, Edmund Sir, 1922, D 22,15:5
Robbins, Edmund Y, 1942, My 31,39:3
Robbins, Edward, 1919, Ja 26,20:4
Robbins, Edward I, 1942, O 18,52:4
Robbins, Edward J, 1950, My 29,17:4
Robbins, Edward R, 1941, N 8,19:2
Robbins, Eli, 1883, Je 23,4:7
Robbins, Eugene, 1943, D 18,15:2
Robbins, Eugene 3d, 1963, Ag 9,23:5
Robbins, F LeBaron Jr, 1945, Jl 4,13:7
Robbins, Frances, 1937, Mr 26,21:2
Robbins, Frances C L Mrs, 1942, O 1,23:5
Robbins, Francis H, 1940, Ag 15,19:1
Robbins, Francis L, 1911, S 9,9:5
Robbins, Francis Le Baron Rev Dr, 1920, Ja 29,9:5
Robbins, Frank G, 1941, My 26,19:3
Robbins, Frank W, 1941, Ag 13,17:4
Robbins, Franklin G, 1939, Ja 2,24:2
Robbins, Franklin H, 1944, Mr 13,15:5
Robbins, Fred A, 1941, Ja 28,19:1; 1947, F 7,23:3
Robbins, Frederick, 1960, S 26,33:2
Robbins, Frederick W, 1939, S 11,19:4
Robbins, G David, 1962, D 4,41:4
Robbins, George J, 1948, D 26,52:4
Robbins, George S, 1942, S 18,21:4; 1947, Ap 1,28:
Robbins, George W, 1923, Ja 13,13:5; 1942, Ja 5,1
Robbins, George W Jr, 1963, Ap 25,33:4
Robbins, Grover C (Je 24 death noted), 1956, D
30:3
Robbins, Harris A, 1940, O 27,45:1
Robbins, Harry P, 1946, Mr 21,25:1
Robbins, Harry P Mrs, 1962, Ap 24,37:2
Robbins, Harry W, 1954, Je 21,23:5
Robbins, Hartley, 1938, My 26,25:2
Robbins, Helen C Mrs, 1949, S 2,17:3
Robbins, Henry Asher, 1914, Ja 23,11:5
Robbins, Henry B, 1943, S 8,23:5
Robbins, Henry E Mrs, 1962, N 22,29:5
Robbins, Henry W, 1904, D 15,9:3; 1942, F 17,21:
Robbins, Herbert D, 1947, Ag 22,15:5
Robbins, Herbert W, 1940, F 25,38:8
Robbins, Herman, 1963, Ag 1,27:1
Robbins, Herman G, 1962, O 23,37:1
Robbins, Howard C, 1952, Mr 21,23:1
Robbins, J Clarke Rev, 1937, Mr 13,19:5
Robbins, J Holden, 1951, Ag 12,76:5
Robbins, J M Capt, 1907, Mr 14,7:5
Robbins, James, 1962, S 28,33:3; 1966, S 27,13:1
Robbins, James M, 1939, F 15,23:5
Robbins, James M Mrs (por), 1942, Jl 6,15:3
Robbins, James Mrs, 1966, S 27,13:1
Robbins, Jane E, 1946, Ag 17,13:2
Robbins, John C, 1958, Ap 8,30:6
Robbins, John J, 1950, O 3,31:5
Robbins, John J (Jack), 1959, D 17,37:1
Robbins, John W, 1942, N 9,23:1
Robbins, Joseph, 1957, D 17,35:4
Robbins, Joseph C, 1962, O 1,31:2
Robbins, Karl, 1960, Mr 14,29:1
Robbins, Kenneth V, 1945, My 26,15:6
Robbins, Larry, 1960, F 8,29:1
Robbins, Laurence S (Oct 1), 1965, O 11,61:4

Robbins, Lawrence B, 1944, O 5,23:2
Robbins, Leonard H, 1947, Je 25,25:1
Robbins, Leonard H Mrs (por), 1945, S 7,24:2
Robbins, Lester D Mrs, 1968, Ja 17,47:1
Robbins, Loring G Mrs, 1968, Je 25,41:3
Robbins, Louis, 1943, S 10,23:4
Robbins, Louis L, 1942, Mr 12,19:2
Robbins, Louis Leland Maj, 1915, Ja 28,9:4
Robbins, Mary L Mrs, 1940, S 29,44:1
Robbins, Merton C (por), 1937, My 21,21:3
Robbins, Merton C Mrs, 1948, Jl 19,19:4
Robbins, Milton, 1910, D 30,11:4
Robbins, Morton J Dr, 1968, Je 25,41:4
Robbins, Nathan G, 1953, O 2,21:2
Robbins, Nathaniel A Dr, 1909, F 18,7:5
Robbins, Oscar, 1965, Ap 26,31:3
Robbins, Percy A, 1938, Ap 25,15:5
Robbins, Philip H, 1943, O 31,49:1
Robbins, Rainard B, 1951, F 13,31:4
Robbins, Ralph S, 1950, S 26,31:2
Robbins, Reginald C, 1955, N 21,29:2
Robbins, Richard Bennett, 1909, F 18,7:5
Robbins, Robert, 1949, S 21,47:2
Robbins, Robert M, 1964, Ap 28,37:3
Robbins, Roy B, 1944, Jl 17,15:3
Robbins, Royal Mrs, 1956, Ja 31,29:1
Robbins, S Howland (funl, S 5,7:6), 1901, S 4,2:2
Robbins, Sabin, 1939, Ap 30,45:1
Robbins, Samuel, 1949, N 28,27:4; 1951, Mr 3,13:5; 1954, Ja 7,31:2
Robbins, Selinda R Mrs, 1916, F 10,11:4
Robbins, Sydney, 1957, F 20,33:5
Robbins, Ted, 1946, Ja 18,8:3
Robbins, Thomas H, 1954, N 15,27:3
Robbins, Thomas P, 1944, Ap 1,13:5
Robbins, Truman, 1949, S 6,27:4
Robbins, Truman Mrs, 1948, Jl 23,20:3
Robbins, W D, 1935, Ap 8,19:1
Robbins, Walter, 1940, My 8,23:5; 1956, Jl 22,60:6
Robbins, Walter G, 1950, My 19,27:3
Robbins, Walter J Dr, 1937, N 23,23:5
Robbins, Warren D Mrs, 1960, My 9,29:4
Robbins, William A, 1947, F 7,24:3
Robbins, William D, 1952, Mr 26,29:3
Robbins, William F, 1947, Ag 1,17:4
Robbins, William H Mrs, 1937, S 21,25:3
Robbins, William H Sr, 1943, Je 5,15:3
Robbins, William J, 1944, Mr 21,20:2
Robbins, William M, 1953, D 9,11:2
Robbins, Winfield S, 1910, N 21,9:5
Robbins, Wolcott P, 1966, Jl 2,23:5
Robe, Charles F Brig-Gen, 1910, Jl 3,II,7:4
Robe, Harold A, 1946, Ap 22,21:4
Robe, Robert S, 1965, D 19,84:6
Robels, Arch Mrs, 1956, Je 12,35:1
Rober, Richard, 1952, My 27,30:2
Roberg, Harry A, 1951, Jl 17,27:2
Roberge, Abijah M Mrs, 1943, Ap 7,26:3
Roberge, Henri A, 1942, F 17,21:1
Roberge, John L, 1940, Jl 31,11:3
Roberson, Clifford H, 1951, Ap 3,27:2
Roberson, Horace K, 1955, Ja 14,21:3
Roberson, Horace 3d, 1953, My 21,31:5
Roberson, S S, 1882, My 30,5:5
Roberson, Samuel A, 1957, Ap 10,33:2
Roberson, William K, 1943, N 19,19:3
Robert, Abraham, 1949, Ap 12,29:3
Robert, Arthur, 1939, Mr 22,23:1
Robert, Bro, 1937, S 21,25:3
Robert, Camille, 1957, Mr 26,33:3
Robert, Christine Mrs, 1918, Je 1,11:8
Robert, E Weston, 1944, Je 20,19:2
Robert, Frederick Mrs, 1923, Ap 16,17:5
Robert, Hans, 1954, My 3,25:2
Robert, Henry M Jr Prof, 1937, Ag 26,21:4
Robert, Henry Martyn Henry Brig-Gen, 1923, My 12, 15:5
Robert, Horace Sgt, 1871, Mr 18,8:4
Robert, J Eugene, 1907, O 5,11:6
Robert, John C Jr, 1956, Je 23,17:3
Robert, Joseph C, 1946, Mr 11,25:2
Robert, L W, 1944, Ag 18,13:4
Robert, Lawrence W 3d, 1962, Je 12,31:7
Robert, Louis, 1938, F 16,21:5
Robert, Louis D, 1948, Mr 2,23:3
Robert, Osmond T, 1945, N 9,19:4
Robert, William P, 1963, S 10,39:2
Roberti, Guerino Countess, 1958, F 24,19:4
Roberti, Lyda, 1938, Mr 13,II,8:5
Roberto, Gabriel, 1947, Ap 21,27:6
Roberto, Josephine, 1951, Jl 25,23:2
Roberto, Mary T Mrs, 1957, Ap 13,19:3
Roberto, Pasquale, 1940, Ap 30,21:3
Roberto, Vincent Mrs, 1943, Je 10,21:1
Roberton, Hugh, 1952, O 8,31:1
Roberts, A, 1933, F 28,19:1
Roberts, A Cledge, 1957, Je 16,84:5
Roberts, A H, 1939, D 21,23:3
Roberts, A M, 1947, Ap 3,25:5
Roberts, Albert, 1948, My 17,19:5
Roberts, Albert C, 1939, My 7,III,6:7
Roberts, Albert E, 1940, My 8,23:3
Roberts, Albert H, 1946, Je 27,21:5
Roberts, Albert J, 1950, F 27,19:4; 1958, Ja 2,29:1
Roberts, Albert Mrs, 1945, F 28,23:5
Roberts, Alex B, 1956, Jl 2,21:6
Roberts, Alfred Mrs, 1953, O 11,89:3
Roberts, Alfred P, 1959, Je 15,27:3
Roberts, Alfred S, 1956, D 4,39:2
Roberts, Algernon B, 1909, Ja 9,9:6
Roberts, Alice A, 1955, S 21,33:4
Roberts, Alice E, 1958, Ag 9,13:5
Roberts, Allan, 1966, Ja 15,27:1
Roberts, Ann C Mrs, 1963, Jl 24,31:2
Roberts, Annabel, 1918, Ja 22,11:4
Roberts, Anthony, 1885, Ja 24,5:4; 1962, Mr 2,30:1
Roberts, Arthur G, 1941, N 19,23:1
Roberts, Arthur J D, 1944, Jl 9,35:2
Roberts, Arthur L, 1952, O 29,29:6; 1962, Mr 30,33:2
Roberts, Arthur O, 1949, F 3,23:2
Roberts, Arthur S Mrs, 1944, F 7,15:4
Roberts, Arthur T, 1956, N 16,28:1
Roberts, Arthur V, 1957, My 7,31:6
Roberts, Basil C, 1957, F 6,25:5
Roberts, Ben, 1922, My 6,11:4
Roberts, Benjamin H (trb, S 21,II,2:1), 1947, S 15, 17:4
Roberts, Benjamin Kearney Gen, 1921, Jl 18,11:7
Roberts, Burt, 1949, O 12,29:1
Roberts, C Bruce, 1941, Je 4,23:4
Roberts, C Wesley, 1946, My 8,25:3
Roberts, C Wilson, 1960, O 2,85:2
Roberts, Calvin S, 1964, Jl 22,33:3
Roberts, Carl G, 1950, Ja 17,27:1
Roberts, Carl Mrs, 1920, D 22,11:4
Roberts, Carlton P, 1956, My 29,27:5
Roberts, Carroll J, 1939, Ap 7,19:3
Roberts, Carroll M, 1965, Ja 25,37:3
Roberts, Cecilia, 1947, My 7,27:4
Roberts, Charles, 1924, Mr 18,21:5
Roberts, Charles A, 1964, Je 2,37:4
Roberts, Charles B, 1962, Mr 13,35:2
Roberts, Charles B 3d, 1951, N 12,25:5
Roberts, Charles D, 1949, F 14,19:5; 1966, O 26,47:2
Roberts, Charles E, 1951, N 12,25:5
Roberts, Charles F, 1920, S 28,13:1
Roberts, Charles G D, 1943, N 27,13:1
Roberts, Charles G Jr, 1950, Ja 9,25:2
Roberts, Charles H, 1913, Ap 10,11:5; 1937, Ag 8,II, 6:3
Roberts, Charles H (por), 1941, S 11,23:3
Roberts, Charles H, 1942, Je 4,19:4; 1945, N 7,23:4; 1967, Ja 3,34:2
Roberts, Charles H Jr, 1941, O 23,23:3
Roberts, Charles H L, 1949, My 24,28:5
Roberts, Charles H Mrs, 1947, N 27,31:1
Roberts, Charles L, 1941, My 31,11:1
Roberts, Charles M, 1967, Mr 20,31:5
Roberts, Charles S, 1948, F 11,27:1; 1951, D 21,27:4; 1965, Ag 10,29:2
Roberts, Charles W, 1947, Jl 29,21:2; 1950, Ap 25,31:2
Roberts, Chester J, 1960, S 8,35:1
Roberts, Chester Mrs, 1948, Mr 12,23:5
Roberts, Chris, 1903, S 22,7:4
Roberts, Clarence, 1942, D 5,15:4
Roberts, Clarence V, 1948, Ja 6,23:4
Roberts, Clarence W Mrs, 1961, O 20,30:5
Roberts, Clarence W P, 1956, O 23,33:5
Roberts, Clifford P, 1949, D 1,31:2
Roberts, Columbus Sr, 1950, Ag 27,89:2
Roberts, Corraine J, 1921, F 2,11:5
Roberts, Cyrus S Brig-Gen, 1917, Mr 20,11:6
Roberts, Daniel C (will, Je 12,23:1), 1940, Je 5,25:4
Roberts, Daniel S, 1907, Ap 10,7:7
Roberts, David, 1942, My 6,19:1; 1943, D 9,28:3; 1954, Mr 11,31:5
Roberts, David E, 1942, Jl 1,25:2; 1955, Ja 5,23:5
Roberts, David H, 1939, Ap 2,III,7:3
Roberts, David S, 1950, Ap 29,15:5
Roberts, Deering J Dr, 1925, Mr 31,19:5
Roberts, Dimon E, 1943, Ag 14,11:5
Roberts, Donald F, 1965, Jl 2,29:1
Roberts, Dorothea K Mrs, 1942, O 6,23:1
Roberts, Douglas J, 1957, Mr 14,29:4
Roberts, Dudley D, 1940, Mr 9,15:6
Roberts, Dudley Mrs, 1952, Ag 21,19:4
Roberts, E A, 1881, Mr 26,5:3
Roberts, E A Mrs, 1953, Ja 6,29:5
Roberts, E E, 1933, D 12,23:4
Roberts, E G, 1881, Jl 26,5:4
Roberts, E Marion, 1963, Jl 18,27:5
Roberts, E Marion Mrs, 1954, Ja 16,15:5
Roberts, E Walter, 1941, My 24,15:3
Roberts, Edward, 1964, Mr 23,29:3
Roberts, Edward A, 1954, F 1,23:3; 1965, Ap 11,93:1
Roberts, Edward D, 1963, D 12,39:1
Roberts, Edward Everett, 1918, Ja 14,11:4
Roberts, Edward F, 1951, S 1,11:5
Roberts, Edward H, 1954, D 15,31:5
Roberts, Edward J, 1953, O 10,17:5
Roberts, Edward K, 1940, Ja 16,23:4
Roberts, Edwin, 1951, D 31,13:5
Roberts, Elizabeth H Mrs, 1948, F 27,21:4
Roberts, Elizabeth M (por), 1941, Mr 14,21:4
Roberts, Ella, 1963, O 25,31:1
Roberts, Ellis H Mrs, 1903, Jl 21,6:5
Roberts, Ellsworth A, 1960, Je 30,29:5
Roberts, Elmer (por), 1937, N 18,23:1
Roberts, Elmer R, 1942, N 7,15:2
Roberts, Elsie S Mrs, 1950, F 2,27:4
Roberts, Elzey Sr, 1962, My 15,39:2
Roberts, Emma (Mrs Chas F Loughead), 1968, S 19, 47:1
Roberts, Ernest A, 1956, Ja 22,88:8
Roberts, Ethel L, 1948, My 18,23:3
Roberts, Eugene, 1950, S 15,25:5
Roberts, Eugene A, 1963, Ag 14,33:1
Roberts, Eugene B Mrs, 1958, My 24,21:3
Roberts, Eugene C, 1944, Ja 3,21:1
Roberts, Eugene P, 1953, Ja 10,17:4
Roberts, Eugene P Mrs (Ruth), 1968, O 3,47:3
Roberts, Ex-President of Siberia, 1876, Mr 18,5:4
Roberts, Ezra C Mrs, 1953, S 24,33:4
Roberts, Florence, 1940, Je 7,23:4
Roberts, Floyd L, 1950, Je 15,2:5
Roberts, Francis E, 1946, Jl 15,25:5
Roberts, Frank, 1967, Jl 25,32:3
Roberts, Frank A, 1942, O 18,55:3; 1949, Ja 2,63:3
Roberts, Frank C Jr, 1966, Mr 29,41:3
Roberts, Frank C Mrs, 1948, D 5,92:4
Roberts, Frank C Sr, 1942, D 2,25:3
Roberts, Frank H, 1945, S 28,21:4
Roberts, Frank L Mrs, 1948, F 12,23:3
Roberts, Frank M, 1937, Jl 14,21:5
Roberts, Frank S Mrs, 1941, Je 6,21:2
Roberts, Frank W, 1950, Ap 7,25:2; 1951, Ap 16,25:3; 1953, Je 4,29:4
Roberts, Fred C, 1940, S 30,17:3
Roberts, Fred R, 1946, Ap 18,27:3
Roberts, Fred T, 1962, Ag 15,31:2
Roberts, Frederick C, 1944, O 13,19:1
Roberts, Frederick H, 1950, Ja 5,26:2
Roberts, Frederick O, 1941, O 25,17:2
Roberts, Frederick W, 1961, Jl 6,29:2
Roberts, G Brinton, 1945, O 19,23:4
Roberts, G S, 1905, F 27,1:3
Roberts, Garrett, 1958, Jl 24,25:5
Roberts, George, 1950, Mr 5,92:5; 1968, Ag 9,35:3
Roberts, George A, 1952, Mr 7,23:2; 1957, D 26,19:2
Roberts, George B Mrs, 1965, N 18,47:2
Roberts, George D Jr, 1966, Ap 5,39:2
Roberts, George E (por), 1948, Je 8,25:3
Roberts, George E, 1952, Ja 15,27:3
Roberts, George F, 1950, N 22,25:5
Roberts, George H, 1915, Ja 2,9:6; 1937, Jl 1,27:3; 1950, Jl 25,27:2
Roberts, George I, 1960, D 29,25:2
Roberts, George I Mrs, 1937, Ap 8,23:4; 1949, N 4, 28:6
Roberts, George J, 1948, F 13,21:3; 1954, S 11,17:5
Roberts, George L, 1941, F 27,19:3
Roberts, George Morrison, 1914, O 29,11:4
Roberts, George Mrs, 1944, Jl 26,19:1
Roberts, George N, 1940, S 13,23:2
Roberts, George S, 1913, Ag 7,7:4; 1940, Ja 20,15:2
Roberts, George W, 1942, Je 11,23:4; 1954, Ja 30,17:3
Roberts, George W B, 1941, N 27,23:2
Roberts, Gilbert W, 1958, Ja 14,33:3
Roberts, Glenn (Fireball), 1964, Jl 3,21:1
Roberts, Grace van B, 1958, Jl 29,23:2
Roberts, Graham, 1954, S 6,15:5
Roberts, Griffith, 1954, S 7,25:2
Roberts, Guy H, 1961, N 2,37:5
Roberts, H Armstrong, 1947, F 13,24:3
Roberts, H F Rev, 1879, Ja 17,2:4
Roberts, H H, 1876, My 31,5:4
Roberts, H Llewelyn, 1967, D 2,39:3
Roberts, Harlow P, 1953, O 16,27:3
Roberts, Harold, 1953, Ag 29,17:1
Roberts, Harold M, 1949, D 28,25:4
Roberts, Harrison B, 1964, Ag 25,33:2
Roberts, Harry, 1946, N 14,29:3
Roberts, Harry Mrs, 1944, D 19,21:5
Roberts, Harvey E, 1917, Je 2,9:6
Roberts, Harvey L, 1919, Je 15,22:5
Roberts, Harvey M, 1949, My 27,22:2
Roberts, Henrietta W Mrs, 1962, Je 29,27:4
Roberts, Henry, 1903, D 16,9:5; 1941, Mr 10,17:4
Roberts, Henry B, 1943, Ag 2,15:3; 1960, Ap 5,37:2
Roberts, Henry C, 1949, Ap 4,23:4; 1966, Ja 25,41:3
Roberts, Herbert R, 1950, D 28,26:2
Roberts, Herbert W Mrs, 1958, D 11,13:5
Roberts, Hereward L, 1947, N 2,72:6
Roberts, Homer B, 1952, Jl 25,17:5
Roberts, Horace E, 1940, F 4,40:4
Roberts, Howard C, 1948, O 5,25:2
Roberts, Howard H, 1948, D 11,15:6
Roberts, Howard S, 1947, F 2,57:2
Roberts, Howland Mrs, 1949, Ap 17,76:3
Roberts, Hugh L, 1943, N 13,13:5
Roberts, Hugh S, 1947, Mr 2,60:5
Roberts, Irven J, 1941, F 15,15:3
Roberts, Isaac, 1942, Ja 17,17:1
Roberts, Isaac Dr, 1904, Jl 19,7:7
Roberts, Isabelle J B Mrs, 1941, N 20,27:3
Roberts, J Louis, 1959, Jl 19,69:2
Roberts, J M Sr Mrs, 1947, My 10,13:4
Roberts, J S Judge, 1903, O 21,9:6
Roberts, Jack, 1955, Je 3,23:6

Roberts, James, 1940, Mr 16,15:6
Roberts, James A, 1940, O 14,19:2; 1943, D 11,15:3; 1946, O 9,27:3; 1967, Mr 19,46:6
Roberts, James Arthur, 1922, N 23,21:6
Roberts, James Henry, 1920, Je 26,11:6
Roberts, James J, 1940, Ag 23,15:5
Roberts, James M, 1949, Jl 15,19:4
Roberts, James Mrs, 1951, O 15,25:1
Roberts, James O, 1952, Ap 19,15:5
Roberts, James S, 1939, S 27,25:5
Roberts, Jane Mrs, 1914, Ja 11,15:5
Roberts, Jennie, 1940, S 23,17:3
Roberts, John, 1938, F 23,23:4; 1938, O 16,45:2; 1943, F 13,11:1
Roberts, John A Jr, 1963, Ap 8,47:1
Roberts, John B Dr, 1924, N 29,13:4
Roberts, John C, 1924, Ap 28,15:4
Roberts, John E, 1946, Ap 13,17:2
Roberts, John G, 1951, Jl 24,25:6; 1955, Ap 30,17:3
Roberts, John G Mrs, 1947, S 27,15:5
Roberts, John H, 1940, My 16,23:4; 1949, D 9,31:5; 1951, Ag 28,23:3; 1954, Mr 30,27:4; 1958, N 20,35:2; 1962, D 18,4:8
Roberts, John H Mrs, 1951, Ag 2,21:5
Roberts, John L, 1952, N 27,31:6
Roberts, John M, 1942, My 19,19:1; 1959, F 22,88:5
Roberts, John Mrs, 1953, D 29,23:2
Roberts, John Pratt, 1906, Jl 8,9:6
Roberts, John S (por), 1938, F 2,19:1
Roberts, John S, 1953, Ap 10,21:6
Roberts, John S Mrs, 1952, Mr 13,30:3
Roberts, John T, 1940, My 3,21:3; 1955, Mr 7,27:4
Roberts, John W, 1946, Mr 8,21:2; 1959, Ap 16,33:5
Roberts, Jonathan W, 1912, N 2,13:5
Roberts, Joseph E, 1950, Je 6,29:5
Roberts, Joseph H Sr, 1954, Ag 15,84:4
Roberts, Joseph Rev Dr, 1921, F 17,11:6
Roberts, Joseph W, 1951, Jl 10,27:5
Roberts, Katherine Eggleston, 1968, Mr 5,41:2
Roberts, Kenneth (will, S 17,26:4), 1957, Jl 22,1:8
Roberts, Kenneth M Mrs, 1963, Ap 24,35:3
Roberts, Kingsley (por), 1947, N 22,15:5
Roberts, Laurence C, 1950, Je 21,27:2
Roberts, Lawrence L, 1956, F 5,86:4
Roberts, Leo B, 1954, Ja 17,93:1
Roberts, Leslie E, 1961, Ag 29,31:2
Roberts, Leslie S, 1939, Ap 27,25:5
Roberts, Llewellyn, 1939, Ap 5,25:6; 1961, Ap 1,17:6
Roberts, Loren B, 1940, S 14,17:6
Roberts, Louis A, 1951, Je 1,26:1
Roberts, Louis M Sr, 1950, O 28,17:6
Roberts, Louise B Mrs, 1950, D 3,88:4
Roberts, Luckey (C Luckeyth Roberts), 1968, F 7, 47:4
Roberts, Luckey Mrs, 1958, S 27,21:1
Roberts, Lucy K, 1961, Ap 17,29:5
Roberts, Luther K, 1964, Je 20,25:6
Roberts, M A, 1938, Je 19,29:2
Roberts, M O, 1880, S 8,1:6
Roberts, Maelor O, 1948, Je 12,15:6
Roberts, Malcolm Mrs, 1951, My 20,89:1
Roberts, Malvern H, 1943, N 28,68:3
Roberts, Margaret (Mrs M Catchpole), 1962, O 24, 39:3
Roberts, Marshall O Mrs, 1874, D 15,1:7
Roberts, Martin A, 1940, Je 16,39:2
Roberts, Mary A Mrs, 1952, Jl 10,31:3
Roberts, Mary L Mrs, 1949, F 28,19:5
Roberts, Mary M, 1959, Ja 12,39:2
Roberts, Maurice G, 1952, S 20,15:6
Roberts, Meredith J, 1960, Je 17,31:2
Roberts, Michael, 1948, D 16,29:4
Roberts, Michael H, 1942, Ja 24,17:5
Roberts, Miles, 1947, O 20,23:3
Roberts, Miles Mrs, 1950, Mr 1,27:3
Roberts, Millard U, 1957, S 15,84:7
Roberts, Montague H, 1957, S 21,19:5
Roberts, Morton, 1964, Ja 20,43:4
Roberts, Munro, 1962, Jl 4,21:6
Roberts, Myron, 1943, Je 22,19:2
Roberts, Ned H, 1948, Jl 21,23:4
Roberts, Nelson A, 1949, O 22,17:6
Roberts, Newell W, 1966, D 21,39:2
Roberts, Nicholas, 1945, My 19,19:6
Roberts, Norman, 1944, Ap 19,23:1
Roberts, Norman K, 1954, N 25,22:1
Roberts, O, 1934, Jl 25,17:3
Roberts, Olan Mrs, 1966, Ja 10,25:5
Roberts, Oliver Everett, 1903, Ag 11,7:7
Roberts, Oren Mrs, 1951, My 4,27:2
Roberts, Osgood, 1958, Ap 28,23:5
Roberts, Owen, 1907, S 22,9:4
Roberts, Owen F, 1955, Ja 10,23:4
Roberts, Owen J (funl plans, My 19,29:5; will, My 27,46:1), 1955, My 18,1:1
Roberts, P Warren, 1965, S 3,27:1
Roberts, Paul, 1950, My 20,15:3; 1962, F 25,89:2; 1967, S 15,47:3
Roberts, Paul Mrs, 1953, N 18,31:3
Roberts, Percival Jr, 1943, Mr 7,38:2
Roberts, Percy W Dr, 1937, N 9,23:1
Roberts, Peter Mrs, 1953, Ja 24,15:3
Roberts, Philip, 1943, Mr 25,21:5
Roberts, Phill T Jr, 1960, S 1,27:4
Roberts, Porter A, 1952, Mr 14,23:1
Roberts, Preston A, 1959, D 30,21:2
Roberts, Quincey F Mrs, 1942, Jl 18,13:3
Roberts, R Lloyd, 1961, D 19,29:5
Roberts, Ralph E, 1957, Je 23,85:1
Roberts, Rankin H, 1939, Je 13,23:6
Roberts, Raymond, 1948, O 20,29:1
Roberts, Raymond M Sr, 1954, Ap 15,29:5
Roberts, Raymond P, 1924, My 8,19:4
Roberts, Reginald E, 1946, D 6,23:2
Roberts, Richard, 1945, Ap 12,23:3
Roberts, Richard B, 1949, F 18,23:3; 1952, S 22,23:3
Roberts, Richard E, 1953, O 7,29:4
Roberts, Richard H, 1968, O 8,47:3
Roberts, Richard L, 1946, Mr 12,25:1; 1956, Jl 30,42:2
Roberts, Richard S, 1907, Je 2,7:5
Roberts, Richards Mrs, 1943, Jl 9,17:2
Roberts, Robert, 1939, F 25,15:5
Roberts, Robert F, 1940, My 16,23:3
Roberts, Rollin W, 1950, N 20,25:3
Roberts, Ronald Mrs, 1962, My 30,19:4
Roberts, Ross E, 1960, Je 4,23:6
Roberts, Roy A (funl, F 28,34:3), 1967, F 24,35:1
Roberts, Roy A Mrs, 1952, Ap 29,27:4
Roberts, Russell J, 1950, Ag 20,77:1
Roberts, Sam E, 1966, Jl 20,41:3
Roberts, Samuel A, 1953, Ja 29,28:6
Roberts, Samuel Judson, 1913, Mr 24,11:5
Roberts, Selwyn W, 1939, Mr 10,23:5
Roberts, Seth B, 1947, Jl 30,21:4
Roberts, Sidney, 1951, Jl 5,25:5
Roberts, Sigfrid, 1939, Ja 14,4:4
Roberts, Spencer, 1958, Ap 28,23:4
Roberts, Stacy L, 1946, O 4,23:1
Roberts, Stanley, 1952, Je 5,31:3
Roberts, Stanley D, 1945, Je 23,13:2
Roberts, Stephen R, 1944, D 3,58:8
Roberts, Stewart R, 1941, Ap 15,23:3
Roberts, T, 1928, D 15,19:5
Roberts, T C, 1928, S 29,19:4
Roberts, Theodore Goodridge, 1953, F 25,27:3
Roberts, Thomas B Sr, 1966, Ja 10,25:2
Roberts, Thomas C, 1950, Je 29,29:2
Roberts, Thomas Mrs, 1959, My 12,35:5
Roberts, Thomas S, 1946, Ap 21,46:1
Roberts, Timothy H Mrs, 1919, F 19,13:3
Roberts, Tobias L, 1956, N 21,27:5
Roberts, Vance C, 1942, F 5,21:2
Roberts, Vincent, 1953, S 2,25:3
Roberts, W Adolph, 1962, S 17,31:3
Roberts, W Blair, 1964, Ap 25,29:2
Roberts, W C Rev, 1903, N 28,9:4
Roberts, W F, 1938, F 11,23:3
Roberts, W M, 1946, Ap 4,25:4
Roberts, W M Col, 1881, Jl 31,2:7
Roberts, Walter, 1947, Je 3,19:5
Roberts, Walter C, 1966, Ja 6,27:3
Roberts, Walter F, 1958, Ja 22,27:3
Roberts, Walter L, 1953, Mr 29,92:1; 1953, N 1,87:1
Roberts, Waters D, 1939, D 10,23:5
Roberts, Weldon, 1945, Mr 26,19:5
Roberts, Wilfred S, 1954, F 26,20:5
Roberts, Willard A, 1942, Jl 26,30:7
Roberts, Willard H, 1950, My 9,29:3
Roberts, William, 1940, Ap 11,25:2; 1948, F 13,21:4; 1952, Mr 5,29:4; 1965, Ag 18,35:5
Roberts, William A, 1945, Ja 5,15:6; 1955, Ap 13,29:1; 1966, Ag 3,37:4
Roberts, William C, 1873, D 11,3:3
RobertS, William C, 1941, N 23,51:5
Roberts, William C, 1947, Je 24,23:3
Roberts, William C Mrs, 1956, O 15,25:5
Roberts, William E, 1944, Ja 3,21:3; 1950, Ag 30,32:2
Roberts, William F, 1947, Je 10,27:2
Roberts, William G, 1938, Ja 23,II,8:8
Roberts, William H, 1940, D 20,25:1; 1943, O 19,19:5; 1944, D 2,13:5; 1946, Jl 30,23:5; 1946, S 29,62:1; 1948, Ag 3,25:3; 1961, My 31,33:3
Roberts, William H Jr, 1958, O 26,88:8; 1963, Jl 1,29:3
Roberts, William H Mrs, 1945, S 28,21:6; 1955, N 25, 27:1
Roberts, William H Sr, 1937, O 17,II,8:8
Roberts, William Henry Dr, 1920, Je 27,18:2
Roberts, William J, 1941, Je 9,19:3; 1944, Mr 5,36:6
Roberts, William M, 1945, Mr 7,22:2; 1949, Mr 17,25:2
Roberts, William N, 1943, Mr 12,17:3
Roberts, William P, 1945, O 25,21:2
Roberts, William R, 1949, Ja 3,23:1
Roberts, Willys H, 1942, S 17,25:2
Roberts, Winfred H, 1946, My 23,21:4
Roberts, Wolcott, 1951, Ag 29,25:4
Roberts-Horsfield, William C, 1950, Jl 29,13:1
Roberts y Fernandez, Hugo, 1948, Je 6,73:1
Roberts y Terry, Mauricio L (Torrehermosa, Marquis de), 1940, F 19,17:3
Robertsen, John, 1873, Jl 7,4:7
Robertshaw, George A, 1965, F 15,27:3
Robertson, A, 1931, Jl 2,27:1
Robertson, A C, 1942, Mr 17,22:3
Robertson, A H, 1930, Jl 14,19:4
Robertson, A Heaton, 1924, Ag 7,15:5
Robertson, A J, 1948, O 31,88:6
Robertson, A James, 1960, Ja 21,31:2
Robertson, A L Chief Justice, 1868, D 20,5:3
Robertson, Agnes, 1916, N 7,11:4
Robertson, Alastair D, 1949, N 20,95:2
Robertson, Albert, 1919, My 4,22:6
Robertson, Albert D, 1955, Ag 25,23:6
Robertson, Alexander, 1923, Ap 8,6:3; 1946, Je 20,2
Robertson, Alexander G M, 1947, Ag 22,15:3
Robertson, Alexander W, 1943, Je 21,17:4
Robertson, Alfred J, 1958, Mr 2,89:1
Robertson, Alma L, 1954, Jl 4,30:7
Robertson, Andrew, 1908, F 17,7:4
Robertson, Andrew W, 1965, D 19,84:4
Robertson, Angus W, 1947, O 24,23:4
Robertson, Arthur L, 1942, Mr 31,21:2
Robertson, Averell S, 1941, Ja 17,17:4
Robertson, Benjamin F, 1943, Jl 3,13:4
Robertson, Beridge L, 1953, S 8,32:3
Robertson, Beverly H, 1910, N 14,9:4
Robertson, Charles, 1941, F 5,19:4
Robertson, Charles A, 1945, Je 25,17:4
Robertson, Charles C, 1965, O 18,35:1
Robertson, Charles E, 1938, F 26,15:6
Robertson, Charles L Sr, 1950, F 23,27:1
Robertson, Charles M Sr, 1961, Ja 24,29:4
Robertson, Charles Mrs, 1947, Ag 6,23:5
Robertson, Charles R, 1948, Mr 2,23:4; 1951, F 19,2
Robertson, Clarence R, 1951, O 30,29:1
Robertson, Claude O, 1953, Jl 14,27:3
Robertson, D Curtis, 1946, N 22,24:2
Robertson, Dan R, 1959, Je 7,86:3
Robertson, Daniel W, 1939, D 16,17:5
Robertson, David, 1918, Ag 15,11:1
Robertson, David A, 1961, Jl 16,68:3
Robertson, David A Mrs, 1941, N 5,23:5
Robertson, David B, 1961, S 28,41:3
Robertson, David E, 1944, F 20,36:2
Robertson, David R, 1961, Jl 14,23:5
Robertson, David S, 1958, Ja 4,15:2
Robertson, Dennis, 1963, Ap 22,27:3
Robertson, Douglas, 1957, Jl 22,19:4
Robertson, E Arnot (Mrs H Turner), 1961, S 24,8
Robertson, E J, 1960, Ap 9,23:5
Robertson, E V (Edw V), 1963, Ap 17,41:5
Robertson, E W, 1928, N 21,29:5
Robertson, Earl E, 1950, O 11,33:5
Robertson, Ed Shafto, 1871, O 23,3:7
Robertson, Edmund (Baron Lochee), 1911, S 14,9
Robertson, Edward, 1925, Ag 2,5:4; 1964, My 1,35
Robertson, Edward A, 1950, My 24,29:4
Robertson, Edward L, 1954, Jl 4,31:2
Robertson, Edward L Justice, 1937, O 17,II,8:8
Robertson, Edwin E, 1951, S 19,31:3
Robertson, Elizabeth, 1952, Jl 14,17:5
Robertson, Eva A Mrs, 1939, Je 24,17:6
Robertson, F H, 1928, Ap 21,17:5
Robertson, Frances (Mrs W Young), 1942, Jl 1,2
Robertson, Frank A, 1949, My 13,23:3
Robertson, Frank C, 1944, Ja 10,17:1
Robertson, Frank H, 1938, Mr 26,15:2
Robertson, Frank J, 1941, O 16,21:2; 1958, N 15,2
Robertson, Frank W, 1938, Ag 28,32:7
Robertson, Fred, 1967, O 5,50:2
Robertson, Frederick, 1968, F 15,43:4
Robertson, Frederick A, 1938, Ag 16,19:5
Robertson, Frederick Sr, 1943, Jl 13,21:4
Robertson, Frederick Y (por), 1938, Jl 13,21:3
Robertson, G Scott, 1948, D 23,19:4
Robertson, Gardner E (por), 1948, Mr 31,25:3
Robertson, George D, 1956, D 31,13:3
Robertson, George F, 1961, D 11,31:5
Robertson, George G, 1948, D 21,25:4
Robertson, George H, 1955, Jl 5,29:1
Robertson, George H Jr, 1945, D 8,17:5
Robertson, George Sir, 1916, Ja 5,13:8
Robertson, George V, 1954, Je 4,23:2
Robertson, Gordon F, 1964, F 8,23:5
Robertson, H Marshall, 1959, My 1,29:2
Robertson, H P, 1961, Ag 28,25:2
Robertson, H W, 1939, F 13,15:4
Robertson, Harold E, 1946, Mr 9,14:2
Robertson, Harold H, 1950, S 20,31:4
Robertson, Harrison, 1939, N 12,48:6
Robertson, Harrison M, 1958, O 27,27:5
Robertson, Harvey H, 1938, Jl 14,21:6
Robertson, Heaton R, 1953, My 10,89:1
Robertson, Helena Mrs, 1952, D 18,29:5
Robertson, Henry, 1881, Ap 11,5:4
Robertson, Henry M Mrs, 1950, Jl 21,19:5
Robertson, Herbert H, 1954, Ap 22,29:5
Robertson, Hezekiah D, 1870, S 20,4:7
Robertson, Horace C H, 1960, Ap 29,31:3
Robertson, Howard, 1963, My 6,29:4
Robertson, Howard E, 1947, Jl 7,17:3
Robertson, Hugh J, 1947, F 18,25:2
Robertson, Hugh S, 1951, Je 25,19:4
Robertson, Hugh Wilfred, 1924, N 3,17:4
Robertson, J B A, 1938, Mr 8,19:2
Robertson, J C G, 1882, D 5,5:7
Robertson, J C Rev, 1882, Jl 11,2:4
Robertson, J D, 1931, Ag 21,17:1
Robertson, J Milton, 1904, F 6,9:6
Robertson, J W, 1930, Mr 21,27:3

Robertson, J Walter, 1953, N 12,43:5
Robertson, James A, 1967, Je 2,41:2
Robertson, James B, 1942, D 15,27:1
Robertson, James F, 1942, My 19,19:5
Robertson, James F Mrs, 1946, Je 21,23:4
Robertson, James Ferguson Capt, 1922, Ag 18,13:3
Robertson, James L, 1942, F 25,19:1; 1968, N 11,47:3
Robertson, James T, 1952, O 20,23:4
Robertson, James W, 1943, N 6,13:3
Robertson, Jason N, 1942, Ap 8,19:4
Robertson, Jeffrey J, 1948, S 27,23:3
Robertson, Jessie, 1944, D 6,23:1
Robertson, Jessie S, 1943, D 29,17:1
Robertson, John, 1941, Ja 7,23:4; 1941, F 20,19:5; 1943, S 22,23:3; 1948, D 15,35:7; 1952, My 15,31:4
Robertson, John A C, 1962, My 29,31:3
Robertson, John C, 1956, F 26,88:4
Robertson, John D, 1950, O 17,26:5
Robertson, John D Mrs, 1950, O 17,26:5
Robertson, John Forbes, 1903, F 26,3:5
Robertson, John McK, 1959, Je 12,27:1
Robertson, John Ross, 1918, Je 1,11:8
Robertson, John S, 1964, N 8,88:6
Robertson, John T, 1966, Ap 16,33:4
Robertson, John W, 1957, O 14,27:1
Robertson, Joseph A, 1939, S 17,48:8
Robertson, Josephine, 1942, Ap 20,21:4
Robertson, Judson H, 1962, Ag 25,19:4
Robertson, Julia M, 1944, Ag 8,17:4
Robertson, Julius (est, O 30,9:5), 1914, O 22,11:4
Robertson, L F, 1882, F 11,8:1
Robertson, Lawson N, 1951, Ja 23,27:5
Robertson, Lloyd P, 1952, My 6,29:6
Robertson, Louis J (por), 1947, Ja 25,17:4
Robertson, Louis J Mrs, 1962, S 18,39:2
Robertson, MacPherson (por), 1945, Ag 21,21:2
Robertson, Malcolm A, 1951, Ap 24,29:3
Robertson, Margaret C, 1954, Je 1,27:5
Robertson, Margaret M Mrs, 1941, S 12,22:3
Robertson, Marion C, 1953, N 21,13:4
Robertson, Matthew H, 1903, D 20,7:6
Robertson, Merle, 1965, S 25,6:1
Robertson, Nathan W, 1950, Ap 5,34:2
Robertson, Nathaniel G Mrs, 1949, Je 25,13:3
Robertson, Norman A, 1968, Jl 18,33:2
Robertson, Norman T, 1960, Jl 21,27:5
Robertson, Orlo L Mrs, 1964, Ag 18,31:4
Robertson, Oswald H, 1966, Mr 25,41:4
Robertson, Peter, 1943, O 15,19:1
Robertson, Peter B, 1953, O 10,17:3
Robertson, Phil W, 1949, F 25,23:1
Robertson, Purcell C, 1952, Ap 9,31:4
Robertson, R C, 1942, O 2,3:3
Robertson, R Ritchie, 1939, N 6,23:6
Robertson, Rae, 1956, N 6,35:2
Robertson, Ralph K, 1964, O 6,39:2
Robertson, Reuben B Jr (funl, Mr 16,53:3; est appr, S 14,22:4), 1960, Mr 14,10:3
Robertson, Reuben Mrs, 1958, S 21,86:5
Robertson, Richard A 3d, 1959, Ag 13,27:5
Robertson, Robert, 1937, Ja 25,19:1; 1949, Ap 29,23:6
Robertson, Robert B, 1938, Jl 13,21:5
Robertson, Robert C, 1945, F 21,19:5
Robertson, Robert H, 1940, D 6,23:4
Robertson, Robert Henderson, 1913, Mr 11,11:3; 1919, Je 5,13:2
Robertson, Robert K, 1946, S 17,7:3
Robertson, Robert S, 1947, N 27,32:2; 1955, My 31, 27:4
Robertson, Ross F, 1939, O 21,15:5
Robertson, Roval W, 1938, Ja 10,17:5
Robertson, Sam A, 1938, Ag 24,21:6
Robertson, Samuel L, 1947, D 16,33:2
Robertson, Samuel N Dr, 1937, O 4,21:6
Robertson, Sherman B Mrs, 1944, Ap 10,19:5
Robertson, Steven Mrs, 1945, Ag 6,15:4
Robertson, Stuart, 1940, My 2,23:2
Robertson, T W, 1871, F 5,1:7
Robertson, Tate MacE Jr, 1963, Jl 14,61:2
Robertson, Thomas, 1905, Ap 3,2:5
Robertson, Thomas A, 1950, F 19,79:3
Robertson, Thomas K, 1938, Mr 6,II,8:2
Robertson, Thomas M, 1962, Ag 3,23:2
Robertson, Thomas W Mrs, 1912, S 4,11:4
Robertson, Tom, 1950, Ja 2,23:5
Robertson, Victor A, 1939, D 23,15:5
Robertson, Victor A Mrs, 1939, D 23,15:5
Robertson, Victor J, 1940, Je 11,25:2
Robertson, Victoria G Mrs, 1947, Ja 8,23:2
Robertson, W A, 1929, Ja 19,17:4
Robertson, W A Mrs, 1964, N 10,47:2
Robertson, W G, 1950, S 10,92:5
Robertson, W Graham, 1948, S 6,13:6
Robertson, W H, 1898, D 7,7:2
Robertson, W Lowell, 1937, Ja 3,II,8:4
Robertson, W R, 1941, Mr 17,17:2
Robertson, W Sir, 1933, F 3,1:2
Robertson, W Spencer, 1958, N 28,30:6
Robertson, Walter K, 1937, S 1,19:5
Robertson, Walter M, 1954, N 23,35:2
Robertson, Wesley Mrs, 1953, O 5,27:6
Robertson, Wilfrid H, 1962, My 16,41:2
Robertson, William, 1949, Ap 2,15:3
Robertson, William D, 1951, N 26,25:1; 1955, S 19, 25:4
Robertson, William E, 1956, Mr 11,88:2
Robertson, William F, 1938, D 22,22:1; 1941, Mr 1, 15:3; 1941, N 9,55:2
Robertson, William G Dr, 1924, Je 22,25:3
Robertson, William G Sir, 1937, Je 29,22:2
Robertson, William H, 1859, Je 6,4:4; 1941, Je 12, 24:2; 1941, N 1,15:4; 1942, Ap 19,43:2; 1944, O 17, 23:1; 1950, N 17,27:5
Robertson, William J, 1937, Ja 27,21:4; 1941, Ap 3, 23:4; 1955, Jl 20,27:6
Robertson, William L, 1949, D 26,29:4
Robertson, William P Mrs, 1958, Ap 9,33:2
Robertz, Charles F, 1945, Jl 11,11:5
Robertz, Henry J, 1947, N 14,23:3
Robeson, Andrew, 1939, Ag 7,15:5
Robeson, Benjamin, 1963, D 2,37:5
Robeson, Benjamin C Mrs, 1957, D 9,35:3
Robeson, Edward J Mrs, 1954, Je 13,88:2
Robeson, Elizabeth W Mrs, 1940, Ap 6,17:5
Robeson, Frank K Mrs, 1949, Je 3,25:4
Robeson, Frank R, 1916, D 28,9:5
Robeson, Harold B, 1960, O 7,35:3
Robeson, Henry Bellows Adm, 1914, Jl 17,9:7
Robeson, Irving S, 1940, Jl 11,19:5
Robeson, Paul Mrs (Eslanda), 1965, D 14,43:4
Robeson, Roscoe J, 1943, O 21,27:1
Robeson, W P, 1881, S 17,5:5
Robeson, William Rotch, 1922, N 23,21:6
Robey, George, 1954, N 30,29:2
Robey, Louis W, 1968, Jl 1,33:1
Robey, William H, 1954, F 24,25:3
Robfogel, Jacob, 1942, My 7,19:4
Robi, Armand, 1925, S 5,13:5
Robichaud, Walter, 1955, N 30,33:4
Robicheau, John L P, 1948, Mr 2,23:6
Robicsek, Hans, 1951, O 26,23:4
Robiczek, Stanley, 1958, Ja 26,88:3
Robideau, Alex, 1950, F 14,25:4
Robider, Dorothea, 1948, Mr 20,13:4
Robie, Charles W, 1949, D 11,93:1
Robie, Edward Dr, 1917, S 24,13:6
Robie, Frederick, 1964, Je 6,23:6
Robie, Frederick Ex-Gov, 1912, F 3,11:4
Robilant, Mario N di, 1943, Jl 30,15:5
Robiliart, Herman, 1963, O 25,31:4
Robillard, Ambolina H Mrs, 1953, Ag 4,21:5
Robillard, Basil Mrs, 1958, Je 24,31:4
Robillard, Charles, 1943, My 22,13:5
Robillard, Gregory L, 1949, Jl 3,26:8
Robillard, Peter A, 1939, F 1,21:5
Robilotti, Joseph G, 1953, Mr 28,17:5
Robin, Edwin J, 1965, Mr 28,92:5
Robin, Mado, 1960, D 11,88:6
Robin, Maurice, 1942, F 8,48:4
Robin, Max, 1967, Jl 11,37:2
Robin, Morris J, 1965, F 14,88:7
Robin, Nathaniel H Mrs, 1961, N 13,31:4
Robin, Phil F, 1940, F 27,21:3
Robin, Raymond, 1954, S 27,21:1
Robina, Florrie, 1953, Je 11,29:1
Robineau, Simon P, 1952, D 10,35:3
Robins, Adolph, 1950, D 20,32:4
Robins, Augustine W (por), 1940, Je 17,15:3
Robins, Barth, 1960, Ja 3,88:5
Robins, Charles R, 1948, O 18,23:3
Robins, Charles R Mrs, 1962, My 19,27:4
Robins, David Mrs, 1958, Mr 22,17:1
Robins, E L C, 1933, Ap 28,17:3
Robins, Edward, 1943, My 22,13:4
Robins, Edward H, 1955, Jl 28,23:3
Robins, Edward M, 1946, Ag 5,21:5
Robins, Elizabeth, 1952, My 9,23:5
Robins, Francis Finch, 1915, S 5,11:4
Robins, Henry R, 1957, Ag 17,15:2
Robins, Jessie S Mrs, 1948, N 6,13:3
Robins, John A, 1959, Jl 11,19:6
Robins, John B, 1940, Ja 8,15:2
Robins, John N, 1923, Mr 27,19:5
Robins, Joseph H, 1961, My 8,35:3
Robins, Kingman Nott, 1923, F 6,19:4
Robins, Louis, 1964, Je 20,25:4
Robins, Max B, 1952, S 11,31:5
Robins, Ralph M, 1951, N 21,25:4
Robins, Raymond Mrs (por), 1945, F 22,27:1
Robins, Robert, 1956, Mr 3,19:6
Robins, Thomas, 1941, Ap 4,21:3; 1957, N 5,31:1
Robins, Thomas E, 1962, Jl 23,21:4
Robins, Thomas Jr Mrs, 1962, Jl 13,23:4
Robins, Thomas Mrs, 1952, S 16,29:4; 1958, My 1,31:4
Robins, Wright, 1882, Mr 30,5:5
Robinsky, Joseph A Sr, 1958, S 28,88:3
Robinson, A G, 1932, Ag 31,17:3
Robinson, A H, 1950, Jl 30,60:4
Robinson, A J Mrs, 1878, Mr 27,10:4
Robinson, Abraham, 1954, O 21,27:3
Robinson, Adeline K, 1943, F 6,13:6
Robinson, Alanson, 1870, My 25,4:7
Robinson, Albert Alonzo, 1918, N 8,15:3
Robinson, Albert G, 1947, Je 26,23:4
Robinson, Albert S, 1952, S 11,31:1
Robinson, Alex, 1938, Je 12,39:3
Robinson, Alex J, 1952, My 27,27:4
Robinson, Alex Mrs, 1903, F 6,1:6
Robinson, Alexander Indian Chief, 1872, Ap 25,1:6
Robinson, Alfred B, 1941, Ja 5,44:4
Robinson, Alice W Mrs, 1952, Jl 5,15:7
Robinson, Allen M, 1947, Je 16,21:5
Robinson, Allyn P Mrs, 1967, S 28,57:3
Robinson, Allyn P Sr, 1959, S 19,23:5
Robinson, Alonzo C, 1957, Ja 10,29:2
Robinson, Alson H Mrs, 1958, Ja 10,26:2
Robinson, Alvin, 1968, Jl 13,27:3
Robinson, Andrew J, 1922, N 10,17:2
Robinson, Andrew R Dr, 1924, Jl 10,21:6
Robinson, Andrew Rose Dr, 1925, N 3,25:5
Robinson, Anna, 1917, O 6,13:6
Robinson, Anna J, 1951, F 6,27:5
Robinson, Annie E Mrs, 1942, Je 3,23:1
Robinson, Archer T, 1960, My 7,23:4
Robinson, Archibald R, 1946, Ag 23,19:3
Robinson, Arthur A, 1955, Ap 23,19:2
Robinson, Arthur E, 1943, Mr 16,19:1
Robinson, Arthur G, 1967, F 1,40:1
Robinson, Arthur G Mrs, 1957, S 11,33:2
Robinson, Arthur J, 1946, My 8,25:2
Robinson, Arthur M, 1942, S 24,27:2
Robinson, Arthur P, 1944, O 1,46:2
Robinson, Arthur R, 1961, My 18,23:3
Robinson, Austin, 1960, Jl 20,29:3
Robinson, Austin F, 1938, My 17,23:1
Robinson, Avery, 1965, My 13,37:2
Robinson, Avery Mrs, 1964, Ja 12,92:4
Robinson, Azariah, 1951, Ag 11,11:4
Robinson, Baylor, 1966, My 9,39:2
Robinson, Benjamin, 1968, Ja 28,76:3
Robinson, Benjamin F, 1939, N 2,23:1
Robinson, Bertrand, 1949, O 31,25:3; 1959, F 5,31:4
Robinson, Beverley Dr, 1924, Je 22,25:1
Robinson, Beverley Mrs, 1940, My 23,23:5
Robinson, Beverley R, 1951, S 22,17:2
Robinson, Beverly, 1876, F 17,1:6
Robinson, Bill (Bojangles), 1949, N 26,1:2
Robinson, Boardman, 1952, S 7,84:3
Robinson, Bradbury N, 1949, Mr 11,25:3
Robinson, Bud, 1942, N 4,24:2
Robinson, C W, 1944, Jl 28,13:5
Robinson, Catherine A Mrs, 1953, Ap 11,17:1
Robinson, Chalfant Mrs, 1957, Je 27,25:3
Robinson, Chalfont, 1947, Ja 2,28:3
Robinson, Charles, 1937, Ag 30,21:4; 1965, N 14,89:1
Robinson, Charles A, 1946, Ap 14,46:7
Robinson, Charles A Jr, 1965, F 24,41:2
Robinson, Charles A Mrs, 1944, My 31,19:6
Robinson, Charles Augustus, 1909, S 28,9:7
Robinson, Charles E, 1944, D 28,20:2; 1951, F 14, 29:3; 1961, Ja 25,33:1
Robinson, Charles E Mrs, 1948, Ja 30,23:2
Robinson, Charles F Sr, 1952, Ag 27,27:1
Robinson, Charles G, 1940, My 15,25:4
Robinson, Charles H, 1940, F 25,39:1; 1940, Ap 14, 45:2
Robinson, Charles K, 1954, Jl 9,17:4
Robinson, Charles K (Sept 23), 1965, O 11,61:4
Robinson, Charles L, 1942, My 9,13:5; 1943, D 6,23:5; 1951, Ag 18,11:6
Robinson, Charles L Mrs, 1951, Ja 4,29:4
Robinson, Charles Leonard Frost Col (funl, Je 8,9:6), 1916, Jl 7,11:6
Robinson, Charles M, 1924, D 7,7:3; 1950, Ja 24,31:4
Robinson, Charles M Mrs (por), 1948, Mr 10,27:3
Robinson, Charles Mulford, 1917, D 31,7:6
Robinson, Charles P, 1962, F 7,37:3
Robinson, Charles S, 1945, Jl 24,23:5
Robinson, Charles W, 1939, Ja 10,19:4
Robinson, Charles W Mrs, 1968, Ap 1,45:1
Robinson, Chester C, 1956, Mr 27,35:4
Robinson, Chris C, 1948, Mr 2,23:4
Robinson, Clare M, 1941, Je 29,33:2
Robinson, Clarence A (left no will), 1954, Mr 9,30:3
Robinson, Clarence W, 1938, Ap 16,13:6
Robinson, Clark S, 1947, My 24,15:3
Robinson, Clarke, 1962, Ja 19,31:2
Robinson, Claude E, 1961, Ag 8,29:1
Robinson, Clifford Mrs, 1967, O 10,47:3
Robinson, Clinton F, 1962, Ap 11,43:3
Robinson, Coleman T, 1872, My 4,2:4
Robinson, Cyrilius L, 1907, N 24,9:6
Robinson, Daisy O, 1942, Mr 14,15:3
Robinson, David, 1940, D 7,17:5; 1952, Ag 27,27:1; 1958, O 29,35:4
Robinson, David Jr, 1947, N 7,23:4
Robinson, David L, 1913, Ja 25,15:5
Robinson, David M, 1952, Jl 8,27:4; 1958, Ja 3,21:4
Robinson, David Taft, 1909, O 23,11:1
Robinson, David W, 1948, F 2,20:3
Robinson, DeLange, 1940, D 1,61:2
Robinson, Dewey R, 1950, D 13,35:3
Robinson, Dlorence V, 1937, Ap 1,23:2
Robinson, Douglas, 1918, S 13,11:3; 1964, My 31,77:3
Robinson, Douglas Mrs, 1906, Ag 24,7:6
Robinson, Duane L, 1965, Ap 30,35:4
Robinson, Duncan S, 1956, N 23,27:4
Robinson, Dwight E Mrs, 1948, Ja 16,21:2
Robinson, Dwight N, 1941, O 31,23:5

Robinson, Dwight P, 1955, Mr 18,27:1
Robinson, E A, 1935, Ap 6,15:1
Robinson, E B, 1880, O 22,5:3
Robinson, E C, 1882, N 12,9:2
Robinson, Earl B, 1949, My 27,21:4
Robinson, Earl H, 1958, D 22,2:4
Robinson, Earl Mrs, 1940, F 17,13:2
Robinson, Edgar M, 1951, Ap 10,28:3
Robinson, Edna A Mrs, 1939, Jl 21,19:2
Robinson, Edward, 1863, Ja 29,8:5
Robinson, Edward A, 1939, Ap 5,25:5
Robinson, Edward H, 1962, Jl 4,21:2
Robinson, Edward H Mrs, 1953, D 11,31:3
Robinson, Edward L, 1943, Ja 17,44:3
Robinson, Edward Moore, 1910, Ja 5,11:4
Robinson, Edward Mrs, 1952, My 26,23:2
Robinson, Edward N, 1945, Mr 11,40:2
Robinson, Edward V Mrs, 1943, F 21,32:7
Robinson, Edward Van Dyke Dr, 1915, D 11,13:6
Robinson, Edward W, 1939, Ja 11,19:3; 1942, My 6, 19:1
Robinson, Edward W Mrs, 1940, D 14,17:2
Robinson, Edwin M, 1946, S 21,15:4
Robinson, Edwin S, 1945, D 8,17:4
Robinson, Edwin S Mrs, 1956, N 12,29:4
Robinson, Eliot H, 1942, N 23,23:1
Robinson, Elizabeth, 1967, N 21,48:1
Robinson, Elizabeth E Mrs, 1947, Ap 3,25:5
Robinson, Elizabeth M Mrs, 1941, N 13,27:1
Robinson, Elizabeth Mrs, 1903, Mr 31,5:4
Robinson, Elkanah S, 1946, Jl 6,15:3
Robinson, Ella A Mrs, 1952, F 4,17:2
Robinson, Ella Mrs, 1942, F 18,19:1
Robinson, Ellis J, 1958, O 6,31:2
Robinson, Elsie, 1956, S 9,84:5
Robinson, Ernest R, 1953, My 28,23:3
Robinson, Ernest W, 1948, Mr 29,21:3
Robinson, Esther L Mrs, 1938, O 28,23:4
Robinson, Ethel B, 1947, Ag 2,13:3
Robinson, Etta W Mrs, 1958, Ag 19,27:1
Robinson, Eugene N, 1916, Je 1,11:6
Robinson, Everett, 1945, N 5,19:4
Robinson, Everett S, 1943, Jl 10,13:5
Robinson, F C, 1927, Ja 6,27:4
Robinson, F deLancey, 1954, Jl 31,13:6
Robinson, F E, 1957, My 4,21:4
Robinson, F L (Yankee), 1884, S 5,4:6
Robinson, Faye, 1948, S 2,23:4
Robinson, Fielding, 1967, D 31,44:6
Robinson, Forrest, 1924, Ja 8,23:3
Robinson, Francis, 1955, Ap 18,23:5
Robinson, Francis D, 1938, N 13,45:2
Robinson, Francis H, 1944, Ag 2,15:4; 1960, Ag 8,21:4
Robinson, Francis M, 1942, N 4,23:3
Robinson, Francis Mrs, 1957, S 8,84:7; 1959, S 23,39:2
Robinson, Frank B, 1948, O 20,29:1
Robinson, Frank Mrs, 1947, O 21,10:5
Robinson, Frank N, 1949, Ag 24,25:4
Robinson, Frank W, 1948, D 11,15:2
Robinson, Franklin C Prof, 1910, My 26,9:5
Robinson, Franklin Mrs, 1945, O 5,23:4
Robinson, Franklin W, 1946, S 17,7:2
Robinson, Fred N, 1966, Jl 22,31:1
Robinson, Fred R Maj, 1923, Jl 23,13:3
Robinson, Frederic H, 1923, Mr 16,17:4
Robinson, Frederic J Mrs, 1962, N 7,39:5
Robinson, Frederick A, 1938, F 12,15:3
Robinson, Frederick B (por), 1941, O 20,17:1
Robinson, Frederick G Mrs, 1949, Je 29,27:3
Robinson, Frederick Oliver (Marquis of Ripon), 1923, S 23,7:5
Robinson, G B, 1880, N 29,1:3
Robinson, G Canby, 1960, S 1,27:1
Robinson, Gardiner W, 1942, My 2,13:6
Robinson, Genevieve, 1951, Ag 28,24:2
Robinson, George, 1940, Mr 6,23:5
Robinson, George B, 1963, S 25,43:4
Robinson, George C, 1957, O 27,87:1
Robinson, George E, 1952, Ag 5,19:2
Robinson, George H, 1906, Jl 5,7:6; 1943, Mr 2,19:1; 1951, O 29,23:4
Robinson, George Hazard, 1919, S 6,11:4
Robinson, George J (por), 1940, My 23,23:4
Robinson, George J Mrs, 1967, Ap 29,35:4
Robinson, George L, 1943, Ap 22,23:5; 1958, D 18,2:5
Robinson, George L Mrs, 1940, F 4,40:4
Robinson, George M, 1937, F 13,13:2; 1959, Jl 31,23:4
Robinson, George R, 1955, F 5,15:6
Robinson, George S, 1953, Jl 15,25:5
Robinson, George W, 1947, O 27,21:5; 1951, D 13,33:1
Robinson, Gerald T Mrs, 1963, Ag 4,81:1
Robinson, Gerson, 1940, D 21,17:5
Robinson, Gilbert P Col, 1908, Je 24,7:5
Robinson, Gilbert W, 1950, My 8,23:6
Robinson, Gov of Vermont, 1860, My 1,1:3
Robinson, Grant, 1951, S 7,29:3
Robinson, Guy N, 1960, O 28,31:4
Robinson, Guy T, 1953, N 25,23:3
Robinson, H Ridgely, 1943, S 11,13:2
Robinson, H Sir, 1930, D 22,19:5
Robinson, H W, 1879, Ap 8,4:7
Robinson, H Wheeler, 1945, My 15,19:5
Robinson, Hamilton Mrs, 1940, D 15,60:2
Robinson, Harold B, 1966, Ap 14,35:6
Robinson, Harold M, 1939, Mr 5,48:4; 1952, Ap 3,35:1
Robinson, Harriet Duer, 1921, Jl 12,13:3
Robinson, Harris C, 1941, S 23,23:3
Robinson, Harry A Mrs, 1957, N 23,19:6
Robinson, Harry E, 1938, O 18,26:4
Robinson, Harry H, 1950, Ap 30,102:6
Robinson, Harry H Sr, 1955, D 13,40:1
Robinson, Harry L, 1946, S 9,9:4
Robinson, Harry L Mrs, 1947, My 2,22:3; 1960, Mr 20,87:1
Robinson, Harry S, 1950, F 20,25:1
Robinson, Harry T, 1954, O 6,25:5
Robinson, Harry W, 1953, N 11,31:4
Robinson, Helen Ring, 1923, Jl 11,19:6
Robinson, Henry A, 1950, Ap 13,29:2
Robinson, Henry C, 1905, Ap 5,9:5
Robinson, Henry Douglas Rev, 1913, D 19,11:4
Robinson, Henry H, 1953, Ja 11,91:3
Robinson, Henry Hollister Prof, 1925, O 21,23:3
Robinson, Henry J, 1952, Ag 1,17:3
Robinson, Henry M (por), 1937, N 4,25:4
Robinson, Henry M, 1949, S 1,21:3; 1961, Ja 14,23:2
Robinson, Henry P, 1958, My 4,88:7
Robinson, Henry S Sr, 1949, D 23,21:2
Robinson, Henry U, 1939, Mr 22,23:3
Robinson, Herbert, 1960, D 13,31:4
Robinson, Herbert A, 1937, Je 9,25:1
Robinson, Herbert G, 1948, Je 20,62:4
Robinson, Herbert H, 1954, Ap 23,27:3
Robinson, Herbert L, 1966, Ag 23,39:4
Robinson, Herbert S Mrs, 1952, Jl 28,15:2
Robinson, Herman (funl, My 12,21:2), 1918, My 11, 13:8
Robinson, Hilbert B, 1959, Je 1,27:3
Robinson, Hiram S, 1952, O 3,23:2
Robinson, Holton D (por), 1945, My 8,19:1
Robinson, Holton D Mrs, 1950, N 24,36:2
Robinson, Homer F, 1939, S 8,23:5
Robinson, Horace E, 1944, Ja 12,23:3
Robinson, Horace E Mrs, 1941, Je 28,15:2
Robinson, Howard P, 1950, Ag 25,21:6
Robinson, Howard T, 1942, D 4,25:3
Robinson, Howard W, 1956, Mr 9,23:2
Robinson, Hugh B, 1945, Jl 2,15:4
Robinson, Ida E, 1940, My 21,23:2
Robinson, Ida Mrs, 1938, F 13,13:3; 1958, Mr 5,28:4
Robinson, Ira E, 1951, O 29,23:2
Robinson, Irving E, 1944, Mr 8,19:3
Robinson, J A, 1901, Je 23,7:6; 1933, My 9,17:2
Robinson, J B, 1929, O 31,25:3
Robinson, J C, 1880, F 12,2:5
Robinson, J E Rev, 1903, My 26,9:6
Robinson, J F, 1882, N 2,5:3
Robinson, J H, 1936, F 17,17:3
Robinson, J Millen, 1939, N 15,23:2
Robinson, J Morris, 1938, Je 29,19:3
Robinson, J N, 1878, S 15,2:4
Robinson, J R Sir, 1903, D 2,9:5
Robinson, J Russel, 1963, O 2,42:1
Robinson, J T, 1877, Ap 8,7:1
Robinson, J Thomas, 1964, Ag 6,29:3
Robinson, J William, 1961, N 8,35:2
Robinson, Jack, 1953, Je 23,29:3
Robinson, Jacob A Mrs, 1949, D 2,29:5
Robinson, James A, 1961, Ap 6,33:1
Robinson, James B, 1942, N 6,23:1; 1963, Jl 26,25:4
Robinson, James D, 1948, F 4,23:3
Robinson, James D Jr, 1967, Jl 28,31:2
Robinson, James F, 1963, O 13,46:7
Robinson, James G Mrs, 1949, Jl 9,13:5
Robinson, James J, 1946, S 24,30:3
Robinson, James K, 1908, My 25,7:2
Robinson, James K Sr, 1949, F 28,19:6
Robinson, James P, 1950, Je 9,23:4; 1951, Je 27,29:2
Robinson, James P Lt-Com, 1875, Jl 21,4:6
Robinson, Jenks B, 1955, Jl 26,25:2
Robinson, Jeremiah, 1907, S 8,7:5
Robinson, Jeremiah Potter, 1916, Jl 4,11:5
Robinson, Jesse, 1947, Jl 28,15:5
Robinson, Jesse C, 1943, Ja 26,19:3
Robinson, Jim, 1906, Mr 20,9:7
Robinson, Joel A, 1960, F 13,19:4
Robinson, John, 1925, Ap 10,19:4; 1947, Mr 5,25:4
Robinson, John A, 1938, Mr 25,19:3
Robinson, John B, 1963, Je 22,23:4
Robinson, John Beverly Prof, 1923, N 14,17:5
Robinson, John C, 1944, F 27,38:4; 1944, S 8,19:3; 1954, Mr 28,40:1
Robinson, John E (funl, My 31.15:5), 1924, My 29, 19:6
Robinson, John E, 1924, My 31,15:5; 1946, S 27,23:3
Robinson, John E Bp, 1925, D 15,25:3
Robinson, John Edward Bp, 1922, F 18,13:3
Robinson, John F, 1921, My 1,22:3
Robinson, John G, 1944, Je 4,42:2
Robinson, John H, 1940, F 10,15:2
Robinson, John J, 1950, Je 19,21:3; 1950, Jl 18,29:3; 1952, Mr 14,23:4
Robinson, John J F, 1961, My 12,29:3
Robinson, John L, 1949, O 15,15:4
Robinson, John M, 1912, Ap 1,13:6; 1949, Je 25,13:1
Robinson, John R, 1941, Je 26,23:2; 1950, Ap 9,87:3; 1953, F 20,20:3
Robinson, John R Mrs, 1956, Jl 29,65:1
Robinson, John S Mrs, 1956, Je 10,88:5
Robinson, John T, 1914, S 12,9:5; 1937, N 28,II,8:6; 1945, F 20,19:6
Robinson, John V Mrs, 1949, O 12,30:2
Robinson, John W, 1941, N 28,23:5
Robinson, John W (por), 1947, Je 7,13:3
Robinson, John W, 1958, Ap 13,84:6
Robinson, John W Mrs, 1950, S 15,25:4
Robinson, Jonah L, 1946, N 28,27:6
Robinson, Joseph, 1968, D 28,27:3
Robinson, Joseph A, 1943, My 17,15:6
Robinson, Joseph C, 1938, Jl 5,17:4
Robinson, Joseph H, 1948, Ag 23,17:4
Robinson, Joseph H Mrs, 1952, Ap 28,19:2
Robinson, Joseph J, 1939, My 29,15:5
Robinson, Joseph Peck, 1914, Ag 25,9:6
Robinson, Joseph T Mrs, 1958, Ag 8,19:3
Robinson, Joseph T Sen, 1937, Jl 15,1:8
Robinson, Julia Jr, 1948, Mr 23,25:3
Robinson, Julian M, 1948, Je 29,23:2
Robinson, Julius J Jr, 1950, Je 14,31:5
Robinson, Kenneth A, 1961, D 21,27:4
Robinson, Kenneth O Mrs, 1956, Ag 18,17:2
Robinson, L L, 1945, Ag 15,19:3
Robinson, L T, 1931, N 5,25:3
Robinson, L W Adm, 1903, F 17,9:6
Robinson, Lansing F, 1943, S 24,23:3
Robinson, Lansing R, 1942, Je 26,21:4
Robinson, Lee, 1962, N 3,25:1
Robinson, Leland R, 1966, N 16,47:1
Robinson, Lennox, 1958, O 15,39:2
Robinson, Leonard G (por), 1947, D 12,27:3
Robinson, Lewis B, 1960, Ap 25,29:4
Robinson, Lora W, 1952, Ja 19,15:6
Robinson, Lorenzo, 1879, Ag 9,1:6
Robinson, Louis, 1945, F 25,37:1
Robinson, Louis H, 1957, S 13,23:2
Robinson, Louis H Mrs, 1946, N 17,68:2
Robinson, Louis M Mrs, 1946, D 14,15:6
Robinson, Louis N, 1952, N 26,23:6
Robinson, Lucius, 1882, Je 9,5:4; 1891, Mr 24,4:7
Robinson, Lucius F Sr, 1941, Je 12,23:6
Robinson, Lucius W, 1941, O 20,17:2
Robinson, Lucy N, 1938, N 30,23:2
Robinson, Lydia, 1920, Mr 14,22:1
Robinson, Lyell B, 1961, Jl 17,21:3
Robinson, M C, 1903, Ag 14,7:6
Robinson, Mabel L (mem ser set, Mr 10,21:2), 19 F 22,25:2
Robinson, Mallie Mrs, 1968, My 23,47:4
Robinson, Margaret A, 1941, Mr 28,23:3
Robinson, Margaret Downing Lanman, 1925, F 23, 17:6
Robinson, Marion C Mrs (will, Mr 31,22:4), 1949, Mr 26,19:8
Robinson, Martin S, 1949, Je 2,27:1
Robinson, Mary, 1950, N 11,15:5
Robinson, Mary E Mrs, 1947, S 14,60:3
Robinson, Mary Knox Mrs, 1923, F 26,13:4
Robinson, Mary Mrs, 1949, Ja 18,23:5
Robinson, Mary O Mrs, 1948, Ap 30,23:3
Robinson, Matilda Mrs, 1949, S 30,23:1
Robinson, Maude, 1960, D 15,44:1
Robinson, Maude A, 1942, My 31,39:2
Robinson, Maurice, 1952, Ja 5,11:6; 1953, N 1,87:
Robinson, Maurice H, 1946, Mr 1,21:2; 1951, Je 2 27:2
Robinson, Maville J, 1948, D 6,25:4
Robinson, Max, 1915, F 1,9:4
Robinson, Max Mrs, 1951, My 21,35:1
Robinson, McMillan, 1949, Ap 7,29:4
Robinson, Merrill H, 1953, Ap 2,27:2
Robinson, Merton A, 1954, F 13,13:5
Robinson, Millard L (por), 1947, Ap 24,25:5
Robinson, Milton, 1967, D 10,87:1
Robinson, Milton H Mrs, 1955, Ap 1,28:3
Robinson, Moncure, 1920, Ag 12,9:2
Robinson, Monroe D, 1944, D 9,15:6
Robinson, Morris, 1952, O 19,89:1; 1962, Jl 30,23:
Robinson, Myron, 1946, N 22,24:2
Robinson, Myron W, 1955, Ag 28,84:4
Robinson, Myron W Maj, 1912, My 28,11:4
Robinson, N T N Maj, 1903, D 11,9:5
Robinson, Nathaniel, 1938, Ja 4,24:3
Robinson, Nathaniel M, 1904, Ja 31,7:6
Robinson, Nehemiah, 1964, Ja 12,92:7
Robinson, Nelson L, 1944, Ap 9,34:3
Robinson, Noel, 1944, Jl 17,15:4
Robinson, Nugent, 1903, D 27,7:5
Robinson, O D, 1955, Ag 20,17:6
Robinson, O James, 1947, D 14,78:4
Robinson, O Pomeroy Jr, 1956, F 28,31:1
Robinson, Olive E, 1949, My 25,29:2
Robinson, Oliver P (por), 1941, D 11,27:3
Robinson, Ora Mrs, 1952, O 16,29:2
Robinson, Orville, 1882, D 2,5:2; 1947, Mr 19,26:
Robinson, Oscar D Prof, 1911, Jl 12,7:6
Robinson, Oscar E, 1939, Mr 28,23:2
Robinson, Otho, 1941, D 7,77:2
Robinson, Otho E C, 1940, Ag 16,15:5
Robinson, Paschal, 1948, Ag 28,15:4

Robinson, Pat, 1964, N 14,29:4
Robinson, Purdon, 1941, My 7,25:4
Robinson, R Bruce, 1953, N 6,27:4
Robinson, R D, 1940, N 22,23:4
Robinson, R E, 1903, F 4,9:5
Robinson, R H, 1933, N 9,21:1
Robinson, R L, 1939, Ja 11,19:5
Robinson, R Leroy, 1944, S 5,19:5
Robinson, Ralph C, 1943, N 9,21:5
Robinson, Ralph H, 1951, Mr 9,25:4
Robinson, Ralph H Mrs, 1952, Ap 15,27:3
Robinson, Ralph P, 1949, D 19,28:2
Robinson, Raymond V, 1951, N 8,29:5
Robinson, Reuben R, 1954, Ap 29,31:4
Robinson, Richard, 1925, O 5,21:4
Robinson, Richard G, 1960, Ag 25,29:6
Robinson, Richard H M, 1951, Ap 24,30:2
Robinson, Riley, 1956, Jl 17,23:1
Robinson, Robert, 1941, Je 21,17:6; 1953, Ag 27,25:2
Robinson, Robert A, 1949, D 10,18:3
Robinson, Robert B, 1952, D 7,88:6
Robinson, Robert H, 1953, Ag 10,23:4
Robinson, Robert P, 1939, Mr 5,48:6
Robinson, Robert W, 1958, D 11,13:5
Robinson, Rodney G, 1939, Ap 16,III,7:3
Robinson, Rodney P, 1950, Ap 3,23:4
Robinson, Roger F Mrs (Mary P), 1965, D 22,31:1
Robinson, Roland Reed 2d, 1968, Jl 22,35:3
Robinson, Rosell Mrs, 1947, Jl 27,44:6
Robinson, Roswell A, 1940, F 25,38:8
Robinson, Roswell R 2d Mrs, 1951, Je 12,29:4
Robinson, Roy L, 1952, S 6,17:4
Robinson, Rufus L Mrs, 1952, Ja 15,27:2
Robinson, Rufus L Sr, 1960, Ap 30,23:5
Robinson, Russell M Mrs, 1949, Mr 19,15:2
Robinson, S A, 1927, Ja 14,19:5
Robinson, S Rev, 1881, O 6,5:3
Robinson, S V Rev, 1918, F 12,11:2
Robinson, Samuel, 1947, S 18,25:5; 1958, S 7,86:2; 1958, O 27,27:4
Robinson, Samuel F, 1937, My 12,23:5
Robinson, Samuel I, 1939, F 22,21:3
Robinson, Samuel J, 1961, Je 16,33:3
Robinson, Sanford, 1942, S 19,15:4
Robinson, Seymour, 1940, Je 10,17:2
Robinson, Sherman A Mrs, 1952, S 29,23:4
Robinson, Sidney C, 1943, Mr 2,19:6
Robinson, Simon Mrs, 1954, Ag 4,21:4
Robinson, Sol, 1966, Ap 24,87:2
Robinson, Sol M, 1967, Ag 23,51:4
Robinson, Solon, 1964, Ap 18,29:6
Robinson, Stanley J, 1959, Ja 8,29:1
Robinson, Stephen Mrs, 1950, Jl 16,69:1
Robinson, Stephen P Jr, 1960, Ag 9,27:2
Robinson, Stewart Douglas, 1909, F 25,7:5
Robinson, Stewart MacM (Sept 22), 1965, O 11,61:4
Robinson, Sue, 1871, Je 18,4:2
Robinson, Sumner, 1948, Ja 1,23:5
Robinson, Sylvester A, 1947, Ja 28,24:2
Robinson, T A, 1934, My 11,21:2
Robinson, T D, 1934, Ap 11,21:1
Robinson, Ted Jr (police rept note was not found, Ag 4,27:4), 1966, Jl 21,30:6
Robinson, Thadeus B, 1940, Ja 22,15:4
Robinson, Theodore D Mrs, 1962, Jl 10,33:4
Robinson, Theodore Mrs, 1950, F 18,15:1
Robinson, Theodore W, 1948, D 31,15:3
Robinson, Thomas A, 1939, F 11,15:5
Robinson, Thomas B Sir, 1939, My 17,23:6
Robinson, Thomas J, 1966, Mr 25,41:2
Robinson, Thomas J B, 1958, Ja 28,27:1
Robinson, Thomas L, 1940, F 21,19:1
Robinson, Thomas M, 1914, Je 1,11:5
Robinson, Thomas P, 1954, N 22,23:2
Robinson, Thomas R, 1948, Mr 1,23:3; 1957, S 14,19:3
Robinson, Thomas Rev, 1873, My 14,1:2
Robinson, Thomas T, 1945, Mr 7,21:5
Robinson, Thomas W, 1942, N 12,25:1
Robinson, Thomas W Mrs, 1939, F 23,23:5
Robinson, Thurman S, 1939, Jl 25,19:2
Robinson, Tom, 1958, Ag 12,29:1
Robinson, Tracey Layard, 1923, O 13,15:4
Robinson, V D L, 1947, Ag 12,23:3
Robinson, V Gilpin, 1942, Mr 28,17:5
Robinson, Vernon C, 1959, Je 22,25:4
Robinson, Victor (por), 1947, Ja 9,23:1
Robinson, W, 1929, Ja 21,21:3
Robinson, W Cortland Mrs, 1951, S 18,31:2
Robinson, W Courtland (por), 1938, Mr 16,23:4
Robinson, W Dean, 1957, Jl 21,60:1
Robinson, W G Dr, 1905, Mr 3,2:5
Robinson, W H, 1883, Jl 22,5:3
Robinson, W L, 1954, Mr 28,88:4
Robinson, W M M, 1950, Ja 9,25:4
Robinson, W Meade, 1965, F 22,21:2
Robinson, W S, 1876, Mr 12,7:5
Robinson, Wade, 1923, Je 7,19:4
Robinson, Wallace F, 1920, F 18,11:2
Robinson, Walter E, 1940, D 1,62:2
Robinson, Walter F, 1940, Ap 29,15:4
Robinson, Walter G, 1940, Ja 25,21:4
Robinson, Walter H, 1943, S 24,23:3
Robinson, Walter O, 1954, Ap 11,86:2
Robinson, Walter S, 1956, Ja 5,33:2
Robinson, Walter S Mrs, 1941, Mr 19,21:4
Robinson, Walter W Sr, 1958, Jl 3,25:4
Robinson, Warren F, 1954, Jl 2,19:6
Robinson, Wilbur J Mrs, 1951, Ag 10,15:5
Robinson, Wilbur S, 1941, O 4,15:6
Robinson, William, 1942, D 8,25:5; 1946, F 26,26:2; 1952, Ag 24,88:2; 1956, My 7,27:3; 1967, Je 9,45:4
Robinson, William A, 1944, Jl 2,20:5; 1950, Ja 1,43:1; 1950, Je 11,92:6; 1951, Ap 28,15:5; 1957, N 17,86:7
Robinson, William B, 1941, Je 14,17:2; 1964, S 24,41:3
Robinson, William B Sr, 1946, Ag 24,11:5
Robinson, William C Dr, 1937, Ag 8,II,6:7
Robinson, William C Mrs, 1950, My 17,29:2
Robinson, William Callyhan Prof, 1911, N 7,13:4
Robinson, William Dr, 1921, Ja 5,13:6
Robinson, William E, 1951, F 8,23:7; 1954, Jl 29,23:2; 1962, My 17,37:4; 1966, Ja 10,25:3
Robinson, William F, 1953, N 26,31:1
Robinson, William H, 1944, S 14,23:4; 1945, Ap 17, 23:3; 1946, O 13,58:6; 1956, D 11,39:1
Robinson, William H Jr Mrs, 1947, Jl 30,21:6
Robinson, William H Mrs, 1956, Ap 12,31:1
Robinson, William J, 1945, Jl 18,27:6; 1950, Ag 17,27:2
Robinson, William L, 1954, Jl 10,13:5; 1955, S 10,17:2
Robinson, William L Mrs, 1954, O 2,17:5
Robinson, William M, 1938, Ja 25,21:2; 1950, My 17, 29:3
Robinson, William Mrs, 1952, Jl 5,15:3
Robinson, William S, 1943, Ap 14,23:3; 1949, Ag 25, 23:3; 1953, Ja 25,84:4; 1963, S 14,25:6
Robinson, William T, 1913, Mr 26,11:3; 1958, Je 20, 23:2
Robinson, William W, 1915, Mr 24,11:6; 1939, D 27, 21:5
Robinson, Willis B, 1942, Jl 20,13:2
Robinson-Duff, Frances, 1951, N 1,29:2
Robinton, John, 1937, Je 30,23:3
Robiscon, Ernest P, 1956, O 17,35:1
Robison, Carson J, 1957, Mr 25,25:2
Robison, Clarence H, 1952, My 23,21:6
Robison, Dennis, 1946, Ag 3,15:5
Robison, Eben, 1962, Jl 20,25:5
Robison, Eben Mrs, 1957, Ap 24,33:2
Robison, Jeannie Mrs, 1937, O 2,21:3
Robison, John K (por), 1938, Jl 16,13:3
Robison, John K Mrs, 1949, Jl 2,15:2
Robison, John L, 1955, O 20,36:1
Robison, L A Mrs, 1950, Ag 4,21:2
Robison, Lyman H, 1952, Je 16,17:2
Robison, Martha E, 1941, N 24,17:5
Robison, Mary Mrs, 1942, S 19,15:5
Robison, Robert, 1950, Jl 22,15:2
Robison, Ross S, 1941, My 30,15:2
Robison, Samuel D, 1942, Jl 30,21:6
Robison, Samuel S, 1952, N 22,23:3
Robison, Samuel S Mrs, 1940, Ag 29,19:5
Robison, Stanley, 1911, Mr 25,11:4
Robison, Willard, 1968, Je 25,41:1
Robison, William F, 1944, Je 5,19:4
Robison, William W, 1939, Mr 27,15:2
Robitaille, Abbe A, 1939, F 1,21:2
Robitaille, Anthony, 1947, Jl 31,21:5
Robitschek, Fritz O, 1962, F 8,31:2
Robitscher, Jonas B, 1956, F 20,23:4
Robitscher, Joseph Mrs, 1924, D 24,15:3
Robitzek, Gustavus, 1914, Ap 4,15:5
Robitzek, Harry Justice (funl, Ap 11,13:4), 1923, Je 9,11:7
Robjohn, William John (Caryl Florio), 1920, N 22, 15:4
Roble, Chet, 1962, N 1,31:4
Roble, Edward D Rear-Adm, 1911, Je 8,11:5
Robles, Bernabe S, 1945, F 20,19:4
Robles, Santos Mrs, 1947, D 26,15:1
Robles, Sebastian T, 1959, Ag 31,21:2
Robles, Serafina, 1951, F 16,25:2
Roblin, Rodman P Sir, 1937, F 17,21:2
Roblin, Stephen H, 1947, D 30,23:2
Robling, Warner T, 1946, Ap 30,21:2
Robnett, A H, 1940, O 2,23:3
Robnett, John D, 1956, D 22,19:4
Robnett, John D Capt, 1937, N 18,23:5
Robnett, Ronald H, 1954, F 18,31:1
Robollio, Charlotte Mrs, 1949, Mr 3,26:2
Robottom, Arthur Mrs, 1946, O 11,23:3
Robottom, Percy, 1950, Ap 2,93:1
Roboz, Hugo G, 1938, N 19,17:1
Robrecht, Edward J Mrs, 1940, My 4,17:4
Robrecht, John J, 1940, D 23,19:5
Robsarte, Lionel, 1937, N 5,23:4
Robsham, Esther Mrs, 1951, O 26,23:1
Robsion, John M, 1948, F 18,27:3
Robson, A Flag, 1942, Ja 31,17:4
Robson, A Roy, 1943, O 29,19:1
Robson, Albert H, 1939, Mr 7,21:4
Robson, Albert N, 1947, Ag 7,21:5
Robson, B R Dr, 1878, Ag 19,8:4
Robson, David Mrs, 1958, Je 25,29:4
Robson, Edmond, 1940, Ap 18,23:5
Robson, Frank E, 1948, Mr 1,23:2
Robson, Frank H, 1937, Mr 23,23:3
Robson, Fred, 1952, N 5,27:3
Robson, Frederick, 1864, Ag 26,3:1
Robson, Frederick E, 1950, Ja 16,26:3
Robson, George E, 1953, My 2,15:6
Robson, George R, 1949, Jl 18,17:4
Robson, H Harris, 1964, Je 20,25:2
Robson, J William Mrs, 1958, Ag 18,19:5
Robson, James, 1939, D 14,27:2
Robson, James A Justice, 1916, F 2,11:6
Robson, James G, 1959, Mr 24,39:3
Robson, Kenneth W, 1941, O 23,23:3
Robson, Leonard, 1948, Je 15,28:2
Robson, Margaret N Mrs, 1946, Mr 23,13:4
Robson, May (por), 1942, O 21,21:1
Robson, Miles, 1959, S 10,35:5
Robson, Stuart, 1903, Ap 30,9:4
Robson, Stuart Mrs, 1924, D 23,19:4
Robus, Hugo, 1964, Ja 15,31:2
Roby, Eben Willard, 1919, Ja 4,11:5
Roby, Henry John, 1915, Ja 5,15:5
Roby, Horace E, 1948, My 14,23:3
Roby, Robert J, 1947, N 22,15:5
Roby, Sidney J, 1961, Mr 25,25:1
Robyn, Louise, 1949, Je 12,76:2
Robyn, Paul Sr, 1953, Ag 19,29:4
Roca, Julio A, 1942, O 9,22:2
Roca, Julio Argentino Gen (funl, O 22,11:6), 1914, O 20,13:6
Roca Niz, Joaquin, 1948, My 29,15:4
Rocamora, William, 1964, S 10,35:4
Rocamora, Wynn, 1959, D 3,13:5
Rocca, Anthony J, 1948, O 20,29:4
Rocca, Francesco N Count, 1940, D 19,25:4
Rocca, R H, 1949, S 7,4:3
Rocchi, Filippo, 1962, N 12,29:3
Rocchietti, Paul J Capt, 1925, O 1,27:4
Rocchio, Thomas A J, 1964, N 15,86:4
Rocco, A, 1935, Ag 29,21:4
Rocco, Emmett, 1961, D 7,43:1
Rocco, Gino, 1941, F 15,15:5
Roces, Antonia de Mrs, 1955, Ap 16,19:3
Roces, Marcos, 1938, Mr 12,17:3
Rocha de Vasconcelos, Camila Mrs, 1942, My 9,13:4
Rocha y Garcia, Juan J, 1938, Jl 31,32:8
Rochambeau, Marquis de, 1941, Ap 13,38:4
Rochas, Marcel, 1955, Mr 15,26:8
Rochat, Louis A, 1958, Ja 10,23:3
Rochat, Marie L, 1946, Ap 13,17:5
Rochdale, Lord, 1945, Mr 25,38:2
Roche, A S, 1935, F 18,15:1
Roche, Alex A Lord, 1956, D 24,13:1
Roche, Alexander, 1921, Mr 11,15:5
Roche, Andrew T Rev, 1919, Ja 27,13:4
Roche, Austin J, 1952, D 14,90:7
Roche, Billy, 1955, Je 19,92:4
Roche, Catherine D Mrs, 1940, Mr 25,15:5
Roche, Charles F, 1948, Ja 20,23:3
Roche, Daniel G (por), 1939, Ja 22,35:1
Roche, Daniel W, 1950, Jl 25,27:3
Roche, David J, 1956, O 23,33:3
Roche, Deirdre M, 1963, D 2,37:4
Roche, Dominick H, 1907, Mr 17,9:5
Roche, Dorothy K, 1939, Ap 2,III,7:2
Roche, E, 1879, F 14,4:7
Roche, Edmund B, 1948, Je 21,21:3
Roche, Edmund Fitz-Edmund (Baron Fermoy), 1920, S 2,9:2
Roche, Edward A, 1941, Mr 30,49:2
Roche, Edward F, 1962, N 28,39:4
Roche, Edward J Mrs, 1955, Ap 10,25:4
Roche, Edward P, 1950, S 24,104:6
Roche, Francis A, 1945, Ap 11,23:2
Roche, Francis G B, 1958, O 31,29:4
Roche, Frank, 1884, Ap 6,7:2; 1949, Jl 20,25:4
Roche, Frank T, 1951, Jl 28,8:8
Roche, Frank W, 1947, Ag 12,23:4
Roche, Fred J, 1955, S 14,35:3
Roche, Garret, 1942, Ja 11,44:1
Roche, Harold, 1953, Ap 2,28:3
Roche, Hugh, 1949, D 20,31:1
Roche, J J, 1916, D 24,15:1
Roche, James, 1869, Jl 7,4:7; 1951, S 25,11:6
Roche, James A (por), 1942, Ap 28,21:2
Roche, James A, 1943, O 14,22:2
Roche, James B B Mrs, 1947, Ja 27,23:3
Roche, James Boothby Burke (Lord Fermoy), 1920, N 1,15:6
Roche, James Connor, 1915, Ag 25,11:5
Roche, James F, 1960, Mr 26,21:2
Roche, James Jeffrey, 1908, Ap 4,9:7
Roche, James M, 1958, S 23,33:1
Roche, James T Jr, 1954, Je 23,25:5
Roche, James T Jr Mrs, 1961, Ja 17,37:3
Roche, Jeffrey Mrs, 1939, My 19,21:2
Roche, John, 1913, S 11,11:6; 1947, My 3,17:3
Roche, John B Mrs, 1942, F 23,21:4
Roche, John D, 1953, O 5,27:5
Roche, John F, 1947, Ap 8,27:2
Roche, John F Sr, 1938, Ja 28,21:3
Roche, John J Rev, 1924, N 28,15:4
Roche, John M, 1947, Ja 25,17:5
Roche, John W, 1967, N 22,47:3
Roche, Lily, 1945, Je 9,13:3
Roche, Margaret E, 1942, Mr 30,17:2

Roche, Marquise de la, 1948, D 30,19:2
Roche, Maurice Mrs, 1944, Jl 9,35:2
Roche, Michael J, 1956, D 14,29:5
Roche, Nicholas, 1937, O 7,27:1
Roche, Patrick J, 1947, D 8,25:4
Roche, Patrick T, 1955, Jl 13,25:6
Roche, Philip Q, 1966, Ag 1,27:3
Roche, Rayson E, 1963, Ap 25,33:3
Roche, Richard F, 1949, S 15,27:4
Roche, Spencer S Mrs, 1950, My 2,29:5
Roche, Thomas A, 1941, My 8,23:2
Roche, Thomas F, 1938, Ja 14,23:2
Roche, Thomas J, 1963, Ag 13,31:4
Roche, Thomas O, 1954, Mr 31,27:2
Roche, William, 1965, Ap 17,19:6
Roche, William F, 1945, My 9,23:3
Roche, William J Dr, 1937, O 1,21:1
Roche, William T, 1960, Jl 15,23:2
Rocheblave, Samuel, 1944, My 6,15:6
Rochefort, Charles de, 1952, F 2,13:2
Rochefort, Henri, 1913, Jl 2,9:4
Rochefort-Lucay, Octave de, 1950, Ja 3,25:4
Rochegrosse, Antoine, 1938, Jl 15,17:1
Rocheleau, Phoebe, 1950, Ja 31,23:4
Rochelle, Eugene, 1914, Mr 10,9:2
Rochelle, T V, 1950, N 6,27:3
Rochelle, Thomas Alfred W, 1965, S 15,47:3
Roches, Charles B, 1953, My 5,29:5
Rochester, Anna, 1966, My 12,45:2
Rochester, Charles, 1956, N 29,35:4
Rochester, Charles E Mrs, 1951, Jl 3,23:5
Rochester, Donald, 1955, Jl 4,11:4
Rochester, Edward S, 1946, Mr 11,25:5
Rochester, Emily N, 1943, Je 8,21:4
Rochester, Gertrude, 1955, N 10,35:1
Rochester, Lord (E H Lamb), 1955, Ja 14,21:4
Rochester, Loretto M, 1959, F 19,31:2
Rochester, Paul A, 1925, S 13,5:1
Rochester, Richmond, 1939, My 19,21:2
Rochester, Robert K (por), 1945, Ag 19,40:4
Rochester, Robert R, 1939, N 2,23:5
Rochester, Thomas W, 1959, Ja 30,27:3
Rochester, William B Mrs, 1905, Ap 27,9:2
Rochester, William Beatty, 1909, N 12,11:6
Rochford, Anna (Sister Dominica Maria), 1940, My 14,23:3
Rochford, Frank M, 1938, Ag 2,19:2
Rochford, James J, 1945, Ag 22,23:4
Rochford, John E, 1960, Jl 20,29:1
Rochford, John J, 1955, Jl 20,27:5
Rochford, Julia C, 1958, Ap 13,84:1
Rochford, Maurice J, 1957, O 21,25:1
Rochford, Richard J Sr, 1951, D 22,15:3
Rochkind, William, 1955, S 5,11:4
Rochlin, Jacob Mrs, 1941, Jl 17,19:3
Rochling, Ernst, 1964, Ja 26,80:6
Rochman, Esther Mrs, 1939, Ap 17,17:4
Rochmis, Oscar, 1946, Ap 3,25:5
Rochon, Dave, 1966, D 1,47:6
Rochon, Rodolph J, 1958, Ag 1,21:4
Rock, Adolph, 1954, F 3,23:4
Rock, Albert G, 1962, Ap 11,43:4
Rock, Alfred V, 1957, Ag 2,19:5
Rock, Charles, 1919, Jl 13,22:4
Rock, Clarence A, 1950, F 8,27:2
Rock, E Lloyd, 1954, O 20,29:2
Rock, E Lloyd Mrs, 1963, Jl 15,29:3
Rock, Edward J, 1961, F 15,35:4
Rock, Edwin J, 1953, F 28,17:4
Rock, Edwin M, 1957, Ap 10,33:2
Rock, Frank J, 1967, N 25,39:3
Rock, Frederick J, 1954, My 15,15:4
Rock, George, 1961, Mr 7,35:3
Rock, George H (por), 1946, Ap 21,46:1
Rock, George H, 1948, Jl 10,15:5
Rock, George H Mrs, 1938, Mr 7,17:5
Rock, Gerald P, 1959, Jl 16,27:3
Rock, Henry J, 1946, S 13,7:3
Rock, Herman A, 1942, Ag 8,11:5
Rock, Isaac Rabbi, 1914, Ag 27,11:5
Rock, James E (por), 1941, Mr 22,15:2
Rock, John B, 1948, N 25,31:5
Rock, John J, 1947, Mr 16,60:1
Rock, Joseph F C, 1962, D 7,39:3
Rock, Leo T, 1956, Ag 21,29:3
Rock, Mathias, 1912, Ag 10,7:6
Rock, P Arthur, 1960, N 16,41:4
Rock, Paul J, 1942, Mr 28,17:5
Rock, Roger J, 1955, O 25,33:3
Rock, Samuel W, 1947, O 18,16:2
Rock, Thomas S, 1958, N 29,21:5
Rock, William, 1922, Je 28,15:6
Rock, William T (est, Ag 3,11:5), 1916, Jl 28,11:7
Rockafellar, Harry Col (funl), 1875, Ag 27,8:5
Rockafellow, Edward W (por), 1946, N 4,25:3
Rockafellow, George, 1949, Ap 19,26:5
Rockafellow, Henry A Mrs, 1944, Ap 15,11:3
Rockafellow, John W, 1947, Mr 18,27:2
Rockart, John R, 1951, O 14,88:3
Rocke, Leo A, 1948, My 30,34:3
Rockefeller, Albert H, 1961, S 3,61:1
Rockefeller, Alden H, 1948, Jl 17,15:3
Rockefeller, Alice M, 1942, S 19,15:2
Rockefeller, Allen C, 1940, Jl 9,21:1
Rockefeller, Amasa P Mrs, 1949, O 15,15:4
Rockefeller, Beveridge J, 1954, Mr 15,25:5
Rockefeller, Eugene Lincoln, 1922, F 17,15:5
Rockefeller, Frank (funl, Ap 17,11:5), 1917, Ap 16, 13:5
Rockefeller, Harry, 1913, Jl 8,7:4
Rockefeller, Harry E, 1966, F 6,92:4
Rockefeller, John D Jr, 1917, D 7,13:5
Rockefeller, John D Jr (private funl planned, My 13,31:4), 1960, My 12,1:4
Rockefeller, John D Jr (est appr), 1964, D 25,1:5
Rockefeller, John D Jr Mrs, 1948, Ap 6,23:1
Rockefeller, John D Mrs (por),(funl, Mr 14,11:1), 1915, Mr 13,13:1
Rockefeller, John D Sr, 1937, My 24,1:7
Rockefeller, P A, 1934, S 26,21:1
Rockefeller, Percy A (will), 1938, Ap 28,14:3
Rockefeller, Richard, 1921, My 27,17:5
Rockefeller, Roy P, 1941, Je 23,17:4
Rockefeller, Stanton, 1942, Je 25,23:5
Rockefeller, Vernard J, 1939, Jl 14,19:4
Rockefeller, William, 1922, Je 27,15:3
Rockefeller, William J, 1949, Ap 6,29:3
Rockefeller, William Mrs, 1920, Ja 18,22:4
Rockefellow, John A, 1947, My 18,60:1
Rockell, Edwin Amasa, 1919, Mr 9,20:5
Rockenstire, Walter C Sr, 1951, F 23,27:2
Rockenstyre, Charles E, 1944, Jl 19,19:3
Rocker, Abraham, 1959, Ap 20,31:2
Rocker, George, 1950, S 3,39:1
Rocker, Rudolph, 1958, S 11,34:1
Rockett, James F, 1948, Ap 2,23:1
Rockett, Patrick A, 1947, O 29,27:1
Rockewitz, Esther Mrs, 1922, Mr 26,27:3
Rockey, Basil S S, 1962, My 2,37:2
Rockey, Charles H Mrs, 1951, O 10,23:6
Rockey, E Huntley, 1962, Jl 30,23:3
Rockey, H, 1934, My 28,19:1
Rockey, Keller Mrs, 1947, Je 17,25:3
Rockfellow, William H, 1915, Jl 4,11:6
Rockhill, Charles S Dr, 1925, Mr 10,21:2
Rockhill, Howell C, 1942, S 19,15:3
Rockhill, Jerome B Sr, 1964, Ag 9,76:1
Rockhill, Margaret H Mrs, 1941, Je 8,48:3
Rockhill, Victor C, 1947, Je 11,27:3
Rockhill, Walter S, 1962, O 14,85:4
Rockhill, William W, 1914, D 9,13:5
Rockhill, William W Mrs, 1946, Ap 7,45:1
Rockley, Lady, 1941, S 15,17:2
Rockley, Lord, 1941, Ap 3,23:3
Rockman, Max, 1962, F 5,31:2
Rockmore, Isaac, 1952, N 27,31:4
Rockne, Knute K Mrs, 1956, Je 3,85:1
Rockne, Louise P, 1959, S 1,30:2
Rockne, Martha Mrs, 1944, My 19,19:5
Rockne, William D, 1960, N 9,35:4
Rockow, Julius, 1962, Mr 18,86:6
Rockstroh, Carl E, 1955, My 17,29:1
Rockstroh, William, 1956, Ap 9,27:4
Rockstroh, William F, 1957, Je 5,35:4
Rockstroh, William Mrs, 1959, Jl 31,23:1
Rockwell, A D, 1933, Ap 13,17:3
Rockwell, Alfonso D Mrs, 1958, My 11,87:1
Rockwell, Alfred Gen, 1903, D 25,7:5
Rockwell, Alice J, 1947, S 4,25:4
Rockwell, Almon F Lt-Col, 1903, Ag 1,2:2
Rockwell, Bertha L, 1963, O 1,39:2
Rockwell, Bertrand Mrs, 1947, D 9,29:3
Rockwell, Camden O, 1925, Mr 12,19:4
Rockwell, Charles B, 1967, Ag 31,33:2
Rockwell, Charles F, 1949, D 27,24:3
Rockwell, Charles H, 1925, N 25,21:4
Rockwell, Charles H Rear-Adm, 1908, Jl 2,9:6
Rockwell, Charles Hull, 1904, Ja 3,24:3
Rockwell, Charles J, 1940, F 12,17:4
Rockwell, Daniel J, 1942, Ap 20,21:2
Rockwell, Dwight, 1963, Je 11,37:4
Rockwell, Edward H, 1943, My 27,25:5
Rockwell, Edwin C, 1962, F 2,29:5
Rockwell, Eliza E Mrs, 1908, Mr 15,9:4
Rockwell, F Berry, 1963, O 31,34:1
Rockwell, Fenton, 1913, Ja 14,17:5
Rockwell, Florence, 1964, Mr 26,35:2
Rockwell, Frederick W, 1942, F 25,19:1
Rockwell, George L, 1947, My 29,21:4; 1954, N 11, 34:5
Rockwell, Guy T, 1953, Ag 2,73:3
Rockwell, Harold A, 1953, O 15,33:6
Rockwell, Harold H, 1939, Ap 23,III,7:2
Rockwell, Harry V, 1951, F 21,27:4
Rockwell, Harry W, 1961, Ja 11,47:4
Rockwell, Harvey G, 1938, O 10,19:5
Rockwell, Henry T, 1956, Jl 26,25:2
Rockwell, Homer M Mrs, 1964, S 18,32:4
Rockwell, Isabel, 1943, Ap 6,21:2
Rockwell, J E Rev, 1882, Jl 31,8:2
Rockwell, J L, 1879, Ja 22,8:2
Rockwell, J S, 1879, Ja 4,5:3
Rockwell, J Waring Mrs, 1953, Mr 7,15:3
Rockwell, L Wilson, 1940, N 26,23:5
Rockwell, Leo L, 1967, Ap 4,43:3
Rockwell, Loren H Mrs, 1949, Jl 21,25:4
Rockwell, Louis D, 1945, O 26,19:4
Rockwell, Mary D Mrs, 1939, Ja 9,15:1
Rockwell, Mary H, 1949, Ap 10,78:4
Rockwell, Nathan L, 1911, Ja 2,9:4
Rockwell, Norman Mrs, 1959, Ag 26,29:2
Rockwell, Park D, 1948, O 5,25:3
Rockwell, Rena, 1947, O 11,17:2
Rockwell, Rob E, 1904, F 13,9:5
Rockwell, Robert E, 1951, Ag 9,21:6
Rockwell, Robert F, 1950, S 30,17:5
Rockwell, Sarah F Mrs, 1953, N 24,29:1
Rockwell, Selden E, 1955, Mr 16,33:2
Rockwell, Thomas G, 1958, My 30,21:4
Rockwell, Tod, 1952, Mr 24,25:2
Rockwell, Walter S, 1942, My 22,21:4
Rockwell, Ward, 1941, D 3,52:3
Rockwell, William E (por), 1940, Ag 17,15:6
Rockwell, William H Dr, 1873, D 10,5:4
Rockwell, William L, 1940, N 29,21:1
Rockwell, William M, 1945, N 29,23:4
Rockwell, William O Mrs, 1948, Ap 28,27:4
Rockwell, William W, 1958, My 31,15:2
Rockwell, Winthrop E, 1947, N 25,32:4
Rockwitt, Jacob L, 1956, Ag 21,29:3
Rockwood, Charles G, 1904, Jl 19,7:6
Rockwood, Charles Greene Jr Prof, 1913, Jl 3,9:4
Rockwood, Edith, 1952, Ag 18,17:2
Rockwood, Edward V, 1941, Mr 8,19:1
Rockwood, Flozari Mrs, 1954, Ap 16,21:1
Rockwood, George Gardner, 1911, Jl 12,7:6
Rockwood, George H Jr, 1948, Ap 24,15:5
Rockwood, George Henry, 1911, F 3,9:5
Rockwood, George O Mrs, 1964, Jl 19,65:3
Rockwood, Ralph K, 1944, Je 12,19:3
Rockwood, W T, 1903, Ap 22,9:5
Rockwood, William B, 1949, F 4,24:3
Rocque, Francois de la (por), 1946, Ap 30,21:1
Rod, Louis Edouard, 1910, Ja 30,II,11:5
Rod, Norman J, 1953, Jl 31,19:2
Roda Roda, Alexander, 1945, Ag 21,21:4
Rodakiewicz, Erla H, 1965, Ja 1,19:4
Rodale, Joseph W, 1952, N 15,17:5
Rodale, Sol, 1956, Ja 27,23:2
Rodan, Victor, 1948, Mr 5,22:2
Rodarte, Jose, 1920, Ag 14,7:7
Rodas, Caballero De Gen (see also D 22), 1875, D 28,1:7
Rodau, Anatol L, 1941, S 2,17:5
Rodcevitch-Plotnitsky, Leon, 1959, Jl 7,33:1
Rodd, William A, 1941, Ap 3,23:4
Roddan, Celestine, 1947, N 8,17:2
Rodden, M, 1877, Jl 1,7:2
Roddenbery, Seaborn A, 1913, S 26,11:6
Roddewig, Louis E, 1947, Je 21,17:5
Roddey, William J, 1945, F 16,23:2
Roddick, Lady, 1954, F 18,31:2
Roddie, Herbert Mrs, 1958, O 9,37:3
Roddie, J W Wesley, 1953, O 24,15:6
Roddie, John W, 1943, Ag 6,15:5
Roddle, W H (Harry), 1943, N 21,57:2
Roddy, Harry J, 1943, S 5,28:8
Roddy, Hugh V Capt, 1920, Ag 31,9:3
Roddy, James P Sr, 1961, S 9,19:6
Roddy, Joseph S, 1950, Ja 15,84:6
Roddy, Maurice, 1949, S 24,13:6
Roddy, Vincent A, 1960, D 10,23:6
Rode, Alfred B, 1950, My 22,21:3
Rode, Frederick Mrs, 1913, S 26,11:4
Rodecker, Alvin, 1960, Je 25,23:6
Rodee, Chuck, 1966, My 15,V,1:2
Rodeheaver, Homer, 1955, D 19,27:5
Rodeheaver, Joseph N, 1946, Ja 29,25:2
Rodel, George, 1955, Je 6,27:3
Rodellec du Porzic, Comtesse de (por), 1941, N 15, 17:4
Rodeman, William, 1872, Je 3,8:3
Rodemeyer, John, 1943, D 20,23:1
Roden, Anna B Mrs, 1957, Ja 11,24:4
Roden, Arthur P, 1953, Ag 28,17:2
Roden, Carl B, 1956, O 27,21:5
Roden, George J, 1953, Mr 19,29:3
Roden, H W, 1963, My 14,39:5
Roden, H W Mrs, 1952, Jl 18,19:5
Roden, Harry R, 1953, D 21,31:6
Roden, Hugh P Dr, 1912, Ja 1,13:4
Roden, Hugh V, 1952, Je 5,31:4
Roden, James, 1947, S 7,60:7
Roden, John J, 1964, Ag 2,77:2
Roden, Lincoln Jr, 1958, Mr 19,31:1
Roden, Max F, 1968, Mr 24,92:8
Roden, Robert B, 1939, F 7,19:2
Roden, Thomas A, 1963, N 26,37:2
Roden, William F Mrs, 1955, My 27,23:1
Rodenbach, William J, 1948, S 12,72:3
Rodenbeck, Adolph J, 1960, Ap 9,23:2
Rodenbeck, Edward T, 1944, Je 6,17:2
Rodenbeck, Edwin J, 1952, My 24,19:6
Rodenberg, Albert S, 1953, D 25,17:2
Rodenberg, August, 1944, Jl 5,11:2
Rodenberg, Gustav L, 1917, Ja 11,15:4
Rodenberg, Gustave Mrs, 1912, Mr 14,11:4
Rodenberg, Jerome J (name incorrectly spelled as Rosenberg), 1954, N 16,29:5

Rodenberg, Julius Dr, 1914, Jl 12,5:4
Rodenberg, William, 1959, D 6,86:5
Rodenberg, William A (por), 1937, S 11,17:1
Rodenberg, William A Mrs, 1942, Je 1,13:2
Rodenbough, Theophilus Francis Brig-Gen, 1912, D 20,15:4
Rodenburg, John T, 1948, Jl 20,23:3
Rodenhurst, Fred S, 1942, Ap 22,23:3
Rodenstein, Louis A Dr, 1915, F 1,9:4
Roderer, John F Dr, 1937, Mr 9,23:1
Roderick, Frank J, 1951, S 13,31:5
Roderick, George W, 1907, Ap 21,9:4
Roderick, Mary, 1909, Ap 17,9:5
Roderick, Raymond R, 1949, D 18,90:4
Roderick, T E, 1955, Ap 8,21:2
Roderick, Thomas E, 1944, S 28,19:3
Roderick, Walter B, 1955, Je 2,29:3
Rodes, Clifton, 1948, F 5,23:3
Rodes, Joseph W, 1953, Mr 20,23:1
Rodes, Lester A, 1944, Je 23,19:4
Rodes, Luis, 1939, Je 8,25:6
Rodes, Peter P, 1966, S 30,47:3
Rodes, T William, 1966, Mr 24,39:1
Rodesk, Maurice, 1953, Ag 18,23:1
Rodesky, Harry, 1943, D 21,27:2
Rodewald, F K, 1964, Ap 1,39:1
Rodewald, Herman N, 1957, S 4,33:4
Rodewald, Winthrop V, 1918, Ap 22,11:8
Rodewig, Louis F, 1952, F 9,13:5
Rodey, Bernard S Jr, 1956, My 12,19:6
Rodger, David R, 1945, Jl 7,13:6
Rodger, David R Mrs, 1943, N 29,19:6
Rodger, James D, 1954, My 5,31:3
Rodgers, Alan M, 1952, Ap 24,31:3
Rodgers, Alex, 1938, D 13,26:1
Rodgers, Arch (por), 1941, O 15,21:3
Rodgers, Bert, 1951, Ap 13,23:3
Rodgers, Charles G, 1950, O 13,29:2
Rodgers, Cleveland, 1956, My 22,33:3
Rodgers, Earl V Mrs, 1964, N 1,89:1
Rodgers, Edward H, 1940, Ap 24,23:5
Rodgers, Elbert Mrs, 1960, Ag 2,29:1
Rodgers, Elizabeth Mrs, 1939, Ag 28,19:2
Rodgers, Frederick G, 1938, Mr 14,15:3
Rodgers, Frederick G Sr, 1952, O 12,89:2
Rodgers, G A, 1942, F 11,21:4
Rodgers, G W Capt, 1863, Ag 24,4:6
Rodgers, George C, 1937, O 21,24:1
Rodgers, H G, 1882, Mr 21,5:3
Rodgers, Harold E, 1949, My 5,28:2
Rodgers, J A, 1933, Mr 3,17:3
Rodgers, J Comdr, 1926, Ag 28,1:6
Rodgers, J Harvey, 1954, D 29,23:1
Rodgers, James B, 1944, Je 30,21:5
Rodgers, James B Mrs, 1945, Ap 26,23:4
Rodgers, James L Jr, 1955, F 26,15:5
Rodgers, James O, 1945, My 17,19:1; 1957, Ag 25,86:4
Rodgers, John C, 1919, Jl 27,22:5
Rodgers, John G, 1923, Ap 12,19:5
Rodgers, John H (will, F 23,17:5), 1940, F 16,19:5
Rodgers, John Kearney, 1919, Jl 9,13:5
Rodgers, John Rear-Adm, 1882, My 6,2:5
Rodgers, Joseph G, 1937, Jl 13,19:4
Rodgers, Joseph M Mrs, 1945, Je 10,32:2
Rodgers, Julia S, 1950, My 28,44:3
Rodgers, Lida, 1963, Je 16,84:6
Rodgers, Louise Mrs, 1944, F 15,17:2
Rodgers, Marion, 1940, Jl 17,21:4
Rodgers, Melissa, 1952, Mr 5,29:1
Rodgers, N Willis, 1918, Ag 3,9:3
Rodgers, Raymond Perry Rear-Adm, 1925, D 29,23:5
Rodgers, Samuel P, 1962, S 29,23:2
Rodgers, Selden S, 1950, Ja 10,29:5
Rodgers, Thomas J Mrs, 1945, S 9,46:4
Rodgers, Viola, 1944, Je 21,19:5
Rodgers, W B Prof, 1882, My 31,5:5
Rodgers, W Ralston Jr, 1949, Je 21,25:4
Rodgers, William A, 1937, My 2,II,9:1; 1948, N 18, 28:3
Rodgers, William C Rev Dr, 1921, Ja 7,13:5
Rodgers, William F, 1957, Je 3,27:6
Rodgers, William H, 1938, Mr 27,II,6:8; 1941, O 2,25:4
Rodgers, William Harrison, 1925, Jl 20,15:7
Rodgers, William J, 1921, S 2,13:3
Rodgers, William L, 1940, Je 18,23:6; 1944, My 8,19:2
Rodgers, William S S, 1965, S 10,35:1
Rodhe, Edward M, 1954, Ap 16,21:4
Rodholen, Soren D, 1951, Ap 12,33:4
Rodic, Slavko, 1949, My 1,88:2
Rodick, Serenus B, 1948, My 18,23:2
Rodie, Gerard A, 1962, My 31,27:3
Rodie, Robert S, 1939, Jl 4,13:6
Rodie, William S, 1911, Jl 14,7:4
Rodier, Charlemagne, 1958, Je 8,88:4
Rodier, Marie G, 1957, S 29,86:6
Rodier, Paul, 1946, Je 21,23:6
Rodiger, Walter G, 1965, D 21,37:1
Rodigrass, Nathan D, 1941, N 30,68:1
Rodin, Alexei G, 1955, Je 2,29:2
Rodin, Auguste, 1917, N 18,3:3
Rodin, Auguste Mrs, 1917, F 17,11:6
Rodin, Bernard E, 1948, O 21,27:2
Rodin, Harry, 1946, O 7,31:4
Rodin, Morris, 1956, Ag 19,92:1
Rodino, Giulio, 1946, F 18,21:4
Rodis, James C Mrs (R Cumming), 1967, Ag 14,31:4
Roditi, Victor, 1942, F 8,50:1
Rodkey, Edith, 1940, Mr 14,23:3
Rodkinson, Michael L Dr, 1904, Ja 8,7:5
Rodkinson, Rudolph M Mrs, 1964, My 14,35:2
Rodman, Albert L, 1950, D 12,34:3
Rodman, Bernece Mrs, 1938, My 17,23:2
Rodman, Burton R, 1961, Ap 1,17:2
Rodman, D C, 1881, O 12,1:6
Rodman, Elizabeth R S Mrs, 1942, O 15,23:5
Rodman, Ernest L, 1948, Mr 4,25:3
Rodman, Erskine M Rev Dr, 1908, Ap 6,7:6
Rodman, Ethel G Mrs, 1950, Jl 29,13:2
Rodman, George A, 1958, N 30,86:2
Rodman, George T, 1956, Je 14,33:2
Rodman, Grover C, 1923, S 15,15:6
Rodman, H H Mrs, 1902, D 23,5:1
Rodman, H Thompson, 1954, Jl 19,19:6
Rodman, Harold S Mrs, 1946, O 3,27:4
Rodman, Harry Dr, 1924, Ap 30,19:3
Rodman, Henrietta, 1923, Mr 22,19:5
Rodman, Hugh (por), 1940, Je 9,45:1
Rodman, John S, 1958, Ap 28,23:2
Rodman, Julia, 1937, D 15,25:5
Rodman, Macy, 1942, Ag 21,19:1
Rodman, Robert F, 1947, S 29,21:5
Rodman, Robert W, 1943, N 1,17:6
Rodman, Roger W, 1950, My 22,21:5
Rodman, Samuel J, 1967, D 12,47:2
Rodman, Thomas H, 1951, D 3,31:3
Rodman, Thomas J Gen, 1871, Je 8,5:5
Rodman, Walter S, 1947, Ja 2,27:2
Rodman, Washington Rev, 1908, Ja 1,9:5
Rodman, William L Dr, 1916, Mr 9,13:7
Rodner, Harold, 1952, Je 5,31:3
Rodney, Archer U Mrs, 1943, S 27,19:4
Rodney, Aubrey Mrs, 1956, Jl 29,64:6
Rodney, Aubrey S, 1963, S 22,86:6
Rodney, Charles C, 1954, Jl 4,31:3
Rodney, David H, 1907, Ja 7,7:4
Rodney, Earle H, 1959, F 18,33:1
Rodney, Earle H Mrs, 1962, S 14,31:5
Rodney, John Henry, 1913, Ag 4,7:4
Rodney, Keith R, 1956, N 26,27:4
Rodney, Keith R Mrs, 1964, D 1,41:1
Rodney, Milton F, 1959, N 28,21:3
Rodomar, Oleg V, 1961, F 2,29:5
Rodomin, Joseph, 1956, Ja 8,86:8
Rodrigues, Jose Carlos, 1923, Je 30,11:5
Rodrigues, Manuel, 1946, Mr 3,46:6
Rodriguez, Abelardo L, 1967, F 14,43:3
Rodriguez, Bastilio A, 1943, N 17,25:1
Rodriguez, Buenaventure, 1940, D 10,19:2
Rodriguez, Ceasar, 1964, Mr 14,23:6
Rodriguez, Edicer N, 1962, O 21,88:5
Rodriguez, Eulogio Sr, 1964, D 9,47:4
Rodriguez, G Mattos, 1948, Ap 26,23:2
Rodriguez, Horacio M, 1961, Ag 20,86:2
Rodriguez, Joaquin F, 1967, S 6,47:2
Rodriguez, Joaquin P Mrs, 1953, Ap 16,29:5
Rodriguez, Jose Ignacio Dr, 1907, F 2,9:3
Rodriguez, Jose L, 1941, S 22,15:4
Rodriguez, Joseph M, 1944, Ag 7,15:5
Rodriguez, Juan, 1964, Je 10,5:6; 1968, D 9,39:4
Rodriguez, Justo L A, 1949, Ag 3,23:4
Rodriguez, Luis, 1954, Jl 2,19:4
Rodriguez, Manuel F, 1947, Jl 27,45:2
Rodriguez, Mayia Gen, 1903, My 26,9:4
Rodriguez, N Gen, 1940, Ag 12,15:4
Rodriguez, Philip R, 1945, O 1,19:4
Rodriguez, Ricardo (funl, N 3,20:2), 1962, N 2,35:1
Rodriguez, Tomas Father, 1921, Ap 14,13:5
Rodriguez Alves, Jose de Paula, 1944, My 7,45:2
Rodriguez Cano, Enrique, 1955, Je 8,29:4
Rodriguez Cerna, Jose, 1952, Jl 22,25:5
Rodriguez Claveria, Joseph, 1958, Mr 21,21:1
Rodriguez Fernandez, Rodrigo, 1941, O 29,12:4
Rodriguez-Morejon, A Gerardo, 1966, Mr 1,37:2
RodriguezFernandez, Hermina, 1944, Ja 16,43:1
Rodriquez, Valmore, 1955, Jl 11,23:3
Rodrock, Harold E, 1948, S 6,13:5
Rodstrom, Charles (por), 1943, Jl 4,20:4
Rodway, Alfred R, 1956, D 6,37:3
Rodyenko, Peter, 1961, N 7,33:4
Rodzevitch, Georges, 1956, Jl 13,19:2
Rodzianko, M, 1924, Ja 28,15:4
Rodzianko, Victor Mrs, 1949, N 4,27:4
Rodzinski, Artur (funl plans, N 29,21:2; funl, D 2,-37:4), 1958, N 28,27:1
Roe, Alex V, 1955, F 12,15:2
Roe, Alexander F, 1967, F 13,33:2
Roe, Arthur, 1942, Ap 18,16:8
Roe, Arthur F, 1947, O 1,29:2
Roe, C G, 1934, Je 29,21:3
Roe, Charles E, 1952, N 19,29:5
Roe, Charles F, 1950, N 9,33:6
Roe, Charles F Mrs, 1921, Ap 16,11:4
Roe, Charles H Mrs, 1958, Ag 17,85:3
Roe, Charles Hamilton, 1925, O 24,15:6
Roe, Chester M, 1950, Ap 30,102:8
Roe, E P Rev, 1888, Jl 21,5:4
Roe, Earle C, 1958, Ja 1,25:2
Roe, Edward L Rev, 1914, Jl 23,9:3
Roe, Edwin P, 1940, F 29,19:3
Roe, Elias P, 1943, S 16,21:4
Roe, Ernest S, 1964, Je 5,31:4
Roe, Eugene T, 1951, N 30,23:4
Roe, F A Adm, 1901, D 29,7:6
Roe, Floyd C, 1953, Mr 12,27:2
Roe, Frank O, 1947, O 27,21:3
Roe, Frederick, 1965, Ag 22,83:2
Roe, Gelston G Mrs, 1947, N 8,17:5
Roe, George H, 1944, Ap 13,19:6
Roe, George R, 1955, D 20,31:2
Roe, Gilbert E Mrs, 1968, Ap 9,48:1
Roe, Grace M Mrs, 1949, Ap 23,13:6
Roe, Henry K, 1950, O 30,27:5
Roe, Herman, 1961, N 19,89:1
Roe, Humphrey V, 1949, Jl 27,23:3
Roe, Irving, 1944, Ja 3,21:4
Roe, Irving L, 1960, Jl 27,29:2
Roe, James A, 1941, D 19,25:4; 1942, Ag 16,45:3; 1945, S 2,32:1
Roe, James A Jr Justice, 1968, S 9,1:1
Roe, James A Sr, 1967, Ap 23,92:2
Roe, James H Mrs, 1945, Ap 1,36:3
Roe, James P, 1948, D 1,29:6
Roe, Jefferson, 1925, N 25,21:5
Roe, John, 1942, Ag 13,19:3
Roe, John C, 1949, Mr 14,19:6
Roe, John C Dr, 1915, D 25,7:6
Roe, John J, 1966, Je 21,43:4
Roe, John J Jr, 1967, Mr 2,35:2
Roe, John J Sr, 1956, Jl 8,64:4
Roe, John L, 1951, Ag 7,25:3
Roe, John W, 1911, Ap 17,11:5
Roe, Joseph B Dr, 1904, F 6,9:5
Roe, Joseph W, 1960, N 11,29:1
Roe, Joseph W Mrs, 1960, Ag 1,23:3
Roe, June R, 1958, F 23,92:1
Roe, Livingston, 1925, Ap 6,19:5
Roe, Louis N Mrs, 1962, F 24,27:4
Roe, Luther M, 1938, My 8,II,6:8
Roe, Nathaniel, 1957, Ja 15,30:2
Roe, Stephen J Capt, 1908, Ag 27,7:6
Roe, Thomas B Mrs, 1944, D 7,25:1
Roe, Thomas Hazard, 1907, Mr 8,9:7
Roe, Thomas W, 1907, Jl 13,7:6
Roe, Walter C Rev Dr, 1913, Mr 14,9:1
Roe, Walter F, 1948, Je 20,60:7
Roe, Wellington, 1952, F 5,29:2
Roe, William Clarke, 1925, Ja 6,25:5
Roe, William E, 1950, S 7,31:4
Roe, William H, 1953, Jl 23,23:2
Roe, William I, 1953, Jl 1,29:5
Roe, William R Mrs, 1953, Mr 13,27:1
Roe, Wilmot O, 1955, D 10,21:5
Roeandt, Augustus, 1944, O 26,23:6
Roeber, Ernest, 1944, D 16,15:4
Roeber, Ernest Mrs, 1953, Jl 11,11:4
Roeber, Eugene F Mrs, 1947, F 15,15:4
Roeber, Eugene P Dr, 1917, O 19,13:7
Roeblind, Ferdinand W 3d Mrs, 1950, My 23,29:1
Roebling, Cornelia W Mrs, 1942, My 3,53:2
Roebling, Donald (will, D 30,19:7), 1959, Ag 30,82:1
Roebling, F W Jr, 1936, My 30,15:4
Roebling, Ferdinand W, 1917, Mr 17,13:5
Roebling, Ferdinand W Jr Mrs, 1960, F 1,27:2
Roebling, George W Mrs, 1959, Ja 27,33:3
Roebling, John A, 1869, Jl 23,4:6
Roebling, John A (will, F 29,21:2), 1952, F 3,85:1
Roebling, John A Mrs, 1914, S 18,9:6
Roebling, Karl G (funl, My 31,15:4), 1921, My 30,9:5
Roebling, Lucia W, 1884, D 30,5:5
Roebling, W A Col, 1926, Jl 22,19:1
Roebling, W A Mrs, 1903, Mr 1,7:7
Roebuck, Alvah C (por), 1948, Je 20,60:4
Roebuck, Arthur H, 1950, N 25,13:2
Roebuck, Charles A, 1949, Je 28,27:3
Roebuck, J A, 1879, D 1,5:4
Roebuck, John A, 1945, Ja 2,19:5
Roebuck, Member of Parliment, 1879, D 2,2:4
Roechling, Hermann, 1955, Ag 26,19:1
Roeck, E C, 1903, My 10,7:6
Roeckel, Charles F, 1957, Ap 7,88:7
Roedder, Edwin C (por), 1945, O 23,17:1
Roedel, Frederick W, 1956, S 21,25:4
Roedel, Karl (por), 1946, F 3,40:1
Roedel, William A, 1937, My 21,22:1
Roedelheim, Alfred M, 1944, Ag 27,33:3
Roedelheimer, Hans, 1966, Je 9,47:3
Roedell, Robert J, 1948, Je 23,27:2
Roeder, Alan T, 1956, My 17,31:4
Roeder, Alex E, 1962, Je 2,19:4
Roeder, Arthur, 1960, My 10,37:4
Roeder, Austin H, 1945, My 2,23:3
Roeder, Benjamin F, 1943, My 5,27:3
Roeder, Benjamin F Mrs, 1918, My 21,13:2
Roeder, Carl M, 1952, Ja 25,22:2
Roeder, Charles B, 1968, Je 29,29:2
Roeder, Charles W, 1948, Ja 15,23:2
Roeder, Edward M, 1939, My 13,15:5
Roeder, Elmer, 1959, Ja 29,27:3
Roeder, Elsa, 1914, Ap 22,15:5

Roeder, Gus C, 1920, My 23,22:4
Roeder, Harry H, 1944, N 3,21:3
Roeder, Jehail M Mrs, 1957, My 19,88:3
Roeder, John W, 1940, Mr 14,23:2
Roeder, Joseph, 1957, Ap 17,31:3
Roeder, Lawrence J, 1943, My 16,43:2
Roeder, William G, 1945, O 13,15:2
Roeder, William K, 1950, Mr 17,24:5
Roediger, Louis F, 1942, Jl 28,17:4
Roediger, T Frederick, 1965, N 5,37:3
Roeding, Frederick F, 1961, D 13,43:4
Roeger, William H, 1963, Je 25,33:3
Roehig, Frederic Louis Otto Prof, 1908, Jl 18,7:6
Roehl, Charles C, 1953, Ja 1,23:2
Roehl, Charles E, 1959, Mr 5,31:2
Roehl, Charles E Mrs, 1962, Je 28,31:5
Roehl, Frank A Jr, 1959, O 23,17:5
Roehm, Charles L Jr, 1946, O 2,29:4
Roehm, Frederick, 1953, Ja 21,31:4
Roehm, Frederick G, 1951, My 21,27:5
Roehm, MacDonell, 1960, Jl 21,27:3
Roehm, William, 1949, Mr 18,25:4
Roehmn, Adolf, 1958, Ja 25,19:4
Roehr, Eduard Franz, 1907, F 19,9:6
Roehr, F E, 1880, Ja 11,7:1
Roehrauer, William, 1949, Ag 27,13:3
Roehrich, Marcel R, 1968, Jl 17,43:3
Roehrig, Emil, 1941, O 29,23:4
Roehrig, G Edward, 1938, Ap 19,21:5
Roehrig, George F, 1948, N 11,27:4
Roehrig, Henry, 1946, Ja 1,28:3
Roehrle, Charles F, 1950, D 16,17:3
Roehrs, Walter E, 1949, N 9,27:3
Roelker, Alfred, 1915, D 23,13:4; 1953, F 17,27:3
Roelker, Charles R Rear-Adm, 1910, S 30,13:6
Roelker, Edward G, 1957, N 2,21:2
Roelker, Eleanor J Mrs, 1910, S 6,9:6
Roelker, William G, 1953, My 30,15:7
Roelker, William G Ex-Sen, 1911, Ja 25,9:5
Roell, Johan H, 1942, O 21,21:2
Roell, John, 1947, Ag 21,23:3
Roeller, Russell S, 1952, N 13,31:2
Roelofs, Henrietta (por), 1942, Ja 28,19:1
Roelofs, Henry, 1943, Mr 11,21:2
Roelofsma, Edmond, 1943, Ap 2,21:6
Roelse, Harold V, 1960, Ja 24,88:4
Roem, Otto, 1943, N 22,19:2
Roemaet, Charles, 1909, Ag 2,7:6
Roember, Charles A, 1951, S 21,23:2
Roemer, Charles G, 1952, Ap 26,23:3
Roemer, Clarence J, 1949, Je 22,31:4
Roemer, Elisabeth, 1961, My 10,45:4
Roemer, Erwin W, 1960, Mr 4,25:4
Roemer, George P, 1943, N 3,25:4
Roemer, Henry C, 1953, N 17,31:1
Roemer, Herbert C, 1940, Jl 6,15:3
Roemer, Herbert T, 1948, Je 30,25:2
Roemer, Hubert, 1942, Ap 7,22:3
Roemer, Irving Mrs, 1954, Ja 7,31:4
Roemer, J Charles (por), 1945, F 16,23:3
Roemer, Jacob (died Je 22, funl plans, Je 27,39:4; cor), 1967, Je 28,45:4
Roemer, Jacob Mrs, 1940, O 19,17:2
Roemer, John L, 1940, Ag 10,13:6
Roemer, John Mrs, 1947, My 16,23:2
Roemer, Joseph, 1955, Jl 3,33:1
Roemer, Phil, 1938, Ja 11,23:5
Roemer, Theodor, 1951, S 10,21:3
Roemer, William B, 1955, Ap 23,19:5
Roemer, William C, 1953, Je 24,25:5
Roemheld, Jules E, 1947, F 18,25:4
Roemle, Edward H, 1944, Jl 17,15:5
Roemmert, George, 1952, Mr 13,29:5
Roenneberg, Hans J, 1941, S 16,23:6
Roentgen, Wilhelm K von, 1923, F 11,6:3
Roepke, Henry F, 1942, Jl 31,15:2
Roepke, John, 1962, F 28,33:4
Roerdam, Archbishop, 1909, S 26,13:6
Roerich, George, 1960, My 23,29:6
Roerich, Nicholas K, 1947, D 16,33:1
Roerink, Garrett Mrs, 1964, Jl 25,19:6
Roes, Frank J, 1944, Je 18,35:1
Roes, William A, 1954, Ja 12,24:3
Roesch, Donald G, 1965, Mr 15,31:4
Roesch, Frank P, 1951, Ap 30,21:4
Roesch, George F, 1917, D 22,11:5
Roesch, J Albert Jr, 1939, Ap 28,25:5
Roesch, Joseph L, 1949, Jl 26,27:3
Roesch, W Eugene, 1952, S 20,15:7
Roese, John B (Bro Jerome), 1959, Je 10,37:1
Roese, William, 1954, Ap 13,31:3
Roesen, Isabella L G Mrs, 1941, Jl 4,13:2
Roesen, Oscar, 1921, My 15,22:3
Roesen, Oscar C (will, Ag 8,22:6), 1951, Jl 29,69:1
Roesen, Robert H, 1924, Ja 20,13:2
Roeser, Charles F, 1949, Jl 15,19:2
Roeser, Ernest A, 1950, My 29,17:3
Roeser, Theodore, 1951, Ap 11,29:3
Roesler, Edward Mrs, 1962, Mr 15,35:4
Roesler, Hugo, 1961, Ap 28,31:2
Roesler De Villiers, Robert A, 1944, O 22,45:1
Roesner, Walt, 1951, S 2,48:8
Roessel, Carl A, 1941, O 10,23:3
Roessel, L Otto E, 1942, Jl 7,19:4
Roessel, Max L, 1958, Mr 2,88:6
Roesser, Henry F, 1904, O 26,9:5
Roesser, Mary K Mrs, 1941, Ap 18,21:8
Roessle, Herman, 1961, F 25,21:2
Roessle, T E, 1904, Ag 11,7:6
Roessle, William, 1947, Mr 5,25:1
Roessler, Carl, 1951, F 24,13:2
Roessler, Harry K, 1960, Mr 31,33:3
Roessler, Rudolf, 1958, D 17,2:6
Roessler, Solomon W, 1945, Ja 19,20:2
Roethke, Julius Sr, 1949, S 13,29:2
Roethke, Theodore, 1963, Ag 2,27:1
Roetken, Oscar H, 1937, Mr 16,23:1
Roetsseau, Norbert, 1939, O 6,25:4
Roetter, Friedrich, 1953, O 27,27:4
Roettger, Friederich Wilhelm, 1946, S 17,8:3
Roettger, Harold E, 1955, Ag 12,20:2
Roettiger, Hans, 1960, Ap 16,17:4
Roey, Joseph E van Cardinal (funl, Ag 11,23:2), 1961, Ag 7,23:2
Roff, Allen A, 1948, Je 29,23:2
Roff, Fred, 1953, Jl 18,13:5
Roff, John A, 1949, D 8,33:2
Roff, Nate, 1907, O 29,11:6
Roff, W Wallace, 1960, Ja 18,27:4
Roffman, Maurice Mrs, 1967, F 7,39:2
Roffman, Samuel W, 1962, Ag 9,25:5
Roffo, Angel H, 1947, Jl 25,17:3
Rofrano, M A, 1932, Jl 4,11:3
Rog, Simon, 1951, Ag 26,79:3
Rogalin, Maurice E, 1966, D 10,38:5
Rogan, Daniel A, 1948, F 8,61:1
Rogan, Edward, 1951, Jl 22,61:1
Rogan, Fred L, 1960, F 9,31:1
Rogan, George F, 1940, O 3,25:5
Rogan, George R, 1941, F 5,19:3
Rogan, Henry A, 1966, Jl 26,35:3
Rogan, James A, 1949, Jl 28,23:4
Rogan, James S, 1954, Je 14,21:5
Rogan, James W Rev Dr, 1916, N 8,13:6
Rogan, John H Mrs, 1957, Ag 8,23:2
Rogan, Nat, 1943, Ag 9,13:6
Rogan, Ralph F Mrs, 1953, S 11,21:4
Rogan, Roger K, 1947, Ja 29,26:3
Roge, Edward H Sr, 1960, N 22,35:3
Roge, Paul A, 1962, D 6,43:1
Rogenski, Walter F, 1955, O 22,19:5
Roger, Alexander Rev, 1914, Ja 10,9:5
Roger, Davenant Col, 1915, Ja 21,9:4
Roger, G H, 1879, S 14,7:3
Roger, George H, 1947, D 11,33:3
Roger, John, 1903, Jl 18,2:6; 1955, Mr 10,27:3
Roger, John E, 1956, N 8,39:5
Roger, Tenor, 1879, S 29,5:1
Rogers, A, 1928, My 10,27:5
Rogers, A George, 1955, Ja 28,19:2
Rogers, A Glenn, 1954, O 11,27:6
Rogers, A L, 1905, Je 23,2:2
Rogers, Agnes E, 1938, My 2,17:4
Rogers, Agnes L, 1943, Jl 23,17:3
Rogers, Al, 1954, My 9,88:5
Rogers, Alan, 1941, S 20,17:5
Rogers, Albert E, 1945, D 24,15:2
Rogers, Albert T, 1937, Ap 11,II,8:8
Rogers, Alex, 1938, F 17,21:3
Rogers, Alex H, 1942, Ag 21,19:4
Rogers, Alex Mrs, 1948, O 18,23:2
Rogers, Alex P, 1950, Je 30,23:1
Rogers, Alexander L, 1944, O 14,13:3
Rogers, Alfred M, 1953, Ja 28,27:1
Rogers, Alfred Mrs, 1955, D 4,88:6
Rogers, Alfred S, 1953, N 1,87:3
Rogers, Allan B, 1962, Je 13,41:3
Rogers, Allan E, 1937, N 6,17:4
Rogers, Allen (por), 1938, N 5,19:7
Rogers, Allen C, 1942, Ag 14,17:2
Rogers, Allen H, 1938, F 15,25:3
Rogers, Annie D Mrs, 1940, S 17,23:3
Rogers, Anson H, 1961, F 24,21:7
Rogers, Anthony S, 1941, N 2,53:3
Rogers, Arthur, 1938, Je 11,15:2; 1951, Mr 1,27:4
Rogers, Arthur P, 1960, Ag 8,21:4
Rogers, Arthur S, 1953, N 17,31:4
Rogers, Arthur W Dr, 1937, Ag 29,II,7:4
Rogers, Augustus, 1953, Mr 17,29:5
Rogers, Augustus Mrs, 1947, Ag 7,21:2
Rogers, B T, 1934, S 22,15:4
Rogers, Belden J, 1909, Ag 7,9:6
Rogers, Belsen J Mrs, 1903, Jl 5,7:5
Rogers, Benjamin Talbot Mrs, 1916, S 1,9:6
Rogers, Bernard, 1968, My 25,35:1
Rogers, Bernard F, 1941, Ja 13,15:2
Rogers, Bernard F Jr, 1937, Ag 30,21:4
Rogers, Bert, 1939, O 16,19:4
Rogers, Bert Mrs, 1960, O 23,88:5
Rogers, Bogart, 1966, Jl 26,32:1
Rogers, Boone L, 1956, N 15,46:8
Rogers, Bruce, 1957, My 19,89:1
Rogers, Bud Mrs, 1955, Je 23,29:1
Rogers, Burton C, 1946, O 8,23:3
Rogers, C D, 1903, My 28,9:6
Rogers, C E, 1905, F 19,1:2
Rogers, C H, 1885, Ja 1,5:4
Rogers, C Milton, 1945, N 5,19:4
Rogers, C O Maj, 1869, Ap 16,1:7
Rogers, C Paul, 1950, Je 30,23:5
Rogers, Cassius C, 1944, Ap 22,15:3
Rogers, Cephas Brainerd, 1919, Mr 21,13:3
Rogers, Charles, 1940, N 8,21:3
Rogers, Charles A, 1940, Mr 28,24:3; 1956, D 22,36:3
Rogers, Charles B, 1937, D 23,21:6
Rogers, Charles Curtis, 1917, D 5,13:5
Rogers, Charles D Mrs, 1955, D 20,31:4
Rogers, Charles E, 1942, Jl 2,21:6; 1946, N 26,29:5
Rogers, Charles E Mrs, 1952, Ag 17,77:3
Rogers, Charles H, 1947, F 20,26:3
Rogers, Charles L, 1941, My 15,23:1
Rogers, Charles Mrs, 1947, Je 26,24:2
Rogers, Charles P, 1943, D 6,23:3; 1960, Je 12,86:6
Rogers, Charles R, 1957, Mr 31,88:7
Rogers, Charles S Col, 1922, N 21,19:4
Rogers, Charles T, 1945, Mr 23,19:4; 1950, S 2,15:4
Rogers, Charles W, 1938, Ja 26,23:2
Rogers, Clarence, 1942, Jl 8,23:4
Rogers, Clarence M, 1950, Ap 28,21:3
Rogers, Clayton, 1943, N 8,19:6
Rogers, Clayton T, 1945, Mr 29,23:5
Rogers, Cornwell B, 1956, Jl 8,65:2
Rogers, Crawford S, 1956, Je 5,35:5
Rogers, Daisy F, 1954, Ja 23,13:3
Rogers, Dan D, 1952, O 18,19:5
Rogers, Daniel F, 1938, My 31,19:4
Rogers, Daniel L, 1945, S 12,25:4
Rogers, David B, 1967, S 9,31:2
Rogers, David G, 1941, D 31,17:4
Rogers, David W, 1968, My 23,47:3
Rogers, De F Rev, 1876, Ja 20,5:5
Rogers, Donald G, 1959, Ja 1,31:2
Rogers, Dumont D, 1949, O 27,27:4
Rogers, Dwight L, 1954, D 2,31:5
Rogers, Dwight L Mrs, 1958, Ja 19,86:6
Rogers, Dwight Mrs (M Tyndall), 1966, Mr 23,48:1
Rogers, E Albert, 1942, Je 27,13:6
Rogers, E Claude, 1943, Mr 30,26:5
Rogers, E Norman (por), 1940, Je 25,23:2
Rogers, E P, 1881, O 25,3:5
Rogers, Earl C, 1941, Ap 15,23:2
Rogers, Edith N, 1960, S 11,82:2
Rogers, Edmund E Capt, 1937, O 14,25:3
Rogers, Edmund P, 1966, S 17,29:1
Rogers, Edmund P Jr, 1966, D 4,88:5
Rogers, Edmund Pendleton, 1919, Mr 18,11:2
Rogers, Edmund W, 1937, N 9,23:4
Rogers, Edward C, 1948, S 27,23:4
Rogers, Edward Covell, 1925, Ap 14,23:5
Rogers, Edward H, 1942, Jl 14,19:5; 1948, Ja 7,25:2
Rogers, Edward I, 1968, Ja 11,37:2
Rogers, Edward J, 1951, O 24,31:3
Rogers, Edward L, 1912, Jl 19,9:5
Rogers, Edward R, 1948, Ag 28,16:3
Rogers, Edward S, 1939, My 7,III,6:8
Rogers, Edward S (por), 1949, My 23,23:5
Rogers, Edward S, 1950, Ag 16,29:2
Rogers, Edward W, 1952, Mr 3,21:3
Rogers, Edwin, 1907, Ag 17,7:6
Rogers, Edwin A, 1946, F 28,23:2
Rogers, Edwin M, 1944, Jl 25,19:5
Rogers, Egbert I, 1947, F 4,26:3
Rogers, Elijah, 1949, My 16,21:2
Rogers, Elisabeth C Mrs (E Cobb), 1959, My 27,3
Rogers, Elmer F, 1943, Mr 21,26:4
Rogers, Elvin H, 1948, Ap 14,28:2
Rogers, Emil Mrs, 1966, Jl 27,39:3
Rogers, Emmett (mem ser, N 4,56:2), 1965, N 2,3
Rogers, Emmett F, 1953, O 1,29:5
Rogers, Ernest A, 1950, Mr 7,27:3
Rogers, Ernest E, 1945, Ja 29,13:1; 1960, Je 12,86:
Rogers, Erskine C (por), 1940, N 4,19:3
Rogers, Eugene C, 1937, Mr 24,25:5
Rogers, Ezra Dr, 1912, D 18,15:2
Rogers, F H, 1923, Jl 21,9:4
Rogers, Fanny E, 1938, Ap 16,13:3
Rogers, Fletcher, 1940, Ja 12,17:4
Rogers, Frances Mrs, 1938, Je 5,45:2
Rogers, Francis, 1915, Jl 7,11:6; 1951, My 16,35:1
Rogers, Francis E, 1940, Ag 15,19:5
Rogers, Francis Mrs, 1958, S 3,33:3
Rogers, Francis Rev, 1951, Ja 14,86:2
Rogers, Frank B Mrs, 1965, Ja 6,39:2
Rogers, Frank C, 1946, My 28,21:3
Rogers, Frank F, 1942, My 1,19:4; 1948, Je 28,19:
Rogers, Frank Fowler, 1923, Jl 3,13:5
Rogers, Frank H, 1951, N 15,29:2
Rogers, Frank J, 1961, S 17,86:7
Rogers, Frank T, 1947, Jl 11,15:4
Rogers, Frank V, 1965, Je 28,29:4
Rogers, Franklin Dr, 1921, My 29,22:4
Rogers, Franklyn H, 1957, Ap 25,31:1
Rogers, Fred A, 1949, Mr 20,76:5
Rogers, Fred E, 1951, F 10,13:2
Rogers, Fred E Jr, 1950, Mr 30,30:2
Rogers, Fred F, 1952, N 7,23:2
Rogers, Fred S, 1953, N 26,31:4
Rogers, Frederick C, 1953, My 25,26:5
Rogers, Frederick J, 1941, D 11,27:6

Rogers, Frederick S, 1942, Je 11,23:4
Rogers, Frederick S Mrs, 1953, Jl 23,23:1
Rogers, G Sherburne, 1919, D 19,15:2
Rogers, G Vernor, 1961, Ag 14,25:5
Rogers, Gardner, 1943, D 20,23:5
Rogers, George, 1951, Ap 15,93:2
Rogers, George A, 1946, S 23,23:4; 1954, N 25,29:5
Rogers, George A Mrs, 1955, Ap 6,29:1
Rogers, George B, 1945, O 12,23:2
Rogers, George B Mrs, 1948, Ag 22,60:7
Rogers, George C, 1940, Jl 12,15:4; 1950, My 5,22:2; 1950, O 21,17:5
Rogers, George D (will), 1949, D 14,42:6
Rogers, George E F Mrs, 1961, Ap 11,5:5
Rogers, George F (por), 1948, N 21,88:1
Rogers, George H, 1948, Ja 15,23:4
Rogers, George M, 1949, S 11,92:1
Rogers, George M Mrs, 1951, Ap 28,15:4; 1967, Mr 30,45:3
Rogers, George R, 1939, O 21,15:3
Rogers, George W, 1904, O 15,9:4; 1958, Ja 11,36:2
Rogers, Gerrit P, 1954, Ja 30,17:6
Rogers, Glenn E, 1965, Je 1,39:1
Rogers, Gordon B, 1967, Jl 3,17:4
Rogers, Grace R Mrs, 1943, My 11,21:3
Rogers, Granville P, 1942, Ag 8,11:5
Rogers, Griffith G, 1945, N 6,19:3
Rogers, Gus, 1908, O 20,9:5
Rogers, Gus Mrs, 1961, My 12,29:4
Rogers, Guy, 1967, Jl 21,31:4
Rogers, H E Mrs, 1945, Ap 11,23:5
Rogers, H H, 1935, Jl 26,15:1
Rogers, H J, 1927, S 30,25:5
Rogers, H T, 1879, Ag 21,1:2
Rogers, H W Judge, 1926, Ag 17,21:5
Rogers, Harold E, 1946, Ja 21,23:2; 1960, F 7,84:6
Rogers, Harriet P Mrs, 1941, Je 24,19:6
Rogers, Harris, 1924, My 20,21:5
Rogers, Harrison S Mrs, 1958, Ag 12,29:4
Rogers, Harry, 1950, Ag 13,76:4; 1961, Ag 19,17:6
Rogers, Harry H, 1957, D 5,35:6
Rogers, Harry L, 1944, N 21,25:4
Rogers, Harry L Gen, 1925, D 15,25:3
Rogers, Harry L Mrs, 1950, Jl 9,69:2
Rogers, Harry S, 1957, Je 7,23:1
Rogers, Harry T, 1939, My 22,17:5
Rogers, Harry W, 1956, D 4,39:4
Rogers, Hattie C Mrs, 1957, N 7,35:3
Rogers, Henry A, 1941, O 31,23:1
Rogers, Henry B, 1964, Je 9,35:2
Rogers, Henry D, 1866, Je 24,1:7
Rogers, Henry E, 1943, Ja 4,15:3
Rogers, Henry F, 1902, N 11,3:5
Rogers, Henry G Mrs, 1954, My 23,88:6
Rogers, Henry H, 1909, My 21,9:6
Rogers, Henry H Jr, 1948, Je 22,25:1
Rogers, Henry H Mrs, 1912, Ag 31,7:3
Rogers, Henry H 3d, 1948, Jl 26,17:6
Rogers, Henry J, 1939, Ag 29,21:5
Rogers, Henry M, 1937, Mr 30,23:5
Rogers, Henry M Mrs, 1937, D 10,25:1
Rogers, Henry Pendleton, 1912, Ag 14,9:4
Rogers, Henry Pendleton Mrs, 1911, Je 14,9:6
Rogers, Henry W, 1940, Ja 2,19:1; 1951, Ja 25,25:1
Rogers, Herbert W, 1964, Ja 26,80:7
Rogers, Herman L, 1957, O 22,33:4
Rogers, Hopewell L, 1948, F 29,60:6
Rogers, Horatio R, 1958, O 25,21:4
Rogers, Howard A, 1946, N 19,31:2
Rogers, Howard J, 1948, S 27,23:5; 1957, F 13,35:6
Rogers, Howard L Mrs, 1949, F 18,23:1
Rogers, Hubert E, 1959, Ja 1,31:3
Rogers, Hubert E Mrs, 1963, S 24,39:3
Rogers, Hugh M Jr, 1954, Je 11,23:4
Rogers, Ida M, 1947, N 11,27:4
Rogers, Ida M Mrs, 1941, O 29,23:4
Rogers, Ira G Sr, 1956, Ag 10,17:6
Rogers, J Dwight, 1938, Jl 9,13:2
Rogers, J Elsworth, 1960, Je 16,33:3
Rogers, J R, 1932, O 8,17:3
Rogers, J R Ex-Gov, 1901, D 27,7:5
Rogers, Jacob H Mrs, 1943, Je 30,21:5
Rogers, James, 1914, Je 23,11:4; 1952, My 1,29:6; 1955, Mr 25,23:3
Rogers, James C, 1907, Ja 8,9:2; 1938, N 5,19:6; 1952, Ja 16,25:2
Rogers, James Clinton Gen, 1907, F 12,9:6
Rogers, James F, 1947, S 26,23:3
Rogers, James G (por), 1947, O 2,27:1
Rogers, James G Mrs, 1942, D 16,25:6
Rogers, James Guinness Rev, 1911, Ag 21,9:7
Rogers, James H, 1940, N 30,17:5
Rogers, James Harmond Mrs, 1968, Ap 8,47:2
Rogers, James J, 1963, Je 8,25:3
Rogers, James S, 1949, Jl 10,56:5; 1955, My 19,29:2
Rogers, James V, 1939, My 3,23:6
Rogers, James Wood, 1912, Ag 21,9:3
Rogers, Janet P, 1940, Ap 16,23:2
Rogers, Jason, 1932, Ap 27,17:5
Rogers, Jason Mrs, 1964, Ap 11,25:4
Rogers, Jennie S Mrs, 1937, Ap 28,23:3
Rogers, Jesse A, 1962, N 22,29:3
Rogers, Jessie, 1938, Ap 3,II,7:2
Rogers, Jessie Mrs, 1949, O 12,30:2
Rogers, Joel A, 1966, Mr 27,86:6
Rogers, Joel E, 1940, Mr 23,13:4
Rogers, John, 1904, Jl 27,7:7; 1939, N 20,19:3; 1948, D 3,26:2; 1952, O 23,31:1
Rogers, John A, 1966, D 13,47:4
Rogers, John C, 1940, Ap 8,20:4
Rogers, John D, 1965, N 2,34:1; 1967, Je 18,76:1
Rogers, John E, 1950, F 28,29:2
Rogers, John F, 1939, Je 7,23:6; 1943, O 28,23:4
Rogers, John H Judge, 1911, Ap 18,11:5
Rogers, John I, 1910, Mr 14,7:4
Rogers, John J (por), 1945, F 13,23:4
Rogers, John Jacob (funl, Ap 1,23:5), 1925, Mr 29,7:1
Rogers, John Jr, 1967, Je 30,37:3
Rogers, John L, 1950, N 26,89:5
Rogers, John M, 1943, O 30,15:4; 1946, Jl 24,27:1; 1948, O 16,15:5
Rogers, John M Jr, 1947, D 31,15:4
Rogers, John Mrs, 1950, D 19,29:3
Rogers, John P, 1962, Ag 31,21:4
Rogers, John R, 1960, N 25,27:3
Rogers, John T (por), 1937, Mr 4,23:2
Rogers, John V Mrs, 1949, O 12,30:2
Rogers, John W, 1908, F 26,7:6; 1946, Ja 1,28:3; 1958, Je 28,17:6; 1965, N 20,35:1; 1968, F 1,37:3
Rogers, Johnson, 1943, Ja 31,46:3
Rogers, Joseph B, 1940, O 14,19:3
Rogers, Joseph E, 1948, Ap 2,23:2; 1951, Ag 28,23:3
Rogers, Joseph L, 1951, S 17,21:6
Rogers, Joseph W, 1952, Jl 10,31:2
Rogers, Josephine C, 1925, S 10,25:6
Rogers, Karl H, 1942, S 14,15:4
Rogers, Katherine W Mrs, 1942, Ja 6,23:4
Rogers, Lawrence H, 1959, O 16,31:4
Rogers, Lawrence J, 1967, Ap 23,94:2
Rogers, Lawrence W, 1962, Ap 22,80:6
Rogers, Leighton W, 1962, Ja 28,76:4
Rogers, Leo J, 1941, Mr 8,19:5
Rogers, Leo M, 1967, Jl 17,29:4
Rogers, Lettie H Mrs, 1957, My 15,35:3
Rogers, Lewis G, 1953, N 23,27:2
Rogers, Lewis G Mrs, 1957, D 28,17:4
Rogers, Lewis L Jr, 1940, Ag 13,19:6
Rogers, Lincoln, 1944, My 6,15:4
Rogers, Lindsay Mrs, 1965, Ja 28,30:6
Rogers, Lora, 1948, D 24,17:2
Rogers, Loraine, 1904, Ja 19,9:5
Rogers, Lorlys E, 1942, Ag 2,39:2
Rogers, Louis A Mrs (L Andrews),(funl plans, My 10,47:2), 1967, My 9,47:3
Rogers, Louise T Mrs, 1962, D 8,27:4
Rogers, Lowell L, 1944, Ap 7,20:3
Rogers, Mable Mrs, 1947, Ap 5,19:4
Rogers, Maggie Mrs, 1953, Jl 23,23:6
Rogers, Mark H, 1941, O 6,17:4
Rogers, Marshall C, 1960, Je 9,33:6
Rogers, Martha M, 1951, My 12,21:1
Rogers, Mary (Mother Mary Joseph), 1955, O 10, 27:1
Rogers, Mary B Mrs, 1956, S 23,84:4
Rogers, Mary E Mrs, 1948, Ja 22,27:5
Rogers, Mary G, 1951, F 28,28:3
Rogers, Mason T, 1954, F 11,29:1
Rogers, Max Mrs, 1955, Je 23,29:1
Rogers, Merrill, 1964, N 11,43:2
Rogers, Michael C, 1952, Ja 28,17:2
Rogers, Michael I, 1938, N 17,4:4
Rogers, Millicent A, 1953, Ja 2,15:1
Rogers, Millicent A Mrs (est tax appr), 1954, Jl 8, 48:5
Rogers, Morgan W, 1949, S 26,25:3
Rogers, Nathaniel P Mrs, 1945, Ap 9,19:1
Rogers, Nathaniel R, 1945, S 10,19:4
Rogers, Naylor, 1952, Mr 15,13:4
Rogers, Neil, 1966, D 5,45:3
Rogers, Nelson W, 1951, Ag 8,25:5
Rogers, Newton H, 1946, O 29,25:4
Rogers, Noah C Mrs, 1958, Ap 24,31:1
Rogers, Norman Phelps, 1914, Ap 9,11:4
Rogers, Norton P, 1965, Ap 19,29:2
Rogers, Oliver H, 1954, Ja 24,84:4
Rogers, Oscar H, 1941, My 18,43:1
Rogers, Oscar S Jr, 1949, Ja 8,15:4
Rogers, Otis J, 1941, Je 9,19:3
Rogers, P L, 1864, Jl 9,3:4
Rogers, Patrick J, 1949, Ap 24,76:8
Rogers, Paul B, 1938, My 25,23:5
Rogers, Paul I, 1967, Mr 19,92:8
Rogers, Pearce, 1948, F 21,13:6
Rogers, Peter F Maj, 1915, My 10,15:6
Rogers, Philip, 1945, O 15,17:6
Rogers, Preston P, 1947, My 3,17:4
Rogers, R E, 1884, S 7,6:7
Rogers, Ralph D Mrs, 1954, Mr 16,29:2
Rogers, Ralph E, 1945, Jl 5,13:5
Rogers, Ralph W, 1956, S 24,27:4
Rogers, Raymond C, 1949, S 29,29:2
Rogers, Raymond Prof, 1968, D 24,20:3
Rogers, Reginald, 1949, N 30,27:3
Rogers, Rex D, 1962, Ap 19,31:5
Rogers, Richard J, 1949, Ap 24,76:3
Rogers, Richard M, 1957, D 7,21:4
Rogers, Richard R, 1949, N 11,26:3
Rogers, Richard R Mrs, 1945, N 4,44:2
Rogers, Richard W, 1962, Ja 27,21:3
Rogers, Robert, 1945, O 18,23:6; 1950, My 3,29:2
Rogers, Robert Cameron, 1912, Ap 21,II,13:4
Rogers, Robert E, 1941, My 14,21:4; 1947, Ap 16,25:2
Rogers, Robert M, 1941, My 14,21:2
Rogers, Robert S, 1946, N 7,31:5
Rogers, Robert W, 1958, Ap 30,33:2
Rogers, Robert W Mrs, 1939, D 5,27:4
Rogers, Robin E, 1952, Ag 25,17:5
Rogers, Roy Mrs, 1946, N 4,25:5
Rogers, Roy R Sr, 1950, Jl 6,27:2
Rogers, Roy S, 1945, Je 11,15:4
Rogers, Roys S, 1955, Je 6,27:4
Rogers, Rufus B, 1947, Ja 15,26:3
Rogers, Russell C Mrs, 1967, Ja 2,19:4
Rogers, S, 1946, Mr 21,25:6
Rogers, Samuel S, 1939, O 29,41:2
Rogers, Sanford, 1944, Je 29,23:4
Rogers, Sarah A (Sister Annette), 1953, Ja 30,22:5
Rogers, Scott M, 1953, S 7,19:5
Rogers, Scott M Mrs, 1946, S 15,9:8
Rogers, Shadow, 1940, My 30,18:3
Rogers, Stanley R H, 1961, Ja 23,23:3
Rogers, Theodore, 1903, N 9,7:6
Rogers, Theodore B Jr, 1940, D 27,14:6
Rogers, Theodore C, 1943, Mr 23,20:3
Rogers, Thomas, 1947, N 11,28:2; 1950, O 17,31:2
Rogers, Thomas J, 1957, O 5,17:2
Rogers, Thornton Lt-Col, 1937, O 20,23:4
Rogers, Tyler S, 1967, O 13,39:2
Rogers, Vance, 1962, Ag 29,14:4
Rogers, Vinnie, 1965, N 3,35:5
Rogers, W, 1935, Ag 17,1:8
Rogers, W A, 1931, O 21,23:3
Rogers, W Clifton, 1956, My 14,25:2
Rogers, W Horace, 1953, My 30,15:4
Rogers, Wallace B Mrs, 1950, D 2,13:5
Rogers, Walter, 1937, Ja 17,II,8:5; 1960, Jl 6,33:2
Rogers, Walter B, 1945, Jl 14,11:6
Rogers, Walter F, 1943, O 24,44:4
Rogers, Walter P, 1948, O 11,23:4
Rogers, Walter S, 1965, O 26,45:1
Rogers, Warren L, 1938, N 7,19:2
Rogers, Watson M Justice, 1911, F 2,11:4
Rogers, Wilbur H, 1945, Ag 15,19:5
Rogers, Wilbur H Mrs, 1949, N 22,29:5
Rogers, Will, 1950, D 20,31:1
Rogers, Will Mrs, 1944, Je 22,19:5
Rogers, Willard H Dr, 1922, S 21,17:5
Rogers, Willard Hall Dr, 1917, F 10,9:3
Rogers, William, 1944, N 22,19:1
Rogers, William A, 1946, Ap 8,27:4; 1954, Mr 23,88:8
Rogers, William A Mrs, 1961, Ja 5,31:4
Rogers, William B, 1923, Ja 26,17:4; 1956, Ja 9,25:4
Rogers, William B rev, 1937, Jl 30,19:3
Rogers, William C, 1922, Je 26,13:6; 1951, Ja 14,84:5; 1951, Ap 17,29:3
Rogers, William Charles, 1912, Jl 9,9:5
Rogers, William Evans, 1913, Mr 11,11:3
Rogers, William F, 1937, N 9,24:2; 1952, Jl 24,27:5
Rogers, William F Jr, 1964, O 22,32:3
Rogers, William G, 1950, Ag 18,21:4
Rogers, William G Mrs, 1951, Mr 10,13:2
Rogers, William H, 1905, Je 13,9:5
Rogers, William H D, 1959, Ap 7,33:4
Rogers, William H Mrs, 1965, Ag 24,31:4
Rogers, William J, 1915, F 2,7:6
Rogers, William J Mrs, 1908, My 11,7:5
Rogers, William L Maj-Gen, 1968, S 7,29:3
Rogers, William L Mrs, 1950, S 14,32:4
Rogers, William M, 1959, Je 23,33:5
Rogers, William O, 1919, D 18,13:3; 1944, Ja 2,38:3
Rogers, William O Jr, 1955, Jl 19,27:2
Rogers, William P, 1946, O 18,23:4
Rogers, William T, 1939, Ag 5,15:6
Rogers, William W, 1954, My 24,27:5
Rogers, Willis P, 1945, N 24,19:3
Rogers, Winifred, 1952, Ag 21,19:3
Rogers, Winthrop L, 1921, D 13,19:4
Rogerson, Charles M, 1944, D 29,15:3
Rogerson, Cuthbert H, 1949, F 12,17:5
Rogerson, James C Mrs, 1938, Je 26,6:5
Rogerson, Kathryn T Mrs, 1940, Ap 27,15:6
Rogerson, Wallace, 1943, F 25,21:4
Roget, Amedee, 1883, O 21,4:4
Roget, Peter Mark, 1869, S 18,4:7
Rogge, John C L, 1955, Ap 2,17:2
Roggen, Harry, 1944, Ag 31,17:2
Roggen, Nathan, 1925, O 14,25:3
Roggeveen, Adriaan P L, 1957, N 8,29:4
Roggs, Montivile, 1952, Ap 18,25:4
Rogick, Mary D, 1964, O 27,39:4
Rogier, Charles, 1885, My 28,5:6
Rogin, Leo, 1947, Jl 24,21:4
Rogin, Morris Mrs, 1948, Je 12,15:2
Roginsky, David N, 1968, Ja 29,31:1
Roglaski, Teodor, 1954, F 8,23:2
Rogoff, George, 1961, Mr 3,27:1
Rogoff, Julius M, 1966, Je 27,35:4
Rogoff, Louis Mrs, 1957, Ja 6,89:2
Rogoff, Rose Mrs, 1937, Mr 12,23:4

Rogokos, Aug, 1942, Ja 29,19:5
Rogosin, Maurice, 1957, Ag 27,29:5
Rogov, Ivan V, 1949, D 7,31:3
Rogovine, M A, 1923, Mr 26,13:4
Rogovine, Wladimir M (funl, Ja 14,17:6), 1924, Ja 12,13:2
Rogow, Allan, 1964, S 10,35:2
Rogow, Harry B, 1949, O 15,15:1
Rogow, Isidor, 1951, Ja 23,27:3
Rogow, Isidor Mrs, 1953, Ja 13,32:4
Rogowsky, David Mrs, 1950, Jl 17,21:5
Rohac, Frantisek, 1952, S 14,86:2
Rohan, Alain Charles Louis de Duke, 1914, Ja 7,11:5
Rohan, de Dowager Duchess, 1926, Ap 14,23:2
Rohan, Jack J, 1963, Jl 9,31:5
Rohan, James A, 1951, D 21,27:1
Rohan, John Mrs, 1968, Ag 6,37:2
Rohan, Patrick J, 1951, O 21,92:3; 1956, Ap 6,25:3
Rohange, Robert, 1949, Je 1,31:6
Rohbeck, John C, 1938, N 2,23:4
Rohde, Aloysius H Rev, 1937, Jl 21,21:6
Rohde, Borge Mrs (funl plans, Jl 29,23:4; funl, Jl 31,13:7), 1954, Jl 27,21:1
Rohde, Emil, 1942, D 16,25:2
Rohde, Gilbert, 1944, Je 17,13:2
Rohde, Henry Mrs, 1947, S 23,25:5
Rohde, James B, 1954, N 30,29:3
Rohde, Kurt, 1957, D 23,23:2
Rohde, Robert H, 1941, F 1,17:2
Rohdenburg, Meta Mrs, 1942, N 13,23:5
Rohe, Alice, 1957, Ap 8,23:4
Rohe, George (Whitey), 1957, Je 12,35:3
Rohe, Julius, 1903, O 18,7:6
Roheim, Geza, 1953, Je 8,29:4
Rohl-Smith, Carl Mrs, 1921, Ag 18,11:6
Rohland, Clarence B, 1954, Ja 12,23:5
Rohleder, Alfred G, 1949, S 9,25:3
Rohleder, John C, 1950, D 26,23:2
Rohlehr, John A, 1962, N 10,25:6
Rohlffs, Louis C Mrs, 1964, Je 24,37:5
Rohlfing, Charles C, 1954, Ap 5,25:4
Rohlfing, John M, 1948, Je 19,15:5
Rohlfs, Henry D G, 1940, My 25,17:6
Rohlfs, John, 1942, F 11,22:2
Rohlfs, John P, 1948, Ag 21,15:6
Rohliffs, August, 1950, Ag 29,27:4
Rohllfs, Herbert E, 1951, Je 1,23:4
Rohlman, Henry P Archbishop, 1957, S 14,19:5
Rohm, F Harland, 1947, My 28,25:4
Rohm, John, 1958, Ja 23,21:5
Rohm, William F, 1959, Ap 11,21:4; 1964, Ap 6,31:1
Rohmer, F J E Dr, 1903, Jl 1,9:6
Rohmer, Sax (A S Ward), 1959, Je 3,35:1
Rohn, Frederick Jr Mrs, 1947, Jl 22,23:4
Rohn, Julius, 1950, S 8,31:4
Rohner, Albert, 1953, F 26,25:2
Rohns, William C, 1951, Je 19,30:4
Rohonczy, Imre, 1956, Jl 27,21:4
Rohout, Albert, 1952, My 17,19:5
Rohr, Charles, 1922, Mr 28,17:4
Rohr, Charles H, 1940, Jl 28,27:4
Rohr, Ernest, 1948, Ag 7,15:4
Rohr, James E, 1952, F 26,27:3
Rohr, John T, 1967, S 18,47:3
Rohr, Leopold M, 1949, Ap 7,30:2
Rohr, Leopold M Mrs, 1958, N 30,86:2
Rohr, Marjorie H, 1941, Ap 4,23:7
Rohrabaugh, Daniel H Mrs, 1955, Ap 10,88:1
Rohrbach, Adolf, 1939, Jl 10,19:4
Rohrbach, Charles C, 1950, D 24,36:1
Rohrbach, Charles H, 1938, S 9,21:2
Rohrbach, David R, 1950, Ja 4,35:1
Rohrbach, James P Mrs, 1960, My 14,23:6
Rohrbach, John F D, 1968, D 27,33:3
Rohrbach, John J, 1953, Jl 31,19:5
Rohrbacher, John, 1951, My 17,31:6
Rohrback, Frederick E, 1948, Je 19,15:4
Rohrbaugh, Emanuel C, 1948, D 31,17:5
Rohrbaugh, Glenn D, 1949, D 6,31:3
Rohrbaugh, Harry J, 1945, F 27,19:5
Rohrbeck, Dorothea, 1921, F 25,11:2
Rohrberg, Clifford R, 1968, Ag 6,37:3
Rohrer, Albert L, 1951, O 19,27:2
Rohrer, Charles H, 1947, S 21,61:1
Rohrer, David J, 1950, Ja 11,23:3
Rohrer, Freeley, 1948, S 8,29:4
Rohrer, Grant, 1916, D 13,15:5
Rohrer, Ida F, 1940, Ja 7,48:2
Rohrer, John A, 1949, O 7,31:3
Rohrheimer, Maurice, 1943, Mr 10,19:3
Rohrig, Frank J, 1942, Mr 6,22:2
Rohrig, Louis L, 1963, Ap 8,9:1
Rohrlich, Abraham, 1953, Ag 30,89:1
Rohrlich, Abraham Mrs, 1953, Je 2,29:4
Rohrmann, Paul Sr, 1947, N 13,27:2
Rohrs, George C, 1951, N 11,89:5
Rohrs, Herman, 1904, Mr 30,9:5
Rohrs, John C, 1956, Jl 12,23:1
Rohrs, Peter, 1949, S 26,25:2
Rohs, Henry F, 1950, F 16,23:2
Rohsenberger, Carl J, 1958, N 20,35:5
Rohtlein, Arnold, 1952, N 2,88:5
Rohwer, Sievert A, 1951, F 14,30:2
Rohwerder, Frederick C, 1950, N 12,92:4
Roig, Alfredo Capt, 1919, My 14,17:6
Roig, Antonio A, 1956, Je 12,35:4
Roig, Julio, 1966, Ja 17,47:1
Roijen, Melza van, 1960, S 22,20:5
Roirdan, David F, 1937, Ag 28,15:4
Roitman, A G, 1964, F 15,23:1
Roitman, David (por), 1943, Ap 5,19:1
Roitman, David Mrs, 1965, Ja 28,29:1
Rojansky, Arnon M, 1966, My 13,38:6
Rojas, Francisco, 1942, Ap 3,21:2
Rojas, Luis M, 1949, F 28,19:3
Rojas, P Ezequiel, 1914, Je 27,7:5
Rojas, Pedro de, 1947, S 5,20:2
Rojas, Richard, 1957, Jl 31,23:4
Rojas, Samuel C, 1939, Ag 11,15:5
Rojas Cruzat, Carlos, 1945, S 21,21:5
Rojas Pinilla, Carlos, 1954, Ag 7,13:4
Rojestvensky, Zinovi Petrovitch, 1908, Jl 21,7:7
Rojo, Julio, 1945, F 8,19:4
Rojo, Vincente, 1966, Je 16,47:3
Rojtman, Marc B, 1967, My 13,33:3
Rokach, Aharon, 1957, Ag 19,19:2
Rokach, Israel, 1959, S 14,29:4
Roke, Daniel J, 1957, D 10,35:1
Rokeby, Ralph Thomas, 1924, My 24,15:3
Rokenbaugh, Henry S, 1943, D 2,27:4
Rokitansky, Paul Prof, 1878, Jl 24,5:6
Rokossovsky, Konstantin K Marshal (funl, Ag 1,-43:2), 1968, Ag 4,68:5
Rokta, Steven, 1953, Je 24,25:5
Roland, Alexander M, 1946, O 2,29:3
Roland, Cornelius F, 1951, Jl 13,21:3
Roland, Dana (Mrs R Barrows), 1959, Mr 28,17:1
Roland, Edward C, 1942, Jl 12,35:3
Roland, Howard W, 1945, Ag 22,23:4
Roland, Ralph, 1952, Je 27,23:1
Roland, Richard Mrs, 1948, D 25,17:1
Roland, Ruth, 1937, S 23,27:1
Roland, S E, 1882, F 13,4:7
Roland, Timothy E, 1941, Jl 31,17:2
Roland, William, 1937, Ap 12,17:2
Roland-Gosselin, Benjamin O, 1952, My 23,21:4
Roland Holst, Richard N Mrs, 1952, N 23,88:3
Roland-Marcel, Pierre, 1939, N 26,42:7
Rolando, H Com, 1869, Mr 24,2:7
Rolandow, Gottfried, 1940, D 7,17:5
Roldan, Enrique, 1954, F 6,19:6
Roldan, Raymond R, 1955, D 25,48:4
Roler, Albert H, 1942, O 11,56:2
Rolerfort, G W Dr, 1903, Ag 8,1:1
Rolf, Charles A, 1957, S 15,85:1
Rolfe, A G, 1959, D 5,23:2
Rolfe, Alfred G, 1942, Je 9,23:2
Rolfe, Benjamin A, 1956, Ap 24,31:1
Rolfe, Clarence W, 1942, Jl 1,25:2
Rolfe, George F, 1937, N 10,25:4
Rolfe, George W, 1942, Je 22,15:5
Rolfe, Herbert, 1937, D 6,27:3
Rolfe, John C, 1943, Mr 28,24:1
Rolfe, John F, 1937, Mr 21,II,8:2
Rolfe, Walter L, 1944, Ja 18,19:4
Rolfe, William A, 1949, S 25,92:5
Rolfe, William James Dr, 1910, Jl 8,7:5
Rolin, Henri E A M (por), 1946, Je 14,21:5
Rolins, Henry P, 1961, My 11,37:5
Rolinson, Harry M, 1942, D 10,25:6
Roll, Carl, 1958, Je 20,23:4
Roll, Edward P Jr, 1964, Je 18,35:5
Roll, Fabian, 1965, Ja 23,25:4
Roll, Frank R, 1949, Ja 12,27:4
Roll, George W, 1947, Jl 13,44:7
Roll, Herman A, 1937, Ag 8,II,7:3
Roll, J Harrison, 1950, Ap 8,13:3
Roll, J Melford, 1943, Je 21,17:5
Roll, John B, 1968, D 13,42:3
Roll, Joseph, 1939, O 28,15:3
Roll, Matthew, 1948, F 26,23:4
Roll, S Ernest, 1956, O 27,21:5
Roll, Sanford F, 1949, N 17,29:2
Rolland, Bugler, 1915, S 17,7:4
Rolland, Eugene, 1946, Jl 18,25:2
Rolland, Jean Damien, 1912, N 17,17:5
Rolland, Jules, 1921, Ap 11,11:3
Rolland, Mary A, 1947, Ap 12,17:2
Rolland, Robert, 1953, Je 15,24:8
Rolland, Romain, 1945, Ja 2,19:1
Rolland, Ross W M, 1960, S 15,37:3
Rolland, Sibyl E, 1948, My 24,19:3
Rolland, William, 1960, Ja 17,86:5
Rolland, William Mrs, 1952, Ag 30,13:5
Rollason, George H S, 1949, Ja 2,60:5
Rollefson, Gerhard E, 1955, N 17,35:4
Roller, Charles, 1944, Ap 9,34:2
Roller, Duane E, 1965, D 25,13:6
Roller, Frank W, 1938, Ag 22,13:2
Roller, Frederick, 1948, Mr 3,24:3
Roller, Jack, 1949, Ap 14,1:1
Rolleston, G Dr, 1881, Je 18,2:4
Rolleston, Humphry D (por), 1944, S 25,17:5
Rolleston, John A, 1961, Jl 15,19:5
Rolleston, Patrick W, 1947, S 12,21:3
Rollet, Paul (por), 1941, Ap 17,23:4
Rollier, Auguste, 1954, O 31,88:3
Rollin, A B, 1878, D 5,5:4
Rollin, Louis, 1952, N 4,30:5
Rollings, George T, 1942, O 17,15:6
Rollings, Harry W Sr, 1941, My 24,15:1
Rollings, James H, 1937, S 19,II,7:3
Rollings, Reginald W H, 1943, Ap 29,21:3
Rollini, Adrian, 1956, My 16,35:4
Rollins, Carl P, 1960, N 21,29:3
Rollins, Carle E, 1956, Ja 4,27:3
Rollins, Carola, 1941, F 26,21:2
Rollins, Charlotte A, 1951, My 25,27:6
Rollins, D G, 1897, Ag 31,1:5
Rollins, Daniel A, 1952, Jl 21,19:4
Rollins, Ernest C, 1951, Ag 26,77:2
Rollins, Frank Dr, 1920, My 12,11:5
Rollins, Frank P, 1962, Je 29,27:5
Rollins, Frank West Ex-Gov, 1915, O 28,11:5
Rollins, George A, 1945, S 11,23:5
Rollins, George B, 1875, My 24,4:7
Rollins, George Mrs, 1951, D 25,31:4
Rollins, Harry T, 1965, O 17,86:7
Rollins, Hyder E, 1958, Jl 27,61:2
Rollins, John F, 1961, S 24,87:1
Rollins, John F Mrs, 1957, S 29,86:7
Rollins, Joseph, 1938, N 28,15:3
Rollins, Kenneth A, 1956, N 11,86:4
Rollins, Marland W, 1950, D 22,23:4
Rollins, Marland W Mrs, 1948, Ap 5,21:4
Rollins, Maurice, 1943, Ag 20,15:2
Rollins, Montgomery, 1918, Ap 19,13:6
Rollins, Phil A, 1950, S 12,27:3
Rollins, Phil A Mrs, 1957, D 23,23:4
Rollins, Robert W, 1943, My 20,21:5
Rollins, Walter G, 1954, Ag 6,17:2
Rollins, Walter H (por), 1939, My 2,23:3
Rollins, William H, 1908, Jl 30,5:4
Rollins, William Jr, 1950, Je 16,25:5
Rollins, William L, 1940, My 7,25:2
Rollinson, Charles, 1937, O 15,23:5
Rollinson, Charles H, 1908, D 31,9:6
Rollinson, Charles Mrs, 1963, D 13,36:8
Rollinson, Henry S, 1946, O 19,21:2
Rollinson, Henry S Mrs, 1950, Je 26,27:2
Rollinson, John A, 1950, Jl 22,15:6
Rollinson, John J, 1955, Ap 18,23:2
Rollinson, John K, 1948, Mr 3,24:3
Rollinson, Reginald H, 1956, F 6,23:6
Rollinson, William H, 1944, S 19,21:5
Rollmann, Max, 1942, S 9,23:1
Rollo, Billy, 1964, My 9,27:4
Rollo, Frederick, 1968, Ja 24,45:3
Rollo, Guy W, 1939, Je 21,23:5
Rollo, Guy W Mrs, 1945, Je 4,19:2
Rollo, Herbert D, 1949, O 12,29:4
Rollo, James, 1952, S 8,21:4
Rollo, Lord, 1947, S 3,26:6
Rollo, Louie C, 1943, Ap 16,22:2
Rollo, Vincent, 1961, O 25,26:4
Rollow, James S Mrs, 1952, F 7,27:5
Rolls, Albert E, 1950, Jl 10,21:4
Rollston, Guy, 1945, Ap 7,15:4
Rolnick, Harry A, 1949, S 10,17:4
Rolnick, Joseph, 1955, Ag 20,17:5
Rolo, Robert, 1944, Jl 12,19:6
Roloff, Carlos Gen, 1907, My 19,7:4
Roloff, Charles F, 1947, S 29,21:5
Roloff, Frederick Jr Mrs, 1963, Je 11,37:3
Rolph, Gordon, 1959, Mr 24,39:1
Rolph, Harold, 1937, S 20,23:5
Rolph, J Jr, 1934, Je 3,1:2
Rolph, James Jr Mrs, 1956, S 25,33:4
Rolph, John G, 1958, N 4,27:4
Rolph, Samuel W, 1962, Ap 9,29:5
Rolph, Thomas, 1956, My 13,86:4
Rolph, W K Mrs, 1953, D 25,17:4
Rolsen, John, 1925, My 7,19:4
Rolsen, Leonard, 1949, Jl 21,25:6
Rolshoven, J, 1930, D 8,21:5
Rolston, Fanny H Mrs, 1940, Jl 25,17:2
Rolston, Henry G, 1951, D 28,21:2
Rolston, Horace W, 1939, Ap 24,17:5
Rolston, James V, 1949, D 2,29:1
Rolston, John H Mrs, 1949, F 2,27:2
Rolston, John J, 1954, S 30,31:5
Rolston, John W C, 1955, D 8,37:2
Rolston, Robert A, 1960, N 17,18:5
Rolston, Tilly Mrs, 1953, O 14,29:4
Rolston, William Henry, 1924, F 25,15:2
Rom, Ralph R, 1958, Ag 18,19:3
Roma, Alexander Count, 1914, Jl 25,7:5
Romagnoli, Ettore, 1938, My 2,17:5
Romagosa, Sebastian B, 1940, Ap 20,17:1
Romaguera, Jose, 1941, My 2,21:1
Romain, Joseph, 1941, S 29,17:3
Romain, Stephen M, 1944, Je 6,17:3
Romain, William Garrett, 1903, O 21,9:6
Romaine, Augustus, 1957, Jl 1,23:3
Romaine, Augustus Mrs, 1957, Jl 1,23:3
Romaine, Demarest, 1957, N 30,21:6
Romaine, Dewitt C, 1939, Je 2,23:4
Romaine, Esther J Mrs, 1937, O 21,24:2
Romaine, Girard, 1947, Ap 17,27:5

Romaine, Henry W, 1956, Jl 26,25:3
Romaine, Herman, 1952, Ja 1,25:5
Romaine, Hunter H Dr, 1968, Ap 22,47:2
Romaine, Isaac, 1901, Je 23,7:6
Romaine, Lily, 1949, Ja 25,23:3
Romaine, Peter A, 1945, Jl 16,11:7
Romaine, Sigourney B Mrs, 1963, N 16,27:6
Romaine, William, 1940, Ja 21,34:8
Romaine, Worthington D Mrs, 1951, N 7,29:3
Romakoff, Vasily, 1945, Mr 6,22:2
Roman, Aurel Mrs, 1962, S 8,19:5
Roman, Desiderio, 1950, S 8,31:2
Roman, Frederick W, 1948, Ap 10,13:6
Roman, J Philip, 1943, Ag 16,15:5
Roman, James B, 1947, O 14,27:3
Roman, John Mrs, 1955, Ap 6,29:4
Roman, Joseph M, 1951, Jl 10,27:3
Roman, Martin L Mrs, 1955, Ap 21,29:4
Roman, Segundo A, 1937, D 9,25:1
Roman, Thomas A, 1949, Ag 24,25:3
Roman, Victoria, 1954, O 25,27:4
Roman y Reyes, Victor M Pres, 1950, My 7,106:3
Romana, Alejandro Lopez de, 1912, My 28,11:4
Romanacce, Luis, 1955, N 4,29:4
Romanach y Guillen, Leopoldo, 1951, S 12,31:3
Romane, Andre, 1941, F 28,19:4
Romanelli, Joseph, 1944, My 20,15:2
Romanelli, Luigi, 1942, Jl 30,21:4
Romanenko, Profkoff L, 1949, Mr 12,18:3
Romani, Romano, 1958, Jl 6,56:3
Romanis, Alfonso de, 1950, Ja 21,17:2
Romano, Anthony M, 1957, Ag 2,19:5
Romano, Armando, 1963, O 14,29:3
Romano, Charles, 1937, Ag 10,19:2
Romano, Enrico, 1939, S 20,27:5
Romano, Frank, 1938, D 13,25:1
Romano, Gennaro, 1949, Mr 24,27:3
Romano, Jacques, 1962, O 15,29:3
Romano, Jacques Mrs, 1958, F 19,27:5
Romano, Jane, 1962, Ag 3,23:2
Romano, Lillian V D Mrs, 1942, Je 25,23:5
Romano, Nicholas, 1941, Ag 30,13:4
Romano, William, 1966, My 28,22:3
Romano, William J, 1944, Mr 11,13:5
Romanoff, Boris, 1957, Ja 31,27:2
Romanoff, George, 1950, Mr 12,57:3
Romanoff, Harry J Mrs, 1951, O 1,23:5
Romanoff, Paul, 1943, D 13,23:5
Romanos, J A Mrs, 1952, F 15,25:1
Romanov, Boris, 1950, Ja 7,17:2
Romanov, Dmitri P Grand Duke (por), 1942, Mr 8, 42:5
Romanov, M F, 1951, Ap 5,29:5
Romanov, Pavel, 1952, Ap 27,91:1
Romany, Marcelino, 1963, Ap 3,47:2
Romanyo, Santi, 1947, N 5,27:3
Romashov, Boris, 1958, My 8,29:5
Romatka, Anton, 1948, Mr 21,60:5
Romayne, Patrick Francis Rev, 1925, Ag 15,11:5
Rombalski, William, 1953, O 21,24:5
Rombauer, Edgar Mrs (Irma S), 1962, O 17,39:4
Rombaur, Raphael G Maj, 1912, S 18,11:4
Romberg, Abraham, 1945, Mr 2,19:4
Romberg, Arnold B, 1952, Jl 11,17:3
Romberg, Baron von (Edmund Coggswell Convetse), 1914, S 30,9:6
Romberg, Shalah S Mrs, 1941, F 18,24:2
Romberg, Sigmund, 1951, N 10,17:1
Romberg, Sigmund (est tax appr), 1957, Ja 16,36:3
Romberger, William R, 1939, My 29,18:8
Rombough, John B, 1942, Ag 11,19:4
Rome, Albert M, 1949, N 6,92:3
Rome, Granville H, 1949, Ap 6,29:4
Rome, James R, 1943, S 25,15:3
Rome, Lena Mrs, 1940, D 30,17:3
Rome, Louis, 1940, Mr 20,34:8
Rome, Russel W, 1959, O 16,31:5
Rome, Sigmund, 1967, Je 7,47:1
Rome, Theodore H, 1965, Ag 23,31:5
Rome, Thomas, 1938, F 11,23:4
Romei, Francesco, 1917, D 19,11:7
Romeike, Henry, 1903, Je 4,9:5
Romel, Adolf, 1949, S 9,25:5
Romeo, Dominic, 1951, Ja 6,30:4
Romeo, Frank, 1952, F 12,27:1
Romeo, James V, 1960, Mr 18,25:3
Romeo, Nicola, 1938, Ag 17,19:6
Romeo, Vincent, 1943, Ap 13,25:1
Romer, Alfred, 1922, N 5,5:3
Romer, Arthur C, 1962, O 26,31:1
Romer, Arthur J, 1940, Ja 29,16:2
Romer, Baron, 1944, Ag 21,15:5
Romer, Caroline S, 1962, F 25,88:8
Romer, Frank, 1939, Ag 10,19:2
Romer, George W, 1948, My 30,34:2
Romer, Henry H, 1945, F 15,19:2
Romer, J R, 1933, Ag 10,17:1
Romer, John A, 1951, D 8,11:5
Romer, John H, 1952, Ap 4,33:6
Romer, John Lockwood, 1920, Mr 20,11:6
Romer, Max L, 1964, Ja 26,81:1
Romer, Sebastian, 1939, Jl 21,19:6
Romer, W Purser, 1946, Ag 31,15:5
Romer, William Sr, 1948, Je 15,27:2
Romero, Don M, 1898, D 31,6:6
Romero, Emanuel A, 1960, D 10,23:5
Romero, Jose R, 1952, Jl 6,49:3
Romero, Juliana Mrs, 1951, S 4,27:2
Romeyn, Charles W, 1904, D 29,7:6; 1942, F 6,19:3
Romeyn, Emma L, 1947, Mr 15,13:2
Romeyn, Jeremiah, 1871, Ja 22,1:5
Romeyn, Radcliffe, 1956, My 28,27:2
Romfh, Edward C, 1952, Ja 17,27:4
Romier, Lucien, 1944, Ja 7,17:4
Romieux, Charles J, 1957, Ap 10,33:3
Romig, Edgar F, 1963, N 13,41:4
Romig, Edwin H, 1942, Ja 18,42:1
Romig, John S, 1951, N 2,23:3
Romig, Joseph H Mrs, 1937, Ja 3,II,8:5
Romilly, B H S Mrs, 1955, F 4,19:4
Romine, E W, 1942, Mr 18,23:1
Romine, Frank, 1939, S 4,19:5
Romine, Samuel E, 1925, D 1,25:5
Romita, Giuseppe, 1958, Mr 15,17:4
Romm, Max, 1947, S 27,15:4
Romm, Milton, 1946, Ap 6,27:2
Romm, Morris Mrs, 1953, Ap 28,27:4
Romme, John H, 1938, Je 9,23:5
Rommel, Charles D, 1952, Jl 8,27:5
Rommel, Daniel J Mrs, 1949, Jl 12,27:5
Rommel, Hattie Mrs, 1941, Ap 21,19:2
Rommel, I Leon, 1952, Ap 11,23:4
Rommel, Juliusz, 1967, S 10,82:3
Rommel, Lewis A Mrs, 1953, Ap 28,27:4
Rommel, William C, 1949, Ag 31,23:6
Rommel, William F Jr, 1937, Jl 13,19:4
Rommel, William P, 1943, Jl 13,21:4
Rommell, Christian F, 1951, Ja 30,25:5
Rommen, Heinrich A, 1967, F 22,29:4
Rommer, Dora Mrs, 1942, Ag 29,15:6
Romney, George Bp, 1920, F 2,13:4
Romney, Kenneth Sr, 1952, Ap 7,25:5
Romo, Luis S, 1947, Ja 6,23:5
Romoda, Joseph J, 1966, D 20,43:1
Romoli, Remo F, 1949, My 4,29:3
Romolo, Samuel A, 1948, Jl 20,23:2
Romond, Clestine Mrs, 1948, Ag 5,21:5
Romondt, Augustinus A F W van, 1947, Mr 13,28:3
Romoser, Amelia K Mrs, 1939, F 26,38:6
Romualdi, Serafino, 1967, N 12,86:6
Romulo, Carlos P Jr (funl, O 17,12:5), 1957, O 12,2:4
Romulo, Carlos P Mrs, 1968, Ja 23,43:5
Romulo, Maria P Mrs, 1948, My 27,25:4
Rona, L Lester, 1957, O 16,32:3
Rona, Lilly (Mrs F Ehrenhaft), 1958, Ap 3,31:4
Rona, Maurice R, 1954, O 15,23:1
Ronaghan, Arthur J, 1939, O 3,23:3
Ronai, Sandor (Sept 28), 1965, O 11,61:5
Ronald, Alex M Mrs, 1949, My 16,21:4
Ronald, Landon (por), 1938, Ag 15,15:2
Ronald, Malcolm B, 1955, Ap 5,29:1
Ronald, W R, 1951, Ap 4,29:1
Ronalds, C C Mrs, 1948, D 18,19:4
Ronalds, Charles C, 1948, My 28,23:3
Ronalds, Francis Sir, 1873, Ag 25,8:6
Ronalds, George L, 1910, O 12,9:4
Ronalds, Peter Lorillard (will, D 17,9:1), 1905, O 24, 9:5
Ronalds, Pierre Lorillard Mrs, 1910, Je 4,9:6
Ronalds, Reginald (funl, N 14,19:6), 1924, N 5,19:4
Ronan, Arthur T, 1946, Ag 3,15:6
Ronan, Bartholomew Mrs, 1957, My 9,19:1
Ronan, Bro, 1948, Jl 7,23:2
Ronan, Daniel V, 1948, Jl 28,23:2
Ronan, Edward S Jr, 1957, Mr 25,25:3
Ronan, Eugene J, 1956, F 28,31:2
Ronan, Francis D, 1948, My 4,25:2
Ronan, Frank J, 1966, Ap 8,31:2
Ronan, John J Sr, 1952, Ja 6,92:4
Ronan, Julia T Mrs, 1953, Jl 13,25:5
Ronan, Julian A, 1965, My 19,47:2
Ronan, Peter Msgr, 1917, My 1,13:6
Ronan, Stephen, 1925, O 4,5:2
Ronan, Thomas E, 1958, S 26,28:1
Ronan, Thomas J Mrs, 1948, S 4,15:5
Ronan, William J, 1966, D 24,19:6
Ronan, William T, 1946, Ja 4,22:2
Ronarc'h, Pierre, 1940, Ap 2,25:5
Ronarch, Pierre de, 1960, D 8,35:4
Ronay, Emil H, 1954, Jl 9,6:3
Roncace, Louis, 1960, Ap 7,35:3
Roncalli, Angelo G (Pope Jno XXIII), 1963, Je 4,1:8
Ronchetti, Robert F, 1953, F 4,27:2
Ronchi, Louis Dr, 1903, N 4,16:2
Ronck, Amos H, 1946, Ja 18,19:2
Ronconi, Signor, 1875, S 17,1:6
Roncovieri, A P, 1874, N 30,5:2
Rondeau, Henry, 1943, My 29,13:1
Rondeau, Henry O, 1946, Ag 19,25:5
Rondeau, Noah J, 1967, Ag 26,28:4
Rondepierre, Jules, 1944, F 3,19:2
Rondon, Candido Mariano da Silva, 1958, Ja 20,23:3
Rondthaler, Howard E, 1956, O 23,33:4
Roney, Daniel H, 1937, Mr 7,II,8:5
Roney, Ernest T, 1951, D 4,33:3
Roney, Garner, 1957, N 22,25:4
Roney, John J Jr, 1947, Ja 7,27:4
Roney, John R Sr, 1953, S 26,17:3
Roney, Newton B T, 1952, S 9,31:6
Roney, Newton B T Mrs, 1965, S 4,21:6
Rongetti, Nicholas E, 1946, Jl 26,21:5
Rongy, Abraham J (por), 1949, O 11,31:5
Rongy, Abraham J Mrs, 1961, S 13,45:4
Rongy, P, 1933, F 16,19:3
Ronin, James F, 1947, Ag 20,21:4
Roninella, Annina C, 1949, Mr 12,18:7
Ronk, Emerson S, 1968, Je 5,47:2
Ronk, George Mrs, 1954, Ja 26,27:1
Ronk, Irwin W Mrs, 1953, Ja 18,93:1
Ronk, Van Etten, 1949, Mr 7,21:5
Ronk, William K Mrs, 1950, Ja 25,27:4
Ronkin, Cassel, 1961, Ja 14,23:3
Ronkin, Samuel H, 1955, Je 28,27:5
Ronne, Charles A Mrs, 1957, Jl 14,72:6
Ronnebeck, Arnold, 1947, N 16,76:4
Ronneberger, Harry, 1945, D 6,27:5
Ronnenberg, Francis E J, 1957, S 24,35:2
Ronner, Edward P, 1950, Mr 30,30:3
Ronner, John H, 1920, D 4,13:4
Ronner, Peter C, 1940, Jl 17,21:3
Ronon, Gerald, 1960, Je 4,23:5
Ronsheim, Joshua Dr, 1968, Jl 12,31:2
Ronzone, Carolina G, 1960, Ja 25,27:3
Ronzoni, Angelo Mrs, 1962, Ag 17,48:1
Ronzoni, Emanuele, 1956, Ag 25,15:2
Ronzoni, Raymond, 1946, Jl 18,25:4
Roob, John R, 1959, Ap 3,27:3
Rooby, George, 1946, Ap 30,21:4
Rood, A Edward, 1961, O 20,33:3
Rood, Alan Mrs, 1943, Ja 23,13:6
Rood, C M, 1958, My 11,86:8
Rood, Carl A, 1957, O 19,21:5
Rood, Chauncey A, 1942, My 5,21:1
Rood, Henry A Dr, 1953, Ja 6,29:4
Rood, Henry C Jr, 1938, O 29,19:2
Rood, Henry E, 1954, Ja 5,27:2
Rood, Kingsland T, 1949, D 25,26:5
Rood, Leo P, 1965, Je 2,45:4
Rood, Leslie L Sr, 1952, N 20,31:3
Rood, Leslie L Sr Mrs, 1944, My 23,23:4
Rood, Louise, 1964, F 9,88:7
Rood, Martin R, 1903, Jl 31,7:6
Rood, O N Prof, 1902, N 13,9:5
Roode, Frederick J, 1947, O 2,27:3
Roodenburg, John, 1957, Ja 2,27:1
Roodkowsky, Dimitry, 1947, Ap 9,25:1
Roodner, Samuel, 1951, S 25,29:4
Roof, Dow G, 1950, Ja 18,31:3
Roof, Orley H, 1953, Ap 12,89:1
Roohan, Leo W, 1953, O 5,27:5
Roohan, Patrick F, 1939, O 29,40:7
Roohan, William F, 1959, Ap 11,21:4
Rook, Charles A, 1946, O 21,31:5
Rook, Edward F, 1960, O 27,37:4
Rook, Edward K, 1964, Ap 16,37:4
Rook, Ralph H, 1939, Ap 28,25:3
Rook, Sherman Frederick, 1915, Ag 2,9:4
Rook, Thomas E, 1957, Jl 10,27:4
Rook, Thomas E Mrs, 1942, F 6,19:4
Rooke, Emma, 1953, My 10,88:5
Rooke, George, 1904, N 1,5:5
Rooke, Margaret L, 1955, Ja 9,87:3
Rooker, Cornelius, 1922, N 4,13:6
Rooker, Frederick Zadok, 1907, S 20,9:6
Rooks, Benjamin D, 1948, My 1,15:5
Rooks, Russel, 1962, F 1,31:3
Rooksby, Edwin J, 1937, Mr 19,23:2
Rookwood, Lord, 1902, Ja 17,7:5
Roome, Abraham R Mrs, 1946, D 22,41:3
Roome, Claudius Monell Rev, 1920, D 14,17:3
Roome, Francis R, 1917, Je 16,11:4
Roome, Henry Clay, 1916, Mr 15,11:4
Roome, Kenneth A Mrs, 1961, Ag 12,17:4
Roome, Reginald (por), 1949, Ag 14,25:5
Roome, W H, 1934, Ja 30,19:3
Roome, Wallace, 1941, O 11,17:4
Roome, William J, 1924, F 12,17:3
Roome, William J Mrs, 1924, Ag 2,9:6
Roome, William P Col, 1925, D 14,21:4
Roon, A T E Von Gen, 1879, F 24,8:2
Roon, Karin R Mrs, 1967, Ap 20,43:3
Rooney, Albert T, 1962, Ja 9,47:3
Rooney, Alexander Joseph Dr, 1922, Ag 3,13:7
Rooney, Arthur C, 1964, N 12,37:4
Rooney, Arthur F, 1938, Ag 2,19:1
Rooney, Austin J, 1938, D 25,14:8
Rooney, Charles A Mrs, 1959, Ja 15,33:4
Rooney, Edward F, 1959, Ag 8,17:5
Rooney, Edward Mrs, 1960, N 4,33:2
Rooney, Edward T, 1947, Ja 20,25:2
Rooney, Eugene F, 1953, Jl 18,13:6
Rooney, Francis, 1951, F 6,27:5
Rooney, Francis X, 1959, My 6,39:2
Rooney, Frank M, 1937, F 11,23:4
Rooney, Frederick J, 1947, D 19,25:2
Rooney, Henry L, 1955, D 17,23:2
Rooney, James, 1948, N 10,30:3
Rooney, James B, 1943, My 18,23:2
Rooney, James D, 1945, D 20,23:3

Rooney, James F, 1951, F 5,23:2
Rooney, James J, 1947, N 14,23:4; 1948, Mr 3,23:2
Rooney, James Mrs, 1949, Jl 1,19:3
Rooney, James P, 1941, F 20,19:4
Rooney, James R, 1954, D 29,23:1
Rooney, John, 1910, My 20,9:6
Rooney, John A, 1941, Ap 7,17:2
Rooney, John J, 1941, Ap 29,19:2; 1944, N 4,15:6; 1948, Je 8,25:2; 1952, Ag 26,25:5; 1953, Mr 13,27:1
Rooney, John J Jr, 1937, N 11,26:3
Rooney, John J Mrs, 1949, D 23,21:3
Rooney, John R, 1952, Ja 29,25:4
Rooney, Joseph F, 1961, D 23,23:4
Rooney, Joseph G Dr, 1904, F 5,16:5
Rooney, L J F, 1936, S 22,27:3
Rooney, Michael, 1948, S 10,23:5
Rooney, Michael J, 1952, Jl 13,60:4
Rooney, P J, 1934, My 12,16:1
Rooney, Pat (funl, S 13,37:2), 1962, S 11,33:1
Rooney, Pat Mrs, 1940, Jl 29,13:3
Rooney, Pat 2d Mrs, 1943, F 7,48:2
Rooney, Patrick J Mrs, 1950, Ag 18,21:2
Rooney, Richard J, 1941, Je 11,21:1
Rooney, Thomas, 1953, Ja 9,21:1
Rooney, Thomas H, 1912, Ja 11,13:4
Rooney, William Mrs, 1950, Ag 14,17:5
Roop, Albert B, 1950, Ag 15,29:3
Roop, Edward de Baron, 1939, Jl 26,19:3
Roope, Fay, 1961, S 16,19:4
Roorbach, G B, 1934, My 24,23:3
Roos, Albert, 1951, Mr 25,74:6; 1951, Ag 10,36:6
Roos, Albert G, 1938, O 2,49:2
Roos, Alfred, 1918, Ja 2,11:5
Roos, Carl, 1958, My 8,29:3
Roos, Charles, 1937, My 11,25:3
Roos, Charles F, 1958, Ja 8,47:4
Roos, Delmar G, 1960, F 14,84:2
Roos, Edward R, 1952, Ap 26,23:5
Roos, Emanuel, 1939, N 9,23:3
Roos, Frank H, 1954, Ag 27,21:4
Roos, George W, 1943, Jl 27,17:4
Roos, Hugo, 1946, D 19,29:4
Roos, J Raymond, 1954, N 23,35:1
Roos, J Raymond Mrs, 1947, N 15,17:5
Roos, John P, 1952, Mr 12,27:5
Roos, Nancy Mrs, 1957, Ap 8,23:6
Roos, Paul, 1948, S 23,29:5
Roos, Paul J, 1968, My 1,47:1
Roos, Sylvain U, 1958, Ag 24,87:1
Roos, William A, 1938, My 27,17:2
Roosa, Benjamin I Mrs, 1948, Mr 26,22:2
Roosa, Charles C, 1948, My 10,21:1
Roosa, Daniel Bennett St John Dr (funl, Mr 10,7:5), 1908, Mr 9,7:3
Roosa, Everett, 1942, Jl 1,25:4
Roosa, I P, 1930, Ap 29,27:5
Roosa, Lewis, 1944, D 18,19:5
Roosa, Margaret C, 1938, My 1,II,6:7
Roosa, Zachariah, 1940, Jl 17,21:5
Roosens, Cyril, 1960, D 18,84:7
Roosevelt, Alice H, 1884, F 17,3:3
Roosevelt, Andre, 1962, Jl 31,27:2
Roosevelt, Blanch (Marchesa d'Alligri), 1898, S 11, 7:6
Roosevelt, C Y, 1883, N 8,2:5
Roosevelt, Cornelia Van Nest (see also F 20), 1876, Ap 24,8:3
Roosevelt, Cornelius Mrs, 1941, Ja 29,17:2
Roosevelt, Cornelius V S, 1871, Jl 18,1:5
Roosevelt, Dirck, 1953, Ja 8,27:4
Roosevelt, Elbert C, 1909, D 26,11:6
Roosevelt, Ellen C, 1954, S 27,21:4
Roosevelt, Franklin D, 1945, Ap 13,1:8
Roosevelt, Franklin D Mrs (funl plans; trb, N 9,1:6), 1962, N 8,1:2
Roosevelt, Franklin D Mrs (est tax appr), 1964, Mr 5,44:8
Roosevelt, Frederick, 1916, Je 16,13:6
Roosevelt, George E, 1963, S 4,39:3
Roosevelt, George E Mrs, 1937, Jl 27,21:2
Roosevelt, George E Mrs (will), 1938, My 27,19:6
Roosevelt, George W, 1907, Ap 16,11:6; 1917, Je 20, 11:5
Roosevelt, Gracie H, 1941, S 26,1:4
Roosevelt, Grant C, 1943, N 29,19:2
Roosevelt, H L, 1936, F 23,1:5
Roosevelt, Henry L Mrs, 1958, Jl 20,64:8
Roosevelt, Henry P, 1946, Ag 18,44:3
Roosevelt, J R, 1927, My 8,29:2
Roosevelt, J West Mrs, 1945, Mr 24,17:3
Roosevelt, James A Mrs, 1912, Ap 14,II,17:3
Roosevelt, James Alfred Maj (funl, Mr 29,13:4), 1919, Mr 27,13:3
Roosevelt, James P, 1947, Ag 13,23:3
Roosevelt, John Aspinwall, 1909, Mr 12,7:5
Roosevelt, John E, 1912, S 27,13:5; 1939, Mr 10,23:4
Roosevelt, John E Mrs, 1943, D 14,27:2
Roosevelt, Kate Shippen Mrs, 1925, Mr 27,19:6
Roosevelt, Kermit, 1943, Je 6,42:2
Roosevelt, Kermit Sr Mrs (funl plans, Mr 31,80:7), 1968, Mr 30,33:1
Roosevelt, Lucy Margaret, 1914, Ja 4,15:4
Roosevelt, Martha B, 1884, F 17,3:3
Roosevelt, Nicholas G, 1965, Je 30,37:2
Roosevelt, Nicholas Mrs, 1961, My 25,37:1
Roosevelt, Oliver W, 1953, Jl 16,21:3
Roosevelt, Phil J, 1941, N 10,17:3
Roosevelt, R B Mrs, 1902, Ja 11,9:5
Roosevelt, Ralph M, 1963, Jl 29,19:2
Roosevelt, Ralph M Mrs, 1959, My 19,33:4
Roosevelt, Robert B Jr, 1922, Ap 5,17:5
Roosevelt, Robert Barnwell (funl, Je 19,9:6; will, Je 20,14:4), 1906, Je 15,9:5
Roosevelt, S Weir, 1870, Mr 27,5:3
Roosevelt, Samuel, 1878, S 4,5:6
Roosevelt, Samuel Montgomery, 1920, Ag 20,9:4
Roosevelt, Sara D (coroner's rept, Ag 14,25:6; funl, Ag 15,1:6), 1960, Ag 13,12:2
Roosevelt, Sara D Mrs, 1941, S 8,1:2
Roosevelt, Simon W, 1965, My 2,83:1
Roosevelt, T, 1878, F 11,4:6
Roosevelt, Theodore Jr Mrs, 1960, My 30,17:4
Roosevelt, Theodore Sr Mrs, 1948, O 1,25:1
Roosevelt, Virginia, 1947, Ja 16,25:2
Roosevelt, W E, 1930, My 16,23:1
Roosevelt, W Rev, 1884, F 13,5:2
Root, Albert K, 1954, Mr 13,15:4
Root, Arthur G, 1939, F 27,15:2
Root, Arthur Lewis Dr, 1921, Ap 27,17:5
Root, Benjamin T, 1956, O 10,39:2
Root, Bill Col, 1903, Ap 13,9:6
Root, Chapman J, 1945, N 21,21:4
Root, Charles A Sr Mrs, 1954, Ap 25,86:4
Root, Charles P, 1938, Je 8,23:5
Root, Charles T, 1938, D 14,25:1
Root, Dorothy Mrs, 1959, Ag 23,93:2
Root, E Mrs, 1928, Je 9,17:5
Root, E Tallmadge, 1948, O 9,19:2
Root, Edward, 1956, D 6,37:1
Root, Edward F, 1956, My 5,19:6
Root, Edward K Dr, 1937, Ag 13,18:3
Root, Edwin F, 1944, S 15,19:2
Root, Edwin P, 1938, F 8,21:3
Root, Elihu Jr, 1967, Ag 28,31:2
Root, Elihu Jr Mrs (will, D 9,68:5), 1951, D 2,90:2
Root, Ella G Mrs, 1942, Ag 20,19:3
Root, Ernest D, 1948, O 13,25:5
Root, F M, 1934, O 22,15:3
Root, Frank C, 1960, O 31,31:2
Root, Frederick J, 1951, Ja 19,25:5
Root, G F Dr, 1895, Ag 8,2:6
Root, George H, 1949, Mr 25,23:2
Root, George V Mrs, 1904, F 26,9:7
Root, Harold P, 1942, Mr 25,21:6
Root, Henry G, 1949, My 21,13:4
Root, Horace E, 1942, My 6,19:5
Root, Howard F, 1967, N 18,37:4
Root, J Eugene, 1948, Ag 15,60:6
Root, Jack, 1963, Je 11,37:2
Root, James M, 1911, D 15,13:5
Root, James Porter, 1918, Mr 3,23:2
Root, John C, 1945, F 4,38:7
Root, John W, 1963, O 25,32:1
Root, Joseph L 3d, 1955, Je 16,31:1
Root, Lewis C, 1941, Mr 4,23:2
Root, Louis C, 1939, F 21,19:5
Root, Lyman, 1953, Je 11,29:5
Root, Max, 1964, Ja 26,80:6
Root, Oren, 1948, Ag 31,23:1
Root, Paul A, 1947, My 13,25:5
Root, Ralph, 1950, S 6,29:2
Root, Ralph E, 1961, S 27,41:2
Root, Robert, 1954, N 19,23:3
Root, Robert K, 1950, N 21,31:1
Root, Robert Keating, 1923, D 4,21:3
Root, Rosamond Dr, 1968, D 17,50:2
Root, Stella Q, 1941, Ap 18,21:5
Root, T Scott, 1949, N 23,29:1
Root, Thatcher W, 1903, S 16,9:6
Root, V Prof, 1885, My 24,2:3
Root, Walter K, 1938, N 5,19:1
Root, Warren S, 1955, N 26,19:1
Root, Wayne A, 1923, My 31,15:4
Root, Wayne A Mrs, 1956, O 16,33:1
Root, William A (por), 1942, O 1,23:4
Root, William D, 1954, Ap 18,89:2
Root, William F S, 1948, Ag 29,60:2
Root, William F S Mrs, 1947, Ja 18,15:4
Root, William H Col, 1937, D 25,15:4
Root, William T, 1945, Ja 25,19:4
Rootes of Ramsbury, Lord (Wm E Rootes),(will), 1965, Ap 24,11:5
Rootes of Ramsbury, William E Lord, 1964, D 13,1:6
Rootham, Cyril B, 1938, Mr 19,15:6
Roothbert, Albert, 1965, O 24,87:1
Roots, Benjamin H, 1943, O 19,19:3
Roots, Logan H, 1945, S 25,25:3; 1964, Ag 15,21:4
Roots, Willard H, 1946, Ap 1,27:4
Rope, John, 1944, Ag 17,17:2
Roper, Amund C, 1964, O 27,39:4
Roper, Anton J, 1968, Ap 15,43:1
Roper, Daniel C (por), 1943, Ap 12,23:1
Roper, Daniel C Mrs (por), 1944, Ja 9,43:2
Roper, Daniel Mrs, 1943, Ap 6,21:1
Roper, Denney W, 1949, O 12,30:3
Roper, Edgar S, 1953, N 20,23:4
Roper, Elmo B Mrs, 1958, S 17,37:1
Roper, Frank E, 1962, O 10,51:6
Roper, Frederick C, 1951, Ja 16,29:5
Roper, George O, 1961, Ag 28,25:5
Roper, J C, 1940, Ja 27,13:2
Roper, Jack, 1966, D 2,39:4
Roper, James G, 1952, Jl 17,23:3
Roper, John, 1968, N 24,87:1
Roper, John S, 1946, Ja 29,25:5
Roper, John W, 1963, S 10,39:3
Roper, Joseph C, 1955, N 20,88:7
Roper, Langdon Heywood, 1968, Ja 19,47:1
Roper, Lewis M, 1939, Ap 27,25:5
Roper, Lonsdale J, 1951, Je 13,29:6
Roper, Mary R, 1939, S 21,23:6
Roper, Morgan E, 1963, O 24,30:4
Roper, Ralph C, 1962, My 18,31:2
Roper, Robert P, 1965, D 23,27:2
Roper, Roswell M, 1954, F 23,27:1
Roper, Thomas A, 1946, Ag 3,15:3
Roper, Thomas C, 1954, F 28,92:2
Roper, W W, 1933, D 11,19:1
Roper, William F Dr, 1937, Ja 14,22:1
Roper, William W Jr Mrs, 1939, Ag 20,33:3
Roper, William W Mrs, 1954, Ja 21,31:5
Ropert, G F Bp, 1903, Ja 6,9:6
Ropes, Charles Joseph H Rev, 1915, Ja 7,13:4
Ropes, E D, 1903, O 31,9:6
Ropes, Ernest C, 1949, O 14,27:5
Ropes, R, 1890, My 19,5:2
Ropes, William T Mrs, 1955, Je 18,17:6
Ropes, William Townsend, 1924, N 29,13:4
Ropp, Alfred de Baron, 1941, Ag 8,15:5
Ropp, Ottily de Baroness, 1937, S 5,II,6:5
Roqueplan, Nestor, 1870, My 15,4:5
Roques, Clement E Cardinal, 1964, S 5,19:3
Roques, Pierre August, 1920, F 27,13:4
Roquet, George F, 1948, D 21,31:1
Roraback, Frederick S, 1938, My 22,II,7:3
Roraback, Robert H, 1949, D 15,35:4
Rorary, Leonard, 1939, My 14,III,7:3
Roray, Albert, 1940, D 18,25:2
Roray, Nelson L, 1943, My 1,15:6
Rorden, Harold L, 1968, Jl 30,39:4
Rorebeck, A C, 1914, O 24,13:4
Rorer, Dwight E, 1962, Je 13,41:2
Rorer, Herbert C, 1962, Ap 21,20:7
Rorer, Jonathan T, 1948, Ag 17,21:2
Rorex, J F, 1951, Mr 23,21:4
Rorex, W David, 1953, F 23,25:2
Rorick, Horton C, 1946, Ag 20,27:1
Rorimer, James J (mem ser, My 17,47:4), 1966, My 12,1:4
Rorimer, Louis, 1939, D 1,23:4
Rorimer, Louis Mrs, 1954, Ja 2,11:5
Rork, Charles H, 1949, Jl 12,27:2
Rork, Glen V, 1960, Ap 23,23:3
Rorke, Alexander I, 1967, Ja 28,25:4
Rorke, Alfred J, 1917, F 15,11:5
Rorke, Cornelius E, 1937, Jl 27,21:4
Rorke, James F, 1959, S 23,35:2
Rorke, Kate, 1945, Ag 1,19:4
Rorke, Louise R, 1949, Jl 25,15:5
Rorke, Mary, 1938, O 13,23:4
Rorke, Raymond A, 1953, Ap 1,29:3
Rorke, Vincent J, 1941, Ag 22,15:3
Rorley, John, 1916, O 24,12:5
Rorty, M C, 1936, Ja 20,19:1
Rorty, Phil A, 1941, Mr 11,24:2
Rorty, Richard M Mrs, 1943, Mr 14,25:2
Ros, Salvador E, 1937, N 23,23:3
Ros, Salvador Mrs, 1941, Mr 15,17:3
Rosa, Carl A N, 1889, My 1,5:5
Rosa, Edward Bennett Dr, 1921, My 18,17:5
Rosa, Francisco G, 1942, S 30,23:4
Rosa, Gerald, 1941, F 3,20:2
Rosa, Gregory J, 1950, My 7,106:5
Rosa, Leon W, 1943, F 14,48:4
Rosa, Philip, 1966, Jl 14,35:2
Rosa, Ralph de, 1942, Ag 11,19:3
Rosai, Ottone, 1957, My 14,35:2
Rosales, Carlos, 1941, Ja 16,21:5
Rosales, H L, 1943, F 17,11:1
Rosales, Lorna, 1957, Ag 31,32:2
Rosalie, Sister (Mary Lenahan), 1923, Ja 13,13:6
Rosall, Jerry E, 1957, Ap 13,19:1
Rosalsky, Alex, 1958, Mr 1,17:4
Rosalsky, Harry W, 1939, O 27,23:4
Rosalsky, Joseph S Justice, 1937, S 5,II,7:1
Rosalsky, O A, 1936, My 12,23:1
Rosalsky, Otto A Mrs, 1956, Ja 5,33:2
Rosalsky, Solomon, 1923, Je 30,11:5
Rosan, Julius H, 1950, S 22,31:2
Rosanbloom, Louis, 1946, O 24,27:3
Rosander, Arthur A, 1951, My 24,35:6
Rosander, Ervin L, 1963, O 18,31:2
Rosanoff, Aaron J, 1943, Ja 8,20:3
Rosanoff, Martin A, 1951, Jl 31,21:1
Rosaria Bianco, Mother, 1947, Ag 25,17:2
Rosas, Eduardo G, 1938, My 17,21:5
Rosas, Enrique de, 1948, Ja 21,25:4
Rosasco, Giovanni B, 1949, Ap 14,25:5
Rosasco, John B, 1959, D 20,60:3

Rosati, Enrico, 1963, O 13,86:4
Rosato, Giuseppe, 1910, O 17,9:4
Rosbach, John W, 1954, D 8,35:2
Rosbash, Alfred, 1954, O 7,23:2
Rosberg, Anitra J G Mrs, 1956, Jl 20,17:4
Rosberg, Magnus, 1952, Je 27,23:4
Rosberg, Magnus Mrs, 1944, Ja 25,19:2
Rosbloom, Julius, 1950, S 28,31:4
Rosbotham, Samuel, 1950, Mr 13,21:2
Rosbotham, Thomas A, 1919, Mr 27,13:3
Rosch, Andrew J, 1940, Ag 8,19:3
Rosch, Andrew J Mrs, 1938, My 20,19:3
Rosch, Fanny M, 1958, Je 10,33:2
Rosch, John, 1949, F 1,25:3
Rosch, John Mrs, 1947, My 1,25:2
Rosch, Joseph, 1967, Ap 1,31:4
Rosch, Joseph Mrs, 1947, Ap 3,25:2
Rosch, Melville C Mrs, 1958, Je 10,33:2
Rosch, Sophia M, 1953, Mr 3,27:3
Roschen, William E, 1963, Ag 3,17:4
Roscher, Clarence J, 1952, Je 25,29:2
Roscher, Frederick, 1968, My 6,47:1
Roscoe, Nelson F, 1918, Mr 19,11:8
Roscoe, P A Mrs, 1946, Ja 8,24:3
Rose, Abraham, 1948, N 1,23:4; 1957, Ja 19,15:3
Rose, Abraham M, 1942, Mr 30,17:2
Rose, Abraham Mrs, 1949, Ag 25,23:3
Rose, Achilles Dr, 1916, Ja 12,13:4
Rose, Albert E, 1940, Mr 26,34:4
Rose, Albert E Mrs, 1956, My 1,33:3
Rose, Alex F Mrs, 1948, Ap 21,27:3
Rose, Anna Perrot (Mrs Arth Wright), 1968, S 5,47:2
Rose, Anton, 1948, S 24,25:4
Rose, Arnold, 1946, Ag 26,23:1
Rose, Arnold M Prof, 1968, Ja 6,27:6
Rose, Arthur, 1937, O 21,24:3
Rose, Arthur B, 1954, N 10,33:5
Rose, Arthur F, 1960, Mr 23,37:2
Rose, Arthur Sir, 1937, Ag 16,19:6
Rose, Augustus F, 1946, Jl 21,40:5
Rose, Barney, 1963, S 28,19:1
Rose, Ben-Hy, 1962, S 20,33:4
Rose, Ben L Mrs (B Howell), 1957, O 23,33:2
Rose, Benjamin, 1962, N 12,29:5
Rose, Bernard, 1948, Ag 11,21:4
Rose, Billy (W S Rosenberg),(will, F 12,16:2; funl, F 14,35:5), 1966, F 11,1:7
Rose, Blanche, 1953, Ja 6,29:4
Rose, C, 1877, Ag 14,5:2
Rose, C Homer, 1937, Ap 17,17:2
Rose, Catherine Sister, 1940, D 10,26:2
Rose, Charles, 1922, Ag 3,13:6; 1947, S 19,23:2; 1966, Mr 28,33:4
Rose, Charles I, 1957, Jl 3,23:6
Rose, Charles O, 1942, Je 5,17:5
Rose, Charles R, 1947, Ja 17,23:3
Rose, Charles Sr, 1962, My 28,29:3
Rose, Charles W, 1942, Mr 8,43:2
Rose, Claude C, 1945, S 4,23:2
Rose, Clifford E, 1961, Ag 6,85:1
Rose, D Kenneth, 1963, Ag 3,17:4
Rose, D S, 1932, Ag 9,17:3
Rose, David, 1942, D 8,25:3
Rose, David Mrs, 1959, Jl 31,23:2
Rose, Deloss M, 1952, D 12,29:4
Rose, Don (Donald F), 1964, F 9,89:1
Rose, Edgar M Dr, 1921, Je 23,17:4
Rose, Edmund B Jr, 1966, Ag 24,51:5
Rose, Edouard Dr, 1937, D 12,II,8:7
Rose, Edward, 1948, F 29,60:4
Rose, Edward E, 1939, Ap 3,15:4
Rose, Edward M, 1939, Mr 7,21:4
Rose, Edwin L, 1940, Mr 18,17:1
Rose, Elbert B, 1964, S 2,37:3
Rose, Elizabeth L, 1958, Ag 9,13:4
Rose, Ella J, 1964, O 17,29:5
Rose, Elmer J, 1965, S 7,39:3
Rose, Fannie, 1967, F 3,28:6
Rose, Flora, 1959, Jl 28,27:4
Rose, Floyd, 1950, Jl 31,17:6
Rose, Frank C, 1962, Jl 6,25:1
Rose, Frank H, 1954, Ap 14,29:2
Rose, Frank S, 1940, O 11,21:5
Rose, Frank W, 1946, N 20,31:3
Rose, Fred, 1954, D 3,27:4
Rose, Frederick B, 1950, F 22,30:7
Rose, Frederick F, 1947, Jl 27,44:6
Rose, Geoffrey, 1959, Je 3,5:6
Rose, George (Arth Sketchley), 1882, N 14,4:7
Rose, George, 1914, Ag 10,7:4; 1946, O 25,23:1
Rose, George A, 1952, My 29,27:4
Rose, George E Sr, 1952, My 2,25:1
Rose, George I, 1954, S 7,25:2
Rose, George K Jr, 1958, D 27,2:8
Rose, Goodman A, 1950, D 19,30:3
Rose, Hans O, 1946, D 16,23:5
Rose, Harold M, 1957, Ap 12,25:2
Rose, Henry B, 1941, Jl 25,12:4
Rose, Henry C, 1938, D 11,60:5
Rose, Henry E, 1963, Je 6,35:2
Rose, Henry J, 1942, Ap 3,21:1
Rose, Henry N, 1955, Ap 15,23:4
Rose, Henry R Mrs, 1958, Ag 14,25:4
Rose, Herbert, 1956, S 12,37:3
Rose, Herbert E, 1960, Mr 20,86:2
Rose, Hudson P Mrs, 1942, My 13,19:2
Rose, Hugh D, 1948, Ja 23,23:2
Rose, Hugh E, 1945, O 15,17:5
Rose, I Joseph, 1948, Mr 26,21:1
Rose, Irl W, 1956, Ap 11,33:3
Rose, Irving, 1963, Je 25,33:4
Rose, Irving K, 1951, Ap 5,29:1
Rose, Ivan M Mrs, 1947, Mr 9,60:6
Rose, Jack, 1964, Ag 25,33:3
Rose, Jacob, 1947, O 9,52:3
Rose, Jacques M, 1939, My 26,23:4
Rose, James A, 1912, My 30,11:5
Rose, James B, 1911, Jl 7,9:6
Rose, James E, 1942, My 15,19:5
Rose, James G, 1945, Ap 20,19:1
Rose, James Graham, 1925, S 23,25:3
Rose, James P, 1948, Ag 31,23:1
Rose, James R, 1916, Je 26,13:7
Rose, Jesse Mrs, 1951, O 9,29:5
Rose, John A, 1962, N 2,31:1
Rose, John B, 1949, Mr 5,18:2
Rose, John H, 1953, O 5,27:4
Rose, John L, 1944, Ap 14,19:6
Rose, John M, 1944, Jl 26,19:4
Rose, John W Mrs, 1940, Mr 24,31:1
Rose, Johnston L, 1945, O 28,43:2
Rose, Joseph B, 1944, Ja 22,13:5
Rose, Joseph H, 1921, Jl 14,15:4
Rose, Joseph J, 1953, N 4,33:3
Rose, Joseph M, 1967, Ja 23,43:1
Rose, Joseph S, 1939, Ap 14,23:5
Rose, Joshua, 1948, Ag 17,21:2
Rose, Joshua Mrs, 1945, D 25,23:4
Rose, Judah L, 1946, F 5,23:4
Rose, Judah L Mrs, 1937, Ap 26,19:3
Rose, Judge, 1871, My 17,1:7
Rose, Layton A, 1940, Ap 30,21:5
Rose, Lee L, 1946, Ap 1,27:4
Rose, Lenox S (will, My 17,20:1), 1937, Ap 26,19:3
Rose, Leo, 1949, D 10,17:4
Rose, Leon H, 1940, F 7,21:2
Rose, Lewis E, 1952, Mr 16,90:2
Rose, Lisle A, 1955, My 25,33:4
Rose, Louis, 1954, My 17,23:5; 1961, Je 22,31:5
Rose, Louis H, 1961, Je 29,33:4
Rose, Louis S, 1942, Je 3,23:4
Rose, Louis S Mrs (will, D 27,11:1), 1947, D 17,29:4
Rose, Luke H, 1958, O 6,31:5
Rose, Lustaw, 1873, Jl 23,1:7
Rose, Lyman O, 1903, D 16,9:5
Rose, Marc A, 1964, Ja 24,27:1
Rose, Marc A Mrs, 1952, Mr 25,27:4
Rose, Mark, 1956, Jl 8,64:6
Rose, Marshall C, 1947, D 17,29:2
Rose, Mary D, 1940, Ag 31,13:5
Rose, Mary D Mrs, 1939, O 15,49:2
Rose, Mary S Mrs, 1941, F 2,46:1
Rose, Maurice, 1946, Ap 22,21:5
Rose, Max, 1951, Ag 22,23:2
Rose, Meyer, 1951, Ag 14,23:5
Rose, Milton R, 1946, Ag 13,27:4
Rose, Milton S, 1938, N 1,23:2
Rose, Morris E, 1967, N 12,86:8
Rose, Mother (H Sweeney), 1957, S 28,17:2
Rose, Norman H, 1967, S 2,25:5
Rose, Norman S, 1944, O 28,15:4
Rose, Oren W, 1939, F 3,15:3
Rose, Parker E, 1942, Ag 21,19:4
Rose, Paul F, 1942, My 15,19:4
Rose, Paul H, 1955, Ja 20,31:2
Rose, Percy A, 1940, Ap 14,45:2
Rose, Philip G, 1947, O 23,25:5
Rose, Philip Mrs, 1961, D 30,19:6
Rose, Philip S, 1962, O 27,25:2
Rose, Raymond C, 1942, My 18,15:5
Rose, Remington E, 1948, N 22,21:5
Rose, Robert A, 1947, Ap 11,25:4
Rose, Robert D Mrs, 1949, S 27,27:2
Rose, Robert S, 1964, F 29,21:5
Rose, Roger P, 1957, Ag 9,19:2
Rose, Rufus, 1914, Ja 22,11:6
Rose, Russell A, 1968, Ja 8,39:3
Rose, Russell K, 1949, Ap 26,25:2
Rose, Samuel, 1945, Jl 12,11:7; 1953, D 23,25:4
Rose, Samuel Allison Dr, 1968, Jl 17,43:5
Rose, Samuel B, 1964, S 6,56:8
Rose, Sanford B, 1967, Mr 18,29:2
Rose, Spencer L, 1940, Jl 24,21:4
Rose, Stanley B, 1962, Ja 3,33:1
Rose, Stanley H, 1954, S 3,17:6
Rose, Stephen D, 1959, Mr 15,89:1
Rose, Theodore T, 1962, Ag 9,25:5
Rose, Thomas A, 1959, Ja 27,33:4
Rose, Thomas L, 1939, My 8,18:2
Rose, Tom Mrs, 1953, Je 11,29:3
Rose, Uncle Tom, 1954, Jl 20,19:5
Rose, Vincent, 1944, My 21,44:5
Rose, W A, 1876, Je 8,5:2
Rose, W C Capt, 1912, D 12,13:2
Rose, W K Dr (Wm K Rose), 1968, O 5,35:3
Rose, Waldemar H, 1952, Jl 21,19:2
Rose, Walter, 1958, S 2,25:3
Rose, Wilbur B, 1957, D 6,29:3
Rose, William, 1946, Ap 13,17:4; 1954, S 20,23:2
Rose, William C, 1949, Jl 3,26:6
Rose, William F Mrs, 1964, Mr 11,39:2
Rose, William H, 1941, F 9,48:7; 1947, D 8,25:2
Rose, William H F, 1953, O 30,23:3
Rose, William I, 1954, Je 10,31:5
Rose, William J (funl), 1871, Ap 9,8:5
Rose, William J, 1937, Mr 9,23:5
Rose, William K, 1942, Ja 20,19:5
Rose, William M, 1959, My 18,27:5
Rose, William S Mrs, 1965, O 26,45:2
Rose, William W, 1950, F 22,29:3
Rose, Wilson S, 1917, Ap 26,13:6
Rose, Winfred Mrs, 1941, My 14,21:1
Rose, Wright R, 1953, F 26,25:4
Rose Alice, Sister (M White), 1942, Ag 18,21:5
Rose Anthony, Sister, 1947, D 10,31:4
Rose De Lima, Sister, 1945, D 17,21:2
Rose Eleanore, Sister (M Karl), 1964, Ap 4,28:4
Rose Frances, Sister (M V Stevenson), 1960, Jl 3, 32:4
Rose Gertrude, Mother (A Hoenighausen), 1962, My 9,43:4
Rose Gertrude, Sister (Sisters of Charity), 1955, Ap 1,28:3
Rose Leontine, Sister, 1937, O 10,II,8:4
Rose Marit, Sister (E Durant), 1966, Ag 12,31:1
Rose Miriam, Sister (Sisters of Charity), 1959, Mr 21,21:3
Rose of Lima, Mother, 1962, Ap 2,31:4
Rose Veronica, Sister, 1958, Ja 3,23:1
Rosebault, Charles J Mrs, 1968, Mr 25,41:4
Rosebault, Leonard W, 1965, Ag 19,31:5
Rosebault, Leonard W Jr, 1955, F 20,89:1
Roseberry, George W, 1954, O 20,29:3
Roseberry, Herbert H, 1947, My 14,25:2
Roseberry, Joseph M, 1942, Ja 25,40:4
Roseberry, Joseph M Mrs, 1952, D 23,23:1
Roseberry, Lewis H, 1949, Mr 18,25:3
Roseberry, Louis H, 1956, Jl 26,25:6
Roseberry, Seymour H Mrs, 1942, My 20,20:3
Roseberry, William A, 1950, Je 15,31:2
Rosebery, Earl of, 1929, My 21,31:1
Roseboro, Viola, 1945, Ja 30,19:3
Rosebrock, Charles, 1958, Ja 3,23:1
Rosebrook, Carrie E, 1952, Ag 11,15:7
Rosebrook, John B Mrs, 1958, F 13,29:4
Rosebury, Richard W F, 1939, Mr 31,21:3
Rosecrans, A L (see also My 12), 1876, Mr 14,2:6
Rosecrans, Benjamin A, 1957, S 24,35:4
Rosecrans, Egbert, 1948, Ja 21,26:2
Rosecrans, Henry J, 1903, N 17,9:6
Rosecrans, James H, 1952, S 7,86:6
Rosecrans, S H Bp, 1878, O 22,1:5
Rosecrans, W S Gen, 1898, Mr 12,7:3
Rosecrantz, Clarke M, 1920, Ja 14,9:1
Rosedale, Max, 1963, D 13,36:2
Rosefeld, George, 1919, O 4,11:4
Roseff, Alex, 1958, My 27,31:1
Roseff, Samuel, 1943, Mr 29,15:3
Rosegger, Peter Dr, 1918, Je 29,11:5
Rosekrans, E H, 1877, My 5,2:5
Rosekrans, I Newton, 1949, Jl 16,13:4
Roseland, Harry, 1950, D 22,23:2
Roselius, Friedrich, 1941, Je 14,17:2
Rosell, Leonard O, 1940, S 10,23:3
Roselle, Charles T, 1960, Mr 20,87:1
Roselle, Edward H, 1958, N 26,29:4
Roselle, John A, 1957, N 30,21:5
Roselle, William, 1945, Je 2,15:6
Roselli, Carlo Mrs, 1949, O 19,29:3
Roseman, Benjamin M, 1940, F 23,15:4
Roseman, Charles E Sr, 1953, F 24,25:3
Roseman, Marcus, 1949, Jl 27,23:1
Roseman, Milo A, 1953, Ja 29,27:2
Rosemeier, Marion Mrs, 1944, Mr 5,35:2
Rosemond, Robert T, 1948, N 26,23:4
Rosen, Aaron, 1962, Mr 19,29:1
Rosen, Aaron H, 1944, D 3,57:3
Rosen, Aaron L, 1947, S 8,21:4
Rosen, Abraham, 1948, D 21,25:5
Rosen, Abraham Mrs, 1964, D 5,31:3
Rosen, Abraham N, 1967, S 28,47:3
Rosen, Abraham N Mrs, 1956, O 26,29:1
Rosen, Abram, 1952, Ap 16,27:4
Rosen, Adam, 1960, Mr 9,33:4
Rosen, Alfred J Mrs, 1956, Ag 8,25:2
Rosen, Arthur, 1965, F 13,21:3
Rosen, Avis, 1942, D 18,27:1
Rosen, B Paul, 1961, Ap 28,31:2
Rosen, Barry, 1965, Jl 19,21:3
Rosen, Ben, 1944, D 25,19:4
Rosen, Ben R, 1956, Ap 11,33:1
Rosen, Benzion Mrs, 1944, D 24,25:2
Rosen, Bernard, 1946, Jl 5,19:5
Rosen, Charles, 1950, Je 22,27:3
Rosen, Charles E, 1960, Ja 20,31:2
Rosen, Charles Mrs, 1960, N 19,21:6
Rosen, Clarence von Count, 1955, Ag 21,93:2
Rosen, David, 1958, Ag 6,25:3; 1960, Mr 10,32:1
Rosen, Ephriam Mrs, 1949, Ja 23,70:3

Rosen, Felix T, 1953, Je 11,29:2
Rosen, Frank, 1954, D 22,23:4
Rosen, Frank E, 1941, F 12,21:4
Rosen, Frederick M, 1967, N 20,47:2
Rosen, George, 1965, Ap 29,35:3
Rosen, George A, 1956, S 15,17:4
Rosen, Goran Count, 1920, F 19,11:4
Rosen, Harold J, 1964, Ag 26,39:1
Rosen, Harry, 1949, O 6,31:3
Rosen, Harry B, 1922, D 30,13:5
Rosen, Henry, 1947, Ja 29,25:5
Rosen, Herman L, 1943, Je 18,21:1
Rosen, Hugo von, 1962, S 26,39:4
Rosen, Hyman, 1937, S 22,27:5
Rosen, I Theodore, 1961, Ja 13,29:2
Rosen, Ira J, 1960, Je 16,33:5
Rosen, Isadore, 1958, Ag 5,27:4
Rosen, Isidor, 1939, Mr 18,17:2
Rosen, Jacob, 1956, My 11,28:2
Rosen, Jacob M, 1961, Ja 1,49:2
Rosen, James, 1940, Je 2,44:6
Rosen, James R, 1962, Ja 30,29:3
Rosen, John, 1958, Ap 7,21:2
Rosen, Joseph, 1953, S 26,17:4
Rosen, Joseph A (por), 1949, Ap 2,15:1
Rosen, Joseph R, 1965, Je 20,72:7
Rosen, Julius, 1944, Ap 12,21:3
Rosen, Kopul, 1962, Mr 16,31:2
Rosen, Leon, 1942, Ag 19,19:1
Rosen, Louis, 1955, F 23,27:3; 1960, My 11,39:1
Rosen, Louis A, 1956, S 19,37:1
Rosen, Lucie Bigelow (Mrs W Rosen), 1968, N 28, 37:2
Rosen, Matty, 1958, Jl 5,17:3
Rosen, Max, 1949, Je 10,28:5; 1949, Ag 18,21:6; 1953, F 27,21:1; 1956, Mr 2,23:3; 1956, D 17,31:3
Rosen, Max Mrs, 1951, Ja 18,27:2
Rosen, Melville S, 1959, My 30,17:4
Rosen, Meyer A, 1951, S 8,17:1
Rosen, Meyer A Mrs, 1963, O 1,39:2
Rosen, Meyer S, 1957, Ja 12,19:5
Rosen, Moe, 1965, Ag 6,27:3
Rosen, Morris H (por), 1945, Mr 3,13:3
Rosen, Moses, 1957, O 14,27:1
Rosen, Nathan A, 1938, S 5,15:5
Rosen, Paul, 1950, Jl 28,21:5
Rosen, Raymond, 1952, Ap 9,31:2
Rosen, Raymond M, 1949, My 20,28:2
Rosen, Roman Romanovitch Baron, 1922, Ja 1,20:3
Rosen, Samuel, 1944, Je 14,19:5; 1953, Je 27,15:5; 1955, My 14,19:6; 1968, Jl 10,39:3
Rosen, Samuel H Mrs, 1967, Ja 2,19:1
Rosen, Samuel R, 1952, My 25,93:1
Rosen, Seymour, 1959, Ja 3,17:3
Rosen, Sidney, 1953, D 23,25:1
Rosen, Sigismund V von, 1949, O 1,13:2
Rosen, Theodore, 1940, Ag 27,21:3
Rosen, Walter T (will), 1951, N 1,34:1
Rosen, William T, 1951, O 17,31:1
Rosen, Zalel Mrs, 1945, F 3,11:4
Rosen, Zavel, 1953, Mr 19,36:7
Rosenak, Ignatz I, 1957, S 14,19:1
Rosenak, Leopold Mrs, 1961, S 8,32:1
Rosenak, Miksa, 1959, S 27,86:1
Rosenau, Gruseff, 1941, My 27,14:6
Rosenau, Joseph F, 1956, D 13,37:4
Rosenau, Leo M, 1964, Je 11,33:4
Rosenau, Milton J (por), 1946, Ap 10,27:1
Rosenau, Walter N, 1964, S 26,23:6
Rosenau, William, 1943, D 10,27:2
Rosenbach, Abraham S W, 1952, Jl 3,1:6
Rosenbach, Joseph B, 1951, N 7,29:2
Rosenbach, Morris, 1937, My 29,17:6
Rosenbach, Philip H, 1953, Mr 6,20:7
Rosenband, Norbert Mrs, 1941, Ag 7,17:5
Rosenbaum, Adolph, 1968, N 13,47:2
Rosenbaum, Alex, 1964, Ap 22,47:3
Rosenbaum, Bernard, 1949, Ja 26,25:1
Rosenbaum, David R Mrs, 1944, S 24,46:2
Rosenbaum, Ed, 1965, Mr 13,25:1
Rosenbaum, Edward P, 1963, Ap 26,35:1
Rosenbaum, Elias, 1937, O 8,23:5
Rosenbaum, Ernst M, 1966, My 27,43:3
Rosenbaum, Francis F, 1967, D 20,45:2
Rosenbaum, Francis S Mrs, 1963, S 29,86:5
Rosenbaum, George D, 1967, Ja 6,35:4
Rosenbaum, Heinrich, 1947, N 21,28:2
Rosenbaum, Henry Mrs, 1957, D 30,23:2
Rosenbaum, Henry W, 1906, Ja 31,11:6
Rosenbaum, Herman, 1956, Ap 21,17:3
Rosenbaum, Irving, 1925, Je 3,23:3
Rosenbaum, Jose Mrs, 1961, F 8,31:1
Rosenbaum, Joseph, 1919, My 23,13:4; 1949, My 26, 29:2
Rosenbaum, Joseph W, 1946, O 18,23:3
Rosenbaum, Joseph 2d, 1942, Mr 4,19:2
Rosenbaum, Lewis N, 1956, Ja 10,31:2
Rosenbaum, Louis, 1959, My 17,84:2
Rosenbaum, Louis M, 1948, F 6,23:4
Rosenbaum, Mayer, 1938, Jl 19,21:5
Rosenbaum, Mervin F, 1955, Ap 30,17:3
Rosenbaum, Morris, 1946, O 1,23:5; 1953, Je 2,29:5
Rosenbaum, Nathan, 1950, My 19,28:2
Rosenbaum, Paul, 1952, Ja 20,85:1
Rosenbaum, Samuel, 1965, Jl 24,21:5
Rosenbaum, Sigmund, 1920, F 18,11:3
Rosenbaum, Sigmund Mrs, 1949, F 4,23:2
Rosenbaum, Sol G (por), 1937, D 27,15:1
Rosenbaum, Sol G (will), 1938, Ja 1,10:7
Rosenbaum, Solomon, 1907, Ja 9,9:5
Rosenbaum, W G, 1949, Ja 13,23:3
Rosenbaum, Walter, 1947, O 24,23:2
Rosenbaum, Walter S, 1920, O 6,15:5
Rosenbaum, William, 1945, O 27,15:4; 1951, S 17,21:5
Rosenberg, A Henry, 1963, N 4,35:2
Rosenberg, A P, 1945, Ap 17,23:2
Rosenberg, Aaron S, 1964, Ja 18,23:3
Rosenberg, Abraham, 1925, Jl 15,17:5; 1954, D 27,17:4
Rosenberg, Abraham Chaim Rabbi, 1925, Ag 9,5:2
Rosenberg, Adolf, 1967, Jl 28,31:2
Rosenberg, Adolph (por), 1946, D 7,21:1
Rosenberg, Adolph M, 1942, D 18,27:3
Rosenberg, Alan R, 1964, O 24,29:3
Rosenberg, Albert S, 1951, D 28,21:5
Rosenberg, Alex, 1952, S 26,22:4
Rosenberg, Alex S Mrs, 1963, Je 24,27:5
Rosenberg, Alfred, 1937, O 7,27:1
Rosenberg, Anna M Mrs, 1952, F 9,13:2
Rosenberg, Anna Mrs, 1961, Jl 19,29:4
Rosenberg, Arthur, 1948, N 17,27:4; 1954, Mr 27,17:6
Rosenberg, Arthur A (por), 1943, F 9,23:3
Rosenberg, Arthur Mrs, 1939, D 13,27:2
Rosenberg, Ben, 1959, Mr 28,17:3
Rosenberg, Ben Mrs, 1950, S 10,92:3
Rosenberg, Benjamin, 1938, My 24,19:4
Rosenberg, Bernard, 1949, Ag 26,19:1; 1957, Jl 26,19:5
Rosenberg, Charles, 1938, My 8,II,6:5; 1942, S 25,21:1
Rosenberg, Charles R Jr, 1951, Ap 5,29:2
Rosenberg, David, 1950, S 21,31:5; 1951, Ap 21,17:2
Rosenberg, David L, 1967, Mr 16,47:1
Rosenberg, E, 1928, Je 24,II,7:1
Rosenberg, Edgar A, 1941, Mr 13,21:3
Rosenberg, Edgar J, 1968, Mr 14,43:2
Rosenberg, Edward Mrs, 1953, Ap 15,31:3; 1958, My 17,19:1
Rosenberg, Elmer, 1951, Ap 12,33:2
Rosenberg, Emil Dr, 1903, N 6,9:6
Rosenberg, Felix Col, 1916, Mr 24,11:4
Rosenberg, Frederic H von (por), 1937, Ag 2,19:3
Rosenberg, Gertrude, 1903, O 2,7:6
Rosenberg, Hans Mrs (Ernestine), 1962, S 18,39:5
Rosenberg, Harry, 1948, N 24,23:2
Rosenberg, Harry W, 1951, My 5,17:3
Rosenberg, Henry, 1923, F 13,21:4; 1955, S 9,23:3
Rosenberg, Henry A, 1955, F 24,27:3
Rosenberg, Henry E, 1962, Ap 1,48:4
Rosenberg, Henry R, 1952, My 13,30:3
Rosenberg, Herman H, 1966, Ap 25,31:5
Rosenberg, Heyman, 1952, Mr 2,92:4
Rosenberg, Heyman Mrs, 1960, D 5,31:1
Rosenberg, Hyman, 1962, Mr 29,33:1
Rosenberg, I B, 1961, My 14,87:1
Rosenberg, I M, 1938, N 22,23:4
Rosenberg, Ida, 1951, Ap 26,32:3
Rosenberg, Ike, 1945, My 20,32:1
Rosenberg, Ike Mrs, 1945, F 2,19:1
Rosenberg, Isaac E, 1961, D 31,48:6
Rosenberg, Isidor, 1955, Je 1,33:3
Rosenberg, Isidore, 1953, Ap 26,85:1
Rosenberg, Israel, 1956, Ja 27,23:1
Rosenberg, Israel A Mrs, 1951, Je 1,26:2
Rosenberg, Jack S, 1968, Jl 15,31:1
Rosenberg, Jacob, 1919, Ap 2,11:3; 1941, Ap 1,23:2; 1946, Ag 1,23:1; 1959, Je 30,31:4
Rosenberg, Jacob H, 1944, Ap 11,19:3
Rosenberg, Jacob Mrs, 1965, O 20,47:4
Rosenberg, Jason Mrs, 1952, Ag 27,27:2
Rosenberg, Jefferson, 1916, S 29,13:5
Rosenberg, Jerome, 1944, Jl 19,19:4
Rosenberg, Jesaiah Dr, 1937, N 9,24:2
Rosenberg, Jonas G, 1955, Je 4,15:4
Rosenberg, Joseph, 1943, N 18,23:4
Rosenberg, Joseph (por), 1944, D 9,15:3
Rosenberg, Joseph, 1945, Mr 16,15:1
Rosenberg, Joseph D, 1941, Ag 17,38:1
Rosenberg, Joseph H, 1949, D 3,15:3
Rosenberg, Josephine Mrs (will), 1945, Jl 27,9:4
Rosenberg, Julius J (por), 1949, Ag 16,23:1
Rosenberg, Kahman, 1922, Mr 2,21:5
Rosenberg, Lazarus, 1956, N 30,23:5
Rosenberg, Lee, 1945, Ap 30,19:4
Rosenberg, Leonard X, 1956, Mr 6,31:3
Rosenberg, Lewis S, 1958, Mr 23,88:6
Rosenberg, Lionel, 1959, F 7,19:3
Rosenberg, Louis, 1939, My 27,15:5; 1948, D 23,19:2; 1954, My 16,88:2; 1955, Jl 21,23:4
Rosenberg, Louis Mrs, 1950, N 24,35:1; 1952, Ja 21, 15:4; 1958, My 17,19:6
Rosenberg, Manuel, 1967, Ap 30,86:8
Rosenberg, Maurice, 1952, N 11,29:4; 1953, S 15,31:5
Rosenberg, Max M, 1955, Ap 11,23:4
Rosenberg, Max Mrs, 1943, Jl 2,19:5; 1951, N 4,87:2
Rosenberg, Melrich V, 1937, D 10,25:4
Rosenberg, Meyer Mrs, 1959, Jl 13,27:4
Rosenberg, Michael M, 1956, O 21,86:4
Rosenberg, Milton, 1954, F 10,29:4
Rosenberg, Morris, 1941, N 24,17:2; 1953, N 10,31:4
Rosenberg, Nathan, 1957, O 1,33:1
Rosenberg, Paul, 1959, Jl 1,31:1
Rosenberg, Phil H, 1957, S 30,31:2
Rosenberg, Philip, 1943, N 16,23:1
Rosenberg, Pierce, 1966, My 20,47:3
Rosenberg, Robert, 1964, Ja 6,47:3
Rosenberg, Robert H, 1966, S 13,47:2
Rosenberg, Sam, 1946, F 17,42:4
Rosenberg, Samuel, 1954, O 8,23:2
Rosenberg, Sanford, 1949, Jl 29,18:5
Rosenberg, Saul, 1967, N 3,45:3
Rosenberg, Sebsal Rabbi, 1913, Ja 3,9:4
Rosenberg, Simon, 1946, Ap 11,25:5
Rosenberg, Theodore, 1959, D 29,25:1
Rosenberg, Werner, 1957, My 5,88:2
Rosenberg, William B, 1946, N 6,23:3
Rosenberg, William S (Billy Rose),(will, F 12,16:2; funl, F 14,35:5), 1966, F 11,1:7
Rosenberg, Zoltan, 1943, S 20,21:3
Rosenberger, Carl, 1957, O 9,35:1
Rosenberger, Charles G, 1944, My 19,9:1
Rosenberger, Gerald E, 1967, F 1,39:3
Rosenberger, Hermann, 1950, N 21,31:3
Rosenberger, Holmes G, 1937, Je 28,19:4
Rosenberger, James M Mrs, 1940, S 2,15:5
Rosenberger, John N, 1939, My 17,23:2
Rosenberger, Martin, 1951, Mr 31,15:5
Rosenberry, Edward S, 1950, My 2,29:1
Rosenberry, Eugene L Sr, 1959, N 20,31:2
Rosenberry, Marvin B, 1958, F 16,86:3
Rosenblad, Victoria Mrs, 1950, Ja 31,23:3
Rosenblate, Adolph J, 1955, O 13,32:1
Rosenblatt, Abraham, 1959, Ag 21,21:2
Rosenblatt, Albert (por), 1944, N 2,19:3
Rosenblatt, Albert Mrs, 1941, Ap 4,21:5
Rosenblatt, Alfred M, 1960, D 31,17:5
Rosenblatt, Bernard A Mrs, 1955, O 10,27:6
Rosenblatt, Charles, 1947, D 23,23:1
Rosenblatt, Edward H, 1961, O 14,23:4
Rosenblatt, G, 1885, Ja 4,2:1
Rosenblatt, Harry, 1950, Ap 27,33:1
Rosenblatt, Herman, 1949, O 14,29:5
Rosenblatt, Irving, 1966, Ap 12,39:2
Rosenblatt, Isaac, 1940, Ag 28,19:1
Rosenblatt, J, 1933, Je 19,15:4
Rosenblatt, Joseph Mrs, 1966, Mr 31,39:4
Rosenblatt, Louis Mrs, 1947, Ap 8,27:4
Rosenblatt, Mandell, 1966, D 8,47:4
Rosenblatt, Max, 1941, Jl 11,15:5
Rosenblatt, Morris S, 1965, Je 6,85:1
Rosenblatt, Murray, 1961, Je 10,23:4
Rosenblatt, Sol (por), 1955, D 25,48:3
Rosenblatt, Sol A (mem ser set, My 9,47:4; will, My 18,23:6), 1968, My 5,87:1
Rosenblatt, William Mrs, 1948, Ap 3,15:2
Rosenblith, Eric Mrs, 1956, F 9,37:8
Rosenbloom, Abraham Mrs, 1939, D 2,17:6
Rosenbloom, Carl W, 1949, Mr 4,21:3
Rosenbloom, Celia Mrs, 1947, Ja 27,23:4
Rosenbloom, Harry, 1953, Ag 14,19:3
Rosenbloom, Harry W, 1940, Je 10,17:5
Rosenbloom, Leo, 1939, F 11,15:4
Rosenbloom, Seymour, 1967, My 24,32:2
Rosenbloom, Sidney G, 1939, F 7,20:1
Rosenbloom, Sol, 1925, N 17,25:4
Rosenbloom, William J Mrs, 1958, O 9,37:1
Rosenblueth, Jacob C, 1943, F 22,17:2
Rosenbluh, Louis, 1965, Ag 5,29:5
Rosenblum, A George Dr, 1968, F 7,47:5
Rosenblum, Abraham H, 1960, My 5,35:5
Rosenblum, Abraham J, 1955, D 31,13:6
Rosenblum, Benjamin W, 1967, Mr 23,35:4
Rosenblum, Bernard, 1940, Ja 17,21:1
Rosenblum, David (por), 1943, Jl 20,19:1
Rosenblum, Dorothy L, 1953, Je 10,29:3
Rosenblum, George M, 1956, S 29,19:3
Rosenblum, Hyman, 1942, Ap 23,23:2
Rosenblum, Irving, 1960, Ag 13,15:5
Rosenblum, Israel, 1946, Mr 27,27:1
Rosenblum, Jacob C, 1943, Je 28,21:3
Rosenblum, Leopold, 1937, N 1,21:6
Rosenblum, Max, 1953, S 7,19:4
Rosenblum, Molly H Mrs, 1940, Jl 8,17:3
Rosenblum, Phil S, 1954, D 14,33:1
Rosenblum, Philip E, 1965, Je 26,29:3
Rosenblum, Roger L, 1948, Ja 3,13:4
Rosenblum, S J, 1934, Ja 6,15:6
Rosenblum, Solomon J Mrs, 1946, Ja 25,24:3
Rosenblum, William, 1944, Je 22,19:6
Rosenblum, William F Rabbi, 1968, F 10,33:4
Rosenbluth, Anna S Dr, 1917, Mr 31,11:6
Rosenbluth, Milton B, 1959, Mr 25,35:1
Rosenbluth, Phineas, 1957, Jl 9,27:5
Rosenburg, John C, 1941, Ap 4,21:4
Rosenburgh, William, 1947, F 11,27:2
Rosencrans, Augustus E, 1950, Je 17,15:2
Rosencrans, Charles, 1944, D 9,15:3
Rosencrans, James H Mrs, 1943, Ja 19,19:4
Rosencrans, John C, 1947, Ja 21,23:1
Rosencrants, Fay H, 1943, Ag 28,11:3
Rosencrantz, Bradley S Mrs, 1958, Ag 11,21:1
Rosencrantz, Esther, 1950, D 19,29:4

Rosencrantz, Frederick, 1879, D 10,5:2
Rosencrantz, Hilliard J, 1943, N 25,25:5
Rosencrantz, James, 1946, N 24,76:6
Rosencrantz, Palle Baron, 1941, O 3,23:2
Rosendahl, Astley, 1937, Ag 17,24:7
Rosendahl, Edward, 1966, Je 4,29:2
Rosendahl, Hannah Mrs, 1941, N 8,19:5
Rosendahl, Louis, 1952, My 29,27:3
Rosendahl, Rear-Adm, 1917, Ag 18,7:4
Rosendale, George, 1944, Ap 7,19:2
Rosendale, Robert W, 1955, D 14,39:4
Rosendale, Simon W (por), 1937, Ap 23,21:3
Rosendale, Simon W Mrs, 1922, Ag 24,15:5
Rosendale, William A Mrs, 1968, F 19,39:2
Rosende, Alfredo, 1951, Ja 30,25:1
Rosenek, Leo Dr, 1968, Ja 22,47:1
Rosener, Henry, 1912, F 29,11:5
Rosenfarb, Joseph, 1955, S 11,85:1
Rosenfeld, Adolph H, 1953, F 5,23:2
Rosenfeld, Arthur, 1959, Jl 25,17:5
Rosenfeld, Arthur R Mrs, 1943, F 20,13:2
Rosenfeld, Barnett, 1958, Mr 28,25:2
Rosenfeld, Benjamin, 1963, N 9,25:4
Rosenfeld, Carl, 1915, Jl 27,9:5
Rosenfeld, E William, 1963, O 6,88:5
Rosenfeld, Edgar, 1939, Jl 17,20:1
Rosenfeld, Edward N H, 1942, S 22,21:3
Rosenfeld, Elizabeth, 1949, Ag 18,21:5
Rosenfeld, Evelyn, 1967, D 17,92:8
Rosenfeld, Francis M, 1942, Ja 13,22:6
Rosenfeld, Francis M Mrs, 1950, Mr 23,29:2
Rosenfeld, Harry, 1939, Ja 2,24:2; 1942, Jl 22,19:4
Rosenfeld, Harry M, 1957, Ja 12,19:1
Rosenfeld, Henry L Sr, 1939, Jl 18,19:6
Rosenfeld, Hersh, 1960, My 21,23:4
Rosenfeld, Hersh Mrs, 1959, Je 19,25:5
Rosenfeld, I Joseph, 1941, N 25,25:3
Rosenfeld, Isaac, 1956, Jl 16,21:4
Rosenfeld, Israel, 1925, O 12,21:5; 1956, Mr 30,19:2
Rosenfeld, John, 1942, Ja 20,20:4; 1948, D 31,15:3
Rosenfeld, John D, 1967, My 7,87:1
Rosenfeld, John J, 1961, N 4,19:5
Rosenfeld, Jonah, 1944, Jl 10,15:4
Rosenfeld, Joseph, 1946, N 9,17:6; 1961, Mr 30,29:1
Rosenfeld, Julius, 1939, Mr 15,23:2
Rosenfeld, Kurt (por), 1943, S 27,19:1
Rosenfeld, Lawrence L, 1961, S 28,41:2
Rosenfeld, Maurice, 1939, F 26,39:3
Rosenfeld, Max, 1943, Jl 18,35:2; 1951, Ap 10,28:3
Rosenfeld, Max S, 1965, D 7,47:3
Rosenfeld, Monroe H, 1918, D 14,17:2
Rosenfeld, Morris, 1938, D 14,25:1; 1957, S 27,19:2; 1968, S 22,88:5
Rosenfeld, Mortimer C, 1943, Ag 29,38:1
Rosenfeld, Paul (por), 1946, Jl 22,21:1
Rosenfeld, Reuben, 1959, Ja 6,33:2
Rosenfeld, Robert, 1966, Mr 18,39:4
Rosenfeld, Rose Mrs, 1941, Ja 28,19:5
Rosenfeld, Sam Mrs, 1965, Jl 3,19:5
Rosenfeld, Samuel, 1942, Mr 27,23:3; 1943, D 11,15:2; 1966, S 20,47:2
Rosenfeld, Theodore, 1907, My 23,9:6
Rosenfeld, William I, 1957, S 10,33:2
Rosenfeld, Zacharia Rabbi (funl, S 12,17:4), 1915, S 11,9:5
Rosenfelder, Charles, 1940, N 25,17:5
Rosenfelder, George L, 1947, F 15,15:1
Rosenfelt, Henry H, 1959, Jl 11,19:6
Rosenfield, Abner B, 1955, Ja 22,11:3
Rosenfield, Abner B Mrs, 1967, O 22,84:6
Rosenfield, Dave, 1949, Ap 2,15:4
Rosenfield, Harold A, 1957, Ja 29,31:1
Rosenfield, Joe Jr Mrs, 1965, Mr 6,25:3
Rosenfield, John Jr, 1966, N 28,39:4
Rosenfield, Jonas A Sr, 1964, D 28,29:2
Rosenfield, Louis D, 1940, Mr 23,13:5
Rosenfield, Morris, 1947, Ag 21,23:3
Rosenfield, Morris Mrs, 1910, Je 1,6:5
Rosenfield, Murray, 1952, S 9,27:7
Rosenfield, Myron (Mike; por), 1955, O 6,29:5
Rosenfield, Walter A, 1959, Jl 30,27:4
Rosenfled, Morris (funl, Je 25,13:6), 1923, Je 22,17:4
Rosengard, Maurice, 1952, Ag 28,23:5
Rosengarten, Adolph G, 1946, Ap 23,21:5
Rosengarten, David, 1948, Mr 7,68:4
Rosengarten, Frank H, 1923, My 8,17:5
Rosengarten, Frederic, 1955, O 30,88:3
Rosengarten, George, 1953, N 25,23:2
Rosengarten, George D Mrs, 1947, O 4,17:2
Rosengarten, Henry, 1944, Ag 21,15:5
Rosengarten, Isaac, 1961, Ap 12,41:2
Rosengarten, Isidore B, 1948, S 21,27:2
Rosengarten, J Clifford, 1938, Jl 10,29:2
Rosengarten, Joseph G Jr, 1959, S 30,37:5
Rosengarten, Mitchell G, 1942, O 15,23:2
Rosengarten, Morris, 1942, F 13,21:3
Rosengarten, Sarah S Mrs, 1940, Ag 21,19:3
Rosengrant, John, 1965, F 6,25:5
Rosengren, Axel Mrs, 1958, Ap 29,29:1
Rosenhain, Bruno Dr, 1968, Mr 2,29:2
Rosenhaus, Harold, 1960, D 9,31:2
Rosenheck, Charles, 1960, Mr 6,86:1
Rosenheim, a Collector of Religions, 1879, Ag 17,5:6
Rosenheim, Abraham H, 1918, Ag 14,9:4
Rosenhirsch, Alfred E, 1967, Je 17,31:4
Rosenhirsch, Clara Mrs, 1947, Je 11,27:3
Rosenhirsch, Leo, 1952, N 8,17:2
Rosenhirsch, N Edward, 1958, S 3,33:5
Rosenholz, Jack, 1951, N 10,17:5
Rosenholz, Jack Mrs, 1952, D 31,15:4
Rosenholz, Mayer, 1963, Ag 18,80:2
Rosenkampff, Arthur H, 1952, N 7,23:1
Rosenker, Michael Mrs, 1962, Ap 3,39:4
Rosenkrans, Addison P, 1952, Jl 3,25:1
Rosenkrans, Allen E, 1941, D 18,27:4
Rosenkrans, William R, 1943, Ag 12,19:5
Rosenkranz, Benjamin G, 1966, Mr 9,41:2
Rosenkranz, J K F Prof, 1879, Je 18,5:6
Rosenmeyer, Benjamin J, 1943, Ja 17,45:2
Rosenmeyer, Bernard J Mrs, 1951, Jl 12,25:3
Rosenmiller, Joseph L Jr Mrs, 1967, My 28,61:2
Rosenof, Samuel, 1957, Jl 21,61:2
Rosenow, Curt, 1959, O 23,29:2
Rosenow, Erwin, 1951, Ap 13,23:3
Rosenow, Henry G, 1943, Ag 14,11:5
Rosenquest, Eugene H Mrs, 1947, N 23,76:2
Rosenquest, J Wesley, 1918, D 15,22:3
Rosenquest, Lewis, 1945, Ag 13,19:5
Rosenquist, Charles Mrs, 1947, S 16,23:2
Rosenquist, Helen A Mrs, 1939, D 3,60:6
Rosenquist, Ivar H, 1954, Ag 10,19:5
Rosenscheim, Herman, 1914, O 4,15:5
Rosenschein, Ben, 1954, Je 14,21:4
Rosenschein, Ben Mrs, 1940, N 19,23:1
Rosenschein, Charles S, 1957, Ap 19,21:4
Rosenshine, Albert A, 1946, Mr 19,27:4; 1950, Mr 17, 23:3
Rosensohn, Meyer, 1953, Ap 27,23:4
Rosensohn, Samuel J (por), 1939, My 12,21:1
Rosensohn, Samuel J Mrs, 1966, S 21,47:2
Rosenson, Alvin C, 1961, My 8,35:3
Rosenson, Isador, 1946, Ja 23,27:4
Rosenson, Isadore Mrs, 1954, D 18,15:2
Rosenson, Morris, 1949, My 27,22:2
Rosenstamm, S S, 1919, Mr 31,13:4
Rosenstein, Aaron, 1958, N 12,37:4
Rosenstein, Abraham, 1948, F 3,26:1
Rosenstein, Abraham F, 1949, O 20,29:3
Rosenstein, Alex, 1955, Mr 7,27:3
Rosenstein, Alfred B, 1945, My 31,15:4
Rosenstein, Benjamin, 1953, N 24,29:6
Rosenstein, Charles, 1955, Mr 4,23:4
Rosenstein, David, 1963, My 9,28:5
Rosenstein, David Mrs, 1956, F 20,23:4
Rosenstein, Filbert L, 1961, Ap 24,29:2
Rosenstein, George L, 1958, Mr 7,24:1
Rosenstein, Harry, 1959, F 1,84:4
Rosenstein, Harry J, 1951, Mr 4,17:4
Rosenstein, Henry, 1949, O 28,24:2
Rosenstein, Herman O, 1958, S 24,27:4
Rosenstein, Jacob, 1959, F 10,33:3
Rosenstein, Jeana Mrs (funl), 1953, Jl 13,25:6
Rosenstein, Louis, 1950, Je 16,25:2
Rosenstein, Marcus Rabbi, 1917, F 9,11:5
Rosenstein, Murray L, 1959, My 3,87:2
Rosenstein, Sophie, 1952, N 12,27:4
Rosenstein, Victor, 1949, Ap 23,13:3
Rosenstiel, David J, 1960, Ja 28,31:1
Rosenstiel, Lewis S Mrs, 1910, S 7,9:6; 1944, D 4,23:1
Rosenstirn, Alfred M, 1950, O 17,31:5
Rosenstock, Henry B, 1944, My 17,19:6
Rosenstock-Huessy, Eugen Mrs, 1959, S 2,29:4
Rosenstrauch, Saul, 1964, Ap 23,39:5
Rosenstraus, Archibald, 1944, F 8,15:2
Rosenstrom, Peter J, 1941, My 10,15:2
Rosensweig, Charles S, 1958, Je 6,23:1
Rosensweig Diaz, Alfonso de, 1963, Ag 6,31:4
Rosenthal, A S, 1940, My 18,15:6
Rosenthal, Abraham, 1937, F 17,21:3; 1958, Ja 23, 21:5; 1963, S 16,35:1
Rosenthal, Abraham M Mrs, 1948, F 1,60:2
Rosenthal, Adolph H, 1962, Jl 22,64:2
Rosenthal, Albert, 1939, F 21,23:5
Rosenthal, Alex, 1939, Mr 24,21:4
Rosenthal, Arnold W, 1924, Je 8,26:1
Rosenthal, Ben, 1953, My 26,29:5
Rosenthal, Benjamin, 1950, O 7,19:4
Rosenthal, C Rev, 1874, My 5,8:3
Rosenthal, Charles, 1937, Ag 20,17:4; 1966, Je 30,39:2
Rosenthal, Charles M, 1958, Jl 21,21:5
Rosenthal, Charles Mrs, 1945, D 17,22:3
Rosenthal, Charles S, 1945, Ap 18,23:3
Rosenthal, Chess Master, 1902, S 30,9:2
Rosenthal, Daniel D, 1957, Ja 22,29:1
Rosenthal, David, 1940, S 15,49:1; 1949, O 21,25:5; 1951, Mr 7,33:2
Rosenthal, David Mrs, 1947, N 25,29:3; 1959, Mr 6, 25:3
Rosenthal, David S, 1954, Ag 19,23:4
Rosenthal, Delphine, 1955, Jl 12,25:2
Rosenthal, Eliot, 1956, D 27,25:3
Rosenthal, Emanuel, 1965, My 18,39:3
Rosenthal, Emil, 1939, D 3,60:8
Rosenthal, Gerald, 1953, O 8,18:6
Rosenthal, Govriel L, 1947, O 16,28:3
Rosenthal, Gustave H, 1941, Ag 19,21:3
Rosenthal, Harold, 1967, F 18,29:4
Rosenthal, Harry, 1909, Je 30,7:2; 1940, Ag 27,21:4; 1947, Ap 8,27:2
Rosenthal, Harry Mrs, 1964, Jl 22,33:4
Rosenthal, Harry T, 1941, N 24,17:4
Rosenthal, Harvey I, 1943, Ap 25,34:2
Rosenthal, Hedwig Mme (rept false, D 7,27:2), 1956, D 6,37:4
Rosenthal, Henry, 1937, Ja 17,II,8:7; 1939, My 14,III, 7:4; 1956, D 20,29:3
Rosenthal, Henry Mrs, 1951, Ag 27,19:1
Rosenthal, Herbert W, 1953, Jl 31,19:5; 1963, O 10, 41:3
Rosenthal, Herman, 1917, Ja 31,11:4
Rosenthal, Ignatius L, 1920, D 1,15:5
Rosenthal, Isadore, 1954, F 12,25:5
Rosenthal, Isidore, 1950, Ja 24,31:4
Rosenthal, Israel H, 1939, O 19,23:4
Rosenthal, Jack, 1942, Mr 29,44:2
Rosenthal, Jack B, 1967, N 2,47:4
Rosenthal, Jacob, 1924, Ja 13,23:1
Rosenthal, Jacob C, 1954, O 25,27:4
Rosenthal, Jake, 1949, D 22,23:5
Rosenthal, Jay J, 1943, Mr 16,19:1
Rosenthal, Jerome, 1952, D 20,17:4
Rosenthal, Joseph, 1938, N 30,24:1; 1946, O 21,31:5
Rosenthal, Joseph (por), 1949, S 25,92:3
Rosenthal, Joseph, 1966, N 24,35:3
Rosenthal, Joseph M, 1941, S 4,21:2
Rosenthal, Joseph Mrs, 1951, Ja 12,27:4; 1961, O 1, 86:4
Rosenthal, Julian (por), 1948, D 8,31:4
Rosenthal, Julius, 1938, Jl 24,28:2
Rosenthal, Julius M, 1955, Jl 12,25:4
Rosenthal, Julius Mrs, 1960, N 17,37:3
Rosenthal, Lazar, 1965, Je 15,41:1
Rosenthal, Leon A Mrs, 1962, Ag 31,21:2
Rosenthal, Leon J Mrs, 1957, Je 2,86:2
Rosenthal, Leon W, 1945, Ja 9,19:3
Rosenthal, Leonard, 1955, Jl 18,21:3
Rosenthal, Lessing, 1949, D 21,29:1
Rosenthal, Lessing (will), 1950, Ja 14,8:4
Rosenthal, Louis Dr, 1922, O 20,17:5
Rosenthal, Louis S (por), 1943, Ja 21,21:1
Rosenthal, Luthier, 1968, D 14,45:1
Rosenthal, M Rev, 1873, Ja 13,2:2
Rosenthal, Max, 1918, Ag 9,11:8; 1940, Jl 6,15:3
Rosenthal, Michael, 1942, N 4,23:2
Rosenthal, Michael C, 1957, Je 10,27:2
Rosenthal, Milton N, 1955, S 14,35:3
Rosenthal, Miriam S, 1963, O 26,27:3
Rosenthal, Moriz, 1946, S 4,23:1
Rosenthal, Moriz Mme, 1959, S 10,35:4
Rosenthal, Morris Mrs, 1945, N 20,21:4
Rosenthal, Morris S, 1958, F 14,23:4
Rosenthal, Morton I, 1937, D 16,27:2
Rosenthal, Moses, 1943, N 21,57:1
Rosenthal, Nathan, 1948, O 26,31:4; 1955, Je 30,25:1
Rosenthal, Nathan Mrs, 1951, N 11,90:5
Rosenthal, Oscar W, 1943, O 3,48:6
Rosenthal, Philip, 1945, Ag 8,23:4
Rosenthal, Philip Mrs, 1963, D 1,85:1
Rosenthal, Rebecca Mrs, 1923, F 14,17:4
Rosenthal, Reuben, 1948, N 15,25:3
Rosenthal, Samuel, 1917, D 18,15:4; 1937, Je 22,23:4; 1950, My 25,29:5
Rosenthal, Samuel C, 1956, Ag 10,17:1
Rosenthal, Saul J, 1962, Ja 6,19:5
Rosenthal, Shephard, 1952, Ag 26,25:5
Rosenthal, Sol, 1949, D 9,32:3
Rosenthal, Sydney, 1955, O 23,86:5
Rosenthal, Toby, 1917, D 29,11:5
Rosenthal, William, 1958, Ap 14,25:1
Rosenthall, Louis S Mrs, 1962, N 17,25:1
Rosenwald, Augusta Mrs, 1921, F 25,11:6
Rosenwald, Benno, 1925, Ap 18,15:5; 1925, Ap 21,21:6
Rosenwald, Benno Mrs, 1955, D 25,48:6
Rosenwald, J, 1932, Ja 7,1:4
Rosenwald, J Mrs, 1929, My 24,27:3
Rosenwald, Julius Mrs, 1949, S 30,24:3
Rosenwald, Max, 1953, S 6,52:3
Rosenwald, Sigmund, 1908, Ag 13,7:4
Rosenwald, T, 1927, Ap 10,II,8:7
Rosenwald, Theodore Jr, 1956, Jl 2,21:5
Rosenwasser, Benjamin B, 1938, Mr 30,21:3
Rosenwasser, Benjamin Dr, 1968, D 24,20:6
Rosenwasser, Henry Mrs, 1953, D 26,13:6
Rosenwasser, Maurice Mrs, 1943, F 2,19:1
Rosenwasser, Morris, 1960, Mr 21,29:3
Rosenweig, David, 1962, Ap 9,29:1
Rosenzweig, Alfred L, 1956, Ja 10,34:2
Rosenzweig, Benjamin, 1957, Ja 31,27:2
Rosenzweig, Charles, 1952, D 31,15:1
Rosenzweig, David, 1946, Mr 17,43:1
Rosenzweig, Henry, 1950, Ap 29,15:5
Rosenzweig, Ira, 1965, Je 9,47:1
Rosenzweig, Irwin, 1961, N 19,88:7
Rosenzweig, Jacob, 1942, D 4,25:3
Rosenzweig, Joseph, 1951, S 11,30:3
Rosenzweig, Leo, 1951, F 27,27:3
Rosenzweig, Louis, 1956, My 22,33:3
Rosenzweig, Louis I, 1939, Je 3,15:6
Rosenzweig, Manheim, 1958, Ap 29,29:2

Rosenzweig, Maxwell, 1950, Ag 15,29:4
Rosenzweig, Mitchell, 1947, Ap 11,25:4
Roser, Charles, 1922, Mr 13,15:2
Roser, Charles G, 1942, Je 10,21:1
Roser, Harold C, 1955, Jl 7,27:3
Roser, Herman, 1947, Mr 7,25:4
Roser, Sarah N Mrs, 1944, Ja 23,38:1
Roser, William J, 1937, O 26,23:1
Rosera, Milton P, 1961, N 12,64:3
Rosett, Joshua, 1940, Ap 5,21:4
Rosett, Joshua Mrs, 1967, Je 10,33:3
Rosett, Leo J, 1952, F 17,84:5
Rosett, Max (por), 1955, S 5,11:4
Rosett, Moritz Mrs, 1923, Mr 9,15:4
Rosette, George A, 1966, Mr 27,87:1
Rosevear, Charles R B Jr, 1963, Ag 28,33:5
Rosevear, Charles W, 1947, Ja 10,21:4
Rosevear, E William, 1945, D 6,27:4
Rosevear, John S, 1953, Mr 22,86:1
Rosevear, Thomas Mrs, 1937, D 7,25:4
Roseward, Edward, 1906, S 1,9:4
Rosewater, Charles C, 1946, O 5,17:3
Rosewater, Victor, 1940, Jl 13,13:3
Rosewell, Edna M Mrs, 1965, O 29,43:5
Roshgolin, Zalman, 1944, Ag 29,17:4
Rosholdt, Erling C, 1956, Jl 17,23:2
Rosier, Alfred M Mrs, 1963, N 18,33:2
Rosier, Joseph, 1951, O 8,21:1
Rosillo Del Toro, Domingo, 1957, N 30,21:1
Rosin, Thomas, 1956, Ag 27,19:4
Rosina Quillinan, Mother, 1943, Ja 18,15:1
Rosing, Bodil, 1942, Ja 3,32:4
Rosing, Nehemiah (Ned), 1956, S 18,35:4
Rosing, Vladimir, 1963, N 27,27:5
Rosinia, Michael L, 1947, S 25,29:6
Rosinoff, Gregory H Dr, 1968, Je 8,31:1
Rosinoff, Gregory H Mrs, 1952, O 10,25:4
Rosinski, Herbert, 1962, F 28,25:4
Rosinski, Stanislaus F, 1962, My 17,37:4
Rosinski, Victor, 1955, Jl 12,25:1
Rosit, Harry A Mrs, 1949, S 21,31:2
Rositi, Alberto, 1906, Je 24,9:6
Roslafsky, Abraham, 1961, Ap 2,76:1
Rosler, Louis J, 1955, My 19,29:5
Rosley, Adrian, 1937, Mr 6,17:5
Rosman, Daniel H, 1950, D 14,35:4
Rosman, Isidor B, 1958, Ap 4,24:1
Rosman, Jed, 1937, F 14,II,8:8
Rosman, Sol, 1950, O 19,31:1
Rosmarin, William, 1954, N 23,35:1
Rosmer, Alfred, 1964, My 7,37:1
Rosnagle, Harry, 1947, Jl 24,21:5
Rosner, Albert A, 1962, Mr 5,23:3
Rosner, David, 1962, Ap 11,43:2
Rosner, Michael M, 1966, O 30,88:7
Rosner, Murray, 1962, Je 9,25:1
Rosner, Oscar Mrs, 1961, Ag 2,29:3
Rosner, Samuel, 1952, O 21,29:6
Rosney, Katherine M, 1950, O 1,104:5
Rosny, J H, 1948, Je 17,25:4
Rosny, Joseph H, 1940, Mr 11,15:5
Roso, Manuel A Mrs, 1903, My 6,9:6
Rosof, Irving L, 1960, N 9,35:1
Rosoff, Max, 1962, My 7,31:1
Rosoff, Max Mrs, 1948, Ja 19,23:2
Rosoff, Meyer L, 1948, O 7,29:1
Rosoff, Samuel, 1950, Jl 15,13:4
Rosoff, Samuel R (will, Ap 20,18:6), 1951, Ap 10, 27:1
Rosoff, Seymour, 1954, S 24,23:4
Rosofsky, Barnet D (B Ross),(funl, Ja 21,23:2), 1967, Ja 19,31:1
Rosov, Phil, 1951, My 16,35:3
Rosovsky, Selik S, 1967, Ap 5,47:1
Rosowsky, Salomo, 1962, Ag 1,31:2
Rospigliosi, Camillo Prince, 1915, Je 7,11:4
Rospigliosi, Giambattista Princess, 1924, N 6,19:4
Rospigliosi, Girolama Prince, 1959, O 2,29:2
Rospigliosi, Mildred Princess, 1946, N 10,62:6
Rospiglosi, Francesco G, 1943, My 21,20:3
Rospondi, Stanislaw, 1958, F 6,27:2
Ross, A, 1878, Mr 10,2:2
Ross, A Franklin Mrs, 1966, Mr 14,31:2
Ross, A Rear Adm, 1926, Ja 24,II,11:2
Ross, A Y, 1922, Ap 5,17:5
Ross, Abram B, 1944, D 27,19:3
Ross, Adam F, 1954, Mr 4,25:2
Ross, Albert M, 1965, Jl 23,29:4
Ross, Alex, 1952, Je 26,29:5
Ross, Alex M, 1957, O 22,33:2
Ross, Alex S, 1939, Ja 14,17:5
Ross, Alexander, 1945, Jl 11,11:7
Ross, Alfonse, 1959, Ja 3,17:3
Ross, Alfred, 1958, S 27,21:5
Ross, Allan C, 1951, My 16,35:4
Ross, Andrew, 1937, Ap 4,II,11:1; 1941, D 30,19:3; 1956, N 24,19:5
Ross, Andrew G, 1955, F 18,21:2
Ross, Anna E, 1942, F 28,17:3
Ross, Anna F, 1942, N 1,52:8
Ross, Anthony, 1955, O 27,33:2
Ross, Art (Arth H), 1964, Ag 6,29:3
Ross, Arthur E, 1952, N 16,88:4
Ross, Arthur H, 1945, O 6,13:5
Ross, Arthur H Mrs, 1953, My 12,27:3
Ross, Arthur L, 1963, My 4,25:5
Ross, Arthur M, 1940, My 3,21:1
Ross, Aubrey C Mrs, 1951, O 22,23:4
Ross, Augustus R, 1963, S 21,21:4
Ross, Austin C, 1960, Ja 9,21:5
Ross, Barney (B D Rosofsky),(funl, Ja 21,23:2), 1967, Ja 19,31:1
Ross, Benjamin A, 1959, Mr 19,33:3
Ross, Benjamin C, 1944, Je 11,45:1
Ross, Benjamin H, 1903, S 28,7:5
Ross, Bertha, 1940, S 24,23:5
Ross, Betty C, 1947, F 3,19:3
Ross, Blair, 1951, My 2,31:3
Ross, Blanche A Mrs, 1958, Ap 22,33:2
Ross, Byers G, 1944, D 24,26:2
Ross, C Ben, 1946, Ap 1,27:5
Ross, C Chandler, 1952, Ja 9,29:2
Ross, C H Capt, 1901, Ag 19,7:6
Ross, Carlyle H, 1952, Jl 23,23:2
Ross, Carlyle N, 1938, Ap 19,21:3
Ross, Carmon (por), 1946, O 14,29:5
Ross, Charles (por), 1942, Je 29,15:1
Ross, Charles, 1949, F 11,23:4
Ross, Charles A Mrs, 1957, F 13,35:5
Ross, Charles C, 1938, S 13,23:1; 1940, Ap 10,25:4
Ross, Charles C Mrs, 1960, Je 19,88:2
Ross, Charles D, 1940, Ap 30,21:4
Ross, Charles E, 1903, D 15,9:5
Ross, Charles G, 1937, Ap 15,23:3; 1950, D 6,1:6
Ross, Charles Mrs, 1949, Mr 24,28:3
Ross, Charles N, 1873, Jl 11,3:2
Ross, Charles R, 1941, Jl 17,19:2; 1955, F 15,27:1
Ross, Charles W, 1940, Je 7,23:1; 1946, D 25,29:5
Ross, Clarence F, 1942, O 20,21:5
Ross, Clarence M, 1949, Mr 1,26:2
Ross, Clark, 1938, My 5,23:6
Ross, Colin G, 1938, N 27,49:2
Ross, Daniel G, 1951, D 4,33:2
Ross, David, 1949, F 10,27:1; 1951, Mr 16,16:5; 1959, Mr 14,23:2; 1965, Mr 18,30:6; 1966, My 6,47:4
Ross, David E, 1943, Je 29,19:5
Ross, David O, 1968, F 10,33:1
Ross, David William, 1925, Je 11,19:3
Ross, Dennis, 1948, O 17,76:4
Ross, Donald G, 1938, Mr 2,19:5; 1939, Mr 18,17:6
Ross, Donald G Mrs, 1948, S 6,13:6
Ross, Donald H, 1959, Ja 26,29:5
Ross, Donald J (por), 1948, Ap 27,25:1
Ross, Donald R, 1964, Je 13,23:2
Ross, Douglas W, 1940, Je 21,21:6
Ross, Douglas W Mrs, 1958, S 6,17:3
Ross, Duncan, 1919, S 9,17:6
Ross, E Clarendon, 1950, Je 26,27:2
Ross, Edmund Gibson, 1907, My 9,9:6
Ross, Edward, 1943, F 26,20:2
Ross, Edward A, 1951, Jl 23,17:5
Ross, Edward D (por), 1940, S 21,19:4
Ross, Edwin, 1944, Je 29,23:4
Ross, Edwin E, 1965, My 8,31:3
Ross, Elizabeth, 1940, Ap 6,17:5; 1953, Ap 18,19:6
Ross, Elizabeth Mrs, 1924, My 4,23:1
Ross, Ella, 1951, S 26,31:5
Ross, Elmer E, 1960, Ag 6,19:6
Ross, Eugene H, 1957, Ja 15,30:1
Ross, F Clair, 1956, Ja 18,31:2
Ross, F W Forbes Dr, 1913, S 20,11:3
Ross, Finley, 1950, Je 30,23:3
Ross, Francis J, 1955, Ag 7,73:1
Ross, Francois-Xavier, 1945, Jl 6,11:6
Ross, Frank, 1966, Ag 13,25:1
Ross, Frank A, 1943, N 18,23:3
Ross, Frank H Jr, 1947, My 7,27:2
Ross, Frank K, 1952, D 4,35:6
Ross, Frank P, 1947, F 25,25:2
Ross, Frank W, 1951, Je 27,29:6
Ross, Fred G, 1942, Ag 19,19:5
Ross, Frederick A, 1951, S 28,31:2
Ross, Frederick A Mrs, 1942, Ja 29,19:3
Ross, Frederick R W, 1955, Ap 23,19:4
Ross, G, 1879, Je 25,4:7
Ross, G A Johnston Rev Dr, 1937, Ja 23,17:4
Ross, Gale H, 1955, F 23,27:4
Ross, George, 1943, O 4,17:5
Ross, George E Mrs, 1941, Mr 31,15:3
Ross, George H, 1950, F 15,27:4; 1956, S 28,27:4
Ross, George J, 1948, N 2,25:2
Ross, George K, 1961, F 6,21:1
Ross, George L, 1941, F 2,44:5
Ross, George M, 1948, S 14,29:2
Ross, George W, 1965, D 8,47:2
Ross, George William, 1914, Mr 8,15:5
Ross, Gilbert N, 1942, My 1,19:1
Ross, Gordon, 1946, D 27,19:1
Ross, H C Dr, 1926, D 21,23:2
Ross, H P, 1882, Ap 14,5:3
Ross, Harold, 1951, D 7,1:2
Ross, Harold C, 1948, Jl 26,17:3
Ross, Harold P, 1949, Ag 30,27:4
Ross, Harper G, 1953, S 8,31:2
Ross, Harry, 1948, Je 6,72:2
Ross, Harry A Mrs, 1943, D 10,28:3
Ross, Harry B, 1955, O 27,33:1
Ross, Harry D Mrs, 1966, Ag 4,33:4
Ross, Helen C, 1937, F 11,23:4
Ross, Helen S B Mrs, 1941, Je 4,23:1
Ross, Henry, 1948, Jl 26,17:4
Ross, Henry A Mrs, 1946, D 9,25:2
Ross, Henry C, 1903, D 12,9:6
Ross, Henry E, 1946, D 25,29:3
Ross, Hervey, 1905, My 1,9:4
Ross, Hilda, 1959, Mr 7,21:3
Ross, Howard H, 1953, D 28,21:3
Ross, Howard S, 1955, F 11,23:2
Ross, Howard V, 1958, My 17,19:6
Ross, Hugh, 1938, Je 4,15:2
Ross, Hugh G, 1950, F 16,23:5
Ross, Isidore, 1960, Ag 17,31:2
Ross, J A, 1927, Ag 25,21:4
Ross, J C, 1941, Mr 28,23:3
Ross, J Elliot, 1946, S 19,31:4
Ross, J Stewart, 1917, Ap 28,13:6
Ross, J Thomas, 1945, F 24,11:5
Ross, Jacob A, 1949, O 11,34:2
Ross, Jacob B, 1960, S 6,33:5
Ross, Jacob J, 1950, Je 6,29:4
Ross, James, 1913, S 21,II,15:5; 1944, Jl 20,19:4
Ross, James A, 1939, Ag 19,15:3; 1949, Ap 28,31:6
Ross, James D, 1939, Mr 15,23:3; 1967, Mr 15,47:1
Ross, James E, 1950, My 20,15:5
Ross, James F, 1957, Jl 6,16:2; 1957, Jl 29,14:8
Ross, James J, 1952, Ap 21,21:5
Ross, James M, 1948, N 7,88:7
Ross, James P, 1965, My 1,31:5
Ross, James W, 1960, Jl 28,27:3
Ross, Janet M (Mrs W B), 1963, D 10,43:2
Ross, Jennie, 1924, D 29,15:3
Ross, Jeremiah K, 1940, My 17,19:3
Ross, Jerry (trb lr, N 20,II,3:4), 1955, N 12,19:1
Ross, Jo J Mrs, 1964, Ap 2,33:3
Ross, John, 1866, Ag 3,5:3; 1923, D 24,11:6; 1942, Jl 10,17:2; 1956, Ja 20,23:2
Ross, John A, 1956, D 23,30:3
Ross, John C, 1951, Mr 4,93:1; 1951, N 15,29:4
Ross, John D, 1939, O 30,17:4
Ross, John E Rev, 1925, Ja 20,21:4
Ross, John F, 1949, S 4,40:5
Ross, John G, 1946, Je 7,20:2
Ross, John J, 1951, O 26,23:2
Ross, John K L, 1951, Jl 27,19:5
Ross, John M, 1940, My 9,23:5; 1944, Ag 3,19:3
Ross, John O, 1966, Je 24,37:1
Ross, John O Mrs, 1960, Jl 25,23:5
Ross, John R, 1962, S 9,84:1
Ross, John S C (King Ross III), 1945, My 24,19:2
Ross, John W Capt, 1937, O 1,21:1
Ross, Jonathan Judge, 1905, F 24,7:6
Ross, Joseph, 1946, Ja 10,23:3; 1952, My 6,29:5; 196 Jl 16,21:1; 1966, D 10,37:2
Ross, Joseph J, 1953, Ap 7,29:5
Ross, Joseph M, 1953, Ap 11,17:6
Ross, Joseph Mrs, 1950, Mr 30,30:2
Ross, Joseph T, 1942, N 19,25:4
Ross, Julia, 1905, Ap 25,11:6
Ross, K, 1939, O 10,8:6
Ross, Laura E Mrs, 1955, Jl 31,69:3
Ross, Lawrence B, 1954, Jl 21,27:6
Ross, Leland H, 1948, F 7,15:5
Ross, Leland M, 1948, Ap 10,13:3
Ross, Leo J, 1968, Ap 19,47:5
Ross, Leonard K, 1963, Je 29,23:5
Ross, Leroy W, 1921, Ag 10,13:6
Ross, Leslie F, 1945, D 23,18:6
Ross, Leslie G, 1937, Ag 20,17:3
Ross, Lester J, 1953, N 15,89:2
Ross, Lewis P, 1953, O 10,17:6
Ross, Lewis T, 1958, S 5,27:1
Ross, Lionel, 1913, Jl 8,7:2
Ross, Llewellyn G, 1955, Ag 19,19:5
Ross, Louis Mrs, 1951, Ag 6,21:4
Ross, Malcolm B, 1957, Ja 1,23:5
Ross, Manuel, 1947, D 21,52:6
Ross, Mario T, 1937, Jl 7,24:1
Ross, Marshall V, 1947, N 14,23:4
Ross, Martin, 1959, My 20,35:3
Ross, Mary K Mrs, 1942, Ap 2,21:3
Ross, McGregor, 1941, Mr 22,15:4
Ross, Merritt K, 1958, My 14,33:3
Ross, Michael, 1963, N 10,87:1
Ross, Michael L, 1968, My 9,47:2
Ross, Mildred E, 1944, D 30,11:3
Ross, Miles, 1903, F 23,7:6
Ross, Milton R, 1961, My 2,37:4
Ross, Molly-Jane Mrs, 1953, N 23,27:1
Ross, Moses P Col, 1903, Ap 29,9:6
Ross, Moses R Lt, 1905, My 8,1:4
Ross, Norman, 1953, Je 21,85:1
Ross, Norman J, 1940, Ja 8,15:1
Ross, Olive C, 1943, Je 27,32:4
Ross, Oscar P Mrs, 1940, Je 14,21:2
Ross, Otto, 1955, Je 2,29:4
Ross, P D, 1949, Jl 6,27:5
Ross, Pearl V Mrs, 1939, Jl 17,19:2
Ross, Percy J, 1948, S 29,29:4
Ross, Perley A (por), 1938, Mr 21,15:4

Ross, Peter, 1902, Je 3,9:5
Ross, Phil J, 1952, S 27,17:1
Ross, Philip L, 1961, O 3,39:2
Ross, Pierre S, 1950, F 21,25:2
Ross, Polk, 1951, Mr 31,15:4
Ross, R Sir, 1932, S 17,15:1
Ross, Randolph Jr, 1939, F 2,19:4
Ross, Raymond S, 1962, F 15,29:4
Ross, Richard V, 1954, F 8,23:2
Ross, Robert, 1904, F 11,9:5; 1943, Ag 14,11:6; 1954, F 25,31:1
Ross, Robert E Jr, 1963, Jl 22,23:5
Ross, Robert L, 1946, Ap 25,21:1
Ross, Robert M, 1942, Mr 26,23:2
Ross, Robert R, 1939, D 24,14:7
Ross, Robert S, 1953, Ag 18,23:3
Ross, Roderick, 1950, Ja 8,76:6
Ross, Roland T, 1955, O 22,19:2
Ross, Ronald M, 1950, Jl 23,57:1
Ross, Roy E, 1945, O 2,23:5
Ross, Roy G, 1964, Mr 8,87:1
Ross, Roy Irving, 1968, Jl 25,33:4
Ross, Roy J, 1956, N 11,87:2
Ross, Rufus E, 1960, Mr 5,19:1
Ross, Ruth A, 1951, Mr 16,16:5
Ross, S, 1877, O 27,4:7
Ross, S Col, 1880, Jl 12,1:6
Ross, Sam, 1960, S 20,39:1
Ross, Samuel, 1943, Je 23,21:4; 1947, Ap 7,24:2
Ross, Sarah A Mrs, 1938, S 10,17:5
Ross, Sarah G, 1962, My 14,29:3
Ross, Sidney F, 1948, Je 1,23:4
Ross, Sidney H, 1961, My 8,35:4
Ross, Sophia L, 1957, Ja 24,29:2
Ross, Stanley H, 1958, My 17,19:3
Ross, Stanley Mrs, 1960, F 6,19:2
Ross, Theodore S Mrs, 1947, Je 20,19:4
Ross, Theodore W, 1949, F 18,24:2
Ross, Thomas, 1938, F 11,24:2; 1951, O 16,31:2; 1953, Ap 13,27:2
Ross, Thomas E (Mar 24), 1963, Ap 1,36:5
Ross, Thomas H, 1956, N 21,27:3
Ross, Thomas K, 1952, S 15,25:2
Ross, Thomas L Mrs, 1940, Ja 30,20:2
Ross, Thomas Mrs, 1953, Jl 5,49:2
Ross, Thomas R, 1869, Jl 1,2:2
Ross, Thomas W, 1958, O 1,37:3; 1959, N 15,86:6
Ross, Thorvald S, 1965, Mr 23,39:3
Ross, Travus, 1908, S 30,7:4
Ross, Victor, 1958, Ag 13,27:3
Ross, W B Gov, 1924, O 3,21:4
Ross, W D, 1947, Je 26,24:2
Ross, W E W Gen, 1907, N 13,9:6
Ross, Walter, 1963, N 21,39:5
Ross, Walter A, 1941, D 17,27:6
Ross, Walter L (por), 1939, Ap 6,25:4
Ross, Walter L, 1943, Jl 24,13:3
Ross, Walter M, 1939, Jl 2,15:3
Ross, Walter S, 1960, S 7,37:7
Ross, Wilbur L, 1958, Jl 28,23:2
Ross, Wilhelmina A, 1945, N 22,35:2
Ross, Will, 1951, Je 2,19:2
Ross, Will E, 1948, Ja 25,56:4
Ross, William, 1879, Mr 2,10:2; 1903, D 2,9:5; 1939, S 8,23:4; 1952, O 20,23:3
Ross, William A, 1912, Jl 12,9:4
Ross, William A (por), 1947, Ap 30,60:6
Ross, William A Mrs, 1958, N 8,21:5
Ross, William B, 1904, Ja 15,9:6
Ross, William B Maj, 1903, O 18,7:6
Ross, William G, 1943, Ag 8,37:3
Ross, William H, 1943, Ap 1,23:2; 1955, My 10,29:1
Ross, William H Mrs, 1939, Ag 17,21:5
Ross, William J, 1946, Ag 13,27:2; 1950, Ag 18,21:4
Ross, William M, 1941, D 25,25:6
Ross, William M Mrs, 1954, S 11,17:4
Ross, William N, 1956, Jl 6,21:2; 1961, F 11,23:6
Ross, William N Mrs, 1940, Je 4,23:2
Ross, William T, 1953, Ja 6,29:3
Ross, William W, 1937, F 20,17:1
Ross-Duggan, John K, 1967, F 4,27:4
Ross-of-Bladensburg, J F G Sir, 1926, Jl 11,24:1
Rossa, J O'Donovan Mrs, 1916, Ag 18,9:4
Rossa, O'Donovan Mrs, 1870, S 5,2:7
Rossano, Antonio, 1948, Ag 24,24:3
Rossbach, Adam J, 1952, S 7,87:1
Rossbach, Edgar H, 1952, N 13,31:5
Rossbach, George E, 1943, Jl 19,15:5
Rossbach, Herman, 1956, Ja 19,33:5
Rossbach, Laurence B Mrs, 1949, Je 2,28:2
Rossbach, Max J H, 1963, Ag 9,23:3
Rossbach, Max J H Mrs, 1967, F 25,27:3
Rossbach, Philip Rev, 1921, Ag 4,15:6
Rossbach, Walter S, 1958, N 30,86:2
Rossbacher, Henry J, 1961, N 11,23:5
Rossbottom, Thomas H, 1959, Ap 19,86:4
Rossby, Carl-Gustav, 1957, Ag 20,27:5
Rossby, Samuel, 1951, Je 20,27:5
Rosse, Earl of (Lawrence Parsons), 1908, Ag 31,7:7
Rosse, Earl of (Wm Edw Parsons), 1918, Je 11,11:5
Rosse, Herman, 1965, Ap 15,34:1
Rosse, Joseph, 1951, O 26,23:2
Rosse, June D, 1949, Mr 12,17:5
Rosse, Matthew R, 1948, O 8,25:3
Rosse, William Lord, 1867, N 2,1:1
Rosseau, G S, 1879, F 9,9:4
Rosseau, Percival L, 1937, D 1,23:4
Rossel, Louis A, 1871, N 29,5:6
Rossell, Arthur D, 1945, Ja 3,17:5
Rossell, Fay V, 1947, N 4,26:2
Rossell, Henry E Mrs, 1964, N 7,27:1
Rossell, John E, 1939, N 10,23:4
Rossell, Nellie C Mrs, 1947, Ja 7,27:1
Rossell, William T, 1960, F 11,36:1
Rossell, William Treat Brig-Gen, 1919, O 13,13:4
Rossell y Arellano, Mariano, 1964, D 12,31:4
Rosselli, Rex, 1941, Jl 25,15:6
Rossen, Robert, 1966, F 19,27:1
Rosser, John E Mrs, 1950, Ja 7,30:1
Rosser, Robert C, 1966, Jl 11,29:1
Rosser, Thomas L Gen, 1910, Mr 30,12:3
Rosser, W W, 1937, D 24,17:3
Rosset, Ephraim M, 1953, Ja 3,15:5
Rosseter, J H, 1936, Ap 30,19:3
Rossett, Abraham, 1949, Mr 25,23:2
Rossetter, Asher Mrs, 1950, F 6,25:4
Rossetter, George W, 1959, S 21,31:4
Rossetti, Constantine, 1885, Ap 21,5:4
Rossetti, D G, 1882, Ap 12,4:7
Rossetti, William Michael, 1919, F 6,11:2
Rossetto, Joseph Mrs, 1962, O 31,37:1
Rossey, Chris C, 1946, Je 22,19:6
Rossi, Alberto A, 1948, D 7,31:3
Rossi, Angela Signora, 1956, Je 11,9:1
Rossi, Angelo J, 1948, Ap 6,23:3
Rossi, Antonio A, 1948, Mr 31,25:3
Rossi, Ercole J (por), 1946, Mr 29,24:2
Rossi, Eugene, 1952, S 18,29:5
Rossi, Frederico G, 1942, Jl 13,15:5
Rossi, Gino, 1947, D 19,25:1
Rossi, Giuseppe, 1948, Ag 14,13:5
Rossi, Karl M, 1949, Je 7,31:3
Rossi, Leopold V, 1953, N 10,31:5
Rossi, Louis J, 1939, Ap 27,25:1
Rossi, Louis M, 1944, My 26,19:6
Rossi, Martino, 1950, F 7,28:2
Rossi, Maurice, 1966, Ag 30,41:1
Rossi, Peter Mrs, 1948, F 27,21:5
Rossi, Raffaele C, 1948, S 18,18:2
Rossi, Vincento, 1949, Je 30,23:5
Rossi, William N, 1947, Ap 2,27:4
Rossi di Montelera, Enrico Count, 1939, O 11,27:3
Rossi di Montelera, Lando, 1967, Jl 13,37:2
Rossi-Diehl, Conrad, 1955, Ja 1,13:5
Rossi Longhi, Roberto, 1957, Jl 5,17:2
Rossie, Grete G Mrs, 1941, Ja 22,21:2
Rossien, Ahbrohm X, 1960, N 11,31:2
Rossier, Edmund, 1945, O 4,23:2
Rossigniani, Luigi, 1948, F 23,25:4
Rossignol, Claude B, 1957, N 28,31:4
Rossin, Alfred S (por), 1947, Je 6,23:3
Rossin, C L Mrs, 1927, D 18,31:1
Rossin, Edgar L (por), 1948, Ag 19,21:5
Rossin, Peter C Sr, 1954, My 8,17:4
Rossing, Gunther, 1965, Ag 4,35:4
Rossini, Mrs, 1878, Mr 24,1:1
Rossini, the Composer (trb, D 7,2:6), 1868, N 15,5:3
Rossiter, Arthur W, 1955, S 17,15:6
Rossiter, C Lawrence, 1956, Jl 6,21:1
Rossiter, Clinton Lawrence, 1925, N 13,19:5
Rossiter, David P, 1947, Ag 15,17:1
Rossiter, E V W (funl, D 13,13:5), 1910, D 12,9:3
Rossiter, Edward Van Wyck, 1925, Ja 15,21:5
Rossiter, Ehrick K, 1941, O 16,21:3
Rossiter, Frank H, 1947, Ja 13,21:5
Rossiter, Fred J, 1964, My 30,17:2
Rossiter, Helen H Mrs, 1939, Je 25,36:8
Rossiter, James P, 1943, S 27,19:2
Rossiter, John J, 1904, Jl 15,7:6
Rossiter, Laurence N, 1957, Mr 27,31:5
Rossiter, P S Mrs, 1954, N 22,23:2
Rossiter, Sidney R, 1968, N 25,47:3
Rossiter, Stealy B Rev Dr, 1914, Je 25,9:6
Rossiter, Walter King, 1910, O 2,II,13:4
Rossiter, Will, 1954, Je 11,23:2
Rossiter, William J Mrs, 1942, N 30,23:4
Rossiter, William W G, 1954, F 15,23:6
Rosskam, Charles, 1954, Jl 30,17:4
Rosskam, Charles H Mrs, 1953, S 3,21:1
Rosskam, William K, 1946, D 27,20:2
Rosslyn, Dowager Countess of, 1933, D 9,15:4
Rosslyn, Earl of (por), 1939, Ag 11,15:3
Rossman, George M Mrs, 1941, Je 9,19:1
Rossman, Grant B, 1918, Je 21,13:4
Rossman, H Herbert, 1964, N 17,41:1
Rossman, Morris, 1958, F 5,18:5
Rossman, Palen P, 1953, S 10,25:1
Rossman, Phil M, 1941, S 11,23:4
Rossman, Sidney, 1946, F 16,13:4
Rossman, William C, 1966, D 17,33:3
Rossmann, Carl O, 1947, My 31,13:2
Rossmann, Louis, 1940, Ap 3,23:3
Rossmassler, Edward C, 1944, Ap 27,23:3
Rossmoore, Emerson E, 1961, Je 22,31:5
Rossmore, Baron, 1874, Mr 29,1:7
Rossnagel, David H, 1951, D 19,31:1
Rossnagel, William E, 1966, O 12,43:1
Rossner, Alex, 1949, Mr 13,76:6
Rossner, Erhard, 1953, F 21,13:1
Rosso, Augusto, 1964, D 21,29:2
Rossomondo, Frank D, 1959, Mr 9,29:3
Rosson, Arthur H, 1960, Je 19,88:5
Rosson, Gladys, 1953, Je 16,27:4
Rosson, Stuart G, 1951, N 13,29:3
Rossoni, Edmondo, 1965, Je 10,36:1
Rossow, Frank C, 1940, Je 26,23:4
Rossow, Robert, 1960, Ap 13,39:3
Rosston, Walter J, 1958, N 4,27:1
Rossum, Charles, 1947, My 26,21:1
Rossum, W van, 1932, Ag 30,17:4
Rost, Anton, 1967, F 20,37:5
Rost, Henry, 1954, Ap 30,23:5
Rost, Henry L, 1960, My 6,31:3
Rost, John M, 1948, D 25,17:4
Rost, W L, 1933, D 5,23:5
Rostaing, Mother Superior, 1937, D 10,25:4
Rostan, Stanley, 1948, Ag 26,21:3
Rostand, Edmond, 1918, D 3,15:3
Rostand, Edmond Mrs, 1953, Jl 9,25:6
Rostand, Eugene, 1915, Ja 21,9:4
Rostand, Henri, 1952, Mr 28,23:2
Rostand, Maurice, 1968, F 23,33:3
Rostang, Pierre de, 1950, D 26,23:4
Rostel, Rudolph B, 1952, Ja 5,11:5
Rosten, Harry, 1964, Mr 5,33:2
Rostenberg, Adolph Sr, 1950, S 6,23:2
Rostern, William J, 1938, N 28,15:1
Rosthal, Fannie Mrs, 1939, My 7,III,6:8
Rosthal, Joseph, 1955, O 10,27:5
Rostock, Frank W, 1960, Jl 20,29:2
Rostovtzeff, Michael I, 1952, O 21,29:1
Rostow, Leo J, 1941, S 4,21:4
Rostowski, Stanley P, 1938, Ap 12,23:4
Rostron, Arthur H (por), 1940, N 6,23:4
Rostron, John B (por), 1944, Je 13,19:4
Roswell, Ross E, 1947, S 7,60:1
Roszel, Clarence A, 1948, Mr 3,23:4
Roszel, Clarence A Mrs, 1950, N 28,31:4
Roszel, Wilfred C, 1962, Jl 10,33:2
Roszel, Wilfred C Mrs, 1955, S 12,25:3
Rota, Ferro Mrs, 1967, D 7,52:2
Rotan, George V, 1943, Ap 18,48:4
Rotan, Julius, 1948, Ja 25,57:1
Rotberg, Harry, 1957, Ag 31,15:5
Rotblat, Louis, 1943, Ja 19,19:2
Rotch, A Lawrence Prof, 1912, Ap 8,11:6
Rotch, Thomas Morgan Dr, 1914, Mr 10,9:5
Rote, Jack T, 1953, S 11,21:1
Rote, Stuart B, 1942, Je 15,19:3
Rotenberg, Maurice, 1952, N 18,31:1
Rotermundt, Fritz, 1939, My 25,25:4
Rotgans, J, 1948, Ap 1,25:6
Roth, Albert C, 1947, O 18,15:2
Roth, Albert J, 1947, S 25,29:3
Roth, Albert Mrs, 1965, My 24,31:5
Roth, Alfred P, 1950, Jl 23,56:4
Roth, Almon E, 1964, Ja 3,23:1
Roth, Andrew W, 1947, Ja 22,23:1
Roth, Ben, 1960, Ja 23,21:1
Roth, Benjamin H, 1955, F 21,21:2
Roth, Bernard Mrs, 1949, N 13,92:4
Roth, Bert W, 1967, Je 28,45:1
Roth, Britain G, 1960, My 21,23:2
Roth, Budd, 1956, O 15,25:6
Roth, Carl, 1943, Ap 5,21:7
Roth, Charles A, 1943, D 30,17:5; 1948, Ja 20,23:4
Roth, Charles F, 1954, Je 25,21:2
Roth, Charles F Mrs, 1956, Jl 23,23:6
Roth, Christian, 1946, Ag 12,21:5
Roth, Claude L, 1952, F 20,29:4
Roth, Conrad, 1941, Ap 25,19:4
Roth, David W Mrs, 1954, D 19,84:6
Roth, Elias E, 1958, N 25,33:4
Roth, Emery, 1948, Ag 21,16:2
Roth, Ernest D, 1964, Ag 22,21:5
Roth, Ernest E, 1963, Jl 17,31:3
Roth, Ernst, 1951, My 15,31:1
Roth, Frank C, 1954, Jl 17,13:7
Roth, Fred, 1949, S 10,17:3
Roth, Frederick, 1944, My 22,19:5
Roth, Frederick G, 1940, Mr 9,15:5
Roth, G J, 1902, D 28,13:6
Roth, G Stuart, 1940, Mr 26,21:5
Roth, Gustave, 1960, My 17,37:5
Roth, Gustave S, 1938, D 27,17:2
Roth, Harry, 1943, Ag 31,17:6; 1946, Ag 8,21:4
Roth, Harry W Mrs, 1957, Ap 11,31:4
Roth, Henry, 1918, Jl 16,13:6; 1937, F 19,13:5; 1949, S 12,21:3
Roth, Henry G, 1958, S 11,34:1
Roth, Herb, 1953, O 28,29:2
Roth, Herman, 1968, F 21,47:2
Roth, Hermine Mrs, 1949, My 27,22:2
Roth, Ignatz, 1947, N 9,74:4
Roth, Irving R, 1957, Je 26,31:5
Roth, Isadore Mrs, 1945, S 28,21:4
Roth, Isidor, 1949, Mr 4,21:4
Roth, Jack L Sr Mrs, 1955, Ag 17,27:2
Roth, Jacob, 1938, Je 17,21:6; 1966, Jl 8,35:1

Roth, Jacob H, 1948, Ap 10,13:4
Roth, Jacob H Mrs, 1955, N 18,25:3
Roth, Jacques H, 1938, Jl 30,13:4
Roth, Joe, 1960, F 18,33:1
Roth, John, 1948, F 22,49:1
Roth, John E, 1949, Je 28,27:2
Roth, Joseph, 1939, Je 7,23:4; 1960, Mr 12,21:4
Roth, Julius, 1914, O 29,11:4; 1942, Ja 11,46:2
Roth, Lawrence V, 1963, S 20,33:4
Roth, Lazar, 1909, Je 24,7:4
Roth, Lena, 1948, O 25,23:5
Roth, Leo L Mrs, 1942, S 27,49:2
Roth, Leon, 1963, Ag 5,47:3
Roth, Leon G, 1963, My 16,35:2
Roth, Leonard Mrs, 1968, N 30,19:2
Roth, Leonard Prof, 1968, N 30,19:2
Roth, Lester, 1952, Ja 27,76:8
Roth, Lillian, 1943, F 17,21:1
Roth, Louis, 1948, D 7,31:1; 1959, Ja 25,92:8; 1961, O 22,86:3
Roth, Louis Mrs, 1955, Je 24,21:3
Roth, Ludwig, 1967, N 2,47:2
Roth, Marcus J, 1937, D 22,25:4
Roth, Mark J, 1944, Ja 28,17:5
Roth, Max, 1903, Je 15,12:2; 1951, Ja 16,29:5; 1965, N 5,37:3
Roth, Michael J, 1952, Ap 14,19:4
Roth, Milton, 1964, F 8,23:4; 1968, N 7,47:2
Roth, Morris, 1950, Ap 20,29:4
Roth, Moses, 1952, Ja 29,25:2
Roth, Oscar, 1943, N 13,13:4
Roth, Oswald H, 1947, F 21,19:3
Roth, Oswald H Jr Mrs, 1942, N 8,51:5
Roth, Phil, 1950, D 14,35:5
Roth, Raymond T, 1952, Ap 6,89:1
Roth, Richard F, 1951, F 20,25:3
Roth, Richard G, 1967, D 5,50:2
Roth, Robert A, 1951, O 25,26:2
Roth, Robert F, 1964, Ja 23,31:3
Roth, Rudolph J, 1946, O 16,27:4
Roth, Sam (Bway Sam),(will, N 14,28:4), 1951, N 1, 29:3
Roth, Samuel, 1943, Ag 29,39:3
Roth, Samuel J (por), 1955, My 17,29:6
Roth, Samuel R, 1958, Ja 25,19:6
Roth, Sanford H, 1962, Mr 6,32:7
Roth, Sigmund, 1958, S 20,19:6
Roth, Theophilus B Rev, 1937, N 17,23:6
Roth, Victor, 1939, Jl 27,19:3; 1962, O 8,23:5
Roth, William, 1939, S 12,25:4; 1946, O 29,15:7; 1966, N 20,88:6
Roth, William F, 1941, Ap 2,23:2
Roth, William H, 1949, Ap 14,25:2
Roth, William P, 1963, F 26,7:2
Rothaar, George W, 1946, N 27,25:3
Rothacker, Douglas D, 1954, N 13,15:1
Rothacker, George F, 1913, Jl 9,7:6
Rothacker, Watterson R, 1960, Ja 27,33:5
Rothafel, Max, 1948, Jl 8,23:2
Rothafel, S L, 1936, Ja 14,21:1
Rothaug, Christian Dr, 1937, N 4,25:5
Rothaug, Edward, 1952, Ap 6,45:3
Rothaus, Charles, 1955, Ja 13,27:3
Rothauser, Charles, 1951, N 26,25:5
Rothberg, Alex Mrs, 1960, Jl 22,23:1
Rothberg, Bernard Mrs, 1943, My 12,25:1
Rothberg, Kalman, 1947, F 2,57:3
Rothberg, Kalman Mrs, 1941, Jl 23,19:5
Rothberg, Lawrence S, 1945, S 29,15:5
Rothberg, Morris Mrs, 1964, Ap 1,39:4
Rothberg, Samuel, 1937, My 5,25:5
Rothberg, Torsten, 1938, N 5,2:7
Rothblatt, Adolphe, 1937, D 12,II,9:1
Rothblum, Benjamin (por), 1949, N 21,25:5
Rothblum, David, 1956, Je 5,35:5
Rothbub, Anne I, 1949, Jl 9,13:2
Rothchild, Edward S, 1943, S 3,19:5
Rothchild, Edward S Mrs, 1945, Ag 4,11:3
Rothchild, Kennon V, 1953, Je 7,83:1
Rothe, Anita, 1944, Ja 11,19:4
Rothe, Arthur, 1946, Jl 19,19:6
Rothe, Augusta L Mrs, 1939, D 13,27:4
Rothe, Lloyd B, 1966, Ag 15,27:4
Rothe, Paul N, 1948, Ap 24,15:6
Rothe, Walter C, 1950, Ja 11,23:1
Rothe, William H, 1957, Mr 4,27:4
Rothenberg, Abraham, 1966, Je 3,39:3
Rothenberg, Adolph Mrs (G Gordon), 1963, Je 8,25:2
Rothenberg, Alex, 1956, Ag 13,19:6
Rothenberg, Alfred E, 1943, Je 18,21:6
Rothenberg, Anna S Mrs, 1960, My 19,37:5
Rothenberg, Herman, 1949, N 7,27:2
Rothenberg, Jack, 1964, My 11,31:2
Rothenberg, Jack Mrs, 1958, Mr 11,29:4
Rothenberg, Joel E, 1958, Ja 26,88:5
Rothenberg, Joseph Mrs, 1953, Jl 19,57:2
Rothenberg, Louis, 1948, Ag 19,21:4
Rothenberg, Louis I Mrs, 1955, Ja 5,23:4
Rothenberg, Meyer D, 1949, N 18,29:3
Rothenberg, Morris, 1950, S 18,23:1
Rothenberg, Morton, 1965, Ag 30,25:5
Rothenberg, Phil, 1955, S 8,31:4
Rothenberg, Samuel, 1951, Ja 23,27:5; 1959, Je 27,23:4
Rothenberg, Sheftel Mrs, 1967, S 2,25:6
Rothenberg, Simon, 1961, Ag 11,23:4
Rothenberg, Simon Mrs, 1948, D 19,76:5
Rothenberg, William, 1960, Mr 24,33:4
Rothenburg, Grover V, 1943, Je 27,32:7
Rothenbusch, Frederick D, 1937, Ag 11,24:3
Rothenfeld, Jack, 1944, D 7,25:6
Rothengast, Conrad H, 1963, N 9,1:2
Rothengast, John Mrs, 1951, Ja 31,25:4
Rothengatter, Emil, 1939, N 6,23:3
Rothenstein, Albert I, 1965, D 4,31:1
Rothenstein, Lady (Mrs W Rothenstein), 1957, Je 17,23:3
Rothenstein, William (por), 1945, F 15,19:5
Rother, Edward T, 1937, Ja 21,23:4
Rotherham, John Sr, 1942, Jl 5,29:2
Rothermel, Amos C, 1946, O 6,59:5
Rothermel, Enoch S, 1957, My 9,31:6
Rothermel, George C, 1952, S 27,17:3
Rothermel, John H, 1922, S 9,13:5
Rothermel, Nelson L, 1956, Jl 26,25:4
Rothermel, Ulla A Mrs, 1957, N 15,27:2
Rothermere, Lady, 1937, Mr 17,25:3
Rothermere, Lord, 1940, N 27,8:1
Rotherwick, Lord (H R Crayzer), 1958, Mr 18,29:4
Rothery, Agnes (Mrs H R Pratt), 1954, Ag 12,25:3
Rothery, John, 1940, My 18,15:6
Rothfeder, Abraham F, 1961, Ap 5,37:4
Rothfeld, Laurence, 1949, D 1,31:3
Rothfeld, Saul, 1955, Ap 27,31:1
Rothfus, John F, 1944, Je 29,23:3
Rothfuss, C Howard Mrs, 1953, Jl 26,69:2
Rothfuss, Gustave A, 1943, Ja 28,19:4
Rothfuss, John T, 1957, Mr 19,37:2
Rothier, Leon, 1951, D 7,27:2
Rothier, Leon Mrs, 1948, Je 14,23:4
Rothing, Harry J, 1937, S 5,II,7:1
Rothkop, Sophie Mrs (cor, Ap 20,84:8), 1958, Ap 18, 23:6
Rothkopf, Julius, 1966, Je 16,47:4
Rothkopf, Morris, 1937, O 13,23:2
Rothlauf, Anthony J, 1962, O 9,42:1
Rothlauf, Theresa A, 1962, O 9,42:1
Rothlein, William, 1954, Ag 9,17:2
Rothlisberger, Harry E, 1966, Ag 13,25:1
Rothmaler, Oswald, 1946, Jl 13,15:3
Rothman, Aaron A, 1961, D 20,33:1
Rothman, Abraham Don, 1968, Ja 13,31:2
Rothman, George, 1959, Ja 19,27:3
Rothman, Henry, 1963, Ag 19,25:2
Rothman, Herman N, 1964, D 17,41:3
Rothman, L, 1938, Ap 16,13:2
Rothman, Leopold M, 1942, O 29,23:1
Rothman, Martin J, 1962, Ag 22,34:5
Rothman, Morris, 1945, D 22,19:3
Rothman, Norman D, 1953, O 6,29:5
Rothman, Stephen, 1963, S 1,56:7
Rothmann, Charles J, 1964, O 28,45:4
Rothmann, Charles Mrs, 1949, Ap 28,31:3
Rothmann, George M, 1949, Ag 14,68:1
Rothmann, Paul Mrs, 1966, F 1,35:1
Rothmann, Peter, 1950, Ag 10,25:1
Rothnagel, David, 1938, F 20,23:4
Rothrock, Harry A Sr, 1957, Ap 6,19:3
Rothrock, Harry W, 1965, F 11,39:4
Rothrock, Ray, 1962, Ag 9,25:3
Rothschild, A M, 1902, Jl 29,3:4
Rothschild, Abe, 1937, My 15,19:5
Rothschild, Adolphe de Baroness, 1907, N 20,9:5
Rothschild, Albert, 1953, Ap 7,29:4
Rothschild, Albert S A Baron, 1911, F 12,12:2
Rothschild, Alonzo, 1915, O 2,11:2
Rothschild, Alphonse de Baron, 1905, My 27,9:1; 1942, S 2,23:1
Rothschild, Anselm Baron, 1874, Ag 28,1:7
Rothschild, Anthony G de, 1961, F 6,23:1
Rothschild, Anthony Sir, 1876, Ja 5,4:7
Rothschild, Arthur Baron, 1903, D 11,9:7
Rothschild, August, 1917, My 29,13:2
Rothschild, Bert C, 1943, O 11,19:2
Rothschild, Bruno, 1964, D 11,39:5
Rothschild, Clarence G, 1949, Jl 31,60:5
Rothschild, Daniel, 1956, Je 16,19:5
Rothschild, Daniel L, 1957, Je 11,35:1
Rothschild, David J Mrs, 1945, My 7,17:2
Rothschild, E J de, 1934, N 3,15:1
Rothschild, Edmond de Baron, 1920, F 12,11:4
Rothschild, Edouard de, 1949, Jl 1,19:1
Rothschild, Edward, 1914, Jl 31,9:5
Rothschild, Edward F, 1937, F 14,II,8:5
Rothschild, Edward L, 1925, Mr 22,7:3; 1953, F 10, 27:3
Rothschild, Eugene de Baroness (por), 1946, O 10, 27:3
Rothschild, Frank Mrs, 1907, S 26,9:5
Rothschild, George F, 1957, Mr 27,31:4
Rothschild, Gunter L, 1951, Jl 24,17:2
Rothschild, Gustave de Baroness, 1912, O 25,13:2
Rothschild, Gustave Samuel James de Baron, 1911, N 29,11:5
Rothschild, H Leonard, 1964, Je 12,32:6
Rothschild, Hans S (por), 1946, My 13,21:4
Rothschild, Harry, 1945, Ap 19,27:4
Rothschild, Harry S, 1945, Ap 6,15:4
Rothschild, Henri de, 1947, O 13,23:3
Rothschild, Hugo, 1962, Ja 29,25:2
Rothschild, Hugo S, 1967, D 27,34:7
Rothschild, Irving S, 1960, Jl 18,27:5
Rothschild, Isidor M, 1968, Jl 14,65:1
Rothschild, J Henry, 1913, D 28,II,15:5
Rothschild, Jacob, 1911, Ap 5,9:5
Rothschild, James A de (will, Jl 23,6:8), 1957, My 37:3
Rothschild, James Baron, 1868, N 17,5:3; 1881, O 26 2:2
Rothschild, James de Mrs, 1964, Jl 4,13:4
Rothschild, Jerome J, 1964, Jl 21,33:2
Rothschild, L O (Leopold), 1968, D 4,47:1
Rothschild, Lambert Baron, 1919, F 1,13:5
Rothschild, Leo, 1941, D 1,19:3
Rothschild, Leo H, 1950, Ja 11,23:1
Rothschild, Leon, 1944, Je 5,19:2
Rothschild, Leopold de, 1917, My 30,9:5
Rothschild, Lionel N De (will, Je 19,1:2), 1879, Je 5:2
Rothschild, Lionel N de, 1942, Ja 29,19:5
Rothschild, Lionel W Baron (por), 1937, Ag 28,15:
Rothschild, Louis de (funl, Ja 31,19:4), 1955, Ja 16 92:6
Rothschild, Louis F, 1957, Je 18,29:2
Rothschild, Louis F Mrs, 1956, D 14,29:4
Rothschild, Louis H, 1943, Ja 28,20:2
Rothschild, M A, 1936, F 17,20:1
Rothschild, M H, 1927, Jl 31,24:1
Rothschild, Marcus, 1962, Je 11,31:4
Rothschild, Marie de Mrs, 1937, Ap 9,21:4
Rothschild, Martin Mrs, 1943, O 30,15:3
Rothschild, Marx, 1904, Mr 10,9:5
Rothschild, Maurice, 1949, Jl 24,52:8
Rothschild, Maurice de Baron, 1957, S 5,29:4
Rothschild, Maurice de Baroness, 1968, Mr 19,47:1
Rothschild, Maurice L, 1941, Ap 24,21:3
Rothschild, Maurice L Mrs, 1922, D 16,15:5
Rothschild, Melville N, 1941, Jl 19,13:5
Rothschild, Meyer D, 1943, Ja 31,46:1
Rothschild, Monroe W, 1946, Ap 28,44:7
Rothschild, Montefiore, 1940, Ja 13,15:3
Rothschild, Morris H, 1939, Je 26,15:4
Rothschild, Morris M, 1943, Mr 1,19:3
Rothschild, Moses, 1937, N 18,23:3
Rothschild, Nathan Mayer Baron (funl, Ap 3,9:4), 1915, Ap 1,15:3
Rothschild, Nathaniel de Baron, 1905, Je 14,9:6
Rothschild, Nelly de (por), 1945, Ja 9,19:1
Rothschild, Ralph, 1948, D 19,76:2
Rothschild, Robert de, 1946, D 26,25:3
Rothschild, Rozsika Mrs, 1940, Jl 4,15:3
Rothschild, S, 1927, Jl 6,25:1; 1954, F 22,19:3
Rothschild, S F, 1936, Ja 6,17:1
Rothschild, Samson, 1939, Je 15,23:4
Rothschild, Samuel, 1962, Ap 19,31:4
Rothschild, Sanford, 1947, Ja 11,19:6
Rothschild, Sigmund, 1907, Jl 16,7:6
Rothschild, Sofia, 1960, Jl 20,29:4
Rothschild, Solomon, 1947, Ag 4,17:5
Rothschild, Solomon Mrs, 1953, Mr 12,25:1
Rothschild, V Henry (funl, My 19,11:4), 1911, My 17,13:5
Rothschild, V Henry, 1917, Ap 28,13:5
Rothschild, V Sydney, 1924, Mr 3,17:6
Rothschild, Walter M, 1955, Ja 23,85:3
Rothschild, Walter N, 1960, O 9,86:1
Rothschild, Wilhelm Baron, 1901, Ja 26,9:6
Rothschild, William, 1910, Ag 31,9:5
Rothschild, William Earl Baroness, 1924, Mr 11,19:
Rothschild, William L, 1964, F 5,35:5
Rothseid, Abraham, 1949, F 25,23:5
Rothseid, Louis B, 1950, Ap 6,29:1
Rothshtein, Fedor A, 1953, S 3,21:2
Rothsteen, Lafayette Mrs, 1945, F 19,17:6
Rothstein, Abe L, 1952, Ja 10,29:2
Rothstein, Abraham E, 1939, N 21,26:1
Rothstein, Adolph, 1904, N 23,2:4
Rothstein, Arthur, 1938, Ap 19,21:3
Rothstein, Herman, 1966, O 18,40:5
Rothstein, Israel Mrs, 1957, My 10,27:2
Rothstein, Julius, 1959, Ja 25,92:2
Rothstein, Justin A, 1967, N 19,85:1
Rothstein, Milton, 1959, Ag 11,27:3
Rothstein, Morris, 1905, Ap 18,20:5
Rothstein, Samuel, 1958, Je 1,86:6
Rothstein, Thor C Dr, 1937, F 21,II,10:6
Rothstein, William, 1957, N 25,31:4
Rothweiler, John Mrs, 1950, Mr 8,25:1
Rothwell, Austin S, 1941, My 29,19:2
Rothwell, Bernard J, 1948, N 29,23:4
Rothwell, Bertram S, 1945, Mr 25,38:2
Rothwell, George R, 1943, N 17,25:4
Rothwell, John J, 1959, F 16,29:2
Rothwell, John J Mrs, 1957, S 8,84:4
Rothwell, Thomas H, 1941, D 9,31:3
Rothwell, Walter, 1949, F 10,27:2
Rothwell, William P, 1939, Je 15,19:4
Roti, Francis, 1953, O 13,29:4
Rotman, David B, 1948, Je 1,23:3
Rotner, Philip, 1944, D 7,25:3

Rotoli, Augusto, 1904, N 27,7:6
Rotondi, Joseph J, 1948, Ja 13,25:3
Rotstein, Charles, 1959, My 16,23:3
Rottach, Richard J, 1953, F 12,28:3
Rottenberg, I M, 1927, Ag 10,23:5
Rottenberg, Julius, 1914, Je 9,11:4
Rottenberg, Marcus Mrs, 1958, My 10,21:6
Rottenberg, Samuel, 1958, Ag 15,21:4
Rottenberg, Solomon, 1950, Je 3,15:4
Rotter, Frederick, 1950, Ap 22,19:3
Rotter-Diefenbach, Johanna (Mrs Rich D L Diefenbach), 1909, Jl 27,7:3
Rotterd, Dr, 1924, O 2,23:3
Rottman, Benjamin, 1955, Ag 24,27:4
Rottman, Martin, 1947, S 27,15:5
Rottmann, John F, 1938, Je 21,19:5
Rottner, Chester D, 1951, Jl 22,60:2
Rotunda, Nicholas, 1925, S 12,15:4
Rotundo, Dominick, 1949, N 17,29:4
Rotundo, Joseph, 1953, Mr 10,29:1
Roty, Lewis Oscar, 1911, Mr 24,11:4
Rotz, Rhiman A, 1967, S 7,33:5
Rouaul, Georges, 1958, F 14,23:2
Roubaud, Louis, 1941, O 18,19:3
Roubik, Joseph, 1962, Mr 23,33:1
Rouclere, Harry Mrs, 1938, Ja 9,43:1
Roudebush, John H Mrs, 1941, O 19,47:2
Roudebush, John Heywood, 1925, Ap 24,19:5
Roudebush, Wallace P, 1956, Ap 16,27:2
Roudiez, Leon S, 1941, Ja 16,23:3
Roudin, Bernard, 1915, My 25,15:5
Rouffe, Alida, 1949, N 23,29:2
Rouge, Charles F, 1955, D 4,88:4
Rough, Frederick, 1914, D 17,13:6
Rough, Lewis W Mrs, 1944, My 31,19:3
Rougier, Francis L, 1945, My 22,19:1
Rouher, E, 1884, F 4,2:4
Rouillard, Irving G, 1950, Jl 23,59:8
Rouillard, Paul R, 1951, D 14,31:2
Rouilliard, Raoul, 1954, My 29,15:3
Rouillion, Louis, 1949, D 8,33:5
Roujou, Henry Francois Joseph, 1914, Je 2,11:2
Rouke, Fabian L, 1965, Ap 29,35:2
Roukey, Kenneth (Bro Canrad), 1963, N 23,29:1
Rouleau, R M, 1931, Je 1,17:5
Roulet, Calvin B, 1951, Mr 20,29:3
Roulette, William U Jr, 1961, Ja 31,29:5
Roulhac, William S, 1954, My 4,29:3
Roullier, Edward, 1920, Mr 20,11:6
Roulston, Florence A, 1959, O 5,31:2
Roulston, Frank J, 1939, Ap 27,25:3
Roulston, Henry D, 1944, Ja 30,38:5
Roulston, Herbert C, 1944, Mr 21,20:3
Roulston, Robert J, 1937, N 28,II,8:8
Roulston, Thomas, 1918, Ap 27,15:8
Roulston, Thomas H (por), 1949, Ag 19,17:1
Roulston, William J, 1954, Ap 13,31:3
Roulstone, William Bradford, 1953, F 14,17:3
Roumefort, Count de, 1953, Ap 22,29:3
Roumfort, A L Gen, 1878, Ag 3,1:4
Round, Charles J, 1942, O 30,19:3
Round, George A Mrs, 1937, D 28,21:3
Round, Henry J, 1966, Ag 19,33:6
Round, William M F, 1906, Ja 6,9:4
Rounds, A C, 1928, D 8,19:5
Rounds, Charles C, 1964, D 4,39:4
Rounds, Charles E, 1944, Ja 11,19:2
Rounds, Charles E Mrs, 1944, Ja 12,23:2
Rounds, Charles R, 1947, Jl 26,13:4; 1948, Ap 4,60:3
Rounds, Christina, 1913, D 13,13:7
Rounds, Frank W, 1951, My 17,31:5
Rounds, George H, 1955, Jl 31,68:5
Rounds, Harry A, 1942, Je 8,15:5
Rounds, Harry T, 1938, My 5,23:2
Rounds, Herbert O, 1942, F 19,19:3
Rounds, Leslie R (Oct 3), 1965, O 11,61:5
Rounds, Lester S, 1967, Je 9,45:3
Rounds, Lester S Mrs, 1966, O 12,43:2
Rounds, Mary Mrs, 1949, O 11,31:4
Rounds, Merton, 1954, My 25,27:1
Rounds, Ralph S, 1948, O 23,15:3
Rounds, Tryphena C Mrs, 1939, S 8,23:5
Roundtree, Herman, 1946, D 10,32:2
Roundtree, Irving W L, 1948, Mr 19,23:3
Roundy, Edward C, 1954, Jl 15,27:5
Roundy, George M, 1948, D 7,31:4
Roundy, Rodney W, 1965, My 1,31:2
Rounsevell, Nelson, 1948, S 27,23:1
Rounseville, Albert, 1951, N 18,90:5
Rounseville, Daniel C, 1939, Mr 1,21:4
Rountree, Albert L, 1906, Ag 20,7:5
Rountree, Charles D, 1956, Jl 29,65:2
Rountree, Earl Mrs, 1949, Je 22,31:3
Rountree, Harry, 1950, S 27,31:4
Rountree, John H, 1958, Jl 26,15:6
Rountree, Russell S, 1937, My 22,15:1
Rountree, William J, 1949, N 26,15:6
Roupp, Leonard M, 1961, Ja 30,23:4
Roure, Remy, 1966, N 9,39:3
Rourke, Barney, 1901, My 29,9:5
Rourke, Bernard J, 1953, Jl 5,49:2
Rourke, Constance M, 1941, Mr 24,17:5
Rourke, Cornelius G, 1968, Ap 18,47:4
Rourke, Elizabeth B Mrs, 1940, Ja 8,15:2
Rourke, Frank M, 1937, S 25,17:4
Rourke, James A, 1938, Mr 27,II,7:3; 1946, Je 19,21:4
Rourke, Joseph B, 1968, Ap 24,47:3
Rourke, Joseph G, 1943, S 28,25:3
Rourke, William B, 1956, My 10,31:2
Rous, Adm, 1877, Jl 2,2:1
Rous, Bernard, 1944, My 30,21:3
Rousby, C M J Mrs, 1879, Ap 22,2:3
Rouse, Arthur B Sr, 1956, Ja 26,29:3
Rouse, Carl, 1948, S 7,25:1
Rouse, Clarence W, 1951, My 9,33:4
Rouse, Edna G Mrs, 1942, Jl 19,30:6
Rouse, Fanny Denham, 1912, Jl 30,9:5
Rouse, Gene, 1956, Ag 27,19:4
Rouse, Grove M, 1940, N 8,21:5
Rouse, Harold A, 1961, Ag 29,31:4
Rouse, Henry C, 1906, My 1,9:6
Rouse, Herbert H, 1944, Ap 4,21:4
Rouse, L H, 1936, Jl 8,19:1
Rouse, Leon H Mrs, 1951, D 21,27:4
Rouse, Merl L Mrs, 1955, My 19,29:3
Rouse, William E, 1945, Je 21,19:3
Rouse, William H, 1937, S 27,21:3
Rouse, William L, 1963, Ag 20,33:4
Rouse, William L Mrs, 1959, Jl 23,27:4
Rouse, William M, 1943, S 5,28:7
Rouse, Wylie J, 1943, Ag 15,38:5
Rousek, Charles E, 1954, Ap 2,27:2
Roush, Carrie M, 1951, Ag 24,15:5
Roush, Jesse A, 1946, S 2,17:5
Roush, Sigel, 1954, D 18,15:4
Roush, Stanley L, 1946, Ag 25,46:5
Roush, Walter E, 1951, Ja 7,76:6
Rousina, Ada M Mrs, 1951, F 3,15:5
Rousmaniere, Edmund S Mrs (will), 1945, Ja 3,20:1
Rousmaniere, John E, 1944, S 7,23:3
Rousmaniere, John E Mrs, 1954, N 26,29:4
Rouss, C B, 1902, Mr 4,9:4
Rousseau, Arthur E, 1947, Ag 13,23:5
Rousseau, G L, 1882, O 8,9:5
Rousseau, H H, 1930, Jl 25,17:3
Rousseau, J R, 1960, Ag 12,19:4
Rousseau, Joseph B, 1950, Ag 27,88:2
Rousseau, L H Maj Gen, 1869, Ja 9,5:1
Rousseau, Leo R, 1965, Ag 26,33:3
Rousseau, Louis, 1949, N 10,31:5
Rousseau, Otto F, 1963, Mr 26,9:8
Rousseau, Paul, 1941, My 26,19:5
Rousseau, R H, 1872, S 20,2:4
Rousseau, Theodore, 1953, Mr 31,31:3
Rousseau, Theodore D Mrs, 1966, Mr 27,86:8
Rousseau, Victor, 1954, Mr 18,31:4
Roussel, Albert (por), 1937, Ag 25,21:1
Roussel, George A Mrs, 1946, Ag 30,17:2
Roussel, Martha Noemie, 1953, F 23,25:3
Rousselle, C, 1938, S 9,2:4
Rousses, Charles, 1951, Ag 24,35:4
Roussey, Leon, 1953, S 7,10:4
Roussillon, Etienne Rev, 1866, N 19,8:5
Roussy de Sales, Francois de, 1943, Jl 8,19:5
Roussy de Sales, Jean de Countess, 1948, O 9,19:3
Roussy de Sales, Raoul de Count, 1942, D 6,76:1
Roussy de Sales, Reine de Countess, 1966, Ja 19,38:1
Roussy de Sales de, Marquis, 1939, Je 13,23:7
Roustan, Theodore, 1906, Ag 9,7:7
Routh, Edward John, 1907, Je 9,9:5
Routh, H de B, 1884, N 25,2:6
Routh, John S, 1968, Je 14,47:1
Routh, Mary Mother, 1962, O 1,31:4
Routhier, Joseph F Capt, 1937, O 13,23:5
Routledge, Scoresby, 1939, Ag 1,19:2
Routley, Frederick W, 1951, F 14,30:6
Routsky, Pierre A, 1953, Jl 18,13:6
Routson, H Ted, 1955, Ja 4,21:2
Routzahn, Evart G (por), 1939, Ap 25,23:5
Routzahn, Evart G Mrs, 1956, D 24,13:6
Routzohn, Harry N, 1953, Ap 15,31:3
Rouverol, Aurania Mrs, 1955, Je 25,15:4
Rouvier, Maurice Sen, 1911, Je 8,11:5
Rouviere, Louis A, 1947, N 27,31:3
Roux, Andre C, 1945, N 5,19:2
Roux, E, 1933, N 4,13:1
Roux, George P, 1937, S 2,21:1
Roux, Jules Charles, 1918, Mr 9,13:5
Roux, Louis A M de, 1943, D 9,27:4
Roux, Maurice G, 1955, F 17,27:4
Roux, William C, 1962, Ja 28,76:2
Rouxel, Gustave A Bp, 1908, Mr 18,7:5
Rouzaud, Nilsson's Husband, 1882, F 23,1:6
Rouzeau, Edgar T, 1958, Ag 12,29:4
Rovai, Ernest, 1943, Ag 23,15:4
Rove, Olaf, 1940, O 9,25:4
Rove, Olaf I Mrs, 1960, O 7,35:1
Rovensky, John E Mrs (will, Ag 25,16:1), 1956, Jl 22,60:8
Rovensky, Joseph C, 1952, D 18,29:1
Rovenstine, Emery A, 1960, N 10,47:1
Rover, Leo A, 1960, N 12,21:3
Rover, William C, 1957, Ag 13,27:4
Roverchio, Rose, 1941, N 14,25:1
Rovere, Signor, 1865, D 14,5:1
Rovereto, Gaetano, 1952, N 27,31:5
Rovillain, Eugene E, 1948, F 22,48:2
Rovinsky, Anton, 1966, Mr 7,27:2
Rovitti, Frederick Dr, 1922, Je 15,19:6
Rovner, Seidel, 1943, Ap 25,34:3
Row, Francis, 1948, N 24,23:4
Row, William, 1942, My 31,38:1
Row, William H, 1961, Mr 12,87:1
Rowalt, Elmer M, 1943, O 10,48:6
Rowan, Alfred G Mrs, 1915, Ja 14,11:4
Rowan, Andrew S (por), 1943, Ja 12,23:1
Rowan, Andrew S Mrs, 1949, Ja 16,68:5
Rowan, Archibald H, 1961, S 23,19:4
Rowan, Arthur J, 1954, My 12,31:1
Rowan, Bartlett J, 1964, F 4,33:2
Rowan, Catherine B Mrs, 1943, Mr 21,26:5
Rowan, Charles A, 1940, S 14,17:5
Rowan, Dorothy M, 1953, Ap 22,29:3
Rowan, Ernest, 1960, O 3,31:3
Rowan, Francis J, 1950, N 16,31:2
Rowan, J C (see also Mr 8), 1878, Mr 11,8:6
Rowan, James P, 1937, Ja 19,23:2
Rowan, James T, 1941, N 21,17:3
Rowan, John A, 1947, N 16,76:4
Rowan, John F, 1953, Jl 13,25:6
Rowan, John S, 1950, D 6,33:2
Rowan, Joseph F Mrs, 1941, Jl 26,16:7
Rowan, M B (funl),(see also My 16), 1876, My 18, 2:4
Rowan, Paul J, 1958, Ja 2,29:3
Rowan, Rae L, 1958, My 14,33:2
Rowan, Raymond, 1963, N 22,37:4
Rowan, Richard W, 1964, Ag 14,27:3
Rowan, Robert H Mrs, 1957, N 7,35:2
Rowan, S C, 1890, Ap 1,2:2
Rowan, Thomas J, 1948, Ap 4,61:1
Rowan, Thomas P, 1951, Mr 23,21:2
Rowan, W A, 1928, Ja 3,25:5
Rowan, William A Sr Mrs, 1952, Ap 6,88:1
Rowan, William J, 1948, Ag 31,26:1; 1952, O 23,31:1
Rowan, William Mrs, 1951, Ap 22,89:2
Rowan, William P, 1946, D 17,31:4
Rowand, Harry H, 1950, Ap 19,30:3
Rowand, Lewis G, 1944, D 4,23:5
Rowand, Louis D, 1947, Mr 18,27:5
Rowand, Phyllis (Mrs S Landau), 1963, Je 17,25:4
Rowbotham, Geoffrey G, 1958, O 31,29:2
Rowbotham, Harry A, 1956, Jl 19,27:4
Rowbotham, J Howard, 1949, Jl 10,56:5
Rowcliff, Gilbert J, 1963, Jl 15,29:2
Rowcliff, Gilbert J Mrs, 1965, Ag 26,33:5
Rowcroft, Samuel D, 1951, Ap 28,15:3
Rowe, A W, 1934, D 7,23:1
Rowe, Adrina K Mrs, 1945, My 29,15:3
Rowe, Albert E, 1946, Ap 19,29:1
Rowe, Alfred, 1966, Ja 1,17:2
Rowe, Allan C, 1959, Jl 1,25:7
Rowe, Arthur H, 1955, My 18,31:5
Rowe, Arthur J, 1948, Mr 2,24:3
Rowe, August, 1946, F 15,26:3
Rowe, Benjamin A, 1937, S 4,15:4
Rowe, Bertha O Mrs, 1945, My 28,19:4
Rowe, Casper S Mrs, 1954, S 21,27:3
Rowe, Charles E, 1942, Jl 31,15:5
Rowe, Charles S, 1947, Mr 3,21:2
Rowe, Charles T, 1908, Ap 26,9:4
Rowe, Clarence E, 1949, Je 10,27:2
Rowe, Clifford, 1938, Ja 21,20:2
Rowe, Cole Y Mrs, 1962, Mr 28,39:3
Rowe, D Alton, 1960, F 15,27:4
Rowe, D Frank, 1954, S 12,84:5
Rowe, Daniel T Mrs, 1947, Mr 29,15:5
Rowe, Daniel T Sr, 1966, Ag 30,36:1
Rowe, Earl, 1948, O 3,67:4
Rowe, Edward D, 1954, Mr 20,15:2
Rowe, Ellis L, 1942, Jl 10,17:5
Rowe, Eugene C, 1947, Ja 1,33:2
Rowe, Frank P, 1957, F 11,29:4
Rowe, Frank W, 1954, O 4,27:2
Rowe, Frank W Mrs, 1949, Jl 6,27:4
Rowe, Frederic R, 1946, Jl 19,19:3
Rowe, Frederick H, 1958, Jl 12,15:1
Rowe, Frederick J, 1945, Je 5,19:4
Rowe, Frederick M, 1946, D 11,31:4
Rowe, Frederick W, 1946, Je 22,19:2
Rowe, G C, 1963, N 15,32:4
Rowe, George A Mrs, 1948, Jl 22,23:1
Rowe, George E, 1952, Ap 17,29:5
Rowe, George E Mrs, 1962, Ja 14,84:5
Rowe, George H, 1947, My 17,15:4; 1963, D 24,17:1
Rowe, George P (funl, Ag 26,5:3), 1873, Ag 21,5:4
Rowe, George T, 1951, N 28,31:2
Rowe, George V Mrs, 1943, Jl 25,31:1
Rowe, Gerhard George, 1923, Jl 11,19:5
Rowe, Guy Mrs (Corinn), 1965, Ap 4,87:2
Rowe, Harold, 1960, O 18,39:3
Rowe, Harry A, 1944, My 24,19:6
Rowe, Helen Sister, 1966, Ja 11,29:1
Rowe, Herbert A, 1939, O 20,23:4
Rowe, Howard M, 1941, Mr 15,17:6
Rowe, Howard V, 1949, F 24,24:2
Rowe, Hubert J, 1943, S 10,23:1
Rowe, Ida W Mrs, 1942, S 10,27:6
Rowe, J Gordon, 1948, N 26,23:3

Rowe, J Staples, 1905, N 3,9:5
Rowe, James E, 1951, S 20,31:3
Rowe, James E Mrs, 1960, F 6,19:1
Rowe, James L, 1947, S 25,29:4
Rowe, James Rev, 1914, Ap 1,13:4
Rowe, Jay D, 1941, Je 16,15:1
Rowe, Jesse L, 1949, Ap 23,13:3
Rowe, John, 1943, Ap 29,21:1
Rowe, John A, 1955, S 21,33:5
Rowe, John C, 1946, D 16,23:4
Rowe, John L, 1941, F 15,15:1
Rowe, John R, 1965, Ap 9,33:1
Rowe, John S (por), 1940, Je 9,44:5
Rowe, John T W, 1940, Je 11,25:4
Rowe, Joseph E, 1939, O 3,23:4
Rowe, Josiah P Jr, 1949, S 8,29:3
Rowe, Leslie, 1904, Jl 8,9:6
Rowe, Louis E, 1937, F 18,21:4
Rowe, Louis H, 1951, F 1,25:5
Rowe, Lynwood T (Schoolboy), 1961, Ja 9,39:1
Rowe, Malcolm, 1951, Ja 25,25:1
Rowe, Mark D, 1942, S 1,20:2
Rowe, Matthew F, 1914, Mr 14,11:5
Rowe, Melvin, 1945, N 7,23:2
Rowe, Merritt C, 1943, My 19,25:3
Rowe, Norman L, 1940, D 1,61:2
Rowe, Orville K, 1952, Ja 21,15:2
Rowe, Perce C Mrs, 1964, Ap 25,29:3
Rowe, Peter T (por), 1942, Je 2,23:4
Rowe, Phil, 1955, Jl 18,21:2
Rowe, Reginald M, 1942, O 8,27:6
Rowe, Reginald P, 1922, Jl 18,11:4
Rowe, Stuart H, 1945, Je 6,21:5
Rowe, Theodore G Sr, 1944, Mr 21,19:1
Rowe, Thomas J, 1940, My 6,17:4
Rowe, Thomas J Jr, 1940, Jl 18,19:6
Rowe, W H, 1928, My 25,25:4
Rowe, Walter J, 1942, My 14,19:4
Rowe, Willard C Mrs, 1951, Je 3,92:7
Rowe, William, 1954, D 24,13:2
Rowe, William F, 1950, F 16,23:5
Rowe, William G, 1951, F 1,25:3
Rowe, William H, 1945, Jl 24,23:4
Rowe, William J, 1946, Ap 12,27:2
Rowe, William J A (por), 1938, Ap 21,19:3
Rowe, William S, 1941, My 21,23:5
Rowell, Charles Emery Dr, 1914, Mr 30,9:4
Rowell, Chester H, 1948, Ap 13,27:1
Rowell, Edgar N, 1966, Mr 8,39:4
Rowell, Edward E, 1938, Je 29,19:5
Rowell, Edward E Jr, 1951, D 3,31:5
Rowell, Ella W Mrs, 1937, D 14,25:4
Rowell, Emma Mrs, 1947, Ap 15,25:2
Rowell, Frank B, 1937, Ap 6,23:1
Rowell, Frank B Mrs, 1962, Mr 16,31:4
Rowell, Frank F Sr, 1952, Jl 21,19:6
Rowell, Fred W, 1952, F 23,11:3
Rowell, Glen (Oct 8), 1965, O 11,61:5
Rowell, Homer H, 1923, D 24,11:6
Rowell, Hugh C Mrs, 1957, N 2,21:1
Rowell, Hugh G, 1963, My 30,17:1
Rowell, John W, 1924, F 14,17:4
Rowell, Kendall B, 1952, D 13,21:3
Rowell, Loren W, 1953, Jl 14,27:2
Rowell, Newton W, 1941, N 23,53:3
Rowell, Warren C, 1941, D 2,23:3
Rowen, George, 1967, F 28,37:1
Rowes, Edward F, 1948, O 27,27:4
Rowlan, Walter, 1952, S 26,21:2
Rowland, Albert L, 1959, N 22,86:8
Rowland, Alvin J, 1950, Ag 15,29:4
Rowland, Amy F, 1953, Mr 12,25:2
Rowland, Arthur Mrs, 1953, F 9,27:5
Rowland, Bo (Jno T), 1964, S 24,41:4
Rowland, C B, 1926, N 2,27:3
Rowland, Charles, 1879, Ag 9,5:2
Rowland, Charles B Mrs, 1938, F 11,23:4
Rowland, Clarence Mrs, 1955, Mr 7,27:5
Rowland, David H, 1937, Ag 12,19:2
Rowland, Edward A, 1940, Jl 11,19:4
Rowland, Edward C H, 1955, Mr 14,23:1
Rowland, Edwin W, 1954, Ap 29,31:3
Rowland, Elmer E, 1966, My 14,31:4
Rowland, Floyd H, 1951, D 8,11:2
Rowland, Frank H Sr, 1948, D 21,25:2
Rowland, Frank L Mrs, 1949, Ja 6,23:5
Rowland, G, 1878, D 13,5:4
Rowland, George, 1907, Jl 9,7:6; 1937, Ap 14,25:2; 1939, O 4,25:4
Rowland, George M, 1941, Mr 15,17:6
Rowland, George M Jr, 1958, Mr 29,17:2
Rowland, George Mrs, 1904, Ja 23,9:5
Rowland, H C, 1933, Je 7,21:1
Rowland, Harold B Mrs, 1948, S 8,29:5
Rowland, Harry T, 1955, Ag 29,19:5
Rowland, Henry, 1953, Ja 28,27:5
Rowland, Henry A, 1962, Ag 8,31:2
Rowland, James, 1914, S 27,15:5
Rowland, James E, 1951, Je 2,19:5
Rowland, James G, 1951, N 30,23:3
Rowland, James K, 1941, Mr 21,21:2
Rowland, James K Mrs, 1946, Ag 18,47:8
Rowland, John, 1941, Ja 3,19:5; 1949, Ap 2,15:6
Rowland, John A (por), 1942, Ap 19,43:1
Rowland, John C, 1964, N 17,42:1
Rowland, John E, 1953, N 10,31:2
Rowland, John R, 1948, D 11,15:1
Rowland, John R Mrs, 1948, N 22,21:5
Rowland, John T, 1945, Ja 24,21:3
Rowland, Kate H Mrs, 1942, Ja 15,19:1
Rowland, Kate Mason, 1916, Je 30,11:6
Rowland, Katherine L Mrs, 1957, Ap 15,29:3
Rowland, Lafe Ex-Sen, 1903, N 3,7:6
Rowland, Leon, 1952, D 3,33:5
Rowland, Louis H, 1942, S 3,19:4
Rowland, Margaretta Mrs, 1940, Ag 13,19:6
Rowland, Peter W, 1943, O 15,19:3
Rowland, Ralph W, 1954, My 18,30:5
Rowland, Ralph W Mrs, 1949, Mr 31,25:2
Rowland, Reginald, 1947, N 8,17:2; 1961, Ap 23,86:7
Rowland, Richard A (por), 1947, My 13,25:1
Rowland, Robert W, 1961, Je 1,35:4
Rowland, Samuel, 1924, O 8,19:3
Rowland, Sherwood L, 1939, Jl 25,19:2
Rowland, Stanley J Sr, 1964, Ag 28,29:3
Rowland, Sydney V, 1966, Ap 28,43:3
Rowland, Thomas F Jr, 1939, Ja 14,17:4
Rowland, Thomas W, 1940, Mr 25,15:3
Rowland, Victor H, 1943, S 12,52:6
Rowland, W L, 1883, Ag 5,7:6
Rowland, W W, 1944, S 4,19:4
Rowland, William, 1937, Ap 12,17:2
Rowland, William C, 1941, Ag 11,13:6
Rowland, William F Mrs, 1957, Ag 21,27:4
Rowland, William P, 1947, Ag 1,17:2
Rowlands, Arch, 1953, Ag 20,27:4
Rowlands, Gwilym, 1949, Ja 17,19:2
Rowlands, Harry E, 1957, Ag 22,27:3
Rowlands, Richard A, 1955, Mr 15,29:3
Rowlands, Walter D, 1953, O 22,29:5
Rowlands, William, 1866, O 30,5:3
Rowlands, William A, 1940, Ap 27,15:1
Rowlands, Willis L, 1955, Ja 17,23:6
Rowles, Albert E, 1944, My 6,19:5
Rowles, Burton J, 1966, Je 11,31:5
Rowles, Malcolm M, 1950, S 25,23:1
Rowlett, Robert, 1937, Ja 4,29:4
Rowley, Alfred M, 1942, Jl 21,20:4
Rowley, Blanche A, 1919, F 26,11:4
Rowley, Clarence W, 1943, My 24,15:6
Rowley, Clayton W, 1953, N 8,89:2
Rowley, Daisy W, 1938, Ap 1,23:3
Rowley, Edwin N, 1957, F 27,27:5
Rowley, F A Mrs, 1950, O 21,17:6
Rowley, Frank S, 1952, Jl 27,56:6
Rowley, Fred N, 1903, Jl 20,7:6
Rowley, Frederick, 1954, N 26,13:5
Rowley, George, 1962, Ja 6,19:3
Rowley, George H, 1953, D 25,17:4
Rowley, George Mrs, 1943, Ap 10,17:2; 1956, Je 10, 89:1
Rowley, Harriet, 1922, N 25,13:5
Rowley, James B, 1938, Ap 30,15:4
Rowley, James F, 1943, Ja 7,19:5
Rowley, Kenneth B (por), 1947, Ap 2,27:6
Rowley, Leslie B, 1937, Jl 22,19:5
Rowley, Lincoln E Mrs, 1946, F 10,40:7
Rowley, Lord (Arth Henderson), 1968, Ag 30,30:2
Rowley, Louis N, 1951, Je 7,33:2
Rowley, M Rita (Very Rev Mother), 1963, Jl 2,29:1
Rowley, Park A (por), 1949, F 1,26:2
Rowley, Paul, 1941, Ap 21,19:2
Rowley, Ridgway L, 1950, Mr 26,94:3
Rowley, Robert B, 1952, Je 10,27:5
Rowley, William H, 1915, Ja 14,11:4
Rowley, William S, 1920, Je 28,15:4
Rowley-Conwy, Rafe G, 1951, Ap 5,29:3
Rowlinson, Asa K, 1948, Ag 15,61:1
Rowlinson, George H Jr, 1944, Je 21,19:3
Rowntree, Arnold S, 1951, My 22,31:2
Rowntree, Benjamin S, 1954, O 8,23:1
Rowntree, Cecil, 1943, O 15,19:2
Rowntree, Joseph S, 1951, Jl 28,11:5
Rowohlt, Ernst, 1960, D 3,23:4
Rowson, Guy, 1937, N 17,23:2
Rowswell, Albe (Rosey), 1955, F 7,21:4
Rowton, Ist Baron, 1903, N 10,9:5
Rox, Henry, 1967, Jl 16,65:1
Rox, John R, 1957, Ag 6,27:2
Roxas, Emilio A, 1965, Jl 7,37:2
Roxas, Hilario A, 1944, My 29,15:6
Roxburgh, E M Lady, 1929, Ja 16,25:4
Roxburgh, John A Sir, 1937, N 24,23:2
Roxburghe, Dowager Duchess of (por),(will, N 21,-38:2), 1937, Ap 27,23:1
Roxby, John B, 1957, Mr 20,37:6
Roxby, Percy M, 1947, F 18,25:4
Roy, Abbe J, 1951, O 1,3:5
Roy, Albert, 1949, Mr 15,27:4
Roy, Alfred, 1950, Ap 22,19:6
Roy, Arthur J, 1948, S 12,72:6
Roy, Basanta K, 1949, Je 8,29:3
Roy, Bidhan C, 1962, Jl 2,29:3
Roy, Camille, 1943, Je 25,17:5
Roy, Edward E, 1956, Ag 31,17:3
Roy, Eugene, 1938, Ag 31,15:5
Roy, Eugene H, 1944, Je 18,36:3
Roy, Ferdinand, 1948, Je 23,27:5
Roy, H L, 1953, S 22,31:2
Roy, Harold E Mrs, 1940, O 1,23:2
Roy, Henri, 1946, D 17,19:6; 1950, Ag 26,13:2
Roy, Henry B, 1962, Ag 18,39:1
Roy, Herbert F, 1939, S 23,17:4
Roy, Herbert F Mrs, 1964, Ap 11,35:5
Roy, Herman T, 1950, D 3,88:4
Roy, Isak M, 1947, Ag 8,17:2
Roy, J Amedee, 1950, My 3,29:2
Roy, J Wilson, 1938, N 26,15:3
Roy, James I, 1955, Ja 6,27:4
Roy, James P Lt-Col, 1874, O 28,4:7
Roy, Jean (funl), 1956, N 16,52:7
Roy, John F Mrs, 1954, S 10,23:2
Roy, John J, 1939, Ja 16,15:4
Roy, Joseph, 1951, Ag 16,27:5
Roy, Joseph A, 1940, Ja 2,19:2
Roy, Malcolm M, 1960, Ja 15,31:2
Roy, Malcolm M Mrs, 1955, Ap 12,29:1
Roy, Mehendranath, 1954, Ja 26,27:3
Roy, Norbert J, 1952, Jl 5,15:5
Roy, Oscar C, 1959, Ag 17,24:1
Roy, P A (por), 1949, Jl 2,15:4
Roy, P E Archbishop, 1926, F 22,17:2
Roy, Phileas, 1939, N 24,23:3
Roy, Philippe, 1948, D 11,15:2
Roy, Pierre, 1950, O 14,19:6
Roy, Robert H Justice (funl, Ap 13,22:5), 1919, Ap 11,11:3
Roy, Sharat J, 1962, Ap 19,31:3
Roy, Stephen, 1948, Mr 23,25:5
Roy, Teddy, 1966, S 1,35:2
Roy, William H, 1958, Je 19,31:2
Roy, William M, 1937, Jl 24,15:6
Roy, William T Mrs, 1948, Ag 28,16:3
Royal, Andrew, 1904, F 5,9:5
Royal, Forrest B, 1945, Je 21,19:1
Royal, Henry W Mrs, 1952, Ap 30,27:2
Royal, James, 1962, Ja 4,33:3
Royal, John A, 1959, Mr 15,89:1
Royal, John F Mrs, 1942, Ja 27,21:6
Royal, Rhoda, 1940, Jl 24,21:3
Royal, Silas I, 1944, Je 27,19:2
Royal, Thomas M, 1947, O 23,25:4
Royal, William L Mrs, 1942, D 25,18:3
Royale, Jonathan C Judge, 1910, Je 7,9:4
Royall, John A Mrs, 1945, S 1,11:2; 1961, Je 8,35:
Royall, Ralph, 1954, Mr 4,25:3
Royall, William L Jr, 1941, Mr 13,21:4
Royce, Albert A, 1959, Ja 16,27:1
Royce, Alexander B, 1967, D 9,47:1
Royce, Alice Carrington Mrs, 1908, F 17,7:4
Royce, Charles Howard, 1921, Ag 6,9:7
Royce, Christian B Mrs, 1937, Ja 31,II,9:2
Royce, Edward, 1963, Jl 9,32:1
Royce, G Fred, 1947, Ja 15,25:3
Royce, H, 1933, Ap 23,29:1
Royce, Henry H, 1941, Ja 12,44:2
Royce, James C, 1946, N 6,23:2
Royce, Josiah Dr, 1916, S 15,11:3
Royce, Lionel, 1946, Ap 4,25:2
Royce, Mary E, 1947, N 19,27:3
Royce, Ralph, 1965, Ag 11,35:4
Royce, Richard H, 1944, Jl 26,19:5
Royce, Robert Mrs, 1942, D 5,15:6
Royce, Rubert S, 1938, Ag 18,20:2
Royce, Stephen, 1954, Je 14,21:4
Royce, W Irving, 1948, S 30,27:3
Royce, William F, 1947, S 26,23:4
Roycraft, George W, 1944, D 18,19:3
Royden, Lord, 1950, N 7,27:2
Royden, Maude (cor, Ag 5,77:1), 1956, Jl 31,23:
Roye, Ruth (Mrs J Kolleeny), 1960, Je 13,27:5
Royen, J H van, 1933, S 1,17:4
Royen, M R van, 1942, S 19,3:8
Royer, Harry B (por), 1946, Ja 8,23:3
Royer, Harry P, 1944, Ag 25,13:5
Royer, Henri, 1938, N 5,19:1
Royer, Wilfred C, 1953, F 24,25:4
Royer, William C, 1941, S 23,23:3
Royes, Robert, 1960, Jl 22,23:1
Roylance, Edward, 1944, Ja 6,23:3
Royle, Edwin M (por), 1942, F 17,21:4
Royle, Edwin M Mrs, 1955, My 16,23:5
Royle, Guy C C, 1954, Ja 6,46:4
Royle, James T, 1939, My 17,23:2
Royle, Joshua, 1881, O 24,5:5
Royle, Vernon E, 1947, S 21,60:5
Roynesdal, Torkell, 1946, Ap 9,27:2
Roys, Charles K Mrs, 1956, O 7,86:4
Roys, Claude A Mrs, 1954, Ja 28,27:2
Roys, Cyrus D Col, 1915, My 20,11:5
Roys, Harold S Mrs, 1950, Jl 20,25:3
Roys, John H, 1940, Ja 9,24:2
Royster, Hubert A, 1959, N 9,31:3
Royster, Lawrence Thomas, 1953, Ja 9,21:4
Royster, Vermont Connecticut, 1922, Ag 9,11:6
Royston, John P, 1957, My 8,37:1
Royston, John R, 1942, Ap 26,39:2
Roystuart, Victor I, 1944, O 20,19:1
Royter, Carl H, 1939, Mr 22,23:2

Roz, Firmin, 1957, N 7,35:3
Rozanka, Stanley, 1946, N 16,19:2
Rozanski, Frank S, 1951, Mr 6,27:3
Rozell, Albert, 1951, Mr 31,15:6
Rozell, Charles, 1941, Ja 29,17:3
Rozell, Gilbert Z, 1943, O 2,13:2
Rozelle, Richard, 1950, Je 5,30:2
Rozen, Abraham A, 1954, Mr 12,22:4
Rozen, I Robert, 1966, N 19,33:4
Rozendaal, Julien DeH, 1963, S 29,87:1
Rozenoer, Mary Mrs, 1941, N 12,23:1
Rozental, Michael, 1966, Ag 17,39:2
Rozet, Albin, 1915, S 17,7:5
Rozier, Frank, 1949, Jl 10,V,3:6
Rozinski, Jadwiga Mrs, 1950, S 29,27:2
Rozman, Gregory, 1959, N 17,35:6
Rozman, Louis, 1957, S 11,33:2
Rozniecki, Karen M Mrs, 1954, Ja 5,27:4
Roznoy, Edwin J, 1967, S 17,84:7
Rozofsky, Louis, 1956, N 26,27:4
Rozofsky, Louis Mrs, 1964, Je 11,33:4
Rozsa, George, 1963, O 16,45:4
Rozsa, Louis, 1922, D 30,13:6
Rozsa, Louis Mrs, 1950, F 7,27:4
Rozwadowski, Eugenieusz (por), 1947, Ap 25,21:3
Rozzo, Felice Mrs, 1944, Jl 25,19:2
Ruane, Garret Mrs, 1949, My 5,27:5
Ruane, Garry J Jr, 1949, Mr 1,25:3
Ruark, Fletcher, 1952, Ja 3,7:5
Ruark, Jenny W Mrs, 1966, Jl 20,41:1
Ruark, Robert C (funl, Jl 9,26:1), 1965, Jl 1,31:1
Ruark, Robert C (will), 1966, Ja 6,17:1
Ruback, John C, 1953, Ap 24,24:5
Ruback, Meyer E, 1956, N 5,31:2
Rubaiz, Samuel K, 1949, Je 16,30:6
Rubano, Peter A, 1939, Mr 11,17:1
Rubanow, Joseph, 1952, D 31,15:4
Rubashoff, Abraham, 1966, S 7,41:5
Rubba, Russell R Mrs, 1947, Ja 14,25:4
Rubbra T C, 1942, O 7,25:5
Rubel, A C, 1967, Je 2,46:4
Rubel, Herbert, 1958, Ag 16,17:3
Rubel, Isadore, 1939, Mr 23,23:3
Rubel, Isadore Mrs, 1958, Jl 20,64:5
Rubel, Jacob A, 1947, F 19,25:2
Rubel, Jacob A Mrs, 1956, S 4,29:2
Rubel, Maurice, 1941, S 18,25:5
Rubel, Samuel (por), 1949, Ap 30,13:3
Rubel, Vere L Dr, 1968, Mr 12,43:2
Rubel, William, 1960, Je 13,27:6
Ruben, Abe, 1959, F 26,31:3
Ruben, Barney, 1959, O 28,37:1
Ruben, Frank, 1947, Ja 31,23:1
Ruben, Isadore S, 1954, Ap 20,29:4
Ruben, J Walter, 1942, S 5,13:5
Ruben, Jacob, 1951, O 12,27:3
Ruben, Max W Mrs, 1963, S 25,43:3
Ruben, Meyer, 1907, Ja 15,7:6
Ruben, Meyer Mrs, 1907, Ja 15,7:6
Rubenfeld, Aaron H, 1948, Ap 8,25:5
Rubenfeld, Isadore, 1948, S 1,48:5
Rubens, A, 1931, Ja 22,23:2
Rubens, Anna Mrs, 1938, My 12,23:5
Rubens, Barney (est tax appr), 1962, Jl 31,25:3
Rubens, Charles (will), 1906, Jl 20,2:3
Rubens, Gilbert E, 1960, Ja 8,23:6
Rubens, Henry A, 1959, O 2,29:1
Rubens, Horatio S (por), 1941, Ap 4,21:1
Rubens, Isaac R, 1943, N 4,23:2
Rubens, Jules J, 1945, D 1,23:2
Rubens, Leon F, 1943, Ag 20,15:5
Rubens, Maury, 1948, Jl 26,17:1
Rubens, Paul Alfred, 1917, F 6,9:4
Rubensohn, Jack, 1964, N 8,88:4
Rubensohn, Samuel, 1966, Mr 20,87:2
Rubenstein, A Harry, 1959, O 3,19:6
Rubenstein, Abraham H, 1952, Ag 2,15:4
Rubenstein, Benjamin H, 1964, Je 25,33:2
Rubenstein, Charles Mrs, 1962, D 2,88:8
Rubenstein, E Ivan, 1955, F 19,15:1
Rubenstein, Edward, 1949, Jl 23,11:1
Rubenstein, Frank, 1953, O 21,29:2
Rubenstein, Fritz, 1944, D 7,20:3
Rubenstein, George, 1957, Ja 10,29:3
Rubenstein, Hyman J, 1945, My 1,23:4
Rubenstein, Isidore A, 1961, N 30,37:3
Rubenstein, Jacob, 1966, N 5,31:4
Rubenstein, Jules Mrs, 1952, Ja 3,46:4
Rubenstein, Julian U, 1941, F 18,23:3
Rubenstein, M Morton, 1963, O 19,25:5
Rubenstein, Max, 1943, Ap 3,15:5
Rubenstein, Max I Mrs, 1948, Mr 14,72:5
Rubenstein, Meyer, 1948, Ja 8,25:2
Rubenstein, Moses Mrs, 1949, D 29,25:2
Rubenstein, Philip, 1963, Ap 18,35:4
Rubenstone, Abraham I, 1961, Ja 24,29:1
Ruberl, Charles A, 1966, Ja 2,72:6
Ruberti, Albert E, 1944, F 9,19:3
Ruberti, Ernest, 1943, O 4,17:2
Ruberton, Rocco, 1949, My 10,25:2
Ruberton, Rocco Mrs, 1945, O 14,44:4
Rubi, Roendo, 1942, Ja 8,21:2
Rubicam, Arthur, 1950, Ap 28,21:2
Rubicam, Harry C, 1941, N 27,23:3
Rubien, Charles, 1937, F 28,II,8:5
Rubien, Frederick W, 1951, Jl 6,23:3
Rubien, Frederick W Mrs, 1939, Ja 29,33:2
Rubien, William H, 1953, Ap 8,29:3
Rubin, A David, 1949, Ag 11,23:2
Rubin, Abraham L, 1961, D 21,27:4
Rubin, Alex, 1955, Mr 5,17:6
Rubin, Barnett, 1949, Jl 8,19:2
Rubin, Benjamin, 1946, Jl 31,27:2; 1953, Ag 13,25:5; 1963, Ag 8,27:5
Rubin, Bernard, 1962, My 25,33:5
Rubin, Bernard D (por), 1948, Jl 7,23:3
Rubin, Channa F E Mrs, 1937, D 21,23:3
Rubin, E Robert, 1955, Mr 29,29:2
Rubin, Edwin, 1939, O 4,25:2
Rubin, Eli H Dr, 1968, Ag 30,30:3
Rubin, Fred H, 1954, Mr 11,34:8
Rubin, George Mrs, 1958, Ag 30,15:5
Rubin, Harold, 1949, My 4,30:2
Rubin, Harold S, 1965, My 19,47:4
Rubin, Harry, 1941, Jl 5,11:5; 1950, S 15,26:3; 1955, F 12,15:5; 1956, Ap 1,89:3
Rubin, Harry M, 1949, Je 5,92:4
Rubin, Henry, 1966, O 1,32:8
Rubin, Herbert, 1956, O 26,29:3
Rubin, Herman, 1952, O 14,31:4; 1962, Jl 22,64:2; 1966, My 19,47:4
Rubin, I Ben, 1953, O 2,21:4
Rubin, I Louis, 1959, S 19,23:4
Rubin, Ida Mrs, 1948, F 1,61:1
Rubin, Isidor C, 1958, Jl 11,23:1
Rubin, Israel, 1955, D 24,13:4
Rubin, J Robert, 1958, S 11,33:1
Rubin, Jacob, 1946, O 4,23:2
Rubin, Joe, 1951, Jl 26,21:4
Rubin, Joseph, 1952, S 5,27:5; 1957, Ap 28,86:2; 1965, Je 16,43:1
Rubin, Joseph M, 1950, Ag 23,29:4
Rubin, Lena Mrs, 1956, F 18,19:4
Rubin, Leo, 1938, Ja 11,23:4; 1949, F 24,23:1
Rubin, Leon, 1958, Ap 12,19:5
Rubin, Leonard, 1948, Je 25,23:4
Rubin, Lewis, 1912, Jl 21,II,11:6
Rubin, Lionel C, 1958, Ag 8,17:5
Rubin, Louis, 1957, Jl 24,25:4; 1959, O 29,33:5; 1961, Mr 2,27:3
Rubin, Maurice, 1957, O 14,27:4
Rubin, Max, 1954, S 22,29:4; 1955, Ag 10,25:4
Rubin, Max J, 1950, Ja 25,27:4
Rubin, Maxwell, 1946, Ag 7,27:2
Rubin, Menachem, 1962, Je 20,35:3
Rubin, Michael (por), 1947, N 3,23:3
Rubin, Morris, 1921, Ag 22,13:4
Rubin, Moses B, 1951, N 17,17:2
Rubin, Oscar, 1937, Ag 29,II,6:7
Rubin, Paul E, 1953, Ja 21,10:3
Rubin, Rabbi H, 1903, D 9,9:5
Rubin, Rebecca Mrs, 1951, Ja 29,19:4
Rubin, Robert S, 1947, Je 21,17:1
Rubin, Samuel, 1949, N 4,28:4; 1954, My 17,24:5
Rubin, Samuel Mrs, 1946, D 11,31:2; 1953, D 10,47:2
Rubin, Sharry, 1958, N 18,37:4
Rubin, Solomon, 1952, Ja 3,27:3
Rubin, William, 1966, Jl 21,33:4
Rubin, William B, 1959, F 4,26:1
Rubinchick, Hyman, 1948, My 11,25:3
Rubinger, Morris, 1947, N 23,72:4
Rubini-Reichlin, Mario, 1968, O 8,44:2
Rubino, Frank, 1962, S 27,37:1
Rubino, Frank Mrs, 1960, My 11,39:4
Rubino, Herman C, 1940, D 15,61:2
Rubino, Thomas J, 1950, F 5,85:1
Rubino, Vedo, 1921, Ag 16,15:2
Rubinoff, Jacob, 1948, N 25,31:5
Rubinoff, Libbie Mrs, 1949, N 1,27:3
Rubinoff, Ruben, 1938, Ap 21,19:6
Rubinow, I M, 1936, S 3,21:3
Rubinow, Isaac M Mrs, 1960, F 26,31:3
Rubinow, Morton L, 1962, S 4,31:5
Rubinow, Saul M, 1943, Ap 15,25:3
Rubinow, William G, 1959, Ja 17,19:4
Rubinow, William G Mrs, 1959, O 17,23:7
Rubinowich, Bernard H, 1962, Ja 21,88:7
Rubinowitz, Adolph J, 1957, O 17,33:1
Rubins, Charles C, 1943, Ap 12,23:4
Rubins, Saul, 1944, Ag 5,11:4
Rubinshtein, Sergei L, 1960, Ja 12,45:5
Rubinsky, William, 1951, S 5,31:2
Rubinsohn, Lewis S Dr, 1920, Ag 20,9:4
Rubinsohn, S Lewis, 1955, My 2,21:3
Rubinstein, A G, 1894, N 21,13:4
Rubinstein, Abraham, 1941, Mr 5,22:3
Rubinstein, Albert, 1955, Ja 15,13:4
Rubinstein, Bernard, 1967, S 2,25:5
Rubinstein, Beryl, 1952, D 30,19:4
Rubinstein, David J, 1951, Ap 26,29:1
Rubinstein, David Mrs, 1950, O 23,23:1
Rubinstein, Harry, 1960, F 18,33:3
Rubinstein, Helena (will, Ap 3,18:2), 1965, Ap 2,1:2
Rubinstein, Henry, 1943, N 30,27:4
Rubinstein, Ida, 1960, O 18,39:4
Rubinstein, Irving, 1953, Je 7,84:4
Rubinstein, Irving B, 1954, Ja 19,26:4
Rubinstein, Marcus, 1952, Mr 13,29:4
Rubinstein, Nikolai L, 1952, Ag 15,15:4
Rubinstein, Serge (est appr filed), 1960, Je 24,12:6
Rubinstein, Simcha Mrs, 1953, O 31,17:3
Rubinton, Samuel, 1956, Ap 27,28:1
Rubio, Emery, 1963, Jl 16,21:1
Rubio, Juan B, 1958, Ag 31,56:7
Rubio, Louis, 1882, Ag 26,5:5
Rubirosa, Porfirio (funl, Jl 9,26:6), 1965, Jl 6,16:3
Rublack, Aug, 1939, Jl 6,23:1
Ruble, Samuel S, 1956, Ap 30,23:5
Rublee, George, 1957, Ap 27,19:4
Rublee, William A, 1910, Ap 16,11:6
Rubluee, Herbert M, 1944, Ap 6,23:6
Rubman, Janice, 1952, F 23,26:6
Rubner, Fred, 1948, F 4,24:1
Rubner, Gustave, 1956, Mr 31,15:4
Rubotton, J W Mrs, 1954, My 2,77:1
Rubsam, C William, 1955, My 28,15:1
Rubsam, Joseph, 1942, Ag 8,11:3
Rubsamen, Ernest B, 1925, F 24,19:4
Rubtsov, Boris, 1952, Je 29,56:4
Ruby, Anna L, 1937, Ap 1,24:1
Ruby, Charles H, 1958, My 3,19:2
Ruby, Doris, 1951, D 17,22:2
Ruby, Emery H, 1965, S 7,39:1
Ruby, Herman, 1959, Jl 31,24:3
Ruby, Jack L (funl, Ja 7,15:5), 1967, Ja 4,1:2
Ruby, Myron M Mrs, 1953, My 4,23:6
Rucci, Giuseppe, 1950, D 12,33:3
Rucellai, Edith M Countessa, 1956, D 6,37:4
Ruch, Andrew Sr, 1952, Je 21,15:4
Ruch, Charles, 1945, Ag 30,21:3
Ruch, Emile H, 1959, N 20,31:2
Ruch, George F (will, Ag 18,21:3), 1938, Ag 9,19:5
Ruch, Howard C, 1940, N 16,17:2
Ruch, Lewis C (por), 1937, Ag 31,23:4
Ruch, Louis, 1941, Ap 27,38:3
Ruch, Titus M, 1939, Jl 7,17:4
Ruch, Valentine, 1941, Mr 31,15:5
Ruch, Ward N, 1952, N 20,31:1
Ruchamkin, Phil, 1954, Mr 21,89:2
Ruchdi Pasha (Mehemet), 1882, Mr 27,5:5
Ruck, Charles E, 1965, O 23,31:3
Ruck, Ernest C A, 1949, Ap 29,23:2
Ruck, John F, 1949, O 15,15:6
Ruck, Samuel, 1967, Ja 9,36:8
Ruck, Silvio von Dr, 1918, Ap 8,15:5
Ruckbeil, Eugene A Sr, 1946, F 20,25:1
Ruckel, J H, 1884, Ap 18,5:4
Ruckel, William, 1938, D 16,25:4
Ruckelshausen, Henry Mrs, 1950, Ja 1,42:4
Rucker, Arthur W Sir, 1915, N 2,11:6
Rucker, C A Col, 1907, Je 29,7:6
Rucker, Casper B, 1948, Ap 1,25:5
Rucker, Daniel H Gen, 1910, Ja 7,9:4
Rucker, John B, 1947, F 8,17:1
Rucker, Joseph T, 1957, O 23,33:4
Rucker, Louis Henry Gen, 1906, Jl 11,7:7
Rucker, Robert E, 1939, S 27,25:3
Rucker, Roy, 1957, Ag 1,25:3
Rucker, Tinsley W Jr, 1941, D 6,17:2
Ruckes, Herbert, 1965, D 25,13:5
Ruckgaber, Paul, 1945, Ag 1,19:6
Rucki, William A, 1943, My 11,21:2
Ruckle, Joseph N, 1937, Jl 11,16:1
Ruckman, John W Gen, 1921, Je 7,17:4
Rucks, Fred J Mrs, 1939, Je 13,23:3
Ruckstuhl, Charles E, 1960, N 15,39:4
Ruckstuhl, John B, 1953, Ap 29,29:4
Ruckstull, Frederick W (por), 1942, My 27,23:1
Rucquoi, Leon G, 1962, Mr 8,31:1
Rud, Anthony M, 1942, D 1,25:4
Rudack, Rudy M, 1951, Jl 12,25:3
Rudas, Laszlo, 1950, Ap 30,102:5
Rudavsky, Jochanon I, 1965, F 10,41:1
Rudberg, David, 1951, O 3,36:3
Rudd, A B, 1944, Ap 4,21:3
Rudd, Alex H, 1949, S 19,23:3
Rudd, Alex H Mrs, 1957, Ja 6,89:1
Rudd, Arthur J, 1940, Mr 29,22:2
Rudd, Augustin Goelet Col, 1968, D 4,47:3
Rudd, Channing, 1920, N 9,15:2
Rudd, Charles E, 1950, Ja 11,23:2
Rudd, E Irvine, 1962, S 13,37:1
Rudd, G H, 1881, F 9,2:5
Rudd, Harold O, 1954, Ap 19,23:4
Rudd, Harris D Mrs, 1947, D 13,15:4
Rudd, Henry A, 1942, My 9,13:4
Rudd, John A, 1963, N 29,34:5
Rudd, John H, 1958, N 15,23:3
Rudd, Joseph H, 1948, F 16,22:3
Rudd, Mary Ann Mrs, 1925, Ja 9,17:3
Rudd, Mary E, 1941, Mr 16,44:8
Rudd, Ralph E, 1953, Ja 20,25:4
Rudd, Robert B Mrs, 1956, N 21,27:4
Rudd, Stephen A Mrs, 1961, Mr 7,35:5
Rudd, Thomas B, 1955, Ap 12,29:3
Rudd, W T, 1903, My 18,7:6
Rudd, Wellmann, 1952, Jl 8,27:1
Rudd, William B, 1947, S 6,17:3
Rudd, William Cullen, 1915, S 9,11:6

Rudd, William G, 1943, My 27,25:4
Rudd, Wortley F, 1950, Jl 28,21:4
Ruddall, Arden K Prof, 1968, My 24,65:3
Ruddell, James C, 1958, Je 15,76:5
Ruddell, Stuart G, 1944, Ja 7,17:5
Rudden, Anna V, 1947, Ja 11,19:3
Rudden, Phil J, 1951, My 30,21:4
Rudden, Thomas E, 1959, F 25,31:2
Rudden, Thomas F Rev, 1937, F 14,II,9:3
Rudderham, John E, 1942, Ap 4,13:5
Rudderow, Edward D, 1959, N 17,35:3
Ruddick, Girard B, 1944, N 7,27:2
Ruddick, Hamilton, 1904, Ja 8,7:5
Ruddick, J Leon, 1950, F 13,21:4
Ruddick, John A, 1953, Mr 6,23:4
Ruddick, John R, 1945, Jl 14,11:4
Ruddick, Nellie, 1952, Ja 6,93:2
Ruddiman, Edsel A, 1954, Mr 23,27:4
Ruddiman, James B, 1953, O 20,29:4
Ruddiman, John, 1919, Mr 4,11:3
Ruddiman, Margaret F Mrs, 1960, Mr 1,33:1
Ruddock, Austin A, 1925, Ag 24,13:6
Ruddock, Malcolm I, 1961, Je 19,27:5
Ruddy, E L, 1954, N 25,29:6
Ruddy, John A, 1962, Ja 14,84:7
Ruddy, Joseph A Sr, 1962, N 12,29:4
Ruddy, Joseph F, 1952, F 29,23:1
Ruddy, Joseph P, 1941, F 18,23:2
Ruddy, Leo J, 1959, O 24,21:6
Ruddy, Michael F, 1952, Je 16,17:3
Ruddy, Raymond L, 1968, Je 21,41:2
Ruddy, Stephen A, 1955, S 28,35:5; 1964, Ja 3,24:1
Ruddy, Thomas A, 1948, Ja 7,25:4
Rude, Benton S, 1945, Ag 3,17:3
Rude, I, 1941, My 21,23:5
Rude-Jacobsen, Hans, 1964, Mr 7,23:1
Rudel, Alexander G, 1967, My 27,31:4
Rudel, Clarence M, 1938, Je 22,23:6
Rudel, Jakob Mrs, 1962, D 4,41:2
Rudenberg, Reinhold, 1961, D 27,27:1
Rudensky, Max, 1953, My 12,27:3
Ruder, Jacob L Mrs, 1967, Je 25,68:7
Ruderman, James, 1966, Ja 28,47:2
Ruderman, Louis A, 1964, Mr 25,41:3
Ruderow, Maurice B, 1938, Ag 2,19:4
Rudersdorff, Ermina M, 1882, F 27,1:5
Rudert, Anton, 1964, Jl 12,68:3
Rudick, Harry J, 1964, Je 1,29:3
Rudin, Edward, 1968, Jl 25,33:3
Rudin, Nathan, 1954, S 18,15:5
Rudin, Samuel, 1958, O 29,35:5
Rudinger, Hugo Mrs, 1962, My 8,39:1
Rudini, Marquis Di, 1908, Ag 8,5:6
Rudinow, Moshe, 1953, N 16,25:3
Rudinsky, Joseph, 1964, F 19,36:1
Rudisill, Earl S Mrs, 1952, Jl 20,53:1
Ruditsky, Barney, 1962, O 19,31:1
Rudkin, Arthur Mrs, 1954, O 16,17:2
Rudkin, Frank H Mrs, 1962, D 6,43:4
Rudkin, Henry A, 1966, Ap 23,31:5
Rudkin, Henry A Mrs, 1967, Je 2,41:1
Rudloff, Edward S, 1946, Mr 5,25:1
Rudloff, Viola Mrs, 1955, N 17,35:4
Rudmose-Brown, Robert N, 1957, Ja 30,29:2
Rudner, Louis, 1944, Ja 10,17:1
Rudnev, Lev V, 1956, N 22,33:3
Rudnick, Henry, 1937, Ag 31,23:5
Rudnick, Max, 1942, D 5,15:4
Rudnick, Morris, 1946, Ag 16,21:6
Rudnick, Rudolph A, 1954, S 7,25:2
Rudo, Stephen L, 1960, Mr 11,26:3
Rudofker, Morris, 1954, S 13,23:2
Rudolf, Albert C, 1944, D 30,11:4
Rudolf, Albert C Mrs, 1937, Ja 24,II,8:2
Rudolf, Chester D, 1951, S 12,31:5
Rudolf, Harry J, 1937, Ja 26,21:2
Rudolf, Philip Sr, 1963, Je 25,33:5
Rudolfs, Willem, 1959, Mr 4,31:5
Rudolph, Alfred, 1942, Ap 26,39:2
Rudolph, Anna Mrs, 1951, Ja 23,27:3
Rudolph, Arthur, 1945, N 2,19:5
Rudolph, Bert E, 1940, My 12,49:2
Rudolph, Charles, 1949, N 20,94:2
Rudolph, Crown Prince of Austria, 1889, Ja 31,1:1
Rudolph, Dick, 1949, O 22,17:4
Rudolph, Edward R Jr, 1948, D 22,23:4
Rudolph, Erwin, 1957, My 20,25:5
Rudolph, Frank M, 1939, My 7,III,6:8
Rudolph, George, 1943, My 24,15:4
Rudolph, George A, 1939, Mr 29,23:6
Rudolph, Harold W, 1963, O 15,39:1
Rudolph, Harry, 1948, Mr 15,23:4
Rudolph, Harry E (Babe McCoy), 1962, Ap 23,29:4
Rudolph, Joseph F, 1952, N 25,29:3
Rudolph, Kalso, 1948, Ag 18,25:2
Rudolph, Louis, 1949, Ja 31,19:4
Rudolph, Mary Adrian Sister, 1916, Ja 18,11:6
Rudolph, Max W, 1952, O 7,29:4
Rudolph, Myron P, 1953, Jl 3,19:2
Rudolph, Otto C, 1956, D 12,39:5
Rudolph, Raymond L, 1948, D 31,15:1
Rudolph, Walter H Mrs, 1961, Ag 4,21:5
Rudolph, William, 1941, Jl 22,19:4; 1947, Ap 7,23:3
Rudolph, William B, 1949, S 21,32:2
Rudrow, William P, 1965, My 2,89:1
Rudtke, Stephan J, 1948, D 1,29:4
Rudulph, Gerald K, 1957, My 16,31:4
Rudy, Joseph K, 1948, Mr 18,28:2
Rudyard, Clarence Mrs, 1938, Ja 18,23:2
Rue, Charles T, 1938, O 8,17:4
Rue, Edgar H, 1951, D 9,91:2
Rue, Floyd E Jr, 1959, Ag 16,82:3
Rue, Henry B Dr, 1937, Ap 4,II,11:1
Rue, J Herbert, 1943, D 4,13:5
Rue, Jacob B Mrs, 1957, N 6,35:4
Rue, Larry, 1965, Jl 13,33:4
Ruebling, Charles J, 1965, Ag 15,82:6
Ruebsam, Charles A, 1955, N 10,35:5
Ruecke, Herman, 1948, F 1,60:6
Rueckel, Frederick A, 1937, Je 14,23:5
Rueckel, Walter C Dr, 1968, My 12,84:5
Rueckheim, Frederick W Jr, 1937, F 7,II,8:8
Ruedemann, Rudolf, 1956, Je 20,31:6
Ruedi, August H, 1946, My 26,32:6
Ruediger, William C, 1947, Jl 5,11:6
Rueff, Paul, 1964, Je 14,84:8
Rueffer, Charles, 1946, F 20,25:5
Ruege, Bernard F, 1945, F 20,19:5
Ruegg, Alfred H, 1941, Ap 23,21:3
Ruegg, Erhart A, 1950, Mr 4,17:6
Ruegg, Ernest J, 1951, Ja 21,76:8
Ruegger, Albert Jr, 1958, F 28,13:4
Ruegger, Charles, 1952, My 3,21:1
Ruegger, Wally, 1946, Je 30,38:3
Ruegsegger, Charles, 1956, Ja 12,27:2
Ruehe, Harrison A, 1953, O 10,17:5
Ruehl, Sebastian Mrs, 1950, My 16,31:1
Ruehl, Theodore C Mrs, 1968, N 30,39:2
Ruehl, Victor E, 1942, Je 17,23:4
Ruekberg, Nathan T, 1949, S 28,27:1
Ruel, Muddy (Herold D), 1963, N 15,32:4
Ruemler, Clement F, 1951, My 3,29:5
Ruemmler, Gerhard G, 1966, My 29,56:4
Ruenzel, Henry G, 1938, Ap 4,17:4
Ruetenik, Fred H, 1955, Ap 24,86:4
Ruetennik, Martin L, 1947, S 25,29:3
Ruether, Richard A, 1956, Jl 3,25:3
Ruetke, Alfred M, 1958, Ja 17,30:1
Ruettgers, Arthur, 1954, Ag 11,25:4
Ruf, Walter, 1951, F 27,27:3
Rufe, Augustin H, 1939, My 22,17:2
Rufenacht, Rodolphe E, 1949, Jl 9,13:7
Rufer, Rudolph, 1944, S 19,21:2
Ruff, Albert E, 1948, D 10,26:2
Ruff, Frederick E, 1968, Ja 16,39:3
Ruff, Herman Mrs, 1962, F 28,25:2
Ruff, John D, 1938, S 26,17:2
Ruff, Robert H, 1942, My 6,19:4
Ruffalo, Anthony P, 1960, Mr 19,21:6
Ruffell, Charles E, 1954, Ap 18,89:2
Ruffier, Joseph P, 1959, Ag 27,17:5
Ruffier, Marino J, 1961, My 26,33:3
Ruffin, Ben A, 1939, N 13,19:4
Ruffin, Edmund S, 1949, Ag 16,23:4
Ruffin, Julian M, 1938, N 12,15:5
Ruffin, Sterling (por), 1949, Je 2,27:3
Ruffing, John T, 1955, S 24,19:4
Ruffini, Ernesto Cardinal, 1967, Je 12,45:1
Ruffini, G D, 1881, N 4,5:3
Ruffle, Harry M, 1942, My 23,13:2
Ruffner, Benjamin F, 1951, O 15,25:6
Ruffner, Charles S, 1939, Ja 22,34:8
Ruffner, Clifford, 1948, F 22,48:3
Ruffo, Titta, 1953, Jl 7,27:1
Ruffridge, George Albert Lt, 1918, My 9,13:5
Ruffside, Viscount (D C Brown), 1958, My 6,35:4
Ruffu, Anth M Mrs, 1956, D 12,39:3
Ruffu, Frank, 1938, Ag 5,17:3
Rufin, S Col, 1885, Ja 10,3:6
Rufino, Garcia, 1943, F 23,21:3
Rufner, Frank T, 1955, Mr 26,15:5
Ruge, A, 1881, Ja 8,2:4
Ruge, Arthur E, 1944, S 5,19:4
Ruge, Clara Mrs, 1937, O 11,21:5
Ruge, Edward P, 1952, Ja 14,19:3
Ruge, Herman J, 1949, Ag 20,11:5
Ruge, Otto, 1961, Ag 16,31:1
Rugen, Frederick C Mrs, 1947, O 18,15:1
Rugen, Louis C, 1944, Mr 19,41:2
Ruger, Henry W, 1948, Mr 23,25:4
Ruger, Theodore, 1910, Ap 20,9:4
Ruger, Thomas Gen, 1907, Je 4,7:5
Ruger, W C, 1892, Ja 15,10:6
Rugg, Addison F, 1954, F 12,25:3
Rugg, Arthur P (por), 1938, Je 13,19:1
Rugg, Charles B, 1962, N 27,37:1
Rugg, Dan M, 1954, Mr 29,19:4
Rugg, Earl M, 1952, My 2,25:5
Rugg, George B C, 1955, Je 20,21:2
Rugg, Harold, 1960, My 18,41:1
Rugg, Harold G, 1957, F 15,23:5
Rugg, Harry J, 1942, F 11,22:2
Rugg, Harry L, 1941, Ag 20,19:4
Rugg, Henry W Rev, 1910, Jl 22,7:6
Rugg, Herb, 1942, Mr 19,21:5
Rugg, Robert B, 1946, My 30,21:2
Rugg, Walter S (por), 1940, Ap 27,15:3
Rugg, Warren F, 1948, Ag 4,21:2
Ruggaber, Martin C, 1945, S 23,46:7
Rugge, Johanna, 1905, Je 24,9:6
Ruggeri, Charles Jr Mrs, 1950, Jl 4,17:6
Ruggeri, Ruggero, 1953, Jl 22,27:4
Ruggi, Giuseppe Prof, 1925, Mr 16,19:3
Ruggieri, Alex, 1951, Jl 7,13:3
Ruggieri, Jean M R, 1965, Ap 6,39:3
Ruggiero, Guido de, 1948, D 30,19:5
Ruggiero, John C, 1938, Ja 21,19:4
Ruggiero, Thomas G, 1963, D 29,43:1
Ruggles, Arthur H, 1961, Ja 3,27:8
Ruggles, Arthur V, 1945, O 22,17:5
Ruggles, Augustus D Dr, 1903, D 30,7:2
Ruggles, Austin C Mrs, 1947, Mr 17,23:3
Ruggles, Burnet R, 1945, My 30,19:2
Ruggles, Burnett R Mrs, 1941, My 14,21:3
Ruggles, Charles A, 1938, S 7,25:3
Ruggles, Clyde O, 1958, Ap 7,21:3
Ruggles, Daniel B, 1942, D 4,25:3
Ruggles, E Wood, 1942, N 9,23:5
Ruggles, Edward Dr, 1867, Mr 12,5:3
Ruggles, Edwin P, 1940, Je 21,22:2
Ruggles, Francis A, 1955, F 10,31:4
Ruggles, Frank E, 1958, Ja 30,23:2
Ruggles, George D Gen, 1904, O 20,7:5
Ruggles, Harry L, 1959, O 25,86:7
Ruggles, Harry W, 1953, Ja 4,76:4
Ruggles, Henry Joseph, 1906, Mr 7,9:5
Ruggles, Horace F, 1944, Mr 13,15:4
Ruggles, James A, 1948, Ag 15,60:3
Ruggles, James H, 1946, Je 16,40:6
Ruggles, May S Mrs, 1953, Ap 13,27:2
Ruggles, Nepean C, 1946, Mr 11,25:5
Ruggles, Ralph C, 1966, Ja 1,17:4
Ruggles, S B, 1881, Ag 29,8:4
Ruggles, S P, 1880, My 31,2:2
Ruggles, William B, 1916, Ja 24,11:3
Rugh, Arthur, 1946, D 19,29:2
Rugh, Arthur (mem ser), 1947, F 21,19:2
Rugh, Charles E, 1938, O 1,17:5
Rugh, James T, 1942, O 13,23:3
Rugh, Verling R, 1951, F 17,15:3
Rugh, William W Rev, 1937, Ja 2,11:5
Rugh, Willie, 1912, O 19,11:6
Rugman, Herbert T, 1942, Jl 12,36:1
Rugoff, Edward N, 1952, S 18,29:5
Ruh, Harold O, 1946, My 21,24:2
Ruh, John J, 1945, Jl 29,40:4
Ruh, Joseph F Msgr, 1922, F 3,15:3
Ruh, Oscar J, 1942, O 7,25:4
Ruh, Peter J Mrs, 1948, O 5,25:2
Ruhe, C H William, 1941, My 20,23:3
Ruhe, Charles, 1941, Ag 22,15:2
Ruhe, Heinz, 1953, Mr 5,27:5
Ruhfel, Edward A, 1964, Ap 17,32:5
Ruhia, Princess, 1948, Ja 31,19:6
Ruhl, Antes S, 1942, My 4,19:5
Ruhl, Christian H, 1937, O 22,19:6
Ruhl, Frederick, 1957, O 29,31:1
Ruhl, Harold J, 1943, Ap 13,25:2
Ruhl, Henry C, 1939, Je 14,23:1
Ruhl, Henry R, 1949, F 24,23:3
Ruhl, James B, 1949, My 17,25:3
Ruhl, James B Mrs, 1925, F 24,19:4
Ruhl, Oscar K, 1958, Ag 11,21:4
Ruhl, Robert W, 1967, Ag 22,34:7
Ruhl, William H, 1947, S 13,11:6
Ruhland, Frederick T, 1945, N 27,23:5
Ruhland, George C, 1958, Ap 16,33:3
Ruhle, Otto, 1943, Je 27,15:6
Ruhlender, Henry, 1944, Ag 3,19:6
Ruhling, Frederick E, 1948, O 13,25:1
Ruhlman, Randall M, 1967, Ja 6,35:4
Ruhm, Herman D, 1957, Mr 10,89:1
Ruhm, Thomas F, 1913, D 5,11:6
Ruhman, Irving C, 1950, F 28,29:2
Ruhman, Louis F, 1945, F 3,11:6
Ruhmann, Benjamin, 1956, Je 15,25:3
Ruhrseitz, Kurt, 1937, Mr 2,21:3
Ruick, Melville Mrs (C Neisen), 1963, O 6,88:8
Ruillier, Marie V, 1941, My 22,21:1
Ruisenada, Count of, 1958, Ap 25,27:1
Ruisi, John E, 1948, My 29,15:6
Ruisi, Nino, 1957, Jl 20,15:2
Ruiz, Antonio Dr, 1925, Ja 7,25:4
Ruiz Guinazu, Enrique, 1967, N 15,47:1
Ruiz Moreno, Isidoro, 1952, S 12,21:4
Ruiz y Rodriguez, Manuel Damata, 1940, Ja 4,24:
Ruiz y Ruiz, Drutos, 1948, My 5,25:1
Rukenbrod, Cornelius J, 1937, Je 28,19:5
Rukeyser, Isaac Mrs, 1961, O 6,35:3
Rukeyser, Lawrence, 1958, My 28,31:1
Rukeyser, Marryle S Mrs, 1964, Ag 23,87:2
Rukeyser, Walter A, 1960, O 19,45:3
Rukin, Abraham, 1964, My 27,39:4
Rukosz, Stanley J, 1964, F 23,85:1
Ruland, Clarence W, 1941, My 4,53:2
Ruland, Frank, 1949, Mr 20,76:5
Ruland, Fred M, 1939, Ap 14,23:6
Ruland, Harold L, 1961, My 5,29:3
Ruland, Lloyd S, 1953, My 18,21:4

Ruland, Manly A, 1907, My 19,7:4
Ruland, Wallace W, 1939, Ap 7,21:4
Ruland, William S, 1956, Jl 2,21:3
Rule, Arthur R, 1950, Je 28,27:4
Rule, Henry, 1958, Mr 23,88:7
Rule, J M, 1950, Ja 11,23:3
Rule, James N, 1938, Ap 12,24:1
Rule, Louis B, 1941, My 4,53:1
Rule, W, 1928, Jl 27,19:5
Rule, Wallace N, 1943, N 26,23:3
Rulison, Howard V, 1947, F 24,19:2
Rulison, Lawrence, 1966, Jl 25,27:4
Rulison, W P, 1939, Mr 30,23:5
Rullman, Augustus Maj, 1878, O 1,5:4
Rullman, Bernard L, 1960, Je 27,25:1
Rullman, Caroline, 1949, F 12,17:2
Rullman, Leo (por), 1946, Ag 23,19:2
Rullman, Walter A, 1962, Mr 20,37:1
Rulman, Ernest, 1952, N 5,27:1
Rulnick, Milton M, 1966, D 8,47:2
Rulon, Philip Justin Prof, 1968, Jl 1,33:3
Rulon, William, 1939, Mr 6,15:2
Rulon-Miller, Berkeley T, 1937, Jl 10,15:6
Rulon-Miller, Sumner, 1951, Ja 9,29:5
Rulter, William, 1906, Ja 19,11:6
Ruman, Sig, 1967, F 16,35:1
Rumanceff, Nicholas A, 1948, My 23,68:7
Rumball, Fred G, 1950, Ag 1,23:5
Rumball-Petre, Edwin A R, 1954, Jl 20,19:3
Rumbarger, John J, 1943, Mr 25,21:3
Rumbaugh, David S Mrs, 1937, D 7,25:3
Rumbaugh, Lynn H, 1964, Mr 12,35:4
Rumbel, Ralph M, 1939, Ag 2,19:4
Rumbold, Daniel C, 1951, Ap 23,25:1
Rumbold, Horace (por), 1941, My 25,37:1
Rumbough, Stanley M, 1961, D 17,82:3
Rumbough, Stanley M Mrs, 1962, My 1,38:1
Rumeau, Francois, 1946, Jl 23,25:4
Rumeau, Joseph, 1940, F 11,48:5
Rumely, Edward A, 1964, N 28,21:1
Rumely, Leo M, 1955, Ja 1,13:5
Rumery, Joseph A, 1940, Mr 23,13:2
Rumery, Ralph R, 1965, Mr 13,25:2
Rumey, Mason P, 1944, Ja 22,13:3
Rumfeldt, W S, 1954, Ja 29,19:5
Rumill, Loren W, 1951, Ag 6,21:4
Rumilly, L M C H G De, 1884, F 1,5:6
Ruml, Beardsley (funl, Ap 21,31:4), 1960, Ap 19,1:1
Ruml, Wentzle, 1943, N 25,25:5
Rumley, Charles S, 1955, Je 29,29:2
Rummage, Leland C, 1956, My 30,21:5
Rummalls, Charles H, 1955, Ag 13,13:5
Rummel, Harry W, 1961, Mr 3,27:2
Rummel, Joseph F, 1964, N 9,33:2
Rummel, Leila M Mrs (por), 1937, D 10,25:3
Rummel, Richard M, 1956, N 4,86:3
Rummel, W Michael, 1966, O 26,47:4
Rummel, Walter M, 1953, My 3,88:5
Rummell, Leslie J Lt, 1919, F 23,18:1
Rummler, Alex J, 1959, Mr 15,88:4
Rummler, Alex J Mrs, 1959, Jl 1,31:3
Rummo, Michael, 1951, Ag 8,25:4
Rumney, Jay, 1957, Ap 9,33:2
Rumney, John G, 1941, Ap 30,19:5
Rumney, Pegeen G (Mrs Ralph Rumney), 1967, Mr 8,37:3
Rumohr, John A, 1937, F 9,23:5
Rump, Henry Mrs, 1938, Mr 16,23:4
Rump, William C, 1938, Mr 10,21:4
Rumpel, John A, 1948, Je 8,26:3
Rumpf, Carl F, 1951, Mr 13,31:2
Rumpf, Ernest F, 1947, My 27,25:4
Rumph, Harry F, 1947, O 1,29:4
Rumph, Ida M, 1958, O 25,21:4
Rumple, J N W, 1903, F 1,7:5
Rumpler, Charles M Mrs, 1948, Jl 20,24:2
Rumpler, Edmund (por), 1940, S 10,23:3
Rumpler, Jonas, 1949, Mr 13,76:3
Rumplik, Rudolph Mrs, 1953, Je 28,60:8
Rumpp, Paul T, 1954, Mr 17,31:1
Rumreich, Alphonsus S, 1964, Ag 19,37:5
Rumrill, Harry B, 1951, Ja 24,27:3
Rumrill, J B, 1885, Ap 9,5:3
Rumrill, James M, 1954, Ja 4,19:3
Rumsey, Benjamin G, 1962, Je 26,33:1
Rumsey, Bronson, 1946, Ag 20,27:1
Rumsey, Charles G, 1940, Ap 24,23:4
Rumsey, David, 1937, Ja 6,23:4
Rumsey, David Mrs, 1922, D 14,21:3
Rumsey, G D, 1881, Je 18,2:4
Rumsey, H S, 1946, Mr 4,23:5
Rumsey, Hiram S, 1871, S 17,5:2
Rumsey, John W, 1960, O 18,40:1
Rumsey, Lee M, 1942, Ag 4,19:5
Rumsey, Maurice C, 1944, Mr 29,21:6
Rumsey, William Judge, 1903, Ja 17,9:4
Rumsey, William L Mrs, 1964, F 26,32:7
Rumshinsky, Joseph M, 1956, F 7,31:3
Runbeck, Margaret L, 1956, O 1,27:2
Runcie, Sylvia D, 1952, Ag 2,15:6
Runciman, Lord, 1937, Ag 14,13:1
Runciman, Phil, 1953, Je 6,17:2
Runciman, Walter Viscount (por), 1949, N 15,25:3

Runco, Albert, 1960, N 22,35:1
Rund, Edwin Mrs, 1953, Ap 9,27:3
Rundall, Charles O, 1953, Je 10,29:5
Rundall, John C, 1940, O 8,25:3
Rundbaken, Frederick J Mrs, 1963, Ap 6,19:5
Runde, Fred J, 1965, Je 21,29:3
Rundell, Charles L, 1944, Mr 31,21:5
Rundell, Charles L Sr, 1952, N 20,18:8
Rundell, Susan E Mrs, 1948, Jl 9,19:1
Rundin, Gustav A, 1959, S 22,35:4
Rundle, Alfred Augustus, 1912, Jl 5,13:6
Rundle, Henry M, 1960, Mr 1,33:5
Rundle, Katherine A, 1939, Ap 16,III,6:8
Rundles, Ralph R, 1951, N 19,23:3
Rundlet, Charles T, 1956, Jl 19,27:2
Rundlett, Emilie V, 1959, N 18,41:2
Rundlett, Henry A Dr, 1904, Mr 10,9:3
Rundlett, Raymond C, 1957, My 6,29:4
Rundquist, Emil A, 1948, Ja 10,15:5
Rundspaden, Charles F, 1953, Jl 18,13:5
Rundstedt, Karl Rudolf Gerd von, 1953, F 25,27:1
Rundstrom, Alfred J, 1942, Ap 7,21:5
Rundstrom, Leonard G, 1957, N 5,31:1
Runge, Albert, 1937, Ag 28,15:6
Runge, Charles V, 1952, Ap 6,88:1
Runge, Edmond J, 1964, F 18,35:1
Runge, Edward, 1916, N 21,11:3
Runge, Edward Mrs, 1923, Ag 10,11:2
Runge, Edward T, 1952, N 2,88:3
Runge, Herman G, 1958, Mr 18,29:5
Runge, Robert F, 1942, Jl 8,23:3
Rungee, Elizabeth, 1939, Ja 24,19:3
Rungeet Singh, Mrs, 1863, Ag 22,2:3
Rungius, Carl, 1959, O 22,37:1
Runk, Arthur H, 1954, Ja 7,31:3
Runk, Casper, 1949, N 6,92:1
Runk, George S, 1956, N 13,37:2
Runk, Louis B, 1954, My 15,15:5
Runk, Louise F Mrs, 1941, N 1,15:4
Runk, Marshall H, 1952, Ja 14,19:5
Runk, Otto A, 1942, Jl 11,13:7
Runk, William N, 1960, S 26,33:3
Runkel, Hermann, 1918, Mr 30,13:5
Runkel, Mortimer H, 1966, Ag 7,81:2
Runkle, Delmer Mrs, 1954, Mr 21,89:1
Runkle, Erwin W, 1941, F 15,15:6
Runkwitz, Karl, 1942, Ja 8,21:4
Runnells, Edward S, 1951, My 4,27:2
Runnells, John E, 1964, Ja 4,23:1
Runnells, John E Mrs, 1953, D 13,86:4
Runnells, William A, 1941, My 19,12:3
Runnels, O E, 1961, Ap 10,31:5
Runner, George M Mrs, 1949, N 29,29:2
Runner, Harvey E, 1961, D 5,43:3
Runner, John Jr, 1951, Ap 17,29:5
Runnion, Ray, 1945, S 7,23:4
Runsdorf, Jacob Mrs, 1964, Ap 4,28:4
Runser, Frank B Mrs, 1962, N 14,39:2
Runyan, Charles D, 1963, Je 24,27:2
Runyan, Edward W, 1937, D 18,21:2
Runyan, Guy W, 1946, My 24,19:3
Runyan, Raymond W, 1948, S 18,17:2
Runyan, William J, 1951, Mr 7,33:3
Runyan, William M, 1957, Jl 31,23:2
Runyan, William W, 1940, Ja 28,32:1
Runyon, A Milton Mrs, 1948, S 13,21:4
Runyon, Albert, 1949, Mr 17,26:2
Runyon, Albert Mrs, 1941, Je 22,32:2
Runyon, Alice S Mrs, 1941, Jl 12,13:2
Runyon, Carman R, 1941, O 22,23:3
Runyon, Carman R Mrs (W Kingston), 1967, F 5, 88:5
Runyon, Carroll T, 1937, Ap 9,21:1
Runyon, Charles (Oct 14), 1903, N 25,9:5
Runyon, Charles, 1945, O 24,21:4; 1946, F 12,25:4
Runyon, Charles A, 1951, Jl 17,27:3
Runyon, Charles W, 1940, D 11,27:4
Runyon, Clarkson, 1945, N 8,19:4
Runyon, Damon, 1946, D 11,31:3
Runyon, Donald M, 1956, D 4,39:3
Runyon, Enos, 1908, My 12,7:6
Runyon, Frederick F, 1944, Mr 14,19:1
Runyon, Frederick O, 1961, My 7,87:2
Runyon, Harold D, 1963, Ap 26,35:4
Runyon, Harry, 1964, O 4,88:8
Runyon, Herman M, 1943, Ap 4,40:4
Runyon, Howard J Mrs, 1945, D 11,25:4
Runyon, James, 1947, My 28,26:2
Runyon, Jennie V Mrs, 1943, Ja 10,50:4
Runyon, John B, 1948, N 30,27:3
Runyon, John C, 1955, O 25,33:3
Runyon, John W, 1967, Ja 21,31:3
Runyon, John W Mrs, 1968, O 4,47:2
Runyon, Katherine Mrs, 1951, Ag 18,11:6
Runyon, Kenneth E, 1946, N 10,63:4
Runyon, M Chase, 1964, S 28,29:6
Runyon, Malvin W Mrs, 1954, S 10,23:1
Runyon, Nelson, 1915, Je 29,13:5
Runyon, Paul M, 1956, F 16,29:1
Runyon, Peter F, 1954, N 10,33:4
Runyon, Ralph C, 1957, F 1,25:4
Runyon, Richard B, 1964, Mr 31,35:4
Runyon, Stanford K, 1947, Mr 2,60:4

Runyon, Theodore, 1896, Ja 27,1:3
Runyon, Tom, 1957, Ap 11,35:3
Runyon, W N, 1931, N 10,34:2
Runyon, William H Mrs, 1951, S 5,31:3
Ruoff, Aloysius J, 1956, F 6,23:2
Ruoff, Charles L, 1946, S 4,23:2
Ruoff, Leonard, 1907, N 2,9:2; 1924, Ag 13,15:3
Ruohomaa, Kosti S, 1961, N 5,89:1
Ruot, Marcel, 1961, Ja 20,29:1
Ruotolo, Onorio, 1966, D 19,37:4
Rupert, Charles G Mrs, 1947, Ja 5,53:2
Rupert, J Leslie, 1950, My 23,29:2
Rupert, Mary P S, 1939, Jl 23,29:2
Rupert, W Earle, 1951, N 19,23:4
Rupert, William B, 1946, Ap 1,27:4
Ruperti, Justus, 1944, Ja 17,19:4
Ruperti, Justus Mrs, 1955, My 24,31:2
Rupertus, William H (por), 1945, Mr 27,19:1
Rupnik, Edna M H Mrs, 1939, Mr 5,48:6
Rupp, Aug Jr, 1942, Jl 11,13:2
Rupp, Charles E, 1960, Ja 29,25:2
Rupp, Charles S, 1948, Ap 15,25:6
Rupp, Fred, 1951, S 11,29:1
Rupp, George F Mrs, 1941, D 4,25:2
Rupp, J George, 1947, Mr 8,13:2
Rupp, John A, 1958, Jl 13,68:5
Rupp, Mary E, 1943, D 30,17:1
Rupp, Nelson, 1948, Ag 11,22:3
Rupp, Waldemar F, 1962, My 1,14:5
Rupp, Werner A, 1963, Ja 3,15:7
Rupp, William L, 1942, N 21,13:3
Ruppel, Frederick F, 1949, O 12,29:3
Ruppel, Henry J Jr, 1948, F 9,17:2
Ruppel, Joseph J, 1947, Ap 10,25:3
Ruppel, Louis, 1958, Ja 25,19:1
Ruppell, Edward A, 1953, N 24,24:3
Ruppersberger, George G, 1937, S 18,19:5
Ruppert, Elsie M Mrs, 1952, N 2,89:2
Ruppert, Frank, 1902, O 22,9:4
Ruppert, Franz, 1883, O 3,2:4
Ruppert, George E, 1948, N 6,13:1; 1959, My 1,29:1
Ruppert, George E Mrs, 1957, N 25,31:3
Ruppert, Jacob, 1915, My 26,13:5; 1939, Ja 14,1:6
Ruppert, Louis L, 1939, Ag 26,15:6
Ruppert, Robert Mrs, 1966, F 24,7:7
Ruppf, Frederick, 1947, Ag 28,23:3
Ruppin, Arthur, 1943, Ja 2,11:3
Rupposki, Edward, 1937, Mr 8,3:1
Rupprecht, Carl H, 1944, S 11,17:3
Rupprecht, Charles H, 1957, Ja 24,29:1
Rupprecht, Crown Prince of Bavaria (funl plans, Ag 4,25:2), 1955, Ag 3,23:3
Rupprecht, Frederick K, 1954, N 30,29:5
Rupprecht, George, 1961, S 3,61:2
Rupprecht, Otto, 1937, D 21,23:3
Ruprecht, Carl F, 1937, Mr 13,II,9:2
Ruprecht, Carl H, 1966, O 29,29:5
Ruprecht, Carl H W Mrs, 1943, Ag 13,17:5
Ruprecht, Leontine, 1946, My 26,32:1
Ruprecht, Louis, 1949, O 14,27:2
Ruprecht, Walter E, 1953, O 29,31:2
Rura, John E, 1949, O 21,25:1
Ruroede, Carl Jr, 1956, O 8,27:4
Rurrill, Randolph, 1937, S 25,17:3
Rus, Joseph A, 1958, Mr 20,29:1
Rusak, Frank (funl, D 12,15:4), 1914, D 7,11:6
Rusakov, Arseni V, 1953, Ap 15,31:4
Rusby, Henry H (por), 1940, N 19,23:4
Rusby, S O, 1938, Ap 22,19:4
Ruscansky, Andrew J, 1954, D 11,13:5
Rusch, Frank, 1941, Ap 12,15:5
Rusch, Henry A, 1938, My 29,II,6:7
Rusch, Joseph L, 1959, Ap 12,86:7
Rusch, Oscar F, 1940, N 26,23:3
Rusch, Robert, 1957, Jl 3,46:1
Rusch, William D, 1951, S 5,31:5
Rusche, Adolphe Jr Mrs, 1957, D 2,27:3
Ruschmeyer, Henry, 1957, Ag 9,19:5
Ruscoe, Ernest C, 1959, My 3,87:1
Ruscoe, Fred W, 1951, D 28,21:4
Ruscoe, George I, 1957, Ag 30,19:3
Ruse, Frank G, 1956, Mr 6,31:4
Rusen, Anthony G, 1954, Ja 26,27:4
Rusg, Harry K, 1952, F 18,19:5
Rush, Alan S, 1946, Ap 13,17:5
Rush, Allan J, 1955, Jl 10,72:6
Rush, Arthur T, 1938, D 1,14:6
Rush, Benjamin (see also Jl 5), 1877, Jl 6,4:6
Rush, Benjamin F, 1942, Ja 20,20:3
Rush, Benjamin Mrs, 1946, My 10,19:1
Rush, Benjamin Sr (por), 1948, Ap 27,25:3
Rush, Charles M, 1942, N 1,52:3
Rush, Daniel V Mrs, 1948, Ag 11,22:3
Rush, David M Sr, 1964, Ag 10,31:3
Rush, Emmett B, 1946, D 29,37:1
Rush, Ephraim W, 1940, O 7,17:4
Rush, Eugene, 1949, F 20,60:2
Rush, Floyd E, 1947, N 25,29:3
Rush, George A, 1948, Ja 17,17:5
Rush, George F, 1944, My 1,15:4
Rush, Harry P, 1951, Je 20,27:1
Rush, Howard M, 1950, Ja 17,28:3
Rush, Isador, 1904, N 15,1:6

Rush, James Dr, 1869, My 30,3:6
Rush, James I, 1953, N 26,31:4
Rush, John (funl, Ap 29,11:5), 1912, Ap 26,11:3
Rush, John A, 1943, N 2,25:3; 1952, S 27,17:3
Rush, John H, 1958, S 2,25:1
Rush, John Sr, 1959, Jl 7,33:4
Rush, Joseph F, 1960, Je 23,29:2
Rush, Julia, 1941, Ap 29,19:2
Rush, Louis H, 1942, F 9,23:8
Rush, Margaret, 1952, F 24,84:2
Rush, Max J, 1951, Ja 3,25:2
Rush, Olive, 1966, Ag 23,39:1
Rush, Ralph L, 1956, O 21,86:8
Rush, Richard, 1859, Ag 2,3:3
Rush, Richard Capt, 1912, F 4,13:4
Rush, Roger, 1951, N 25,79:4
Rush, Sam, 1961, Ap 19,39:2
Rush, T E, 1927, Je 4,17:3
Rush, Walter A, 1938, Ap 3,II,7:3; 1954, S 28,29:2
Rush, William N, 1954, D 27,17:2
Rush, William R, 1940, Ag 4,32:8
Rushbrook, Walter F, 1951, F 24,13:5
Rushbrooke, J H Mrs, 1944, S 12,19:4
Rushbrooke, James H (por), 1947, F 2,57:1
Rushby, Horace, 1916, Je 18,18:5
Rushby, William G, 1951, Jl 19,23:4
Rushcliffe, Lord (H B Betterton), 1949, N 19,17:2
Rushford, George, 1958, Ja 11,17:6
Rushfort, Walter, 1952, D 23,23:1
Rushforth, Thomas, 1942, S 24,27:5
Rushkin, saml, 1937, Ap 8,23:3
Rushmore, Arthur W, 1955, S 16,23:5
Rushmore, C E, 1931, O 31,17:6
Rushmore, David B (por), 1940, My 7,25:4
Rushmore, Edmund, 1958, S 12,26:1
Rushmore, Edwin H (por), 1941, F 10,20:2
Rushmore, George R, 1964, F 19,39:3
Rushmore, Jane P, 1958, Je 14,21:5
Rushmore, Jaques C, 1949, S 4,40:5
Rushmore, Maurice L Mrs, 1957, Je 29,17:5
Rushmore, Perry M, 1953, F 1,88:1
Rushmore, Samuel W, 1948, Ag 17,21:3
Rushmore, Stephen, 1960, N 1,39:4
Rushmore, Thomas H, 1955, Ag 7,72:7
Rushmore, Townsend, 1948, Ja 2,23:2
Rushmore, Virginia O Mrs, 1953, Mr 26,31:6
Rushton, Herbert J, 1947, D 13,15:5
Rushton, J Harry, 1939, S 21,23:3
Rushton, Joe, 1964, Mr 4,37:2
Rushton, Joseph A, 1956, O 1,27:5
Rushton, Joseph Rev, 1917, F 21,11:5
Rushton, Kenneth F, 1921, S 3,9:6
Rushton, Margaret P Mrs, 1938, N 16,23:1
Rushton, Richard H, 1910, Ja 23,II,11:3
Rushton, Robert, 1952, Ap 24,31:2
Rushton, Urban J, 1949, D 28,25:2
Rushworth, Frank, 1952, Je 28,19:2
Rushworth, Leroy A Mrs, 1951, Jl 24,25:4
Rusie, Amos, 1942, D 7,27:4
Rusk, Henry J, 1941, Jl 13,28:8
Rusk, Henry P, 1954, Ja 11,25:4
Rusk, J McL, 1893, N 22,5:5
Rusk, Michael Y Mrs, 1966, Mr 17,39:3
Rusk, Paul, 1962, My 1,37:2
Rusk, Ralph L, 1962, Jl 1,56:4
Rusk, William S Mrs (Evelyn C), 1964, D 8,45:2
Rusk, Wilmer N, 1950, N 17,27:1
Ruska, George J, 1949, S 20,29:3
Ruskay, Cecil B, 1955, O 4,35:2
Ruskay, Samuel S, 1922, D 11,17:5
Ruskin, Jacob, 1944, Ap 23,43:3
Ruskin, Jacob S, 1962, N 7,39:5
Ruskin, Jerrold H, 1968, Jl 2,41:2
Ruskin, John, 1900, Ja 21,7:1
Ruskin, Leonard L Mrs, 1961, F 14,37:1
Ruskin, Philip H, 1944, Je 7,19:4
Ruskin, Sigmund C, 1943, Ag 31,17:3
Ruskin, Simon L, 1958, Ja 2,29:2
Ruskis, Clarence J, 1959, F 5,31:5
Rusko, Paul, 1950, Jl 7,19:4
Ruslander, David, 1940, F 24,13:2
Rusling, Clifford Mrs, 1950, O 11,33:5
Rusling, Gershon, 1914, Je 6,9:3
Rusling, James W, 1947, F 1,15:1
Rusling, Van Dyck, 1956, Jl 19,27:1
Rusmisel, R Raymond, 1967, O 18,47:4
Rusnak, Herman, 1951, O 29,23:5
Ruspini, Angelo, 1959, Jl 21,30:6
Ruspoli, Carlo M Prince, 1947, Je 21,17:2
Ruspoli, Eugenia Princess, 1951, Ja 27,13:6
Ruspoli, Katherine Q Princess, 1956, F 13,27:1
Ruspoli, Rosalie Princess, 1914, Jl 10,9:4
Ruspoll, Enrico Prince, 1909, D 6,9:4
Russ, Carl R, 1961, N 17,35:2
Russ, Carolyn H, 1944, F 15,17:6
Russ, Caus Capt, 1916, F 10,11:2
Russ, Charles, 1909, Ja 1,11:6
Russ, Charles A Mrs, 1950, Ja 28,13:3
Russ, Edward, 1912, F 3,11:4
Russ, F A, 1933, N 11,15:4
Russ, F Howard Jr Mrs, 1954, D 1,31:3
Russ, Hermann, 1942, F 5,22:3
Russ, Howard C, 1939, N 30,21:2
Russ, J D, 1881, Mr 2,5:5
Russ, Joel, 1961, Mr 11,21:4
Russ, Joel Mrs, 1958, Ag 3,80:5
Russ, John J, 1957, My 30,19:2
Russ, John T, 1955, Ja 1,13:1
Russ, Kate P, 1952, S 5,27:2
Russ, Ulmer C, 1937, Mr 3,23:4
Russ, W Arthur, 1953, Ap 8,29:2
Russ, Wallace A, 1949, Ja 18,23:1
Russ, Walter V (por), 1943, Jl 27,17:2
Russ-Suchard, Carl, 1925, F 15,7:2
Russbach, Jacob, 1950, Jl 23,56:1
Russe, Ellen (Mrs L G van der Velden Vygh), 1942, O 7,25:3
Russeine, Kamil, 1921, Mr 23,13:5
Russek, Frank (por), 1948, D 11,15:1
Russek, Frank Mrs, 1955, Mr 29,30:3
Russek, I H, 1947, Je 2,25:5
Russel, Abraham D Judge, 1870, Ap 27,5:5
Russel, Albert L, 1952, S 3,29:4
Russel, Albert W, 1949, Mr 22,25:3
Russel, Anne D, 1943, Je 3,21:5
Russel, Edward J, 1958, Mr 8,17:6
Russel, Edward Richard Baron, 1920, F 21,13:5
Russel, Fred B Mrs, 1941, Ja 20,17:3
Russel, George B, 1947, S 5,19:5
Russel, George H, 1915, My 18,13:4
Russel, Henry, 1920, F 26,11:4
Russel, Mary L, 1940, Je 26,23:5
Russell, A, 1936, Ja 17,19:1
Russell, A David, 1955, Je 6,27:5
Russell, A Le Barron, 1948, O 7,29:2
Russell, A Y, 1940, Je 29,15:3
Russell, Adaline Du Bois, 1883, Ap 27,8:2
Russell, Addison Peale, 1912, Jl 26,9:6
Russell, Albert (King of the Bowery), 1910, F 10,7:4
Russell, Albert H, 1960, F 15,27:4
Russell, Albert I, 1954, Je 25,21:5
Russell, Alex H, 1949, Je 20,19:5
Russell, Alexander, 1876, Jl 19,4:7
Russell, Alexander G, 1911, N 12,II,15:5
Russell, Alexander Wilson Rear-Adm, 1908, N 27,9:3
Russell, Alfred, 1906, My 9,9:5
Russell, Alice H Mrs, 1940, N 20,21:4
Russell, Alice M, 1956, O 17,35:5
Russell, Alys Mrs, 1951, Ja 22,17:3
Russell, Andrew A, 1942, O 22,21:4
Russell, Andrew A Mrs, 1942, O 22,21:4
Russell, Andrew H Col, 1915, Je 15,13:6
Russell, Angeline Roome, 1913, D 11,11:4
Russell, Annie E Mrs, 1943, O 13,23:4
Russell, Archibald, 1871, Ap 21,8:4
Russell, Archibald D Mrs, 1918, F 13,13:4
Russell, Archibald Douglas, 1919, N 30,22:4; 1968, My 28,47:2
Russell, Arthur H K, 1960, F 3,33:2
Russell, Arthur Mrs, 1967, Ap 22,31:4
Russell, Arthur P, 1946, O 18,23:2
Russell, Arthur S, 1939, Ja 29,33:2
Russell, Baron, 1900, Ag 11,6:7
Russell, Barrett B Jr, 1961, My 18,35:2
Russell, Barrett B Jr Mrs, 1960, N 23,29:4
Russell, Benee, 1961, Jl 2,32:7
Russell, Benjamin C, 1945, Ja 29,14:2
Russell, Benjamin F, 1908, O 27,9:5
Russell, Benjamin F Mrs, 1944, Ja 13,21:1
Russell, Bernard F, 1966, N 8,39:4
Russell, Bruce, 1963, D 19,33:3
Russell, Byron (Patk J), 1963, S 7,19:2
Russell, Byron Mrs, 1963, Ag 20,33:4
Russell, C A, 1902, O 24,9:5
Russell, C D, 1963, O 25,31:1
Russell, C H, 1884, Ja 22,5:2
Russell, C N, 1926, O 26,27:1
Russell, C Sir, 1883, Ap 15,9:3
Russell, C T, 1903, F 18,9:6
Russell, Charles, 1875, N 3,4:5; 1957, N 4,29:3
Russell, Charles A (por), 1937, Jl 11,5:2
Russell, Charles B, 1948, O 27,27:1
Russell, Charles C, 1942, O 9,21:5; 1954, Ag 14,15:5
Russell, Charles E, 1943, N 13,13:3; 1960, D 1,35:3
Russell, Charles E Mrs, 1967, Je 8,47:4
Russell, Charles H, 1940, S 17,23:2; 1965, O 15,45:2
Russell, Charles H Mrs, 1949, Ja 29,13:1
Russell, Charles Hazen, 1912, Mr 15,9:4
Russell, Charles Howland (funl, F 23,13:6), 1921, F 20,22:1
Russell, Charles L, 1945, F 11,38:5
Russell, Charles Mills, 1923, Ag 13,13:4
Russell, Charles Mrs, 1922, Mr 12,30:3
Russell, Charles S (por), 1941, Ag 24,21:1
Russell, Charles T, 1958, Ja 3,21:4
Russell, Charles Taze, 1916, N 1,11:5
Russell, Chris, 1948, My 23,68:5
Russell, Clarence K, 1941, Ja 24,17:3
Russell, Clifford H, 1956, Ag 9,25:5
Russell, Clinton F, 1961, S 26,39:4
Russell, Clinton W, 1943, Mr 26,19:1
Russell, Daniel (por), 1947, F 11,27:1
Russell, Daniel B, 1943, Mr 26,19:4
Russell, Daniel Mrs, 1944, F 28,17:5
Russell, David, 1903, Ap 15,9:6
Russell, David Brown, 1915, D 28,11:4
Russell, David E, 1939, N 6,23:5
Russell, Donald J, 1952, Jl 14,17:3
Russell, Doris A, 1962, Ap 25,39:2
Russell, Dwight E, 1948, Jl 24,15:6
Russell, E H Mrs (Rose), 1965, Ja 3,84:5
Russell, E Wirt, 1957, My 10,27:4
Russell, Earl, 1931, Mr 5,25:3
Russell, Earl B, 1941, S 29,17:3
Russell, Earl T, 1943, Je 10,21:2
Russell, Earle L, 1947, Ag 6,23:4
Russell, Edgar Gen, 1925, Ap 28,21:3
Russell, Edmund A, 1944, O 26,23:2
Russell, Edward, 1916, Je 4,21:5
Russell, Edward A, 1951, O 2,28:3; 1955, Je 28,27:4
Russell, Edward B, 1949, Ap 25,23:5
Russell, Edward C, 1958, Je 16,23:4
Russell, Edward L, 1937, O 27,31:1
Russell, Edward L Col, 1911, Ja 29,11:1
Russell, Edward S, 1959, D 23,27:1
Russell, Edward T, 1937, S 30,23:2
Russell, Edward W, 1959, Je 2,35:4
Russell, Edwin E, 1938, Je 7,23:2
Russell, Elbert, 1951, S 23,86:1
Russell, Elijah T, 1953, S 23,31:4
Russell, Elizabeth C G, 1939, Ap 6,25:2
Russell, Emmett B Mrs, 1947, F 6,23:6
Russell, Ernest B, 1945, Mr 22,23:3
Russell, Ernest H, 1955, Ag 14,81:2
Russell, Ernest J, 1956, Jl 13,19:1
Russell, Erneste S, 1945, Ag 10,15:4
Russell, Ethel H Mrs, 1953, Jl 5,49:2
Russell, Eugene F, 1941, Ap 27,38:3
Russell, Eugene F Mrs, 1948, Jl 7,23:3
Russell, F, 1931, N 21,17:1
Russell, Fanny E Mrs, 1937, F 15,17:3
Russell, Faris R, 1968, S 10,47:2
Russell, Faris R Mrs, 1954, O 6,25:4
Russell, Floyd M, 1957, O 2,33:4
Russell, Francis William, 1871, S 1,1:2
Russell, Frank, 1925, Ag 13,19:5
Russell, Frank C, 1962, Jl 22,64:5
Russell, Frank H, 1947, Ag 5,23:1
Russell, Frank J, 1947, Mr 19,25:4
Russell, Frank P, 1937, Jl 2,21:3
Russell, Frank S, 1943, S 10,23:1
Russell, Fraser, 1952, Mr 29,15:4
Russell, Fred (Thos F Parnell), 1957, O 15,30:2
Russell, Fred, 1958, Ja 11,17:2
Russell, Frederick (por), 1945, O 27,15:3
Russell, Frederick, 1961, Ap 16,86:7
Russell, Frederick A (por), 1946, Mr 30,15:4
Russell, Frederick C, 1952, Ap 13,76:4
Russell, Frederick F, 1960, D 30,19:4
Russell, Frederick G, 1948, My 19,28:3
Russell, G W, 1935, Jl 18,19:1
Russell, Gail, 1961, Ag 28,21:3
Russell, George, 1924, N 25,23:3
Russell, George A, 1953, N 26,32:4
Russell, George B Dr, 1903, S 1,7:6
Russell, George D Col, 1923, Ja 20,13:6
Russell, George E, 1925, O 19,21:3; 1953, D 14,31
Russell, George F, 1951, Ap 14,16:2
Russell, George H, 1944, My 19,19:5
Russell, George J, 1948, Ag 22,62:4
Russell, George L, 1946, O 21,31:6
Russell, George L Jr (por), 1947, Mr 5,25:1
Russell, George M (por), 1938, Ag 19,19:4
Russell, George O, 1938, S 11,II,11:2
Russell, George W Dr, 1937, F 5,21:3
Russell, George W Sr, 1942, O 31,15:5
Russell, Gertrude, 1939, N 27,17:1
Russell, Gertrude M Mrs, 1948, Jl 22,23:4
Russell, Gordon H, 1938, Ap 26,21:5
Russell, Grace L, 1949, Ag 14,68:7
Russell, H Lawton, 1941, S 26,23:2
Russell, Harold H, 1956, Jl 24,25:1
Russell, Harold L, 1954, Ap 12,29:4
Russell, Harold Mrs (A Dwyer), 1952, Jl 5,15:6
Russell, Harry A, 1921, My 23,13:6
Russell, Harry Alton, 1921, My 22,22:4
Russell, Harry V, 1953, Ap 15,45:1
Russell, Helen G, 1968, O 26,37:5
Russell, Helen G Mrs, 1953, Ja 6,29:5
Russell, Henri Tosti, 1968, O 12,37:4
Russell, Henry, 1916, F 22,11:5; 1937, O 12,25:5; 1944, Jl 22,15:6
Russell, Henry B, 1945, N 27,23:6
Russell, Henry E, 1962, N 2,31:4
Russell, Henry N (funl, F 22,21:4), 1957, F 19,3
Russell, Henry P, 1943, Mr 4,19:3
Russell, Henry P Mrs, 1966, Jl 19,39:4
Russell, Henry R, 1940, Mr 3,45:2
Russell, Henry W, 1944, Mr 4,13:5
Russell, Herbert, 1944, Mr 27,19:6
Russell, Herbert D, 1943, F 21,32:5
Russell, Herbert L, 1943, Ap 3,15:6
Russell, Herman, 1956, Mr 15,31:4
Russell, Horace, 1913, Je 15,IV,5:5
Russell, Howard H, 1946, Jl 2,25:4
Russell, Howard H Mrs, 1939, D 22,19:4
Russell, Howard L, 1954, O 28,35:5
Russell, Hugh, 1939, Mr 21,24:2
Russell, Hugh L Dr, 1925, Je 10,23:4

Russell, Hugh M, 1966, Ja 16,83:1
Russell, Hugh W, 1962, Ja 20,45:1
Russell, Irving L Mrs, 1944, Je 27,19:6
Russell, Irwin, 1879, D 24,5:3
Russell, Isaac F Mrs, 1958, Je 1,86:3
Russell, Israel, 1866, Mr 21,5:3
Russell, Israel C Prof, 1906, My 2,9:5
Russell, J D Mrs, 1902, Ja 7,7:4
Russell, J Elmer, 1941, N 21,17:2
Russell, J F Rev, 1884, Ap 11,5:3
Russell, J Hervey, 1925, Mr 26,23:5
Russell, J J, 1922, O 20,17:5
Russell, J Louis Mrs, 1947, D 10,31:4
Russell, J S, 1882, Je 10,4:7; 1935, Mr 29,21:2
Russell, J Stuart, 1960, Ag 5,8:6
Russell, J Thomas, 1963, Je 27,33:1
Russell, J Townsend, 1962, Je 23,23:4
Russell, J Townsend Mrs, 1947, Ag 16,13:4
Russell, J Warren, 1961, D 19,33:4
Russell, Jack Rev, 1883, My 20,10:2
Russell, James, 1914, F 1,5:5; 1938, My 28,15:7
Russell, James A, 1960, Ag 16,29:5
Russell, James B, 1956, D 29,15:4
Russell, James Capt, 1879, Jl 18,4:7
Russell, James Carew, 1913, Mr 21,13:2
Russell, James E (por), 1945, N 5,19:1
Russell, James E Mrs, 1954, N 9,27:2; 1958, Ag 13, 27:5
Russell, James H, 1940, Ap 1,19:4
Russell, James I (por), 1944, F 15,17:1
Russell, James J, 1953, Ag 2,72:6
Russell, James M, 1941, S 15,17:4
Russell, James P, 1954, Je 13,88:2
Russell, James P Mrs, 1958, Ap 5,15:5
Russell, James S Mrs, 1965, Ap 19,29:3
Russell, James S R, 1939, Mr 21,23:5
Russell, Jane A (Mrs A E Wilhelmi), 1967, Mr 14, 47:1
Russell, Jean F, 1964, O 26,31:4
Russell, John, 1874, D 28,1:7; 1883, My 3,3:1
Russell, John (funl, My 12,23:5), 1925, My 5,21:4
Russell, John, 1938, Jl 21,21:3; 1939, Jl 8,15:4; 1956, Mr 8,29:4; 1965, Jl 15,29:5
Russell, John A, 1938, Je 10,21:5
Russell, John C, 1949, Jl 11,17:2
Russell, John D, 1950, Ag 1,23:2
Russell, John E, 1903, O 29,9:4
Russell, John Edward Prof, 1917, F 27,11:4
Russell, John F, 1946, Ja 9,24:2
Russell, John F Jr, 1956, Ag 29,29:3
Russell, John Father, 1912, N 5,13:5
Russell, John H, 1913, Je 18,9:4; 1947, Mr 7,25:1
Russell, John H Mrs, 1967, Ap 1,31:5
Russell, John J, 1952, Ja 29,25:3
Russell, John L, 1937, S 22,27:2
Russell, John Lord, 1878, My 29,1:7
Russell, John M Mrs, 1958, Ap 18,23:2
Russell, John N, 1941, Ja 21,22:2; 1943, N 6,13:5
Russell, John W, 1954, N 11,31:4; 1959, N 7,23:6
Russell, John W Mrs, 1964, F 13,31:4
Russell, John William, 1918, F 5,13:5
Russell, Joseph, 1876, Ag 24,4:7
Russell, Joseph A, 1958, N 23,88:6
Russell, Joseph E Judge, 1911, Ap 8,13:5
Russell, Joseph H, 1950, My 2,29:3
Russell, Joseph W, 1943, F 28,48:1
Russell, Jules P, 1967, Ap 17,37:2
Russell, Justin W, 1952, Ag 1,18:4
Russell, Karl M Mrs, 1949, Ag 20,11:6
Russell, Kate S Mrs, 1939, O 2,17:6
Russell, Katherine, 1937, N 13,19:2
Russell, Katherine L, 1951, S 5,31:1
Russell, Kenneth L, 1967, My 28,61:1
Russell, L E Dr, 1917, Ag 3,9:2
Russell, L W Judge, 1903, F 4,9:5
Russell, Lady, 1941, F 10,17:5
Russell, Lawrence, 1938, Mr 18,19:5
Russell, Lee M, 1943, My 18,23:5
Russell, Leroy, 1953, Ap 7,29:5
Russell, Lewis, 1961, N 16,39:4; 1965, Ap 18,80:7
Russell, Lillian (funl), 1922, Je 8,19:4
Russell, Lindsay, 1949, O 9,95:3
Russell, Lord, 1946, D 22,41:2
Russell, Louis Arthur, 1925, S 7,11:6
Russell, Louis J, 1966, Ja 21,48:1
Russell, Louisa, 1940, Ag 7,19:5
Russell, Lucius T (por), 1948, Je 22,25:1
Russell, Luis, 1963, D 14,27:2
Russell, Lyman E, 1959, D 16,41:4
Russell, Margaret C, 1947, Ap 13,60:1
Russell, Marie L, 1946, Jl 4,19:6
Russell, Marshall H Mrs, 1944, Jl 5,17:4; 1947, D 7, 76:2
Russell, Martha Le Barron, 1911, Ag 21,9:7
Russell, Mary Holbrook, 1968, D 3,47:2
Russell, Mary M Mrs, 1942, Ag 27,19:4
Russell, Matthew Rev, 1912, S 13,9:6
Russell, Maurice E, 1950, Ja 26,27:5
Russell, May Irene Mrs, 1925, Ag 24,13:5
Russell, McKay Mrs, 1950, Ja 19,28:4
Russell, Meigs B, 1952, F 12,27:2
Russell, Milton D, 1956, S 24,27:3
Russell, Morgan, 1953, My 31,72:1
Russell, Nancy C Mrs, 1940, My 25,17:4
Russell, Ned (funl, N 6,37:4), 1958, N 3,37:3
Russell, Nelson V, 1951, O 14,88:5
Russell, Neville N Mrs, 1937, F 7,II,9:2
Russell, Norman, 1965, F 1,23:2
Russell, Norman F S, 1954, F 25,31:5
Russell, Odo, 1884, Ag 26,5:2
Russell, Oscar V, 1955, Je 6,27:5
Russell, Paris S, 1948, Jl 13,27:2
Russell, Parvin M Sr, 1954, Je 16,31:4
Russell, Patrick W, 1948, Mr 31,25:2
Russell, Paul, 1960, Ag 31,29:1
Russell, Paul G, 1963, Ap 7,86:2
Russell, Paul S, 1950, Ja 9,25:1
Russell, Percy, 1949, Ja 1,13:2
Russell, Phil J, 1939, S 23,17:4
Russell, Phil W (por), 1941, Ag 25,15:5
Russell, Pierce H, 1952, Je 4,27:1
Russell, Pierce H Mrs, 1946, S 7,15:2
Russell, R Blake, 1966, My 27,43:2
Russell, Ralph P, 1954, Ja 1,23:5
Russell, Richard B (por), 1938, D 4,60:4
Russell, Richard B Mrs, 1953, Ag 31,18:3
Russell, Richard G, 1950, F 7,27:4
Russell, Richard H, 1949, Je 23,27:4
Russell, Richard J, 1943, F 7,49:3
Russell, Robert E, 1957, My 16,31:3
Russell, Robert H, 1950, Ag 23,29:3
Russell, Robert L, 1923, Mr 24,13:5; 1955, Ja 19,27:3
Russell, Robert L Jr (funl), 1965, Je 17,22:1
Russell, Robert M, 1958, Ap 23,33:5
Russell, Robert P, 1965, My 29,27:3
Russell, Robert V Rev Dr, 1968, S 17,94:3
Russell, Roy E, 1959, Mr 9,29:1
Russell, Ruth A, 1948, N 12,23:1
Russell, S P, 1881, Ap 27,5:4
Russell, Salem Towne, 1914, D 5,13:6
Russell, Sally, 1951, O 21,92:5
Russell, Samuel B, 1938, D 29,19:1
Russell, Samuel M, 1946, O 30,27:2
Russell, Samuel R, 1943, Jl 9,17:1
Russell, Sarah B, 1955, D 3,17:5
Russell, Scott, 1882, Jl 4,2:3
Russell, Sol Smith, 1902, Ap 29,9:5
Russell, Sol Smith Mrs, 1923, Ja 4,19:4
Russell, Stanley A, 1959, Ja 1,31:5
Russell, Stanley A Mrs, 1951, S 17,21:4
Russell, T Edward, 1960, F 27,19:5
Russell, T H, 1881, N 21,3:7
Russell, T Macdonald Mrs, 1962, N 11,88:8
Russell, Thomas, 1911, N 8,13:5; 1938, Ap 9,17:6
Russell, Thomas A, 1940, D 30,17:3
Russell, Thomas E, 1946, N 3,63:2
Russell, Thomas H (por), 1947, Ap 6,60:5
Russell, Thomas H, 1947, S 9,31:4; 1955, Mr 7,27:3
Russell, Thomas Sir, 1920, My 3,13:4
Russell, Thomas W (Russell Pasha), 1954, Ap 11, 86:3
Russell, Victor H, 1946, Ag 3,15:5
Russell, Vincent L, 1950, Ja 28,13:4
Russell, W Duncan, 1959, Jl 19,68:5
Russell, W E, 1896, Jl 17,5:3
Russell, W H, 1885, My 20,5:4
Russell, Waldo P, 1947, Ag 14,23:5
Russell, Walter, 1963, My 20,31:3
Russell, Walter B, 1940, Jl 15,15:4
Russell, Walter C, 1954, Mr 11,31:3
Russell, Walter G, 1943, Ja 20,19:4
Russell, Walter S, 1955, N 9,33:4
Russell, Walter W, 1949, Ap 22,23:1
Russell, Whitney C, 1963, Ag 9,23:4
Russell, William (Duke of Bedford), 1872, My 28,1:5
Russell, William, 1940, Ag 13,19:5
Russell, William A, 1949, Jl 9,13:5; 1956, Mr 21,37:3
Russell, William C, 1944, My 24,19:3
Russell, William Clarke, 1911, N 9,11:5
Russell, William D (por), 1937, Ja 6,23:2
Russell, William D Mrs, 1955, N 28,31:3
Russell, William E Mrs, 1960, My 5,35:2
Russell, William F, 1946, Ap 2,28:3; 1953, Jl 9,25:1
Russell, William F (mem ser, Ap 13,25:2), 1956, Mr 27,35:1
Russell, William G, 1953, Ja 18,92:4
Russell, William H (funl, Ag 9,7:6), 1907, Jl 25,7:5
Russell, William H, 1947, D 17,29:5; 1953, Jl 4,11:6; 1958, O 20,29:4
Russell, William H C, 1942, My 26,21:3
Russell, William H Mrs, 1944, Je 22,19:5
Russell, William Henry Rev, 1912, My 28,11:4
Russell, William Hepburn, 1911, N 22,13:3
Russell, William Howard Sir, 1907, F 11,9:5
Russell, William I, 1949, N 1,27:6
Russell, William Ingraham, 1925, Mr 6,19:5
Russell, William J, 1942, O 14,25:1; 1963, Jl 3,25:1
Russell, William L, 1945, Ja 31,21:5; 1951, Ap 1,92:1
Russell, William Maj, 1914, Je 18,11:6
Russell, William P, 1959, S 17,39:6
Russell, William R, 1946, D 25,29:4
Russell, William Walker, 1924, Ap 7,17:6
Russell, Wortington S, 1938, Ag 16,19:5
Russell, Zenas H, 1955, Ja 16,93:2
Russell-Murray, John, 1945, Ja 9,19:4
Russett, James J, 1941, My 10,15:6
Russhon, Annie G Mrs, 1950, Je 26,27:2
Russhon, Joseph, 1942, Jl 14,19:5
Russian Grand Duchess, Maria Nicolaievna, 1876, F 22,5:6
Russo, Amedeo, 1953, O 30,23:2
Russo, Anthony, 1948, Je 15,28:2; 1950, Jl 27,25:3
Russo, Carmine, 1945, Mr 10,17:3
Russo, Dan J, 1943, D 15,27:3
Russo, Danny, 1956, S 6,25:3
Russo, Dominick, 1954, S 25,15:4
Russo, Dominick V Sr, 1955, N 10,35:4
Russo, Francis A, 1949, S 28,27:3
Russo, Frank, 1950, S 21,31:2
Russo, Frank A, 1964, N 5,45:4
Russo, Fritz, 1943, Ja 9,13:5
Russo, George J, 1963, N 12,41:4
Russo, Gioacchina, 1953, My 9,19:3
Russo, Giuseppe, 1955, Mr 3,27:5
Russo, James, 1949, Je 21,25:1; 1955, Jl 14,23:5
Russo, Jerry A, 1951, Mr 1,27:1
Russo, Jimmy, 1949, Ap 6,29:5
Russo, Joseph, 1947, Ap 6,60:1; 1947, N 5,27:4; 1959, S 19,23:5
Russo, Leonardo Rev, 1925, F 19,19:5
Russo, Marie R, 1960, F 13,19:5
Russo, Mario, 1952, Ag 18,17:3
Russo, Michele, 1937, O 31,II,11:3
Russo, Nic, 1902, Ap 2,9:7
Russo, Ralph, 1947, Ag 18,17:5; 1952, Ja 17,27:4
Russo, Thomas S, 1938, O 24,17:6
Russo, Vincent P, 1954, O 14,29:3
Russoman, Emil, 1945, O 30,19:5
Russomanno, Joseph, 1941, Mr 29,15:4
Russotto, Alex C, 1953, Mr 26,31:4
Russotto, Irving H, 1939, Ap 9,III,7:1
Russp, Paul, 1942, My 7,19:2
Russum, Raymond C, 1945, Mr 15,23:3
Russum, Thomas B, 1938, Ja 15,15:5
Russum, William A R, 1942, Ag 25,23:4
Rust, Albert C Mrs, 1943, S 17,21:4
Rust, Alfred H, 1966, Jl 7,37:1
Rust, Carl E, 1951, Ja 4,29:2
Rust, Carl H, 1951, Ag 20,19:4
Rust, David L, 1940, N 4,19:4
Rust, Donald E, 1961, Ja 13,27:1
Rust, E J Lee, 1939, Mr 4,15:1
Rust, Edward Gray, 1925, D 26,15:6
Rust, Edward H, 1944, F 11,19:5
Rust, Ellsworth M, 1946, Jl 27,17:4
Rust, Fred W, 1949, Mr 8,25:2
Rust, Harold N, 1938, Jl 30,13:5
Rust, Harry C, 1939, Ja 23,13:2
Rust, Harry L, 1938, Ag 23,17:6
Rust, Horatio Nelson Maj, 1906, N 15,9:6
Rust, John D, 1954, Ja 22,27:1
Rust, Murray, 1954, Ja 30,17:3
Rust, Peter C Gen, 1913, Mr 16,IV,7:4
Rust, William, 1949, F 4,8:5
Rust, William F, 1940, O 30,23:4
Rust, William Mrs, 1952, Jl 24,27:4
Rust, William R, 1942, F 17,21:5
Rust-Oppenheim, August, 1967, F 2,35:1
Rustad, Brice M, 1965, Je 3,35:4
Rustako, Joseph J, 1950, S 17,105:1
Ruste, Martha Mrs, 1955, My 15,86:4
Rustem, Pasha, 1895, N 20,5:1
Rustem Bey, Alfred, 1934, S 25,21:1
Rustgard, John, 1950, F 14,25:3
Rustin, Henry, 1906, F 28,9:7
Ruston, Charles, 1954, Je 13,88:3
Ruston, Hiram H, 1946, Jl 17,23:5
Ruston, J E, 1932, F 2,25:1
Ruston, Martha, 1950, Jl 11,31:4
Ruston, Monteath, 1957, Ag 20,27:2
Rustvedt, Sigurd B, 1954, O 6,25:4
Ruszas, Joseph, 1956, Ap 27,27:5
Ruszkiewicz, Joseph C, 1937, O 12,25:4
Ruszkiewicz, Roselia Mrs, 1940, Ag 10,13:1
Ruta, G, 1932, O 27,19:1
Rutan, Albert C, 1951, Mr 1,27:3
Rutan, Charles H, 1914, D 18,13:5
Rutan, Frank C, 1922, Ap 28,17:6
Rutan, Harold D, 1956, N 15,35:5
Rutan, Melville M, 1950, O 6,27:3
Rutan, Richard, 1947, D 3,29:4
Rutan, T B, 1903, Ja 7,9:5
Rutan, Walter, 1937, D 29,21:3
Rutchick, Sol, 1965, O 19,43:3
Rute, Harry, 1950, F 15,27:1
Rutelli, Mario, 1941, N 6,23:6
Rutenberg, Pinhas, 1942, Ja 4,48:3
Ruter, John H, 1938, Je 6,17:2
Rutgers, Nicholas G, 1937, O 19,25:4; 1951, N 22,31:2
Rutgers, Nicholas G Mrs, 1961, N 24,31:2
Rutgers, Victor H, 1945, Ap 29,37:1
Ruth, Charles A, 1938, Mr 14,15:5
Ruth, Charles H, 1949, O 21,25:4
Ruth, Christian W, 1941, My 28,25:5
Ruth, David N Mrs, 1952, Ag 6,21:2
Ruth, Edgar K, 1949, My 20,27:3
Ruth, Elmer Sr, 1948, Mr 26,21:1
Ruth, Henry S, 1956, Je 9,17:5
Ruth, Jacob, 1937, Ag 27,19:5

Ruth, John N, 1954, Mr 8,27:4
Ruth, Sanderson S, 1951, N 27,31:4
Ruth, Stephen E, 1948, Mr 12,23:2
Ruth Clare, Sister, 1962, Ag 7,29:3
Ruth Kreuzer, Sister, 1945, My 11,19:3
Ruthberg, Oscar Mrs (cor, Jl 25,17:1), 1959, Jl 23, 27:2
Ruthenberg, C E, 1927, Mr 3,23:3
Ruthenburg, Ottelia T Mrs, 1938, S 16,21:4
Ruthenburg, Walter J, 1965, S 11,27:3
Rutherfoord, John, 1942, N 8,51:5
Rutherford, A G (por), 1941, Ag 11,13:6
Rutherford, Alex C, 1941, Je 12,23:2
Rutherford, Alex H, 1955, Jl 23,17:4
Rutherford, Forest, 1938, F 2,19:5
Rutherford, Forrest S, 1948, S 15,32:3
Rutherford, Frank P, 1942, Ag 4,20:2
Rutherford, Franklin B, 1937, D 10,25:3
Rutherford, George A, 1950, D 23,15:4
Rutherford, George H, 1966, Ag 5,31:2
Rutherford, George P Mrs, 1943, D 16,27:4
Rutherford, Henry H, 1951, Ja 20,15:6
Rutherford, Isabella Brooks Mrs, 1903, Jl 29,7:6
Rutherford, J C, 1866, Ag 24,2:6
Rutherford, J Kenneth, 1960, F 11,36:1
Rutherford, James W, 1939, F 28,20:3
Rutherford, John, 1923, O 17,19:3
Rutherford, John B, 1953, Jl 21,23:4
Rutherford, John C, 1938, O 16,45:2
Rutherford, John M, 1966, Ag 17,36:5
Rutherford, John M L Mrs, 1946, Ja 24,21:5
Rutherford, Joseph F, 1942, Ja 11,46:3
Rutherford, Lady, 1954, Ja 22,27:2
Rutherford, Livingston, 1940, O 26,15:2
Rutherford, Lord, 1937, O 20,1:2
Rutherford, Louis P, 1947, Je 4,27:2
Rutherford, Mark (Wm Hale White), 1913, Mr 16, IV,7:4
Rutherford, Martin C, 1942, O 4,53:2
Rutherford, Morris, 1944, Ja 9,42:4
Rutherford, Morris Mrs, 1951, Jl 15,60:5
Rutherford, Paul, 1959, Mr 7,21:3
Rutherford, Raymond H Mrs, 1958, Je 28,17:5
Rutherford, Richard George Mrs, 1916, O 14,11:3
Rutherford, Robbins S, 1951, Mr 26,23:4
Rutherford, Robert A Mrs, 1937, S 11,17:4
Rutherford, Robert C Mrs, 1956, Ja 17,33:1
Rutherford, S, 1932, F 5,6:1
Rutherford, Thomas A, 1955, D 24,13:3
Rutherford, Villa, 1922, S 25,15:6
Rutherford, Walter, 1915, Ag 1,15:6
Rutherford, Walter E, 1959, S 15,39:4
Rutherford, William J, 1949, F 26,15:5
Rutherford, William T, 1940, S 19,23:5
Rutherford, Winthrop, 1944, Mr 21,19:3
Rutherford, Winthrop Mrs, 1917, Je 21,13:4
Rutherfurd, Barbara Mrs, 1939, Ag 6,37:2
Rutherfurd, Douglas, 1968, D 7,47:4
Rutherfurd, John, 1965, My 21,35:1
Rutherfurd, John A, 1920, F 14,11:4
Rutherfurd, Lewis Morton, 1920, F 5,9:3
Rutherfurd, Robert W, 1904, Mr 4,9:6
Rutherfurd, Winthrop Mrs, 1948, Ag 1,56:6
Ruthford, S W Col, 1867, Ap 22,1:7
Ruthman, Adolph G, 1960, My 2,29:4
Ruthrauff, Wilbur B, 1941, Mr 14,21:5
Ruthven, John, 1939, My 4,23:3
Ruthven, Lady, 1885, Ap 25,3:5
Rutkins, Harry B, 1962, Jl 26,27:1
Rutkowski, Albert, 1945, D 8,17:4
Rutkowski, Miecislas de, 1941, Ap 6,48:5
Rutland, Dowager Duchess of, 1938, F 18,12:5
Rutland, Duke of (Jno James Robert Manners), 1906, Ag 5,9:6
Rutland, Duke of (Hy Jno Brinsley), 1925, My 9,15:5
Rutland, Duke of, 1940, Ap 22,17:5
Rutland, Violet Dowager Duchess, 1937, D 28,21:2
Rutland, William Mrs, 1952, F 7,27:2
Rutledge, Alice J Mrs, 1940, Ag 24,13:6
Rutledge, Charles D, 1941, Ja 31,19:2
Rutledge, Edward B, 1947, Ag 19,23:5
Rutledge, F A Bishop, 1866, N 15,2:5
Rutledge, Frank E, 1952, Ap 21,21:2
Rutledge, Fred J, 1957, O 18,23:1
Rutledge, George, 1940, S 22,49:3
Rutledge, J Flemming (por), 1955, Je 4,15:3
Rutledge, J Howard, 1959, F 9,29:3
Rutledge, Jack Mrs, 1953, N 19,31:3
Rutledge, John J, 1946, Jl 28,40:3
Rutledge, Joseph B, 1949, Ap 9,17:4
Rutledge, Joseph L, 1957, Mr 14,29:5
Rutledge, Joseph N, 1944, O 13,19:3
Rutledge, Ormsby T, 1949, N 11,25:3
Rutledge, Paul W Mrs, 1952, Ag 6,21:2
Rutledge, R L, 1939, Ag 28,19:4
Rutledge, Richard, 1940, Ap 10,25:4
Rutledge, Richard E, 1942, Mr 7,17:5
Rutledge, Sallie Mrs, 1922, My 4,19:6
Rutledge, Samuel A, 1941, Ag 16,15:2
Rutledge, Somers M, 1954, D 20,29:4
Rutledge, Thomas G, 1963, Je 23,29:8
Rutledge, Wiley B, 1949, S 11,1:2
Rutledge, William E, 1947, Jl 21,17:3
Rutledge, William P, 1950, Mr 9,29:3
Rutledge-Smith, Albert, 1952, Je 19,27:3
Rutquist, Arne, 1952, Jl 25,17:5
Rutsky, Morton S, 1952, S 21,89:2
Rutstein, Harry Mrs, 1949, Jl 1,19:4
Rutstein, Jacob, 1946, F 28,23:2
Rutstein, Leo Mrs, 1955, Ag 4,25:4
Rutstein, Louis M, 1968, Ap 30,47:1
Ruttan, George R, 1939, Ag 8,17:5
Rutten, John Rev, 1925, Ag 19,19:7
Ruttenber, Edward M, 1907, D 6,11:4; 1957, D 19,31:5
Ruttenberg, Benjamin A, 1964, Ag 25,33:1
Ruttenberg, Nelson, 1959, S 13,83:3
Rutter, Frank V P, 1937, Ap 19,21:6
Rutter, Frederick P, 1949, Je 25,13:2
Rutter, J H, 1885, Je 13,5:3
Rutter, J H Mrs, 1885, Je 13,5:3
Rutter, Joseph D Col, 1968, D 16,47:6
Rutter, Joseph W, 1957, Ag 23,19:4
Rutter, Josiah B, 1951, Ja 29,19:4
Rutter, Mary E H Mrs, 1941, Ap 16,23:5
Rutter, Mary E H Mrs (will), 1942, Mr 25,23:5
Rutter, N Edward C, 1947, Ap 16,25:2
Rutter, Owen, 1944, Ag 4,13:6
Rutter, Richard A Mrs, 1948, N 11,27:4
Rutter, William I Jr, 1952, My 13,30:1
Rutter, William M, 1955, D 2,27:5
Rutter, William W, 1937, Ag 26,21:3
Ruttkay, George, 1955, O 22,19:2
Ruttledge, Hugh, 1961, N 10,35:1
Ruttledge, Patrick J, 1952, My 9,23:4
Rutty, Charles P, 1954, Jl 14,27:2
Rutz, Andrew J, 1938, F 28,15:2
Rutz, Edward D, 1948, Je 22,25:5
Rutz, Frank A, 1941, F 25,23:4
Rutz, John, 1923, F 12,13:5
Rutzen, Albert de Sir, 1913, S 23,11:7
Rutzler, Enoch, 1908, Mr 3,7:5
Ruutz-Rees, Caroline, 1954, F 16,25:1
Ruvane, Joseph J, 1961, S 15,33:2
Ruvolo, Peter H, 1943, Ja 29,19:2
Ruwe, Edward C, 1957, F 7,27:1
Ruwe, Horace A, 1940, S 13,23:5
Ruwol, Gustav A, 1952, Mr 26,29:2
Ruxton, Edgar T, 1952, N 16,89:1
Ruxton, Edward J, 1956, N 8,39:4
Ruxton, Philip, 1945, Ja 9,19:1
Ruxton, William V C, 1958, O 10,31:1
Ruygrok, Leo, 1944, Ja 5,17:3
Ruysdael, Basil, 1960, O 12,39:1
Ruzicka, D J, 1960, O 1,19:6
Ruzicka, Joseph F, 1957, O 5,17:3
Ruzicka, Stevan, 1950, Ag 4,21:2
Ryablov, Mikhail F, 1954, O 9,17:2
Ryall, Ernest L, 1958, Ap 23,33:1
Ryall, Eugene F, 1953, Mr 7,16:6
Ryall, John M, 1938, Ja 26,23:2
Ryall, W B (W Bolitho), 1930, Je 4,27:3
Ryan, A C, 1927, Je 24,23:3
Ryan, Abraham H Col, 1903, D 30,7:2
Ryan, Abram, 1941, S 19,24:3
Ryan, Adrian J Mrs, 1946, Jl 18,25:6
Ryan, Agnes Gonzaga Mother, 1917, Je 16,11:4
Ryan, Agnes L, 1955, Ag 23,23:5
Ryan, Allan A (por), 1940, N 27,23:1
Ryan, Allan A Mrs, 1949, O 12,30:5
Ryan, Ambrose A, 1968, Ag 1,31:5
Ryan, Andrew W, 1960, Jl 21,27:1
Ryan, Anna B Mrs, 1955, D 3,17:6
Ryan, Anna Maria Mrs, 1925, D 31,15:5
Ryan, Anne, 1954, Ap 18,89:1
Ryan, Anne C, 1959, Ag 5,27:3
Ryan, Arthur J, 1960, O 30,87:1
Ryan, Arthur R, 1951, Jl 25,23:3
Ryan, B, 1878, D 4,3:2
Ryan, Basil A (will, My 25,13:8), 1946, My 13,21:4
Ryan, Belle M, 1949, Mr 28,21:5
Ryan, Ben (Bennett A Ryan), 1968, Jl 6,21:4
Ryan, Benvenute, 1953, Jl 4,11:7
Ryan, Bessie, 1948, Ap 27,25:1
Ryan, Byford, 1924, Ap 23,21:4
Ryan, C Denis, 1958, N 19,37:1
Ryan, C E, 1939, Je 5,19:3
Ryan, Charles, 1951, Ja 16,29:5
Ryan, Charles B, 1943, Jl 22,19:1
Ryan, Charles E, 1943, Ja 12,24:2; 1952, Mr 13,29:5
Ryan, Charles F, 1950, Ag 20,76:2
Ryan, Charles G, 1937, O 30,19:3
Ryan, Charles M, 1941, F 16,41:2
Ryan, Charles W Jr, 1954, My 27,27:3
Ryan, Charlotte, 1946, Ja 16,23:2
Ryan, Clarence C, 1956, Mr 15,31:5
Ryan, Clarke S (funl, S 16,29:6), 1954, S 13,23:3
Ryan, Clendenin J (final est acctg), 1961, Jl 7,25:4
Ryan, Clendenin J Mrs, 1946, Ja 9,40:4
Ryan, Columbus, 1882, Ap 5,2:7
Ryan, Cornelius J, 1967, Mr 25,23:2
Ryan, Cyril C, 1966, Ja 15,27:6
Ryan, Daniel E, 1965, Ap 3,29:5
Ryan, Daniel H, 1945, Ap 28,15:2
Ryan, Daniel J, 1943, N 10,23:2
Ryan, Daniel L, 1951, S 11,29:3
Ryan, Daniel P, 1949, Ja 25,23:4
Ryan, Daniel R, 1961, Ap 9,86:5
Ryan, Daniel S, 1950, My 16,31:5
Ryan, David A, 1953, Ja 17,15:4
Ryan, David C, 1952, S 13,8:2
Ryan, David F, 1954, My 24,27:3
Ryan, David L, 1949, F 21,23:4
Ryan, Dennis J, 1954, Ja 13,31:1
Ryan, Donald E, 1943, Ap 25,34:6
Ryan, Dorothy A, 1946, F 16,13:3
Ryan, E G, 1880, O 20,8:6
Ryan, Edgar E, 1952, F 17,86:4
Ryan, Edith G, 1961, Jl 1,17:3
Ryan, Edward A, 1946, S 24,29:4; 1964, N 19,39:5
Ryan, Edward F, 1921, O 13,15:4; 1956, N 5,31:5
Ryan, Edward J, 1940, Ap 2,25:2; 1943, D 6,23:3; 1952, My 2,25:2; 1953, F 5,23:3; 1960, F 6,19:5
Ryan, Edward R, 1946, D 25,29:5
Ryan, Edward S, 1948, D 18,19:3
Ryan, Edward Sir, 1875, Ag 25,1:4
Ryan, Edward W Col, 1923, S 21,4:7
Ryan, Edwin, 1960, Ap 6,41:2
Ryan, Edwin M, 1946, Mr 2,13:4
Ryan, Elizabeth A, 1939, D 15,25:1
Ryan, Elizabeth C Mrs, 1954, F 10,29:5
Ryan, Ella T, 1952, F 26,27:1
Ryan, Ellis W, 1966, Ag 12,31:3
Ryan, Elmer J, 1958, F 3,15:6
Ryan, Emma, 1948, My 11,25:3
Ryan, Emma H, 1952, Ag 15,15:2
Ryan, Emma H Mrs, 1957, S 1,56:4
Ryan, Eric J, 1962, Jl 13,23:2
Ryan, F H Mrs, 1937, S 9,48:4
Ryan, Francis, 1940, Mr 31,45:3
Ryan, Francis A, 1956, S 18,35:2; 1963, My 22,41:
Ryan, Francis C, 1943, F 25,21:2
Ryan, Francis J, 1943, Ag 27,17:6; 1944, Je 15,19: 1949, O 3,17:4; 1951, Ap 11,29:4; 1958, O 13,29: 1963, Jl 15,29:1
Ryan, Francis P, 1943, O 22,17:1
Ryan, Frank, 1951, Ap 27,23:4; 1951, Jl 26,21:5; 1 Mr 3,41:5
Ryan, Frank A (por), 1937, F 24,23:3
Ryan, Frank C, 1952, Je 19,27:5
Ryan, Frank H, 1954, N 5,21:2
Ryan, Frank J, 1947, Ag 13,23:2; 1949, Mr 13,76:7 1949, Je 19,68:4; 1955, Je 1,33:4; 1961, D 31,48:
Ryan, Frank P, 1955, F 18,22:1
Ryan, Frank W, 1950, Ap 8,13:4
Ryan, Franklin Mrs, 1943, D 5,64:4
Ryan, Fred M, 1945, Je 13,23:4
Ryan, Frederick B (por), 1955, D 1,35:1
Ryan, Frederick D, 1950, Mr 21,29:3
Ryan, Frederick Hamilton, 1918, O 28,11:2
Ryan, Frederick J, 1944, N 7,27:6
Ryan, Frederick R, 1952, O 16,29:3
Ryan, G P, 1877, D 7,5:5
Ryan, Gabriel J, 1952, S 18,29:4
Ryan, Gannon F, 1962, D 7,39:3
Ryan, George, 1951, Jl 5,25:5; 1964, Ja 11,23:5
Ryan, George E, 1940, Ag 22,20:2
Ryan, George F (will, Ag 18,6:6), 1949, Ap 12,2
Ryan, George F, 1957, O 6,84:7
Ryan, George J (por), 1949, O 5,29:1
Ryan, George J Mrs, 1957, Ag 26,23:4
Ryan, George W, 1939, N 7,25:3
Ryan, George W Mrs, 1947, S 3,25:2
Ryan, Gerald A, 1950, D 22,23:4
Ryan, Gerald H Sir, 1937, My 28,21:2
Ryan, Harry A, 1938, Je 7,23:2
Ryan, Harry J, 1950, O 3,31:4
Ryan, Harry W, 1953, Ag 1,11:5
Ryan, Heber H Sr, 1950, D 28,25:2
Ryan, Helen M, 1940, F 22,23:6
Ryan, Henrietta Mrs, 1940, My 12,49:1
Ryan, Henry M, 1955, Je 22,29:3
Ryan, Henry W, 1950, Je 21,27:1
Ryan, Herbert J Mrs, 1945, S 27,21:2
Ryan, Howard J, 1950, My 14,106:8
Ryan, Hubert W, 1958, N 7,28:5
Ryan, Ignatius, 1963, O 31,34:1
Ryan, J Barry Sr Mrs, 1947, Jl 28,15:2
Ryan, J D, 1933, F 12,1:2
Ryan, J Frank, 1952, O 29,29:4
Ryan, J Frank Mrs, 1938, D 11,61:1
Ryan, J Harold, 1961, Je 7,38:5
Ryan, Jack Mrs, 1952, Je 27,23:5
Ryan, James, 1913, Ja 6,9:4; 1941, O 12,53:1
Ryan, James A, 1949, My 20,27:3; 1949, S 15,27: 1950, S 24,105:1; 1956, Ja 15,93:1
Ryan, James B, 1949, Jl 7,26:2; 1952, S 18,31:7
Ryan, James Bp, 1923, Jl 3,13:5
Ryan, James C, 1968, F 20,47:2
Ryan, James E, 1947, Jl 4,13:4
Ryan, James F, 1910, N 24,11:2; 1956, Ap 21,17:
Ryan, James F Sr, 1953, Jl 14,27:5
Ryan, James H, 1939, My 2,23:4; 1947, N 24,23:1
Ryan, James H Mrs, 1945, D 1,23:3
Ryan, James J, 1944, Ja 24,17:3; 1948, N 13,15:4; 1956, Ja 20,23:3; 1956, Ag 30,25:5; 1964, S 23,4
Ryan, James J Mrs, 1960, N 23,29:1
Ryan, James J Sr Mrs, 1949, D 20,31:4
Ryan, James Mrs, 1949, Ag 8,15:3
Ryan, James P, 1939, Mr 17,21:3

Ryan, James T, 1954, Ag 22,92:1; 1968, Ap 24,47:2
Ryan, James W, 1953, D 9,11:3
Ryan, Jere F (por), 1948, Ap 3,15:1
Ryan, Jeremiah (por), 1937, Je 4,23:4
Ryan, Jeremiah D, 1922, N 28,21:3
Ryan, John, 1960, D 7,43:1
Ryan, John A (por), 1945, O 13,15:4
Ryan, John A, 1967, Ag 14,31:2
Ryan, John B, 1941, O 22,23:1; 1942, F 10,20:2; 1944, N 2,19:2; 1966, Ja 25,41:2
Ryan, John C, 1938, Jl 11,17:4; 1956, My 24,31:4
Ryan, John C (Blondy),(funl, D 2,43:4), 1959, N 29, 86:1
Ryan, John D, 1959, Ag 13,27:2
Ryan, John D Mrs, 1960, Je 7,35:4
Ryan, John E, 1938, D 17,15:4; 1947, Mr 18,27:1
Ryan, John E (por), 1949, O 1,13:4
Ryan, John F, 1937, O 2,21:5; 1938, F 25,17:2; 1941, Jl 10,19:4; 1942, Ag 29,15:5; 1943, Je 3,21:4; 1948, Mr 24,25:3; 1949, Ag 10,21:4; 1950, D 22,23:5
Ryan, John F Rev, 1924, My 5,15:2
Ryan, John G Mrs, 1952, F 27,27:3
Ryan, John H, 1948, Mr 27,13:4
Ryan, John J, 1924, My 28,23:4; 1937, Ja 8,19:2; 1937, S 16,25:5; 1938, Ag 29,13:4; 1942, Ja 24,17:2; 1942, My 9,13:2; 1943, Ja 3,38:6; 1943, O 2,13:2; 1944, N 29,23:4; 1946, Ap 3,25:4; 1947, My 1,25:1; 1949, Ap 9,17:5; 1950, Ja 20,25:2; 1950, Ja 30,17:3; 1950, Ap 9,84:5; 1950, Ap 17,23:3; 1952, O 14,31:2; 1953, O 16,27:3; 1953, O 17,15:3; 1955, O 22,19:7; 1957, Ap 9,33:4
Ryan, John J Jr, 1963, My 15,39:2
Ryan, John J Jr Mrs, 1947, My 11,60:6
Ryan, John J Mrs, 1945, F 6,19:1; 1948, My 20,29:2; 1954, Je 28,19:5
Ryan, John L, 1967, Mr 3,35:3
Ryan, John M (cor, S 2,15:3), 1940, S 1,21:3
Ryan, John N, 1938, F 11,23:5; 1951, Jl 11,23:4
Ryan, John P, 1940, Je 27,23:4; 1945, Ag 15,19:3; 1945, N 16,19:4; 1947, Jl 8,23:1; 1948, S 20,25:4
Ryan, John P J Com, 1918, S 9,13:2
Ryan, John T, 1937, Je 10,23:4; 1941, F 21,19:4; 1946, D 29,35:2
Ryan, John W, 1958, Jl 17,27:1
Ryan, John W Mrs, 1951, My 2,31:3
Ryan, Joseph A, 1956, N 2,27:4; 1957, N 17,87:1
Ryan, Joseph C, 1944, O 12,27:3
Ryan, Joseph D, 1963, S 23,29:3
Ryan, Joseph F, 1956, O 25,33:3
Ryan, Joseph J, 1920, N 26,13:4; 1951, O 7,87:1
Ryan, Joseph M, 1950, O 26,31:3; 1960, Jl 23,19:4
Ryan, Joseph P, 1953, N 10,31:3
Ryan, Joseph P (funl plans, Je 28,29:3; funl, Jl 2,29:2), 1963, Je 27,33:4
Ryan, Joseph T, 1952, F 21,27:3
Ryan, Joseph T Mrs, 1924, D 11,23:4; 1943, Jl 26,19:3
Ryan, Laurence, 1923, O 15,15:5
Ryan, Lawrence Brendan Capt (funl plans), 1968, Jl 11,87:3
Ryan, Lawrence F, 1960, F 11,35:4
Ryan, Leo E, 1953, Je 1,23:4
Ryan, Leo J, 1937, F 8,17:3
Ryan, Leo R, 1966, Je 28,42:2
Ryan, Leonard Osborne, 1953, F 26,25:2
Ryan, Lewis A, 1940, S 10,23:1
Ryan, Lewis C, 1961, My 11,37:1
Ryan, Lillian Mrs, 1911, S 30,13:4
Ryan, Lillie Eldridge Mrs, 1920, Ag 19,9:4
Ryan, Loretta E Mrs, 1952, Ja 24,27:2
Ryan, Lorne M, 1949, Ja 3,23:3
Ryan, M Edward, 1966, D 23,25:1
Ryan, Margaret (Sister M Eustelle), 1942, Ap 6,15:4
Ryan, Margaret Mrs, 1948, Ja 15,23:1
Ryan, Martha F, 1943, Ap 6,21:1
Ryan, Martin C, 1939, My 22,17:3
Ryan, Martin P, 1941, My 26,19:6
Ryan, Marvin, 1874, Ag 17,1:6
Ryan, Mary, 1948, O 3,67:4
Ryan, Mary C, 1959, N 16,31:1
Ryan, Mary E, 1938, Ap 23,15:2
Ryan, Mary H, 1947, Ag 27,23:3
Ryan, Mary J Mrs, 1937, Ag 11,23:4
Ryan, Mary T Mrs (will, Ag 17,17:4), 1937, Jl 3,15:5
Ryan, Mary V Sister, 1954, Je 19,15:4
Ryan, Matthew P, 1903, Ap 23,9:5
Ryan, Matthew R, 1959, Ja 1,31:2
Ryan, Matthew W, 1949, N 16,29:4
Ryan, Maud, 1949, O 29,33:5
Ryan, Maxwell D, 1950, Je 13,27:5
Ryan, Michael, 1909, My 19,9:5; 1915, N 7,21:5; 1953, D 9,11:7
Ryan, Michael A, 1949, Jl 11,17:5
Ryan, Michael C, 1964, Mr 13,33:5
Ryan, Michael J, 1943, S 8,24:2; 1951, S 22,17:5
Ryan, Michael J Rear-Adm, 1953, F 26,25:2
Ryan, Michael R, 1941, D 9,31:1
Ryan, Morgan M L, 1962, Jl 19,27:5
Ryan, Norman A, 1945, N 6,20:3
Ryan, O'Neil Mrs, 1967, Ap 2,93:1
Ryan, P J, 1947, F 11,27:4
Ryan, P Leon, 1957, N 7,35:5
Ryan, Patricia, 1949, F 19,15:3
Ryan, Patrick, 1925, N 8,5:1
Ryan, Patrick J, 1917, D 26,9:3; 1940, Mr 2,13:2; 1964, F 14,33:6
Ryan, Patrick J B, 1964, Je 1,29:4
Ryan, Patrick John Archbishop (funl, F 17,9:5), 1911, F 12,12:1
Ryan, Patrick L, 1961, Ja 23,23:3
Ryan, Patrick Mrs, 1965, Mr 24,43:1
Ryan, Patrick T Bp, 1937, Ap 16,23:3
Ryan, Patrick V, 1967, Mr 7,41:2
Ryan, Paul C, 1944, N 15,27:3
Ryan, Paul G, 1965, F 2,33:1
Ryan, Paul M, 1957, My 22,33:5
Ryan, Peter, 1921, D 28,15:5
Ryan, Peter J, 1950, N 2,31:1
Ryan, Philip H, 1945, D 19,25:2
Ryan, Ray, 1958, Ag 11,21:4
Ryan, Raymond F, 1958, S 11,33:4
Ryan, Reuben W, 1940, Ap 1,19:2
Ryan, Richard A, 1949, My 14,13:1
Ryan, Richard N, 1949, S 19,23:5
Ryan, Richard P, 1945, S 6,25:2
Ryan, Richard T Rev, 1937, N 19,23:4
Ryan, Richard W, 1943, Je 24,21:4
Ryan, Robert J, 1947, S 15,17:4
Ryan, Robert L, 1967, Jl 10,31:1
Ryan, Rogar Msgr, 1912, Ja 10,17:4
Ryan, Royal W Mrs, 1963, Je 12,43:1
Ryan, Rupert, 1952, Ag 27,27:4
Ryan, Russell E, 1948, D 11,30:3
Ryan, S F Rev, 1903, My 23,9:3
Ryan, S V Right Rev, 1896, Ap 11,3:7
Ryan, Sally (will, Ag 9,9:1), 1968, Je 30,52:3
Ryan, Samuel J, 1939, Ap 5,25:2
Ryan, Samuel Mrs, 1952, O 17,27:4
Ryan, Sarah Mrs, 1937, Ap 25,II,9:1
Ryan, Sophie, 1952, N 27,31:3
Ryan, Stanley M, 1957, Mr 10,89:1
Ryan, Stephen M, 1963, D 5,45:3
Ryan, Stephen V, 1942, N 3,23:6
Ryan, Stetson K, 1956, S 18,35:2
Ryan, Susan Mrs, 1925, Mr 28,15:4
Ryan, Sylvester A, 1966, S 4,64:6
Ryan, T Emmett, 1955, Je 7,33:5
Ryan, T F, 1928, N 24,1:3
Ryan, T G, 1936, My 25,19:2
Ryan, Terrence C, 1956, Jl 7,13:5
Ryan, Th, 1903, Mr 6,9:5
Ryan, Thomas, 1879, My 6,10:3; 1914, Ap 7,9:6; 1916, Ap 30,19:5; 1943, Je 19,13:2; 1948, Mr 13,15:6
Ryan, Thomas A, 1943, Ap 29,21:4
Ryan, Thomas F, 1943, Je 10,21:2; 1944, Jl 5,17:6; 1950, Ja 17,28:3; 1951, My 4,27:3; 1951, S 19,31:5; 1958, F 12,29:3
Ryan, Thomas F Rev, 1937, S 25,17:6
Ryan, Thomas F 2d, 1954, My 1,15:7
Ryan, Thomas Fortune, 1924, O 1,19:2
Ryan, Thomas Fortune Mrs, 1917, O 18,15:3
Ryan, Thomas H, 1938, F 9,19:2
Ryan, Thomas J, 1941, Je 29,33:1; 1947, Je 27,22:3; 1950, D 19,29:3; 1959, Mr 10,35:1
Ryan, Thomas J F, 1946, Ap 19,29:4
Ryan, Thomas J Jr, 1947, F 21,19:4
Ryan, Thomas Jefferson, 1968, N 11,47:2
Ryan, Thomas Joseph, 1921, Ag 2,9:4
Ryan, Thomas L L, 1953, Jl 31,19:5
Ryan, Thomas M, 1943, F 1,15:3
Ryan, Thomas Mrs, 1948, D 27,21:3
Ryan, Thomas P, 1907, D 26,7:5; 1957, Ja 24,29:4
Ryan, Timothy, 1945, Ja 13,11:5; 1956, Jl 19,27:3
Ryan, Timothy Jr, 1940, Jl 14,31:2
Ryan, Timothy Mrs, 1968, Ja 31,41:2
Ryan, Tommy (por), 1948, Ag 4,21:4
Ryan, Vincent J, 1951, N 12,25:1
Ryan, W D, 1934, Mr 15,24:1
Ryan, W M, 1902, Ap 23,9:1
Ryan, Walter A, 1942, Ja 5,2:6; 1948, S 4,15:6; 1962, O 26,32:1
Ryan, Walter B, 1967, D 25,21:2
Ryan, Walter G H, 1959, Ap 23,31:5
Ryan, Walter S, 1941, Ag 6,17:4; 1945, Mr 29,23:4
Ryan, Wilfred A, 1962, Mr 24,25:4
Ryan, Will C, 1942, My 9,13:3
Ryan, Will Carson Dr, 1968, Je 2,76:7
Ryan, William, 1921, Ag 29,11:4; 1924, S 8,15:2; 1925, F 19,19:5; 1940, N 8,21:3; 1956, Mr 4,88:4
Ryan, William A, 1941, Ja 16,21:5; 1947, N 1,15:2; 1950, N 21,31:4
Ryan, William B Sr, 1948, My 21,23:4
Ryan, William C, 1942, S 3,19:3
Ryan, William D, 1951, Ag 21,27:1
Ryan, William D Sr, 1949, N 18,29:2
Ryan, William F, 1952, Mr 29,15:1; 1956, D 30,32:5
Ryan, William F Mrs, 1951, Ag 6,21:5
Ryan, William H, 1938, N 11,25:3; 1939, N 19,38:7; 1945, F 20,19:4; 1957, O 2,33:4; 1961, N 14,39:2
Ryan, William H Jr, 1939, F 22,21:4
Ryan, William I, 1967, Jl 31,27:4
Ryan, William J, 1942, F 21,19:2; 1945, Ap 21,13:6; 1950, N 22,25:4; 1951, My 24,35:4; 1955, Mr 17, 45:4; 1956, Jl 14,15:4
Ryan, William J Jr, 1948, Mr 4,25:4
Ryan, William J Mrs, 1941, Mr 25,23:5
Ryan, William J Rev, 1937, Mr 25,25:6
Ryan, William K, 1906, O 9,7:5
Ryan, William M, 1938, Ja 5,21:2
Ryan, William P, 1958, D 3,37:4
Ryan, William R, 1944, F 16,17:1; 1951, D 22,15:3; 1955, S 17,15:4
Ryan, William T, 1943, Mr 9,23:2
Ryazanov, Vasily G, 1951, Jl 11,23:6
Ryazhskii, Georgii, 1952, O 23,31:4
Ryba, Adolph, 1954, Ap 11,86:5
Ryba, Jim, 1950, F 17,24:3
Ryba, Peter Mrs, 1950, Ja 26,27:4
Rybak, Francis J, 1951, O 31,29:3
Rybakoff, Nicholas P, 1963, Ap 10,39:5
Rybalko, P S (por), 1948, Ag 29,56:5
Rybb, Daniel, 1956, Jl 17,23:4
Ryberg, Victor, 1945, Ja 13,11:4
Rybicki, Edward C (por), 1946, Je 24,31:1
Rybkin, Piotr N, 1948, Ja 11,58:4
Rybner, Cornelius M Mrs, 1943, O 26,23:2
Rybner, Dagmar de C, 1965, Jl 24,21:3
Rybner, M C (por), 1929, Ja 22,29:1
Rybolt, W L, 1951, Ag 21,27:1
Ryburn, James F, 1951, D 29,11:4
Ryce, Lucius C, 1949, Ap 26,26:2
Rychman, Paul O, 1912, D 1,II,17:2
Ryckmans, Pierre, 1959, F 19,31:5
Rydberg, P A, 1931, Jl 26,II,4:3
Rydell, Alex B, 1958, F 15,17:3
Rydell, Louis, 1947, N 12,27:5
Rydell, Melville B, 1946, My 26,32:7
Rydell, Swen J, 1939, My 4,23:3
Ryden, George H, 1941, O 13,17:3
Ryden, Henning, 1938, D 28,26:5
Ryden, Roy W, 1956, Ag 21,29:4
Ryder, Adrian H, 1957, My 16,31:1
Ryder, Aimee T Mrs, 1963, Jl 21,65:1
Ryder, Albert P, 1917, Mr 29,13:5
Ryder, Alice A, 1954, Jl 1,25:3
Ryder, Andrew J, 1941, O 28,23:5
Ryder, Arthur W, 1938, Mr 22,21:5
Ryder, C H D, 1945, Jl 17,13:4
Ryder, Carroll D, 1947, Ja 23,23:2
Ryder, Charles A, 1951, Mr 30,24:2
Ryder, Charles Jr, 1958, Ag 8,19:5
Ryder, Charles K, 1956, Je 1,23:2
Ryder, Charles L, 1924, Mr 20,19:5
Ryder, Charles W, 1960, Ag 19,23:1
Ryder, Chauncey F, 1949, My 19,29:4
Ryder, Clarence W, 1943, D 11,15:1
Ryder, Clayton, 1954, O 28,35:6
Ryder, Clayton Mrs, 1948, Je 16,29:4
Ryder, Dudley Earl of Harrowby, 1882, N 21,5:2
Ryder, E Dean, 1952, N 30,88:7
Ryder, Earl A, 1948, N 29,23:4
Ryder, Edgar G, 1949, S 21,31:3
Ryder, Elisabeth A, 1941, Mr 16,44:6
Ryder, Ella Mrs, 1944, Jl 12,19:5
Ryder, Elmer A, 1949, Jl 23,11:5
Ryder, Everett Mrs, 1948, O 27,27:1
Ryder, George H, 1946, Ag 28,27:3
Ryder, H R, 1937, D 30,40:4
Ryder, Harrison M, 1950, Ja 6,21:2
Ryder, Henry D, 1950, Je 7,29:2
Ryder, Henry E, 1953, S 3,21:3
Ryder, James C, 1945, F 21,19:5
Ryder, John, 1947, Jl 22,23:1
Ryder, John A, 1953, Mr 14,15:2
Ryder, John H D (Earl of Harrowby), 1956, Mr 31, 15:6
Ryder, John L, 1957, Je 26,31:4
Ryder, John W, 1955, F 11,23:3
Ryder, Joseph S, 1947, Ap 14,27:4
Ryder, Laura E Mrs, 1942, S 21,15:4
Ryder, Mary E Mrs, 1961, S 7,35:3
Ryder, Maude C, 1954, Je 15,29:3
Ryder, Oliver A Dr, 1937, N 28,II,9:2
Ryder, Patrick J, 1907, Je 15,9:6
Ryder, Raymond R, 1948, Mr 16,27:3
Ryder, Samuel Mrs, 1955, Ap 27,31:4
Ryder, Stephen J, 1948, Mr 15,23:4
Ryder, Stephen M, 1946, S 2,17:3
Ryder, Thomas (will), 1939, N 17,13:4
Ryder, Thomas B, 1942, N 1,53:1
Ryder, Thomas F, 1962, N 7,39:2
Ryder, William, 1951, Je 27,19:6
Ryder, William C, 1956, O 28,88:2
Ryder, William L Mrs, 1943, S 25,15:2
Ryder, Worth, 1960, F 20,23:5
Rydgren, Gustave, 1948, My 13,25:5
Ryding, Herbert C, 1946, Ap 13,17:6
Rydstrom, Alvah W, 1948, Ag 30,25:2
Rydzinski, Felix S, 1947, O 5,71:1
Ryer, Alfred A, 1943, Ja 26,19:5
Ryer, Bertsill, 1944, Jl 27,17:1
Ryer, Fanny Mrs, 1953, N 11,31:1
Ryer, Frank E, 1946, N 24,79:4
Ryer, Girard, 1951, My 7,45:2
Ryer, Henry L, 1962, O 28,88:7
Ryer, J B Col, 1884, Ag 1,5:3
Ryer, John A, 1955, Je 14,29:4
Ryer, Thomas A, 1946, Mr 24,46:7
Ryer, Thomas J, 1903, D 17,9:4
Ryers, George M C, 1940, S 30,17:3

Ryers, L R Ex-Alderman, 1867, Ap 25,5:4
Ryerson, Abraham, 1943, D 1,21:5
Ryerson, Anna L Mrs, 1940, Ap 22,17:4
Ryerson, Carrie H Mrs, 1937, S 6,17:5
Ryerson, Egerton, 1882, F 20,5:4
Ryerson, George H, 1939, Je 18,37:2
Ryerson, George Sterling Maj-Gen, 1925, My 21,23:5
Ryerson, H G, 1879, Mr 20,5:4
Ryerson, Helen O Mrs, 1942, Ja 5,20:1
Ryerson, Ira, 1873, S 9,5:5
Ryerson, Joseph E, 1940, Jl 29,13:5
Ryerson, Joseph T (will, D 20,10:1), 1947, D 8,26:3
Ryerson, M A, 1932, Ag 12,15:5
Ryerson, Martin Ex-Judge (see also Je 12), 1875, Je 15,6:5
Ryerson, Mary M Mrs (will), 1939, N 30,18:5
Ryerson, Richard V, 1956, Ja 4,27:5
Ryerson, U Cutler, 1945, Ap 10,19:2
Rygel, John (por), 1955, O 20,36:1
Rygg, Andreas N, 1951, S 22,17:6
Ryker, George C, 1938, Ag 4,17:4
Rylance, Elmer A, 1964, Mr 7,23:6
Ryland, Alex F, 1941, S 18,25:4
Ryland, Edwin P, 1957, S 15,83:1
Ryland, John, 1937, Jl 31,15:3; 1938, N 26,16:2
Ryland, Robert K, 1951, N 11,90:5
Ryland, Samuel, 1941, S 27,17:3
Rylander, Charles A, 1948, S 3,19:4
Rylander, Paul N, 1952, N 30,31:2
Rylands, Peter, 1948, O 25,23:5
Ryle, Arthur Mrs, 1952, O 9,31:2
Ryle, Fred C, 1960, Mr 4,25:1
Ryle, Graham, 1946, Ag 15,25:3
Ryle, Herbert Edward, 1925, Ag 21,13:6
Ryle, J Joseph, 1960, D 6,37:3
Ryle, Jane F Mrs, 1944, My 1,17:1
Ryle, John F, 1958, Ja 3,21:4
Ryle, John J, 1933, F 16,19:4
Ryle, John J Sr, 1938, N 27,4:1
Ryle, Joseph P Mrs, 1958, Ag 9,13:6
Ryle, Thomas J, 1954, Ap 27,21:5
Ryle, W, 1881, N 6,7:4
Ryle, William, 1906, Mr 30,9:4
Ryley, James, 1946, D 23,23:3
Rylsky, Maxim F, 1964, Jl 26,56:2
Ryman, Herbert, 1954, My 28,23:2
Ryman, Leslie S Mrs, 1946, Mr 26,29:1
Rymer, Lyuba, 1961, Je 15,43:5
Rymon, Benjamin, 1947, D 14,78:4
Rynar, Joseph D, 1951, Je 10,93:2
Rynd, Charles E Dr, 1937, Ja 14,22:1
Rynd, Charles E Mrs, 1948, Ap 3,15:3
Rynders, Isaiah, 1885, Ja 14,1:7
Rynehart, Henry M, 1937, F 24,23:6
Ryner, Han, 1938, Ja 8,15:4
Ryniese, Harry, 1940, Ja 27,13:4
Rynne, Thomas, 1955, F 13,86:6
Ryno, Eleanor A, 1949, Mr 6,72:5
Ryno, George W, 1949, S 29,29:4
Ryno, Harry, 1950, N 17,28:2
Rynveld, Herman, 1956, Mr 19,31:1
Ryon, Augustus M, 1949, Je 10,28:2
Ryon, Henry, 1941, Ag 2,15:6
Ryon, Walter G, 1925, D 7,21:4
Rypins, Harold (por), 1939, Ag 26,15:3
Ryrie, Gordon A, 1953, Mr 12,27:4
Ryrie, Granville Maj-Gen, 1937, O 4,21:3
Rysavy, Frank, 1956, Jl 2,21:2
Rysiakiewcz, Stanislaus, 1950, Ja 31,23:4
Ryso, Ellis, 1908, Jl 12,9:6
Rystrom, Charles, 1939, Ag 7,15:5
Ryswick, Stephen, 1950, My 30,17:3
Ryther, Julie de, 1915, Mr 15,11:5
Ryti, Risto H, 1956, O 26,29:1
Ryttenberg, Madeline, 1957, O 4,13:1
Rytter, Aage L, 1961, F 13,27:4
Ryu, Shintaro, 1967, D 5,50:4
Ryweck, Charles Mrs, 1948, N 28,92:3
Ryzhov, Alex, 1950, D 17,85:1
Ryzymowski, Wincenty, 1950, My 3,29:5
Rzeckowska, Juliana Mrs, 1943, N 30,27:5

S

Sa Chen-ping, 1952, Ap 14,19:5
Saadi, Mohammed, 1962, F 25,88:6
Saafield, Albert G, 1959, F 10,33:2
Saal, Catherine P Mrs, 1950, Mr 21,32:2
Saal, Chris G, 1940, N 8,21:5
Saalberg, Jerome, 1945, Ja 8,17:5
Saalborn, Louis A, 1957, Je 21,25:3
Saalfield, Richard A, 1912, D 4,13:3
Saar, Adolph F, 1941, Jl 10,19:2
Saar, Louis V Dr, 1937, N 25,31:6
Saar, Oscar A, 1957, Ja 19,15:4
Saar, William, 1864, My 8,8:1
Saarbach, Louis, 1954, My 4,29:4
Saarinen, Eero, 1961, S 2,15:1
Saarinen, Eliel, 1950, Jl 3,15:3
Saarinen, Eliel Mrs (died Ap 21; not reptd), 1968, My 6,46:6
Saarup, fred C, 1947, D 11,33:1
Saas, Charles, 1949, F 21,23:5
Saathoff, George W, 1956, N 12,29:6
Saathoff, George W Mrs, 1948, S 18,17:4
Saavedra, Abdon, 1942, Ja 7,19:5
Saavedra, Juan B, 1939, Mr 3,24:2
Saavedra, Tomas de Baron, 1956, Ja 25,31:5
Saavedra Lamas, Carlos, 1959, My 6,39:4
Sabarts, Jaime, 1968, F 17,29:1
Sabata, Victor de, 1967, D 12,47:1
Sabatello, Joseph, 1940, Jl 1,19:4
Sabath, Adolph J, 1952, N 6,1:6
Sabath, Albert, 1950, O 6,27:3
Sabath, Joseph, 1956, My 4,25:1
Sabath, Joseph Mrs, 1955, My 27,23:2
Sabath, Rudolph, 1943, Mr 1,19:5
Sabatier, Paul, 1941, Ag 16,15:5
Sabatier, Raoul, 1939, D 16,17:1
Sabatini, Attilio B, 1952, Mr 11,27:3
Sabatini, Guglielmo, 1949, Ag 1,17:3
Sabatini, John C Mrs, 1964, Ja 5,92:7
Sabatini, Rafael, 1950, F 14,25:1
Sabatino, C Frank Dr, 1968, Ap 20,33:4
Sabatino, Carmela Mrs, 1956, Ja 6,24:6
Sabatino, John B, 1949, Ja 7,22:3
Sabatino, Nicholas S, 1963, D 24,17:4
Sabatino, Samuel V Mrs, 1959, Je 18,31:4
Sabattini, Amadeo, 1960, Mr 1,10:8
Sabattis, Joseph D, 1951, S 26,31:2
Sabatucci, Antonio, 1921, Ja 15,13:2
Sabbatino, Anth, 1948, Jl 6,23:1
Sabbatino, Anthony Mrs, 1943, My 13,21:3
Sabbatino, Louis, 1940, N 21,29:2
Sabbaton, Frederic A, 1949, O 13,27:5
Sabbia, John, 1943, Je 20,34:7
Sabel, Josephine, 1945, D 25,23:3
Saben, Mowry, 1950, O 8,104:8; 1950, O 26,16:3
Saberski, Leopold, 1944, My 11,19:5
Sabia, Cajetan, 1953, Je 6,17:3
Sabia, Theodore de Joly de, 1914, O 24,13:6
Sabin, Albert B Mrs, 1966, Ag 27,29:3
Sabin, Alvah H, 1940, Jl 12,15:4
Sabin, C H, 1933, O 12,25:1
Sabin, Charles Dwight, 1923, Jl 12,17:3
Sabin, D M, 1902, D 24,9:5
Sabin, Edwin A, 1942, Mr 14,15:4
Sabin, Ellen C, 1949, F 3,23:2
Sabin, Florence R, 1953, O 4,89:1
Sabin, Frances E, 1943, Ja 11,15:3
Sabin, H D, 1939, F 26,38:7
Sabin, Helen D Mrs, 1943, My 20,21:2
Sabin, Henry P, 1956, S 21,25:1
Sabin, Jesse, 1960, Ag 19,23:4
Sabin, Louis C, 1950, D 31,42:8
Sabin, Milton H, 1949, Ag 19,17:3
Sabin, Oliver C, 1914, Ja 15,9:5
Sabin, Stewart B, 1951, N 16,25:2
Sabin, Wallace A, 1937, D 10,25:3
Sabin, William, 1945, D 8,17:4
Sabine, E, 1883, Je 27,1:6
Sabine, E Sir, 1883, Jl 9,3:5
Sabine, Edward G, 1943, N 1,18:2
Sabine, George H, 1961, Ja 20,26:3
Sabine, Jane D, 1950, Mr 1,27:1
Sabine, Paul E, 1958, D 30,35:2
Sabine, Wallace C Dr, 1919, Ja 11,13:5
Sabine, William Tufnell Bp, 1913, Ag 12,7:6
Sabino, Antonio, 1946, Ag 15,25:3
Sabino Lopez, Manuel, 1947, Jl 1,25:3
Sabins, Mary A Mrs, 1923, Ja 18,15:5
Sabinus, Bro (J J Herbert), 1955, My 14,19:4
Sabio, Vincent, 1953, O 27,27:5
Sabiston, Colin J, 1938, Je 19,28:6
Sable, Catherine S Mrs, 1945, Ag 9,23:7
Sable, John C, 1949, N 19,17:5
Sable, Louis A, 1955, My 15,86:4
Sable, Thaddeus T, 1968, D 11,41:1
Sabline, Eugene, 1949, My 3,25:3
Sablosky, Abraham, 1959, My 26,35:4
Sablosky, Lewis, 1967, Ja 15,84:4
Sablosky, Thomas, 1955, Ap 20,33:2
Sablow, Joseph N, 1947, F 22,13:4
Sabo, Alexander J Mrs, 1947, F 11,27:4
Sabo, Ladis W, 1953, O 12,27:5
Saboi, Andrew, 1952, Mr 21,23:3
Sabol, John, 1950, Jl 26,25:2; 1953, F 14,17:2
Sabol, John G, 1950, F 28,29:4
Sabol, Joseph, 1949, Ag 14,69:1
Sabot, John, 1937, My 6,25:1
Sabourin, Edward E, 1947, D 8,25:5
Sabrella, Nicholas D, 1967, Ja 19,31:5
Sabry Pasha, Hassan, 1940, N 15,5:4
Sabsovich, H L Prof, 1915, Mr 24,11:6
Sabu (S Dastagir),(funl plans, D 4,47:4), 1963, D 3, 43:2
Sacasa, Joaquin N, 1941, Ap 6,48:6
Sacasa, Juan B (por), 1946, Ap 18,27:1
Sacasa, Roberto, 1961, F 13,27:5
Sacastin, Joseph, 1948, Mr 29,21:4
Saccamanno, Nicola, 1911, F 22,9:4
Saccardo, Pietro, 1903, N 20,9:6
Sacco, Anthony G, 1964, F 24,25:1
Sacco, Charles S, 1968, Ap 11,45:2
Sacco, Nicholas, 1947, Je 1,60:3
Saccone, Andrea, 1966, Je 13,39:4
Saccone, Giuseppe, 1939, Jl 7,17:2
Sacerdote, Edoardo, 1938, O 19,23:4
Sacerdote, Rene Mrs, 1954, My 30,44:6
Sachar, Samuel, 1949, Mr 19,15:4
Sacher, Frank, 1954, S 14,27:4
Sacher, Harry, 1963, My 23,37:2
Sacher, Louis, 1953, S 8,31:3
Saches, Leopold, 1961, Ap 5,37:3
Sachmatov, A A Dr, 1920, Ag 29,20:5
Sachnow, Morris, 1964, Mr 10,37:2
Sachs, Adolph, 1955, My 4,29:3
Sachs, Bernard (por), 1944, F 9,19:1
Sachs, Bernard Mrs, 1940, S 30,17:4
Sachs, Carl, 1962, Ap 21,20:8
Sachs, Charles N, 1959, O 18,86:5
Sachs, Curt, 1959, F 6,25:1
Sachs, Daniel M, 1943, O 24,45:1; 1967, Je 21,47:3
Sachs, David, 1961, F 3,25:5
Sachs, Eddie, 1964, My 31,V,1:3
Sachs, Emanuel, 1940, F 1,21:4
Sachs, Ernest, 1958, D 3,37:2
Sachs, George, 1960, O 31,31:2
Sachs, George M, 1939, Ap 6,25:6
Sachs, Hanns, 1947, Ja 11,19:4
Sachs, Henry, 1952, Ap 16,27:5
Sachs, Herman, 1940, N 13,23:3
Sachs, Isaac, 1942, D 19,19:5; 1945, F 1,23:5
Sachs, Israel (por), 1949, S 30,23:1
Sachs, Israel Mrs, 1960, Ap 14,37:3
Sachs, J, 1934, F 3,13:3
Sachs, Jacob, 1950, F 24,24:2
Sachs, Josef, 1949, Je 24,23:3
Sachs, Joseph, 1946, N 16,19:6
Sachs, Julius, 1942, Ja 17,17:3
Sachs, Leonard, 1942, O 28,23:5; 1964, F 27,31:2
Sachs, Louis, 1952, F 4,17:5
Sachs, Louis B, 1962, My 8,39:2
Sachs, Louis K, 1961, Ja 14,23:5
Sachs, Louis Mrs, 1942, N 8,53:2
Sachs, Ludwig, 1941, Ap 16,6:2
Sachs, Mary, 1960, Je 25,21:4
Sachs, Max, 1961, F 9,31:2
Sachs, Melville F (will, Jl 4,21:7), 1946, Je 18,25:4
Sachs, Michael, 1952, Ag 12,19:5
Sachs, Morris B, 1957, S 24,35:1
Sachs, Morris Nelson Mrs, 1968, Ja 6,29:4
Sachs, Nathan S, 1956, My 7,27:3
Sachs, Nathaniel L, 1967, O 14,27:1
Sachs, Paul J, 1965, F 19,35:1
Sachs, Paul J Mrs, 1960, D 26,23:4
Sachs, Phil, 1953, O 2,21:2
Sachs, Rosa Mrs, 1940, F 27,21:5
Sachs, Samuel, 1954, F 5,19:2
Sachs, Samuel J, 1959, Mr 10,35:3
Sachs, Samuel Mrs, 1949, Ap 28,31:6
Sachs, Teviah, 1959, Jl 22,28:1
Sachs, Wulf, 1949, Je 24,23:5
Sachtleben, Arthur F, 1953, F 16,35:2
Sacia, C, 1880, Ap 21,8:2
Sack, Alex N, 1955, My 31,27:3
Sack, Benjamin, 1966, F 13,84:7
Sack, David, 1958, Ja 16,30:1
Sack, Isidor, 1961, My 26,33:3
Sack, Isidor Mrs, 1957, Mr 25,25:4
Sack, Israel, 1959, My 5,33:1
Sack, Leo R, 1956, Ap 17,31:5
Sack, Nathaniel, 1966, Jl 5,37:3
Sackersdorff, Augustus Count, 1908, Ag 26,7:6
Sackerson, Charles M, 1948, S 15,31:4
Sacket, D B Gen, 1885, Mr 9,5:6
Sacket, Harry, 1950, My 18,29:1
Sackett, Albert B, 1905, S 11,7:7
Sackett, Albert H, 1939, My 6,17:3
Sackett, Augustine, 1914, My 11,11:6
Sackett, Charles T, 1946, Ap 13,17:3
Sackett, Clarence, 1938, Ag 18,19:6
Sackett, Edward T, 1953, Ja 13,27:3
Sackett, Franklin W, 1941, Mr 18,23:2
Sackett, Frederic M Mrs, 1948, D 20,25:5
Sackett, Frederick M (por), 1941, My 19,17:3
Sackett, George S, 1962, D 7,34:3
Sackett, George T, 1951, O 25,29:5
Sackett, George V, 1865, Je 18,4:4
Sackett, Harry P, 1939, F 17,19:2
Sackett, Helen L, 1941, Mr 15,17:2
Sackett, James L, 1940, Je 23,31:2
Sackett, Jeanette E Mrs, 1952, Ag 18,17:1
Sackett, John B, 1937, Je 23,25:4
Sackett, Marion Mrs, 1921, F 16,9:6
Sackett, Ray P, 1955, Mr 6,89:1
Sackett, Robert L (por), 1946, O 7,31:3
Sackett, Sheldon F, 1968, S 3,43:2
Sackett, Stephen J, 1951, Ja 3,27:2
Sackett, W E, 1926, N 19,25:3
Sackett, William L, 1945, Mr 30,15:3
Sackett, William P, 1946, D 7,21:4
Sackheim, Max B Mrs, 1948, D 13,23:5
Sackin, David, 1963, S 17,35:4
Sacking, Mae, 1951, S 5,31:4
Sackley, John B Jr, 1947, N 23,75:1
Sackman, Charles, 1946, My 19,42:2
Sackman, Hannah, 1946, Ja 8,23:3
Sackman, Harry, 1951, Je 1,15:1
Sackrider, Rosabelle, 1943, Je 3,21:3
Sacks, David, 1944, My 27,15:7
Sacks, Emanuel (funl, F 12,29:4), 1958, F 10,23:1
Sacks, Harry N Mrs, 1965, N 19,47:1
Sacks, Jacob, 1954, N 7,89:1
Sacks, James J Mrs, 1959, Je 2,35:4
Sacks, Joseph L, 1952, My 20,25:5
Sacks, Louis, 1925, S 12,15:6; 1950, Ag 19,13:6
Sacks, Paul, 1961, F 21,35:4
Sacks, Raymond, 1965, Je 6,85:1
Sacks, Reuben R, 1956, Ja 7,17:4
Sacks, Robert, 1961, D 4,37:2
Sacks, Samuel, 1952, S 13,17:3
Sacks, Samuel Mrs, 1950, N 12,93:1
Sacks, William, 1937, Mr 26,22:1
Sackville, Anne, 1961, Ja 11,47:2
Sackville, Gilbert George Reginald (Earl de la Warr), 1915, D 18,11:5
Sackville, Lord, 1928, Ja 29,29:4
Sackville, Lord (Chas J Sackville-West), 1962, My 9,43:4
Sackville, Lord (Edw C Sackville-West), 1965, Jl 6, 34:1
Sackville, V, 1936, Ja 31,19:1
Sackville-West, Lionel Sackville, 1908, S 4,7:6
Sackville-West, Victoria (Mrs H Nicolson), 1962, Je 3,88:3
Saco, J A, 1880, Ag 22,7:2
Sacy, S De, 1879, F 15,4:7
Sadak, Necmeddin, 1953, S 22,31:5
Sadaka, Namy A, 1941, Ap 27,38:1
Sadako, Dowager Empress, 1951, My 18,27:3
Sadanand, Swaminathan, 1953, N 18,32:4
Sadden, Harry A, 1941, Mr 24,17:3
Sadden, William H, 1944, Jl 25,19:4
Saddler, Alex, 1952, D 16,31:1
Saddler, Frank, 1921, Mr 29,15:6
Sadeh, Itzhak, 1952, Ag 21,19:7
Sadek, Fahmi, 1950, Mr 3,25:2
Sadek, Hassan, 1949, My 27,21:1
Sadeleer, Louis de, 1918, Ap 5,15:5
Sadenwater, Harry, 1961, Ag 31,27:3
Sadi, Subhi M, 1966, O 14,40:1
Sadimas, John G, 1961, Jl 17,21:2
Sadinoff, Isack, 1939, My 17,23:1
Sadkin, Irving, 1959, O 7,43:5
Sadlak, William V, 1953, Mr 14,15:5
Sadler, Alfred J, 1955, Jl 18,21:6
Sadler, Anne Houstoun, 1968, Mr 13,53:2
Sadler, Charles R, 1950, Mr 24,26:2
Sadler, Daniel K Sr, 1960, Ap 3,86:3
Sadler, Eda Mrs, 1954, F 20,17:6
Sadler, Edward, 1947, D 11,33:2
Sadler, Edward T, 1949, Ap 14,25:6
Sadler, Eugene H, 1962, F 6,35:3
Sadler, Everit J (por), 1947, O 29,27:4
Sadler, Everit J Mrs, 1953, My 10,89:2
Sadler, Frank H Mrs, 1951, Je 20,27:1
Sadler, Henry R, 1912, D 3,15:5
Sadler, Herbert C, 1948, D 16,29:2
Sadler, James E Mrs, 1946, Jl 11,23:2
Sadler, John M Mrs, 1950, My 7,108:2
Sadler, John W, 1950, My 13,17:6
Sadler, Lena K, 1939, Ag 9,17:6
Sadler, McGruder E, 1966, S 12,45:3
Sadler, Michael (por), 1943, O 15,19:1
Sadler, Michael, 1957, D 16,29:1
Sadler, Nettie M, 1955, Ap 6,29:2
Sadler, R Watson, 1955, D 29,23:2
Sadler, Ray F Jr, 1965, N 12,47:1
Sadler, Rich, 1965, Ap 5,31:4
Sadler, Thomas H, 1937, Jl 17,15:2

Sadler, Walter Dendy, 1923, N 14,17:5
Sadler, Walter L, 1948, Je 18,23:1
Sadler, Walter L Mrs, 1948, Je 18,23:1
Sadler, Wilbur F, 1920, Jl 5,9:3
Sadler, Wilbur F Adj-Gen, 1916, N 12,23:1
Sadler, William M, 1952, My 2,25:3
Sadlier, Ailbe, 1949, Ag 23,23:1
Sadlier, Denis, 1885, F 5,5:4
Sadlier, Francis J, 1947, My 24,15:4
Sadlier, Francis X, 1939, Je 9,21:6
Sadlier, James E, 1939, O 11,27:3
Sadlo, George W, 1960, Mr 2,37:2
Sadlo, William J Jr, 1959, Ag 9,89:3
Sadlow, Joseph, 1947, Ag 12,24:3
Sadoc, Prince, 1955, O 7,6:8
Sadoff, Louis, 1953, Ja 20,25:3; 1957, Mr 12,33:4
Sadoff, Louis Mrs, 1963, Jl 6,15:3
Sadona, Paul G, 1953, Je 21,85:1
Sadousky, August Mrs, 1958, Ag 23,15:3
Sadoveanu, Mihail, 1961, O 22,86:6
Sadovsky, Prov, 1947, My 5,23:3
Sadowski, George G, 1961, O 11,47:4
Sadowsky, David, 1960, Ag 22,25:3
Sadowsky, David R, 1957, My 29,27:1
Sadowsky, Hirsch, 1939, Ap 5,25:2
Sadowsky, Nathan, 1954, Je 15,29:4
Sadowsky, Reuben (por), 1944, Ap 7,19:1
Sadowsky, Solomon, 1946, N 1,23:4
Sadtler, Harry A L, 1939, Je 20,21:5
Sadtler, Howard P Jr, 1960, S 4,69:2
Sadtler, Otis K, 1954, Je 7,23:4
Sadtler, Philip B, 1964, My 29,29:2
Sadtler, Samuel S, 1954, N 4,31:3
Sadvoransky, Julius, 1939, N 14,23:4
Sadwin, Louis, 1956, Jl 20,17:5
Saecker, Edward F, 1946, N 16,19:4
Saeger, Gellert Edwin, 1907, F 17,9:6
Saeger, Wilford C, 1944, Je 10,15:5
Saegusa, Hitoro, 1963, N 11,4:6
Saeki, Tadasu, 1959, N 30,31:6
Saenger, August, 1950, My 19,28:3
Saenger, Eugen, 1964, F 11,39:1
Saenger, Helene K Mrs, 1938, O 27,23:3
Saenger, Herbert J Mrs, 1945, Ag 20,19:3
Saenger, Samuel, 1944, My 10,19:1
Saenger, Stella, 1950, Je 18,76:1
Saenger, Walter, 1943, My 20,21:4
Saenz, Moises, 1941, O 25,17:2
Saerchinger, Cesar Mrs, 1962, Ag 26,83:1
Saether, Mathias N, 1957, Ja 9,31:1
Safberg, B Frederick, 1944, F 13,41:2
Safe, Hope S, 1946, N 5,25:2
Safe, Kenneth S, 1956, Jl 10,31:3
Safer, Maxwell S, 1944, N 30,23:5
Saffe, E L, 1909, S 5,9:6
Saffer, Abraham J, 1961, F 13,27:5
Saffer, Ansel L, 1964, My 27,39:1
Saffer, Isadore L, 1962, Jl 30,23:4
Saffer, Samuel, 1941, Mr 3,15:5
Saffir, Abraham, 1962, N 20,35:3
Safford, Arthur T, 1944, N 11,13:2
Safford, Carlton R Mrs, 1963, N 21,39:2
Safford, Charles, 1925, Ap 16,21:5
Safford, Charles L, 1944, Je 9,15:4; 1952, Jl 19,15:6
Safford, Charles N, 1950, Jl 24,17:2
Safford, David Bigelow, 1914, My 26,11:5
Safford, Edwin, 1948, Mr 27,13:5
Safford, Edwin R Mrs, 1943, O 26,23:3; 1945, Mr 6, 21:5
Safford, Frank K, 1941, Ap 8,25:1
Safford, Frederick H, 1950, O 31,27:5
Safford, Frederick S, 1945, My 21,19:3
Safford, Granville R, 1937, N 11,25:2
Safford, Harold, 1960, O 20,35:2
Safford, Harry R (por), 1943, Ap 11,48:2
Safford, Henry B, 1956, S 18,35:4
Safford, Henry T, 1941, N 12,23:2
Safford, T H Prof, 1901, Je 14,7:6
Safford, Theodore Lee Rev, 1924, Ap 11,21:5
Safford, Thomas S Mrs, 1952, N 11,30:3
Saffran, Morris, 1942, D 9,27:1
Saffran, Morris Mrs, 1959, F 3,31:1
Saffron, Abram N Mrs, 1961, F 22,25:5
Saffron, Andrew L, 1951, Ag 8,25:4
Safir, Leo C, 1951, D 30,25:2
Safley, J Clifford, 1953, O 24,13:1
Safonoff, Wassili, 1918, Mr 14,13:6
Safran, Anni H, 1967, F 20,37:2
Safran, Benjamin, 1954, Ag 11,25:4
Safran, Bruno D, 1950, F 11,15:5
Safran, Charles, 1948, Jl 31,15:1; 1951, O 27,19:3
Safran, Charles Mrs, 1950, Ag 30,31:3
Safranski, Kurt, 1964, Mr 2,27:4
Safrazyan, Leon B, 1954, Ag 16,17:4
Safron, Harry, 1964, F 16,92:3
Safronov, Arseny M, 1957, O 14,27:4
Safstrom, John O, 1951, N 14,31:5
Safvet, Pasha, 1883, N 19,5:1
Sagal, William Mrs, 1939, Ag 1,19:5
Sagalowitch, Jacob M, 1943, D 31,16:7
Sagaphi, Mirza M K, 1942, O 24,15:2
Sagar, J Edgar, 1949, Ap 14,25:3
Sagar, William S, 1952, Mr 14,23:3
Sagarin, Max J, 1959, Ja 4,88:3
Sàgarna, Antonio, 1949, Jl 29,21:3
Sage, Andrew G C, 1952, F 5,29:5
Sage, Annie W, 1951, S 18,31:3
Sage, C E, 1903, Ag 14,7:6
Sage, Charles G, 1967, F 5,89:2
Sage, Charles J, 1940, O 19,17:4
Sage, David W Mrs, 1943, F 21,32:7
Sage, Dean, 1902, Je 24,9:6
Sage, Dean (por), 1943, Jl 2,19:1
Sage, Dean, 1963, N 3,89:3
Sage, Dean Mrs, 1941, Je 4,23:3
Sage, Edmund E, 1944, My 26,19:6
Sage, Edward E, 1920, N 10,13:6
Sage, Eloise H Mrs, 1963, N 12,38:1
Sage, Francis P, 1871, Ja 29,5:5
Sage, G A, 1882, Ag 24,2:7
Sage, H W, 1897, S 19,13:5
Sage, Henry, 1938, Ag 13,13:3
Sage, Henry A 3d, 1937, S 22,27:4
Sage, J D, 1928, D 5,31:2
Sage, James, 1906, Je 15,1:4
Sage, John C Bp, 1919, O 4,11:4
Sage, John H, 1925, Ag 18,19:5
Sage, Leon W, 1962, Jl 19,27:5
Sage, Lillian B, 1915, Ap 7,13:4
Sage, Louise H Mrs, 1913, D 25,9:4
Sage, Mary Mrs, 1916, Ag 17,11:5
Sage, Merton W, 1958, N 12,37:5
Sage, Nathaniel M, 1956, My 16,35:2
Sage, Omar V Col, 1917, Ja 9,13:3
Sage, R F, 1878, Ja 8,8:1
Sage, Robert, 1962, O 28,88:6
Sage, Robert H, 1944, Mr 8,19:3
Sage, Russell (funl, Jl 26,1:1; will Jl 28,1:7), 1906, Jl 23,1:7
Sage, Russell Mrs (funl, N 7,15:4), 1918, N 4,13:1
Sage, Sylvester B, 1905, Je 15,9:6
Sage, William D, 1951, F 19,23:1
Sage, William H (por), 1942, F 13,21:3
Sage, William H Brig-Gen, 1922, Je 6,17:3
Sage, William H Mrs, 1943, F 1,15:2; 1961, F 4,19:6
Sage, William Jr (por), 1946, D 3,31:3
Sagebeer, Joseph E, 1940, D 19,25:5
Sagehorn, Herman G, 1949, Jl 20,25:4
Sageman, Annie M, 1950, D 6,33:1
Sageman, Lewis M, 1945, N 6,19:4
Sagen, A K Bp, 1907, F 10,7:6
Sagendorff, Josephine, 1944, Je 13,19:4
Sagendorph, Frank J, 1957, S 29,86:6
Sager, A Dr, 1877, Ag 9,4:7
Sager, Clarence L, 1955, Jl 16,15:7
Sager, Clarence L Mrs, 1945, D 20,23:4
Sager, Edwin A, 1944, N 29,23:2
Sager, Elmer C, 1959, My 7,33:5
Sager, Garrie A, 1944, Ap 12,21:2
Sager, George J, 1914, Ja 28,9:5
Sager, Hiram N, 1924, O 30,19:5
Sager, John, 1952, F 14,27:1
Sager, Lewis A, 1951, Mr 12,25:4
Sagerquist, Eric, 1944, S 12,19:6
Sagert, Carl M, 1951, My 24,35:5
Sagi, Alex Z, 1956, My 16,35:4
Sagi, Eugene S, 1958, My 16,25:3
Sagi Barba, Alicante E, 1949, Ag 9,26:3
Sagmeister, Joseph, 1957, Ap 25,31:4
Sagner, Stanley, 1964, Jl 17,27:5
Sagolowitz, Samuel, 1941, F 21,19:1
Sagor, Albert L, 1960, Ja 24,88:3
Sague, John K, 1957, N 10,86:4
Saha, Meghnad, 1956, F 17,23:2
Sahadi, Abraham A, 1952, O 9,31:1
Sahadi, Emil, 1962, Ja 31,31:1
Sahagian, Alsan, 1904, F 10,9:6
Sahlberg, August, 1903, My 7,9:5
Sahle Selassie, Prince of Ethiopia, 1962, Ap 25,39:4
Sahler, George C Mrs, 1948, F 15,60:5
Sahler, Helen G, 1950, D 4,29:5
Sahlin, Axel, 1937, Je 11,23:2
Sahlin, Henry, 1956, Ja 19,33:3
Sahlin, Nils Mrs, 1941, S 25,25:5
Sahlstrom, Gosta, 1946, N 20,31:2
Sahm, Heinrich (por), 1939, O 4,25:3
Sahm, John C Mrs, 1960, Jl 4,15:6
Sahn, George Cortelyou, 1907, Jl 18,7:6
Sahner, Victor P, 1956, S 5,27:4
Sahni, Birbal, 1949, Ap 10,76:1
Sahradnik, John A, 1949, O 7,31:2
Sahud, Moses, 1947, S 29,21:4
Saibara, Seito, 1939, Ap 12,23:2
Said, Boris, 1941, Je 6,21:2
Sa'id, Majed F, 1966, S 8,47:1
Saida, Aiko, 1954, S 23,33:2
Saidla, Leo E A, 1961, Je 22,31:6
Saier, Herman, 1940, O 14,19:2
Saier, John Mrs, 1945, Ap 30,19:5
Saifuddin, Syedna, 1965, N 13,29:4
Saigai, Todamu, 1947, Ag 16,13:6
Saigh, Maximos IV Cardinal, 1967, N 6,47:4
Saigo, Marquis, 1902, Jl 19,9:5
Saile, Edward H, 1958, My 10,21:6
Saile, Frank A, 1958, Ap 12,19:4
Saile, Joseph C, 1939, Ja 13,19:5
Sailer, A Jackson, 1956, F 14,29:3
Sailer, Arthur H, 1944, Ja 23,38:2
Sailer, J, 1929, Ja 2,27:5
Sailer, Joseph, 1883, Ja 16,5:5
Sailer, Joseph Mrs, 1963, Jl 27,17:5
Sailer, Louis F, 1954, Mr 2,25:3
Sailer, Rudolph W, 1945, Je 2,15:5
Sailer, T H P, 1962, Ag 2,25:2
Sailer, T H P Mrs, 1960, Jl 10,72:1
Sailer, William A, 1937, S 20,23:6
Saillant, Maurice-Edmond, 1956, Jl 23,31:4
Saillard, L E, 1881, D 29,5:5
Sailor, Robert W, 1949, O 25,27:2
Sain, Martin, 1961, F 3,25:2
Sain, Tony, 1907, Ja 30,9:6
Sainbury, William R, 1948, O 2,15:2
Saindon, Roy J, 1951, D 11,33:4
Sainsbury, John B, 1956, My 24,9:4
Sainsbury, William C, 1956, F 9,31:1
Saint, Lawrence B, 1961, Je 18,88:7
St Agnes, Sister, 1925, D 2,25:4
St Agnes, Sister (F Finn), 1951, Ja 16,29:5
St Albans, Duke of, 1934, S 21,23:4
St Albans, Duke of (O de V Beauclerk), 1964, Mr 35:2
St Aldwyn, Earl, 1916, My 1,11:5
St Alwyn, Harry, 1943, F 3,19:4
St Andrassy, George Sr, 1947, N 4,25:3
St Andre, Arthur F, 1955, O 26,31:2
St Anthony, Rev Mother, 1937, Jl 4,II,7:2
St Auban, Emile de B de, 1947, My 3,17:6
St Aubin, Avide de (por), 1943, Ja 28,19:4
Saint-Aulaire, Charles D de, 1954, S 28,29:5
Saint-Beuve, C A, 1869, O 14,7:3
St Catherine, Mother, 1948, Je 11,23:4
St Catherine, Mother (Sisters of Jesus Marie), 195 Mr 17,31:2
St Charles, William P, 1943, D 17,27:4
St Clair, David F, 1947, F 2,57:2
St Clair, Duncan R, 1957, S 16,31:4
St Clair, Harold J, 1941, Je 6,21:3
St Clair, Harold W, 1949, N 3,3:1
St Clair, Harry H, 1953, D 13,87:1
St Clair, Harry P, 1961, Ja 2,25:4
St Clair, Helene A Mrs (cor, Jl 22,17:4), 1951, Jl 1 27:2
St Clair, James W, 1945, My 5,15:2
St Clair, Jerry W, 1941, Ag 27,19:4
St Clair, Labert, 1949, D 18,90:3
St Clair, Leonard P, 1960, Je 23,29:3
St Clair, Malcolm, 1952, Je 3,29:4
St Clair, Milton, 1940, Mr 19,28:7
St Clair, Norman, 1912, Mr 8,13:5
St Clair, Thomson, 1943, Ja 31,44:5
St Clair, Wilbur F, 1949, N 8,31:2
St Clair, William G, 1942, F 24,21:3
St Clair, William S, 1908, Ag 18,9:6
St Clair-Erskine, Millicent Fanny (Duchess of Sutherland), 1955, Ag 21,93:1
St Cloud, Alphonse, 1948, Mr 20,13:4
St Croix, D E Rev, 1871, Ap 22,2:6
St Cyr, Charles de, 1940, Je 5,25:5
St Cyr, Johnny, 1966, Je 18,31:3
St Damase, Mother (A Trudeau), 1955, O 3,27:5
St Davids, Lord, 1938, Mr 29,21:6
St Denis, Ruth, 1968, Jl 22,1:1
St Denis, Walter, 1947, F 16,57:1
St Denis, Walter Mrs, 1944, N 8,17:4
St Dennis, George, 1942, F 19,19:4
St Edward, Sister, 1948, D 12,93:1
St Firmin, Mother, 1949, F 19,15:4
St Francis Hieronyme, Sister (Sisters of St Joseph), 1953, Ja 8,27:3
Saint Gaudens, Augustus (funl, Ag 5,7:6), 1907, Ag 4,7:1
Saint-Gaudens, Louis, 1913, Mr 10,9:4
Saint-Gaudens, Louis Mrs, 1943, Ap 7,26:3
St George, Armin V, 1943, N 21,56:6
St George, Chris R Mrs, 1904, Ag 24,7:5
St George, George B, 1957, O 6,84:4
St George, Gertrude K, 1951, Ja 16,29:3
St George, Howard B, 1940, F 18,43:5
St George, Howard B Mrs, 1938, S 17,17:3
St George, J F, 1876, Jl 23,12:6
St George, Julia, 1903, N 17,7:5
St George, Robert C C, 1948, D 12,92:4
St George-Smith, Frederick Mrs, 1956, D 11,39:2
Saint Georges, dossin de, 1954, D 7,33:1
Saint-Georges, M de, 1876, Ja 8,1:7
St Georges, Maubert, 1955, Mr 10,27:2
St Germaine, Thomas L, 1947, O 10,25:2
St Germans, Earl of, 1881, Mr 21,5:3
St Germans, Earl of (M C Eliot), 1960, S 20,39:3
Saint-Gudens, Homer S, 1958, D 9,38:3
St. Heliers, Lord, 1905, Ap 10,9:5
Saint-Hilaire, B, 1895, N 26,5:3
St Hill, Ralph W, 1950, D 29,20:3
Saint-Huentin, Rene D de, 1961, Mr 17,31:1
Saint-Jacques, Maurice Mrs, 1946, N 19,21:1
St Jane, Sister, 1948, Mr 16,27:4
St Jean, Idola, 1945, Ap 7,15:4
St John, Adrian, 1955, Ja 14,19:8
St John, Al (Fuzzy Q Jones), 1963, Ja 23,7:5
St John, Ann, 1955, N 16,35:3

St John, Archer, 1955, Ag 14,71:4
St John, Arthur, 1944, Ap 14,19:5
St John, Byron D, 1953, D 16,35:4
St John, C Wardell, 1968, Jl 5,25:1
St John, Charles E, 1954, D 22,23:4
St John, Charles Elliott, 1916, F 26,9:5
St John, D Dr Mrs, 1903, S 9,7:6
St John, Earl, 1968, F 28,47:4
St John, Edward A, 1937, N 6,17:3
St John, Everitte, 1908, Ap 22,9:6
St John, Florence, 1912, Ja 31,11:4
St John, Francis C, 1964, F 26,35:1
St John, Francis G, 1947, F 18,25:1
St John, Gamaliel C Mrs, 1956, Mr 2,23:2
St John, George C, 1950, My 31,29:3; 1966, Ja 20,35:1
St John, George C Mrs, 1940, Ag 29,19:4; 1958, Jl 8, 27:3
St John, Guy, 1948, Je 2,29:4
St John, Henrietta, 1946, N 14,29:5
St John, J R, 1880, My 16,5:5
St John, Jane L Mrs (Jane Lee), 1957, Mr 20,37:4
St John, John, 1950, My 30,18:2
St John, John Pierce Ex-Gov, 1916, S 1,9:6
St John, Joseph Wesley, 1907, Ap 8,9:6
St John, Leigh E, 1965, Mr 29,33:1
St John, Lynn W, 1950, O 1,104:1
St John, Margaret G, 1965, Ja 25,37:5
St John, Marguerite, 1940, O 17,25:2
St John, Merle I, 1960, Jl 16,5:8
St John, Mother, 1942, O 23,22:3
St John, Richard R, 1954, F 18,31:4
St John, S R, 1880, F 10,3:4
St John, T Raymond, 1958, N 5,35:4
St John, T Raymond Mrs, 1963, Jl 21,65:1
St John, W P, 1897, F 16,12:3
St John, Walter S, 1955, Je 22,29:5
St John, William A, 1940, My 21,23:4
St John, William M, 1952, S 28,77:2
St John-Brenon, 1915, D 20,11:4
St Johnston, Reginald Sir, 1950, Ag 30,31:4
St Just, Eustache L de, 1952, Jl 28,15:2
St Just, L L, 1881, Ja 30,7:2
St Just, Lord (por), 1941, N 29,17:3
St Laurent, Louis Mrs, 1966, N 15,47:1
St Lawrence, William, 1960, Je 5,86:5
St Leger, Roderick C, 1949, D 17,17:4
St Levan, Lord, 1940, N 12,24:3
St Lifer, David, 1957, O 25,27:1
St Louis, Albert J Sr, 1964, My 2,27:3
St Louis, Antoine, 1911, N 1,11:5
St Marc, Cardinal Archbishop, 1878, F 28,4:7
St Marie, Henry B, 1874, S 12,7:3
St Mart, Lucienne de, 1953, Mr 30,21:5
St Mary Edith, Mother (T Turner), 1949, Je 11,18:4
St Maude, Sister (Sisters of St Joseph of Carondolet), 1960, N 3,39:1
St Maur, Kate V Mrs, 1942, S 29,23:6
St Mildred, Mother (Sisters of St Joseph), 1958, Mr 4,29:2
St Norbert, Sister, 1938, Ag 20,15:4
St Pere, Edouard, 1950, F 1,30:3
St Peter, Wilfred N, 1951, Jl 21,13:3
St Phalle, Raoul de Comte, 1913, Mr 25,13:4
Saint-Pierre, Henri, 1951, O 10,23:3
St Placidie, Sister, 1943, F 26,19:2
Saint-Prix, Amable Maille, 1924, Ja 21,17:5
St Reginald, Mother, 1940, Ag 25,35:3
St Rose Marie, Mother (M Barron), 1950, Je 15,31:4
Saint-Saens, Camillo, 1921, D 17,13:4
St Seigne, Giuseppi de Mrs, 1925, Jl 27,13:3
St Stanislaus, Sister (H Donnelly), 1958, Jl 31,23:1
St Sure, Adolphus F, 1949, F 6,76:7
St Sure, J Paul, 1966, S 26,41:3
St Veran, Countess de, 1907, N 28,7:5
St Victor, Paul de, 1881, Jl 10,7:2
St Vigeans, Lord, 1948, Je 2,30:3
St Vincent, Viscount, 1940, F 18,41:2
St Vincent Ferrer, Mother (Religious of Jesus and Mary), 1955, S 24,19:4
St Winnifred, Rev Mother, 1940, Ja 19,19:3
Saintbury, H A, 1939, Je 20,21:4
Sainte Croix, Eugenie A de, 1939, Mr 23,23:6
Sainte-Marie, Henriette, 1964, D 16,46:3
Sainton-Dolby, Charlotte H, 1885, F 19,2:4
Saintsbury, G, 1933, Ja 29,24:1
Sainz, Juan M, 1939, Mr 7,21:2
Saionji, Kimmochi Prince, 1940, N 25,8:3
Saisset, French Adm, 1879, My 26,5:5
Sait, Edward M, 1943, O 28,23:1
Saitbaev, Rachman A, 1953, Jl 18,5:5
Saito, Hirosi, 1939, F 27,15:1
Saito, Takao, 1949, O 8,13:1
Saitta, Charles A, 1960, Je 14,37:3
Saitz, Simon, 1955, Je 19,93:1
Saiz, Francis, 1948, Ja 23,25:3
Saiz, Giusto, 1938, Ja 21,20:2
Sajben, Charles Jr, 1966, N 24,35:2
Sajous, C E de M, 1929, Ap 28,24:1
Sajous, L T De M, 1929, Ja 17,25:2
Saka, Hasan, 1960, Jl 31,68:2
Sakai, Seiji, 1947, Mr 1,15:1
Sakala, John, 1943, Je 26,13:4
Sakall, S Z, 1955, F 14,19:2
Sakamoto, Tamao, 1944, Jl 7,15:3
Sakas, Peter D, 1946, My 13,21:4
Sakata, Jujir, 1919, N 28,13:2
Sakatani, Yoshiro, 1941, N 14,23:2
Sakel, Manfred J, 1957, D 3,35:1
Sakele, Assad, 1951, D 14,31:1
Sakharov, A, 1951, Ap 12,33:5
Sakhri, Prince of Kuwait, 1961, S 13,17:2
Sakin, Benjamin M, 1958, F 19,27:3
Sakin, Genia I, 1960, S 12,29:3
Saklatvala, Mae Mrs, 1939, Ja 7,15:5
Saklatvala, Nowroji Sir, 1938, Jl 23,13:6
Saklatvala, S, 1936, Ja 17,19:3
Sakoh, Shuichi, 1949, Jl 24,53:1
Sakolski, Aaron M, 1955, D 31,14:7
Sakonskaya, Nina P, 1951, Jl 11,23:4
Sakovits, Joseph, 1947, My 5,25:7
Sakow, Max, 1956, F 1,31:3
Sakowicz, Stanley, 1951, O 24,32:2
Saks, Andrew, 1912, Ap 9,11:3
Saks, Andrew Mrs, 1938, Ap 3,II,7:1
Saks, Arthur, 1961, F 24,21:8
Saks, Edward, 1957, Ap 27,19:4
Saks, Horace A, 1925, N 29,13:2
Saks, Horace A Mrs, 1960, Ja 29,25:1
Saks, I, 1933, S 14,23:1
Saks, Joseph I, 1939, O 26,23:6
Saks, Max J, 1952, O 21,29:5
Saks, Sanford, 1959, O 14,43:3
Sala, Antoine de Count (por), 1946, Je 21,23:3
Sala, Charles B, 1949, Ap 9,17:4
Sala, G A, 1895, D 9,5:1
Sala, J Roland, 1963, N 3,89:1
Sala, John, 1954, S 6,15:3
Sala, John Mrs, 1951, My 23,35:3
Sala, Joseph, 1948, O 16,15:5
Sala, Laura, 1961, F 27,27:3
Sala, Maximilian Mrs, 1952, Jl 21,19:4
Sala, Thomas Msgr, 1968, F 29,37:3
Saladino, Sebastian, 1963, My 11,25:5
Saladrigas, Augusto, 1940, Ag 8,19:6
Saladrigas y Zayas, Carlos, 1956, Ap 16,27:6
Salaj, Djuro (funl, My 23,23:4), 1958, My 21,33:4
Salajan, Leontin, 1966, Ag 29,29:5
Salaman, Euston A Lt, 1916, F 20,15:4
Salamanca, D, 1935, Jl 18,19:4
Salamar Serrera, Tiberio de J, 1942, Mr 7,17:4
Salamon, John D, 1945, N 14,19:3
Salamon, Nicholas, 1942, Mr 10,19:4
Salamowitz, Gilbert, 1954, Jl 9,9:4
Salandi, John, 1950, Ja 20,25:1
Salandra, A, 1931, D 9,25:1
Salant, Aaron B, 1967, Jl 30,64:5
Salant, Aaron B Mrs, 1960, D 10,23:2
Salant, Louis, 1958, F 4,26:4
Salant, Nathan N, 1949, Jl 2,15:2
Salant, Samuel Rabbi, 1909, Ag 17,9:5
Salant, William, 1943, D 12,68:2
Salant, William A, 1966, Jl 5,27:2
Salas Arzuaga, Justo, 1956, Ag 12,84:1
Salas-Asalariado, Jose S, 1955, O 18,37:4
Salat, Joseph J, 1942, F 25,19:1
Salata, Francesco, 1944, Mr 13,15:5
Salata, Kalman, 1958, S 14,84:3
Salay, Emil, 1937, Jl 17,15:2
Salay, Julius, 1956, F 26,88:6
Salazar, Abel L, 1946, D 30,22:2
Salazar, Demetrio Sarsfield Count, 1968, S 11,51:1
Salazar, Gonzalo, 1949, F 12,17:5
Salazar, Marco A, 1958, O 15,39:2
Salazar Gomez, Eduardo, 1958, F 9,88:6
Salch, Edward H, 1944, N 17,19:3
Salchow, Ulrich, 1949, Ap 20,27:3
Salciccia, Raffaele, 1951, Je 26,29:4
Salcius, Petras, 1958, Ap 24,31:2
Saldana, James T (por), 1947, Ag 25,17:6
Saldanha, Duke of, 1876, N 22,5:5
Sale, B Le Roy, 1941, S 9,23:6
Sale, C, 1936, N 8,II,8:6
Sale, F O Mrs, 1940, Ag 30,19:5
Sale, William W, 1938, O 19,23:4
Saleeby, C W, 1940, D 12,27:2
Saleeby, George N, 1925, N 5,23:5
Saleh, Chaerul, 1967, F 9,11:1
Salem, Andrew G Sr, 1950, Mr 14,25:2
Salem, Gamal, 1968, My 31,29:4
Salem, Salah, 1962, F 19,31:3
Salem, Toufic, 1959, F 24,29:2
Salembier, Albert R, 1965, S 13,35:3
Salembier, Rene R, 1942, S 14,15:2
Salemme, Attilio, 1955, Ja 26,25:1
Salengro, R, 1936, N 19,1:2
Salerano, Sclopis de Count, 1878, Mr 9,2:6
Salering, William, 1959, Ja 28,31:4
Salerno, Andrew C, 1961, D 9,27:5
Salerno, Arthur A, 1965, Ap 27,37:2
Salerno, Edward, 1961, O 24,37:4
Salerno, John J, 1959, S 12,21:2
Salerno, Marie G, 1942, Ag 25,23:3
Sales, Fred J, 1952, Mr 25,27:4
Sales, George Sr, 1946, N 21,32:2
Sales, Joseph A, 1954, Je 10,31:5
Sales, Pierre, 1914, Ap 10,13:6
Sales, Richard G Jr, 1951, Jl 11,23:6
Sales Diaz, Jose, 1951, N 12,25:1
Saleski, Gdal, 1966, O 9,86:4
Salesky, Bernard L (Feb 2), 1963, Ap 1,36:5
Salesky, Joseph M, 1959, Jl 24,25:1
Salfisberg, Leroy L, 1950, Ap 22,19:2
Salgado, Nicolas F, 1942, F 24,21:3
Salganik, Jassa, 1937, Ag 1,II,7:2
Saliba, Mike, 1939, My 15,17:2
Saliege, Jules G, 1956, N 6,35:2
Saliklis, Michael, 1958, Mr 1,17:5
Salim, Ahmed, 1949, S 12,21:3
Salim, Hadji A, 1954, N 5,15:1
Salimbene, Anthony, 1960, F 1,27:1
Salin, John W, 1967, My 23,47:1
Salinas, Pedro, 1951, D 5,36:2
Saline, Samuel, 1968, S 6,43:1
Salines, Vincent J, 1962, My 16,41:1
Salinger, Allan B, 1956, D 29,15:4
Salinger, Alvin, 1950, Ja 6,21:2
Salinger, Benjamin I, 1949, N 2,27:3
Salinger, Charles, 1941, Ap 29,19:3
Salinger, Harry, 1951, Ap 9,25:3
Salinger, Sidney, 1963, Ap 13,19:4
Salins, Sol, 1949, O 11,34:2
Saliquet, Andres, 1959, Je 24,31:4
Salis, Charles F De, 1942, Ja 26,15:5
Salis, Emil, 1920, My 27,11:3
Salisbury, Andrew A, 1941, S 18,25:2
Salisbury, Bert E, 1946, O 21,31:4
Salisbury, Bp of (Jno Wordsworth), 1911, Ag 17,7:6
Salisbury, C Birney, 1954, Mr 6,15:3
Salisbury, Charles Fox, 1905, My 24,9:6
Salisbury, Donald W, 1954, Ag 4,21:4
Salisbury, Dowager Marchioness of, 1955, F 6,89:1
Salisbury, Edgar T, 1949, O 5,29:2
Salisbury, Everett Mrs, 1948, N 30,27:3
Salisbury, Frank O, 1962, S 1,19:1
Salisbury, Frederick Stephen, 1908, Je 15,7:6
Salisbury, George B, 1950, My 25,29:4
Salisbury, George J Justice, 1920, S 25,13:4
Salisbury, Gerald H, 1968, F 27,43:3
Salisbury, Harold M, 1952, S 20,15:3
Salisbury, Henry W Mrs, 1950, S 8,31:2
Salisbury, Henry W Sr, 1955, My 11,31:3
Salisbury, Javan Butterfield Col, 1907, Jl 12,7:6
Salisbury, John R, 1945, My 25,19:4
Salisbury, Lloyd M, 1956, F 3,23:1
Salisbury, Lord (pir), 1947, Ap 5,19:1
Salisbury, Morse, 1962, O 6,25:5
Salisbury, Moses B, 1951, Ja 1,17:4
Salisbury, Nate, 1902, D 25,7:5
Salisbury, Orange J, 1907, Je 19,7:5
Salisbury, Peter F, 1964, N 8,88:2
Salisbury, Philip, 1967, Jl 21,31:2
Salisbury, Richard, 1961, My 20,23:2
Salisbury, Robert V, 1964, S 28,29:5
Salisbury, Rollin D Prof, 1922, Ag 17,13:4
Salisbury, S, 1884, Ag 25,4:7
Salisbury, Stanton W, 1966, Mr 15,39:3
Salisbury, Stephen (will, N 12, 1:6), 1905, N 17,9:5
Salisbury, W Burton Sr, 1966, F 7,29:3
Salisbury, W Randall, 1942, N 13,23:4
Salisbury, William H, 1946, D 2,25:2
Salisian, Aram, 1961, Mr 22,41:3
Salit, Charles R, 1959, N 10,47:3
Salit, Michael, 1941, Ja 7,23:5
Salit, Norman, 1960, Jl 22,23:4
Salk, Daniel, 1959, N 26,38:1
Salk, Daniel Mrs, 1964, S 27,86:5
Salkeld, Andrew D, 1951, F 20,25:3
Salkover, Meyer Dr, 1968, Mr 16,31:3
Salkowe, Thomas M, 1951, Ag 4,15:6
Sall, Jacob, 1952, S 9,31:2
Sallade, Charles H, 1950, O 30,27:3
Sallaway, Francis X, 1950, My 4,27:4
Sallaway, T Harry, 1949, N 18,29:4
Sallay, William, 1959, D 10,39:5
Salle, Albert, 1937, Ap 16,23:4
Salle, George V, 1955, O 21,27:2
Sallee, A C, 1951, Je 18,23:4
Sallee, Harry, 1950, Mr 23,36:3
Sallee, W H, 1957, S 18,24:6
Sallenger, Hilarion W, 1955, My 19,29:2
Salles, John M, 1939, N 27,17:4
Salles, Maurice, 1954, S 23,33:4
Salley, Edward M, 1943, D 12,68:3
Salley, Michael Rev, 1914, N 1,17:4
Salling, John B, 1959, Mr 17,33:2
Sallinger, Nathan, 1942, F 9,15:2
Sallis, Frank, 1882, Jl 11,8:2
Sallows, Ben J, 1950, D 18,31:5
Salls, David M A, 1957, Ag 7,27:4
Salls, Harry B, 1949, Ap 7,29:3
Salls, Samuel G Mrs, 1954, N 19,23:2
Sallume, Najib N, 1938, Jl 2,13:4
Sally, Frank, 1954, Ag 7,13:4
Salm, Louise M, 1951, Je 20,29:5
Salm, Mary E Mrs, 1948, Ag 10,22:3
Salm-Salm, Agnes Princess, 1912, D 22,15:5
Salmaggi, Alfredo Jr Mrs, 1967, S 21,47:2
Salmaggi, Edward A, 1959, My 9,21:2
Salman, Ernest O, 1960, D 8,35:4

Salman, George F, 1966, Je 2,43:4
Salman, Phinehas, 1961, O 1,86:2
Salman ibn Hamad al Khalifa, Sheik, 1961, N 3,6:4
Salmanowitz, Jules M, 1968, Je 17,39:1
Salmans, Levi B, 1938, F 2,19:3
Salmans, Levi B Mrs, 1925, Je 18,21:5
Salmeron, Jose, 1938, Ag 2,19:2
Salminen, Carl H, 1962, N 16,31:1
Salmini, Manuel F, 1951, O 30,29:1
Salmon, A C, 1931, My 16,17:5
Salmon, Albert K, 1950, S 1,21:2
Salmon, Carl F Sr, 1951, Jl 25,24:2
Salmon, Charles Carty, 1917, S 17,13:4
Salmon, Charles D, 1959, Mr 13,22:3
Salmon, Clarke, 1959, Mr 29,80:7
Salmon, Edward, 1965, Ap 8,39:1
Salmon, Edward B Sr, 1944, Je 18,35:2
Salmon, Edward H Dr, 1937, Mr 1,19:1
Salmon, Edward M, 1953, Ag 8,11:2
Salmon, Edwin A, 1965, F 24,41:4
Salmon, F Horace, 1951, D 5,35:2
Salmon, Ferd S (will), 1937, Ag 7,13:2
Salmon, Fred D, 1962, Jl 13,23:4
Salmon, George E, 1949, Je 30,23:4
Salmon, George E Mrs, 1947, F 4,26:3
Salmon, George Rev Dr, 1904, Ja 23,9:4
Salmon, Hamilton H, 1943, D 12,68:3
Salmon, Hamilton H Jr, 1962, S 16,86:7
Salmon, Harry, 1950, O 14,19:5
Salmon, Harry G, 1952, Jl 8,27:5
Salmon, Henry S, 1937, O 28,25:3
Salmon, Isidore (por), 1941, S 17,23:5
Salmon, Jere B, 1940, My 17,19:4
Salmon, Jesse R (will, Ag 9,6:3),(por), 1938, Jl 29, 17:6
Salmon, John L, 1947, Ap 13,60:4
Salmon, John R, 1952, Jl 27,57:2
Salmon, Jonas H, 1955, D 29,23:1
Salmon, Joseph, 1942, Ag 6,19:6
Salmon, Joseph A, 1939, Je 18,37:2
Salmon, Joseph W, 1939, Je 15,23:3
Salmon, Joshua R, 1947, Jl 14,21:4
Salmon, L, 1927, F 15,25:2
Salmon, Leon A, 1957, Ja 14,23:3
Salmon, Louis (Red), 1965, S 29,3:7
Salmon, Louis J A, 1961, Ag 31,27:4
Salmon, Maurice, 1947, Je 9,21:4
Salmon, Miner R, 1955, Ja 8,13:5
Salmon, Mortimer R, 1942, My 22,21:5
Salmon, Nathan, 1941, Je 18,21:5
Salmon, Nowell Sir, 1912, F 15,11:4
Salmon, Russell O, 1955, F 26,15:2
Salmon, Thomas, 1903, Ja 10,9:6
Salmon, Thomas W Mrs, 1953, Ja 16,23:2
Salmon, Udall J, 1963, Jl 11,29:2
Salmon, W R Dr (por), 1896, My 12,5:6
Salmon, Walter J, 1953, D 26,13:1
Salmon, William C, 1939, Ja 1,24:8
Salmon, William L, 1958, Ap 29,29:3
Salmond, Felix, 1952, F 20,30:2
Salmond, G Sir, 1933, Ap 28,17:1
Salmond, James J, 1937, N 5,23:5
Salmond, John Sir, 1968, Ap 17,32:4
Salmond, Mary E, 1952, Ja 12,13:4
Salmond, S D F Rev, 1905, Ap 21,9:5
Salmony, Alfred, 1958, My 3,19:5
Salmony, Paul, 1967, Mr 13,37:1
Salmore, Michael Mrs, 1946, Mr 15,21:4
Salmore, Michael N, 1949, Ap 19,25:1
Salmowitz, Samuel, 1954, Je 21,23:3
Salneron, Nicolas de, 1908, S 22,9:6
Salny, David S, 1942, F 18,19:2
Salo, Johnny Mrs, 1956, S 27,35:5
Salom, Leandro, 1962, Ja 11,33:3
Salom, Pedro G, 1946, Ja 3,20:3
Salome, Charles, 1942, Ja 29,19:5
Salomon, Albert, 1966, D 19,37:3
Salomon, Alberto, 1959, Ap 10,29:4
Salomon, Alfred V, 1957, Mr 6,31:3
Salomon, Alice (por), 1948, S 1,23:1
Salomon, Bernard J, 1914, F 13,9:7
Salomon, Charles S (por), 1944, N 24,24:2
Salomon, H Bennett, 1961, Ja 28,19:5
Salomon, H Bennett Mrs, 1959, Jl 28,27:2
Salomon, Henry, 1958, F 2,86:5
Salomon, Herbert, 1951, Mr 8,29:6
Salomon, Jacob E, 1922, Jl 29,7:6
Salomon, Mark M, 1916, Ja 6,13:3
Salomon, Martin L, 1943, Mr 19,19:4
Salomon, Mateus M, 1952, Ag 30,13:6
Salomon, Max, 1944, Ag 13,35:3
Salomon, Moritz M Dr, 1937, D 16,27:3
Salomon, Otto J, 1956, D 25,25:5
Salomon, Percy F, 1960, Ap 9,23:3
Salomon, Richard G, 1966, F 4,31:3
Salomon, Rochus L, 1945, Ap 21,13:4
Salomon, Schachna M, 1948, Ag 13,15:3
Salomon, Sir, 1873, Ag 3,6:4
Salomon, William, 1919, D 15,15:3
Salomonski-Rosen, Moritz, 1952, Jl 12,13:3
Salonen, Wesley, 1951, O 28,V,6:7
Salopoulos, Nicholas A, 1940, F 4,40:5
Salote, Queen of Tonga (funl, D 24,17:5), 1965, D 16,47:1
Salotti, Carlo, 1947, O 25,19:3
Salottolo, Alex Mrs, 1958, Ag 25,21:1
Salou, Louis, 1948, O 22,25:4
Salpeter, Benjamin Mrs, 1965, F 14,88:6
Salpeter, David, 1956, O 22,29:5
Salpeter, Harry, 1967, N 14,43:1
Salpeter, Morris, 1941, Ja 30,21:2
Salsbery, Charles, 1939, Jl 8,15:6
Salsburg, Abram, 1948, O 17,76:6
Salsburg, John, 1940, F 6,21:3
Salsbury, David M, 1957, Ja 30,29:4
Salsbury, Henry L, 1947, D 26,15:2
Salsbury, Joseph E, 1967, D 2,39:5
Salsgiver, Paul L, 1954, Jl 13,23:6
Salsich, LeRoy, 1957, O 29,31:1
Salsich, Neil S, 1954, F 5,20:3
Salsieder, Christian R, 1956, My 28,27:5
Salsinger, H G, 1958, N 28,27:3
Salson, Francois, 1901, S 29,9:2
Salt, Albert L (por), 1945, O 1,19:3
Salt, Edwin E, 1944, S 16,13:6
Salt, Henry S, 1939, Ap 20,23:3
Salt, John, 1947, D 27,13:3
Salt, Joseph J, 1959, D 23,27:6
Salt, T Sir, 1877, Ja 13,2:2
Saltas, Arsenios (funl), 1955, D 21,29:5
Salten, Felix (por), 1945, O 9,22:2
Salter, Alfred, 1945, Ag 25,11:5
Salter, Alfred Mrs, 1942, D 6,76:2
Salter, Borbert, 1942, Ja 7,20:2
Salter, C Edward W, 1948, N 27,17:1
Salter, David, 1956, S 29,19:4
Salter, David I Mrs, 1951, N 2,24:4
Salter, Edward A, 1948, Je 10,25:2
Salter, Fannie P Mrs, 1940, O 20,50:2
Salter, Fred C Sr, 1937, D 15,25:2
Salter, George, 1967, N 1,47:3
Salter, Harry B, 1938, Ag 7,32:8
Salter, Jack, 1947, Je 9,21:2
Salter, Jasper C, 1945, D 10,21:4
Salter, John A, 1941, S 23,23:1
Salter, Lawrence C, 1961, D 6,47:4
Salter, Leslie E, 1964, F 21,27:3
Salter, Louis, 1939, S 23,17:3
Salter, Oliver L, 1956, Mr 9,23:3
Salter, R Newton Mrs, 1957, Je 15,17:4
Salter, R Newton Rev, 1937, Jl 21,21:7
Salter, Robert M, 1955, S 14,35:2
Salter, Stanley, 1940, My 26,34:3
Salter, Stephen, 1937, S 17,25:3
Salter, Sumner, 1944, Mr 6,19:6
Salter, Suzanna M Mrs, 1961, Mr 18,23:5
Salter, Thomas J Rev, 1872, F 27,5:2
Salter, W M, 1931, Jl 19,22:3
Salter, William F, 1964, D 4,40:3
Salter, William T, 1952, Jl 31,23:5
Salterini, John B, 1952, D 16,31:4
Saltford, William G, 1938, F 6,II,9:2
Salthe, Ole, 1952, S 11,31:4
Saltis, Joseph, 1947, Ag 3,46:6
Saltonstall, Dudley W, 1945, N 26,21:5
Saltonstall, Endicott P, 1943, N 8,19:5
Saltonstall, Endicott P Mrs, 1951, O 14,88:4
Saltonstall, John L, 1959, Je 8,27:3
Saltonstall, John L Mrs, 1947, O 23,25:4
Saltonstall, L W Rev, 1904, My 22,2:5
Saltonstall, Leverett Jr, 1966, Ap 28,43:2
Saltonstall, Richard M Mrs, 1961, O 23,29:2
Saltpeter, Henry L, 1939, Ag 4,13:3
Saltus, Edgar, 1921, Ag 2,9:3
Saltus, Freeman M, 1950, N 19,92:5
Saltus, J Sanford, 1922, Je 25,26:3
Saltus, John Sanford (funl), 1922, Jl 22,7:5
Saltus, Lloyd S, 1954, Je 21,23:3
Saltus, R Sanford Mrs, 1938, Ap 25,15:1
Saltus, Rollin S Mrs, 1949, Ja 10,25:6
Saltus, Winthrop N, 1948, F 12,21:5
Saltz, Harry, 1959, O 4,87:1
Saltza, Carl Frederik von, 1905, D 11,2:4
Saltzer, Harry J, 1958, Jl 25,19:3
Saltzgiver, Ambrose M, 1941, Ap 26,15:3
Saltzman, Auguste L, 1948, Ap 8,25:4
Saltzman, Benjamin, 1968, Ap 10,47:2
Saltzman, Carl C, 1964, Je 12,32:6
Saltzman, Charles M (por), 1942, N 26,27:1
Saltzman, Harry, 1948, O 25,23:5
Saltzman, Herman (Jack Curley), 1958, Ag 27,29:3
Saltzman, Irving, 1954, S 28,29:3; 1966, Jl 19,39:4
Saltzman, Jeol E, 1967, F 7,39:1
Saltzman, Julius, 1958, Jl 22,27:2
Saltzman, Louis H, 1950, My 27,17:3
Saltzman, Louis H Mrs, 1950, Jl 8,13:5
Saltzman, Rubin, 1959, Mr 16,31:4
Saltzman, Shephard, 1955, Ag 10,25:1
Saltzman, William, 1954, D 25,11:4
Saltzstein, A L, 1947, Mr 22,13:1
Salumu, Bernard, 1965, O 2,3:8
Salus, Herbert W Sr, 1959, Je 28,69:1
Salus, Joseph W, 1938, My 3,23:6
Salus, Samuel W, 1945, D 30,14:3
Salustri, David, 1946, Ag 13,27:6
Salvador, d'Avernas Baroness, 1919, Je 1,22:4
Salvador, James E, 1966, My 2,27:1
Salvador, John P, 1949, Jl 13,28:4
Salvadore, Anthony J, 1940, Ap 2,25:5
Salvage, Mary Lady (Mrs S A Salvage), 1964, Ja 5 92:6
Salvage, Samuel A (por), 1946, Jl 11,23:1
Salvail, Adolph L, 1937, Jl 23,19:5
Salvaj, Jean, 1965, Je 10,35:2
Salvati, Leo H, 1958, F 15,17:4
Salvator, Franz, 1939, Ap 22,17:3
Salvator, Ludwig Archduke, 1915, O 15,11:6
Salvatore, Biagio, 1942, S 6,30:5
Salvatore, Paul J, 1960, O 20,35:3
Salvatore, Victor, 1965, Ap 12,35:3
Salvatori, William, 1937, F 8,17:3
Salvemini, Gaetano (trb lr, S 15,IV,12:6), 1957, S 7 19:6
Salvesen, Edward T, 1942, F 25,19:5
Salvey, Harold M, 1953, Ap 7,20:4
Salvi, Giunio, 1952, Mr 19,29:2
Salviati, A M B, 1959, O 6,39:1
Salvin, Arthur A, 1947, N 20,29:3
Salvin, Sam, 1952, Ap 28,19:6
Salvini, Alexander, 1896, D 16,5:1
Salvini, Mario, 1940, F 1,21:5
Salvini, Maud D, 1944, N 26,58:4
Salvini, Tommasso, 1916, Ja 1,11:6
Salvo, Carlo (Calogero Salvaggio), 1968, Ap 16,47
Salvo, T J Santo, 1948, Ap 21,27:1
Salway, Benjamin, 1962, Mr 4,86:3
Salwen, Emanuel (por), 1949, Ap 5,29:4
Salwen, Nathan, 1951, Je 17,86:1
Salyards, Henry F, 1944, N 6,19:6
Salyer, J Clark, 1966, Ag 18,32:5
Salz, Adolph, 1925, D 13,13:1
Salz, Ignatz, 1958, Je 20,23:4
Salzano, Raffaele, 1949, N 7,27:2
Salzberg, Abraham H, 1949, F 5,15:4
Salzberg, Charles, 1942, Jl 24,19:2
Salzberg, Harry E, 1948, Jl 7,23:3
Salzberg, Herbert, 1962, S 24,29:5
Salzberg, Max, 1962, Jl 18,29:5
Salzberg, Philip L, 1963, S 29,86:8
Salzberg, Samuel, 1938, Ag 12,34:6
Salzberg, Saul, 1955, N 8,31:3
Salzedo, Carlos, 1961, Ag 18,21:1
Salzer, Benjamin, 1956, N 13,37:3
Salzer, Eugene, 1964, Ja 30,29:2
Salzer, Moses, 1952, Ja 8,27:3
Salzer, William, 1940, F 11,48:3
Salzman, Adolph L, 1944, Je 30,21:3
Salzman, Barnett, 1956, O 13,19:5
Salzman, Charles, 1949, S 7,29:3
Salzman, George J, 1948, Jl 16,19:4
Salzman, Harry A, 1963, N 9,25:1
Salzman, Henry, 1947, Ag 23,13:6
Salzman, Joseph, 1956, O 31,33:2
Salzman, Lena Mrs, 1938, Jl 3,12:7
Salzman, Milton Mrs, 1957, My 21,35:3
Salzmann, John, 1950, D 2,13:4
Salzmann, Joseph M, 1938, Jl 24,29:4
Salzmann, Joseph Sr Mrs, 1949, Ap 7,30:3
Salzmann, Louis H, 1939, My 16,23:3
Salzmann, Rafael L, 1956, Mr 7,33:4
Sam, Charles, 1945, Je 24,22:5
Samalman, Alex, 1956, Ja 22,89:1
Samanamud, Pelayo, 1948, N 16,29:3
Samanez Ocampo, David, 1947, Jl 15,23:3
Samara, Robert, 1953, Ja 9,21:3
Samary, Marie, 1941, Jl 2,21:1
Sambrook, Russell, 1956, O 25,33:5
Samdperil, George Mrs, 1954, S 5,50:1
Samec, Hinko Mrs, 1964, Jl 22,33:1
Samek, Arthur E, 1956, Ja 1,50:4
Samek, Emil, 1958, Ag 25,21:5
Samek, Hans H, 1966, Mr 8,39:1
Samela, Charles L, 1950, Je 21,27:5
Samelson, Lester Mrs, 1961, D 9,27:4
Samenfeld, Joseph Dr, 1937, S 7,21:1
Samer, Adam, 1949, Je 17,24:4
Samer, Frederick Sr, 1947, Jl 2,23:3
Sames, Albert S, 1958, Mr 18,29:2
Samet, Jerome, 1958, Je 24,31:1
Sameth, Eugene H, 1948, N 28,92:5
Sameth, Maurice E, 1961, Je 5,31:4
Sameth, Nathan N, 1955, F 22,21:4
Sametini, Leon, 1944, Ag 22,17:2
Samfield, Max Rabbi, 1915, S 28,11:3
Samford, W J Gov, 1901, Je 12,1:4
Saminsky, Lazare (mem ser, S 26,23:5), 1959, Jl 25:3
Saminsky, Lazare Mrs, 1945, My 29,15:5
Samit, S Martin, 1968, My 8,47:1
Samler, Louis, 1948, N 9,27:3
Sammann, Paul E, 1942, S 2,23:4
Sammarco, Arthur G, 1952, My 2,25:1
Sammarco, Faust W, 1950, Ap 11,31:5
Sammarco, John B Mrs, 1946, O 30,27:5
Sammet, Harry, 1963, Jl 10,35:4
Sammet, Joel E, 1968, S 29,80:8
Sammet, Julian M, 1958, Ag 26,29:3
Sammis, A Clifford, 1942, Mr 11,19:3
Sammis, Addison W, 1948, Je 6,72:7

Sammis, Aldrich J, 1958, My 21,33:5
Sammis, Charles E, 1937, D 31,16:1
Sammis, Donald Stuart, 1968, Mr 22,47:2
Sammis, Edson B, 1953, S 10,25:3
Sammis, Ezra, 1947, Ap 27,60:7
Sammis, J Newell Mrs, 1949, F 1,25:3
Sammis, Jesse F, 1952, Je 23,19:4
Sammis, John M, 1908, O 18,VII,11:6
Sammis, John S, 1965, O 18,35:4
Sammis, Joseph H, 1941, D 4,25:4
Sammis, Louise A, 1944, My 25,21:4
Sammis, Royal A, 1910, D 9,11:4
Sammis, Russell Mrs, 1949, Je 13,19:5
Sammis, Samuel C, 1941, My 17,15:3
Sammis, Theron H, 1942, Ja 18,43:2
Sammon, Howard F, 1965, Mr 1,27:3
Sammon, Joseph, 1945, N 23,23:3
Sammon, Joseph A, 1938, O 29,19:5
Sammon, Mollie F, 1948, O 17,76:2
Sammon, Patrick J, 1948, Jl 31,15:2
Sammon, William J, 1956, Ja 25,31:5; 1962, Mr 19,29:3
Sammond, Herbert S, 1964, Ap 30,35:2
Sammond, John E, 1947, O 7,27:1
Sammons, Albert, 1957, Ag 26,23:4
Sammons, Annie Mrs, 1940, S 2,15:3
Sammons, F Elmer, 1958, Mr 26,37:1
Sammons, F Elmer Mrs, 1938, S 5,15:4
Sammons, J Rufus, 1944, Ag 26,11:2
Sammons, James (Fur), 1960, My 22,41:8
Sammons, Melvin, 1949, Ja 7,21:3
Sammons, W H Mrs, 1955, Ja 13,27:5
Sammons, Warren, 1947, F 7,23:4
Sammons, Wheeler Sr, 1956, F 22,27:3
Sammons, William H, 1944, Ja 8,13:5; 1951, F 6,27:2
Samnick, Samuel Mrs, 1958, F 2,86:8
Samninatelli, Cardinal, 1910, N 25,11:6
Samoan King, Malietoa Lagupepa, 1898, Ag 30,1:2
Samoilov, Fyodor, 1952, Je 15,84:5
Samokhin, Alex G, 1955, Jl 28,23:2
Samolis, John F Mrs, 1947, Ap 29,27:2
Samonisky, Harris, 1951, Je 23,15:5
Samons, W C, 1905, Je 13,9:6
Samossoud, Jacques A, 1966, Je 15,47:5
Samossoud, Jacques A Mrs, 1962, N 21,30:1
Samosud, Samuil A, 1964, N 10,47:4
Sampaix, Leon, 1948, Je 23,27:4
Samper, Joaquin Mrs, 1943, N 2,25:3
Samper, Julio, 1961, O 28,21:4
Samper, Riccardo de, 1954, F 25,31:2
Sampers, Harry P, 1949, F 12,17:3
Sampey, John R (por), 1946, Ag 20,27:3
Sampietro, Faustino, 1941, D 18,27:4
Sample, Charles H, 1953, Je 19,22:3
Sample, George B, 1948, Je 18,23:3
Sample, George E Mrs, 1954, Je 21,23:4
Sample, John J, 1954, O 17,84:5
Sample, Matthias W, 1961, Ag 7,23:3
Sample, Paul, 1958, Ja 29,27:3
Sample, Paul L, 1953, D 10,47:1
Sample, Wilton W, 1937, Mr 14,II,9:1
Sampliner, Philip A, 1944, N 28,23:5
Sampognaro, Vigilio, 1945, N 4,44:2
Sampsell, Marshall E, 1940, Ap 5,21:6
Sampson, Albert D Capt, 1925, Ap 16,21:5
Sampson, Albert R Mrs, 1941, Jl 6,27:1
Sampson, Alden, 1925, Ja 7,25:4
Sampson, Archibald J Gen, 1921, D 25,20:3
Sampson, Archibald T, 1957, Ap 19,21:5
Sampson, Charles B, 1940, Mr 3,44:1
Sampson, Charles E, 1946, Ja 22,27:2
Sampson, Charles H, 1957, Jl 7,60:6
Sampson, David, 1947, Ag 19,23:6
Sampson, David V, 1955, S 26,23:4
Sampson, Davis W, 1952, Ag 16,15:6
Sampson, Edgar, 1944, F 26,13:4
Sampson, Edward Mrs, 1943, My 7,19:4
Sampson, Flem D, 1967, My 27,31:3
Sampson, Frank J, 1967, O 20,47:2
Sampson, George P, 1952, Mr 6,31:4
Sampson, Harry O, 1958, Jl 3,25:2
Sampson, Harvey E, 1964, Jl 3,21:3
Sampson, Henry, 1914, My 25,11:5
Sampson, Henry A Mrs, 1947, My 9,21:5
Sampson, Henry J, 1951, S 6,31:1
Sampson, Henry Jr, 1940, Ja 24,21:2
Sampson, Homer L, 1945, My 17,19:5
Sampson, John A, 1946, D 24,17:2; 1954, Mr 20,15:2
Sampson, John S, 1942, D 25,17:3
Sampson, John Sr Mrs, 1949, Ja 1,13:4
Sampson, Julia F, 1957, Jl 26,19:3
Sampson, Lyndon E, 1948, Je 19,15:4
Sampson, M W, 1930, Ag 24,II,6:3
Sampson, Ralph A, 1939, N 11,15:3
Sampson, Ralph B, 1949, Ap 3,76:3
Sampson, S L R Mrs, 1902, My 20,9:5
Sampson, Samuel, 1952, S 4,27:3
Sampson, Thomas F, 1951, N 25,87:1
Sampson, W T Adm, 1902, My 7,1:7
Sampson, Walter C, 1940, My 20,17:3
Sampson, William, 1922, Ap 6,17:4
Sampson, William H, 1957, Mr 15,26:1
Sampter, Charles, 1942, Ap 23,23:1
Sampter, Jessie E, 1938, N 26,16:3
Samra, Victor M, 1960, Ag 11,27:1
Samras, Karl, 1948, Ap 14,27:4
Samrock, Samuel, 1951, S 20,31:3
Sams, Conway Whittle Judge, 1909, S 6,7:6
Sams, Earl C, 1950, Jl 24,17:1
Sams, Earl C Mrs, 1953, S 6,52:6
Sams, William, 1872, S 19,9:6
Samson, Charles F, 1964, N 12,37:5
Samson, Charles Louis, 1910, N 9,9:2
Samson, David N Mrs, 1948, D 24,17:3
Samson, David T, 1964, S 14,33:1
Samson, Edward A, 1945, Mr 28,23:6
Samson, Edward J, 1951, S 19,31:1
Samson, Harry G, 1948, My 24,19:3
Samson, Harry G Mrs, 1947, Je 1,62:4
Samson, Henry T, 1964, Jl 2,31:4
Samson, Hudson, 1903, Jl 16,7:6
Samson, Joseph W, 1961, Ag 3,23:2
Samson, Leon L, 1951, F 17,15:2
Samson, Samuel M, 1948, Mr 21,60:2
Samson, Walter J, 1942, N 8,50:4
Samson, William Holland, 1917, Je 26,13:5
Samsonoff, Margaret T Mrs, 1963, Je 2,84:1
Samstag, Frederick, 1946, Ag 6,28:7
Samstag, Henry F, 1940, F 24,13:4
Samstag, Julia R Mrs, 1953, Ja 2,15:4
Samstag, L Albert, 1937, Je 11,23:4
Samstag, Nicholas, 1968, Mr 28,47:1
Samstag, Nicholas Mrs, 1968, Mr 29,41:3
Samter, Benjamin, 1946, F 27,25:4
Samter, Samuel Mrs, 1959, Je 11,33:2
Samuel, Alex L, 1942, N 20,23:4
Samuel, Allen T, 1942, My 6,19:2
Samuel, Bernard (est acctg, Mr 24,18:6), 1954, Ja 13,32:3
Samuel, Elizabeth I Dr, 1937, Ja 7,21:4
Samuel, Ephraim, 1944, Jl 13,17:6
Samuel, Frank E (por), 1943, Jl 26,19:6
Samuel, H J Rev, 1926, Je 24,21:5
Samuel, Harold (por), 1937, Ja 16,17:1
Samuel, Harry, 1962, Ja 13,21:1
Samuel, Herbert L, 1963, F 6,4:7
Samuel, Howard, 1961, My 8,7:1
Samuel, John E, 1962, Mr 9,29:1
Samuel, Lawrence M, 1952, Ap 25,23:3
Samuel, Lionel Mrs, 1953, Ja 16,23:2
Samuel, Marcus, 1942, Mr 4,19:4
Samuel, Mary A, 1945, Ja 21,40:2
Samuel, Max, 1949, O 27,27:2
Samuel, Ralph E (mem ser set, O 19,47:3), 1967, O 17,47:1
Samuel, Robert M, 1937, N 3,23:1
Samuel, Rudolf, 1949, F 5,15:2
Samuel, S M Sir, 1926, My 15,21:2
Samuel, sigmund, 1962, Ap 30,27:2
Samuel, Sigmund Mrs, 1951, D 28,21:3
Samuel, Snowden, 1939, Jl 17,19:5
Samuel, Victor, 1961, Ag 20,86:1
Samuel, William S, 1937, Ap 23,21:1
Samuel-Montagu, Montagu (Baron Swaythling), 1911, Ja 13,9:3
Samuelian, Varton S, 1941, Mr 4,23:4
Samuels, Aaron, 1940, F 17,13:4
Samuels, Abe O, 1966, My 31,43:2
Samuels, Abraham S, 1960, Ap 24,88:8
Samuels, Ansyl T Mrs, 1964, D 1,41:3
Samuels, Arthur H (por), 1938, Mr 21,15:1
Samuels, Arthur S, 1946, O 5,17:5
Samuels, Benjamin, 1961, Mr 31,33:4
Samuels, Bernard, 1959, Jl 28,27:1
Samuels, Bernard Mrs, 1961, Je 20,33:2
Samuels, Bertrand B, 1937, Mr 13,19:4
Samuels, Charles H Mrs, 1938, F 14,17:3
Samuels, Collins W, 1947, N 9,72:4
Samuels, David, 1944, Je 18,36:3
Samuels, Donald L, 1948, N 3,27:2
Samuels, Elsie C Mrs, 1942, Ja 4,48:7
Samuels, Emanuel, 1922, N 12,6:4
Samuels, Frank E, 1942, D 29,21:2
Samuels, Frank Jr, 1957, Jl 8,23:1
Samuels, Fred E, 1952, Ag 8,17:6
Samuels, George E Judge, 1925, D 28,15:3
Samuels, Harry A, 1949, Ja 3,23:2
Samuels, Harry I, 1963, S 20,33:2
Samuels, Harry L Mrs, 1968, Ja 10,43:3
Samuels, Harry R, 1963, S 24,39:4
Samuels, Henry C, 1941, Ag 9,15:2; 1952, Mr 21,24:4
Samuels, Homer, 1956, O 15,25:5
Samuels, Jack J, 1954, Ap 3,15:6
Samuels, James, 1909, Jl 16,7:6
Samuels, Jerome, 1951, Ja 20,15:2
Samuels, Joseph (will, F 22,21:2), 1939, F 14,20:2
Samuels, Joseph, 1941, S 1,15:4
Samuels, Joseph Mrs, 1940, Ag 26,15:5
Samuels, Lester Mrs, 1953, D 21,31:3
Samuels, Levi, 1915, My 9,18:4
Samuels, Louis, 1937, Ja 4,29:4
Samuels, Louis (mem ser, Mr 8,26:4), 1956, F 1,31:2
Samuels, Louis (P Burton), 1959, Ap 29,33:4
Samuels, Louis C, 1872, O 31,7:3
Samuels, Louis M, 1947, O 9,25:1
Samuels, Mark, 1953, Jl 13,16:1
Samuels, Martin Mrs, 1961, Jl 25,27:4
Samuels, Maurice M, 1949, Ja 30,60:5
Samuels, Michael, 1957, F 27,27:2
Samuels, Mitchell, 1959, N 30,31:2
Samuels, Otto A, 1968, F 7,47:4
Samuels, Phil, 1953, Ja 28,27:1
Samuels, Robert, 1962, Ap 9,29:1
Samuels, S N, 1936, F 4,21:5
Samuels, Samuel Capt, 1908, My 19,7:3
Samuels, Saul S, 1961, N 2,37:1
Samuels, Sem A, 1949, F 17,23:3
Samuels, Sidney L, 1958, N 30,87:1
Samuels, Sigmund, 1943, Ag 9,13:5
Samuels, Victor, 1950, Ag 5,15:5
Samuelson, Aaron, 1965, Mr 20,27:4
Samuelson, Bess, 1946, D 27,19:3
Samuelson, Clarence F, 1955, O 1,19:3
Samuelson, Enoch E Mrs, 1962, Ja 31,31:4
Samuelson, Estelle E, 1955, O 23,86:2
Samuelson, G B, 1947, Ap 20,60:2
Samuelson, Joel S, 1947, N 20,30:2
Samuelson, Magnus, 1947, My 27,26:2
Samuelson, Roy C, 1968, F 7,47:2
Samuelson, S Harold, 1962, D 4,41:4
Samuelson, Samuel, 1951, O 27,19:2
Samwick, Harry A, 1953, Jl 28,19:3
Samwick, Samuel, 1953, F 13,21:2
Samworth, Robert P Mrs, 1944, My 9,19:3
San, Louis J, 1952, N 11,30:3
San Donato, Duke, 1901, O 29,1:2
San Faustino, Princess of, 1938, Je 24,19:6
San Giacomo, Thomas S, 1962, N 16,32:1
San Giovanni, Edoardo Dr, 1918, O 24,13:1
San Jules, Floyd C, 1952, N 21,25:4
San Marco, Baron of (Sen P Libertini), 1940, Je 5, 25:2
San Martin, Julio W, 1954, Ap 19,23:3
San Miguel, Antonio, 1940, Ag 10,13:6
San Pietro, Louis J, 1958, N 7,27:2
San Salvador, Archbishop of (J A Belloso y Sanchez), 1938, Ag 11,17:5
San Simon y Ortega, Luis Count, 1938, Jl 28,19:6
San Souci, E J, 1936, Ag 11,21:1
Sanabria, Nicolas, 1945, D 2,46:2
Sanabria y Martinez, Victor M, 1952, Je 10,27:6
Sanatescu, Constantin, 1947, N 9,74:3
Sanborn, Caleb C, 1947, Ja 20,25:1
Sanborn, Charles H, 1940, D 9,19:3
Sanborn, Edward G, 1941, D 8,23:2
Sanborn, Edward H Jr, 1949, S 2,17:5
Sanborn, Elmer E, 1949, Ap 22,23:1
Sanborn, Elwin R, 1947, D 20,17:1
Sanborn, Eugene B, 1954, Ja 5,27:3
Sanborn, Francis A, 1941, Jl 30,18:3
Sanborn, Francis B, 1954, F 28,92:1
Sanborn, Frank B, 1958, My 17,19:4
Sanborn, Franklin B, 1917, F 25,19:2
Sanborn, Franklin J, 1875, My 30,7:1
Sanborn, Fred E, 1961, Mr 11,21:6
Sanborn, Frederick R Dr, 1968, Ag 29,35:5
Sanborn, Frederick R Mrs, 1959, N 27,29:3
Sanborn, G H, 1881, Ja 28,8:1
Sanborn, G Walter, 1950, D 23,15:3
Sanborn, Harvey D, 1955, S 11,85:1
Sanborn, Henry C, 1939, N 1,23:2
Sanborn, Herbert W Mrs, 1948, S 27,23:1
Sanborn, J S, 1903, My 13,9:5
Sanborn, James F, 1949, N 13,94:3
Sanborn, John A, 1953, Je 30,23:2
Sanborn, John B, 1940, Je 30,32:6; 1964, Mr 8,86:6
Sanborn, John P, 1915, D 31,9:8
Sanborn, Katherine A, 1941, F 25,23:5
Sanborn, Katz Abbott, 1917, Jl 10,13:5
Sanborn, Lauren M, 1953, Ap 9,27:2
Sanborn, Lawrence M, 1944, Ap 1,13:3
Sanborn, Lewis E B Dr, 1911, S 25,9:4
Sanborn, Lloyd W, 1949, Ap 27,27:2
Sanborn, Mabel Y Mrs, 1950, S 22,31:4
Sanborn, Noel B, 1914, Ag 15,9:6
Sanborn, Olin Mrs, 1951, O 31,29:2
Sanborn, Oren C Mrs, 1947, Ja 19,53:3
Sanborn, Paul C, 1948, Jl 15,23:5
Sanborn, Phil, 1940, N 10,57:2
Sanborn, Pitts (por), 1941, Mr 8,19:1
Sanborn, Ruth B, 1942, Je 30,21:5
Sanborn, Victor P, 1967, My 10,47:4
Sanborn, Victor P Mrs, 1966, Je 21,43:2
Sanborn, W H, 1928, My 11,25:3
Sanborn, Walter L, 1947, O 22,29:4
Sanborn, Walter L Mrs, 1945, D 31,17:1
Sanborn, William H, 1955, Je 2,29:3
Sanbourne, Linley, 1910, Ag 4,7:6
Sanbourne, Maurice R, 1952, Ap 27,90:4
Sancer-Santich, Karlo, 1961, D 5,43:1
Sancha y Hervas, Ciriaco Maria Cardinal, 1909, F 26,7:3
Sanche, Ruby D, 1952, S 21,89:2
Sancher, Harold A, 1953, O 17,15:1
Sanchex, Francisco, 1952, D 9,33:3
Sanchez, Alberto Carlos, 1915, My 24,11:5
Sanchez, Carl N Jr, 1955, Ap 25,23:5
Sanchez, Carlos N, 1952, Ap 30,27:4
Sanchez, Edward J, 1941, Je 18,21:4
Sanchez, Eloy, 1952, Ja 3,27:1

Sanchez, Francis J, 1952, F 24,84:6
Sanchez, Jesus, 1954, Mr 26,21:2
Sanchez, Joaquin M, 1966, S 14,39:3
Sanchez, Manuel L, 1946, Ap 26,21:4
Sanchez, Marshall Mrs, 1949, S 22,31:2
Sanchez, Paul F Jr, 1957, Je 4,35:1
Sanchez, Salvador S, 1945, O 17,19:5
Sanchez, Thomas, 1915, S 4,7:1
Sanchez Agramonte, Armando, 1938, O 11,25:2
Sanchez de Fuentes, Eduardo, 1944, S 8,19:4
Sanchez Guerra, J, 1935, Ja 27,27:3
Sanchez Guerra, Rafael (Bro Rafael), 1964, Ap 3, 33:2
Sanchez Pessino, Mario, 1946, N 28,27:2
Sanchez Roman, Filipe, 1956, Ja 24,31:2
Sanchez Sorondo, Matias G, 1959, F 13,27:1
Sanchez Taboada, Rodolfo, 1955, My 3,31:2
Sancho, Rupert C, 1967, My 26,47:2
Sancken, John, 1946, D 20,24:2
Sancoucy, A Eugene, 1950, Ap 16,6:2
Sanctis, Gaetano de, 1957, Ap 10,33:5
Sancton, George E, 1910, Mr 23,11:4
Sand, Christian H, 1867, Mr 10,5:6
Sand, Frederick J, 1961, Ja 7,19:6
Sand, Gabrielle, 1909, Jl 3,7:4
Sand, George (see also Je 9), 1876, Je 22,1:7
Sand, Isaac Mrs, 1959, My 2,23:4
Sand, J Henry (Heinie), 1958, N 5,35:5
Sand, Jacob, 1945, Ag 17,17:3
Sand, John H E Dr, 1937, D 4,17:4
Sand, Joseph H, 1964, Je 18,35:2
Sand, Martin B, 1951, N 25,86:1
Sand, Rene, 1953, Ag 26,27:2
Sandager, Harry, 1955, D 25,48:6
Sandahl, Charles F, 1943, D 25,13:3
Sandalls, George Jr, 1953, Mr 31,31:5
Sandalls, George T, 1937, Jl 29,19:6
Sandalls, George T Mrs, 1946, Mr 27,27:1
Sanday, William D S, 1952, Mr 31,19:2
Sandberg, C Peter, 1941, Je 29,32:7
Sandberg, Eddy, 1948, O 3,64:4
Sandberg, Jonkheer J N R, 1944, D 30,11:5
Sandberg, Maurice H, 1953, S 9,29:2
Sandberg, Russell V Sr, 1951, N 24,11:2
Sandberg, Samuel S, 1945, D 24,16:3
Sandblom, Charles A, 1944, Ja 8,13:2
Sandblom, Gustave A, 1948, D 22,24:3
Sandbrook, John A, 1942, F 14,15:5
Sandburg, Carl (ed trb, Jl 23,IV,8:2; funl, Jl 25,32:1), 1967, Jl 23,1:2
Sande, Earl, 1968, Ag 21,45:1
Sande, Thomas, 1943, My 15,15:3
Sandeau, Jules (see also, My 8), 1883, Ap 25,4:7
Sandefer, Jefferson D (por), 1940, Mr 23,13:3
Sandel, William D, 1947, Jl 29,22:3
Sandelin, G Lincoln, 1967, Jl 18,37:4
Sandelson, Herman, 1942, Ap 26,39:1
Sandeman, Nairne S Sir, 1940, Ap 24,23:2
Sandemose, Aksel, 1965, Ag 7,21:2
Sanden, Andrew P Capt, 1909, My 18,9:5
Sanden, Arthur L, 1950, My 3,29:2
Sander, Daniel, 1949, Jl 1,19:3
Sander, Frances (Sister Mary Tryphosa), 1958, My 27,31:2
Sander, Fred, 1943, Ja 13,23:5
Sander, Hugo Mrs, 1956, O 8,27:4
Sander, Monroe H, 1956, S 18,35:3
Sander, Philip, 1965, Ja 4,29:2
Sander, Theodore Jr Mrs, 1964, S 7,19:2
Sander, Theodore Mrs, 1951, Ap 26,29:3
Sander, Walter D, 1958, Ap 16,33:1
Sander, William, 1946, Je 30,38:4
Sanderford, John R, 1962, Jl 26,27:1
Sanderl, Alphonse B, 1948, S 5,40:5
Sandermann, Charles, 1938, D 6,23:5
Sanders, Albert, 1924, Ap 29,17:2
Sanders, Alex, 1951, Mr 27,29:2
Sanders, Alvin E, 1952, My 27,27:5
Sanders, Alvin H, 1948, Jl 19,19:4
Sanders, Archie D (por), 1941, Jl 16,17:4
Sanders, Arthur, 1908, S 6,9:2
Sanders, Arthur C, 1938, Ap 11,15:4
Sanders, Bernard, 1967, Ja 22,77:2
Sanders, Bert, 1957, Ap 7,88:8
Sanders, C W, 1889, Jl 6,5:2
Sanders, Carl R, 1948, Ja 29,23:5
Sanders, Carl T, 1965, Ap 30,40:2
Sanders, Charles, 1938, S 8,23:3
Sanders, Charles B, 1943, Je 7,13:3
Sanders, Charles H, 1956, Ap 24,31:1
Sanders, Charles Walton Dr, 1918, Jl 23,13:5
Sanders, Constance B, 1937, Ag 3,23:3
Sanders, Ed, 1954, D 13,37:2
Sanders, Ed (inquest rept), 1955, Ja 15,17:2
Sanders, Edwin L Mrs, 1938, My 13,19:1
Sanders, Everett, 1950, My 13,17:3
Sanders, Everett M, 1964, F 1,23:6
Sanders, Frederick M, 1944, Ag 20,34:2
Sanders, George N, 1873, Ag 13,8:2
Sanders, George P, 1957, O 14,27:4
Sanders, Gerard A F, 1941, Mr 12,21:3
Sanders, Gilbert, 1955, Ap 20,33:5
Sanders, Gregory, 1958, N 19,37:4

Sanders, H George Mrs, 1945, Ag 12,40:6
Sanders, Harold F, 1959, Ap 15,33:2
Sanders, Harry L, 1950, O 24,29:5
Sanders, Henry A, 1956, N 18,88:3
Sanders, Henry E, 1949, O 21,21:4
Sanders, Henry Martin Rev Dr, 1921, Jl 23,7:6
Sanders, Henry N, 1943, My 23,42:8
Sanders, Henry R (Red),(services, Ag 19,27:2), 1958, Ag 15,21:3
Sanders, Henry S Mrs (H Slade), 1958, Jl 20,65:1
Sanders, Horace W, 1968, F 13,43:2
Sanders, Ivan W, 1957, Jl 18,25:3
Sanders, J Glen (will), 1961, Ja 19,21:6
Sanders, J Y Jr, 1960, D 1,35:4
Sanders, James P, 1904, D 19,9:5
Sanders, James W, 1937, Ap 3,19:2
Sanders, Jared Y, 1944, Mr 24,19:1
Sanders, Jo, 1965, My 16,87:3
Sanders, Joe Mrs, 1947, F 14,21:1
Sanders, John C, 1947, D 21,52:4
Sanders, John G, 1937, Jl 14,21:4
Sanders, Joseph, 1960, Ag 23,29:1
Sanders, Lawrence H, 1964, Ap 26,88:5
Sanders, Leo, 1955, Je 16,31:5; 1962, Je 16,19:6
Sanders, Leon Judge, 1937, Ag 23,19:5
Sanders, Leonard G, 1940, Jl 13,14:8
Sanders, LeRoy, 1961, O 9,35:2
Sanders, Leslie E, 1951, Ag 11,11:3
Sanders, Lewis, 1967, Mr 21,46:3
Sanders, Mary M H V Mrs, 1957, Je 24,23:5
Sanders, Maurice, 1967, F 2,36:1
Sanders, Max E, 1959, Ap 8,37:1
Sanders, Michael E, 1942, D 5,15:5
Sanders, Morgan G, 1956, Ja 8,87:1
Sanders, Murray, 1961, My 22,31:3
Sanders, Nathan, 1940, Mr 21,25:5
Sanders, Nathaniel S H, 1949, Ap 9,17:3
Sanders, Newell, 1939, Ja 27,20:2
Sanders, Omar, 1959, Mr 31,29:1
Sanders, Paul C, 1955, O 29,19:2
Sanders, Philip J, 1960, Ag 28,83:1
Sanders, Robert, 1964, N 26,33:3
Sanders, Roy, 1950, Ja 18,31:4
Sanders, Rudolph, 1959, My 1,29:3
Sanders, Samuel, 1943, My 4,23:2
Sanders, Samuel S, 1950, Ag 31,26:2
Sanders, Sydney A, 1948, My 27,25:3
Sanders, Theodore M, 1965, Ag 12,27:5
Sanders, Thomas J, 1946, D 27,19:4
Sanders, Troy, 1959, My 4,29:5
Sanders, Valentine, 1942, Ja 23,19:4
Sanders, W W Col, 1883, Ja 27,2:2
Sanders, Walter, 1947, Je 8,60:3
Sanders, Walter F, 1938, Jl 22,17:2
Sanders, Walter J, 1955, Jl 18,21:5
Sanders, Wiley, 1937, Ag 23,19:4
Sanders, William A, 1945, O 2,23:5
Sanders, William A Mrs, 1949, Ap 24,76:7
Sanders, William H, 1947, My 31,13:3
Sanders, William S, 1941, F 6,22:2
Sanders, William W, 1947, D 28,40:6
Sanderson, Albert C D, 1942, S 9,23:5
Sanderson, Arch J, 1954, Ag 27,21:5
Sanderson, Benjamin S, 1943, Mr 13,13:5
Sanderson, Charles D, 1956, Ag 29,29:4
Sanderson, Charles R, 1956, Jl 25,29:6
Sanderson, David, 1910, F 21,9:5
Sanderson, Dudley E Mrs, 1963, O 3,35:1
Sanderson, Dwight, 1944, S 28,19:6
Sanderson, E L, 1876, O 23,2:7
Sanderson, E N, 1932, N 11,22:2
Sanderson, Edward F Mrs, 1917, Je 1,9:4
Sanderson, Emilie, 1950, Mr 19,92:3
Sanderson, Frank S, 1942, Jl 8,23:6
Sanderson, George, 1951, Jl 18,29:5
Sanderson, George A, 1925, Ap 25,15:5; 1959, Ap 15, 33:2
Sanderson, George Rev, 1923, Mr 1,15:2
Sanderson, H A, 1932, F 27,17:5
Sanderson, Harris V Mrs, 1949, F 3,23:5
Sanderson, Harry, 1871, S 28,4:7
Sanderson, Harry M, 1953, Ap 12,88:3
Sanderson, Harry Schley, 1922, Ap 27,17:4
Sanderson, Herbert H, 1949, My 7,13:6
Sanderson, J O G, 1963, Ag 30,21:2
Sanderson, James V, 1945, N 28,27:3
Sanderson, James W Mrs, 1946, N 18,23:5
Sanderson, John, 1958, D 8,31:4
Sanderson, John C, 1948, N 16,29:2
Sanderson, John W, 1925, N 8,5:1
Sanderson, Joseph, 1952, Mr 21,23:5
Sanderson, Joseph H, 1956, S 20,33:2
Sanderson, Joseph Rev Dr, 1915, O 29,13:6
Sanderson, L B, 1926, O 25,19:3
Sanderson, Lord, 1939, Mr 26,III,7:1
Sanderson, Lyle W, 1917, Jl 16,9:4
Sanderson, Marshall, 1909, O 11,9:5
Sanderson, O, 1926, D 27,15:3
Sanderson, Orville P, 1950, Mr 13,21:4
Sanderson, Paul T, 1944, O 11,21:5
Sanderson, Percy Sir, 1919, Jl 15,11:2
Sanderson, Richard, 1955, Mr 8,27:3
Sanderson, Richard P C, 1942, Jl 12,36:8

Sanderson, Robert Louis Prof, 1922, N 7,17:4
Sanderson, Rowe, 1951, N 29,33:3
Sanderson, Sybil, 1903, My 17,7:5
Sanderson, Thomas C, 1950, F 14,25:4
Sanderson, Thomas Henry Baron, 1923, Mr 22,19:5
Sanderson, William E, 1952, O 27,27:4
Sanderson, William W, 1951, O 6,19:2
Sanderspree, William A, 1958, My 8,29:4
Sandes, Flora, 1956, D 2,86:5
Sandford, C O Col, 1883, N 30,4:7
Sandford, C W Maj-Gen, 1878, Jl 26,5:5
Sandford, Charles W, 1945, S 9,45:1
Sandford, Clarence R, 1961, Je 21,37:6
Sandford, Edward, 1921, F 20,22:1
Sandford, Frank W, 1948, Ap 25,72:1
Sandford, James A, 1938, N 20,39:1
Sandford, John H, 1962, O 27,25:5
Sandford, Margaret C Mrs, 1923, Ap 16,17:5
Sandford, Percy Mrs, 1960, N 18,31:2
Sandford, Peregrine, 1884, N 16,2:6
Sandford, Rollin, 1879, D 3,2:6
Sandford, W F, 1880, D 14,8:4
Sandford, William H Jr, 1956, Mr 12,27:3
Sandham, Elijah, 1944, My 10,19:5
Sandham, Henry (trb, Je 23,7:4), 1910, Je 22,9:4
Sandham, John C, 1959, D 10,39:1
Sandhaus, Benjamin, 1955, S 7,31:2
Sandhaus, Max Mrs, 1953, Ag 20,27:5
Sandhurst, Lord, 1876, Jl 6,2:1
Sandhurst, Viscount (Wm Mansfield), 1921, N 3,
Sandiford, Marie (Sister M Raymond), 1959, S 1
Sandiford, Peter, 1941, O 13,17:4
Sandino, Gregorio, 1947, F 15,15:3
Sandison, John S, 1948, Ap 14,27:2
Sandizzi, Clementia S, 1944, Ap 4,21:6
Sandkam, Claude H, 1938, D 14,25:4
Sandkam, Donald C, 1953, My 5,29:1
Sandker, Eugene W, 1954, O 1,23:3
Sandland, William H, 1938, Ja 2,42:1
Sandler, Aaron, 1945, Mr 30,15:4
Sandler, Albert (por), 1948, Ag 31,26:2
Sandler, Arthur J, 1952, S 2,23:4
Sandler, Bernard H, 1958, Je 3,31:1
Sandler, J K, 1931, Mr 1,25:1
Sandler, Jack, 1957, Ag 12,19:5
Sandler, John J (funl;trb, Mr 7,35:1), 1961, Mr
Sandler, Maurice, 1955, Ja 23,85:1
Sandler, Max, 1960, Ap 11,31:1
Sandler, Morris, 1955, D 16,30:1
Sandler, Philip, 1954, Ag 30,17:6
Sandler, Rickard J, 1964, N 13,36:1
Sandlin, Willie, 1949, My 30,13:5
Sandman, Morris, 1941, S 20,17:3
Sandmeyer, John H, 1957, Ja 28,23:5
Sandmeyer, William E, 1966, Ap 24,86:4
Sando, Michael F, 1945, S 12,25:6
Sandonato, Louis, 1959, My 9,21:2
Sandor, Hungarian Robber King, 1878, D 15,2:3
Sandor, Mathias, 1920, N 4,13:3
Sandor, Samuel, 1944, Ag 29,17:1
Sandoval, Aurello, 1925, Ja 2,15:4
Sandoval, Gen, 1907, Jl 12,7:5
Sandoval, Jose M, 1952, F 27,27:1
Sandoval, Miguel, 1953, Ag 25,21:1
Sandoval, Oscar, 1957, Mr 26,22:5
Sandow, Eugene, 1925, O 15,23:5
Sandoz, Jules Mrs, 1938, Ag 20,15:6
Sandoz, Mari, 1966, Mr 11,33:3
Sandoz, Maurice Y, 1958, Je 16,23:5
Sandrich, Mark R (por), 1945, Mr 6,21:4
Sandritter, William G, 1952, My 17,19:4
Sandrow, Edward, 1956, Jl 5,25:4
Sands, A C, 1925, N 15,13:1
Sands, A J Dr, 1877, D 26,1:3
Sands, Alex H Jr, 1960, Ap 23,23:4
Sands, Andrew H, 1904, F 6,9:6
Sands, Anne A, 1945, Ja 31,21:4
Sands, Austin L, 1966, My 31,43:4
Sands, Austin L Mrs, 1952, S 10,29:6
Sands, B F Adm, 1883, Jl 2,5:1
Sands, Benjamin Aymar, 1917, My 2,11:5
Sands, Charles E, 1945, Ag 12,39:3
Sands, Charles H, 1953, Ap 8,29:4
Sands, Charles P, 1939, D 25,23:4
Sands, Daniel E, 1939, S 1,12:7
Sands, Dave, 1952, Ag 12,26:2
Sands, David, 1942, Mr 26,23:4
Sands, Edward Van V, 1962, F 11,87:2
Sands, Elijah M, 1954, F 21,68:3
Sands, Esther, 1903, Ag 14,7:6
Sands, Frank E, 1943, Jl 12,15:6; 1951, Je 10,9
Sands, Frederic P Jr Mrs, 1944, Ja 20,19:1
Sands, Frederick P, 1905, D 23,7:5
Sands, Frederick P Mrs, 1946, O 30,27:5
Sands, Frederick W, 1966, D 27,32:2
Sands, G Winthrop (funl, Ag 2,7:6), 1908, Jl
Sands, George, 1943, F 23,21:4
Sands, George J, 1922, Je 19,15:6
Sands, George W, 1953, Je 4,29:5
Sands, Harold A, 1951, My 30,21:5
Sands, Henry M, 1913, N 11,13:5
Sands, Howard E, 1945, Je 28,19:4; 1964, Mr
Sands, Howard Mrs, 1964, S 15,37:1

Sands, Howard T, 1938, F 14,17:2
Sands, Irving J, 1958, O 23,31:1
Sands, J A, 1883, O 4,2:4
Sands, J R, 1883, O 5,8:2
Sands, James Hoban, 1911, O 28,13:6
Sands, John, 1944, S 18,19:4
Sands, Joseph F, 1946, Mr 8,21:3
Sands, Julius, 1903, Je 9,9:6
Sands, Kenneth F, 1959, Mr 14,23:1
Sands, Lewis E, 1942, Ja 24,15:7
Sands, Merrill B, 1951, Mr 28,29:4; 1963, O 1,39:1
Sands, Norton J Dr, 1915, N 14,19:5
Sands, R A, 1879, Ag 1,5:2
Sands, R M Col, 1903, N 19,9:7
Sands, Robert, 1874, Ag 22,5:3
Sands, Robert M, 1937, My 22,15:4
Sands, Simon R, 1950, D 14,35:3
Sands, Tucker K Mrs, 1948, N 30,27:3
Sands, Walter H, 1947, Je 28,13:5
Sands, William A, 1950, Jl 27,25:5
Sands, William A Jr, 1959, Ap 2,31:5
Sands, William E, 1937, F 14,II,9:1
Sands, William F, 1946, Je 19,21:1
Sands, William H, 1920, Jl 17,7:7
Sands, William J, 1945, Je 3,32:4
Sands, William L, 1943, Je 26,13:4
Sands, William P, 1912, Mr 15,9:5
Sands, William Richardson, 1908, Mr 25,9:4
Sandson, Sidney, 1967, Ag 24,37:4
Sandstroem, Johan, 1947, Ja 13,21:5
Sandstrom, Claude W, 1947, D 21,54:1
Sandstrom, Earl R, 1956, F 26,88:2
Sandstrom, Emil, 1962, Jl 8,64:2
Sandstrom, Henry F, 1945, F 3,11:2
Sandt, Benjamin F Dr, 1937, Jl 1,27:4
Sandt, Frank R, 1938, Ap 6,23:6
Sandt, Lloyd O Mrs, 1959, N 7,23:3
Sandt, Robert A, 1953, O 13,29:4
Sandt, Russell L, 1951, Mr 13,31:3
Sandus, Alfred P, 1948, S 22,31:2
Sandusky, Fred H, 1951, F 10,13:4
Sandusky, John W, 1937, N 22,19:5
Sandwell, Arnold H, 1940, Mr 11,15:4
Sandwell, Bernard K, 1954, D 9,33:5
Sandwich, Countess of, 1951, O 24,31:3
Sandwich, Earl of (G C Montagu), 1962, Je 17,81:2
Sandwich, Lord, 1916, Je 27,11:7
Sandwina, Kati (Mrs M Heyman), 1952, Ja 22,29:3
Sandy, William C, 1957, S 9,25:4
Sandy, William E, 1956, Mr 7,33:3
Sandys, Baron, 1948, Ag 6,17:1
Sandys, Edwin, 1906, O 27,9:6
Sandzen, Birger, 1954, Je 20,86:2
Sandzen, Sigurd C Mrs, 1953, N 27,27:3
Sanefur, James F, 1955, Ag 23,23:3
Saner, Robert E L (por), 1938, N 1,23:3
Sanes, Kay I Dr, 1925, My 11,17:4
Sanford, Aaron K Rev Dr, 1910, F 23,9:4
Sanford, Arthur B Mrs, 1945, D 18,27:2
Sanford, Arthur E Mrs, 1954, My 11,29:4
Sanford, Baylis, 1875, N 30,5:5
Sanford, Bert, 1953, F 12,27:4
Sanford, C H, 1928, D 25,23:4
Sanford, C Hamilton, 1942, F 17,22:3
Sanford, Carleton F, 1907, O 27,9:5
Sanford, Charles Edwin Dr, 1914, Ap 28,13:6
Sanford, Charles F Judge, 1881, O 22,5:3
Sanford, Charles W, 1941, D 10,25:5
Sanford, Clarke A, 1964, My 17,86:5
Sanford, Cornelia M Mrs, 1942, D 1,25:2
Sanford, Daniel S Mrs, 1956, Ja 23,25:1
Sanford, David L, 1939, F 6,13:5
Sanford, David L Mrs, 1944, O 5,23:5
Sanford, De W C, 1881, Je 18,2:4
Sanford, Delerue, 1951, Ag 2,21:1
Sanford, Della M, 1924, Ja 4,13:4
Sanford, Dent W, 1956, Ag 8,25:5
Sanford, Desiree M, 1952, D 1,23:5
Sanford, E B, 1932, Jl 4,11:1
Sanford, E S, 1882, S 10,7:3
Sanford, E Starr, 1917, Jl 19,11:5
Sanford, E T, 1930, Mr 9,1:6
Sanford, E W Dr, 1918, Jl 24,11:4
Sanford, Edgar A, 1942, Je 14,45:1
Sanford, Edgar L, 1945, O 17,19:2
Sanford, Edmund C Dr, 1924, N 23,7:1
Sanford, Edwin W, 1953, Ja 29,28:3
Sanford, Edwin W Mrs, 1945, Ja 1,21:5
Sanford, Emma C, 1937, Ap 3,19:3
Sanford, Ernest H, 1937, O 7,27:1
Sanford, Eugene B Mrs, 1942, F 14,15:2
Sanford, Eva M, 1954, Mr 27,17:4
Sanford, Ezra, 1883, Ag 16,1:7
Sanford, Ezra T, 1912, Ag 24,9:7
Sanford, F H Capt, 1926, F 19,21:4
Sanford, Ferdinand D (por), 1943, Mr 4,19:4
Sanford, Fillmore H, 1967, Ag 7,29:5
Sanford, Floyd S Jr, 1950, O 20,27:6
Sanford, Francis B, 1949, Mr 25,23:5
Sanford, Francis T, 1960, Je 21,33:3
Sanford, Francis T Mrs, 1960, Jl 11,29:4
Sanford, Frank B Mrs, 1941, N 15,17:4
Sanford, Frank C, 1948, Mr 31,26:2
Sanford, G Foster Mrs, 1961, S 17,86:8
Sanford, George Bliss Col, 1908, Jl 14,5:6
Sanford, George D Gen, 1917, Mr 15,11:5
Sanford, George F, 1938, My 24,19:1
Sanford, George H, 1871, N 27,1:2
Sanford, Graham, 1942, Ja 22,18:3
Sanford, H C, 1928, Ap 23,23:5
Sanford, H Rev, 1882, Ag 6,9:4
Sanford, Harold, 1945, Ja 21,40:6
Sanford, Harold W, 1950, Ap 6,29:3
Sanford, Harry, 1905, Ap 22,11:6; 1942, Mr 3,23:3
Sanford, Henry, 1903, S 8,7:5; 1940, Je 18,23:5
Sanford, Henry G Mrs, 1963, Jl 29,19:3
Sanford, Henry L, 1938, F 6,II,8:7
Sanford, Henry Mrs, 1903, Je 20,7:6
Sanford, Homer R, 1947, Ap 9,25:3
Sanford, Howard Mrs, 1958, N 9,88:5
Sanford, Hugh W S, 1961, N 16,39:1
Sanford, J Edgar, 1949, My 3,25:2
Sanford, James H, 1952, F 15,25:3
Sanford, Jared, 1903, F 5,9:4
Sanford, John, 1939, S 27,25:1
Sanford, John Mrs, 1924, N 14,19:3
Sanford, John Ramsey Com, 1919, My 4,22:5
Sanford, John W, 1939, Jl 13,19:7
Sanford, John W Mrs, 1956, Ja 4,27:4
Sanford, John W Sr, 1942, D 5,15:6
Sanford, Jonathan B, 1939, My 15,17:5
Sanford, Joseph W, 1952, F 7,27:1
Sanford, Leigh, 1949, N 15,26:3
Sanford, Lemuel C, 1947, My 23,23:2
Sanford, Leonard C, 1950, D 8,29:3
Sanford, Lewis W, 1947, Je 20,19:2
Sanford, Lillias R Mrs, 1940, Ap 17,23:4
Sanford, Louis C, 1948, Ag 12,21:3
Sanford, Luman, 1944, Ja 13,21:5
Sanford, Lutie W Mrs, 1939, Jl 7,17:1
Sanford, Marcelline H Mrs, 1963, D 10,43:2
Sanford, Margaret L Mrs, 1938, Jl 27,17:2
Sanford, Maria L, 1920, Ap 22,11:4
Sanford, Mary E Mrs, 1948, Mr 20,13:2
Sanford, Mary R, 1947, D 21,52:4
Sanford, Maude, 1943, S 28,25:4
Sanford, Myron R, 1939, Ja 16,15:5
Sanford, Philip Gerard, 1917, Mr 26,11:5
Sanford, Rollin, 1957, My 17,51:2
Sanford, Roswell G R Mrs, 1948, My 23,68:6
Sanford, Samuel S Prof (mem), 1910, Mr 17,9:4
Sanford, Samuel Simons Prof, 1910, Ja 7,9:4
Sanford, Sarah Elizabeth, 1924, Ap 9,21:2
Sanford, Selden B, 1958, O 8,35:2
Sanford, Steadman V (por), 1945, S 16,43:1
Sanford, Stephen, 1913, F 14,15:3
Sanford, Thaddeus, 1867, My 10,1:2
Sanford, Trent E, 1952, Je 26,29:5
Sanford, Wallis A Mrs, 1949, N 28,27:4
Sanford, Walter, 1922, N 27,15:4; 1942, Ag 4,19:6
Sanford, Walter B, 1942, Ag 13,19:4
Sanford, Walter S, 1948, Ag 9,19:3
Sanford, Warren B, 1955, Ap 29,23:1
Sanford, Watson E, 1953, Ag 18,23:2
Sanford, Willard C, 1938, D 13,26:2
Sanford, William A Mrs, 1959, Je 24,31:5
Sanford, William F Mrs, 1962, F 19,31:5
Sanford, William H, 1941, My 1,23:2; 1946, Ag 11,46:1
Sanford, William Moore, 1920, Ja 30,15:5
Sang, Don Dr, 1903, Mr 11,9:5
Sang, Joseph R, 1965, Ag 18,35:5
Sanger, Alan B, 1963, D 27,25:1
Sanger, Bertram J Mrs, 1960, Ap 19,37:4
Sanger, Charles A Mrs, 1962, My 2,37:3
Sanger, Charles Robert Dr, 1912, F 26,11:4
Sanger, David, 1953, O 22,29:5
Sanger, Eugene B, 1904, D 28,7:6; 1946, F 25,25:3
Sanger, George, 1947, F 1,15:3
Sanger, Henry H, 1956, Ja 5,34:1
Sanger, Herbert H, 1967, O 30,45:4
Sanger, Isaac Mrs (died Je 23; funl), 1967, Je 29,43:4
Sanger, Isaac S, 1939, Ag 20,33:4
Sanger, J P Maj Gen, 1926, Mr 16,25:1
Sanger, John B, 1955, Ag 25,23:3
Sanger, John P, 1951, F 12,23:2
Sanger, Lester N, 1953, F 24,25:4
Sanger, Louis P, 1955, Mr 3,27:4
Sanger, Margaret, 1940, N 21,29:5
Sanger, Margaret (Mrs J Noah H Slee),(mem ser, S 9,45:1), 1966, S 7,1:1
Sanger, Milton J, 1916, N 11,9:1
Sanger, Paul W Dr, 1968, S 10,47:1
Sanger, Prentice Mrs, 1952, Je 22,68:1
Sanger, Richard, 1957, Ja 20,92:5
Sanger, Robert E, 1949, D 16,31:3
Sanger, Roderick MacLean Dr, 1911, Ap 17,11:6
Sanger, Sabin P, 1938, Jl 9,13:6
Sanger, Sigmond, 1946, D 29,35:7
Sanger, William C Mrs, 1952, My 14,27:1
Sanger, William Carey Col, 1921, D 7,17:6
Sangmeister, Henry J, 1956, My 6,87:1
Sangnier, Marc, 1950, My 29,17:4
Sangree, L Alan, 1924, Mr 3,17:5
Sangster, Donald, 1967, Ap 12,47:4
Sangster, George M, 1946, My 28,21:2
Sangster, James R, 1905, Ap 5,9:6
Sangster, John M, 1941, Je 1,41:1
Sangster, Margaret E Mrs, 1912, Je 5,11:5
Sangster, William E R, 1960, My 25,39:1
Sanguily, Julio Gen, 1906, Mr 24,9:6
Sanguily, Manuel Col, 1925, Ja 25,7:1
Sanhedrai, Israel Rabbi, 1968, Ag 16,33:1
Sania, Albert, 1962, N 18,85:8
Sanial, Albert D, 1957, F 11,29:5
Sanin, Alex, 1956, My 10,31:1
Sanine, Alex A Mrs, 1939, F 9,21:3
Sanjo, Kimiteru, 1945, N 12,21:2
Sanjule, Carl K, 1946, Je 7,19:2
Sankey, Ira D (funl, Ag 16,7:4), 1908, Ag 15,7:5
Sankey, Ira D Mrs, 1910, S 26,13:5
Sankey, Viscount (por), 1948, F 8,60:3
Sankley, Ira S, 1915, D 31,9:8
Sankowsky, Nicholas A, 1948, O 5,25:1
Sanks, William R Mrs, 1951, Je 18,23:6
Sanky, Paul G, 1939, D 7,27:1
Sann, Paul Mrs, 1961, N 13,31:1
Sanna, Serfino, 1958, N 20,35:4
Sanno, James M J Gen, 1907, My 5,9:6
Sano, Tsuneha, 1956, Ja 27,23:3
Sansburn, John, 1948, N 19,27:1
Sansbury, Marvin O, 1962, F 23,29:1
Sansel, B Frank Sr, 1959, D 1,39:2
Sansevere, Frank J, 1947, D 18,30:3
Sansevere, Joseph J Mrs, 1959, Je 20,21:4
Sanso, Salvatore, 1959, Jl 17,21:5
Sansom, Charles H, 1943, Mr 17,21:2
Sansom, Edward M Sr, 1949, Jl 7,25:3
Sansom, Herbert B, 1963, My 22,41:4
Sansom, John W, 1942, My 12,19:2
Sansom, Richard A Judge, 1923, F 17,13:5
Sansom, Walter C, 1943, Ap 25,34:8
Sanson, Pierre E, 1955, Ja 17,23:6
Sanson, Stanton D, 1964, D 22,29:4
Sansone, Filomeno, 1958, N 16,88:4
Sansone, Francis X, 1962, Ag 4,19:5
Sansone, Frank, 1952, Je 20,23:2
Sansone, Joseph B, 1958, My 20,33:4
Sansone, Ralph C, 1953, N 6,27:2
Sansoni, Guido, 1942, D 21,23:5
Sanstrom, Ragnhild Mrs, 1960, D 8,35:4
Sansum, William D, 1948, Ja 7,26:2
Sant, James, 1916, Jl 13,11:5
Santa, Michael, 1959, F 2,25:4
Santa Anna, A L de, 1876, Jl 7,4:7
Santa Anna, Mary A (Sister of Mary of St Felix), 1960, S 2,23:3
Santa Cruz, Marquis of, 1940, S 14,17:5
Santa Elena, Duke of, 1939, Ja 25,21:3
Santa Maria, Marceliano, 1952, O 13,21:5
Santacruz, Blanca E de Mrs, 1940, Mr 22,19:2
Santaella, Antonio, 1948, Ja 29,23:5
Santaella, Raymond, 1947, Ap 7,41:8
Santamaria, Giuseppe, 1964, F 13,31:2
Santamarina, Enrique, 1937, Ap 19,21:3
Santander, Luis A, 1920, O 20,13:4
Santander, Manuel Msgr, 1907, F 15,11:4
Santangelo, Earl, 1945, Je 7,19:4
Santangelo, Leo B, 1944, D 28,20:2
Santangelo, Michael, 1951, Mr 24,13:6
Santangelo, Michael Mrs, 1950, Ap 3,23:1
Santangelo, Paul E, 1949, Ap 26,26:3
Santaniello, Severino, 1944, Mr 2,17:4
Santarelli, Loretto, 1944, O 12,27:1
Santayana, George, 1952, S 28,1:2
Santee, Alvin C, 1949, Ja 14,23:3
Santee, Harry A, 1951, Ap 26,29:5
Santee, Martha P Mrs, 1937, My 31,15:4
Santee, Ross, 1965, Jl 1,31:3
Santell, Al Mrs, 1944, S 15,19:5
Santelli, Salvatore M, 1955, D 23,18:2
Santens, Remi H, 1943, Mr 6,13:3
Santer, Morris, 1952, Ap 25,23:1
Santhouse, Herman Mrs, 1948, N 19,28:2
Santhouse, Ralph, 1944, Ag 23,19:5
Santi, Fabio, 1956, O 25,33:2
Santiago, Pedro, 1966, F 12,27:3
Santiesteban y Ochoa, Teodoro, 1950, D 6,33:4
Santillo, Giovanni, 1959, Je 16,35:2
Santina, Peter D, 1955, Jl 10,75:1
Santini, Albina B, 1962, O 17,39:4
Santini, August, 1964, Ja 6,47:3
Santini, Frank, 1957, Je 6,31:1
Santini, Gabriele, 1964, N 14,29:3
Santini, George A, 1956, Je 8,25:4
Santini, Giuselio C, 1957, S 8,84:3
Santini, Godfrey E, 1956, Je 23,17:6
Santini, Paride L, 1954, Ja 2,11:2
Santini, Randolph R, 1940, Ap 15,17:4
Santini, Ruggero, 1963, Je 10,31:3
Santley, Charles, 1922, S 23,15:4
Santley, Fredric, 1953, My 16,19:2
Santley, Kate, 1923, Ja 19,17:6
Santly, Harry, 1955, F 26,15:5
Santly, Joseph, 1962, Ag 30,29:3
Santmier, Arthur, 1951, D 18,31:1
Santo, Emery J Mrs, 1968, Jl 19,35:2
Santo, John, 1950, Ja 4,35:4
Santo, Vincenzo de, 1923, D 17,17:4
Santopoli, Joseph, 1942, My 30,8:2

Santoro, Daniel, 1954, D 2,31:2
Santoro, Edward J, 1968, O 18,20:5
Santoro, Frank A, 1960, Ag 30,29:4
Santoro, George R, 1966, Ap 2,29:4
Santoro, John A Mrs, 1967, My 23,47:1
Santoro, Pasquale L, 1955, Ap 28,29:3
Santoro, Ralph A Mrs, 1962, O 7,82:7
Santoro, Raymond V, 1962, F 18,93:1
Santoro, Tobias, 1943, S 3,19:2
Santos, Carlos, 1965, S 29,3:6
Santos, Demitro, 1956, Ap 10,31:4
Santos, Eduardo Sra, 1960, Mr 28,29:5
Santos, Maria, 1949, D 25,12:5
Santos, Rafael, 1947, F 5,26:1
Santos, Richard S, 1953, Ag 1,11:5
Santos, Samuel, 1942, Mr 29,45:2
Santos, Valentin de los, 1967, Ag 25,35:2
Santos-Dumont, A, 1932, Jl 25,15:1
Santos Montejo, Guillermo, 1948, N 8,21:1
Santos y Oliveira, Balbino, 1953, F 15,92:2
Santosbraga, Emilia, 1949, D 30,19:5
Santosiossoa, Ralph, 1949, Ap 18,25:5
Santry, Augustus B, 1949, Ap 24,76:5
Santry, Edward J, 1941, D 3,25:5
Santry, Harry, 1916, O 8,23:3
Santry, Jeremiah J Jr, 1958, F 5,28:2
Santry, Joseph V, 1967, My 10,44:5
Santucci, Edward D, 1964, Jl 4,13:4
Santullo, Louis Mrs, 1968, Ag 15,37:3
Santvoord, Sloat Van, 1882, Je 1,5:5
Sanville, Henry F, 1941, My 26,19:4
Sanville, L Frederic, 1951, F 17,15:5
Sanvito, Charles, 1953, O 2,21:6
Sanwald, Robert, 1947, Ap 27,60:2
Sanz, Louis B, 1943, Ap 4,40:3
Sanz y Tovar, Emilio Count, 1959, N 20,31:3
Sap, Gustavus, 1940, Mr 20,27:2
Saperstein, Aaron, 1938, Jl 11,17:2
Saperstein, Abe, 1966, Mr 19,45:2
Saperstein, Abraham L, 1948, Ap 23,23:4
Saperstein, Bernard H Mrs, 1959, D 15,39:6
Saperstein, David, 1959, Jl 13,27:4
Saperstein, Luis, 1950, My 9,29:2
Saperstein, Rocky, 1951, Ja 16,29:2
Saperstein, Sidney, 1958, S 10,33:2
Saperstone, Isaac, 1941, Mr 14,21:2
Sapey, Ernest E, 1957, Je 12,35:4
Saphar, Farris D, 1951, My 23,35:2
Saphier, Sol J, 1967, D 4,47:3
Saphir, Joseph F, 1959, N 27,26:6
Saphir, Otto, 1963, N 27,37:1
Saphirstein, Jacob (funl, Je 3,13:6), 1914, Je 2,11:6
Saphore, Edwin W (por), 1944, My 24,19:4
Saphore, Peter E, 1942, N 15,58:1
Saphra, Ivan, 1957, O 8,35:1
Sapieha, Adam S, 1951, Jl 24,25:1
Sapieha, Eustace Prince, 1963, F 21,9:7
Sapienza, Nunzio J Mrs, 1957, N 12,37:2
Sapin, Ruth (Mrs H Hurwitz), 1961, Je 19,27:2
Sapinsky, Simon M, 1948, My 15,15:5
Sapio, Romualdo, 1943, S 24,23:4
Sapio, Romualdo Mrs (C D de Vere), 1954, Ja 20, 27:5
Sapir, Edward, 1939, F 5,40:6
Sapiro, Aaron L (trb lr, D 4,30:5), 1959, N 25,29:1
Sapiro, David, 1955, D 11,88:6
Sapiro, Phil H, 1955, Je 25,15:5
Saporiti, Allesandro, 1941, Jl 22,19:5
Saporito, Frank, 1940, S 4,23:1
Saporito, Frank A, 1943, Ja 19,19:4
Saportas, Edward, 1885, F 2,5:6
Saposs, David J, 1968, N 16,37:1
Sapp, Alva C, 1962, Jl 29,61:1
Sapp, Arthur H, 1946, Ag 10,13:3
Sapp, Clyde C, 1959, Ap 7,33:4
Sapp, Edward H, 1942, D 16,25:4
Sapp, Fred A, 1955, My 4,29:4
Sapp, Fred A Mrs, 1951, D 7,27:2
Sapp, Warren H, 1945, Mr 5,19:4
Sapper, Louis, 1962, Jl 23,21:3
Sappington, Clarence O, 1949, N 7,27:3
Sappington, John C, 1942, Jl 14,20:2
Sappington, Samuel W, 1951, My 17,31:1
Sapru, Tej B, 1949, Ja 21,21:5
Sar, Samuel L, 1962, Je 22,25:1
Sar, Samuel L Mrs, 1961, Ag 18,21:4
Sara, George M Mrs, 1955, O 22,19:1
Saracco, Guiseppe, 1907, Ja 20,7:3
Saraceni, Adele T Mrs, 1947, N 16,76:2
Sarachek, Joseph, 1953, Je 16,27:6
Saracin, William V, 1941, Ja 6,15:2
Saracino, Donato, 1943, Mr 28,24:3
Saracoglu, Sukru, 1953, D 28,21:1
Sarafiance, Alex, 1962, Jl 28,19:5
Sarasate, Pablo de, 1908, S 22,9:6
Sarasohn, Abraham H, 1940, Je 21,22:2
Sarasohn, E, 1933, Ag 16,17:4
Sarasohn, K H, 1905, Ja 13,6:1
Sarasohn, Kasryel Mrs, 1913, Je 2,7:5
Sarason, Abraham, 1968, S 27,47:2
Sarason, Samuel D, 1946, S 12,7:4
Saravanamuttu, Ratnajothi, 1949, S 13,29:1
Saraz (Bro Michael Damian), 1958, N 30,86:4

Sarcey, M Francisque, 1899, My 16,7:2
Sard, Marion K, 1944, S 9,15:6
Sard, Russell E, 1948, Ag 12,21:6
Sardeson, Orville A, 1957, Ag 21,27:4
Sardi, V Msgr, 1920, Ag 13,9:5
Sardou, Victorien, 1908, N 9,7:4
Sardou, Victorien Mrs, 1923, Ap 16,17:5
Sardy, Helen L, 1958, Ap 25,27:3
Sare, Paul F L, 1952, N 5,25:3
Saretsky, Max, 1953, Mr 14,15:6
Sarett, Lew S, 1954, Ag 18,29:3
Sarg, Tony, 1942, Mr 8,42:2
Sarg, Tony Mrs, 1950, Je 28,27:1
Sargant-Florence, Mary Mrs, 1954, D 17,31:1
Sargeant, Earl S, 1958, Ja 24,21:1
Sargeant, Edmund K, 1903, D 24,9:5
Sargeant, Frank W, 1954, F 11,29:5
Sargeant, Frederick D, 1942, Jl 15,19:4
Sargeant, George L Mrs, 1948, Mr 17,25:3
Sargeant, Leonard R, 1944, My 22,19:4
Sargeant, William J, 1954, Jl 7,31:3
Sargeant, Winthrop W Mrs, 1957, Ag 12,19:3
Sargeaunt, Frank W, 1943, Jl 1,19:5
Sargent, Albert E Mrs, 1946, O 12,2:2
Sargent, Allston, 1939, Ap 17,17:5
Sargent, Benjamin F Jr, 1957, D 28,17:5
Sargent, Casius J, 1947, D 26,15:3
Sargent, Charles C Jr, 1913, Ag 27,7:5
Sargent, Charles Chapin, 1922, N 26,6:3
Sargent, Charles F, 1952, D 10,35:2
Sargent, Charles H, 1949, Ag 27,13:5
Sargent, Charles M, 1952, Ap 24,31:4
Sargent, Charles S, 1959, F 16,29:4
Sargent, Christopher S, 1946, D 25,29:4
Sargent, Daniel R, 1952, My 17,19:5
Sargent, David C, 1942, Je 28,33:2
Sargent, Dom H, 1944, O 16,19:3
Sargent, Dudley A Dr, 1924, Jl 22,15:3
Sargent, Eaton D, 1944, Mr 28,19:5
Sargent, Edward H, 1954, O 11,27:5
Sargent, Edward R, 1940, Je 21,21:2
Sargent, Elmer P Jr, 1939, Jl 4,13:2
Sargent, Epes, 1881, Ja 1,5:5; 1902, Ap 5,9:4
Sargent, Epes W, 1938, D 8,27:3
Sargent, Ernest S, 1948, O 11,23:3
Sargent, Fitz W, 1937, Jl 27,21:4
Sargent, Fitzwilliam, 1955, Mr 15,29:1
Sargent, Florence W Mrs, 1938, Ja 11,23:3
Sargent, Frank P, 1908, S 5,7:4; 1908, S 7,5:7
Sargent, Franklin D, 1945, O 4,23:5
Sargent, Franklin H, 1923, S 3,13:5
Sargent, Fred M, 1948, Ag 7,15:5
Sargent, Fred W (will, F 24,9:2),(por), 1940, F 5,17:3
Sargent, Frederick, 1919, Jl 27,22:6
Sargent, G H, 1931, Ja 15,23:3
Sargent, George, 1946, O 2,29:3; 1962, Je 19,35:3
Sargent, George B, 1954, F 12,25:2
Sargent, George K (will, Jl 13,9:4), 1937, Je 26,17:2
Sargent, George L, 1944, F 6,42:4
Sargent, George L Mrs, 1915, Je 30,11:6
Sargent, George P T, 1960, Ap 25,29:5
Sargent, Georgiana, 1946, Je 8,21:4
Sargent, Gorham P, 1945, Ag 23,23:5
Sargent, H W, 1882, N 11,5:1
Sargent, Harriett M Mrs, 1942, Ja 6,23:2
Sargent, Helen D, 1959, D 27,61:1
Sargent, Henry, 1951, N 13,29:4
Sargent, Henry B, 1967, Mr 27,33:3
Sargent, Horace B Gen, 1908, Ja 10,7:5
Sargent, Isaac, 1946, F 12,25:4; 1956, Ap 9,27:5
Sargent, J Ray, 1925, O 7,27:3
Sargent, James B, 1907, Jl 16,7:6
Sargent, Jane I, 1955, Ag 27,15:6
Sargent, John A, 1954, Ja 9,15:2
Sargent, John G (por), 1939, Mr 6,15:1
Sargent, John G Mrs, 1938, S 29,25:4
Sargent, John Mrs, 1952, D 30,19:4
Sargent, John Singer, 1925, Ap 18,15:5
Sargent, John William, 1920, S 25,13:2
Sargent, Joseph A, 1939, Ap 21,23:3; 1950, Jl 6,27:4
Sargent, Laura, 1946, D 24,17:1
Sargent, Laura D, 1961, Ja 16,27:5
Sargent, Lester A, 1958, Mr 20,29:4
Sargent, Lucius Manlius, 1867, Je 4,5:5
Sargent, Malcolm, 1967, O 4,47:1
Sargent, Margherita (Mrs A Duncan), 1964, S 11, 33:2
Sargent, Merritt W, 1946, Ap 12,27:1
Sargent, Norman V, 1958, My 15,29:2
Sargent, Porter, 1951, Mr 28,29:4
Sargent, Raymond F, 1960, D 12,29:4
Sargent, Robert H, 1944, Ag 1,15:5
Sargent, S Harold, 1959, Jl 7,33:3
Sargent, S Harold Mrs, 1967, Ap 20,43:4
Sargent, Samuel E, 1951, My 13,89:1
Sargent, Samuel L, 1953, D 16,35:3
Sargent, Samuel W, 1953, Jl 30,23:4
Sargent, Sullivan A, 1940, Ja 9,23:5
Sargent, Walter F, 1939, Mr 17,21:4
Sargent, William A B, 1949, D 18,88:6
Sargent, William D, 1940, F 16,19:2; 1965, N 25,35:1
Sargent, William D Mrs, 1963, Jl 15,29:5
Sargent, Winthrop, 1916, S 8,7:4; 1963, Jl 21,64:8

Sargent, Winthrop Mrs, 1942, D 9,27:2
Sargent, Ziegler, 1955, O 14,27:4
Sargint, Herman J, 1951, N 28,31:4
Sargison, Frederick W, 1949, N 16,29:4
Sarin, Max K, 1967, Ja 20,42:1
Sarit Thanarat, Premier (funl, D 10,12:2), 1963, D 9, 1:1
Sarit Thanarat (will), 1964, Ap 26,9:1
Sarjeant, Herbert W, 1948, Jl 15,23:5
Sarjeant, Joseph J, 1950, Ap 3,23:2
Sarjeant, Leon F, 1949, S 26,25:4
Sarjeantson, Kate (Kate Sarjeantson Power), 1918, F 18,11:6
Sarkadi, Leo, 1947, Mr 27,28:3
Sarkar, Benoy, 1949, N 25,31:2
Sarkar, Nalini R, 1953, Ja 26,22:7
Sarkis, Eleazer D, 1957, Ag 18,82:6
Sarkisian, Dickran M (por), 1947, D 11,33:3
Sarkisian, Hagop, 1957, Ja 24,29:4
Sarkizov-Serazini, Ivan, 1964, Mr 22,76:8
Sarles, Harold A, 1948, N 26,23:4
Sarles, J W Rev, 1903, Ag 26,7:6
Sarles, Tyler D, 1948, N 9,27:2
Sarly, Albert, 1947, S 30,25:1
Sarma, P J, 1943, Ja 23,13:2
Sarmiento, Fernando, 1939, O 19,23:4
Sarnataro, Salvatore Mrs, 1939, Je 24,17:1
Sarnecka, Joseph Mrs, 1942, S 17,27:7
Sarnecky, Alex, 1958, Je 6,23:4
Sarnella, Eugenio, 1956, S 13,35:2
Sarno, Achille Mrs, 1955, Jl 14,23:4
Sarno, Anthony J, 1967, D 31,44:3
Sarno, Hector V, 1953, D 18,29:2
Sarno, Herman B, 1965, Mr 28,92:1
Sarno, James J, 1962, Jl 28,19:4
Sarnoff, Irving, 1948, Je 10,25:2; 1961, Mr 20,29:2
Sarnoff, Jacob, 1961, Jl 1,17:6
Sarnoff, Jacob M, 1965, Je 7,37:4
Sarnoff, Rae Mrs, 1944, Mr 29,21:3
Sarnoff, Simon, 1950, S 3,38:6
Sarokin, Samuel O, 1967, Ag 6,76:5
Sarolea, Charles, 1953, Mr 12,27:2
Saroli, Franceso L, 1954, N 24,23:6
Saroni, Alfred B Mrs, 1962, N 15,37:2
Sarony, Napoleon, 1896, N 10,9:5
Sarony, Otto, 1903, S 14,7:5
Saros, Peter, 1948, F 16,21:1
Saroyan, Takoohi Mrs, 1950, F 27,19:4
Sarp, Alfred C H, 1956, F 8,33:4
Sarper, Selim, 1968, O 13,84:3
Sarrall, M, 1929, Mr 24,4:1
Sarratt, James A, 1938, My 7,15:5
Sarraut, Albert, 1962, N 27,37:4
Sarraut, Maurice, 1943, D 4,13:5
Sarrazin, Gregor Dr, 1915, N 5,13:4
Sarre, Gordon Mrs, 1965, S 7,39:2
Sarre, John, 1909, Mr 16,9:5
Sarria, Romualdo, 1941, Ap 19,15:2
Sarrocchi, Gino, 1950, My 29,17:5
Sarruf, Neguib Bey, 1949, Mr 26,17:4
Sarsen, William J, 1946, My 30,21:3
Sarsfield, Patrick, 1949, My 25,29:2
Sartain, Harriet, 1957, Mr 6,31:4
Sartain, William, 1924, O 26,7:2
Sartelle, Edward J Mrs, 1943, Mr 14,26:2
Sarther, John M, 1957, O 8,35:1
Sartin, Paul, 1944, Ap 10,19:2
Sarto, Angelo, 1916, Ja 11,11:5
Sarton, George, 1956, Mr 23,27:1
Sartor, Thomas J, 1948, S 7,25:5
Sartorelli, Albert P Mrs, 1965, Je 22,35:2
Sartori, Joseph F, 1946, O 7,31:2
Sartori, Joseph J, 1949, Ag 28,72:5
Sartorio, Antonio, 1958, Jl 11,23:4
Sartoris, Adelaide Kemole, 1879, Ag 31,10:6
Sartoris, Ellen (Nellie Grant), 1879, Ag 16,5:2
Sartoris, George B, 1949, N 21,25:6
Sartoris, Harry M, 1961, O 28,21:2
Sartorius, Augustus, 1915, Jl 13,11:4
Sartorius, G R Sir, 1885, Ap 14,2:4
Sartorius, Herman U, 1960, My 12,35:3
Sartorius, Irving A, 1959, Jl 10,25:2
Sartorius, Irving A Mrs, 1941, Jl 12,13:2
Sartorius, Louis R, 1957, Mr 23,19:5
Sartorius, Otto W, 1939, My 27,15:7
Sarubbi, Michael Rev, 1937, Jl 28,19:1
Sarubbi, Pancrazio A, 1953, Ja 24,15:3
Sarubbi, Paul F, 1946, N 29,25:1
Sarubbi, Peter, 1957, D 15,86:7
Sarubbi, Peter Mrs, 1944, Je 12,19:3
Sarvarfelsovidek, Bertalyan S von, 1943, Je 4,21:5
Sarver, Charles, 1944, N 11,13:6
Sarver, Will P, 1941, My 15,23:4
Sarvis, James Capt, 1905, Je 5,9:3
Sarvis, Robert G, 1954, O 9,17:6
Sarvis, William E, 1950, Ap 9,84:3
Sarwate, Manohar B, 1967, F 20,37:4
Sarzenski, Lawrence, 1951, O 31,29:2
Sasaki, Paul S, 1946, D 22,41:8
Sasaki, Shigetsu Mrs, 1967, O 25,47:3
Sasaki, Sokei-an, 1945, My 19,19:5
Saseon, Robert A, 1944, D 28,19:2
Saslaff, Morris, 1950, O 31,27:4

Saslaff, William E, 1942, Ag 17,15:4
Saslavsky, Alexander, 1924, Ag 4,13:4
Saslavsky, Nicholas L, 1965, Ag 29,84:6
Saslaw, Ruth, 1954, Ja 17,93:1
Saslawsky, Boris, 1955, S 16,23:3
Sason, Frederick C, 1957, O 13,86:4
Sasorith, Katay Don, 1959, D 30,21:2
Sass, Adolph H, 1952, Jl 2,25:6
Sass, Alex E, 1953, O 11,89:3
Sass, Herbert R, 1958, F 20,25:2
Sass, Hugo V, 1953, F 15,93:1
Sass, Julius A, 1943, Je 1,23:3
Sass, Moe J, 1964, My 2,27:1
Sassano, Joseph, 1965, Ag 26,33:5
Sassano, Pasquale Mrs, 1952, Ja 23,27:2
Sasscer, Ernest, 1955, Jl 9,15:6
Sasscer, Lansdale G, 1964, N 7,27:2
Sasse, Hannah, 1944, Je 17,13:3
Sasse, Ralph I, 1954, O 17,86:4
Sassen, K C J M, 1948, F 20,27:3
Sasser, John W, 1938, O 17,15:5
Sasser, Samuel, 1941, Mr 1,15:5
Sasserath, Albert R, 1942, O 25,46:2
Sasseville, Alphonse R, 1966, My 16,37:3
Sassi, Michael F, 1949, Ja 28,21:5
Sassman, William H, 1940, Ap 30,21:2
Sasso, Theodore J, 1949, F 6,76:6
Sassoli-Ruata, Ada, 1946, D 4,31:3
Sassone, Rosalie Mrs, 1922, Ja 17,17:3
Sassoon, Arthur Abraham, 1912, Mr 14,11:5
Sassoon, David E, 1938, My 23,17:6
Sassoon, Phil Sir (will, Ag 16,9:3), 1939, Je 3,15:3
Sassoon, Siegfried, 1967, S 3,53:1
Sassoon, Victor (funl plans, Ag 14,25:5), 1961, Ag 13,88:6
Sassulitch, Vera, 1921, Jl 19,15:5
Sastre, Juan, 1949, Mr 24,27:4
Sastri, Shakuntala R, 1961, My 8,35:3
Satchel, William F, 1941, Ap 25,19:3
Satchell, Nelson, 1945, Ja 14,39:2
Satcher, Herbert B, 1966, My 15,88:2
Satchwell, Harry H, 1938, Ap 7,23:5
Satchwell, Ida Mrs, 1943, Je 5,15:3
Satenstein, Bernard, 1959, My 2,23:6
Satenstein, David L, 1943, F 27,13:2
Satenstein, Edward, 1968, Je 6,48:3
Satenstein, Jesse, 1965, S 9,41:2
Satenstein, Louis (por), 1947, My 27,25:3
Satenstein, Sidney, 1961, F 24,29:3
Sater, J, 1881, Je 6,5:5
Sater, John E, 1937, Jl 19,16:2
Sater, Melvin H, 1940, Jl 31,17:4
Sater, Ola T, 1960, S 8,35:3
Saterlee, Gerald B, 1957, Ap 8,24:1
Satie, Erik, 1925, Jl 4,11:6
Sating, Martin H, 1947, N 18,29:1
Satinsky, Sol, 1966, N 6,88:2
Satko, Paul, 1957, Ap 6,19:4
Sato, A, 1934, Ja 13,13:1
Sato, Ichiro, 1958, Ap 13,84:6
Sato, O K, 1921, Mr 25,15:5
Sato, Sankichi, 1943, Je 19,13:1
Sato, Shiro, 1946, Ag 18,5:4
Satre, Magnus, 1955, Ja 15,13:4
Satterfield, Clavin Jr, 1941, S 10,23:3
Satterfield, Dave E Jr (por), 1946, D 28,16:2
Satterfield, Howard W, 1959, Ag 13,27:2
Satterfield, John P, 1955, My 9,23:5
Satterfield, William R, 1941, Ap 13,38:3
Satterlee, Charles E, 1912, Je 18,11:5
Satterlee, Churchill Rev, 1904, F 17,9:7
Satterlee, Edmund Rathbone, 1903, N 29,7:6
Satterlee, Edward, 1878, My 13,10:2
Satterlee, F L, 1935, D 4,23:1
Satterlee, Francis L Mrs, 1955, D 12,31:3
Satterlee, Francis LeRoy Dr, 1917, N 13,13:5
Satterlee, G, 1880, Mr 14,12:2
Satterlee, George B, 1903, S 19,7:6
Satterlee, Helen F Mrs, 1942, Ap 28,21:5
Satterlee, Henry Yates B (por),(funl, F 24,7:4), 1908, F 23,7:5
Satterlee, Henry Yates Rev, 1916, Je 17,11:5
Satterlee, Herbert L Mrs (por), 1946, O 8,23:5
Satterlee, Hugh, 1963, Jl 16,31:2
Satterlee, Livingston K, 1949, S 1,21:6
Satterlee, Neil, 1939, Ja 1,24:8
Satterlee, R S, 1880, N 11,5:4
Satterlee, Richard Sherwood Capt, 1917, F 16,11:6
Satterlee, Walter, 1908, My 29,7:4
Satterley, Charles E Mrs, 1940, Je 14,21:1
Satterly, C Scott Mrs, 1952, D 1,23:5
Satterly, Courtlandt, 1904, Ja 1,7:6
Satterthawaite, Pennington, 1946, Ap 28,44:2
Satterthwait, John J, 1941, D 20,19:1
Satterthwaite, Alba, 1944, Ja 6,23:2
Satterthwaite, Pennington Mrs, 1958, O 29,35:5
Satterthwaite, Rosalie P Mrs, 1942, Ja 26,15:4
Satterthwaite, T E, 1934, S 20,23:3
Satterthwaite, Thomas C, 1950, F 28,30:2
Satterthwaite, Thomas E Mrs, 1955, Je 29,29:3
Satterwhite, B O Rev, 1911, Mr 12,II,13:3
Satterwhite, Preston P, 1948, D 28,21:3
Satterwhite, Robert B, 1956, N 25,88:7
Satterwhite, Susan B, 1943, Mr 17,21:3
Satti, C John, 1968, My 8,44:4
Satti, C John Mrs, 1960, S 29,35:1
Sattig, John A, 1955, D 21,29:5
Sattler, Benjamin W, 1963, Jl 10,35:1
Sattler, George, 1964, S 3,45:5
Sattler, George A, 1958, S 29,27:3
Sattler, Harry A, 1945, S 11,23:1
Sattler, Jack, 1961, F 4,19:5
Sattler, Katherine E Mrs, 1940, Ap 16,23:1
Sattler, Otto, 1950, Mr 16,32:2
Sattler, Peter, 1960, N 15,39:2
Sattler, Thomas G, 1953, O 29,31:4
Sattler, William G, 1946, Ap 14,46:3
Sattler, Willis, 1948, S 29,29:4
Sattley, Frederick L, 1942, N 23,23:5
Satulsky, Emanuel M Mrs, 1964, Jl 30,27:4
Saturinski, Masloff, 1918, Mr 15,13:5
Saturnelli, John F, 1949, S 9,26:4
Satyamurti, S, 1943, Mr 28,24:7
Satz, David M, 1959, N 7,23:2
Satz, Max Mrs (Dorothy), 1968, Ag 24,27:8
Satz, Sidney, 1958, Ap 30,15:6
Sauber, Helen, 1951, Ag 10,36:6
Saucedo Vargas, Lorenza, 1952, Jl 8,27:1
Sauder, Adolph, 1937, F 25,23:5
Sauder, Harry N Mrs, 1942, D 15,27:2
Sauer, Anthony M, 1952, F 16,13:4
Sauer, Anton, 1873, Je 20,5:6
Sauer, Arthur, 1908, My 31,9:5
Sauer, Arthur A, 1943, S 4,13:4
Sauer, C F Jr, 1953, Ja 19,23:1
Sauer, Carl J Sr, 1949, N 2,27:5
Sauer, Charles J, 1912, S 29,13:5
Sauer, Ella M, 1937, Ap 1,24:1
Sauer, Emil von, 1942, Ap 30,19:1
Sauer, Ferdinand N Dr, 1913, Jl 9,7:6
Sauer, Frederick C, 1942, Ap 1,21:3
Sauer, G Winfield, 1953, N 13,27:2
Sauer, George, 1884, Jl 18,2:4; 1959, Mr 3,33:5
Sauer, George F, 1941, My 19,17:3
Sauer, George F Mrs, 1956, N 3,23:6
Sauer, Gustave, 1942, Ap 30,19:5
Sauer, Hans D, 1948, D 2,29:4
Sauer, Harold J, 1961, Jl 22,21:4
Sauer, Heinrich, 1952, O 12,86:3
Sauer, Henry A, 1937, F 6,17:5
Sauer, J Leo, 1919, Je 10,13:3
Sauer, Joseph J Mrs, 1947, O 24,23:4
Sauer, Joseph S, 1940, Ja 31,19:3
Sauer, Louis J, 1952, Ag 31,44:6
Sauer, Mary T Mrs, 1940, Mr 25,15:3
Sauer, Max, 1954, Je 28,19:4
Sauer, McKinley H Mrs, 1949, S 15,27:1
Sauer, Nicholas, 1947, D 27,13:2
Sauer, Oscar A, 1957, Je 8,19:4
Sauer, Paul, 1949, O 22,17:2
Sauer, Paul K, 1957, D 7,21:3
Sauer, Paul Mrs, 1938, My 13,19:1
Sauer, Phil F, 1951, Ja 30,25:3
Sauer, Rudolph Mrs, 1947, Mr 12,25:2
Sauer, Werner, 1947, Ag 5,47:3
Sauer, William, 1950, Jl 18,30:2
Sauer, William B Mrs, 1954, Ag 2,17:2
Sauer, William E, 1955, S 6,25:1
Sauerbier, William, 1937, D 1,23:1
Sauerborn, Joseph, 1937, Mr 18,25:4
Sauerbrey, Paul N, 1940, Mr 5,23:2
Sauerbruch, Ferdinand, 1951, Jl 2,23:1
Sauerbrun, Alfred H, 1963, Ag 22,27:1
Sauerbrun, William H, 1949, N 24,31:3
Sauerbrunn, John J, 1961, Jl 23,68:3
Sauerbrunn, William M, 1944, O 30,19:3
Sauerbrunn, William M Mrs, 1950, Je 25,68:3
Sauerland, Henry, 1948, Je 16,29:4
Sauerwein, George F Sr, 1948, O 14,30:2
Sauerwein, John, 1962, O 11,39:1
Sauerwein, Joseph, 1945, F 26,19:4
Sauerwen, Frank P, 1910, Je 15,9:5
Saufley, Michael C Judge, 1910, Ag 13,7:5
Saufley, Shelton M Sr, 1942, My 25,15:4
Saufley, Victor, 1953, D 14,1:1
Saul, Alex L, 1948, Ag 6,17:5
Saul, C Dudley, 1947, Ja 9,24:2
Saul, Charles R, 1948, Ja 29,24:3
Saul, J Patrick Capt, 1968, Je 24,37:5
Saul, Monroe, 1965, Mr 13,25:5
Saul, Richard, 1965, D 2,41:3
Saul, Theodore C, 1941, Je 19,21:3
Saul, Walter B, 1966, S 1,35:2
Sauler, Babetta E Mrs (will), 1937, D 22,3:3
Sauliere, Frank, 1963, My 19,86:8
Saulnier, Henry E, 1907, Mr 15,9:6
Saulnier, Nicholas J, 1962, O 17,39:3
Saulpaugh, Arthur, 1944, Ag 31,17:1
Saulpaugh, Edwin J, 1953, Jl 31,19:3
Sauls, Henry C, 1947, Jl 16,23:4
Saulsbury, Gove, 1881, Ag 2,5:3
Saulsbury, W, 1927, F 21,17:4
Saulstein, Murray, 1939, F 9,21:2
Saultz, Frank E Sr, 1956, Je 12,35:3
Saumenig, Charles, 1912, N 11,11:5
Saunder, Eugene D Judge, 1914, O 28,13:4
Saunders, A A Mrs, 1937, Ja 4,29:3
Saunders, A Edward, 1964, S 18,32:6
Saunders, Albert, 1956, Ap 3,29:6
Saunders, Albert D, 1945, S 20,23:4
Saunders, Alec, 1939, Mr 4,15:2
Saunders, Alexander, 1916, F 2,11:4
Saunders, Alfred C, 1943, Ap 18,48:5
Saunders, Alfred H, 1937, Je 7,19:3
Saunders, Anna, 1946, Ag 19,25:5
Saunders, Annabell Mrs, 1956, N 25,89:2
Saunders, Arthur C, 1939, O 6,25:4; 1958, O 23,31:4
Saunders, Arthur H, 1956, Ja 13,23:4
Saunders, Arthur L, 1956, D 9,88:6
Saunders, Arthur P, 1953, Ag 15,15:2
Saunders, Arthur P Mrs, 1961, S 24,86:5
Saunders, Augusta E, 1947, D 6,15:5
Saunders, Bertram H, 1956, Ja 19,33:5
Saunders, Blanche, 1964, D 10,47:2
Saunders, Boyd G, 1945, S 4,23:5
Saunders, C J W, 1939, Ag 6,37:4
Saunders, Carl Mrs, 1952, S 3,29:2
Saunders, Carleton E, 1949, Jl 20,25:5
Saunders, Catherine, 1943, Ja 20,19:4
Saunders, Charles Dr, 1937, Jl 26,19:3
Saunders, Charles E Mrs, 1950, Ap 15,15:2
Saunders, Charles Mrs, 1946, F 16,13:3
Saunders, Charles O Mrs, 1951, My 7,25:5
Saunders, Charles R, 1941, O 19,45:2
Saunders, Charles Sr Mrs, 1952, Ja 5,11:2
Saunders, Clarence, 1953, O 15,33:4
Saunders, Clyde W, 1939, My 23,23:4
Saunders, Douglas, 1961, N 11,23:3
Saunders, Edmund A, 1944, F 2,21:4
Saunders, Edward, 1946, Ja 18,19:3
Saunders, Edward M, 1962, Ja 4,33:3
Saunders, Edward W, 1957, Ag 5,19:1
Saunders, Edward Watts Justice, 1921, D 17,13:5
Saunders, Edwin E, 1957, N 22,25:1
Saunders, Ervin, 1909, F 19,9:5
Saunders, Frank, 1938, F 21,19:5
Saunders, Frank B, 1946, S 17,7:5; 1948, D 24,17:4
Saunders, Frank H, 1954, My 27,27:1
Saunders, Frederick, 1902, D 14,7:6
Saunders, Frederick A, 1963, Je 10,31:3
Saunders, Frederick K, 1938, N 2,23:4
Saunders, G Walton, 1937, D 21,23:2
Saunders, George, 1922, S 11,17:7
Saunders, H Elmer, 1956, D 11,39:1
Saunders, Harry, 1951, N 16,36:2
Saunders, Harry C, 1949, N 30,27:4
Saunders, Harry L, 1963, Jl 10,35:4
Saunders, Henry, 1951, N 1,29:5
Saunders, Henry D, 1952, S 21,88:1
Saunders, Hilary A S, 1951, D 18,31:2
Saunders, Irving M, 1960, Ag 15,23:5
Saunders, J Dr (Mrs Walter Cronk), 1926, Je 16,25:2
Saunders, James M, 1957, Jl 13,17:4
Saunders, Jesse G, 1949, Ap 15,23:3
Saunders, John A, 1945, F 22,27:1
Saunders, John D Mrs, 1966, F 24,37:4
Saunders, John F, 1946, D 21,19:4
Saunders, John H, 1940, N 9,17:4
Saunders, John N, 1961, Ag 1,21:4
Saunders, John P, 1945, My 23,19:2
Saunders, John R, 1964, My 5,43:1
Saunders, John S (Bro Arnold Edward), 1952, D 29, 19:1
Saunders, John S Gen, 1904, Ja 20,9:7
Saunders, Joseph H, 1946, F 10,42:1
Saunders, Joseph T, 1942, N 9,23:6
Saunders, Lawrence, 1968, Ag 28,47:3
Saunders, Leonard T, 1945, Je 12,19:3
Saunders, Margaret M, 1947, F 17,19:4
Saunders, Mary E, 1945, D 27,20:2
Saunders, Minott, 1947, D 10,31:1
Saunders, Orris W, 1946, Ja 15,23:5
Saunders, Paul H, 1947, Ap 14,27:1
Saunders, Peter, 1945, Jl 25,23:6
Saunders, Reginald A Mrs, 1945, D 4,29:5
Saunders, Reginald A Sr, 1946, Ja 6,40:5
Saunders, Richard L, 1950, My 17,29:3
Saunders, Richard L Sr, 1963, D 12,39:1
Saunders, Richardson, 1939, O 27,23:5
Saunders, Ripley D, 1915, Mr 17,11:5
Saunders, Robert C, 1959, Ap 11,21:4
Saunders, Robert E, 1957, D 7,21:1
Saunders, Robert H, 1955, Ja 17,5:3
Saunders, Robert L Sr, 1958, My 27,29:1
Saunders, Robert S, 1937, Jl 28,19:2
Saunders, Robert Sr Mrs, 1952, Je 13,25:5
Saunders, Samuel A, 1952, D 12,29:1
Saunders, Samuel J, 1950, Mr 28,31:2
Saunders, Stanley G, 1959, My 11,27:3
Saunders, T Laurence, 1965, S 3,27:5
Saunders, Theodosia, 1920, Ja 10,11:4
Saunders, Thomas H, 1944, Ja 18,20:2; 1952, Ap 21, 21:5; 1953, Je 7,85:1
Saunders, Truman L Mrs, 1949, Jl 30,15:6
Saunders, W E, 1944, Ag 12,11:5
Saunders, W L, 1931, Je 26,23:3
Saunders, Wilbour E Mrs, 1950, S 17,104:6
Saunders, Wilbur T, 1940, D 25,27:5
Saunders, William, 1951, Mr 17,15:5

Saunders, William D Mrs, 1948, Mr 1,23:3
Saunders, William Duncan, 1922, Ja 24,15:4
Saunders, William E G, 1947, Ja 20,25:1
Saunders, William G, 1957, Ag 11,80:8
Saunderson, Jason M, 1950, F 18,15:6
Saunier, Edward M, 1939, Jl 4,13:4
Sauntry, William, 1953, Ag 26,27:5
Saupe, Alfred M W, 1948, N 11,27:2
Saur, Louis O, 1938, N 1,23:5
Saurat, Denis, 1958, Je 10,33:1
Saurel, P L, 1934, Ja 23,19:3
Saurino, Benedict, 1952, My 10,21:6
Saurman, Wilbur W Mrs, 1942, Ja 15,19:3
Sause, Clifton A, 1952, Mr 1,15:2
Sause, Oliver L, 1954, Mr 17,31:6
Sauser, Michael H (will), 1938, F 23,25:6
Sausser, Warren L, 1958, Ap 26,19:5
Saussier, Felix G Gen, 1905, D 21,9:5
Sauter, Albert J, 1925, S 6,13:2
Sauter, Arthur Dr, 1937, N 12,22:1
Sauter, Fred Jr, 1959, Mr 24,39:3
Sauter, Frederick W, 1919, My 18,22:5
Sauter, George, 1937, D 29,22:1
Sauter, Herbert W, 1955, S 9,48:1
Sauter, James E (will, My 29,15:2), 1958, Mr 19,31:1
Sauter, Martin, 1905, Je 25,1:4
Sauter, Otto, 1951, Je 3,92:7
Sauter, Robert, 1943, Ag 22,36:3
Sautner, John T Mrs, 1963, Je 20,33:5
Sautter, Carl M, 1946, N 4,25:4
Sautter, Charles F, 1943, D 10,27:4
Sautter, James B, 1955, O 27,33:4
Sauvage, George, 1951, Mr 10,13:6
Sauvageot, Elle Mrs, 1962, Jl 30,3:1
Sauvalle, Edouard J Capt, 1921, F 22,13:2
Sauve, Arthur, 1944, F 7,15:2
Sauve, Paul (funl, Ja 6,5:2), 1960, Ja 3,88:1
Sauveur, Albert, 1939, Ja 27,19:5
Sauzade, John S, 1879, S 24,5:4
Sauzedde, Rene E, 1963, N 9,25:4
Sava, George, 1951, My 29,25:4
Savacool, James E, 1960, N 15,39:1
Savacool, John K Mrs, 1967, D 21,37:2
Savacool, Leon B, 1956, Jl 5,25:4
Savada, Elias, 1950, Mr 1,27:5
Savadge, Kenneth L, 1944, D 1,24:2
Savadskaya, Nadia D, 1954, N 2,27:4
Savage, A J, 1941, D 21,40:7
Savage, A O (Alf Orville Savage), 1968, N 2,37:3
Savage, Albert L (will), 1943, Jl 9,14:8
Savage, Albert R Justice, 1917, Je 15,9:5
Savage, Alfred H Mrs, 1964, Je 29,27:4
Savage, Augusta, 1962, Mr 27,37:3
Savage, B Jermain, 1952, Je 18,27:4
Savage, Belle, 1943, F 13,11:5
Savage, Bernard, 1954, Ap 22,29:4
Savage, Brooks E, 1951, O 8,21:1
Savage, Charles C, 1907, N 10,9:6; 1907, N 12,9:7; 1942, D 28,20:3
Savage, Charles J, 1943, Je 22,19:2
Savage, Charles W, 1949, D 2,29:2
Savage, Clair R, 1953, Ja 20,25:4
Savage, Cornelius B, 1952, D 11,33:1
Savage, Courtenay, 1946, Ag 24,11:4
Savage, Donald, 1961, D 27,27:2
Savage, Donald M, 1945, Mr 7,22:2
Savage, Edward H, 1949, Mr 25,23:4
Savage, Edward S, 1947, Ag 25,17:3
Savage, Elmer S, 1943, N 23,25:3
Savage, Emma L, 1955, Ag 12,19:3
Savage, Eric D, 1963, Je 17,25:4
Savage, Ernest M, 1950, S 16,19:6
Savage, Frank A, 1959, Ag 4,27:2
Savage, Frank M, 1949, Je 20,19:4
Savage, George A, 1960, Je 6,29:2
Savage, George E, 1949, Ja 1,13:3
Savage, George H (por), 1940, Jl 19,19:2
Savage, George W, 1950, Ja 13,24:3
Savage, H N, 1934, Je 25,15:4
Savage, H W, 1927, N 30,25:3
Savage, Harlow D (por), 1942, F 10,19:3
Savage, Harlow D Mrs, 1956, D 28,21:3
Savage, Harry K, 1938, Ja 15,15:2
Savage, Henry B Dr, 1937, F 2,23:5
Savage, Henry E, 1939, Ap 20,23:3
Savage, Herbert K, 1954, O 1,23:2
Savage, Howard P, 1944, My 8,19:6
Savage, James, 1952, N 2,89:2
Savage, James J, 1949, Ap 17,78:5
Savage, James R, 1951, Ap 5,29:2
Savage, Jennie L Mrs, 1945, Ap 27,19:2
Savage, Jeremiah J, 1957, Mr 9,19:5
Savage, John, 1953, N 10,31:5
Savage, John H, 1946, Ap 24,25:3; 1953, Je 30,23:4
Savage, John J, 1958, Ja 31,22:8
Savage, John L, 1967, D 29,27:2
Savage, John M, 1938, Mr 19,15:2
Savage, John R, 1922, F 26,26:3
Savage, John W (por), 1941, Jl 10,19:4
Savage, Jose R F, 1939, My 4,23:5
Savage, Joseph E Maj, 1921, Mr 30,13:6
Savage, Joseph K, 1956, Mr 12,27:6
Savage, Leo A, 1945, Je 30,17:6
Savage, Leon, 1967, Ap 30,86:7
Savage, Leon Mrs, 1960, Ap 7,35:4
Savage, Leslie H Jr, 1958, My 28,31:4
Savage, Lizzie, 1952, Mr 8,13:6
Savage, M J, 1940, Mr 27,21:1
Savage, M W Mrs, 1948, Ja 4,52:1
Savage, Margene, 1965, My 3,20:6
Savage, Maria G M Mme, 1957, Je 29,17:4
Savage, Marion A (por), 1947, Ap 10,26:2
Savage, Marion Dutton, 1923, Mr 21,17:4
Savage, Maxwell, 1948, N 5,26:2
Savage, May G, 1963, Ap 20,27:5
Savage, Michael, 1923, Mr 19,17:5
Savage, Michael J, 1941, Mr 24,17:6
Savage, Patrick, 1951, Je 2,19:5
Savage, Paul W, 1958, N 5,39:1
Savage, Porter C, 1951, My 26,17:3
Savage, Richard H, 1937, Je 2,23:5
Savage, Richard Mrs, 1910, Jl 8,7:5
Savage, Robert, 1943, Jl 24,13:6
Savage, S, 1884, D 12,3:4
Savage, Sol H, 1941, My 31,11:3
Savage, Theodore F, 1957, F 16,17:5
Savage, Thomas F, 1947, N 15,17:6
Savage, Thomas J, 1945, Ap 22,36:2
Savage, Troy, 1961, N 11,12:5
Savage, Valere G, 1961, N 21,39:2
Savage, W L, 1931, Ja 12,19:3
Savage, Walter P, 1952, D 30,19:2
Savage, Watson L Mrs, 1944, Ag 4,21:5
Savage, William E, 1945, D 9,44:6
Savage, William H, 1948, Ag 11,21:1
Savage, William H Mrs, 1961, S 18,29:5
Savage, William J, 1962, Jl 6,25:2
Savage, William L Mrs, 1950, F 26,76:4
Savage, William T, 1940, O 31,23:4
Savanack, Mary Mrs, 1939, Ja 28,13:6
Savanella, Vito, 1923, My 29,15:5
Savard, Frank D, 1949, O 22,17:5
Savareid, Alfred E, 1953, O 28,29:3
Savarese, Ferdinand B, 1961, Ja 7,19:5
Savarese, Martin L, 1962, Ja 9,48:1
Savarese, Ralph, 1941, Je 11,21:5
Savarkar, Vinayak D, 1966, F 27,85:1
Savedoff, William M, 1957, Jl 24,26:6
Savell, Walter L, 1965, Ja 3,84:8
Savell, Walter L Jr, 1958, N 9,88:1
Savelson, Barnett Mrs, 1964, Ja 30,30:1
Savelyev, Boris V, 1965, S 22,3:8
Saveniers, Jean, 1960, Jl 25,30:7
Savercool, Ellen K Mrs, 1948, Ap 9,23:4
Saverese, Anthony P, 1965, N 3,39:3
Saveri, Francesco, 1961, D 10,88:6
Savery, Albert H, 1939, Ap 1,19:1
Savery, Clyde W, 1939, Ag 15,19:3
Savery, James R, 1938, Ja 30,II,8:2
Savidge, Eugene Coleman Dr, 1924, O 11,15:5
Savidge, F R, 1928, Ja 31,25:5
Savidge, Reuben, 1938, D 16,25:4
Savile, John Mrs, 1912, O 17,11:5
Saville, Adam L, 1943, D 7,27:4
Saville, Bruce W, 1939, F 28,19:4
Saville, Caleb M, 1960, F 17,35:2
Saville, Charles O, 1942, Ap 23,23:5
Saville, Clark Mrs, 1959, N 19,39:5
Saville, Cornelius M, 1944, My 9,19:4
Saville, Foster H, 1942, Ap 12,44:1
Saville, George, 1905, Mr 25,9:6
Saville, John G, 1910, Je 4,9:6
Saville, Mathew E, 1942, Jl 5,29:2
Saville, Randolph M, 1966, Jl 30,25:6
Saville, Robert L, 1949, F 15,23:2
Saville, William G S, 1964, Mr 5,33:4
Savin, Ralph B, 1951, O 16,31:4
Savine, Alex, 1949, Ja 21,22:3
Savine, Richard, 1944, Jl 21,19:3
Savini, Carlo, 1947, S 12,21:4
Savini, Carlo Mrs, 1946, N 29,25:4
Savini, Robert M, 1956, Ap 30,23:5
Savino, Carmine S Mrs, 1938, Mr 14,15:5
Savino, Carmine Sr, 1962, N 29,37:2
Savinsky, Daniel, 1949, O 24,23:5
Savio, Manuel N (por), 1948, Ag 2,21:5
Savitsch, Eugene C de, 1959, O 17,23:4
Savitsky, Nathan, 1953, S 5,15:5
Savitt, Jan (por), 1948, O 5,25:4
Savitz, Jerohn J, 1951, D 7,28:3
Savitz, Jerohn J Mrs, 1952, Ja 18,27:4
Savitz, Julius H, 1947, Jl 11,15:3
Savitz, Samuel A, 1950, D 1,27:6
Savitz, Solomon I, 1949, My 23,23:3
Savner, Herman, 1950, D 5,31:2
Savo, Jimmy (will, N 4,7:7), 1960, S 7,41:1
Savoia, Umberto, 1954, Je 5,17:2
Savolaine, John H, 1950, D 7,33:6
Savord, Ruth, 1966, F 27,84:8
Savornin, Lohman Bonifacius C de, 1946, Mr 19,28:2
Savory, Herbert W Mrs, 1944, My 18,19:4
Savory, Philip M H, 1965, Je 12,31:4
Savotsky, Stanley Sr, 1947, D 18,29:3
Savoy, Bert (funl, Je 30,11:4), 1923, Je 29,17:2
Savoy, Eddie A (por), 1943, Ag 28,11:1
Savoy, George A, 1951, Ag 16,27:6
Savoy, Hubert, 1951, Ja 25,25:4
Savoy, Prew, 1956, D 8,39:3
Saw, Premier, 1942, Ag 7,8:8
Sawada, Kosaku, 1968, Ap 17,32:8
Sawade, Richard, 1947, F 13,23:3
Sawall, John G, 1948, Ag 17,22:3
Sawall, Walter, 1953, F 2,21:3
Sawan, Nakhorn, 1944, F 25,17:4
Saward, Frederick Edward, 1917, D 6,13:5
Saward, Frederick W (por), 1940, Ap 24,23:3
Saward, Frederick W Mrs, 1960, Jl 25,23:4
Sawaska, Joseph J Mrs, 1967, F 25,27:2
Sawatikat, Sawat, 1952, My 19,17:4
Sawday, Charle B, 1945, Ja 24,21:4
Sawdon, W N, 1952, Ap 2,33:3
Sawhill, Donald V, 1955, D 25,48:2
Sawicki, Anthony M, 1961, Mr 25,25:5
Sawicki, Frank, 1950, My 28,45:1; 1953, F 6,20:4
Sawicki, Michael, 1951, Jl 14,13:3
Sawicz, Boris T Mrs, 1958, S 14,84:2
Sawin, Edward A, 1946, Ja 17,23:3
Sawin, George A, 1961, N 30,34:6
Sawin, George H, 1961, Mr 2,27:4
Sawin, Harry B, 1950, D 29,19:1
Sawitz, William G, 1957, Ap 23,31:3
Sawitzky, William (por), 1947, F 3,19:3
Sawler, W C B, 1909, Mr 7,11:5
Sawmelle, Cyrille H Mrs, 1952, F 17,85:2
Sawmelle, Michael S, 1941, Ja 1,23:3
Sawtelle, Charles E Rev, 1917, N 30,13:6
Sawtelle, Charles G Brig-Gen, 1913, Ja 5,17:2
Sawtelle, Edmund M Mrs, 1955, My 10,29:4
Sawtelle, George, 1967, S 5,43:2
Sawtelle, Raymond, 1949, Jl 12,27:6
Sawtelle, William O, 1939, S 25,20:1
Sawvel, Leonard F, 1961, Mr 28,35:5
Sawyer, Alan F, 1937, Mr 12,24:1
Sawyer, Albert H, 1941, Ap 20,43:2
Sawyer, Albert P, 1903, N 22,7:5
Sawyer, Amanda Nye Mrs, 1923, F 2,15:5
Sawyer, Ansley W, 1955, O 2,86:4
Sawyer, Arch D, 1937, Ap 21,23:4
Sawyer, Arthur, 1966, Je 26,73:1
Sawyer, Arthur T, 1942, Jl 13,16:4
Sawyer, Benjamin A, 1938, Ag 3,19:5
Sawyer, C Adrian Jr, 1952, Ja 31,27:2
Sawyer, Charles B, 1964, Mr 26,35:1
Sawyer, Charles B Dr, 1937, My 8,19:4
Sawyer, Charles D, 1955, Jl 12,25:4
Sawyer, Charles E Brig-Gen, 1924, S 24,19:3
Sawyer, Charles F, 1938, D 28,26:4
Sawyer, Charles Henry, 1908, Ja 19,11:4
Sawyer, Charles M, 1944, D 12,23:3
Sawyer, Charles P Mrs, 1949, F 15,23:1
Sawyer, Charles R, 1960, Je 18,23:4
Sawyer, Cleon J, 1948, Ja 6,23:5
Sawyer, Cleon J Mrs, 1940, My 3,21:5
Sawyer, Clifford P, 1954, Jl 25,69:2
Sawyer, Daniel, 1937, Jl 7,23:2
Sawyer, Donald H, 1941, Je 24,19:2
Sawyer, Edward, 1924, Ja 23,17:4
Sawyer, Elizabeth R, 1949, Ap 7,29:2
Sawyer, Elmer P, 1942, Ag 15,11:5
Sawyer, Elmer W, 1954, Ag 17,21:2
Sawyer, Eugene D, 1964, Mr 27,28:1
Sawyer, Eugene M Mrs, 1957, N 22,25:1
Sawyer, Eugene T, 1924, O 30,19:4
Sawyer, Frank E Com, 1912, Ap 19,15:5
Sawyer, Fred A, 1938, Ja 13,22:1
Sawyer, Frederick A Col, 1908, N 29,11:5
Sawyer, G Y, 1882, Je 16,5:4
Sawyer, George A, 1948, D 23,19:3; 1962, Jl 22,64:4
Sawyer, George C, 1943, S 22,23:4
Sawyer, George H, 1955, Ja 5,23:1
Sawyer, George L, 1948, D 3,25:1
Sawyer, Gordon H, 1942, N 10,27:5
Sawyer, Gordon L, 1939, F 28,19:2
Sawyer, H, 1877, My 8,7:7
Sawyer, H A, 1946, N 19,21:1
Sawyer, Harold, 1953, Ap 14,27:1
Sawyer, Harold A P, 1939, Je 16,23:5
Sawyer, Harold M, 1961, F 7,35:4
Sawyer, Harold R, 1944, S 10,46:1
Sawyer, Henry B, 1950, Ap 16,104:8
Sawyer, Herbert E, 1952, D 30,19:3
Sawyer, Howard, 1953, Ja 12,27:2
Sawyer, Jacob H, 1961, O 24,37:4
Sawyer, James, 1944, Ag 9,17:6
Sawyer, James D, 1943, S 20,21:5
Sawyer, James D Mrs, 1948, N 12,23:1
Sawyer, James Estcourt Gen, 1914, My 30,11:7
Sawyer, James P, 1957, Ja 7,25:4
Sawyer, John, 1882, Ag 11,8:4; 1942, Ap 9,19:4
Sawyer, John F, 1939, Mr 26,III,6:8
Sawyer, Joseph A, 1964, D 25,29:1
Sawyer, Katherine Agnes, 1914, My 18,9:6
Sawyer, Lawrence J, 1945, F 13,23:2
Sawyer, Lee A, 1953, Ag 23,89:2
Sawyer, Leonard A, 1951, Ap 30,21:3
Sawyer, Margaret J Mrs, 1937, Jl 8,23:1
Sawyer, Mary A, 1942, Je 12,22:2
Sawyer, Miles S, 1946, S 20,31:1
Sawyer, Milo C, 1949, N 28,27:4

Sawyer, Moses E, 1941, S 12,21:3
Sawyer, Nathaniel P Col, 1903, N 25,9:5
Sawyer, Paul B (por), 1946, Ap 9,27:4
Sawyer, Perley W, 1947, Ap 5,19:1
Sawyer, Phil (por), 1949, My 22,88:1
Sawyer, Phil A, 1949, Mr 10,27:5
Sawyer, Phil H Mrs, 1941, Ja 27,15:2
Sawyer, Phil H Sr, 1941, Je 24,19:2
Sawyer, Prince E, 1954, Ja 18,23:2
Sawyer, Ralph W, 1942, S 2,24:3
Sawyer, Raymond T, 1938, Je 23,21:3
Sawyer, Robert K, 1955, F 12,15:4
Sawyer, Robert W 3d, 1964, Jl 23,27:5
Sawyer, Robert W 3d Mrs, 1951, D 21,27:4
Sawyer, Rollin A, 1960, O 26,39:2
Sawyer, Rollin Augustus Rev, 1915, Ja 19,9:5
Sawyer, S J Mrs, 1939, O 26,23:4
Sawyer, S T Maj, 1865, D 17,3:2
Sawyer, Samuel M, 1961, N 2,37:1
Sawyer, Samuel N, 1939, My 2,23:5
Sawyer, Sherwood D, 1944, Ja 13,21:2
Sawyer, W E, 1883, My 17,3:1
Sawyer, Walter E Mrs, 1959, S 21,31:1
Sawyer, Warren L, 1922, N 1,19:5
Sawyer, Warren L Mrs, 1953, Ja 19,23:1
Sawyer, Wells, 1960, Mr 22,37:2
Sawyer, Wilbur A, 1951, N 13,29:1
Sawyer, Wilbur A Mrs, 1965, Ag 20,29:3
Sawyer, William, 1903, My 22,9:4; 1908, Ja 1,9:5
Sawyer, William B Jr, 1948, Jl 27,25:2
Sawyer, William D, 1922, N 13,15:5
Sawyer, William H, 1938, Ag 20,15:2
Sawyer, William T, 1953, My 28,23:4
Sax, Ada, 1946, Ag 21,28:2
Sax, Carol M, 1961, O 2,31:5
Sax, Charles, 1943, O 19,19:5
Sax, Julius, 1916, Jl 21,9:8
Sax, Percival M, 1954, F 25,31:4
Saxe, Albert, 1949, D 9,31:3
Saxe, Alfred J, 1943, O 17,49:1
Saxe, Charles J, 1943, F 6,13:4
Saxe, Herbert K, 1946, Mr 13,30:2
Saxe, Herbert W, 1960, Ja 24,88:2
Saxe, Herman, 1960, S 11,82:3
Saxe, J G, 1887, Ap 1,5:2
Saxe, John B, 1959, F 16,29:1
Saxe, John E, 1939, N 4,15:4
Saxe, John G, 1953, Ap 18,19:1
Saxe, John G (est tax appr), 1955, F 5,17:2
Saxe, John H, 1961, Ap 18,37:3
Saxe, Julian T, 1938, D 27,17:3
Saxe, Leonard S, 1968, Jl 1,33:2
Saxe, Martin, 1967, F 6,29:1
Saxe, Mary L M Mrs, 1940, Ag 9,15:5
Saxe, Michael, 1955, My 28,15:2
Saxe, Samuel D, 1949, N 20,95:3
Saxe, Sigmond, 1944, F 29,17:6
Saxe, Thomas, 1938, D 17,15:7
Saxe, William H, 1903, Ag 9,7:6
Saxe, William W, 1953, S 7,19:4
Saxe-Altenbourg, Duke of (Prince Ernst), 1908, F 7, 7:6
Saxe-Altenburg, Alexandra Mary Wilhelmina Princess, 1907, Ja 10,9:4
Saxe-Coburg, Duke of, 1900, Ag 1,6:6
Saxe-Meiningen, Charlotte Duchess of, 1919, O 4,11:4
Saxe-Weimar, Edward Princess, 1904, Ap 4,9:6
Saxe-Weimar, Wilhelm Ernst of, 1923, Ap 25,21:5
Saxe-Weimer, Grand Duchess, 1905, Ja 18,2:2
Saxen, Benjamin H, 1954, F 18,31:2
Saxer, Edward J, 1945, Mr 23,19:3
Saxer, Paul, 1950, F 10,23:5
Saxer, William H L, 1945, D 26,19:3
Saxl, Josef, 1957, N 6,35:2
Saxman, Edwin F, 1938, Ap 7,23:3
Saxon, Arthur Sr, 1942, O 24,15:5
Saxon, Avon, 1909, Mr 25,9:4
Saxon, Benjamin F, 1940, N 27,23:2
Saxon, Eugene F Mrs, 1965, F 11,39:3
Saxon, Herman, 1939, D 17,49:2
Saxon, John A, 1947, F 18,25:4
Saxon, John Jr, 1941, Ja 14,21:3
Saxon, Louis, 1968, Jl 12,31:4
Saxon, Louis R, 1952, Mr 17,21:4
Saxon, Lyle (por), 1946, Ap 10,28:2
Saxon, Mack, 1949, My 10,25:4
Saxon, Marie, 1941, N 13,27:2
Saxon, Mary B Mrs, 1966, N 23,39:4
Saxon, O Glenn, 1962, O 7,82:3
Saxon, Pauline, 1949, N 1,27:5
Saxony, George King, 1904, O 15,9:4
Saxony, King of P, 1873, O 30,1:7
Saxstein, J Harry, 1939, My 8,17:4
Saxton, C T Judge, 1903, O 24,9:5
Saxton, Edward H, 1937, My 16,II,8:4
Saxton, Ernest L, 1955, Ap 17,86:5
Saxton, Eugene F (por), 1943, Je 27,32:3
Saxton, George A, 1942, S 15,23:6
Saxton, Homer P, 1942, Je 16,23:4
Saxton, Joseph, 1873, O 29,6:7; 1903, Ag 4,7:6
Saxton, Louis H, 1949, Jl 18,17:4
Saxton, Lynn M, 1941, S 23,23:6
Saxton, Robert W, 1951, O 13,17:5
Saxton, Rufus Brig-Gen, 1908, F 24,7:4
Saxton, S W, 1933, Mr 21,20:1
Saxton, Samuel, 1908, N 18,9:2
Saxton, William A, 1939, Mr 31,21:2
Saxton, William H, 1954, F 15,23:4
Say, Allan B Prof, 1915, Jl 7,11:5
Say, Leon, 1896, Ap 22,5:5
Sayaji Rao, Maharajah (Gaekwar of Baroda), 1939, F 7,19:1
Sayanov, Vissarion, 1959, Ja 25,93:1
Sayao, Maria J Mrs, 1966, Je 1,47:3
Saybolt, William H, 1944, Je 21,19:4
Sayce, A R, 1933, F 5,28:1
Saydah, Antoon W, 1949, N 20,92:4
Saydah, Khaleel W, 1948, N 28,94:4
Saydah, Khaleel W Mrs, 1960, My 15,85:3
Saydam, Refik, 1942, Jl 8,23:1
Saye, Geoffrey L, 1959, Mr 7,22:1
Saye and Sele, Baron, 1937, F 3,23:3
Saye and Sele, Lord, 1907, O 9,11:6
Saye and Sele, Lord (G R C Twisleton-Wykeham-Fiennes), 1949, F 19,15:7
Sayed, Mehrem, 1943, S 28,25:5
Sayegh, Ignatius, 1941, F 25,23:5
Sayen, Clarence N, 1965, Ag 18,25:7
Sayen, William H Jr, 1966, Ja 31,39:3
Sayen, William H Mrs, 1953, F 20,19:3
Sayenni, Donald L Mrs (N Purviance), 1960, D 24, 15:4
Sayer, Albert H (cor on age, Je 19,29:1), 1965, Je 18,35:4
Sayer, Arthur S, 1949, F 23,28:2
Sayer, Elizabeth, 1942, N 9,23:6
Sayer, Eugene Y, 1937, Ag 7,15:4
Sayer, F A, 1877, My 22,8:5
Sayer, Grover C, 1956, F 7,31:1
Sayer, Henry D, 1968, N 22,47:2
Sayer, James, 1939, Jl 18,19:5
Sayer, Mary C D Mrs, 1953, Ag 25,21:1
Sayer, Raymond, 1917, Ja 11,15:4
Sayer, Robert A, 1945, S 27,21:2
Sayer, Stanley W, 1954, My 5,31:4
Sayer, Thomas Mrs, 1952, D 22,25:6
Sayer, William H, 1951, O 31,29:3
Sayers, Dorothy L (Mrs O L Fleming), 1957, D 19, 29:5
Sayers, Douglas R, 1967, Ag 22,34:5
Sayers, Fred T Mrs, 1947, Je 16,21:4
Sayers, H Schieffelin, 1943, D 4,13:1
Sayers, Henry J Mrs, 1943, Ap 16,22:3
Sayers, John, 1939, O 16,19:5
Sayers, Lucile N Dame, 1959, N 5,35:5
Sayers, S R Jr Dr, 1906, My 30,1:2
Sayers, Warner, 1949, Ag 26,19:1
Sayers, William D, 1947, N 8,17:5
Sayers, William L, 1959, F 22,89:2
Sayford, P Maxwell Mrs, 1947, F 11,27:3
Sayia, Anthony A, 1947, Jl 12,13:6
Sayid Abdul Ahad, Emir of Bokhara, 1911, Ja 6,9:4
Saylan, Charles A, 1939, Ja 2,24:3
Sayle, Harry H, 1958, N 5,35:4
Sayle, Robert G, 1940, Ag 2,15:5
Sayler, Henry (por), 1939, Jl 7,17:2
Sayler, Jane W Mrs, 1948, F 22,48:5
Sayler, Oliver M, 1958, O 20,29:5
Sayles, Alex, 1953, Mr 5,27:3
Sayles, Ethel M, 1946, Ap 9,27:2
Sayles, F C, 1903, Ja 6,9:5
Sayles, Frank A Mrs, 1946, Jl 29,21:4
Sayles, Frederic C Mrs, 1955, Ja 10,23:5
Sayles, Halsey, 1958, Ja 17,25:1
Sayles, Harry A, 1952, Ja 8,27:3
Sayles, John, 1947, My 10,13:6
Sayles, John M, 1956, D 4,39:2
Sayles, Rort W, 1942, O 24,15:4
Sayles, Sol, 1909, O 25,7:5
Saylor, Curwen S, 1941, S 17,23:2
Saylor, Frank, 1950, D 13,35:5
Saylor, Harry T Mrs, 1939, Ja 25,22:1; 1953, N 8,88:6
Saylor, Henry D, 1947, F 9,61:5
Saylor, Henry H, 1967, Ag 23,45:4
Saylor, J Abner, 1957, My 22,33:1
Saylor, John C, 1948, Je 28,19:3
Saylor, Milton, 1937, F 10,23:2
Saylor, Parry D, 1942, F 21,19:3
Saylor, Port L, 1953, S 4,34:3
Saylor, Roger B, 1957, D 19,31:1
Saylor, Sam E, 1958, D 14,2:5
Saylor, W Jay, 1954, Ja 25,19:3
Saylor, Warren K, 1949, D 5,23:3
Sayman, Albert, 1961, Ja 29,85:2
Sayman, Thomas M, 1937, S 7,21:1
Saymon, Benjamin H, 1954, Jl 18,57:1
Sayour, Elias, 1961, Je 27,33:5
Saypol, Louis Mrs, 1946, S 19,31:4
Sayre, A Nelson Mrs, 1955, N 12,19:1
Sayre, Annie W M Mrs, 1948, Jl 30,18:5
Sayre, Austin B Sr, 1967, Jl 7,31:2
Sayre, C H H, 1880, Ap 6,5:1
Sayre, Caryl H, 1963, D 5,45:1
Sayre, Charles Eugene, 1915, N 24,13:6
Sayre, D M, 1876, Ag 4,4:7
Sayre, Edwin H, 1937, Ja 22,21:4
Sayre, Eugene, 1953, D 11,34:4
Sayre, F B Mrs, 1933, Ja 16,15:5
Sayre, Fred G, 1939, Ja 3,17:1
Sayre, George, 1947, O 11,17:4
Sayre, Hannah M (will), 1949, Ja 15,2:2
Sayre, Harry, 1958, Ja 15,39:1
Sayre, Homer D Mrs, 1961, Ja 21,21:4
Sayre, Howell E, 1959, S 19,23:4
Sayre, James R Jr, 1908, S 16,9:5
Sayre, Joel G Mrs, 1963, D 24,17:2
Sayre, Joel Mrs, 1960, Ag 3,29:6
Sayre, Joseph D, 1939, Ap 1,19:5
Sayre, Joseph Monell, 1915, S 10,11:6
Sayre, Leslie C Mrs, 1955, Ap 6,29:3
Sayre, Louis T, 1937, My 6,25:2
Sayre, Lucius Elmer, 1925, Jl 22,19:6
Sayre, M, 1936, Je 16,25:1
Sayre, Marion E, 1945, D 21,21:1
Sayre, Martha N Mrs, 1918, Ag 16,7:3
Sayre, Morris, 1953, Mr 8,90:1
Sayre, Morris Mrs, 1960, S 19,31:2
Sayre, R H, 1929, My 30,19:3
Sayre, Raymond, 1954, My 25,27:3
Sayre, Robert H, 1907, Ja 5,9:5
Sayre, Robert H Jr, 1904, F 14,7:6
Sayre, Theodore B, 1954, N 22,23:1
Sayre, Theodore H, 1908, Mr 23,7:6
Sayre, William C, 1937, F 26,21:4
Sayre, Woodburn J, 1954, Jl 14,27:4
Sayres, Edwin A, 1952, S 29,23:4
Sayres, Gilbert Barker, 1922, Ap 27,17:4
Sayres, Philip C, 1963, Je 6,35:4
Sayres, Stanley S, 1956, S 18,35:1
Sayres, William S Rev Dr, 1916, My 6,11:7
Sayward, Joseph T, 1954, Ja 8,21:5
Sazonoff, S, 1927, D 26,23:3
Sbarbaro, John A, 1960, Mr 18,11:1
Sbarra, Pauline Mrs, 1945, S 12,25:4
Sbarretti, Donato (por), 1939, Ap 2,III,7:1
Sbicca, Frank, 1953, N 16,25:4
Sbinowitz, Morris, 1956, Ja 12,27:4
Sbriglla, Giovanni, 1916, Mr 13,9:3
Scacco, Jack, 1947, S 13,11:5
Scacheri, Mario, 1940, Ag 2,15:5
Scadding, Charles Bp, 1914, My 28,13:6
Scadron, Louis, 1963, D 15,86:1
Scadron, Louis H Mrs, 1953, N 3,31:4
Scaer, Paul H, 1967, Ap 25,43:5
Scaff, Albert N, 1947, Ap 10,25:1
Scaff, Jack H Mrs, 1962, O 11,39:1
Scaff, William D, 1945, F 16,23:3
Scaffa, Noel C (por), 1941, S 1,17:8
Scaffi, Maurice, 1957, D 15,86:5
Scafford, Justus M, 1947, F 8,17:3
Scafuro, Francis X, 1968, Mr 19,44:1
Scafuro, Victor E, 1965, Ag 23,31:5
Scaife, Alan M, 1958, Jl 25,19:3
Scaife, Alan M Mrs (Sarah), 1965, D 29,29:1
Scaife, Arthur L, 1955, O 20,35:2
Scaife, O P Sr, 1903, Mr 16,9:6
Scaife, Roger L, 1951, O 20,15:3
Scaife, William B Mrs, 1946, O 27,63:1
Scaine, Richard P, 1946, Ap 29,22:3
Scaison, Herman, 1946, D 13,23:3
Scala, Eugene D, 1964, Mr 29,61:1
Scala, F M Prof, 1903, Ap 20,7:4
Scala, Gerard, 1959, My 12,35:4
Scalera, Paul S, 1953, Ja 10,17:4
Scalero, Rosario, 1954, D 29,29:1
Scales, Albert F, 1959, Ja 24,19:5
Scales, Arthur T, 1949, Jl 16,13:4
Scales, E G, 1928, Je 6,25:3
Scales, Jefferson Dr, 1919, Ap 15,11:4
Scales, Victor H, 1959, N 19,39:5
Scales, William J, 1940, N 6,10:4
Scalettar, Louis W, 1966, Je 9,47:2
Scali, Vincent J, 1948, Ja 27,26:3
Scalian, William, 1883, O 14,9:3
Scalli, James Sr, 1948, N 25,31:1
Scallon, James B, 1951, N 23,29:1
Scallon, John Mrs, 1949, Mr 16,28:2
Scallon, Robert I Sir, 1939, My 2,24:3
Scallon, William, 1951, Jl 7,13:6
Scally, Francis M, 1968, My 23,47:3
Scally, John J Msgr, 1968, Je 22,33:3
Scalon, Michael A, 1914, Ag 17,7:6
Scalvini, Andrea, 1946, O 5,17:6
Scalzi, John A Jr, 1962, S 28,33:1
Scalzo, Pasquale, 1954, D 15,31:3
Scambio, Peter, 1948, My 9,68:6
Scamman, Clarence L, 1965, Je 27,64:7
Scammell, Arnold D, 1937, Je 5,17:3
Scammell, Charles H Mrs, 1948, Mr 19,24:2
Scammell, Frank G, 1947, D 7,76:2
Scammell, Matthew J, 1953, Je 16,27:3
Scammell, Scott, 1954, O 21,27:2
Scammell, William K, 1965, My 3,33:4
Scammell, William K Mrs, 1960, N 6,89:1
Scanandoah, Elias, 1948, Ap 26,23:3
Scandlon, William S, 1951, Mr 28,29:2
Scandrett, Henry A, 1957, Mr 22,23:1
Scandrett, Richard B Mrs, 1953, N 25,23:4
Scank, Jack Mrs, 1963, Jl 25,25:4

Scanlan, Anthony J, 1965, F 14,89:1
Scanlan, Carmel J, 1952, Ja 16,25:5
Scanlan, Charles V, 1964, My 3,86:8
Scanlan, Cornelias T, 1948, Ag 11,21:1
Scanlan, D Ward, 1960, S 19,31:2
Scanlan, Edward, 1949, S 1,21:3
Scanlan, Elizabeth G (Sept 21), 1965, O 11,61:5
Scanlan, George A, 1952, Jl 15,21:2; 1952, N 22,23:4
Scanlan, Gertrude F, 1959, D 9,45:4
Scanlan, James C, 1945, O 19,23:2
Scanlan, James E, 1948, Ap 10,13:4
Scanlan, James J, 1940, Ja 9,23:2
Scanlan, James M Mrs, 1958, My 18,87:1
Scanlan, Jeremiah J Mrs, 1951, O 2,27:3
Scanlan, John J, 1950, F 9,29:4
Scanlan, John J Mrs, 1951, My 22,31:2
Scanlan, Joseph D, 1939, Ag 10,19:2
Scanlan, Kickham, 1955, Mr 7,27:5
Scanlan, Laurence Bp, 1915, My 11,15:4
Scanlan, M W, 1960, D 24,15:3
Scanlan, Mark J, 1962, Je 16,19:5
Scanlan, Martin A, 1963, Jl 25,25:2
Scanlan, Michael J, 1957, F 19,31:1
Scanlan, Michael J Justice, 1923, Mr 24,13:5
Scanlan, Michael J Mrs, 1950, My 20,15:4
Scanlan, Philip, 1915, Ag 31,9:6
Scanlan, Raymond J, 1947, N 25,29:5
Scanlan, Raymond J Mrs, 1959, Ag 21,21:2
Scanlan, Ross, 1961, Ap 17,29:3
Scanlan, Stuart J, 1965, O 22,43:1
Scanlan, Thomas, 1961, Ja 2,25:3
Scanlan, William D, 1949, My 31,23:2
Scanlan, William D Jr, 1958, My 10,21:2
Scanlan, William J, 1957, My 26,92:5
Scanlan, William J Mrs, 1950, Jl 4,17:3
Scanland, Francis W, 1946, O 17,23:5
Scanlin, James A, 1949, Ja 22,13:4
Scanlon, Annie, 1924, Je 5,21:6
Scanlon, Arthur L, 1945, Jl 12,11:6
Scanlon, C Rev, 1927, Mr 22,27:3
Scanlon, Charles A, 1951, My 19,15:3
Scanlon, Charles M, 1940, F 16,19:4; 1946, N 6,23:2
Scanlon, Elizabeth W Dr, 1968, S 10,47:1
Scanlon, Frank J, 1957, Jl 23,25:1
Scanlon, James A, 1940, Mr 29,21:1
Scanlon, James F, 1959, Jl 11,19:6
Scanlon, Jeremiah J, 1944, S 14,23:5
Scanlon, John J, 1924, Jl 20,20:4; 1937, Je 27,II,7:1; 1944, Mr 29,21:4; 1951, S 10,21:4
Scanlon, John T Sr Mrs, 1946, Ja 9,23:4
Scanlon, Joseph A, 1957, Ap 23,31:4
Scanlon, Joseph L (Bro Jasper),(por), 1944, F 21,15:1
Scanlon, Joseph N, 1956, F 11,17:5
Scanlon, Laurence H, 1965, My 19,47:1
Scanlon, Leon, 1922, S 11,17:5
Scanlon, Mary, 1947, Ag 24,57:1
Scanlon, Michael L, 1961, S 12,33:4
Scanlon, Oscar T, 1943, Jl 24,13:4
Scanlon, Thomas, 1938, O 25,23:2; 1955, Ag 10,25:1
Scanlon, Thomas F, 1952, Ag 9,13:3
Scanlon, Thomas J, 1940, Mr 23,13:4
Scanlon, William A, 1953, Ja 30,22:3
Scanlon, William G, 1958, Mr 15,17:2
Scanlon, William J, 1962, Ag 18,19:5
Scannell, Austin J, 1960, D 3,23:6
Scannell, Austin J Mrs, 1950, Mr 7,28:3
Scannell, Daniel D, 1967, Jl 16,64:5
Scannell, Edward J, 1950, Ap 13,29:3
Scannell, George F, 1912, S 19,11:3
Scannell, James A, 1950, Mr 4,17:6
Scannell, Jeremiah J, 1946, D 15,77:1; 1967, S 14,47:3
Scannell, Jeremiah Mrs, 1961, Je 26,31:5
Scannell, John Jay, 1918, Mr 6,7:3
Scannell, John P, 1948, S 15,31:2
Scannell, Richard Bp, 1916, Ja 9,17:6
Scannell, Robert L Mrs, 1954, Jl 21,27:4
Scantlebury, Howard B, 1940, S 9,15:4
Scapigliati, Alex, 1952, Je 25,29:2
Scapinelli di Leguigno, R Card, 1933, S 18,19:1
Scarabec, Henry, 1949, S 21,44:6
Scaramelli, Henry, 1961, Je 28,35:2
Scaramelli, Louis J, 1957, F 2,19:4
Scarante, Antonio, 1944, D 29,15:4
Scarboro, Lewis F, 1940, F 2,17:1
Scarborough, Alfred, 1952, S 16,59:3
Scarborough, Alonzo, 1943, O 27,23:5
Scarborough, Andrew J, 1949, Ag 16,23:3
Scarborough, Benjamin P, 1958, S 11,33:3
Scarborough, George Mrs, 1951, D 17,31:3
Scarborough, H Sargeant Rev Dr, 1925, S 24,25:4
Scarborough, Henry, 1949, Je 28,27:4; 1952, D 31,15:1
Scarborough, Howard O, 1949, Je 24,23:5
Scarborough, John B Mrs, 1956, S 7,23:2
Scarborough, John Bp, 1914, Mr 15,7:5
Scarborough, John Mrs, 1909, D 20,9:3
Scarborough, Lee R, 1945, Ap 11,23:5
Scarborough, William B, 1964, F 10,27:4
Scarbrough, Lord, 1945, Mr 5,19:2
Scarburgh, Robert S, 1950, My 15,21:2
Scarcello, Jerome, 1951, Ja 22,12:4
Scardaoni, Francesco, 1951, F 9,25:5
Scardino, Antonio, 1949, N 8,31:4
Scardon, Paul, 1954, Ja 20,27:4

Scarff, Paul B, 1940, Ja 22,15:4
Scarfiotti, Lodovico, 1968, Je 9,V,1:8
Scaricabarozzi, Roberto, 1949, My 3,25:4
Scarlet, James, 1920, F 26,11:4
Scarlett, Andrew, 1947, Ja 7,27:3
Scarlett, Charles C, 1944, My 10,19:2
Scarlett, Charles E, 1940, Mr 17,51:2
Scarlett, George B, 1952, D 19,31:2
Scarlett, Hugh R, 1943, Jl 22,19:6
Scarlett, Hunter, 1954, D 24,13:5
Scarlett, James C, 1966, Jl 12,43:2
Scarlett, James Yorke Sir, 1871, D 8,1:7
Scarlett, P C, 1881, Jl 18,5:2
Scarola, Pasquale N, 1956, O 6,21:3
Scarpino, David A, 1954, S 11,17:5
Scarpino, Phil, 1940, N 27,23:3
Scarpitta, Salvatore C, 1948, Ag 19,21:6
Scarpone, Daniel, 1940, My 22,23:3
Scarpulla, Norman C, 1958, F 6,27:4
Scarr, J H, 1936, F 15,15:1
Scarritt, Daniel, 1961, My 2,37:4
Scarritt, Ellett G, 1952, N 6,29:1
Scarritt, Horace S, 1949, My 17,26:2
Scarritt, William R, 1943, N 1,17:3
Scarritt, William R Mrs, 1942, Ag 24,15:2
Scarritt, Winthrop E, 1911, D 8,13:4
Scarritt, Winthrop E Mrs, 1946, S 4,23:5
Scarritt, Winthrop T, 1955, Ag 4,25:4
Scarry, Jack, 1957, Mr 11,25:2
Scarsdale, Baron (Rev Alf Curzon), 1916, Mr 24,11:6
Scarselli, Oliver A, 1952, S 25,31:4
Scarseth, George D, 1962, Mr 22,35:5
Scarsten, Christian P, 1948, Ap 26,23:3
Scatcherd, Winifred, 1911, Ap 1,13:6
Scates, John C, 1949, My 12,31:5
Scattergood, Alfred G, 1954, Ag 11,25:4
Scattergood, Alfred M Sr, 1957, My 2,31:4
Scattergood, Ezra F, 1947, N 17,22:3
Scattergood, J Henry, 1953, Je 16,27:4
Scattergood, John K, 1941, Ja 17,17:4
Scattergood, Joseph, 1949, Mr 19,15:1
Scattergood, Joseph Jr, 1948, Je 6,72:6
Scattergood, Samuel F, 1960, Ag 24,29:1
Scattergood, Thomas Mrs, 1946, N 13,27:4
Scatuorchio, Michael A, 1946, N 28,27:4
Scavarda, Caesar J, 1955, F 22,21:1
Scavenius, Erik, 1962, N 30,33:3
Scavullo, Angelo C, 1965, F 9,37:3
Scavuzzo, Rudolph J, 1950, O 11,33:4
Scearce, James P, 1941, F 17,15:5
Scearce, W Eugene, 1954, Jl 3,11:5
Sceery, Edward W, 1951, N 24,11:4
Scelle, Georges, 1961, Ja 12,29:4
Scerbo, Frank C Mrs, 1960, My 3,39:3
Scervini, Frank, 1962, Mr 9,29:2
Sceureman, Floyd A, 1948, My 19,27:2
Schaab, Louis Sr, 1944, S 14,23:6
Schaack, Harry C, 1947, Jl 29,21:2
Schaack, John M, 1938, Jl 20,19:6
Schaad, Carl E, 1952, My 2,25:4
Schaad, Cornelius, 1939, F 12,45:2
Schaad, David, 1880, O 10,7:5
Schaad, Henry D, 1913, Jl 19,7:6
Schaad, Jacob, 1952, Je 8,86:6
Schaad, Julius A, 1938, O 26,23:2
Schaaf, Albert E, 1950, Je 9,23:3
Schaaf, Edward O, 1939, Je 27,23:2
Schaaf, George L, 1944, Ap 7,19:1
Schaaf, Hugh K, 1952, O 18,19:3
Schaaf, Royal A, 1964, Ap 15,39:3
Schaafsma, Albert, 1967, F 7,39:2
Schaal, Edwin G, 1950, O 5,31:1
Schaal, John G, 1949, Mr 26,17:3
Schaal, Kenneth R, 1960, Ja 16,21:4
Schaap, Abraham, 1944, Je 14,19:4
Schaap, Herman M, 1938, My 3,23:4
Schaap, Irving E, 1948, N 24,23:2
Schaap, Joseph M, 1956, Ag 7,27:1
Schaap, Joseph M Mrs, 1940, S 1,20:6
Schaap, Michael, 1957, D 24,34:1
Schaar, Adolph Mrs, 1960, Mr 3,29:1
Schaar, Gustav Mrs, 1947, Jl 27,45:1
Schaar, Henry F, 1947, Ag 26,23:5
Schabehorn, Henry E, 1940, Ag 8,19:5
Schabelitz, Rudolph F, 1959, Jl 3,17:4
Schaberg, Roy R, 1956, O 25,33:2
Schabinger, Otto W, 1948, Ag 28,16:2
Schachat, Abraham B, 1943, N 5,19:5
Schachat, Edward K, 1957, Ag 2,19:2
Schachel, William H, 1953, My 28,23:1
Schacher, Alfred, 1960, Mr 2,37:3
Schacher, Gerhard, 1953, D 25,17:5
Schachleiter, Albanus Rev, 1937, Je 21,19:2
Schachner, Aug, 1941, Jl 11,15:2
Schachner, Nathan, 1955, O 3,27:3
Schacht, Adolph, 1942, Ja 24,17:2
Schacht, Charles A, 1954, My 26,29:2
Schacht, Elmer W, 1952, Mr 31,19:2
Schacht, Gustav, 1943, O 12,27:2
Schacht, Henry (H Sharp), 1964, Ja 11,23:5
Schacht, Hjalmar Mrs, 1940, My 28,23:4
Schacht, Mayer, 1967, My 29,25:3
Schacht, Samuel, 1952, Ja 15,27:1

Schacht, Samuel Mrs, 1957, Je 17,23:1
Schachtel, Bernard Mrs, 1959, Mr 14,23:2
Schachtel, Sol H, 1950, O 24,29:4
Schachtel, Victor R, 1960, D 20,33:1
Schachter, Esther Mrs, 1947, Ag 8,17:3
Schachter, Max F, 1952, Ap 12,11:2
Schachter, Morris, 1952, Jl 25,18:4
Schachter, Sadie V Mrs, 1939, Jl 17,19:2
Schack, George W von Gen, 1909, Ja 18,9:2
Schack, O W C, 1875, S 5,12:3
Schack, William G, 1941, F 8,15:2
Schackno, Henry G, 1950, Ag 24,27:2
Schacterle, Louis G, 1949, My 14,13:3
Schactman, Irving Mrs, 1963, Jl 18,27:5
Schad, Edith H, 1942, F 4,19:4
Schad, J Harry, 1948, O 12,25:2
Schad, Theodore G, 1965, N 15,37:1
Schada, Marie, 1954, Ag 15,85:1
Schade, Caroline (will), 1954, S 29,55:1
Schade, Fred, 1954, Ap 20,29:3
Schade, Henry, 1937, Ap 9,21:2
Schade, Henry N, 1961, Mr 23,33:1
Schade, John D, 1966, Ja 10,25:2
Schade, Palmer W Sr Mrs, 1954, Jl 5,11:5
Schade, William T, 1968, Je 11,47:3
Schadenko, Efim A, 1951, S 7,29:2
Schader, Frederic, 1962, Ap 4,43:5
Schadle, Chester L, 1950, O 3,31:1
Schadler, Adolph Sr, 1944, N 7,27:5
Schadt, Frederick W, 1942, My 20,19:2
Schadt, George, 1957, F 28,27:4
Schadt, George C, 1957, N 8,29:3
Schadt, Oliver G J, 1939, Ja 6,21:2
Schaeberle, John M, 1924, S 20,15:5
Schaeck, Theodore Col, 1911, My 3,13:5
Schaedle, George W, 1922, O 20,17:5
Schaedle, Matilda A, 1941, F 16,40:8
Schaedle, Thomas G, 1949, O 2,51:6
Schaeer, Peter J, 1944, Mr 13,15:1
Schaefer, A, 1943, Je 2,25:4
Schaefer, Albert, 1947, O 25,19:5
Schaefer, Augustus H, 1955, Ap 20,33:5
Schaefer, Benjamin, 1962, F 18,93:1
Schaefer, Charles A, 1952, F 3,84:1
Schaefer, Charles G, 1946, Ag 8,21:6
Schaefer, Charles H, 1922, Mr 3,13:4
Schaefer, Charles J, 1960, D 28,27:3
Schaefer, Charles J Jr, 1955, F 17,27:1
Schaefer, Christian L, 1957, Ja 27,84:1
Schaefer, D, 1929, Ja 14,23:4
Schaefer, David, 1950, Ja 12,27:1
Schaefer, E George, 1962, Mr 30,33:2
Schaefer, E Paul, 1948, N 26,23:3
Schaefer, Edgar F, 1954, My 4,29:4
Schaefer, Edmund, 1953, Ja 3,15:1
Schaefer, Edward C, 1921, D 21,19:5
Schaefer, Edward E, 1948, D 5,92:7
Schaefer, Elizabeth, 1959, D 2,43:4
Schaefer, Elsie L, 1951, Je 21,27:5
Schaefer, Emil, 1905, Mr 25,9:5
Schaefer, Emma W Mrs, 1942, Mr 6,22:2
Schaefer, Ernest R, 1954, Ap 22,29:5
Schaefer, Everett B, 1958, Jl 11,23:4
Schaefer, Ferdinand, 1953, Ap 21,27:1
Schaefer, Frank C, 1948, Ja 24,16:2
Schaefer, Fred C, 1952, S 30,31:3
Schaefer, Frederic, 1955, F 22,21:4
Schaefer, Frederick C A, 1954, Je 17,29:6
Schaefer, Frederick L, 1912, Jl 31,9:5
Schaefer, Frederick W, 1941, Ja 8,19:2; 1947, O 1 21:3
Schaefer, George, 1946, O 24,27:3
Schaefer, George A, 1944, N 4,15:4
Schaefer, George J, 1944, My 5,19:4
Schaefer, George Jr, 1940, Ag 27,21:3
Schaefer, George L, 1941, My 3,15:2; 1950, O 8,1
Schaefer, George P, 1964, Je 18,35:2
Schaefer, George W, 1947, Mr 27,27:3; 1960, F 8
Schaefer, George Washington Capt, 1913, N 6,11:
Schaefer, Henry (funl, N 27,19:3), 1924, N 26,1
Schaefer, Henry G, 1946, Mr 21,25:1
Schaefer, Henry Jr, 1942, N 13,23:3
Schaefer, Herbert W, 1947, Mr 26,25:5
Schaefer, Hugo E, 1967, S 29,47:3
Schaefer, J L, 1927, F 6,II,11:1
Schaefer, J Louis Mrs, 1955, Ap 15,23:3
Schaefer, Jacob, 1910, Mr 9,9:2
Schaefer, Jacob Mrs, 1945, Je 7,19:3
Schaefer, John A, 1957, Jl 25,23:1
Schaefer, John Dr, 1913, Jl 20,II,11:4
Schaefer, John H, 1941, Je 7,17:5
Schaefer, John T, 1968, N 27,47:4
Schaefer, John V, 1937, O 22,19:4
Schaefer, John W, 1945, Ag 16,19:4
Schaefer, Joseph A, 1945, Ja 16,19:3
Schaefer, Joseph F, 1954, Ap 24,17:4
Schaefer, Joseph J, 1958, Ap 12,19:2
Schaefer, Louis, 1944, O 8,43:1
Schaefer, Louis E Dr, 1968, Mr 12,43:3
Schaefer, Ludwig (will, Mr 20,29:7), 1947, F 23
Schaefer, Marie C Mrs, 1939, My 13,15:3
Schaefer, Marie T Mrs, 1937, D 29,21:3
Schaefer, Nicholas, 1949, Mr 26,18:6

Schaefer, Oskar, 1939, Ag 30,17:5
Schaefer, Otto E (por), 1939, Ag 25,15:3
Schaefer, Paul E, 1958, F 1,19:4
Schaefer, Paul F, 1949, O 11,31:1
Schaefer, Paul H Capt, 1937, My 13,25:4
Schaefer, Phil F, 1942, D 9,27:5
Schaefer, Phil Mrs, 1955, Mr 12,19:4
Schaefer, Robert M, 1946, Ag 24,11:4
Schaefer, Rudolf J Mrs, 1966, D 24,19:3
Schaefer, Rudolph J, 1923, N 13,21:4
Schaefer, Rudolph Jay, 1923, N 11,23:3
Schaefer, Samuel (por), 1949, Ap 21,25:3
Schaefer, Solomon W, 1967, Ag 11,31:3
Schaefer, Sydney L, 1958, Je 3,31:5
Schaefer, Theodore, 1959, F 26,31:4
Schaefer, Walter, 1961, My 9,39:4
Schaefer, Wilhelm, 1952, Ja 21,15:1
Schaefer, William, 1945, O 2,23:3; 1950, N 19,93:2; 1955, Ap 22,25:2
Schaefers, John M Rev, 1908, My 6,7:5
Schaeffer, Adolph, 1904, Ap 17,1:2
Schaeffer, Alvah O, 1947, Mr 11,27:3
Schaeffer, Benjamin L, 1957, F 19,31:5
Schaeffer, Carl A, 1956, O 31,33:5
Schaeffer, Carl E, 1955, My 5,33:4
Schaeffer, Carroll, 1957, Ja 7,25:4
Schaeffer, Charles, 1953, O 10,17:6
Schaeffer, Charles B, 1950, Jl 16,69:1
Schaeffer, Daniel W, 1945, Ap 4,21:4
Schaeffer, Edmund B, 1950, S 5,27:4
Schaeffer, Emil, 1952, N 18,31:5
Schaeffer, Francis J Capt, 1937, Ja 8,20:2
Schaeffer, Fred J, 1959, My 15,58:3
Schaeffer, Frederick, 1953, Jl 2,23:4
Schaeffer, Frederick Mrs, 1949, S 15,27:2
Schaeffer, Fritz, 1967, Mr 30,40:1
Schaeffer, G Ray, 1948, S 17,26:2
Schaeffer, George, 1950, Mr 15,29:4
Schaeffer, George S, 1962, Mr 6,32:8
Schaeffer, Hanns S, 1967, My 3,42:4
Schaeffer, Hans, 1967, Mr 25,23:2
Schaeffer, J Nevin, 1942, Je 11,23:6
Schaeffer, John A, 1941, Ap 8,26:2
Schaeffer, John H Dr, 1937, My 19,23:6
Schaeffer, John Rev, 1907, D 28,7:7
Schaeffer, Joseph H Rev, 1937, N 14,II,11:3
Schaeffer, Joseph M, 1956, S 9,84:1
Schaeffer, Joseph W Dr, 1925, My 5,21:4
Schaeffer, Ledru G, 1947, Jl 26,13:3
Schaeffer, Louis F, 1950, S 26,31:5
Schaeffer, Louis J, 1958, S 28,88:3
Schaeffer, Nathan C Dr, 1919, Mr 16,20:4
Schaeffer, Richard E, 1954, Ja 30,17:4
Schaeffer, Rupert C Jr, 1947, O 25,19:6
Schaeffer, Sam, 1952, Jl 9,27:3
Schaeffer, William B, 1951, D 12,37:3
Schaeffler, Frank C, 1942, Ap 13,15:4
Schaeffler, Frank C Mrs, 1939, Mr 29,23:2
Schaeffler, Frederick A (por), 1937, F 25,23:3
Schaeffner, Anthony, 1946, Mr 13,29:4
Schaeffner, William C Rev Dr, 1921, Ap 17,23:4
Schaefle, Louis J, 1955, Mr 9,27:2
Schaeken, Alphonse M Rev, 1915, O 23,11:5
Schaen, Jack M, 1951, F 24,13:2
Schaerer, Eduardo, 1941, N 13,28:4
Schaerer, Walter G, 1962, Mr 1,31:4
Schaerf, Adolf (funl plans;trb, Mr 2,35:5; funl, Mr 6,25:3), 1965, Mr 1,27:2
Schaerf, Adolf Mrs, 1956, Je 22,23:5
Schaerges, Robert J, 1951, Ap 3,27:4
Schaerges, Robert J Mrs, 1942, My 9,13:4
Schaetzel, Francois J, 1940, Ag 13,19:5
Schaetzle, Max, 1949, Ag 23,23:1
Schaetzle, Max J Sr, 1947, D 25,21:2
Schafer, Algernon S, 1942, F 13,22:2
Schafer, Alvin J, 1940, Ap 28,36:4
Schafer, Anthony, 1940, D 16,23:3
Schafer, Charles E, 1916, Je 8,13:7
Schafer, Charles E Mrs, 1954, Ja 9,15:4
Schafer, Edward, 1937, My 8,19:3
Schafer, Edward Jr, 1952, Mr 8,13:6
Schafer, Ernest, 1941, N 10,17:3
Schafer, Fred G Mrs, 1945, S 22,17:3
Schafer, Frederick G, 1950, Je 5,23:4
chafer, Henry Y, 1944, D 2,13:4
chafer, Irving H Mrs, 1953, Ja 14,31:2
chafer, Jacob R, 1950, Ap 29,15:5
chafer, John C, 1962, Je 11,31:4
chafer, John H, 1942, My 17,47:4
chafer, John P Sr Mrs, 1950, S 7,31:4
chafer, Joseph, 1941, Ja 28,19:1
chafer, Martin F, 1945, F 2,19:3
chafer, Martin F Mrs, 1952, D 25,29:5
chafer, Myron, 1951, S 13,31:3
chafer, Oscar S, 1961, N 24,28:6
chafer, Roy A, 1943, Mr 28,24:6; 1963, Ag 9,9:2
chafer, Samuel M, 1918, Ja 14,11:4
chafer, William, 1914, Je 2,11:7
chaff, A Edwin, 1941, S 28,48:5
chaff, Charles E, 1945, N 6,19:5
chaff, David S, 1941, Mr 3,15:5
chaff, David S Mrs, 1947, O 1,29:5
chaff, Frederic A, 1950, F 9,29:1
Schaff, Frederic A Mrs, 1950, My 28,44:6
Schaff, George H, 1956, D 17,31:5
Schaff, Harold H, 1945, S 1,11:5
Schaff, P Rev Dr, 1893, O 21,2:1
Schaff, Sebastian, 1939, Ap 6,25:1
Schaff, Valentine (mem mass, NYC, D 4,13:1),(por), 1946, D 2,25:6
Schaff, William, 1905, My 22,9:6
Schaffer, Albert R Mrs, 1942, D 29,21:4
Schaffer, Aug, 1942, Ag 9,43:2
Schaffer, Benjamin, 1958, Mr 30,88:8
Schaffer, Daniel, 1937, F 2,23:2
Schaffer, David, 1950, My 26,23:5
Schaffer, David R, 1961, O 26,35:5
Schaffer, Donald N, 1946, D 17,38:7
Schaffer, Edna V, 1960, N 30,37:4
Schaffer, Eugene P, 1947, D 17,29:3
Schaffer, Franklin P, 1966, Ja 31,39:3
Schaffer, Frederick J, 1953, S 20,87:2
Schaffer, Henry, 1944, Ja 1,13:1; 1953, Ag 20,27:3
Schaffer, Howard W, 1943, F 12,19:5
Schaffer, Jacob I, 1948, My 20,29:2
Schaffer, Jay M, 1942, My 10,42:6
Schaffer, John Henry, 1912, Ag 6,9:6
Schaffer, John J Sr, 1957, O 19,21:5
Schaffer, John S, 1961, N 30,37:4
Schaffer, Julius, 1966, S 15,43:4
Schaffer, Karl F, 1949, N 23,29:4
Schaffer, Louis, 1953, O 21,30:5
Schaffer, Louis Mrs, 1948, Mr 16,27:4
Schaffer, Nathan, 1966, Ja 7,27:6
Schaffer, Otto C, 1950, N 28,31:4
Schaffer, Ralph, 1941, Ja 21,21:2
Schaffer, Sylvester (por), 1941, Ap 27,40:1
Schaffer, Walter L Mrs, 1947, My 2,21:3
Schaffer, William I, 1953, Ja 16,23:3
Schaffernoth, Charles A, 1961, Mr 18,23:5
Schaffhausen, Joseph F, 1960, O 11,45:4
Schaffner, Abraham, 1920, D 9,13:3
Schaffner, Abraham J Mrs, 1940, N 28,23:5
Schaffner, Carl F, 1957, Je 30,86:7
Schaffner, John H, 1939, Ja 28,13:5
Schaffner, Joseph (funl, Ap 22,11:8), 1918, Ap 20, 13:8
Schaffner, Joseph H Mrs, 1960, S 25,86:3
Schaffner, Joseph Mrs (will, My 16,29:6), 1957, My 10,27:5
Schaffner, Martin, 1965, O 8,6:1
Schaffner, Phil M, 1942, Jl 17,15:4
Schaffner, Robert C, 1946, N 14,29:2
Schaffnit, Charles T, 1953, S 9,29:5
Schafhauser, Ernest Mrs, 1960, Mr 19,21:5
Schafman, Joseph, 1962, Ja 20,21:5
Schafmeister, Henry Mrs, 1953, O 14,29:1
Schafran, Gregor Mrs, 1954, Ja 3,88:5
Schafran, Samuel, 1954, Je 12,15:4
Schagemann, Joseph, 1961, Ap 13,35:4
Schager von Eckartsau, Albin Baroness, 1950, D 8, 30:3
Schagrin, Charles W, 1940, Ja 3,22:4
Schah, Vladimir, 1949, Jl 12,27:4
Schaible, Charles C Sr, 1951, Mr 23,21:4
Schaible, Rudolph F, 1949, My 6,25:3
Schaick, S D Van, 1876, Ap 7,4:6
Schaidt, Leander, 1943, Je 7,13:1
Schaik, Willem T van, 1946, Ag 18,44:4
Schaikewitz, Nahum Meir, 1905, N 27,9:3
Schaill, William M, 1944, S 17,42:3
Schain, Morris L, 1956, S 29,19:2
Schak, Frank J, 1948, Ja 30,24:2
Schak, William, 1961, D 1,30:3
Schal, George, 1952, D 4,35:6
Schalau, Mabel V, 1943, Je 24,21:2
Schalk, F, 1931, S 4,19:3
Schalk, Henry, 1908, My 3,11:4
Schalk, Herbert B, 1941, Ag 31,23:3
Schalk, Herman, 1945, O 30,19:3
Schalk, J Rupert (will), 1964, Mr 20,20:8
Schalk, J Ruppert, 1962, O 26,31:3
Schalk, Oscar, 1924, F 10,23:2
Schalk, Otto B, 1956, Ap 29,86:6
Schall, Aly I, 1948, S 8,29:4
Schall, Gordon W, 1964, F 15,23:4
Schall, Herman, 1946, N 4,25:4
Schall, J Hubley Mrs, 1961, Jl 4,19:4
Schall, John H, 1947, Jl 12,13:4
Schall, T D Sen, 1935, D 23,1:5
Schall, William A, 1947, My 3,17:1
Schallek, Max L, 1941, N 29,17:4
Schallenberger, James M, 1944, My 23,23:4
Schaller, Carleton, 1947, O 8,25:1
Schaller, George J, 1964, Jl 17,27:3
Schaller, Jacob J, 1945, Jl 18,27:5
Schaller, Waldemar T, 1967, O 3,47:3
Schallitz, Walter G, 1958, O 28,35:4
Schallmann, Hyman H, 1952, Ap 11,23:3
Schambach, Robert P, 1954, Ap 1,31:3
Schamberg, Morris J, 1953, My 21,31:3
Schamburg, Frank D Mrs, 1943, S 12,53:1
Schamerhorn, A J (por), 1946, Ag 6,25:3
Schamus, John B, 1944, O 21,17:6
Schanandoah, Chapman, 1953, F 23,25:6
Schanbacher, Charles A, 1953, Je 12,27:3
Schanbeck, Jordan, 1958, Jl 3,8:5
Schanberger, Frederick C, 1947, N 29,13:1
Schanck, George E, 1943, O 24,44:4
Schanck, George H, 1961, Ap 13,35:2
Schanck, James L, 1939, Je 22,23:6
Schanck, Thomas E, 1945, Mr 28,23:2
Schanck, Will H, 1955, Je 17,23:5
Schanck, Will H Mrs, 1945, Mr 13,23:2
Schandel, John J Rev, 1910, F 20,II,9:1
Schanerman, Philip G, 1966, O 19,38:6
Schanfarber, Edwin, 1944, Jl 3,11:5
Schanfarber, Tobias, 1942, Mr 5,24:2
Schang, Frederick, 1945, Je 1,15:5
Schang, Wally (Walter H), 1965, Mr 7,82:6
Schank, Charles F, 1966, Ja 24,35:3
Schanker, Abraham, 1945, S 13,23:5
Schantz, F M, 1951, Ap 4,29:5
Schantz, Horace W, 1937, Ja 29,19:5
Schantz, Lorin, 1940, S 18,23:2
Schantz, Orpheus M, 1951, S 4,27:5
Schantz, Philip Mrs, 1945, Ja 19,19:2
Schanze, Fred M, 1938, O 25,23:5
Schanzer, Edward A, 1965, Je 20,72:4
Schaper, Samuel Mrs, 1962, Ag 17,23:2
Schapira, Maurice Judge, 1968, F 26,37:3
Schapira, S W, 1936, N 22,II,8:6
Schapiro, Harry, 1968, O 29,47:2
Schapiro, Jacob, 1958, Ja 5,86:3; 1962, Jl 4,21:2
Schapiro, Jacques J, 1959, D 28,23:2
Schapiro, John M, 1966, Ap 27,47:3
Schapiro, Joseph, 1945, N 14,19:3
Schapiro, Louis, 1947, Ap 2,27:3
Schapiro, Maxim, 1958, Jl 21,21:2
Schapiro, Peter D, 1963, O 2,41:3
Schapiro, Simon, 1957, O 30,29:4
Schappa, Walter J, 1948, Mr 15,23:2
Schappert, Anthony F X Mrs, 1959, Ja 29,27:4
Schappert, George W Mrs, 1951, Jl 27,19:5
Schappert, N L, 1948, Mr 11,27:3
Schappert, Philip L, 1947, Ja 20,25:2
Scharbauer, John, 1941, O 22,23:1
Schardien, Adam, 1955, F 15,27:3
Schardien, John A, 1948, D 8,31:4
Schare, David Mrs, 1959, O 17,23:6
Scharf, Charles, 1965, F 19,36:4
Scharf, Emily E, 1948, D 4,19:1
Scharf, Gregory, 1949, F 20,60:1
Scharf, Herman, 1953, O 13,29:4
Scharfe, Paul, 1942, Jl 31,15:4
Scharfenberg, Theodore J, 1904, F 9,9:6
Scharfer, Solomon S, 1966, D 29,31:2
Scharff, Alex, 1950, N 18,15:3
Scharff, Bernard W, 1941, Ag 20,19:2
Scharff, Joseph Mrs, 1949, S 30,24:3
Scharff, Maurice R, 1967, Ap 9,92:6
Scharffenberg, Paul, 1938, Je 30,23:4
Scharffin, Leo, 1952, O 27,27:3
Scharfman, Abraham, 1950, Jl 7,19:4
Scharfman, Isidore Mrs, 1957, Mr 11,25:1
Scharfman, Martin H, 1948, Ag 10,21:1
Scharl, Josef, 1954, D 9,33:2
Scharles, Gus, 1960, O 19,45:2
Scharlin, Harold E, 1957, My 25,21:3
Scharlin, Harold E Mrs, 1951, N 2,23:2
Scharmann, August C, 1917, My 9,11:2
Scharmann, Gustav, 1942, Mr 7,17:2
Scharmann, Herman B, 1920, Ag 4,11:3
Scharmann, Walter G, 1949, Ag 26,19:5
Scharnagel, Isabel M, 1953, N 26,31:4
Scharping, Russell A, 1943, Ap 1,23:1
Scharps, Abraham, 1904, F 19,9:6
Scharps, Albert Mrs, 1953, Ja 29,27:3
Scharps, Albert T, 1959, My 29,23:3
Scharps, Benjamin, 1943, Mr 5,17:5
Scharps, Charles E T, 1955, Ap 3,86:7
Scharps, Tessie K, 1938, O 28,23:2
Scharps, Victor, 1913, My 31,11:6
Scharrer, Ernst A, 1965, Ap 30,35:1
Scharrott, Charles, 1948, N 11,20:5
Scharschug, George, 1958, Ap 28,23:4
Schartenberg, Charles S, 1939, Je 30,19:4
Scharton, William R, 1948, Jl 9,19:2
Scharule, Louis, 1917, Je 24,19:4
Scharwachter, Albert A, 1958, F 18,21:4
Scharwath, John A, 1956, Ja 4,27:2
Scharwenka, Xaver, 1924, D 9,25:4
Schary, Ben, 1951, N 24,11:2
Schary, Herman Mrs, 1948, My 3,21:4
Scharzkoff, Ernst W, 1937, D 15,25:5
Scharzwald, Milton, 1950, Mr 3,25:2
Schasberger, Otto C, 1941, F 1,17:2
Schasseur, Michael, 1946, Je 25,21:5
Schattan, Elsie T, 1943, D 18,15:1
Schattle, Conrad F, 1958, Je 28,17:4
Schattman, Murray, 1952, Ja 3,27:4
Schatvet, Einar, 1939, Ja 28,13:5
Schatz, B, 1932, Mr 24,21:1
Schatz, Charles, 1954, Mr 15,25:3
Schatz, George J, 1959, Jl 26,69:2; 1959, S 14,29:2
Schatz, H A, 1942, Mr 17,21:2
Schatz, Louis, 1953, O 23,23:2
Schatz, Louis B, 1954, F 8,23:3
Schatz, Ralph H, 1937, F 13,13:5

Schatz, William F, 1951, N 27,31:4
Schatzel, Robert, 1950, O 17,34:2
Schatzer, Joseph M Sr, 1947, Ja 12,59:3
Schatzin, Solomon, 1944, Ap 25,23:4
Schatzkin, Harvey, 1958, S 29,27:5
Schatzkin, Henry A, 1949, My 20,27:4
Schatzman, Benjamin S, 1958, Mr 12,31:2
Schatzov, Lewis, 1963, Ag 24,19:4
Schau, William, 1948, Mr 3,23:1
Schaub, Abinah K Mrs, 1938, My 21,15:6
Schaub, August, 1954, My 18,29:2
Schaub, Edward L, 1953, My 27,31:6
Schaub, F Carter, 1956, O 30,37:2
Schaub, Gordon C, 1966, Mr 14,31:2
Schaub, Howard C, 1947, D 3,29:3
Schaub, Howard C Mrs, 1959, Ja 28,31:5
Schaub, Jacob, 1940, Ap 23,23:3
Schaub, Jacob Mrs, 1948, N 12,23:5
Schaub, Robert C, 1958, Ja 18,15:2
Schaub, Stanley J, 1963, Je 11,37:4
Schaubel, Charles W, 1939, F 26,38:7
Schauble, Edward Mrs, 1950, Je 1,27:2
Schauble, P Otto, 1938, My 7,15:3
Schauble, Peter L, 1952, O 12,89:1
Schauble, Toby, 1962, Jl 19,27:4
Schauble, William, 1947, N 12,56:3
Schauer, Anthony V, 1946, Ag 9,17:4
Schauer, Carl F, 1941, F 5,19:4
Schauer, Ernest, 1947, Mr 3,21:5
Schauer, John F, 1947, D 28,40:4
Schauer, Joseph, 1953, S 31,25:4
Schauer, Marie, 1951, Ag 4,15:6
Schaufele, Everett, 1948, Mr 2,19:7
Schauffler, Adolph Frederick Rev Dr, 1919, F 19,13:5
Schauffler, Alfred Theodore, 1915, Je 13,15:5
Schauffler, Frederick H, 1940, Je 27,23:3
Schauffler, Frederick H Jr, 1955, F 20,89:2
Schauffler, Julia M P Mrs, 1937, Jl 7,23:2
Schauffler, Lilian M B Mrs, 1941, O 10,23:1
Schauffler, Robert H, 1964, N 25,37:2
Schauffler, W G, 1933, My 1,15:4
Schauffler, William G Jr, 1951, O 23,29:3
Schaufler, Aloys H, 1949, S 4,40:8
Schaufler, Frederick, 1949, Mr 23,27:4
Schaufler, Walter A, 1962, S 16,86:8
Schaul, Harry W, 1944, Ap 5,19:4
Schaum, Otto W, 1947, D 10,31:4
Schaumann, Jorgen N, 1953, Ag 21,27:1
Schaumberger, Charles, 1953, Ag 11,27:4
Schaumburg, Charles H, 1944, O 23,19:2
Schaumburg, Charles H Sr, 1948, Ag 22,61:1
Schaumburg, Clarence W, 1948, N 10,29:3
Schaupp, Henry, 1940, F 17,13:4
Schaupp, Henry R, 1961, D 24,36:3
Schaus, Harold J, 1956, My 16,35:4
Schaus, Hermann, 1911, F 10,9:5
Schaus, William J Mrs, 1940, Ap 25,23:4
Schauss, Hayyim, 1953, O 6,29:4
Schauss, Stanley L, 1951, Ja 25,25:2
Schauss, William (career), 1946, Mr 25,27:3
Schautz, George J Sr, 1946, Je 25,21:6
Schautz, William A, 1942, S 25,21:4
Schavel, John, 1941, F 7,19:5
Schayer, George F Col, 1914, N 22,3:7
Schebera, Ernst H, 1949, F 8,25:3
Schechner, Abraham, 1967, Jl 13,37:3
Schechter, Abraham, 1937, O 19,26:2
Schechter, Eliot, 1953, Mr 26,31:4
Schechter, Frank I, 1937, S 27,21:1
Schechter, Irving, 1953, Ag 13,25:4
Schechter, Isidore Mrs, 1960, Ap 27,25:5
Schechter, Israel, 1952, Mr 6,31:2
Schechter, Jack, 1966, My 15,88:8
Schechter, Jack Mrs, 1963, Ap 15,29:4
Schechter, Jacob, 1951, Ja 16,29:5
Schechter, Joseph, 1960, Ja 27,30:6
Schechter, Meyer Mrs, 1951, Ag 4,15:4
Schechter, Solomon Dr (funl, N 21,19:4), 1915, N 20, 13:1
Schechter, Solomon Mrs (funl, Ag 29,11:5), 1924, Ag 28,17:5
Schechter, Victor, 1959, Ja 21,31:2
Schechterman, Hyman, 1948, My 18,23:4
Schechtman, Gustave, 1948, N 22,22:2
Scheck, Emanuel P, 1956, S 2,57:1
Scheck, Emanuel P Mrs, 1956, Je 1,23:2
Scheck, Julius, 1961, Jl 13,29:6
Scheck, Morris, 1962, Je 15,27:3
Scheckenburger, Walter W, 1951, F 3,15:3
Scheckler, Howard T, 1948, Ag 18,25:4
Schecter, Samuel B, 1963, Ag 5,29:4
Schecter, Saul N, 1962, Ap 27,35:1
Schecter, Solomon P, 1963, Ap 28,87:3
Schede, Fred C, 1952, Ap 16,27:3
Schediegger, Fred Mrs, 1949, Ja 21,22:2
Scheding, William L, 1947, Je 29,48:7
Schedler, Alfred J, 1950, Ap 26,29:5
Schedler, Augusta B Mrs, 1950, Jl 27,25:4
Schedler, Carl R, 1965, Jl 8,28:4
Schedler, Erich, 1958, Ag 14,29:3
Scheehle, Harold G, 1955, N 16,35:1
Scheehle, J Evans, 1965, Ag 31,33:4
Scheel, Arthur B, 1948, Ag 30,25:1
Scheel, Fritz, 1907, Mr 14,7:5
Scheel, Henry VanRiper Mrs (Anna Stnekoo), 1968, My 30,25:3
Scheele, George C, 1957, O 21,25:4
Scheele, George H, 1954, D 10,28:2
Scheele, Walter T Dr, 1922, Mr 6,13:5
Scheeler, Irwin, 1945, Je 29,15:3
Scheeler, John C, 1942, D 16,25:6
Scheepers, John T (por), 1938, S 24,17:3
Scheer, Alex G, 1958, Ap 21,23:6
Scheer, Edward A, 1960, Mr 2,37:1
Scheer, Edward W (por), 1949, Je 17,23:1
Scheer, Henry C Sr, 1956, N 19,31:3
Scheer, Horace F, 1948, Jl 5,15:3
Scheer, Joseph, 1938, Ja 3,10:7
Scheer, Max, 1953, Mr 5,27:5
Scheer, Otto J, 1967, Ag 11,31:4
Scheer, R, 1928, N 27,31:1
Scheer, Robert H, 1956, Ag 9,25:4
Scheer, Walter G, 1960, My 5,35:4
Scheer, William, 1946, O 25,24:2
Scheer, William N Mrs, 1964, Jl 23,27:5
Scheerer, Aloysius L, 1966, Ja 29,27:4
Scheerer, Gertrude R Mrs, 1947, My 10,13:2
Scheerer, Harold Mrs, 1966, Mr 20,86:8
Scheerer, Hugo E, 1941, Mr 21,21:3
Scheerer, Joseph D Sr Mrs, 1966, Ap 15,39:2
Scheerer, Martin, 1961, O 20,30:4
Scheerer, Maud, 1961, S 13,45:2
Scheerer, Paul R Sr, 1965, Je 16,43:3
Scheerer, William, 1944, O 28,15:5
Scheetz, Francis H, 1968, S 27,47:3
Scheetz, George, 1944, Jl 5,17:3
Scheetz, John F Mrs, 1942, Ap 6,15:1
Scheetz, William C Mrs, 1950, My 6,15:3
Schefer, Anton H, 1950, Ag 6,73:2
Schefer, Carl, 1916, F 16,11:7
Scheff, Frederick, 1962, S 21,29:2
Scheff, Fritzi (will, My 14,16:3), 1954, Ap 9,23:3
Scheff, Fritzi (est acctg), 1955, F 4,16:8
Scheff, Mary A Mrs, 1938, My 26,25:5
Scheffel, William, 1952, My 2,25:3
Scheffer, Gordon L, 1949, D 2,29:5
Scheffer, Jeannette M, 1946, O 25,23:4
Scheffer, John H, 1939, Ja 27,19:2
Scheffer, Ralph W, 1954, Ag 10,19:2
Scheffer, William J, 1952, Ag 11,15:6
Scheffey, Frank L, 1954, F 5,19:2
Scheffey, Frank L Mrs, 1950, O 29,92:1
Scheffey, Heston S, 1955, Jl 22,23:4
Scheffey, Ralph N, 1945, O 17,19:3
Scheffler, Arthur, 1940, Jl 13,15:5
Scheffler, Eugene Mrs, 1946, N 11,27:2
Scheffler, Samuel, 1950, My 26,23:3
Scheffmeyer, Charles A, 1938, Ja 7,19:1
Scheffmeyer, Wayne, 1951, Ja 10,27:3
Scheflen, Albert E, 1954, F 19,27:1
Scheflin, Christian, 1904, Ja 11,7:6
Schefmeyer, Robert T, 1940, Ap 10,25:5
Schefrin, Jacob, 1940, Mr 19,25:3
Scheftel, Adolph, 1909, S 15,9:5
Scheftel, Adolph Mrs, 1921, Mr 15,11:4
Scheftel, Herbert A, 1914, S 16,11:7
Scheftel, Walter M, 1917, My 27,19:4
Scheftel, Yetta, 1940, S 10,23:2
Schehl, John A, 1937, O 11,21:4
Schehl, Leila S Mrs, 1940, Mr 16,15:4
Schei, A G, 1965, F 20,25:2
Scheib, Eleanor W, 1944, Je 5,19:4
Scheib, Phil A Mrs, 1952, Mr 25,27:3
Scheibe, Alphons, 1959, Je 17,35:4
Scheibe, Charles F, 1963, My 19,86:8
Scheibel, John C, 1939, Ja 13,19:1
Scheibell, William O, 1947, N 21,27:4
Scheiber, Irving M, 1957, O 17,33:3
Scheiberling, Edward N, 1967, S 11,45:1
Scheibert, Justus Maj, 1903, Jl 19,5:2
Scheible, John M, 1942, O 2,25:4
Scheid, Collistus, 1954, Ap 15,29:1
Scheid, Frederick, 1968, N 22,47:3
Scheide, Charles E Maj, 1916, Ag 19,9:6
Scheide, John H, 1942, S 30,23:2
Scheide, Lester B, 1953, Mr 2,23:4
Scheidemann, Phil (por), 1939, N 30,21:1
Scheidenhelm, Frederick W, 1959, O 19,29:3
Scheider, Alfred M, 1952, Ja 24,27:4
Scheider, Alfred M Mrs (por), 1948, F 2,19:3
Scheider, Charles G, 1944, S 21,19:5
Scheider, Frank C Mrs (M C Thompson), 1953, Ap 13,27:1
Scheider, Fred M, 1939, Ja 20,19:1
Scheider, J Conrad, 1961, Mr 23,33:4
Scheidlinger, Herman, 1959, Ag 3,25:5
Scheidt, Karl F, 1966, Jl 6,42:2
Scheidt, Max S, 1962, S 28,33:2
Scheidt, Vernon, 1951, Ja 20,15:5
Scheifley, Wilfred L, 1954, D 25,11:3
Scheil, Richard, 1879, N 11,5:3
Scheim, Charles S, 1961, Ja 17,27:4
Schein, Annette (Mrs B Jaslow), 1967, Ja 29,76:7
Schein, Ernest, 1967, Je 11,87:1
Schein, George L, 1942, O 3,15:2
Schein, Herbert Dr, 1953, F 1,88:4
Schein, Mandel, 1951, Je 9,19:4
Schein, Marcel, 1960, F 21,92:6
Schein, Nathan, 1943, Ja 10,50:3
Schein, Sigmund, 1954, Ag 25,27:1
Scheinberg, Justin S (Jesse), 1953, S 21,25:4
Scheinberg, Samuel, 1952, S 9,31:4
Scheiner, George, 1959, Jl 29,29:3
Scheiner, Robert, 1949, Jl 29,21:3
Scheingross, Aron Rabbi, 1937, Ja 20,21:4
Scheinis, Joseph L, 1957, S 29,87:1
Scheinkman, Bernard Dr, 1924, Jl 22,15:5
Scheinman, Benjamin J, 1954, F 19,34:2
Scheinpflugova, Olga (Mrs Karel Capek), 1968, Ap 17,47:2
Scheirich, Henry J, 1968, Je 22,33:6
Scheitlin, Emil, 1946, My 3,22:2
Schekman, Emanuel, 1953, Je 23,30:5
Schelhorn, Herbert F, 1960, My 22,86:5
Schelke, Anton J, 1963, My 29,33:1
Schelke, Fred, 1949, Ja 30,60:3
Schelke, Simon, 1947, S 9,31:6
Schelker, Walter G, 1957, N 6,35:4
Schell, Andrew J, 1952, Ag 26,25:3
Schell, Augustus, 1884, Mr 28,5:3
Schell, Edward Mrs, 1951, Jl 29,68:4
Schell, Eleanor, 1955, My 26,31:1
Schell, Erwin H, 1965, Ja 5,33:1
Schell, Frank C, 1942, F 24,21:5
Schell, Frank R, 1959, D 6,86:7
Schell, Frederick B Mrs, 1946, My 21,23:5
Schell, George J, 1937, Jl 30,19:6
Schell, Harmon F, 1950, D 1,25:6
Schell, Harry, 1960, My 14,21:2
Schell, Herman W, 1940, My 17,19:4
Schell, Lillian Mrs, 1920, My 6,11:3
Schell, Nathan, 1957, Mr 20,37:5
Schell, Orville H, 1964, Ja 11,23:4
Schell, Orville H Mrs, 1942, Mr 1,45:3
Schell, Oswald H, 1950, Je 15,31:2
Schell, Richard, 1949, S 13,29:1
Schell, Richard M, 1924, Jl 29,15:5
Schell, Selim L, 1939, O 20,23:3
Schellas, Adam E, 1945, Ag 11,13:4
Schellen, Wilbur, 1940, N 14,23:5
Schellenberg, Chris, 1948, F 18,27:2
Schellenberg, Edward J, 1959, Je 16,35:2
Schellenberg, Frank L, 1941, Ja 19,41:2
Schellenberg, John L, 1948, D 16,29:2
Schellendorf, Bronsart von Gen, 1914, D 17,13:6
Schellenger, William A Mrs, 1947, N 29,13:4
Schellens, Christopher A, 1957, Je 14,25:1
Scheller, John A, 1960, My 23,29:1
Schellet, Arnold E, 1952, Mr 14,20:8
Schellhammer, Fred M, 1954, Je 6,86:3
Schellhase, C H Otto, 1954, O 5,27:5
Schellhorn, Adam J, 1944, Mr 1,19:3
Schelling, Charles E W, 1940, N 7,25:4
Schelling, Clinton W, 1965, O 30,35:3
Schelling, Clinton W Mrs, 1937, S 7,21:4
Schelling, Ernest H, 1939, D 9,15:1
Schelling, Ernest Mrs, 1938, F 5,15:3
Schelling, Felix E (por), 1945, D 16,40:3
Schelling, Henry L, 1941, Ap 13,38:2
Schelling, Julia E, 1950, Ag 10,25:4
Schellinger, Rial B, 1954, Ap 25,87:2
Schellings, Joseph W, 1965, Mr 16,39:4
Schelper, Caspar A, 1950, Mr 16,31:1
Schelz, George J Mrs, 1954, D 16,37:5
Schem, A J Prof, 1881, My 24,5:2
Schemenauer, George J, 1958, Ag 5,27:3
Schemke, Hugo, 1955, S 9,23:1
Schemm, Ferdinand R, 1955, My 18,31:3
Schemmelfennig, Gen, 1865, S 8,1:4
Schempf, John L, 1943, Je 12,13:5
Schenardi, Louis Mrs, 1943, S 5,28:7
Schenberg, Joseph, 1946, Jl 21,39:2
Schenck, Albert S, 1938, Ag 31,15:3
Schenck, Aletta, 1942, Je 15,19:4
Schenck, Aletta V, 1941, F 25,23:5
Schenck, Anna C Mrs, 1942, F 4,19:4
Schenck, Archibald A, 1946, F 21,21:4
Schenck, B, 1928, Ja 5,29:5
Schenck, C Newton Jr, 1957, Ja 20,93:1
Schenck, Carl A, 1955, My 17,29:3
Schenck, Charles A, 1957, Mr 20,37:5
Schenck, Charles D, 1941, D 4,25:2
Schenck, Charles L, 1959, O 8,42:4
Schenck, Charles L Mrs, 1942, Je 27,13:4
Schenck, Charles N, 1945, Mr 14,19:4
Schenck, Charles S, 1914, F 16,7:5
Schenck, Daniel S, 1949, O 25,27:5
Schenck, David, 1948, Mr 8,23:2
Schenck, Douglas S, 1947, Ja 30,25:3
Schenck, Edgar C, 1959, N 17,35:1
Schenck, Elliott, 1939, Mr 6,15:5
Schenck, Emil, 1943, Je 6,42:3
Schenck, Ernest G H, 1955, Ja 19,27:4
Schenck, Eunice M, 1955, My 10,29:5
Schenck, Frederic Prof, 1919, Mr 1,13:2
Schenck, Frederick Brett, 1913, My 22,11:4
Schenck, Frederick P, 1959, My 3,86:5
Schenck, George H, 1947, Mr 6,25:5
Schenck, Gerret R Mrs, 1950, S 24,104:5

Schenck, Gilbert V, 1946, Mr 25,25:5
Schenck, Gilbert V Mrs, 1941, Je 25,21:4
Schenck, Harold W, 1960, My 12,35:4
Schenck, Hattie O, 1944, S 3,26:6
Schenck, Henry, 1956, N 17,21:6
Schenck, Henry A, 1922, F 21,17:3
Schenck, Hollister V, 1960, S 25,88:7
Schenck, Isaac Van Wert Rev Dr, 1913, D 17,11:6
Schenck, J, 1930, Je 29,II,6:1
Schenck, J Fred, 1905, F 10,7:4
Schenck, James S, 1952, S 3,29:4
Schenck, Joe Mrs, 1946, Mr 30,15:3
Schenck, John Cornell, 1909, O 1,9:5
Schenck, John E, 1918, N 14,13:2
Schenck, John G, 1905, Je 9,9:5
Schenck, Joseph M, 1940, D 12,27:4
Schenck, Joseph M (funl plans, O 26,35:2; funl, O 28,21:4), 1961, O 23,1:2
Schenck, Louis Mrs, 1949, Ja 27,24:3
Schenck, M E Rev Dr, 1903, D 16,9:5
Schenck, M Theodora Mrs, 1942, N 13,23:5
Schenck, Martin, 1949, Ag 12,17:2
Schenck, Martin A, 1956, F 1,31:4
Schenck, Mary E Mrs, 1942, D 17,29:2
Schenck, Matilda B, 1941, O 22,23:5
Schenck, May A Mrs, 1942, Mr 15,43:3
Schenck, N H, 1885, Ja 5,5:3
Schenck, Nora V, 1963, Ap 13,19:5
Schenck, Otto J, 1938, Je 10,21:4
Schenck, Peter H, 1911, Mr 20,9:4
Schenck, Peter Lawrence Dr, 1920, Mr 7,22:3
Schenck, R C, 1890, Mr 24,1:7
Schenck, R Percy, 1940, My 22,23:5
Schenck, Ralph E, 1952, Ja 22,29:3
Schenck, Reginald H, 1956, O 21,86:3
Schenck, Samuel B, 1965, N 27,31:5
Schenck, Samuel C, 1952, Jl 11,17:3
Schenck, Samuel C Jr, 1950, My 7,108:3
Schenck, Spotswood D, 1908, Je 27,9:4
Schenck, Stewart C, 1944, F 20,36:2
Schenck, Vincent R, 1942, S 26,15:5
Schenck, Warren R, 1944, Ag 27,33:1
Schenck, Willard P, 1940, Mr 8,22:3
Schene, Louis H, 1953, D 31,19:3
Schenesky, Henry J, 1948, Ag 27,18:4
Schenider, Edwin J, 1947, F 3,19:2
Schenk, C Milton, 1938, Ja 4,23:3
Schenk, Carl A, 1939, S 2,17:6
Schenk, Ferdinand S, 1938, Mr 2,19:4
Schenk, Henry F, 1960, O 8,23:5
Schenk, Hubert G, 1960, Je 21,33:3
Schenk, Karl, 1947, O 4,17:2
Schenk, Karl Mrs, 1958, Jl 6,56:1
Schenk, Robert J, 1962, My 18,31:4
Schenkel, D Prof, 1885, My 23,5:4
Schenkel, Edward C, 1945, S 27,21:3
Schenker, Alfred, 1958, F 14,23:4
Schenker, Benjamin, 1959, Ap 28,35:2
Schenker, Clara E, 1957, Je 17,23:2
Schenkman, Israel, 1960, O 12,43:2
Schenley, E W H Mrs, 1903, N 6,9:5
Schenuit, Frank G, 1948, Mr 31,25:4
Schepp, Christiaan L, 1948, F 14,13:6
Schepp, L, 1926, Mr 12,19:1
Schepp, Phil H, 1957, Ja 31,27:3
Scheps, Henry Mrs, 1946, Je 30,38:2
Scher, Edward, 1964, O 9,40:3
Scher, Jacob, 1961, S 29,35:2
Scher, Joseph S, 1949, N 5,13:2
Scher, Louis S, 1957, D 1,88:7
Scher, Maurice A, 1953, Mr 29,95:3
Scher, Robert J Mrs, 1937, N 5,23:2
Scher, Sidney M Mrs, 1963, Jl 11,29:2
Scherb, Henry, 1943, S 20,21:5
Scherbatoff, Mara (funl plans, Jl 1,56:6), 1956, Je 30,19:4
Scherbatow, Boris Prince, 1949, O 18,27:4
Scherbatow, Boris Princess (A M C Worden), 1956, Je 26,29:4
Scherbatow, Kyril Princess, 1968, Jl 25,33:3
Scherbaty, Harry, 1954, Jl 26,17:1
Scherchen, Hermann, 1966, Je 13,39:1
Schere, Irving S, 1965, D 31,21:1
Schereck, Leon H, 1921, N 17,17:4
Scherer, Adolph, 1952, D 26,15:3
Scherer, Alice M C Mrs, 1938, D 8,27:5
Scherer, Daniel, 1949, N 9,27:1
Scherer, Ernest K, 1967, Mr 2,35:3
Scherer, George F, 1948, N 27,18:2
Scherer, Henry, 1949, Jl 31,60:4
Scherer, Isidor, 1945, N 1,23:3
Scherer, James A B, 1944, F 17,19:6
Scherer, John, 1967, My 24,47:2
Scherer, John J Jr, 1956, Ja 15,92:6
Scherer, Marvin H, 1965, Jl 30,25:3
Scherer, Moses, 1924, Ag 29,11:5
Scherer, Nathan Mrs, 1963, My 16,35:1
Scherer, Robert P, 1960, Jl 29,25:1
Scherer, Victor Mrs, 1962, Ap 18,39:1
Scherer, W J D Mrs, 1949, Mr 30,25:5
Scherer, Walter H, 1951, My 15,31:1
Schereschewsky, Joseph W, 1940, Jl 11,19:1
Scherf, Chrisman G Dr, 1968, Mr 5,41:1
Scherf, Margaret L, 1953, Mr 5,27:3
Scherff, George, 1951, N 1,29:1
Scherff, George Mrs, 1944, D 2,13:5; 1946, Jl 19,19:5
Scherger, George L, 1941, Ap 1,23:6
Scheri, Saverio Mrs, 1955, My 15,86:3
Schering, Richard, 1942, Ag 14,17:1
Scherk, Ludwig, 1946, Ag 6,25:2
Scherl, Archer, 1958, My 4,88:4
Scherl, August, 1921, Ap 19,17:4
Scherl, Sam A, 1959, O 26,29:5
Scherman, Katherine H Mrs, 1943, Ag 20,15:3
Scherman, William S Mrs, 1950, D 19,29:4
Schermerhorn, A Coster, 1956, My 3,31:5
Schermerhorn, A F, 1933, S 4,11:3
Schermerhorn, Alfred E Mrs, 1946, D 22,41:4
Schermerhorn, Arthur F Mrs, 1956, O 23,33:6
Schermerhorn, Avery M, 1946, Ja 30,25:4
Schermerhorn, Bernard T, 1947, N 6,27:3
Schermerhorn, C Fred, 1941, N 5,23:5
Schermerhorn, C Howard, 1925, D 11,23:3
Schermerhorn, Charles Augustus, 1914, O 3,11:6
Schermerhorn, Charles H, 1910, Mr 3,9:4
Schermerhorn, Edward G, 1943, Je 29,19:1; 1949, N 7, 27:4
Schermerhorn, Edwards F, 1957, Ja 26,19:2
Schermerhorn, Frances Serrill Mrs, 1915, Ag 9,7:6
Schermerhorn, Frank E, 1957, D 17,35:1
Schermerhorn, Frederick Augustus, 1919, Mr 21,13:3
Schermerhorn, George S, 1923, N 9,17:4; 1956, Je 27, 31:3
Schermerhorn, George Stevens, 1914, D 10,13:6
Schermerhorn, Grace, 1925, Ja 12,15:3
Schermerhorn, Harvey O, 1958, Jl 4,19:1
Schermerhorn, Herman M Mrs, 1954, My 16,87:2
Schermerhorn, Howard F Mrs, 1960, Mr 28,29:2
Schermerhorn, J A, 1944, Ag 4,13:6
Schermerhorn, J Egmont Mrs, 1907, F 4,9:5
Schermerhorn, J P (funl), 1877, Je 22,8:3
Schermerhorn, James, 1941, D 3,25:3
Schermerhorn, Jane F Mrs, 1937, N 4,25:3
Schermerhorn, John, 1876, Ja 19,4:1
Schermerhorn, John Edgmont, 1906, Je 22,7:6
Schermerhorn, John R, 1938, My 17,24:4
Schermerhorn, John R Mrs, 1949, Ap 6,29:2
Schermerhorn, Julian J, 1953, N 10,31:3
Schermerhorn, Lyman G, 1960, Ap 21,31:5
Schermerhorn, M K Mrs, 1909, F 20,7:4
Schermerhorn, Marvin B, 1940, Je 28,19:3
Schermerhorn, Phil G, 1952, O 8,31:1
Schermerhorn, Richard Jr, 1962, S 29,23:2
Schermerhorn, Sarah Mrs (see also Jl 31), 1903, Ag 1,7:6
Schermerhorn, W C, 1903, Ja 2,1:3
Schermerhorn, William Colford Mrs, 1907, F 15,11:4
Schermerhorn, William G, 1921, Mr 26,13:5
Schermerhorn, William Henry, 1921, D 4,22:3
Scherp, Henry, 1911, O 10,13:6
Scherpenberg, J P A, 1947, Jl 8,23:2
Scherr, Emilius W Mrs (A L Hull), 1959, F 14,21:2
Scherr, Joseph, 1947, N 26,23:2
Scherr, Louis, 1950, Je 9,23:3
Scherr, Sheldon, 1955, S 4,56:6
Scherrer, Franklin J, 1941, Je 10,23:5
Schertzinger, Victor (por), 1941, O 27,17:3
Schery, Ferdinand M, 1952, S 18,29:4
Scherza, Charles, 1952, O 21,29:4
Scherzer, Karl von, 1903, F 21,9:5
Scherzer, Mack M, 1950, Ja 22,76:3
Scherzer, Mack M Mrs, 1954, Mr 31,27:5
Schesler, Charles, 1953, N 21,13:2
Schetky, John Christian, 1874, F 23,5:5
Schettino, Dominic, 1954, Ap 8,27:3
Schetzer, Lawrence G, 1948, N 27,17:3
Scheuer, Arnold L, 1944, Ag 9,17:4
Scheuer, Cecile Mrs, 1950, N 1,35:2
Scheuer, Charles, 1941, F 1,17:6
Scheuer, Charles P, 1963, N 8,31:4
Scheuer, Henry, 1953, Je 2,29:4
Scheuer, Lewis M, 1965, N 5,37:3
Scheuer, Moses, 1946, N 10,63:3
Scheuer, Nicholas Mrs, 1950, Ap 8,13:3
Scheuer, Ray N Mrs, 1939, Jl 6,23:2
Scheuer, Selig Mrs, 1959, Ja 10,17:2
Scheuer, Simon, 1909, S 30,9:4
Scheuer, William, 1948, S 30,27:1
Scheuerle, Joe, 1948, Ap 9,23:5
Scheuerle, Lewis, 1948, Jl 12,19:5
Scheuerman, Henry W Mrs, 1952, Ap 30,27:5
Scheuermann, George C, 1968, Je 21,41:1
Scheuermann, Gregory, 1939, S 6,23:5
Scheuermann, Hugo E, 1957, Ap 2,31:2
Scheulke, Ernest R, 1952, S 16,29:2
Scheumaker, Walter M, 1952, Jl 19,15:6
Scheumann, Walter W, 1958, O 8,35:2
Scheunemann, Curtis R, 1940, D 16,23:6
Scheurer, Christian G, 1950, O 9,25:3
Scheurer, Robert E, 1945, D 21,21:2
Schevill, Ferdinand, 1954, D 11,13:4
Schevill, Rudolph, 1946, F 19,25:3
Schey, Robert (por), 1942, My 6,19:3
Scheyer, David, 1948, F 3,25:5
Scheyer, Emanuel, 1939, Jl 6,23:2
Scheyer, William J, 1956, My 17,31:4
Scheyhing, Herman K Mrs, 1955, Ap 8,21:3
Scheyven, Baudouin Dr (requim mass, Ag 30,33:1), 1968, Ag 21,42:2
Schiadaresis, Constantine, 1964, Mr 20,33:4
Schiaffino, Giovanni, 1938, Ja 4,23:4
Schiaparelli, Giovanni V Prof, 1910, Jl 6,7:6
Schiavazzi, Piero, 1949, My 28,15:6
Schiavon, Beniamino, 1968, N 19,47:1
Schiavone, James, 1941, F 18,4:4
Schiavone, Michael, 1940, Ja 4,24:4
Schiavone, Saul Mrs, 1957, N 16,19:5
Schibel, Charles W, 1942, S 3,19:4
Schibley, Dewey A, 1948, O 14,29:2
Schiby, Allegra, 1963, O 25,31:2
Schicho, John, 1963, My 25,25:4
Schick, Bela, 1967, D 7,1:1
Schick, Charles W, 1940, Ap 3,23:5
Schick, Frederick Mrs, 1951, My 17,31:5
Schick, Gustav G Mrs, 1950, D 20,31:4
Schick, Herman J Mrs, 1957, Jl 2,27:2
Schick, Jacob Lt-Col (por), 1937, Jl 4,II,7:1
Schick, John, 1943, My 23,42:6
Schick, John M Rev, 1913, Jl 23,7:6
Schick, Joseph, 1938, Mr 18,19:4
Schick, Michael J, 1947, My 28,25:3
Schick, Phil, 1937, F 4,21:3
Schick, William, 1943, Ap 23,17:2
Schick, William A Jr, 1937, Ap 8,23:3
Schick, William Mrs, 1943, Ap 5,19:4
Schick Gutierrez, Rene President (funl, Ag 6,8:6), 1966, Ag 4,13:1
Schickerling, Alfred T, 1941, F 12,21:2
Schickle, Julia L, 1943, O 30,15:1
Schicks, George C, 1961, Jl 18,29:2
Schidrowitz, Philip, 1960, My 19,37:5
Schiebel, Henry J, 1938, Mr 19,15:2
Schiebelhuth, Fred C, 1961, O 10,43:2
Schiebler, Joseph P D Mrs, 1950, Ja 31,24:2
Schied, Charles F J, 1953, My 22,27:3
Schied, Otto, 1949, My 31,25:7
Schief, G Adolph, 1958, My 18,87:1
Schieferstein, Frederick Sr, 1951, Mr 28,29:3
Schieferstein, Henry, 1945, D 5,25:3
Schieffelin, Bradhurst, 1909, Mr 11,9:5
Schieffelin, Cooper Mrs (funl, Jl 18,68:8), 1965, Jl 16,1:5
Schieffelin, Edgar, 1903, Mr 22,7:5
Schieffelin, Edgar Mrs, 1914, My 13,11:5
Schieffelin, Eugene, 1906, Ag 16,7:4
Schieffelin, Frederick A, 1946, F 28,23:4
Schieffelin, George R D, 1950, Je 21,27:2
Schieffelin, George R Mrs, 1915, Mr 29,9:4
Schieffelin, Julia C Mrs, 1939, Ap 14,23:4
Schieffelin, P, 1883, Je 14,4:7
Schieffelin, S Dorthy, 1945, Ag 10,15:3
Schieffelin, William Henry Mrs, 1916, Ja 14,9:4
Schieffelin, William J, 1955, My 1,88:1
Schieffelin, William J Mrs (por), 1948, Ag 19,21:1
Schiefflin, J L, 1880, S 12,2:4
Schiel, Boer Col, 1903, Ag 9,7:6
Schiel, Edward G, 1937, Jl 20,23:4
Schiel, Father, 1940, O 10,25:2
Schiel, Frank A Mrs, 1941, O 28,23:2
Schielinger, Adolph C, 1939, Mr 10,23:2
Schier, Fred D, 1940, Ja 11,23:2
Schier, Helwig, 1952, Jl 15,21:4
Schierbaum, A E, 1950, Ap 22,19:5
Schierbrand, Wolf von, 1920, D 3,15:4
Schierege, ERnest, 1951, My 17,31:4
Schieren, Charles A, 1915, Mr 11,11:5
Schieren, Charles A Mrs (funl, Mr 13,13:6), 1915, Mr 12,11:6
Schieren, G Arthur, 1944, D 8,21:2
Schieren, George A Jr, 1951, N 3,17:3
Schieren, George A Mrs, 1950, F 5,84:6
Schieren, Harrie V, 1954, Mr 1,25:4
Schierenbeck, Arthur O, 1953, S 27,84:5
Schierenbeck, John H, 1947, Je 12,25:4
Schierenberg, August C, 1947, D 3,30:3
Schierholz, Emil C, 1948, Jl 31,15:1
Schiettinger, Katherine Mrs, 1944, Ja 25,19:5
Schiff, A G Mrs, 1932, Jl 8,17:1
Schiff, Abraham, 1945, F 22,28:2
Schiff, Adolph Mrs, 1947, Ag 20,21:4
Schiff, Arthur J, 1958, Mr 5,31:4
Schiff, Charles Mrs, 1922, Ja 28,13:4
Schiff, Efraim, 1958, Ag 7,25:4
Schiff, Frank, 1957, Ja 16,31:3
Schiff, Fritz, 1940, Jl 31,17:4
Schiff, Harry, 1939, O 21,15:4
Schiff, Herbert, 1924, Jl 16,11:5; 1962, Ag 11,17:4
Schiff, Herman S, 1954, S 4,11:7
Schiff, Hyman, 1950, Mr 15,29:5
Schiff, J H Mrs, 1933, F 26,20:5
Schiff, Jacob H, 1911, Je 12,11:4
Schiff, Jacob R (will, Ja 19,25:5), 1949, Ja 11,27:1
Schiff, Josef, 1946, Ap 27,17:1
Schiff, Julian G, 1952, O 5,89:1
Schiff, Leo, 1953, Jl 3,19:5
Schiff, Louis, 1958, N 8,21:2
Schiff, Louis N, 1949, D 19,27:2
Schiff, M L, 1931, Je 5,1:2
Schiff, Morris, 1949, Je 17,23:2

Schiff, Morton, 1952, Je 7,19:5
Schiff, Nathan S, 1959, Jl 29,29:3
Schiff, Otto M, 1952, N 18,31:4
Schiff, Paul H, 1944, Mr 18,13:2
Schiff, Philip, 1925, Ap 8,21:5; 1958, F 15,17:2
Schiff, Rose, 1951, My 9,33:1
Schiff, Samuel, 1950, S 30,17:4
Schiff, Simon, 1949, Ja 2,60:6
Schiff, Solomon E, 1959, Ag 6,27:4
Schiff, Terry, 1941, O 8,23:5
Schiff, Victor, 1959, D 17,37:3
Schiff, William, 1964, N 20,37:4
Schiff, William G, 1962, My 10,37:2
Schiff, William Mrs, 1943, Ag 28,11:4
Schiffel, Carolyn, 1943, Mr 11,21:4
Schiffer, Alfred, 1908, Mr 1,9:4
Schiffer, Don, 1964, My 19,37:2
Schiffer, Eugen, 1954, S 6,15:2
Schiffer, Henry M, 1955, F 20,88:7
Schiffer, Herbert M, 1952, F 2,13:6
Schiffer, Leslie L, 1967, My 17,47:4
Schiffer, Myron B, 1948, Ja 24,15:2
Schiffer, Walter A, 1962, Ap 10,43:1
Schifferdecker, Charles H, 1939, Ap 11,24:2
Schifferdecker, George, 1948, Jl 3,15:2
Schifferil, F X, 1925, S 9,25:5
Schifferli, Paul P, 1954, F 19,34:2
Schiffl, Charles, 1963, O 13,86:8
Schiffler, Charles, 1943, Jl 24,13:5
Schiffman, David Mrs, 1952, O 16,29:4
Schiffman, Isadore, 1937, F 11,23:6
Schiffman, Julius C, 1954, Jl 10,13:5
Schiffman, Max, 1952, Je 8,87:2
Schiffman, Philip, 1966, S 25,84:4
Schiffman, Samuel, 1939, D 21,23:2
Schiffres, Stanley S, 1958, Ag 31,57:2
Schiffrin, Max, 1943, O 11,19:4
Schifran, Abraham, 1940, Ja 15,17:3
Schifreen, Clement S, 1967, Je 4,87:1
Schifrin, Isidor Mrs, 1955, Ja 24,23:2
Schifrin, Solomon Mrs, 1946, D 5,31:5
Schifrin, Solomon S, 1948, Je 16,29:2
Schifter, B, 1946, Ag 27,29:3
Schildecker, Charles B, 1945, N 13,21:2
Schilder, Edgar F, 1963, Ag 27,31:4
Schildge, W John Dr, 1913, Jl 3,9:4
Schildhauer, Edward, 1953, My 25,25:1
Schildknecht, Charles, 1953, S 24,33:3
Schildknecht, Frederick L, 1941, D 3,25:2
Schildkraut, Joseph, 1964, Ja 22,37:1
Schildkraut, R, 1930, Jl 16,23:3
Schildkraut, Sadie Mrs, 1937, Je 5,17:6
Schildkraut, Sol, 1959, S 25,29:2
Schildman, Robert R M, 1952, Jl 25,17:2
Schildwachter, Frederick H, 1954, Ja 20,27:5
Schile, Romeo H, 1939, My 2,23:5
Schilero, Vito, 1952, Mr 6,31:2
Schilke, Walter, 1942, Je 13,15:2
Schill, Edward, 1963, Ag 11,84:6
Schill, Joseph J, 1948, My 9,68:7
Schill, Mainard C, 1943, My 13,21:5
Schill, Maxwell, 1957, My 5,88:2
Schill, Nicholas von, 1943, Jl 11,35:1
Schill, Otto K, 1959, D 29,25:1
Schill, Walter J, 1945, Mr 8,23:3
Schill, William N, 1938, Ja 13,21:6
Schille, William H, 1960, N 15,39:2
Schiller, A Noah, 1942, D 19,20:3
Schiller, Benjamin, 1953, Ag 18,23:4
Schiller, Bianca, 1944, N 6,19:4
Schiller, Edward A, 1945, N 13,21:3
Schiller, Edward L, 1954, D 8,35:2
Schiller, Edwin, 1948, N 21,88:4
Schiller, Ferdinand C S Dr, 1937, Ag 8,II,6:5
Schiller, Frank K, 1950, F 7,27:2
Schiller, Frederick A Mrs, 1958, Ag 30,15:6
Schiller, George A, 1937, Ap 15,23:4; 1961, Ap 1,17:3
Schiller, Gustave Mrs, 1952, F 1,21:2
Schiller, Jay A, 1956, O 27,21:4
Schiller, John F, 1954, Je 18,23:4
Schiller, John Mrs, 1955, Ap 3,86:8
Schiller, Joseph F, 1951, Ja 9,29:1
Schiller, Louis J, 1942, Ja 21,18:2
Schiller, Max, 1952, Jl 31,23:5
Schiller, Oscar, 1948, Mr 26,21:4
Schiller, Walter, 1960, My 5,35:5
Schiller (Last Descendant), 1877, My 11,1:6
Schillerstrom, Curtis G, 1959, Ap 9,31:4
Schilling, Arthur O, 1958, Je 24,31:2
Schilling, August E, 1957, Je 17,23:3
Schilling, Carolina Mrs, 1938, Jl 24,29:4
Schilling, Clergue G, 1954, Ja 23,13:6
Schilling, David C (funl, Ag 24,19:3), 1956, Ag 15,8:4
Schilling, Elias H, 1874, Ag 16,1:4
Schilling, Francis A, 1964, S 29,43:5
Schilling, Frederick E, 1959, D 4,32:1
Schilling, Frederick K, 1952, Mr 12,27:4
Schilling, George E, 1938, Ja 28,21:1
Schilling, Gustav J, 1961, My 6,31:6
Schilling, Jacob H, 1948, F 6,23:4
Schilling, Joseph, 1904, F 24,5:2
Schilling, Joseph M, 1954, Ag 9,17:4
Schilling, Lawrence R, 1939, Jl 30,29:4
Schilling, Louis, 1943, O 16,13:5
Schilling, Louis F (por), 1948, F 7,15:1
Schilling, Mary S K, 1940, Mr 13,23:4
Schilling, Mildred, 1943, D 25,13:3
Schilling, Peter Mrs, 1943, D 23,19:4
Schilling, Philip V, 1960, Mr 1,33:2
Schilling, William, 1945, Ag 12,39:2
Schilling, William F, 1962, O 3,41:3
Schilling, William H Mrs, 1949, Ja 2,60:5
Schillinger, Arnold A, 1965, Jl 17,25:5
Schillinger, Benjamin, 1944, My 19,19:4
Schillinger, George J, 1951, My 26,17:6
Schillinger, Joseph (por), 1943, Mr 24,23:3
Schillinger, Raphael, 1967, O 29,84:4
Schillings, C G Prof, 1921, F 1,11:2
Schillings, Charles E, 1940, Ja 22,15:6
Schillings, Elbert I, 1954, Ja 9,15:5
Schillings, M von, 1933, Jl 25,19:1
Schilplin, Fred Mrs, 1949, Ag 30,27:3
Schilplin, Frederick C, 1949, Ap 29,25:1
Schilthuis, Pieter W, 1947, Jl 11,15:2
Schimberg, Albert P, 1949, N 23,29:5
Schimerka, Francis S, 1939, D 20,25:1
Schimko, Charles, 1940, Ap 12,23:2
Schimmel, Augustus H, 1949, Jl 12,27:3
Schimmel, Charles F, 1942, Ja 2,23:4
Schimmel, Walter E, 1947, Jl 23,23:6
Schimmel, Willem C, 1944, Jl 7,15:3
Schimmelpfennig, Robert D, 1938, Ag 11,17:5
Schimoler, August A, 1946, F 6,23:2
Schimper, G P, 1880, Mr 30,2:3
Schimpf, Wallace B, 1960, Ap 8,31:2
Schimpf, William, 1944, Ap 13,19:5; 1948, Ag 11,21:2
Schimpfle, Frank Mrs, 1961, Jl 15,19:5
Schimps, Lizzetta Mrs, 1937, F 8,3:7
Schinasi, S Leon, 1962, Je 2,19:3
Schinbein, Austin B, 1950, N 3,27:2
Schinckel, Maximilian H von, 1938, N 12,15:2
Schinco, Frank, 1951, Jl 17,27:1
Schindel, Aaron J, 1950, Mr 26,23:3
Schindel, Abraham, 1939, D 22,19:5
Schindel, George Mrs, 1948, Mr 11,27:4
Schindel, John R, 1941, O 30,23:2
Schindel, Lester, 1940, F 9,19:4
Schindel, S J B Col, 1921, Mr 12,11:6
Schindl, Frank, 1965, Mr 16,39:4
Schindler, Bill, 1952, S 21,V,3:7
Schindler, Clarence M, 1954, D 8,35:1
Schindler, Ewald Mrs, 1962, Jl 26,27:3
Schindler, Hans J, 1952, Ap 22,29:4
Schindler, Irvin, 1952, S 27,17:1
Schindler, John A, 1957, N 17,85:1
Schindler, Joseph W Sr, 1952, F 27,27:1
Schindler, Kurt Mrs, 1919, Ja 29,13:5
Schindler, Leon A Mrs, 1950, Ag 24,27:4
Schindler, Lizzie Mrs, 1904, F 15,14:2
Schindler, Phil Mrs, 1956, N 28,35:1
Schindler, Philip A, 1945, F 1,23:3
Schindler, Raymond C, 1959, Jl 2,26:1
Schindler, Rudolf Dr, 1968, S 9,47:4
Schindler, Solomon Rabbi, 1915, My 6,13:6
Schindler, Walter S, 1954, S 15,33:5
Schine, James T, 1955, Ap 25,23:5
Schine, Louis W, 1956, N 7,31:3
Schingel, Herman E, 1947, My 10,13:5
Schinnen, Conrad Mrs, 1949, Mr 31,25:6
Schinner, Augustine F Bp, 1937, F 8,17:6
Schinner, Carl A, 1949, N 20,93:1
Schinz, Albert, 1943, D 20,23:4
Schinz, Georgette, 1940, S 27,23:1
Schiochetti, Luigi, 1961, My 11,37:2
Schiott, Christian, 1960, D 30,20:1
Schiott, Johannes, 1944, F 26,13:2
Schiott, Mary Esther Mrs, 1911, Mr 27,11:5
Schipa, Tito (mem ser set, D 19,84:6), 1965, D 18, 29:1
Schipani, Mary Mrs, 1951, Ja 23,27:3
Schipper, Herman C Mrs, 1950, Ap 26,29:4
Schippers, Joseph, 1949, F 17,23:2
Schirano, Louis V, 1964, N 14,29:4
Schireman, Henry, 1912, Je 3,9:4
Schirm, Ralph F, 1962, Ja 2,30:3
Schirmer, Charles L, 1947, My 9,21:2
Schirmer, Edward, 1957, Ja 17,29:1
Schirmer, Frank A, 1942, N 18,25:5
Schirmer, Frank G, 1925, D 16,25:4
Schirmer, Gustave, 1965, My 30,51:1
Schirmer, Harry, 1966, Ag 18,35:2
Schirmer, L A, 1884, Mr 2,2:6
Schirmer, Mary A Mrs, 1938, Mr 4,23:5
Schirmer, Max, 1941, Ag 1,15:3
Schirmer, Paul J, 1959, Je 5,27:2
Schirmer, Rens E, 1960, Ja 5,31:4
Schirmer, Robert, 1947, S 24,23:3
Schirmer, W Dr, 1878, Jl 9,5:4
Schirmer, Walter F, 1941, Jl 11,15:1
Schiro, Louis, 1951, My 31,27:6
Schirp, Francis M, 1941, Ap 21,19:6
Schirrmann, Richard, 1961, D 16,25:5
Schisane, Charles F, 1938, Ap 20,23:3
Schissler, Paul, 1968, Ap 18,47:5
Schive, Henry T, 1949, D 13,31:4
Schive, Henry T Jr, 1946, D 1,76:3
Schiverea, Ferdinand Rev, 1937, Ag 30,21:5
Schiverin, Isaac Mrs, 1921, D 30,15:6
Schjerven, Oscar N, 1947, D 28,40:3
Schlabach, Asa L, 1950, Ap 21,23:2
Schlabach, Ross P, 1951, Ag 27,19:2
Schlacht, Edes Mrs, 1940, Mr 5,24:3
Schlacht, Harry H, 1961, My 4,37:3
Schlacks, Charles H, 1941, Mr 4,23:1
Schlacter, Robert Mrs, 1952, Ag 19,23:1
Schladermundt, Herman T, 1937, Ja 27,21:6
Schladermundt, Herman T Mrs, 1963, Je 6,35:2
Schlaeger, Victor L, 1949, Ap 2,15:2
Schlaet, Arnold S, 1946, N 17,68:5
Schlafer, Mildred, 1951, D 13,34:3
Schlag, William C, 1945, N 20,21:5
Schlagenhauf, Milton J, 1961, Ap 30,86:7
Schlager, Charles, 1871, D 22,1:4
Schlager, Frank L, 1943, N 27,13:2
Schlager, Robert R Jr, 1952, Je 15,84:2
Schlager, Simon S (por), 1943, F 23,21:1
Schlageter, George, 1951, Jl 17,27:1
Schlagintweit, H, 1882, Ja 20,5:6
Schlaich, Henry C, 1952, D 7,88:4
Schlaifer, Abraham, 1948, Ag 12,21:5
Schlaifer, Israel, 1953, N 21,13:2
Schlaifer, Ziril Mrs, 1948, O 20,29:3
Schlake, William, 1940, My 7,25:5
Schlakman, Julius A, 1968, F 4,81:1
Schlamm, Nathaniel G, 1950, Ja 4,35:1
Schlang, Harry, 1919, My 8,17:3
Schlange-Schoeningen, Hans, 1960, Jl 25,23:4
Schlank, Fares J, 1953, F 19,23:2
Schlapak, Stephen A Mrs, 1948, Ja 18,60:3
Schlapak, Stephen J, 1950, Ja 24,31:2
Schlapp, M G, 1928, Mr 5,27:1
Schlarman, Joseph H, 1951, N 11,90:3
Schlater, John R P (por), 1949, Ag 27,13:4
Schlater, Myron F, 1950, Ja 1,42:5
Schlatter, Charles H, 1909, O 22,7:4
Schlatter, Edward H, 1951, O 28,84:5
Schlatter, Francis Mrs, 1922, O 18,19:4
Schlauch, William S, 1953, Ja 31,15:3
Schlech, Walter F, 1967, O 15,85:4
Schlech, Walter F Mrs, 1964, Ja 13,35:4
Schlecht, Carl F, 1952, Ja 13,89:2
Schleck, Alols J, 1959, Ja 24,19:4
Schleck, Joseph E, 1947, O 5,71:3
Schleck, Richard C Sr, 1958, My 24,21:3
Schlecter, John F, 1957, S 27,19:3
Schlee, A Frederick, 1941, S 21,42:2
Schlee, Edward F Mrs, 1954, F 28,93:2
Schlee, George (funl, O 8,43:2), 1964, O 5,42:2
Schleede, Charles, 1946, Ag 6,25:5
Schleede, Karl, 1950, Je 27,29:3
Schleede, Martin J, 1948, Ag 25,25:3
Schleer, Gordon U, 1960, O 5,41:3
Schlefer, Albert, 1966, Mr 30,45:1
Schlegel, Carl, 1945, Ap 6,15:4
Schlegel, Carl Mrs, 1944, F 27,38:2
Schlegel, Christian C, 1949, F 12,27:2
Schlegel, Franklin K, 1946, O 8,23:1
Schlegel, Frederick C, 1946, Ja 1,27:4
Schlegel, George C, 1945, D 7,22:2; 1954, Ap 1,31
Schlegel, H F, 1941, Ap 30,19:1
Schlegel, James R Mrs, 1951, N 5,31:4
Schlegel, John W, 1955, Ja 14,21:2
Schlegel, Julius, 1958, Ag 9,13:5
Schlegel, Katherine Mrs, 1913, Ap 3,9:4
Schleger, Frederic S, 1967, S 23,31:4
Schleger, Hans E, 1957, Ja 9,31:3
Schlegman, Mrs, 1941, S 12,22:3
Schlegman, Saul, 1954, Ap 11,86:6
Schleich, Daniel, 1943, My 30,26:7
Schleich, Michel, 1945, Ap 28,15:6
Schleicher, Congressman, 1879, Ja 11,1:2
Schleicher, Henry M, 1966, Je 2,43:2
Schleicher, John C, 1940, Jl 30,19:5
Schleichkorn, Henry, 1954, D 20,29:3
Schleif, William, 1951, Ja 30,25:3
Schleifer, Arnold, 1950, S 24,104:3
Schleifer, Jacob Mrs, 1954, Ja 26,27:4
Schleifer, Louis, 1956, Ja 18,31:4
Schleifstein, Joseph, 1962, Mr 11,86:2
Schleigh, William B, 1959, Ag 30,83:2
Schlein, David, 1954, S 20,23:1
Schlein, Julius, 1953, My 9,19:3
Schlein, Louis Mrs, 1949, Ap 26,25:2
Schlein, William, 1960, S 25,88:7
Schleisner, Solomon, 1949, Je 30,23:4
Schleisner, William H, 1962, N 8,39:1
Schleissner, Paul, 1949, F 13,76:6
Schleiter, Howard G, 1947, F 6,23:2
Schlemmer, Aug W Mrs, 1940, O 25,21:5
Schlemmer, August W, 1947, D 2,29:2
Schlemmer, Emil Mrs, 1959, Ja 15,33:2
Schlemmer, William F Mrs (will, D 7,29:2), 195
N 28,35:4
Schlemmer, William H, 1945, Ag 19,40:3
Schlenker, Charles F, 1967, My 13,33:2
Schlenker, Eda B, 1945, Jl 20,19:5
Schlenker, George, 1941, S 19,23:2
Schlenker, Henry W, 1958, Je 7,19:3
Schlenker, Henry W Mrs (will, O 27,37:6), 1950
O 21,17:4

Schlenker, John, 1946, Je 23,40:4
Schlenker, John F Sr Mrs, 1949, N 10,31:1
Schlenker, John Mrs, 1946, Jl 4,19:4
Schlepegrell, Hermann, 1876, Ap 12,8:6
Schlesier, Gustave P, 1952, Jl 6,49:1
Schlesinger, Arthur, 1953, My 10,89:1
Schlesinger, Arthur M Sr (mem ser set, N 1,41:4), 1965, O 31,86:2
Schlesinger, B, 1932, Je 7,19:1
Schlesinger, Benjamin Mrs, 1959, My 8,27:2
Schlesinger, Bert L (B Lewis), 1960, Ap 27,37:5
Schlesinger, David Mrs, 1954, Je 16,31:4
Schlesinger, E, 1929, F 21,27:3
Schlesinger, Edgar L, 1966, O 21,41:4
Schlesinger, Edwin J, 1957, Jl 9,27:1
Schlesinger, Falk Dr, 1968, Ag 29,35:6
Schlesinger, Ferdinand, 1921, Ja 5,13:6
Schlesinger, Ferdinand G Mrs, 1964, Ap 16,37:4
Schlesinger, Frank (por), 1943, Jl 12,15:3
Schlesinger, Frank, 1943, N 11,30:3
Schlesinger, Frederick S, 1917, Mr 11,21:3
Schlesinger, George F, 1939, D 2,17:5
Schlesinger, Gus S, 1948, Ja 4,52:4
Schlesinger, Harold L, 1942, N 26,27:5
Schlesinger, Harold L Mrs, 1939, Mr 7,21:3
Schlesinger, Herman I Mrs, 1957, D 23,23:1
Schlesinger, Hermann I, 1960, O 4,43:4
Schlesinger, Humboldt, 1940, Ap 25,23:3
Schlesinger, I H, 1953, Je 23,29:2
Schlesinger, I H Mrs, 1954, S 11,13:2
Schlesinger, Isadore W (por), 1949, Mr 12,17:4
Schlesinger, Jacob, 1955, N 12,19:2
Schlesinger, Joseph, 1949, N 28,27:6
Schlesinger, Julius, 1960, D 12,29:5
Schlesinger, Leo, 1924, F 28,19:5
Schlesinger, Leon, 1949, D 26,29:3
Schlesinger, Leonard S (por), 1948, Mr 30,23:5
Schlesinger, Louis (por), 1942, S 16,23:3
Schlesinger, Louis Mrs, 1937, My 20,21:3
Schlesinger, Ludwig, 1959, Ag 15,17:5
Schlesinger, Maurice F, 1961, F 20,27:1
Schlesinger, Max, 1943, S 20,21:2
Schlesinger, Max A, 1953, F 26,25:3
Schlesinger, Max Mrs, 1954, Ap 22,29:2
Schlesinger, Max Rev, 1919, D 29,9:3
Schlesinger, Monroe, 1951, D 29,11:6
Schlesinger, Morris S, 1944, My 24,19:6
Schlesinger, Robert, 1966, Ja 10,25:3
Schlesinger, Samuel B, 1965, Ag 28,21:3
Schlesinger, Sol Hunt, 1913, Ja 18,13:6
Schlesinger, William A Mrs, 1966, O 12,43:4
Schless, Jacob T, 1955, N 24,29:2
Schless, Maurice J, 1961, D 5,43:3
Schleswig-Holstein, Albrecht Prince of (Prince of Albrecht), 1948, Ap 24,15:6
Schleswig-Holstein, Princess Feodora of, 1910, Je 22, 9:5
Schleth, Matilda Mrs, 1942, My 28,17:5
Schlette, Harry L, 1946, Ja 26,13:5
Schleusing, Carl A, 1953, Mr 13,25:4
Schleusner, Richard R, 1942, Mr 11,19:1
Schleussner, Robert C, 1968, Ja 27,29:2
Schlevogt, Andrew, 1952, Ap 5,15:3
Schley, B H, 1882, Je 8,5:4
Schley, B Jr, 1926, N 15,21:3
Schley, Buchanan Col, 1916, O 13,11:4
Schley, Charles E, 1949, S 10,17:3
Schley, Evander B, 1952, D 3,33:2
Schley, Evander B Mrs, 1950, Ag 16,29:1
Schley, Evander H, 1907, Mr 29,9:6
Schley, Fayette E Dr, 1908, F 9,11:5
Schley, George, 1916, Ja 24,11:3
Schley, Grant B, 1917, N 23,11:5
Schley, Gustave A, 1947, Ap 9,25:2
Schley, Henry S, 1953, N 1,86:5
Schley, Henry S Mrs, 1954, Ag 5,23:6
Schley, J Montfort Dr, 1924, O 23,21:4
Schley, James Montfort Jr, 1922, Ap 14,17:6
Schley, Julian L, 1965, Mr 31,40:1
Schley, Kenneth B, 1944, Je 13,19:3
Schley, Kenneth B Mrs, 1965, Ag 12,27:2
Schley, R Montford, 1948, My 6,25:4
Schley, Reeve, 1960, Je 27,25:4
Schley, Sturges M, 1950, S 11,23:4
Schley, Thomas F Maj, 1917, My 17,13:5
Schley, William, 1872, Mr 2,1:6
Schley, Winfield Scott Adm, 1920, N 18,15:4
Schley, Winfield Scott Rear-Adm (por),(funl, O 6,-13:5), 1911, O 3,13:1
Schleyen, Erwin, 1961, My 11,37:4
Schleyer, Father, 1888, O 10,1:3
Schleyer, Johann Martin, 1912, Ag 21,9:6
Schlich, C Edward, 1941, N 19,23:3
Schlich, Frederick J, 1968, Ag 30,33:2
Schlich, Theodore R, 1963, S 19,27:4
Schlicht, Louisa Mrs, 1939, F 27,15:2
Schlichter, Charles F, 1951, F 15,31:4
Schlichter, Charles H (por), 1948, Ap 30,23:5
Schlichter, Charles H Mrs, 1948, O 23,15:6
Schlichter, Charles S, 1946, O 5,17:4
Schlichter, Fred C, 1943, Ja 31,46:2
Schlichter, Henry W, 1944, Ja 16,41:6
Schlichter, Rudolf, 1955, My 6,23:2
Schlichter, William R, 1957, O 19,21:6
Schlichting, Emil, 1941, D 29,15:2
Schlichtmann, Walter H, 1959, Ja 4,87:2
Schlick, Henry Col, 1905, Ap 13,11:5
Schlick, Louis F, 1960, My 9,29:4
Schlick, Otto, 1913, Ap 11,9:6
Schlick, Roy N, 1948, Ja 27,26:2
Schlicker, Charles J, 1939, Ap 10,14:1
Schlieckert, Charles W, 1949, My 8,76:5
Schlieder, Frederick W, 1953, Ja 15,27:1
Schlieder, Howard A, 1953, N 17,31:3
Schliemann, H Dr, 1890, D 27,3:6
Schliemann, Hosias Dr, 1911, Mr 11,13:5
Schliemann, John, 1911, N 15,11:5
Schliep, Louis C, 1937, Ap 11,II,9:2
Schliep, Louis C Mrs, 1951, N 18,91:3
Schlieper, Gustav, 1937, Ag 25,21:4
Schliesman, John J, 1960, D 2,29:2
Schlim, Joseph H, 1945, Jl 18,27:3
Schlimme, Lucille, 1944, Ja 19,19:4
Schlimmer, Jacob, 1943, Ag 21,11:4
Schlimmer, Jacob Mrs, 1947, Mr 16,60:2
Schling, Frederick Mrs, 1948, Ja 17,17:1
Schling, Max (por), 1943, F 13,11:1
Schling, Max Mrs, 1955, N 29,29:4
Schlingplesser, Aug, 1940, My 23,24:2
Schlining, George A, 1966, Ap 18,29:3
Schlintz, John, 1960, Ap 1,33:4
Schlitter, Marquis H, 1945, D 15,17:5
Schlittler, Henry, 1948, D 4,13:2
Schlitz, Joseph A, 1953, F 21,13:1
Schlitzer, Victor J, 1948, Ja 6,23:3
Schlivek, Kaufman, 1955, Ap 1,28:2
Schlobohm, Carl J, 1952, Mr 29,15:3
Schlobohm, Frederick H, 1937, Mr 31,11:2
Schlobohm, Friedericke L Mrs, 1940, O 1,23:1
Schlobohm, Harriet, 1952, N 18,32:4
Schlobohm, John R, 1919, D 9,17:3
Schlobohm, William A, 1949, D 31,15:6
Schlochauer, Ernst J, 1961, Mr 3,27:4
Schlock, John, 1953, Ap 28,27:5
Schlockow, Oswald, 1954, Jl 7,31:5
Schloeman, Edward, 1911, S 16,7:5
Schloen, John, 1905, Je 6,4:3
Schloerb, Rolland W, 1958, Mr 16,87:1
Schloessinger, Max, 1944, My 11,19:6
Schloh, Henry L, 1957, Ja 23,29:4
Schlomann, Alfred F, 1952, Mr 30,94:2
Schlomer, William B, 1942, My 20,19:1
Schloo, Henry, 1938, S 25,39:2
Schlorff, Paul, 1942, N 20,24:4
Schlos, Samuel, 1914, Ag 3,11:4
Schlosberg, Harold, 1964, Ag 6,29:5
Schlosberg, Samuel, 1940, F 27,21:3
Schloss, Benjamin, 1940, Ap 14,45:1
Schloss, Emil, 1952, Ap 6,89:2
Schloss, Herbert W, 1968, Ja 18,40:1
Schloss, Jacob, 1938, N 24,27:3
Schloss, Jennie Mrs, 1942, O 27,25:3
Schloss, Jerome E Mrs, 1958, D 1,29:4
Schloss, Moritz, 1952, S 13,17:3
Schloss, Myron J, 1966, S 2,31:4
Schloss, Norman P S, 1956, F 8,33:1
Schloss, Oscar M, 1952, O 14,31:1
Schloss, Samuel W, 1905, Ja 7,7:6
Schloss, Tony Mrs, 1937, Ag 1,II,7:3
Schloss, Walter J, 1923, Je 5,21:4
Schloss, William L, 1944, Je 13,19:2
Schlossberg, Ben, 1968, N 12,47:3
Schlossberg, Irving B, 1968, F 3,29:4
Schlossberg, William, 1961, Je 30,25:3
Schlosser, Alex L, 1943, F 11,19:2
Schlosser, Frank J, 1943, N 20,13:5
Schlosser, Fred, 1956, My 9,33:1
Schlosser, Jack, 1966, Mr 10,33:2
Schlosser, Jacob, 1945, My 17,19:4
Schlosser, Jacques B, 1960, Ap 20,39:3
Schlosser, John C, 1959, S 9,41:2
Schlosser, Mortimer M, 1961, D 23,23:3
Schlosser, William A, 1958, N 2,88:4
Schlosshauer, Eleanor R Mrs, 1954, Ag 6,17:4
Schlossmacher, Stephan J, 1959, Mr 7,21:4
Schlossman, Arthur, 1950, Je 15,31:6
Schlossman, Bernard, 1946, Ja 29,25:1
Schlotheim, Ethel von Baroness, 1948, Jl 11,53:1
Schlotman, Joseph B, 1951, N 26,25:5
Schlotter, John M, 1952, Mr 27,29:1
Schlotter, Robert, 1957, Jl 13,17:2
Schlotter, Robert Mrs, 1963, Jl 21,64:8
Schlotterer, George H Sr, 1948, My 19,27:1
Schlotterer, Ray C, 1966, D 30,25:4
Schlottman, R H, 1955, Ap 12,29:4
Schlottman, William H, 1944, F 26,13:2
Schlottmann, Edward L, 1947, Mr 20,27:2
Schlubach, Herbert, 1940, Ap 24,23:2
Schlubach, Herbert B, 1965, D 1,47:2
Schluderberg, Henry, 1947, Ap 29,27:1
Schluderberg, William F, 1957, Mr 4,27:4
Schlueter, Edward H, 1957, Ap 3,31:4
Schlueter, Henry C Rev, 1937, N 3,23:4
Schlueter, Herman, 1919, Ja 31,11:5
Schlueter, Robert E, 1955, F 13,86:5
Schlueter, Sophia Mrs, 1948, D 26,52:5
Schlumberger, Dewitt Mrs, 1924, O 26,7:2
Schlumberger, Jean, 1968, O 27,82:6
Schlumbohm, Peter, 1962, N 7,39:2
Schlumper, Samuel Jr, 1913, Ag 14,9:3
Schlumpf, Joseph, 1941, Jl 18,19:5
Schlund, Fidel, 1882, Ap 3,5:2
Schlung, Benjamin B, 1942, N 27,23:2
Schlusing, Christian W, 1968, Mr 27,47:4
Schlusnus, Heinrich, 1952, Je 20,23:4
Schluter, Fred H Mrs, 1963, O 19,25:2
Schluter, Wilhelm H F, 1967, F 3,31:1
Schlutz, Frederic, 1944, Mr 9,17:4
Schlyen, Samuel M Mrs, 1965, F 6,25:1
Schmacher, Helene, 1944, Ja 18,19:3
Schmahl, Julius A, 1955, Ap 11,23:4
Schmahl, Lydia von, 1915, Ja 9,11:4
Schmalacker, Joseph M Mrs, 1960, F 6,19:1
Schmalenbach, Herman, 1950, N 6,27:3
Schmalenberger, Adam, 1925, Mr 31,19:6
Schmalheiser, Samuel, 1939, Ag 24,19:1
Schmalholz, Edward B, 1953, Ja 17,15:7
Schmaling, George P, 1961, Ja 16,27:5
Schmall, Katherine E, 1956, O 31,33:4
Schmalstich, Henry D, 1940, Ja 25,21:5
Schmalz, Edward H, 1940, D 14,17:4
Schmalz, Gerard, 1945, Ja 11,23:1
Schmalz, Julia M Mrs, 1938, Ag 23,17:2
Schmalz, William, 1947, Ag 22,15:2
Schmalz, William Mrs, 1952, F 5,29:1
Schmalzer, Peter 3d, 1963, O 11,37:1
Schmand, J Phil, 1942, Jl 9,21:2
Schmandt, L Frank, 1951, O 8,21:2
Schmauch, Walter W, 1957, My 31,19:4
Schmauk, Theodore Emanuel Dr, 1920, Mr 24,9:5
Schmaus, Harold E, 1944, Mr 19,41:1
Schmavonian, A B, 1940, Ag 6,22:6
Schmeck, Herbert P, 1956, O 24,37:4
Schmeckenbecher, Joseph, 1958, Ap 2,31:4
Schmedeman, Albert G (por), 1946, N 27,25:1
Schmedeman, Albert G Mrs, 1948, N 14,76:8
Schmedlin, Carl E Mrs, 1948, O 13,25:4
Schmeelk, Garrett E, 1941, O 18,19:3
Schmehl, Walter J, 1942, Ap 21,23:1
Schmeidel, Frederick, 1948, Mr 4,25:1
Schmeidler, Daniel, 1959, Ap 8,37:4
Schmeiser, Charles, 1917, Jl 20,9:6
Schmeiser, Frederick, 1917, Jl 20,9:6
Schmeisser, William C, 1941, Jl 2,21:2
Schmelke, William D, 1940, Ap 25,23:2
Schmella, J M, 1960, Jl 19,29:1
Schmelz, Henry L Mrs, 1946, Mr 11,25:2
Schmelzel, Annie L Mrs, 1940, Ja 24,44:1
Schmelzel, George, 1921, Jl 25,13:5
Schmelzel, James H, 1939, Ja 13,19:2
Schmelzel, John G, 1944, S 3,26:7
Schmenger, John P, 1904, Ja 14,9:5
Schmering, Albert J, 1946, Ap 6,17:6
Schmerl, Abraham, 1948, F 25,23:4
Schmerling, Abraham, 1947, D 6,15:3
Schmertz, M Mrs, 1940, N 30,32:1
Schmertz, Max, 1943, S 10,23:4
Schmerzler, Samuel, 1962, Ja 4,33:4
Schmetz, Walter, 1949, Ag 29,17:5
Schmick, William F, 1963, Mr 16,7:2
Schmid, Albert, 1920, Ja 1,15:2
Schmid, Alfred L, 1956, Ja 2,3:8
Schmid, Aug F, 1939, Ja 10,19:2
Schmid, Augusta B Mrs, 1952, Je 17,28:5
Schmid, Charles P, 1956, D 12,39:5
Schmid, Cornelius A, 1950, Ap 19,29:3
Schmid, Frank L, 1951, Jl 14,13:2
Schmid, Herman, 1949, N 9,27:1
Schmid, J O Von, 1913, N 4,9:7
Schmid, Johann C, 1951, Mr 10,13:5
Schmid, John M, 1947, Mr 30,56:1
Schmid, Joseph K, 1959, Je 3,35:4
Schmid, Julius Jr, 1960, My 7,23:1
Schmid, Julius Sr Mrs, 1956, D 31,13:1
Schmid, Max H, 1967, Jl 7,31:6
Schmid, Richard G, 1937, Je 7,19:5
Schmid, Samuel L, 1966, S 12,45:3
Schmid, William F, 1950, Ap 25,31:2
Schmid, William G, 1951, Ja 2,23:4
Schmidlapp, Carl J, 1960, My 14,23:4
Schmidlapp, Carl J Mrs, 1967, N 30,47:2
Schmidlapp, Jacob Godfrey, 1919, D 19,15:2
Schmidlin, Edward J, 1951, O 16,31:1
Schmidlin, Joseph, 1944, Ja 29,4:4
Schmidling, Charles S, 1957, D 30,23:3
Schmidling, W E Jr, 1944, Ja 28,17:3
Schmidt, A Gero, 1924, D 26,15:5
Schmidt, Adam, 1960, S 17,23:4
Schmidt, Adolf, 1948, Ag 6,17:5; 1958, F 16,86:4
Schmidt, Albert A, 1956, O 6,21:6
Schmidt, Alex, 1949, Je 21,25:4
Schmidt, Alfred J, 1943, Ja 12,23:2
Schmidt, Alfred M Mrs, 1957, N 25,31:4
Schmidt, Anna M, 1950, Ag 19,13:5
Schmidt, Anna Mrs, 1942, Jl 9,12:8
Schmidt, Arnold M (por), 1939, Je 15,23:3
Schmidt, Arthur R Mrs, 1948, Ja 23,23:3
Schmidt, Aug W Jr, 1938, Je 5,45:2

Schmidt, Augusto F, 1965, F 10,42:1
Schmidt, Bache McEvers, 1903, N 29,7:6
Schmidt, Benedict Rev, 1923, N 29,21:3
Schmidt, Benjamin F, 1954, Ja 13,31:4
Schmidt, Bernard, 1940, F 10,15:5
Schmidt, Bernard 2d, 1943, Mr 13,13:5
Schmidt, Bruno, 1956, Ag 8,25:2
Schmidt, Bruno C, 1941, My 14,21:1
Schmidt, Carl, 1904, Ja 19,9:6
Schmidt, Carl C, 1941, Ja 7,28:8
Schmidt, Carl Capt, 1921, My 1,22:3
Schmidt, Carl G, 1938, S 22,23:5
Schmidt, Carl T, 1958, O 18,21:6
Schmidt, Charles, 1958, Je 1,87:1
Schmidt, Charles E, 1946, O 19,21:5; 1949, Jl 26,27:4
Schmidt, Charles F, 1959, Ag 2,81:2
Schmidt, Charles J, 1952, S 5,27:2
Schmidt, Charles M, 1938, Ja 8,15:2; 1962, N 15,37:4
Schmidt, Charles P, 1940, Mr 5,23:4
Schmidt, Christian, 1950, Jl 6,28:3
Schmidt, Christian H, 1937, Ap 16,23:4
Schmidt, Christian M, 1962, Jl 25,33:5
Schmidt, Christian R, 1946, My 7,21:4
Schmidt, Christian W, 1948, D 11,15:4; 1967, Mr 10, 39:2
Schmidt, Conrad, 1952, Ag 29,23:1
Schmidt, Dorothea, 1948, Ag 29,60:1
Schmidt, E, 1939, Ap 13,3:3
Schmidt, Edward, 1943, Ag 18,19:3
Schmidt, Edward A, 1944, Jl 13,17:3
Schmidt, Edward C, 1942, Mr 23,15:4
Schmidt, Edward C Mrs, 1937, Ag 5,23:4
Schmidt, Edwin G, 1958, Ja 19,87:1
Schmidt, Elizabeth A Mrs, 1940, Ag 18,37:2
Schmidt, Ella S Mrs, 1948, Mr 4,25:1
Schmidt, Erich F, 1964, O 5,33:2
Schmidt, Erwin R, 1961, Jl 11,31:4
Schmidt, Erwin R Mrs, 1963, S 1,56:4
Schmidt, Eugene, 1959, Ja 1,31:5
Schmidt, Evelyn C, 1963, S 2,15:3
Schmidt, F G, 1878, N 16,8:3
Schmidt, Ferdinand, 1964, Mr 25,41:2
Schmidt, Florence M, 1953, S 10,25:1
Schmidt, Florian E, 1953, S 11,21:4
Schmidt, Frank, 1949, My 25,29:3
Schmidt, Frank A Mrs, 1950, Ag 1,15:2
Schmidt, Frank M, 1937, Ap 16,23:3
Schmidt, Frank Mrs, 1948, Je 7,19:6
Schmidt, Frank W, 1960, S 15,37:3
Schmidt, Fred, 1939, O 30,12:5
Schmidt, Fred J Jr, 1958, O 18,21:7
Schmidt, Frederic E, 1943, F 6,13:3
Schmidt, Frederick, 1951, F 20,25:3
Schmidt, Frederick C, 1952, My 16,24:3
Schmidt, Frederick G Mrs, 1965, Ap 19,29:1
Schmidt, Frederick J A, 1949, S 13,29:3
Schmidt, Frederick W, 1946, O 24,28:2; 1949, Ag 22, 21:1; 1953, S 5,15:5
Schmidt, Fritz G, 1937, Ap 13,25:5
Schmidt, G Peter, 1948, F 24,25:2
Schmidt, George, 1946, Mr 12,25:1
Schmidt, George A, 1945, O 31,23:4
Schmidt, George A (will), 1957, Jl 21,13:1
Schmidt, George A, 1961, N 29,41:2
Schmidt, George C, 1962, Ap 9,29:3
Schmidt, George E, 1957, Jl 24,25:4
Schmidt, George F, 1942, Ap 30,42:6
Schmidt, George H, 1941, Ja 12,46:1; 1947, O 10,25:4; 1959, O 10,21:6
Schmidt, George J, 1959, Ja 20,35:2
Schmidt, George Jr, 1941, O 10,23:1
Schmidt, George K, 1939, Ja 2,23:1
Schmidt, George L, 1941, Ag 20,19:1; 1947, S 19,23:5
Schmidt, George T, 1954, F 28,93:2
Schmidt, George X, 1941, O 24,24:3
Schmidt, Glenn, 1952, Jl 15,21:2
Schmidt, Guido, 1957, D 7,21:3
Schmidt, Gustav, 1949, Ja 6,23:4
Schmidt, Gustave, 1951, My 26,17:4
Schmidt, Gustave A, 1947, F 4,25:2
Schmidt, Hans, 1946, Jl 13,15:6
Schmidt, Hans Mrs, 1962, Je 4,29:2
Schmidt, Harold, 1962, S 14,31:3
Schmidt, Harold C, 1957, F 12,27:2
Schmidt, Harry, 1945, Ap 9,19:3
Schmidt, Harry F, 1950, F 1,29:3
Schmidt, Harry Gen, 1968, F 11,92:7
Schmidt, Harry J, 1955, Ja 13,27:4
Schmidt, Henry, 1939, Ag 20,32:5; 1950, O 30,27:3
Schmidt, Henry Dr, 1949, Ag 7,61:2
Schmidt, Henry F, 1949, N 4,27:4
Schmidt, Henry Jr, 1904, F 1,1:2
Schmidt, Henry Mrs, 1958, Ja 14,30:4; 1960, S 25,88:8
Schmidt, Henry Sr, 1949, Ag 1,17:5
Schmidt, Henry W, 1961, O 26,35:4
Schmidt, Herbert, 1959, Ja 11,88:4
Schmidt, Herbert W, 1966, Ap 10,79:5
Schmidt, Herman F, 1952, O 2,29:2
Schmidt, Herman L A, 1955, F 12,15:5
Schmidt, Hugh E, 1947, D 12,27:3
Schmidt, Hugo, 1954, S 30,31:2
Schmidt, J E R, 1954, Ag 19,23:3
Schmidt, Jacob W, 1944, Ag 12,11:3; 1950, Ap 29,15:2
Schmidt, James H, 1962, F 21,41:4
Schmidt, James M, 1952, My 20,25:2
Schmidt, John E, 1913, N 25,11:6
Schmidt, John H, 1943, N 25,25:6; 1957, S 5,29:4; 1966, Ap 9,25:2
Schmidt, John H Mrs, 1939, Ag 14,15:4
Schmidt, John Mrs, 1950, Je 8,31:2
Schmidt, John Prof, 1901, Jl 7,5:6
Schmidt, Joseph, 1963, Je 12,43:3
Schmidt, Joseph J, 1945, N 7,23:4
Schmidt, Julius E A, 1953, S 22,31:1
Schmidt, Julius F, 1952, F 1,21:1
Schmidt, Julius W, 1955, Ja 21,23:2
Schmidt, Karl, 1938, Jl 5,2:5; 1950, O 8,104:4
Schmidt, Karl P (death ruled accidental, O 5,10:5), 1957, S 27,15:6
Schmidt, Lawrence M, 1947, My 6,28:3
Schmidt, Leo J, 1947, D 2,29:4
Schmidt, Leopold C, 1958, Mr 1,17:5
Schmidt, Louis, 1913, N 25,11:6; 1938, Je 11,15:2; 1940, Ap 4,23:1; 1945, Ag 24,19:4; 1953, Ag 9,77:4
Schmidt, Louis E, 1957, Jl 13,17:6
Schmidt, Louis H Sr, 1956, Mr 24,19:6
Schmidt, Louis J, 1944, Ap 9,33:1
Schmidt, Louis M, 1947, D 27,13:1
Schmidt, Ludvig O, 1941, Je 24,19:5
Schmidt, Lydia M, 1951, N 3,17:3
Schmidt, Mae D Mrs, 1965, Mr 13,25:5
Schmidt, Maria Olga Mrs, 1911, Je 3,11:6
Schmidt, Martin, 1961, Je 17,21:2
Schmidt, Maude N Mrs, 1947, Je 11,27:4
Schmidt, Milton H, 1968, Ag 23,39:3
Schmidt, Minnie, 1950, Mr 17,23:2
Schmidt, Moses B, 1954, N 13,15:6
Schmidt, Mott B Mrs, 1955, Je 30,25:2
Schmidt, Nathaniel, 1939, Jl 1,17:3
Schmidt, Nicholas C, 1953, My 11,27:4
Schmidt, Norman L, 1960, Jl 21,27:4
Schmidt, Oscar C Mrs, 1961, S 26,39:4
Schmidt, Oswald W, 1939, Mr 3,24:2
Schmidt, Otto, 1940, My 23,23:5
Schmidt, Otto Y, 1956, S 9,85:1
Schmidt, Parbury P, 1964, Je 4,37:5
Schmidt, Paul, 1925, F 23,17:6; 1951, S 19,31:5
Schmidt, Paul J, 1949, S 13,29:4
Schmidt, Peter J, 1944, O 27,23:4
Schmidt, Petrus J, 1952, D 3,33:1
Schmidt, Phil H, 1942, D 30,23:4
Schmidt, Phil Sr, 1940, Ja 15,15:6
Schmidt, Raymond C, 1944, N 2,19:2
Schmidt, Richard E, 1959, O 18,86:8
Schmidt, Richard Mrs, 1959, My 24,88:4
Schmidt, Sylvester Rev, 1908, Je 10,7:5
Schmidt, Theodore, 1947, Je 18,25:5
Schmidt, Theodore J, 1943, Jl 22,19:5
Schmidt, Thomas B, 1950, O 8,104:7
Schmidt, Thomas P (funl plans, Ag 15,27:5), 1966, Ag 13,19:7
Schmidt, Victor E, 1965, Jl 5,17:5
Schmidt, Vincent, 1962, O 23,37:4
Schmidt, Walt S, 1957, Jl 17,27:1
Schmidt, Walter O, 1950, Je 28,27:2
Schmidt, William, 1905, Ja 10,7:6; 1942, S 15,23:3
Schmidt, William A, 1951, F 19,23:4
Schmidt, William C, 1945, Ag 27,19:2
Schmidt, William H, 1922, O 2,17:6; 1942, Jl 17,15:5; 1950, Ja 30,17:4; 1957, F 17,93:2; 1965, Ap 18,81:3
Schmidt, William J, 1947, N 2,72:6
Schmidt, William Jr, 1955, F 20,89:1
Schmidt, William Mrs, 1944, Jl 25,19:5
Schmidt, William R, 1966, Jl 20,41:5
Schmidt, William Sr, 1948, D 29,21:4
Schmidt-Barker, Adele Elma Mrs, 1920, Jl 22,11:5
Schmidt-Degener, Frederick, 1941, N 22,19:3
Schmidtman, Theodore, 1945, S 28,21:2
Schmiedel, George N, 1963, My 10,33:3
Schmieder, Charles, 1950, O 12,31:4
Schmieder, E Henry, 1954, Mr 9,27:5
Schmieder, Louis, 1944, Ap 2,39:1
Schmieder, Paul, 1953, Ja 10,17:1
Schmier, Harry, 1961, Je 2,32:3
Schmier, Pinkas, 1955, Ap 7,27:5
Schmier, William, 1955, D 28,23:3
Schminke, Eberhardt A, 1948, O 13,25:5
Schmits, Thoo J, 1941, Mr 10,17:5
Schmitt, Albert H, 1948, Ja 10,15:4
Schmitt, Alex H, 1958, O 14,37:4
Schmitt, Alex H Mrs, 1949, Je 23,27:4
Schmitt, Alphonse R, 1959, Ag 29,17:4
Schmitt, Anthony Jr, 1941, D 10,25:4
Schmitt, Bertha Mrs, 1944, Je 6,17:4
Schmitt, Carrie, 1950, Ag 27,88:8
Schmitt, Charles A, 1957, Mr 17,86:5
Schmitt, Charles H, 1958, My 2,27:3
Schmitt, Charles W, 1941, Je 14,17:3
Schmitt, Conrad, 1940, D 30,17:5
Schmitt, David Mrs, 1946, My 4,15:5
Schmitt, Edgar W, 1959, N 1,86:5
Schmitt, Eugene A, 1958, Mr 19,31:1
Schmitt, Florent, 1958, Ag 19,28:4
Schmitt, Frank J, 1945, Ja 4,19:4; 1956, Mr 15,31:3
Schmitt, Frederick E, 1964, My 29,29:3
Schmitt, Frederick J, 1951, N 14,31:3
Schmitt, G Phil, 1954, D 2,31:2
Schmitt, George, 1939, S 28,25:6
Schmitt, George W, 1940, Ag 12,15:5
Schmitt, Hans H, 1955, Ag 28,85:1
Schmitt, Harold, 1965, F 2,33:1
Schmitt, Henry, 1939, Ap 11,13:1; 1945, Mr 7,21:5; 1964, O 18,89:2
Schmitt, Henry J, 1941, S 30,23:4
Schmitt, Henry M, 1946, Jl 8,29:3
Schmitt, Jacob, 1947, O 11,17:7
Schmitt, John, 1952, Ag 24,88:5
Schmitt, John A, 1950, S 26,31:1
Schmitt, John J (will, N 30,15:7), 1940, N 25,17:5
Schmitt, John J, 1952, O 29,29:4
Schmitt, John P, 1938, Ja 21,19:3
Schmitt, Joseph H, 1959, Ja 12,39:2
Schmitt, K Walter, 1958, S 21,86:5
Schmitt, Katherine, 1950, Ja 12,27:2
Schmitt, Louis A, 1937, N 24,23:5
Schmitt, Matthew, 1948, Ja 15,23:3
Schmitt, Oscar C, 1953, Ap 22,29:4
Schmitt, Phil F, 1939, Ag 16,23:5
Schmitt, Richard B, 1945, Ag 12,39:2
Schmitt, Saladin, 1951, Mr 16,31:3
Schmitt, Stanley W, 1952, Ag 26,25:2
Schmitt, William, 1942, Mr 4,19:3; 1962, Ja 25,31:4
Schmitt, William J, 1941, Jl 18,19:5
Schmittberger, Max F (funl, O 2,15:6), 1917, N 1, 15:3
Schmittberger, William G, 1939, Mr 30,23:4
Schmitter, Dean M Mrs, 1958, Jl 17,53:4
Schmitter, Elizabeth H, 1920, My 31,11:2
Schmitter, Ferdinand, 1950, Je 30,23:2
Schmitter, Lyle L, 1958, Ap 13,84:1
Schmitthenner, John W Rev Dr, 1937, S 14,23:5
Schmittmann, William, 1950, My 21,104:3
Schmitz, Andrew B, 1941, N 30,69:2
Schmitz, Andrew J Mrs, 1963, Ap 19,43:3
Schmitz, Bruno Prof, 1916, Ap 28,11:6
Schmitz, C F, 1883, My 23,4:7
Schmitz, Carl L, 1967, My 14,86:6
Schmitz, Clarence E, 1961, Ag 3,23:5
Schmitz, E, 1928, N 22,29:3
Schmitz, E Robert, 1949, S 7,29:1
Schmitz, Elizabeth Mrs, 1941, F 21,19:4
Schmitz, Frank, 1966, S 5,20:7
Schmitz, Henry, 1939, Ap 18,23:1
Schmitz, Henry (biog data, F 2,33:5), 1965, Ja 31, 18:1
Schmitz, Herbert E, 1960, Ap 18,29:2
Schmitz, Herbert W, 1960, D 18,84:2
Schmitz, Hermann, 1960, O 11,45:5
Schmitz, John H, 1948, Ap 19,23:4
Schmitz, Max, 1924, My 28,23:3
Schmitz, Richard, 1954, Ap 28,31:2
Schmitz, Ronald C, 1960, Jl 8,21:3
Schmitzer, John, 1953, Ja 7,31:2
Schmoeger, Fred A, 1955, S 10,17:5
Schmoker, Caroline, 1942, O 25,44:2
Schmolkova, Marie Mrs, 1940, Mr 29,21:3
Schmoll, Armand, 1945, Je 19,19:4
Schmoll, Armand Jr, 1944, N 17,19:4
Schmoll, Frank, 1945, D 8,17:2
Schmolze, Mildred C, 1960, Mr 7,29:1
Schmon, Arthur A, 1964, Mr 19,33:2
Schmon, Arthur A Mrs, 1963, Ap 22,27:1
Schmoyer, Herbert L, 1943, Ag 30,15:5
Schmuck, Allen J C, 1955, Ap 24,86:8
Schmuck, J C, 1936, My 22,23:5
Schmuck, Peter (mem ser, S 21,27:2), 1954, Ag 2[illegible] 17:1
Schmucker, Beale M, 1937, D 24,17:1
Schmucker, Samuel C, 1943, D 28,17:2
Schmuckler, Samuel C Mrs, 1946, Je 25,21:3
Schmugler, Albert D, 1964, Ap 29,41:4
Schmukler, Jacob, 1965, Ap 18,80:8
Schmukler, Jacob J, 1960, Jl 28,27:3
Schmulen, Leon B, 1961, Jl 22,21:3
Schmults, Henry E, 1967, Ja 21,43:1
Schmutz, Ernest G, 1956, D 29,15:4
Schmutz, Frederick J, 1942, N 25,23:2
Schmutzer, J I J M, 1946, S 28,17:4
Schnabel, Arthur, 1951, Ag 16,27:1
Schnabel, Artur Mme, 1959, F 2,26:5
Schnabel, Charles, 1965, Mr 8,29:2
Schnabel, Ellis A, 1955, Ap 13,29:4
Schnabel, Ellis A Mrs, 1958, Jl 12,15:5
Schnabel, Richard A, 1924, Mr 10,15:4
Schnabel, Robert C, 1954, F 15,23:4
Schnacke, Mahlon K, 1938, N 5,19:4
Schnackel, George C, 1944, Je 18,36:1; 1946, N 12
Schnackenberg, Elmer J Judge, 1968, S 17,47:3
Schnader, William A, 1968, Mr 19,44:1
Schnaer, Samuel, 1915, N 15,11:6
Schnaker, Stanley T, 1953, N 22,88:1
Schnaper, Edward, 1938, S 5,15:3
Schnarendorf, Alfred, 1941, Ag 8,15:4
Schnaring, Walter L, 1943, Jl 18,34:8
Schnautz, Robert W, 1945, Ja 27,11:3
Schnavel, Barbara Mrs, 1925, My 18,15:5
Schnebbe, F H, 1941, Mr 13,21:2
Schnebel, Daniel Rev, 1912, Jl 27,7:6
Schneberger, Henry Rev Dr, 1916, N 3,13:4

Schnebly, Keith G, 1957, S 4,33:3
Schneck, John J, 1947, Mr 11,27:4
Schneck, Max, 1965, Jl 24,21:5
Schneder, David B, 1938, O 6,23:2
Schnee, Albert F, 1953, Ag 5,23:5
Schnee, Berthold, 1940, My 20,17:3
Schnee, Charles, 1962, N 30,33:2
Schnee, Murray, 1958, Je 29,69:1
Schneeberger, Frederick W, 1946, My 13,21:5
Schneer, Frederick H, 1943, My 5,27:4
Schneer, Jacob B, 1959, My 2,23:4
Schneer, Max R, 1959, My 18,27:5
Schneersohn, Joseph I, 1950, Ja 30,2:3
Schneerson, Chana Mrs, 1964, S 13,86:2
Schneeweiss, Oliver P, 1940, N 26,23:1
Schnefel, Peter M, 1953, My 15,24:5
Schnehen, Wolfgang J Mrs, 1958, S 5,27:1
Schneidawin, Anna Mrs, 1922, F 20,11:5
Schneidenbach, Oscar R, 1955, S 14,35:3
Schneider, A E R, 1954, My 19,31:3
Schneider, Adam T, 1943, Ap 9,21:3
Schneider, Adolph J, 1963, D 4,47:3
Schneider, Albert, 1957, My 25,21:5
Schneider, Albert C, 1946, D 29,37:3
Schneider, Albert K, 1952, Je 9,23:4
Schneider, Alfred D, 1940, Ap 26,21:2
Schneider, Alfred E, 1966, O 26,47:4
Schneider, Alfred E Mrs, 1946, My 19,42:3
Schneider, Arthur, 1958, My 14,33:4
Schneider, Arthur F, 1942, F 8,48:1
Schneider, August F, 1946, F 7,23:3
Schneider, B Aubrey, 1960, S 24,23:3
Schneider, Ben (por), 1946, Jl 15,25:1
Schneider, Benjamin B, 1957, S 3,28:1
Schneider, Carl A, 1962, O 11,39:3
Schneider, Carol C S Mrs, 1954, D 19,85:1
Schneider, Charles (cor, Ag 9,27:1), 1960, Ag 7,84:6
Schneider, Charles A, 1951, Ap 11,29:2
Schneider, Charles T, 1944, Jl 26,19:2
Schneider, Conrad, 1941, O 12,52:1; 1954, N 18,33:3
Schneider, Edward F, 1950, Jl 2,24:7
Schneider, Edward J, 1952, O 7,29:1
Schneider, Edwin C, 1954, O 4,27:5
Schneider, Edwin J, 1968, Ap 12,35:3
Schneider, Emelia J, 1949, F 25,24:2
Schneider, Ernst, 1957, Mr 14,29:1
Schneider, Esther Mrs, 1953, Jl 29,23:5
Schneider, Eugene, 1875, N 28,1:4; 1942, N 18,25:1
Schneider, Eugene H, 1946, Ag 1,23:3
Schneider, Everett J, 1943, Ag 1,39:1
Schneider, Francis A, 1949, D 28,25:3
Schneider, Franz James Rev, 1907, Mr 13,9:5
Schneider, Frederick, 1944, Jl 23,36:2
Schneider, Frederick C, 1958, N 26,29:3
Schneider, Frederick E, 1941, D 31,17:3
Schneider, Frederick F, 1947, Mr 7,26:2
Schneider, Frederick W, 1941, D 20,19:2; 1946, D 30, 19:6
Schneider, Frederick W Mrs, 1938, O 26,23:2
Schneider, George, 1939, My 7,III,7:2; 1950, Ag 30, 32:2; 1959, My 8,27:1
Schneider, George A, 1955, Ja 11,25:4
Schneider, George E, 1961, Jl 4,19:1
Schneider, George H, 1941, N 19,23:3
Schneider, George J, 1939, My 12,III,6:5; 1943, Mr 19, 20:2
Schneider, George W, 1966, S 28,47:3
Schneider, Georges, 1963, S 11,43:2
Schneider, Gustave, 1948, Jl 17,15:5
Schneider, Gustave A, 1948, O 15,23:4
Schneider, Gustave J, 1961, Ap 11,37:2
Schneider, Hannes, 1955, Ap 27,31:4
Schneider, Harold O, 1959, Ap 30,31:2
Schneider, Harry, 1937, Je 26,17:6
Schneider, Henry, 1945, S 22,17:4; 1952, F 21,27:4; 1960, F 10,38:1
Schneider, Henry G, 1946, S 15,9:7
Schneider, Henry I, 1958, O 22,35:3
Schneider, Henry P, 1953, O 20,29:1
Schneider, Herman (por), 1939, Mr 29,23:3
Schneider, Herman C, 1941, My 30,15:1
Schneider, Herman Mrs, 1947, N 24,23:3
Schneider, Hortense, 1920, My 7,11:3
Schneider, J, 1928, My 2,25:1
Schneider, John, 1938, Jl 6,25:6; 1950, Ap 27,29:4; 1952, Jl 16,25:1
Schneider, John G, 1956, Ja 11,31:2; 1964, F 4,30:8
Schneider, John Mrs, 1946, O 12,19:3
Schneider, John R, 1952, Mr 27,29:5
Schneider, Jonathan, 1947, My 13,25:2
Schneider, Joseph, 1953, Ag 23,89:3; 1966, D 1,47:5
Schneider, Joseph Mrs, 1948, N 14,76:4
Schneider, Kalman W Mrs, 1949, Ag 5,19:5
Schneider, Karl J, 1955, N 10,35:4
Schneider, Kenneth R, 1961, N 20,31:6
Schneider, Leo V, 1963, N 14,35:5
Schneider, Leonard (Lenny Bruce), 1966, Ag 4,33:2
Schneider, Lou, 1966, My 14,31:5
Schneider, Louis, 1951, N 8,29:2
Schneider, Louis F, 1942, S 23,25:2
Schneider, Louis M, 1939, Ja 8,42:7
Schneider, Louis Prof, 1906, N 27,2:6
Schneider, Margaret, 1937, N 27,17:2
Schneider, Marguerite, 1947, My 28,25:5
Schneider, Maurice, 1956, S 21,25:3
Schneider, Max, 1962, Ap 28,25:3
Schneider, Max J Mrs, 1937, N 14,II,10:2
Schneider, Mendel Mrs, 1942, Ag 15,11:4
Schneider, Michael, 1949, O 5,29:3
Schneider, Miss, 1871, F 22,5:5
Schneider, Mitchel, 1959, O 23,29:1
Schneider, Morris, 1939, O 29,40:8
Schneider, Oscar, 1915, Ag 11,9:5
Schneider, Otto C, 1938, Jl 21,21:5
Schneider, Paul O, 1950, Ag 8,29:5
Schneider, Perry L (por), 1948, Ap 24,15:1
Schneider, Peter O, 1960, Ja 17,86:5
Schneider, Phil J, 1951, D 23,22:4
Schneider, Philip, 1962, Jl 25,33:6
Schneider, Ralph E, 1964, N 3,31:4
Schneider, Raymond, 1959, Ap 17,25:2
Schneider, Reinhard, 1904, Ja 15,9:6
Schneider, Robert, 1951, Mr 24,26:2
Schneider, Samuel, 1951, Mr 9,10:3; 1952, Je 3,29:1; 1966, Jl 26,35:4
Schneider, Samuel H, 1939, Mr 18,17:5
Schneider, Samuel R, 1965, O 26,45:4
Schneider, Theodore D, 1955, N 2,35:5
Schneider, Walter A, 1956, N 22,33:6
Schneider, William, 1950, N 14,31:3
Schneider, William A, 1940, O 1,23:2; 1961, Je 14,19:3
Schneider, William A Mrs, 1957, Ag 5,19:1
Schneider, William F, 1941, O 23,23:4
Schneider, William L (por), 1944, Je 1,19:5
Schneider, William N, 1947, O 17,21:1
Schneider, William S, 1941, D 3,25:3
Schneider-Paas, Alfred J, 1957, D 14,21:1
Schneiderhahn, Maximilian, 1923, N 26,17:4
Schneiderman, Jacob (J Kelly), 1965, D 5,89:1
Schneiderman, Louis Mrs, 1950, Mr 16,32:3
Schneiders, Henry Mrs, 1958, S 17,37:2
Schneidkraut, Louis, 1950, My 23,29:1
Schneier, Alfred Mrs, 1954, N 5,21:3
Schneier, Alfred Sr, 1963, S 17,35:1
Schneier, Emil H, 1957, Ap 4,33:3
Schneiker, Charles F, 1912, Ap 5,13:5
Schneir, David, 1961, Ap 1,17:3
Schneir, Jack S Mrs, 1966, D 29,31:4
Schneir, Max, 1957, D 22,41:1
Schneir, Solomon, 1950, F 24,23:3
Schneirla, Richard (Donn), 1961, Ja 12,12:5
Schneirla, Theodore C Dr, 1968, Ag 21,42:1
Schnell, Frederick W, 1951, My 27,68:7
Schnell, George, 1952, O 10,25:1
Schnell, Harry J, 1942, N 30,23:6
Schnell, John, 1962, S 23,87:1
Schnell, Leo, 1951, Ap 26,32:3
Schnell, Phil, 1954, Jl 30,17:5
Schnell, Richard A, 1942, N 4,23:5
Schnelle, Frederick J Mrs, 1952, S 29,23:5
Schnelle, Henry J, 1940, D 8,68:3
Schneller, Andrew H Sr, 1964, D 26,17:5
Schneller, Charles J, 1942, Ag 2,39:3
Schneller, Charles J Mrs, 1941, Ap 18,21:5
Schneller, Frank J, 1954, S 13,23:5
Schneller, Fred, 1949, O 29,15:3
Schneller, Frederic A, 1960, Ag 3,29:2
Schneller, Julius, 1945, Ja 9,19:3
Schneller, Louis, 1939, S 8,23:4
Schneller, Robert W, 1952, D 7,89:1
Schneller, Rudolph, 1937, Je 21,19:5
Schnepel, George A, 1946, Mr 13,29:2
Schnepel, Herman H, 1952, Ag 6,21:2
Schnepf, G Leonhard, 1939, Mr 13,21:3
Schnepper, Frederick H, 1946, Mr 8,21:4
Schner, Charles Jr, 1963, D 4,47:4
Schnering, Otto, 1953, Ja 12,27:5
Schnerring, J George, 1950, F 9,29:4
Schnetter, Joseph Dr, 1903, S 6,7:6
Schneyer, Chiam (C S Hamerow), 1961, Jl 27,31:4
Schneyer, Edward Mrs, 1954, Jl 21,27:3
Schneyer, Samuel, 1915, N 13,11:5
Schnibbe, Frederick, 1949, Je 21,25:3
Schnieder, T Franklin, 1965, Ap 9,33:2
Schnier, August, 1943, N 23,26:3
Schniewind, Carl, 1957, Ag 30,19:4
Schniewind, Ewald H, 1943, Ag 11,19:4
Schniewind, H Z, 1953, O 22,29:5
Schniewind, Henry, 1962, Ap 6,35:3
Schnipelsky, Louis A, 1951, My 28,21:2
Schnittger, Herman J, 1957, D 13,27:3
Schnitzer, Charles, 1952, Ja 11,21:3
Schnitzer, EDw M, 1950, F 4,15:5
Schnitzer, Henry J, 1941, Jl 8,19:5
Schnitzer, Herriman, 1938, N 4,3:3
Schnitzer, Joseph I (por), 1944, Jl 22,15:2
Schnitzer, Joseph M, 1941, D 9,31:3
Schnitzer, Louis, 1954, Ag 19,23:5
Schnitzer, Max, 1959, S 1,30:1
Schnitzler, A, 1931, O 22,23:1
Schnitzler, Emil F Mrs, 1966, Ja 25,41:4
Schnitzler, George, 1925, S 11,23:6
Schnitzler, Louis C, 1961, N 20,31:4
Schnizer, Winthrop L, 1963, Ap 9,31:3
Schnizer, Winthrop L Mrs, 1962, O 21,88:8
Schnoeller, Anton, 1940, N 4,19:2
Schnoor, Herman H, 1951, S 19,31:5
Schnorr, Joseph Rev, 1918, My 25,13:4
Schnur, Baruch H, 1957, F 21,27:4
Schnur, Baruch H Mrs, 1944, Je 21,19:3
Schnur, Charles Mrs, 1950, Mr 5,92:5
Schnur, David, 1948, Mr 17,25:4
Schnur, Jacob, 1959, S 16,39:5
Schnurer, Bert, 1958, Ap 30,33:2
Schnurmacher, Lippman Mrs, 1960, F 3,33:2
Schnurr, Barbara B Mrs, 1941, S 24,23:6
Schnurr, Martin K, 1965, Ap 15,33:2
Schnyder, Paul, 1952, Jl 25,17:2
Schnyder, Walter, 1964, Jl 10,29:3
Schoaf, Ira B Dr, 1937, D 10,26:1
Schobel, Benjamin, 1951, Je 8,27:4
Schober, Albert F, 1951, O 21,92:3
Schober, Henry Mrs, 1946, O 11,23:5
Schober, Irby L, 1951, Jl 12,25:5
Schober, J, 1932, Ag 20,13:1
Schober, John, 1939, D 15,19:3
Schober, John L, 1945, Je 30,17:4
Schoch, Amos Z, 1939, Ap 15,19:3
Schoch, Charles H, 1954, S 3,17:4
Schoch, Eliza J, 1953, F 20,19:3
Schoch, George H Mrs, 1961, D 24,36:5
Schoch, Gustave Mrs, 1948, Je 5,15:6
Schoch, James G, 1953, S 11,21:2
Schoch, Layton M, 1940, Ja 19,19:4
Schoch, Marion S, 1946, D 15,76:1
Schoch, Mathilde C Mrs, 1938, Jl 19,22:2
Schoch, Milton G, 1965, Mr 27,27:5
Schoch, Parke H, 1938, O 16,45:3
Schoch, Paul A, 1950, My 28,44:2
Schoch, Walter, 1968, Mr 1,37:1
Schochet, Louis J, 1939, Ja 17,21:4
Schock, Arthur P, 1943, S 11,13:6
Schock, Clarence (por), 1955, My 31,27:2
Schock, Frederick F, 1949, F 21,23:5
Schock, John, 1953, N 9,35:5
Schocke, Henry, 1938, N 26,15:4
Schocken, Salman, 1959, Ag 8,17:4
Schockert, Nathan, 1961, Jl 20,27:4
Schocky, S A von, 1928, N 15,29:5
Schoder, Rex F, 1959, Jl 6,27:4
Schoder, Stewart A Mrs, 1960, Je 1,39:4
Schoeck, Frederick, 1944, N 20,21:4
Schoeck, Othmar, 1957, Mr 28,31:4
Schoedel, Frederick, 1942, N 15,58:2
Schoedel, Louis, 1947, Ja 3,22:3
Schoedler, Ulrich Mrs, 1946, S 13,7:2
Schoefer, Thomas, 1949, Ap 16,15:4
Schoeffel, Francis H, 1957, S 17,35:1
Schoeffel, George J Gen, 1921, D 22,15:5
Schoeffel, John B, 1918, S 1,17:1; 1940, F 28,21:2
Schoeffel, John B Mrs (Agnes Booth), 1910, Ja 3,9:5
Schoeffel, Sarah C Mrs, 1937, N 27,17:3
Schoeffler, Herman, 1944, Ag 12,11:5
Schoefield, Sydney, 1955, My 17,29:4
Schoelcher, V, 1893, D 27,5:2
Schoelkopf, C P H, 1928, F 25,17:5
Schoelkopf, Frederick, 1950, Ag 12,13:5
Schoeller, Ewald S, 1964, S 3,29:4
Schoeller, G Phil Mrs, 1956, Ag 7,27:1
Schoeller, William, 1946, S 13,7:3
Schoelles, William Mrs, 1940, Ja 9,23:4
Schoellkopf, Alfred H (will, S 17,11:6),(por), 1942, S 10,28:2
Schoellkopf, Jacob F Jr (will, D 24,15:7), 1952, D 17,33:1
Schoellkopf, Jacob F Jr Mrs, 1958, Ap 20,84:3
Schoellkopf, Jacob F Mrs, 1938, S 17,17:4
Schoellkopf, Jacob F Sr (will, S 17,11:6),(por), 1942, S 11,21:1
Schoellkopf, Olive A Mrs (est appr), 1959, O 22,37:1
Schoellkopf, Paul A (por), 1947, O 1,29:1
Schoellkopf, Walter H Mrs, 1950, S 3,38:7
Schoelwer, William B, 1955, F 16,29:4
Schoemaker, Daniel M, 1951, My 20,25:2
Schoemaker, William H, 1938, N 22,23:5
Schoemer, Joseph J, 1950, Je 3,15:4
Schoemer, Lewis A, 1961, Jl 22,21:5
Schoen, Andre, 1950, F 3,23:2
Schoen, Arthur, 1963, N 30,27:4
Schoen, August C, 1954, Ja 23,13:6
Schoen, Charles T, 1917, F 5,11:6
Schoen, Edward C, 1957, Jl 1,23:4
Schoen, Eugene, 1957, Ag 17,15:2
Schoen, Frank J, 1955, F 25,21:2
Schoen, Fred, 1963, Je 15,23:3
Schoen, George, 1953, Ag 23,88:5
Schoen, George J, 1951, My 9,33:4
Schoen, Harold H, 1951, Jl 5,25:4
Schoen, Harry J, 1958, Je 19,31:6
Schoen, Jacob, 1913, Je 30,7:5; 1942, D 15,27:3
Schoen, Louis, 1958, D 4,39:1
Schoen, Mac E, 1957, Ja 10,29:3
Schoen, Max, 1968, Ag 10,27:5
Schoen, Nelson J, 1952, Jl 19,15:6
Schoen, W von, 1933, Ap 25,17:1
Schoen, William F, 1946, N 24,79:5
Schoen, William H Mrs, 1956, Ja 25,31:4
Schoen-Rene, Anna E (por), 1942, N 15,57:1
Schoen-Rene, Eugene, 1967, O 13,39:4

Schoenaich, Paul von, 1954, Ja 8,22:3
Schoenaich-Carolath, Heinrich Prince, 1920, Je 22,11:4
Schoenaich-Carolath, Wanda, 1925, Jl 3,13:7
Schoenau, Carl Mrs, 1956, O 28,88:3
Schoenau, Carl W, 1954, N 13,15:4
Schoenbach, Emanuel B, 1952, S 7,85:1
Schoenbaum, Irving, 1950, N 15,31:2
Schoenberg, Albert J, 1960, N 2,39:2
Schoenberg, Alex Mrs, 1949, Ap 20,27:4
Schoenberg, Arnold, 1951, Jl 15,1:2
Schoenberg, Arnold Mrs, 1967, F 16,35:2
Schoenberg, Hyman, 1952, My 31,17:4
Schoenberg, Isaac (Jan 25), 1963, Ap 1,36:5
Schoenberg, Joseph E, 1910, S 1,9:5
Schoenberg, Louis Mrs, 1954, Jl 28,23:4
Schoenberg, Mark J (por), 1945, F 17,13:1
Schoenberg, Martin W, 1951, Ap 26,32:3
Schoenberg, Phil, 1950, My 25,29:3
Schoenberg, William, 1958, Jl 3,25:4
Schoenberg, William Mrs, 1948, S 17,25:4
Schoenberger, Ludwig, 1941, F 11,23:4
Schoenborn, Frederick W, 1945, O 24,21:5
Schoenborn, K L Max Mrs, 1949, F 1,26:3
Schoenborn, Laura F, 1959, D 27,61:2
Schoenbrun, Irving, 1960, O 20,35:5
Schoendorf, Solomon, 1955, Jl 20,27:2
Schoeneck, Charles C, 1940, Ja 11,23:2
Schoeneck, Edward, 1951, Je 23,15:3
Schoenefeld, Jacob M, 1943, Mr 10,19:3
Schoenegan, John, 1944, Ag 17,17:5
Schoenen, Percy L, 1953, Je 16,27:2
Schoenenberger, Frederick J Dr, 1920, F 21,13:4
Schoener, Francis Mrs, 1951, My 28,21:3
Schoener, George M A, 1941, F 11,23:5
Schoener, John G, 1943, D 7,27:4
Schoener, John J, 1938, D 2,23:3
Schoener, William F, 1959, Je 2,35:2
Schoenewaldt, Arthur C, 1953, N 19,31:1
Schoenfeld, Aug D Sr, 1941, Mr 19,21:3
Schoenfeld, August D Jr, 1945, D 30,14:4
Schoenfeld, Berman Sr, 1940, O 16,23:2
Schoenfeld, Frank E, 1962, S 25,37:4
Schoenfeld, Frank H, 1955, F 19,15:5
Schoenfeld, Frederick A, 1952, Mr 4,27:5
Schoenfeld, Harry, 1960, N 16,41:2
Schoenfeld, Henry Mrs, 1950, F 24,23:2
Schoenfeld, John L, 1956, S 13,35:5
Schoenfeld, Joseph Mrs, 1961, F 10,24:2
Schoenfeld, L Kenneth, 1954, Mr 23,27:2
Schoenfeld, Lazar Mrs, 1950, Ja 18,31:2
Schoenfeld, Morris, 1947, S 26,23:1; 1948, Ja 11,56:2; 1950, Mr 15,29:3
Schoenfeld, Moses Mrs, 1956, Jl 27,21:2
Schoenfeld, Nathan, 1945, D 17,21:3; 1950, Ag 29,27:4
Schoenfeld, Phil (will), 1954, My 12,37:1
Schoenfeld, Phil, 1957, Ag 21,27:3
Schoenfeld, Samuel, 1956, Mr 4,88:6; 1968, My 26,84:1
Schoenfeld, Siegfried, 1953, N 17,25:2; 1962, N 1,31:3
Schoenfeld, William A, 1959, N 15,87:1
Schoenfeld, William Mrs, 1951, Ja 2,23:3
Schoenfeld, William Rev, 1919, Jl 31,9:2
Schoenfeldt, Herbert S, 1956, Jl 3,25:4
Schoenfield, Otto B, 1938, Ag 27,13:5
Schoenherr, Gus Mrs, 1944, F 21,15:1
Schoenherr, Henry, 1957, Ag 10,15:2
Schoenherr, Karl, 1943, My 15,15:2
Schoenherr, Oscar, 1937, D 26,II,7:2
Schoenhof, Carl, 1911, My 29,9:6
Schoenhof, Jacob, 1903, Mr 15,7:5
Schoenhof, Madeleine T, 1966, Ag 7,80:3
Schoenhoff, William G, 1943, D 4,13:3
Schoenholtz, Samuel S, 1948, N 22,22:3
Schoenholz, Benjamin J, 1952, Ap 8,29:2
Schoenhut, Albert F, 1950, S 13,27:3
Schoeni, Arnold, 1946, Ag 31,15:5
Schoenijahn, William C, 1939, Mr 29,23:4
Schoening, George W, 1924, D 12,21:4
Schoening, J Jacob, 1951, Je 23,15:5
Schoenkopf, Archie, 1951, Je 5,31:5
Schoenlank, Walter, 1950, Je 29,29:3
Schoenle, Frederick L, 1952, Je 20,23:5
Schoenlein, August J, 1958, Jl 19,15:5
Schoenrod, Edward J, 1968, Mr 2,29:1
Schoenstein, Emil O Mrs, 1953, Ag 29,17:4
Schoentag, Christian I, 1949, F 11,23:5
Schoenwald, Emanuel, 1909, Ag 4,7:3
Schoenwalder, Max A, 1968, N 3,89:1
Schoenweiss, Charles J, 1951, Ap 11,29:5
Schoenwisner, Charles M, 1948, Mr 3,23:3
Schoenwolf, Louis E, 1944, Ja 26,19:2
Schoepf, Albin K, 1954, Mr 22,27:4
Schoepf, Charles L, 1946, My 29,24:2
Schoeppel, Andrew F (funl plans, Ja 23,33:2), 1962, Ja 22,23:4
Schoepperle, Victor F, 1962, Ja 13,21:3
Schoettle, Edwin J, 1947, D 25,21:2
Schoettle, Jacob, 1945, F 10,11:1
Schoettle, Louise W Mrs, 1956, Ja 16,13:1
Schoettle, Ralph J, 1944, Je 23,19:5
Schoettle, William C, 1948, F 6,23:4
Schoettler, Robert J, 1966, F 12,25:4
Schoew, Frederick L, 1939, Ja 21,15:2
Schoff, Albert S, 1946, Ap 12,27:1
Schoff, Hannah K, 1940, D 12,27:2
Schoffel, Louis A, 1946, Jl 9,21:2
Schofield, Albert, 1937, Je 4,23:1
Schofield, Anne S Mrs, 1960, Jl 4,15:6
Schofield, Arnold S, 1945, Mr 19,19:5
Schofield, Arthur, 1883, Ja 20,2:5
Schofield, Arthur C, 1952, My 23,21:2
Schofield, Aubrey W, 1950, S 1,1:7
Schofield, Charles E, 1951, Je 29,21:3; 1956, Mr 23, 28:3
Schofield, Charles I, 1940, Mr 14,23:6
Schofield, Edgar, 1966, Mr 29,41:1
Schofield, Edward B, 1937, S 18,19:2
Schofield, Edward L, 1951, D 8,11:2
Schofield, Frank H (por), 1942, F 22,27:1
Schofield, Frank M, 1947, Je 29,48:6
Schofield, Frederick, 1943, O 31,48:6
Schofield, Frederick S, 1963, Ap 11,33:4
Schofield, G W Lt-Col, 1882, D 19,5:1
Schofield, George Mrs, 1949, Ja 14,24:3
Schofield, Graham L, 1953, D 11,31:4
Schofield, H C, 1941, S 25,25:5
Schofield, Harrison D, 1956, Ja 20,23:2
Schofield, Harvey A, 1941, Ag 4,13:5
Schofield, James D, 1959, Ag 10,27:5
Schofield, John, 1908, O 19,9:6
Schofield, John A, 1949, Mr 20,77:1
Schofield, John C, 1944, Ja 23,38:2
Schofield, John H, 1957, Je 9,89:1
Schofield, John M Lt-Gen (funl, Mr 8,9:4), 1906, Mr 5,9:5
Schofield, Joseph A Jr, 1955, Ap 26,29:1
Schofield, Joseph Mrs, 1961, Ap 24,29:5
Schofield, Lemuel B, 1955, Jl 4,11:6
Schofield, Loomis (cor, Mr 2,13:4), 1940, F 27,21:2
Schofield, Paul, 1962, F 12,23:1
Schofield, Rachel Mrs, 1940, My 23,23:2
Schofield, Robert J, 1939, N 17,21:4
Schofield, Theodore R, 1951, O 18,29:2
Schofield, Thomas, 1957, S 14,19:5
Schofield, W Allen, 1953, Ap 5,76:5
Schofield, Walter E, 1944, Mr 3,15:5
Schofield, William H, 1939, D 21,23:3
Schofield, William H Mrs, 1943, Ja 11,15:3; 1948, Ag 28,15:5
Schofield, William H Prof, 1920, Je 25,11:5
Schofield, William J, 1950, O 19,31:6
Schofield, William R, 1950, Je 15,31:4
Schofield, William T, 1960, Jl 18,27:5
Schofield, William U, 1950, My 2,29:4
Schoham, Robert O, 1955, D 30,19:6
Schohl, William F, 1938, Ag 12,17:6
Scholding, Christopher E Mrs, 1950, Jl 31,17:5
Scholefield, Herbert, 1950, N 17,27:2
Scholer, Walter E, 1961, O 29,88:6
Scholes, Arthur O, 1953, N 24,29:5
Scholes, John L, 1949, Jl 6,27:5
Scholes, Lou, 1942, Ap 20,13:8
Scholes, Percy A, 1958, Ag 3,81:1
Scholey, Charles M, 1940, F 13,23:2
Scholl, Albert A, 1965, My 4,44:1
Scholl, Aurelian, 1902, Ap 17,9:5
Scholl, Charles, 1947, My 20,25:3
Scholl, Edward, 1946, My 15,21:3
Scholl, Frank J, 1967, F 16,39:1
Scholl, Fred, 1942, O 7,25:4
Scholl, Louis A Jr, 1953, S 24,33:2
Scholl, William M Dr, 1968, Mr 30,33:2
Schollaert, Eleanor, 1965, Ja 7,31:1
Schollaert, M J, 1917, Jl 2,9:6
Schollderfer, Leonard, 1946, N 26,29:3
Scholle, Abraham, 1880, Mr 16,8:4
Scholle, Albert W, 1917, D 5,13:5
Scholle, Charles, 1903, Je 14,7:6
Scholle, Gustave, 1937, My 21,21:2
Scholle, Gustave Mrs, 1946, Je 5,23:5
Scholle, Jaques A, 1962, O 15,29:3
Scholle, Phil F, 1938, N 30,24:1
Scholle, William, 1913, My 17,11:6
Scholle, William D, 1961, D 11,31:3
Scholler, Adolph, 1939, F 13,15:5
Scholler, Frederick C, 1957, O 7,27:5
Schollhorn, Frank J, 1949, Mr 18,25:3
Schollmeyer, Herman Mrs, 1944, Ag 17,17:5
Scholten, Arthur, 1947, N 16,76:5
Scholten, Paul, 1946, My 3,22:3
Scholtz, Carlos A, 1946, My 14,21:2
Scholtz, Charles G (por), 1949, O 4,27:2
Scholtz, J Henrique, 1954, S 24,23:5
Scholtz, Moses, 1942, S 1,19:2
Scholz, Carl, 1953, N 16,25:4
Scholz, Emil M, 1948, F 1,60:5
Scholz, Ernest A, 1946, My 6,21:4
Scholz, Frederick W, 1952, Je 13,23:4
Scholz, Karl W H, 1962, My 10,37:4
Scholz, Lawrence, 1945, Je 3,32:6
Scholz, Leopold, 1946, My 14,21:2
Scholz, Leopold Mrs (B Kinney), 1959, Ag 28,23:5
Scholz, Paul F, 1947, S 25,29:4
Scholz, Richard F Dr, 1924, Jl 24,13:4
Scholz, Samuel B Jr, 1949, Mr 8,25:4
Scholze, Olga, 1938, My 24,19:4
Scholze, Robert, 1907, Ap 9,9:6
Schomburg, Arthur A, 1938, Je 11,15:6
Schomer, Abraham S, 1946, Ag 17,13:7
Schomer, Alexander, 1967, N 13,47:2
Schomer, Henry, 1957, O 8,35:1
Schomp, Albert L, 1957, Jl 9,29:4
Schomp, Albert L Mrs, 1951, D 18,31:1
Schomp, John J, 1964, Ja 26,81:1
Schon, Henry Mrs, 1951, Ja 2,23:3
Schon, Pierre, 1944, Ag 4,13:3
Schonberg, Chris M, 1957, Je 17,23:3
Schonberg, Jackson R, 1954, O 21,27:3
Schonberg, Max, 1946, Ap 10,27:4; 1960, Jl 20,29:2
Schonberg, Philip, 1945, Ja 10,23:4
Schonberg, Samuel, 1949, Ja 20,27:2
Schonberger, Henry Mrs (P Einstein), 1967, O 14, 27:1
Schonbrun, Alan B, 1961, Ag 1,31:4
Schoncke, William, 1939, Ap 6,25:4
Schonewald, George A, 1939, Mr 11,17:2
Schoney, Lazarus Dr, 1914, F 19,9:4
Schonfarber, Gordon, 1951, N 17,17:5
Schonfeld, Max, 1966, O 4,47:1
Schongut, Sidney, 1960, Jl 27,29:2
Schonhardt, Henry A, 1954, My 23,88:5
Schonhart, Andrew J, 1956, F 18,19:5
Schonher, Irving, 1957, D 25,31:5
Schonrock, Henry M, 1956, Ag 30,25:4
Schonstadt, Henry, 1946, F 11,29:2
Schontzer, George, 1920, Jl 2,11:5
Schonwald, Philip, 1947, D 23,23:6
Schoo, Clarence J, 1966, O 5,42:8
School, Charles Jr, 1955, Mr 17,45:1
School, Otto, 1938, O 15,17:3
Schooland, Klass, 1938, S 24,17:4
Schoolcraft, J Teller, 1937, F 13,13:5
Schoolcraft, John, 1966, Ap 22,29:6
Schooler, Harry N, 1948, F 3,25:3
Schooley, Arthur B, 1945, Mr 23,19:4
Schooley, Harry B, 1953, S 7,19:5
Schooley, Herbert R, 1959, Ja 10,17:3
Schooley, Raymond H, 1948, Ag 15,60:2
Schooley, Sherman R, 1952, Jl 31,23:6
Schoolfield, John H, 1950, O 23,23:4; 1955, Mr 16,33:3
Schoolfield, John H Mrs, 1954, D 29,23:4
Schoolhouse, Jacob, 1937, Ag 3,23:4
Schoolhouse, Lena Mrs, 1912, Jl 26,9:5
Schoolman, Irving M, 1961, Jl 15,19:2
Schoonhoven, John J Mrs, 1958, Mr 15,17:1
Schoonmaker, Archie C, 1944, N 29,23:2
Schoonmaker, Catherine J Mrs, 1938, Ja 11,23:5
Schoonmaker, Edwin D, 1940, My 6,17:3
Schoonmaker, Edwin D Mrs, 1965, O 28,43:2
Schoonmaker, Ellis, 1940, Ap 20,17:3
Schoonmaker, Emma W Mrs (will), 1938, F 17,19:2
Schoonmaker, Eva A, 1945, S 20,23:4
Schoonmaker, Francis K, 1925, My 14,19:2
Schoonmaker, Frank, 1954, Ap 16,21:2
Schoonmaker, Frank Laying, 1925, F 14,13:5
Schoonmaker, Fred W, 1944, Jl 17,15:4
Schoonmaker, Gerrit L, 1954, My 24,27:2
Schoonmaker, Hortense B G Mrs, 1940, O 8,25:1
Schoonmaker, Irving R, 1951, S 16,84:4
Schoonmaker, Jacob H, 1943, O 3,48:5
Schoonmaker, Jacob H Mrs (will, Mr 5,19:1), 1937, F 27,17:3
Schoonmaker, James J, 1950, D 15,31:4
Schoonmaker, James M Jr (por),(will, D 13,23:7), 1941, D 2,24:3
Schoonmaker, James Mrs, 1950, D 29,19:1
Schoonmaker, James O Mrs, 1952, O 20,23:3
Schoonmaker, Jason, 1944, My 19,19:4
Schoonmaker, John, 1904, Ja 2,9:4; 1940, N 7,25:2
Schoonmaker, John H, 1951, O 27,19:6
Schoonmaker, John J, 1950, My 10,31:1
Schoonmaker, John V V, 1960, F 26,27:1
Schoonmaker, Justin U, 1940, Jl 17,21:3
Schoonmaker, Leon M, 1950, My 31,29:3
Schoonmaker, Mary Mrs, 1909, Je 1,9:6
Schoonmaker, Milton J, 1960, Jl 29,25:1
Schoonmaker, Paul G Sr, 1960, Ap 28,35:5
Schoonmaker, Ralph J, 1948, D 21,15:4
Schoonmaker, Robert, 1948, Ja 9,21:2
Schoonmaker, Samuel V, 1965, D 7,47:2
Schoonmaker, Scott M, 1945, S 6,25:4
Schoonmaker, Sylvanus Lathrop, 1918, Ag 19,9:5
Schoonmaker, Theodor R, 1967, My 3,42:5
Schoonmaker, Theodore B, 1925, Ap 5,5:2
Schoonmaker, Thomas (por), 1948, Ap 8,25:4
Schoonmaker, Thomas, 1968, Ag 27,41:4
Schoonmaker, Wilbur R, 1952, O 27,27:2
Schoonmaker, William H, 1941, Jl 19,13:4
Schoonover, Hiram G, 1945, Jl 31,19:1
Schoonover, Ira, 1942, F 13,21:4
Schoonover, John H, 1943, Ap 7,25:2
Schoonover, Romaine H Mrs, 1938, F 4,21:3
Schoonover, Warren Dr, 1919, Je 5,13:4
Schoonover, Wear K Mrs, 1949, Ap 3,77:1
Schopbach, Charles H, 1947, Je 26,23:3
Schopen, Emil Mrs, 1947, Je 30,19:4
Schopp, Frederick J, 1943, Je 26,13:1
Schopp, Ludwig, 1949, Je 17,24:2
Schoppmeyer, William G, 1948, Ap 14,27:5
Schopps, Edward M, 1953, F 1,88:4

Schor, Ilya, 1961, Je 8,35:2
Schorenstein, Hyman, 1953, F 4,27:1
Schorer, Herman, 1950, D 22,23:4
Schork, George, 1952, Mr 27,29:4
Schork, George J, 1956, N 17,21:4
Schork, Joseph F, 1954, O 7,23:4
Schorkopf, Max, 1962, Ja 7,88:5
Schorlemer-Lieser, Baron, 1922, Jl 8,11:7
Schorling, Raleigh, 1950, Ap 23,95:3
Schorn, Julian, 1940, Ap 18,23:5
Schorn, William F, 1966, Jl 13,43:4
Schorndorfer, Edward F, 1942, N 21,13:2
Schorner, Carrie, 1959, F 3,31:1
Schornstein, Harry Mrs, 1966, My 19,47:3
Schorpp, Louis, 1953, Ap 9,27:2
Schorr, Anshel, 1942, Je 1,13:3
Schorr, Charles, 1960, O 9,86:5
Schorr, Friedrich, 1953, Ag 15,15:1
Schorr, Friedrich Mrs, 1951, D 19,31:2
Schorr, George J, 1946, O 18,23:5
Schorr, Harold V, 1949, Jl 10,57:2
Schorr, Henry F Mrs, 1951, Ja 16,29:3
Schorr, Israel Mrs, 1961, Jl 21,23:2
Schorr, Joseph, 1952, Mr 19,29:1
Schorr, Leopold, 1966, Jl 15,31:1
Schorr, Lewis G, 1966, Je 3,39:1
Schorr, Morris Mrs, 1966, Ap 10,79:5
Schorr, Walter A Sr, 1947, D 16,33:4
Schorsch, Alex P, 1957, Ag 12,19:5
Schorsch, Emanuel I, 1950, Ap 10,19:4
Schorsch, Isaac, 1950, O 13,29:4
Schorsch, Jacob E (will), 1954, N 25,26:8
Schorske, Theodore, 1948, Ap 28,27:5
Schortje, Nicholas, 1952, My 11,92:8
Schosberg, Eugene L, 1965, My 5,47:2
Schosberg, Max, 1957, Jl 27,17:6
Schotland, Joseph J, 1963, Jl 4,17:2
Schotland, Philip J, 1947, N 11,27:3
Schott, C A, 1901, Ag 1,2:2
Schott, Earl A, 1954, D 1,31:4
Schott, Frederick W, 1958, Mr 30,88:8
Schott, Harry S (por), 1937, S 2,21:3
Schott, John, 1958, Ap 1,31:6
Schott, Max (por), 1955, N 11,25:1
Schott, Ralph P, 1922, Je 7,19:6
Schott, Robert C, 1953, Je 12,27:3
Schott, Walter, 1938, S 4,16:6
Schott, Walter E, 1956, Ap 30,23:6
Schott, William F, 1958, F 5,27:3
Schottenfels, Sara X, 1958, N 5,35:2
Schotter, Howard W, 1958, Jl 29,23:4
Schotters, Frank A, 1951, Ag 1,23:6
Schotthoefer, Conrad Father, 1916, N 28,13:4
Schottland, Mary E, 1955, O 4,70:4
Schotz, John F, 1941, Ag 1,15:3
Schou, Axel H, 1952, Ja 8,27:3
Schou, Eugene, 1938, D 25,15:2
Schou, Kenneth, 1950, O 13,29:3
Schou, Magnhild Mrs, 1952, S 18,29:2
Schou, Sidney, 1964, O 5,33:3
Schou, Sidney Mrs, 1939, S 28,25:4
Schoubye, O Robert, 1955, F 3,23:3
Schoudel, Albert W, 1951, O 12,27:3
Schouler, John Adm, 1917, D 27,11:6
Schouler, William Gen, 1872, O 25,4:7
Schoulten, Gertrude Mrs, 1909, My 19,9:6
Schouten, Charles A, 1941, S 9,23:3
Schouten, Sterling B, 1952, Jl 2,25:2
Schowe, Frank, 1948, Mr 31,25:5
Schoyen, A Robert, 1967, Ja 20,43:3
Schoyer, Alfred McGill, 1924, Ag 27,17:6
Schoyer, Balkan, 1910, Ap 3,II,11:2
Schrack, Ephrem, 1951, Ap 30,21:5
Schrade, Henry, 1953, S 4,34:7
Schrade, Henry J, 1943, Ag 13,17:4
Schrade, J Louis, 1960, D 5,31:4
Schrader, Albert R Mrs, 1951, Je 8,27:3
Schrader, Edward D, 1956, Ap 7,19:4
Schrader, Ellen, 1941, N 4,23:3
Schrader, F J, 1952, Jl 15,23:1
Schrader, Franz, 1962, Mr 23,33:1
Schrader, Fred B, 1938, Ag 14,32:6
Schrader, Frederick, 1938, F 2,19:4
Schrader, Harry, 1946, S 18,31:5
Schrader, Henry C, 1907, F 13,9:2
Schrader, Martin H Mrs, 1954, Jl 4,23:1
Schrader, Robert M, 1953, Ap 25,15:4
Schradieck, Henry Prof, 1918, Mr 27,13:7
Schradzke, Harold R, 1949, Mr 20,76:5
Schraedel, Raymond, 1941, Je 12,23:3
Schraeder, Frank, 1940, N 17,50:1
Schraffenberger, Strieder, 1962, O 16,39:2
Schrafft, Albert G Mrs, 1951, Je 6,31:5
Schrafft, Arthur Sr, 1962, S 26,39:3
Schrafft, George F Mrs, 1956, F 10,21:6
Schrafft, Nelson H, 1947, N 22,15:5
Schrafft, William E, 1963, Je 6,35:5
Schraft, Oscar A, 1949, Ag 3,23:5
Schrag, Carl I, 1958, Ja 23,27:4
Schrag, Louis, 1945, Ap 15,14:5
Schrage, Benjamin L, 1958, My 21,33:1
Schrage, Walter E, 1941, O 10,23:1
Schrager, Jean, 1939, Jl 5,11:3
Schrager, Tina Mrs, 1942, Ag 19,19:1
Schrager, Victor L, 1944, O 16,19:6
Schrager, Victoria L (por), 1943, O 26,24:2
Schraig, James V, 1961, S 13,45:3
Schram, Daniel Mrs, 1911, Ag 2,7:6
Schram, Emil A, 1944, N 20,21:2
Schram, Frank E, 1939, Ja 18,19:1
Schram, Herman, 1958, F 8,19:5
Schram, Jack A, 1961, Ap 22,25:6
Schram, Louis B, 1921, Ag 15,13:7
Schram, Walter E, 1945, Je 28,19:5
Schramm, Adolf Mrs, 1951, Mr 7,33:2
Schramm, Albert, 1946, O 29,25:3
Schramm, Anna, 1916, Je 3,13:7
Schramm, Charles V, 1916, Je 3,13:4
Schramm, chas E, 1951, My 12,12:7
Schramm, Frank E E, 1949, O 21,25:1
Schramm, Frank E E Mrs, 1952, O 22,27:2
Schramm, Gustav L, 1959, S 6,72:4
Schramm, J P A, 1884, F 27,5:2
Schramm, Louis, 1957, Ag 12,19:3
Schramm, Louis Sr, 1947, Ja 12,59:6
Schramme, L M T, 1883, Ag 28,5:5
Schrank, John Flammang, 1943, S 17,23:4
Schrank, Max C, 1964, Ap 5,86:6
Schrank, Pincus, 1948, S 27,23:5
Schranz, Frederick G, 1950, Mr 7,27:5
Schratt, Heinrich, 1940, S 11,25:3
Schratt, Katharina, 1918, Ja 12,11:4
Schratt, Katharina (Mrs Maria M K von Kiss de Ittebe), 1940, Ap 19,21:5
Schratter, Julius, 1946, Je 21,23:5
Schratwieser, Christian H Sr, 1948, D 28,22:3
Schraub, Frederick C, 1938, O 7,23:4
Schraubstadter, Oswald, 1955, Ja 21,23:1
Schraudenbach, Frederick, 1949, O 10,23:3
Schrauder, Frank F, 1949, Mr 7,21:2
Schrauff, Charles J, 1962, S 21,30:1
Schrauth, William H, 1945, Ap 20,19:4
Schrayman, William, 1955, Jl 12,25:1
Schrecher, Frederick, 1948, N 18,28:2
Schreck, Henry, 1956, Ja 31,29:3
Schreck, William J, 1950, N 10,27:2
Schrecker, Paul, 1963, D 27,25:2
Schreckinger, Abraham B, 1955, D 15,37:3
Schreeder, Lemuel, 1943, N 25,25:5
Schrei, Fred J, 1947, Ja 29,26:2
Schreiber, Albert, 1940, N 15,21:4
Schreiber, Andrew, 1941, D 16,27:2
Schreiber, Anna F, 1965, N 26,37:3
Schreiber, Anthony, 1938, N 9,23:5
Schreiber, Barbara Mrs, 1925, S 8,21:5
Schreiber, Benjamin F Mrs, 1949, Ja 23,68:4
Schreiber, Bernard J, 1948, D 31,15:2
Schreiber, Carl F, 1960, Mr 3,29:3
Schreiber, Charles, 1963, Ag 30,12:4
Schreiber, Collinwood Sir, 1918, Mr 24,13:1
Schreiber, Cornell, 1945, Ja 14,39:2
Schreiber, Dora L Mrs, 1940, F 2,17:4
Schreiber, Elwood L, 1948, Ap 15,25:3
Schreiber, Frank P Sr Mrs, 1954, My 16,87:1
Schreiber, Frederick W, 1959, D 5,23:2
Schreiber, George E, 1960, N 29,37:1
Schreiber, George F, 1950, N 10,27:4
Schreiber, George G, 1941, Mr 15,17:2
Schreiber, George J, 1954, S 1,27:4
Schreiber, Harry Mrs, 1950, My 9,29:1
Schreiber, Henry C, 1967, N 28,47:4
Schreiber, Henry J, 1938, O 12,27:2
Schreiber, Herbert, 1967, Ja 4,43:2
Schreiber, Jane S, 1949, Ap 29,23:1
Schreiber, John C, 1907, N 10,9:6
Schreiber, John M, 1941, Jl 20,31:2
Schreiber, Julius, 1948, Ag 9,19:5
Schreiber, Karl O, 1948, O 6,29:4
Schreiber, Leroy Mrs, 1959, My 25,29:2
Schreiber, Lew, 1961, F 8,31:3
Schreiber, Louis, 1965, Jl 19,27:5
Schreiber, Max, 1959, My 21,31:4
Schreiber, Milton, 1941, Je 7,17:5; 1963, Jl 10,35:3
Schreiber, Olga, 1959, Mr 6,25:2
Schreiber, Otto, 1945, Ag 10,15:6
Schreiber, Otto L Mrs, 1948, My 4,25:2
Schreiber, Samuel Mrs, 1956, F 10,10:6
Schreiber, Siegfried M Mrs, 1964, Je 26,29:3
Schreiber, Walther, 1958, Jl 2,29:4
Schreiber, William, 1958, F 20,25:4; 1961, Ag 19,18:1
Schreiber, William F, 1946, Ap 3,25:5
Schreiber, William L, 1949, O 16,88:4
Schreiber, William Mrs, 1965, N 4,47:5
Schreibersdorf, Nathan, 1942, Ag 2,38:8
Schreibman, Jacob, 1944, My 26,19:5
Schreider, Frank Mrs, 1944, Ag 31,17:5
Schreier, Max, 1951, Ap 13,23:5
Schreiner, Anthony Sr, 1951, N 14,31:2
Schreiner, Bernard F, 1951, My 10,31:2
Schreiner, Berthold J, 1939, Mr 21,23:3
Schreiner, Bess D, 1959, D 9,42:2
Schreiner, Francis C L Dr (por), 1937, Ag 9,19:3
Schreiner, Francis Mrs, 1949, D 6,32:6
Schreiner, George A, 1942, Ja 22,17:1
Schreiner, Helen R, 1945, My 30,19:3
Schreiner, Joseph, 1963, Ag 25,83:1
Schreiner, Marie V, 1964, D 11,39:1
Schreiner, Olive, 1920, D 13,15:6
Schreiner, Osmond Harvey, 1914, F 15,5:3
Schreiner, Otto, 1952, Ap 18,25:4
Schreiner, Samuel, 1958, Mr 15,17:2
Schreiner, William C, 1937, Mr 12,23:1
Schreiner, William Philip, 1919, Je 29,22:4
Schreiter, Charles D, 1939, S 7,25:2
Schreiter, Henry, 1919, S 17,13:2
Schreker, F, 1934, Mr 23,23:1
Schrembs, Joseph (por), 1945, N 3,15:1
Schremp, Hilbert P, 1951, D 24,13:5
Schrempp, Vincent, 1941, Je 1,41:2
Schrenkeisen, Frank G, 1946, Ja 12,15:2
Schrenkeisen, Hilda P, 1957, Ja 19,15:4
Schrenkeisen, Martin H, 1944, S 25,17:3
Schrenkeisen, Ralph R, 1946, Mr 14,25:5
Schrenkeisen, Ralph R Mrs, 1950, Jl 6,28:3
Schrepfer, Frank A, 1940, Mr 20,27:4
Schreur, Clara T Mrs, 1940, Ap 10,25:4
Schrever, James A, 1945, Mr 2,19:2
Schreyvogel, Charles, 1912, Ja 29,11:5
Schriber, Louis, 1952, Ap 20,92:3
Schribner, Fred C Jr Mrs, 1958, F 13,29:3
Schricker, Henry F, 1966, D 29,31:2
Schrider, Peter P, 1966, My 2,37:3
Schrier, Harry, 1937, Mr 13,19:4
Schrier, Harry A, 1938, N 2,24:3
Schrier, Heyman, 1958, Jl 25,19:2
Schrier, Isaac, 1960, Jl 11,29:3
Schrift, Jonas, 1955, Ag 18,23:3
Schriftman, Jay B, 1940, My 27,19:5
Schrimer, Ellis L, 1960, S 10,21:1
Schrimger, John Rev Dr, 1915, Ag 9,7:6
Schrimpf, Adam, 1943, Mr 13,19:4
Schriver, Andrew Rev Dr, 1920, O 10,22:2
Schriver, Charles (Hank), 1968, Ap 30,47:1
Schriver, Howard M, 1950, Je 13,27:3
Schriver, James C, 1948, F 6,26:5
Schriver, L Howard, 1968, N 28,37:3
Schriver, Otto S, 1946, Ja 29,25:2
Schriver, William H, 1937, Jl 15,19:2
Schrock, Clarence W, 1954, Jl 18,57:1
Schroder, Bruno Baron (por), 1940, D 11,28:2
Schroder, Charles W, 1939, F 7,19:5
Schroder, George H, 1966, S 13,47:1
Schroder, Walter (cor, Jl 30,21:5), 1942, Jl 29,17:2
Schroder, William F, 1957, Ja 1,23:4
Schroder, William H, 1948, N 12,23:3
Schroedel, Edward C, 1966, Ag 3,37:3
Schroedel, Edward C Mrs, 1953, N 15,88:1
Schroedel, Frederick H, 1951, Ag 22,23:5
Schroeder, Arthur, 1963, Je 16,84:4
Schroeder, August H, 1966, N 26,36:6
Schroeder, Carl, 1947, Ja 22,23:3
Schroeder, Carl A, 1965, Ag 5,29:4
Schroeder, Carl F, 1955, Jl 23,17:6
Schroeder, Carl R, 1958, Ap 26,19:3
Schroeder, Charles J Mrs, 1951, N 28,31:2
Schroeder, Conrad E Mrs, 1955, D 15,37:5
Schroeder, D Heinrich, 1948, Ja 11,56:2
Schroeder, Edgardo von, 1956, Ja 30,27:4
Schroeder, Edward, 1904, F 22,5:6
Schroeder, Elbrecht von, 1943, My 21,20:2
Schroeder, Elmer H, 1963, O 17,32:6
Schroeder, Ernest, 1941, My 27,23:5
Schroeder, Ernest P, 1960, S 29,35:1
Schroeder, F Aug, 1941, F 11,23:4
Schroeder, Fradk H, 1917, Ja 13,11:3
Schroeder, Francis D, 1952, D 30,19:6
Schroeder, Fred A, 1899, D 2,9:3
Schroeder, Frederick T, 1960, My 21,23:1
Schroeder, Frederick T Mrs, 1960, D 24,15:2
Schroeder, G Baker, 1955, Ja 19,16:3
Schroeder, G W Capt, 1914, Mr 4,11:5
Schroeder, George W, 1942, My 5,21:1
Schroeder, Gerhard, 1966, My 27,43:1
Schroeder, Gillat, 1914, D 12,15:4
Schroeder, Gilliat D, 1942, O 5,19:4
Schroeder, Gilliat Mrs, 1925, O 13,23:4
Schroeder, Harry C Mrs, 1955, S 10,17:5
Schroeder, Harry Jr, 1959, F 23,23:2
Schroeder, Henry, 1947, D 30,24:2; 1952, D 23,23:4
Schroeder, Henry A, 1943, Je 5,15:4
Schroeder, Henry F, 1959, Ja 24,19:2
Schroeder, Henry J, 1942, My 9,13:3
Schroeder, Henry J L, 1941, F 14,17:5
Schroeder, Henry R, 1964, F 23,85:2
Schroeder, Henry W, 1914, Je 1,11:4
Schroeder, Irving M, 1959, F 15,86:8
Schroeder, J Langdorn, 1949, F 15,24:2
Schroeder, James L Mrs, 1956, D 5,39:5
Schroeder, John C, 1954, N 17,31:3
Schroeder, John F, 1953, O 20,29:3
Schroeder, John F Mrs, 1907, Je 19,7:5
Schroeder, John G, 1948, Ap 7,25:1
Schroeder, John H, 1951, F 9,19:7
Schroeder, John H W Sir, 1910, Ap 22,9:5
Schroeder, John Mrs, 1954, O 17,87:2
Schroeder, Joseph, 1942, S 2,23:2
Schroeder, Joseph A, 1948, Ja 29,23:5
Schroeder, Joseph Msgr, 1903, S 20,7:6
Schroeder, Karl T F, 1944, F 8,15:3

Schroeder, L von, 1933, Jl 24,15:1
Schroeder, Leila B Mrs, 1955, N 22,35:1
Schroeder, Leroy C, 1945, Ap 4,21:5
Schroeder, Leslie E, 1948, Je 5,15:6
Schroeder, Lloyd L, 1959, S 1,29:1
Schroeder, Louis C, 1938, F 26,15:5
Schroeder, Louis H, 1956, Je 13,37:4
Schroeder, Louise, 1957, Je 5,35:4
Schroeder, Mae C, 1947, D 10,31:1
Schroeder, Margaret L, 1946, Mr 28,25:5
Schroeder, Mary G, 1952, N 17,25:4
Schroeder, Ophir O Mrs, 1952, N 11,29:3
Schroeder, Paul L, 1966, O 28,31:2
Schroeder, Reginald, 1920, Ap 24,15:4
Schroeder, Robert, 1950, F 7,27:3
Schroeder, Robert A, 1952, My 30,15:2
Schroeder, Robert G, 1925, S 8,21:7
Schroeder, Robert H Mrs, 1952, Ja 7,19:4
Schroeder, Roy, 1949, S 2,17:3
Schroeder, Rudolf A, 1962, Ag 23,29:2
Schroeder, Rudolph W, 1952, D 30,19:2
Schroeder, Seaton, 1965, My 7,41:2
Schroeder, Seaton Rear-Adm, 1922, O 20,17:5; 1925, Jl 13,17:6
Schroeder, Theodore, 1950, Ja 30,17:2
Schroeder, Theodore A, 1953, F 12,27:4
Schroeder, Walter, 1961, O 21,21:1
Schroeder, Walter A, 1959, O 19,29:4
Schroeder, Werner W (will, D 13,20:1), 1960, D 3, 23:2
Schroeder, William, 1948, My 3,21:5; 1952, N 5,27:5
Schroeder, William A, 1941, N 22,19:5; 1953, My 21, 31:6; 1961, My 1,29:4
Schroeder, William E, 1950, Je 18,76:8
Schroeder, William H, 1940, My 25,17:4
Schroeder, William Mrs, 1959, Mr 10,36:1
Schroedern, Gustavo, 1950, Ag 2,25:3
Schroedinger, Erwin, 1961, Ja 6,27:1
Schroepfer, Robert, 1947, D 16,33:3
Schroer, Alice M, 1961, Mr 7,35:4
Schroer, Maria Mrs, 1940, Je 19,23:4
Schroeter, Carl W, 1956, Ag 23,27:3
Schroeter, Cornelius O, 1941, Ap 6,48:5
Schroeter, Frank B, 1963, Jl 28,64:5
Schroeter, Otto H, 1957, Ag 13,27:3
Schroeter, Victor F, 1961, Ag 25,25:5
Schroff, Charles T, 1941, S 24,23:4
Schroff, Joseph, 1967, N 15,47:1
Schroff, Karl G, 1949, N 25,31:3
Schroll, Ditlow, 1949, D 6,31:1
Schroll, Louise K, 1944, Mr 13,15:1
Schroller, Henry Harmon Mrs, 1903, D 26,7:7
Schropp, John K R, 1943, F 19,19:2
Schropp, Raymond J, 1949, Je 24,23:1
Schroppe, Charles G, 1948, Ja 13,25:4
Schror, Adolph, 1956, Ap 23,27:4
Schroth, Charles E, 1952, O 17,27:4
Schroth, Godfrey W, 1959, D 19,27:4
Schroth, Peter J, 1950, My 28,44:8
Schrowang, Caroline H Mrs, 1941, S 22,15:5
Schrowang, Henry H, 1950, N 8,29:5
Schroyer, Fred, 1938, Je 12,3:5
Schruble, Joseph H, 1943, Jl 24,13:4
Schruefer, Joseph G, 1947, O 16,27:4
Schrymser, W, 1910, Mr 28,9:3
Schryver, Edson B, 1959, N 13,29:2
Schryver, George O, 1953, Ja 9,21:4
Schryver, Harold G, 1944, Mr 28,19:6
Schryver, Harry E, 1940, Ap 25,23:5
Schuander, Max, 1953, Mr 26,31:5
Schuartz, Julius, 1909, N 20,11:1
Schubart, Henry A Mrs (F Kilbourne), 1961, S 8,31:4
Schubart, Louis Mrs, 1957, Je 27,25:2
Schubart, William H, 1953, O 8,29:6
Schube, Charles J, 1951, Mr 31,15:1
Schubel, Anton, 1965, Je 11,31:4
Schuberg, John A, 1953, D 16,35:2
Schuberg, Theodore C W, 1947, O 23,25:5
Schubert, Alwyn K, 1942, Ag 11,19:5
Schubert, Bernard E, 1940, Ap 5,21:3
Schubert, Carl von, 1947, Je 28,14:2
Schubert, Christian J, 1953, O 16,27:1
Schubert, Edmund J, 1944, Ap 22,15:2
Schubert, Frank, 1942, F 5,21:4
Schubert, Frank J, 1937, Ja 29,19:2
Schubert, Frederick S, 1964, Ap 18,29:3
Schubert, Gus, 1953, F 27,21:2
Schubert, Hans von Gen, 1945, Ap 9,3:2
Schubert, J Paul Mrs, 1958, Je 17,29:4
Schubert, Quentin M, 1956, Ag 26,84:4
Schubert, Roy H, 1954, N 8,21:3
Schubert, Walter A Sr, 1963, O 27,88:4
Schubert, William C Mrs, 1963, Jl 15,29:2
Schucart, Herman, 1968, N 6,47:1
Schucatowitz, Mordecai, 1946, Ja 16,23:2
Schuch, Edward A, 1952, N 13,31:6
Schuch, Ernst von, 1914, My 11,11:5
Schuch, Fred, 1940, S 1,20:6
Schuchard, Carl B, 1943, Ja 4,15:3
Schuchardt, William H, 1958, Ap 18,23:2
Schuchat, Isidor, 1944, Ja 29,13:2
Schuchert, Charles (por), 1942, N 22,53:1
Schuchman, Robert M, 1966, Mr 14,31:3
Schuck, Arthur A, 1963, F 25,16:7
Schuck, Arthur F Mrs, 1954, Ag 31,21:3
Schuck, Augustus, 1942, Ag 23,42:2
Schuck, Donald J, 1966, Je 4,29:3
Schuck, Frank, 1952, Ja 26,13:4
Schuck, Frank W, 1951, F 17,15:2
Schuck, Franz, 1958, Ja 20,23:4
Schuck, George, 1966, Jl 6,42:5
Schuck, George W, 1943, Je 1,23:3
Schuck, Harry Mrs, 1945, O 4,23:5
Schuck, Henrik (por), 1947, O 5,68:7
Schuck, Maurice W, 1944, F 21,15:1
Schuck, Traugott, 1952, My 17,19:6
Schuckman, Ferdinand, 1907, Ja 21,9:1
Schudt, Charles, 1954, Ja 26,27:2
Schudt, William A, 1961, D 7,43:4
Schuecker, Edmund, 1911, N 10,11:4
Schuecking, W, 1935, Ag 27,19:3
Schueddekopf, 1920, Jl 8,11:3
Schueg, Enrique, 1950, Ag 12,13:6
Schuelein, Fritz Mrs, 1954, D 19,84:1
Schuelein, Hermann Mrs, 1950, Je 22,27:1
Schuelein, Julius, 1959, Ap 22,33:1
Schueler, Anthony L, 1956, D 15,25:4
Schueler, Augusta M Mrs (A Marschall), 1942, Jl 8, 23:4
Schueler, Charles T, 1937, S 7,21:5
Schueler, Else L, 1945, Ja 23,19:2
Schueler, Ernest, 1961, N 15,43:3
Schueler, Herbert Mrs, 1964, F 19,39:1
Schuelke, Eric, 1941, Ja 29,17:5
Schueller, Rudolph, 1949, Ag 3,23:2
Schuenemann, Alex P Jr, 1955, S 8,31:3
Schuengel, Heinz (por), 1939, Ap 11,24:2
Schuenzel, Reinhold (cor, S 16,29:3), 1954, S 14,27:3
Schuessler, Anton, 1955, N 12,21:8
Schuessler, Oswald, 1940, My 15,25:1
Schuessler, William Mrs, 1947, O 30,25:3
Schuette, Bernard G Rev, 1937, D 23,21:4
Schuette, E H Johann, 1940, Ap 2,25:5
Schuette, Louis, 1946, N 9,17:3
Schuette, Oswald F, 1953, O 9,27:4
Schuette, Paul, 1941, S 5,22:2
Schuette, Walter E, 1955, Ag 12,19:1
Schuette, William D Jr, 1908, Je 19,9:7
Schuette, William H, 1959, N 10,47:4
Schuette, William Jr, 1967, S 28,47:2
Schuettler, Herman F, 1918, Je 7,13:6
Schuetz, Frederick F, 1964, Jl 20,25:4
Schuetz, Harry W, 1951, Mr 3,13:5
Schuetz, Herman, 1943, Mr 3,24:2
Schuetz, Leonard, 1944, F 14,17:3
Schuetz, Ludwig H, 1941, Mr 24,17:2
Schuetze, Arthur, 1937, N 27,17:4
Schuetzendorf, Gustav, 1937, Ap 30,21:4
Schuff, William, 1959, F 15,85:5
Schug, John A, 1940, Je 16,38:7
Schugens, William, 1938, S 5,11:1
Schugt, Henry P, 1956, Ja 31,29:4
Schuh, Henry F, 1965, D 22,31:4
Schuhler, Albert A, 1956, Je 19,29:5
Schuhmann, George H, 1910, Ja 24,9:4
Schukin, Boris V, 1939, O 8,48:8
Schul, Charles, 1925, Ap 13,19:4
Schulbaum, Marcel Mrs, 1963, Je 12,43:4
Schulberg, Benjamin P, 1957, F 27,27:3
Schuld, George J, 1952, Mr 5,29:3
Schulder, Israel M, 1945, Je 24,22:2
Schulder, Joseph, 1964, My 23,23:4
Schulder, William, 1949, O 2,81:2
Schulder, William Mrs, 1961, N 26,88:2
Schuldt, Gus A, 1939, Mr 12,III,6:7
Schuldt, Walter S, 1950, D 5,31:4
Schule, John J Mrs, 1966, Je 26,73:3
Schulederberg, Carl G, 1938, Ap 10,II,6:2
Schulenberg, Friedrich von, 1939, My 20,15:2
Schuler, Adam F, 1943, Ag 27,17:2
Schuler, Andrew J, 1952, D 12,29:2
Schuler, Anthony J, 1944, Je 4,42:1
Schuler, Eric, 1937, Ag 8,II,7:3
Schuler, Frank, 1946, Ag 2,19:2
Schuler, Frank Mrs, 1951, Ja 17,27:2
Schuler, Gaspard, 1946, Ja 28,19:4
Schuler, George H, 1954, Jl 15,27:6
Schuler, George T, 1948, Ag 11,22:2
Schuler, Henry C, 1960, O 25,35:1
Schuler, John, 1951, My 15,31:4
Schuler, Loring Ashley, 1968, Je 6,47:4
Schuler, Louis W, 1946, Jl 9,21:4
Schuler, Malcolm W, 1938, Ap 25,15:5
Schuler, Oswald Mrs, 1949, F 3,23:3
Schuler, Otto, 1963, Ag 27,31:1
Schuler, Valentine, 1945, Ja 6,11:2
Schuler, William F, 1955, O 14,36:7
Schuler, William J, 1950, Ja 15,84:3
Schulgen, George F, 1955, F 18,22:1
Schulhafer, Herbert J, 1957, Ja 15,29:1
Schulhof, Andrew, 1960, F 9,31:2
Schulhof, William Mrs, 1961, D 14,43:1
Schulhofer, Samuel Mrs, 1938, O 25,23:4
Schulhoff, William K, 1943, Ag 4,17:5
Schuling, Gustav Mrs, 1924, Jl 21,11:5
Schulke, Robert W, 1962, S 19,39:3
Schulkind, Edward B Mrs, 1960, Jl 1,25:1
Schulkind, Paul D, 1942, My 15,19:2
Schuller, Erwin, 1967, Jl 9,61:1
Schullinger, James K, 1957, D 13,27:2
Schulmaier, Adlai T, 1952, Ap 17,29:5
Schulman, Abraham, 1942, Jl 20,13:2; 1964, Ja 4,23:1
Schulman, Abraham S, 1954, Ag 8,85:2
Schulman, Edmund, 1958, Ja 10,23:2
Schulman, Frank, 1964, Mr 6,31:1
Schulman, Frank Mrs, 1962, My 4,34:1
Schulman, Gabriel, 1950, O 13,29:5
Schulman, Harry, 1958, N 9,88:2
Schulman, Jack H, 1967, Je 21,47:4
Schulman, Jacob, 1950, Je 25,70:1
Schulman, Joseph, 1946, Je 8,21:2
Schulman, Leroy, 1955, Ja 28,19:1
Schulman, Louis D, 1948, O 10,76:4
Schulman, Mitchell, 1946, Jl 17,23:4
Schulman, Nathan, 1967, Ja 4,43:1
Schulman, Robert, 1917, Je 24,19:4; 1941, My 19,17:6
Schulman, Samuel (funl, N 7,29:4), 1955, N 4,29:1
Schulman, Samuel Mrs, 1945, Ag 23,23:2
Schulman, Sidney G, 1948, Je 17,25:3
Schulman, Victor, 1951, Ag 29,25:3
Schulman, William B Mrs, 1965, N 24,39:1
Schulman, Yetta Mrs, 1909, My 21,9:7
Schulmann, Henry Mrs, 1946, Mr 7,25:4
Schulmerich, Anthony, 1948, Ag 22,61:1
Schulte, Anthony, 1904, S 28,9:5
Schulte, Arthur D Mrs, 1954, Je 24,19:3
Schulte, Augustine J Rev, 1937, My 24,19:4
Schulte, David A (will, Ag 16,25:7), 1949, Jl 30,15:3
Schulte, Edmund, 1943, N 27,13:6
Schulte, George B Mrs, 1954, F 25,31:1
Schulte, George J, 1949, F 7,19:4
Schulte, Godfrey, 1939, Mr 5,49:2
Schulte, Henry, 1944, N 3,21:5
Schulte, Henry F, 1944, O 19,23:4
Schulte, Henry G, 1938, Je 28,19:4
Schulte, Herman A, 1947, F 4,25:2
Schulte, Joseph M, 1946, N 11,27:2
Schulte, Karl (por), 1941, Mr 12,22:2
Schulte, Theodore E, 1950, My 4,27:3
Schulte, Theodore E Mrs, 1959, N 21,23:6
Schulte, Theodore J, 1948, Ja 17,17:3
Schulten, Adolf, 1960, Mr 23,37:4
Schulten, J W, 1875, D 29,4:5
Schulten, Leo B, 1948, My 23,68:4
Schulter, Henry N, 1946, S 12,7:4
Schultes, John, 1940, Ap 18,23:1
Schultes, Leonard H, 1962, Jl 3,23:2
Schultes, Martin F, 1951, Mr 8,29:1
Schultheis, Adam H, 1961, Jl 11,31:5
Schultheis, Henry, 1948, N 30,27:4
Schultheis, Leo, 1940, N 29,21:3
Schultheiss, Carl M, 1961, D 9,27:5
Schultheiss, Emily M Mrs, 1967, My 18,47:1
Schultheiss, Gustav Mrs, 1960, N 4,33:1
Schulthess, Albert, 1947, My 31,26:5
Schulthess, Edmund, 1944, Ap 23,41:1
Schults, Charles A Sr Mrs, 1949, D 29,26:2
Schultz, Abraham, 1949, Ja 3,23:1; 1951, Ap 14,15:2
Schultz, Albert B, 1952, Ag 27,27:5
Schultz, Albert J, 1945, Mr 16,15:2
Schultz, Albert M Mrs, 1945, Ag 24,19:2
Schultz, Alexander H, 1867, My 2,5:4
Schultz, Andrew G, 1956, Jl 16,21:4
Schultz, Anthony, 1951, Je 11,25:5
Schultz, Arthur W, 1957, Ja 6,88:7
Schultz, Ben, 1967, F 8,31:2
Schultz, Benjamin, 1963, Ap 25,33:4
Schultz, Birl E, 1955, N 10,35:5
Schultz, Caroline, 1947, N 3,23:1
Schultz, Charles, 1948, F 24,25:3
Schultz, Charles A, 1947, Ag 19,23:4
Schultz, Charles E, 1924, S 25,23:5; 1954, S 22,29:2
Schultz, Charles F, 1961, Jl 2,33:2
Schultz, Charles H, 1950, Mr 16,32:2
Schultz, Charles L, 1940, F 19,17:3
Schultz, Charles P, 1957, O 6,85:2
Schultz, Charles Prof, 1920, Ag 14,7:5
Schultz, Charlotte S Mrs, 1953, S 10,25:3
Schultz, Clifford G, 1958, Mr 23,88:8
Schultz, David, 1963, Je 12,43:1
Schultz, Dorothy A, 1961, F 9,31:1
Schultz, Edward, 1964, N 9,33:2
Schultz, Edward J, 1950, O 11,33:6
Schultz, Edward S, 1942, N 19,25:5
Schultz, Edwin M Mrs, 1950, F 20,25:5
Schultz, Edwin W Mrs, 1953, Ja 5,21:3
Schultz, Emil, 1961, D 9,27:4
Schultz, Eugene G, 1960, N 5,23:6
Schultz, Frank, 1939, Ja 8,43:1
Schultz, George H, 1952, D 9,33:2
Schultz, George R, 1958, Mr 6,27:4
Schultz, Gerard A, 1939, F 19,39:3
Schultz, Germany A, 1951, Ap 15,93:1
Schultz, Gertrude, 1946, S 17,7:2
Schultz, Gertrude M Mrs, 1942, F 22,26:5
Schultz, Gustav J, 1949, Jl 8,19:5
Schultz, Hall Mrs, 1965, Ap 28,45:5
Schultz, Harold, 1966, Ja 12,21:1
Schultz, Harry O, 1952, D 31,15:1

Schultz, Henry F, 1944, Ag 22,17:6
Schultz, Henry J, 1941, F 10,17:3
Schultz, Herman, 1950, My 10,35:2
Schultz, Herman E, 1945, Mr 2,19:2
Schultz, Herman Mrs, 1960, D 18,84:1
Schultz, Hugo J Mrs, 1950, F 10,23:4
Schultz, Hyman Mrs, 1952, Mr 5,29:4
Schultz, Ignac, 1954, O 9,17:6
Schultz, Irwin William Judge, 1909, My 18,9:4
Schultz, J S, 1891, Mr 2,5:4
Schultz, J S Mrs (see also N 6), 1877, N 8,8:5
Schultz, Jack (Jno J), 1967, Ja 9,36:6
Schultz, Joe Sr, 1941, Ap 14,17:5
Schultz, John, 1923, Jl 26,15:4; 1939, Mr 19,III,7:3; 1963, Jl 30,29:2
Schultz, John C, 1956, Jl 13,19:2
Schultz, John D, 1954, Ap 20,29:4
Schultz, Joseph, 1903, Jl 6,5:3; 1913, Jl 29,7:7; 1949, Ap 6,29:3; 1965, D 14,43:4
Schultz, Joseph F, 1945, Jl 26,19:5
Schultz, Katherine Mrs, 1944, F 27,38:3
Schultz, Kristian, 1953, Ap 23,29:4
Schultz, Leo (por), 1944, Ag 20,34:3
Schultz, Lester J Dr, 1968, S 3,43:2
Schultz, Lockhart Mrs, 1960, F 1,27:3
Schultz, Louis, 1949, Ja 3,23:5
Schultz, Malina B Mrs, 1944, Ja 18,19:1
Schultz, Martin E, 1945, Jl 3,13:4
Schultz, Mary Mrs, 1954, Ag 31,14:4
Schultz, Mathilda J Mrs, 1947, Je 9,21:1
Schultz, Max, 1961, Mr 23,33:1
Schultz, Milly, 1943, D 12,68:6
Schultz, Moritz, 1904, D 18,7:6
Schultz, Mrs, 1865, O 3,5:3
Schultz, Oscar, 1937, Je 15,23:5
Schultz, Otto H, 1956, Je 19,29:4
Schultz, P Richard Mrs, 1937, Mr 30,23:1
Schultz, Paul W, 1944, N 28,23:2
Schultz, Raymond, 1948, Jl 3,15:4
Schultz, Raymond A, 1942, N 10,27:5
Schultz, Robert S Jr, 1960, N 9,35:4
Schultz, Schuyler C, 1944, Ja 16,43:2
Schultz, Theodore A, 1949, N 15,25:3
Schultz, Thomas H, 1937, D 14,25:3
Schultz, Thomas Mrs, 1950, S 25,12:3
Schultz, Thomas S, 1961, Mr 4,23:5
Schultz, Walter H, 1961, F 3,25:3
Schultz, William, 1904, Jl 15,7:6
Schultz, William F Jr, 1950, F 3,23:4
Schultz, William F Sr, 1943, D 16,28:3
Schultz, William H, 1955, Jl 26,25:4
Schultz, William J, 1949, F 25,23:4
Schultz, William L, 1950, N 14,31:4
Schultz, William L Mrs, 1965, O 15,45:5
Schultz, William Mrs, 1967, My 23,47:3
Schultz, William R Mrs, 1943, My 16,42:4
Schultz, William W, 1948, Ja 9,21:2
Schultz, Willy, 1907, F 12,9:2
Schultz, Wolfgang Mrs, 1948, D 6,25:5
Schultz-Shultzenstein, Dr, 1871, Ap 12,1:2
Schultzberg, Anselm, 1945, F 28,23:3
Schultze, Al, 1947, Ag 12,23:5
Schultze, Carl E, 1939, Ja 19,42:1
Schultze, Edward Mrs, 1916, Je 6,13:6
Schultze, Ernest F, 1946, S 1,35:1
Schultze, George A, 1962, F 6,35:1
Schultze, Howard C, 1965, Ag 31,33:4
Schultze, John S Gen, 1912, Ap 9,11:4
Schultze, Leonard, 1951, Ag 26,76:3
Schultze, Leonard Mrs, 1954, N 30,29:5
Schultze, Louis F, 1938, Ap 1,23:5
Schultze, Louis W Dr, 1922, Mr 25,11:3
Schultze, O H, 1934, Jl 5,18:2
Schultze, Walter F, 1965, Je 11,31:4
Schultze, William A R, 1954, Mr 31,27:2
Schulum, Joseph, 1906, F 5,9:6
Schulum, Lafayette, 1906, O 17,9:4
Schulum, Raphael, 1937, N 20,17:2
Schulz, Albert, 1954, Mr 27,17:1
Schulz, Edward H, 1951, Mr 4,94:1
Schulz, Frank F, 1941, Ap 8,25:4
Schulz, G M S, 1930, Ap 8,26:1
Schulz, George S, 1961, S 6,37:2
Schulz, George W, 1940, S 21,19:5
Schulz, Gustav F, 1951, N 6,29:3
Schulz, Henry T, 1948, S 28,27:5
Schulz, Louis, 1951, My 21,27:3
Schulz, Ludwig J, 1955, D 28,23:4
Schulz, Paul, 1959, Je 16,35:5
Schulz, Sigmund J, 1958, Ap 22,33:1
Schulz, William F Father, 1953, F 15,92:2
Schulze, Adolf, 1944, Ja 1,13:2; 1957, S 25,29:1
Schulze, Andrew L, 1950, Ja 18,31:4
Schulze, August F, 1954, O 12,27:3
Schulze, E C L Rev Dr, 1918, O 11,11:3
Schulze, Fred J, 1950, Ap 17,23:5
Schulze, Frederick H, 1958, Ja 3,23:3
Schulze, G Albert, 1958, Jl 25,19:4
Schulze, John Ducasse, 1943, Je 19,13:1
Schulze, Paul Sr, 1948, Ag 15,60:6
Schulze, Theodore, 1962, D 24,8:5
Schulze, Theodore A Mrs, 1949, S 20,29:1
Schulze-Gaewernitz, Gerhardt von, 1943, Jl 23,17:1

Schumacher, Albert, 1955, Ap 2,17:1
Schumacher, Arthur W, 1920, N 28,22:4
Schumacher, Charles, 1904, N 11,9:2
Schumacher, Charles H, 1952, N 13,31:4
Schumacher, Charles Mrs, 1950, Ag 14,17:4
Schumacher, Conrad R, 1939, D 21,23:2
Schumacher, Curtis Mrs, 1968, Jl 24,50:4
Schumacher, Edward F Sr, 1958, O 8,35:1
Schumacher, Edward T, 1952, Mr 24,25:3
Schumacher, Edwin F Mrs (M Hurter), 1956, F 10, 21:2
Schumacher, Frederick W, 1957, Je 5,35:2
Schumacher, Gustav, 1944, Ja 19,19:2
Schumacher, Henry, 1949, Ag 23,23:1
Schumacher, Henry C, 1915, Ap 21,13:6
Schumacher, Herman H, 1958, My 25,86:5
Schumacher, Herman Mrs, 1950, Mr 16,31:4
Schumacher, Hiram S, 1948, Jl 15,23:5
Schumacher, J Harry, 1946, Je 24,31:4
Schumacher, John, 1938, Jl 24,II,9:2
Schumacher, John F, 1965, Ja 6,39:1
Schumacher, John H, 1941, Ap 2,23:3
Schumacher, John J, 1944, S 20,23:3
Schumacher, Joseph H, 1946, Je 6,21:5
Schumacher, Kurt, 1952, Ag 21,1:4
Schumacher, Lock, 1952, Ag 14,23:5
Schumacher, Matthew A, 1966, Je 15,47:4
Schumacher, Oscar J, 1940, Je 13,23:6
Schumacher, Richard, 1955, Jl 8,23:3
Schumacher, Roland H, 1964, Mr 26,35:4
Schumacher, Rudolph, 1944, Mr 21,19:1
Schumacher, Thomas M, 1948, F 27,21:4
Schumacher, Walter A, 1955, Ag 11,21:2
Schumacher, Wilbert A, 1942, S 19,15:2
Schumacher, William, 1953, Ja 14,31:2
Schumaher, John W, 1942, F 6,19:4
Schumaker, Edward E, 1949, N 5,13:4
Schumaker, Henry Mrs, 1943, S 18,17:6
Schumaker, L J, 1948, Ja 4,52:1
Schuman, Arthur, 1963, Jl 25,25:3
Schuman, Edward A, 1952, Ja 16,25:1
Schuman, Harry, 1941, Ag 18,13:1; 1953, F 7,15:4
Schuman, Henry, 1962, S 20,33:1
Schuman, Herman, 1950, F 25,17:3
Schuman, Isidore, 1959, N 2,31:4
Schuman, Jacob P, 1941, Ag 15,17:5
Schuman, Michael, 1959, Ap 3,27:2; 1965, F 15,27:4
Schuman, Robert (funl, S 8,86:6), 1963, S 5,1:8
Schuman, Samuel, 1950, D 1,25:4
Schumanis, Vilis, 1948, O 29,25:3
Schumann, Adam, 1946, My 4,15:2
Schumann, Arthur R Mrs, 1956, D 20,29:1
Schumann, Carl G A, 1944, Mr 21,19:2
Schumann, Carl Prof, 1904, Mr 26,9:7
Schumann, Charles, 1950, My 7,108:2
Schumann, Clara, 1896, My 22,5:5
Schumann, Donald F, 1942, Ag 2,38:7
Schumann, Edward C, 1957, Ap 13,19:5
Schumann, Elisabeth, 1952, Ap 24,31:1
Schumann, Frank J, 1939, F 4,15:6
Schumann, George H, 1912, O 23,13:6
Schumann, Giles V B, 1949, S 28,27:3
Schumann, Gustav, 1923, F 16,13:5
Schumann, Henrietta A, 1949, S 20,29:4
Schumann, Hugo, 1913, Je 13,9:4
Schumann, Ilya M, 1952, Ap 11,23:2
Schumann, John, 1952, Ag 24,88:2
Schumann, John H, 1914, Ja 1,15:4
Schumann, John J Jr, 1964, Ag 13,29:3
Schumann, John J Mrs, 1958, Ja 17,25:1
Schumann, Max H, 1959, Ja 13,47:3
Schumann, Meta, 1937, O 4,21:5
Schumann, Oscar, 1951, S 20,31:5
Schumann, Theodore E, 1960, Ag 4,25:6
Schumann, Theodore K, 1950, My 24,29:4
Schumann, Walter, 1958, Ag 22,21:4
Schumann, William H, 1958, Jl 27,61:2
Schumann-Heink, E, 1936, N 18,1:2
Schumann-Heink, Ferdinand C, 1958, S 17,32:6
Schumann-Heink, Hans, 1916, Ja 6,13:5
Schumann-Heink, Henry, 1951, Mr 30,24:3
Schumate, Frederick O, 1950, Ag 10,25:5
Schumb, Karl F, 1958, Ap 22,33:1
Schumer, Henry, 1959, S 23,35:2
Schumer, Julius, 1955, D 19,27:6
Schumer, Karl J, 1967, My 25,47:3
Schumm, Fred H, 1947, D 23,24:3
Schumm, George, 1941, S 15,17:4
Schumpelt, Karl, 1966, Je 9,47:5
Schumpeter, Joseph A, 1950, Ja 9,25:1
Schumpeter, Joseph A Mrs, 1953, Jl 19,57:2
Schunk, Herman J, 1952, Ja 25,21:4
Schunk, Joseph, 1958, Je 26,27:5
Schupler, Louis Mrs, 1955, My 5,33:4
Schupp, Ernest, 1950, O 7,17:1
Schupp, Herman A, 1940, My 19,42:3
Schupp, Philmina Mrs, 1916, O 10,11:5
Schuppe, Henry G, 1950, D 27,28:3
Schupper, Meyer, 1954, N 11,33:7
Schupper, Rayle, 1963, Ap 9,32:1
Schur, Arthur L, 1951, O 6,19:5
Schur, Robert P, 1954, S 18,7:6
Schur, Robert P Jr, 1945, Mr 28,23:3

Schurch, Jack, 1965, Ap 7,43:3
Schurff, Hans, 1939, Mr 29,23:1
Schuricht, Carl, 1967, Ja 8,88:6
Schurig, Charles, 1883, Je 10,7:3
Schurig, Friedrich W, 1967, Je 22,39:2
Schurig, Hugo, 1946, F 23,13:2
Schurman, Albert Jeremiah Dr, 1903, Jl 30,7:6
Schurman, Emil W, 1960, Mr 14,29:3
Schurman, Ferdinand, 1952, Ap 4,33:5
Schurman, Ferdinand Mrs, 1959, My 7,33:5
Schurman, George W Mrs, 1955, Ap 16,19:5
Schurman, Jacob G (por), 1942, Ag 13,19:1
Schurman, Jacob G, 1961, S 22,33:1
Schurman, James A, 1942, Jl 21,19:2
Schurman, John H, 1960, Ap 15,7:2
Schurmann, F Aug, 1949, Je 3,25:1
Schurmann, Howard, 1953, O 15,33:3
Schurr, Burlingham, 1951, Jl 14,13:3
Schurr, Joseph, 1942, Mr 28,17:2
Schurtz, Perry Dr, 1924, N 18,25:3
Schurz, Agatha, 1915, Jl 19,9:4
Schurz, Carl (funl plans, My 17,9:6; funl, My 18,9:1), 1906, My 15,9:1
Schurz, Carl L, 1924, Je 16,15:4
Schurz, Carl Lincoln, 1924, My 22,17:5
Schurz, Carl Mrs (see also Mr 17), 1876, Mr 19,12:2
Schurz, William L, 1962, Jl 27,25:4
Schurz, William Mrs, 1963, N 21,39:3
Schuschnigg, Arthur, 1938, O 22,8:5
Schuschnigg, Kurt von Mrs, 1959, S 19,23:6
Schussheim, Solomon Dr, 1968, My 26,84:7
Schussler, Hugh Dr, 1916, Ap 17,11:4
Schustek, George, 1941, Ap 26,15:2
Schuster, A Paul, 1954, D 31,13:5
Schuster, Addison B, 1953, O 11,88:6
Schuster, Barnet, 1946, My 22,21:4
Schuster, Barnet Mrs, 1945, Ja 16,20:2
Schuster, Charles A, 1945, Mr 9,19:3
Schuster, Christian F, 1957, Je 27,25:4
Schuster, Clement Mrs, 1950, Jl 7,19:3
Schuster, Edward, 1954, N 15,27:6
Schuster, Edwin, 1967, Mr 21,46:2
Schuster, Ellwood D, 1952, My 2,25:1
Schuster, Emile G, 1949, D 25,26:5
Schuster, Ernest J, 1924, D 11,23:4
Schuster, F, 1936, My 15,28:2
Schuster, Frank, 1949, Ap 7,29:3
Schuster, Frederick W, 1954, My 30,44:2
Schuster, George C, 1940, O 23,23:5
Schuster, George D, 1957, O 9,35:3
Schuster, Ildefonso Cardinal, 1954, Ag 31,21:4
Schuster, Ira, 1946, O 11,23:4
Schuster, Joseph, 1959, Je 11,33:5
Schuster, Leo, 1952, Je 27,23:4
Schuster, Leonard B, 1945, O 23,17:3
Schuster, Lord (cor, Jl 3,25:1), 1956, Je 30,17:3
Schuster, Martin V B, 1940, Mr 17,48:7
Schuster, Max, 1966, Ap 14,35:7
Schuster, Michael, 1914, Ag 20,11:4
Schuster, Michael R, 1968, F 17,26:1
Schuster, Paul (more details, Je 7,21:2; mem ser, Je 8,47:3), 1967, Je 6,16:6
Schuster, Ralph A, 1953, Ja 31,15:1
Schuster, Richard, 1950, Ap 28,21:4
Schuster, Theodore G, 1947, Jl 11,15:2
Schuster, William, 1951, O 9,29:5
Schutt, Arthur, 1965, F 2,33:4
Schutt, Edwin H Mrs, 1943, N 30,27:5
Schutt, Erle M, 1950, Jl 27,25:3
Schutt, Harold S, 1963, Ag 6,31:5
Schutt, Louis P Mrs, 1943, N 16,23:3
Schutt, Sadie E, 1952, Jl 22,25:5
Schutt, Warren E, 1955, F 10,31:5
Schutte, Louis H, 1957, Ap 19,21:5
Schutte, Stephen R Jr, 1948, N 4,29:3
Schutte, William, 1947, Ja 23,23:5
Schutz, Alfred, 1959, My 23,25:5
Schutz, August Mrs, 1922, Jl 10,13:5
Schutz, Bernard, 1924, F 8,19:5
Schutz, C Daniel, 1963, Ag 19,25:5
Schutz, Ervin A, 1966, D 17,33:4
Schutz, John G, 1945, S 20,23:4
Schutz, John P, 1945, Je 28,19:6
Schutz, Maver, 1884, Jl 20,2:2
Schutz, Milton W, 1957, Mr 19,37:2
Schutz, Peter A, 1952, S 20,15:1
Schutz, Philip W, 1947, Mr 8,13:2
Schutze, Martin, 1950, Jl 21,19:1
Schutzendorf, Charles W, 1939, S 16,17:3
Schutzendorf, Guion L, 1944, Ap 11,19:2
Schutzer, Jacob, 1952, Jl 30,23:1
Schutzman, Julius, 1962, Jl 30,23:2
Schutzman, Leo, 1962, Mr 18,86:8
Schutzman, Louis, 1952, Ap 23,29:5
Schutzman, William, 1966, D 8,47:3
Schuyler, Charles E Mrs, 1949, D 3,15:2
Schuyler, Daniel J, 1909, Ap 2,9:6
Schuyler, E, 1890, Jl 19,5:3
Schuyler, Edythe B, 1958, S 12,25:3
Schuyler, Elmer L, 1946, Mr 25,25:4
Schuyler, Fred J (por), 1942, Ap 14,21:3
Schuyler, G L, 1890, Ag 1,1:5
Schuyler, Georgina, 1923, D 26,15:5

Schuyler, Gertrude, 1924, D 20,15:5
Schuyler, Gertrude L, 1948, Ap 24,15:2
Schuyler, H, 1933, Ja 24,19:5
Schuyler, Henry C, 1962, S 1,19:2
Schuyler, Herman P Capt, 1909, Ag 15,7:3
Schuyler, James Everett, 1925, Je 23,19:4
Schuyler, L L, 1926, O 11,21:4
Schuyler, L S Rev, 1878, S 29,7:4
Schuyler, Livingston R Mrs, 1952, D 9,33:1
Schuyler, Marion R, 1961, Je 7,19:5
Schuyler, Montgomery, 1955, N 2,35:5
Schuyler, Montgomery Mrs, 1914, Jl 8,9:3
Schuyler, Montgomery Roosevelt, 1924, Ja 2,17:3
Schuyler, Oakley, 1919, Ap 22,17:2
Schuyler, Peter V R Jr, 1965, Je 30,37:3
Schuyler, Phil, 1942, Mr 18,23:4
Schuyler, Philip Gen (funl, D 2,4:1), 1906, N 30,1:7
Schuyler, Philip L, 1962, Ja 7,89:1
Schuyler, Philip Mrs, 1915, O 26,11:6
Schuyler, Philip Van R, 1958, Ag 21,25:4
Schuyler, Philippa D (funi, My 19,39:2), 1967, My 10,1:5
Schuyler, Robert L, 1966, Ag 16,39:2
Schuyler, Robert L Mrs, 1957, Ag 23,19:2
Schuyler, Rose, 1924, Ag 6,13:3
Schuyler, Sarah E, 1958, Mr 7,23:3
Schuyler, Theophilus, 1938, F 6,II,9:1
Schuyler, Van Rensselaer, 1946, Je 16,40:3
Schuyler, W G, 1927, F 1,27:3
Schuyler, William, 1914, Jl 9,7:4
Schuyler, William B, 1956, F 5,87:1
Schuyler, William M, 1950, Ap 24,25:5
Schuyler, Willis Middleton, 1922, D 30,13:6
Schuyler, Wilton S, 1949, F 4,23:3
Schuylke, Julius A Dr, 1903, Ag 8,5:4
Schvervisky, Alex, 1919, Ag 16,7:5
Schwaab, Walter W, 1937, Je 1,23:4
Schwab, Abraham, 1920, Mr 17,11:3
Schwab, Adolph E, 1937, O 27,31:4
Schwab, Alfred, 1947, Jl 14,21:5
Schwab, Anton L, 1941, Mr 29,15:1
Schwab, Anton L Mrs, 1951, N 26,25:5
Schwab, Armand, 1961, F 18,19:2
Schwab, Carl A, 1937, My 3,19:3
Schwab, Charles, 1947, D 21,52:4
Schwab, Charles A, 1950, N 4,17:4
Schwab, Charles H, 1919, Ja 20,15:5
Schwab, Charles M, 1939, S 19,1:2; 1957, My 13,31:2
Schwab, Charles M Mrs, 1908, Je 29,7:6; 1939, Ja 13, 19:3
Schwab, Charles S, 1947, O 13,23:4
Schwab, Daniel, 1949, D 24,16:2
Schwab, David E, 1965, Ap 3,29:5
Schwab, Edward C, 1955, Ap 2,17:6
Schwab, Emily, 1950, Mr 9,29:3
Schwab, Frank, 1949, Ag 6,17:7; 1967, F 16,44:3
Schwab, Frank J (Dutch), 1965, D 14,43:3
Schwab, Frank X, 1946, Ap 24,25:3
Schwab, Frank X Mrs, 1943, Ap 17,17:4
Schwab, Gabriel, 1909, Jl 15,7:4
Schwab, Gustav, 1945, O 11,23:2
Schwab, Gustav H Mrs, 1911, Mr 10,9:4
Schwab, Gustave H (funl, N 15,13:4), 1912, N 13, 15:3
Schwab, Irving, 1943, Ap 18,48:6
Schwab, John A, 1924, My 14,19:5; 1962, Je 18,25:5
Schwab, John C Mrs, 1922, Ag 13,28:4
Schwab, John Christopher, 1916, Ja 13,11:4
Schwab, John J Sr, 1940, N 1,25:5
Schwab, Joseph E, 1922, F 18,13:3
Schwab, Joseph E Mrs, 1922, Ag 29,15:6
Schwab, Joseph F, 1945, Jl 14,11:5
Schwab, Joseph S, 1939, Ap 18,23:5
Schwab, Kate de V Mrs, 1950, Jl 18,29:4
Schwab, Laurence, 1951, My 30,21:3
Schwab, Laurence Henry Rev, 1911, My 30,11:5
Schwab, Lee W Mrs, 1944, S 6,19:5
Schwab, Lewis M, 1942, My 2,13:6
Schwab, Lucie C Mrs, 1940, Mr 4,15:4
Schwab, Martin C, 1947, Ja 4,15:1
Schwab, Norman Von P (cor on role in ch work, Jl 2,29:3), 1965, Je 28,29:2
Schwab, P Mrs, 1936, Mr 31,21:1
Schwab, Robert W, 1945, F 6,19:1
Schwab, Samuel S (por), 1949, N 23,29:3
Schwab, Sidney I, 1947, N 13,27:6
Schwab, Sidney I Mrs, 1947, F 6,23:5
Schwab, Simon, 1925, O 16,21:5
Schwab, W Waters, 1965, Ap 7,43:3
Schwab, W Waters Mrs, 1953, Ja 10,17:6
Schwab, Wilfred, 1954, D 16,37:5
Schwab, William A, 1949, Je 18,13:2
Schwab, William H, 1951, My 1,29:4
Schwab, William K, 1956, Ja 7,17:5
Schwaba, Peter H, 1957, Ap 16,33:1
Schwabacher, Albert E, 1963, N 16,27:1
Schwabacher, Leo H, 1946, Mr 16,13:5
Schwabacher, Wolfgang S, 1951, Ag 30,23:1
Schwabe, George, 1952, Ap 3,35:4
Schwabe, Henry August, 1916, F 10,11:4
Schwabe, Oscar A, 1948, My 11,26:3
Schwabe, Oscar A Mrs, 1937, My 5,25:3
Schwabe, William C, 1948, Ap 17,15:2
Schwachheim, Helen, 1961, F 20,27:4
Schwacke, John H, 1942, F 22,26:3
Schwaeber, Martin, 1964, O 18,89:2
Schwaeber, William Mrs, 1948, S 2,24:2
Schwager, Charles H, 1945, S 16,44:2
Schwager, Mortimer, 1965, My 5,47:4
Schwager, Phil, 1951, N 20,31:1
Schwager, Solomon, 1948, D 1,29:2
Schwagerl, Walburgher Mrs, 1909, Mr 2,9:7
Schwagerman, Anthony F, 1942, N 5,25:5
Schwalb, Charles Mrs, 1961, Jl 16,68:4
Schwalb, Emanuel Mrs, 1951, My 3,29:4
Schwalb, Fincus, 1911, O 4,13:5
Schwalb, Fincus Mrs, 1911, O 4,13:5
Schwalb, Otto, 1942, Ag 19,19:4
Schwalbach, Eduardo, 1946, D 9,25:3
Schwalbach, John B, 1937, Mr 6,17:1
Schwalbach, John H, 1957, My 28,33:1
Schwalbe, Jacob Mrs, 1967, S 9,31:2
Schwalje, Walter J, 1955, D 16,29:2
Schwam, John, 1957, S 16,31:4
Schwamb, Herbert H, 1960, D 9,31:4
Schwamm, Harvey L, 1958, Ag 16,1:8
Schwamm, Henry, 1943, Jl 23,17:3
Schwamm, Saul Mrs, 1948, Je 5,15:4
Schwan, Paul F Rev, 1937, Mr 21,II,8:1
Schwanda, Benedict Jr, 1948, Mr 23,25:3
Schwandt, William F, 1950, Ag 19,13:3
Schwanebach, Charles von, 1908, S 29,9:5
Schwaner, Aug P, 1948, S 21,27:4
Schwanewede, Henry, 1948, O 30,15:1
Schwanhausser, Frederick, 1943, S 8,23:6
Schwank, James L, 1946, O 25,23:2
Schwank, James O, 1938, Je 6,17:5
Schwann, Theodore, 1882, Ja 21,2:6
Schwannecke, Coroner, 1912, My 4,13:6
Schwar, Oscar, 1946, N 28,27:2
Schwarcz, Leonard B, 1950, Jl 1,15:2
Schwark, Joseph J, 1962, My 19,27:5
Schwark, Julius, 1939, N 20,19:4
Schwaroch, Louis, 1940, My 14,23:3
Schwarting, John H (por), 1938, Ap 26,21:1
Schwarting, William V, 1967, Mr 28,39:5
Schwartje, Herman J, 1947, D 28,40:1
Schwartman, Moses, 1946, Ap 6,17:4
Schwarts, John S, 1939, N 15,23:2
Schwartz, A Charles, 1967, N 16,47:1
Schwartz, Aaron Mrs, 1955, Ja 8,13:5
Schwartz, Abe, 1963, My 9,37:4
Schwartz, Abe Mrs, 1950, Je 21,27:4
Schwartz, Abraham, 1956, My 6,87:2; 1959, O 28,37:2
Schwartz, Abraham H, 1938, S 10,17:6
Schwartz, Abraham N Rabbi, 1937, F 5,21:2
Schwartz, Abraham T, 1945, Ja 12,15:1
Schwartz, Albert, 1950, Jl 11,31:5; 1964, Je 16,39:4
Schwartz, Albert E, 1944, Je 9,15:3; 1958, F 16,85:3
Schwartz, Albert I, 1949, D 6,31:3
Schwartz, Albert V, 1959, Ja 6,33:3
Schwartz, Alex, 1958, D 31,5:2
Schwartz, Alex J, 1962, Jl 12,29:3
Schwartz, Alfred A, 1952, Ja 15,27:3
Schwartz, Allen M, 1940, O 2,23:6
Schwartz, Alois, 1945, Ap 25,23:3
Schwartz, Amelia Mrs, 1925, O 19,21:4
Schwartz, Andrew T, 1942, S 18,21:4
Schwartz, Arnold A, 1964, O 3,29:3
Schwartz, Arnold A Mrs, 1942, F 17,21:3
Schwartz, Arnold J, 1954, Jl 2,19:3
Schwartz, Arthur, 1959, Mr 13,26:8
Schwartz, Arthur D, 1955, Ag 15,15:2
Schwartz, Arthur Z, 1950, S 28,31:4
Schwartz, Augustus Mrs, 1953, N 10,31:2
Schwartz, Barney Mrs, 1941, My 16,23:4
Schwartz, Benjamin, 1964, Mr 27,28:1
Schwartz, Bernard M, 1967, Ja 14,31:5
Schwartz, Bertha, 1961, O 17,39:4
Schwartz, Bessie, 1955, Ja 9,87:4
Schwartz, Carleton, 1947, Ag 27,23:6
Schwartz, Cecil, 1951, Je 9,19:6
Schwartz, Charles, 1957, S 6,31:2; 1959, Je 11,33:3
Schwartz, Charles E, 1951, F 23,27:4
Schwartz, Charles W, 1957, O 31,31:5
Schwartz, Christian Mrs, 1943, Jl 16,17:2
Schwartz, Conrad, 1965, D 2,41:2
Schwartz, Craigie, 1961, Mr 31,53:2
Schwartz, David, 1944, N 22,19:1; 1950, Mr 22,27:4; 1961, N 5,89:1
Schwartz, David H, 1957, F 19,31:2
Schwartz, David Mrs, 1945, S 1,11:5
Schwartz, Delmore (funl plans, Jl 16,25:5), 1966, Jl 14,35:1
Schwartz, Earle Mrs, 1946, Ap 18,27:5
Schwartz, Edward, 1947, Ja 25,17:1
Schwartz, Edward E, 1950, Ag 31,26:2
Schwartz, Elmer H, 1943, F 22,17:4
Schwartz, Emanuel, 1967, O 2,47:1
Schwartz, Emanuel H Mrs, 1957, Je 25,29:2
Schwartz, Eugene B, 1961, Ja 8,86:3
Schwartz, Frank, 1946, Ag 12,21:5
Schwartz, Frank B, 1953, Ap 15,45:2
Schwartz, Frank J, 1957, Ap 24,33:4
Schwartz, Frank M, 1966, O 9,86:1
Schwartz, Frederick G, 1953, Jl 1,29:1
Schwartz, G William, 1950, N 14,31:1
Schwartz, George, 1962, Ja 21,88:4
Schwartz, George D, 1944, S 4,19:4
Schwartz, George J, 1949, N 23,29:5
Schwartz, George M, 1942, Ag 5,19:4
Schwartz, Gertrude Mrs, 1942, Ag 15,11:5
Schwartz, Hans J, 1956, F 16,29:5
Schwartz, Harry, 1950, N 7,27:6; 1953, D 15,39:4; 1954, Mr 13,15:2; 1960, D 31,17:3
Schwartz, Harry E Mrs, 1944, My 13,19:5
Schwartz, Harry F, 1959, Jl 18,15:4
Schwartz, Harry H, 1955, Ap 26,29:6
Schwartz, Harvie E, 1948, My 18,23:2
Schwartz, Harwood M, 1945, S 13,23:6
Schwartz, Henry, 1946, Mr 7,25:3
Schwartz, Herbert A Sr, 1964, Mr 8,87:1
Schwartz, Herbert J, 1955, Ap 12,29:1
Schwartz, Herman, 1965, Ag 7,21:5
Schwartz, Herman N, 1953, F 6,19:3
Schwartz, Hyman S, 1964, Je 20,25:6
Schwartz, Ignatius N, 1955, N 12,19:2
Schwartz, Ira M, 1951, N 20,31:2
Schwartz, Irving, 1950, Mr 14,25:2
Schwartz, Isaac F, 1937, Mr 3,23:3
Schwartz, Isaie, 1952, Jl 22,25:3
Schwartz, Isidore, 1957, Jl 14,73:2
Schwartz, Jacob, 1953, Je 8,29:3; 1957, O 14,27:1; 1958, F 4,29:1
Schwartz, Jacob R, 1964, F 9,88:5
Schwartz, James, 1965, Mr 11,33:1
Schwartz, Jean, 1956, D 1,21:4
Schwartz, Jeannette Mrs, 1915, S 4,7:4
Schwartz, Jesse, 1963, Ag 21,33:4
Schwartz, Jesse D, 1950, Ap 9,87:1
Schwartz, John, 1952, Mr 13,29:1
Schwartz, John J, 1953, My 8,25:2
Schwartz, John P, 1940, F 24,13:1
Schwartz, John R, 1967, S 26,47:3
Schwartz, John W, 1952, My 1,29:4
Schwartz, Joseph, 1937, Mr 10,23:4; 1941, F 6,21: 1946, O 28,27:5; 1948, Ag 11,22:2; 1960, Ag 21, 1961, Ja 8,86:6
Schwartz, Joseph A, 1962, Ag 16,27:1
Schwartz, Joseph H, 1953, Ap 2,28:3
Schwartz, Joseph L, 1948, My 1,15:5; 1952, Ja 4,2
Schwartz, Joseph M, 1944, Je 29,23:4
Schwartz, Joseph P, 1958, Ag 9,13:6
Schwartz, Julien J, 1938, Ja 6,19:4
Schwartz, Julius, 1946, Jl 25,21:4; 1957, Je 19,35: 1964, S 9,43:4
Schwartz, Julius Mrs, 1946, My 18,19:5
Schwartz, Karl K, 1955, Jl 15,21:4
Schwartz, Karl Mrs, 1950, Ja 31,23:1
Schwartz, Kathryn H, 1945, Ap 18,23:2
Schwartz, Laszlo, 1966, S 17,29:5
Schwartz, Leo, 1951, O 3,36:3
Schwartz, Leo B, 1951, Je 11,25:5
Schwartz, Leo Mrs, 1958, O 15,39:4
Schwartz, Leo S (por), 1948, D 31,16:4
Schwartz, Lewis H, 1950, D 4,29:3
Schwartz, Lewis M, 1945, O 6,13:1
Schwartz, Louis, 1943, N 29,19:3; 1963, D 21,23: 1966, Jl 19,39:2; 1968, Je 22,33:5
Schwartz, Louis Dr, 1963, F 27,16:1
Schwartz, Louis G, 1951, My 10,31:1
Schwartz, Louis J, 1962, F 4,82:4; 1968, Ag 18,88
Schwartz, Louis S, 1955, Ja 27,23:2
Schwartz, Manfred Mrs, 1964, N 11,43:3
Schwartz, Manuel, 1958, N 19,37:1
Schwartz, Mary L, 1938, O 20,23:3
Schwartz, Maurice (funl plans, My 13,31:6), 196 My 11,39:2
Schwartz, Maurice A, 1957, Je 2,87:1
Schwartz, Maurice I, 1967, D 10,86:8
Schwartz, Maurice R, 1950, F 21,25:3
Schwartz, Max, 1918, Ag 10,7:5
Schwartz, Max (por), 1939, Ap 5,25:1
Schwartz, Max, 1967, Je 3,31:4
Schwartz, Max L, 1957, F 16,17:4
Schwartz, Max Mrs, 1949, N 8,31:2
Schwartz, Milton, 1944, Je 7,19:2; 1967, My 23,4
Schwartz, Morton L, 1953, Ja 12,27:4
Schwartz, Moses, 1923, D 21,17:5
Schwartz, Nathan, 1965, Je 17,33:1; 1967, Je 7,47
Schwartz, Nathan T, 1959, Mr 9,29:4
Schwartz, Numan, 1953, Ap 19,90:4
Schwartz, O G, 1938, F 21,19:1
Schwartz, Paul, 1966, N 12,29:2
Schwartz, Paul E, 1950, N 19,93:1
Schwartz, Peter, 1957, N 24,87:1
Schwartz, Peter S, 1956, D 27,25:3
Schwartz, Phil L, 1960, D 21,31:5
Schwartz, Pincus, 1956, Jl 18,27:4
Schwartz, Pinkhos, 1963, D 16,33:3
Schwartz, Ralph H Jr, 1954, Je 25,21:2
Schwartz, Ray F Mrs (por), 1949, Jl 11,17:5
Schwartz, Robert Dr, 1968, Je 20,45:1
Schwartz, Robert L, 1952, My 13,30:2
Schwartz, Robert S, 1964, Ap 14,34:7
Schwartz, Rudolph J, 1953, Mr 24,42:3
Schwartz, Russian Adm, 1905, Ap 14,9:6
Schwartz, S Nicoll, 1950, D 13,35:1
Schwartz, Samuel, 1943, D 9,27:3; 1959, Ag 5,27

Schwartz, Samuel H, 1960, Ja 7,29:2; 1960, My 10, 37:4; 1966, Ja 24,35:5
Schwartz, Samuel L, 1954, F 9,27:4; 1964, S 23,47:4
Schwartz, Samuel L Mrs, 1962, Ja 7,88:4
Schwartz, Samuel M, 1952, My 13,30:2; 1953, Ap 23, 29:4
Schwartz, Samuel X, 1951, Ag 10,15:3
Schwartz, Selig, 1963, Ag 7,33:4
Schwartz, Simon I, 1956, Ap 25,35:3
Schwartz, Solomon, 1950, S 13,27:1
Schwartz, Walter, 1949, Ap 19,26:6
Schwartz, William, 1953, Ag 22,15:4; 1958, Ag 21,25:3
Schwartz, William B, 1949, S 10,17:1
Schwartz, William J, 1942, F 24,21:1
Schwartz, William S, 1960, F 12,27:2
Schwartz, William W Mrs, 1955, Ap 19,31:4
Schwartz, Yetta, 1925, My 31,5:1
Schwartzbard, Samuel, 1938, Mr 4,23:4
Schwartzenberg, Samuel, 1947, Ja 30,25:2
Schwartzer, Max, 1957, Ja 12,19:1
Schwartzer, Morris, 1956, Jl 3,25:5
Schwartzhaupt, Emil, 1950, Mr 31,31:3
Schwartzkopf, William, 1954, Ag 17,21:4
Schwartzman, Daniel B, 1959, S 26,23:5
Schwartzman, Gregory Mrs, 1961, Mr 18,23:5
Schwartzman, Joseph Mrs (Selma H), 1965, Mr 30, 47:1
Schwartzmann, John G, 1965, My 23,85:1
Schwartzstein, Samuel, 1952, O 24,23:1
Schwartzwalder, Michael Mrs, 1961, D 8,42:6
Schwarz, Adolph C, 1944, N 8,17:6
Schwarz, Alexis von, 1953, S 29,29:2
Schwarz, Arthur, 1939, Ap 17,17:5
Schwarz, Arthur D, 1966, My 23,41:1
Schwarz, Augustine, 1946, Ap 28,42:7
Schwarz, Charles A, 1946, Ja 7,19:2
Schwarz, Charles D, 1966, Je 25,31:5
Schwarz, Charles G, 1951, D 19,31:1
Schwarz, Ernst, 1957, N 2,21:4
Schwarz, Eugene, 1945, Ag 9,21:2
Schwarz, F X, 1947, D 15,2:4
Schwarz, Frank H, 1951, S 7,29:4
Schwarz, Fred Jr, 1951, Ja 7,78:5
Schwarz, George, 1962, Ag 4,19:3
Schwarz, Gottwald, 1959, F 27,52:2
Schwarz, H Stanley, 1955, My 18,31:5
Schwarz, Harry F, 1925, My 17,6:1
Schwarz, Harry L Mrs, 1960, Ja 4,29:5
Schwarz, Henry, 1903, O 13,9:7
Schwarz, Henry F Mrs, 1967, Ap 3,33:4
Schwarz, Herbert F, 1960, O 3,31:4
Schwarz, Herbert H, 1956, Jl 23,23:4
Schwarz, Herman, 1945, My 20,32:5
Schwarz, Hermann, 1952, Ja 14,19:4
Schwarz, Hugo I, 1952, S 12,21:3
Schwarz, Imre M Mrs, 1961, Je 23,29:1
Schwarz, Ira D, 1946, D 4,31:4
Schwarz, Ira D Mrs, 1961, My 7,86:5
Schwarz, J, 1926, N 11,25:3
Schwarz, Jacob L, 1937, Ap 9,21:3
Schwarz, Julius, 1950, Mr 6,21:2
Schwarz, Karl, 1956, O 19,27:1
Schwarz, Leo W, 1967, D 3,84:5
Schwarz, Louis, 1940, D 17,25:3
Schwarz, Mary Mrs, 1937, Ag 11,6:7
Schwarz, Max (por), 1940, F 23,15:1
Schwarz, Milton A, 1959, F 22,89:1
Schwarz, Moritz E, 1952, O 14,31:4
Schwarz, Otto H, 1950, Ag 21,19:6
Schwarz, Paul, 1951, Ag 28,24:2
Schwarz, Paul M, 1948, Jl 29,21:3
Schwarz, Percy I, 1952, O 31,25:2
Schwarz, Philipin Mrs, 1942, Mr 6,21:2
Schwarz, Richard T, 1957, O 19,21:2
Schwarz, Robert, 1948, Je 25,23:3
Schwarz, Rudolph J, 1952, S 7,86:3
Schwarz, Sigmund, 1938, D 3,19:6
Schwarz, Solomon M Mrs (V Alexandrova), 1966, O 3,47:5
Schwarz, Vera, 1964, D 5,31:4
Schwarz, Victor W, 1954, O 12,27:4
Schwarz, Walter M, 1960, F 13,19:2
Schwarz, William E, 1952, O 5,89:1
Schwarzbach, Carl H, 1948, N 10,30:3
Schwarzbach, William, 1950, F 14,26:5
Schwarzbart, Isaac, 1961, Ap 27,21:2
Schwarzchild, Fritz, 1967, Je 10,33:3
Schwarzchild, Leopold, 1950, O 2,23:3
Schwarze, C Theodore Mrs, 1941, Ja 1,23:5
Schwarze, Carl A, 1956, My 11,27:2
Schwarze, Carl T, 1956, Jl 1,56:3
Schwarze, Julius W, 1946, Je 12,27:4
Schwarze, Linus A, 1952, My 4,90:3
Schwarze, Reinhardt Mrs, 1944, Je 1,19:3
Schwarze, William N, 1948, Mr 16,28:2
Schwarzenbach, Alfred, 1940, N 19,23:5
Schwarzenbach, Ernest B, 1968, S 4,47:1
Schwarzenbach, George, 1939, Ap 24,17:4
Schwarzenbach, Walter H, 1948, O 21,27:4
Schwarzenberg, Louis H, 1951, S 29,17:6
Schwarzenberg, von Cardinal, 1885, Mr 28,3:4
Schwarzer, Paul F, 1951, Ja 17,27:3
Schwarzkopf, Albert B, 1945, Ja 28,38:1
Schwarzkopf, H Norman (funl plans, N 28,30:4), 1958, N 27,29:4
Schwarzkopf, Leopoldine Mrs, 1940, S 29,44:1
Schwarzler, Albert J, 1941, N 10,17:5
Schwarzman, Samuel, 1957, My 15,35:3
Schwarzmann, Adolph, 1904, F 5,3:3
Schwarzmann, Emil, 1966, Ag 17,36:6
Schwarzmann, Emil Mrs (Gertrude T), 1962, My 14, 29:2
Schwarzschild, Harry, 1951, Ap 29,89:2
Schwarzschild, Sol M, 1957, Ja 21,25:5
Schwarzschild, William H, 1952, Je 10,27:3
Schwarzstein, Eugene, 1954, F 24,25:2
Schwarzstein, Joseph Mrs, 1965, N 5,37:2
Schwarzwalder, Henry, 1915, My 11,15:4
Schwasta, William A, 1958, Mr 17,29:5
Schwatka, Frederick Lt, 1892, N 3,1:3
Schweb, Otto W, 1948, Ap 28,27:4
Schwebel, Isador, 1938, S 16,21:2
Schwebel, Robert, 1959, Ja 21,31:4
Schwebel, Rudolph W, 1960, D 7,44:6
Schwebemeyer, Henry, 1956, My 5,19:6
Schweber, Elijahu Mrs, 1966, Mr 3,33:4
Schwed, Emil H Mrs (will), 1948, Ag 5,23:7
Schwed, Fred Jr, 1966, My 11,47:4
Schwed, Isidore, 1948, S 9,27:4
Schwed, Laurence I, 1966, Jl 7,37:1
Schwed, Leo H, 1959, S 9,41:3
Schwed, Moses, 1944, N 20,21:4
Schwedel, John B, 1966, My 28,27:3
Schwedenberg, Theodore, 1952, Je 26,29:3
Schwedersky, Herve, 1959, S 22,35:4
Schwedersky, Oscar, 1940, O 26,15:1
Schwedtman, F Charles (will, F 29,25:2), 1952, F 3, 84:3
Schweers, Ambrose Mrs, 1946, N 7,31:4
Schweeters, Dr, 1903, N 15,9:2
Schweeters, Dr Mrs, 1903, N 15,9:2
Schwefel, Charles R, 1954, Jl 1,25:4
Schwefel, Charles W (funl, Ag 25,15:2), 1956, Ag 22, 29:1
Schwefler, Frederick A, 1949, Mr 11,25:2
Schwehr, Will L, 1951, N 7,29:5
Schweich, Albert, 1962, Ap 29,86:5
Schweickert, Peter, 1920, Mr 30,11:4
Schweig, George E, 1948, My 12,28:2
Schweigardt, Frederick W (por), 1948, S 22,32:2
Schweiger, Ludwig Mrs, 1947, Ja 23,23:5
Schweiger, Nathan, 1944, Je 28,23:1
Schweigert, William, 1939, O 25,23:5
Schweikert, Charles, 1959, Jl 4,15:2
Schweikert, William L, 1958, Ja 19,86:7
Schweinfest, George F, 1949, Je 10,27:2
Schweinfest, William J, 1943, Ap 16,22:2
Schweinfest, William Mrs, 1948, S 18,17:4
Schweinfurth, Georg, 1925, S 21,19:6
Schweingruber, Joseph, 1914, Ag 20,11:4
Schweinhaut, Frank A, 1944, Ag 10,17:6
Schweinitz, Emil A de Dr, 1904, F 16,9:6
Schweinitz, H L Gen, 1901, Je 25,7:7
Schweinler, Carl L, 1968, Ap 24,47:3
Schweinler, Charles Mrs, 1949, Ag 30,27:5
Schweis, Etta M, 1950, Mr 3,25:2
Schweisguth, William, 1941, Jl 26,15:3
Schweitzer, Albert (mem set, NYC, S 8,47,1; mem ser NYC, S 10,35:4), 1965, S 6,1:3
Schweitzer, Albert Mme, 1957, Je 2,86:2
Schweitzer, Arthur R, 1957, Je 15,17:6
Schweitzer, Charles W, 1957, My 19,88:2
Schweitzer, Daniel, 1953, N 24,29:1
Schweitzer, Dell A, 1950, Ag 7,19:6
Schweitzer, Freddie, 1950, N 18,15:3
Schweitzer, Frederick, 1952, Mr 21,23:2
Schweitzer, Harold C, 1967, Ap 1,32:6
Schweitzer, Harold C Jr, 1965, Ja 26,37:3
Schweitzer, Harry, 1959, S 8,43:2
Schweitzer, J A, 1941, Mr 13,21:2
Schweitzer, John P H, 1959, Mr 12,31:4
Schweitzer, Marguerite, 1959, Ap 11,21:6
Schweitzer, Nathan (por), 1949, My 9,25:5
Schweitzer, Nelson B Mrs, 1914, Ag 20,11:5
Schweitzer, Nicholas J, 1950, Je 22,27:1
Schweitzer, Otto H, 1952, O 27,27:3
Schweitzer, Peter J, 1922, N 28,21:4
Schweitzer, Peter J Mrs, 1938, Mr 21,16:1
Schweitzer, William H, 1945, F 24,11:3
Schweitzka, Walter, 1946, S 23,23:5
Schweizer, Carl L, 1955, Mr 11,25:5
Schweizer, Frederick Mrs, 1956, My 20,87:1
Schweizer, Gustave, 1957, Ap 21,89:1
Schweizer, J Otto, 1955, D 3,17:5
Schweizer, Robert Mrs, 1955, Jl 9,7:3
Schweizer, Roman G, 1961, Je 24,21:2
Schweizer, William Mrs, 1948, Mr 4,25:4
Schwellenbach, Edgar W, 1957, S 24,35:3
Schwellenbach, Lewis B, 1948, Je 11,1:2
Schwellenbach, Martha B Mrs, 1948, Jl 15,23:4
Schwemmer, Oscar E, 1942, O 28,23:4
Schwenck, Fred W, 1947, Mr 29,15:5
Schwendler, Richard H, 1946, Ag 13,27:6
Schwener, Clement J, 1962, S 11,33:2
Schwengel, Frank R Mrs, 1961, F 19,86:7
Schwenger, Gustav J, 1954, N 24,23:4
Schwengerdt, William E, 1956, Mr 4,88:3
Schweninger, Ernst Dr, 1924, Ja 15,19:4
Schwenk, Alfons, 1960, Ap 15,24:1
Schwenk, Henry Mrs, 1945, Ag 29,23:2
Schwenk, Leon M, 1940, Ag 30,19:4
Schwenk, Norris H, 1965, Ap 4,87:2
Schwenk, Walter W (por), 1945, Mr 13,23:3
Schwenker, Alfred, 1948, Jl 13,27:6
Schwenker, Carl F, 1941, F 16,40:2
Schwenker, Carl F Mrs, 1962, Ag 31,21:1
Schwenker, Harry R, 1942, O 10,15:4
Schwenter, Albert P, 1955, D 17,23:5
Schwenter, Nicholas, 1955, D 17,23:5
Schwentker, Francis S, 1954, N 9,27:2
Schwenzer, William, 1949, N 16,29:3
Schwep, C Frank, 1946, Ap 18,27:5
Schweppe, Charles H Mrs, 1937, Ap 21,23:6
Schweppe, Charles H Mrs (will), 1938, Je 14,14:2
Schweppe, Eugene P, 1949, My 29,36:4
Schweppe, Richard J, 1940, My 13,17:5
Schweppe, William H, 1961, Je 20,33:2
Schwer, John J, 1943, S 30,21:4
Schwerd, Frederick M Mrs, 1941, N 18,25:5
Schwerd, Friedrich, 1953, Ag 7,19:2
Schwerdt, Eugene, 1940, Ap 26,21:6
Schwerdtfeger, Otto M, 1960, F 20,23:4
Schwerer, Paul Mrs, 1966, Ja 25,41:2
Schwerin, Arthur, 1962, Ag 25,19:1
Schwerin, Clarence M, 1944, O 29,44:2
Schwerin, Clarence M Jr, 1956, Je 5,35:2
Schwerin, Count von, 1914, N 7,11:6
Schwerin, Ernst Mrs, 1966, Je 9,36:1
Schwerin, James P, 1942, O 31,15:2
Schwerin, Richard C, 1941, Ap 6,48:8
Schweriner, Herman, 1948, My 20,29:1
Schwersenski, Simon, 1915, Ag 26,9:5
Schwert, Pius L, 1941, Mr 12,22:3
Schwertner, Aug J (por), 1939, O 3,23:5
Schwertz, Alfred R, 1948, Ja 6,23:4
Schwerzmann, Leon Sr, 1949, N 30,27:3
Schwetje, George, 1950, Ja 8,77:1
Schwetje, Gustave J, 1952, My 19,17:1
Schwetje, John, 1941, Ag 14,17:2
Schweyer, Alberto L, 1942, Ag 13,19:2
Schwickert, Joseph, 1949, Ag 16,23:2
Schwidetzky, Oscar O R, 1963, O 11,37:1
Schwieger, Hans Mrs, 1944, Jl 7,15:3
Schwieker, Fred, 1948, Je 18,23:2
Schwill, Julius, 1938, Jl 10,31:3
Schwimbersky, Charles, 1938, S 1,23:2
Schwimmer, Rosika, 1948, Ag 4,21:1
Schwimmer, Samuel, 1945, S 12,25:5; 1959, Mr 4,31:3
Schwin, John B, 1942, Jl 23,19:3
Schwind, Donald, 1965, Ap 3,29:6
Schwind, Harold P, 1947, N 7,23:2
Schwind, Jacob, 1907, S 1,7:6
Schwind, Joseph L, 1948, My 22,15:5
Schwind, Thomas, 1946, Jl 16,23:5
Schwinden, Catherine (Sister Eliz Pierre), 1964, D 24,19:1
Schwindinger, Edward C, 1944, Mr 14,19:2
Schwindinger, George C, 1951, My 2,31:2
Schwing, Casper W Mrs, 1953, O 19,21:6
Schwing, Leopold, 1940, Jl 24,21:3
Schwingel, Vincent J, 1967, O 18,47:1
Schwinges, C, 1934, Ap 24,23:2
Schwinhart, Josiah B, 1953, S 29,29:4
Schwinn, Charles, 1946, Mr 29,23:4
Schwinn, John S, 1940, Jl 27,13:7
Schwinn, Karl C, 1938, My 2,17:6
Schwinn, Sidoine J, 1963, D 31,39:4
Schwitalla, Alphonse M, 1965, My 27,37:3
Schwitter, Louise, 1947, D 11,34:2
Schwitzer, Louis H, 1967, My 11,47:2
Schwob, Henri Mrs, 1944, S 23,13:6
Schwob, Jules, 1949, Je 3,25:3
Schwob, Louis A, 1949, Ag 20,11:2
Schwob, Simon, 1954, Ag 9,17:3
Schwoegler, Anthony W, 1955, Ag 30,27:4
Schwolsky, Louis, 1954, Ja 30,17:2
Schworer, Francis E, 1946, Jl 16,23:1
Schwortzer, Karl H, 1959, Mr 29,80:2
Schwotzer, Albert F, 1950, Ap 2,92:5
Schwyzer, Gustav, 1951, F 4,77:2
Schyberg, Birger, 1953, Je 5,5:4
Schylander, Axel R, 1957, My 17,26:2
Scialoja, Carlo, 1947, My 27,25:5
Scialoja, V, 1933, N 20,15:1
Sciaraffa, Ercole P, 1956, S 12,37:4
Sciaretta, Joseph J, 1941, O 18,19:2
Sciaretti, Alberto V, 1962, Ag 3,23:3
Sciarretti, Salvatore, 1948, N 22,21:4
Scidmore, George H, 1922, N 28,21:5
Scidmore, Wright, 1957, Ja 26,19:5
Sciepura, Benjamin E, 1951, Ap 20,29:4
Scileppi, Francis P Mrs, 1953, Je 17,27:5
Sciorsci, Edward F Dr, 1968, N 6,39:3
Sciorsci, Roger S, 1959, N 24,34:1
Sciortino, Frank, 1946, Ja 26,13:5
Sciple, Carl E, 1953, Ag 7,19:1
Scism, Don, 1954, Mr 3,21:8
Scism, Don Mrs, 1954, Mr 3,21:8
Sciuto, Frank Mrs, 1951, N 28,31:4

Sclafani, Anthony J, 1965, D 25,13:3
Sclater, William L Mrs, 1942, Ja 9,21:4
Scleininger, Charles A, 1947, D 7,76:2
Sclev, Simon I, 1951, Mr 12,25:1
Sclove, A Bernard, 1954, O 14,29:2
Scobell, Ernest C, 1940, D 12,27:4
Scobell, John, 1955, Mr 4,23:3
Scobey, Bob, 1963, Je 14,29:2
Scobey, Harry C, 1954, Mr 20,15:4
Scobey, Samuel S Mrs, 1955, Ja 22,11:1
Scobie, Alex G, 1949, Ag 16,23:4
Scobie, Florence Y Mrs, 1940, D 20,25:4
Scobie, John C, 1944, Ag 1,15:5
Scoble, Thomas D, 1946, My 7,21:3
Scoble, Thomas D Jr, 1957, Ap 13,19:1
Scoble, William H, 1920, My 27,11:3
Scoca, Salvatore, 1962, My 11,31:1
Scocca, Carmine, 1947, Ag 19,23:2
Scocozza, Anthony Mrs, 1959, D 6,86:4
Scoefield, George E, 1939, S 30,17:7
Scofield, Cahs Ansel, 1904, N 3,9:5
Scofield, Calvin E, 1953, F 21,13:4
Scofield, Charles E, 1947, My 19,21:3
Scofield, Charles H Sr, 1947, My 18,60:8
Scofield, Cyrus Ingerson Rev Dr, 1921, Jl 25,13:5
Scofield, Daniel R, 1954, S 15,33:2
Scofield, Edson M, 1939, D 30,15:4
Scofield, Edward, 1925, F 4,21:4
Scofield, Edward F, 1951, O 16,31:2
Scofield, Edward R Mrs, 1949, Jl 19,29:2
Scofield, Edwin L, 1918, Ja 15,13:2
Scofield, Ellsworth S, 1937, Mr 16,23:5
Scofield, Frank L, 1947, N 12,27:4
Scofield, Fred R, 1953, N 24,29:4
Scofield, Frederic C, 1943, N 18,23:2
Scofield, Frederick H, 1943, Ap 9,21:1
Scofield, George A, 1951, Je 22,25:2
Scofield, George E, 1950, Jl 4,17:3
Scofield, George S, 1941, Jl 9,21:5
Scofield, George Starr Jr, 1920, Ja 8,17:3
Scofield, Gilbert J, 1954, Je 4,23:2
Scofield, Glenni W, 1947, Ja 31,23:2
Scofield, Herbert L Sr, 1957, Jl 28,61:3
Scofield, Hiram Gen, 1907, Ja 1,9:5
Scofield, Howard, 1945, Ap 24,19:4
Scofield, Irving F, 1949, O 21,25:2
Scofield, Isaac, 1939, F 26,38:7
Scofield, Isaac M, 1940, Mr 23,13:6
Scofield, James C, 1950, Ja 4,35:2
Scofield, John H, 1944, O 12,27:6
Scofield, John H Mrs, 1942, Ag 15,11:7
Scofield, Leonard, 1960, D 5,31:5
Scofield, Lewis N, 1946, N 23,15:5
Scofield, Louis A, 1961, Je 16,33:3
Scofield, Louis F, 1953, F 28,17:5
Scofield, Philo W, 1914, N 7,11:6
Scofield, Ralsey B, 1961, My 30,17:4
Scofield, Richard C, 1943, N 22,19:6
Scofield, Russell E, 1962, Je 5,41:4
Scofield, Sarah B Mrs, 1939, F 15,23:4
Scofield, Sherman W, 1942, Ag 6,19:5
Scofield, Stanley T (por), 1937, D 2,25:6
Scofield, Walter K Rear-Adm, 1910, Ag 6,7:6
Scofield, Walter W, 1951, Mr 27,29:5
Scofield, William A, 1942, Jl 4,17:4
Scofield, William M, 1942, Jl 5,29:2
Scofield, William R, 1941, My 9,21:4
Scofield, Wilson B, 1949, O 8,13:3
Scoggan, H J, 1903, Ag 21,6:5
Scoggin, Margaret Clara, 1968, Jl 13,27:1
Scoggins, Charles E, 1955, D 7,39:5
Scoglio, Felix, 1962, N 7,39:3
Scognamiglio, Gennaro (G Cardenia), 1965, N 24, 39:2
Scognamillo, Enrico, 1921, O 4,15:6
Scola, Dominick Mrs, 1924, Jl 18,13:3
Scoledes, Nicholas G, 1967, My 15,43:3
Scoles, Dwight L, 1967, N 8,47:2
Scoll, David S Mrs, 1965, Ja 4,29:4
Scollard, C, 1932, N 20,29:1
Scollard, Clinton Mrs, 1948, S 30,28:3
Scolley, Jennie E, 1950, N 30,33:4
Scolnick, Abraham, 1966, Je 27,35:3
Scolponeti, Joseph A, 1959, D 20,60:8
Scoon, Thompson M, 1953, Jl 28,19:4
Scope, Mortimer, 1948, F 9,17:3
Scopelleti, Valentine T, 1960, Jl 7,31:3
Scopp, Maurice, 1965, Mr 27,27:2
Scoppa, Joachim, 1943, Je 12,13:3
Scoppa, Salvatore J, 1950, Je 3,15:6
Scoralick, Frederick B, 1941, F 7,19:4
Score, Herbert A, 1957, N 10,85:2
Score, J N R, 1949, S 28,27:3
Score, Stanley G, 1944, N 21,25:4
Scorgie, John, 1944, Ja 21,17:5
Scotland, Eda Mrs, 1924, Ja 7,9:1
Scotland, Felix A, 1961, Ag 17,27:2
Scott, A C Sr, 1940, O 28,17:3
Scott, A H, 1962, N 17,28:2
Scott, A Lincoln, 1953, My 28,23:4
Scott, A Louis, 1952, N 8,17:5
Scott, Albert, 1938, Ja 17,19:4
Scott, Albert L (por), 1946, Mr 3,46:5
Scott, Albert L Mrs, 1946, Mr 20,23:3
Scott, Albert M, 1957, My 2,31:4
Scott, Albert W Jr, 1942, S 5,13:3
Scott, Alex, 1942, F 3,19:3; 1953, Mr 1,92:4
Scott, Alex H, 1940, My 21,23:5
Scott, Alexander Dr, 1925, Jl 29,21:6
Scott, Alexis P Mrs, 1949, F 8,25:3
Scott, Alfred B, 1908, Ja 10,7:5
Scott, Alfred I, 1951, Mr 13,31:4
Scott, Alfred J, 1940, Ap 18,23:4
Scott, Alfred W, 1943, N 14,56:4; 1959, Ag 3,25:6
Scott, Alice H, 1954, Ja 8,21:3
Scott, Allan, 1954, Mr 26,21:2
Scott, Allen C, 1964, My 2,27:3
Scott, Ambrose, 1953, Ja 5,21:5
Scott, Andrew C Mrs, 1951, Ja 27,13:6
Scott, Andrew R, 1941, My 2,21:4
Scott, Andrew Sir, 1939, N 11,15:3
Scott, Anna B Mrs, 1945, Ag 9,21:2
Scott, Anna D, 1946, D 21,19:5
Scott, Annie M Mrs, 1938, O 6,23:5
Scott, Arthur H Mrs, 1960, Jl 21,27:4
Scott, Arthur P, 1961, F 13,27:5
Scott, Austin, 1954, Je 28,27:5
Scott, Austin Dr, 1922, Ag 17,13:4
Scott, B L, 1955, Je 4,15:6
Scott, B L Mrs, 1950, Ja 14,15:5
Scott, Ben, 1959, Ag 8,17:4
Scott, Benjamin F, 1954, S 2,21:2
Scott, Bertrand W, 1940, Ja 16,23:2
Scott, Bessie B, 1947, S 3,25:1
Scott, Bruce, 1939, Mr 16,24:2
Scott, Byron, 1944, My 2,19:2
Scott, C P, 1932, Ja 1,29:1
Scott, Campbell, 1960, Mr 14,29:3
Scott, Campbell Mrs, 1949, Je 30,23:3
Scott, Carey, 1941, O 24,23:3
Scott, Carroll C, 1937, N 25,31:4
Scott, Carroll L, 1946, Ap 9,27:4
Scott, Cecil O, 1946, F 17,42:3
Scott, Charles A, 1941, D 7,79:2
Scott, Charles A (por), 1944, N 27,23:3
Scott, Charles A Maj, 1907, D 23,9:5
Scott, Charles B, 1940, N 7,25:2
Scott, Charles Col, 1916, Mr 15,11:5
Scott, Charles D, 1956, Mr 12,27:3
Scott, Charles E, 1950, F 7,27:4; 1956, Ja 14,19:5; 1961, N 28,37:3
Scott, Charles F, 1938, S 20,23:3; 1942, My 28,17:3; 1944, D 19,21:3
Scott, Charles H, 1943, D 3,23:1; 1945, Ja 29,13:5; 1958, Ag 17,85:3
Scott, Charles H Jr, 1952, My 4,90:5
Scott, Charles I, 1950, F 17,24:2
Scott, Charles Jr, 1922, Ag 22,17:6
Scott, Charles L, 1954, N 29,25:5
Scott, Charles L Mrs, 1964, S 5,19:2
Scott, Charles R, 1954, Ag 5,23:5
Scott, Charles R Mrs, 1938, S 4,16:6
Scott, Charles Taylor, 1906, Mr 1,9:6
Scott, Charles W, 1939, Ap 12,23:6
Scott, Chester O Mrs, 1954, Ap 28,31:2
Scott, Clarence N, 1939, Ja 26,21:4
Scott, Clement, 1904, Je 26,7:5; 1941, S 17,23:4
Scott, Clyde P, 1950, Je 14,31:6
Scott, Clyde R, 1941, S 5,22:3
Scott, Cornelius W, 1967, Ag 24,37:2
Scott, Cyril (por), 1945, Ag 18,11:5
Scott, Cyrus H, 1944, Jl 21,19:3
Scott, D A Rev, 1879, Ap 4,4:7
Scott, Daniel J, 1950, Ja 3,25:2
Scott, Daniel L, 1950, N 22,25:2
Scott, David, 1954, O 24,89:2
Scott, David C, 1951, My 14,25:4
Scott, David E, 1957, Jl 30,23:4
Scott, David F Mrs, 1954, F 14,92:5
Scott, David H Col, 1919, Mr 18,11:2
Scott, David L, 1958, Ag 13,27:5
Scott, David T, 1943, My 10,19:5
Scott, Dewitt Mrs, 1947, F 18,25:3
Scott, Don O, 1959, Mr 24,39:3
Scott, Donald, 1957, Jl 19,19:5; 1967, Ap 7,37:3
Scott, Donald L, 1943, N 22,19:5
Scott, Douglas G, 1941, Je 30,17:3
Scott, Dred, 1858, S 21,4:2
Scott, Duncan C, 1947, D 20,17:2
Scott, E Greenough Mrs, 1937, Ag 7,15:5
Scott, E Irvin Mrs, 1949, Je 13,19:4
Scott, E Raymond, 1946, Je 15,21:5
Scott, E Walcott Jr Brig-Gen, 1968, O 16,47:4
Scott, Earl S, 1953, Ap 13,27:3
Scott, Earle R, 1956, Jl 8,65:2
Scott, Edgar Mrs, 1941, O 16,21:2
Scott, Edith W, 1948, Ag 20,17:6
Scott, Edward A Jr Mrs, 1957, Ag 29,27:4
Scott, Edward H Mrs, 1950, Jl 22,15:1
Scott, Edward R, 1945, Jl 6,11:3
Scott, Edward W, 1908, Ag 5,5:4; 1953, N 4,16:7
Scott, Edwin A, 1955, Je 27,21:6
Scott, Edwin C, 1937, S 9,23:5
Scott, Ellis, 1956, Je 3,86:8
Scott, Elmer, 1954, Ap 21,29:4
Scott, Emily, 1946, Je 28,21:5
Scott, Emily M Mrs, 1915, Ap 10,11:5
Scott, Emmett J, 1957, D 14,21:4
Scott, Ernest F, 1954, Jl 22,23:1
Scott, Ernest H, 1951, O 30,29:1
Scott, Ernest L, 1966, Ja 20,35:4
Scott, Ernest R, 1948, O 20,29:1
Scott, Eula L, 1949, O 11,34:2
Scott, Everett B, 1954, F 12,25:2
Scott, Everett Sr, 1960, N 3,39:2
Scott, Fanny W Mrs, 1942, Ja 6,23:3
Scott, Ferris Rev, 1879, My 12,8:4
Scott, Florence M (Sister Florence Marie), 1965, Ag 23,31:3
Scott, Frances P Mrs, 1942, Je 1,13:4
Scott, Francis, 1952, Jl 27,57:2
Scott, Francis Ex-Judge, 1923, Je 15,19:5
Scott, Francis Markoe, 1922, F 6,13:3
Scott, Frank, 1949, N 30,4:4
Scott, Frank A, 1949, Ap 16,15:1
Scott, Frank C, 1937, D 2,25:4
Scott, Frank D, 1954, Ap 15,29:6
Scott, Frank E Mrs, 1945, Jl 4,13:7
Scott, Frank Hall, 1912, N 26,15:4
Scott, Frank L Jr Mrs, 1941, Ja 20,17:5
Scott, Frank M, 1942, Jl 20,13:5
Scott, Frank Mrs, 1949, N 30,4:4
Scott, Frank P, 1955, My 31,27:4
Scott, Frank W, 1946, D 22,41:2
Scott, Franklin W, 1950, Ja 12,27:3
Scott, Frederic W, 1939, S 25,19:3
Scott, Frederick A, 1957, Ap 26,25:3
Scott, Frederick G, 1944, Ja 20,19:6
Scott, Frederick G Mrs, 1943, Jl 14,19:5
Scott, Frederick H, 1942, S 2,23:6; 1958, Mr 16,86:
Scott, Frederick H Jr, 1961, O 14,23:4
Scott, Frederick T, 1942, F 24,21:1
Scott, Frederick W, 1950, D 28,25:4; 1965, N 11,47
Scott, G, 1929, Ag 15,23:3
Scott, G C, 1879, D 20,5:2
Scott, G G Sir (see also Mr 28), 1878, Ap 7,2:1
Scott, G H Rear-Adm, 1882, Mr 25,5:3
Scott, G Howard, 1958, D 1,29:3
Scott, Garfield, 1955, Je 19,92:8
Scott, Gen, 1866, My 30,1:2
Scott, George, 1943, Ja 14,21:5; 1945, My 22,19:4
Scott, George A, 1952, D 10,35:5
Scott, George A Jr, 1951, F 13,31:1
Scott, George A Sr, 1952, F 7,27:4
Scott, George B, 1949, Ag 31,23:4
Scott, George C, 1947, F 18,25:5; 1948, O 7,29:1
Scott, George D Brig-Gen, 1911, F 21,11:5
Scott, George E, 1939, Ja 13,19:4
Scott, George G Mrs, 1958, Je 26,27:4
Scott, George H, 1937, Je 6,II,9:1; 1942, Ap 14,21 1950, N 17,27:1
Scott, George H Col, 1937, D 15,25:4
Scott, George Isham, 1915, O 31,7:4
Scott, George Mrs, 1937, D 10,26:4
Scott, George R, 1946, Ap 10,27:2
Scott, George T Mrs, 1957, Ag 4,81:2
Scott, George W, 1943, Jl 18,35:1; 1944, Je 5,19:6; 1953, S 15,31:1
Scott, George W Brig-Gen, 1922, O 27,17:4
Scott, George W Col, 1903, O 4,7:6
Scott, Georgiana H, 1947, Mr 28,23:1
Scott, Gilbert L, 1944, Je 30,21:4
Scott, Giles G, 1960, F 10,37:3
Scott, Grant E, 1954, Ap 13,31:2
Scott, Guy T Maj, 1920, D 3,15:5
Scott, H L, 1934, My 1,23:1
Scott, Hamilton, 1951, F 19,23:4
Scott, Hamilton G (por), 1943, N 2,25:4
Scott, Harlan M, 1965, My 13,37:3
Scott, Harley J, 1942, N 23,23:3
Scott, Harold, 1951, Ap 30,29:3
Scott, Harold B, 1938, N 23,21:3
Scott, Harold M, 1954, Ap 8,27:4
Scott, Harris P Sr, 1954, D 30,17:4
Scott, Harry, 1947, Je 23,23:4; 1964, Je 1,29:5
Scott, Harry P, 1945, Mr 6,21:3
Scott, Harry R, 1952, Mr 25,27:2
Scott, Harry S, 1956, My 27,88:5
Scott, Harry W, 1951, N 12,25:4
Scott, Harvey W Col, 1910, Ag 8,7:5
Scott, Henri G, 1942, Ap 5,41:1
Scott, Henry, 1947, Ag 12,23:5; 1956, My 9,33:2
Scott, Henry B, 1948, Mr 22,23:2
Scott, Henry D, 1947, Ap 23,25:2
Scott, Henry E, 1944, Ja 27,19:2
Scott, Henry G Mrs, 1956, D 2,87:1
Scott, Henry H, 1939, D 22,19:2
Scott, Henry L, 1937, D 1,23:5
Scott, Henry M, 1961, My 30,17:2
Scott, Henry Mrs, 1940, Je 27,23:1
Scott, Henry P Jr, 1950, Ag 3,23:2
Scott, Henry P Jr Mrs, 1942, Jl 27,15:4
Scott, Herbert A, 1962, Ap 12,35:2
Scott, Herbert Van W, 1965, Je 26,29:3
Scott, Herman, 1959, Ja 29,27:3
Scott, Howard Mrs, 1942, Mr 3,24:2
Scott, Hugh, 1940, S 1,21:3
Scott, Hugh D, 1952, Je 24,29:3
Scott, I Grant, 1964, N 18,47:3

Scott, I S, 1952, Ja 28,17:5
Scott, Ida G, 1938, N 9,23:3
Scott, Ira D, 1951, Ag 3,21:5
Scott, Irene E B Mrs, 1941, N 4,26:6
Scott, Irvin L, 1952, N 2,88:3
Scott, Irving M, 1903, Ap 29,9:6
Scott, Irving V, 1947, Jl 29,21:1
Scott, Irving W, 1952, Ja 9,29:1
Scott, Isaac M, 1942, Ap 28,21:4
Scott, Isbon B, 1944, Ag 12,11:3
Scott, Ivan E, 1963, O 24,30:4
Scott, Ivy, 1947, F 4,26:2
Scott, J B, 1903, Ja 26,9:5
Scott, J Douglas Mrs, 1939, Ja 18,20:4
Scott, J Edward, 1956, Je 20,31:1
Scott, J H, 1935, Jl 28,24:1
Scott, J Hutchinson Jr, 1952, Ja 6,92:2
Scott, J J, 1881, O 8,5:5
Scott, J Murray, 1950, D 30,13:6
Scott, J Thomas, 1948, F 4,23:2
Scott, J W, 1895, Ap 15,1:3
Scott, Jack, 1950, S 9,17:5
Scott, Jack G, 1956, My 3,31:3
Scott, Jack V, 1956, Jl 25,29:5
Scott, Jack V Mrs, 1964, F 15,23:4
Scott, James, 1885, Mr 7,5:2; 1907, My 6,9:3; 1944, Jl 6,15:6
Scott, James A, 1949, O 18,27:3; 1949, N 9,27:2; 1960, S 3,17:5
Scott, James B, 1943, Je 27,32:5
Scott, James Capt, 1903, Je 24,9:6
Scott, James G, 1937, Ag 5,23:3
Scott, James H, 1939, Ja 25,21:3
Scott, James J, 1963, Ap 18,35:5
Scott, James J Mrs, 1948, Je 23,27:2
Scott, James M, 1956, Ap 22,86:8
Scott, James R, 1945, Ja 4,19:2
Scott, James R Mrs, 1948, Mr 23,25:3
Scott, James T, 1963, My 28,28:5
Scott, James W, 1937, Je 6,II,8:7
Scott, Jeannette, 1937, N 17,23:1
Scott, Jefferson, 1907, Ag 7,7:6
Scott, John, 1908, Ag 12,5:5; 1939, D 16,17:1; 1951, S 24,27:5
Scott, John A, 1939, Mr 7,21:3; 1947, O 28,25:6; 1948, D 3,25:4; 1950, N 14,31:1; 1952, F 26,27:2
Scott, John C, 1945, Jl 27,15:3
Scott, John F, 1948, S 21,27:3; 1955, O 31,25:2
Scott, John F R, 1954, Jl 30,17:2
Scott, John G, 1953, N 3,31:5
Scott, John H, 1941, O 13,17:5
Scott, John J K, 1941, Ja 28,19:3
Scott, John J Mrs, 1938, Mr 7,17:4
Scott, John L, 1938, O 27,23:4; 1964, D 18,33:2
Scott, John M, 1939, Je 10,17:4; 1944, F 12,13:5; 1945, O 28,44:2
Scott, John M Mrs, 1937, Jl 22,19:6; 1949, F 21,23:4
Scott, John Morrin (will, O 12,16:6), 1945, O 4,23:6
Scott, John Mrs, 1942, Jl 16,19:2
Scott, John R, 1949, Ap 6,30:2
Scott, John R K, 1945, D 10,21:4
Scott, John W, 1941, My 27,23:6; 1953, Ag 29,17:5; 1958, Je 24,31:4
Scott, John W A, 1907, Mr 5,9:6
Scott, John W Jr, 1964, Ag 5,33:1
Scott, John Walter, 1919, Ja 6,13:1
Scott, Jonathan F, 1942, My 31,38:3
Scott, Joseph, 1951, F 23,27:4; 1961, S 11,27:3; 1962, Ap 7,25:4
Scott, Joseph D, 1954, O 13,31:1
Scott, Joseph F, 1953, Ag 7,19:5; 1960, Je 19,88:2
Scott, Joseph F Col, 1918, D 15,22:4
Scott, Joseph L, 1958, Mr 25,33:2
Scott, Joseph M, 1938, Ja 9,43:2
Scott, Julia Green Mrs, 1923, My 1,21:4
Scott, Julian Col, 1901, Jl 5,7:4
Scott, Julian F, 1953, N 18,32:4
Scott, K Hazen, 1958, D 28,2:5
Scott, Kenneth D, 1950, Ja 23,23:4
Scott, Kenneth S, 1960, Mr 2,37:5
Scott, L Bruce, 1952, Ag 19,23:3
Scott, L Parkin Judge, 1873, O 14,1:4
Scott, Lawrence E, 1942, O 1,23:3
Scott, Lee Mrs, 1951, Mr 9,25:2
Scott, Leonard H, 1952, S 6,17:2
Scott, Leroy Mrs, 1944, Ja 7,17:5
Scott, Leslie, 1950, My 20,15:3
Scott, Lester F (cor, Ap 19,25:8), 1954, Ap 18,26:3
Scott, Lester F Mrs, 1943, F 27,13:5
Scott, Lester F Mrs (cor, Ap 19,25:8), 1954, Ap 18, 26:3
Scott, Levi, 1882, Jl 14,5:3
Scott, Lewis M, 1959, Ap 5,86:8
Scott, Lida W Mrs, 1955, Ap 24,87:1
Scott, Lillian M, 1950, Je 30,23:5
Scott, Llewellyn D, 1939, Je 6,23:3
Scott, Lloyd N, 1966, F 20,88:4
Scott, Lorne A, 1948, N 25,31:2
Scott, Lucy A Mrs, 1937, Jl 7,23:5
Scott, Lucy Jameson Mrs, 1920, F 4,11:4
Scott, Lucy P Mrs, 1937, N 12,22:1
Scott, Luther C, 1956, N 3,23:6
Scott, Mabel, 1941, D 17,27:4
Scott, Margaret P, 1942, Ap 27,15:4
Scott, Margaret S Mrs, 1946, My 31,24:3
Scott, Marsden G, 1923, Mr 6,21:4
Scott, Marthe, 1937, N 1,21:2
Scott, Martin J, 1954, N 29,25:1
Scott, Martin Jr Mrs, 1965, Jl 15,29:3
Scott, Mary, 1966, My 18,47:2
Scott, Mary E M, 1941, Ag 28,19:4
Scott, Mary M Mrs, 1951, Ja 23,27:2
Scott, Mary P, 1938, S 14,48:4
Scott, Mary W Mrs, 1940, N 20,21:4
Scott, Max L, 1947, N 4,25:3
Scott, Melinda, 1954, Ag 10,19:3
Scott, Michael, 1958, My 31,15:4; 1959, Ja 11,89:1
Scott, Michael S, 1938, F 5,15:2
Scott, N Stone, 1940, D 25,27:2
Scott, Natalie, 1957, N 20,35:4
Scott, Nathan Bay, 1924, Ja 3,17:4
Scott, Norman, 1968, S 23,35:4
Scott, Norman M, 1950, Mr 31,32:5
Scott, Oliver, 1949, F 25,23:2
Scott, Orlando F, 1950, Mr 23,36:3
Scott, Owen F, 1953, D 14,31:5
Scott, Paul, 1943, Ja 26,19:2
Scott, Paul W, 1950, D 29,20:2
Scott, Percy Sir Adm (funl, O 22,21:5), 1924, O 19, 7:1
Scott, Philip B, 1961, My 8,35:3
Scott, Preston H, 1966, My 10,39:8
Scott, R Hunter, 1945, N 24,19:3
Scott, R M, 1953, Jl 11,11:4
Scott, Ralph, 1909, Ap 28,9:4
Scott, Randolph J, 1945, Mr 16,15:2
Scott, Reginald H, 1959, F 13,27:4
Scott, Reuben E Sr, 1957, Mr 28,31:1
Scott, Richard Daniel, 1907, Mr 30,9:7
Scott, Richard H, 1944, Mr 12,37:3
Scott, Richard S, 1943, F 19,19:1
Scott, Richard Sir, 1913, Ap 24,11:2
Scott, Robert, 1942, Ja 16,21:2; 1942, Ag 26,19:4; 1946, Ap 16,25:5; 1949, My 8,76:4; 1951, Mr 19,27:3
Scott, Robert B, 1940, O 5,15:5; 1948, Ag 2,21:4
Scott, Robert Crozier, 1923, Jl 6,13:6
Scott, Robert D, 1949, N 19,17:4
Scott, Robert E, 1968, Mr 12,43:1
Scott, Robert G, 1947, Ja 22,23:1; 1957, Je 10,27:5; 1965, Ap 29,35:4
Scott, Robert I, 1964, Ag 24,27:4
Scott, Robert J, 1942, F 19,19:2
Scott, Robert L, 1953, Ap 11,17:3
Scott, Robert L Mrs, 1950, Je 13,28:2
Scott, Robert Mrs, 1945, My 5,16:2
Scott, Robert T, 1939, Ag 14,15:4; 1942, S 19,15:5
Scott, Roland F, 1959, F 18,33:4
Scott, Ronald W, 1958, Jl 16,29:4
Scott, Roy W, 1957, My 27,31:4
Scott, Roy W Mrs, 1942, N 16,19:3
Scott, Ruby T, 1943, Mr 18,19:1
Scott, Rufus W, 1962, Ag 28,31:3
Scott, S Horace, 1952, Jl 15,21:3
Scott, Samuel B, 1941, Ap 7,17:4
Scott, Samuel H, 1871, Mr 7,1:2
Scott, Samuel L Mrs, 1954, Ag 26,27:6
Scott, Samuel W, 1948, Je 5,15:2
Scott, Sarah E, 1939, D 23,15:2
Scott, Seaton M Mrs, 1949, Mr 19,15:2
Scott, Sidney, 1937, Ap 14,26:1
Scott, Stevenson, 1945, O 7,43:1
Scott, T, 1928, O 5,25:5
Scott, T A, 1881, My 22,1:7
Scott, T L, 1881, F 24,5:6
Scott, T Parkin Mrs, 1925, S 3,25:6
Scott, Temple, 1939, O 1,53:3
Scott, Thomas, 1903, N 9,7:7; 1940, Ap 30,21:6; 1949, Ag 6,17:3
Scott, Thomas A, 1958, S 14,84:3; 1961, Ap 6,33:3
Scott, Thomas A Capt, 1907, F 18,9:5
Scott, Thomas D, 1940, Ja 20,15:2
Scott, Thomas J (Tom), 1961, Ag 13,88:5
Scott, Thomas M, 1959, Je 30,31:4
Scott, Thomas Mrs, 1945, D 14,17:5; 1958, Jl 16,29:5
Scott, Thomas P, 1949, Ja 25,23:3
Scott, Thomas W, 1947, My 6,27:3
Scott, Vincent E, 1956, Je 30,17:6
Scott, Virginia Mrs, 1955, Mr 20,89:2
Scott, Virginia N Mrs, 1956, Mr 4,88:2
Scott, W, 1935, N 29,19:1
Scott, W B, 1885, Ja 18,7:3
Scott, W Edward, 1958, Je 11,36:1
Scott, W L, 1891, S 21,5:4
Scott, Wainwright Capt, 1866, F 12,5:2
Scott, Walter, 1907, S 15,9:5; 1938, Mr 24,23:5; 1944, F 13,42:1
Scott, Walter A Sr Mrs, 1949, Ag 17,23:5
Scott, Walter C, 1964, D 9,50:5
Scott, Walter E (Death Valley Scotty), 1954, Ja 6, 31:2
Scott, Walter F, 1940, Mr 6,23:2
Scott, Walter F Mrs, 1953, Ja 18,92:6
Scott, Walter G, 1944, D 31,25:1
Scott, Walter J, 1939, Ap 24,17:2; 1941, O 18,19:2
Scott, Walter J Mrs, 1948, Je 23,27:4
Scott, Walter L, 1951, Ag 18,11:2
Scott, Walter M, 1943, N 26,23:3
Scott, Walter Quincey Rev Dr, 1917, My 11,11:1
Scott, Walter S, 1948, O 30,15:4
Scott, Walter V, 1946, O 7,31:2
Scott, Walter W, 1964, Jl 7,22:4
Scott, Warwick L, 1952, Je 20,23:4
Scott, Waterbury M, 1959, My 26,35:2
Scott, Wilbur S, 1944, Ag 17,17:4
Scott, Willard J, 1964, D 27,64:1
Scott, William, 1909, My 14,9:5; 1914, O 14,11:6; 1953, O 20,29:5
Scott, William A, 1940, Ag 30,19:2
Scott, William A Mrs, 1960, O 14,33:4
Scott, William B (por), 1947, Mr 30,56:5
Scott, William B Mrs, 1953, Jl 4,11:6
Scott, William C, 1951, O 13,17:1
Scott, William C Dr, 1937, O 19,25:4
Scott, William E, 1940, Mr 5,23:5
Scott, William Earl Dodge, 1910, Ag 24,9:5
Scott, William F, 1943, S 20,21:6
Scott, William F Mrs, 1948, Mr 14,73:1
Scott, William G, 1903, O 2,7:6; 1953, Mr 21,17:5
Scott, William H, 1938, Jl 22,18:4; 1955, Mr 18,27:2
Scott, William H Dr, 1937, Ja 13,24:3
Scott, William J, 1940, Ap 14,45:2; 1940, Jl 1,19:3; 1940, Jl 31,17:3; 1960, S 13,37:1
Scott, William J Mrs, 1949, Mr 22,25:4; 1952, Ap 12, 11:4
Scott, William J Sr, 1952, Ap 5,15:3
Scott, William K (funl, Ap 19,21:6), 1958, Ap 17,31:1
Scott, William L, 1941, Jl 21,15:4; 1951, D 3,31:4
Scott, William M, 1942, Ja 20,19:5
Scott, William M Mrs, 1958, O 1,37:4
Scott, William M Sgt, 1918, Jl 14,21:4
Scott, William Mrs, 1951, Ap 27,23:5
Scott, William P, 1942, My 21,19:2; 1950, D 8,29:1
Scott, William S, 1941, S 1,15:5
Scott, William S Mrs, 1954, F 7,88:2
Scott, William Sr, 1943, My 8,15:5
Scott, William Sr Mrs, 1950, My 28,44:5
Scott, William W, 1947, D 8,25:3
Scott, William Wallace, 1909, Ap 4,13:4
Scott, Willis H, 1960, Je 23,29:3
Scott, Winfield, 1921, Ja 10,11:5; 1953, D 28,22:5; 1954, Ja 28,27:4
Scott, Winfield H, 1947, D 16,33:3
Scott, Winfield Townley, 1968, Ap 29,43:2
Scott, Wisner G, 1941, S 17,23:3
Scott, Zachary, 1965, O 4,4:1
Scott, Zachary T, 1964, Ja 20,43:3
Scott, Zona J, 1947, N 18,29:3
Scott-Gatty, Alex, 1937, N 8,23:3
Scott-Moncrieff, Colin Campbell Sir, 1916, Ap 8,15:6
Scott-Moncrieff, George Maj-Gen, 1924, Je 7,13:4
Scott-Paine, Hubert, 1954, Ap 15,29:5
Scott-Siddons, M F, 1896, N 20,5:6
Scotten, S C, 1920, Ag 7,5:7
Scotti, A, 1936, F 29,8:1
Scotti, D William, 1966, S 22,47:1
Scotti, John, 1957, O 19,21:3
Scotti, Louis P, 1942, D 6,76:3
Scotti, William Mrs, 1942, O 26,15:3
Scottino, Albert J, 1965, Ja 23,25:4
Scotto, Antonio L, 1946, F 6,23:5
Scotto, Charles (por), 1937, O 25,19:5
Scotto, Vincent, 1952, N 16,87:2
Scouler, Ambrose A, 1950, S 19,29:5
Scouten, Dan G, 1913, Ag 23,7:5
Scovel, James M, 1904, D 3,9:3
Scovel, Mary C, 1941, O 21,23:5
Scovel, Sylvester, 1905, F 13,2:5
Scovel, Sylvester F Rev, 1910, N 30,11:4
Scovell, Earl L, 1947, F 4,25:6
Scovern, Jones Mrs, 1966, D 3,39:3
Scovil, Charles B, 1946, Jl 13,15:6
Scovil, E Medley, 1949, S 8,29:2
Scovil, Thomas Simpson, 1905, Ap 13,11:5
Scovill, Carlos P, 1904, Ap 28,9:6
Scovill, Edward E, 1946, Je 2,44:6
Scovill, Edward E Mrs, 1956, Ja 18,31:5
Scovill, H Lamson, 1937, O 31,II,11:2
Scovill, Irene C R Mrs, 1945, Je 28,19:3
Scovill, Lester R, 1966, N 28,39:3
Scovill, Robert B, 1965, Ag 30,25:5
Scoville, Addison B Sr, 1963, Jl 1,29:3
Scoville, Anne E N Mrs, 1938, Jl 17,27:3
Scoville, Annie, 1953, Mr 15,92:2
Scoville, Charles A, 1938, Ja 15,15:3
Scoville, Charles A Mrs, 1948, S 2,24:2
Scoville, Charles O, 1947, Je 6,23:2
Scoville, Clifford E, 1938, F 2,19:3
Scoville, Edwin R, 1941, Mr 26,23:5
Scoville, George A, 1940, Ja 15,15:4
Scoville, Herbert, 1937, Mr 13,19:4
Scoville, Herbert Mrs, 1967, Ag 9,39:4
Scoville, J B, 1878, Ag 3,2:7
Scoville, John Hasbrouck, 1915, Jl 26,9:4
Scoville, John W, 1949, Ja 4,40:3
Scoville, Lewis P Jr, 1950, S 24,104:4
Scoville, Lila S Mrs, 1945, My 7,17:4
Scoville, Samuel A, 1962, N 14,39:3
Scoville, Samuel Jr, 1950, D 5,31:1
Scoville, William H, 1943, D 31,16:6

Scoville, William H Mrs, 1949, Je 2,27:5
Scowcroft, Edward T, 1941, Ja 8,19:4; 1959, Ja 24,19:4
Scowcroft, William J, 1943, Ap 18,48:4
Scown, William J, 1938, Ag 1,13:3
Scozza, Lou, 1967, D 1,47:3
Scozzaro, Carmela Mrs, 1950, Ap 10,19:5
Scragg, Harold A, 1952, D 8,41:5
Scragg, Robert E, 1955, My 19,29:4
Scram, Abraham W, 1948, S 6,13:6
Scranton, Asa R, 1960, Ag 15,23:1
Scranton, Benjamin H Mrs, 1951, D 22,15:2
Scranton, Charles W, 1941, F 26,21:3
Scranton, DeHart G, 1963, Ap 23,37:1
Scranton, E C, 1866, D 30,1:6; 1867, D 29,3:7
Scranton, George Whitefield, 1861, Mr 26,4:6
Scranton, Harry R, 1945, D 14,28:3
Scranton, I Elbert, 1950, Jl 27,25:4
Scranton, J Perry, 1951, Ja 6,15:6
Scranton, James A, 1908, O 14,9:5
Scranton, William D, 1950, O 2,23:4
Scranton, William W, 1916, D 4,13:4
Scranton, Worthington, 1955, F 14,20:3
Scranton, Worthington Mrs, 1960, Je 25,21:2
Screvane, Joseph J, 1968, Ag 11,72:5
Scriabin, Alexander N, 1915, Ap 28,13:4
Scribe, Augustin Eugene, 1861, Mr 11,4:5
Scriber, Adelbert M, 1948, Ag 14,13:5
Scriber, Bert B, 1942, Mr 26,23:2
Scriber, Jacob L, 1953, Je 11,29:5
Scribner, A H, 1932, Jl 4,11:6
Scribner, Arthur H Mrs, 1949, N 9,28:6
Scribner, C, 1930, Ap 20,1:4
Scribner, Charles, 1871, Ag 28,4:6
Scribner, Charles (funl, S 30,2:7), 1871, S 23,5:2
Scribner, Charles, 1952, F 12,27:1
Scribner, Charles E, 1968, Mr 17,80:8
Scribner, Charles H, 1952, Ag 16,15:2
Scribner, Charles Mrs, 1948, O 1,25:2
Scribner, Charles W, 1945, Ap 1,36:2
Scribner, David A, 1911, F 9,7:6
Scribner, Ernest V Dr, 1918, Je 15,11:5
Scribner, Frank J, 1966, F 2,35:4
Scribner, Frank J Mrs, 1956, Jl 20,17:4
Scribner, Frederick P, 1944, Jl 18,19:4
Scribner, George K, 1963, Ag 4,80:4
Scribner, Gilbert H, 1910, Ja 6,9:3; 1967, Ja 1,52:5
Scribner, Gilbert H Mrs, 1950, F 5,84:4
Scribner, H F, 1882, S 17,14:7
Scribner, Henry S, 1945, Ja 5,15:4
Scribner, Hilton, 1961, Ag 17,27:2
Scribner, Howard, 1944, D 9,15:4
Scribner, Howard Mrs, 1945, F 15,19:5
Scribner, J B (funl, Ja 24,8:3), 1879, Ja 21,5:4
Scribner, J W, 1880, Ja 29,3:2
Scribner, John M, 1908, Je 17,9:5
Scribner, Norman, 1952, S 2,23:3
Scribner, Russell O, 1959, Mr 22,87:1
Scribner, Sam A (por), 1941, Jl 9,21:4
Scribner, Sam A Mrs, 1940, Je 23,31:2
Scriggins, Edwin J, 1942, D 4,25:3
Scrimgeour, Archibald, 1945, Ja 16,19:5
Scrimgeour, James A, 1954, Je 16,31:3
Scrimgeour, James Mrs, 1903, Mr 22,7:5
Scrimgeour, William R, 1950, D 12,33:4
Scrimger, F A C Dr, 1937, F 15,17:3
Scrimshaw, A D, 1943, My 12,25:5
Scrimshaw, Ernest R, 1944, Je 23,19:3
Scripps, Dolla B, 1953, N 26,31:3
Scripps, E B, 1932, Ag 4,19:3
Scripps, F Tudor Jr, 1963, D 21,23:5
Scripps, G H Mrs, 1951, F 1,25:4
Scripps, James E, 1906, My 30,7:7
Scripps, James E 2d, 1925, O 3,15:6
Scripps, James G, 1921, Ja 8,11:6
Scripps, James G Mrs, 1959, N 17,35:2
Scripps, John L, 1866, O 1,2:4
Scripps, Robert P, 1938, Mr 4,23:1
Scripps, William E, 1952, Je 13,23:3
Scripps, William J, 1965, D 12,87:1
Scripture, Harry E, 1948, F 4,24:2
Scripture, Parker F, 1939, Ap 21,23:5
Scrivani, Robert Mrs, 1963, N 27,37:4
Scriven, George P (por), 1940, Mr 8,22:2
Scrivener, Harry S, 1937, Ag 18,19:1
Scroggie, Eugene R, 1959, F 22,89:2
Scroggs, William O, 1957, Ag 23,19:2
Scruggs, Anderson M, 1955, Ja 30,85:2
Scrugham, Eleanor B, 1947, S 10,27:3
Scrugham, James G, 1945, Je 24,22:3
Scrugham, Mary, 1943, Mr 4,19:4
Scrugham, William W, 1944, Jl 20,19:3
Scrugham, William W Judge, 1867, Ag 10,5:3
Scrugham, William W Mrs, 1947, Je 6,23:5
Scruton, William A, 1944, Mr 24,19:1
Scrutton, James H, 1938, Je 30,23:6
Scrutton, T, 1934, Ag 21,17:1
Scrymgeour, Edwin (por), 1947, F 2,57:6
Scrymser, James A, 1918, Ap 22,11:1
Scrymser, John Phillips, 1921, My 19,15:4
Scuccimarra, Mose, 1948, D 28,22:2
Scudamore, F I, 1884, F 9,5:3
Scudamore, Herbert F, 1938, S 10,17:4
Scudamore, William E Mrs, 1960, S 18,85:4
Scudder, Alanson H, 1949, N 9,27:6
Scudder, Antoinette Q, 1958, Ja 28,28:1
Scudder, Barry, 1943, Je 11,19:2
Scudder, Benjamin N, 1924, N 8,15:5
Scudder, Charles E Rev, 1937, F 11,23:3
Scudder, Charles J, 1940, Ja 31,19:3; 1956, Jl 25,29:6
Scudder, Charles L, 1949, Ag 21,68:3
Scudder, Charles M, 1953, Je 21,84:8
Scudder, Edward M, 1944, S 6,19:5
Scudder, Edward W Mrs, 1962, My 31,27:2
Scudder, Edward Wallace, 1953, F 21,13:3
Scudder, Eliot R, 1954, S 22,29:2
Scudder, Ellen C, 1938, Ap 11,15:5
Scudder, Eugene T, 1957, O 5,17:6
Scudder, Frank D, 1942, F 9,15:5
Scudder, Frank H, 1944, Ja 6,23:3
Scudder, Frederick F, 1949, My 22,89:1
Scudder, Frederick J, 1962, N 26,29:5
Scudder, Frederick P, 1919, N 29,11:4
Scudder, H E, 1902, Ja 12,7:4
Scudder, Halstead, 1909, Ap 5,7:4
Scudder, Harold H, 1951, Ap 20,29:5
Scudder, Harry Mrs, 1948, S 5,40:4
Scudder, Henry D Jr, 1941, O 6,17:5
Scudder, Henry J, 1955, My 6,23:3
Scudder, Henry J Mrs, 1957, D 3,35:5
Scudder, Henry T Rev, 1937, Jl 14,21:2
Scudder, Hewlett, 1918, Ja 18,9:5
Scudder, Hewlett (por), 1942, Ag 1,11:3
Scudder, Ida S, 1960, My 25,39:3
Scudder, Isaac L, 1943, O 29,19:4
Scudder, Janet (por), 1940, Je 11,25:1
Scudder, Laurence, 1967, My 4,44:5
Scudder, Lawrence W, 1941, My 19,17:5
Scudder, Lewis W, 1939, Ag 22,19:2
Scudder, Louisa W Mrs, 1937, Mr 5,21:2
Scudder, Moses L, 1917, O 31,13:5
Scudder, Phil J (Jack), 1950, Ap 24,27:4
Scudder, S D Dr, 1877, D 27,8:3
Scudder, Samuel, 1911, My 18,11:4
Scudder, Samuel D, 1953, Je 23,29:4
Scudder, Sophia Weld Mrs, 1925, S 2,23:5
Scudder, Susan S, 1946, Je 13,28:2
Scudder, Theodore T, 1953, Ja 17,15:3
Scudder, Townsend, 1874, Ag 5,5:5; 1960, F 23,31:4
Scudder, Vida D, 1954, O 11,27:6
Scudder, W M, 1931, F 25,25:1
Scudder, Wallace M Mrs, 1953, Jl 29,23:1
Scudder, Walter T, 1948, S 7,25:3
Scudi, Michael A, 1937, F 7,II,8:6
Scull, A Penrose 3d, 1961, Jl 12,31:3
Scull, C Mulford, 1953, Je 1,26:6
Scull, C O, 1927, O 5,27:3
Scull, Carl A, 1957, Jl 1,23:4
Scull, Carl B J, 1950, Jl 27,25:2
Scull, D Chester, 1942, Ap 2,21:5
Scull, David, 1907, N 23,9:5
Scull, E Marshall, 1952, My 30,15:5
Scull, Edward B, 1942, O 18,55:1
Scull, Eleanor, 1947, D 20,17:3
Scull, George E, 1939, O 24,23:3
Scull, George F, 1942, D 12,15:4
Scull, Guy Hamilton, 1920, O 30,11:1
Scull, Lewis B, 1937, Mr 20,19:5
Scull, Lewis M Sr, 1954, O 16,17:3
Scull, Robert B, 1937, N 5,23:4
Scull, Roy N, 1940, F 18,41:3
Scull, Samuel B, 1939, F 22,21:5
Scull, William C Mrs, 1960, O 29,23:5
Scull, William E Mrs, 1937, S 24,21:4
Scull, William S, 1953, My 14,29:2
Scullen, James, 1871, Ag 17,6:2
Scullen, William, 1943, Mr 27,13:5
Sculley, Gertrude L, 1940, Mr 15,23:1
Sculley, John D, 1954, O 27,29:4
Sculley, Joseph V, 1919, Ja 16,13:2
Scullin, Augustus A, 1966, Ag 9,37:1
Scullin, Harry, 1947, F 16,57:2
Scullin, James H, 1953, Ja 29,27:2
Scullin, Robert E, 1960, Mr 2,37:5
Scullin, Terance, 1948, Ap 1,26:3
Scullin, Virginia, 1959, O 11,86:7
Scullion, James H J, 1920, Jl 15,7:3
Scully, Arthur M, 1948, Jl 3,15:2
Scully, Bernard R, 1944, Je 10,15:4
Scully, C Alison, 1954, N 10,33:4
Scully, Charles B, 1959, Je 14,86:1
Scully, Charles J, 1952, Ag 6,21:3
Scully, Cornelius D, 1952, S 23,33:4
Scully, Cornelius D Mrs, 1952, O 16,29:4
Scully, Daniel H, 1939, Ag 28,19:4
Scully, Daniel J, 1910, F 18,7:4
Scully, Daniel J Dr, 1913, Je 17,11:4
Scully, David H, 1908, Ag 20,7:5
Scully, Don, 1958, Ag 20,27:4
Scully, Edward, 1947, Jl 12,13:3
Scully, Edward F Sr, 1949, My 15,90:2
Scully, Edward P, 1955, Jl 25,19:4
Scully, Edwin T, 1951, Mr 6,27:4
Scully, Emily M, 1966, Jl 25,27:5
Scully, Frank, 1964, Je 25,33:1
Scully, Frederick, 1942, O 30,19:4
Scully, George E, 1939, Jl 20,19:4
Scully, Harold J V, 1952, D 21,53:1
Scully, Hugh Day, 1968, Ap 19,47:4
Scully, Irvin J, 1946, Ja 12,15:3
Scully, J Aylward, 1944, Je 14,19:5
Scully, James E, 1963, N 17,87:2
Scully, John, 1943, F 3,19:5
Scully, John E, 1954, F 6,19:5; 1955, Mr 13,86:1
Scully, John E Jr, 1951, S 6,31:5
Scully, John J, 1947, Ap 7,23:4; 1956, My 20,86:6; 1966, F 23,39:1
Scully, John J Capt, 1924, Ag 27,17:6
Scully, John Loftus Rev, 1914, Mr 12,9:5
Scully, John Rev, 1917, D 27,11:5
Scully, John T Mrs, 1962, F 28,33:2
Scully, John Thomas, 1968, Ja 13,31:1
Scully, Joseph B, 1956, Ap 23,27:2
Scully, Mary Mrs, 1940, Mr 17,51:3
Scully, Mary S Mrs, 1941, Ja 26,36:2
Scully, Michael, 1958, Ag 27,29:1
Scully, Myles Mrs, 1947, S 28,60:6
Scully, Norbert J, 1963, N 12,41:3
Scully, Patrick F, 1944, Ag 28,11:5
Scully, Patrick J, 1921, My 4,10:5; 1921, My 5,17:5
Scully, Peter F, 1943, Ag 20,15:3
Scully, Peter F Mrs, 1950, Ap 4,29:5
Scully, Raymond J, 1925, F 12,19:4
Scully, Richard Mrs, 1945, Ag 5,37:1
Scully, Thomas A, 1961, Jl 13,29:1
Scully, Thomas J, 1921, D 15,19:4; 1937, Ja 31,II,8:7; 1955, S 13,31:4
Scully, Thomas P, 1950, F 26,76:8
Scully, Vincent A, 1943, Ja 10,50:1; 1953, F 8,88:4
Scully, Vincent J, 1962, Ap 28,25:2
Scully, William, 1906, O 19,9:5
Scully, William E, 1965, N 4,47:5
Scully, William J, 1937, Ja 4,29:4; 1949, My 3,25:4; 1950, Ja 21,18:3
Scultz, Shorb B, 1940, Ja 12,17:4
Sculy, J McC, 1883, D 31,5:2
Scutari, Ferdinand A, 1962, O 20,25:4
Scutt, Franklin W, 1940, Jl 27,13:4
Sea, Antonio, 1943, Mr 8,15:2
Sea, Phil N, 1941, Je 25,21:4
Seaback, Charles, 1947, N 9,72:6
Seaber, Louis E, 1964, Ja 25,23:4
Seaberg, Carl, 1960, Ag 20,19:4
Seaberg, Gust, 1954, Ja 20,27:3
Seaberg, O Walter, 1951, O 12,92:5
Seaberg, Oscar F, 1944, Ja 4,17:1
Seabough, James Sr, 1951, N 11,90:6
Seabranch, John P, 1947, N 20,29:1
Seabring, Cornelius O, 1941, My 29,19:1
Seabrook, Albert M, 1948, F 18,27:2
Seabrook, Belford L Mrs, 1959, My 24,88:5
Seabrook, Charles F, 1964, O 21,47:1
Seabrook, Charles F Mrs, 1968, Ja 25,40:1
Seabrook, Edwin L, 1940, Ag 9,15:1
Seabrook, Henry H, 1952, Ap 13,77:1
Seabrook, Nicholas, 1872, O 23,2:3
Seabrooke, Thomas Quigley, 1913, Ap 4,9:2
Seaburg, Anna, 1952, D 13,21:5
Seaburg, Ernest J, 1957, F 7,27:5
Seabury, Adam, 1914, N 10,11:5
Seabury, Charles B, 1943, N 9,21:2
Seabury, Charles L, 1922, Ap 8,15:5
Seabury, David, 1960, Ap 3,86:4
Seabury, Dr, 1872, O 17,8:3
Seabury, Edwin M, 1957, N 4,29:2
Seabury, Elmer F, 1954, N 17,31:1
Seabury, Florence G Mrs, 1951, O 8,21:2
Seabury, George T (por), 1945, My 26,15:1
Seabury, Howland, 1968, O 5,35:5
Seabury, J M, 1880, N 15,5:7
Seabury, Mary B, 1943, F 10,25:2
Seabury, Nathaniel N, 1954, Ja 17,93:2
Seabury, R, 1877, Mr 10,2:6
Seabury, Robert, 1915, D 27,9:5
Seabury, Robert B, 1961, Jl 15,19:2
Seabury, Robert Capt, 1864, My 21,2:6
Seabury, Robert Mrs, 1915, D 30,13:4
Seabury, Ruth I, 1955, Jl 31,69:3
Seabury, Samuel (funl plans, My 8,29:5; funl, My 10,21:3), 1958, My 7,1:2
Seabury, Samuel Mrs, 1950, Jl 22,15:1
Seabury, Samuel Rev, 1872, O 11,8:5
Seabury, William Jones Dr, 1916, Ag 31,9:3
Seabury, William Jones Rev Dr, 1916, S 3,19:7
Seacord, Andrew W, 1941, My 17,15:4
Seacord, Annie, 1948, My 18,23:4
Seacord, Charles C Mrs, 1959, F 13,27:2
Seacord, Chester C, 1951, O 1,23:6
Seacord, Daniel Freeman, 1968, Ja 3,47:1
Seacord, Frederick H, 1949, Ap 16,15:3
Seacord, Frederick H Mrs, 1942, Je 25,23:6
Seacord, Moses, 1938, My 21,15:5
Seacrest, Joseph C (por), 1942, Ap 22,23:5
Seadler, Sials F Mrs, 1963, My 26,92:5
Seagar, Cedric H, 1959, F 19,31:1
Seage, Clarence E, 1950, F 8,27:3
Seager, Allan, 1968, My 11,35:4
Seager, Charles A, 1948, S 10,23:3
Seager, George, 1962, Mr 22,35:3
Seager, George L (Lord Leighton), 1963, O 18,31:2

Seager, H R, 1930, Ag 24,II,6:1
Seager, John C Mrs, 1962, O 14,86:8
Seager, Lawrence H Bp, 1937, Ag 31,23:5
Seager, Oscar, 1966, D 13,47:2
Seager, Richard B, 1925, My 14,19:3
Seager, Warren A, 1952, Je 16,17:4
Seager, William, 1941, Mr 11,23:2
Seagers, Harrison M, 1956, Jl 28,17:3
Seagle, Nathan A, 1957, Ja 27,84:3
Seagle, Oscar, 1945, D 21,21:3
Seagram, Edward F, 1937, F 2,23:4
Seagram, Joseph E, 1919, Ag 19,13:4
Seagram, Wilfred (por), 1938, My 29,II,6:6
Seagrave, Arthur E, 1956, Ap 9,27:4
Seagrave, Charles B, 1941, My 25,36:8
Seagrave, Edwin L, 1968, S 25,47:3
Seagrave, F E, 1934, Ag 16,17:1
Seagrave, Gordon S (funl, Ap 1,35:1), 1965, Mr 29, 1:1
Seagrave, Gordon S Mrs, 1966, F 6,93:1
Seagrave, Grace, 1951, Ag 21,4:5
Seagraves, Hal E Mrs, 1954, D 29,29:1
Seagriff, Luke V, 1946, Ag 10,13:3
Seagrist, Francis W Jr, 1908, F 15,7:5
Seagrove, Gordon K, 1963, S 4,39:4
Seaholm, Charles H Mrs, 1948, Jl 1,23:4
Seaight, James Capt, 1911, Ja 15,13:3
Seakins, William B, 1946, Mr 25,26:2
Seal, Brajendranath, 1938, D 3,20:1
Seal, Harry E, 1939, F 21,19:1
Seal, John F, 1964, Ap 8,43:2
Seal, John H Mrs, 1949, Ag 12,17:4
Seale, Claude L, 1960, Je 18,23:4
Seale, Irene E, 1948, Je 3,25:4
Sealey, Frank G, 1949, Ap 1,25:4
Sealock, Robert R, 1951, Ag 21,27:4
Seals, Eugene D, 1955, Jl 19,27:1
Seals, Mary E Mrs, 1948, Ja 9,21:3
Sealy, Frank L, 1938, D 14,25:4
Sealy, Frank L Mrs, 1955, S 18,86:2
Sealy, George, 1944, N 5,54:6
Sealy, J, 1926, F 20,15:3
Seaman, Alfred P W (por), 1940, Mr 30,15:3
Seaman, Allen B, 1903, S 26,9:4
Seaman, Augusta H, 1950, Je 5,23:6
Seaman, Benjamin W, 1955, F 12,15:3
Seaman, C Merton, 1966, D 11,89:2
Seaman, Charles E, 1937, Ag 20,17:3
Seaman, Charles F M, 1950, Ag 14,17:4
Seaman, Charles F Mrs, 1956, Jl 9,23:5
Seaman, Charles K, 1949, Jl 6,30:3
Seaman, Claude, 1951, Ag 8,25:6
Seaman, David S, 1954, Ag 11,25:2
Seaman, E B, 1876, O 11,4:5
Seaman, E C, 1879, Jl 20,2:3
Seaman, Earl F, 1955, Mr 6,88:1
Seaman, Edwin H, 1947, Je 30,19:4
Seaman, Emily C, 1962, Ag 20,23:4
Seaman, Emily V Mrs, 1937, Ap 6,23:2
Seaman, Frank, 1939, Mr 26,III,6:8
Seaman, Frank Mrs, 1954, Ag 28,15:6
Seaman, Fred, 1951, My 6,93:1
Seaman, Frederick A, 1914, O 29,11:4
Seaman, Furman, 1941, Mr 19,21:2
Seaman, George, 1872, Mr 29,5:3; 1956, Ap 3,35:2
Seaman, George G Col, 1937, My 16,II,9:2
Seaman, George S, 1943, Mr 7,38:5
Seaman, George W, 1942, Ja 28,19:2
Seaman, Gerald L, 1959, N 10,47:2
Seaman, Gilbert E, 1941, My 27,23:6
Seaman, H Clayton Jr, 1953, D 20,77:1
Seaman, Halleck W, 1941, D 16,27:4
Seaman, Hannah T, 1944, Ap 28,19:4
Seaman, Hayward A, 1951, F 26,24:2
Seaman, Hayward A Mrs, 1941, Je 29,32:8
Seaman, Helen R, 1943, S 29,21:2
Seaman, Henry B, 1940, O 25,21:3
Seaman, Herbert D, 1942, F 28,17:3
Seaman, Herbert H Mrs, 1953, S 7,19:6
Seaman, Herbert R, 1944, Ja 24,17:3
Seaman, Herbert W, 1955, Ja 14,21:2
Seaman, Horace M, 1942, Je 5,17:1
Seaman, Howard L, 1944, N 28,23:2
Seaman, J M, 1884, N 9,9:5
Seaman, James A, 1951, Ap 22,89:1
Seaman, James M, 1920, F 18,11:3
Seaman, John Ferris, 1915, Ag 29,15:5
Seaman, John Sr, 1950, Je 21,27:2
Seaman, Joseph B, 1947, Je 3,26:3
Seaman, Joseph H, 1948, Jl 23,19:1
Seaman, Joseph H Mrs, 1944, My 2,19:6
Seaman, Julian H, 1942, Mr 11,19:5
Seaman, Katherine W, 1956, Ap 30,23:4
Seaman, Kenneth L, 1962, Mr 13,32:2
Seaman, L L, 1932, F 1,17:1
Seaman, Lawrence Mrs, 1964, Mr 30,29:2
Seaman, Lindlay F, 1905, Mr 26,9:4
Seaman, Mary E U Mrs, 1955, Jl 18,21:2
Seaman, Max, 1925, My 15,19:5
Seaman, Noah, 1911, Mr 19,II,11:2
Seaman, O, 1936, F 3,17:1
Seaman, Otis R, 1966, F 7,29:3
Seaman, Paul E, 1965, Jl 2,29:2
Seaman, Phineas A, 1937, Ap 2,23:1
Seaman, Ralph E, 1939, N 24,23:4
Seaman, Robert, 1904, Mr 13,8:7
Seaman, Robert G, 1962, My 28,29:3
Seaman, Samuel J, 1954, D 31,13:3
Seaman, Stephen, 1947, My 5,23:3
Seaman, Susan L Mrs, 1942, F 26,19:2
Seaman, Thomas B, 1916, Jl 19,9:5
Seaman, Valentine, 1899, Mr 30,7:5
Seaman, William H, 1951, F 14,30:2; 1954, Ja 3,88:3
Seaman, William H Judge, 1915, Mr 9,9:4
Seaman, William H Mrs, 1951, F 13,31:3
Seaman, William I Mrs, 1950, N 21,31:3
Seaman, William S, 1951, Je 24,72:5
Seamans, Clarence M, 1939, Jl 21,19:5
Seamans, Clarence Walker, 1915, My 31,7:6
Seamans, Frank, 1955, Ap 3,87:1
Seamans, Frank M, 1940, F 26,15:3
Seamans, Ida G Mrs, 1937, Ja 19,23:3
Seamans, William S, 1949, Je 16,30:5
Seamans, William Shepard Dr, 1917, F 7,13:5
Seamon, Leonard, 1948, O 15,24:3
Seamon, Phil, 1951, My 25,27:5
Seamon, Raymond G, 1949, Ag 24,76:2
Seaone, Consuelo A, 1964, Jl 7,32:6
Sear, Joseph J, 1966, Ag 8,27:4
Searby, Ira R, 1949, Mr 31,25:4
Searcy, Charles L, 1940, F 25,39:2
Searcy, William N Mrs, 1947, Ja 17,23:4
Searer, Jay C, 1967, Je 26,33:4
Seares, Frederick H, 1964, Jl 22,33:5
Searight, Clarence L, 1959, F 15,86:6
Searing, Adolphus H Mrs, 1949, Mr 4,29:1
Searing, Annie E P Mrs, 1942, Ap 23,24:3
Searing, Augustus V, 1953, Jl 3,19:5
Searing, Charles E, 1944, F 10,15:3
Searing, Edward M, 1947, O 23,25:5
Searing, Frederick L, 1948, My 21,23:1
Searing, Henry, 1937, Ap 11,II,8:4
Searing, Hudson R (funl, Je 30,69:2), 1957, Je 27,25:3
Searing, J A, 1876, My 8,5:4
Searing, John T, 1945, F 16,23:4
Searing, Joseph C, 1958, Ja 11,17:1
Searing, Leonard H, 1960, Mr 27,86:7
Searing, Throckmorton V, 1957, N 5,35:6
Searl, Clifford H, 1961, N 15,43:1
Searl, Kelly S, 1942, Ap 29,21:5
Searle, Arthur Prof, 1920, O 25,15:7
Searle, August J, 1955, F 3,23:4
Searle, Augustus L Mrs, 1942, Ja 15,19:3
Searle, Charles A, 1956, Ap 15,88:8
Searle, Clarence E, 1965, My 14,37:2
Searle, Clinton, 1952, Ag 14,23:3
Searle, D Francis, 1943, S 7,23:5
Searle, Edward Van Vechten Rev, 1907, F 12,9:6
Searle, Franklin E, 1916, Ap 23,19:5
Searle, Franklin H, 1955, Ag 3,23:3
Searle, Frederick A, 1940, F 2,17:2
Searle, George J, 1954, O 21,27:5
Searle, George M Rev, 1918, Jl 8,11:6
Searle, George W, 1949, O 12,29:1
Searle, H R, 1882, O 23,5:3
Searle, Harold E, 1966, F 3,31:2
Searle, Hayward, 1943, N 28,15:3
Searle, John P Mrs, 1950, Mr 18,13:3
Searle, John P Rev, 1922, Jl 28,13:4
Searle, Lewen F, 1940, Ja 25,21:5
Searle, Robert W, 1967, Je 18,76:3
Searle, Roy L, 1949, My 15,90:2
Searle, S T Rev, 1903, My 15,9:6
Searle, Susan A, 1951, O 27,19:7
Searle, Thomas, 1937, Mr 2,21:1
Searle, Truman G, 1949, D 19,27:2
Searle, Walter, 1953, S 1,23:1
Searle, Z, 1880, My 13,5:6
Searles, Albert R, 1942, My 7,19:5
Searles, Albert V, 1942, S 29,23:2
Searles, Charles E, 1947, F 6,15:3
Searles, Charles K, 1947, Ap 8,27:3
Searles, Charles M, 1951, Je 19,29:4
Searles, Charles N, 1954, F 3,23:5
Searles, E F Mrs (Mrs Mark Hopkins), 1891, Jl 26, 1:5
Searles, Edward Francis, 1920, Ag 7,5:5
Searles, Ellis, 1945, F 16,24:3
Searles, Harry M, 1953, Ap 21,27:3
Searles, Herbert N, 1952, Je 16,17:4
Searles, Howard A, 1962, Ag 4,19:5
Searles, Howard B, 1955, Jl 20,27:5
Searles, Jennie H, 1949, My 3,25:1
Searles, John Ennis, 1908, O 25,13:5
Searles, Leonard, 1940, F 22,23:4
Searles, Paul C, 1947, My 18,60:4
Searles, Paul J, 1958, S 11,33:2
Searles, Raymond R, 1944, My 29,15:4
Searles, Wallace, 1946, N 5,25:5
Searles, Walter H, 1950, Ag 12,13:2
Searles, William E, 1949, Mr 26,17:3
Searls, Charles E, 1925, Jl 15,17:5
Searls, Edmund D, 1951, Ag 26,77:2
Searls, Fred Jr, 1968, O 23,47:2
Searry, Michael Mrs, 1948, Mr 12,23:5
Sears, Albert F, 1958, Mr 23,88:3
Sears, Allan D, 1942, Ag 21,19:2
Sears, Amelia, 1946, Mr 28,25:4
Sears, Andrew C, 1943, My 10,19:1
Sears, Andrew M, 1953, Ja 13,27:2
Sears, Arthur, 1940, My 4,17:4
Sears, Augustus T, 1949, Jl 1,19:3
Sears, B, 1880, Jl 7,5:2
Sears, Benjamin, 1947, N 23,76:1
Sears, Blanche E Mrs, 1939, Ag 9,17:2
Sears, Caroline Mrs, 1938, O 12,27:2
Sears, Celia P Mrs, 1947, D 23,24:3
Sears, Charles B, 1946, Ag 1,23:5; 1950, D 18,31:1
Sears, Charles B Mrs, 1939, O 5,23:2
Sears, Charles E Col, 1904, F 26,9:6
Sears, Charles H (por), 1943, My 4,23:1
Sears, Charles M Mrs, 1953, N 12,31:1
Sears, Charles Payne, 1908, Je 25,9:5
Sears, Charles S, 1948, Ap 13,27:2
Sears, Charles W, 1903, O 6,9:6
Sears, Clara E, 1960, Mr 26,21:1
Sears, David, 1923, D 23,20:3
Sears, Delbert R, 1951, D 20,31:3
Sears, E H Rev :r, 1876, Ja 19,4:7
Sears, Edgar F, 1942, Jl 25,13:5
Sears, Edmund H, 1942, Jl 31,15:5
Sears, Edward H, 1948, Ja 16,21:1
Sears, Edward Mrs, 1944, Je 18,36:1
Sears, Eleonora Randolph, 1968, Mr 27,37:1
Sears, Emily C, 1946, Ap 4,25:2
Sears, Francis B, 1914, Ag 27,11:5; 1943, Ag 13,17:3
Sears, Frank H Mrs, 1947, N 29,13:5
Sears, Frank M Maj, 1921, Mr 9,13:4
Sears, Frank Mrs, 1956, F 2,25:4
Sears, Fred, 1957, D 1,88:4
Sears, Fred C, 1949, O 11,31:2
Sears, Frederick R, 1947, Ja 6,23:3
Sears, George G, 1940, My 29,23:4
Sears, Gradwell L, 1956, N 23,27:3
Sears, Grant H, 1950, N 22,25:5
Sears, Harold C, 1948, Jl 14,23:4
Sears, Harriet A Mrs, 1937, O 20,23:2
Sears, Harry L Mrs, 1953, Ap 24,23:1
Sears, Helen W, 1956, Ap 16,27:1
Sears, Henry D, 1942, My 24,43:2
Sears, Henry F, 1942, Ja 3,19:4
Sears, Herbert M, 1942, F 20,17:5
Sears, I L, 1942, Jl 18,13:5
Sears, Ida M Mrs, 1939, Jl 9,30:5
Sears, Ike U, 1937, D 19,II,8:7
Sears, J Boyd Judge, 1937, Ja 3,II,8:2
Sears, J Henry Capt, 1912, My 28,11:4
Sears, J Montgomery, 1908, Ag 13,7:3
Sears, J Thacher, 1958, Je 29,69:1
Sears, Jefferson D, 1946, Mr 15,22:3
Sears, John R, 1941, Jl 27,30:4
Sears, John W (Ziggy), 1956, D 17,31:2
Sears, Joseph D, 1959, Je 8,27:2
Sears, Joseph H, 1946, F 17,42:3
Sears, Joseph H Mrs, 1937, S 28,23:4
Sears, Judah H, 1938, S 21,25:3
Sears, Kenneth, 1951, O 15,25:1
Sears, Kenneth C, 1961, D 26,25:4
Sears, Laurence M, 1958, F 17,23:2
Sears, Leo, 1964, Ja 22,37:3
Sears, Lester M, 1967, F 22,29:2
Sears, Lorenzo Dr, 1916, Mr 1,11:5
Sears, Marcus C, 1947, O 14,27:2
Sears, Nancy L Mrs, 1938, N 17,25:5
Sears, Nathan P, 1946, F 26,25:5
Sears, Richard, 1943, S 3,19:5; 1962, Ap 28,25:3
Sears, Richard D Sr, 1943, Ap 10,17:3
Sears, Richard W, 1955, N 12,19:6
Sears, Richard W Mrs, 1946, My 29,24:2
Sears, Richard Warren, 1914, S 29,11:6
Sears, Richard 2d, 1949, Ja 9,72:6
Sears, Robert G Mrs, 1964, Ag 27,33:4
Sears, Samuel P, 1964, N 18,47:1
Sears, Seymour N, 1941, Mr 20,22:2; 1954, Mr 4,25:3
Sears, Taber, 1950, O 19,31:3
Sears, Taber Mrs, 1960, Je 8,39:1
Sears, Thomas D, 1954, Je 17,29:5
Sears, Thomas E, 1958, O 22,35:5
Sears, Thomas F, 1944, Ap 21,19:4
Sears, Walter J Com, 1913, Ap 13,IV,7:6
Sears, Walter Lincoln, 1915, D 16,15:5
Sears, Warren W, 1955, S 21,33:5
Sears, Wesley M, 1948, My 3,21:4
Sears, William H, 1951, Ap 21,17:3
Sears, William J (por), 1944, Mr 31,21:2
Sears, William R, 1941, Ap 21,19:5
Sears, Z, 1935, F 20,19:1
Searson, Joseph M, 1953, Ja 5,16:7
Searson, Robinson P, 1943, O 24,44:3
Seary, Elmer E, 1953, Jl 2,23:1
Sease, Virgil B, 1962, My 7,31:2
Seashore, Carl E, 1949, O 18,27:2
Seashore, Harold G, 1965, Je 14,33:2
Seashore, Robert H, 1951, Ap 28,23:5
Seasongood, Albert Sr, 1955, Je 8,29:6
Seasongood, Alfred Mrs, 1941, Ja 12,46:1
Seasongood, Edwin A, 1953, Ag 17,15:4
Seasongood, Emil W Mrs, 1949, F 15,24:3
Seasongood, Lewis Gen, 1914, N 30,9:6

Seastrom, Victor (V Sjoestroem), 1960, Ja 4,29:3
Seater, Samuel Scott Ex-Sen, 1916, N 20,13:5
Seath, Gordon H, 1952, S 1,8:5
Seaton, Anthony, 1955, Ap 12,29:3
Seaton, Arthur E, 1937, Ja 25,19:2
Seaton, Clarence J, 1953, Ja 19,23:3
Seaton, Edward P, 1966, Je 7,47:2
Seaton, Fay N, 1952, D 5,28:3
Seaton, Frank P, 1952, F 28,27:2
Seaton, George M Mrs, 1955, O 4,35:1
Seaton, George W, 1944, Ag 29,17:6
Seaton, James B, 1938, My 27,17:5
Seaton, John E, 1949, F 24,23:4
Seaton, John L, 1961, Ja 29,84:6
Seaton, Kenner Mrs, 1952, Ja 9,29:4
Seaton, Tom, 1940, Ap 12,23:5
Seaton, W W Col, 1866, Je 17,4:6
Seatree, V Ernest, 1945, N 3,15:6
Seaver, Charles H, 1964, Mr 22,76:8
Seaver, Florence M Mrs, 1940, F 21,19:5
Seaver, George W, 1939, D 4,23:6
Seaver, Guy J, 1938, O 18,25:2
Seaver, Jay W Dr, 1915, My 7,13:5
Seaver, John W Mrs, 1949, My 19,29:3
Seaver, Lucas, 1866, My 13,1:7
Seaver, Roscoe A, 1937, Jl 3,15:3
Seaver, Thomas C, 1950, Jl 22,15:3
Seaver, W A, 1883, Ja 8,5:5
Seaver, William Col, 1871, Ag 30,4:7
Seaver, William P Mrs, 1947, O 3,25:5
Seaverns, Annie W, 1942, D 4,25:2
Seaverns, Charles F T, 1956, Jl 12,23:2
Seaverns, Charles F T Mrs, 1947, F 20,25:3
Seaverns, George A, 1942, Mr 6,21:5
Seaverns, George A Mrs, 1944, Jl 7,15:5
Seaverns, Houghton, 1938, Ag 7,33:2
Seaverns, Joel H, 1923, N 13,21:5
Seavey, Arthur Dodge Mrs, 1912, Ja 9,13:6
Seavey, Clude L (por), 1943, Ag 7,11:3
Seavey, James Arthur, 1924, Ag 6,13:4
Seavey, Warren A, 1966, Ja 19,41:3
Seavy, Marion J, 1951, Ap 17,29:4
Seawell, Aaron A F, 1950, O 15,104:5
Seawell, Emmett, 1939, Jl 8,15:5
Seawell, Jerrold L, 1952, O 22,27:3
Seawell, Molly Elliot, 1916, N 16,11:5
Seawright, Robert M, 1956, F 10,21:5
Seawson, Loton H, 1924, My 5,15:3
Seay, A J Ex-Judge, 1915, D 24,9:4
Seay, Adrian V, 1947, N 27,31:2
Seay, Cornelius J, 1948, Ap 25,71:3
Seay, Edward L Mrs, 1956, Ja 30,27:4
Seay, Edward M, 1953, F 26,25:2
Seay, Frank, 1940, Jl 17,43:1
Seay, George J, 1952, N 13,31:4
Seay, Samuel Maj, 1913, D 7,19:3
Seay, Sue K Mrs, 1963, S 20,33:1
Seayden, James L, 1924, F 26,17:2
Seazer, Dolly, 1943, D 17,19:2
Seazer, Ellen, 1943, D 17,19:2
Sebag-Montefiore, Charles, 1960, My 9,29:1
Sebald, W W, 1967, Mr 17,41:3
Sebast, Frederick M, 1955, Jl 16,15:5
Sebastian, Dorothy, 1957, Ap 10,33:2
Sebastian, Jerome D, 1960, O 12,39:4
Sebastian, John, 1914, Mr 2,9:4
Sebastiani, Alfred D, 1948, My 3,21:1
Sebelin, Fred W, 1950, Je 20,27:3
Sebestyen, Charles, 1942, Ag 27,19:4
Sebok, Louis L, 1950, Ag 9,29:4
Sebold, Charles, 1942, O 28,23:6
Sebold, Charles E, 1941, N 26,23:1
Sebold, Phil, 1952, N 24,23:2
Sebrechts, Joseph M A A, 1948, Ap 1,25:5
Sebree, Uriel Rear-Adm, 1922, Ag 7,13:5
Sebring, Capt of Police, 1867, N 21,2:5
Sebring, Emma G, 1952, S 9,31:3
Sebring, H O, 1950, O 24,29:1
Sebring, Harold L Judge, 1968, Jl 27,27:2
Sebring, Lewis B, 1950, O 12,31:2
Sebring, Lewis B Mrs, 1953, Ap 30,31:2
Sebsow, R Murray, 1957, Jl 5,17:1
Secchi, Angelo, 1878, F 27,4:7
Seccomb, Edward O, 1943, My 13,21:3
Seccomb, Milo L, 1946, My 17,22:3
Seccor, Stanislaus J, 1950, F 7,27:2
Sechist, Frank K Dr, 1921, D 9,17:5
Sechler, J H Rev Dr, 1905, Ap 13,11:3
Sechny, John A, 1954, My 7,23:2
Sechrest, William B, 1951, F 1,13:6
Sechrist, Henry T, 1950, Ag 20,76:1
Sechrist, Theodore O, 1950, Ap 3,23:4
Seckel, Frederick W, 1961, D 20,33:1
Seckel, George T, 1954, O 14,29:5
Seckel, Thomas, 1952, Mr 28,23:2
Seckendorf, Theodore W, 1952, F 3,84:5
Seckendorff, Goetz von Count, 1910, Mr 3,9:5
Seckendorff, Maximillian von Count, 1911, Ag 29,7:3
Seckinger, A D, 1955, My 6,23:4
Seckler, Lillian, 1958, Jl 22,27:4
Seckler-Hudson, Catheryn (Mrs R G Steinmeyer), 1963, My 5,86:7
Seckles, Isadore, 1955, F 18,22:1
Seckner, Edgar C, 1945, Ag 22,23:3
Secolo, Floriano del, 1949, Je 22,31:4
Secon, Norman, 1958, Ag 24,87:1
Secor, Audubon J, 1946, F 10,40:7
Secor, C F, 1881, Mr 10,5:5
Secor, Daniel O, 1953, Jl 20,17:5
Secor, David Pell, 1909, Mr 31,11:4
Secor, Frank B, 1937, Ap 24,19:4
Secor, Frederick, 1945, N 6,19:2
Secor, Helen L Mrs, 1939, Mr 12,III,6:8
Secor, Horace D, 1951, Ja 16,29:4
Secor, J D, 1882, Je 23,5:6
Secor, Jay K, 1960, Mr 21,11:7
Secor, William, 1942, Je 29,15:6; 1944, Ja 20,19:3
Secord, Frank G, 1950, N 9,33:4
Secord, Wallace T, 1939, Jl 16,31:2
Secord, Warren D, 1938, My 5,23:3
Secord, William H, 1944, N 9,27:4
Secrest, Edmund, 1949, N 30,27:2
Secrist, Horace, 1943, Mr 6,13:1
Secrist, Walter D, 1942, D 5,15:2
Secunda, William, 1962, Ag 2,25:3
Securcher, Frank J Sr, 1943, O 10,48:4
Sedam, Robert W, 1957, Jl 11,25:4
Sedam, Walter C, 1945, O 27,15:4
Sedden, J A, 1880, Ag 20,4:7
Seddon, James A, 1939, Je 1,25:2
Seddon, Richard John Prim Min, 1906, Je 11,4:2
Seddon, Scott, 1949, N 4,27:3
Seddon, William L, 1937, Jl 13,19:1
Seddon, William P, 1958, Ap 20,85:1
Seddons, Peter J, 1955, Ja 25,25:4
Seder, Richard, 1940, Jl 18,19:2
Sederholm, Harriet Mrs, 1955, My 17,29:4
Sederholm, J, 1934, Je 28,23:5
Sedgeman, William, 1907, F 3,7:6
Sedgewick, Garnet C, 1949, S 5,17:4
Sedgewick, George H, 1939, Mr 15,23:4
Sedgewick, James A, 1937, N 28,II,8:5
Sedgley, Reginald F, 1938, Mr 30,21:2
Sedgman, William J, 1939, Ag 23,21:5
Sedgwick, Adam Rev, 1873, Ja 29,5:3
Sedgwick, Arthur H, 1948, S 12,72:3
Sedgwick, Augustus V, 1941, Je 12,23:3
Sedgwick, C B, 1883, F 8,5:2
Sedgwick, C F, 1882, Mr 10,5:1
Sedgwick, Catherine Maria, 1867, Ag 1,4:6
Sedgwick, Charles H, 1959, My 2,23:4
Sedgwick, Dwight R, 1950, Mr 29,29:4
Sedgwick, Earl H, 1947, N 28,27:2
Sedgwick, Edward M, 1953, My 8,25:3
Sedgwick, Edward V, 1939, S 12,25:4
Sedgwick, Ellery (will, My 5,33:3), 1960, Ap 22,31:1
Sedgwick, Ellery Mrs, 1937, Mr 7,II,8:2
Sedgwick, George E, 1947, O 8,25:2
Sedgwick, Harry, 1959, Mr 8,87:2
Sedgwick, Henry, 1916, S 30,11:4
Sedgwick, Henry D, 1903, D 27,7:5; 1957, Ja 7,25:4
Sedgwick, Henry Dwight Mrs, 1919, Ja 27,13:4
Sedgwick, Henry R, 1946, Ag 16,21:6
Sedgwick, Hubert M, 1950, N 12,93:1
Sedgwick, John, 1945, N 1,23:2
Sedgwick, John H, 1941, S 25,25:5
Sedgwick, John Maj-Gen, 1864, My 11,4:4
Sedgwick, Mary D G Mrs, 1954, F 18,31:3
Sedgwick, R Minturn Mrs, 1948, S 7,25:6
Sedgwick, Robert, 1922, F 14,17:5; 1953, F 9,27:2
Sedgwick, S J Prof, 1920, Ap 22,11:3
Sedgwick, T D, 1879, Ap 27,10:4
Sedgwick, Theodore, 1859, D 10,1:4; 1939, Ap 30,44:7; 1951, My 23,35:4
Sedgwick, Theodore Mrs, 1949, F 10,27:3; 1963, Jl 23, 29:5
Sedgwick, Walter N, 1944, F 26,13:6
Sedgwick, Walter N Mrs (por), 1949, F 13,77:1
Sedgwick, William E, 1942, F 16,17:2
Sedgwick, William T Prof, 1921, Ja 27,13:4
Sedinger, Thomas E Jr, 1951, S 13,31:4
Sedlacek, Ernst Mrs, 1951, Je 15,24:2
Sedlacek, Milo J, 1955, S 21,33:2
Sedley, Henry Mrs, 1871, Je 16,8:5
Sedlis, Elias, 1957, S 15,84:7
Sedlor, Joseph Sr, 1948, Je 22,25:3
Sedoff, Leon, 1938, F 17,5:1
Sedol, Jacob S, 1945, D 20,23:5
Sedric, Eugene H, 1963, Ap 6,19:3
Sedway, Moe, 1952, Ja 5,11:3
Sedwick, William P Jr, 1952, D 25,29:4
See, Alonzo B, 1941, D 17,27:3
See, Amos L, 1906, Mr 15,9:6
See, Arthur M, 1953, Mr 6,23:2
See, Charles A, 1949, N 7,27:2
See, Edmund T, 1965, F 22,21:2
See, Elliott M Jr (mem ser, Mr 3,33:3; funl, Mr 5,9:2), 1966, Mr 1,1:4
See, Francena S Mrs, 1940, Jl 25,17:5
See, Frank G Mrs, 1956, Jl 18,27:1
See, George N, 1939, D 24,15:3
See, Grace, 1913, Mr 25,13:5
See, Herbert G Mrs, 1950, My 16,31:3
See, J Benedict, 1908, Ap 11,7:4
See, J M Mrs, 1955, Ja 1,13:4
See, John Sir, 1907, F 1,9:4
See, Milton, 1920, O 29,15:5
See, Orley, 1957, N 28,31:3
See, Samuel D, 1941, O 16,21:2
See, Thomas, 1944, N 13,19:2
See, Thomas J J, 1962, Jl 5,23:4
Seebach, George J, 1948, N 17,27:2
Seebach, Julius F, 1950, S 11,23:5
Seebach, Julius F Mrs, 1948, O 21,27:2
Seebach, Oscar, 1939, My 29,15:6
Seebach, Otto, 1948, S 13,21:5
Seebacker, George, 1944, Ja 16,42:4
Seebeck, Edward F Rev, 1917, Jl 30,9:5
Seeber, Charles G, 1966, Ja 1,17:2
Seeber, Constance, 1949, Ja 23,68:6
Seeber, Elizabeth, 1964, Je 28,56:6
Seeber, George Mrs, 1944, Ap 29,15:5
Seebode, Otto C H, 1943, My 21,19:1
Seebohm, Hans C, 1967, S 18,47:1
Seebold, Amelia, 1952, Mr 25,27:4
Seebold, Edward M, 1942, Mr 17,21:5
Seeburger, Frank, 1942, O 4,52:4
Seeckt, H von, 1936, D 28,17:1
Seed, Allen H, 1961, Ja 22,84:3
Seed, Edward C, 1954, Mr 15,25:4
Seed, Edward C Mrs, 1963, My 1,39:1
Seed, Miles A, 1913, D 6,11:6
Seeders, Gerald F, 1958, O 5,87:2
Seeds, Blair C, 1946, Ap 26,21:2
Seeds, Enos L, 1944, Ja 23,37:1
Seeds, Jacob J Mrs, 1937, S 24,21:5
Seefeldt, Ruth E, 1959, Ag 13,3:7
Seegal, Morris, 1953, S 4,15:2
Seegar, J K B, 1945, Ag 25,11:5
Seeger, A F H Mrs, 1941, F 9,48:2
Seeger, Albert H F, 1945, Je 17,26:2
Seeger, Charles L, 1943, N 7,56:7
Seeger, Charles L Mrs, 1947, S 20,15:3
Seeger, Charles Mrs, 1953, N 20,23:3
Seeger, Christian Mrs, 1948, Mr 23,25:5
Seeger, Eugene, 1941, O 1,21:2
Seeger, Ferdinand Dr, 1923, F 28,17:4
Seeger, Henry C, 1948, S 14,29:5
Seeger, John Mrs, 1950, Ap 19,29:4
Seeger, Ludwig, 1905, Mr 14,9:5
Seeger, Stanley J, 1952, Je 21,15:3
Seegers, Gustave, 1947, Je 6,23:2
Seeherman, Max, 1944, O 13,19:2
Seekamp, Arthur A, 1958, S 18,31:4
Seekamp, Henry H, 1948, Je 21,21:4
Seekell, Ulysses L, 1944, F 2,21:1
Seel, George J 3d, 1945, Ag 6,15:4
Seeland, Howard F, 1950, Ap 7,25:1
Seeland, William J Sr, 1957, O 16,35:2
Seelaus, Henry K Dr, 1937, F 15,17:4
Seelbach, Alfred C, 1944, S 26,23:4
Seeldrayers, Rodolphe W, 1955, O 9,86:5
Seelen, Mark B, 1958, My 25,87:1
Seeler, Frederick Mrs, 1948, N 20,13:6
Seeler, Harrison G, 1944, Ja 6,23:2
Seeley, Charles F, 1941, N 9,52:2
Seeley, Charles F Mrs, 1946, Jl 20,13:4
Seeley, Clinton B, 1958, Mr 18,29:3
Seeley, Clinton B Mrs, 1957, N 12,34:2
Seeley, Frank B, 1951, D 27,21:1
Seeley, George C Mrs, 1909, Mr 8,7:6
Seeley, George P, 1960, N 29,37:1
Seeley, Gerard U, 1946, O 23,27:5
Seeley, Halstead H, 1952, Ap 20,92:5
Seeley, Henry Gouvier Prof, 1909, Ja 9,9:6
Seeley, Henry J Col, 1937, N 17,23:2
Seeley, Henry S, 1913, O 5,IV,17:6
Seeley, Herbert Barnum, 1914, Jl 9,7:6
Seeley, I C Rev, 1874, D 28,1:6
Seeley, Isaac, 1937, O 20,23:5
Seeley, Isaac Mrs, 1954, D 7,33:4
Seeley, James, 1943, F 16,19:1
Seeley, John H, 1947, F 10,29:5
Seeley, John J, 1945, Mr 9,19:2
Seeley, Lamar Dr, 1907, Je 15,9:6
Seeley, Milton J, 1943, My 30,26:2
Seeley, Nathan, 1916, Je 28,11:3
Seeley, Nathaniel S, 1958, S 14,85:1
Seeley, R S K, 1957, Ag 4,80:8
Seeley, Robert E, 1959, Je 14,86:4
Seeley, Storrs H Mrs, 1939, O 7,17:6
Seeley, W Parker, 1953, Ja 4,76:3
Seeley, W W Dr, 1903, N 8,7:7
Seeley, Ward, 1960, Jl 24,64:3
Seeley, William W, 1961, Mr 23,33:2
Seelhorst, George, 1948, Je 26,17:5
Seelhozer, Berthold Mrs, 1939, O 6,25:4
Seelig, Alfred E, 1942, S 14,15:2
Seelig, Gustave A F, 1944, O 15,45:2
Seelig, Major G, 1953, Mr 12,27:3
Seeligsberg, Leonard, 1943, N 5,19:2
Seeligson, Emma L Mrs, 1939, My 24,23:5
Seeling, Charles R, 1951, O 16,31:3
Seelman, Caroline R, 1956, S 26,33:5
Seelman, Maurice S, 1943, Mr 9,23:3
Seels, William, 1908, F 18,7:6
Seely, Aaron K, 1951, Mr 22,31:5
Seely, Aaron K Mrs, 1947, Ap 28,23:4
Seely, Florence C, 1949, Ap 4,23:5

Seely, Fred L, 1942, Mr 15,42:6
Seely, Grace A, 1948, My 25,27:5
Seely, Harry G, 1961, Ag 21,23:5
Seely, Hart I, 1951, N 24,28:8
Seely, Henry M, 1917, My 5,13:6
Seely, Henry S Mrs, 1945, Jl 24,23:1
Seely, Herman B, 1941, F 26,21:4
Seely, Homer R, 1956, Je 25,23:6
Seely, I Wesley, 1925, N 19,25:5
Seely, Leslie B, 1954, N 10,33:2
Seely, Lewis S, 1945, O 3,19:3
Seely, Roy B, 1958, Ja 14,33:4
Seely, Walter E, 1954, Mr 28,89:2
Seely, Weeden R, 1942, Ja 13,19:3
Seely, William C Mrs, 1944, S 3,26:5
Seely, William H, 1939, Ap 7,21:4; 1952, N 16,88:5
Seelye, Burt P, 1937, O 15,23:5
Seelye, Caroline A, 1937, Ap 25,II,9:2
Seelye, Elwyn E, 1959, D 29,26:1
Seelye, Henrietta Chapin Mrs, 1925, S 15,25:4
Seelye, J H Prof, 1895, My 13,2:3
Seelye, L Clark Dr, 1925, S 13,5:2
Seelye, Laurens H, 1960, Ag 22,25:3
Seelye, Laurenus Clark, 1924, O 13,17:4
Seelye, Mary M Mrs, 1940, D 12,27:4
Seelye, Theodore E Mrs, 1948, Je 29,23:2
Seem, Ralph B, 1941, My 15,23:4
Seeman, Alois, 1950, S 1,21:5
Seeman, Clare H Mrs, 1944, S 15,19:4
Seeman, Frederick C, 1914, O 20,13:5
Seeman, Isaac W, 1947, D 26,15:3
Seeman, Joseph (por), 1941, Ap 24,21:5
Seeman, Robert, 1943, Jl 19,15:3
Seeman, William, 1961, Je 7,41:1
Seep, J, 1928, Ap 2,21:5
Seery, Francis J, 1947, Jl 28,15:4
Seery, Frank L, 1918, Ja 22,11:4
Seery, Irving P, 1966, Ja 13,25:4
Seery, James E, 1953, Ap 7,29:3
Seery, James K, 1956, O 7,87:1
Seery, John J (por), 1944, O 2,19:3
Seery, Joseph J Sr, 1956, N 13,37:5
Seery, Matthew J, 1955, My 26,31:3
Seery, Peter, 1922, D 16,15:5
Seery, Peter S, 1946, My 22,21:1
Seery, William F, 1953, Mr 26,31:3; 1958, Ag 21,25:5
Seery, William M, 1944, My 24,19:4
Sees, Edward W, 1952, S 4,27:5
Sees, John H, 1955, Jl 16,15:6
Sees, John V, 1946, S 3,19:3
Seese, Edwin Rohn, 1953, F 21,13:6
Seese, George, 1955, Ja 19,27:2
Seested, A F, 1928, O 3,31:1
Sefa, Suat Mrs, 1960, Jl 4,15:4
Seff, Isadore, 1941, D 21,40:8
Sefferino, Peter Mrs, 1948, Je 24,25:1
Sefrit, Charles Green, 1925, Ag 25,17:5
Sefrit, Frank I, 1950, My 28,45:1
Sefton, Earl of, 1901, D 3,9:5
Sefton, Edwin, 1943, Je 29,20:3
Sefton, Frederick, 1938, F 5,15:5
Sefton, J O, 1881, S 6,2:2
Sefton, John, 1868, S 20,5:3
Sefton, John E, 1945, Ag 23,33:5
Sefton, Maria A D Mrs, 1941, O 11,17:6
Sefton, Stanley L, 1954, Ap 22,29:2
Sefton, Thomas J Mrs, 1956, O 8,27:5
Sefton, W Harry, 1966, Je 19,85:1
Sefton, William J, 1912, Jl 8,9:5
Sefton, William Mrs, 1952, Ja 31,27:3
Segal, Abe L, 1955, My 31,27:1
Segal, Abraham, 1957, Mr 25,25:4
Segal, Abraham D, 1963, Ap 21,86:7
Segal, Alfred, 1968, Mr 5,41:2
Segal, Arthur, 1949, Mr 27,76:1
Segal, Ben, 1961, N 2,37:2
Segal, Bernard, 1967, D 16,41:2
Segal, Charles, 1962, S 15,25:2
Segal, Charles M Mrs, 1961, N 8,35:5
Segal, Harry, 1964, Ap 22,47:4
Segal, Henry C Mrs, 1954, Ag 5,23:5
Segal, Herbert I, 1962, Ag 25,44:5
Segal, Jacob, 1951, Mr 4,92:3
Segal, Jacob I, 1954, Mr 9,27:3
Segal, Jacob M, 1953, Ja 6,29:1
Segal, Joseph, 1953, S 4,33:4
Segal, Joseph P, 1954, My 5,31:4
Segal, Keeva, 1941, F 10,17:4
Segal, Louis, 1958, Ap 1,31:2; 1964, Je 17,43:2
Segal, Louis Mrs, 1958, N 3,37:3
Segal, Marek, 1958, D 9,41:4
Segal, Maurice, 1951, My 4,27:4
Segal, Morris S, 1960, F 7,84:2
Segal, Myer, 1955, S 10,17:3
Segal, Paul M, 1968, My 25,35:1
Segal, Paula Mrs, 1939, My 3,23:5
Segal, Philip, 1967, My 8,41:4
Segal, Samuel, 1964, Mr 7,23:4
Segal, Samuel I, 1958, Ag 21,25:4
Segal, Samuel M, 1954, F 23,27:4; 1961, Ag 29,31:1
Segal, Samuel Mrs, 1957, Jl 5,17:2
Segal, Sigmund L, 1953, S 28,25:5
Segalas, Anthony S, 1964, My 7,37:2
Segall, Abraham, 1938, N 1,23:2
Segall, Charles, 1953, O 30,23:2
Segall, Herman, 1961, S 28,41:5
Segall, Jose, 1952, Je 18,27:3
Segall, Joseph M, 1956, Jl 19,27:4
Segall, Julius, 1925, Ja 21,21:3
Segall, Louis S, 1937, Ap 23,21:2
Segall, Morris, 1940, Je 25,23:2
Segall, Samuel, 1950, S 19,31:3
Segaloff, Abraham, 1946, N 20,31:5
Segalovitch, Zusman, 1949, F 22,23:3
Seganti, Mario, 1962, Jl 28,19:4
Segar, Abe, 1958, N 18,37:2
Segar, Elzie C (por), 1938, O 14,23:3
Segar, J E, 1880, My 1,5:4
Segar, Minnie A, 1959, Ag 20,25:2
Segar, Ralph Mrs, 1954, D 1,31:3
Segarra, Consuelo, 1946, Ap 30,21:4
Segarra, Pedro, 1951, Jl 27,19:6
Segault, Leon, 1941, My 1,23:3
Segel, Rubin Mrs, 1949, Ap 13,29:4
Segelcke, John F, 1951, D 5,35:1
Segelcke, Otto, 1908, S 3,7:5
Segelken, Rose C Mrs, 1942, O 28,23:4
Seger, Arthur A, 1954, F 15,23:4
Seger, Charles B, 1940, N 12,23:3
Seger, George N, 1940, Ag 27,21:4
Seger, Gerhart H, 1967, Ja 22,76:4
Seger, John P, 1958, My 26,51:3
Segerblom, Wilhelm, 1941, N 11,23:3
Segers, George A, 1953, F 18,31:2
Segerstedt, Torgny, 1945, Ap 1,36:5
Segerstrom, Henry C, 1958, S 24,27:4
Seggerman, Frederick T, 1961, N 1,43:6
Seggerman, Frederick T Mrs, 1941, O 29,23:3
Seggerman, Kenneth Mrs, 1946, F 28,23:3
Seggerman, Virginia T Mrs, 1940, Jl 19,19:4
Seghers, Paul D Mrs, 1958, Mr 16,87:1
Segison, Herbert S Mrs, 1961, O 2,31:2
Seglie, Paul, 1938, F 4,21:2
Segner, Charles A, 1952, D 27,9:1
Segner, Lajos, 1956, D 27,25:1
Segond, Paul Dr, 1912, O 28,11:5
Segovia, Fernando, 1954, Mr 30,27:5
Segrave, Francis D, 1946, Ja 29,25:5
Segrave, John R, 1938, S 22,23:5
Segraves, James E, 1949, S 22,31:4
Segre, Alfredo, 1960, O 1,19:5
Segreto, Dominick, 1949, Je 17,23:1
Segriff, James F, 1958, My 13,29:4
Segrin, Oscar E, 1953, Jl 2,23:3
Segschneider, Rudolph Mrs, 1944, Je 9,15:3
Segsworth, Walter E, 1945, Jl 22,38:2
Segui, Henriette L Mrs, 1938, D 1,23:4
Segui, M Charles, 1965, Je 26,29:6
Seguin, Anne, 1888, Ag 25,4:6
Seguin, E, 1879, O 10,5:2; 1880, O 29,2:3
Seguin, Marc, 1937, Ag 2,19:5
Seguin de Reynies, Antoine de, 1942, Je 13,15:5
Seguine, Edward M, 1938, Je 11,15:4
Seguine, Edward M Mrs, 1949, D 16,31:4
Seguine, Edward S, 1947, Ap 18,21:4
Seguine, Henry H, 1951, S 23,87:2
Seguine, Joseph, 1941, Jl 7,15:5
Seguine, Joseph C, 1944, Mr 8,19:5
Seguine, Lester W, 1946, Ap 30,21:2
Seguine, William, 1940, My 13,17:4
Segur, Guillaume de, 1945, N 9,19:2
Segur, Hollis D, 1939, Jl 24,13:4
Segur, Pierre Marie Maurice Henri de, 1916, Ag 15,9:4
Segur, Willard B, 1939, Ja 28,15:2
Segura y Seanz, Pedro (funl plans, Ap 9,33:4; funl, Ap 12,25:3), 1957, Ap 8,23:1
Segurola, Andreas de, 1953, Ja 23,19:1
Seherr-Thoss, Hermann Mrs, 1943, My 4,23:4
Sehinasi, Solomon, 1919, O 5,22:4
Sehnert, Henry B Mrs, 1945, O 10,21:3
Sehres, Ephraim Mrs, 1963, D 13,35:2
Sehwarz, Frederick A O, 1911, My 18,11:6
Seibel, Carl F, 1951, F 27,27:4
Seibel, Chris W, 1947, Jl 1,25:1
Seibel, Edwin A, 1957, S 11,33:3
Seibel, George, 1958, Jl 27,61:4
Seibel, Harry C, 1941, Ap 9,25:3
Seibel, I, 1932, Ag 3,15:1
Seibels, Edwin G, 1954, D 23,19:2
Seiber, Abram E, 1938, Ag 25,19:4
Seiber, Matyas, 1960, S 27,6:6
Seiberlich, Edward B, 1948, Je 18,60:1
Seiberling, Charles W, 1946, S 21,15:1
Seiberling, Edith A Mrs, 1952, O 7,29:5
Seiberling, Frank A, 1955, Ag 12,19:1
Seiberling, Frank A Mrs (por), 1946, Ja 9,23:4
Seiberling, John F Sr, 1962, Jl 16,23:5
Seibert, Albert E, 1955, O 22,19:2
Seibert, Charles A, 1949, Jl 29,21:2
Seibert, Charles L, 1920, Je 30,13:4
Seibert, Edward C Dr (por), 1937, N 9,23:2
Seibert, Frank A Mrs, 1950, O 21,17:3
Seibert, Henry, 1909, Mr 15,9:7
Seibert, Herbert, 1938, O 28,23:4
Seibert, J Frank, 1953, F 6,20:4
Seibert, Jacob Mrs, 1948, D 19,76:2
Seibert, James W, 1963, Ag 6,31:4
Seibert, Katherine B Mrs, 1940, D 6,23:5
Seibert, Kenneth S, 1948, N 22,21:4
Seibert, Philip J, 1946, S 10,7:2
Seibert, Walter E Sr, 1961, Je 11,86:5
Seibert, Walter R, 1965, D 24,17:2
Seibert, Walter W, 1948, D 15,33:5
Seibig, Arthur H, 1954, My 20,31:2
Seibold, Harry C, 1960, Ja 5,31:3
Seibold, John L, 1948, Ag 18,25:5
Seibold, Louis (por), 1945, My 11,19:1
Seibold, Louis Mrs, 1925, Jl 20,15:5
Seibold, Philip W, 1964, Ja 14,31:4
Seibold, Stewart F, 1949, O 15,15:2
Seiby, Edward, 1942, Ja 21,18:3
Seid, Reuben, 1951, Jl 10,27:2
Seidband, Harry, 1945, F 5,15:3
Seide, Gustav A Mrs, 1945, Ag 8,23:4
Seide, Harold, 1953, S 15,27:6
Seide, Herman, 1943, My 26,23:4
Seide, I Lincoln, 1939, Jl 9,31:1
Seide, I Lincoln Mrs (por), 1948, F 9,17:5
Seide, Jack, 1967, Jl 10,28:6
Seide, Joseph C, 1967, O 28,31:4
Seide, Max, 1948, F 24,26:2
Seidel, Albert E, 1957, N 10,86:8
Seidel, Albin, 1947, S 2,21:3
Seidel, Alfred E Sr, 1957, S 22,86:2
Seidel, Arthur, 1961, F 4,19:1
Seidel, Charles, 1948, My 25,27:2
Seidel, Emil, 1947, Je 26,23:2
Seidel, Ewald, 1949, F 16,26:2
Seidel, Frederick, 1949, Jl 6,30:3
Seidel, Hanns, 1961, Ag 6,84:4
Seidel, Horace Y, 1950, Jl 5,31:1
Seidel, Kaspar H, 1962, Ap 12,36:1
Seidel, Leon, 1968, My 20,47:4
Seidel, Richard, 1942, S 14,15:4
Seidel, Titania Mrs, 1925, Ap 29,21:6
Seidelman, Joseph H, 1968, Mr 20,47:4
Seidelson, Max, 1954, Ja 28,27:2
Seideman, Morris H, 1958, Ja 15,29:4
Seiden, Frank (cor, N 15,27:3), 1957, N 14,33:2
Seiden, Harry G, 1955, Ja 23,85:2
Seiden, Ira, 1964, Ja 25,23:6
Seiden, Leon, 1962, Je 27,35:4
Seiden, Louis, 1956, Ap 3,35:1
Seiden, Michael M, 1947, Mr 29,15:3
Seidenberg, Harry Mrs, 1960, Mr 26,21:4
Seidenberg, Samuel, 1924, Ja 5,13:5
Seidenman, Charles, 1966, Je 17,45:1
Seidenspinner, Earle A, 1949, Je 15,29:4
Seidenstein, Benjamin, 1940, Ja 24,21:2
Seidenstein, Harold, 1960, Ja 11,45:1
Seidensticker, Charles A, 1940, Je 21,21:2
Seidensticker, Louis J, 1958, Mr 21,21:2
Seider, Joseph H, 1960, O 7,35:1
Seiderman, Elias, 1937, Jl 18,II,7:2
Seiderman, Jack, 1954, My 6,33:5
Seiders, George M, 1915, My 27,11:6
Seiders, Joseph F, 1950, Mr 28,31:3
Seides, Harry M, 1948, Jl 19,19:2
Seidl, Anton, 1898, Mr 29,1:3
Seidl, Johanna E Mrs, 1944, D 27,19:1
Seidl, John H, 1966, O 20,43:4
Seidl-Kraus, Auguste Mrs (cor, Jl 25,19:5), 1939, Jl 17,19:4
Seidler, Alex Sr, 1960, Jl 13,35:4
Seidler, Charles J, 1957, Jl 18,25:2
Seidler, Ernest W, 1950, Ap 9,85:1
Seidler, Frederick A, 1961, N 4,19:2
Seidler, George E, 1955, Ja 1,13:3
Seidler, George M, 1951, Mr 24,13:5
Seidler, Russell, 1948, O 16,15:1
Seidler, Victor B, 1961, Je 13,35:2
Seidlin, Samuel M, 1955, Ja 4,21:3
Seidling, Oscar, 1947, S 2,21:2
Seidlitz, Baroness Frieda von, 1951, Ja 9,29:2
Seidlitz, Maurice Mrs, 1953, Ja 13,32:3
Seidman, Edwin A, 1962, O 12,32:3
Seidman, Henry L, 1963, My 16,35:1
Seidman, Herman (cor, F 28,29:2), 1964, F 26,35:3
Seidman, Louis, 1954, O 17,87:1
Seidman, Maximilian L, 1963, O 3,35:4
Seidman, Maxwell E, 1950, N 19,93:1
Seidman, Nathan H, 1948, Mr 11,27:5
Seidman, Simon, 1959, S 13,84:6
Seidman, William I, 1948, Ap 3,15:3
Seidmann, Henry P, 1954, My 6,33:5
Seidner, Jacob H, 1960, Jl 21,27:3
Seif, George, 1940, D 12,27:3
Seif El Islam Mutahar, 1952, Ap 27,90:3
Seifart, Fritz, 1964, O 5,33:4
Seifer, Morris, 1967, F 8,31:2
Seiferheld, Freda Mrs, 1951, My 18,32:8
Seiferheld, Sigmund, 1937, F 7,II,9:2
Seifert, Albert C, 1949, My 21,13:5
Seifert, Charles W, 1954, N 20,17:2
Seifert, Hettie W, 1956, Mr 6,31:2
Seifert, John, 1950, S 27,31:1
Seifert, Joseph A, 1950, Ja 7,17:2
Seifert, Marie E Mrs, 1949, Mr 1,25:2
Seifert, Mathias J, 1947, F 2,57:7

Seifert, Theodore, 1951, N 18,51:5
Seiff, Arthur N Mrs, 1955, Mr 10,27:1
Seiffer, Morris Mrs, 1945, O 11,23:5
Seiffert, Edward O, 1961, F 16,31:5
Seiffert, Frank M, 1948, Je 28,19:1
Seiffert, Moses, 1922, F 8,17:5
Seiffert, William R, 1963, My 26,92:7
Seifriz, William C, 1955, Jl 17,11:1
Seifts, Jacob, 1953, Mr 28,17:6
Seigel, Eugene, 1948, My 4,25:5
Seigel, Henry, 1873, S 3,8:5
Seigel, Henry F, 1938, Ap 19,21:5
Seigel, Janet S, 1960, Mr 19,21:1
Seigel, Joshua Rabbi (funl, F 25,7:5), 1910, F 23,9:3
Seigel, Max Mrs, 1959, F 26,31:3
Seigel, Paul D, 1948, D 17,27:4
Seigel, Samuel, 1954, My 23,88:5
Seiger, Sol Mrs (Lee), 1968, Ag 22,37:2
Seigh, Clarence C, 1957, F 19,31:6
Seigle, William R (por), 1938, D 27,17:1
Seignobos, Charles, 1942, Ap 30,19:4
Seikel, Oscar C, 1949, Ja 11,31:2
Seil, Gilbert E, 1946, S 13,7:2
Seil, Harvey A, 1951, Ja 6,15:5
Seiler, Alexander Dr, 1920, Mr 8,9:6
Seiler, Charles E, 1951, F 16,25:3
Seiler, Edward, 1952, Ja 2,12:1
Seiler, Fred, 1962, Ja 6,19:2
Seiler, George W, 1950, Ap 26,29:5
Seiler, Gustave W, 1941, Jl 10,19:5
Seiler, Isaac W Mrs, 1960, O 6,41:5
Seiler, James, 1946, Ja 5,13:2
Seiler, John G, 1946, My 26,32:6
Seiler, Joseph L, 1952, Ag 5,19:2
Seiler, Karl Sr, 1946, Ag 24,11:6
Seiler, Martin Mrs, 1940, D 31,15:1
Seiler, Otto E, 1951, D 7,27:1
Seiler, Peter W, 1941, S 27,17:4
Seiler, Ralph G, 1963, Jl 10,35:1
Seiler, William A, 1953, Ap 25,15:5
Seilern, Countess, 1901, S 24,7:6
Seilheimer, Henry, 1959, Ap 27,27:3
Seilikovitch, Sol, 1940, N 19,23:6
Seiller, H A, 1944, S 24,46:1
Seilliere, Ernest, 1955, Mr 16,33:2
Seims, William, 1944, F 15,17:5
Seinard, George, 1873, O 1,1:7
Seinecke, Ferdinand, 1914, Ap 20,9:2
Seinfel, Henry, 1938, Ag 1,13:6
Seinosuke Go, Baron, 1942, Ja 20,19:2
Seinsheimer, Louis A, 1951, Jl 11,23:5
Seip, Frank T, 1947, Je 21,17:4
Seip, Howard S, 1939, D 24,14:4
Seip, Jacob G, 1954, O 22,27:4
Seip, Theodore L Dr, 1903, N 30,7:6
Seipel, Rudolph B, 1954, F 17,31:2
Seiple, Bernard A, 1961, My 28,64:5
Seiple, William Mrs, 1952, F 2,13:4
Seipmann, Otto, 1947, Ja 12,21:2
Seipp, Henry G Mrs, 1956, N 3,23:5
Seipp, John, 1945, O 18,23:1
Seipp, William C, 1962, Jl 27,25:3
Seiser, Louis J, 1944, O 15,44:3
Seiser, Louis Mrs, 1945, O 28,44:4
Seiter, Charles J Col, 1910, O 10,9:6
Seiter, Joseph C, 1941, F 10,17:5
Seiter, Karl, 1958, F 1,19:2
Seiter, William A, 1964, Jl 28,29:5
Seither, Fred J, 1951, My 18,27:2
Seitman, Charles E Mrs, 1940, Jl 29,13:3
Seits, Edward O, 1954, S 15,33:1
Seitz, Arthur, 1943, Je 3,21:5
Seitz, C, 1935, D 5,25:1
Seitz, Don C Mrs, 1924, Ag 6,13:4
Seitz, Edmund V, 1948, S 30,27:2
Seitz, Edward F Mrs, 1957, Ja 22,29:5
Seitz, Frank F, 1938, S 5,15:5
Seitz, Frederick J, 1946, Ap 24,26:3
Seitz, George A, 1947, O 26,70:5
Seitz, George B, 1944, Jl 9,35:3
Seitz, George W, 1945, Jl 12,11:5
Seitz, Gothold W, 1949, N 21,25:5
Seitz, J J, 1940, Ja 13,15:2
Seitz, Jay A, 1956, Ag 28,27:4
Seitz, John, 1947, Ap 23,25:5
Seitz, John A, 1941, O 23,23:5
Seitz, John F R Mrs, 1953, Ja 11,90:3
Seitz, Josiah A Rev, 1922, O 1,28:4
Seitz, Karl, 1950, F 4,15:3
Seitz, Louis J Sr, 1950, Je 21,27:5
Seitz, Ludovico Prof, 1908, S 12,7:6
Seitz, Mary, 1940, F 14,21:2
Seitz, Messick V, 1943, Mr 30,21:4
Seitz, Myra Tolins, 1968, My 7,41:4
Seitz, Rebecca J Mrs, 1924, N 23,7:1
Seitz, Robert, 1957, O 3,29:3
Seitz, Roland F, 1946, D 31,17:5
Seitz, Selma H Mrs, 1940, Ap 8,19:2
Seitzick, Samuel, 1966, S 30,47:1
Seiver, George O, 1964, Ap 14,37:5
Seivert, Emil G, 1959, Ap 9,31:3
Seiwell, Donald R, 1963, N 21,39:5
Seiwell, H R, 1951, Mr 8,31:4
Seixas, Arch, 1950, N 28,31:3
Seixas, Edward F (por), 1945, Ja 10,23:3
Seixas, Edward W Mrs, 1961, N 10,35:3
Seixas, Ernest P, 1952, Jl 14,61:1
Seixas, Everett M, 1949, D 12,34:4
Seixas, Myler L, 1918, S 12,11:2
Sejour, Victor, 1874, S 22,4:7
Sekel, Andrew, 1946, Je 15,21:1
Sekine, Hunter E, 1942, S 13,45:5
Sekine, Ioji B, 1948, S 5,40:5
Sekine, Ioji B Mrs, 1957, My 17,25:1
Sekiya, Toshiko, 1941, N 24,17:4
Seksaria, Gobindam G, 1946, My 23,21:5
Sekulich, Steve, 1956, O 31,25:4
Selander, Harry W Mrs, 1955, Jl 29,17:4
Selander, Sture, 1949, Ag 29,23:2
Selander, Wilbur M, 1967, N 16,47:5
Selangor, Sultan of, 1938, Ap 1,23:3
Selangor, Sultan of (Paramount Ruler of Malaya), 1960, S 1,27:4
Selbach, Albert K (Kip), 1956, F 18,19:4
Selbert, Edwin, 1950, O 5,31:1
Selbie, Evelyn, 1950, D 9,15:3
Selbit, Percy, 1938, N 21,19:5
Selborne, Earl of, 1942, F 27,18:2
Selby, Charles E, 1949, My 29,36:5
Selby, Clarence D, 1967, F 28,34:3
Selby, Ernest, 1957, O 18,23:4
Selby, G Terrell, 1958, S 3,33:2
Selby, George L L, 1950, My 18,29:3
Selby, Howard W, 1953, Ag 26,27:3
Selby, James A, 1940, D 5,25:3
Selby, Jo, 1955, Mr 20,75:5
Selby, Nathaniel E, 1965, S 2,31:2
Selby, Paul, 1913, Mr 21,13:2
Selby, Viscount (Wm Court Gully), 1909, N 7,13:5
Selby, Walford H M, 1965, Ag 9,25:4
Selby, William E Mrs, 1948, F 16,22:2
Selby, William E Sr, 1957, D 27,19:4
Selby, William G, 1956, D 6,37:5
Selch, Fred G Jr Mrs, 1947, O 26,68:4
Selchow, Charles E, 1938, F 4,21:4
Selcow, Eva Mrs, 1942, O 27,30:7
Selcow, Merrill, 1942, O 27,30:7
Selden, A Kenneth, 1940, O 5,15:3
Selden, Charles, 1871, Ag 1,5:2
Selden, Charles A, 1949, F 10,27:1
Selden, Charles A Mrs, 1952, Jl 3,25:5
Selden, Edward G, 1938, Je 23,21:2
Selden, Ethelinda Mrs, 1864, Jl 17,6:2
Selden, G Dudley, 1960, Ap 22,31:2
Selden, George B, 1922, Ja 18,17:2
Selden, John T, 1964, My 31,76:7
Selden, Lynde Mrs, 1966, Jl 1,35:2
Selden, S L, 1876, S 22,5:1
Selden, Samuel, 1959, O 27,37:3
Selden, Samuel Mrs, 1960, Ap 21,31:5
Selden, William C Mrs, 1946, Jl 3,25:4
Seldes, Gilbert Mrs, 1954, Ja 29,19:1
Seldes, Karen, 1957, Jl 16,53:5
Seldin, Alex, 1949, N 27,104:6
Seldin, Jules B Mrs (N Gordani), 1966, Ja 21,47:4
Seldner, Arthur H, 1955, Mr 26,15:4
Seldner, Isaac, 1947, F 10,29:5
Seldte, Franz, 1947, Ap 2,27:3
Seldwyn, Arch, 1959, Je 23,33:3
Selecman, Charles C, 1958, Mr 29,17:1
Selee, Frank, 1909, Jl 6,7:6
Selee, Marion (Mrs T E Williams), 1961, S 19,35:3
Seleiman, Abdul H, 1945, F 14,19:5
Selekman, B M Mrs, 1954, Jl 9,17:5
Selekman, Benjamin M, 1962, Ap 8,86:8
Selesnick, Sydney, 1967, F 7,39:2
Seletzky, Anatoli, 1938, My 12,23:4
Selevan, Aaron, 1954, My 14,23:2
Seley, Jacob, 1944, O 23,19:4; 1955, Ja 11,25:4
Seley, Moses H, 1967, F 25,28:1
Seley, Simon, 1962, My 31,27:2
Seleznev, O P Y, 1949, Mr 8,25:5
Self, Edward, 1923, D 27,13:2
Self, Edward D, 1952, Ja 13,88:2
Self, James C, 1955, Jl 22,23:1
Self, Lucian Mrs, 1947, D 1,22:2
Self, Lucien Jr, 1950, D 28,25:3
Selfridge, Adm, 1902, O 16,3:4
Selfridge, Harry G (por), 1947, My 9,21:1
Selfridge, Harry Gordon Mrs, 1918, My 14,13:5
Selfridge, James L, 1937, F 12,15:5
Selfridge, Minnie L Mrs, 1924, N 23,7:1
Selfridge, Russell, 1944, Mr 25,15:6
Selfridge, Susan W K Mrs, 1940, Ag 29,19:3
Selgas, Alfredo, 1940, Mr 27,21:4
Selheimer, Charles A, 1945, D 7,21:4
Seliers, Salome Mrs, 1909, Ja 11,9:6
Selig, Albert L, 1946, Jl 31,27:1
Selig, Albert S, 1955, Ja 3,27:2
Selig, August, 1943, Jl 5,15:3
Selig, Bernard, 1939, Mr 22,23:1
Selig, Ely K, 1938, Ja 8,15:3
Selig, George R, 1960, S 13,74:4
Selig, Harris L, 1960, Ap 18,29:5
Selig, Jack, 1951, Je 11,25:4
Selig, Marcus M, 1946, Ag 6,25:3
Selig, Samson Mrs, 1950, Je 22,27:2
Selig, Seth (por), 1941, N 4,23:3
Selig, Sigmund, 1903, O 25,7:6
Selig, William N, 1948, Jl 17,15:3
Seliger, Robert V, 1953, Ap 26,85:3
Seligman, A, 1933, S 26,21:5
Seligman, A R Mrs, 1902, My 29,16:4
Seligman, Achille, 1941, O 13,17:3
Seligman, Addie B Mrs, 1937, Mr 28,II,9:1
Seligman, Alfred Lincoln (funl), 1912, Je 28,13:6
Seligman, Alice F, 1904, S 10,9:6
Seligman, Arthur R, 1925, O 6,27:5
Seligman, Charles D, 1954, D 12,89:2
Seligman, Charles G, 1940, S 21,19:4
Seligman, Edmond, 1915, Ap 24,11:6
Seligman, Edwin R A, 1939, Jl 19,19:1
Seligman, Edwin R A Mrs, 1953, Mr 27,23:2
Seligman, F J, 1939, My 5,23:5
Seligman, Harold B, 1966, N 8,39:5
Seligman, Henrietta Hellman, 1909, Ag 6,7:4
Seligman, Henry, 1909, F 21,7:5; 1915, Ja 13,9:4
Seligman, Isaac N Mrs, 1956, Je 15,25:5
Seligman, Isaac Newton (funl), 1917, O 3,13:1
Seligman, J, 1880, Ap 27,2:3
Seligman, Jacob, 1907, Mr 8,9:6
Seligman, Jacob Mrs, 1905, Ja 24,19:6
Seligman, James (funl, Ag 24,9:3), 1916, Ag 21,11:3
Seligman, James Mrs, 1907, D 18,9:6
Seligman, Jefferson, 1937, Je 19,17:1
Seligman, Jesse, 1894, Ap 24,5:5; 1903, D 29,9:6
Seligman, Jesse Mrs, 1909, Jl 24,7:4
Seligman, Julia Wormser Mrs, 1921, Mr 29,15:5
Seligman, Leopold, 1911, D 6,13:4
Seligman, Max, 1953, Mr 10,29:4
Seligman, Minnie (funl, Mr 5,11:4), 1919, Mr 2,21:4
Seligman, Roger Mrs, 1955, O 2,87:1
Seligman, Samuel J, 1909, Ag 20,7:5
Seligman, Sidney, 1962, Je 6,41:4
Seligman, Theodore, 1907, S 11,9:6
Seligman, Violet, 1918, Ap 2,13:4
Seligman, William, 1910, Ja 7,9:3; 1956, Ag 30,25:4
Seligman, William Mrs, 1904, O 4,9:6
Seligmann, Andre J, 1945, Jl 18,27:6
Seligmann, Arthur R, 1946, D 3,31:5
Seligmann, Carl, 1954, O 7,23:4
Seligmann, Erich, 1954, Ja 3,88:1
Seligmann, George A, 1951, O 31,29:1
Seligmann, Herbert J Mrs, 1964, Ag 24,27:3
Seligmann, Jacques, 1923, N 1,21:3
Seligmann, Jacques Mrs, 1940, Ap 3,23:4
Seligmann, Kurt, 1962, Ja 3,24:5
Seligmann, Rene, 1940, Jl 22,17:4
Seligmann, Rudolph A, 1941, Ja 19,40:8
Seligsberg, A F, 1933, Mr 18,13:1
Seligsberg, Abraham, 1914, F 16,7:4
Seligsberg, Albert J, 1947, Jl 2,23:1
Seligsberg, Alice L, 1940, Ag 29,19:1
Seligsberg, Walter N, 1945, Jl 6,11:7
Seligsohn, Julius L, 1942, My 2,6:5
Seligson, Abraham A, 1961, Mr 19,89:1
Seligson, Charles Mrs, 1963, Ag 30,21:2
Seligson, David D, 1962, F 24,27:3
Seligson, Emanuel, 1953, My 7,31:4
Seligson, Maurice, 1944, Ja 6,23:1
Seligson, Seymour A, 1951, Jl 24,25:2
Selim, Hussein K, 1962, Jl 31,27:2
Selim El-Bichri, 1917, S 24,13:6
Selincourt, B de Mrs, 1935, Jl 22,15:1
Selinger, David Mrs, 1968, Ap 14,76:4
Selinger, Jean Paul, 1909, S 12,9:4
Seliskar, James M, 1947, S 25,29:5
Seliskar, Paul J, 1949, N 6,92:4
Selivanova, Nina N Mrs, 1953, N 8,88:6
Selke, Aug F, 1941, My 19,17:5
Selkirk, Alex Mrs, 1939, Jl 31,13:3
Selkirk, George R, 1942, My 17,45:2
Selkirk, William, 1949, S 26,20:6
Sell, Casper, 1942, Ap 9,21:6
Sell, Casper Mrs, 1942, Ap 9,21:6
Sell, Charles F A, 1947, My 7,27:4
Sell, Frances D, 1948, Jl 26,17:3
Sell, Frederic C, 1956, Ag 13,19:4
Sell, Frederick W, 1958, Jl 11,23:5
Sell, G William, 1941, S 8,15:3
Sell, George D, 1957, Ap 24,33:2
Sell, Ida J Mrs, 1954, F 10,29:5
Sell, J Wesley, 1940, Ja 24,21:3
Sella, Quintino, 1884, Mr 15,4:7
Selland, Arthur, 1963, D 6,72:1
Sellar, Robert F, 1951, D 20,31:2
Sellars, Fred M, 1946, Je 11,23:3
Sellars, Joseph B, 1952, My 27,27:4
Sellars, Joseph B Mrs, 1951, F 6,27:2
Sellars, Lacy H, 1943, O 30,15:5
Sellbini, Lalla, 1942, F 14,15:2
Selle, Raymond M, 1960, Je 1,39:4
Selleck, Albert F, 1943, My 4,23:1
Selleck, Charles M Rev, 1909, Mr 23,9:5
Selleck, Cynthia J Mrs, 1937, Ap 20,25:5
Selleck, George H, 1949, Mr 27,78:4
Selleck, Isaac Mrs, 1950, O 19,31:2
Selleck, Nathaniel B, 1959, Ap 25,21:6
Selleck, Preston, 1937, Ap 28,23:1

Selleck, Virgil D, 1945, O 14,42:6
Selleck, William, 1947, Ja 14,26:2
Selleck, William J (will), 1957, F 12,20:5
Selleg, D N, 1903, Je 19,9:5
Sellen, Bert C, 1938, Ja 16,3:6
Sellenings, Albert E Mrs, 1941, Ag 10,37:1
Sellentine, Robert J, 1952, N 29,13:4
Seller, F P, 1927, N 3,27:3
Seller, Henry, 1949, Jl 13,27:2
Seller, Monroe D, 1953, Ja 13,27:2
Seller, Thomas, 1949, Jl 30,15:5
Sellers, Charles C Mrs, 1951, F 14,30:2
Sellers, Charles E Mrs, 1954, N 23,35:1
Sellers, Coleman Dr, 1907, D 29,9:5
Sellers, Coleman 3d, 1957, S 4,34:2
Sellers, David F, 1949, Ja 28,21:1
Sellers, David Mrs, 1954, Ag 4,21:2
Sellers, Edward J, 1946, Ja 13,44:3
Sellers, James C Jr Mrs, 1945, My 12,13:5
Sellers, James C Mrs, 1942, O 24,15:2
Sellers, John A, 1956, Ap 28,17:6
Sellers, John A Mrs, 1956, Jl 22,61:2
Sellers, Lee West Lt, 1919, Je 13,15:3
Sellers, M K Mrs (Dr M Stanley-Brown), 1958, Je 13,23:1
Sellers, Montgomery P, 1942, D 6,76:7
Sellers, Morris, 1946, Ap 22,21:5
Sellers, Paul, 1953, Ja 18,93:2
Sellers, Paulding F, 1950, Ag 6,73:2
Sellers, Robert H, 1948, My 21,23:1
Sellers, Robert R, 1939, Mr 14,21:4
Sellers, Sandford Sr, 1938, Mr 5,17:5
Sellers, Thomas F, 1940, D 24,15:4
Sellery, George C, 1962, Ja 22,23:3
Sellet, Nelson E, 1948, Ap 25,68:6
Sellew, Frank S, 1953, Mr 2,23:5
Sellew, Frederick S Dr, 1912, D 29,15:2
Sellew, Ralph, 1884, Ja 16,4:6
Sellew, Robert C, 1951, Je 1,26:1
Sellew, Timothy Gibson, 1912, S 20,11:6
Sellew, W A, 1929, Ja 17,25:3
Sellew, W Welles, 1962, Ag 10,19:5
Sellew, Welles H, 1968, My 31,29:3
Sellew, William H, 1939, Ja 31,21:2
Selliaas, Johannes, 1955, Jl 6,28:1
Sellick, Frank, 1957, Jl 16,27:1
Sellig, Charles E, 1946, F 10,40:5
Selling, Julius, 1950, Jl 6,28:2
Selling, Lowell S, 1955, Ja 19,27:3
Sellinger, Carl F, 1953, Mr 21,17:3
Sellinger, John M, 1945, O 13,15:6
Sellinger, Samuel, 1952, D 20,17:5
Sellman, Christian H, 1946, Jl 3,25:3
Sellman, Edward A, 1950, S 1,21:3
Sellman, Folke E, 1955, D 13,39:3
Sellman, Leland, 1947, Ja 15,26:2
Sellman, Nils T, 1962, Ag 31,21:5
Sellman, Raymond, 1961, Ap 5,37:4
Sellmayer, Frank J Jr, 1958, S 24,27:4
Sellmer, Robert, 1963, Ag 11,85:2
Sellner, George C, 1940, D 23,19:3
Sellner, Harry R, 1949, O 15,15:5
Sellner, Joseph J, 1954, Je 13,89:1
Sellon, Charles H Mrs, 1962, Je 2,19:4
Sells, Arthur G, 1968, S 15,84:7
Sells, Bernice R Mrs, 1937, F 3,3:5
Sells, Charles H Mrs, 1965, My 31,17:2
Sells, Elijah, 1924, Mr 20,19:6
Sells, Jennie Mrs, 1947, Ag 21,23:5
Sells, John, 1918, Ja 4,11:5
Sells, Louis, 1907, S 7,9:6
Sells, Murray C, 1953, F 9,27:3
Sells, Peter, 1904, O 6,1:5
Sells, Simeon W, 1965, Mr 17,45:5
Sells, William S, 1963, Ag 20,33:1
Sellstedt, Lars G, 1911, Je 5,11:6
Sellvine, Hugo E, 1953, D 26,13:5
Selman, John, 1944, D 30,11:4
Selman, Joseph, 1958, O 2,37:5
Selman, Samuel N, 1947, Mr 15,13:5
Selmanowitz, Louis, 1957, N 19,33:2
Selmer, William L, 1937, Jl 13,20:2
Selmes, John Henry, 1916, O 25,11:5
Selmi, William, 1957, My 18,19:2
Selner, Charles H, 1942, N 3,23:3
Selnick, Stanley G, 1964, Ag 29,21:6
Selover, Cornelius S Mrs, 1945, S 22,17:2
Selover, James V, 1956, O 22,29:2
Selover, Walton B, 1955, Ja 29,15:2
Selover, William O, 1951, My 7,25:4
Selsam, John P, 1950, My 26,23:3
Selsdon, Lord, 1938, D 25,14:6
Selser, George M, 1959, N 19,39:1
Selten, Morton, 1939, Jl 28,17:5
Selton, Hugo D, 1959, Ap 19,86:4
Seltz, Harry, 1947, Je 20,19:1
Seltz, Samuel Mrs, 1947, Je 29,48:7
Seltzer, Arthur, 1960, O 12,39:1
Seltzer, Benjamin P, 1941, F 17,15:5
Seltzer, Charles A, 1942, F 10,20:4; 1955, S 20,31:5
Seltzer, Charles A Mrs, 1956, Mr 23,27:2
Seltzer, George S, 1950, Jl 25,27:1
Seltzer, Harold K, 1939, N 27,17:4
Seltzer, Harry G, 1938, Je 7,23:5
Seltzer, Harry G Mrs, 1955, My 15,86:6
Seltzer, J George, 1945, S 20,23:2
Seltzer, Jacob Mrs, 1957, Ag 29,27:4
Seltzer, Louis Mrs, 1965, D 2,41:5
Seltzer, Meyer, 1951, O 2,27:4
Seltzer, Morris Mrs, 1962, My 14,29:2
Seltzer, Richard J, 1959, My 16,23:4
Seltzer, Sherman S, 1952, D 7,89:1
Seltzer, Theodore, 1943, O 3,49:1; 1957, Ja 2,27:2
Seltzer, Thomas, 1943, S 29,21:3
Selva, Ezio, 1957, D 30,28:1
Selvage, Clarence E, 1937, N 3,24:4
Selvage, Harry N, 1943, Mr 29,15:5
Selvage, Watson, 1943, Mr 13,13:2
Selver, Henry, 1957, S 22,86:6
Selverstone, Arthur W, 1963, D 25,33:1
Selves, J G C de, 1934, Ja 14,28:1
Selves, Marquis de, 1942, F 9,15:5
Selvig, Conrad G, 1953, Ag 4,21:6
Selvig, John N, 1958, Ap 23,33:1
Selvig, John N Mrs, 1958, D 11,13:4
Selwood, William V, 1948, D 11,15:5
Selwyn, Edgar (por), 1944, F 14,17:1
Selwyn, G A, 1878, Ap 13,4:7
Selwyn, J H, 1873, F 5,2:5
Selwyn, Michael (por), 1938, Ap 28,23:5
Selye, Lewis, 1883, Ja 28,7:3
Selz, Abraham K (est tax appr), 1957, F 26,15:2
Selz, Emanuel F, 1940, Ap 29,15:4
Selzer, Eugene R, 1944, Ja 11,20:3
Selzer, Frederick J Mrs, 1944, S 8,19:4
Selzer, Robert J, 1956, Ap 11,33:1
Selznick, David O (mem ser, Je 26,29:3), 1965, Je 23,1:4
Selznick, L J, 1933, Ja 26,17:3
Selznick, Lewis J Mrs, 1959, Mr 8,86:5
Selznick, Myron (por), 1944, Mr 24,20:2
Semal, Charles, 1958, O 21,33:4
Seman, Irving Mrs, 1955, O 30,88:7
Seman, Phil L, 1957, S 27,19:1
Semancik, John Jr, 1952, Jl 5,15:4
Semans, Henry, 1951, N 9,27:4
Semans, Josiah T, 1966, Mr 1,37:4
Semansky, Peter J, 1951, Mr 17,15:4
Semashko, Nikolai A, 1949, My 20,27:2
Sembach, William E, 1939, Ag 20,32:2
Sembat, Marcel, 1922, S 6,15:1
Sembat, Marcel Mrs, 1922, S 7,17:5
Sembower, Charles J, 1947, Ap 27,60:6
Sembower, Jasper T, 1941, Ja 27,15:4
Sembrich, M, 1935, Ja 12,16:1
Semel, Bernard, 1959, Jl 1,31:3
Semel, Guttman, 1942, Ap 1,21:1
Semel, Lewis, 1961, F 15,35:3
Semel, Meyer M, 1955, O 3,27:5
Semel, Souhie Mrs, 1951, N 13,20:6
Semery, Henry L, 1945, Je 15,19:2
Semet, Esther Mrs, 1956, F 5,87:1
Semetkovsky, Emil, 1950, Jl 12,29:2
Seminick, Wasil, 1952, F 19,29:1
Seminick, Wassil Mrs, 1950, My 1,25:1
Semisch, Frederick, 1950, My 31,24:2
Semke, Henry F, 1951, Ap 23,25:4
Semke, Henry J, 1937, Ja 13,23:4
Semken, George H (will, S 28,15:6), 1946, S 17,7:1
Semken, Gerd H, 1959, Ag 23,93:2
Semken, Harry, 1948, My 6,25:5
Semlar, William, 1950, D 14,35:3
Semle, Frances, 1948, F 17,25:5
Semler, Albert P, 1941, Ja 7,23:2
Semler, G Herbert, 1954, N 11,31:4
Semler, George, 1937, S 2,21:4
Semmel, Dora Mrs, 1937, N 19,23:4
Semmeles, Charles W Sr, 1943, N 9,21:4
Semmes, Harry H, 1962, My 31,27:3
Semmes, John E, 1967, N 27,47:2
Semmes, Matilda, 1881, Je 19,2:5
Semmes, Oliver J Judge, 1918, Ja 20,17:1
Semmes, R, 1877, Ag 31,4:7
Semmes, T J, 1902, D 2,9:4
Semmes-Ives, Eugene Ex-Sen, 1917, Ag 30,11:6
Semmig, Ernest J, 1962, Jl 22,64:5
Semmins, William H, 1925, Jl 20,15:5
Semon, Eric (cor, My 22,13:6), 1943, My 21,19:3
Semon, John, 1925, Mr 13,19:3
Semon, John H, 1945, D 6,27:5
Semon, Kurt M Mrs, 1943, F 19,19:5
Semon, L, 1928, O 9,31:3
Semon, Simon H, 1910, S 7,9:5
Semones, Arthur M, 1952, Je 19,27:5
Semper, Godfrey, 1879, My 19,5:2
Sempier, John, 1941, Je 22,32:2
Sempill, Lord (Wm Francis Forbes-Sempill), 1965, D 30,23:4
Semple, Allan, 1945, N 21,21:3
Semple, Arthur, 1948, Je 1,23:3
Semple, Charles C, 1946, Je 1,13:5
Semple, David Sir, 1937, Ja 8,20:1
Semple, Ellen, 1959, Ag 31,21:2
Semple, George H, 1955, Mr 2,27:3
Semple, Henry Churchill Rev, 1925, Je 29,13:6
Semple, Jack, 1959, Ap 20,31:5
Semple, Jacob C, 1952, Mr 24,25:2
Semple, James A, 1916, Je 11,21:5
Semple, John B, 1947, N 14,23:2
Semple, Lorenzo, 1962, Ja 7,88:7
Semple, Mary M Mrs, 1942, D 1,25:3
Semple, Parlan Mrs, 1941, Mr 2,42:3
Semple, Samuel, 1947, O 23,25:6
Semple, T Darrington Mrs, 1944, My 20,15:4; 1956, O 11,39:5
Semple, Walter Hart Rev, 1925, Ag 16,5:2
Semple, William A Mrs, 1959, Je 22,25:3
Semple, William J, 1955, Jl 16,15:2
Semple, William T Mrs (will), 1961, Ap 8,13:5
Sempliner, Abram W, 1949, Jl 15,19:4
Sen, Usha Nath, 1959, Ap 20,31:4
Senac, Louis, 1948, Mr 7,68:5
Senac, Regis, 1908, Ag 18,9:6
Senanyake, Don S, 1952, Mr 23,93:1
Senarens, Luis P, 1939, D 28,21:1
Senator, David W, 1953, N 4,33:5
Senator, Herman Prof, 1911, Jl 15,7:4
Senatore, Vincent, 1947, Ag 9,13:6
Sencenbaugh, Charles W, 1950, D 9,15:2
Sencer, Joseph, 1939, N 15,23:2
Sencer, Philip, 1964, F 7,32:1
Sencer, Sidney J, 1958, Ap 20,84:5
Sendak, Philip Mrs, 1968, Ag 21,45:4
Sendar, Morris, 1947, Ap 5,19:6
Sendel, Aaron, 1954, D 20,29:2
Senden-Bibran, Gustav von Adm, 1909, N 24,9:4
Sender, Arthur C, 1962, Mr 30,33:3
Sender, Toni, 1964, Je 27,25:4
Sendericker, Henry J, 1937, O 28,25:1
Senderling, George W, 1941, Je 23,17:2
Sendon, Nathan J, 1948, D 22,23:3
Senear, Francis E, 1958, F 13,29:1
Seneca, Pasquale, 1952, D 13,21:4
Senecal, James N, 1953, Ja 20,25:2
Senecal, Leo P, 1950, Je 29,29:3
Senekoff, Morris, 1955, Jl 1,21:2
Sener, Harry, 1948, F 24,25:3
Senesey, Nicholas Mrs, 1966, S 4,64:6
Senesi, Aristide, 1960, Jl 4,15:3
Seney, Clyde C, 1967, N 9,61:5
Seney, G I, 1893, Ap 8,1:6
Seney, George F, 1905, Je 12,9:5
Seney, George Ingraham Mrs, 1904, Ja 19,9:6
Seney, Henry W Judge, 1909, S 3,9:5
Senf, Frederic M, 1963, O 30,39:3
Senf, Louis, 1940, F 25,X,6:3
Senff, Charles H, 1911, Ag 24,7:5
Senff, L Dr, 1885, Ja 21,5:5
Senft, Frederick H Dr, 1925, N 26,23:5
Senft, Lawrence, 1940, N 17,50:1
Seng, Frank J, 1946, Ag 21,27:2
Senger, Frederick Mrs, 1943, N 9,21:5
Senger, Herbert, 1953, Ag 8,11:7
Senger, Louis C, 1940, Mr 13,23:3
Senger, Martin, 1903, Jl 4,7:6
Senger, Oscar, 1940, Ap 27,15:5
Senges, August J, 1944, Mr 7,17:5
Sengier, Edgar, 1963, Jl 30,29:1
Sengman, A, 1885, Ja 21,5:5
Sengst, John, 1950, Ja 1,42:7
Sengstaken, Charles W, 1968, Ag 3,25:3
Sengstaken, John H, 1967, Je 3,31:2
Senie, Louis, 1960, D 8,35:3
Senie, Louis Mrs, 1956, O 21,86:4
Senigo, Mary E, 1957, Ja 30,29:2
Senior, Abram G, 1943, Jl 15,21:2
Senior, Augustus W, 1938, Ag 13,13:6
Senior, Bertha Mrs, 1940, Mr 16,15:4
Senior, Charles A Jr, 1950, Ja 29,68:5
Senior, Charles L, 1941, D 27,19:5
Senior, Eugene, 1966, F 14,29:3
Senior, Frank H, 1952, S 23,33:5
Senior, Frank S, 1942, N 30,23:4
Senior, George R, 1903, S 10,7:5
Senior, Harold B, 1948, D 6,25:1
Senior, Harold D (por), 1938, Ag 8,13:6
Senior, Harvey C, 1947, F 6,23:4
Senior, Henry C Mrs, 1940, My 11,19:5
Senior, Hester A Mrs, 1953, Mr 23,23:5
Senior, John L, 1946, My 1,26:2
Senior, Joseph H, 1949, O 17,23:3
Senior, Leon S, 1940, F 5,17:6
Senior, Richard L, 1958, Ja 22,27:2
Senior, Russell C, 1963, Ja 9,8:3
Senior, Samuel P Sr, 1962, O 16,39:2
Seniour, W F, 1903, My 17,7:6
Senk, Charles, 1946, My 22,21:3
Senk, Henry, 1950, Ja 26,27:5
Senk, Philip M, 1944, O 20,19:3
Senkbeil, Otto, 1946, My 28,21:4
Senker, Louis H, 1945, Ap 8,36:3
Senkowsky, Frank, 1946, O 22,25:4
Senkus, W Vincent, 1948, Jl 28,23:4
Senn, Charles E, 1944, Je 2,15:4
Senn, Emanuel J (will), 1948, Ja 6,26:4
Senn, George, 1954, Mr 7,90:6
Senn, Gould A, 1946, S 28,17:5
Senn, Nicholas Dr, 1908, Ja 3,9:4
Senn, Thomas J (por), 1947, F 13,23:3

Senn, William, 1907, O 8,11:5
Senner, Joseph Henry (funl, O 1,9:6), 1908, S 29,9:7
Senner, Joseph O, 1951, Ap 24,29:2
Sennet, Samuel, 1964, D 8,45:4
Sennett, Albert, 1959, Jl 26,68:1
Sennett, Eugene B, 1950, D 16,17:5
Sennett, Mack (funl, N 9,18:4), 1960, N 6,1:3
Sennett, William E, 1942, S 23,25:5
Sennhauser, Edwin H Mrs, 1958, S 21,87:2
Sennhauser, Walter, 1949, Ja 5,25:3
Senning, Frederick W, 1945, F 4,38:6
Senning, John P, 1954, D 5,88:4
Senno, Anthony A, 1955, S 27,35:4
Senole, William Mrs, 1952, Ap 15,27:3
Senor, Louis H, 1953, Ap 8,29:2
Senor Manzano, Capt-Gen of Cuba, 1867, S 25,1:7
Senoret, Octavio de, 1941, Mr 12,22:2
Senour, Harry C, 1954, Jl 20,19:1
Sensale, Robert, 1966, N 18,43:3
Sensbach, John, 1957, Je 6,31:4
Senseman, Margaretta K Mrs, 1940, N 24,51:2
Sensemann, Harley L, 1946, O 25,23:2
Sensenbrenner, Frank J, 1952, Jl 23,23:1
Sensenbrenner, Frank J (est acctg), 1954, N 6,13:2
Sensenderfer, J P, 1903, My 4,7:6
Sensenderfer, Robert E, 1957, Ja 3,33:2
Senseney, George E, 1943, N 19,19:2
Senseney, Mary T Mrs, 1939, N 18,17:6
Sensenich, Roscoe L (Jan 18), 1963, Ap 1,36:5
Sensenig, Peter A, 1954, Ag 6,17:5
Sensor, Thomas Dorr, 1921, F 22,13:5
Senst, William G, 1949, N 20,92:4
Sentelle, Mark E, 1949, Ap 14,25:1
Senter, Alex, 1951, Mr 7,33:5
Senter, Meyer, 1945, F 17,13:2
Senter, Ralph T, 1948, Ja 25,56:8
Senter, Ralph T Mrs, 1953, Mr 27,23:2
Senterman, Charles V, 1951, Ja 2,23:4
Sentilhes, Theophile, 1940, Ja 9,24:3
Sentner, Irving, 1958, Ap 19,21:4
Sentner, Marion D Mrs, 1966, Ja 17,47:3
Sentner, Matthew B, 1946, Je 14,21:3
Sentz, Anton E, 1947, My 22,27:4
Senutovitch, Andre Mrs, 1965, Je 11,31:3
Senville, Isidore, 1959, F 19,31:3
Senz, Adolf, 1955, Ja 27,23:2
Senz, Fred J, 1950, Ja 5,25:2
Seoane, Consuelo A Mrs, 1951, Ja 14,84:3
Seoane, Manuel A, 1963, S 11,43:4
Sep, Louis, 1964, O 25,89:1
Sep, Ludwig, 1943, N 5,19:5
Sepenuk, Abraham, 1964, Ap 12,86:7
Sepersky, Alex, 1963, O 18,31:2
Sephton, John Rev, 1968, Jl 9,39:1
Sepp, J, 1909, Je 11,9:7
Seppala, Leonard, 1967, Ja 29,77:1
Seppelt, Franz X, 1956, Jl 31,23:2
Septier, Gaston Rev, 1937, Ja 31,II,8:6
Sepulveda, Matias S, 1951, F 10,13:2
Sequine, William Mrs, 1950, Jl 20,25:2
Serafimovich, Alex, 1949, Ja 20,27:2
Serafin, Felix, 1966, Ag 11,33:1
Serafin, Tullio, 1968, F 4,80:6
Serafini, Camillo, 1952, Mr 22,13:4
Serafini, Domenico Cardinal, 1918, Mr 8,11:5
Serafini, G (por), 1938, Jl 17,26:6
Serafini, Giovananna, 1947, O 21,23:4
Serafinowicz, Jan L, 1956, Je 9,40:7
Serafis, Stephen, 1957, Je 1,8:6
Serano, Juna E Mrs, 1923, Jl 2,15:6
Serao, M, 1927, Jl 28,19:3
Seraphim, Mother, 1940, Jl 6,15:3
Seraphine, Phil J, 1957, O 20,86:8
Seraphine, Rev Mother, 1917, Ap 14,13:4
Serapia, Sister, 1942, Mr 30,17:5
Serapinto, Carlota, 1949, Ja 13,24:3
Serat, Mortimer E, 1949, D 20,31:3
Serbe, Frederick W, 1959, Ag 5,27:4
Serbe, George F, 1950, Ag 3,23:1
Serben, Jacob J, 1958, O 21,33:5
Serber, Gilbert M (cor, D 2,88:7), 1962, D 1,25:2
Serbin, Alex, 1950, N 16,31:3
Serbury, William M (por), 1949, N 9,27:1
Serck, Max H, 1948, F 3,25:4
Sercus, Charles A, 1968, My 21,47:1
Serdobin, Paul Michael Baron, 1915, N 19,11:4
Sere, Julien, 1955, D 28,24:6
Serebrakian, Leon, 1954, Mr 6,15:4
Serebrenik, Robert, 1965, F 12,29:4
Serena, Alex R, 1961, My 23,39:2
Serena, Josephine Mrs, 1956, O 4,33:5
Serena, Samuel H, 1964, N 8,88:8
Serenbetz, George B, 1951, F 14,31:2
Sereni, Angelo P, 1967, Ap 6,39:4
Serent, Arman F H, 1952, O 1,33:4
Seres, Georges, 1951, Je 27,29:5
Seres, Louis G, 1948, N 27,17:2
Seres, Louis G Mrs, 1949, F 3,23:4
Sergant, James C, 1954, O 8,23:4
Serge, Victor, 1947, N 20,30:2
Sergeant, Adeline, 1904, D 6,9:3
Sergeant, Alfred E, 1940, Mr 24,30:8
Sergeant, Bernard de Santelys, 1912, Je 24,9:4
Sergeant, Edgar M, 1958, Mr 2,88:5
Sergeant, Elizabeth S, 1965, Ja 28,29:2
Sergeant, Henry C, 1907, F 1,9:4
Sergeant, W, 1878, Ap 28,7:2
Sergel, Joseph P, 1967, Mr 1,43:3
Sergent, Emile, 1943, My 25,23:4
Sergenti, Marcellinus, 1949, Jl 1,19:3
Serger, Frederick B, 1965, N 4,47:6
Sergescu, Pierre, 1954, D 23,19:2
Sergi, Pasquale J (Pat), 1954, Ap 14,29:4
Sergine, Vera, 1946, Ag 25,46:2
Sergison, Herbert S, 1953, O 28,29:4
Sergius, Metropolitan, 1944, My 16,21:3
Serieix, Clodoald, 1948, Mr 9,23:2
Serjeant, D M Sir, 1929, Ja 14,23:3
Serkowich, Benjamin H, 1954, My 9,89:1
Serkus, Michael, 1952, Jl 19,15:4
Serle, Hester B, 1945, Ag 7,23:1
Serlen, Murray, 1955, D 7,39:5
Serles, Earl R, 1957, Mr 15,25:3
Serlin, Abraham (will), 1960, Mr 6,2:7
Serlin, Edward, 1968, F 9,27:3
Serlin, Fannie Mrs, 1948, Mr 26,22:2
Serling, Joseph L, 1941, Mr 2,42:4
Serly, Lajos, 1939, F 2,19:3
Serly, Lajos Mrs, 1951, Ag 10,15:2
Sermolino, Anacleto, 1937, Ja 16,15:2
Sermon, Roger T, 1950, Ja 24,31:5
Sermoneta, Duchess of (M C Caetani), 1963, D 19, 33:3
Sermoneta, Duke of (Onorato Caetani), 1917, S 4, 11:5
Sernander, Rutger, 1944, N 1,23:4
Serniak, Stephen, 1955, S 2,17:3
Serol, Albert, 1961, My 10,45:2
Seronde, Joseph Mrs, 1945, O 1,19:2
Serota, David, 1954, S 18,15:5
Serov, Vladimir Aleksandrovich, 1968, Ja 21,76:5
Serova, Sonia, 1943, My 10,19:5
Serpentini, Ernest, 1953, My 25,25:5
Serper, Harry, 1966, N 29,39:4
Serpico, Frank, 1955, Jl 24,47:3
Serpico, James C, 1956, Mr 3,15:6
Serpico, John, 1950, Ag 26,13:3
Serpico, Thomas, 1961, N 21,39:1
Serpollet, Leon, 1907, F 12,9:6
Serra, Eugene, 1956, Je 12,70:2
Serra, John F, 1959, Mr 11,35:1
Serra, Joseph, 1942, Mr 27,23:2
Serradell, Valentine Mrs, 1954, Ag 19,4:5
Serrano, F S yD, 1885, N 27,5:3
Serrano, Jose, 1941, Mr 9,40:8
Serrano Palma, Jose (funl plans, Je 22,25:3), 1959, Je 20,21:2
Serrati, Meriggio, 1945, D 18,27:5
Serrato, Jose, 1960, S 8,35:1
Serraz, John F, 1944, N 2,19:5
Serre, Albert, 1941, N 19,23:3
Serre, Eugene A, 1949, Ja 18,23:3
Serre, John C, 1947, D 9,29:3
Serre, Louis, 1939, Ja 9,15:2
Serre, Louis H, 1946, My 10,19:5
Serrell, Edward P Mrs, 1940, Jl 3,17:2
Serrell, Harrison Mrs, 1962, Je 28,31:4
Serrell, John J, 1939, Ja 13,19:1
Serrell, Wellman Gen, 1906, Ap 26,11:6
Serri, Frank R, 1968, D 11,41:1
Serrick, John, 1946, S 4,23:2
Serrick, William F, 1940, Ap 22,17:6
Serrill, Joseph L, 1951, F 9,91:3
Serrill, William W, 1958, Mr 21,21:4
Serruys, Daniel, 1950, Ja 19,28:4
Sert, Jose M, 1945, N 28,27:1
Sert, Jose M Mrs, 1938, D 18,48:5
Servais, Jean, 1946, D 10,31:1
Servais, Louis J, 1942, Ap 16,21:5
Servan-Schreiber, Emile, 1967, D 30,23:3
Serven, Abram R, 1942, Jl 13,15:6
Serven, Harry D, 1942, Je 17,23:2
Serven, J Kenneth Mrs, 1963, Ap 4,47:2
Serven, James, 1903, Jl 26,7:6
Serven, William A, 1923, F 1,11:4
Serventi, Charles, 1951, F 23,27:2
Server, Edward A, 1924, My 31,15:5
Servey, Claude E, 1951, D 27,21:6
Service, Charles A, 1942, Je 24,19:2
Service, George H, 1941, Ja 12,44:2
Service, John A, 1950, O 20,27:2
Service, Robert Mrs, 1937, Je 28,19:3
Service, Robert W (funl, S 17,32:3), 1958, S 13,1:6
Service, Sarah E Mrs (will), 1937, O 20,21:2
Service, William S, 1946, N 30,15:2
Servin, Abram F, 1940, Je 29,15:4
Servis, Cora S Mrs, 1940, S 22,49:2
Servis, David S, 1945, Mr 4,36:5
Serviss, Garrett P Mrs, 1906, Ja 20,9:5
Servoss, George S Capt, 1907, D 13,11:4
Servoss, Henry, 1951, Ja 27,13:3
Serwer, Samuel, 1938, Ag 10,13:1
Serwer, Zachary, 1961, My 18,35:1
Seryogin, Vladimir S Col, 1968, Mr 28,1:2
Sesak, Frank A, 1954, Jl 29,23:5
Seskind, Morris, 1958, S 7,87:2
Seskis, Irving J, 1951, Mr 7,33:5
Sesky, Max, 1956, N 20,37:2
Sesler, Ray, 1953, Jl 11,11:6
Sesnan, James B, 1945, Ag 29,23:5
Sesselberg, Arthur W, 1954, Jl 23,17:2
Sesselberg, Henry A, 1948, My 13,25:1
Sesselman, Henry J, 1951, Je 16,15:5
Sesselman, John Mrs, 1957, F 13,35:1
Sessions, Albert L, 1937, My 1,19:3
Sessions, Archibald L Mrs, 1946, D 3,31:3
Sessions, Charles H, 1942, D 26,11:2
Sessions, Frank M Mrs, 1947, My 15,25:4
Sessions, Harriet E, 1920, F 20,15:4
Sessions, Harry A, 1948, Mr 16,27:2
Sessions, James M, 1962, N 16,31:3
Sessions, Joseph B, 1941, N 2,52:6
Sessions, Richard, 1958, My 17,39:5
Sessions, William E, 1920, Ag 28,7:5
Sessions, William J, 1950, Ja 9,25:1
Sessions, William J Mrs, 1952, F 9,13:2
Sessler, Belle K Mrs, 1938, S 5,15:3
Sessler, J Leonard, 1951, My 4,27:5
Seta, Allessandro della, 1945, My 26,15:2
Seth, Frank W, 1947, O 12,76:3
Seth, James Dr, 1924, Jl 26,9:7
Sethe, Paul, 1967, Je 23,31:3
Setjanegara, Sunardi S, 1955, Mr 27,86:4
Setley, Albert Van W, 1959, Mr 19,33:4
Seto Mee Tong, 1955, My 9,23:1
Setoguchi, Tokichi, 1941, N 9,52:1
Seton, A L, 1902, D 8,9:4
Seton, Archbishop, 1927, Mr 23,25:3
Seton, Elizabeth, 1906, D 22,6:4
Seton, Ernest T (por), 1946, O 24,27:1
Seton, Flavia Lady, 1959, O 15,39:4
Seton, Grace G T Mrs, 1959, Mr 20,31:1
Seton, Henry Maj, 1904, S 7,7:6
Seton, S W, 1869, N 23,5:2
Seton-Karr, Heywood W, 1938, Ja 14,23:2
Seton-Pattison, E Dr, 1924, S 4,19:6
Seton-Watson, Robert W, 1951, Jl 28,11:7
Sette, Alfred J, 1955, Mr 15,29:2
Settel, Isaac, 1941, O 19,45:3
Settel, Mary K, 1952, N 14,23:2
Settel, Nathan, 1965, F 10,41:4
Settele, Frank H Jr, 1957, Mr 24,86:7
Settell, Clary, 1949, F 24,24:3
Setterfield, Hugh E, 1953, Mr 18,31:4
Setti, Giulio (por), 1938, O 4,25:1
Setti, St John, 1963, N 7,37:5
Settle, Allan E, 1968, N 29,45:4
Settlemayer, Frank A, 1942, My 10,42:8
Settlemayer, Frank A Mrs, 1956, Mr 31,15:5
Settlemyer, Charles Mrs, 1946, Je 18,25:3
Setze, J A Mrs, 1958, F 13,29:5
Setze, Julius A, 1955, My 27,23:6
Setzer, Bernhard, 1949, Mr 8,25:5
Setzer, Fred, 1953, Mr 13,27:2
Setzler, Henry, 1940, Jl 5,13:2
Seubert, Edward G (por), 1949, N 19,17:6
Seubert, John, 1940, My 17,19:3
Seubert, Louis Henry, 1916, Je 20,11:6
Seubert, William L, 1959, Ag 12,29:2
Seufert, William M, 1957, S 24,35:3
Seuffert, George Sr, 1964, N 11,43:5
Seulowitz, Warren S, 1967, Ja 7,27:4
Seum, Otto, 1948, Ap 9,23:2
Seuss, Mrs (Mrs T S Geisel), 1967, O 24,47:3
Seute, Ernst, 1956, D 16,86:4
Seutter, Benjamin G, 1945, Jl 21,11:6
Sevag, Manesseh G, 1967, N 26,84:7
Sevastopoulo, Mathieu, 1947, Ap 6,60:4
Sevebeck, Judson E Mrs, 1961, Ja 16,27:3
Sevenoak, Frank L, 1938, Mr 16,23:6
Sever, Joel V, 1953, Ap 10,21:5
Sever, Werther, 1940, Mr 16,15:4
Severa, W F, 1938, Mr 31,23:2
Severage, Frank A, 1950, Ap 23,93:1
Severance, Caroline M Mrs, 1914, N 11,13:6
Severance, Charles D, 1942, Je 26,21:3
Severance, Claude M, 1939, Je 17,15:3
Severance, Cordenio A, 1925, My 7,19:5
Severance, Cordenio A Mrs, 1925, S 26,17:5
Severance, Edwin, 1941, Ap 22,21:6
Severance, H Craig (por), 1941, S 3,23:1
Severance, Lena L H Mrs, 1942, S 16,23:6
Severance, Robert N, 1955, Mr 12,19:5
Severeid, Hank, 1968, D 19,47:3
Severence, Henry L, 1948, N 13,15:2
Severence, Juliet Dr, 1919, S 4,13:3
Severgnini, Alberto, 1962, My 29,31:2
Severin, E Mrs, 1911, D 23,9:5
Severin, Huldah, 1943, D 4,13:3
Severin, Nils P, 1945, Mr 27,19:4
Severin, Sten V, 1953, Ag 23,88:4
Severing, Carl, 1952, Jl 24,27:3
Severinghause, Willard L (por), 1947, Ag 29,17:1
Severini, Gino, 1966, F 28,27:1
Severini, I S, 1885, F 15,2:2
Severino, Thomas, 1941, N 8,19:5
Severn, Edmund, 1942, My 16,13:6
Severn, J Millett, 1942, Jl 21,19:4
Severn, Walter, 1904, S 23,9:7

Severn, William E, 1941, Jl 30,17:4
Severne, Frank W, 1959, D 30,21:2
Severo, G, 1943, O 25,15:4
Severs, Enoch W, 1948, F 17,25:3
Severs, Isabelle G, 1943, Je 29,19:2
Severs, John A, 1960, Ag 7,84:4
Severs, Mary A Mrs, 1942, Ja 28,19:2
Severs, Ralph K, 1957, Ag 15,21:6
Seversmith, Herbert F, 1967, Ag 17,37:3
Severson, Charles F, 1951, F 19,23:3
Severson, Charlotte J, 1943, D 6,23:4
Severson, Earl M, 1952, Mr 25,27:3
Severson, Harry A, 1957, Ap 21,88:2
Severson, Herman, 1950, S 3,38:3
Severson, Lloyd J, 1965, N 27,31:1
Severson, Louis N, 1950, D 13,35:1
Severson, Siguird B, 1952, S 24,33:3
Severy, B Franklin, 1954, Jl 28,23:4
Severy, Lewis W Mrs, 1949, Ap 10,76:6
Severy, Luther, 1903, D 4,9:5
Sevick, O, 1934, Ja 19,19:4
Sevier, Henry H, 1940, Mr 11,15:4
Sevier, Joseph R, 1944, O 17,23:1
Sevier, O'Neil, 1950, Ag 6,72:8
Sevigny, Albert, 1961, My 15,31:2
Sevilla, Ramon, 1953, Ag 5,23:6
Seville, John, 1939, O 14,19:4
Sevin, Hector Irenaeus, 1916, My 5,11:6
Sevin, Isadore, 1945, O 31,23:1
Seving, Frederick T Sr, 1965, Mr 13,25:1
Sevitzky, Fabien (cor, F 6,29:2), 1967, F 5,88:5
Sevrin, Louis, 1941, N 17,19:5
Sewall, Arthur, 1900, S 6,7:6
Sewall, Arthur E, 1956, Ja 13,37:4
Sewall, Arthur W, 1939, Ag 2,19:2
Sewall, Arthur 2d, 1962, Je 25,29:2
Sewall, Carolyn T, 1946, O 9,27:1
Sewall, Charles G Mrs, 1937, N 30,23:5
Sewall, Duer I, 1960, F 19,27:2
Sewall, Edgar D, 1952, My 4,91:2
Sewall, Edmund D, 1923, Mr 31,13:5
Sewall, Harold M, 1924, O 29,21:4
Sewall, Henry Foster, 1920, Je 18,11:4
Sewall, J N, 1884, Ap 13,8:7
Sewall, James W, 1946, Jl 22,21:3
Sewall, Karl H, 1949, S 13,29:2
Sewall, Loyall F, 1958, Ap 8,29:5
Sewall, Mary H (Mother Theresa), 1878, F 17,9:2
Sewall, May Wright Mrs, 1920, Jl 24,9:7
Sewall, Oscar T, 1914, Ja 20,9:6
Sewall, R K, 1903, Ap 18,9:4
Sewall, Samuel Green Dr, 1911, D 31,II,11:4
Sewall, Sumner, 1965, Ja 26,34:4
Sewall, William G (por), 1941, Jl 16,17:6
Sewall, William J, 1957, F 19,31:2
Sewall, William Mrs, 1914, Jl 17,9:4
Seward, A H, 1876, S 12,1:6
Seward, Anne L, 1956, S 1,15:4
Seward, C A, 1939, F 1,21:3
Seward, Carlos E, 1944, My 11,19:3
Seward, E Clarkson, 1968, N 7,47:1
Seward, Edwin J, 1947, Mr 2,60:2
Seward, Edwin P, 1872, Ap 24,1:6
Seward, F W Sr Dr, 1925, O 2,23:5
Seward, Fannie, 1866, O 30,4:7
Seward, Fanny L, 1937, Je 15,23:5
Seward, Franklin D, 1938, S 21,25:5
Seward, Frederic K, 1943, D 8,23:1
Seward, Frederick W, 1960, Mr 7,29:4
Seward, Frederick W Mrs, 1919, My 3,15:7
Seward, Frederick William (por), 1915, Ap 26,9:1
Seward, George F, 1910, N 29,11:3
Seward, Herbert L, 1966, Jl 15,31:1
Seward, John, 1941, My 30,15:5
Seward, Mary Louisa, 1879, S 8,4:7
Seward, Matie C, 1952, F 27,27:1
Seward, Mr, 1873, Ja 30,2:6
Seward, Olive Risley, 1908, N 29,11:5
Seward, Robert B, 1966, F 22,23:3
Seward, Robert Mrs, 1952, My 23,21:6
Seward, Samuel Swayze Rev Dr, 1916, F 23,13:5
Seward, T F, 1902, S 1,7:6
Seward, Thomas F Mrs, 1919, S 3,13:5
Seward, Thomas J, 1955, Je 9,29:2
Seward, W H Mrs (funl, Je 25,4:5), 1865, Je 22,4:5
Seward, William, 1940, Ag 2,15:2
Seward, William Gen, 1905, Ag 17,7:7
Seward, William H (trb, O 28,5:3), 1872, O 11,4:7
Seward, William H Dr, 1968, N 13,47:1
Seward, William H Gen, 1920, Ap 27,9:4
Seward, William H Mrs, 1913, N 10,9:3
Seward, William H 3d (will, F 24,15:3), 1951, F 17, 15:4
Sewards, Jerome N, 1955, Ja 1,13:3
Sewecke, Walter F, 1958, Ag 6,25:1
Sewell, Albert H, 1924, Jl 14,15:4
Sewell, Anna M, 1937, Ap 9,21:4
Sewell, Arthur, 1947, N 14,23:5
Sewell, Ashton L, 1957, O 27,86:7
Sewell, Barton, 1915, Ja 8,11:4
Sewell, Charles S, 1955, Mr 29,30:2
Sewell, Charles T, 1951, Mr 27,29:1
Sewell, Dee Clinton, 1968, My 22,47:2
Sewell, E George (por), 1940, Ap 3,23:1
Sewell, Frank Rev Dr, 1915, D 8,15:5
Sewell, George F, 1948, S 8,29:2
Sewell, Helen, 1957, F 26,29:3
Sewell, Horace S, 1953, D 30,23:3
Sewell, J W Mrs, 1957, N 12,37:3
Sewell, James C, 1941, D 12,25:2
Sewell, John, 1938, D 2,23:1
Sewell, John I, 1952, O 11,19:6
Sewell, Maggie E Mrs, 1944, Ap 9,34:4
Sewell, Mary H L Mrs, 1937, Mr 8,19:2
Sewell, Millard F, 1945, Je 6,21:2
Sewell, Oscar, 1879, Mr 22,8:2
Sewell, P W Mrs, 1951, Jl 19,23:5
Sewell, Robert, 1939, Jl 16,30:4
Sewell, Robert Van Vorst, 1924, N 20,23:5
Sewell, Sara, 1904, N 20,7:5
Sewell, W J Mrs, 1906, D 6,1:2
Sewell, William E, 1947, My 22,27:2
Sewell, William E Ex-Gov, 1904, Mr 18,9:1
Sewell, William Grant, 1862, Ag 11,4:6
Sewell, William J, 1944, O 1,46:2
Sexsmith, Edward A, 1940, Ja 2,19:4
Sexson, John A, 1952, Ap 15,27:4
Sexson, W Mark, 1953, D 22,31:5
Sexton, Ada M Mrs, 1925, Ap 19,7:1
Sexton, Andrew R, 1952, Ja 16,25:3
Sexton, Charles B, 1952, Ag 18,17:4
Sexton, Charles E, 1947, Ap 9,25:5
Sexton, Charles E Mrs, 1946, Ap 18,27:3
Sexton, Charles F, 1954, Mr 31,27:4
Sexton, Charles F Mrs, 1948, N 7,88:6
Sexton, Daniel E, 1948, O 2,15:4
Sexton, Daniel F, 1959, Ap 8,37:2
Sexton, Edward B Mrs, 1945, Ag 8,23:5
Sexton, Emory, 1944, S 20,23:3
Sexton, Francis J, 1960, S 27,37:2
Sexton, Frank J, 1938, Ja 6,19:6
Sexton, Frederick H, 1955, Ja 14,21:1
Sexton, George E, 1960, Mr 8,24:3
Sexton, George L, 1955, Mr 16,33:4
Sexton, George P, 1947, F 8,17:3
Sexton, Helen, 1953, D 15,39:1
Sexton, Herbert B, 1951, Mr 27,29:5
Sexton, J E (will), 1958, Mr 9,58:3
Sexton, J Frederick, 1946, Jl 10,23:6
Sexton, James, 1938, D 28,21:3
Sexton, James J (por), 1947, Ag 25,17:3
Sexton, James J Jr, 1964, Jl 22,33:2
Sexton, James J Mrs, 1950, Jl 23,56:3
Sexton, Jere A, 1950, S 11,23:4
Sexton, John, 1904, F 20,9:5; 1951, F 24,13:2
Sexton, John B (funl, Ap 4,9:1), 1910, Ap 2,11:5
Sexton, John E, 1949, Mr 9,25:4; 1960, F 1,27:1
Sexton, John J, 1957, N 17,86:2
Sexton, John L, 1955, F 8,27:4
Sexton, John Mrs, 1951, D 29,11:5
Sexton, Joseph P, 1947, My 18,60:7
Sexton, Lawrence Eugene, 1919, Ag 31,22:2
Sexton, Leo, 1968, S 7,29:2
Sexton, Mary J F Mrs, 1942, D 12,17:2
Sexton, Michael, 1924, O 23,21:5
Sexton, Michael H, 1937, Ja 19,23:3
Sexton, Morgan H, 1949, Mr 28,21:2
Sexton, P J, 1903, O 30,9:6
Sexton, Pliny Titus, 1924, S 6,11:6
Sexton, Richard Mrs, 1956, Ap 14,17:6
Sexton, Richard P Mrs, 1968, N 14,47:3
Sexton, Robert, 1944, Jl 4,19:2
Sexton, Robert H, 1945, S 6,25:2
Sexton, Robert L Mrs, 1948, N 21,88:7
Sexton, S B, 1903, Ap 20,7:5
Sexton, Sherman J, 1956, Mr 14,33:5
Sexton, Vincent Mrs, 1951, D 24,13:3
Sexton, Walton R, 1943, S 10,23:5
Sexton, William L, 1940, Mr 29,22:2; 1948, Ap 30,23:4
Sexton, William T, 1955, Ja 13,27:1
Seybert, H, 1883, Mr 4,9:5
Seybold, Frank E, 1951, My 1,29:2
Seybold, Frederick J, 1913, Ag 24,II,11:3
Seybold, George H, 1955, Jl 30,17:5
Seybold, Thomas E, 1948, Ja 18,60:4
Seybolt, Eleanor Mrs, 1947, S 18,25:4
Seydel, Herman, 1955, O 15,15:6
Seydel, Victor, 1948, O 4,23:5
Seyden, Alfred, 1942, S 26,15:4
Seyden, Joseph, 1903, Jl 27,7:6
Seydl, Ernst, 1952, S 30,31:2
Seyes, John Rev, 1872, F 12,1:3
Seyfang, Frank G, 1963, F 11,7:5
Seyfang, William G, 1955, N 2,35:5
Seyfert, Carl K, 1960, Je 15,15:2
Seyfert, Samuel R, 1939, F 14,20:1
Seyfert, Stanley S, 1939, D 12,27:2
Seyfert, W M, 1902, Ja 19,9:6
Seyfert, William H, 1953, F 7,15:3
Seyffert, Leopold, 1956, Je 14,33:5
Seyfferth, Jacob, 1941, Je 2,17:4
Seyfried, Gordon, 1918, D 2,13:3
Seyfried, Herman, 1951, Mr 3,13:1
Seyfried, John G, 1955, S 24,19:4
Seyfrit, Michael, 1955, S 2,7:3
Seyler, Julius, 1949, S 23,23:2
Seymour, Ainsworth W, 1951, Ja 14,84:4
Seymour, Allen L Mrs, 1944, Jl 31,13:4
Seymour, Arthur B, 1952, F 18,19:5
Seymour, Arthur Mrs, 1948, Ap 6,23:4
Seymour, Burge M, 1967, Ap 11,47:1
Seymour, Burge M Mrs, 1964, Mr 22,76:8
Seymour, C Lansing, 1946, D 24,18:2
Seymour, Charles, 1883, Mr 11,9:4; 1963, Ag 12,21:1
Seymour, Charles B (funl, My 6,5:6), 1869, My 3,5:1
Seymour, Charles R, 1952, Ap 29,27:4
Seymour, Clarine E, 1920, Ap 26,13:4
Seymour, Cornelia C Mrs, 1937, F 18,21:5
Seymour, Daniel, 1925, Ap 13,19:4
Seymour, David (funl), 1956, N 16,52:7
Seymour, David B, 1939, D 1,23:4
Seymour, David L, 1867, O 12,1:4
Seymour, Dudley D, 1950, Mr 8,27:2
Seymour, E (see also Ap 30), 1877, My 2,8:2
Seymour, E Rev, 1879, Je 23,5:2
Seymour, Edith G Mrs, 1941, Ja 12,44:2
Seymour, Edmund, 1949, D 18,89:1
Seymour, Edward L D, 1956, Ag 4,15:3
Seymour, Edward P, 1948, N 12,23:3
Seymour, Edward Palmer, 1968, S 29,80:1
Seymour, Effie T Mrs, 1938, Ag 6,13:5
Seymour, Ernest, 1951, Je 15,24:2
Seymour, Eugene S, 1957, Mr 18,27:4
Seymour, Evelyn F E (Duke of Somerset), 1954, Ap 27,29:3
Seymour, F, 1869, Jl 11,3:3
Seymour, Fielding A, 1952, S 21,89:2
Seymour, Frances I, 1954, D 18,15:4
Seymour, Frank, 1942, S 2,23:3
Seymour, Frank B, 1939, My 7,III,7:3
Seymour, Frank L, 1959, F 28,19:3
Seymour, Frank Mrs, 1937, N 10,25:1
Seymour, Frank W, 1944, Mr 31,21:4
Seymour, Fred, 1947, Ja 3,22:3
Seymour, Fred B, 1943, S 30,21:6
Seymour, Frederick, 1924, My 30,15:5
Seymour, Frederick P, 1952, N 22,23:5
Seymour, Frederick W, 1941, S 12,22:2
Seymour, Frederick W Mrs, 1949, D 6,31:4
Seymour, G H Sir, 1880, F 4,3:4
Seymour, George D, 1945, Ja 22,17:3
Seymour, George Franklin, 1906, D 9,7:6
Seymour, George S, 1945, S 9,45:1
Seymour, Gideon D, 1954, My 21,28:3
Seymour, H G, 1883, Je 18,8:3
Seymour, H M, 1876, D 3,9:7
Seymour, H T Rev, 1917, O 27,17:6
Seymour, Harold J, 1953, S 17,29:5; 1968, Ap 11,45:2
Seymour, Harold M, 1959, F 12,27:4
Seymour, Harry, 1944, Ag 30,15:3
Seymour, Harvey B, 1923, D 14,21:5
Seymour, Helen C, 1941, S 13,17:5
Seymour, Henry T, 1938, Mr 23,23:4
Seymour, Henry T Mrs, 1962, N 2,31:1
Seymour, Herbert A, 1947, D 11,33:3
Seymour, Horace L, 1940, Ap 23,23:5
Seymour, Horatio, 1872, S 19,1:6; 1886, F 13,1:7
Seymour, Horatio Mrs, 1915, Ja 8,11:3
Seymour, Horatio Winslow, 1920, D 18,13:4
Seymour, Hugh B, 1937, D 19,II,9:2
Seymour, Hugh de Gray (Marquis of Hertford), 1912, Mr 24,15:3
Seymour, Isaac N, 1873, Ja 27,5:6
Seymour, J S, 1875, D 4,4:7
Seymour, James, 1925, D 25,17:5
Seymour, James A (por), 1943, Je 29,19:1
Seymour, James A Mrs, 1949, Ap 19,25:3
Seymour, James F, 1938, Ag 20,15:6
Seymour, James M, 1905, Ap 2,9:6
Seymour, James M Jr, 1940, S 4,23:5
Seymour, James Sherwood, 1924, Ag 12,11:4
Seymour, Jane (J S Lair), 1956, Ja 31,29:2
Seymour, John B Mrs, 1958, Jl 20,65:2
Seymour, John G, 1950, O 5,31:2
Seymour, Julius Mrs, 1917, O 24,15:5
Seymour, Kate, 1903, S 8,7:6
Seymour, Katherine, 1945, F 12,20:3
Seymour, Lee J, 1943, Ja 19,19:2
Seymour, Leofwine R, 1940, N 18,19:4
Seymour, M T, 1885, Je 1,5:2
Seymour, Martha P Mrs, 1937, Ap 20,25:3
Seymour, Martin A, 1874, Ap 24,1:4
Seymour, May D, 1967, O 6,39:2
Seymour, Morris Woodruff Ex-Judge, 1920, O 29,15:5
Seymour, Nan G, 1940, My 28,23:4
Seymour, O S, 1881, Ag 10,4:7
Seymour, Orange Stoddard, 1903, Jl 18,7:6
Seymour, Origen S (por), 1940, My 23,23:3
Seymour, R W Col, 1884, Mr 19,1:5
Seymour, R W Mrs, 1952, My 3,21:5
Seymour, Reginald, 1938, O 3,15:4
Seymour, Robert G Rev, 1912, S 21,11:6
Seymour, Robert P, 1920, Je 30,13:4
Seymour, Samuel J, 1956, Ap 14,17:4
Seymour, Stewart M, 1956, Je 21,31:5
Seymour, Sydney D, 1943, Jl 27,17:3
Seymour, Theodius, 1945, Je 23,13:4
Seymour, Thomas Day Prof, 1908, Ja 1,9:5
Seymour, Thomas G Mrs, 1954, Je 26,13:3

Seymour, Thomas H Ex-Gov, 1868, S 4,4:5
Seymour, Tot (Mrs Harold Seymour), 1966, S 1,35:3
Seymour, Truman Mrs, 1919, D 17,17:2
Seymour, W F, 1928, Ap 26,5:4
Seymour, W Jr, 1882, Ja 10,5:4
Seymour, W Mrs, 1927, F 11,21:3
Seymour, W N, 1881, Je 7,8:3
Seymour, Walter, 1953, S 7,19:4
Seymour, Walter B, 1944, Je 10,15:3
Seymour, Walter F Mrs, 1955, F 26,15:2
Seymour, Walton Mrs, 1960, D 7,43:4
Seymour, William E Gen, 1915, F 11,9:5
Seymour, William H, 1950, N 11,15:6
Seymour, William J, 1945, Ag 5,37:2
Seymour-Jones, Frank L, 1953, Jl 3,19:6
Seymour-Lloyd, John Sir, 1939, Jl 27,19:3
Seymoure, C Orvas, 1949, Je 7,31:2
Seys, John O, 1938, Ja 24,23:2
Seyssel-d'Aix, Count, 1880, Ap 30,2:2
Seyyid Khalifah, Sultan of Zanzibar, 1890, F 14,2:5
Sforza, Ascania, 1944, O 20,20:2
Sforza, Carlo Count, 1952, S 5,1:3
Sforza, Giovanni Count, 1922, O 2,17:6
Sforza, S R Cardinal, 1877, O 1,5:5
Sgambati, Giovanni, 1914, D 15,13:6
Sghia, Otto T, 1959, F 4,26:1
Sgiers, Martin J Mrs, 1938, Ap 13,25:4
Shaak, Walter D, 1958, S 11,33:1
Shabecoff, Sidney Mrs, 1968, Jl 12,31:1
Shaber, Samuel, 1941, D 3,25:4
Shachtman, Oizer, 1955, D 9,27:2
Shack, David N, 1957, Jl 7,60:8
Shack, Ferdinand, 1908, Ja 12,9:5
Shack, Jacob H, 1967, F 12,93:1
Shackeford, Dorothy Mae (Mrs Stanley A Tucker), 1968, D 30,31:2
Shackelford, Eleanor A, 1925, Jl 14,21:5
Shackelford, Emmett, 1945, My 17,19:2
Shackelford, George R, 1948, Ag 18,25:5
Shackelford, J W, 1883, Ja 19,5:2
Shackelford, James Gen, 1909, S 8,9:4
Shackelford, Larkin M, 1964, Jl 25,19:5
Shackell, Stanton M, 1956, S 21,25:2
Shackford, John E Capt, 1905, Je 24,9:5
Shackford, Moses A C, 1944, D 23,13:1
Shackford, William G Capt, 1907, O 23,11:6
Shackford, William M Mrs, 1952, Ja 16,25:3
Shackiston, Parker, 1923, S 1,11:6
Shacklady, William Mrs, 1943, F 13,11:4
Shackleford, Malcolm, 1940, Je 9,44:4
Shackleton, David (por), 1938, Ag 2,19:3
Shackleton, Horace E Mrs, 1937, O 30,19:5
Shackleton, Robert, 1923, F 26,13:4
Shackleton, Robert W, 1956, Je 22,23:4
Shackleton, William E Mrs, 1948, Mr 30,23:5
Shacklock, Floyd Mrs, 1943, O 28,23:1
Shackson, Roland, 1939, Jl 13,19:6
Shacter, Joseph A, 1954, N 26,14:6
Shad, Conrad, 1953, Jl 9,25:4
Shadd, Henry L, 1952, Mr 23,93:2
Shaddock, Richard, 1943, F 28,48:2
Shaddock, Seranus B, 1938, N 2,23:2
Shaddrick, Lawrence D, 1958, O 2,37:3
Shade, Billy, 1951, D 12,37:5
Shade, George, 1952, F 2,13:5
Shade, H Edgar, 1951, Je 3,92:6
Shade, James E, 1954, Je 11,23:3
Shader, George (Mickey), 1953, Mr 31,31:4
Shader, Louisa F Mrs, 1942, Ag 2,39:3
Shader, Virgil C, 1948, O 7,29:2
Shadid, Michael A, 1966, Ag 15,27:4
Shadwell, Henry C, 1951, Ag 29,25:5
Shaefer, Lesley G, 1956, Ap 16,27:4
Shaeffer, Craig R, 1961, Jl 10,13:1
Shaeffer, Grant, 1947, Ja 15,26:3
Shaeffer, Joseph R, 1953, Jl 1,29:4
Shaeffer, Rebecca Mrs, 1954, Mr 12,22:3
Shaen, Harry B, 1920, N 22,15:4
Shafer, Anna J, 1942, Ja 10,15:6
Shafer, Audrey B, 1951, Jl 9,27:7
Shafer, Austin C, 1944, Ag 17,17:3
Shafer, Billy, 1909, Ag 30,7:5
Shafer, Burr, 1965, Je 16,43:2
Shafer, Charles, 1948, D 24,18:3
Shafer, Chester J, 1951, Ja 19,25:1
Shafer, Clark S Rev, 1937, My 18,23:5
Shafer, Claude, 1962, My 25,33:3
Shafer, David W, 1954, Je 22,27:2
Shafer, F Culver, 1950, Ag 31,25:3
Shafer, Francis H, 1953, Ag 25,21:2
Shafer, Frank G, 1948, D 19,76:4
Shafer, Fremont K Mrs, 1954, My 12,31:3
Shafer, George F, 1948, Ag 14,13:4
Shafer, Gustavus A, 1952, O 8,31:5
Shafer, Harry H, 1950, Ap 21,23:3
Shafer, Helen A, 1894, Ja 20,8:2
Shafer, Henry W, 1949, Je 23,27:4
Shafer, Jay E, 1950, O 25,35:4
Shafer, John F, 1941, N 24,17:1
Shafer, Leon A, 1940, Ap 20,17:5
Shafer, Luman J, 1958, Ja 3,23:2
Shafer, Mervin M, 1957, Ag 30,19:6
Shafer, Michael H, 1943, Ap 21,25:5
Shafer, Morgan R, 1943, Ag 29,39:2
Shafer, Paul F, 1959, Je 9,37:5
Shafer, Paul W, 1954, Ag 18,29:1
Shafer, Paul W Mrs, 1954, Jl 6,23:5
Shafer, Ralph, 1950, F 7,27:5
Shafer, Robert, 1956, Ja 7,17:1
Shafer, Rudolph J, 1956, O 31,33:3
Shafer, Samuel Jr, 1946, F 6,23:2
Shafer, Samuel W, 1959, O 11,86:4
Shafer, Willard H, 1948, O 13,25:5
Shafer, William, 1966, F 20,88:3
Shafer, William C, 1940, D 22,30:8
Shaff, C Dell, 1940, D 30,17:3
Shaff, Carl Mrs, 1956, Ja 15,92:1
Shaffer, Aaron H, 1965, Mr 3,41:3
Shaffer, Albert B, 1947, F 17,19:2
Shaffer, Almon, 1942, F 21,20:2
Shaffer, C Norman, 1962, Je 9,25:1
Shaffer, Charles, 1947, My 10,13:4
Shaffer, Charles Ashford, 1916, Ja 17,11:2
Shaffer, Charles B, 1943, Jl 19,15:2
Shaffer, Charles G, 1953, D 15,39:1
Shaffer, Charles M, 1952, S 16,29:2
Shaffer, Duncan E, 1940, Mr 26,21:6
Shaffer, Edward F, 1941, Ap 1,23:2
Shaffer, Edward H, 1944, Ap 4,21:1
Shaffer, Ferenc (por), 1949, F 1,25:5
Shaffer, Frank J, 1948, F 17,26:2
Shaffer, Frank L, 1942, D 29,22:3
Shaffer, George E, 1955, Ap 7,27:5
Shaffer, I, 1952, Mr 23,4:3
Shaffer, Ines V Mrs, 1955, My 17,29:5
Shaffer, J W Gov, 1870, N 10,2:6
Shaffer, John C, 1943, O 6,23:3
Shaffer, Kent, 1925, Ap 6,19:5
Shaffer, Lester D, 1937, F 6,17:2
Shaffer, Lloyd L, 1937, Ag 10,19:4
Shaffer, Morris, 1942, F 21,19:4
Shaffer, N M, 1928, Ja 4,25:3
Shaffer, Nathan L, 1952, My 30,15:1
Shaffer, Newton H, 1962, S 18,39:1
Shaffer, Philip, 1960, D 5,31:4
Shaffer, Robert, 1906, Jl 13,4:2
Shaffer, Samuel S, 1938, S 5,15:2
Shaffer, Stanley N, 1956, S 17,27:2
Shaffer, Theodore J, 1942, My 5,21:1
Shaffer, Theodore L, 1954, F 14,93:2
Shaffer, Thomas C, 1960, Ap 9,23:6
Shaffer, William R, 1964, N 4,39:4
Shafner, Harris, 1965, My 5,47:3
Shafran, David Mrs (R Renee), 1967, My 12,47:3
Shafritz, Morris, 1953, S 12,17:1
Shafroth, John F, 1967, S 3,52:5
Shafroth, John F Ex-Sen, 1922, F 21,17:3
Shaftel, Maurice B, 1957, Ag 16,19:1
Shaftel, Samuel Dr, 1968, Jl 3,32:3
Shafter, William Rufus Maj-Gen, 1906, N 13,3:3
Shaftesbury, Earl of (A Ashley Cooper), 1961, Mr 27,31:2
Shafto, Harold M, 1956, Je 27,31:4
Shafto, M E, 1940, Ap 27,15:6
Shaftoe, Joseph T, 1953, N 23,27:3
Shah, Persian, 1896, My 2,1:7
Shahan, George A, 1939, Ja 8,42:5
Shahani, Ranjee, 1968, D 21,31:5
Shaheen, Phil J, 1957, Ja 23,29:1
Shaheen, Shaheen A, 1946, My 8,25:5
Shaheen, Shaheen A Mrs, 1949, N 1,27:2
Shaible, Maude S Mrs, 1941, Mr 25,23:3
Shaifer, Carl H Jr, 1964, F 15,23:4
Shailer, Fisk A, 1966, F 1,35:2
Shailer, Gladys T, 1955, Jl 27,23:4
Shailer, Russell H, 1938, Mr 8,19:4
Shain, Jesse, 1906, Ap 27,11:5
Shain, Mendy, 1953, Je 9,27:1
Shainblum, Benjamin Mrs (Julia),(cor, My 29,27:6), 1965, My 28,33:2
Shaine, Louis, 1954, My 16,86:6
Shaine, Maurice L, 1945, N 25,48:4
Shaine, William, 1951, S 14,25:4
Shainline, Harry S, 1951, Ja 13,15:4
Shainmark, David, 1961, Ja 21,21:6
Shainmark, Ephraim J, 1960, Je 10,31:5
Shainwald, Ralph Louis, 1919, D 11,13:3
Shainwald-von Ahlefeldt, Ilse B Mrs, 1940, My 1,23:5
Shair, David H, 1962, S 3,15:5
Shairp, Mordaunt, 1939, Ja 19,19:4
Shakespear, J H, 1902, Ap 23,9:4
Shakespeare, Charles B, 1916, Ag 1,9:6
Shakespeare, Edward O Jr, 1937, Mr 2,21:3
Shakespeare, Edward O Mrs, 1946, Ja 21,23:2
Shakespeare, Franklin H, 1950, F 24,23:2
Shakespeare, Geoffrey Mrs, 1950, F 15,27:5
Shakespeare, Monroe, 1945, Ag 31,17:3
Shakespeare, William, 1965, Mr 16,39:1
Shakespeare, William Mrs, 1947, My 6,27:3
Shakib Arslan, Emir, 1946, D 11,32:3
Shaklee, George R, 1941, Ap 28,15:5
Shaklee, Warren J, 1951, Ja 9,29:2
Shako, George K Sr, 1944, Ja 11,19:1
Shalamon, Nicholas Mrs (J T Patton), 1963, Je 18, 37:3
Shale, Jacob B (por), 1937, Ap 1,23:5
Shalen, Samuel H, 1950, Mr 2,27:5
Shaler, Alexander Gen, 1911, D 28,9:3
Shaler, Bessie (E Brice), 1965, Ja 26,37:2
Shaler, Charles B, 1948, D 3,25:2
Shaler, Charles Gen, 1915, Mr 27,11:5
Shaler, Edward C, 1943, S 6,18:3
Shaler, James R Col, 1910, S 8,9:4
Shaler, Millard, 1942, D 16,25:2
Shaler, Nathaniel Southgate Dean, 1906, Ap 11,11:4
Shalett, Benjamin, 1946, S 21,15:3
Shalett, Sidney, 1965, Jl 3,19:4
Shalian, Artin K, 1964, N 5,45:3
Shallcross, Cecil F, 1947, Ap 10,25:3
Shallcross, Cecil F Mrs, 1940, F 11,49:1
Shallcross, John W, 1967, Ja 20,43:2
Shallcross, Joseph Sr, 1951, Ja 3,27:2
Shallcross, Joseph W, 1956, Ja 20,23:4
Shallcross, Thomas Jr, 1960, O 15,23:6
Shallenberger, Ashton C (por), 1938, F 23,23:5
Shallenberger, Martin C, 1951, F 13,31:4
Shallenberger, Thomas M, 1946, My 13,21:6
Shallenberger, W F, 1944, D 18,19:4
Shallenberger, William S, 1914, Ap 16,9:4
Shaller, William C, 1938, Ag 9,19:4
Shallew, John F (Bro Alban Faber), 1956, O 17,35
Shallot, William R, 1949, S 4,40:4
Shallow, E B, 1927, F 9,19:5
Shallow, Frank L, 1955, D 28,23:4
Shallow, Thomas A, 1955, D 27,24:3
Shalom, Isaac, 1968, Jl 25,33:2
Shalsky, Michael, 1946, Ap 23,21:5
Shaltout, Mahmoud, 1963, D 14,27:2
Shalut, Harry, 1939, Ap 5,25:5
Shamaskin, Arnold, 1966, S 3,23:5
Shambaugh, George E, 1947, D 2,30:3
Shamberg, Alex J, 1941, N 21,17:3
Shamberg, Gustave H, 1940, N 20,21:3
Shambler, William A, 1949, Jl 16,13:6
Shambroom, Henry, 1942, D 11,24:2
Shamos, Abraham, 1966, My 10,39:4
Shampaine, Abraham, 1962, Jl 29,60:1
Shampan, Joseph, 1961, D 16,25:3
Shampnois, Austin D, 1950, O 24,29:1
Shamsey, John K, 1956, Ap 19,31:4
Shamy, Killel, 1947, D 23,23:5
Shanafelt, Dick, 1967, N 11,33:3
Shanahan, Anna L Mrs, 1941, Jl 6,26:2
Shanahan, David, 1942, O 18,55:4
Shanahan, Dennis J, 1958, F 13,29:6
Shanahan, Edward T, 1942, Je 14,45:2
Shanahan, George A Mrs, 1957, My 9,31:4
Shanahan, James F, 1949, Ag 6,17:4
Shanahan, John J, 1942, Mr 20,19:5
Shanahan, John N Mrs, 1951, N 19,23:6
Shanahan, John Rev, 1870, Ag 21,6:5
Shanahan, John W Bp, 1916, F 20,15:4
Shanahan, Mabel, 1952, Ja 22,29:1
Shanahan, Mary M, 1937, Mr 15,23:3
Shanahan, Patrick, 1937, D 9,25:6
Shanahan, Patrick E, 1964, N 14,29:4
Shanahan, Paul R, 1966, Ap 15,39:5
Shanahan, Richard J, 1940, F 29,19:2
Shanahan, Robert H, 1955, Ap 27,31:3
Shanahan, Robert H Mrs, 1948, O 1,25:3
Shanahan, Roger F, 1951, Jl 27,19:4
Shanahan, Samuel E, 1942, D 8,25:4
Shanahan, Thomas A, 1939, My 2,23:2; 1963, Je 27 33:2
Shanahan, Thomas J, 1963, Mr 8,12:1
Shanahan, W M, 1949, Jl 16,13:1
Shanahan, Walter E, 1953, Je 16,27:1
Shanahan, William F, 1937, S 19,II,6:7; 1946, Ap 2 27:3
Shanahan, William J, 1943, D 23,19:4; 1958, My 2 33:4
Shanahan, William S, 1947, Mr 30,56:2
Shanahan, William T, 1951, Ja 28,77:2
Shanaman, William F, 1939, Ag 22,19:2
Shanbacker, Edward F, 1943, F 12,19:3
Shanck, Roy B, 1967, Ap 20,43:2
Shand, George J Jr, 1937, Mr 2,21:4
Shand, James G Mrs, 1942, Je 22,15:4
Shand, Richings J, 1939, Mr 27,15:2
Shand, Robert G, 1966, N 26,35:1
Shand, S James, 1957, Ap 22,25:5
Shandelle, Henry Rev, 1925, N 28,15:5
Shandley, E J (see also Jl 28), 1876, Jl 31,8:1
Shands, Milo C, 1951, Jl 19,23:4
Shane, Dennis, 1924, D 16,25:3
Shane, Hyman, 1956, Jl 3,25:2
Shane, Theodore Mrs, 1965, S 5,57:3
Shane, Theodore S, 1967, Je 17,31:2
Shane, Thomas Mrs, 1952, Ag 8,17:3
Shanefield, Benjamin, 1966, S 2,31:4
Shaner, Albert L, 1945, D 8,17:4
Shaner, Carl L, 1949, Jl 3,27:1
Shaner, Frank J, 1954, Ap 9,24:4
Shaner, Samuel R, 1960, Ag 12,19:4
Shanes, Abraham M, 1963, O 13,86:7
Shanfield, Louis, 1957, O 18,23:1
Shangle, Milton A, 1958, F 8,19:6
Shanhart, Frederick D, 1949, F 24,23:5
Shanholt, Henry H, 1949, D 13,31:4

Shank, Burt O, 1940, F 13,23:5
Shank, Donald J, 1967, Jl 30,64:7
Shank, George, 1920, D 27,13:5
Shank, L D, 1943, Jl 19,15:5
Shank, Louis W, 1959, Mr 28,17:2
Shank, Reed A Sr, 1953, N 27,27:2
Shank, Robert F, 1968, Ap 13,25:1
Shank, S L, 1927, S 25,26:1
Shank, William, 1920, D 27,13:5
Shank, William C, 1953, S 5,11:4
Shankey, Ann G, 1942, D 29,21:1
Shankey, John F Mrs, 1950, O 9,25:2
Shankey, Joseph I, 1954, Ja 7,31:5
Shankey, Victor J, 1966, O 10,41:2
Shankland, Arch D, 1949, Ja 7,21:5
Shankland, Edward Clapp, 1924, Je 5,21:5
Shankland, Palmer K, 1939, Ap 9,III,6:8
Shankland, Sherwood D (por), 1947, My 29,22:2
Shanklin, George B, 1961, N 22,33:2
Shanklin, John Gilbert, 1903, Ag 7,7:6
Shanklin, Radford C, 1951, My 17,31:4
Shanklin, Robert G Mrs, 1953, F 7,15:4
Shanklin, William A Mrs, 1946, N 8,23:3
Shanklin, William Arnold Dr (funl, O 9,23:5), 1924, O 7,23:4
Shankman, Harry L, 1952, N 23,88:2
Shankman, Max, 1965, Jl 8,28:2
Shankman, Samuel B, 1952, O 25,17:3
Shankroff, Louis, 1955, Je 4,15:5
Shanks, David C (por), 1940, Ap 11,25:1
Shanks, Edward, 1953, My 5,29:4
Shanks, Elsie, 1960, F 7,84:5
Shanks, Howard, 1941, Ag 1,15:6
Shanks, J Crawford, 1955, Je 7,33:3
Shanks, James Mrs, 1951, S 29,17:5
Shanks, Lucian H, 1963, My 29,33:1
Shanks, Maria G, 1950, S 6,30:3
Shanks, Mary L, 1948, Ja 23,23:3
Shanks, Milo, 1940, F 11,49:2
Shanks, Sanders Jr (por), 1949, Je 12,78:3
Shanks, W F G, 1905, F 24,7:5
Shanks, W G, 1864, My 21,1:4
Shanks, William R, 1907, F 22,9:6
Shanley, Abigail, 1909, Ag 27,7:6
Shanley, Andrew E, 1919, Ja 28,9:4
Shanley, Anna, 1951, O 11,37:1
Shanley, Bernard M Jr, 1924, O 7,23:4
Shanley, Bernard M Mrs, 1946, My 5,44:2
Shanley, Charles A, 1949, F 4,24:3
Shanley, Edward J, 1952, My 7,27:1
Shanley, F Sheppard, 1949, D 26,29:2
Shanley, Francis, 1943, O 4,17:1
Shanley, Frank N, 1958, Jl 14,21:4
Shanley, G Frank, 1949, Mr 6,72:2
Shanley, James, 1937, Ag 25,21:2; 1940, Je 16,38:6
Shanley, James A, 1965, Ap 6,39:4
Shanley, James J, 1951, Je 28,25:5
Shanley, John F, 1911, D 19,13:4; 1943, Jl 18,34:1
Shanley, John F Mrs, 1965, Je 15,41:1
Shanley, Margaret (Sister Mary Luana), 1954, D 1, 31:4
Shanley, Michael F, 1938, F 28,15:5
Shanley, Patrick, 1941, D 9,31:4
Shanley, Patrick J, 1947, Ag 20,22:2; 1948, O 11,23:5
Shanley, Patrick Mrs, 1960, Ap 24,88:4
Shanley, Peter F, 1950, Mr 3,25:1
Shanley, Richard B, 1938, Ag 28,33:3
Shanley, T J, 1932, O 8,17:4
Shanley, Timothy, 1923, Ag 6,11:2
Shanley, Walter J, 1919, My 5,13:5
Shanley, William F, 1951, Ja 17,28:2
Shann, Frederick C, 1920, S 24,15:2
Shann, Oscar A, 1967, S 2,22:7
Shannahan, cornelius M, 1957, F 21,27:4
Shannahan, John N, 1938, Ag 18,19:3
Shannahan, William P Msgr, 1937, O 23,15:8
Shannan, M G Mrs, 1951, Ag 25,11:7
Shanno, Ralph, 1951, F 16,25:2
Shannon, Andrew F, 1956, My 23,31:6
Shannon, Angus R Sr, 1958, Jl 20,64:5
Shannon, Arthur E, 1940, Je 14,21:1
Shannon, Charles, 1937, Mr 19,24:1; 1947, S 21,60:6
Shannon, Charles B, 1946, S 29,60:3
Shannon, Chester A, 1944, F 21,15:2
Shannon, Clarence D, 1950, Mr 5,92:5
Shannon, Donald E, 1937, Je 5,17:1
Shannon, Earl of, 1868, D 26,1:1
Shannon, Earl of (R H Boyle), 1963, D 30,2:3
Shannon, Edgar F, 1938, My 3,23:3
Shannon, Edward, 1943, Ap 9,21:5
Shannon, Edward C, 1946, My 21,23:2
Shannon, Edward P, 1955, Jl 4,11:5
Shannon, Effie, 1954, Jl 25,69:1
Shannon, Erwin V, 1959, Ja 31,19:2
Shannon, Eugene Mrs, 1945, Jl 3,13:2
Shannon, Fern L, 1953, O 20,29:4
Shannon, Frank A, 1952, Jl 29,21:4
Shannon, Frank P, 1961, O 29,88:8
Shannon, Fred, 1965, S 1,37:4
Shannon, Fred A, 1963, F 7,7:4
Shannon, Frederick F, 1947, Ap 15,25:2
Shannon, George S, 1941, S 4,21:3
Shannon, George W, 1951, S 26,31:6
Shannon, Grace Mrs (G Cunard), 1967, Ja 24,37:2
Shannon, Harold D (por), 1943, F 17,21:1
Shannon, Harry, 1940, F 24,13:1
Shannon, Herbert, 1940, Ja 17,21:5
Shannon, Hugh Mrs (B Sundmark), 1959, Ag 19,29:2
Shannon, J Vincent, 1957, Jl 13,17:6
Shannon, James B, 1964, O 21,47:3
Shannon, James B Mrs (Lardner), 1960, My 6,31:2
Shannon, James E, 1948, Je 29,24:2
Shannon, James I, 1950, S 10,92:3
Shannon, James J Sir, 1923, Mr 7,15:4
Shannon, James P, 1940, D 15,61:2
Shannon, John, 1940, Mr 16,15:5
Shannon, John J, 1948, N 14,76:1
Shannon, John M, 1943, F 7,48:3; 1946, Jl 9,22:2
Shannon, John P, 1943, N 10,23:2; 1949, Ap 22,24:6; 1949, D 29,25:4
Shannon, John R, 1941, Ap 21,19:3; 1942, Jl 5,30:3
Shannon, John W, 1955, N 17,35:4
Shannon, Joseph B, 1943, Mr 29,15:3
Shannon, Joseph G, 1949, O 1,13:5
Shannon, Joseph W, 1937, Mr 28,II,8:8
Shannon, Lavinia, 1945, Ap 27,19:4
Shannon, Lincoln V, 1955, Jl 13,25:5
Shannon, Martha A, 1938, O 26,23:2
Shannon, Mary Mrs, 1941, D 6,17:2
Shannon, Matthew, 1938, D 6,23:4
Shannon, Matthew E, 1945, Je 6,21:5
Shannon, P (see also Mr 27), 1878, Mr 30,8:4
Shannon, Patrick, 1945, My 12,13:4
Shannon, Patrick J Mrs, 1945, N 14,19:4; 1967, Mr 29, 45:1
Shannon, Paul E V, 1957, My 25,21:2
Shannon, Peggy, 1941, My 12,17:3
Shannon, Philip F, 1960, My 8,88:5
Shannon, R G (Boss), 1956, D 26,21:1
Shannon, Ralph E, 1962, My 16,41:2
Shannon, Ralph W Sr, 1949, My 8,76:4
Shannon, Raymond D, 1952, F 9,13:7
Shannon, Robert, 1966, D 9,47:2
Shannon, Robert K, 1964, Ja 10,43:2
Shannon, Sallie, 1911, O 9,11:5
Shannon, Stephen A, 1947, O 29,27:2
Shannon, Stephen S, 1952, Mr 25,18:1
Shannon, T W, 1883, Jl 15,7:2
Shannon, Theodore J Gen, 1912, S 23,13:6
Shannon, Thomas, 1925, My 16,17:7; 1939, F 2,19:5
Shannon, Thomas B Rev, 1911, O 15,II,15:4
Shannon, Thomas E, 1950, N 20,25:3
Shannon, Thomas F, 1941, Mr 3,15:3
Shannon, Thomas F Jr, 1951, Ap 25,29:3
Shannon, Thomas W, 1941, Ag 31,23:2
Shannon, W Ex-Gov, 1877, S 1,4:7
Shannon, W W, 1948, N 16,29:2
Shannon, Walter Mrs, 1941, Ap 24,21:6
Shannon, Walter W, 1937, Ag 17,19:2
Shannon, Warren, 1948, Mr 27,13:6
Shannon, William H, 1959, D 13,86:3
Shannon, William J, 1943, Jl 30,15:3
Shannon, William N, 1925, D 3,25:4
Shannon, William P, 1940, My 18,15:5
Shannon, William W, 1939, F 19,39:3
Shannon (Bro Justin), 1961, Je 25,76:6
Shanor, H A Ralph, 1954, N 7,88:3
Shanor, Perry A, 1939, N 7,28:4
Shanton, G R, 1930, S 25,25:1
Shantz, Edgar, 1943, O 31,48:4
Shantz, Harold, 1967, S 4,21:5
Shantz, Homer L, 1958, Je 24,31:5
Shantz, Katy J, 1946, F 17,44:1
Shanz, John J, 1962, D 17,15:8
Shao Li-tzu, 1967, D 30,23:1
Shape, Robert L, 1941, Je 18,21:1
Shaper, Ray, 1955, Jl 17,60:4
Shapera, Archie Mrs, 1962, Je 2,19:3
Shapera, Morris L, 1938, F 28,15:4
Shapiro, A Alver, 1960, O 22,23:5
Shapiro, A M Mrs, 1944, Mr 16,19:4
Shapiro, Aaron A, 1961, S 8,32:1
Shapiro, Aaron S, 1938, Jl 10,29:2
Shapiro, Abraham, 1940, Mr 10,49:2; 1942, Jl 17,15:6; 1949, F 19,15:3; 1950, Mr 27,11:2; 1965, D 29,26:5; 1967, Mr 12,86:8
Shapiro, Abraham M, 1947, Je 8,60:8
Shapiro, Abraham Mrs, 1950, Mr 27,11:2
Shapiro, Abram, 1960, Ag 3,29:5
Shapiro, Anne, 1945, Mr 4,38:5
Shapiro, Anne R, 1955, S 25,92:6
Shapiro, Arnold, 1958, S 15,21:5
Shapiro, Barnett M, 1957, O 28,27:4
Shapiro, Benjamin, 1955, D 4,88:5
Shapiro, Benjamin D, 1956, Ja 29,92:2
Shapiro, Bennett M, 1959, F 23,23:4
Shapiro, Bernard, 1952, N 29,17:3
Shapiro, Bernard H, 1962, Ja 20,21:6
Shapiro, Carl Mrs, 1953, Mr 24,31:1
Shapiro, Chaim E, 1937, My 13,25:2
Shapiro, Charles, 1966, My 2,37:3; 1968, D 26,37:2
Shapiro, Daniel, 1941, Ja 31,19:1
Shapiro, Daniel S Mrs, 1948, Ag 31,23:2
Shapiro, David (por), 1940, N 3,56:4
Shapiro, David, 1954, My 4,29:3; 1958, S 11,33:1
Shapiro, David I, 1961, My 31,33:1
Shapiro, David Mrs, 1958, N 11,29:4
Shapiro, Elliott, 1956, F 3,23:3
Shapiro, Esther Mrs, 1937, S 18,19:4
Shapiro, Harry, 1945, Je 27,19:2; 1953, Jl 30,23:2; 1964, Jl 26,56:7; 1967, D 2,39:5
Shapiro, Harry L Mrs, 1962, Ap 26,33:4
Shapiro, Harry Mrs, 1951, S 20,31:2
Shapiro, Henry, 1953, Je 1,23:5
Shapiro, Henry A, 1954, D 2,31:2
Shapiro, Herbert R, 1952, My 9,23:6
Shapiro, Herman, 1961, Je 14,19:4
Shapiro, Hyman, 1968, D 13,42:1
Shapiro, Ira J, 1948, Jl 18,52:6
Shapiro, Irving, 1955, Mr 30,29:4
Shapiro, Isadore, 1956, My 23,31:3
Shapiro, Israel E, 1942, Ap 29,21:3
Shapiro, Jacob, 1942, S 19,15:1; 1947, Je 10,56:1
Shapiro, Jerome N, 1968, Ap 10,47:3
Shapiro, Jesse, 1968, Mr 23,31:5
Shapiro, Jonas J, 1954, Jl 8,23:5
Shapiro, Joseph, 1904, N 8,6:2; 1948, Jl 27,25:2; 1949, F 9,28:2; 1960, Jl 20,29:3; 1964, Ja 23,31:3; 1968, Ja 25,37:1
Shapiro, Joseph I, 1962, My 24,35:5
Shapiro, Joseph L, 1965, N 23,45:3
Shapiro, Joseph M, 1968, Jl 31,41:3
Shapiro, Joseph Mrs, 1961, Ag 28,25:3
Shapiro, Julius, 1910, O 28,9:5
Shapiro, Lawrence M, 1953, Ag 27,25:6
Shapiro, Leo, 1952, Jl 11,17:5
Shapiro, Lionel S B, 1958, My 28,31:2
Shapiro, Louis, 1957, Ja 14,23:5; 1965, F 10,41:1
Shapiro, Louis J, 1968, Mr 28,47:2
Shapiro, Louis L, 1966, O 29,29:5
Shapiro, Maurice, 1945, D 1,23:2; 1966, Ja 11,27:3
Shapiro, Max J, 1949, My 20,27:3
Shapiro, Max S, 1949, O 15,15:5
Shapiro, Melvin Mrs, 1952, My 22,27:4
Shapiro, Mordecai Mrs, 1955, N 25,28:1
Shapiro, Morris, 1943, N 30,27:5; 1945, Jl 10,11:5; 1954, O 19,27:5
Shapiro, Morris L, 1949, S 16,27:3
Shapiro, Mortimer F Mrs, 1959, D 29,25:2
Shapiro, Moses Rabbi, 1907, O 25,11:5
Shapiro, Murray, 1955, Mr 14,23:2
Shapiro, Nathan, 1937, Ja 15,22:2
Shapiro, Nathan Mrs, 1951, F 7,29:4
Shapiro, Nathaniel, 1954, D 30,17:4
Shapiro, Nathaniel J, 1960, Ap 19,37:4
Shapiro, Phil Mrs, 1956, My 7,27:2
Shapiro, Phil S, 1956, S 22,17:3
Shapiro, Pincus, 1962, F 20,36:1
Shapiro, Robert, 1967, Ja 10,40:3
Shapiro, Rose Mrs, 1947, Ap 18,21:2
Shapiro, Sadie, 1967, My 3,45:3
Shapiro, Samuel, 1941, F 19,21:2; 1959, Jl 2,25:4; 1960, S 28,39:1; 1968, F 21,47:2
Shapiro, Samuel (cor, D 1,86:2), 1968, N 30,39:3
Shapiro, Samuel M, 1958, Jl 6,56:5
Shapiro, Samuel Mrs (Sammy Spear), 1968, Je 29, 29:2
Shapiro, Samuel S, 1954, O 28,35:2
Shapiro, Seymour L, 1961, D 10,88:4
Shapiro, Shabsi, 1947, Ja 30,25:2
Shapiro, Shepard, 1966, Je 13,39:4
Shapiro, Solomon A, 1964, N 18,47:4
Shapiro, Solomon Mrs, 1952, N 15,17:4
Shapiro, William, 1953, F 23,25:3
Shapiro, William M, 1958, F 2,86:8
Shaplan, Joseph, 1946, Je 5,23:4
Shapleigh, Alfred L, 1945, D 25,23:6
Shapley, George A Rev, 1957, S 7,19:6
Shapley, Joseph S, 1942, Mr 25,21:2
Shapley, Philina Mrs, 1918, Ag 10,7:5
Shapley, Rufus E, 1906, F 12,7:4
Shaporin, Yuri, 1966, D 11,88:7
Shaposhnikoff, Boris, 1945, Mr 27,19:5
Shapre, Guy W, 1957, Ap 24,33:4
Shapter, George L, 1967, O 28,31:4
Shapter, Margaret A, 1948, My 17,19:2
Shapter, Richard S Sr, 1947, Je 17,25:3
Sharapov, Ydshi D, 1963, Mr 13,7:6
Shard, Kate, 1942, Ja 6,23:1
Shardlow, Eliza (will), 1938, Ja 25,22:4
Share, George A, 1957, D 17,35:4
Share, Hamnet H Sir, 1937, Je 28,19:6
Share, Henry Pruett, 1905, Je 22,9:6
Share, Simon S, 1962, F 10,23:4
Share, William W Dr, 1937, Ap 22,23:2
Sharett, Moshe (funl plans, Jl 9,26:5; funl, Jl 10,25:6), 1965, Jl 8,31:1
Sharff, Morris, 1943, My 28,21:2
Sharfin, Zelik, 1962, Mr 24,25:5
Sharfstein, Harry, 1967, Mr 22,47:3
Sharfstein, Samuel, 1949, My 27,21:4
Shargorowska, Tua, 1950, Ap 10,19:3
Sharick, Andrew J, 1950, N 17,27:2
Sharick, Peter S, 1966, Ap 25,31:4
Shark, John C Mrs, 1951, Mr 5,16:5
Sharkey, Adolph, 1954, D 23,19:4
Sharkey, Alice M Mrs, 1954, D 4,17:4
Sharkey, Bartholomew F, 1956, O 17,35:3
Sharkey, Bert, 1953, My 8,25:2

Sharkey, Catherine T Mrs, 1941, Mr 29,15:1
Sharkey, Charles, 1937, Jl 23,20:6
Sharkey, Charles J, 1940, D 20,25:5
Sharkey, Edward J Mrs, 1947, O 5,68:5
Sharkey, Edwin J, 1952, My 26,23:4
Sharkey, Harold S, 1939, Mr 28,23:4
Sharkey, Henry W, 1924, Mr 27,19:5
Sharkey, John C, 1946, D 5,31:5
Sharkey, John F, 1949, D 28,25:2
Sharkey, John J, 1961, Ap 18,37:4
Sharkey, John M, 1950, Jl 7,19:4
Sharkey, Joseph E, 1958, Mr 30,88:4
Sharkey, Joseph E Mrs, 1956, Jl 5,25:4
Sharkey, Lawrence F, 1940, S 14,17:4
Sharkey, Luke F, 1955, Ag 29,19:4
Sharkey, Mary Agnes Sister, 1940, Ja 2,19:3
Sharkey, Mary M, 1947, O 29,27:4
Sharkey, Owen H Sr, 1949, Je 9,31:2
Sharkey, R A, 1928, My 20,II,8:1
Sharkey, Robert E Mrs, 1953, Jl 4,11:4
Sharkey, Sue, 1925, N 19,25:5
Sharkey, Terence C, 1962, My 12,23:5
Sharkey, Thomas A, 1965, Ja 29,29:3
Sharkey, Thomas H Sr, 1964, F 13,31:1
Sharkey, Thomas J (Sailor Tom), 1953, Ap 18,19:3
Sharkey, Will R, 1948, Jl 26,17:3
Sharkey, William L Ex-Gov, 1873, Ap 30,7:5
Sharland, Joseph Bennett, 1909, Mr 23,9:6
Sharlock, Herbert L, 1954, O 19,27:2
Sharlow, Benjamin, 1954, Je 12,15:3
Sharman, Harrison O, 1963, D 18,41:2
Sharman, Harry E, 1955, F 3,23:2
Sharman, Lyon (Mrs H B Sharman), 1957, Ag 13, 27:2
Sharman, William E, 1957, Mr 4,27:4
Sharon, Clark W, 1947, My 1,25:3
Sharon, Fred B, 1949, Jl 11,17:4
Sharon, Frederic C Mrs, 1961, O 3,39:2
Sharon, Samuel Mrs, 1946, Ap 6,17:3
Sharon, W Sen, 1885, N 14,5:1
Sharp, Albert, 1961, Ap 9,86:5
Sharp, Albert E, 1956, Ag 10,17:5
Sharp, Alex A, 1942, D 7,27:3
Sharp, Alex Mrs, 1904, D 28,7:6
Sharp, Alpheus P, 1909, O 11,9:5
Sharp, Alton B, 1961, Jl 11,31:3
Sharp, Amanda, 1909, Ag 8,9:5
Sharp, Archie, 1956, Mr 28,31:3
Sharp, Barton F, 1946, D 8,77:4
Sharp, Baxter C, 1939, Ap 29,17:3
Sharp, Benjamin Dr, 1915, Ja 26,9:6
Sharp, Bessie D, 1960, Ag 30,29:3
Sharp, Boyd, 1947, F 10,29:3
Sharp, Carl G, 1953, Ag 22,15:6
Sharp, Charles C 2d, 1953, Ap 30,31:5
Sharp, Charles E, 1947, Jl 30,21:3
Sharp, Charles H, 1948, N 28,92:4
Sharp, Clayton H, 1942, My 14,19:6
Sharp, David B, 1943, F 9,23:5
Sharp, Earl L, 1952, Mr 16,90:8
Sharp, Edgar A (por), 1948, N 28,96:2
Sharp, Edgar A Mrs, 1958, Ag 20,27:4
Sharp, Edward R, 1961, Jl 25,27:3
Sharp, Ernest P, 1940, Je 2,44:6
Sharp, Evelyn, 1955, Je 22,29:3
Sharp, Francis R, 1948, My 19,28:3
Sharp, Frank, 1943, O 7,23:4
Sharp, Frank C, 1943, My 6,19:2
Sharp, Frank R, 1946, Jl 21,40:2
Sharp, Frederick Capt, 1904, Jl 23,2:2
Sharp, G F, 1882, O 26,5:5
Sharp, George G, 1960, O 22,23:3
Sharp, George W, 1919, Ja 9,11:3; 1951, Ag 4,15:6
Sharp, H Cecil, 1944, Ja 25,19:4
Sharp, H Rodney Mrs, 1946, D 18,29:1
Sharp, Harry, 1946, Mr 1,21:1
Sharp, Harry C, 1940, N 1,25:4
Sharp, Henry (H Schacht), 1964, Ja 11,23:5
Sharp, Henry D, 1948, N 16,29:2
Sharp, Henry S, 1947, Mr 5,25:5; 1961, Ag 9,33:3
Sharp, Hunter, 1923, D 18,19:3
Sharp, Ira P, 1944, S 12,19:3
Sharp, Isaac Ex-Gov, 1903, D 26,7:7
Sharp, Isaac W, 1946, N 11,27:4
Sharp, J Clarence, 1946, Ja 18,19:2
Sharp, J Frank, 1949, Ja 12,27:3
Sharp, Jacob, 1888, Ap 6,5:1
Sharp, James C, 1952, D 6,21:6
Sharp, James H Mrs, 1952, Ja 5,11:1
Sharp, James R, 1943, S 12,52:5
Sharp, Jesse (por), 1941, N 8,19:2
Sharp, John, 1938, Ja 29,15:4
Sharp, John E, 1947, O 13,23:4
Sharp, Joseph H, 1951, Je 26,29:4
Sharp, Joseph W Jr, 1950, O 22,92:3
Sharp, Lewis I, 1945, Ja 19,19:1
Sharp, Lloyd B, 1963, D 6,36:1
Sharp, Louis R, 1951, N 22,32:3
Sharp, Manson, 1951, N 25,86:2
Sharp, Maude, 1946, Je 25,22:3
Sharp, R S, 1932, Mr 9,21:1
Sharp, Rich, 1950, My 3,31:3
Sharp, Robert M, 1939, Ja 22,34:7

Sharp, Samuel A, 1955, Ja 19,27:3
Sharp, Sarah P, 1945, S 11,23:2
Sharp, Sidney W, 1922, F 3,15:3
Sharp, Sydney T, 1953, O 1,29:3
Sharp, Thomas E, 1959, D 1,39:5
Sharp, U S Grant, 1949, D 27,24:2
Sharp, W F, 1947, Mr 31,23:3
Sharp, W Howard, 1958, D 18,2:5
Sharp, Warren R, 1948, Je 18,23:2
Sharp, William (Fiona Macleod), 1905, D 15,2:3
Sharp, William, 1961, Ap 2,76:2
Sharp, William E Mrs, 1938, Mr 10,21:5
Sharp, William G, 1919, Jl 2,13:4
Sharp, William Graves, 1922, N 18,15:5
Sharp, William J, 1948, Ap 26,23:5
Sharp, William L, 1950, D 23,15:5
Sharp, William S Col, 1906, Je 28,7:6
Sharp, William W, 1956, F 16,29:4
Sharp, William W Mrs, 1951, Ag 9,21:2
Sharpe, Albert E, 1955, O 5,35:3
Sharpe, Albert H, 1966, My 19,47:1
Sharpe, Alex, 1942, Ap 29,21:4
Sharpe, Archibald J M, 1956, O 5,25:3
Sharpe, Carl M, 1948, Je 18,23:3
Sharpe, Charles T, 1950, O 29,92:1
Sharpe, Charles T Mrs, 1953, F 14,17:2
Sharpe, Christian, 1874, Mr 14,6:7
Sharpe, D L, 1929, N 30,19:6
Sharpe, Earl, 1960, F 24,37:4
Sharpe, Edward, 1909, Ap 16,9:1
Sharpe, Frank M, 1938, S 16,21:4
Sharpe, Harold T, 1952, D 14,90:4
Sharpe, Harry (por), 1949, Ap 14,25:3
Sharpe, Henry, 1947, Jl 14,21:6
Sharpe, Henry D, 1954, My 18,29:2
Sharpe, Henry G Mrs, 1941, Mr 25,23:3
Sharpe, Hugh H, 1953, Jl 25,11:2
Sharpe, John, 1939, N 14,19:5
Sharpe, John A, 1947, O 27,21:4
Sharpe, John C, 1942, Mr 19,21:3
Sharpe, John C Mrs, 1937, D 14,25:4
Sharpe, Leo N, 1939, Ag 16,23:5
Sharpe, M C Mrs, 1929, My 31,13:1
Sharpe, Mary Mrs, 1937, F 8,3:7
Sharpe, Richard 6th, 1937, S 20,23:1
Sharpe, Samuel, 1881, Ag 11,5:1
Sharpe, Theodore Maj, 1920, Jl 25,20:4
Sharpe, W H, 1942, Ap 20,21:4
Sharpe, William, 1960, Mr 30,37:1
Sharpe, William C, 1924, Ja 21,17:3; 1948, Ag 13,15:5
Sharpe, Wilmer S, 1950, Jl 15,13:6
Sharpey-Schafer, Edward P, 1963, O 27,88:8
Sharpey-Shafer, E, 1935, Mr 30,15:2
Sharples, Bill, 1945, Ja 31,21:4
Sharples, Philip M, 1944, Ap 15,11:5
Sharples, Winston S Jr Mrs, 1960, Jl 8,21:2
Sharpless, Aldred, 1903, D 8,9:4
Sharpless, Edward F, 1937, S 3,17:5
Sharpless, Evan B, 1949, S 16,27:4
Sharpless, Frederick F, 1951, Ap 13,23:5
Sharpless, Frederick F Mrs, 1939, My 16,23:4
Sharpless, G Walter, 1953, Mr 4,27:4
Sharpless, Isaac Dr, 1920, Ja 17,11:4
Sharpless, S Franklin, 1939, N 6,23:5
Sharpless, Townsend, 1940, O 16,23:4
Sharpless, William, 1938, Je 4,15:2
Sharpless, William H, 1939, O 13,23:2
Sharpless, William T, 1947, O 21,23:3
Sharpley, Percy A, 1937, Je 27,II,6:7
Sharpley, Samuel J, 1954, Je 9,31:6
Sharpley, Thomas Howard, 1908, Jl 13,7:5
Sharpsteen, William C, 1949, S 22,31:3
Sharrard, Hallock C, 1941, D 29,15:3
Sharrett, Clinton J Mrs, 1955, N 17,35:4
Sharrett, Horatio J, 1946, N 12,29:2
Sharretts, Edward P Sr, 1953, Ag 6,21:4
Sharretts, Lucy P Mrs, 1942, D 13,72:2
Sharretts, Mary E P Mrs, 1937, Ja 8,19:2
Sharrocks, Alfred M Mrs, 1950, My 14,106:3
Sharron, Albert, 1943, Mr 10,19:4
Sharswood, G, 1883, My 29,5:4
Sharton, Alexander R (por), 1943, F 1,15:5
Sharts, Thaddeus R Mrs, 1950, Ag 12,13:3
Sharwell, Samuel G, 1943, Ja 10,49:1
Sharwood, Robert W, 1954, Ap 21,29:3
Shary, William, 1952, Jl 27,57:2
Shashkov, Gregor I, 1955, N 16,35:2
Shashoua, Stanley, 1964, D 11,39:4
Shaskan, E Felix, 1943, Ag 25,19:6
Shaskan, George, 1950, S 19,31:2
Shastid, Thomas H, 1947, F 16,57:6
Shastri, Harihar N, 1953, D 13,86:8
Shastri, Lal Bahadur Prime Min (funl, Ja 12,1:4), 1966, Ja 11,1:1
Shatelen, Mikhail A, 1957, F 3,77:1
Shaterian, William S, 1964, Mr 16,31:1
Shatford, Almar H, 1955, Ap 30,17:6
Shatraw, Athol Mrs, 1956, S 20,24:6
Shatsky, Boris, 1941, Ja 23,21:3
Shatsky, Nikolai, 1960, Ag 3,29:5
Shattenstein, Nikol, 1954, S 7,26:3
Shatto, Carl W, 1959, Je 22,25:4
Shatto, Clare R Mrs, 1942, Mr 11,19:5

Shatton, Wladyslaw J, 1946, D 7,21:3
Shattuck, Albert R (por), 1925, N 5,23:3
Shattuck, Albert R, 1925, N 7,15:4
Shattuck, Arthur, 1951, O 17,32:2
Shattuck, Charles, 1955, F 6,88:1
Shattuck, Clifford P, 1944, Je 9,15:5
Shattuck, Corrina, 1910, My 24,9:5
Shattuck, Edward, 1947, Ag 15,17:2
Shattuck, Edward S, 1965, D 15,47:1
Shattuck, Edward S Mrs, 1961, Jl 20,27:2
Shattuck, Edwin P, 1964, O 24,29:5
Shattuck, Edwin P Mrs, 1961, S 1,17:2
Shattuck, F C, 1929, Ja 12,17:4
Shattuck, Florence, 1966, N 22,45:2
Shattuck, Frank G, 1937, Mr 15,23:1
Shattuck, Frank G (will), 1938, O 8,9:2
Shattuck, Frank G Mrs, 1947, F 23,53:4
Shattuck, Frank M, 1959, S 3,27:4
Shattuck, George B Dr, 1923, Mr 14,19:4
Shattuck, Grace Mrs, 1944, N 8,9:5
Shattuck, Harriette R Mrs, 1937, Mr 23,23:3
Shattuck, Jane M (por), 1948, S 26,76:3
Shattuck, John G, 1964, F 15,23:3
Shattuck, John G Mrs, 1941, Je 3,21:1
Shattuck, Katherine M, 1950, Ap 18,31:2
Shattuck, L Hubbard, 1945, Mr 30,15:5
Shattuck, Lillian, 1940, Je 26,23:6
Shattuck, Mayo A, 1952, N 5,27:2
Shattuck, Myron, 1953, F 10,27:3
Shattuck, Ray H, 1946, Ja 3,19:4
Shattuck, Raymond A, 1961, O 21,21:4
Shattuck, Ross Mrs (M Ettinger), 1967, Ja 14,31:
Shattuck, Thomas L, 1967, N 30,47:3
Shattuck, Truly, 1954, D 10,27:1
Shattuck, Walter F, 1948, D 15,33:3; 1954, Ja 9,15:
Shattuck, Wilfred C, 1961, N 9,35:1
Shatuck, Clarence D, 1948, Ja 26,19:4
Shatzer, Charles G, 1959, S 13,84:6
Shatzkes, Moses, 1958, D 30,32:3
Shatzky, Jacob, 1956, Je 14,33:3
Shaub, Howard C, 1955, Jl 22,23:1
Shaud, Edward G, 1955, D 19,27:4
Shauger, Florence A Mrs, 1942, Jl 14,19:3
Shaughnessay, John S, 1919, Ag 11,11:4
Shaughnessey, Margaret Mrs, 1938, Je 9,23:3
Shaughnessey, Michael W, 1947, O 27,21:3
Shaughnessy, Charles S, 1946, Jl 16,23:5
Shaughnessy, Edward H Col, 1922, F 3,15:4
Shaughnessy, Frank Mrs, 1958, O 26,88:8
Shaughnessy, Gerald, 1950, My 19,28:4
Shaughnessy, John D, 1953, Jl 20,17:5
Shaughnessy, John F, 1944, D 12,23:5
Shaughnessy, John J, 1962, Mr 30,33:2; 1965, Ag 33:2
Shaughnessy, John P, 1945, Je 1,15:2
Shaughnessy, Lady, 1937, My 9,II,11:1
Shaughnessy, Laurie, 1953, Ap 24,24:4
Shaughnessy, Letitia J Mrs, 1941, My 11,45:1
Shaughnessy, Lord (por), 1938, O 5,23:3
Shaughnessy, M J, 1916, Jl 9,19:5
Shaughnessy, Michael, 1943, F 7,48:7
Shaughnessy, Michael Q, 1957, N 25,31:4
Shaughnessy, Stanley H, 1955, Jl 22,23:4
Shaughnessy, Thomas George Lord (por),(funl, De 12,21:3), 1923, D 11,21:3
Shaughnessy, Thomas H, 1947, N 1,15:2
Shaughnessy, Thomas J, 1965, Mr 9,35:2
Shaughnessy, Valentine J, 1949, S 10,17:1
Shaughnessy, William K, 1964, D 22,29:3
Shaugnessy, Edward J, 1968, N 5,47:1
Shaul, Elmer B, 1958, Jl 14,21:6
Shaul, Frederick G, 1955, S 15,33:3
Shaul, Frederick G Mrs, 1959, Je 28,69:2
Shaul, Harry F, 1947, Ap 21,27:5
Shaunessy, Winifred (N Rambova),(will, Ag 6,15: 1966, Je 8,47:1
Shaurman, N, 1880, Jl 13,5:5
Shavelenko, Isidor, 1952, N 20,31:3
Shavelsky, George, 1951, O 9,29:3
Shaver, Bill, 1951, Ag 2,21:2
Shaver, Clem L, 1954, S 3,17:1
Shaver, Clem L Mrs, 1944, My 12,19:4
Shaver, Dorothy (funl, Jl 1,31:2), 1959, Je 29,1:
Shaver, Harry L, 1940, Ag 8,19:6
Shaver, James D, 1951, Mr 16,31:2
Shaver, James R, 1949, D 25,26:6
Shaver, Manila G, 1947, F 23,53:3
Shaver, Price A Mrs, 1946, Jl 18,25:1
Shaver, Raleigh, 1937, Mr 18,25:1
Shaver, Roy B, 1951, F 8,33:2
Shaver, Roy William, 1961, My 10,45:5
Shavick, Emanuel, 1959, Ja 8,29:2
Shavitch, Vladimir, 1947, D 27,13:1
Shavitz, Frank, 1954, Ag 14,15:3
Shavitz, Irving, 1964, Ag 4,29:1
Shavuo, Isaiah Mrs, 1955, Ja 26,25:1
Shaw, Adam E, 1950, Ap 12,28:3
Shaw, Adele M, 1941, D 5,23:2
Shaw, Albert, 1947, Je 26,23:1; 1950, O 31,27:5
Shaw, Albert D, 1952, N 18,31:3
Shaw, Albert E, 1963, Ag 22,27:3
Shaw, Albert H, 1942, F 3,19:2
Shaw, Albert J, 1958, Je 27,25:3

Shaw, Albert W, 1940, Ja 30,20:3
Shaw, Alex Maj, 1902, D 14,8:3
Shaw, Allena B Mrs, 1941, Ap 9,25:2
Shaw, Amy, 1949, O 14,27:1
Shaw, Anna H Dr (funl, Je 6,20:4), 1919, Jl 3,13:1
Shaw, Anna M, 1940, Mr 20,15:5
Shaw, Arch, 1940, Ag 1,21:3
Shaw, Arch W, 1962, Mr 11,86:1
Shaw, Archer H, 1962, Ag 3,23:2
Shaw, Arthur, 1946, Mr 24,46:2
Shaw, Arthur E, 1945, D 30,14:6
Shaw, Arthur H, 1941, Je 19,21:4
Shaw, Arvin B Jr, 1953, Ja 30,21:2
Shaw, Arvin 3d Mrs, 1967, D 27,37:2
Shaw, Avery A (por), 1949, Mr 19,15:3
Shaw, B W, 1881, Mr 30,5:3
Shaw, Benjamin I, 1947, O 19,66:4
Shaw, Benjamin W, 1942, O 31,15:6
Shaw, Burton C, 1945, My 24,19:2
Shaw, Carroll H, 1960, Mr 15,39:1
Shaw, Charles B, 1962, Ja 30,29:5
Shaw, Charles D, 1875, My 15,4:7; 1907, S 13,7:4
Shaw, Charles D Rev Dr, 1909, N 13,11:5
Shaw, Charles F, 1954, D 2,31:5; 1958, Mr 15,17:5
Shaw, Charles Gray, 1949, Jl 29,21:6
Shaw, Charles H, 1941, S 10,23:2; 1958, Jl 1,31:4
Shaw, Charles H Dr, 1910, Ag 10,11:5
Shaw, Charles J, 1968, O 25,47:2
Shaw, Charles K, 1941, Ap 12,15:2
Shaw, Charles L Mrs, 1963, My 24,31:4
Shaw, Charles O, 1942, D 4,25:3
Shaw, Charles R, 1941, Ap 12,15:1
Shaw, Christopher C, 1959, D 7,31:2
Shaw, Clement B, 1938, Ja 15,15:3
Shaw, Clifford, 1963, Ap 5,48:1
Shaw, Clifford E, 1949, Ap 26,25:5
Shaw, Clinton A, 1953, S 15,31:4
Shaw, Clinton E, 1947, Ag 14,23:2
Shaw, Clyde M, 1939, Ag 6,37:2
Shaw, Cyrus C, 1948, S 2,23:4
Shaw, Daniel, 1937, Jl 17,15:4; 1952, S 24,33:5
Shaw, David, 1954, Ja 9,15:1
Shaw, David B, 1939, O 16,19:5
Shaw, David Capt, 1925, N 14,15:4
Shaw, David F, 1956, O 12,29:2
Shaw, Donald A, 1962, Ag 18,19:4
Shaw, E Lester, 1959, Je 17,35:3
Shaw, E Paul Mrs, 1960, O 2,84:6
Shaw, E R Prof, 1903, F 12,9:6
Shaw, Ed E, 1940, F 17,13:2
Shaw, Edgar W, 1939, D 10,68:1
Shaw, Edmund Sr, 1939, D 14,27:4; 1952, D 2,36:5
Shaw, Edward A, 1924, O 8,19:4
Shaw, Edward L, 1943, F 7,48:8
Shaw, Edward W, 1948, N 23,29:2
Shaw, Edwin A, 1951, Ja 10,27:1
Shaw, Ellsworth V, 1954, O 14,29:1
Shaw, Elmer, 1937, N 20,17:2
Shaw, Elton S, 1954, Ja 25,19:1
Shaw, Elwyn R, 1950, Jl 19,32:2
Shaw, Emma S, 1938, F 6,II,8:1
Shaw, Eugene, 1953, N 18,31:3
Shaw, Eva E Mrs, 1951, Ag 9,21:2
Shaw, F Dickinson, 1961, O 8,87:1
Shaw, F G, 1882, N 9,5:3
Shaw, F G Mrs, 1902, D 31,9:6
Shaw, F T, 1907, Ja 11,9:3
Shaw, Ferdon, 1953, My 11,27:1
Shaw, Frances W Mrs, 1937, O 13,23:1
Shaw, Francis, 1958, Ap 7,21:1
Shaw, Frank A, 1948, F 21,13:4
Shaw, Frank D, 1952, Ap 13,77:2
Shaw, Frank H, 1959, S 2,29:3
Shaw, Frank L, 1958, Ja 25,19:5
Shaw, Frank S, 1959, D 24,19:5
Shaw, Frank W Dr, 1904, Ja 10,7:5
Shaw, Franklin W, 1943, D 9,27:2
Shaw, Frederick, 1953, Je 30,23:3
Shaw, Frederick B, 1957, Mr 3,84:4
Shaw, Frederick W, 1945, My 30,19:1; 1949, S 28,27:3
Shaw, G Arnold, 1937, F 10,23:4
Shaw, G Howland, 1965, Ag 17,33:2
Shaw, G W Hudson, 1944, D 3,57:3
Shaw, G W V, 1951, Ja 24,27:1
Shaw, George B, 1947, Je 14,15:2; 1962, Jl 10,33:4
Shaw, George B Mrs (por), 1943, S 14,23:5
Shaw, George E, 1938, Je 16,23:5; 1956, Jl 6,21:1
Shaw, George F, 1954, Ap 27,29:3
Shaw, George H, 1956, Ap 25,35:1
Shaw, George H Mrs, 1963, D 20,29:1
Shaw, George H Mrs (will), 1964, Ja 9,28:8
Shaw, George K Maj, 1915, S 1,9:4
Shaw, George P, 1966, Jl 16,25:4
Shaw, George V, 1944, My 25,21:5
Shaw, George W, 1943, Mr 4,19:3; 1947, Ja 27,23:4
Shaw, Godfrey B, 1916, Mr 24,11:7
Shaw, Guthrie, 1967, My 24,47:4
Shaw, Guthrie Mrs, 1968, Ja 15,47:4
Shaw, H Cooper, 1956, N 30,23:2
Shaw, H Van D, 1926, My 8,17:4
Shaw, H W (Josh Billings), 1885, O 15,1:6
Shaw, H Walter, 1924, D 9,25:3
Shaw, Harlan P, 1940, Ja 18,23:6
Shaw, Harold A, 1913, Ag 13,9:3
Shaw, Harry, 1938, O 17,15:6; 1959, N 9,31:2
Shaw, Henry, 1943, Jl 20,19:3
Shaw, Henry A, 1958, O 20,29:3
Shaw, Henry C, 1918, My 31,13:2
Shaw, Henry G Col, 1907, Mr 13,9:6
Shaw, Henry L K, 1941, Mr 27,23:2
Shaw, Henry P, 1937, S 20,23:1
Shaw, Herbert B Mrs, 1943, Mr 11,21:5
Shaw, Herbert I, 1961, O 25,37:2
Shaw, Herbert P, 1942, Ja 3,32:3
Shaw, Herman, 1950, My 6,15:4
Shaw, Holger M, 1955, S 13,31:3
Shaw, Howard B, 1943, D 16,27:5
Shaw, Howard D, 1952, Je 17,27:2
Shaw, Howard E, 1924, S 27,16:4
Shaw, Humphrey S, 1960, Jl 23,19:6
Shaw, Isaac H, 1943, N 5,19:5
Shaw, J A, 1927, Mr 20,II,9:1
Shaw, J Byam, 1919, Ja 27,13:5
Shaw, J M, 1928, D 16,30:6
Shaw, J W, 1934, N 3,15:6
Shaw, James, 1943, F 23,21:3; 1945, Jl 27,15:4
Shaw, James D, 1947, Ag 19,23:5
Shaw, James F, 1922, N 14,19:5; 1948, Ja 13,25:1
Shaw, James F Mrs, 1958, D 29,15:6
Shaw, James G Mrs, 1943, S 7,23:4
Shaw, James J, 1954, Ap 6,30:3
Shaw, James K, 1924, My 28,23:4
Shaw, James M, 1960, My 11,39:3
Shaw, James O, 1951, Ap 30,21:3
Shaw, James R, 1952, Ap 1,29:2
Shaw, James T, 1939, Ag 1,19:5
Shaw, James W, 1864, D 25,4:6
Shaw, Jane F, 1939, S 6,23:4
Shaw, Janet, 1925, Ag 22,11:5
Shaw, Jed F, 1952, Jl 27,56:3
Shaw, Jerome B, 1949, N 30,1:8
Shaw, Jerome T, 1954, My 27,27:2
Shaw, John, 1881, N 21,1:6; 1940, N 16,17:4
Shaw, John A, 1965, D 8,43:5
Shaw, John B, 1959, Jl 30,27:2
Shaw, John C, 1912, Jl 6,7:6; 1955, Jl 20,27:5
Shaw, John G, 1950, D 23,16:2
Shaw, John H, 1937, Jl 30,19:5; 1955, D 8,37:4
Shaw, John J, 1941, Je 25,21:3; 1948, My 25,27:4
Shaw, John K, 1943, My 15,15:6
Shaw, John Oakes, 1909, Mr 17,9:3
Shaw, John P Mrs, 1948, My 13,25:1
Shaw, John S, 1952, Ap 27,90:4
Shaw, Joseph A Mrs, 1957, S 2,13:4
Shaw, Joseph B Sr, 1961, Mr 13,9:2
Shaw, Joseph J, 1953, Ja 28,27:3
Shaw, Joseph N, 1903, Je 25,7:6
Shaw, Joseph T, 1952, Ag 3,61:2
Shaw, Joseph V, 1951, Mr 26,23:2
Shaw, Joshua A, 1907, My 13,9:6
Shaw, Justin H, 1944, Ap 11,19:4
Shaw, Kate S, 1949, O 22,17:3
Shaw, L D Capt, 1884, F 1,5:6
Shaw, L M, 1932, Mr 28,15:1
Shaw, Leo J (Sept 18), 1965, O 11,61:5
Shaw, Leon, 1940, Ag 12,15:5
Shaw, Louis, 1937, D 13,27:2
Shaw, Louis A, 1940, Ag 28,19:4
Shaw, Louis Dr, 1903, Jl 26,16:3
Shaw, Louis V, 1947, Je 20,19:3
Shaw, M, 1929, My 19,27:2
Shaw, Mabel S Mrs, 1955, Mr 8,27:5
Shaw, Maria de la C C S B Mrs (Conchita), 1940, Je 16,38:5
Shaw, Mark, 1907, Ag 28,7:6
Shaw, Martin F, 1958, O 26,88:5
Shaw, Mary R, 1940, My 20,17:1
Shaw, Matilda, 1909, Ap 3,9:5
Shaw, Merrill, 1954, Ap 26,25:2
Shaw, Milton G, 1903, D 19,9:4
Shaw, Milton M Mrs, 1944, Ja 29,13:2
Shaw, Munson G, 1951, Je 14,27:4
Shaw, Munson G Jr, 1953, Jl 15,25:4
Shaw, Munson G Mrs, 1954, Ap 29,31:3
Shaw, Murray M, 1968, Ap 4,47:3
Shaw, Nathaniel, 1967, My 9,47:2
Shaw, Norman, 1912, N 19,15:4
Shaw, Olive V Mrs, 1952, N 27,31:5
Shaw, Oliver W, 1913, F 3,11:4
Shaw, Osborn, 1959, D 4,31:2
Shaw, Osborn Mrs, 1939, N 25,17:3
Shaw, Oscar, 1967, Mr 8,45:3
Shaw, Oscar Mrs, 1964, Ap 1,39:2
Shaw, Percy H, 1951, Je 12,29:3
Shaw, Percy L, 1957, Je 25,29:3
Shaw, Percy Mrs, 1941, N 11,23:5
Shaw, Phil L, 1955, Je 14,29:4
Shaw, Phil M, 1941, Ag 16,15:3
Shaw, Phillip E, 1966, Ap 4,31:3
Shaw, Phillips B, 1937, F 2,23:5; 1947, N 11,27:5
Shaw, Plato E, 1947, Ag 6,23:3
Shaw, Plato E Mrs, 1958, Ag 13,27:3
Shaw, Quincy A, 1960, My 9,29:4
Shaw, Quincy Admas Mrs, 1917, F 11,23:4
Shaw, Ralph M, 1949, My 4,30:2
Shaw, Ralph W, 1961, N 25,23:2
Shaw, Ransford W, 1945, Mr 15,23:5
Shaw, Ray, 1957, D 10,35:1
Shaw, Reeves, 1952, Mr 18,27:2
Shaw, Reuben T, 1949, O 26,27:6
Shaw, Richard, 1876, Ja 20,1:7
Shaw, Robert, 1912, Jl 19,9:6; 1941, S 13,17:3; 1955, O 23,86:6
Shaw, Robert A, 1941, Ag 3,34:2
Shaw, Robert A (por), 1948, S 10,23:1
Shaw, Robert Findley, 1968, Je 22,33:5
Shaw, Robert G Col, 1863, Jl 25,2:5
Shaw, Robert Mrs (will), 1944, S 7,17:6
Shaw, Robert Rushton, 1905, My 5,8:6
Shaw, Robert Rushton Mrs, 1905, My 5,8:6
Shaw, Robert S, 1953, F 9,27:5; 1960, O 25,35:3
Shaw, Robert S Mrs, 1947, S 25,29:1
Shaw, Roger, 1959, F 23,23:3
Shaw, Samuel, 1947, Je 22,52:4; 1949, F 24,23:5
Shaw, Samuel C Judge, 1937, Ag 4,19:5
Shaw, Samuel D, 1964, Jl 22,33:1
Shaw, Samuel E, 1945, D 18,27:4
Shaw, Samuel J, 1944, Mr 1,19:2
Shaw, Samuel Jr Mrs, 1948, S 18,17:2
Shaw, Samuel T (por), 1945, F 11,38:4
Shaw, Samuel T Jr, 1945, Ag 14,21:1
Shaw, Samuel T Mrs, 1940, Ap 2,26:2
Shaw, Theodore A, 1941, N 10,17:4
Shaw, Thomas, 1958, Ja 16,30:1
Shaw, Thomas A, 1949, Mr 6,72:2
Shaw, Thomas M, 1949, S 8,29:5; 1965, F 20,25:2
Shaw, Tom, 1938, S 27,21:3
Shaw, Vincent D, 1967, Ja 24,28:7
Shaw, Walden W, 1962, S 29,23:3
Shaw, Walter C Sr, 1962, Ja 11,33:2
Shaw, Walter F, 1950, Mr 25,11:8
Shaw, Walter K, 1954, S 12,85:1
Shaw, Walter L Rev, 1937, O 18,17:4
Shaw, Walter R, 1968, Ag 11,73:1
Shaw, Walter S Sir, 1937, Ap 25,II,9:1
Shaw, Warwick A, 1937, O 19,25:4
Shaw, Wilbur (funl, N 3,29:4), 1954, O 31,1:3
Shaw, Wilbur D, 1940, N 25,17:2
Shaw, Wilfred W Rev Dr, 1937, Ja 1,23:2
Shaw, William, 1940, Mr 4,15:6; 1941, D 5,23:1; 1956, Je 25,23:5; 1957, Ag 24,15:1
Shaw, William B, 1953, Jl 29,23:5
Shaw, William D Col, 1909, Ag 26,9:6
Shaw, William D Mrs, 1964, Je 22,27:1
Shaw, William E, 1947, F 23,54:4
Shaw, William F, 1942, D 19,19:3
Shaw, William J, 1951, Jl 16,21:6
Shaw, William M, 1963, Ag 31,17:2
Shaw, William N, 1945, Mr 26,19:2
Shaw, William S, 1942, F 22,26:5
Shaw, William T, 1948, My 14,23:3
Shaw, William W, 1939, My 1,23:3; 1940, F 10,15:6
Shaw, Winslow A, 1949, N 11,25:1
Shaw-Kennedy, David V, 1945, My 15,19:6
Shaw-Stewart, Hugh, 1942, Je 30,21:2
Shawe, Loyal P, 1941, S 24,23:1
Shawhan, Benjamin P, 1937, O 1,21:4
Shawhan, Romer Mrs, 1956, Ag 6,23:3
Shawkey, Morris P, 1941, F 8,15:4
Shay, Arthur J, 1951, F 21,27:4
Shay, Charles H, 1909, Mr 23,9:5
Shay, Charles Oscar, 1917, D 3,13:5
Shay, Clarence D, 1950, S 6,29:2
Shay, Dennis H, 1950, F 15,27:2
Shay, Eli M, 1949, S 11,96:3
Shay, Ernest A, 1938, Mr 18,19:3
Shay, Ernest E, 1954, Ag 12,25:5
Shay, Frank, 1954, Ja 15,19:1
Shay, Harry, 1963, Jl 31,29:3
Shay, Henry D, 1950, N 7,27:5
Shay, John P, 1940, Jl 10,19:5
Shay, Joseph A, 1951, Ag 2,21:3
Shay, Mary A (will), 1940, Mr 12,23:2
Shay, Matthew H, 1915, Jl 3,7:6
Shay, Samuel M, 1947, Mr 25,25:2
Shay, William F, 1937, Ap 4,11:2
Shayler, Ernest V, 1947, Je 27,21:2
Shaylor, Grace T Mrs, 1940, My 8,23:5
Shayne, Alex, 1957, Jl 27,17:2
Shayne, C C, 1906, F 23,9:3
Shayne, Martin L, 1964, N 4,39:2
Shchelkin, Kirill I, 1968, N 14,47:3
Shcherbakoff, Alexander S, 1945, My 11,19:2
Shcherbakov, Dmitry I, 1966, My 27,46:1
Shcherbinina, Ekaterina E, 1955, F 19,27:1
Shchusev, Alexei V, 1949, My 26,30:2
Shea, A Evelyn, 1967, N 9,61:6
Shea, A J, 1946, N 30,15:1
Shea, Albert E, 1949, Ja 7,21:3; 1968, Mr 11,41:3
Shea, Anna, 1948, Je 28,19:2
Shea, Arthur B, 1942, O 5,19:5
Shea, Benedict A, 1948, My 17,19:3
Shea, Bernard V, 1960, Mr 26,21:6
Shea, Charles A, 1942, Ja 26,15:5; 1946, Je 20,23:3
Shea, Charles L, 1951, Mr 12,25:2
Shea, Christian B, 1961, Ja 6,27:3
Shea, Clara B Mrs, 1939, Je 8,25:3
Shea, Cornelius, 1954, Ap 27,29:4
Shea, Cornelius F, 1938, Jl 17,26:5

Shea, Daniel A, 1965, D 5,89:1
Shea, Daniel E, 1948, Ap 6,23:3
Shea, Daniel J, 1948, F 17,26:2
Shea, Danny Sr, 1959, D 16,41:1
Shea, Dennis A, 1964, D 15,43:2
Shea, Dennis F, 1925, F 6,17:5
Shea, Eddie, 1947, F 13,23:5
Shea, Edward L, 1963, D 12,39:1
Shea, Edward L Mrs, 1947, Ap 24,25:4
Shea, Edward T, 1962, Jl 4,21:4
Shea, Emmett J, 1944, Jl 27,17:4
Shea, Francis E, 1950, My 30,17:3
Shea, Frank A, 1950, Ag 28,17:6
Shea, Frank E, 1941, Ap 27,38:3
Shea, Frank E Mrs, 1946, S 5,27:3
Shea, Frederick C, 1958, O 28,15:6
Shea, George F, 1960, Ap 28,35:3
Shea, Hamilton P, 1943, Ag 6,15:6
Shea, Harold A, 1948, Mr 19,23:4
Shea, Isaac M, 1874, S 1,8:5
Shea, J H, 1928, D 23,19:2
Shea, James, 1941, S 7,50:2
Shea, James A, 1955, My 12,29:4; 1966, Ap 1,35:3
Shea, James F, 1964, O 2,37:4
Shea, James H, 1937, D 22,25:2; 1943, Mr 14,24:7
Shea, James L, 1954, Ja 16,15:6
Shea, James Mrs, 1951, S 24,27:3
Shea, James P, 1950, O 2,23:3
Shea, Jeremiah, 1943, D 14,27:3
Shea, Jerome P, 1943, Je 27,32:4
Shea, Jerry, 1939, My 1,23:4
Shea, John, 1937, Mr 10,23:2; 1957, F 20,33:1
Shea, John A, 1949, F 7,19:2; 1949, Ag 14,68:4
Shea, John B, 1906, Ja 25,9:6
Shea, John F, 1951, O 3,36:2; 1965, O 25,37:2
Shea, John J, 1946, Jl 14,37:1; 1949, My 29,36:4; 1958, Je 28,17:4
Shea, John Joseph, 1903, N 2,7:4
Shea, John L, 1956, Mr 12,27:3
Shea, John Mrs, 1948, Ap 12,21:5; 1959, Mr 31,29:3
Shea, John P, 1952, O 22,27:3
Shea, John S, 1944, Jl 6,15:5
Shea, John T, 1943, N 19,19:3
Shea, John W, 1954, Ag 22,92:2
Shea, Joseph A, 1939, D 14,27:1
Shea, Joseph E, 1942, Je 6,13:1; 1948, F 18,27:4
Shea, Joseph F, 1953, F 6,9:4
Shea, Joseph F Mrs, 1953, Je 21,85:2
Shea, Joseph P, 1942, Mr 5,24:4
Shea, M, 1934, My 17,23:3
Shea, Martin F, 1959, D 29,25:1
Shea, Mary C, 1944, F 20,35:2
Shea, Mary F, 1942, Je 24,19:5
Shea, Maurice A, 1940, O 20,49:1
Shea, Merv, 1953, Ja 29,28:4
Shea, Michael F, 1948, D 23,20:2
Shea, Michael J, 1940, Ag 20,19:5
Shea, Michael P, 1938, My 9,17:2
Shea, Mortimer J, 1956, My 12,19:5
Shea, Nelly I, 1954, Ja 19,26:6
Shea, Norman J Jr, 1963, N 9,25:4
Shea, Pat, 1941, Ap 19,15:1
Shea, Patrick F, 1922, Ag 24,15:5; 1947, O 2,27:4
Shea, Raymond A, 1949, My 5,27:6
Shea, Richard E, 1945, N 7,23:5
Shea, Richard J, 1964, O 9,40:1
Shea, Robert, 1949, O 11,31:2
Shea, Robert E, 1957, Mr 1,23:4
Shea, Robert E Mrs, 1940, Mr 11,15:3
Shea, Sidney M, 1967, Ap 24,33:2
Shea, Steve, 1954, O 30,17:6
Shea, T J, 1933, N 12,34:1
Shea, Thomas E, 1940, Ap 24,23:5
Shea, Thomas F, 1916, F 11,11:6
Shea, Thomas J, 1937, Jl 20,23:6; 1948, D 31,16:4; 1953, Ja 14,31:2
Shea, Timothy, 1948, My 8,15:5
Shea, Timothy F, 1923, Jl 22,24:5
Shea, Vincent P, 1968, Ap 2,47:3
Shea, William, 1946, Je 21,23:1
Shea, William D Rev, 1906, Mr 16,9:5
Shea, William G, 1953, S 19,15:1
Shea, William H, 1945, Jl 18,27:5; 1958, S 19,28:1
Shea, William J, 1940, F 28,21:2; 1965, F 6,25:3
Sheacraft, Edward, 1950, N 1,35:4
Sheaf, Joseph, 1937, Ag 25,21:3
Sheafe, Charles Dr, 1873, Ap 24,5:2
Sheafe, Charles M Jr, 1959, Je 27,23:2
Sheaffer, Charles M, 1943, D 5,64:3
Sheaffer, Lawrence E, 1946, Jl 26,21:3
Sheaffer, Walter A, 1946, Je 20,23:5
Sheaffer, Walter A Mrs, 1961, Ja 7,19:4
Sheahan, David J, 1937, F 15,17:3
Sheahan, Emmet, 1947, My 24,15:7
Sheahan, J F, 1934, N 3,15:3
Sheahan, J W, 1883, Je 18,5:2
Sheahan, John J Mrs, 1952, Ja 23,27:4
Sheahan, Michael J, 1938, N 15,23:3
Sheahan, Richard T, 1941, F 19,21:6
Sheahan, Richard T Mrs, 1955, N 9,33:1
Sheahan, T Ambrose, 1950, Ag 8,29:3
Sheak, R M, 1880, S 29,5:2
Sheakly, James Ex-Gov, 1917, D 12,15:6

Shealer, Cleason Sr, 1945, Ap 24,19:4
Shealey, Terence J Rev, 1925, S 3,25:5
Shealy, James T, 1944, Jl 24,15:6
Shealy, Terence J Rev, 1922, S 6,15:1
Shealy, William B Mrs, 1958, Ap 25,27:1
Shean, Al (por), 1949, Ag 13,11:1
Shean, Al Mrs, 1944, Je 28,23:6
Shean, David W, 1963, My 24,31:1
Shean, Harry A, 1961, Ag 31,27:5
Shean, J Fred, 1943, Jl 20,19:4
Sheane, Francis L, 1947, D 15,28:6
Shear, Cornelius L, 1956, F 3,23:1
Shear, Jack, 1954, S 19,88:3
Shear, John K, 1958, Ja 11,17:3
Shear, Sidney B, 1961, N 29,41:2
Shear, Theodore L (por), 1945, Jl 5,13:4
Sheard, Alfred J, 1942, Ap 4,13:5
Sheard, George A, 1943, Ap 27,23:4
Sheard, Titus, 1904, Ap 14,9:6
Sheard, Walter G, 1943, Je 11,19:5
Shearer, Alfred M (funl plans), 1961, Jl 5,33:4
Shearer, Andrew, 1944, F 9,14:2
Shearer, Andrew A Mrs, 1958, Jl 12,15:5
Shearer, Andrew Mrs, 1958, Jl 3,25:1
Shearer, Augustus H, 1941, Je 1,40:1
Shearer, Chester T, 1937, D 2,25:4
Shearer, Chris, 1939, My 2,23:4
Shearer, Conrad, 1948, O 10,76:2
Shearer, Edward P, 1952, N 5,27:4
Shearer, Edwin, 1948, Je 24,25:6
Shearer, Francis J, 1953, Mr 8,88:3
Shearer, Fred W, 1957, F 28,27:2
Shearer, Frederick E Rev Dr, 1912, Jl 21,II,11:4
Shearer, George L, 1946, Mr 20,23:5
Shearer, George L Mrs, 1952, Ja 3,46:3
Shearer, George Lewis Rev Dr, 1919, Mr 11,11:2
Shearer, Harold H (por), 1938, N 13,45:1
Shearer, Henry, 1947, N 24,23:2
Shearer, Jerry S, 1953, Ag 27,25:4
Shearer, John B, 1963, Je 18,41:5
Shearer, John S Dr, 1922, My 19,17:6
Shearer, Jon P Mrs, 1950, Je 14,31:4
Shearer, Joseph E, 1945, S 29,15:4
Shearer, Leander H Mrs, 1941, O 30,23:5
Shearer, Mary B, 1953, Ja 14,31:5
Shearer, Robert B, 1948, O 17,76:1
Shearer, Thomas L, 1912, Mr 5,11:4; 1946, D 14,15:2
Shearer, William A, 1950, Mr 28,31:2
Shearer, William B, 1958, S 27,22:1
Shearer, William J Mrs, 1955, F 26,15:3
Shearing, Alex, 1960, Jl 16,19:3
Shearler, William, 1954, Ap 2,77:1
Shearman, Frank E Sr, 1942, Ag 8,11:1
Shearman, George, 1876, N 2,4:7
Shearman, Lawrence H (por), 1941, Mr 15,17:1
Shearman, Thomas G, 1900, S 30,1:5
Shearn, Bettie M Mrs, 1938, Mr 10,21:4
Shearn, Clarence J, 1953, F 13,21:1
Shearn, Clarence J Jr, 1961, Mr 30,29:1
Shearn, Clarence J Mrs, 1938, O 31,15:2
Shearn, Mary C Mrs, 1937, S 14,23:2
Shearn, William B, 1938, Ja 14,23:3
Shearon, Clarence G, 1945, N 18,44:2
Shearon, Lowe, 1948, O 2,15:6
Shearon, Lowe Mrs, 1950, Ja 10,29:5
Shearon, Will H Jr, 1963, O 1,39:4
Shears, Edith E, 1948, Ag 18,25:4
Shears, George P Dr, 1915, D 13,13:3
Shears, George P Mrs, 1954, F 7,88:2
Shears, Joseph A Dr, 1925, O 3,15:6
Shears, Lambert A, 1962, Ap 26,33:4
Shearson, Charles Arindell, 1910, Ja 24,9:4
Shearson, Edward, 1950, N 1,35:4
Shearwood, Robert W, 1947, D 26,15:4
Sheary, Joseph E Sr, 1943, D 7,27:4
Sheather, Albert, 1956, Jl 20,17:1
Sheats, C O Col, 1904, My 28,1:6
Sheats, William, 1943, Ag 10,19:4
Sheatz, John, 1922, Je 26,13:6
Shebalin, Vissarion Y, 1963, My 31,25:2
Shebanin, Vassily I, 1955, Jl 14,23:5
Shechner, David, 1958, My 9,23:4
Sheckard, James T, 1947, Ja 16,25:5
Sheckell, Thomas O, 1943, Mr 4,20:2
Sheckles, Jesse H, 1942, O 6,23:4
Sheckman, Herman, 1964, Je 21,84:8
Sheckter, Samuel J (por), 1942, N 5,25:4
Shecora, Michael, 1955, F 24,10:4
Shedaker, Benjamin D, 1940, F 20,21:4
Shedd, Frances H Mrs, 1939, Ja 22,35:1
Shedd, Fred F (por), 1937, Ap 3,19:1
Shedd, George C, 1937, Ja 10,II,10:7
Shedd, Harrison P, 1949, N 3,29:3
Shedd, Harry C, 1942, F 21,20:3
Shedd, Harry M, 1949, Mr 21,23:4
Shedd, J G, 1926, O 23,17:5
Shedd, Jarvis A, 1958, N 1,19:5
Shedd, John A Mrs, 1948, O 17,78:4
Shedd, Llewellyn F, 1955, Ja 29,15:1
Shedd, Mary P Mrs, 1942, Ap 19,44:4
Shedd, Paul C, 1960, Ja 4,29:5
Shedd, William C, 1903, Jl 30,7:6
Shedd, William E, 1953, D 9,11:2

Sheddan, William B (cor, Ja 23,29:1), 1957, Ja 22, 29:1
Shedden, J W, 1884, Ja 25,3:4
Shedden, John S, 1960, Ag 10,31:5
Shedden, Lewis, 1941, O 24,24:2
Shedden, Lucian L Ex-Judge, 1912, Ja 18,13:5
Shedletzky, Nathan, 1949, Jl 21,25:5
Shee, Ouk Lonn, 1953, Ja 10,2:7
Sheean, Thomas, 1943, Jl 28,15:3
Sheebs, Lawrence C, 1951, F 13,31:5
Sheeder, Vincent, 1939, N 18,17:3
Sheedy, Anna (Sister Maureen), 1963, O 19,25:1
Sheedy, Bryan D Mrs, 1957, N 14,33:2
Sheedy, D M Dr, 1914, N 1,17:5
Sheedy, Daniel M Mrs, 1949, Ja 14,23:4
Sheedy, Dennis, 1923, O 17,19:3
Sheedy, James F Mrs, 1944, F 15,17:3
Sheedy, John J, 1942, F 10,19:4; 1954, D 8,35:3
Sheedy, Joseph E, 1955, Ja 25,25:1
Sheedy, Joseph Mrs, 1962, Ag 3,23:3
Sheedy, Michael J, 1965, Ag 15,82:6
Sheedy, Morgan M, 1939, O 26,23:2
Sheedy, Patrick F, 1942, O 27,25:2
Sheedy, Patrick Francis, 1909, D 16,9:5
Sheedy, Thomas J, 1940, O 9,25:4
Sheedy, William, 1949, D 26,29:5
Sheedy, William J, 1938, Mr 17,21:2
Sheeham, James J, 1953, Ja 14,31:2
Sheehan, Albert M, 1943, Je 24,22:2
Sheehan, Andrew E, 1961, Mr 28,35:5
Sheehan, Arthur J, 1953, F 8,88:1
Sheehan, C M, 1936, O 12,27:5
Sheehan, Catherine, 1943, D 17,27:1
Sheehan, Charles V, 1967, O 7,29:3
Sheehan, Clarence J, 1948, Jl 9,19:5
Sheehan, Cornelius, 1956, My 1,33:4
Sheehan, Cornelius J, 1966, Ja 4,27:3
Sheehan, Daniel, 1939, Mr 2,21:3; 1940, Ag 20,19:2
Sheehan, Daniel F, 1942, S 21,15:5
Sheehan, Daniel Mrs, 1940, Ag 20,19:2
Sheehan, Daniel Sr, 1951, Ag 29,25:6
Sheehan, David A, 1925, Ag 26,19:5
Sheehan, Dennis, 1937, Ja 30,17:2
Sheehan, Donal, 1964, Jl 20,25:2
Sheehan, E M, 1949, Je 1,31:3
Sheehan, Edward, 1937, Ja 4,29:1; 1950, Jl 27,25:5
Sheehan, Edward A, 1944, Ag 12,11:5; 1949, Ja 23, 68:8
Sheehan, Edward J, 1944, Jl 4,23:1
Sheehan, Edward S, 1940, Mr 14,23:3
Sheehan, Edward S Dr, 1915, Ap 26,9:6
Sheehan, Elizabeth, 1906, F 25,9:6
Sheehan, Ernest, 1949, Mr 15,27:5
Sheehan, Frank, 1938, D 27,17:5; 1966, Ap 27,47:3
Sheehan, George A, 1953, Je 7,84:2
Sheehan, George P, 1968, Ag 28,44:4
Sheehan, Harold J, 1949, D 10,17:4
Sheehan, Henry H, 1939, My 4,23:5
Sheehan, Henry J, 1941, Mr 27,23:4
Sheehan, Hubert J, 1951, Ja 14,84:5
Sheehan, J Eastman, 1951, Ja 9,29:5
Sheehan, James E, 1948, Je 26,18:2
Sheehan, James J, 1955, D 22,23:3
Sheehan, James J Rev, 1921, My 24,15:4
Sheehan, James T, 1954, Mr 25,29:5
Sheehan, Jane F, 1957, Mr 3,84:8
Sheehan, Jeremiah A, 1944, Ja 30,37:1
Sheehan, Jeremiah P, 1955, Ag 5,19:4
Sheehan, John C, 1916, F 13,15:4; 1939, Mr 26,III,6:8
Sheehan, John H, 1939, Jl 1,17:3
Sheehan, John J, 1949, Mr 1,1:5; 1952, F 16,13:4; 1954, D 29,23:5
Sheehan, John P, 1938, O 6,23:4; 1945, Ag 28,19:3
Sheehan, John R Mrs, 1961, D 18,35:2
Sheehan, John S, 1948, Ja 6,23:5
Sheehan, John T, 1948, S 30,27:4; 1952, N 15,17:1; 1954, O 18,25:5; 1956, Ja 26,29:4
Sheehan, Joseph B, 1958, Ja 6,39:3
Sheehan, Joseph F, 1949, N 19,17:4
Sheehan, Joseph H, 1955, Ap 29,23:5
Sheehan, Joseph J, 1947, Je 26,24:3
Sheehan, Joseph M, 1959, Mr 8,87:1
Sheehan, Joseph M Mrs, 1962, My 14,29:3
Sheehan, Joseph R, 1940, Mr 29,21:3
Sheehan, Lulu V, 1959, My 16,23:5
Sheehan, Marion Turner, 1968, D 12,47:3
Sheehan, Mary E, 1953, Ag 16,76:7; 1954, S 24,23:1
Sheehan, Mary E Mrs, 1909, N 17,9:3
Sheehan, Matthew, 1937, S 2,21:3
Sheehan, Matthew J, 1955, S 1,23:4
Sheehan, Michael, 1912, F 16,9:4; 1945, Mr 2,19:2
Sheehan, Michael F, 1944, F 3,19:5
Sheehan, Michael J, 1920, Je 7,15:4; 1947, F 13,23:3
Sheehan, Michael V, 1941, S 13,17:3
Sheehan, Mike, 1965, Ag 17,14:8
Sheehan, Milton P, 1941, Ag 13,17:2
Sheehan, Patrick Augustine Rev Dr, 1913, O 7,13:6
Sheehan, Perley P, 1943, O 2,13:5
Sheehan, Raymond C, 1941, D 11,27:4
Sheehan, Richard, 1939, My 23,23:1; 1951, Ag 30,2
Sheehan, Robert F, 1947, Ap 17,27:1
Sheehan, Robert J, 1962, Mr 1,31:4
Sheehan, Sarah I Mrs, 1941, Ag 16,15:3

Sheehan, Thomas B, 1937, Ag 30,21:6
Sheehan, Thomas C, 1938, D 16,25:2; 1954, Mr 17,31:3
Sheehan, Tim, 1965, Ag 17,14:8
Sheehan, Timothy J, 1941, N 27,23:6
Sheehan, Walter B, 1964, Je 29,27:3
Sheehan, William, 1940, Jl 6,15:6
Sheehan, William A, 1956, F 12,88:8
Sheehan, William C, 1951, Ap 15,92:1
Sheehan, William E, 1951, Mr 7,33:4
Sheehan, William F, 1945, Ja 11,23:2; 1949, Jl 11,17:4; 1959, Ap 13,31:3; 1960, Mr 9,33:1; 1963, O 9,43:2
Sheehan, William F Mrs, 1946, O 4,23:3
Sheehan, William Francis (funl, Mr 16,11:5), 1917, Mr 15,11:3
Sheehan, William J, 1939, Ap 8,15:1; 1939, N 10,23:1
Sheehan, William Mrs, 1943, Jl 21,15:1
Sheehan, William P, 1948, Ap 28,27:6
Sheehan, Winfield H (will), 1945, S 1,9:8
Sheehan, Winfield R (por), 1945, Jl 26,19:3
Sheehe, Thomas J, 1962, Mr 1,31:4
Sheehy, Daniel F, 1965, D 20,35:3
Sheehy, Edward C Lt, 1917, D 20,11:3
Sheehy, Edward Mrs, 1945, Ap 4,21:5
Sheehy, Edward S, 1942, Jl 28,17:3
Sheehy, Harry B Mrs, 1944, D 12,23:3
Sheehy, Harry C, 1962, Jl 30,23:3
Sheehy, James J, 1962, F 17,19:3
Sheehy, James J Mrs, 1947, O 23,25:5
Sheehy, James S, 1958, D 2,38:1
Sheehy, John, 1941, F 25,23:2
Sheehy, John D, 1966, S 23,37:1
Sheehy, John E (por), 1945, F 3,11:5
Sheehy, John J, 1943, Je 23,21:2; 1952, D 12,29:4; 1959, Jl 24,25:2; 1959, N 3,31:2; 1968, Je 8,31:3
Sheehy, John J Mrs, 1944, S 15,19:1
Sheehy, M J, 1944, Jl 5,17:5
Sheehy, Manus J (rites, D 7,34:4), 1962, D 4,41:4
Sheehy, Martin, 1953, N 23,27:3
Sheehy, Michael J, 1949, Mr 12,18:3
Sheehy, Michael J Sr, 1958, D 7,88:1
Sheehy, Thomas M, 1959, Ap 19,86:1
Sheehy, William H, 1924, S 12,21:5
Sheekley, Gilbert J, 1949, Jl 26,27:4
Sheelen, Augustus, 1947, S 21,60:7
Sheeler, Charles, 1965, My 8,31:1
Sheeley, Raymond N, 1950, My 21,104:3
Sheeline, Paul C Mrs, 1962, O 11,39:4
Sheely, Earl, 1952, S 18,29:2
Sheen, Frederick R, 1947, O 10,25:1
Sheen, James M Mrs, 1961, Jl 22,21:5
Sheen, Marion J, 1955, Mr 23,31:4
Sheen, Milton R, 1947, Ap 5,19:5
Sheen, Newton M, 1944, Ap 26,19:6
Sheen, Newton Mrs, 1943, Mr 30,21:3
Sheenan, Daniel M, 1961, D 11,31:4
Sheepshanks, John Bp, 1912, Je 4,11:5
Sheer, Jacob L, 1955, My 21,17:6
Sheeran, Bernard J, 1955, N 8,31:2
Sheeran, Daniel W, 1952, Je 8,85:1
Sheeran, Francis Michael Rev, 1912, Ja 20,13:6
Sheeran, Gerard F, 1949, My 18,27:2
Sheeran, Gertrude C, 1945, My 30,19:4
Sheeran, Hugh J (por), 1938, F 25,17:1
Sheeran, James J Mrs, 1957, Jl 18,25:5
Sheeran, John A, 1937, Ag 31,23:1
Sheeran, John F, 1956, D 8,19:1
Sheeran, Joseph A (por), 1942, Mr 31,21:3
Sheeran, Thomas B, 1956, Ja 21,21:6
Sheeran, Vincent J, 1956, Mr 7,33:2
Sheerer, Louis B, 1949, F 9,27:2
Sheerin, Charles W (por), 1948, Ap 6,24:2
Sheerin, John J, 1965, Je 2,45:3
Sheerin, Maria (will), 1940, Mr 23,8:1
Sheerin, Simon P, 1905, Je 21,7:3
Sheerr, Maurice J, 1964, Mr 7,23:3
Sheerr, Phil L, 1952, Je 29,56:5
Sheeser, Frank R Mrs, 1949, My 26,29:1
Sheesley, Frederick K, 1941, Ap 9,15:6
Sheesley, John M, 1944, O 29,43:2
Sheets, Arthur B, 1946, Ja 24,21:3
Sheets, Charles J, 1944, Je 13,19:2
Sheets, Elmer A, 1946, Je 8,21:4
Sheets, Elmer A Jr Mrs, 1939, Ja 24,19:5
Sheets, Elmer A Mrs, 1939, Ap 3,15:2
Sheets, Frank T, 1951, N 5,31:6
Sheets, George A, 1954, Je 24,27:5
Sheets, George T, 1911, My 3,13:2
Sheets, Harold F Mrs, 1948, D 15,33:2; 1955, Ja 14, 21:1
Sheets, Henry M, 1956, Jl 26,25:6
Sheets, John M, 1940, D 31,15:5
Sheets, John P L, 1947, Ag 16,13:1
Sheets, Vaughn L, 1950, F 3,23:3
Sheetz, George W, 1949, O 11,34:4
Sheetz, John A, 1941, S 17,23:3
Sheetz, William C, 1945, N 21,21:5
Shefer, Viola, 1957, Je 25,29:5
Sheffeld, Charles A, 1939, Ap 15,19:1
Sheffeld, William M, 1968, O 30,47:4
Sheffer, Burton H, 1951, Ag 19,85:1
Sheffer, Garrett H, 1962, Jl 6,25:1
Sheffer, Henry M, 1964, Mr 18,41:3
Sheffer, Homer F, 1962, Ja 6,19:6
Sheffer, Homer L (cor, S 22,39:1), 1964, S 21,31:5
Sheffer, Richard W, 1940, Mr 10,51:6
Shefferman, Nathan W, 1968, F 5,35:2
Sheffers, Peter W, 1949, Ap 6,29:2
Sheffield, Alfred D Mrs, 1943, O 3,48:3
Sheffield, Archibald, 1903, Ag 1,7:6
Sheffield, Baron (Edw Lyulph Stanley), 1925, Mr 19, 21:3
Sheffield, Berkley D G, 1946, N 27,25:5
Sheffield, Charles J, 1958, Jl 2,27:1
Sheffield, Charles J Mrs, 1942, Mr 17,21:2
Sheffield, Clarence G, 1946, D 21,19:4
Sheffield, Duncan S, 1957, D 3,35:4
Sheffield, Earl, 1876, Ap 6,5:4
Sheffield, Edward H Capt, 1923, Ag 24,11:6
Sheffield, Florence B Mrs, 1940, F 20,21:1
Sheffield, George D, 1958, Ja 26,88:6
Sheffield, George St John, 1924, D 15,17:5
Sheffield, J E, 1882, F 17,5:2
Sheffield, J Langdon, 1947, Je 6,23:1
Sheffield, James Mrs, 1956, Je 16,19:2
Sheffield, James R (will, S 15,23:3), 1938, S 3,13:3
Sheffield, John B, 1965, Ja 1,19:3
Sheffield, Joseph B, 1958, Je 7,19:4
Sheffield, Joseph C, 1942, S 27,48:8
Sheffield, Julie M, 1948, My 19,28:2
Sheffield, M E, 1864, Je 14,2:2
Sheffield, Mable R, 1952, My 31,17:3
Sheffield, Maurice, 1956, Ja 26,29:2
Sheffield, Reginald, 1957, D 9,35:3
Sheffield, Rena Mrs, 1948, Ag 12,21:3
Sheffield, Robert H, 1954, D 22,23:3
Sheffield, Robert Mrs, 1964, S 23,47:4
Sheffield, Thomas C, 1961, Ap 9,86:4
Sheffield, Tom, 1952, D 10,35:3
Sheffield, Wesley F, 1946, F 15,25:2
Sheffield, William (Bro Benignus Joseph), 1953, D 30,23:1
Sheffield, William H, 1949, Jl 27,23:5
Sheffield, William M, 1941, Mr 13,21:2
Sheffield, William P, 1919, O 20,15:6
Sheffield, William Payne, 1907, Je 3,7:6
Sheffield, William T, 1944, Ja 23,8:3
Sheffler, Bill, 1949, Je 29,27:2
Sheffler, Hattie Mrs, 1938, N 11,25:5
Sheffler, Simon, 1949, Ag 4,23:6
Shehadi, Beshara, 1955, Je 22,30:1
Shehadi, Shehadi A, 1943, My 7,19:4
Shehan, Alice A, 1947, My 28,26:3
Shehan, Hoyt R, 1942, Ja 11,46:2
Shehan, Michael R (por), 1938, Ag 20,30:5
Shehan, W Mason, 1940, Ag 26,15:6
Sheibley, Bertram H, 1950, Ag 12,13:4
Sheide, Frederick, 1944, Mr 13,15:3
Sheier, John H, 1943, Mr 15,13:4
Sheifer, Emanuel Mrs, 1951, Ag 3,21:5
Sheifer, Saul, 1954, O 24,89:1
Sheik, Harry S, 1955, S 8,31:3
Sheil, Denis R, 1945, Ja 12,15:2
Sheil, Frank J, 1947, F 6,23:2
Sheil, Frank J Mrs, 1943, F 4,23:3
Sheil, John, 1941, Ja 9,21:4
Sheil, P A, 1927, N 21,1:7
Sheilds, Charles A, 1941, My 17,15:2
Sheils, George K, 1953, N 24,29:2
Sheils, John F M, 1940, Ag 10,13:5
Sheils, John L, 1941, My 25,36:6
Sheils, Thomas, 1916, N 3,13:5
Sheils, William J (por), 1940, Je 19,23:5
Shein, Benjamin, 1957, My 21,35:4
Shein, Philip, 1964, O 7,47:1
Shein, Robert P, 1968, Jl 2,26:1
Sheinauf, Abraham, 1957, Mr 25,25:4
Sheinberg, Arthur, 1967, Jl 21,31:4
Sheinberg, Frank B, 1967, Mr 2,35:4
Sheinberg, Samuel, 1945, F 10,11:6
Sheiner, Sidney, 1961, Je 10,23:4
Sheinfeld, Meyer, 1962, N 15,37:2
Sheinin, Lev, 1967, My 12,47:3
Sheinman, Louis, 1954, Ag 3,19:4
Sheinwald, Julius M, 1953, Ja 14,31:4
Sheip, Henry L, 1942, My 24,42:2
Sheirr, Charles M, 1967, Jl 31,27:3
Sheitlis, Benjamin E, 1954, O 18,25:6
Sheitlis, David, 1952, Ag 12,19:4
Sheketoff, Ekehile, 1947, Ja 24,22:2
Shekleton, A, 1941, Mr 2,42:4
Shelanski, Herman A, 1954, Ap 15,29:3
Shelare, Alphonse A, 1964, Jl 7,35:1
Shelburne, James M, 1951, O 28,84:6
Shelby, David D Judge, 1914, Ag 23,13:5
Shelby, Edmund P, 1943, S 24,23:1
Shelby, Evan, 1965, Ap 29,35:3
Shelby, J Gen, 1897, F 14,20:7
Shelby, Jeanne, 1964, N 3,31:1
Shelby, Joseph P, 1951, Ap 11,29:2
Shelby, Robert E, 1955, D 9,27:1
Shelden, Allan, 1905, My 2,11:6
Shelden, Charles N, 1951, Je 13,29:4
Shelden, Henry D, 1941, D 9,31:5
Sheldon, A James, 1955, N 6,87:1
Sheldon, Addison E, 1943, N 26,23:5
Sheldon, Adelaide, 1942, S 11,21:2
Sheldon, Allan, 1951, Mr 25,74:7
Sheldon, Andrew Flint Dr, 1914, Ja 5,9:6
Sheldon, Artemas B, 1954, Ag 31,21:2
Sheldon, August Mrs, 1950, Je 18,76:4
Sheldon, Bernard P Capt, 1917, N 29,13:5
Sheldon, Butler Mrs, 1959, D 9,42:1
Sheldon, Caroline A, 1961, Jl 17,21:5
Sheldon, Charles I, 1949, My 6,25:4
Sheldon, Charles M (cor, Mr 1,22:2), 1946, F 25,25:1
Sheldon, E H, 1940, Jl 12,15:3
Sheldon, E W, 1934, F 16,19:1
Sheldon, Edward B, 1946, Ap 2,27:1
Sheldon, Edward M, 1949, Ag 6,17:5
Sheldon, Edward Stevens, 1925, O 17,15:5
Sheldon, Eugene E, 1906, Je 29,9:7
Sheldon, Frederick, 1907, N 23,9:5; 1908, Ja 4,9:4; 1908, Ja 30,7:5
Sheldon, G Rev, 1881, Je 18,2:4
Sheldon, George B, 1942, Jl 9,21:3
Sheldon, George L, 1960, Ap 6,41:3
Sheldon, George O, 1944, Ja 19,19:3
Sheldon, George R (funl, Ja 18,11:4), 1919, Ja 15, 11:3
Sheldon, George W, 1949, Mr 7,21:2
Sheldon, George William, 1914, Ja 30,9:5
Sheldon, Georgiana R, 1946, O 2,29:5
Sheldon, H K, 1902, Mr 3,9:5
Sheldon, Harold H, 1964, D 24,19:1
Sheldon, Harold P, 1951, S 1,11:4
Sheldon, Harry, 1925, D 9,27:3
Sheldon, Harry A, 1946, My 27,23:1
Sheldon, Harry D, 1948, N 8,21:6
Sheldon, Harry E (por), 1937, F 11,23:1
Sheldon, Harry W, 1942, S 8,23:2
Sheldon, Harry W Mrs, 1958, Mr 5,31:1
Sheldon, Henry, 1950, Ag 28,17:6
Sheldon, Henry D, 1946, F 7,23:2
Sheldon, Herb, 1964, Jl 22,33:3
Sheldon, James C Mrs, 1964, D 2,50:4
Sheldon, James O, 1907, Ap 25,9:5
Sheldon, James R, 1966, Ap 28,43:3
Sheldon, Jennie M Mrs, 1938, Ja 16,II,9:1
Sheldon, John, 1958, N 7,23:1
Sheldon, John H, 1940, Je 22,15:5
Sheldon, John M, 1967, F 13,33:3
Sheldon, Kenneth J, 1940, My 15,25:2
Sheldon, L Grant, 1943, Je 20,34:6
Sheldon, Lewis, 1880, Mr 12,8:4; 1939, My 15,1:2
Sheldon, Martin A, 1961, F 16,31:2
Sheldon, Martin J, 1917, S 23,23:3
Sheldon, Porter, 1908, Ag 16,7:6
Sheldon, Ralph, 1952, D 25,29:6
Sheldon, Ralph C, 1937, S 17,25:4
Sheldon, Ralph C Mrs, 1951, My 8,31:3
Sheldon, Raymond H, 1966, Ap 6,43:1
Sheldon, Raymond Mrs (M Stewart), 1961, Ja 28, 19:2
Sheldon, Rex P, 1952, Ag 17,76:3
Sheldon, Samuel, 1915, S 11,9:6
Sheldon, Samuel Prof, 1920, S 6,7:5
Sheldon, Sara E A Mrs, 1941, Mr 18,23:4
Sheldon, Sarah, 1947, N 21,27:1
Sheldon, Smith, 1884, S 2,4:6
Sheldon, Suzanne, 1924, Mr 24,15:4
Sheldon, Theodore Sr Mrs, 1949, O 10,23:5
Sheldon, Vilas P, 1941, Ja 2,27:6
Sheldon, Wilfred, 1951, Ap 15,92:2
Sheldon, William H, 1963, D 22,34:3
Sheldrake, Charles K, 1959, N 10,47:1
Sheldrick, Joseph T, 1958, Ap 8,30:6
Sheley, Abram T, 1949, Ap 6,29:5
Sheley, Vernon, 1952, D 19,31:1
Shelford, Melvia T, 1941, S 16,23:6
Shelhorse, James B, 1952, D 2,31:5
Shelko, Morris L, 1961, N 6,37:3
Shell, Emma K Mrs, 1941, N 2,53:1
Shell, Jacob K, 1940, D 12,27:4; 1945, S 13,29:4
Shell, John, 1952, Mr 4,27:3
Shell, John F Mrs, 1963, Je 22,23:4
Shell, Robert, 1953, Jl 5,49:2
Shell, Thomas, 1951, D 1,13:4
Shellabarger, Fred, 1940, F 25,39:1
Shellabarger, Samuel, 1954, Mr 22,27:1
Shellabear, William G, 1947, Ja 17,24:3
Shellaberger, Edward F, 1947, F 15,15:6
Shelland, Harry, 1959, D 4,32:2
Shelland, Harry Mrs, 1955, My 29,44:2
Shellard, Philip H, 1947, Mr 18,27:5
Shellenberger, J Frank, 1946, S 14,7:6
Shellenberger, William H, 1958, My 23,23:2
Shellens, Michael, 1944, Ap 23,41:1
Sheller, Charles W, 1951, Mr 17,15:3
Shelley, Bridget, 1908, D 18,9:7
Shelley, C Raymond, 1937, Ja 23,17:2
Shelley, Charles W, 1941, Ap 28,15:3
Shelley, Clement H, 1946, Mr 17,45:1
Shelley, Frank D, 1919, Ja 28,9:2
Shelley, Frank H, 1947, S 9,31:5
Shelley, Frank H Mrs, 1949, Ap 26,25:2
Shelley, Frederick M, 1942, Jl 28,17:6
Shelley, Frederick W, 1958, Je 24,31:3
Shelley, George L, 1959, Ag 27,27:4
Shelley, George W, 1940, Ja 17,21:4

Shelley, Harry R (por), 1947, S 13,11:1
Shelley, Harry R Mrs, 1950, F 10,23:4
Shelley, Henry T, 1955, Ap 5,29:2
Shelley, Henry V, 1959, My 28,31:5
Shelley, Howard M (B Beekman), 1956, D 12,39:2
Shelley, James E Mrs, 1913, F 11,13:5
Shelley, John, 1939, Ag 16,23:2
Shelley, John A Mrs, 1944, F 10,15:1
Shelley, John F Mrs, 1952, S 29,23:6
Shelley, Patrick J, 1948, Ap 19,23:2
Shelley, Percy B, 1953, S 27,85:6
Shelley, Samuel M Mrs, 1951, Jl 4,17:3
Shelley, Thomas A, 1940, Mr 20,27:5
Shelley, William F, 1968, Je 12,47:1
Shelley, William H (por), 1944, D 28,20:2
Shelling, David H, 1938, My 18,21:1
Shellman, Mary B, 1938, O 6,23:2
Shelly, John F, 1955, Je 12,86:5
Shelly, Joseph V Capt, 1937, Jl 18,II,6:5
Shelly, Kate, 1912, Ja 22,9:4
Shelly, Oswin H, 1937, Mr 27,15:1
Shelly, Patrick J, 1953, Ja 19,23:4
Shelly, Patrick J Mrs, 1946, F 19,25:3
Shelly, Percy V D, 1943, Je 28,21:4
Shelly, Samuel, 1912, Jl 19,9:6
Shelly, Sophia R Mrs, 1937, Je 20,II,6:7
Shelly, W Dayton Mrs, 1950, Ja 9,25:2
Shelly, William A, 1938, My 4,23:2
Shelmire, Horace Mrs, 1946, Je 11,23:3
Shelnitz, Louis E, 1957, O 16,35:1
Shelp, James H, 1949, My 16,21:4
Shelton, Ben, 1945, Ja 7,37:1
Shelton, Carroll, 1963, D 31,19:3
Shelton, Charles E, 1940, My 14,24:2
Shelton, Charles G, 1941, O 2,25:3
Shelton, Clement A, 1938, Mr 18,19:5
Shelton, Don O (por), 1941, Ja 30,21:1
Shelton, Don O Mrs, 1941, My 14,21:3
Shelton, Edward M, 1944, D 12,23:4
Shelton, Edwin C, 1949, D 20,31:5
Shelton, Frances E (will), 1940, Ap 5,26:8
Shelton, Frank M, 1951, D 3,31:5
Shelton, Frederick D, 1943, Mr 24,23:1
Shelton, Frederick De Witt, 1956, Jl 14,15:7
Shelton, George H Col, 1920, N 4,13:3
Shelton, George M, 1949, Ja 19,27:3
Shelton, Henry T, 1950, Ap 11,31:2
Shelton, I E, 1954, N 19,28:7
Shelton, Ida E S Mrs, 1942, Jl 28,17:4
Shelton, Kenneth E, 1962, Ag 17,23:1
Shelton, Richard, 1963, Ja 22,15:5
Shelton, Robert M Jr, 1956, Mr 7,33:4
Shelton, Ted, 1965, Ja 7,31:4
Shelton, W C, 1879, F 25,3:3
Shelton, W Rev, 1883, O 12,4:7
Shelton, William A, 1937, Ja 1,19:5
Shelton, William H, 1912, Mr 16,13:5; 1955, O 6,29:4
Shelvin, Bernard, 1941, N 29,17:6
Shelvin, John J, 1944, S 20,23:4
Shemeley, William G, 1958, S 20,19:4
Shemin, David Mrs, 1962, Ap 22,80:4
Shemin, Louis Mrs, 1959, Ag 1,17:2
Shen Chun-ju, 1963, Je 12,43:2
Shenandoah, Ocias, 1939, N 24,23:5
Shenberg, Irving, 1955, My 12,29:1
Shenesky, Frank J, 1952, O 28,31:4
Shenhar, Itzhak, 1957, Je 20,29:5
Shenk, John, 1959, Ag 4,27:4
Shenk, Joseph, 1923, F 3,13:5
Shenkar, Aryeh, 1959, O 5,31:1
Shenkel, William T Mrs, 1961, Mr 29,33:2
Shenkman, Harry A, 1963, S 5,31:5
Shenlin, Thomas L, 1915, D 30,13:4
Shenton, Clarence G, 1954, Ag 14,15:4
Shenton, Herbert N Dr (por), 1937, Je 8,19:1
Shenton, William A, 1953, Mr 5,27:4
Shepard, Augustus D, 1955, O 2,87:2
Shepard, Augustus D Mrs, 1914, F 5,9:5
Shepard, Augustus Dennis, 1913, S 30,13:5
Shepard, Barbara M Mrs, 1964, Mr 20,24:8
Shepard, Benjamin Mrs, 1966, F 11,33:3
Shepard, Bertram D, 1966, Ap 5,39:4
Shepard, Charles D Dr, 1904, O 9,9:5
Shepard, Charles E, 1942, D 22,26:2
Shepard, Charles F, 1941, My 16,23:1
Shepard, Charles N, 1961, Je 20,33:3
Shepard, Charles O Mrs, 1951, Ag 12,78:4
Shepard, Charles R, 1937, Je 10,23:3
Shepard, Charles S, 1948, N 18,27:2; 1956, Ap 26,33:5
Shepard, Charles T, 1942, Ap 9,20:2
Shepard, Daniel W, 1941, N 11,23:5
Shepard, David, 1963, S 28,19:1
Shepard, Donald D, 1946, Ap 28,42:2
Shepard, E B Mrs, 1876, Ag 10,2:3
Shepard, E F Col, 1893, Mr 25,1:7
Shepard, E M Adm, 1904, Ag 20,7:6
Shepard, E W, 1933, Ja 12,17:5
Shepard, Earl D Rev Dr, 1937, F 9,23:4
Shepard, Edward Dwight, 1912, Ja 14,II,16:1
Shepard, Edward M (funl, Ag 1,9:6; est, Ag 9,9:3), 1911, Jl 30,9:6
Shepard, Edward M Prof (mem), 1911, S 19,13:2
Shepard, Edward M Prof (mem), 1911, O 30,11:3
Shepard, Edward V, 1937, F 10,23:5
Shepard, Eliza L Mrs, 1939, S 30,17:4
Shepard, Elliott F Mrs (funl, Mr 7,15:4), 1924, Mr 4, 19:3
Shepard, Elmer W, 1963, My 4,25:2
Shepard, Eugene M, 1953, My 27,31:3
Shepard, Eugene M Mrs, 1956, Je 12,35:4
Shepard, Finley J (will, Ag 26,19:1), 1942, Ag 22,13:4
Shepard, Finley J Mrs, 1938, D 21,1:2; 1946, S 4,23:1
Shepard, Fitch, 1881, Ag 24,2:4
Shepard, Francis H, 1957, Je 23,84:8
Shepard, Frank H, 1913, F 16,II,7:4
Shepard, Frank P Jr, 1959, O 15,39:3
Shepard, Frank T, 1947, N 6,28:3
Shepard, Frederic W, 1954, Ap 26,25:5
Shepard, Frederick D Dr, 1916, Ja 11,11:5
Shepard, Frederick M, 1913, Jl 1,9:4
Shepard, Frederick S, 1940, O 11,21:4
Shepard, George A, 1903, Ap 29,9:6
Shepard, Gerald F, 1937, My 1,19:4
Shepard, Gertrude B Mrs, 1940, O 8,25:2
Shepard, Guy C, 1938, S 6,21:2
Shepard, Harold E, 1953, Ag 29,17:4
Shepard, Henry L, 1956, Mr 24,19:4
Shepard, Herman A, 1944, S 22,19:2
Shepard, Horace B, 1944, S 7,23:4
Shepard, Irwin Dr, 1916, Ap 18,13:4
Shepard, James E, 1947, O 7,27:4
Shepard, James O, 1952, D 18,29:4
Shepard, Jean E, 1941, S 4,21:5
Shepard, Jesse S, 1947, My 20,25:2
Shepard, John Jr, 1948, D 22,23:3
Shepard, John W, 1911, Jl 16,II,9:3; 1944, Je 11,45:3; 1954, Ag 14,15:6
Shepard, John 3d, 1950, Je 12,27:4
Shepard, Leroy F, 1960, Mr 2,37:4
Shepard, Leslie M Mrs (Margt), 1966, D 13,47:2
Shepard, M van R, 1947, My 17,16:2
Shepard, Marshall L, 1967, F 22,29:3
Shepard, Mary, 1944, S 29,21:5
Shepard, Michael Mrs, 1951, Jl 24,25:5
Shepard, Myron Mrs, 1951, Jl 13,21:4
Shepard, O M, 1909, Je 2,7:4
Shepard, Odell, 1967, Jl 20,37:1
Shepard, Oscar C, 1951, Ja 28,76:4
Shepard, Otis N, 1949, O 17,23:5
Shepard, Percy W Mrs, 1955, O 13,31:5
Shepard, Peter L Mrs, 1916, S 24,19:3
Shepard, R F, 1927, Ap 11,21:3
Shepard, Raymond A Jr, 1968, F 12,39:4
Shepard, Raymond E, 1958, Ap 19,21:1
Shepard, Richard Mrs, 1940, S 24,23:2
Shepard, S E Rev, 1877, O 13,5:4
Shepard, Samuel B, 1960, My 25,39:1
Shepard, Seth, 1921, Jl 9,9:6
Shepard, Simeon F, 1945, O 25,21:2
Shepard, Theodore A, 1954, D 6,27:5
Shepard, Thomas G, 1905, Ap 26,11:5
Shepard, Tona Mrs, 1940, Ja 24,21:2
Shepard, W E, 1905, Ap 5,6:4
Shepard, Walter A, 1959, O 26,29:2
Shepard, Whiting N, 1965, Ja 17,88:4
Shepard, William C Mrs, 1953, Mr 23,23:2
Shepard, William K, 1958, Ja 24,23:4
Shepard, William P, 1948, N 16,29:3
Shepard, Woolsey A, 1960, Ag 31,29:4
Shepardson, Benjamin E, 1954, My 15,15:3
Shepardson, Frank L, 1952, Ag 20,25:4
Shepardson, Frank L Mrs, 1952, Jl 13,60:3
Shepardson, Frank O, 1939, N 21,26:3
Shepardson, Ira L, 1903, D 4,9:5
Shepardson, Whitney H, 1966, Je 1,47:1
Shepardson, Whitney H Mrs, 1964, Mr 18,41:5
Sheperd, Cornelius Dr, 1903, O 8,9:5
Sheperd, Frederick J, 1948, Je 10,25:3
Sheperd, John W, 1937, Ap 6,23:4
Sheperd, William Edgar, 1925, Ja 29,19:3
Shephard, C J, 1876, My 12,2:3
Shephard, Charles F Mrs, 1954, D 23,19:3
Shephard, E Olcott Gen, 1903, Ap 29,9:5
Shephard, Firth, 1949, Ja 5,25:3
Shephard, L Mrs (Lulu Van Pelt), 1877, F 7,8:2
Shephard, Sidney, 1953, N 27,27:2
Shephard, Thomas Mrs (will), 1945, My 12,15:4
Shepheard, Frederick H, 1946, N 3,64:3
Shepheard, J K, 1883, Ag 30,8:4
Shepherd, A R, 1902, S 13,9:5
Shepherd, A Warner Dr, 1907, S 10,7:5
Shepherd, Alexander R, 1943, F 26,19:4
Shepherd, Arthur, 1958, Ja 14,30:5
Shepherd, B Morgan, 1949, S 7,29:4
Shepherd, Bert, 1955, Mr 23,31:4
Shepherd, Bruce E, 1966, S 26,41:4
Shepherd, Calvin N, 1964, Jl 14,33:1
Shepherd, Charles, 1924, Ag 19,15:5
Shepherd, Charles E, 1946, N 17,68:2
Shepherd, Charles Upham Dr, 1915, Jl 7,11:5
Shepherd, Clara S, 1956, Jl 3,25:1
Shepherd, Clinton O, 1950, O 14,19:3
Shepherd, Edward P, 1951, Ap 28,15:4
Shepherd, Elizabeth, 1947, Jl 11,15:4
Shepherd, Ernest S, 1949, O 2,80:7
Shepherd, Francis K, 1966, S 22,47:2
Shepherd, Frank W, 1945, O 19,23:4
Shepherd, Fred S, 1954, My 4,29:5
Shepherd, Frederick M, 1919, S 18,13:5
Shepherd, George, 1911, My 10,11:4
Shepherd, George B, 1939, Ap 25,23:2
Shepherd, George F, 1948, Ag 10,21:5
Shepherd, George Lord, 1954, D 5,88:4
Shepherd, George R, 1947, F 25,25:3
Shepherd, George R Mrs, 1943, Je 11,19:4
Shepherd, George W, 1959, Ja 19,27:4
Shepherd, Harry T, 1948, F 20,27:4
Shepherd, Henry A Mrs, 1948, Ja 5,20:2
Shepherd, Henry R, 1954, O 20,29:2
Shepherd, Henry Sr, 1952, S 23,33:5
Shepherd, Howard O, 1962, O 13,25:3
Shepherd, Isabella, 1948, N 21,88:2
Shepherd, J Linwood, 1945, D 27,19:3
Shepherd, Jack, 1955, Mr 15,29:2
Shepherd, James A, 1946, My 12,44:1
Shepherd, James F, 1943, Ag 16,15:4
Shepherd, John J, 1945, My 6,37:1
Shepherd, John P, 1948, Mr 21,60:2
Shepherd, John W, 1955, Jl 1,21:3
Shepherd, Julian C, 1953, O 19,21:6
Shepherd, Leland H, 1956, N 23,27:3
Shepherd, Louis Mrs, 1949, Ap 26,25:2
Shepherd, Margaret M Mrs, 1939, Ap 15,19:4
Shepherd, Mary E, 1950, N 19,92:5
Shepherd, Meyer J, 1954, D 21,13:4
Shepherd, Nathan G, 1869, My 24,2:5
Shepherd, Oliver W, 1937, O 5,25:4
Shepherd, Orrin W, 1942, Jl 16,19:3
Shepherd, R Bowden, 1941, S 6,15:2
Shepherd, R T, 1955, Mr 2,27:4
Shepherd, Ray C, 1961, Mr 16,37:1
Shepherd, W G, 1933, N 5,33:1
Shepherd, W R, 1934, Je 7,23:1
Shepherd, Walter R, 1961, F 17,28:1
Shepherd, William G, 1945, Ja 22,17:3
Shepherd, William H, 1945, Je 13,23:5
Shepherd, William Mrs, 1950, Jl 19,31:3
Shepherd-Darron, Dorothy Mrs, 1953, F 21,3:3
Shepherdson, Francis W Dr, 1937, Ag 10,19:2
Sheplar, Adele E, 1944, F 12,13:2
Shepler, Harry, 1943, Mr 3,23:5
Shepler, Joseph R, 1951, N 8,29:4
Shepley, G F Judge, 1878, Jl 22,5:3
Shepley, George Foster, 1903, Jl 19,7:6
Shepley, George L Col, 1924, Ag 4,13:4
Shepley, Henry R, 1962, N 26,29:1
Shepley, Ruth, 1951, O 17,31:2
Shepp, Daniel B, 1940, O 30,23:1
Sheppard, Albert, 1959, Ap 6,27:4
Sheppard, Alfred T, 1947, My 11,62:3
Sheppard, Bernard J, 1963, O 4,35:1
Sheppard, C C, 1949, N 6,94:4
Sheppard, C T Rev, 1903, O 10,9:6
Sheppard, Charles E, 1939, F 19,39:1; 1952, My 13, 23:1; 1965, F 19,35:1
Sheppard, Daniel J Sr, 1939, F 2,19:1
Sheppard, Edgar F, 1952, F 21,27:4
Sheppard, Edgar K, 1956, Mr 8,29:1
Sheppard, Edgar Rev, 1921, Ag 31,13:5
Sheppard, Erle Jr, 1954, Je 26,17:7
Sheppard, Ernest J, 1943, N 18,23:3
Sheppard, Frank, 1951, S 24,27:4
Sheppard, George, 1912, F 23,11:4; 1966, D 18,84:8
Sheppard, George Q, 1945, Ja 16,19:5
Sheppard, George R, 1911, Jl 21,9:6
Sheppard, George S, 1945, S 28,21:5
Sheppard, George W, 1946, S 28,17:4
Sheppard, H D, 1879, F 26,4:1
Sheppard, H R L Rev Dr, 1923, F 13,21:4
Sheppard, Harper D, 1951, O 11,37:3
Sheppard, Harry S, 1954, D 15,31:4
Sheppard, Henry, 1917, F 4,19:3
Sheppard, Herbert N, 1945, My 26,15:3
Sheppard, Hugh R L Canon, 1937, N 1,22:1
Sheppard, Irene, 1960, F 4,31:3
Sheppard, J C, 1931, O 18,30:3
Sheppard, J Stanley, 1955, Ag 20,17:3
Sheppard, J Warren, 1943, Ja 6,27:2
Sheppard, James J, 1914, Mr 14,11:4
Sheppard, John A Msgr, 1925, Ja 20,21:5; 1925, Ja 2 19:4
Sheppard, John Evans Dr, 1915, S 14,11:5
Sheppard, John H, 1957, S 16,31:6
Sheppard, John S, 1948, My 15,15:4
Sheppard, John S Mrs, 1953, Ap 17,25:1
Sheppard, John T Capt, 1907, N 2,9:2
Sheppard, Joseph A, 1949, Je 29,28:2
Sheppard, Joseph Mrs, 1944, N 8,17:6
Sheppard, Josiah F, 1873, Ag 23,2:3
Sheppard, Laurence B, 1968, F 27,43:3
Sheppard, Lawrence B Jr, 1949, Je 16,31:5
Sheppard, Melvin, 1942, Ja 4,48:5
Sheppard, Morris, 1941, Ap 10,23:1
Sheppard, Peter C, 1960, O 15,23:5
Sheppard, Richard A (funl, Ja 21,12:6; will, Ja 29,-30:4), 1955, Ja 19,11:1
Sheppard, Robert A, 1943, D 1,21:1
Sheppard, S Clayton, 1960, My 12,35:4
Sheppard, Samuel E (por), 1948, S 30,27:1

Sheppard, Stanford M, 1952, O 9,31:1
Sheppard, Stanley R, 1961, D 27,25:6
Sheppard, Thomas T, 1948, Jl 6,23:4
Sheppard, Walter L, 1943, O 17,48:6
Sheppard, Walter L Mrs, 1958, Ja 4,15:4
Sheppard, Warren (por), 1937, F 23,27:3
Sheppard, William H, 1942, Mr 9,19:4
Sheppard, William H G, 1953, Jl 24,13:4
Sheppard, William Mrs, 1947, Ap 9,25:4
Shepperd, George M, 1942, S 2,23:1
Shepperd, Gwynn R, 1941, Je 22,32:4
Shepperd, Walter, 1949, S 15,27:2
Shepperson, Archibald B, 1962, Jl 25,33:5
Sheps, Eliash A (E A Almi), 1963, S 25,43:1
Sheps, Irving, 1953, O 7,29:4
Sheps, William G, 1943, F 15,15:4
Sheptin, Max, 1960, F 19,54:1
Shequen, Louise B, 1925, Je 10,23:5
Sher, Adolph, 1960, Mr 23,37:3
Sher, Benjamin R, 1953, Je 12,27:4
Sher, David, 1945, S 17,19:3
Sher, Edward, 1937, My 25,27:3
Sher, Elizabeth M, 1962, O 24,39:3
Sher, J J, 1965, Mr 7,83:1
Sher, Julius Mrs, 1956, Jl 8,65:2
Shera, James C, 1951, F 7,29:3
Sherard, Robert H, 1943, F 2,19:4
Sherbo, Duilio, 1950, Ap 27,29:2
Sherburn, George W, 1962, N 29,38:3
Sherburne, Harry, 1954, O 26,27:2
Sherburne, John, 1949, My 25,30:2
Sherburne, John C Mrs, 1962, D 5,47:2
Sherburne, John H, 1959, Jl 26,68:4
Sherburne, Nelson E, 1952, Ja 24,27:1
Sherby, Daniel, 1954, Ag 16,17:2
Sherdel, William H (Wee Willie), 1968, N 16,37:3
Shere, O M Dr, 1922, O 21,13:5
Shere Ali, Ameer, 1879, Mr 2,7:3
Sherek, Henry, 1967, S 25,45:1
Sheremetrov, Boris I, 1952, Mr 26,29:4
Sherer, Arthur L, 1938, O 1,17:5
Sherer, Dunham B, 1965, Ja 20,39:4
Sherer, Ernest, 1952, S 26,21:1
Sherer, Harvey C, 1938, O 30,41:2
Sherer, Henry C Mrs, 1957, N 12,34:2
Sherer, John A Mrs, 1948, Ag 29,56:4
Sherer, Joseph P, 1950, S 30,17:5
Sherer, Louise H Mrs, 1951, My 25,27:3
Sherer, Prescott, 1920, Ag 13,9:5
Sherer, William, 1921, N 21,15:5
Shereshewsky, David S, 1951, Mr 20,29:1
Sheresky, Harry S, 1953, O 21,29:4
Sherfesee, Emily B Mrs, 1939, D 30,15:2
Sherfesee, Louis Jr, 1953, S 1,24:4
Sheridan, Algernon Thomas Brinsley Mrs, 1918, Ja 15,13:3
Sheridan, Amy, 1878, N 14,5:2
Sheridan, Ann (Mrs S McKay),(funl, Ja 23,43:4), 1967, Ja 22,77:1
Sheridan, Ann Mrs, 1942, My 31,22:8
Sheridan, Annie G Mrs, 1937, F 24,24:2
Sheridan, Arthur, 1911, Je 11,II,11:5
Sheridan, Arthur V, 1952, Je 20,48:1
Sheridan, Bernard M, 1951, N 13,29:4
Sheridan, Bernard O Rev, 1903, Je 22,7:6
Sheridan, Billy, 1960, My 4,45:4
Sheridan, C Mac, 1924, Ap 17,19:4
Sheridan, Charles J, 1958, Jl 30,29:4
Sheridan, Charles P (por), 1938, Je 28,19:4
Sheridan, Christopher T, 1962, N 14,39:2
Sheridan, Cornelius A, 1942, Jl 15,19:5
Sheridan, Edward J, 1907, D 8,11:5; 1940, N 1,25:3
Sheridan, Edwin A, 1945, S 21,21:2
Sheridan, Eugene J, 1949, Jl 6,27:4
Sheridan, Farrell T, 1950, O 16,27:3
Sheridan, Francis A Sr, 1952, Jl 18,19:3
Sheridan, Francis J, 1948, S 29,29:1
Sheridan, Frank, 1943, N 28,68:7; 1962, Ap 17,35:5
Sheridan, Frank J, 1942, O 27,25:2
Sheridan, Frank J Jr, 1937, My 1,19:3
Sheridan, Gail, 1950, Jl 16,69:2
Sheridan, George A, 1952, Ap 3,35:2
Sheridan, George J Mrs, 1944, Ag 1,15:4
Sheridan, George T, 1940, Jl 7,25:3
Sheridan, George V, 1963, Ag 27,31:4
Sheridan, George W, 1947, My 15,25:3
Sheridan, Henry B Mrs, 1943, My 29,13:1
Sheridan, Homer, 1939, Ap 21,23:4
Sheridan, Honor A, 1952, D 16,31:5
Sheridan, Howard J, 1944, Mr 23,19:3
Sheridan, Irene, 1964, D 8,45:1
Sheridan, Irene R Mrs, 1938, F 25,17:5
Sheridan, J Harold, 1962, Je 16,19:4
Sheridan, J Morton, 1952, My 6,29:2
Sheridan, James A, 1939, Ja 2,24:2; 1947, My 7,31:2
Sheridan, James B, 1965, O 15,45:4
Sheridan, James C Sr Mrs, 1945, My 9,23:2
Sheridan, James E, 1938, My 2,17:5
Sheridan, James J Sr, 1941, Ap 24,21:5
Sheridan, James M, 1950, My 2,29:4
Sheridan, Jerome F, 1967, Ag 22,34:8
Sheridan, John, 1875, My 8,3:7; 1914, S 23,9:4
Sheridan, John A, 1944, N 27,23:6
Sheridan, John B, 1942, Mr 31,21:3
Sheridan, John E, 1948, Jl 5,16:2
Sheridan, John F, 1949, Ja 14,24:2
Sheridan, John F X, 1961, Ja 3,27:7
Sheridan, John H, 1945, Mr 18,42:5
Sheridan, John J, 1950, Ja 5,25:4; 1953, Jl 22,27:5; 1954, Ja 25,19:2
Sheridan, John S, 1953, S 6,50:2
Sheridan, John V, 1947, O 15,27:5
Sheridan, John W, 1944, F 6,42:1
Sheridan, Joseph F, 1947, Mr 9,60:7
Sheridan, Joseph P, 1948, N 16,29:2
Sheridan, Joseph W, 1959, Mr 4,31:4
Sheridan, Lawrence A, 1954, O 18,25:1
Sheridan, Leo Mrs, 1952, D 23,23:3
Sheridan, Lula W Mrs, 1946, Ja 29,25:3
Sheridan, Marie (Mrs S Cibelli), 1954, Ap 26,25:5
Sheridan, Martin J Sr, 1939, My 19,21:4
Sheridan, Mary, 1959, My 24,89:2
Sheridan, Mary Clotilde Mother, 1955, Ap 12,29:2
Sheridan, Mary Sister, 1942, F 4,19:1
Sheridan, Matthias A Rev, 1937, Ap 12,17:4
Sheridan, Max, 1959, Jl 26,68:1
Sheridan, Michael V Brig-Gen, 1918, F 22,11:5
Sheridan, Nicholas Mrs, 1948, S 28,27:3
Sheridan, P H Gen, 1888, Ag 6,1:6
Sheridan, P J, 1918, Ja 3,9:2
Sheridan, Patrick E, 1942, Ap 5,42:1
Sheridan, Paul M, 1965, Ap 1,35:3
Sheridan, Peter Mrs, 1940, F 9,19:6
Sheridan, Phil L Mrs, 1952, Ag 12,19:6
Sheridan, Philip Henry Maj, 1918, F 19,13:5
Sheridan, Philip J, 1960, Ja 19,35:1
Sheridan, Raymond C, 1962, S 26,39:1
Sheridan, Raymond F, 1939, Mr 15,23:1
Sheridan, Richard B, 1937, Ja 20,15:2; 1939, Ja 23, 13:2; 1951, My 27,68:2
Sheridan, Richard J, 1962, S 27,37:1
Sheridan, Richard J Sr, 1961, Jl 28,21:5
Sheridan, Stephen F Jr Mrs, 1963, My 30,17:4
Sheridan, Thomas F, 1951, Mr 13,31:4
Sheridan, Thomas I (Jan 31), 1963, Ap 1,36:6
Sheridan, Thomas I Mrs, 1955, My 20,25:5
Sheridan, Thomas P, 1938, My 17,23:5
Sheridan, Thomas P Mrs, 1955, O 6,29:1
Sheridan, Thomas W, 1964, Je 28,57:1
Sheridan, Viola L, 1948, N 24,23:2
Sheridan, W P, 1934, D 18,21:1
Sheridan, William H, 1942, Je 23,20:2; 1947, D 23,23:5
Sheridan, William J, 1954, Ag 22,92:2
Sheridan, William J Mrs, 1941, Je 8,49:1
Sheriff, Meyer, 1939, S 4,19:4
Sheriff, Meyer Mrs, 1939, S 4,19:4
Sheriff, Paul, 1960, S 29,35:5
Sherill, Edwin S, 1945, D 31,17:2
Sherin, Arthur H, 1967, Je 20,39:3
Sherin, Clarence E, 1911, S 26,9:5
Sherin, G H, 1928, My 4,9:3
Sherin, Henry, 1937, Mr 5,21:4
Sheringham, George, 1937, N 12,21:5
Sherinyan, Elizabeth, 1947, Ja 26,53:6
Sherley, Brannin C Mrs, 1939, Ja 9,15:3
Sherley, Swager (por), 1941, F 14,17:1
Sherlock, David E, 1938, F 18,19:4
Sherlock, Frank M, 1946, Jl 15,25:6
Sherlock, James J, 1924, Ap 3,21:6
Sherlock, Louise T Mrs, 1937, Mr 27,15:3
Sherlock, William P, 1950, O 23,23:1
Sherman, A M, 1880, Ag 10,5:5
Sherman, Adah, 1942, My 13,19:5
Sherman, Alfred L, 1938, F 28,15:3
Sherman, Allton L, 1940, Ja 10,23:1
Sherman, Alonzo D Mrs, 1944, F 15,17:5
Sherman, Alpheus, 1866, Ja 15,8:4
Sherman, Alson Smith, 1903, S 23,7:5
Sherman, Alvin, 1924, D 20,15:4
Sherman, Anna W Mrs, 1941, My 10,15:3
Sherman, Arthur L, 1941, Ag 25,15:3
Sherman, Arthur M, 1953, Mr 21,17:2
Sherman, Arthur Mrs, 1951, Jl 27,19:5
Sherman, Arthur O, 1949, S 24,13:2
Sherman, Augustus F, 1925, F 21,11:5
Sherman, B B, 1885, My 3,2:2
Sherman, Brant C, 1940, F 25,39:1
Sherman, C A, 1883, Ja 15,5:3
Sherman, C Bezalel Mrs, 1960, Je 3,31:3
Sherman, C L, 1879, Ap 20,2:5
Sherman, C T, 1879, Ja 2,5:1
Sherman, Carl (funl, Jl 20,17:5), 1956, Jl 18,27:2
Sherman, Charles A, 1950, F 25,17:2
Sherman, Charles Augustus, 1917, Ap 25,11:6
Sherman, Charles Celestine, 1864, D 25,4:6
Sherman, Charles D, 1950, Ap 30,102:5
Sherman, Charles E Mrs, 1925, Ap 30,21:5
Sherman, Charles L, 1954, D 23,19:3; 1965, O 18,35:2
Sherman, Charles M Mrs, 1955, F 9,27:2
Sherman, Charles P, 1944, Ja 22,13:4
Sherman, Charles R, 1953, O 18,86:6
Sherman, Charles S, 1951, My 23,35:2
Sherman, Chester E, 1940, D 11,27:5
Sherman, Clarence R, 1939, D 14,27:6
Sherman, Clifton L, 1946, F 7,23:4
Sherman, Clifton W, 1955, N 26,19:2
Sherman, Clinton T, 1947, N 3,23:3
Sherman, Davis T, 1945, Ag 9,21:4
Sherman, De Witt H, 1940, F 3,13:2
Sherman, Donald P, 1967, Ja 16,41:5
Sherman, Eber C, 1949, Ap 23,13:4
Sherman, Edward A, 1940, Mr 29,21:4; 1954, My 15, 15:1; 1966, O 11,47:1
Sherman, Edward J, 1950, F 3,23:2
Sherman, Elbert S, 1959, S 13,85:1
Sherman, Eliezer L, 1946, Mr 8,21:2
Sherman, Elizabeth, 1925, Ap 8,21:4
Sherman, Elizabeth M, 1941, My 20,23:4
Sherman, Ellen B, 1956, Ja 16,21:4
Sherman, Emma, 1948, F 14,13:5
Sherman, Emma L Mrs, 1942, Ap 17,17:5
Sherman, Forrest P, 1951, Jl 23,1:8
Sherman, Frances, 1955, Mr 26,15:2
Sherman, Francis T Gen, 1905, N 10,9:4
Sherman, Frank Asbury Prof, 1915, F 27,11:5
Sherman, Frank Dempster Prof, 1916, S 20,9:5
Sherman, Frank J, 1945, F 25,38:1
Sherman, Frank M, 1960, My 12,35:4
Sherman, Frank P, 1949, Ap 14,25:4
Sherman, Franklin A Dr, 1903, Ap 23,9:6
Sherman, Franklin C, 1942, Je 9,24:3
Sherman, Fred, 1947, Ap 9,25:2
Sherman, Frederic F, 1940, O 25,21:2
Sherman, Frederick, 1966, Ap 16,33:1
Sherman, Frederick C, 1957, Jl 28,60:2
Sherman, Frederick D, 1942, Mr 8,42:1
Sherman, Frederick T Jr, 1951, F 4,76:5
Sherman, Gardiner, 1907, Ja 12,11:4
Sherman, George D, 1957, My 1,37:5
Sherman, Grace A Mrs, 1948, Ap 21,27:1
Sherman, H L, 1933, Jl 12,17:1
Sherman, Harold C, 1949, F 1,25:3
Sherman, Harold M Jr, 1966, Ap 16,33:3
Sherman, Harold T, 1954, Ag 13,15:5
Sherman, Harry, 1952, Mr 5,29:5; 1952, S 27,17:2; 1961, O 8,87:1
Sherman, Harry B, 1956, Mr 30,19:4
Sherman, Harry T, 1941, Mr 7,21:3
Sherman, Helen I Mrs, 1946, O 29,15:7
Sherman, Henry, 1964, N 29,86:5
Sherman, Henry C, 1955, O 8,19:5
Sherman, Henry D, 1955, D 6,37:4
Sherman, Henry J, 1952, Jl 31,23:1
Sherman, Henry J Mrs, 1946, My 14,21:3
Sherman, Henry L Mrs, 1962, N 11,88:8
Sherman, Herbert A, 1919, Ja 15,11:2
Sherman, Hiram M, 1940, Ja 21,34:8
Sherman, Howard, 1912, Je 8,11:4
Sherman, Hoyt, 1904, Ja 26,9:7; 1962, O 17,39:2
Sherman, Irvin I, 1966, Jl 8,35:3
Sherman, Irving P, 1949, My 7,13:4
Sherman, Isaac, 1881, Ja 23,7:2
Sherman, Isaac J, 1955, Jl 6,27:4
Sherman, Isaac Mrs, 1903, O 13,9:5
Sherman, J Clifford, 1950, S 19,32:2
Sherman, J Ellen, 1968, Ap 24,47:3
Sherman, J W, 1865, Ag 23,4:6
Sherman, Jack, 1960, N 2,39:3
Sherman, Jacob, 1954, Mr 23,27:3
Sherman, Jacob D, 1944, Ja 27,19:4
Sherman, Jacob Mrs, 1954, Ag 13,15:6
Sherman, Jacob P, 1958, My 13,29:3
Sherman, Jacob T, 1950, Ja 8,77:1
Sherman, James H, 1941, D 23,21:6
Sherman, James W Jr Mrs, 1950, My 3,29:3
Sherman, John, 1879, Ja 5,1:2; 1900, O 23,5:1
Sherman, John B, 1944, Mr 25,15:4
Sherman, John C, 1942, Ap 13,15:5
Sherman, John D, 1960, Ap 18,29:3
Sherman, John D Jr Mrs, 1953, Ja 3,15:2
Sherman, John E, 1938, Jl 1,19:1
Sherman, John F, 1952, S 9,31:2
Sherman, John Mrs, 1949, N 27,105:1
Sherman, John T 2d Mrs, 1942, N 3,23:2
Sherman, John Thomas, 1921, Mr 16,9:4
Sherman, John W, 1939, Jl 29,15:4
Sherman, John W Mrs (B Fowler), 1942, O 29,23:3
Sherman, Joseph, 1954, D 20,29:3
Sherman, Joseph H, 1955, N 24,29:2
Sherman, Joseph R, 1950, F 26,78:2
Sherman, Julius, 1945, O 12,23:2
Sherman, Karl M, 1940, Ap 13,17:2
Sherman, L, 1934, D 29,15:1
Sherman, L E Gen, 1912, F 18,II,13:4
Sherman, Larry, 1964, O 3,9:1
Sherman, Lawrence, 1958, Jl 15,25:1
Sherman, Lawrence F, 1946, My 14,21:4
Sherman, Lawrence Y, 1939, S 16,17:3
Sherman, Leslie W Mrs, 1942, F 24,21:4
Sherman, Louis R, 1953, Ag 1,11:5
Sherman, Lu Ligermore, 1943, S 4,13:3
Sherman, Lucius B, 1945, Ja 25,19:4
Sherman, Lydia, 1878, My 17,1:6
Sherman, M H, 1932, S 10,9:4
Sherman, M Mortimer, 1951, Je 23,15:6
Sherman, Marilla B Mrs, 1946, F 19,25:5
Sherman, Marvin, 1950, Jl 21,19:4
Sherman, Maurice Mrs, 1950, Mr 15,29:2
Sherman, Maurice S, 1947, Je 28,13:2

Sherman, Max, 1964, S 8,29:3
Sherman, Max Mrs, 1949, Je 1,31:3
Sherman, Melhado, 1959, S 2,29:4
Sherman, Mildred P, 1961, N 18,23:6
Sherman, Minnie Mrs, 1923, N 26,17:4
Sherman, Moe, 1949, S 21,31:1
Sherman, Myron Mrs, 1948, F 3,25:1
Sherman, Nathan, 1944, Ag 16,19:3
Sherman, Otis W, 1944, F 11,19:4
Sherman, Phil D, 1957, Ja 11,23:1
Sherman, Philemon T, 1941, D 7,79:4
Sherman, Port W, 1944, F 12,13:1
Sherman, Ralph, 1941, N 22,19:3
Sherman, Ray W Mrs, 1959, Ag 8,17:4
Sherman, Richard, 1926, My 24,19:4; 1962, Ja 10,29:7
Sherman, Richard U, 1950, D 18,31:3
Sherman, Robert J, 1939, Ag 9,17:6
Sherman, Robert L, 1952, S 19,23:3
Sherman, Robert T, 1961, Mr 18,23:3
Sherman, Roger, 1954, S 6,15:5
Sherman, Roger F, 1944, S 17,42:2
Sherman, Roger M, 1905, O 27,9:4
Sherman, Ruth T, 1965, Ap 7,43:2
Sherman, S P, 1926, Ag 22,1:2
Sherman, Samuel, 1948, F 2,21:3; 1964, Je 17,43:2
Sherman, Samuel R, 1946, O 9,27:4
Sherman, Sidney Gen, 1873, Ag 3,1:6
Sherman, Solomon Mrs, 1966, F 10,34:1
Sherman, T W Gen, 1879, Mr 18,5:6
Sherman, T W Mrs, 1879, Mr 13,15:4
Sherman, Thomas A, 1950, O 27,30:5; 1961, D 6,47:1
Sherman, Thomas C, 1941, D 23,22:3
Sherman, Thomas M, 1944, Mr 1,19:4
Sherman, Thomas M Mrs, 1953, Ap 7,29:5
Sherman, W C H, 1882, Jl 21,5:1
Sherman, W T Gen, 1891, F 15,1:6
Sherman, W T Mrs, 1888, N 29,5:4
Sherman, W W Mrs, 1884, Mr 4,8:3
Sherman, Waldo L, 1956, Ap 13,25:2
Sherman, Walter J, 1937, Ap 16,23:2
Sherman, Warren A, 1949, D 23,21:3
Sherman, Watts, 1865, Mr 12,6:2
Sherman, Watts Mrs, 1947, Je 29,48:4
Sherman, William, 1941, Mr 25,23:2
Sherman, William A, 1943, Ag 6,15:2
Sherman, William D, 1952, D 2,36:4
Sherman, William H, 1950, D 25,19:3; 1961, Ap 16, 87:1
Sherman, William O, 1954, Je 22,27:5
Sherman, William S, 1944, My 24,19:4
Sherman, William T, 1938, S 21,25:4; 1945, O 5,23:3
Sherman, William Watts (funl, Ja 27,11:5), 1912, Ja 23,11:4
Sherman, William Winslow, 1908, Jl 20,9:5
Shern, Daniel H, 1947, Je 26,24:2
Sherndal, Alfred E, 1958, Je 13,23:3
Sherndal, Alfred E Mrs, 1959, F 15,86:6
Shernoff, Mark Mrs, 1951, D 7,27:1
Shero, Lucius Rogers Dr, 1968, Je 2,89:2
Shero, William F, 1943, My 13,21:5
Sherover, Max, 1959, Je 17,35:4
Sherover, Max Mrs, 1958, N 21,29:3
Sherow, Alonzo B, 1961, S 30,25:6
Sherow, Edith K Mrs, 1941, F 25,23:2
Sherow, Norman W, 1938, S 17,17:5
Sherower, Robert, 1961, Ja 29,84:7
Sherpick, Eugene A, 1944, S 1,13:5; 1964, F 17,31:4
Sherr, David, 1939, Ja 3,17:4
Sherr, Ivens Mrs, 1953, Ag 30,88:2
Sherrard, Earl C, 1944, O 7,13:2
Sherrard, Glenwood J, 1958, Ag 13,27:5
Sherrard, Henry Gray Prof, 1909, N 14,13:4
Sherrard, J Alfred, 1937, D 23,22:3
Sherre, Martin A, 1966, Ja 5,31:4
Sherrer, Frank L, 1944, O 20,19:2
Sherrerd, William D, 1951, F 11,88:2
Sherrerd, William D Mrs, 1958, O 29,35:3
Sherres, Isaac H, 1945, Ap 10,19:3
Sherri, Andre, 1924, O 22,21:4
Sherrier, Henry H, 1961, Ja 29,84:7
Sherriff, George R, 1966, My 4,47:3
Sherriff, Virginia L Mrs, 1941, Ja 15,23:5
Sherrill, Allen G, 1938, Jl 6,23:5
Sherrill, Arthur M, 1963, Jl 6,15:2
Sherrill, C H, 1936, Je 26,19:1
Sherrill, Charles H Mrs, 1948, My 11,25:4
Sherrill, Gibbs W, 1957, Jl 28,60:4
Sherrill, Howard W Mrs, 1962, My 14,29:4
Sherrill, James W, 1955, Ja 6,27:5
Sherrill, Lewis J, 1957, Ja 30,29:4
Sherrill, Richard E, 1952, N 27,31:3
Sherrill, Stephen H, 1956, Je 30,17:3
Sherrill, William H, 1944, My 29,15:4
Sherrill, William M, 1947, Jl 6,41:1
Sherring, Conrad V Mrs, 1949, S 22,31:2
Sherrington, Charles, 1952, Mr 6,31:3
Sherris, Bernard H, 1960, Ap 2,23:4
Sherritt, Frank, 1940, Ja 15,15:3
Sherritt, William N, 1942, S 1,20:2
Sherrod, Robert L Mrs, 1958, D 22,2:4
Sherry, David Mrs, 1956, F 19,92:2
Sherry, Edward P, 1941, Ag 7,17:5
Sherry, Edward P Mrs, 1947, Ap 19,16:2
Sherry, Ernest Mrs, 1967, F 6,29:4
Sherry, Henry Mrs, 1944, D 25,19:5
Sherry, J Barney, 1944, F 23,19:4
Sherry, James A, 1955, Jl 20,27:5
Sherry, Joseph, 1968, Je 1,27:4
Sherry, L, 1926, Je 10,25:1
Sherry, Louis F, 1905, My 7,7:3
Sherry, Marie B Mrs, 1941, Jl 2,21:2
Sherry, Nathan, 1954, My 31,13:6
Sherry, Peter Mrs, 1939, My 5,23:3
Sherry, Phil, 1950, My 17,29:2
Sherry, Ralph E, 1951, O 4,33:1
Sherry, Ralph E Mrs, 1951, F 24,13:4
Sherry, Robert E, 1957, Ap 30,19:6
Sherry, William J Mrs, 1961, My 5,29:4
Sherry, William L, 1951, Je 16,15:5
Shershin, Frank W, 1959, O 8,39:4
Shershin, Michael W, 1947, Mr 2,60:6
Sherstyok, Gavril, 1954, Ja 7,31:1
Shertel, Anton (funl), 1913, Mr 17,11:4
Shertzer, Tyrell B, 1951, D 6,34:3
Sherwell, G Butler, 1963, My 1,39:3
Sherwell, Louis N, 1937, Ja 28,25:5
Sherwell Dr, 1926, Jl 8,25:5
Sherwen, James E, 1952, My 29,27:3
Sherwin, Abraham L, 1959, Mr 25,35:2
Sherwin, Belle, 1955, Jl 10,73:2
Sherwin, Charles F Dr, 1953, F 14,17:5
Sherwin, Donald G, 1942, F 13,21:4
Sherwin, Harold B, 1939, My 13,15:6
Sherwin, Howard H, 1951, Mr 18,88:7
Sherwin, J Sr, 1934, Ja 17,19:3
Sherwin, Mark, 1962, My 15,39:2
Sherwin, Robert W, 1959, Je 17,35:2
Sherwin, Thomas Gen, 1914, D 20,15:5
Sherwood, A, 1933, N 2,21:5
Sherwood, A M, 1928, Je 3,II,7:1
Sherwood, Absalom F, 1943, Je 9,21:5
Sherwood, Albert, 1868, F 18,5:5
Sherwood, Alfred A, 1945, My 20,32:1
Sherwood, Alida M Mrs, 1942, Ag 29,15:2
Sherwood, Arthur M, 1951, Je 30,15:7
Sherwood, Arthur M Mrs, 1948, Ja 20,24:3
Sherwood, Benjamin E, 1968, D 4,47:2
Sherwood, Byron P, 1950, N 3,27:3
Sherwood, Carroll P, 1955, D 24,13:2
Sherwood, Catherine Wadsworth Mrs, 1911, O 6,13:3
Sherwood, Charles, 1908, Ja 19,11:4
Sherwood, Charles A, 1947, Ap 6,60:6
Sherwood, David B, 1954, Jl 1,25:1
Sherwood, Edgar F, 1920, Mr 16,9:5
Sherwood, Edward C, 1953, S 16,33:2
Sherwood, Edward L, 1955, D 5,31:2
Sherwood, Elizabeth F Mrs, 1938, D 12,19:2
Sherwood, Elizabeth J, 1963, Jl 28,65:1
Sherwood, Ellsworth H Mrs, 1959, F 11,39:2
Sherwood, Eugene Mrs, 1946, D 16,23:2
Sherwood, Floyd Mrs, 1949, Jl 24,53:2
Sherwood, Frank B, 1964, F 5,35:3
Sherwood, Frank D Mrs, 1961, S 11,27:1
Sherwood, Frank S, 1954, My 18,29:2
Sherwood, Franklin D Ex-Sen, 1907, S 15,9:6
Sherwood, George, 1903, My 26,9:6
Sherwood, George F J, 1939, D 17,49:3
Sherwood, George G, 1951, S 16,84:5
Sherwood, George H, 1949, Ag 4,23:5
Sherwood, George H Dr (por), 1937, Mr 19,23:3
Sherwood, Gertrude A, 1948, S 23,29:5
Sherwood, Gilbert, 1947, Jl 29,21:2
Sherwood, Glenn O, 1948, Ag 15,61:2
Sherwood, H N, 1883, F 2,3:3
Sherwood, H W, 1939, N 2,23:2
Sherwood, Harold B, 1946, O 29,25:5
Sherwood, Harold H, 1964, S 25,41:4
Sherwood, Harry E, 1905, My 2,1:4
Sherwood, Harry R, 1966, Ag 24,51:6
Sherwood, Harry S Mrs, 1946, S 7,15:3
Sherwood, Henry, 1875, Jl 24,4:6
Sherwood, Howard C (will, F 9,10:3), 1957, Ja 20, 92:5
Sherwood, Howard M, 1943, F 21,32:8
Sherwood, Howard W, 1951, Mr 20,29:2
Sherwood, Isaac R, 1925, O 16,21:3
Sherwood, Isaac R Mrs, 1914, F 16,7:5
Sherwood, J P, 1883, Ag 5,7:1
Sherwood, James C H, 1940, Ap 14,45:1
Sherwood, James C Mrs, 1953, My 18,21:3
Sherwood, James D, 1961, Mr 6,25:4
Sherwood, John B Mrs, 1938, Ag 8,13:4
Sherwood, John Dickinson, 1919, N 25,11:4
Sherwood, John Dickinson Mrs, 1919, N 25,11:4
Sherwood, John F, 1959, Mr 20,32:1
Sherwood, John J, 1946, Jl 4,19:4
Sherwood, Jonathan, 1944, Ja 22,13:2
Sherwood, Lorenzo, 1869, My 13,4:7
Sherwood, Louis, 1942, F 13,22:3
Sherwood, Margaret P, 1955, S 26,23:4
Sherwood, Mary E W, 1903, S 15,9:6
Sherwood, Maud (Mrs E H Jewett), 1953, Ap 18,19:4
Sherwood, N, 1882, N 1,4:7
Sherwood, Oliver P Lt, 1918, Ja 23,9:5
Sherwood, Percy, 1940, O 16,23:2
Sherwood, Ralph A, 1949, My 4,29:5
Sherwood, Raymond P, 1948, My 13,25:3
Sherwood, Richard H, 1961, Ja 29,85:1
Sherwood, Richard H Mrs, 1947, F 15,15:1
Sherwood, Robert E, 1946, Mr 11,25:1
Sherwood, Robert E (funl, N 17,35:1), 1955, N 15,1
Sherwood, Samuel, 1862, N 13,3:1
Sherwood, Sidney Mrs, 1963, Je 26,39:2
Sherwood, Sidney Prof, 1901, Ag 7,7:6
Sherwood, Simon C, 1906, Mr 16,9:5
Sherwood, Stanley L, 1957, Ap 28,86:5
Sherwood, Sterling C Mrs, 1960, Ja 31,92:2
Sherwood, Thomas D Justice, 1875, My 27,2:4
Sherwood, W C, 1950, N 20,25:3
Sherwood, W De Forest, 1942, Mr 28,17:2
Sherwood, W Leigh, 1965, Mr 28,92:4
Sherwood, Walter K, 1949, N 15,26:4
Sherwood, Walter S, 1950, N 21,31:2
Sherwood, Warner Mrs, 1925, S 14,19:5
Sherwood, Warren G, 1947, My 31,13:5
Sherwood, Wilbur R, 1944, F 29,17:5
Sherwood, William A, 1951, Ag 14,23:2; 1953, Ag 2 27:1
Sherwood, William C, 1957, Je 11,35:2
Sherwood, William D, 1959, F 3,27:1
Sherwood, William J, 1953, Ag 29,17:2
Sherwood, William L Lt, 1873, Ap 17,1:7
Sherwood, William R, 1960, Ag 14,92:6
Sherwood, Winifred, 1954, D 4,17:5
Shesa, Louis, 1952, S 15,25:2
Shesta, Ivan, 1949, Ja 21,21:2
Shestokas, Joseph, 1958, D 1,29:4
Shethar, Prentice, 1951, O 25,29:2
Shethar, Samuel, 1940, Ap 26,21:6
Shetterly, C Russel Mrs, 1966, Ja 24,35:3
Shettle, Arthur F, 1961, F 18,19:4
Shettler, Edward W, 1949, Ag 27,13:6
Shetzer, Simon, 1947, My 30,21:2
Shetzline, Charles A, 1939, Mr 1,21:3
Shevack, George F, 1955, O 8,19:4
Shevaldin, Trifom I, 1954, Jl 7,31:4
Shevell, Jacob, 1949, My 23,23:2
Shevelove, Jacob J, 1949, Ja 26,25:1
Shevikiar Ibrahim, Princess, 1947, F 18,25:1
Shevkunenko, Victor, 1952, Jl 6,49:2
Shevlin, Arthur L, 1946, Ag 6,25:5
Shevlin, Charles A, 1940, F 7,21:2
Shevlin, Eddie (J Prendergast), 1959, F 8,86:8
Shevlin, Edwin L, 1950, O 14,19:5
Shevlin, George H, 1961, D 21,27:3
Shevlin, James, 1924, N 25,23:4
Shevlin, James Mrs, 1914, Jl 18,7:6
Shevlin, Mary G, 1938, S 21,25:4
Shevlin, Thomas H, 1912, Ja 16,13:3
Shevlin, William A, 1943, Jl 16,17:5
Shew, Robert, 1948, N 27,14:4
Shewan, Edwin A (por), 1945, Mr 7,22:2
Sheward, Caleb M, 1946, O 6,56:5
Shewbridge, Peter E, 1950, My 21,104:6
Shewell, George D, 1938, S 18,44:5
Shewell, L D Mrs, 1871, Ap 15,1:3
Shewell, Livingston R, 1873, F 4,4:7
Shewfelt, Gordon, 1940, Ja 18,23:4
Shewhart, Walter A, 1967, Mr 13,37:4
Shewmon, Dan D, 1953, Mr 18,31:3
Shewmon, Dan Mrs, 1941, Je 11,21:4
Sheyer, Mary, 1907, Ag 16,7:5
Shiarrella, Nicholas W, 1946, Mr 16,13:4
Shiba, Sometaro, 1949, Jl 17,57:2
Shibata, Tsunematsu, 1945, Mr 8,13:2
Shibe, Herbert B, 1947, Ja 11,19:3
Shibe, John B, 1937, Jl 12,18:2
Shibe, Thomas S Mrs, 1952, My 14,28:4
Shibe, Thomas S Mrs (will), 1953, My 16,9:4
Shiber, Etta K Mrs, 1948, D 25,18:2
Shibley, Fred W (por), 1944, Mr 2,17:1
Shibusaw, Keizo, 1963, O 26,27:3
Shibusawa, E, 1931, N 10,34:4
Shibusawa, Masao, 1942, S 11,21:5
Shich, Benea, 1960, Je 22,35:2
Shick, Frederick A, 1958, Ja 20,23:1
Shick, Frederick A Mrs, 1951, O 25,29:5
Shick, Horace V, 1942, Ag 8,11:6
Shick, Lloyd L, 1951, N 19,23:2
Shick, Robert P, 1947, Ja 26,53:4
Shidehara, Kijuro, 1951, Mr 11,92:1
Shideler, Albert L, 1949, My 27,21:1
Shideler, Paul, 1962, Jl 22,64:2
Shideler, William H, 1958, D 19,2:6
Shidlovsky, Sarah Mrs, 1938, S 16,22:4
Shiebler, Francis Q, 1963, My 19,86:5
Shiebler, George F, 1939, Ja 3,17:2
Shiebler, Howard A, 1960, F 18,33:1
Shiebler, Marvin, 1944, O 20,19:3
Shiefler, Carl G, 1942, Ap 3,21:2
Shiel, Alfred J N, 1946, O 3,27:5
Shiel, Jefferson, 1945, My 8,19:4
Shiel, Matthew P, 1947, F 18,25:4
Shield, John J, 1951, N 19,29:6
Shield, Lansing P, 1960, Ja 7,29:1
Shield, Lansing P Mrs, 1947, Ap 6,60:2
Shield, Leroy B (Roy), 1962, Ja 11,33:5
Shield, Morris, 1953, Mr 17,29:1
Shield, Walter B, 1939, My 28,III,7:2

Shields, A S L Dr, 1916, Ja 20,9:4
Shields, Addis M, 1957, S 22,86:2
Shields, Albert W, 1956, Ja 27,23:2
Shields, Alexander, 1907, S 14,9:7
Shields, Alexander J, 1947, My 28,25:3
Shields, Charles J, 1953, Ag 28,17:4
Shields, Charles W Prof, 1904, Ag 27,7:6
Shields, Clarence, 1951, Ap 29,88:6
Shields, Claude S, 1951, Ag 2,21:6
Shields, Curtis W, 1952, Ap 21,21:3
Shields, Donald A, 1946, Je 12,27:2
Shields, Dorothy A, 1951, Jl 31,21:3
Shields, E H Mrs, 1955, S 23,25:3
Shields, Edmund C, 1947, Ja 7,27:2
Shields, Edward E, 1943, N 21,56:6
Shields, Edward J, 1957, Ap 30,29:2
Shields, Edwin W, 1920, Ja 7,19:3
Shields, Ella, 1952, Ag 6,21:2
Shields, Ella L, 1955, Je 7,33:1
Shields, Francis H, 1939, S 15,23:5
Shields, Frank, 1939, N 19,38:6
Shields, Frank B, 1946, O 17,23:6
Shields, G O, 1925, N 13,19:4
Shields, George, 1908, My 29,7:3
Shields, George S, 1952, D 28,48:5
Shields, George W Mrs, 1946, Ap 29,22:3
Shields, Helen (Mrs W Kemp), 1963, Ag 8,27:2
Shields, Henry, 1874, Mr 17,2:7
Shields, Henry G, 1955, S 24,19:5
Shields, Henry G Mrs, 1945, N 8,19:5
Shields, J Frank, 1947, Ap 3,25:1
Shields, J Franklin Mrs, 1938, Ap 4,17:3
Shields, J K, 1934, O 1,17:1
Shields, J W, 1903, Ag 25,7:6
Shields, James, 1879, Je 3,5:1
Shields, James A, 1949, Ag 12,17:3
Shields, James E, 1948, Ap 25,71:3
Shields, James J, 1944, Ja 6,23:1
Shields, James K, 1950, F 21,25:5
Shields, James L, 1951, O 3,33:2
Shields, James P, 1953, Je 30,23:1
Shields, James S, 1944, Ja 11,19:3
Shields, James V, 1954, Ag 11,25:4
Shields, Jane, 1916, F 18,11:7
Shields, Jesse W, 1965, Ag 12,27:2
Shields, Jessie M, 1949, My 3,25:2
Shields, Joanna B Mrs, 1965, F 5,31:6
Shields, John, 1964, Je 14,85:1
Shields, John A, 1914, Jl 8,9:5
Shields, John F, 1947, O 2,27:2; 1959, Mr 6,25:4
Shields, John J, 1954, S 19,89:2
Shields, John R Mrs, 1956, Jl 28,17:4
Shields, John William, 1920, Jl 31,7:6
Shields, Joseph J, 1964, N 4,39:3
Shields, Joseph V Mrs, 1959, Ag 1,17:2
Shields, Lawrence J, 1953, N 23,27:2
Shields, Leonard, 1938, O 27,23:5
Shields, Louis G, 1954, Ap 15,29:3
Shields, Lowell W, 1945, O 16,23:1
Shields, M J, 1939, Ja 24,19:5
Shields, Mark, 1953, My 14,29:2
Shields, Matthew J, 1954, Ja 31,88:1
Shields, Michael Rev, 1923, O 24,19:5
Shields, Nelson Jr Mrs, 1938, Jl 21,21:4
Shields, Nelson T, 1940, Jl 16,17:4
Shields, Nelson T Mrs, 1940, Ap 1,19:2
Shields, Patrick Henry, 1912, N 6,15:5
Shields, Paul V Mrs, 1958, O 30,31:2
Shields, R McCormick, 1964, S 18,35:2
Shields, Ren, 1913, O 26,15:6
Shields, Robert C, 1946, D 13,23:1
Shields, Robert J, 1958, D 3,37:1
Shields, Robert M Jr, 1958, Jl 30,29:4
Shields, Russell G, 1947, My 6,27:3
Shields, Samuel L Mrs, 1960, My 17,37:4
Shields, Sandra, 1967, Mr 22,47:2
Shields, Sydney, 1960, S 21,37:1
Shields, Sydney T, 1964, S 29,43:2
Shields, Thomas A, 1964, Mr 10,37:1
Shields, Thomas A Mrs, 1937, My 14,23:1
Shields, Thomas I, 1954, Ag 17,21:2
Shields, Thomas T, 1955, Ap 6,29:3
Shields, Thomas W, 1920, S 22,15:2
Shields, Walter C, 1944, Mr 11,13:4
Shields, Walter G Jr, 1941, Jl 22,19:4
Shields, William, 1962, My 12,23:3
Shields, William G, 1942, Jl 12,36:7; 1947, Mr 14,24:3
Shields, William I, 1942, Jl 1,25:2
Shields, William J (B Fitzgerald),(funl, Ja 8,86:7), 1961, Ja 5,31:2
Shiels, Albert, 1940, Mr 15,23:1
Shiels, Albert Mrs, 1955, Jl 11,23:3
Shiels, George, 1949, S 21,32:2
Shiels, William E, 1948, F 2,19:2
Shienbloom, Charles, 1954, S 17,27:4
Shieneman-Sharon, Samuel, 1957, Ja 3,33:5
Shientag, Bernard L, 1952, My 24,1:4
Shiff, Madelon, 1941, F 3,20:1
Shiffel, Ralph W, 1949, Ja 25,23:5
Shiffer, Anthony J, 1954, Ap 26,25:4
Shiffer, Joseph D, 1955, Ap 20,33:4
Shifferens, William E, 1939, Mr 24,21:1
Shiffman, Henry, 1960, Ap 27,37:3
Shiffman, Louis, 1960, D 11,88:7
Shiffman, Mack L, 1963, Je 21,29:3
Shiffman, Rose, 1954, S 24,23:4
Shiftman, Abraham, 1958, Ag 12,29:3
Shifty, Harry, 1958, Mr 12,31:3
Shiga, Kiyoshi, 1957, Ja 26,19:6
Shigemitsu, Mamoru, 1957, Ja 26,19:4
Shih-chang, Hsu, 1939, Je 7,23:6
Shih Chao-Ying, 1956, Je 26,29:1
Shiland, Andrew, 1914, Mr 25,11:6; 1962, F 23,29:3
Shiland, Andrew Jr, 1963, Jl 1,29:2
Shiland, Andrew R Lt, 1918, Ja 28,13:4
Shiland, Finley H, 1954, S 11,17:5
Shilanse, Arnold W, 1952, O 23,31:4
Shildkret, Samuel, 1964, Ja 28,31:4
Shildkret, Samuel Mrs, 1946, Ag 1,23:1
Shiley, Ralph U Mrs, 1959, Je 21,92:4
Shilin, Alan D, 1955, D 24,13:3
Shilkret, Jack, 1964, Je 17,43:5
Shilkret, Rose Mrs, 1937, Ag 18,19:3
Shill, Arthur E, 1963, O 21,31:4
Shill, Claude E, 1945, Ap 11,23:2
Shill, Richard A Mrs, 1955, Ap 7,27:1
Shillaber, B P (Mrs Partington), 1890, N 26,1:6
Shillaber, William, 1920, My 1,15:2; 1938, Ag 11,17:4
Shillady, John R, 1943, S 7,23:5
Shillard-Smith, Charles Mrs, 1955, O 13,31:2
Shiller, Samuel, 1959, Jl 26,69:1
Shilliday, William J, 1948, F 21,13:2
Shilling, Albert A, 1949, Ja 9,72:1
Shilling, Alex, 1937, Ja 22,22:3
Shilling, Carroll H, 1950, Ja 13,23:1
Shilling, David W, 1955, Ap 8,21:6
Shilling, Ray E, 1947, D 4,31:2
Shilling, William, 1956, Jl 29,65:1
Shilling, William K, 1939, S 14,23:2
Shillingford, George W, 1944, My 3,19:2
Shillinglaw, J M, 1945, Mr 15,23:3
Shillinglaw, Richard, 1946, F 10,40:6
Shillito, Alfred, 1939, Ja 17,22:3
Shillito, Edward, 1948, Mr 12,23:1
Shillito, John, 1879, S 11,5:1
Shillito, Stewart, 1925, Je 10,23:5
Shillito, Wallace, 1905, Mr 21,11:4
Shiloah, Reuven, 1959, My 11,27:5
Shilovsky, Eugene, 1952, My 30,15:3
Shilowitz, Charles, 1968, S 27,47:2
Shilstone, Hugh P, 1959, Ja 20,35:1
Shima Mura, Hayao Adm, 1923, Ja 9,23:4
Shimada, Saburo, 1923, N 17,13:4
Shimazaka, Toson, 1943, Ag 23,15:2
Shimberg, Mandell, 1950, Je 27,29:5
Shimer, A Burton, 1943, Ap 24,13:1
Shimer, Charles E, 1946, F 3,40:1
Shimer, E D, 1933, Ap 6,17:3
Shimer, Floyd A, 1951, Ap 22,88:3
Shimer, Hervey W, 1965, D 14,39:4
Shimer, Howard, 1943, My 16,42:8
Shimer, Ira A Dr, 1909, Mr 14,11:6
Shimer, William I, 1915, Ap 1,15:4
Shimizu, Sojiro, 1952, Ag 15,16:5
Shimizu, Sojiro Mrs, 1954, My 21,27:3
Shimkin, Sarah, 1948, Ja 10,15:2
Shimkin, Victor I, 1967, Ap 23,92:8
Shimko, Anthony J, 1963, My 10,33:3
Shimko, John J, 1955, Ap 3,86:3
Shimkus, Peter S, 1941, S 5,21:3
Shimm, Abraham S, 1951, Jl 7,13:7
Shimmon, Claude W, 1948, S 21,27:1
Shimmon, Elia, 1954, Je 15,29:5
Shimmon, Florence L A Mrs, 1951, Je 8,27:4
Shimomura, Hiroshi, 1957, D 10,35:3
Shimoni, David, 1956, D 13,37:3
Shimose, Masuchika, 1911, S 7,9:5
Shimp, Byron W, 1964, Ap 19,84:7
Shimp, Hayes G, 1966, S 16,37:2
Shimp, Herbert G, 1943, Ap 5,19:2
Shimshi, Zvi I, 1953, N 5,31:3
Shimura, Shunzo, 1882, Ap 3,2:4
Shinawi, Mamoun al, 1950, S 5,27:1
Shinborn, Mark, 1916, F 14,13:4
Shind, Zeev, 1953, D 22,31:3
Shindler, James, 1904, Mr 12,9:4
Shindler, Margaret A Mrs, 1954, Jl 7,31:2
Shine, Charles M, 1953, O 28,29:4
Shine, Cornelius D Sr, 1939, My 29,15:2
Shine, Francis Eppes Dr, 1922, S 22,15:5
Shine, Francis W (por), 1941, S 25,25:1
Shine, Francis X, 1953, Jl 24,13:6
Shine, George E, 1940, My 10,23:3
Shine, Giles, 1912, Mr 1,11:5
Shine, J L, 1930, O 17,23:5
Shine, James A, 1953, Ag 10,23:6
Shine, James H, 1920, N 9,15:3
Shine, John, 1953, Ap 20,25:4
Shine, John J, 1953, S 23,32:3
Shine, Joseph M, 1944, F 3,19:5
Shine, Louis M Mrs, 1939, S 25,19:2
Shine, Michael J, 1938, Jl 10,31:3
Shine, Thomas, 1955, N 23,23:5
Shine, Timothy J, 1941, Ap 5,17:1; 1955, Je 19,92:6
Shine, W L Dr, 1885, F 18,5:6
Shine, William A, 1961, F 8,31:4
Shine, William H Mrs, 1952, Ja 30,26:3
Shineman, Elmer A, 1950, Je 8,32:3
Shiner, Ronald, 1966, Jl 2,23:5
Shingler, Don G, 1963, N 1,34:7
Shingler, John J Mrs, 1948, Je 29,23:5
Shinicky, P H, 1956, My 5,19:2
Shinjo, Shinzo, 1938, Ag 2,19:4
Shinkle, A Clifford Jr, 1950, F 5,84:7
Shinkle, A Clifford Mrs, 1951, Ag 11,11:2
Shinkle, Albert T, 1949, F 26,15:6
Shinkman, Samuel, 1937, F 13,13:4
Shinn, Arthur T, 1948, N 24,24:2
Shinn, Byron L, 1955, Jl 21,23:2
Shinn, David B, 1962, S 24,29:4
Shinn, Elizabeth C Mrs, 1938, Ap 16,13:6
Shinn, Everett, 1953, My 3,89:1
Shinn, F A Mrs, 1933, Je 25,22:1
Shinn, Florence S Mrs, 1940, O 18,21:5
Shinn, George Wolfe Rev, 1910, D 8,13:3
Shinn, James T, 1907, O 5,11:6
Shinn, Joseph H, 1942, S 11,21:4
Shinn, Joseph H Jr, 1939, N 27,17:2
Shinn, Millicent W, 1940, Ag 15,19:4
Shinn, N G N J Col, 1903, Jl 22,7:5
Shinn, Owen L, 1941, Je 12,24:3
Shinn, Richard R, 1950, Je 21,27:4
Shinn, Robert C, 1946, Mr 23,13:5
Shinn, Wilson B, 1941, F 28,19:2
Shinner, Ernest G, 1963, Ag 22,27:5
Shinner, H R, 1938, N 7,19:4
Shinners, Arthur J M Jr, 1953, N 15,88:3
Shinnick, Mary M, 1938, D 23,19:3
Shinnick, William C, 1957, Ag 12,19:4
Shinnick, William L, 1960, My 17,37:2
Shinolt, Perry, 1947, My 10,13:6
Shinsheimer, Joseph, 1950, O 6,27:3
Shinwell, Emanuel Mrs, 1954, N 5,21:3
Shinwell, Samuel, 1955, F 11,23:1
Shiono, Suehiko, 1949, Ja 10,25:4
Shiozawa, Koichi (por), 1943, N 18,23:3
Shiozawa, Shotei, 1945, Jl 14,11:4
Ship, Moses L Dr, 1937, N 5,23:4
Shipe, Calvin E, 1953, F 27,21:2
Shipe, Claude, 1942, N 3,23:5
Shiplacoff, A I, 1934, F 8,19:1
Shiple, George J, 1958, My 21,33:3
Shipler, Guy Emery Rev Dr, 1968, Ap 20,33:1
Shipley, Agnes G E Mrs, 1937, O 18,17:5
Shipley, Alfred E, 1959, S 7,15:4
Shipley, Alfred E Mrs, 1937, Jl 30,19:5
Shipley, Charles R, 1961, Mr 14,35:1
Shipley, Elberta K, 1937, My 8,19:5
Shipley, Elizabeth, 1903, F 9,2:3
Shipley, Esther, 1877, Ja 16,4:6
Shipley, Frank F, 1958, Jl 31,23:2
Shipley, Frederick W, 1945, F 13,23:5
Shipley, Frederick W van D Mrs (Ruth), 1966, N 5, 31:2
Shipley, George, 1944, My 7,46:3
Shipley, James E, 1948, My 12,27:5
Shipley, James L Rev, 1937, Je 14,23:4
Shipley, Jay R, 1945, Jl 18,27:2
Shipley, Jay R Mrs, 1955, F 17,27:3
Shipley, Napoleon, 1904, S 17,5:5
Shipley, Richard L, 1947, N 26,23:4
Shipley, Walter C, 1966, Je 6,41:1
Shipley, Walter P, 1942, F 18,19:3
Shipley, William E Mrs, 1962, Mr 23,33:4
Shipley, William S, 1951, Ja 15,17:1
Shipman, Andrew Jackson, 1915, O 18,9:5
Shipman, Arthur L, 1937, O 18,17:1
Shipman, Bertram F, 1963, N 23,29:4
Shipman, Bertram F Mrs, 1968, Jl 26,31:2
Shipman, Charles M, 1947, My 15,26:3
Shipman, Ellen B Mrs, 1950, Mr 29,29:2
Shipman, Evan B, 1957, Je 25,29:5
Shipman, Frank W, 1941, S 21,44:1
Shipman, Frederic W, 1961, S 4,15:3
Shipman, Frederick E, 1904, S 24,9:6
Shipman, Frederick H, 1920, F 3,15:3
Shipman, G E Mrs, 1903, Ap 26,7:6
Shipman, Herbert A, 1906, Ja 28,2:7
Shipman, J L, 1884, Mr 9,2:3
Shipman, J S Rev, 1905, F 24,7:6
Shipman, Jehiel G, 1944, Ag 31,17:5
Shipman, L E, 1933, Ag 3,17:4
Shipman, Leroy T, 1944, D 28,19:5
Shipman, Natalie (Mrs G S Worcester), 1967, My 15,43:4
Shipman, Nathan Judge Mrs, 1903, My 25,9:6
Shipman, Nathaniel, 1906, Je 27,7:6
Shipman, Paul R, 1917, Mr 22,11:6
Shipman, Paul R Mrs, 1917, Ap 5,13:4
Shipman, Samuel (por), 1937, F 10,23:1
Shipman, Thomas, 1963, O 15,40:1
Shipman, Walter Mrs, 1940, Je 3,15:5
Shipman, Wayne M, 1944, Ja 25,19:4
Shipp, Cameron, 1961, Ag 21,23:4
Shipp, E Maltby, 1955, O 22,19:6
Shipp, Edward M Dr, 1914, Je 21,15:6
Shipp, John F Capt, 1925, S 19,15:4
Shipp, S W G Judge, 1937, Jl 23,19:2
Shipp, Thomas R, 1952, F 11,25:6

Shipp, Vladimir L Dr, 1968, Je 6,48:1
Shippard, Sidney Sir, 1902, Mr 30,7:4
Shippee, Carl C, 1951, F 18,76:2
Shippee, David N, 1943, Ap 8,23:1
Shippee, Lester B, 1944, F 10,15:1
Shippen, Edward, 1904, Mr 15,9:6; 1911, Je 18,11:2
Shippen, Ettie, 1953, Ag 1,11:4
Shippen, J, 1883, My 13,9:2
Shippen, John M, 1968, My 22,47:3
Shippen, William H Jr, 1953, N 25,23:3
Shippen, William W, 1922, Je 2,17:6
Shipper, James H, 1948, D 30,19:1
Shippers, John J Mrs, 1948, Je 10,25:3
Shippey, Elizabeth K Mrs, 1937, F 20,17:5
Shippey, Jacob J, 1955, S 12,25:3
Shippy, Frank C, 1946, O 26,17:3
Shipstead, Henrik, 1960, Je 27,25:2
Shipton, A W Mrs, 1952, D 13,21:5
Shipway, William R, 1965, Jl 7,37:1
Shiras, George, 1942, Mr 25,21:6
Shiras, George Jr, 1924, Ag 3,24:4
Shiras, Oliver P Ex-Judge, 1916, Ja 8,9:7
Shiratori, Toshio, 1949, Je 4,5:4
Shirayma, Shim, 1945, Je 8,19:3
Shircliffe, Arnold, 1952, S 22,23:2
Shirè, Albert C, 1958, S 11,33:5
Shire, Nathaniel N, 1922, F 24,12:5
Shireff, William P, 1959, Ap 22,33:2
Shirer, J T Mrs, 1945, N 28,27:5
Shires, Art, 1967, Jl 14,29:1
Shires, Henry H, 1961, Ap 30,86:8
Shirey, Walter G, 1951, Ap 20,29:4
Shirk, A Urban, 1956, O 22,29:6
Shirk, Charles F, 1955, My 14,19:5
Shirk, Christian H, 1946, F 20,25:2
Shirk, George S, 1957, Je 17,23:4
Shirk, James W Com, 1873, F 11,1:5
Shirk-Johnstone, Hermona Mrs (Virginia Dale), 1957, S 6,21:1
Shirkey, George J, 1955, D 9,27:2
Shirlaw, Walter, 1909, D 30,9:5
Shirley, Arthur, 1925, Ag 23,7:3
Shirley, E P, 1882, O 15,2:7
Shirley, Edward J, 1955, F 5,15:4
Shirley, Edward J Mrs, 1952, S 23,33:2
Shirley, F Ellen, 1946, D 16,23:4
Shirley, Farnandis G, 1957, Je 29,17:6
Shirley, Henrietta Mrs, 1940, Jl 24,11:6
Shirley, Henry G, 1941, Jl 17,19:4
Shirley, John B, 1954, D 10,27:3
Shirley, John J, 1953, Je 11,29:4
Shirley, Marion, 1925, Jl 9,19:4
Shirley, Oliver H, 1943, Ag 6,15:1
Shirley, Paul Commodore, 1876, N 26,7:2
Shirley, Queenie H, 1955, F 3,23:1
Shirley, R Kirby, 1956, Ja 25,31:3
Shirley, Robert W (Earl Ferrers), 1954, O 13,31:4
Shirley, Sylvia, 1966, S 24,23:5
Shirley, Thomas, 1959, S 22,39:2
Shirley, Thomas P, 1962, Ja 25,31:2
Shirley, W F, 1903, N 13,1:6
Shirley, W F Mrs, 1903, N 13,1:6
Shirley, Walter T (Jan 29), 1963, Ap 1,36:6
Shirley, William J, 1952, S 16,29:1
Shirley, William M, 1962, My 27,92:6
Shirley, William R, 1952, My 23,21:5
Shirley-Fox, John, 1939, Je 4,49:2
Shirmer, Gustave, 1907, Jl 17,9:6
Shirmer, R E, 1919, Ag 21,11:4
Shiroky, Nicholas A, 1968, O 1,48:1
Shirras, George F, 1955, Je 24,21:5
Shirreff, Miss, 1884, Ja 18,3:6
Shirrefs, Russell A, 1947, Jl 16,23:5
Shirrefs, Russell A Mrs, 1959, S 6,72:2
Shirshov, Pytor Petrovich, 1953, F 19,23:2
Shisgal, Abraham I, 1952, D 19,31:4
Shishkin, A D, 1954, S 10,23:5
Shishmarev, Vladimir F, 1957, N 24,86:3
Shislaner, Elizabeth Mrs, 1924, Ap 7,17:5
Shissler, Simon E, 1951, Ap 5,29:4
Shitreet, Behor, 1967, Ja 29,76:8
Shive, Hannah Mrs, 1943, Ag 5,15:3
Shivelhood, David K, 1944, S 14,23:5
Shively, Benjamin F Sen (funl, Mr 17,11:7), 1916, Mr 15,11:1
Shively, Bernie A, 1967, D 11,47:5
Shively, Carlton A, 1952, Jl 10,31:4
Shively, Robert R, 1956, O 28,88:1
Shively, Samuel B, 1953, Jl 26,69:1
Shiverick, Asa, 1937, Jl 2,21:4
Shivers, C Walter, 1940, Jl 13,13:7
Shivers, Herbert M, 1949, Mr 14,19:5
Shivers, Robert L, 1950, Je 29,29:4
Shivers, William, 1925, My 16,17:5
Shiverts, Benjamin, 1947, N 3,23:1
Shivitz, Max H, 1955, D 27,23:2
Shivley, William, 1946, N 16,19:5
Shkiryatov, Matvei F, 1954, Ja 19,25:2
Shlakman, Saul A, 1954, N 7,89:2
Shlefstein, Isaac, 1942, Ap 5,42:1
Shlemon, Abraham, 1942, N 25,23:1
Shlenker, Milton A, 1957, D 3,35:5
Shlensky, Morris, 1946, Ja 3,19:1
Shlepianov, Ilya Y, 1951, D 23,22:6
Shlifer, Solomon, 1957, Ap 2,31:5
Shlionsky, Herman, 1966, Je 3,39:3
Shlisky, Josef Z, 1955, F 15,27:2
Shluger, Alexander L, 1944, Ag 14,15:5
Shmidheiser, Edward G, 1948, S 27,23:5
Shmidheiser, Edward G Mrs, 1961, O 24,37:1
Shnayerson, Edward F, 1958, Ap 11,25:1
Shneour, Zalman (cor, F 22,88:5), 1959, F 21,21:3
Shniper, Isidor Mrs, 1949, Ag 19,17:3
Shnyder, Frederick E, 1955, Ap 9,13:4
Shoaf, Alston, 1944, S 17,41:1
Shoals, F P, 1881, O 12,5:6
Shoals, George R, 1960, Ap 22,29:1
Shoban, Matthew, 1946, D 1,76:2
Shober, Francis E, 1919, O 9,15:4
Shober, Frank W, 1955, D 4,88:5
Shober, Reginald K, 1948, Mr 8,23:5
Shober, Samuel L, 1938, Jl 20,19:2
Shobert, Dallas C, 1948, Mr 18,27:2
Shoch, George Q, 1937, O 2,21:1
Shochet, Moses Rev, 1937, Ag 27,19:4
Shock, Donald P, 1966, Ag 14,88:1
Shock, James Rev, 1912, Ag 11,II,11:5
Shock, Thomas M, 1962, O 5,36:5
Shockley, August W, 1956, My 12,19:4
Shockley, E Gordon, 1961, Ap 2,77:1
Shockley, Francis M, 1944, Ap 27,23:1
Shockley, Frank W, 1954, Ja 15,19:2
Shockley, Lawrence, 1907, Ag 16,7:5
Shoemake, Arah, 1955, D 8,37:4
Shoemaker, A C, 1938, Mr 17,21:4
Shoemaker, A H Mrs, 1951, Jl 24,25:4
Shoemaker, Abraham D, 1944, F 12,13:3
Shoemaker, Aletha, 1953, My 26,29:6
Shoemaker, Bernard M, 1962, Jl 28,19:2
Shoemaker, C C Mrs, 1922, Ag 1,19:3
Shoemaker, Charles C, 1937, My 23,II,11:2
Shoemaker, Clifton B Jr, 1948, S 1,23:2
Shoemaker, Davis W, 1947, O 14,27:6
Shoemaker, Dudley, 1948, Ja 3,13:1
Shoemaker, Eleanor C, 1940, O 21,17:6
Shoemaker, George G, 1944, My 15,19:3
Shoemaker, George J, 1959, Jl 20,25:4
Shoemaker, George W, 1947, Mr 30,56:6
Shoemaker, Guy W, 1948, S 20,25:1
Shoemaker, Harry, 1939, O 24,23:2
Shoemaker, Harry B, 1950, F 15,27:3
Shoemaker, Harry L, 1954, D 21,27:2
Shoemaker, Henry Francis, 1918, Jl 4,13:2
Shoemaker, Henry W, 1958, Jl 16,29:1
Shoemaker, J L, 1876, D 28,4:6
Shoemaker, Jack C, 1954, Ap 16,21:1
Shoemaker, James, 1939, N 30,21:4
Shoemaker, James M, 1956, Je 3,85:1
Shoemaker, Jane A (will, Mr 29,21:2), 1938, Mr 23, 23:1
Shoemaker, John F, 1948, My 13,25:1
Shoemaker, Jonathan E Mrs, 1937, My 16,II,8:4
Shoemaker, Joseph H, 1943, My 5,27:3
Shoemaker, Joseph M, 1948, S 25,17:5
Shoemaker, Louis J, 1949, Mr 30,25:4
Shoemaker, Mary E, 1943, Mr 27,13:5
Shoemaker, Michael, 1924, Ag 12,11:4
Shoemaker, Murray M Mrs, 1965, Ag 18,35:4
Shoemaker, Percy E Rev, 1925, O 5,21:4
Shoemaker, Perry M Mrs, 1964, Je 28,57:2
Shoemaker, R M, 1885, F 11,5:5
Shoemaker, Ray H, 1959, Ag 27,27:2
Shoemaker, Robert Henry, 1915, Jl 29,9:6
Shoemaker, S M, 1884, Je 2,5:4
Shoemaker, Samuel M, 1963, N 2,25:5
Shoemaker, Samuel Mrs, 1907, Je 30,7:7
Shoemaker, Walter S, 1939, O 27,23:2
Shoemaker, Wayne A, 1962, Jl 20,25:3
Shoemaker, Wheeler, 1945, Je 28,19:5
Shoemaker, William B, 1906, Je 22,5:3
Shoemaker, William E, 1950, F 24,23:4
Shoemaker, William M, 1951, Ag 2,21:5
Shoemaker, William R, 1938, My 31,19:3
Shoemaker, William T, 1942, N 27,23:4
Shoenberg, Moses Col, 1925, Jl 20,15:6
Shoenke, Austin J, 1946, Mr 3,46:6
Shoffner, Charles P, 1946, My 6,21:4
Shoffstall, Hugh F, 1960, F 1,27:5
Shofner, Howard B, 1941, Ap 15,23:1
Shoghi, Effendi, 1957, N 6,35:2
Shogren, Herbert C, 1953, Ap 24,24:6
Shohan, Jacob B, 1957, Ja 26,19:2
Shohan, Leo B, 1966, Je 28,45:3
Shohat, James A, 1944, O 10,23:5
Shohat, James A Mrs, 1948, Mr 7,68:3
Shohet, David M, 1961, S 27,42:1
Sholar, William J, 1949, Jl 7,25:5
Sholes, A E, 1931, Jl 30,19:1
Sholes, Benjamin, 1904, Ja 26,9:6
Sholes, Earl H, 1961, D 30,19:4
Sholes, Frank L, 1951, N 16,25:3
Sholes, Justin G, 1952, O 29,29:5
Sholes, Steven, 1968, Ap 23,47:1
Sholes, Walter H Mrs, 1961, O 17,39:4
Sholk, Barnett, 1967, Je 14,47:3
Sholl, Anna M, 1956, Ap 3,29:6
Sholl, Edward Pearson, 1923, N 19,15:3
Shollenberger, H R, 1951, Jl 13,21:1
Sholler, George W, 1947, F 5,23:2
Sholod, Morris L, 1967, Ag 16,41:4
Sholtz, David, 1953, Mr 22,86:3
Sholtz, Leo, 1941, F 2,45:2
Sholtz, Michael, 1952, Ag 2,15:2
Sholtz, Michael Mrs, 1954, S 17,27:2
Shonberg, Isidore I, 1944, S 16,13:4
Shone, Charles W, 1905, Ap 17,9:6
Shone, Terence, 1965, O 31,86:5
Shoneman, Louis, 1941, F 16,41:1
Shoneman, Saul Mrs, 1950, Ja 17,27:6
Shong, Albert C, 1939, O 2,17:2
Shongood, Charles, 1945, Je 12,19:5
Shongut, Donald I Mrs, 1963, D 30,21:3
Shongut, Jacob, 1940, My 9,23:6
Shongut, Morris Mrs, 1963, S 1,57:1
Shoninger, Alex S Mrs, 1942, My 17,47:5
Shoninger, Bernard J, 1941, F 15,15:4
Shonk, H B, 1930, S 27,17:5
Shonle, Horace A, 1947, F 25,25:5
Shonnard, Horatio S, 1946, O 12,19:2
Shonsey, Mich, 1954, Ag 7,13:6
Shonts, Henry Daniel, 1910, Ja 11,9:4
Shonts, Henry Daniels Mrs, 1915, Jl 13,11:4
Shonts, Theodore P (funl, S 24,17:3), 1919, S 22,11:3
Shontz, Charles L, 1937, S 14,23:5
Shontz, Harry B, 1954, Ap 21,29:4
Shontz, Orfa J, 1954, My 7,23:5
Shontz, Vernon L, 1954, O 17,86:8
Shook, Alfred F Mrs, 1950, My 16,31:4
Shook, Alfred M Col, 1923, Mr 19,17:6
Shook, Doreen, 1944, Ja 11,11:1
Shook, Francis M, 1940, D 28,15:3
Shook, Glenn A, 1954, Ag 28,15:6
Shook, J Purman, 1956, S 13,35:1
Shook, Sheridan, 1899, Ap 28,7:4
Shoong, Joe, 1961, Ap 16,86:8
Shoop, Duke, 1957, Ap 28,87:1
Shoop, Jesse E, 1939, F 7,20:1
Shoop, John D, 1918, Ag 10,7:5
Shoop, Max, 1956, O 30,37:4
Shoosmith, Stephen N, 1956, D 5,39:3
Shoots, Lewis J, 1951, O 28,85:2
Shope, Richard E, 1966, O 3,47:2
Shope, Samuel Z Mrs, 1946, Je 20,23:1
Shope, Simeon Ex-Justice, 1920, Ja 26,7:1
Shor, George G, 1967, Je 21,47:3
Shor, I L, 1949, S 16,27:2
Shorb, Paul E, 1950, Jl 3,15:5
Shordiche, Thomas F, 1951, Ja 19,25:5
Shore, A Bernard, 1957, Je 16,84:4
Shore, Alfred E, 1951, N 28,31:4
Shore, Ben R, 1944, Ag 21,15:4
Shore, Edward J Mrs, 1945, S 18,23:2
Shore, Howard J, 1952, Je 21,15:6
Shore, Joseph R, 1946, Mr 6,27:3
Shore, Justin O, 1965, F 13,21:4
Shore, Maurice J, 1961, Jl 15,19:6
Shore, Robert D, 1937, O 2,21:6
Shore, Samuel, 1946, D 5,31:2
Shore, Solomon A, 1945, My 15,19:3
Shore, William F, 1960, Mr 16,37:1
Shores, Byron L, 1957, N 15,28:3
Shores, Robert J, 1950, Ja 7,17:2
Shorey, Albert C, 1946, S 9,9:2
Shorey, Eva L, 1964, Jl 3,21:3
Shorey, Frederick Mrs, 1958, My 5,29:1
Shorey, George H, 1944, Je 21,19:5
Shorey, Harry S, 1953, Ag 13,25:2
Shorey, Henry A Jr, 1952, Ja 6,93:2
Shorin, Joseph E, 1959, D 10,39:2
Shorn, Ira, 1955, S 9,23:6
Shorr, Abraham, 1951, My 15,31:2
Shorr, Harold M, 1953, D 18,36:8
Shorr, Isaac, 1964, Ap 26,88:8
Short, Albert E, 1937, Ag 11,24:1; 1951, Mr 5,21:1
Short, Alfred, 1938, Ag 25,19:6
Short, Benjamin J, 1947, Mr 25,25:3
Short, Byron, 1937, O 17,II,8:8
Short, Carlton B (por, Je 16,40:6), 1946, Je 15,21:5
Short, Charles W, 1954, Ap 17,13:5
Short, Clarence A, 1947, Mr 24,25:4
Short, Donald I, 1952, N 17,25:4
Short, Esther I, 1940, F 4,41:2
Short, Everett J, 1949, F 10,27:4
Short, Floyd T, 1944, D 17,38:3
Short, Francis J, 1946, N 5,25:2
Short, Frank, 1945, Ap 24,19:2
Short, Frank L, 1949, Je 15,30:2
Short, Frank R, 1949, N 5,13:3
Short, Frederick Henry, 1907, Ag 26,7:7
Short, Harold H, 1957, Ap 5,27:2
Short, Harry, 1943, Ag 19,19:2
Short, Harvey B, 1943, Ag 6,15:3
Short, Hassard (mem ser set, N 21,27:4), 1956, O 10,39:1
Short, Hassard (will), 1957, Ja 10,26:2
Short, Helen Mrs, 1942, O 7,25:6
Short, Henry S, 1938, D 13,26:2
Short, J C, 1946, Ja 3,19:1
Short, Jacob, 1950, Mr 14,25:3

Short, James, 1941, Mr 22,15:4
Short, James A, 1947, My 2,21:3; 1958, Ap 24,31:3
Short, James M Sr, 1954, S 11,17:6
Short, Joseph C, 1951, Jl 1,51:2
Short, Joseph D, 1946, Ag 25,46:2
Short, Joseph H Jr, 1952, S 19,1:7
Short, Katherine C, 1961, Ap 15,21:5
Short, Livingston L, 1963, N 2,25:1
Short, Luther, 1925, D 31,15:5
Short, Mac V (por), 1948, Ag 14,13:3
Short, Marion L L Mrs, 1966, O 29,34:2
Short, Martin, 1904, Jl 26,1:5
Short, Martin T, 1941, Ag 4,13:3
Short, Melissa Mrs, 1908, D 19,9:4
Short, Pat Col, 1911, My 20,13:4
Short, Peter, 1907, Ap 7,9:6; 1915, S 20,9:6
Short, Ralph C, 1954, Ag 4,21:4
Short, Raymond L, 1945, Je 17,26:6
Short, Raymond W, 1966, Ja 30,84:1
Short, Reginald Mrs, 1942, N 24,25:5
Short, Robert, 1941, Ap 13,39:2
Short, Samuel Dr, 1912, Ja 26,11:5
Short, Sarah L, 1948, Ag 25,25:4
Short, Stanley, 1956, N 16,31:2
Short, Sue M Mrs, 1939, D 11,23:4
Short, Thomas A, 1954, My 27,27:4
Short, Van Courtlandt, 1958, My 1,31:1
Short, Wallace M, 1953, Ja 4,78:4
Short, Walter C, 1949, S 4,40:3
Short, William B, 1958, S 4,29:2
Short, William Mrs, 1948, F 4,23:4
Short, William Rev Dr, 1905, O 28,9:6
Shortall, Edward P, 1941, D 1,19:2
Shortau, Robert O, 1943, Mr 20,15:4
Shortell, James, 1937, My 29,17:6
Shortell, John J, 1952, Ag 26,25:3
Shortell, Joseph, 1952, Ag 8,17:2
Shortell, Joseph H, 1951, F 4,76:4
Shorter, Bert D, 1948, S 21,27:5
Shorter, C K, 1926, N 20,17:5
Shorter, John U, 1904, Mr 14,9:6
Shorter, William, 1952, My 25,94:5
Shortess, William G, 1942, F 6,19:2
Shorthouse, J H, 1903, Mr 5,9:5
Shortle, Mae A, 1968, Ap 5,47:1
Shortledge, Joseph Prof, 1911, D 11,11:3
Shortlidge, Raphael J, 1962, Je 16,19:6
Shortlidge, Raymond S, 1964, Je 5,31:2
Shortliffe, J Melbourne, 1954, D 15,31:1
Shortreed, William J, 1943, Mr 20,15:4
Shortridge, N Parker, 1915, Ja 4,11:5
Shortridge, Samuel M, 1952, Ja 16,25:1
Shorts, Bruce C, 1945, Mr 31,19:4
Shortt, Adam Mrs, 1949, Ja 15,17:6
Shortt, Alexis D, 1939, Ap 24,17:6
Shortt, Alfred H, 1941, My 17,15:1
Shortt, Lucy E L Mrs, 1941, O 4,15:4
Shortt, Thomas C, 1951, Je 23,15:3
Shortt, William A, 1915, Mr 10,13:6
Shortwell, Thomas J, 1940, My 10,23:2
Shortz, Edwin Jr, 1953, Je 23,29:4
Shoshano, Rose, 1968, N 3,89:1
Shoskes, Henry, 1964, My 7,37:5
Shostak, Michael Mrs, 1961, Ap 2,76:1
Shostak, Rebecca Mrs, 1952, S 14,86:2
Shostakovich, Dimitri Mrs, 1954, D 9,33:5
Shotland, Henry M, 1957, F 23,17:6
Shotland, Leisor Rabbi, 1937, D 28,21:1
Shotlander, Alex, 1952, S 13,17:5
Shotmeyer, Albert Mrs, 1963, O 28,27:4
Shott, Hugh I, 1953, O 13,29:6
Shott, Jim, 1957, Ja 27,84:5
Shotter, Spencer O, 1952, Mr 16,91:2
Shotton, Burton E Sr (Barney), 1962, Jl 31,27:4
Shotts, John C Col, 1919, Ag 28,11:3
Shotts, Sarah M Mrs, 1939, Ja 7,15:5
Shotwell, Abram R, 1949, Mr 20,76:5
Shotwell, Carl C, 1947, D 30,24:3
Shotwell, Edmund B, 1962, N 8,39:1
Shotwell, Fred C, 1950, Ja 14,15:4
Shotwell, Frederick C, 1946, Je 13,27:2
Shotwell, George M, 1916, Jl 29,9:7
Shotwell, Henry T, 1941, O 24,24:2
Shotwell, James S Mrs, 1965, Jl 10,25:5
Shotwell, James T, 1965, Jl 17,1:8
Shotwell, Raymond, 1953, F 15,93:2
Shotwell, Thomas C, 1957, D 15,86:8
Shoudy, Loyal, 1950, Ag 31,25:1
Shoudy, Theodore, 1962, D 2,88:7
Shoulberg, William Mrs, 1961, S 28,41:3
Shoulders, Harrison H Sr, 1963, N 18,33:2
Shoulders, Louis, 1962, My 12,5:4
Shouldice, E Earle, 1965, Ag 23,31:5
Shoup, Alonzo D, 1949, D 3,15:3
Shoup, Arthur C, 1942, Ap 9,19:4
Shoup, Daniel L, 1962, N 26,29:1
Shoup, Earl L Dr, 1953, F 1,88:6
Shoup, Eldon C, 1954, O 11,27:3
Shoup, George L Sen, 1904, D 22,9:4
Shoup, Merrill E, 1964, Jl 17,27:5
Shoup, Oliver H, 1940, O 1,23:2
Shoup, Paul, 1946, Jl 31,27:5
Shoup, Samuel R, 1940, Ja 6,13:6
Shoup, William F, 1952, Ag 26,25:1
Shour, Isaac, 1964, Je 6,23:5
Shourds, Frank H, 1942, Ja 14,21:2
Shourds, Merrill E, 1961, My 6,31:5
Shouse, James D, 1965, Ag 22,82:4
Shouse, James D Mrs, 1958, S 27,21:6
Shouse, Jouett, 1968, Je 3,45:3
Shouse, Len B, 1957, S 30,31:3
Shousha, Aly T, 1964, Je 2,37:3
Shove, Benjamin J, 1940, Ap 4,23:6
Shove, Eugene P, 1939, F 18,15:6
Shovitz, Phillip, 1945, Ap 19,27:3
Shovlin, Patrick A, 1944, N 25,13:4
Showalter, Hiram M, 1938, N 13,45:2
Showalter, Victor E, 1939, N 7,25:5
Showalter, William D, 1920, Ap 5,15:4
Showell, Lemuel Mrs, 1943, S 21,24:3
Showers, Harding, 1954, S 16,29:1
Showers, James L, 1940, Mr 21,22:2
Showers, Lee, 1947, Je 17,25:5
Showers, Phil H, 1937, F 21,II,11:1
Showles, Jacob, 1912, Ja 2,11:5
Showman, Harry M, 1943, Je 26,13:5
Shoyer, Frederick J, 1940, Ag 29,19:4
Shozo, Mori, 1953, Ja 12,27:1
Shpall, Leo, 1964, O 12,29:3
Shrader, E Roscoe, 1960, Ja 21,31:1
Shrader, James E, 1947, Je 20,19:3
Shrader, James F, 1962, Mr 22,35:4
Shrader, Ralph R, 1967, My 1,37:3
Shrader, William T, 1957, My 23,33:4
Shrady, Arthur M, 1939, Ja 15,38:4
Shrady, Arthur M Mrs, 1960, Ja 8,23:5
Shrady, Charles D, 1954, Je 20,85:2
Shrady, George F Dr, 1907, D 1,11:5
Shrady, George F Mrs, 1945, Ja 13,11:1
Shrady, Henry M Mrs, 1946, Ag 1,23:5
Shrady, Henry Merwin, 1922, Ap 13,19:5
Shrady, John Dr, 1914, N 12,13:4
Shrage, Robert I R, 1959, Mr 5,31:4
Shrager, Herman L, 1952, My 30,15:3
Shred, Charles F, 1949, Ap 3,77:1
Shreeve, Herbert E, 1942, Ap 26,39:3
Shreffler, Arthur L, 1951, Ag 11,11:5
Shreiner, Charles W, 1964, O 30,37:1
Shreve, Benjamin D, 1957, Jl 26,19:3
Shreve, Charles T, 1954, Ja 8,21:4
Shreve, Charles T Mrs, 1954, Jl 13,23:4
Shreve, Charles U Mrs, 1942, D 6,76:1
Shreve, Ephraim Mrs, 1953, My 13,29:3
Shreve, Eugene S, 1949, Ja 12,27:5
Shreve, Harriet, 1951, N 16,25:3
Shreve, Kate M (will), 1949, N 4,5:1
Shreve, Milton W, 1939, D 24,14:7
Shreve, Richmond H (por),(funl, S 13,7:6; will, S 18,21:6), 1946, S 11,7:1
Shreve, Richmond H Mrs, 1960, S 6,35:3
Shreve, S H, 1884, N 29,2:6
Shreve, Wickliffe W, 1964, N 20,37:2
Shreves, Melvin L, 1962, Ag 4,19:3
Shrewsbury, Kenneth O, 1964, F 22,21:3
Shrewsbury, Roy R, 1957, F 5,23:1
Shrewsbury, William E, 1952, O 21,29:4
Shrewsbury, William J Dr, 1923, Jl 20,13:5
Shridharani, Krishnalal, 1960, Jl 24,64:4
Shrier, Martin, 1954, D 24,13:6
Shrier, Samuel (will), 1945, O 31,16:5
Shrigley, Alfred R, 1940, Mr 4,15:5
Shriner, Blanchard U, 1952, F 24,84:4
Shriner, Charles A, 1945, Mr 27,19:5
Shriner, J C, 1915, F 23,13:3
Shriner, Wilber L, 1953, D 25,17:5
Shripka, Harold F, 1954, Ja 15,19:1
Shrive, John George Rev, 1908, Mr 29,9:7
Shrive, William G Sr, 1940, Mr 28,23:6
Shriver, Alfred, 1963, Mr 8,12:1
Shriver, Alfred J, 1939, S 4,19:5
Shriver, Charles F, 1948, Je 24,25:2
Shriver, Charles M (por), 1949, O 3,17:3
Shriver, Christopher C, 1921, O 31,15:6
Shriver, Clarence, 1923, Ap 20,17:3
Shriver, Frank J, 1940, Jl 29,13:4
Shriver, George M, 1942, My 12,19:1
Shriver, Henry, 1947, Ja 1,33:4
Shriver, John B, 1915, Ap 12,9:6
Shriver, Robert S, 1942, Je 13,15:4
Shriver, William P, 1957, F 25,25:3
Shroder, William J, 1952, Jl 12,13:5
Shroeder, Harmon, 1908, Ap 3,9:6
Shrope, Newton, 1940, Ja 22,15:4
Shrope, Roy F, 1952, Ag 5,19:2
Shropshire, Elmo, 1959, Ja 26,29:4
Shropshire, Elmo Mrs, 1959, Ja 24,40:3
Shrubb, Alfie, 1964, Ap 25,29:3
Shrycock, William A, 1955, D 17,23:6
Shryer, Clarence L, 1938, Ja 5,21:2
Shryock, John K, 1947, Ag 26,23:4
Shryock, John K Rev, 1953, F 7,15:2
Shryock, Joseph G, 1956, Ag 31,17:5
Shryock, Thomas Gen, 1918, F 4,9:6
Shtafman, Jacob H, 1958, Je 18,33:4
Shteppa, Konstantin, 1958, N 20,35:5
Shtykov, Terenty F, 1964, O 28,45:4
Shu Shi-ying, 1964, O 14,3:2
Shuart, William H, 1944, N 19,50:5
Shub, Boris, 1965, Ag 21,54:3
Shubert, David, 1913, Ag 30,7:6
Shubert, Earl, 1948, Ja 31,19:5
Shubert, Edward E, 1918, My 6,13:2
Shubert, George E, 1946, My 11,27:1
Shubert, Harold, 1955, S 2,17:4
Shubert, Jacob J (funl, D 30,21:4), 1963, D 27,1:8
Shubert, Jacob J (will), 1964, Ja 7,37:1
Shubert, John (funl plans, N 19,31:1; funl, N 22,45:4), 1962, N 18,1:6
Shubert, John (will), 1964, Ja 30,18:1
Shubert, John J (will), 1963, Ag 9,1:1
Shubert, Joseph S, 1947, O 14,28:2
Shubert, Katherine Mrs, 1914, N 30,9:6
Shubert, Lee, 1953, D 26,1:4
Shubert, Milton I, 1967, Mr 8,46:1
Shubert, Sam S, 1905, My 13,2:5
Shubin, Alex, 1951, Je 2,19:5
Shubin, Murray J, 1956, Jl 26,25:3
Shubrick, W B Rear-Adm, 1874, My 28,4:6
Shuck, Otto C Mrs, 1939, My 29,15:4
Shuck, William C, 1954, My 13,29:2
Shudderth, Shelly E, 1962, O 8,23:3
Shue, Albert Mrs, 1961, Mr 11,21:5
Shueler, Frederick W, 1950, N 2,31:2
Shufeldt, Augustus W, 1952, N 12,27:5
Shufeldt, R W Adm, 1895, N 8,10:3
Shufelt, Frank, 1938, N 22,23:5
Shuff, John L, 1940, N 23,17:5
Shuffleton, Wilford P, 1943, My 22,13:1
Shuford, Forrest H, 1954, My 20,31:5
Shufro, Samuel, 1950, My 5,4:8
Shugar, Frank, 1964, Ag 7,29:3
Shugarts, Sadie Mrs, 1953, Ja 6,29:2
Shugg, Carleton Mrs, 1967, N 20,47:3
Shuglin, Nicholas, 1937, Ja 17,II,8:3
Shugrue, John, 1949, Ja 21,22:2
Shugrue, John J, 1946, S 19,31:5
Shugrue, Joseph A, 1961, My 12,26:5
Shugrue, Michael J, 1965, O 28,43:4
Shukuris, Avraam, 1953, Je 19,21:2
Shuler, Frank, 1944, O 3,23:5
Shuler, Frank J Mrs (por), 1939, D 3,60:6
Shuler, George K, 1942, O 17,15:2
Shulgin, Paul, 1952, My 27,27:3
Shulhof, Arthur, 1962, N 17,25:2
Shulhof, Otto B (por), 1940, Ja 5,19:1
Shuling, Jacobus J, 1952, S 9,31:4
Shulkin, Anatol, 1961, N 22,33:5
Shull, Charles A, 1962, S 24,29:5
Shull, Charles E Mrs, 1944, D 31,26:4
Shull, Deloss C, 1938, Je 9,23:4
Shull, Elliott C, 1964, D 17,41:2
Shull, George H, 1954, S 30,31:1
Shull, James W, 1937, My 13,25:6
Shull, Joseph H, 1944, Ag 9,17:2
Shull, Samuel E, 1945, Je 5,19:3
Shulman, Abraham, 1959, N 23,31:6
Shulman, Albert, 1968, Ag 8,33:4
Shulman, Alexander, 1945, Ja 13,11:6
Shulman, Charles E Rabbi (funl plans, Je 4,47:1), 1968, Je 3,45:1
Shulman, Emanuel, 1950, My 30,17:5
Shulman, Fred Mrs, 1965, Jl 3,19:5
Shulman, Harry, 1955, Mr 21,25:1
Shulman, Harry G, 1952, Ag 26,27:6
Shulman, Herbert Mrs, 1962, Jl 24,27:3
Shulman, Herman, 1945, Jl 24,23:2
Shulman, Isaac, 1944, Ag 4,13:6
Shulman, Julius, 1953, Ap 18,19:2
Shulman, Mark H, 1956, N 11,86:3
Shulman, Marshall D, 1956, N 5,31:5
Shulman, Matthew Mrs, 1956, S 3,29:4
Shulman, Max Mrs, 1963, My 18,13:2
Shulman, Ralph, 1940, D 23,19:5
Shulman, Samuel, 1945, O 8,15:5; 1962, Mr 6,35:1
Shulock, Barney B, 1948, Je 24,25:5
Shulsky, Louis, 1947, Ag 1,17:1
Shulter, H V, 1932, S 29,21:1
Shultis, Felix, 1938, Je 30,23:3
Shultis, George M, 1951, My 5,17:4
Shultis, Myron, 1950, F 1,29:3
Shultis, Roland A, 1948, F 12,23:3
Shultis, Wallace, 1944, Ag 27,33:1
Shultis, William K, 1943, N 17,25:3
Shultise, Samuel J Jr, 1946, D 7,21:4
Shults, Clyde C, 1963, N 5,31:4
Shults, Clyde E, 1952, Je 13,23:4
Shults, Fred P Mrs, 1958, F 20,25:4
Shults, John H, 1914, D 12,15:4
Shultz, Charles E, 1945, Ag 10,15:4
Shultz, Clifford G Mrs, 1962, Ag 18,19:5
Shultz, Leonard, 1952, F 2,13:6
Shultz, Maurice L, 1941, My 24,15:3
Shultz, Morris, 1952, N 5,27:1; 1961, Mr 14,35:2
Shultz, Paul T, 1954, S 12,84:8
Shulze, Martin B, 1955, Ag 15,9:2
Shumaker, Samuel, 1944, My 30,21:1
Shumaker, W H, 1958, Ap 30,33:3
Shuman, Abraham, 1918, Je 27,11:6
Shuman, Arno, 1939, Mr 28,23:3

Shuman, Bertram A, 1962, Ja 4,33:4
Shuman, David, 1957, D 5,35:3
Shuman, Davis, 1966, S 1,35:1
Shuman, Edwin A, 1942, Ja 8,21:5
Shuman, Edwin L, 1941, D 14,68:3
Shuman, Harry M, 1967, F 18,29:4
Shuman, Ik (Isaac), 1965, Je 17,33:4
Shuman, John B, 1956, Ap 9,27:5
Shuman, Paul, 1946, Ag 23,19:5
Shuman, Royal L, 1957, Mr 29,21:4
Shuman, Waldo I, 1957, Ja 28,23:4
Shumate, Frank B, 1953, F 18,31:1
Shumate, Hiram, 1948, Ja 2,23:2
Shumate, Nannie C Mrs, 1953, Ag 29,17:2
Shumate, Roger V, 1954, My 24,27:1
Shumberger, John C, 1958, S 17,37:1
Shumeyko, Stephen, 1962, Ag 14,31:2
Shumshere, Bishnu Prince, 1946, F 5,24:2
Shumshere, Rudra, 1963, F 14,14:4
Shumsky, Morris, 1953, Mr 13,27:2
Shumway, Daniel B, 1940, Ja 13,15:3
Shumway, Edward J, 1952, My 21,27:3
Shumway, Eric, 1951, My 29,18:8
Shumway, Everett W, 1940, Ag 28,19:3
Shumway, Franklin P, 1941, Ja 13,15:4
Shumway, H C (funl), 1884, My 9,8:6
Shumway, Lowell Mrs, 1950, Jl 20,25:6
Shumway, Milton A Ex-Justice, 1923, O 22,19:4
Shumway, Waldo, 1956, Mr 10,17:3
Shumway, Walter B Mrs, 1943, N 25,25:2
Shunfenthal, Benjamin, 1959, Ap 26,86:8
Shunfenthal, Chaim, 1953, D 11,31:2
Shunk, William F, 1907, Je 23,7:6
Shunway, Robert C, 1940, N 10,57:2
Shupe, Harry R, 1960, Ap 14,31:2
Shupe, Harry R Mrs, 1948, N 21,88:3
Shupp, Fred G, 1956, Ap 19,31:4
Shupp, Paul F, 1950, Ag 15,30:3
Shur, Benjamin C, 1948, Mr 15,23:4
Shurcliff, Arthur A, 1957, N 13,35:2
Shurcliff, Arthur A Mrs, 1959, Mr 2,27:4
Shure, Irving, 1968, Jl 23,39:2
Shure, Joseph, 1966, Ag 8,27:2
Shure, Joseph Mrs, 1960, D 23,19:2
Shure, Thomas P, 1951, Jl 10,27:4
Shurina, Stephen L, 1960, Jl 19,29:3
Shurkin, Jacob M, 1963, Jl 23,29:5
Shurr, Louis (funl plans, N 7,39:4), 1967, N 3,48:3
Shurter, Edwin D, 1946, O 16,27:4
Shurter, Elijah T, 1950, My 30,17:1
Shurter, Howard C, 1959, Jl 6,27:4
Shurtleff, Charles A, 1941, Ap 15,23:3
Shurtleff, Ernest W Rev, 1917, Ag 28,7:4
Shurtleff, Eugene K Mrs, 1943, F 4,23:5
Shurtleff, Harold R, 1938, D 7,23:2
Shurtleff, Harold R Mrs, 1951, S 2,48:6
Shurtleff, Harry C, 1949, N 17,29:6
Shurtleff, Maurice E, 1951, Ag 3,21:3
Shurtleff, N B Dr, 1874, O 19,5:6
Shurtleff, Roswell Morse, 1915, Ja 7,13:4
Shurtleft, Dwight W, 1940, Ja 18,23:5
Shurts, Frank E, 1958, Je 19,31:5
Shushan, Joseph Mrs, 1948, Mr 9,23:3
Shuster, Benjamin H, 1961, O 3,39:2
Shuster, Earle M, 1952, O 25,17:6
Shuster, George F, 1952, S 24,33:4
Shuster, Harry, 1958, Mr 20,29:5
Shuster, Howard B, 1950, Je 27,29:4
Shuster, P Atkins Mrs, 1952, Jl 18,19:2
Shuster, Theodore D, 1955, N 28,31:4
Shuster, W Morgan, 1960, My 27,31:4
Shuster, Wilbur D, 1964, Ag 6,29:1
Shuster, William, 1948, Ja 21,25:1
Shusterman, Harry L, 1952, Mr 6,31:2
Shute, Berrian R, 1961, Je 19,27:5
Shute, Berrian R Mrs, 1966, F 28,27:2
Shute, Daniel K Mrs, 1943, My 3,17:5
Shute, Emmett R, 1965, Jl 22,31:4
Shute, Frank F, 1944, Mr 20,17:2
Shute, Henry A, 1943, Ja 26,19:2
Shute, Hermon B, 1948, N 11,27:4
Shute, John, 1948, S 14,29:5
Shute, Katherine H, 1939, Ja 22,35:1
Shute, Nevil (N S Norway),(funl plans, Ja 14,33:1), 1960, Ja 13,47:1
Shuter, E Mortimer, 1939, N 12,48:8
Shuter, William T, 1945, O 2,23:4
Shuter, William T Mrs, 1947, Mr 18,27:2
Shutes, Mary A, 1951, My 23,35:3
Shutorev, Nicolay, 1948, S 22,31:1
Shutt, George M (por), 1938, Je 9,23:2
Shutt, George M Mrs, 1943, Ag 6,15:4
Shutt, George P, 1958, Je 14,21:6
Shutt, William E, 1924, Ja 26,13:2
Shutta, Charles, 1944, Ja 16,43:1
Shutta, Jack, 1957, Je 30,69:2
Shutter, William J, 1943, Ap 10,17:1
Shuttleworth, Arthur W, 1940, Ja 28,32:1
Shuttleworth, E Irving, 1949, D 13,38:3
Shuttleworth, Edwin, 1949, F 11,24:2
Shuttleworth, Lord, 1939, D 22,19:4
Shuttleworth, W A Col (funl), 1871, O 2,8:4
Shuttleworth, Walter W, 1952, Mr 26,29:2

Shutts, Frank B (por), 1947, Ja 8,23:5
Shutz, Earl L, 1961, Jl 17,21:2
Shutz, Lawrence J, 1922, Ap 17,17:6
Shuvlin, Anthony C, 1943, N 7,56:6
Shuyler, Thomas Capt, 1866, O 1,2:4
Shvernik, Nikolai M Mme, 1959, Ja 23,26:1
Shvetsov, Arkadii D, 1953, Mr 23,23:2
Shvetsov, Vasily I, 1958, O 4,21:4
Shwalberg, Alfred W Mrs, 1950, O 24,29:4
Shwartzman, Gregory, 1965, Jl 24,21:4
Shwitzer, Samuel D, 1967, Mr 24,31:1
Shy, G Milton, 1967, S 26,47:3
Shy, Gus, 1945, Je 17,26:8
Shydlower, Nathan, 1955, Ag 11,21:5
Siam, King of, 1868, N 17,5:3
Siani, Severino, 1964, Je 9,35:1
Siano, Frank E, 1955, D 15,37:5
Siantos, George, 1947, My 21,25:5
Sias, William H Mrs, 1951, S 25,29:2
Sibal, Charles L Mrs, 1961, D 30,19:2
Sibbald, Reginald M, 1942, Ap 19,44:7
Sibbald, Robert A, 1940, Mr 12,23:5
Sibbel, Joseph, 1907, Jl 12,7:6
Sibbern, F K, 1901, O 6,4:7
Sibbers, Louis Mrs, 1945, Jl 14,11:4
Sibbons, H, 1941, Jl 18,19:6
Sibelis, Andrew Bro, 1941, O 1,21:3
Sibelius, Jean (funl plans, S 22,69:4; funl, O 1,34:1), 1957, S 21,1:3
Sibenaler, Charles, 1940, Je 20,23:5
Sibenman, Henry A, 1939, S 17,48:7
Siber, Sidney Sr Mrs, 1944, F 15,17:5
Sibert, W L, 1935, O 17,23:1
Siberts, Samuel W Rev Dr, 1908, Mr 6,7:5
Sibilia, Enrico, 1948, Ag 5,21:3
Sible, John F, 1956, F 12,88:7
Sibler, Charles J, 1959, Mr 14,23:6
Sibley, A H Maj, 1878, Jl 11,8:1
Sibley, Charles L, 1946, Je 4,23:4
Sibley, Charles T, 1957, S 6,21:5
Sibley, E Forrest, 1943, Ag 29,39:2
Sibley, E S Col, 1884, Ag 15,4:7
Sibley, Edward C, 1949, Ja 8,15:2
Sibley, Eugene B Mrs, 1948, Ja 2,23:2
Sibley, F Haviland, 1953, Jl 27,19:2
Sibley, Florence, 1952, Ag 30,13:4
Sibley, Frank P, 1949, N 16,29:6
Sibley, Frederick H, 1941, Ap 4,21:3
Sibley, Frederick W Gen, 1918, F 19,13:6
Sibley, H, 1888, Jl 13,5:1
Sibley, Harper, 1959, Ap 26,86:5
Sibley, Harper (est tax appr), 1961, Ap 7,40:1
Sibley, Homer W, 1939, O 17,25:2
Sibley, J C, 1926, My 20,25:3
Sibley, J Ross, 1965, O 21,47:2
Sibley, John H, 1948, S 29,29:6
Sibley, John R (Oct 8), 1965, O 11,61:5
Sibley, Margaret D H Mrs, 1939, My 29,15:4
Sibley, Robert L, 1957, Ag 21,27:3
Sibley, Robert P, 1957, N 4,29:4
Sibley, Walter G, 1958, Mr 1,17:6
Sibley, Walter K, 1949, Mr 13,77:1
Sibole, Barton P, 1945, Je 7,19:2
Sibour, Mary de Countess, 1912, Ag 12,9:6
Sibray, William W, 1924, N 2,7:1
Sibson, Denis E Mrs, 1946, Ag 29,27:2
Sibson, Horace E, 1946, S 20,31:4
Sibson, Walter W Jr, 1964, Ag 26,39:1
Sica, Louis J, 1944, Ag 21,15:6
Sica, Samuel L Mrs, 1943, Jl 18,35:2
Sicard, Adrian Mrs, 1955, D 1,35:2
Sicard, Boland, 1968, D 17,47:1
Sicard, Charles L, 1937, N 20,17:5
Sicard, George M, 1942, Ja 8,21:2
Sicard, Montgomery Rear Adm, 1900, S 15,6:6
Sicard, Nicolas, 1920, Ja 4,23:3
Sicardo, Rafael L Dr, 1937, D 23,22:4
Sicari, William, 1962, F 15,29:3
Sicault, Charles, 1947, Je 8,60:4
Sicca, Michele, 1945, Mr 25,38:1
Sichberg, Joseph P Mrs, 1943, Ap 24,13:3
Sichel, Arthur A, 1949, Ja 12,28:3
Sichel, Charles H, 1963, O 17,35:2
Sichel, Eugene, 1949, Je 8,30:5
Sichel, Eugene A, 1963, S 20,33:1
Sichel, Ferdinand, 1957, O 25,27:3
Sichel, Ferdinand Mrs (Etta K), 1962, O 11,39:5
Sichel, Franz W, 1967, O 24,47:1
Sichel, Moritz F, 1965, Mr 29,36:2
Sichel, Walter Mrs, 1960, Ag 5,23:2
Sicher, David E, 1914, Ja 24,9:4
Sicher, Dudley D (por), 1939, D 30,15:1
Sicher, Dudley D (ed), 1940, Ja 1,22:3
Sicher, Dudley D Mrs, 1938, Jl 1,19:3
Sicher, Dudley F, 1957, N 16,19:3
Sicher, Lydia, 1962, Ap 4,43:1
Sicher, Samuel A, 1940, Ja 2,19:4
Sichert, Paul O, 1954, Jl 1,25:2
Sichler, Jacob, 1942, Mr 31,21:5
Sicignano, Antonio, 1909, Ag 21,7:2
Siciliano, Domenico, 1938, My 7,5:6
Siciliano, Samuel, 1955, Mr 2,27:5
Sick, Frederick, 1953, N 20,23:1

Sickel, Edward W, 1941, My 20,23:3
Sickel, Welling G, 1911, Jl 16,II,9:5
Sickels, Avery C, 1938, F 7,15:3
Sickels, Elizabeth Mrs (Grandma), 1910, Ap 19,9:5
Sickels, Irvin (por), 1943, Ag 6,15:2
Sickels, John S, 1957, D 6,29:4
Sickels, Martha O P Mrs, 1939, My 30,17:2
Sickels, Walter N, 1952, Ja 19,15:4
Sicker, Joseph, 1950, My 24,29:4
Sickert, Walter R (por), 1942, Ja 24,17:1
Sickinger, Kenneth W, 1953, Ag 20,27:3
Sickle, Horatio G 3d, 1947, F 14,21:3
Sickler, Barclay J, 1950, Mr 16,31:4
Sickler, Charles A, 1940, Jl 23,19:4
Sickler, William A, 1943, Ja 20,19:1
Sickles, A Leon, 1953, N 25,23:4
Sickles, Arthur B, 1950, S 1,21:2
Sickles, Capt, 1872, Ja 15,1:6
Sickles, Charles, 1955, Ap 26,29:2
Sickles, Charles T Mrs, 1949, Ja 16,69:2
Sickles, Daniel E Maj-Gen, 1914, My 10,IV,7:6
Sickles, Daniel Mrs, 1919, Jl 19,9:6
Sickles, David B Mrs, 1911, F 12,12:5
Sickles, David Banks, 1918, Jl 20,9:8
Sickles, Eugene C, 1946, Ap 13,17:4
Sickles, Frederick J, 1964, Ja 31,27:1
Sickles, George S, 1939, F 19,39:3
Sickles, Grandon, 1940, O 24,25:5
Sickles, H George, 1955, Jl 18,21:1
Sickles, J B, 1876, My 12,7:5
Sickles, Julia Mrs, 1942, F 13,21:2
Sickles, Lloyd N, 1962, My 29,31:5
Sickles, Solomon, 1944, D 8,21:1
Sickles, Willard J, 1938, Jl 1,19:6
Sickley, Cyrus W Mrs, 1943, Ap 1,23:2
Sickley, Elmer, 1959, Ja 28,31:2
Siclis, Charles, 1942, My 10,42:6
Sicuranza, Michael, 1951, My 29,19:8
Sidamon-Eristoff, George Prince, 1953, Ja 25,85:1
Sidamon-Eristoff, Simon C Prince, 1964, S 15,37:2
Siddall, Hugh, 1948, Je 29,23:4
Siddall, Thomas G, 1945, Jl 29,40:7
Siddeley, John D (Lord Kenilworth), 1953, N 4,3
Siddik el Mahdi, Sayed, 1961, O 3,39:3
Siddiqui, Abdur R, 1953, My 27,31:5
Siddons, F L, 1931, Je 20,17:1
Side, Joseph, 1956, Ag 25,15:3
Sidebotham, Herbert, 1940, Mr 20,34:7
Sidebotham, Thomas D, 1915, Ag 27,9:6
Sidell, W H Gen, 1873, Jl 2,4:7
Sideman, Monte Mrs, 1958, O 4,21:5
Sidenberg, George M, 1943, Mr 31,19:6; 1954, Jl 2 17:4
Sidenberg, Gustavus, 1915, Ja 23,11:5
Sidenberg, Henry, 1925, F 6,17:5
Sidenberg, Joseph W, 1964, Ag 1,21:5
Sidenberg, William R, 1961, F 20,27:1
Sidenberg, William R Mrs, 1941, Ag 7,17:1
Sidener, Fred E, 1950, Jl 11,31:3
Sidener, Merle, 1948, My 11,25:5
Siders, Walter R, 1961, Ap 6,33:3
Sides, Arthur C, 1962, D 7,34:4
Sides, Nettie A Mrs, 1941, F 27,19:4
Sides, Samuel, 1946, My 14,21:4
Sides, W Herman Mrs, 1940, Mr 21,25:5
Sides, Winfield M, 1959, Ja 11,88:3
Sidford, Aubrey J, 1951, N 17,17:6
Sidford, Henry G, 1942, D 27,34:4
Sidford, Henry G Mrs, 1954, S 29,31:3
Sidford, Noel D, 1950, Je 30,23:2
Sidford, Noel D Mrs, 1940, Ag 14,19:2
Sidgreaves, Arthur F, 1948, Je 8,25:2
Sidgwick, Nevil V, 1952, Mr 17,21:4
Sidgwick, Rose (funl, D 31,11:4), 1918, D 30,9:2
Sidgwick, Rose (funl, Ja 2,9:2), 1919, Ja 1,17:2
Sidi Ahmed II, Bey of Tunis (por), 1942, Je 20,1
Sidis, Boris Dr, 1923, O 25,19:6
Sidis, Sarah, 1959, Jl 12,72:8
Sidis, William J, 1944, Jl 18,21:4
Sidky, Fatma H, 1946, N 19,31:6
Sidky Pasha, Ismail, 1950, Jl 10,21:3
Sidley, John, 1903, Mr 19,9:5
Sidley, John (daughter of), 1903, Mr 19,9:5
Sidley, Maybelle H Mrs, 1938, Jl 8,2:4
Sidley, William H (death laid to heart attack, Ag 23,51:2), 1963, Ag 14,8:5
Sidlo, Thomas L, 1955, My 28,15:2
Sidlowski, Carol, 1963, Jl 31,57:7
Sidman, Alfred G, 1965, F 17,43:3
Sidman, C A, 1928, Ja 11,29:3
Sidman, Henry L, 1944, Mr 8,19:1
Sidman, Samuel, 1948, Ja 4,52:3
Sidmouth, Viscount (G W Addington), 1953, Ap 19:5
Sidner, Alvan V, 1951, Jl 24,25:5
Sidney, Carl, 1958, F 2,86:6
Sidney, Clara, 1924, My 29,19:6
Sidney, Fred H, 1951, Ap 17,29:3
Sidney, Frederick W Mrs, 1946, S 18,31:2
Sidney, George, 1945, Ap 30,19:2
Sidney, Louis K, 1958, F 23,92:2
Sidney, Robert, 1939, F 21,19:4
Sidney, Sigmund, 1961, F 18,19:1

Sido, George H, 1955, Ap 1,28:2
Sidonia, Thomas, 1954, Je 17,29:2
Sidor, Karol, 1953, O 22,29:5
Sidore, Saul O, 1964, Ja 8,37:4
Sidway, Chester, 1950, Ag 15,29:1
Sidway, Frank S, 1938, Ja 18,23:4
Siebel, Frederick P, 1957, Je 18,33:1
Siebel, John W, 1942, O 12,19:6
Siebel, Peter, 1949, Mr 5,17:4
Sieben, Bernard F, 1946, S 12,7:4
Sieben, Isabelle N Mrs, 1949, Ap 11,25:5
Sieben, Jean, 1942, Ap 18,15:4
Siebenberg, Louis, 1959, My 1,29:3
Siebeneichen, Carl W, 1941, Ag 10,37:2
Siebens, Allen C, 1966, S 26,41:4
Siebenthaler, Clarence O, 1950, O 12,31:4
Sieber, J O, 1959, Je 7,86:3
Sieberg, Jacob, 1963, Ag 22,27:4
Sieberg, Jacob Mrs, 1940, Je 9,45:2
Sieberg, William H J, 1911, Ag 4,7:6
Siebern, Emil, 1942, Je 15,19:4
Siebern, Milton Mrs, 1964, N 4,39:1
Siebert, Amanda Mrs, 1940, N 28,25:3
Siebert, Carl J Mrs, 1952, Ag 2,15:6
Siebert, Donald W, 1955, Mr 13,87:1
Siebert, Edward S, 1944, F 1,19:5
Siebert, Frank A, 1948, D 21,31:1
Siebert, Jacob A Capt, 1912, S 15,II,15:6
Siebert, Louis P Col, 1914, N 27,11:6
Siebert, Louis P Mrs, 1915, Je 23,11:4
Siebert, Ludwig, 1942, N 2,21:6
Siebert, Otto, 1941, Ag 23,13:6
Siebert, William C, 1956, My 3,31:4
Siebert, William H, 1950, Je 23,25:4
Siebott, Henry D E, 1954, Je 16,31:4
Siebrecht, H A, 1934, Je 20,21:3
Siebrecht, William H, 1939, Ag 20,33:3
Sieburg, Charles, 1952, O 21,29:5
Sieck, J Henry, 1962, S 4,31:6
Sieck, Louis J, 1952, O 15,31:4
Siedenberg, George H, 1955, F 6,88:1
Siedenburg, Frederic, 1939, F 21,19:1
Siedenburg, George R, 1941, Ap 6,48:3
Siedenburg, Henry D, 1950, S 22,31:4
Siedenburg, Reinhard Mrs, 1967, F 13,33:1
Sieder, Aug, 1940, F 22,23:5
Siedle, Edward (funl, Ap 1,23:4), 1925, Mr 31,19:3
Siedle, Edward Mrs, 1907, F 28,9:6
Siedle, Edward V, 1965, Jl 7,37:1
Siedler, Charles W, 1960, Ja 22,27:4
Siedler, Howard D, 1955, F 22,13:5
Sieferman, William Mrs, 1953, Ap 17,26:4
Sieferstorpff, John C, 1944, D 7,25:1
Siefert, Francis, 1947, My 19,21:3
Sieff, Lady (Mrs Israel M), 1966, Ja 9,56:5
Siefken, George R, 1951, Jl 21,13:6
Siegal, Dora Mrs, 1948, Ag 28,15:2
Siegal, Moses, 1956, S 15,17:4
Siegal, William, 1956, Ag 31,17:3
Siegartel, Morris, 1964, F 22,21:4
Siegbert, Henry, 1967, My 6,31:2
Siegbert, Julius, 1948, My 22,15:1
Siegbert, Samuel, 1905, F 23,12:7; 1905, Mr 16,9:7
Siegel, Abraham, 1939, D 12,27:2; 1963, Ap 12,27:2
Siegel, Abraham H, 1958, F 13,29:2
Siegel, Abraham M, 1960, N 4,33:2
Siegel, Abraham Mrs, 1950, O 30,27:1
Siegel, Alexander B, 1954, Ja 30,17:3
Siegel, Alfred E, 1949, Je 25,13:1
Siegel, Amanda F Mrs, 1945, Ag 10,17:3
Siegel, Benjamin, 1921, Ap 11,11:3; 1954, Je 14,21:5
Siegel, Caroline W Mrs, 1916, Ja 27,11:2
Siegel, Chaim H, 1942, Ja 31,17:1
Siegel, Charles H, 1949, Ap 5,30:5
Siegel, Charles J (por), 1948, D 23,19:3
Siegel, Charles M, 1953, My 13,29:2
Siegel, Chester A, 1943, Ap 4,40:5
Siegel, David I Mrs, 1956, N 7,31:1
Siegel, David P, 1958, Je 19,31:6
Siegel, David P Mrs, 1962, S 24,29:3
Siegel, Edward L, 1962, Mr 2,30:2
Siegel, Ferdinand Dr, 1920, My 27,11:4
Siegel, Francis E, 1950, Ap 9,86:5
Siegel, Frederick Mrs, 1949, Jl 23,11:5
Siegel, Gerson Mrs, 1907, N 12,9:5
Siegel, Henry, 1966, S 30,47:1
Siegel, Henry Mrs, 1946, Jl 3,25:5
Siegel, Henry W, 1943, D 31,15:1
Siegel, Isadore, 1954, F 27,13:5
Siegel, Isidor, 1957, Ag 18,83:1
Siegel, Jacob, 1938, D 13,25:4; 1942, Ap 9,19:2
Siegel, Jacob J, 1960, S 14,43:3
Siegel, Jacob Mrs, 1956, Je 6,33:4
Siegel, Jerome, 1940, S 16,19:5
Siegel, John, 1941, F 28,19:2
Siegel, Joseph, 1913, Je 28,7:5; 1938, D 10,17:3; 1941, Ja 18,15:2; 1941, F 20,19:5; 1947, S 14,60:8
Siegel, Joseph E, 1959, Ap 20,31:3
Siegel, Joseph G, 1962, O 31,37:3
Siegel, Joseph H, 1951, O 26,23:5
Siegel, Kaufman Mrs, 1949, Ja 30,60:4
Siegel, Leah G Mrs, 1940, F 14,21:5
Siegel, Leo Mrs, 1967, Ja 28,27:4
Siegel, Lou G, 1965, My 18,39:4
Siegel, Louis, 1939, Ja 30,14:1; 1955, Je 25,15:5; 1962, Ja 9,47:2
Siegel, Louis A Mrs, 1948, D 24,17:1
Siegel, Louis H, 1949, Ag 24,25:1
Siegel, Louis J, 1966, S 27,47:4
Siegel, Max, 1952, F 10,93:1
Siegel, Max (trb lr, N 30,II,3:7), 1958, N 17,31:6
Siegel, Max, 1966, S 28,47:2
Siegel, Milton R, 1964, N 12,37:4
Siegel, Morris A, 1964, S 2,37:4
Siegel, Morris H, 1945, F 9,15:3
Siegel, Morris J, 1948, Ag 31,23:4
Siegel, Morris W, 1956, Mr 4,88:3
Siegel, Mortimer Mrs, 1950, Mr 8,27:3
Siegel, Moses, 1958, Ja 10,26:3
Siegel, Norman, 1961, Ja 25,20:7
Siegel, Philip, 1964, Je 2,37:4
Siegel, Robert, 1959, O 5,31:1
Siegel, Samuel T, 1948, F 18,27:3
Siegel, Sarah Mrs, 1941, Ag 19,21:6
Siegel, Sidney, 1961, D 3,88:4
Siegel, Sol, 1964, Je 6,23:4
Siegel, Sol C Mrs, 1962, Ap 2,31:2
Siegel, William, 1966, My 24,43:6
Siegelack, Francis O, 1943, D 8,23:4
Siegelack, John W Mrs, 1954, Je 6,86:5
Siegele, August Jr, 1967, F 22,29:4
Siegelstein, Pierre A Dr, 1922, Ag 10,11:6
Sieger, Charlie, 1951, Mr 30,23:4
Siegert, A F, 1883, N 4,5:3
Siegert, William P, 1948, O 22,25:1
Siegfried, Andre, 1959, Mr 30,31:3
Siegfried, Clarence S, 1957, Mr 14,29:5
Siegfried, Frederick H, 1918, My 27,13:5
Siegfried, Harry D, 1952, O 25,17:1
Siegfried, Howard J, 1939, Je 29,23:6
Siegfried, Lute L, 1951, F 5,23:1
Siegk, Arthur M, 1937, Je 17,23:2
Siegle, Arthur, 1964, D 9,50:8
Siegler, Abraham J, 1968, S 30,47:1
Siegler, C Louis, 1946, N 25,27:3
Siegler, Caroline D Mrs, 1938, My 18,21:4
Siegler, George B, 1963, Jl 22,23:3
Siegler, Joseph, 1957, My 18,19:6
Siegler, Samuel L, 1953, S 16,33:5
Siegman, Charles, 1946, My 21,23:2
Siegman, Charles Mrs, 1945, My 16,19:1
Siegman, Emil J, 1949, Ja 12,27:3
Siegman, Peter P, 1949, D 29,26:2
Siegman, Sidney B, 1951, O 17,31:4
Siegmann, John F P, 1940, O 11,21:2
Siegmeister, Isaac, 1967, F 11,29:3
Siegmeister, Isador, 1945, Ja 25,19:1
Siegmund, G F, 1884, F 26,5:3
Siegmund, Humphreys O, 1957, Je 7,24:2
Siegmund, Reinhold O, 1951, Ap 14,15:2
Siegried, Alfred, 1944, Je 25,30:2
Siegrist, David W, 1946, Jl 18,25:3
Siegrist, Henry G, 1962, Mr 18,86:4
Siegrist, Mary, 1953, Mr 17,29:1
Siegrist, William Jr, 1943, S 17,21:4
Siehl, Walter H, 1955, My 31,27:1
Siehr, Ernest, 1946, Ja 28,19:1
Sieker, Otto, 1940, S 6,21:3
Siekert, Hugo P, 1947, S 30,25:4
Sielcken, Hermann, 1917, N 23,11:4
Sielski, Stanley, 1952, Je 12,33:3
Siemann, Charles R, 1941, N 18,25:2
Siemens, arnold von, 1918, My 1,13:5
Siemens, C W Dr, 1883, N 21,4:6
Siemens, Carl F von, 1941, Jl 11,15:1
Siemens, E W Dr, 1892, D 7,5:3
Siemens, Wilhelm von, 1919, O 17,17:5
Siemer, August, 1924, Jl 9,19:6
Siemer, Frederick J, 1938, Ag 2,19:4
Siemer, Henry, 1946, Ag 4,46:1
Siemer, John A, 1946, S 20,31:1
Siemering, Henry Mrs, 1945, Ag 12,39:1
Siemering, Rudolf, 1905, Ja 25,9:5
Siemers, Gustav F, 1959, Ap 14,35:3
Siemers, Julius, 1941, Ag 1,15:6
Siemers, Theodore, 1922, D 11,17:4
Sieminski, Edmund, 1955, My 5,33:2
Sieminski, Henry, 1941, Je 2,17:4
Sieminski, Stanley, 1940, D 15,61:3
Sieminski, Stanley Mrs, 1968, Mr 10,92:4
Siemiradzki, Thomas, 1940, Mr 27,21:5
Siemon, George, 1947, Ap 16,25:2
Siemon, William F, 1948, Jl 9,19:5
Siemonn, George, 1952, N 22,24:5
Siemonn, George Mrs (M Garrison), 1963, Ag 22, 27:3
Siemons, Josiah M, 1948, My 2,76:5
Siems, August W, 1946, Ap 26,21:3
Siems, Chester P, 1918, O 24,13:1
Siems, Valentine B, 1946, F 16,13:3
Siemsen, Frederick, 1957, Ap 20,17:2
Siemund, Henry L, 1955, Ag 26,19:3
Siener, Edward A, 1958, F 14,23:5
Sienkiewicz, Henryk, 1916, N 17,9:1; 1924, O 27,19:5
Sientz, Michael I, 1958, Je 29,68:8
Sieper, Ernst, 1916, Ja 8,9:5
Siepert, Albert F, 1947, My 1,25:5
Sierck, Herbert C, 1938, D 9,25:4
Sierichs, Henry, 1916, F 9,11:5
Siering, Eugene R, 1960, O 6,41:5
Siering, Eugene R Mrs, 1960, Ja 24,88:3
Siering, Walter A, 1957, D 2,27:5
Sierks, Charles H, 1954, Jl 10,13:6
Sierks, Ted, 1959, S 6,72:8
Sieroty, Adolph, 1937, Mr 3,23:4
Sierra, Guadalupe Mrs, 1943, Ap 13,8:6
Sierra, Justo, 1912, S 14,13:6
Sierra, Margarita, 1963, S 7,19:4
Sierra Berdecia, Fernando, 1962, Ja 22,23:2
Sierstorpff, Johannes Count, 1917, Ja 15,9:5
Siesel, Harold J, 1955, Ap 17,86:6
Siesel, Harold J Mrs, 1965, N 28,88:5
Siesel, William F, 1952, My 31,17:3
Siess, Charles W Mrs, 1955, F 27,86:3
Siess, George P, 1942, S 27,49:2
Siess, Henry Mrs, 1946, S 3,19:4
Siess, Mildred H, 1950, My 16,31:2
Siessel, George C, 1949, Je 7,32:7
Siet, Solomon, 1937, My 18,23:2
Sievering, Philip, 1943, My 6,19:4
Sievers, Charles, 1954, Ap 16,21:3
Sievers, Harry, 1939, Ja 3,17:4
Sievers, Herman, 1947, D 20,17:1
Sievers, Maurice J Mrs, 1956, O 20,21:2
Sievers, Walter R, 1953, Jl 12,65:1
Sievers, William H, 1942, Je 21,37:2
Sievert, Henry S, 1939, F 14,19:4
Sievert, Leo E, 1962, My 3,33:2
Sievier, Robert S, 1939, O 9,19:4
Siewek, Walter J, 1951, Mr 7,33:3
Siewerts, Frederick E B, 1937, S 26,II,8:4
Siexas, Claude L, 1954, My 6,33:5
Siff, H A, 1954, N 11,31:2
Siff, Henry, 1939, Je 21,23:5
Siff, Hilda, 1966, Je 22,47:3
Siffert, George D, 1938, Je 15,23:5
Siffken, F E, 1880, F 12,2:5
Sifton, Arthur Lewis, 1921, Ja 22,11:4
Sifton, C, 1929, Ap 18,29:5
Sifton, Clifford Lady, 1925, F 20,17:3
Sifton, Clifford MacLean, 1953, F 27,21:1
Sifton, Elizabeth A B, 1950, F 27,19:4
Sifton, Victor, 1961, Ap 22,25:3
Sigal, Herman N Mrs, 1954, S 18,15:5
Sigala, Marcus, 1950, Mr 14,25:1
Sigall, Joseph, 1953, S 18,23:5
Sigall, Louis M, 1960, N 10,47:1
Sigaloff, Eugene, 1960, Ja 17,86:8
Sigel, Albert J Mrs, 1949, Ja 8,15:6
Sigel, Eleanor R Mrs, 1952, Ja 4,23:4
Sigel, Frank Gen, 1902, Ag 22,9:5
Sigel, Franz, 1922, F 20,11:4
Sigel, Franz Mrs, 1910, Ja 18,11:4
Sigelstein, Nathan, 1951, Ag 18,11:4
Sigendall, George S, 1949, N 24,31:1
Sigerist, Henry E, 1957, Mr 18,27:3
Sigerson, George Dr, 1925, F 18,19:3
Sigerson, John J Sr, 1959, Ja 18,88:2
Sigfried, Clara A Mrs, 1942, Jl 21,20:4
Siggins, Ernest L Mrs, 1951, Mr 31,30:6
Sigismondi, Pietro, 1967, My 27,31:1
Sigl, Alphonse J, 1966, Ag 11,33:2
Sigler, Charles E, 1959, Mr 30,31:1
Sigler, Frank, 1949, My 12,31:3
Sigler, Henry, 1962, Je 5,41:1
Sigler, Isaac, 1937, My 25,27:4
Sigler, Jay C, 1948, Jl 16,19:1
Sigler, Kim, 1953, D 1,2:7
Sigler, Kim Mrs, 1963, O 25,31:2
Sigler, Maurice, 1961, F 7,33:4
Sigler, Russell V, 1952, Ag 13,21:4
Sigler, Thomas H, 1960, My 29,56:3
Sigman, Abraham N, 1959, D 25,21:3
Sigman, George A, 1937, D 3,23:5
Sigman, Harry, 1959, F 2,25:3
Sigman, J William, 1954, D 10,27:3
Sigman, James G, 1940, S 15,49:2
Sigman, Louis K, 1953, My 4,23:4
Sigman, M, 1931, Jl 21,21:1
Sigman, Morris Mrs, 1946, Ag 25,46:1
Sigmans, Arnold, 1949, F 6,77:1
Sigmond, Sven O (por), 1944, Ja 14,19:2
Sigmund, Benjamin J, 1956, S 1,15:4
Sigmund, Carl F, 1952, D 9,33:4
Sigmund, Paul E, 1959, Je 15,27:2
Signer, Isador, 1953, Ja 9,21:2
Signor, Charles G, 1960, S 14,43:2
Signor, William, 1951, Ap 17,29:4
Signoret, Gabriel, 1937, Mr 17,26:2
Signoriello, Pelligrino, 1945, Mr 11,39:1
Signorini, Giovanni, 1954, D 24,13:3
Sigourney, Andrew W, 1941, D 31,17:4
Sigourney, L H Mrs (funl, Je 16,4:1), 1865, Je 12,8:2
Sigourney, Louis, 1940, Je 29,15:6
Sigray, Antal Count, 1947, D 28,40:7
Sigray, Antal Countess, 1950, Je 1,27:2
Sigretto, Joseph L, 1940, O 17,25:5
Sigsbee, Charles Dwight Rear-Adm (por), 1923, Jl 20,13:4

Sigurdsson, Joseph, 1880, Ja 24,2:3
Sigurdsson, Sigurgeir, 1953, O 14,29:3
Sihler, Ernest G, 1942, Ja 8,21:3
Siihring, Albert, 1939, D 10,69:2
Siino, Salvatore, 1963, O 9,43:2
Sikelianos, Angelos Mrs, 1952, Je 5,31:1
Sikes, Clara O Mrs, 1953, F 25,27:4
Sikes, Enoch W, 1941, Ja 9,21:5
Sikes, Franklin V, 1954, N 12,21:1
Sikes, Frederick Jr, 1957, D 7,21:3
Sikes, J V, 1964, My 21,35:4
Sikes, Lincoln Y, 1944, F 27,38:3
Sikevich, Vladimir, 1952, Jl 29,21:2
Sikkim, Maharaja of (Namgyal), 1963, D 3,3:1
Sikora, Alexander, 1946, N 24,79:7
Sikorski, John J, 1950, S 20,31:4
Silagy, Joseph M, 1968, Ja 20,29:3
Silance, Louis M, 1955, N 5,19:5
Silber, Samuel, 1961, D 30,19:6
Silber, Samuel S, 1951, My 10,31:5
Silber, Saul, 1946, S 2,17:6
Silber, Sol Mrs, 1949, S 21,31:5
Silber, William B Dr, 1906, My 7,9:6
Silberbach, Martha, 1954, Ap 15,29:5
Silberbauer, Charles (Boom Boom), 1953, My 22,27:1
Silberberg, Abraham A, 1941, N 11,23:2
Silberberg, Alex, 1952, Mr 9,92:5
Silberberg, Mendel B, 1965, Je 30,37:1
Silberberg, Willy, 1959, N 26,37:5
Silberblatt, Theodore, 1967, Ap 30,87:1
Silberfarb, Jacob I, 1967, Ag 2,37:2
Silberfeld, John, 1913, O 20,7:4
Silberfeld, Julius, 1957, D 27,19:3
Silberg, Murray, 1964, Mr 12,35:4
Silbergleit, J Charles, 1943, S 18,17:4
Silbergleit, Jasper Mrs, 1962, Ag 31,21:5
Silberling, Louis J, 1962, S 24,29:3
Silberman, Abris, 1968, D 24,20:1
Silberman, Alfred M, 1948, D 22,23:4
Silberman, Alfred M Mrs, 1951, F 19,23:5
Silberman, Benedict, 1961, Ja 10,47:3
Silberman, Benjamin, 1966, Mr 28,33:2
Silberman, Charles S, 1950, Ap 26,29:5
Silberman, David, 1943, Mr 17,21:4
Silberman, Elkan, 1952, My 16,23:3
Silberman, Isadore, 1960, D 22,26:3
Silberman, Isidore M, 1961, My 19,31:4
Silberman, J D, 1966, S 24,23:6
Silberman, Max, 1952, Mr 9,93:1
Silberman, Tanchum, 1944, Je 7,19:6
Silbermann, Jesse (por), 1947, My 18,60:1
Silbermann, Milton, 1952, N 18,31:3
Silbernagel, Raoul P, 1949, O 29,3:2
Silberrad, Oswald J, 1960, Je 18,23:4
Silbersack, Walter F, 1960, Je 8,39:2
Silberstein, Adolf, 1958, Jl 29,17:4
Silberstein, Adolf Mrs, 1958, Jl 29,17:4
Silberstein, Alfred J, 1957, O 14,27:4
Silberstein, David Mrs, 1953, S 4,15:3
Silberstein, Emanuel I, 1939, S 2,17:7
Silberstein, Harry, 1957, F 12,27:6
Silberstein, Herman B, 1937, Ap 28,23:5
Silberstein, John I, 1904, My 4,9:6
Silberstein, Joseph, 1956, Ag 12,84:1
Silberstein, Ludwik, 1948, Ja 18,60:5
Silberstein, Michael E, 1950, Ja 26,28:3
Silberstein, Murray L, 1968, S 18,47:3
Silberstein, Nathan, 1966, O 25,48:1
Silberstein, Sydney G, 1956, Ap 11,33:5
Silberstein, Wolf H, 1948, N 25,31:3
Silberston, Michel, 1966, Ap 26,45:1
Silbert, Charles, 1967, O 23,45:2
Silbert, Jacob, 1937, Ap 20,25:5
Silbert, Julius, 1949, Mr 14,19:4
Silbert, Lisa, 1965, N 30,41:2
Silbert, Richard H, 1939, Jl 19,19:4
Silbert, Samuel, 1959, Jl 11,19:5
Silberta, Rhea, 1959, D 8,45:3
Silbon, Cornelius E, 1966, Jl 10,69:2
Silbon, Edward, 1948, S 24,25:4
Silby, Reginald M, 1954, Ja 14,29:4
Silcott, Arthur E, 1948, My 22,15:1
Silcox, Claris E, 1961, My 10,45:1
Silcox, Ferdinand A, 1939, D 21,23:3
Silcox, J Evart D, 1945, F 2,20:2
Silen, Bertrand, 1958, D 15,2:5
Silenzi, Guglielmo, 1947, D 19,26:3
Sileo, James V, 1961, Ag 12,17:4
Siler, Adam T, 1953, N 17,31:4
Siler, Frank Mrs, 1939, Ja 28,15:5
Siler, George, 1908, Je 14,11:5
Siler, J Hammond Sr, 1949, F 24,24:2
Siler, Joseph F, 1960, F 10,37:2
Siles, Hernando, 1942, N 24,25:5
Sili, Cardinal, 1926, F 28,28:3
Siliaev, Andrei, 1952, Ap 19,15:4
Silieri, Sante, 1949, Ap 8,25:2
Silingardi, I Dario, 1943, Je 30,21:2
Silk, Edward A, 1955, N 20,88:5
Silk, Floyd I Mrs, 1957, Ap 4,33:3
Silk, Gerald, 1966, F 23,39:1
Silk, Louis, 1961, S 27,41:1
Silk, Louis A, 1937, S 21,25:3
Silk, Morris G, 1952, Mr 3,21:2
Silk, Samuel, 1965, S 7,39:3
Silke, Cornelius A Rev, 1937, D 26,II,7:1
Silke, James Freeman, 1913, Jl 21,7:7
Silke, John B, 1953, N 1,87:2
Silke, Patrick M, 1953, S 29,29:4
Silkin, Lady, 1963, Je 26,39:3
Silkman, Aaron Dr, 1937, Ag 14,13:3
Silkman, Charles H, 1940, D 21,17:6
Silkman, John B, 1875, My 18,1:6
Silkman, Theodore H, 1910, Ag 23,9:6
Silknitter, George F, 1954, Ja 30,17:4
Silkowski, Henry, 1941, D 24,17:2
Silkworth, Myron A, 1944, N 9,27:6
Silkworth, William D, 1951, Mr 23,21:5
Sill, Allan P, 1957, F 12,27:3
Sill, Frederick H, 1952, Jl 18,19:1
Sill, George Griswold, 1907, My 21,9:6
Sill, Jerry Mrs, 1942, My 22,21:2
Sill, Louise M Mrs, 1961, Ap 1,17:2
Sill, Richard N Mrs, 1938, Ag 3,19:4
Sill, Susan S Mrs, 1942, Je 5,17:1
Sill, Thomas H Rev, 1910, Ap 7,11:4
Sill, Walter G, 1958, S 2,25:4
Sill, William Raymond, 1922, D 2,13:5
Sillanpaa, Frans E, 1964, Je 4,37:2
Sillanpaa, Miina, 1952, Ap 9,31:4
Sillari, Eugene, 1950, S 17,105:2
Sillbereysen, William (por), 1939, O 19,23:5
Sillcock, J J, 1882, Ag 16,2:6
Sillcocks, Millicent, 1950, O 10,31:2
Sillcox, Luise M, 1965, Je 29,32:6
Silleck, Charles H Mrs, 1950, Ap 29,15:3
Silleck, Frank U, 1952, D 7,89:1
Silleck, Henry G Mrs, 1951, F 13,31:3
Silleck, Henry Jr Mrs, 1952, Ap 28,19:5
Silleck, Wallace V, 1950, My 29,17:3
Silleck, Walter Mandeville, 1925, F 17,23:5
Siller, Edward F, 1954, My 20,31:6
Siller, Edward H, 1956, Ja 6,23:4
Siller, Edward H Mrs, 1955, S 18,87:1
Siller, William Mrs, 1959, Jl 6,27:5
Sillers, Walter, 1966, S 25,84:5
Sillick, Fletcher H, 1940, N 28,23:4
Sillig, Oscar Prof, 1910, N 27,II,13:4
Silliman, A E, 1884, My 31,2:2
Silliman, B D, 1901, Ja 25,7:3
Silliman, B Prof, 1885, Ja 15,5:3
Silliman, Benjamin Sr Prof (funl, D 1,8:5), 1864, N 25,4:5
Silliman, Charles, 1949, O 31,25:2
Silliman, Frank Jr, 1945, Je 14,19:2
Silliman, Grover, 1948, Ap 28,28:3
Silliman, Harper, 1951, O 1,23:5
Silliman, Horace H, 1955, Jl 7,27:1
Silliman, Joseph E, 1955, Jl 23,17:1
Silliman, Leland L, 1964, S 8,29:4
Silliman, Reuben D, 1961, N 13,31:5
Silliman, Reuben D Mrs, 1944, Je 20,19:4
Silliman, William Col, 1865, Ja 5,2:1
Sillins, Benjamin, 1957, S 5,29:3
Sillitoe, Percy J, 1962, Ap 6,35:4
Sillivan, Daniel M (por), 1949, Jl 14,28:3
Sillivan, Dennis, 1950, Je 28,27:5; 1952, Ap 16,27:4
Sillman, Archie, 1937, Ap 1,23:5
Sillman, Claire L, 1938, Mr 17,21:4
Sillman, John H, 1967, My 22,43:2
Sills, Charles Morton Rev, 1924, My 1,19:3
Sills, Edmund, 1957, Ag 5,21:5
Sills, Gwladys W Mrs, 1964, N 27,36:5
Sills, Howard L, 1947, S 13,11:2
Sills, Kenneth C M, 1954, N 16,27:1
Sills, Leonard H Mrs, 1967, My 10,47:4
Silman, Irving, 1962, Ap 8,86:6
Silo, James P, 1922, F 2,17:4
Silodor, Sidney, 1963, Ag 5,29:3
Silos, Samuel, 1942, N 7,15:2
Siloti, Alexander (por), 1945, D 10,21:1
Silsbe, John Nelson, 1917, My 15,13:1
Silsbe, Sherman, 1940, N 6,9:2
Silsbee, George S, 1907, O 12,9:6
Silsby, Joseph C, 1903, S 18,7:3
Silten, Adolph M, 1941, N 5,23:4
Silva, Antonio M da, 1950, O 15,104:2
Silva, Arthur Mrs, 1950, Ja 29,68:7
Silva, Frank J, 1954, S 18,15:6
Silva, Luigi, 1961, N 30,37:2
Silva, Manuel J, 1951, F 6,27:2
Silva, Plinio, 1948, Je 8,25:4
Silva, Rudolf A, 1954, Ap 21,29:2
Silva, Silvio, 1955, Ap 17,87:1
Silva, Simone, 1957, D 1,82:5
Silva, William P, 1948, F 11,27:4
Silva Joacham, Jorge, 1945, O 9,21:2
Silva Vildosola, Carlos, 1939, D 23,15:4
Silveira, Roberto, 1961, Mr 1,33:3
Silveira Sampaio, Jose de, 1964, N 25,37:4
Silver, A Robert, 1961, Ja 6,27:1
Silver, Abba H (mem ser, D 2,37:5), 1963, N 29,1:1
Silver, Ann R, 1968, F 4,80:7
Silver, Bernard, 1949, Jl 31,61:1; 1963, Ag 30,21:5
Silver, Bertram E, 1949, Ap 27,27:6
Silver, Boris W, 1941, Ja 10,11:4
Silver, Charles A, 1963, D 13,36:5
Silver, Charles A Mrs, 1916, F 18,11:5
Silver, Charles H Mrs, 1961, My 15,31:4
Silver, Charles Mrs, 1963, Ag 24,19:4
Silver, Charles S, 1949, Mr 17,25:4
Silver, David, 1955, F 7,21:5; 1968, Jl 4,19:3
Silver, David H, 1946, Mr 3,45:2
Silver, Edgar O, 1909, N 19,11:4
Silver, Edwin H, 1956, S 17,27:2
Silver, Eliezer Rabbi, 1968, F 9,27:1
Silver, Ernest L, 1949, Ja 5,25:3
Silver, Frank, 1960, Je 15,41:2
Silver, G, 1935, Jl 29,15:3
Silver, George A, 1944, Ja 8,13:6
Silver, H P, 1934, D 16,II,9:1
Silver, Harold I, 1946, F 7,23:4
Silver, Henry, 1949, Ja 18,23:5
Silver, Henry A, 1954, N 8,21:4
Silver, Henry M (por), 1945, S 29,15:1
Silver, Henry M, 1965, Mr 1,27:2
Silver, Herbert D, 1963, D 7,27:3
Silver, Isaac, 1940, D 2,23:4
Silver, Isador, 1954, D 3,27:3
Silver, Isadore, 1946, Ja 10,23:4
Silver, James F, 1954, Ap 26,25:5
Silver, John Archer Prof, 1916, F 6,15:4
Silver, Jules, 1951, D 10,29:2
Silver, Larry, 1965, Mr 17,45:1
Silver, Leo, 1958, F 13,29:2
Silver, Louis, 1957, Ap 10,33:5; 1966, F 3,32:1
Silver, Louis H, 1963, O 28,27:5
Silver, Mark, 1965, Ja 24,80:8
Silver, Maurice A, 1960, Mr 27,86:4
Silver, Maxwell, 1966, O 10,41:1
Silver, Michael, 1958, F 11,31:2
Silver, Morris, 1947, My 7,27:2
Silver, Morris S, 1950, Je 3,15:5
Silver, Moshe, 1949, Ja 13,24:3
Silver, N, 1939, My 11,22:1
Silver, Robert, 1943, F 11,19:3
Silver, S Sidney, 1965, My 9,86:3
Silver, Samuel, 1958, Je 20,23:4
Silver, Samuel E, 1963, O 3,35:5
Silver, Samuel Mrs, 1956, S 14,23:3
Silver, Sanford, 1967, F 23,35:5
Silver, Saul Mrs, 1960, Je 17,31:3
Silver, Sol S, 1946, Ag 25,46:4
Silver, Sol S Mrs, 1966, Je 4,29:1
Silver, Thomas H, 1951, D 6,33:4
Silvera, Victor A, 1961, S 3,60:4
Silverberg, Harry M, 1968, Ag 29,35:4
Silverberg, Mark, 1965, Ap 17,19:5
Silverberg, Morris, 1953, Ap 19,90:8
Silverberg, Naftala H, 1945, Jl 20,19:4
Silverberg, Stanley M, 1953, N 14,17:4
Silverberg, William V, 1967, O 12,45:2
Silverburgh, Roy Mrs, 1963, D 23,25:1
Silverbush, Sam, 1952, Ja 26,13:3
Silvercruys, F X B, 1936, Je 23,24:2
Silverhtorne, Spencer V, 1962, N 24,1:2
Silverius de Santa Teresa, 1954, Mr 12,22:4
Silverman, Abraham, 1953, D 23,25:3; 1954, F 17,31:
Silverman, Abraham J, 1943, O 26,23:2
Silverman, Albert G Mrs, 1968, O 14,47:3
Silverman, Albert J, 1951, Ag 22,23:6
Silverman, Benjamin, 1957, F 20,33:1
Silverman, Bernard, 1923, Je 25,13:5
Silverman, Charles H, 1953, Mr 8,88:3
Silverman, David, 1959, Jl 29,29:2
Silverman, Edith Mrs, 1948, N 24,23:4
Silverman, Edith Roberta, 1909, Je 4,7:5
Silverman, Edmund G Mrs, 1955, D 23,17:4
Silverman, Edward, 1945, Mr 6,22:2
Silverman, Edward B (cor, S 1,23:2), 1955, Ag 31, 25:2
Silverman, Edwin H, 1951, Ap 17,23:3
Silverman, Estelle L, 1946, Ag 6,25:2
Silverman, George, 1955, O 20,36:2
Silverman, Harriet, 1940, Je 1,15:5
Silverman, Harry (por), 1948, O 27,27:2
Silverman, Harry, 1958, Ap 14,25:4
Silverman, Harry L, 1959, My 25,29:4
Silverman, Henry D, 1937, Ja 25,19:5
Silverman, Herbert R Mrs, 1965, D 15,47:1
Silverman, Herman, 1951, My 13,88:8; 1957, D 29, 48:7; 1958, Ap 11,26:1
Silverman, Herman Mrs, 1908, Ap 13,7:4
Silverman, I Jerome Dr, 1968, S 5,47:4
Silverman, Irving, 1955, D 10,21:6; 1967, Ag 27,89:1
Silverman, Irving I Mrs, 1956, Jl 16,21:2
Silverman, Irving Mrs, 1949, Mr 30,25:5
Silverman, Isaac H, 1941, My 13,23:6
Silverman, J, 1930, Jl 27,23:3
Silverman, John, 1948, N 15,25:6
Silverman, Joseph, 1956, Jl 27,21:5
Silverman, Julius, 1962, F 4,82:5
Silverman, Lazarus, 1909, Je 10,7:5
Silverman, Leslie, 1966, Mr 5,27:3
Silverman, Max, 1953, F 14,17:3; 1954, O 31,50:8
Silverman, Mel, 1966, S 17,29:2
Silverman, Meyer H, 1943, Jl 1,19:2
Silverman, Meyer M, 1954, O 5,27:3
Silverman, Milton S, 1962, F 6,32:6

Silverman, Mordecai Mrs, 1957, Mr 1,37:1
Silverman, Morris Mrs, 1911, Mr 16,9:5
Silverman, Morris R, 1959, F 25,31:4
Silverman, Moses, 1965, S 9,41:4
Silverman, Norman J, 1951, Ja 10,27:3
Silverman, Rachel Mrs, 1939, F 5,41:3
Silverman, Rashe Mrs, 1940, Je 25,25:6
Silverman, Robert M, 1946, S 24,30:2
Silverman, S, 1933, S 23,15:1
Silverman, Samuel, 1965, Mr 31,39:3
Silverman, Samuel Mrs, 1941, Ag 8,15:3
Silverman, Samuel T, 1938, S 9,22:5
Silverman, Sid (will, Mr 21,31:4), 1950, Mr 11,15:1
Silverman, Sidney H, 1957, Je 25,25:1
Silverman, Sydney, 1968, F 10,33:1
Silverman, Wolf Mrs, 1954, F 4,25:2
Silvermaster, Nathan G, 1964, O 15,39:2
Silvernail, Andrew J, 1951, S 15,15:5
Silvernail, Charles H, 1952, Ap 30,27:4
Silvernail, Clarence L, 1950, N 28,31:2
Silvernail, Egbert Mrs, 1965, D 11,33:4
Silvers, Earl R (por), 1948, Mr 27,13:1
Silvers, Elihu Brittin Dr, 1914, Ap 3,11:5
Silvers, Evelyn R Mrs, 1940, O 10,25:1
Silvers, Harry, 1959, Ag 26,29:4
Silvers, Homer I, 1948, Ap 8,25:3
Silvers, Joseph, 1953, Je 25,27:2
Silvers, Joseph F, 1923, Ja 26,17:3
Silvers, Louis, 1954, Mr 28,88:3
Silvers, Mary Mrs, 1941, F 20,19:5
Silversmith, Charles, 1966, N 26,36:3
Silversmith, Joseph H, 1954, F 8,23:2
Silverson, Harry, 1963, Ag 5,29:2
Silverson, Joseph, 1958, N 5,35:1
Silversteen, Joseph S, 1958, O 19,87:2
Silversteen, Stanley A, 1955, Jl 29,17:5
Silverstein, Benjamin J, 1966, Jl 22,21:3
Silverstein, Benjamin R, 1959, S 16,39:1
Silverstein, Bernard, 1968, Je 12,47:2
Silverstein, David F, 1944, Jl 7,15:4
Silverstein, Hannah M, 1952, Ag 15,15:4
Silverstein, Harry G, 1966, Je 26,73:3
Silverstein, Hyman, 1948, F 11,28:2
Silverstein, Jacob, 1957, Je 4,35:1
Silverstein, Jacob H, 1961, Ap 30,86:8
Silverstein, Joseph, 1954, Mr 26,21:2
Silverstein, Joseph Mrs, 1948, D 22,23:2
Silverstein, Joshua, 1951, S 23,87:2
Silverstein, Lazar, 1962, My 9,43:5
Silverstein, Louis M, 1962, My 13,88:7
Silverstein, Max, 1955, Ag 11,21:4; 1962, Mr 24,25:3
Silverstein, Michael I, 1964, My 20,43:4
Silverstein, Morris, 1939, Jl 13,19:5
Silverstein, Nathan, 1949, Jl 1,19:1
Silverstein, Paul R, 1965, Mr 23,39:4
Silverstein, Samuel, 1949, Mr 25,23:4; 1953, My 1, 14:1; 1954, Jl 30,17:6
Silverstein, William R, 1941, Je 22,32:7
Silverstone, Abraham, 1951, Ja 10,27:1
Silverstone, Harry T Mrs, 1943, Ap 1,23:3
Silverstone, Louis, 1938, F 22,21:5
Silverstone, Wolf Mrs, 1914, Je 6,9:4
Silvert, Jack M, 1950, O 13,29:3
Silverthau, Benjamin, 1944, F 16,17:5
Silverthorn, Katherine V Mrs, 1942, D 15,27:4
Silverthorne, Louise M Mrs, 1958, My 23,23:4
Silverthorne, Spencer V, 1964, My 18,29:2
Silverthorne, Spencer V Mrs, 1954, O 15,23:4
Silvertone, Arthur J, 1956, D 23,30:5
Silvertsen, Peter M L, 1962, O 31,37:1
Silvery, William Maj, 1872, Je 23,3:5
Silvester, Francis, 1903, D 8,9:4
Silvester, Lindsay M, 1963, Ag 7,33:2
Silvestri, George, 1967, Ap 15,31:4
Silvestri, Giovanni, 1940, My 28,23:1
Silvestri, Ottavio, 1950, Ag 8,30:2
Silvestri, Pietro Di Cardinal, 1875, N 20,1:1
Silvestris, Jane Mother, 1958, Mr 5,31:1
Silveti, Juan, 1956, S 12,37:4
Silvette, Ellis M, 1940, O 23,23:3
Silveus, Frank F, 1950, Mr 24,26:2
Silvey, Ben, 1948, F 8,60:2
Silvey, Harry A, 1955, O 31,25:2
Silvey, Helene Mrs (Helene Carter), 1961, Ja 2,25:5
Silvia, Frank M, 1948, F 25,24:2
Silvia, John S, 1940, Ag 7,19:5
Silvia, Joseph, 1955, Ja 29,15:3
Silving, Bert, 1948, F 11,27:2
Silvioni, Aniceto, 1950, Ap 1,15:2
Silvis, Richard S, 1960, My 8,88:3
Silz, August, 1921, Mr 29,15:6
Silzer, George S (por), 1940, O 17,25:1
Silzer, George S Mrs, 1957, F 19,31:5
Silzer, William, 1956, Mr 27,35:2
Sim, Charles W, 1941, Mr 16,45:3
Sim, John Robert, 1925, D 24,13:4
Sim, Malcolm, 1956, D 25,25:3
Sim, Robert J, 1941, S 1,15:6
Sim, Robert L, 1950, Ap 13,29:4
Sim, Robert P, 1966, My 29,56:5
Simandl, Harold, 1950, Ja 25,27:2
Simandl, Lester A, 1953, Mr 31,31:4
Simandl, Sidney, 1957, Ja 23,29:1
Simard, Georges, 1956, N 4,87:3
Simard, J Edouard, 1960, S 23,29:1
Simavi, Sedat, 1953, D 12,19:3
Simberkoff, Louis L, 1968, Jl 26,33:4
Simberloff, Martin K, 1957, My 2,31:4
Simcerbox, William D, 1949, O 14,27:5
Simcox, Frederick B, 1960, Jl 23,19:2
Sime, Frank, 1940, O 19,17:6
Sime, Richard, 1959, Ap 19,86:5
Sime, Thomas, 1939, O 3,23:5
Simels, Louis, 1967, Je 3,31:2
Simeon, Archbishop, 1937, O 24,II,8:8
Simeon, Omer, 1959, S 18,25:4
Simeone, Augustin J M, 1940, O 25,21:4
Simeoni, Giovanni Cardinal, 1892, Ja 15,9:4
Simer, Dorr M, 1955, F 5,15:3
Simeral, Charles D, 1947, Je 19,21:1
Simet, Anthony G, 1948, Je 16,29:5
Simiansky, Bella Mrs, 1939, Ag 14,15:2
Simiansky, Morris, 1939, Mr 6,15:4
Simila, Martti, 1958, Ja 10,26:1
Simington, Milton, 1943, Ja 18,21:3
Simis, Albert V, 1962, Mr 14,39:4
Simister, May P Mrs, 1941, Je 30,17:5
Simken, John R, 1944, D 7,25:1
Simkhovitch, Simka, 1949, F 26,15:2
Simkhovitch, Stephen K, 1939, Jl 2,15:1
Simkhovitch, Vladimir G, 1959, D 10,39:1
Simkhovitch, Vladimir G Mrs, 1951, N 16,25:1
Simkins, Daniel, 1953, N 17,31:3
Simkins, Samuel, 1956, Jl 13,19:4
Simler, Henry, 1954, Je 27,68:6
Simler, William A, 1958, S 12,26:1
Simm, Isaac A, 1937, Ja 20,21:1
Simmat, Franz, 1950, Ap 11,32:3
Simmel, Ernst, 1947, N 13,27:2
Simmelkjaer, Harold E, 1956, Je 26,29:5
Simmen, Charles A Mrs, 1952, Je 27,23:4
Simmen, John J, 1944, D 21,22:2
Simmen, Paul J, 1941, Jl 2,21:2
Simmenroth, John W, 1951, Je 19,29:2
Simmer, John Mrs, 1944, O 7,13:2
Simmerer, Eugene, 1948, Ag 1,58:2
Simmering, S L, 1940, Ja 28,32:1
Simmern, Ernst L von, 1942, N 22,52:5
Simmers, Hugh, 1949, Ag 28,72:8
Simmonds, Albert C Jr, 1963, Je 24,27:4
Simmonds, Albert P, 1953, N 14,17:2
Simmonds, Annette (Lady Dangan), 1959, O 30,2:8
Simmonds, Arthur E, 1950, O 29,92:1
Simmonds, C Leo, 1951, N 17,17:5
Simmonds, Edward B, 1944, S 2,11:4
Simmonds, Edward Mrs, 1945, My 3,23:2
Simmonds, Frank W Mrs, 1938, My 1,6:8
Simmonds, H G Mrs, 1903, Ag 30,7:6
Simmonds, Lawrence H, 1961, Ap 2,77:1
Simmonds, Lionel J, 1961, N 13,31:1
Simmonds, Newton M, 1955, S 11,84:8
Simmonds, Robert L, 1952, Ja 11,21:4
Simmonds, Roy, 1954, Je 23,25:5
Simmons, A R Capt (funl), 1910, Jl 3,II,7:4
Simmons, Al (funl, My 30,21:4), 1956, My 27,88:4
Simmons, Albert C, 1950, My 26,23:2
Simmons, Albert L, 1960, F 9,31:3
Simmons, Albert V, 1959, Ja 6,33:4
Simmons, Alvin, 1937, D 26,27:2
Simmons, Benjamin, 1954, Ja 15,19:2
Simmons, Benjamin D, 1956, Jl 25,29:2
Simmons, Bert Mrs, 1959, Ja 6,33:4
Simmons, Carlton E, 1948, Je 8,25:3
Simmons, Channing C, 1953, Ag 17,15:5
Simmons, Charles A Sr, 1963, O 10,41:4
Simmons, Charles E, 1942, Jl 15,19:3; 1953, Ap 9,27:5
Simmons, Charles E Dr, 1917, My 4,11:5
Simmons, Charles F, 1961, S 25,33:2
Simmons, Charles H (por), 1945, Je 12,19:3
Simmons, Charles J, 1952, My 29,27:1
Simmons, Charles P, 1905, F 26,8:5
Simmons, chas L, 1940, Ap 18,23:2
Simmons, Cheston, 1956, Ap 22,86:6
Simmons, Claude, 1962, O 31,37:5
Simmons, Daniel Dr, 1914, Mr 20,11:5
Simmons, David A, 1951, Mr 25,72:5
Simmons, Don A, 1964, Ag 19,37:2
Simmons, Donald M, 1961, Ja 28,19:5
Simmons, E, 1931, N 18,23:5
Simmons, E A, 1931, O 2,25:3
Simmons, E Henry H, 1955, My 22,88:8
Simmons, E Henry H Mrs, 1942, Je 21,36:6
Simmons, E Henry Mrs, 1920, Je 19,13:6
Simmons, Edward A Mrs, 1951, S 22,17:3
Simmons, Edward B, 1951, Je 2,19:1
Simmons, Edward D Mrs, 1945, Mr 18,42:3
Simmons, Edward P, 1951, F 19,23:2
Simmons, Edwin S Mrs, 1948, D 2,29:5
Simmons, Eleanor B, 1950, Ja 22,76:4
Simmons, Elizabeth W Mrs, 1941, Ja 17,17:3
Simmons, Elmer J, 1954, D 4,17:6
Simmons, Emmett P, 1940, Mr 14,23:4
Simmons, Ernest R, 1954, Mr 8,27:3
Simmons, Fielding Jr, 1955, Ag 24,27:3
Simmons, Francis E, 1967, F 22,29:2
Simmons, Francis Tolles, 1920, Jl 6,15:1
Simmons, Frank A, 1959, O 21,44:1
Simmons, Frank E, 1954, O 18,25:5
Simmons, Frank H, 1937, Ap 12,17:5
Simmons, Franklin, 1913, D 9,11:4
Simmons, Frederick F, 1949, O 3,17:5
Simmons, Furnifold M, 1940, My 1,23:1
Simmons, George C Mrs, 1904, D 11,7:6
Simmons, George E, 1949, F 23,27:2
Simmons, George F, 1955, Jl 22,23:6
Simmons, George H Dr (por), 1937, S 2,21:1
Simmons, George M, 1945, Mr 28,23:5
Simmons, Georges M, 1963, Je 12,43:3
Simmons, Gordon H, 1951, Je 8,27:1
Simmons, Grant G Mrs, 1968, Je 3,45:2
Simmons, Harold B, 1949, F 15,23:1
Simmons, Harrison S, 1943, S 12,53:2
Simmons, Harry, 1938, S 1,23:5; 1940, My 15,25:2
Simmons, Harry D Mrs, 1957, F 26,29:2
Simmons, Harry Sr Mrs, 1959, Je 9,37:5
Simmons, Helena N Mrs, 1942, O 13,24:3
Simmons, Henry Mrs, 1962, Je 28,31:4
Simmons, Henry R Mrs, 1953, O 23,23:1
Simmons, Homer C, 1951, D 24,13:5
Simmons, Isaac, 1941, Jl 10,19:6
Simmons, J Andrew, 1966, F 24,38:1
Simmons, James F, 1864, Jl 17,3:6
Simmons, James S, 1954, Ag 2,17:3
Simmons, James W Mrs, 1948, S 6,13:2
Simmons, John B, 1937, Mr 25,25:4
Simmons, John F, 1968, Ja 3,47:1
Simmons, John G, 1947, My 10,13:6
Simmons, John P (por), 1946, O 31,25:3
Simmons, John S, 1938, Mr 7,17:3
Simmons, John Sir, 1903, F 15,7:5
Simmons, John W, 1939, S 24,44:7
Simmons, Joseph F, 1937, Jl 8,23:4
Simmons, Joseph I Mrs, 1939, S 14,23:5
Simmons, Joshua A, 1919, Je 3,13:3
Simmons, Leonhard W, 1923, O 19,19:5
Simmons, Lucretia V, 1942, Ag 29,15:2
Simmons, M Theodore, 1952, Ja 19,15:4
Simmons, Marion E, 1954, Jl 4,30:7
Simmons, Maurice, 1958, S 16,27:3
Simmons, Merrill, 1948, My 26,25:1
Simmons, Myron H, 1945, Jl 19,23:4
Simmons, Nellie K Mrs, 1939, Ja 27,19:5
Simmons, Oliver, 1903, N 12,9:5
Simmons, Oliver W, 1958, Ja 12,86:3
Simmons, P N, 1949, Ap 20,27:2
Simmons, Pearl B Mrs, 1955, S 11,56:6
Simmons, Peter Mrs, 1950, Je 25,70:1
Simmons, Ralph, 1938, Mr 19,15:4; 1955, Ag 28,85:1
Simmons, Ralph H, 1941, Mr 15,17:3
Simmons, Ralph T, 1945, D 22,19:6
Simmons, Richard J, 1956, Jl 19,27:1
Simmons, Richard W, 1939, Je 26,15:6
Simmons, Robert, 1960, S 28,39:2
Simmons, Robert B Y, 1950, Mr 14,25:3
Simmons, Robert L, 1953, Mr 27,23:3
Simmons, Roscoe C, 1951, Ap 29,88:5
Simmons, Samuel J, 1946, Ja 26,13:3
Simmons, Sarah Mrs, 1943, My 20,21:1
Simmons, Sidney C Mrs, 1953, O 18,86:8
Simmons, T Karl, 1943, O 27,23:3
Simmons, Theodore P, 1951, My 20,88:8
Simmons, Thomas J, 1942, Mr 18,23:2; 1949, S 4,40:6
Simmons, Thomas W, 1951, Ap 23,25:3; 1952, My 21, 27:1
Simmons, Virgil M, 1958, F 20,25:2
Simmons, Waldeman Moe, 1915, S 30,11:6
Simmons, Walter D Mrs, 1948, Jl 27,25:1
Simmons, Ward A, 1948, Ja 5,19:4
Simmons, Ward W, 1916, Ag 15,9:6
Simmons, Warren S, 1944, My 3,19:5
Simmons, Will, 1949, Ja 2,63:3
Simmons, Willard F, 1952, F 27,27:2
Simmons, Willard L, 1960, Je 24,27:2
Simmons, William, 1941, Ap 28,15:3; 1955, S 16,23:3
Simmons, William C Prof, 1907, Mr 26,9:6
Simmons, William D M, 1939, Mr 19,III,6:5
Simmons, William E (Skipper), 1924, N 8,15:5
Simmons, William H, 1949, S 17,17:2
Simmons, William H Jr, 1944, Je 4,42:2
Simmons, William J (por), 1945, My 22,19:2
Simmons, Z G, 1934, Ap 27,21:4
Simmons, Zalmon G 3d, 1960, My 14,23:6
Simms, Albert G, 1964, D 30,23:1
Simms, Charles C Mrs, 1946, O 31,25:5
Simms, Charles E, 1947, S 14,60:6
Simms, Charles H, 1903, Ag 31,7:6
Simms, Edward F, 1938, D 7,23:1
Simms, Elizabeth W Mrs, 1937, Je 9,25:5
Simms, Florence, 1923, Ja 7,7:3
Simms, Frederick R, 1944, Ap 24,19:5
Simms, H C Dr, 1883, F 14,5:1
Simms, Harry, 1942, D 14,23:1
Simms, Harry Mrs, 1945, F 20,19:4
Simms, J Ed, 1946, S 23,23:4
Simms, J R, 1883, Je 3,2:3
Simms, John F Sr, 1954, F 13,13:5
Simms, Lillie L Mrs, 1938, Ja 9,42:3
Simms, Lyman L Maj, 1937, Ap 6,23:5
Simms, Ruth H M Mrs, 1945, Ja 1,21:3

Simms, Stephen C (por), 1937, Ja 29,19:3
Simms, Willard, 1917, My 4,11:6
Simms, William Gilmore, 1870, Je 13,5:6
Simms, William P, 1957, Ja 17,29:5
Simon, Aaron J, 1960, Je 24,27:5
Simon, Abraham H, 1963, N 14,35:4
Simon, Abram, 1938, D 25,14:7
Simon, Abram Mrs, 1961, Mr 4,23:5
Simon, Adolph L, 1956, Ag 4,15:4
Simon, Alfred, 1968, My 1,47:1
Simon, Anton, 1942, Mr 11,19:1
Simon, Arthur, 1948, N 6,13:6; 1963, Jl 3,25:4
Simon, Arthur J, 1968, My 31,29:4
Simon, Benjamin, 1942, N 23,23:4
Simon, Bernard D, 1953, Ap 19,86:5
Simon, Carleton, 1951, F 19,23:3
Simon, Chaim J Rabbi, 1937, Ap 12,17:4
Simon, Charles, 1966, Mr 10,33:1
Simon, Charles Jr, 1964, Je 5,31:2
Simon, Charles L, 1955, Ag 24,27:3
Simon, Charles Mrs, 1951, F 23,27:5; 1954, O 16,17:5
Simon, David M, 1961, My 21,87:3
Simon, David M Mrs, 1966, S 21,47:1
Simon, David Mrs, 1962, Je 18,25:1
Simon, Dowager Viscountess, 1955, Mr 28,27:4
Simon, Edward P (por), 1949, My 10,25:3
Simon, Edward W, 1946, O 12,19:1
Simon, Eli, 1961, Ja 10,47:5
Simon, Emil J, 1963, S 15,86:5
Simon, Ernest, 1945, Je 26,19:5
Simon, F, 1934, O 5,23:1
Simon, Francis, 1956, N 1,39:2
Simon, Franklin Mrs, 1949, My 1,88:3
Simon, George, 1957, N 24,86:6; 1963, My 1,39:4
Simon, George C, 1952, Mr 11,27:5
Simon, George D, 1944, My 18,19:3
Simon, Georges S, 1961, Mr 14,35:1
Simon, H, 1926, D 3,23:4
Simon, Harris, 1948, Ja 27,26:2; 1960, S 24,23:3
Simon, Harris Mrs, 1944, My 26,19:4
Simon, Harry W, 1958, Jl 8,27:1
Simon, Henry, 1957, N 3,89:1
Simon, Henry M, 1949, My 17,25:4
Simon, Herman, 1913, S 28,7:6
Simon, Herman Mrs, 1950, D 17,84:6
Simon, Hugo F, 1958, Ag 21,25:3
Simon, I J, 1947, Ag 12,23:1
Simon, Ike, 1953, O 18,86:5
Simon, Irving, 1948, Ja 10,15:4
Simon, Irving M, 1953, S 4,34:3
Simon, Isadore, 1947, Jl 30,21:5
Simon, Jack B, 1948, Je 12,15:1
Simon, Jacob, 1954, Ag 24,21:4
Simon, John, 1949, F 11,23:4
Simon, John A, 1954, Ja 12,23:1
Simon, John Sir, 1904, Jl 24,5:6
Simon, Joseph Dr, 1968, F 6,43:4
Simon, Joseph T Mrs, 1952, Ag 20,25:5; 1964, Ap 20, 29:3
Simon, Joseph W, 1952, Ja 31,27:4
Simon, Jules, 1896, Je 8,5:1
Simon, Julius, 1938, Ap 3,II,7:3
Simon, Lee R, 1948, S 28,27:3
Simon, Leo, 1966, O 9,86:3
Simon, Leo J, 1952, F 9,13:5
Simon, Leo L, 1959, Je 11,33:2
Simon, Leon, 1965, Ap 28,45:4
Simon, Leon G, 1953, F 19,23:1
Simon, Leopold K, 1952, O 3,23:3
Simon, Lester S, 1968, My 16,48:1
Simon, Louis, 1946, Ja 21,23:2; 1953, My 3,88:6
Simon, Louis A, 1958, My 14,33:3
Simon, Louis Mrs, 1965, D 30,23:1
Simon, Lucien, 1945, O 17,19:5
Simon, Marian, 1937, Mr 30,23:4
Simon, Matthew Dr, 1968, Ag 19,37:1
Simon, Maurice Mrs (will), 1947, Je 26,26:1
Simon, Max, 1961, F 4,19:6
Simon, Max L, 1965, F 21,76:7
Simon, Max M Mrs, 1962, Ag 15,31:3
Simon, Milton Mrs, 1960, S 27,37:2; 1966, N 17,47:3
Simon, Moe, 1954, O 2,17:5
Simon, Monroe L Mrs, 1949, Je 3,25:1
Simon, Morris, 1959, O 27,37:1
Simon, Morris L, 1942, S 2,24:3
Simon, Mortimer R, 1958, Mr 29,17:4
Simon, Moses C, 1967, Jl 3,17:5
Simon, Myer, 1952, Jl 17,23:6
Simon, Nelson B, 1923, Ag 19,26:5
Simon, Paul, 1937, N 17,23:2; 1955, Mr 30,29:1
Simon, Peter M, 1941, F 18,23:1
Simon, Philip, 1961, My 24,41:3
Simon, R E, 1935, S 8,39:1
Simon, Ralph M, 1961, Je 2,32:2
Simon, Reuben Mrs, 1949, D 27,23:4
Simon, Richard L, 1960, Jl 30,17:2
Simon, Robert, 1966, Ja 17,47:5
Simon, Robert E Sr Mrs, 1964, D 3,49:2
Simon, Ronnie, 1944, Jl 19,19:4
Simon, S J, 1948, Jl 28,23:2
Simon, S Sylvan, 1951, My 19,15:6
Simon, Sam, 1939, N 17,21:4
Simon, Sam (Uncle Sam), 1953, O 17,13:2
Simon, Sam S, 1964, O 13,43:3
Simon, Samuel, 1907, Ja 26,9:5
Simon, Samuel B, 1947, My 23,23:4; 1953, Ja 18,93:1
Simon, Samuel Dr, 1968, N 2,37:4
Simon, Samuel O, 1943, N 18,23:4
Simon, Sidney, 1959, My 25,29:4
Simon, Sidney H, 1962, F 22,25:4
Simon, Sidney S, 1938, D 9,25:2
Simon, Sol, 1939, S 25,19:6; 1940, Ap 27,15:5
Simon, Solomon Mrs, 1945, D 2,45:2
Simon, Stephen, 1943, Mr 10,19:4
Simon, Sylvia B, 1952, O 10,25:4
Simon, T Frantisek, 1942, D 23,19:4
Simon, Ulrich, 1910, Ag 24,9:6
Simon, Wilfred, 1957, F 6,25:5
Simon, William, 1964, Je 8,29:3
Simon, William A, 1954, Jl 1,25:2
Simon, William Dr, 1916, Jl 21,9:8
Simon, William Mrs, 1965, Ja 3,84:6
Simon, Yves R, 1961, My 12,26:4
Simon of Wythenshawe, Ernest D Lord, 1960, O 4,43:1
Simonaitis, Joseph J Rev, 1953, F 6,19:2
Simond, Maynard E, 1963, O 12,23:5
Simondetti, Ernest T Mrs, 1950, My 11,29:4
Simonds, Alvan T (will, O 5,38:4),(por), 1941, S 3, 23:4
Simonds, Caspar L, 1909, F 14,11:3
Simonds, Charles G Mrs, 1943, Ap 13,26:3
Simonds, Ellen G Mrs, 1937, O 2,21:6
Simonds, F H, 1936, Ja 24,19:1
Simonds, Francis M, 1939, N 17,22:2; 1961, Jl 12,32:2
Simonds, Fred W, 1941, Mr 29,15:2
Simonds, Frederic P, 1944, Ap 21,19:6
Simonds, Frederick W, 1955, Ag 4,25:5
Simonds, George S (por), 1938, N 2,23:1
Simonds, Gifford K, 1941, Mr 21,21:5
Simonds, Godfrey B, 1952, N 27,31:3
Simonds, Grant H, 1950, D 22,23:5
Simonds, Harlan K, 1962, My 21,33:3
Simonds, Henry D, 1946, Mr 11,26:2
Simonds, Justin D, 1967, N 5,86:7
Simonds, Lawrence B, 1946, Mr 11,25:4
Simonds, Lewis C, 1916, F 17,11:7
Simonds, Olivia E Mrs, 1938, Ap 8,19:4
Simonds, William Henry, 1919, Mr 28,13:3
Simone, Antonio, 1919, Je 21,15:6
Simone, Edgardo (por), 1948, D 20,25:4
Simone, Harry C, 1951, Ap 19,31:6
Simone, Paul M, 1961, Ag 6,85:1
Simone, Vincenzo J, 1948, D 3,25:1
Simonelli, Pasquale I, 1960, S 9,29:2
Simonet, Lucien R, 1952, My 8,31:2
Simonette, Paul F, 1951, My 15,31:4
Simonetti, Anthony, 1945, D 1,23:3
Simonetti, Ernest A, 1958, Mr 10,23:5
Simoni, Aristeo, 1958, F 18,27:2
Simoni, Charles Mrs, 1958, F 19,27:4
Simoni, Renato, 1952, Jl 6,48:6
Simoni, Romano, 1961, F 16,31:2
Simonin, Eugene B, 1966, Jl 20,41:4
Simonov, Ruben, 1968, D 6,47:2
Simons, Abram Mrs, 1944, O 18,21:1
Simons, Albert H, 1959, Jl 1,25:5
Simons, Algie M, 1950, Mr 12,93:1
Simons, Algie M Mrs, 1948, D 5,92:5
Simons, Charles C, 1964, F 3,27:3
Simons, Claude, 1943, N 6,13:5
Simons, E Naudain, 1954, S 20,23:4
Simons, E Ray, 1947, D 22,21:2
Simons, Edward L, 1952, Mr 28,23:1
Simons, Ernest, 1945, D 27,19:4
Simons, Frederick F, 1956, Ag 18,17:3
Simons, George A, 1952, Ag 3,60:3
Simons, George E, 1960, S 6,35:1
Simons, George J, 1939, Jl 15,15:1
Simons, George V, 1953, S 29,29:3
Simons, Gerard J, 1948, My 26,25:2
Simons, Guy O, 1962, Ag 19,88:2
Simons, Harry, 1944, Mr 27,19:6; 1967, Je 28,45:2
Simons, Harry E, 1949, N 10,31:5
Simons, Herb, 1968, S 14,31:1
Simons, Herbert, 1952, S 24,33:4
Simons, Irving, 1951, N 12,25:1
Simons, J, 1879, My 16,4:7
Simons, John Mrs, 1950, F 17,23:3
Simons, Langdon S, 1967, S 27,47:3
Simons, Lao G, 1949, N 26,15:5
Simons, Leroy E, 1948, D 17,27:4
Simons, Minot (por), 1941, My 26,19:3
Simons, Minot Mrs, 1944, N 4,15:5
Simons, Moises (por), 1945, Je 29,15:3
Simons, Molly Mrs, 1939, Ap 14,23:5
Simons, Morris, 1954, N 21,86:8
Simons, Radcliffe M, 1948, Mr 13,15:3
Simons, Rodger L, 1965, Ap 17,19:7
Simons, Russell M, 1942, Je 7,42:4
Simons, S A Lt, 1877, D 7,2:4
Simons, Seward C, 1952, D 27,10:4
Simons, Seymour, 1949, F 13,76:7
Simons, Thomas A, 1955, Ja 20,31:1
Simons, Walther Dr (por), 1937, Jl 16,19:1
Simons, William B, 1939, Ap 5,25:4; 1961, Mr 14,35:3
Simons, William H Mrs (F Hennock), 1960, Je 21, 33:4
Simonsen, Alfred P, 1949, My 25,29:3
Simonsen, Fred A, 1964, F 1,23:5
Simonsen, Jesper, 1957, My 26,92:5
Simonsen, Mario, 1965, Mr 25,37:4
Simonsen, Nels E, 1939, Ap 20,23:5
Simonsen, Read B Mrs, 1950, Jl 15,13:2
Simonsen, Roberto, 1948, My 26,25:4
Simonsen, Wallace C, 1955, Je 7,33:4
Simonson, Catherine C Mrs, 1941, Ap 22,21:2
Simonson, Charles E, 1951, D 7,27:3
Simonson, Charles F, 1939, S 21,23:4
Simonson, Cortelyou L, 1962, F 12,23:2
Simonson, David, 1946, N 21,31:4
Simonson, George H, 1945, Ja 22,17:6
Simonson, George M, 1938, Ja 9,42:8
Simonson, Harold J, 1958, Ja 24,23:2
Simonson, Henry J, 1967, N 27,47:2
Simonson, Howard M, 1950, S 14,31:4
Simonson, J S, 1881, D 7,5:4
Simonson, J W, 1882, D 30,5:3
Simonson, Jacob, 1958, Ja 10,26:3
Simonson, Jacob Dr, 1937, N 13,19:5
Simonson, James A, 1946, N 5,25:6
Simonson, Jeremiah T, 1944, O 2,19:6
Simonson, John E, 1939, D 18,23:2
Simonson, Joseph, 1922, O 28,13:6
Simonson, Lee (trb lr, F 5,II,14:7), 1967, Ja 24,28:4
Simonson, Louis, 1949, S 5,17:4
Simonson, Lucy C, 1951, Ap 19,31:5
Simonson, Marshall L, 1950, D 5,31:3
Simonson, Martha J Y Mrs, 1942, Ag 10,19:5
Simonson, Miguel, 1945, My 23,19:2
Simonson, Otto G, 1922, Je 25,26:3
Simonson, Read B, 1955, S 14,35:2
Simonson, Roger A Sr, 1944, Ja 8,13:3
Simonson, Selie, 1925, N 12,25:5
Simonson, Simon, 1943, F 23,21:1
Simonson, Stephen N, 1906, D 3,9:4
Simonson, William A, 1937, Mr 6,17:1
Simonson, William A Mrs, 1950, Mr 12,93:1
Simonson, William I, 1945, Mr 8,23:2
Simont, Jose, 1968, N 21,47:3
Simonton, Catherine M, 1945, O 11,23:4
Simonton, Frank F Mrs, 1964, Ja 23,31:4
Simonton, I V, 1931, Jl 6,17:3
Simonton, J W, 1882, N 1,5:2
Simonton, William A, 1951, O 10,23:6
Simonyi, Laszlo, 1963, Jl 11,29:4
Simopoulos, Charalambos, 1942, O 25,44:5
Simovic, Dusan, 1962, Ag 28,31:1
Simpich, Frederick, 1950, Ja 26,27:6
Simpkins, N S Jr, 1883, O 19,4:7
Simpkins, Tudor J, 1938, O 14,23:4
Simpkins, Willard S, 1967, O 1,84:4
Simpkins, Willard S Mrs, 1961, Je 18,88:8
Simpkins, William J, 1946, S 10,7:2
Simpkins, William J Mrs, 1945, D 25,23:1
Simpler, Roy D Mrs, 1943, D 29,17:4
Simpson, Albert B Rev, 1919, O 30,13:3
Simpson, Albert E, 1964, Mr 7,23:3
Simpson, Alex, 1953, Jl 21,23:2
Simpson, Alex D, 1949, Jl 13,27:4
Simpson, Alexander, 1947, Je 29,48:1
Simpson, Alexander Russell, 1916, Ap 8,15:6
Simpson, Alexander T, 1943, S 1,19:5
Simpson, Alexander T Mrs, 1943, Jl 24,13:1
Simpson, Alfred B, 1938, D 3,19:5
Simpson, Alfred D, 1955, Ag 26,19:6
Simpson, Alfred L, 1914, N 27,11:6
Simpson, Alfred W, 1941, Ag 6,17:5
Simpson, Anna Mrs, 1907, D 4,9:6
Simpson, Arthur G R, 1940, Ja 1,23:3
Simpson, Arthur Mrs, 1944, N 14,23:5
Simpson, Arthur P, 1965, Je 13,85:1
Simpson, Augustus P, 1957, Ag 31,15:6
Simpson, B L, 1930, N 12,20:2
Simpson, Benjamin G, 1942, Je 28,33:1
Simpson, Bernard Mrs, 1944, Je 20,19:5
Simpson, Bethel W, 1955, F 18,21:2
Simpson, Burton T, 1946, Mr 6,27:4
Simpson, C L, 1944, My 25,21:6
Simpson, Carnegie, 1947, D 23,23:1
Simpson, Caroline S, 1938, S 23,27:3
Simpson, Charles E, 1957, Ja 28,23:2
Simpson, Charles E S, 1941, Ag 17,39:3
Simpson, Charles H, 1949, Ja 13,23:5
Simpson, Charles J, 1967, Jl 6,29:5
Simpson, Charles L, 1945, My 17,19:4; 1946, My 28, 21:2
Simpson, Charles W, 1942, S 17,25:2
Simpson, Christopher G, 1947, Je 26,23:2
Simpson, Clara H, 1957, F 13,35:2
Simpson, Colin C, 1961, O 29,88:8
Simpson, David B, 1924, N 29,13:3
Simpson, David P, 1959, Ap 6,27:3
Simpson, David P Mrs, 1942, D 21,23:2
Simpson, Dwight S, 1962, O 8,23:5
Simpson, E, 1877, Ap 1,7:4
Simpson, Edward R, 1939, Jl 16,30:3
Simpson, Edward R Mrs, 1939, Jl 16,30:3
Simpson, Edwin A Mrs, 1938, Mr 26,15:3
Simpson, Edwin J, 1965, Ja 29,34:2

Simpson, Elihu C, 1939, My 6,17:1
Simpson, Elliot E, 1954, S 23,33:5
Simpson, Elliot H, 1960, Ag 6,19:5
Simpson, Ellsworth T, 1958, Mr 12,31:1
Simpson, Elwyn W, 1963, Je 22,23:4
Simpson, Ernest, 1958, N 30,86:3
Simpson, Ernest A Mrs (por), 1941, O 4,15:6
Simpson, Ernest C, 1946, My 22,21:4
Simpson, Ernest L, 1947, Ag 16,13:1
Simpson, Ernest S, 1941, Ag 15,17:2
Simpson, Erwin M, 1950, Mr 27,23:5
Simpson, Etta G Mrs, 1940, S 25,27:2
Simpson, Eva B, 1966, O 14,43:3
Simpson, Eva H, 1951, Jl 18,29:6
Simpson, Eyler N (por), 1938, Jl 2,13:3
Simpson, Fanny A, 1949, O 4,27:1
Simpson, Frank E, 1948, D 15,33:3
Simpson, Frank F, 1948, F 12,24:3
Simpson, Frank Jr, 1956, Mr 17,19:6
Simpson, Frank L, 1954, S 3,24:8
Simpson, Frank M, 1957, Ap 11,31:1
Simpson, Fred B, 1939, S 24,44:1
Simpson, Fred W, 1945, O 9,21:5
Simpson, Frederick B, 1956, N 29,35:1
Simpson, Frederick Sr, 1944, Jl 5,17:5
Simpson, George, 1903, N 12,9:5; 1921, Ag 23,15:6; 1940, My 21,23:2; 1953, Ja 13,27:4; 1961, D 4,37:4
Simpson, George F, 1950, Ja 6,21:3
Simpson, George H, 1954, Mr 3,27:5; 1957, Mr 27,31:3
Simpson, George J, 1950, Je 23,25:4
Simpson, George R, 1941, Mr 22,15:4
Simpson, George S, 1939, Jl 21,19:2
Simpson, George W, 1951, F 2,23:1; 1951, Ag 18,11:2
Simpson, George Washington, 1912, D 30,7:4
Simpson, George Washington Rev Dr, 1912, Ag 19,9:6
Simpson, Glenn W, 1948, D 31,16:3
Simpson, H A L, 1938, D 22,21:3
Simpson, H Pierce Rev, 1968, N 20,47:3
Simpson, Harold B, 1957, D 9,35:2
Simpson, Harold G, 1939, Je 15,23:6
Simpson, Harry, 1949, N 1,27:5
Simpson, Helen (por), 1940, O 16,23:5
Simpson, Henry E, 1922, Je 1,19:5
Simpson, Herbert E, 1966, My 7,31:4
Simpson, Herbert Mrs, 1941, Ja 29,17:3
Simpson, Herbert S, 1957, N 5,31:4
Simpson, Herman Mrs, 1957, Ja 13,84:6
Simpson, Herman P, 1937, D 14,25:5
Simpson, Hester, 1951, Jl 23,17:4
Simpson, Homer N, 1943, F 6,13:5
Simpson, Ida Mrs, 1947, Mr 1,15:4
Simpson, Isidor, 1948, S 13,21:3
Simpson, Isidore H, 1952, Ag 31,45:2
Simpson, Ivan, 1951, O 14,89:1
Simpson, J, 1878, D 8,2:5
Simpson, J A, 1880, My 7,5:6
Simpson, J H Gen, 1883, Mr 3,5:3
Simpson, J S Capt, 1923, Ja 30,17:4
Simpson, J Y, 1934, My 22,23:1
Simpson, James, 1918, Mr 21,13:5
Simpson, James (por), 1939, N 26,43:1
Simpson, James, 1941, N 29,17:1; 1953, S 17,29:6
Simpson, James C, 1944, Ap 21,19:2; 1949, Jl 26,27:2
Simpson, James H, 1947, Ag 29,17:4
Simpson, James Jr, 1960, Mr 1,33:2
Simpson, James K Dr, 1937, My 20,21:3
Simpson, James M, 1948, My 15,15:4
Simpson, James V, 1947, S 20,15:5
Simpson, James V Mrs, 1950, Ap 12,27:3
Simpson, James W, 1943, D 28,17:3
Simpson, Jeremiah, 1905, O 24,7:2
Simpson, John, 1944, Je 19,19:4
Simpson, John B, 1943, O 15,19:3
Simpson, John B Mrs, 1957, Je 28,23:5
Simpson, John F, 1941, Ja 1,23:6
Simpson, John Gen, 1914, N 1,17:4
Simpson, John M, 1946, O 23,27:2
Simpson, John M Sr, 1949, D 1,31:5
Simpson, John R, 1956, D 6,37:3
Simpson, John T, 1962, Ap 12,36:1
Simpson, John W, 1950, Ja 18,32:2; 1967, O 13,39:4
Simpson, John W Mrs, 1943, Ja 12,23:4
Simpson, John Woodruff, 1920, My 17,15:1
Simpson, Joseph, 1939, Ja 31,21:1
Simpson, Joseph Cairn, 1906, My 28,9:6
Simpson, Joseph E, 1938, Ap 16,13:6
Simpson, Joseph F, 1941, Ag 1,15:2
Simpson, Joseph Sir, 1968, Mr 21,47:4
Simpson, Joseph W, 1944, Je 11,46:1; 1952, D 9,34:3
Simpson, Joseph W Sr, 1946, Je 25,21:4
Simpson, Kenneth F, 1941, Ja 26,1:5
Simpson, Kenneth M, 1951, Ja 14,84:7
Simpson, Kirke L Mrs, 1952, O 19,88:4
Simpson, Leo F, 1955, N 1,31:3
Simpson, Leon, 1944, My 26,19:4
Simpson, Leon G, 1942, Jl 18,13:4
Simpson, Leonard J, 1940, Ag 19,17:6
Simpson, Lusby, 1954, Je 1,27:3
Simpson, Lynn C, 1944, Jl 18,19:2
Simpson, M Bp (funl), 1884, Je 19,4:7
Simpson, Mabel, 1938, Ja 16,II,8:6
Simpson, Mabel E, 1938, Ap 6,23:2
Simpson, Mae, 1952, D 19,31:4

Simpson, Margaret Mrs, 1939, Ja 4,21:5
Simpson, Marie L, 1941, Ap 16,23:5
Simpson, Marshall, 1958, D 1,29:4
Simpson, Martha P Mrs, 1942, Jl 29,17:4
Simpson, Maxwell G, 1945, Ja 3,17:1
Simpson, Merlin, 1947, F 21,19:1
Simpson, Milton, 1941, Mr 4,23:1
Simpson, Mortimer L, 1947, Ag 3,52:3
Simpson, Napoleon B, 1950, Ag 13,76:1
Simpson, Nathaniel W, 1944, F 3,19:5
Simpson, Norma P, 1956, Je 29,21:2
Simpson, Paul E, 1950, F 9,29:4
Simpson, Percy B, 1903, Jl 5,7:5
Simpson, Quintus I, 1940, F 17,13:3
Simpson, R A, 1903, Ja 10,9:6
Simpson, Richard H, 1945, O 10,21:4
Simpson, Richard M (funl, Ja 10,86:7), 1960, Ja 8, 25:1
Simpson, Richard M Mrs, 1945, Mr 8,23:5
Simpson, Richard W, 1953, My 31,74:2; 1953, N 14, 17:5
Simpson, Robert, 1915, Ag 31,9:6; 1950, Mr 12,93:2; 1952, Ag 22,21:4
Simpson, Robert C, 1955, Ag 17,27:3
Simpson, Robert E, 1938, Mr 7,17:6; 1952, Ag 14,23:3
Simpson, Robert H Mrs, 1947, My 23,23:3
Simpson, Robert R, 1940, Mr 10,48:2
Simpson, Robert S Mrs, 1963, Je 30,56:3
Simpson, Robert Tennent, 1912, Ag 13,9:5
Simpson, Russell, 1959, D 13,86:4
Simpson, S Dr, 1926, Mr 4,21:3
Simpson, Sid, 1958, O 27,27:3
Simpson, Sidney P (por), 1949, O 7,31:1
Simpson, Sol, 1952, Je 6,9:2
Simpson, Stanley W, 1946, D 9,25:1
Simpson, Stephen M Sr, 1965, My 30,50:8
Simpson, Stephen Price Rev Dr, 1913, Jl 4,7:4
Simpson, Sumner, 1953, Je 15,29:5
Simpson, Sumner Mrs, 1940, D 29,24:8
Simpson, Sylvester, 1963, Ap 10,39:2
Simpson, T, 1932, Jl 21,17:3
Simpson, Theodore M, 1937, N 26,21:1
Simpson, Thomas, 1885, Ja 26,2:4
Simpson, Thomas B, 1948, O 27,27:4
Simpson, Thomas Hargrove, 1923, Ja 23,21:5
Simpson, Thomas I, 1939, Ja 16,15:1
Simpson, Thomas J, 1939, Ap 25,23:1
Simpson, Thomas S Mrs, 1937, Ja 14,22:1
Simpson, Tommy, 1947, F 7,23:2
Simpson, W, 1879, Ap 10,9:4
Simpson, W J R, 1931, S 22,27:1
Simpson, W L Hope Mrs, 1956, Ja 13,23:2
Simpson, W Percy, 1938, F 21,19:5
Simpson, W Ray, 1949, Ja 10,25:2
Simpson, W S, 1947, Mr 30,56:2
Simpson, Waller S, 1950, Jl 11,31:4
Simpson, Walter B, 1953, My 6,31:4
Simpson, Walter F, 1953, O 26,21:5
Simpson, Walter S Mrs, 1950, S 19,31:3
Simpson, Wendell E, 1959, N 3,31:1
Simpson, Wilford C, 1952, My 16,23:5
Simpson, William, 1916, D 7,13:5
Simpson, William (will, Ja 14,11:7), 1956, Ja 3,31:3
Simpson, William A, 1945, N 12,22:2; 1948, Je 27,52:4
Simpson, William E, 1938, Ap 2,15:2; 1951, Ap 30, 21:6; 1958, My 17,19:5
Simpson, William G, 1946, Jl 12,17:5
Simpson, William H, 1945, Ja 31,21:5
Simpson, William Henry, 1924, O 6,19:5
Simpson, William Kelly Dr, 1914, F 7,11:5
Simpson, William M, 1963, My 3,31:2
Simpson, William Mrs, 1949, Ja 25,24:2
Simpson, William P, 1953, Jl 3,19:2
Simpson, William R, 1944, Ap 7,19:3; 1957, D 10,35:2
Simpson, William S, 1948, N 3,27:3
Simrall, Josephine P, 1949, Jl 5,23:4
Simrell, George W, 1943, D 2,27:3
Sims, Alfred V, 1944, Ja 22,13:6
Sims, C, 1928, Ap 17,29:5
Sims, C Frank, 1957, My 9,31:5
Sims, Charles, 1953, D 24,15:5
Sims, Edward, 1946, S 9,9:1
Sims, Edward C, 1942, Ap 30,19:4
Sims, Edwin M, 1948, Je 17,25:5
Sims, Frank Mrs (Marian), 1961, Jl 10,21:5
Sims, Frank S, 1951, D 22,15:6; 1955, F 13,86:3
Sims, Frederick G, 1948, Ja 8,25:3
Sims, George H Sr, 1955, Ja 7,22:3
Sims, George R, 1922, S 6,15:3
Sims, Hall B, 1944, Mr 2,17:2
Sims, Harold H, 1940, My 7,25:5
Sims, Harry Mrs, 1949, Mr 29,25:4
Sims, Henry U, 1961, N 2,37:4
Sims, Hugo S Sr, 1951, N 4,86:4
Sims, J Isabelle, 1952, Mr 12,28:3
Sims, J M Dr, 1883, N 14,2:1
Sims, James D, 1948, My 21,23:5
Sims, James W, 1943, D 20,23:3
Sims, Jesse O, 1966, O 19,38:5
Sims, Joseph P, 1953, Mr 30,21:3
Sims, Lee, 1966, My 9,39:5
Sims, Marjorie, 1950, Ap 5,31:5
Sims, P Hal (por), 1949, F 28,19:1

Sims, P Hal Mrs (Dorothy R), 1960, Mr 25,27:1
Sims, Paul, 1959, D 31,21:1
Sims, Robert F, 1959, S 13,84:2
Sims, Robert P, 1944, Ap 26,19:3
Sims, Ross B, 1938, Ag 26,17:5
Sims, Russell S (por), 1949, Ag 4,23:5
Sims, Thetus W, 1939, D 18,23:4
Sims, Thetus W Mrs, 1946, F 19,25:6
Sims, Van Buren, 1967, Je 30,37:4
Sims, Victor, 1953, Jl 7,27:3
Sims, W S, 1936, S 29,1:3
Sims, William, 1871, N 27,1:6; 1941, Ap 30,19:5
Sims, William E, 1959, Jl 22,27:5
Sims, Winfield S, 1918, Ja 8,15:8
Simson, A G, 1960, Ag 14,92:8
Simson, Alex L Mrs, 1964, O 3,29:4
Simson, Eugen, 1957, N 28,31:2
Simson, Frances, 1940, F 14,21:5
Simson, George F, 1949, F 9,27:3
Simson, Hugh J, 1941, My 30,15:6
Simson, Julius, 1953, Ja 30,21:3
Simson, Walter A, 1950, O 5,31:5
Simunek, Charles J, 1960, My 4,45:2
Sinapi, John, 1954, Ja 29,6:5
Sinatra, Frank, 1948, Ap 10,13:3
Sinauer, Alan B, 1964, My 19,37:1
Sinauer, Otto, 1937, Je 24,25:5
Sinbine, William H, 1952, Jl 21,19:5
Sincell, Benjamin H, 1947, Ja 12,59:2
Sincerbeaux, Charles S, 1956, O 1,27:4
Sincerbeaux, Frank H Mrs, 1962, S 22,25:5
Sincere, Ben E, 1941, O 6,17:4
Sincere, Charles, 1937, Ap 21,23:5
Sincere, Victor W, 1955, S 29,33:5
Sincero, L, 1936, F 8,15:2
Sinclair, Alex, 1955, My 31,27:4
Sinclair, Angus Dr, 1919, Ja 3,9:1
Sinclair, Archibald G, 1959, Ap 18,23:4
Sinclair, Arthur, 1941, Je 4,23:3; 1951, D 16,90:3
Sinclair, Arthur B, 1953, F 3,25:4
Sinclair, Bessie T Mrs, 1941, Ja 27,15:1
Sinclair, Beverley K, 1947, Jl 6,40:8
Sinclair, Calder P, 1959, N 16,31:5
Sinclair, Carroll T, 1965, D 30,21:4
Sinclair, Catharine, 1864, Ag 25,3:2
Sinclair, Charles G Jr (cor, Ap 15,33:2), 1958, Ap 13,84:7
Sinclair, Crawford C, 1950, Mr 28,31:1
Sinclair, D G C, 1933, Ag 18,15:3
Sinclair, Daniel A, 1947, Jl 18,17:4
Sinclair, Daniel M Mrs, 1950, O 3,31:2
Sinclair, Duncan, 1939, Jl 25,19:3; 1962, My 19,27:4
Sinclair, E W Mrs, 1952, O 12,89:2
Sinclair, Earle W (por), 1944, S 22,19:6
Sinclair, F R, 1912, Ag 24,9:7
Sinclair, Francis MacD Mrs, 1965, Mr 10,30:2
Sinclair, Francis MacDonald, 1918, D 16,15:2
Sinclair, Frank D, 1961, O 21,21:1
Sinclair, Frazer V, 1965, Je 15,41:3
Sinclair, Fred A Sr, 1953, D 18,29:3
Sinclair, George D Mrs, 1955, D 5,31:1
Sinclair, George H, 1959, Ag 6,27:5
Sinclair, Gerritt V, 1955, D 25,48:3
Sinclair, Graham M, 1907, S 14,9:5
Sinclair, Guy V Sr, 1957, S 8,84:5
Sinclair, Harold, 1966, My 25,47:1
Sinclair, Harry F (funl plans, N 12,29:3), 1956, N 11,1:3
Sinclair, Harry F MRs, 1964, My 16,25:6
Sinclair, Henry Harbinson, 1914, S 3,7:7
Sinclair, Horace, 1949, F 20,60:5
Sinclair, Hugh, 1962, D 31,4:5
Sinclair, James, 1960, O 2,84:2
Sinclair, James A, 1942, Ja 24,17:2
Sinclair, James R (Earl of Caithness), 1965, My 9, 87:2
Sinclair, John, 1949, Mr 29,25:3; 1949, S 20,29:4
Sinclair, John E, 1949, D 24,15:3
Sinclair, John F, 1948, My 13,25:4
Sinclair, John J, 1916, S 16,11:6; 1954, Ag 4,21:6
Sinclair, John M, 1953, F 2,3:7; 1961, S 29,35:2
Sinclair, John Mrs, 1946, Jl 22,21:4
Sinclair, Joseph H, 1946, My 26,32:5
Sinclair, May (por), 1946, N 15,23:3
Sinclair, Percival C, 1954, Ja 2,11:4
Sinclair, Peter, 1869, Mr 1,2:4
Sinclair, Prior, 1961, Jl 15,19:3
Sinclair, Richard, 1946, Ag 17,13:1
Sinclair, Robert Mrs, 1945, My 5,15:4
Sinclair, Robert Ring, 1907, F 25,9:4
Sinclair, Robert S (por), 1937, Ja 19,23:2
Sinclair, Robert S, 1937, My 16,II,9:2
Sinclair, Scott, 1950, N 3,27:5
Sinclair, Scott Mrs, 1956, N 22,33:5
Sinclair, T M, 1881, Mr 25,2:1
Sinclair, Thomas, 1940, N 26,23:2
Sinclair, Thomas S D, 1951, Ag 2,21:2
Sinclair, Thomas W, 1940, Ap 12,23:1
Sinclair, Upton, 1968, N 26,1:6
Sinclair, Upton Mrs, 1961, Ap 27,21:2; 1967, D 21,37:2
Sinclair, Walrond, 1952, Ag 31,44:6
Sinclair, William E, 1947, N 27,31:3
Sinclair, William Gen, 1905, O 4,2:3

Sinclair, William R, 1965, Ap 24,29:1
Sinclaire, Thomas Dr, 1865, Ag 25,3:2
Sinclari, Frank, 1964, O 31,29:5
Sincoff, Abraham, 1939, Ja 17,21:5
Sincoff, Jacob, 1965, My 20,43:3
Sindall, Frank G, 1947, S 4,25:4
Sindall, Robert A, 1947, S 4,25:5
Sindeband, Irwin L, 1953, N 26,31:1
Sindeband, Samuel J, 1962, F 28,25:2
Sindelar, James S, 1951, Jl 29,69:3
Sinding, Christian, 1941, D 4,25:5
Sindler, Morris, 1954, Ja 8,22:3
Sindler, Thomas, 1947, S 2,21:3
Sindt, Harry E, 1952, Ag 18,17:1
Sindt, Henry E, 1955, Je 2,29:5
Sinek, William J, 1964, Jl 7,35:2
Sinenberg, Robert L, 1960, F 14,84:4
Siner, Emanuel, 1957, N 10,86:7
Siner, Leandro C, 1942, Mr 16,15:4
Sines, John H, 1943, Ja 1,23:1
Sinexon, Justus, 1938, D 29,20:3
Siney, Edward F, 1959, Ap 17,25:3
Siney, Wildey V, 1959, F 11,39:5
Sing, C B Rev, 1878, Mr 4,8:3
Singe, Gurcharan, 1942, D 16,25:5
Singer, A Alex, 1953, Ap 25,15:6
Singer, Aaron H, 1966, S 24,23:4
Singer, Abraham S, 1949, O 11,34:3
Singer, Al, 1961, Ap 21,33:4
Singer, Albert, 1955, Ap 14,29:3
Singer, Alfred Mrs, 1948, Ap 6,23:6
Singer, Arion, 1908, Jl 25,5:6
Singer, Arthur G, 1942, N 12,25:5
Singer, Arthur J, 1953, Je 22,21:2
Singer, Barney, 1925, My 18,15:5
Singer, Benjamin, 1951, N 29,33:5; 1963, My 30,17:1
Singer, Benjamin J, 1948, Je 13,68:7
Singer, Benny, 1944, Mr 29,21:5
Singer, Caroline H Mrs, 1937, O 28,25:4
Singer, Cecil M, 1952, Ja 30,25:4
Singer, Charles, 1942, Je 30,21:4; 1960, Je 13,27:6
Singer, Charles A Mrs, 1943, Ag 17,17:4
Singer, Charles E, 1956, D 27,25:4
Singer, Charles I, 1951, D 11,33:5
Singer, Charles Jr, 1940, Je 27,23:1
Singer, Charles L, 1954, Ja 26,27:5
Singer, Daniel J, 1924, S 29,15:2
Singer, Edgar A Jr, 1955, Ap 5,29:3
Singer, Elizabeth M Mrs, 1966, Je 30,34:1
Singer, Emanuel, 1967, N 7,39:3
Singer, Emil, 1952, Jl 16,25:3
Singer, Eugene T, 1956, Mr 30,19:1
Singer, Franklin M, 1939, Ag 12,13:6
Singer, Franz, 1953, Jl 23,23:1
Singer, Frederick Rear-Adm, 1923, Ja 6,13:5
Singer, George A, 1958, Ag 27,29:2
Singer, Gerald, 1968, S 4,47:3
Singer, H Douglas, 1940, Ag 30,19:1
Singer, Harry, 1967, My 27,31:2
Singer, Hayward, 1967, Ag 21,31:2
Singer, Hazel, 1922, Je 6,17:4
Singer, Henach Mrs, 1958, Je 4,33:4
Singer, Henry B Mrs, 1952, O 29,29:6
Singer, Herbert J, 1966, Mr 2,41:1
Singer, I A, 1902, S 26,9:6
Singer, Isaac L, 1943, S 18,17:6
Singer, Isaac Merritt, 1875, Jl 25,6:6
Singer, Israel J (por), 1944, F 11,19:1
Singer, J J, 1954, Ap 15,29:4
Singer, Jack, 1938, F 1,42:2; 1949, N 7,27:1
Singer, Jacob, 1956, F 1,31:4; 1964, Ag 6,29:1
Singer, Jacob M, 1949, S 30,23:2
Singer, Jacques, 1949, Mr 18,25:2
Singer, John G, 1957, F 22,21:2
Singer, Joseph, 1958, Je 7,19:1
Singer, Joseph C, 1966, Jl 16,25:3
Singer, Joseph F, 1953, S 21,25:5
Singer, Joseph G, 1955, Ag 11,21:3
Singer, Joseph L, 1953, My 26,29:5
Singer, Julius, 1942, O 26,15:5
Singer, Karl, 1956, Jl 14,15:5
Singer, Kenneth M, 1962, Jl 31,27:3
Singer, Lawrence H, 1946, N 7,31:2
Singer, Louis (will, Mr 3,19:2), 1937, F 16,23:5
Singer, Louis C, 1966, D 31,19:4
Singer, Louis N, 1954, Mr 16,29:4
Singer, M Meyer, 1956, Jl 14,15:3
Singer, Marian, 1924, N 22,15:5
Singer, Martha, 1950, Ag 15,29:5
Singer, Martin, 1955, D 23,17:2
Singer, Martin H (will), 1944, Ap 17,38:4
Singer, Max, 1943, Ag 16,15:5; 1966, Je 26,73:2
Singer, Mayer, 1957, O 27,86:8
Singer, Michael, 1953, N 18,26:7
Singer, Michael (M Kantor), 1958, N 30,87:2
Singer, Morgan, 1938, Ap 29,21:1
Singer, Mort H, 1944, Mr 30,21:6
Singer, Morton, 1957, My 23,33:4
Singer, Mose, 1947, Mr 22,13:2
Singer, Murry M, 1966, Ja 4,27:3
Singer, Nathaniel, 1963, Ag 17,19:3
Singer, P E, 1932, Je 25,13:1
Singer, Paris G, 1953, D 15,39:5
Singer, Paris Mrs, 1951, Mr 9,25:3
Singer, Paul, 1911, F 1,11:5
Singer, Richard, 1940, Mr 1,21:4
Singer, Ronald, 1953, D 21,39:2
Singer, Ronald Mrs, 1953, D 21,39:2
Singer, Ruth, 1953, Ja 12,27:1
Singer, Ruth Mrs, 1960, Jl 1,25:4
Singer, Samuel, 1952, Mr 9,82:6; 1960, My 6,31:2
Singer, Samuel W, 1945, Ap 9,19:5
Singer, Saul, 1948, Mr 2,23:2
Singer, Sidney, 1960, N 2,39:4
Singer, Sidney K, 1940, Jl 18,19:4
Singer, Sol, 1962, Ag 25,19:3
Singer, Sumer, 1945, Je 6,21:2
Singer, Victor E Dr, 1968, F 17,29:4
Singer, W M G, 1934, F 12,15:4
Singer, Walter O, 1954, F 5,13:5
Singer, Werner Mrs (P Novikova), 1967, Ag 24,37:3
Singer, William, 1955, Jl 18,21:5
Singer, William H, 1909, S 5,9:6; 1944, Mr 22,19:6
Singerly, W M, 1898, F 28,7:5
Singerman, Bruno A, 1968, Mr 24,92:8
Singh, Amarjit, 1944, S 24,45:2
Singh, Baldev, 1961, Je 30,25:1
Singh, Ganga, 1943, F 2,19:3
Singh, Hari, 1961, Ap 27,21:4
Singh, Jagajit Maharajah, 1949, Je 20,19:3
Singh, Jogendra, 1946, D 4,31:3
Singh, Pertab Gen, 1922, S 5,17:6
Singh, Prince, 1926, Ag 16,15:4
Singh, Rajah Ravi S, 1947, Ja 7,27:2
Singh, Tara, 1967, N 22,47:3
Singha, Prince, 1947, O 19,66:3
Singhji, Sajjan, 1947, F 4,25:5
Singiser, Frank I Mrs, 1949, Mr 2,26:2
Singiser, Frank K, 1949, F 2,27:4
Single, Forrest E, 1949, Mr 1,25:3
Singlehurst, John, 1940, N 22,23:2
Singletary, Benjamin H, 1964, Ap 1,39:1
Singleton, Albert O, 1947, Je 13,23:3
Singleton, Alex H, 1955, Ap 30,17:6
Singleton, Amy E, 1938, S 26,17:2
Singleton, Asa L (por), 1943, Je 8,21:3
Singleton, Asa L Mrs, 1939, O 15,49:2
Singleton, Edward, 1950, Mr 31,31:3
Singleton, Edward J, 1942, Mr 10,19:3
Singleton, Francis T, 1950, O 24,29:5
Singleton, Frederick A, 1947, N 13,28:3
Singleton, Frederick W, 1941, Ap 2,23:2
Singleton, Henry M, 1951, O 21,92:3
Singleton, Horace L Rev, 1910, Jl 14,7:1
Singleton, J Edward, 1958, Mr 9,86:6
Singleton, J Edward Mrs, 1950, O 16,27:2
Singleton, J William Sr, 1948, N 15,25:2
Singleton, John W, 1940, N 16,17:3
Singleton, Jouett P Mrs, 1949, Ag 25,23:4
Singleton, Kate, 1904, N 1,9:6
Singleton, Marvin E, 1938, Ja 30,II,8:5
Singleton, Milton R, 1943, Jl 29,19:4
Singleton, Milton R Mrs, 1941, D 17,27:5
Singleton, Shelby M, 1938, O 30,41:3
Singleton, Timothy P, 1961, Ja 1,48:7
Singleton, Walter C, 1962, O 6,25:4
Singleton, William H, 1938, S 9,21:1
Singley, Lloyd Mrs, 1947, Je 25,26:2
Singley, Robert J, 1943, Je 20,34:4
Singman, Joseph, 1946, Ap 15,27:3
Singmaster, Elsie (Mrs E S Lawars), 1958, O 1,37:2
Singmaster, J A Rev Dr, 1926, F 28,II,9:1
Singmaster, James A, 1962, Ap 13,35:1
Singsen, Frederick M, 1962, Mr 29,33:3
Singstad, Ole Mrs, 1964, Jl 9,33:1
Sinha, Dowager Lady, 1938, O 17,15:6
Sinisi, James, 1950, F 9,29:2
Sinistorie, Antoinette Mrs, 1962, Ag 26,83:1
Sink, Charles L, 1951, O 21,92:6
Sink, Emory W, 1965, Ap 7,43:2
Sink, John D, 1948, N 8,21:1
Sink, Robert F, 1965, D 15,47:3
Sinkinson, Charles D, 1939, F 20,17:1
Sinkler, Caroline, 1949, My 6,25:1
Sinkler, Charles, 1952, Ja 14,19:3
Sinkler, Wharton 2d, 1952, Ja 18,27:3
Sinks, Albert E (por), 1940, Je 2,44:8
Sinks, Albert E Mrs, 1954, Ja 8,21:3
Sinlcair, William E, 1946, D 31,17:5
Sinn, Francis P, 1967, Mr 17,41:3
Sinn, Francis P Mrs, 1954, My 5,31:4
Sinn, Frank J, 1947, Ja 23,23:1
Sinn, Joseph A, 1917, S 26,13:5
Sinn, Samuel, 1908, My 14,9:6
Sinn, William, 1948, Jl 1,23:5
Sinn, William B, 1950, O 24,29:4
Sinn, William E Col, 1899, Ag 10,5:1
Sinn, William H Mrs, 1945, Jl 27,15:4
Sinnamon, George, 1947, Mr 12,25:4
Sinnamon, Henry H, 1949, D 22,23:4
Sinnamon, Henry H Mrs, 1958, Ap 6,88:3
Sinner, Emanuel, 1950, F 13,21:3
Sinner, Kurt M, 1956, F 24,25:3
Sinnett, Thomas J, 1958, O 8,35:1
Sinnickson, Clement Hall, 1919, Jl 26,9:7
Sinnickson, J Forman, 1939, F 24,19:5
Sinnigen, Charles E, 1949, Mr 12,17:3
Sinnigen, James C, 1959, O 20,39:2
Sinnock, John R, 1947, My 15,25:3
Sinnock, William D, 1909, F 5,7:3
Sinnot, Delia E Mrs, 1937, Ag 26,21:4
Sinnot, Edwin M (por), 1944, F 16,17:5
Sinnott, Alfred A, 1954, Ap 19,23:2
Sinnott, Arthur J (por), 1944, Ag 9,17:3
Sinnott, Arthur J Mrs, 1948, Ag 3,25:4
Sinnott, Carroll J, 1955, Jl 8,23:5
Sinnott, Charles P, 1943, O 18,15:4
Sinnott, Edmund T, 1962, Mr 6,35:1
Sinnott, Edmund W Dr, 1968, Ja 7,84:6
Sinnott, Edward A Mrs, 1968, Je 15,35:2
Sinnott, Francis J (funl, S 21,25:3), 1956, S 17,27:5
Sinnott, Frank J, 1950, Jl 19,31:5
Sinnott, George Mrs, 1948, Ag 3,25:6
Sinnott, George Rev, 1921, Ap 25,11:4
Sinnott, Gilbert J, 1950, S 5,27:5
Sinnott, J J, 1928, Ja 27,21:3
Sinnott, J P, 1880, S 21,8:3; 1928, S 11,27:3
Sinnott, James P, 1948, S 18,17:1; 1955, S 15,33:3
Sinnott, James P Msgr, 1925, D 23,19:4
Sinnott, John F, 1946, Jl 11,23:3; 1954, Ag 31,21:2
Sinnott, John J, 1918, My 3,15:5
Sinnott, Lawrence J, 1949, Je 21,25:6
Sinnott, Michael P, 1960, Je 20,31:5
Sinnott, Patrick, 1951, S 1,11:1
Sinnott, Peter, 1955, N 26,19:2
Sinnott, Peter Mrs, 1938, Ag 16,19:5
Sinnott, Philip J, 1944, Je 4,42:3
Sinnott, Sabina R, 1951, Ja 30,25:4
Sinnott, William J, 1965, Mr 31,39:1
Sinott, John J, 1943, Ja 28,19:4
Sinram, George F, 1951, D 13,35:7
Sinram, Henry D, 1954, Ja 12,23:4
Sinran, John V, 1951, Je 6,44:8
Sinsabaugh, Christopher G, 1943, Ja 27,21:3
Sinsabaugh, Clifford, 1943, Ag 28,39:2
Sinsabaugh, John V, 1941, D 16,27:4
Sinsabaugh, Robert W, 1961, My 20,23:6
Sinsabaugh, Willard K, 1951, Ag 16,27:6
Sinsheimer, Alex L Mrs (will), 1958, Jl 4,21:4
Sinsheimer, Arthur, 1949, My 26,29:3
Sinsheimer, Benjamin L, 1959, S 2,29:3
Sinsheimer, Bernard, 1947, Ja 7,28:2
Sinsheimer, Michael L, 1943, Ja 15,17:4
Sinsheimer, Solomon, 1943, Jl 31,13:4
Sinsheimer, Walter J, 1921, Ag 2,9:4
Sinsheimer, Warren A, 1952, N 29,13:4
Sinske, Morris M, 1959, Mr 31,29:3
Sintenis, Renee Mrs, 1965, Ap 24,29:3
Sinton, Arthur C Jr Dr, 1937, N 7,II,9:4
Sinton, Stanley H, 1954, S 10,23:1
Sinz, Walter A Mrs, 1945, Ag 30,21:5
Sioberg, Charles F, 1948, Ja 18,60:8
Sioka, Frank, 1948, O 6,29:4
Sioris, P A Mrs, 1945, Mr 27,19:5
Sioussat, A M Mrs, 1942, Mr 18,23:3
Sioussat, St George L, 1960, S 1,27:5
Sipe, Ben, 1948, N 12,23:2
Sipe, Samuel Mrs, 1917, F 9,11:5
Siper, Benjamin, 1964, D 5,31:3
Sipkin, Joseph Mrs, 1949, F 28,19:6
Siple, Paul Allman Dr, 1968, N 26,47:1
Sipley, James T, 1940, F 4,40:4
Sipley, Louis Walton Dr, 1968, O 19,37:4
Sipp, Frank Mrs, 1942, Mr 14,15:6
Sipp, John L, 1943, S 16,21:5; 1945, N 9,19:4
Sippel, John F Mrs, 1943, Jl 11,34:6
Sippel, Max, 1958, N 27,29:3
Sippel, Otto, 1946, O 15,25:1
Sippel, William E, 1947, Jl 6,42:8
Sipperley, Ellis Mrs, 1949, N 15,25:1
Sipple, Ernest W, 1961, Ag 5,17:5
Sippley, Joseph, 1949, Ag 2,19:2
Sipser, Josef N, 1954, F 21,69:2
Siqueland, Tryggve Col, 1937, F 8,17:4
Sir Johnny (Lt Jno J Dunn), 1910, Ja 24,9:1
Siracusa, Anthony J Jr (por), 1938, Ja 14,23:5
Siracusa, Frank J, 1957, Ap 24,33:2
Siragusa, Dominic R, 1950, O 30,27:3
Siragusa, Matteo, 1957, D 31,17:4
Sircom, Frank R Mrs, 1940, D 19,25:4
Sircom, Rupert, 1962, Ap 23,29:4
Sire, Albert I Mrs, 1903, O 30,1:5
Sire, Henry B, 1917, Ja 18,11:3
Sire, Lillian Mrs, 1945, N 24,19:5
Sirianni, Guiseppe, 1955, Ag 17,27:4
Sirignano, Alfonso Mrs, 1957, Jl 2,27:2
Sirken, Charles S, 1959, Jl 6,27:4
Sirkey, Louis, 1949, N 30,27:3
Sirmay, Albert, 1967, Ja 17,39:4
Siro, James, 1958, O 26,88:7
Sirois, Joseph, 1941, Ja 18,15:5
Siron, Ernest, 1910, F 2,9:4
Sironi, Mario, 1961, Ag 14,25:3
Sirot, John O, 1967, Ap 8,31:5
Sirota, Abraham, 1967, O 16,45:1
Sirota, Leo, 1965, F 25,31:1
Sirota, Maurice, 1956, Ja 26,29:2
Sirota, Samuel L, 1965, N 25,35:3
Sirota, William, 1961, Ja 29,85:2

Sirotiak, Lazor, 1949, F 19,15:7
Sirovatka, Frank J, 1945, S 5,23:2
Sirovich, William I, 1939, D 18,23:1
Sirrine, Joseph E, 1947, Ag 8,17:2
Sirrine, William, 1944, My 28,34:2
Sirry, Hussein, 1961, Ja 8,86:1
Sirtl, Sumner, 1947, O 15,27:4
Sirvent, Harry Jr, 1955, Jl 21,23:4
Sisakyan, Norair M, 1966, Mr 13,86:8
Sisavang Vong, King of Laos, 1959, O 30,27:3
Sisavang Vong, King of Laos (cremation), 1961, Ap 30,3:5
Sisca, Alessandro, 1940, Ag 27,21:5
Sisca, Marziale, 1968, F 5,35:4
Sisca, Marziale Mrs, 1967, Mr 14,47:1
Sisco, Andrew, 1942, Ag 2,39:3
Sisco, Frank T, 1965, Ja 14,35:1
Sisco, Frederick A, 1950, Ap 1,15:4
Sisco, George M, 1953, Je 25,27:2
Sisco, Gordon A, 1953, D 17,37:3
Sisco, H N, 1943, Ag 5,15:3
Sise, Charles F, 1918, Ap 10,13:5; 1960, N 11,31:1
Sise, Edward F (por), 1943, Jl 4,20:6
Sise, Lincoln F, 1942, Ap 30,19:3
Sise, Paul F, 1951, Ag 3,21:4
Siser, Theodore, 1967, Je 22,39:2
Sisholz, Benjamin H, 1965, Ap 29,35:2
Sisinni, Gerard, 1952, Jl 12,13:3
Sisk, Bernard E, 1945, F 28,23:2
Sisk, Berry J, 1963, Je 26,39:2
Sisk, David A, 1946, Je 7,20:2
Sisk, James H, 1938, D 6,23:4
Sisk, Patrick H, 1945, F 4,38:4
Sisk, Robert J Mrs, 1967, Mr 9,39:2
Sisk, Robert Mrs, 1957, N 18,31:1
Siskind, Alexander L, 1944, My 6,19:5
Sisley, Edward J, 1956, S 25,33:1
Sisley, John M, 1954, O 21,27:1
Sisley, William R, 1959, N 21,23:1
Sisos, Catherine R, 1939, O 18,26:2
Sisowath, King, 1927, Ag 11,21:5
Sisowath Monipong, Prince of Cambodia, 1956, S 1, 15:5
Sisowath Monivong, Prea Bat Samdach Prea King of Cambodia, 1941, Ap 25,19:5
Sissano, Michael, 1945, O 27,15:5
Sisserson, James F, 1952, S 27,17:3
Sisserson, W Wilson, 1948, S 3,19:2
Sission, Lewis H, 1953, N 28,15:5
Sissman, Peter, 1941, O 1,21:6
Sisson, Albert T, 1952, Ap 16,27:5
Sisson, Arthur O, 1948, Mr 15,23:3
Sisson, Charles H, 1941, Mr 14,21:2
Sisson, Charles H Mrs, 1950, Ag 8,29:2
Sisson, Charles J, 1874, Ag 23,8:1
Sisson, Charles P, 1947, Ag 3,52:4
Sisson, Delmar F, 1954, Mr 17,31:4
Sisson, Edgar G, 1948, Mr 13,15:3
Sisson, Edgar G Mrs, 1963, Jl 12,25:5
Sisson, Edward O, 1949, Ja 25,23:4
Sisson, Edwin C, 1941, N 19,23:4
Sisson, Elliot H, 1940, D 21,17:4
Sisson, Elmer S, 1947, S 2,21:3
Sisson, F H, 1933, S 18,1:4
Sisson, Francis T Sr, 1955, O 13,31:4
Sisson, Frederick J (por), 1949, O 23,84:1
Sisson, Frederick R, 1962, F 2,29:1
Sisson, Frederick R Jr, 1957, Ag 15,21:2
Sisson, George W, 1954, F 8,23:5
Sisson, Grace L Mrs, 1939, Ag 17,21:5
Sisson, Harry D, 1938, N 5,19:5
Sisson, Harry R, 1951, F 23,27:2
Sisson, Harry T, 1938, Jl 10,29:5
Sisson, Harvey Albert, 1953, F 21,13:4
Sisson, Herbert S, 1961, Ja 3,29:2
Sisson, Horace F, 1942, Mr 11,19:2
Sisson, J Nolan Mrs, 1948, My 25,27:2
Sisson, John P, 1949, O 10,23:3
Sisson, Lewis, 1944, Ag 30,17:6
Sisson, Perry L, 1938, Jl 13,21:5
Sisson, Rufus L Sr, 1937, Ja 2,11:2
Sisson, Rufus Mrs, 1947, Je 5,26:3
Sisson, Samuel B, 1947, N 23,74:5
Sisson, Thomas Upton, 1923, S 27,7:3
Sisson, W Lee, 1924, My 21,19:2
Sisson, Warren B, 1949, D 9,31:2
Sisson, Wesley, 1937, Ja 26,21:4
Sisson, William M Jr, 1954, Jl 22,23:6
Sisson, William W, 1937, My 17,19:5
Sistare, Elvira, 1948, My 28,23:4
Sistare, G K, 1880, Ja 26,8:4
Sistare, William H M Col, 1915, N 27,15:5
Sister Dolores, Irene Marshall, 1902, O 25,1:6
Sister Mary Cleophas, 1903, My 24,7:4
Sister Mary Ursula, 1874, Ap 11,1:6
Sister Serena (Miss Gilman), 1871, Ja 11,2:5
Sisto, John F, 1957, Je 16,84:2
Sisto, Louis J, 1961, Mr 25,25:4
Sitarsky, John J, 1956, N 4,87:1
Sitarz, Hans, 1958, Ja 9,33:1
Sitchevska, Constantine Mrs, 1958, My 21,33:3
Sitehouse, George A, 1939, Ap 15,19:3
Siteman, Arthur, 1956, O 4,33:2
Siteman, John H Jr, 1944, Ag 25,13:6
Siter, Elijah H, 1941, S 6,15:6
Sites, Clement M L, 1958, F 19,27:3
Sites, Frederick R, 1947, Ap 30,25:2
Sitgreaves, Beverly (por), 1943, Jl 15,21:1
Sitgreaves, Edward A, 1953, Ja 17,15:5
Sitgreaves, Julius A Capt, 1912, Ja 24,11:4
Sitgreaves, Marion, 1961, F 4,19:3
Sitland, William, 1942, Ap 19,43:2
Sitler, Joseph M, 1964, Ap 21,37:2
Sitler, William R Dr, 1937, F 6,17:4
Sitrin, Charles T, 1942, Jl 25,13:2
Sitsen, Pieter H W, 1945, Ja 23,19:5
Sittenfield, Maurice J (por), 1938, D 3,19:5
Sittenham, William, 1938, S 30,21:6
Sitter, Stephen C, 1959, S 14,29:5
Sitter, W de, 1934, N 22,21:1
Sitterding, Frederick B Jr, 1961, Jl 28,21:5
Sitterley, Augustus T, 1938, F 23,23:5
Sitterley, Harry E, 1952, Jl 15,21:3
Sitterley, James E, 1945, Mr 24,17:2
Sitterly, Charles F, 1945, N 10,15:2
Sittig, Albert J, 1942, F 14,15:1
Sittig, Charles A, 1949, Ja 10,25:4
Sittig, Edmund F, 1946, My 4,15:4
Sitwell, Edith, 1964, D 10,1:2
Sitwell, Ida Lady, 1937, Jl 13,20:3
Sitwell, Sidney A H, 1956, Ja 22,88:8
Siudinski, Marion R, 1944, My 9,19:5
Sivian, Leon J, 1947, S 24,23:5
Sivick, Andrew, 1952, F 9,13:4
Siviero, Carlo, 1953, S 12,17:2
Sivitz, Dorothy J, 1955, O 8,19:6
Six, Harry Sylvester, 1924, Je 17,19:4
Six, J Harry, 1948, D 5,92:3
Six, Walter, 1951, N 28,31:3
Six, Willie, 1950, Ja 13,25:7
Sixbury, Robert, 1873, O 26,4:7
Sixta, Boza, 1949, Jl 19,29:4
Sixta, Ernest F, 1959, O 10,24:4
Sixtus, Prince, 1934, Mr 15,26:3
Sizer, Henry S Sr Mrs, 1947, Ag 7,21:4
Sizer, J M Col, 1882, N 3,5:5
Sizer, Mary T Mrs, 1941, O 29,23:2
Sizer, Robert R, 1947, Ja 17,23:3
Sizer, Robert Ryland, 1925, Jl 4,11:5
Sizer, T Carroll, 1954, Ag 1,85:2
Sizer, Winston, 1967, Je 29,43:2
Sizoo, Joseph R, 1966, Ag 29,29:2
Sjaardema, Hendrikus, 1958, O 4,21:1
Sjahrir, Sutan (funl plans, Ap 17,3:5; funl, Ap 20,8:3), 1966, Ap 10,76:1
Sjauken, George E, 1950, My 5,21:2
Sjoblom, Axel T, 1937, O 23,15:8
Sjoblom, Einar, 1954, O 2,17:5
Sjodahl, Janne M, 1939, Je 25,36:7
Sjoden, Erick O, 1939, F 3,15:3
Sjoestroem, Victor (V Seastrom), 1960, Ja 4,29:3
Sjogren, Tage, 1939, Ja 11,19:4
Sjoqvist, Olof, 1954, D 7,33:2
Sjostrom, Carl, 1941, Ap 12,15:2
Sjostrom, Otto A, 1949, Je 18,13:3
Sjovik, Amund, 1957, Ja 23,29:2
Skaggs, L S, 1950, Mr 19,94:5
Skahan, Vincent A, 1942, Jl 14,20:2
Skakel, George Jr (funl plans, S 26,41:3), 1966, S 25, 1:3
Skakel, George Jr Mrs, 1967, My 19,40:1
Skala, Frank J, 1945, Mr 30,15:2
Skala, Steven, 1949, Ja 19,27:5
Skalak, Rudolph, 1962, Mr 27,37:4
Skall, David G, 1965, Ja 18,35:1
Skalmer, Morris, 1957, O 23,33:2
Skalski, Clement, 1957, D 5,35:5
Skapier, Joseph, 1952, Ag 17,77:3
Skarda, Edward, 1943, S 18,17:4
Skarde, William J, 1947, Jl 26,13:6
Skariatina, Irina (Mrs V F Blakeslee), 1962, N 18, 86:5
Skarl, Joseph Sr, 1951, S 21,24:2
Skarstrom, William, 1951, Mr 26,23:2
Skavlan, Einar, 1954, Ag 17,21:4
Skea, Alfred, 1946, My 20,23:4
Skeat, Walter W Rev Dr, 1912, O 8,13:3
Skebelsky, James W, 1938, Je 3,21:2
Sked, Otis S, 1948, D 3,25:2
Skeehan, Edward M, 1950, Je 27,29:1
Skeel, Burt E Capt, 1924, O 6,19:2
Skeel, Frank D Dr, 1923, Ja 18,15:5
Skeel, H Robertson (por), 1942, Mr 24,19:4
Skeel, Roswell Jr Mrs, 1958, F 8,19:2
Skeele, Amos Rev Dr, 1915, N 6,11:6
Skeele, John W (cor, S 19,11:6), 1912, S 18,11:6
Skeele, Otis G Mrs, 1942, Mr 23,15:4
Skeeles, Fannie Mrs, 1940, Ap 7,45:1
Skeels, Ella M Mrs, 1945, N 14,19:4
Skeels, Homer G, 1954, Ja 4,19:3
Skeels, Homer L Mrs, 1944, Je 1,19:4
Skeels, Irving T, 1954, S 14,27:3
Skeels, James S, 1948, N 16,29:3
Skeels, John G, 1940, Jl 26,17:5
Skeer, Jacob, 1953, Mr 12,27:4
Skeet, George, 1937, Mr 9,3:2
Skeffington, Francis S Mrs, 1946, Ap 21,46:5
Skeffington, James J, 1962, N 17,25:4
Skeffington, Patrick J, 1950, Je 3,15:5
Skeffington, Robert, 1938, Ap 8,19:3
Skeggs, John H, 1959, Ag 30,83:1
Skehan, John E Mrs, 1941, My 20,23:3
Skehan, John J, 1955, S 8,31:2
Skehan, Paul A, 1954, Ag 7,13:5
Skeldon, Frank L, 1948, My 27,25:2
Skellenger, William E, 1943, S 29,21:5
Skelley, Mary C, 1946, F 11,29:3
Skelley, William C, 1950, S 15,25:5
Skellinger, Harvey L, 1945, F 2,19:4
Skelly, Daniel J, 1949, Mr 1,25:3
Skelly, Hugh P, 1943, Ja 25,14:2
Skelly, Jack, 1953, My 26,29:6
Skelly, James E, 1961, Jl 22,21:7
Skelly, James Mrs, 1939, Jl 26,19:3; 1955, Ap 21,29:4
Skelly, John F, 1925, Ja 12,15:3
Skelly, John J, 1959, D 21,27:3
Skelly, John P, 1967, Jl 31,27:3
Skelly, Joseph A, 1963, Jl 9,32:1
Skelly, Joseph P, 1937, Mr 10,23:3
Skelly, Margaret C, 1948, D 7,31:2
Skelly, Mary B Mrs, 1949, F 4,23:3
Skelly, Oliver B, 1946, Ja 7,19:4
Skelly, William G, 1957, Ap 12,25:3
Skelly, William J (est appr), 1958, S 7,114:1
Skelton, Daniel, 1920, Je 18,11:4
Skelton, Denny I, 1943, Je 7,13:2
Skelton, Eugene W, 1941, N 1,15:5
Skelton, Frank A, 1942, Ag 15,11:2
Skelton, Frederick, 1955, Je 1,33:5
Skelton, Horace W, 1953, Mr 30,21:5
Skelton, Jesse F, 1948, S 1,24:3
Skelton, Julia G Mrs, 1951, S 13,31:1
Skelton, L J, 1929, Ja 11,23:2
Skelton, Oscar D (por), 1941, Ja 29,17:1
Skelton, Pierson A, 1945, Je 1,15:5
Skelton, Richard (funl plans, My 12,50:2), 1958, My 11,27:1
Skelton, Robert T, 1950, Je 14,31:2
Skelton, William B, 1964, F 2,89:1
Skene, Davis M, 1948, N 10,29:4
Skene, Don, 1938, My 17,23:5
Skene, Frederick, 1943, Ag 25,19:1
Skene, George M, 1949, Je 7,32:7
Skene, Philip G M, 1944, D 15,19:4
Skerberg, Karl, 1952, Jl 24,27:4
Skeritt, Harry H, 1952, S 17,31:3
Skern, Abraham N, 1956, Jl 9,23:4
Skerrett, Delamere, 1939, My 19,21:4
Skerrett, Harry H, 1939, My 24,23:5
Skerrett, J S Adm, 1897, Ja 2,1:4
Skerrett, Joseph R A, 1937, S 15,23:6
Skevington, Samuel J, 1944, Ap 26,19:6
Skevington, Samuel J Mrs, 1944, Ja 26,19:3
Skevington, William, 1944, D 2,13:5
Skewes, James H, 1958, My 7,35:1
Skey, Harvey F, 1958, D 7,88:6
Skiba, John, 1962, O 1,31:4
Skiddy, Francis, 1879, My 2,2:7
Skiddy, Lawrence J, 1951, Jl 8,60:5
Skiddy, W W, 1929, O 8,31:3
Skidell, Sidney H, 1964, F 7,32:1
Skidgell, William A Mrs, 1952, Jl 25,18:4
Skidmore, Abram W, 1958, F 7,21:2
Skidmore, Abram W Mrs, 1947, D 13,15:2
Skidmore, Arba R, 1961, F 4,19:2
Skidmore, David V, 1950, Mr 8,25:3
Skidmore, Douglass W, 1955, F 6,88:7
Skidmore, Francis Mrs, 1952, N 14,23:1
Skidmore, George R, 1948, O 26,32:2
Skidmore, Grace G, 1943, My 14,19:1
Skidmore, Harry B Jr Mrs, 1949, N 24,31:2
Skidmore, Henry, 1942, My 22,21:6
Skidmore, Hugh W, 1953, O 20,29:3
Skidmore, J, 1877, N 29,5:3
Skidmore, J R, 1882, F 31,2:4
Skidmore, Joel L, 1955, O 5,35:2
Skidmore, John D, 1903, N 16,7:6
Skidmore, Joseph P, 1947, S 16,24:3
Skidmore, Lemuel, 1921, Jl 24,22:4; 1964, D 18,34:6
Skidmore, Lewis P, 1955, Je 14,29:1
Skidmore, Louis, 1962, S 29,23:4
Skidmore, Marguerite, 1939, Ap 27,25:3
Skidmore, Samuel T, 1947, F 28,23:3
Skidmore, William B, 1905, Mr 2,9:6
Skidmore, William C Mrs, 1952, Ap 26,23:3
Skidmore, William Lemuel, 1916, O 30,9:4
Skidmore, Zenas, 1875, S 21,5:6
Skierski, Stefan, 1948, F 4,24:1
Skiff, Arthur R, 1953, Ag 7,19:4
Skiff, David T, 1948, Ag 31,24:2
Skiff, Frank V Mrs, 1951, Ap 8,93:2
Skiff, Frederick James V Dr, 1921, F 25,11:6
Skiff, J Victor, 1964, S 16,31:4
Skiffington, George B, 1950, S 4,17:6
Skifter, Hector R, 1964, Jl 27,31:1
Skifter, Hector R Mrs, 1961, D 7,43:3
Skifter, Jens A, 1948, N 10,29:4
Skiles, Burney B, 1938, S 27,21:2
Skiles, Hugh P, 1944, Je 3,13:4

Skiles, William V, 1947, S 11,27:2
Skiles, William W, 1904, Ja 10,7:5
Skillin, Carroll B, 1952, Je 2,22:3
Skillin, Edward S, 1947, Jl 3,21:4
Skillin, Silas F, 1949, Ap 9,17:2
Skilling, Arthur W, 1965, Mr 21,86:5
Skilling, Chauncey F, 1945, F 15,19:2
Skilling, Daniel H, 1938, Je 21,19:3
Skilling, John M, 1964, My 23,23:4
Skillings, D N, 1880, Mr 12,4:7
Skillings, Joseph K, 1953, Jl 10,19:5
Skillings, Stephen H, 1946, Ja 1,28:3
Skillman, Anita M, 1948, D 29,21:1
Skillman, Charles A, 1944, My 28,34:1
Skillman, Charles V, 1939, S 7,25:2
Skillman, Frank F, 1947, Ap 14,27:3
Skillman, George, 1949, F 16,25:2
Skillman, Harry S, 1944, N 17,19:2
Skillman, Lillian D, 1941, Je 14,17:4
Skillman, Merle R, 1947, D 28,40:3
Skillman, Robert H, 1945, S 13,23:1
Skillman, Russell W, 1956, Ja 25,31:4
Skillman, Theodore W, 1944, Mr 25,15:6
Skillman, Thomas J (por), 1939, S 25,20:1
Skillman, Walter M, 1953, S 17,29:3
Skillman, William F, 1964, F 5,35:3
Skillman, William T, 1957, My 12,86:2
Skilton, Adah S G Mrs (por), 1940, D 21,17:4
Skilton, Charles Avery, 1904, F 21,7:6
Skilton, Charles S, 1941, Mr 13,21:6
Skilton, Elizabeth R, 1952, Je 2,22:3
Skilton, George S, 1921, Ja 11,11:4
Skilton, Harry I, 1947, Ag 27,23:4
Skilton, John D, 1951, Jl 10,27:3
Skilton, Joseph R, 1958, Jl 10,27:3
Skimmin, George H, 1941, Ap 13,39:1
Skinker, J Hampson Mrs, 1943, D 27,19:4
Skinner, A W Mrs, 1884, O 24,8:4
Skinner, Adrian A, 1947, F 24,19:2
Skinner, Albert M, 1948, Ag 13,15:6
Skinner, Alburn E, 1958, Je 5,31:2
Skinner, Alburn E Mrs, 1938, N 18,21:5
Skinner, Alice W, 1947, S 10,27:5
Skinner, Alvah H, 1952, Ap 25,23:1
Skinner, Amelia Mrs, 1938, D 30,16:4
Skinner, Arthur A, 1950, Mr 25,11:7
Skinner, Avery, 1876, N 27,8:4
Skinner, Avery W Dr, 1937, D 14,25:5
Skinner, B, 1928, Ap 9,21:3
Skinner, Barton Dwight Dr, 1917, Je 24,19:3
Skinner, C R, 1928, Jl 1,25:4
Skinner, Calvin Dr, 1903, S 25,7:4
Skinner, Charles E, 1939, F 20,17:4; 1950, My 14,108:1
Skinner, Charles E Mrs, 1944, F 25,17:4
Skinner, Charles F, 1953, F 5,23:1
Skinner, Charles M, 1907, D 21,9:5
Skinner, Charles R Dr, 1937, Ja 3,II,8:4
Skinner, Clarence E, 1947, Ap 26,13:4; 1949, My 17, 26:2
Skinner, Clarence R (por), 1949, Ag 28,73:1
Skinner, Claude H, 1950, O 17,31:2
Skinner, Constance L (por), 1939, Mr 28,24:2
Skinner, David A Mrs, 1939, Je 4,49:3
Skinner, David L Mrs, 1960, Ap 27,37:1
Skinner, Donald B, 1947, Jl 14,21:5
Skinner, E Darwin Mrs, 1952, S 8,21:5
Skinner, Edmond N, 1957, Ap 29,25:5
Skinner, Edmond N Mrs, 1948, S 9,27:3
Skinner, Edna L, 1958, Jl 12,15:2
Skinner, Edward A, 1956, N 25,89:1
Skinner, Edward H, 1953, Ja 13,27:4
Skinner, Edward M, 1939, Ap 3,15:3
Skinner, Ella H Mrs, 1938, F 1,21:3
Skinner, Erasmus D Dr, 1915, S 23,13:4
Skinner, Ernest M, 1960, N 29,37:5
Skinner, Eugene W, 1954, Mr 2,25:5
Skinner, F W, 1932, D 26,21:1
Skinner, Francis, 1914, My 8,13:7
Skinner, Frank, 1968, O 12,37:5
Skinner, Franklin E, 1944, My 29,15:5
Skinner, Fred B, 1946, F 1,23:3
Skinner, Fred G Mrs, 1954, Je 1,27:1
Skinner, Frederick S, 1955, Ja 22,11:1
Skinner, Garnett C, 1952, Ap 21,21:5
Skinner, George D Mrs, 1943, O 16,13:3
Skinner, George H, 1949, F 20,60:3
Skinner, George L, 1949, N 16,30:3
Skinner, George Mrs, 1947, Jl 12,26:1
Skinner, Halcyon N Mrs, 1947, Je 8,60:2
Skinner, Harold B, 1945, D 29,13:4
Skinner, Harold S, 1967, Ag 14,31:3
Skinner, Harris E, 1945, Ap 26,23:3
Skinner, Harry A, 1952, Ap 15,27:2
Skinner, Harry C, 1950, My 19,27:1
Skinner, Harry W, 1943, Ja 30,15:2
Skinner, Henry Dr, 1926, My 31,15:4
Skinner, Henry W, 1941, S 5,21:6
Skinner, Herbert W B (trb lr, F 3,32:6), 1960, Ja 22, 25:1
Skinner, Howard A, 1956, N 8,39:3
Skinner, Hubert N Dr, 1916, Je 5,11:6
Skinner, James, 1940, Ja 19,19:1
Skinner, James Avery Rev, 1917, N 28,13:6
Skinner, James D, 1959, Mr 1,87:1
Skinner, James G, 1950, O 21,17:4
Skinner, James M (will, F 26,23:1), 1953, F 15,93:1
Skinner, James Mrs, 1956, Ag 8,25:5
Skinner, James N, 1956, Ap 16,27:3
Skinner, James R, 1946, Jl 9,21:3
Skinner, John, 1952, Je 1,84:4
Skinner, John C, 1957, N 28,31:1
Skinner, John H, 1942, Ap 29,21:6
Skinner, John R Mrs, 1944, Ap 22,15:4
Skinner, Joseph A, 1946, S 7,15:2
Skinner, Joseph J Mrs, 1942, Ap 16,21:5
Skinner, Laura A, 1944, N 3,21:3
Skinner, Lila, 1924, Jl 25,13:5
Skinner, Lloyd, 1940, Mr 17,51:2
Skinner, Louis H, 1949, N 22,29:3
Skinner, Mabel, 1946, Jl 4,19:6
Skinner, Mark A, 1942, D 3,25:5
Skinner, Mary, 1944, Mr 17,17:3
Skinner, Mary Mrs, 1940, Mr 18,17:3
Skinner, Mercein, 1941, Je 1,40:2
Skinner, Morris C, 1964, Jl 23,27:4
Skinner, Neil M, 1959, Je 27,23:4
Skinner, Neil M Mrs, 1953, Ja 14,31:4
Skinner, Otis, 1942, Ja 5,17:1
Skinner, Owen L, 1953, O 22,29:4
Skinner, Prescott O, 1951, F 17,15:1
Skinner, Prescott O Mrs (A Van L Carrick), 1961, N 26,88:4
Skinner, Richard D (por), 1941, N 7,24:4
Skinner, Richard D Mrs, 1958, Ja 5,86:2
Skinner, Robert, 1953, My 2,15:3
Skinner, Robert C, 1967, Ja 9,39:3
Skinner, Robert M, 1967, Mr 23,35:2
Skinner, Robert P, 1960, Jl 3,32:3
Skinner, Robert P Mrs, 1956, Ja 28,17:6
Skinner, Robert W, 1953, O 13,29:2
Skinner, Robert W Jr, 1957, Ag 9,19:4
Skinner, Ross H, 1958, Ag 17,86:6
Skinner, Sidney Mrs, 1942, N 22,52:5
Skinner, St J B L Gen, 1872, Jl 11,1:6
Skinner, Sydney M (por), 1941, Mr 6,21:4
Skinner, T H Dr, 1884, My 12,4:7
Skinner, T M, 1880, Mr 24,4:7
Skinner, T Sir, 1926, My 13,25:6
Skinner, Theodore H, 1944, S 6,19:4
Skinner, Thomas C, 1955, Mr 12,19:5
Skinner, Thomas H Rev, 1871, F 2,5:4
Skinner, Thomas Rev, 1871, My 8,5:2
Skinner, Walter J Sr, 1950, Jl 24,17:3
Skinner, Warren C, 1954, Je 3,27:5
Skinner, William, 1940, D 15,60:3; 1947, O 18,15:5
Skinner, William A, 1950, Ja 2,23:4; 1951, O 30,29:2
Skinner, William B, 1968, Je 20,45:5
Skinner, William C, 1922, Mr 9,17:4
Skinner, William E Ex-Judge, 1915, Mr 10,13:6
Skinner, William H, 1945, F 25,37:1
Skinner, William S, 1905, Mr 19,9:4
Skinner, William T, 1951, D 7,28:2
Skinner, William W, 1965, D 16,50:8
Skinrood, Carle O, 1954, My 20,31:2
Skippon, William A Jr, 1961, Ap 24,29:5
Skipton, Pitt M Mrs, 1945, O 31,23:2
Skipworth, Alison, 1952, Jl 7,21:3
Skipworth, Vance D, 1945, D 21,21:3
Skirball, Miriam F Dr, 1937, Ja 10,II,10:7
Skirde, Herbert W, 1966, My 4,47:1
Skirm, Joseph G, 1955, S 12,25:4
Skirm, William H Gen, 1905, O 8,9:6
Skirrow, John F, 1952, D 17,33:4
Skirven, Percy G, 1941, My 6,21:1
Skitt, Alfred, 1939, N 22,24:8
Skivington, George J Sr, 1961, Jl 1,17:5
Sklar, Aaron, 1960, Jl 2,17:6
Sklar, Ezak, 1947, My 31,13:4
Sklar, Phil, 1956, S 27,35:4
Sklar, Solomon I, 1964, O 8,43:3
Sklarew, Albert Mrs, 1947, Ag 1,17:5
Sklaroff, Albert, 1950, F 28,29:2
Skobeleff, Russian Gen, 1882, Jl 8,5:1
Skobline, Nadine (La Plevitskaia), 1940, O 5,15:4
Skochinsky, Aleksandr A, 1960, O 8,23:2
Skoda, J Dr, 1881, Je 14,5:4
Skoda, Von K, 1929, Ja 12,17:2
Skofield, Ray L, 1958, N 29,21:1
Skofield, Ray L Mrs, 1940, Je 2,44:5
Skoglund, Ludwig, 1948, Je 14,23:4
Skoglund, Robert W, 1949, Ja 2,60:5
Skogmo, P W Mrs, 1951, Mr 23,21:4
Skogmo, Phil W, 1950, Ja 2,23:4
Skold, Otte, 1958, N 11,29:1
Skoldberg, Ernest Mrs, 1965, Mr 8,29:5
Skolianik, John, 1949, F 16,26:2
Skolkin, David, 1949, Jl 7,26:2
Skolowec, Andrew, 1943, O 20,21:6
Skolsky, Mildred A Mrs, 1942, D 10,25:5
Skoropadsky, Danilio, 1957, F 27,27:5
Skoss, Solomon L (will, Ag 14,17:4), 1953, Ap 7,29:3
Skottsberg, Carl, 1963, Je 18,41:6
Skouras, Charles P (funl, O 26,27:1; will, N 2,30:7), 1954, O 23,15:1
Skouras, George P (funl, Mr 20,33:2), 1964, Mr 17, 35:1
Skouras, George P Mrs, 1965, My 4,43:1
Skoutelsky, Boris, 1938, Ag 17,19:2
Skov, Bunde V, 1955, D 16,29:5
Skov, Villads B, 1959, Ap 2,31:2
Skowron, William J Sr, 1962, Jl 26,27:5
Skowronski, Benjamin C, 1950, N 9,33:2
Skowronski, Felix J, 1948, Mr 6,13:5
Skowronski, Frank, 1946, Ja 11,22:3
Skrabik, Andrej, 1950, Ja 10,30:2
Skrainka, Fred, 1940, Jl 2,21:5
Skraly, Myron, 1966, Ap 16,33:4
Skrbensky, Leo de (por), 1938, D 25,15:1
Skredsvig, Christian, 1924, Ja 21,17:5
Skrobisch, Jean, 1966, F 22,23:3
Skrotzki, Bernard G A, 1963, N 15,35:5
Skuce, Lou, 1951, N 22,31:4
Skulme, Otto, 1967, Mr 24,31:3
Skulsky, Abraham, 1959, N 23,31:6
Skultety, Arpad, 1950, O 19,31:5
Skum, Nils N, 1951, D 28,22:2
Skuse, James Richard, 1907, O 2,11:6
Skutch, Ira, 1945, S 17,19:5
Skvarla, John A, 1957, D 20,24:6
Skwirsky, Joseph, 1955, S 17,15:6
Skyberg, Victor O, 1944, D 27,19:3
Skyles, William N, 1939, F 26,38:8
Skylstead, Ralph F, 1939, Ja 24,19:3
Slaback, Lawrence, 1938, Mr 31,23:2
Slabey, John M, 1958, My 26,29:2
Slabok, Marian, 1965, My 27,37:1
Slaby, Adolf Prof, 1913, Ap 7,9:6
Slacer, John W, 1963, D 17,39:4
Slach, Peter J, 1949, D 20,31:2
Slack, Beekman C, 1966, D 16,47:1
Slack, Bertram L, 1950, N 21,31:2
Slack, Charles W, 1945, D 22,19:1
Slack, E E, 1920, F 16,11:5
Slack, E Munsey, 1939, D 8,25:4
Slack, Edgar P, 1962, Ag 6,25:1
Slack, Edward S, 1907, Ag 28,7:6
Slack, Frank V, 1961, D 13,43:4
Slack, Frederic S, 1942, Ap 12,44:8
Slack, Frederick T Mrs, 1945, Jl 19,23:5
Slack, Harry R Jr, 1957, D 14,21:4
Slack, John T, 1939, Ja 20,19:1
Slack, John W, 1958, Ja 26,88:8
Slack, Leighton P, 1938, Ap 3,II,7:3
Slack, Lemuel E, 1952, F 26,27:4
Slack, Marguerite H, 1956, Ja 17,33:2
Slack, Robert, 1948, Ap 15,25:5
Slack, T Mrs, 1932, Jl 2,15:1
Slack, William J, 1946, Mr 16,13:4
Slade, Alex T Mrs, 1953, My 4,23:5
Slade, Benjamin, 1951, N 2,24:2
Slade, Caleb A, 1961, D 18,35:5
Slade, Charles B, 1942, Ag 26,19:4
Slade, Edward, 1885, Mr 30,5:6; 1941, N 23,53:1
Slade, Everett N, 1948, N 13,15:3
Slade, F Louis, 1944, O 5,23:6
Slade, F Louis Mrs (trb lr, Ja 17,26:7), 1951, Ja 15:3
Slade, Frank A, 1960, N 19,21:6
Slade, George T, 1941, Ja 25,15:3
Slade, George T Mrs, 1923, D 15,13:4
Slade, Guy V H, 1949, Je 8,29:3
Slade, Helen (Mrs Hy S Sanders), 1958, Jl 20,65
Slade, Henry L, 1924, Jl 12,9:7
Slade, Henry Lewis, 1924, Jl 11,13:6
Slade, Howard, 1965, D 14,43:1
Slade, J M, 1882, D 6,5:3
Slade, John Mrs, 1960, Ag 22,25:4
Slade, Lawrence, 1942, Ap 13,16:2
Slade, Leon D, 1948, F 24,25:4
Slade, Lester P, 1960, Mr 22,37:4
Slade, M B C, 1882, Ap 16,2:7
Slade, Margaret B, 1939, Je 20,21:5
Slade, Marshall P, 1950, N 1,35:1
Slade, Marshall P Mrs, 1953, Ja 10,17:6
Slade, Sam I, 1942, N 24,25:2
Slade, William, 1948, Jl 18,53:2
Slade, William A, 1950, My 18,29:3
Sladem, Douglas (por), 1947, F 14,21:3
Sladen, Arthur F, 1944, Mr 7,17:5
Sladen, Fred W (por), 1945, Jl 11,11:3
Sladen, Frederick W Mrs (Oct 6), 1965, O 11,6
Slader, William T, 1962, Ap 13,35:2
Sladky, George, 1950, Jl 15,13:1
Sladowsky, Samuel, 1962, My 8,39:2
Slafer, William E, 1921, Ag 3,13:5
Slaff, Florence (Mrs Saml Mamlet), 1964, N 4,
Slaff, Frank Mrs, 1962, My 13,88:4
Slaff, Max A, 1953, N 26,31:3
Slaff, Samuel, 1944, Jl 18,19:3
Slager, Walter D, 1952, F 8,23:2
Slagg, Joseph L, 1965, Mr 12,33:2
Slaght, Arthur T, 1940, Ap 16,23:1
Slaght, George W, 1947, N 27,32:3
Slaght, Kenneth K, 1949, N 23,29:4
Slagle, Eleanor C Mrs (por), 1942, S 20,41:3
Slagle, Samuel A, 1940, N 7,25:4
Slaight, G Wilmer Jr, 1957, Ag 2,19:4
Slaight, Herbert A, 1949, Jl 4,13:6
Slaight, Sherwood S, 1951, N 5,31:2

Slama, Gilbert F, 1952, Ag 19,23:5
Slaman, Andrew, 1952, Jl 19,15:4
Slane, James J, 1954, Je 23,26:4
Slane, Sarah, 1871, Ap 9,8:5
Slane, Willis H Jr, 1965, S 10,35:4
Slanetz, Charles A, 1964, F 5,35:5
Slany, Paul Peter, 1953, F 10,27:4
Slape, John C, 1947, N 3,23:2
Slape, William Stevens, 1909, F 5,7:4
Slark, Maria A T Mrs, 1947, O 13,23:2
Slate, Alex R, 1949, Je 15,29:2
Slate, Anna M W Mrs (Tillie Baldwin), 1958, O 24, 33:3
Slate, Arthur W Mrs, 1953, Ja 7,31:4
Slate, Edmund J, 1948, O 22,25:3
Slate, George, 1945, O 26,19:1
Slate, George R Mrs, 1952, O 29,29:6
Slate, John H, 1967, S 20,47:2
Slater, A James, 1967, Ag 13,80:1
Slater, Albert H, 1961, Je 12,29:5
Slater, Albert H Mrs, 1954, F 24,25:4
Slater, Alexander, 1967, Je 19,35:2
Slater, B Cecilia Mrs, 1942, S 3,19:2
Slater, Benjamin J, 1948, D 6,25:3
Slater, Bernard, 1950, F 15,27:4
Slater, Bill (Wm E), 1965, Ja 26,34:1
Slater, Charles, 1941, O 4,15:2
Slater, Edward, 1946, N 19,31:4
Slater, Edward J, 1959, O 12,19:3
Slater, Edward S, 1957, Ag 3,15:4
Slater, Edward W Mrs (Princess Marina Torlonia), 1960, S 16,3:3
Slater, Esther Mrs, 1951, S 8,17:2
Slater, Frank, 1965, Ag 24,31:2
Slater, Frank J, 1940, Ap 21,43:1
Slater, Fred W, 1966, Ag 16,39:5
Slater, Frederick J, 1943, Ag 21,11:4
Slater, Frederick S, 1940, N 5,34:2
Slater, George A Mrs, 1950, F 9,29:3
Slater, George A Surrogate, 1937, F 24,23:5
Slater, Gilbert, 1938, Mr 10,21:2
Slater, Harry, 1953, Je 26,19:3
Slater, Harry C, 1960, D 31,17:3
Slater, Herbert W, 1947, Ag 14,23:5
Slater, Horatio Nelson, 1968, My 2,47:3
Slater, Howard A, 1949, Ap 8,25:5
Slater, J F, 1884, My 8,5:5
Slater, J Harold, 1944, Jl 8,11:4
Slater, James A, 1955, My 30,13:6
Slater, John (por), 1948, D 30,19:4
Slater, John E Sr, 1949, D 24,15:4
Slater, John R, 1965, Je 23,41:3
Slater, Joseph H, 1948, Mr 9,23:5; 1948, My 16,68:6
Slater, Lucius K, 1945, My 16,19:2
Slater, Lucy (Modern Diana), 1879, O 7,2:3
Slater, Mabel H Mrs, 1942, N 28,13:4
Slater, Montagu, 1956, D 22,19:6
Slater, Mortimer (por), 1943, D 13,23:2
Slater, Mortimer B, 1939, O 6,25:6
Slater, Noble B, 1953, Je 5,27:4
Slater, Ora, 1945, F 2,19:2
Slater, Oscar, 1948, F 1,60:3
Slater, Ransford, 1940, Ap 25,23:3
Slater, Robert S, 1964, Jl 12,68:3
Slater, Thomas G, 1961, N 19,89:1
Slater, Thomas H, 1965, Ja 30,27:5
Slater, Thomas M, 1951, Je 7,33:5
Slater, W S, 1882, My 29,6:2
Slater, Wallis, 1949, F 10,27:3
Slater, Walter, 1952, My 25,94:3
Slater, Washington I, 1950, Je 17,15:5
Slater, William, 1960, Je 20,31:5
Slater, William D Commodore, 1869, Ja 5,5:5
Slater, William H, 1945, Ja 25,19:2
Slater, William H Mrs, 1941, O 9,23:4
Slater, William J, 1946, Ja 31,21:5; 1955, My 18,31:6
Slater, William Mrs, 1953, Mr 16,19:4
Slater, William P, 1948, S 9,27:3
Slatin, Pasha, 1932, O 5,21:4
Slatkin, Constance W Mrs, 1953, Mr 2,23:3
Slatkin, Felix, 1963, F 11,7:5
Slatkin, Herman R, 1956, F 10,21:1
Slatkin, Joseph, 1958, Ap 6,89:1
Slatnick, William, 1943, Je 24,21:2
Slaton, John M Mrs, 1945, F 26,19:2
Slatter, Leonard, 1961, Ap 17,29:2
Slattery, Aloysius C, 1950, S 7,31:2
Slattery, Arthur E, 1958, D 4,39:3
Slattery, C L, 1930, Mr 13,25:1
Slattery, Cyril A, 1952, N 25,29:1
Slattery, Daniel G, 1964, Je 30,33:3
Slattery, Dennis H, 1941, Ap 24,21:4
Slattery, Edmund J, 1953, D 9,11:4
Slattery, Edward J, 1946, Mr 15,21:3
Slattery, Eugene, 1872, S 26,2:7
Slattery, Frank J, 1954, Ap 28,31:2
Slattery, Frank P Sr, 1949, D 21,29:5
Slattery, George N, 1951, Mr 28,29:3
Slattery, Harry (cor, S 9,25:3), 1949, S 2,17:5
Slattery, J R, 1932, S 24,15:1
Slattery, J Warren, 1968, Je 22,33:5
Slattery, Jack, 1912, N 20,15:4
Slattery, James, 1953, My 31,72:8
Slattery, James F, 1947, My 14,25:5
Slattery, James M (por), 1948, Ag 31,23:3
Slattery, Jimmy, 1960, Ag 31,29:3
Slattery, John, 1940, Je 6,25:1
Slattery, John J, 1938, Ag 1,13:2; 1961, Je 23,29:2
Slattery, John M, 1916, Jl 1,11:6
Slattery, John R Mrs, 1949, Ag 20,11:5
Slattery, John T (will, My 15,II,5:2), 1938, Mr 28, 15:3
Slattery, John T, 1949, Jl 18,17:5; 1952, F 23,11:2
Slattery, John W, 1938, D 23,19:2; 1946, My 21,23:3
Slattery, Lawrence J, 1945, F 7,21:5
Slattery, Lillian C Mrs, 1939, Ag 4,13:5
Slattery, Michael T, 1944, Ap 15,11:6
Slattery, Robert A Mrs, 1946, F 16,13:2
Slattery, Thomas C, 1937, F 16,24:1
Slattery, Thomas D, 1960, My 3,39:2
Slattery, Thomas F, 1940, F 24,13:6
Slattery, Thomas P, 1951, Jl 12,25:4
Slattery, Thomas S, 1942, O 2,25:6
Slattery, Vincent J, 1939, D 31,18:7; 1952, F 5,29:3
Slattery, William, 1947, N 24,23:4
Slaught, Herbert E Dr, 1937, My 23,II,10:5
Slaught, James W, 1937, Mr 6,17:5
Slaughter, Benjamin G, 1940, S 19,23:4
Slaughter, C Denton, 1952, Ap 17,29:4
Slaughter, Charles, 1953, O 30,23:1
Slaughter, Donald, 1952, Je 7,19:3
Slaughter, Evans G, 1950, Ja 19,27:3
Slaughter, Franklin V, 1943, Ag 29,39:3
Slaughter, Gerald (J Gans), 1959, Ap 21,35:4
Slaughter, Harry Delorme, 1903, Ap 15,9:6
Slaughter, Harvey L, 1961, D 2,23:6
Slaughter, Homer H, 1953, D 23,25:3
Slaughter, Joseph C, 1964, D 10,58:1
Slaughter, Marion Mrs, 1950, O 27,29:5
Slaughter, Rochester B, 1939, Ag 31,19:5
Slaughter, William H, 1941, Je 5,23:4
Slauson, Clarence M, 1937, Ja 23,17:3
Slauson, Henry M, 1964, Ja 4,23:2
Slauson, Henry M Mrs, 1968, N 28,37:5
Slauson, J Wesley, 1946, My 1,25:4
Slauson, Mary R, 1949, O 12,30:4
Slauson, Robert R, 1958, N 29,21:4
Slaven, H Bartholomew, 1904, D 5,7:4
Slaven, Matthew W, 1955, Ja 19,27:3
Slavenski, Josip, 1955, D 1,35:3
Slaviansky, Validimir B Mrs, 1964, O 11,88:4
Slavicek, William, 1949, Ag 14,68:1
Slavikout, Bruno, 1955, Je 21,38:5
Slavin, Abraham, 1966, D 19,37:5
Slavin, Charles, 1954, Ag 24,21:4
Slavin, Dennis J, 1943, D 11,15:3
Slavin, Eugene Mrs (G Tyven), 1966, F 15,39:2
Slavin, Harry, 1956, Ja 11,29:1
Slavin, Hugh H, 1952, D 18,29:4
Slavin, John C, 1940, Ag 29,19:2
Slavin, Leon Mrs, 1959, Jl 19,69:2
Slavin, Patrick J, 1950, My 27,17:3
Slavin, Robert J, 1961, Ap 25,35:2
Slavin, Vincent D, 1945, D 17,22:3
Slavitt, Alex, 1952, O 28,31:5
Slavyanov, Nikolai N, 1958, O 20,29:3
Slawoj-Skladkowski, Felicien, 1962, S 10,29:4
Slawson, Chester B, 1964, Mr 14,23:4
Slawson, George L, 1944, O 28,15:7
Slawson, Harry H, 1954, O 6,25:3
Slawson, John Mrs, 1945, D 29,13:3
Slawson, John W Sr, 1958, Ap 14,25:1
Slawson, Mary B Mrs, 1941, Mr 18,23:4
Slawson, Robert N, 1958, Ja 21,26:5
Slawson, Roe B, 1950, O 7,17:4
Slawson, Ward W, 1941, Ag 7,17:6
Slay, Ronald J, 1948, S 20,25:1
Slayback, David H, 1942, Ja 27,22:2
Slayback, Edward F, 1916, Je 1,11:5
Slayback, John D, 1924, Mr 3,17:4
Slayback, Nellie H Mrs, 1941, My 25,36:5
Slayback, Russell B, 1950, D 31,43:2
Slaybaugh, Harvey B Mrs, 1959, Ja 27,33:1
Slaymaker, Samuel R, 1939, My 4,23:5; 1940, N 30, 17:3
Slaymaker, William W, 1940, F 20,21:2
Slayter, Games, 1964, O 16,39:4
Slayton, G Noyes, 1944, F 2,21:2
Slayton, John C F, 1922, Ja 5,15:4
Slayton, Louis E, 1942, D 2,25:1
Slayton, Ralph E Mrs, 1942, My 7,19:5
Slazenger, Frank L, 1938, Ag 10,19:5
Slear, James A, 1961, O 12,29:4
Sleath, Arthur R, 1949, Je 3,25:2
Sleator, James S, 1950, Ja 20,25:2
Slechta, Emanuel, 1960, Mr 19,21:1
Slechtner, Joseph, 1953, Mr 13,29:3
Sleckman, Frederick, 1966, F 18,33:4
Sledd, Andrew W, 1939, Mr 17,21:1
Sledd, Benjamin F, 1940, Ja 5,19:2
Sledge, Norfleet R Judge, 1937, Mr 12,28:2
Slee, George H, 1951, S 25,29:4
Slee, J Noah H, 1943, Je 23,21:3
Slee, J Noah H Mrs (M Sanger),(mem ser, S 9,45:1), 1966, S 7,1:1
Slee, John B, 1947, Ja 15,25:2
Slee, Norman S, 1942, Je 12,21:2
Slee, Richard, 1945, Ap 10,19:3
Sleepeck, William H, 1941, Ap 27,38:2
Sleeper, A E, 1934, My 14,17:1
Sleeper, Benjamin A, 1951, F 23,27:4
Sleeper, Elizabeth A N, 1949, Ag 11,23:1
Sleeper, George M, 1939, D 26,19:2
Sleeper, Harold R, 1960, N 11,31:1
Sleeper, Harold R Mrs, 1954, N 29,17:2; 1966, Mr 13, 41:4
Sleeper, Helen J, 1959, F 24,29:4
Sleeper, Henry D, 1948, Ja 30,23:2
Sleeper, James T, 1942, S 20,41:1
Sleeper, Josiah, 1946, Ag 24,11:2
Sleeper, Mabel A Mrs, 1940, F 17,13:6
Sleeper, Oliver S, 1940, Ag 9,15:1
Sleeper, William A, 1950, Mr 10,27:3
Sleeth, John J, 1949, Ag 28,72:3
Sleeth, Robert L, 1946, Ap 19,29:6
Sleicher, John A, 1919, D 8,15:4
Sleicher, John Albert, 1921, My 6,13:5
Sleicher, William, 1919, My 1,17:5
Sleicher, William N, 1950, Ap 19,29:1
Sleigh, Arthur Mrs, 1942, F 25,19:2
Sleigh, William L, 1945, My 7,17:4
Sleight, Benjamin H, 1942, My 17,47:2
Sleight, Charles H, 1938, N 9,23:5
Sleight, Elizabeth Cowan Dr, 1918, N 6,17:3
Sleight, Harry L, 1952, Jl 15,21:1
Sleight, Walter, 1947, F 19,25:1
Sleight, William P, 1904, Jl 11,7:6
Slemp, C Bascom (por), 1943, Ag 8,37:1
Slemp, Campbell, 1907, O 14,9:4
Slensby, Joseph P Mrs, 1957, D 15,86:4
Slep, Daniel N, 1953, Mr 26,31:3
Slep, William H Jr, 1960, Ja 21,31:3
Slepack, Moses J, 1956, S 12,37:5
Slepin, Max, 1952, Jl 18,2:6
Slesinger, Anthony, 1946, Mr 17,43:1
Slesinger, Anthony Mrs, 1952, Ja 7,19:4
Slesinger, Laurence A, 1960, Ap 4,29:5
Slesinger, Stephen, 1953, D 18,29:2
Slesinger, Tess, 1945, F 22,27:3
Slevin, James J, 1914, F 14,11:6
Slevin, Joseph Mrs, 1960, D 30,20:1
Slevin, Joseph W Mrs, 1937, F 5,21:1
Slevin, William E, 1953, D 24,15:5
Slevin, William E Jr, 1967, N 28,51:8
Slewin, Regina Mrs, 1925, N 14,15:3
Sleyster, Rock, 1942, Mr 8,43:2
Slezak, Leo, 1946, Je 17,19:3
Slezak, Stanislaus, 1948, Ap 3,15:2
Slicer, Thomas Roberts Rev Dr, 1916, My 30,9:5
Slichter, Sumner H, 1959, S 29,39:1
Slichter, Walter I, 1958, O 15,39:3
Slichter, Walter I Mrs, 1959, Je 8,27:6
Slick, Edwin E, 1952, Je 11,29:3
Slick, Frank F, 1944, Mr 24,19:4
Slick, Thomas B, 1962, O 8,23:3
Slick, Thomas W, 1959, Ja 5,29:3
Slickers, Albert C Sr, 1953, N 15,89:1
Slidell, John (trb, Ag 8,4:7), 1871, Jl 31,5:4
Slider, Walter A, 1951, Je 20,27:5
Slifer, Belding S, 1959, Jl 30,27:2
Slifer, Hiram J Lt-Col, 1919, F 14,13:5
Slifer, Michael, 1961, Ap 13,35:5
Slifkin, Lester L, 1957, Jl 6,15:6
Slifman, Samuel Mrs, 1955, N 25,27:1
Sliger, Herbert B, 1954, D 21,27:4
Slight, Frederick A, 1953, N 22,88:1
Slight, George Mrs, 1957, Ja 6,88:1
Sligo, Marquess of (A H Browne), 1951, My 29,25:1
Sliker, J Ellsworth, 1954, O 14,29:3
Slimmon, Haddow, 1962, O 18,39:1
Sliney, John R, 1953, S 17,29:5
Slinger, Joseph Rev, 1909, Ap 12,7:4
Slingerland, Ernest, 1945, S 29,15:1
Slingerland, Frederick A, 1947, Ja 25,17:5
Slingerland, Henry B, 1950, Ja 17,28:2
Slingerland, Mark Vernon Prof, 1909, Mr 12,7:4
Slingland, George, 1952, D 5,27:1
Slingluff, Frank, 1947, Ap 1,28:2
Slingluff, Hambleton, 1937, Ap 11,II,8:3
Slinker, Clay D, 1943, D 16,28:3
Slinn, Clarence, 1951, S 6,34:3
Sliosberg, Henry Dr, 1937, Je 9,25:2
Slipher, Earl C, 1964, Ag 9,76:4
Slipper, J A, 1882, Jl 26,5:6
Slipyan, Alvin, 1960, Jl 6,33:1
Sliter, Harold M, 1956, My 4,25:3
Sliter, John P, 1954, Je 25,21:4
Sloame, Milton L, 1960, Je 28,31:5
Sloan, A E Prof, 1902, Mr 21,9:7
Sloan, A P Sr, 1932, Ag 31,17:1
Sloan, Albert L, 1947, Je 20,19:2
Sloan, Alexander K, 1944, D 11,23:6
Sloan, Alexander N Mrs, 1945, N 8,20:2
Sloan, Alexander N Sr, 1943, N 7,56:5
Sloan, Alfred P Jr (funl, F 20,88:3; will, F 24,1:1), 1966, F 18,1:3
Sloan, Alfred P Jr Mrs, 1956, F 14,29:4
Sloan, Andrew, 1943, Ap 23,17:4
Sloan, Andrew J, 1904, Ja 10,7:6

Sloan, Arthur L, 1946, My 15,21:3
Sloan, Benson B Sr, 1958, D 30,35:3
Sloan, Bernard, 1942, Ag 23,43:1
Sloan, Charles G Jr, 1951, My 30,21:5
Sloan, Chester L Mrs, 1943, D 4,13:4
Sloan, Clarence V, 1954, N 13,15:4
Sloan, Clark A, 1953, N 21,13:5
Sloan, David B, 1966, N 6,88:7
Sloan, Douglas Mrs, 1946, O 23,27:2
Sloan, E Hamilton, 1938, D 1,23:3
Sloan, Edgar J, 1942, S 29,23:3
Sloan, Fergus M Sr, 1963, S 13,29:2
Sloan, Frank H Mrs, 1950, Mr 2,27:4
Sloan, Frank T, 1940, Jl 7,25:3
Sloan, George, 1943, N 28,68:3
Sloan, George A (funl plans, My 22,88:6; funl, My 24,31:4), 1955, My 21,1:5
Sloan, George Beale, 1904, Jl 11,7:6
Sloan, George Beale (est), 1914, Ag 15,9:7
Sloan, George L B, 1947, Ja 25,17:3
Sloan, Gordon, 1964, Je 27,25:6
Sloan, Harold P, 1961, My 23,39:1
Sloan, Harry M, 1941, Ja 1,23:4
Sloan, Herbert A, 1940, D 5,25:5
Sloan, J Alex, 1937, Mr 11,24:1
Sloan, J Frederick, 1947, Ap 18,21:4
Sloan, J Seymour, 1966, D 17,33:2
Sloan, James J, 1952, D 4,35:3
Sloan, James Jr, 1945, D 27,19:5
Sloan, Jane deK Mrs, 1958, Jl 23,23:6
Sloan, John, 1924, Ap 12,15:3; 1951, S 9,1:2; 1954, Je 26,13:3
Sloan, John F, 1941, Ap 9,25:4
Sloan, John Mrs, 1943, My 5,27:5; 1960, Je 8,39:1
Sloan, John Y, 1946, Mr 15,21:4
Sloan, Kellogg, 1955, D 13,39:3
Sloan, Laurence H (por), 1949, My 7,13:5
Sloan, Leroy H, 1961, Je 4,86:6
Sloan, Malachi W, 1955, Ja 12,27:2
Sloan, Marianna, 1954, Mr 21,88:4
Sloan, Mary A, 1925, D 22,21:5
Sloan, Matthew, 1947, O 14,28:2
Sloan, Matthew S (por), 1945, Je 15,19:3
Sloan, Matthew S Mrs, 1951, My 25,27:3
Sloan, Maurice W Jr, 1955, My 19,29:5
Sloan, Paul L Mrs, 1954, S 10,23:4
Sloan, Ralph Sr, 1954, Ap 15,29:1
Sloan, Raymond P, 1959, Ja 6,33:1
Sloan, Robert B, 1946, D 12,29:2
Sloan, Robert H, 1954, D 18,15:2
Sloan, Robert J, 1964, O 16,39:1
Sloan, Ruell, 1951, Je 19,29:1
Sloan, Samuel (funl, S 26,9:5), 1907, S 25,9:5
Sloan, Samuel (por), 1939, N 27,17:5
Sloan, Samuel, 1945, Mr 31,19:2; 1949, D 14,31:3
Sloan, Samuel Mrs, 1913, O 13,9:4; 1951, Jl 19,23:6
Sloan, St Clair, 1942, My 12,19:4
Sloan, T Dwight, 1948, Ja 11,56:1
Sloan, T E Col (funl, Je 28,7:6), 1901, Je 24,1:3
Sloan, Thomas R, 1950, N 4,17:5
Sloan, Will, 1958, Ap 9,33:1
Sloan, William C, 1942, Je 9,23:4
Sloan, William D, 1952, Ap 20,92:3
Sloan, William E, 1942, Ag 30,43:1
Sloan, William G, 1960, Ap 23,23:2
Sloan, William J, 1938, Jl 3,13:2; 1941, Ap 2,23:2; 1945, N 11,42:7
Sloan, William K Mrs, 1945, Je 24,22:2
Sloan, William Mrs, 1949, O 21,25:3
Sloan, William S, 1961, Ag 3,23:5
Sloane, Alfred Baldwin (funl, F 23,17:6), 1925, F 22, 19:2
Sloane, Arthur J, 1956, S 7,24:3
Sloane, Arthur J Mrs, 1937, F 18,21:1
Sloane, Benjamin, 1941, Jl 15,19:6
Sloane, Charles B, 1948, Jl 11,53:2; 1955, F 5,15:4
Sloane, David Mrs, 1940, S 24,23:4
Sloane, Douglas 2d Mrs, 1959, N 16,31:3
Sloane, George, 1946, S 30,25:4
Sloane, George B, 1958, Jl 17,27:1
Sloane, Harry, 1961, Mr 5,87:1
Sloane, Henry T (will, O 6,7:2), 1937, S 19,II,7:1
Sloane, Howard A, 1958, My 3,19:6
Sloane, Isabel D Mrs, 1962, Mr 11,86:2
Sloane, James R, 1955, N 14,27:3
Sloane, John, 1905, D 10,7:6
Sloane, John J Jr, 1941, S 22,15:5
Sloane, John J Mrs, 1949, Ja 2,60:6
Sloane, John Mrs, 1911, My 15,11:6; 1947, Ag 20,21:3
Sloane, Joseph T, 1951, D 15,13:3
Sloane, Joseph T Mrs, 1940, Ja 25,21:4
Sloane, Malcolm Douglas, 1924, S 7,31:2
Sloane, Marian P Mrs, 1954, Ja 18,23:3
Sloane, Morris H Sr, 1950, S 22,31:2
Sloane, Parker (will), 1939, Je 28,22:3
Sloane, Reginald G, 1957, Je 11,35:2
Sloane, Robert R, 1955, Ap 5,29:2
Sloane, Samuel, 1963, D 24,17:3
Sloane, T O'Conor Mrs, 1952, Ap 9,31:4
Sloane, Thomas M, 1959, Mr 21,21:2
Sloane, Thomas O'C (por), 1940, Ag 8,19:4
Sloane, W M, 1928, S 12,27:3
Sloane, Walter H, 1939, Ag 6,37:2
Sloane, William, 1879, My 24,12:2; 1922, Ag 12,9:6; 1922, Ag 16,9:5
Sloane, William D, 1942, S 20,40:1
Sloane, William Douglas, 1915, Mr 20,13:3
Sloane, William J Mrs, 1948, N 27,17:6
Sloane, Winifred E, 1966, F 16,43:4
Sloat, Benjamin F, 1949, N 13,94:2
Sloat, Edwin C, 1956, S 20,33:1
Sloat, Ernest H, 1953, N 19,31:2
Sloat, Maitland B, 1937, F 24,24:1
Sloat, Mary J, 1946, Mr 13,29:2
Sloat, Nell V, 1939, My 24,23:3
Sloat, Stephen F, 1937, Ap 28,23:3
Sloat, Stephen F Mrs, 1943, S 25,15:4
Sloat, Wallace H, 1961, My 18,35:3
Sloat, William H, 1941, S 4,22:2
Sloate, Barnet, 1948, S 19,76:5
Sloate, G Barbara, 1959, N 5,35:5
Sloate, Herbert D, 1943, Ag 11,19:4
Slobey, Joseph, 1950, Ap 20,29:2
Slobin, Hermon L, 1951, F 24,13:5
Slobins, Simon, 1949, My 14,13:4
Sloboda, Edward, 1948, S 18,17:2
Sloboda, Paul S, 1967, S 8,40:3
Slobodien, Leo, 1966, My 15,88:7
Slobodin, Harry L, 1951, D 27,21:2
Slobodkin, Simon, 1956, F 6,23:5
Sloca, Charles Mrs, 1952, D 13,21:4
Slochowsky, Morris, 1960, Mr 15,39:4
Slocomb, Charles E, 1943, My 2,44:6
Sloctemeyer, Hugo F Rev, 1937, F 9,23:5
Slocum, Alfred J, 1958, Ja 10,26:1
Slocum, Arthur W, 1937, N 21,II,8:7
Slocum, Benjamin Mrs, 1944, S 1,13:5
Slocum, C Jonathan, 1950, Ja 29,68:5
Slocum, Chester A, 1942, S 23,26:2; 1959, Ap 8,37:3
Slocum, Chester C, 1964, Jl 14,33:1
Slocum, Edward R, 1937, My 2,II,9:3
Slocum, Elisha, 1937, F 20,17:2
Slocum, Ernest E Mrs, 1962, Je 29,27:5
Slocum, Everett, 1937, Je 22,23:3
Slocum, Frederick, 1944, D 5,23:4
Slocum, George F, 1939, S 9,17:2
Slocum, George M, 1949, O 30,85:1
Slocum, George W, 1961, Je 21,37:4
Slocum, H W Gen, 1894, Ap 15,16:1
Slocum, Harold, 1962, F 2,30:3
Slocum, Harold W, 1956, Ja 29,93:2
Slocum, Harry B, 1957, D 20,27:2
Slocum, Harvey, 1961, N 12,86:1
Slocum, Harvey F, 1943, My 9,40:6
Slocum, Henry W, 1949, Ja 23,68:3
Slocum, Herbert J, 1948, F 3,25:2
Slocum, Herbert J Mrs, 1910, Mr 24,9:3
Slocum, Herbert Spencer, 1916, Je 30,11:5
Slocum, J C, 1879, F 25,5:5
Slocum, J Howard, 1943, N 23,25:2
Slocum, Jeremiah D Col, 1907, Mr 13,9:6
Slocum, John Palmer, 1925, Ap 2,21:5
Slocum, John W, 1938, My 23,17:2
Slocum, Joseph Jermain Col, 1924, O 3,21:4
Slocum, Kenneth M, 1940, D 12,27:3
Slocum, Laura (will), 1948, O 30,13:1
Slocum, Leslie A, 1949, N 14,27:4
Slocum, Lois T, 1951, My 26,17:6
Slocum, Lorimer B, 1957, N 21,30:1
Slocum, Louis W, 1941, Je 25,21:2
Slocum, Myles S, 1956, Je 9,17:6
Slocum, P Warren, 1946, F 16,13:2
Slocum, Phil H, 1939, F 8,23:3
Slocum, Ralph D, 1950, O 18,33:3
Slocum, Richard W (trb, Ap 2,31:4; mem ser, Ap 4,33:3), 1957, Ap 1,25:1
Slocum, S L'H, 1933, D 15,23:1
Slocum, Stephen E, 1960, S 23,29:3
Slocum, Thomas W (will, Jl 22,17:4),(por), 1937, Je 25,21:4
Slocum, Victor, 1949, D 12,33:2
Slocum, Walter W Mrs, 1938, Ap 4,17:4
Slocum, William J (por), 1943, My 7,19:5
Slocum, William J Mrs, 1943, Ja 16,13:1
Slocum, William J Mrs (Ann Gillis), 1957, D 17,35:2
Slocum, William J Msgr, 1908, O 23,9:4
Slocumb, Rufus C, 1962, F 11,86:7
Sloley, Herbert Sir, 1937, S 23,27:4
Sloman, David W, 1963, D 28,23:3
Sloman, Ernest G, 1952, My 2,25:6
Sloman, Frank, 1922, Ja 4,13:4
Sloman, Jerome, 1948, Mr 21,60:6
Sloman, Mark J, 1966, D 31,19:4
Sloman, Michael H, 1957, Ja 2,27:3
Slomka, Mathilde Mrs, 1942, Jl 20,13:5
Slomka, Sidney S, 1962, Jl 30,23:3
Slomski, Joseph S, 1963, Jl 22,23:2
Slonaker, James R, 1954, Ja 5,27:2
Slonaker, Louis V, 1937, Je 19,17:5
Slonaker, William C, 1948, Ag 3,26:3
Slone, Joseph, 1955, S 28,35:2
Slone, L Caney, 1953, Ap 8,29:4
Slonim, Irving, 1957, O 13,85:3
Slonim, Irving M, 1956, F 5,86:3
Slonim, Joel, 1944, O 28,15:4
Slonim, Max P, 1959, O 15,39:5
Sloop, Eustace H, 1961, F 9,31:4
Sloop, Eustace H Mrs, 1962, Ja 15,27:3
Sloper, A J, 1933, Je 3,13:6
Sloper, Charles W Mrs, 1954, D 30,17:4
Sloper, Ezekiel, 1945, F 27,19:4
Sloper, Harold T, 1945, Mr 3,13:4
Sloper, Leslie A Mrs (M Lloyd), 1960, Mr 2,37:2
Slorah, George W, 1946, My 4,15:4
Sloss, Leon Jr, 1947, D 18,30:2
Sloss, Marcus C, 1958, My 18,86:6
Slosson, Ex-Judge, 1872, D 27,2:3
Slosson, Frank S, 1950, Ja 21,17:2
Slosson, Harrison T, 1944, S 24,46:1
Slosson, Henry Lawrence, 1903, N 15,7:5
Slosson, J S, 1903, Ap 9,9:5
Slosson, Mary P Mrs, 1943, N 27,13:2
Slosson, Stewart, 1941, Ja 8,19:4
Slote, Aaron, 1949, D 15,35:3
Slote, Benjamin, 1949, Je 4,19:1
Slote, Daniel, 1882, F 14,5:4
Slote, Edgar A, 1916, N 24,13:3
Slote, Henry Lowery, 1906, Ja 23,9:5
Slote, Jerome J, 1953, D 14,31:5
Slote, Samuel, 1961, D 15,37:3
Slotkin, Samuel, 1965, O 31,87:1
Slotky, Samuel, 1961, Je 1,35:3
Slotnick, Jacob L, 1961, Mr 11,21:6
Slotnick, Michael N, 1938, O 28,23:5
Slotnick, Morris M, 1956, My 9,33:3
Slotnick, Murray, 1951, O 7,36:4
Slott, Mollie (Mrs C Levinson), 1967, Ja 25,43:2
Slott, Toni Mrs, 1953, Ap 25,10:6
Slottman, George V, 1958, Ap 23,33:1
Slough, Ephraim F, 1949, D 24,15:4
Slovak, Marty, 1950, Mr 23,29:3
Slover, Charles F, 1948, N 19,27:3
Slover, George F, 1941, F 19,21:5
Slover, Peter, 1943, N 9,21:5
Slover, Samuel L, 1959, N 30,31:4
Slover, William M, 1939, S 24,44:1
Sloves, Herman J, 1957, D 11,31:3
Sloves, Joseph, 1961, Ja 16,27:4
Slowey, George P, 1954, Ja 23,13:2
Slowey, John C Sr, 1961, Ag 6,84:4
Slowey, Joseph F, 1956, Jl 9,23:2
Slowey, T, 1878, D 24,8:3
Sloyan, Jerome J Mrs, 1954, Mr 16,29:6
Sloyan (Sister Mary Thos Aquinas), 1964, Ag 17, 25:2
Sluder, Greenfield Mrs, 1951, Ja 11,26:3
Sludock, Michael P, 1963, Jl 18,27:3
Slugg, Clarence H, 1944, D 21,21:5
Slugg, Ruth M, 1954, Je 29,27:5
Slugg, Thomas L Mrs, 1947, F 13,24:2
Sluja, John, 1952, Ja 3,27:4
Slusarev, Boris D, 1961, Ag 8,29:1
Sluss, Alfred H, 1944, Ap 19,23:5
Slusser, Charles E, 1963, D 4,47:3
Slusser, Clifton (por), 1949, Mr 26,17:5
Sluter, Henry C, 1920, F 20,15:4
Sluter, Henry C Mrs, 1920, F 20,15:4
Sluter, Randolph, 1943, D 31,15:4
Slutsky, Joseph, 1958, N 24,29:4
Slutsky, Nathan I, 1949, My 13,24:2
Slutz, Frank D, 1956, D 18,31:4
Slutz, Lillian B, 1955, Je 17,23:3
Slutzkin, Jacob H, 1956, F 16,29:4
Slutzky, William, 1961, Mr 11,21:5
Sluyter, Henry, 1940, Ag 14,19:5
Sluyter, Ross E, 1953, N 19,31:3
Sly, Frederick S, 1952, Je 29,59:3
Sly, H Belden, 1951, Mr 13,31:1
Sly, John F, 1965, Ap 28,45:1
Slye, Andrew Mrs, 1958, N 6,37:3
Slye, Maud, 1954, S 18,15:2
Slyman, Joseph V, 1960, Ap 27,37:4
Smadbeck, Warren, 1965, Jl 30,25:1
Smadel, Joseph E, 1963, Jl 23,29:3
Smagley, Philip, 1960, Ja 9,21:2
Smailer, Albert L, 1956, Ja 19,33:1
Smalbach, Emanuel, 1956, Ag 2,25:3
Smale, Henry C, 1949, Ja 17,19:4
Smale, Ira O, 1960, Je 30,29:2
Smales, Holbert, 1881, Mr 18,3:4
Small, Abraham M, 1950, D 30,13:4
Small, Alex, 1965, My 19,47:2
Small, Alonzo P, 1904, Je 16,9:2
Small, Alvah R, 1954, O 10,84:2
Small, Ben J, 1957, Ap 15,29:3
Small, Carlton L, 1951, Ag 2,21:1
Small, Charles A, 1943, Ap 18,48:5
Small, Charles C, 1956, My 22,33:1
Small, Charles P, 1947, S 27,15:3
Small, Charlie A, 1953, Ja 15,27:1
Small, Daniel, 1951, Ap 16,25:2
Small, E Wallace, 1962, My 27,92:6
Small, Edgar P, 1960, Ja 4,29:5
Small, Edward L, 1947, Ag 8,21:5
Small, Edward Mrs, 1947, Jl 3,21:4
Small, Elisha H, 1944, Ja 18,19:1
Small, Elizabeth W Mrs, 1941, Mr 21,21:1
Small, Ernest G, 1944, D 27,19:5
Small, Eugene W Mrs, 1958, Ap 26,19:4

Small, Fenwick B, 1941, F 24,15:3
Small, Fessenden H, 1925, S 29,27:4
Small, Florence, 1953, Mr 20,23:6
Small, Frank B, 1953, Jl 29,23:6
Small, Fred G Mrs, 1962, Ag 6,25:6
Small, Fred Mrs, 1958, Ja 2,29:4
Small, Frederick A, 1965, Ja 18,35:4
Small, Frederick F, 1941, O 7,23:1
Small, Frederick P, 1958, Mr 3,27:2
Small, George D, 1949, N 20,92:5
Small, George G, 1948, N 16,29:3
Small, George W, 1951, S 2,48:6
Small, George W Mrs, 1956, O 6,21:3
Small, Grant D I, 1942, Ap 15,21:4
Small, Harold G, 1953, Ap 4,13:5
Small, Herbert, 1903, D 13,7:5
Small, Howard L, 1943, O 18,15:3
Small, J H, 1909, F 15,7:4
Small, Jack, 1962, Ap 30,27:3
Small, James C, 1948, Ja 5,19:4
Small, John, 1961, O 6,35:2
Small, John H, 1946, Jl 15,25:5
Small, John K (por), 1938, Ja 21,19:3
Small, L, 1936, My 18,17:5
Small, Leslie C, 1957, Ja 12,19:4
Small, Maurice, 1903, Je 12,9:6
Small, Mitchell, 1959, D 6,86:5
Small, Osgood L, 1955, F 2,27:1
Small, Paul, 1954, Ag 7,13:5
Small, Paul Mrs, 1961, D 17,82:4
Small, Percy L, 1955, Ap 24,86:6
Small, Phil, 1948, Ag 22,60:4
Small, Reuel, 1937, F 28,II,9:1
Small, Richard Dr, 1937, S 12,II,6:7
Small, Roy L, 1951, N 24,11:2
Small, S W, 1931, N 22,30:1
Small, Samuel H, 1948, Ja 3,13:2
Small, Solomon, 1943, Ja 3,43:1
Small, Vivian B, 1946, My 16,21:5
Small, Willard S, 1943, F 2,20:2
Small, William R Mrs, 1945, Ja 12,15:2
Smallbrook, John H, 1947, N 11,28:3
Smalle, Edwin J Jr, 1957, Mr 27,31:5
Smallens, Alex Mrs, 1958, D 8,31:4
Smalley, Albert, 1943, My 5,27:2
Smalley, Albt Mrs, 1953, F 11,29:5
Smalley, August H, 1947, D 3,29:3
Smalley, Bradley B, 1909, N 7,13:6
Smalley, Emerson, 1945, Ag 20,19:4
Smalley, Evelyn G, 1938, Mr 26,15:5
Smalley, George O, 1956, Ja 17,33:3
Smalley, George W, 1916, Ap 5,13:7
Smalley, George W Mrs, 1923, F 7,15:5
Smalley, Harold R, 1945, Mr 1,21:3
Smalley, Harvey S Sr, 1946, Ag 16,21:5
Smalley, Henry C, 1953, Ap 4,13:4
Smalley, Joseph B, 1942, Jl 6,15:3
Smalley, Kenneth E, 1961, Ap 1,17:4
Smalley, Newton B Mrs, 1944, F 13,41:2
Smalley, Paul C, 1955, Je 10,25:4
Smalley, Ralph J (funl, Ja 25,31:4), 1956, Ja 22,88:1
Smalley, Ralph T, 1950, Ja 17,27:3
Smalley, Robert A, 1958, O 12,86:7
Smalley, Robert C, 1954, Mr 29,19:5
Smalley, Sara D, 1952, Ag 8,17:6
Smalley, Vincent R, 1966, Ap 13,40:4
Smalley, W E, 1880, Jl 9,8:4
Smalley, William, 1947, Mr 5,25:2
Smalley, William C, 1952, D 29,19:5
Smalley, William L, 1955, O 28,25:3
Smalley, William W, 1916, D 28,9:4
Smallheiser, Albert L, 1957, F 4,19:2
Smallman, Alfred W, 1949, D 29,25:1
Smallman, Clinton I, 1941, Mr 27,23:2
Smallman, Isadore, 1957, Mr 23,19:4
Smallman, James, 1941, D 12,25:4
Smallman, John, 1937, D 21,23:1
Smallman, Samuel J, 1966, Je 29,47:4
Smalls, Edward L, 1942, S 14,15:5
Smallwood, Arthur N, 1942, O 29,23:2
Smallwood, Edward, 1952, F 27,27:1
Smallwood, Hugh M, 1953, Ap 29,29:4
Smallwood, Joseph, 1941, Jl 20,30:1
Smallwood, Robert F, 1965, Ag 11,35:3
Smallwood, Robert G, 1949, Mr 18,25:3
Smallwood, William M, 1949, N 21,25:2
Smally, D A, 1877, Mr 11,7:2
Smalth, John H, 1941, Ap 13,38:3
Smaney, George F, 1949, Mr 4,21:2
Smart, Alfred, 1951, F 5,23:4
Smart, Allen R, 1940, F 9,19:5
Smart, Billy, 1966, S 26,41:2
Smart, Borlase, 1947, N 4,25:5
Smart, C A Brig-Gen, 1937, Je 5,17:2
Smart, Charles A, 1967, Mr 13,37:2
Smart, Charles Col, 1905, Ap 25,11:6
Smart, David A, 1952, O 17,27:1
Smart, Edmund H, 1942, N 16,19:2
Smart, Floyd G Mrs, 1941, S 7,51:4
Smart, Frederick R, 1920, O 29,15:5; 1953, Ag 4,21:2
Smart, G T, 1928, Mr 15,25:3
Smart, George J, 1958, O 1,37:1
Smart, George Mrs (Lucy A), 1960, S 8,35:3
Smart, George T Mrs, 1952, Je 3,29:5
Smart, Gino, 1959, S 11,27:2
Smart, Guy Mrs, 1955, Mr 26,15:1
Smart, Henry C, 1937, Ja 15,21:4
Smart, Isabelle T, 1943, D 12,68:1
Smart, Isaiah H, 1938, N 23,21:4
Smart, J Scott, 1960, Ja 16,21:2
Smart, James D, 1950, Ag 5,15:3
Smart, James H, 1945, Ag 20,19:5
Smart, John C Mrs, 1950, Ap 30,102:7
Smart, John H, 1952, Ja 4,40:3
Smart, Josephine Mrs, 1960, Je 2,23:2
Smart, Oliver M Mrs, 1942, Je 15,19:5
Smart, R, 1928, Ap 9,21:5
Smart, Robert F, 1947, Ag 2,13:4
Smart, Robert Mrs, 1947, Ap 10,25:3
Smart, Roy H, 1953, Ap 27,23:4
Smart, Sidney J, 1952, Ap 19,15:3
Smart, Thomas W Sr, 1952, F 3,84:4
Smart, V I, 1940, D 4,27:3
Smart, William C, 1940, N 28,23:1
Smart, William F (por), 1947, Ap 13,60:3
Smarzo, William S, 1945, Ja 3,17:4
Smathers, Benjamin F, 1942, D 11,23:5
Smathers, Charles B, 1940, O 30,23:6
Smathers, E E, 1928, Ja 12,27:1
Smathers, Elmer E Mrs, 1947, O 4,17:1
Smathers, Eugene Rev Dr, 1968, Ag 18,89:1
Smathers, James F, 1967, Ag 10,37:3
Smathers, Joseph B, 1960, Ja 6,35:4
Smathers, William H, 1955, S 25,92:4
Smead, Edwin R, 1948, Ja 27,25:1
Smead, Harold, 1938, O 9,45:4
Smead, Wesley Dr, 1871, Ja 7,1:3
Smeade, George Gordon Rev, 1922, D 30,13:5
Smeallie, John M (por), 1947, N 25,32:3
Smeallie, John M Jr, 1939, Jl 23,29:3
Smeallie, John V, 1949, Mr 26,17:1
Smeathers, Eugene G, 1950, Ja 24,31:4
Smeaton, Edna, 1942, Jl 16,19:3
Smeaton, James V, 1938, Jl 21,21:4
Smed, Peer, 1943, N 20,13:6
Smedberg, Carl G Mrs, 1949, N 16,29:3
Smedberg, Edmund M, 1938, O 1,17:5
Smedberg, William R Jr, 1942, O 10,15:4
Smedley, Agnes, 1950, My 9,29:1
Smedley, Constance, 1941, Mr 13,21:5
Smedley, Frederick George, 1907, D 14,9:4
Smedley, Graham, 1954, Je 18,23:2
Smedley, Harvey L, 1962, My 27,92:8
Smedley, Howard B, 1956, S 19,37:2
Smedley, J Harvey, 1925, Jl 6,11:5
Smedley, M Harvey, 1968, N 28,37:1
Smedley, Perry A, 1948, Ag 8,56:5
Smedley, Ralph C, 1965, S 12,87:1
Smedley, Will L, 1957, S 20,25:3
Smedley, William H, 1942, D 22,25:3
Smedley, William Mrs, 1946, Mr 13,30:2
Smedley, William P, 1953, Mr 12,25:2
Smedley, William T, 1920, Mr 27,13:3
Smedt, Leon J de, 1951, D 28,2:7
Smeed, Henry A, 1937, D 6,27:2
Smejkal, Frank J, 1950, Ag 13,77:1
Smellie, Ernest, 1944, Ja 25,19:3
Smellie, Harold, 1966, O 11,43:5
Smelo, William M, 1950, Ag 5,15:6
Smelter, Alfred E, 1946, Ag 18,46:6
Smeltz, George W, 1967, Ja 6,35:5
Smeltz, William N (Billy Newton), 1954, F 16,25:5
Smeltzer, John Rev, 1937, S 12,II,7:1
Smeraldi, John D, 1947, My 15,26:3
Smeraldo, Ferdinand, 1953, Je 30,23:4
Smeriglio, Rocco, 1952, Ap 10,29:4
Smet, Charles A, 1944, Ap 10,19:3
Smetanka, Jarsolav F, 1937, D 29,21:5
Smeterlin, Jan, 1967, Ja 20,43:1
Smethurst, Arthur F, 1954, Ja 25,19:4
Smethurst, Frank, 1941, S 19,23:3
Smethurst, William A, 1938, Ag 13,13:3
Smiddy, Charles L, 1950, Jl 4,17:5
Smiddy, Thomas W, 1965, N 5,37:4
Smidl, Joseph C, 1968, Mr 26,46:1
Smidovitch, P, 1935, Ap 17,23:4
Smidt, Raymond G, 1961, Ag 21,16:5
Smidt, Theodore, 1871, Ag 9,5:2
Smidt, Thomas, 1940, Ag 31,13:5
Smietan, Simon, 1945, Mr 7,22:2
Smigel, Joseph O, 1967, N 20,47:2
Smilansky, Moshe, 1953, O 8,29:4
Smilde, Lubertus, 1964, D 16,43:4
Smiles, Gertrude E, 1938, D 30,15:5
Smiles, Norman T, 1939, O 7,17:3
Smiles, Samuel, 1904, Ap 17,7:6
Smiley, Albert Keith, 1912, D 3,15:4
Smiley, Daniel Mrs, 1951, My 15,31:5
Smiley, David B Mrs, 1945, Je 21,19:1
Smiley, David E, 1960, O 28,31:2
Smiley, David E Mrs, 1955, Mr 27,86:3
Smiley, Edward, 1966, N 9,39:4
Smiley, Edward A, 1945, O 15,17:4
Smiley, George H, 1943, Mr 9,24:3
Smiley, George W, 1954, Ja 2,11:4
Smiley, John C, 1946, N 28,27:4
Smiley, John M, 1953, O 20,29:4
Smiley, Joseph W, 1945, D 4,30:2
Smiley, Raymond W, 1938, Mr 5,17:5
Smiley, Robert Irving, 1911, O 7,13:6
Smiley, U Franklin, 1938, Ap 8,19:6
Smiley, Virgil D, 1948, O 26,31:3
Smiley, William H, 1950, Mr 9,30:2
Smillie, Charles F, 1914, N 23,11:6
Smillie, Charles Van V, 1960, F 1,27:4
Smillie, G H, 1880, D 31,8:1
Smillie, George Henry, 1921, N 11,13:5
Smillie, James David, 1909, S 15,9:4
Smillie, Ralph, 1960, F 17,35:5
Smillie, Robert, 1940, F 17,13:2
Smilo, Daniel, 1940, My 19,43:1
Smilo, Maurice, 1948, Je 2,29:2
Smingler, August, 1943, Ja 31,45:1
Smink, Frank C, 1920, Mr 4,11:5
Smink, Ray B, 1966, Mr 1,37:2
Smink, Simon, 1964, D 19,29:1
Smirke, Charles Mrs, 1954, N 8,21:5
Smirnov, Nikolai I, 1962, Je 19,2:4
Smirnow, Louis M, 1948, F 25,23:4
Smissaert, Leonard A, 1953, Mr 25,31:2
Smit, Johannes J Sr, 1965, Ap 15,33:3
Smit, Leonard J A, 1953, Ap 23,29:3
Smit, Piet, 1964, Mr 8,87:1
Smit, Rodolphe J, 1950, D 17,85:1
Smitchel, Louis, 1937, Ag 25,21:6
Smith, A (see also D 30), 1876, D 31,1:5
Smith, A, 1878, N 7,8:1; 1933, Je 29,19:1
Smith, A A, 1876, Jl 8,5:1; 1931, Je 26,23:1
Smith, A Alexander Dr, 1915, D 14,13:5
Smith, A Arthur, 1968, N 2,37:3
Smith, A C Dr, 1909, Mr 21,11:6
Smith, A D Rev Dr, 1877, Ag 17,4:6
Smith, A Dr, 1884, F 20,5:3
Smith, A Edward, 1962, Je 6,42:2
Smith, A F, 1879, Jl 25,1:3; 1939, O 5,23:2
Smith, A Frank, 1962, O 7,83:1
Smith, A G, 1928, Je 6,25:5
Smith, A Herbert, 1958, F 14,24:4
Smith, A Homer, 1949, Ag 29,18:2
Smith, A L, 1934, My 21,17:1
Smith, A Marguerite, 1959, Jl 6,27:5
Smith, A McKay, 1937, My 23,II,11:1
Smith, A Morton, 1957, Ap 8,24:1
Smith, A Vincent, 1951, Ap 4,29:4
Smith, A W, 1866, Mr 30,8:5
Smith, A Wesley, 1939, Je 3,15:5
Smith, Aaron, 1947, Je 22,52:6; 1963, Je 26,39:5; 1966, D 15,47:3
Smith, Abbie H, 1948, F 5,23:5
Smith, Abbott P, 1943, Mr 19,20:3
Smith, Abbott P Mrs, 1949, My 18,27:3
Smith, Abby H, 1878, Jl 25,5:5
Smith, Abe Mrs, 1950, Jl 10,21:4
Smith, Abel I, 1949, O 25,27:5
Smith, Abiel L, 1946, Ap 26,21:3
Smith, Abraham E, 1915, Ja 20,9:4
Smith, Abraham I, 1956, O 4,33:4
Smith, Abraham Mrs, 1944, O 19,23:1
Smith, Abram B, 1945, D 8,17:5
Smith, Adam E, 1949, Jl 28,23:5
Smith, Addison, 1942, Je 3,23:4
Smith, Addison Jr, 1962, F 14,35:1
Smith, Addison R, 1946, N 6,23:6
Smith, Addison T, 1956, Jl 6,21:3
Smith, Addison T Mrs, 1947, F 11,27:2
Smith, Adela J, 1947, Mr 3,21:5
Smith, Adelaine, 1907, My 31,9:6
Smith, Adrian W, 1874, N 27,5:6; 1955, N 25,27:2
Smith, Al (funl), 1909, O 12,9:6
Smith, Alan R, 1961, Jl 12,31:5
Smith, Albanus L, 1938, N 25,23:5
Smith, Albert (funl), 1860, Je 9,2:2
Smith, Albert, 1922, D 25,13:2
Smith, Albert B Mrs (M Nybloc), 1962, Ja 15,27:2
Smith, Albert D, 1962, O 3,41:2
Smith, Albert D Mrs, 1956, D 20,29:4
Smith, Albert Dodge, 1913, O 18,13:4
Smith, Albert E, 1941, Ag 27,19:4; 1943, Ja 5,19:4; 1958, Ag 3,80:3
Smith, Albert F, 1948, Jl 23,19:4
Smith, Albert H, 1940, Ap 11,25:5; 1940, N 5,25:2; 1943, O 15,19:4; 1946, Ja 4,21:1; 1950, Je 13,27:1
Smith, Albert H Mrs, 1950, Ja 18,31:4
Smith, Albert J, 1952, Ag 9,13:5
Smith, Albert M, 1910, F 28,9:5
Smith, Albert Mrs, 1917, Jl 30,9:7
Smith, Albert R, 1950, O 21,17:5
Smith, Albert T, 1959, Ja 29,27:3
Smith, Albert U, 1942, O 23,21:2
Smith, Albert V, 1955, N 27,88:8
Smith, Albert W, 1942, Ag 17,15:6; 1946, Ag 26,23:5
Smith, Albert W Mrs, 1960, Mr 14,23:5
Smith, Albertus, 1949, O 9,93:1
Smith, Albridge C, 1951, Je 5,31:2
Smith, Albridge C Mrs, 1964, D 17,41:2
Smith, Alex, 1941, F 19,21:1; 1959, Ja 15,33:1
Smith, Alex C, 1963, My 13,29:4
Smith, Alex F, 1939, D 3,60:5
Smith, Alex K Mrs, 1950, N 30,33:2

Smith, Alex M, 1958, Je 25,29:2
Smith, Alex Mrs, 1954, Jl 3,11:5
Smith, Alex W, 1958, Mr 1,17:6
Smith, Alexander, 1867, Ja 22,4:6
Smith, Alexander Bailey, 1915, D 27,9:5
Smith, Alexander J, 1924, Ap 8,19:3
Smith, Alexander L, 1947, Jl 3,21:5
Smith, Alexander Prof, 1922, S 10,28:3
Smith, Alfred, 1941, Ja 7,23:5
Smith, Alfred B, 1943, Jl 16,17:6
Smith, Alfred B Mrs, 1941, D 15,19:4; 1955, Ap 5,29:1
Smith, Alfred D, 1940, Ja 4,23:5
Smith, Alfred E, 1938, O 8,17:6; 1943, D 24,13:1; 1944, O 4,1:1; 1950, My 9,59:3; 1959, Je 11,33:3
Smith, Alfred E Jr, 1968, N 17,86:5
Smith, Alfred E Mrs, 1944, My 5,19:1
Smith, Alfred F Mrs, 1940, Je 24,15:6
Smith, Alfred G, 1939, F 17,19:5
Smith, Alfred H, 1910, O 26,9:5
Smith, Alfred H (funl, Mr 11,19:1), 1924, Mr 10,15:5
Smith, Alfred P, 1944, Ag 9,17:4
Smith, Alfred T, 1939, N 29,23:2; 1948, N 13,15:2
Smith, Alfred T Gen, 1905, My 24,9:5
Smith, Alice, 1947, Mr 14,23:4
Smith, Alice L, 1947, Je 7,13:2
Smith, Alice W Mrs, 1942, Je 7,43:3
Smith, Alison, 1943, Ja 8,19:5
Smith, Allan, 1941, F 24,15:4
Smith, Allan A, 1959, D 22,31:6
Smith, Allan M, 1947, O 26,68:3
Smith, Allen A, 1953, S 25,21:5
Smith, Allen V, 1949, Ja 25,24:2
Smith, Almeron W Mrs, 1967, Ap 28,41:3
Smith, Alonzo, 1948, F 25,23:5
Smith, Alonzo D, 1917, O 18,15:3
Smith, Alpheus D Mrs, 1938, O 22,17:6
Smith, Alvarez H, 1939, My 24,23:5
Smith, Alvert W, 1949, O 30,84:3
Smith, Alvin A, 1943, Ag 26,17:6
Smith, Alvin G, 1942, N 30,23:3
Smith, Alzamora, 1950, Ag 17,27:1
Smith, Amanda Mrs, 1915, Mr 6,11:6
Smith, Amanda W Mrs, 1941, N 6,23:3
Smith, Amaroy J Mrs, 1941, Ap 24,21:3
Smith, Ambrosia W Mrs, 1946, Mr 19,27:4
Smith, Amina E, 1949, Ag 2,20:2
Smith, Amos T, 1942, N 24,25:1
Smith, Amos Tyler Mrs, 1968, Ja 7,84:8
Smith, Amzi, 1907, Ag 25,7:5
Smith, Andrew, 1918, Ag 7,9:8
Smith, Andrew A, 1949, Je 29,27:1
Smith, Andrew A Jr, 1958, Mr 26,27:3
Smith, Andrew B, 1938, Je 3,21:3
Smith, Andrew E, 1937, Ap 6,23:6
Smith, Andrew G, 1939, Ja 28,15:3
Smith, Andrew H Dr, 1910, Ap 9,11:4
Smith, Andrew J, 1951, Ap 3,27:5
Smith, Andrew J Col, 1903, Ap 28,9:6
Smith, Andrew Jackson Col, 1913, S 2,7:7
Smith, Andrew W, 1954, Je 14,21:5
Smith, Andy W Jr, 1966, Ag 9,37:1
Smith, Ann K, 1951, Ag 8,25:5
Smith, Anna E, 1945, N 22,35:4
Smith, Anna F Mrs, 1945, My 15,19:2
Smith, Anna J, 1946, Je 13,27:3; 1948, F 18,27:2
Smith, Anna L Mrs, 1949, N 10,31:1
Smith, Anna S Mrs, 1958, O 24,33:2
Smith, Anna W, 1943, Ag 4,17:3
Smith, Annie Mrs, 1948, Ja 21,25:4
Smith, Another, 1951, Jl 7,13:6
Smith, Appleton W, 1952, S 15,25:1
Smith, Arabella Eugenia, 1916, Jl 25,9:5
Smith, Arch H Mrs, 1937, Mr 14,II,8:7
Smith, Arch W, 1950, Ag 2,25:2
Smith, Archibald Cary, 1911, D 9,13:4
Smith, Archibald D, 1945, N 24,20:2
Smith, Archibald J, 1951, My 3,29:4
Smith, Archibald W, 1962, F 28,33:5
Smith, Archie, 1939, F 5,38:1
Smith, Armide, 1907, Ap 21,9:3
Smith, Arnold B, 1949, D 25,26:3
Smith, Arrender, 1944, N 20,21:5
Smith, Arthur, 1947, S 6,17:6; 1951, Jl 8,20:5
Smith, Arthur B, 1946, Jl 17,23:4; 1956, S 18,24:2
Smith, Arthur B Mrs, 1956, S 24,27:1
Smith, Arthur C (por), 1938, Ja 7,19:4
Smith, Arthur C, 1945, S 4,23:3
Smith, Arthur D, 1939, F 21,19:4; 1944, Ap 23,43:4
Smith, Arthur D H, 1945, D 19,25:5
Smith, Arthur E, 1945, F 21,19:3
Smith, Arthur Eugene, 1925, Je 10,23:5
Smith, Arthur G Prof, 1916, N 7,11:4
Smith, Arthur J, 1944, My 12,19:4
Smith, Arthur J Rev, 1937, Ap 25,II,8:3
Smith, Arthur L, 1951, D 19,31:1; 1967, O 5,39:2
Smith, Arthur L J, 1946, D 18,29:3
Smith, Arthur Mrs, 1949, My 13,23:1
Smith, Arthur Mumford Judge, 1968, N 21,47:3
Smith, Arthur R, 1948, Ja 20,23:1; 1953, Ja 2,15:4
Smith, Arthur S (por), 1942, Mr 28,17:4
Smith, Arthur T, 1937, Mr 24,25:2; 1947, N 4,25:3; 1952, S 19,23:2; 1953, F 5,23:5
Smith, Arthur W, 1940, F 12,17:4; 1946, D 20,23:4; 1955, S 8,31:4
Smith, Arthur W Mrs, 1954, Mr 17,31:1
Smith, Asa, 1907, O 1,11:5
Smith, Asa B, 1950, Mr 14,25:3
Smith, Asa Francis, 1925, Ja 18,7:1
Smith, Ashley A, 1949, Ag 30,27:4
Smith, Aubrey, 1957, O 7,27:2
Smith, Audley L, 1954, S 11,17:4
Smith, August C, 1952, Mr 1,15:2
Smith, Augusta L Mrs, 1946, Ja 27,42:4
Smith, Augustine, 1952, Mr 29,15:7
Smith, Augustine C, 1928, Je 16,17:3
Smith, Augustine J Mrs, 1953, N 7,17:5
Smith, Augustus, 1914, Jl 29,9:5
Smith, Augustus Ledyard, 1924, D 21,5:2
Smith, Augustus S, 1938, Ja 15,15:1
Smith, Austin R, 1941, N 16,57:1
Smith, Axel T, 1954, Jl 7,31:4
Smith, Azariah, 1902, Ja 15,9:5
Smith, B, 1935, Mr 28,21:5
Smith, B B Bp, 1884, Je 1,3:4
Smith, B Herbert, 1939, O 23,19:2
Smith, B K Bp, 1881, Jl 29,1:5
Smith, B Pressley, 1943, D 13,23:3
Smith, Baldwin B, 1952, Ag 10,61:2
Smith, Bancroft, 1937, Mr 23,II,10:8
Smith, Barney, 1903, My 17,7:6
Smith, Barrett P, 1953, My 30,15:5
Smith, Barry C, 1952, Ap 1,29:4
Smith, Bayard M, 1942, Je 30,21:3
Smith, Beasley, 1968, My 16,47:3
Smith, Beatrice, 1948, D 22,28:2
Smith, Beaumont, 1901, Ag 16,6:7
Smith, Ben, 1964, My 6,47:1
Smith, Ben V, 1955, Ja 22,11:6
Smith, Ben W, 1942, Ap 9,20:2
Smith, Benjamin, 1959, Je 6,21:6
Smith, Benjamin A Capt, 1923, My 9,19:4
Smith, Benjamin Eli Dr, 1913, F 25,11:3
Smith, Benjamin G, 1945, Ja 17,21:4
Smith, Benjamin H Mrs, 1945, Ja 31,21:1
Smith, Benjamin J Jr, 1947, D 23,23:5
Smith, Benjamin L, 1951, Ja 15,17:2
Smith, Benjamin T, 1959, Je 28,69:1
Smith, Benjamin W, 1942, Jl 29,17:5
Smith, Bernard E, 1961, My 12,29:1
Smith, Bernard H, 1952, Jl 6,49:1
Smith, Bert E, 1938, Mr 21,15:1
Smith, Bert V, 1964, Mr 7,23:5
Smith, Bertha W, 1957, Ag 7,27:3
Smith, Bertram, 1959, Je 5,27:1
Smith, Bertram E, 1952, Mr 1,15:4
Smith, Bertram L Judge, 1924, N 5,19:4
Smith, Bertrand L, 1957, Mr 6,31:2
Smith, Bertrand L Sr, 1965, N 15,37:1
Smith, Beverly W, 1940, O 15,23:1
Smith, Bevier, 1954, D 16,39:5
Smith, Billy, 1937, O 16,19:4
Smith, Bina C, 1919, Ag 12,9:6
Smith, Blaine S, 1955, O 28,25:3
Smith, Bracewell, 1966, Ja 13,25:4
Smith, Bradford, 1964, Jl 15,35:2
Smith, Brainard S, 1959, Ag 23,93:2
Smith, Breedlove, 1914, D 7,11:6
Smith, Bro Owen, 1942, O 30,19:5
Smith, Browning Mrs, 1953, S 13,84:6
Smith, Bruce, 1955, S 19,25:3; 1967, Ag 29,37:2
Smith, Bruce D, 1952, My 30,15:5
Smith, Bryan H, 1912, Mr 28,11:4
Smith, Bryce B, 1962, My 23,45:2
Smith, Burgess, 1958, Ap 16,33:2
Smith, Burns L, 1941, Ja 15,23:3
Smith, Burton, 1944, O 6,23:1
Smith, Burton J, 1954, Mr 27,17:5
Smith, Burton M, 1940, Mr 19,25:5
Smith, Byron Laflin, 1914, Mr 23,11:4
Smith, Byron P, 1955, F 15,27:4
Smith, C A Capt, 1877, D 28,1:3
Smith, C Arch, 1947, N 19,28:2
Smith, C Arthur, 1964, N 21,29:5
Smith, C Aubrey, 1948, D 21,25:1
Smith, C B Mrs, 1931, Jl 1,25:1
Smith, C E, 1903, Ag 22,5:5
Smith, C Edward, 1942, F 11,21:5; 1948, F 27,21:2
Smith, C Edward Mrs, 1939, N 10,23:1
Smith, C Elliot (por), 1947, D 3,29:1
Smith, C F Capt, 1921, Je 12,22:2
Smith, C Frank (will), 1950, O 21,7:3
Smith, C Franklin, 1951, My 24,35:3
Smith, C H (Bill Arp), 1903, Ag 25,7:6
Smith, C H, 1933, F 15,21:5
Smith, C Henry, 1948, O 20,29:4
Smith, C Howard Mrs, 1937, Mr 30,23:4
Smith, C M, 1881, Ap 5,5:2
Smith, C Ney, 1942, O 6,23:1
Smith, C P (see also F 14), 1877, F 16,4:6
Smith, C P, 1881, Jl 25,8:6; 1948, D 27,21:1
Smith, C Philip, 1943, S 24,23:2
Smith, C Ross, 1955, Ja 19,27:3
Smith, C S, 1959, O 16,31:4
Smith, C Stanley, 1959, Ag 18,29:4
Smith, C Walter, 1943, Mr 19,19:2
Smith, C Warner, 1953, N 17,31:3
Smith, C Wenham, 1920, S 8,11:2
Smith, Caleb B, 1864, Ja 8,1:5
Smith, Calvin A, 1903, D 29,9:5
Smith, Calvin B Mrs, 1962, Ap 28,25:5
Smith, Carey, 1939, My 1,23:5
Smith, Carl, 1950, Ag 23,29:5
Smith, Carl D Mrs, 1953, F 2,22:6; 1958, Ap 2,31:1
Smith, Carl H, 1946, Mr 8,21:1; 1964, Jl 21,33:4
Smith, Carl P, 1943, Jl 13,21:5
Smith, Carleton G, 1944, F 27,38:4
Smith, Caroline B Mrs, 1940, Je 4,23:2
Smith, Caroline F, 1907, Jl 19,7:6
Smith, Caroline P, 1938, S 13,23:2
Smith, Carrie B Mrs (will), 1939, Mr 21,19:1
Smith, Carrington Shepard, 1916, Je 2,11:5
Smith, Carroll D Sr, 1956, Mr 4,88:1
Smith, Carroll S, 1941, My 9,21:6
Smith, Caswell M, 1960, S 9,29:1
Smith, Caswell M Mrs, 1946, Mr 25,25:2
Smith, Catherine L, 1941, N 25,25:5
Smith, Catherine M (will, Mr 22,44:1), 1938, Mr 12, 17:3
Smith, Catherine Mrs, 1925, My 18,15:5
Smith, Cecil, 1950, O 24,29:1; 1956, My 30,21:2
Smith, Cecil Brunswick, 1912, Jl 2,11:3
Smith, Cecil Clementi Sir, 1916, F 7,11:3
Smith, Cecil Mrs, 1962, My 30,19:5
Smith, Cecile Gardner A C Mrs, 1924, Ag 19,15:5
Smith, Cedric E, 1937, Je 12,15:6
Smith, Chandler, 1948, Mr 20,13:5
Smith, Chandler Mrs, 1954, Jl 21,27:3
Smith, Channing G, 1952, D 23,23:2
Smith, Charles, 1945, O 9,21:1; 1947, My 20,25:1; 1947, N 4,25:2; 1962, N 6,33:4
Smith, Charles A, 1938, Mr 2,19:2; 1939, Jl 13,19:6; 1939, Jl 16,31:1; 1941, Mr 25,23:1; 1941, Jl 21,15:3; 1942, Jl 11,13:6; 1948, Mr 12,23:4; 1949, S 3,13:5; 1953, O 15,33:3; 1963, D 8,86:5
Smith, Charles A Mrs, 1945, Mr 24,17:6
Smith, Charles Alvin Rev, 1908, Mr 9,7:4
Smith, Charles B, 1937, Ja 25,19:1
Smith, Charles B (por), 1939, My 22,17:3
Smith, Charles B, 1939, N 29,23:4; 1957, Ag 19,19:4
Smith, Charles C, 1940, Jl 11,19:5; 1947, F 5,23:2; 1948, F 12,23:4; 1950, Ag 14,17:5; 1954, Ag 9,17:4
Smith, Charles C Mrs, 1954, Ja 4,19:4
Smith, Charles D, 1940, F 29,19:2
Smith, Charles Dr, 1923, Mr 31,13:5
Smith, Charles E, 1940, Mr 16,15:6; 1947, D 2,30:3; 1949, D 9,31:1; 1967, Ap 21,39:3
Smith, Charles E Mrs, 1943, Jl 22,19:3; 1947, Je 3,25:4
Smith, Charles F, 1938, F 23,23:4; 1938, D 5,23:2
Smith, Charles F (por), 1941, S 29,17:5
Smith, Charles F, 1942, D 5,15:2; 1943, N 10,23:5; 1944, Ap 20,19:2; 1949, D 3,15:2; 1950, F 16,23:5; 1951, S 1,11.4; 1958, Ja 15,39:3
Smith, Charles G, 1938, Je 23,21:4; 1949, My 3,25:4; 1953, S 24,33:4
Smith, Charles H, 1907, Ap 20,9:6; 1937, O 2,21:6; 1938, O 5,23:3; 1939, Ap 9,III,7:2; 1939, My 14,III, 7:2; 1941, Ja 25,15:3; 1942, Jl 25,13:1; 1942, O 2, 25:5; 1946, S 5,27:5; 1949, O 18,27:4; 1950, D 17, 85:1; 1955, F 6,88:4
Smith, Charles Hendee Dr, 1968, Jl 27,27:2
Smith, Charles Herbert, 1924, N 22,15:5
Smith, Charles I, 1948, O 19,27:1
Smith, Charles J, 1911, Jl 15,7:4; 1914, Jl 21,9:6; 1947 D 20,17:4; 1948, Ja 4,52:4; 1967, Mr 10,39:3
Smith, Charles J Mrs, 1942, S 17,25:3
Smith, Charles John, 1925, Ap 23,21:3
Smith, Charles L, 1957, N 15,27:3
Smith, Charles M (por), 1937, Ag 13,18:2
Smith, Charles M, 1938, Ja 9,42:3; 1939, Je 13,23:4; 1952, Mr 17,21:3
Smith, Charles M Mrs, 1948, S 19,78:4
Smith, Charles Maurice, 1903, S 19,7:6
Smith, Charles Mrs, 1945, My 16,19:1
Smith, Charles N, 1967, F 11,29:3
Smith, Charles P, 1937, S 23,27:4; 1948, Jl 8,23:2; 1955, F 5,15:3
Smith, Charles R, 1937, Ag 9,20:2; 1949, D 10,17:6; 1952, My 4,91:1
Smith, Charles R Mrs, 1945, Ap 8,35:1
Smith, Charles S, 1942, My 22,21:3; 1949, My 12,31:4 1960, Jl 26,29:2; 1962, S 18,39:4; 1964, Ag 25,33:4
Smith, Charles S Prof (mem), 1910, Ap 7,11:4
Smith, Charles Sidney Gen, 1922, N 20,17:2
Smith, Charles Sprague (funl), 1910, Ap 11,7:5
Smith, Charles Stewart (funl, D 2,9:5), 1909, D 1,9:3
Smith, Charles T, 1946, My 14,21:3; 1948, S 22,31:4; 1964, S 2,37:4
Smith, Charles V, 1947, Ap 13,60:4; 1950, Ja 24,31:2
Smith, Charles W, 1942, Je 10,21:4
Smith, Charles W (por), 1943, Ag 23,15:4
Smith, Charles W, 1943, S 7,23:6; 1945, F 21,19:4; 1949, F 21,23:2; 1949, Ap 3,76:7; 1952, O 30,31:5; 1952, N 2,89:2; 1955, Ja 12,27:3
Smith, Charles W Mrs, 1947, N 3,23:4; 1949, O 28, 23:3; 1950, S 12,28:6
Smith, Charles W Sr, 1964, Je 16,39:1
Smith, Charles William Bp, 1914, N 1,17:4
Smith, Charlie, 1966, Ja 17,47:5
Smith, Charlotte C, 1959, Je 7,85:2

Smith, Charlotte F, 1951, Mr 22,31:3
Smith, Charlotte Mrs, 1942, D 17,29:5
Smith, Chester A, 1947, O 29,28:2; 1961, D 1,30:3
Smith, Chester F, 1964, D 31,17:3
Smith, Chester M, 1949, Mr 25,23:3; 1958, F 6,27:4
Smith, Chester T, 1968, Ag 2,33:3
Smith, Chris C, 1939, S 10,48:8
Smith, Christopher K, 1952, Ja 12,13:3
Smith, Clair E, 1956, Ap 16,27:2
Smith, Clara E, 1943, My 14,19:5
Smith, Clarence A, 1967, Je 17,31:2
Smith, Clarence B, 1925, Je 5,17:4; 1948, S 20,25:5; 1960, My 22,86:4
Smith, Clarence C, 1956, Ap 6,25:2
Smith, Clarence E, 1940, S 21,19:5; 1959, Je 21,92:5
Smith, Clarence H (por), 1947, O 7,27:3
Smith, Clarence H, 1954, Jl 30,17:4; 1956, F 3,23:5
Smith, Clarence H Jr, 1948, S 15,31:1
Smith, Clarence H Mrs, 1960, O 25,35:4
Smith, Clarence J, 1940, Ag 29,19:3; 1962, Ag 2,25:4
Smith, Clarence M, 1959, Je 13,21:5
Smith, Clarence M Mrs, 1953, S 4,15:3
Smith, Clarence R, 1948, S 14,29:2
Smith, Claribel, 1953, Mr 16,19:2
Smith, Claude, 1948, Ja 26,19:2
Smith, Clay S, 1947, Mr 19,25:4
Smith, Clayton, 1964, Ja 25,10:7
Smith, Clayton F, 1962, Jl 21,19:5
Smith, Clement A Mrs, 1960, O 10,31:4
Smith, Clement H, 1942, Jl 15,19:6
Smith, Clement L, 1961, Ja 5,31:4
Smith, Clement Lawrence Prof, 1909, Jl 2,7:4
Smith, Cleveland E, 1940, N 11,19:4
Smith, Clifford, 1937, S 18,19:1
Smith, Clifford A, 1941, Jl 16,17:3
Smith, Clifford P (por), 1945, Ag 10,15:3
Smith, Clifton, 1939, Mr 26,III,7:3
Smith, Clifton H Mrs, 1952, Ag 5,19:5
Smith, Clinton B Judge, 1923, O 30,19:3
Smith, Clinton B Mrs, 1945, N 15,19:5
Smith, Clinton De Witt Prof, 1916, Ag 5,9:5
Smith, Clinton F, 1955, Jl 6,28:1
Smith, Clinton H Maj, 1913, D 25,9:4
Smith, Clovis Mrs, 1956, Ap 20,25:2
Smith, Clyde E, 1950, N 21,31:2
Smith, Clyde H, 1940, Ap 9,23:3; 1952, D 25,29:5
Smith, Clyde W, 1952, Mr 20,29:1
Smith, Colin D, 1952, Ap 25,23:1
Smith, Constance, 1939, N 28,25:5
Smith, Constance M, 1959, My 19,33:1
Smith, Copeland E, 1940, O 1,23:1
Smith, Cora C, 1950, O 12,31:4
Smith, Cornelia L, 1955, Jl 29,17:4
Smith, Cornelius, 1918, F 1,9:5; 1950, Ag 6,73:2
Smith, Cornelius Bp Rev Dr, 1913, Je 24,11:6
Smith, Cornelius H, 1938, Mr 2,19:3
Smith, Cornelius J, 1939, D 21,26:4
Smith, Cornelius M, 1965, O 25,37:4
Smith, Cornelius T Capt, 1937, D 13,27:3
Smith, Court, 1957, Jl 2,27:4
Smith, Courtland H 2d, 1952, Mr 13,29:3
Smith, Crapo C (will), 1948, My 11,23:2
Smith, Crawford C, 1940, My 7,25:3
Smith, Crawford L, 1946, Ag 6,25:1
Smith, Curtis B, 1951, Ja 20,15:3
Smith, Curtis R, 1963, Ap 27,25:4
Smith, Cyril, 1950, Ja 9,26:3; 1963, Mr 6,4:5
Smith, Cyril H, 1952, F 12,16:8
Smith, Cyril L, 1942, N 15,57:1
Smith, D Burt, 1941, My 16,23:4
Smith, D Franklin, 1939, F 5,40:3
Smith, D Nathan R, 1938, Ap 1,23:4
Smith, D Nevin, 1964, Ap 15,39:3
Smith, Damion S, 1951, D 8,11:1
Smith, Daniel, 1940, My 29,23:2; 1948, D 12,92:5
Smith, Daniel A Rev, 1921, D 15,19:4
Smith, Daniel B, 1907, F 26,11:5
Smith, Daniel C (por), 1945, Je 25,17:3
Smith, Daniel E, 1949, S 18,95:3
Smith, Daniel H, 1908, Je 13,7:4
Smith, Daniel H Dr, 1912, Jl 11,9:5
Smith, Daniel L, 1950, N 3,27:2
Smith, Daniel P, 1940, F 29,19:3
Smith, Daniel S, 1941, D 4,25:2
Smith, Daniel W Mrs, 1938, Ap 13,25:4
Smith, Darrell H, 1951, Je 13,29:3
Smith, Darwin R, 1951, Je 2,19:6
Smith, David, 1873, N 8,3:6; 1954, Ja 24,84:6; 1957, F 11,29:6; 1965, My 25,41:5
Smith, David A, 1944, Ap 28,19:2; 1952, Ap 7,25:5
Smith, David Cady, 1908, Ja 30,7:5
Smith, David D Mrs, 1948, N 2,25:3
Smith, David E (por), 1944, Jl 30,35:3
Smith, David G, 1938, Ap 29,21:2
Smith, David H, 1949, D 9,32:2
Smith, David P, 1956, Ap 25,35:1
Smith, David S, 1949, D 18,90:8; 1950, Ap 13,29:1
Smith, David W, 1948, S 4,15:5
Smith, De Witt C, 1916, Mr 31,11:6
Smith, Dean C, 1939, S 8,23:5
Smith, Delavan, 1922, Ag 26,11:6
Smith, Deloss, 1939, Mr 18,17:5
Smith, Dennis R, 1953, N 9,35:6
Smith, Denys H, 1962, O 30,35:2
Smith, Dexter, 1909, N 30,9:4; 1947, Ag 3,52:4
Smith, Dilman M K, 1968, Je 20,45:5
Smith, Donald B, 1955, S 8,31:1; 1959, D 19,27:6
Smith, Donald D, 1955, S 14,23:5
Smith, Donald E, 1945, Ap 8,36:2
Smith, Donald H, 1953, S 1,23:1; 1964, Ag 18,31:4
Smith, Donald J, 1964, Je 2,37:2
Smith, Donald M, 1941, F 28,19:4; 1948, Jl 29,21:4; 1956, D 5,39:3
Smith, Donald M Mrs, 1959, Jl 20,25:4
Smith, Donald P, 1957, Ag 4,80:6; 1967, D 23,23:1
Smith, Donald V, 1952, O 8,31:2
Smith, Donald Y, 1953, D 18,29:3
Smith, Dorcas, 1956, Ja 21,21:3
Smith, Dorman H, 1956, Mr 2,23:1
Smith, Dorothy H (Mrs P Barlow), 1955, D 18,92:6
Smith, Douglas, 1951, Ja 20,8:5
Smith, Douglas C, 1938, Je 16,23:5
Smith, Douglas G, 1954, S 12,84:2
Smith, Douglas Y, 1965, N 30,41:5
Smith, Duane G, 1964, F 5,35:2
Smith, Dudley C, 1950, S 2,15:6; 1960, Je 12,86:7
Smith, Durward S, 1951, Mr 22,31:2
Smith, Dwight, 1949, Je 1,32:4; 1967, My 15,59:5
Smith, E A, 1940, Ap 3,23:2; 1947, D 11,33:4
Smith, E Allen, 1951, N 10,17:4
Smith, E B Mrs, 1870, My 30,2:4
Smith, E Baird, 1945, F 10,11:2
Smith, E Capt, 1875, S 5,12:2
Smith, E D (see also Ap 13), 1878, Ap 17,2:2
Smith, E D, 1883, N 12,5:2
Smith, E D Rev, 1883, Mr 29,5:5
Smith, E de Forest Mrs, 1952, Je 9,23:3
Smith, E Eugene, 1943, Jl 1,19:4
Smith, E F, 1928, My 4,25:3
Smith, E Franklin Dr, 1917, Je 18,9:6
Smith, E H, 1927, Ja 29,15:5
Smith, E K Gen, 1893, Mr 29,4:7
Smith, E Lovell, 1955, F 16,29:1
Smith, E Norman, 1957, O 19,21:3
Smith, E O, 1960, O 29,23:5
Smith, E Otheman Mrs, 1955, F 9,25:3
Smith, E P, 1876, Ag 16,4:7; 1882, O 23,5:3
Smith, E Percy, 1954, Ap 14,29:1
Smith, E S, 1901, Je 10,2:5
Smith, E T, 1940, S 30,17:1
Smith, E Terry Mrs, 1965, Je 16,44:5
Smith, E W, 1882, Je 13,5:1; 1883, My 22,5:5
Smith, Earl A (will, D 6,5:6),(por), 1938, N 30,23:3
Smith, Earl B, 1956, Mr 8,29:1
Smith, Earl D, 1947, Je 20,19:1
Smith, Earl E T Mrs (F Pritchett), 1965, N 11,47:1
Smith, Earl H, 1950, D 7,67:4
Smith, Earl O, 1943, Mr 15,13:1
Smith, Earl R, 1943, O 10,48:6
Smith, Earl S, 1963, Je 11,37:5
Smith, Earl W, 1955, Ap 27,31:3
Smith, Earle, 1948, S 3,40:7
Smith, Earle C, 1960, My 21,23:3
Smith, Earnest E, 1947, Mr 14,24:3
Smith, Eben B, 1956, O 1,27:4
Smith, Eckert A, 1947, Je 9,21:3
Smith, Ed Arthur, 1910, D 3,11:5
Smith, Ed C, 1952, Ap 20,92:4
Smith, Edgar B, 1948, Je 30,25:3; 1964, Jl 22,33:3
Smith, Edgar F Mrs, 1953, Ag 9,76:5
Smith, Edgar L, 1944, N 25,13:3
Smith, Edgar L Mrs, 1957, Ag 15,21:2
Smith, Edgar M, 1910, Ap 10,13:2; 1938, Mr 9,23:1; 1938, S 5,15:3
Smith, Edgar M Mrs, 1946, My 17,21:4
Smith, Edgar Mrs, 1937, Ag 3,23:3
Smith, Edgar S, 1941, Ag 31,23:1
Smith, Edgar V, 1953, Mr 3,27:1
Smith, Edgar W (trb lr, S 27,36:6), 1960, S 18,86:1
Smith, Edgeworth, 1952, O 31,25:4
Smith, Edith, 1942, Ja 13,22:3
Smith, Edith B Mrs (est acctg), 1964, Ag 1,21:2
Smith, Edith I, 1964, My 23,23:3
Smith, Edith M, 1945, D 16,40:5; 1950, Ag 12,13:4
Smith, Edmund, 1874, Mr 14,7:2
Smith, Edmund Banks Rev Dr, 1924, D 23,19:5
Smith, Edmund H, 1939, Jl 14,19:6
Smith, Edric B, 1959, My 30,17:6
Smith, Edric B Mrs, 1944, D 13,23:4
Smith, Edward A, 1954, Ap 7,31:2
Smith, Edward B, 1918, Ja 8,15:6
Smith, Edward C, 1937, My 18,23:4; 1940, Je 2,44:5; 1945, Mr 12,19:5; 1964, Ag 21,29:4
Smith, Edward C Mrs, 1947, Ja 27,23:1; 1954, Ja 14, 29:4
Smith, Edward D Mrs, 1949, Ap 27,27:2
Smith, Edward E, 1956, S 10,27:1
Smith, Edward Elmer, 1965, S 2,31:2
Smith, Edward Everett, 1965, Ja 3,84:6
Smith, Edward F, 1940, Mr 21,25:4
Smith, Edward G, 1956, My 3,31:3
Smith, Edward H, 1938, S 2,17:2; 1942, F 12,23:4; 1961, O 31,31:1
Smith, Edward H Mrs, 1938, D 1,23:5
Smith, Edward Hull, 1921, Ap 8,13:4
Smith, Edward Hunting, 1961, D 28,27:5
Smith, Edward I, 1937, S 19,II,7:2
Smith, Edward Iungerick, 1912, Ap 9,11:4
Smith, Edward J, 1945, Ja 12,15:1; 1957, O 11,27:3
Smith, Edward J Mrs, 1961, Ag 22,29:5
Smith, Edward M, 1944, Ag 31,17:4; 1950, Mr 20,21:3; 1955, Ap 5,29:4
Smith, Edward M Jr, 1946, Ag 10,13:6
Smith, Edward Mrs, 1950, Mr 3,25:3
Smith, Edward N, 1943, Mr 26,19:3; 1954, Je 13,88:5
Smith, Edward O, 1949, O 11,34:3
Smith, Edward P, 1948, Je 10,25:4; 1949, F 7,19:4
Smith, Edward R, 1968, O 10,47:5
Smith, Edward R Mrs, 1943, O 29,19:1
Smith, Edward S, 1944, My 30,21:4
Smith, Edward T, 1921, Jl 3,18:2
Smith, Edward W, 1940, Ag 28,19:2; 1956, Ap 15,88:6
Smith, Edward W Mrs, 1954, F 1,23:3; 1956, S 8,17:3
Smith, Edwin, 1912, D 3,15:4
Smith, Edwin Burritt, 1906, My 10,9:4
Smith, Edwin C, 1947, D 1,21:4; 1952, O 26,88:6
Smith, Edwin D, 1943, Ja 18,15:2
Smith, Edwin D Mrs, 1952, Ja 10,29:3
Smith, Edwin F, 1941, S 4,22:2; 1944, Mr 29,21:3
Smith, Edwin Holden, 1908, Mr 19,7:4
Smith, Edwin K, 1945, Je 22,15:2
Smith, Edwin Rev, 1903, O 17,9:6
Smith, Edwin T, 1947, Ag 14,23:3
Smith, Edwin T Mrs, 1941, Ap 18,21:4
Smith, Edwin W (will, N 29,25:1), 1937, N 18,23:6
Smith, Edwin W, 1950, My 12,27:3
Smith, Egbert W, 1944, Ag 27,33:1
Smith, Eleanor, 1942, Jl 1,25:6
Smith, Eleanor Lady (por), 1945, O 21,46:1
Smith, Eleanor T Mrs, 1937, O 2,21:2
Smith, Eleanor W Mrs, 1943, Ja 9,13:3
Smith, Elgin C, 1939, Jl 5,17:6
Smith, Eli A, 1948, Ja 16,21:2
Smith, Elias A C, 1949, Je 27,27:3
Smith, Eliza J, 1940, My 29,23:4
Smith, Elizabeth J, 1950, Ag 19,13:6
Smith, Elizabeth M, 1952, S 12,21:3
Smith, Elizabeth M Mrs, 1941, Ap 19,15:5
Smith, Elizabeth T, 1948, F 22,48:6
Smith, Elizur Y, 1950, Ja 13,23:2
Smith, Ella S Mrs, 1937, Mr 25,25:1
Smith, Ellen C Mrs, 1939, D 20,25:1
Smith, Elleroy M, 1953, Ja 21,31:2
Smith, Elliott, 1944, Ap 1,13:3
Smith, Elliott B, 1946, O 2,29:4
Smith, Ellison D, 1944, N 18,13:1
Smith, Ellsworth C Mrs, 1951, My 29,25:1
Smith, Elmer A, 1947, Jl 17,19:3; 1953, D 30,23:3
Smith, Elmer D, 1939, N 11,15:2
Smith, Elmer E, 1937, D 24,20:2
Smith, Elmer F, 1952, Ag 31,44:8
Smith, Elmer J, 1937, Je 4,23:3
Smith, Elmer W, 1950, O 12,31:2
Smith, Elmo, 1968, Jl 17,43:4
Smith, Elmore G, 1952, Ap 30,27:3
Smith, Eloise H Mrs, 1940, My 4,17:2
Smith, Elvet V, 1946, Jl 26,21:4
Smith, Elward, 1947, O 17,21:4
Smith, Elward B Mrs, 1957, Ap 22,25:4
Smith, Emelius W, 1941, Ja 20,17:2
Smith, Emerson J, 1950, My 16,31:4
Smith, Emily, 1949, Je 23,27:4
Smith, Emily W, 1956, Jl 29,64:8
Smith, Emily W Mrs, 1940, Jl 7,25:2
Smith, Emma Becknell Mrs, 1911, My 25,11:6
Smith, Emma M, 1943, F 12,19:3
Smith, Emma Victoria, 1917, My 3,15:4
Smith, Emmet, 1905, Mr 13,7:7
Smith, Emmett F, 1959, F 1,85:5
Smith, Emmons S, 1937, O 29,21:5
Smith, Emory B, 1950, O 16,27:2
Smith, Emory E, 1943, My 2,44:4
Smith, Enos B, 1905, Je 12,9:5
Smith, Ephraim J, 1944, Ap 2,40:1
Smith, Erastus G Dr, 1937, Je 20,II,6:4
Smith, Eric M, 1951, Ag 14,23:3
Smith, Erle J, 1953, Jl 17,17:5
Smith, Ernest (cor, Je 10,45:1), 1968, Je 9,84:8
Smith, Ernest A, 1947, Mr 16,60:1
Smith, Ernest B, 1941, N 29,17:4
Smith, Ernest B (E Bramah), 1942, Je 28,32:5
Smith, Ernest E, 1944, F 18,17:5
Smith, Ernest F, 1940, D 8,71:3
Smith, Ernest G (por), 1945, D 29,13:4
Smith, Ernest G Mrs, 1958, Ag 18,19:3
Smith, Ernest K, 1954, My 12,31:2
Smith, Ernest L, 1963, Mr 27,4:6
Smith, Ernest M, 1946, Ag 9,17:5
Smith, Ernest S, 1949, D 5,23:3
Smith, Ernest V Sr, 1950, Je 19,21:5
Smith, Erneste V, 1940, Ap 18,23:2
Smith, Erskine M, 1940, Mr 13,23:2
Smith, Erwin Z, 1963, Jl 23,29:3
Smith, Esther M, 1942, Mr 20,19:5
Smith, Ethel M, 1951, Mr 25,74:7
Smith, Ethelbert W, 1958, Je 10,33:5
Smith, Eugene, 1952, D 18,30:5
Smith, Eugene D, 1945, D 22,19:4
Smith, Eugene F, 1955, S 16,23:4

Smith, Eugene H, 1963, My 28,28:5
Smith, Eugene H Mrs, 1963, N 24,22:6
Smith, Eugene Hanes, 1925, My 10,6:1
Smith, Eugene K, 1943, F 14,49:1
Smith, Eugene L, 1937, My 22,15:5
Smith, Eugene N, 1950, Jl 14,21:3
Smith, Eugene R, 1938, Ja 16,II,8:6
Smith, Eugenie A T (will, Mr 10,26:4), 1954, Mr 6, 15:6
Smith, Eugenie M Raye Mrs, 1914, Jl 10,9:4
Smith, Eunice A, 1961, D 10,88:6
Smith, Eva F, 1943, O 1,19:2
Smith, Eva L, 1950, Ag 27,88:8
Smith, Evalena M Mrs, 1953, N 14,17:6
Smith, Evan C E, 1950, O 19,31:3
Smith, Evan J Dr, 1937, F 14,II,9:2
Smith, Everett, 1945, F 26,19:3; 1958, O 17,29:3
Smith, Everett B, 1949, D 6,31:4
Smith, Everett L, 1950, O 22,93:1
Smith, Everett Pepperell Rev Dr, 1968, Ag 3,25:5
Smith, Everett W, 1941, O 23,23:5; 1959, Ag 11,27:2; 1961, F 13,27:2
Smith, F B, 1936, S 5,15:1
Smith, F Bascom, 1945, Ap 27,19:3
Smith, F Delysle Mrs, 1948, Ap 3,15:5
Smith, F Edward, 1938, F 11,23:4
Smith, F G Prof, 1878, Ap 9,5:3
Smith, F Gordon, 1964, F 15,23:6
Smith, F H, 1903, Ap 26,7:6
Smith, F Harold (funl plans, N 25,39:2), 1967, N 24, 43:1
Smith, F Hopkinson (funl, Ap 12,9:6), 1915, Ap 8, 13:5
Smith, F Hopkinson, 1949, Ja 1,13:5
Smith, F Howard, 1954, Jl 13,23:4
Smith, F Lee, 1949, Ag 13,11:2
Smith, F M, 1931, Ag 28,15:1
Smith, F M Mrs, 1906, Ja 2,9:4
Smith, F O, 1924, Ja 30,19:3
Smith, F Osgood, 1961, Je 5,31:3
Smith, F R, 1901, Je 29,9:6
Smith, Fannie A, 1945, My 14,17:4
Smith, Fannie B Mrs, 1940, Je 1,15:3
Smith, Fanny M, 1940, Je 10,17:3
Smith, Fanny R, 1942, Je 23,19:6
Smith, Felix F Mrs, 1955, Ja 10,23:2
Smith, Felix Willoughby, 1920, Ja 13,13:3
Smith, Ferdinand, 1961, Ag 16,31:3
Smith, Ferris N, 1957, S 20,25:3
Smith, Fine W, 1955, N 12,19:5
Smith, Fitzhugh, 1914, Mr 28,13:5
Smith, Fletcher C, 1947, O 20,23:1
Smith, Fletcher L, 1938, Jl 11,17:4
Smith, Flora C, 1943, D 24,13:2
Smith, Florence E, 1958, S 3,33:1
Smith, Florence G, 1938, Ap 17,II,6:5
Smith, Florence M (will), 1957, Ap 13,17:3
Smith, Florence Mother, 1951, Jl 30,17:4
Smith, Floyd B, 1951, S 26,31:5
Smith, Floyd R, 1942, Ja 4,48:2
Smith, Floyd R Jr, 1947, N 10,29:3
Smith, Floyd T, 1939, Jl 14,19:2
Smith, Forest J, 1952, Je 22,69:2
Smith, Forrest, 1962, Mr 9,19:3
Smith, Forrest R, 1958, Ag 12,29:2
Smith, Forrest S, 1958, O 12,86:8
Smith, Forrest V, 1947, D 27,13:4
Smith, Frances, 1939, O 20,23:2
Smith, Frances C, 1948, N 30,27:1
Smith, Frances C Mrs, 1942, Ag 20,19:1
Smith, Frances G Mrs, 1951, Ag 18,11:2
Smith, Frances V, 1950, Je 22,27:1
Smith, Frances V Mrs, 1951, Mr 12,25:4
Smith, Francis, 1916, Jl 3,9:6
Smith, Francis A, 1962, My 9,43:1
Smith, Francis E Mrs, 1947, D 25,21:2; 1965, F 10,41:1
Smith, Francis G, 1956, My 11,27:3
Smith, Francis H, 1906, Ag 15,7:5
Smith, Francis J, 1964, S 1,36:1
Smith, Francis M, 1955, Ja 8,13:5
Smith, Francis P Mrs, 1947, N 23,72:3
Smith, Francis R, 1958, Ag 12,29:2
Smith, Francis Retell Sir, 1874, F 18,5:6
Smith, Francis V, 1944, Mr 3,15:2
Smith, Francis X, 1939, Mr 8,21:4
Smith, Frank, 1938, D 25,18:5; 1940, F 29,19:5; 1940, D 27,19:5; 1942, F 5,21:2; 1949, N 18,29:3; 1954, N 17,31:2; 1960, Ja 11,45:1; 1960, My 15,86:7
Smith, Frank A, 1942, Ap 27,15:4; 1948, Ja 5,20:2; 1952, Ja 15,27:2
Smith, Frank A Mrs, 1961, Mr 25,25:5
Smith, Frank B, 1939, My 20,15:5; 1949, Je 8,30:2; 1953, D 15,39:3; 1957, Ja 31,27:5
Smith, Frank C, 1937, Jl 2,21:1; 1953, Ap 21,27:3
Smith, Frank D, 1960, Je 27,25:2
Smith, Frank D L, 1949, F 12,18:2
Smith, Frank E, 1940, My 15,25:5; 1943, S 28,25:2; 1944, N 13,19:6; 1947, O 17,21:2; 1948, N 20,13:4; 1952, N 5,27:2; 1963, D 18,37:8
Smith, Frank G, 1937, Ja 8,19:4; 1939, N 5,49:2; 1945, D 10,21:3; 1966, N 18,43:4
Smith, Frank H, 1937, Ag 11,23:4; 1941, O 4,15:6; 1950, Jl 19,31:2; 1957, Jl 8,23:5; 1957, Jl 21,60:2
Smith, Frank H Mrs, 1958, Mr 11,29:4
Smith, Frank I, 1951, N 1,29:3
Smith, Frank J, 1941, O 17,23:5; 1941, N 5,23:2; 1949, Je 13,19:6; 1950, O 6,27:1; 1964, O 31,29:5
Smith, Frank L, 1938, F 12,15:4; 1942, Ap 15,21:3; 1950, Ag 31,25:4; 1953, F 9,27:4; 1955, Je 29,29:5
Smith, Frank L Mrs, 1965, Jl 5,17:3
Smith, Frank M, 1941, F 24,15:3; 1941, Jl 31,17:5; 1943, My 22,13:1; 1951, Ap 9,25:4; 1957, Ag 24,15:5; 1966, Ag 8,27:2
Smith, Frank M Mrs, 1950, My 25,29:5
Smith, Frank Mrs, 1953, Ja 26,19:3
Smith, Frank N Mrs, 1952, Ja 7,19:4
Smith, Frank P, 1960, Mr 9,33:3
Smith, Frank R, 1909, D 31,9:6; 1941, My 4,53:2; 1950, Jl 3,15:3
Smith, Frank R Sr, 1938, S 27,21:6
Smith, Frank S (por), 1946, Jl 23,25:1
Smith, Frank Sullivan, 1920, N 16,15:1
Smith, Frank T, 1950, Ap 16,105:1
Smith, Frank W, 1939, Ap 3,15:3; 1943, F 12,19:2; 1945, F 24,11:6; 1946, Je 6,21:3; 1953, Mr 4,27:5; 1955, N 1,31:4; 1956, Ag 9,25:2
Smith, Frank W Col, 1937, D 4,17:6
Smith, Frank W Mrs, 1937, Jl 19,15:3; 1957, My 17, 25:1
Smith, Franklin E, 1952, Jl 20,52:3
Smith, Franklin G Brig-Gen, 1912, O 8,13:6
Smith, Franklin H, 1946, My 20,23:4
Smith, Franklin L Mrs, 1945, N 26,21:4
Smith, Franklin W, 1968, Ja 4,34:3
Smith, Franklin Waldo Mrs, 1915, Je 16,11:4
Smith, Fred A, 1940, O 27,45:3; 1943, Ap 25,34:4; 1951, Je 29,16:7
Smith, Fred C, 1955, Mr 31,27:4
Smith, Fred D, 1953, Jl 19,56:3
Smith, Fred D Sr, 1950, Mr 5,93:1
Smith, Fred E, 1952, F 23,11:3; 1953, D 22,31:6; 1957, Jl 20,15:3
Smith, Fred F, 1920, O 1,11:3
Smith, Fred G, 1959, S 1,30:1
Smith, Fred J, 1952, D 7,89:2
Smith, Fred M, 1962, F 9,29:2
Smith, Fred Mrs, 1943, Ja 1,23:5; 1945, N 2,19:3
Smith, Fred N Mrs, 1955, O 3,27:4
Smith, Fred O, 1939, Ja 23,13:6
Smith, Fred W, 1961, N 22,33:3
Smith, Frederic W, 1938, F 21,19:6
Smith, Frederick, 1925, Ag 2,5:4; 1941, N 4,6:4; 1948, N 21,88:4; 1951, Ja 29,19:2
Smith, Frederick A, 1943, N 18,23:5; 1944, N 15,27:6
Smith, Frederick A Maj, 1937, Mr 4,23:6
Smith, Frederick Appleton Brig-Gen, 1922, F 5,22:3
Smith, Frederick B, 1940, O 30,23:3
Smith, Frederick C, 1956, Jl 17,23:3; 1960, O 1,19:1
Smith, Frederick C Mrs, 1947, Jl 24,21:4
Smith, Frederick D, 1946, Ja 27,42:2
Smith, Frederick G, 1948, S 15,31:3
Smith, Frederick G C Sr, 1945, Je 18,19:2
Smith, Frederick Hoffman Jr, 1916, Ag 5,9:5
Smith, Frederick J, 1941, Ap 16,23:6; 1941, Ag 6,17:5; 1954, D 2,31:1
Smith, Frederick J Jr, 1945, Ap 16,23:1
Smith, Frederick J Mrs, 1952, D 25,41:1
Smith, Frederick L, 1937, O 19,25:3; 1942, Ja 19,20:1; 1946, Ap 11,25:4; 1949, N 11,25:3; 1965, Ap 14,41:4
Smith, Frederick L Mrs, 1950, O 10,31:4
Smith, Frederick M (por), 1946, Mr 21,25:3
Smith, Frederick M, 1951, D 13,33:3
Smith, Frederick S, 1944, N 21,25:5
Smith, Frederick U, 1938, Ap 15,19:3
Smith, Frederick V, 1947, O 6,21:2
Smith, Frederick W, 1941, Ag 9,15:2; 1944, Jl 14,13:5; 1953, Ja 13,27:5; 1957, F 26,29:4
Smith, Frederick William Dr, 1923, My 25,21:5
Smith, Freeborn Garrison, 1911, O 10,13:5
Smith, Freeman A, 1946, Ja 8,23:1
Smith, Freeman W, 1949, S 27,27:2
Smith, Friend W, 1943, Mr 20,15:2
Smith, G, 1880, Jl 24,5:6
Smith, G A, 1875, S 10,8:6; 1876, N 6,5:2
Smith, G Albert, 1959, S 4,21:2
Smith, G B, 1879, S 22,2:6
Smith, G Butler, 1922, Ap 11,19:4
Smith, G Butler Mrs, 1961, S 1,17:1
Smith, G E, 1874, Jl 21,5:3; 1905, F 2,7:1
Smith, G Foster (por), 1940, My 27,19:3
Smith, G Goodhue, 1948, S 29,29:4
Smith, G Harold, 1949, Mr 14,19:4
Smith, G Harrison, 1949, F 18,24:2
Smith, G Morris, 1962, Ja 21,89:1
Smith, G Stanley Brig-Gen, 1968, S 6,43:1
Smith, G Steward, 1948, D 10,25:2
Smith, G W, 1876, O 29,9:4
Smith, Gaillard B, 1957, O 25,27:1
Smith, Garret, 1954, O 14,29:5
Smith, Gaston, 1937, Ag 23,19:4
Smith, Gaylord U, 1956, Jl 27,21:5
Smith, Geddes, 1953, Je 17,27:2
Smith, Gene Mrs, 1964, Ag 15,21:2
Smith, George, 1876, S 6,5:4; 1876, O 1,10:4; 1925, D 5,19:4; 1938, Je 15,23:4; 1939, Ja 5,23:2; 1940, D 10,26:3; 1956, Ja 17,33:3; 1956, F 22,27:4
Smith, George A, 1937, Ja 20,21:4
Smith, George A (por), 1942, Ja 7,19:4
Smith, George A, 1942, Mr 4,20:2; 1942, Mr 21,17:4 1945, F 10,11:5; 1946, N 2,15:3; 1949, Ap 5,29:5; 1951, Mr 7,33:2; 1951, Ap 5,29:1; 1954, Jl 13,23:2; 1955, My 19,29:4; 1962, Je 13,41:2; 1965, Ja 10,92
Smith, George A H Dr, 1923, F 11,6:2
Smith, George A Mrs, 1953, Ja 16,23:4; 1954, O 16, 17:3
Smith, George B, 1945, O 20,11:3; 1950, Ag 26,13:4; 1953, N 17,31:3
Smith, George B Mrs, 1946, Jl 31,27:3
Smith, George Bernard, 1920, F 9,9:4
Smith, George C, 1943, My 6,19:5; 1966, O 18,40:3
Smith, George C Jr, 1937, Ap 8,23:2
Smith, George Carson, 1916, My 31,13:4
Smith, George D, 1920, Mr 5,13:3; 1953, O 28,29:3; 1963, Ag 10,17:4
Smith, George D (Sept 24), 1965, O 11,61:5
Smith, George De Forest Dr, 1921, Jl 31,22:4
Smith, George E, 1945, D 13,29:4; 1953, Ja 4,77:1; 1959, Jl 21,29:5
Smith, George E Mrs, 1952, O 13,21:5
Smith, George F, 1915, S 26,15:4; 1945, N 27,23:4; 1952, Jl 23,23:4; 1952, D 18,29:3; 1954, O 5,27:1; 1965, F 28,88:3
Smith, George G, 1963, S 20,33:3
Smith, George H, 1937, Ja 5,23:3; 1939, Je 26,15:5; 1941, Jl 7,15:6; 1941, D 15,19:5; 1944, Ap 16,41:2; 1945, Ja 30,19:3; 1947, F 25,25:2; 1949, F 8,25:4; 1951, My 27,69:1; 1952, Jl 9,27:3
Smith, George H E, 1962, D 4,41:1
Smith, George H Mrs, 1950, Je 30,23:4; 1954, Ap 1, 31:4
Smith, George Herbert, 1924, D 20,15:5
Smith, George I, 1950, Je 22,11:6
Smith, George J, 1904, Ja 10,7:6
Smith, George J (por), 1938, O 30,41:1
Smith, George J, 1939, Mr 28,23:4; 1953, N 20,23:3
Smith, George J Mrs, 1940, Ag 1,19:4
Smith, George J Sr, 1951, N 23,29:4
Smith, George K, 1947, Jl 10,21:1; 1949, F 19,15:5; 1962, O 22,29:4
Smith, George L, 1959, N 16,31:3; 1962, S 8,19:4
Smith, George M, 1942, Je 3,24:5; 1943, Je 27,33:1; 1951, N 26,25:4; 1952, N 25,29:4
Smith, George M Dr, 1951, F 27,28:2
Smith, George M Gen, 1915, Je 22,15:5
Smith, George M Mrs, 1944, N 3,21:5; 1963, Ag 26, 27:1
Smith, George McLeod (por),(funl, N 25,15:5), 192 N 23,13:4
Smith, George Mrs, 1957, N 12,34:1
Smith, George O (por), 1944, Ja 11,19:1
Smith, George P, 1948, S 6,13:2
Smith, George P F, 1962, Ap 18,39:2
Smith, George R, 1950, D 27,27:4
Smith, George S, 1960, S 7,37:5
Smith, George Stuart, 1920, Jl 29,9:4
Smith, George T, 1939, Mr 19,III,7:2; 1940, D 20,25 1948, Ja 6,23:6; 1955, D 8,37:2
Smith, George T Msgr, 1968, D 29,52:4
Smith, George V, 1938, N 24,27:5; 1943, Je 25,17:2; 1953, D 18,29:2
Smith, George W, 1940, Ap 16,23:6; 1943, Ap 28,23 1943, D 30,18:2; 1944, Jl 2,20:6; 1945, N 21,21:5; 1946, My 11,27:2; 1947, N 19,27:2; 1948, Jl 14,23: 1957, N 11,29:4; 1960, Jl 3,32:4; 1964, Jl 8,35:2
Smith, George W Col, 1907, Ap 25,9:5
Smith, George W Jr, 1965, Mr 9,35:3
Smith, George W L, 1911, Ag 1,9:6
Smith, George W Mrs, 1946, Ap 2,29:5; 1948, O 28, 29:4
Smith, George Warren, 1923, Ja 1,15:5
Smith, George Wells, 1915, Ag 11,9:4
Smith, George Willard, 1968, Mr 19,44:2
Smith, George Williamson Rev Dr, 1925, D 28,15:3
Smith, George Wilson, 1921, F 20,22:1
Smith, Gerald C, 1951, N 15,29:6
Smith, Gerald E, 1964, My 23,23:3
Smith, Gerald H, 1955, Je 20,21:3
Smith, Gerard T, 1949, D 6,32:2
Smith, Gerrit (trb, D 30,8:1), 1874, D 29,1:1
Smith, Gerrit, 1915, My 5,13:5
Smith, Gerrit Dr, 1912, Jl 22,7:6
Smith, Gertrude M, 1945, Ag 1,19:2
Smith, Gertrude R Mrs, 1963, O 23,41:1
Smith, Gilbert B L, 1957, Ag 31,15:4
Smith, Gilbert D, 1941, F 25,23:2; 1950, Mr 14,25:1
Smith, Gilbert M, 1940, My 27,19:6; 1959, Jl 14,29:
Smith, Gilbert M Mrs, 1938, Ja 11,23:4
Smith, Gilbert P, 1959, S 18,31:4
Smith, Gilbert S, 1957, S 30,31:5
Smith, Gilbert S Jr, 1959, Ag 27,27:3
Smith, Gipsy R, 1947, Ag 6,23:1
Smith, Glenn M, 1938, Je 13,19:2
Smith, Goldie, 1938, Je 28,19:5
Smith, Goldwin Mrs, 1909, S 10,9:6
Smith, Goldwin Prof (funl, Je 12,13:4), 1910, Je 8,
Smith, Gomer, 1953, My 27,31:3
Smith, Gordon A, 1944, My 8,19:5
Smith, Gordon H, 1962, Ja 28,76:4; 1965, Ja 14,35:4
Smith, Gordon M Mrs, 1959, Jl 25,17:6

Smith, Gordon S, 1944, Ap 10,19:5
Smith, Grace E, 1955, Ag 18,23:2
Smith, Grafton F, 1939, Mr 16,23:5
Smith, Granville Byan, 1907, D 12,11:5
Smith, Granville M Mrs (Evelyn D), 1965, Mr 13, 25:4
Smith, Griffin, 1955, Ap 30,17:7
Smith, Gus, 1943, Ag 5,15:1
Smith, Gustavus E, 1948, Ag 10,21:6
Smith, Gustavus R, 1937, Jl 9,21:4
Smith, Guy Lincoln, 1968, N 22,47:4
Smith, H, 1931, N 28,17:1
Smith, H A, 1928, D 18,31:5
Smith, H A Mrs, 1950, D 18,31:4
Smith, H A Rev, 1883, Mr 9,5:6
Smith, H Alexander, 1966, O 28,41:1
Smith, H Alexander Jr, 1964, Mr 5,33:1
Smith, H Alexander Mrs, 1967, D 1,47:3
Smith, H Armour Mrs, 1952, Ag 2,15:5
Smith, H Augustine, 1952, Mr 18,27:5
Smith, H B, 1877, F 8,5:3; 1932, F 10,23:3
Smith, H Carl, 1949, N 19,17:3
Smith, H Chandler Jr, 1963, N 4,35:5
Smith, H Dean Mrs, 1957, D 15,86:5
Smith, H E, 1928, O 6,19:5
Smith, H Farmer, 1949, Ja 11,27:4
Smith, H H, 1908, S 15,9:6
Smith, H Hilliard, 1948, My 25,27:5
Smith, H K, 1931, D 18,23:4
Smith, H Lester, 1951, O 8,21:1
Smith, H Lincoln, 1949, Jl 22,19:1
Smith, H Mart, 1958, Ag 7,25:5
Smith, H Mrs, 1929, Ja 5,19:5
Smith, H P, 1927, F 27,30:4
Smith, H Raymond, 1949, My 29,36:4
Smith, H Stacy, 1938, N 8,23:6
Smith, H Stacy Mrs, 1962, F 23,29:4
Smith, H Warren, 1950, Ap 13,29:3
Smith, Hal H, 1944, D 22,17:6; 1953, Ja 16,23:1
Smith, Hal H Mrs, 1952, Mr 13,29:2
Smith, Hamilton, 1941, O 30,23:4
Smith, Hamilton L Prof, 1903, Ag 2,7:5
Smith, Hamlin A, 1956, Ja 16,21:5
Smith, Hamlin A Mrs, 1943, Ag 7,11:5
Smith, Hanford L, 1948, Jl 19,19:4
Smith, Hank, 1874, F 24,5:2
Smith, Hannah, 1939, Ja 13,19:3
Smith, Hannah Whithall Mrs (Mrs Robt Pearsall Smith), 1911, My 8,11:5
Smith, Harder, 1959, O 19,29:2
Smith, Hardy H, 1956, O 22,29:4
Smith, Harlan I, 1940, Ja 29,15:2
Smith, Harold, 1949, N 24,31:5; 1952, F 6,29:5
Smith, Harold A, 1940, My 15,25:3; 1950, Ap 9,85:1; 1964, N 10,47:2
Smith, Harold B, 1949, Mr 17,25:3; 1952, Ag 13,21:1; 1967, Ja 16,41:3
Smith, Harold D, 1947, Ja 24,21:5
Smith, Harold D W, 1947, F 14,21:2
Smith, Harold E, 1942, Jl 8,23:6; 1943, Jl 19,15:2; 1954, Jl 25,69:3
Smith, Harold H, 1950, Ap 27,29:1
Smith, Harold I, 1923, Je 1,19:6
Smith, Harold J, 1943, Ap 1,23:5
Smith, Harold K, 1963, O 31,33:3
Smith, Harold M Mrs, 1966, O 11,43:6
Smith, Harold R, 1957, D 17,35:4
Smith, Harold S, 1949, O 17,23:4
Smith, Harold T, 1956, My 5,19:6
Smith, Harold T N, 1947, Je 3,25:4
Smith, Harold W, 1961, Ag 20,86:7
Smith, Harradon S, 1944, Ap 11,19:2
Smith, Harris King, 1908, Ap 16,9:4
Smith, Harrison, 1941, Jl 28,13:2; 1952, Ag 23,13:3
Smith, Harrison B, 1948, Ag 7,15:5
Smith, Harrison P, 1947, Ag 25,17:2
Smith, Harrison W, 1947, Ja 29,23:8
Smith, Harry, 1944, Jl 20,19:5; 1948, F 17,26:2; 1949, N 17,29:1
Smith, Harry A, 1939, N 11,15:6; 1944, Ja 9,43:1; 1947, F 5,23:1; 1954, Jl 11,73:2
Smith, Harry A Mrs, 1945, Je 6,21:4
Smith, Harry B, 1948, Jl 20,24:2; 1951, D 15,13:4
Smith, Harry C, 1946, N 22,23:3; 1950, F 26,77:1; 1958, N 20,25:3
Smith, Harry C Mrs, 1958, My 23,23:3
Smith, Harry Chauncey, 1949, Mr 10,54:2
Smith, Harry D, 1937, Ap 11,II,8:6; 1943, F 4,23:2; 1950, O 18,33:4
Smith, Harry D Mrs, 1950, O 7,17:1
Smith, Harry E, 1939, Ja 12,19:2; 1944, Je 27,19:6; 1951, O 23,29:4; 1952, Mr 16,90:1; 1952, N 11,29:4
Smith, Harry E Capt, 1937, My 24,19:4
Smith, Harry G, 1938, Ap 6,23:4; 1948, Jl 30,18:2
Smith, Harry H Mrs, 1940, S 7,15:6
Smith, Harry James, 1918, Mr 18,13:3
Smith, Harry K, 1957, Ja 11,24:1
Smith, Harry L, 1942, Jl 3,17:3
Smith, Harry M, 1945, Ap 2,19:4; 1953, N 7,17:6; 1954, S 7,26:1; 1960, S 13,37:2
Smith, Harry N, 1939, D 20,25:3
Smith, Harry P, 1939, Mr 20,17:3; 1953, F 19,23:2
Smith, Harry Sr, 1950, My 30,17:5
Smith, Harry T, 1940, Jl 5,13:5
Smith, Harry T (funl plans, N 1,27:5), 1954, O 31, 89:1
Smith, Harry T, 1955, S 9,23:3
Smith, Harry W (por), 1945, Ap 6,15:3
Smith, Harry W, 1949, Ag 3,23:3; 1955, F 26,15:4; 1959, My 28,31:4
Smith, Harvey A, 1955, Mr 4,23:3
Smith, Harvey F, 1962, N 13,38:1
Smith, Harvey M, 1949, O 9,93:1
Smith, Harvey N, 1939, O 29,40:5
Smith, Harvey S, 1953, Mr 19,29:4
Smith, Harwood B, 1918, S 21,9:8
Smith, Hattie L Mrs, 1951, Ja 13,15:3
Smith, Hawley A, 1943, Ap 20,23:2
Smith, Hay W, 1940, Ja 21,35:2; 1966, Je 14,47:2
Smith, Helen B, 1951, Ap 20,29:2
Smith, Helen C, 1951, Jl 9,25:6
Smith, Helen J, 1958, Ag 7,25:2
Smith, Helen M, 1955, Ja 17,23:2
Smith, Helen V, 1964, Ja 20,43:1
Smith, Helen W Mrs, 1954, O 14,29:4
Smith, Heman Page Col, 1921, Ja 18,11:4
Smith, Henry, 1872, Ja 15,8:2; 1939, O 26,23:4
Smith, Henry A, 1950, My 17,29:2; 1954, S 4,11:2
Smith, Henry Allan, 1920, F 14,11:3
Smith, Henry B, 1945, Je 1,15:4; 1947, F 24,19:2
Smith, Henry Bascom Maj, 1916, Ja 5,13:4
Smith, Henry C, 1949, Je 16,29:3
Smith, Henry D, 1918, Jl 7,21:3
Smith, Henry DeW, 1962, O 22,29:3
Smith, Henry E, 1912, F 29,11:5; 1950, My 27,17:6
Smith, Henry F, 1940, O 18,21:5
Smith, Henry G, 1942, Ap 17,17:6; 1959, Je 4,31:1
Smith, Henry H, 1941, D 31,17:1
Smith, Henry H Dr, 1937, F 25,23:5
Smith, Henry J, 1924, Jl 31,13:7; 1940, O 9,25:4; 1941, O 19,47:1; 1947, F 2,57:8; 1952, F 1,29:3; 1955, Ag 12,19:2
Smith, Henry J Mrs, 1954, D 31,13:5
Smith, Henry K, 1943, Je 12,28:3
Smith, Henry L, 1944, My 16,21:3; 1951, F 28,27:1; 1957, Ja 11,23:1; 1963, O 27,88:7
Smith, Henry Leavitt, 1918, S 8,23:1
Smith, Henry Mrs, 1946, Mr 6,27:4; 1947, D 18,30:3
Smith, Henry N, 1967, Jl 4,19:1
Smith, Henry P, 1907, O 18,11:5; 1939, Ja 25,21:2; 1947, O 2,27:4; 1951, F 13,31:4
Smith, Henry R W, 1949, D 28,25:1
Smith, Henry T, 1947, Ja 19,53:5
Smith, Henry W (por), 1943, D 5,64:2
Smith, Henry Wesley, 1916, N 5,23:4
Smith, Herbert, 1908, Mr 3,7:4
Smith, Herbert (por), 1938, Je 17,21:4
Smith, Herbert, 1941, Je 24,19:5; 1941, N 10,17:3; 1942, Ap 4,13:6; 1953, D 21,31:6
Smith, Herbert A, 1944, Jl 23,35:2
Smith, Herbert B, 1947, Ja 3,21:4; 1967, Jl 15,25:3
Smith, Herbert C, 1950, N 3,27:3
Smith, Herbert D, 1947, F 7,23:4
Smith, Herbert E, 1938, F 15,25:4; 1968, Ja 27,29:3
Smith, Herbert E Mrs, 1946, O 14,29:5
Smith, Herbert H, 1959, Ap 23,31:3
Smith, Herbert M, 1949, F 16,25:3; 1951, Ja 12,27:1
Smith, Herbert R, 1955, F 13,86:1
Smith, Herbert S, 1944, Je 5,19:6
Smith, Herbert W, 1948, Je 6,72:5; 1956, N 6,35:3; 1961, D 28,27:1; 1965, Mr 24,43:2
Smith, Herbert W Mrs, 1953, Ap 11,17:5
Smith, Herman, 1959, Je 3,35:4
Smith, Herman E Sr, 1946, Je 25,22:3
Smith, Herman H, 1957, Mr 5,31:3
Smith, Herman J, 1959, Ag 20,25:2
Smith, Herndon, 1943, My 17,15:1
Smith, Hewlett R, 1939, Mr 12,III,6:7
Smith, Hezekiah, 1957, Ja 11,23:4
Smith, Hinsdale, 1959, Mr 9,29:5
Smith, Hiram, 1937, Ag 22,II,7:2
Smith, Hiram H, 1946, Jl 1,31:3
Smith, Hirman M, 1946, Jl 18,25:1
Smith, Hoke, 1940, Jl 13,13:5
Smith, Holland M (funl, Ja 16,41:4), 1967, Ja 13,23:2
Smith, Hollis F Mrs, 1945, F 22,27:5
Smith, Homer A A, 1940, Mr 22,19:5
Smith, Homer A A Mrs, 1945, Mr 28,23:3
Smith, Homer B, 1953, Ap 13,27:5
Smith, Homer C, 1947, S 16,23:4
Smith, Homer E, 1949, Je 4,13:4
Smith, Homer F, 1957, My 22,33:5
Smith, Homer T, 1952, N 11,29:3
Smith, Homer W, 1948, S 6,13:4; 1962, Mr 26,31:4
Smith, Horace, 1957, Ag 29,27:2
Smith, Horace B, 1939, Mr 6,15:5; 1957, F 9,19:2
Smith, Horace E, 1939, Je 18,37:1
Smith, Horace F, 1940, Je 2,45:2
Smith, Horace F Jr, 1961, O 7,23:5
Smith, Horace H Mrs, 1962, F 26,27:4
Smith, Horatio D Capt, 1918, My 5,23:1
Smith, Horatio E, 1946, S 10,7:4
Smith, Horton, 1963, O 15,39:2
Smith, Houghton C, 1954, Je 15,29:4
Smith, Howard, 1941, N 25,25:2; 1950, Mr 23,29:3; 1968, Ja 11,33:1
Smith, Howard A, 1963, S 11,43:2
Smith, Howard B, 1953, Ja 9,22:3
Smith, Howard B Mrs, 1947, O 28,25:2
Smith, Howard C, 1941, My 6,21:5; 1965, Ja 31,88:4
Smith, Howard C Mrs, 1952, Ja 12,13:6
Smith, Howard E, 1944, Je 29,23:6; 1945, O 1,19:5
Smith, Howard G E, 1946, O 21,31:5
Smith, Howard Irving, 1906, Ja 25,9:6
Smith, Howard L (will), 1941, Je 9,15:1
Smith, Howard L, 1949, N 21,25:3
Smith, Howard L Mrs, 1967, Je 26,33:3
Smith, Howard M, 1924, Jl 10,21:5; 1967, Mr 19,92:6
Smith, Howard Mapes, 1920, F 26,11:4
Smith, Howard Mrs, 1953, S 21,25:3; 1965, Ap 17,19:4
Smith, Howard N, 1944, Ap 5,19:1
Smith, Howard P, 1951, My 9,33:3; 1958, My 15,29:2; 1967, Je 19,35:2
Smith, Howard S, 1938, F 20,II,8:5
Smith, Howard W, 1951, D 29,11:4; 1953, F 4,27:2
Smith, Howard W Mrs, 1959, Mr 24,39:2
Smith, Hoxie W, 1938, Ap 6,23:2
Smith, Hubert S, 1946, O 6,59:4
Smith, Hugh C, 1946, Ap 2,27:4
Smith, Hugh G, 1948, Ap 6,23:5
Smith, Hugh L, 1943, Ja 19,20:3; 1947, O 25,19:6
Smith, Hugh M, 1964, N 29,16:5
Smith, Hugh M Mrs, 1946, N 27,26:2
Smith, Hugh M Rev, 1937, F 22,17:5
Smith, Hugh Mrs, 1965, Ja 2,19:4
Smith, Hugh R, 1949, Ja 17,19:2
Smith, Hurlbutt W, 1951, D 17,31:5
Smith, Hyde, 1967, Ag 13,80:7
Smith, Ida B W Mrs, 1952, F 17,85:1
Smith, Ida C, 1946, Ja 16,23:4
Smith, Ida C Mrs, 1938, Mr 13,II,8:5
Smith, Ignatius (funl, Mr 13,31:2), 1957, Mr 9,19:4
Smith, Ira E, 1954, Ap 29,31:2
Smith, Ira P Dr, 1905, My 27,9:4
Smith, Ira R, 1943, Je 12,13:2
Smith, Ira R Mrs, 1951, D 22,15:4
Smith, Ira R T, 1955, Jl 7,27:1
Smith, Irene Mrs (I Bentley), 1940, Je 4,23:5
Smith, Irving, 1959, F 1,33:5
Smith, Irving H, 1940, F 24,13:5
Smith, Irving J, 1954, My 2,88:4
Smith, Irving R, 1954, Mr 25,29:1
Smith, Isaac B, 1941, N 29,17:1; 1966, F 14,29:1
Smith, Isaac Capt, 1907, N 7,9:6
Smith, Isaac E, 1940, S 30,17:4
Smith, Isaac H, 1937, Mr 10,23:3
Smith, Isaac Townsend, 1906, Mr 31,9:5
Smith, Isabel C E Mrs, 1942, Je 2,23:5
Smith, Isabella, 1938, S 15,25:2
Smith, Isabelle K, 1948, N 3,27:5
Smith, Isom Mrs, 1948, Mr 10,27:1
Smith, Ison, 1948, Mr 10,27:1
Smith, Israel A, 1958, Je 15,76:1
Smith, Israel Mrs, 1950, O 10,31:3
Smith, J, 1877, Ja 18,5:2; 1877, F 25,8:2
Smith, J A G, 1942, Ap 21,23:2
Smith, J A Rev, 1881, Je 10,2:7
Smith, J Alexander, 1964, Ja 5,93:1
Smith, J Allen, 1937, S 12,II,6:6
Smith, J Allen Dr, 1924, Ja 31,15:5
Smith, J Andre, 1959, Mr 4,31:2
Smith, J Augustus, 1950, F 15,27:4
Smith, J B, 1945, Ja 1,21:1
Smith, J B Lt, 1874, N 26,1:7
Smith, J Bruce Mrs, 1943, Ap 24,13:4
Smith, J C, 1884, Mr 28,5:3
Smith, J C (G H A), 1884, Mr 31,2:4
Smith, J C Col, 1883, N 10,5:2
Smith, J Campbell, 1940, Ja 5,20:2
Smith, J Clarence, 1938, F 9,19:6
Smith, J Cotton, 1882, Ja 10,5:4
Smith, J Edgar, 1942, D 29,22:3
Smith, J Edward, 1950, O 3,31:2
Smith, J Edward Mrs, 1967, N 4,33:4
Smith, J Emil Mrs, 1955, N 5,19:1
Smith, J Ernest (por), 1948, Je 3,25:1
Smith, J F, 1928, O 1,23:4
Smith, J Francis, 1949, D 29,25:4; 1959, F 6,25:1
Smith, J George, 1943, F 24,22:2
Smith, J Gordon, 1951, S 30,73:1
Smith, J Grove, 1939, Ap 4,25:3
Smith, J H Dean, 1903, Ap 18,2:6
Smith, J Hamilton, 1943, Je 9,22:2
Smith, J Harper, 1911, D 27,11:4
Smith, J Harvey, 1945, My 18,19:4
Smith, J Henry, 1951, Je 27,29:5
Smith, J Hopkins Mrs, 1939, Mr 21,23:4
Smith, J Howard, 1951, Mr 14,33:2
Smith, J L, 1883, O 13,2:2
Smith, J L B Prof, 1968, Ja 9,32:4
Smith, J Lambert, 1948, F 2,19:2
Smith, J Le Roy, 1949, N 2,27:5
Smith, J M C, 1903, Ag 26,7:5; 1923, Mr 31,13:5
Smith, J M P, 1932, S 28,19:2
Smith, J Macdonald, 1949, Ja 6,23:4
Smith, J Melvin, 1948, Ap 21,27:2
Smith, J Middleton Mrs, 1962, Mr 20,37:4
Smith, J Morton, 1961, F 5,81:1
Smith, J Mrs, 1882, N 25,2:2

Smith, J Neelands, 1943, My 31,17:3
Smith, J O Dr, 1885, F 1,7:3
Smith, J Otis, 1944, D 22,17:3
Smith, J Owen, 1953, S 5,16:4
Smith, J P Mrs, 1947, Ja 28,23:3
Smith, J Paul, 1955, My 6,23:4
Smith, J Philip Mrs, 1968, Ap 29,43:3
Smith, J Q, 1882, My 13,2:3
Smith, J Q H, 1942, Ag 19,19:2
Smith, J Roger Rev, 1937, S 30,23:4
Smith, J Russell, 1950, My 26,23:2; 1966, F 27,84:6
Smith, J Russell Mrs, 1962, Jl 8,65:1
Smith, J S, 1882, O 7,5:4
Smith, J Somers, 1956, Mr 7,33:4
Smith, J Spencer, 1953, N 10,31:2
Smith, J Stanley, 1950, O 3,31:3
Smith, J T Mrs, 1877, N 1,4:1
Smith, J Thomas, 1964, My 16,25:2
Smith, J Van C, 1879, Ag 22,5:3
Smith, J W, 1879, Ja 26,5:5; 1933, O 16,17:1
Smith, J Wentworth, 1949, Ap 8,25:2
Smith, J Willett, 1945, D 8,17:1
Smith, Jack, 1940, O 24,25:2; 1947, Jl 21,17:4; 1950, My 14,106:5
Smith, Jack C, 1944, Ja 17,19:5
Smith, Jack S Mrs, 1950, O 4,31:1
Smith, Jack W, 1949, Ja 9,72:1
Smith, Jackson D, 1937, Ap 20,25:2
Smith, Jacob, 1949, Ap 3,76:2; 1958, D 6,23:5
Smith, Jacob G, 1958, O 29,35:2
Smith, Jacob Hurd Gen, 1918, Mr 3,23:1
Smith, James, 1883, N 22,8:4; 1937, O 3,II,8:6; 1937, N 20,17:4; 1941, Ag 28,19:1; 1942, S 1,19:1; 1944, N 1,13:3; 1951, O 18,29:5; 1953, S 4,17:7
Smith, James A, 1959, Mr 2,27:5; 1961, F 10,24:2
Smith, James A Father, 1905, Ap 8,9:5
Smith, James A Jr, 1953, Mr 26,31:3
Smith, James Allwood, 1920, O 4,13:2
Smith, James B, 1941, Ag 1,15:1
Smith, James C, 1946, N 9,17:5; 1961, Mr 18,23:4
Smith, James Clinch Mrs, 1913, Ag 21,9:7
Smith, James D, 1948, D 18,19:1; 1949, F 22,23:5; 1951, Ap 22,88:2; 1955, O 19,33:5
Smith, James E, 1949, D 8,33:4; 1950, Je 1,27:5; 1961, O 13,35:5
Smith, James E Mrs, 1943, Ap 30,21:2; 1949, Ag 26, 19:1
Smith, James F, 1939, My 31,23:4
Smith, James F (por), 1940, Ap 9,23:4
Smith, James F, 1942, My 15,19:4; 1950, Ap 3,24:2; 1957, My 7,35:3
Smith, James F Dr, 1919, O 20,15:6
Smith, James G, 1946, N 29,25:3
Smith, James H, 1967, O 3,47:1
Smith, James Henry, 1907, Mr 29,9:6; 1907, Mr 30, 9:7; 1907, My 3,7:4
Smith, James Hinman, 1914, Je 7,5:6
Smith, James J, 1942, Ap 17,17:3; 1942, Ag 19,19:2; 1945, F 24,11:2; 1947, N 25,32:4; 1951, My 17,31:2; 1954, F 28,92:1
Smith, James J Col, 1913, O 10,11:6
Smith, James J R Lt, 1937, Ja 22,21:1
Smith, James Jr, 1927, Ap 2,17:3
Smith, James Jr Mrs, 1910, F 13,II,11:4
Smith, James K, 1961, F 19,86:3
Smith, James L, 1948, Jl 31,15:4; 1955, Ja 11,25:1; 1960, D 21,31:4
Smith, James M, 1949, My 28,7:1; 1952, S 3,29:2; 1965, D 2,41:1
Smith, James M Col, 1915, D 12,19:6
Smith, James Mrs, 1947, Jl 22,23:4; 1966, F 13,84:3
Smith, James P, 1940, Ag 1,21:2
Smith, James P Rev, 1923, Ag 12,26:5
Smith, James Power Rev Dr, 1923, Ag 7,17:3
Smith, James R, 1945, F 22,28:3; 1945, Mr 10,17:2
Smith, James R Mrs, 1952, D 13,21:2
Smith, James S, 1958, My 18,86:5
Smith, James T (por), 1942, F 6,19:5
Smith, James T, 1946, My 13,21:4
Smith, James T Mrs, 1947, D 10,31:5
Smith, James Thorne Commodore, 1920, Ag 24,9:3
Smith, James W, 1942, Mr 11,19:5; 1943, Ja 8,19:4; 1944, F 10,15:1; 1948, Ag 15,60:6; 1948, N 18,27:1; 1949, N 24,31:3; 1951, Mr 24,13:3; 1955, O 26,31:1
Smith, James W A Sr, 1952, O 26,88:5
Smith, James W Mrs, 1960, O 5,41:2
Smith, Jarvis Mrs, 1943, N 15,19:4
Smith, Jarvis P, 1949, Ap 26,25:3
Smith, Jay B, 1943, Ag 4,17:6; 1953, S 2,25:2
Smith, Jeanette, 1958, Ag 13,27:4
Smith, Jeff (J V Jefferds), 1962, F 4,82:3
Smith, Jennie, 1924, S 4,19:4
Smith, Jennie D, 1961, D 30,19:2
Smith, Jennie L Mrs, 1949, Ja 11,31:7
Smith, Jere S, 1960, Ag 25,29:4
Smith, Jeremiah Dr, 1921, S 5,11:6
Smith, Jerry, 1953, Ja 11,90:4
Smith, Jesse A B, 1967, F 6,29:3
Smith, Jesse E, 1941, S 4,22:2
Smith, Jesse J, 1947, Ap 18,21:3
Smith, Jesse L, 1951, D 24,1:1
Smith, Jesse S, 1957, Je 21,25:4
Smith, Jessie A, 1948, F 22,48:6
Smith, Jessie A Mrs, 1946, F 10,40:6
Smith, Jimmy, 1948, Mr 29,21:6
Smith, Joan M, 1965, F 18,42:6
Smith, Joan Mrs, 1940, F 10,15:2
Smith, Joe L Sr, 1962, Ag 24,25:3
Smith, Joel West, 1924, My 10,13:3
Smith, John, 1911, My 16,13:6; 1911, N 8,13:5; 1914, Ag 23,13:5; 1922, F 8,17:4; 1937, Mr 9,23:6; 1941, Ag 24,35:2; 1948, Ja 20,23:2; 1949, Mr 27,76:2; 1950, D 28,26:3; 1954, O 10,87:1
Smith, John A, 1937, Mr 20,19:2; 1943, My 14,19:6; 1953, N 13,28:3
Smith, John B, 1943, Ja 5,19:5; 1948, Ja 1,23:1
Smith, John Bernhardt, 1912, Mr 13,11:5
Smith, John C, 1946, Je 20,23:5; 1948, Ap 10,13:2; 1951, My 18,27:4
Smith, John C Gen, 1911, Ja 2,9:6
Smith, John C Mrs, 1948, Ja 27,25:1
Smith, John Coddington, 1917, Jl 22,15:3
Smith, John D Mrs, 1955, Jl 9,15:4
Smith, John E, 1940, O 27,45:1; 1948, F 7,15:2; 1948, Ap 22,27:4; 1950, N 12,93:2; 1958, Ap 21,23:3
Smith, John E Mrs, 1949, Jl 1,19:2
Smith, John F (Phenomenal), 1952, Ap 4,33:7
Smith, John F Mrs, 1957, Mr 20,37:5
Smith, John Frederick, 1952, My 6,29:1
Smith, John H, 1920, N 13,11:6; 1941, Ja 6,18:2; 1941, N 25,25:5; 1942, F 10,19:4; 1951, Mr 11,95:1; 1951, N 17,17:5
Smith, John Henry, 1911, O 14,13:4
Smith, John I J, 1948, Mr 7,68:3
Smith, John J, 1941, Ja 8,19:4; 1957, My 23,33:4; 1960, Mr 4,25:3; 1966, O 9,86:6
Smith, John J C, 1914, My 13,11:5
Smith, John J C Mrs, 1912, N 19,15:4
Smith, John L, 1946, F 20,25:5; 1950, Jl 11,31:1; 1958, O 8,35:2
Smith, John L Mrs, 1947, Je 4,27:4
Smith, John M, 1945, Ag 7,23:5; 1946, Ja 9,23:3; 1947, Ag 19,23:3; 1963, S 25,43:4
Smith, John Mrs, 1937, N 28,II,9:1; 1948, Ja 18,60:3
Smith, John N, 1951, S 4,27:4
Smith, John N Jr, 1953, Je 14,84:2
Smith, John O, 1942, F 9,15:3
Smith, John P, 1938, My 15,II,7:2; 1944, Ap 15,11:4; 1947, F 21,19:2; 1948, N 5,25:1; 1954, Mr 7,91:3; 1956, Je 27,31:4
Smith, John P Mrs, 1945, O 13,15:1
Smith, John R, 1940, Ap 25,23:2; 1948, Ag 6,17:2
Smith, John R Ex-Gov, 1914, Ag 11,9:6
Smith, John S, 1921, Ap 22,13:6; 1947, O 23,25:5
Smith, John T, 1925, Ag 27,19:5; 1938, Mr 29,21:4; 1938, My 22,II,6:6; 1947, S 29,21:6
Smith, John T (will), 1947, O 3,30:2
Smith, John T C, 1943, Ap 2,21:4
Smith, John T Mrs, 1943, Mr 6,13:5
Smith, John U, 1948, Ap 20,27:3
Smith, John V, 1941, My 21,23:6; 1951, Ja 4,29:5
Smith, John V Dr, 1950, Jl 15,13:5
Smith, John V W, 1952, Je 29,59:4
Smith, John W, 1937, Mr 9,23:4; 1938, Jl 6,23:3; 1940, Ja 22,15:2; 1941, Mr 15,17:4; 1942, Je 18,21:4; 1944, F 11,19:2; 1944, Mr 3,15:4; 1947, D 8,25:2; 1950, F 8,27:1; 1953, O 19,21:6; 1959, Ag 23,92:5; 1965, F 27,25:4
Smith, John W Mrs, 1941, N 5,23:2
Smith, John Walter Ex-Sen, 1925, Ap 20,17:5
Smith, John William, 1912, Ap 27,13:4
Smith, Joseph, 1914, N 28,13:5
Smith, Joseph (funl, D 14,11:4), 1914, D 11,13:5
Smith, Joseph, 1942, My 9,13:4; 1945, F 27,19:2; 1952, O 12,89:1; 1953, My 31,73:1
Smith, Joseph A, 1950, F 14,26:3; 1953, O 15,33:1; 1963, My 20,31:3; 1966, N 29,43:1
Smith, Joseph B, 1939, Mr 15,23:5; 1943, My 28,22:3
Smith, Joseph C, 1945, O 2,23:2; 1960, Ja 19,35:2
Smith, Joseph D, 1909, S 22,9:4
Smith, Joseph E, 1940, Ag 23,15:4; 1946, N 19,21:1
Smith, Joseph F, 1918, N 20,15:3; 1939, Ap 25,23:3; 1943, My 25,23:6; 1949, O 14,27:3; 1954, Ag 31,21:4; 1955, Jl 9,15:3; 1963, Je 17,25:1
Smith, Joseph G, 1937, Mr 10,10:1
Smith, Joseph H, 1949, Ap 11,25:4
Smith, Joseph J, 1939, F 10,23:1
Smith, Joseph J Mrs, 1957, O 22,33:4
Smith, Joseph L, 1950, O 20,27:5; 1952, Ap 19,15:3
Smith, Joseph L Mrs, 1965, Je 28,29:5
Smith, Joseph Mather Dr, 1866, Ap 23,5:5
Smith, Joseph Mrs, 1961, O 12,29:1; 1967, Mr 24,31:4
Smith, Joseph N, 1958, Jl 23,27:4
Smith, Joseph P, 1958, N 21,29:4; 1964, Ja 7,33:2
Smith, Joseph R, 1967, My 24,32:2
Smith, Joseph Rowe Brig-Gen, 1911, F 12,12:2
Smith, Joseph S, 1950, Ag 24,27:2
Smith, Joseph T, 1965, My 28,33:2
Smith, Joseph W, 1954, D 25,11:6
Smith, Josephine C (will, Ja 29,13:5), 1941, Ja 14, 21:4
Smith, Josephine D Mrs, 1937, Jl 1,27:3
Smith, Josephine M Mrs, 1941, Ap 2,23:3
Smith, Josephine S Mrs, 1947, Jl 25,18:2
Smith, Joshua, 1938, Mr 27,II,6:5
Smith, Josiah, 1875, Je 25,10:7
Smith, Judson Rev Dr, 1906, Je 30,7:6
Smith, Jules M, 1960, Mr 7,29:2
Smith, Julia H Mrs, 1939, Mr 17,21:1
Smith, Julian C, 1939, Je 25,37:4; 1941, Ap 5,17:3
Smith, Julian P, 1957, Ag 29,27:3
Smith, Julie P Mrs, 1883, S 8,1:4
Smith, Juliet M, 1947, F 7,23:4
Smith, June C, 1947, F 8,17:1
Smith, K Wesley, 1961, Ag 18,21:6
Smith, Karl B, 1957, My 12,87:1
Smith, Karl B C, 1947, N 11,28:3
Smith, Karl L, 1949, N 7,27:1
Smith, Kate Adams, 1903, D 13,4:7
Smith, Katherine B, 1955, D 4,89:2
Smith, Kathryn C K, 1942, Mr 15,42:4
Smith, Kay, 1967, My 15,59:5
Smith, Keith, 1955, D 20,31:2
Smith, Kenneth G (will, D 19,15:1), 1945, D 5,25:3
Smith, Kenneth L (por), 1948, Ja 22,27:6
Smith, Kenneth L, 1957, Jl 2,27:1
Smith, Kenneth O, 1951, My 11,27:3
Smith, Kenneth S, 1962, My 23,45:1
Smith, King, 1944, Ag 19,11:4
Smith, King Mrs, 1954, Jl 15,27:5
Smith, Kirby, 1903, Ap 12,1:5
Smith, Kirby Flower Dr, 1918, D 7,15:5
Smith, Knowles A, 1955, N 2,35:3
Smith, Kurt A, 1959, D 10,39:1
Smith, L Gerard, 1940, Mr 15,23:3
Smith, L Winfield, 1952, Je 27,23:2
Smith, Lamar Mrs, 1955, Je 13,23:6
Smith, Lancelot A Sr, 1957, Ja 6,89:2
Smith, Landon P, 1946, F 26,25:3
Smith, Langdon, 1908, Ap 9,9:6
Smith, Langdon C, 1956, O 5,25:4
Smith, Langley C Mrs, 1945, Ja 3,17:5
Smith, Lansing F, 1948, Ag 25,25:3
Smith, Larry M, 1949, Je 15,29:4
Smith, Latimer P, 1937, D 25,15:4
Smith, Laura D, 1961, N 21,39:4
Smith, Laurence D, 1952, S 6,17:7
Smith, Lavern, 1952, Ap 23,29:4
Smith, Lawrence, 1946, Mr 7,26:2; 1954, Jl 22,23:6
Smith, Lawrence A, 1958, Ja 23,27:1
Smith, Lawrence B, 1945, Ap 24,19:2
Smith, Lawrence D, 1958, Ja 29,27:1
Smith, Lawrence J, 1946, F 26,25:4
Smith, Layton F, 1937, F 21,II,11:2
Smith, Le Montte Dinwiddle, 1912, Ap 29,11:5
Smith, Le Roy, 1938, N 13,44:6; 1952, Jl 14,17:2
Smith, Lee O, 1942, Ap 8,19:4
Smith, Lee T, 1963, D 9,35:1
Smith, Leigh Travis, 1946, Mr 19,13:7
Smith, Leland, 1944, D 25,19:6
Smith, Lemon L, 1954, N 25,29:6
Smith, Lemuel, 1903, Ag 23,7:5
Smith, Lemuel C, 1965, N 4,47:4
Smith, Lemuel F, 1951, N 26,25:5; 1956, O 16,33:4
Smith, Lena R Mrs, 1942, Je 12,21:4
Smith, Lenox, 1924, Ja 29,19:3
Smith, Leo A, 1952, S 12,21:4
Smith, Leo J, 1945, My 3,23:3
Smith, Leo O, 1938, F 9,19:4
Smith, Leo R, 1963, O 10,41:3
Smith, Leon, 1959, O 4,86:6
Smith, Leon B Dean, 1937, My 5,25:1
Smith, Leon D, 1960, Ja 27,33:5
Smith, Leon F Mrs, 1943, Mr 10,19:5
Smith, Leon L, 1946, N 11,27:3
Smith, Leonard, 1947, O 22,29:1
Smith, Leonard B, 1957, Ap 27,19:2
Smith, Leonard C L, 1943, F 5,21:2
Smith, Leonard F, 1941, My 9,21:2
Smith, Leonard H, 1959, O 15,39:2
Smith, Leonard H Jr, 1950, Je 4,92:6
Smith, Leonard H Mrs, 1952, Mr 24,25:2
Smith, Leonard J, 1944, F 13,42:1
Smith, Leonard K, 1955, Jl 28,23:3
Smith, Leonard M, 1943, O 14,21:4
Smith, Leonard S Jr, 1960, My 1,87:1
Smith, Leroy H, 1954, Je 27,68:3
Smith, LeRoy L, 1961, O 16,29:3
Smith, Leslie, 1940, Jl 5,13:4
Smith, Leslie Col, 1907, Ag 31,7:6
Smith, Lester, 1949, Jl 28,23:5
Smith, Lester H, 1938, Ap 16,13:4
Smith, Lester Rev, 1925, Ag 13,19:5
Smith, Lewis E, 1941, N 1,15:4
Smith, Lewis H, 1955, Ap 2,17:5
Smith, Lewis J, 1947, Ag 16,13:5; 1954, Jl 13,23:5
Smith, Lewis P, 1952, Ap 20,94:5
Smith, Lewis W, 1952, D 20,17:6
Smith, Lillian, 1966, S 29,47:1
Smith, Lillian A, 1957, Je 28,23:3
Smith, Lillian H E Mrs, 1940, Je 23,31:3
Smith, Lillian R, 1949, Ap 15,23:3
Smith, Lily L Mrs, 1950, F 4,15:4
Smith, Littleton E H, 1943, My 15,15:5
Smith, Livingston, 1961, Ag 22,29:6
Smith, Livingston M, 1953, N 9,35:3
Smith, Lizzie D Mrs, 1938, S 4,17:1
Smith, Lloyd E, 1950, Jl 15,13:6; 1950, Jl 17,21:4; 1960, N 29,37:4

Smith, Lloyd G, 1958, S 11,33:2
Smith, Lloyd L, 1948, N 14,76:5
Smith, Lloyd M Mrs, 1955, Je 18,17:6
Smith, Lloyd R, 1944, D 24,25:1
Smith, Lloyd W (will, Jl 31,51:1), 1955, Jl 3,32:6
Smith, Logan P, 1946, Mr 3,45:1
Smith, Lon K, 1946, D 26,25:2
Smith, Lothair, 1940, Je 8,15:2
Smith, Louis A, 1957, S 19,29:2
Smith, Louis E, 1948, Je 11,23:4
Smith, Louis G, 1952, Ja 11,21:3; 1955, Jl 13,25:2
Smith, Louis G Mrs, 1950, N 14,32:2
Smith, Louis J, 1949, F 20,61:1; 1949, Jl 19,29:1
Smith, Louis Joseph, 1968, O 24,47:4
Smith, Louis L, 1964, Ja 15,31:3
Smith, Louis P, 1957, D 6,29:1
Smith, Louis R, 1950, My 19,27:1
Smith, Louis R Mrs, 1946, Ja 22,27:2
Smith, Louis Sir, 1939, Mr 16,23:5
Smith, Louis W, 1947, Mr 5,25:3
Smith, Louisa Mrs, 1906, O 25,9:2
Smith, Louise, 1954, My 9,88:6
Smith, Louise H Mrs, 1942, O 28,23:4
Smith, Louise L, 1964, S 13,86:5
Smith, Loyal L, 1908, F 12,7:6
Smith, Lucian E Mrs, 1954, D 27,17:2
Smith, Lucy A H, 1949, Je 29,27:4
Smith, Lucy B Mrs, 1947, Mr 2,52:5
Smith, Lucy H Mrs, 1939, N 20,19:2
Smith, Lucy P Woods Mrs, 1906, D 9,7:6
Smith, Luther E, 1951, Ap 3,27:1
Smith, Luther J, 1949, S 9,25:5
Smith, Lybrand P, 1948, N 26,23:5
Smith, Lyman, 1944, Je 21,19:3
Smith, Lyman A, 1950, Ja 4,35:1
Smith, Lyman C, 1910, N 6,II,13:3
Smith, M Cliston, 1952, Je 8,87:1
Smith, M Dr, 1926, Ap 14,23:3
Smith, M H, 1879, N 8,8:4
Smith, M J, 1928, Ag 28,23:5
Smith, M L, 1884, Ag 15,4:7
Smith, M L Dr (funl), 1871, My 26,8:2
Smith, M L Gen, 1866, Ag 5,3:6; 1874, D 30,5:6
Smith, M Louise, 1961, F 21,35:3
Smith, M Marion, 1953, F 8,88:5
Smith, Mabel E, 1959, Ag 6,27:5
Smith, Mabel G, 1952, S 27,17:5
Smith, MacDonald, 1949, S 1,21:1
Smith, Madeleine W (cor, Mr 18,27:2), 1955, Mr 17, 45:5
Smith, Madeline B Mrs, 1952, D 17,33:1
Smith, Madeline D, 1943, D 10,27:2
Smith, Magill Mrs (J Keegan), 1966, Ag 27,29:5
Smith, Mahlon B, 1937, Ap 7,25:5
Smith, Major, 1954, O 27,29:4
Smith, Malcolm K, 1952, F 15,25:1
Smith, Manning J Jr, 1966, Ap 5,39:1
Smith, Marco C Jr, 1961, F 24,29:2
Smith, Marcus A Ex-Sen, 1924, Ap 8,19:2
Smith, Margaret, 1938, My 12,23:5
Smith, Margaret A, 1954, O 31,89:1
Smith, Margaret E, 1937, Jl 16,19:2
Smith, Margaret G Mrs, 1937, D 10,25:2
Smith, Margaret Mrs, 1947, Ag 28,25:4; 1950, Mr 24, 25:4
Smith, Margaret P, 1947, O 29,27:3
Smith, Margot N Mrs, 1949, S 25,92:6
Smith, Maria Fox, 1902, N 5,9:3
Smith, Marian W (Mrs H F Alehurst), 1961, My 4, 37:5
Smith, Marie, 1957, N 15,27:2
Smith, Marie F K Mrs, 1954, D 26,63:4
Smith, Marion, 1947, S 11,27:1
Smith, Marjorie, 1956, O 28,89:2
Smith, Mark, 1874, Ag 27,5:7; 1903, S 22,7:5; 1944, My 10,19:4
Smith, Mark J, 1949, Mr 28,21:2
Smith, Marshall B, 1962, F 18,92:2
Smith, Martha R, 1960, Ag 23,29:3
Smith, Martha T Mrs, 1939, Ja 26,21:3
Smith, Martin E, 1941, Je 1,40:6; 1952, My 10,21:4
Smith, Martin F, 1954, O 27,29:2
Smith, Martin F Mrs, 1949, My 21,13:3
Smith, Mary Almira Dr, 1923, Ag 12,26:4
Smith, Mary B Mrs, 1952, Mr 23,92:2
Smith, Mary C, 1950, My 1,25:2
Smith, Mary D Mrs, 1941, Ag 7,17:5
Smith, Mary E, 1918, My 25,13:5
Smith, Mary E Mrs, 1938, Mr 17,21:3
Smith, Mary G, 1948, D 31,15:4
Smith, Mary H, 1966, Je 15,47:5
Smith, Mary L, 1939, Ag 21,13:6; 1945, S 5,23:4; 1965, Jl 29,27:2
Smith, Mary M, 1950, Mr 23,29:5
Smith, Mary Mrs, 1952, Mr 12,27:3
Smith, Mary R, 1938, F 7,15:1
Smith, Mary S, 1955, Mr 24,31:1
Smith, Mason R Mrs, 1965, N 11,50:1
Smith, Mathew A, 1938, F 1,21:1
Smith, Mathew C, 1941, Mr 13,21:1
Smith, Matthew, 1953, Mr 17,29:3; 1958, F 27,27:3; 1959, S 30,37:2
Smith, Matthew I, 1958, Je 27,25:2
Smith, Matthew J, 1960, Je 17,31:3
Smith, Maxwell J, 1948, S 29,29:1
Smith, Mayme Mrs, 1947, Jl 22,23:4
Smith, Maynard D, 1948, Jl 6,23:1
Smith, McCauley, 1947, S 13,11:4
Smith, Melborne, 1964, O 13,39:5
Smith, Melville, 1962, Jl 18,29:3
Smith, Melville R, 1950, N 3,27:1
Smith, Merritt H Mrs, 1949, Mr 19,15:5
Smith, Michael, 1946, D 6,24:3
Smith, Michael A, 1947, Mr 16,60:4
Smith, Michael H, 1966, Ag 27,29:6
Smith, Michael J, 1941, Mr 11,23:3
Smith, Michael Mrs, 1950, Je 12,27:2
Smith, Michael T, 1950, Ja 1,42:5
Smith, Milburn D, 1963, D 31,19:3
Smith, Mildred C, 1964, My 27,39:3
Smith, Mildred E, 1946, F 9,13:5
Smith, Millard Fillmore, 1911, N 22,13:4
Smith, Miller A, 1939, Ja 4,21:2
Smith, Milton, 1942, My 4,19:5
Smith, Milton G, 1941, Ag 21,17:6
Smith, Milton Hannibal, 1921, F 23,13:6
Smith, Milton S, 1964, Mr 31,35:4
Smith, Minnie Colvin, 1916, Je 5,11:4
Smith, Minor C, 1944, S 17,42:1
Smith, Miranda B, 1946, My 11,27:2
Smith, Moe, 1960, D 16,33:2
Smith, Montague M, 1937, Je 17,23:2
Smith, Montgomery C, 1938, S 21,25:2
Smith, Morgan S, 1940, N 14,23:3
Smith, Morris, 1941, Je 15,37:1; 1951, Ap 20,29:3; 1964, Jl 17,27:6
Smith, Morris K, 1950, Jl 3,15:6
Smith, Mortimer A, 1940, O 10,25:5
Smith, Mortimer F, 1940, Ap 28,36:4
Smith, Morton B, 1916, My 18,11:6
Smith, Morton Fitz Lt-Col, 1916, Je 17,11:6
Smith, Moses, 1964, Jl 29,33:4
Smith, Moses E, 1952, Ap 6,88:4
Smith, Mulford D, 1948, S 11,15:4
Smith, Munroe Mrs, 1949, Ja 23,70:4
Smith, Myra E Mrs, 1940, Jl 2,21:6
Smith, Myron C, 1945, N 8,19:3
Smith, Myron H, 1950, S 14,31:2
Smith, Myron J, 1943, Jl 21,15:3
Smith, N A, 1934, F 2,17:5
Smith, N Blanchard, 1954, D 10,27:5
Smith, N J Mrs, 1940, D 12,38:2
Smith, N Mansfield, 1938, N 13,45:3
Smith, N Mrs (Ida Greely), 1882, Ap 12,8:2
Smith, N R, 1877, Jl 4,4:6
Smith, Nan D, 1938, Ag 10,19:5
Smith, Naomi R (Mrs E Milton), 1964, Jl 29,33:1
Smith, Nathan, 1878, Ap 26,5:5
Smith, Nathan A, 1939, N 30,21:5
Smith, Nathaniel B, 1954, Je 13,88:3
Smith, Nathaniel Stevens, 1912, Mr 24,II,15:3
Smith, Nelson, 1916, Mr 1,11:6; 1946, F 21,23:1
Smith, Nelson J, 1949, Ja 11,31:5
Smith, Newell N, 1948, My 7,23:1
Smith, Newton B, 1956, S 26,33:5
Smith, Nicholas Col, 1911, Ja 20,11:4
Smith, Nicholas T Capt, 1907, Ap 25,9:5
Smith, Nixola Greeley (Mrs Andrew W Ford), 1919, Mr 10,11:4
Smith, Noel W, 1947, Ap 13,60:6
Smith, Norman, 1959, Ag 15,17:4; 1965, Jl 4,37:4
Smith, Norman E Sr Mrs, 1951, Ag 12,78:7
Smith, Norman F, 1965, F 12,29:4
Smith, Norman F Mrs, 1965, F 12,29:4
Smith, Norman L, 1962, Ja 12,23:5
Smith, Norman M Rear-Adm, 1968, N 27,47:4
Smith, O, 1926, Jl 20,19:3
Smith, O G, 1933, Ap 18,15:3
Smith, O Warren, 1941, S 24,23:2
Smith, Olin W, 1938, My 30,11:4
Smith, Oliver B, 1945, Ja 9,19:2
Smith, Oliver D Mrs, 1942, F 3,19:2
Smith, Oliver H, 1954, Ja 29,19:1
Smith, Oney P, 1950, Ja 7,18:2
Smith, Ora L, 1941, N 20,27:2
Smith, Orison H, 1941, My 19,17:4
Smith, Orland Gen, 1903, O 4,7:6
Smith, Orlando L, 1941, F 26,22:2
Smith, Orlando Maj, 1908, D 21,9:4
Smith, Orrin Randolph, 1913, Mr 5,17:4
Smith, Orville, 1946, N 12,29:5
Smith, Orville C, 1940, Ja 11,23:4
Smith, Oscar B, 1938, S 27,21:5; 1950, F 25,17:6
Smith, Oscar F, 1944, My 18,19:2
Smith, Oscar J, 1937, F 19,19:5
Smith, Oscar M, 1954, Ja 26,27:2
Smith, Oscar W, 1938, F 8,21:5
Smith, Oskaloosa H Col, 1910, Mr 24,9:5
Smith, Otis, 1923, S 4,17:2
Smith, Otis Leroy, 1910, Ja 25,9:4
Smith, Otto T, 1953, Ap 4,13:5
Smith, Owen, 1943, Jl 31,13:5; 1943, N 12,21:4
Smith, Owen Mrs, 1953, Ap 10,21:3
Smith, P B, 1885, Mr 30,1:6
Smith, P Bryant, 1961, Je 9,33:2
Smith, P C, 1903, My 19,9:6
Smith, P H, 1885, Ap 2,5:2
Smith, P Holly Dr, 1920, Ja 23,13:2
Smith, P L O, 1961, S 20,29:5
Smith, Page R L, 1949, Jl 28,23:4
Smith, Palmer, 1955, Ap 19,31:3
Smith, Patrick G, 1949, Ja 31,19:6
Smith, Patrick H, 1947, F 27,21:4
Smith, Patrick J Mrs, 1950, Mr 26,92:3
Smith, Patrick S, 1943, My 14,19:4
Smith, Paul, 1950, Mr 25,13:4; 1952, Je 1,84:5
Smith, Paul E Dr, 1968, Mr 19,47:3
Smith, Paul H, 1949, Mr 12,17:3
Smith, Paul K, 1960, O 8,23:5
Smith, Paul M, 1957, My 8,37:1
Smith, Paul Mrs, 1953, D 26,13:5; 1955, Jl 9,15:4
Smith, Paul R, 1948, S 12,72:1
Smith, Paul T, 1948, O 29,25:3
Smith, Paul W, 1961, Ap 15,21:6
Smith, Paul W J, 1953, Ap 16,29:2
Smith, Pemberton Mrs, 1951, Je 20,27:4
Smith, Percival M, 1952, Ap 20,94:5
Smith, Percival O, 1950, Mr 24,25:5
Smith, Percival P, 1946, Jl 1,31:3
Smith, Percy J D, 1948, N 3,27:1
Smith, Percy N, 1950, Jl 30,60:6
Smith, Percy W, 1940, Je 29,15:3; 1967, N 4,33:1
Smith, Perry D, 1967, F 6,29:4
Smith, Perry L, 1951, My 31,27:4
Smith, Perry M, 1955, Mr 22,31:4
Smith, Persifor F Jr, 1939, Ap 6,25:1
Smith, Peter A, 1940, D 2,23:6
Smith, Peter F, 1965, Ja 6,39:2
Smith, Peter H, 1949, F 15,23:2
Smith, Peter J, 1937, Mr 8,19:2
Smith, Peter J Mrs (por), 1943, Ag 10,19:6
Smith, Peter Mrs, 1942, Mr 28,17:6
Smith, Peter P, 1960, F 4,31:3
Smith, Peter V, 1949, F 2,27:5
Smith, Phelps (will, Ja 24,II,1:4), 1937, Ja 19,23:3
Smith, Phil B, 1953, D 18,29:2
Smith, Phil C Sir, 1937, N 6,17:5
Smith, Phil J Sr, 1952, Ag 15,15:4
Smith, Phil M, 1952, S 2,23:1
Smith, Phil S, 1949, My 11,29:5
Smith, Philemon H F, 1946, Mr 30,15:1
Smith, Philip, 1943, D 8,23:3; 1961, Jl 19,29:1
Smith, Philip E, 1963, S 3,33:2
Smith, Philip H W, 1946, S 2,17:5
Smith, Philip L, 1943, Ag 28,11:5
Smith, Philip M, 1960, F 27,19:1
Smith, Philip T, 1943, N 19,19:4
Smith, Philred C, 1950, O 13,104:3
Smith, Pierre J, 1946, Ja 17,23:4
Smith, Powel J, 1942, Ag 11,19:2
Smith, Preserved, 1941, My 16,23:4
Smith, Preston H, 1945, D 17,21:4
Smith, Preston R, 1967, Ja 17,39:4
Smith, Pryor T Mrs, 1942, Mr 1,44:6
Smith, Q L Sir, 1901, O 22,9:6
Smith, R A C, 1933, Jl 28,15:1
Smith, R C, 1947, Ap 18,23:5
Smith, R Ernest, 1947, Je 30,19:4
Smith, R Gibson, 1923, D 7,21:5
Smith, R Gordon, 1952, Ja 16,25:4
Smith, R H, 1933, D 12,24:1
Smith, R H Mrs, 1949, Je 2,27:5
Smith, R Jasper, 1962, Ja 9,47:2
Smith, R Kendrick, 1946, Ag 30,17:3
Smith, R Leslie, 1960, Ag 29,25:4
Smith, R Mayo Prof, 1901, N 12,1:7
Smith, R S, 1877, Ja 25,2:6
Smith, Ralph, 1945, S 12,25:2
Smith, Ralph C, 1962, Ap 20,27:2; 1965, D 26,68:7
Smith, Ralph D, 1951, D 29,11:1
Smith, Ralph E, 1953, D 17,37:3
Smith, Ralph E Mrs, 1961, My 13,19:3
Smith, Ralph G, 1957, Jl 16,25:3
Smith, Ralph H (por), 1943, O 16,13:3
Smith, Ralph H, 1945, S 25,25:3; 1947, Ja 4,15:3; 1948, Ja 13,25:1
Smith, Ralph M, 1951, O 10,23:4
Smith, Ralph Mrs, 1953, F 22,34:3
Smith, Ralph P, 1947, Je 15,62:5
Smith, Ralph S, 1956, O 10,39:3
Smith, Randolph M, 1962, Mr 8,31:4
Smith, Ransom C, 1946, S 14,7:7
Smith, Ravil, 1941, Ap 26,15:3
Smith, Ray Mrs, 1938, N 19,17:4
Smith, Raymond, 1958, Ja 21,26:6; 1958, O 12,86:4
Smith, Raymond A, 1955, Ap 18,23:5
Smith, Raymond B, 1939, D 29,15:5
Smith, Raymond B Mrs, 1947, O 19,64:2
Smith, Raymond D, 1955, Ag 18,23:5
Smith, Raymond E, 1947, Ja 10,22:3; 1955, Ap 12, 29:5; 1957, O 2,33:3
Smith, Raymond F Mrs, 1958, Ja 14,30:5
Smith, Raymond F Sr, 1964, O 30,38:1
Smith, Raymond H Mrs, 1939, Jl 13,19:6
Smith, Raymond I, 1967, My 25,42:6
Smith, Raymond L, 1942, Je 7,43:1
Smith, Raymond M, 1958, Ja 23,27:1
Smith, Raymond P Mrs, 1956, F 15,31:4
Smith, Raymond W, 1947, O 28,25:1

Smith, Raynor Rock, 1907, My 19,7:4
Smith, Reardon Lady, 1939, Ag 10,19:4
Smith, Reed, 1943, Jl 25,31:2
Smith, Reginald G, 1946, Ag 27,27:2
Smith, Reginald H, 1966, O 24,39:4
Smith, Reginald John, 1916, D 29,9:5
Smith, Reginald K Dr, 1937, Ap 20,26:1
Smith, Reuben B, 1955, Ap 22,25:3
Smith, Reuben F, 1913, Mr 13,11:5
Smith, Rex W D Jr (funl plans, My 19,33:3), 1959, My 18,27:1
Smith, Richard, 1918, Je 18,13:6; 1922, S 4,13:7
Smith, Richard B, 1937, F 27,1:6
Smith, Richard C, 1957, Mr 2,21:5
Smith, Richard Cayuga, 1921, O 6,17:5
Smith, Richard H, 1937, D 30,19:5; 1942, D 26,11:1
Smith, Richard Herbert Justice, 1920, Ja 27,15:3
Smith, Richard L, 1949, Ag 27,13:7
Smith, Richard M, 1958, Ap 28,23:2
Smith, Richard R, 1951, Mr 14,33:4; 1957, Ag 10,15:3
Smith, Richard S, 1953, My 21,31:4; 1968, S 28,33:5
Smith, Richard W, 1954, S 1,27:3
Smith, Robert, 1908, Jl 31,5:4; 1942, Mr 19,21:2; 1954, O 8,23:2; 1955, Ag 3,23:4
Smith, Robert A (por), 1942, F 5,15:3
Smith, Robert A (trb lr, N 14,20:6), 1959, N 12,35:4
Smith, Robert A Mrs, 1959, Je 9,37:4
Smith, Robert B, 1944, D 17,38:3; 1946, Jl 12,17:5; 1951, My 22,31:2; 1951, N 7,29:3; 1956, S 12,37:4; 1965, Jl 24,21:4
Smith, Robert C, 1939, Mr 10,23:4; 1940, Ap 24,23:2; 1951, Je 17,84:5; 1961, D 7,43:3; 1962, Ag 16,27:5
Smith, Robert C W, 1939, Mr 26,III,7:3
Smith, Robert D, 1948, N 17,27:3; 1958, F 1,19:3
Smith, Robert E, 1914, Ag 17,7:1; 1941, F 2,44:8; 1957, N 2,21:1; 1965, My 23,85:1
Smith, Robert E Jr, 1949, O 16,88:3
Smith, Robert F, 1954, F 2,27:2; 1963, My 25,25:6; 1964, Je 19,31:2
Smith, Robert G, 1940, Ja 9,23:2; 1957, F 21,27:1
Smith, Robert H, 1950, N 17,28:2; 1951, My 30,21:2; 1955, D 8,37:5; 1960, Je 19,88:2; 1962, Je 18,25:4
Smith, Robert H Capt, 1923, F 22,15:4
Smith, Robert L, 1951, Ja 20,15:5; 1961, O 7,23:6; 1962, Ja 9,47:3; 1968, Ag 13,36:5
Smith, Robert L Mrs, 1965, F 22,21:4
Smith, Robert M, 1938, D 16,25:6; 1952, Mr 27,29:3
Smith, Robert M Dr, 1952, Ja 16,31:6
Smith, Robert P, 1955, D 15,37:4; 1961, My 13,19:5
Smith, Robert Pearsall Mrs (Mrs Hannah Whithall Smith), 1911, My 8,11:5
Smith, Robert R Sr, 1954, F 1,23:3
Smith, Robert S, 1923, D 19,19:4; 1939, Ja 16,15:5; 1947, Ja 11,19:5
Smith, Robert W, 1948, Ja 20,24:2; 1952, Jl 27,57:2; 1966, D 22,33:3
Smith, Robert W Mrs, 1946, Ag 13,27:4
Smith, Robert Z, 1950, Ap 1,15:5
Smith, Roberta L, 1956, O 9,35:4
Smith, Robin, 1962, Jl 31,8:1
Smith, Robinson, 1966, N 10,47:1
Smith, Roderick W, 1950, Ap 12,27:5
Smith, Rodney Brig-Gen, 1915, N 13,11:6
Smith, Rodney H, 1956, Mr 12,27:3
Smith, Rodney J, 1953, Ap 3,23:2
Smith, Rodney Jr (Gipsy), 1951, Ag 26,77:3
Smith, Roger McE Sr, 1965, N 23,38:1
Smith, Roland C Mrs, 1943, F 2,19:2
Smith, Ronald B, 1961, D 10,88:8
Smith, Rosina E, 1958, O 7,35:1
Smith, Roswell D Rev, 1910, Mr 21,9:5
Smith, Rowland, 1942, F 21,19:2
Smith, Roy B, 1940, D 26,19:2
Smith, Roy C, 1940, Ap 12,23:4; 1953, Ap 22,29:5
Smith, Roy C Jr, 1946, Je 3,21:5
Smith, Roy E, 1947, F 14,22:3
Smith, Roy G, 1953, Ja 17,15:3
Smith, Roy H, 1951, S 5,31:5; 1952, Ap 26,23:6
Smith, Roy K, 1957, Ag 2,19:3
Smith, Roy L, 1963, Ap 22,27:4
Smith, Royal H Mrs, 1937, S 5,II,7:2
Smith, Royall, 1966, S 2,31:2
Smith, Ruel P, 1937, Jl 31,15:4
Smith, Ruel Perley Mrs, 1920, Jl 27,13:5
Smith, Ruel S Mrs, 1956, My 10,31:4
Smith, Rufus, 1947, Ag 4,17:2
Smith, Rufus D, 1954, Ja 3,90:3
Smith, Rufus E, 1946, D 16,23:2
Smith, Rufus J Mrs, 1953, Mr 11,29:3
Smith, Russell H, 1947, D 4,31:2
Smith, Russell P Sr, 1955, S 17,15:5
Smith, Ryerson H, 1938, Ap 6,23:3
Smith, S, 1935, O 21,21:7
Smith, S Archibald, 1954, S 20,23:5
Smith, S Dimon, 1943, Ap 5,19:5
Smith, S E, 1950, D 2,13:2
Smith, S F Dr, 1895, N 17,16:1
Smith, S Fahs, 1942, Ja 21,18:2
Smith, S Homer, 1950, Je 17,15:4
Smith, S I, 1926, My 7,19:2
Smith, S Leroy, 1956, Mr 27,35:3
Smith, S Newton, 1907, D 25,7:5
Smith, S Sidney, 1967, Ja 30,29:1
Smith, S Stephenson, 1961, O 4,45:3
Smith, S W, 1932, Ja 5,28:6
Smith, S Wallace, 1948, D 15,33:2
Smith, S Willard, 1949, Jl 9,13:5
Smith, Samuel, 1872, My 21,2:3; 1947, N 30,76:7; 1957, F 24,84:5; 1959, O 6,39:3
Smith, Samuel A, 1957, Mr 2,21:4
Smith, Samuel B, 1965, Jl 14,37:1
Smith, Samuel C, 1939, Ag 1,19:1
Smith, Samuel D Jr, 1942, N 29,64:7
Smith, Samuel I, 1944, Ja 29,13:3
Smith, Samuel J, 1940, Jl 20,15:5; 1941, D 11,27:3; 1948, Je 26,17:4
Smith, Samuel J Jr, 1960, N 4,33:1
Smith, Samuel K, 1954, N 24,23:4
Smith, Samuel L Dr, 1937, F 16,23:1
Smith, Samuel O, 1955, Ag 14,81:2
Smith, Samuel W, 1940, O 25,21:2
Smith, Samuel W J, 1948, Ag 23,17:4
Smith, Sanford C, 1962, Ag 13,25:4
Smith, Saqui, 1924, Ap 20,22:1
Smith, Sara R, 1946, Jl 7,36:4
Smith, Sarah A Mrs, 1939, F 28,19:5
Smith, Sarah Adams Mrs, 1907, N 16,9:5
Smith, Sarah M Mrs, 1941, S 20,17:3
Smith, Sarah Mrs, 1937, Jl 15,19:1
Smith, Sayle E, 1959, Jl 20,25:4
Smith, Scott L, 1957, Jl 31,23:5
Smith, Scott L Mrs, 1953, My 16,19:3
Smith, Seneca S, 1946, Jl 12,17:5
Smith, Sheldon P, 1966, My 1,87:1
Smith, Shepherd F, 1955, N 27,89:1
Smith, Sherman K, 1954, S 8,31:4
Smith, Sherrill, 1951, Ap 11,29:2
Smith, Sherrod M, 1949, S 14,31:5
Smith, Shirley, 1964, N 18,47:2
Smith, Shirley W, 1959, F 17,31:2
Smith, Sidney, 1953, Ja 27,25:3
Smith, Sidney A, 1940, N 17,50:1; 1953, N 16,25:2
Smith, Sidney Capt, 1924, Jl 6,21:3
Smith, Sidney D, 1944, Ag 12,11:4
Smith, Sidney E, 1944, F 6,42:2
Smith, Sidney E (funl, Mr 20,32:1), 1959, Mr 18,37:1
Smith, Sidney F Mrs, 1952, Mr 26,29:2
Smith, Sidney V, 1953, Je 12,27:3
Smith, Sidney W, 1966, Mr 20,86:7
Smith, Simon H, 1943, Je 4,21:3
Smith, Sinclair, 1938, My 20,19:4
Smith, Sion B, 1954, F 1,23:2
Smith, Sol (will, F 24,2:6), 1869, F 16,5:3
Smith, Sol, 1884, Jl 4,2:3
Smith, Sol Mrs (Mrary Sedley Smith), 1917, Je 16, 11:4
Smith, Solomon A Mrs (Fredrika), 1968, Mr 8,39:4
Smith, Solwin W, 1958, F 21,23:2
Smith, Spencer, 1938, Jl 17,27:4; 1951, Mr 14,33:4
Smith, Spencer H, 1917, N 29,13:5; 1957, D 27,19:3
Smith, Spencer P, 1939, My 20,15:6
Smith, St Clair, 1945, N 29,23:2
Smith, St Clair Dr, 1923, My 2,19:2
Smith, St John, 1944, Ja 3,21:4
Smith, Stafford (por), 1944, Je 21,19:6
Smith, Stanley H, 1963, Ag 25,82:8
Smith, Stanley P, 1945, Ja 7,38:5
Smith, Stanley R, 1943, Ag 18,19:6
Smith, Stanley W, 1947, D 19,25:3
Smith, Stephen A Jr, 1940, My 15,25:5; 1947, Je 29, 48:8
Smith, Stephen C, 1937, F 3,23:2
Smith, Stephen D, 1944, N 23,31:3
Smith, Stephen Dr, 1922, Ag 27,28:4
Smith, Stephen G, 1959, N 19,39:4
Smith, Stephen H, 1941, Ag 22,15:5
Smith, Stephen J, 1962, Jl 30,25:1
Smith, Stephen L, 1947, Je 11,27:4
Smith, Stephen M, 1961, N 2,37:4; 1967, F 20,37:2
Smith, Stephen T, 1915, My 5,13:6
Smith, Stephen T Mrs, 1951, My 21,27:4
Smith, Stephen W, 1944, Ap 13,19:5
Smith, Stewart W, 1907, My 11,7:4
Smith, Stuart F, 1951, Mr 6,27:3
Smith, Stuart F Mrs, 1938, O 8,23:1
Smith, Stuart G, 1958, N 21,29:4
Smith, Stuff (Hezekia L G Smith), 1967, O 2,48:1
Smith, Susan, 1953, Jl 27,19:1
Smith, Swire Sir, 1918, Mr 19,11:8
Smith, Sydney A, 1947, Jl 15,23:4
Smith, Sydney J, 1949, O 14,28:4
Smith, Sydney U, 1949, O 12,29:5
Smith, Sylvester C Jr Mrs, 1958, Mr 2,89:2
Smith, Sylvester C Mrs, 1948, F 3,25:4
Smith, Sylvester D, 1925, S 21,19:4
Smith, Sylvester L, 1950, N 2,31:3
Smith, T, 1934, D 11,23:1
Smith, T Garland, 1946, F 9,13:5
Smith, T H Col, 1914, Ap 12,15:4
Smith, T P, 1883, D 27,2:4
Smith, T Thomas, 1949, O 25,27:5
Smith, T Wade, 1952, Ap 28,19:4
Smith, T York, 1937, Mr 24,25:3
Smith, Th Ralston Rev, 1903, S 6,7:6
Smith, Theodore C, 1960, N 20,87:1
Smith, Theodore E, 1941, N 4,26:7; 1952, Mr 1,15:4
Smith, Theodore G, 1953, N 6,27:4
Smith, Theodore H, 1945, Je 28,19:5; 1966, Mr 26,29:4
Smith, Theodore H Mrs, 1948, My 3,21:1
Smith, Theodore J, 1943, D 5,66:7
Smith, Theodore Jr, 1941, F 24,15:2
Smith, Theodore Mrs, 1945, Jl 31,19:5; 1949, Mr 26, 17:2
Smith, Theodore R, 1954, S 11,17:6
Smith, Theodore W E, 1940, D 17,26:3
Smith, Thomas, 1883, My 22,5:5; 1914, Jl 20,7:2; 1925, F 26,21:4
Smith, Thomas A, 1906, Ja 23,9:5; 1951, Ja 17,27:3; 1955, Je 10,25:1
Smith, Thomas Allison Dr (trb, N 22,15:4), 1924, N 20,23:3
Smith, Thomas B, 1949, Ap 18,25:1
Smith, Thomas E Sr, 1948, S 4,15:3
Smith, Thomas F (funl, Ap 12,15:4), 1924, Ap 7,17:5
Smith, Thomas F, 1950, O 23,23:2; 1957, N 12,34:2
Smith, Thomas F Dr, 1916, Je 8,13:7
Smith, Thomas F Mrs, 1950, Ap 4,29:2
Smith, Thomas H, 1957, O 17,33:4
Smith, Thomas J, 1921, Ja 25,11:4; 1938, Jl 6,23:2; 1941, S 2,18:3; 1945, Mr 27,19:4; 1945, Je 20,23:5; 1950, Je 21,27:4
Smith, Thomas K, 1942, D 8,25:5
Smith, Thomas L, 1957, Mr 6,31:2
Smith, Thomas L Mrs, 1947, O 14,28:3
Smith, Thomas M, 1874, Ag 12,4:7; 1954, My 23,88:7
Smith, Thomas M Capt, 1905, Je 25,7:2
Smith, Thomas Mrs, 1948, Jl 23,19:3
Smith, Thomas P, 1947, Je 21,17:5; 1967, Jl 7,31:2
Smith, Thomas R, 1942, Ap 12,44:4
Smith, Thomas S, 1940, Ap 27,15:4; 1943, Je 16,21:3; 1950, S 14,31:4
Smith, Thomas T Mrs, 1949, F 9,27:4
Smith, Thomas V, 1964, My 25,33:3
Smith, Thomas W, 1938, F 26,15:3; 1939, Jl 16,30:7; 1941, O 22,23:5
Smith, Thompson Rev, 1903, N 24,9:5
Smith, Thornton, 1942, D 28,20:2
Smith, Tim Cpl, 1916, Ag 25,7:6
Smith, Titus K Mrs, 1946, O 25,23:3
Smith, Tom, 1953, F 28,17:2; 1957, Ja 24,29:4
Smith, Tony, 1941, Ja 15,23:3
Smith, Truman, 1884, My 6,5:5
Smith, Tucker P, 1951, F 5,24:2
Smith, Ulysses Grant, 1924, Jl 24,13:4
Smith, Ulysses S, 1946, Je 23,40:4
Smith, Uselma C, 1939, Ap 12,23:4
Smith, V Roy E, 1958, Ja 23,21:5
Smith, Valentine W, 1941, Je 27,18:2
Smith, Verne L Mrs, 1948, Ag 18,25:4
Smith, Vernon L, 1948, S 28,28:2; 1951, Ag 23,23:2
Smith, Versal T, 1968, S 19,47:1
Smith, Victor, 1909, Mr 15,9:7
Smith, Victor A, 1960, Ja 5,31:2
Smith, Victor K, 1954, D 30,17:3
Smith, Victor M, 1938, Je 19,28:7
Smith, Victor R, 1947, N 22,15:4
Smith, Vilance B, 1949, Ja 21,21:4
Smith, Vincent G, 1939, Ap 3,15:1
Smith, Vincent W, 1964, Ap 12,86:6
Smith, Vine H, 1957, Ap 21,89:1
Smith, Virginia T, 1949, Ag 7,60:3
Smith, Virginia W, 1939, D 4,23:3
Smith, Vivian B, 1952, D 6,21:4
Smith, Vivian H (Lord Bicester), 1956, F 18,19:3
Smith, Vivian T, 1946, Ja 3,20:3
Smith, W (see also Mr 6), 1878, Mr 8,2:2
Smith, W, 1933, Je 11,30:3
Smith, W A, 1903, Ap 14,9:6; 1932, O 12,23:3
Smith, W B, 1865, Mr 10,4:3; 1903, Ap 1,3:3; 1934, Ag 7,17:6
Smith, W Dulty, 1965, Ag 19,31:5
Smith, W E, 1939, My 26,23:5; 1940, Je 6,25:5
Smith, W Everett, 1955, Ap 3,86:5
Smith, W F Dr, 1903, Ap 15,9:6
Smith, W F Gen (Baldy), 1903, Mr 2,9:5
Smith, W H, 1873, Ap 18,1:6; 1891, O 7,1:5; 1903, My 13,9:5; 1907, Jl 9,7:6
Smith, W H (Pop), 1953, My 2,15:5
Smith, W Halsey, 1953, Ag 31,17:1
Smith, W Harry, 1951, Jl 12,25:2
Smith, W Hinckle, 1943, Ja 30,15:2
Smith, W J, 1878, Ag 25,2:1
Smith, W L, 1928, Mr 7,25:3; 1945, Jl 18,27:2
Smith, W Nelson, 1960, D 7,43:2
Smith, W Palmer, 1949, Ap 29,23:4
Smith, W Palmer Mrs, 1947, N 11,27:2
Smith, W R, 1934, F 20,21:3
Smith, W R C, 1941, O 8,23:6
Smith, W Schuyler, 1951, Ag 23,23:5
Smith, W Scott, 1939, Je 24,17:6
Smith, W Shaffer, 1954, Ja 12,23:4
Smith, W Stebbins, 1937, Jl 3,15:6
Smith, W Wallis, 1951, Mr 5,21:3
Smith, W Ward, 1965, My 2,88:6
Smith, W Wickham, 1912, F 28,11:3
Smith, W Wilberforth, 1943, F 27,13:2
Smith, Waldron, 1954, D 10,28:3
Smith, Walker Breese, 1925, Je 4,19:5
Smith, Wallace, 1937, F 1,19:4

Smith, Wallace H, 1938, Jl 25,15:7
Smith, Wallace J, 1948, Mr 24,25:6
Smith, Wallace W, 1956, My 16,35:5
Smith, Walter A, 1945, Mr 2,20:2; 1963, Je 23,84:7
Smith, Walter A Mrs, 1961, Ap 3,30:2
Smith, Walter B, 1939, Ja 16,15:4; 1945, Ap 3,19:3; 1948, Ag 30,17:2; 1949, Je 11,18:5
Smith, Walter B (funl plans, Ag 11,23:2; funl, Ag 15,29:4), 1961, Ag 10,1:2
Smith, Walter B Mrs, 1963, Ag 24,19:6
Smith, Walter C, 1943, Ag 18,19:4
Smith, Walter C Sr, 1960, Ap 8,31:3
Smith, Walter D, 1955, S 22,31:2
Smith, Walter E, 1953, D 10,47:4
Smith, Walter F, 1951, F 5,23:3
Smith, Walter F Jr (por), 1949, F 10,27:3
Smith, Walter F Mrs, 1952, Ag 30,13:6
Smith, Walter George, 1924, Ap 5,15:4
Smith, Walter H B, 1959, Ap 6,27:2
Smith, Walter J Mrs, 1966, Ag 12,31:4
Smith, Walter J Sr, 1953, Je 25,27:6
Smith, Walter M, 1907, N 29,9:6; 1937, My 2,II,9:1; 1938, Ap 21,19:3
Smith, Walter M Mrs, 1953, Jl 26,19:1
Smith, Walter P, 1938, N 6,48:8
Smith, Walter P Mrs, 1957, Ap 26,25:1
Smith, Walter R, 1955, O 3,27:5
Smith, Walter S, 1945, Ag 2,19:6; 1953, Ja 27,25:1
Smith, Walter T, 1940, N 12,24:2; 1947, Ag 6,23:3
Smith, Walter T Mrs, 1949, S 13,29:2; 1951, O 7,87:2
Smith, Walter W, 1949, Ap 27,27:5; 1950, Ag 3,23:4
Smith, Walter W Mrs, 1967, F 20,37:4
Smith, Walton W, 1966, N 21,45:2
Smith, Ward W Sr, 1943, My 29,13:4
Smith, Warren A, 1964, O 1,35:3
Smith, Warren B, 1965, My 23,85:2
Smith, Warren D, 1950, Jl 19,31:2
Smith, Warren H, 1942, Ag 11,19:2
Smith, Warren M, 1951, O 19,27:2
Smith, Warren Mrs, 1937, F 21,II,11:1
Smith, Warren P Mrs, 1957, Jl 10,27:4
Smith, Washington R, 1955, Ag 20,17:5
Smith, Wayne C, 1964, N 14,29:2; 1966, D 24,19:6
Smith, Wayne C Jr, 1948, D 21,25:3
Smith, Wayne Dr, 1915, N 13,11:5
Smith, Wendell Mather, 1925, N 14,15:5
Smith, Wesley, 1942, My 12,19:6
Smith, Wesley C, 1939, Jl 18,19:2
Smith, Wesley L, 1944, F 20,13:6
Smith, Wesley L (Feb 7), 1963, Ap 1,36:6
Smith, Wesley S, 1950, Ja 18,31:2
Smith, Wiatt, 1950, My 28,44:5
Smith, Wikoff, 1940, My 3,21:4
Smith, Wikoff Mrs, 1944, F 10,15:3
Smith, Wilbert A, 1952, Je 29,58:3
Smith, Wilbert L, 1937, Ag 29,II,6:8
Smith, Wilbur A, 1940, Je 21,21:4
Smith, Wilbur C, 1952, Jl 5,15:5
Smith, Wilbur F, 1940, Ag 11,31:4
Smith, Wiley S, 1947, Mr 26,26:2
Smith, Will C, 1951, Mr 21,33:2
Smith, Willard C, 1962, O 6,25:6
Smith, Willard E Dr, 1937, Mr 24,25:4
Smith, Willard H Mrs, 1953, Ag 13,25:1
Smith, Willard M, 1960, F 23,32:1
Smith, Willard P, 1954, My 18,29:3
Smith, William, 1872, Jl 5,5:4; 1912, F 8,11:4; 1948, Mr 3,23:2; 1948, Ag 8,57:3; 1949, F 8,26:2; 1952, S 25,31:3
Smith, William A, 1871, Ap 25,4:2; 1913, S 26,11:6; 1938, Ja 16,II,8:6; 1940, D 18,25:4; 1953, S 6,50:3; 1958, Je 11,35:2; 1967, Ap 3,33:4
Smith, William A Mrs, 1954, Ag 21,17:5; 1958, S 18, 31:2
Smith, William A Sir, 1914, My 12,11:5
Smith, William Alden Sr, 1920, Ap 30,13:5
Smith, William Alexander, 1911, Je 2,11:6
Smith, William Austin Rev Dr, 1922, S 28,21:4
Smith, William B, 1937, Mr 4,23:4; 1944, S 5,19:4; 1947, Mr 25,26:2; 1951, Jl 25,23:4; 1951, N 30,23:6; 1952, Ag 20,25:5
Smith, William B Mrs, 1959, Je 23,33:4
Smith, William Brig-Gen, 1912, Ja 18,13:5
Smith, William Burns, 1917, N 24,13:5
Smith, William C, 1937, Mr 14,II,9:2; 1940, Ap 9,23:3; 1940, D 18,25:3; 1942, Ja 6,24:4; 1943, S 8,23:5; 1944, Ag 14,15:4; 1945, Mr 3,13:2; 1947, Je 24,23:4; 1952, Ja 9,29:1
Smith, William C Mrs, 1942, Ap 1,21:3
Smith, William Capt, 1928, Ap 16,23:5
Smith, William Columbus, 1903, S 29,9:5
Smith, William Commodore, 1873, My 2,5:5
Smith, William D, 1939, F 6,13:4; 1952, Mr 30,93:1
Smith, William D Jr, 1944, Je 6,17:5
Smith, William D Mrs, 1943, My 24,15:2
Smith, William DeG, 1958, S 27,21:1
Smith, William E, 1943, Ap 4,40:6; 1943, O 25,15:4; 1944, S 12,19:2; 1946, O 3,27:4; 1948, Ja 18,60:4; 1948, My 19,27:2; 1950, F 25,17:4; 1950, Je 23,26:2; 1957, My 9,31:4; 1957, N 1,27:4
Smith, William E Ex-Gov, 1883, F 14,5:2
Smith, William E Mrs, 1949, F 5,15:6
Smith, William Emmet Mrs, 1924, Ap 3,21:6
Smith, William F, 1943, Ja 31,46:2; 1943, F 25,21:4; 1950, Jl 27,25:4; 1953, S 26,17:5; 1956, My 29,27:2
Smith, William F Judge, 1968, F 27,43:1
Smith, William G, 1942, Ja 17,17:5; 1943, D 26,32:3; 1945, Mr 29,23:4
Smith, William G Mrs, 1942, F 25,19:2
Smith, William G Sr, 1951, Je 21,27:5
Smith, William H, 1903, N 17,9:5; 1911, Je 29,11:4; 1914, Je 25,9:5; 1916, Ap 15,13:5; 1938, My 3,23:2; 1942, Mr 22,49:1; 1942, Ag 19,19:4; 1943, Mr 2,19:4; 1944, Jl 13,17:3; 1949, Mr 19,15:1; 1950, S 26,31:2; 1953, Ap 16,29:2; 1954, Ap 13,31:4; 1960, D 2,29:2
Smith, William H Jr, 1943, N 30,27:2
Smith, William H Mrs, 1954, N 27,14:3; 1962, F 25, 88:8
Smith, William H Sedley, 1872, Ja 20,5:3
Smith, William Harvey Mrs, 1968, Ja 29,31:2
Smith, William J, 1906, N 23,9:3; 1913, N 30,IV,7:6; 1920, N 4,13:3; 1937, D 27,16:3; 1938, N 26,15:2; 1939, Ap 14,23:3; 1943, F 21,32:8; 1944, O 22,46:6; 1948, Ja 23,23:3; 1950, Ag 16,29:2; 1954, Mr 8,27:2; 1954, Mr 24,27:2; 1955, My 29,45:1; 1955, Je 9,29:5
Smith, William J (Willie the Midge), 1966, Ag 6,23:2
Smith, William J Mrs, 1949, Ap 14,25:3
Smith, William J Rev, 1954, S 30,31:4; 1968, Ja 11,33:2
Smith, William J Sr, 1953, My 9,19:2
Smith, William J T, 1954, Jl 6,23:4
Smith, William K, 1948, O 17,76:4
Smith, William L, 1939, Mr 19,III,7:2; 1944, Je 24, 13:4; 1947, F 23,53:6; 1948, F 17,26:2
Smith, William L Mrs, 1948, Ap 5,21:5
Smith, William M, 1937, Je 6,II,5:1; 1941, Jl 1,23:4; 1946, Ja 14,19:2; 1948, My 30,34:3; 1950, Jl 4,17:3; 1964, F 17,31:3
Smith, William M Mrs, 1947, My 10,13:3
Smith, William P, 1956, N 9,29:5
Smith, William Prescott, 1872, O 2,5:3
Smith, William R, 1912, Jl 8,9:5; 1938, F 14,17:4; 1940, Ap 6,17:3
Smith, William R (por), 1941, Jl 16,17:1
Smith, William R, 1945, Mr 14,19:3; 1946, F 1,24:2
Smith, William R Mrs, 1941, O 16,21:2; 1946, Ag 20, 27:4; 1948, S 23,29:3
Smith, William S, 1940, D 11,27:2; 1944, Ap 19,23:5
Smith, William S A, 1953, Mr 6,20:5
Smith, William St Elmo Rev (funl, My 2,11:4), 1911, Ap 29,13:6
Smith, William T, 1952, Mr 23,21:4
Smith, William T Mrs, 1937, D 13,27:4
Smith, William Thayer Prof, 1909, S 18,9:6
Smith, William V, 1952, Ja 2,25:2; 1957, F 20,33:1
Smith, William Van Renselaer, 1911, N 3,11:5
Smith, William W, 1913, N 16,IV,7:6; 1924, Je 26,23:5; 1942, Mr 4,19:4; 1946, Mr 28,25:4; 1950, Je 1,27:2; 1950, Jl 22,15:5
Smith, William W (est tax appr), 1958, Ap 17,37:4
Smith, William W, 1966, Je 2,43:1
Smith, William W Jr, 1940, Mr 4,15:1
Smith, William W 2d, 1955, Mr 7,27:2
Smith, William Warren, 1951, F 5,23:1
Smith, William Watt (funl), 1907, Ja 6,II,9:7
Smith, William Watts, 1906, D 29,3:3
Smith, William Waugh Dr, 1912, N 30,13:3
Smith, William Weir, 1951, Ap 8,93:1
Smith, Williard W, 1950, My 23,29:3
Smith, Willie (Wm McSmith), 1967, Mr 9,39:3
Smith, Willis, 1953, Je 27,15:1
Smith, Wilmot M (funl plans, Mr 31,9:5), 1906, Mr 29,9:4
Smith, Wilson F, 1937, N 30,23:6
Smith, Winfield S, 1955, My 8,89:2
Smith, Winford H, 1961, N 14,36:1
Smith, Winfred L, 1937, D 16,27:2
Smith, Wing R, 1924, Je 10,11:4
Smith, Winifred, 1967, O 29,84:4
Smith, Winthrop, 1938, O 5,23:3
Smith, Winthrop H, 1961, Ja 11,48:1
Smith, Woodruff, 1942, Ap 27,15:5
Smith, Wuanita, 1959, F 20,26:1
Smith, Young B, 1960, Je 25,21:3
Smith, Yvonne, 1956, Ag 16,53:4
Smith (Mother Marie du Sacre Coeur), 1964, Mr 12, 35:4
Smith-Dorrien, H Sir, 1930, Ag 13,19:5
Smith-Merle, Wilton Mrs, 1943, Ag 31,17:5
Smith-Petersen, Marius N, 1953, Je 17,38:3
Smith-Petersen, Nils, 1953, D 24,15:1
Smith y Miyares, Alberto, 1942, Je 29,15:4
Smithe, Ferdinand L, 1938, O 19,23:2
Smithe, Ferdinand L Mrs, 1956, Ja 26,29:3
Smithells, Arthur, 1939, F 9,21:6
Smither, Henry C Mrs, 1950, Je 14,31:4
Smither, Robert N, 1945, My 13,20:2
Smithers, C, 1928, Mr 19,21:5
Smithers, Christopher D, 1952, My 28,29:4
Smithers, Christopher D Mrs, 1957, Jl 2,27:2
Smithers, Edward W, 1939, Ja 30,14:1
Smithers, Ernest L, 1940, Je 6,25:5
Smithers, Francis S, 1919, N 30,22:3
Smithers, Francis S Mrs, 1952, Ja 27,76:4
Smithers, Francis Sydney Rev, 1925, O 21,23:3
Smithers, Henry L, 1966, S 26,41:1
Smithers, John F, 1961, S 5,35:4
Smithers, John P (funl), 1912, O 14,15:5
Smithers, William W, 1947, Mr 21,22:2
Smithies, Frank Dr, 1937, F 10,23:6
Smithies, Frank Mrs, 1967, Ja 20,43:3
Smithies, John T, 1968, Ja 18,39:1
Smithline, Morris Mrs, 1942, N 15,59:3
Smithman, Frederick E, 1946, Ap 2,27:4
Smithman, Frederick Mrs, 1948, D 28,21:3
Smithson, Frank Mrs (Phoebe Coyne), 1942, Ap 9, 19:4
Smithson, George M, 1946, N 1,23:5
Smithson, Harry P Mrs, 1948, F 4,23:2
Smithson, O W, 1941, O 14,23:5
Smithton, Harry L, 1951, Ag 6,21:5
Smithy, Horace G, 1948, O 29,25:1
Smitke, T Stephen, 1955, Je 13,23:4
Smitley, Robert L, 1964, S 24,41:5
Smitley, Robert Mrs, 1949, Ap 12,29:5
Smits, Bastian Mrs, 1953, O 6,29:5
Smits, Jeanette Mrs, 1957, D 29,49:1
Smits, Lawrence A V, 1966, Ag 30,41:2
Smits, R E, 1949, S 14,31:3
Smits, Theodore A, 1964, Ja 16,26:1
Smitter, Wessel, 1951, N 9,27:4
Smock, Grant H, 1948, Jl 3,15:3
Smock, Harry Mrs, 1955, My 2,21:4
Smock, Harry W, 1941, Ag 6,17:3
Smock, Harry W Jr, 1952, F 20,29:4
Smock, Harry W Jr Mrs, 1948, N 29,23:4
Smock, Martin Van B, 1962, S 11,33:2
Smock, Ray F, 1951, N 22,32:3
Smock, William E, 1961, Jl 4,19:2
Smodlaka, Josip, 1956, Je 2,20:1
Smoira, Moshe, 1961, O 9,35:4
Smoke, Albert, 1944, D 22,17:2
Smoke, Fred, 1963, O 19,25:5
Smoker, Amos D, 1951, Je 22,25:4
Smolak, George, 1959, Ap 15,33:5
Smolczynski, Karol M, 1954, Jl 21,27:5
Smolen, John S, 1957, D 30,23:5
Smolen, Samuel M, 1951, Ap 26,32:3
Smolens, Joseph B, 1968, My 15,47:4
Smolenski, John, 1953, Je 1,23:3
Smolenski, John Mrs, 1961, S 17,86:3
Smolensky, Joseph, 1925, Ja 30,17:4
Smoler, Boris Mrs, 1949, O 17,23:2
Smoler, Maurice A, 1966, Ap 27,47:4
Smoley, Constantine K, 1952, O 22,27:1
Smoley, Seymour, 1964, Ja 11,23:5
Smolian, Charles, 1962, Jl 28,19:4
Smolianinoff, Andre V, 1955, Mr 14,23:3
Smolianinoff, Vladimir N, 1942, Ag 9,43:4
Smolik, Anthony, 1944, Jl 22,15:4
Smolka, Robert, 1966, Ja 31,39:3
Smoller, Phineas, 1952, D 14,90:4
Smolowe, Louis, 1962, Ap 22,80:8
Smoluchowski, Marjan Mrs, 1959, My 7,33:1
Smoot, Albert M, 1941, Ap 20,43:1
Smoot, B R, 1946, D 17,31:4
Smoot, Gerald W C Mrs, 1938, F 6,II,8:3
Smoot, James S, 1941, Ap 12,15:3
Smoot, Joseph M, 1955, F 16,29:2
Smoot, Lalla P Mrs, 1940, S 1,21:2
Smoot, Perry M, 1960, Ja 4,29:2
Smoot, Reed (por), 1941, F 10,17:1
Smoot, Thomas A Rev, 1937, Ag 30,21:6
Smothers, Isaac A, 1939, O 17,25:4
Smott, John M, 1941, N 29,17:4
Smoyer, Henry, 1943, F 20,13:3
Smucker, Jerome M, 1948, Mr 22,23:3
Smukler, Abram, 1952, Je 13,23:3
Smukler, Maximilian E, 1940, Ap 24,23:1
Smukler, Moe, 1959, Jl 28,27:4
Smulders, Francis Mrs (M C Gay), 1957, S 13,23:2
Smull, J Barstow, 1962, D 5,47:5
Smull, John A, 1879, Jl 11,2:2
Smullen, Edward A, 1959, My 6,39:3
Smullen, Georgiana M, 1962, My 25,33:5
Smullen, William J, 1954, My 3,25:1
Smuller, H W, 1881, O 16,8:6
Smullyan, Benjamin, 1959, Ap 30,31:5
Smullyan, Isidore, 1953, Jl 22,27:5
Smullyan, Isidore Mrs, 1961, Jl 19,29:4
Smullyan, Susan, 1963, My 28,41:6
Smulski, J F, 1928, Mr 19,10:3
Smulyan, Martin Y, 1957, O 23,33:3
Smurl, David, 1940, F 26,15:5
Smurl, Jane L Mrs, 1940, D 2,23:3
Smurthwaite, Henry, 1955, Ag 23,23:4
Smutney, Theodore J, 1955, Mr 23,31:1
Smutny, Rudolf Mrs, 1968, My 15,47:2
Smuts, A M, 1952, Ja 22,29:5
Smuts, Jacob D, 1948, O 12,25:6
Smuts, Jan C, 1950, S 12,1:7
Smuts, Jan C Mrs (funl, Mr 2,25:2), 1954, F 26,19:4
Smuts, John, 1939, Je 12,17:6
Smuts, Tobias Gen, 1916, Ag 13,15:6
Smyer, John J Mrs, 1953, Jl 21,23:2
Smyers, Bert H Sr, 1953, Je 19,21:1
Smykal, Richard, 1958, Ap 5,15:2
Smykowski, Bronislaw D Dr, 1953, F 6,20:4
Smylie, Adolphe E, 1937, Ja 8,19:3
Smylie, Arthur Elmore Dr, 1917, F 6,9:3

Smylie, Russell A, 1959, Ag 21,21:4
Smyllie, R Marie, 1954, S 12,84:8
Smyth, Albert H Prof, 1907, My 5,9:6
Smyth, Bernard T J, 1959, Je 13,21:5
Smyth, Bill, 1966, N 7,47:4
Smyth, Callender, 1948, O 16,15:3
Smyth, Casimir, 1944, Ja 24,17:2
Smyth, Charles H Jr Dr, 1937, Ap 5,20:1
Smyth, Clifford (por), 1943, D 2,27:1
Smyth, Clifford Mrs, 1967, Ap 20,43:2
Smyth, Constantine J, 1924, Ap 16,23:5
Smyth, Cornelius J, 1950, D 6,33:1
Smyth, David J, 1954, D 6,27:4
Smyth, David J Mrs, 1939, Ag 22,19:6
Smyth, David W, 1949, S 6,27:1
Smyth, David W Mrs (est tax appr), 1958, Ag 5,29:3
Smyth, Delos D, 1950, Mr 25,11:6
Smyth, Douglas, 1909, Ag 1,9:7
Smyth, Egbert C Mrs, 1904, F 5,3:3
Smyth, Ellison A, 1942, Ag 4,19:6
Smyth, Ellison A Jr, 1941, Ag 20,19:4
Smyth, Ethel M (por), 1944, My 10,19:3
Smyth, Francis J, 1965, F 8,25:4
Smyth, Frank J Mrs, 1940, Jl 5,13:3
Smyth, Frederic H, 1960, Ap 18,29:4
Smyth, Frederick H, 1949, Ap 2,15:5
Smyth, G Ogden, 1944, Je 2,15:6
Smyth, George Alexander, 1920, Ag 13,9:5
Smyth, George H, 1942, Mr 14,15:1; 1959, Ag 26,29:4
Smyth, George H Mrs, 1951, F 13,31:3
Smyth, George J, 1917, Ap 19,15:5
Smyth, Glen M, 1947, Je 5,25:1
Smyth, Gordon R Mrs, 1954, Je 12,15:2
Smyth, Harold M, 1956, D 21,23:1
Smyth, Harper G, 1945, Ag 26,43:2
Smyth, Henry F Sr, 1954, O 18,25:1
Smyth, Henry G, 1964, Ap 3,33:4
Smyth, Henry L, 1944, Ap 5,19:7
Smyth, Herbert C (por), 1944, Ja 16,42:1
Smyth, Herbert C Mrs, 1945, F 26,19:4; 1964, Ag 11, 33:5
Smyth, Herbert W, 1937, Jl 17,15:3
Smyth, Hugh J Msgr, 1921, F 5,11:4
Smyth, Hugh P Rev, 1908, Jl 13,7:7
Smyth, Isaac S Jr, 1939, Jl 22,15:1
Smyth, J P A, 1957, N 7,35:4
Smyth, J W Mrs, 1903, Je 17,9:6
Smyth, James, 1940, Mr 27,21:6; 1950, N 4,17:4
Smyth, James A, 1949, Ap 3,76:4
Smyth, James E, 1946, S 6,22:2
Smyth, James P, 1958, S 17,32:6
Smyth, James W, 1950, Ja 30,17:4
Smyth, John C, 1959, Ap 18,23:2
Smyth, John M, 1948, S 11,15:6
Smyth, Joseph P, 1954, N 14,89:2
Smyth, Julian Kennedy Rev, 1921, Ap 6,15:5
Smyth, Lawrence, 1960, N 24,29:1
Smyth, Margaret H, 1958, Ja 1,25:5
Smyth, Marie C, 1955, Je 15,31:1
Smyth, Miriam, 1967, Ag 7,29:3
Smyth, Muir C, 1945, Mr 25,37:2
Smyth, Nathan A, 1956, D 8,19:3
Smyth, Nevill, 1941, Jl 24,17:5
Smyth, Newman Dr, 1925, Ja 7,25:5
Smyth, Newman Mrs, 1939, Ja 8,42:8
Smyth, Osmond N, 1952, Ag 16,5:1
Smyth, P J, 1885, Ja 14,5:5
Smyth, Patrick E Msgr, 1922, O 13,17:6
Smyth, Patrick H, 1947, Ap 10,25:2
Smyth, Patrick J, 1949, Jl 9,13:4
Smyth, Peter F, 1951, O 19,27:4
Smyth, Raphael J, 1939, S 17,49:3
Smyth, Richard H, 1965, Ag 26,33:3
Smyth, Robert I, 1956, Je 17,92:5
Smyth, Robert L, 1960, Ag 25,29:4
Smyth, S Gordon, 1942, Ja 24,15:8
Smyth, Stuart W, 1941, Ap 5,17:2
Smyth, Susie B Mrs, 1952, Je 14,15:2
Smyth, Walter W, 1961, Ag 5,17:4
Smyth, William A, 1919, Ag 13,11:4; 1967, My 26,39:8
Smyth, William G, 1921, S 16,17:4
Smyth, Winfield S, 1940, Je 9,44:2
Smythe, Charles W, 1945, F 1,23:1
Smythe, Edward J, 1955, Ag 17,20:2
Smythe, Francis S, 1949, Je 29,27:4
Smythe, Frederick W, 1938, Ap 16,13:6; 1940, Jl 23, 19:2
Smythe, Frederick W R Mrs, 1950, S 22,31:2
Smythe, George, 1909, Ja 22,7:6
Smythe, J H, 1933, O 27,19:6
Smythe, J Henry, 1956, Ag 16,25:2
Smythe, J Herbert, 1951, O 16,31:4
Smythe, R, 1878, D 5,2:2
Smythe, Raymond F, 1947, F 21,19:1
Smythe, Stewart, 1951, Je 14,27:2
Smythe, William Ellsworth, 1922, O 8,30:4
Smythe, William F Mrs, 1946, Mr 12,25:3
Snackenberg, John C, 1923, N 17,13:4
Snader, Howard B, 1950, N 15,32:2
Snagge, Harold, 1949, Mr 23,27:4
Snape, John, 1941, S 6,15:5
Snare, Frederick, 1946, S 23,23:4
Snare, Frederick Jr, 1942, N 28,13:1
Snavely, Charles C, 1943, D 17,27:4
Snavely, Charles G, 1953, Jl 26,69:1
Snavely, Evelyn L, 1942, Mr 7,17:4
Snavely, Francis B, 1948, My 23,70:1
Snavely, Guy E Mrs, 1948, O 30,15:1; 1963, My 12, 86:2
Snavely, Jerome C, 1937, Je 7,19:3
Snavely, John, 1949, Ag 28,73:1
Snavely, John J, 1952, F 13,29:4
Snavely, Marion E, 1955, D 29,23:2
Snead, Alfred C, 1961, Mr 5,86:4
Snead, B Chandler, 1939, Ja 29,32:8
Snead, Claybourne G, 1957, Ja 6,89:2
Snead, Edgar M, 1950, D 31,43:1
Snead, Harry Valrin, 1924, S 21,29:1
Snead, Herbert S Mrs, 1949, O 3,17:4
Snead, J T Col, 1881, D 18,2:2
Snead, Udolpho, 1921, Ap 21,13:5
Sneath, Anna S C Mrs (will, S 4,18:2), 1937, Ag 31, 23:3
Sneath, William H, 1962, Je 22,25:3
Sneckner, J Leroy, 1940, D 4,27:3
Snedaker, Bradford C, 1941, Ap 28,15:5
Sneddon, David L, 1950, N 6,27:5
Sneddon, J Stuart, 1955, D 16,30:2
Sneddon, James P Mrs, 1949, F 16,25:6
Sneddon, Jean, 1946, Ag 1,23:5
Sneddon, Robert W, 1944, Mr 10,15:5
Snedecor, Eugene T, 1959, Mr 4,31:2
Snedecor, Frank B, 1967, Ja 20,43:4
Snedecor, Fred E, 1952, My 24,19:3
Snedecora, Charles C, 1923, Jl 28,7:6
Snedeker, Alfred M, 1947, Ag 31,37:1
Snedeker, Alfred W, 1949, Jl 1,19:1
Snedeker, Edward S, 1959, Je 4,31:4
Snedeker, Edwin L, 1957, Jl 8,23:1
Snedeker, Henry H, 1938, Ag 6,13:5
Snedeker, J S, 1875, O 2,4:7
Snedeker, John A Mrs, 1943, D 29,17:4
Snedeker, Milton, 1960, O 25,35:4
Snedeker, Milton Mrs, 1965, Jl 2,29:3
Sneden, Albert T, 1940, Mr 12,23:3
Sneden, Arthur D, 1942, Ja 25,41:1
Sneden, George V, 1915, D 25,7:6
Sneden, Melville R, 1939, Ap 1,19:2
Snedes, William S, 1905, Ap 15,11:5
Snediker, George W, 1940, F 3,30:4
Snediker, Isaac, 1905, Ap 18,11:5
Snediker, Morton O, 1951, Jl 21,13:3
Snediker, Walter J, 1956, S 18,35:1
Snee, James Mrs, 1943, D 17,27:1
Snee, Thomas J Rev, 1968, N 21,47:3
Sneeburg, Harvey, 1959, Ap 14,35:5
Sneed, Albert L, 1967, N 27,47:4
Sneed, Beverly L, 1944, N 28,23:6
Sneed, Byard, 1938, Mr 29,21:4
Sneed, Charles W, 1955, D 3,17:4
Sneed, Edward M, 1964, Je 28,56:8
Sneed, William J, 1949, Mr 25,23:3
Snegireff, Leonide S, 1963, S 6,29:1
Snegireff, Sergius, 1947, S 26,23:4
Snegoff, Esther, 1924, D 16,25:4
Sneider, Abram M, 1956, My 20,86:4
Sneider, Charles, 1947, N 4,25:4
Sneider, Charles Mrs, 1958, Jl 22,27:2
Sneider, Leopold J Mrs, 1967, Ap 11,41:4
Sneidesgar, Emijean Mrs, 1951, D 24,1:1
Snelgrove, Herbert C, 1944, Je 24,13:6
Snelham, John S, 1964, Mr 28,19:2
Snelham, John S Mrs, 1968, Je 10,45:3
Snell, Albert M, 1960, F 8,29:1
Snell, Albert S, 1954, D 12,88:3
Snell, Arthur V, 1968, S 7,29:1
Snell, Baron, 1944, Ap 21,19:6
Snell, Bertrand H, 1949, Je 27,27:4
Snell, Bertrand H (trb, F 4,29:2), 1958, F 3,23:1
Snell, Bertrand H Mrs, 1964, S 28,29:1
Snell, Cora, 1950, Mr 18,13:2
Snell, Daniel D, 1941, N 18,25:3
Snell, E L, 1876, S 19,4:7
Snell, Elton R, 1950, Ja 20,25:3
Snell, Eugene L, 1949, Ap 30,13:4
Snell, Fannie C Mrs, 1939, My 11,25:6
Snell, George B, 1956, S 5,27:5
Snell, George W, 1962, My 23,45:3
Snell, George W Mrs, 1962, My 23,45:3
Snell, Henry B, 1943, Ja 18,15:5
Snell, Henry B Mrs, 1946, Ja 21,23:4
Snell, Jacob, 1905, D 23,7:6
Snell, James P, 1946, Mr 15,21:4
Snell, John, 1938, Jl 7,19:4
Snell, Joseph E, 1958, Ja 30,23:1
Snell, Kimball J, 1937, S 25,17:4
Snell, Manning A, 1954, N 19,32:2
Snell, Merwin Arthur Dr, 1921, S 25,22:4
Snell, Raymond F Mrs, 1951, Mr 4,93:1
Snell, Roswell O, 1945, Ja 10,23:3
Snell, T, 1931, My 7,23:5
Snell, Thomas C B, 1937, S 4,15:5
Snell, W H, 1954, Mr 28,88:4
Snell, William J Sr, 1953, F 22,60:4
Snellenberg, Abraham Mrs, 1949, N 1,28:3
Snellenberg, Joseph H, 1950, F 1,29:1
Snellenburg, Abraham, 1950, My 4,27:3
Snellenburg, Harry H, 1953, Jl 10,19:5
Snellenburg, Joseph N, 1941, Ap 28,15:3
Snellenburg, Morton E, 1959, Ja 27,33:1
Snellenburg, Samuel, 1923, Ag 18,9:6
Snellens, Gerald, 1959, My 10,87:2
Snelling, Charles M, 1939, S 20,27:6
Snelling, Harry G, 1938, Je 13,19:2
Snelling, Harry G Mrs, 1950, My 18,29:3
Snelling, John Herbert, 1920, Ja 2,11:2
Snelling, Louis R Jr, 1963, N 17,86:6
Snelling, Percy N, 1949, Ag 11,23:2
Snelling, Walter O, 1965, S 11,27:3
Snelling, William H, 1946, S 28,17:3
Snellings, Milton, 1921, Je 10,13:6
Snepvangers, Rene, 1967, Je 28,45:4
Sneudaira, Harry J, 1919, F 17,13:3
Snevily, Henry M, 1954, Ja 25,19:4
Snevily, Robert S Mrs, 1959, Ag 18,29:4
Snevily, Robert St C, 1966, D 27,32:5
Snibbe, George W, 1925, N 27,17:4
Snider, Benjamin, 1960, Jl 8,21:1
Snider, Charles A, 1944, Ag 27,33:1
Snider, Clarence A, 1955, S 6,25:2
Snider, Denton J Dr, 1925, N 26,23:5
Snider, Frank T, 1940, My 15,25:2
Snider, Guy E, 1940, Ja 11,23:5
Snider, Henry B, 1941, O 12,52:1
Snider, Joseph L, 1955, Mr 6,88:7
Snider, Leon, 1960, S 7,42:1
Snider, Lora O, 1950, S 13,27:1
Snider, Marguerite, 1955, Je 25,15:2
Snider, Ward Mrs, 1955, D 27,23:1
Snider, William P, 1961, Ap 9,86:5
Snider, William T, 1955, Ap 17,87:1
Sniff, William W, 1941, S 19,23:2
Sniffen, Charles J, 1918, Ja 6,18:5
Sniffen, Charles P, 1958, Mr 6,27:4
Sniffen, Culver C Mrs, 1907, D 29,9:4
Sniffen, D Austin, 1950, F 2,27:4
Sniffen, D Austin Mrs, 1945, My 16,19:2
Sniffen, Ellen R Mrs, 1939, O 20,23:2
Sniffen, Elmer, 1956, Jl 26,25:3
Sniffen, Eugene, 1938, Ja 17,19:3
Sniffen, Frank L Mrs, 1957, Ap 22,25:5
Sniffen, Grover C, 1942, S 17,25:2
Sniffen, Henry O, 1941, Ag 25,15:6
Sniffen, Irving C, 1945, D 24,15:2
Sniffen, John, 1942, Ap 3,21:3
Sniffen, Robert D Mrs, 1938, N 7,19:5
Sniffen, Robert D P, 1949, Ap 5,30:3
Sniffen, Thomas E, 1956, Je 6,33:5
Sniffen, William L, 1966, Ja 13,25:5
Sniffin, Elisha, 1953, Ap 17,25:6
Sniffin, Matthew K, 1942, Jl 28,17:2
Snigg, John P, 1952, D 18,29:3
Snijders, Cornelis J, 1939, My 27,15:5
Snipes, Roscoe, 1958, Je 10,33:1
Snite, Albert P, 1960, D 7,44:6
Snite, Fred B Jr (funl, N 18,33:3; will, N 25,17:1), 1954, N 13,20:6
Snitkin, L A, 1929, Ja 20,29:3
Snitzer, Emma, 1947, Ap 26,13:4
Snitzler, Fred A, 1952, Je 5,31:3
Snitzler, John L, 1950, Jl 16,69:1
Snively, Alfred D, 1954, N 24,23:3
Snively, C E, 1937, S 22,27:2
Snively, Mansfield B, 1951, Je 11,25:2
Snively, Richard K, 1965, N 12,48:1
Snively, Richard K Mrs, 1965, Jl 6,33:2
Snivley, Summerfield Rev, 1914, F 9,7:5
Snoddy, James, 1963, Jl 7,52:5
Snoddy, Leland B, 1950, N 13,28:2
Snodgrass, David E, 1963, Jl 12,25:2
Snodgrass, George, 1951, N 15,29:3
Snodgrass, George M, 1939, Ja 14,17:6
Snodgrass, J H Mrs, 1909, Mr 27,9:4
Snodgrass, James C, 1960, Je 4,23:4
Snodgrass, John H, 1943, D 19,48:8
Snook, Curtis P, 1947, D 24,21:4
Snook, H Clyde, 1942, S 24,27:1
Snook, John, 1946, F 23,13:3
Snook, Samuel B, 1915, Mr 15,11:5
Snook, Thomas E, 1953, Ag 15,15:4
Snooks, E H, 1882, N 18,2:2
Snopeck, Walter Mrs, 1954, My 10,9:4
Snouder, Arthur H, 1956, Ag 22,29:3
Snouder, Imogene C Mrs, 1942, Jl 31,15:5
Snover, Frederick W, 1942, F 25,19:4
Snover, James B Mrs, 1948, Mr 23,25:4
Snow, A Chester, 1942, N 11,25:2
Snow, A J Russell, 1937, O 22,23:1
Snow, Albert W, 1939, Ja 7,15:3
Snow, Alpheus Henry, 1920, Ag 20,9:6
Snow, Anna B Mrs, 1932, Ag 6,11:3
Snow, Archie H, 1941, Ap 8,26:3
Snow, Arthur L, 1943, My 24,15:6
Snow, B S, 1903, Je 5,9:6
Snow, Benjamin B, 1948, Ag 15,60:4
Snow, Bernard W, 1941, Ag 3,35:2
Snow, C Preston, 1958, S 30,31:4
Snow, Carmel, 1961, My 9,39:2
Snow, Charles, 1960, Je 7,35:3

Snow, Charles H, 1957, O 30,29:5
Snow, Charles L Mrs, 1967, Ag 13,80:6
Snow, Charles T, 1945, Ja 11,23:2
Snow, Chauncey D, 1964, S 5,19:5
Snow, Christine Mrs, 1949, Ap 13,29:2
Snow, Clarence E, 1952, Jl 10,31:3
Snow, Donald H, 1957, Je 13,31:2
Snow, E G 3d, 1926, Je 3,1:2
Snow, Eben H, 1945, Ap 4,21:2
Snow, Edgar D, 1945, Je 19,19:4
Snow, Edith H, 1960, Mr 31,33:2
Snow, Edward J, 1959, Ap 4,19:4
Snow, Edward N, 1966, My 3,47:1
Snow, Edward Taylor, 1913, S 28,IV,7:5
Snow, Elbridge G, 1941, D 30,19:3
Snow, Elbridge Gerry (funl, N 12,25:4), 1925, N 9, 19:5
Snow, Elbridge Gerry Mrs, 1920, O 28,15:5
Snow, Elliott, 1939, N 28,25:5
Snow, Elmer H, 1952, Je 13,23:5
Snow, F Herbert, 1942, O 30,19:5
Snow, Frances M Mrs, 1941, F 18,23:4
Snow, Frances U Mrs, 1939, Ja 1,25:2
Snow, Francis, 1949, F 8,25:3
Snow, Franklin A, 1942, Mr 21,17:2
Snow, Franklin C, 1945, Mr 3,13:5
Snow, Frederick B, 1954, D 12,88:4
Snow, Frederick W, 1940, Ja 31,19:5
Snow, George M, 1866, S 28,4:7; 1937, F 23,28:1
Snow, George T, 1952, O 14,34:3
Snow, George W, 1903, O 1,6:4
Snow, Harold E, 1942, D 21,25:7
Snow, Harold R, 1957, Ag 1,25:4
Snow, Harry G, 1913, Ja 14,17:5
Snow, Howard V, 1937, Ap 16,24:1
Snow, Jane Elliott Mrs, 1922, Ag 24,15:5
Snow, Jane P Mrs, 1947, Je 8,60:1
Snow, Jesse B, 1947, Je 18,25:1
Snow, John E, 1958, Ap 20,85:1
Snow, John F, 1956, Jl 14,15:7
Snow, John I, 1948, Mr 8,23:1
Snow, Lehella M, 1945, Ap 29,38:1
Snow, Leslie P Mrs, 1948, S 1,48:4
Snow, Leslie W, 1958, Ag 17,86:8
Snow, Levi T, 1949, Je 22,31:2
Snow, Lillian M, 1946, My 15,21:4
Snow, Lorenzo, 1901, O 11,9:3
Snow, Lorenzo L, 1954, My 8,17:3
Snow, Marshall S, 1916, My 29,11:4
Snow, Mary L, 1947, Jl 12,13:4
Snow, Mary P Mrs, 1937, S 17,25:2
Snow, Mason, 1954, D 22,23:4
Snow, Morton, 1956, Ja 7,17:5
Snow, Morton M Mrs, 1954, Je 10,31:1
Snow, Neely Mrs, 1958, F 18,27:4
Snow, Nora E, 1943, Ja 9,13:2
Snow, Philip C, 1946, Ja 28,19:4
Snow, Ralph H, 1952, O 16,29:1
Snow, Robert, 1913, Jl 11,9:5
Snow, Robert A, 1944, Jl 23,36:1
Snow, Robert O, 1948, N 25,31:3
Snow, Roger V Sr, 1953, Ap 2,27:5
Snow, Samuel 2d, 1942, Ja 9,21:5
Snow, Shirley R Sr, 1944, Mr 9,17:2
Snow, Sidney A, 1959, Ag 28,23:2
Snow, Sydney, 1958, N 25,33:1
Snow, Sydney B, 1944, Ap 8,13:4
Snow, Sydney B Mrs, 1949, F 9,28:3
Snow, Thad, 1955, Ja 17,23:3
Snow, Warren H Mrs, 1948, S 26,76:6
Snow, Warren H Sr, 1963, My 8,39:4
Snow, William, 1951, N 17,17:6
Snow, William A, 1940, S 27,23:6
Snow, William B, 1949, Ja 1,11:8
Snow, William D, 1910, F 12,9:5
Snow, William E, 1941, N 25,25:6
Snow, William F, 1950, Je 13,27:4
Snow, William F Mrs, 1962, S 30,86:7
Snow, William G, 1945, O 12,23:3
Snow, William H, 1944, Ag 10,17:6
Snow, William J, 1947, Mr 1,15:4
Snow, William P, 1957, Ja 26,19:3
Snow, William W, 1943, Ja 6,25:4
Snowball, Jabez Bunting, 1907, F 25,9:5
Snowball, James W Dr, 1919, My 15,17:6
Snowber, Michael F, 1964, N 27,36:4
Snowden, A Louden Col, 1912, S 7,11:6
Snowden, Alex O Dr, 1937, S 21,25:2
Snowden, Arthur K, 1955, F 11,23:2
Snowden, C A Col, 1922, Ja 5,15:4
Snowden, Charles Randolph, 1913, F 3,11:5
Snowden, Frederick A, 1945, Ja 7,38:1
Snowden, George G Mrs, 1943, My 28,21:5
Snowden, Harold W Sr Mrs (E Evans), 1962, O 13, 25:2
Snowden, Harry, 1940, Ap 8,19:5
Snowden, Harry Mrs, 1956, Ja 31,29:4
Snowden, J R, 1878, Mr 23,1:5
Snowden, Joanna Mrs, 1941, O 2,25:1
Snowden, Louis W Mrs, 1961, N 22,33:1
Snowden, R Brinkley, 1942, O 13,23:5
Snowden, Robert B Col, 1909, O 8,9:3
Snowden, Sarah W, 1952, My 29,27:1
Snowden, Thomas Mrs, 1909, Mr 30,9:6
Snowden, Viscountess, 1951, F 24,13:6
Snowden, William, 1944, My 4,19:6
Snowden of Ickornshaw, Viscount, 1937, My 16,1:2
Snowdon, Charles L, 1937, F 22,17:4
Snowdon, Howard J, 1960, Jl 2,17:2
Snowdon, Walter A, 1943, S 16,21:2
Snure, Dale, 1961, My 26,33:3
Snydacker, Arthur G, 1954, Je 11,23:3
Snydacker, Joseph G, 1920, O 14,13:2
Snydecker, Isaac E, 1942, Ap 14,21:5
Snyder, A Cecil, 1959, Je 30,31:2
Snyder, A Thomas, 1951, Je 9,19:5
Snyder, Albert B, 1954, D 5,88:1
Snyder, Albert F, 1948, Ag 17,21:5
Snyder, Alexander C, 1924, Ja 1,23:2
Snyder, Alexander Mrs, 1944, Jl 1,15:5
Snyder, Alfred D, 1948, Ap 8,25:3
Snyder, Alice D, 1943, F 18,23:3
Snyder, Anthony, 1950, Jl 4,17:5
Snyder, Arnold F, 1967, Je 5,43:2
Snyder, Arrietta, 1952, D 31,15:1
Snyder, Arthur, 1964, S 30,43:4
Snyder, Baird, 1946, My 20,23:5
Snyder, Benjamin F, 1942, D 15,28:2
Snyder, Benton L, 1942, F 27,18:3
Snyder, Bert M Lt-Com, 1920, F 10,9:1
Snyder, Burwell C (Sept 24), 1965, O 11,61:5
Snyder, C Joseph Mrs, 1953, Jl 16,21:4
Snyder, Carl (por), 1946, F 17,44:1
Snyder, Carl M (por), 1943, Ag 15,39:1
Snyder, Charles, 1938, S 8,24:2; 1951, F 3,15:2
Snyder, Charles E, 1941, Ap 20,42:6; 1950, My 22,21:2
Snyder, Charles F, 1949, N 29,29:2; 1952, Mr 5,29:2
Snyder, Charles O, 1940, D 24,8:5
Snyder, Charles P, 1964, D 6,88:4
Snyder, Charles R, 1946, N 28,27:4
Snyder, Charles S, 1938, My 15,II,7:2
Snyder, Charles T, 1964, F 28,29:3
Snyder, Charles W, 1952, N 30,86:4
Snyder, Chauncey E, 1946, F 20,25:6
Snyder, Chester, 1946, S 19,31:3
Snyder, Christopher H, 1955, Jl 11,23:3
Snyder, Clarence, 1938, N 25,23:4
Snyder, Clarence T Mrs, 1945, Ap 30,19:1
Snyder, Clarence W, 1948, D 13,23:2
Snyder, Clayton A Maj, 1924, Ja 23,17:4
Snyder, Clifford E, 1967, F 11,29:4
Snyder, Daniel F, 1944, O 27,23:4
Snyder, Daniel J, 1949, Je 5,92:3
Snyder, Donald F, 1949, My 14,13:3
Snyder, Edgar A, 1959, Ja 20,35:5
Snyder, Edith (will), 1939, Ag 31,14:1
Snyder, Edward C, 1948, Jl 26,17:2
Snyder, Edward E, 1953, O 9,27:1
Snyder, Edward G Mrs, 1952, Mr 17,21:3
Snyder, Edward H (por), 1944, Jl 2,20:1
Snyder, Edward Lawton, 1913, F 22,11:4
Snyder, Edward M, 1951, N 5,31:3
Snyder, Edward P, 1961, Ap 20,33:3
Snyder, Edward R, 1959, D 14,31:3
Snyder, Eldredge, 1967, Mr 28,39:2
Snyder, Electa P, 1955, D 26,19:4
Snyder, Ellen Mrs, 1948, F 21,13:1
Snyder, Ellen S T Mrs, 1942, Je 12,21:5
Snyder, Frank, 1946, N 22,23:3
Snyder, Frank C, 1947, N 2,72:5
Snyder, Frank J, 1962, Ja 6,19:4
Snyder, Frank L, 1946, Mr 13,29:6
Snyder, Frank M, 1939, Mr 6,15:4; 1942, Je 24,19:2
Snyder, Frank S, 1950, Ag 12,13:4
Snyder, Franklyn B, 1958, My 12,29:2
Snyder, Freas, 1962, Ap 17,35:2
Snyder, Fred B, 1951, F 15,31:4
Snyder, Frederic A, 1954, O 21,27:3
Snyder, Frederic S, 1956, Je 14,33:4
Snyder, Frederick L, 1944, O 6,23:1
Snyder, Gene, 1953, Ap 17,25:4
Snyder, George, 1960, Mr 26,21:6
Snyder, George B, 1903, Jl 10,7:6
Snyder, George D Col, 1921, O 22,13:6
Snyder, George D Jr, 1958, Je 21,19:2
Snyder, George F, 1943, D 25,13:3
Snyder, George P, 1965, Ja 11,45:2
Snyder, George 3d, 1944, Mr 4,13:4
Snyder, Glenn H, 1942, D 13,72:2
Snyder, H J, 1944, O 16,19:6
Snyder, H M Jr, 1903, O 17,9:6
Snyder, Harlan H, 1946, Jl 11,23:4
Snyder, Harold B, 1962, Ja 17,33:3
Snyder, Harold M, 1955, Je 1,33:2
Snyder, Harry L, 1949, Ja 5,26:2
Snyder, Harry M, 1953, Ap 22,29:1
Snyder, Harry P, 1964, Mr 26,35:1; 1966, Je 11,31:3
Snyder, Hartland S, 1962, My 24,35:1
Snyder, Helen, 1953, O 20,29:1
Snyder, Henry B, 1967, Ja 4,26:3
Snyder, Henry Dr, 1923, Jl 28,7:6
Snyder, Henry M, 1958, My 25,86:4
Snyder, Henry Mrs, 1954, O 31,89:3
Snyder, Henry N, 1949, S 19,23:3
Snyder, Henry S, 1941, O 2,25:1
Snyder, Henry S Mrs, 1949, F 20,61:1
Snyder, Herbert O, 1949, D 20,31:3
Snyder, Herbert R, 1945, Ap 15,14:5
Snyder, Homer P (por), 1937, D 31,15:3
Snyder, Horace M, 1962, Ap 6,36:1
Snyder, Howard, 1963, Ap 16,35:4
Snyder, Howard P Mrs, 1964, My 10,83:2
Snyder, Irving, 1955, N 14,27:5
Snyder, J Buell, 1946, F 25,25:3
Snyder, J Charles, 1938, Ja 16,II,9:1
Snyder, J D, 1943, Je 17,21:5
Snyder, J H Mrs, 1952, My 14,28:3
Snyder, J Leroy, 1962, Ag 27,23:2
Snyder, J Ralph, 1960, F 12,27:2
Snyder, James E, 1949, D 7,31:2
Snyder, James G, 1946, Ap 16,25:4
Snyder, James K, 1942, S 22,21:2
Snyder, James L, 1938, N 23,21:1
Snyder, John A, 1938, My 8,II,6:8
Snyder, John A Sr, 1953, Mr 5,27:1
Snyder, John C, 1941, O 1,21:4
Snyder, John H, 1941, Ag 6,17:4
Snyder, John I, 1965, Jl 18,68:7
Snyder, John I Jr Mrs, 1966, Ap 7,39:3
Snyder, John I Mrs, 1964, Je 6,23:3
Snyder, John J, 1946, F 14,25:4
Snyder, John M, 1945, O 10,36:3
Snyder, John M Mrs, 1946, Ja 8,24:2
Snyder, John P Jr Mrs, 1960, Je 1,39:3
Snyder, John Rev, 1914, Ag 13,9:6
Snyder, John T, 1956, O 14,86:2
Snyder, John T Jr, 1965, Ap 25,88:4
Snyder, John T Mrs, 1962, My 5,27:5
Snyder, John W, 1949, Ja 1,11:8; 1950, Ag 9,29:2
Snyder, John W Mrs, 1956, My 21,25:4; 1960, Jl 14, 27:4
Snyder, Joseph C, 1952, F 18,19:3
Snyder, Joseph G, 1951, D 18,31:1
Snyder, Joseph J Mrs (K Harding), 1958, F 3,23:2
Snyder, Joseph L K, 1965, Mr 2,35:2
Snyder, Joseph W, 1948, Jl 17,15:4
Snyder, Julian M, 1961, Ja 7,19:6
Snyder, Leland C, 1947, N 13,28:2
Snyder, Leonard Mrs, 1951, Jl 21,13:3
Snyder, Leroy E, 1944, F 17,19:5
Snyder, Leslie J, 1950, O 27,30:2
Snyder, Lester R, 1950, Ag 18,21:3
Snyder, Livingston A, 1944, S 30,13:3
Snyder, Lloyd H, 1957, N 16,19:2
Snyder, Louis, 1944, Ja 27,19:3
Snyder, M Vernon, 1941, Ja 3,19:1
Snyder, Marshall, 1966, Ap 19,41:1
Snyder, Marty Mrs, 1964, N 12,37:5
Snyder, Mary D, 1949, Ap 24,76:3
Snyder, Meredith P, 1937, Ap 8,23:4
Snyder, Meredith P Mrs, 1937, F 8,17:3
Snyder, Mesier R Mrs, 1949, Mr 22,25:1
Snyder, Michael, 1949, Ja 23,68:6; 1968, S 23,35:5
Snyder, Milton C, 1948, F 8,60:6
Snyder, Milton J, 1904, My 30,6:2
Snyder, Milton V, 1938, Jl 17,27:3
Snyder, Morton, 1964, Ag 3,25:3
Snyder, Nicholas, 1951, N 25,86:5
Snyder, Nicholas H, 1956, D 19,31:3
Snyder, Oscar J, 1947, Je 12,25:2
Snyder, Otto, 1942, N 25,23:4
Snyder, Paul, 1949, Je 18,13:1
Snyder, Paul R, 1952, N 10,25:1
Snyder, Paul W, 1947, Ap 27,60:3
Snyder, Phil J, 1952, My 29,27:1
Snyder, R Garfield, 1944, F 26,13:6
Snyder, R S, 1955, Jl 1,21:5
Snyder, Ray P, 1941, O 17,23:2
Snyder, Reginald C, 1941, O 4,15:3
Snyder, Robert A, 1915, Jl 28,9:6
Snyder, Robert H Mrs, 1950, Mr 25,13:5
Snyder, Samuel J, 1954, Ag 17,21:2
Snyder, Silas W, 1947, Ag 18,17:1
Snyder, Simon Brig-Gen, 1913, Ap 15,11:2
Snyder, Stanley, 1950, Ja 5,26:5
Snyder, Stratton A Mrs, 1945, O 10,36:2
Snyder, Susan W, 1945, S 28,21:4
Snyder, Susie C Mrs, 1938, F 15,25:3
Snyder, Sydney S, 1964, S 2,37:4
Snyder, Ted, 1965, Jl 21,37:4
Snyder, Theodore Mrs, 1956, My 3,31:3
Snyder, Thomas, 1907, F 15,11:4
Snyder, Thomas E, 1941, O 31,23:2
Snyder, Thomas J, 1954, F 27,13:2
Snyder, Thomas K, 1940, F 17,13:1
Snyder, Thomas M, 1948, Mr 27,13:2
Snyder, Valentine P Mrs (will), 1944, Mr 1,15:7
Snyder, Virginia, 1955, Ap 27,31:1
Snyder, W, 1934, Ap 26,23:3
Snyder, W Harry, 1946, Ag 6,25:5
Snyder, W Irving, 1914, Jl 30,9:6
Snyder, W Percival, 1938, S 26,17:1
Snyder, W V, 1910, My 7,9:6
Snyder, Walter, 1944, F 8,15:2
Snyder, Walter C, 1948, Ag 26,22:3
Snyder, Walter M, 1948, S 1,48:4
Snyder, Wellington J Jr, 1940, Je 7,23:2
Snyder, William A Mrs, 1948, Jl 20,23:2
Snyder, William B Mrs, 1948, Jl 27,25:3

Snyder, William C, 1948, F 16,21:3
Snyder, William E, 1966, Ap 3,84:1
Snyder, William F, 1961, Mr 31,27:4
Snyder, William H, 1939, O 21,15:5; 1948, N 14,78:5
Snyder, William H Mrs, 1952, Ap 2,33:2
Snyder, William H Sr, 1953, Ja 12,27:3
Snyder, William Mrs, 1950, Mr 12,92:2
Snyder, William P Jr, 1967, Je 13,47:2
Snyder, William Penn, 1921, F 4,11:3
Snyder, William S, 1952, Mr 19,29:3
Snyder, William T, 1937, O 19,25:2
Snyder, William Taylor Mrs, 1916, Ap 11,13:6
Snyder, Z X Dr, 1915, N 12,11:6
Snygg, Donald, 1967, F 2,35:1
Snyman, W W Gen, 1916, O 27,9:5
Soans, Leonard W, 1961, Mr 19,88:5
Soare, William, 1940, Mr 5,23:4
Soares, Claude, 1940, Ag 20,19:4
Soaysmith, Kenneth Charles, 1917, Mr 29,13:4
Sobanski, Antoni Count, 1941, Ap 22,21:6
Sobel, Aaron Mrs, 1953, Ap 4,13:3
Sobel, Abraham, 1957, O 7,27:4
Sobel, Albert E, 1967, Je 16,43:1
Sobel, Bernard, 1964, Mr 13,33:1
Sobel, George, 1946, D 4,31:2
Sobel, Hattie L Mrs, 1941, Jl 27,31:2
Sobel, Henry, 1966, Mr 21,33:2
Sobel, Herman D, 1958, S 1,13:5
Sobel, Isaac, 1961, N 4,19:2
Sobel, Isador, 1939, O 27,23:3
Sobel, Isidore, 1940, My 4,17:4
Sobel, Jack Mrs, 1954, Mr 12,21:1
Sobel, Jacob, 1942, S 16,23:6; 1954, Jl 26,17:5
Sobel, Joseph, 1960, S 17,23:6; 1964, S 27,85:5
Sobel, L Sylvester Dr, 1937, Ja 30,17:4
Sobel, Leon, 1939, S 24,43:2
Sobel, Louis H (funl; trb), 1955, Ag 17,27:5
Sobel, Louis H Mrs (funl; trb), 1955, Ag 17,27:5
Sobel, Meyer, 1965, D 9,47:2
Sobel, Nathan, 1962, O 7,83:1
Sobel, Nathan Dr, 1962, O 18,39:5
Sobel, Samuel P, 1942, F 14,15:3
Sobel, Simon, 1905, F 14,10:4
Soberances, Pearl (Mrs G S Linn), 1941, F 24,15:3
Sobering, Reint, 1937, S 25,17:4
Soberski, Barend L, 1940, S 10,23:6
Sobieski, J, 1927, N 13,31:2
Soble, Kenneth D, 1966, D 18,84:6
Soble, Morris, 1955, O 11,39:5
Soblen, Robert A Dr, 1962, S 12,1:2
Sobo, Joseph, 1939, S 13,25:2
Sobo, Leslie M, 1952, Je 27,23:5
Sobodnik-Sloden, Michael, 1953, O 14,29:2
Sobol, Alfred, 1955, F 13,86:2
Sobol, Bernard, 1958, Jl 2,29:3
Sobol, Edward, 1962, Mr 12,31:3
Sobol, Louis Mrs, 1948, Ja 20,23:1
Sobolev, Arkady A, 1964, D 3,45:1
Sobolev, Ivan A, 1952, D 1,23:5
Sobon, August S, 1963, S 18,40:1
Sobotka, Hans, 1947, O 31,23:5
Sobotka, Harry H, 1965, D 28,25:1
Sobotka, Ignaz Mrs, 1949, Mr 26,17:6
Sobotka, Ruth, 1967, Je 19,35:2
Sobrinho, Edward E, 1949, Mr 6,72:6
Sobta, John S, 1955, Mr 24,31:1
Socarras, Cayetano, 1947, Ap 1,28:3
Socarras, Regla de Sra, 1960, Mr 4,25:1
Socha, Peter, 1959, Ap 5,86:8
Socin, Jay M, 1968, Je 21,41:3
Socolof, Joseph, 1961, Ag 14,25:5
Socolow, Adolph Mrs, 1968, N 13,47:1
Socolow, Harry J, 1937, Ag 28,15:6
Socolow, Harry J Mrs, 1957, S 4,34:4
Soddy, Frederick, 1956, S 23,85:1
Soden, Alfred, 1943, Ap 14,23:5
Soden, Catherine Mrs, 1942, Je 22,15:4
Soden, Charles E, 1941, D 25,25:1
Soden, Charlotte V Mrs, 1944, Je 13,19:3
Soden, David F, 1960, N 27,86:5
Soden, Harry F, 1958, N 2,89:2
Soden, Jean, 1941, Mr 11,25:7
Soden, John G, 1940, Ap 10,13:6
Soder, Walter, 1918, My 20,11:4
Soderberb, Theodore, 1943, D 11,15:2
Soderberg, Donna J, 1950, My 7,96:5
Soderberg, Fred W, 1939, Ag 20,32:3
Soderland, Arthur A, 1954, S 18,35:4
Soderman, Harry, 1956, Mr 18,88:3
Sodero, Cesare (por), 1947, D 17,29:3
Sodero, Cesare Mrs, 1961, Ap 24,29:3
Sodero, Dominick, 1940, Ja 11,23:5
Soderstam, Julius T, 1942, Ja 12,15:4
Soderstrom, Carl, 1964, F 16,92:6
Sodt, William G, 1955, F 26,15:6
Soeder, Henry, 1949, N 2,27:5
Soehl, Joseph E, 1955, Mr 27,86:6
Soehring, Hans J, 1960, O 11,3:6
Soejono, Pangeran, 1943, Ja 6,27:1
Soemann, John, 1944, S 12,19:5
Soenning, Arthur G, 1941, Ja 5,44:4
Soep, Abraham, 1953, Ap 27,23:6
Soerensen, S P L, 1939, F 13,15:4
Soergel, Edwin W, 1949, Ag 22,21:5
Soergel, Hermann, 1952, D 31,15:5
Soerheide, George W, 1945, Je 7,19:3
Soerlie, A G, 1928, Ag 29,21:5
Soete, Pierre de, 1948, Ag 17,22:3
Soetemon, Winfield S, 1952, Ag 16,15:4
Soetemon, Winfield S Mrs, 1949, Mr 13,76:4
Soffel, Catherine A, 1942, Mr 14,15:3
Soffel, Conrad P, 1937, Je 12,15:5
Soffel, George F, 1966, Ap 6,43:1
Soffer, Henry A, 1951, O 28,85:1
Soffici, Ardengo, 1964, Ag 21,29:4
Sofge, Benjamin H, 1952, D 2,36:5
Sofia, Aurelius, 1949, Ap 6,29:3
Sofia, Peter, 1952, O 23,31:3
Sofia, Theodore C, 1955, Mr 1,25:3
Sofia, Theresa Mrs, 1941, Je 3,21:4
Sofia Pia, Princess of Savoy, 1941, Ja 14,21:3
Sofield, Edward S, 1953, F 22,60:5
Sofield, Frank A, 1962, Ap 28,25:1
Sofield, Franklin D, 1957, D 17,35:2
Sofield, Stephen B, 1947, Mr 31,23:2
Sofield, William W, 1948, Je 2,29:5
Sofman, Archie, 1963, D 24,17:4
Softer, Elizabeth (Mrs E S Mann), 1963, F 12,4:6
Softness, Burt H, 1953, Jl 11,11:5
Sog, Nestor Mrs, 1949, D 30,20:2
Sogard, Vernon R, 1956, Mr 10,17:6
Soheily, Ali, 1958, My 2,27:3
Sohier, William D, 1938, O 16,44:4
Sohl, Frank B, 1958, Ja 25,20:1
Sohl, George, 1940, S 24,23:4
Sohl, Webster L, 1946, S 27,23:2
Sohmer, Bernard, 1958, Mr 27,33:5
Sohmer, Edwin H, 1957, Je 24,16:2
Sohmer, Harry J Mrs, 1954, O 24,88:8
Sohmer, Isador, 1918, Ag 13,9:4
Sohn, George W, 1950, F 1,29:1
Sohn, J, 1935, Mr 17,37:3
Sohn, Monte W, 1955, N 6,86:7
Sohns, John A A, 1951, Ja 10,27:1
Sohon, Harry, 1961, N 26,87:3
Sohon, Michel D, 1945, S 16,44:2
Sohrab, Mirza A, 1958, Ap 22,33:2
Sohst, Helen H, 1965, Je 8,41:2
Soicher, Max, 1954, Je 8,12:6
Soifer, Max E, 1953, Ja 9,21:2
Soifer, Samuel, 1958, D 5,31:2
Soiland, Albert, 1946, My 16,21:5
Soithetman, Mordecai, 1948, F 12,23:4
Sojourner, Truth, 1883, N 27,2:5
Sokal, Saul, 1964, S 8,29:4
Sokalner, Arthur J, 1950, N 15,31:3
Sokerka, John, 1950, N 19,93:1
Sokhey, Lady, 1947, My 31,13:3
Sokol, George, 1950, Ja 13,23:1
Sokol, John A, 1943, D 24,13:3
Sokol, Joseph, 1947, Ap 3,25:4
Sokol, Julius, 1942, Jl 29,17:2
Sokol, Morton Mrs, 1952, Mr 28,24:4
Sokol, N Robert, 1961, Jl 18,29:3
Sokoler, Henry, 1952, Jl 13,60:4
Sokoloff, John, 1955, My 4,29:4
Sokoloff, Michael, 1949, Jl 8,19:5
Sokoloff, Nikolai G (Sept 24), 1965, O 11,61:5
Sokoloff, Nikolai Mrs, 1955, Jl 21,23:1
Sokoloff, Vladimir, 1962, F 16,27:1
Sokolov, Alexei, 1952, N 15,17:3
Sokolov-Skalya, Pavel, 1961, Ag 4,21:1
Sokolove, F Milton, 1960, Ap 23,23:4
Sokolovsky, Vasily D Marshal, 1968, My 11,25:3
Sokolow, Benjamin D, 1966, Jl 30,25:5
Sokolow, N, 1936, My 18,17:3
Sokolowski, Rose Mrs, 1946, Ag 3,15:3
Sokolski, Albert, 1950, S 1,21:4
Sokolski, Irving Mrs, 1964, Mr 15,86:6
Sokolski, Samuel, 1966, Ag 3,37:3
Sokolsky, George E, 1962, D 14,16:7
Sokolsky, Michel, 1946, Mr 30,15:6
Sol, Vincente, 1953, D 30,23:1
Sola, Gerard S, 1946, Ja 4,21:4
Sola, Mendoza de Reo, 1918, Ap 30,13:4
Solak, Annie Mrs, 1920, Ag 10,13:4
Solalinde, A G Prof, 1937, Jl 15,19:2
Solan, Robert F Mrs, 1950, N 25,13:2
Solan, William H, 1938, N 12,15:2
Solandt, Donald Y, 1955, Ap 2,17:2
Solano, Angel A, 1950, Mr 2,27:1
Solano, Armando, 1953, N 4,33:2
Solano, Bro, 1942, Mr 8,42:8
Solar, Israel E, 1966, My 15,88:5
Solar, Severao S, 1938, Ja 26,23:2
Solari, Arturo, 1951, Je 20,27:4
Solari, Joseph, 1966, My 3,47:1
Solari, Luigi, 1937, D 4,17:5
Solari, Robert J, 1965, Mr 25,37:4
Solari, Tomas J, 1954, My 14,23:3
Solberg, Thor, 1967, F 28,34:2
Solberg, Thorvald, 1949, Jl 16,13:1
Solbert, Oscar N, 1958, Ap 17,31:2
Solbrig, Oscar A Mrs, 1954, D 30,17:5
Solchaga, Jose, 1953, S 28,25:5
Sold, Charles M, 1953, N 10,31:3
Soldan, F Louis, 1908, Mr 28,9:4
Soldo, Daniel, 1960, My 25,39:4
Soldwedel, Frederic A, 1958, S 20,19:6
Soleau, Charles J Mrs, 1943, F 11,19:4
Solem, Erik Justice, 1949, Jl 16,13:5
Solenberger, Edwin D, 1964, Mr 19,33:1
Solender, Samuel S, 1960, F 15,27:3
Solensten, Rudolph T, 1952, N 3,27:5
Soler, Emanuele, 1940, Ja 26,17:5
Soler, Paul, 1945, O 18,23:2
Soler, Urbici, 1953, Ja 17,15:1
Soler y Guardilla, Pablo, 1941, N 10,17:5
Soleri, Marcello, 1945, Jl 24,23:4
Soles, T F Mrs, 1940, D 6,27:3
Soles, Wesley D, 1944, Ja 28,17:1
Solether, Pliny L, 1952, Ja 4,23:4
Soley, Anna L Mrs, 1937, F 8,17:5
Soley, James Russell, 1911, S 12,11:5
Soley, Paul, 1951, N 20,31:1
Solf, W, 1936, F 7,19:3
Solganick, Esther, 1954, O 14,29:1
Solh, Samies, 1968, N 7,47:4
Solick, Alexander, 1946, N 22,23:2
Soliday, Joseph H, 1947, D 18,29:6
Solimando, Frederick, 1952, My 5,23:5
Solimene, Joseph, 1962, Mr 22,35:5
Solin, Jack, 1940, Ap 21,43:2
Solinger, Nathan, 1957, My 10,27:2
Solinger, Walter B, 1957, S 11,33:2
Solis, Isaac N, 1909, F 14,11:3
Solis-Cohen, J, 1927, D 23,19:5
Solis-Cohen, Leon, 1965, My 8,31:4
Solis-Cohen, Leon M, 1944, Je 10,15:2
Solis-Cohen, Myer, 1960, Ja 9,21:4
Solis-Cohen, Solomon, 1948, Jl 13,27:3
Soll, Louis, 1942, N 23,23:2
Sollar, Max, 1950, D 9,15:5
Solleder, George J Sr, 1953, F 19,23:2
Sollenberg, John B, 1967, Ag 30,43:4
Sollenberger, George A, 1937, Ap 6,23:5
Soller, Jack, 1951, Mr 12,25:4
Sollers, Joseph S Mrs, 1951, Ja 29,19:5
Solley, Frank D Dr, 1937, Ap 25,II,9:1
Solley, Fred P, 1950, S 8,31:5
Solley, Frederick W, 1961, S 11,27:3
Solley, John B Jr, 1947, Mr 4,26:3
Solley, Theodore H, 1938, Je 22,23:3
Sollfrey, Clarence Mrs, 1968, Je 5,47:2
Sollier, J F, 1938, Ap 29,21:5
Sollmann, F Wilhelm, 1951, Ja 8,17:3
Sollmann, Torald H, 1965, F 13,21:3
Sollott, Ralph P, 1953, Jl 11,11:6
Solly, David A, 1940, Ja 17,21:5
Solman, Alfred, 1937, N 24,23:4
Solmson, Meyer B, 1938, Ja 17,19:5
Solny, Norman, 1946, F 14,25:3
Solo, David H, 1947, Ag 31,36:8
Solo, Sultan of (Mangkoe Negoro VII), 1944, Jl 2 19:5
Solomon, A Alfred Mrs, 1963, Je 11,37:2
Solomon, Aaron M, 1948, S 10,23:4
Solomon, Abraham, 1957, O 6,84:5
Solomon, Alex Mrs, 1957, D 2,27:4
Solomon, Arthur L Mrs, 1949, Mr 24,27:4
Solomon, Aunt Rosa, 1904, D 21,2:2
Solomon, Charles, 1955, S 16,23:5; 1961, Mr 1,33: 1963, D 10,43:1
Solomon, Chick, 1961, F 11,23:6
Solomon, Cooley L, 1947, My 27,26:2
Solomon, David, 1957, My 31,19:4
Solomon, Edward Philip Sir, 1914, N 22,3:7
Solomon, Elias, 1948, Jl 20,23:4
Solomon, Elizabeth (will), 1938, Ag 4,14:6
Solomon, Felix Mrs, 1950, My 6,15:4
Solomon, Frederick, 1924, S 10,21:4
Solomon, Gabriel R Mrs, 1956, F 17,23:3
Solomon, George, 1940, Ag 26,15:2
Solomon, George J, 1943, My 15,15:1
Solomon, Harold W, 1967, Ja 15,84:5
Solomon, Henry Mrs, 1948, O 2,15:6
Solomon, Hiram, 1950, Ap 11,31:2
Solomon, Ida B Mrs, 1940, S 11,25:5
Solomon, Irving, 1957, Jl 12,21:1; 1965, S 4,21:6
Solomon, Irwin L, 1968, D 21,37:5
Solomon, Isaac, 1943, D 8,23:4
Solomon, Isidore, 1950, Mr 26,96:2
Solomon, Isidore Mrs (Sadie), 1965, Ag 2,29:3
Solomon, Izler Mrs, 1959, D 16,41:3
Solomon, Jack, 1956, Jl 13,19:5; 1963, Jl 19,25:2
Solomon, Jack Mrs, 1943, Ap 7,25:1
Solomon, Jacob, 1959, My 11,27:2; 1965, My 15,
Solomon, Jacob P, 1909, My 27,9:6
Solomon, John A, 1950, O 14,19:1
Solomon, John W, 1961, My 19,31:2
Solomon, Joseph, 1945, Jl 1,19:4
Solomon, Joseph Mrs, 1966, Ja 9,56:4
Solomon, Julius E, 1940, Jl 4,15:5
Solomon, Kalman Rabbi, 1937, O 30,19:4
Solomon, Kenneth, 1954, N 3,29:3
Solomon, Lee, 1957, Ap 25,31:3
Solomon, Leo M Mrs, 1950, F 2,27:3; 1956, F 12
Solomon, Lep, 1957, Ag 17,15:2
Solomon, Lester, 1947, Ap 22,27:1

Solomon, Lester H, 1965, Jl 6,34:1
Solomon, Louis, 1962, Ap 28,25:4
Solomon, Louis H, 1964, F 24,25:3
Solomon, Louis Mrs, 1960, O 16,88:7
Solomon, Mark K, 1942, S 14,15:4
Solomon, Mary E Mrs, 1938, Jl 7,19:3
Solomon, Max, 1952, Ap 12,11:3
Solomon, Meyer, 1953, Ja 1,23:3
Solomon, Meyer C, 1947, F 3,20:3
Solomon, Michael, 1961, Ja 2,25:3
Solomon, Milton A, 1965, My 17,35:3
Solomon, Morris, 1908, Ja 18,9:6; 1958, Mr 3,27:4
Solomon, Morris J (Moish), 1967, Ja 23,43:1
Solomon, Nathan, 1948, D 12,92:3
Solomon, Oscar, 1925, Ap 17,21:4
Solomon, Phil, 1950, My 20,15:5
Solomon, Richard Sir, 1913, N 11,13:6
Solomon, S J, 1927, Jl 28,19:4
Solomon, Samuel, 1924, Je 13,19:6
Solomon, Saul, 1946, F 21,21:5
Solomon, Seymour J, 1962, O 3,41:3
Solomon, Sidney J, 1948, Ja 29,24:2
Solomon, Sigmund, 1948, My 19,27:3
Solomon, Sydney, 1955, My 23,23:1
Solomon, William J, 1947, O 16,27:5; 1955, N 7,29:1
Solomon, Winfield S, 1954, S 14,27:1
Solomonoff, Senia, 1954, S 9,32:2
Solomons, Adolph Simeon (mem, Ap 15,9:2), 1910, Mr 22,11:2
Solomons, Edward, 1963, Ja 29,7:6
Solomons, Henry, 1965, N 8,3:3
Solomons, J R Mrs, 1944, Je 7,19:5
Solomons, Joseph R, 1940, Mr 26,21:3
Solomonson, David T, 1949, F 5,15:3
Solomonson, J K A Wortheim, 1922, S 17,30:2
Solon, Harry, 1958, Ag 7,25:5
Solon, Stanley J, 1957, S 19,29:2
Solonche, Louis H, 1956, F 9,31:1
Solonitsym, Nikolai, 1951, Je 7,33:4
Solorzano Diaz, Ernesto, 1946, O 22,25:4
Solotaire, George, 1965, Ja 25,37:1
Solovay, Hyman U, 1966, My 12,45:3
Solove, Abraham, 1966, Ap 28,43:2
Solove, Rubin, 1966, Je 20,33:1
Soloveichik, Moses Mrs, 1967, Ja 3,34:1
Soloveichik, Samuel, 1967, F 27,29:2
Soloveitchik, Moses, 1941, F 1,18:3
Soloveitchik, Simchah, 1941, N 17,19:2
Solovetzik, Solomon, 1938, O 11,25:2
Soloviev, Alex P, 1954, My 6,33:2
Soloviev, Y N, 1955, N 25,48:1
Solovioff, Nicholas N, 1960, S 10,21:2
Solovitz, Joseph Mrs, 1967, S 15,47:2
Solovitz, Louis, 1954, Ag 16,17:5
Solovitz, Louis Mrs, 1952, N 2,89:2
Solow, Herbert, 1964, N 27,35:2
Solow, Joseph, 1924, O 23,21:4
Solow, Samuel, 1939, Ap 16,III,6:8
Soloway, Herman Mrs, 1965, Ja 19,33:5
Solowey, Sol, 1966, D 17,33:5
Solski, Ludwik, 1954, D 20,29:3
Soltan, Andrzej, 1959, D 12,23:4
Soltanitzky, Joseph, 1953, Ap 9,27:4
Soltanovsky, Boris P, 1954, Ap 26,25:4
Soltau, Amelia, 1944, Ag 20,34:3
Soltau, Samuel, 1945, O 14,42:2
Soltes, Mordecai, 1957, Je 29,17:3
Soltis, Joseph, 1945, Ja 11,23:4
Soltykoff, Prince, 1903, N 22,7:5
Solvay, Ernest, 1922, My 27,13:6
Solway, Maurice, 1960, Je 23,29:2
Solworth, Lee, 1962, Ag 22,34:3
Som, Max L Mrs, 1961, Je 28,35:2
Somach, Alex E, 1951, S 8,17:4
Somach, Irving, 1958, N 29,21:5
Somach, Rebecca Mrs, 1944, D 18,19:3
Soman, Bernard, 1959, N 6,30:2
Sombart, Werner (por), 1941, My 20,23:4
Somdej Phra Wanarat, Patriarch, 1962, Je 18,11:1
Somer, Raymond, 1950, S 11,32:5
Somerervell, Brehon, 1955, F 14,19:1
Somerfield, Benjamin Mrs, 1962, N 9,26:2
Somerford, Fred A, 1965, Mr 2,3:3
Somerindyke, William F, 1954, Ap 27,29:2
Somerndike, John M, 1939, Mr 15,24:2
Somers, A S, 1932, Ja 7,23:1
Somers, Andrew L, 1949, Ap 7,29:1
Somers, Arthur G, 1966, My 22,86:7
Somers, Daniel E C, 1961, N 26,88:6
Somers, Daniel McLean, 1912, Ag 30,9:6
Somers, Debroy, 1952, My 29,27:3
Somers, Edgar L, 1907, Ap 22,9:5
Somers, Edwin R, 1944, Jl 5,17:5
Somers, Elbert M, 1942, F 10,20:3
Somers, Elbert M Mrs, 1943, S 20,21:4
Somers, Eugene, 1951, F 27,28:2
Somers, Frank C, 1961, Jl 21,23:5
Somers, Frank D, 1943, D 30,18:2
Somers, Frank E Mrs, 1962, Ap 5,33:1
Somers, Frank W, 1903, S 5,7:6
Somers, George W, 1941, Ja 26,36:1
Somers, Harold D, 1956, Je 21,31:4
Somers, Harry L, 1950, Jl 14,21:1
Somers, James A, 1939, N 21,23:2
Somers, James M, 1957, Ag 5,21:5
Somers, James T, 1947, Jl 11,15:3
Somers, Joe R Mayor, 1949, Jl 21,26:3
Somers, John A Mrs, 1958, Ap 13,84:2
Somers, John E, 1942, Ag 22,13:5
Somers, John J, 1949, D 17,17:5
Somers, John Mrs, 1946, F 12,27:4
Somers, Joseph R Capt, 1908, F 3,9:4
Somers, Lord (por), 1944, Jl 15,13:2
Somers, Paul J, 1939, N 26,43:1
Somers, Ralph C J, 1961, Ja 4,33:4
Somers, Robert D, 1960, F 12,27:1
Somers, Roy Mrs, 1948, D 12,92:5
Somers, Sutphen M, 1959, Je 24,31:2
Somers, Willard, 1946, Je 3,21:4
Somerset, Bobby (H R S F de V), 1965, Mr 1,13:1
Somerset, Duke of, 1931, My 7,23:1
Somerset, Duke of (E F E Seymour), 1954, Ap 27, 29:3
Somerset, FitzRoy R (Lord Raglan), 1964, S 15,37:1
Somerset, Henry Adelbert Wellington (Duke of Beaufort), 1924, N 28,15:4
Somerset, Henry Lady, 1921, Mr 12,11:6
Somervell, Arthur Sir, 1937, My 3,19:2
Somervell, Brehon B Mrs, 1942, Ja 27,21:3
Somervell of Harrow, Lord (Donald B Somervell), 1960, N 21,29:2
Somerville, A, 1885, Je 20,1:6
Somerville, Albert A, 1959, S 21,31:2
Somerville, Albert A Mrs, 1951, O 14,89:2
Somerville, Colina E M, 1940, Ja 14,43:1
Somerville, Daniel G, 1938, Jl 2,13:5
Somerville, Douglas G, 1960, Ag 11,27:4
Somerville, Frederick H, 1937, Ag 18,19:2
Somerville, Harry P, 1960, O 26,39:5
Somerville, Henderso Middleton, 1915, S 16,11:5
Somerville, Howard, 1952, Jl 5,15:4
Somerville, Ina B Mrs, 1949, N 9,28:2
Somerville, Irwin B, 1944, D 1,24:2
Somerville, James (por), 1949, Mr 21,23:3
Somerville, James A, 1939, Jl 8,15:4
Somerville, James P, 1962, N 21,30:1
Somerville, John F, 1943, S 25,15:5
Somerville, Mary, 1963, S 2,15:3
Somerville, Mary Fairfax Mrs, 1872, D 2,1:3
Somerville, Maxwell Prof, 1904, Mr 7,9:6
Somerville, Milo L, 1967, S 5,43:3
Somerville, Nellie N Mrs, 1952, Jl 30,23:1
Somerville, Randolph, 1958, S 7,87:1
Somerville, Richard V, 1948, Ja 24,15:5
Somerville, William A Sr, 1961, My 11,37:4
Somes, Dana, 1953, My 24,89:3
Somes, Glenn H, 1950, O 15,104:2
Somma, Bonaventura, 1960, O 24,29:2
Somma, Richard E, 1951, Ja 14,84:6
Somma, Rose, 1948, Ja 4,35:1
Sommar, Leo A, 1940, Je 7,23:3
Sommar, Vincent A, 1954, O 16,17:1
Sommaripa, Alexis Mrs, 1964, Mr 15,86:4
Sommaripa, George G, 1964, F 4,33:1
Sommer, Barbara Mrs, 1938, S 6,21:1
Sommer, Carl E, 1965, S 3,27:2
Sommer, Charles Sr, 1954, O 7,23:6
Sommer, Frank, 1942, Ap 2,21:2
Sommer, Frank C, 1952, O 28,31:3
Sommer, Frank C Mrs, 1943, S 1,19:4
Sommer, Frederick, 1948, Ja 6,24:2
Sommer, G J M Mrs, 1903, My 19,16:2
Sommer, Gustav Rev, 1923, My 19,13:6
Sommer, Gustavus F, 1943, N 27,13:5
Sommer, Harry F, 1947, N 17,21:1
Sommer, Henry G, 1952, Ag 31,44:7
Sommer, Henry J Dr, 1937, Jl 12,18:1
Sommer, Henry P, 1945, O 1,19:4
Sommer, Herbert R, 1946, My 2,22:3
Sommer, Herman B, 1948, Ja 24,15:6
Sommer, Isidor, 1963, Je 6,35:3
Sommer, J W E, 1952, O 18,19:4
Sommer, Julius V, 1954, D 7,33:3
Sommer, Karl M, 1953, D 27,60:5
Sommer, Kenneth W, 1951, Je 29,21:3
Sommer, Lena W Mrs, 1938, Ap 23,15:5
Sommer, Louise, 1964, Je 6,23:4
Sommer, Luther A, 1946, Mr 4,23:4
Sommer, Max, 1953, N 20,23:4
Sommer, Reuben E, 1961, O 9,35:1
Sommer, Roger, 1965, Ap 16,29:2
Sommer, Walter M, 1949, Jl 15,19:4
Sommer, William, 1949, Je 22,31:5
Sommer, William F, 1941, Ja 30,21:3
Sommer, William M, 1950, Mr 9,30:5
Sommerer, Harry L, 1956, N 30,24:1
Sommerer, John P, 1964, Mr 17,35:1
Sommerfeld, Arthur H, 1958, N 9,88:2
Sommerfelt, Alfred, 1965, O 13,47:2
Sommerfield, Adolph W, 1957, Je 20,29:2
Sommerfield, Adolph W Mrs, 1941, Mr 3,15:3
Sommerfield, Alvan B, 1966, Je 10,45:2
Sommerfield, Arnold, 1951, Ap 28,5:3
Sommerfield, George H, 1950, Je 6,29:2
Sommerfield, Martin, 1939, Jl 28,17:4
Sommerich, Edwin, 1938, Mr 11,19:5
Sommerich, Otto C, 1968, Ja 12,34:5
Sommers, Benjamin, 1943, F 24.21:1
Sommers, Charles, 1941, Mr 10,9:7
Sommers, Charles E, 1945, Ag 28,19:5
Sommers, Edwin A, 1953, Ag 2,73:1
Sommers, Edwin Mrs, 1940, Mr 26,21:4
Sommers, Frank H, 1957, Ag 20,27:1
Sommers, Harry, 1968, Ap 13,25:5
Sommers, Harry G, 1953, My 16,19:6
Sommers, Henry C, 1919, Mr 25,13:3
Sommers, Jack, 1963, O 11,37:1
Sommers, Martin, 1963, Jl 18,27:3
Sommers, Paul B, 1958, Je 23,23:4
Sommers, Seymour T, 1961, Jl 13,29:4
Sommerstein, Emil, 1957, My 28,34:4
Sommerville, Norman, 1941, Jl 5,11:2
Sommerville, Robert, 1954, Ja 2,12:3
Sommier, Edme, 1945, Jl 18,27:6
Somnes, George, 1956, F 10,22:1
Somogyi, Imre, 1951, S 21,24:3
Somogyi, Stephen F, 1949, Jl 27,23:3
Somoza Debayle, Luis A (funl, Ap 17,37:2), 1967, Ap 14,39:2
Somyak, Arthur J, 1967, My 8,41:1
Somyak, John, 1960, My 10,37:4
Son, Abraham V, 1937, Ap 20,26:1
Sonastine, W Gil, 1955, Ag 16,23:4
Sonberg, Charles E, 1939, Ap 6,25:5
Sonberg, Kenneth T, 1940, Ap 16,23:5
Sondak, Harry, 1957, Jl 11,25:4
Sondergaard, Laurits, 1938, Mr 30,21:1
Sonderling, Jacob, 1964, O 1,35:2
Sonderman, John, 1937, My 23,II,10:6
Sondern, Frederic Jr, 1966, Ag 5,31:4
Sondheim, Herbert, 1966, Ag 2,33:2
Sondheim, Mabel, 1960, S 15,37:1
Sondheim, Phineas, 1943, Jl 24,13:2
Sondheim, Phineas Mrs, 1944, S 22,19:4
Sondheimer, Albert, 1942, Jl 14,19:4
Sone, Arasuke Viscount, 1910, S 14,9:5
Sonen, Robert W Rev, 1968, Je 26,47:5
Sones, A Merlin, 1964, S 3,29:4
Sonfield, Charles, 1967, My 28,61:1
Sonfield, Joseph, 1961, S 22,34:1
Songcrant, Herbert N (Jack Herbert), 1957, Je 12, 35:5
Sonken, Abraham H, 1958, Ap 13,84:2
Sonken, Sidney, 1948, Ag 30,17:3
Sonkin, Jack, 1964, O 16,39:4
Sonkin, Simon, 1965, Ag 31,33:4
Sonn, Albert E, 1968, My 25,35:2
Sonn, Harold A, 1963, D 4,47:4
Sonn, Henry, 1940, Ag 7,19:5
Sonnabend, Abraham M, 1964, F 12,33:2
Sonne, Otto L, 1953, Ap 14,27:2
Sonneborn, Ferdinand, 1953, Je 10,32:2
Sonneborn, Ferdinand Mrs, 1958, N 23,88:7
Sonneborn, John G, 1957, Ja 10,29:4
Sonneborn, Myer, 1912, N 5,13:5
Sonneborn, Siegmund B, 1940, S 20,23:6
Sonneborn, Siegmund B Mrs, 1961, N 19,88:3
Sonnek, Frank, 1943, Mr 11,23:5
Sonnemann, Leopold, 1909, N 1,11:4
Sonnenberg, Gus (por), 1944, S 13,19:2
Sonnenberg, Hudson B (cor, Mr 23,27:3), 1956, Mr 22,47:8
Sonnenberg, John J, 1955, My 15,86:4
Sonnenberg, Louis, 1953, Mr 19,29:2
Sonnenberg, Max Hugo Liebermann von, 1911, S 19, 13:2
Sonnenblick, Harry, 1944, Jl 16,31:2
Sonnenfeld, Walter J, 1964, My 20,43:2
Sonnenreich, Charles Mrs, 1961, Je 10,23:6
Sonnenschein, Harry D, 1950, Je 29,29:6
Sonnenschein, Henry, 1952, Mr 31,19:5
Sonnenschein, Hugo, 1939, D 3,60:5; 1956, S 3,13:6
Sonnenschein, Joseph L, 1965, Je 16,43:1
Sonnenschein, Louis, 1946, Jl 16,23:5
Sonnenschein, Paul, 1968, Je 9,84:8
Sonnenstrahl, Ely N, 1923, My 1,21:3
Sonnenthal, Adolph Ritter von, 1909, Ap 5,7:4
Sonnenthell, Jacob, 1908, O 21,9:5
Sonner, Edwin B, 1966, O 24,39:3
Sonner, Hans, 1946, Ap 16,25:1
Sonner, Joel P Mrs, 1945, My 17,19:4
Sonnhalter, Aaron L, 1948, D 12,93:1
Sonnino, Baron, 1921, Mr 24,17:6
Sonnino, Giorgio Sen, 1921, D 4,22:3
Sonnino, Sidney Baron, 1922, N 24,17:3
Sonntag, Alfred E, 1965, Ap 14,41:3
Sonntag, Alfred Mrs, 1962, Jl 17,25:4
Sonntag, Charles G, 1937, F 21,II,10:3
Sonntag, Willy, 1943, D 15,27:1
Sonquist, Robert G, 1965, Ag 1,77:1
Sonsteby, John J, 1941, Ap 16,23:4
Sontag, George, 1946, D 24,17:2
Sontag, William, 1952, S 12,21:4
Sontum, Ewald, 1946, Je 8,21:2
Sontup, Sholem, 1968, Jl 19,35:4
Sontupe, Louis, 1962, F 26,27:1
Sook, Bentley P, 1958, Jl 9,27:3
Sookne, Morris A, 1940, S 3,17:2
Sooloo Islands, Sultan, 1881, Ap 20,1:4

Soons, Percy E, 1942, Je 25,23:5
Soons, Sydney G, 1959, Jl 21,29:2
Sooy, Raymond R, 1938, D 21,23:1
Sooy, William F, 1947, O 11,17:6
Sooysmith, Charles, 1916, Je 2,11:5
Sooysmith, William Brig-Gen, 1916, Mr 7,11:5
Soper, A W, 1901, D 2,9:5
Soper, Arthur, 1946, F 4,25:4
Soper, Arthur R, 1953, Ag 1,11:4
Soper, Arthur R Mrs, 1946, O 15,25:4
Soper, Caroline J Mrs, 1941, S 16,23:5
Soper, Cornelia T Mrs (June Atherton),(Sereno), 1912, My 29,11:4
Soper, Daniel R, 1949, Je 8,29:4
Soper, Dudley E Mrs, 1951, My 17,31:2
Soper, Edmund D, 1961, O 24,37:5
Soper, Frederick Davey, 1922, Ap 26,19:5
Soper, George A, 1948, Je 18,23:1
Soper, Harry W Sr, 1952, Ag 17,77:2
Soper, Horace W, 1953, S 30,31:5
Soper, Howard K, 1940, Ag 20,19:5
Soper, Leslie B, 1951, S 28,31:3
Soper, Mahlon E, 1937, Mr 28,II,9:1
Soper, Royal R, 1906, N 24,5:2
Soper, Wayne W, 1956, Mr 31,15:3
Soper, Willard B, 1939, O 31,23:4
Soper, Willard P, 1963, Jl 12,25:2
Sophia, Archduchess of Austria, 1872, My 29,1:6
Sophia, Queen of the Netherlands, 1877, Je 4,5:2
Sophian, Lawrence H, 1959, Jl 9,27:2
Sophie, Former Queen of Greece, 1932, Ja 14,21:1
Sophie, Princess of Orleans, 1928, O 12,25:4
Sophn, Franklin E, 1948, Jl 23,19:3
Sophocles, E A, 1883, D 18,5:2
Sophoulis, Lucie, 1946, Ja 22,27:2
Sophoulis, Themistocles Premier, 1949, Je 25,1:2
Soppitt, Rendel K, 1952, Ja 7,19:5
Sorabji, Cornelia, 1954, Jl 9,17:3
Soracco, Frank A, 1959, D 6,86:2
Sorangelo, Michael, 1954, O 27,29:4
Soranno, Saverio, 1966, N 10,47:2
Soranzo, Julio Federico, 1923, Je 28,15:5
Sorapure, Cornelius E, 1965, Ap 20,39:2
Soraya, Ex-Queen of Afghanistan, 1968, Ap 21,80:8
Sorchan, Victor, 1944, Ja 19,19:4
Sorcher, Jerome, 1966, F 24,37:3
Sorden, Hannah, 1947, Mr 28,24:2
Soref, Harry E, 1957, Mr 3,84:6
Soreiano, Felix, 1959, O 23,29:3
Sorel, Albert E, 1938, N 27,49:1
Sorel, Cecile, 1966, S 4,65:1
SoRelle, Boyd R, 1957, D 8,87:4
Sorelle, Rupert P, 1937, D 15,25:6
Sorelle, Vivian, 1951, F 2,24:2
Sorensen, Abel R Mrs (Wendy), 1965, My 26,47:3
Sorensen, Alfred W Mrs, 1951, D 7,27:3
Sorensen, Carl C, 1965, My 8,31:4
Sorensen, Charles E, 1968, Ag 14,43:3
Sorensen, Charles E Mrs, 1959, Mr 5,31:4
Sorensen, Henrik, 1962, F 27,33:4
Sorensen, Henry R, 1951, Je 18,23:4
Sorensen, Henry R Mrs, 1941, Je 21,17:4
Sorensen, Holger, 1948, Ja 12,19:2
Sorensen, Jens H, 1956, Ap 29,17:2
Sorensen, Max H, 1960, O 14,33:2
Sorensen, Niels A, 1944, Mr 9,17:6
Sorensen, Oluf T, 1949, My 6,25:2
Sorensen, Royal W, 1965, O 28,43:3
Sorensen, Samuel P, 1958, My 8,29:4
Sorensen, Sigurd, 1962, Ag 6,25:5
Sorensen, Thor C (por), 1949, Ag 10,22:2
Sorensen, Zeda E, 1938, Ag 22,13:4
Sorenson, Abraham, 1954, Ag 25,27:2
Sorenson, Alfred, 1939, N 2,23:1
Sorenson, Arthur A, 1959, O 4,86:2
Sorenson, Bernhardt, 1941, N 24,17:2
Sorenson, C A, 1947, D 7,76:2
Sorenson, Edward A, 1955, My 10,29:3
Sorenson, Hal T, 1952, O 29,29:5
Sorenson, Harvey L, 1961, S 11,27:6
Sorenson, Sofos M, 1945, Jl 6,11:5
Soresi, Angelo L, 1951, D 12,37:3
Sorey, William Fletcher, 1914, My 24,IV,7:4
Sorfia, Raffaelo, 1941, Je 6,21:3
Sorg, Charles A Jr, 1940, Jl 1,19:5
Sorg, Edmond P, 1947, Jl 1,25:1
Sorg, H Theodore, 1955, D 11,89:1
Sorg, Louis R, 1961, F 25,21:2
Sorg, Paul Arthur, 1913, My 5,9:2
Sorger, Anton F, 1949, Ag 16,23:1
Sorger, Fred J, 1955, D 28,24:7
Sorgie, Charles S, 1948, Ag 22,60:5
Sorhagen, James C, 1960, Ap 16,17:4
Soria, Guido, 1962, Ag 25,22:1
Soriano, Andres, 1964, D 31,19:1
Soriano, Nicola, 1943, D 2,27:3
Sorieri, Antonio A, 1967, Jl 13,37:4
Sorin, Herbert Mrs, 1966, Ag 31,40:5
Sorin, Louis, 1961, D 16,25:5
Sorine, Savely, 1953, N 23,27:5
Sorisi, Charles P, 1949, Jl 31,61:2
Sorisi, Marion C Mrs, 1958, My 15,29:4
Sork, Benjamin, 1957, Jl 6,15:6
Sorkin, Abraham J Mrs, 1957, Je 15,17:5
Sorkin, David, 1956, S 15,17:3
Sorkin, Samson Z, 1967, Ag 7,29:4
Sorley, Lewis S, 1966, Ag 17,39:4
Sorlin, Victor E, 1912, N 21,13:5
Sormani, Joseph S, 1947, Ag 15,17:2
Soroch, Morris, 1960, F 27,19:4
Soroka, Louis, 1962, F 10,23:4
Soroka, Mary O, 1956, Ap 7,19:5
Sorokin, Pitirim A Prof, 1968, F 11,92:5
Sorokin, Vassily, 1945, N 12,21:3
Sorokoff, Hyman, 1954, Ag 29,89:1
Sorolla, Joaquin, 1923, Ag 12,26:4
Soronsen, Christian B, 1945, N 19,21:4
Sorotzkin, Zalman, 1966, Je 28,45:2
Sorrell, Donald W, 1958, Je 26,27:3
Sorrell, John H, 1948, Mr 1,23:5
Sorrells, John H (por), 1948, F 26,23:1
Sorrells, John H Sr Mrs, 1956, O 21,86:3
Sorrells, Walter, 1946, O 17,23:2
Sorrenti, Gennaro (will), 1957, Ja 11,25:7
Sorrentino, Anna di Duchess, 1951, My 20,88:2
Sorrentino, Luigi (Luigi the Tomb), 1961, Ja 31,7:5
Sorrentino, Umberto B, 1959, Mr 29,80:4
Sorrentino, Vincent Mrs, 1949, Mr 13,76:2
Sorrentino, Vincent Rev, 1920, Je 15,11:4
Sorrick, Warde W, 1949, Mr 6,72:5
Sorries, Frederick J Mrs, 1941, F 28,19:2
Sorrin, Isaiah, 1942, Mr 5,23:3
Sors, Ivan, 1950, Mr 17,23:3
Sorsby, William R, 1912, Mr 28,11:4
Sorso, Cardinal, 1878, Mr 31,1:7
Sorter, Alfred, 1959, Ap 1,37:4
Sorter, Frank G, 1937, My 28,21:3
Sortor, William H, 1937, Ag 6,17:2
Sortore, Emerson J, 1945, S 11,23:4
Sortwll, Alvin F, 1946, Jl 18,25:6
Sorvall, Ivan, 1952, N 11,29:2
Sory, Henry W, 1947, S 4,25:4
Sorzano, Joseph L T, 1938, O 4,25:5
Sorzano y Jorrin, Leonardo, 1950, Jl 25,27:2
Sosa, John, 1942, D 24,15:5
Sosa Molina, Humberto, 1960, Ap 12,33:2
Soskin, William, 1952, Mr 25,27:4
Sosman, Merrill C, 1959, Mr 29,80:3
Sosman, Robert B, 1967, N 1,47:3
Sosner, Benjamin, 1949, N 4,31:2
Sosnoff, Leon, 1966, Ja 24,35:3
Sosnowski, Narcissus S, 1941, F 17,15:3
Sosro, Mme, 1958, S 13,19:5
Sossner, Abraham J, 1956, Mr 1,34:4
Sossner, Theodore T, 1967, Ja 11,25:3
Sossnitz, Issac, 1967, N 29,40:7
Sossnitz, Joseph L, 1910, Mr 3,9:5
Sossong, Raymond A, 1940, Jl 1,19:2
Sostman, Emil M (por), 1948, Ja 25,56:3
Sotak, Frank W, 1940, Jl 23,19:3
sotheran, Charles A Mrs, 1919, D 17,17:2
Sothern, E A (funl, Ja 26,1:4), 1881, Ja 22,5:3
Sothern, E A Mrs, 1882, Ja 17,2:6
Sothern, E H, 1933, O 30,1:2
Sothern, Harry, 1957, F 23,17:4
Sothman, Peter W Dr (por), 1937, Je 26,17:5
Sothoron, Allan (por), 1939, Je 19,15:4
Sotis, Gino, 1960, Mr 16,37:4
Soto, Celestina M de Mrs, 1940, Mr 13,23:4
Soto, Jeanne, 1955, Ap 27,20:4
Soto, Luis A, 1953, My 8,25:1
Soto, Maximiliani F, 1957, Mr 13,31:5
Soto, Pedro P, 1948, O 26,31:4
Soto, Roberto, 1960, Jl 19,29:3
Sotogras, Francisco, 1937, My 15,19:3
Sotomayor, Duke of (P Martinez de Irujo y Caro), 1957, S 8,84:7
Sotomayor, Luna Manuel, 1949, O 17,23:3
Sott, Walter, 1949, S 5,17:3
Sotter, George, 1953, My 7,31:3
Sotter, Phil, 1937, Jl 19,15:6
Sottong, Frederick V, 1947, F 20,25:4
Sottong, Lois S Mrs, 1948, Je 6,72:6
Sottong, Peter, 1958, Ap 2,31:5
Soubiran, Robert, 1949, F 6,76:3
Soucek, Apollo, 1955, Jl 23,17:1
Soucek, Apollo Mrs, 1951, N 14,31:3
Soucek, Myrrah, 1939, S 30,17:4
Souchon, Marion, 1954, Ap 3,16:5
Soucy, Cleophas, 1950, Je 23,25:5
Soudarskaya, Raissa Mrs, 1942, Ja 1,25:5
Soudeikine, Serge, 1946, Ag 13,27:1
Souden, Alex G, 1952, F 22,21:5
Souden, O M, 1944, S 30,13:3
Souder, Alfred I, 1939, F 22,21:4
Souder, Edwin M, 1947, Jl 25,17:1
Souder, Harrison (por), 1938, Je 2,23:3
Souder, Harrison Mrs, 1944, Ap 19,23:2
Souder, Harry J, 1956, D 3,29:3
Souder, John D, 1942, S 15,24:2
Souder, Max E, 1960, D 14,35:2
Souders, Martin W, 1964, O 30,37:4
Souers, Casper J, 1942, Mr 4,19:5
Souhami, Allen A, 1941, Mr 5,21:3
Soukop, John C, 1946, O 17,23:4
Soukup, William F, 1953, Je 27,15:6
Soulas, Marie E, 1948, Je 4,23:4
Soulbury, Lady, 1954, F 21,29:2
Soule, Bishop, 1867, Mr 7,1:7
Soule, David, 1966, O 10,41:2
Soule, Edith L, 1948, O 11,23:1
Soule, Edward, 1942, S 8,23:5
Soule, Frank, 1882, Jl 5,2:1
Soule, Frank C, 1942, Mr 15,43:2
Soule, Frank E, 1937, O 30,19:4
Soule, Frank L, 1953, D 29,23:4
Soule, H Percy, 1937, D 25,15:3
Soule, Henri (burial plans, Ja 29,27:1; will, Mr 15,-41:8), 1966, Ja 28,44:1
Soule, James W, 1952, S 29,23:5
Soule, Louis H, 1951, O 9,29:5
Soule, Pierre, 1870, Mr 27,5:3
Soule, Richard H Mrs, 1944, Mr 23,19:1
Soule, Robert H, 1952, Ja 27,76:5
Soule, Rufus A 3d, 1950, Je 15,31:1
Soule, Sherrod, 1951, S 21,23:5
Soule, Thomas P, 1938, Mr 15,23:4
Soule, Winsor 3d, 1954, Jl 2,19:5
Soule Echeverria, Carlos, 1954, Ag 18,31:8
Soulen, Henry J, 1965, O 23,31:5
Soulice, M Gabriel, 1940, Jl 30,19:4
Soulier, Henry P, 1940, S 12,25:5
Soulis, Wilbur T, 1950, O 11,33:3
Soulsby, William Sir, 1937, F 15,17:3
Soupios, Spero V, 1965, F 2,33:3
Sour, Bernard, 1941, My 8,23:3
Sourbier, Charles J Mrs, 1939, Mr 8,21:2
Sourdille, Gabriel P, 1956, Ag 20,21:4
Souren, Y (por), 1949, O 7,27:3
Sourian, Zareh M, 1967, Ap 17,37:1
Sours, Alvin, 1951, F 8,23:8
Sours, Fred C, 1947, Jl 4,13:4
Sousa, J P, 1932, Mr 6,1:3
Sousa, Jane P, 1958, O 30,31:4
Sousa, John P Jr, 1937, My 19,23:5
Sousa, John P Jr Mrs, 1961, N 22,33:1
Sousa, John P Mrs, 1944, Mr 12,38:5
Sousa, Joseph Mrs, 1949, N 27,105:1
Sousa Dias, Anibel de, 1961, Ag 23,33:1
Sousa Horta Ecosta, L M de, 1946, Mr 11,26:3
Sousauva, Joao, 1949, Je 14,31:4
Sousloff, Alexis, 1945, Ap 25,23:3
Soutar, Andrew, 1941, N 25,25:4
Soutar, Richard G Jr, 1964, N 18,47:1
Souter, Alex, 1949, Ja 18,23:1
Souter, Alwin F, 1958, F 25,27:2
Souter, Lex K, 1957, O 17,33:1
Souter, Norman N, 1948, Je 8,25:1
South, Charles M, 1939, My 26,23:4
South, Eddie, 1962, Ap 26,33:3
South, James Sir, 1867, O 25,1:1
South, John G, 1940, My 14,23:5
Southack, Frederick, 1907, N 20,9:6
Southack, J W, 1882, Ja 23,5:4
Southack, John W, 1915, My 11,15:4
Southack, Tilden W, 1955, Ap 11,23:5
Southall, Edward W, 1941, N 14,23:3
Southall, James P C, 1962, Ag 25,19:4
Southall, William B, 1944, Ag 13,35:2
Southall, William Richardson Abbot, 1968, D 24,20:4
Southam, F N, 1946, Mr 19,27:4
Southam, F N Mrs, 1944, F 23,19:4
Southam, Henry S, 1954, Mr 28,87:3
Southam, John D, 1954, N 30,29:3
Southam, Richard, 1937, Ap 26,19:1
Southam, William J, 1957, My 23,33:2
Southam, William W, 1950, Ap 3,23:1
Southam, Wilson M, 1947, Ag 25,17:5
Southam, Wilson M Mrs, 1950, Ag 31,25:3
Southampton, Baron (Chas H Fitzroy), 1958, D 10, 39:3
Southard, Albert W, 1943, Ap 3,15:5
Southard, Charles Zibeon Mrs, 1924, Mr 20,19:5
Southard, Daniel B, 1950, Ag 1,23:3
Southard, Daniel Mrs, 1958, Je 11,35:3
Southard, Elmer Ernest Dr, 1920, F 9,9:3
Southard, George H, 1913, Ja 14,17:5
Southard, H H Mrs, 1903, Ap 12,2:3
Southard, Harry D, 1939, Ap 29,17:6
Southard, Henry F, 1958, D 2,38:1
Southard, J Valentine, 1943, D 18,15:2
Southard, James B Jr, 1955, Ag 15,15:3
Southard, Kittie Mrs, 1938, O 27,23:3
Southard, Mary E, 1946, Mr 30,15:5
Southard, Milton I, 1905, My 5,9:4
Southard, Paul J, 1961, D 4,37:2
Southard, Vera R (Mrs A Petersen), 1964, S 23,47:
Southard, Walter P, 1950, Mr 27,23:2
Southard, William A Mrs, 1955, Je 19,93:2
Southborough, Lord, 1947, Ja 18,15:2
Southe, Paul, 1946, Ag 26,23:6
Southee, Earl R, 1967, N 18,37:3
Southee, George R, 1940, My 11,19:6
Souther, A F Lt, 1918, Jl 20,9:8
Souther, Carl E, 1956, O 27,21:4
Souther, George Sr, 1949, N 11,25:4
Souther, J William, 1925, Ja 13,19:5; 1925, F 25,19:
Souther, John, 1911, S 13,9:5
Southerland, A Francis, 1924, O 14,23:3

Southerland, Darwin B, 1940, Ag 25,35:3
Southerland, Leonard B, 1958, N 16,1:7
Southerland, Leonidas, 1946, S 10,7:5
Southerland, S B Rev Dr, 1907, S 6,9:6
Southerland, W H H, 1933, Ja 31,17:3
Southern, Allen C, 1967, Ja 24,28:7
Southern, Harold C, 1956, Je 24,77:1
Southern, Lee P, 1943, Ap 22,23:5
Southern, Myles F, 1949, Je 2,28:6
Southern, Sam, 1920, Mr 26,13:4
Southern, William N Jr, 1956, F 12,88:6
Southers, Henry C Maj, 1917, Ag 16,11:7
Southers, Nathaniel, 1944, Jl 28,10:1
Southerton, Joseph E, 1940, Je 2,45:2
Southesk, countess of, 1945, D 15,17:3
Southesk, Earl of, 1905, F 22,7:6; 1941, N 11,23:5
Southey, Alan L, 1925, N 14,15:4
Southey, H H W Maj, 1917, My 10,13:4
Southey, Katherine, 1864, Ag 30,2:4
Southey, Wilbur J, 1940, O 14,19:5
Southgate, Herbert J, 1939, D 26,19:3
Southgate, Horatio Mrs, 1909, F 24,9:5
Southgate, J F, 1941, Ag 9,15:4
Southgate, James Haywood, 1916, S 30,11:4
Southgate, Richard H, 1912, Mr 4,11:4
Southgate, Rodney W, 1944, D 1,24:2
Southmayd, H, 1877, F 25,7:1
Southmayd, Henry J, 1959, Mr 31,29:3
Southmayd, Leon N, 1937, Jl 31,15:5
Southward, Robert D, 1955, Mr 16,33:1
Southwell, E P Rev, 1922, My 12,19:5
Southwell, Fred H, 1946, Ag 6,25:2
Southwell, George C, 1954, O 12,27:4
Southwell, Harry J, 1958, Ja 6,39:4
Southwell, Raymond J, 1951, Jl 16,21:4
Southwick, Alfred L, 1949, Mr 10,27:2
Southwick, Charles M, 1903, D 20,7:6
Southwick, Clarence T, 1942, Jl 25,13:3
Southwick, Everett C, 1957, D 31,18:2
Southwick, Frank, 1952, S 14,87:1
Southwick, George N, 1912, O 18,11:4
Southwick, Hanna Mrs, 1903, Ap 24,1:2
Southwick, Horace Claflin, 1925, Ja 5,21:4
Southwick, J A, 1881, Je 1,2:5
Southwick, Odile Hamersley Mrs, 1920, Ag 24,9:3
Southwood, Lady (Mrs J S Elias), 1951, Mr 8,29:5
Southwood, Lord, 1946, Ap 11,25:3
Southworth, Andrew S J, 1953, F 23,25:2
Southworth, Charles A, 1943, Ja 14,21:3
Southworth, Chester Mrs, 1950, D 30,13:4
Southworth, Constant, 1952, Jl 10,31:4; 1955, O 17, 27:4
Southworth, E D E N Mrs, 1899, Jl 1,7:5
Southworth, Edward, 1943, My 19,25:4
Southworth, Edward B, 1940, Ja 19,19:4
Southworth, Edward B Jr, 1949, S 17,17:6
Southworth, Edward F, 1946, N 21,31:5
Southworth, Francis B, 1941, Ag 13,17:6
Southworth, Franklin C, 1944, My 23,23:5
Southworth, Franklin C Mrs, 1948, Ag 26,21:2
Southworth, Frederick A, 1938, My 13,19:3
Southworth, Frederick A Mrs, 1949, Mr 28,21:5
Southworth, George, 1947, Mr 26,25:3
Southworth, George C S Dr, 1918, F 21,11:7
Southworth, George W, 1941, N 17,19:2
Southworth, Irving, 1950, Ap 15,15:6
Southworth, Jack, 1956, O 18,33:2
Southworth, Louis R, 1919, D 1,15:2
Southworth, Melvin D, 1967, Ap 12,47:4
Southworth, Stacy B, 1965, Je 17,33:2
Southworth, Thomas S, 1940, N 15,21:5
Southworth, W S, 1875, S 1,1:6
Southworth, William A, 1911, S 7,9:1
Southworth, William H, 1941, N 16,56:8
Souto, Alcio, 1948, S 6,13:5
Souto, Baldwin V, 1948, D 4,13:4
Souttar, Henry, 1964, N 14,29:5
Soutter, James T, 1949, D 27,23:4
Soutter, James T Mrs, 1942, Ag 27,19:3
Soutter, William H Mrs, 1951, F 23,27:5
Souvaine, Henry, 1954, Ja 31,89:2
Souvaine, Mabel Drouet Hill Mrs, 1968, Jl 7,52:7
Souweine, Arthur J, 1951, D 1,13:3
Souza, Antone J, 1949, Je 16,29:2
Souza, Frederick W Mrs, 1945, O 24,21:2
Souza Bandeira, Luis de, 1963, F 9,8:6
Souza Costa, Arthur de, 1957, Ap 13,19:3
Souza Coutinho, Maria S R de (Countess of Funchal), 1961, My 8,35:6
Souza Dantas, Louis de, 1954, Ap 17,13:1
Sovak, Francis W (por), 1939, O 28,15:3
Sovatkin, Edward J, 1965, My 19,47:3
Sovatkin, Joseph S, 1942, Ap 7,21:3
Sovel, Harry A, 1957, N 17,86:7
Soveral, Marquis de, 1922, O 7,15:6
Sovereign, Otto E, 1954, My 16,87:1
Soverel, Elmer V, 1950, F 7,27:3
Soverel, Herbert F Mrs, 1958, Jl 3,26:1
Soverel, M De Forrest, 1956, My 14,25:4
Soverel, Stanley R, 1965, Ag 31,33:3
Soverel, Stanley R Mrs, 1946, N 19,31:5
Sovey, Raymond, 1966, Je 28,45:2
Soviero, James, 1962, Jl 9,31:1
Soviero, Thomas, 1955, My 19,29:5
Sovinski, Vic, 1960, D 21,31:2
Sowa-Sowinski, Zygmunt, 1954, S 14,27:5
Sowden, Lee, 1947, Jl 30,21:5
Sowder, James, 1955, N 18,16:6
Sowders, William J, 1951, F 5,23:2
Sowdon, Arthur J C, 1911, Je 4,II,11:5
Sowdon, Joseph A, 1956, D 12,39:4
Sowdon, Joseph A Mrs, 1948, S 18,17:4
Sowdon, William K, 1953, D 13,87:1
Sowell, Ashley B, 1945, Jl 11,11:7
Sowell, Ingram C, 1947, D 23,23:1
Sowell, Norman B, 1942, O 4,52:8
Sowerby, Arthur D, 1954, Ag 18,29:5
Sowerby, Leo, 1968, Jl 8,39:2
Sowers, Alva B, 1952, S 1,17:5
Sowers, Aubern D, 1955, N 30,33:4
Sowers, Clinton A, 1952, O 5,88:3
Sowers, Frank, 1967, Je 3,31:5
Sowers, Irvin P Mrs, 1948, O 10,76:4
Sowers, Joseph H, 1941, S 18,25:3
Sowerwine, John W Mrs, 1959, My 11,27:3
Sowles, Melvin, 1951, Ja 6,15:1
Sowles, W L, 1878, My 31,4:6
Sowter, George J, 1942, F 11,21:2
Soybel, Esther W Mrs, 1958, N 12,37:1
Soybel, George W, 1958, N 12,37:1
Soybel, Meyer M, 1967, Jl 19,39:2
Soye, J N, 1882, O 7,5:4
Soyer, Abraham, 1940, Ja 14,42:6
Soyer, Nicholas, 1937, My 16,II,8:6
Soyeshima, Michimasa, 1948, O 15,23:2
Soyez, Philippe C, 1942, F 10,19:1
Soyza, Guanesena de, 1961, O 13,35:2
Sozek, Maximilian Mrs, 1966, Mr 27,86:3
Spaak, Paul-Henri Mrs, 1964, Ag 18,31:2
Spaak, Paul Mrs, 1960, Mr 9,33:2
Spaander, Leendert, 1955, Jl 5,29:1
Space, James A, 1958, S 17,32:4
Space, Z A Rev, 1920, N 13,11:6
Spach, John G Sr, 1957, Mr 3,84:4
Spack, Frank, 1952, O 7,29:4
Spackman, Cyril S, 1963, My 18,27:6
Spackman, G Donald, 1957, Ap 16,33:3
Spackman, H B, 1957, Ag 22,27:3
Spackman, Horace B, 1938, D 12,19:2
Spackman, Mae F Mrs, 1948, Ag 1,59:1
Spackpole, Harrison Mrs, 1937, Jl 29,19:4
Spada, John M, 1950, N 27,25:4
Spadafora, Emil V, 1964, Ja 16,25:1
Spadaro, Francis S, 1955, D 19,27:4
Spadaro, Frank P, 1949, Jl 27,23:4
Spadaro, Joseph, 1952, O 26,88:5
Spadelman, Joseph M S J, 1941, Ap 27,39:2
Spader, Alice M Mrs, 1940, O 17,26:3
Spader, Serena L Mrs, 1907, O 20,9:6
Spadola, Anthony C, 1955, F 2,27:2
Spadone, Alfred A, 1945, F 27,19:1
Spaens, Jan Pieter, 1968, My 27,47:2
Spaeth, Adolph Rev Dr, 1925, My 8,19:4
Spaeth, Dorothea D, 1964, D 25,29:1
Spaeth, Henry Douglas Rev, 1920, F 11,11:4
Spaeth, Herbert A, 1959, Jl 2,25:1
Spaeth, J Belle, 1959, Mr 11,35:2
Spaeth, J Duncan Mrs, 1937, Ap 9,21:5
Spaeth, John D, 1954, Jl 28,23:1
Spaeth, Otto L, 1966, O 9,86:1
Spaeth, Sigmund, 1965, N 13,29:2
Spaeth, Sigmund Mrs, 1965, Ag 1,77:3
Spaeth, Walter M, 1939, Mr 20,17:4
Spaeth, Walter T, 1954, My 12,31:4
Spaeth, William T, 1957, Jl 27,17:5
Spafford, Edward E, 1941, N 14,23:5
Spafford, Edward E Mrs, 1964, D 24,20:2
Spafford, Joseph H, 1945, F 11,40:5
Spafford, Lewis B, 1941, D 16,27:3
Spafford, Milton, 1953, Ap 5,76:4
Spagiari, Stephen B Count, 1915, D 29,11:5
Spagna, Francis D, 1949, D 9,31:1
Spagna, Joseph, 1948, D 14,29:5
Spagna, Vincenzo, 1958, Ag 21,25:4
Spagnoli, Dominic J, 1966, N 30,47:3
Spagnoli, James M, 1962, Mr 19,29:2
Spahn, Curtis B, 1950, F 17,23:2
Spahn, Otto J, 1940, Jl 11,19:3
Spahn, Peter Dr, 1925, S 2,23:5
Spahn, Philip Mrs, 1968, Ap 12,35:4
Spaho, Mehmed, 1939, Je 30,19:7
Spahr, Anna B, 1937, F 17,21:3
Spahr, Clarence S, 1951, Jl 7,13:5
Spahr, Elizabeth B Mrs, 1947, Ap 10,25:1
Spahr, Herman L, 1953, Je 17,27:3
Spaid, William W (por), 1938, My 22,II,7:3
Spaidal, Donald M, 1950, S 19,29:2
Spaide, Rolland L, 1945, F 3,11:6
Spain, Batt T Sr Mrs, 1963, My 16,35:4
Spain, Charles L, 1950, F 24,24:1
Spain, John F, 1955, Mr 3,27:5
Spain, John J Jr, 1947, O 15,27:3
Spain, Purvis A, 1940, Jl 14,31:3
Spain, Will C, 1956, My 13,86:5
Spair, Daniel A, 1956, O 17,35:2
Spala, Vaclav, 1946, My 16,21:2
Spalding, A G, 1915, S 10,11:7
Spalding, Albert, 1953, My 27,31:1
Spalding, Archbishop, 1872, F 8,5:6
Spalding, Arthur C, 1954, Ja 11,25:3
Spalding, Charles, 1885, F 10,8:3
Spalding, Charles F, 1909, O 25,7:5
Spalding, Charles F Mrs, 1949, Jl 14,27:1
Spalding, Charles H, 1950, F 4,15:1
Spalding, Charles Mrs, 1956, O 8,27:2
Spalding, Edward B, 1960, D 27,29:2
Spalding, Ely P, 1948, Mr 25,27:5
Spalding, Ely P Mrs, 1950, Mr 11,15:3
Spalding, F S Bp, 1914, S 26,11:3
Spalding, Frank C, 1949, Jl 26,27:4
Spalding, Fred M, 1944, Ja 27,19:3
Spalding, George A Mrs, 1945, S 19,25:1
Spalding, George B Dr, 1914, Mr 14,11:5
Spalding, George R, 1962, Je 30,19:5
Spalding, Henry, 1938, D 19,23:5
Spalding, J F Bp, 1902, Mr 10,9:6
Spalding, Jack J, 1938, D 9,26:1
Spalding, James A, 1938, F 28,15:4
Spalding, James R, 1872, O 12,7:2
Spalding, John, 1943, Ag 1,39:1
Spalding, John Lancaster Archbishop, 1916, Ag 26,7:5
Spalding, Keith, 1961, Je 26,31:5
Spalding, Leonard A Jr, 1964, N 7,27:2
Spalding, Lewis, 1922, Jl 28,13:4
Spalding, Lyman A 3d, 1949, F 16,25:3
Spalding, Lyman J, 1946, My 16,21:4
Spalding, Mathias Dr, 1865, My 26,4:1
Spalding, Maurice J, 1952, D 18,29:4
Spalding, Melvin P, 1951, D 25,31:2
Spalding, Phil L, 1938, D 5,23:3
Spalding, Phil W, 1956, Mr 7,67:2
Spalding, Robert H, 1904, D 12,9:5
Spalding, Sam S, 1961, N 26,88:7
Spalding, Sam S Mrs, 1956, Jl 31,23:4
Spalding, Samuel A, 1945, My 27,26:1
Spalding, Samuel C, 1962, F 10,23:3
Spalding, Samuel H Dr, 1937, Ag 31,23:4
Spalding, Vaughan C, 1949, Mr 26,17:5
Spalding, Walter R, 1962, F 12,23:2
Spalding, William, 1905, Ja 20,1:6
Spalding, William A, 1941, S 8,15:4
Spalding, William G, 1938, Ap 27,23:2
Spalding, William W, 1945, D 18,27:1
Spalt, George, 1946, O 2,29:5
Spalt, George Jr, 1943, Ja 1,23:3
Spalter, Edward J, 1959, O 8,39:4
Spalter, Maurice, 1967, My 20,35:4
Spamer, Carol O Mrs, 1954, Je 7,23:4
Spamer, Richard, 1938, Ag 25,19:5
Span, Noel, 1964, S 8,29:4
Spang, Charles H, 1919, F 17,13:2
Spang, Henry A, 1943, Je 14,17:4
Spang, Julius, 1951, Ja 2,23:1
Spang, Norman, 1922, D 9,13:4
Spang, William, 1951, Mr 29,27:2
Spang, William L, 1948, Ap 6,23:4
Spangehl, Louis W, 1924, N 13,21:4
Spangenberg, Caroline E Mrs, 1941, Ap 13,38:3
Spangenberg, Roy R, 1964, D 23,27:2
Spangler, Charles A, 1951, Mr 4,93:1
Spangler, Edward W, 1907, Ap 24,9:5
Spangler, Harrison E, 1965, Jl 29,27:4
Spangler, Henry H, 1940, O 25,21:4
Spangler, Henry Wilson Dr, 1912, Mr 19,11:3
Spangler, J Miller, 1952, N 11,29:1
Spangler, J Miller Mrs, 1964, Jl 18,19:5
Spangler, John M, 1945, O 3,19:1; 1954, F 28,92:2
Spangler, Martha Mrs, 1951, N 8,29:5
Spanien, Samuel, 1952, S 10,2:2
Spanier, Muggsy (Francis J Spanier), 1967, F 13,33:2
Spanish Infanta (Maria del Pilar), 1879, Ag 6,1:2
Spanjaardt, Peter, 1937, Ap 8,23:5
Spann, Charles W, 1955, Jl 27,23:3
Spann, Floyd M, 1952, O 16,29:3
Spann, McLain C, 1955, Ap 19,31:1
Spannaus, Fred, 1949, F 10,28:2
Spano, Frank, 1966, D 23,25:2
Spano, Nicola, 1949, S 22,31:3
Spanslack, Sally Mrs, 1948, Ag 8,56:5
Spanuth, August Mrs, 1950, S 29,27:4
Spanutius, Frederick W, 1915, Je 21,9:4
Spar, Samuel, 1968, N 5,44:7
Spara, Frank, 1951, D 4,33:3
Sparacino, Philip, 1962, S 23,86:7
Sparano, Luiz, 1951, S 5,31:1
Spare, Arthur F, 1950, N 26,90:8
Spare, Austin O, 1956, My 16,35:1
Spare, Reuben Y, 1940, My 26,34:2
Sparenberg, Edward J, 1923, Ag 14,15:4
Spargo, Edward C Sr, 1953, Jl 7,27:2
Spargo, Eugene, 1939, F 13,15:3
Spargo, James A Sr, 1947, N 15,17:2
Spargo, John, 1966, Ag 18,35:1
Spargo, John Mrs, 1953, F 19,23:2
Spargo, John R, 1940, O 23,23:3
Spargo, William Mrs, 1957, Je 11,35:2
Spargue, George A, 1963, N 10,86:4
Sparkes, Boyden R, 1954, My 20,31:2
Sparkes, John G, 1942, Ag 21,19:5

Sparking, Georgia A Mrs, 1950, S 22,31:1
Sparkman, Drake H, 1964, Mr 21,25:5
Sparkman, Drake H Mrs, 1948, My 17,19:5
Sparkman, J D, 1876, Je 4,5:2
Sparkman, James D, 1924, Je 11,21:5
Sparkman, James D Mrs, 1966, Ja 14,39:2
Sparkman, Thorne Mrs, 1955, Ja 13,27:1
Sparks, A Benjamin, 1941, Je 20,21:5
Sparks, Adah F Mrs, 1940, Ag 30,19:2
Sparks, Arthur A, 1962, Mr 15,32:1
Sparks, Arthur W, 1919, Ag 6,9:1
Sparks, Ashley, 1964, My 22,35:3
Sparks, Benjamin C, 1946, Ag 15,25:5
Sparks, Catherine V Mrs, 1957, F 6,25:3
Sparks, Charles I, 1937, My 1,19:6
Sparks, Chauncey, 1968, N 7,47:3
Sparks, David R, 1968, Je 8,31:3
Sparks, Earl S, 1959, Ap 13,31:5
Sparks, Edward G, 1937, Jl 15,19:3
Sparks, Edward G Mrs, 1946, O 22,25:2
Sparks, Edwin B, 1939, D 7,27:4
Sparks, Edwin E Dr, 1924, Je 16,15:4
Sparks, Elsie Mrs, 1949, S 16,27:1
Sparks, Fannie J, 1919, Ag 9,9:7
Sparks, Frank C, 1944, D 26,19:4
Sparks, Frank H, 1965, Ja 1,19:4
Sparks, Frank M, 1950, Mr 9,30:4
Sparks, Frederick W, 1943, Je 27,32:8
Sparks, Gar, 1954, S 9,31:5
Sparks, George M, 1958, O 30,31:2
Sparks, Harvey R, 1951, O 28,85:1
Sparks, Jared, 1866, Mr 15,5:4
Sparks, Joe, 1947, Ja 17,24:3
Sparks, John B, 1949, D 24,15:6
Sparks, John G, 1922, My 6,11:6
Sparks, John Gov, 1908, My 23,9:3
Sparks, Joseph A, 1956, Je 28,29:3
Sparks, Laban, 1943, Ja 6,25:4
Sparks, Ned (funl, Ap 7,89:2), 1957, Ap 4,33:5
Sparks, Robert S, 1963, Jl 23,29:2
Sparks, Rupert D, 1961, My 10,45:4
Sparks, Ruth L, 1947, D 25,21:2
Sparks, Sarah H, 1947, Ja 4,15:4
Sparks, T Ashley Mrs, 1958, Mr 29,17:3
Sparks, Thomas A, 1953, N 11,31:3
Sparks, Vernon A, 1946, My 19,40:6
Sparks, Will M, 1950, Ja 8,78:1
Sparks, William, 1943, My 14,19:2
Sparks, William A, 1940, O 11,21:4; 1944, Mr 18,13:3
Sparks, William A Mrs, 1945, O 16,23:5
Sparks, William C, 1951, Je 1,26:1
Sparks, William E, 1957, Ag 10,15:6
Sparling, Earl, 1951, F 16,25:2
Sparling, Edith Mrs, 1944, F 12,13:2
Sparling, Melvin A, 1951, Ap 12,33:3
Sparling, William J, 1949, S 29,29:2
Sparr, B F Dr, 1871, Je 8,2:6
Sparr, David, 1879, S 20,8:2
Sparre, Christian, 1940, D 4,27:1
Sparre, Fin, 1944, O 9,23:4
Sparre, Louis, 1964, O 27,39:2
Sparrow, Allen, 1951, Ja 16,29:1
Sparrow, Charles A, 1944, S 21,19:3
Sparrow, Edward G, 1967, Mr 16,47:4
Sparrow, Edward W Mrs, 1958, Jl 23,27:3
Sparrow, Frederick K, 1943, Ap 10,17:1
Sparrow, James A, 1950, S 8,32:2
Sparrow, John Edward, 1916, O 17,13:5
Sparrow, Ray F, 1961, My 27,23:5
Sparrow, Sol E Capt, 1903, Jl 15,5:2
Sparrow, Stanwood W, 1952, Ag 15,17:3
Sparrow, Thomas, 1937, D 5,II,9:3
Sparrow, W Fred, 1963, Je 14,29:1
Sparrow, William Rev, 1874, Ja 18,4:6
Sparrow, William W K, 1939, N 8,23:2
Sparry, Eugene E, 1945, Ag 4,11:2
Sparti, Aldo Mrs, 1945, Mr 13,23:5
Spasokukotey, Sergeo I, 1943, N 19,19:5
Spat, Gabriel, 1967, My 6,31:4
Spatcher, Thomas, 1954, Mr 31,27:5
Spate, Edward, 1950, My 30,18:3
Spates, Lorenzo S, 1967, Jl 21,31:4
Spates, Lorenzo S Mrs, 1949, My 20,27:2
Spath, George B, 1941, F 27,19:4
Spath, John J, 1954, F 18,31:2
Spatola, Joseph Sr, 1954, Mr 24,27:3
Spatz, Charles R Mrs, 1947, Ja 17,23:4
Spatz, Harold A, 1941, S 20,17:6
Spatz, Irving, 1955, S 21,33:3
Spatz, John P, 1940, Je 30,32:6
Spatz, Max, 1945, D 6,27:4
Spaugh, Lonnie F, 1945, F 2,19:1
Spaulding, Albert C, 1903, S 13,7:5
Spaulding, Alexander, 1876, F 21,1:3
Spaulding, Arthur, 1943, Ap 28,23:2
Spaulding, Charles C, 1952, Ag 2,15:5
Spaulding, Charles C Mrs, 1949, F 5,15:3
Spaulding, Clifford L Mrs, 1956, My 15,31:3
Spaulding, David J, 1948, Ja 26,19:5
Spaulding, Donald G, 1960, O 27,37:2
Spaulding, E Jack, 1953, Ap 3,24:5
Spaulding, Edna C, 1952, Ja 25,21:3
Spaulding, Edward A, 1944, My 2,19:4
Spaulding, Edward G (por), 1940, F 1,21:3
Spaulding, Edward G Mrs, 1954, S 2,21:3
Spaulding, Edwin J, 1959, Mr 12,31:2
Spaulding, Elliott J, 1956, Je 15,25:3
Spaulding, Eugene R, 1966, D 27,32:4
Spaulding, Frank E, 1960, Je 8,39:1
Spaulding, Frederick D, 1908, Ag 3,5:6
Spaulding, Gene Mrs, 1966, Ap 10,76:8
Spaulding, George L, 1921, Je 3,15:4
Spaulding, George R Mrs, 1954, N 20,17:3
Spaulding, H F, 1903, Ag 14,7:6
Spaulding, Harry V, 1954, O 23,15:4
Spaulding, Helim G, 1943, F 25,21:1
Spaulding, Henry A, 1904, F 10,16:3
Spaulding, Henry A Mrs, 1918, Ap 2,13:5
Spaulding, Hollon C Mrs, 1954, D 12,88:8
Spaulding, Howard, 1940, F 24,13:3
Spaulding, Hugh W, 1944, Ap 3,21:5
Spaulding, Huntley N Mrs, 1954, Ag 2,17:5
Spaulding, Jess H Mrs, 1953, Ap 18,19:1
Spaulding, Jesse H, 1951, S 12,31:5
Spaulding, John T, 1948, Ja 25,56:4
Spaulding, Marquis O, 1942, F 11,21:3
Spaulding, Myrtle, 1960, Mr 10,32:1
Spaulding, N W, 1903, O 9,7:4
Spaulding, Nuntley N, 1955, N 15,33:4
Spaulding, Oliver L, 1947, Mr 30,56:2
Spaulding, Oliver Lyman Brig-Gen, 1922, Ag 1,19:4
Spaulding, Randall, 1916, O 25,11:6
Spaulding, Renna Z, 1956, O 14,87:1
Spaulding, Renna Z Mrs, 1953, Ja 23,19:1
Spaulding, Rolland H, 1942, Mr 15,43:3
Spaulding, Roy H Mrs, 1951, Jl 14,13:5
Spaulding, Royal Mrs, 1961, D 17,83:2
Spaulding, Sumner, 1952, Ap 11,23:4
Spaulding, Sumner Mrs, 1955, Ap 16,49:3
Spaulding, Wickliffe J, 1948, S 7,25:4
Spaulding, William Dixon, 1925, Jl 28,13:7
Spaulding, William S, 1937, Ag 16,19:2
Spaulding, William S Mrs, 1950, Ag 18,21:2
Spaunhurst, John F, 1942, Je 12,21:2
Spaur, Teresa Countess, 1873, Je 16,2:2
Spaven, George Mrs, 1941, O 14,24:3
Spawn, Richard P, 1946, F 20,25:2
Spayth, Annis S Mrs, 1957, My 30,19:2
Speaight, Frederick W, 1942, N 17,25:5
Speak, Alfred J O, 1966, Je 17,45:2
Speake, John W, 1941, Jl 31,17:4
Speaker, George M, 1937, Jl 20,23:5
Speaker, Mark Mrs, 1957, My 1,37:5
Speaker, Tris, 1958, D 9,1:5
Speaker, Tris Mrs, 1960, N 3,39:3
Speakman, C A, 1941, Ap 8,25:2
Speakman, Frank M, 1956, Ag 4,15:4
Speakman, G Dixon, 1956, N 12,29:4
Speakman, Harry E, 1939, Ap 29,17:3
Speaks, Charles E, 1965, O 24,86:8
Speaks, Edna L Mrs, 1943, D 8,23:3
Speaks, John, 1965, Ja 11,45:4
Speaks, John C, 1945, N 7,23:2
Speaks, Oley, 1948, Ag 28,16:2
Spealler, Louis H, 1937, D 20,27:4
Spear, Alex, 1952, Ap 7,25:5
Spear, Alfred, 1964, Je 27,25:5
Spear, Ellis Gen, 1917, Ap 6,13:7
Spear, Ellwood B, 1943, My 3,17:6
Spear, Fitzhugh C, 1954, N 20,17:3
Spear, Foster C, 1948, Ja 28,23:2
Spear, Frederick W Mrs, 1950, Ap 17,23:5
Spear, Furman D, 1942, Ja 22,17:3
Spear, George, 1937, S 9,23:1
Spear, George F, 1960, Ap 15,23:2
Spear, H Kirk Mrs, 1946, Ja 31,21:5
Spear, James, 1902, Ja 31,9:5
Spear, John J, 1867, Jl 24,5:4
Spear, John W, 1943, F 9,23:3
Spear, Joseph H, 1944, Mr 19,42:1
Spear, Laura Mrs, 1947, Jl 24,21:4
Spear, Lawrence Y, 1950, S 27,31:1
Spear, Lawrence Y Mrs, 1954, D 4,17:3
Spear, Levi, 1913, Jl 27,II,9:4
Spear, Lewis E, 1953, Mr 3,27:3
Spear, Maurice R Mrs, 1966, My 22,86:7
Spear, Maurice W, 1938, Ap 22,19:5
Spear, May P, 1937, Ja 12,16:3
Spear, Maynard H, 1937, Mr 20,21:4
Spear, Monroe, 1943, Ja 27,21:1
Spear, Nathaniel (por), 1947, Je 20,19:5
Spear, Phil H, 1953, Jl 21,23:3
Spear, Raymond Capt, 1937, S 30,23:3
Spear, Sammy Mrs (Saml Shapiro), 1968, Je 29,29:2
Spear, Samuel S Gen, 1875, My 5,7:3
Spear, Simon Mrs, 1955, Ag 6,15:1
Spear, Thelma, 1968, Je 17,39:4
Spear, Thomas I, 1873, F 21,2:4
Spear, Walter E (por), 1940, Mr 30,15:5
Spear, Warner E, 1938, S 20,23:3
Spear, Wilfred S, 1954, D 5,88:3
Spear, William H, 1937, D 27,15:3
Spear, William M, 1944, Ag 10,17:3
Spear, William T Ex-Justice, 1913, D 9,11:5
Speare, Alden, 1902, Mr 24,9:6
Speare, Charles F, 1961, Ap 7,31:4
Speare, Dorothy, 1951, F 5,23:1
Speare, Edward R, 1960, Ap 11,32:1
Speare, Frank P, 1954, My 30,45:3
Spearin, H L, 1903, My 2,9:5
Spearing, James O, 1937, Ja 10,II,11:1
Spearing, James O Mrs, 1954, Mr 26,22:3
Spearing, Jessie Mrs, 1938, F 25,17:5
Spearl, G, 1948, F 19,23:4
Spearman, Charles E, 1945, S 19,25:5
Spearman, Edward, 1960, F 2,35:1
Spearman, Frank H (por), 1937, D 31,16:1
Spearman, Leonard, 1945, Jl 24,23:2
Spears, Claude W, 1939, Je 6,23:4
Spears, Doc (Clarence W), 1964, F 2,88:7
Spears, George E, 1950, Je 11,92:1
Spears, George W, 1945, D 1,23:5
Spears, Harry A, 1949, Je 11,18:4
Spears, Harry D, 1914, S 18,9:6
Spears, James, 1923, Jl 27,13:6
Spears, John W, 1940, S 23,17:2
Spears, Leo L, 1956, My 17,31:3
Spears, Lewis R, 1916, F 24,13:4
Spears, Raymond S, 1950, Ja 27,23:5
Spears, Seymour M Jr, 1948, S 16,29:6
Spears, Zarel C, 1967, My 4,44:5
Spease, Edward, 1957, O 14,27:1
Specce, Ralph P, 1959, D 28,23:3
Specht, Anton, 1951, D 11,33:5
Specht, Charles J Mrs, 1951, N 18,91:1
Specht, Frank Mrs, 1958, N 28,30:3
Specht, George H, 1962, N 4,88:3
Specht, Harry M, 1946, Je 4,23:2
Specht, Harry M Mrs, 1946, Ag 9,17:6
Specht, Joseph, 1902, S 14,7:5
Specht, Joseph B, 1924, O 29,21:2
Specht, Louise F, 1958, N 29,21:1
Specht, Paul L, 1954, Ap 12,29:2
Specht, Roselyn, 1945, Ag 31,17:5
Specht, William, 1965, O 11,39:3
Specht, William H, 1949, My 23,23:4
Spechter, Rose Mrs, 1952, My 4,91:1
Speciner, I Jonas Mrs, 1955, F 12,15:1
Speck, Emil, 1945, My 11,19:4
Speck, Frank G, 1950, F 8,27:3
Speck, Harry L, 1948, Je 26,17:4
Speck, W A, 1928, O 10,29:3
Speck, William, 1953, Ag 30,88:5
Specker, Henry, 1957, My 4,21:4
Specker, Richard H, 1959, Mr 12,31:3
Speckler, Herman A, 1952, S 30,31:2
Speckman, John W, 1947, Ag 20,21:2
Spector, Abraham, 1967, S 27,47:2
Spector, Abram L, 1966, My 14,31:1
Spector, Clifford, 1961, Jl 30,69:3
Spector, Edward, 1964, Mr 15,86:6
Spector, Emanuel, 1952, F 21,27:5
Spector, Maurice, 1959, O 27,37:4; 1968, Ag 2,33:1
Spector, Michael, 1952, My 4,90:3
Spector, Mordecai, 1925, Mr 18,21:5
Spector, Morris Mrs, 1938, Mr 27,II,6:6
Spector, Nathaniel Mrs, 1939, My 9,23:5
Spector, Samuel, 1941, Jl 19,13:4
Spector, Samuel D, 1966, Jl 25,27:4
Spector, Samuel Mrs, 1956, S 23,84:6
Spectorsky, Isaac, 1944, Je 10,15:2
Spedden, Edgar Mrs, 1908, S 26,7:6
Spedden, Frederic Mrs, 1950, F 11,15:2
Spedden, Frederic O, 1947, F 4,27:1
Spedden, George W, 1938, Jl 1,19:4
Spediel, George J, 1948, Jl 27,25:2
Speed, Harold S, 1957, Ja 10,29:2
Speed, James, 1887, Je 26,5:2
Speed, James B, 1912, Jl 8,9:5; 1957, Jl 14,72:4
Speed, John W, 1946, S 8,44:4
Speed, Keats, 1952, Mr 2,93:1
Speed, Keats Mrs, 1950, F 12,85:1
Speed, Kellogg, 1955, Jl 4,11:5
Speed, P Maj, 1882, N 3,5:5
Speed, Philip, 1915, D 9,15:6
Speed, Philip K Mrs, 1883, S 11,5:2
Speed, Robert H, 1951, O 26,23:5
Speed, Sherwood B, 1955, Jl 18,21:5
Speed, U G, 1940, Mr 25,15:2
Speed, William S, 1955, D 9,27:5
Speel, Virginia W Mrs, 1945, Ap 14,15:4
Speer, Alfred, 1910, F 17,9:6
Speer, Alfred Mrs, 1921, N 26,13:6
Speer, C D Maude, 1938, My 25,23:2
Speer, Charles Edward, 1905, My 3,9:5
Speer, Edmund M, 1955, Ja 19,27:2
Speer, Edmund M Mrs, 1965, Jl 6,33:1
Speer, Eleanor B V Mrs, 1938, Ja 7,19:4
Speer, Emma W Mrs, 1939, Ja 14,17:1
Speer, Frank, 1938, Je 11,15:5
Speer, Helen L, 1953, Je 8,29:4
Speer, Herbert W Lt, 1912, Ag 25,II,11:6
Speer, Herman, 1903, Ap 24,9:6
Speer, Horace S, 1949, My 31,23:4
Speer, Howard B, 1942, Ja 3,32:2
Speer, Howard B Mrs, 1940, O 5,15:5
Speer, Irving, 1948, Ag 31,26:1
Speer, J Fred, 1961, O 19,35:3
Speer, James, 1880, F 19,5:4

Speer, James A, 1961, S 20,29:2
Speer, James R, 1944, O 3,23:3
Speer, John, 1906, D 16,7:6
Speer, John H Jr, 1949, N 2,27:4
Speer, John R, 1953, Ag 11,27:1
Speer, Joseph A, 1946, N 1,23:3
Speer, Peter M Mrs, 1943, F 20,13:3
Speer, Robert E Mrs (mem ser set, O 3,36:5), 1961, Ap 26,39:3
Speer, Robert K, 1959, Ag 11,27:3
Speer, Robert P, 1959, Mr 31,29:3
Speer, Stephen J, 1938, D 15,27:4
Speer, Victor, 1909, Je 28,7:5
Speer, Walter G, 1954, Ap 11,86:4
Speer, William H, 1948, My 4,25:1; 1959, Jl 9,27:6
Speer, William H Jr, 1939, Ja 31,21:4
Speer, William H Mrs, 1956, Jl 8,65:1
Speer, William M Mrs, 1961, F 26,92:6
Speer, William McMurtrie, 1923, Ap 3,23:5
Speers, Alex, 1949, Je 22,31:1
Speers, Alice M Mrs, 1941, Ja 21,22:2
Speers, James A, 1952, Ja 8,27:2
Speers, James M (por), 1941, Jl 25,15:1
Speers, James M Jr, 1962, Jl 4,21:4
Speers, Leland C (por), 1946, Je 24,31:3
Speers, Robert J, 1955, Jl 20,27:2
Speers, Theodore C, 1964, S 29,43:3
Speers, Wallace C, 1963, Ap 2,47:1
Speers, William E, 1960, D 23,19:1
Speers, William E Mrs, 1943, D 5,64:6
Speers, William J, 1954, Mr 13,15:7
Spees, Erwin S, 1954, N 1,27:5
Spees, Francis C, 1949, Ja 13,23:5
Speh, Edwin J Sr, 1950, F 22,30:2
Speh, Herman A, 1938, My 12,23:4
Spehr, Otto H, 1950, D 1,25:5
Speich, Frank A, 1953, Ag 11,27:2
Speich, Rodolphe, 1961, Ag 15,29:5
Speicher, Eugene Mrs, 1959, N 11,35:5
Speicher, Harvey J, 1939, Ap 17,17:5
Speicher, Paul E, 1947, O 1,30:3
Speidel, Eli H, 1948, Ja 17,17:1
Speidel, George J Mrs, 1937, O 12,25:1
Speidel, Henry C, 1944, F 8,15:3
Speidel, Merritt C, 1960, Mr 21,29:3
Speidel, Thomas D, 1957, D 2,27:3
Speidel, William E, 1962, Je 6,41:1
Speidell, Charles F, 1951, Je 15,23:5
Speidell, Charles F Mrs, 1951, Je 15,23:5
Speidell, Elsie Mrs, 1939, Mr 5,13:2
Speidell, Louis G, 1937, Ja 22,21:4
Speiden, C, 1926, My 26,27:5
Speiden, Clement C, 1954, Jl 20,19:3
Speiden, Clement L, 1946, Je 3,21:4
Speiden, Clement L Mrs, 1965, Jl 4,37:2
Speiden, Marion, 1949, My 22,88:3
Speier, Herman, 1939, Ja 24,19:5
Speier, Moritz, 1963, Je 18,37:3
Speiermann, Henrik O, 1948, Jl 4,27:1
Speight, Earl, 1963, Jl 13,17:5
Speight, F C (see also Mr 21), 1877, Mr 24,3:6
Speight, Harold E B Mrs, 1966, O 7,43:3
Speight, Henry, 1946, Mr 26,29:3
Speight, J S, 1874, Ja 12,1:6
Speight, John, 1951, Ag 24,15:5
Speight, John J, 1943, Ap 5,19:3
Speights, Charles H, 1958, Ag 8,17:6
Speir, Archibald W, 1910, Ap 1,11:5
Speir, Francis, 1904, F 19,9:5
Speir, Louis D Mrs, 1965, Ap 14,41:4
Speir, Oswald (funl, F 5,11:4), 1921, F 3,7:4
Speir, Robert W Jr, 1948, F 17,25:2
Speir, Robert W Mrs, 1956, Je 19,29:6
Speirs, James A, 1942, N 20,23:3
Speiser, Ephraim A, 1965, Je 17,33:1
Speiser, Herbert A, 1947, Je 26,24:2
Speiser, Irwin, 1944, Ag 11,15:3
Speiser, Maurice J, 1948, Ag 6,17:1
Speiser, Mortimer D, 1967, F 26,85:1
Speiser, Paul, 1947, N 9,72:5
Speiser, Raymond A, 1959, My 3,86:3
Speiser, Robin G Mrs, 1948, S 11,15:6
Speizer, Saul, 1958, My 9,23:2
Speke, Capt, 1864, O 9,2:3
Spektorsky, Eugene V, 1951, Mr 5,21:2
Spelke, Abram, 1945, N 10,15:5
Spelke, Max, 1962, F 24,27:1
Spelke, Sarah Mrs, 1938, Ja 29,15:3
Spellacy, Martin M, 1937, Ap 13,25:5
Spellacy, Thomas J, 1957, D 6,29:3
Spellani, Giovanni, 1949, Ja 13,24:3
Speller, Edward, 1943, F 4,23:2
Spellissy, Dennis Aloysius, 1918, N 6,17:3
Spellman, Arthur F, 1958, N 5,35:4
Spellman, Benjamin F, 1952, Ap 26,23:3
Spellman, Charles A, 1949, Mr 31,25:1
Spellman, Francis J Cardinal (funl, D 8,1:2), 1967, D 3,1:2
Spellman, George F, 1941, O 20,17:3
Spellman, Irwin S, 1965, D 6,37:1
Spellman, J S, 1883, N 5,8:2
Spellman, James A, 1942, My 16,13:2
Spellman, John H, 1904, N 19,9:5
Spellman, John L, 1938, Ag 14,32:6
Spellman, Leo F, 1965, Ap 28,45:4
Spellman, Martin H Mrs, 1962, N 5,31:5
Spellman, Mary, 1945, Ap 6,15:2
Spellman, Mary F (Sister Mary Francis), 1957, S 27, 19:4
Spellman, Peter W, 1945, N 20,21:4
Spellman, Raymond, 1944, Ag 31,17:5
Spellman, William (funl, N 15,29:4), 1955, N 12,19:3
Spellman, William H, 1961, N 28,37:4
Spellmeyer, Henry W Bishop, 1910, Mr 13,II,11:3
Spelman, Anna R, 1941, N 3,19:1
Spelman, Henry B, 1960, Ag 17,31:3
Spelman, John R, 1943, F 28,49:2
Spelman, Joseph J Mrs, 1944, My 19,19:5
Spelman, Joseph W Mrs, 1957, N 5,31:1
Spelman, Lucy Maria, 1920, F 9,9:4
Spelman, Mark Rollo, 1920, Jl 2,11:4
Spelman, Thomas J, 1952, Jl 25,18:6
Spenadel, Irving, 1941, Ap 8,25:4
Spence, Albert W, 1940, N 8,21:2
Spence, Arthur E, 1941, Ap 7,17:4
Spence, Bernard L, 1944, Ag 21,15:4
Spence, Brent, 1967, S 19,47:1
Spence, Brent Mrs, 1950, Je 2,24:3
Spence, Catherine H, 1910, Ap 4,9:4
Spence, Charles L, 1963, S 19,27:5
Spence, Clara B (funl, Ag 11,9:6), 1923, Ag 10,11:4
Spence, Clarence S, 1938, O 5,23:1
Spence, David, 1940, F 14,21:3; 1957, S 26,25:5
Spence, Edward, 1949, Jl 31,V,7:3
Spence, Edward C, 1948, D 31,16:4
Spence, Edward E, 1941, My 19,17:6
Spence, Frederick O, 1951, S 4,27:2
Spence, Gene P, 1954, Ap 12,29:5
Spence, George M, 1951, My 22,31:5
Spence, George W, 1942, F 7,17:3
Spence, Gordon R Mrs, 1962, Ap 4,43:3
Spence, Henry, 1945, N 23,23:2
Spence, Hubert D Mrs, 1948, F 24,26:2
Spence, James, 1882, Je 7,5:4; 1954, My 27,27:2
Spence, James H, 1939, F 22,21:3
Spence, James R, 1958, S 16,27:2
Spence, Jay, 1940, N 14,23:2
Spence, John A, 1946, F 6,23:2
Spence, John E, 1964, My 5,43:2
Spence, Kenneth M, 1957, Ap 21,88:6
Spence, Kenneth M Mrs, 1939, My 23,23:3
Spence, Kenneth W, 1967, Ja 14,31:4
Spence, Leonard, 1947, N 11,28:2
Spence, Lewis (Jas L T C), 1955, Mr 4,21:1
Spence, Margaret, 1940, Je 27,23:1
Spence, Newton W, 1942, Ap 1,21:5
Spence, Peter C (por), 1939, Jl 25,19:3
Spence, Ralph, 1949, D 22,23:2
Spence, Robert J, 1951, N 30,23:3
Spence, Thomas B, 1940, Je 20,23:4
Spence, Thomas H, 1948, My 12,27:4
Spence, Thomas W, 1912, F 25,II,11:2
Spence, Walter, 1958, O 17,41:3
Spence, Wells W, 1965, Ap 25,88:6
Spence, William G, 1954, Mr 14,89:3
Spence, William J, 1952, Mr 20,29:3
Spence, William T, 1958, O 4,21:5
Spenceley, Joseph Winfred, 1908, O 19,9:7
Spencer, A R, 1885, Ap 29,8:3
Spencer, Abbott K, 1966, Mr 24,39:2
Spencer, Alfred C, 1948, Ja 16,21:3
Spencer, Alfred L, 1953, Ap 3,24:3
Spencer, Ambrose P, 1951, Mr 3,13:5
Spencer, Arnold F, 1953, Je 26,19:3
Spencer, Arthur C, 1942, My 26,21:3
Spencer, B W, 1931, Jl 29,19:1
Spencer, Beecher M, 1954, O 21,27:2
Spencer, Benjamin M, 1958, O 3,29:1
Spencer, Bertrand E, 1941, Ja 24,17:3
Spencer, C, 1927, Ap 10,30:3
Spencer, C G, 1940, My 17,19:6
Spencer, C Luther, 1960, O 26,39:2
Spencer, Cecil O, 1949, Mr 7,21:3
Spencer, Charles B, 1956, Ja 8,86:3
Spencer, Charles C, 1947, F 24,19:5
Spencer, Charles E, 1938, N 1,23:5
Spencer, Charles E Jr, 1953, Ja 19,23:3
Spencer, Charles F, 1942, D 2,25:2
Spencer, Charles G, 1948, Ag 17,21:1; 1952, My 20, 25:2
Spencer, Charles Griswold, 1906, N 19,9:4
Spencer, Charles H, 1940, Ja 24,21:3
Spencer, Charles H Sr, 1940, D 26,19:4
Spencer, Charles J Mrs, 1943, D 3,23:4
Spencer, Charles L, 1921, S 22,17:6
Spencer, Charles M, 1954, Ja 10,86:3
Spencer, Charles W Mrs, 1942, Ja 8,21:4
Spencer, Chester, 1938, N 11,25:4
Spencer, Christopher, 1922, Ja 15,22:4
Spencer, Clarence G, 1964, Mr 29,61:1
Spencer, Clarence G Mrs, 1954, Ap 4,87:1
Spencer, Clarissa H Y Mrs, 1939, Ag 23,21:4
Spencer, David Rev Dr, 1924, Jl 30,13:4
Spencer, Duncan M Mrs, 1951, Ag 24,15:5
Spencer, Earl, 1922, S 27,19:4
Spencer, Earl W Jr, 1950, My 30,17:2
Spencer, Earl W Jr (will), 1950, Jl 12,26:7
Spencer, Edgar A Justice, 1911, My 6,13:6
Spencer, Edward, 1883, Jl 18,4:7
Spencer, Edward B T, 1945, O 29,19:4
Spencer, Edward B T Mrs, 1968, My 27,47:2
Spencer, Edward D, 1941, N 22,19:1
Spencer, Edward V, 1950, Ja 17,27:1
Spencer, Edward W, 1939, Ap 26,23:3
Spencer, Edwards, 1911, D 31,II,11:4
Spencer, Edwards Mrs, 1940, Ap 30,21:5
Spencer, Elias J, 1945, F 14,20:2
Spencer, Elizabeth, 1956, O 28,89:1
Spencer, Elwin, 1954, Ap 5,25:2
Spencer, Eugene, 1925, Ag 20,19:7
Spencer, Eugene J, 1938, S 23,27:3
Spencer, F Gilman, 1950, O 25,35:5
Spencer, Fanny, 1943, Ap 10,17:5
Spencer, Frank A, 1943, Mr 2,19:2
Spencer, Frank Capt, 1916, F 21,11:6
Spencer, Frank E, 1952, N 8,17:3
Spencer, Frank N Sr, 1963, N 4,35:4
Spencer, Frank W, 1918, Ag 17,7:8; 1953, My 23,15:5
Spencer, Frederick B, 1959, Ja 30,27:3
Spencer, Garrick M, 1942, Ag 5,19:5
Spencer, George F, 1941, N 14,23:4; 1956, S 24,27:5
Spencer, George F A, 1952, N 19,29:6
Spencer, George H Mrs, 1949, F 16,25:4
Spencer, George O, 1947, My 6,28:3
Spencer, George V, 1966, Ap 11,29:3
Spencer, George W, 1953, O 24,15:6; 1958, O 16,37:2
Spencer, Girard Mrs, 1961, Ap 3,30:4
Spencer, Guy R, 1945, D 28,16:2
Spencer, Gwendoline Mrs, 1941, Jl 8,19:5
Spencer, Gwladys, 1947, N 25,29:3
Spencer, Harold C, 1955, O 23,86:8
Spencer, Harry, 1964, Ap 1,39:1
Spencer, Harry A, 1948, Jl 26,17:5
Spencer, Harry P, 1943, Ap 10,17:5
Spencer, Hazelton, 1944, Jl 29,13:2
Spencer, Henry B, 1956, Jl 6,21:4
Spencer, Henry C, 1955, N 4,29:2
Spencer, Henry F, 1964, Je 2,37:1
Spencer, Henry Furman (funl, D 29,13:6), 1923, D 27,13:3
Spencer, Henry J, 1944, Je 12,19:5
Spencer, Henry J Mrs, 1948, Ag 30,17:1
Spencer, Herbert, 1903, D 9,8:6; 1944, Ag 28,11:5; 1945, D 26,19:2
Spencer, Herbert L, 1960, Ja 31,92:1
Spencer, Herbert L Mrs, 1968, Ap 28,83:1
Spencer, Herbert Mrs, 1938, S 3,13:4
Spencer, Howard B, 1967, My 7,87:1
Spencer, Howland, 1957, Ag 27,29:2
Spencer, Ira T, 1955, N 24,29:4
Spencer, J Beaumont, 1952, D 26,15:2
Spencer, J C ex-Judge, 1901, D 23,7:4
Spencer, J E, 1938, D 21,23:5
Spencer, J Poyntz Earl, 1910, Ag 14,II,9:5
Spencer, James B, 1959, N 19,39:4
Spencer, James C, 1937, S 12,II,7:1
Spencer, James H, 1950, D 14,35:1
Spencer, Janet, 1948, My 20,29:4
Spencer, Jervis Jr, 1940, F 21,19:4
Spencer, John, 1957, O 31,31:2
Spencer, John E Col, 1937, Ap 2,23:1
Spencer, John G, 1942, Ap 2,21:6
Spencer, John M, 1965, Jl 19,33:3
Spencer, John O, 1947, My 26,22:3
Spencer, John T Mrs, 1939, N 27,17:3
Spencer, John Thompson, 1924, Jl 17,15:5
Spencer, John Walton, 1912, O 25,13:2
Spencer, Joseph E, 1948, Jl 6,23:4
Spencer, Joseph W, 1963, D 20,26:8
Spencer, Josephine H Mrs, 1938, Jl 7,19:4
Spencer, Kate T Mrs, 1941, D 14,69:2
Spencer, Kenneth (por), 1946, Jl 27,17:4
Spencer, Kenneth A, 1960, F 20,23:4
Spencer, Leon E, 1940, Je 30,32:5
Spencer, Leonard Garfield, 1914, D 16,15:5
Spencer, Leontine G, 1964, Ag 26,39:3
Spencer, Leslie V, 1967, S 9,31:2
Spencer, Lillian W Mrs, 1953, Je 25,27:6
Spencer, Lily B Mrs, 1942, D 25,17:3
Spencer, Lily M, 1902, My 23,9:4
Spencer, Lloyd L, 1956, Ap 9,27:5
Spencer, Lorillard, 1912, Mr 15,9:5
Spencer, Lorillard (will, Je 28,23:3),(por), 1939, Je 10,17:1
Spencer, Lorillard Mrs, 1948, Ap 7,25:3; 1956, S 9,84:4
Spencer, Luella R Mrs, 1947, Jl 30,21:2
Spencer, Lyle M, 1968, Ag 22,37:4
Spencer, Lyman P, 1915, Je 12,11:5
Spencer, Mary A Mrs, 1943, S 18,17:5
Spencer, Mary B Mrs, 1942, Jl 3,17:2
Spencer, Mary H Mrs, 1942, Ja 24,15:7
Spencer, Max, 1949, Je 7,32:6
Spencer, Maxwell, 1907, D 28,7:7
Spencer, N S, 1934, Jl 1,24:4
Spencer, Nelson E, 1941, F 4,22:2
Spencer, Newton H Mrs, 1946, My 6,21:2
Spencer, Niles, 1952, My 17,19:6
Spencer, Norma R J Mrs, 1944, Mr 8,19:1
Spencer, Oliver E, 1958, O 7,35:1

Spencer, Oliver W, 1944, Je 19,19:6
Spencer, Orrin S, 1946, Mr 12,25:4; 1951, Ja 30,25:1
Spencer, Page, 1946, S 19,31:4
Spencer, Paul M (mem ser, Jl 3,16:5), 1950, Je 20, 27:3
Spencer, Paul R, 1953, Ja 10,17:2
Spencer, Percival F, 1938, F 18,19:4
Spencer, Ralph H, 1948, Ap 21,27:3
Spencer, Ray A, 1941, Ap 5,17:2
Spencer, Ray S Mrs, 1949, Ja 10,25:2
Spencer, Raymond A, 1939, N 27,17:1
Spencer, Raymond D, 1941, O 7,23:1
Spencer, Richard, 1962, Ja 23,33:1
Spencer, Richard S Mrs, 1952, D 5,28:3
Spencer, Robert C, 1953, S 11,21:2
Spencer, Robert E, 1946, S 15,9:7
Spencer, Robert L, 1945, O 11,23:2
Spencer, Robert N Mrs, 1954, Jl 31,13:5
Spencer, Robert S, 1953, Ap 11,17:4
Spencer, Robert W, 1949, Mr 30,25:3
Spencer, Samuel (funl, D 3,9:1; will D 8,8:2), 1906, N 30,1:7
Spencer, Samuel Mrs, 1919, S 11,15:4
Spencer, Selden P Sen, 1925, My 21,23:4
Spencer, Squire, 1954, S 6,15:1
Spencer, Stanley, 1906, Ja 27,9:5; 1959, D 15,40:2
Spencer, T Seldon Rev, 1914, D 2,13:6
Spencer, Theodore (por), 1949, Ja 19,27:3
Spencer, Thomas P, 1953, N 23,27:3
Spencer, Thomas W, 1938, Je 22,23:3
Spencer, Victor, 1960, F 23,31:2
Spencer, Virginia A Mrs, 1940, My 13,17:2
Spencer, W Vaughan, 1940, O 18,21:4
Spencer, Walter B, 1943, S 20,21:5; 1944, Je 1,19:3
Spencer, Walter G, 1940, O 31,23:6
Spencer, William B, 1938, S 26,17:3; 1948, Jl 27,25:5
Spencer, William C, 1940, Mr 17,48:8
Spencer, William G, 1960, N 25,27:4
Spencer, William H, 1942, Je 10,21:1; 1966, My 30, 19:4
Spencer, William T Jr, 1937, S 6,17:3
Spencer, Willie (Wm G), 1963, O 3,35:6
Spencer, Willing, 1952, S 19,23:2
Spencer, Winifred, 1909, N 2,9:3
Spencer-Kelly, James, 1944, My 5,19:3
Spencer-Mounsey, Creighton Rev, 1937, Ap 10,19:4
Spender, E H, 1926, Ap 16,23:3
Spender, Frederick J, 1950, O 19,31:2
Spender, Harold Mrs, 1922, Ja 21,13:5
Spender, J Alfred (por), 1942, Je 22,15:3
Spender-Clay, Herbert H Col, 1937, F 16,23:6
Spengler, Arthur W, 1953, O 31,17:4
Spengler, Francis J, 1944, Je 14,19:4
Spengler, Henry M, 1961, O 12,2:5
Spengler, John A, 1949, Ag 13,11:6
Spengler, Louis, 1949, O 16,88:2
Spengler, Luther C, 1944, O 25,21:6
Spengler, O, 1936, My 9,15:5
Spennato, Phil, 1956, D 22,19:5
Speno, Frank, 1950, Mr 2,27:3
Speno, Tommy (R F Pinzino), 1959, Je 24,31:3
Sper, Felix, 1954, F 15,23:2
Sper, Winona W Mrs, 1940, Ap 28,37:3
Spera, Keidner Maj, 1921, Ap 15,15:4
Sperandei, Louis, 1938, Ap 22,19:3
Sperandeo, Vincent, 1959, Mr 23,31:2
Sperans, Samuel R, 1959, Ja 15,33:2
Speransky, Aleksi, 1961, Jl 26,31:4
Speranza, Gino Mrs, 1951, My 25,27:2
Sperati, Carlo A, 1945, S 13,23:4
Sperbeck, Oscar, 1948, N 17,27:2
Sperber, Emil O, 1965, Jl 18,68:7
Sperber, Herman Mrs, 1954, F 7,88:3
Sperber, Irving J, 1946, N 16,19:3
Sperber, Jacob, 1963, Ap 22,27:2
Sperber, Marcus M, 1962, Ap 2,31:2
Sperber, Meyer, 1957, Jl 2,27:1
Spering, Irving G, 1958, Mr 21,21:1
Sperl, August G, 1957, Je 5,35:4
Sperl, Edmund A, 1959, Jl 14,29:5
Sperl, George W, 1958, O 25,21:5
Sperle, John, 1954, Mr 14,89:1
Sperle, John Mrs, 1952, S 26,22:4
Sperling, Charles P, 1938, Ap 30,15:5
Sperling, Elrika A Mrs, 1937, S 8,23:1
Sperling, Frederick W, 1963, My 14,39:3
Sperling, H A, 1940, My 8,23:4
Sperling, Harry, 1948, O 22,25:3; 1961, My 9,39:4
Sperling, Phil Mrs, 1953, N 20,23:1
Sperling, Walter J, 1946, Jl 19,19:5
Sperling, William, 1955, Mr 11,25:3
Sperling, William R, 1959, Je 3,35:2
Spero, Harold L, 1967, My 10,47:1
Spero, Herbert, 1954, Ja 9,16:3
Spero, Robert, 1948, D 14,29:3
Spero, Robert Mrs, 1940, Ja 19,19:3
Sperrle, Hugo, 1953, Ap 8,29:3
Sperry, Charles S Rear-Adm (funl, F 4,13:5), 1911, F 2,11:5
Sperry, Davis A, 1953, My 3,89:3
Sperry, Don E, 1957, D 16,29:5
Sperry, E A, 1930, Je 17,27:3
Sperry, Edith M Mrs, 1938, N 18,21:5
Sperry, Edward Beck, 1925, S 20,7:2
Sperry, Edward G, 1945, N 8,19:3
Sperry, Elmer Ambrose Jr, 1968, D 24,20:6
Sperry, Eugene E Mrs, 1957, N 8,29:5
Sperry, Francis Lewis, 1906, Ap 18,11:5
Sperry, Frederick N, 1950, S 9,17:6
Sperry, George T, 1947, Ag 24,56:1
Sperry, Helen, 1956, F 2,25:5
Sperry, Howard A, 1940, Ap 23,23:4
Sperry, James A, 1915, Ja 15,11:4
Sperry, John Mrs, 1950, Ap 19,29:4
Sperry, Joseph, 1925, S 26,17:6
Sperry, Lawrence B, 1924, F 13,19:4
Sperry, Leavenworth P, 1958, N 23,89:1
Sperry, Leonard M, 1963, S 13,29:3
Sperry, Margaret G Mrs, 1940, F 18,41:1
Sperry, Mark L Mrs, 1945, Jl 17,13:4
Sperry, Nehemiah D, 1911, N 14,13:5
Sperry, Phil (por), 1949, Ja 25,23:3
Sperry, Richard E, 1951, My 10,31:3
Sperry, Theodore H, 1944, Mr 27,19:4
Sperry, Thomas A, 1913, S 3,9:7
Sperry, Willard L, 1954, My 16,87:1
Sperry, William L, 1938, Ap 12,23:3
Sperry, William M Mrs, 1955, Mr 8,27:4
Sperry, William M 2d, 1952, F 5,29:3
Speth, Aribert Mrs (F Alberti), 1955, D 23,17:3
Speth, Leon C, 1956, My 9,33:2
Speth, Reuben C, 1947, S 17,25:2
Spetrino, Francesco, 1948, Jl 27,25:5
Spette, Albert E, 1961, N 21,39:1
Spetter, Ies, 1959, S 19,23:2
Spettigue, George B, 1940, Mr 1,21:2
Spewachek, Frank, 1950, Je 1,27:3
Spewack, Noel, 1963, Jl 5,16:8
Spewack, Noel Mrs, 1950, N 17,27:1
Speyer, E, 1932, F 18,21:3
Speyer, Eugene, 1910, Je 18,9:2
Speyer, Everett G, 1954, D 29,23:2
Speyer, George, 1902, Ap 26,9:5
Speyer, James J, 1941, N 1,15:1
Speyer, James Mrs, 1918, F 22,11:5
Speyer, James Mrs (funl, F 24,13:6), 1921, F 23,13:1
Speyer, Leonora, 1956, F 11,17:3
Speyer, Wilhelm, 1952, D 3,33:5
Speyers, A (Black Friday), 1880, D 24,2:4
Speyers, A G P Mrs, 1903, S 20,7:6
Speyers, Arthur B Rear-Adm, 1918, N 20,15:4
Speyers, Bayard, 1964, Jl 11,25:4
Spezi, Pio, 1940, Ja 5,20:3
Sphears, Wellington B, 1959, My 28,31:3
Spiak, John, 1948, S 8,29:2
Spice, Robert Treat, 1920, Ap 11,22:2
Spice, William H, 1953, D 23,25:2
Spicehandler, Abraham, 1968, Ja 27,29:3
Spicer, Arthur L, 1943, F 26,20:2
Spicer, C B, 1878, S 19,2:5
Spicer, Clarence W, 1939, N 22,21:4
Spicer, E Grant, 1953, D 11,34:4
Spicer, Evan Sir, 1937, D 23,22:2
Spicer, Harold L Sr, 1958, Mr 3,27:4
Spicer, Henry R Maj-Gen, 1968, D 5,47:1
Spicer, Hiram E Mrs, 1938, F 16,21:2
Spicer, Howard C, 1947, Jl 2,23:1
Spicer, Isaac F, 1950, D 16,17:6
Spicer, Phoebe W Mrs, 1942, N 29,65:2
Spicer, W F Commodore, 1878, N 30,2:4
Spicer, William A, 1952, O 18,19:5
Spicer, William A Jr, 1950, O 31,27:3
Spicer, William Sr, 1946, O 3,27:3
Spickard, Anderson, 1950, My 29,28:7
Spicker, Max (funl, O 18,11:4), 1912, O 16,13:5
Spickers, William, 1907, Mr 27,9:6; 1945, D 30,14:2
Spickett, Rufus, 1903, Je 10,9:6
Spickschen, Henry F, 1956, O 4,33:5
Spidel, Otto W, 1938, My 26,25:3
Spidell, Roscoe C, 1949, My 7,13:3
Spiecker, Carl, 1953, N 17,31:5
Spiegel, Adolph, 1957, Ap 9,33:1
Spiegel, Arthur H, 1916, Ap 8,15:7
Spiegel, Arthur M, 1947, O 4,17:4
Spiegel, B Edgar, 1962, Je 22,25:2
Spiegel, Charles R, 1941, O 20,17:5
Spiegel, Emanuel M, 1956, Je 17,92:4
Spiegel, Herman A, 1950, N 7,27:6
Spiegel, Isaac L, 1939, F 12,45:1
Spiegel, J R, 1945, F 4,37:1
Spiegel, Jacob, 1951, S 4,27:2
Spiegel, Joseph, 1957, Ja 21,25:5
Spiegel, Leo, 1951, D 18,31:5
Spiegel, Louis, 1965, My 12,47:2
Spiegel, Max, 1966, Je 13,39:3
Spiegel, Max J (por), 1949, Ja 6,23:2
Spiegel, Max Mrs, 1965, Ap 10,30:1
Spiegel, Modie J, 1943, Ja 10,48:5
Spiegel, Pauline S Mrs, 1941, S 19,23:5
Spiegel, Reisel Mrs, 1959, F 8,86:7
Spiegel, Samuel, 1958, D 8,31:3
Spiegel, Samuel Mrs (por), 1948, F 16,21:4
Spiegel, Saul, 1953, N 25,23:5
Spiegel, Simon, 1960, O 24,29:3
Spiegel, Tommy, 1945, N 10,15:2
Spiegel, Walter E, 1948, S 7,25:3
Spiegelberg, Ernest, 1962, S 18,39:2
Spiegelberg, Frederick Jr, 1925, N 9,19:6
Spiegelberg, Frederick Justice, 1937, Jl 11,II,4:4
Spiegelberg, Isaac Mrs, 1943, S 2,19:3
Spiegelberg, Levi, 1906, Ap 4,1:3
Spiegelberg, W I, 1932, Ja 19,21:1
Spiegelberg, William Mrs, 1943, D 9,27:1
Spiegelberger, Henry, 1946, Je 20,23:5
Spiegelglass, Abraham B, 1956, N 15,35:4
Spiegelhalter, Andrew G, 1959, My 27,35:1
Spiegelman, Eva Mrs, 1947, Je 16,21:4
Spiegelman, William Z, 1949, My 16,21:5
Spiegl, Ludwig, 1940, My 18,15:4
Spiegle, Frederick M, 1942, D 30,23:1
Spiegle, Grace E, 1949, Mr 19,15:1
Spiegler, Adele Mrs, 1940, D 28,15:2
Spiegler, Frederick, 1961, My 1,29:3
Spiegler, Louis, 1968, N 9,33:3
Spiehler, Adolph M, 1956, Jl 14,15:3
Spieker, George F Rev Dr, 1913, S 9,7:6
Spiekerman, Kraft Mrs (H Behnee), 1963, S 29,86:
Spiekerman, Louis P, 1951, My 12,21:5
Spiel, George, 1951, Ap 18,31:3
Spielberg, Harold, 1940, Ag 1,21:5
Spielberg, Israel, 1962, Je 15,27:4
Spielberger, Arthur, 1940, Mr 4,15:4
Spielberger, Louis, 1945, Ap 18,23:6
Spielberger, Morris, 1954, Je 28,19:4
Spielberger, William J, 1944, N 20,21:3
Spieles, Margaret Mrs, 1939, Ja 24,19:4
Spielfogel, Herman, 1943, D 1,21:2
Spielhagen, Friedrich, 1911, F 26,II,11:4
Spielman, Adolph, 1947, F 6,23:6
Spielman, Daniel, 1956, D 12,39:5
Spielman, Emeric M, 1952, My 14,27:4
Spielman, Gernand I, 1949, D 8,33:3
Spielman, Gustave, 1956, S 15,17:1
Spielman, Joseph, 1962, Ag 1,31:3
Spielman, Joseph J, 1943, Ja 11,15:5
Spielman, Marvin A, 1957, Jl 13,17:3
Spielman, Samuel, 1967, Ja 23,43:2
Spielmann, Isidore Sir, 1925, My 11,17:4
Spielmann, Marion H, 1948, O 5,25:2
Spielmann, Marion H Mrs, 1938, My 2,17:4
Spielter, Herman, 1925, N 12,25:4
Spielvogel, Siegfried W, 1959, D 16,41:1
Spier, Fannie Mrs, 1939, O 25,23:4
Spier, George W, 1924, My 4,23:2
Spier, Harry F, 1945, Jl 9,11:7
Spier, Harry R, 1952, Ja 21,15:2
Spier, Larry, 1956, N 11,86:3
Spier, Larry Mrs, 1967, N 17,47:3
Spier, Leopold A, 1937, Ag 12,19:6
Spier, Oscar A, 1951, Mr 10,13:2
Spier, Richard, 1949, Jl 20,25:4
Spier, Sydney, 1939, N 15,23:5
Spier, William J, 1941, F 8,15:5
Spiering, Theodore, 1925, Ag 14,13:5
Spierling, Frank W, 1968, Je 30,52:8
Spiero, Milton H, 1961, Je 14,19:3
Spiers, Alex G H Dr, 1937, D 17,25:5
Spiers, Fred M Dr, 1923, Ag 16,15:5
Spiers, Harry S Mrs, 1949, Je 12,76:6
Spiers, Jane Mrs, 1940, Je 22,15:6
Spiers, R Phene, 1916, O 5,11:3
Spies, Albert, 1910, Ag 17,7:5
Spies, Edwin A Dr, 1937, Mr 23,24:1
Spies, Franklin C, 1938, N 1,23:4
Spies, Gottfried L, 1939, Jl 7,17:4
Spies, Henry, 1920, F 20,15:5
Spies, Louise B Mrs, 1941, Ag 26,19:2
Spies, Peter, 1906, F 1,9:5
Spies, Tom D (cor, Mr 5,19:1), 1960, F 29,27:1
Spiesberger, Herbert T, 1960, Mr 12,21:2
Spiess, William, 1942, D 31,15:5
Spigel, Herbert B, 1951, D 13,33:3
Spiker, Laurence J, 1950, N 6,27:4
Spikins, F R G, 1951, My 14,3:2
Spilberg, Alex, 1963, Ap 23,37:1
Spilberg, Thomas F Mrs, 1946, Ap 23,21:2
Spiliadis, Basil, 1953, N 20,23:4
Spilka, Jack, 1952, F 10,92:4
Spilker, Antonio (Sister M Stanislaus), 1959, Ag 27:1
Spillane, James J, 1949, N 26,15:5
Spillane, James R, 1952, My 14,27:3
Spillane, John, 1941, My 31,11:3
Spillane, Lawrence W, 1963, S 23,29:2
Spillane, Maurice, 1950, Mr 14,25:4
Spillane, Michael J, 1949, S 25,92:3
Spillane, Michael J Mrs, 1937, My 18,23:4
Spillane, William J (por), 1942, Ap 8,19:3
Spillane, William J, 1947, N 4,25:4
Spiller, Fred, 1953, S 16,33:4
Spiller, Jesse B, 1967, Ag 13,81:1
Spiller, Leslie J, 1939, O 28,15:2
Spiller, Rell J, 1946, D 5,31:2
Spiller, T Boyd, 1942, Ja 11,44:1
Spiller, William G, 1940, Mr 19,25:4
Spiller, William H, 1949, F 24,23:4
Spilliaert, Leon, 1946, D 9,25:5
Spillinger, Frank, 1940, F 2,17:2
Spillman, Albert, 1949, F 3,23:5

Spillman, Harry C, 1948, Ap 26,23:5
Spillman, Max, 1945, Je 24,21:1
Spillman, O S, 1941, Mr 25,23:5
Spilman, Bernard W, 1950, Mr 27,23:4
Spilman, Charles H, 1940, Mr 8,21:5
Spilman, Charles W, 1941, My 7,25:2
Spilman, Lucretia, 1943, Ap 18,49:1
Spilman, Richard W, 1937, S 27,21:2
Spilner, Alexander, 1946, Ja 15,23:3
Spilo, Leon A, 1956, F 9,32:2
Spilo, William A, 1949, N 15,25:4; 1949, N 16,29:4
Spilsbury, Edmund Gybbon, 1920, My 30,22:3
Spilsbury, P G, 1952, My 5,23:4
Spilsbury, Raymond G, 1958, N 13,33:4
Spina, Domenick, 1948, Ag 27,19:3
Spina, John A, 1952, S 4,27:4
Spina, Phil, 1937, Je 23,25:2
Spindel, Bernard, 1959, Mr 13,26:6
Spindell, Harold W, 1952, O 8,31:3
Spinden, Herbert J, 1967, O 24,44:1
Spindler, Alfred W C, 1953, N 8,88:5
Spindler, George A Mrs, 1949, Mr 16,27:2
Spindler, Henry, 1961, Mr 2,27:3
Spindler, John M, 1944, D 24,25:1
Spindler, Leo O, 1956, Ag 7,27:4
Spindler, Lorenz G, 1947, Jl 4,13:3
Spindler, Walter E, 1951, Jl 21,13:4
Spindt, Herman A, 1960, Mr 20,86:8
Spinelli, Louis, 1949, Je 18,13:2
Spinelli, P Dalton, 1947, My 11,60:3
Spinello, Edward J, 1968, My 9,47:2
Spingard, Joel E (will, Ag 12,17:8),(por), 1939, Jl 27, 19:1
Spingarn, Alexander, 1943, My 24,15:4
Spingarn, Harry, 1947, S 11,27:6
Spingarn, Herman, 1959, Ag 1,17:5
Spingarn, Leopold, 1951, Jl 2,23:4
Spingarn, Samuel, 1943, F 20,13:5
Spingarn, Samuel H, 1913, N 29,13:6
Spingold, Nate B, 1958, Je 15,77:1
Spining, George Lawrence Rev Dr, 1923, S 28,7:3
Spink, Benjamin Franklin, 1914, Mr 21,13:4
Spink, Bernard Mrs, 1952, Jl 27,57:1
Spink, Ernest W, 1956, Ag 18,17:6
Spink, Erwin S, 1937, F 28,II,8:5
Spink, Erwin S Jr, 1965, My 28,33:4
Spink, Harold B, 1950, Mr 20,21:2
Spink, J G Taylor, 1962, D 8,27:1
Spink, James F, 1950, Je 3,15:6
Spink, S L, 1881, S 25,5:4
Spink, Urban, 1952, Jl 7,21:4
Spinks, Lewis, 1946, F 17,42:3
Spinks, Marcellus G, 1943, N 30,27:6
Spinner, Charles, 1872, O 27,1:6
Spinner, F E Gen, 1891, Ja 1,5:1
Spinney, Charles J Mrs, 1946, Ag 27,27:6
Spinney, George F Mrs, 1948, F 16,21:1
Spinney, George W, 1948, F 2,19:4
Spinney, Hazen P, 1954, Ap 11,86:6
Spinney, John A, 1937, Mr 12,23:3
Spinney, Joseph, 1882, Je 28,5:4
Spinney, Louis B, 1951, Ja 26,23:5
Spinney, Mabel F Mrs, 1951, Ag 26,77:1
Spinney, William, 1924, O 2,23:3
Spinney, William Rev, 1924, My 6,21:5
Spinning, Everett T, 1956, Mr 30,19:3
Spinning, Louis N, 1952, D 27,9:4
Spinning, Seymour E, 1952, F 3,85:1
Spino, Pasquale, 1916, Jl 24,9:3
Spinola, F B Gen, 1891, Ap 14,5:3
Spinrad, Abraham, 1945, N 6,20:3
Spinrad, Abraham Mrs, 1966, F 11,30:4
Spira, Isaac, 1964, Ja 7,33:4
Spirer, Abe Mrs, 1956, S 11,35:3
Spiritoso, Gennaro, 1946, O 14,29:1
Spiro, Abraham I, 1943, D 21,27:4
Spiro, Albert, 1968, Je 4,44:3
Spiro, Amster, 1956, Ag 25,15:5
Spiro, Benjamin, 1951, Ag 15,27:3
Spiro, Bob, 1954, Je 7,23:2
Spiro, Cecilia Mrs, 1938, Mr 31,23:1
Spiro, Jack, 1963, Ag 11,84:3
Spiro, Jacob N, 1954, Jl 17,13:3
Spiro, Joseph A, 1949, Ap 30,13:5
Spiro, Max, 1959, S 24,37:1
Spiro, Samuel, 1966, Jl 3,34:8
Spiro, Walter Mrs, 1962, My 3,33:2
Spisak, John G Sr, 1949, S 2,17:4
Spisak, John Mrs, 1944, Mr 17,17:5
Spisak, Joseph W, 1949, F 16,25:4
Spissak, William, 1937, Ap 22,2:7
Spissinger, John G, 1957, Jl 9,29:3
Spitaleri, Frank, 1965, Ag 5,29:5
Spitaleri, Louis N, 1958, Mr 21,21:4
Spitaleri, Rosario, 1964, Ja 15,31:3
Spitalny, Dora Mrs, 1939, S 16,17:4
Spitalny, Rachel Mrs, 1949, Ja 21,21:3
Spitler, Paul A, 1968, S 25,47:1
Spitta, Edmund Johnson, 1921, Ja 26,7:4
Spittal, Dave, 1938, N 22,24:7
Spittel, Herman E, 1948, Jl 20,23:5
Spitteler, Carl, 1924, D 30,17:6
Spitz, Abram A, 1954, F 11,29:5
Spitz, Arthur, 1950, Ja 25,27:3
Spitz, Bertha C Mrs, 1937, Je 5,17:5
Spitz, Charles B, 1937, My 5,25:4
Spitz, Henry H, 1949, Jl 18,17:6
Spitz, Jack, 1966, F 9,39:3
Spitz, Joseph, 1958, Ap 30,33:2
Spitz, Leo, 1956, Ag 17,31:1
Spitz, Leon, 1959, N 29,86:2
Spitz, Morry W, 1949, F 6,76:3
Spitz, Rene A Mrs, 1961, Ag 13,88:4
Spitz, Sophie (Mrs A C Allen), 1956, Ag 11,13:4
Spitzer, A Lewis, 1966, Jl 19,39:2
Spitzer, Alvin C, 1944, Je 12,19:5
Spitzer, Benjamin L, 1968, F 18,80:4
Spitzer, Blanche W Mrs, 1964, S 8,29:4
Spitzer, Cellan M, 1919, F 25,11:2
Spitzer, Edgar, 1949, Ag 2,20:5
Spitzer, Frank Mrs, 1955, N 17,35:3
Spitzer, Herman, 1956, O 3,33:2
Spitzer, Horton, 1959, Mr 24,39:4
Spitzer, Joseph, 1956, Ap 30,23:4
Spitzer, Leo, 1960, S 18,86:7
Spitzer, Max, 1949, Ag 9,25:4
Spitzer, Morris, 1957, Mr 26,33:1
Spitzer, Paul, 1966, Jl 28,33:1
Spitzer, Robert, 1938, Ag 26,17:4
Spitzer, Samuel E, 1950, N 1,35:2
Spitzer, Sigmund Mrs, 1949, Mr 11,25:2
Spitzer, Solomon, 1882, Ap 15,5:4
Spitzform, Harold, 1959, F 24,29:5
Spitzhoff, Carl, 1941, N 25,25:1
Spitzig, Edmund W, 1957, Jl 27,17:4
Spitzka, Edward Dr, 1922, S 6,15:4
Spitzka, Henry, 1925, F 16,19:4
Spitzler, Theodore, 1958, Je 29,69:1
Spitzmiller, George W, 1924, Ap 26,15:5
Spitznagle, Stephen A, 1957, D 9,35:4
Spitzyn, Georgi G, 1948, My 9,68:7
Spivack, Ephraim, 1948, F 13,21:3
Spivack, Rudie, 1964, Ja 12,92:3
Spivack, victor, 1957, S 9,25:5
Spivacke, Charles A, 1943, N 24,21:4
Spivacke, Charles A Mrs, 1939, Ja 1,24:3
Spivak, Elie, 1960, Jl 25,23:3
Spivak, Hyman Mrs, 1964, Je 20,25:5
Spivak, Max Mrs, 1965, Jl 25,69:2
Spivak, Minnie Mrs, 1952, O 23,31:2
Spivak, Munroe L Mrs, 1965, My 18,39:4
Spivak, Samuel, 1949, My 25,29:4
Spivak, William B Mrs, 1957, Mr 9,19:5
Spivey, Thomas S, 1938, N 9,23:2
Spiwak, Max, 1949, Je 2,27:2
Spizman, Leib, 1963, Je 22,23:6
Splain, James F, 1960, D 21,31:1
Splain, John J, 1940, F 26,15:2
Splain, Maurice J, 1951, N 10,17:4
Splaine, Michael J, 1951, O 7,86:7
Splan, Edward J, 1959, Ja 16,27:2
Splane, John, 1940, Ja 21,34:6
Splett, Carl M, 1964, Mr 6,28:2
Splint, Frederic W, 1950, Ja 10,29:1
Splint, Sarah F, 1959, D 27,61:2
Splitdorf, Charles F, 1940, Mr 4,15:3
Splitdorf, Henry, 1916, O 18,11:6
Splitdorf, J M, 1934, O 25,23:1
Splivalo, Ray, 1937, Ag 29,II,6:8
Spock, Benjamin I Mrs, 1968, Ja 18,40:1
Spock, Jasper, 1947, S 26,23:4
Spockman, William M, 1925, N 19,25:5
Spoder, John, 1949, F 9,27:1
Spoehr, Herman A, 1954, Je 23,25:5
Spoer, H Henry, 1951, O 4,33:4
Spoerer, George R, 1950, Ag 19,13:6
Spoerl, Edwin W, 1956, My 2,31:3
Spoerl, Elmo E, 1961, O 3,39:1
Spoerl, Howard D, 1957, Ap 25,31:4
Spoffard, Judson G, 1950, Je 18,76:4
Spofford, Ainsworth R, 1908, Ag 13,7:4
Spofford, Charles A, 1921, Mr 7,11:5
Spofford, Edward V, 1940, My 23,23:6
Spofford, Edward W, 1946, Ja 6,40:3
Spofford, Ellen B Mrs, 1942, Ja 31,17:5
Spofford, Ernest, 1945, Je 8,19:3
Spofford, Florence M, 1944, N 24,23:2
Spofford, Florence P, 1939, Ja 17,22:4
Spofford, H M, 1880, Ag 22,7:5
Spofford, Paul, 1869, O 29,4:7
Spofford, Paul Nelson, 1912, S 8,II,13:4
Spofford, Phillip A, 1953, Jl 8,27:5
Spofford, Richard S Mrs (Harriet P Spofford), 1921, Ag 16,15:4
Spohler, John Mrs, 1960, N 11,31:5
Spohn, George, 1943, N 10,23:3
Spohn, Howard Mrs, 1946, Jl 12,17:1
Spohn, John, 1953, Mr 22,86:5
Spohn, Marion W, 1954, Ag 28,15:5
Spohn, Robert C, 1958, My 17,19:2
Spohn, Robert C Mrs, 1955, F 1,29:2
Spohn, William C Jr, 1967, Ja 7,27:5
Spohr, Howard A, 1955, Ag 16,23:2
Spohr, Kurt A, 1954, My 11,29:2
Spohrer, Gregory J, 1962, O 31,37:4
Spokesfield, William Mrs, 1964, Mr 25,41:4
Spon, William E, 1953, O 22,29:4
Sponenberg, Frank, 1938, S 16,21:6
Sponer-Franck, Hertha Dr, 1968, F 19,39:4
Spong, Hilda, 1955, My 17,29:4
Spong, Victor, 1949, D 29,25:5
Spongaugle, S Woodrow, 1967, My 1,37:4
Spongberg, Charles O, 1959, D 10,39:1
Spongberg, Fred, 1959, My 13,37:4
Sponholz, Albert E, 1944, Ap 27,23:2
Sponholz, Richard C, 1951, Ag 9,21:5
Sponland, Ingeborg, 1951, D 5,35:5
Sponsler, Clayton, 1920, D 17,17:4
Sponsler, O L, 1953, Mr 16,22:5
Spooner, A J, 1881, Ag 4,5:6
Spooner, Bernard, 1957, Jl 23,27:4
Spooner, David Brainerd Dr, 1925, F 2,17:3
Spooner, E B, 1876, N 21,8:5
Spooner, Edna M, 1953, Jl 16,21:3
Spooner, Henry J, 1918, F 10,17:1
Spooner, Henry S, 1938, My 11,19:5
Spooner, Herbert T, 1958, Jl 5,17:2
Spooner, John, 1963, S 4,39:5
Spooner, John A Jr, 1964, Mr 20,43:1
Spooner, John Colt (funl, My 12,15:5), 1919, Je 11, 15:1
Spooner, Joseph, 1883, Je 29,5:3
Spooner, Malcolm G, 1956, O 31,33:4
Spooner, Mary G Mrs, 1940, Ap 13,17:6
Spooner, Robert K, 1941, Je 28,15:3
Spooner, W A, 1930, S 1,13:1
Spooner, William, 1963, S 20,33:3; 1966, Jl 16,25:4
Spooner, William B Jr, 1956, Ap 8,84:5
Spoor, B G, 1928, D 24,13:6
Spoor, George K, 1953, N 25,23:1
Spoor, Marvin K, 1951, D 5,35:2
Spoor, Marvin Mrs, 1947, D 16,34:3
Spoor, Ralph E Jr Mrs, 1965, Je 18,35:2
Spoor, Seward G, 1955, Ja 30,84:7
Spoor, Simon H, 1949, My 26,29:3
Spor, Madeline (Mother Teresa), 1966, Ag 6,23:5
Sporborg, Henry J Mrs, 1939, Ag 15,19:3
Sporborg, William D Mrs (funl, Ja 5,31:4), 1961, Ja 3,29:2
Spordina, Benjamin, 1953, Ag 1,13:3
Sporkin, Albert L, 1957, Je 20,29:3
Sporkin, David, 1953, N 6,27:1
Sportell, Paul N, 1962, Je 11,31:4
Sposato, Anthony J, 1946, F 16,13:5
Spoth, Edward P, 1908, Ag 28,7:5
Spoto, Joseph C, 1948, F 16,21:4
Spottiswood-Mackin, Sarah, 1923, Ag 22,15:6
Spottiswoode, George, 1923, Je 14,19:4
Spottiswoode, George E, 1942, D 15,28:3
Spottiswoode, William, 1883, Je 28,4:7
Spottiswoode, 1883, Jl 12,3:1
Spottke, Albert, 1948, O 30,15:4
Spotts, J H Rear-Adm, 1882, Mr 24,5:4
Spotts, S Dale, 1952, F 2,13:4
Spottswood, James (por), 1940, O 12,17:3
Spozel, Ralph Mrs, 1948, O 8,26:2
Sprackling, Nelson, 1950, Ap 2,94:4
Sprackling, Nelson Mrs, 1963, Je 26,39:4
Spradling, Ralph D (Turk), 1955, N 19,19:1
Sprafke, Anna M Mrs, 1947, Je 2,25:4
Sprague, A A Mrs, 1916, Mr 29,11:6
Sprague, Abram M, 1948, Je 6,72:2
Sprague, Adelbert W, 1956, Ap 20,25:4
Sprague, Albert A (por), 1946, Ap 8,27:1
Sprague, Albert Arnold, 1915, Ja 12,9:4
Sprague, Arthur R Jr Prof, 1968, Je 22,33:3
Sprague, Augustus B, 1910, My 18,11:4
Sprague, Austin Velorous Milton, 1916, Ja 29,9:4
Sprague, Beecher W, 1949, O 6,31:1
Sprague, C A F, 1955, Ap 12,29:2
Sprague, C F, 1902, Ja 31,9:5
Sprague, Carl O, 1946, Jl 30,23:2
Sprague, Carleton, 1916, N 20,13:5
Sprague, Chandler, 1955, N 16,35:4
Sprague, Charles, 1939, Ap 30,44:8
Sprague, Charles Ezra Col (funl, Mr 25,11:5), 1912, Mr 22,9:4
Sprague, Charles James, 1903, Ag 6,7:6
Sprague, Clarence A, 1957, My 11,21:5
Sprague, Clarence H, 1955, Ap 10,89:1
Sprague, Claribel, 1942, Ag 1,11:3
Sprague, David H, 1945, N 28,27:2
Sprague, Dering J Mrs, 1954, D 17,31:1
Sprague, Dewitt C Col, 1908, O 12,9:7
Sprague, Edward E, 1924, O 4,13:4
Sprague, Edward Mrs, 1955, N 12,19:5
Sprague, Edward W Mrs, 1948, N 9,27:5
Sprague, Embert H, 1940, Mr 10,48:2
Sprague, Ernest L, 1944, N 30,23:2
Sprague, Ernest M, 1938, My 10,21:6
Sprague, Ezra K, 1943, F 3,19:6
Sprague, Ezra K Mrs, 1943, Ja 15,17:5
Sprague, F J, 1934, O 26,21:1
Sprague, F W, 1938, F 27,II,8:8
Sprague, Florence E, 1955, Ag 4,25:5
Sprague, Frank M, 1940, Ap 28,36:4
Sprague, Franklin H Mrs, 1923, Ap 11,21:4
Sprague, Franklin K Mrs, 1947, Je 4,27:3
Sprague, Frederick G Sr, 1952, N 23,89:1

Sprague, George C, 1966, Je 14,47:1
Sprague, George C Mrs, 1954, Ja 25,19:4
Sprague, George E, 1949, Je 28,21:3
Sprague, Gilbert S Mrs, 1939, Ap 8,15:4
Sprague, Harold T, 1949, Ja 7,22:7
Sprague, Henry, 1949, Je 26,35:2
Sprague, Henry Elliot, 1918, Ja 31,9:5
Sprague, Henry H, 1937, My 30,19:2
Sprague, Hester N B Mrs, 1937, S 25,17:4
Sprague, Homer Baxter Dr, 1918, Mr 24,13:1
Sprague, Hugh A, 1939, Jl 12,19:2
Sprague, Inez Mrs, 1938, Ja 23,II,8:1
Sprague, J B Col, 1878, D 4,2:6
Sprague, Jesse R, 1946, S 6,23:1
Sprague, John C Mrs, 1951, My 27,68:3
Sprague, John F, 1949, Jl 28,23:3
Sprague, John T, 1950, Ja 20,25:4
Sprague, Joseph, 1948, F 7,15:1
Sprague, Julian K, 1960, S 28,39:4
Sprague, Kenneth A, 1955, Jl 1,21:1
Sprague, Kenneth B, 1967, Ag 12,25:4
Sprague, Leslie W, 1938, O 29,19:6
Sprague, Lester B Mrs, 1949, D 9,31:1
Sprague, Lucian C, 1960, Ag 4,25:2
Sprague, Maud A Mrs, 1922, My 15,17:7
Sprague, Merton C, 1953, S 25,21:5
Sprague, N T Col, 1903, My 24,3:2
Sprague, Oliver M W, 1953, My 25,25:3
Sprague, Oliver M W Mrs, 1942, Ag 6,19:5
Sprague, Patricia D, 1966, Ag 19,33:2
Sprague, Phil G, 1951, S 25,29:5
Sprague, Phineas W, 1943, Je 30,21:2
Sprague, R L, 1934, O 17,23:1
Sprague, R W, 1928, My 25,25:5
Sprague, Ralph J Capt, 1924, Mr 21,19:3
Sprague, Robert J Mrs, 1956, My 18,25:4
Sprague, Seth, 1941, Mr 21,21:6
Sprague, Seth B, 1947, N 24,23:5
Sprague, Shirley E, 1957, F 2,19:5
Sprague, Smith, 1939, D 14,27:1
Sprague, Smith Mrs, 1946, Ag 5,21:4
Sprague, Talbert W, 1965, D 27,23:8
Sprague, Thomas S, 1937, Ag 15,II,7:2
Sprague, Victor D, 1941, My 10,15:4
Sprague, W B (funl), 1876, My 12,8:4
Sprague, W Edward, 1942, My 8,21:3
Sprague, W Edward Mrs, 1939, Mr 29,23:5
Sprague, Wallace E, 1947, D 29,17:1
Sprague, Wheeler S, 1950, My 10,31:1
Sprague, William, 1915, S 12,17:5
Sprague, William D, 1947, Ag 6,23:2
Sprague, William W, 1960, My 18,41:3
Sprague-Smith, Charles Mrs, 1950, D 29,20:2
Spraker, Benjamin F, 1940, N 5,25:4
Spraker, Ferdinand W, 1942, Ja 9,21:2
Spraker, George V, 1946, S 28,17:2
Spraker, John C Jr, 1950, N 28,31:3
Spranger, Eduard, 1963, S 18,39:1
Spratling, William, 1967, Ag 9,39:2
Spratling, William P Dr, 1915, D 24,9:4
Spratt, Daniel R, 1944, D 27,19:2
Spratt, Daniel R Mrs, 1937, Jl 31,15:5
Spratt, George V L, 1941, Ja 8,19:1
Spratt, Jack, 1959, O 5,31:2
Spratt, John J Mrs, 1945, My 2,23:4
Spratt, Joseph J, 1949, D 17,17:4
Spratt, Michael J, 1938, F 24,19:6
Spratt, Nathan W, 1942, D 27,34:2
Spratt, T, 1928, O 20,17:5
Spratt, Theodore H, 1949, Mr 9,25:5
Spratt, Thomas A, 1952, Jl 12,13:6
Spratt, William R Jr (por), 1938, Je 21,19:4
Spraul, Clarence, 1948, Je 5,15:6
Spray, Joseph H, 1962, F 24,27:1
Sprayregen, Richard H, 1959, S 26,23:4
Sprecher, Samuel Rev, 1906, Ja 12,9:6
Sprecher, Samuel Rev Dr, 1910, O 4,11:5
Spreckels, Adolph, 1924, Je 30,15:3
Spreckels, Adolph Bernard Mrs (Alma), 1968, Ag 8, 33:3
Spreckels, Claus A (por), 1946, N 10,62:1
Spreckels, Howard, 1939, Je 10,17:3
Spreckels, John D Jr, 1921, Ag 9,9:4
Spreckels, Rudolph, 1958, O 5,86:4
Spreckles, Adolph B 2d (death ruled accidental, N 1,14:1), 1961, O 29,79:5
Spreckles, Claus, 1908, D 27,9:5
Spreckles, J D, 1926, Je 8,25:3
Spreckles, Rudolph Mrs, 1949, F 23,27:6
Spreng, Samuel P, 1946, Ap 20,13:2
Sprenger, Arthur L, 1952, My 24,19:4
Sprenger, Henry P, 1951, Je 10,92:8
Sprengling, Martin, 1959, S 8,35:4
Sprenkle, Charles W Lt, 1953, F 5,23:3
Sprickman, Fred C, 1948, Mr 19,23:2
Sprigg, Gist, 1948, Mr 3,24:2
Sprigg, James C, 1947, S 21,60:5
Sprigg, James C Mrs, 1949, Ap 22,24:3
Sprigg, John Gordon Sir, 1913, F 6,11:4
Sprigg, Louis R, 1962, Je 26,33:3
Sprigg, William, 1913, O 27,9:4
Sprigge, Squire Sir, 1937, Je 18,21:1
Spriggins, Walter H, 1950, S 24,104:6
Spriggs, Charles J Dr, 1948, Ag 28,15:2
Spriggs, James A, 1938, N 3,23:5
Sprigle, Ray, 1957, D 23,13:4
Spring, Alfred Justice, 1912, O 23,13:5
Spring, Amasa, 1905, Ap 6,11:6
Spring, Arthur F, 1960, N 15,18:3
Spring, Arthur J, 1967, O 15,85:2
Spring, Ernest B, 1940, F 16,19:2
Spring, Gardiner Rev, 1873, Ag 20,4:7
Spring, George E, 1917, Ja 26,9:2; 1940, Ap 3,23:1
Spring, George W, 1956, Jl 2,21:6
Spring, Harry B, 1964, Ja 27,23:2
Spring, Henry P, 1950, F 22,29:2
Spring, Herbert A, 1949, Mr 22,25:4
Spring, Herman, 1963, Ap 7,85:7
Spring, Howard, 1965, My 4,43:3
Spring, Jesse, 1942, Mr 27,23:3
Spring, Leverett Wilson Prof, 1917, D 25,15:4
Spring, Mary Mrs, 1923, F 3,13:4
Spring, Matthew, 1952, O 30,31:6
Spring, Morton A, 1967, Ag 14,31:4
Spring, Romney, 1949, D 2,29:2
Spring, S Anthony Mrs, 1954, Je 1,27:5
Spring, Samuel N, 1952, F 5,29:4
Spring, Sylvester O, 1940, Ja 28,32:2
Spring, Thomas A, 1938, Ag 5,18:2
Spring, Thomas H, 1923, F 3,13:4
Spring, William A (por), 1940, N 24,48:1
Spring, William A, 1959, My 27,35:1
Spring, William A Mrs, 1954, Ap 22,29:2
Spring, William M, 1943, F 11,19:1
Spring-Rice, Cecil Arthur Sir (funl, F 22,11:5), 1918, F 15,9:1
Spring-Rice, Dominick, 1940, N 14,23:1
Springer, Ada L Mrs, 1942, Ag 15,11:3
Springer, Arthur H, 1956, D 20,29:5
Springer, Cornelius Rev, 1875, Ag 19,4:6
Springer, Durand W, 1943, My 19,25:3
Springer, Edward K, 1938, O 30,V,2:7
Springer, Elwell L, 1937, Je 5,17:1
Springer, Eugene Mrs, 1940, My 4,17:4
Springer, Floyd H, 1953, Mr 1,92:2
Springer, Francis C, 1951, Jl 13,21:1
Springer, Fred E, 1945, Ap 9,19:2
Springer, Fred W, 1948, S 15,31:4
Springer, George W, 1950, Je 9,23:6
Springer, J A, 1934, Ja 18,21:1
Springer, James E Mrs, 1945, Mr 26,19:2
Springer, John H, 1925, Ap 17,21:4
Springer, John M Mrs (por), 1949, Ag 26,19:5
Springer, John McK, 1963, D 8,86:3
Springer, Lewis A, 1945, F 9,15:4
Springer, Louis, 1948, D 8,31:4
Springer, Louis A, 1940, Ja 7,48:2
Springer, Louis A Mrs, 1953, Jl 18,13:4
Springer, Maxwell Mrs, 1943, Jl 6,21:4
Springer, Nathaniel N, 1962, S 15,25:5
Springer, R R, 1884, D 11,2:5
Springer, Raymond S, 1947, Ag 29,17:2
Springer, Robert L, 1963, Je 20,33:5
Springer, Ruter W, 1937, Mr 20,19:4
Springer, Ruter W Mrs, 1951, N 16,25:5
Springer, Sarah H Mrs, 1943, S 8,24:2
Springer, Walter I, 1949, My 17,25:4
Springer, Walter I Mrs, 1948, Ja 6,23:4
Springer, William E Dr, 1912, Mr 14,11:4
Springer, William J, 1941, F 11,23:5
Springer, William M Judge, 1903, D 5,9:1
Springett, E J, 1955, Je 13,23:6
Springett, Leslie E, 1959, F 10,33:2
Springford, Herbert H, 1942, Ap 2,21:3
Springhall, Douglas F, 1953, S 8,3:1
Springhorn, Frederick, 1941, O 1,21:2
Springhorn, Herman J, 1940, S 7,15:5
Springmann, Edward, 1938, Je 26,27:2
Springmeyer, Charles E, 1948, S 29,29:3
Springmeyer, Charles E Mrs, 1946, Jl 18,25:4
Springorum, Fritz, 1942, Ap 19,43:2
Springorum, Hans W, 1965, D 28,25:2
Springovics, Antonio, 1958, O 5,87:2
Springs, Albert A, 1943, F 27,13:5
Springs, E B, 1933, Ap 15,13:1
Springs, Elliot W (est appr filed), 1960, My 21,14:3
Springs, Elliott W (will, O 25,60:8), 1959, O 16,31:1
Springs, Lena J Mrs, 1942, My 19,19:4
Springs, Richard A, 1944, Je 30,21:3
Springs, Richard A Jr, 1959, F 8,86:1
Springstead, Charles B, 1952, N 5,27:4
Springstead, Egbert E, 1946, S 26,25:1
Springstead, Elizabeth M Mrs, 1943, Jl 28,15:5
Springstead, Joseph A, 1963, S 22,87:1
Springsted, James W, 1946, S 18,31:3
Springsted, Johnson A, 1953, Ag 2,73:1
Springsteel, Garret A, 1942, F 22,26:3
Springsteel, John M Sr, 1952, S 23,33:4
Springsteen, George W, 1954, O 6,25:1
Springsteen, Howard D, 1952, Ap 7,25:4
Springsteen, Levi, 1910, O 24,9:6
Springsteen, Nelson J, 1961, Mr 6,25:1
Springsteen, William H, 1943, Je 27,32:5
Sprintz, Henry, 1955, D 25,49:1
Sprinz, Joseph Mrs, 1964, F 10,27:4
Sprinz, Samuel B, 1951, Je 28,25:6
Sprinzak, Joseph, 1959, Ja 29,27:1
Sproat, Elric S, 1951, D 30,25:1
Sproat, Eric, 1950, Ja 20,26:3
Sproat, Harris L, 1952, S 26,21:1
Sproedt, Gustav A, 1949, S 4,41:1
Sproesser, William C, 1958, F 1,19:5
Sprogiani, Henrico (Rhum), 1953, O 23,23:5
Sprong, Severn D, 1946, Je 30,38:2
Spronghorn, Frederick J, 1947, Ja 28,23:5
Spross, Charles G, 1961, D 25,23:6
Spross, Walter J, 1953, O 22,29:4
Sprott, Albert, 1951, D 20,18:4
Sprott, Jarl S, 1949, F 13,76:2
Sproul, Albert E, 1946, Jl 7,36:1
Sproul, Alphonzo Jr, 1950, D 5,31:3
Sproul, Arthur E, 1940, Mr 18,17:1
Sproul, George, 1925, N 24,25:2
Sproul, John J, 1942, Mr 10,19:4
Sproul, John R, 1949, O 10,23:2
Sproul, Joseph S, 1959, Ag 26,29:3
Sproul, Mary S Mrs, 1943, Ag 10,19:5
Sproul, Merrill F Jr, 1965, Je 8,41:1
Sproul, S Everett, 1940, S 20,23:6
Sproul, W C, 1928, Mr 22,25:5
Sproul, William C, 1946, Ap 9,27:5
Sproule, Charles D, 1950, Ap 26,29:2
Sproule, Charles J R, 1952, Jl 1,23:3
Sproule, Dorothy, 1963, Ja 4,4:4
Sproule, W, 1935, Ja 2,25:1
Sproull, Edward I, 1956, Ag 17,19:4
Sproull, Gormly J, 1940, Ag 30,19:5
Sproull, S Everett Mrs, 1940, Mr 26,21:1
Sprouls, Estelle R, 1956, O 24,37:4
Sprouse, Claude W, 1952, S 9,29:1
Sprout, Warren A Sr, 1945, Ag 25,11:4
Sprowl, Annie H Mrs, 1941, Mr 3,15:2
Sprowl, Edward A, 1941, Mr 11,23:1
Sprowl, James H, 1949, F 17,23:2
Sprowle, M J, 1903, Ag 15,7:6
Sprowles, M Reba, 1951, Jl 20,21:4
Spruance, Benton M, 1967, D 7,52:7
Spruance, Gilbert, 1944, Ja 2,38:6
Spruance, John S, 1945, Jl 5,13:1
Spruance, William C Ex-Justice, 1913, Mr 13,11:3
Spruill, Addison W, 1950, S 13,27:3
Sprung, Martin K Mrs, 1961, Ja 31,29:2
Sprung, May I, 1950, N 21,31:2
Sprunt, Alex Rev Dr, 1937, D 16,27:6
Sprunt, James, 1924, Jl 11,13:6
Spruth, Erwin, 1952, O 31,25:3
Spry, Constance Mrs, 1960, Ja 5,31:5
Spry, Walter, 1953, S 27,86:4
Spuechler, M U Mrs, 1912, Ap 21,II,13:3
Spurdle, Alfred, 1949, S 12,21:2
Spurdle, Henry, 1940, O 4,23:1
Spurgeon, Arthur, 1938, Je 10,21:5
Spurgeon, Caroline F E (por), 1942, O 25,44:3
Spurgeon, Charles H Rev, 1892, F 1,1:7
Spurgeon, J J, 1930, F 20,25:1
Spurgeon, Louis, 1956, Je 19,29:3
Spurgeon, Thomas Rev, 1917, O 22,15:5
Spurgeon, William P, 1920, Je 5,15:5
Spurgeon's, Ch H Rev, 1903, O 23,7:6
Spurling, Nancy J Mrs, 1925, N 23,21:4
Spurling, Stanley, 1961, Ja 12,29:4
Spurney, A B, 1950, My 4,27:3
Spurney, Albert F, 1943, Ap 17,17:4
Spurr, Albert R, 1950, O 14,19:2
Spurr, E Willard, 1938, F 16,21:1
Spurr, Ethel M, 1960, F 20,23:5
Spurr, Joseph G, 1950, Je 8,32:3
Spurr, Josiah E, 1950, Ja 13,24:2
Spurrier, Henry, 1964, Je 19,31:1
Spurrier, Samuel, 1940, N 10,57:2
Spurway, Hubert V, 1944, Ag 1,15:3
Spyglass, J Elmer, 1957, F 22,21:5
Spykman, Nicholas J, 1943, Je 27,33:1
Spykman, Nicholas J Mrs, 1965, Ag 8,64:8
Spyr, Lawrence Nelson, 1953, F 22,60:4
Spyridon, Vlahos Archbishop, 1956, Mr 21,3:6
Spyropolous, Andrew Mrs, 1937, Ap 6,23:5
Spyropoulos, Andrew, 1955, Ag 23,24:1
Spyschalski, Sam J, 1903, Jl 29,2:6
Squadron, Howard M Mrs, 1967, O 31,49:3
Square, William H, 1951, D 19,31:3
Squarewood, Ida D, 1950, S 2,15:6
Squarey, Edward M, 1957, D 28,17:3
Squibb, George L P, 1944, My 4,19:6
Squibb, George S, 1951, F 21,27:4
Squibb, John, 1953, Ap 30,31:1
Squibbs, Henry A, 1946, D 30,19:3
Squier, Albert J, 1949, F 12,17:4
Squier, Anderson P, 1940, Je 2,44:8
Squier, Carl B, 1967, N 7,43:1
Squier, Charles B, 1904, O 7,9:6
Squier, Clarence T, 1951, Ja 28,76:4
Squier, Cyrus W, 1944, Mr 9,18:2
Squier, E G, 1888, Ap 18,8:3
Squier, E M, 1926, N 10,27:1
Squier, Frank, 1908, S 27,11:6
Squier, Frederick C, 1937, Ag 30,21:5
Squier, Harriet M, 1946, Je 8,21:3
Squier, Herbert, 1948, Mr 3,23:2

Squier, J Bentley, 1924, F 14,17:4; 1948, Mr 2,23:1; 1967, N 2,47:3
Squier, J Bentley Mrs, 1956, Ag 10,17:4
Squier, Joel H Mrs (cor, Ag 5,27:5), 1958, Ag 3,81:3
Squier, Joel J, 1955, O 9,86:7
Squier, John J, 1938, Je 22,23:5
Squier, Lucien B, 1904, Ja 5,9:6
Squier, Miles P Dr, 1866, Jl 15,3:7
Squier, Minnie S Mrs, 1938, S 10,17:5
Squier, S C, 1926, N 7,II,9:1
Squier, William, 1945, Ap 12,23:4
Squiers, Arnon L Justice (funl, O 30,22:3), 1921, O 29,13:6
Squiers, Harry, 1952, Mr 26,29:3
Squiers, Herbert G, 1911, O 21,13:3
Squiers, John M, 1949, My 17,25:3
Squiers, William H T, 1948, Ap 21,27:3
Squinobal, George B, 1952, Ag 13,21:2
Squire, Abiram F Dr, 1925, O 5,21:4
Squire, Amos O (por), 1949, F 12,17:1
Squire, Amos O Mrs, 1944, O 6,23:2
Squire, Belle, 1939, Ap 18,23:6
Squire, Edward J, 1967, S 30,33:1
Squire, Frank W, 1953, Jl 9,25:5
Squire, G O, 1934, Mr 25,29:3
Squire, George H, 1950, Ja 20,25:1
Squire, Gouverneur P, 1944, Ap 28,20:2
Squire, Irving, 1940, Ja 3,21:2
Squire, J H, 1956, S 19,37:3
Squire, John, 1958, D 29,15:6
Squire, John P Mrs (E Purviance), 1958, Ja 16,29:1
Squire, John R, 1947, Jl 23,23:4
Squire, Julius Mrs, 1965, My 28,33:1
Squire, Latham C, 1962, Ja 6,19:2
Squire, Margaret S Mrs, 1938, Ja 19,23:3
Squire, Marguerite, 1925, Jl 8,17:5
Squire, Paul C, 1966, N 23,39:2
Squire, R M, 1899, Mr 14,7:6
Squire, Roger J, 1960, My 2,29:4
Squire, Ronald, 1958, N 17,31:5
Squire, Rose E, 1938, Ap 18,15:4
Squire, Samuel, 1937, Ap 12,18:1
Squire, W C Col, 1926, Je 9,23:3
Squire, W H, 1942, Mr 18,28:3
Squire, W L, 1903, Je 20,7:6
Squire, Walter, 1959, D 30,21:2
Squire, William R, 1951, Mr 26,23:4
Squire, William W T, 1952, O 29,29:5
Squires, Alvin, 1943, Jl 2,19:3
Squires, Alvin E, 1937, Ja 2,14:1
Squires, Arthur C, 1956, Ja 17,33:3
Squires, Benjamin M Mrs, 1937, Mr 14,42:3
Squires, Boyd T, 1955, Je 9,29:4
Squires, Charles A, 1942, Mr 23,15:5
Squires, Charles W, 1941, Ap 26,15:5
Squires, Clarence, 1915, Jl 9,11:5
Squires, Cyrenius N, 1906, Ag 21,7:6
Squires, Edith L, 1939, Je 3,15:6
Squires, Ernest K Lt-Gen, 1940, Mr 4,15:2
Squires, Ethel J, 1952, D 7,88:3
Squires, Etta, 1952, F 16,13:3
Squires, F Donald, 1966, S 19,43:2
Squires, Frederic W, 1952, Ag 28,23:6
Squires, G, 1928, D 11,31:5
Squires, George F, 1956, N 19,31:3
Squires, H W, 1876, My 9,3:3
Squires, Harry, 1953, Mr 9,29:5
Squires, Harry D, 1960, D 20,33:4
Squires, Henry, 1907, Ja 15,7:6
Squires, Herbert W Mrs, 1937, Je 2,23:2
Squires, John N, 1950, D 25,19:5
Squires, Joseph C, 1909, N 15,9:3
Squires, Leander E, 1949, D 31,15:2
Squires, Lewis Mrs, 1956, Ag 6,23:5
Squires, Maurice, 1944, O 16,19:4
Squires, Paul C, 1958, N 26,29:5
Squires, Richard A Sir, 1940, Mr 26,21:2
Squires, Stephen, 1905, Mr 25,9:3
Squires, Thomas W, 1954, Je 18,23:3
Squires, Warren M Mrs, 1949, Je 1,31:2
Squires, William A, 1953, Jl 21,23:1
Squires, William Dr, 1937, Ja 8,19:3
Squittieri, Albert, 1947, Mr 2,60:8
Squyres, Scott P, 1946, My 19,42:5
Srafford, Helen G, 1958, Je 13,23:3
Sramek, Jan, 1955, Ag 25,3:7
Srebnik, Abraham, 1948, Ja 7,25:5
Srebnik, Philip, 1946, N 13,27:3
Sreenivasachar, Puttaparthi, 1963, N 29,34:5
Srholez, Joseph Jr, 1957, N 10,86:8
Srinivasa Sastri, V S, 1946, Ap 18,27:2
Srinivasan, C R, 1962, Ja 31,31:2
Srinivasan, Kasturi, 1959, Je 22,25:2
Srobar, Vavro, 1950, D 7,33:2
Sroka, Stanislaw, 1967, Ag 14,31:4
Sruh, Sam F, 1952, My 27,27:3
Srulovitz, Morris J, 1959, Mr 9,29:1
Srulowitz, Harry J, 1964, D 24,19:3
Srybnik, Aaron G, 1952, Ag 26,25:2
Sszk, Josef G, 1947, Jl 7,17:4
Staab, Charles F Sr, 1948, Je 18,23:2
Staab, Harold B, 1949, N 20,93:1
Staab, Robert G, 1963, F 5,4:7
Staab, William F, 1957, S 12,31:4
Staab, William J, 1952, Ap 3,36:3
Staack, Peter, 1952, Jl 12,13:7
Staaf, Karl Albert, 1915, O 5,11:6
Staake, William H Judge, 1924, Jl 31,13:5
Staates, Chris F, 1939, F 21,19:1
Staats, Bergen B, 1942, Je 28,32:4
Staats, Charles B, 1942, O 28,23:2
Staats, Frederick T, 1956, Ap 26,33:3
Staats, Grace, 1948, N 14,76:7
Staats, Herbert W, 1950, Mr 31,31:3
Staats, Ludwig, 1949, Ap 2,15:2
Staats, Phil, 1913, My 12,9:4
Staats, Robert Parker, 1920, Ag 20,9:5
Staats, W P B Dr, 1871, Jl 11,5:3
Staats, Walter J Sr Mrs, 1956, Jl 4,19:2
Stabb, Mrs, 1903, F 16,14:2
Stabell, Frederick P, 1954, Ag 21,17:1
Staber, Ernest H, 1966, S 10,29:5
Staber, George, 1914, N 21,13:4
Stabert, William H Mrs, 1943, N 18,23:4
Stabile, Ralph B, 1951, F 8,33:1
Stableford, Richard G, 1938, Ja 27,21:4
Stablein, Frank J, 1956, O 18,33:1
Stabler, C Norman Mrs (Mae W), 1965, N 27,31:1
Stabler, Clara M K Mrs, 1941, Je 17,21:6
Stabler, E, 1883, S 6,4:7
Stabler, Francis, 1948, My 9,68:3
Stabler, Frederick, 1950, O 20,28:3
Stabler, Frederick Sr, 1945, Ap 30,19:3
Stabler, Herman, 1942, N 26,27:2
Stabler, J Paul, 1968, Ag 20,41:2
Stabler, John G (por), 1940, Ja 4,24:3
Stabler, Jordan, 1916, Je 23,11:7
Stabler, Jordan H, 1938, D 31,15:3
Stabler, Laird J, 1939, N 27,17:3
Stabler, Walter, 1937, Mr 17,25:4
Stabley, Edna A, 1952, Ap 21,21:2
Staborahy, Viscount, 1872, F 12,1:2
Stace, Arthur W, 1950, Ja 12,27:4
Stace, Walter T, 1967, Ag 5,21:5
Stacey, Alfred E (por), 1940, Mr 11,15:6
Stacey, Charles E, 1956, N 11,86:3
Stacey, Delia, 1945, Ag 4,11:2
Stacey, Frank, 1946, D 22,42:2
Stacey, Herbert R, 1957, O 29,31:4
Stacey, John W, 1951, N 13,29:5
Stacey, M H Mrs, 1918, Ja 22,11:5
Stacey, Sidney, 1967, My 20,35:5
Stacey, Sidney G, 1953, Ja 11,91:2
Stacey, Sidney J, 1966, Ap 6,43:2
Stacey, Stephen L, 1937, O 30,19:2
Stachel, Jacob A, 1966, Ja 2,73:1
Stachnik, Edward P, 1965, Ap 29,35:4
Stachnik, Victor S, 1950, N 15,31:4
Stack, Arthur J, 1948, F 19,23:1
Stack, Bridget Mrs, 1938, N 27,5:1
Stack, Edward W, 1941, Mr 12,21:1
Stack, Emmett J, 1968, Je 23,73:1
Stack, Frank T Mrs, 1942, D 25,17:4
Stack, Garrett M, 1950, Ja 14,15:6
Stack, Gene, 1942, Je 28,V,3:1
Stack, Herbert J, 1967, Ap 1,31:5
Stack, James A, 1951, F 9,25:3
Stack, James M, 1942, D 26,11:5
Stack, John G, 1949, F 4,23:2
Stack, John J, 1955, F 21,21:3
Stack, Joseph C, 1949, Jl 29,21:5
Stack, Joseph F X, 1943, F 18,23:2
Stack, Joseph M, 1952, Mr 8,13:2
Stack, Lee P, 1968, Ag 16,33:2
Stack, Loyola J Mrs, 1940, N 28,23:5
Stack, Maurice F, 1960, O 21,33:5
Stack, Michael J, 1960, D 16,33:1
Stack, Morton M, 1967, D 30,23:2
Stack, Richard, 1945, N 3,15:5
Stack, Richard Mrs, 1943, My 10,19:1
Stack, Thomas V, 1946, Ja 23,27:2
Stack, William J, 1961, Mr 3,27:2
Stackhouse, Clarence, 1945, S 9,46:8
Stackhouse, D Trueman, 1938, Ap 14,23:3
Stackhouse, Edwin S, 1951, O 11,37:3
Stackhouse, G E, 1903, Ja 31,9:6
Stackhouse, Glenn W, 1958, Ap 3,31:4
Stackhouse, P, 1927, F 5,15:6
Stackpole, Alice Mrs, 1949, Ja 9,64:4
Stackpole, Caroline E, 1957, Mr 16,19:3
Stackpole, Charles B Col, 1937, Ja 26,21:2
Stackpole, Chester S Mrs, 1963, My 25,25:4
Stackpole, Gordon, 1941, Ap 9,25:3
Stackpole, J Lewis, 1953, Ag 5,23:4
Stackpole, John Col, 1873, Ag 10,1:6
Stackpole, John F, 1949, S 30,23:3
Stackpole, Joseph L, 1904, Ja 3,9:5
Stacom, Matthew J, 1954, F 26,19:4
Stacpoole, Henry D, 1951, Ap 13,23:1
Stacton, David, 1968, Ja 24,42:1
Stacy, Charles L, 1963, Je 8,25:1
Stacy, Gardner W, 1944, Ag 9,17:5
Stacy, George Edward, 1925, My 18,15:5
Stacy, N Winchell, 1939, S 23,17:2
Stacy, Orville Brigs Prof, 1912, Jl 13,9:5
Stacy, Paul F, 1950, S 15,26:3
Stacy, Richard G, 1949, O 2,81:1
Stacy, Thomas, 1951, Ag 19,V,3:1
Stacy, Walter P, 1951, S 14,25:3
Stacy, Wilbur H, 1950, Je 24,13:2
Stad, Ben, 1946, Ag 20,27:5
Stad, Ben Mrs, 1958, Mr 1,17:3
Stadelman, Otto R, 1958, Mr 16,86:5
Stadelman, W A, 1910, Jl 7,7:4
Stader, Anna M (Sister M Angela), 1952, S 28,77:2
Stader, Otto, 1962, S 14,31:1
Stadie, William C, 1959, S 13,84:3
Stadler, A Lincoln, 1938, Jl 3,12:8
Stadler, John, 1948, F 29,61:1
Stadler, Lewis J, 1954, My 14,23:5
Stadler, Max, 1910, Jl 13,7:5
Stadler, Phil J, 1958, Ag 14,29:5
Stadmuller, Ellen S, 1941, N 27,23:6
Stadtfeld, Joseph, 1943, D 13,23:2
Stadtfeld, Nicolaas T F, 1964, Mr 20,33:3
Stadthagen, David, 1948, Jl 16,19:3
Stadtlander, Elizabeth L, 1958, Je 15,76:6
Stadtlander, George, 1943, Ja 9,13:2
Stadtmueller, Frank H, 1918, Ja 12,11:4
Stadtmuller, C Frederick, 1956, Je 11,31:5
Staedter, Robert E, 1943, Mr 18,15:4
Staeger, Anna Mrs, 1937, Ja 20,21:1
Staeger, Henry C, 1966, S 13,47:2
Staehle, Arthur J Sr, 1956, My 15,31:4
Staehle, Cyrus H, 1950, Jl 21,19:2
Staehle, Hans H L, 1961, Ja 4,33:4
Staehle, John L, 1950, O 21,17:5
Staehle, Richard H Dr, 1968, My 22,47:5
Staehlin, Gustavus, 1916, Ap 19,13:4
Stael, Nicolas de, 1955, Mr 23,31:5
Staempfli, Jacob, 1879, My 16,5:6
Staff, Aaron S, 1960, Je 17,31:1
Staff, Clement, 1958, Mr 27,33:3
Staff, Leopold, 1957, Je 6,31:5
Staff, Louis A (por), 1949, Ap 8,25:4
Staff, Mary E (will), 1938, D 13,8:3
Staff, Oscar H, 1949, O 16,90:4
Staff, Pauline Mrs, 1947, Ag 26,23:3
Staff, Samuel G, 1965, Ja 14,35:4
Staff, Samuel I, 1954, Ja 9,16:3
Staffa, Frank, 1949, O 20,29:2
Staffa, Frank Mrs, 1938, Jl 2,13:3
Staffelli, Louis Mrs, 1954, My 22,15:2
Stafflinger, Charles N, 1942, Jl 14,19:2
Stafford, Archibald S, 1943, O 13,23:5
Stafford, Arthur N Mrs, 1946, N 4,25:4
Stafford, Bernard L, 1955, Ap 26,29:1
Stafford, Bert L, 1941, Jl 30,17:5
Stafford, Charles M, 1913, O 24,11:5
Stafford, Clarence Mrs, 1945, N 7,23:1
Stafford, Denis J Dr, 1908, Ja 4,9:4
Stafford, Elmore H, 1951, Ja 26,23:1
Stafford, Frank B, 1947, Mr 20,28:3
Stafford, Frank B Mrs, 1963, O 21,31:2
Stafford, Frank S, 1951, Ap 23,15:3
Stafford, Frank S Mrs, 1951, Ap 23,15:3
Stafford, Franklin H, 1950, Ap 7,25:4
Stafford, Geoffrey W, 1958, O 28,35:1
Stafford, George A, 1937, D 15,25:3
Stafford, George D Mrs, 1952, N 6,29:4
Stafford, George L, 1946, Mr 15,21:1
Stafford, Grover C Mrs, 1950, N 25,13:4
Stafford, Hanley, 1968, S 11,47:3
Stafford, Harlow H Mrs, 1959, Jl 16,27:4
Stafford, Harold C, 1948, Je 10,25:3
Stafford, Harriet, 1904, F 6,9:6
Stafford, Hattie Mrs, 1923, My 21,15:5
Stafford, Helen Ford, 1939, My 1,23:4
Stafford, Henry, 1938, N 20,39:1
Stafford, Hiram M, 1941, O 13,17:6
Stafford, James Dr, 1909, Ag 5,7:6
Stafford, James J, 1941, Ap 7,17:5
Stafford, John A, 1923, O 18,19:3; 1952, N 5,27:5
Stafford, John A Msgr, 1913, Ja 22,11:4
Stafford, John E, 1946, My 20,23:2
Stafford, John P, 1942, F 17,21:6
Stafford, John P Sr, 1943, N 1,17:3
Stafford, John T, 1944, S 1,13:1
Stafford, Leonard D, 1949, Mr 18,25:2
Stafford, Lord, 1941, S 30,23:2
Stafford, Marian Mrs, 1953, Mr 7,15:4
Stafford, Mary Mrs, 1940, My 5,53:2
Stafford, Morgan H, 1940, N 21,30:2
Stafford, Morton O, 1942, O 24,15:3
Stafford, Nathaniel H, 1950, Ap 25,31:3
Stafford, Ralph S, 1966, Ja 19,41:3
Stafford, Richard L, 1947, Je 6,23:4
Stafford, Robert K, 1940, O 15,23:2
Stafford, Roy D, 1942, D 17,29:4
Stafford, Russell Mrs, 1954, Ja 10,86:1
Stafford, Sarah Mrs, 1937, Jl 19,15:2
Stafford, Sarah S, 1880, Ja 13,4:7
Stafford, Thomas D, 1953, O 3,17:6
Stafford, W H Mrs, 1949, D 28,25:3
Stafford, William, 1941, Ja 10,19:4
Stafford, William A, 1956, Ja 14,19:6
Stafford, William B, 1955, Mr 8,27:2; 1964, Je 2,37:4
Stafford, William Frederick, 1918, D 6,15:4

Stafford, William S, 1943, N 7,57:2
Stafsholt, Theodore, 1942, Mr 18,23:1
Staft, Emanuel W, 1968, Ja 2,41:4
Stage, Vern, 1948, D 28,21:2
Stager, A Gen, 1885, Mr 23,1:2
Stager, Adolph, 1949, O 22,17:2
Stager, Francis T, 1938, Je 13,19:5
Stager, Luke L, 1962, Ja 20,21:5
Stager, Stanley R Mrs, 1941, Mr 31,15:4
Stagg, Amos A (funl, Mr 22,33:3), 1965, Mr 18,1:8
Stagg, Amos A Mrs, 1964, Jl 24,27:2
Stagg, Annie E Mrs, 1916, My 6,11:4
Stagg, Chester A, 1951, Ja 23,27:1
Stagg, Henry P, 1925, N 2,23:5
Stagg, Ida C Mrs, 1940, Ja 16,23:2
Stagg, James H, 1937, Ja 5,23:4
Stagg, Mary, 1878, O 25,2:7
Stagg, Paul L, 1944, Ag 22,17:5
Stagg, Peter Gen, 1884, D 28,2:2
Stagg, Thomas L, 1952, O 24,23:2
Stagg, W De P, 1883, Mr 30,5:4
Stagg, Washington I, 1941, My 18,45:1
Stagg, William B Mrs, 1945, Mr 28,23:2
Stagg, William H, 1951, Ap 3,27:2
Stagias, George, 1947, My 5,23:1
Stagich, Bozo N, 1949, Je 14,31:3
Stagmaier, John, 1944, F 16,17:4
Stagmeier, Arthur F, 1965, D 29,26:7
Stagmer, E Bronson, 1948, Je 15,27:5
Stagni, P F Msgr, 1918, O 24,13:1
Stahel, Julius H Gen, 1912, D 5,17:3
Stahl, A Clark, 1945, Ag 3,17:5
Stahl, A M, 1926, N 28,II,11:1
Stahl, Adolph, 1940, S 18,23:5
Stahl, Albert W, 1942, S 20,39:2
Stahl, Benjamin F, 1944, Mr 21,19:4
Stahl, Charles E, 1938, Ja 14,23:4
Stahl, Charles E Sr, 1953, O 10,17:7
Stahl, Charles J, 1942, Ag 8,11:6
Stahl, Charles N Sr, 1954, D 18,15:3
Stahl, E C Col, 1921, Je 25,11:6
Stahl, Emil P, 1951, My 22,31:2
Stahl, Frank M, 1937, Mr 5,21:2
Stahl, Fred C, 1938, Ap 10,II,6:5
Stahl, Frederick L, 1941, Ja 5,44:6
Stahl, Friedrich, 1940, Jl 14,30:8
Stahl, Gustav A, 1953, Je 5,27:5
Stahl, Gustave A Mrs, 1945, O 11,23:3
Stahl, Heinrich, 1942, N 28,6:7
Stahl, Henry A, 1953, Ja 30,21:3
Stahl, Henry A Mrs, 1953, Ap 16,29:6
Stahl, Henry W, 1954, Mr 8,27:2
Stahl, Jasper B, 1943, N 14,57:1
Stahl, John M, 1944, O 19,23:2; 1950, Ja 14,15:3
Stahl, Joseph J, 1962, Mr 5,23:2
Stahl, Julius J, 1944, Je 11,46:1
Stahl, Karl F, 1946, Ag 27,27:5
Stahl, Leo J, 1960, Jl 8,21:3
Stahl, Lionel A, 1937, Mr 8,19:1
Stahl, Louis, 1940, N 14,23:4
Stahl, Nicholas, 1943, Ja 2,11:5
Stahl, Otto, 1957, Ja 29,31:4
Stahl, Otto Mrs, 1945, Mr 5,19:5
Stahl, Robert H, 1954, Mr 10,25:5
Stahl, Roy E, 1940, Ap 27,15:5
Stahl, Sidney, 1959, My 17,84:8
Stahl, Vincent J, 1945, Jl 29,40:5
Stahl, W, 1942, Ag 25,18:3
Stahl, W Albert, 1960, S 1,27:3
Stahl, William M Sr, 1956, D 12,35:6
Stahl, Willy, 1963, Ap 13,19:4
Stahlberg, Emil, 1941, My 24,15:1
Stahlberg, Frederick, 1937, Jl 24,15:7
Stahlberg, Gideon, 1967, My 27,31:5
Stahlberg, Kaarlo J S, 1952, S 23,33:2
Stahler, Horace C, 1961, O 21,21:6
Stahley, Cass Mrs, 1950, Mr 7,27:5
Stahlin, Charles E F, 1945, O 31,23:1
Stahlin, Charles E F Mrs, 1953, Ja 20,25:2
Stahlman, E B, 1930, Ag 13,19:1
Stahlman, Edward C Mrs, 1938, My 22,II,7:2
Stahlman, Frank C, 1949, My 5,28:2
Stahlman, James G Mrs, 1952, Mr 8,5:4
Stahlnecker, Elizabeth F Mrs, 1942, N 9,23:5
Stahlschmidt, Arthur E, 1942, Mr 13,19:4
Stahnke, August J, 1945, D 4,29:3
Stahr, Elvis J Sr, 1963, D 26,28:4
Stahr, Frederick C, 1946, Mr 11,25:5
Stahr, Henry I, 1962, Je 1,28:1
Stahr, John M (por), 1944, Ag 17,17:5
Stahr, Paul, 1953, Ja 6,29:2
Stahr, Theodora, 1949, Ja 30,60:4
Staib, Charles, 1941, Ag 16,15:1
Staib, Phil C, 1949, Mr 7,21:6
Staier, Julius C, 1945, Mr 22,23:3
Staiger, Hugo M, 1943, O 27,23:2
Staigers, Del, 1950, Jl 15,13:4
Staigg, R M, 1881, O 12,5:6
Stailing, Robert L, 1950, F 12,85:1
Stain, L Dr, 1882, D 7,5:1
Stainach, Armand R Count, 1911, O 18,11:5
Stainach, Stephen Mrs (S Perry), 1959, Ja 23,25:3
Stainback, Charles L Jr, 1959, O 6,39:3
Stainback, Ingram M, 1961, Ap 13,35:3
Stainback, Ingram M Mrs, 1949, O 13,27:4
Staines, Charles T Sr, 1953, Ja 30,22:5
Staines, Glenn S, 1951, Jl 8,60:3
Stainsby, William, 1906, Je 21,7:6
Stainton, C Raymond, 1943, My 30,26:3
Stainton, Charles D, 1941, Ag 28,19:2
Stair, Arthur C, 1961, S 7,35:1
Stair, Bird, 1957, My 12,87:1
Stair, Carl E, 1966, Jl 9,27:2
Stair, E D Jr, 1950, Ag 1,23:1
Stair, Earl of, 1903, D 4,9:4
Stair, Earl of (Jno Hew North Gustav Hamilton), 1914, D 3,13:3
Stair, Edward, 1945, O 5,23:4
Stair, Edward D, 1951, My 23,35:2
Stair, Edward D Mrs, 1947, Ap 14,27:2
Stair, Edwin B, 1961, F 16,31:1
Stair, Harry, 1952, My 19,17:5
Stair, Henry, 1906, Je 23,7:2
Stair, Sidney, 1938, S 13,23:1
Stajer, Sidney, 1940, D 12,16:6
Stake, Edward Judge, 1902, N 17,9:5
Stake, Emil A, 1944, D 20,23:3
Stake, J Edward, 1939, My 4,23:4
Stake, Walter W, 1964, F 27,31:2
Stakes, Wilbur S, 1957, Mr 16,19:6
Stakgold, Henri, 1966, Jl 5,27:3
Staknevich, John, 1961, D 18,35:3
Stalb, Walter A, 1963, S 21,21:2
Stalberg-Wernigerode, Udo von Count, 1910, F 20,II, 9:1
Stalbridge, Lord (H Grosvenor), 1949, D 25,26:7
Stalcup, Benjamin F, 1949, F 22,23:1
Staley, Allan C, 1960, D 6,41:3
Staley, Allen C Jr Mrs, 1961, Ja 18,33:4
Staley, Augustus E Sr, 1940, D 27,20:3
Staley, Cass F, 1939, O 22,40:7
Staley, Donald, 1954, Mr 26,21:3
Staley, Ellis J, 1943, F 9,23:4
Staley, Frank S, 1943, Jl 7,19:5
Staley, George R, 1961, My 13,19:4
Staley, Gilbert Mrs, 1953, O 30,23:1
Staley, Harry M Mrs, 1956, F 5,86:4
Staley, Harvey B, 1949, N 18,29:1
Staley, J H, 1959, S 2,29:5
Staley, John R, 1964, N 8,88:2
Staley, Marion T, 1938, Mr 27,18:1
Staley, Orville H, 1943, Mr 11,21:5
Staley, Raymond M, 1943, Mr 7,38:4
Stalfort, John A, 1954, Jl 15,27:5
Stalheber, Walter J Sr, 1952, My 28,29:1
Stalin, Joseph V Premier, 1953, Mr 6,1:8
Stalions, B R, 1955, O 1,19:6
Stalker, Benjamin, 1949, Ap 18,25:5
Stalker, John R, 1958, O 29,35:4
Stalker, John W, 1950, Ap 9,84:4
Stall, Albert B, 1953, F 27,21:3
Stall, Edward, 1948, Ap 22,27:4
Stall, Karl, 1947, Je 17,28:4
Stall, Roy L, 1922, Ag 24,15:6
Stall, Sylvanus Dr, 1915, N 7,21:5
Stallard, George F, 1964, Jl 25,19:6
Stallard, Henry C, 1955, My 6,23:3
Staller, Isadore Mrs, 1957, F 16,17:6
Stalley, Richard E, 1946, Ag 5,21:5
Stallforth, Federico, 1960, Ag 30,29:2
Stalling, Edward E Mrs, 1945, D 3,21:4
Stallings, G T, 1929, My 14,34:8
Stallings, L Tucker Mrs, 1943, D 2,27:3
Stallings, Laurence, 1968, F 29,37:1
Stallings, William H, 1954, Ja 20,27:4
Stallknecht, Charles P, 1941, Ja 21,21:3
Stallknecht, E P, 1903, D 9,9:5
Stallknecht, F S, 1875, D 21,4:6
Stallknecht, Thorwald (por), 1940, Mr 20,27:4
Stallknect, William C, 1947, Je 12,25:5
Stallman, Benjamin F, 1968, N 1,47:1
Stallman, Maxamilian M, 1966, D 16,47:4
Stallo, Edward K, 1947, Mr 18,27:3
Stallone, Richard, 1949, Jl 29,18:5
Stallsmith, Thomas H, 1937, Mr 21,II,8:7
Stallwood, Harold A, 1903, My 6,9:6
Stallworth, Robert B, 1943, F 9,23:5
Stalnaker, Luther W, 1954, Jl 14,8:4
Staloff, Max, 1955, D 24,13:4
Stals, Albert J, 1951, F 6,27:2
Stalter, Brewster, 1943, My 30,26:1
Stalter, Charles Cooper, 1968, Mr 22,44:4
Stalter, Edmund G, 1937, Ap 11,II,8:7
Stam, Colin F, 1966, Ja 7,29:3
Stamato, Frank, 1939, O 20,23:3
Stamato, Frank G Mrs, 1968, O 16,47:4
Stambaugh, Armstrong A, 1961, Jl 12,32:3
Stambaugh, Lynn U Mrs, 1955, Mr 26,15:5
Stambaugh, William F, 1952, Ag 24,88:3
Stambler, Benedict S, 1967, Jl 5,41:3
Stambler, Benjamin, 1962, My 3,33:2
Stambul, Joseph, 1959, Ap 12,86:5
Stamen, Harry C, 1941, My 6,21:2
Stamer, Frank F, 1961, O 26,35:5
Stames, Mary Mrs (Aunt Molly Jackson), 1960, S 3, 17:4
Stamford, Eva M W Mrs, 1945, Ap 17,23:3
Stamford, Leland A, 1945, S 18,24:2
Stamfordham, Lord, 1931, Ap 1,29:3
Stamler, Charles J, 1965, My 11,39:3
Stamler, John J, 1938, Mr 14,15:5
Stamler, Samuel, 1946, Ja 7,20:3
Stamler, Samuel Mrs, 1958, F 9,88:4
Stamm, A Carson, 1939, F 10,23:5
Stamm, Alex C, 1961, F 15,35:4
Stamm, Bernard J, 1966, Ag 2,33:1
Stamm, Christian Mrs, 1947, N 13,27:3
Stamm, Earle W, 1963, Je 5,41:4
Stamm, Ernest, 1951, Ag 19,49:6
Stamm, Frederick K, 1961, F 25,21:3
Stamm, George L, 1961, Ag 24,29:3
Stamm, Henry, 1941, F 24,15:2
Stamm, John H, 1959, Ja 31,19:4
Stamm, John S, 1956, Mr 7,33:2
Stamm, Paul, 1961, My 28,35:3
Stamm, W T, 1938, Ap 1,23:2
Stamm, Walter G, 1938, O 6,23:4
Stamm-Rodgers, Estelle, 1921, S 14,19:4
Stammel, John, 1947, Je 12,25:4
Stammel, John H, 1947, O 17,21:1
Stammel, Nellie K Mrs, 1943, Ja 22,19:4
Stammer, Peter (por), 1946, Je 15,21:3
Stammers, Alfred H, 1949, O 12,29:1
Stammers, Frank, 1921, Jl 4,9:7
Stammers, Thomas F, 1940, Mr 3,45:2
Stamp, Charles E Mrs, 1925, O 10,15:4
Stamp, Dudley, 1966, Ag 10,41:1
Stamp, Ernest, 1942, D 28,20:3
Stamp, Sidney A, 1951, Ag 29,25:3
Stampa, George L, 1951, My 27,68:4
Stampalia, Anthony, 1968, Ag 9,35:3
Stampar, Andrija, 1958, Je 27,25:1
Stamper, Carter D, 1939, O 7,17:3
Stamper, Dave, 1963, S 19,27:5
Stampfer, Friedrich, 1957, D 2,27:5
Stampfer, J F, 1937, O 12,25:3
Stampfli, Walther, 1965, O 13,47:4
Stampleman, Jeffries E, 1962, Jl 25,33:2
Stamps, Frank, 1965, Ap 13,37:1
Stamps, Thomas D, 1964, Ap 13,29:3
Stamy, David L, 1944, D 8,21:4
Stan, Anisoara, 1954, Ja 23,13:3
Stanaback, Jacob B, 1948, F 26,23:3
Stanacker, Lewis H, 1957, O 26,21:4
Stanage, Brooks H, 1944, F 5,15:5
Stanard, Edwin Obed, 1914, Mr 12,9:5
Stanard, Sidney R, 1961, D 30,19:2
Stanbery, Henry, 1881, Je 27,5:4; 1953, S 4,34:1
Stanbrough, Edward M, 1939, My 3,24:2
Stanbury, William S, 1962, N 8,39:1
Stanchfield, John B, 1921, Je 27,13:5
Stanchfield, Oliver O, 1945, My 25,19:2
Stancliffe, Elizabeth J Mrs, 1939, F 7,19:3
Stancliffe, Noah A, 1944, Ja 28,17:1
Stancliffe, William L, 1949, Ja 18,23:6
Stanco, Italo, 1954, Mr 12,21:3
Stancook, Joseph C, 1960, Ag 19,23:2
Stanculeanu, George Dr, 1917, Jl 17,9:6
Stand, Bert, 1967, Ap 27,45:1
Stand, E J, 1882, Jl 13,3:5
Stand, Leon Mrs, 1940, Ja 2,20:1
Stand, Murray W (funl, My 21,25:5), 1956, My 25:1
Stand, Rudolph, 1963, Ap 11,33:1
Standart, Frank W, 1941, N 9,55:4
Stander, Arthur M, 1963, Jl 22,23:4
Stander, Henriqus J (por), 1948, My 4,25:1
Standerwick, Bertrand F, 1951, Mr 12,25:4
Standerwick, De Sales, 1967, Je 24,18:1
Standerwick, Henry F, 1943, Ja 6,27:3
Standerwick, Henry F Dr, 1953, F 4,27:6
Standeven, Herbert L, 1942, Ag 30,42:5
Standiford, Frank B, 1943, O 15,19:2
Standiford, Harry R, 1952, Je 4,27:4
Standige, Harry S, 1947, Mr 26,25:3
Standing, G, 1936, Ap 6,22:1
Standing, Guy Sir (por), 1937, F 25,23:1
Standing, Herbert, 1923, D 6,19:3; 1955, S 24,19:
Standing, William, 1959, D 1,39:1
Standing Bear, Luther, 1939, F 23,23:5
Standing Bear, 1908, S 6,9:6
Standish, Annie E Mrs, 1938, Ja 7,19:5
Standish, Burt L (por), 1945, Ja 17,21:3
Standish, C Dyas Mrs, 1951, F 16,25:5
Standish, Charles, 1937, Ap 29,21:5
Standish, Clifford T, 1962, S 9,84:5
Standish, Frank B, 1954, Mr 30,27:5
Standish, Granville S, 1953, O 25,89:2
Standish, Granville S Jr, 1953, N 18,32:3
Standish, James D Jr, 1967, My 3,42:6
Standish, Jared B, 1961, N 21,39:2
Standish, John C, 1966, Jl 23,25:1
Standish, John Miles, 1871, D 6,2:7
Standish, Joseph W, 1943, O 28,23:4
Standish, Miles, 1952, N 11,30:3
Standish, Myles, 1915, Jl 2,11:6; 1940, N 29,21: 1950, Jl 31,17:4; 1953, D 9,11:5
Standish, Norman S, 1944, Ag 14,15:4
Standish, Richard, 1943, O 20,21:4; 1949, Ag 7,

Standish, Willard L, 1938, Je 23,21:4
Standley, William H, 1963, O 26,27:4
Standring, Benjamin, 1941, Ja 31,19:1
Standt, Carl F, 1947, O 7,27:2
Stanek, George, 1954, S 23,33:6
Stanek, John A, 1954, My 17,23:3
Stanelis, Ray, 1938, Ag 4,17:5
Stanfield, Clarkson, 1867, Je 9,3:1
Stanfield, Cora Leopold Mrs, 1921, Ja 23,22:3
Stanfield, Douglas M, 1950, My 2,29:1
Stanfield, Harry, 1949, O 4,27:3
Stanfield, Henry J, 1960, F 19,27:3
Stanfield, J Fisher, 1958, My 9,23:2
Stanfield, Otto M, 1946, O 7,31:2
Stanfield, Robert N (por), 1945, Ap 16,23:2
Stanfield, Theodore (will, Jl 17,11:3), 1938, Jl 6,23:4
Stanford, A P Col, 1903, My 7,9:5
Stanford, Alan, 1961, Jl 24,23:2
Stanford, Edward V, 1966, F 19,27:5
Stanford, Frank, 1947, N 7,23:2
Stanford, George J, 1943, Ap 3,15:2
Stanford, Gorham E, 1941, Je 20,21:3
Stanford, Gorham E Mrs, 1956, My 7,27:1
Stanford, Grattan T (por), 1946, Ap 29,21:5
Stanford, Henry, 1921, F 19,11:5
Stanford, Jane Lathrop Mrs, 1905, Mr 2,1:7
Stanford, Joseph B, 1906, Jl 6,4:1
Stanford, Joseph V, 1960, Ap 29,31:1
Stanford, Julius T, 1954, Jl 21,27:2
Stanford, Kenneth J, 1953, O 14,29:4
Stanford, Lady, 1941, Ja 23,21:4
Stanford, Leland, 1943, F 27,13:1
Stanford, Leland D W, 1949, Je 22,31:2
Stanford, Leland Sir, 1893, Je 22,1:7
Stanford, Leland V, 1966, My 2,37:4
Stanford, Nicholas, 1964, Jl 22,33:4
Stanford, Richard S, 1944, Jl 9,36:1
Stanford, Samuel P, 1943, Jl 5,15:4
Stanford, Spencer C, 1950, Ag 12,13:4
Stanford, Wesley M Rev Dr, 1923, Ap 9,17:4
Stang, Arthur J, 1954, N 2,27:6
Stang, Bp, 1907, F 3,7:5
Stang, Frederick, 1948, O 24,76:3; 1966, Ap 7,36:2
Stang, Fredrik, 1941, N 16,57:3
Stang, Marvin Mrs (Judith), 1968, S 29,80:7
Stange, Stanislaus, 1917, Ja 3,11:5
Stangel, Charles, 1949, F 4,23:3
Stangel, Charles G, 1950, Ja 16,26:3
Stanger, Arthur E, 1945, S 23,44:4
Stanger, Christian G, 1954, Ag 16,17:4
Stanger, George H, 1958, Mr 3,27:5
Stanger, John V, 1943, D 7,27:3
Stanger, Julius, 1947, Ag 27,23:6
Stanger, Wesley A, 1961, Jl 8,19:5
Stanger, William D, 1941, F 28,19:5
Stangland, Benjamin F, 1940, Mr 27,21:5
Stangland, Robert S, 1953, D 17,37:1
Stangle, John L Mrs, 1961, Ja 12,29:1
Stanhope, Countess, 1940, S 20,23:6
Stanhope, George W, 1909, My 22,7:5
Stanhope, James R Earl, 1967, Ag 16,41:3
Stanhope, John R Capt, 1873, Ja 28,2:5
Stanhope, Lord, 1905, Ap 20,9:7
Stanhope, Olin L, 1950, Je 23,25:1
Stanhope, Philip Henry 5th Earl, 1875, D 25,4:7
Stanhope, William F, 1960, Jl 8,21:5
Stanier, Arthur, 1965, S 29,3:5
Staniford, Arthur F, 1953, Ja 17,15:1
Staniford, Charles W, 1948, O 31,88:4
Staniford, Charles W Mrs, 1957, Ap 7,88:6
Staniford, Foye F, 1964, My 23,23:5
Staniford, Robert H, 1965, Jl 5,17:5
Staniland, Albert E, 1946, Je 30,38:5
Stanion, Thomas, 1944, Ja 5,17:1
Stanislaus, John N, 1962, N 11,88:6
Stanislaus, Mary Rev Mother (Mary S K Schilling), 1940, Mr 13,23:4
Stanislaus, Sister (M Zerhussen), 1950, D 16,17:4
Stanislavsky, Constantin S (por), 1938, Ag 8,13:1
Stanislaw, Paul, 1960, Ja 16,21:4
Staniszewski, John Mrs, 1958, Je 20,23:1
Stankard, Edward J, 1951, Jl 28,11:1
Stanke, Louis E, 1945, Ap 22,36:2
Stankoff, Dimitri, 1940, Mr 26,7:5
Stankov, Ivan D, 1949, Ja 23,68:6
Stankovitch, Radenko, 1956, D 7,27:2
Stanlaws, Penrhyn, 1957, My 20,20:3
Stanley, A A, 1932, My 20,19:3
Stanley, A P Dean (funl, Jl 26,1:5), 1881, Jl 19,5:3
Stanley, Alfred T, 1965, D 31,21:4
Stanley, Alix W, 1953, D 29,23:3
Stanley, Arthur, 1947, N 5,27:3
Stanley, Arthur C, 1940, My 1,23:2
Stanley, Arthur V, 1967, My 19,39:2
Stanley, Augusta Lady (see also Mr 2), 1876, Mr 10,1:5
Stanley, Augustus O, 1958, Ag 13,27:5
Stanley, Ben, 1938, Ap 15,19:3
Stanley, Charles A, 1953, My 1,21:3
Stanley, Charles V, 1954, O 13,31:4
Stanley, Clarence L, 1951, My 24,35:3
Stanley, Donald C Mrs, 1954, Ap 4,87:1
Stanley, Douglas, 1958, Ap 21,23:4
Stanley, Douglas E, 1950, Jl 18,29:2
Stanley, Edgar S, 1952, S 30,31:5
Stanley, Edmund A, 1956, F 4,19:2
Stanley, Edward D Mrs, 1959, S 26,23:4
Stanley, Edward F, 1959, S 10,35:4
Stanley, Edward H, 1951, Mr 30,23:3
Stanley, Edward Lyulph (Baron Sheffield), 1925, Mr 19,21:3
Stanley, Edward R, 1948, Je 3,25:3
Stanley, Elizabeth, 1940, S 14,17:5
Stanley, Elizabeth Mrs, 1925, My 2,15:5; 1940, Ap 19, 21:3
Stanley, Emory D, 1968, F 10,34:2
Stanley, Ethan B Mrs, 1952, O 10,25:3
Stanley, Fabius, 1882, D 7,5:1
Stanley, Forrester C, 1949, N 7,27:5
Stanley, Frank Grant, 1921, Jl 6,15:6
Stanley, Fred, 1949, My 28,15:6
Stanley, Frederick Arthur (Earl of Derby), 1908, Je 15,7:4
Stanley, Frederick C, 1953, Jl 21,23:2
Stanley, Freelan O, 1940, O 3,25:4
Stanley, Genevieve M, 1964, Mr 8,87:2
Stanley, George, 1938, Jl 2,13:3
Stanley, George C, 1962, My 12,23:6
Stanley, George J, 1960, S 9,29:2
Stanley, Gilbert, 1968, D 8,86:3
Stanley, Gordon, 1965, D 24,17:2
Stanley, Grant Dr, 1913, Mr 24,11:5
Stanley, Harold, 1963, My 15,39:3
Stanley, Harris M, 1944, Ap 27,23:1
Stanley, Harry, 1947, S 17,25:5
Stanley, Harry E, 1958, F 25,27:3
Stanley, Harry L, 1949, F 10,28:2
Stanley, Henry M, 1904, My 10,1:4
Stanley, Herbert, 1955, Je 6,27:2
Stanley, Hugh W, 1955, F 8,27:5
Stanley, I J Jr, 1950, D 14,35:4
Stanley, Ira Nelson, 1904, S 24,9:4
Stanley, Irvin, 1939, My 20,15:4
Stanley, J E, 1940, O 26,15:3
Stanley, Jack, 1913, Jl 16,7:6
Stanley, James, 1961, My 30,17:6
Stanley, James J Mrs, 1948, Je 28,19:4
Stanley, James N Mrs, 1945, Ja 11,23:5
Stanley, Jane C Mrs, 1940, N 1,25:4
Stanley, Joe (Sailor), 1957, My 18,9:4
Stanley, John C, 1947, Jl 26,13:5
Stanley, John J, 1954, O 21,27:2
Stanley, John M, 1872, Ap 14,2:4
Stanley, John Mrs, 1950, Ja 17,28:3
Stanley, John T, 1959, S 3,27:2
Stanley, John W, 1954, Je 15,29:4
Stanley, K (Dead Shot), 1927, My 14,19:5
Stanley, Lila C Mrs, 1938, D 7,23:3
Stanley, Lord, 1869, Je 17,5:4
Stanley, Lord (will, N 29,19:3),(por), 1938, O 16,44:3
Stanley, Lord of Alderley, 1903, D 11,9:7
Stanley, Louise, 1954, Jl 16,21:3
Stanley, Mary E, 1939, My 4,23:3
Stanley, Mary L Mrs, 1939, D 3,21:1
Stanley, Matilda, 1878, S 16,1:4
Stanley, Maureen Lady, 1942, Je 22,15:5
Stanley, Maurice, 1967, Mr 13,37:1
Stanley, Mervin C, 1907, F 4,9:6
Stanley, Merwin C, 1907, F 2,9:3
Stanley, Mortimer D, 1939, D 8,25:1
Stanley, Oliver F, 1950, D 12,34:2
Stanley, Paul, 1909, Mr 17,9:3
Stanley, R De Witt, 1945, S 10,19:3
Stanley, R H, 1875, N 29,2:1
Stanley, Ray M, 1944, My 4,19:3
Stanley, Richard B, 1943, D 7,27:2
Stanley, Richard B Mrs, 1964, Ap 8,43:3
Stanley, Richard C, 1958, Ag 14,29:4
Stanley, Robert C, 1951, F 13,31:3
Stanley, Robert Francis, 1968, Ap 13,25:2
Stanley, Robert H, 1954, Je 15,29:3
Stanley, Russell W, 1951, Ag 11,11:3
Stanley, Sherwood B, 1948, D 3,25:1
Stanley, Stanley T, 1955, My 19,29:4
Stanley, Stephen, 1952, Ja 22,29:1
Stanley, Stuart M, 1956, S 22,17:4
Stanley, Thomas J, 1946, Je 20,23:2
Stanley, W E Ex-Gov, 1910, O 14,11:6
Stanley, W P, 1938, My 26,25:1
Stanley, Walter, 1925, S 30,23:4
Stanley, Walter L, 1943, Jl 5,15:4
Stanley, Walter P, 1949, O 28,23:3
Stanley, Walter T, 1950, D 12,33:2
Stanley, William, 1916, My 15,9:5; 1946, Jl 21,40:3
Stanley, William E 3d, 1966, Je 30,26:8
Stanley, William H, 1967, O 20,47:1
Stanley, William L, 1939, Je 13,23:6
Stanley, William W, 1952, Ap 1,29:5; 1955, Ag 10,25:4
Stanley-Brown, Joseph, 1941, N 3,19:2
Stanley-Brown, Joseph Mrs, 1947, D 31,15:4
Stanley-Brown, M, 1942, O 6,23:5
Stanley-Brown, Margaret (Mrs M K Sellers), 1958, Je 13,23:1
Stanley-Brown, Rudolph, 1944, F 9,19:4
Stanley of Alderley, Baron, 1931, Ag 23,27:1
Stanmore, Baron (Arth Hamilton Gordon), 1912, Ja 31,11:5
Stannard, Ambrose B, 1919, Ag 21,11:4
Stannard, E Tappan, 1949, S 10,1:2
Stannard, Edson, 1950, N 29,33:4
Stannard, Edward D, 1955, Mr 23,31:1
Stannard, William J, 1950, Jl 14,21:1
Stanovsky, Otto, 1945, D 7,21:5
Stansbury, Alfred L, 1949, F 8,25:4
Stansbury, E, 1883, D 20,4:7
Stansbury, E A, 1873, N 5,7:2
Stansbury, Franklin B, 1941, D 28,28:1
Stansbury, Gilbert, 1943, Ap 23,17:4
Stansbury, Harold E, 1954, D 18,15:5
Stansbury, Henry H, 1937, S 23,27:4
Stansbury, Jane Beaumont, 1913, Mr 27,11:5
Stansbury, William F, 1915, D 30,13:3
Stansfield, Clarence W, 1952, My 18,93:1
Stansfield, George E, 1954, Ja 28,27:6; 1955, S 23,25:2
Stansfield, Harold W, 1952, D 25,29:3
Stansfield, Herbert, 1941, Ap 4,21:3
Stansfield, Sarah J Mrs, 1953, O 29,31:3
Stansfield, William H, 1920, Jl 12,9:4
Stansgate, Viscount (Wm W Benn),(cor, N 19,21:5), 1960, N 18,31:4
Stansky, Lyman Mrs, 1967, Je 7,47:3
Stanten, Arthur G, 1956, N 15,35:4
Stantial, Robert S, 1953, My 19,30:4
Stanton, Albert H, 1946, S 7,15:3
Stanton, Alden D, 1963, O 23,41:3
Stanton, Arch B, 1946, F 23,13:5
Stanton, Arthur, 1948, D 20,25:4
Stanton, Benjamin Ex-Gov, 1872, Je 5,1:6
Stanton, Benjamin Prof, 1874, Jl 21,8:3
Stanton, C E, 1933, My 9,17:1
Stanton, Charles E, 1951, F 4,77:1; 1953, Ap 11,17:5
Stanton, Charles E Mrs, 1962, Mr 14,39:3
Stanton, Charles N, 1941, Jl 12,13:6
Stanton, Charles S, 1947, Ag 1,17:1
Stanton, Charlotte E Mrs, 1942, Ag 5,19:3
Stanton, Clara H Mrs, 1914, O 13,11:6
Stanton, Clifford H, 1959, My 23,25:4
Stanton, David Col, 1871, N 6,8:3
Stanton, David L Gen, 1919, D 27,9:5
Stanton, Dr, 1871, N 13,2:5
Stanton, E M Mrs, 1873, N 19,1:6
Stanton, E S, 1877, Ag 31,5:4
Stanton, Earle W, 1953, Je 11,29:3
Stanton, Edgar, 1943, Ap 15,25:2
Stanton, Edmund C, 1948, S 2,24:2
Stanton, Edward J, 1939, S 16,17:4
Stanton, Edward L, 1962, Ja 19,31:3
Stanton, Edward R, 1938, Ja 7,19:5
Stanton, Edwin F, 1968, Ag 31,23:1
Stanton, Edwin M, 1869, D 25,3:1
Stanton, Elmer E, 1944, Mr 23,19:2
Stanton, Emanuel Mrs, 1952, My 22,27:4
Stanton, Emma B, 1947, Ag 21,23:5
Stanton, Ernie, 1944, F 8,16:3
Stanton, F L, 1927, Ja 8,17:3
Stanton, F McMillan, 1916, S 13,9:6
Stanton, Forrest Q, 1953, F 28,17:1
Stanton, Francis R, 1939, My 29,15:3
Stanton, Frank C, 1944, D 16,15:5
Stanton, Frank L (por), 1939, My 27,15:4
Stanton, Frank M, 1963, Jl 5,19:3
Stanton, Frederick E, 1959, F 19,31:4
Stanton, Frederick L, 1945, Ja 2,19:4
Stanton, Frederick Mrs, 1967, N 25,39:3
Stanton, G A, 1938, S 30,21:4
Stanton, G S, 1927, Ap 25,23:5
Stanton, G W, 1883, My 2,5:5
Stanton, George E, 1958, N 20,35:5
Stanton, George F, 1947, Mr 7,25:2
Stanton, Gilman S, 1954, My 8,17:3
Stanton, Grove A, 1961, Mr 24,31:1
Stanton, H B, 1887, Ja 15,2:1
Stanton, Hazel, 1966, Jl 5,27:1
Stanton, Henry, 1903, D 6,7:6
Stanton, Henry T, 1954, O 8,23:5
Stanton, Henry W, 1942, F 9,10:2
Stanton, Herbert A, 1958, Ag 30,15:7
Stanton, Horace Hale, 1914, S 15,11:5
Stanton, Howard, 1947, Ag 25,17:4
Stanton, Irving G, 1943, Jl 10,48:6
Stanton, Irwin, 1947, S 5,20:2
Stanton, J Frank, 1945, Ja 6,11:2
Stanton, J William Mrs, 1947, My 6,27:2
Stanton, James E Jr, 1939, Ja 27,19:4
Stanton, John, 1906, F 24,9:5
Stanton, John A Mrs, 1959, My 7,33:5
Stanton, John J, 1940, Mr 15,23:4
Stanton, John Livingston, 1920, F 26,11:4
Stanton, John P, 1952, Ja 24,27:1; 1966, Ap 27,47:3; 1968, S 21,33:2
Stanton, Joseph, 1954, Ja 4,19:1
Stanton, Joseph A, 1943, N 7,56:5
Stanton, Joseph M, 1950, Mr 16,31:3
Stanton, Lawrence M, 1950, Ja 7,17:6
Stanton, Lawrence P, 1946, Ja 30,25:2
Stanton, Lewis B, 1942, Jl 17,15:4
Stanton, Lewis H, 1938, Ap 25,15:4
Stanton, Lewis P, 1957, Je 30,69:2
Stanton, Louis Lee, 1911, My 12,11:4

Stanton, Lucius M, 1919, F 17,13:3
Stanton, Martin Mrs, 1952, O 25,17:2
Stanton, Michael B Mrs, 1959, My 8,27:3
Stanton, Michael Bernard, 1912, Ag 16,9:5
Stanton, Nathaniel B, 1946, O 19,21:1
Stanton, Oscar F, 1924, Jl 7,15:4
Stanton, Owen, 1961, Ja 1,49:2
Stanton, Philip A, 1945, S 9,45:2
Stanton, R L Rev, 1885, My 30,1:1
Stanton, Richard P Mrs, 1950, Ja 17,28:2
Stanton, Robert C, 1949, Mr 8,25:2
Stanton, Robert T (por), 1943, Ap 12,23:3
Stanton, Samuel C, 1949, Ja 27,24:2
Stanton, Samuel M, 1946, S 20,31:2
Stanton, Stephen B, 1954, N 12,21:3
Stanton, Stephen Keyes, 1914, Ap 4,15:4
Stanton, Styles Franklin, 1907, Je 17,7:7
Stanton, Thaddeus Mrs, 1916, Jl 8,9:4
Stanton, Theodore, 1925, Mr 2,17:6
Stanton, Thomas, 1938, Ja 26,23:1
Stanton, Thomas J, 1941, D 9,31:3
Stanton, Walter R, 1941, N 9,52:1
Stanton, Walter X, 1960, F 22,17:1
Stanton, William A, 1919, S 30,19:2; 1955, O 2,87:2
Stanton, William J, 1941, F 24,15:1
Stanton, William L, 1945, Ag 22,23:5
Stanton, William O, 1959, N 14,21:7
Stanton, Zed S Justice, 1921, Ag 16,15:4
Stanwich, Jacob, 1907, N 3,9:5
Stanwix, George B, 1954, D 25,11:5
Stanwix, Minnie U Mrs, 1939, My 21,III,7:3
Stanwood, Arthur G, 1907, D 31,7:6
Stanwood, Daniel C, 1951, Jl 29,69:4
Stanwood, Edward, 1923, O 12,17:3
Stanwood, George E, 1942, My 27,23:2
Stanwood, Isaac Augustus, 1914, Mr 6,11:4
Stanwood, Louise R, 1961, Ja 30,15:8
Stanwood, Samuel J, 1954, Jl 7,31:4
Stanworth, Charles S, 1937, F 4,21:5
Stanwyck, Jay, 1967, S 18,47:2
Stanyan, Frank H, 1942, D 3,25:5
Stanyer, J M, 1927, Jl 22,19:3
Stanyon, Herbert H, 1946, Ag 30,17:5
Stanz, William F, 1965, S 4,21:6
Stanziale, Charles A, 1962, O 5,33:2
Stanzione, Gustavo, 1968, O 12,37:4
Stanzler, Abraham, 1937, S 4,15:2
Staord, Guy C, 1944, Ag 9,17:4
Stapelfeld, Wilfred P, 1962, My 10,37:5
Stapledon, R George, 1960, S 17,23:4
Stapledon, William O, 1950, S 8,31:3
Stapler, Charles Mrs, 1944, D 7,25:5
Stapler, Henry B B, 1906, D 2,7:4
Stapler, Henry B B Mrs, 1958, O 11,23:4
Staples, Abram P, 1951, Mr 22,31:4
Staples, Alex R, 1940, Mr 12,23:5
Staples, Alvah S, 1958, O 8,35:4
Staples, Arthur, 1952, My 3,21:4
Staples, Arthur G, 1940, Ap 3,23:2
Staples, Arthur G Mrs, 1938, D 16,25:2
Staples, Bert Edwin, 1917, My 18,13:5
Staples, C E, 1903, My 9,9:5
Staples, Charles J, 1949, Ap 27,27:4
Staples, Charles J Mrs, 1955, Ap 16,19:6
Staples, Charles S, 1944, Je 13,19:4
Staples, Elial M Mrs, 1952, N 4,29:3
Staples, Elliott E, 1957, Ja 13,85:1
Staples, Eugene A, 1964, Jl 3,21:3
Staples, Frances Wright, 1922, Mr 31,17:5
Staples, Henry B, 1958, D 7,88:4
Staples, Horace A, 1941, Ag 26,19:6
Staples, J Clark, 1958, Ja 29,27:2
Staples, John J, 1925, Ap 28,21:3
Staples, John N, 1947, My 9,22:2
Staples, Leonard C, 1942, O 28,23:5
Staples, Mary E W Mrs (will, N 4,25:4), 1942, O 20, 21:2
Staples, Mrs (Mary Wells) (see also Jl 17), 1878, Jl 20,5:2
Staples, Owen, 1949, D 7,31:2
Staples, Percy A, 1956, Jl 24,25:3
Staples, Phil C (por), 1949, Je 30,23:5
Staples, Richard T, 1962, Jl 26,27:4
Staples, Robert G, 1937, N 5,23:3
Staples, Seth P, 1861, N 8,4:6
Staples, Stowell S, 1949, Ap 13,29:2
Staples, Thomas J, 1940, My 5,53:1
Staples, W J, 1883, Jl 7,5:5
Stapleton, B F, 1941, Mr 10,17:2
Stapleton, Benjamin F, 1950, Mr 24,29:5
Stapleton, C H, 1946, Ap 4,25:5
Stapleton, Clarence A, 1951, O 26,24:3
Stapleton, Daniel, 1941, Ag 23,13:6
Stapleton, David L, 1947, My 25,60:5
Stapleton, Edward A, 1947, Je 13,23:2
Stapleton, Edward J, 1919, My 4,22:5
Stapleton, Elsie Mrs, 1949, Je 16,29:1
Stapleton, Frank H, 1945, Ja 19,19:3
Stapleton, Guy W Mrs, 1951, Ap 23,25:2
Stapleton, James H, 1961, D 13,43:2
Stapleton, John, 1947, Mr 1,15:2
Stapleton, John A, 1938, Ap 14,23:4
Stapleton, Luke D, 1923, F 13,21:3
Stapleton, Luke D Jr, 1948, Je 28,19:3
Stapleton, Luke D Mrs, 1943, Ag 2,15:5
Stapleton, Margaret F, 1942, Mr 16,15:4
Stapleton, Michael A, 1937, Je 3,25:4
Stapleton, Percy T, 1962, My 15,39:2
Stapleton, Percy T Mrs, 1950, F 10,23:2
Stapleton, T Ray Sr, 1952, Jl 24,27:2
Stapleton, Thomas, 1925, Ap 1,23:4
Stapleton, Thomas J, 1944, My 31,19:4
Stapleton, Timothy R, 1966, D 16,47:2
Stapleton, Walter F, 1943, S 13,19:5
Stapleton, Walter J Mrs, 1951, Jl 20,21:2
Stapleton, William B (cor, F 24,29:4), 1968, F 21,47:3
Stapleton, William R, 1957, Ap 7,89:1
Stapley, Lewis G, 1938, Je 26,27:1
Stapperfenne, Henry, 1950, Je 27,29:3
Starace, Carl S, 1952, Ag 8,17:6
Starace, Giovanni, 1917, Ag 2,9:4
Starace, Louis J Mrs, 1960, Je 27,25:2
Starbird, Beecher, 1939, Je 10,17:2
Starbird, Isaac W Gen, 1907, F 3,7:6
Starbranch, Nels P, 1950, My 1,25:4
Starbuck, Caleb B, 1938, D 30,15:1
Starbuck, Calvin W, 1870, N 16,5:2
Starbuck, Charles A, 1925, My 30,9:4
Starbuck, Charles L, 1941, Ja 29,17:4
Starbuck, Edward B, 1949, Ag 1,17:4
Starbuck, Edwin D, 1947, N 19,27:4
Starbuck, Frank R, 1951, O 2,27:3
Starbuck, G Fred, 1925, F 18,19:4
Starbuck, George S Mrs, 1951, F 26,23:1
Starbuck, J F, 1880, D 12,2:3
Starbuck, Jesse D, 1946, S 10,7:5
Starbuck, John C, 1961, F 5,81:2
Starbuck, Kathryn H, 1965, N 20,35:3
Starbuck, Leonard M, 1953, D 21,31:3
Starbuck, Raymond D, 1965, Ag 17,33:3
Starbuck, William D L, 1954, My 3,25:4
Starchenko, Vasili, 1948, Jl 19,19:5
Starck, Albert G Mrs, 1945, O 16,23:1
Starck, Carl A, 1939, N 8,23:3
Stare, Frederick J Mrs, 1957, My 22,33:4
Starek, Herbert, 1955, O 3,27:5
Staren, John E, 1966, Mr 1,37:3
Starets, John, 1957, Ja 7,25:5
Starhemberg, Ernst R von Prince, 1956, Mr 16,23:1
Starhope, Charles Augustus (Lord Harrington), 1917, F 6,9:3
Starichevsky, Sergei, 1959, Mr 2,7:5
Starin, Arthur A, 1955, N 17,35:4
Starin, J H, 1883, S 16,6:6
Starin, James Henry, 1924, Ag 7,15:5
Starin, John H Mrs, 1906, D 19,11:5
Starin, John Henry, 1909, Mr 23,9:4
Starin, William Henry, 1917, Mr 8,11:4
Staring, William H, 1950, Jl 23,56:1
Starjawakki, Joseph, 1907, S 12,7:7
Stark, A Maurice, 1951, O 7,86:6
Stark, Abraham I Mrs, 1967, Jl 18,37:4
Stark, Alex D, 1956, D 18,31:4
Stark, Arthur W, 1962, Ja 19,31:4
Stark, Charles, 1873, Ag 20,4:7
Stark, Charles W, 1941, Je 5,23:5
Stark, Clifford, 1944, S 17,42:1
Stark, Dolly, 1968, Ag 25,88:5
Stark, Eugene J, 1958, Je 13,23:5
Stark, Francis R, 1956, N 26,27:5
Stark, Frank F, 1967, Jl 12,43:5
Stark, Freddie, 1961, My 31,33:3
Stark, Frederic W Mrs, 1945, Ja 4,19:5
Stark, Frederick Mrs, 1937, Ap 18,II,8:7
Stark, George, 1947, S 10,27:1
Stark, H J Lutcher, 1965, S 3,27:2
Stark, H J Lutcher Mrs, 1939, O 13,23:5
Stark, Harry R, 1941, My 2,21:3
Stark, Harry R Mrs, 1953, Ap 29,29:5
Stark, Helene H, 1909, Ap 7,11:5
Stark, Henry, 1943, My 27,28:7
Stark, Henry I, 1946, D 14,15:6
Stark, Herman, 1943, O 17,48:5; 1953, O 7,29:2
Stark, Hubert H, 1963, My 14,39:3
Stark, Isaac, 1915, Je 29,13:4
Stark, Jack G, 1950, D 3,88:3
Stark, Jacob P Mrs, 1967, My 4,44:5
Stark, Jacob W, 1954, N 11,31:4
Stark, James H, 1941, S 22,15:6; 1945, D 11,25:5
Stark, James H Mrs, 1941, D 13,21:4; 1953, Jl 1,29:5
Stark, Jerome J, 1950, Jl 4,17:5
Stark, Jesse D Mrs, 1965, D 30,21:4
Stark, Johannes, 1957, Je 22,15:6
Stark, John, 1943, Ag 31,17:5
Stark, John B, 1941, Mr 31,15:2
Stark, John C, 1968, Jl 16,39:2
Stark, John C Mrs, 1962, My 4,33:3
Stark, John R, 1949, O 18,28:2
Stark, Joseph W, 1954, Ap 30,24:3
Stark, Julius, 1955, Ap 9,5:2
Stark, Lawrence E Jr, 1957, D 21,19:5
Stark, Lou, 1954, Mr 18,31:2
Stark, Louis (funl, My 20,31:5), 1954, My 18,29:4
Stark, Louise Mrs, 1946, Ag 6,25:2
Stark, Lucien, 1949, Ja 12,27:3
Stark, Mack, 1959, Ag 22,17:6
Stark, Meyer M Mrs, 1963, N 15,35:2
Stark, Michael S, 1967, Ja 8,88:3
Stark, Nathan N, 1960, O 25,35:1
Stark, O, 1926, Ap 15,27:5
Stark, Paul E, 1945, D 15,17:2
Stark, Peter, 1951, Ag 8,25:3
Stark, Rodney J, 1954, Ja 23,13:5
Stark, Sadie (cor, Jl 7,35:1), 1946, Jl 3,25:5
Stark, Sanford W, 1966, Jl 27,39:3
Stark, Sebastian, 1956, F 24,25:3
Stark, Sigmar Dr, 1925, Jl 17,15:5
Stark, Walter E, 1963, N 30,27:1
Stark, William, 1873, N 1,5:6
Stark, William A, 1956, O 29,29:4
Stark, William A Rev, 1907, Ap 6,7:7
Starke, Christian, 1941, Je 3,21:3
Starke, Konrad Mrs, 1914, S 10,9:6
Starke, William, 1948, Ja 17,18:3
Starker, Jennie, 1949, Jl 15,19:5
Starkey, Benjamin, 1949, F 17,23:4
Starkey, Bernard, 1940, Ap 21,42:2
Starkey, Catherine C Mrs, 1942, Je 6,13:2
Starkey, Herbert A Dr, 1903, N 22,7:5
Starkey, Jack B, 1945, Ap 25,23:4
Starkey, James L, 1938, Ap 3,II,7:2
Starkey, James T, 1952, Ag 25,11:4
Starkey, Jay R, 1951, Ap 6,25:2
Starkey, John F, 1945, S 1,11:6
Starkey, John R, 1940, N 15,21:1
Starkey, Roland W, 1953, Ag 10,23:5
Starkey, T A Bp, 1903, My 18,1:3
Starkey, William C, 1949, Jl 6,30:5
Starkey, William R, 1949, Ja 20,27:1
Starkey, William U, 1942, S 25,21:5
Starkie, Thomas J, 1952, D 22,25:3
Starkman, Harold R, 1964, Ag 17,25:4
Starkman, Samuel, 1955, Ap 6,29:2
Starks, B M, 1923, N 29,21:3
Starks, Charles D, 1950, Je 15,31:5
Starks, Gerald, 1951, Ap 25,37:3
Starks, James W, 1949, F 4,23:5
Starks, Thomas F, 1952, F 23,11:5
Starks, W Frederick, 1939, N 2,23:3
Starkus, Ignas, 1956, S 12,37:3
Starkweather, Edd V, 1961, F 9,31:4
Starkweather, Edd V Mrs, 1956, S 29,19:1
Starkweather, G A Jr, 1883, N 22,2:5
Starkweather, G B, 1878, O 16,2:4
Starkweather, H H, 1875, Ag 23,4:6; 1876, Ja 29,5:2
Starkweather, H W, 1946, My 20,24:2
Starkweather, James C, 1937, My 9,II,11:2
Starkweather, Jeannette N Mrs, 1937, N 15,23:5
Starkweather, John G, 1952, Ja 18,27:2
Starkweather, Louis P, 1911, Ja 10,11:5; 1958, Ag 25, 21:2
Starkweather, S Anna Mrs, 1941, Jl 14,13:3
Starkweather, W Dana, 1942, Jl 2,21:5
Starlight, Alex, 1941, Ja 30,21:1
Starlight, Marks, 1915, My 6,13:5
Starling, Charles W, 1943, My 20,21:4
Starling, Edmund W, 1944, Ag 4,13:1
Starling, Edmund W Mrs, 1946, O 14,29:3
Starling, Paul N, 1950, Je 7,30:2
Starling, Samuel W, 1950, Ap 20,29:5
Starlings, A Knox, 1960, Ja 27,33:4
Starmont, Leon, 1952, F 6,29:2
Starner, Albert J, 1950, S 24,104:5
Starner, Fidellas A, 1951, O 20,15:5
Starner, O H, 1961, F 13,27:4
Starnes, A B (will), 1947, Ag 13,21:6
Starnes, Joe, 1962, Ja 10,47:1
Starobin, Abraham, 1957, S 17,35:1
Starobin, Mort, 1942, Je 14,46:1
Starostin, M I, 1948, N 17,27:3
Starr, Alfred, 1956, O 16,33:2
Starr, Alfred Russell, 1924, O 28,23:3
Starr, Alice D Mrs (will, D 24,7:2), 1942, F 19,19:2
Starr, Allen A, 1954, My 28,23:1
Starr, Ambrose M, 1948, Mr 25,27:4
Starr, Anna Mrs, 1947, Ag 29,17:2
Starr, Charles, 1925, Ag 2,5:4
Starr, Clifford J, 1950, Je 3,15:4
Starr, Cornelius Vander, 1968, D 21,37:2
Starr, Daniel, 1945, Ag 21,21:4
Starr, Daniel H, 1940, Ap 4,23:7
Starr, Dillwyn P Lt, 1916, S 27,11:7
Starr, Edgar P Mrs, 1903, O 12,7:7
Starr, Edward C (por), 1941, Ja 18,15:3
Starr, Ellen G, 1940, F 11,49:3
Starr, F, 1933, Ag 15,17:1
Starr, Ferdinand M, 1938, Ja 28,21:4
Starr, Florence C Mrs, 1963, Jl 17,31:5
Starr, Frank, 1961, Ja 26,29:4
Starr, Frederick E, 1951, Jl 23,17:6
Starr, George, 1904, My 3,9:6; 1945, Ag 29,23:4
Starr, George E, 1945, Ag 2,19:4
Starr, George H, 1916, Jl 31,9:6
Starr, George Mrs, 1917, N 25,23:4
Starr, George O, 1915, S 10,11:7
Starr, George R Dr (por), 1937, D 8,25:4
Starr, Graham, 1951, Ap 13,23:4
Starr, H, 1942, Mr 18,23:6
Starr, Harriston B, 1925, Mr 16,19:3

Starr, Helen Mrs, 1937, D 26,II,7:3
Starr, Henry, 1937, Ap 5,19:3
Starr, Herman, 1958, Mr 25,33:4; 1965, Ja 9,25:4
Starr, Howard M, 1948, Ja 10,15:1
Starr, Howard M Mrs, 1950, D 30,13:6
Starr, Howard W, 1946, N 30,15:5
Starr, Hughie, 1938, F 27,II,8:4
Starr, Ida M Mrs, 1938, F 4,21:4
Starr, James, 1948, Mr 14,72:5
Starr, James Mrs, 1956, Ag 21,29:5
Starr, John B, 1947, My 25,60:4
Starr, John F, 1904, Ag 10,7:6
Starr, John V, 1959, D 8,45:5
Starr, Joseph, 1952, F 27,27:4
Starr, Joseph Mrs, 1959, N 16,31:3
Starr, Lillian, 1958, Ap 1,27:2
Starr, Louis (cor, My 4,25:3), 1956, Ap 22,87:2
Starr, Louis E, 1967, My 5,39:4
Starr, Louisa A Mrs, 1942, My 19,20:3
Starr, M A, 1932, S 5,11:3
Starr, Malcolm W, 1949, Mr 25,23:4
Starr, Martin, 1967, Ap 28,41:4
Starr, Milton P, 1946, Ag 15,25:2
Starr, Muriel, 1950, Ap 20,29:1
Starr, Orrin S, 1937, N 27,17:3
Starr, Pete, 1925, My 4,19:5
Starr, Russell W, 1954, Ap 9,24:3
Starr, Sara A Mrs, 1924, D 30,17:5
Starr, Saul, 1964, D 18,34:4
Starr, Sidney, 1925, O 5,21:4
Starr, Solomon, 1944, Jl 7,15:4
Starr, Theodore B, 1907, My 10,7:4
Starr, Thomas A, 1940, Ja 23,21:5
Starr, Walter L Mrs, 1918, Ag 3,9:6
Starr, William E, 1939, Ag 5,15:7
Starr, William M, 1908, F 16,11:5
Starr, William T, 1964, O 17,29:6
Starr-Hunt, Jack (J Brackenridge), 1951, Jl 20,21:6
Starrett, Cummins A, 1940, Jl 16,17:5
Starrett, Frank, 1918, Ja 7,13:1
Starrett, Goldwin, 1918, My 10,11:5
Starrett, Harold G, 1968, Ap 11,45:3
Starrett, Jay E, 1967, O 17,47:1
Starrett, Milton G, 1942, S 19,15:2
Starrett, Paul, 1957, Jl 6,15:1
Starrett, Paul Jr, 1943, F 26,19:2
Starrett, Rosell H, 1949, F 10,28:3
Starrett, Roswell H Mrs, 1953, F 24,25:2
Starrett, Saul, 1953, S 5,16:4
Starrett, Theodore, 1917, O 10,11:6
Starrett, W A Col, 1932, Mr 27,II,4:1
Starrett, W Kamp, 1952, Jl 10,31:6
Starring, David S Mrs, 1960, F 9,31:1
Starring, George A, 1949, N 20,92:8
Starring, Mason B Mrs, 1947, Ag 4,17:5
Starrs, Percy F (funl, My 3,5:2), 1925, My 2,15:5
Starrs, William Very Rev, 1873, F 7,8:6
Start, Albert H, 1950, N 7,27:2
Start, George P, 1948, My 27,25:2
Start, J H, 1941, Ap 29,19:4
Startup, Charles H, 1955, O 8,19:3
Startup, Clifford I Mrs, 1955, Ap 15,23:2
Startz, Irving S, 1954, Ag 23,17:6
Stary, Joseph (will), 1958, Mr 14,50:3
Stary, Ladd, 1946, S 24,29:1
Starzynski, Thad A, 1951, D 27,21:1
Starzynski, Theophilus, 1952, Je 10,27:6
Stash, John F, 1954, Ag 26,27:2
Stashower, Morris Mrs (Ida), 1968, My 30,25:4
Stasinskas, Vytautas, 1967, Jl 16,64:4
Stasio, Arnaldo, 1942, F 10,19:3
Stasio, Arnaldo Mrs, 1959, N 4,41:6
Staskevicius, Jonas, 1950, My 20,15:2
Stasney, Emanuel, 1961, Mr 16,37:3
Stasova, Yelena D, 1967, Ja 2,19:4
Stassa, Peter, 1945, S 8,15:4
Stassen, A H, 1959, Ap 4,19:3
Stassen, William A, 1962, Ja 14,84:5
Stassen, William Mrs, 1959, Je 1,27:4
Stasser, Edward L Sr, 1946, Jl 12,17:3
Stastny, John J, 1948, O 23,15:3
Stasz, Michael, 1952, N 1,21:6
States, Agatha Mme, 1874, S 4,5:4
States, William Gaynor Dr, 1919, O 7,19:2
Statesir, William H, 1907, F 2,9:3
Stathakis, Angel Mrs, 1947, O 7,27:4
Stathes, George, 1948, F 7,15:5
Stathopoulo, Epiminondas A, 1943, Je 8,21:3
Statile, Leonard, 1956, S 20,33:4
Station, Lavina Mrs, 1950, S 28,64:5
Statler, DeCamp, 1962, S 15,25:1
Statler, E M, 1928, Ap 17,29:3
Statler, Ellsworth M Mrs, 1925, O 29,25:5
Statler, Osceola A Mrs, 1958, Ja 7,47:2
Staton, Adolphus, 1964, Je 6,23:3
Staton, Harry, 1959, Jl 6,27:5
Staton, Harry M, 1948, Ag 23,17:2
Staton, Henry, 1952, Mr 25,27:4
Staton, L L Dr, 1921, Jl 2,9:6
Stats, Daniel, 1958, Mr 12,31:2
Statt, Herbert M, 1945, D 31,17:5
Stattini, Ulisse, 1947, My 22,27:3
Statton, Arthur B Bp, 1937, D 9,25:3
Statzer, Augusta M Mrs, 1941, My 21,23:1
Staub, Albert W, 1953, Ja 7,31:4
Staub, Anton, 1948, N 13,15:5
Staub, E Elmer, 1950, N 28,31:2
Staub, Francis R, 1965, S 7,39:2
Staub, George E Dr, 1937, N 25,31:2
Staub, Gordon J, 1958, Ja 28,27:4
Staub, Hugo, 1942, O 30,19:3
Staub, J Howard, 1960, Ja 11,45:6
Staub, John L, 1959, Mr 14,23:2
Staub, Maurice, 1939, Jl 12,19:5
Staub, Nicholas, 1907, Ja 6,II,9:6
Staub, Walter A, 1945, N 5,19:2
Staub, Walter A Mrs, 1945, Je 8,19:4
Staub, William E, 1941, O 30,23:2
Staub, William J, 1946, Ja 23,27:2
Staubach, William, 1968, Ag 5,39:3
Staubach, William T, 1959, D 23,27:1
Stauber, Adolph J, 1951, O 12,27:3
Stauble, Charles L, 1947, Ja 7,27:3
Stauch, L, 1929, Ap 5,25:3
Stauder, Lewis M, 1956, F 13,27:1
Stauderman, Herbert H, 1958, Ja 16,29:1
Staudinger, Hans Mrs, 1966, Mr 13,86:2
Staudinger, Hermann, 1965, S 10,35:1
Staudinger, James E, 1966, My 10,25:1
Staudt, August K, 1958, Ag 17,86:7
Staudt, Calvin K, 1951, Ap 4,29:6
Staudt, Calvin K Mrs, 1952, My 9,23:3
Staudt, Corneille, 1957, O 6,84:7
Staudt, Richard W, 1955, My 10,29:4
Stauff, August F, 1950, F 20,5:5
Stauff, John H, 1940, Mr 3,44:8
Stauffacher, Edward L, 1966, Ag 30,41:2
Stauffacher, Frank A, 1955, Jl 28,23:4
Stauffen, Ernest Jr, 1950, N 30,34:2
Stauffen, Ernest Jr Mrs, 1962, Ja 19,31:4
Stauffen, Ernst, 1939, Ag 28,19:4
Stauffen, Ralph M, 1955, Ag 30,27:4
Stauffenberg, Schenck Baron, 1901, Je 4,9:6
Stauffer, Allen M, 1956, F 29,31:2
Stauffer, Amos F, 1937, Jl 5,17:6
Stauffer, Byron Rev Dr, 1922, O 3,21:5
Stauffer, Cleveland H, 1944, Ja 1,13:2
Stauffer, Donald A, 1952, Ag 9,13:3
Stauffer, E E, 1951, O 1,23:5
Stauffer, Edgar E, 1955, Ag 31,25:2
Stauffer, Edna P, 1956, Ag 29,29:3
Stauffer, Florence V, 1949, F 7,19:6
Stauffer, Frank R, 1937, N 6,17:5
Stauffer, Grant (por), 1949, Ap 1,25:3
Stauffer, Harry F, 1937, F 10,23:5
Stauffer, Henry E, 1946, Je 29,19:5
Stauffer, J Barr, 1953, Ag 28,17:3
Stauffer, John, 1940, Mr 5,23:3
Stauffer, John K, 1952, Jl 8,27:2
Stauffer, Joseph R, 1960, F 9,31:4
Stauffer, Milton F, 1952, N 4,29:5
Stauffer, Nathan P, 1959, Je 7,86:5
Stauffer, Oscar F Mrs, 1964, Jl 12,68:4
Stauffer, Ralph D, 1957, Ja 1,23:5
Stauffer, Ralph F, 1949, Ap 2,15:3
Stauffer, Wallace W, 1938, Ag 24,21:5
Stauffer, Wilfred L, 1943, D 16,27:5
Stauffer, William H, 1945, Ja 12,15:5
Stauhs, Charles J, 1967, Je 23,31:1
Stauning, Thorvald, 1942, My 11,15:4
Staunton, Henry C F, 1957, O 16,35:3
Staunton, Howard, 1874, Je 27,4:6
Staunton, John A, 1944, My 25,21:4
Staunton, Mildred Mrs, 1945, Ap 26,23:4
Staunton, Sidney A, 1939, Ja 12,19:4
Staus, Andrew Col, 1912, F 26,11:4
Stauss, Emil G von, 1942, D 12,17:6
Stave, Benjamin, 1951, D 20,31:4
Stave, Carl N, 1944, F 22,23:3
Stavenitz, Alex R, 1960, F 13,19:5
Staver, Elery H, 1938, N 29,23:1
Staver, Henry C, 1907, N 13,9:7
Staver, Wilson W, 1941, Ja 10,19:1
Stavert, William Sir, 1937, D 31,15:5
Staves, William H, 1962, Ap 8,87:2
Stavey, Nicholas H Lt, 1921, Mr 1,13:4
Stavin, Nathan M, 1950, Ja 12,28:3
Staving, William A, 1941, Mr 6,21:6
Stavini, Amando, 1925, Ap 1,23:4
Stavisky, Abraham M, 1953, N 16,25:5
Stavisky, Benedict M, 1940, N 6,23:3
Stavitsky, Michael A, 1967, F 18,29:1
Stavnheim, Laurits, 1940, Ja 21,34:6
Stavra, Countess (Mabel F Tilton), 1910, F 23,9:4
Stavrides, Michael, 1951, Jl 13,21:5
Stay, Jay D, 1946, My 12,44:3
Stayer, Edgar S, 1959, Je 12,27:4
Stayton, Norris Col, 1937, Ag 22,II,7:2
Stayton, S Herbert, 1945, Ap 10,19:2
Stayton, Tom V, 1966, N 25,37:3
Stayton, William H (por), 1942, Jl 14,19:1
Steacie, Edgar W R, 1962, Ag 29,29:1
Stead, Alfred, 1907, D 16,9:4
Stead, Alfred H Brig-Gen, 1920, Ja 2,11:2
Stead, Arthur, 1946, Mr 26,29:2
Stead, Frank A, 1954, S 4,11:2
Stead, Frank A Mrs, 1946, My 7,21:4
Stead, Franklin, 1951, F 26,23:3
Stead, J E, 1923, N 2,17:3
Stead, John, 1949, F 20,60:4
Stead, John H, 1904, Ja 19,9:6
Stead, T J, 1933, My 11,17:3
Stead, William H, 1959, Je 13,21:3
Stead, William M, 1966, Ap 29,29:3
Stead, William T (trb), 1912, Je 7,13:4
Steadman, Christopher, 1946, F 26,25:4
Steadman, Cornelius H, 1943, Ap 5,19:2
Steadman, Frank, 1939, S 14,23:6
Steadman, J J, 1941, Ap 20,42:5
Steadman, John M, 1945, D 22,19:5
Steadman, William A, 1964, My 21,35:1
Steadwell, Bert S, 1947, Ap 7,23:1
Steagall, Henry B, 1943, N 23,25:5
Stealey, Watterson, 1944, Mr 21,20:2
Stearly, George R, 1947, Je 4,27:1
Stearly, Wilson R (por), 1941, N 9,52:1
Stearly, Wilson R Mrs, 1961, Ag 12,41:4
Stearly, Wilson W, 1947, Ag 18,17:2
Stearly, Wilson W Mrs, 1950, Jl 27,25:5
Stearman, Arthur O, 1949, Jl 1,19:3
Stearman, Walter, 1949, N 26,15:5
Stearn, Albert, 1944, Ja 7,17:4
Stearne, Edwin, 1937, N 10,25:5
Stearnes, Reaumur C, 1945, My 29,15:5
Stearns, A Warren, 1959, S 25,29:1
Stearns, Adelaide, 1924, Je 8,26:1
Stearns, Albert L, 1952, My 13,23:4
Stearns, Albert L Mrs, 1960, N 20,86:7
Stearns, Alfred E, 1949, N 16,29:5
Stearns, Arthur J Mrs, 1953, Ag 9,77:3
Stearns, Benjamin, 1913, Ag 28,9:3
Stearns, Bernice M Mrs, 1940, S 12,25:6
Stearns, Charles F, 1946, S 4,23:4
Stearns, Charles H, 1948, Mr 30,23:4
Stearns, Clark D Mrs, 1958, Ap 2,31:1
Stearns, Don Abel, 1871, Ag 25,4:1
Stearns, E Ward, 1953, Mr 20,23:5
Stearns, Edgar W Jr, 1958, N 2,88:3
Stearns, Edith B Mrs (mem ser set), 1961, N 29,41:4
Stearns, Edith F Mrs, 1956, Je 29,21:4
Stearns, Edward B, 1944, Ja 7,17:4
Stearns, Edward R, 1939, Ja 21,15:2
Stearns, Edwin I, 1947, Mr 2,60:4
Stearns, Edwin W Lt, 1923, F 1,11:4
Stearns, Ex-Gov, 1878, D 29,7:4
Stearns, Florence D Mrs, 1958, F 3,23:4
Stearns, Foster, 1956, Je 5,35:5
Stearns, Frank B, 1953, Jl 23,23:5
Stearns, Frank W (will, Mr 11,6:1),(por), 1939, Mr 7,21:1
Stearns, Frederick S, 1951, My 12,21:4
Stearns, George, 1956, Je 16,19:6
Stearns, George L Maj, 1867, Ap 15,5:4
Stearns, George Mrs, 1947, N 14,23:3
Stearns, George R, 1944, Je 5,19:5
Stearns, Gilbert P, 1961, N 24,28:5
Stearns, Gustav, 1951, Ap 22,88:4
Stearns, Harold E (por), 1943, Ag 14,11:3
Stearns, Harold G, 1958, N 1,19:4
Stearns, Harry L, 1939, Jl 11,19:5
Stearns, Henry C Mrs, 1948, Jl 12,19:3
Stearns, Henry F, 1966, N 10,47:3
Stearns, Henry S (por), 1942, Ap 3,21:3
Stearns, J Brenton, 1965, N 25,35:1
Stearns, Jessie L Mrs, 1950, O 25,35:2
Stearns, John C, 1955, My 31,27:3
Stearns, John N, 1947, Jl 1,25:5
Stearns, John Noble, 1907, Mr 16,9:5
Stearns, Joseph T, 1949, Ja 20,27:1
Stearns, Josiah O, 1867, Ag 30,5:3
Stearns, Joyce C, 1948, Je 12,15:4
Stearns, Kendall, 1963, N 18,33:4
Stearns, Lester O, 1947, Ag 3,52:6
Stearns, Louis, 1940, My 19,42:6
Stearns, Louis A, 1960, Mr 6,86:2
Stearns, Louise A, 1940, Mr 4,15:3
Stearns, Lutie E, 1943, D 27,19:2
Stearns, Malcolm, 1958, Je 24,31:2
Stearns, Malcolm Mrs, 1955, D 27,24:4
Stearns, Marshal, 1943, Ja 23,13:5
Stearns, Marshall W, 1966, D 19,37:3
Stearns, Maurice H, 1951, O 26,23:3
Stearns, Monroe M Mrs, 1961, Jl 13,29:4
Stearns, Ranald M, 1950, My 13,17:7
Stearns, Raymond E, 1956, D 18,31:1
Stearns, Richard H, 1909, Ag 17,9:5
Stearns, Robert B, 1944, Jl 14,13:6; 1954, D 15,31:2
Stearns, Robert L, 1939, N 3,21:3
Stearns, Roger, 1958, F 23,92:5
Stearns, Russell B Mrs, 1950, F 22,29:1
Stearns, Saul, 1938, Je 7,44:6
Stearns, Sherman D, 1965, Ja 12,37:5
Stearns, Svlenda M Mrs, 1938, D 21,23:4
Stearns, Thomas G, 1916, Ja 28,9:5
Stearns, Thornton, 1967, Jl 7,33:1
Stearns, Tilden H, 1943, D 27,20:2
Stearns, Timothy R, 1961, Mr 6,25:1
Stearns, W A, 1876, Je 9,4:6
Stearns, Walter C, 1965, Jl 3,19:5

Stearns, Walter M, 1957, Je 25,29:2
Stearns, Wayland E, 1937, Ap 23,21:5
Stearns, Wilbur M, 1946, Mr 23,13:3
Stearns, William B, 1937, My 8,19:4
Stearns, William F Rev, 1923, F 5,15:6
Stearns, William O, 1945, F 3,11:2
Stearns, William R Bro, 1959, Ap 12,86:8
Stearns, William S, 1937, D 13,27:2
Stearns, William W, 1905, Mr 2,9:6
Stebbings, George T, 1939, N 22,21:4
Stebbins, Albert K, 1937, N 12,22:1
Stebbins, Allen E, 1941, Ja 26,35:8
Stebbins, Arthur W, 1963, Jl 14,61:2
Stebbins, C S, 1884, N 27,5:4
Stebbins, Carrie M, 1951, S 26,31:2
Stebbins, Charles L, 1946, Ag 5,21:4
Stebbins, Charles M, 1937, N 24,23:4
Stebbins, Delia, 1956, S 2,57:2
Stebbins, E Vail, 1950, N 28,31:4
Stebbins, Edwin A, 1954, Je 7,23:6
Stebbins, Edwin A Mrs, 1954, O 2,17:5
Stebbins, F G (funl), 1883, Mr 7,5:6
Stebbins, F Lansing, 1948, Mr 29,21:1; 1959, Ja 19, 27:4
Stebbins, George C (por), 1945, O 7,44:1
Stebbins, George C Mrs, 1915, S 2,9:4
Stebbins, George L, 1952, N 21,25:4
Stebbins, George M, 1942, Jl 13,15:6
Stebbins, George Mrs, 1902, D 28,7:7
Stebbins, George T, 1917, D 7,13:5
Stebbins, H G, 1881, D 11,2:5
Stebbins, Henry H Jr, 1952, Jl 19,15:3
Stebbins, Homer A, 1962, N 6,33:5
Stebbins, Horace C, 1947, Je 3,25:3
Stebbins, Howard L Mrs, 1958, Ja 31,21:4
Stebbins, Kathleen B Mrs, 1962, Jl 26,27:5
Stebbins, Leo A, 1946, Ja 5,13:2
Stebbins, Marion (Sister Mary Austin), 1957, Ja 1,8:5
Stebbins, Olive G F Mrs, 1938, Jl 31,33:3
Stebbins, Orson B, 1943, F 15,15:5
Stebbins, R Sr, 1878, Jl 12,2:6
Stebbins, Roswell O Dr, 1910, My 25,9:4
Stebbins, Rowland, 1948, D 13,23:1
Stebbins, S Schieffelin, 1912, My 10,11:5
Stebbins, Theodore, 1941, O 15,21:2
Stebler, William J, 1960, Ag 1,23:6
Stebner, Louis, 1949, Mr 25,23:4
Stecher, Alois, 1916, Ap 14,9:1
Stecher, Alois Msgr, 1916, Ap 11,13:6
Stecher, Anton, 1954, O 11,27:4
Stecher, Edward, 1950, N 4,17:5
Stecher, Fred J, 1948, My 17,19:4
Stecher, Frederick H Jr Mrs, 1948, Mr 3,23:4
Stecher, Russell P Mrs, 1950, S 4,17:6
Stechschulte, Victor C, 1955, Mr 4,23:2
Steck, Augustus R, 1943, D 28,18:2
Steck, Daniel F, 1951, Ja 2,23:4
Steck, Leo J, 1950, Je 21,27:4
Steckbeck, David W, 1956, O 16,33:2
Steckel, Abram P, 1954, Ag 21,17:4
Steckel, Elmer A, 1949, Ap 5,29:4
Steckel, Harry A, 1962, Jl 14,21:4
Steckel, Harry B, 1953, Je 6,17:6
Steckel, Samuel W, 1949, Ap 13,29:2
Stecker, H Freeman Dr, 1923, O 31,15:3
Stecker, Henry J, 1954, My 29,15:5
Stecker, Jesse J, 1944, D 20,23:5
Stecker, Leroy H, 1965, Ap 21,45:2
Stecker, Louis, 1945, Je 15,19:5
Stecker, Robert D, 1959, D 17,37:2
Steckert, William, 1925, O 17,15:4
Steckle, Roy E, 1950, N 15,31:2
Steckler, A, 1929, Je 11,29:3
Steckler, Alfred Mrs, 1907, N 19,9:5
Steckler, Alfred R Jr Mrs, 1956, D 10,31:1
Steckler, Benjamin, 1924, Ja 16,19:6
Steckler, C, 1927, O 16,31:2
Steckler, David, 1942, O 6,23:2
Steckler, David Mrs, 1938, Ja 28,21:2
Steckler, Edward L (por), 1949, Jl 31,61:1
Steckler, Edward L, 1949, Ag 2,20:6
Steckler, Frank, 1961, D 7,43:3
Steckler, Herman Dr, 1901, D 1,7:1
Steckler, Louis, 1941, Je 7,17:4
Steckler, Samuel P, 1963, Ag 15,29:1
Steckman, Albert, 1962, O 9,42:1
Stecz, Joseph F, 1950, D 11,25:5
Stedler, Alwin W, 1940, F 11,48:1
Stedler, Mary R Mrs, 1941, F 5,19:5
Stedler, Robert C, 1956, Je 5,35:4
Stedler, Robert C Mrs, 1954, F 16,25:4
Stedler, William, 1943, F 3,19:5
Stedman, Arthur G, 1908, S 17,7:6
Stedman, Bayard J, 1941, Ja 27,15:3
Stedman, C M, 1930, S 24,23:1
Stedman, Charles, 1908, Ja 20,9:2
Stedman, Charles S, 1940, O 1,23:3
Stedman, Edward M, 1939, O 17,25:4
Stedman, Emory A, 1937, O 17,II,9:1
Stedman, Ernest W, 1957, Mr 28,31:1
Stedman, Francis W Mrs, 1945, D 1,23:6
Stedman, Frank A, 1939, N 11,15:6
Stedman, Frank H, 1939, N 11,15:2
Stedman, Fred H, 1946, My 22,21:2
Stedman, Frederick, 1906, Ja 23,2:3
Stedman, George W, 1954, N 24,23:5
Stedman, Giles C, 1961, Ap 11,37:1
Stedman, H R Dr, 1926, F 21,18:4
Stedman, James H, 1950, N 14,31:2
Stedman, John M, 1949, N 7,27:3
Stedman, John W, 1952, D 27,9:4
Stedman, Joseph F, 1944, S 22,19:5
Stedman, Joseph F (por), 1946, Mr 24,44:4
Stedman, Lincoln, 1948, Mr 23,25:5
Stedman, Myrtle Mrs, 1938, Ja 9,42:4
Stedman, Samuel L, 1961, S 3,61:1
Stedman, Seymour, 1948, Jl 10,15:4
Stedman, Theodore W, 1959, O 18,86:3
Stedman, Thomas L, 1938, My 27,17:4
Stedman, William G, 1942, Ja 9,21:3
Stedman, William M Mrs, 1949, Jl 26,27:2
Steeb, John Mrs, 1941, S 27,17:5
Steeb, Olga, 1941, D 31,17:1
Steeble, William H, 1951, My 14,25:5
Steed, Charles W, 1947, D 29,17:2
Steed, Emma C Mrs, 1949, D 18,90:2
Steed, Henry W, 1956, Ja 14,19:1
Steed, Leonard L, 1953, Je 17,38:3
Steed, Robert L (funl, Ja 23,11:5), 1922, Ja 19,17:5
Steedle, Robert E, 1937, My 13,25:6
Steedman, J B, 1883, O 19,4:7
Steedman, Rosa, 1903, Je 10,5:2
Steeg, Herman B, 1949, O 14,27:3
Steeg, Theodore, 1950, D 11,25:3
Steege, Otto P, 1952, Ag 15,16:6
Steegman, Phil, 1952, F 19,31:8
Steegmuller, Charles A A, 1957, Mr 4,27:2
Steegmuller, Francis Mrs, 1961, Jl 1,17:5
Steel, Alfred G B, 1949, Je 8,29:1
Steel, Byron, 1965, Ja 4,29:4
Steel, Charles F (see also Ja 3), 1904, Ja 4,9:3
Steel, Charles L, 1938, Je 13,19:5
Steel, Gerald, 1957, S 15,83:1
Steel, James Mrs (will), 1960, Jl 13,37:8
Steel, James W, 1947, D 7,76:3
Steel, John, 1950, Mr 23,36:2; 1965, D 3,35:7
Steel, John Judge, 1905, Ap 28,9:4
Steel, John W, 1950, Ja 11,23:3
Steel, Matthew, 1952, Mr 17,21:2
Steel, Phil S, 1941, Mr 25,23:1
Steel, Reginald, 1947, My 11,60:4
Steel, Reginald A, 1949, Jl 10,57:1
Steel, Robert, 1952, Ap 24,31:2
Steel, Samuel W, 1957, My 31,19:1
Steel, Thomas Sedgewick, 1903, S 11,5:6
Steel, William, 1954, Jl 28,23:4
Steel, William J, 1915, Ap 24,11:5
Steel, William W, 1939, Ja 31,21:4
Steelberg, Wesley R, 1952, Jl 9,27:5
Steele, Alfred N (funl, Ap 23,31:5), 1959, Ap 20,31:1
Steele, Alfred N (est acctg), 1961, F 3,12:7
Steele, Allen D, 1941, My 15,23:1
Steele, Blanche L Mrs, 1937, Je 22,23:4
Steele, Boyd M, 1948, Jl 27,25:3
Steele, Charles (will, Ag 11,16:5), 1939, Ag 6,37:1
Steele, Charles H, 1925, Ap 14,23:3
Steele, Charles M, 1943, Jl 19,15:4
Steele, Chester I, 1967, Jl 21,31:1
Steele, Clarence A, 1953, Ag 11,27:5
Steele, Clarence A Mrs, 1953, Ap 11,17:3
Steele, D A, 1931, Jl 20,17:4
Steele, Daniel Rev, 1914, S 3,7:5
Steele, David M, 1945, F 27,20:2
Steele, Domhnall A, 1953, Je 19,21:2
Steele, Edward E, 1953, O 24,15:2
Steele, Edward H Mrs, 1947, N 28,27:3
Steele, Edward S, 1942, Ja 6,24:3
Steele, Eli S, 1959, Ja 26,29:2
Steele, Ellessdie J, 1947, D 12,27:2
Steele, Eugene E, 1951, O 4,33:2
Steele, Eugene F Mrs, 1945, D 16,40:3
Steele, Florence M, 1948, O 23,15:3
Steele, Francis J, 1950, Ag 29,27:4
Steele, Francis R C, 1955, Ag 9,25:3
Steele, Fred E, 1943, D 11,15:4
Steele, Fred W, 1949, My 21,13:5
Steele, Frederic D, 1944, Jl 7,15:5
Steele, Frederic D Mrs, 1957, Ja 7,25:4
Steele, Frederic T, 1942, Ap 3,21:2
Steele, Frederick A Mrs, 1946, N 7,31:3
Steele, Frederick Gen, 1868, Ja 15,1:3
Steele, Frederick W, 1943, F 4,23:5
Steele, Gayle A, 1938, Ja 30,II,9:2
Steele, George, 1906, N 11,9:6
Steele, George A, 1953, My 13,29:5
Steele, George F, 1937, Ap 1,23:6; 1939, Je 27,23:5; 1944, My 31,19:2
Steele, George F Mrs, 1950, Je 1,27:4
Steele, George G Sr, 1959, Ag 6,27:4
Steele, George L Dr, 1953, F 16,21:5
Steele, George W, 1955, F 11,23:5
Steele, George W Maj, 1922, Jl 14,13:6
Steele, Gilbert V, 1950, N 3,27:3
Steele, Gordon, 1961, S 9,19:6
Steele, H Roy, 1946, Je 18,25:3
Steele, Harold J, 1957, Ap 12,25:1
Steele, Harry L (por), 1938, Ap 2,15:3
Steele, Heath M, 1956, F 22,27:1
Steele, Helen M, 1950, O 18,33:3
Steele, Henry Dr, 1924, S 27,16:3
Steele, Hiram M, 1958, Ja 6,39:4
Steele, Howard C, 1948, O 15,24:3
Steele, Ida, 1944, My 17,19:2
Steele, Irwin B (por), 1946, Ap 23,21:5
Steele, J A, 1928, D 7,29:5
Steele, J Dalmus, 1942, O 4,52:2
Steele, J N, 1933, Mr 8,13:2
Steele, J Nevett Rev Dr, 1916, Ag 24,9:4
Steele, Jacob H Sr, 1954, Je 4,23:4
Steele, James, 1962, Je 12,37:2
Steele, James K, 1937, D 27,15:3
Steele, Jennie P, 1954, Ja 28,27:4
Steele, John Dutton Dr, 1908, My 18,7:5
Steele, John L, 1956, S 30,86:5
Steele, John N, 1955, S 17,15:4
Steele, John Nelson, 1968, Je 7,39:2
Steele, John S, 1947, Ja 8,24:2
Steele, Joseph M, 1957, Mr 31,88:8
Steele, Judge, 1873, Jl 29,4:5
Steele, Kyle B, 1942, Je 19,23:6
Steele, Leo M, 1952, F 4,17:4
Steele, Leon C, 1945, F 11,38:6
Steele, Mark V, 1948, F 5,23:2
Steele, Mary A Mrs, 1941, S 25,25:3
Steele, Matthew A, 1938, My 13,19:4
Steele, N M G, 1882, Je 20,8:6
Steele, O R, 1875, O 4,4:6
Steele, Porter, 1966, D 21,39:1
Steele, R B, 1944, D 14,23:2
Steele, Ray, 1949, S 13,29:2
Steele, Robert, 1939, Mr 2,21:4
Steele, Robert P, 1944, O 24,23:1
Steele, Robert W Justice, 1910, O 13,11:4
Steele, Robert William, 1912, Mr 2,13:5
Steele, Roswell H, 1943, O 23,13:5
Steele, Ruth B (will), 1957, Jl 19,21:7
Steele, S Tagart, 1967, O 13,36:2
Steele, Sam Genl, 1919, Ja 31,11:5
Steele, Samuel B, 1950, O 20,28:2
Steele, Samuel B Mrs Lady, 1951, Ap 3,27:1
Steele, Sanford H (funl, D 22,11:5), 1920, D 20,13:5
Steele, Sherman, 1945, Ap 19,27:3
Steele, Thomas B, 1938, Mr 20,II,9:2
Steele, Thomas B Dr, 1905, Je 23,7:1
Steele, Thomas C Mrs, 1950, D 31,43:2
Steele, Thomas L Sr, 1950, Ag 22,27:4
Steele, Thomas M (por), 1944, Jl 31,13:6
Steele, Thomas W Mrs, 1947, D 5,25:4
Steele, Vernon, 1955, Jl 25,19:6
Steele, W Donald, 1968, D 9,47:3
Steele, W Harry Sr, 1955, Mr 31,27:5
Steele, Walter P, 1953, N 6,28:4
Steele, Walter S, 1960, Mr 4,25:4
Steele, Warren C, 1944, Jl 7,15:6
Steele, Wilbur D Mrs (N Mitchell), 1967, My 30,19:5
Steele, William, 1949, O 21,18:6; 1955, O 25,33:3
Steele, William D, 1964, My 12,37:6
Steele, William J, 1938, Ap 23,15:3
Steele, William L, 1940, O 27,45:2
Steele, William M, 1940, Ag 26,15:2; 1955, Jl 1,21:1
Steele, William P, 1951, Ap 8,92:7
Steele, William 3d, 1960, Ag 14,92:7
Steeley, Joseph A, 1964, S 17,43:4
Steelholm, Hardy, 1961, Je 24,21:6
Steell, Susan (Mrs A Allen), 1959, N 14,21:6
Steell, Willis, 1941, F 1,18:4
Steelman, Andrew J, 1964, My 19,37:3
Steelman, Andrew J Mrs (por), 1945, Je 17,26:4
Steelman, Chester N, 1951, N 28,31:3
Steelman, Fred G, 1950, Mr 17,23:2
Steelman, Jonas, 1939, Jl 20,19:4
Steelman, Mathias Mrs, 1957, S 8,84:5
Steelman, P C, 1950, My 30,17:3
Steelman, Raymond E, 1949, Ap 17,76:6
Steelman, Somers R, 1965, F 2,33:4
Steelsmith, Linden, 1942, S 1,20:2
Steen, Alfred R, 1949, Mr 8,25:4
Steen, Burnside, 1948, N 22,21:3
Steen, Cecil A S, 1956, Ag 3,20:2
Steen, Christian A, 1940, N 9,17:4
Steen, Daniel, 1958, Ag 28,27:3
Steen, Daniel Mrs, 1960, Je 26,72:5
Steen, Edward D, 1950, F 7,27:2
Steen, Elizabeth K, 1938, Jl 14,21:3
Steen, James, 1949, Je 26,60:2
Steen, John E, 1955, O 10,27:2
Steen, John F (por), 1938, Mr 30,21:1
Steen, John F Mrs, 1946, Ap 26,21:4
Steen, Olaf, 1954, S 25,15:5
Steen, Patricia H, 1946, S 17,7:3
Steen, Robert Sevice, 1908, Ap 19,9:6
Steen, Sigvart J Dr, 1968, D 22,52:4
Steenberg, Christian, 1954, S 28,29:2
Steenberghe, A F M, 1947, F 18,26:2
Steenbock, Harry, 1967, D 27,37:1
Steenbock, Henry Mrs, 1946, Mr 8,21:2
Steene, W Vernon, 1939, Mr 21,23:6
Steene, William, 1965, Mr 25,37:5
Steengrafe, Gustave O, 1954, O 6,25:1

Steenken, Charles D Dr, 1937, Jl 31,15:6
Steensby, Prof, 1920, O 22,15:5
Steensen, J Howard, 1955, S 4,56:3
Steenstra, Peter Henry Rev, 1911, Ap 28,13:4
Steenstrup, Christian, 1955, N 30,33:1
Steenstrup, Peter A, 1942, Jl 17,15:4
Steenwijk, W L de vos van, 1947, Ap 13,60:2
Steep, Thomas, 1944, S 4,19:2
Steer, Bernard A, 1952, Jl 19,15:6
Steer, Charles, 1958, F 18,27:1
Steer, Ebenezer, 1952, Ag 5,19:6
Steer, Edward, 1956, Je 6,33:3
Steer, G L Mrs, 1937, Ja 30,17:4
Steer, Henry, 1937, O 16,9:2
Steer, Joseph B, 1940, D 8,68:2
Steer, P Wilson, 1942, Mr 22,49:2
Steere, Edward Rev, 1882, Ag 30,4:7
Steere, Jonathan M, 1958, S 23,33:1
Steere, Jonathan M Mrs, 1956, D 19,31:4
Steere, Lloyd R, 1961, Ja 30,23:4
Steere, Richard, 1947, Ja 17,24:2
Steere, Sayles B, 1958, My 22,29:2
Steere, Thomas E (por), 1949, F 25,23:4
Steergren, George G, 1951, Jl 28,11:1
Steers, Abraham, 1960, S 22,27:3
Steers, Abraham Mrs, 1941, Ja 21,22:3
Steers, Alfred E (por), 1948, Mr 3,23:3
Steers, C R Coster, 1952, Ap 24,31:3
Steers, Francis F, 1964, Ap 28,37:2
Steers, H Treadwell, 1937, Je 3,25:4
Steers, Henry C, 1947, N 6,27:3
Steers, Henry Mrs, 1946, S 29,60:3
Steers, Henry V, 1917, N 2,15:6
Steers, J Rich, 1964, My 9,27:1
Steers, J Richard Mrs, 1948, O 27,28:3
Steers, Newton I (por), 1944, My 17,19:3
Steers, T Capt, 1884, Je 14,5:4
Steers, William H, 1944, Je 1,19:2; 1957, D 21,19:6
Steese, Edward S Mrs, 1961, O 6,35:2
Steese, James G, 1958, Ja 12,86:7
Steeve, John A, 1956, Ap 28,17:5
Steeves, Alfred T, 1951, S 11,29:2
Steeves, Charles P Dr, 1937, O 3,II,8:3
Steeves, E M Mrs, 1951, D 31,13:2
Steeves, Henry L, 1950, O 26,31:5
Stefan, Anthony R, 1964, Mr 25,41:1
Stefan, J Sutton, 1964, F 1,23:3
Stefan, Karl, 1951, O 3,33:1
Stefan, Paul (por), 1943, N 13,13:3
Stefan, Roger, 1955, D 28,23:1
Stefanescu, Gheorges, 1950, Ja 6,21:3
Stefanic, John, 1951, Ag 28,23:4
Stefanic, John (Bugs Brown), 1958, S 30,10:5
Stefanik, Andrew J, 1945, D 31,17:5
Stefanini, Francois, 1948, Mr 30,23:3
Stefano, Mario di, 1963, S 17,35:2
Stefanovic, Lazar, 1950, Ap 8,13:6
Stefanowicz, Michael A, 1956, Je 5,35:5
Stefanowicz, Zygmunt Mrs, 1950, O 17,31:5
Stefansky, George, 1957, D 25,31:5
Steffan, Michael Mrs, 1949, N 22,29:4
Steffanson, Hokan B, 1962, My 23,45:2
Steffanson, Hokan Mrs, 1953, D 14,31:2
Steffen, Albert, 1963, Jl 15,29:3
Steffen, Alma M Mrs, 1938, S 12,17:2
Steffen, Eugene C, 1959, O 12,19:2
Steffen, Frederick L, 1958, O 17,29:1
Steffen, J Hall (por), 1937, Ap 14,25:3
Steffen, Julius, 1923, Je 25,13:4
Steffen, Walter A, 1965, Ap 17,19:1
Steffen, Walter P Judge (will, Ap 2,3:4), 1937, Mr 10,23:2
Steffens, Afred P, 1944, Ja 9,42:1
Steffens, Fritz, 1964, Ap 20,41:4
Steffens, Gustave R, 1963, Jl 12,25:1
Steffens, Harold M, 1955, Je 1,33:5
Steffens, John, 1942, S 15,23:4
Steffens, L, 1936, Ag 10,19:1
Steffens, Lincoln Mrs, 1911, Ja 9,13:5
Steffer, Louise Mrs, 1940, Je 18,23:6
Stefferson, Raymond E, 1964, Mr 16,31:5
Steffes, Joseph M, 1940, Ap 12,23:3
Steffner, Wayne R, 1957, F 25,25:2
Steffy, George W, 1964, S 1,36:6
Stegall, Glynn, 1963, Ag 11,85:2
Stegelske, Francis S, 1937, Jl 10,15:3
Stegeman, Gebhard, 1949, S 7,29:3
Stegeman, Herman J, 1939, O 23,19:2
Stegemann, Edward Jr, 1937, F 4,21:4
Stegemeyer, Andrew J, 1939, S 19,25:3
Stegemeyer, Fred E, 1948, Je 16,29:1
Stegen, Edward F, 1965, Jl 6,33:1
Steger, Anthony J Mrs, 1955, My 14,19:3
Steger, Chris G, 1944, Ag 11,15:3
Steger, Frederick J, 1938, S 3,13:2
Steger, Harry Peyton, 1913, Ja 6,9:4
Steger, John H, 1957, Je 6,31:3
Steger, John Valentine, 1916, Je 12,11:6
Steger, John W, 1948, O 4,23:1
Steger, Julius, 1959, Mr 3,33:5
Steger, Robert C, 1952, Ja 12,7:1
Stegerwald, Adam, 1945, D 7,21:4
Steggerda, Morris, 1950, Mr 16,31:1
Stegler, Richard Peter, 1922, N 13,15:5
Stegmaier, Charles Mrs, 1946, D 10,32:3
Stegmaier, George J, 1956, Mr 2,23:2
Stegman, Fred, 1938, D 28,22:3
Stegman, Harold G, 1952, Jl 7,21:6
Stegman, Harold G Mrs, 1963, My 19,86:3
Stegman, Lewis R Col, 1923, O 8,17:4
Stegmann, George H, 1944, Ja 4,17:5
Stegmeyer, William John, 1968, Ag 22,37:2
Stehfest, Herman W, 1951, F 18,78:4
Stehl, Frederick S, 1940, Ja 12,17:2
Stehl, John H, 1937, My 29,17:2
Stehle, Augustine Rev, 1913, N 5,13:6
Stehle, Florence M Mrs, 1940, Ag 11,31:4
Stehli, Emil J, 1945, My 22,19:5
Stehli, H E, 1955, D 9,27:5
Stehli, Henry J, 1943, Ag 1,39:3
Stehling, George T, 1947, Je 25,25:1
Stehling, Joseph J, 1949, Ag 4,23:3
Stehman, Frederick F, 1967, My 22,43:1
Stehman, Walter K, 1947, O 2,27:2
Steibling, John, 1910, Mr 30,12:3
Steichen, Clara Mrs, 1952, O 18,19:5
Steichen, Edward Mrs, 1957, F 21,27:5
Steidel, Florence, 1962, Ap 7,25:6
Steidel, John H, 1938, Ag 10,19:4
Steidle, George J, 1954, Mr 12,21:5
Steiert, Alois, 1941, Je 19,21:4
Steiert, Louise A Mrs, 1942, Mr 20,19:4
Steif, B Leo, 1953, S 22,31:3
Steif, Jonathan, 1958, Ag 28,27:3
Steig, Joseph, 1955, Mr 28,27:4
Steig, Joseph Mrs (Laura), 1965, My 28,33:3
Steiger, Adolf, 1925, Mr 2,17:6
Steiger, Albert, 1938, S 10,17:5
Steiger, Harry, 1950, D 20,31:3
Steiger, Howard A, 1966, D 19,37:4
Steiger, Phil C, 1952, O 30,31:1
Steiger, Walter C, 1958, Mr 14,25:3
Steigers, William C, 1923, My 26,15:6
Steigerwald, Frank J, 1960, F 27,19:6
Steigerwald, Gustav J, 1943, Jl 1,19:5
Steiglitz, Julius O Prof (por), 1937, Ja 11,19:3
Steiglitz, Matty, 1940, My 19,42:3
Steiguer, Louis R de, 1947, Ap 20,63:3
Steikelis, Moshe, 1967, Mr 14,47:3
Steiker, Aaron L, 1968, D 11,47:1
Steimer, Ferdinand, 1940, D 11,28:2
Steimle, Augustus Rev Dr, 1937, O 1,21:3
Steimle, Mildred, 1964, S 23,47:2
Stein, A Frank Mrs, 1950, S 29,27:3
Stein, Abram N, 1911, D 31,II,11:4
Stein, Abram N (funl, Ja 3,13:4), 1912, Ja 2,11:6
Stein, Adolphe, 1938, F 28,15:3
Stein, Albert C, 1946, My 8,25:2
Stein, Albert C Mrs, 1954, Je 17,29:4
Stein, Alex Mrs (por), 1948, Ap 27,26:2
Stein, Alfred A, 1961, O 31,31:3
Stein, Alfred A Jr, 1964, S 9,43:3
Stein, Alfred A Mrs, 1953, S 17,29:4
Stein, Alvin B, 1954, S 5,51:2
Stein, Anthony H Msgr, 1921, Ag 23,15:7
Stein, Arthur, 1962, Ja 18,29:2
Stein, Aug Dr, 1937, S 7,21:4
Stein, Aurel, 1943, O 29,19:2
Stein, Barnet M, 1957, S 16,31:5
Stein, Benjamin F, 1960, O 28,31:4
Stein, Bertha Mrs, 1948, Mr 15,23:4
Stein, Boris E, 1961, Mr 20,29:5
Stein, Carl J, 1952, Ap 1,29:5
Stein, Charles F, 1939, My 6,17:2
Stein, Charles H, 1952, Mr 22,13:4; 1957, My 1,37:4
Stein, Charles H Mrs, 1948, O 21,27:2
Stein, Charles Mrs, 1947, Jl 20,44:6
Stein, Christopher E, 1950, Jl 27,25:4
Stein, Christopher E Mrs, 1944, O 18,21:2
Stein, Conrad, 1904, Ja 19,9:6
Stein, David, 1946, Ag 9,36:8; 1954, N 29,25:3; 1959, F 27,25:3; 1959, Je 21,93:1
Stein, David B, 1953, Ag 1,11:3
Stein, David Mrs, 1961, Ag 17,27:2
Stein, Edward, 1915, N 25,13:5; 1920, Jl 20,7:4
Stein, Edwin, 1959, S 2,29:4
Stein, Elias, 1947, D 20,17:1
Stein, Elias Mrs, 1955, O 5,35:4
Stein, Elizabeth P, 1966, My 26,47:3
Stein, Elsy, 1961, Ja 12,29:4
Stein, Emil, 1960, Mr 27,87:1
Stein, Emil Mrs, 1956, F 26,88:5
Stein, Emma H Mrs, 1937, Ja 17,II,2:4
Stein, Estelle A Mrs, 1941, Ag 9,15:3
Stein, Everett, 1963, D 29,42:5
Stein, Ewald, 1957, F 4,19:3
Stein, Francis R, 1967, Ag 26,28:6
Stein, Frank, 1948, Ap 27,25:3
Stein, Frank J, 1948, Ja 11,58:6
Stein, Fred, 1957, Ja 28,23:6; 1958, Jl 24,25:5; 1967, S 24,84:3
Stein, Fred M, 1950, Ap 26,29:1
Stein, Fred M Mrs, 1958, S 10,33:5
Stein, Frederick J, 1943, D 4,13:5
Stein, Frederick W, 1955, Ja 30,84:6
Stein, George F, 1938, O 11,25:2
Stein, Gerson, 1958, N 28,30:3
Stein, Gertrude, 1946, Jl 28,40:1
Stein, Gervin C, 1958, Ap 13,84:5
Stein, Gilbert F, 1956, Mr 12,27:3
Stein, Gustav, 1946, N 30,15:4
Stein, H von Gen, 1927, My 28,17:5
Stein, Harold, 1966, My 10,45:1
Stein, Harold J, 1941, S 10,23:1
Stein, Harry, 1952, O 26,88:6; 1959, O 12,19:2
Stein, Harry M, 1940, N 16,17:2
Stein, Harry N, 1959, Mr 18,37:2
Stein, Henry, 1942, S 14,15:5; 1953, S 7,19:3
Stein, Henry B, 1960, F 6,19:6
Stein, Henry G, 1967, N 30,47:1
Stein, Henry Mrs, 1949, My 18,27:1
Stein, Herbert E, 1954, Ag 23,17:6
Stein, Herman, 1941, O 10,23:5; 1949, My 10,25:2
Stein, Herman H, 1919, Mr 20,13:3
Stein, Herman M, 1960, O 13,37:1
Stein, Hyman, 1950, Ap 20,29:3
Stein, I Melville, 1965, Ja 25,37:1
Stein, Irving, 1954, N 13,34:8
Stein, Irving L, 1966, My 15,88:4
Stein, Isadore, 1957, F 26,29:3
Stein, Isidor F, 1956, F 10,22:1
Stein, Israel, 1957, Jl 21,61:1
Stein, J I, 1880, Jl 5,5:5
Stein, Jacob, 1956, My 19,19:6
Stein, Jacob A, 1949, Ap 2,15:4
Stein, Jacob B, 1946, Mr 16,13:3
Stein, Jacob J, 1939, O 4,25:5
Stein, Jacob Mrs, 1965, Mr 14,87:1
Stein, John, 1946, S 13,7:2; 1951, D 28,21:4
Stein, John B, 1947, My 17,15:4; 1960, O 30,86:3
Stein, Joseph, 1949, O 5,29:5
Stein, Joseph A, 1940, Je 21,21:6
Stein, Joseph Mrs, 1945, Je 13,23:1; 1947, S 15,17:3
Stein, Joseph W, 1940, Ag 26,15:6
Stein, Julian, 1937, Ja 16,17:2
Stein, Julius Mrs, 1947, Mr 31,23:4
Stein, L, 1930, Jl 15,23:1
Stein, Leo (por), 1939, Mr 28,23:1
Stein, Leo, 1947, Jl 31,21:5; 1951, O 17,31:3
Stein, Leon, 1937, S 13,21:6
Stein, Lewis, 1958, Je 19,31:4
Stein, Lewis A, 1954, Je 4,23:3
Stein, Louis, 1923, Ap 11,21:5
Stein, Louis F, 1963, Ap 29,31:2
Stein, Louis N, 1918, O 2,13:4
Stein, Ludwig, 1944, Ja 6,23:1
Stein, Malvin F, 1954, N 10,33:4
Stein, Max, 1947, N 23,76:1
Stein, Max Mrs, 1953, Ap 3,23:1
Stein, Maximillian J Mrs, 1944, My 14,46:2
Stein, Meyer A Mrs, 1942, Jl 14,19:4
Stein, Meyer J, 1925, F 19,19:3
Stein, Modest, 1958, F 27,27:5
Stein, Morris, 1948, Je 29,23:5; 1965, Ja 25,37:1
Stein, Morton, 1944, Mr 2,17:1
Stein, Moshe Mrs, 1966, My 15,88:7
Stein, Nathan, 1908, Je 5,7:4
Stein, Otto Jr, 1949, Mr 17,25:4
Stein, Paul, 1958, O 23,32:1; 1962, Ja 18,29:4
Stein, Phil, 1955, Mr 30,29:5
Stein, Raymond J, 1946, N 15,24:3
Stein, Robert, 1943, S 22,23:3
Stein, Robert M Mrs, 1958, Ja 14,33:4
Stein, Rose Mrs, 1938, Ag 25,2:6
Stein, S Sidney, 1945, O 30,19:5
Stein, Samuel, 1967, D 3,84:7; 1968, Jl 31,27:1
Stein, Samuel S, 1943, Ja 16,13:6
Stein, Sidney, 1939, S 30,17:3; 1963, D 28,23:4
Stein, Sidney J, 1954, O 30,17:4
Stein, Sidney S, 1943, N 11,23:5
Stein, Simon N, 1945, F 2,20:2
Stein, Sophie A Mrs, 1938, N 15,23:5
Stein, Sydney M Mrs, 1964, Ja 25,23:4
Stein, Walter J, 1964, Mr 27,27:4
Stein, William, 1949, F 16,25:2
Stein, William A, 1948, Je 30,25:1
Stein, William B, 1954, D 29,23:2
Stein, William D, 1943, Je 22,19:4
Stein, William H, 1943, My 16,42:6
Stein, William J, 1938, My 20,19:3
Stein, William L, 1948, My 26,25:3
Stein, William P, 1953, O 7,29:5
Steinach, Eugen, 1944, My 15,19:3
Steinach, William, 1946, Mr 22,21:2
Steinacher, Gustavo Sr, 1947, Je 29,48:8
Steinam, Abraham, 1914, Ja 18,5:4
Steinam, Edward S Mrs, 1964, Mr 19,33:4
Steinam, Nathan, 1905, Je 17,4:2
Steinbach, A D, 1946, O 17,23:4
Steinbach, Arthur C, 1954, O 6,25:5
Steinbach, Bernard A, 1957, O 25,27:1
Steinbach, D Frederick, 1951, O 15,25:4
Steinbach, George W, 1944, Ap 17,23:5
Steinbach, Gustav M, 1945, Ag 31,17:3
Steinbach, Jacob, 1954, Jl 6,23:5
Steinbach, Larry, 1967, Jl 1,23:5
Steinbach, M Maxim, 1950, F 2,27:5
Steinbach, Robert C, 1955, Ap 22,25:1
Steinback, Gustave E, 1959, S 25,24:7

Steinbaker, Abraham, 1946, O 20,60:4
Steinbeck, John (funl, D 24,20:5), 1968, D 21,1:3
Steinbeck, William A, 1944, My 9,19:4
Steinberg, A Ralph, 1959, Ag 2,80:5
Steinberg, Abe, 1964, Je 2,37:3
Steinberg, Abraham, 1956, My 31,27:5
Steinberg, Adolph, 1910, S 3,7:6
Steinberg, Alvin, 1959, Jl 7,33:4
Steinberg, Benjamin, 1966, Ag 11,33:1
Steinberg, Benjamin B, 1951, F 24,13:2
Steinberg, Benjamin L, 1942, F 23,21:1
Steinberg, Bernhard, 1940, Ap 27,15:4
Steinberg, David Mrs, 1943, Mr 11,21:3
Steinberg, Gregory, 1961, D 3,88:1
Steinberg, Harold B, 1952, O 30,31:3
Steinberg, Harry, 1949, O 14,28:3; 1954, Ag 1,84:3
Steinberg, Herman, 1947, D 20,17:3; 1957, Ja 19,15:2
Steinberg, Herman L, 1957, Je 15,17:4
Steinberg, Irwin A, 1950, S 19,29:1
Steinberg, Isaac, 1939, Je 15,23:4; 1957, Ag 3,15:6
Steinberg, Isaac N, 1957, Ja 3,33:5
Steinberg, Isidor, 1949, S 1,21:4
Steinberg, Israel, 1956, Jl 20,17:5
Steinberg, Israel K, 1950, Mr 2,27:2
Steinberg, Jacob I Mrs, 1959, F 7,19:3
Steinberg, James P, 1941, N 29,17:1
Steinberg, Julius, 1922, O 11,19:5; 1945, N 28,27:3
Steinberg, Louis, 1958, Mr 8,17:2
Steinberg, Louis J, 1953, O 18,87:1
Steinberg, Mark C, 1951, O 22,23:3
Steinberg, Mark C (will), 1955, Ja 29,7:5
Steinberg, Max, 1957, Je 4,35:5
Steinberg, Max J, 1963, Ap 10,39:2
Steinberg, Michael Mrs, 1959, S 14,29:3
Steinberg, Milton (mem rites, My 15,21:3), 1950, Mr 21,29:1
Steinberg, Mollie B, 1942, My 30,8:6
Steinberg, Morris, 1955, D 24,13:6
Steinberg, Moses, 1941, N 29,17:1
Steinberg, Nathan V, 1953, Mr 22,86:6
Steinberg, Robert, 1948, Jl 22,23:4
Steinberg, Sadie, 1948, Ag 10,22:2
Steinberg, Samuel, 1947, Jl 30,21:5
Steinberg, Samuel Sidney, 1968, F 12,39:4
Steinberg, William, 1961, D 5,39:4
Steinberg, William Mrs, 1967, Jl 8,25:2
Steinberger, Harry E, 1957, Ag 7,27:5
Steinberger, Simon Mrs, 1915, Mr 6,11:6
Steinbock, David A, 1963, My 7,43:1
Steinbock, Frederick W, 1938, N 8,23:5
Steinbock, Henry A, 1943, O 15,19:6
Steinbock, Max Mrs, 1958, Ap 26,19:1
Steinbrecher, Paul, 1937, Ja 16,17:2
Steinbrenner, Ernest, 1960, Jl 13,35:5
Steinbrenner, George E Mrs, 1950, Jl 21,19:3
Steinbrenner, George M, 1949, Ag 8,15:4
Steinbrink, Jac, 1944, O 7,13:6
Steinbrink, Joseph, 1948, F 17,25:3
Steinbrink, Meier, 1967, D 8,42:4
Steinbrink, Stuart H Mrs, 1961, My 19,31:3
Steinbronn, Stanley, 1960, N 3,36:4
Steinbugler, Frank J Sr, 1939, S 16,17:2
Steinbugler, John L Mrs, 1957, My 26,92:3
Steinbugler, Lawrence, 1946, My 23,21:6
Steinbugler, William F C, 1957, Ap 8,23:6
Steindecker, Otto H, 1952, Mr 24,25:6
Steindel, Bruno K, 1949, My 6,25:4
Steindler, David M, 1923, Ag 29,17:3
Steindler, Max, 1966, N 18,43:2
Steindorff, Georg, 1951, Ag 29,25:4
Steineke, Max, 1952, Ap 17,29:1
Steinel, Ben F, 1938, Ja 7,19:4
Steinel, Joseph, 1956, Je 20,31:1
Steinem, Pauline Mrs, 1940, Ja 7,49:3
Steinen, William, 1965, F 13,21:5
Steiner, Abraham, 1937, Je 15,23:5
Steiner, Adelaide W Mrs, 1938, My 8,II,6:5
Steiner, Arpad, 1944, Ja 11,20:2
Steiner, Bernard, 1965, Mr 17,45:4
Steiner, Burghard, 1923, Mr 10,13:4
Steiner, Carl, 1948, Ja 16,21:2
Steiner, Charles, 1946, Je 29,19:4
Steiner, Charles A, 1953, S 6,50:3
Steiner, Charles E, 1951, Jl 17,27:2
Steiner, Christian, 1946, N 2,15:2
Steiner, Clarence S, 1950, Je 27,29:2
Steiner, Edgar, 1958, My 23,23:3
Steiner, Edward A, 1956, Jl 2,21:3
Steiner, Edward C, 1963, Jl 1,29:4
Steiner, Edwin, 1961, F 28,33:2
Steiner, Emanuel, 1904, Ja 20,9:6
Steiner, Erwin L, 1962, Mr 8,31:1
Steiner, Ferenz J, 1941, O 24,23:1
Steiner, Frank, 1944, D 9,15:3
Steiner, Franz, 1954, N 8,21:6
Steiner, Frederick G, 1968, Ag 27,41:2
Steiner, Gabor C, 1944, S 10,45:2
Steiner, Gary, 1966, Ja 18,75:3
Steiner, George, 1967, Je 24,29:4
Steiner, George H, 1950, My 21,108:1
Steiner, Gordon J, 1966, Je 24,37:3
Steiner, Harry E, 1951, N 27,31:5
Steiner, Henry (por), 1949, Jl 8,19:1
Steiner, Herb, 1964, Mr 19,33:5
Steiner, Herman, 1955, N 27,89:1
Steiner, J Frederick, 1952, Ja 7,19:3
Steiner, Jacob, 1924, D 2,25:4
Steiner, John A, 1952, Mr 7,23:3
Steiner, John F, 1943, Jl 8,19:3
Steiner, John P, 1953, Ja 21,31:3
Steiner, Joseph, 1937, Ja 2,14:1; 1952, Ja 12,13:5
Steiner, Joseph M Dr, 1937, Ja 28,25:2
Steiner, Joseph Mrs, 1952, O 26,89:1
Steiner, Maurice, 1964, Mr 20,33:2
Steiner, Paul, 1948, Jl 30,17:2
Steiner, Paul W, 1942, Ap 8,19:5
Steiner, Phil, 1938, My 20,19:5
Steiner, Robert L, 1954, Mr 10,25:4
Steiner, Roland Dr, 1906, Ja 14,9:6
Steiner, Rudolf Dr, 1925, Mr 31,19:5
Steiner, Sam S, 1955, D 31,13:6
Steiner, Samuel, 1953, Mr 15,92:1
Steiner, Thomas A, 1962, Ja 2,30:5
Steiner, Walter R, 1942, N 6,23:1
Steiner, William H, 1966, Je 3,40:1
Steiner-Prag, Hugo (por), 1945, S 11,23:3
Steinert, Alexander Mrs, 1924, Ag 9,11:5
Steinert, Ambrose M, 1940, F 27,21:5
Steinert, Bryan, 1944, D 7,25:2
Steinert, Edward G, 1948, Ag 14,13:6
Steinert, Henry M Justice, 1913, F 3,11:4
Steinert, Leopold, 1949, Ap 1,25:1
Steinert, Morris, 1912, Ja 22,9:5
Steines, Gabriel, 1941, S 3,23:1
Steinetz, Bernard G, 1966, My 13,41:3
Steinfalt, Henry W, 1954, Jl 31,13:5
Steinfeld, Arnold L, 1960, O 30,86:1
Steinfeld, Jacob B, 1966, Ap 1,35:3
Steinfeld, Lewis, 1963, D 19,33:2
Steinfels, Mortimer, 1943, O 4,17:4
Steinfirst, Louis, 1941, Je 11,21:2
Steinglass, Abraham Mrs, 1964, My 9,27:3
Steinglass, Charles, 1961, F 2,29:4
Steingrube, C Roy, 1958, D 4,39:4
Steingut, Irwin, 1952, S 27,1:5
Steingut, Simon, 1919, Mr 12,11:4
Steingut, Simon Mrs, 1957, Je 24,23:5
Steinhacker, William Mrs, 1956, F 2,25:4
Steinhammer, Bertha, 1883, D 2,4:4
Steinhardt, Amelia Mrs, 1938, Ag 27,13:4
Steinhardt, Arnold, 1959, O 22,37:4
Steinhardt, Benjamin, 1907, Je 18,7:5
Steinhardt, Charles S, 1961, My 7,86:6
Steinhardt, Ellis L, 1947, F 1,15:5
Steinhardt, Frederick J, 1954, S 9,31:4
Steinhardt, Gustav, 1953, D 18,29:2
Steinhardt, Irving D, 1942, F 26,19:4
Steinhardt, J H, 1926, D 11,17:3
Steinhardt, Karl (Jan 21), 1963, Ap 1,36:6
Steinhardt, Laurence A, 1950, Mr 29,1:3
Steinhardt, Lawrence R, 1966, My 18,47:3
Steinhardt, Milton, 1957, Jl 27,17:6
Steinhardt, Samuel I, 1925, F 7,15:5
Steinhardt, Sigmund, 1938, O 18,25:4
Steinhardt, William B, 1955, Ja 5,23:3
Steinhart, Frank (por), 1938, D 10,17:3
Steinhart, Frank Sr Mrs, 1937, Ja 23,17:5
Steinhart, Jesse, 1965, Mr 28,93:1
Steinhart, John W, 1952, Ap 5,15:5
Steinharter, Paul, 1957, My 15,35:2
Steinharter, Sigwart, 1962, Ja 16,33:2
Steinharter, Stephen, 1956, My 12,19:4
Steinhauer, Rubert M, 1950, Ap 2,94:4
Steinhauer, William F, 1940, O 8,25:5
Steinhaus, Oscar Mrs, 1949, D 7,31:5
Steinhausen, Theodore D, 1944, Ap 19,23:2
Steinheuer, J Louis, 1940, Ag 4,33:2
Steinhilper, Anthony, 1952, S 12,21:3
Steinhof, Eugene G, 1952, Jl 13,60:5
Steinhoff, Francis M, 1954, O 26,27:3
Steinhoff, Samuel Mrs, 1964, D 27,64:4
Steinholz, Reuben Mrs, 1967, Mr 13,37:2
Steinhorst, Frederick C, 1950, Ja 6,21:4
Steinhorst, Henry O, 1956, N 28,35:4
Steinhorst, Theodore F, 1947, Mr 11,27:3
Steinhouse, Irving, 1965, N 28,88:8
Steinhuber, Andreas Cardinal, 1907, O 16,9:5
Steinigans, William J, 1918, Ja 30,9:8
Steininger, George, 1944, Mr 2,17:5
Steinitz, Ernst, 1942, F 2,17:3
Steinitz, William, 1897, F 22,2:2; 1900, Ag 14,5:7
Steinkamp, Christopher, 1959, S 26,23:4
Steinkamp, J C Harold, 1954, S 29,31:5
Steinkamp, Joseph G, 1948, O 22,26:3
Steinkamp, William H, 1940, D 18,25:4
Steinke, Frank Dr, 1925, N 6,23:6
Steinke, Rudolph, 1948, Ag 8,57:1
Steinke, Rudolph Mrs, 1964, Je 3,43:1
Steinke, William Sr, 1958, Ja 30,23:4
Steinkellner, Peter, 1947, N 10,29:4
Steinkemper, Oscar, 1939, Ap 27,25:3
Steinkemper, Paul Mrs, 1951, Ag 7,25:4
Steinkraus, John H, 1961, O 29,88:7
Steinlauf, Edward, 1965, O 31,86:6
Steinle, Majella, 1944, N 11,13:1
Steinlen, Theophile A, 1923, D 15,13:4
Steinman, Ansel, 1945, Mr 29,23:5
Steinman, Caroline Mrs, 1946, O 13,58:6
Steinman, David B, 1960, Ag 23,29:2
Steinman, George W, 1956, O 21,86:4
Steinman, Ignatz, 1946, Ag 27,27:3
Steinman, Joseph Mrs, 1954, D 28,25:2
Steinmann, Emil, 1949, Ag 4,23:2
Steinmann, Herman, 1905, Ap 15,20:3
Steinmeier, Bertha F Mrs, 1937, Ja 16,15:2
Steinmety, Eloise Mrs, 1910, My 7,9:4
Steinmetz, Bruce I, 1951, Ag 8,25:6
Steinmetz, C F von, 1877, Ag 5,6:6
Steinmetz, Charles G Jr, 1957, My 30,19:4
Steinmetz, Charles Proteus Dr, 1923, O 30,19:3
Steinmetz, Deacon, 1951, S 11,29:4
Steinmetz, Edwin S, 1967, My 25,47:3
Steinmetz, Francis C, 1946, O 19,21:2
Steinmetz, Frederick C, 1939, Ja 23,13:4
Steinmetz, George N, 1915, D 20,11:4
Steinmetz, Henry A, 1950, O 7,17:1
Steinmetz, J A, 1928, Jl 12,23:3
Steinmetz, John A, 1944, Jl 3,11:4
Steinmetz, Mary O Mrs, 1948, D 27,21:1
Steinmetz, Michael, 1941, N 27,23:2
Steinmetz, Norman R, 1968, S 13,47:2
Steinmetz, Philip J, 1945, N 14,19:6
Steinmetz, Robert H, 1952, Mr 9,92:6
Steinmetz, Samuel, 1954, O 25,27:3
Steinmeyer, Frederick W, 1954, S 30,31:3
Steinmeyer, Reuben G, 1965, Ap 27,37:2
Steinmeyer, Reuben G Mrs (C Seckler-Hudson), 1963, My 5,86:7
Steinmiller, Frank E, 1941, Mr 13,21:2
Steinmuller, Bernard A Mrs, 1956, Mr 5,23:4
Steinmuller, William A Mrs, 1952, O 31,25:2
Steinreich, George W Mrs, 1954, Jl 24,13:2
Steinreich, Kenneth P, 1965, Ja 10,92:4
Steinreich, Kenneth P Mrs (funl, My 8,67:2), 1956, My 4,25:3
Steinrock, Charles M, 1949, Ag 30,27:2
Steinrock, Charles M Mrs, 1951, S 6,31:1
Steinschneider, Richard, 1966, Mr 28,33:4
Steinschreiber, Herman, 1951, D 5,35:3
Steinschreiber, Hermann Mrs, 1940, Mr 26,21:3
Steinthal, Carl F, 1938, Je 22,23:5
Steinthal, F W, 1951, Ag 23,23:6
Steintorf, Paul, 1957, D 24,15:1
Steinway, A (see also My 15), 1877, My 17,8:4
Steinway, C F T, 1889, Mr 27,5:5
Steinway, Charles, 1865, Ap 27,4:4
Steinway, Charles Herman, 1919, O 31,13:5
Steinway, Charles Herman Mrs (Marie Lefebvre), 1924, Je 25,23:5
Steinway, F T, 1927, Jl 18,17:1
Steinway, Frederick T Mrs (trb lr, F 28,20:6), 1958, F 22,17:2
Steinway, Henry, 1865, Mr 15,8:4; 1871, F 8,5:5
Steinway, Henry W T (will, Jl 11,16:6), 1939, Je 28, 21:6
Steinway, Theodore E, 1957, Ap 9,33:4
Steinway, William, 1896, D 1,9:1
Steinway, William R, 1960, S 23,29:4
Steinweg, Arthur, 1947, My 17,15:3
Steinweg, Arthur Mrs, 1943, Ag 4,17:2
Steinwehr, A Von, 1877, F 26,5:3
Steitz, George W, 1941, F 4,22:2
Steitz, Howard, 1951, O 20,15:6
Steitz, John J Jr Mrs, 1964, Ag 11,33:4
Steiwer, Frederick W (por), 1939, F 4,15:1
Stekel, Wilhelm, 1940, Je 28,19:3
Steketee, Frank W, 1951, D 27,21:4
Steketee, Lewis B, 1949, F 3,23:5
Stekhoven, J H S, 1941, N 22,19:5
Steling, Bernard F, 1954, My 24,27:2
Steljes, John H, 1943, N 16,23:4
Stell, Elizabeth H Mrs, 1937, Ap 14,25:4
Stella, Giovanni, 1951, N 1,29:2
Stella, Guido B, 1941, Ag 18,13:4
Stella, Guy T, 1954, Ap 28,31:5
Stella, John S (probe, F 4,13:4), 1955, F 3,1:8
Stella, Joseph, 1946, N 6,23:4
Stella Margt, Sister (M F Malone), 1942, Ja 30,20:3
Stellakis, Leonidas N, 1963, Je 18,41:8
Stellara, Gregorio U di Mrs, 1949, Jl 14,28:2
Stellato, Otto J, 1958, Je 4,31:2
Stelle, Alex Mrs, 1954, Ap 26,25:4
Stelle, Charles C, 1964, Je 12,35:1
Stelle, Clarkson P, 1952, Mr 6,31:2
Stelle, Gustav C, 1948, F 28,15:5
Stelle, John, 1962, Jl 7,17:4
Stelle, Peter R, 1948, D 31,16:2
Stelle, Robin, 1944, D 12,23:2
Stellhorn, E F William, 1941, N 30,69:3
Stelling, Albert, 1949, Ap 24,76:4
Stellingwerf, Cornelius, 1954, Jl 30,17:5
Stellman, Wilhelm E, 1937, S 7,21:4
Stellwagen, Frederick L, 1945, Ja 7,37:1
Stelver, Saul, 1923, D 28,15:6
Stelwagon, Joseph, 1940, Jl 14,31:1
Stelzer, George H, 1965, Mr 31,39:4
Stelzer, Louis E, 1945, Ag 22,23:4
Stelzer, Michael, 1950, O 23,23:2
Stelzle, Charles (por), 1941, F 28,19:1

Stelzle, Lawrence G, 1949, F 13,76:1
Stelzner, Hugo J, 1951, Je 28,25:2
Stem, A H, 1931, My 21,27:3
Stem, Allen H Mrs, 1954, Ja 9,15:2
Stem, Almer C, 1939, Je 21,23:5
Stem, Arthur Mrs, 1945, Jl 27,15:4
Stem, Frank O, 1940, F 7,21:5
Stem, Harry E, 1940, Je 27,23:1
Stem, James E, 1952, Je 27,23:3
Steman, Louis J, 1947, D 16,33:2
Stembel, Charles P G, 1939, D 17,48:8
Stembel, Clarence Mrs, 1954, Ap 21,29:4
Stemberg, Oscar, 1960, Jl 20,29:1
Stemer, David H, 1958, S 8,29:3
Stemm, Norma C Mrs, 1957, Ap 17,31:5
Stemmler, Arthur R, 1959, Ag 11,27:4
Stemmler, John B, 1943, F 19,19:4
Stemmler, Theodor W Mrs, 1946, Ap 20,13:4
Stemmons, Walter C, 1965, Je 27,64:7
Stemmyer, William, 1945, My 6,38:1
Stempel, Guido H, 1955, D 24,13:6
Stempel, Guido H Mrs, 1951, O 9,29:4
Stemper, Henry T, 1939, Jl 11,19:3
Stemper, John H, 1947, Ap 22,27:1
Stempf, Victor H (por), 1946, Ap 19,29:3
Stenberg, Charles, 1947, S 26,23:1
Stenberg, John J, 1953, Jl 10,19:1
Stenbuck, Joseph, 1951, Je 2,19:6
Stendel, Theodore, 1956, D 16,87:1
Stender, Albert W Sr, 1967, O 7,29:3
Stender, Hugo E, 1951, F 10,13:5
Stender, Hugo Mrs, 1956, F 17,21:1
Stender-Petersen, Adolf, 1963, Ap 17,41:4
Stendrup, Harry A, 1950, O 27,30:2
Steneken, Charles A, 1949, Je 16,29:4
Stenerson, Harry W, 1961, F 3,23:1
Stenerson, William N, 1918, Jl 24,11:4
Stengel, Alfred (por), 1939, Ap 11,23:1
Stengel, Arthur W, 1964, N 1,89:1
Stengel, Charles E H Mrs, 1956, Ja 25,31:5
Stengel, Frederick W, 1949, S 17,17:2
Stengel, George F, 1916, S 23,7:2
Stengel, George J, 1937, N 21,II,8:7
Stengel, George J Mrs, 1946, Ag 29,27:3
Stengel, Guillaume (funl, My 17,13:6), 1917, My 16, 13:6
Stengel, H G L von Baron, 1919, My 7,15:6
Stengel, Jennie J Mrs, 1938, D 6,23:2
Stengel, Marcel W Mrs, 1961, Ja 31,29:2
Stengele, Harry E Jr, 1945, Ag 16,19:2
Stenger, John H, 1945, N 28,27:5
Stenger, Louis J, 1964, Ap 27,31:3
Stengle, Charles I, 1953, N 24,29:4
Stengle, Robert L, 1942, Ja 2,23:3
Stenhouse, Robert H, 1962, Jl 2,29:4
Stenhouse, Robert H Mrs, 1951, F 15,31:1
Stenhouse, William P, 1949, My 19,29:3
Stenius, Arthur C, 1955, My 26,31:2
Stenken, George H, 1942, Jl 19,30:7
Stensgaard, Anton C, 1953, Jl 25,11:3
Stensgaard, William L, 1965, My 4,43:1
Stenson, Charles E, 1954, F 14,92:2
Stenson, Samuel, 1925, Mr 11,21:4
Stenson, Walter T, 1943, D 9,27:3
Stenstrom, David G, 1952, F 2;13:5
Stentz, Lewis, 1949, Je 30,23:3
Stentzel, R Theodore, 1947, Ag 13,23:5
Stenz, Carl J, 1959, D 25,21:2
Stenz, Edward F, 1950, Ag 2,25:1
Stenz, Edward J, 1938, N 2,23:3
Stenzel, Roland, 1963, N 19,41:3
Stenzler, Benjamin, 1954, My 13,29:4
Stepanek, Joseph, 1955, My 14,19:4
Stepansky, Nachum, 1964, F 17,31:5
Stepat, Frederick, 1959, S 11,28:1
Stephan, Carl J, 1948, Ag 26,21:2
Stephan, Charles Rev, 1922, Mr 7,13:5
Stephan, Frederick, 1944, N 25,13:6
Stephan, Henry C, 1952, My 4,91:1
Stephan, Hilary J, 1961, Ap 2,77:1
Stephan, John F, 1948, N 12,24:2
Stephan, John H, 1960, Ap 19,37:2
Stephan, Joseph A, 1957, N 7,35:4
Stephan, Msgr, 1901, S 13,7:6
Stephan, Oscar, 1946, O 23,27:4
Stephan, Paul R, 1941, Ja 4,13:1
Stephan, Robert S, 1949, F 22,23:1
Stephan, Werner, 1957, Ag 18,8:2
Stephan, Wilhelmina P, 1947, Ag 31,36:8
Stephani, Franz von, 1939, Ap 27,25:4
Stephani, James, 1945, S 15,15:1
Stephanidis, Stephen D, 1955, Mr 24,31:2
Stephanidis, Stephen D Mrs, 1964, Ap 27,31:4
Stephanie, Grand Duchess of Baden, 1860, F 16,2:3
Stephanie, Mother (Dominican Sisters), 1954, S 20, 23:4
Stephanie, Princess, 1945, S 9,47:4
Stephanie, Queen of Portugal, 1859, Ag 4,2:5
Stephano, C Charles, 1964, D 28,15:1
Stephano, Constantine Sr (por), 1944, Jl 28,13:2
Stephano, Stephen C, 1965, Mr 19,35:4
Stephano, Stephen X, 1956, O 10,39:3
Stephano, Stephen X Mrs, 1947, Ag 16,13:5
Stephans, Frederick J, 1963, My 13,29:5
Stephany, William A, 1937, Ag 14,13:2
Stephen, A M, 1942, Jl 3,17:6
Stephen, Alexander Condie Sir, 1908, My 12,7:6
Stephen, Charles, 1938, Mr 15,23:3
Stephen, Donald B, 1957, Ap 1,25:4
Stephen, George (Lord Mount Stephen), 1921, D 1, 17:6
Stephen, George, 1955, F 1,29:4
Stephen, George C Mrs, 1950, My 15,21:5
Stephen, John M, 1952, N 16,88:3
Stephen, John Mrs, 1941, Mr 20,21:3
Stephen, Leslie, 1873, Mr 23,5:4
Stephen, Leslie Sir, 1904, F 23,7:2
Stephen, Mount Lord (Geo Stephen), 1921, D 1,17:6
Stephen, Robert A Mrs, 1955, Mr 3,27:5
Stephen, Thomas, 1953, S 12,17:6
Stephen, William G, 1938, F 20,II,8:6
Stephen, William Mrs, 1954, Jl 2,19:5
Stephens, A B, 1927, F 13,II,11:1
Stephens, A H, 1883, Mr 4,1:7
Stephens, Albert E, 1939, S 6,23:3
Stephens, Albert L, 1965, Ja 17,89:2
Stephens, Alexander W, 1943, D 17,27:2
Stephens, Ann S, 1886, Ag 21,2:3
Stephens, Anna M Mrs, 1938, Ja 5,21:4
Stephens, Annie L W Mrs, 1941, Ap 17,23:1
Stephens, Ardenah L Mrs, 1944, N 28,23:5
Stephens, Benjamin F, 1903, O 18,7:6
Stephens, Carl F, 1953, N 15,88:4
Stephens, Catherine, 1953, Ja 13,27:1
Stephens, Charles A Mrs, 1945, Ja 14,39:1
Stephens, Charles E, 1946, N 21,31:2
Stephens, Charles E Capt, 1905, My 24,9:5
Stephens, Charles H, 1940, Ap 2,26:3
Stephens, Charles R, 1946, My 1,25:1
Stephens, Charles S, 1961, Ap 26,39:4
Stephens, Clinton, 1915, O 4,9:6
Stephens, D Mallory, 1961, Ja 13,29:2
Stephens, D Owen, 1937, Je 24,25:3
Stephens, Dan V, 1939, Ja 14,17:5
Stephens, Dana R Mrs, 1946, S 21,15:4
Stephens, Davy, 1925, S 12,15:5
Stephens, Doran J, 1941, Mr 20,22:2
Stephens, E B, 1882, N 11,5:1
Stephens, E Browning, 1875, My 2,6:6
Stephens, E Sydney, 1948, O 18,23:5
Stephens, Edward P, 1965, My 16,88:7
Stephens, Edward W, 1950, My 10,31:2
Stephens, Edward W T, 1947, D 4,31:1
Stephens, Elizabeth S Mrs, 1937, F 23,27:4
Stephens, Elliot M, 1948, My 10,22:2
Stephens, Fitch H, 1950, F 5,85:2
Stephens, Francis J, 1948, Ap 22,27:5
Stephens, Frank H, 1946, O 11,23:5
Stephens, Franklin M, 1946, O 22,25:6
Stephens, Franklin M Dr (por), 1937, My 21,22:1
Stephens, Fred J, 1941, N 9,52:1
Stephens, Frederick L, 1939, D 17,49:3
Stephens, Frederick Mrs, 1948, My 8,15:3
Stephens, George, 1946, Ap 2,27:3
Stephens, George W, 1940, My 15,25:5; 1942, F 8, 50:1; 1952, Ag 13,21:2
Stephens, Goldsmith C, 1946, Ja 30,25:3
Stephens, H L, 1882, D 14,5:2
Stephens, Harold D, 1950, Ap 18,31:4
Stephens, Harold M, 1955, My 29,44:3
Stephens, Harry G, 1956, Je 14,33:5
Stephens, Harry G Mrs, 1961, Mr 13,29:6
Stephens, Henry G, 1946, Ja 19,13:4
Stephens, Henry Jr Mrs, 1944, My 14,46:5
Stephens, Henry M (por), 1941, S 26,23:6
Stephens, Henry Morse Prof, 1919, Ap 17,11:4
Stephens, Howard V, 1952, O 13,21:2
Stephens, Hubert D (por), 1946, Mr 15,21:3
Stephens, Isabel, 1960, Ap 20,39:1
Stephens, J J, 1885, Mr 25,5:5
Stephens, James, 1950, D 27,27:3
Stephens, James B, 1946, Je 22,19:4; 1954, Mr 14,88:2
Stephens, James Brown, 1918, O 28,11:2
Stephens, John Edmonson Brig-Gen, 1919, Ja 11,13:2
Stephens, John L, 1913, D 19,11:4
Stephens, Joseph, 1952, Ja 12,13:5
Stephens, Joseph T, 1954, Mr 17,31:4
Stephens, Kate, 1938, My 13,19:5
Stephens, Kate Dowager Countess of Essex, 1882, Mr 17,3:7
Stephens, Kenneth, 1954, N 8,21:4
Stephens, Kenneth Mrs, 1965, Ag 13,29:4
Stephens, L Walter (por), 1948, O 2,15:1
Stephens, Leonard W, 1940, Ja 28,32:1
Stephens, Lon V Ex-Gov, 1923, Ja 11,21:5
Stephens, Louis E, 1966, D 7,47:3
Stephens, Louis L, 1960, N 20,86:8
Stephens, M E Jr, 1954, O 7,23:3
Stephens, Marguerite D Mrs, 1941, O 11,17:4
Stephens, Marshall Mrs (and 4 children), 1961, D 9, 33:5
Stephens, Michael J, 1958, N 21,29:2
Stephens, Michael J Jr, 1945, F 26,19:5
Stephens, Olga W, 1964, O 25,88:4
Stephens, Percy R (por), 1942, Je 17,23:5
Stephens, R Allan, 1942, Jl 27,15:5
Stephens, Richmond, 1958, Mr 18,29:4
Stephens, Robert, 1963, O 13,39:4
Stephens, Robert Mrs, 1950, Ag 6,72:7
Stephens, Robert Neilson, 1906, Ja 21,7:6
Stephens, Roger, 1955, D 13,39:3
Stephens, Roscoe G, 1949, Ja 31,19:2
Stephens, Roy (por), 1947, O 15,27:4
Stephens, Roy Mrs, 1961, Jl 13,29:3
Stephens, Russell F, 1958, O 3,29:2
Stephens, S D Sr, 1883, Mr 2,5:2
Stephens, Sam, 1925, Ja 16,17:3
Stephens, Stephen D Judge, 1911, Ap 20,11:5
Stephens, Thomas C, 1945, N 21,21:1
Stephens, Thomas C Mrs, 1943, Ja 21,21:4
Stephens, Thomas E, 1966, Ja 5,31:5
Stephens, Thomas M, 1959, F 24,29:2
Stephens, Vern, 1968, N 5,47:1
Stephens, Virgila T, 1954, Je 28,19:4
Stephens, W H, 1873, D 31,8:1
Stephens, W R, 1902, D 23,9:6
Stephens, Ward, 1940, S 13,23:3
Stephens, William A Mrs (por), 1947, Ap 24,25:4
Stephens, William C, 1941, N 25,25:3
Stephens, William D (por), 1944, Ap 26,19:1
Stephens, William E, 1946, My 12,44:4
Stephens, William F, 1950, F 28,29:1
Stephens, William H, 1938, D 5,23:2; 1940, O 7,17:2
Stephens, William L, 1952, S 23,33:2
Stephens, William P (por), 1946, My 11,27:3
Stephens, William W, 1938, Ap 22,19:2
Stephens, Yorke, 1937, F 6,17:4
Stephenson, A E, 1954, My 15,15:5
Stephenson, Annie L, 1925, My 7,19:4
Stephenson, B C, 1906, Ja 23,9:5
Stephenson, Barton K, 1949, F 16,25:5
Stephenson, Bertram S Mrs, 1960, F 11,35:2
Stephenson, Burnette F, 1954, My 15,15:6
Stephenson, C S, 1880, Mr 22,4:7
Stephenson, Carl, 1954, O 6,25:3
Stephenson, Charles S, 1965, F 12,29:4
Stephenson, Chester A, 1945, D 23,18:7
Stephenson, Claudine W Mrs, 1944, Mr 6,19:6
Stephenson, David T, 1948, O 10,76:2
Stephenson, Edward C, 1956, O 10,39:5
Stephenson, Edward P, 1945, F 17,13:3
Stephenson, Edward T, 1944, Jl 23,36:1
Stephenson, F Kenneth, 1954, Ap 2,27:3
Stephenson, Frank, 1953, Jl 25,11:2
Stephenson, Frank Bryan, 1925, F 5,19:5
Stephenson, Fred, 1943, Jl 28,15:6
Stephenson, Frederick Gen Sir, 1911, Mr 24,11:4
Stephenson, Geoffrey D, 1954, N 10,12:4
Stephenson, George, 1865, N 20,8:4; 1955, S 28,35:4
Stephenson, George B, 1947, S 27,15:5
Stephenson, George W, 1955, Ja 26,25:1
Stephenson, Gordon A, 1956, My 6,87:2
Stephenson, H R, 1881, Ja 14,5:4
Stephenson, Harold F, 1953, O 15,33:4
Stephenson, Harry W, 1954, Ja 13,31:3
Stephenson, Henrietta Mrs, 1909, My 30,9:2
Stephenson, Henry (funl plans, Jl 26,25:3), 1956, Ap 25,35:3
Stephenson, Henry, 1961, Ag 26,17:3
Stephenson, Henry K, 1947, S 21,61:1
Stephenson, Hugh M, 1951, S 12,31:3
Stephenson, Isaac, 1918, Mr 16,13:3
Stephenson, J Fred, 1938, Ap 6,23:4
Stephenson, James (por), 1941, Jl 30,17:1
Stephenson, John, 1954, Jl 3,11:6
Stephenson, John Lt, 1910, Je 22,9:4
Stephenson, John W, 1945, Ja 16,19:5
Stephenson, L E, 1940, N 2,15:2
Stephenson, L Oren, 1960, My 25,39:1
Stephenson, Lewis, 1945, My 26,15:4
Stephenson, Lowry B, 1939, Jl 12,19:6
Stephenson, Lyle A, 1941, D 1,19:2
Stephenson, Marion, 1951, Jl 4,17:2
Stephenson, Marjory, 1948, D 13,23:4
Stephenson, Mary E Mrs, 1953, Ag 8,11:6
Stephenson, Orlistus B, 1940, Jl 25,17:3
Stephenson, Ralph A, 1962, Je 12,37:1
Stephenson, Ralph A Mrs, 1966, S 1,35:4
Stephenson, Ray W, 1942, O 3,15:2
Stephenson, Richard A, 1956, Ja 17,33:1
Stephenson, Richard B, 1944, Jl 18,19:5
Stephenson, Richard W, 1950, N 19,93:2
Stephenson, Robert (funl, N 7,2:2), 1859, O 26,2:3
Stephenson, S M, 1907, Ag 1,7:6
Stephenson, Sarah, 1945, Mr 29,23:3
Stephenson, Stuart A, 1938, S 2,17:4
Stephenson, Thomas, 1938, N 5,19:1
Stephenson, victor L, 1955, Ag 7,73:3
Stephenson, William L (will, O 2,2:4), 1963, My 10, 33:1
Stephenson, William M, 1967, Ap 29,35:2
Stephenson, William Mrs, 1959, Ag 6,27:3
Stephenson, William P, 1945, D 7,22:2
Stephenson, William S, 1950, Jl 4,17:6
Stephenson, William W, 1953, Ja 3,15:3
Stephenson, William W Mrs, 1957, Je 18,29:4
Stephenson, Winfield S, 1937, Ap 2,23:5
Stephos, Arthur G, 1965, N 7,88:6
Stepinac, Aloysius (funl plans, F 12,9:5), 1960, F 11, 1:5

Stepler, Irving F, 1942, F 9,15:2
Stepniak, 1895, D 24,1:6
Stepnickova, J, 1952, Ag 23,15:7
Steppe, Frank E, 1941, D 28,28:6
Stepper, Christian F, 1944, O 13,19:3
Stept, Sam H, 1964, D 3,49:4
Stepura, Walter, 1950, D 11,25:2
Sterba, Ernest J, 1939, Ap 26,23:2
Steren, Aaron M, 1961, Ja 28,19:1
Sterenbuch, S Alex, 1964, Mr 2,27:4
Sterett, Dwight, 1961, Ap 11,37:2
Sterett, William G Col, 1924, O 8,19:4
Sterki, V, 1933, Ja 27,22:2
Sterley, Harry C, 1948, Ap 29,23:3
Sterling, Ada, 1939, S 3,19:4
Sterling, Albert M, 1941, F 14,17:2
Sterling, Andrew B, 1955, Ag 12,19:2
Sterling, Bowman S, 1954, O 1,23:4
Sterling, Calvin, 1951, O 3,33:1
Sterling, Charles A, 1952, My 11,93:2
Sterling, Charles A Col, 1913, S 7,II,13:6
Sterling, Clara C, 1940, Ja 7,48:7
Sterling, Clarence I, 1956, Ap 12,31:4
Sterling, David, 1943, My 15,15:3
Sterling, David W, 1955, N 1,31:1
Sterling, Donald J, 1954, Je 16,31:5
Sterling, Duncan, 1947, S 27,15:6
Sterling, Duncan Mrs, 1955, S 15,33:4
Sterling, Edith, 1947, Mr 22,30:6
Sterling, Edward Canfield, 1911, F 27,9:3
Sterling, F E, 1934, F 11,40:1
Sterling, Ford, 1939, O 14,19:1
Sterling, Frank W, 1937, O 4,21:5
Sterling, Frederick A, 1957, Ap 22,25:3
Sterling, Frederick A Mrs, 1950, S 9,17:3
Sterling, G, 1926, N 18,2:5
Sterling, George K, 1913, Ag 9,7:7
Sterling, George Mrs, 1956, N 3,23:6
Sterling, George Waring, 1925, Jl 3,13:4
Sterling, Gilbert Henry Rev Dr, 1912, N 9,11:6
Sterling, Harry L, 1939, Mr 2,21:1; 1944, F 27,38:4
Sterling, Howard T, 1967, N 19,85:2
Sterling, J W, 1881, Jl 9,5:3
Sterling, James G, 1952, S 2,23:4
Sterling, John, 1956, D 11,39:1
Sterling, John B, 1939, N 9,23:4
Sterling, John C, 1964, Mr 25,41:1
Sterling, John W, 1918, Jl 10,13:5
Sterling, Joseph, 1945, Mr 3,13:4; 1964, Je 25,33:3
Sterling, Julian H, 1924, F 5,23:3
Sterling, Leslie S, 1945, Je 3,31:1
Sterling, Louis S, 1958, Je 3,31:2
Sterling, Louis S (will), 1959, F 3,63:3
Sterling, Louis V, 1942, Ja 2,23:4
Sterling, Mary I Mrs, 1937, O 14,25:4
Sterling, Montaigu M (por), 1945, Jl 10,11:4
Sterling, Oliver J Mrs, 1964, Mr 23,29:5
Sterling, Paul, 1942, F 9,15:3
Sterling, Paul R, 1947, Ap 17,27:1
Sterling, Reuben W, 1951, F 27,27:3
Sterling, Richard (A G Leggett), 1959, Ap 16,33:2
Sterling, Robert D Mrs, 1966, Je 12,86:6
Sterling, Ross S, 1949, Mr 26,17:4
Sterling, Susan A, 1946, O 15,25:1
Sterling, Thomas E Mrs, 1954, Mr 19,23:6
Sterling, Walter C, 1949, D 13,31:3
Sterling, Warner S, 1956, Jl 15,61:2
Sterling, Warner S Mrs, 1952, O 4,17:4
Sterling, Wilbur F, 1966, D 14,47:4
Sterling, William, 1950, F 6,25:2
Sterling, William H Gen, 1918, Ja 31,9:5
Sterling, William T, 1951, Mr 25,72:3
Sterlini, Victor, 1949, My 27,21:5
Sterman, Moses, 1938, D 11,61:1
Stern, A J, 1933, Mr 22,17:1
Stern, A R (por), 1941, My 9,21:3
Stern, Abe, 1965, S 8,47:4
Stern, Abraham B, 1943, N 17,25:2
Stern, Abraham I, 1967, Ja 21,31:5
Stern, Abraham M, 1955, Ja 31,19:3
Stern, Adolph, 1939, Mr 4,15:5; 1958, Ag 23,15:5
Stern, Albert (por), 1941, Je 14,17:6
Stern, Albert, 1945, My 8,19:4; 1964, Ap 7,32:3
Stern, Albert Mrs, 1944, D 20,23:4
Stern, Alex A, 1938, F 28,15:1
Stern, Alfred W (will, My 18,10:8), 1960, My 5,35:4
Stern, Arnold E, 1958, My 10,21:4
Stern, Arthur, 1940, N 23,17:2; 1959, O 27,37:1
Stern, Arthur J, 1959, Mr 31,29:2
Stern, B, 1933, Mr 9,13:3
Stern, B Albert, 1958, Ja 5,86:3
Stern, Ben, 1919, Mr 28,13:2
Stern, Benjamin, 1948, Mr 12,23:2
Stern, Benjamin F, 1943, Je 12,13:4
Stern, Benjamin H, 1950, F 20,25:1
Stern, Benjamin S, 1965, F 13,21:2
Stern, Bernhard, 1945, Ag 18,11:4; 1949, Ja 20,27:2
Stern, Bernhard J, 1956, N 24,19:2
Stern, Bertram, 1963, N 17,86:4
Stern, Charles J, 1953, Ap 12,88:4
Stern, Charles K (por), 1948, Mr 27,13:3
Stern, D, 1939, Ja 23,13:1
Stern, Daniel, 1938, D 1,23:3
Stern, David, 1952, Mr 13,29:1; 1955, Mr 8,3:3
Stern, De Witt H Mrs, 1967, O 27,45:2
Stern, Dewitt H, 1938, Ap 3,II,6:7
Stern, Edgar B (funl plans, Ag 27,27:3), 1959, Ag 26, 30:5
Stern, Edgar Mrs, 1966, Je 22,47:2
Stern, Edward, 1883, Ja 2,5:4; 1953, N 7,17:2
Stern, Edward A, 1908, O 9,9:4
Stern, Edwin H, 1949, N 30,27:2
Stern, Edwin Hyman Ex-Gov, 1968, Mr 10,92:8
Stern, Edwin M Mrs, 1948, Ap 25,68:7
Stern, Elias L, 1966, Ja 29,27:4
Stern, Elizabeth G Mrs (Eleanor Morton), 1954, Ja 10,86:1
Stern, Emanuel, 1950, F 1,29:3
Stern, Emanuel Mrs, 1957, O 17,33:2
Stern, Emil, 1954, S 6,15:4
Stern, Emil E Mrs, 1955, Jl 8,23:4
Stern, Ernest E, 1964, Mr 30,29:4
Stern, Felix, 1949, S 5,17:3
Stern, Frances, 1947, D 25,21:6
Stern, Frederick, 1952, Jl 11,17:5
Stern, Frederick D, 1960, Ap 5,37:3
Stern, Frederick S Mrs, 1941, Mr 16,45:2
Stern, Fritz S, 1941, D 3,25:3
Stern, Gedalie Mrs, 1937, D 7,25:4
Stern, Gustave, 1964, D 3,45:5
Stern, Hans J, 1961, O 11,47:2
Stern, Harold, 1960, D 13,31:2
Stern, Harry, 1954, My 9,88:2
Stern, Harry I, 1956, My 8,33:4
Stern, Harry I Mrs, 1964, Jl 18,19:5
Stern, Heinrich, 1951, F 10,13:5
Stern, Heinrich Dr, 1918, F 2,11:4
Stern, Henrietta, 1941, My 6,21:5
Stern, Henry E, 1937, S 26,II,8:3
Stern, Henry M, 1950, S 1,21:4
Stern, Henry R, 1966, Mr 15,39:1
Stern, Herbert (Baron Michelham), 1919, Ja 8,11:2
Stern, Herbert L, 1966, Jl 24,60:8
Stern, Herman, 1953, Ja 13,27:3; 1967, Jl 30,64:8
Stern, Herman W, 1964, Ja 17,43:1
Stern, Hyman, 1956, Ag 13,19:4
Stern, I Foster, 1966, Je 12,86:5
Stern, Irving B Mrs, 1955, O 20,36:2
Stern, Isaac (funl, D 8,13:4), 1910, D 6,13:4
Stern, Isaac, 1937, Ja 20,21:2; 1967, S 13,47:1
Stern, Isaac L, 1941, S 4,21:4
Stern, Isadore A, 1953, Ja 31,15:5
Stern, J Ernest, 1950, N 21,31:4
Stern, J L, 1932, My 4,19:1
Stern, Jack, 1950, Ja 15,84:3
Stern, Jacob (por), 1949, Ag 7,60:4
Stern, James J, 1952, My 21,27:4
Stern, John F, 1944, Jl 11,15:3
Stern, John F Mrs, 1957, F 6,25:4
Stern, Jonas, 1954, Ag 2,17:2
Stern, Joseph, 1919, Ap 29,15:4; 1945, S 18,24:3
Stern, Julius, 1941, N 11,23:4
Stern, Julius L, 1964, Jl 5,43:3
Stern, Karl F, 1954, N 13,15:5
Stern, Kurt M, 1962, Ap 17,35:4
Stern, L, 1928, D 30,20:1
Stern, Lehman, 1945, Ja 23,19:3
Stern, Leo, 1904, S 12,9:6
Stern, Leo C, 1962, D 5,47:4
Stern, Leo Mrs, 1965, N 1,41:3
Stern, Leo S, 1943, Ap 17,17:2
Stern, Leopold, 1914, Je 30,11:6
Stern, Lina Solomonova Prof, 1968, Mr 9,29:3
Stern, Lionel M, 1951, Ja 13,15:4
Stern, Louis (por),(funl, Je 24,13:6), 1922, Je 23,17:1
Stern, Louis, 1941, F 17,15:4; 1957, S 13,23:4
Stern, Louis E, 1962, Ja 12,35:3
Stern, Louis Mrs, 1905, N 28,9:4; 1964, Je 16,39:4
Stern, Louis Rabbi, 1920, Ap 30,13:5
Stern, Louis W, 1938, Mr 28,15:2
Stern, Lucie, 1938, My 16,17:5
Stern, Ludwig, 1942, O 9,22:3
Stern, M S, 1929, O 29,31:3
Stern, Maurice E, 1951, Ag 25,11:4
Stern, Max, 1941, F 17,15:2; 1944, Mr 9,17:4
Stern, Max E, 1958, Je 21,19:3
Stern, Max M, 1946, O 21,31:3
Stern, Max Mrs, 1945, Je 30,17:5; 1946, Ap 26,21:1; 1957, My 22,33:4; 1967, Ag 8,39:2
Stern, Max W, 1950, Ag 27,88:4
Stern, Maximilian, 1920, F 24,13:5; 1946, Ja 22,28:2
Stern, Maximilian Mrs (cor, F 27,21:3), 1953, F 26, 25:3
Stern, Meyer, 1938, Ja 31,19:3
Stern, Meyer E, 1960, N 7,35:3
Stern, Milton, 1958, Jl 20,64:8
Stern, Milton M, 1949, Ag 28,72:3
Stern, Mordecai A, 1963, D 23,25:2
Stern, Morley A, 1939, F 19,39:2
Stern, Morton F, 1956, Ja 31,29:1
Stern, Morton M, 1966, Ap 26,45:1
Stern, N D, 1932, S 16,21:1
Stern, Nathan (por), 1945, Ja 25,19:1
Stern, Nathan J, 1946, S 16,5:4
Stern, Oscar, 1943, Ag 20,15:3
Stern, Paul, 1962, S 3,15:6
Stern, Percy W, 1952, Ja 26,13:6
Stern, Peter, 1965, F 9,37:4
Stern, Peter A, 1947, Ap 7,23:3
Stern, Philip M, 1960, Ap 12,33:5
Stern, Philip M Mrs, 1960, Mr 31,33:5
Stern, Renee B, 1940, My 20,17:6
Stern, Roman, 1943, N 4,23:5
Stern, Rudolf A, 1962, N 11,89:1
Stern, Samuel, 1940, D 9,19:4; 1942, F 19,19:3; 1946 Je 16,40:5; 1948, D 22,24:2; 1961, D 25,23:6; 1963 Je 8,25:6; 1968, Je 20,45:4
Stern, Samuel Mrs, 1953, Je 8,29:3; 1966, My 31,43
Stern, Sidney E, 1964, Ja 9,31:2
Stern, Sidney M (Oct 7), 1965, O 11,61:5
Stern, Siegfried, 1952, O 7,29:5; 1961, Jl 26,31:2
Stern, Sigmund, 1940, My 6,17:2; 1951, N 19,23:4; 1960, Jl 20,29:4; 1966, Ja 8,26:5
Stern, Sigmund Mrs, 1956, F 10,21:5
Stern, Simon H Mrs, 1937, Je 27,II,7:1
Stern, Simon T, 1942, My 19,19:3
Stern, Walter D, 1964, Jl 6,29:3
Stern, Walter E, 1968, Ap 13,25:6
Stern, Walter T, 1952, Mr 25,27:3
Stern, William, 1958, My 18,63:5; 1964, Ja 2,27:2
Stern, William A 2d, 1965, Je 9,47:5
Stern, William E, 1957, Mr 27,31:3
Stern, William Mrs, 1947, Ap 30,25:3
Sternbach, Louis Mrs, 1958, F 7,21:1
Sternbach, Maurice, 1924, Ap 8,19:3
Sternbach, Nathan, 1952, Jl 1,23:1
Sternberg, Adolph, 1955, N 18,25:5
Sternberg, Adolph Mrs, 1949, Ag 28,75:2
Sternberg, Carl, 1957, Jl 4,19:2
Sternberg, Charles H, 1943, Jl 23,17:5
Sternberg, Charles Mrs, 1938, D 25,14:4
Sternberg, Donald P, 1953, Jl 25,11:5
Sternberg, Edward A, 1948, Mr 13,15:1
Sternberg, Ferdinand, 1937, Mr 27,15:2
Sternberg, George H, 1948, D 4,19:1
Sternberg, George Miller Gen, 1915, N 4,11:5
Sternberg, H Sumner, 1963, N 28,39:3
Sternberg, Helen (H Stevens), 1966, N 14,41:4
Sternberg, Irving, 1961, D 16,25:6
Sternberg, Jules Mrs, 1943, F 9,23:4
Sternberg, Louis, 1958, S 17,37:1; 1963, D 21,23:2
Sternberg, Maurice D, 1947, Je 5,25:6
Sternberg, Milton, 1955, My 10,29:5
Sternberg, Natalie C Mrs (will), 1950, D 14,23:2
Sternberg, Norman, 1963, Je 24,27:5
Sternberg, Phil, 1948, Je 19,15:5
Sternberg, Ralph, 1949, D 14,32:3
Sternberg, Samuel H, 1950, Mr 28,31:4
Sternberg, Walter, 1966, My 5,47:4
Sternberger, Edwin Dr, 1924, N 5,19:5
Sternberger, Henry, 1951, Ap 17,29:4
Sternberger, Henry Mrs, 1959, D 19,27:2
Sternberger, Henry S, 1953, Je 14,84:5
Sternberger, Joseph A, 1937, Je 17,23:3
Sternberger, Leon J, 1956, S 17,27:5
Sternberger, Lionel C, 1964, Ja 31,27:4
Sternberger, Louis, 1947, Je 26,24:3
Sternberger, Marcel, 1956, O 27,21:6
Sternberger, Mayer, 1915, Ag 22,13:5
Sternbergh, J Hervey, 1949, Ap 4,23:5
Sternbergh, J Hervey Mrs, 1950, N 29,36:6
Sternbergh, Van Renssalaer H, 1953, Mr 13,27:2
Sternburg, James A Speck von, 1916, Ja 27,11:2
Sternburgh, Machlin E, 1961, Ap 20,33:2
Sterndale, Lord, 1923, Ag 18,9:6
Sterndale-Bennett, T C, 1944, My 18,19:6
Sterne, Abraham L Mrs, 1954, D 6,27:6
Sterne, Eugene H, 1955, My 20,25:4
Sterne, Katherine, 1944, S 1,13:1
Sterne, Louis, 1924, Je 2,17:6
Sterne, Maurice, 1957, Jl 24,25:4
Sterne, Maurice Mrs, 1963, N 4,35:1
Sterne, Morris E, 1909, Ag 16,7:5
Sterne, Niel P, 1939, F 14,19:6
Sterne, Robert, 1957, My 28,34:6
Sterne, Robert L, 1954, Ap 25,87:2
Sterne, Simon (funl, S 26,9:6), 1901, S 23,9:6
Sterner, Albert (por), 1946, D 17,31:3
Sterner, Harry B, 1952, My 20,25:4
Sterner, L Parvin, 1951, N 14,31:3
Sterner, Willard J, 1941, S 11,23:6
Sternfels, Florence Mrs, 1965, Ap 20,39:1
Sternhage, John M, 1954, S 26,86:6
Sternheim, Carl, 1943, Mr 14,26:2
Sternova, Miroslava, 1955, Mr 11,10:3
Sternroyd, Vincent, 1948, N 4,30:2
Sterns, Fred H, 1951, Mr 8,29:5
Sterns, H, 1939, D 30,15:3
Sterns, M Richard, 1960, Mr 20,86:7
Sterns, Mary A, 1942, S 1,19:5
Sterns, William E, 1957, Mr 26,33:2
Sterns, William S Sr, 1948, O 7,29:4
Sterphone, Joseph, 1949, Ap 3,76:3
Sterrett, Cliff Mrs, 1948, S 22,32:2
Sterrett, Frank W Mrs, 1961, My 24,41:1
Sterrett, H Willard, 1951, O 24,32:3
Sterrett, Harold R, 1942, Ap 29,21:6
Sterrett, J E, 1934, Mr 23,23:5

Sterrett, John K, 1953, O 13,29:4
Sterrett, John Robert Sitlington Prof, 1914, Je 17,11:6
Sterrett, Joseph E Mrs, 1950, Jl 31,17:5
Sterrett, Robert J, 1943, O 17,48:3
Sterrett, Samuel, 1939, N 26,43:1
Sterrett, Walter E Mrs, 1963, Ag 2,4:6
Sterritt, James E, 1947, Ag 23,13:4
Sterritte, Frank G, 1965, Mr 9,35:1
Sterrry, F, 1933, Jl 12,17:4
Sterry, C N, 1903, My 23,9:3
Sterry, Frederic Mrs, 1959, D 9,45:2
Sterry, Leland, 1923, S 1,11:6
Sterzelbach, Abraham, 1953, Ap 4,13:1
Stetansson, Vilhjalmur (funl plans, Ag 30,29:3), 1962, Ag 27,1:4
Stetler, Henry A, 1950, Ap 16,104:8
Stetser, Herbert F, 1952, D 11,33:3
Stetser, Jesse R, 1938, N 9,23:4
Stetser, Oliver J, 1950, O 31,27:1
Stetser, William H, 1953, S 8,31:2
Stetson, A E Mrs, 1928, O 13,15:3
Stetson, Alex M Maj, 1903, S 29,9:4
Stetson, Augusta Rice Mrs, 1916, O 21,11:3
Stetson, Bertram C, 1965, Je 14,33:3
Stetson, C A Jr, 1882, Ag 10,8:4
Stetson, C R, 1932, Je 16,21:1
Stetson, C W, 1911, Jl 22,7:6
Stetson, Charles, 1883, Mr 28,5:3
Stetson, Clarence, 1915, Ja 7,13:4
Stetson, Clarence A, 1938, D 16,25:1
Stetson, Clarence C, 1950, Ag 14,17:4
Stetson, E C, 1908, N 11,9:6
Stetson, Eugene W, 1959, Jl 21,30:2
Stetson, Francis Lynde (por), 1920, D 6,15:1
Stetson, Frank E, 1938, O 21,23:1
Stetson, Franklin, 1924, My 21,19:2
Stetson, Franklin D Sr, 1965, Ap 6,39:1
Stetson, George A, 1959, Je 21,93:1
Stetson, Halbert G, 1943, S 16,21:1
Stetson, Harold S, 1955, N 26,19:3
Stetson, Harry, 1905, Mr 16,9:6
Stetson, Henry C, 1955, D 5,32:1
Stetson, Henry T Mrs, 1954, My 8,17:2
Stetson, J B, 1909, Ag 22,9:6
Stetson, James D, 1953, F 9,27:4
Stetson, John B, 1906, F 19,9:5
Stetson, John B Jr, 1952, N 16,88:3
Stetson, John B 3d, 1944, Jl 19,19:4
Stetson, John H, 1938, N 11,25:1
Stetson, Joshua, 1879, Mr 12,2:2
Stetson, Lucretia H Mrs, 1939, Je 4,48:8
Stetson, Oscar F, 1948, Ag 14,13:2
Stetson, Paul C Dr (por), 1937, Je 2,23:3
Stetson, Raymond H, 1950, D 5,31:2
Stetson, Reuben K, 1948, Ap 28,27:3
Stetson, Rufus E, 1967, N 15,47:4
Stetson, Stephen L, 1947, S 24,23:3
Stetson, Walter H, 1951, O 16,31:3
Stetson, William P, 1945, Je 22,15:4
Stetson, Willis K, 1942, Ja 10,15:5
Stettauer, James, 1903, Mr 7,1:5
Stettauer, Louis, 1952, Ag 2,15:6
Stetten, DeWitt, 1951, N 11,91:1
Stettenbenz, Miles D, 1947, O 5,68:5
Stettenheim, Daisy B Mrs, 1949, Jl 28,23:3
Stettenheim, Frederic R, 1952, D 17,33:5
Stettheimer, Ettie, 1955, Je 3,23:2
Stettheimer, Florine, 1944, My 14,46:1
Stettheimer, Walter W, 1954, O 16,17:2
Stettheimer, Walter W Mrs, 1961, S 14,31:1
Stettinius, Edward R (por), 1925, S 4,21:4
Stettinius, Edward R Jr, 1949, N 1,1:3
Stettinius, John L, 1924, Ap 30,19:2
Stettinius, Judith C Mrs, 1938, D 6,23:3
Stettinius, William C (por), 1937, Jl 21,21:4
Stettler, Marvin H, 1949, Mr 14,19:5
Stetzer, John J, 1957, Jl 9,29:2
Stetzer, Raymond, 1964, Jl 15,35:3
Steuart, Edith, 1951, N 11,90:4
Steuart, John P, 1944, Jl 4,19:2
Steuart, Richard D, 1951, O 16,31:5
Steuben, Baron Von, 1864, Je 10,2:2
Steuben, John, 1957, My 10,27:4
Steubenbord, Conrad, 1913, Jl 23,7:6
Steubner, Gustavus L, 1923, S 13,19:3
Steuer, Bernard, 1966, Je 5,86:7
Steuer, Max, 1944, Ja 24,17:6
Steuer, Max D, 1940, Ag 22,1:3
Steuer, O H, 1903, Ap 5,11:3
Steuer, Samuel, 1954, N 3,29:3
Steuermann, Edward, 1964, N 13,32:7
Steuernagel, Herman, 1951, O 31,29:4
Steuernagel, Philip, 1945, S 13,23:3
Steup, Adolph G, 1948, F 13,21:2
Steup, Martin L, 1951, N 30,23:1
Steup, William H, 1947, N 29,13:5
Steur, Johannes A C, 1948, Jl 28,23:6
Steur, van der (Pa), 1945, S 28,21:5
Steurer, Albert J, 1937, Ag 24,21:4
Steurer, Charles D Jr, 1965, Je 8,41:3
Steurer, Charles D Mrs, 1949, F 13,76:4
Steurer, John A, 1942, Ag 8,11:2
Steuri, Fritz, 1950, D 8,30:3
Steurnagel, George M, 1949, S 6,27:4
Steurnagel, William P, 1950, D 27,27:1
Steurwald, John E, 1917, N 6,13:4
Steutel, Thomas, 1950, Jl 24,17:5
Stevanowich, John, 1949, S 1,21:4
Steven, Andrew R, 1942, Je 22,15:2
Steven, Harold C, 1948, Ja 22,27:5
Steven, Mary M, 1943, My 1,15:5
Stevens, A Leo, 1944, My 9,19:4
Stevens, Abbot, 1958, My 17,19:4
Stevens, Abby W, 1939, Jl 22,15:5
Stevens, Abram Walter Rev, 1924, F 12,17:3
Stevens, Albert M, 1945, Ag 12,39:3
Stevens, Albert P, 1914, Ap 5,15:1
Stevens, Albert W, 1949, F 9,27:2
Stevens, Albert W (por), 1949, Mr 27,76:3
Stevens, Albion M Mrs, 1947, Ja 14,26:2
Stevens, Alden, 1968, Ap 29,43:4
Stevens, Alexander H, 1916, Jl 11,9:7
Stevens, Alexander R Dr, 1968, Je 7,36:3
Stevens, Alfred, 1906, Ag 25,7:6
Stevens, Alice P, 1958, Ag 28,27:5
Stevens, Almira E, 1946, Ag 6,25:3
Stevens, Alton E, 1924, Ja 22,17:4
Stevens, Alviso B, 1940, Ja 27,13:3
Stevens, Ambrose, 1880, D 30,1:7
Stevens, Ann Mrs, 1952, Je 27,23:1
Stevens, Annie K Mrs, 1939, Mr 17,21:2
Stevens, Arthur A, 1944, Je 12,19:4
Stevens, Arthur F, 1940, Ja 15,15:4
Stevens, Arthur K, 1968, Ap 10,43:5
Stevens, Ashton, 1951, Jl 13,21:3
Stevens, Augustus C, 1948, S 21,27:4
Stevens, B F, 1902, Mr 7,9:5
Stevens, Basil M, 1957, N 9,27:3
Stevens, Benjamin, 1913, O 23,11:6
Stevens, Benjamin F, 1908, Ap 12,7:6
Stevens, Bernard, 1953, Ap 13,27:5
Stevens, Bertha, 1947, Ap 12,17:6
Stevens, Blanchard B, 1949, Jl 31,60:4
Stevens, Byan Kerby, 1911, D 13,11:4
Stevens, C Brooks, 1949, Je 27,27:6
Stevens, C Guy, 1945, Ag 16,19:2
Stevens, C K, 1934, F 9,19:1
Stevens, Calvin G, 1946, Jl 18,25:2
Stevens, Carleton H, 1943, S 29,21:4
Stevens, Carlyle, 1961, O 4,45:4
Stevens, Caroline H, 1952, Ja 3,27:2
Stevens, Caroline W, 1948, D 6,25:4
Stevens, Catherine Mrs, 1925, S 9,25:5
Stevens, Charles, 1942, Ap 20,21:2
Stevens, Charles B Dr, 1924, My 15,19:4
Stevens, Charles D, 1955, Ag 26,19:5
Stevens, Charles F, 1941, Ap 2,23:6
Stevens, Charles H, 1944, F 3,19:2; 1945, Jl 19,23:3
Stevens, Charles J Mrs, 1953, F 5,23:4
Stevens, Charles L, 1962, O 8,23:4
Stevens, Charles N, 1940, My 9,23:5
Stevens, Charles S, 1950, N 18,15:4; 1960, F 2,35:3
Stevens, Charles W, 1937, Ja 4,29:1; 1943, Mr 16,19:2; 1949, F 16,26:2
Stevens, Chester H, 1966, Mr 15,39:2
Stevens, Clarence, 1960, Mr 24,33:1
Stevens, Clarence S, 1939, Ja 10,19:4
Stevens, Clarence W, 1949, S 16,27:3
Stevens, Clifford E, 1961, Jl 12,31:1
Stevens, Clinton S, 1943, F 12,19:6
Stevens, Corwin E, 1954, Je 3,27:1
Stevens, Daniel L, 1903, Jl 22,1:3
Stevens, David D Mrs, 1948, Mr 6,13:5
Stevens, David J, 1957, S 20,25:3
Stevens, Delmar A, 1959, Mr 6,25:2
Stevens, Donald B Mrs, 1961, N 29,41:5
Stevens, Donald R, 1963, N 27,37:4
Stevens, Doris, 1963, Mr 25,7:4
Stevens, E, 1928, Ja 3,10:2
Stevens, E A (funl; will, S 20,5:4), 1868, S 17,2:3
Stevens, Earl K Mrs, 1940, N 15,21:5
Stevens, Earle E, 1948, N 2,25:1
Stevens, Edgar H, 1955, Jl 3,32:2
Stevens, Edmund, 1916, Mr 19,19:6
Stevens, Edmund H, 1939, Mr 15,23:2; 1952, Ag 24, 89:2
Stevens, Edmund H Mrs, 1940, S 17,23:4
Stevens, Edmund Mrs, 1960, Ap 3,86:2
Stevens, Edward, 1966, Mr 21,33:3
Stevens, Edward A, 1942, Ja 23,19:2; 1957, Mr 12,33:5
Stevens, Edward B, 1960, D 27,29:2
Stevens, Edward B Mrs, 1955, Je 25,15:2
Stevens, Edward F, 1946, Mr 1,22:3
Stevens, Edward I Mrs, 1945, O 11,23:1
Stevens, Edward Lawrence, 1914, Ap 4,15:4
Stevens, Edwin A, 1868, Ag 11,8:2
Stevens, Edwin A Col, 1918, Mr 9,13:3
Stevens, Edwin A 3d, 1954, D 2,31:1
Stevens, Edwin A 4th, 1959, S 27,86:7
Stevens, Edwin F Jr (por), 1945, D 21,21:1
Stevens, Edwin Mrs (Lillia), 1966, Jl 6,42:5
Stevens, Elbert C, 1947, S 27,15:2
Stevens, Elgin H Mrs, 1948, S 5,40:6
Stevens, Elisha M, 1942, N 29,65:2
Stevens, Elizabeth D Mrs, 1941, My 10,15:3
Stevens, Ellen A, 1947, Ag 12,24:3
Stevens, Ernest L, 1964, Ap 5,86:7
Stevens, Ernest N, 1960, Ja 12,45:5; 1961, Je 3,23:3
Stevens, Erskine C, 1951, Jl 26,21:4
Stevens, Eugene M (por), 1937, Ja 23,18:1
Stevens, Eugene S, 1952, F 10,92:3
Stevens, Evarts C, 1956, N 10,19:2
Stevens, Evelyn O Mrs, 1960, Je 15,41:1
Stevens, F, 1926, N 29,19:4
Stevens, F G, 1946, Ag 11,46:1
Stevens, F J, 1905, Ap 8,1:6
Stevens, F Paul, 1949, Mr 18,25:4
Stevens, F W, 1926, N 3,23:4; 1928, Ja 21,17:5
Stevens, Flinn W, 1943, Mr 24,23:4
Stevens, Frances J Mrs, 1939, Jl 12,19:6
Stevens, Francis B, 1908, My 24,9:4
Stevens, Francis Bowes Mrs, 1916, Jl 7,11:5
Stevens, Francis K (por), 1945, Ag 29,23:3
Stevens, Francis K Mrs, 1951, Ap 22,88:4
Stevens, Frank, 1958, S 20,19:2
Stevens, Frank G, 1937, Ja 8,19:4
Stevens, Frank H, 1937, Ap 22,23:4
Stevens, Frank K Mrs, 1950, F 11,15:5
Stevens, Frank L, 1941, My 20,23:2
Stevens, Frank M, 1947, Ap 3,25:1; 1965, Ja 4,29:2
Stevens, Frank M Mrs, 1954, N 23,35:2
Stevens, Frank S Jr, 1944, D 5,23:3
Stevens, Franklin A, 1956, Je 23,17:4
Stevens, Franklin C, 1949, My 9,25:5
Stevens, Fred O, 1937, Ap 10,19:1
Stevens, Frederic B, 1947, Je 23,23:2
Stevens, Frederic C, 1939, D 2,17:2
Stevens, Frederick, 1958, Ag 16,17:4
Stevens, Frederick C, 1916, Mr 16,13:4
Stevens, Frederick William, 1919, N 7,13:1
Stevens, George A, 1939, Mr 11,17:2; 1952, My 1, 29:4; 1954, Ap 21,29:2
Stevens, George A Mrs, 1945, Ja 13,11:1
Stevens, George Asher, 1920, S 18,9:4
Stevens, George Barker Rev, 1906, Je 23,7:4
Stevens, George C, 1941, Ap 11,21:2; 1951, O 30,29:2
Stevens, George E, 1966, N 23,39:4
Stevens, George H, 1955, Jl 26,25:3
Stevens, George J, 1945, S 28,21:3
Stevens, George M, 1953, S 24,33:4; 1956, D 22,19:6
Stevens, George S, 1940, Ag 22,20:3
Stevens, George Thomas Dr, 1921, Ja 31,9:4
Stevens, George W (funl, N 6,13:3), 1920, N 4,13:4
Stevens, Gerard M, 1903, D 31,9:5
Stevens, Gertrude M, 1948, Mr 8,23:3
Stevens, Gilbert B, 1957, O 29,31:3
Stevens, Grace, 1950, Mr 21,29:1
Stevens, Guy, 1944, Je 12,19:5
Stevens, H M, 1934, My 4,21:1
Stevens, H R, 1881, My 24,5:2
Stevens, Harley C, 1959, D 28,23:5
Stevens, Harold, 1964, Je 27,25:3
Stevens, Harold A, 1961, N 16,39:1
Stevens, Harold A Mrs, 1963, S 13,30:1
Stevens, Harold R G, 1961, Ja 2,25:4
Stevens, Harold W, 1937, D 22,25:4
Stevens, Harriet S Mrs, 1948, F 16,21:2
Stevens, Harry A, 1942, N 19,25:5
Stevens, Harry E, 1949, N 1,27:3
Stevens, Harry M Mrs, 1941, Je 8,49:2
Stevens, Helen (H Sternberg), 1966, N 14,41:4
Stevens, Henry, 1867, Ag 4,3:7; 1939, D 5,10:1
Stevens, Henry E, 1944, D 10,54:8
Stevens, Henry M, 1953, Ag 13,25:1
Stevens, Henry W, 1960, Ja 6,35:2
Stevens, Hiram T, 1953, N 14,17:1
Stevens, Hobart M, 1951, Je 2,19:3
Stevens, Horace, 1950, N 18,15:6
Stevens, Horace A, 1967, F 4,27:1
Stevens, Horace F Mrs, 1965, Jl 22,31:4
Stevens, Horace M Jr (will), 1951, Ag 8,22:8
Stevens, Horace N, 1951, Jl 20,21:4
Stevens, Horace S, 1954, Mr 4,25:2
Stevens, Howard D, 1948, D 29,21:4
Stevens, Howard E, 1954, My 27,27:2
Stevens, Howard R, 1940, Jl 9,21:1
Stevens, Howard R Mrs, 1951, Ja 3,27:2
Stevens, I N, 1920, F 12,11:4
Stevens, Irving T, 1949, Mr 22,25:4
Stevens, Isabelle, 1948, Ag 24,25:6
Stevens, J Crawford, 1955, Ag 18,23:2
Stevens, J F, 1942, Jl 23,19:5
Stevens, J Frank, 1950, Ja 20,25:4
Stevens, J Hubert, 1950, N 27,25:2
Stevens, James A (funl), 1873, O 11,8:2
Stevens, James A, 1938, Je 12,39:4
Stevens, James E, 1951, S 18,31:4
Stevens, James G, 1950, N 13,28:3
Stevens, James H, 1956, F 14,29:5
Stevens, James M, 1937, Ag 24,22:2
Stevens, James R, 1952, O 15,31:2
Stevens, James S, 1940, Mr 25,16:2; 1946, Ap 17,25:5
Stevens, Jennie L Mrs, 1938, Mr 7,17:4
Stevens, John, 1882, Ap 25,8:2; 1950, Ja 31,23:3
Stevens, John A, 1916, Je 18,18:5; 1925, My 20,23:3; 1950, S 7,31:5
Stevens, John Austin, 1874, O 20,4:7
Stevens, John Austin (funl, Je 19,11:4), 1910, Je 17, 7:4

Stevens, John Austin Mrs, 1911, D 8,13:4
Stevens, John B, 1940, Jl 10,19:2; 1946, Ap 27,17:2
Stevens, John C, 1938, Jl 11,17:4
Stevens, John D, 1944, D 22,17:1
Stevens, John E, 1957, F 24,85:1
Stevens, John F, 1943, Je 3,21:3
Stevens, John H, 1943, Je 24,22:2; 1959, D 19,27:6
Stevens, John L, 1895, F 9,9:3
Stevens, John M, 1948, D 6,25:3
Stevens, John O, 1919, F 15,11:4
Stevens, John P Mrs, 1964, Ag 31,25:2
Stevens, John Rhinelander Mrs, 1914, Ap 19,IV,7:5
Stevens, John W, 1963, D 11,47:4
Stevens, John 7th, 1941, Ap 17,23:2
Stevens, Joseph C, 1946, Jl 4,19:5
Stevens, Joseph E, 1961, Ap 12,41:5
Stevens, Joseph M, 1967, S 19,51:3
Stevens, Joseph O Sr, 1960, Jl 4,15:6
Stevens, Joseph T, 1949, Ap 1,25:4
Stevens, Junius, 1947, Mr 31,23:5
Stevens, Landers, 1940, D 21,17:4
Stevens, Laurence, 1902, Mr 26,9:6
Stevens, Leon K, 1938, Jl 22,17:2
Stevens, Leonard, 1937, O 11,21:2
Stevens, LeRoy, 1954, My 27,27:3
Stevens, Leslie C, 1956, D 1,21:3
Stevens, Leslie W, 1954, O 20,29:1
Stevens, Lester C, 1937, D 29,21:4
Stevens, Louis, 1943, My 8,15:3
Stevens, Louise C Mrs, 1937, My 30,19:
Stevens, Ludlow W Mrs, 1943, Jl 9,17:5
Stevens, Lydia Mrs, 1953, Ag 14,19:2
Stevens, Lyndon Hoyt, 1910, Je 23,7:5
Stevens, Maltby, 1955, Je 30,25:5
Stevens, Margaret T, 1955, Ap 1,27:4
Stevens, Marion E, 1962, Mr 26,31:3
Stevens, Marion L M Mrs, 1967, Ap 3,33:2
Stevens, Mary B Mrs (will), 1943, N 7,7:7
Stevens, Mary P Mrs, 1938, O 17,15:6
Stevens, Mary T, 1949, Ap 17,76:3
Stevens, Matthew K, 1957, F 23,17:4
Stevens, Maud L, 1949, N 12,15:1
Stevens, Maurice K, 1962, Ap 29,86:1
Stevens, Melbourne, 1949, Ag 28,72:6
Stevens, Merton P, 1962, Mr 23,33:6
Stevens, Michael Mrs (Lillian M N Stevens), 1914, Ap 7,9:6
Stevens, Montague, 1953, D 18,29:1
Stevens, Morton L, 1959, Ag 6,27:6
Stevens, Moses T, 1948, F 5,23:5
Stevens, Moses Tyler, 1907, Mr 26,9:6
Stevens, Nat D, 1939, D 15,25:2
Stevens, Nathaniel, 1946, Je 17,21:5
Stevens, Neil C, 1952, D 29,19:4
Stevens, Neil E, 1949, Je 30,23:3
Stevens, Nelson M, 1938, F 9,19:4
Stevens, Oscar E, 1937, O 12,25:4
Stevens, Oscar L, 1958, F 23,94:1
Stevens, Paran, 1872, Ap 26,1:3
Stevens, Paran Mrs, 1895, Ap 4,1:5
Stevens, Patricia (Mrs E W Muntz), 1959, Je 26,25:5
Stevens, Percy C, 1948, O 2,15:5
Stevens, Philip H, 1966, Je 6,41:1
Stevens, R Cuyler Jr, 1965, Je 14,33:1
Stevens, Ralph C, 1950, S 4,17:5
Stevens, Ralph L, 1949, O 27,27:6
Stevens, Ralph T, 1952, Jl 18,19:2
Stevens, Ray P, 1966, Je 5,85:1
Stevens, Ray P Mrs, 1961, F 16,31:4
Stevens, Raymond B, 1942, My 19,19:3
Stevens, Raymond F, 1957, Ag 15,21:6
Stevens, Rebecca Mrs, 1940, D 31,15:5
Stevens, Richard, 1919, My 19,17:6
Stevens, Richard T, 1941, Jl 13,29:1
Stevens, Robert H, 1956, F 27,4:4
Stevens, Robert L, 1937, N 30,23:5
Stevens, Robert L Mrs, 1950, Mr 10,28:2; 1964, Ja 29, 33:4
Stevens, Robert M Mrs, 1946, S 8,46:4
Stevens, Robert S, 1918, Jl 23,13:5
Stevens, Robert Sproule Dean, 1968, N 18,47:1
Stevens, Roderick G, 1939, My 9,23:3
Stevens, Roland E, 1957, N 17,87:2
Stevens, Romlett Prof, 1922, Ag 8,11:4
Stevens, S P, 1902, D 21,7:6
Stevens, S S, 1905, Je 24,9:5
Stevens, Samuel N, 1966, My 15,88:3
Stevens, Sara, 1904, S 9,7:6
Stevens, Shepherd, 1962, F 12,23:3
Stevens, Sidney W Mrs, 1952, D 8,41:5
Stevens, T H Adm, 1896, My 16,9:2
Stevens, Thaddeus (funl, Ag 18,1:4), 1868, Ag 12,4:6
Stevens, Thaddeus Col, 1874, N 4,2:3
Stevens, Theodore F (por), 1938, D 18,49:2
Stevens, Theodosius, 1959, F 11,39:2
Stevens, Theodosius Mrs, 1967, Je 5,43:2
Stevens, Thomas Brig-Gen, 1864, My 13,2:4
Stevens, Thomas D, 1949, D 9,31:4
Stevens, Thomas H Capt, 1914, O 6,11:3
Stevens, Thomas Hood Prof, 1920, Mr 12,13:5
Stevens, Thomas P, 1955, D 29,23:3
Stevens, Thomas W (por), 1942, Ja 30,20:2
Stevens, Tyler A, 1945, Ag 31,17:4
Stevens, Velma S Mrs, 1942, My 25,15:4
Stevens, W, 1883, Je 9,1:6
Stevens, W B Bishop, 1887, Je 12,5:2
Stevens, W Bertrand, 1947, Ag 23,13:6
Stevens, W F, 1923, Jl 19,15:4
Stevens, Wallace, 1955, Ag 3,23:1
Stevens, Walter, 1903, Je 14,7:6
Stevens, Walter B, 1939, Ag 29,21:4
Stevens, Walter C, 1954, O 25,12:1
Stevens, Walter L Mrs, 1942, F 7,17:6
Stevens, Walter P, 1954, My 27,27:4
Stevens, Walter T, 1947, Ap 23,26:2
Stevens, Walter Y, 1949, N 23,29:4
Stevens, Ward Mrs, 1957, Jl 29,19:3
Stevens, Ward P, 1949, F 4,23:3
Stevens, Wayne E, 1959, Jl 21,29:5
Stevens, Weld M, 1941, F 23,39:5
Stevens, Wesley P, 1959, Jl 26,68:2
Stevens, Willard E, 1963, D 15,87:1
Stevens, Willet H, 1958, Ja 30,23:4
Stevens, William A, 1941, Mr 10,17:1
Stevens, William C, 1939, My 16,23:6
Stevens, William C (por), 1942, D 31,15:3
Stevens, William C (will, Ja 16,9:7), 1943, Ja 3,42:8
Stevens, William Coppee, 1903, S 22,7:4
Stevens, William D, 1956, Ap 29,86:4; 1960, D 7,43:4
Stevens, William H, 1937, Mr 22,23:5
Stevens, William H Maj, 1937, S 2,21:5
Stevens, William H Mrs, 1944, S 24,46:1; 1963, O 6, 88:6
Stevens, William J, 1940, N 2,15:2
Stevens, William Mrs, 1949, Mr 9,25:2
Stevens, William O, 1955, Ja 16,92:5
Stevens, Woodland D, 1938, Ag 17,19:2
Stevenson, A Rev, 1881, Je 26,7:3
Stevenson, Adlai E (trb; funl, Je 17,11:5), 1914, Je 16,9:6
Stevenson, Adlai E (service, Washington, DC, Jl 17,1:5), 1965, Jl 15,1:8
Stevenson, Albert L, 1960, My 27,31:2
Stevenson, Alex G, 1939, Mr 14,21:2
Stevenson, Alex Mrs, 1952, Jl 31,23:1
Stevenson, Alexander R (por), 1946, Ag 29,27:6
Stevenson, Archibald E, 1961, F 11,23:5
Stevenson, Archie M, 1922, N 28,21:5
Stevenson, Beulah, 1965, Mr 19,35:3
Stevenson, Burton E, 1962, My 15,39:4
Stevenson, C A, 1929, Jl 3,21:3
Stevenson, Candace Thurber, 1968, Ag 2,33:3
Stevenson, Charles G Mrs, 1948, Mr 14,72:3
Stevenson, Charles J, 1965, O 15,45:2
Stevenson, Charles J Jr, 1945, My 17,19:2
Stevenson, Charles L, 1947, Mr 7,26:2
Stevenson, Charles R, 1964, F 6,30:1
Stevenson, Clinton Dr, 1913, Ja 23,11:4; 1913, Ja 26, 17:1
Stevenson, Coke R Mrs, 1942, Ja 4,48:6
Stevenson, Cornelia Mrs, 1921, N 15,19:3
Stevenson, D W, 1904, Mr 19,9:4
Stevenson, Daniel M, 1944, Jl 12,19:3
Stevenson, David, 1919, Mr 31,13:4; 1950, N 23,35:6
Stevenson, David K, 1948, Ag 30,25:1
Stevenson, Dwight H, 1945, Ap 19,27:3
Stevenson, E, 1928, My 23,25:3
Stevenson, E Robert Mrs, 1950, Je 26,27:4
Stevenson, E Vicar Mrs, 1949, Mr 2,26:2
Stevenson, Earle W, 1958, Ap 15,33:4
Stevenson, Edgar T, 1956, D 10,31:5
Stevenson, Edmund, 1961, Jl 15,19:4
Stevenson, Edward A, 1937, Ja 1,23:1
Stevenson, Edward F, 1960, N 7,35:4
Stevenson, Edward L, 1944, Jl 17,15:3
Stevenson, Edward L Mrs, 1945, Ap 17,23:1
Stevenson, Edward V, 1949, Jl 5,23:2
Stevenson, Elliott G, 1925, Mr 9,17:4
Stevenson, Emma L Mrs, 1939, Ag 8,17:4
Stevenson, Emmett A, 1949, N 16,29:1
Stevenson, Faber Mrs, 1953, O 17,15:3
Stevenson, Francis L, 1946, F 16,13:5
Stevenson, Frank E, 1953, Jl 10,19:4
Stevenson, Franklin L, 1952, My 14,27:1
Stevenson, Frederick A (por), 1937, D 18,21:1
Stevenson, Frederick A (por), 1948, Jl 30,18:4
Stevenson, Frederick A Mrs, 1950, Ja 21,18:2
Stevenson, Frederick B, 1938, Ag 5,18:2
Stevenson, Frederick H, 1950, Ap 18,32:2
Stevenson, Frederick Mrs, 1965, Ap 23,35:4
Stevenson, Frederick S, 1949, D 2,29:4
Stevenson, George, 1925, S 29,27:4
Stevenson, George E, 1943, Mr 21,26:6
Stevenson, George H, 1946, Jl 3,25:6; 1959, N 30,31:1
Stevenson, George L, 1966, N 19,33:2
Stevenson, George Sr, 1954, S 21,27:4
Stevenson, George W, 1937, S 3,17:4
Stevenson, Gethryn C, 1967, D 10,87:1
Stevenson, Gordon Mrs, 1960, F 8,29:1
Stevenson, H D, 1953, My 24,88:6
Stevenson, H Godwin, 1960, O 9,86:4
Stevenson, H W, 1944, Je 14,19:5
Stevenson, Harriet L M Mrs, 1937, My 14,23:5
Stevenson, Harry, 1948, Ag 25,25:5; 1965, O 23,31:5
Stevenson, Harry F, 1939, N 10,23:5
Stevenson, Harry Mrs, 1958, Mr 2,89:2
Stevenson, Herbert R, 1958, My 12,29:4
Stevenson, Holland N 2d, 1959, Ja 13,47:1
Stevenson, Howard, 1945, Ag 10,18:1
Stevenson, Howard G, 1943, O 31,48:3
Stevenson, J A Col, 1884, Je 29,6:6
Stevenson, J Baron, 1926, Je 11,21:5
Stevenson, J G, 1883, N 12,5:2
Stevenson, J Roland, 1948, D 9,33:4
Stevenson, J Ross, 1939, Ag 14,15:3
Stevenson, J Ross Mrs (funl plans, Je 27,31:2), 1956, Je 24,77:2
Stevenson, James A, 1937, O 6,25:2; 1943, Jl 10,13:3
Stevenson, James H, 1948, F 24,25:2
Stevenson, James J, 1941, My 12,17:1
Stevenson, James Mrs, 1915, Je 25,11:6
Stevenson, James R, 1957, Je 15,17:5; 1962, Ag 15, 31:4
Stevenson, James R Mrs, 1948, Mr 6,13:4
Stevenson, John, 1948, My 21,23:6
Stevenson, John A, 1945, F 9,15:5; 1949, S 1,21:3
Stevenson, John C, 1910, Ap 17,II,11:4
Stevenson, John F, 1952, Mr 21,23:3
Stevenson, John J, 1924, Ag 11,13:5
Stevenson, John J Mrs, 1959, My 16,23:4
Stevenson, John Jr, 1938, Jl 22,17:4
Stevenson, John S, 1941, Mr 9,40:5
Stevenson, John W, 1955, D 31,13:4
Stevenson, L G, 1929, Ap 6,17:3
Stevenson, L L, 1953, F 8,88:1
Stevenson, Lewis W, 1953, Ag 12,31:2
Stevenson, Louis T, 1966, F 20,88:4
Stevenson, Malcolm, 1953, Jl 10,19:3
Stevenson, Marion H, 1943, F 8,20:2
Stevenson, Markley, 1960, D 4,88:7
Stevenson, Martin Mrs, 1948, Jl 22,23:2
Stevenson, Mary A Mrs (Mary Gannon), 1868, F 23,4:6
Stevenson, Mary E (will), 1957, S 28,14:6
Stevenson, Mary V, 1948, Mr 14,73:1
Stevenson, Mary V (Sister Rose Frances), 1960, Jl 3,32:4
Stevenson, Maxwell, 1951, F 10,13:6
Stevenson, Mayor, 1874, Je 18,5:4
Stevenson, Oren C, 1950, S 24,104:3
Stevenson, Paul E, 1910, D 21,11:2
Stevenson, Philip, 1961, Jl 9,77:2
Stevenson, Philip (Sept 28), 1965, O 11,61:5
Stevenson, R Helen, 1948, Mr 20,13:5
Stevenson, R Macaulay, 1952, S 21,89:1
Stevenson, Ralph C, 1955, Mr 9,27:1
Stevenson, Richard C, 1958, My 3,19:2
Stevenson, Richard W, 1967, Ap 18,41:1
Stevenson, Robert, 1903, Ag 24,7:7; 1938, S 18,45:2; 1951, D 15,13:3
Stevenson, Robert A, 1948, Ap 24,15:1
Stevenson, Robert H Jr, 1955, S 25,95:4
Stevenson, Robert L, 1894, D 18,9:1
Stevenson, Robert Livingston, 1907, Ap 27,9:6
Stevenson, Robert Louis Mrs, 1914, F 20,9:4
Stevenson, Samuel M, 1940, Mr 8,22:2
Stevenson, Samuel O, 1941, D 15,19:2
Stevenson, Sarah Hackett Dr, 1909, Ag 15,7:4
Stevenson, Stuart R Mrs, 1960, O 24,29:4
Stevenson, Susan Dilsham Mrs, 1919, Ag 23,7:7
Stevenson, T P Rev, 1912, O 4,13:4
Stevenson, Thomas, 1953, O 11,89:1
Stevenson, Thomas H, 1948, Ag 26,15:6
Stevenson, Thomas J Mrs, 1961, Ag 14,25:1
Stevenson, Thomas J Sr, 1968, Ja 29,31:1
Stevenson, Thomas W, 1937, S 13,21:2; 1958, F 23,92:1
Stevenson, V K, 1884, O 18,5:2
Stevenson, Vernon Mrs (S Graf), 1965, Mr 7,82:1
Stevenson, W F, 1883, N 30,4:7
Stevenson, W H, 1951, Ja 8,17:2
Stevenson, W Wesley, 1941, Jl 25,15:6
Stevenson, W Wesley Mrs, 1953, Je 19,21:1
Stevenson, Walter C, 1941, Je 17,21:3
Stevenson, Wilbur H, 1950, Jl 6,27:5
Stevenson, William, 1874, My 18,1:7; 1947, Ag 13, 23:5; 1951, My 23,35:2; 1960, Jl 10,72:4; 1967, My 9 40:8
Stevenson, William C, 1942, Ap 19,44:8
Stevenson, William D, 1966, Ap 1,35:5
Stevenson, William F, 1942, D 13,21:3
Stevenson, William H, 1943, Ja 16,13:6; 1947, Mr 16, 60:6
Stevenson, William J, 1938, Mr 13,II,8:4
Stevenson, William M, 1938, Je 14,21:6; 1945, My 2, 23:4
Stevenson, William P (por), 1941, D 31,17:5
Stevenson, William T, 1957, My 23,33:5
Stever, Ralph H, 1952, D 7,89:1
Steves, James Mrs, 1953, Mr 31,31:3
Steves, Walter E Mrs, 1947, F 19,25:2
Stevick, Crist H, 1953, D 24,15:2
Stevick, David W Mrs, 1967, S 19,47:2
Steward, C R, 1950, Mr 26,94:4
Steward, Campbell Mrs, 1951, Ap 27,23:5
Steward, Edwin J, 1941, Ap 14,17:2
Steward, George H, 1948, S 4,15:6
Steward, Harold D, 1960, Mr 13,31:2
Steward, Harry M, 1948, Ja 4,52:6
Steward, John, 1923, Ja 5,11:6; 1957, Ap 30,13:3

Steward, John W, 1947, Ja 10,21:5
Steward, Leroy T, 1944, Ap 28,19:5
Steward, Mary, 1943, Ap 2,21:4
Steward, Orlando T Rev Dr, 1937, Ap 17,17:2
Stewart, A, 1878, O 8,5:6
Stewart, A C, 1916, Ap 23,19:4
Stewart, A T, 1876, Ap 11,1:1
Stewart, Adelbert T, 1963, Je 2,84:3
Stewart, Albert A, 1941, Ag 7,17:1
Stewart, Albert F, 1944, Ja 29,13:5
Stewart, Alex, 1961, D 29,23:1
Stewart, Alex M (por), 1939, D 22,19:1
Stewart, Alex M, 1955, D 25,49:1
Stewart, Alex Mrs, 1948, Mr 4,25:5
Stewart, Alexander, 1912, My 25,13:6; 1946, S 17,7:1
Stewart, Alexander P Gen, 1908, Ag 31,7:7
Stewart, Alfred K, 1947, My 28,25:2
Stewart, Alfred L, 1956, N 18,89:3
Stewart, Alonzo H, 1955, F 16,29:2
Stewart, Alva D, 1961, Je 29,33:5
Stewart, Andrew, 1872, Jl 17,1:6; 1938, Jl 6,23:4
Stewart, Andrew G, 1964, My 9,27:5
Stewart, Andrew M, 1942, S 25,21:4
Stewart, Angus, 1953, Ja 17,15:1
Stewart, Anita (funl, My 10,45:2), 1961, My 5,29:3
Stewart, Annie M Mrs, 1940, Mr 19,26:2
Stewart, Arch H, 1941, Ap 30,19:5
Stewart, Arch M Dr, 1916, Ja 13,11:3
Stewart, Archibald A, 1945, My 25,19:3
Stewart, Archibald K Mrs, 1965, Ja 23,25:5
Stewart, Arthur A A, 1940, O 4,23:1
Stewart, Arthur E, 1948, Ag 31,23:3
Stewart, Arthur L, 1961, Ag 18,21:4
Stewart, Arthur M, 1955, Ag 13,13:6
Stewart, Athole C, 1940, O 23,23:6
Stewart, Bayard M, 1944, My 17,19:6
Stewart, Bayard Mrs, 1944, Ap 24,19:5
Stewart, Belle K, 1950, Mr 16,32:4
Stewart, Bill (Wm J), 1964, F 19,39:4
Stewart, Blanche P Mrs, 1952, Jl 26,13:6
Stewart, Bryce M, 1956, N 14,35:1
Stewart, Bryce M Mrs, 1967, F 22,29:2
Stewart, C A, 1952, O 2,29:5
Stewart, C B, 1881, Ja 5,1:5
Stewart, C S Rev, 1870, D 19,5:3
Stewart, Carl K, 1958, Je 28,17:6
Stewart, Cecil P, 1945, My 30,19:1
Stewart, Charles, 1946, D 7,21:5; 1949, S 2,17:3; 1959, Ag 10,27:6
Stewart, Charles A, 1953, Jl 8,27:4
Stewart, Charles A Jr, 1957, Ap 28,87:1
Stewart, Charles E, 1950, Jl 5,32:3; 1960, Ag 5,23:3
Stewart, Charles E Mrs, 1968, My 4,39:2
Stewart, Charles H, 1946, O 1,23:4; 1951, N 13,29:4
Stewart, Charles I, 1958, Ap 20,84:4
Stewart, Charles I Mrs, 1959, D 2,43:4
Stewart, Charles J, 1941, Ja 29,17:3
Stewart, Charles J Mrs, 1966, Ja 31,39:4
Stewart, Charles L, 1947, Mr 16,60:2
Stewart, Charles M 3d Mrs, 1960, Mr 21,29:5
Stewart, Charles Mrs, 1951, Jl 26,21:2; 1961, O 17,39:1
Stewart, Charles R, 1920, S 1,13:2
Stewart, Charles W, 1943, Mr 27,14:7
Stewart, Christine (Mrs R Magera), 1966, Je 17,45:3
Stewart, Clay H, 1953, My 23,15:4
Stewart, Colin C, 1944, Ja 23,37:3
Stewart, Cornelia M, 1886, O 26,1:3
Stewart, D, 1877, Jl 18,4:7
Stewart, D E (Danny), 1958, My 6,35:1
Stewart, David, 1952, F 17,84:3
Stewart, David C, 1937, Ja 25,19:5; 1944, Je 27,19:6
Stewart, David J, 1966, D 27,32:3
Stewart, David Samuel, 1916, Je 3,13:6
Stewart, David V, 1954, F 2,15:3
Stewart, De Lisle, 1941, F 10,20:2
Stewart, Don, 1954, S 7,25:4
Stewart, Donald F, 1945, O 31,23:3
Stewart, Donald G, 1957, Ag 4,81:2
Stewart, Dorothy S, 1954, Je 20,84:7
Stewart, Douglas R, 1939, F 3,15:4
Stewart, Duncan M, 1938, Mr 3,21:3; 1939, Ja 4,21:2
Stewart, Duncan Mrs, 1948, My 12,27:1; 1956, Mr 15, 31:5
Stewart, E, 1933, Mr 1,17:3; 1936, O 14,25:4
Stewart, Earl R Brig-Gen, 1923, My 2,19:2
Stewart, Edgar W, 1955, Ap 10,88:5
Stewart, Edward J, 1951, Je 7,33:3
Stewart, Edward M, 1955, D 17,23:6
Stewart, Edwin F Dr, 1955, F 13,86:4
Stewart, Edwin F Rev, 1955, My 28,15:1
Stewart, Eleanor, 1945, Je 19,19:1
Stewart, Eliza D Mrs, 1908, Ag 8,5:6
Stewart, Elizabeth Mrs, 1937, Jl 13,20:3
Stewart, Ellen, 1902, O 12,13:2
Stewart, Ellery V, 1953, O 11,88:5
Stewart, Elliott A Mrs, 1962, N 7,39:2
Stewart, Elsie R, 1937, Ag 26,21:4
Stewart, Eugene L, 1937, Mr 20,19:1
Stewart, Fenwick J, 1924, Ag 8,13:6
Stewart, Findley, 1965, Ap 11,92:4
Stewart, Frances D Mrs, 1957, N 3,89:2
Stewart, Francis B, 1961, N 29,41:1
Stewart, Francis E, 1941, F 21,19:2
Stewart, Francis E Mrs, 1938, Ja 22,18:1
Stewart, Francis J, 1962, Je 17,80:7
Stewart, Frank B, 1953, Ap 25,15:4
Stewart, Frank H, 1948, O 15,23:1
Stewart, Frank Y, 1947, Je 6,23:1
Stewart, Fred A, 1945, Je 6,21:2
Stewart, Fred C, 1946, Ap 27,17:1
Stewart, Fred De P, 1942, Jl 24,20:2
Stewart, Frederick, 1950, Mr 11,15:6
Stewart, Frederick F Capt, 1937, S 14,23:5
Stewart, Frederick M, 1958, S 6,17:3
Stewart, G B Mrs, 1903, Jl 4,7:6
Stewart, G B Rev, 1871, My 1,8:1
Stewart, G D, 1933, Mr 10,15:1
Stewart, G E, 1943, Jl 6,21:2
Stewart, George, 1955, Ap 21,29:1
Stewart, George C Bp (por), 1940, My 3,21:1
Stewart, George E, 1952, Mr 19,29:2
Stewart, George F, 1953, O 29,31:2
Stewart, George H Gen, 1903, N 23,7:3
Stewart, George L, 1945, My 9,23:3
Stewart, George M, 1944, My 27,15:5
Stewart, George Mrs, 1957, Jl 20,15:6
Stewart, George S Jr, 1949, D 27,24:2
Stewart, George T, 1940, Jl 26,17:2; 1951, Ja 20,15:3
Stewart, George W, 1940, Ja 26,17:2; 1956, Ag 18,17:3
Stewart, Gilbert H, 1957, Ag 5,19:2
Stewart, Glenn, 1957, N 6,35:3
Stewart, Gordon (por), 1937, Ja 28,25:1
Stewart, Graeme, 1905, Je 28,9:2
Stewart, Graham M, 1950, Ag 31,26:2
Stewart, Gustav L, 1941, D 7,76:1
Stewart, H Carleton, 1943, N 29,19:5
Stewart, Hal W, 1964, Ag 10,31:3
Stewart, Halley Sir, 1937, Ja 28,25:5
Stewart, Harold A, 1966, Mr 1,37:4
Stewart, Harold M, 1966, Ap 6,43:2
Stewart, Harold W, 1943, D 7,27:3
Stewart, Harry B, 1938, Ja 13,21:4; 1949, N 1,27:2
Stewart, Harry E, 1948, Ja 8,25:6
Stewart, Harry H, 1958, D 7,88:1
Stewart, Harry J Mrs, 1947, N 6,28:3
Stewart, Harvey R, 1942, Ag 16,44:7
Stewart, Helen (Mrs Wm W Morrison), 1961, My 7, 87:1
Stewart, Henry, 1942, Ap 1,21:1
Stewart, Henry J, 1951, Ag 9,21:5
Stewart, Henry M, 1961, D 9,27:3
Stewart, Henry W, 1951, S 25,29:3
Stewart, Herbert L, 1953, S 22,31:2
Stewart, Herbert W Mrs, 1940, Mr 10,49:2
Stewart, Horace G, 1957, D 26,19:4
Stewart, Horatio Seymour, 1908, Jl 13,7:6
Stewart, Houston Sir Vice-Adm, 1875, D 13,4:7
Stewart, Howard C, 1955, My 28,15:3
Stewart, Howard D (por), 1947, Ap 5,19:4
Stewart, Howard T, 1951, Ja 19,25:2
Stewart, Hugh H, 1954, Ag 1,84:4
Stewart, Hugh R Judge, 1921, Jl 26,15:5
Stewart, Isabel M, 1963, O 7,31:3
Stewart, J, 1878, F 28,4:7; 1929, Jl 2,27:3
Stewart, J A, 1926, D 18,17:1; 1928, N 2,25:5
Stewart, J B, 1934, S 28,23:1
Stewart, J E, 1949, O 28,23:4
Stewart, J M, 1880, O 8,2:5
Stewart, J Ross, 1940, Ag 23,15:4
Stewart, J W, 1938, S 25,38:7; 1943, Ap 26,19:3
Stewart, James, 1883, D 3,8:4; 1941, D 2,23:4; 1947, Ap 28,23:4
Stewart, James A, 1949, F 11,23:4; 1968, Mr 3,88:7
Stewart, James A Mrs, 1954, My 6,33:5
Stewart, James B Mrs, 1943, N 24,21:5
Stewart, James C (por), 1942, Ja 18,43:1
Stewart, James C, 1954, F 9,27:3
Stewart, James D Lt, 1919, Ag 16,7:4
Stewart, James F, 1904, Ja 22,9:5; 1943, O 1,19:1; 1949, D 6,32:2
Stewart, James F M, 1954, O 5,27:3
Stewart, James G, 1959, Ap 4,19:3
Stewart, James H, 1951, Je 5,31:1
Stewart, James M, 1955, F 13,87:2
Stewart, James Maj, 1905, Ap 23,9:5
Stewart, James N, 1950, N 24,36:3
Stewart, James R, 1944, My 22,19:6
Stewart, James S, 1938, O 20,23:1
Stewart, James T, 1946, D 31,17:5
Stewart, Jessie, 1958, Ag 30,15:5
Stewart, Jim, 1918, S 27,13:7
Stewart, John, 1874, D 20,5:7; 1945, Ag 23,23:3; 1948, D 6,25:4
Stewart, John A, 1922, O 9,15:6; 1959, Mr 17,33:1
Stewart, John A Jr, 1946, O 29,25:2
Stewart, John A Mrs, 1944, Jl 2,20:1; 1960, Ja 25,27:5
Stewart, John C, 1955, Mr 3,27:5
Stewart, John D, 1938, Ag 4,17:3; 1959, N 7,23:5
Stewart, John D Mrs, 1953, My 15,23:2
Stewart, John F, 1943, Mr 14,24:4
Stewart, John G, 1943, F 9,23:1; 1954, Ja 22,28:4
Stewart, John H, 1914, Mr 10,9:5; 1939, N 2,23:3; 1950, S 12,27:3
Stewart, John J, 1967, D 4,47:3
Stewart, John Jr, 1903, S 28,7:5
Stewart, John K, 1919, Je 28,9:4; 1941, N 30,69:3
Stewart, John L (por), 1940, Je 1,15:5
Stewart, John L, 1950, O 12,31:4; 1961, Jl 2,33:1
Stewart, John N, 1945, Ja 24,22:2
Stewart, John R, 1949, O 21,25:4; 1954, O 2,17:4
Stewart, John S, 1958, O 15,39:3
Stewart, John T, 1961, F 11,23:5
Stewart, John W, 1947, Ap 1,27:4; 1959, Ag 25,31:6
Stewart, John W Ex-Sen, 1915, O 30,13:7
Stewart, Johnston Jr, 1961, Ja 24,29:2
Stewart, Joseph A, 1943, S 17,22:2
Stewart, Joseph B Jr, 1949, N 12,15:3
Stewart, Joseph N, 1948, Mr 22,23:3
Stewart, Joseph W, 1954, N 26,29:2
Stewart, Joseph W A, 1947, Je 28,14:2
Stewart, Josephine I Mrs, 1941, F 13,19:4
Stewart, Karl W, 1957, My 21,35:2
Stewart, Katherine, 1949, Ja 26,25:2
Stewart, Katherine W (will, D 27,17:2), 1940, My 12,48:2
Stewart, Keith, 1914, My 21,11:5
Stewart, Kilton R, 1965, My 19,47:1
Stewart, L, 1927, O 16,31:1
Stewart, L H, 1940, Ap 23,24:3
Stewart, Lawrence R, 1940, N 26,23:4
Stewart, Lee, 1941, S 18,25:2
Stewart, Levi M, 1910, My 4,11:4
Stewart, Lewis B, 1948, D 2,29:3
Stewart, Lila A, 1937, Ja 29,19:4
Stewart, Lizabeth J Mrs, 1951, Ap 18,31:5
Stewart, Louis, 1940, D 1,60:1
Stewart, Lyman, 1923, S 29,7:2
Stewart, M B, 1934, Jl 4,15:3
Stewart, Maco, 1950, D 18,31:4
Stewart, Malcolm L, 1959, Ag 31,21:2
Stewart, Margaret G, 1945, N 27,23:1
Stewart, Margaret K, 1950, Jl 25,27:1
Stewart, Marian, 1947, Je 24,23:4
Stewart, Marion, 1940, Ap 6,17:3
Stewart, Marshall B, 1956, Jl 30,21:6
Stewart, Martha A Mrs, 1940, N 5,25:4
Stewart, Mary (Mrs R Sheldon), 1961, Ja 28,19:2
Stewart, Mary A Mrs (will), 1947, N 21,29:8
Stewart, Mary E, 1939, Ja 4,21:5
Stewart, Mary Mrs, 1937, Jl 10,16:1
Stewart, Matthew, 1944, Ja 4,17:2
Stewart, Matthew C, 1947, O 15,27:5
Stewart, Maud, 1885, My 26,8:4
Stewart, Morris A, 1961, O 17,39:4
Stewart, Murray, 1949, My 21,13:2
Stewart, N Coe Prof, 1921, Mr 1,13:5
Stewart, Nels, 1957, Ag 22,27:4
Stewart, O W, 1950, S 24,104:3
Stewart, Oliver W Dr, 1937, F 16,23:4
Stewart, Oliver W Mrs, 1945, F 2,19:1
Stewart, P H Mrs, 1933, Ja 31,17:1
Stewart, Patrick A, 1942, Ja 20,19:5
Stewart, Paul, 1925, Ap 10,19:5; 1941, Je 12,23:4
Stewart, Paul M, 1957, Ag 26,23:2
Stewart, Paul W, 1955, F 26,15:3
Stewart, Percy H, 1951, Jl 1,51:1
Stewart, Percy M, 1951, F 28,27:3
Stewart, Peter, 1941, S 11,23:2
Stewart, R G, 1881, O 30,9:3
Stewart, Ralph A Mrs, 1957, My 31,19:1
Stewart, Ralph H, 1939, Ja 1,25:1
Stewart, Ray M, 1964, Jl 1,35:4
Stewart, Rear Adm (funl, N 11,1:6), 1869, N 8,5:3
Stewart, Reid T, 1945, Ja 14,40:2
Stewart, Rex, 1967, S 11,45:4
Stewart, Richard F, 1939, S 3,19:2
Stewart, Robert, 1922, O 18,19:4; 1941, Ag 12,19:2
Stewart, Robert A, 1950, Ja 20,26:2
Stewart, Robert B, 1943, O 23,13:2; 1960, Ap 22,31:3
Stewart, Robert Bowman, 1960, Je 18,23:3
Stewart, Robert G, 1948, F 24,25:4; 1962, Je 11,31:3
Stewart, Robert J, 1961, S 19,35:1
Stewart, Robert J Jr, 1943, My 22,13:6
Stewart, Robert L, 1946, My 9,21:5
Stewart, Robert M, 1954, S 4,11:6
Stewart, Robert S, 1946, Jl 30,23:5
Stewart, Robert T, 1965, O 23,31:6
Stewart, Robert W (por), 1947, F 26,25:1
Stewart, Robert W (will), 1947, Mr 5,43:4
Stewart, Roger P (will, D 6,18:6), 1952, D 4,1:5
Stewart, Rolland M, 1963, Je 13,33:4
Stewart, Ronald, 1919, My 22,15:6
Stewart, Rowe, 1940, My 13,17:3
Stewart, Roy R, 1949, F 28,19:4
Stewart, Rudolph W, 1958, S 8,29:1
Stewart, Russell C, 1942, F 6,19:1
Stewart, Ruth D Mrs, 1938, N 23,21:3
Stewart, Ruth L, 1961, N 30,37:4
Stewart, S J, 1939, My 26,23:6
Stewart, S Lurman, 1947, N 21,28:2
Stewart, Sammy, 1960, Ag 7,85:2
Stewart, Samuel B, 1943, D 26,32:6
Stewart, Samuel C, 1939, Mr 31,21:5
Stewart, Samuel G, 1950, Ag 31,25:5
Stewart, Samuel J Jr Mrs, 1962, F 18,92:7
Stewart, Samuel M, 1951, Je 5,31:4
Stewart, Samuel T Mrs, 1946, Jl 20,13:6
Stewart, Samuel V, 1939, S 16,17:2
Stewart, Sarah A, 1947, Ap 30,26:3

Stewart, Seth Thayer, 1913, Ap 16,11:4
Stewart, Sheldon M, 1964, Je 20,25:6
Stewart, Spencer W, 1964, Je 24,37:3
Stewart, Susan B F Mrs, 1941, Je 23,18:2
Stewart, T, 1884, S 13,2:5
Stewart, T Bruen, 1902, S 21,7:5
Stewart, T Frank, 1946, S 17,7:4
Stewart, T S, 1878, O 26,8:2
Stewart, Thomas A Mrs, 1948, Ag 20,17:1
Stewart, Thomas B Mrs, 1950, Ag 3,23:1
Stewart, Thomas C, 1946, My 25,15:3
Stewart, Thomas D, 1958, F 7,21:3
Stewart, Thomas Douglas, 1915, Ag 21,7:6
Stewart, Thomas E, 1904, Ja 10,7:5
Stewart, Thomas J, 1917, S 12,11:5; 1940, O 7,18:2
Stewart, Thomas K, 1939, Ap 7,21:3
Stewart, Thomas M, 1952, F 29,23:4
Stewart, Thomas R, 1953, Je 25,27:6; 1961, N 23,31:1
Stewart, Thomas S, 1949, F 21,23:4
Stewart, Thomas W, 1968, D 29,52:1
Stewart, W A, 1938, F 12,15:5
Stewart, W E Jr, 1901, Mr 6,1:6
Stewart, W J, 1885, Ap 28,2:2
Stewart, W Plunket, 1948, D 24,17:1
Stewart, W Plunket Mrs, 1948, N 4,29:2
Stewart, W R, 1878, Ja 27,6:7; 1929, S 5,29:1
Stewart, Walter, 1942, My 8,21:2; 1958, N 19,37:2
Stewart, Walter D, 1959, Ja 28,31:5
Stewart, Walter Mrs, 1946, O 14,29:5
Stewart, Walter P Dr, 1937, Je 23,25:4
Stewart, Walter S, 1943, O 24,44:5
Stewart, Walter W (funl, Mr 9,86:8), 1958, Mr 7,23:1
Stewart, Wilfred, 1952, Ag 30,15:4
Stewart, William, 1937, Ap 28,23:2; 1953, D 24,15:4
Stewart, William A, 1937, S 20,11:1; 1953, Ap 11,17:2; 1966, Ja 22,29:1
Stewart, William A W, 1960, O 24,29:4
Stewart, William B, 1922, Ag 9,11:6; 1943, O 10,III, 4:1; 1947, O 24,23:2
Stewart, William D, 1942, N 2,21:4
Stewart, William E, 1948, S 2,23:3
Stewart, William G, 1941, Jl 19,13:6
Stewart, William H, 1946, Ag 21,27:2; 1949, Ap 30, 13:2; 1954, Ja 10,87:1; 1954, O 14,29:5; 1966, S 9, 45:5
Stewart, William H Mrs, 1959, Je 28,68:2
Stewart, William J, 1946, Je 27,21:4; 1947, My 3,17:3
Stewart, William J Jr, 1942, Ag 28,19:4
Stewart, William J Mrs, 1941, S 12,21:2
Stewart, William James, 1925, My 6,23:4
Stewart, William K, 1944, My 12,19:1; 1946, F 4,25:3
Stewart, William Kirkwood, 1953, F 28,17:3
Stewart, William L, 1952, Ag 11,15:7
Stewart, William L Jr, 1963, Ag 31,17:4
Stewart, William M, 1909, Ap 24,7:3; 1940, Mr 25,16:2
Stewart, William Mrs, 1949, D 28,32:4
Stewart, William R (por), 1942, Ja 11,45:2
Stewart, William R (por), 1945, Jl 3,13:3
Stewart, William R, 1948, Ja 14,25:4; 1948, My 6,25:3
Stewart, William S, 1952, Ag 14,23:2
Stewart, William Shaw Dr, 1903, N 26,2:4
Stewart, William T, 1962, O 2,39:4
Stewart, William W, 1942, Ap 2,21:2; 1948, Mr 30,23:4
Stewart, Winifred B, 1957, Ag 21,27:4
Stewart, Wood Mrs (lr), 1939, Mr 19,XI,6:6
Stewart, Woodford T Mrs, 1953, Ja 14,32:4
Stewart-Murray, James Lord (Duke of Atholl), 1957, My 9,31:1
Stewart-Murray, John James (Duke of Atholl), 1917, Ja 21,17:2
Stewart-Richardson, Robert M Mrs, 1943, N 15,19:4
Stewartson, Jerome H, 1951, Ja 8,17:3
Steyn, Colin F, 1959, Ap 24,27:4
Steyn, Martinus Mrs, 1955, Ja 4,21:4
Steyn, Martinus T, 1916, N 30,13:3
Steyskal, Anthony O, 1947, S 21,60:3
Sthamer, F, 1931, Jl 1,25:5
Stiansen, Erling, 1948, S 9,27:2
Stiassni, Ernest, 1962, My 22,38:1
Stiassny, Robert, 1943, O 25,15:3
Stiastny, L J, 1881, My 31,5:5
Stibal, Leona (Mrs E C Mills), 1960, N 26,21:4
Stibbs, Harry L, 1945, D 25,23:3
Stibbs, Oliver C, 1937, D 16,27:2
Stibbs, Pierre, 1967, F 5,27:1
Stibbs, Thomas C, 1942, Ag 19,19:2
Stibr, Joseph, 1951, N 15,29:5
Stich, Benjamin, 1942, Ag 12,19:3
Stich, Louis, 1960, O 1,19:3
Stichler, Asher D, 1952, D 24,17:4
Stichman, Herman T, 1967, S 2,22:4
Sticht, Frank H, 1950, Mr 29,29:1
Sticht, John L, 1943, My 25,23:2
Stick, Frank, 1966, N 14,41:6
Stickel, James P, 1940, Je 24,16:2
Stickel, Lester W, 1959, My 18,27:4
Stickel, William A, 1944, My 5,19:4
Stickel, William J, 1955, Jl 9,15:4
Stickelmaier, Henry C, 1951, Mr 10,13:5
Stickelman, Clifford C, 1943, S 17,21:1
Stickels, Byron C, 1956, Ag 14,25:5
Stickle, Charles W, 1941, Mr 9,40:5
Stickle, Frank B, 1941, Je 26,23:3
Stickle, Lina J Mrs, 1942, My 18,15:5
Stickle, Walter A, 1957, F 7,27:3
Stickler, J W, 1903, Ja 20,9:5
Stickles, Claire Hazard Mrs (Mrs Howard Stickles), 1968, F 12,53:5
Stickles, Frank A, 1950, Ja 11,23:2
Stickles, Robert O, 1961, Mr 30,29:4
Stickley, Gustave, 1942, Ap 22,24:2
Stickney, A B, 1916, Ag 10,9:3
Stickney, Albert, 1908, My 5,7:6; 1955, F 3,23:2
Stickney, Amos Brig-Gen, 1924, O 26,7:2
Stickney, Benjamin R, 1946, Ja 23,27:2
Stickney, Burnham C, 1937, Je 12,15:3
Stickney, Charles B, 1948, F 5,23:4
Stickney, Charles D, 1916, Mr 10,9:3
Stickney, Charles D Mrs, 1911, F 24,9:4
Stickney, Earle H, 1945, Je 9,13:4
Stickney, Edward P, 1950, Mr 29,29:2
Stickney, Emily A C Mrs, 1941, Mr 21,21:2
Stickney, Frederic A, 1952, Ap 4,33:6
Stickney, George E, 1950, Ap 30,102:6
Stickney, Henry A, 1958, N 28,30:4
Stickney, Henry H, 1962, Ag 22,34:5
Stickney, James E, 1944, Ag 29,17:1
Stickney, John E, 1938, Ag 30,17:2
Stickney, Joseph, 1903, D 22,9:5
Stickney, Joseph L, 1907, My 29,7:5
Stickney, Louis R, 1957, S 17,35:2
Stickney, Raymond D, 1967, Ja 22,76:5
Stickney, Richard C Col, 1952, D 15,25:2
Stickney, W W, 1932, D 16,19:1
Stickney, William Dr, 1924, D 3,11:3
Stickney, William R, 1916, My 9,11:5
Stidger, William L, 1949, Ag 8,15:5
Stidham, Melissa, 1957, Ap 11,31:1
Stidham, Tom E, 1964, Ja 30,29:5
Stidley, Leonard A, 1958, My 29,27:3
Stidworthy, Earl W Mrs, 1945, Ja 30,20:3
Stiebeling, Alfred H Dr, 1937, Jl 13,42:2
Stiedle, Joseph C, 1954, Jl 22,23:3
Stiefel, Adele L Mrs, 1943, F 18,23:5
Stiefel, Benjamin W, 1953, Ap 19,90:7
Stiefel, Carl J, 1946, O 29,25:1
Stiefel, Frederick A, 1949, D 27,23:5
Stiefel, Isaac, 1939, Ap 24,17:2
Stiefel, J K, 1903, Ag 25,7:6
Stiefel, Jacob, 1949, Mr 4,21:2
Stiefel, Otto A, 1943, Ap 10,17:2
Stiefel, Ralph C, 1938, Mr 17,21:6
Stiefel, Samuel H, 1958, N 22,21:4
Stiefel, Samuel Mrs, 1947, Jl 13,44:1
Stieff, Frederick P, 1964, Ja 27,23:2
Stiefler, Robert M, 1966, O 15,29:4
Stieg, Hermann M, 1962, My 5,27:1
Stiegler, Richard, 1967, Ap 12,42:7
Stiegler, William G, 1938, Ap 7,23:5
Stieglitz, Abraham, 1940, F 9,19:3
Stieglitz, Albert (will), 1938, S 27,24:2
Stieglitz, Alfred, 1946, Jl 14,38:1
Stieglitz, Clarence, 1952, Mr 13,29:1
Stieglitz, Edward J, 1958, Je 13,23:1
Stieglitz, Emmeline Mrs, 1953, S 21,25:5
Stieglitz, Hyman, 1959, Mr 13,26:8
Stieglitz, Leopold, 1956, O 8,27:2
Stieglitz, Marcel H, 1962, F 28,25:2
Stieglitz, William H, 1957, O 26,21:4
Stier, Albert A, 1965, N 18,47:5
Stier, Anna M Mrs, 1949, D 18,89:1
Stier, Conrad W, 1951, Jl 17,27:3
Stier, George P, 1964, Ja 2,28:1
Stier, Hugh D, 1964, F 5,35:4
Stier, J Henry, 1941, O 10,23:5
Stierer, Maurice Jr, 1961, Je 6,37:2
Stieri, Emanuele, 1959, S 27,86:2
Stiernstedt, Marika, 1954, O 27,29:2
Stiers, Frank A, 1943, Jl 8,19:2
Stifel, Edward W Sr, 1947, My 15,25:3
Stiff, Bertram, 1958, Ap 3,31:1
Stiff, John T, 1948, Je 29,23:1
Stiff, John T Mrs, 1948, Ja 29,23:2
Stiff, William D, 1904, Ja 30,9:5
Stifler, Francis C, 1962, N 29,37:1
Stifler, James M, 1949, Ap 8,25:4
Stifler, William W, 1954, D 3,27:2
Stigall, John B, 1942, Jl 8,23:3
Stiger, Augustus K, 1949, Je 26,60:4
Stiger, Charles W, 1942, Ap 24,17:5
Stiger, William Edwin, 1925, Ag 26,19:5
Stigers, Morton Mrs (Marie H), 1964, N 9,33:5
Stigler, Joseph S, 1949, Ag 27,13:5
Stigler, William G, 1952, Ag 22,21:1
Stiglitz, Andrew H, 1957, Ja 25,21:5
Stiles, Arthur, 1908, Ap 1,7:4; 1941, D 18,27:6
Stiles, Bert W, 1957, Ag 24,15:3
Stiles, Bruce, 1959, Jl 18,15:1
Stiles, Charles A, 1962, Ap 2,31:5
Stiles, Charles E, 1954, N 21,87:3
Stiles, Charles G, 1965, Je 10,36:3
Stiles, Charles M, 1944, Ja 29,13:4
Stiles, Charles P, 1941, Mr 18,23:3
Stiles, Charles W, 1941, Ja 25,15:1
Stiles, Corliss P, 1952, Mr 22,13:1
Stiles, Edith M, 1943, F 23,21:3
Stiles, Esmond, 1954, Jl 9,17:5
Stiles, Frank Gardiner, 1916, O 5,11:6
Stiles, Frank L, 1922, Je 10,11:5; 1944, F 4,16:2
Stiles, Frank L Mrs, 1957, Mr 30,19:5
Stiles, Franklin L, 1941, My 15,23:5
Stiles, G Warren, 1951, Ja 9,30:3
Stiles, Harold S, 1948, Je 14,23:4
Stiles, Harris S, 1950, F 12,33:3
Stiles, Harry L, 1961, Ja 2,25:4
Stiles, Henry Reed Dr, 1909, Ja 10,13:6
Stiles, Henry W, 1944, S 6,19:5
Stiles, Henry W Mrs, 1938, Je 5,45:1
Stiles, Herbert G Jr, 1949, Ag 30,27:1
Stiles, Howard R, 1937, Je 18,21:3
Stiles, James E, 1960, Ag 5,23:5
Stiles, James E Mrs, 1960, Ap 27,37:4
Stiles, James O, 1952, Je 22,69:1
Stiles, John A, 1958, N 30,87:1
Stiles, John W, 1947, Ag 21,23:5
Stiles, John W Mrs, 1946, Ja 18,19:4
Stiles, Joseph T, 1948, N 3,27:3
Stiles, Karl A Dr, 1968, My 17,47:2
Stiles, Kent B (trb lr, Mr 15,38:6), 1961, Mr 9,29:3
Stiles, Louis E, 1947, Ag 29,17:3
Stiles, Mark D (por), 1942, My 5,21:1
Stiles, Meredith N, 1937, Je 27,II,7:1
Stiles, Russell, 1951, Ag 1,23:3
Stiles, Samuel W Dr, 1937, Ap 13,25:3
Stiles, Simon, 1941, S 5,21:3
Stiles, Sumner B, 1938, N 20,38:8
Stiles, T Beveridge, 1951, Ja 27,13:4
Stiles, Thomas W, 1941, Mr 29,15:6
Stiles, Vernon, 1947, D 12,28:2
Stiles, W A, 1897, O 7,5:3
Stiles, William B, 1949, O 19,29:2
Stiles, William C I, 1945, F 7,21:4
Stiles, William Curtis Rev, 1916, N 30,13:3
Stiles, William Curtis Rev Dr, 1911, Ag 16,7:6
Stiles, William H, 1942, My 24,43:1
Stiles, William R Mrs, 1950, N 7,27:6
Stilgenbauer, George H, 1952, Ja 15,27:2
Stilgoe, Thomas, 1938, Ag 3,19:4
Stilinovich, Marian, 1959, D 8,45:4
Still, A T Dr, 1917, D 13,13:4
Still, Alanson S, 1942, Ap 9,19:3
Still, Benjamin F, 1949, S 14,31:3
Still, Charles, 1955, Jl 8,23:1
Still, Charles E (por), 1949, Je 22,31:4
Still, Cora, 1946, N 26,29:4
Still, Frederic, 1941, Jl 1,23:3
Still, Frederick R, 1940, F 16,19:4
Still, George W, 1938, Je 16,23:5
Still, John A, 1923, N 13,21:4
Still, Nelson H, 1943, Ap 9,21:4
Still, Pauline D Mrs, 1950, S 3,38:5
Still, Robert S, 1953, Je 15,29:4
Still, Sidney A, 1949, O 26,27:5
Still, Timothy (funl, Jl 19,35:3), 1968, Jl 15,31:2
Still, William (Freedman), 1902, Jl 15,2:6
Stille, F Carroll, 1958, My 29,27:3
Stille, Julius L, 1947, Mr 11,27:2
Stilley, George, 1947, Jl 2,23:3
Stilley, Ken, 1968, Mr 24,92:8
Stillgebauer, Harry J, 1949, Mr 13,76:6
Stillger, Walter F, 1951, N 11,89:5
Stillhamer, William H, 1954, Ap 21,29:3
Stillings, Charles E, 1962, Je 26,33:4
Stillings, Kemp, 1967, My 2,47:2
Stillings, William E (funl, Jl 16,9:5), 1911, Jl 14,7:5
Stillman, Albert L, 1959, F 8,86:1
Stillman, Amos B (funl, Jl 12,13:4), 1921, Jl 10,22:4
Stillman, C, 1933, N 17,19:1
Stillman, C C, 1926, Ag 17,1:7
Stillman, C O, 1933, N 19,34:2
Stillman, Charles A, 1906, Ja 22,7:6; 1941, S 7,50:1
Stillman, Charles C, 1952, Ja 7,19:1
Stillman, Charles Chauncey, 1925, S 25,21:6
Stillman, Charlotte R (will), 1954, D 23,19:1
Stillman, Clara E Mrs, 1959, F 26,31:3
Stillman, David B, 1963, Ap 26,35:5
Stillman, Donald, 1949, Ap 21,25:2
Stillman, E W, 1942, S 8,23:5
Stillman, Edgar, 1967, Ag 26,28:3
Stillman, Edgar Mrs, 1967, O 31,49:3
Stillman, Emma P Mrs, 1938, D 18,49:2
Stillman, Ernest G, 1949, D 17,17:1
Stillman, Ernest G Mrs, 1950, Ag 23,29:1
Stillman, Francis H, 1912, F 19,9:6
Stillman, Franklin W, 1924, F 1,17:4
Stillman, Frederick D, 1951, Jl 25,23:5
Stillman, George L, 1938, O 15,17:6
Stillman, George S, 1964, S 9,43:3
Stillman, George Schley, 1907, Mr 16,9:5
Stillman, James, 1918, Mr 19,11:3
Stillman, James A, 1944, Ja 14,19:5
Stillman, James A (will), 1944, F 12,28:8
Stillman, James A Mrs, 1951, Je 11,25:1
Stillman, James Mrs, 1925, N 30,19:3; 1925, D 1,25:5
Stillman, John Maxson Dr, 1923, D 14,21:5
Stillman, Joseph F Mrs, 1952, Ag 14,23:4
Stillman, Kamaka Mrs, 1924, Jl 27,23:4
Stillman, King, 1944, D 21,21:5
Stillman, Lisa (lr), 1946, F 27,24:6

Stillman, Louis B, 1964, O 9,39:4
Stillman, Marie Mrs, 1957, Ja 29,31:1
Stillman, Phil T, 1939, O 16,19:5
Stillman, Phillip T Mrs, 1945, Ap 10,19:2
Stillman, Ralph G, 1950, N 18,15:4
Stillman, Regina L Mrs, 1961, Ag 4,21:3
Stillman, Thomas B, 1948, S 29,29:4
Stillman, Thomas Bliss Prof, 1915, Ag 11,9:3
Stillman, Thomas E, 1906, S 5,9:5
Stillman, W J, 1901, Jl 9,7:6
Stillman, Walter, 1937, Mr 21,II,8:7
Stillman, Walter Mrs, 1946, N 24,79:4
Stillman, Walter N, 1956, Ja 7,17:3
Stillman, William, 1952, N 27,31:2
Stillman, William M (por), 1937, Mr 3,24:1
Stillman, William O Dr, 1924, Mr 16,23:2
Stillpass, John, 1955, Je 17,23:2
Stillson, J B, 1880, D 27,5:6
Stillson, L B, 1883, S 17,5:5
Stillwell, Addison, 1942, Mr 22,48:5
Stillwell, Arthur L, 1958, Ag 4,21:4
Stillwell, Charles, 1939, Mr 31,21:2
Stillwell, Charles Mrs, 1947, S 28,60:5
Stillwell, Charles R (will), 1954, N 14,119:4
Stillwell, Eugenie, 1942, F 28,17:5
Stillwell, Fletcher, 1952, F 26,27:3
Stillwell, Frederick W, 1948, Mr 10,27:2
Stillwell, G W Col, 1901, D 10,9:4
Stillwell, Harry C, 1943, Je 17,21:5
Stillwell, J J, 1884, D 16,2:6
Stillwell, John L, 1943, D 2,27:3
Stillwell, Lewis B (por), 1941, Ja 20,17:1
Stillwell, Lewis B Mrs, 1960, F 16,37:4
Stillwell, Peter, 1942, Mr 11,19:3
Stillwell, R E, 1885, Mr 24,2:5
Stillwell, Richard Mrs, 1957, Ap 9,33:1
Stillwell, Roy P, 1941, Jl 29,15:5
Stillwell, Staats C, 1942, Ja 18,44:1
Stillwell, Wellesley H, 1951, Ja 1,17:5
Stillwill, Clarence L, 1955, Ja 12,27:1
Stilson, Colby, 1966, Jl 5,37:1
Stilson, Earl N, 1940, Ag 26,15:5
Stilson, Florence C Mrs, 1940, O 1,23:5
Stilson, Palmer H, 1942, Mr 3,23:1
Stilwagen, Stephen W, 1951, Mr 11,94:4
Stilwell, A E, 1928, S 27,29:2
Stilwell, Abner J, 1962, Ja 21,88:6
Stilwell, Albert, 1947, Je 19,21:5
Stilwell, Clifford S, 1941, N 20,27:4
Stilwell, Clyde S, 1950, Ap 21,24:4
Stilwell, Clyde S Mrs, 1953, S 3,21:1
Stilwell, Frank W (Bob Mills), 1968, F 7,47:3
Stilwell, Harry E, 1942, O 31,15:5
Stilwell, John, 1963, Jl 27,17:3
Stilwell, John Mrs, 1958, Jl 15,25:4
Stilwell, Joseph W, 1946, O 13,1:4
Stilwell, Lewis D, 1963, Ap 6,19:6
Stilwell, Mary A P Mrs, 1942, Je 23,19:3
Stilwell, Mary D Mrs, 1925, N 15,13:1
Stilwell, Richard E, 1947, Ja 3,21:1
Stilwell, Sidney W, 1947, F 22,13:4
Stilwell, Smith, 1881, Ja 21,5:1
Stilwell, Stephen J, 1942, Ap 22,16:2
Stilwell, T K P, 1942, Ja 12,15:5
Stilwill, Augustus H, 1955, Ja 8,13:4
Stilz, Joseph, 1957, O 8,35:1
Stilz, Wallace C, 1961, My 14,86:4
Stimer, David, 1966, Mr 4,33:4
Stimis, Chris, 1903, Je 4,9:6
Stimmel, Walter S, 1948, N 16,29:3
Stimmell, Jean G, 1944, N 30,23:6
Stimming, C, 1931, N 8,II,7:1
Stimpson, Fred H, 1873, D 15,1:4
Stimpson, George, 1952, S 28,78:2
Stimpson, Harold W, 1943, S 13,19:5
Stimpson, Harry F, 1941, D 11,27:4
Stimpson, Lydia C Mrs, 1941, O 6,17:4
Stimpson, Mary S Mrs, 1939, N 7,28:3
Stimpson, Wallace I, 1939, N 22,24:8
Stimson, Alice B Mrs (por), 1937, O 29,21:1
Stimson, Bernard N, 1954, Je 28,19:5
Stimson, Boudinot, 1940, Je 29,15:4
Stimson, Candace C (will, F 22,19:1), 1944, F 10,15:1
Stimson, Candace C (will), 1945, D 6,25:2
Stimson, Daniel MacMartin Dr, 1922, F 21,17:3
Stimson, Frank T, 1909, F 14,11:6
Stimson, Frederic J (por), 1943, N 21,57:1
Stimson, H A, 1936, Jl 19,II,7:3
Stimson, Harry P, 1920, Mr 4,11:5
Stimson, Henry B, 1948, Mr 3,24:3
Stimson, Henry C, 1908, Jl 17,7:5
Stimson, Henry L, 1950, O 21,1:2
Stimson, Henry L Mrs, 1955, D 4,89:1
Stimson, Herbert, 1964, S 7,19:6
Stimson, John F, 1958, N 1,19:4
Stimson, Joseph J Mrs (por), 1940, N 17,50:3
Stimson, Julia C (por), 1948, O 1,26:3
Stimson, Lewis Atterbury Dr, 1917, S 18,9:6
Stimson, Margaret, 1916, D 22,9:3
Stinchcomb, Harry W, 1956, Jl 10,31:2
Stinchcomb, James, 1945, Jl 15,15:6
Stinchcomb, William A, 1959, Ja 18,88:2
Stinchfield, Frederick H, 1950, Ja 17,27:3
Stindberg, Auguste, 1912, My 15,11:4
Stine, Albert E, 1960, Jl 21,27:2
Stine, Charles C Mrs, 1955, S 27,35:4
Stine, Charles M, 1954, My 29,15:6
Stine, Consuelo Mrs, 1940, F 22,23:1
Stine, John R, 1939, N 9,23:4
Stine, W M, 1934, Jl 5,18:4
Stine, W Vigil, 1965, F 23,33:5
Stine, Walter R, 1949, Jl 4,13:4
Stine, Walter W, 1955, Je 2,29:5
Stiner, J H Judge, 1902, S 21,7:7
Stiner, Jacob (funl, Ja 16,8:3), 1874, Ja 14,1:1
Stiner, Jacob Daughter of (funl, Ja 16,8:3), 1874, Ja 14,1:1
Stiner, Jacob Mrs (funl, Ja 16,8:3), 1874, Ja 14,1:1
Stiner, John S, 1949, My 24,27:1
Stiner, Max, 1904, Je 1,9:6
Stiner, Oscar, 1919, Ap 22,17:4
Stiner, S, 1884, Je 27,5:4
Stiness, John Henry Ex-Justice, 1913, S 7,II,13:5
Stinger, Philip, 1943, F 7,48:1
Stingo, John R (J A Macdonald), 1964, N 6,37:1
Stinnes, Adeline Mrs, 1925, Mr 11,21:4
Stinson, Alfred, 1939, N 25,17:1
Stinson, Arthur F, 1961, N 20,31:3
Stinson, Charles A, 1939, My 9,23:3
Stinson, Col, 1866, Mr 1,4:7
Stinson, Frank T, 1945, D 16,40:5
Stinson, Harry C, 1947, O 4,17:5
Stinson, John T, 1958, Je 22,29:2
Stinson, John W, 1957, My 30,19:3
Stinson, Richard E Mrs, 1940, N 2,15:1
Stinson, Roy A, 1948, Mr 15,23:2
Stinson, Thomas Mrs, 1949, My 24,27:1
Stinson, William J, 1950, Ja 31,24:4
Stinson, William S, 1940, Je 4,23:5
Stipe, John H, 1950, My 28,44:4
Stirbey, Barbu Prince, 1946, Mr 25,26:2
Stires, Ernest M, 1951, F 13,31:1
Stires, Ernest M Mrs, 1955, D 7,39:2
Stires, Manning 2d, 1962, Jl 22,64:5
Stirling, Alex W, 1943, Ag 18,19:3
Stirling, Antoinette, 1904, Ja 11,7:5
Stirling, Charles B, 1945, F 3,11:5
Stirling, E Mrs (Lady Gregory), 1895, D 31,5:4
Stirling, Edmund, 1948, N 24,23:2
Stirling, Edward R Sr, 1949, D 25,26:4
Stirling, Gordon Sheffield Capt, 1917, Ja 14,19:3
Stirling, Grote, 1953, Ja 19,23:2
Stirling, Norman W Sr, 1950, O 16,27:4
Stirling, Robert F Mrs, 1941, S 1,15:5
Stirling, Thomas H, 1952, My 3,21:2
Stirling, W Edward, 1948, Ja 14,25:4
Stirling, William, 1881, Jl 13,5:4
Stirling, Yates Jr, 1948, Ja 28,23:1
Stirling-Maxwell, W Sir, 1878, Ja 17,4:6
Stirn, Ferdinand Roebling, 1968, N 5,44:4
Stirn, Louis A, 1962, Mr 8,31:5
Stirn, Louis A Mrs, 1943, O 30,15:5
Stirnweiss, George (funl, S 20,19:5), 1958, S 17,30:6
Stirrat, David H, 1945, Ja 28,38:4
Stirrup, Frank A Sr, 1964, O 11,89:2
Stirton, John, 1944, O 11,21:4
Stitch, Nathaniel I, 1968, Ja 4,34:3
Stitch, Rudell, 1960, Je 6,14:2
Stitch, Thomas, 1950, O 2,25:4
Stiteler, Allen M F, 1942, F 13,22:2
Stites, Edgar Page, 1921, Ja 9,23:2
Stites, John, 1938, D 2,23:2
Stites, Joseph, 1948, Ag 24,23:2
Stites, Sells, 1951, Ja 22,17:1
Stith, Van B, 1963, Jl 4,17:3
Stitt, Adelaide F Mrs, 1944, Je 19,19:5
Stitt, David, 1949, Mr 31,25:6
Stitt, E W, 1927, Jl 15,17:1
Stitt, Edward W Jr Mrs, 1957, Je 6,31:2
Stitt, George Folsom, 1915, My 11,15:5
Stitt, Helen S, 1939, Ag 12,13:4
Stitt, Henry J, 1937, My 26,25:2
Stitt, Herbert D, 1943, F 20,13:4
Stitt, James Alexander, 1925, Ag 2,5:4
Stitt, Jesse W Mrs, 1959, Je 3,35:5
Stitt, Phil H, 1961, Je 17,21:6
Stitt, Theodore, 1952, Ag 24,89:3
Stitt, William C Dr, 1904, Ja 4,9:6
Stitzel, Frederick, 1924, S 19,23:5
Stitzel, Herbert H Mrs, 1952, D 16,31:5
Stitzel, Melville J, 1953, Ja 2,15:3
Stitzer, James A G, 1948, Mr 20,13:1
Stitzer, Louis, 1946, S 22,63:1
Stitzer, Sibyl M, 1949, Mr 30,25:5
Stiven, Frederic B, 1947, Ja 22,23:2
Stiver, Charles W, 1941, D 19,25:6
Stivers, Alonzo G, 1949, Je 17,23:5
Stivers, Culver, 1955, S 7,33:8
Stivers, Edwin J Maj, 1921, F 7,11:5
Stivers, Elmer E, 1955, S 10,17:5
Stivers, Fred E, 1937, D 8,25:1
Stivers, George L Mrs, 1957, My 16,31:2
Stivers, John D Mrs, 1951, O 29,23:1
Stivers, John R Dr, 1913, S 19,9:4
Stivers, Schuyler C, 1953, Ap 18,19:5
Stix, Charles A, 1916, S 6,9:4
Stix, Ernest W, 1955, S 30,25:3
Stix, Henry, 1908, S 21,7:6
Stix, Henry A, 1957, N 26,30:1
Stix, Otto L, 1942, N 18,25:6
Stix, Sylvan L, 1960, S 2,23:1
Stix, Walter H, 1963, Je 4,39:3
Stixrud, Thomas T, 1942, D 31,15:5
Stixt, William M, 1954, Ja 23,13:3
Stjernsward, Carl Mrs, 1941, Mr 12,21:4
Stnekoo, Anna (Mrs Hy VanRiper Scheel), 1968, My 30,25:3
Stobbs, George R, 1966, D 24,19:4
Stober, George W, 1950, N 4,17:5
Stober, J A, 1910, Ja 11,9:5
Stobie, Robert H, 1940, Mr 15,23:1
Stobo, A, 1878, D 7,2:4
Stock, Alex, 1942, Mr 19,21:4; 1953, S 16,33:2; 1961, Ja 2,25:1
Stock, Alvin M, 1959, My 30,17:6
Stock, Archie F, 1942, O 21,21:6
Stock, Archie F Mrs, 1959, Ag 15,17:1
Stock, Bane, 1961, Je 23,29:3
Stock, Bernard A, 1952, My 30,15:4
Stock, Chester, 1950, D 8,30:4
Stock, Fred, 1950, S 15,25:2
Stock, Fred J, 1945, F 26,19:1
Stock, George E, 1949, O 21,25:3
Stock, Harry T, 1958, Ag 31,56:6
Stock, Jacques F, 1947, Jl 24,21:5
Stock, John J, 1947, D 2,29:4
Stock, John P, 1952, N 14,23:2
Stock, Nicholas, 1938, Mr 18,19:3
Stock, P V, 1943, My 18,23:4
Stock, Richard W, 1951, O 10,30:7
Stock, Samuel, 1949, My 16,21:3
Stock, Wallace C, 1958, Ag 25,21:2
Stock, Wallace T, 1944, N 7,27:1
Stockard, Charles R (por), 1939, Ap 8,15:5
Stockard, Lester N, 1960, Ap 15,23:2
Stockbarger, Donald C, 1952, F 25,21:5
Stockbridge, Basil, 1951, Ja 28,76:3
Stockbridge, Carl W, 1942, D 22,26:2
Stockbridge, F B Sen, 1894, My 1,1:3
Stockbridge, Frank P (por), 1940, D 8,69:1
Stockbridge, Frank P Mrs, 1950, O 25,35:1
Stockbridge, George H, 1916, Ap 27,13:5
Stockbridge, Henry L, 1944, O 16,19:5
Stockbridge, Morton G, 1938, Jl 18,13:6
Stockbridge, Winfield Scott Mrs, 1923, D 3,17:3
Stockdale, Allen A, 1956, O 10,39:2
Stockdale, Charles, 1943, Ap 3,15:5
Stockdale, Frank, 1949, Ag 4,23:1
Stockdale, John H, 1965, Mr 4,31:1
Stockdale, Wallace J, 1940, Ja 5,20:4
Stockdale, William A, 1950, N 17,27:3
Stockdall, Bertha D Mrs, 1954, F 9,27:2
Stockder, Archiblad H, 1967, Jl 3,17:6
Stocke, Otto R, 1944, O 3,23:4
Stockel, Samuel, 1952, S 25,31:5
Stockelbach, Frits E E, 1948, Ap 27,25:4
Stockelberg, Charles, 1945, My 14,17:5
Stocker, Arthur B, 1945, Je 25,17:3
Stocker, Charles F, 1958, F 28,13:3
Stocker, Edward G, 1957, D 14,21:1
Stocker, Evelyn H, 1942, Jl 22,19:6
Stocker, Fred A, 1954, S 28,29:5
Stocker, Howard C, 1965, Ap 5,31:4
Stocker, Monroe J, 1951, Ap 4,29:3
Stocker, Robert Rear-Adm, 1937, My 4,25:2
Stocker, William A, 1966, O 5,47:1
Stockett, M Letitia, 1949, Mr 15,27:4
Stockett, Norman, 1943, D 1,21:4
Stockey, William F Sr, 1950, D 24,35:1
Stockfield, Betty, 1966, Ja 29,27:2
Stockfisch, Charles P Mrs, 1952, Ag 7,21:3
Stockfleth, Charles, 1940, F 22,23:2
Stockham, Alice Bunker Dr, 1912, D 4,13:4
Stockham, George T, 1950, Ag 26,13:5
Stockham, Thomas B, 1948, Je 6,72:5
Stockhammer, Nicholas J, 1956, Ag 27,19:6
Stockheim, Asher, 1960, Ap 29,31:2
Stockheimer, Arthur, 1943, S 16,21:2
Stockhoff, Walter W, 1968, Ap 4,47:1
Stockholm, Franklyn E, 1946, Ja 24,21:4
Stockholm, Frederick, 1909, S 3,9:5
Stocking, Frank H Mrs, 1947, S 10,27:3
Stocking, George Edward Mrs, 1921, Ap 24,22:4
Stocking, Harvey C, 1961, Ap 30,87:1
Stocking, J T, 1936, Ja 28,20:1
Stocking, Lucy M, 1942, Mr 3,24:3
Stocking, Thomas M, 1943, My 5,27:5
Stocking, Vaughn D, 1957, Jl 12,21:1
Stocking, Wilbur F, 1875, Jl 2,5:4
Stocking, Willard Y, 1963, Ag 1,27:4
Stocking, William R, 1942, Ja 23,19:4
Stockinger, George A, 1953, Jl 27,19:6
Stockinger, Minnie M Mrs, 1952, Ag 7,21:5
Stockinger, William, 1949, D 3,15:1
Stockley, James, 1954, Mr 6,15:4
Stockley, W F P, 1943, Ag 15,38:8
Stockly, Walter D, 1955, Mr 31,27:5
Stockman, Alfred M, 1938, N 12,15:5
Stockman, Carl O, 1940, D 28,15:5

Stockman, Frank J, 1955, Ap 19,31:4
Stockman, George H, 1957, F 9,19:5
Stockman, Henry, 1938, D 16,25:3
Stockman, Julius W Jr, 1963, S 14,25:1
Stockman, Lowell, 1962, Ag 11,17:5
Stockman, O S, 1946, D 7,21:3
Stockman, Robert Mrs, 1951, Mr 14,33:3
Stockman, S Sir, 1926, Je 4,23:3
Stockmeyer, Harry S, 1949, My 27,21:1
Stocks, J S, 1951, Jl 28,11:5
Stocks, John L, 1937, Je 14,23:2
Stockschlader, David (will), 1942, Je 23,21:7
Stockschlaeder, Mary Mrs, 1945, Ja 22,17:3
Stockslager, David S, 1956, My 5,19:6
Stockton, Alfred H, 1910, Ap 12,11:5
Stockton, Alfred H Mrs, 1910, Ap 12,11:5
Stockton, B, 1928, My 19,13:5
Stockton, Bayard Mrs, 1949, O 27,27:1
Stockton, Charles H Rear-Adm, 1924, Je 2,17:7
Stockton, Charles Stacey Dr, 1912, S 10,9:5
Stockton, Charles W, 1940, S 6,21:2
Stockton, Edward A Jr, 1948, Jl 14,24:2
Stockton, Edwin F Sir, 1939, F 5,27:4
Stockton, Elmer E, 1938, My 10,21:5
Stockton, Eric W, 1952, Ap 18,25:1
Stockton, Ernest L, 1954, N 5,21:3
Stockton, Frank R, 1902, Ap 21,9:3
Stockton, Frank R Mrs, 1906, N 20,9:6
Stockton, H Reeve, 1943, Ap 19,19:3
Stockton, Herbert K, 1939, Ja 3,18:2
Stockton, Isaac, 1941, N 25,25:4
Stockton, J D (see also N 5,7), 1877, N 8,5:2
Stockton, Jack P, 1953, N 18,31:2
Stockton, James L, 1942, Ja 7,19:5
Stockton, John L, 1953, S 9,29:4
Stockton, John Thor, 1923, Je 26,19:5
Stockton, Joseph D, 1960, N 15,39:2
Stockton, Joseph Gen, 1907, Mr 18,7:5
Stockton, Kenneth E, 1950, My 12,27:1
Stockton, Lawrence, 1918, Mr 28,11:8
Stockton, Lee F, 1957, Je 26,31:2
Stockton, Leila, 1938, Ap 21,19:4
Stockton, Mary H Mrs, 1938, Ja 14,23:5
Stockton, Miriam K Mrs, 1941, Je 2,17:6
Stockton, Mitchell M, 1938, O 21,23:3
Stockton, Phil (por), 1940, F 12,17:3
Stockton, Richard, 1876, Ap 6,4:6; 1952, My 2,25:4
Stockton, Richard 3d, 1944, F 10,15:5
Stockton, Richard 6th, 1961, N 15,43:5
Stockton, Robert F 3d Mrs, 1957, My 19,88:3
Stockton, Robert Field Commodore, 1866, O 9,1:5
Stockton, Sanford D, 1965, N 24,39:1
Stockton, Sarah A M Mrs, 1941, My 11,44:5
Stockton, William L, 1908, Ag 3,5:3
Stockton, William S Col, 1913, Ag 30,7:6
Stockweather, A Grant, 1938, Mr 11,19:1
Stockwell, Burt G, 1947, D 8,25:4
Stockwell, D W, 1912, My 19,II,15:5
Stockwell, Eleanor Louise Sister, 1909, My 8,7:4
Stockwell, F E, 1933, Je 22,19:4
Stockwell, Florence C Mrs, 1942, F 12,23:4
Stockwell, Frank C (por), 1946, D 30,19:3
Stockwell, Frederick E, 1949, Mr 1,25:3
Stockwell, Frederick E Mrs, 1951, Jl 9,25:2
Stockwell, Herbert G, 1937, Mr 6,17:2
Stockwell, John I, 1961, O 25,37:2
Stockwell, John Nelson Dr, 1920, My 19,11:5
Stockwell, Joseph F, 1943, Ja 29,19:3
Stockwell, Rupert K, 1944, Ag 26,11:6
Stockwell, S N, 1881, Ap 10,1:3
Stockwell, William R, 1961, Jl 30,69:2
Stockwell, William R Mrs (H L Cohen), 1957, Jl 20, 15:4
Stockwell Alden B, 1905, My 3,9:5
Stocky, Maria L Mrs, 1941, O 18,19:2
Stocton, Hannah E B Mrs, 1941, Ja 26,37:1
Stoddard, Alex J, 1965, O 19,43:4
Stoddard, Alfred B, 1957, S 18,33:5
Stoddard, Belle, 1950, D 14,35:4
Stoddard, Benjamin R, 1937, D 11,19:1
Stoddard, Bode M, 1941, Jl 17,19:3
Stoddard, C F, 1933, Ja 17,19:3
Stoddard, Charles A, 1946, F 18,21:3
Stoddard, Charles Augustus Dr, 1920, Je 4,13:3
Stoddard, Charles C, 1961, D 21,27:2
Stoddard, Charles F, 1958, My 1,31:3
Stoddard, Charles N Jr, 1967, N 18,37:4
Stoddard, Charles R, 1958, Mr 27,33:2
Stoddard, Charles W, 1909, Ap 25,11:5
Stoddard, Clifford I, 1951, D 1,13:3
Stoddard, E B Col, 1903, S 26,9:4
Stoddard, Edward L Mrs, 1943, Ag 7,11:3
Stoddard, Elijah Woodrow Rev Dr, 1913, O 31,11:6
Stoddard, Emma E L Mrs, 1937, Ag 11,23:5
Stoddard, Florence, 1903, Je 20,7:6
Stoddard, Francis R, 1957, O 13,86:1
Stoddard, Francis Russell, 1923, S 3,13:4
Stoddard, Frank K, 1937, F 13,13:5
Stoddard, Frederick L, 1940, F 25,38:5
Stoddard, George E, 1944, Jl 20,19:6
Stoddard, Henry, 1941, F 10,20:3
Stoddard, Henry B, 1953, My 22,27:1
Stoddard, Henry L, 1947, D 14,76:3
Stoddard, Henry L Mrs, 1951, Ag 26,77:1
Stoddard, Henry Mrs, 1952, Jl 7,21:4
Stoddard, J Morgan, 1948, Ja 19,23:5
Stoddard, J P, 1954, Mr 6,15:5
Stoddard, Jennie, 1954, F 25,31:2
Stoddard, John M, 1916, Mr 30,13:5
Stoddard, John Tapan Prof, 1919, D 10,13:1
Stoddard, John W, 1917, S 19,13:6
Stoddard, John W Mrs, 1945, Ja 9,19:3
Stoddard, Le Roy, 1943, Mr 20,15:3
Stoddard, Lincoln W, 1952, O 15,31:4
Stoddard, Lorimer, 1901, S 1,5:6
Stoddard, Louis E (por), 1948, Mr 10,27:1
Stoddard, Louis E, 1951, My 10,31:2
Stoddard, Louis E Mrs, 1945, F 23,17:5
Stoddard, Mayvilla Mrs, 1954, Je 27,69:2
Stoddard, Mortimer J Dr, 1953, F 24,25:5
Stoddard, Paul W, 1966, Jl 4,15:2
Stoddard, Percy D, 1957, Ap 20,17:4
Stoddard, R H, 1903, My 13,9:4
Stoddard, R H Mrs, 1902, Ag 2,9:3
Stoddard, Ralph, 1945, F 22,28:3
Stoddard, Ralph Mrs, 1943, F 13,11:1
Stoddard, Raymond R, 1949, Je 20,19:6
Stoddard, Reba, 1956, Ap 24,31:4
Stoddard, Robert, 1952, Ap 9,31:4
Stoddard, Sanford, 1952, Jl 12,13:4
Stoddard, Theodore L, 1950, My 2,29:2
Stoddard, W J, 1940, Ap 24,23:1
Stoddard, Wallace E, 1959, My 10,86:8
Stoddard, Warren J, 1944, Mr 13,15:4
Stoddard, William Mrs, 1949, Je 15,29:2
Stoddard, William O (funl), 1925, Ag 31,15:6
Stoddard, William O, 1965, F 1,23:4
Stoddart, Alex R, 1940, Ap 3,23:3
Stoddart, Arch P, 1939, D 20,25:4
Stoddart, Arthur W, 1944, Ja 20,19:3
Stoddart, George W Mrs, 1911, My 1,11:5
Stoddart, James, 1942, F 26,19:2
Stoddart, James Henry, 1907, D 10,9:5
Stoddart, John C, 1961, S 14,31:3
Stoddart, Joseph M, 1921, F 27,22:3
Stoddart, Molly, 1953, F 14,17:5
Stoddart, Samuel S, 1963, Ap 23,37:3
Stoddart, Walter E, 1940, Ja 1,23:2
Stoddart, William C, 1962, Jl 24,27:2
Stoddart, William L, 1940, O 3,25:2
Stoddartt, George B, 1925, Ap 18,15:5
Stodder, Anne B Mrs (will), 1942, N 4,28:3
Stodder, Frank F, 1942, Jl 15,19:4
Stodder, Louis N Capt, 1911, O 10,13:5
Stoddert, Robert B Mrs, 1949, Ag 6,17:3
Stodel, Andrew J, 1945, Jl 25,23:1
Stodolsky, Jacob, 1962, Ja 23,33:1
Stoebener, Harry W, 1946, My 12,44:2
Stoeber, Emmeran, 1945, D 25,23:6
Stoebling, Charles F, 1953, Ja 20,25:5
Stoeckel, Carl, 1925, N 2,23:6
Stoeckel, Christopher, 1954, Ja 26,27:1
Stoeckel, Ellen B Mrs, 1939, My 6,17:4
Stoeckel, Gustave Jacob, 1907, My 18,7:4
Stoeckel, H Fred Mrs, 1942, S 17,25:5
Stoeckel, Robbins B, 1951, O 16,31:1
Stoeckel, Robbins B Mrs, 1938, D 27,17:1
Stoecker, Adolf, 1909, F 9,7:5
Stoecker, Adolf Dr, 1909, F 9,7:5
Stoecker, Frederick, 1946, Je 7,19:5
Stoecker, Helene, 1943, F 26,20:2
Stoecker, Henry D, 1962, My 2,37:3
Stoecker, Leo J Mrs, 1960, My 17,37:1
Stoecker, Louis, 1958, Je 15,77:1
Stoecker, Magdalen, 1938, Jl 5,17:4
Stoeckle, Erwin R, 1938, Mr 16,23:5
Stoeffler, Charles W, 1967, O 21,31:3
Stoeffler, Henry W, 1943, Ag 5,15:4
Stoeger, Alexander F, 1945, Ag 24,19:3
Stoeher, Charles A, 1957, Jl 25,23:1
Stoehr, Edith A (por), 1946, Mr 7,25:5
Stoehr, Max W, 1953, S 30,31:5
Stoehr, Moriz, 1944, Ja 24,17:5
Stoehr, Ruth M, 1962, S 7,29:2
Stoelting, Hugh H, 1948, Je 15,27:3
Stoeltzing, Harry E, 1949, N 18,29:5
Stoenesco, Eustatiu, 1957, S 15,82:6
Stoer, Edmund M, 1948, N 9,27:1
Stoerm, William C, 1960, Ag 26,25:4
Stoermer, Carl F, 1957, Ag 14,25:1
Stoerzer, Charles H, 1949, D 26,29:2
Stoes, Paul H, 1955, Jl 24,65:3
Stoess, William C, 1953, S 27,85:7
Stoessel, Albert, 1943, My 13,1:2
Stoessel, Albert Mrs, 1957, Jl 6,15:1
Stoessel, Anatole M Gen, 1915, Ja 18,9:1
Stoesser, Henry, 1938, S 27,21:2
Stoesser, Raymond A, 1957, O 30,29:4
Stoessler, Karl, 1953, Ap 7,29:3
Stoetzner, Fridel, 1967, S 23,31:4
Stoever, Anne M Mrs, 1939, F 18,15:5
Stofel, Ernest, 1967, N 11,33:1
Stofer, Alfred J, 1938, Ja 8,15:2
Stofer, M Webster, 1950, Ap 20,29:5
Stoffel, Mary, 1944, Ja 26,19:5
Stoffer, Bryan S, 1961, Mr 20,29:1
Stoffer, David, 1960, O 24,29:2
Stoffer, Ross, 1954, Ja 24,85:1
Stoffers, Charles H, 1965, My 12,47:2
Stoffers, Herman Jr, 1946, Ja 1,28:3
Stofflet, Herbert M, 1959, F 20,25:2
Stofflet, James P, 1938, Ag 24,21:6
Stofflet, John E, 1944, Ja 15,13:2
Stoffregen, Carl H, 1951, D 21,27:3
Stofko, John T Sr, 1949, Je 1,31:3
Stofko, Michael Jr, 1952, Je 7,19:4
Stogsdall, Ralph, 1940, D 11,27:3
Stohl, John Sr, 1949, Mr 31,25:2
Stohldreier, Henry E, 1958, Je 23,23:3
Stohldrier, William C, 1954, Jl 15,27:2
Stohlman, Leroy G, 1956, Jl 5,25:3
Stohlman, W Frederick, 1966, Ja 20,35:4
Stohn, Emil, 1963, Je 8,25:5
Stohr, Frank H, 1949, Mr 30,25:1
Stohr, Richard J, 1967, D 21,37:3
Stohs, Eldon R Rev, 1968, Jl 7,33:2
Stoiber, Adolphus H, 1916, Mr 12,19:5
Stoiber, Frederick J, 1943, D 22,23:4
Stoil, Ted, 1967, D 26,33:3
Stoilof, Stoil, 1941, F 4,21:1
Stojka, Alexander, 1943, Je 15,21:5
Stojowski, Sigismond, 1946, N 6,23:1
Stokeley, W S, 1902, F 23,7:6
Stokely, John B, 1946, N 26,29:2
Stokely, Joseph Mrs, 1943, S 9,25:4
Stokely, Will B, 1945, My 27,26:2
Stoker, Bram, 1912, Ap 23,13:5
Stoker, Frederick, 1918, N 30,11:4
Stoker, Walter G Mrs, 1963, S 7,19:4
Stokes, Alfred A, 1939, Ag 11,15:5
Stokes, Alfred E, 1940, Je 27,23:5
Stokes, Anson P (mem ser set, Ag 16,17:5), 1958, Ag 15,21:4
Stokes, Anson P Mrs, 1962, My 26,25:4
Stokes, Anson Phelps (est appr, Ag 2,7:5), 1913, Je 29,5:6
Stokes, Arthur, 1940, N 1,25:5
Stokes, C F, 1931, O 30,23:3
Stokes, Caroline, 1909, Ap 28,9:4
Stokes, Charles, 1921, Ap 7,15:6
Stokes, Charles A, 1944, S 16,13:5
Stokes, Charles E Mrs, 1945, O 20,11:4
Stokes, Charles E Sr, 1946, D 26,25:3
Stokes, Clifford, 1944, My 20,15:5
Stokes, Dorys-Mary Mrs, 1954, N 3,29:2
Stokes, Earl B, 1945, Ap 30,19:1
Stokes, Edna W Mrs, 1952, S 8,21:5
Stokes, Edward C (por), 1942, N 5,25:1
Stokes, Edward H, 1912, N 6,15:4
Stokes, Edward L, 1964, N 9,33:4
Stokes, Edward S, 1958, F 2,86:4
Stokes, Ellen, 1960, My 30,17:5
Stokes, Ellen C Mrs, 1942, F 21,19:3
Stokes, Ellwood H Mrs, 1913, S 12,11:4
Stokes, Everard C, 1951, F 8,23:5
Stokes, Francis C Mrs, 1953, Ja 8,27:5
Stokes, Francis J, 1955, Ag 2,23:3
Stokes, Frank Mrs, 1951, Je 26,29:2
Stokes, Frank W, 1955, F 15,27:3
Stokes, Frederick A (por), 1939, N 17,21:1
Stokes, Frederick B, 1946, Je 9,40:4
Stokes, G G Sir, 1903, F 2,8:6
Stokes, George W, 1925, Je 25,21:6
Stokes, H C, 1903, My 25,9:6
Stokes, Helen O P, 1945, D 28,15:4
Stokes, Henry B, 1914, Ja 3,11:6
Stokes, Henry W, 1938, D 1,23:1
Stokes, Horace Sheldon Dr, 1924, D 20,15:5
Stokes, Horace W, 1950, Ja 19,27:5
Stokes, Howard G, 1963, S 22,87:1
Stokes, I N Phelps (por), 1944, D 19,21:1
Stokes, I N Phelps Mrs (will, Jl 16,17:6), 1937, Je 13,II,7:2
Stokes, Isaac N P Mrs, 1965, N 3,39:2
Stokes, J G Phelps, 1960, Ap 9,23:4
Stokes, J Stogdell, 1947, S 28,61:1
Stokes, James, 1881, Mr 10,8:1; 1881, Ag 3,5:4; 1918 O 5,13:4
Stokes, James B, 1955, N 4,29:2
Stokes, James Mrs, 1920, Ag 29,20:4
Stokes, James S Jr, 1937, S 5,II,6:4
Stokes, Jeremiah, 1954, N 1,27:5
Stokes, Jeremiah Mrs, 1966, My 1,88:4
Stokes, John C, 1937, D 10,25:4
Stokes, John Dunlap Rev, 1921, My 29,22:3
Stokes, John Gen, 1902, N 18,9:4
Stokes, John H, 1961, F 25,21:2
Stokes, John P, 1939, Ap 11,23:2
Stokes, John W, 1907, Ap 7,9:6; 1944, Ja 13,21:4; 1948, Ap 10,13:2; 1950, Jl 25,27:2
Stokes, John W Rev, 1937, N 12,21:4
Stokes, Joseph, 1947, Ap 8,28:2
Stokes, Joseph Mrs, 1955, F 15,27:2
Stokes, Louis J, 1949, F 10,27:4
Stokes, Marcus B Mrs, 1961, My 21,87:2
Stokes, Martin C, 1949, Ap 7,30:2
Stokes, Matilda G Mrs, 1911, Je 14,9:6
Stokes, Morgan G, 1949, O 25,27:2
Stokes, Morris Mrs, 1958, O 10,31:4

Stokes, N Newlin Dr, 1905, Ap 20,9:7
Stokes, Nicholas L, 1941, Ja 21,19:4
Stokes, R P, 1933, Je 21,17:1
Stokes, Richard L, 1957, Ag 2,19:3
Stokes, Richard R, 1957, Ag 4,81:1
Stokes, Robert J, 1938, O 21,23:6
Stokes, Robert T, 1908, Jl 30,5:4
Stokes, Solomon Mrs, 1945, My 6,38:1
Stokes, Stephen, 1948, Ag 15,60:3
Stokes, Sydney, 1953, N 7,17:2
Stokes, Thomas, 1915, S 8,13:6; 1920, O 10,22:2; 1952, Ag 28,23:4
Stokes, Thomas H, 1938, Jl 27,17:4
Stokes, Thomas L, 1950, S 4,17:5
Stokes, Thomas L Jr (funl, My 17,19:1), 1958, My 15,29:3
Stokes, Una P, 1940, F 19,17:4
Stokes, W Cheston, 1957, My 4,21:5
Stokes, W E D, 1926, My 20,25:1
Stokes, W Standley, 1948, Jl 21,23:5
Stokes, W Stanley Mrs, 1944, D 31,26:7
Stokes, Walter C, 1924, My 23,19:3
Stokes, Walter W, 1960, Mr 28,29:4
Stokes, Warren, 1968, F 22,32:6
Stokes, William, 1948, Jl 10,15:6
Stokes, William A Brig-Gen, 1923, Je 6,21:4
Stokes, William A Mrs, 1904, Ja 17,7:6
Stokes, William C, 1938, O 17,15:4
Stokey, Fred E, 1956, Jl 16,21:6
Stokke, Peter L (por), 1947, Ap 18,21:1
Stokley, Edward G, 1961, Mr 6,25:5
Stokley, John H, 1944, N 9,27:5
Stokley, Thomas P, 1950, Ja 5,26:7
Stokley, William B Jr, 1966, O 18,45:3
Stokowski, Olga S Mrs, 1948, My 18,23:1
Stokum, William F, 1952, Je 21,15:6
Stolba, Nestor W, 1951, D 27,21:5
Stolberg, Benjamin, 1951, Ja 22,17:5
Stolberg, Emil C, 1949, My 5,28:3
Stolberg, Margaret K H Mrs, 1941, Mr 22,15:5
Stolberg, Prince, 1903, Ja 28,2:4
Stoldt, John F, 1946, Ag 26,23:5
Stoleschnikoff, V K, 1908, Ja 31,7:5
Stolese, Frank P, 1964, Ag 27,33:4
Stolfi, Alex Mrs, 1953, O 5,27:6
Stoliar, Matias, 1951, Jl 16,21:5
Stoliarsky, Raphael G, 1960, My 31,31:2
Stoliker, Phil, 1948, Ja 26,19:3
Stoll, Abraham Jr, 1950, D 12,33:5
Stoll, Albert F, 1966, Je 27,35:3
Stoll, Bernard, 1964, Ap 21,33:3
Stoll, Charles C, 1943, S 6,17:2
Stoll, Charles T, 1938, D 12,19:5
Stoll, David Mrs, 1948, N 12,24:2
Stoll, Emile, 1951, Ap 2,25:5
Stoll, Ernest, 1957, My 21,35:5
Stoll, Frederick H, 1956, O 8,27:4
Stoll, George, 1961, S 17,87:1
Stoll, George M, 1964, Ag 5,33:4
Stoll, George M Mrs, 1957, Je 10,27:4
Stoll, George W, 1943, Mr 21,26:5
Stoll, Henry (por), 1943, D 7,27:1
Stoll, John G, 1959, Ag 27,27:5
Stoll, Julius W, 1937, Mr 9,23:5
Stoll, Karl L, 1951, D 19,31:5
Stoll, Karl W, 1939, D 12,27:2
Stoll, Lottie C Mrs, 1938, N 2,23:1
Stoll, Louis F, 1940, Ja 5,20:2
Stoll, Louis H, 1916, My 5,11:6
Stoll, Meyer, 1957, Ag 13,27:3
Stoll, Moses, 1949, Ja 1,13:3
Stoll, Oswald, 1942, Ja 10,18:1
Stoll, R P Mrs, 1946, F 6,23:3
Stoll, Richard C, 1949, Je 27,27:2
Stoll, S D Mrs, 1925, My 12,23:5
Stoll, William, 1907, O 28,9:5
Stolla, Otto, 1956, Ja 4,27:1
Stollberg, Agnes A Mrs, 1938, D 1,23:2
Stollberg, Charles (por), 1937, S 24,21:5
Stollberg, Robert L, 1957, Ap 22,25:3
Stolle, Edwin F, 1950, O 11,33:6
Stolle, John O, 1947, Mr 25,25:3
Stoller, Hugh M, 1947, N 18,29:5
Stoller, James, 1955, Je 6,27:4
Stoller, Morton J, 1963, Je 14,29:1
Stollmack, David J, 1950, D 17,84:4
Stollman, Abe Mrs, 1949, S 20,29:5
Stolls, Samuel D, 1950, O 25,35:3
Stolls, Samuel D Mrs, 1951, F 3,15:5
Stoloff, Benjamin, 1954, F 7,88:2
Stoloff, I Arthur, 1950, D 20,31:3
Stolpe, Hilda Eleanor, 1915, Ag 14,7:5
Stolpe, Moritz, 1938, Jl 17,26:6
Stolper, David B, 1960, Mr 13,86:3
Stolper, Gustav (por), 1947, D 28,40:1
Stolt, Andreas, 1944, Ag 8,17:5
Stolte, Harry J, 1947, Mr 26,25:4
Stolts, Julius W, 1924, Je 2,17:6
Stoltz, Frank L, 1945, S 8,15:2
Stoltz, James L, 1940, S 4,23:2
Stoltz, James L Mrs, 1944, F 5,15:3
Stoltz, Raymond E, 1952, Ag 9,13:3
Stolz, Alex Mrs, 1948, Mr 21,60:5
Stolz, Alexander, 1947, N 27,31:6
Stolz, August, 1957, Jl 24,25:1
Stolz, Benjamin, 1937, My 30,19:2
Stolz, Benjamin Mrs, 1955, D 1,35:1
Stolz, Henry J, 1938, Mr 17,21:2
Stolz, Joseph, 1941, F 8,15:6
Stolz, Joseph Mrs, 1953, Ja 12,27:2
Stolz, Karl R, 1943, Mr 31,19:2
Stolz, Leon, 1968, O 15,47:1
Stolz, Louis H, 1940, Mr 16,15:5
Stolz, Melville, 1938, Mr 10,21:1
Stolz, Robert K, 1967, Ap 9,92:7
Stolzenbach, Conrad, 1912, N 18,11:5
Stolzenberg, Jacob, 1963, D 2,37:5
Stolzenberger, Henry, 1952, Jl 27,57:2
Stolzman, Maurice, 1951, D 2,90:5
Stommel, Aug W, 1939, O 6,25:5
Stonaker, Cornelia V, 1940, F 18,43:6
Stonaker, Edwin R, 1937, Ja 19,23:2
Stonaker, Harry R, 1959, Ap 23,31:4
Stonaker, Voorhees, 1958, N 9,88:1
Stonaker, William H, 1960, N 7,35:4
Stone, A, 1931, Ap 23,25:4
Stone, A P, 1865, Ag 13,3:1
Stone, Abraham, 1959, Mr 27,35:2
Stone, Abraham Dr (funl, Jl 7,33:5), 1959, Jl 4,15:1
Stone, Ala M, 1953, F 7,15:5
Stone, Albert E, 1959, O 9,29:2
Stone, Albert G, 1949, Ap 6,29:5
Stone, Albert J, 1950, O 7,19:4
Stone, Albert Jr (will), 1959, O 7,30:1
Stone, Alice D Mrs, 1938, N 19,17:4
Stone, Allison, 1940, S 12,25:3
Stone, Andrew J Mrs, 1946, Ag 20,27:2
Stone, Annie, 1921, O 24,15:4
Stone, Archibald R, 1947, Ap 14,27:1
Stone, Archie W, 1946, Jl 25,21:3
Stone, Arnold, 1948, Jl 31,15:2
Stone, Arthur B, 1943, Je 9,21:4
Stone, Arthur D, 1937, Ap 27,23:5
Stone, Arthur F, 1944, S 3,26:7
Stone, Arthur K, 1952, Ag 1,17:2
Stone, Arthur P, 1943, Ap 21,25:3
Stone, Arthur T, 1940, S 6,21:1
Stone, Arthur W, 1949, Ap 1,25:3
Stone, Avery J, 1953, Ap 19,91:2
Stone, B S Lt-Col, 1878, D 17,5:2
Stone, Ben, 1962, S 14,31:4
Stone, Benjamin Bellows Grant Col, 1906, Ag 12,7:7
Stone, Benjamin C, 1953, Mr 10,29:4
Stone, Benjamin H, 1953, F 8,88:1
Stone, Benjamin Lady, 1914, Jl 7,9:6
Stone, Benjamin Sir, 1914, Jl 3,9:6
Stone, Berkley C, 1953, Mr 24,31:1
Stone, Bernard, 1942, F 23,21:4
Stone, Bernard M, 1937, Ja 5,23:3
Stone, Burtis A, 1920, D 13,15:4
Stone, C G F, 1954, Je 1,27:5
Stone, C Henry, 1943, Mr 25,21:2
Stone, C P Gen, 1887, Ja 25,5:4
Stone, Caleb, 1967, My 28,61:1
Stone, Calvin P, 1954, D 30,17:3
Stone, Carrie H Mrs, 1947, F 9,61:3
Stone, Charles A, 1940, N 4,19:4
Stone, Charles A (por), 1941, F 26,21:1
Stone, Charles A, 1944, Ag 16,19:2
Stone, Charles A Mrs, 1940, O 8,25:5
Stone, Charles C, 1951, Ja 1,17:2
Stone, Charles E, 1945, O 10,36:3; 1953, S 1,24:4; 1956, D 21,23:4
Stone, Charles F, 1910, Ap 29,9:6; 1910, My 11,9:5
Stone, Charles Francis Judge, 1910, Jl 26,7:6
Stone, Charles L, 1961, D 6,47:1; 1967, Ja 14,31:6
Stone, Charles T, 1942, Je 5,17:2
Stone, Charles W, 1912, Ag 17,9:6; 1938, F 4,21:5
Stone, Clarence D Mrs (J Dransfield), 1957, Jl 19, 19:2
Stone, Claude U, 1957, N 15,27:3
Stone, Clyde, 1948, Ja 15,23:3
Stone, Cornelia H, 1958, Ap 20,84:2
Stone, Cyrus Maynard, 1904, Ap 25,9:5
Stone, D Grace L (Mrs Wm T), 1964, Je 8,29:1
Stone, David, 1950, Ap 28,21:2
Stone, David M, 1895, Ap 3,2:5
Stone, Dwight C, 1956, Mr 3,19:4
Stone, E C, 1878, D 23,4:7
Stone, E M, 1927, D 15,29:5
Stone, Earle, 1943, S 16,21:1
Stone, Eaton, 1903, Ag 10,7:6
Stone, Edgar H, 1959, Jl 16,27:3
Stone, Edgar P Mrs, 1946, D 6,23:1
Stone, Edith C Mrs, 1941, My 10,15:4
Stone, Edward H, 1940, F 12,17:5
Stone, Edward R, 1939, F 19,39:4
Stone, Elihu D, 1952, Mr 23,92:2
Stone, Elijah Rev, 1904, Je 21,7:6
Stone, Eliza, 1939, O 11,30:3
Stone, Ellis S, 1956, F 27,23:4
Stone, Elmer E Mrs, 1943, Mr 9,23:3
Stone, Elsie W, 1946, Ja 5,13:1
Stone, Emerson L, 1953, Ja 12,27:6
Stone, Emma G, 1957, Jl 13,17:6
Stone, Everett E, 1943, My 27,25:5
Stone, Everett W, 1947, O 3,25:4
Stone, F Lee, 1960, Ag 3,29:5
Stone, Fenn O (will), 1941, O 1,17:7
Stone, Ferne Mrs, 1950, My 30,17:4
Stone, Ferris D, 1945, Je 20,23:2
Stone, Florence, 1950, Ag 27,89:3
Stone, Florence O Mrs, 1956, S 27,35:5
Stone, Floyd M, 1955, O 30,88:3
Stone, Francis L, 1946, Mr 12,25:3
Stone, Frank F, 1939, Ag 14,15:2
Stone, Frank R, 1921, O 5,17:4
Stone, Frank W, 1949, Ja 15,17:4
Stone, Franklin A, 1944, Mr 6,19:5
Stone, Franklyn M, 1961, O 18,43:1
Stone, Fred, 1951, Ag 29,16:3
Stone, Fred (funl, Mr 12,31:4), 1959, Mr 7,1:3
Stone, Fred L Mrs, 1962, S 17,31:1
Stone, Fred W, 1950, Mr 10,27:4
Stone, Frederick E, 1954, D 23,19:5
Stone, Frederick L, 1942, Ag 19,19:4
Stone, G Charles, 1946, F 23,13:5
Stone, G F, 1902, Ja 19,1:7
Stone, Galen L Mrs (will, Ag 7,20:4), 1945, Jl 30,19:3
Stone, George, 1939, Jl 11,19:4; 1961, Ag 24,29:4
Stone, George A, 1953, N 2,25:6
Stone, George C, 1941, O 30,23:1
Stone, George D Maj, 1913, N 10,9:3
Stone, George E, 1941, My 29,19:6; 1967, My 29,25:2
Stone, George G, 1961, Ag 16,31:4
Stone, George H Maj, 1913, N 13,11:5
Stone, George L F, 1955, Ja 22,11:4
Stone, George R, 1945, Ja 8,17:4
Stone, George W, 1965, Ja 18,35:1
Stone, Hannah M (por), 1941, Jl 11,15:4
Stone, Harlan F, 1946, Ap 23,1:2
Stone, Harlan F Mrs, 1958, N 25,33:2
Stone, Harold, 1946, Je 2,44:6
Stone, Harold B, 1955, O 4,35:4
Stone, Harry C, 1913, Mr 5,17:4
Stone, Harry Z, 1961, D 1,30:3
Stone, Henry A, 1956, F 7,31:6
Stone, Henry P, 1952, Je 5,31:4
Stone, Herbert, 1915, Je 1,15:6
Stone, Herbert K, 1945, Je 22,15:5
Stone, Herbert L, 1955, S 29,33:3
Stone, Herbert L Mrs, 1952, My 16,23:5
Stone, Herbert S Mrs, 1955, Je 12,86:5
Stone, Hope H, 1949, O 17,23:1
Stone, Horace M, 1944, Mr 8,19:6
Stone, Horace O, 1923, Ap 11,21:5
Stone, Horatio (see also S 22), 1875, S 24,4:6
Stone, Hubbard G, 1910, Ja 8,9:4
Stone, Hugh L, 1967, Mr 25,23:5
Stone, I Frank, 1920, My 6,11:3
Stone, Ira, 1950, S 20,31:3; 1968, N 7,47:2
Stone, Ira A, 1946, N 15,23:2
Stone, Irvin L, 1950, Ap 29,15:2
Stone, Irving I, 1948, O 25,23:4
Stone, Irving L, 1925, Jl 30,19:6
Stone, Isaac, 1905, Je 6,6:2
Stone, J O, 1876, Je 8,5:2
Stone, J S Rev, 1882, Ja 15,5:5
Stone, J Summer, 1938, F 19,15:2
Stone, Jacob C Mrs, 1962, Mr 13,35:2
Stone, James A, 1946, D 14,15:5
Stone, James C, 1949, D 4,109:1
Stone, James H, 1938, Jl 10,29:2
Stone, Jerry C, 1953, F 28,17:5
Stone, Jesse, 1902, My 12,9:6
Stone, Jesse I, 1945, Mr 9,19:1
Stone, John, 1961, Je 4,86:7
Stone, John A, 1962, Ap 29,29:2
Stone, John C, 1940, My 23,23:1
Stone, John G M Mrs, 1948, N 17,27:4
Stone, John H, 1948, Mr 18,27:2
Stone, John J, 1946, S 2,17:4; 1958, O 17,29:2
Stone, John Lt, 1919, Mr 28,13:2
Stone, John Mrs, 1946, Jl 23,25:2
Stone, John S, 1943, My 21,19:6
Stone, John T, 1954, Je 29,27:5
Stone, Joseph, 1957, Ap 13,19:5
Stone, Joseph E, 1952, F 8,23:2
Stone, Joseph Parker, 1919, F 27,11:2
Stone, Judson F, 1958, F 21,24:1
Stone, Julius F (por), 1947, Jl 27,44:4
Stone, Julius F Mrs, 1950, F 21,26:2
Stone, Kate, 1940, O 6,49:2
Stone, Kenneth F, 1952, Ap 6,88:3
Stone, Kent R, 1962, S 6,31:1
Stone, Kimbrough, 1958, Mr 1,17:5
Stone, L Mrs, 1932, F 12,21:3
Stone, L P, 1885, Ja 1,5:4
Stone, L T, 1933, Mr 14,15:3
Stone, Lauson, 1948, O 9,17:4
Stone, Lawrence J Mrs, 1962, S 13,37:4
Stone, Le Pine, 1950, Je 4,92:3
Stone, Leon, 1947, Ja 31,23:2
Stone, Leonard, 1966, Je 1,47:2
Stone, Lester A, 1967, Ag 13,80:6
Stone, Lester B (trb lr, Ap 10,14:7), 1954, Ap 6,30:4
Stone, Lewis, 1943, Ap 13,25:3; 1953, S 13,84:4
Stone, Lewis H, 1947, Ja 3,26:2
Stone, Lillian S Mrs, 1955, F 27,86:4

Stone, Louis, 1953, Ja 4,78:1
Stone, Louis A, 1961, Jl 12,32:1; 1967, Je 27,39:2
Stone, Louis H, 1953, Ap 18,19:4
Stone, Louis T, 1958, Ja 3,44:7
Stone, M E, 1929, F 16,1:3
Stone, Mamie R Mrs, 1958, Je 8,88:6
Stone, Marcus, 1921, Mr 26,13:6
Stone, Marie A Mrs, 1951, D 11,33:2
Stone, Martin V, 1939, F 20,17:4
Stone, Mary, 1954, D 31,13:5
Stone, Mary Grace, 1919, Je 26,9:2
Stone, Mason Albert Col, 1923, Jl 5,15:4
Stone, Mason S, 1940, Jl 14,31:4
Stone, Maud L Mrs, 1951, Ja 27,13:5
Stone, Maurice L, 1955, F 21,21:5
Stone, Medad E, 1946, Jl 25,21:4
Stone, Melville E Jr, 1918, Ja 4,11:5; 1918, Ja 5,9:2
Stone, Melville E Jr (funl), 1918, My 19,23:2
Stone, Meyer, 1948, Mr 20,13:3
Stone, Meyrick, 1952, D 12,29:2
Stone, Michael, 1965, My 14,37:1
Stone, Morris, 1968, Ja 19,44:3
Stone, Morris J, 1952, D 15,25:5
Stone, Nahum I, 1966, O 26,47:1
Stone, Nat, 1955, Mr 20,88:5
Stone, Nathan H, 1962, Ap 12,35:3
Stone, Naylor, 1959, Ap 26,86:6
Stone, Percy N Sr, 1959, Ap 11,21:5
Stone, Phil, 1967, F 22,29:2
Stone, R E, 1939, Je 6,23:5
Stone, Ralph, 1944, Jl 13,17:6; 1956, My 13,86:4
Stone, Ralph E, 1961, F 8,31:4
Stone, Ralph T, 1950, O 16,27:2
Stone, Ralph W, 1950, N 3,27:5
Stone, Raymond W, 1955, Mr 18,28:4
Stone, Robert, 1968, Je 6,48:8
Stone, Robert A, 1938, D 11,61:3
Stone, Robert B, 1945, Mr 12,19:2
Stone, Robert L Mrs, 1965, D 21,37:1
Stone, Robert R, 1962, F 21,45:2
Stone, Roy Gen, 1905, Ag 7,7:6
Stone, Roy Mrs, 1925, S 30,23:4
Stone, Russell E Dr, 1937, Je 20,II,7:1
Stone, S M, 1940, My 23,24:2
Stone, Samuel B, 1941, My 8,23:3
Stone, Samuel H Col, 1909, Ap 5,7:4
Stone, Samuel M, 1959, D 11,33:4
Stone, Shelton P Mrs, 1959, Ag 23,92:6
Stone, Silas W, 1940, Ag 17,15:2
Stone, Stephen, 1938, N 15,23:5
Stone, Thomas, 1939, My 21,III,6:8
Stone, Thomas A, 1965, Jl 27,33:1
Stone, Thomas A Mrs, 1961, O 25,37:2
Stone, Thomas C, 1940, My 23,24:2
Stone, Thomas L, 1945, Ja 18,19:2
Stone, Ulysses B, 1945, Ja 20,11:3
Stone, Virgil H Mrs, 1954, S 6,15:3
Stone, W Raymond, 1947, Ja 5,53:4
Stone, Wallace D, 1951, Ap 22,89:2
Stone, Wallace D Mrs, 1951, Ap 22,89:2
Stone, Walter B (ruled suicide, Mr 14,5:2), 1959, Mr 13,9:7
Stone, Walter K, 1949, Je 22,31:3
Stone, Walter P Mrs, 1945, F 6,19:1
Stone, Walter R, 1937, F 23,27:3
Stone, Walter R Mrs, 1948, D 1,29:5
Stone, Wilbur Fisk Ex-Justice, 1920, D 28,11:5
Stone, Wilbur M, 1941, D 22,17:2
Stone, William, 1941, F 22,15:5; 1958, O 27,27:3
Stone, William A Mrs, 1919, D 12,17:1; 1950, N 7,27:6
Stone, William Alexis Ex-Gov, 1920, Mr 2,11:3
Stone, William C, 1939, F 25,15:5
Stone, William E Jr, 1957, Jl 24,25:1
Stone, William G, 1944, Ap 13,19:6
Stone, William Joel (funl, Ap 18,13:8), 1918, Ap 15, 15:1
Stone, William Leete Col, 1908, Je 12,7:6
Stone, William M Dr, 1937, O 30,19:5
Stone, William N, 1937, Ag 2,19:4
Stone, William R, 1942, Ja 3,19:2
Stone, William R Dr, 1937, Ap 6,23:1
Stone, William S, 1946, Je 28,21:3
Stone, William S Gen, 1968, D 3,50:6
Stone, Witmer, 1939, My 25,25:2
Stoneall, Frederick R, 1959, Ja 1,31:1
Stoneback, Frank A, 1946, Ap 2,27:2
Stonebank, Truletta, 1915, D 12,19:3
Stonebreaker, Joseph R, 1903, O 26,7:6
Stonebridge, William G, 1937, My 29,17:3
Stoneburner, W Earl, 1954, F 12,25:3
Stoneham, C A, 1936, Ja 7,21:1
Stoneham, Charles A Mrs, 1951, F 21,27:2
Stoneham, E Harold, 1951, D 13,33:3
Stoneham, Horace A, 1950, Mr 28,31:2
Stoneham, Horace A Mrs, 1948, D 23,20:3
Stonehaven, Viscount (por), 1941, Ag 21,17:1
Stonehill, Ben, 1965, D 28,25:1
Stonehill, George, 1943, My 8,15:5
Stonehill, George Mrs, 1951, F 13,31:3
Stonehill, William M Rev Dr, 1908, F 7,7:6
Stonehouse, J B Gen, 1885, N 25,1:2
Stonehouse, Ned B, 1962, N 20,36:1
Stonehouse, Thomas, 1946, My 2,21:4

Stonelake, Charles A, 1941, D 2,23:2
Stoneman, Bertha, 1943, My 1,15:5
Stoneman, David, 1948, O 7,29:5
Stoneman, Earle J, 1950, Ja 9,25:6
Stoneman, Edgar A Mrs, 1951, N 23,29:3
Stoneman, Edwin C, 1958, Jl 27,60:8
Stoneman, Ernest V (Pop), 1968, Je 15,35:3
Stoneman, Frank B, 1941, F 2,44:3
Stoneman, Frank E, 1906, Je 28,1:6
Stoneman, James J, 1947, F 16,57:1
Stoneman, Kate, 1925, My 22,19:7
Stoneman, Lewis H, 1945, Ap 8,36:2
Stoneman, Louis, 1956, N 8,39:2
Stonemetz, Harry M, 1950, Jl 6,27:3
Stoner, C Birch Mrs, 1961, D 23,23:3
Stoner, Clarence, 1937, Ap 10,19:2
Stoner, Dayton, 1944, My 9,19:5
Stoner, Frank, 1965, My 13,37:3
Stoner, Harry, 1960, F 22,17:3
Stoner, James Buchanan Col, 1925, Jl 23,19:5
Stoner, John A, 1956, Je 24,77:1
Stoner, Lewis E, 1941, Jl 2,21:2
Stoner, Ralph F J Mrs (Lady Camoys), 1961, N 22, 33:1
Stoner, Raoul J, 1962, Ap 13,35:1
Stoner, Thurman W, 1942, My 21,19:4
Stoner, W Gordon, 1942, Ag 20,19:1
Stoner, Willard C, 1939, N 17,21:3
Stoner, William D, 1966, Ja 13,25:4
Stoner, William R, 1942, Ap 23,23:3
Stonesifer, J Ross, 1962, Ja 1,23:5
Stonesifer, J Ross Mrs, 1950, Jl 17,21:5
Stoneson, Ellis L, 1952, Ag 24,88:3
Stoneson, Henry, 1959, Ja 1,31:1
Stonestreet, Nicholas, 1943, F 12,19:4
Stonewski, John, 1962, N 7,39:4
Stoney, Alfred Bedle, 1907, Ja 24,9:5
Stoney, Frank B, 1947, Je 5,25:2
Stoney, Frank E A Dr, 1917, My 16,13:6
Stoney, Frank Mrs, 1917, Ja 14,19:3
Stoney, G Johnstone, 1911, Jl 6,9:4
Stoney, G M M Commander, 1905, My 1,2:2
Stong, Phil, 1957, Ag 27,19:3
Stong, Phil Mrs (Virginia), 1968, Ap 9,47:2
Stonier, Harold, 1957, Je 4,35:3
Stonier, J William, 1951, Ap 8,92:5
Stonington, Edgar H L, 1954, My 5,31:4
Stonner, G Marinus, 1941, Mr 30,49:1
Stonor, Edmund Rev, 1912, Mr 1,11:5
Stonor, Harry Sir, 1939, My 6,17:5
Stonor, Ralph Francis Julian (Lord Camoys), 1968, Ag 4,69:1
Stoody, Charles E, 1940, Je 24,15:6
Stookey, Byron, 1966, O 21,41:3
Stookey, Lyman D, 1940, F 16,19:3
Stoops, Herbert M, 1948, My 20,29:4
Stoops, John P, 1947, Je 10,27:5
Stoops, Todd, 1951, Jl 17,27:2
Stoothoff, Ella Mrs, 1940, Je 26,23:4
Stoothoff, Millard F, 1940, Je 19,23:5
Stopes, Marie C, 1958, O 3,29:1
Stopford, Harry B, 1940, Ja 6,13:4
Stopford, James R N (Earl of Courtown), 1957, Ja 26,3:1
Stopford, Lord (J S Bach), 1961, Mr 7,35:2
Stopher, Emmet C, 1948, Je 19,15:2
Stopher, William H, 1949, Mr 24,28:2
Stoppani, Charles F, 1941, Ja 19,40:7
Stoppani, Mario, 1959, S 22,35:3
Stoppione, Harry, 1960, N 24,29:4
Stoppione, Harry Mrs, 1960, N 24,29:4
Stoppleworth, Louis M, 1951, Ag 21,27:2
Stora, Raphael, 1963, Ag 23,25:5
Storandt, John W, 1923, Je 11,13:4
Storch, Alfons C, 1954, D 2,31:4
Storch, Charles C, 1947, Ag 8,17:5
Storch, Henry H, 1961, N 21,39:3
Storch, Nathan, 1957, N 29,29:2
Storch, Nathan Mrs, 1947, My 4,60:5
Storch, Samuel, 1947, Je 6,23:4
Storck, Arthur Mrs, 1947, My 18,60:5
Storck, Carl, 1950, Mr 14,25:2
Storck, Frank C, 1956, Ap 13,31:3
Storck, George H, 1943, Jl 29,19:5
Storck, Herman I, 1962, F 8,31:2
Storck, William A, 1945, S 5,23:4
Storcy, H K Mrs, 1873, Ja 22,1:6
Stordahl, Axel, 1963, Ag 31,17:6
Storer, Agnes C, 1943, S 5,28:6
Storer, Bellamy, 1922, N 14,19:5
Storer, Charles N, 1939, Ap 2,III,6:8
Storer, David A, 1966, F 6,92:6
Storer, David A Mrs, 1943, My 24,15:4
Storer, Francis E, 1943, Mr 24,23:1
Storer, Francis Humphreys Prof, 1914, Jl 31,9:5
Storer, Henry A Mrs, 1955, F 12,15:3
Storer, Horatio P Dr, 1922, S 19,19:4
Storer, James, 1951, Ap 2,25:4
Storer, Jane L Mrs, 1964, F 22,21:1
Storer, John H, 1946, S 10,7:4
Storer, Sarah Sherman Mrs, 1907, Jl 25,7:5
Storey, Arthur D, 1944, O 13,19:5
Storey, Elizabeth C, 1939, Mr 21,23:4

Storey, Fred G, 1937, O 24,II,8:3
Storey, George Adolphus, 1919, Jl 30,9:3
Storey, George F, 1941, D 17,27:5
Storey, Homer W, 1937, O 13,23:3
Storey, J Walker, 1956, Jl 6,21:4
Storey, John, 1921, O 6,17:6
Storey, John De R, 1957, Ap 18,29:1
Storey, John J, 1938, O 17,15:5
Storey, John S, 1955, Jl 4,11:5
Storey, Margaret, 1960, O 19,45:3
Storey, Robert Jr, 1962, Ap 20,27:3
Storey, Thomas A, 1943, O 29,19:2
Storey, Thomas J Mrs, 1950, Ag 18,21:4
Storey, W F, 1884, O 28,5:1
Storey, Walter R, 1953, N 27,27:1
Storey, William A, 1942, Ap 24,17:4
Storey, William B (por), 1940, O 25,21:1
Storey, William G, 1941, Ja 16,21:2
Storey, William H, 1954, D 23,19:5
Storey, William R, 1941, Mr 13,21:3
Storey, Williard M, 1949, S 11,95:3
Storfer, Adolf J, 1945, Ja 25,19:4
Storgoff, Florence Mrs, 1964, S 13,87:1
Storing, James A, 1967, F 11,29:3
Stork, Alex S A Mrs, 1948, Ap 8,25:3
Stork, Laura, 1940, My 24,19:4
Stork, Louis Mrs, 1947, S 17,25:3
Stork, Theophilus B (will, D 8,52:3), 1937, O 14,25:5
Stork, Wilford L, 1962, O 7,82:8
Storke, Arthur D, 1949, S 10,1:2
Storke, Harold G, 1961, Ap 30,86:7
Storke, Murray M, 1938, Ag 16,19:3
Storke, Murray W Mrs, 1945, Ap 4,21:4
Storks, Henry K Sir, 1874, S 10,3:6
Storm, Annie B Mrs, 1937, S 12,II,7:4
Storm, Ashley V, 1943, O 28,23:2
Storm, Clarence, 1915, Mr 25,11:5
Storm, Cornelia V, 1939, O 29,40:5
Storm, Edward, 1950, S 24,106:2
Storm, Fred, 1939, O 25,23:6
Storm, George B, 1914, N 14,11:6
Storm, George E Mrs, 1948, Ap 2,23:2
Storm, George L, 1925, Jl 12,7:3
Storm, George Wilkinson, 1903, S 29,9:5
Storm, Harry F, 1945, Jl 4,13:7
Storm, Irving G, 1940, Mr 3,45:1
Storm, Isaac, 1948, S 20,25:3
Storm, Isabel H Mrs, 1937, My 25,27:3
Storm, John J, 1953, Ap 6,19:5
Storm, John Mrs, 1957, F 12,27:2
Storm, Julius Mrs, 1958, Ap 5,15:4
Storm, Marion Mrs, 1950, Jl 4,19:2
Storm, Raymond W, 1951, Ap 18,31:3
Storm, Rufus K, 1941, F 20,20:3
Storm-Petersen, Robert, 1949, Mr 7,21:4
Stormer, J J, 1911, Ag 21,9:6
Stormer, Paul, 1954, Ja 9,15:3
Storms, Alice, 1965, Je 30,37:3
Storms, Charles E, 1953, Ag 20,27:4
Storms, Charles H, 1948, S 6,13:5
Storms, Edward W, 1939, F 11,15:6
Storms, Edwin, 1946, My 25,15:2
Storms, Estelle V, 1955, Mr 2,27:1
Storms, Francis L, 1941, F 22,15:5
Storms, George A Mrs, 1947, My 11,60:6
Storms, Harold A, 1956, F 5,86:6
Storms, Sylvester L, 1940, Ja 24,21:4
Storms, Sylvester L Mrs, 1957, Je 13,32:1
Storms, Walter G, 1954, Ag 29,89:1
Storni, Andre Mrs, 1952, F 17,85:1
Storni, Segundo, 1954, D 7,33:2
Storr, Vernon F, 1940, O 27,44:1
Storrie, Robert S, 1945, Je 30,17:5
Storrie, William, 1955, Je 2,29:4
Storrier, Charles R, 1951, N 24,28:6
Storrier, Ruth, 1953, My 27,31:5
Storrow, J J, 1926, Mr 14,II,11:1
Storrow, James J Jr Mrs, 1945, Mr 22,23:4
Storrs, Blanche F, 1941, D 16,27:4
Storrs, Burton W, 1954, O 1,23:2
Storrs, Charles, 1884, S 3,2:2
Storrs, Charles L, 1952, Mr 23,92:1
Storrs, Charles P, 1958, O 5,87:1
Storrs, Frank V, 1939, Mr 9,21:5
Storrs, Frank V (will), 1940, F 24,11:6
Storrs, Frank V Mrs, 1954, F 10,29:2
Storrs, Frederick A, 1951, Je 22,25:5
Storrs, Gertrude C Mrs, 1940, D 10,26:2
Storrs, Harry C, 1961, Ag 27,84:4
Storrs, Henry J, 1947, Ap 23,25:2
Storrs, John, 1956, Ap 26,33:5
Storrs, Lewis A, 1945, Jl 6,11:4
Storrs, Lucius S, 1957, Ja 23,29:3
Storrs, Norman, 1941, N 26,23:3
Storrs, Richard S, 1939, Ag 11,15:2
Storrs, Richard Salter Rev, 1873, Ag 14,4:7
Storrs, Richard Salter Rev Dr, 1900, Je 6,7:1
Storrs, Richard W Mrs, 1912, My 7,11:4
Storrs, Ronald, 1955, N 2,35:3
Storrs, S D, 1883, Jl 7,2:5
Story, Albert E Jr, 1948, My 24,19:3
Story, Albert Mrs, 1945, F 3,11:2
Story, Allen L, 1963, Je 11,37:3

Story, Anna Warren, 1913, Je 15,IV,5:5
Story, Arthur H, 1950, N 18,15:4
Story, Christopher, 1960, Je 23,29:1
Story, Clifford M, 1937, D 18,21:2
Story, Douglas, 1921, Jl 11,11:5
Story, Douglas T, 1952, Ap 23,29:6
Story, Duane Mrs, 1924, Mr 6,17:4
Story, Edward H, 1939, S 4,19:4
Story, Edwin B Prof, 1909, Jl 28,9:4
Story, Enoch F, 1954, Ag 25,27:4
Story, Fred L, 1949, Jl 15,19:2
Story, G N, 1882, F 25,8:1
Story, George Henry, 1922, N 25,13:5
Story, Hanford L, 1939, Je 19,15:4
Story, Harold R, 1961, Ap 9,86:5
Story, John G, 1941, Je 1,41:2
Story, John P Gen, 1915, Mr 26,13:3
Story, John S, 1966, Ap 5,39:4
Story, Julian, 1919, F 25,11:3
Story, Russell M, 1942, Mr 28,17:7
Story, T Waldo, 1915, O 24,17:5
Story, Theodore L, 1949, Ag 10,21:5
Story, W C Mrs, 1932, Jl 16,11:1
Story, W W, 1895, O 8,5:3
Story, Walter P, 1957, Je 20,29:3
Story, Walter S, 1955, Je 25,15:6
Story, William O, 1938, Ja 15,15:6
Story, William O Mrs, 1953, F 14,17:2
Storz, Ferdinand, 1952, D 23,23:2
Storz, Frank, 1950, D 5,31:4
Storz, Joseph, 1948, Je 30,25:2
Storz, Leo, 1965, Ag 27,29:5
Storz, Todd, 1964, Ag 14,34:8
Stote, Amos, 1954, O 1,23:5
Stotesbury, Charles C, 1921, Mr 10,13:6
Stotesbury, Edward T, 1938, My 17,1:4
Stotesbury, Edward T (will), 1940, Je 1,31:6
Stotesbury, Edward T Mrs (will, My 30,23:1),(por), 1946, My 24,19:1
Stotesbury, Herbert, 1953, F 19,23:4
Stotesbury, Louis W (por), 1948, Je 26,17:3
Stotesbury, Louis W Mrs, 1957, My 24,26:1
Stotesbury, Wellington, 1944, Ap 4,21:4
Stothart, Herbert (por), 1949, F 2,27:1
Stothart, Herbert Mrs, 1924, D 20,15:5
Stothers, Clifford A, 1944, S 9,15:6
Stothers, Edward M, 1954, Mr 8,27:5
Stotler, Joseph H, 1957, O 15,33:2
Stotsenburg, Evan B, 1937, Ag 1,II,7:3
Stott, Asa J, 1941, O 3,23:1
Stott, Clarence A Lt, 1907, D 18,9:6
Stott, Edward, 1918, Mr 21,13:5
Stott, Edward B, 1941, Ag 18,13:1
Stott, George H, 1952, Mr 10,21:4
Stott, Henry Gordon, 1917, Ja 17,9:4
Stott, John, 1923, Ag 6,11:2
Stott, Louis L, 1964, S 5,19:1
Stott, Norman M, 1964, Ap 9,31:3
Stott, Phil S Sir, 1937, Ap 2,23:5
Stott, Robert D, 1965, O 25,37:1
Stott, William Taylor Dr, 1918, N 2,15:4
Stotter, Henry B, 1954, S 14,27:2
Stotter, Herbert J, 1967, Je 5,43:2
Stotter, Jack P, 1949, S 24,13:6
Stotter, Patricia Mrs, 1956, Mr 6,33:7
Stotter, Raymond Mrs, 1950, My 3,29:5
Stottlar, Frank, 1954, Ja 28,29:7
Stottmeister, Walter, 1963, Ap 22,27:5
Stotz, Timothy A, 1948, Ja 29,23:2
Stotzfus, Sarah Mrs, 1946, N 26,32:7
Stoudt, John, 1940, Ja 7,48:8
Stoudt, John B, 1944, Ap 9,34:3
Stoudt, John K, 1957, Mr 12,33:4
Stouffer, George C Capt, 1873, My 7,5:4
Stouffer, Gordon A, 1956, Je 7,31:6
Stouffer, Karl J, 1942, S 5,13:5
Stouffer, Robert A, 1945, N 7,23:2
Stouffer, Samuel A, 1960, Ag 25,29:1
Stough, Mulford Mrs, 1955, My 12,29:2
Stough, William L, 1945, N 12,21:3
Stoughton, A B, 1875, N 27,1:3
Stoughton, Arthur A, 1955, Ja 14,19:5
Stoughton, Arthur A Mrs, 1961, D 29,23:2
Stoughton, Bradley, 1959, D 31,21:1
Stoughton, Charles W, 1945, Ja 9,19:5
Stoughton, Dorothy R Mrs, 1956, Ja 26,29:4
Stoughton, Dwight H, 1944, D 18,19:2
Stoughton, E H Gov, 1868, D 29,4:6
Stoughton, E M, 1882, Ja 8,7:2
Stoughton, Edward N, 1952, Ap 23,29:6
Stoughton, Edward P, 1938, O 4,25:5
Stoughton, Frederick A, 1961, N 23,31:6
Stoughton, Grace W, 1940, Jl 20,15:3
Stoughton, Henry E, 1949, F 15,23:6
Stoughton, Marion W, 1945, Ag 12,40:3
Stoughton, Milton W, 1951, N 2,23:2
Stoughton, Roy, 1961, Ja 10,47:3
Stoughton, Roy S, 1953, F 2,21:4
Stoupa, George J, 1961, Mr 31,27:3
Stourdza, M, 1884, My 10,5:3
Stourton, William M (Lord Mowbray and Stourton), 1965, My 8,31:5
Stout, A V, 1883, S 6,4:7
Stout, Althea W Mrs, 1947, N 19,27:3
Stout, Andrew V, 1953, Mr 30,21:6
Stout, Andrew V Mrs, 1965, My 6,39:1
Stout, Arlow B, 1957, O 13,86:3
Stout, Arthur P, 1967, D 21,37:2
Stout, Arthur P Mrs, 1955, D 24,13:5
Stout, C Bartlette, 1903, Je 26,9:6
Stout, C Frederick C, 1952, Ja 31,27:4
Stout, C H, 1928, Mr 16,23:5
Stout, Charles H Mrs, 1958, F 18,27:2
Stout, Charles T Mrs, 1960, Ag 1,23:6
Stout, David H, 1941, Ag 7,17:4
Stout, Dora D Mrs, 1947, Jl 13,44:4
Stout, Edmund Mrs, 1945, Ap 7,15:5
Stout, Edward M, 1949, Ap 15,23:4
Stout, Edward P (por), 1945, O 31,23:3
Stout, Edwin, 1958, N 27,29:3
Stout, Ernest C, 1938, Ap 16,13:3
Stout, Eugene E, 1940, Ja 27,13:3
Stout, Frank, 1955, Ap 12,29:3
Stout, Frank D Mrs, 1949, Ag 17,23:3
Stout, Garrett I, 1944, F 24,15:2
Stout, George C Jr, 1957, Ap 6,19:3
Stout, George W, 1939, Ap 29,17:4
Stout, Harry E, 1954, Ja 5,27:5
Stout, Harry H, 1949, Ap 14,25:6
Stout, Harry H Mrs, 1944, Ap 10,19:4
Stout, Henrietta Mrs, 1942, Ja 22,18:4
Stout, Henry P, 1942, O 8,27:5
Stout, Howard A, 1959, My 20,35:2
Stout, Howard D, 1949, S 29,29:2
Stout, Isaac H Dr, 1903, N 10,9:5
Stout, Israel W, 1938, O 21,23:5
Stout, J Robert, 1965, Mr 14,86:6
Stout, Jacob, 1907, Jl 9,7:6
Stout, James Huff, 1910, D 9,11:4
Stout, Jesse F, 1964, N 18,47:2
Stout, John, 1923, S 5,15:4; 1946, D 29,35:5
Stout, John E, 1942, D 22,25:3
Stout, John P, 1950, N 22,25:2; 1952, My 22,27:3
Stout, John W, 1903, N 25,9:5
Stout, Joseph J, 1943, N 25,25:2
Stout, Joseph S, 1904, Je 30,9:6
Stout, Loren, 1942, Jl 10,17:4
Stout, Lucetta T Mrs, 1940, D 12,27:2
Stout, Marcus B, 1940, Ap 4,23:3
Stout, Mary E Mrs, 1941, N 5,23:6
Stout, Mary-Jane N Mrs, 1957, Je 1,17:5
Stout, Merrell L, 1964, Je 24,37:2
Stout, Newton E, 1925, Mr 14,13:5
Stout, Phil S, 1938, N 4,23:5
Stout, R Van Rensslaer H, 1954, Ag 28,15:7
Stout, Richard C, 1938, F 25,17:4
Stout, Richard W, 1941, F 8,15:1
Stout, Roy Mrs, 1948, Ag 15,60:5
Stout, Royal C, 1958, Ap 3,31:4
Stout, S S H Dr, 1903, S 19,7:6
Stout, W C, 1901, Je 14,7:6
Stout, Warren B, 1943, D 19,48:2
Stout, William B, 1956, Mr 21,37:1
Stout, William H, 1944, O 14,13:4
Stout, William J, 1945, N 20,21:5; 1955, Ap 19,31:3
Stoute, John M, 1952, Ag 26,25:5
Stoutenburgh, Albert E, 1962, Ja 26,31:1
Stoutenburgh, Mary A, 1946, Jl 12,17:5
Stoutenburgh, Robert Mrs, 1903, S 23,7:6
Stouter, Frank Mrs, 1945, Ag 23,23:3
Stoutt, Paul H, 1966, S 28,47:3
Stovall, George, 1951, N 6,29:6
Stovall, Harold S, 1953, Ag 25,21:5
Stovall, J Willis, 1953, Jl 25,11:2
Stovall, Pleasant A Mrs, 1951, Ja 2,23:1
Stovall, William F, 1950, Ap 17,23:2
Stoveken, William, 1946, N 29,25:1
Stovel, Edith V, 1943, Ap 16,21:4
Stovel, Everett F, 1952, D 23,23:5
Stovel, Russell W, 1954, D 22,23:2
Stovell, Cuthbert J, 1958, Ag 22,21:1
Stover, C B, 1929, Ap 26,25:3
Stover, C Jaspar, 1944, My 3,19:3
Stover, Charles, 1940, Ap 10,25:6
Stover, Charles C, 1948, Jl 29,21:2
Stover, E C, 1927, Jl 11,19:3
Stover, Edgar S, 1965, Ap 18,81:2
Stover, Edward J, 1961, N 29,41:4
Stover, Fannie C Mrs, 1938, N 8,23:3
Stover, Franklin F, 1958, Ja 4,15:3
Stover, Fred, 1947, F 19,25:1
Stover, George C, 1944, O 27,23:3
Stover, George H, 1946, My 24,19:2; 1949, N 15,25:2
Stover, George H Mrs, 1944, Ja 14,19:1
Stover, Henry A, 1954, Ja 29,19:1
Stover, Holly, 1963, Jl 26,25:1
Stover, John S, 1959, Je 4,31:6
Stover, Joseph W, 1920, O 1,11:5
Stover, Josiah A, 1942, S 27,48:1
Stover, Martin L Ex-Justice, 1921, Je 9,15:5
Stover, Miles E, 1944, D 25,19:5
Stover, Russell, 1954, My 12,31:5
Stover, Sarah Mrs, 1945, Jl 31,19:2
Stover, Theodore M, 1953, Ap 11,17:5
Stover, Walter A, 1955, S 21,33:4
Stover, Walter E, 1950, D 23,15:5
Stover, Weller E, 1949, Jl 1,19:3
Stover, Willis W, 1941, Je 13,19:5
Stovin, Samuel S, 1938, Ja 25,21:5
Stovroff, Jacob, 1953, Jl 7,27:4
Stow, Baron Rev, 1869, D 28,5:5
Stow, Bond, 1940, Ap 1,19:5
Stow, Bond Mrs, 1943, O 16,13:5
Stow, Charles, 1907, Ag 23,7:4
Stow, Charles M, 1952, My 16,23:4
Stow, Franklyn B, 1953, Jl 19,56:4
Stow, Herbert, 1941, Mr 2,42:7
Stowbridge, Robert W, 1965, D 17,39:1
Stowe, A Monroe, 1952, Jl 18,19:4
Stowe, Alfred, 1941, Ja 3,19:2
Stowe, Allen B, 1957, F 24,73:1
Stowe, Benjamin L, 1943, Ja 31,44:7
Stowe, C E, 1934, Jl 26,19:2
Stowe, Frederick A, 1938, My 4,23:4
Stowe, George (por), 1941, O 7,23:4
Stowe, Harriet B, 1896, Jl 1,1:6
Stowe, Harry, 1937, S 21,25:2
Stowe, Harry Welsh, 1915, O 28,11:5
Stowe, Herbert L, 1949, Ap 28,31:1
Stowe, Julia, 1955, O 26,31:2
Stowe, Leroy, 1950, O 26,31:1
Stowe, Leslie, 1949, Jl 19,29:1
Stowe, Lewis R, 1957, N 6,35:2
Stowe, Lucy B, 1946, Je 27,21:2
Stowe, Lyman B, 1963, S 26,35:2
Stowe, Lyman B Mrs, 1965, Ja 4,29:4
Stowe, Lyman M, 1965, Je 3,35:4
Stowe, Mary G, 1944, S 17,42:2
Stowe, Raymond T M, 1944, F 15,17:4
Stowe, Wilbur F, 1938, Je 2,23:2
Stowe, William C, 1952, Ag 17,77:2
Stowe-Gullen, Augusta Mrs, 1943, S 26,48:1
Stowell, Ben L, 1946, Ap 11,25:4
Stowell, Clarence (por), 1940, N 27,23:4
Stowell, Ellery C, 1958, Ja 3,23:4
Stowell, Frank C, 1941, F 2,44:2
Stowell, George A, 1937, N 25,31:5
Stowell, Harley L, 1942, Ja 21,17:3
Stowell, Harold B, 1951, Mr 17,15:5
Stowell, Henry W, 1947, D 10,31:5
Stowell, Jay S, 1966, O 7,43:2
Stowell, John S Mrs, 1945, F 21,19:5
Stowell, Leland E, 1957, Ap 16,33:4
Stowell, Mary Jane, 1916, Je 26,13:7
Stowell, Ruben, 1941, My 14,21:4
Stowell, Stanley A, 1951, D 2,91:2
Stowell, William A, 1950, My 31,29:4
Stowell, William A Mrs, 1943, Ja 7,19:4
Stowell, William Henry Harrison, 1922, Ap 28,17:5
Stowell, William V N, 1945, S 18,23:2
Stowers, Edward J, 1944, My 14,46:4
Stowitts, Earl O, 1953, Je 30,23:3
Stowitts, George P, 1938, Mr 6,II,8:6
Stoy, Franklin Pierce, 1911, Jl 23,9:5
Stoy, Lyda K Mrs, 1939, N 15,23:4
Stoyadinovitch, Milan, 1961, O 25,37:1
Stoyanov, Petko, 1951, Ag 28,23:2
Stoyanovitch, Kosta Dr, 1921, Ja 8,11:5
Stoye, Karl H, 1943, D 15,27:2
Stoyl, Richard, 1905, Je 29,9:3
Stozingen, Fedele de, 1947, Ja 10,22:2
Strabel, Thelma (Mrs D P Godwin), 1959, My 29, 23:4
Strabolgi, Lord, 1953, O 9,27:5
Strabolgi, Lord (will), 1954, Mr 7,86:3
Stracciari, Riccardo, 1955, O 11,39:2
Strachan, Arthur, 1941, N 26,23:6
Strachan, Bishop Rt Rev, 1867, N 2,1:4
Strachan, Donald C, 1957, N 15,27:1
Strachan, Douglas H, 1953, Ap 3,23:4
Strachan, James A, 1940, N 20,21:2
Strachan, James F, 1939, Ap 6,25:1
Strachan, Joseph J, 1948, Ap 4,60:4
Strachan, Malcolm, 1960, S 23,29:4
Strachan, Mary A Mrs, 1940, D 25,27:5
Strachan, R Kenneth, 1965, F 26,29:1
Strachan, Robert W, 1950, O 26,31:5
Strachan, Thomas C Jr, 1957, S 24,35:1
Strachan-Davidson, James Leigh, 1916, Mr 29,11:4
Strachen, Earle K, 1939, N 22,24:8
Strachey, J St L, 1927, Ag 27,13:5
Strachey, Joan P, 1951, D 20,31:2
Strachey, John, 1963, Jl 16,31:1
Strachey, L, 1932, Ja 22,19:1
Strachovsky, Nitaka, 1948, D 10,25:1
Strachstein, Abraham, 1960, Ap 5,37:4
Strack, Frank P, 1937, Jl 8,23:2
Strack, George J, 1955, Ag 13,13:6
Strack, Henry D, 1947, My 13,25:3
Strack, Henry D Mrs, 1941, O 28,23:6
Strack, J H, 1880, Je 22,5:4
Strack, Jerome A, 1947, Je 13,23:4
Strack, Meinard J, 1948, O 23,15:5
Stradbroke, Earl of (por), 1947, D 21,52:3
Stradbroke, Lady, 1949, Ap 15,23:4
Strader, Bernard E (por), 1949, Ja 5,25:5
Strader, Norman (Red), 1956, My 27,89:1
Strader, P W, 1881, F 27,7:3
Strader, Ralph M, 1957, Je 24,23:1

Strader, William L, 1957, Je 23,84:3
Stradley, Benjamin F, 1938, Ja 4,23:2
Stradley, Bland L, 1957, Ag 5,19:1
Stradley, Leighton P, 1956, Ap 20,25:5
Stradley, Shermer H, 1950, Ja 11,23:2
Stradling, Fred P, 1956, N 11,86:6
Stradling, Reginald, 1952, Ja 29,25:4
Straehle, Charles E, 1941, F 9,49:1
Straehley, Erwin Sr, 1947, N 8,17:5
Straeten, Francois A van der, 1948, Ap 8,25:2
Straeter, Ted (Theo A), 1963, Ap 3,47:3
Strafaci, Giuseppe, 1955, My 18,31:5
Strafaci, Joseph Mrs, 1949, F 2,27:2
Strahan, Albert E Mrs, 1952, Jl 22,25:3
Strahan, Charles, 1947, D 29,17:3
Strahan, John H, 1939, F 8,23:4
Strahan, John W, 1911, Ag 17,7:6
Strahan, Joseph C J, 1956, F 7,31:5
Strahan, Martin A, 1953, D 15,39:2
Strahan, R H, 1884, O 2,5:5
Strahan, Robert, 1951, Ap 16,25:4
Strahan, Robert H (por), 1947, O 3,26:3
Strahan, Samuel A S, 1942, N 17,25:2
Strahan, Thomas Mrs, 1954, D 19,84:1
Strahan, Thomas R, 1956, D 30,33:1
Strahl, Egbert H A, 1966, My 11,47:3
Strahl, Jacob S, 1965, Ja 24,81:1
Strahl, Joseph Mrs, 1956, S 22,17:2
Strahl, Milton I, 1967, F 7,39:2
Straight, Albert F, 1948, Ja 20,23:4
Straight, Albert F Mrs, 1938, Je 13,19:4
Straight, Benjamin E, 1951, F 27,28:2
Straight, Douglas Sir, 1914, Je 5,11:4
Straight, Edward B, 1949, F 24,24:3
Straight, Edward H, 1948, Jl 30,17:4
Straight, Willard D Maj, 1918, D 2,13:1
Strain, Chalmer B, 1942, Ap 29,21:4
Strain, Earle, 1953, Je 3,31:2
Strain, James H, 1941, Je 21,17:6
Strain, John, 1947, N 26,23:5
Strain, John D, 1947, O 1,29:4
Strain, John J, 1938, F 4,21:4
Strain, Joseph B Mrs, 1947, S 20,15:3
Strain, Richard H, 1965, Mr 27,27:4
Strain, W Ralph, 1939, Ja 5,23:3
Strain, William A, 1949, My 21,13:4
Strainline, George, 1939, Jl 16,30:6
Strait, Burton A Mrs, 1948, Je 13,69:1
Strait, Edmund T Rev, 1968, Ja 27,29:1
Strait, Edward N, 1951, D 24,13:5
Strait, Ernest C, 1941, F 26,21:3
Strait, Wesley, 1942, D 17,37:5
Strait, William B, 1968, S 13,47:4
Strait, Worthington G, 1961, Je 15,43:3
Straith, Claire L, 1958, Jl 15,25:2
Straiton, Alex, 1955, S 24,19:5
Straiton, Robert, 1962, S 18,39:4
Straka, John, 1939, Ag 19,15:6
Strakacz, Sylwyn Mrs, 1950, N 14,31:2
Straker, Robert L, 1959, D 8,45:2
Strakhovsky, Leonid, 1963, Ap 26,35:1
Strakosch, Carl, 1916, O 24,12:6; 1946, D 26,25:5
Strakosch, Celia L Mrs, 1961, My 10,45:3
Strakosch, Claire (Julia C H), 1963, Ap 16,35:2
Strakosch, Henry, 1943, N 1,17:5
Strakosch, Henry (will), 1944, F 6,1:2
Strakosch, M, 1887, O 10,5:5
Strakosch, Maurice Mrs, 1915, D 15,15:5
Strakosch, Max, 1892, Mr 18,1:6
Strakosch, Phoebe, 1952, N 8,17:5
Straley, John A, 1907, O 28,9:5
Straley, John A Jr, 1966, D 20,43:3
Straley, May W, 1947, Ag 31,36:3
Straley, Sebastian, 1950, My 10,31:1
Stralia, Elsa, 1945, S 1,11:6
Stralla, Anthony C (T Cornero), 1955, Ag 1,38:3
Stranacher, Rudolph R, 1947, O 14,27:2
Stranahan, Frank D, 1965, N 12,47:2
Stranahan, Frank D Mrs, 1954, D 18,15:2
Stranahan, J S Mrs, 1905, Ja 23,7:5
Stranahan, J S T, 1898, S 4,7:5
Stranahan, James A Jr, 1964, My 12,37:4
Stranahan, Olin A, 1911, S 10,II,13:4
Stranahan, Robert A Mrs, 1968, My 13,43:1
Stranahan, Robert A Sr, 1962, F 10,23:2
Stranahan, Robert A 3d, 1968, S 28,33:4
Stranahan, Smith, 1904, N 15,9:3
Strand, C Oscar, 1946, Ap 8,27:3
Strand, Charles J, 1960, Je 8,39:4
Strand, Ludwig C, 1945, Je 4,19:4
Strand, William C, 1950, O 30,27:4
Strandberg, C Bert, 1949, O 28,24:2
Strandberg, Herbert L, 1939, F 25,15:2
Strandell, Harry G, 1952, Jl 24,27:5
Strandt, Gustav, 1940, D 19,25:4
Strang, Arthur I, 1941, N 22,19:5
Strang, Benjamin B, 1963, Ag 29,29:3
Strang, Burton Mrs, 1949, Mr 25,24:2
Strang, Charles D, 1937, N 19,23:1
Strang, Edward, 1939, Mr 12,22:4
Strang, George Mrs, 1953, Jl 13,25:6
Strang, Herbert M, 1948, D 30,19:3
Strang, Herbert M Mrs, 1946, Ag 1,23:4
Strang, Hickson K, 1953, Ja 5,21:1
Strang, James N Mrs, 1945, Ag 27,19:4
Strang, John C, 1937, Ag 21,15:2
Strang, John C Mrs, 1945, Jl 16,11:7
Strang, Mary, 1947, Ja 28,24:2
Strang, May, 1952, Je 11,29:3
Strang, P O, 1883, Je 1,5:2
Strang, Samuel B, 1954, S 3,17:5
Strang, Walter W, 1944, Ap 15,11:2
Strang, William, 1921, Ap 14,13:4
Strang, William F, 1960, Je 27,25:4
Strang, William H, 1939, Ja 9,15:6; 1943, Ag 31,17:4
Strang, William H Jr, 1953, Mr 9,29:6
Strang, William M (Jeff), 1956, F 27,23:5
Strang, William N, 1949, N 20,92:4
Strange, A Bruton Mrs, 1968, F 10,33:2
Strange, Albert B, 1937, Mr 15,23:4
Strange, Alvin A, 1950, Ap 2,94:3
Strange, E B, 1881, Ap 30,8:5
Strange, Hugh M, 1945, Jl 17,13:7
Strange, Michael (will, D 3,63:3), 1950, N 6,27:3
Strange, Robert, 1949, O 15,15:2
Strange, Robin T, 1944, Ap 11,19:1
Strange, Thaddeus S, 1951, S 26,31:2
Strangeway, Walter D, 1945, Je 26,19:4
Strangmeier, Ernst C, 1944, Ja 21,17:3
Strangward, William J, 1955, S 8,31:2
Stransky, Franklin J, 1960, Ag 5,23:4
Stransky, Franklin U, 1959, Jl 6,27:4
Stransky, Gustave, 1960, D 21,31:4
Stransky, J, 1936, Mr 7,15:3
Stransky, Josef Mrs, 1954, F 3,23:4
Stransky, Ludek, 1950, O 12,31:2
Stransky, Victor, 1963, S 18,39:2
Straphy, Kathleen R Mrs, 1947, S 3,25:1
Strasberg, Abraham, 1948, O 17,76:4
Strasberg, Moe, 1950, S 16,19:3
Strasberg, Paula (Mrs Lee Strasberg),(funl, My 2,37:2), 1966, My 1,87:3
Strasbourger, Peter, 1961, Mr 13,59:5
Strasbourger, Samuel (por), 1943, N 5,19:3
Strasburg, Paul Stephen Jr Mrs (Mary), 1968, Ag 7, 43:3
Strasburger, Adele F, 1948, Ap 10,13:5
Strasburger, Alvin L, 1914, D 31,9:6
Strasburger, Henryk, 1951, My 4,27:2
Strasburger, Irwin, 1953, Je 18,29:4
Strasburger, Katherine M Mrs, 1940, D 11,27:1
Strasburger, Montrose, 1952, Ap 23,29:2
Strashun, Isidore Mrs, 1949, Ag 29,17:2
Strashun, John J, 1945, Ag 19,40:2
Strashun, Paul, 1941, N 22,19:2
Strassburg, Max Mrs, 1966, Jl 18,27:4
Strassburger, Aloysius J, 1967, D 14,47:2
Strassburger, Ernest J, 1949, S 14,31:4
Strassburger, Isaac, 1941, N 22,19:3
Strassburger, Karel, 1953, My 10,86:4
Strassburger, Lionel, 1951, Ja 10,27:4
Strassburger, Perry B, 1954, O 23,15:1
Strassburger, Peter F, 1942, Je 3,24:3
Strassburger, Ralph B, 1959, F 28,19:4
Strassburger, Raymond C Dr, 1968, Ja 26,47:3
Strasser, Albert, 1948, F 2,19:5
Strasser, Arthur L, 1967, Mr 10,39:1
Strasser, August Adrian Dr, 1918, N 21,15:4
Strasser, Benjamin, 1955, S 21,33:2
Strasser, Christopher, 1946, My 19,40:5
Strasser, John W, 1957, Je 15,17:6
Strasser, Roger, 1965, Jl 20,20:8
Strasser, William, 1944, Jl 7,15:6
Strasser, William W, 1941, N 12,23:3
Strassheim, Arthur G, 1946, My 31,23:2
Strassle, Charles T, 1955, Mr 16,33:2
Strassman, Max, 1955, Je 30,25:1
Strassman, Ralph K, 1960, Je 16,33:5
Strassman, Samuel, 1954, Jl 8,23:4
Strassmann, Antonie, 1952, Ja 10,29:2
Strassner, Raymond C, 1944, F 11,19:5
Stratas, Emanuel Mrs, 1963, S 12,37:3
Stratchan, James D, 1944, Ja 12,23:4
Strate, Walter V, 1959, Jl 22,27:5
Strateman, Emil, 1952, O 7,29:4
Strateman, Emil Mrs, 1949, F 12,17:2
Straten-Ponthoz, Claudine van der, 1959, O 18,1:7
Strater, Charles G, 1937, S 27,21:2
Strater, William J, 1947, Ag 22,15:3
Strates, James E, 1959, O 12,19:3
Stratford, Arthur C, 1937, Ap 24,19:3
Stratford, Herbert R, 1907, F 28,9:6
Stratford, James, 1952, Ja 18,27:5
Stratford, Ralph B, 1962, Ag 30,29:5
Stratford, William, 1908, Ja 26,9:5
Strathcarron, Baron (por), 1937, Ag 15,II,7:1
Strathclyde, Baron, 1928, O 3,31:3
Strathcona, Baroness, 1926, Ag 19,19:5
Strathcona, Isabella Sophia Lady, 1913, N 13,11:5
Strathearn, E Baron Gordon, 1879, S 23,4:7
Strathearn, G Hobart, 1959, Ap 22,33:3
Strathern, Annie White, 1920, O 24,22:4
Strathmore, Countess of (will, O 28,16:4),(por), 1938, Je 23,21:1
Strathmore, Countess of (M B Brennan), 1967, S 9, 31:5
Strathmore, Ralph, 1962, Ag 23,29:4
Strathmore and Kinghorn, Countess of, 1946, Je 19, 21:4
Strathmore and Kinghorne, Earl of (P Bowes-Lyon), 1949, My 26,29:1
Strathspey, Lord, 1948, N 14,76:3
Stratigos, George Mrs, 1946, Mr 28,25:1
Stratmann, Charles Francis Dr, 1925, Mr 30,17:6
Stratmann, Ernst, 1940, Je 20,23:6
Stratmeyer, Julius S, 1948, My 7,23:4
Straton, J R, 1929, O 30,25:1
Straton, John C, 1966, My 23,41:4
Straton, Warren B Mrs, 1943, Je 27,32:4
Stratt, Kent, 1937, Ap 20,25:4
Stratti, Frank, 1921, My 30,9:5
Stratton, Albert E, 1942, D 16,25:6
Stratton, Arthur G, 1966, Jl 27,39:3
Stratton, Asa Evans, 1925, Ag 15,11:6
Stratton, C H, 1883, Jl 16,8:7
Stratton, Charles G, 1940, Jl 7,25:3
Stratton, Charles T, 1957, Ag 24,15:4
Stratton, Clifton J Jr, 1967, O 4,47:2
Stratton, Collin J Mrs, 1948, My 4,25:3
Stratton, E, 1933, D 3,39:3
Stratton, E Platt Mrs, 1920, Je 2,11:4
Stratton, Edgar Mrs, 1950, F 15,27:4
Stratton, Edgar W, 1952, Ap 6,88:3
Stratton, Edward Mrs, 1949, N 26,15:2
Stratton, F A, 1904, Jl 1,5:4
Stratton, F E, 1928, Je 5,29:2
Stratton, F N, 1879, Jl 20,2:3
Stratton, Francis A, 1946, Mr 5,26:2
Stratton, Frederick L, 1951, N 16,25:2
Stratton, George B, 1948, Mr 15,23:5
Stratton, George M, 1957, O 10,33:4
Stratton, Gerald, 1941, Ja 12,46:2
Stratton, Harold L, 1948, F 2,19:3
Stratton, Harold Mulford Gen, 1911, My 18,11:4
Stratton, Helen L, 1955, Jl 27,23:5
Stratton, Henry B, 1958, O 31,29:3
Stratton, Henry Prof, 1903, S 17,3:2
Stratton, Herbert C, 1952, F 20,29:3
Stratton, James M, 1949, F 13,77:2
Stratton, John G, 1953, Mr 16,22:4
Stratton, Joseph M, 1937, S 26,II,8:6
Stratton, Leslie C, 1964, Ap 9,31:4
Stratton, Lloyd, 1961, Jl 13,29:3
Stratton, Margaret, 1925, D 19,17:5
Stratton, Paul, 1942, O 12,17:2
Stratton, Percy F, 1950, Ja 5,25:2
Stratton, Ralph R, 1940, F 12,17:4
Stratton, Rienzie H, 1951, Ap 21,17:5
Stratton, Riley E, 1867, F 3,3:6
Stratton, Rosecrans, 1944, D 3,57:2
Stratton, S W, 1931, O 19,21:1
Stratton, Samuel S Mrs, 1964, Ja 11,23:1
Stratton, Vernon D, 1945, Je 23,13:3
Stratton, W E, 1902, S 15,9:6
Stratton, Walter W, 1943, N 12,21:1
Stratton, William D, 1919, S 26,13:4
Stratton, William H, 1903, Ag 14,7:7; 1943, Je 5,15:4
Stratton, William J, 1938, My 9,17:5
Straub, A Frank, 1948, D 17,27:2
Straub, Annie, 1940, O 1,23:1
Straub, Anthony F, 1954, Mr 3,27:3
Straub, Carl A, 1955, Ap 14,36:2
Straub, Carlyle F, 1950, F 25,30:5
Straub, Francis P, 1950, F 11,15:3
Straub, Frank J Mrs, 1924, Jl 9,19:6
Straub, Fridolin, 1948, Ag 9,19:3
Straub, Herbert L, 1944, Ja 28,18:2
Straub, James M, 1961, Mr 16,37:4
Straub, John E, 1956, F 16,29:2
Straub, Joseph E, 1958, Mr 6,27:3
Straub, Lorenz G, 1963, O 29,35:1
Straub, Oscar A, 1964, N 24,39:3
Straub, Paul A, 1958, D 10,39:2
Straub, Paul F Col, 1937, N 26,21:4
Straub, Roger C (will), 1966, My 4,47:1
Straub, Walter F, 1964, Jl 13,29:2
Straub, Walter J, 1952, D 16,31:6
Straub, William L, 1939, Ap 11,24:3
Straube, Karl, 1950, My 3,29:3
Straube, Leopold P, 1949, Jl 22,19:4
Straube, William, 1871, My 11,8:5
Straubenmuller, G, 1934, My 14,17:4
Strauch, Jacob, 1952, Jl 8,27:5
Strauchen, Edmund R, 1963, Je 30,56:5
Straughn, Archie D, 1948, O 28,29:4
Straughn, Charles T, 1942, Ap 19,44:3
Straughn, William Dr, 1947, Je 2,25:2
Straus, Aaron, 1958, Ja 21,29:2
Straus, Abraham, 1951, My 1,29:4
Straus, Addie O Mrs, 1937, O 30,19:2
Straus, Adolph Delisle, 1925, My 1,19:5
Straus, Arthur, 1962, N 18,86:6
Straus, Arthur W (will), 1938, Ja 28,4:6
Straus, Burnett W Mrs, 1953, Mr 13,27:2
Straus, David, 1943, S 6,18:3
Straus, David J (will), 1938, S 2,19:7
Straus, Edwin G, 1953, O 6,29:3
Straus, Eli M, 1945, O 13,15:5
Straus, Emanuel, 1937, Ja 19,24:2

Straus, Everett M, 1967, N 24,46:8
Straus, Fredinand A, 1959, D 18,29:2
Straus, H N, 1933, Ap 7,19:1
Straus, Harold H (por), 1947, Ja 5,53:6
Straus, Harry H, 1951, F 28,27:4
Straus, Harry H Mrs, 1951, Ag 12,76:7
Straus, Henry A, 1957, S 24,35:4
Straus, Henry L, 1949, O 26,21:5
Straus, Henry W Dr, 1937, N 22,19:5
Straus, Hiram, 1915, Mr 22,9:4
Straus, Hugh G, 1961, N 12,86:5
Straus, Isidor (funl), 1912, My 9,11:4
Straus, J I, 1936, O 5,1:4
Straus, James, 1959, Ja 1,33:3
Straus, Joe, 1943, O 5,25:5
Straus, Joseph, 1943, Ag 11,19:2
Straus, Julian G, 1940, D 18,25:4
Straus, Marcus Mrs, 1923, My 23,21:5
Straus, Martin L 2d, 1958, Jl 18,21:2
Straus, Martin 3d, 1950, Ag 3,25:6
Straus, Moses, 1910, Jl 21,7:4; 1944, Jl 21,19:3
Straus, N, 1931, Ja 12,1:6
Straus, N Mrs, 1930, My 5,23:1
Straus, Nathan (funl plans, S 15,33:2; funl, S 16,19:2), 1961, S 14,1:3
Straus, Noel (trb, N 12,29:3), 1959, N 7,23:1
Straus, Oscar S Mrs, 1945, N 10,15:3
Straus, Oskar (funl plans, Ja 15,19:1), 1954, Ja 12, 23:3
Straus, Percy Mrs, 1957, F 8,23:2
Straus, Percy S, 1944, Ap 8,13:1
Straus, Ralph, 1950, Je 7,29:4
Straus, Raymond I, 1940, Jl 5,13:5
Straus, Roger W (funl plans, Jl 30,23:3; funl, Ag 1,25:1), 1957, Jl 26,1:3
Straus, S W, 1930, S 8,1:4
Straus, Samuel J, 1942, D 30,23:4
Straus, Simon W Mrs, 1966, Jl 2,23:3
Straus, Thomas C, 1939, Ag 5,15:6
Strausberg, Samuel (por), 1947, My 25,60:3
Strause, George, 1912, Jl 3,11:6
Strausnan, Rebecca Mrs, 1923, Ap 21,11:4
Strauss, A, 1929, Mr 29,23:3
Strauss, Abraham, 1946, F 1,23:2; 1958, Mr 4,29:5; 1960, Ag 26,25:5; 1961, D 21,27:4; 1967, Jl 14,31:3
Strauss, Adolph, 1962, Je 15,27:6
Strauss, Albert, 1964, F 3,27:3
Strauss, Albert I, 1925, Ap 30,21:3
Strauss, Albert L, 1918, O 23,13:1
Strauss, Ansel L Mrs, 1959, Mr 10,35:4
Strauss, Arthur W, 1937, F 27,17:3; 1946, F 23,13:4
Strauss, Ben, 1962, Ja 19,31:5
Strauss, Benjamin F, 1949, Ja 1,13:1
Strauss, Benjamin M, 1950, Mr 14,25:5
Strauss, Bernard, 1938, F 5,15:4
Strauss, Berthold Mrs, 1960, Jl 25,45:8
Strauss, C, 1934, Ap 12,23:1
Strauss, C Frank, 1967, Ap 29,35:4
Strauss, Cecil W, 1939, Ag 12,13:5
Strauss, Charles A, 1943, Mr 1,19:4
Strauss, Charles H, 1957, N 7,35:1
Strauss, Daniel, 1945, My 9,23:2
Strauss, David, 1967, Ag 2,37:2
Strauss, David Frederick, 1874, F 10,5:2
Strauss, David Mrs, 1957, F 7,27:1
Strauss, Eduard, 1952, Ag 25,17:2
Strauss, Edward A, 1939, Mr 27,15:5
Strauss, Emil, 1960, Ag 12,19:5
Strauss, Emil L, 1918, D 13,15:3
Strauss, Eugene, 1911, S 15,9:5
Strauss, Ferdinand, 1946, Ap 15,27:3
Strauss, Frederick (will, Ag 22,II,4:8),(por), 1937, Ag 12,19:3
Strauss, Hellmuth, 1963, S 12,37:5
Strauss, Henry, 1915, N 4,11:4
Strauss, Henry C, 1952, Jl 17,23:3
Strauss, Henry X, 1939, Mr 15,23:4
Strauss, Herbert H Mrs, 1963, D 4,47:2
Strauss, Herman, 1947, D 6,15:1
Strauss, Irving, 1955, Ap 14,36:5
Strauss, Irwin P, 1967, Ap 26,47:3
Strauss, Israel Mrs, 1960, Je 18,23:4
Strauss, Jerome A, 1955, Je 14,29:2
Strauss, Johann, 1899, Je 4,4:4; 1939, Ja 15,38:7
Strauss, John A, 1938, Mr 17,21:3
Strauss, Joseph (por), 1948, D 31,15:1
Strauss, Joseph, 1949, Je 15,29:2; 1959, O 16,31:3
Strauss, Joseph B (por), 1938, My 17,23:1
Strauss, Joseph G, 1940, Jl 3,17:4
Strauss, Jules C, 1956, Ap 21,17:5
Strauss, Julius, 1920, D 4,13:4; 1961, Mr 9,29:5
Strauss, Laurence, 1951, D 14,31:3
Strauss, Lawrence L, 1951, S 10,21:5
Strauss, Lawrence M, 1965, D 20,35:4
Strauss, Leon, 1964, F 9,89:1
Strauss, Leon Mrs, 1942, O 19,19:5
Strauss, Leopold, 1952, O 5,89:1
Strauss, Lester W Mrs, 1949, Mr 9,25:4
Strauss, Lewis S, 1937, Jl 24,15:5
Strauss, Lillian J, 1959, O 7,43:1
Strauss, Louis, 1940, F 28,21:5; 1941, O 22,23:4; 1944, Ag 18,13:2; 1968, My 25,35:3
Strauss, Louis A, 1938, S 28,25:1
Strauss, Louis M, 1938, Je 16,23:2
Strauss, Manny, 1957, D 22,42:3
Strauss, Manny Mrs, 1940, Ap 20,17:3
Strauss, Martin Mrs, 1954, N 9,27:5
Strauss, Maurice D, 1941, Ja 19,41:2
Strauss, Maurice J, 1958, F 4,29:2
Strauss, Max, 1942, D 5,15:1; 1944, S 12,19:4; 1946, S 3,19:5
Strauss, Max Dr, 1968, S 8,84:7
Strauss, Michael, 1943, Mr 25,21:3
Strauss, Morris L, 1953, S 14,27:2
Strauss, Morton, 1961, My 2,37:4
Strauss, Moses, 1905, Je 21,7:7; 1913, Ja 31,11:5; 1938, Jl 15,17:5
Strauss, Norman, 1955, F 7,21:3
Strauss, O S, 1926, My 4,7:1
Strauss, Oscar R Sr, 1939, Jl 21,19:3
Strauss, Richard, 1949, S 9,25:1
Strauss, Richard M, 1967, S 28,47:3
Strauss, Richard Mrs, 1950, My 14,106:4
Strauss, Samuel, 1953, Ap 13,27:3; 1957, Ja 8,31:3
Strauss, Samuel M, 1965, D 30,23:4
Strauss, Samuel Mrs, 1949, N 11,25:2
Strauss, Samuel S, 1937, Ja 9,17:4
Strauss, Seligman J Mrs, 1968, Ap 4,47:3
Strauss, Seymour A, 1953, My 26,29:4
Strauss, Sidney H, 1961, Ja 27,23:2
Strauss, Sidney L, 1947, O 25,19:2
Strauss, Sig, 1947, My 25,60:7
Strauss, Sigmund, 1940, N 11,19:4; 1942, Mr 30,17:3
Strauss, Simon, 1951, Ap 10,28:3
Strauss, Sol, 1967, D 14,68:7
Strauss, Sophie Mrs, 1941, Mr 16,45:1
Strauss, William, 1903, N 2,7:5; 1960, F 7,84:6
Strauss, William M, 1952, S 18,29:4
Strauss, William S, 1967, Je 1,43:1
Strauss, William T, 1941, Jl 15,19:4
Straussberg, Marcus, 1954, Je 25,21:4
Straussenburg, A von, 1935, Jl 2,21:1
Strausser, Clayton E, 1956, O 12,29:2
Straut, Frank, 1950, Ja 25,27:2
Strauwen, Jean, 1947, Ja 14,25:5
Stravelli, John M, 1962, Je 29,27:5
Straw, A Gale Mrs, 1955, O 3,27:5
Straw, Charles S, 1941, O 17,23:3
Straw, Charles W, 1949, Ap 14,25:5
Straw, E A, 1882, O 24,5:2
Straw, Ezekial A, 1941, S 8,15:6
Straw, H Ellis, 1950, N 5,94:5
Straw, Luther C, 1949, Mr 14,19:7
Strawbridge, Anne W, 1941, S 10,23:3
Strawbridge, Charles H, 1939, My 16,23:5
Strawbridge, Edwin, 1957, O 31,28:4
Strawbridge, Francis R, 1965, My 12,47:4
Strawbridge, Francis R Jr, 1966, Mr 17,39:1
Strawbridge, Frederic H Mrs, 1946, N 13,27:3
Strawbridge, George H Mrs, 1950, Ja 14,15:4
Strawbridge, George Mrs, 1953, Ag 2,72:5
Strawbridge, I R Mrs, 1938, Ag 14,33:3
Strawbridge, Isaac R, 1942, Ap 14,21:2
Strawbridge, John Mrs, 1952, My 4,91:2
Strawbridge, Katherine M Mrs, 1962, N 28,39:1
Strawbridge, Robert E, 1963, D 25,33:4
Strawbridge, Robert E Mrs, 1942, Jl 21,19:3
Strawinski, Raymond J, 1961, Ja 28,9:1
Strawn, Harold V, 1937, Je 8,25:2
Strawn, Jacob, 1865, Ag 31,4:6
Strawn, Lester H, 1949, My 28,15:7
Strawn, Silas H (por), 1946, F 5,23:3
Strawn, Taylor, 1938, D 25,15:2
Strayer, Edward R, 1951, D 18,31:1
Strayer, Franklin R, 1954, S 3,17:2
Strayer, George D, 1962, O 1,31:2
Strayer, George D Mrs, 1957, F 2,19:6
Strayer, Luther M Sr, 1951, N 19,23:4
Strayer, Meyer, 1966, My 4,47:2
Strayer, Paul J, 1961, Jl 25,27:5
Strayer, Paul M Mrs, 1966, Ja 19,41:5
Strayer, Seibert I, 1941, S 28,48:5
Strayhorn, Billy (Wm T),(funl, Je 6,49:1), 1967, Je 1, 43:4
Strazhesko, Nikolai, 1952, Je 29,56:4
Strazza, P Henry, 1962, Ag 9,25:4
Streaker, George H, 1949, My 7,13:6
Stream, Eloise, 1940, Mr 30,15:3
Stream, John G, 1940, Je 26,23:2
Streamer, A C, 1950, My 5,22:2
Streamer, Volney, 1915, Ap 15,13:4
Strean, Maria J, 1949, Jl 15,19:1
Streat, Hearn W (por), 1946, F 20,25:6
Streat, Herbert G, 1948, Ag 27,19:2
Streatfeild, Henry, 1938, Jl 27,17:4
Streator, George W, 1955, Jl 29,17:3
Strebeigh, Harold Mrs, 1938, Ja 26,23:1
Strebeigh, Lefferts, 1916, F 11,11:4
Strebeigh, Waring C, 1950, O 4,31:2
Strebel, George W, 1948, Mr 19,23:4
Strebel, Gustave A (por), 1945, N 28,27:3
Strebel, Ralph F, 1959, F 9,29:3
Strebelcock, W P, 1947, S 8,21:5
Strebig, James J, 1951, O 20,15:6
Streble, Joseph Jr, 1956, Jl 6,21:3
Streck, Kalman, 1946, Je 15,21:1
Streck, Louis Jr, 1945, N 8,20:2
Strecker, Edward, 1938, My 10,21:4
Strecker, Edward A, 1959, Ja 3,17:3
Strecker, Henry A, 1941, O 1,21:2
Streckert, Henry R, 1950, Ja 2,23:2
Streckfus, John Capt, 1925, O 14,25:2
Streckfus, John N, 1948, Mr 9,23:1
Streckfus, Victor H Mrs, 1946, O 8,23:3
Streckmest, Alvin A, 1941, O 17,23:3
Streckus, Ludwig A, 1945, O 25,21:5
Streed, W I, 1950, F 18,15:4
Streep, John, 1949, F 5,15:6
Streepey, George W, 1965, F 14,88:1
Streepy, William M, 1953, F 3,25:4
Streeruwitz, Ernst, 1952, O 20,23:2
Street, Alvin M, 1964, My 19,37:1
Street, Arthur, 1951, F 25,86:4
Street, Arthur I, 1923, My 15,19:5
Street, Arthur Wray, 1919, Jl 11,11:4
Street, Augustus R, 1866, Je 24,1:7
Street, Charles E, 1950, O 15,104:1
Street, Charles E (Gabby), 1951, F 7,29:1
Street, Charles Larrabee Bishop, 1968, Ag 15,37:2
Street, Charles S, 1939, Ag 16,23:5
Street, Claude E, 1945, Ja 12,15:3
Street, Daniel B, 1952, O 23,31:6
Street, Edwin T, 1948, Ja 8,25:2
Street, Emeline A, 1963, S 7,19:3
Street, F S, 1883, Ap 16,5:2
Street, Frank, 1944, N 29,23:6
Street, Frank A, 1946, N 29,25:1
Street, Frederick G Mrs (Eleanor C), 1965, Ap 14, 41:4
Street, G E, 1881, D 19,2:5
Street, George Edward Rev, 1903, D 27,7:6
Street, George L, 1960, Mr 20,86:6
Street, Gus C Sr, 1948, My 18,24:3
Street, H Louis, 1943, Ag 10,19:4
Street, Harris N, 1956, Je 7,31:4
Street, Henry A, 1956, Mr 17,19:6
Street, Herbert R, 1953, F 17,27:3
Street, Herman E Dr, 1919, Ag 19,13:4
Street, J Fletcher, 1944, S 20,23:6
Street, J Fletcher Mrs, 1944, N 30,23:6
Street, J Harry, 1951, Je 4,27:5
Street, James, 1957, D 31,17:4
Street, James H, 1954, S 29,31:3
Street, John P, 1938, S 23,27:2
Street, Julian (por), 1947, F 20,25:1
Street, Katherine D, 1957, O 25,27:2
Street, Lottie E, 1942, Ja 22,17:2
Street, Mary D, 1951, N 12,25:5
Street, Murray C, 1951, F 22,31:4
Street, O Dickinson, 1955, Je 12,86:8
Street, Philip W, 1938, S 12,17:5
Street, R P, 1903, Ja 13,9:3
Street, Richard H, 1960, Ag 23,29:3
Street, Robert Rev, 1903, F 2,1:3
Street, Susan W, 1956, D 11,32:6
Street, T A, 1936, Mr 18,23:1
Street, T C, 1872, S 8,1:6
Street, Thomas N, 1942, Jl 31,15:6
Street, W D, 1911, O 18,11:4
Street, W G, 1932, S 17,15:5
Street, Wade L, 1941, My 5,17:2
Street, William, 1918, Mr 22,13:4
Street, William Augustus, 1924, My 22,17:6
Street, William B, 1940, Jl 6,15:4
Street, William D, 1958, D 30,35:3
Street, William E, 1919, My 18,22:5
Streeter, A Newton, 1943, N 28,68:8
Streeter, Arch L, 1952, Ag 26,25:4
Streeter, E L, 1936, O 19,19:5
Streeter, Edward C, 1947, Je 18,25:5
Streeter, Edward C Mrs, 1964, N 6,37:3
Streeter, Elford D, 1946, My 29,23:6
Streeter, Ferdinand D Dr, 1937, Ja 22,21:3
Streeter, Frank Sherwin, 1922, D 12,19:4
Streeter, Frederick B, 1955, Ag 26,19:2
Streeter, Frederick G, 1925, Mr 8,5:3
Streeter, George L, 1948, Jl 29,21:5
Streeter, Helen W, 1957, Ag 13,27:1
Streeter, John William Dr, 1905, Je 6,9:5
Streeter, Leo, 1952, N 7,25:2
Streeter, Lewis B, 1952, Mr 12,27:5
Streeter, Milford B, 1940, My 28,23:2
Streeter, O F, 1864, Ag 28,4:6
Streeter, Samuel S, 1951, D 17,32:4
Streeter, Thomas W, 1965, Je 13,85:1
Streeter, Wilfrid A, 1962, Ap 19,31:4
Streeter, William W, 1961, Jl 21,23:4
Streeton, James W, 1915, Ag 29,15:6
Streetor, W Day Mrs, 1952, O 25,17:6
Streett, David Dr, 1915, Ag 1,15:5
Streett, Katherine B Mrs, 1941, Je 18,21:6
Streever, Fred S, 1955, F 25,21:3
Streever, Lester V, 1954, N 13,15:2
Strehan, Charles L, 1950, O 31,27:1; 1956, O 17,35:5
Strehan, George E, 1963, Ap 23,37:1
Strehl, Charles E, 1959, Ag 12,29:2
Strehl, Joseph P, 1940, F 13,23:2
Strehl, Joseph P Mrs, 1953, S 15,31:5
Strehle, Malcolm W, 1949, Je 8,29:3

Streibert, Henry, 1942, Jl 29,17:3
Streibert, Jacob A, 1942, O 2,25:5
Streich, Ernest Mrs, 1948, My 2,76:6
Streich, Herman L Rev, 1937, N 15,23:5
Streich, Paul E, 1944, Jl 13,17:3
Streicher, Charles, 1944, D 17,38:3
Streicher, Jack, 1961, Mr 13,19:4
Streicher, Samuel, 1967, N 1,51:1
Streicher, Victor M, 1959, Ap 10,26:7
Streicher, William, 1958, Mr 8,17:3
Streight, A D Col, 1864, Ag 21,5:3
Streight, Everett, 1955, Je 3,23:4
Streight, Howard, 1912, O 22,11:5
Streight, Levina Mrs, 1910, Je 7,9:4
Streisel, George D Sr, 1956, Je 20,31:2
Streisel, George J, 1946, Ag 1,23:1
Streissguth, Thomas O, 1950, D 23,15:6
Streit, Albert C, 1942, N 7,15:4
Streit, Claire, 1939, My 25,25:2
Streit, Emil A, 1950, N 9,33:3
Streit, Frank W, 1949, Je 13,19:5
Streit, Henry E, 1951, F 23,27:4
Streit, Nettie Mrs, 1937, D 2,25:4
Streit, Raymond A, 1937, Jl 11,II,4:6
Streitcher, Michael H, 1956, F 10,21:2
Streithorst, Thomas J, 1965, Ap 14,41:2
Strelecki, Marie, 1944, D 1,9:1
Strelecki, Martha de Countess, 1959, Mr 19,33:4
Strelitz, Charles, 1949, Je 6,19:3
Strelsin, William, 1965, O 18,35:2
Strelsky, Nikander, 1946, Je 21,23:4
Strelz, Elias, 1945, Mr 31,19:4
Stremlay, Emil Mrs, 1956, Ja 25,31:1
Strene, Edward, 1949, F 3,24:2
Streng, J Truman, 1953, Ap 9,27:3
Strenger, Stanley, 1949, Mr 16,27:3
Strenz, Charles F, 1954, Jl 6,23:4
Stret, Edwin, 1909, Ja 26,9:3
Stretch, Albert T, 1961, Ag 3,23:4
Stretch, Charles C, 1940, Ag 22,20:3
Stretch, Harold A, 1951, F 2,23:4
Stretch, Harry J, 1966, Ja 14,39:4
Stretch, Henry L Mrs, 1940, S 28,17:4
Stretch, William M, 1943, Ag 31,17:4
Stretton, John, 1943, F 16,19:2
Stretz, Frank, 1955, N 7,29:4
Stretz, George Mrs, 1948, Ap 1,25:3
Streubel, Ernest J, 1963, S 17,35:3
Streuber, Karl L, 1948, D 21,31:1
Streufert, Frank C, 1953, S 18,23:5
Streuli, Alfred F H, 1942, Ja 18,44:4
Streusand, Bernard L Mrs, 1967, Jl 18,37:4
Streusand, Harry, 1950, Je 8,31:3
Strevell, Clarence, 1939, Ja 7,15:3
Strever, Fred H, 1945, S 12,25:5
Streyckmans, Felix J, 1953, F 9,27:2
Stribley, Robert J, 1954, Jl 5,11:5
Stribling, C K Rear-Adm, 1880, Ja 21,2:7
Stribling, H M Mrs, 1876, Mr 24,4:7
Stribling, Herbert G, 1967, Ja 6,35:4
Stribling, P T, 1913, Ag 19,9:7
Stribling, Thomas S, 1965, Jl 9,26:2
Stribling, William L, 1956, O 15,25:2
Stribling, William L Sr, 1959, My 5,33:1
Strichter, Joseph T (Bro Wm), 1963, N 21,39:4
Strick, Frank, 1951, N 24,11:4
Strick, Frank C, 1943, Ja 17,45:2
Stricker, Adam A, 1937, Ap 2,23:5
Stricker, August D, 1964, D 5,31:2
Stricker, Fritz, 1949, Jl 10,56:5
Stricker, George J, 1945, O 10,8:2
Stricker, Henry, 1953, Ag 27,25:5
Stricker, Paul F, 1963, N 26,37:4
Stricker, Paul F Mrs, 1946, F 15,25:1
Strickland, Agnes, 1874, Jl 14,8:5
Strickland, Alice, 1874, Jl 15,4:6
Strickland, Arthur B, 1952, N 3,27:4
Strickland, Arthur H G, 1942, N 28,13:1
Strickland, Clarence W, 1967, My 6,31:5
Strickland, Claude H (por), 1945, Ap 3,19:1
Strickland, David J, 1956, O 14,87:1
Strickland, Dean A, 1953, My 14,29:4
Strickland, Edward P, 1951, Je 26,29:5
Strickland, Edward W, 1944, S 18,19:5
Strickland, Emma J Mrs, 1937, Ag 14,13:5
Strickland, Francis L, 1959, Ag 27,27:4
Strickland, George G, 1945, D 29,13:1
Strickland, George W, 1940, O 4,23:4
Strickland, Gerald Lord, 1940, Ag 23,15:5
Strickland, Helen, 1938, Ja 15,15:4
Strickland, Lloyd A, 1951, D 11,33:1
Strickland, Mark B Mrs, 1964, F 1,23:5
Strickland, Mary E Mrs, 1941, Je 25,21:1
Strickland, Norman L, 1960, Jl 4,15:5
Strickland, Robert (por), 1946, Ag 9,17:5
Strickland, Ruric H, 1942, D 31,15:4
Strickland, Sidney T, 1954, Jl 12,19:5
Strickland, Walter C, 1952, S 16,29:3
Strickland, Walter W, 1938, Ag 12,17:2
Strickland, William P Jr, 1952, Jl 28,15:4
Strickland, William R, 1950, Mr 23,29:3
Strickler, Albert, 1953, N 9,35:5
Strickler, Alfred S, 1955, Mr 31,27:2
Strickler, Charles S, 1966, Ja 1,17:6
Strickler, Gratz B, 1950, S 15,25:4
Strickler, Henry W, 1941, D 14,68:4
Strickler, Homer E, 1955, S 27,35:2
Strickler, John L, 1949, Jl 27,23:4
Strickler, Thomas J Mrs, 1958, F 1,19:2
Strickler, Virgil Osmond, 1921, S 1,15:4
Stricklett, Elmer G, 1964, Je 9,35:3
Strickling, C W, 1952, Je 17,27:2
Strickrott, Alfred C, 1942, N 14,15:5
Stridsberg, Gustaf, 1943, N 10,23:4
Striebel, John H, 1962, My 23,45:5
Strief, George A, 1946, Ap 3,25:2
Strife, Clarence J, 1953, My 25,25:2
Strife, Cyril F, 1965, O 28,43:4
Striffler, Edward C, 1939, Mr 22,23:3
Striffler, Frederick W, 1939, Ag 25,15:2
Strigner, John H, 1958, Mr 14,25:1
Strigner, Valerie, 1949, Ap 10,77:1
Strijdom, Johannes G (funl plans, Ag 26,9:8; funl, Ag 31,56:7), 1958, Ag 24,86:1
Strike, Clifford J, 1948, F 12,24:2
Striker, A K, 1883, Mr 27,5:4
Striker, Edith, 1949, Je 8,29:3
Striker, Fran, 1962, S 5,40:1
Striker, Laura P, 1959, D 24,20:2
Strimaitis, Constantine, 1949, N 10,31:2
Strindberg, August Mrs, 1943, Jl 3,13:5
Strine, Charles, 1907, Ap 7,9:5
String, Jesse H, 1943, F 23,21:2
Stringer, Arthur, 1950, S 15,25:3
Stringer, Desmond E, 1959, Ap 25,21:3
Stringer, Elizabeth, 1940, Jl 13,14:6
Stringer, John A, 1953, Jl 30,23:2
Stringer, William C, 1938, Ja 27,21:5
Stringfellow, Douglas R, 1966, O 21,41:1
Stringfellow, Elzie E, 1939, Ja 22,35:2
Stringfellow, George E Mrs, 1961, D 29,23:3
Stringfellow, Henry A, 1942, N 6,23:4
Stringfield, Lamar E, 1959, Ja 23,26:1
Stringham, Ernest J, 1940, Je 9,45:2
Stringham, Irving, 1909, O 6,9:4
Stringham, Irving J, 1943, Ap 5,19:3
Stringham (funl),(see also F 8), 1876, F 11,2:3
Strippel, Andrew, 1949, My 28,15:6
Strippel, G Capt, 1883, Ja 23,3:5
Strippel, Otto, 1966, D 23,25:1
Strippel, William, 1947, S 21,60:7
Strisik, Samuel R, 1958, S 8,29:2
Stritch, Richard, 1962, Jl 5,25:1
Stritch, Robert E Sr, 1948, Je 6,72:4
Stritch, Samuel A (funl plans, My 28,15:1; funl, Je 4,33:4), 1958, My 27,1:6
Stritch, Thomas H (por), 1943, Ja 23,13:4
Stritt, William, 1916, Jl 3,9:6
Strittar, John J, 1946, Ag 20,27:1
Strittmatter, Alvin R, 1953, Jl 14,27:1
Strittmatter, Isidor P, 1938, Ap 15,19:3
Strittmatter, Louis E, 1952, N 3,27:2
Stritzinger, Frederick G Jr Col, 1937, Ja 24,II,8:5
Strobel, Alfred J, 1947, My 2,21:2
Strobel, Daniel F, 1948, Ja 1,23:5
Strobel, Edward H, 1908, Ja 16,9:6
Strobel, Frederick, 1937, S 6,17:5
Strobel, George Rev, 1874, O 30,4:7
Strobel, John, 1953, Ap 18,19:5
Strobel, Walter E, 1950, Ag 3,23:3
Strobell, Caro L Mrs, 1940, S 19,23:5
Strobell, George H, 1925, O 6,27:5
Strobing, Samuel, 1945, Ja 8,17:4
Strobridge, Frank S, 1918, Jl 23,13:5
Strobridge, Richard L, 1955, Ag 8,21:3
Strobridge, Stuart A, 1951, Ap 30,21:5
Strobridge, Vivian, 1946, Jl 4,19:6
Strodach, Paul Z Rev Dr, 1947, Je 1,60:5
Strode, George K, 1958, O 29,35:1
Strode, George K Mrs, 1937, O 6,25:3
Strode, Harry G, 1962, Ap 12,35:3
Strodel, Earl J, 1954, Ap 26,25:2
Strodel, Frederick C, 1968, Jl 26,31:1
Strodl, George T, 1963, Jl 9,31:4
Stroebe, Lilian L, 1959, Ap 7,34:1
Stroebel, George A, 1966, Ap 4,24:6
Stroemberg, Johansen, 1946, Ja 27,42:7
Stroffolino, George Mrs, 1950, F 5,84:5
Stroh, Claire, 1953, O 27,27:5
Stroh, Donald A, 1953, D 22,31:3
Stroh, Edwin H, 1963, Jl 10,35:2
Stroh, Grant, 1949, Jl 27,23:3
Stroh, Herbert J, 1959, My 6,39:4
Stroh, Herman C, 1945, F 10,11:2
Stroh, John, 1937, Ja 26,21:3
Stroh, Simon, 1944, N 30,23:5; 1948, Mr 14,72:2
Strohbach, William, 1949, My 26,29:3
Strohbeck, Charles W, 1951, Je 1,23:3
Strohbeck, Charles W Mrs, 1949, Ja 3,23:4
Stroheim, Salo J, 1924, Mr 6,17:3
Strohl, George A, 1950, Jl 18,29:2
Strohl, Leroy S Sr, 1958, Jl 1,31:4
Strohl, Russell B, 1952, N 13,31:5
Strohle, Jacob, 1907, S 10,7:5
Strohm, Clarence R, 1937, F 18,21:2
Strohm, John, 1884, D 13,5:2
Strohmenger, Frederick G, 1952, Ag 8,17:3
Strohmenger, Paul H, 1955, S 18,86:1
Strohmeyer, Charles, 1946, Jl 13,15:6
Strohmeyer, George D, 1965, F 11,39:4
Strohmeyer, Henry A, 1943, F 26,19:5
Strohmeyer, Lillian D, 1965, Mr 1,27:4
Strok, Awsay (cor, Jl 4,19:2), 1956, Jl 3,25:4
Stroker, Jack E, 1961, Je 24,21:1
Stroll, Charles, 1946, Ja 20,42:2
Strollo, Angelo, 1941, D 22,17:4
Strollo, James, 1950, Jl 31,17:3
Strollo, Michael H, 1954, S 6,15:5
Strom, Eugene N, 1937, Ja 11,19:2
Strom, Paul H, 1959, D 16,41:3
Strom, Sverre A, 1950, Je 18,76:5
Strombach, Victor H, 1943, Ja 5,19:4
Stromberg, Asbury G E, 1963, Ap 14,92:8
Stromberg, C H, 1903, O 17,9:5
Stromberg, Eugene, 1939, Jl 22,6:7
Stromberg, Hunt, 1968, Ag 25,88:6
Stromberg, Hunt Mrs, 1951, Mr 16,31:2
Stromberg, Leonard, 1941, Jl 4,16:5
Stromberg, Paul G, 1952, N 5,27:4
Stromberg, William T, 1951, Je 25,19:3
Strome, Frank P, 1952, Jl 30,23:4
Stromenger, Richard P Mrs, 1964, My 18,29:2
Strommer, Sigfrid, 1944, O 6,23:1
Stromquist, Walter G, 1948, S 14,29:3
Stroms, T Harold D, 1955, N 29,29:4
Stronach, Carl L, 1946, My 28,21:4
Strong, Alan H, 1925, F 4,21:4
Strong, Alonijah, 1879, D 10,5:2
Strong, Andy, 1951, Je 17,V,2:4
Strong, Ann G, 1957, Je 24,23:1
Strong, Ann Hervey, 1925, Je 20,13:6
Strong, Arch M, 1941, Jl 22,19:6
Strong, Archange S Mrs, 1937, Ja 5,23:2
Strong, Augustus H Mrs, 1938, D 1,23:3
Strong, Augustus Hopkins Rev Dr (funl, D 1,19:6), 1921, D 3,13:5
Strong, Austin, 1952, S 18,29:1
Strong, B, 1928, O 17,29:1
Strong, Benjamin, 1915, N 7,21:6
Strong, Benjamin Woodhull, 1904, Ja 31,2:5
Strong, Bertha F, 1941, Ap 6,48:5
Strong, Carl H, 1944, Ap 6,23:3
Strong, Chapman E, 1938, My 19,21:3
Strong, Charles A (will, F 4,44:1), 1940, Ja 25,21:1
Strong, Charles Augustus Mrs, 1906, N 15,9:5
Strong, Charles H, 1949, Jl 31,60:1; 1951, My 12,21: 1960, My 27,31:1
Strong, Charles S, 1962, O 12,31:1
Strong, Clinton A, 1938, D 2,23:4
Strong, Cornelia L V Mrs, 1956, Ag 5,77:1
Strong, David, 1914, Ap 30,11:6
Strong, Donaldson, 1950, Ag 6,75:1
Strong, Dudley B, 1950, O 22,93:1
Strong, Edward E, 1948, My 5,25:4
Strong, Edward F, 1953, Jl 31,19:5
Strong, Edward K, 1963, D 6,35:2
Strong, Edward P, 1948, Ja 22,27:5
Strong, Edward T, 1955, N 13,88:3
Strong, Edward Trask Rear-Adm, 1909, Mr 19,9:5
Strong, Edward W, 1939, S 15,23:4
Strong, Edwin D Mrs, 1943, D 8,23:3
Strong, Edwin J, 1954, My 24,27:3
Strong, Elizabeth B, 1952, My 16,23:4
Strong, Emerson E, 1957, My 25,21:4
Strong, Emma M Mrs, 1959, Jl 26,68:2
Strong, Ernest M, 1961, Ag 31,27:1
Strong, Ernest W Maj, 1937, Jl 5,17:4
Strong, Evelina K, 1944, Mr 18,13:4
Strong, Frank J Maj, 1903, Jl 26,7:6
Strong, Frederick S, 1940, D 3,25:2
Strong, Frederick W, 1946, F 16,13:5
Strong, G C Gen, 1863, Jl 31,1:6
Strong, George F, 1957, F 28,27:5
Strong, George H, 1943, N 16,23:5
Strong, George J, 1965, Ag 21,24:2
Strong, George L, 1924, F 4,19:4
Strong, George T, 1948, Je 29,23:3
Strong, George Templeton, 1875, Jl 22,4:6
Strong, George V, 1946, Ja 12,15:1
Strong, Harold F, 1964, F 15,23:5
Strong, Harry J, 1943, N 12,21:3
Strong, Henry A, 1919, Jl 27,22:5
Strong, Henry A Mrs, 1950, Je 7,30:2
Strong, Henry B Mrs, 1946, Mr 12,25:5
Strong, Henry M, 1915, S 2,9:5
Strong, Henry T, 1949, Mr 21,23:3
Strong, Henry W, 1943, Ja 26,19:5
Strong, Herbert T, 1951, Je 13,29:6
Strong, Howard M, 1949, D 26,29:4
Strong, Hugh J, 1964, S 12,25:5
Strong, Irving E, 1940, D 27,19:3
Strong, J Claud F, 1947, My 21,25:2
Strong, J H, 1882, N 29,5:4
Strong, J Montgomery, 1938, F 12,15:3
Strong, Jacob H, 1960, Mr 17,33:5
Strong, Jacob H Jr, 1958, Ja 20,23:4
Strong, James A, 1951, F 3,15:3
Strong, James B, 1942, N 11,25:2
Strong, James G, 1938, Ja 13,21:1

Strong, James M, 1943, F 13,11:3; 1949, N 10,31:1
Strong, James M Mrs, 1950, F 22,29:3
Strong, James R, 1940, O 26,15:3
Strong, James R Mrs, 1961, D 4,37:3
Strong, Jane S, 1955, O 7,25:3
Strong, Jay M, 1917, Mr 14,9:4
Strong, John, 1941, N 14,23:2; 1952, O 14,31:1
Strong, John E, 1965, Je 16,43:1
Strong, John S Sr, 1949, D 10,17:3
Strong, John W, 1904, Ja 4,9:6
Strong, John Y, 1942, N 14,16:3
Strong, Joseph F, 1959, My 13,37:4
Strong, Joseph H, 1941, Ag 6,17:5
Strong, Josiah Mrs, 1918, F 19,13:6
Strong, Josiah Rev Dr, 1916, Ap 29,11:5
Strong, Julia E Mrs, 1951, D 30,24:5
Strong, Julius L, 1872, S 8,5:4
Strong, Katherine C Mrs, 1937, Ja 20,22:1
Strong, L C, 1879, D 19,4:7
Strong, L Corrin, 1966, S 20,47:1
Strong, Lee A (por), 1941, Je 3,21:4
Strong, Leonard A G, 1958, Ag 19,27:3
Strong, Louis E, 1948, Mr 10,27:3
Strong, Lydia (Mrs D M Pond), 1966, F 3,31:1
Strong, Margaret D, 1947, Je 25,25:5
Strong, Marguerite G Mrs (will), 1938, D 11,2:6
Strong, Martin, 1945, My 24,19:5
Strong, Miriam C, 1964, Jl 17,27:4
Strong, Nathan L, 1939, D 15,25:3
Strong, Oliver S, 1951, F 24,13:2
Strong, Olyphant Mrs, 1949, Ap 23,13:5
Strong, Paul E, 1947, N 8,17:6
Strong, Phil A, 1948, Jl 3,15:4
Strong, Phil A Mrs (cor, My 28,23:6), 1940, My 26, 35:1
Strong, Porter, 1923, Je 12,19:2
Strong, Prentice Sr, 1960, F 13,19:5
Strong, Pritchard H, 1937, Ag 30,21:4
Strong, Pritchard H Mrs, 1937, Ag 30,21:4
Strong, Putnam B, 1945, N 17,17:4
Strong, Rebecca Mrs, 1944, Ap 27,23:3
Strong, Richard A (por),(will, Ap 30,16:4), 1937, Ap 7,25:1
Strong, Richard P (por), 1948, Jl 5,15:3
Strong, Richard U, 1958, O 19,87:2
Strong, Robert C, 1946, Je 9,40:5
Strong, Robert Jr Mrs, 1953, Je 23,29:2
Strong, Samuel D, 1941, Ag 20,19:5
Strong, Samuel M, 1946, F 3,39:1
Strong, Selah B, 1945, Je 20,23:4
Strong, Selah B Mrs, 1956, F 19,93:1
Strong, Sidney Mrs, 1903, O 15,9:1
Strong, Solomon C, 1950, O 15,104:4
Strong, Sydney, 1939, Ja 1,24:7
Strong, Theodore, 1953, N 3,28:3
Strong, Theron G, 1924, D 7,7:1
Strong, Theron R Judge, 1873, My 15,4:7
Strong, Theron R Mrs, 1955, D 16,30:1
Strong, Thomas B, 1944, Je 11,45:2
Strong, Thomas S, 1960, N 3,39:1
Strong, Tracy, 1968, Mr 5,41:1
Strong, W A, 1931, My 11,19:1
Strong, W M, 1884, Mr 29,5:3
Strong, Walter, 1954, N 5,15:3
Strong, Walter A Sr Mrs (will, O 4,34:1), 1961, O 1, 86:2
Strong, Wendell M, 1942, Mr 31,21:5
Strong, Wendell M Mrs, 1956, Ag 19,92:8
Strong, William A, 1947, S 8,21:2
Strong, William Barstow, 1914, Ag 4,11:6
Strong, William D, 1962, Ja 30,29:2
Strong, William E S, 1947, F 25,25:5
Strong, William Judge, 1895, Ag 20,9:5
Strong, William L, 1900, N 3,14:1; 1939, D 29,15:2
Strong, William L Mrs, 1921, Jl 28,13:4
Strong, William M, 1941, Mr 27,23:6; 1947, Ap 13,60:2
Strong, William S, 1903, S 13,7:5
Strong, William T Mrs, 1948, O 24,76:4
Strong, William V D, 1950, F 24,23:4
Strong, Winifred I, 1960, O 23,89:1
Strong, Woodbridge, 1907, Ag 24,7:4
Stronge, Francis Sir, 1924, Ag 21,11:4
Strongheart, Nipo, 1967, Ja 6,35:3
Strongilos, John, 1960, D 18,85:1
Strongin, Harry Mrs, 1951, S 22,17:2
Strongin, Isidor Mrs, 1945, F 11,40:5
Strongin, Theodore M Mrs, 1954, Mr 9,27:3
Strongman, Richard H, 1940, D 29,24:7
Stronski, Stanislaw, 1955, N 3,31:3
Stroock, Ely (por), 1949, O 8,13:5
Stroock, Irving S, 1943, Je 13,45:1
Stroock, James E, 1965, Jl 23,29:1
Stroock, Joseph Mrs (por), 1948, Ag 15,60:2
Stroock, Louis S, 1925, Mr 30,17:5
Stroock, M J, 1931, O 28,23:1
Stroock, Samuel, 1939, Jl 1,17:4
Stroock, Sol M, 1941, S 12,21:1
Stroock, Sol M Mrs (will, Ag 3,15:8),(por), 1945, Jl 30,19:4
Stroock, Stephen J, 1956, S 10,27:5
Stroock, Sylvan I, 1952, My 18,93:1
Strook, Joseph, 1946, Ag 27,27:3
Strootman, John, 1937, My 5,25:2
Stropp, Leon E, 1961, Ap 3,30:3
Strosnider, Charles A, 1952, F 28,27:5
Stross, Barnett, 1967, My 15,43:2
Stross, Ines Mrs (will), 1942, Jl 30,18:4
Stross, William, 1965, D 30,23:4
Strother, F, 1933, Mr 13,13:1
Strother, James F Mrs, 1947, N 29,13:4
Strother, T Nelson, 1939, My 23,23:3
Strother, Theodosia, 1882, D 12,3:5
Strothmann, Frederick, 1958, My 14,33:2
Strothotte, Maurice A, 1937, O 24,II,9:3
Strott, George G, 1953, Ap 8,29:3
Strotz, Charles N Mrs, 1948, F 23,25:4
Strotz, Sidney N, 1963, N 8,43:4
Stroub, John L, 1959, Mr 15,88:5
Stroud, Ben K, 1950, Mr 4,17:6
Stroud, E Homan, 1954, Je 26,13:4
Stroud, Elsworth W, 1953, O 15,33:2
Stroud, George M, 1875, Je 30,4:6
Stroud, George S, 1961, S 27,42:1
Stroud, Harry W Sr, 1949, N 19,17:3
Stroud, Herbert K L, 1958, Jl 29,23:4
Stroud, Herbert K Mrs, 1939, Ap 29,17:3
Stroud, Morris W, 1941, Ja 8,19:5
Stroud, R W, 1875, D 3,4:7
Stroud, Robert, 1963, N 22,37:1
Stroud, William, 1938, My 28,15:5
Stroud, William D, 1959, Ag 20,25:3
Stroud, William D Jr, 1950, Ap 10,35:5
Stroud, William F, 1941, S 14,49:2
Strough, Allen C, 1941, Ja 3,20:2
Stroup, F Neff, 1938, Mr 10,21:5
Stroup, Freeman P, 1952, Jl 20,52:6
Stroup, George Y, 1947, Jl 31,21:6
Stroup, J Harry, 1938, Ag 21,32:6
Stroup, Jasper D, 1957, D 23,23:2
Stroup, Robert T, 1962, N 21,33:4
Stroup, Samuel B, 1947, Mr 27,27:1
Stroup, Sarah D Mrs, 1942, Ja 24,15:8
Stroup, Thomas A, 1943, Ag 29,39:3
Stroup, Walter M, 1957, My 8,37:1
Strousberg, B H Dr, 1884, Je 16,2:3
Strouse, Alfred N Dr, 1923, F 14,17:5
Strouse, Isaac, 1912, D 13,15:4
Strouse, Leopold, 1904, F 23,7:6
Strouse, M, 1878, F 12,5:3
Strouse, William F, 1945, D 6,27:5
Strousland, John I, 1956, O 16,33:2
Strouss, Charles L Sr, 1958, Mr 2,88:8
Strousse, Leo, 1940, D 1,62:4
Strout, A C, 1880, Jl 3,8:5
Strout, Edwin A, 1952, Mr 30,92:5
Strout, George M, 1945, My 20,32:1
Strout, Henry M, 1959, Jl 6,27:5
Strout, Lewis F, 1946, Je 23,40:2
Strout, Sewell Cushing, 1914, Ag 11,9:6
Strout, William A, 1950, Ap 17,24:2
Strow, Frederick, 1940, D 21,11:7
Strowd, Wallace H, 1946, Mr 15,21:2
Strowger, Frank O, 1951, Mr 16,31:5
Stroyden, Basil M, 1956, Ag 13,19:4
Stroyen, Basil M Mrs, 1951, D 12,37:4
Stroz, Harold C, 1959, O 31,23:3
Strozier, Robert M, 1960, Ap 21,31:1
Strub, Charles H, 1958, Mr 29,17:6
Strub, Charles H Mrs, 1968, Ag 14,39:3
Strub, Joseph F, 1963, S 9,27:1
Strube, Gustav Dr, 1953, F 3,25:3
Strube, Sidney, 1956, Mr 5,23:2
Strubel, George, 1947, O 5,68:3
Strubel, John L, 1940, N 14,23:2
Struber, Charles F, 1951, O 26,23:1
Strubin, Paul, 1951, Ag 21,27:3
Strubing, John K Jr, 1961, Ja 30,23:4
Struble, Amos, 1942, F 22,26:2
Struble, Clyde W, 1948, D 4,13:4
Struble, Dale B, 1952, Ap 23,29:3
Struble, George, 1938, Mr 30,21:4
Struble, Stanley, 1955, F 4,21:2
Struch, Anna Mrs, 1944, My 13,19:3
Struck, Charles J, 1948, S 5,40:4
Struck, Harry C Sr, 1949, Je 5,92:6
Struck, Henrietta (will), 1967, Mr 17,46:8
Struck, Henriette, 1941, Ja 8,19:2
Struck, Hermann, 1944, Ja 15,13:4
Struck, Kuno H, 1947, Mr 6,25:3
Struck, Otto T, 1942, My 6,19:3
Struckmann, H, 1933, N 18,15:1
Strudee, Doveton Sir, 1925, My 12,23:5
Strufe, Adolph, 1940, O 13,49:2
Strug, Andrew, 1937, D 10,25:4
Strugnell, Warren C, 1947, S 29,21:1
Strugstad, Oscar, 1953, Mr 16,19:3
Struhl, Morris, 1952, Jl 27,57:2
Struhs, Arno J, 1965, F 12,29:1
Strum, Arthur L, 1947, Ag 13,23:6
Strum, Fred A, 1947, Jl 10,21:5
Strum, Hyman, 1964, Ag 2,77:1
Strum, Louie, 1954, Jl 27,21:5
Strum, Nellie A, 1947, Je 12,25:5
Strum, Werner Mrs, 1955, Ja 4,21:5
Strumer, Samuel (por), 1940, D 10,25:4
Struminski, Gustaw, 1954, Mr 14,88:4
Strumpen-Darrie, Jacques, 1953, Jl 3,19:5
Strumpf, Dorothy, 1962, Mr 15,32:4
Strunk, Elmer F Sr, 1961, Ja 17,37:4
Strunk, Grover I, 1953, My 14,29:5
Strunk, Harry D, 1960, Ag 7,85:1
Strunk, Peter H, 1954, S 2,21:6
Strunk, William, 1946, S 27,23:3
Strunsky, Albert, 1942, Ja 2,34:3
Strunsky, Albert Mrs, 1962, Jl 20,25:1
Strunsky, Anna (Mrs W E Walling), 1964, F 26,35:4
Strunsky, Hyman, 1942, Ap 13,15:2
Strunsky, Maurice I, 1954, My 4,29:3
Strunsky, Max, 1957, D 2,27:5
Strunsky, Simeon, 1948, F 6,23:1
Strunz, Clara E, 1942, Mr 4,19:5
Strupper, Everett, 1950, F 5,84:6
Struss, Carl M, 1960, F 12,27:1
Struss, William K, 1937, S 14,23:6
Strusser, Harry, 1954, My 19,32:4
Strut, A B, 1881, Je 3,5:4
Strut, Elias Mrs, 1943, Ja 26,19:1
Struther, Jan, 1953, Jl 21,23:1
Struthers, Clayton P, 1950, Ap 18,31:4
Struthers, George H, 1966, Mr 17,39:2
Struthers, John Jr, 1953, S 21,25:4
Struthers, John Walter Wood, 1916, N 14,11:2
Struthers, Joseph, 1924, F 19,15:2
Struthers, Marie D Mrs, 1938, Ap 16,20:3
Struthers, Robert, 1951, My 11,27:4
Struthers, W E Mrs, 1946, Je 13,27:4
Struthers, William W Jr, 1961, My 29,19:4
Strutt, Henry (Baron Belper), 1914, Jl 27,7:7
Strutt, John William (Lord Raleigh), 1919, Jl 2,13:3
Strutt, William, 1915, Ja 5,15:5
Struve, Gustave, 1870, Ag 31,8:1
Struve, Otto (cor, Ap 10,39:1), 1963, Ap 9,31:2
Struve, Vasily V, 1965, S 17,6:1
Struven, Paul, 1968, N 2,37:5
Struycken, A A H Prof, 1923, Jl 29,6:5
Struyk, John A, 1967, Jl 22,26:1
Struyk, John S, 1937, Ap 16,24:1
Strybing, Henry Sr, 1942, My 4,19:6
Strydio, Charles H, 1958, Jl 17,27:4
Stryjak, Joseph, 1952, D 20,17:6
Stryker, Arthur W, 1951, Ap 5,29:3
Stryker, Burdett, 1941, Ja 11,17:3
Stryker, Carol, 1944, My 7,47:1
Stryker, Charles, 1950, O 24,29:1
Stryker, Clarence W, 1955, Ja 4,21:4
Stryker, Daniel, 1964, F 9,88:5
Stryker, Daniel Mrs, 1951, Ap 24,29:1
Stryker, Edward B, 1939, D 21,23:6
Stryker, Elsie G, 1953, Jl 14,27:4
Stryker, Eugene F Sr, 1958, O 6,31:4
Stryker, Fred, 1948, O 14,29:1
Stryker, Frederick H, 1939, Ap 23,III,7:2
Stryker, Garrett V, 1952, Ja 1,25:5
Stryker, George B Mrs, 1949, Ja 8,15:4
Stryker, Gustave, 1943, Je 4,21:3
Stryker, Julius B B, 1957, Ap 28,87:2
Stryker, Leonard W S, 1959, F 11,39:3
Stryker, Lloyd P (will, Jl 15,40:4), 1955, Je 22,29:1
Stryker, Margaret T Mrs, 1939, Ag 4,13:2
Stryker, Max, 1951, Mr 20,29:4
Stryker, Raymond C, 1955, F 2,27:4
Stryker, Richard Daniel, 1907, Ag 13,7:6
Stryker, Russell A, 1964, N 30,33:5
Stryker, Russell F, 1966, O 24,39:2
Stryker, Sidney S, 1951, Ag 20,19:4
Stryker, William A, 1945, My 17,19:2
Strype, Frederick C Sr, 1959, Ap 12,86:3
Strzelecki, John H Msgr, 1918, D 9,13:4
Stuart, A C, 1949, Ag 1,17:3
Stuart, A H, 1912, F 12,11:5
Stuart, Aaron C, 1938, My 25,23:5
Stuart, Alexander, 1879, D 24,5:3
Stuart, Alfred O Mrs (Ruth McEnery Stuart), 1917, My 8,11:5
Stuart, Allison E, 1950, S 10,92:3
Stuart, C E, 1881, Ja 16,8:2
Stuart, Charles, 1939, Ag 18,19:4; 1939, S 6,23:5
Stuart, Charles A, 1962, O 19,20:6
Stuart, Charles E, 1937, F 7,II,8:1
Stuart, Charles E (por), 1943, Je 21,17:3
Stuart, Charles E Sr, 1951, Ag 1,24:4
Stuart, Charles H, 1950, D 22,24:3
Stuart, Charles J B, 1964, S 20,88:4
Stuart, Charles M, 1954, My 18,30:3
Stuart, Charles M Mrs, 1940, F 26,15:4
Stuart, Charles T, 1958, Jl 30,29:3
Stuart, Charles W, 1948, Ag 15,60:2; 1951, O 2,27:2
Stuart, Clyde, 1961, F 11,23:2
Stuart, D D V Mrs, 1940, O 17,25:3
Stuart, Dan A, 1909, N 16,9:5
Stuart, David G, 1954, Ap 6,30:8
Stuart, David Mrs, 1914, Je 28,15:6
Stuart, Donald C, 1943, Je 3,21:2
Stuart, Duane R, 1941, Ag 30,13:6
Stuart, Duane R Mrs, 1962, F 24,27:4
Stuart, E N, 1879, Jl 28,2:6
Stuart, Edward P, 1955, F 3,23:2
Stuart, Edward T, 1940, D 13,23:6
Stuart, Edwin S (por), 1937, Mr 22,23:3

Stuart, Elbridge A, 1944, Ja 15,13:3
Stuart, Elbridge H Mrs, 1937, Ag 22,II,7:1
Stuart, Francis H Dr, 1910, S 5,7:5
Stuart, George, 1943, N 20,13:5
Stuart, George B, 1962, Jl 12,29:4
Stuart, George F, 1946, My 28,21:2
Stuart, George L, 1951, N 6,29:3
Stuart, George R, 1964, O 15,39:3
Stuart, George S, 1957, S 29,86:7
Stuart, George 3d, 1944, Jl 12,19:6
Stuart, H L, 1879, S 6,3:2; 1928, Ag 27,19:5
Stuart, Harold L (will filed, Jl 7,49:6), 1966, Jl 1,35:1
Stuart, Helen K Mrs, 1956, Mr 13,86:7
Stuart, Henry C (por), 1938, My 14,15:5
Stuart, Henry J, 1950, Ja 25,27:3
Stuart, Inglis, 1942, My 17,47:3
Stuart, Isla M T Mrs, 1955, My 28,15:5
Stuart, J Bruce Sr, 1957, D 24,15:4
Stuart, J C, 1945, Mr 17,13:5
Stuart, J E, 1931, Mr 9,21:1
Stuart, J Leighton (funl plans, S 21,30:5; mem ser, D 1,15:6), 1962, S 20,33:4
Stuart, J Martin, 1953, Ap 26,85:3
Stuart, James, 1879, Mr 27,2:4; 1942, Ja 16,21:4; 1960, Je 3,31:4
Stuart, James A, 1950, N 24,35:3
Stuart, James E, 1941, Ja 4,13:6
Stuart, James Edwin, 1968, D 26,37:3
Stuart, James M, 1952, F 26,28:3
Stuart, James Marshall, 1925, Ja 5,21:4
Stuart, Janet Erskine, 1914, O 22,11:4
Stuart, John C, 1914, Mr 5,9:4
Stuart, John H, 1957, D 25,31:4
Stuart, John L, 1966, Mr 27,86:6
Stuart, John M, 1939, Ag 13,29:1
Stuart, John McH Mrs, 1965, F 10,41:2
Stuart, John Sobieski Chevalier, 1872, Mr 2,5:1
Stuart, John V, 1952, S 4,27:4
Stuart, John W, 1958, Ag 21,25:2
Stuart, Joseph, 1874, N 19,4:6; 1944, Ja 16,43:1
Stuart, Josephine B, 1940, N 10,57:2
Stuart, Kenneth, 1945, N 5,19:4
Stuart, Kenneth E, 1951, My 25,27:3
Stuart, Lincoln A, 1940, F 4,40:4
Stuart, Louis C, 1953, D 25,17:3
Stuart, Lyman K, 1964, Je 29,27:4
Stuart, Malcolm, 1925, O 8,27:4
Stuart, Mary Mrs, 1873, Mr 24,4:6
Stuart, Mildred G Mrs, 1950, Jl 11,31:1
Stuart, Minnie P, 1953, Ag 16,77:1
Stuart, Neil, 1961, N 16,39:1
Stuart, Paul M, 1949, O 30,56:1
Stuart, Percy C, 1948, N 30,27:1
Stuart, R L, 1882, D 13,5:1
Stuart, Ralph, 1915, S 14,11:5
Stuart, Ralph E, 1965, Mr 27,27:3
Stuart, Ralph R, 1952, N 5,27:3
Stuart, Ray R, 1949, My 2,25:2
Stuart, Robert Mrs, 1953, S 25,21:4
Stuart, Robert P W Mrs, 1946, F 22,25:2
Stuart, Robert Watson, 1920, My 9,22:4
Stuart, Rodney B (cor, Ag 29,29:1), 1956, Ag 28,27:3
Stuart, Ronald N, 1954, F 11,29:2
Stuart, Ruth Y Mrs, 1937, Ag 8,II,6:2
Stuart, Serene D Mrs, 1941, My 31,11:4
Stuart, Sidney H, 1871, S 17,5:3
Stuart, Silas, 1908, S 12,7:6
Stuart, Sinclair, 1908, F 12,7:6
Stuart, Sterling M, 1905, Ap 22,11:2
Stuart, Theodore M, 1946, Ja 16,23:1
Stuart, Thomas Anderson Sir, 1920, Mr 4,11:5
Stuart, Thomas H, 1940, Jl 21,28:8
Stuart, W (E O'Flaherty), 1886, D 29,1:5
Stuart, W (E O'Flaherty), 1887, Ja 1,3:2
Stuart, W Harry, 1948, Je 5,15:5
Stuart, W Harry Mrs, 1950, N 29,33:3
Stuart, W Searight, 1947, F 12,25:3
Stuart, Walter, 1942, D 26,11:5
Stuart, William C, 1919, N 15,11:4
Stuart, William G, 1954, Mr 12,21:4
Stuart, William H, 1942, S 20,41:4; 1962, F 13,35:4
Stuart, William J C, 1937, F 18,21:5
Stuart, William M, 1957, Ap 13,19:4
Stuart, William P Mrs, 1957, O 3,29:4
Stuart, William Rev, 1916, My 9,11:5
Stuart, William Whitewright, 1914, Ap 1,13:5
Stuart, Wilmer, 1921, Ja 31,9:4
Stuart-Bullock, Wayne, 1965, Jl 24,21:5
Stuart-Jones, Henry Sir, 1939, Je 30,19:5
Stuart-Linton, Adolphus F Mrs, 1944, F 19,14:8
Stuart-Linton, Charles E T, 1962, D 4,41:1
Stuart-Richardson, Henry James Sir (Earl of Castlestewart), 1914, Je 7,5:6
Stuart-Wortley, E, 1934, Mr 20,23:3
Stubb, Quincy, 1937, F 22,17:2
Stubbings, Samuel W, 1944, F 11,19:2
Stubbins, Howard, 1957, Ap 2,31:1
Stubbins, Robert C, 1941, N 8,19:2
Stubblebine, Albert N, 1941, Ag 12,19:4
Stubblefield, D W Mrs, 1959, Ag 20,25:4
Stubblefield, Edward M, 1959, F 1,84:4
Stubblefield, George W, 1940, Ag 30,19:2
Stubblefield, John R, 1963, S 25,43:1
Stubbs, Beulah, 1910, Mr 28,9:4
Stubbs, David D, 1908, S 8,9:4
Stubbs, Edgar S, 1945, Jl 8,11:5
Stubbs, Frederick D, 1947, F 10,29:2
Stubbs, George E Dr, 1937, D 28,21:5
Stubbs, Harry, 1948, Ja 12,19:5
Stubbs, Henry E, 1937, Mr 1,20:1
Stubbs, Joseph Edward Stubbs Dr, 1914, My 28,13:5
Stubbs, Leslie L, 1952, Mr 2,92:1
Stubbs, Lewis S, 1958, My 14,33:5
Stubbs, Mary F Mrs, 1953, Jl 1,29:5
Stubbs, Ralph S (por), 1948, Ap 28,27:5
Stubbs, Ralph S Mrs, 1939, Ja 22,35:1
Stubbs, Reginald E, 1947, D 9,29:3
Stubbs, Richard Mrs, 1948, Mr 19,23:2
Stubbs, Robert L, 1950, My 3,29:1
Stubbs, Robert S, 1925, Mr 20,19:5
Stubbs, Roscoe Mrs, 1954, Je 9,31:3
Stubbs, W R, 1929, Mr 26,31:3
Stubbs, William B Mrs, 1939, Je 13,23:4
Stubenbord, William, 1939, My 25,25:1
Stubenrauch, Arnold V Prof, 1917, F 14,9:5
Stubenrauch, Eugene A, 1953, N 16,25:3
Stuber, Adolph Mrs, 1953, F 8,89:2
Stuber, G H Mrs, 1951, Ja 30,25:3
Stuber, James W, 1955, N 25,27:2
Stuber, William G, 1959, Je 19,25:1
Stubins, Jacob R, 1955, Mr 30,29:4
Stubling, Frederick J, 1942, Ja 6,23:5
Stuchell, John E, 1947, D 21,52:4
Stuchell, William T, 1952, N 12,27:5
Stuchin, Max, 1951, Ap 14,15:3
Stuck, Hudson Rev, 1920, O 13,15:3
Stucke, John F, 1940, Ag 2,15:6
Stucken, F Van Der, 1929, Ag 20,27:3
Stuckenberg, J H W Rev, 1903, My 31,7:6
Stuckert, Harry, 1952, Mr 6,31:1
Stuckert, Howard M, 1956, Mr 2,23:3
Stuckey, Charles N, 1954, Mr 22,27:2
Stuckey, Merrill M, 1947, F 1,15:4
Stuckgold, Jacques, 1953, My 6,31:3
Stucki, Arnold, 1948, Ja 12,19:4
Stucki, Juerg, 1943, O 21,27:4
Stucki, Walter, 1963, O 10,41:2
Stucklen, Regina Mrs, 1909, N 23,9:4
Stuckless, E Cranford, 1950, N 15,31:5
Stucky, Charles J, 1938, D 29,19:2
Stucky, William M (funl plans, Ja 3,27:8; funl, Ja 8,86:3), 1961, Ja 2,25:1
Studd, John E K, 1944, Ja 15,13:5
Studd, Ronald G, 1956, Ja 18,31:4
Studdiford, Andrew D, 1954, Je 22,27:4
Studdiford, Andrew D Mrs, 1964, Ja 22,37:4
Studdiford, Hervey, 1957, Ja 2,27:1
Studdiford, Hervey Mrs, 1956, O 13,19:2
Studdiford, William E Jr, 1964, My 30,17:4
Studdiford, William Emory Dr, 1925, N 18,23:3
Studds, Colin, 1915, S 12,17:4
Stude, Henry, 1951, S 23,86:1
Studebaker, Adele, 1959, D 1,39:2
Studebaker, Clement, 1901, N 28,7:5
Studebaker, George M, 1939, Ag 29,21:3
Studebaker, J M Jr, 1947, Ap 28,23:6
Studebaker, J M Jr Mrs, 1952, S 21,88:1
Studebaker, J M 3d, 1945, N 9,19:3
Studebaker, John Mohler, 1917, Mr 17,13:4
Studebaker, John W Mrs, 1956, Mr 21,38:2
Studebaker, Maria, 1925, My 26,21:4
Studebaker, Thomas H, 1940, N 2,15:3
Studebaker, Thomas H Mrs, 1947, D 20,17:4
Studebaker, Wilbur F, 1905, O 15,9:7
Studenski, Paul, 1961, N 3,36:1
Student, Alex, 1959, Je 1,27:4
Studer, Augustus C, 1922, Je 10,11:6
Studer, Augustus C Jr (funl plans, Ja 6,89:2), 1957, Ja 5,17:5
Studer, Augustus C Mrs, 1943, Mr 10,19:4
Studer, Charles E, 1950, S 13,27:4
Studer, Friedrich, 1945, Ag 14,21:2
Studer, Jacob H, 1904, Ag 8,7:5
Studiford, Grace, 1947, O 24,23:4
Studin, Charles H, 1950, Mr 7,27:2
Studley, Elmer E (por), 1942, S 7,19:3
Studley, Garson, 1940, N 7,25:3
Studley, James D, 1912, Ag 18,II,11:6
Studley, John B, 1910, Ag 9,9:5
Studley, Lucy A, 1962, Ag 19,88:3
Studley, Robert L, 1937, Mr 31,23:2
Studley-Herbert, Derek, 1960, Mr 27,86:7
Studner, David M Mrs, 1959, Jl 21,29:1
Studt, Frederick L, 1947, S 15,17:2
Studt, Frederick R, 1948, N 10,29:1
Studt, Henry F, 1956, F 20,23:3
Studwell, Augustus, 1937, Je 15,23:3
Studwell, Edwin A, 1942, Ja 22,17:4
Studwell, Harry S Mrs, 1938, Je 27,17:3
Studwell, J J, 1884, D 13,5:2
Studwell, Joseph H, 1945, My 22,19:4
Studwell, S Frederic B, 1938, Ap 6,23:4
Studwell, Theodore R, 1959, F 25,31:4
Studwell, William G, 1940, Mr 17,48:7
Study, Jackson W, 1950, Mr 18,13:2
Studzinski, Joseph, 1954, D 5,89:2
Stuebi, Edward C, 1952, D 16,31:2
Stueck, Phillip J, 1958, Je 26,27:5
Stuelpnagel, Benno von (por), 1940, F 21,19:2
Stuerenburg, Casper, 1909, Mr 27,9:4
Stuerhof, John, 1922, Ag 25,13:5
Stuerm, Frank J, 1949, Jl 12,27:6
Stuers, A L E Dr, 1919, My 6,15:6
Stuhl, Nicolas, 1943, D 13,23:5
Stuhldreher, Harry A (funl, Ja 31,V,7:7), 1965, Ja 27, 1:2
Stuhldreher, William J, 1939, O 2,17:3
Stuhler, Charles H, 1951, Ap 13,23:2
Stuhler, Robert, 1961, S 15,30:6
Stuhlmiller, Elizabeth O Mrs, 1948, F 22,48:4
Stuhrmann, Henry A, 1951, Ja 5,21:2
Stuiber, William A Sr, 1948, N 6,13:5
Stuke, Emmy, 1953, Ap 7,29:4
Stukels, Edward, 1956, Ag 3,20:2
Stukes, Taylor H, 1961, F 21,35:3
Stukhart, F F, 1943, Mr 27,13:5
Stulack, Michael J, 1949, D 11,93:1
Stulginskis, Bruce A, 1955, S 24,19:5
Stull, Arthur G, 1960, O 5,41:2
Stull, Arthur L, 1942, My 23,13:5
Stull, Benjamin S, 1951, O 15,25:4
Stull, De Forest, 1938, D 11,60:6
Stull, H C, 1905, Ap 26,2:3
Stull, Henry, 1913, Mr 19,13:3
Stull, John M, 1939, Ag 3,19:6
Stull, Leon E, 1940, F 10,15:4
Stull, Ray T, 1944, Ja 7,17:4
Stulman, Samuel, 1962, Ag 27,23:6
Stultes, Elias D, 1954, D 11,13:1
Stults, Annie K Mrs, 1944, D 2,13:6
Stults, Austin W, 1953, My 31,72:7
Stults, Grover C, 1950, O 27,29:3
Stults, Horace, 1948, D 25,17:6
Stults, Robert H, 1946, D 10,31:5
Stults, Robert M Mrs, 1947, S 22,23:5
Stultz, Charles E, 1952, My 17,19:4
Stultz, Henry B, 1957, Jl 21,60:4
Stultz, Vernon L D Dr, 1937, D 31,15:3
Stumberg, J H, 1933, Ja 22,24:3
Stumer, L V, 1919, Jl 15,11:2
Stumm, Ferdinand von, 1923, Ag 3,15:4
Stumm, Louis C, 1911, My 24,11:4
Stump, A Welles, 1958, F 24,19:2
Stump, Albert, 1958, Ag 5,27:5
Stump, George F, 1925, Ap 23,21:3
Stump, Horace E, 1939, Jl 12,19:6
Stump, J Henry, 1949, Je 16,30:4
Stump, John S Jr, 1953, Ap 22,29:5
Stump, William Mrs, 1959, D 14,31:4
Stumpe, O Arthur, 1956, Jl 14,15:6
Stumpf, Arthur J, 1948, Mr 30,23:5
Stumpf, Charles, 1939, S 27,25:2; 1943, S 8,24:2
Stumpf, Donald L, 1967, Ag 13,81:1
Stumpf, Eileen, 1950, Ja 15,41:4
Stumpf, Frederick, 1950, Ja 15,41:4
Stumpf, Gustav A, 1952, S 2,23:4
Stumpf, Henry, 1923, Ap 24,21:4
Stumpf, Jacob W, 1954, Je 30,27:3
Stumpf, John F, 1941, D 29,15:5
Stumpf, Reinhard A, 1963, Je 26,39:2
Stumpfel, William H, 1940, Jl 25,17:3
Stumpp, George E M, 1943, S 5,28:4
Stumvoll, Ernest W, 1955, Ap 22,25:2
Stumwasser, Samuel, 1953, Mr 9,29:2
Stunkard, Horace W Mrs, 1968, My 19,86:1
Stunkard, Monroe, 1940, Ag 26,15:4
Stuntz, Homer Bp, 1924, Je 4,23:5
Stuntz, John E, 1957, N 28,31:4
Stuntz, John E Mrs, 1954, Ag 16,17:5
Stunzi, Hans, 1925, Jl 28,13:6
Stunzi, 1947, N 24,23:4
Stupart, Frederick, 1940, S 28,17:5
Stupell, Norman J, 1963, Jl 15,29:5
Stupka, Vincent P, 1959, Mr 10,36:1
Stupp, Louis F, 1937, Ap 13,25:4
Stupp, Mary A Mrs, 1938, S 4,17:3
Stur, Louis S Mrs (G Whitney), 1963, S 14,25:2
Sturani, Giuseppe, 1940, Ja 18,23:1
Sturchio, Eugenio, 1965, Mr 18,33:3
Sturcke, Albert Sr, 1941, Jl 4,13:5
Sturcke, Herman, 1962, O 12,31:1
Sturcke, Matilda M, 1951, N 6,29:3
Sturdee, E T, 1940, F 9,19:1
Sturdevant, Albert G, 1947, D 19,25:3
Sturdevant, Clarence L, 1958, Ap 2,31:2
Sturdevant, Edward W, 1952, O 9,31:2
Sturdevant, Elijah, 1953, Je 4,29:5
Sturdevant, Fred E, 1954, O 14,29:5
Sturdevant, George A, 1950, N 7,27:5
Sturdevant, George U Mrs, 1947, Mr 27,27:3
Sturdevant, James H, 1948, D 24,17:2
Sturdevant, Jessie T, 1951, My 15,31:2
Sturdevant, William L, 1952, Jl 3,25:1
Sturdy, Carlton F, 1946, Jl 27,17:2
Sturdy, Charles F, 1937, Je 22,23:3
Sturedee, Frederick Doveton, 1925, My 8,19:5
Sturegeon, Ben, 1943, Jl 2,19:6
Sturge, J Howard, 1937, S 27,21:3
Sturgeon, D, 1878, Jl 5,6:3

Sturgeon, John D, 1957, F 22,21:3
Sturgeon, Robert M, 1941, S 25,25:1
Sturgeon, William A Mrs (E V Berg), 1960, Ja 26, 33:3
Sturgeon, William E, 1950, S 6,29:2
Sturgeon, William S, 1943, Ap 30,21:6
Sturges, Alfred B, 1950, Ja 28,13:5
Sturges, Arthur Pemberton, 1919, Jl 1,13:3
Sturges, Charles M, 1954, Jl 24,13:2
Sturges, Dwight C, 1940, S 9,15:4
Sturges, Edward A, 1943, My 4,23:4
Sturges, Edward E, 1949, Je 3,25:3
Sturges, Fred S Mrs, 1951, Je 12,29:4
Sturges, George W, 1939, D 12,27:2
Sturges, Harry W, 1959, S 26,23:1
Sturges, Henry G, 1939, D 8,25:3
Sturges, Hollister Mrs, 1960, Jl 3,32:4
Sturges, Howard, 1955, O 9,87:2
Sturges, Howard C, 1920, Jl 6,15:2
Sturges, Jonathan, 1874, N 30,5:2; 1911, Je 10,13:4
Sturges, Kenneth, 1959, My 12,35:4
Sturges, Norman D Mrs, 1961, Je 23,29:2
Sturges, Perry MacK, 1960, Mr 10,32:1
Sturges, Philemon F, 1940, Ja 10,21:2
Sturges, Philemon F Mrs, 1939, F 12,44:6
Sturges, Preston (funl, Ag 9,88:5), 1959, Ag 7,23:1
Sturges, Purdy H Mrs, 1945, Ag 22,23:3
Sturges, Ralph A, 1959, Jl 3,17:5
Sturges, Rush Mrs, 1954, F 17,31:1
Sturges, Thomas R, 1943, D 10,28:3
Sturges, Ward L, 1951, Ap 20,29:4
Sturges, Wesley A, 1962, N 11,88:3
Sturges, William C, 1906, S 17,9:6
Sturgess, Charles M, 1948, O 13,25:4
Sturgess, Edward L, 1941, Ja 28,19:2
Sturgess, Sara H Mrs, 1949, Ja 15,17:4
Sturgess, William J, 1945, Jl 1,17:3
Sturgill, Walter S, 1948, Ja 17,17:1
Sturgis, Allan R, 1909, F 28,11:4
Sturgis, Charles I, 1952, Ap 25,23:3
Sturgis, Cony, 1954, Mr 13,15:2
Sturgis, D Farrand, 1939, Mr 17,21:5
Sturgis, David, 1957, Mr 2,21:5
Sturgis, Edward B, 1946, Jl 3,25:3
Sturgis, F K, 1932, Je 16,21:3
Sturgis, Fanny T, 1941, D 27,19:3
Sturgis, Frank K, 1922, Mr 17,17:6
Sturgis, Fred E, 1963, N 21,39:1
Sturgis, Fred E Mrs, 1954, Ap 16,21:4
Sturgis, Frederic Russell, 1919, My 7,15:4
Sturgis, George, 1944, D 22,17:4
Sturgis, H Herbert, 1943, Mr 5,17:5
Sturgis, H S, 1944, F 23,19:4
Sturgis, Julian, 1904, Ap 14,9:5
Sturgis, Julie, 1942, Jl 4,17:2
Sturgis, Lyman B, 1944, F 4,15:1
Sturgis, Norman R, 1947, F 3,20:3
Sturgis, Parker B, 1940, D 8,71:4
Sturgis, Reginald H, 1961, S 14,31:3
Sturgis, Russell, 1872, My 8,4:7; 1909, F 12,13:5
Sturgis, Ruth L, 1955, Ja 30,84:4
Sturgis, S Warren, 1952, Ap 24,31:2
Sturgis, Samuel D Jr, 1964, Jl 6,29:1
Sturgis, Samuel D Mrs, 1955, Je 13,23:4
Sturgis, Thomas, 1914, F 27,11:5; 1939, N 29,23:5
Sturgis, William, 1964, Je 20,25:5
Sturgis, William A, 1954, N 3,29:4
Sturgis, William A Mrs, 1968, O 22,47:3
Sturgis, William B, 1951, Ap 9,25:6
Sturgis, William C, 1942, S 30,23:4
Sturgis, William F, 1955, D 14,39:1
Sturgis, William J, 1968, Jl 20,27:3
Sturgis, William P, 1925, N 9,19:5
Sturim, Edward I, 1953, O 20,29:2
Sturk, L W, 1955, Je 15,31:5
Sturken, Carl A, 1938, O 15,17:3
Sturley, Albert A Dr, 1922, O 25,19:5
Sturm, Abraham, 1965, Ag 29,85:1
Sturm, Alex M, 1951, N 14,31:3
Sturm, Alex M Mrs (death ruled accidental, Mr 7,59:2), 1957, Ja 28,23:1
Sturm, Andreas, 1945, N 6,19:1
Sturm, Ferdinand, 1945, Mr 23,19:3
Sturm, Frank, 1958, Ag 2,17:6
Sturm, Henry O, 1942, F 4,19:4
Sturm, John E, 1948, Jl 10,15:6
Sturm, Justin, 1967, Ag 8,39:2
Sturm, Samuel, 1948, Ap 14,27:2
Sturm, Sanford Z, 1959, Ja 13,47:2
Sturm, William F, 1937, Ag 27,19:4
Sturman, Everett N, 1964, F 9,89:2
Sturman, Joseph Mrs, 1952, Ja 31,27:4
Sturmer, Julius W, 1952, My 6,29:2
Sturn, Henry A, 1938, S 28,25:4
Stursberg, Alma B, 1954, My 29,15:2
Stursberg, Carl L, 1955, Ag 23,23:5
Stursberg, Herbert J, 1959, D 1,39:4
Sturt, A T, 1923, Ja 25,19:6
Sturtevant, Charles F, 1906, Ja 13,9:5
Sturtevant, Chester D, 1950, Mr 3,26:2
Sturtevant, Chester O, 1941, D 5,23:6
Sturtevant, Edgar H, 1952, Jl 2,25:5
Sturtevant, Edward, 1939, Ja 17,22:3
Sturtevant, Edwin M, 1948, N 14,76:4
Sturtevant, Girard, 1938, My 20,19:1
Sturtevant, Helena, 1946, N 10,64:1
Sturtevant, John L, 1939, My 18,25:5; 1946, My 2,21:5
Sturtevant, Joseph L, 1958, O 17,29:2
Sturtevant, Louisa C, 1958, My 4,89:2
Sturtevant, Lydia, 1938, Jl 28,19:3
Sturtevant, Malcolm E, 1938, O 31,15:5
Sturtevant, Melville H Mrs, 1949, Mr 16,27:5
Sturtevant, Mills, 1945, O 30,19:3
Sturtevant, Oscar W, 1859, Ap 4,4:6
Sturtevant, Paul, 1957, N 29,29:1
Sturtevant, Sarah M (por), 1942, D 19,19:5
Sturtevant, Thomas J, 1944, Ap 22,15:4
Sturtevant, Watkins P, 1956, My 27,89:1
Sturtridge, Lewis O, 1940, Jl 31,17:4
Sturtz, Edward E, 1947, Ap 22,27:3
Sturtz, Theodore I, 1957, D 25,31:2
Sturz, Carrie Mrs, 1942, O 26,15:2
Sturz, Charles F, 1937, Ap 28,23:6
Sturz, Louis, 1958, F 14,24:1
Sturzenegger, A J, 1949, Ap 10,76:5
Sturzo, Luigi, 1959, Ag 9,89:1
Stutchbury, Herbert A, 1937, Je 24,25:4
Stutchkoff, Nahum, 1965, N 9,43:3
Stutsman, Harry R, 1943, N 22,19:2
Stutsman, Martin B, 1947, My 20,25:2
Stutt, Alex, 1939, Je 9,24:5
Stuttaford, Richard, 1945, O 23,17:2
Stutts, Sebastian Rev, 1924, My 20,21:5
Stutz, Charles E, 1959, Ag 11,27:4
Stutz, Frank, 1950, F 19,79:3
Stutz, George F Rev, 1916, Ja 16,17:5
Stutz, Harry G, 1954, N 18,33:3
Stutz, John J, 1945, O 24,21:4
Stutz, Ulrich, 1938, Jl 8,17:5
Stutzer, H, 1933, My 13,13:6
Stutzlen, Frank C Mrs, 1950, F 31,42:6
Stutzlen, Leon H, 1954, Jl 28,23:3
Stutzman, Frederick, 1941, Mr 10,17:2
Stutzmann, Rudolph, 1946, Ja 27,42:3
Stutzmann, Rudolph Jr, 1964, Jl 19,64:3
Stuyck, Maurice E, 1948, O 27,27:3
Stuyresant, Augustus Van Horne, 1918, D 29,18:8
Stuyt, Giancomo, 1955, O 15,15:3
Stuyvesant, Alan R, 1954, F 10,13:1
Stuyvesant, Anne W, 1938, My 3,23:2
Stuyvesant, Augustus van Horne Jr (funl, Ag 15,15:5), 1953, Ag 12,31:1
Stuyvesant, Catherine E S, 1924, O 7,23:3
Stuyvesant, Gerard, 1921, Je 22,15:3
Stuyvesant, Helen Mrs, 1873, Ag 21,8:4
Stuyvesant, Henry, 1919, Ag 30,7:6
Stuyvesant, Lewis R, 1944, S 8,19:3
Stuyvesant, Robert, 1907, D 19,9:5
Stuyvesant, Robert Van Rensselaer, 1918, O 31,13:3
Stuyvesant, Rutherford, 1909, Jl 5,7:5
Stybel, Abraham J, 1946, S 17,7:4
Stybel, Abraham J Mrs, 1962, S 5,40:1
Styer, Henry C, 1944, My 13,19:3
Stygall, James H, 1959, O 19,29:5
Styka, Adam, 1959, S 24,37:1
Styka, Tade, 1954, S 12,84:7
Styler, Jesse T, 1952, Ap 8,29:4
Styler, Louis, 1950, Mr 3,25:3
Styler, Louis Mrs, 1950, Mr 4,17:4
Styler, William L Sr, 1951, Ja 23,27:5
Styles, Charles, 1940, O 14,19:1
Styles, Elmer L Dr, 1915, Ag 4,11:5
Styles, Ernest B, 1941, F 22,15:1
Styles, Frank B, 1952, Ap 26,23:2
Styles, Harry C, 1947, My 23,23:1
Styles, Jacob Mrs, 1947, Jl 19,13:2
Styles, Jean E, 1961, Ap 15,21:5
Styles, Philip M, 1964, N 25,37:2
Styles, R K, 1881, O 28,5:2
Styles, Samuel D, 1910, Jl 3,II,7:4
Styles, Walter E, 1955, Ja 20,31:4
Styles, William A, 1949, Ap 15,23:4
Styles, William J, 1949, Mr 22,26:4
Styles, William J Mrs, 1950, Ja 5,25:1
Styles, William S, 1943, Ja 30,15:4
Stymus, George S, 1953, O 29,31:1
Stymus, William P (will), 1944, Ap 21,20:3
Stypulkowski, Joseph, 1941, Jl 7,32:2
Styres, Earle E, 1966, Ag 7,81:1
Styri, Haakon, 1955, S 15,33:1
Styron, Norma C, 1954, Ja 24,84:6
Suardo, Giacomo Count, 1947, My 21,25:6
Suares, Andre, 1948, S 8,29:4
Suarez, Gabriel, 1918, O 24,13:2
Suarez, Justo, 1938, Ag 11,17:3
Suarez, Pablo, 1952, Mr 29,15:4
Suarez, Roberto Mrs, 1949, F 3,24:2
Suarez, Tino, 1962, O 13,25:5
Suarez de Cordoba, Ramona Mrs, 1952, N 19,4:4
Suarez Gutierrez, Miguel, 1945, Mr 25,38:3
Suavet, Henry E, 1956, Ja 21,21:2
Suba, Miklos, 1944, Jl 20,19:5
Subasic, Ivan, 1955, Mr 25,23:3
SubbaRow, Yellapragrada (por), 1948, Ag 11,21:5
Subbaroyan, Paramasiva, 1962, O 7,82:4
Subber, Saul, 1958, Ja 12,86:7
Suber, Carl G, 1951, My 27,38:5
Subercaseaux, Ramon, 1937, Ja 20,22:2
Subers, Robert S, 1946, Jl 23,25:4
Subert, Rodolfo, 1958, S 4,29:3
Subirats, Ramon, 1942, F 9,15:3
Subkoff, A Frau, 1929, N 13,7:1
Subkow, Phil, 1957, Je 16,84:4
Sublett, Hugh W, 1941, N 4,26:5
Sublett, James I Mrs, 1958, Ja 30,23:1
Subroto, Gatot, 1962, Je 12,37:3
Sucato, Carlo, 1951, My 21,27:5
Succob, Paul H, 1942, Ag 27,19:2
Succop, Bertram L, 1948, O 13,25:4
Such, Miguel, 1952, Ag 25,17:4
Suchena, Michael, 1961, F 23,27:4
Sucher, Carle F, 1948, Ja 1,23:1
Sucher, Harry F, 1957, N 6,35:2
Sucher, R, 1927, Ap 20,25:3
Sucher, Ralph G Mrs (Nellie), 1966, D 5,45:5
Suchman, Harry, 1965, My 22,32:3
Suchomel, William, 1950, Ap 16,104:4
Suchorski, Vincent A, 1951, N 21,25:3
Suckert, Curzio (C Malaparte), 1957, Jl 20,15:3
Suckert, Enoch D, 1945, Mr 10,17:4
Suckley, Henry E Montgomery, 1917, Mr 28,13:6
Suckow, Ruth (Mrs F Nuhn), 1960, Ja 24,88:1
Sudak, Frederick N, 1966, F 5,29:5
Sudarsky, Charles, 1966, Ja 26,37:4
Sudarsky, John, 1960, D 20,33:2
Sudarsky, Mendel I, 1952, Ja 1,25:4
Sudbring, Christian Mrs, 1957, N 28,31:6
Sudbury, Edward H, 1957, Ap 3,31:1
Suddards, Frank R Jr, 1952, Ag 10,61:1
Suddards, W Rev, 1883, F 21,2:4
Sudduth, Hugh Thomas, 1922, Jl 5,19:6
Sudekum, Anthony, 1946, Ap 30,22:3
Sudell, Harold, 1954, Mr 11,31:4
Suder, Karl H, 1947, Ap 16,25:2
Sudermann, H, 1928, N 22,29:5
Suderow, George E, 1961, My 1,29:3
Sudhoff, Karl, 1938, O 15,17:5
Sudik, Vincent, 1940, Je 30,33:2
Sudirman, R, 1950, Ja 30,17:4
Sudler, Arthur E, 1968, Ap 7,92:5
Sudler, Hyman, 1965, Ap 8,39:1
Sudour, Maurice, 1941, F 25,23:2
Sudro, William F, 1957, O 2,33:3
Suedmeyer, Armin A, 1957, N 19,33:1
Suehsdorf, Adolph Jr, 1961, Ja 7,19:4
Suering, R, 1951, Ja 8,17:4
Suerken, Hermann P, 1952, Jl 12,13:5
Suermondt, Berthold J, 1944, Jl 20,19:4
Sueskind, Philip R, 1962, Je 23,23:3
Suess, David, 1953, F 13,22:4
Sueter, Murray F, 1960, F 5,28:1
Sueter, William H, 1949, Jl 8,19:4
Suetsugu, Nobumasa (por), 1944, D 30,11:6
Sueyro, Saba H, 1943, Jl 18,34:7
Suffern, Arthur E, 1959, Jl 6,27:4
Suffern, Edward C, 1937, D 15,25:2
Suffern, Edward E, 1952, O 25,17:2
Suffern, Edward Lee, 1925, Ap 14,23:3
Suffern, J Louis, 1939, S 27,25:4
Suffern, John Cassidy, 1908, Jl 16,7:6
Suffern, John D, 1921, My 3,17:4
Suffern, Philip S, 1959, Ja 3,17:2
Suffield, Charles Harbord, 1914, Ap 11,11:5; 1924, F 11,15:4
Suffield, Lord, 1946, My 30,21:2
Suffield, Lord (R M Harbord-Hammond), 1951, F 3, 15:2
Suffield, William H, 1943, N 16,23:1
Suffin, Harry, 1947, N 5,27:5
Suffir, Lewis Jr, 1953, S 19,15:3
Suffness, Robert, 1948, Ap 13,27:6
Suffolk and Berkshire, Dowager Countess of (M Crawford), 1966, F 24,37:4
Suffren, Charles Carroll, 1917, D 18,15:4
Sufrin, Oscar J, 1949, D 5,23:2
Sugarman, Abraham J, 1948, Ap 1,25:1
Sugarman, David B, 1968, My 22,47:2
Sugarman, David B Mrs, 1961, N 29,41:4
Sugarman, George, 1941, D 11,27:2
Sugarman, Herbert, 1957, Jl 1,23:6
Sugarman, J J, 1951, Ag 27,19:3
Sugarman, Joseph, 1947, Ag 20,22:2
Sugarman, Louis L, 1951, Je 15,23:1
Sugarman, M Henry (por), 1946, O 13,60:1
Sugarman, Max, 1955, Ag 27,15:5
Sugarman, Morris Mrs, 1957, Ag 20,27:4
Sugarman, Samuel, 1951, My 21,27:4
Sugarman, Samuel Z, 1948, Je 10,25:4
Sugarman, William, 1940, D 7,17:6
Sugarman, William H, 1948, Je 24,25:5
Sugden, Cecil, 1963, Mr 28,16:5
Sugden, John H, 1944, My 6,15:3
Sugden, Leonard S Dr, 1923, Je 9,11:7
Sugden, Raymond S (Tampa the magician), 1939, Jl 21,19:5
Sugden, Robert P, 1953, Ag 15,15:4
Sugden, Walter S, 1938, Jl 8,17:2
Sugerman, Barnet, 1964, Ap 12,86:5
Sugerman, Samuel Z, 1963, O 31,34:1

Sugg, Thomas, 1956, My 17,31:3
Suggars, Harold J, 1943, Mr 10,19:6
Suggett, Allen H, 1955, Mr 9,27:3
Suggia, Guilhermina (will, Ag 2,30:1), 1950, Ag 1, 23:5
Suggs, N C, 1907, S 7,9:6
Sughrue, John J, 1952, D 11,33:2
Sughrue, Timothy G, 1963, Ap 30,35:4
Sugi, Magoshichiro Viscount, 1920, My 7,11:2
Sugimoto, Etsu Mrs, 1950, Je 22,27:2
Sugimura, Yotaro, 1939, Mr 24,21:3
Suglia, Joseph, 1940, Jl 31,17:5
Suglia, Lucia T Mrs, 1944, F 7,15:5
Sugrue, Daniel F, 1949, Jl 15,19:3
Sugrue, Thomas, 1953, Ja 7,31:3
Suhard, Emmanuel C, 1949, My 30,13:4
Suhl, Frederick W, 1942, Mr 30,17:5
Suhl, Rudolph L (por), 1946, Je 11,23:6
Suhling, Johannes, 1923, N 15,19:3
Suhr, Arthur J, 1948, S 21,27:4
Suhr, Fred W, 1941, O 28,23:2
Suhr, Frederic J, 1941, S 14,50:3
Suhr, Henry B, 1957, Ag 29,27:3
Suhr, Otto, 1957, Ag 31,15:5
Suhr, Robert C, 1944, S 14,23:6
Suhr, William E, 1945, Ja 24,21:2
Suhrawardy, Huseyn S (funl, D 9,35:4), 1963, D 6, 35:3
Suhrhoff, Carrie E, 1942, Jl 14,19:5
Suhrie, Ambrose L, 1956, F 21,33:1
Sui Wang, 1948, Ja 18,60:8
Suida, William E, 1959, O 30,27:2
Suisman, Michael Mrs, 1953, Ag 29,17:4
Suite, Benjamin, 1923, Ag 7,17:3
Suiter, Augustus W Dr, 1925, My 29,17:6
Suiter, George, 1940, My 17,19:4
Suitor, Harry D, 1945, Mr 26,19:5
Suits, Elliott L, 1954, S 22,30:1
Suits, George A Jr, 1944, Mr 24,19:3
Suits, Herman M, 1940, Mr 10,49:3
Suits, Willard J, 1959, Ap 29,33:4
Sujet, Peter Jr, 1946, Ap 14,46:1
Sukenik, Eliezer L, 1953, Mr 1,93:1
Sukloff, Samuel, 1962, Ag 11,17:3
Sukoenig, Abraham Mrs, 1959, Jl 18,15:3
Sukoenig, Sidney, 1961, O 16,29:2
Sukul, Deva R, 1965, N 15,37:3
Sukuna, Lala, 1958, My 31,15:5
Sukys, Paul A, 1949, My 4,29:5
Sulaiman, Shah M, 1941, Mr 13,21:6
Suleiman, Pasha, 1883, Ap 22,8:7
Sulentic, S A, 1951, Jl 19,23:3
Sulger, Frank, 1883, N 30,5:4
Sulima, Adam, 1940, D 8,71:4
Suling, John W, 1966, Je 17,45:3
Sulka, Amos (por), 1946, Ap 15,27:6
Sullard, Arthur B, 1957, F 22,21:4
Sullau, Frederick W, 1955, N 21,29:4
Sullavan, Cornelius H, 1950, Ap 12,28:2
Sullavan, Margaret (Mrs K A Wagg),(funl plans, Ja 3,53:1), 1960, Ja 2,1:2
Sullebarger, Elmer T, 1958, Ag 2,17:6
Sullens, Frederick, 1957, N 21,33:5
Sullivan, A Gilman, 1953, Mr 15,93:1
Sullivan, A M, 1884, O 18,5:1
Sullivan, A S, 1887, D 5,1:7
Sullivan, Adeline Mrs, 1901, N 24,7:6
Sullivan, Adrian S Mrs, 1948, D 12,92:6
Sullivan, Alan, 1947, Ag 7,21:4
Sullivan, Albert J, 1948, F 12,23:3
Sullivan, Albert W, 1938, Mr 28,15:4
Sullivan, Alex, 1940, N 12,23:3; 1956, O 19,27:3
Sullivan, Alex M, 1959, Ja 10,17:3
Sullivan, Alex Mrs, 1903, D 29,9:4
Sullivan, Alexander, 1913, Ag 22,9:6
Sullivan, Alexander D, 1946, F 2,13:2
Sullivan, Alice S, 1966, My 19,47:1
Sullivan, Amelia O Mrs, 1938, F 22,21:5
Sullivan, Andrew T (por), 1942, Ag 27,19:1
Sullivan, Arthur, 1957, O 23,33:4
Sullivan, Arthur B, 1941, Mr 14,21:1; 1956, O 23,33:5
Sullivan, Arthur C, 1948, O 5,25:5
Sullivan, Arthur F, 1951, S 13,31:1
Sullivan, Arthur J, 1950, Ap 25,31:4
Sullivan, Arthur J Sr (cor, My 12,35:4), 1959, My 11,27:2
Sullivan, Arthur Sir, 1900, N 23,7:3
Sullivan, Arthur T, 1912, Ja 7,II,15:5; 1955, D 23,17:3
Sullivan, Arthur W, 1957, Ja 7,25:5
Sullivan, Barry, 1891, My 4,5:2
Sullivan, Bart, 1968, F 26,32:8
Sullivan, Benjamin, 1949, Je 7,31:4
Sullivan, Caroline H, 1938, Mr 20,II,9:2
Sullivan, Cassian, 1943, S 10,23:3
Sullivan, Charles B, 1952, Jl 24,27:3
Sullivan, Charles E, 1943, O 24,44:2
Sullivan, Charles F J, 1962, Ag 26,82:5
Sullivan, Charles Hardin, 1968, Je 14,47:4
Sullivan, Charles L, 1951, S 9,88:4
Sullivan, Charles L Jr, 1948, Ja 28,23:6
Sullivan, Charles P, 1956, Jl 19,27:1
Sullivan, Chris D, 1942, Ag 4,19:1
Sullivan, Clarence P, 1948, Ag 18,25:3

Sullivan, Corliss E, 1939, F 15,23:5
Sullivan, Corliss E Mrs, 1951, S 11,29:2
Sullivan, Cornelius, 1946, Je 12,27:5; 1956, Ag 1,23:1
Sullivan, Cornelius A, 1941, O 2,25:3
Sullivan, Cornelius B, 1941, My 18,45:2
Sullivan, Cornelius F, 1967, My 11,47:2
Sullivan, Cornelius F J, 1956, Mr 28,31:5
Sullivan, Cornelius J, 1937, F 2,23:1; 1941, Ag 16,15:6; 1946, F 4,25:5; 1960, D 14,39:3
Sullivan, Cornelius J Mrs, 1939, D 6,25:4
Sullivan, Cornelius P, 1951, Jl 13,21:4; 1953, Je 21,85:1
Sullivan, Dan, 1954, D 10,27:1
Sullivan, Dan J, 1948, Ja 18,60:4
Sullivan, Daniel, 1924, My 31,15:5; 1942, S 9,23:3; 1945, Ag 4,11:7; 1947, Jl 11,15:3; 1954, S 14,27:3
Sullivan, Daniel A, 1944, Ap 19,23:3
Sullivan, Daniel A J, 1941, Ja 29,17:3
Sullivan, Daniel C, 1948, D 21,25:3; 1964, Je 7,87:1
Sullivan, Daniel E, 1942, Mr 27,23:3; 1944, Ja 24, 17:6; 1949, Je 26,60:4
Sullivan, Daniel F, 1949, Ja 29,13:4
Sullivan, Daniel F X Bro, 1940, Ja 2,20:1
Sullivan, Daniel G, 1947, Ap 9,25:5; 1955, Je 29,29:4
Sullivan, Daniel J, 1922, Mr 13,15:4; 1937, F 24,23:3; 1941, My 16,23:1; 1952, My 14,27:1; 1954, N 11, 31:3; 1954, D 1,31:4
Sullivan, Daniel J F, 1938, Ja 12,21:2
Sullivan, Daniel J Mrs, 1946, Ag 8,21:3
Sullivan, Daniel Maj, 1925, O 2,23:6
Sullivan, Daniel Mrs, 1944, O 12,27:4
Sullivan, Daniel P, 1945, F 11,38:3
Sullivan, Daniel P (por), 1947, My 6,27:3
Sullivan, Daniel V, 1966, Ja 9,56:7
Sullivan, Daniel W, 1945, Ap 22,35:1
Sullivan, David J, 1961, Jl 18,29:3
Sullivan, Deliah Mrs, 1944, N 26,56:4
Sullivan, Denis A, 1942, O 10,15:5
Sullivan, Denis E, 1941, Je 27,17:2
Sullivan, Denis S, 1908, D 19,9:5
Sullivan, Denis T, 1960, My 21,23:3
Sullivan, Dennis A, 1951, F 12,23:4
Sullivan, Dennis D, 1941, F 1,17:4
Sullivan, Dennis E, 1942, Jl 4,17:6
Sullivan, Dennis J, 1940, F 2,17:1
Sullivan, Donald, 1907, Mr 4,9:5
Sullivan, E B Lt, 1918, Jl 8,11:4
Sullivan, E F, 1938, Je 26,27:2
Sullivan, E Mark, 1957, My 27,31:5
Sullivan, Edmund B, 1962, Ap 5,33:4
Sullivan, Edmund C, 1949, O 8,13:4
Sullivan, Edward, 1951, Je 9,19:5
Sullivan, Edward A, 1944, F 27,38:3; 1946, D 31,17:4
Sullivan, Edward C, 1952, My 21,27:5
Sullivan, Edward D, 1938, Ap 5,21:2
Sullivan, Edward F, 1938, Mr 28,15:1; 1943, Jl 15, 21:5; 1943, S 13,19:6
Sullivan, Edward J, 1944, D 3,58:4; 1956, Ap 12,31:2; 1961, My 17,37:1
Sullivan, Edward M, 1942, Mr 21,17:1; 1942, Jl 16,19:4
Sullivan, Edward Mrs, 1944, Ja 26,19:3; 1948, Je 3, 25:6
Sullivan, Edward O Sr Mrs, 1953, Ap 10,21:3
Sullivan, Edward R, 1954, D 15,31:4
Sullivan, Edward Sir, 1885, Ap 14,2:4
Sullivan, Edward T, 1952, My 10,21:7
Sullivan, Edwin W, 1943, O 29,19:4
Sullivan, Elgar J (J B Colleano), 1957, Mr 8,21:1
Sullivan, Elizabeth C Mrs, 1941, S 16,23:2
Sullivan, Elizabeth E, 1941, O 19,45:2
Sullivan, Eugene A, 1950, Je 2,24:3
Sullivan, Eugene B (cor, D 11,31:5), 1953, D 10,47:3
Sullivan, Eugene C, 1962, My 13,88:5
Sullivan, Eugene C Mrs, 1943, D 9,27:3
Sullivan, Eugene C P, 1947, Ja 9,23:3
Sullivan, Eugene P, 1963, S 2,15:4
Sullivan, Eugene R Mrs, 1954, O 2,17:2
Sullivan, Florence J, 1909, Je 28,7:3; 1941, Jl 31,17:5; 1956, Mr 22,35:1
Sullivan, Florence J Mrs, 1959, N 22,86:6
Sullivan, Francis, 1946, Je 26,25:2; 1948, My 18,23:5
Sullivan, Francis A, 1960, Ja 15,31:3
Sullivan, Francis de C, 1957, Jl 2,27:5
Sullivan, Francis G, 1950, N 13,28:5
Sullivan, Francis J (por), 1940, O 15,23:2
Sullivan, Francis J, 1941, Ap 19,15:4; 1946, S 17,7:5; 1955, N 21,29:4
Sullivan, Francis J Mrs, 1939, D 14,27:4
Sullivan, Francis J Rev (funl, O 14,11:6), 1915, O 13,15:4
Sullivan, Francis L, 1956, N 20,37:3
Sullivan, Francis M, 1954, Ja 26,27:2
Sullivan, Frank A, 1942, D 1,25:3
Sullivan, Frank B, 1945, Mr 23,19:4
Sullivan, Frank D, 1949, Ja 21,21:2
Sullivan, Frank J, 1925, D 15,25:3; 1944, Jl 8,11:1; 1956, Je 15,25:2
Sullivan, Frank L, 1938, O 24,17:6
Sullivan, Frank Mrs, 1959, Je 27,25:8
Sullivan, Frank O, 1940, Jl 1,19:4
Sullivan, Frank V, 1940, Ja 29,15:1
Sullivan, Frank X, 1952, My 8,31:3; 1958, Je 28,17:5
Sullivan, Franklin C, 1948, Jl 11,53:1
Sullivan, Fred D, 1956, Ag 5,77:2

Sullivan, Frederick J, 1950, Ap 27,29:3
Sullivan, Gael E (funl plans, O 29,29:3), 1956, O 28, 88:2
Sullivan, George, 1955, My 14,19:4; 1956, Ag 23,27:4
Sullivan, George F, 1944, Ap 15,11:3
Sullivan, George H, 1956, N 16,27:1
Sullivan, George L, 1937, Mr 26,13:6; 1949, D 31,15:4
Sullivan, George M Jr, 1968, Jl 26,33:1
Sullivan, George P, 1941, O 14,23:6; 1954, My 22,15:2
Sullivan, George R, 1952, F 27,27:5
Sullivan, George T, 1938, Ja 21,19:4; 1956, O 14,86:3
Sullivan, Gerard, 1947, Je 28,14:2
Sullivan, Gray B, 1947, F 4,25:2
Sullivan, Grey, 1948, O 23,15:5
Sullivan, Harold D, 1960, Ja 20,31:5
Sullivan, Harry J, 1950, Ja 28,13:5
Sullivan, Harry J Mrs, 1959, F 25,31:2
Sullivan, Harry P, 1953, Ja 18,92:3
Sullivan, Harry S (por), 1949, Ja 16,68:5
Sullivan, Hazen P, 1940, Ja 7,49:3
Sullivan, Henry A, 1951, Jl 24,26:3
Sullivan, Henry F, 1955, F 24,13:5
Sullivan, Henry F Mrs, 1943, D 25,13:3
Sullivan, Humphrey Jr Mrs, 1950, O 28,17:3
Sullivan, Irving L, 1945, O 23,17:2
Sullivan, Isaac N, 1938, F 1,21:3
Sullivan, J, 1931, O 9,23:3
Sullivan, J A, 1952, Ag 12,19:6
Sullivan, J Edward, 1950, Ap 30,102:7
Sullivan, J Frank, 1942, Jl 25,13:5
Sullivan, J J, 1927, Mr 4,21:4; 1928, D 12,31:5
Sullivan, J Stacey, 1957, N 19,33:4
Sullivan, J T, 1879, F 22,8:2; 1904, Je 21,7:5
Sullivan, J W N, 1937, Ag 13,18:2
Sullivan, Jack, 1947, S 6,17:3
Sullivan, James, 1948, Je 11,23:2; 1956, D 23,17:2
Sullivan, James A, 1960, Ap 25,29:1; 1961, Jl 7,25:2
Sullivan, James C, 1948, F 3,25:5
Sullivan, James E, 1914, S 17,9:5; 1951, F 12,23:1
Sullivan, James E Sr, 1942, Je 15,19:3
Sullivan, James F, 1910, My 30,11:7; 1945, F 18,34:1; 1948, Je 11,23:4
Sullivan, James F Mrs, 1959, D 13,87:1
Sullivan, James H, 1949, Ap 23,13:3; 1954, O 9,17:5; 1962, My 12,23:4
Sullivan, James H Mrs, 1954, D 29,23:3
Sullivan, James J, 1938, D 29,19:2; 1945, Je 14,19:3; 1962, Ja 10,47:3; 1966, Ag 5,31:4
Sullivan, James J Father, 1916, Je 10,11:7
Sullivan, James Mark, 1920, Ag 24,9:1
Sullivan, James Mrs, 1944, Ap 13,19:3
Sullivan, James P, 1937, Jl 14,22:3
Sullivan, James R, 1961, Ap 16,86:5
Sullivan, James S, 1959, Je 30,31:5
Sullivan, James T, 1945, Mr 6,22:2
Sullivan, James W, 1938, S 29,25:4
Sullivan, Jean, 1954, N 28,87:2
Sullivan, Jere F, 1950, Ja 16,25:5
Sullivan, Jeremiah (Bro Bertin Leo), 1955, Jl 11,23:3
Sullivan, Jeremiah A, 1948, O 14,30:2; 1950, My 12, 28:2
Sullivan, Jeremiah B Dr, 1937, S 2,21:5
Sullivan, Jeremiah D, 1952, D 6,21:5
Sullivan, Jeremiah E, 1943, My 13,21:5
Sullivan, Jeremiah J Jr, 1954, N 12,21:4
Sullivan, Jeremiah L, 1950, Ag 1,23:4
Sullivan, Jeremiah Mrs, 1948, S 28,27:4
Sullivan, Jeremiah P, 1968, Ag 14,39:2
Sullivan, Jerry B, 1948, Ap 19,23:1
Sullivan, Jesse V, 1953, N 21,13:4
Sullivan, Johanna R Mrs, 1937, O 18,17:4
Sullivan, John, 1921, Mr 20,22:2; 1924, F 5,23:3; 193 Ja 17,II,8:5; 1942, Jl 16,19:3
Sullivan, John (por), 1943, Ja 29,19:3
Sullivan, John, 1952, O 24,23:3; 1955, Ap 29,23:5
Sullivan, John (Spike), 1956, My 13,86:6
Sullivan, John A, 1925, Jl 13,17:6; 1938, Ja 21,19:5; 1947, D 5,26:2; 1949, Ap 17,76:7; 1950, Ja 6,21:4; 1950, Mr 15,29:4; 1954, N 1,27:6; 1959, My 3,87:1; 1964, S 3,29:2
Sullivan, John A Mrs, 1955, Ag 16,23:4
Sullivan, John B, 1951, Ja 30,25:4
Sullivan, John C, 1917, O 24,15:5
Sullivan, John D, 1944, My 4,19:6; 1961, My 7,87:1; 1967, Je 22,39:1
Sullivan, John D Dr, 1925, My 17,6:1
Sullivan, John E, 1937, F 17,21:3; 1945, D 18,27:2; 1950, S 21,31:4; 1951, Je 6,31:3; 1954, My 29,15:4
Sullivan, John F, 1939, Mr 13,17:3; 1942, Ja 5,20:1; 1947, Jl 1,25:5; 1949, My 21,21:3; 1951, Ag 10,15: 1954, S 4,11:5; 1961, Ja 22,85:1; 1962, N 4,88:3; 1964, Jl 28,29:1
Sullivan, John F Jr, 1948, My 23,68:6
Sullivan, John F Jr Mrs, 1946, Je 26,25:4
Sullivan, John G, 1938, Ag 9,19:5
Sullivan, John H, 1943, Ag 13,17:3; 1948, Ja 8,25:5; 1950, F 11,15:1
Sullivan, John H Mrs, 1953, N 9,35:4
Sullivan, John J, 1937, Ag 21,15:2; 1939, Je 2,23:3; 1943, Ja 25,13:4; 1943, Mr 19,20:2; 1943, Ap 15,2 1946, Ja 17,23:2; 1947, My 17,15:6; 1950, Ja 5,25: 1950, Ja 27,24:5; 1950, Mr 25,13:2; 1951, F 2,23:2 1951, My 27,68:4

Sullivan, John J (SI), 1951, Je 2,19:4
Sullivan, John J, 1953, S 19,15:4; 1957, Ag 16,19:5; 1958, My 1,31:4; 1960, S 2,23:2; 1964, Mr 28,19:4; 1967, Mr 25,23:5
Sullivan, John L, 1941, S 10,23:4; 1948, Mr 23,25:2; 1950, Jl 26,25:5; 1951, D 19,31:5; 1953, D 17,37:5; 1959, Ja 3,17:4; 1960, F 25,29:5; 1963, Ap 12,27:5
Sullivan, John M, 1949, Mr 10,27:3
Sullivan, John P, 1955, O 1,19:5; 1968, Ja 24,42:4
Sullivan, John R, 1946, Ag 13,27:3
Sullivan, John R Mrs, 1951, Ja 9,29:5
Sullivan, John S, 1946, O 16,27:1; 1949, Ap 13,29:4
Sullivan, John T, 1947, S 28,61:1
Sullivan, John W, 1951, O 9,29:2
Sullivan, Joseph, 1946, N 2,15:5
Sullivan, Joseph A, 1953, Ap 18,19:2; 1954, Jl 7,31:5
Sullivan, Joseph Aloysius Rev, 1912, Ap 19,15:5
Sullivan, Joseph B, 1940, Ap 4,23:1; 1947, S 14,60:5
Sullivan, Joseph D, 1959, Ap 30,31:1
Sullivan, Joseph F, 1939, Ap 25,23:2
Sullivan, Joseph F (funl plans, D 17,29:3), 1942, D 14,28:1
Sullivan, Joseph F, 1950, S 12,27:5; 1954, S 3,17:5
Sullivan, Joseph H, 1954, F 11,29:1
Sullivan, Joseph J, 1960, Jl 20,29:3
Sullivan, Joseph M, 1941, D 12,25:5
Sullivan, Joseph P, 1966, Ja 4,31:3
Sullivan, Joseph T P Mrs, 1940, Ap 21,43:3
Sullivan, Joseph V, 1966, Ag 18,35:2
Sullivan, Julia E, 1951, Ag 20,19:5
Sullivan, Katherine H, 1957, Ap 17,31:1
Sullivan, L G, 1949, O 4,27:5
Sullivan, Laurence F, 1949, O 14,27:2
Sullivan, Lawrence, 1968, Mr 9,29:4
Sullivan, Leo L, 1937, O 12,25:1
Sullivan, Leo M, 1949, F 12,17:2; 1968, Mr 31,81:2
Sullivan, Leonard, 1956, Jl 18,27:5
Sullivan, Leonard Mrs, 1967, Jl 11,37:2
Sullivan, Lillie, 1903, Je 28,2:4
Sullivan, Louis Henri, 1924, Ap 16,23:5
Sullivan, Lulue R N Mrs, 1939, Ja 30,13:3
Sullivan, M M Mrs, 1933, Je 10,13:1
Sullivan, Mark, 1952, Ag 15,15:1
Sullivan, Mark A, 1964, Jl 27,31:3
Sullivan, Mark Mrs, 1940, D 7,17:4
Sullivan, Marshall P, 1952, Mr 5,29:5
Sullivan, Martin F, 1955, Jl 11,23:4
Sullivan, Mary, 1946, My 26,32:7
Sullivan, Mary (Sister Mary Hilarion), 1957, Mr 29, 21:3
Sullivan, Mary A Mrs, 1950, S 12,28:4
Sullivan, Mary M Mrs, 1938, Ap 30,15:4
Sullivan, Mary Mrs, 1909, My 9,11:7
Sullivan, Mary O M, 1952, Ag 6,21:1
Sullivan, Mason S, 1957, Ag 19,19:4
Sullivan, Matt I, 1937, Ag 8,II,7:3
Sullivan, Matthew G, 1952, Ag 10,60:5
Sullivan, Matthew J, 1960, Ag 29,25:1
Sullivan, Maurice, 1953, Ag 11,27:5
Sullivan, Maurice D, 1943, Ag 1,39:4
Sullivan, Maurice J, 1961, My 18,35:1
Sullivan, Michael, 1903, D 28,5:3
Sullivan, Michael A, 1949, Ja 8,15:6
Sullivan, Michael A Rev, 1937, Mr 16,23:1
Sullivan, Michael E Mrs, 1937, Ja 29,19:4
Sullivan, Michael F, 1905, Ap 20,9:7; 1965, Jl 7,37:1
Sullivan, Michael J, 1915, Je 12,11:6; 1925, D 11,23:3; 1946, Ja 28,19:4; 1947, S 20,15:5; 1948, My 6,25:4; 1952, My 21,27:4; 1955, Jl 27,23:2
Sullivan, Michael J Mrs, 1949, Ja 20,27:5
Sullivan, Michael Joseph Bro, 1904, Ja 17,7:5
Sullivan, Michael L, 1942, N 16,19:5
Sullivan, Michael Mrs, 1903, My 9,9:6; 1952, S 11,31:3
Sullivan, Michael Rev, 1955, Je 23,29:3
Sullivan, Michael T, 1951, Je 11,25:4
Sullivan, Michael X, 1963, My 5,86:8
Sullivan, Mike, 1937, N 1,22:2
Sullivan, Mildred M, 1958, Ag 31,56:1
Sullivan, Mortimer A, 1949, Jl 14,27:6; 1956, Mr 2,23:1
Sullivan, Myles E (Bro Eliphus Victor), 1962, Ap 1, 86:5
Sullivan, Nahum, 1884, S 27,5:2
Sullivan, Neil, 1967, N 30,47:4
Sullivan, Neil J, 1953, My 21,31:5
Sullivan, Neil Mrs, 1955, Jl 24,64:1
Sullivan, Nellie L Mrs (por), 1938, Ja 22,15:5
Sullivan, Noel, 1956, S 18,35:2
Sullivan, Owen Mrs, 1945, My 29,15:5
Sullivan, P J, 1947, Ja 1,33:4
Sullivan, Patrick, 1948, D 31,15:1
Sullivan, Patrick Capt, 1914, Mr 29,5:5
Sullivan, Patrick F, 1960, F 9,31:3
Sullivan, Patrick H, 1944, F 28,17:2; 1956, Jl 8,64:1
Sullivan, Patrick H Mrs, 1951, My 1,29:1
Sullivan, Patrick H Sr, 1939, Je 17,15:6
Sullivan, Patrick J, 1944, F 25,17:4; 1945, My 2,23:5; 1945, D 26,19:2; 1950, Mr 15,29:3; 1957, S 24,35:4
Sullivan, Patrick Mrs, 1912, Jl 4,7:5
Sullivan, Paul J, 1968, F 2,35:1
Sullivan, Paul T, 1955, Je 13,23:6; 1959, Mr 28,17:5
Sullivan, Peter A, 1950, Ap 5,31:4
Sullivan, Peter J, 1938, D 22,21:3; 1944, Je 21,19:1; 1953, My 10,89:1
Sullivan, Phil H, 1952, Mr 31,19:3
Sullivan, Phil J, 1950, S 6,29:3
Sullivan, Philip L, 1960, Je 13,27:3
Sullivan, R O D, 1955, Jl 11,23:4
Sullivan, R Paul, 1941, Ja 12,46:1
Sullivan, Raymond P, 1963, Ap 22,27:2
Sullivan, Richard H Dr, 1905, Mr 29,9:3
Sullivan, Richard L, 1958, D 4,39:3
Sullivan, Robert B, 1955, S 22,31:1
Sullivan, Robert F, 1948, O 3,64:4
Sullivan, Robert P, 1954, Ja 6,31:3
Sullivan, Roger, 1942, Ag 15,11:5
Sullivan, Roger C (funl, Ap 18,22:3), 1920, Ap 15, 11:4
Sullivan, Roy A, 1951, O 31,29:3
Sullivan, Russell M, 1962, Ja 16,33:3
Sullivan, Simon A, 1955, Jl 6,27:3
Sullivan, Stephen K, 1943, Ja 24,42:5
Sullivan, T, 1880, My 13,5:6
Sullivan, T H, 1947, F 12,25:3
Sullivan, T J Jr, 1944, S 24,46:7
Sullivan, T Russell, 1916, Je 29,11:6
Sullivan, Teresa, 1947, My 23,23:5
Sullivan, Terry, 1951, Ag 21,30:5
Sullivan, Thomas, 1937, Ap 15,23:2; 1940, D 23,19:2
Sullivan, Thomas F (cor, D 1,23:5), 1938, N 27,49:1
Sullivan, Thomas F, 1942, Je 22,15:5; 1951, Ja 12, 27:2; 1957, Ag 28,27:3; 1961, D 7,43:4; 1965, Mr 3, 41:4
Sullivan, Thomas H, 1942, S 12,13:2; 1949, Mr 21, 23:5; 1967, O 3,47:3
Sullivan, Thomas J, 1912, My 20,9:5; 1942, Je 7,41:1; 1943, Ag 17,19:7; 1956, Mr 31,15:5; 1957, My 30,19:3
Sullivan, Thomas P, 1965, My 8,31:2
Sullivan, Thomas T, 1958, D 2,37:4
Sullivan, Timothy, 1943, N 19,19:5; 1945, Je 20,23:1; 1949, Mr 30,25:4
Sullivan, Timothy B, 1957, Jl 13,17:4
Sullivan, Timothy D (funl), 1913, S 15,9:1
Sullivan, Timothy D, 1941, Jl 7,15:5; 1946, N 6,23:2; 1960, Ap 15,23:2
Sullivan, Timothy Daniel, 1914, Ap 1,13:5
Sullivan, Timothy F, 1954, Ap 10,15:5
Sullivan, Timothy F Sr, 1951, Je 15,23:4
Sullivan, Timothy F X, 1960, Je 27,25:5
Sullivan, Timothy J, 1939, D 11,23:5; 1942, S 9,23:4; 1951, D 14,31:1
Sullivan, Timothy J Mrs, 1939, Mr 13,17:4; 1953, O 22,29:2
Sullivan, Timothy Mrs, 1967, Mr 7,41:3
Sullivan, Timothy V, 1961, Je 29,33:1
Sullivan, Victor, 1949, N 20,92:7
Sullivan, W L, 1935, O 7,15:6
Sullivan, Walter, 1963, Jl 15,29:3
Sullivan, Walter B, 1921, O 6,17:5
Sullivan, Walter C, 1952, F 3,84:2
Sullivan, Walter C T, 1959, O 17,23:3
Sullivan, Walter D, 1945, Jl 21,11:4
Sullivan, Walter S (por), 1937, N 10,25:4
Sullivan, Walter S, 1949, S 7,29:3
Sullivan, Walter T, 1953, O 30,23:2
Sullivan, Ward, 1947, D 11,33:4
Sullivan, Warren, 1941, Mr 17,17:5
Sullivan, Welby L Dr, 1937, Je 28,19:3
Sullivan, William, 1946, N 14,29:3
Sullivan, William A, 1937, O 5,15:2; 1946, My 25, 15:4; 1956, Jl 17,23:5; 1957, D 1,88:3
Sullivan, William A (death ruled accidental, Jl 29,-43:2), 1959, Jl 28,54:6
Sullivan, William A, 1962, Ap 19,31:4
Sullivan, William A Mrs, 1958, Ja 18,15:5
Sullivan, William C, 1948, Ag 16,19:5
Sullivan, William D, 1946, Ja 31,21:4; 1947, Ja 19,53:2
Sullivan, William E, 1948, D 12,92:2; 1950, My 6,15:3
Sullivan, William F, 1941, N 22,19:1
Sullivan, William H, 1951, Jl 18,29:4; 1962, O 30,35:3; 1966, S 6,48:1
Sullivan, William H Mrs, 1965, S 13,35:3
Sullivan, William J, 1939, D 22,19:6; 1943, Ja 15,17:5; 1948, Mr 13,15:6; 1949, Ja 2,60:5; 1951, N 18,90:6; 1953, Je 15,15:6; 1956, D 22,19:4; 1964, Jl 9,33:5
Sullivan, William L, 1944, S 2,11:5; 1951, Ap 25,29:1
Sullivan, William M, 1939, Mr 24,21:2; 1947, Je 3,25:4
Sullivan, William V, 1946, Je 26,25:2
Sullivan, William W, 1947, Ag 29,17:4
Sullivant, M L, 1879, F 3,3:6
Sully, A Gen, 1879, Ap 29,4:7
Sully, Albert W Mrs, 1947, D 22,21:2
Sully, Alfred, 1909, My 30,9:5
Sully, D L, 1930, S 20,17:3
Sully, Dan, 1910, Je 26,II,9:4
Sully, Lew, 1945, S 21,21:4
Sully, Reginald A, 1948, N 3,27:3
Sully, Thomas, 1872, N 13,4:4; 1939, Mr 16,23:5
Sully, Wilberforce, 1942, Ag 21,19:3
Sully-Prudhomme, Rene Francois Armand, 1907, S 8, 7:6
Sulner, Laszlo, 1950, O 23,23:1
Suloff, Noah, 1939, O 24,23:3
Sulouff, S Henry, 1945, N 3,15:5
Sulouff, S Henry Mrs, 1948, Ap 13,27:2
Sultan, Daniel I, 1947, Ja 15,25:1
Sultan, Joseph, 1962, Je 15,27:3
Sultan, Max Mrs, 1944, N 27,23:5
Sulton, Frederick L, 1944, Mr 24,19:5
Sulton, Malle Mrs, 1944, S 2,11:5
Sultzer, Norman W, 1951, Ag 13,17:6
Sultzer, William F, 1954, Je 15,29:4
Sulu, Sultan of, 1936, Je 9,29:1
Sulu, Sultan of (J Abirin), 1950, O 16,27:5
Sulvano, Joseph, 1948, D 20,1:8
Sulzach, Joseph, 1944, My 19,19:2
Sulzberger, Arthur Hays (mem ser plans, D 13,43:4), 1968, D 12,1:2
Sulzberger, C L, 1932, My 1,II,5:1
Sulzberger, Carl F, 1964, Ag 4,29:3
Sulzberger, Cyrus S Mrs (por), 1938, F 11,23:3
Sulzberger, David H, 1962, S 3,15:4
Sulzberger, Ferdinand, 1915, Ag 7,7:7
Sulzberger, Frank L Mrs, 1964, Jl 16,31:5
Sulzberger, L, 1926, F 1,19:3
Sulzberger, Marcel, 1941, Ja 2,23:2
Sulzberger, Mayer Judge, 1923, Ap 21,11:5
Sulzberger, Milton, 1951, O 9,29:2
Sulzberger, Myron, 1956, S 17,27:3
Sulzberger, Myron Mrs, 1967, Je 22,39:2
Sulzberger, Nathan, 1954, Je 7,23:6
Sulzberger, Solomon L Mrs, 1960, My 16,31:6
Sulzer, Albert F, 1944, Ag 7,15:6
Sulzer, Charles A, 1919, Ap 17,11:3
Sulzer, Clara, 1904, Ag 9,2:1
Sulzer, David, 1940, D 18,25:5
Sulzer, Hans, 1959, Ja 5,29:4
Sulzer, William (died intestate, D 13,23:8),(por), 1941, N 7,23:3
Sulzer, William Mrs, 1948, N 26,23:4
Sulzman, Frank M, 1966, Ag 1,27:4
Suman, Frank T, 1946, O 10,27:6
Sumerfield, Vincent P, 1955, Jl 9,15:5
Sumersby, George W, 1948, Je 17,25:6
Sumerwell, Penelope, 1962, Ag 19,89:2
Sumichrast, F C de, 1933, F 11,10:1
Summer, Nathan, 1958, Mr 6,27:3
Summer, Samuel N, 1949, Mr 3,25:5
Summerall, Charles P (funl, My 18,31:5), 1955, My 15,87:1
Summerbell, Martyn, 1939, S 13,25:4
Summerfeldt, John R, 1941, O 12,53:2
Summerfield, David W, 1965, N 6,29:5
Summerfield, Elias, 1924, N 1,15:3
Summerfield, Hugo, 1943, Mr 11,22:2
Summerfield, Maurice, 1944, Jl 23,36:2
Summerfield, Maurice Mrs, 1949, F 26,15:5
Summerfield, Myron L, 1962, O 21,88:8
Summerfield, Solon E (por), 1947, S 4,25:3
Summerhayes, John W Lt-Col, 1911, Mr 9,11:4
Summerhays, Jared W, 1953, Je 11,29:4
Summerill, Frederick Mrs, 1958, N 19,37:3
Summerill, Kate H Mrs, 1952, S 9,31:5
Summerill, William A, 1943, Ja 4,15:2
Summerlin, George T (por), 1947, Jl 2,23:1
Summerlin, Laurence G, 1948, Ap 17,15:3
Summers, Albert A, 1939, Jl 15,15:6
Summers, Alphonsus J A M, 1948, Ag 11,21:4
Summers, Andrew Rowan, 1968, Mr 15,39:1
Summers, Bill (Wm R), 1966, S 13,47:1
Summers, C, 1878, N 18,8:5
Summers, Charles B Mrs, 1962, Mr 8,31:3
Summers, Ellen, 1878, My 27,8:2
Summers, Emma Mrs, 1941, N 28,23:3
Summers, Ezra T, 1957, Je 12,35:4
Summers, George W, 1952, N 6,29:5
Summers, Harry M V, 1959, Mr 23,31:2
Summers, Henry E, 1949, D 14,31:1
Summers, Herbert G, 1937, F 26,21:5
Summers, J Mills, 1957, Ja 6,89:2
Summers, James E, 1941, Jl 7,15:2
Summers, James J, 1940, Mr 3,44:4
Summers, James K, 1943, Je 23,21:3
Summers, John A, 1952, Je 4,27:3
Summers, John Edward Brig-Gen, 1908, O 3,9:2
Summers, John N, 1938, O 12,27:5
Summers, John W, 1937, S 27,21:5; 1947, Ag 6,23:2
Summers, Katherine W Mrs, 1958, N 18,37:5
Summers, L L, 1927, Mr 11,21:3
Summers, Leland L Mrs, 1949, O 13,27:4
Summers, Llewelyn B, 1948, Mr 24,25:3
Summers, Maddin, 1918, My 6,13:4
Summers, Moses, 1882, Je 16,5:4
Summers, Oren E, 1953, My 13,29:3
Summers, Oscar, 1958, My 18,87:1
Summers, Owen Gen, 1911, Ja 23,7:4
Summers, Patrick, 1914, Ap 24,13:6
Summers, Robert D, 1938, Mr 14,15:5
Summers, Robert G (por), 1943, S 17,21:1
Summers, Snowden Mrs, 1937, S 14,23:2
Summers, Theodore N, 1954, Mr 18,31:2
Summers, Walter G (por), 1938, S 26,17:1
Summers, William H, 1911, Ag 28,7:5; 1951, Mr 19, 27:4
Summers, William M, 1916, N 14,11:2
Summers, Willis M, 1954, O 5,27:1
Summerson, Beverly D, 1942, My 2,13:2
Summerson, Eugene P, 1946, Jl 2,25:5
Summerton, Walter A, 1937, Mr 13,19:2
Summerville, A, 1934, Ja 22,15:3

Summerville, Donald, 1963, N 20,40:1
Summerville, George J (Slim), 1946, Ja 7,19:1
Summey, David L Mrs, 1950, S 29,27:2
Summey, George Sr, 1954, F 23,27:1
Summit, Alphons, 1950, Ap 2,92:7
Summitt, J G, 1935, F 9,15:4
Summy, C D, 1945, F 2,19:5
Sumner, A De Witt, 1942, Jl 14,20:4
Sumner, A E Dr, 1882, S 1,8:2
Sumner, A I Prof (cor, Ap 8,5:6), 1873, Ap 7,5:5
Sumner, A J, 1933, D 3,38:3
Sumner, Adam C (funl), 1873, D 15,5:2
Sumner, Alanson A, 1910, D 4,13:4
Sumner, Albert E, 1940, N 2,15:6
Sumner, Augusta Mrs, 1907, Je 26,7:2
Sumner, Benedict H, 1951, Ap 26,29:2
Sumner, Caroline L, 1947, N 27,31:4
Sumner, Charles K, 1948, My 28,23:2
Sumner, Charles P, 1921, Ap 13,15:6
Sumner, Charles P Mrs, 1950, Jl 31,17:6
Sumner, Charles Sen, 1874, Mr 12,1:1
Sumner, Clarence W, 1952, N 23,88:1
Sumner, Clifford W Dr, 1937, Mr 21,II,8:8
Sumner, Cyril, 1944, F 8,16:3
Sumner, E V Brig-Gen (funl, S 3,11:4), 1912, Ag 25, II,11:6
Sumner, E V Lt-Col, 1919, Je 14,13:5
Sumner, Edward A, 1913, S 23,11:6; 1948, My 3,21:3
Sumner, Eliot, 1941, Ja 30,21:6
Sumner, Francis G, 1954, Ja 12,23:4
Sumner, Frank C, 1924, D 10,23:2
Sumner, Fred, 1942, Ja 13,19:1
Sumner, G Lynn, 1952, Ap 8,29:1
Sumner, George W, 1865, Ag 20,6:2
Sumner, George Watson Rear-Adm, 1924, F 21,17:5
Sumner, Graham Mrs, 1937, Je 2,23:2
Sumner, H W Mrs, 1880, D 11,3:3
Sumner, Humphrey, 1951, My 3,29:4
Sumner, Irving E, 1942, N 10,28:3
Sumner, James B, 1955, Ag 13,13:1
Sumner, John D, 1953, My 5,29:4
Sumner, John O, 1938, F 21,19:6
Sumner, Maj-Gen, 1863, Mr 29,3:5
Sumner, Richard E, 1966, F 3,31:3
Sumner, Robert E, 1941, S 18,25:3
Sumner, Steve, 1946, Mr 6,27:4
Sumner, Viscount, 1934, My 26,18:3
Sumner, William A, 1960, Ja 11,45:4
Sumner, William G Prof, 1910, Ap 13,11:3
Sumners, Hatton W, 1962, Ap 20,27:4
Sumpter, James E, 1960, N 29,37:2
Sumstine, David R, 1965, Ap 20,39:4
Sun, Gus (G F Klotz), 1959, O 2,29:3
Sun, John K, 1941, Ap 3,23:1
Sun Lu, 1952, S 8,21:5
Sun Yat-sen, Dr, 1924, My 15,19:3
Sun Yat-Sen, Dr, 1925, Mr 12,19:1
Sunada, Shigemasa, 1957, D 29,49:2
Sunbury, Maurice Mrs, 1948, Ag 10,21:3
Sundaram, M S, 1959, Je 25,29:3
Sunday, Billy Mrs, 1957, F 21,27:2
Sunday, David W, 1943, Ap 21,25:2
Sunday, W A, 1935, N 7,1:3
Sunday, William A Jr, 1938, Ap 3,II,6:7
Sundback, Gideon, 1954, Je 22,27:5
Sundberg, Agard V, 1951, Ag 29,25:5
Sundberg, August, 1944, D 20,23:4
Sundberg, Carl A, 1962, Ag 11,17:6
Sundberg, John C Dr, 1912, N 21,13:5
Sundberg, Paul C, 1964, O 27,39:4
Sundby-Hansen, Harry, 1946, S 17,7:1
Sunde, Tenold R, 1959, Mr 26,34:6
Sundelius, Gustav, 1946, Jl 11,23:4
Sundelius, Gustave Mme, 1958, Jl 4,19:3
Sundelson, J Wilner Mrs, 1949, D 29,25:5
Sundelson, Ray W Mrs, 1951, Mr 1,27:3
Sunderhauf, Fred A, 1955, Ja 17,23:4
Sunderlal, Felicia, 1961, S 12,33:2
Sunderland, Earl of (J D I Spencer-Churchill), 1955, My 16,9:3
Sunderland, Edson R, 1959, Mr 30,31:4
Sunderland, Edwin S S, 1964, N 7,27:4
Sunderland, L E, 1939, N 22,21:3
Sunderland, Paul U, 1958, O 11,23:4
Sunderland, William A, 1963, Ag 24,19:5
Sunderlin, Fred A, 1949, F 27,68:6
Sunderlin, Louis K, 1947, Jl 7,17:1
Sundermann, Fred S, 1954, Ap 23,27:2
Sundh, Aug, 1940, Mr 5,23:3
Sundheim, Harry C, 1956, D 4,39:4
Sundheim, Sidney, 1937, D 19,II,8:6
Sundheimer, Henry, 1944, D 18,19:4
Sundholm, L Robert Mrs, 1945, Ja 9,19:2
Sundin, Peter O, 1938, N 30,23:4
Sundmark, Betty (Mrs H Shannon), 1959, Ag 19,29:2
Sundock, Benjamin, 1949, N 29,29:1
Sundquist, Edward, 1961, O 13,35:3
Sundquist, Eric E, 1961, F 9,31:3
Sundra, Steve, 1952, Mr 24,25:4
Sundstedt, Hugo, 1966, Jl 9,27:3
Sundstrom, Newton Mrs, 1954, N 18,33:5
Sundstrom, Swan R, 1956, Ag 15,29:5
Sundt, Guy M, 1955, O 26,31:2
Sundwall, John, 1950, D 15,31:1
Sunheim, Joseph H, 1943, My 22,13:5
Suni, Grikor M, 1939, D 20,25:4
Sunley, Bernard, 1964, N 22,85:4
Sunley, William T, 1949, My 24,27:5
Sunn, William J, 1951, N 27,31:5
Sunny, B E Mrs, 1922, D 28,17:5
Sunny, Bernard E, 1943, O 6,23:2
Sunol, Abbot G M, 1946, O 29,26:3
Sunshine, Charles K, 1947, My 1,25:4
Sunshine, Nathaniel L, 1965, Ja 5,33:1
Sunshine, William, 1941, Jl 23,19:3
Sunstrom, Mark A, 1960, N 1,39:4
Suolahti, V Hugo, 1944, F 25,17:5
Suomela, Isaac A, 1948, Jl 17,15:5
Suominen, John S, 1948, Jl 18,52:6
Supensky, John A Mrs, 1953, Ja 3,15:3
Super, Charles W, 1939, O 11,27:5
Super, Paul (por), 1949, Mr 18,25:5
Super, Ralph C Prof, 1937, D 18,21:5
Superior, Ira E, 1959, D 2,43:2
Supernau, Clarence J, 1961, Ja 8,86:1
Supervia, C, 1936, Mr 31,22:1
Supine, Edward I, 1949, O 29,3:2
Supino, Davide Prof, 1937, My 11,26:3
Supinski, Paul C, 1966, Mr 31,39:1
Supiyalat, Queen, 1925, N 25,21:4
Suplee, Frank L, 1939, S 11,19:5
Suplee, Walter S, 1946, D 30,19:3
Suppe, F von, 1895, My 23,5:2
Supple, Eva, 1948, O 1,25:3
Supple, Frank J, 1942, Ja 29,19:3
Supple, James O, 1950, Jl 28,4:5
Supple, Joseph R Jr, 1953, Mr 15,10:4
Supple, Leo F, 1955, Mr 24,31:5
Supplee, C Henderson Mrs, 1943, Je 30,21:2
Supplee, Frederick M, 1945, Ja 26,21:2
Supplee, H Clay M, 1956, D 31,13:4
Supplee, J Frank Col, 1923, Ap 17,21:5
Supplee, J Frank Judge, 1937, Ap 3,19:3
Supplee, Litta M Mrs, 1964, O 6,43:7
Supplee, Samuel G Mrs, 1944, Ap 5,19:3
Supples, Sarah Mrs, 1922, My 12,19:4
Suprenant, Valmore J, 1950, My 16,31:2
Sura, Michael Mrs, 1962, Jl 14,21:4
Suraci, Frank A, 1954, F 2,27:4
Surakarta, Sultan of, 1939, F 21,19:2
Surbaugh, John S Mrs, 1954, D 11,13:2
Surber, Thaddeus, 1949, O 10,23:2
Surber, Wilfred A, 1948, Je 11,23:3
Surbrug, J R, 1882, Jl 29,2:7
Surburg, Carlotta G E Mrs, 1937, Ag 6,17:5
Surburg, John W, 1946, Mr 2,13:4
Surcht, Leo C, 1946, S 8,44:2
Surdam, I Burke, 1963, Mr 9,7:5
Sure, Barnett, 1960, Je 5,86:5
Sureth, Theodore, 1944, My 7,47:1
Surette, Thomas W, 1941, My 20,23:3
Surface, Frank M, 1965, S 1,37:3
Surface, Harvey A, 1941, Jl 10,19:6
Surguy, Henry, 1949, Ag 23,23:2
Suri Castillo, Emilio, 1951, S 2,13:1
Suriano, Joseph, 1953, Mr 3,27:4
Surin, Sergei, 1952, Ap 17,29:4
Suringer, Conrad B Dr, 1924, N 8,15:5
Suritz, Jakob, 1952, Ja 5,11:5
Surkin, Samuel D, 1942, Jl 11,13:3
Surles, Alexander D, 1947, D 7,77:1
Surles, Carson C, 1940, Jl 29,30:6
Surnamer, Isaac Dr, 1937, Ap 24,19:2
Surnburger, George G, 1941, N 26,23:3
Suro, Guillermo A, 1961, My 13,19:6
Surosky, William, 1952, My 6,29:2
Surovitch, Boris, 1953, My 25,25:6
Surovsky, Celia, 1959, Jl 12,72:6
Surpless, Abner C, 1960, Mr 12,21:3
Surpless, James, 1946, Ap 3,25:3
Surpless, Thomas J, 1911, D 25,7:6
Surprenant, E J E, 1951, S 21,23:4
Surprenant, Laurent Mrs (B Bennett), 1958, Ag 10, 93:1
Surratt, Isaac D, 1907, N 4,9:4
Surratt, John Harrison, 1916, Ap 22,11:6
Surre, Anning F, 1949, Ap 21,25:2
Surrey, Frank M, 1952, D 2,31:3
Surrey, Pauline S Mrs, 1964, Mr 2,27:2
Sursa, Charles V, 1951, My 1,29:2
Sursock, Michael, 1954, Jl 8,23:2
Surut, Louis, 1950, O 6,27:2
Survage, Leopold, 1968, N 2,37:2
Surveyer, Arthur, 1961, Ap 19,39:2
Surveyer, E Fabre, 1957, My 22,33:4
Susaikov, Ivan Z, 1962, Jl 15,61:2
Susan, Robert, 1957, Ap 5,27:2
Susini, Signor, 1883, D 29,5:5
Suski, Thaddeus, 1966, Mr 21,33:3
Suskin, Albert I, 1965, Ag 9,25:4
Suskind, Harris, 1951, Ja 10,27:3
Suskind, Harry, 1957, Ja 20,92:4
Suskind, Leonard R, 1948, S 14,29:4
Suslak, Sigmund, 1960, Je 12,86:8
Suslin, Dimitri I, 1954, O 4,27:5
Susman, Harry, 1949, Je 1,31:4
Susmann, Julius H, 1937, Ap 12,17:4
Susmann, Sievers W, 1954, My 26,29:3
Susong, Bruce I, 1939, N 6,23:5
Sussdorff, Edwin S Jr, 1968, Ja 21,76:7
Sussdorff, Louis A Mrs, 1952, F 16,13:1
Susseles, Abraham, 1967, N 4,33:4
Sussillo, Nicholas P, 1955, Je 16,31:3
Susskind, Anson, 1953, Ap 8,29:2
Susskind, Arthur, 1967, Mr 11,29:2
Sussking, Louis, 1940, D 30,17:4
Sussman, Aaron P, 1951, F 27,27:4
Sussman, Abraham, 1949, N 11,26:3; 1951, N 27,31:5
Sussman, Abram L, 1938, Ja 16,II,9:1
Sussman, Albert L, 1962, O 26,31:4
Sussman, Barnett Mrs, 1950, Ja 10,29:2
Sussman, Charles M, 1949, Ja 26,25:4
Sussman, Edward A, 1942, D 31,15:3
Sussman, Harold P (cor, Jl 25,17:4), 1952, Jl 24,27:4
Sussman, Harris, 1940, Ap 25,23:2
Sussman, Harry, 1945, D 15,17:1
Sussman, Henry A, 1938, O 17,15:5
Sussman, Herbert B, 1960, F 17,35:2
Sussman, Herbert W, 1944, O 19,23:1
Sussman, Herman, 1954, D 31,6:1
Sussman, Jennie, 1968, My 31,29:4
Sussman, Joseph, 1938, N 18,21:4; 1960, Ap 30,23:6
Sussman, Lena Mrs, 1941, Je 4,23:5
Sussman, LeRoy, 1966, F 4,31:4
Sussman, Morris, 1944, My 30,21:5; 1950, O 20,28:2
Sussman, Nathan, 1952, My 8,31:2; 1955, S 3,15:4
Sussman, Nathan Mrs, 1951, O 22,23:5
Sussman, Nye N, 1962, S 19,39:1
Sussman, Otto, 1947, F 4,25:1
Sussman, Phil, 1938, S 24,8:6
Sussman, Phil N, 1954, O 26,27:3
Sussman, Rubin Mrs, 1957, Je 8,19:4
Sussman, Rudolph, 1959, Jl 14,29:4
Sussman, Samuel, 1945, S 29,15:3; 1951, Mr 10,13:3
Sussman, Samuel Ernest, 1968, Ja 2,41:4
Sussman, Simon W Mrs, 1966, N 11,43:2
Sussman, Sol, 1959, Ag 15,17:2
Sussman, William, 1968, O 8,47:2
Sussman, William S, 1950, My 11,30:3
Sutch, Frank E, 1958, Ag 31,56:8
Sutcliffe, Arthur, 1937, O 22,24:1; 1951, Ja 20,15:5
Sutcliffe, Charles E, 1939, Ja 12,19:4
Sutcliffe, Denham, 1964, Mr 1,83:2
Sutcliffe, Eli D, 1939, O 14,19:3
Sutcliffe, Frank, 1955, Je 16,31:4
Sutcliffe, George H, 1949, Jl 4,13:2
Sutcliffe, John, 1910, Jl 24,7:5; 1945, Ap 23,19:4
Sutcliffe, Samuel, 1943, Ag 14,11:6
Sutcliffe, William G, 1963, S 7,19:5
Suter, Alfred, 1947, O 25,19:1; 1956, Jl 16,12:5
Suter, Eugene, 1956, Ap 24,31:2
Suter, Frank F, 1951, D 11,33:2
Suter, Herman, 1946, N 1,23:3
Suter, James E, 1941, N 30,68:2
Suter, John T, 1945, D 13,29:4
Suter, John W (por), 1942, Ap 12,44:7
Suter, John W Mrs, 1949, My 24,28:2
Suter, Louis, 1945, Ja 3,17:2
Suter, Phil H Mrs, 1939, F 21,19:4
Suter, Russell, 1953, O 30,23:3
Sutermeister, Edwin, 1958, Ag 1,21:2
Suters, Thomas, 1953, Ag 13,25:1
Sutfin, John C, 1941, N 14,23:6
Sutherland, A G, 1911, Ag 1,9:6
Sutherland, Abby A (Mrs W F Brown), 1961, Mr 30, 29:2
Sutherland, Alan L, 1960, My 25,39:4
Sutherland, Albert (funl, F 24,9:4), 1911, F 22,9:4
Sutherland, Allan, 1962, Ag 15,31:5
Sutherland, Anne (por), 1942, Je 24,19:1
Sutherland, Arthur, 1948, S 21,27:4; 1953, Mr 31,31:5; 1953, O 1,29:5
Sutherland, Arthur E, 1949, Je 13,19:5
Sutherland, Arthur E Mrs, 1958, Ja 4,15:4
Sutherland, Charles R, 1946, Mr 31,46:4
Sutherland, Charles W, 1943, D 8,23:3
Sutherland, Chief R J, 1903, Mr 12,9:7
Sutherland, Christine S Mrs, 1939, My 5,23:4
Sutherland, Clarke S, 1950, Je 5,23:4
Sutherland, Conrad J, 1961, Jl 30,69:2
Sutherland, Dan A, 1955, Mr 26,15:4
Sutherland, Donald, 1949, Ja 3,23:1
Sutherland, Donald R, 1953, Mr 3,27:5
Sutherland, Dowager Duchess of, 1868, O 29,1:1
Sutherland, Duchess of, 1943, Ag 25,19:1
Sutherland, Duchess of (Lady Millicent Fanny St Clair-Erskine), 1955, Ag 21,93:1
Sutherland, Duke of, 1913, Je 27,9:6
Sutherland, Duke of (G G S Leveson-Gower),(Feb 1 1963, Ap 1,36:6
Sutherland, Duncan H, 1952, S 27,17:4
Sutherland, E D Maj, 1923, Ja 9,23:4
Sutherland, E G, 1883, My 18,5:4
Sutherland, Edward, 1948, N 30,27:5
Sutherland, Edward A, 1955, Je 22,29:3; 1957, S 15, 83:1
Sutherland, Edwin H, 1950, O 13,29:3
Sutherland, Eliza (Mrs M Cooper), 1960, Mr 1,33:
Sutherland, Erwin, 1950, My 9,29:3

Sutherland, Francis W, 1959, S 28,31:2
Sutherland, Fred B, 1939, Ag 15,19:2
Sutherland, Fred G, 1951, F 12,23:1
Sutherland, Fred W, 1939, Ag 11,15:4
Sutherland, Frederick P Mrs, 1952, D 27,10:4
Sutherland, George, 1942, Jl 19,31:1; 1943, D 13,23:5; 1951, My 12,21:4
Sutherland, George A, 1912, N 21,13:4
Sutherland, George F, 1954, D 7,33:1
Sutherland, George Mrs, 1946, Ap 5,25:5
Sutherland, Gordon A, 1957, Ag 13,27:1
Sutherland, H Lloyd, 1945, Je 27,19:5
Sutherland, Henry, 1879, Mr 26,2:7; 1959, Ja 15,33:3
Sutherland, Henry H, 1940, Je 1,15:4
Sutherland, Howard, 1950, Mr 13,22:2
Sutherland, Howard Mrs, 1944, F 21,15:4
Sutherland, J Arthur, 1952, Je 12,34:6
Sutherland, J L, 1904, Ja 9,9:2
Sutherland, J P Mrs (Evelyn Greenleaf Sutherland), 1908, D 25,7:5
Sutherland, James A, 1955, Jl 1,21:2
Sutherland, James R, 1951, O 31,29:3
Sutherland, Jim, 1955, S 18,87:1
Sutherland, John, 1921, S 2,13:3; 1945, Ag 7,23:2
Sutherland, John B, 1948, Ap 12,26:6
Sutherland, John J, 1947, Ap 10,25:2
Sutherland, John P, 1941, F 23,40:3
Sutherland, John Ross Rev, 1918, Ja 12,11:4
Sutherland, Kenneth F (will, D 14,50:4), 1954, N 15, 27:1
Sutherland, Kenneth F Mrs, 1953, D 18,29:5; 1957, Mr 22,23:3
Sutherland, Kenneth L, 1910, My 26,9:4
Sutherland, Laura A Mrs, 1938, Mr 18,19:2
Sutherland, Leslie, 1945, Je 7,19:1
Sutherland, Leslie Mrs, 1950, F 11,15:5
Sutherland, Mary, 1939, My 14,III,6:7
Sutherland, Mary Mrs, 1949, O 6,31:3
Sutherland, Meade R, 1944, F 15,17:4
Sutherland, Norman R, 1963, S 2,15:6
Sutherland, Norris, 1937, Mr 19,23:2
Sutherland, Oscar, 1944, S 5,19:6
Sutherland, P D, 1943, Ag 6,15:4
Sutherland, R T Rev Dr, 1915, S 13,9:5
Sutherland, Richard K, 1966, Je 26,73:1
Sutherland, Robert C, 1937, N 2,25:4
Sutherland, Robert F, 1922, My 24,19:5
Sutherland, Roderick Dhu, 1915, O 19,11:5
Sutherland, Ruth, 1949, Je 22,31:1
Sutherland, S F, 1910, Je 1,6:5
Sutherland, Spencer J, 1952, F 26,27:5
Sutherland, Spencer K Mrs, 1944, D 9,15:6
Sutherland, Stuart B Sr, 1951, Mr 12,25:2
Sutherland, Thomas F, 1938, My 30,11:5
Sutherland, Vernette, 1946, S 7,15:5
Sutherland, W J, 1934, My 11,31:5
Sutherland, William, 1949, S 20,29:4
Sutherland, William A, 1908, Mr 12,7:6
Sutherland, William G, 1948, F 3,25:3
Sutherland, William P, 1951, S 16,83:6
Sutherland, William S, 1952, Mr 16,91:2
Sutherland, William W, 1948, N 7,88:5
Sutherland, William W Dr, 1947, Je 1,60:7
Sutherlen, Victor H, 1959, O 27,37:1
Sutherlin, Kane Patrick Mrs, 1911, Ja 14,11:4
Sutio, Rosa, 1883, Ag 5,7:6
Sutley, Frank K, 1943, Ja 17,44:5
Sutley, Margaret H, 1947, Jl 18,17:5
Sutliff, Fred A, 1950, Ap 22,19:3
Sutliff, Joseph W, 1956, Je 30,17:6
Sutliff, Milo J, 1964, S 23,47:1
Sutliff, Roy M, 1948, O 14,29:2
Sutliffe, I H, 1936, D 31,18:1
Sutliffe, Raymond V, 1948, N 29,23:3
Sutliffe, Robert S, 1950, O 26,31:1
Sutlive, Carey, 1950, Mr 18,13:5
Sutlive, W E, 1940, Je 7,23:1
Suto, Paul, 1946, Mr 16,13:3
Sutor, Adele, 1952, Mr 29,15:5
Sutphen, Anne J, 1952, My 24,19:3
Sutphen, Duncan Dunbar, 1953, F 25,27:4
Sutphen, Ernest M, 1956, O 19,27:4
Sutphen, Frederick C Dr, 1915, S 13,9:4
Sutphen, Gertrude C, 1903, Jl 23,7:6
Sutphen, Henry B, 1956, Ap 14,17:4
Sutphen, Henry R, 1950, D 11,25:1
Sutphen, Henry R Mrs, 1956, F 23,27:2
Sutphen, Herbert S, 1939, Ap 22,17:5
Sutphen, John S, 1954, O 2,17:4
Sutphen, John S Mrs, 1949, S 25,93:1
Sutphen, John Schureman, 1925, My 24,7:1
Sutphen, John W, 1954, Ag 5,23:3
Sutphen, Joseph J, 1943, Ap 9,21:6
Sutphen, Margaret P, 1948, Mr 6,13:3
Sutphen, Oliver Mrs, 1924, My 29,19:5
Sutphen, Wallace D, 1962, Ag 12,81:1
Sutphen, William G, 1945, S 21,21:4
Sutphen, William P Mrs, 1961, My 19,31:5
Sutphen, William R, 1944, O 10,23:4
Sutphin, Aaron R Capt, 1924, F 19,15:2
Sutphin, Edwin A, 1945, O 1,19:5
Sutphin, Edwin J, 1937, Ag 4,19:5
Sutphin, Henry, 1954, Ja 28,27:1
Sutphin, Jack, 1958, Ja 23,27:3
Sutphin, James R, 1954, Jl 11,73:1
Sutphin, John H, 1907, Jl 22,7:5; 1907, Jl 25,7:5
Sutphin, William, 1944, F 29,17:2
Sutphin, William H Mrs, 1956, Ja 6,23:2
Sutro, A, 1933, S 13,19:1
Sutro, A H J, 1898, Ag 9,7:5
Sutro, Alfred, 1945, Mr 11,40:1
Sutro, Edward S, 1908, O 4,9:4
Sutro, Florentine S (will, D 30,8:3),(por), 1939, D 21, 26:2
Sutro, Frederick C, 1964, Je 13,23:3
Sutro, Rose L, 1957, Ja 12,19:1
Sutro, T, 1927, Ag 29,17:3
Sutro, Theodore Mrs, 1906, Ap 28,11:5
Sutro, Victor, 1954, Jl 30,17:2
Sutter, Allan Mrs (Rita), 1968, Ag 16,33:4
Sutter, Edward C, 1956, Ag 28,27:1
Sutter, Frederic E Mrs, 1954, N 20,17:4
Sutter, H Gerard Mrs, 1946, Jl 13,15:6
Sutter, Harry B, 1957, N 30,21:6
Sutter, Henry S, 1950, F 23,27:5
Sutter, J A, 1880, Je 20,7:3
Sutter, Otto H, 1957, Mr 13,31:1
Sutter, William, 1951, S 18,31:2
Sutterby, Floyd H, 1944, O 30,19:3
Sutterly, Wilmont G, 1946, Ag 6,25:4
Suttie, Roscoe H, 1956, Ag 1,23:5
Suttle, William G Jr, 1944, Mr 6,19:3
Suttles, J C Mrs, 1949, D 10,18:2
Suttleworth, Frank K, 1958, My 10,21:2
Sutton, Agnes M, 1939, Jl 13,19:5
Sutton, Alfred, 1954, O 5,27:2
Sutton, Anna M B Mrs, 1937, D 9,25:3
Sutton, Arthur E, 1948, Jl 25,48:3
Sutton, Arthur P, 1942, Ja 27,21:1
Sutton, Belle Mrs, 1961, Jl 20,27:4
Sutton, Bertine E, 1946, O 1,23:5
Sutton, C Oscar, 1957, Je 19,35:1
Sutton, Catherine, 1925, S 3,25:4
Sutton, Charles Mrs, 1952, F 9,13:2
Sutton, Charles W, 1949, My 20,28:3
Sutton, Clarence E Rev, 1937, Ap 30,21:5
Sutton, David, 1938, N 9,23:4
Sutton, David M Mrs, 1954, My 11,29:1
Sutton, Donn, 1960, Ja 16,21:4
Sutton, E W, 1954, S 5,50:1
Sutton, Eli L, 1945, Ap 19,27:6
Sutton, F Marvin Mrs, 1959, F 4,33:2
Sutton, Florence L, 1944, Ag 6,37:2
Sutton, Frank, 1957, F 18,27:5
Sutton, Frederick, 1945, D 28,15:1
Sutton, Frederick J H, 1958, Mr 11,29:4
Sutton, Frederick T, 1957, N 16,19:5
Sutton, George, 1948, F 18,27:1
Sutton, George A, 1947, N 8,17:6
Sutton, George E, 1944, Ja 26,19:2
Sutton, George H, 1938, My 16,17:2; 1952, Je 28,19:3
Sutton, George H Jr Mrs, 1950, Ap 6,29:4
Sutton, George W Jr, 1958, Ja 3,23:3
Sutton, Glenn W, 1965, F 12,29:4
Sutton, Harry E, 1947, S 7,60:4
Sutton, Henry C Mrs, 1944, D 16,15:5
Sutton, Henry M, 1942, Je 1,13:1
Sutton, Howard A, 1942, Mr 22,48:6; 1948, Ap 13,27:2
Sutton, Howard Mrs, 1946, My 17,21:4
Sutton, Howard P Mrs, 1942, N 22,53:1
Sutton, Irving D, 1952, F 12,27:2
Sutton, J P, 1903, Ag 21,9:6
Sutton, James E, 1967, Ja 4,43:2
Sutton, James Fountain, 1915, N 25,13:5
Sutton, James G, 1923, F 6,19:4
Sutton, John, 1906, N 17,9:7
Sutton, John B, 1944, N 25,13:1
Sutton, John D, 1941, Mr 31,15:3
Sutton, John E, 1941, Ap 18,21:3; 1967, S 26,47:1
Sutton, John G, 1967, Ja 11,25:3
Sutton, John H Mrs, 1951, S 23,86:3
Sutton, John R, 1938, Mr 15,23:1
Sutton, Joseph Ford Rev Dr, 1912, Je 1,11:4
Sutton, Joseph W, 1958, O 24,33:3
Sutton, Josephine M, 1954, Ja 16,15:1
Sutton, Joshua P, 1941, N 20,27:6
Sutton, Katherine A, 1949, F 11,23:2
Sutton, L H, 1905, Ap 29,11:6
Sutton, Larry, 1956, S 8,17:2
Sutton, Laurus E, 1943, F 15,15:4
Sutton, Lawrence, 1949, Jl 18,17:4
Sutton, Leslie A Mrs, 1953, Ja 5,21:1
Sutton, Leslie C, 1953, D 29,23:2
Sutton, Linton B, 1911, Je 12,11:4
Sutton, Lucy P (por), 1938, D 24,15:6
Sutton, Mabel R, 1954, My 8,17:5
Sutton, N Howard Mrs, 1959, Ja 4,88:3
Sutton, Norborne, 1925, Ag 26,19:5
Sutton, Norman, 1953, Ag 27,25:2
Sutton, Paul B, 1940, Ja 4,24:2
Sutton, R, 1878, Jl 15,5:4
Sutton, Raleigh M, 1956, D 28,21:1
Sutton, Richard H D, 1941, Je 30,17:1
Sutton, Richard M, 1966, Mr 30,45:2
Sutton, Robert C Mrs, 1959, Jl 9,27:6
Sutton, Susan M, 1955, N 17,35:5
Sutton, Sydney R Mrs, 1955, Ap 6,29:1
Sutton, Thomas H Ex-Judge, 1913, N 20,11:5
Sutton, Thomas R, 1953, Mr 3,27:3
Sutton, Vida R, 1956, Jl 28,17:3
Sutton, W Dale Mrs, 1967, F 7,39:4
Sutton, Wilbur E, 1949, S 17,17:4
Sutton, William, 1882, Ap 20,5:2
Sutton, William F, 1949, Ap 12,29:5
Sutton, William H Jr, 1954, Ja 29,19:1
Sutton, William H Jr Mrs, 1940, D 5,25:1
Sutton, William Henry, 1921, My 8,22:3
Sutton, William J Mrs, 1949, D 14,31:5
Sutton, Willis A, 1960, Jl 30,17:4
Suttonsiner, Ada Mrs, 1949, Je 16,29:1
Sutzman, Lloyd L, 1961, S 9,19:6
Suullivan, B O, 1956, N 23,27:4
Suur, Hemmo F, 1943, Mr 19,19:2
Suval, Albert N, 1951, Ap 20,29:4
Suvorin, Alexis, 1912, Ag 25,II,11:5
Suydam, Albert, 1937, S 19,II,6:8
Suydam, Bernard, 1919, D 14,22:4
Suydam, Bernard Mrs, 1950, Ja 15,84:1; 1952, F 29, 23:4
Suydam, Charles Crooke Dr, 1911, N 10,11:4
Suydam, D L, 1884, D 21,2:5
Suydam, Edward H, 1940, D 24,15:5
Suydam, Edwin E, 1957, Jl 10,27:3
Suydam, Elijah R, 1949, Ja 16,68:2
Suydam, Eliza G, 1942, F 16,17:5
Suydam, Emily H, 1963, Je 8,25:4
Suydam, Frederick D, 1960, Ag 24,29:2
Suydam, George H, 1914, Ag 15,9:6
Suydam, Harry T, 1947, Mr 24,25:1
Suydam, Hendrick R, 1961, S 10,86:5
Suydam, Henry, 1955, D 12,31:1
Suydam, Henry Mrs, 1955, O 16,86:1
Suydam, J Howard Rev Dr, 1908, O 18,VII,11:5
Suydam, John R, 1882, My 16,5:3
Suydam, Lambert, 1916, Ja 19,11:5; 1924, Mr 31,17:2
Suydam, Lambert C, 1951, My 29,25:3
Suydam, Matthew, 1943, D 22,23:4
Suydam, Stephen, 1951, Je 5,31:1
Suydam, Walter L Jr, 1951, Ja 3,27:3
Suydam, Walter L Mrs, 1951, Mr 18,88:4
Suydan, John H, 1951, S 8,17:5
Suykes, George E, 1950, D 7,33:1
Suzannet, Mary de Countess, 1920, Mr 6,11:5
Suzio, Leonardo, 1945, Mr 17,13:3
Suzor-Cote, Marc A de F, 1937, Ja 31,II,8:8
Suzuki, Daisetsu, 1966, Jl 12,43:4
Suzuki, Kantaro, 1948, Ap 18,68:3
Suzuki, Kisaburo, 1940, Je 25,23:5
Suzuki, Saschichi, 1958, Ap 5,15:4
Suzuki, Soroku, 1940, F 20,21:3
Suzuki, Umetaro, 1943, S 21,24:3
Suzzallo, H, 1933, S 26,21:3
Svampa, Domenico Cardina, 1907, Ag 11,7:6
Svanda, Anthony, 1959, Mr 22,87:2
Svanholm, Set, 1964, O 6,39:3
Svaton, Joseph, 1954, My 29,15:6
Svecenski, L, 1926, Je 19,15:5
Svecenski, Louis Mrs, 1959, N 25,29:3
Svedberg, Elof, 1939, Je 29,23:4
Svedrofsky, Henry, 1949, F 23,27:1
Svehla, A, 1933, D 13,23:6
Svendsen, Johann, 1911, Je 15,9:5
Svendsen, Kester Dr, 1968, O 10,47:5
Svendsen, Walter R, 1952, S 1,17:5
Svenningsen, Anders P, 1954, My 29,15:4
Svenningson, Karl F, 1947, Mr 22,13:1
Svenson, Gust, 1961, O 26,35:3
Svenson, Hulda Mrs, 1940, Ap 13,2:3
Svenson, Sven H, 1953, Ag 27,25:2
Svensson, Patrik, 1960, Jl 19,29:3
Sverdlik, Aaron, 1948, Jl 6,23:3
Sverdlin, Frank J Mrs, 1963, Je 9,86:6
Sverdlove, Harry R, 1966, D 18,84:7
Sverdrup, Harald U, 1957, Ag 22,27:1
Sverdrup, O, 1930, N 27,25:4
Sves, Charles Jr, 1961, Mr 30,29:3
Svet, Mandell, 1953, O 20,29:2
Svet, Mendell Mrs, 1958, Je 17,29:1
Svetkey, Edward R, 1966, O 23,88:2
Svetlov, Mikhail A, 1964, S 29,43:1
Svevola, Victor de, 1950, Ap 1,15:3
Svimonov, Victor C, 1946, Mr 5,26:2
Svinhufvud, Pehr E, 1944, Mr 1,19:3
Sviridov, Vladimir P, 1963, My 8,36:5
Sviridov, Yefimovich, 1955, N 25,27:2
Svirsky, Herman, 1961, Ap 24,29:4
Svoboda, Jacob, 1937, D 4,19:7
Svoboda, Vincent A, 1961, Mr 19,88:8
Svolos, Alex, 1956, F 24,25:4
Swaab, Maurice B, 1957, N 3,88:8
Swaab, Solomon M, 1947, Je 14,15:3
Swab, Daniel Cooper, 1922, S 4,13:6
Swabey, Carlisle, 1952, F 12,27:3
Swabey, Wilfred S, 1939, S 14,23:4
Swackhamer, Egbert W, 1942, O 3,15:4
Swackhamer, Frank R Mrs, 1947, Ja 8,23:1
Swackhamer, Harry J, 1944, Je 27,19:5
Swackhamer, R J, 1903, My 25,9:6
Swackhamer, Samuel S, 1955, O 11,39:4

Swaen, John A Sr, 1948, Mr 24,25:1
Swaffer, Hannen, 1962, Ja 17,33:2
Swaffield, Harold A, 1961, Je 20,33:5
Swaffield, Millicent, 1939, S 1,17:5
Swaffield, W J Mrs, 1947, F 10,29:5
Swafford, James, 1952, Ja 1,27:5
Swaim, H Nathan, 1957, Jl 31,23:2
Swaim, Loring T, 1964, Mr 6,28:5
Swaim, Verne F, 1954, Ja 6,31:4
Swain, C Raymond, 1950, Ag 11,19:1
Swain, Charles, 1874, S 24,6:7
Swain, Chester O (por), 1937, Ap 22,23:1
Swain, David W, 1947, F 25,25:4
Swain, David W Mrs, 1940, Ap 26,21:2
Swain, Donaldson Mrs, 1940, Ag 16,15:5
Swain, Edward A, 1909, Mr 11,9:6
Swain, Edwin O, 1965, Mr 21,86:6
Swain, Florence T Mrs, 1949, S 3,13:2
Swain, Frank K, 1954, Mr 21,89:2
Swain, George, 1871, Mr 13,3:3
Swain, George R, 1941, My 25,36:7
Swain, Harold, 1955, My 23,23:4
Swain, Harold Mrs, 1947, Mr 24,25:3
Swain, Henry L, 1940, Ja 12,17:3
Swain, Homer, 1945, My 23,19:4
Swain, Homer Mrs, 1947, F 12,25:5
Swain, Howard T Mrs, 1946, Je 27,21:4
Swain, J, 1927, My 20,19:5
Swain, James R, 1957, Ap 24,33:5
Swain, John D, 1964, Jl 20,25:4
Swain, Joseph W, 1948, F 16,21:2
Swain, Kathryn D, 1958, Ja 10,26:2
Swain, Lewis C, 1963, Ap 15,29:4
Swain, Philip, 1943, My 30,26:1
Swain, Philip W, 1958, Ap 28,23:3
Swain, R, 1931, Ap 10,25:3
Swain, R B, 1872, Je 16,8:1
Swain, Richard L, 1940, Mr 29,21:2
Swain, Robert E, 1961, Je 1,35:2
Swain, S E, 1882, N 1,4:7
Swain, Samuel, 1950, Ap 29,15:6
Swain, William H, 1949, Ja 4,40:3
Swain, William M, 1940, Mr 23,13:2
Swain, William T, 1937, D 18,21:3
Swaine, James M, 1955, N 12,19:3
Swaine, Robert T, 1949, S 26,25:1
Swaine, Robert T Mrs, 1966, Ja 8,26:5
Swainson, Swain J, 1954, O 26,27:5
Swal, Phil, 1942, F 21,20:2
Swales, A B, 1952, S 27,17:5
Swales, Francis S, 1962, N 8,39:1
Swales, Fred K, 1954, Ag 31,21:3
Swallen, William L, 1954, My 11,29:2
Swalley, Chattie W Mrs, 1951, Mr 1,27:2
Swallow, Alan, 1966, N 28,39:3
Swallow, Arthur G, 1938, Ag 16,19:6
Swallow, Chandler E, 1952, My 11,93:1
Swallow, Joseph G, 1939, Ja 17,22:4
Swallow, Rebecca S Mrs, 1937, Je 26,17:7
Swalm, Albert W, 1922, Ag 25,13:6
Swalm, Charles J, 1949, Ja 2,63:3
Swalm, William A, 1950, Ag 13,76:2
Swaltek, Joseph, 1953, Ap 22,29:4
Swalwell, Kenneth E, 1949, O 30,87:4
Swan, Abram Jr, 1939, Jl 18,19:4
Swan, Alden S, 1917, F 24,9:5
Swan, Annie S, 1943, Je 19,13:7
Swan, Benjamin Sr, 1953, Mr 14,29:4
Swan, Byron L, 1950, S 28,31:4
Swan, Carroll J Mrs, 1946, Ag 31,15:6
Swan, Charles A, 1937, F 18,21:4
Swan, Charles E Jr, 1956, D 25,25:4
Swan, Charles E Mrs, 1954, Ap 10,15:6
Swan, Charles S, 1945, Ja 1,21:6
Swan, Clinton C, 1967, Ag 20,88:3
Swan, Dallas DeW, 1966, Mr 31,39:3
Swan, Donnell, 1911, S 14,9:6
Swan, Edward H, 1903, Ag 31,7:6
Swan, Eugene L, 1957, D 3,35:3
Swan, Frederick T, 1956, D 23,30:4
Swan, George L, 1944, N 15,27:2
Swan, Gustavus, 1903, Jl 3,9:6
Swan, Halstead, 1966, Jl 7,37:3
Swan, Harriet R, 1943, Ap 10,17:5
Swan, Harry E, 1950, Mr 11,15:2
Swan, Henry T, 1942, F 14,15:3
Swan, Howard W, 1950, O 10,31:2
Swan, Hylton, 1960, D 17,23:5
Swan, Isabel T Mrs, 1942, My 23,13:2
Swan, James, 1925, Mr 20,19:6; 1944, F 11,19:3
Swan, John H, 1957, My 31,19:1
Swan, John J, 1963, S 14,25:4
Swan, John L, 1956, My 5,19:5
Swan, John M, 1910, F 16,9:4; 1949, N 23,29:3
Swan, Joseph, 1908, F 20,7:6
Swan, Joseph E C, 1960, Je 22,35:4
Swan, Joseph R, 1948, S 14,29:4; 1965, N 11,50:1
Swan, Joseph R Mrs, 1965, Ap 14,41:1
Swan, Joseph S, 1909, Mr 23,9:5
Swan, Joseph Wilson Sir, 1914, My 28,13:5
Swan, Kingsley, 1918, Ag 3,9:6
Swan, Marie V H Mrs, 1942, F 9,15:1
Swan, Mary E, 1937, F 24,24:1
Swan, Mary Ella, 1912, O 24,11:6
Swan, Oscar H, 1945, Jl 15,15:3
Swan, Patrick J, 1937, O 31,II,11:1
Swan, Paul Mrs, 1951, Je 15,23:3
Swan, Philip H, 1967, Ja 3,37:2
Swan, Robert, 1916, O 16,11:2
Swan, Robert Mrs, 1937, My 26,25:4
Swan, Robert O, 1953, Ja 17,15:2
Swan, Rodolphus A Mrs, 1952, S 21,89:1
Swan, Roy C, 1964, Ap 11,25:5
Swan, Russell, 1943, Mr 7,38:3
Swan, Russell G, 1949, Ap 28,31:2
Swan, Samuel B Mrs, 1948, S 6,13:5
Swan, Thomas E, 1956, Mr 9,23:3
Swan, Thomas W, 1948, Mr 17,25:3
Swan, W B, 1903, Ap 15,9:6
Swan, W Dana Mrs, 1957, Ag 22,27:3
Swan, W G, 1884, Ja 18,5:4
Swan, Walter S, 1907, Ap 1,9:8
Swan, Willard A, 1954, F 1,23:5
Swan, William A, 1943, Ap 21,25:3
Swan, William F, 1938, Ag 2,19:2
Swan, William J, 1903, Je 18,9:7
Swan, William L, 1925, N 9,19:6
Swan, William U, 1942, Mr 24,19:6
Swanberg, Curt O, 1959, Mr 18,37:4
Swander, George J, 1947, S 24,23:4
Swaner, William J, 1959, Ap 9,31:3
Swaney, Clarke R, 1950, O 14,19:6
Swaney, William B, 1945, Jl 29,39:2
Swank, Jesse, 1943, Je 16,21:2
Swank, John, 1944, D 26,19:5
Swank, Paul E Jr, 1965, F 4,31:3
Swank, Paul F, 1954, S 3,17:1
Swank, Thaddeus H, 1940, Je 4,23:4
Swann, Arthur, 1959, N 13,29:1
Swann, Arthur Mrs, 1947, O 14,27:5
Swann, Arthur W Dr, 1914, My 29,11:5
Swann, David V, 1954, F 15,23:5
Swann, Donovan, 1954, Mr 1,25:5
Swann, E G, 1876, Ap 27,6:7
Swann, Edward, 1945, S 21,21:1
Swann, Edward Mrs, 1955, Ja 17,23:2
Swann, Edwin D Mrs (Caroline B), 1964, D 7,35:3
Swann, James, 1903, My 2,9:5
Swann, Oliver, 1948, Mr 8,23:4
Swann, Samuel V, 1937, O 11,21:4
Swann, Theodore, 1955, F 6,88:3
Swann, Thomas, 1883, Jl 23,1:6
Swann, William F G, 1962, Ja 30,29:2
Swann, William F G Mrs, 1954, My 26,29:2
Swanson, Albert S, 1957, S 22,86:7
Swanson, Alex, 1949, Ja 8,15:1
Swanson, Antone B, 1950, N 26,89:5
Swanson, Arnold Mrs, 1948, F 16,21:1
Swanson, Carl, 1949, O 10,23:5
Swanson, Charles E, 1940, Mr 24,30:7
Swanson, Charles Mrs, 1950, Mr 4,17:5
Swanson, Claude A, 1939, Jl 8,1:3
Swanson, Claude A Mrs, 1953, Jl 18,13:1
Swanson, Douglas H, 1948, O 9,19:3
Swanson, Earl G, 1942, Je 24,19:2
Swanson, Edgar F, 1948, S 14,29:3
Swanson, Fred B, 1961, My 20,23:2
Swanson, Fred R, 1955, F 21,21:5
Swanson, Fred W Sr, 1956, N 30,23:4
Swanson, Fritz J, 1967, Ja 19,31:5
Swanson, Gilbert C Mrs, 1959, O 22,37:3
Swanson, Gilbert Carl, 1968, Mr 10,92:3
Swanson, Harold A, 1954, O 13,31:2
Swanson, Harry K, 1947, O 23,25:4
Swanson, Harry R, 1948, Jl 26,17:3
Swanson, Henry W, 1956, N 21,27:3
Swanson, John, 1956, Ja 28,17:4
Swanson, John E, 1961, Je 25,76:7
Swanson, John T, 1949, O 1,13:6
Swanson, John V Mrs, 1951, Jl 13,21:4
Swanson, Joseph, 1961, Mr 14,35:1
Swanson, Leonard E, 1960, S 29,35:3
Swanson, O Frederick, 1949, My 30,13:5
Swanson, Paul F, 1963, S 18,39:3
Swanson, Paul L, 1945, Ag 18,11:4
Swanson, Reynolds, 1949, Jl 20,25:5
Swanson, Robert W, 1959, D 24,19:5
Swanson, Sarah Mrs, 1944, Ap 25,23:1
Swanson, Sigurd B, 1956, F 12,89:2
Swanson, Verne J, 1950, S 2,17:2
Swanson, W Clarke, 1961, Ap 16,86:8
Swanson, Walter B, 1952, Mr 20,29:3
Swanson, William A, 1954, O 17,87:1
Swanstrom, Arthur M, 1940, O 5,15:6
Swanstrom, Carl A, 1940, Mr 14,23:3
Swanstrom, Francis W, 1914, Jl 11,7:4
Swanstrom, Gustave A Mrs, 1959, Jl 14,29:3
Swanstrom, J Edward, 1911, F 16,11:5
Swanstrom, J Edward (mem), 1911, Mr 26,II,15:4
Swanton, Gerald F, 1955, Ap 10,88:2
Swanton, Hobart P, 1956, My 21,25:6
Swanton, Robert G, 1964, F 1,23:5
Swanton, Roy J, 1943, Je 5,15:2
Swanton, Susan Mrs, 1948, My 16,68:3
Swanton, Thomas J, 1940, My 9,23:5
Swanwick, Charles H, 1956, S 16,84:4
Swanwick, Curtis C, 1941, F 23,41:2
Swanwick, Leo S, 1938, Ja 8,15:4
Swanwick, Morrison, 1946, Mr 29,23:1
Swapp, Albert D, 1949, F 24,23:5
Swapp, Charles W, 1944, Jl 29,13:5
Swarer, Theodore F Mrs, 1948, My 4,25:3
Swart, Charles M Mrs, 1954, Jl 6,23:6
Swart, Elmer E, 1945, Ja 6,11:6; 1951, N 24,11:6
Swart, George R, 1961, Ja 29,85:1
Swart, Gilbert, 1965, D 19,84:2
Swart, H N A, 1946, Ag 28,27:6
Swart, Harmon V, 1965, S 2,31:4
Swart, John A, 1962, My 2,37:4
Swart, R Emerson (por), 1947, My 8,25:1
Swart, R M, 1947, My 11,60:2
Swart, Samuel A, 1953, O 10,17:5
Swart, W Burton, 1941, S 6,15:4
Swart, Walter G, 1946, Ap 20,13:3
Swart, William J Mrs, 1962, My 25,33:3
Swartchild, Jacob K, 1945, Ja 19,20:2
Swartenberg, Abraham, 1956, Ag 7,27:5
Swarthout, Donald M, 1962, Je 13,41:3
Swarthout, Leon L, 1954, My 16,86:1
Swarthout, Max V Mrs, 1952, S 17,31:4
Swarthout, Ruth Mrs, 1954, Ap 8,27:2
Swartley, Henry R, 1942, D 6,77:2
Swartley, Henry R Jr, 1958, Mr 12,31:3
Swartley, William B, 1955, N 17,35:5
Swartley, Wilmer C, 1950, Ja 25,28:4
Swartout, Albert S, 1938, O 24,17:5
Swartout, William J, 1942, Ag 14,17:6
Swarts, Anna C Mrs, 1943, N 16,23:4
Swarts, Margaret Mrs, 1941, S 5,21:1
Swartsberg, Jerome, 1966, My 28,27:2
Swartsel, Samuel C, 1958, O 13,29:3
Swartsfager, Vern, 1957, O 28,27:3
Swartwood, Howard A, 1965, My 21,35:3
Swartwout, Egerton (por), 1943, F 19,19:1
Swartwout, F Robert, 1954, D 3,27:3
Swartwout, F Robert Mrs, 1949, My 12,31:3
Swartwout, Frank G, 1947, Jl 24,21:6
Swartwout, Henry B Dr, 1937, F 6,17:2
Swartwout, Richard H, 1938, Jl 22,17:5
Swartwout, William H, 1941, O 15,21:4
Swarty, Edward J, 1910, Je 5,II,11:4
Swartz, Abraham, 1962, F 28,33:2
Swartz, Arthur L, 1940, My 15,25:4
Swartz, Charles B, 1951, F 4,77:1
Swartz, Charles C, 1947, Jl 27,45:3
Swartz, Charles F, 1940, My 25,17:3
Swartz, Charles K, 1949, N 30,27:1
Swartz, Charles K Mrs, 1957, N 4,29:5
Swartz, Christian S, 1953, D 30,24:3
Swartz, David J, 1963, D 6,36:3
Swartz, Harry R, 1945, Je 11,15:3
Swartz, Helen M, 1959, My 26,35:1
Swartz, Howard V, 1957, Jl 12,21:5
Swartz, Joel Rev Dr, 1914, Mr 17,11:5
Swartz, John B, 1942, O 20,21:4
Swartz, John G, 1942, Jl 10,17:3
Swartz, Junior G, 1963, Ag 10,17:3
Swartz, Leo, 1950, My 11,29:5
Swartz, Louis, 1959, Ag 24,21:1
Swartz, Mabel R, 1958, Ap 2,31:4
Swartz, Maud O Mrs (por), 1937, F 23,28:1
Swartz, Nelle, 1952, Mr 6,31:1
Swartz, Peter C, 1938, D 17,15:5
Swartz, Philip A, 1962, O 31,37:1
Swartz, William K, 1957, N 22,25:2
Swartz, William P Mrs, 1940, Ja 27,13:6
Swartzel, Karl D, 1941, N 1,15:3
Swarzenski, Georg, 1957, Je 16,84:5
Swasey, Albert L, 1956, Ja 8,86:6
Swasey, Ambrose Dr (por), 1937, Je 16,24:3
Swasey, Carleton F, 1952, Jl 25,18:6
Swasey, Edgar M, 1954, Ja 2,18:5
Swasey, John H Dr, 1907, S 13,7:6
Swatland, Donald C, 1962, Ap 4,43:1
Sway, David, 1954, S 1,27:2
Swayne, Alfred H (will, Ap 30,16:6),(por), 1937, Ap 17,17:1
Swayne, C H Col, 1925, Ag 23,7:4
Swayne, Charles Judge, 1907, Jl 6,7:4
Swayne, David L, 1868, Ag 28,5:3
Swayne, Eleanor, 1967, Ap 13,43:4
Swayne, Eugene, 1941, Ag 16,15:3
Swayne, N H, 1884, Je 10,5:3
Swayne, Noah H, 1950, O 6,27:4
Swayne, Rawley K, 1942, Jl 13,15:1
Swayne, W S, 1941, Jl 2,21:2
Swayne, Wager, 1952, Ag 11,15:4
Swayne, Wager Gen, 1902, D 19,9:4
Swaynes, Charles R C, 1943, Jl 18,34:7
Swaythling, Baron, 1927, Je 12,25:5
Swaythling, Montagu Baron (Samuel-Montagu), 1911, Ja 13,9:3
Swayze, Charles F, 1954, O 11,27:6
Swayze, Clara M Mrs (will), 1951, Mr 10,11:5
Swayze, Francis J Mrs, 1951, Mr 8,29:3
Swayze, Francis S, 1946, Ap 24,25:3
Swayze, Frank H, 1947, Ja 6,23:4
Swayze, J L, 1881, Je 9,1:7
Swayze, John L, 1922, Ag 13,28:5

Swayze, John L Jr, 1967, O 23,45:3
Swaziland, Queen Mother of, 1957, F 18,27:1
Swchrstzuwysky, Edward, 1964, D 28,7:1
Sweadner, Walter R, 1951, Ja 15,17:2
Swearer, William K, 1946, D 5,31:4
Swearingen, H C, 1932, Je 3,19:1
Swearingen, Joseph M Judge, 1937, Mr 28,II,8:5
Swears, Clifford W, 1951, F 23,27:3
Sweasy, George H Mrs, 1950, F 8,27:4
Sweatman, Wilbur C, 1961, Mr 10,27:1
Sweatt, Harold W Mrs, 1966, My 2,37:2
Sweazey, George B, 1946, Ag 11,46:3
Swebilius, Carl G (por), 1948, O 19,27:3
Sweda, Michael, 1952, Ag 21,19:4
Swedberg, Ruben G, 1957, Je 10,27:5
Sweden, Queen of, 1871, Mr 31,1:2
Swedlin, Abraham, 1964, Jl 21,33:2
Sweedler, Benjamin, 1965, Ja 25,37:1
Sweedler, Edward L, 1954, Ja 11,25:3
Sweedler, Nathan, 1960, Ag 26,25:2
Sweedler, Samuel, 1942, Jl 21,19:5
Sweedy, Theodore S, 1967, Jl 25,35:1
Sweek, William O, 1940, Mr 3,44:1
Sweemer, William, 1947, Je 24,23:3
Sweeney, Algernon T, 1959, O 29,33:5
Sweeney, Alvin R, 1954, Ap 20,29:3
Sweeney, Angela M, 1949, S 9,25:5
Sweeney, Bartholomew P, 1948, My 21,23:5
Sweeney, Berton F, 1967, Ja 28,25:4
Sweeney, Caroline C Mrs, 1940, Ja 19,19:2
Sweeney, Charles, 1967, Mr 2,35:4
Sweeney, Charles L Mrs, 1925, O 3,15:6
Sweeney, Charles P, 1924, D 12,21:5; 1954, Ap 24,17:6
Sweeney, Daniel, 1958, Jl 24,19:2
Sweeney, Daniel C Mrs, 1952, Je 25,29:3
Sweeney, Daniel J, 1937, Mr 19,23:3; 1941, D 7,76:2
Sweeney, Daniel J Mrs, 1952, My 2,25:2
Sweeney, Daniel P, 1938, D 14,25:2
Sweeney, David G Mrs, 1961, D 13,43:4
Sweeney, Dennis, 1917, S 12,11:5
Sweeney, Dennis F, 1941, Ag 25,15:2; 1959, Ap 2,31:3
Sweeney, Dennis P, 1951, Ja 3,27:4
Sweeney, Edmund B, 1940, D 27,19:2
Sweeney, Edward C, 1967, Ag 15,39:3
Sweeney, Edward F, 1967, S 9,31:3
Sweeney, Edward F Mrs, 1944, Jl 22,15:4
Sweeney, Edward J, 1959, Jl 23,27:4
Sweeney, Edwin M, 1947, Mr 3,21:4
Sweeney, Elizabeth, 1920, N 3,11:2
Sweeney, Eugene V Jr, 1951, Ja 24,27:1
Sweeney, Frances, 1944, Je 20,19:2
Sweeney, Frank A, 1960, S 27,37:4
Sweeney, Frank J, 1941, Mr 31,15:3
Sweeney, George, 1940, D 23,19:3
Sweeney, George J Mrs, 1946, F 21,21:5
Sweeney, George N, 1942, Ap 28,21:2
Sweeney, George W (por), 1940, D 14,17:1
Sweeney, Harold J, 1959, O 11,87:1
Sweeney, Helen (Mother Rose), 1957, S 28,17:2
Sweeney, Henry M, 1961, Jl 14,23:4
Sweeney, Henry W, 1967, S 3,52:6
Sweeney, J A, 1923, Ja 5,11:5
Sweeney, J Monroe, 1950, Ja 31,23:1
Sweeney, J Raymond, 1966, Je 4,29:4
Sweeney, James H, 1949, D 13,31:1
Sweeney, James J, 1950, S 6,29:1
Sweeney, James P, 1961, F 1,35:1; 1962, F 11,86:8
Sweeney, James T, 1946, F 26,25:5
Sweeney, John, 1951, N 29,24:2
Sweeney, John A, 1951, F 16,25:2
Sweeney, John C, 1939, S 24,44:8
Sweeney, John D, 1950, F 7,27:2
Sweeney, John F, 1938, S 25,38:8; 1951, Mr 8,29:5
Sweeney, John F Mrs, 1954, Je 14,21:4
Sweeney, John J, 1937, Mr 9,23:2; 1942, Mr 1,45:2; 1944, Je 28,23:3; 1948, Jl 29,21:5; 1952, Ap 20,93:1; 1956, N 3,23:5; 1960, Ja 27,33:3
Sweeney, John M, 1947, Je 20,20:2
Sweeney, John R Mrs, 1956, Ja 15,92:7
Sweeney, John W, 1948, S 12,72:5; 1964, O 3,29:3
Sweeney, John W Sr, 1958, Ag 21,25:2
Sweeney, Joseph A, 1959, Ap 25,21:4; 1966, N 29,43:2
Sweeney, Joseph B, 1951, F 10,13:3
Sweeney, Joseph L Mrs, 1961, Ag 13,88:3
Sweeney, Julia Mrs, 1942, Mr 31,21:5
Sweeney, Leo, 1944, Ag 28,11:4
Sweeney, Leo A, 1967, Ag 10,37:3
Sweeney, Lizzie A Mrs, 1939, S 19,25:3
Sweeney, Manus M, 1941, S 27,17:6
Sweeney, Margaret Dr, 1920, N 20,15:4
Sweeney, Mark A, 1954, Mr 23,27:1
Sweeney, Martin L, 1960, My 2,29:5
Sweeney, Matthew J, 1960, N 12,21:1
Sweeney, Michael F, 1940, O 19,17:7; 1947, Ag 16, 13:1; 1949, My 6,25:3
Sweeney, Michael T, 1905, Mr 19,9:4
Sweeney, Miriam T, 1947, Je 3,25:3
Sweeney, Morris M, 1941, F 25,23:4
Sweeney, Orland R, 1958, Ap 23,33:1
Sweeney, Patrick, 1964, Ap 15,39:5
Sweeney, Patrick Mrs, 1952, N 6,29:2
Sweeney, Raymond W, 1961, Ja 13,27:1
Sweeney, Richard W Jr, 1966, Ja 24,35:3
Sweeney, S Beauregard, 1949, Ap 2,15:4
Sweeney, Samuel H (funl), 1965, O 15,45:4
Sweeney, Samuel H Mrs (funl), 1965, O 15,45:4
Sweeney, Stanley W, 1955, O 26,31:5
Sweeney, Terrance A, 1941, D 19,25:3
Sweeney, Thomas, 1955, Ap 23,19:1
Sweeney, Thomas B Mrs, 1959, D 7,31:3
Sweeney, Thomas B Sr, 1957, F 3,76:2
Sweeney, Thomas J, 1922, N 6,15:4
Sweeney, Thomas M, 1961, F 9,31:2
Sweeney, Thomas P, 1950, N 21,31:5
Sweeney, Thomas W, 1966, S 21,47:4
Sweeney, Thompson, 1942, My 8,21:5
Sweeney, Vaiden B, 1937, Ag 4,19:2
Sweeney, Vincent D, 1967, My 22,43:1
Sweeney, Walter C, 1963, Ap 11,33:3
Sweeney, Walter C Jr, 1965, D 23,27:2
Sweeney, Walter J, 1949, My 12,31:4
Sweeney, William, 1957, Ap 19,21:2
Sweeney, William A, 1939, Ja 27,19:3
Sweeney, William E, 1963, My 24,31:4
Sweeney, William F, 1952, Jl 12,13:4; 1965, My 20, 43:4
Sweeney, William H, 1941, N 2,52:7
Sweeney, William J, 1945, Ap 23,19:5; 1947, Ja 1, 33:3; 1948, My 28,23:4; 1958, Ja 27,27:1; 1958, Je 29,68:8
Sweeney, William J Mrs, 1945, Ja 25,19:3; 1946, Ag 15,25:4
Sweeney, William R, 1960, Ag 2,29:4
Sweeney, Winfield H, 1959, Ap 7,27:5
Sweeney, Winifred (Sister Mary Antonia), 1952, Mr 30,94:1
Sweeney, Z T Mrs, 1944, F 4,15:1
Sweenie, Phil J, 1940, Ja 10,21:2
Sweeny, Arthur Mrs, 1960, Je 11,21:6
Sweeny, Bo, 1917, Jl 17,9:5
Sweeny, Charles A, 1968, D 17,50:2
Sweeny, E Arthur, 1947, My 19,21:3
Sweeny, Edward C, 1945, Ap 20,19:4
Sweeny, Edward F, 1951, Jl 6,23:4
Sweeny, Edwin F Rev, 1923, N 27,19:2
Sweeny, Francis J, 1966, D 3,39:2
Sweeny, James F, 1940, S 19,23:4
Sweeny, James M, 1875, Je 8,7:3
Sweeny, John P, 1957, D 17,35:5
Sweeny, Joseph Mrs, 1944, F 16,17:4
Sweeny, Martin C, 1950, Ja 22,76:3
Sweeny, Martin Mrs, 1952, Mr 15,13:4
Sweeny, Perry J, 1953, My 25,25:2
Sweeny, Peter B, 1911, S 1,7:4
Sweeny, Robert, 1945, D 18,27:2
Sweeny, Robert Mrs, 1941, Jl 30,17:2
Sweeny, Thomas, 1916, O 11,11:4
Sweeny, William M, 1945, Je 2,15:6
Sweerts de Landas Wyborgh, Arthur M D Baron, 1944, Mr 17,17:4
Sweet, A Raymond, 1956, Ag 19,92:6
Sweet, Albert C, 1945, My 14,17:5
Sweet, Alex T, 1956, Jl 11,29:5
Sweet, Alfred H, 1950, Ap 24,25:4
Sweet, Alfred N Dr, 1912, D 9,11:4
Sweet, Andrew B, 1938, S 7,25:3
Sweet, Arthur H Mrs, 1944, Je 20,19:1
Sweet, Arthur W, 1964, Mr 23,29:3
Sweet, B G Gen, 1874, Ja 2,5:5
Sweet, Birdsall, 1950, Ap 18,26:2
Sweet, Burton E, 1957, Ja 5,17:6
Sweet, C Parker, 1947, N 4,26:2
Sweet, Carroll F Sr, 1955, S 27,35:4
Sweet, Chandos, 1960, Mr 2,37:1
Sweet, Charles A (por), 1947, Ja 12,59:5
Sweet, Charles C, 1963, Ag 12,21:5
Sweet, Charles E, 1963, Ja 17,8:6
Sweet, Charles F, 1953, O 20,29:5
Sweet, Cornelius, 1940, Ja 21,34:6
Sweet, E Fred, 1965, My 20,43:2
Sweet, E Tracy, 1945, S 3,23:4
Sweet, Earl H, 1946, My 8,25:5
Sweet, Earl V, 1954, Mr 12,21:2
Sweet, Edward S, 1942, Ap 4,13:4
Sweet, Elizabeth, 1949, Mr 11,26:2
Sweet, Eln, 1903, Ja 28,9:6
Sweet, Forest G, 1956, Mr 25,92:6
Sweet, Fred A, 1947, S 13,11:6
Sweet, Frederick B, 1941, My 11,45:1
Sweet, George C, 1953, Ag 7,19:4
Sweet, George H Col, 1912, Ag 9,7:5
Sweet, George L, 1949, Ja 12,28:3
Sweet, George S, 1965, N 7,89:3
Sweet, George Sullivan, 1920, D 7,13:3
Sweet, George W, 1958, Mr 23,88:8
Sweet, Harold A, 1956, Jl 1,57:1
Sweet, Harold R, 1958, Jl 11,23:2
Sweet, Helen M, 1941, Ag 4,13:2
Sweet, Henry, 1939, S 19,25:3
Sweet, Henry H, 1941, Mr 30,49:1
Sweet, Herbert R Mrs, 1948, My 29,15:4
Sweet, Hogarth S, 1957, O 15,30:3
Sweet, Homer N, 1948, My 20,29:3
Sweet, Hubert R, 1961, My 11,37:2
Sweet, I S, 1932, Jl 1,21:3
Sweet, Jacob, 1951, Jl 31,21:2
Sweet, James A, 1961, Ja 20,26:1
Sweet, John Byron Dr, 1923, Ja 22,15:6
Sweet, John H Jr, 1950, Jl 31,17:3
Sweet, Joshua E, 1957, Ap 10,33:5
Sweet, Joshua E Mrs, 1942, Ja 4,48:2
Sweet, Leon, 1960, F 9,31:2
Sweet, Leona H Mrs, 1941, N 23,52:1
Sweet, Lewis K, 1950, S 26,31:5
Sweet, Louis M, 1950, O 5,31:5
Sweet, Louis M Mrs, 1948, D 11,15:2
Sweet, Monroe H, 1961, S 9,46:5
Sweet, O J, 1928, Ja 6,23:5
Sweet, Philip W K, 1946, Ag 13,15:6
Sweet, Ralph A, 1949, F 27,69:1
Sweet, Reginald L, 1950, Ja 13,23:5
Sweet, Richard H, 1962, Ja 14,84:3
Sweet, Robert V Jr, 1954, Jl 27,21:4
Sweet, Ruth P, 1958, Ag 24,87:2
Sweet, Stanley A, 1952, Ag 4,15:3
Sweet, Stanley A (est tax appr), 1955, N 29,46:4
Sweet, Stanley A Mrs, 1955, My 24,31:3
Sweet, Stephen S, 1941, Ag 8,15:2
Sweet, T C, 1928, My 2,1:7
Sweet, Thaddeus P, 1954, N 11,36:7
Sweet, W Glenn, 1944, Ja 21,17:4
Sweet, Walter I, 1937, S 17,25:3
Sweet, Willard H, 1949, Ap 26,25:2
Sweet, William A, 1904, Ja 31,7:6
Sweet, William B, 1952, N 18,31:5
Sweet, William E, 1942, My 10,42:6
Sweet, William H, 1945, N 26,21:2
Sweet, William H Mrs, 1945, N 2,19:3
Sweet, William I Mrs, 1967, N 9,47:3
Sweet, William J, 1955, F 8,27:2
Sweet, William L (por), 1949, F 5,15:3
Sweet, William W, 1959, Ja 5,29:1
Sweet, Willis, 1925, Jl 10,17:7
Sweet, Winfield (por), 1942, My 22,21:3
Sweet-Escott, Ernest B, 1941, Ap 11,21:3
Sweeter, John H, 1904, Mr 5,9:5
Sweeting, Louise B Mrs, 1940, Jl 28,27:2
Sweetland, Cornelius Sowle, 1923, My 31,15:4
Sweetland, Edwin R, 1950, O 22,92:4
Sweetland, Ernest J, 1950, N 17,27:5
Sweetland, Frank W, 1943, Ap 15,25:3
Sweetlove, Ellen Mrs, 1949, D 17,17:3
Sweetman, Henry, 1944, Je 10,15:6
Sweetman, James T, 1943, D 14,28:3
Sweetman, William E, 1949, D 6,31:2
Sweets, Henry W, 1952, F 27,27:4
Sweetser, Arthur (trb lr, F 10,32:4), 1968, Ja 21,77:1
Sweetser, E Leroy, 1951, Ja 27,13:4
Sweetser, Frank E, 1938, Ja 1,19:1
Sweetser, Frank L, 1952, D 29,19:3
Sweetser, George E, 1944, O 19,23:4
Sweetser, Harold T, 1944, Ag 21,15:5
Sweetser, Harry P, 1952, D 28,49:1
Sweetser, Horatio B, 1950, Je 1,27:6
Sweetser, John A, 1944, Ag 19,11:6
Sweetser, Kate D, 1939, Mr 23,23:5
Sweetser, Moses, 1903, Mr 11,9:6
Sweetser, Robert Chauncey, 1924, Jl 6,21:2
Sweetser, William A, 1924, S 2,19:1
Sweetser, William J, 1939, O 17,25:6
Sweetzer, Charles E, 1871, Ja 5,1:3
Sweetzer, Henry E, 1870, F 18,5:3
Sweezey, Claude B, 1939, S 23,17:5
Sweezy, Charles L, 1944, Jl 14,13:4
Sweezy, Clarence E, 1939, Mr 13,17:4
Sweger, George Mrs, 1945, D 1,23:2
Swehla, Benjamin, 1945, O 18,23:1
Sweig, Max, 1937, D 1,23:5
Sweikert, Bob (funl, Jl 22,29:4), 1956, Je 18,31:2
Sweinhart, Henry L, 1949, Mr 18,25:2
Sweinhart, James, 1953, N 22,88:3
Sweitzer, Channing E (por), 1937, O 6,25:1
Sweitzer, Morris K, 1914, Mr 16,9:4
Sweitzer, Robert M, 1938, Ap 7,23:4
Swem, Charles L, 1956, D 28,21:3
Swem, Lee A, 1954, My 25,21:4
Swenarton, James H Mrs, 1958, N 5,35:4
Swenarton, James T, 1957, My 24,25:2
Swenarton, Jane J, 1965, Ag 13,29:3
Swenarton, W Hastings, 1960, Ja 15,31:2
Swenehart, John, 1951, Je 18,23:5
Sweney, F W, 1938, Ja 20,23:4
Swengel, Uriah F Bp, 1921, Mr 9,13:4
Swensen, Charles, 1964, N 20,37:1
Swensen, Joel, 1961, Ja 7,19:5
Swensen, Johan, 1940, Ag 8,19:6
Swensen, S Roy, 1961, Ap 21,33:2
Swenson, Albert, 1955, Je 29,29:2
Swenson, Alfred G, 1941, Mr 29,15:1
Swenson, Andrew C, 1958, Jl 20,64:8
Swenson, August J Mrs, 1945, O 28,44:3
Swenson, Axel J, 1952, Ag 20,25:6
Swenson, Bernard V, 1948, Jl 25,48:4
Swenson, Carl A, 1967, Ap 10,35:1
Swenson, Carl A Dr (see also F 17), 1904, F 18,9:6
Swenson, Carl J, 1951, F 14,29:1
Swenson, Charles Mrs, 1948, S 24,25:3
Swenson, David F, 1940, F 13,23:4
Swenson, Edward F, 1947, My 30,21:2

Swenson, Edward F Mrs, 1963, Ag 1,27:4
Swenson, Edwin, 1956, My 15,31:1
Swenson, Emma Mrs, 1941, Je 3,21:2
Swenson, Eric P (por), 1945, Ag 15,19:3
Swenson, Ernest S, 1960, N 29,37:4
Swenson, George F, 1955, F 21,21:4
Swenson, John A, 1944, My 3,19:6
Swenson, John O, 1937, Mr 22,23:5
Swenson, Jonas W, 1959, My 1,29:3
Swenson, Kristie Mrs, 1925, O 24,15:6
Swenson, Laurita S Mrs, 1912, My 8,11:4
Swenson, Lauritz, 1947, N 5,28:3
Swenson, M, 1936, Mr 30,19:2
Swenson, Marie C, 1940, My 28,23:3
Swenson, Michael J, 1944, F 29,17:2
Swenson, N Werner, 1955, Ap 22,25:2
Swenson, O Clement, 1957, Je 5,35:6
Swenson, Oliver, 1959, Ag 7,23:2
Swenson, Oliver A, 1957, Ja 31,27:1
Swenson, Oscar F, 1952, My 1,29:5; 1957, Mr 6,31:5
Swenson, Oscar W (por), 1948, D 18,19:3
Swenson, Svante M, 1966, N 11,43:1
Swenson, Swen R, 1965, Je 14,33:2
Swensson, Otto J, 1957, Je 14,25:1
Sweny, Harry Roy, 1914, My 28,13:6
Swepston, John E, 1961, O 26,35:4
Swerdlow, Irving, 1955, My 14,38:6
Swerdlow, Maurice E, 1950, D 3,88:5
Swerling, Samuel, 1955, My 16,23:4
Swersey, John S, 1953, S 23,31:3
Swertfager, Charles H Mrs, 1948, N 10,29:5
Swertfager, Walter M, 1961, My 29,19:4
Swet, Gershon, 1968, Jl 20,27:2
Swete, Henry B Rev Dr, 1917, My 11,11:1
Swetland, Horace M, 1924, Je 16,15:4
Swetlow, George I, 1956, Ag 22,29:2
Swetnick, George (funl, Jl 4,19:3), 1968, Jl 2,41:1
Swetnick, Samuel, 1965, Je 3,35:4
Swett, Arthur H, 1953, Je 29,21:5
Swett, Bert L, 1949, My 15,90:5
Swett, Charles N, 1945, My 7,17:3
Swett, Eddy B, 1951, F 25,84:5
Swett, Elmer J, 1940, My 10,23:2
Swett, Emily F Dr, 1937, Mr 30,24:2
Swett, Francis H, 1943, F 12,19:6
Swett, Herbert L, 1945, O 21,45:1
Swett, John A, 1948, Mr 17,25:1
Swett, Joseph A, 1956, F 24,25:4
Swett, Lucy E, 1961, Jl 15,19:6
Swett, Lyman R, 1939, D 10,69:1
Swett, Paul F, 1922, Mr 8,15:6
Swett, Paul P, 1950, Ag 4,21:5
Swett, Trevor W Mrs, 1925, D 27,7:1
Swett, William O Jr, 1938, O 16,45:2
Swett, William R Mrs, 1954, S 25,15:5
Swettenham, Frank, 1946, Je 13,27:3
Sweyd, Mike, 1952, N 14,23:4
Swezey, Arthur M, 1954, N 25,29:5
Swezey, Carroll M, 1965, Ja 27,35:1
Swezey, Edward G Mrs, 1951, Ja 21,76:6
Swezey, Elvira M Mrs, 1938, Mr 27,II,7:3
Swezey, Frederick P Mrs, 1943, Jl 17,13:6
Swezey, H Chester, 1955, Mr 19,15:4
Swezey, Isaac R, 1952, My 17,19:3
Swezy, C M Mrs, 1953, Je 6,17:2
Swick, Charles F Mrs, 1946, Ag 25,45:1
Swick, Charles F Sr, 1948, D 21,25:4
Swick, Clarence E, 1942, Ja 5,20:1
Swick, Frank, 1949, Mr 31,25:3
Swick, George W, 1950, Je 25,70:1
Swick, Jacob H, 1949, Ja 26,25:1
Swick, Lester J, 1949, O 29,15:3
Swick, Minor Rev, 1921, S 21,15:6
Swick, Thomas F, 1944, S 14,23:4
Swickard, Joseph, 1940, Mr 3,44:6
Swickard, Ray Mrs, 1959, D 22,31:5
Swicker, Lester C, 1958, Ja 10,23:2
Swickerath, Robert, 1948, D 16,29:2
Swid, Arthur, 1944, N 10,19:5
Swid, Mollie, 1938, Ap 27,23:4
Swidler, Phil, 1952, F 2,13:6
Swieder, Frederick, 1949, F 18,23:2
Swieder, Henry A Sr, 1952, F 9,13:4
Swieder, John A, 1952, Je 5,31:4
Swienty, Wilhelm, 1960, Jl 15,23:5
Swift, Alfred M, 1962, O 15,29:3
Swift, Alice M, 1941, Jl 21,15:4
Swift, Allan A, 1964, F 13,31:2
Swift, Archie D, 1961, S 30,25:7
Swift, Arthur L, 1938, Ag 6,13:2
Swift, Belle W Mrs, 1937, My 5,25:4
Swift, Bob (Robt V), 1966, O 18,45:4
Swift, C, 1877, N 20,4:7
Swift, C Addison, 1938, N 11,25:5
Swift, Charles F, 1944, O 11,21:5; 1962, Ap 27,35:1
Swift, Charles H (will, O 9,5:2), 1948, O 1,25:3
Swift, Charles N, 1938, Ap 12,23:4
Swift, Charles W, 1938, D 19,23:2
Swift, Daniel E, 1925, F 8,7:1
Swift, David J, 1944, Ja 13,21:6
Swift, Donald A, 1956, Ja 26,29:2
Swift, Douglas, 1946, F 17,42:7
Swift, E J, 1932, Ag 31,17:5
Swift, Eben, 1938, Ap 26,21:3
Swift, Edith E Mrs, 1945, D 14,16:3
Swift, Edith L, 1945, Ja 4,19:5
Swift, Edward L, 1944, N 30,23:4
Swift, Edward P, 1938, Ja 17,19:4
Swift, Edward S, 1949, F 12,33:4
Swift, Edwin C, 1906, Ap 5,9:3
Swift, Edwin E Mrs (will), 1943, Jl 15,11:7
Swift, Elijah K, 1959, Jl 19,69:1
Swift, Elizabeth P Mrs, 1942, N 11,25:5
Swift, Ellen, 1952, Mr 4,28:4
Swift, Ernest F, 1968, Jl 25,33:2
Swift, Ernest J (por), 1941, O 20,17:3
Swift, Eugene E C, 1944, N 14,23:4
Swift, Eva M, 1943, N 13,13:6
Swift, Everett M, 1940, Mr 20,27:2
Swift, Francis H, 1947, O 11,17:1
Swift, Frank E, 1941, Ap 4,21:1
Swift, Fred J Mrs, 1948, My 1,15:6
Swift, Frederick C, 1938, S 11,II,11:3
Swift, Frederick R, 1940, Ja 23,21:5
Swift, Frederick T, 1953, Ja 10,17:2
Swift, G F, 1903, Mr 30,1:2
Swift, George B, 1912, Jl 3,11:6
Swift, George H, 1951, Mr 11,93:1
Swift, George Montague Dr, 1925, D 27,7:1
Swift, George R, 1945, Mr 17,13:6
Swift, George S, 1952, Ag 21,19:5
Swift, George W, 1960, My 19,37:3
Swift, George W Mrs, 1950, Ja 12,28:4
Swift, Gustavus F, 1922, My 20,15:6
Swift, Gustavus F (por), 1943, O 30,15:1
Swift, Harold H (will, Je 21,27:4; est acctg, N 14,-36:3), 1962, Je 9,25:3
Swift, Harry L Mrs, 1949, Ag 25,23:2
Swift, Harry P, 1954, N 17,31:4
Swift, Harry P Mrs, 1939, Ag 25,15:3
Swift, Harry R Capt, 1937, Ag 11,23:1
Swift, Henry A, 1942, Ag 21,19:5
Swift, Henry M, 1944, Ag 20,33:2
Swift, Homer F, 1953, S 25,21:3
Swift, Innis P, 1953, N 4,33:1
Swift, Isaac C Rev, 1937, N 20,17:4
Swift, J D, 1881, My 25,4:7
Swift, J Otis, 1948, My 15,15:3
Swift, J Otis Mrs, 1950, N 2,31:4
Swift, J W Commodore, 1877, Jl 31,2:3
Swift, James C, 1938, F 1,21:2
Swift, James J Mrs, 1952, Jl 2,25:3
Swift, James J Sr, 1963, Je 29,23:1
Swift, James L, 1940, Mr 26,21:4
Swift, James M, 1946, Jl 14,37:2
Swift, James Mrs, 1949, Ap 15,23:1
Swift, Jesse G, 1949, N 27,104:6
Swift, Jireh Jr, 1941, D 26,14:2
Swift, John E Mrs, 1947, N 10,29:2
Swift, John J, 1952, Ja 4,40:3
Swift, John J Msgr, 1916, Ap 21,11:3
Swift, John T, 1940, Je 19,23:4; 1957, Je 6,31:3
Swift, John T Mrs, 1949, N 26,15:1
Swift, Lawrence, 1966, Ja 25,41:4
Swift, Lewis Dr, 1913, Ja 6,9:5
Swift, Linton B (por), 1946, Ap 12,27:1
Swift, Louis F (will, N 27,9:8),(por), 1937, My 13, 25:1
Swift, Louis F Mrs, 1922, Ap 6,17:4
Swift, Lynn G, 1955, My 15,86:5
Swift, Mary Mrs, 1946, Ag 10,13:2
Swift, Nathan B, 1953, Ag 2,73:1
Swift, Nelson, 1955, O 7,25:2
Swift, Oscar W, 1940, Jl 1,19:5
Swift, Parton, 1952, Ap 18,25:4
Swift, Polemus H Mrs, 1947, Ag 7,21:2
Swift, Richard E, 1951, Mr 2,26:3
Swift, Rigby Sir (por), 1937, O 20,23:3
Swift, Robert, 1872, My 10,1:3
Swift, Robert W, 1950, Mr 10,27:2
Swift, Samuel, 1914, Jl 22,9:4; 1953, Je 1,23:4
Swift, Samuel E, 1944, O 10,23:3
Swift, Sarah J Mrs, 1942, N 21,13:6
Swift, Stanley, 1941, F 6,21:2
Swift, Susan (Sister Imalda Teresa), 1916, Ap 24, 13:5
Swift, Thomas P, 1967, Ap 6,39:4
Swift, Vance, 1947, My 19,22:3
Swift, Virginie M Mrs (will), 1942, O 7,25:2
Swift, Walker E, 1953, D 22,31:2
Swift, Walter B, 1942, My 5,21:2
Swift, Willard E, 1947, Ja 15,25:2
Swift, William B, 1938, D 21,23:3
Swift, William E, 1937, Mr 25,25:5; 1953, Mr 2,23:3
Swift, William E Jr Mrs, 1954, Ja 8,21:4
Swift, William F, 1946, N 11,27:5
Swift, William Mrs, 1953, Jl 14,27:3
Swift, William Rear-Adm, 1919, Jl 1,13:3
Swig, Simon, 1939, Jl 31,13:3
Swigart, Otto S, 1943, Mr 24,23:2
Swigart, Robert E Dr, 1915, Je 28,9:6
Swigart, W Emmert, 1949, D 18,88:4
Swiger, Arlen G, 1960, Ag 23,30:1
Swigert, Frank L, 1938, Ap 7,23:2
Swiggett, Douglas W, 1950, F 14,25:2
Swiggett, Glen L, 1961, Je 28,35:3
Swiggett, Howard, 1957, Mr 8,25:2
Swiggett, Howard Mrs, 1957, Ap 14,87:1
Swiggum, E N, 1956, D 22,19:5
Swiler, Mary F Mrs, 1941, F 11,23:4
Swim, Bobby, 1878, O 13,1:6
Swim, Joseph B, 1950, Ap 8,13:2
Swimm, Charles T, 1939, Ag 20,32:7
Swin, Frances M, 1947, Ag 6,23:5
Swin, Herbert T, 1967, Mr 22,47:4
Swin, Thomas P Mrs, 1938, Mr 30,21:5
Swin, William E, 1942, My 27,23:1
Swinburne, Algernon Charles, 1909, Ap 11,11:1
Swinburne, George Knowles Dr, 1921, Jl 24,22:4
Swinburne, James, 1958, Mr 31,27:4
Swinburne, John Sir, 1914, Jl 17,9:7
Swinburne, Rhodes D, 1955, Je 17,23:4
Swinburne, Samuel F, 1938, My 16,17:2
Swinburne, W, 1883, N 6,8:2
Swindall, Charles, 1939, Je 20,21:4
Swindell, Bertha, 1951, Ap 2,25:4
Swindells, Eugenia P Mrs, 1941, Ap 2,23:5
Swindells, Frederick, 1937, S 20,23:4
Swindells, Walter, 1948, Ja 29,23:5
Swinderen, Rene D van, 1955, Ja 18,27:4
Swindlehurst, Frederick, 1957, Je 19,35:2
Swindler, Mary H, 1967, Ja 18,43:4
Swinehart, Gerry, 1966, N 1,41:4
Swinehart, Lester E, 1944, Jl 29,13:6
Swineheart, Joseph R, 1944, Ja 12,23:5
Swiney, Merrill A, 1946, D 8,78:5
Swinfen, Charles Baron, 1919, N 16,22:4
Swinford, M C, 1952, S 16,29:1
Swing, Albert T Mrs, 1944, Jl 25,19:4
Swing, Charles W, 1938, S 18,44:6
Swing, E Coates, 1938, Jl 6,23:6
Swing, Philip D, 1963, Ag 10,17:6
Swing, R Hamill D, 1950, My 12,27:4
Swing, R Hamill D Mrs, 1942, Je 28,15:6
Swing, Raymond, 1968, D 24,23:1
Swingle, Walter T, 1952, Ja 20,85:1
Swink, William J, 1939, Ag 25,15:3
Swinley, Ion, 1937, S 17,25:5
Swinnerton, Allyn C, 1952, Jl 7,21:4
Swinnerton, George B, 1950, Ag 20,76:1
Swinnerton, Radcliffe, 1960, N 13,88:4
Swinnerton, Radcliffe Mrs, 1964, Ja 14,31:4
Swinney, E F, 1946, O 25,24:2
Swinney, John B, 1948, S 8,29:4
Swinsky, Albert Jr, 1943, Jl 7,19:4
Swinsky, R P, 1947, S 16,23:3
Swint, Benjamin H, 1946, S 8,44:1
Swint, Curran, 1953, F 8,89:2
Swint, Samuel H, 1962, F 15,29:4
Swint, Wendel R, 1958, Ap 12,19:5
Swinton, Agnes Mrs, 1924, F 28,19:6
Swinton, Alex A, 1950, S 25,23:3
Swinton, Ernest, 1951, Ja 17,27:1
Swinton, George S C Capt, 1937, Ja 18,6:4
Swinton, John, 1901, D 18,9:5; 1968, F 1,37:3
Swinton, John D, 1944, Je 4,42:3
Swinton, Marion, 1939, F 14,20:1
Swinton, Ralph S, 1950, Jl 22,15:2
Swinton, Ralph S Mrs, 1949, O 5,29:1
Swinton, Roy S, 1956, O 22,29:4
Swintz, Robert H, 1954, Je 6,86:5
Swinyard, Thomas, 1915, F 26,9:6
Swirbul, Leon A, 1960, Je 29,33:1
Swiren, David B, 1944, Mr 4,13:2
Swirlbul, Frederick Mrs, 1949, F 15,23:3
Swirnow, Irving, 1964, My 16,25:4
Swirsky, Harry, 1959, N 9,31:2
Swirsky, Israel A, 1959, O 18,87:1
Swisher, Carl Brent Dr, 1968, Je 16,68:3
Swisher, Charles C, 1940, F 9,19:6
Swisher, Harold, 1951, Mr 17,15:4
Swisher, John H, 1944, F 3,19:5
Swisher, Paul L, 1958, Mr 11,29:4
Swisshelm, Jane G, 1884, Jl 23,5:1
Swisstack, Peter, 1950, Ja 24,31:3
Swits, Mary A, 1941, S 8,15:3
Switzer, Andrew Jackson, 1912, F 26,11:4
Switzer, Carl (Alfalfa),(death ruled murder, Ja 23,-13:2), 1959, Ja 22,28:4
Switzer, Clarence, 1963, S 24,39:4
Switzer, Frederick Sr, 1949, O 25,27:2
Switzer, George (por), 1940, O 9,25:5
Switzer, George L, 1958, Mr 17,29:1
Switzer, Herbert, 1950, Ag 10,25:2
Switzer, James G, 1944, O 1,46:1
Switzer, James G Mrs, 1946, My 3,21:4
Switzer, James K, 1948, Ag 3,25:2
Switzer, John J, 1947, S 10,27:3
Switzer, John J Mrs, 1945, N 20,21:1
Switzer, John M (will), 1938, D 14,28:6
Switzer, Merritt A, 1948, N 8,21:3
Switzer, Robert M, 1956, My 1,33:4
Switzer, Sam, 1967, Je 6,47:3
Switzer, Sam L, 1960, Ap 16,17:3
Switzer, William H, 1958, Je 3,31:2
Switzer, William S, 1938, F 24,3:1
Switzgable, Elvin C Mrs, 1954, Ag 30,17:5
Switzky, Abraham, 1950, Je 30,23:6
Switzler, W F Col, 1906, My 25,11:5

Switzler, William F, 1967, Je 11,87:1
Swoboda, Gustave, 1942, N 18,26:2; 1956, S 5,27:5
Swoboda, Hans O Mrs, 1958, Ag 9,13:6
Swoboda, Joseph, 1903, Ja 8,3:3; 1942, Je 23,15:2
Swoboda, Vecheslav, 1948, Ag 25,25:2
Swody, Edward, 1952, Ja 4,23:3
Swody, Valentine, 1937, My 9,II,10:1
Swope, Charles B, 1960, S 25,23:1
Swope, Charles S, 1959, Je 1,27:1
Swope, Edwin B, 1955, D 27,23:2
Swope, Ethel, 1937, My 28,21:3
Swope, Gerald Mrs, 1955, O 29,19:2
Swope, Gerard (trb lr, N 29,28:6; will, D 4,41:4), 1957, N 21,33:1
Swope, Henry B, 1874, F 17,5:3
Swope, Herbert B (funl, Je 23,23:5; mem meeting, S 18,36:4), 1958, Je 21,1:6
Swope, Herbert B Mrs, 1967, N 24,43:1
Swope, Horace M, 1939, O 11,27:3
Swope, Isaac G, 1957, Je 5,35:2
Swope, John C, 1907, Ag 10,7:5
Swope, King, 1961, Ap 25,25:2
Swope, Meier, 1940, O 2,23:6
Swope, Thomas H, 1909, O 4,9:6
Swope, Tom Mrs, 1946, Ag 12,21:6
Swor, Bert, 1943, D 1,21:2
Swords, Albert T, 1958, My 13,29:3
Swords, Charles Rob, 1916, Ag 30,9:6
Swords, Edward J, 1940, S 8,49:2
Swords, G H, 1877, Je 28,8:5
Swords, Henry Catheal (funl, Fe 10,23:1), 1924, F 7, 17:6
Swords, Joseph F, 1962, Ja 22,23:4
Swords, William V, 1952, My 22,27:3
Swoyer, Alfred P, 1941, S 30,23:2
Swyer, Sol P, 1953, Mr 27,23:2
Sybel, Katherine Mrs, 1952, Mr 31,20:4
Sybesma, William R, 1957, Jl 13,17:5
Sychrava, Lev, 1958, Ja 7,47:1
Sycle, Leon, 1938, S 25,39:3
Sydell, Rose, 1941, Ag 5,19:2
Sydenham, Laura M, 1952, O 19,88:7
Sydenham, Lord, 1933, F 8,22:1
Sydenstricker, E, 1936, Mr 21,17:1
Sydmeth, Louise, 1938, N 27,48:5
Sydney, Basil, 1968, Ja 11,33:3
Sydney, Elias C, 1963, Ap 30,35:4
Sydney, Manuel G, 1959, My 18,27:2
Sydney, William O'Connor Col, 1873, Jl 1,5:1
Sydnor, Charles S, 1954, Mr 3,27:3
Sydnor, Harold, 1958, N 28,27:4
Sydnor, Henry M, 1951, Ja 19,25:1
Sygietynski, Tadeusz, 1955, Je 2,29:4
Sykes, Alfred, 1956, N 13,37:2
Sykes, Bernard G, 1943, Jl 1,20:5
Sykes, Charles, 1950, N 17,27:4
Sykes, Charles H, 1942, D 20,44:6
Sykes, Charles S, 1915, N 1,11:6
Sykes, Clarence, 1953, F 15,92:4
Sykes, David A, 1942, D 1,25:2
Sykes, Edward, 1943, O 3,48:4
Sykes, Edward C, 1945, O 21,46:3
Sykes, Edward S Jr, 1941, Ag 12,19:6
Sykes, Emery H, 1956, N 8,39:5
Sykes, Eugene O (por), 1945, Je 22,15:3
Sykes, Frank C, 1943, My 14,19:2
Sykes, Frank H, 1944, D 25,19:5
Sykes, Frank W, 1951, Je 22,25:3
Sykes, Frederick G Mrs, 1941, Ap 26,15:5
Sykes, Frederick H, 1954, O 2,17:3
Sykes, Frederick Henry, 1917, O 15,13:4
Sykes, G Frederick, 1955, D 8,37:2
Sykes, George, 1903, D 24,9:5
Sykes, George B, 1941, Ag 1,15:2
Sykes, George Gen, 1880, F 10,5:5
Sykes, George Maj, 1919, Ag 23,7:7
Sykes, Godfrey, 1948, D 24,18:3
Sykes, Henry B, 1940, My 8,23:3
Sykes, Howard C, 1966, F 22,23:1
Sykes, J Russell, 1946, N 11,27:4
Sykes, James G, 1939, My 9,23:4
Sykes, Jerome, 1903, D 30,7:1
Sykes, John P, 1942, Ag 18,21:4
Sykes, John T, 1937, Je 6,II,8:7
Sykes, Lawrence G, 1955, My 12,29:5
Sykes, M L Mrs, 1881, My 12,5:1
Sykes, M'Cready, 1952, F 1,21:3
Sykes, Mark Col, 1919, F 18,11:6
Sykes, Martin L, 1907, Ap 18,11:6
Sykes, Percy, 1945, Je 13,23:3
Sykes, Richard E, 1942, O 3,15:3
Sykes, Robert B, 1946, N 15,24:3
Sykes, Robert W, 1954, O 21,27:2
Sykes, Roy A Mrs, 1937, O 8,23:6
Sykes, Tatton Sir, 1913, My 5,9:2
Sykes, Walter A, 1950, Ap 4,29:3
Sykes, Wilfred, 1964, My 4,29:5
Sykes, William L, 1941, My 7,25:6
Sykes, William W, 1941, Ag 23,13:2
Sykora, Bogumil, 1953, Ja 20,25:4
Sylcox, Albert, 1946, My 19,40:6
Syles, William W, 1941, Ap 3,23:2
Sylva, Carmen (por), 1916, Mr 3,11:1
Sylva, Eloi, 1919, S 10,11:1
Sylva, Marguerite, 1957, F 22,21:5
Sylvain, Georges, 1925, Ag 4,19:5
Sylvaine, Vernon, 1957, N 24,86:8
Sylvan, Tage P, 1937, My 11,25:2
Sylvania, Frank C, 1963, O 29,36:2
Sylvano, Frank, 1964, S 2,37:2
Sylvern, Henry, 1964, Jl 5,43:3
Sylvester, Allie L, 1962, Ja 28,76:5
Sylvester, Arthur D, 1963, D 3,43:1
Sylvester, Arthur Mrs, 1957, Mr 24,86:7
Sylvester, Carl A, 1951, Ag 25,11:6
Sylvester, Charles B, 1941, D 20,19:4
Sylvester, Charles P Dr, 1937, Ag 7,15:2
Sylvester, Dana S, 1942, Je 6,13:5
Sylvester, Edith R Mrs, 1940, Jl 10,19:3
Sylvester, Edmund Q, 1942, S 24,27:5
Sylvester, Edward J Sr, 1965, Ag 18,35:5
Sylvester, Evander W, 1960, Ag 6,19:6
Sylvester, Francis R, 1944, My 2,19:6
Sylvester, Frank W, 1961, Ap 16,86:7
Sylvester, George Mrs, 1951, Mr 10,13:2
Sylvester, George W, 1941, Mr 27,23:4
Sylvester, Harry A, 1964, My 4,29:4
Sylvester, J Wilson, 1948, Mr 24,25:1
Sylvester, Jerry A, 1968, O 25,47:3
Sylvester, John, 1946, Je 20,23:1
Sylvester, John M, 1956, Mr 1,33:4
Sylvester, John Mrs, 1948, Ja 11,58:5
Sylvester, Kate, 1951, Jl 23,17:2
Sylvester, Miriam Mrs, 1923, Ag 28,17:5
Sylvester, R, 1930, D 12,25:4
Sylvester, Rachel S Mrs, 1944, Ja 12,23:2
Sylvester, Robert F, 1950, Mr 1,27:3
Sylvestre, Martin Rev, 1937, O 21,23:3
Sylvia, Manuel K, 1944, Mr 29,21:4
Sylvis, William M, 1947, O 3,25:4
Syman, Stanley, 1967, O 21,31:5
Symanski, Chester F, 1951, D 29,11:3
Syme, Campbell, 1942, Je 17,23:4
Syme, Geoffrey, 1942, Ag 1,11:6
Syme, M Herbert, 1956, Ag 19,92:6
Syme, Margaret, 1948, S 12,72:3
Syme, Sydney A, 1957, Jl 25,23:1
Symes, J Foster, 1951, Ap 6,25:1
Symes, John T, 1950, F 24,24:2
Symes, Marty, 1953, Je 20,17:4
Symington, Albert Mrs, 1944, Ja 18,19:2
Symington, Allwyn E Mrs, 1958, Mr 9,86:5
Symington, Charles J Mrs, 1958, N 7,28:5
Symington, Diedre H, 1967, Je 12,25:4
Symington, Donald, 1944, My 23,23:6
Symington, E Harrison, 1912, S 6,9:6
Symington, Frederick S, 1962, S 1,19:2
Symington, Gilbert J, 1961, N 6,37:4
Symington, James M, 1961, My 30,17:3
Symington, Jeanie A Mrs, 1942, Mr 25,21:1
Symington, Powers, 1957, N 19,33:1
Symington, Thomas A, 1953, N 20,23:3
Symington, W Stuart Maj, 1912, Je 11,9:6
Symmers, Douglas, 1952, Ap 20,93:1
Symmers, James K Mrs, 1965, D 8,47:2
Symmers, Lawrence A, 1948, N 1,23:2
Symmers, W St Clair, 1937, O 5,25:2
Symmes, Cleve Mrs, 1921, F 26,11:6
Symmes, Ernest M, 1949, Je 17,23:1
Symmes, F W Jr Mrs, 1939, N 8,23:3
Symmes, John C, 1945, F 13,23:1
Symmes, Joseph Gaston Rev, 1916, Ap 6,13:6
Symmes, William B Jr (por), 1942, Ag 18,21:1
Symmonds, Charles J (por), 1941, Jl 19,13:2
Symmons, J H, 1936, F 14,19:1
Symms, Ronald T, 1963, N 2,25:1
Symnes, Charles H Mrs, 1937, F 13,13:3
Symon, Burk, 1950, F 22,29:3
Symonds, Alfred G, 1953, D 31,19:6
Symonds, Brandreth Dr, 1924, Ag 12,11:3
Symonds, Charles, 1941, Ap 3,23:5
Symonds, Charles J Mrs, 1959, N 20,31:3
Symonds, Edward L, 1944, Ja 12,23:3
Symonds, Gene (funl plans, My 20,25:3; funl, My 24,31:5), 1955, My 14,1:3
Symonds, Harvey D (por), 1947, Je 17,28:1
Symonds, James E, 1946, Ag 29,27:5
Symonds, Joseph H A, 1961, D 25,23:5
Symonds, Joseph W Ex-Justice, 1918, S 29,21:1
Symonds, Maurice, 1956, Ag 15,29:4
Symonds, Nathaniel G, 1951, Ja 21,77:2
Symonds, Percival M, 1960, Ag 8,21:2
Symonds, Uriah, 1924, O 29,21:1
Symons, Arthur, 1945, Ja 26,21:5
Symons, Charles D, 1949, O 20,29:1
Symons, Claude T, 1937, Ap 7,25:2
Symons, Dan (funl, Ap 25,8:4), 1871, Ap 23,1:6
Symons, Roland J, 1954, S 29,31:5
Symons, Thomas W Col, 1920, N 28,22:4
Symons, Walter F, 1948, D 6,25:4
Symporien, Bro, 1954, Ap 21,25:2
Syms, Hugh F Sr, 1947, N 12,27:3
Syms, Robert Howard Prof, 1912, D 9,11:4
Syms, William J Sr, 1957, Ap 6,19:6
Synan, James A, 1952, My 27,27:2
Syngalowski, Aron, 1956, O 9,35:2
Syngalowski, Aron Mrs, 1956, My 23,31:3
Synge, Robert Sir, 1920, Ja 23,13:2
Synnestvedt, Arthur, 1965, Jl 10,25:1
Synnestvedt, Paul, 1950, Mr 2,27:2
Synnott, James B, 1964, F 26,32:6
Synnott, John Msgr, 1921, O 21,15:6
Synnott, Peter, 1941, Ag 12,19:5
Synnott, Thomas W, 1941, Mr 20,21:4
Synott, Francis A, 1945, O 14,44:6
Syoen, Henry, 1941, N 8,19:3
Sypher, Alex M, 1950, My 23,30:2
Sypher, Francis J, 1960, N 21,29:3
Sypher, Grace Mrs, 1937, Ja 24,31:2
Sypher, Harry W, 1940, Je 27,23:3
Sypherd, Herman M, 1950, Jl 10,21:5
Sypherd, Walter H, 1954, Ag 27,21:3
Sypherd, Wilbur O, 1955, N 4,29:2
Syphers, Grant E, 1968, F 6,43:1
Syracuse, Countess of, 1874, F 21,4:5
Syracuse, Violet, 1937, Je 23,25:3
Syrek, Mitchell R, 1945, N 11,42:1
Syrell, Laurence, 1953, S 13,34:5
Syrett, Allen L, 1957, O 19,21:4
Syrett, Frank Harold, 1968, Ja 10,43:2
Syrett, Netta, 1943, D 19,48:6
Syrjala, Jan, 1968, F 17,29:3
Syrkin, Froim E, 1941, Mr 27,23:2
Syrkin, Nachman Dr, 1924, S 8,15:2
Syron, Thomas, 1945, D 18,27:4
Syrop, William, 1958, N 8,21:5
Syska, Adolph G, 1961, My 12,29:1
Sysol, Joseph, 1947, Ja 2,27:3
Sysoyev, Ivan G, 1957, Mr 23,19:7
Syssoeff, Boris, 1955, Ag 8,21:5
Syverston, Albert J, 1947, Ja 1,34:3
Syverton, Jerome T, 1961, Ja 29,84:4
Syvertsen, August Mrs, 1958, Je 14,21:5
Syvertsen, Rolf C, 1960, Ja 30,22:1
Syz, John, 1883, D 25,8:2
Syze, Frederick C, 1937, F 4,21:2
Szabados, Miklos, 1962, F 14,35:1
Szabados, Zador, 1939, Mr 31,21:2
Szabo, Arthur, 1953, Mr 7,15:3
Szabo, Bila, 1904, Ap 28,9:3
Szabo, Nicholas M, 1961, O 10,43:5
Szabo, Stephan, 1924, N 4,21:1
Szacszay, Emmerich, 1939, My 24,23:4
Szakacs, Gabor, 1937, Jl 25,II,7:4
Szakasits, Arpad, 1965, My 4,43:2
Szalay, Stephen C, 1956, N 20,37:3
Szalkowski, Stanley K, 1948, Je 17,25:2
Szaniawski, Henry, 1964, N 1,88:6
Szanto, Bela, 1951, Je 5,31:5
Szanto, Louis, 1952, N 10,25:1
Szanto, Louis P, 1965, Mr 16,39:5
Szapary, Julius Count, 1905, Ja 22,9:3
Szapiro, Gerson Mrs, 1965, D 11,33:5
Szapiro, Jerzy, 1962, Je 2,19:5
Szaro, Edward, 1948, Ap 2,23:4
Szarski, Martin Mrs, 1955, S 2,17:3
Szarvasy, Frederick A, 1948, Jl 5,15:6
Szary, William J, 1950, S 9,17:5
Szasz, Geza, 1942, Ap 24,17:3
Szasz, Otto, 1952, S 21,88:1
Szczepanik, Edward, 1964, Mr 3,21:6
Sze, Fred C, 1953, Jl 6,17:5
Sze, Sao-ke Alfred, 1958, Ja 5,87:1
Szebenyei, Joseph, 1953, F 26,25:4
Szebenyei, Joseph Mrs, 1952, Mr 22,13:1
Szechenyi, Gabrielle, 1924, S 9,19:3
Szechenyi, Laszlo (por), 1938, Jl 6,23:1
Szechenyi, Laszlo Countess (Gladys Vanderbilt),(cor, Ja 31,89:1), 1965, Ja 30,27:4
Szecskay, George, 1958, My 29,27:5
Szekat, Arthur, 1944, D 26,21:7
Szekely, Izso, 1966, O 3,47:4
Szekely, William, 1966, O 26,47:4
Szemes, Dezso, 1962, Je 29,27:4
Szenes, Sigmond, 1951, O 13,17:6
Szenkovits, Gustav C, 1953, Ja 27,25:2
Szepesi, Eugene, 1966, Ap 10,76:7
Szepinski, George W, 1958, Jl 4,19:4
Szeptycki, Andreas R, 1944, N 5,54:5
Szereszowski, Raphael, 1948, Ap 27,25:5
Szerlip, Sidney, 1966, My 29,56:7
Szeszol, Francis J, 1966, Je 18,31:5
Szewczuk, Mirko, 1957, Je 4,35:5
Szigeti, Dezso D, 1963, Ap 19,43:1
Szigeti, Geza, 1952, D 13,21:3
Szilagyi, Moritz Mrs, 1962, Ap 2,31:3
Szilard, Leo, 1964, My 31,1:6
Szilard, Marcel, 1962, Ag 1,31:4
Szinnyey, Stephen I, 1919, Mr 18,11:2
Szirmai, Oscar Mme, 1958, My 17,19:5
Szlanda, Stanley, 1957, Je 25,29:4
Szlapka, Stephen S, 1962, N 26,29:4
Szmania, Lillian, 1959, Je 21,92:4
Szoke, Louis, 1948, Mr 6,13:4
Szold, Bernard, 1960, N 17,37:2
Szold, Henrietta, 1945, F 14,19:1
Szold, Norman Ferdinand Dr, 1968, S 7,29:2
Szoldaties, Giorgio, 1955, Je 30,25:1
Szorc, Lawrence F, 1944, Je 15,19:4

Szpiech, Thomas P, 1949, Mr 3,25:2
Szpinalski, Stanislaw L, 1957, Je 19,35:4
Sztucko, Casimir, 1949, Ag 13,11:3
Sztybel, Thaddeus, 1959, Ap 14,35:4
Sztykgold, Konrad, 1959, My 20,35:2
Szubzda, Emil, 1955, Ap 22,25:1
Szudrowicz, Ignatius P, 1946, O 30,27:3
Szulc, Henry, 1966, D 15,47:1
Szupa, Stanislaus, 1944, Ap 14,19:6
Szwajkart, Stanislas, 1918, My 16,13:6
Szweda, Franciske Mrs, 1940, My 23,23:3
Szwiebel, William J, 1967, N 16,47:1
Szyfman, Arnold, 1967, Ja 14,31:4
Szyk, Arthur, 1951, S 14,25:1
Szymanowski, Karol, 1937, Mr 30,24:1
Szymanski, Agnes Mrs, 1954, N 28,87:1
Szyszko, Michal, 1946, Ja 16,23:4

T

Taafe, L, 1879, Mr 18,8:3
Taafe (Mother Mary Josephine), 1965, Ja 9,25:5
Taafee, E F J Count, 1895, N 30,5:2
Taaffe, Frank A, 1949, Jl 8,19:4
Taaffe, James A, 1939, Ja 16,15:2
Taaffe, John P, 1924, My 28,23:4
Taaffe, John P Mrs, 1946, Je 7,19:3
Taaffe, Rose A, 1960, Je 21,33:1
Taaffe, T G, 1936, Ap 30,19:5
Taaffe, Thomas Msgr, 1920, D 2,11:4
Taaffe, William P, 1968, N 21,47:5
Taaning, A Vedel, 1958, S 29,27:1
Taba, Hilda, 1967, Jl 8,25:2
Tabachinsky, Benjamin, 1967, Ag 8,39:2
Tabachneck, Abraham, 1942, N 21,11:5
Tabachnick, Abraham W, 1957, My 12,86:3
Tabachnik, Moses, 1966, O 12,43:3
Tabachnik, Moses Mrs, 1961, N 20,31:3
Tabakovich, Eugene, 1952, Ja 7,19:5
Tabasso, Rocco A, 1938, Jl 22,17:3
Tabb, B West, 1941, Ag 8,15:6
Tabb, Herbert L Mrs, 1960, Je 13,27:5
Tabb, Robert H, 1951, N 9,27:2
Tabbs, John C, 1939, Ap 28,25:3
Tabe, David S, 1915, Ja 2,9:6
Tabeling, John J, 1954, F 14,92:1
Tabell, Edmund W, 1965, S 15,47:1
Taber, A M Capt, 1911, Ja 30,9:4
Taber, Arthur H, 1941, Ap 2,23:5
Taber, Charles R, 1944, Ag 22,17:1
Taber, Charles Seymour, 1916, F 27,17:5
Taber, Edgar F, 1951, Ap 27,23:5
Taber, Edgar F Jr, 1950, Ja 23,23:2
Taber, Eliza H Mrs, 1942, My 29,17:3
Taber, Frank A, 1964, O 24,29:5
Taber, Frank M, 1939, S 3,19:2
Taber, George A, 1951, D 1,13:2
Taber, George E, 1941, S 13,17:4
Taber, George H Jr, 1954, Ag 21,17:7
Taber, Gerald H Mrs, 1951, Mr 14,33:5
Taber, Grieg, 1964, Ap 11,25:4
Taber, Harry B Sr, 1952, Mr 21,23:3
Taber, John, 1965, N 23,45:1
Taber, John A Dr, 1937, Je 5,17:4
Taber, John Mrs, 1964, Ja 27,23:5
Taber, Leslie R, 1963, O 24,33:5
Taber, Louis J, 1960, O 17,29:1
Taber, Norman S, 1952, Jl 16,25:5
Taber, Richard, 1957, N 18,31:3
Taber, S Birdsall, 1946, Ag 2,19:3
Taber, William, 1953, Jl 1,17:5
Taber, William C, 1945, N 15,19:2
Taberer, William, 1947, Jl 29,21:4
Tabernilas, Jose D, 1945, O 25,21:2
Taberski, Frank (por), 1941, O 24,23:3
Tabet, Ayoub, 1947, F 16,57:1
Tabian, Isaac, 1925, Ag 10,13:6
Tabibian, Dickran, 1945, D 7,21:3
Tabibian, Edward, 1963, S 16,35:3
Tablada, Jose J, 1945, Ag 4,11:5
Tableporter, Lewis J (Lew Porter), 1956, Ja 30,27:2
Tableporter, Morris, 1939, O 23,19:5
Tabler, James F, 1950, O 3,31:3
Tabner, J Gordon, 1957, D 24,15:3
Tabolt, Jacob J, 1959, Je 2,35:4
Tabor, Alice P, 1959, Mr 7,21:6
Tabor, Carl N, 1953, F 2,21:2
Tabor, Desiree, 1957, My 26,93:2
Tabor, Edward O, 1948, Jl 28,23:2
Tabor, Ernest G, 1954, Ap 21,29:1
Tabor, Francis H, 1925, O 13,23:4
Tabor, Gilbert S, 1957, Ap 6,19:5
Tabor, Gilbert S Mrs, 1946, Ap 27,17:3
Tabor, Horace J, 1945, Ap 16,23:6
Tabor, Jim, 1953, Ag 23,89:2
Tabor, Lee L, 1911, D 26,9:6
Tabor, Merritt E, 1913, Ag 31,11:4
Tabor, Myron, 1962, F 24,27:2
Tabor, Ray, 1940, Ja 14,42:7
Tabor, S J W, 1883, My 15,2:6
Tabuteau, George G Maj Gen, 1940, My 22,5:3
Tabuteau, Marcel, 1966, Ja 7,29:3
Tacan, Necati, 1958, Jl 29,23:1
Taccetta, Anthony C, 1957, D 24,15:3
Tacchi Venturi, Pietro, 1956, Mr 19,31:3
Tachau, Hanna, 1942, Mr 6,21:4
Tache, E P Sir, 1865, Ag 1,4:5
Tack, Augustus V, 1949, Jl 22,19:2
Tack, Lum, 1915, O 14,11:6
Tack, Robert F, 1949, Ap 8,25:2
Tack, Theodore E, 1914, Ag 15,9:6
Tack, Theodore Edward Mrs, 1919, O 26,22:3
Tacke, Carl A, 1962, Je 21,31:1
Tackenberg, Charles W, 1948, Ag 11,21:3
Tacker, Gustave E, 1940, N 15,21:4
Tacker, John E, 1967, Mr 10,36:2
Tackett, Virgil, 1951, D 27,27:8
Tackett, William C, 1958, Ap 28,23:1
Tackie, Daniel G, 1954, Ag 15,84:5
Tackman, Julius, 1944, Ap 3,21:4
Tackney, Peter C, 1939, D 13,27:4
Tada, So, 1941, Mr 27,23:3
Taddei, Paolino Sen, 1925, O 18,5:1
Taddeo, Andrew J, 1948, D 26,52:5
Taddeo, Bartolmeo, 1951, Mr 3,15:4
Taddeo, Carmine, 1951, Mr 3,15:4
Taddiken, Paul G, 1952, My 3,21:2
Taddington-Schigorin, James S, 1948, Ja 26,19:2
Taddlini, Giovani, 1873, Ja 6,5:3
Tadlock, Charles W, 1942, My 10,42:7
Tadross, Nami Mrs, 1964, Ag 14,27:5
Taesas, Lorenzo, 1947, Je 27,21:4
Taeubler, Eugene, 1953, Ag 14,19:4
Taeusch, Carl F, 1961, S 23,19:5
Tafel, Louis L, 1941, Mr 3,15:1
Tafel, Samuel, 1963, Je 18,37:2
Tafelov, Louis G, 1964, O 8,43:2
Taff, Alfred E, 1952, Je 29,58:4
Taff, David Jones, 1916, Ag 31,9:4
Taff, Frederick A, 1939, Jl 7,17:4
Taff, Walter E, 1943, My 24,15:2
Taffe, John, 1884, Mr 15,4:7
Taffe, Stephen P Mrs, 1944, Ap 24,19:5
Taffet, Alfred, 1958, Ja 28,27:2
Taffinder, Sherwood A, 1965, Ja 26,37:3
Tafsun, Julian, 1937, Mr 22,23:5
Taft, A, 1891, My 22,4:7
Taft, A S Mrs, 1931, F 1,II,8:1
Taft, Arthur N, 1967, F 28,34:3
Taft, C A Dr, 1884, Je 30,1:7
Taft, C E Mrs, 1933, N 19,35:3
Taft, C P, 1930, Ja 1,29:1
Taft, Charles P Mrs, 1961, Ag 29,31:2
Taft, David G, 1962, S 28,25:5
Taft, Dorcas M Mrs, 1925, Jl 14,21:6
Taft, Earl D, 1960, Ag 7,85:2
Taft, Edward P Jr, 1950, Ap 19,29:5
Taft, Elijah D Capt, 1915, Mr 2,9:4
Taft, Enos N, 1903, D 21,7:4
Taft, Eugene S, 1949, Ag 3,23:4
Taft, Frank, 1947, O 17,21:2
Taft, Frank E, 1939, Mr 14,21:3
Taft, Frank Mrs, 1942, N 15,58:1
Taft, Frederick C, 1914, N 6,11:5
Taft, George A, 1952, D 9,33:3
Taft, George S, 1940, My 1,23:1
Taft, George W, 1939, Ja 22,35:2
Taft, Harrison S, 1942, Ap 5,42:2
Taft, Harry, 1939, O 20,23:1
Taft, Harry D, 1956, Jl 17,23:4
Taft, Henry D, 1940, N 8,21:2
Taft, Henry W (funl plans, Ag 13,19:2; funl, Ag 15,19:4), 1945, Ag 12,39:1
Taft, Henry W Mrs, 1942, D 10,30:1
Taft, Horace D (por), 1943, Ja 29,19:1
Taft, Hulbert (est inventory, O 20,48:7), 1959, Ja 20, 35:3
Taft, Hulbert Jr, 1967, N 11,15:4
Taft, Irwin B, 1961, O 5,37:3
Taft, Isabel L, 1954, F 13,13:6
Taft, James C, 1947, Jl 26,13:3
Taft, Jane Mrs, 1922, N 4,13:6
Taft, Jesse A Mrs, 1909, Jl 21,7:6
Taft, Jessie, 1960, Je 8,39:2
Taft, John H, 1940, F 3,7:1; 1941, Ap 19,15:3
Taft, Jonathan, 1903, O 17,9:6
Taft, Jules J, 1940, Jl 22,17:5
Taft, L, 1936, O 31,19:1
Taft, Lorado Mrs, 1950, Ap 30,102:8
Taft, Louisa M Mrs (funl, D 11,11:3), 1907, D 9,7:2
Taft, Lt-Col, 1864, Ja 24,6:4
Taft, Orray, 1937, Ag 7,15:4
Taft, R S Judge, 1902, Mr 23,7:6
Taft, Rebecca, 1914, Jl 23,9:3
Taft, Robert A, 1953, Ag 1,1:8
Taft, Robert A (est acctg), 1954, Ja 23,15:5
Taft, Robert A Mrs (trb; funl plans; will, O 4,21:6), 1958, O 3,29:3
Taft, Robert B, 1951, Ap 17,29:2
Taft, Robert Jr Mrs, 1968, Je 29,29:3
Taft, Robert McLean, 1921, Ag 9,9:4
Taft, Roger B, 1938, Jl 25,15:5
Taft, Royal, 1943, O 2,13:3
Taft, Royal C, 1942, Ap 2,21:4
Taft, Royal C Ex-Gov, 1912, Je 5,11:6
Taft, Theodore M, 1945, Ja 10,23:2
Taft, W H, 1930, Mr 9,1:8
Taft, W Y, 1880, Jl 30,8:1
Taft, Walbridge S, 1951, Ja 3,27:1
Taft, Willard C, 1947, D 16,33:5
Taft, William E, 1939, Mr 31,21:3
Taft, William H Mrs (por),(will, Je 9,23:5), 1943, My 23,43:1
Taft, William H 2d, 1952, F 11,25:4
Taft, William H 2d Mrs, 1958, My 5,29:4
Taft, William Pitts, 1913, F 18,13:5
Tafuri, Louis, 1955, Ag 16,49:3
Tagawa, Daikichiro, 1947, O 10,25:2
Tager, Israel, 1957, My 20,25:2
Tager, Marcus, 1955, Ap 5,29:3
Tagg, Harry B, 1960, D 29,25:3
Taggard, Edward T, 1959, Ja 5,29:5
Taggard, Genevieve (por), 1948, N 9,28:2
Taggart, Alonzo B Mrs, 1950, Ja 22,77:1
Taggart, Arthur F, 1959, Ag 23,93:1
Taggart, Arthur F Mrs (cor, Ap 28,35:2), 1959, Ap 27,27:3
Taggart, Bert, 1941, Ap 7,17:3
Taggart, Byron B, 1941, Ap 14,17:6
Taggart, Byron B Mrs, 1958, Je 25,29:2
Taggart, D M Capt, 1918, O 17,15:2
Taggart, Edward T, 1915, D 12,19:6
Taggart, Eugene F, 1951, Mr 22,31:1
Taggart, Eva B Mrs, 1937, Jl 31,15:5
Taggart, Everett J, 1952, Mr 12,27:3
Taggart, Frank F, 1945, Jl 25,23:5
Taggart, Frederick S, 1941, Mr 12,21:2
Taggart, G R, 1931, S 16,3:1
Taggart, George, 1945, Je 8,19:4
Taggart, George C, 1940, D 19,25:1
Taggart, Herbert F, 1962, Ap 23,29:4
Taggart, Hugh Thomas, 1914, O 9,9:4
Taggart, Ida K Mrs, 1939, Je 18,37:3
Taggart, John J, 1942, O 3,15:3
Taggart, John P, 1951, N 24,11:3
Taggart, John T, 1925, Ag 13,19:5
Taggart, Laurence D, 1942, Ap 4,13:1
Taggart, Marion A, 1945, Ja 21,40:3
Taggart, Matthew H, 1942, Jl 24,20:3
Taggart, Moses, 1883, F 20,5:4
Taggart, Pearl S Mrs, 1941, S 6,15:4
Taggart, Ralph E, 1951, My 2,31:2
Taggart, Robert C, 1912, F 26,11:4
Taggart, Robert M, 1912, Ja 25,11:5
Taggart, Rush, 1922, S 29,19:6; 1965, D 28,25:3
Taggart, Rush Mrs, 1966, O 2,86:6
Taggart, Sylvester A Sr Mrs, 1961, Je 25,77:1
Taggart, Thomas D Jr, 1949, Ja 8,15:3; 1950, S 6,29:1
Taggart, Walter T, 1938, Ap 11,15:2
Taggart, William S, 1949, Ap 13,29:5
Tagge, Hans J, 1946, Ja 27,42:8
Tagiuri, Pier L, 1949, Ja 23,68:5
Tagliabue, Angelo, 1961, My 22,31:4
Tagliabue, Felix A, 1960, Jl 13,35:2
Tagliabue, G, 1878, My 8,2:1
Tagliapietra, Gino, 1954, Ag 9,17:4
Tagliapietra, Giovanni, 1921, Ap 12,17:5
Tagliavia, Aida, 1922, Jl 2,16:4
Tagliavini, Arbara, 1951, Ja 5,21:4
Taglioni, Maria (denial, Ap 26,1:5), 1873, Ap 23,6:7
Taglioni, Maria, 1884, Ap 25,5:5
Taglioni, Marie, 1891, Ag 30,13:4
Tagney, Vincent G, 1958, O 20,29:4
Tagore, Rabindranath, 1941, Ag 8,15:1
Tague, Peter F, 1941, S 18,26:4
Taha, Sayed (Brig), 1953, F 6,20:5
Tai Hsu Tai, 1947, Mr 18,27:4
Tai-Koon, Emperor, 1859, Ja 5,8:2
Taiano, Eugene Sr, 1951, Mr 6,27:4
Taibi, Calogero (Chas), 1968, Ja 6,29:2
Taibosh, Franz, 1940, S 2,15:3
Tailer, Agnes Suffern Mrs, 1917, Mr 19,11:4
Tailer, Edward N, 1917, F 16,11:5
Tailer, H A (see also Mr 16), 1878, Mr 18,8:4
Tailer, Henry P Mrs, 1946, Ap 25,21:1
Tailer, J Lee Mrs, 1943, N 12,21:5
Tailer, Robert W, 1915, My 30,13:4
Tailer, T S, 1928, D 26,17:5
Tailer, T Suffern Mrs, 1962, Ag 31,21:2
Tailer, William H Mrs, 1909, My 16,9:5
Taillandier, R G E, 1879, F 25,5:5
Taillefer, Germaine, 1925, F 2,17:3
Taillon, Angus D, 1953, My 10,88:3
Taillon, Leon A, 1948, S 20,25:1
Taine, Hippolyte, 1893, Mr 6,5:1
Tainsly, Adrian, 1941, Ag 1,15:6
Tainter, Charles S, 1940, Ap 22,18:2
Tainter, Frank S, 1941, S 26,23:4
Taintor, Charles Newhall, 1920, Mr 13,9:6
Taintor, E C, 1879, Ap 23,2:4
Taintor, Frederic B, 1938, My 9,17:6
Taintor, Giles, 1882, Mr 8,5:5
Taintor, Giles E, 1919, Ja 13,11:2
Taintor, Giles E Mrs, 1914, Jl 20,7:4
Taintor, Henry Fox, 1908, N 10,9:5
Taintor, Lolotte C, 1937, Jl 31,15:4
Tairov, Alex Y, 1950, S 28,31:3
Taishoff, Jerome, 1964, D 21,29:1
Tait, A C Archbishop of Canterbury, 1882, D 4,5:2
Tait, Aldo, 1967, Mr 13,27:7
Tait, Arthur A, 1958, O 7,35:1
Tait, Arthur Fitz William, 1905, Ap 29,11:5
Tait, Arthur J B, 1949, Ap 27,27:4
Tait, Charles M, 1950, Jl 2,25:1
Tait, Don, 1958, S 16,28:1
Tait, Edward H, 1947, Jl 1,25:1
Tait, Edward J, 1947, Jl 13,44:5

Tait, Edwin E, 1954, My 12,31:5
Tait, Frank M, 1962, F 26,27:2
Tait, Galen L, 1953, S 28,25:4
Tait, George, 1940, N 5,25:2; 1952, Ag 25,17:4
Tait, George F Maj, 1919, Je 1,22:4
Tait, George G, 1940, S 21,19:4
Tait, Harold, 1920, N 30,11:4
Tait, J Nevon Mrs, 1939, Ja 19,19:4
Tait, James, 1944, Jl 5,17:4
Tait, John H, 1955, S 24,19:6; 1959, Ap 14,35:2
Tait, John R, 1909, Jl 30,7:5
Tait, Melbourne Sir, 1917, F 11,23:4
Tait, P G Prof, 1901, Jl 5,7:5
Tait, R S, 1877, N 9,8:5
Tait, Robert, 1937, F 3,23:5
Tait, Robert C Jr, 1943, Ja 6,16:4
Tait, Thomas, 1940, Jl 26,17:4
Tait, Thomas S, 1954, Jl 20,19:1
Tait, Thomas W, 1939, D 15,25:4
Tait, Walter W, 1941, N 29,17:2
Tait, William J, 1956, Ja 18,31:5
Tait, William O, 1966, Jl 16,25:3
Tait, William T, 1951, Ag 9,21:5
Taitinger, Nich, 1944, Jl 4,19:1
Taitt, Francis M, 1943, Jl 18,34:8
Taittinger, Francois, 1960, O 8,5:3
Taittinger, Pierre C, 1965, Ja 26,37:1
Tajiri, Seigo, 1944, Jl 24,15:5
Tak, Max, 1967, Ag 8,39:4
Takach, Basil, 1948, My 14,23:4
Takahashi, Charles T, 1920, Ja 16,9:5
Takahashi, Hitoshi, 1965, Ag 12,27:1
Takahashi, Motokichi, 1920, N 28,22:3
Takahashi, Riichi, 1963, Jl 30,29:3
Takahashi, Sakue Prof, 1920, S 15,9:1
Takaishi, Shingoro, 1967, F 27,29:1
Takaki, Shunzo, 1919, Ja 30,13:3
Takakusu, Junjiro, 1945, Je 30,17:5
Takami, Jun, 1965, Ag 18,35:4
Takami, Mark R, 1967, Ja 16,41:3
Takami, Masahiko Mrs, 1938, Mr 11,19:3
Takami, Ralph M Mrs, 1952, Ag 10,61:2
Takami, Toyohiko C, 1945, My 19,19:6
Takamine, Eben T, 1953, Ag 29,17:6
Takamine, Jokichi Dr, 1922, Jl 25,11:6
Takano, Iwanaburo, 1949, Ap 7,29:4
Takarabe, Takeshi, 1949, Ja 14,23:4
Takasaki, Tatsunosuke, 1964, F 24,25:1
Takasukasa, Toshimachi, 1966, Ja 29,5:1
Takeda, Masako Princess, 1940, Mr 8,22:4
Takenaka, Katsuo, 1959, Ja 27,33:4
Takeshita, Isamu, 1949, Jl 7,25:4
Takis, Nicholas, 1964, Mr 6,28:5
Takla Pasha, Gabriel, 1943, Jl 7,19:4
Takoi, Oskari Mrs, 1963, O 6,88:6
Taks, Alexander L, 1945, N 3,15:3
Talaat, Mahmoud, 1951, N 29,33:5
Talalay, Joseph A, 1961, O 17,39:3
Talamantes, Rofrigo, 1939, Ap 27,25:3
Talamo-Rossi, Ralph J, 1937, My 30,19:2
Talbert, Ansel D Mrs, 1952, Je 25,29:4
Talbert, Ansel Dixie, 1953, F 3,25:2
Talbert, Benjamin G, 1917, D 8,15:4
Talbert, Ernest L Mrs, 1960, Jl 15,23:2
Talbert, Joseph Truitt, 1920, My 9,22:3
Talbert, Rezin, 1952, Ja 17,27:1
Talbert, William E Mrs, 1952, D 2,31:2
Talbot, Abbie M, 1954, O 14,29:2
Talbot, Ada M, 1949, Mr 16,27:5
Talbot, Adolphus R, 1944, Ja 30,38:5
Talbot, Alfred W, 1949, Jl 13,27:3
Talbot, Anna H, 1943, Ag 23,15:5
Talbot, Arthur Mrs, 1952, Mr 22,13:5
Talbot, Arthur N (por), 1942, Ap 4,13:5
Talbot, Benjamin, 1947, D 18,30:2
Talbot, Benjamin M Sr, 1964, O 22,32:4
Talbot, Benjamin Mrs, 1962, Je 28,31:3
Talbot, C C, 1885, Mr 11,5:6
Talbot, Charles A, 1874, D 7,5:3
Talbot, Charles A P Capt, 1903, D 12,9:5
Talbot, Charles N (cor, Je 17,29:5), 1954, Je 16,31:3
Talbot, D Earl Mrs, 1959, Je 18,31:3
Talbot, E Bishop, 1928, F 28,25:1
Talbot, Ebenezer C, 1945, F 21,19:3
Talbot, Edward A, 1959, O 25,85:5
Talbot, Edward M, 1958, Ag 18,19:2
Talbot, Egan F, 1955, O 21,27:5
Talbot, Elisha H, 1923, My 23,21:6
Talbot, Ellen Bliss, 1968, Ja 26,47:3
Talbot, Ellen C, 1954, Ag 1,85:2
Talbot, Ethelbert, 1924, F 19,15:3
Talbot, Francis X, 1953, D 10,47:5
Talbot, Gayle, 1956, Mr 30,19:3
Talbot, Gayle Sr Mrs, 1950, Mr 11,15:1
Talbot, George, 1938, Jl 14,21:2
Talbot, George A, 1943, O 8,19:2
Talbot, George F, 1938, Ja 17,19:2
Talbot, Gilbert P, 1966, O 19,38:8
Talbot, Gilman S, 1949, F 19,15:2
Talbot, Grace M Mrs, 1940, S 9,15:4
Talbot, H, 1928, S 13,27:4
Talbot, H P, 1927, Je 19,23:1
Talbot, Hammond, 1946, Jl 9,21:4
Talbot, Harriette S Mrs, 1952, Ja 27,76:8
Talbot, Henry D Mrs, 1938, Ap 2,15:4
Talbot, Howard, 1948, D 21,31:2
Talbot, J C, 1883, Ja 16,5:5
Talbot, J Thomas, 1944, Je 8,21:5
Talbot, James B, 1948, Ag 23,18:2
Talbot, James E, 1956, Ap 25,35:2
Talbot, John A, 1962, D 27,7:5
Talbot, Joseph E, 1966, My 2,37:3
Talbot, Laurie H Mrs, 1944, D 9,15:5
Talbot, Lester J, 1948, Je 6,72:3
Talbot, Louis A Mrs, 1950, D 31,42:8
Talbot, Lowell Capt, 1907, Jl 26,7:6
Talbot, Marion, 1948, O 21,27:3
Talbot, Martha B B Mrs, 1941, Mr 3,15:3
Talbot, Mignon, 1950, Jl 20,25:3
Talbot, Montgomery H, 1943, Ap 24,13:5
Talbot, Nellie R, 1946, Mr 8,21:1
Talbot, Neville S, 1943, Ap 4,40:6
Talbot, Newton, 1904, F 4,9:6
Talbot, Paul A, 1956, S 21,25:4
Talbot, Ralph L, 1948, S 21,28:3
Talbot, Robert Bancker Dr, 1921, Jl 17,22:4
Talbot, Robert Rev Dr, 1923, My 18,19:3
Talbot, Susan, 1938, Jl 28,19:2
Talbot, Thomas, 1954, D 13,27:4
Talbot, Thomas L, 1940, Ja 3,22:2
Talbot, Thomas Lt-Col, 1910, F 26,7:4
Talbot, W F H, 1877, S 22,5:3
Talbot, Walter C, 1955, N 20,89:2
Talbot, William, 1949, Ag 30,27:4
Talbot, William B, 1965, Jl 2,29:4
Talbot, William C, 1941, Je 3,21:5
Talbot-Perkins, Rebecca C Mrs, 1956, N 3,23:4
Talbott, C C, 1937, Ap 9,21:1
Talbott, Charles F, 1937, Mr 7,II,8:3
Talbott, Charles G, 1961, D 24,37:2
Talbott, E Guy, 1945, F 6,19:3
Talbott, Earl G, 1967, S 25,45:4
Talbott, Edward W, 1945, F 14,19:5
Talbott, Harold E (funl, Mr 5,31:5), 1957, Mr 3,1:1
Talbott, Harold E Mrs, 1962, Jl 16,13:1
Talbott, J Dan, 1950, My 18,29:4
Talbott, Nelson S, 1952, Jl 8,27:1
Talbott, Paul Rev Dr, 1937, Mr 29,19:5
Talbott, William H Mrs, 1937, O 19,26:3
Talburt, Harold M, 1966, O 23,88:1
Talbut, Blaine I, 1954, Ap 10,15:6
Talcott, Agnew A, 1955, Mr 26,15:4
Talcott, Albert L, 1937, Je 10,23:4
Talcott, Allen B Mrs, 1956, F 7,31:5
Talcott, August Belmont, 1908, My 18,7:1
Talcott, Carlton H, 1948, Ja 14,25:5
Talcott, Charles Andrew, 1920, F 29,22:3
Talcott, Chester W, 1940, Ja 14,42:8
Talcott, Dennison L, 1955, Ja 5,23:4
Talcott, Edward B, 1941, Ap 7,17:3
Talcott, Edwin C, 1905, Je 22,9:6
Talcott, F L, 1884, N 3,10:2
Talcott, Fred L, 1946, Je 19,21:3
Talcott, George S, 1957, Ap 16,33:2
Talcott, Harry P, 1955, Ap 20,33:3
Talcott, Henrietta E Francis Mrs, 1921, D 16,17:5
Talcott, J Frederick, 1944, F 7,15:3
Talcott, J Frederick (trb), 1944, Ap 20,13:2
Talcott, J Frederick Mrs, 1956, Mr 8,29:1
Talcott, James (funl, Ag 23,9:4), 1916, Ag 22,9:4
Talcott, John G, 1944, N 3,21:2
Talcott, Mancel, 1958, Mr 14,25:3
Talcott, Seth, 1961, O 16,29:3
Talcott, Wait, 1943, Jl 4,20:4
Talcott, William E, 1947, Ja 14,25:5
Taleisnik, Joseph, 1961, N 18,23:5
Taleisnik, Joseph Mrs, 1956, F 25,19:5
Talensky, Nikolai A, 1967, Jl 26,39:3
Taley, Stanley B, 1941, O 1,21:2
Talfor, Edward A, 1954, Je 20,86:1
Taliaferro, A Pendleton Jr, 1942, Jl 8,23:2
Taliaferro, C O Col, 1916, Mr 3,11:4
Taliaferro, Edith (Mrs H B Jameson), 1958, Mr 3, 27:3
Taliaferro, Eugene S, 1963, Ag 5,29:5
Taliaferro, Felix T, 1955, O 24,27:3
Taliaferro, Harry Monroe, 1968, D 28,27:4
Taliaferro, Henry B, 1958, N 7,27:3
Taliaferro, Lucene G Mrs, 1958, Ja 30,23:3
Taliaferro, Phil B, 1938, Je 26,27:3
Taliaferro, Thomas H, 1941, S 27,17:5
Taliaferro, Thomas S Jr, 1940, Ag 18,37:3
Taliaferro, Thomas W, 1940, Jl 13,14:6
Taliaferro, W Perrin, 1938, Ja 4,23:4
Taliaferro, Windsor L, 1943, Ap 17,17:3
Talich, Vaclav, 1961, Mr 22,41:1
Talihade, Laurent, 1919, N 4,15:1
Talimer, Bernard, 1938, Ag 6,13:4
Talimer, Bernard Mrs (Mattie O), 1963, My 26,91:4
Talks, Josephine Mrs, 1944, Jl 15,13:2
Talladay, George S, 1941, S 24,23:4
Tallamy, Bertram F, 1944, My 14,46:2
Tallant, Alice W, 1958, Je 1,86:4
Tallant, Hugh, 1952, D 9,33:2
Tallant, Hugh Mrs, 1945, Je 24,21:1
Tallant, Robert, 1957, Ap 3,31:3
Tallard, Henry S, 1937, Ja 4,29:4
Tallarigo, Albert M, 1938, Mr 7,17:4
Tallau, Karl R, 1957, F 28,27:3
Tallchief, Alec (Alec Jos Tall Chief), 1959, O 13,39:3
Tallentine, Thomas L, 1947, N 5,28:3
Tallentire, Norman H, 1953, N 9,35:4
Tallents, Stephen, 1958, S 14,84:5
Tallerday, George C Jr, 1952, Ja 21,15:4
Tallerday, Howard G, 1946, Ja 27,42:5
Talleur, Alex, 1957, S 23,27:3
Talleur, Gustav J, 1950, Ja 25,27:4
Talley, Alfred J, 1952, Ja 19,15:1
Talley, Charles M, 1937, O 24,II,8:3
Talley, Charlotte W Mrs, 1948, Ag 19,21:5
Talley, Dickson L, 1937, D 5,II,9:2
Talley, Dora Alex Mrs, 1953, F 27,21:2
Talley, Edwin J, 1949, Ja 5,25:4
Talley, Frank A, 1955, My 2,21:4
Talley, Hailman P, 1939, Mr 10,23:2
Talley, J Courtney Mrs, 1950, Jl 1,15:1
Talley, James C, 1943, F 2,19:1
Talley, James E, 1941, Jl 5,11:6
Talley, Lynn P, 1942, O 9,21:4
Talley, Robert, 1953, Jl 12,65:2
Talley, Tazewell T, 1952, Je 29,58:5
Talley, Truman H (por), 1942, Ja 19,17:1
Talley, W Warren Mrs, 1940, Jl 23,19:3
Talley, William W, 1951, N 13,29:5
Talleyrand, Duke of (por), 1937, O 27,31:1
Talleyrand et Sagan, Duchess de, 1905, O 13,4:5
Talleyrand-Perigord, Charles Maurice (Duke de Dino), 1917, Ja 6,13:4
Talleyrand-Perigord, Duchess of (cors, D 1,33:4; D 6,47:4), 1961, N 30,37:1
Talleyrand-Perigord, Duchess of (Anna Gould), 1967, Je 3,29:5
Tallmadge, David F, 1910, O 12,9:4
Tallmadge, Edward S Jr, 1957, N 19,18:4
Tallmadge, F Samuel, 1904, Je 22,9:6
Tallmadge, Frederick A, 1869, S 18,4:7
Tallmadge, Gov, 1864, N 13,2:6
Tallmadge, Henry O, 1948, S 4,15:3
Tallmadge, John E, 1944, Mr 17,17:1
Tallmadge, Joseph, 1941, O 5,48:1
Tallmadge, Orville R, 1955, D 20,31:5
Tallmadge, Spencer, 1944, Ja 21,17:2
Tallmadge, Thomas D, 1943, F 4,23:6
Tallmage, William H Col, 1924, D 23,19:4
Tallman, Albert V W, 1939, Ap 27,25:5
Tallman, Alfred W, 1944, Jl 4,19:1
Tallman, Alison, 1966, Ja 10,45:1
Tallman, Edmund M, 1964, Ag 9,76:4
Tallman, Frank F Jr, 1952, Ag 28,23:1
Tallman, Frederick G, 1938, Ap 2,15:1
Tallman, Grant C, 1955, S 14,35:3
Tallman, Herbert Mrs, 1950, My 19,28:2
Tallman, John F, 1965, Ag 10,29:3
Tallman, John F Capt (funl, Ag 20,8:5), 1875, Ag 15 6:7
Tallman, John H, 1864, Ag 20,8:4; 1957, Ag 13,27:4
Tallman, Leroy A, 1924, D 2,25:5
Tallman, Oliver G, 1961, Ap 11,37:2
Tallman, Stephen Mrs, 1947, Ag 13,23:4
Tallman, Walter B, 1938, Ap 23,15:3
Tallman, William B, 1945, F 5,15:3
Tallman, William D, 1961, Ag 20,86:3
Tallman, William P, 1959, Je 13,21:4
Tallman, William S, 1961, Je 12,29:5
Tallman, Wilson J, 1945, My 12,13:6
Tallmer, Albert F, 1949, O 27,27:2
Tallon, James H, 1937, Ja 5,23:4
Tallon, Lawrence T, 1951, D 18,31:1
Tallon, Thomas W, 1942, Ja 13,19:5
Tallon, William T, 1956, O 14,87:1
Tally, Jesse L, 1950, Ja 26,28:2
Tally, Joseph M, 1937, Ag 31,23:1
Tally, Reuben, 1960, Je 27,25:6
Tally, Thomas L, 1945, N 25,50:4
Tally, William F, 1964, O 14,45:3
Tally, William P, 1944, Ag 19,11:5
Talmadge, Arthur T, 1952, Ap 8,29:3
Talmadge, Eugene, 1946, D 22,1:6
Talmadge, Ezra E, 1951, Ja 23,27:6
Talmadge, Harry S, 1947, D 12,27:2
Talmadge, Henry, 1907, Mr 20,9:6
Talmadge, Henry P, 1937, My 10,19:2
Talmadge, Howard A, 1937, My 12,23:3
Talmadge, J Parker, 1962, O 20,25:5
Talmadge, Joseph, 1952, Jl 3,25:5
Talmadge, Martin, 1945, My 14,17:5
Talmadge, Norma (Mrs C James),(funl, D 29,48:7), 1957, D 25,31:1
Talmadge, Norma (Mrs C M James),(will, Ja 2,22:4; cor), 1958, Ja 6,22:2
Talmadge, T Markham Mrs, 1940, O 22,23:3
Talmadge, William B Mrs, 1951, O 16,31:4
Talmage, Algernon, 1939, S 15,23:4
Talmage, Archibald A Mrs, 1956, S 19,37:4; 1961, Jl 16,69:1
Talmage, David H, 1944, S 20,23:5
Talmage, De Witt C, 1942, Mr 4,19:2
Talmage, Edward T H, 1964, Je 29,27:4
Talmage, Edward T H Mrs, 1940, N 10,57:2

Talmage, Edward Taylor Hunt, 1922, O 6,23:4
Talmage, Frank Dewitt Rev, 1912, F 10,11:6
Talmage, George E, 1944, Jl 28,13:3
Talmage, George E Jr Mrs, 1937, Ja 21,23:2
Talmage, Gertrude B Mrs, 1938, Ap 15,19:2
Talmage, Goyn, 1939, N 23,27:2
Talmage, Henry R, 1951, Ja 30,25:2
Talmage, Katherine M, 1938, N 13,45:3
Talmage, Louis T D Mrs (will, Mr 31,14:6), 1937, Mr 20,19:5
Talmage, Mary B Mrs, 1943, My 24,15:3
Talmage, robt S, 1953, Mr 11,29:2
Talmage, Samuel Dr, 1903, N 22,7:6
Talmage, T De W Mrs, 1895, Ag 6,4:7
Talmage, T DeW Jr (funl, Ja 10,5:4), 1881, Ja 8,8:4
Talmage, Tunis Van Pelt, 1909, N 29,9:5
Talman, E Lee, 1964, F 12,33:4
Talman, Elbert, 1939, My 20,15:6
Talman, G F, 1883, Je 12,4:7
Talman, Howard P, 1961, Mr 24,31:4
Talman, Pierre Courtney, 1907, Ap 20,9:6
Talman, William, 1968, Ag 31,23:3
Talmey, George Mrs, 1959, Ag 2,80:4
Talmey, Max, 1941, N 7,24:2
Talner, Leonard, 1941, D 1,19:4
Talt, Lawrence F, 1940, My 2,24:3
Taltavall, Thomas R, 1918, S 4,11:2
Talty, Patrick J, 1948, Ap 11,72:3
Talva, Galina (Mrs Galina Tzvetckoff Volkov), 1968, D 28,27:1
Tam, J S Col, 1905, Mr 21,11:4
Tamagnini, Arthur, 1940, Jl 11,19:6
Tamagno, Francesco, 1905, S 1,9:6
Tamany, John W, 1960, Je 13,27:1
Tamar, Julius, 1953, D 31,19:3
Tamari, Melvin J, 1954, O 13,31:3
Tamarkin, Jacob D, 1945, N 22,35:2
Tamasese, ex-King of Samoa, 1891, Ap 29,8:6
Tamasson, Solfest, 1941, Ag 16,15:7
Tamayo, Francisco, 1957, Ap 20,17:4
Tamayo, Franz, 1956, Jl 31,23:5
Tamayo, Jose L, 1947, Jl 8,23:3
Tamberlik, H, 1889, Mr 15,2:1
Tamberlik, Henry, 1883, F 3,5:4
Tamblyn, Albert T, 1954, Jl 5,11:6
Tamblyn, Edward, 1957, Je 25,29:2
Tamblyn, Edward C, 1938, Je 7,23:2
Tamblyn, Egbert J, 1941, Ja 16,21:2
Tamblyn, Evan Lynn, 1920, Mr 26,13:4
Tamblyn, George A Mrs, 1943, Jl 10,13:7
Tamblyn, George O, 1947, N 4,25:6
Tamblyn, Gerald M, 1947, Je 9,21:3
Tamblyn, Jere D, 1958, S 1,13:3
Tamblyn, John B, 1943, F 6,13:3
Tambo, Edgar Mrs, 1947, Ja 9,24:2
Tambo, Edgar W, 1959, Je 16,35:2
Tamboer, Marinus C, 1944, D 23,13:6
Tambon, Auguste M, 1952, Mr 4,27:4
Tamborini, Jose P, 1955, S 26,23:6
Tambroni, Fernando, 1963, F 19,8:8
Tamburina, Anthony Mrs, 1949, Jl 1,19:4
Tamburina, Joseph J, 1956, Je 13,37:5
Tamburini, Alessandro, 1954, S 24,23:1
Tamburini, Antonio, 1876, N 12,6:7
Tamburnia, Rocco, 1949, F 19,15:1
Tameling, Albert, 1940, D 31,15:1
Tameling, Gerard P, 1942, Ap 2,21:3
Tamer, Louis G, 1952, S 24,33:6
Tamiris, Helen (Mrs D Nagrin), 1966, Ag 5,31:1
Tamis, Louis, 1948, Ag 28,15:4
Tamke, George R F, 1964, D 12,31:1
Tamlyn, Arthur C, 1955, O 10,27:5
Tamlyn, George H, 1937, D 15,25:2
Tamlyn, Walter J, 1953, F 22,60:7
Tamm, George E, 1941, My 18,45:2
Tammany, Roman Mrs, 1954, Ja 20,27:3
Tammany, William F, 1951, Je 30,15:6
Tammany, William P, 1942, Mr 25,21:4
Tamme, Charles, 1956, Mr 25,92:1
Tammen, Agnes R Mrs, 1942, Jl 3,17:6
Tammen, Harry, 1924, Jl 20,20:4
Tammen, Henry C, 1961, Jl 7,25:3
Tammen, William H, 1938, Ap 28,23:3
Tampa, the magician (R S Sugden), 1939, Jl 21,19:5
Tampone, Joseph, 1944, N 5,53:1
Tamraz, William H, 1954, S 1,27:5
Tams, A W, 1927, Je 26,II,9:1
Tams, J F, 1928, My 28,25:5
Tams, J Frederick Mrs, 1944, S 13,19:3
Tams, William H, 1952, F 3,84:4
Tamsen, E J H, 1907, Jl 25,7:5
Tan, Edith, 1949, D 22,23:2
Tan, Prince, 1917, Je 14,11:6
Tan Ping-shan, 1956, Ap 3,35:4
Tanahashi, Ayako Mrs, 1939, S 24,43:2
Tanahey, Martin F Mrs, 1943, Ap 20,23:2
Tanaka, G Baron, 1929, S 29,31:1
Tanakadate, Aikitsu, 1952, My 22,27:3
Tananbaum, Harry Mrs, 1947, Ap 10,25:3
Tananbaum, Oscar, 1952, S 11,31:4
Tanburn, Stephen, 1952, O 23,31:3
Tanch, Joseph W, 1950, Ja 18,31:2
Tancinco, Tiburcio, 1952, D 19,31:1
Tandardini, A, 1879, Mr 29,5:3
Tandler, Joseph, 1948, Ja 31,19:5
Tandler, Samuel, 1937, O 2,21:2
Tandon, Purshottamdas, 1962, Jl 2,29:3
Tandourjian, Kopernick, 1964, S 6,56:5
Tandy, Arthur H, 1964, O 23,39:1
Tandy, David L, 1966, D 22,33:4
Tandy, Frederick S, 1951, Je 28,25:4
Tandy, John A, 1950, F 28,29:5
Tandy, Vertner W, 1949, N 8,31:4
Tandy, W Warren, 1958, Je 5,31:4
Tanejeff, Sergius, 1915, Je 21,9:4
Tanenbaum, Barnett, 1951, Mr 12,25:3
Tanenbaum, Harry, 1951, Jl 17,27:1
Tanenbaum, Jerome, 1947, N 8,17:4
Tanenbaum, Leon, 1923, Mr 30,17:5
Tanenbaum, Moses, 1937, O 11,21:4
Tanenbaum, Samuel A, 1968, S 16,47:4
Taney, Chief Justice, 1864, O 14,4:6
Taney, Francis J, 1937, O 13,23:3
Taneyhill, Carrie A Mrs, 1939, Jl 8,15:6
Tang, Bernhard G, 1954, S 18,15:4
Tangeman, Charles, 1949, D 11,92:6
Tangeman, Cora H Mrs, 1924, S 3,17:1
Tangeman, George Patterson, 1919, D 7,22:3
Tangeman, Robert S, 1964, S 27,86:5
Tangeman, Walter W, 1966, O 14,40:3
Tanger, Jacob, 1951, D 20,31:4
Tangil y Angulo, Fernando S de, 1964, S 7,19:3
Tangney, John F, 1965, Mr 29,33:5
Tango, Egisto, 1951, O 6,19:6
Tangora, Charles, 1942, F 21,20:2
Tangorra, John, 1959, Ag 1,17:5
Tangorra, Vincenzo Prof, 1922, D 22,15:5
Tanguay, Eva, 1947, Ja 12,59:1
Tanguy, Yves, 1955, Ja 16,92:8
Tangye, Florence P Mrs, 1942, Jl 29,17:6
Tanhauser, Sigmond S (Si), 1953, D 31,19:2
Tani, Masayuki, 1962, O 27,25:3
Tani, Yukio, 1950, Ja 27,24:2
Taniguchi, Tsuneji, 1945, Ag 7,24:2
Tanis, Hubert E Sr, 1944, Ag 9,17:5
Tanis, John C Sr, 1952, N 2,88:2
Tanizaki, Junichiro, 1965, Jl 3,21:2
Tankel, Jesse, 1958, N 23,89:1
Tankel, Stanley B, 1968, Ap 1,45:3
Tankoos, Robert, 1956, Ag 14,25:5
Tankoos, Samuel J (por), 1949, F 9,27:3
Tankoos, Samuel J Mrs, 1963, D 8,86:2
Tanlkawa, Selji Lt-Col, 1918, O 13,23:2
Tann, Baron von der Gen, 1881, Ap 27,5:4
Tann, Georgia, 1950, S 16,19:3
Tannahill, R, 1883, N 28,5:5
Tannahill, Sallie B, 1947, Ja 30,25:6
Tannar, Harold Drake, 1968, Ag 8,33:4
Tanne, John, 1953, F 18,31:2
Tannebaum, Israel, 1948, O 21,27:2
Tannehill, Jesse, 1956, S 23,84:3
Tannen, Daniel, 1953, F 7,15:5
Tannen, Julius, 1965, Ja 5,33:2
Tannenbaum, Abner, 1913, Jl 20,II,11:4
Tannenbaum, Adelaide E, 1945, O 25,21:5
Tannenbaum, Alexander, 1960, Ag 14,93:1
Tannenbaum, David, 1952, D 15,25:3; 1959, Ag 30, 82:2
Tannenbaum, Elk, 1961, Je 13,35:4
Tannenbaum, Ferdinand, 1953, N 2,16:4
Tannenbaum, Ferdinand Mrs, 1953, N 2,16:4
Tannenbaum, Harold J, 1943, O 8,19:1
Tannenbaum, Helen Sarah Mrs, 1922, Ap 21,13:4
Tannenbaum, Herbert, 1958, O 10,31:3
Tannenbaum, Louis, 1958, Ag 1,21:4
Tannenbaum, Max, 1955, Ag 14,81:1; 1961, Mr 2,27:2
Tannenbaum, Norton A, 1966, Ap 5,39:4
Tannenbaum, Samuel, 1955, O 8,19:6
Tannenbaum, Samuel A (por), 1948, N 1,23:3
Tannenbaum, Simon Dr, 1937, Mr 2,21:3
Tannenbaum, William, 1954, O 24,88:8
Tannenbaum, William Mrs, 1954, O 24,88:8
Tannenberger, Henry E, 1946, Mr 31,46:3
Tannenwald, Theodore, 1959, N 22,87:1
Tannenwald, Theodore Mrs, 1956, Ag 14,25:3
Tanner, A H, 1882, Ja 15,5:5
Tanner, Amelia J, 1912, N 14,11:6
Tanner, Annie Louise, 1921, Mr 1,13:4
Tanner, Arden S, 1947, My 5,23:1
Tanner, Benjamin T Bp, 1923, Ja 16,21:3
Tanner, Charles, 1955, Ja 21,23:6
Tanner, Charles E, 1946, Ja 14,19:3
Tanner, Charles H, 1947, Jl 6,40:6; 1952, Ag 17,76:3
Tanner, Charles J Sr, 1947, O 8,25:4
Tanner, Charles Mrs, 1954, Jl 20,19:4
Tanner, Daniel W, 1953, Mr 19,29:4
Tanner, DeWitt C (por), 1948, O 21,27:1
Tanner, E J Selby Lt, 1916, Jl 15,9:7
Tanner, Edward E, 1940, Je 28,19:4
Tanner, Edward E Mrs, 1939, Ja 28,13:5
Tanner, Elmer F, 1941, O 15,21:3
Tanner, Emmeline M, 1955, Ja 9,87:2
Tanner, Ernest K, 1952, Ag 31,44:5
Tanner, Floyd O, 1947, N 29,13:2
Tanner, Frank, 1938, D 18,48:8
Tanner, Fred W, 1957, F 25,25:2
Tanner, Frederick C, 1963, Je 25,33:1
Tanner, H Belden, 1951, Jl 25,23:2
Tanner, Harold B, 1968, D 28,27:3
Tanner, Henry I Mrs, 1949, Ap 29,23:3
Tanner, Henry O, 1937, My 26,26:4
Tanner, Inez, 1951, N 6,29:5
Tanner, Ivins S, 1952, F 6,29:2
Tanner, J, 1927, O 3,23:5
Tanner, J Roy Mrs, 1945, N 14,19:5
Tanner, Jack (John F), 1965, Mr 5,33:1
Tanner, James C, 1952, F 7,27:5
Tanner, James Mrs, 1906, Je 30,1:6
Tanner, John H, 1940, Mr 12,23:1
Tanner, John R Mrs, 1946, Jl 1,31:4
Tanner, John S, 1956, Ja 31,29:3
Tanner, Joseph Mrs, 1941, Jl 28,15:1
Tanner, Josephine, 1959, Jl 16,27:5
Tanner, Laura V, 1941, Ap 24,19:5
Tanner, Marie R Mrs, 1957, Jl 7,61:1
Tanner, Morton S, 1947, O 16,28:2
Tanner, Murray G, 1953, Ja 13,32:3
Tanner, Norman D, 1959, Je 19,25:4
Tanner, Olaf John, 1918, Jl 22,11:6
Tanner, Philip, 1967, Ap 23,92:6
Tanner, Richard J (por), 1943, Jl 4,21:1
Tanner, Richard Mrs, 1943, S 24,23:4
Tanner, Robert A Jr, 1949, Je 6,19:2
Tanner, Rollin H, 1952, Ap 25,23:3
Tanner, Thomas B, 1965, D 15,47:2
Tanner, Vaino A, 1966, Ap 20,47:1
Tanner, W E Mrs, 1940, Mr 10,49:1
Tanner, Willard B, 1946, My 22,21:4
Tanner, William E, 1941, N 30,68:2; 1965, Ap 18,80:6
Tanner, William Fitch, 1919, S 3,13:4
Tanner, William Fitch Mrs, 1919, S 3,13:4
Tanner, William S, 1950, O 11,33:4
Tanner, Z L Capt, 1906, D 17,11:5
Tannert, Carl H, 1963, My 11,25:2
Tannery, George B, 1948, N 18,28:2
Tannery, Jean (por), 1939, Jl 8,15:3
Tannous, Richard H, 1968, Ap 22,47:1
Tanomogi, Keikichi, 1940, F 20,21:5
Tanous, Azeez J, 1937, N 28,II,8:4
Tanquary, M C, 1944, O 26,23:5
Tansey, Bernard J, 1947, Ag 1,17:2
Tansey, James, 1950, N 5,93:2
Tansey, Joseph E, 1945, D 1,23:4
Tansey, Michael, 1948, S 21,27:3
Tansey, Peter T Mrs, 1960, O 24,29:4
Tansey, William A, 1943, Ap 6,21:3
Tansil, John B, 1950, D 12,33:3
Tansill, Charles C, 1964, N 14,29:1
Tansill, Frederic T Mrs, 1961, My 3,37:2
Tansill, J Fred, 1941, O 8,24:3
Tansky, Dmitri, 1950, Mr 18,14:2
Tansley, Charles, 1957, N 4,29:4
Tansley, Henry J, 1938, D 28,21:2
Tansley, Iohn Oscroft Dr, 1905, Mr 26,9:4
Tant, Walter F, 1947, Mr 12,25:3
Tantaquidgeon, John W, 1949, Ap 2,15:3
Tantau, Clarence A, 1943, Ap 22,23:4
Tantleff, Hyman, 1956, Ag 19,92:7
Tanton, Herbert A, 1938, S 13,24:2
Tantum, Emma, 1952, Je 12,34:6
Tantum, Frank, 1945, My 29,15:3
Tantum, Horace, 1949, Ap 8,25:2
Tanz, Isadore, 1940, Ja 10,21:5
Tanz, Louis, 1942, S 27,48:8
Tanzer, Helen H, 1961, D 24,36:6
Tanzer, John M, 1943, Mr 30,21:3
Tanzer, Julius, 1963, S 17,35:2
Tanzer, Laurence A, 1963, Jl 10,35:1
Tanzer, Laurence A Mrs, 1964, Mr 13,33:3
Tanzer, William, 1944, F 24,15:3
Tao Meng-ho, 1960, Ap 19,37:1
Taormina, Louis J, 1964, O 25,89:1
Tapalow, Samuel B, 1956, Ag 16,25:5
Tapert, Robert T, 1942, My 9,13:5
Tapia, Jose Luis, 1957, S 7,19:2
Tapie, Father, 1939, O 9,19:3
Tapley, Alice P, 1942, Ap 13,15:2
Tapley, H Mark, 1953, N 14,17:2
Tapley, Jesse F, 1910, My 14,9:4
Tapley, Rose, 1956, F 26,88:4
Tapley, Thomas S, 1951, Je 17,86:2
Tapley, William, 1950, Ag 2,25:5
Tapley, William T Mrs, 1944, D 4,23:2
Tapley, William W, 1943, F 12,19:2
Taplin, Charles F, 1964, Ag 26,39:2
Taplin, Frank E (por), 1938, Je 8,23:1
Taplinger, John, 1960, Ag 4,25:6
Taplinger, Lewis (por), 1939, Jl 30,29:4
Taplitz, Benjamin, 1967, Ap 30,86:7
Tapp, Jesse W, 1967, Ja 19,35:1
Tapp, John R, 1950, D 12,33:3
Tappan, Arch D, 1942, Ap 3,21:5
Tappan, Benjamin Rear-Adm, 1919, D 19,15:3
Tappan, H P, 1881, N 17,5:2
Tappan, J N, 1884, S 6,5:2
Tappan, James C Gen, 1906, Mr 21,9:5
Tappan, John B, 1941, D 3,26:2
Tappan, Lewis, 1873, Je 23,5:3
Tappan, Mary A, 1941, Ja 27,15:3

Tappan, Paul W, 1964, Jl 10,30:3
Tappan, Robert, 1961, My 30,17:2
Tappan, Samuel Forster Col, 1913, Ja 9,9:5
Tappan, W Bruce, 1957, Je 11,35:3
Tappe, Anna Mrs, 1937, My 4,25:5
Tappe, Herman P, 1954, S 21,27:5
Tappe, Herman P Mrs, 1917, S 23,23:2; 1947, Ag 5, 23:4
Tappen, Eugene R, 1950, My 14,106:6
Tappen, F D, 1902, Mr 1,1:3
Tappen, Frank J, 1937, Ag 9,20:2
Tappen, Fred B, 1944, Ja 2,38:5
Tappen, George (Fish), 1956, Ap 6,25:3
Tappen, George H, 1946, N 25,27:3
Tappen, Joseph E, 1952, Ja 19,15:6
Tappen, Minnie, 1873, N 24,5:5
Tappen, Ray, 1946, Ap 7,44:2
Tappen, Sophie R, 1938, Ja 28,21:3
Tappen, Walter B, 1942, O 15,24:2
Tappen, William J, 1956, Jl 29,64:7
Tappenden, Arthur K, 1949, D 26,29:3
Tappenden, Richard L, 1949, Mr 17,25:3
Tapper, Bono, 1938, Ap 6,23:6
Tapper, George J Mrs, 1954, Ap 17,13:6
Tapper, Thomas, 1958, F 25,27:1
Tapper, William R Mrs, 1963, Ag 25,82:8
Tappert, Carl R, 1950, Ap 4,29:3
Tappert, Ernst A, 1957, Jl 5,17:2
Tappert, Gustav, 1943, Mr 15,13:2
Tappert, John G, 1959, Je 17,35:3
Tappin, Charles, 1941, Ap 14,17:4
Tappin, Delmar Mrs, 1957, N 28,31:2
Tappin, Harold, 1957, My 6,29:4
Tappin, Huntington Mrs, 1959, Ja 6,33:4
Tappin, John F, 1917, Ap 24,11:4
Tappin, John L, 1964, D 26,17:4
Tappin, Lindsley, 1937, Ap 1,24:1
Tappins, James G, 1947, Ap 1,27:2
Tappouni, Ignatius Gabriel Cardinal, 1968, Ja 30,38:3
Tapscott, Kenneth A, 1939, Ag 23,21:3
Tapscott, Ralph H, 1967, Mr 31,37:3
Taqi, Mirza Mohammed, 1968, Je 23,73:2
Tara, Paul W, 1955, Ap 29,23:2
Tara, Peter, 1946, S 28,17:1
Tarachow, Sidney, 1965, D 6,37:4
Taracido, Joseph G, 1967, S 5,43:3
Taracouzio, Timothy A, 1958, Mr 5,31:4
Tarafa, Antonio, 1951, Ag 30,23:6
Tarafa, J M, 1932, Jl 25,15:3
Tarafa, Jaime S, 1941, Jl 14,13:4
Taran, Leo M, 1959, S 12,21:5
Taranger, Edward Mrs, 1954, O 5,15:4
Taranto, Thomas S, 1955, D 22,23:4
Tarantous, Harry A, 1955, D 19,27:3
Tarantous, Harry A Mrs, 1954, S 9,31:5
Tarasoff, Ivan, 1954, S 12,84:8
Tarasov, Alex P, 1958, My 22,29:5
Tarasov, Stepan N, 1955, S 9,23:4
Tarbell, Arthur W, 1946, N 26,29:3
Tarbell, Charles E Mrs, 1950, D 31,43:1
Tarbell, Edmund C, 1938, Ag 2,19:1
Tarbell, Esther McCullough, 1917, S 3,7:6
Tarbell, Farran S, 1947, D 28,40:1
Tarbell, Frank B Prof, 1920, D 5,22:4
Tarbell, G E, 1936, S 6,II,7:3
Tarbell, Gordon H, 1950, My 19,27:1
Tarbell, Harlan E, 1960, Je 17,31:3
Tarbell, Harlan Mrs, 1947, Ja 29,25:8
Tarbell, Harry S, 1944, Mr 28,19:5
Tarbell, Ida M, 1944, Ja 7,17:1
Tarbell, Martha, 1948, O 28,29:4
Tarbell, Sarah, 1953, S 17,29:4
Tarbell, William W, 1941, Mr 14,21:5
Tarbell, William W Mrs, 1946, Je 25,22:3
Tarbert, Arlie W, 1946, N 28,27:3
Tarbet, Grace B, 1949, Mr 1,25:5
Tarbill, John W, 1953, Je 3,31:3
Tarble, Albert Mrs (L Lowe), 1957, Je 25,29:3
Tarbox, Harry R, 1950, My 28,44:5
Tarbox, Roscoe D Sr, 1950, Mr 5,92:5
Tarbox, Russell L, 1955, Je 26,77:1
Tarbox, William, 1943, Jl 16,17:4
Tarbox, William H, 1937, F 16,23:4
Tarcher, Jack D (cor, S 7,41:2), 1960, S 6,33:6
Tarchiani, Alberto, 1964, D 1,41:4
Tarcov, Oscar, 1963, O 17,35:3
Tarde, Antoine, 1942, Ag 30,43:2
Tardella, Frank, 1956, S 19,37:1
Tardieu, Andre (por), 1945, S 18,23:1
Tardif, Joseph L Rev, 1937, S 21,25:4
Tardini, Domenico Cardinal (funl plans;trb, Jl 31,-19:5), 1961, Jl 30,1:7
Tardit, Michel, 1937, Mr 11,23:3
Tardov, Seymour S, 1952, F 26,27:1
Tareyle, Julia Mrs, 1943, N 22,20:3
Targ, William Mrs, 1965, F 8,25:4
Targett, Arthur B Jr, 1961, Mr 5,86:8
Tark, Marcus B, 1954, Ap 30,23:1
Tarkhanov, Mikhail, 1948, Ag 19,21:4
Tarkington, Booth, 1946, My 20,23:1
Tarkington, Booth Mrs, 1966, Ja 13,25:2
Tarkington, Booth Mrs (will filed), 1967, Ag 2,19:4
Tarkington, Elizabeth Booth Mrs, 1909, Ap 18,11:3
Tarkington, Laurel, 1923, Ap 14,13:5
Tarlau, Jacob, 1942, O 4,52:2
Tarle, Eugene, 1955, Ja 7,22:2
Tarleau, Lisa Y Mrs, 1952, O 10,25:2
Tarler, George C, 1945, D 28,15:2
Tarleski, John, 1939, S 3,8:2
Tarleton, J M, 1880, D 25,2:7
Tarlov, Harry A, 1957, Ap 20,17:6
Tarlow, Leo, 1953, My 8,25:2
Tarlowe, Meyer, 1966, Ja 19,41:2
Tarlowe, Nathan, 1952, S 20,15:1
Tarlton, Jere L, 1939, S 27,25:4
Tarn, Al, 1952, Mr 30,92:6
Tarnahan, William C Jr, 1943, Ja 23,13:2
Tarnavsky, Philemon, 1948, S 25,17:6
Tarnow, Harold B, 1958, Mr 17,29:3
Tarnow, Samuel A, 1958, My 22,29:4
Tarpey, John F, 1956, O 26,29:3
Tarpey, Leo A, 1967, S 26,47:4
Tarpey, Leo E Mrs, 1968, F 27,43:2
Tarpey, Patrick J, 1951, Je 10,92:4
Tarpey, Patrick Mrs, 1944, Ag 15,17:5
Tarpgaard, Andreas J, 1950, Je 5,23:3
Tarpgaard, Andreas J Mrs, 1947, Ja 5,53:2
Tarquini, Cardinal, 1874, F 15,5:3
Tarr, Carrie R Mrs, 1940, Ag 1,21:3
Tarr, D Sherman, 1939, Ap 29,17:6
Tarr, Edgar J, 1950, N 9,33:5
Tarr, Florence, 1951, My 24,35:3
Tarr, Frederick C, 1939, S 1,17:5
Tarr, Frederick H, 1944, My 14,46:4
Tarr, Harry M, 1952, Ag 14,23:2
Tarr, Horace G A Capt, 1922, Mr 3,13:5
Tarr, Kate S Mrs, 1939, My 15,17:5
Tarr, Katherine S Mrs (will), 1940, Je 25,26:2
Tarr, Mary R Mrs (will), 1941, O 5,40:6
Tarr, Ralph S Prof, 1912, Mr 22,9:5
Tarr, Robert B, 1958, N 16,89:2
Tarr, William A, 1939, Jl 29,15:4
Tarrant, Robert, 1943, N 14,57:2
Tarrant, Samuel E, 1943, Ag 3,19:4
Tarrant, Thomas A, 1940, S 19,23:3
Tarrant, William P, 1938, Mr 17,21:4
Tarrara, Paul L, 1955, Jl 30,17:5
Tarre, Sam, 1950, O 23,23:2
Tarrell, John, 1923, Ja 18,15:4
Tarrey, Franklin B, 1913, N 9,7:6
Tarry, J Holloway, 1965, Mr 4,31:2
Tarsches, Jacob E, 1952, D 24,17:2
Tarsey, B R, 1941, Ap 7,17:3
Tarshes, George, 1962, Jl 24,28:1
Tarshes, Max, 1951, F 26,23:4
Tarshes, Max Mrs, 1954, D 14,33:2
Tarshis, Elias, 1963, D 6,35:2
Tarshis, Ralph, 1966, S 3,23:6
Tarshish, Jacob, 1960, D 24,15:5
Tarskey, Benjamin J, 1950, N 18,15:6
Tart, Aaron B, 1951, O 23,29:4
Tartaglione, Salvatore, 1911, Ag 21,9:6
Tartakower, Xavier, 1956, F 7,31:5
Tartamella, John, 1966, Jl 14,35:5
Tartaud, Frits, 1947, Ja 2,27:4
Tarte, Eugene, 1958, Ja 11,17:2
Tarte, J Israel, 1907, D 19,9:5
Tarter, Lena Mrs, 1925, Je 22,15:6
Tarter, Solomon S, 1963, My 14,39:5
Tartiere, Raymond F, 1950, Ag 17,27:1
Tartikoff, George, 1959, Jl 23,27:2
Tartikoff, Louis, 1961, D 22,23:1
Tartikoff, Morris, 1958, Ag 27,29:1
Tartikoff, Morris Mrs, 1945, Ja 12,15:3
Tartikoff, Sidney, 1958, D 14,2:8
Tartter, Jean, 1950, Jl 13,25:5
Tartter, Jean Mrs, 1950, Jl 13,25:5
Tartufoli, Amor, 1963, My 12,86:2
Tarver, Malcolm C, 1960, Mr 7,29:3
Tarvin, James Pryor Judge, 1907, Ag 21,7:7
Tarvin, Pryor G, 1950, N 20,25:4
Tarvin, Samuel W, 1937, F 10,23:4
Tas, Emile, 1955, F 17,27:4
Tasch, William L, 1940, Mr 17,48:6
Taschereau, Louis A, 1952, Jl 7,21:6
Taschereau, Maurice, 1961, Mr 26,92:7
Taschman, Max, 1966, O 5,47:3
Tasco, Anthony, 1951, N 8,29:5
Tascon, Tulio Enrique, 1954, Ag 24,21:4
Tash, Earl R, 1958, Ap 23,33:2
Tashiro, Kanichiro Lt-Gen, 1937, Jl 17,6:3
Tashiro, Sohei, 1943, D 10,27:2
Tashjian, Armen H, 1947, Ap 5,19:6
Tashjian, Onnik H, 1956, Ap 12,84:7
Tashkovich, Gligor, 1963, Ag 23,25:2
Tashman, L, 1934, Mr 22,21:4
Tashman, Phil, 1949, Jl 3,27:1
Task, Morton E, 1963, D 6,36:2
Tasker, Arthur M, 1938, F 25,38:1
Tasker, Cyril, 1953, My 30,15:4
Tasker, Frank G, 1953, Ja 31,15:2
Tasker, Frederick H, 1942, D 18,27:3
Tasker, Joshua B, 1945, O 10,21:4
Tasker, Lawrence H, 1945, Jl 26,20:2
Tasker, Stephen P M, 1937, Jl 15,19:3
Taskey, Harry L, 1958, My 12,29:2
Tasman, Eric M, 1967, Ap 16,82:7
Tasman, George, 1949, O 2,80:8
Tasny, Fred W, 1925, Ja 26,17:3
Tassano, Julius, 1959, F 19,31:1
Tasse, Joseph C E, 1951, N 25,87:2
Tassel, Philip J, 1943, Ap 17,17:3
Tassin, Algernon de V (por), 1941, N 4,26:4
Tassin, Wirt du Vivier, 1915, N 3,13:6
Tassman, I S, 1966, Je 12,86:6
Tassone, Don A, 1943, O 14,21:3
Tata, Jamsetjee Prince, 1904, My 20,9:6
Tata, Paul M Sr, 1962, Ap 2,31:5
Tatam, Harold, 1948, Jl 9,19:2
Tatanis, Peter P, 1959, D 29,25:3
Tatarescu, Gheorghe, 1957, Ap 2,31:1
Tatarsky, Morris, 1939, Je 13,23:6
Tatarsky, Morris Mrs, 1945, D 3,21:4
Tataryan, Hovsep, 1960, F 7,84:3
Tate, A C Maj, 1903, Ja 1,9:5
Tate, Alfred O, 1945, Ap 6,16:2
Tate, Arthur F, 1950, O 19,31:6
Tate, Augustus C Mrs, 1909, Ap 24,7:3
Tate, Benjamin E, 1968, Mr 17,80:7
Tate, Caroline L, 1937, Ap 13,25:2
Tate, Charles H, 1949, Jl 15,19:5; 1955, Ja 2,77:2
Tate, Charles S Mrs, 1956, Je 2,20:1
Tate, Dale S, 1957, Jl 11,25:2
Tate, Dale S Mrs, 1955, S 12,25:5
Tate, Frank, 1939, Je 29,23:5
Tate, Geoffrey M, 1964, Jl 22,33:2
Tate, George E, 1961, Ag 25,25:1
Tate, George H H, 1953, D 28,21:4
Tate, George V, 1955, O 1,19:5
Tate, H Theodore, 1960, O 25,35:1
Tate, H Theodore Mrs, 1952, Jl 16,25:2
Tate, Harry J, 1937, F 21,II,10:3
Tate, Henry, 1909, N 8,7:6
Tate, Henry C, 1955, Ag 21,93:3
Tate, Henry Sir, 1899, D 6,8:6
Tate, Hugh M, 1938, My 30,11:4
Tate, J Waddy (por), 1938, Ja 12,21:4
Tate, Jack B, 1968, Mr 22,47:3
Tate, James L, 1949, Ap 16,15:5
Tate, James W Mrs (Lottie Collins), 1910, My 3,13:6
Tate, James William, 1922, F 6,13:3
Tate, Joe, 1938, N 29,23:5
Tate, John, 1953, Mr 11,29:1
Tate, John T, 1950, My 28,44:4
Tate, Joseph S, 1942, My 21,19:4
Tate, Luther H, 1966, Je 29,47:3
Tate, Magnus A, 1940, D 8,69:2
Tate, Mercer B Jr, 1943, O 22,17:2
Tate, Nelson D, 1963, N 28,39:1
Tate, P S, 1949, N 13,71:5
Tate, Ralph H Mrs, 1956, S 26,33:1
Tate, Robert A, 1949, Je 14,32:3
Tate, Robert W, 1964, N 29,86:2
Tate, Sam, 1938, O 12,27:4
Tate, Thomas Mrs, 1955, S 2,17:5
Tate, Ulysses Simpson, 1968, D 15,86:3
Tate, Walter I, 1958, Jl 16,29:4
Tate, Walter K, 1946, My 13,21:3
Tate, William (Bill), 1953, Ag 12,31:5
Tate, William E, 1949, F 25,23:4
Tate, William K Prof, 1917, F 8,13:5
Tatekawa, Yoshitsugu, 1945, S 12,25:6
Tatem, Henry R, 1938, Ap 15,19:1
Tatem, Percy C, 1951, Je 17,84:6
Taten, Harry E, 1967, Je 19,35:3
Tater, Alfreda H, 1963, Ap 13,19:6
Tatge, Marion Mrs, 1950, Ag 3,23:3
Tatham, Blake B, 1946, My 15,21:1
Tatham, Charles, 1939, S 25,19:2
Tatham, Cora L, 1943, O 7,23:6
Tatham, Sarah P Mrs, 1940, Ap 14,44:7
Tatham, William, 1913, S 13,11:3
Tatigian, John H, 1967, D 29,28:2
Tatje, Dietrich H, 1950, Ja 22,76:5
Tatler, Henry L, 1955, Ap 2,17:4
Tatlock, H Woodruff Mrs, 1952, Ag 11,15:5
Tatlock, Henry, 1942, N 1,53:2
Tatlock, Jessie M, 1961, S 9,19:6
Tatlock, John S P, 1948, Je 25,24:3
Tatlock, W Gerard, 1956, O 28,89:1
Tatman, Charles T, 1945, D 24,15:4
Tatnall, Commodore, 1871, Je 16,1:6
Tatnall, Edward C, 1954, Ja 1,23:5
Tatnall, George, 1957, Jl 12,21:4
Tatnall, Henry, 1939, Mr 2,21:3
Tatnall, Walter G Jr, 1949, Ja 17,19:2
Tatoian, Mardiros, 1939, Ap 10,17:6
Tator, Charles W, 1940, S 20,23:4
Tatro, Wynne J, 1950, Mr 27,23:2
Tatsch, Jacob H, 1939, Jl 19,19:3
Tattam, Catherine A L Mrs, 1946, Ja 21,23:1
Tattersall, Edmond S, 1942, O 28,23:5
Tattersall, Edmund, 1898, Mr 6,5:2
Tattersall, Frederick, 1949, Mr 30,25:5
Tattersall, Phil K, 1942, Ja 11,45:2
Tattersall, Richard, 1949, Ap 8,25:2
Tattersall, S Leslie, 1954, Je 13,88:3
Tattersall, Samuel H, 1910, Ja 31,7:7
Tattersall, Walter, 1943, O 7,23:2

Tattersall, William, 1914, O 23,11:4
Tatton, Harold, 1965, Ap 15,34:1
Tatu, Elizabeth A, 1944, My 9,19:4
Tatum, Art (funl, N 11,86:6), 1956, N 6,35:4
Tatum, Bethel B, 1943, Ja 14,21:1
Tatum, Charles A, 1920, N 15,15:5
Tatum, E, 1883, My 16,5:1
Tatum, Edward H Mrs, 1941, F 24,15:4
Tatum, Frederick C, 1967, Je 11,87:2
Tatum, Goose Jr, 1966, Ap 4,38:1
Tatum, James M (Jim),(funl, Jl 26,68:3), 1959, Jl 24, 25:1
Tatum, Jessica Mrs, 1956, Je 11,31:5
Tatum, John C, 1916, Ap 25,11:5
Tatum, John J, 1961, Mr 30,29:4
Tatum, Reese (Goose),(funl, Ja 21,23:2), 1967, Ja 19,31:3
Tatum, Robert G, 1964, Ja 28,31:4
Tatum, Walter A Sr Mrs, 1940, D 24,15:2
Tatum, Warde D Mrs, 1964, Ap 23,39:5
Tatzenspein, Alfred, 1956, My 22,42:6
Taub, Alex, 1964, My 30,17:1
Taub, Arthur, 1950, Mr 14,25:1
Taub, Billy, 1950, Jl 19,31:4
Taub, Harry, 1945, D 21,22:2
Taub, Herman, 1947, Mr 30,56:2
Taub, Isadore, 1954, Je 30,27:4
Taub, Israel Z, 1950, S 4,17:5
Taub, Jacob H Mrs, 1959, Mr 26,34:7
Taub, Jacob Mrs, 1945, My 11,19:2
Taub, Joseph, 1952, Je 4,27:2
Taub, Leon, 1940, S 12,25:5
Taub, Sam Mrs, 1955, Je 25,15:2
Taub, Samuel, 1951, Ag 3,21:5
Taub, Siegfried (por), 1946, My 2,21:4
Taube, F A Count, 1916, O 16,11:5
Taube, Harry R, 1945, Ja 14,39:2
Taube, Mortimer, 1965, S 7,39:4
Taubel, Clarence H, 1940, Mr 31,44:2
Taubele, Edward Mrs, 1949, Jl 2,15:1
Taubenberger, William J, 1948, D 19,76:7
Taubenhaus, Cantor J, 1941, Je 27,18:2
Taubenhaus, Jacob J Dr (por), 1937, D 15,25:4
Tauber, Joseph, 1963, D 4,47:5
Tauber, Maurice F Mrs, 1964, My 17,87:1
Tauber, Richard, 1948, Ja 9,21:3
Taubert, Mark, 1956, My 13,86:7
Taubert, Mark Mrs, 1948, Ja 25,56:7
Taubert, William H, 1953, Ag 9,77:2
Taubert, William H Mrs, 1948, My 8,15:4
Taubkin, Irvin S Mrs, 1963, My 21,37:5
Taubman, Herman P, 1960, S 16,28:5
Taubman, Leo, 1966, Jl 18,27:1
Tauch, Edward R Jr, 1954, Ag 6,33:3
Tauchnitz, C B von Baron, 1895, Ag 15,5:2
Tauchnitz, Christian von, 1921, Jl 9,9:6
Tauder, Elias, 1951, D 27,21:1
Tauffkirchen, Max E von, 1961, F 23,27:4
Taufflieb, Emile A, 1938, D 3,19:4
Taufflier, Emile Mrs, 1947, D 21,54:1
Taugher, William J, 1943, F 26,24:4
Taulane, Joseph J, 1952, Ag 11,15:4
Taulbee, Joseph F, 1938, My 1,II,7:2
Taunton, W D, 1938, Ag 6,13:4
Taupier, Wilfred, 1951, Mr 21,33:2
Tausch, J Franklin, 1950, Ja 22,78:1
Tauscher, Hans, 1941, S 6,17:6
Tausek, Maxwell, 1940, D 2,23:2
Tausig, Karl, 1968, D 2,47:3
Tausk, Alfred A, 1951, S 29,17:3
Tausky, Alex A, 1954, O 24,89:2
Tausky, Herman Rev, 1922, F 4,13:4
Taussig, Charles A, 1949, O 20,29:4
Taussig, Charles W, 1948, My 11,25:1
Taussig, Edward D Rear-Adm, 1921, Ja 30,22:4
Taussig, Frank W (por), 1940, N 12,23:1
Taussig, Fred J, 1943, Ag 23,15:4
Taussig, George W Mrs, 1946, Ja 1,28:3
Taussig, Harriet Holmes, 1924, My 23,19:4
Taussig, James E, 1949, O 4,27:1
Taussig, Joseph K, 1947, O 30,25:5
Taussig, Julius, 1957, Je 25,29:4
Taussig, Louis F, 1946, My 20,23:4
Taussig, Noah W Mrs, 1950, Je 5,23:5
Taussig, Oscar F, 1953, Ap 7,29:3
Taussig, Oscar F Mrs, 1953, Ap 7,29:3
Taussig, Sophia B Mrs, 1939, F 17,19:4
Taussig, William, 1913, Jl 11,9:5
Taussky, Hertha H, 1965, N 9,43:4
Tausz, Jenoe E, 1953, F 21,13:3
Tavarez, Eliza, 1960, Ap 5,37:4
Tavender, Walter J, 1938, F 24,19:4
Taveniere, Louis, 1951, Je 14,27:3
Taveniere, Louis Mrs, 1943, My 3,17:3
Tavenner, Clyde H, 1942, F 8,49:3
Tavenner, Frank S Jr, 1964, O 22,35:3
Tavenor, Thomas, 1937, Ag 4,19:6
Tavera, Charles J, 1939, N 1,23:2
Taverna, Emanuel, 1952, D 14,91:1
Taverne, Bernardus, 1944, Mr 11,13:5
Taverner, Percy A, 1947, My 11,63:3
Taves, Paul, 1912, Ja 18,13:5
Tavlin, Barney, 1959, F 14,21:2
Tavolacci, Frank M Sr, 1966, Jl 2,23:4
Tavorse, Joseph, 1939, Jl 18,6:6
Tawara, Magoichi, 1944, Je 19,19:6
Tawney, Guy A, 1947, Ja 7,27:5
Tawney, James A, 1919, Je 13,15:5
Tawney, Pliny O, 1963, D 22,34:1
Tawney, Richard H (trb lr, Ja 25,30:6), 1962, Ja 17, 33:4
Tawresey, John G, 1943, F 18,23:1
Tawresey, John G Mrs, 1940, S 24,23:2
Tawse, Herbert B, 1940, N 15,21:4
Tax, Abraham, 1946, N 3,61:1
Taxier, Al, 1960, D 18,84:1
Taxter, Claude, 1951, Ja 3,27:2
Taxter, Edward S, 1944, O 5,23:3
Taxter, Odell, 1948, Mr 2,23:5
Tay, Charles H Col, 1871, Ag 24,8:5
Tayler, Edward, 1959, D 18,29:4
Taylor, A, 1878, Jl 10,8:4
Taylor, A A, 1931, N 26,27:3
Taylor, A F, 1883, Je 29,5:3
Taylor, A Merritt, 1937, Je 8,25:3
Taylor, Aaron H Col, 1913, Ja 29,11:5
Taylor, Adeline A Mrs, 1938, Ja 29,15:5
Taylor, Agnes Chalmers Mrs, 1921, Ja 13,13:5
Taylor, Alan Mrs, 1961, Ag 23,33:5
Taylor, Albert B, 1946, Ja 24,21:5
Taylor, Albert D, 1951, Ja 9,30:3
Taylor, Albert H, 1961, D 13,43:2
Taylor, Albert H Mrs, 1961, D 14,43:2
Taylor, Albert S, 1956, F 14,29:2
Taylor, Alec, 1943, Ja 29,19:2
Taylor, Alex A, 1952, My 22,27:6
Taylor, Alex J, 1940, F 28,21:5
Taylor, Alex L, 1955, Mr 3,27:3
Taylor, Alex M, 1958, Ap 4,21:4
Taylor, Alexander, 1946, Je 7,19:2
Taylor, Alexander L Mrs, 1946, N 6,23:3
Taylor, Alexander O'D, 1910, Ap 11,7:4
Taylor, Alfred, 1947, My 5,23:4
Taylor, Alfred A, 1941, D 8,23:3
Taylor, Alfred E, 1945, N 2,19:1
Taylor, Alfred J T, 1945, Jl 21,11:5
Taylor, Alfred K Mrs, 1951, Je 15,23:2
Taylor, Alfred S (por), 1942, Ja 17,17:5
Taylor, Alfred T, 1944, Mr 29,21:1
Taylor, Alice B Mrs, 1942, Je 24,19:4
Taylor, Allen, 1942, Je 1,13:3
Taylor, Almon N, 1937, O 17,II,8:6
Taylor, Alonzo E, 1949, My 21,13:2
Taylor, Andrew M, 1945, My 15,19:2
Taylor, Andrew S, 1949, N 22,29:2
Taylor, Andrew Sir, 1937, D 6,27:5
Taylor, Anna, 1921, My 1,22:3
Taylor, Anna G Mrs, 1941, Mr 3,15:4
Taylor, Anna Goldsmith, 1921, Ag 18,11:6
Taylor, Anson W H, 1948, Ja 26,19:3
Taylor, Anthony W, 1956, S 18,35:1
Taylor, Archibald Dr, 1903, My 13,9:5
Taylor, Archibald W, 1953, S 26,17:5
Taylor, Arthur, 1951, Je 20,27:3
Taylor, Arthur M, 1951, N 16,25:3
Taylor, Arthur N, 1949, Je 16,29:4
Taylor, Arthur Noble, 1905, My 2,11:6
Taylor, Arthur S (por), 1937, O 31,II,11:2
Taylor, Arthur V, 1941, Ag 31,22:6
Taylor, Arthur V Mrs, 1955, Ap 29,23:4
Taylor, Ashby C, 1967, O 29,84:8
Taylor, Aubrey E, 1947, Ap 23,25:5
Taylor, Augusta B Mrs, 1941, Ap 9,25:6
Taylor, Austin C (funl, N 4,50:1), 1965, N 3,39:1
Taylor, B (funl), 1879, Mr 14,8:1
Taylor, B B Capt, 1883, Ap 23,5:4
Taylor, B C Rev, 1881, F 3,8:3
Taylor, B F (funl, De 23,1:2), 1878, D 20,1:7
Taylor, Barnard C Rev Dr, 1937, S 26,II,8:8
Taylor, Bayard Mrs, 1925, Jl 10,17:6
Taylor, Ben M, 1952, My 28,29:1
Taylor, Benjamin I, 1946, S 6,21:1
Taylor, Benjamin L, 1950, My 2,29:1
Taylor, Benjamin M, 1947, O 20,23:3
Taylor, Benjamin W Mrs, 1956, Jl 4,19:1
Taylor, Bert L Mrs, 1953, S 25,21:3
Taylor, Bert Leston, 1921, Mr 20,22:2
Taylor, Bertha M Mrs, 1941, F 18,23:2
Taylor, Bertram L, 1958, Mr 13,29:3
Taylor, Bismark H, 1951, S 11,29:1
Taylor, Blair, 1955, Ap 20,33:2
Taylor, Brice W, 1952, My 30,15:3
Taylor, Burt C, 1950, O 14,19:2
Taylor, C E Col, 1903, Ag 21,9:6
Taylor, C F, 1961, D 23,23:2
Taylor, C Marshall, 1957, N 12,37:3
Taylor, C R H, 1953, Ag 24,23:4
Taylor, C Stanley, 1944, Ag 17,17:2
Taylor, Carl, 1942, Mr 9,20:2
Taylor, Caroline P Mrs, 1939, Ag 9,17:4
Taylor, Carrie, 1951, S 20,31:4
Taylor, Carson, 1962, Ag 2,25:4
Taylor, Casimir, 1939, Je 13,23:4
Taylor, Cathleen, 1953, O 8,29:3
Taylor, Cecelia Mrs, 1925, Jl 4,11:6
Taylor, Cecil H, 1958, F 12,29:5
Taylor, Cecil R, 1941, Mr 12,21:5
Taylor, Charles, 1952, F 22,21:4
Taylor, Charles (Bud), 1962, Mr 10,21:1
Taylor, Charles A, 1942, Mr 22,48:8; 1944, Ja 28,17:2; 1966, O 19,38:6
Taylor, Charles B, 1940, S 22,49:1; 1961, Je 3,23:2
Taylor, Charles C, 1942, O 1,23:5
Taylor, Charles E, 1956, F 1,31:4; 1958, Ag 28,27:2
Taylor, Charles Edgar Rev, 1922, N 2,19:4
Taylor, Charles F, 1938, Ja 11,23:5; 1941, Ag 22,15:2; 1942, D 1,25:2
Taylor, Charles G, 1955, Ja 10,23:2; 1960, N 18,31:2
Taylor, Charles G Jr, 1953, Je 10,29:1
Taylor, Charles H (por), 1921, Je 23,17:3
Taylor, Charles H, 1941, Ag 19,21:1
Taylor, Charles H Gen, 1921, Je 20,13:2
Taylor, Charles Henry, 1968, N 23,47:3
Taylor, Charles I, 1937, D 5,II,9:3
Taylor, Charles L, 1922, F 4,13:4; 1944, Mr 31,21:3
Taylor, Charles M, 1955, Ap 1,27:5
Taylor, Charles Mrs, 1937, Mr 6,17:2
Taylor, Charles S, 1939, S 22,23:2; 1954, Mr 24,27:5
Taylor, Charles V, 1946, F 23,13:3
Taylor, Charles W Mrs, 1958, N 18,37:2
Taylor, Charles Z, 1937, Mr 4,23:4
Taylor, Clara F Mrs, 1954, S 1,27:2
Taylor, Clarence, 1938, Je 26,27:3
Taylor, Clarence B, 1943, O 12,27:5
Taylor, Clarence L, 1945, O 11,23:4
Taylor, Clifford F, 1940, Mr 23,13:4
Taylor, Clifton, 1960, Ja 15,31:1
Taylor, Clifton O Mrs, 1955, Je 10,25:1
Taylor, Clinton E, 1924, Ag 30,9:1
Taylor, Clinton T, 1950, Mr 9,29:1
Taylor, Clinton T Mrs, 1939, My 7,III,6:7
Taylor, Clyde B, 1958, Mr 25,33:1
Taylor, Colin C, 1938, Ap 2,15:5
Taylor, Conrad B, 1960, Je 19,88:4
Taylor, Constance Mrs, 1950, S 19,26:3
Taylor, Corydon F, 1962, Jl 30,23:4
Taylor, D F Mrs (M McDonald), 1965, O 22,44:1
Taylor, Daniel, 1940, D 4,27:6; 1945, My 1,23:3; 1946, Je 13,27:2
Taylor, Daniel A, 1937, D 19,II,8:8
Taylor, Daniel M Col, 1907, Mr 27,9:7
Taylor, Daniel Mrs, 1940, F 6,21:3
Taylor, David, 1923, Ag 23,15:4; 1965, Jl 2,29:4
Taylor, David A, 1945, Ja 3,17:4
Taylor, David C, 1941, N 8,19:3
Taylor, David F, 1952, N 26,23:2
Taylor, David H, 1961, D 29,24:7
Taylor, David W (por), 1940, Jl 29,13:1
Taylor, Deacon R, 1951, Je 27,29:3
Taylor, Deems (funl plans, Jl 5,27:2), 1966, Jl 4,1:1
Taylor, Dennis, 1962, Je 3,V,1:5
Taylor, Dixon C, 1951, Je 21,27:2
Taylor, Dodge, 1950, My 15,21:6
Taylor, Don, 1965, Ja 7,18:4
Taylor, Donald B, 1948, Ja 15,23:3
Taylor, Donald F, 1957, F 3,76:8
Taylor, Donald S, 1962, Ap 28,25:4
Taylor, Donald W, 1955, D 26,19:2
Taylor, Dorr K, 1950, Ag 1,23:3
Taylor, Douglas, 1912, S 13,9:6
Taylor, Duncan A, 1948, Ap 1,25:5
Taylor, Duncan W, 1955, D 20,31:4
Taylor, E E L Rev, 1874, Ag 19,1:5
Taylor, E Leland, 1948, F 17,25:5
Taylor, Earl A, 1965, N 19,39:3
Taylor, Earl B, 1946, N 19,31:4
Taylor, Earl S, 1954, My 26,29:4
Taylor, Ed L, 1944, F 21,15:5
Taylor, Edith, 1946, N 27,25:2
Taylor, Edith H Mrs, 1943, S 23,21:3
Taylor, Edith V Mrs, 1955, Ja 24,23:5
Taylor, Edmund B, 1947, Ag 29,17:1
Taylor, Edmund C, 1956, Mr 10,17:2
Taylor, Edward, 1903, Ag 23,1:5; 1911, D 25,7:5; 1950, F 19,76:1; 1954, S 21,27:3
Taylor, Edward C, 1940, Je 25,23:3
Taylor, Edward D Mrs, 1943, D 24,13:5
Taylor, Edward E, 1947, Mr 12,25:3
Taylor, Edward G, 1945, S 21,21:2
Taylor, Edward G W, 1962, F 6,35:1
Taylor, Edward H, 1944, S 4,19:2; 1965, O 30,35:1
Taylor, Edward I, 1958, Ap 18,23:5
Taylor, Edward J Mrs, 1945, Ag 8,23:4
Taylor, Edward L, 1943, My 18,23:4; 1955, My 30, 13:4
Taylor, Edward M, 1938, Ja 19,23:1
Taylor, Edward T, 1941, S 4,21:1
Taylor, Edwin C Mrs, 1948, Je 18,23:3
Taylor, Edwin S, 1956, Jl 4,19:1
Taylor, Edyth E, 1953, Ja 12,27:4
Taylor, Elbert J, 1955, Ja 25,25:2
Taylor, Elisha E L, 1961, Ja 16,27:4
Taylor, Elizabeth B, 1912, My 14,11:4; 1952, O 11, 19:4
Taylor, Ellery K, 1954, Jl 27,21:4
Taylor, Elliott, 1953, D 27,60:6
Taylor, Ellis W, 1951, Ja 22,17:4
Taylor, Elmer Z, 1949, My 23,23:3
Taylor, Emerson, 1913, Ap 9,9:4

Taylor, Emily, 1943, My 16,42:6
Taylor, Emily D, 1952, Je 20,23:5
Taylor, Emma G Mrs, 1941, My 13,23:4
Taylor, Emma L, 1941, Jl 18,19:6
Taylor, Ernest E, 1955, Ag 17,27:5
Taylor, Ernest Mrs, 1949, My 29,36:6
Taylor, Erwin A, 1950, Ja 16,26:3
Taylor, Estelle, 1958, Ap 16,33:1
Taylor, Estes P, 1945, N 25,48:4
Taylor, Ethel C (por, Jl 19,15:6), 1937, Jl 18,II,7:1
Taylor, Eunice C Mrs, 1942, My 22,21:6
Taylor, Evan, 1963, Ja 17,8:7
Taylor, Everitt K, 1952, Mr 22,13:6
Taylor, Ezra S, 1963, Jl 16,21:3
Taylor, F, 1928, F 26,II,7:1
Taylor, F Carroll, 1949, D 21,29:1
Taylor, F G, 1940, Ja 3,21:1
Taylor, F M, 1932, Ag 9,17:1
Taylor, F W Bp, 1903, Ap 28,9:5
Taylor, F W Howard, 1943, Jl 4,20:2
Taylor, Fannie K, 1949, O 7,31:3
Taylor, Father (funl, Ap 8,1:4), 1871, Ap 6,4:2
Taylor, Fenton (por), 1948, My 27,25:3
Taylor, Fielding Jr, 1965, F 25,31:1
Taylor, Fielding L (por), 1942, Je 23,19:4
Taylor, Fielding L Mrs, 1959, Ap 30,31:2
Taylor, Floyd, 1951, Ag 25,11:1
Taylor, Floyd P, 1952, Ag 16,16:4
Taylor, Floyd T, 1943, Ja 10,50:1
Taylor, Frances L Mrs, 1941, O 20,17:5
Taylor, Francis, 1916, O 3,11:4
Taylor, Francis A Jr, 1939, F 20,17:1
Taylor, Francis B, 1940, My 27,19:5
Taylor, Francis E, 1943, N 23,25:2
Taylor, Francis H, 1953, Ja 15,27:1; 1957, N 23,19:4
Taylor, Francis H L, 1959, N 1,42:1
Taylor, Francis H L Mrs, 1959, N 1,42:1
Taylor, Francis R, 1947, Mr 14,23:4
Taylor, Frank A, 1947, O 9,25:2
Taylor, Frank Brig-Gen, 1920, My 22,15:3
Taylor, Frank F, 1959, N 6,29:4
Taylor, Frank H, 1950, N 23,35:6
Taylor, Frank H Mrs, 1959, Ja 25,92:3
Taylor, Frank J, 1958, My 8,29:1
Taylor, Frank L, 1944, Ja 17,19:3; 1962, Ag 29,29:3
Taylor, Frank M, 1938, N 15,23:5; 1958, O 24,33:2
Taylor, Frank M Mrs (B Davenport), 1957, Jl 31, 23:4
Taylor, Frank P, 1948, S 16,29:3
Taylor, Frank W, 1937, Ag 16,19:4; 1961, Ja 17,37:3
Taylor, Frank W Jr Mrs, 1938, Je 6,17:3
Taylor, Franklin, 1948, My 1,15:3
Taylor, Franklin Mrs, 1961, Jl 19,29:4
Taylor, Franklin V, 1960, Mr 16,37:5
Taylor, Fred C, 1968, Ag 26,39:4
Taylor, Fred G, 1950, F 17,23:2
Taylor, Fred S, 1943, Je 6,42:5
Taylor, Frederic W, 1944, Ja 15,13:3
Taylor, Frederick A, 1944, Jl 26,19:2
Taylor, Frederick A Mrs, 1955, Ap 30,17:5
Taylor, Frederick B, 1950, Je 30,23:3
Taylor, Frederick C (Col Stoopnagle), 1950, My 30, 17:1
Taylor, Frederick C, 1963, D 24,17:2
Taylor, Frederick E, 1959, F 21,21:4
Taylor, Frederick W, 1945, Ag 17,17:3; 1963, Mr 12, 7:7
Taylor, Frederick Winslow, 1915, Mr 22,9:5
Taylor, Freeman P, 1953, Ja 7,31:1
Taylor, G F, 1881, Je 17,4:7
Taylor, G Herbert, 1943, Ag 26,17:2; 1946, Jl 24,27:5
Taylor, G W, 1879, Mr 25,8:4
Taylor, G W Capt, 1879, S 20,2:5
Taylor, Gardner W, 1949, N 2,12:1
Taylor, Gardner W Mrs, 1953, O 7,29:2
Taylor, Garner W, 1965, F 27,25:3
Taylor, George, 1871, N 15,1:6; 1881, Ja 18,5:4; 1939, My 11,25:4
Taylor, George A, 1909, Mr 23,9:6; 1925, Ag 4,19:5; 1939, D 22,19:3
Taylor, George A Mrs, 1951, Mr 18,88:3
Taylor, George B, 1905, N 3,9:5; 1942, Mr 10,19:3; 1952, N 6,29:5; 1968, D 31,27:1
Taylor, George Boardman Rev Dr, 1907, O 5,11:6
Taylor, George C (funl, S 21,9:4), 1907, S 18,9:6
Taylor, George Chadbourne (funl, N 21,19:4), 1923, N 19,15:3
Taylor, George D, 1938, S 28,25:3; 1945, Je 30,17:5
Taylor, George Dr, 1867, Ag 10,6:2
Taylor, George F, 1947, My 15,25:2; 1948, O 30,15:1; 1958, O 17,30:1
Taylor, George G, 1954, Ag 24,17:5
Taylor, George H, 1922, Je 13,19:6; 1945, O 18,23:5; 1950, O 2,23:4; 1951, D 23,23:1; 1961, Ja 21,21:5
Taylor, George H Jr, 1958, N 19,37:3
Taylor, George H Jr Mrs, 1942, Je 19,23:5
Taylor, George H Mrs, 1942, Jl 11,13:2
Taylor, George J, 1911, O 29,II,15:5; 1952, My 17,19:3
Taylor, George L, 1950, O 2,23:5; 1952, Ap 12,11:3
Taylor, George L Mrs, 1924, S 6,11:7
Taylor, George M, 1937, O 22,24:2; 1959, S 3,27:5
Taylor, George M Capt, 1909, Ap 2,9:6
Taylor, George R, 1949, Ja 18,23:2
Taylor, George Stetson, 1915, O 21,11:5
Taylor, George T, 1962, F 13,35:3
Taylor, George V, 1945, Ap 3,19:4
Taylor, George Vallance Capt, 1916, N 24,13:4
Taylor, George W, 1951, Ag 18,11:1; 1958, F 26,27:4
Taylor, George W Col, 1916, Mr 2,11:5
Taylor, George W Mrs, 1944, F 27,37:1; 1945, Je 11, 15:3
Taylor, Gerald Mrs, 1940, Mr 5,24:4
Taylor, Gladys Axman, 1968, F 1,37:4
Taylor, Gordon, 1966, D 17,33:2
Taylor, Gove S, 1951, Je 27,29:4
Taylor, Grace A, 1963, N 6,41:4
Taylor, Grace D, 1948, F 12,24:3
Taylor, Grace L Mrs, 1940, Ap 9,24:4
Taylor, Grace T, 1949, F 7,19:6
Taylor, Graham, 1938, S 27,21:5
Taylor, Graham Mrs, 1918, Jl 23,13:5
Taylor, Graham R (por), 1942, Ag 31,17:3
Taylor, H (see also My 21), 1878, My 23,8:5
Taylor, H B (Pete), 1950, F 25,17:6
Taylor, H Birchard, 1959, D 31,21:3
Taylor, H Bruce, 1943, Ag 8,37:2
Taylor, H Furness Jr, 1963, Ap 16,35:1
Taylor, H G, 1928, Jl 9,19:6
Taylor, H J, 1903, S 9,7:6
Taylor, H P, 1903, My 14,9:7
Taylor, H S, 1884, My 22,5:2
Taylor, H Williams, 1959, S 12,21:5
Taylor, Hannis, 1922, D 27,17:3
Taylor, Harden F, 1966, F 5,29:5
Taylor, Harold E, 1960, N 24,29:2
Taylor, Harold M Sr, 1959, My 19,33:1
Taylor, Harriet, 1938, F 11,23:1
Taylor, Harris, 1952, Jl 15,21:2
Taylor, Harry, 1952, My 29,27:4
Taylor, Harry Andrew, 1925, F 18,19:4
Taylor, Harry E, 1948, Ag 6,17:6
Taylor, Harry G (por), 1938, Ag 12,17:4
Taylor, Harry L, 1955, Jl 13,25:3
Taylor, Harry M, 1949, S 2,17:2; 1957, Mr 3,85:1
Taylor, Harry N, 1937, My 15,19:6
Taylor, Harry N Mrs, 1956, Jl 21,15:2
Taylor, Harry R, 1951, S 9,90:4
Taylor, Harry Sr, 1956, F 27,23:4
Taylor, Harry W, 1939, F 9,21:1
Taylor, Hartley, 1951, S 22,17:2
Taylor, Helen C Mrs, 1937, Ap 4,II,11:1
Taylor, Helen D, 1953, D 10,47:3
Taylor, Henry, 1937, D 31,15:1
Taylor, Henry A C, 1921, My 29,22:3
Taylor, Henry C, 1966, F 3,31:4
Taylor, Henry E, 1938, Ap 4,17:4
Taylor, Henry Fitch, 1925, S 12,15:6
Taylor, Henry L, 1939, Ag 20,32:3
Taylor, Henry O (will, Ap 19,9:7),(por), 1941, Ap 14,17:1
Taylor, Henry O Mrs, 1939, Mr 7,21:3
Taylor, Henry R, 1925, D 6,13:1
Taylor, Henry W, 1943, O 5,25:2; 1958, Jl 15,25:1
Taylor, Henry W Mrs, 1949, Je 3,25:2
Taylor, Herbert, 1948, F 17,25:4
Taylor, Herbert A (por), 1948, Je 29,23:6
Taylor, Herbert A G, 1954, D 9,33:4
Taylor, Herbert B, 1945, Jl 31,19:4
Taylor, Herbert C, 1952, Je 7,19:4
Taylor, Herbert E, 1940, Ja 31,19:3
Taylor, Herbert F, 1968, Ap 27,39:5
Taylor, Herbert J, 1959, O 25,86:5
Taylor, Herbert K, 1957, D 17,35:2
Taylor, Herbert Mrs, 1967, My 23,47:3
Taylor, Herbert N, 1961, S 5,35:2
Taylor, Herbert S Mrs, 1946, Ag 5,21:3
Taylor, Herman C, 1940, Ap 29,15:5
Taylor, Hiram W, 1960, F 16,37:2
Taylor, Hobart, 1937, S 23,27:1
Taylor, Holman, 1947, D 6,15:4
Taylor, Horace A, 1910, Ag 6,7:5; 1946, Mr 28,25:5
Taylor, Horace Clifton Dr, 1903, D 22,9:5
Taylor, Horace F, 1950, O 7,19:3
Taylor, Horace J, 1954, Je 27,69:2
Taylor, Horace Mrs, 1957, D 1,88:2
Taylor, Horace N Mrs, 1957, Ja 11,23:4
Taylor, Howard, 1920, N 27,13:6
Taylor, Howard B Jr, 1948, N 24,23:4
Taylor, Howard C, 1949, Mr 28,21:2; 1958, Ag 16,17:3
Taylor, Howard D, 1941, Je 13,19:3
Taylor, Howard F, 1942, Ap 27,15:3; 1962, Ja 17,33:4
Taylor, Howard P, 1916, Jl 8,9:7
Taylor, Hudson, 1906, N 18,7:5
Taylor, Hugh, 1952, Ja 10,29:4
Taylor, Hugh A, 1942, N 24,25:2
Taylor, Hugh K, 1939, F 26,39:3
Taylor, I Baron, 1879, S 7,2:5
Taylor, Ida, 1946, Ap 6,17:6
Taylor, Irene F, 1951, My 24,35:3
Taylor, Irene Mrs, 1960, F 22,38:8
Taylor, Irving G Mrs, 1953, Ap 21,27:1
Taylor, Irving H (por), 1949, Je 10,28:4
Taylor, Irving K, 1939, Mr 25,15:4
Taylor, Irving M, 1938, S 23,27:2
Taylor, Irwin S, 1939, Ap 6,25:3
Taylor, Isaac, 1944, My 3,19:5
Taylor, Ivon B, 1943, S 21,23:3
Taylor, J, 1887, Jl 27,1:5
Taylor, J A, 1903, Ag 21,9:6
Taylor, J Alfred Sr, 1956, Je 10,88:6
Taylor, J Blyth, 1968, Mr 27,47:2
Taylor, J Coard (por), 1946, Je 26,25:3
Taylor, J D, 1932, N 26,15:4
Taylor, J E, 1901, Je 23,3:4
Taylor, J Gurney, 1956, D 2,87:2
Taylor, J H Gen, 1885, Mr 15,2:3
Taylor, J Hibberd, 1944, Ag 25,13:5
Taylor, J Hibberd Mrs, 1959, Ap 23,31:5
Taylor, J Lanning, 1940, D 6,27:2
Taylor, J M, 1931, O 5,21:3
Taylor, J McL Col, 1875, N 22,4:7
Taylor, J Richard, 1957, Je 20,29:5
Taylor, J T Dr, 1878, O 1,5:5
Taylor, J W, 1864, Ap 3,1:3; 1883, Mr 2,5:2
Taylor, J Will, 1939, N 15,23:3
Taylor, Jackson, 1946, Ja 22,27:3; 1966, Ag 21,93:1
Taylor, Jackson Q, 1948, Ap 11,72:1
Taylor, Jacob B, 1962, Mr 15,35:4
Taylor, Jacob H, 1949, Ja 2,63:5
Taylor, James A, 1940, Ag 3,15:4
Taylor, James B (funl, Ag 26,1:4), 1870, Ag 24,4:7
Taylor, James B, 1943, F 18,23:2; 1954, Ag 26,27:3; 1956, Mr 27,35:3
Taylor, James C, 1904, F 1,7:3
Taylor, James D, 1939, My 4,23:2
Taylor, James D Mrs, 1957, Ja 6,88:2
Taylor, James F, 1922, Jl 1,13:7
Taylor, James H, 1944, Ap 18,21:6; 1957, Ag 8,23:2
Taylor, James Henry Rev, 1907, O 15,9:4
Taylor, James J, 1940, S 18,23:1
Taylor, James L, 1917, O 4,13:5; 1954, F 9,27:4
Taylor, James L Mrs, 1947, N 18,29:1
Taylor, James Loockerman Col, 1925, Jl 17,15:5
Taylor, James Monroe Rev Dr, 1916, D 20,13:3
Taylor, James R, 1949, D 20,31:3
Taylor, James R 2d, 1957, My 14,35:3
Taylor, James S, 1948, Ag 3,25:5
Taylor, James S Capt, 1937, S 17,25:2
Taylor, James S Com, 1922, Ag 28,11:6
Taylor, James Spottiswoode Mrs, 1922, Ag 31,15:3
Taylor, James Wilson, 1925, Ja 22,19:4
Taylor, Jane L Mrs, 1942, Ag 5,19:2
Taylor, Jaquelin P, 1950, S 2,15:5
Taylor, Jay, 1903, Ap 24,9:6
Taylor, Jay C, 1952, Ag 17,76:4
Taylor, Jean P, 1951, Je 27,29:3
Taylor, Jerome Mrs, 1949, Jl 25,15:5
Taylor, Jimmy (Bud), 1952, O 6,31:7
Taylor, John, 1943, F 12,19:5; 1948, Ja 30,23:3; 1953, Je 23,29:3
Taylor, John A, 1944, O 23,19:4; 1947, Ag 14,23:2; 1949, N 24,31:1
Taylor, John A Mrs, 1946, Ag 2,19:6
Taylor, John B, 1939, Mr 16,23:5; 1963, D 21,23:3
Taylor, John B Dr, 1937, Ja 23,18:8
Taylor, John C, 1958, O 18,21:6; 1967, Mr 25,23:3
Taylor, John C Jr, 1961, Mr 8,33:2
Taylor, John C R, 1937, Ap 27,23:5
Taylor, John D Mrs, 1952, Ap 16,27:2
Taylor, John E, 1952, Ag 29,23:2
Taylor, John E M, 1962, F 4,82:3
Taylor, John E Mrs, 1948, Jl 28,23:5
Taylor, John Edwards, 1914, N 24,13:6
Taylor, John H, 1948, My 4,26:3; 1948, Ag 18,25:2; 1955, O 21,27:1; 1963, F 11,7:5
Taylor, John H Jr, 1940, F 1,21:1
Taylor, John Henry, 1911, F 28,11:4
Taylor, John I, 1938, Ja 27,21:6
Taylor, John I Mrs, 1950, Mr 26,94:4
Taylor, John J, 1950, Ap 4,29:2; 1954, Ap 27,29:3
Taylor, John K, 1949, Je 19,68:1
Taylor, John L, 1942, D 8,26:2; 1946, Mr 28,25:1
Taylor, John M, 1918, N 8,15:2; 1924, Ap 2,19:5; 1951, S 15,15:5; 1954, Ja 27,27:1; 1958, Mr 8,17:6
Taylor, John Mrs, 1953, Mr 26,31:5
Taylor, John P Gen, 1914, Je 30,11:5
Taylor, John P Mrs, 1946, Je 21,23:6
Taylor, John Phelps, 1915, S 14,11:5
Taylor, John R, 1947, D 29,17:2; 1960, S 21,37:4
Taylor, John T, 1940, F 6,22:2; 1960, Ag 15,23:3; 1965, My 22,31:4
Taylor, John V, 1946, My 4,15:5
Taylor, John W, 1938, O 13,23:2; 1960, D 7,43:4
Taylor, John W Mrs, 1960, N 19,21:4
Taylor, Jonathan, 1883, Ag 12,9:2
Taylor, Joseph, 1941, Je 12,23:5
Taylor, Joseph E, 1937, Ap 13,25:5; 1941, Mr 3,15:1 1948, Mr 14,72:3
Taylor, Joseph F, 1952, D 2,36:4; 1956, Je 14,33:4; 1956, Jl 1,57:1; 1963, My 8,36:4
Taylor, Joseph H, 1949, Ja 27,23:3; 1950, N 5,92:5
Taylor, Joseph Henry, 1908, Ap 10,9:5
Taylor, Joseph I, 1944, Ja 10,17:5
Taylor, Joseph J, 1943, My 25,23:5; 1947, Ap 8,27:4
Taylor, Joseph P, 1949, S 28,27:6
Taylor, Joseph P Brig-Gen, 1864, Jl 3,3:3
Taylor, Joseph R, 1944, Mr 31,21:1; 1945, Ja 19,19: 1955, Ag 14,81:3; 1961, Ap 15,21:5
Taylor, Joseph S Mrs, 1946, Mr 26,29:2

Taylor, Joshua C, 1946, Ja 15,23:2
Taylor, Julia I Mrs (will), 1939, Mr 12,III,5:3
Taylor, K Allan, 1967, Ap 15,31:3
Taylor, Kathleen D, 1949, N 6,93:1
Taylor, Kenneth, 1963, Mr 5,16:1
Taylor, Kenneth L, 1941, Je 5,24:4
Taylor, Kenneth Mrs, 1960, Je 30,29:4
Taylor, Kimber C, 1947, Je 19,21:2
Taylor, Knox, 1922, Ap 5,17:4
Taylor, L D, 1946, Je 5,23:2
Taylor, Lady (Mrs Hugh S), 1958, Jl 8,28:1
Taylor, Larry R Sr, 1955, Jl 20,27:1
Taylor, Laura K Mrs, 1939, O 1,53:2
Taylor, Laurette, 1946, D 8,78:2
Taylor, Lee H Mrs, 1956, F 9,31:5
Taylor, Lee H Sr, 1948, F 24,25:4
Taylor, Leila, 1923, Jl 2,15:6
Taylor, Leland R, 1967, D 23,23:4
Taylor, Leon R, 1924, Ap 3,21:5
Taylor, Leroy A, 1946, O 28,27:4
Taylor, Leslie A, 1952, Mr 13,29:3
Taylor, Leslie R, 1951, Ja 29,19:2
Taylor, Lewis H, 1940, Ap 1,19:4
Taylor, Lewis Mrs, 1950, Ag 22,27:5
Taylor, Lewis W, 1947, Jl 19,13:3
Taylor, Livingston L, 1941, F 9,48:2
Taylor, Lloyd, 1944, Ja 9,43:2
Taylor, Lloyd K Mrs, 1946, N 23,15:5
Taylor, Loren A, 1950, N 23,35:5
Taylor, Louis, 1958, S 13,19:4
Taylor, Louis H, 1954, D 10,28:5; 1960, N 4,33:4
Taylor, Louise, 1965, Mr 21,86:2
Taylor, Louise C, 1947, Mr 23,60:7; 1956, Ap 17,31:2
Taylor, Lovell A, 1946, Ap 13,17:5
Taylor, Luther, 1958, Ag 24,86:8
Taylor, M, 1928, My 27,26:1
Taylor, M Corwin, 1942, O 11,56:4
Taylor, Mahlon B, 1951, D 18,31:1
Taylor, Malcolm, 1961, Jl 14,23:4
Taylor, Marcus Barnes Rev Dr, 1919, D 5,15:2
Taylor, Margaret I Mrs, 1942, Ja 12,15:3
Taylor, Marie, 1947, D 25,21:1
Taylor, Marion S (por), 1942, F 2,16:4
Taylor, Mark W Mrs, 1948, Je 17,25:5
Taylor, Marriott S Mrs, 1958, Je 3,31:2
Taylor, Marsh N, 1953, Ag 16,76:5
Taylor, Marshall, 1948, Ag 29,60:1
Taylor, Marshall W, 1937, Je 1,23:6
Taylor, Martin, 1880, Ap 4,2:6
Taylor, Mary (Mrs D Montgomery), 1957, Ag 19, 19:6
Taylor, Mary A Mrs, 1941, My 27,23:5
Taylor, Mary I, 1938, Ag 29,13:4
Taylor, Mary M Mrs, 1909, Mr 29,7:4; 1938, S 7,25:1
Taylor, Matt, 1966, S 12,45:5
Taylor, Matthew, 1940, S 7,1:2
Taylor, Matthew Ambrose Msgr (funl, Ag 23,13:5), 1914, Ag 22,7:4
Taylor, Matthew H, 1923, Mr 9,15:4
Taylor, Max, 1957, O 10,33:3
Taylor, Merritt H Sr, 1963, Mr 18,15:2
Taylor, Mervyn R, 1953, My 2,15:3
Taylor, Millard F, 1949, F 25,24:3
Taylor, Minnie F, 1938, Je 8,23:5
Taylor, Minnie L, 1947, F 12,25:6
Taylor, Miriam L, 1957, S 7,19:4
Taylor, Montgomery M, 1952, O 22,27:3
Taylor, Mort F, 1903, Jl 20,2:4
Taylor, Mortimer S, 1944, Ja 7,17:5
Taylor, Moseley, 1952, F 26,27:5
Taylor, Moses, 1882, My 24,10:1
Taylor, Myron C (funl, My 10,86:4), 1959, My 7,1:8
Taylor, Myron C Mrs, 1958, D 29,15:6
Taylor, N G, 1904, Ja 30,9:5
Taylor, Nathan S, 1942, Ja 1,25:3
Taylor, Nelson E Jr, 1960, N 13,88:2
Taylor, Noble, 1921, Mr 30,13:6
Taylor, Norman, 1967, N 9,47:4
Taylor, O S, 1885, Ap 27,5:2
Taylor, Olin P Mrs, 1948, Mr 6,13:4
Taylor, Oliver C, 1950, Ag 27,88:8
Taylor, Oliver F, 1954, D 29,23:4
Taylor, Ora A, 1961, Mr 23,33:3
Taylor, Otis J, 1947, Je 29,48:1
Taylor, Otto F, 1964, N 26,33:3
Taylor, P E, 1926, D 28,19:3
Taylor, Paul F, 1949, Jl 6,27:3
Taylor, Paul H, 1943, Ag 10,19:2
Taylor, Paul S Mrs (D Lange), 1965, O 14,47:2
Taylor, Percy H, 1942, Ag 8,11:2
Taylor, Percy L, 1959, My 13,37:1
Taylor, Permelia Mrs, 1940, D 16,23:4
Taylor, Peter G, 1871, D 23,8:4
Taylor, Phil, 1959, N 1,85:3
Taylor, Presley M Mrs, 1941, F 10,20:2
Taylor, Quintard, 1951, Ag 31,15:2
Taylor, R E Lee, 1952, Je 24,29:3
Taylor, R L (see also F 14), 1878, F 15,3:3
Taylor, R W, 1878, F 26,1:2
Taylor, Ralph C Mrs, 1947, Ap 23,25:4
Taylor, Ralph F, 1968, Jl 6,21:3
Taylor, Ralph G, 1948, N 12,23:4
Taylor, Ralph L Capt, 1917, Ag 6,9:2
Taylor, Randolph S, 1956, N 25,88:5
Taylor, Raymond G, 1958, Jl 1,31:1
Taylor, Raymond R, 1952, D 12,29:5
Taylor, Reese H, 1962, Je 23,23:4
Taylor, Reuben J, 1906, My 31,1:5
Taylor, Rex H, 1944, Ag 6,37:4
Taylor, Richard, 1879, Ap 13,2:3
Taylor, Richard A, 1950, Jl 11,31:4
Taylor, Richard M, 1965, Ja 18,35:3
Taylor, Richard T Mrs, 1944, Jl 11,15:5
Taylor, Richard V (por), 1939, D 23,15:4
Taylor, Richard W, 1947, Ap 13,60:3
Taylor, Robert, 1911, Jl 3,7:5; 1944, Jl 6,15:5; 1951, My 31,27:4
Taylor, Robert B, 1948, Ja 29,23:1
Taylor, Robert C, 1942, O 30,19:5; 1955, Jl 12,25:4
Taylor, Robert Darius Lt-Com, 1923, My 9,19:4
Taylor, Robert E, 1948, Ag 17,21:4; 1949, Ja 29,13:2
Taylor, Robert J, 1943, F 1,15:3; 1954, Jl 20,19:5; 1955, O 30,89:1
Taylor, Robert J Mrs, 1959, D 1,39:1
Taylor, Robert L, 1945, F 11,40:6
Taylor, Robert L Sr Mrs, 1965, N 26,37:3
Taylor, Robert Longley Dr, 1923, My 28,15:4
Taylor, Robert Love (funl, Ap 6,11:6), 1912, Ap 2, 12:5
Taylor, Robert R, 1940, Ag 6,20:3; 1957, Mr 2,21:4
Taylor, Robert W, 1908, Ja 7,7:5
Taylor, Roland L, 1943, Je 24,21:4
Taylor, Rose A Mrs, 1940, Mr 6,23:3
Taylor, Rose F Mrs, 1962, Ag 14,31:2
Taylor, Rose T Mrs, 1940, O 23,23:5
Taylor, Roy J, 1954, Jl 10,13:3
Taylor, Roy M, 1959, F 16,29:1
Taylor, Ruth (Mrs E Klein), 1961, Ja 22,85:1
Taylor, Ruth I, 1961, Ap 29,23:1
Taylor, S, 1926, My 20,25:4
Taylor, S Frederic, 1941, N 27,23:4
Taylor, S Gregory, 1948, F 24,26:3
Taylor, S W S Hall, 1946, Ap 24,25:4
Taylor, Sadie M, 1954, Mr 7,90:4
Taylor, Sam, 1958, Mr 8,17:3
Taylor, Samuel A, 1950, Ag 21,19:5
Taylor, Samuel J Mrs, 1940, Ag 20,19:5
Taylor, Samuel M, 1921, S 14,19:5
Taylor, Samuel Priestly (funl), 1875, Jl 19,4:6
Taylor, Samuel S, 1939, Ja 20,19:4
Taylor, Samuel W, 1949, Ag 4,23:6; 1955, F 13,87:1
Taylor, Sarah E, 1954, O 6,25:4
Taylor, Sarah Wood Mrs, 1941, Mr 7,21:4
Taylor, Sidney W (Bro Dominic), 1960, Je 24,27:1
Taylor, Simon, 1953, N 7,17:4
Taylor, Sloan (por), 1944, F 12,13:4
Taylor, Sofie Q Mrs, 1940, F 6,22:2
Taylor, Stella M Dr, 1937, O 14,25:5
Taylor, Stephen L, 1938, Jl 28,19:4
Taylor, Stevenson Lt-Com, 1918, Mr 6,7:4
Taylor, Stewart B, 1940, Mr 27,21:5
Taylor, Sutherland G, 1924, Ag 30,9:1
Taylor, T Allan, 1968, Je 17,39:2
Taylor, T Griffith, 1963, N 6,36:3
Taylor, T Henry, 1947, Je 10,27:6
Taylor, T J, 1960, O 23,89:1
Taylor, Talbot J, 1938, Ap 3,II,6:8
Taylor, Tell, 1937, N 24,23:4
Taylor, Theodore C, 1952, O 20,23:1
Taylor, Thomas, 1942, F 20,17:2; 1942, O 24,15:2
Taylor, Thomas D, 1942, D 28,19:3
Taylor, Thomas Emerson, 1922, D 28,17:6
Taylor, Thomas F, 1941, F 23,40:6
Taylor, Thomas F Mrs, 1947, Ap 8,27:1
Taylor, Thomas H Mrs, 1954, F 17,31:1
Taylor, Thomas H Rev Dr, 1867, S 11,5:2
Taylor, Thomas J, 1952, Ag 26,25:2
Taylor, Thomas J Jr, 1959, N 2,31:5
Taylor, Thomas L C, 1956, Ap 7,19:4
Taylor, Thomas Mrs, 1940, D 13,23:4
Taylor, Thomas P, 1913, My 27,11:5; 1949, Mr 14,19:5
Taylor, Thomas R, 1945, Ag 9,21:4
Taylor, Thomas S, 1939, My 16,23:6
Taylor, Thomas U, 1941, My 29,19:5
Taylor, Tom, 1880, Jl 13,5:4; 1880, Jl 26,5:2
Taylor, Uriah, 1952, Ja 31,27:3
Taylor, Valentine, 1943, My 5,27:2
Taylor, Vera C Mrs, 1951, Ja 17,28:2
Taylor, Victor V, 1944, S 23,13:3
Taylor, W B, 1871, F 14,5:5
Taylor, W Edward, 1937, Mr 25,25:1; 1956, D 1,21:3
Taylor, W F, 1880, Mr 13,8:4; 1926, Je 12,15:4
Taylor, W G Langworthy, 1941, Jl 8,19:3
Taylor, W S, 1928, Ag 3,17:5
Taylor, W Sir, 1933, Ja 31,17:5
Taylor, Wade A, 1923, F 19,15:4
Taylor, Walter, 1947, F 23,54:4; 1960, Ap 9,23:2
Taylor, Walter H, 1957, N 16,19:5
Taylor, Walter K, 1964, Ja 21,29:1
Taylor, Walter L, 1952, Mr 18,27:3
Taylor, Walter P, 1940, Ja 21,35:1
Taylor, Walter R, 1949, D 23,21:1
Taylor, Walter W Sr, 1951, Mr 29,27:5
Taylor, Warren P Mrs, 1944, Ag 19,11:4
Taylor, Washington P, 1941, S 25,25:6
Taylor, Wayne C, 1967, N 23,33:2
Taylor, Wiley, 1954, Jl 10,13:5
Taylor, Will Samuel, 1968, D 8,86:6
Taylor, Willard U, 1940, Ap 20,17:3
Taylor, William, 1937, Mr 2,7:2; 1938, Ag 13,13:4; 1943, Mr 12,17:2; 1951, D 29,11:4; 1962, F 18,92:4
Taylor, William A, 1939, Mr 27,15:3; 1949, F 10,28:2; 1954, S 7,26:1; 1956, Ag 6,23:4; 1958, F 28,21:1; 1962, S 27,37:1
Taylor, William A Jr, 1938, Ja 11,23:6
Taylor, William Alexander, 1905, D 10,7:6
Taylor, William B A Mrs, 1961, My 7,87:1
Taylor, William Bp, 1902, My 20,9:5
Taylor, William C, 1958, N 3,37:5
Taylor, William D, 1942, D 7,27:2; 1949, Ja 19,27:3
Taylor, William E, 1937, D 10,25:5; 1944, O 7,13:2
Taylor, William E Mrs, 1967, F 7,39:3
Taylor, William F, 1919, N 24,15:2
Taylor, William F Mrs, 1965, Ag 16,27:5
Taylor, William H, 1942, My 6,19:4; 1943, S 2,19:6; 1945, O 10,21:3; 1950, Ag 27,88:5; 1953, Mr 31,31:2; 1962, Mr 16,31:3; 1966, Ja 8,25:4
Taylor, William H Mrs, 1948, Mr 4,25:1
Taylor, William Henry, 1925, Ap 21,21:6
Taylor, William Hickok, 1914, F 8,15:5
Taylor, William Howell Rev, 1914, My 14,11:4
Taylor, William J, 1925, Jl 18,13:5; 1939, Ap 18,23:4; 1944, Mr 29,21:2; 1949, Mr 16,27:4
Taylor, William J Jr, 1937, O 11,21:5
Taylor, William K Mrs, 1943, O 16,13:3
Taylor, William L, 1949, Jl 5,23:4; 1964, My 12,37:4
Taylor, William M, 1951, Ag 10,15:4
Taylor, William N, 1945, Ap 9,19:2
Taylor, William O, 1946, N 23,15:5; 1950, D 2,13:4
Taylor, William O (funl, Jl 17,60:1), 1955, Jl 16,15:3
Taylor, William O Mrs, 1944, My 25,21:6
Taylor, William P Rev Dr, 1937, My 11,25:5
Taylor, William R, 1941, Je 2,17:2
Taylor, William S, 1909, Mr 14,11:6
Taylor, William W, 1951, Ap 5,29:5; 1959, Jl 27,25:6
Taylor, Winthrop Mrs, 1937, Ap 22,23:4
Taylor, Wyatt W, 1957, My 14,35:3
Taylor, Wyatt W Mrs, 1964, Ag 8,19:1
Taylor, Yantis H (Buck), 1956, O 24,37:2
Taylor, Zachary, 1948, N 11,27:1
Taylor, Zebulon S, 1939, My 29,15:3
Taylor, Zenobia, 1954, My 16,86:1
Taylour, Geoffrey T, 1943, Ja 30,15:4
Tayntor, Albert O, 1957, Je 7,23:3
Tays, George, 1958, F 28,13:3
Tazi, Mohammed, 1948, F 14,13:5
Tchelitchew, Pavel, 1957, Ag 2,19:1
Tchenkeli, Akaki, 1959, Ja 9,25:1
Tcherepnine, Nicholas (por), 1945, Je 29,15:5
Tcherikower, Elias Mrs, 1963, Jl 9,31:1
Tcherkauky, Prince, 1878, Mr 25,1:7
Tchernichovsky, Saul, 1943, O 15,19:5
Tchernowitz, Chaim, 1949, My 16,21:3
Tchertkoff, I G Mrs, 1961, O 1,86:1
Tchertkoff, Iekoussiel G, 1958, Je 2,27:2
Tchertkoff, Michel Foanovitch, 1905, N 2,9:5
Tcheyshvili, Alex N, 1962, S 15,25:4
Tchienov, Jechiel Dr, 1918, F 5,13:8
Tchitcherin, G V, 1936, Jl 8,19:3
Tchkotoua, Virginia H Princess, 1958, Ag 18,19:4
Tchok, Ivan M (por), 1948, Je 19,15:6
Tchor-Baj-Oglu, Euthimios, 1964, F 12,33:1
Tchou, M Thomas, 1965, D 28,25:1
Te Mou Hsi, 1952, Ja 25,21:4
Te-Ping Hsi, 1968, Mr 19,44:3
Teabeau, Ralph, 1947, Jl 22,24:2
Teachout, H Arthur, 1939, Mr 7,21:3
Teaff, Charles A, 1941, S 27,17:6
Teagarden, Jack (Weldon I),(funl, Ja 21,25:2), 1964, Ja 16,25:3
Teagle, Ernest W, 1942, O 8,27:4
Teagle, John Mrs, 1943, My 26,23:1
Teagle, Walter C (will, F 15,19:4), 1962, Ja 10,47:2
Teagle, Walter C Jr, 1960, O 6,41:5
Teague, Charles, 1942, Ap 5,42:3
Teague, Charles C, 1950, Mr 22,27:2
Teague, Henry N, 1951, O 3,36:2
Teague, Marshall, 1959, F 12,35:6
Teague, Walter D, 1960, D 6,41:4
Teague, William M, 1945, Jl 28,11:3
Teague, William T, 1958, S 3,33:5
Teal, C T, 1914, D 14,11:4
Teal, Homer Mrs, 1943, Jl 20,19:5
Teal, John J, 1958, S 30,31:2
Teal, Ralph W, 1961, S 15,30:6
Teal, William, 1950, My 30,18:2
Teale, Charles E (funl, Jl 24,9:3), 1919, Jl 22,9:2
Teale, Earle G, 1919, My 16,15:4
Teale, Jennie M Mrs, 1956, O 16,33:1
Teale, Willis E, 1964, Ap 3,33:2
Teall, Arthur Mrs (Edna), 1968, Jl 26,33:4
Teall, Dorothy J, 1946, N 20,31:2
Teall, Edward H Col, 1937, S 10,23:4
Teall, Edward N, 1947, F 19,25:4
Teall, F Horace, 1923, F 28,17:3
Teall, Francis A, 1957, N 11,29:4
Teall, Gardner C, 1956, Jl 24,25:2
Teall, Henry P, 1954, F 1,23:3
Teall, Oliver Sumner, 1906, Je 8,9:2

Teaman, Sam, 1945, S 13,23:3
Teany, Mattie G Mrs, 1937, S 24,21:2
Teare, Julia R, 1953, Je 24,25:3
Tearle, Conway, 1938, O 2,48:6
Tearle, Godfrey, 1953, Je 10,29:5
Tearle, Noel, 1913, F 6,11:2
Tears, Nelson J, 1946, Jl 24,27:3
Tears, William W, 1940, S 20,23:3
Teas, Paul, 1946, O 8,23:1
Teasdale, George, 1953, Ja 7,31:4
Teasdale, Harry B, 1948, D 28,21:5
Teasdale, John S, 1962, Jl 3,23:4
Teasdale, Reginald, 1943, D 23,19:3
Teat, Robert H, 1946, O 30,27:5
Teates, Chester A Mrs, 1951, O 12,27:5
Teator, Milton H, 1948, My 26,25:2
Teatsorth, Ralph C, 1966, F 26,25:4
Teaz, George B, 1950, F 10,24:3
Tebaldi, Teobaldo, 1967, N 12,87:1
Tebaldi, Teobaldo Mrs (funl, D 4,39:5), 1957, D 1, 88:4
Tebaldino, Giovanni, 1952, My 13,30:2
Tebbets, Frederick, 1941, Ja 29,17:1
Tebbetts, Abbie L Mrs, 1948, Ja 7,25:5
Tebbetts, Leon O, 1942, Ag 5,19:2
Tebbetts, Stanley W, 1949, Jl 19,29:1
Tebbs, George E, 1948, Ap 20,27:2
Tebbs, Leroy, 1958, Ja 24,21:1
Tebbs, Robert W Sr, 1945, My 25,19:4
Tebbutt, Harry K Jr, 1949, Je 9,31:1
Tebbutt, James G Mrs, 1943, O 25,15:6
Tebbutt, Marshall W Jr, 1948, N 5,25:2
Tebeau, Albert, 1944, Mr 15,19:5
Tebeau, Isaac J, 1911, D 21,11:5
Tebeau, J F, 1930, My 7,27:1
Tebeau, Joseph Mrs, 1948, Jl 28,23:5
Tebo, Clarence W, 1941, Ag 29,17:2
TeBow, Lillian C, 1944, Ja 21,17:5
Techel, Hans, 1944, Mr 2,17:5
Techow, Hans, 1945, F 23,17:3
Teck, Duchess of, 1897, O 28,7:1
Teck, Francis Joseph Leopold of Prince (funl, O 26,9:5), 1910, O 23,II,13:4
Tedaldi, Dante J, 1962, Ja 1,23:4
Tedcastle, Agnes B V Mrs, 1942, My 13,19:3
Tedcastle, Arthur W, 1938, O 3,15:3
Tedder, Arthur W Lord (will, Ag 26,3:6), 1967, Je 4, 86:2
Teden, Herbert E, 1958, Ag 12,29:1
Tedesche, Leon G, 1956, My 1,33:4
Tedesche, Sidney S, 1962, My 19,27:3
Tedeschini, Federico (funl, N 7,23:2), 1959, N 3,31:2
Tedesco, Louis S, 1954, N 13,15:5
Tedesco, Rudolph S, 1967, Je 7,51:1
Tedford, Robert H, 1945, Je 27,19:5
Tedoff, Samuel R, 1954, S 27,21:1
Tedrini, Louise Mother, 1938, O 19,23:4
Tee-Van, John, 1967, N 6,47:1
Teed, Charles M, 1946, Je 5,23:2
Teed, Cyrus R, 1908, D 25,7:7
Teed, Dexter, 1961, N 8,35:4
Teed, Francis J, 1960, Ja 28,31:3
Teed, Frank B, 1954, Ja 11,25:4
Teed, Lewis C Mrs, 1947, N 6,18:6
Teed, Mary E, 1965, O 24,86:4
Teed, Mary Mrs, 1905, Je 14,9:6
Teed, Ralph H, 1958, My 19,25:2
Teegarden, Bonnard, 1938, Je 30,23:4
Teegarden, Harold B, 1953, N 19,31:4
Teegarden, Jesse L, 1952, Ja 27,76:3
Teegarden, Lindsey W Mrs, 1956, Ag 4,15:6
Teegarden, Robert W, 1963, S 8,87:2
Teel, Frank, 1946, D 5,31:4
Teel, George W, 1952, Mr 6,31:3
Teel, H V, 1938, My 28,15:5
Teele, Arthur W (por), 1940, Ja 31,19:1
Teele, Fred W, 1939, Ja 22,34:6
Teele, Stanley F, 1967, My 30,21:2
Teener, James W, 1966, Jl 30,25:6
Teeple, Andrew H, 1948, D 9,33:1
Teeple, Clarence D, 1954, Ag 25,27:2
Teeple, David S, 1964, Ap 30,35:4
Teeple, John E, 1931, Mr 24,27:5
Teeple, Lina P Mrs, 1938, Ap 7,23:4
Teeple, Percy Mrs, 1951, Ja 2,23:4
Teer, Nello L, 1963, Ag 30,21:4
Teer, Robert Mrs, 1956, Ap 20,25:4
Tees, D Frank, 1950, D 6,29:1
Tees, Francis H, 1951, O 6,19:2
Tees, Walter F, 1958, Jl 16,29:3
Teese, Jesse W, 1949, Jl 12,27:5
Teeter, Albert A, 1953, S 4,34:2
Teeter, Charles E, 1963, My 19,86:7
Teeter, Fred Jr, 1951, Jl 9,23:2
Teeter, John H, 1966, Ap 13,40:3
Teeter, John N, 1938, Mr 6,II,8:2
Teeters, Wilber J, 1959, D 16,41:2
Teetor, Charles N, 1937, My 4,25:1
Teetor, John H, 1939, Mr 10,23:5
Teetor, Lothair, 1962, Ap 7,25:4
Teets, Clarence, 1953, Ap 21,27:4
Teets, Harley O, 1957, S 3,28:3
Teets, Harry R, 1953, Ja 6,29:4
Teets, Henry W, 1943, N 13,13:4
Teets, Herbert M, 1942, Ag 18,21:4
Teets, Sylvanus G, 1920, N 5,15:6
Teetsel, Albert E, 1945, D 20,23:4
Teevan, Thomas L, 1954, O 12,27:4
Tefet, J R E, 1937, Ja 17,II,8:6
Teffner, Gordon B, 1965, O 21,47:1
Tefft, Bert A, 1952, Jl 4,13:5
Tefft, Byron Mrs (Jane), 1966, F 12,27:2
Tefft, C Forrest, 1952, Ap 13,77:2
Tefft, C G, 1877, Jl 13,4:6
Tefft, Charles E, 1951, S 21,23:4
Tefft, Edwin Bassett Dr, 1916, Ag 7,9:6
Tefft, Frank G, 1903, N 11,6:2
Tefft, George H, 1938, My 12,23:5
Tefft, Grant J, 1948, Ja 30,23:3
Tefft, L B Rev, 1926, D 1,27:5
Tefft, Mary E Mrs, 1944, D 9,15:5
Tefft, Thomas A, 1860, F 25,1:3
Tefft, W E, 1903, F 20,9:5
Tefft, W E Mrs, 1903, Je 4,9:7
Tefft, Walter C Mrs, 1958, Ja 29,27:3
Tefft, William H, 1938, Jl 2,13:3
Tefft, William R, 1949, Jl 29,21:6
Teft, James Mrs, 1908, Ag 31,7:2
Tegemeyer, J B, 1901, Jl 5,7:4
Tegen, William A, 1948, N 8,21:5
Teger, Edgar, 1949, Je 5,92:5
Tegetoff, Baron, 1871, Ap 8,1:2
Tegeugh, Tasfaye, 1950, Ja 20,3:1
Tegtmeyer, Archie, 1946, Mr 8,21:3
Tegtmeyer, Charles E, 1963, S 12,37:4
Tegtmeyer, Charles W, 1955, Jl 2,15:4
Tegtmeyer, Theobald, 1950, Jl 13,25:4
Tehan, Edmund G Mrs, 1957, Ja 16,31:1
Tehan, Margaret A, 1952, O 9,31:4
Tehon, Leo R, 1954, O 18,25:2
Teich, Frederick J, 1946, F 16,13:2
Teicher, Maxwell M, 1964, Mr 28,19:6
Teicher, Maxwell M Mrs, 1966, D 29,31:1
Teicher, Sydney J, 1953, Ap 18,19:6
Teichert, Adolph Jr, 1953, My 8,25:1
Teichert, Paul, 1948, Jl 4,27:1
Teichholtz, Ben Mrs, 1960, Mr 3,30:1
Teichman, Abraham, 1947, F 11,30:3
Teichman, Arthur, 1949, Ja 4,19:4
Teichman, John D, 1954, Ap 22,29:5
Teichman, Joseph G, 1965, F 24,42:1
Teichmann, Richard, 1925, Je 16,21:6
Teichmann, William C, 1942, Mr 31,21:3
Teichner, Miriam, 1963, Mr 28,16:3
Teichner, Rudolph J, 1950, N 23,35:2
Teichner, William I, 1960, S 6,35:1
Teigan, Henry, 1941, Mr 13,21:4
Teigan, Martin J, 1940, Je 25,23:1
Teiger, Milton J, 1954, Ja 4,11:1
Teilhard de Chardin, Pierre, 1955, Ap 12,29:5
Teillard, Dorothy Mrs, 1953, Ja 22,23:3
Teimer, Theodor, 1938, O 13,23:5
Teisare, Alberto, 1963, S 12,37:5
Teitel, Jacques, 1939, F 22,21:3
Teitelbaum, Aaron, 1950, Ag 17,27:2
Teitelbaum, Abraham, 1947, O 17,21:3
Teitelbaum, Edward, 1955, Jl 12,25:3
Teitelbaum, Isidor, 1968, Ag 2,33:4
Teitelbaum, Jack, 1957, Ag 4,83:6
Teitelbaum, Jack (J Lane), 1964, Ja 21,29:2
Teitelbaum, Leo Mrs, 1961, Ap 16,86:5
Teitelbaum, Max Mrs, 1937, Ag 8,II,6:7; 1968, My 29, 36:3
Teitelbaum, Michael H, 1956, Ag 12,85:1
Teitelbaum, Norman, 1946, Jl 30,23:2
Teitelbaum, Perry D, 1966, Jl 2,23:4
Teitlebaum, Leib, 1941, F 27,19:4
Teitler, Morris Mrs, 1946, O 12,19:5
Teitz, Abraham B, 1956, O 2,35:4
Teitz, Emanuel, 1948, Ja 3,13:2
Teitz, Leo, 1951, Jl 13,21:2
Tejada, A G de, 1880, D 13,1:4
Tejada, Miguel L, 1941, My 27,23:2
Tekirian, Benon O, 1948, N 14,76:2
Tekulski, Carrie G, 1943, F 1,15:5
Tekulsky, Nathan, 1940, N 25,17:3
Telberg, George G, 1954, F 22,19:4
Telberg, Ina G, 1962, Ja 22,23:2
Teleky, Ludwig, 1957, Ag 28,27:5
Telesca, Anthony W, 1944, Ap 13,19:3
Telesco, Michael, 1955, O 2,65:5
Telese, Peter M, 1962, My 19,27:3
Teleshova, Elizabeth, 1943, Jl 12,15:1
Teleszky, John, 1939, Je 14,23:4
Telfair, Samuel F, 1959, Ja 30,27:2
Telfair, W D, 1942, N 2,21:2
Telfair, William G, 1941, Jl 16,17:5
Telfener, Countess, 1910, My 2,9:4
Telfer, Alex M, 1962, Ag 13,25:5
Telfer, Arthur J, 1954, D 10,27:2
Telfer, Francis G, 1948, Ag 9,20:3
Telfer, Gladys G Mrs, 1949, D 17,32:4
Telfer, John, 1959, Mr 26,34:7
Telfer, John Mrs, 1968, D 31,27:2
Telfer, Peter, 1939, D 3,60:8
Telfer, Thomas A, 1944, Ja 3,21:3
Telfer-Smollett, A P D, 1954, O 10,87:3
Telfeyan, Albert G, 1959, N 6,29:1
Telfeyan, John G, 1924, Ag 11,13:5
Telford, Clarence F, 1955, Ja 4,21:4
Telford, James H, 1949, S 14,31:4
Telford, John H, 1939, D 22,19:3
Telford, Marshall H, 1944, S 13,19:7
Tell, Alma, 1938, Ja 1,19:4
Tell, Irving J, 1959, Ja 3,17:2
Tell, Olive (Mrs H M Hobart), 1951, Je 9,19:4
Tell, Ralph Martin, 1968, Ap 1,45:2
Tellcampf, Dr, 1876, F 17,5:2
Telleen, S Frederick, 1955, F 17,27:4
Tellefson, George, 1937, O 7,27:5
Teller, Albert J (funl), 1911, Mr 16,9:3
Teller, Alfred, 1951, O 27,19:6
Teller, Andrew, 1950, My 18,29:2
Teller, C M Mrs, 1901, N 18,7:4
Teller, Charles R, 1957, My 29,27:5
Teller, Chester J, 1962, My 21,33:4
Teller, Edgar E, 1941, D 12,25:2
Teller, Emma F Mrs, 1954, My 9,89:1
Teller, Frank Mrs, 1953, Jl 23,23:5
Teller, Frederic, 1954, Ap 12,29:5
Teller, Frederick H, 1950, Mr 28,32:3
Teller, George L, 1942, N 14,16:3
Teller, Harry A, 1944, My 31,19:4
Teller, Harvey E, 1955, S 14,35:2
Teller, Henry Moore Ex-Sen, 1914, F 24,11:3
Teller, John, 1945, O 25,21:3
Teller, John D, 1922, Ja 20,15:4
Teller, Morris, 1966, N 28,39:5
Teller, Myron S, 1959, My 10,87:1
Teller, William R, 1944, F 22,24:2; 1953, My 4,23:4
Teller, William R Jr, 1961, Je 28,35:4
Teller, Woolsey, 1954, Mr 12,21:5
Tellez, Julio C, 1958, O 26,88:5
Tellez, Manuel C (por), 1937, My 24,19:5
Tellier, Charles, 1913, O 21,9:7
Tellier, Harry A, 1944, Mr 31,19:5
Tellier, Joseph M, 1952, O 19,89:1
Telligrine, L G, 1919, N 29,11:2
Telling, William E, 1938, Ja 27,21:3
Tellman, Daniel, 1943, Ag 28,11:3
Tellman, Edwin T, 1944, Jl 19,19:1
Tello, Julio C, 1947, Je 5,26:2
Tello, Manly, 1905, Ap 5,9:6
Telmo, Continelli, 1948, S 20,25:5
Telschow, John H, 1941, Ja 26,37:2
Telsey, Jacob, 1958, D 10,40:1
Telsey, Samuel A, 1960, Jl 30,17:4
Telsey, Samuel A Mrs, 1960, S 9,29:1
Telsner, Alex, 1950, Jl 11,31:3
Telva, Marion (M Toucke), 1962, O 24,39:2
Telyakov, Nikolai M, 1950, Ag 28,17:5
Tem Eick, Arthur R, 1946, Ag 2,19:5
Temel, Semih, 1946, O 26,17:5
Temkin, Max M, 1948, O 25,23:5
Temkin, Morris, 1925, Ag 6,19:6
Temkin, Samuel Mrs, 1948, Je 24,26:2
Temme, Arthur, 1949, Je 5,92:3
Temperley, Arthur C (por), 1940, Ap 8,19:6
Temperley, Harold W, 1939, Jl 12,19:5
Tempest, Adolphus Vane Lord, 1864, Jl 3,3:3
Tempest, Marie (por), 1942, O 16,19:1
Tempestini, Maurizio, 1960, Ag 4,25:5
Temple, Alice, 1946, Ja 7,19:3
Temple, Charles D, 1954, Ap 11,42:2
Temple, Charles H, 1943, Je 2,25:3
Temple, Earl, 1940, F 20,21:5
Temple, Edward A Bp, 1924, Ja 12,13:2
Temple, Edward B, 1949, Mr 14,19:5
Temple, Edward L Mrs, 1968, Jl 20,27:1
Temple, Edward P, 1921, Je 24,15:6
Temple, F P F, 1880, My 14,2:4
Temple, Francis J Sr, 1955, S 1,23:3
Temple, Fred Dr Archbishop, 1902, D 24,9:5
Temple, Grace E, 1944, My 13,19:6
Temple, H C, 1951, My 10,31:1
Temple, H F Capt, 1925, Jl 28,13:5
Temple, Harold F, 1961, Jl 11,31:3
Temple, Henry W, 1955, Ja 12,27:4
Temple, Ira F, 1951, Ap 14,15:5
Temple, James H Mrs, 1942, Je 14,45:2
Temple, James Mrs, 1945, F 16,23:4
Temple, Jean B Mrs, 1945, Ja 16,19:2
Temple, John R, 1948, D 1,29:4
Temple, Judge, 1902, D 27,9:5
Temple, Lady, 1943, S 14,23:1
Temple, Larry, 1943, N 18,23:2
Temple, Richard, 1912, O 20,II,15:4; 1954, O 17,87
Temple, Richard Sir, 1902, Mr 18,9:6
Temple, Robert D, 1948, N 30,27:2
Temple, Robert M, 1937, Mr 4,23:4
Temple, Seth J, 1949, Je 5,92:3
Temple, Thomas, 1950, Ap 15,15:3
Temple, Thomas F, 1944, Ap 17,23:5; 1955, O 29,1
Temple, Thomas M, 1943, My 9,40:8
Temple, Thomas P, 1923, S 20,4:5
Temple, Thomas P Mrs, 1923, S 20,4:5
Temple, Walter P, 1938, N 16,23:6
Temple, Wayne N, 1949, S 14,31:4
Temple, William, 1863, My 31,3:6; 1939, D 10,68:4
1944, O 27,23:1

Temple, William C, 1948, F 26,23:4
Temple, William Chase, 1917, Ja 9,13:2
Temple, William F Jr, 1942, D 27,34:6
Temple, William H, 1937, Mr 11,23:1
Temple, William H Col, 1922, Je 9,15:5
Temple of Stowe, Dowager Countess of, 1941, Mr 4, 23:3
Templeman, Samuel H, 1945, Mr 10,17:5
Templeman, William, 1950, F 10,23:4
Templemore, Lord (A C S Chichester), 1953, O 5, 27:4
Templer, Earl B, 1952, D 12,29:3
Templeton, Alec A, 1963, Mr 29,7:6
Templeton, Allan A, 1954, F 19,27:3
Templeton, Andrew, 1958, Ap 13,83:4
Templeton, Charles A, 1955, Ag 16,49:2
Templeton, Clarence R, 1951, S 28,31:3
Templeton, Eleanor K, 1943, D 23,19:3
Templeton, Ernest G, 1947, F 3,19:1
Templeton, Eugene Mrs (Kathryn), 1968, Je 3,45:1
Templeton, Fay (por), 1939, O 4,25:1
Templeton, George, 1945, N 18,44:2
Templeton, Harry C, 1965, D 29,26:8
Templeton, Hoyt D, 1949, Je 22,31:5
Templeton, James, 1947, Ag 29,17:5
Templeton, James S Mrs, 1947, Jl 15,23:2
Templeton, John, 1907, D 12,11:5; 1938, Jl 5,17:6
Templeton, John Hubert Campbell, 1968, Je 8,31:3
Templeton, John I, 1952, Ag 20,27:1
Templeton, John M Mrs, 1951, F 28,21:5
Templeton, Joseph C, 1951, N 24,11:5
Templeton, Martha Mrs, 1949, Ja 20,27:1
Templeton, Max A, 1942, F 17,21:3
Templeton, Michael A, 1945, O 24,21:5
Templeton, Nelson G, 1963, Jl 4,17:5
Templeton, Norman C, 1949, Ja 18,23:4
Templeton, Payne Mrs, 1956, Je 6,33:5
Templeton, Richard H, 1953, Ja 19,23:5
Templeton, Robert L (Dink), 1962, Ag 8,31:3
Templeton, Rosamund D Mrs, 1937, Je 22,23:3
Templeton, Stuart J, 1958, Je 10,33:4
Templeton, Watson G, 1945, F 4,38:6
Templeton, William J, 1911, D 3,15:5
Templeton, William W, 1945, Ja 10,23:4
Templetown, Viscount, 1939, O 3,23:4
Templewood, Viscount (S J G Hoare), 1959, My 9, 21:4
Templin, Edward M, 1967, Ja 4,43:1
Templin, Ernest H, 1961, Jl 22,21:6
Templin, Walter Mrs, 1951, D 31,13:6
Templin, Walter W, 1966, F 3,31:3
Tempski, Armine von, 1943, D 3,23:4
Ten Broeck, Carl, 1966, N 6,89:1
Ten Broeck, Charles W, 1951, Je 16,15:3
Ten Broeck, Dora W Mrs, 1940, N 19,23:2
Ten Broeck, Minnie N S Mrs, 1940, S 26,23:3
Ten Broeck, Samuel, 1938, Mr 9,23:4
Ten Broeck, W A, 1903, My 21,9:4
Ten Cate, Daudin, 1942, D 20,44:6
Ten Eick, Arthur R Mrs, 1949, Mr 23,27:2
Ten Eick, William A, 1956, Ap 14,17:4
Ten Eick, William A Jr, 1968, Jl 10,39:3
Ten Eick, William A Mrs, 1953, Jl 5,49:1
Ten Eyck, Benjamin L, 1948, F 6,26:5
Ten Eyck, Chauncey B Mrs, 1945, Ap 15,14:5
Ten Eyck, Culyer, 1938, Ap 3,II,7:3
Ten Eyck, Edward, 1956, S 11,35:4
Ten Eyck, Helen G Mrs, 1938, F 25,17:4
Ten Eyck, J C, 1879, Ag 26,5:4
Ten Eyck, Jacob H, 1872, O 12,1:2
Ten Eyck, Jacob L, 1942, Mr 31,21:2
Ten Eyck, James A (por), 1938, F 12,15:1
Ten Eyck, Jay (por), 1943, O 23,13:3
Ten Eyck, Jay Mrs, 1957, Je 20,29:4
Ten Eyck, John C Mrs, 1946, D 1,78:6
Ten Eyck, John Mrs, 1921, Ag 19,13:4
Ten Eyck, Joshua J, 1947, Ag 26,23:2
Ten Eyck, Martilou, 1939, N 25,17:3
Ten Eyck, Mary Mrs, 1945, Mr 10,17:6
Ten Eyck, Mills, 1957, Ag 15,21:5
Ten Eyck, Otto W, 1965, My 6,39:3
Ten Eyck, Peter, 1953, O 15,33:3
Ten Eyck, Peter G (por), 1944, S 3,26:6
Ten Eyck, Peter Mrs, 1963, Ap 13,19:6
Ten Eyck, Walter, 1943, F 12,19:2
Ten Eyck, William H, 1919, O 14,17:3
Ten Eyck, William H Mrs, 1944, Ja 18,19:4
Ten Eycke, S R, 1902, F 18,9:5
Ten Hagen, Oliver J, 1946, N 20,31:3
Ten Have, Jean, 1952, Ag 28,23:3
Ten Kate, Geertruidas B, 1947, N 7,23:3
Ten Weeges, Charles H, 1941, Ja 17,17:3
Tenani, Mario, 1955, My 2,21:5
Tenbroeck, Edward B Col, 1912, Je 17,9:6
Tenbroeck, G, 1934, F 12,17:5
Tenbroeck, May, 1908, D 6,13:4
tenBroek, Jacobus Dr, 1968, Mr 28,47:4
Tenbrook, Harry W, 1951, O 16,31:3
Tenby, Viscount (G Lloyd George), 1967, F 15,45:1
Tench, Frederick (por), 1944, O 28,15:3
Tench, W Bernard, 1944, O 5,23:2
Tencza, Joseph P, 1946, S 5,27:3
Tendler, Alex D, 1951, Ap 16,25:2
Tenell, G, 1936, O 5,21:3
Tenen, Paul S, 1955, Jl 10,72:3
Tenenbaum, Charles, 1967, My 10,44:7
Tenenbaum, Harry, 1955, Mr 15,29:3
Tenenbaum, Joseph L, 1961, D 11,31:2
Tenenbaum, Leslie, 1947, Ja 26,53:3
Tenenbaum, Samuel, 1960, Ag 12,19:3
Tener, Alexander C, 1965, N 6,29:5
Tener, George E Mrs, 1952, Ag 17,77:2
Tener, Hampden E, 1948, Ag 28,15:2
Tener, John K (por), 1946, My 20,23:3
Tener, John K Mrs, 1937, O 10,II,9:1
Tener, Kinley J, 1947, My 12,21:5
Tener, Stephen W, 1940, My 26,35:2
Tener, Wilfred A, 1954, Ja 1,23:1
Teneyck, Edward G, 1943, S 1,19:3
Tengwald, Victor J, 1949, O 25,27:5
Tenhaeff, N B, 1943, F 3,19:4
Teninga, Cornelius, 1953, Jl 19,57:1
Tenjost, William C, 1941, S 2,18:3
Tenjost, William C Mrs, 1941, Ag 30,13:1
TenKate, James, 1950, O 2,23:4
Tenke, Julius, 1942, Je 29,15:5
Tennant, A Wiley, 1949, N 15,26:3
Tennant, Andrew, 1951, Ja 1,17:2
Tennant, Brydon Mrs, 1907, N 18,7:6
Tennant, Charles Grant Lt, 1915, Je 19,9:5
Tennant, Charles L, 1949, Ja 29,13:2
Tennant, Colin M, 1940, N 11,19:3
Tennant, Dorothy, 1942, Jl 4,17:3
Tennant, Edward Priauix (Lord Glenconner), 1920, N 22,15:4
Tennant, George B, 1939, Ag 11,15:2
Tennant, George G, 1948, F 4,23:5
Tennant, George G Mrs, 1938, Mr 10,21:3
Tennant, George W, 1953, F 16,21:5
Tennant, James Emerson Sir, 1869, Mr 21,5:1
Tennant, Joseph A, 1948, D 16,29:5
Tennant, Martha B Mrs, 1937, Ap 23,21:3
Tennant, Maurice E, 1951, O 1,23:6
Tennant, Raymond I, 1952, Ag 12,19:3
Tennant, William, 1963, Jl 27,17:4
Tennant, William B, 1940, D 4,27:2
Tennen, Joseph S Dr, 1937, D 15,25:1
Tennent, David H, 1941, Ja 15,23:3
Tennent, Henry M, 1941, Je 12,24:3
Tenner, Oscar, 1948, D 26,52:4
Tennes, Mont (will, S 7,38:2), 1941, Ag 7,17:5
Tenney, Albert B, 1948, D 7,31:3
Tenney, Alvan A Mrs, 1952, F 3,84:1
Tenney, Arthur D, 1949, Ja 17,19:4
Tenney, Charles H, 1951, F 8,33:2
Tenney, D I, 1881, N 25,5:6
Tenney, Daniel G, 1951, Mr 12,25:3
Tenney, Frank M, 1957, S 18,33:3
Tenney, Fred, 1952, Jl 4,13:4
Tenney, Frederick W, 1960, Mr 31,33:5
Tenney, George A, 1947, N 4,25:4
Tenney, George C, 1913, Ja 2,11:4
Tenney, George C Mrs, 1958, Ja 11,17:3
Tenney, Gordon E, 1966, N 13,88:8
Tenney, Grace E, 1950, Je 14,31:4
Tenney, Harral S, 1949, D 11,92:6
Tenney, Harral S Mrs, 1965, Ap 26,31:3
Tenney, Henriette M, 1916, S 14,7:5
Tenney, John F (por), 1949, S 7,29:4
Tenney, John W G, 1967, D 26,33:2
Tenney, Julius S, 1966, Mr 27,86:7
Tenney, Malcolm, 1957, Ap 12,25:1
Tenney, Parker G, 1953, Ag 23,89:3
Tenney, S Prof (funl), 1877, Jl 15,2:7
Tenney, Samuel M, 1939, D 24,14:5
Tenney, Sanborn Gove, 1923, Ja 11,21:6
Tenney, Theodore S Mrs, 1960, S 22,27:2
Tenney, W J, 1883, S 22,4:7
Tenney, Walter C, 1947, My 20,25:4
Tenney, Willis A, 1948, Je 13,68:4
Tenney, Willis R, 1948, My 3,21:5
Tenniel, John Sir, 1914, F 27,11:4
Tennis, Charles O, 1950, Mr 11,15:5
Tennis, Emilie L Mrs, 1943, O 24,44:3
Tennis, John L, 1938, Mr 24,23:5
Tenny, Adrian C, 1957, Ja 24,20:6
Tennyson, H Lord, 1928, D 3,27:4
Tennyson, Lionel H Lord, 1951, Je 7,33:6
Tennyson-D'Eyncourt, Eustace, 1951, F 2,23:2
Tenopyr, Joseph, 1961, N 19,88:4
Tenorio, Jorge, 1958, Ja 1,25:3
Tenschert, William P, 1956, O 6,21:4
Tense, William F, 1945, S 15,15:5
Tenterden, Lord, 1882, S 23,2:4
Tenterden, Lova, 1870, Ap 14,5:4
Tenu, Adrian, 1901, Jl 3,2:4
Tenzer, Michael, 1952, O 19,88:3
Tenzer, Michael Mrs, 1953, N 13,27:3
Tenzer, Milton, 1955, Ag 2,23:1
Teodorescu, Gregorie, 1925, O 15,23:5
Tepikian, Zaven Bill, 1956, Jl 11,29:2
Teplin, Benetal Mrs, 1943, S 26,48:1
Teplitz, David, 1942, F 11,21:3
Tepp, David, 1953, My 20,29:6
Tepper, Abram S, 1959, Ap 15,33:4
Tepper, Adolph, 1949, S 7,29:5
Tepper, Emanuel, 1951, S 17,21:5
Tepper, Hyman, 1951, Ag 15,27:5
Tepper, Jacob, 1944, Je 15,19:3; 1959, D 9,45:4
Tepper, Leo, 1952, N 9,91:2
Tepper, Max, 1937, My 1,19:6
Tepper, Morris, 1941, Mr 11,23:5
Tepperman, Adolph, 1957, S 18,33:2
Tepuea Herangi, Princess of Maori, 1952, O 14,31:1
Ter Braake, B G D, 1948, F 13,21:1
Ter Bush, Emery B, 1953, N 23,27:3
Ter Bush, Frank V, 1944, Ag 21,15:4
Ter Kulle, Jacob, 1910, F 16,9:4
Ter Meulen, Carel E, 1937, N 16,23:3
Teran, Ramon Gen, 1906, Ja 13,9:5
Teraspulsky, Aaron, 1955, Ag 5,19:4
Terauchi, Ex-Premier of Japan, 1919, N 4,15:1
Terauchi, Juichi, 1946, Je 13,27:5
Terauchi, Seiki Count, 1919, O 22,17:3
Terazzo, Louis Mrs, 1914, S 14,9:3
Terbasket, Paul, 1956, F 26,89:2
Terbush, Elmer Mrs, 1945, Ag 3,17:4
Tercek, John, 1942, Je 29,15:4; 1951, F 18,22:6
Terchout, Adele (La Comete), 1881, Mr 28,2:3
Tercijonas, Vincas, 1964, S 14,33:6
Terence, Bro, 1940, Jl 14,31:3
Teresa, Mother (M Spor), 1966, Ag 6,23:5
Teresa, Sister (M L Brink), 1954, Jl 2,19:5
Teresa Aquin, Sister, 1948, Je 29,23:4
Teresa Clare, Sister, 1948, S 4,15:2
Teresa Gertrude, sister (Benedictine Sisters), 1965, Ap 22,33:1
Teresa Joseph, Sister (Whitehead), 1955, Je 28,27:3
Teresa of Jesus, Mother (Discalced Carmelite Nuns), 1961, Ja 12,29:1
Teresa Vincent, Mother (K T Harney), 1954, D 1, 31:3
Terezopoulos, S C, 1956, F 13,27:1
TerHeun, DeWitt M, 1963, D 3,43:4
Terheun, DeWitt M Mrs, 1959, Mr 9,29:5
Terhune, Albert D, 1954, O 28,35:5
Terhune, Albert P (por), 1942, F 19,19:1
Terhune, Albert P (will), 1942, Mr 5,25:7
Terhune, Albert P Mrs, 1964, N 10,47:3
Terhune, Allan Gilmore, 1907, Je 9,9:5
Terhune, Ann E Mrs, 1948, Je 26,17:5
Terhune, Beekman R, 1958, O 31,29:2
Terhune, Bertholf W, 1941, F 1,17:2
Terhune, Charles B Mrs, 1952, O 11,19:3
Terhune, Charles Mrs, 1924, Ap 7,17:6
Terhune, E Malcolm Mrs, 1949, S 21,31:2
Terhune, Edward Payson Mrs (Marion Harland), 1922, Je 7,19:5
Terhune, Edward Payson Rev Dr, 1907, My 26,7:2
Terhune, Everit B, 1956, Jl 25,29:3
Terhune, George A, 1951, N 8,29:3
Terhune, Harry R, 1947, Ja 25,17:3
Terhune, Henry S, 1942, Ja 13,19:2
Terhune, Herman V, 1938, F 7,15:5
Terhune, Jacob H, 1954, Je 6,86:5
Terhune, John, 1943, F 2,19:2
Terhune, Leroy, 1951, Ja 15,17:5
Terhune, Lewis C, 1944, D 7,25:4
Terhune, Nicholas (por), 1947, S 26,23:5
Terhune, Richard A Dr, 1906, F 6,16:1
Terhune, Walter S, 1938, F 12,15:5
Terhune, Walter S Sr, 1950, Mr 2,27:3
Terhune, Wilhelmina D Mrs, 1942, Ap 17,17:1
Terkel, Meyer, 1958, Ap 2,31:4
Terkelsen, Alfred T, 1963, My 9,37:2
Terker, Harry J, 1959, Ja 4,88:3
Terkuhle, Alois, 1959, O 28,37:1
Terlinde, William G, 1962, S 24,29:3
Terman, Lewis M, 1956, D 23,31:1
Ternes, Albert P, 1943, Jl 22,19:2
Ternina, Milka, 1943, Mr 18,19:3
Terp, Christian M, 1944, Je 10,15:5
Terpening, Albert, 1951, S 22,17:2
Terpening, George H Sr, 1954, Je 27,69:1
Terpening, Henry T Sr, 1941, My 10,15:5
Terpening, Roscoe C, 1943, Ja 1,23:4
Terpenning, Charles W, 1946, O 26,17:3
Terpenning, Walter A, 1965, Ja 20,39:5
Terpenning, Walter A Mrs, 1965, Ja 20,39:5
Terpeny, Eugene F, 1914, D 1,13:6
Terpigorev, Aleksander, 1959, N 11,35:1
Terpning, Bert E, 1946, F 25,25:2
Terra, Gabriel (por), 1942, S 16,23:1
Terradell, William F, 1946, Ja 31,21:5
Terrail, Claude, 1954, Ja 17,92:3
Terral, Tom J, 1946, Mr 10,46:6
Terranova, Nicholas, 1955, Mr 16,33:2
Terranova, Peter E, 1968, S 4,44:3
Terranova, William M, 1963, O 18,31:3
Terranova, William M Mrs, 1957, N 2,21:6
Terrart, P Du, 1878, Mr 25,2:4
Terrassi, Alberto, 1951, Mr 20,29:3
Terrazas, Luis Gen, 1923, Je 16,11:5
Terrazas, Luis Jr, 1917, Mr 17,13:4
Terreforte, John W, 1961, S 3,60:4
Terrell, Allan G, 1940, O 10,25:3
Terrell, Alton T, 1938, Ja 23,II,8:2
Terrell, Claude M Mrs, 1939, Mr 6,15:1

Terrell, Edmonds Mrs, 1948, Mr 6,13:5
Terrell, Edward E, 1947, O 4,17:4
Terrell, Edwin H, 1910, Jl 3,II,7:4
Terrell, Frank S, 1948, O 25,23:4
Terrell, Fred N, 1942, F 25,20:2
Terrell, George B, 1947, Ap 19,15:6
Terrell, George K, 1965, N 18,47:4
Terrell, Glenn, 1964, Ja 13,35:4
Terrell, Harrison, 1906, Jl 7,7:6
Terrell, Herbert Leslie, 1909, N 11,9:5
Terrell, James P, 1950, N 7,27:3
Terrell, Joseph M Ex-Sen, 1912, N 18,11:4
Terrell, Katherine H P N Mrs, 1940, F 29,19:5
Terrell, Lyman W Mrs, 1957, O 15,33:2
Terrell, Maude P Mrs, 1947, Ag 10,53:1
Terrell, Robert Mrs, 1954, Jl 29,23:4
Terrell, T C, 1881, My 19,3:2
Terrell, Theodore E Mrs, 1957, Mr 31,88:6
Terrell, Virgil J, 1945, F 19,17:4
Terrell, William H, 1946, N 12,29:3
Terrell, Zack, 1954, Ag 6,17:5
Terrence, William J, 1961, D 6,47:5
Terrett, Courtenay, 1950, Ap 6,29:5
Terriberry, G Gilson, 1968, My 22,47:2
Terriberry, George H, 1948, O 21,27:5
Terriberry, Joseph F Mrs, 1946, Ag 16,21:5
Terriberry, William S, 1948, O 15,23:4
Terriberry, William S Mrs, 1948, N 18,27:4
Terrien, Edmond A Mrs, 1950, My 17,29:4
Terrien, Felix, 1940, F 19,17:1
Terril, Mortimer C, 1944, Mr 26,42:2
Terrill, A J N, 1947, Mr 5,25:4
Terrill, Arthur P, 1949, Mr 28,21:3
Terrill, Frank E, 1949, Jl 13,27:2
Terrill, Frank V, 1954, S 18,15:1
Terrill, Harold M, 1945, N 26,21:4
Terrill, James H, 1943, Jl 29,19:2
Terrill, James H Mrs, 1943, My 23,43:2
Terrill, John, 1953, O 25,89:3
Terrill, Ralph P, 1967, Je 7,47:2
Terrill, Rogers, 1963, Mr 4,6:6
Terrill, Schuyler C, 1946, Je 22,19:2
Terrill, Schuyler C Jr, 1949, Ap 19,25:1
Terrill, Stewart R, 1966, Jl 31,72:4
Terrill, W R Gen, 1863, F 8,3:1
Terrington, Lord (H M Woodhouse), 1961, Ja 8,86:2
Terris, Arthur, 1945, Ag 29,23:3
Terris, Louis H, 1943, Jl 2,19:4
Terriss, Tom Mrs (M Devere), 1964, Ja 4,23:4
Terro (Bro Alban Raymund), 1964, Je 28,57:1
Terrone, Catello, 1950, Mr 30,29:2
Terrott, William J, 1944, F 29,17:4
Terry, A, 1946, S 10,7:2
Terry, A H Gen, 1890, D 17,5:3
Terry, Albert S, 1939, N 7,25:5
Terry, Amy R P Mrs, 1941, Jl 31,17:3
Terry, Anna Prentice Mrs, 1906, Ja 15,9:6
Terry, Anne, 1952, N 13,31:2
Terry, Arden P, 1949, Mr 1,25:5
Terry, Arthur, 1939, Jl 30,29:2
Terry, Arthur H Mrs, 1939, Ap 12,23:2
Terry, Arthur H Sr, 1941, D 27,19:5
Terry, Arthur Mrs, 1947, N 10,29:4
Terry, C A, 1903, Ja 10,1:2
Terry, C S, 1936, N 6,25:3
Terry, Carleton L, 1938, My 25,23:5
Terry, Carrie M C Mrs, 1940, O 14,19:3
Terry, Charles A, 1939, F 20,17:5
Terry, Charles A Mrs, 1944, O 10,23:3
Terry, Charles C, 1962, Mr 10,22:1
Terry, Charles E, 1943, Ag 27,17:2
Terry, Charles G, 1962, Mr 2,30:1
Terry, Charles H, 1910, My 8,II,13:4; 1938, Mr 12, 17:6; 1952, Ag 23,13:3
Terry, Charles H Dr, 1912, Ja 19,11:6
Terry, Charles T, 1923, F 20,17:3
Terry, Charles T Mrs, 1965, Je 9,47:2
Terry, D Rev, 1883, Mr 10,2:6
Terry, Donald M, 1947, F 18,25:1
Terry, E C, 1882, F 28,3:4
Terry, Edna Dr, 1913, S 27,13:5
Terry, Edward, 1882, Je 3,5:4; 1912, Ap 3,13:1
Terry, Edward C, 1954, N 5,15:4
Terry, Edward F, 1924, My 13,21:5
Terry, Edward F Mrs, 1949, My 3,25:5
Terry, Edward M, 1955, F 13,86:2
Terry, Edwin B, 1951, Ag 8,25:4
Terry, Eliphalet B Rev, 1922, O 10,21:3
Terry, Ellis T Mrs, 1937, Ap 26,19:3
Terry, Everett R Mrs, 1959, Ja 29,27:4
Terry, F S, 1926, Jl 24,11:4
Terry, Florence Mrs, 1906, Ap 23,11:5
Terry, Francis H, 1939, My 28,III,7:3
Terry, Frank E, 1940, S 10,23:5
Terry, Frederick, 1944, S 13,19:2
Terry, George C, 1950, O 27,29:4
Terry, George D, 1941, S 29,17:6
Terry, George D Mrs, 1947, Je 15,60:2
Terry, George F, 1948, S 26,76:3
Terry, George S, 1911, Ap 15,13:4
Terry, Harry L, 1943, Ag 27,17:4
Terry, Henry C, 1917, D 1,13:7
Terry, Herbert I, 1950, D 1,25:3
Terry, Herbert L, 1941, Ja 26,37:2
Terry, Ira L, 1939, My 7,III,6:8
Terry, Irving L Mrs, 1942, D 14,28:6
Terry, Isaiah F, 1946, My 18,19:2
Terry, J David, 1945, My 14,17:3
Terry, J E Harold, 1939, Ag 11,15:1
Terry, J William, 1966, Mr 15,39:4
Terry, James, 1912, O 19,11:5
Terry, James A, 1951, Je 15,23:2
Terry, James G, 1954, Jl 13,23:1
Terry, James G Mrs, 1937, Jl 22,19:4
Terry, James L Dr, 1915, My 3,11:2
Terry, James T, 1949, Jl 11,17:5
Terry, James W, 1941, Mr 22,15:6
Terry, Jay L, 1941, F 23,41:3
Terry, Jessie F Mrs, 1947, Ja 12,31:3
Terry, John, 1959, Mr 24,39:4
Terry, John H, 1944, S 14,23:4
Terry, John H Mrs, 1941, Ap 4,21:2
Terry, John Mrs, 1947, N 12,27:2
Terry, John N, 1951, D 21,27:2
Terry, John S, 1953, Jl 5,36:3
Terry, John T, 1942, Je 1,13:6
Terry, John Taylor, 1913, My 5,9:3
Terry, Jose A, 1954, Ap 22,29:3
Terry, Joseph F Sr, 1949, Mr 29,25:5
Terry, Killey E, 1950, Ap 2,92:3
Terry, Leon, 1967, Je 24,29:4
Terry, Leonard S, 1956, Mr 28,31:5
Terry, Lucy J Mrs, 1923, Ja 6,13:6
Terry, M, 1930, Ag 22,15:1
Terry, M O, 1933, O 13,19:1
Terry, Mahala Miss, 1902, D 30,9:5
Terry, Marshall O Mrs, 1912, Ag 18,II,11:6
Terry, Marshall O Mrs (will), 1947, My 6,29:2
Terry, Melville W, 1950, Ag 26,13:2
Terry, Minnie R Mrs, 1942, My 30,15:5
Terry, Nathaniel M, 1938, O 14,23:4
Terry, Orrin, 1941, O 23,23:1
Terry, Oscar F, 1955, Je 29,29:4
Terry, P A, 1884, Ag 26,1:4
Terry, R, 1933, D 29,21:5
Terry, Ralph D, 1949, Mr 19,15:5
Terry, Randall B, 1955, My 28,15:1
Terry, Rensselaer G, 1951, My 24,35:2
Terry, Rex, 1964, Jl 17,27:4
Terry, Richard R, 1938, Ap 19,21:2
Terry, Robert E H, 1953, Je 2,29:4
Terry, Roderick Jr, 1951, Je 8,27:2
Terry, Roger V, 1948, Ja 10,9:6
Terry, Ruth Mrs, 1940, O 23,23:4
Terry, Samuel B, 1953, O 12,27:6
Terry, Samuel H, 1947, D 24,21:3
Terry, Sarah A, 1954, O 17,87:2
Terry, Sarah A H Mrs, 1937, F 17,21:4
Terry, Schuyler B, 1945, Mr 21,23:4
Terry, Septer E, 1946, Mr 2,13:4
Terry, Silas W Rear-Adm, 1911, F 10,9:6
Terry, Simon, 1953, O 7,29:3
Terry, Theodore L, 1946, S 30,25:5
Terry, Thomas A, 1963, Ap 25,33:3
Terry, W E Sr, 1941, My 26,19:5
Terry, Wallace S, 1943, Je 10,21:5
Terry, Walter H Sr, 1950, Ag 8,29:2
Terry, Walter M, 1963, Ap 20,27:5
Terry, Walter O, 1947, Ag 30,15:3
Terry, Watt, 1961, Ap 26,39:3
Terry, William E, 1955, Jl 8,23:4
Terry, William Mrs (Blanche), 1965, N 30,41:3
Terry, William S, 1950, Ja 25,27:5
Terry, William T, 1938, S 3,13:4
Terry, Willis T, 1943, S 2,19:3
Terry, Wilson G, 1946, Ap 27,17:4
Terry, Wyllys, 1949, Ap 22,24:2
Teruzzi, Attilio, 1950, Ap 27,29:2
Tervo, Penna, 1956, F 27,23:6
Terwilleger, Benjamin F, 1946, Jl 5,19:5
Terwilliger, Anna Mrs, 1937, O 18,17:1
Terwilliger, Arner L, 1962, N 22,29:4
Terwilliger, Benjamin, 1950, Ag 27,89:2
Terwilliger, Carrie Mrs, 1941, Jl 20,31:4
Terwilliger, Charles, 1924, Ap 12,15:4
Terwilliger, Charles B Mrs, 1945, Ag 2,19:6
Terwilliger, Charles I, 1946, Jl 20,13:5
Terwilliger, Clarence W, 1940, Je 19,23:4
Terwilliger, Cornelius G, 1946, My 25,15:1
Terwilliger, Daniel F, 1950, Jl 9,69:2
Terwilliger, Emily Mrs, 1942, My 17,47:5
Terwilliger, Frederick R, 1947, F 8,17:5
Terwilliger, Gilbert S, 1953, O 20,29:5
Terwilliger, Halsey R, 1946, Ap 3,25:4
Terwilliger, Hiram, 1942, Mr 10,19:3
Terwilliger, John E, 1940, Ag 21,19:6
Terwilliger, Joseph F, 1950, Jl 23,56:3
Terwilliger, Lansing Mrs, 1944, Je 3,13:6
Terwilliger, Norbury, 1950, Mr 29,29:4
Terwilliger, Richard T, 1924, Je 30,15:3
Terwilliger, Robert H, 1941, Je 8,48:3
Terwilliger, William B Mrs, 1945, Je 6,21:3
Terwilliger, William F, 1951, D 30,24:2
Terwilliger, William G, 1954, My 25,27:1
Tery, G, 1928, Je 22,23:4
Terzaghi, Karl, 1963, O 26,27:2
Terzano, Stefano, 1959, Mr 30,31:1
Terzi, Louisa, 1948, S 29,31:1
Terzian, Bedros G, 1968, N 18,47:3
Terzian, Harutyun G, 1941, S 4,21:6
Tesauro, Thomas H, 1968, Ap 28,83:1
Tesch, Albert J, 1947, Ag 4,17:3
Tesch, Alfred R, 1956, Ag 1,23:1
Tesch, Robert, 1938, Ap 5,21:3
Teschemacher, Carl A Sr Mrs, 1961, Ag 20,86:3
Teschner, Bruno S, 1958, Je 4,33:4
Teschner, Paul A, 1945, My 27,26:2
Teschner, Victor, 1956, Mr 7,33:3
Tesio, Federico, 1954, My 2,88:5
Teske, Charles E Mrs, 1943, N 25,25:1
Teske, J William, 1951, Ap 8,92:4
Teske, Karl Mrs, 1952, O 30,31:3
Teske, William A, 1953, My 6,31:4
Teske, William B, 1953, Ap 18,19:6
Teskey, Harry W Mrs, 1955, N 7,29:2
Teskey, Stanley, 1957, S 1,57:2
Tesla, Nikola (por), 1943, Ja 8,19:1
Tesler, Ezra, 1939, F 2,19:4
Tesreau, Charles M, 1946, S 25,27:3
Tesseler, Barbara Mrs, 1943, Ag 15,39:1
Tessier, Albert P, 1954, Ja 19,26:3
Tessier, Auguste, 1938, F 11,23:2
Tessier, Gaston, 1960, Ag 9,27:6
Tessier, Robert, 1950, N 29,36:4
Test, C H, 1884, O 12,2:5
Test, Clarence L Lt-Col, 1925, My 6,23:3
Test, Clayton Sr, 1956, Ap 20,25:3
Test, Frederick C, 1939, Mr 19,III,7:1
Test, Frederick C Mrs, 1937, S 14,23:5
Test, Louis A, 1943, Ap 24,13:2
Test, Merlin, 1959, O 29,33:1
Test, Robert J, 1962, Ja 16,33:1
Testa, Gaetano, 1950, My 2,29:1
Testa, George G, 1944, Jl 6,15:5
Testa, Giacomo, 1962, S 30,86:8
Testerman, Charles C, 1956, S 21,25:3
Teston, Jules, 1955, Jl 26,25:4
Teta, Thomas A, 1959, My 27,35:3
Tetaz, Frederick F, 1949, N 17,29:1
Tetelman, Alex J, 1954, N 26,29:2
Tetelman, Louis L, 1952, Ag 26,25:4
Tetelman, Michael M, 1953, Ap 1,29:3
Teter, Charles K, 1959, My 31,76:4
Teter, James Mrs, 1951, Ag 17,17:4
Teter, John W, 1956, Ja 28,17:4
Teter, Lucius, 1950, O 23,23:2
Teter, W C, 1929, Ja 15,29:5
Teter, William C, 1954, N 21,87:3
Tether, Floyd E, 1939, O 10,23:3
Tether, Walter T, 1947, S 17,25:5
Tetley, Thomas R, 1938, Mr 23,23:2
Tetlow, Edwin J, 1951, F 6,27:2
Tetlow, Percy, 1960, N 22,35:3
Teto, William H, 1955, O 11,39:3
Tetor, Fred A, 1954, Ap 7,31:5
Tetrault, E A, 1952, D 12,29:4
Tetrault, Laurent, 1951, Mr 16,31:3
Tetrault, Napoleon, 1942, S 12,13:3
Tetrazzini, Luisa Mrs, 1940, Ap 29,15:1
Tetreault, Alvege Mrs, 1960, Mr 20,50:4
Tetreault, Edward P, 1955, Jl 9,15:1
Tetreault, George A, 1952, Ja 22,29:1
Tetreault, Theodore A, 1961, My 27,23:4
Tetrick, Guy, 1956, Jl 17,23:5
Tets van Goudriaan, G C W Van, 1948, F 7,15:3
Tettelbach, John E, 1950, My 6,15:5
Tetter, Charles Mrs, 1950, D 2,13:5
Tettofrezzo, Luigi, 1946, O 16,29:5
Tetzel, George J, 1965, Mr 3,41:3
Teuber, August P, 1959, Je 26,25:5
Teubner, Fred W, 1954, N 2,27:4
Teufel, Alex E, 1961, S 18,29:4
Teufel, Frederick G, 1953, Jl 8,27:4
Teufel, John, 1945, My 24,19:6
Teufel, Morris, 1950, F 2,27:5
Teuscher, Arthur C, 1968, Ja 4,37:3
Teusler, R B, 1934, Ag 11,13:1
Teveluwe, William A, 1956, S 20,33:4
Teves, Frederick W, 1951, F 7,29:4
Teves, Paul A, 1947, My 16,24:2
Tevis, Hugh, 1901, Je 8,9:5
Tevis, Lansing K, 1957, N 5,31:1
Tevlin, C J, 1966, D 4,88:8
Tevlin, Joseph F, 1939, Mr 17,21:3
Tevnan, Michael J, 1959, D 25,21:5
Tevosyan, Ivan F, 1958, Ap 1,31:6
Tevriz, Edward T, 1968, Ja 18,40:1
Tew, Benjamin T Mrs, 1944, Ja 20,19:2
Tew, J Dinsmore 2d, 1955, D 10,22:5
Tew, Oliver C, 1943, Mr 14,26:1
Tew, William H, 1939, Jl 6,23:2
Tew, William Henry Mrs (Eleanor), 1968, Mr 16, 31:4
Tewes, William A Col, 1953, F 23,25:2
Tewfik Nessim, Pasha, 1938, Mr 8,19:1
Tewfik Pasha, Ahmed, 1936, O 9,25:1
Tewhill, William F, 1945, My 7,17:5
Tewksbury, Donald G, 1958, D 10,39:1
Tewksbury, Elwood G (por), 1945, N 9,19:3

Tewksbury, James W, 1946, D 7,21:1
Tewksbury, Lewis G, 1910, F 12,9:3
Tewksbury, William Mrs, 1943, Mr 1,19:4
Tews, Albert R Jr, 1958, Je 15,77:2
Tewson, William O, 1947, Mr 15,13:1
Texel, Carl J, 1958, Mr 27,33:2
Texier, Edmond A, 1954, N 19,23:5
Texier, Hippolyte, 1948, Ag 3,25:2
Texiere, Jacob, 1944, My 2,19:3
Textor, Emil, 1937, My 6,25:4
Textor, George C, 1968, O 11,47:1
Textor, Gordon E, 1955, Mr 21,25:2
Textor, Lucy E, 1958, Je 30,19:5
Teytand, August P, 1956, Mr 9,23:3
Thach, Charles C, 1966, Jl 2,23:6
Thach, James H Jr, 1962, Jl 5,25:2
Thach, Robert G, 1955, My 30,13:5
Thacher, Amos B, 1946, Ja 14,19:5
Thacher, Archibald G, 1952, Ja 3,27:3
Thacher, Edwin, 1920, S 23,13:5
Thacher, Frank W, 1943, S 3,19:6
Thacher, Henry B, 1952, N 12,27:3
Thacher, Henry C, 1956, O 31,33:5
Thacher, John B, 1957, Ap 27,19:1
Thacher, John Boyd, 1909, F 26,7:3
Thacher, John S Mrs, 1962, Ja 31,31:1
Thacher, John Seymour Dr, 1922, O 31,15:4
Thacher, Louis B, 1952, O 10,25:3
Thacher, Sherman Mrs, 1944, O 25,21:5
Thacher, Thomas, 1919, Jl 31,9:3
Thacher, Thomas A (funl; cor, My 19,33:4), 1959, My 18,27:4
Thacher, Thomas C, 1945, Ap 12,23:6
Thacher, Thomas D, 1950, N 13,27:3
Thacher, Thomas D Mrs, 1943, Ja 20,19:2
Thacher, Thomas O, 1941, D 6,17:3
Thacher, Walter H, 1951, Ja 4,29:3
Thackara, Alex M, 1937, Ja 19,23:4
Thackara, Alexander M, 1921, D 28,15:6
Thackara, Alexander M Mrs, 1915, Jl 19,9:4
Thackara, Charles V, 1942, O 1,23:3
Thackara, Robert C, 1940, S 11,25:4
Thacker, Carl W, 1948, Je 5,15:3
Thacker, Herbert C, 1953, Je 4,29:2
Thacker, James K Mrs, 1946, Je 9,40:3
Thacker, James M, 1939, My 2,23:1
Thacker, William R, 1947, Ag 20,21:2
Thackeray, E T Sir, 1927, S 8,27:2
Thackeray, William Makepeace, 1864, Ja 9,1:1
Thackery, Joseph Rev, 1937, S 28,23:2
Thackery, Lance, 1916, Ag 12,9:7
Thackray, George E, 1944, S 26,23:6
Thackrey, Elizabeth Mrs, 1945, Mr 17,13:4
Thackrey, Lyman A, 1955, Ap 16,19:4
Thadden, Eberhard von, 1964, N 20,8:4
Thaike, Sao S, 1962, N 23,29:1
Thain, Emma J Mrs, 1939, Je 5,17:6
Thain, Francis J, 1947, Je 26,23:2
Thairs, George F Lt-Col, 1924, Jl 31,13:6
Thake, William E, 1951, Je 29,21:3
Thakkar, Amritlal V, 1951, Ja 20,15:1
Thakur Das, Andres Mrs, 1960, Mr 19,21:4
Thal, Albert J, 1953, S 29,26:3
Thal, Isidore, 1939, Je 20,11:3
Thal, Max, 1964, D 18,33:4
Thalberg, I G, 1936, S 15,29:3
Thalberg, Sigismund, 1871, Ap 30,5:2
Thalberg, William Mrs, 1945, N 26,21:5
Thalbert, Henry, 1905, Ja 6,1:4
Thale, Charles J, 1938, S 28,25:4
Thaler, Joseph A, 1938, Mr 6,II,8:2
Thalheimer, Alvin, 1965, Jl 10,25:4
Thalhimer, William, 1961, S 12,33:4
Thalimer, Clarence M, 1941, O 18,19:6
Thall, David V, 1953, Jl 23,23:4
Thallon, Robert, 1882, My 13,2:3
Thalmann, Edward E, 1942, Je 30,21:2
Thalmann, Ernest Mrs, 1962, S 23,86:7
Thalmann, Ernst (funl, F 29,11:5), 1912, F 27,9:2
Thalmann, Rene, 1957, O 18,12:6
Thalmessinger, Meger, 1906, Ap 28,11:6
Thams, Jacob T, 1954, Jl 29,23:4
Than Thai, Ex-Emperor of Annam, 1954, Mr 21,89:1
Thanhouser, Edwin, 1956, Mr 23,27:4
Thanhouser, Edwin Mrs, 1951, My 31,27:5
Thankerton, Baron, 1948, Je 14,24:3
Thant, Tin Maung (funl, My 24,8:4), 1962, My 22, 14:4
Tharaldsen, Conrad E (por), 1944, My 22,19:3
Tharaud, Jean, 1952, Ap 10,29:3
Tharaud, Jerome, 1953, Ja 29,28:5
Tharp, Alfred J Mrs, 1945, My 23,19:2
Tharp, Blucher S, 1954, N 14,88:8
Tharp, William H, 1948, F 17,25:2
Tharp, William J, 1958, O 5,87:2
Tharpe, William H, 1968, N 2,37:3
Thatcher, Allen R, 1948, Je 7,19:3
Thatcher, Arlington B, 1950, Ag 5,15:3
Thatcher, Charles J, 1958, Je 23,23:2
Thatcher, Chauncey F, 1944, N 1,23:4
Thatcher, Edward J, 1953, Ag 19,29:3
Thatcher, Edwin H, 1940, O 8,25:5; 1953, Jl 8,27:6
Thatcher, Frank H, 1940, N 13,23:2
Thatcher, G W, 1902, D 25,7:7
Thatcher, George, 1913, Je 26,9:5
Thatcher, George B, 1946, O 17,23:2
Thatcher, George F, 1957, S 30,31:3
Thatcher, H K Rear-Adm, 1880, Ap 6,5:4
Thatcher, Harry C, 1945, Mr 2,19:1
Thatcher, Hervey D Dr, 1925, My 26,21:4
Thatcher, John (funl), 1912, Je 22,13:6
Thatcher, John C, 1949, Ja 30,60:8
Thatcher, John M P Mrs, 1966, Ap 12,39:1
Thatcher, John S, 1966, Je 25,14:6
Thatcher, John T, 1909, Mr 5,9:3
Thatcher, Joseph R, 1941, F 21,19:3
Thatcher, Linden A, 1944, Je 27,19:3
Thatcher, Mahlon Daniel, 1916, F 23,13:4
Thatcher, Mary H Mrs, 1940, Je 10,17:5
Thatcher, Moses, 1909, Ag 24,9:6
Thatcher, Norman H, 1947, Ja 1,33:5
Thatcher, Oliver J Prof, 1937, Ag 24,21:5
Thatcher, R W, 1933, D 7,23:3
Thatcher, Ralph H, 1943, Ja 19,19:2
Thatcher, Raymond L, 1957, My 19,88:3
Thatcher, Russell N Sr, 1952, Ja 5,11:3
Thatcher, S, 1868, Ag 11,2:7
Thatcher, T F, 1879, Jl 2,5:2
Thatcher, Walter E, 1959, Ja 8,29:3
Thatcher, William D, 1941, Mr 12,21:2
Thatcher, William H, 1953, Jl 21,23:4
Thatcher, William L, 1951, S 27,31:5
Thaten, Max, 1943, Ag 27,17:5
Thau, Sigmund, 1946, My 27,23:5
Thaulow, Fritz, 1906, N 6,9:5
Thavenot, Charles V, 1966, Je 14,48:1
Thaw, Alex B, 1937, O 6,25:6
Thaw, B Mrs, 1931, N 14,17:3
Thaw, Benjamin, 1937, Mr 6,17:6
Thaw, Florence D Mrs, 1940, Mr 6,23:2
Thaw, Harry K, 1947, F 23,53:1
Thaw, Josiah C, 1944, Mr 16,19:3
Thaw, Josiah C Mrs, 1947, F 25,26:3
Thaw, Lawrence C, 1965, Je 28,29:3
Thaw, Mary Copley Mrs, 1929, Je 10,25:3
Thaw, W 2d, 1934, Ap 23,17:1
Thaw, William Jr Mrs, 1948, O 4,23:3
Thaw, William 3d, 1948, Ag 26,21:3
Thaw, William 3d Mrs, 1956, Ja 16,21:1
Thaw, William 4th, 1948, Mr 8,23:5
Thawley, Wilbur W, 1950, Je 8,31:3
Thaxter, Celia, 1894, Ag 28,5:2
Thaxter, E R, 1881, Ag 9,3:4
Thaxter, John C, 1968, S 15,84:8
Thaxter, Roger L, 1958, Jl 18,21:4
Thaxter, Sidney St F Mrs, 1966, Ag 2,31:5
Thaxton, Sidney W Maj, 1908, N 11,19:7
Thayer, A, 1927, Ag 17,23:1
Thayer, Abbott Handerson, 1921, My 30,9:5
Thayer, Alfred V, 1952, N 10,25:1
Thayer, Amos Madden Judge, 1905, Ap 25,11:5
Thayer, Annie M, 1955, My 10,29:2
Thayer, B B, 1933, F 23,17:1
Thayer, Bayard, 1916, N 30,13:4
Thayer, Bayard Mrs, 1941, Ap 1,23:2
Thayer, C P, 1879, My 27,5:4
Thayer, Carroll, 1938, O 19,23:4
Thayer, Charles A, 1950, O 11,33:3; 1953, Mr 10,29:3
Thayer, Charles R, 1953, D 12,19:4
Thayer, Clarence A, 1937, S 19,II,7:1
Thayer, Don O, 1968, D 23,39:2
Thayer, Edgar R, 1954, N 11,31:3
Thayer, Edward C, 1949, F 8,25:2
Thayer, Edward Darlong, 1907, Jl 18,7:6
Thayer, Edward N Mrs, 1873, Jl 24,5:7
Thayer, Edwin P, 1943, F 3,19:2
Thayer, Eliza P, 1964, N 10,47:1
Thayer, Elizabeth B C Mrs, 1941, Ja 3,19:3
Thayer, Ernest L, 1940, Ag 22,19:1
Thayer, Eugene V (will, Ja 16,21:4), 1937, Ja 2,11:5
Thayer, Eugene V (will), 1938, D 1,21:2
Thayer, Eugene V R, 1907, D 21,9:6
Thayer, Everett Henry, 1905, Ap 2,9:6
Thayer, F A, 1883, Mr 27,5:4
Thayer, F S, 1880, N 27,5:4
Thayer, Frank G, 1950, My 28,37:3
Thayer, Frederick A, 1942, My 22,21:4
Thayer, Frederick D, 1948, N 8,21:1
Thayer, Frederick M, 1956, N 17,21:4
Thayer, George A, 1937, My 16,II,8:7
Thayer, George A Dr, 1925, O 5,21:5
Thayer, George C Col, 1923, Ap 5,19:6
Thayer, George C Jr, 1952, Ap 22,30:5
Thayer, George C Mrs, 1964, My 28,37:4
Thayer, George W, 1946, F 22,25:4
Thayer, Gerald A, 1943, N 10,23:3
Thayer, Gerald H, 1939, Je 8,25:4
Thayer, H B, 1936, S 4,19:5
Thayer, Henry, 1916, Mr 25,13:3
Thayer, Henry W, 1940, My 13,17:5
Thayer, Horace H Jr, 1959, F 20,25:2
Thayer, J B Prof, 1902, F 15,9:5
Thayer, J H Rev, 1901, N 27,9:5
Thayer, James J, 1923, Jl 9,13:5
Thayer, James Lyman, 1909, F 23,9:2
Thayer, John B Mrs, 1944, Ap 15,11:4
Thayer, John M Gen, 1906, Mr 20,9:5
Thayer, John R, 1916, D 20,13:4
Thayer, John V (por), 1940, D 6,27:2
Thayer, Joseph F, 1912, Ap 11,11:3
Thayer, Lewis P, 1937, S 24,21:3
Thayer, Lillian A, 1939, Mr 6,15:2
Thayer, Louis E, 1956, S 12,37:2
Thayer, Lucius E, 1968, Ap 11,45:3
Thayer, Lucius F, 1919, Ag 11,11:4
Thayer, Lyman E, 1942, Jl 24,19:6
Thayer, Maude, 1955, Je 18,17:4
Thayer, N, 1883, Mr 8,5:4
Thayer, N Mrs, 1934, S 30,35:1
Thayer, Nathan, 1884, S 25,5:7
Thayer, Nathan P, 1943, S 19,48:1
Thayer, Nathan R, 1874, Je 27,4:6
Thayer, Nathaniel, 1911, Mr 22,11:5
Thayer, Nelson W Mrs, 1948, Je 24,25:1
Thayer, Philip H, 1968, Ag 15,37:4
Thayer, Philip W, 1966, D 20,43:1
Thayer, Raymond L, 1955, N 16,35:4
Thayer, Robert W, 1956, D 18,31:4
Thayer, Rufus G, 1965, O 17,87:1
Thayer, Rufus Hildreth Judge, 1917, Jl 13,9:5
Thayer, Russell Jr, 1955, Ja 2,77:3
Thayer, S W Dr, 1882, N 15,5:4
Thayer, Samuel R, 1909, Ja 8,9:5
Thayer, Seth, 1961, Je 29,33:5
Thayer, Simon Willard, 1925, S 8,21:6
Thayer, Stephen F Mrs, 1937, Je 21,19:4
Thayer, Stephen Henry, 1919, D 18,13:4
Thayer, Stephen Henry Mrs, 1907, Ja 2,7:5
Thayer, Stephen Van Rensselaer, 1907, Je 26,7:5
Thayer, Sylvanus Gen, 1872, S 18,5:4
Thayer, Thomas Redmond, 1968, Jl 12,31:3
Thayer, Tiffany (funl plans, Ag 26,29:5), 1959, Ag 24,21:1
Thayer, W, 1933, Ap 19,17:1
Thayer, W B, 1907, Ap 1,9:7
Thayer, W N Jr, 1936, Ja 7,21:3
Thayer, Walter N Jr Mrs, 1958, Jl 2,29:1
Thayer, Warren B, 1939, Ja 8,43:3
Thayer, Warren T, 1956, Mr 10,17:2
Thayer, Wendell G, 1957, Ja 7,25:2
Thayer, William, 1944, Ap 24,19:4
Thayer, William A, 1952, Ja 26,13:5
Thayer, William E, 1953, Mr 21,17:3
Thayer, William G Mrs, 1962, N 18,86:1
Thayer, William H, 1939, D 31,18:8
Thayer, William Roscoe, 1923, S 8,13:5
Theaker, T C, 1883, Jl 17,4:7
Theall, Elisha S Col, 1921, Ja 29,11:5
Theall, Francis M Jr, 1945, Je 1,15:5
Theban, Theodore A, 1944, Je 6,17:6
Theban, Theodore Adrian, 1925, Je 9,21:4
Thebaud, Edward P Mrs, 1955, Je 17,23:4
Thebaud, Julius, 1876, O 21,10:5
Thebaud, Louis A (por), 1939, Ap 3,15:3
Thebaud, Mathilde E R Mrs, 1938, Je 6,17:5
Thebaud, Paul G Sr, 1925, Je 22,15:5
Thebaud, Paul Gilbert Sr, 1925, Je 23,19:4
Thebaud, Paul L Mrs, 1901, Jl 4,7:4
Thebault, William L, 1951, D 24,13:5
Thebes, de Mme, 1937, D 10,26:3
Thebom, Caroline E Mrs, 1953, Ag 23,89:1
Thecauld, Rene G I, 1954, N 22,23:4
Thedenat, Henri, 1916, N 1,11:6
Theders, Clarence G, 1948, Ja 20,23:3
Thedford, George W, 1914, D 15,13:6
Thedford, Harry W, 1956, Ja 4,29:5
Thee, Joseph, 1951, Ag 28,23:1
Theebaw, King of Burmah, 1880, Ap 9,5:6
Theidge, William, 1948, S 9,27:6
Theile, Frederick C, 1944, D 6,23:3
Theile, William, 1944, F 5,15:5
Theilhaber, Felix A, 1956, Ja 27,23:4
Theimer, Eugene, 1952, My 7,27:4
Theimer, Eugene Mrs, 1954, Jl 4,31:1
Theimer, Gustave, 1941, F 26,21:5
Theimer, Max, 1950, Jl 22,15:4
Theimer, Max Mrs, 1949, My 20,28:6
Theis, Edward F, 1965, Jl 16,27:3
Theis, Edward H, 1937, N 25,31:6
Theis, Frank A, 1965, N 26,37:1
Theis, Grover, 1950, O 9,25:5
Theis, Kenneth G, 1941, O 17,23:4
Theis, Leroy W, 1948, N 18,27:1
Theis, Samuel C, 1947, Je 26,23:4
Theis, Sophie V (trb lr, Ap 13,18:6), 1957, Ap 8,23:5
Theis, Stanley J, 1950, F 17,24:2
Theis, Victor, 1947, S 11,27:4
Theise, Fannie, 1947, My 31,13:4
Theise, Mortimer D, 1945, O 16,23:5
Theisen, J J, 1945, Mr 30,15:4
Theisen, John L, 1947, O 13,24:2
Theisinger, Earl F, 1960, Jl 30,17:4
Theiss, John H, 1950, N 24,36:4
Theiss, Joseph, 1944, Ja 28,17:5
Theiss, Lewis E, 1963, My 23,37:2
Theiss, Paul S, 1956, Je 5,35:2
Theissling, Louis Rev, 1925, My 3,5:2
Thelander, Ramon O, 1964, F 11,39:1
Thelen, Harvey P, 1946, Ag 29,27:5

Thelen, William J, 1937, Ag 11,24:1
Thelin, Ernst, 1945, N 10,15:3
Theller, Erling C, 1953, F 20,20:3
Thellusson, Adeline, 1937, D 4,17:3
Thellusson, Charles F, 1949, Ja 30,60:6
Themelis, Alex, 1950, Jl 10,13:6
Themelis, Nicholas S, 1947, Je 27,21:5
Then, Joseph B, 1944, Mr 17,17:2
Thenaud, Franc, 1945, N 24,19:4
Thenault, Georges T (por), 1948, D 22,23:1
Thenen, Solomon L, 1945, Ja 9,19:6
Thenon, Georges, 1941, My 27,23:4
Theobald, Carl, 1961, Mr 3,27:2
Theobald, Carl E, 1945, D 16,39:2
Theobald, Edward P, 1941, N 4,26:5
Theobald, H, 1934, Je 9,15:4
Theobald, Harry J, 1955, S 10,17:6
Theobald, Henry, 1924, Jl 14,15:4
Theobald, Jacob, 1968, S 26,47:1
Theobald, Jacob Mrs, 1955, Mr 4,23:2
Theobald, John J, 1955, Jl 7,27:4
Theobald, Robert A, 1957, My 14,35:1
Theobald, Thomas Alexander, 1923, Je 8,19:5
Theoclitos, Archbishop, 1962, Ja 9,47:1
Theodor, Karl Duke, 1909, D 1,9:5
Theodor, Martha, 1949, Ja 27,23:3
Theodore, Charles Prince of Bavaria, 1875, Ag 17,4:6
Theodore, Davilmar Gen, 1917, Ja 29,11:5
Theodore, Edward G, 1950, F 10,23:3
Theodore, Jennie J Mrs, 1940, F 19,17:3
Theodore, Millard E, 1964, Ag 8,19:2
Theodorowych, Epiphanius B, 1958, F 4,29:3
Theofel, John, 1948, Ja 8,25:3
Theofel, John Mrs, 1946, Je 15,21:2
Theophane Lawrence, Bro, 1960, D 25,42:2
Theophylacots, Archbishop, 1958, Ag 3,9:1
Theopold, Edward T, 1959, N 18,41:2
Theotokis, G N, 1916, Ja 26,11:2
Theresa, Sister (Annie Walker), 1885, Ja 22,5:3
Theresa Mary, Sister, 1956, Mr 7,33:4
Theresa of Breganza , Princess, 1909, D 18,13:4
Theriault, Alphonse N, 1958, Jl 12,15:3
Theriot, Albert, 1915, Ag 4,11:5
Therkelsen, Erid, 1941, F 16,40:2
Therkelsen, Larry, 1951, F 1,25:3
Therkildson, Wro F, 1944, Mr 13,15:2
Theroux, Ernest G, 1955, D 28,23:2
Therrien, Pierre Rev, 1951, Jl 15,61:3
Therry, John J, 1956, Ja 7,17:1
Therry, Stephen, 1909, Je 13,9:5
Thery, Edmund, 1925, My 9,15:4
Thesiger, A H Lord Justice, 1880, O 21,5:4
Thesiger, Ernest, 1961, Ja 15,86:6
Thesterton, Frank H, 1923, Ag 27,11:3
Thetford, William E, 1903, N 26,7:6
Theuer, Bernard L, 1953, Ja 7,31:3
Theuer, Will A, 1960, Ja 17,86:7
Theunis, Georges, 1966, Ja 6,27:1
Theurer, Anna M, 1952, Mr 2,92:1
Theurer, Charles, 1946, Mr 29,23:3
Theurer, E F Charles, 1951, O 31,29:2
Theurer, Erich G, 1952, Jl 9,27:6
Thevenow, Tommy, 1957, Jl 30,23:4
Thevi, Leon, 1953, Ja 28,27:1
Thew, Clarence Mrs, 1950, N 20,25:3
Thew, Robert G, 1964, Mr 3,35:1
Thewlis, Malford W, 1956, Je 4,29:5
Thewman, Samuel, 1940, Mr 23,13:5
Thexton, Joseph R, 1961, Ag 26,17:3
Theysohn, Charles Mrs, 1947, Mr 12,25:3
Theyson, Louis, 1946, D 7,21:2
Thibaud, Jean, 1960, My 23,29:4
Thibaudeau, Alphonse A, 1949, Ap 7,29:4
Thibault, Harold F, 1938, Mr 6,II,8:4
Thibault, Lorenzo H, 1944, S 9,15:6
Thibault, Onesime C, 1947, Ja 27,23:5
Thibault, Zephirin, 1953, N 15,88:8
Thibaut, M H Mrs (will), 1939, Je 11,16:2
Thibaut, Richard E, 1957, S 18,33:1
Thibbitts, Aloysius B, 1942, Je 12,21:3
Thibodeau, Joseph D, 1947, Mr 28,23:3
Thiboust, Lambert, 1867, Jl 26,2:6
Thickens, Richard, 1954, Mr 23,27:2
Thickitt, William E, 1939, Mr 12,III,7:3
Thicknesse, Francis N, 1946, Ap 14,46:2
Thickstun, Ann, 1950, O 12,31:1
Thiebeault, Charles J, 1944, Je 30,21:5
Thiede, Michael C, 1952, F 20,29:2
Thiede, William F, 1964, D 22,29:4
Thiehoff, William F, 1953, Mr 22,86:7
Thieisen, Albert A, 1940, Jl 26,17:3
Thiel, Emil E, 1954, My 13,29:4
Thiel, Ernest H, 1948, Ja 11,56:2
Thiel, Howard, 1961, O 10,43:4
Thiel, Louis, 1949, Je 9,14:3
Thiel, Max, 1953, Mr 25,31:5
Thielbar, Frances C, 1962, Mr 24,25:4
Thielbar, Frederick J, 1941, N 16,56:3
Thiele, Arthur R, 1950, Jl 3,15:5
Thiele, Edward B, 1957, Mr 6,31:6
Thiele, John E, 1957, O 19,21:4
Thiele, Julius, 1952, D 13,21:2
Thieleman, Charles H, 1942, D 11,23:6
Thieler, Edward F, 1956, Mr 21,37:4
Thiell, Annandale K Mrs, 1954, My 15,15:3
Thielpape, John H, 1945, Ag 24,19:4
Thiem, Adolph O, 1949, S 16,27:3
Thieman, Otto, 1963, My 19,86:3
Thieme, Christian W, 1944, My 3,19:1
Thieme, Hugo P, 1940, Je 4,23:5
Thieme, Theodore F, 1949, Ag 12,17:2
Thien, Henry G, 1941, My 22,21:5
Thien, Herbert, 1961, Mr 23,33:1
Thien, Herbert Mrs, 1943, Jl 9,17:5
Thien, John H, 1940, Ja 15,15:4
Thien, R R, 1903, My 30,7:5
Thienemann, Johannes W, 1938, Ap 14,23:2
Thienes, Elmer T, 1950, F 7,27:1
Thienes, Henry, 1946, F 25,26:2
Thienes, Patrick Philip, 1968, My 1,47:4
Thier, J Ernest, 1959, O 10,21:5
Thierbach, George C, 1952, D 4,35:2
Thierbach, Russell P, 1947, Jl 17,19:4
Thieriot, Charles H, 1941, Ja 11,17:2
Thieriot, Ferdinand M, 1956, Jl 28,6:1
Thieriot, Ferdinand M Mrs, 1919, Jl 26,9:6; 1956, Jl 28,6:1
Thieriot, Ferdinand Mrs, 1954, Ap 5,25:2
Thieriot, Fred Melly, 1904, Je 28,9:6
Thierot, Charles H Mrs, 1957, My 2,31:4
Thierry, Amedee-Simon Dominique, 1873, Mr 28,5:5
Thierry, Edward M, 1944, Ap 18,21:3
Thierry, Joseph, 1918, S 24,13:4
Thiers, L A (see also S 4), 1877, S 5,1:5
Thiers, Louise G Mrs, 1938, My 4,23:1
Thiers, M Daughter of, 1873, Ap 1,1:5
Thiers, Mme, 1880, D 13,1:4
Thiersch, Friedrich Prof, 1860, Je 15,2:1
Thiery, Charles W, 1958, Mr 18,29:5
Thies, Henry F, 1941, N 4,23:5
Thies, John A, 1944, Ja 9,43:1
Thies, William F, 1949, Ag 21,69:2
Thiesing, Edward H, 1938, Ag 17,19:4
Thiesing, Henry G, 1946, D 1,79:4
Thiesing, Henry G Mrs, 1942, O 6,24:2
Thiesing, Karl H, 1965, Ja 17,89:1
Thiesing, Karl H Mrs, 1937, Jl 19,15:1
Thiess, Charles J, 1943, Ja 4,15:2
Thiess, Emil Capt, 1917, S 25,11:7
Thiessen, Herman, 1952, F 27,27:3
Thiffault, Alphonse E, 1947, O 20,23:1
Thijssen, Johan N J E H, 1944, Ja 16,43:1
Thikoupis, Nicholas, 1959, F 28,19:6
Thil, Marcel, 1968, Ag 15,37:2
Thill, Frank A, 1957, My 23,33:4
Thilly, Frank Mrs, 1953, S 22,31:1
Thilly, John E Mrs, 1967, Jl 7,31:5
Thimayya, Kondendera S (more details, D 19,85:1), 1965, D 18,29:6
Thimig, Hugo, 1944, S 27,21:4
Thimmes, James G, 1955, Ja 17,23:5
Thirer, Irene (Mrs Z Freedman), 1964, F 20,29:5
Thirkell, Angela, 1961, Ja 30,23:5
Thirkield, W P, 1936, N 9,19:1
Thirlkeld, Harold W, 1953, N 18,32:4
Thirlwall, J, 1879, N 6,5:4
Thirwall, Connop Bp, 1875, Jl 28,4:6
Thiry, Emil, 1944, Je 26,15:3
Thiry, John H, 1911, Je 24,9:5
Thistle, Edward B, 1948, O 17,76:1
Thistle, Robert K, 1954, Je 2,31:3
Thistlethwaite, Glenn F, 1956, O 7,86:4
Thistlethwaite, Joseph L, 1946, Ja 19,13:4
Thistlethwaite, Mark, 1947, Ja 15,26:2
Thistlethwaite, Mark Mrs, 1950, Ja 21,17:3
Thitchener, Conrad K, 1946, N 20,31:4
Thitchener, William H, 1942, O 21,21:2
Thobe, Daniela, 1940, Jl 30,19:4
Thoburn, Isabella, 1901, S 4,7:7
Thoburn, James M Bp, 1922, N 29,17:5
Thodd, Albert E, 1918, Mr 13,11:3
Thode, E Frederick, 1939, D 16,17:2
Thode, E K, 1962, O 22,29:3
Thode, Henry, 1920, N 11,13:5
Thoenebe, George L, 1938, Ag 9,19:3
Thoener, Charles H, 1924, My 24,15:4
Thoens, Harry, 1952, Ap 25,23:1
Thoens, Margaret J R Mrs, 1937, Ap 2,23:2
Thoeny, John, 1948, O 26,31:5
Thoeny, William, 1949, My 4,29:1
Thoericht, Isabella M Mrs, 1943, D 30,17:1
Thoernberg, Ernst H, 1961, N 15,43:4
Thol, Henry, 1944, Jl 29,13:6
Thole, Henry, 1945, D 14,27:2
Tholl, C Harold, 1949, Je 15,29:2
Tholuck, A, 1877, Jl 4,4:6
Thom, Charles, 1956, My 27,88:3
Thom, Charlotte M Mrs, 1939, Ag 21,8:4
Thom, Corcoran, 1956, Ja 19,33:3
Thom, Daniel M B Dr, 1915, D 19,17:5
Thom, Douglas A, 1951, F 24,13:5
Thom, Douglas L, 1962, N 5,31:5
Thom, George A, 1954, D 4,17:4
Thom, James, 1953, F 27,21:3
Thom, John, 1950, Ag 26,13:7
Thom, John H, 1937, Ja 8,19:4
Thom, W H D W, 1932, Ag 7,24:1
Thom, William B, 1964, O 7,47:5
Thom, William R, 1960, Ag 29,25:4
Thoma, Abraham M, 1947, S 3,25:3
Thoma, Albert W, 1967, Mr 26,68:8
Thoma, Caroline (will), 1945, Ag 11,13:2
Thoma, Charles O, 1941, Jl 21,28:3
Thoma, Hans, 1924, N 8,15:5
Thoma, Ludwig F Dr, 1912, Je 23,17:4
Thoma, Ritter von, 1948, My 1,15:4
Thoma, Roswell F, 1962, N 17,25:5
Thoma, Theodore A, 1952, Ag 27,27:4
Thoma, William L, 1966, Jl 17,68:3
Thoman, William F, 1959, Mr 7,21:4
Thomann, Eugene, 1941, My 6,21:2
Thomann, Frederick C, 1952, Ja 23,27:1
Thomann, William F, 1955, S 18,86:6
Thomas, A, 1934, Ag 13,1:5
Thomas, A D, 1939, N 8,23:2
Thomas, A J, 1903, Ap 25,9:4
Thomas, Aaron S, 1915, O 23,11:6
Thomas, Abel C, 1945, F 23,17:4
Thomas, Abner C (funl, Ja 21,13:5), 1911, Ja 18,9:5
Thomas, Adam, 1946, Ag 4,45:1
Thomas, Addison C, 1923, Ja 24,13:6
Thomas, Addison Col, 1908, Jl 29,7:4
Thomas, Adolph A, 1951, D 30,24:5
Thomas, Adolph A Mrs, 1951, D 27,19:3
Thomas, Adolph E, 1960, Ap 3,86:2
Thomas, Alan M, 1957, Ja 18,7:1
Thomas, Albert, 1966, F 16,43:2
Thomas, Albert D, 1925, N 15,13:1
Thomas, Albert E, 1939, N 2,23:2
Thomas, Albert E (por), 1947, Je 19,21:1
Thomas, Albert E Mrs, 1963, Ap 14,92:6
Thomas, Albert L, 1942, My 11,15:5
Thomas, Alexander T, 1947, O 29,27:4
Thomas, Alfred H Dr, 1937, Ap 16,23:5
Thomas, Alfred V, 1950, S 12,27:5
Thomas, Allen C, 1952, N 25,29:2
Thomas, Allen Clapp, 1920, D 16,17:4
Thomas, Allen Gen, 1907, D 5,9:4
Thomas, Allen Mrs, 1949, Mr 22,25:2
Thomas, Ambrose L, 1906, N 11,9:6
Thomas, Andrew J, 1913, Ja 12,II,17:1; 1965, Jl 27, 33:3
Thomas, Anna F Mrs, 1942, N 15,59:2
Thomas, Anne T Mrs, 1938, Ap 6,23:2
Thomas, Art, 1951, Je 5,31:1
Thomas, Arthur E, 1948, Mr 11,27:4
Thomas, Arthur E Mrs, 1948, My 4,25:3
Thomas, Arthur F, 1953, S 1,23:1
Thomas, Arthur H, 1942, S 1,19:2
Thomas, Arthur L, 1944, O 5,23:2
Thomas, Arthur N, 1954, Ap 11,86:3
Thomas, Arthur R, 1967, O 25,47:1
Thomas, Arthur S, 1956, S 12,37:2
Thomas, Augustus K, 1937, S 28,23:4
Thomas, Augustus Mrs, 1949, O 31,25:4
Thomas, B S, 1878, S 28,5:4
Thomas, Bajulus, 1941, Mr 15,17:5
Thomas, Benjamin, 1921, Ja 7,13:5
Thomas, Benjamin F, 1914, Je 26,13:6; 1958, Ja 28, 28:2
Thomas, Benjamin J, 1949, Mr 18,25:3
Thomas, Berkley A, 1952, Mr 5,29:2
Thomas, Bertram, 1950, D 30,13:1
Thomas, Bond, 1920, Ja 26,7:2
Thomas, Brandon, 1914, Je 20,9:6
Thomas, Bruce, 1954, N 4,34:8
Thomas, Brunwell, 1948, Ja 25,56:6
Thomas, C G M, 1926, Mr 21,28:3
Thomas, C L A, 1896, F 13,9:5
Thomas, C Maj-Gen, 1878, F 4,4:7
Thomas, C S, 1934, Je 25,15:1
Thomas, C Wesley, 1907, Je 15,9:6
Thomas, C Y, 1879, F 14,4:7
Thomas, Calvin, 1944, Mr 4,13:5
Thomas, Calvin Dr, 1919, N 5,15:1
Thomas, Calvin L, 1964, S 27,87:1
Thomas, Calvin Mrs, 1940, Ap 19,21:1; 1951, Ap 19, 31:4
Thomas, Camp C, 1951, N 17,17:5
Thomas, Cantidius Rev (por), 1937, F 21,II,11:3
Thomas, Carey S, 1956, Ja 11,31:3
Thomas, Carl C, 1938, Je 6,17:5
Thomas, Caroline W Mrs, 1939, My 15,17:6
Thomas, Catherine Mrs, 1946, S 7,15:3
Thomas, Cecil, 1960, O 28,31:2
Thomas, Cecil B, 1956, Je 12,35:1
Thomas, Cecil V, 1947, N 29,13:3
Thomas, Charles, 1905, Ap 9,4:3
Thomas, Charles A, 1950, Jl 7,19:1
Thomas, Charles C, 1903, Jl 22,7:6; 1959, Ap 7,33:3
Thomas, Charles D Mrs, 1955, D 6,37:3
Thomas, Charles E, 1937, F 14,II,9:2
Thomas, Charles F, 1943, Ap 3,15:5
Thomas, Charles H, 1944, Ap 24,19:5
Thomas, Charles J, 1949, Mr 9,26:3
Thomas, Charles M Dr, 1916, Ja 15,9:6
Thomas, Charles M Rear-Adm, 1908, Jl 13,7:7
Thomas, Charles McG Jr, 1966, Jl 21,33:3
Thomas, Charles N, 1937, Ja 24,II,9:1; 1946, N 5,25:3

Thomas, Charles R, 1948, O 30,13:2
Thomas, Charles S, 1943, Je 28,21:1; 1945, Jl 18,27:3
Thomas, Charles T, 1948, Ag 1,58:2
Thomas, Charles W, 1946, Jl 20,13:5
Thomas, Chauncey Rear-Adm, 1919, My 16,15:4
Thomas, Clarence W, 1938, F 21,19:4
Thomas, Claude A, 1949, D 31,15:5
Thomas, Clifford C, 1958, O 17,29:4
Thomas, Clinton G, 1950, N 13,27:2
Thomas, Conover A, 1946, Je 4,23:3
Thomas, Cornelius F, 1941, F 12,21:2
Thomas, Craig R, 1957, Je 3,27:1
Thomas, Cullen F, 1938, D 9,25:6
Thomas, Cyrus Prof, 1910, Je 28,7:6
Thomas, D D Rev Dr, 1917, O 26,15:5
Thomas, Daniel, 1948, Je 17,25:2; 1950, F 8,28:2
Thomas, Daniel C, 1943, Ap 23,17:2
Thomas, Daniel L, 1940, Ag 10,13:2
Thomas, David, 1882, Je 21,5:5
Thomas, David Alfred (Viscount Rhonddd), 1918, Jl 4,13:3
Thomas, David J, 1952, Jl 20,53:1
Thomas, David L, 1952, N 13,31:2
Thomas, David O Mrs, 1952, S 16,29:2
Thomas, DeWitt V B Mrs, 1959, O 18,86:6
Thomas, Dorothea Mrs, 1953, Ap 14,27:4
Thomas, Douglas H, 1919, Mr 13,11:3
Thomas, Dylan, 1953, N 10,31:1
Thomas, E Eldridge, 1966, Ja 20,35:2
Thomas, E R, 1926, Jl 7,25:3; 1936, S 14,27:3
Thomas, Earl B, 1960, Je 16,33:2
Thomas, Earl B Mrs, 1938, Mr 23,23:2
Thomas, Earl Denison Brig-Gen, 1923, My 11,17:5
Thomas, Earl Roger, 1968, Mr 8,39:3
Thomas, Eben Briggs, 1919, S 5,11:1
Thomas, Edgar C, 1949, My 19,29:5
Thomas, Edith M, 1925, S 15,25:6
Thomas, Edmund E Mrs, 1955, My 10,29:4
Thomas, Edmund W, 1958, F 25,27:2
Thomas, Edson, 1902, D 17,9:6
Thomas, Edward, 1962, N 18,86:1
Thomas, Edward A, 1954, Ja 26,27:4
Thomas, Edward A Sr, 1943, Mr 24,23:2
Thomas, Edward Dr, 1904, F 4,5:3
Thomas, Edward H, 1937, D 12,II,8:4
Thomas, Edward J, 1954, N 20,17:3
Thomas, Edward J Mrs, 1961, Ap 1,17:4
Thomas, Edward M, 1951, Ap 15,92:5
Thomas, Edward R, 1939, Je 27,23:5
Thomas, Edward S, 1913, Ag 21,9:6
Thomas, Edward W, 1943, Ag 15,38:5; 1966, Je 22, 47:1
Thomas, Edwin, 1924, Ag 18,13:3; 1939, Jl 5,17:5
Thomas, Edwin J, 1950, Ja 11,23:5
Thomas, Edwin L, 1908, D 9,13:3
Thomas, Edwin S, 1952, Ja 22,29:6
Thomas, Elbert D Comr (funl, F 15,92:7), 1953, F 12,27:1
Thomas, Elbert D Mrs, 1942, My 1,19:5
Thomas, Eleazur Rev Dr, 1873, Ap 16,1:7
Thomas, Elisabeth F Mrs, 1955, Je 29,29:2
Thomas, Elmer (Sept 19), 1965, O 11,61:5
Thomas, Elmer J, 1952, S 26,21:1
Thomas, Elmer W, 1946, Ag 12,21:4
Thomas, Emma L Mrs, 1939, Jl 14,19:4
Thomas, Enoch H Sr, 1955, Ja 7,21:1
Thomas, Eric, 1959, Ap 4,38:6; 1963, Ja 19,7:2
Thomas, Ernest B, 1942, N 12,25:2
Thomas, Ernest E, 1939, F 12,45:1
Thomas, Ernest K, 1941, N 11,23:1
Thomas, Ethan M, 1940, Je 16,38:5
Thomas, Ethel W Mrs (will), 1953, N 28,10:6
Thomas, Eugene A Mrs, 1951, Mr 24,13:5
Thomas, Eugene P, 1950, Ag 24,27:5
Thomas, Eugene P Mrs, 1948, F 17,25:2
Thomas, Evan, 1905, Ja 29,20:7
Thomas, Evan A, 1958, N 1,19:5
Thomas, Evans, 1947, S 5,19:4
Thomas, Evans A Mrs, 1954, Je 15,29:4
Thomas, Everett E, 1966, Mr 2,41:4
Thomas, Felix, 1966, Ja 26,37:4
Thomas, Florence E D Mrs, 1949, O 16,89:1
Thomas, Florence Mrs, 1958, Ag 18,19:5
Thomas, Francis, 1876, Ja 25,4:7
Thomas, Francis D, 1954, Ja 4,19:5
Thomas, Francis J, 1940, Ja 10,21:3
Thomas, Francis L, 1946, Mr 12,44:1
Thomas, Frank, 1903, Jl 22,7:6; 1954, My 11,29:1; 1954, Je 6,87:2
Thomas, Frank A, 1938, S 7,25:3
Thomas, Frank D, 1949, Ja 10,25:3
Thomas, Frank E, 1958, O 12,86:5
Thomas, Frank H, 1907, Ap 14,9:6; 1952, S 26,21:1
Thomas, Frank S, 1937, Ja 27,21:4; 1943, S 25,15:1
Thomas, Frank Sr, 1938, Je 28,19:5
Thomas, Frank W, 1950, Je 16,25:3
Thomas, Franklin, 1954, Je 17,29:4
Thomas, Franz, 1901, D 23,7:5
Thomas, Fred A, 1964, My 9,27:1
Thomas, Fred A Mrs, 1950, Ja 10,29:2
Thomas, Fred B, 1955, S 7,31:2
Thomas, Fred W, 1945, Ja 19,19:4
Thomas, Frederic C, 1967, S 4,21:5
Thomas, Frederick A Lt-Col, 1908, D 8,9:4
Thomas, Frederick G, 1939, Mr 12,III,6:8
Thomas, Frederick H, 1940, S 15,48:6
Thomas, Frederick W, 1958, F 5,27:3
Thomas, Friend K Mrs, 1952, N 23,88:3
Thomas, G, 1879, Ja 16,8:4
Thomas, G C, 1882, D 5,7:4
Thomas, G Revere, 1940, O 19,17:6
Thomas, G W, 1903, Ap 30,2:4
Thomas, G Y, 1940, My 13,17:5
Thomas, George, 1948, Ap 19,23:5; 1951, Ap 12,33:6; 1952, Ap 29,27:5
Thomas, George A, 1946, O 2,6:4; 1968, O 24,47:2
Thomas, George B, 1954, D 7,33:1
Thomas, George C, 1909, Ap 22,9:4; 1946, N 17,68:3
Thomas, George E, 1950, S 3,39:1; 1955, S 6,25:4
Thomas, George Edward, 1908, Mr 10,7:5
Thomas, George F, 1872, F 25,3:4
Thomas, George G, 1944, Jl 1,15:4
Thomas, George H (R Eden), 1962, S 17,31:5
Thomas, George H Maj-Gen (funl, Ap 9,1:4), 1870, Mr 30,5:2
Thomas, George H Sr, 1949, Ap 20,27:4
Thomas, George P, 1940, F 1,21:4; 1961, Ap 15,21:4
Thomas, George R (por), 1944, Ap 30,45:1
Thomas, George R, 1948, Jl 23,20:2
Thomas, George R Mrs (F Vandamm), 1966, Mr 16, 45:1
Thomas, George S, 1955, Ap 3,86:4
Thomas, George W, 1943, Je 21,17:3; 1960, N 3,39:1
Thomas, Georgine H Mrs (will), 1940, Mr 9,8:7
Thomas, Giles W, 1944, Ja 13,21:3
Thomas, Glen W, 1953, S 24,33:5
Thomas, Glenn H Mrs, 1962, O 4,39:3
Thomas, Glyn A, 1954, Ap 25,86:4
Thomas, Gustave, 1946, O 15,26:2
Thomas, Guy A, 1946, Mr 10,47:2
Thomas, H C, 1945, D 10,21:4
Thomas, H H Gen, 1904, Mr 18,9:2
Thomas, H L Dr, 1903, D 22,9:5
Thomas, H Mark, 1957, Ap 3,31:4
Thomas, Haddam, 1967, D 30,23:1
Thomas, Harold A, 1953, Ap 14,27:4
Thomas, Harold B, 1953, O 24,15:1
Thomas, Harold E, 1959, Mr 16,31:2
Thomas, Harold O, 1961, N 28,32:6
Thomas, Harold S, 1947, Je 26,23:4
Thomas, Harriet M Mrs, 1946, D 29,35:6
Thomas, Harrison M, 1956, N 10,19:5
Thomas, Harry B, 1940, Mr 11,15:5; 1964, N 5,45:1
Thomas, Harry F, 1953, Ag 21,18:4
Thomas, Harry F Mrs, 1938, O 12,27:4
Thomas, Harry G, 1952, My 8,31:4
Thomas, Harry H, 1945, D 11,25:3; 1954, Ja 22,28:4
Thomas, Harry H Mrs, 1961, My 18,35:2
Thomas, Harry Mrs, 1966, S 29,47:4
Thomas, Harry S, 1950, Je 13,27:1
Thomas, Harry T, 1943, Ap 29,21:3
Thomas, Harvey M Mrs, 1941, Jl 22,20:3
Thomas, Hector Mrs, 1945, Ag 23,23:2
Thomas, Helen L, 1959, Ja 19,27:3
Thomas, Henry, 1957, O 15,30:1
Thomas, Henry B, 1940, Ap 15,17:3
Thomas, Henry G, 1963, Je 3,29:3
Thomas, Henry M Dr, 1925, Je 22,15:4
Thomas, Henry S, 1958, O 11,23:5
Thomas, Henry W, 1945, Ap 25,23:3; 1951, Ap 17,29:2
Thomas, Herbert, 1947, My 21,25:2
Thomas, Herbert S, 1945, N 18,44:2
Thomas, Herbert W Mrs, 1948, Mr 10,27:2
Thomas, Hiram S, 1907, Jl 10,7:5
Thomas, Homer H, 1947, Ja 7,27:1
Thomas, Horace T, 1947, D 21,54:1
Thomas, Howell H, 1937, Je 10,23:5
Thomas, Ifor O, 1956, Ap 11,33:5
Thomas, Ira, 1958, O 13,29:5
Thomas, Ira Mrs, 1948, D 27,21:2
Thomas, Isaac, 1952, O 18,19:6
Thomas, Isaac Mrs, 1952, Ja 22,29:4
Thomas, Isabel R Mrs, 1939, N 4,15:6
Thomas, J Albert, 1957, Ap 13,19:5
Thomas, J B Maj, 1922, Mr 3,13:5
Thomas, J C, 1950, N 7,27:3
Thomas, J Elmer, 1949, Ag 23,23:1
Thomas, J H, 1876, Ag 9,4:7; 1881, Jl 16,5:3
Thomas, J J, 1948, Ap 17,15:6
Thomas, J Quincy, 1944, Jl 28,13:5
Thomas, J R, 1901, Ag 29,7:6
Thomas, J R Jr, 1933, Ag 11,15:1
Thomas, J S Ladd, 1959, Jl 15,30:1
Thomas, J S Ladd Mrs, 1951, My 30,21:4
Thomas, Jacob W, 1949, Ja 27,23:4
Thomas, James A, 1925, D 22,21:4
Thomas, James A (por), 1940, S 11,25:3
Thomas, James A, 1957, N 15,27:3
Thomas, James A (cor, Ap 6,43:1), 1966, Ap 5,39:4
Thomas, James A 4th Mrs, 1945, Mr 14,19:1
Thomas, James B, 1946, Mr 19,27:5
Thomas, James C, 1937, N 8,23:4; 1958, Ag 14,29:4
Thomas, James C Mrs, 1956, Jl 28,17:7
Thomas, James F, 1911, Je 1,11:5
Thomas, James H (por), 1949, Ja 22,13:1
Thomas, James J, 1955, F 23,27:3
Thomas, James L Mrs, 1947, Jl 27,44:6
Thomas, James M Judge, 1904, N 9,9:6
Thomas, James P L (Viscount Cilcennin), 1960, Jl 14,27:2
Thomas, Jameson (por), 1939, Ja 11,19:3
Thomas, Jason P, 1946, Ja 25,23:4
Thomas, Jay, 1955, Ap 29,23:3
Thomas, John, 1940, Jl 21,29:1; 1943, N 14,56:6; 1945, N 11,42:1; 1956, S 4,30:1
Thomas, John A, 1946, Je 25,21:4
Thomas, John B, 1949, D 6,31:6
Thomas, John C (funl, D 18,84:1), 1960, D 14,39:3
Thomas, John D, 1951, N 18,91:1
Thomas, John F, 1937, Ag 9,19:3; 1940, N 21,30:2; 1951, F 10,13:4; 1960, N 8,29:5
Thomas, John G, 1939, D 14,27:3; 1947, Ap 25,22:2; 1952, Ja 16,25:4
Thomas, John H, 1937, Mr 10,23:1; 1938, Ap 6,23:6; 1945, F 21,19:2; 1959, O 5,31:3
Thomas, John H Jr, 1944, Ag 4,13:7
Thomas, John H Mrs, 1949, Ap 28,31:3
Thomas, John J, 1952, Ap 24,31:4
Thomas, John L, 1949, O 24,23:1
Thomas, John L Mrs, 1943, Jl 9,17:6
Thomas, John Lloyd, 1925, F 7,15:5
Thomas, John M, 1951, Ap 9,25:4; 1952, F 27,27:3; 1957, My 16,31:1
Thomas, John M Mrs, 1953, Ap 28,27:3
Thomas, John M Sr, 1951, Mr 15,29:2
Thomas, John Mrs, 1943, My 16,43:1
Thomas, John N, 1944, S 20,23:4
Thomas, John P, 1944, Ag 10,17:4
Thomas, John R, 1954, Mr 8,27:1
Thomas, John R Jr Mrs, 1952, Ja 30,25:4
Thomas, John W, 1948, S 7,25:2; 1951, N 27,31:1
Thomas, John W Jr, 1913, D 19,11:4
Thomas, Joseph, 1910, Jl 3,II,7:4
Thomas, Joseph B, 1909, Ag 6,7:4; 1939, F 25,15:2; 1955, Jl 15,21:6; 1959, Ja 25,92:3
Thomas, Joseph D Mrs, 1947, Ap 21,21:4
Thomas, Joseph E, 1947, Jl 25,18:2
Thomas, Joseph Jr, 1951, Ja 10,27:4
Thomas, Joseph P, 1948, D 11,15:1
Thomas, Joseph S, 1955, F 17,27:5
Thomas, Josiah M Mrs, 1961, Ag 1,31:1
Thomas, Julian B, 1948, Ap 24,15:6
Thomas, Julius H, 1937, Ja 28,25:1
Thomas, Kate, 1950, Mr 4,17:1
Thomas, Leon E, 1958, N 13,33:5
Thomas, Leonard E, 1959, Jl 26,69:3
Thomas, Leonard M (will, S 19,38:7), 1937, S 1,19:5
Thomas, Lewin H, 1945, O 6,13:6
Thomas, Lewis, 1880, Mr 18,8:5
Thomas, Lewis V, 1965, O 23,31:4
Thomas, Lloyd C, 1952, Ja 22,29:3
Thomas, Lloyd M, 1941, F 23,41:1
Thomas, Lot, 1905, Mr 18,11:5
Thomas, Lucien B, 1961, Je 1,35:4
Thomas, Luke G, 1949, Mr 26,17:4
Thomas, Luke G Mrs, 1956, N 27,37:2
Thomas, Luther A, 1951, Ag 5,72:5
Thomas, Lyla Mrs, 1951, F 25,87:4
Thomas, M C, 1935, D 3,25:4
Thomas, Mabel, 1964, Ap 30,35:4
Thomas, Maceo A Mrs, 1965, D 29,26:8
Thomas, Malcolm G, 1941, D 10,25:2
Thomas, Marie, 1949, F 20,60:1
Thomas, Marion P, 1950, Ja 21,17:4
Thomas, Mark C, 1950, Je 18,76:4
Thomas, Martha G, 1942, Je 28,32:7
Thomas, Mary E, 1940, Jl 25,17:2; 1958, Ag 17,86:2
Thomas, Mary L, 1941, O 4,15:4
Thomas, Maurice, 1948, D 9,34:3
Thomas, Maurice G, 1954, D 11,13:1
Thomas, Maurice J, 1967, N 6,47:2
Thomas, Mike H, 1943, Ap 4,40:5
Thomas, Morgan H, 1961, Ag 18,21:3
Thomas, Morris A, 1903, Je 13,9:6
Thomas, Nathan L, 1948, N 2,25:5
Thomas, Nathaniel S Bp, 1937, Ap 1,23:4
Thomas, Newell E, 1963, My 1,39:2
Thomas, Norman, 1968, D 20,1:2
Thomas, Norman Mrs (por), 1947, Ag 2,13:1
Thomas, Olive, 1920, S 25,13:4
Thomas, Oren R Sr, 1955, Mr 31,27:1
Thomas, Orlando F, 1918, S 17,13:4
Thomas, Orpha M, 1954, N 7,88:1
Thomas, Oscar B, 1921, N 25,15:4
Thomas, Parry Rev, 1909, Jl 2,7:4
Thomas, Paul, 1962, Jl 15,61:1
Thomas, Percy, 1941, D 31,17:3
Thomas, Percy C Mrs, 1942, Jl 7,20:2
Thomas, Percy H, 1957, Mr 19,37:3
Thomas, Perry C, 1943, Ap 20,24:2
Thomas, Phil H, 1949, Jl 25,15:3
Thomas, Phillips, 1958, Je 14,8:4
Thomas, Preston E, 1952, O 7,29:2
Thomas, Prudence Mrs, 1949, D 26,29:2
Thomas, Purdon C, 1968, Jl 30,39:3
Thomas, R H, 1881, Je 9,8:2
Thomas, R J, 1967, Ap 19,45:4
Thomas, Ralph B Dr, 1968, F 29,37:5
Thomas, Ralph E, 1937, My 2,II,9:2

Thomas, Ralph Hill, 1915, Ja 2,9:7
Thomas, Ralph L, 1965, N 20,35:3
Thomas, Ralph P, 1948, N 24,23:2
Thomas, Ransom H, 1939, N 14,23:1
Thomas, Ranson H, 1922, O 20,17:5
Thomas, Raymond E, 1962, N 25,86:4
Thomas, Reuen Rev Dr, 1907, N 10,9:5
Thomas, Richard C P, 1939, N 12,48:6
Thomas, Richard H Mrs, 1947, F 12,25:2
Thomas, Richard J, 1967, Jl 22,25:5
Thomas, Richard M, 1950, Jl 18,30:3
Thomas, Richard M Lt-Col, 1925, Jl 29,21:6
Thomas, Richard R, 1954, D 22,23:3
Thomas, Richard S, 1923, Jl 9,13:5
Thomas, Richard Simms, 1923, Jl 12,17:3
Thomas, Richard W, 1940, Je 25,23:5
Thomas, Robert J, 1949, F 25,24:2; 1951, S 28,31:2
Thomas, Robert M, 1950, Ja 20,25:5
Thomas, Robert McK Mrs, 1966, D 5,45:2
Thomas, Robert Mrs, 1950, Ja 27,23:3
Thomas, Robert Newton, 1925, D 27,7:1
Thomas, Robert R, 1960, D 26,23:3
Thomas, Robert S, 1941, My 12,17:2
Thomas, Robert W, 1965, D 16,47:2
Thomas, Robert Y Jr, 1925, S 4,21:6
Thomas, Roberts B (por), 1945, Ja 24,22:2
Thomas, Roscoe C, 1948, Ja 31,19:1
Thomas, Rosemary, 1961, Ap 9,86:4
Thomas, Ross R, 1967, Ap 26,47:4
Thomas, Roy E, 1949, N 12,15:3
Thomas, Royal D, 1960, My 30,17:2
Thomas, Rudolph, 1965, Ap 8,39:2
Thomas, Rupert B, 1956, F 29,31:4
Thomas, Rupert B Mrs, 1953, Ap 17,25:4
Thomas, Russell Mrs, 1960, O 22,23:5
Thomas, Ruth S Mrs, 1942, Je 12,21:4
Thomas, S E Jr, 1932, Je 8,19:3
Thomas, S Seymour, 1956, Mr 1,33:4
Thomas, Samuel, 1939, My 4,23:4
Thomas, Samuel Alden, 1865, F 13,8:6
Thomas, Samuel B, 1943, O 12,27:6
Thomas, Samuel Brown Com, 1912, Mr 4,11:6
Thomas, Samuel Gen, 1903, Ja 12,1:3
Thomas, Samuel H Mrs, 1940, O 7,17:3
Thomas, Samuel K, 1954, My 17,23:4
Thomas, Samuel Winter, 1913, N 26,11:6
Thomas, Sarah, 1967, F 12,92:3
Thomas, Sarah J, 1946, F 11,29:4
Thomas, Sarah Mrs, 1942, O 4,53:2
Thomas, Seabrook S, 1937, O 31,II,10:7
Thomas, Seth, 1859, F 7,3:1; 1910, F 9,7:5; 1944, Je 27,19:1; 1962, F 4,82:4
Thomas, Shenton, 1962, Ja 18,29:4
Thomas, Stephen G, 1937, N 17,23:1
Thomas, Stephen Gen, 1903, D 19,9:5
Thomas, Susie H Mrs, 1942, Ap 14,21:5
Thomas, T Bahn, 1941, Ja 1,23:5
Thomas, T Foster 2d, 1956, N 26,27:1
Thomas, T J, 1955, Jl 13,25:3
Thomas, T Lewis, 1951, Ap 28,15:5
Thomas, T Rowland, 1923, O 28,23:3
Thomas, Theodore, 1905, Ja 5,7:3
Thomas, Theodore H, 1958, Mr 17,29:5
Thomas, Theodore L, 1948, Ag 9,19:2
Thomas, Theodore S Mrs, 1943, Ag 20,15:2
Thomas, Thomas F, 1950, Ap 16,104:4
Thomas, Thomas Mrs, 1947, Je 10,27:2
Thomas, Thomas P, 1944, Jl 29,13:5
Thomas, Tommy, 1956, Ag 27,19:4
Thomas, Upton B, 1938, D 4,61:2
Thomas, W A, 1946, Ja 28,19:4
Thomas, W Edward, 1952, S 8,21:3
Thomas, W Everett, 1939, N 15,23:6
Thomas, W H Maj, 1908, O 7,9:4
Thomas, W Herbert, 1951, D 19,31:5
Thomas, W T, 1907, My 8,7:6
Thomas, W W, 1927, Ap 26,27:3
Thomas, Wallace S, 1955, Ja 18,27:4
Thomas, Walter H, 1948, My 5,25:5
Thomas, Walter T, 1950, O 23,23:1
Thomas, Wendell M, 1956, Ja 26,29:3
Thomas, Wendell Mrs, 1954, Ag 24,21:4
Thomas, Wilbur H, 1949, O 24,23:2
Thomas, Wilbur K, 1953, Ap 18,19:5
Thomas, Wilfred W H, 1953, Jl 3,19:4
Thomas, Will W Mrs, 1916, Ja 27,11:4
Thomas, William, 1872, Je 23,5:5
Thomas, William A Jr, 1948, O 13,25:3
Thomas, William Appleton, 1903, D 6,7:5
Thomas, William B, 1940, N 19,23:1
Thomas, William C, 1945, N 13,21:1; 1954, Jl 19,19:5; 1959, Jl 14,29:2
Thomas, William C Mrs, 1957, O 24,33:1
Thomas, William D, 1943, Ag 19,19:1; 1961, Jl 18,29:4
Thomas, William Frye Dr, 1925, Ap 10,19:4
Thomas, William G, 1947, Ag 12,23:4
Thomas, William Grasett, 1910, N 20,II,13:4
Thomas, William H, 1913, Ag 17,II,9:3; 1914, Ag 16, 15:6; 1950, F 18,15:4; 1953, Ap 24,23:4
Thomas, William Henry Griffith REV Dr, 1924, Je 3,17:3
Thomas, William I, 1947, D 7,78:3
Thomas, William J, 1939, O 5,23:5; 1961, Ap 7,31:3; 1966, D 14,47:4
Thomas, William Jacob, 1907, F 5,9:6
Thomas, William M, 1915, Jl 2,11:5; 1956, Ag 12,84:4
Thomas, William M M, 1951, S 20,31:1
Thomas, William M'K, 1962, Ag 25,22:1
Thomas, William P, 1956, Je 30,17:5
Thomas, William R, 1943, Ja 10,50:2; 1950, Ja 25,27:2
Thomas, William R Sr, 1956, My 25,23:5
Thomas, William Reed Rev Dr, 1913, Ap 14,9:4
Thomas, William S, 1941, D 22,17:6
Thomas, William S Mrs, 1953, Ap 16,29:4
Thomas, William T, 1960, My 4,45:2
Thomas, William W, 1937, N 23,23:5; 1946, My 25, 15:2; 1956, F 17,21:2
Thomas, William W D, 1950, N 27,25:4
Thomas, William W Mrs, 1960, Jl 12,35:2
Thomas, Winburn T Mrs, 1959, Jl 7,33:3
Thomas Francis, Sister (Natarianni), 1962, O 29,29:5
Thomas Maria, Sister, 1956, Ja 15,92:7
Thomaschefsky, Philip, 1913, D 21,IV,5:5
Thomashefsky, Boris, 1939, Jl 10,19:3
Thomashefsky, Boris Mrs, 1962, Jl 8,65:2
Thomason, Arthur, 1944, My 3,19:4
Thomason, D R, 1879, S 19,5:6
Thomason, Diana M Mrs, 1942, O 26,15:2
Thomason, Edgar, 1937, Mr 7,II,8:4
Thomason, George Mrs, 1947, Ag 29,17:1
Thomason, H D, 1936, F 28,21:1
Thomason, John E Mrs, 1965, D 17,39:3
Thomason, John W, 1944, Mr 13,15:6
Thomason, L P, 1957, N 24,87:1
Thomason, Samuel E (will, Ap 22,13:4), 1944, Mr 20,17:3
Thomason, Samuel E Mrs, 1952, S 20,15:4
Thomasset, Mary K Mrs, 1960, S 22,27:4
Thombs, P R Dr, 1902, Ap 29,9:5
Thomds, Warren La Rue, 1914, N 25,11:6
Thome, Francis, 1909, N 17,9:5
Thome, Frank P Jr, 1944, N 7,27:2
Thomee, Erik A, 1947, Ap 1,27:2
Thomen, August A, 1943, S 12,53:1
Thomen, Luis F, 1967, Jl 12,43:2
Thomen, Otto J, 1952, Jl 18,19:5
Thomes, Robert S Mrs, 1958, N 20,35:1
Thomison, Harry E, 1959, D 17,37:4
Thomlinson, William, 1943, My 18,23:4
Thommasson, Augustus R, 1953, Ap 14,27:5
Thommen, Ernest, 1948, Jl 22,23:5
Thommes, Anthony, 1940, Je 27,23:1
Thompkins, William H, 1949, D 2,29:1
Thompkins, William J, 1944, Ag 5,11:4
Thompon, D E Mrs, 1911, Jl 22,7:6
Thompsno, Harry LeRoy Sr, 1953, Ag 20,27:2
Thompson, A, 1880, S 15,8:2
Thompson, A Robert, 1946, N 17,68:2
Thompson, Aaron D, 1946, Ap 6,17:5
Thompson, Abby S B Mrs, 1939, My 31,23:3
Thompson, Adalyn, 1944, O 19,23:3
Thompson, Alan, 1953, O 29,31:5
Thompson, Alanson R, 1924, F 19,15:3; 1924, F 22, 15:4
Thompson, Albert, 1948, N 12,24:3; 1952, Ap 18,25:1
Thompson, Albert A, 1967, O 18,47:2
Thompson, Albert C, 1941, N 23,52:1
Thompson, Albert C Judge, 1910, Ja 27,9:4
Thompson, Albert J, 1949, F 17,23:5
Thompson, Albert M, 1961, D 4,37:4
Thompson, Albert W H Rev, 1922, Ja 12,17:5
Thompson, Alex, 1949, F 11,24:2
Thompson, Alex M, 1948, Mr 27,13:7
Thompson, Alex W, 1953, Je 9,27:4
Thompson, Alexander Dr, 1869, O 2,7:2
Thompson, Alexander F, 1945, Mr 12,19:3
Thompson, Alexander Ramsay, 1922, Jl 6,19:5
Thompson, Alexis, 1954, D 21,27:2
Thompson, Alfred C, 1963, N 6,41:2
Thompson, Alfred H, 1951, Ja 4,29:4
Thompson, Alfred J, 1937, D 28,22:2
Thompson, Alfred P, 1950, F 27,19:2
Thompson, Alice, 1947, Jl 25,17:3
Thompson, Allan D, 1961, Jl 28,21:3
Thompson, Allen T, 1868, Jl 19,4:7
Thompson, Andrew, 1913, My 23,13:4; 1920, Ja 27, 15:2; 1938, O 19,23:4
Thompson, Andrew H, 1946, Ap 20,23:6
Thompson, Andrew T, 1939, Ap 21,23:2
Thompson, Angeline, 1939, Ag 9,19:3
Thompson, Anna A, 1940, Ja 1,23:4
Thompson, Anson R, 1940, Mr 19,25:2
Thompson, Arch B, 1941, Ap 19,15:1
Thompson, Arch L, 1948, Jl 24,15:4
Thompson, Arthur, 1945, O 31,23:5
Thompson, Arthur C, 1958, Ag 29,23:5
Thompson, Arthur F, 1951, D 30,24:3
Thompson, Arthur F Sr, 1950, Ja 29,69:1
Thompson, Arthur Graham, 1925, F 3,13:4
Thompson, Arthur J, 1940, S 22,49:1
Thompson, Arthur van R, 1967, N 4,33:3
Thompson, Arthur W, 1965, Jl 14,37:4
Thompson, Asa, 1944, N 23,31:2
Thompson, Ashley I, 1954, Jl 20,19:4
Thompson, Augustus P, 1939, N 8,23:6
Thompson, Augustus S, 1951, Ap 9,25:6
Thompson, Austin, 1951, Ag 31,15:1
Thompson, Avery J 2d, 1949, O 16,88:2
Thompson, Benjamin, 1948, Ap 8,25:2
Thompson, Benton Mrs, 1948, Je 24,25:5
Thompson, Beresford H Dr, 1937, D 12,II,9:1
Thompson, Betty, 1952, Ja 9,21:3
Thompson, Bob, 1966, Je 8,47:3
Thompson, Bruce K, 1947, Jl 9,23:4
Thompson, Bryan, 1955, Ap 18,28:1
Thompson, Burton, 1939, Jl 8,15:5
Thompson, C C, 1883, Ja 29,5:6
Thompson, C E, 1933, O 5,21:1
Thompson, C H (Butch), 1902, Ag 20,14:2
Thompson, Calvin M, 1944, Jl 11,15:2
Thompson, Cameron S Jr, 1962, F 4,82:5
Thompson, Carl D, 1949, Jl 5,23:3
Thompson, Carl T, 1951, D 4,33:5
Thompson, Carmi A (por), 1942, Je 23,19:1
Thompson, Carmi A Mrs, 1953, O 17,15:6
Thompson, Carroll R, 1946, F 23,13:5
Thompson, Cecil V R, 1951, Je 13,29:1
Thompson, Charles A, 1915, Ja 5,15:4
Thompson, Charles A Mrs, 1955, Ap 30,17:3
Thompson, Charles B, 1962, Ja 8,39:2
Thompson, Charles Baker Dr, 1968, D 6,47:3
Thompson, Charles C, 1948, Ja 24,15:2
Thompson, Charles Col, 1924, S 26,21:5
Thompson, Charles D, 1959, Mr 8,86:4
Thompson, Charles E, 1941, Jl 25,15:4
Thompson, Charles F, 1937, Ag 23,19:4; 1954, Je 19, 15:4
Thompson, Charles Griswold, 1919, D 9,17:4
Thompson, Charles H, 1941, Mr 9,40:6; 1946, F 11, 29:4; 1950, Ag 4,21:2
Thompson, Charles I, 1958, Ag 4,21:3
Thompson, Charles J, 1952, Mr 7,24:3
Thompson, Charles L Rev Dr (funl, Ap 17,19:4), 1924, Ap 15,21:3
Thompson, Charles M, 1941, D 20,19:5; 1943, D 27, 19:4
Thompson, Charles Mrs, 1937, Ag 25,21:4
Thompson, Charles O, 1961, F 3,25:2
Thompson, Charles R, 1966, Ag 13,25:4
Thompson, Charles T, 1925, Ap 19,7:1
Thompson, Charles W, 1939, S 2,17:6; 1946, S 9,9:3
Thompson, Charles W Mrs, 1960, Ag 25,29:2
Thompson, Charles W Rep, 1904, Mr 21,9:6
Thompson, Charlotte, 1919, F 11,11:3
Thompson, Chuck, 1966, Jl 4,22:1
Thompson, Clara, 1958, D 21,2:5
Thompson, Clarence E, 1946, O 6,57:1
Thompson, Clarence S, 1945, My 4,19:2
Thompson, Claude A, 1962, N 12,29:2
Thompson, Claude A Mrs, 1954, O 18,25:5
Thompson, Clifford E, 1956, O 15,25:1
Thompson, Clinton, 1956, O 13,23:8
Thompson, Clyde K, 1938, S 28,25:2
Thompson, Clyde S (por), 1939, O 23,19:5
Thompson, Collins, 1953, D 17,37:1
Thompson, Constance C Mrs, 1937, Ap 24,19:1
Thompson, D'Arcy, 1948, Je 22,25:1
Thompson, Daniel G, 1948, N 11,27:1
Thompson, David, 1871, F 24,4:7; 1907, Ja 1,9:5
Thompson, David A, 1951, Ap 10,27:4
Thompson, David D, 1922, Jl 22,7:5
Thompson, De Lloyd, 1949, Ja 30,60:5
Thompson, De Witt, 1947, Ag 14,23:2
Thompson, De Witt B, 1943, Ag 28,11:4
Thompson, De Wolf, 1967, D 31,44:7
Thompson, Dean Mrs, 1961, Ag 21,23:4
Thompson, Denman, 1911, Ap 15,13:5
Thompson, Denman Mrs, 1904, O 3,9:2
Thompson, Dewinel F, 1919, Ap 20,22:2
Thompson, Donald G, 1950, O 1,104:5
Thompson, Donald H, 1949, O 14,28:3
Thompson, Dorothy (trb lr, F 9,30:5; will, Ap 25,21:6 1961, F 1,35:4
Thompson, Douglas H Mrs, 1960, F 11,35:3
Thompson, E C Mrs, 1939, S 8,23:1
Thompson, E Patrick, 1948, My 13,25:3
Thompson, E Philip, 1962, F 22,25:5
Thompson, E R, 1928, Ap 11,29:5
Thompson, E R Commodore, 1879, F 13,5:4
Thompson, Earl C, 1937, Ag 26,21:3
Thompson, Earle, 1967, Mr 24,31:1
Thompson, Eben F, 1939, D 3,61:2
Thompson, Ebenezer, 1912, Mr 9,13:6
Thompson, Edgar, 1909, My 11,9:6
Thompson, Edgar A (por), 1938, S 24,17:5
Thompson, Edith B Mrs, 1937, D 2,25:5
Thompson, Edith B Mrs (will), 1941, S 12,17:1
Thompson, Edmund A, 1921, Ap 2,11:4
Thompson, Edmund B Dr, 1918, Ja 23,9:5
Thompson, Edward, 1945, N 9,19:4
Thompson, Edward A, 1942, Ag 30,43:1
Thompson, Edward B, 1944, Jl 28,13:5
Thompson, Edward C, 1945, F 17,13:6
Thompson, Edward C Mrs, 1946, O 26,17:1
Thompson, Edward Capt, 1923, Ap 20,17:4
Thompson, Edward Gardiner, 1912, F 12,11:5
Thompson, Edward H, 1943, Ja 21,21:5; 1951, Ag 2 23:6
Thompson, Edward J, 1946, Ap 29,21:4; 1959, Je 1C 37:2

Thompson, Edward L, 1938, F 7,15:3
Thompson, Edward M, 1941, Jl 20,31:3
Thompson, Edward Middleton Dr, 1918, O 18,13:1
Thompson, Edward P, 1942, N 5,25:2
Thompson, Edward S Mrs, 1940, F 8,23:2
Thompson, Edward W, 1951, N 14,31:4
Thompson, Edwin L, 1967, Mr 4,27:1
Thompson, Edwin S, 1947, Ap 16,25:6; 1948, D 7,31:2
Thompson, Elias W, 1951, Ja 3,25:2
Thompson, Elizabeth, 1913, N 18,11:7; 1942, Ja 20, 19:3
Thompson, Elizabeth H Mrs, 1951, My 5,17:4
Thompson, Elizabeth Mrs, 1939, Ap 12,23:2
Thompson, Elmer L, 1950, Ap 4,29:3
Thompson, Elmer T, 1950, Mr 22,27:2
Thompson, Elmore E Sr, 1943, O 4,17:3
Thompson, Elwood, 1941, D 14,69:3
Thompson, Ernest, 1938, D 1,23:3
Thompson, Ernest Mrs (M Peterson), 1952, O 9,31:3
Thompson, Ernest O, 1966, Je 29,47:1
Thompson, Ethan W, 1943, D 3,23:4
Thompson, Eugene A Mrs, 1939, Mr 18,17:2
Thompson, Eugene E, 1944, Mr 13,15:2
Thompson, Eugene V, 1944, Je 27,19:3
Thompson, Evarard, 1924, My 2,19:5
Thompson, Everett E, 1962, Mr 25,88:7
Thompson, Ezekiel R, 1913, D 21,IV,5:5
Thompson, F Leslie, 1965, Mr 28,93:1
Thompson, Ferris, 1913, F 20,11:3
Thompson, Finton, 1951, D 4,33:4
Thompson, Floyd E, 1960, O 20,35:5
Thompson, Floyd G, 1954, O 31,89:2
Thompson, Floyd S, 1947, Mr 16,60:1
Thompson, Fountain L, 1942, F 25,19:2
Thompson, Francis, 1907, N 20,9:7
Thompson, Francis E, 1939, Je 5,17:6
Thompson, Francis N, 1948, S 29,29:5
Thompson, Frank, 1938, Je 29,19:5; 1957, Ja 9,31:4; 1959, F 11,39:4
Thompson, Frank A, 1958, F 8,19:5
Thompson, Frank B, 1947, Jl 2,23:4; 1947, Ag 30,15:4
Thompson, Frank C, 1940, My 6,17:2
Thompson, Frank D, 1940, Je 14,21:2
Thompson, Frank Edgar, 1923, Ag 2,15:4
Thompson, Frank F Jr, 1966, D 29,31:2
Thompson, Frank G, 1949, My 25,29:3
Thompson, Frank H, 1957, N 18,31:1
Thompson, Frank H Mrs, 1925, F 13,17:4
Thompson, Frank J, 1946, D 11,31:4
Thompson, Frank L, 1949, Je 11,17:5
Thompson, Frank V, 1921, O 24,15:5; 1954, F 16,25:2
Thompson, Frank William, 1913, My 31,11:6
Thompson, Fred, 1949, Ap 12,29:6
Thompson, Fred D, 1957, Ag 13,27:4
Thompson, Fred D Mrs, 1949, Ap 23,13:4
Thompson, Fred E, 1940, Ag 16,15:4
Thompson, Fred H 3d, 1961, S 24,86:4
Thompson, Fred L, 1948, F 29,60:4
Thompson, Frederic, 1919, Je 7,13:5
Thompson, Frederic L, 1953, Je 12,27:4
Thompson, Frederick A, 1920, Ag 27,11:4
Thompson, Frederick B, 1940, Jl 5,13:5
Thompson, Frederick E Mrs, 1951, F 1,25:5
Thompson, Frederick Ferris Mrs, 1923, Jl 29,6:3
Thompson, Frederick H, 1937, Je 2,23:4; 1939, D 15, 25:5; 1947, N 16,77:1
Thompson, Frederick I, 1952, F 20,29:2
Thompson, Frederick N, 1963, Ag 29,29:5
Thompson, Frederick R, 1939, Jl 25,19:5
Thompson, Frederick W, 1956, Je 27,31:4
Thompson, Fresco, 1968, N 21,47:1
Thompson, Fuller, 1948, O 28,30:2
Thompson, G, 1878, O 14,5:1
Thompson, G A, 1948, Mr 30,23:3
Thompson, G Albert, 1962, Ja 5,29:2
Thompson, G David, 1965, Je 27,65:1
Thompson, G J Sterling, 1947, Mr 15,13:6
Thompson, G W, 1884, Ja 9,4:7
Thompson, Gale (will), 1959, O 2,8:1
Thompson, Geoffrey J, 1951, D 15,13:5
Thompson, George, 1903, D 3,1:6; 1909, D 28,9:4; 1945, Ag 10,15:5; 1947, F 28,23:2; 1947, My 31,13:2; 1952, Je 19,27:4; 1955, Ap 16,19:1; 1960, Mr 27,V,1:2
Thompson, George A, 1938, Mr 19,15:2; 1943, Je 16, 21:3; 1944, Jl 12,19:3
Thompson, George A Mrs, 1939, Mr 29,23:1
Thompson, George C, 1942, F 27,17:4
Thompson, George D, 1950, Jl 16,68:4; 1950, D 7,33:5
Thompson, George E, 1937, Ag 5,23:6
Thompson, George F, 1948, Je 14,24:2
Thompson, George Fayette, 1906, Ja 7,7:6
Thompson, George H, 1953, Mr 9,29:2
Thompson, George H Col, 1868, My 12,5:4
Thompson, George J, 1957, Ja 10,29:5
Thompson, George K, 1946, S 22,63:1
Thompson, George L, 1941, S 2,18:2
Thompson, George M, 1949, D 21,29:4
Thompson, George N, 1944, S 3,26:5
Thompson, George O, 1949, My 23,23:1
Thompson, George R, 1949, O 1,13:5
Thompson, George T, 1942, My 23,13:6; 1950, Ag 23, 29:4; 1961, D 19,33:3
Thompson, George V Col, 1910, Ja 17,7:4
Thompson, George W, 1948, Mr 23,25:4; 1959, Mr 27, 23:3; 1962, Ap 8,86:7
Thompson, Gerald R, 1940, F 25,39:2
Thompson, Geraldine M Mrs, 1967, S 10,82:4
Thompson, Gilbert A, 1941, O 3,23:2
Thompson, Gilbert F, 1947, N 8,17:3
Thompson, Gladys J, 1968, Ap 8,47:3
Thompson, Gladys Mrs, 1950, My 11,33:2
Thompson, Gordon L, 1939, Je 7,23:2
Thompson, Griswold A, 1945, N 25,49:1
Thompson, Griswold A Mrs, 1959, My 10,86:6
Thompson, Gustave W (por), 1942, Ap 23,23:5
Thompson, Guy, 1968, Je 1,27:5
Thompson, Guy A, 1958, Ja 28,27:1
Thompson, Guywood F, 1952, My 23,21:3
Thompson, H, 1931, Ag 6,19:1
Thompson, H C, 1925, N 30,19:5
Thompson, H G, 1903, Je 8,7:6
Thompson, H H, 1880, Mr 13,8:4
Thompson, H M Bp, 1902, N 19,9:5
Thompson, H O, 1886, Jl 27,1:7
Thompson, Hannah D Mrs, 1942, Ag 12,19:4
Thompson, Hannah E Mrs, 1940, D 18,25:4
Thompson, Harlan, 1966, O 30,88:5
Thompson, Harold G, 1950, S 30,17:3
Thompson, Harold I, 1954, Ap 29,31:3
Thompson, Harold J Mrs, 1943, N 6,13:4
Thompson, Harold W, 1964, F 22,21:2
Thompson, Harriet F T Mrs, 1939, Mr 10,23:5
Thompson, Harry, 1951, F 17,15:4
Thompson, Harry A, 1940, O 19,17:5
Thompson, Harry B, 1939, Je 7,23:4
Thompson, Harry C, 1925, S 5,13:5; 1947, S 16,24:2
Thompson, Harry L, 1942, S 4,23:2; 1943, Je 24,22:2
Thompson, Harvey I, 1949, Jl 31,60:5; 1949, Ag 1,17:6
Thompson, Hayes G, 1965, Ag 18,35:4
Thompson, Hayward S, 1954, S 20,23:1
Thompson, Helen G, 1953, S 21,25:5
Thompson, Helen R, 1948, Ag 25,25:4
Thompson, Helen T Mrs, 1940, O 12,17:5
Thompson, Henrietta T Mrs, 1940, Ja 16,23:2
Thompson, Henry, 1951, N 13,29:5
Thompson, Henry B, 1939, S 19,26:4
Thompson, Henry B Mrs, 1947, Ap 3,25:3
Thompson, Henry C, 1940, D 24,15:3
Thompson, Henry D, 1967, Ap 30,87:2
Thompson, Henry G, 1946, N 28,27:2
Thompson, Henry J, 1937, N 13,19:3
Thompson, Henry K Jr, 1941, Mr 3,15:4
Thompson, Henry L, 1937, Je 1,23:3; 1939, Mr 23,23:5
Thompson, Henry M, 1947, D 18,29:2
Thompson, Henry M Mrs, 1946, Mr 11,25:2
Thompson, Henry O, 1937, Ag 5,23:6
Thompson, Henry S, 1944, Ag 7,15:5
Thompson, Henry S (por), 1947, Ap 6,60:3
Thompson, Herbert, 1944, My 30,21:3
Thompson, Herbert A, 1948, Ag 30,17:1; 1968, Ag 3, 25:4
Thompson, Herbert E, 1941, O 21,23:5
Thompson, Herbert F, 1951, Mr 18,89:1
Thompson, Hobart W, 1944, S 23,13:5
Thompson, Hobart W Mrs, 1937, F 6,21:4
Thompson, Holland, 1940, O 22,23:6
Thompson, Hollis R (por), 1944, Jl 8,11:3
Thompson, Horace, 1880, Ja 29,1:4
Thompson, Horace E, 1955, Jl 22,23:5
Thompson, Howard B, 1954, Jl 30,17:3
Thompson, Hugh A, 1955, Ap 7,27:1
Thompson, Hugh L, 1949, F 15,24:3
Thompson, Hugh S Mrs, 1909, Jl 10,7:4
Thompson, Hugh Smith, 1904, N 21,7:2
Thompson, Hugh W, 1943, N 19,19:2
Thompson, Ira F, 1937, Ag 6,17:5
Thompson, Isabelle H, 1943, Ap 24,13:6
Thompson, J A, 1878, Ag 14,8:2; 1948, Mr 30,23:3
Thompson, J B, 1919, S 19,13:4
Thompson, J C Dr, 1903, Je 7,7:7
Thompson, J Campbell, 1919, Mr 29,13:2
Thompson, J De M, 1928, Ja 29,II,7:1
Thompson, J Derwood, 1948, Ap 3,15:5
Thompson, J Ernest, 1944, F 27,38:1
Thompson, J G, 1903, Ag 22,9:7
Thompson, J P, 1879, S 22,5:3
Thompson, J R, 1927, Je 18,17:5
Thompson, J Van K, 1933, S 28,21:5
Thompson, J Vance, 1947, O 8,25:5
Thompson, J W, 1881, S 25,5:4; 1907, S 13,7:5
Thompson, J Walter, 1951, D 30,24:6; 1952, Ja 1,25:3
Thompson, J Walter Mrs, 1946, Jl 7,35:1
Thompson, J Wilmer, 1948, Ap 4,60:4
Thompson, Jack, 1946, Ap 12,27:2
Thompson, Jacob, 1885, Mr 25,5:5
Thompson, Jacob J, 1919, Ap 10,11:1
Thompson, Jacob K, 1948, Ap 8,25:2
Thompson, James, 1913, Ag 10,II,11:5; 1921, Ap 7, 15:5; 1939, S 9,17:5
Thompson, James (por), 1944, N 15,27:3
Thompson, James A, 1937, Ag 11,24:1; 1949, Ja 28, 21:3
Thompson, James D, 1952, Mr 2,92:2
Thompson, James Ex-Chief-Justice, 1874, Ja 29,1:6
Thompson, James F, 1956, Ja 19,33:1; 1967, D 23,23:2
Thompson, James G, 1957, Ag 12,19:6
Thompson, James G 3d, 1968, Mr 31,48:1
Thompson, James H, 1945, Ja 1,21:5; 1949, Ja 12, 28:3; 1953, Ag 27,25:4
Thompson, James J, 1965, Ag 26,33:2
Thompson, James J Mrs, 1951, Ap 14,16:2
Thompson, James L, 1938, My 17,21:4
Thompson, James M, 1946, F 4,25:5; 1948, Ja 11,56:2
Thompson, James McNaughton, 1908, D 27,9:4
Thompson, James N, 1962, Jl 13,20:4
Thompson, James O Jr, 1940, Ag 19,17:5
Thompson, James P, 1949, D 10,17:5; 1958, Ja 10,26:2
Thompson, James R, 1948, Mr 12,23:4
Thompson, James S, 1939, Ag 25,15:5; 1951, Ag 7, 25:4; 1965, My 5,47:3
Thompson, James S Mrs, 1951, D 24,13:4
Thompson, James V, 1952, Jl 2,25:2
Thompson, James W, 1941, O 1,21:3
Thompson, Jean M Mrs, 1944, Mr 8,19:5
Thompson, Jeanette E, 1952, Ap 22,29:3
Thompson, Jennie Condit Mrs, 1953, F 3,25:3
Thompson, Jesse Burgess Rev Dr, 1915, Je 8,13:7
Thompson, Joe C, 1961, Je 12,29:5
Thompson, John, 1938, O 19,23:4; 1944, S 20,23:6; 1958, Ap 19,21:3
Thompson, John A, 1940, F 10,15:3; 1941, Ja 12,45:2
Thompson, John Ambrose, 1968, Ja 28,76:4
Thompson, John B, 1874, Ja 10,5:1; 1938, Je 7,23:4; 1940, Ag 22,20:2; 1942, D 18,27:3
Thompson, John B Jr Mrs, 1941, N 14,23:4
Thompson, John B Mrs, 1952, Ja 30,26:5
Thompson, John Bodine Rev Dr, 1907, S 7,9:6
Thompson, John C, 1872, O 8,8:4; 1910, Ap 9,11:4; 1952, F 10,92:4
Thompson, John E, 1915, S 27,9:6; 1939, Jl 3,13:7; 1941, Ja 14,21:4
Thompson, John Edgar, 1874, My 29,4:6
Thompson, John F (por), 1944, F 21,15:5
Thompson, John F, 1949, Ap 5,29:1; 1965, Ag 14,23:3
Thompson, John F Mrs, 1947, N 1,15:4
Thompson, John Fairfield Dr, 1968, Jl 14,65:1
Thompson, John G, 1940, N 1,25:3
Thompson, John H, 1944, D 18,19:5; 1949, Ap 17,76:8; 1951, My 30,22:2; 1951, Ag 10,15:3
Thompson, John H Dr, 1919, Je 8,20:4
Thompson, John H Mrs, 1939, Je 11,45:2
Thompson, John J, 1937, D 1,23:1; 1941, Je 13,19:4; 1955, Ap 10,10:1; 1960, Ja 4,29:1
Thompson, John M, 1948, Ag 21,15:1; 1967, My 22, 43:1
Thompson, John M Brig-Gen, 1922, Ap 8,15:5
Thompson, John M Mrs, 1966, Ap 27,47:1
Thompson, John N, 1963, Ag 9,23:1
Thompson, John P, 1938, F 15,25:5
Thompson, John Q, 1913, F 27,13:4
Thompson, John R, 1873, My 1,5:5; 1917, Je 23,9:6
Thompson, John R Jr, 1940, D 7,17:2
Thompson, John R Mrs, 1951, O 27,19:3
Thompson, John Rey Rev, 1904, Jl 23,3:2
Thompson, John S, 1939, Ja 9,15:5
Thompson, John S (por), 1948, Jl 16,19:4
Thompson, John S, 1956, My 17,31:3; 1956, S 4,30:1
Thompson, John S (Sept 28), 1965, O 11,61:5
Thompson, John S D Sir, 1894, D 13,1:7
Thompson, John S Mrs, 1946, Ap 12,27:2
Thompson, John T (por), 1940, Je 22,15:1
Thompson, John T, 1948, Ap 24,15:3; 1966, My 14,31:4
Thompson, John W, 1937, Ja 6,23:3; 1951, Mr 10,13:3; 1965, Ag 24,36:3
Thompson, Joseph, 1940, Ag 24,13:7
Thompson, Joseph B, 1937, O 23,17:2
Thompson, Joseph C, 1940, Jl 7,25:3; 1942, Mr 12, 19:4; 1942, N 2,21:3
Thompson, Joseph E, 1950, Ap 19,29:2
Thompson, Joseph H, 1954, Je 26,13:5
Thompson, Joseph H Mrs, 1959, Ag 27,27:4
Thompson, Joseph Henry, 1918, Mr 7,11:4
Thompson, Joseph J, 1952, Mr 21,23:1
Thompson, Joseph Mrs, 1908, Jl 30,5:4
Thompson, Joseph N, 1953, Jl 19,56:3
Thompson, Joseph P, 1955, N 27,88:6
Thompson, Joseph R, 1952, D 23,23:2
Thompson, Joseph W, 1946, Ja 6,23:5
Thompson, Josephine L, 1943, Ag 21,11:5
Thompson, Judson M, 1908, S 4,7:4
Thompson, Julian F, 1939, Ap 22,17:3
Thompson, Julian F Mrs, 1953, O 26,21:4
Thompson, Juliet H, 1956, D 6,37:5
Thompson, Katherine C, 1943, O 28,23:1
Thompson, Kenneth I, 1959, Je 29,29:5
Thompson, Kenneth K, 1956, Jl 11,29:5
Thompson, Kennington L, 1943, Jl 14,19:4
Thompson, L Gordon, 1939, Ap 20,23:5
Thompson, L Milton, 1954, Je 12,15:5
Thompson, L P, 1883, Jl 13,4:7
Thompson, L S, 1936, Mr 26,23:1
Thompson, LaMarcus Adna, 1919, Mr 9,20:4
Thompson, Lang S, 1957, Jl 12,21:5
Thompson, Laura A, 1949, Ap 24,78:1
Thompson, Lena B Mrs, 1942, Ap 20,21:6
Thompson, Leon L, 1957, Ja 16,31:5
Thompson, Leroy Mrs, 1953, Mr 5,27:3
Thompson, Leslie H, 1955, My 1,88:6
Thompson, Lester C, 1944, My 24,19:4

Thompson, Lester H, 1948, F 28,15:4
Thompson, Lester Seymour, 1968, Ja 24,45:2
Thompson, Lewis C, 1949, D 11,92:8
Thompson, Lewis R, 1954, N 14,88:5
Thompson, Lewis S Jr, 1965, Je 12,31:6
Thompson, Lewis W, 1954, Ag 29,88:5
Thompson, Lillian, 1950, Jl 4,17:2
Thompson, Lincoln E, 1944, S 20,23:6
Thompson, Lloyd, 1948, S 5,40:5
Thompson, Lloyd Mrs, 1947, Jl 25,17:2
Thompson, Lloyd O Dr, 1937, Jl 17,15:3
Thompson, Loren O, 1939, My 31,23:3
Thompson, Loy D, 1967, Ag 16,41:5
Thompson, Lydia, 1908, N 19,9:5
Thompson, Lynn W, 1920, D 10,15:4; 1921, Ja 9,23:2
Thompson, M C, 1876, Ja 16,2:7
Thompson, M George, 1948, O 8,25:4
Thompson, M White Mrs, 1965, My 12,47:3
Thompson, Mabel S, 1948, Je 13,69:1
Thompson, Malcolm M, 1920, Ja 27,15:2
Thompson, Malvina C (Mrs F J Scheider),(trb lr, Ap 15,30:6), 1953, Ap 13,27:1
Thompson, Maney L, 1958, Ap 18,23:1
Thompson, Mangle Minthorne, 1864, Ag 13,4:6
Thompson, Marcellus H, 1939, O 18,25:1
Thompson, Maria T B Mrs, 1940, D 6,23:3
Thompson, Mark A, 1953, O 4,88:6
Thompson, Martha S, 1948, Ag 26,21:4
Thompson, Martin T, 1942, O 30,19:2
Thompson, Marvin J, 1958, Ap 18,23:2
Thompson, Mary E Mrs, 1953, Ap 15,31:3
Thompson, Mary V Mrs, 1937, Mr 8,19:2
Thompson, Matthew R, 1961, Jl 4,19:5
Thompson, Maud, 1962, S 27,37:3
Thompson, Maurice, 1901, F 16,7:5
Thompson, Maxwell M, 1955, S 25,92:7
Thompson, May C Mrs, 1939, Je 25,37:3
Thompson, Michael J, 1939, My 31,23:4
Thompson, Milo M, 1945, Mr 27,19:3
Thompson, Milton T, 1942, Ag 10,19:5
Thompson, Moreton R, 1951, S 28,31:1
Thompson, Morrill D Mrs, 1944, Jl 8,11:2
Thompson, Morris S, 1915, Je 15,13:6
Thompson, Mortimer, 1875, Je 26,5:2
Thompson, Mortimer W Mrs (M Leslie), 1965, Jl 23, 26:6
Thompson, Morton H Sr, 1953, Jl 8,27:4
Thompson, Mr, 1879, Ja 3,2:4
Thompson, Mrs, 1879, Ja 3,2:4
Thompson, N A Col, 1874, Ap 12,1:4
Thompson, O T, 1947, O 28,25:6
Thompson, Oco, 1959, N 23,31:4
Thompson, Ole M, 1950, Mr 4,17:5
Thompson, Oliver, 1945, Ja 16,19:5
Thompson, Orville, 1945, Mr 6,21:1
Thompson, Oscar (trb), 1945, Jl 4,13:5
Thompson, Oscar, 1953, Ap 28,86:8
Thompson, Oscar A, 1959, D 8,45:4
Thompson, Oswald, 1866, Ja 24,5:5
Thompson, Otis A, 1968, Ap 17,32:8
Thompson, Paul, 1940, N 28,23:3; 1942, D 14,23:5
Thompson, Paul E, 1948, Jl 5,15:3
Thompson, Pell, 1943, S 30,21:5
Thompson, Percival, 1943, Ja 16,13:5
Thompson, Peter, 1946, Ap 6,27:3; 1950, Ap 20,29:4
Thompson, Philip B Jr, 1909, D 16,9:5
Thompson, Philip E, 1924, Ap 10,23:4
Thompson, Philip L Mrs, 1943, O 16,13:1
Thompson, Phillips B, 1951, F 20,25:2
Thompson, Phineas C, 1952, Je 23,19:3
Thompson, R A, 1878, S 9,2:2
Thompson, R Ellison, 1949, Jl 24,53:2
Thompson, R H Dr, 1864, N 23,2:3
Thompson, R Lloyd, 1961, Jl 15,19:2
Thompson, R M, 1930, S 6,15:3
Thompson, Racia Mrs, 1956, Je 30,17:6
Thompson, Ralph, 1925, Jl 24,13:6
Thompson, Ralph E, 1952, S 16,29:1; 1960, Mr 11,25:4
Thompson, Ralph H, 1945, F 16,23:3
Thompson, Ralph W, 1948, Ja 13,25:3
Thompson, Ralph Wardlaw Rev Dr, 1916, Je 13,11:4
Thompson, Ray, 1946, Ag 14,25:6
Thompson, Ray C, 1955, O 25,33:3
Thompson, Ray W, 1954, Ja 1,23:2
Thompson, Ray W Mrs (Christine), 1968, F 19,39:3
Thompson, Raymond B, 1954, Mr 28,87:4
Thompson, Reginald C, 1941, My 27,23:5
Thompson, Reuben R, 1952, Ap 26,23:2
Thompson, Rhoda Augusta, 1908, My 2,9:5
Thompson, Richard A, 1952, Mr 22,17:5
Thompson, Richard C, 1961, O 21,21:1
Thompson, Richard C Mrs, 1952, Je 14,15:1
Thompson, Richard L, 1950, Mr 6,21:4
Thompson, Richard S, 1954, Jl 30,17:2
Thompson, Richard W, 1943, D 19,48:2
Thompson, Richard W Col, 1900, F 9,1:6
Thompson, Robert, 1945, Ap 3,19:4
Thompson, Robert A, 1965, O 17,86:2
Thompson, Robert B Mrs, 1956, F 7,31:3
Thompson, Robert D, 1951, S 1,11:6
Thompson, Robert Ellis Dr, 1924, O 20,17:6
Thompson, Robert F Justice, 1937, Ap 8,23:5
Thompson, Robert H B, 1942, Ag 4,19:5
Thompson, Robert L Dr, 1937, Ag 31,23:6
Thompson, Robert Means Col, 1924, O 19,7:1
Thompson, Robert P, 1948, D 14,29:4
Thompson, Robert R, 1965, Ag 8,64:4
Thompson, Robert S Mrs, 1962, Mr 14,39:2
Thompson, Robert W, 1951, F 5,24:2
Thompson, Roby C, 1960, Jl 30,17:6
Thompson, Rodney I, 1945, Ap 25,23:2
Thompson, Rollin W Mrs, 1953, O 15,33:5
Thompson, Rose S Mrs, 1941, Mr 25,26:1
Thompson, Ross H, 1941, F 13,19:4
Thompson, Roy, 1966, Ja 6,27:3
Thompson, Roy L, 1947, O 20,23:1; 1955, Ag 3,23:6
Thompson, Roy S, 1965, F 10,42:1
Thompson, Russell I, 1957, O 21,25:4
Thompson, S C, 1884, Ap 11,3:1
Thompson, S D Judge, 1904, Ag 13,7:6
Thompson, S H Mrs, 1949, Ja 18,24:3
Thompson, S P Mrs, 1929, My 7,8:1
Thompson, Sam H, 1956, Ap 23,27:3
Thompson, Samuel A, 1939, Je 18,37:2
Thompson, Samuel D, 1955, Ja 14,21:3
Thompson, Samuel E, 1952, Ag 4,15:6
Thompson, Samuel Gustine Ex-Judge, 1909, S 11,9:4
Thompson, Samuel H, 1941, F 18,23:5; 1952, O 28, 31:2; 1960, Ap 14,31:3
Thompson, Samuel R, 1948, D 14,29:5
Thompson, Samuel W, 1937, Mr 29,19:4
Thompson, Sanford E, 1949, F 27,68:3
Thompson, Sarah, 1924, My 27,21:4
Thompson, Sherley C, 1967, Mr 23,35:5
Thompson, Sidney E, 1958, Ja 26,88:4
Thompson, Silas C, 1964, Ag 27,33:5
Thompson, Silvanus Phillips, 1916, Je 14,13:6
Thompson, Smith Mrs, 1950, O 9,25:5
Thompson, Stanley, 1953, Ja 6,29:4
Thompson, Stanley G, 1959, F 21,21:2
Thompson, Stanley H, 1951, N 5,31:4
Thompson, Stephen B E, 1954, Mr 20,15:2
Thompson, Stephen C, 1955, Ap 25,23:5
Thompson, Stephen J, 1955, Ap 23,19:2
Thompson, Stewart H, 1946, O 14,29:2
Thompson, Sumner E, 1948, F 14,13:4
Thompson, Sydney, 1951, D 2,91:2
Thompson, Sydney A, 1961, Jl 4,19:1
Thompson, Sylvester T, 1942, Je 9,23:2
Thompson, T Ashton, 1965, Jl 2,15:2
Thompson, T Barney, 1967, S 8,39:1
Thompson, T P Jr, 1945, N 2,19:1
Thompson, Terry B, 1945, Mr 8,23:5
Thompson, Theodore, 1942, Ja 11,45:1
Thompson, Theodore C, 1941, My 14,21:2
Thompson, Thomas, 1920, F 5,9:4; 1943, Ja 24,42:8
Thompson, Thomas B, 1941, D 11,27:1
Thompson, Thomas E, 1957, D 27,19:3
Thompson, Thomas G, 1942, Ap 3,21:2; 1961, Ag 12, 17:3
Thompson, Thomas J, 1937, F 16,23:1
Thompson, Thomas Mrs, 1955, S 21,33:2
Thompson, Thomas O, 1956, O 18,33:3
Thompson, Uldric Jr (por), 1947, Ag 20,21:5
Thompson, Uldrick Mrs, 1945, Je 17,26:1
Thompson, Uldrick Sr (por), 1942, Je 26,21:3
Thompson, Vance, 1925, Je 8,15:4
Thompson, Vera R, 1962, N 6,33:4
Thompson, Vernon P, 1961, Jl 23,68:3
Thompson, Vida I, 1939, D 25,23:2
Thompson, Violet E, 1938, My 7,7:2
Thompson, Virginia Campbell Mrs, 1908, Mr 7,7:6
Thompson, W (Bendigo), 1880, Ag 25,5:6
Thompson, W B, 1875, D 28,4:7; 1930, Je 28,15:3
Thompson, W E, 1933, Mr 22,17:5
Thompson, W Edward, 1956, Ja 5,6:5
Thompson, W G, 1927, O 28,23:3; 1935, S 13,21:3
Thompson, W Grant (por), 1940, Mr 31,44:1
Thompson, W H, 1928, F 10,23:3
Thompson, W Harvey Mrs, 1957, D 27,20:2
Thompson, W Henry, 1949, Ap 13,29:1
Thompson, W Leland, 1957, O 14,27:4
Thompson, W Norman, 1944, Ap 8,13:3
Thompson, W O, 1933, D 9,15:6
Thompson, W Stuart, 1968, Ap 3,52:1
Thompson, W T, 1882, Mr 25,5:3
Thompson, W V, 1938, O 2,48:7
Thompson, Waddy, 1939, Mr 20,17:6
Thompson, Wallace, 1952, Ja 23,27:2
Thompson, Walter, 1939, Ap 28,25:3; 1955, Jl 31,69:1
Thompson, Walter B, 1946, Ap 29,22:2
Thompson, Walter Carter, 1918, S 24,13:5
Thompson, Walter E, 1957, D 30,23:4
Thompson, Walter G, 1939, Ja 9,15:5
Thompson, Walter L, 1941, F 3,20:2
Thompson, Walter M, 1952, Ja 6,92:4
Thompson, Walter R, 1964, My 29,29:6
Thompson, Walter T, 1938, S 18,45:1
Thompson, Walter W, 1940, Ap 26,21:3
Thompson, Warren R Col, 1937, S 28,23:4
Thompson, Warren S, 1950, Mr 30,29:4
Thompson, Wilfred G E, 1952, Ap 3,35:4
Thompson, Wilfred J, 1963, S 27,29:4
Thompson, Wilfred M 2d, 1955, Ap 7,27:2
Thompson, Wilfred Mrs, 1903, S 4,7:7
Thompson, Will, 1949, N 23,29:4
Thompson, Will L, 1909, S 21,9:6
Thompson, Will S Mrs, 1953, Je 16,27:2
Thompson, Willard C, 1954, Ja 13,31:5
Thompson, Willard O, 1954, Mr 25,29:2
Thompson, Willard T, 1940, S 4,23:1
Thompson, William, 1879, D 8,3:5; 1903, Je 8,7:7; 1903, D 11,9:6; 1945, Ja 31,21:2; 1946, Ag 21,27:3; 1947, F 9,62:8; 1951, S 11,29:2
Thompson, William A, 1943, O 18,15:5; 1953, Jl 7,27:1
Thompson, William Andrew Jr, 1922, Jl 25,11:6
Thompson, William B, 1941, F 13,19:1
Thompson, William B Mrs, 1950, Ag 28,17:5
Thompson, William Baker, 1919, Ag 17,22:4
Thompson, William C, 1941, S 14,51:6; 1961, D 2,23:2
Thompson, William Corporal, 1872, Mr 14,8:5
Thompson, William D, 1960, Je 29,33:4
Thompson, William Dean Lt, 1918, My 3,15:3
Thompson, William E (por), 1940, F 20,21:1
Thompson, William G, 1953, O 2,21:4; 1966, Mr 24, 39:3
Thompson, William G Deputy Warden, 1953, F 10, 27:3
Thompson, William H, 1921, Mr 22,17:4; 1923, F 5, 15:6; 1937, Je 7,19:2; 1942, F 14,15:6; 1944, F 29, 17:5; 1944, Mr 20,17:1; 1946, F 19,25:4; 1956, D 5, 39:2
Thompson, William H Mrs, 1943, Ja 1,23:4; 1958, O 10,32:1
Thompson, William H Sr, 1945, Jl 26,19:4
Thompson, William J (Duke of Gloucester), 1911, Jl 3,7:5
Thompson, William J, 1944, N 26,58:3; 1948, D 15, 33:2; 1949, Jl 21,25:3; 1954, Ag 14,15:4; 1960, N 29, 37:1
Thompson, William J Mrs, 1959, My 4,29:5; 1959, S 2, 29:3; 1960, Mr 24,37:1
Thompson, William L, 1942, Ag 16,45:2
Thompson, William Lawton Dr, 1918, Ag 29,7:3
Thompson, William M, 1943, Ap 13,26:2
Thompson, William McL, 1966, D 28,37:3
Thompson, William Mrs, 1946, Ja 13,43:1
Thompson, William O, 1942, D 10,25:2
Thompson, William P, 1948, Ag 11,22:3
Thompson, William P Mrs, 1941, S 2,17:1
Thompson, William Payne, 1922, S 21,17:5
Thompson, William R, 1942, N 3,24:2; 1952, Mr 19, 29:3; 1959, S 2,29:4
Thompson, William R Mrs, 1944, S 13,19:6
Thompson, William Reed, 1906, Je 19,9:6
Thompson, William S, 1954, N 13,15:2
Thompson, William Stevely Sr, 1953, Mr 1,93:2
Thompson, William T, 1939, Je 21,23:3; 1951, Ap 6, 25:3
Thompson, Wilmot H, 1950, S 10,92:4
Thompson, Wilmot H Mrs, 1949, N 17,29:5
Thompson, Winfield M, 1946, My 31,24:2
Thompson, Winfield Mrs, 1946, O 1,23:4
Thompson, Woodman, 1955, S 2,17:5
Thompson (Sister Loretto Francis), 1960, Jl 24,64:6
Thoms, C Harry, 1950, Mr 2,27:4
Thoms, Charles M, 1941, Mr 5,21:4
Thoms, David C, 1948, N 29,23:1
Thoms, Frank R, 1950, N 13,27:6
Thoms, Frederic, 1955, Ja 5,23:3
Thoms, George, 1959, N 10,47:1
Thoms, John B, 1908, N 6,7:3
Thoms, Joseph C, 1957, Je 19,35:4
Thoms, Kelcey, 1953, Ja 17,15:5
Thoms, William E, 1939, Ag 11,15:2
Thomsen, Christian L, 1951, O 4,33:2
Thomsen, Frank, 1943, Mr 8,15:3
Thomsen, Hugo Adelberto, 1918, Mr 1,11:3
Thomsen, Lars C, 1946, D 29,35:2
Thomsen, William E Mrs, 1954, Je 16,31:2
Thomson, Adeline, 1906, D 8,1:4
Thomson, Albert R Mrs, 1942, Ap 22,23:3
Thomson, Alex, 1939, Je 28,21:1; 1942, N 22,52:5; 1949, Ja 6,23:4; 1950, N 14,31:4
Thomson, Alex D, 1937, My 17,19:5
Thomson, Alex D Mrs, 1948, My 21,23:5
Thomson, Alex G, 1952, Ja 16,25:1
Thomson, Alex J, 1954, N 23,25:1
Thomson, Alex N, 1950, Jl 6,27:3
Thomson, Alexander Jr, 1944, Je 19,19:3
Thomson, Alice P, 1951, Ag 28,23:4
Thomson, Andrew S, 1951, N 24,11:4
Thomson, Anne (will, Ag 6,10:1), 1954, Jl 24,13:2
Thomson, Anne S, 1950, Je 19,23:1
Thomson, Annie, 1960, Ag 15,23:1
Thomson, Arthur C, 1946, D 17,31:4
Thomson, Barry, 1960, Ag 20,19:2
Thomson, Basil (por), 1939, Mr 27,15:5
Thomson, Bernard C, 1941, Je 3,21:4
Thomson, Bernard W S Capt (por), 1937, F 27,17:1
Thomson, Bert, 1937, S 18,19:3
Thomson, Bertha V, 1939, My 16,23:6
Thomson, C M Sir, 1882, Mr 11,5:3
Thomson, Charles A, 1961, Ap 8,19:2
Thomson, Charles A Dr, 1968, My 30,25:4
Thomson, Charles A Mrs, 1953, Ag 25,21:4
Thomson, Charles G Col, 1937, Mr 24,25:5
Thomson, Charles J, 1948, Mr 4,25:4
Thomson, Charles Jr Dr, 1937, O 18,17:5

Thomson, Charles L, 1945, O 8,15:5; 1966, My 29,56:1
Thomson, Charles M, 1943, D 31,16:7
Thomson, Charles W, 1947, O 28,25:1
Thomson, Clarke, 1940, F 9,19:2
Thomson, Clifford Maj, 1912, S 30,13:2; 1912, O 2,13:6
Thomson, David, 1953, N 19,31:4
Thomson, David C, 1942, N 17,26:4; 1954, O 13,31:2
Thomson, David S, 1958, S 17,37:3
Thomson, E S, 1931, Ja 13,25:3
Thomson, Edith P Mrs, 1941, N 4,23:4
Thomson, Edward, 1938, S 13,23:2
Thomson, Edward William, 1924, Mr 7,15:5
Thomson, Elihu Prof, 1937, Mr 14,II,8:1
Thomson, Eliot C, 1957, S 9,25:5
Thomson, Elnora E, 1957, Ap 27,19:5
Thomson, Eugene Mrs, 1917, Jl 8,15:5
Thomson, Francis Vernon Sir, 1953, F 10,27:1
Thomson, Francus du P, 1959, O 17,23:2
Thomson, Frank G (will, O 31,25:4), 1941, S 14,51:3
Thomson, George, 1941, Ja 7,23:3; 1943, O 8,19:4
Thomson, George F, 1959, D 31,21:6
Thomson, George G, 1923, D 13,21:5; 1946, Ja 8,23:2
Thomson, George G Mrs, 1968, D 30,31:4
Thomson, George J, 1947, My 19,22:3
Thomson, George M, 1952, Ja 17,27:3
Thomson, George Mrs, 1944, N 28,23:2
Thomson, George P, 1965, Ja 26,37:1
Thomson, George R Sr, 1963, N 18,33:1
Thomson, Helen, 1951, O 2,28:2
Thomson, Herbert B, 1953, O 13,29:2
Thomson, Herbert S, 1940, D 17,25:2
Thomson, Hugh, 1920, My 9,22:4
Thomson, Isabel J Mrs, 1941, Ag 12,19:2
Thomson, J A, 1933, F 13,15:3
Thomson, J Archie, 1958, N 3,37:6
Thomson, J B, 1883, Je 23,4:7
Thomson, J Cameron, 1966, Ja 23,88:6
Thomson, J Earle, 1950, F 5,84:5
Thomson, J Edgar Mrs, 1903, N 26,1:4
Thomson, J F Gordon Mrs (por), 1947, Ag 15,17:3
Thomson, James, 1941, F 20,19:1
Thomson, James A, 1951, Je 26,29:3
Thomson, James B F Mrs, 1949, D 28,32:2
Thomson, James L, 1966, Jl 24,61:4
Thomson, James M, 1959, S 26,23:2
Thomson, James McArthur, 1913, Ja 16,17:5
Thomson, James R, 1963, Ap 18,35:5
Thomson, James Renwick, 1968, D 30,31:2
Thomson, James S, 1949, Je 5,92:5
Thomson, James W Rear-Adm, 1914, Mr 18,11:6
Thomson, Jane, 1937, My 16,II,8:7
Thomson, Jennie L, 1957, Ja 22,29:4
Thomson, John, 1916, F 24,13:6
Thomson, John A, 1954, My 23,88:8
Thomson, John D, 1944, Jl 11,15:3
Thomson, John E, 1947, Ag 30,15:5
Thomson, John G Prof, 1937, Ag 15,II,6:4
Thomson, John Jr, 1943, O 22,17:4
Thomson, John Mrs, 1952, O 12,89:1
Thomson, John R Sen, 1862, S 16,5:2
Thomson, John W, 1937, My 6,25:3; 1951, Mr 12,25:2
Thomson, Joseph, 1940, S 5,23:5
Thomson, Joseph J (por), 1940, Ag 31,13:1
Thomson, Joseph John Sir, 1918, F 9,15:8
Thomson, Joseph Mrs, 1910, N 8,9:4
Thomson, Julia V Mrs, 1938, Je 11,15:6
Thomson, Karl J, 1965, D 19,84:5
Thomson, Keith, 1960, D 10,23:4
Thomson, Kenneth, 1967, Ja 27,45:3
Thomson, Logan G Mrs, 1961, Mr 3,27:4
Thomson, Mary J, 1944, O 23,19:4
Thomson, McLeod, 1968, Jl 5,25:2
Thomson, Paul J, 1938, O 16,44:5
Thomson, Peter, 1946, Ap 7,44:2
Thomson, Peter A, 1956, O 27,21:6
Thomson, Peter G, 1960, Mr 27,86:5
Thomson, Polly (funl, Mr 24,33:1), 1960, Mr 22,37:4
Thomson, Quincy A Mrs, 1957, O 24,33:1
Thomson, Robert, 1938, Ap 24,II,7:1
Thomson, Robert B, 1947, Ag 1,17:1
Thomson, Robert C, 1957, F 23,17:5
Thomson, Robert M, 1947, Ja 7,27:2
Thomson, Robert Mrs, 1918, F 20,9:4
Thomson, Robert R, 1944, O 7,13:4
Thomson, Robert W Mrs, 1950, F 10,24:2
Thomson, Roy H Mrs, 1951, F 23,27:5
Thomson, Samuel C, 1940, Jl 14,31:3
Thomson, Samuel M, 1958, Ag 3,81:2
Thomson, Sara P Mrs, 1940, D 22,30:7
Thomson, Sidney, 1943, D 25,13:5
Thomson, Stuart Capt, 1919, Mr 26,15:4
Thomson, Stuart R M, 1955, Jl 31,68:3
Thomson, T Kennard, 1952, Jl 2,25:1
Thomson, T Kennard Mrs, 1955, Ag 28,85:1
Thomson, Thomas N, 1954, F 6,19:2
Thomson, Tommy, 1940, Mr 21,26:4
Thomson, Walter S, 1947, My 24,15:4
Thomson, Wilfrid F H, 1939, Ja 30,14:1
Thomson, William, 1916, N 18,11:5; 1924, D 2,25:4
Thomson, William (funl), 1924, D 14,7:2
Thomson, William, 1947, Ag 7,21:6; 1948, O 29,25:1
Thomson, William A, 1945, S 30,45:1
Thomson, William E, 1954, Ag 4,21:3
Thomson, William H, 1946, My 3,21:2
Thomson, William Hanna Dr, 1918, Ja 19,11:4
Thomson, William J, 1949, S 20,29:3
Thomson, William Judah Rear-Adm, 1909, Ag 14,7:5
Thomson, William T, 1941, Ja 17,17:1; 1967, Ag 11, 31:1
Thomson-Walker, John Sir, 1937, O 7,27:1
Thon, Joseph, 1959, Ja 9,27:3
Thone, Frank, 1949, Ag 26,19:3
Thonet, Oscar L, 1912, Je 7,13:4
Thoorsell, Emilia A, 1937, Ap 30,22:3
Thor, Aug E, 1940, Jl 19,19:5
Thor, Fritz, 1953, N 17,31:3
Thor, John F, 1953, F 24,25:4
Thorbeck, Jan Rudolph, 1872, Je 6,7:6
Thorburn, Alfred Macdonald, 1924, O 15,23:4
Thorburn, Grant, 1863, Ja 25,6:5; 1909, My 4,9:4
Thorburn, Howard B, 1940, N 25,17:5
Thorburn, Joseph Col, 1864, O 23,4:5
Thorburn, Robert Sir, 1906, Ap 14,11:4
Thorburn, Samuel J Jr, 1958, S 4,29:3
Thorburn, Samuel J Mrs, 1950, D 8,29:2
Thorburn, Thomas R, 1962, Mr 9,19:3
Thord-Gray, Frances, 1941, Ap 10,23:4
Thord-Gray, Ivor, 1964, Ag 20,29:4
Thordarson, Chester H, 1945, F 8,19:4
Thordorovich, Theodore Dr, 1910, S 24,11:5
Thore, Wendell P, 1941, Mr 15,17:4
Thoren, B J, 1943, Mr 12,17:4
Thoren, Fred J, 1945, Ap 3,19:5
Thoren, Roy W Mrs, 1966, O 20,43:5
Thoresen, John Mrs, 1942, D 13,75:4
Thorex, Max, 1960, Ja 27,33:3
Thorez, Maurice (trb, Jl 13,29:3; funl, Jl 17,2:7), 1964, Jl 13,1:1
Thorington, James, 1944, O 30,19:4
Thorkelson, Jacob, 1945, N 21,21:4
Thorlakson, Edward J Mrs, 1965, Je 12,31:4
Thorley, Charles (funl, N 13,21:4), 1923, N 12,17:6
Thormahlen, Herbert E, 1955, F 9,27:1
Thorman, Jack, 1958, My 28,31:4
Thorn, Adolph G P, 1944, Je 20,19:4
Thorn, Alice G, 1942, O 3,15:6
Thorn, Amelia V, 1946, Ja 25,23:3
Thorn, Amos P, 1944, D 14,23:5
Thorn, Benjamin C, 1957, Mr 27,31:4
Thorn, Charles E, 1954, N 23,35:4
Thorn, Chessman W, 1944, Jl 8,11:3
Thorn, Conde R, 1944, My 3,19:4
Thorn, Conde R Mrs, 1961, My 17,37:1
Thorn, Elizabeth C Mrs, 1907, O 19,9:6
Thorn, Ernest F Mrs, 1946, N 22,23:4
Thorn, Frank B, 1944, Ap 2,39:2
Thorn, George B, 1956, My 17,31:5
Thorn, George B Mrs, 1903, N 4,9:6
Thorn, George W, 1937, My 26,25:3
Thorn, Harold W, 1943, Ja 21,21:3
Thorn, Harvey K, 1945, Jl 16,11:6
Thorn, Henry C, 1962, Ap 18,39:2
Thorn, Herman, 1859, Ag 2,4:5
Thorn, J Paul, 1964, My 24,93:1
Thorn, John I Mrs, 1948, S 1,24:2
Thorn, John W, 1939, F 22,21:5
Thorn, L Mortimer, 1909, Ag 20,7:3
Thorn, L Mortimer Jr, 1912, S 3,11:6
Thorn, Louis F, 1959, Mr 21,21:2
Thorn, Oscar, 1945, O 21,46:4
Thorn, Percy M, 1944, O 19,23:5
Thorn, Phil R, 1953, Ag 24,23:5
Thorn, Thomas R, 1940, Jl 14,30:8
Thorn, Walter, 1920, Ag 1,22:3; 1945, F 18,33:1
Thorn, Walter M Sr, 1947, My 25,60:3
Thornberry, Otto S Rev, 1937, F 28,II,8:7
Thornberry, Risher W Col, 1937, Mr 22,23:1
Thornborrow, John W H, 1950, D 20,32:5
Thornburg, Charles L, 1944, O 16,19:4
Thornburg, E H Mrs, 1937, O 27,31:3
Thornburg, Edgar H, 1939, Ap 4,25:3
Thornburg, John A, 1940, Mr 31,45:1
Thornburg, Robert A, 1944, N 29,23:3
Thornburg, Thomas P, 1958, O 30,31:5
Thornburgh, Charles G, 1951, D 6,33:3
Thornburgh, Maj, 1879, O 5,2:5
Thornburgh, Robert S, 1939, F 18,15:4
Thornbury, Ethel, 1967, Ja 22,76:6
Thornbury, Theresa, 1948, D 17,27:4
Thorndike, A H, 1933, Ap 18,1:2
Thorndike, Ashley H Mrs, 1959, Ag 18,30:6
Thorndike, Augustus, 1940, Ag 24,13:5
Thorndike, Edward L, 1949, Ag 10,21:1
Thorndike, Edward L Mrs, 1959, F 24,29:3
Thorndike, Edward R Rev, 1920, Ag 19,9:3
Thorndike, Lynn, 1965, D 29,29:2
Thorndike, Oliver, 1954, Ap 16,21:1
Thorndike, Paul, 1939, My 30,17:5
Thorndike, W T Sherman, 1958, O 12,86:5
Thorndike, Willis H, 1940, Mr 20,34:8
Thorndyke, Elizabeth, 1947, D 4,31:4
Thorndyke, John, 1952, Jl 3,25:2
Thorne, Albert E, 1947, Ap 26,13:5
Thorne, Albert M Jr, 1957, Jl 19,19:5
Thorne, Benjamin P, 1958, Mr 11,29:4
Thorne, C R Jr (funl), 1883, F 11,7:2
Thorne, Carolyne G, 1958, Mr 1,17:6
Thorne, Charles H, 1938, Ag 6,13:3; 1948, O 11,23:5
Thorne, Charles S Mrs, 1948, Ja 7,25:4
Thorne, Clifford, 1923, N 14,17:4
Thorne, Edith A, 1946, D 4,31:2
Thorne, Edward A, 1955, Je 7,33:3
Thorne, Edwin S, 1960, Je 16,33:6
Thorne, Elizabeth P, 1942, N 13,23:2
Thorne, Ellen Cobb, 1925, My 26,21:5
Thorne, F Mrs (Lily Davenport), 1878, Ja 15,1:5
Thorne, Francis B, 1950, D 18,31:4
Thorne, Francis B Mrs, 1959, Je 12,27:3
Thorne, Frederick W, 1960, N 27,86:2
Thorne, George R, 1918, S 25,13:4
Thorne, George Winthrop, 1904, F 3,9:5
Thorne, Gilbert (por), 1938, O 2,48:8
Thorne, Gordon C, 1938, Ja 29,15:4
Thorne, Gordon C Mrs, 1966, D 20,44:1
Thorne, H P, 1916, Ap 20,13:5
Thorne, Harold B, 1952, D 10,35:3
Thorne, Harold B Jr, 1951, Mr 27,29:2
Thorne, Harold B Mrs, 1950, D 1,25:3
Thorne, Henry S, 1959, Jl 22,27:1
Thorne, J, 1884, O 10,2:4
Thorne, J Russell, 1965, F 16,35:3
Thorne, James S, 1866, Jl 22,5:4
Thorne, James W Mrs, 1966, Je 27,35:2
Thorne, John A, 1937, Ap 9,21:2
Thorne, John C (por), 1941, S 17,23:3
Thorne, Julia E, 1954, Mr 6,15:6
Thorne, Landon K, 1964, S 14,33:4
Thorne, M S, 1921, Ap 7,15:6
Thorne, Montgomery W, 1954, Je 21,23:1
Thorne, Nellie, 1960, My 14,23:6
Thorne, O M, 1879, D 10,5:2
Thorne, Oakleigh, 1948, My 24,19:1
Thorne, Oakleigh Mrs, 1952, N 11,29:2
Thorne, Olive, 1918, D 27,11:6
Thorne, Perley L, 1967, Ap 8,31:5
Thorne, R, 1934, Mr 7,19:1
Thorne, R Harrison, 1949, My 21,13:5
Thorne, R J, 1882, N 5,8:7
Thorne, Ralph W, 1945, N 1,23:2
Thorne, Robert, 1965, Jl 6,33:2
Thorne, Robert J, 1955, Mr 21,25:5
Thorne, S B, 1930, Je 4,27:5
Thorne, Samuel, 1915, Jl 6,9:5; 1963, O 5,25:5
Thorne, Samuel Mrs, 1923, O 10,21:3; 1937, Ap 29, 21:4
Thorne, Sylvia, 1922, My 11,17:4
Thorne, T W, 1885, Mr 21,8:1
Thorne, Therese K Mrs, 1937, D 26,II,6:8
Thorne, Thomas J, 1947, S 11,27:3
Thorne, Thomas P, 1922, Ja 13,15:6
Thorne, Thomas Wood, 1913, F 4,11:5
Thorne, V B, 1935, Ag 2,17:4
Thorne, Van B, 1935, Ag 2,17:4
Thorne, Victor C, 1948, Ja 19,23:1
Thorne, Will (por), 1946, Ja 3,19:3
Thorne, William, 1956, Ja 11,29:1
Thorne, William Cobb, 1917, Ap 16,13:6
Thorne, William H, 1945, F 23,17:2
Thorne, William Mrs, 1943, Ag 2,15:5
Thorne, William V S, 1920, F 7,11:3
Thorne-Rider, Frederic, 1963, My 18,27:3
Thornell, Henry L, 1939, My 11,25:4
Thornell, L T, 1880, Mr 23,2:7
Thorner, Benjamin, 1943, My 7,19:6
Thorner, Samuel G, 1949, D 21,29:3
Thorner, William, 1948, Je 5,15:2
Thorner, William Mrs, 1961, D 18,35:1
Thorngate, Royal R, 1948, Ja 19,24:2
Thorngreen, Frederick, 1957, Ap 28,87:1
Thornhill, Beecher Mrs, 1953, F 28,17:5
Thornhill, Chester C, 1948, N 28,96:5
Thornhill, Claude, 1965, Jl 2,29:4
Thornhill, Claude E (Tiny), 1956, Jl 1,57:1
Thornhill, Claude E Mrs, 1940, Mr 4,15:1
Thornhill, David C (por), 1942, D 18,27:1
Thornhill, John S, 1946, D 31,17:3
Thornhill, Robert E, 1961, Ap 17,29:6
Thornley, Frank H (funl), 1914, Je 3,13:6
Thornley, J Harry, 1964, Ja 19,76:7
Thornley, John M Mrs, 1955, O 20,36:1
Thornley, Josiah P Dr, 1937, Jl 22,19:3
Thornquist, Arne, 1944, F 22,24:3
Thornschein, Isidor, 1947, Ap 15,25:1
Thornthwaite, Charles W, 1963, Je 12,43:4
Thornton, Alfred, 1939, F 21,19:5
Thornton, Amasa Pierce, 1917, Ja 24,9:3
Thornton, Anne F, 1949, D 31,15:2
Thornton, Annie G Mrs, 1955, My 24,31:3
Thornton, Anthony Mrs, 1912, Ag 10,7:6
Thornton, Archie, 1957, O 21,25:3
Thornton, Augustus Mrs, 1945, F 23,17:2
Thornton, Bonnie, 1920, Mr 14,22:4
Thornton, Carroll, 1947, Jl 22,24:2
Thornton, Edward, 1940, Ag 21,19:5
Thornton, Edward B, 1962, My 6,38:5
Thornton, Edward Q, 1945, Ja 19,19:4
Thornton, Edward Sir, 1906, Ja 27,9:5
Thornton, Emily S, 1961, D 4,37:5
Thornton, Francis M J, 1960, Ap 21,31:4

Thornton, Grant, 1966, Ag 6,23:4
Thornton, H W, 1933, Mr 15,17:1
Thornton, Harry P, 1944, My 18,19:6
Thornton, J S Capt, 1875, My 15,4:7
Thornton, James, 1903, S 17,7:6
Thornton, James (cor, Ag 3,14:3),(por), 1938, Jl 29, 17:5
Thornton, James C Col, 1937, Ja 26,21:5
Thornton, James F, 1954, D 2,31:5
Thornton, James J, 1965, N 24,39:1
Thornton, James M, 1962, O 20,25:5
Thornton, John, 1940, Ap 27,15:1
Thornton, John H, 1943, N 20,13:4
Thornton, John L Mrs, 1946, My 7,21:4
Thornton, John O, 1947, Ag 5,23:5
Thornton, John R, 1945, My 24,19:5
Thornton, John R Ex-Sen, 1917, D 29,11:4
Thornton, L C, 1952, S 11,31:5
Thornton, Lawrence D, 1958, Ja 17,25:2
Thornton, Lawrence E, 1950, N 22,25:3
Thornton, Leonard F, 1955, My 25,33:4
Thornton, Lewis H, 1945, My 10,23:3
Thornton, Mary, 1937, F 7,II,8:5
Thornton, Matthew A, 1940, Ap 9,23:4
Thornton, Michael J, 1956, Jl 24,25:1
Thornton, Owen F, 1953, Jl 17,17:2
Thornton, Richard B, 1951, O 29,23:3
Thornton, Robert D, 1944, Mr 25,15:2
Thornton, Robert L, 1964, F 16,93:1
Thornton, Samuel S, 1948, D 29,21:2
Thornton, Susie, 1937, O 30,19:3
Thornton, Thomas A, 1955, S 9,23:2
Thornton, Virginia L, 1903, D 6,5:5
Thornton, W T, 1880, Je 18,2:3
Thornton, William D, 1953, Je 10,32:1
Thornton, William E, 1951, D 19,31:1
Thornton, William G, 1955, Ap 8,21:1
Thornton, William J, 1955, Mr 3,27:4
Thornton, William L, 1915, D 30,13:4
Thornton, William M Jr, 1953, S 24,33:3
Thornton, William T, 1916, Mr 17,11:6
Thornton, William W, 1939, Ap 23,III,7:1
Thornton, Willis, 1965, My 22,31:4
Thornycroft, J I Sir, 1928, Je 29,25:5
Thornycroft, John E, 1960, N 22,35:4
Thornycroft, Tom, 1955, Je 8,29:4
Thorold, William J, 1941, N 20,27:3
Thorp, Arthur, 1952, Jl 13,61:2; 1956, Jl 17,23:4
Thorp, Benjamin S, 1952, Ja 30,25:4
Thorp, C F, 1903, Ag 26,7:6
Thorp, Charles M, 1942, D 15,28:2
Thorp, Chester C, 1950, Jl 26,25:5
Thorp, Compton B Mrs, 1944, Je 27,19:1
Thorp, E J, 1934, Je 24,24:1
Thorp, Ervin H, 1943, Je 6,44:4
Thorp, Francis Q, 1963, D 22,34:4
Thorp, Frederick Potter, 1913, D 22,9:6
Thorp, George G, 1953, Ja 21,31:5
Thorp, Geral, 1946, Ag 24,11:5
Thorp, Job Mrs, 1951, Jl 24,25:1
Thorp, John, 1961, Ag 14,3:4
Thorp, John R, 1908, Jl 6,7:5
Thorp, John S, 1950, Mr 7,27:4; 1957, Je 1,17:4
Thorp, L Ashton, 1940, O 19,17:6
Thorp, Leon E, 1942, Je 9,23:3
Thorp, Rene-William, 1967, F 5,27:1
Thorp, Tom, 1942, Jl 7,19:5; 1942, Jl 10,17:2
Thorp, Vaughn P, 1945, S 6,25:6
Thorpe, Alonzo V, 1939, Jl 15,15:7
Thorpe, Anna M, 1953, D 22,31:5
Thorpe, Bradley W, 1951, Jl 14,13:2
Thorpe, E Everett, 1953, Ag 17,15:4
Thorpe, Earl T, 1951, Mr 1,27:5
Thorpe, Edward Sir, 1925, F 24,19:2
Thorpe, Freeman Col, 1922, O 21,13:5
Thorpe, Henry, 1913, D 11,11:4
Thorpe, Herbert Mrs, 1948, Ap 9,23:5
Thorpe, Hilton, 1954, Ap 10,15:4
Thorpe, Howard S, 1951, S 13,31:5
Thorpe, James, 1949, F 24,23:5
Thorpe, James B, 1949, Ja 30,60:3
Thorpe, James H, 1955, Mr 27,35:5
Thorpe, James Mrs, 1961, F 21,35:3
Thorpe, Jim, 1953, Mr 29,1:1
Thorpe, John E S, 1950, F 25,17:5
Thorpe, John W, 1949, Jl 30,15:6
Thorpe, Malcolm R, 1958, Je 26,27:6
Thorpe, Merle, 1955, N 1,31:1
Thorpe, Philip N, 1946, N 18,23:4
Thorpe, Prescott H Mrs, 1963, Jl 15,29:3
Thorpe, Ray V, 1948, Mr 26,21:2
Thorpe, Richard S, 1941, O 19,45:1
Thorpe, Robert J (Bobby), 1960, Mr 19,44:5
Thorpe, Rose H Mrs (por), 1939, Jl 21,19:3
Thorpe, S B, 1878, S 20,5:3
Thorpe, Stanley H, 1950, O 16,27:3
Thorpe, Stephen, 1945, Jl 17,13:5
Thorpe, Stephen S, 1965, Mr 11,33:2
Thorpe, Thomas P Msgr, 1907, Mr 18,7:6
Thorpe, Warren, 1958, My 30,21:1
Thorpe, William E, 1949, Ag 12,17:2
Thorpe, William R, 1953, Je 18,29:1
Thors, Olafur, 1965, Ja 1,17:1
Thors, Thor, 1965, Ja 12,37:3
Thorsch, Hugo, 1939, Je 11,45:1
Thorsen, Bill, 1955, Jl 13,25:5
Thorsen, George, 1947, O 22,29:1
Thorsen, J Mitchell, 1951, F 6,27:5
Thorsen, James B, 1937, Ja 3,II,8:2
Thorsgaard, Karl L, 1940, N 26,23:5
Thorson, Truman C, 1966, D 11,89:2
Thorsson, F W, 1925, My 6,23:4
Thorsteinson, Johan M, 1948, Ag 26,22:2
Thorwarth, Peter H, 1951, F 6,27:2
Thorwort, Friedrich, 1912, O 5,13:6
Thorworth, William J, 1949, Mr 14,19:5
Thourot, Harry J, 1965, D 21,37:3
Thousand, Robert E, 1956, N 23,27:1
Thouvenal, M, 1866, O 20,1:5
Thrall, Charles H, 1950, F 5,84:5
Thrall, Fred H, 1941, Je 6,21:5
Thrall, Howard C, 1951, Mr 16,31:5
Thrall, Robert M, 1942, Ja 8,21:4
Thrall, W R Maj, 1916, My 25,13:6
Thrall, William H, 1956, F 17,21:2
Thralls, Jerome Jr, 1955, O 5,33:1
Thralls, Zoe A, 1965, My 24,31:3
Thran, Leslie, 1941, Je 10,23:5
Thrash, Mark (por), 1943, D 18,10:2
Thrasher, Allen W, 1953, Ja 17,15:6
Thrasher, Frederic M, 1962, Mr 27,38:1
Thrasher, James A, 1951, Mr 16,31:3
Thrasher, Milton F, 1964, Ap 1,39:5
Thrasher, Roy, 1941, O 11,17:3
Thrasher, Sam P, 1871, Ap 13,1:5
Thrasher, Samuel P, 1925, S 12,15:5
Thrasher, William E, 1952, O 30,27:7
Thraves, William V, 1946, D 23,23:4
Threkeld, A L, 1967, N 10,43:1
Threshie, George, 1952, Mr 27,29:2
Threshie, Phil H, 1954, Je 2,31:4
Thrift, Chester R, 1943, O 6,23:5
Thro, Fred H, 1949, Mr 11,25:1
Thro, Samuel W, 1944, S 7,23:5
Thro, William C (por), 1939, Ap 7,21:3
Throckmorton, Alwyn A, 1963, Je 19,37:4
Throckmorton, Arch H, 1938, My 23,17:4
Throckmorton, Archibald H Mrs, 1961, Jl 10,21:5
Throckmorton, B W, 1882, N 20,5:6
Throckmorton, Barbarie, 1870, Ja 24,5:6
Throckmorton, C D, 1875, Je 15,6:5
Throckmorton, Charles W, 1941, My 11,44:7
Throckmorton, Charles W Mrs, 1947, Mr 14,23:2
Throckmorton, Cleon, 1965, O 25,37:5
Throckmorton, Edmund W Mrs, 1911, N 9,11:4
Throckmorton, George K, 1953, Ap 5,76:4
Throckmorton, H W, 1882, F 9,3:3
Throckmorton, James B, 1943, Ja 15,17:2
Throckmorton, James S, 1947, N 28,27:4
Throckmorton, John E, 1947, Mr 12,26:3
Throckmorton, Joseph Albert, 1907, Ap 21,9:3
Throckmorton, R Fred, 1955, F 20,89:2
Throckmorton, Robert J, 1956, Ja 30,27:4
Throckmorton, Tyler W, 1907, Ap 23,9:4
Throckmorton, William Nathan, 1908, My 2,9:5
Throm, Thomas, 1956, S 28,27:2
Thron, Francis J, 1951, Mr 18,88:7
Throne, William C, 1952, O 10,25:4
Throop, Enos T, 1874, N 2,5:3
Throop, Frank D, 1943, Mr 5,17:4
Throop, George H, 1938, Ag 10,19:5
Throop, George H Mrs, 1950, N 21,31:2
Throop, George R, 1949, N 13,94:2
Throop, H N Capt, 1884, Ag 8,1:2
Throop, Leo E, 1919, N 6,13:3
Throop, S G, 1877, F 17,2:3
Throp, Alice A, 1955, My 15,87:2
Thropp, Clara, 1960, Mr 1,33:2
Thropp, Harry A, 1955, S 3,15:6
Thropp, John E, 1938, D 19,23:2
Thropp, Joseph W, 1937, Jl 29,19:3
Thrower, Fred M Mrs, 1961, Jl 18,29:5
Thrum, Arno R, 1947, Ja 7,27:3
Thrush, Morris C, 1950, Ja 19,28:3
Thruston, Rogers C B, 1946, D 31,18:2
Thudium, William R, 1944, Jl 22,15:4
Thuer, Frank E Mrs, 1949, F 25,23:1
Thuerk, Hugh C, 1955, O 7,25:5
Thuliez, Louise, 1966, O 15,29:4
Thulin, Einar, 1963, O 21,31:1
Thum, Ernest E, 1961, Ap 12,41:5
Thum, Joseph (por), 1937, Ja 10,II,10:6
Thum, Louis Sr, 1948, O 1,26:2
Thum, Otto, 1943, N 13,13:4
Thum, Otto C, 1952, Je 24,29:5
Thuma, Margaret, 1939, S 20,27:5
Thuman, J Herman, 1960, Ag 14,92:7
Thumas, Francisco E, 1945, O 31,23:1
Thumm, Martin, 1938, Ja 19,23:1
Thummel, Warren F, 1938, D 11,61:2
Thun, Ferdinand, 1949, Mr 26,18:4
Thun, Ferdinand Mrs, 1948, O 28,29:5
Thunder, H G, 1881, D 16,5:2
Thunder, Henry G, 1958, Mr 21,21:2
Thunder, William S, 1954, S 10,23:5
Thunderbird, Richard D, 1946, Ap 7,44:7
Thundercloud, Chief, 1916, Mr 14,11:4
Thundercloud, Chief (V Daniel), 1955, D 3,17:6
Thunderwater, Chief (O Niagara), 1950, Je 11,92:2
Thunell, Carl A, 1955, Mr 16,33:4
Thuon, Raymond J, 1952, N 15,17:2
Thuras, Albert L, 1945, S 9,45:2
Thurber, A Edward Sr, 1958, Ja 8,47:3
Thurber, Abram, 1942, My 15,19:1
Thurber, Alfred E, 1962, S 5,39:3
Thurber, Alfred E Mrs, 1946, F 5,23:2
Thurber, C C, 1930, Je 3,31:3
Thurber, Charles H, 1938, D 10,17:5
Thurber, Charles Mrs, 1955, D 21,29:4
Thurber, Donald H, 1942, S 13,53:1
Thurber, Dwight W, 1922, Jl 28,13:4
Thurber, Edward J Rev Dr, 1913, N 9,IV,7:5
Thurber, Ella F Mrs, 1938, Ag 14,33:4
Thurber, Elmer A, 1968, Je 14,47:4
Thurber, Francis B Jr Mrs, 1957, O 28,27:3
Thurber, Francis B 3d, 1967, Jl 14,31:4
Thurber, Francis Beattie, 1907, Jl 5,7:6
Thurber, Fred C, 1943, Jl 6,21:5
Thurber, H F, 1928, Ap 22,31:1
Thurber, H T, 1904, Mr 18,9:4
Thurber, Hallett E, 1951, Ag 21,27:5
Thurber, Harry R, 1967, S 22,47:3
Thurber, J Kent, 1957, My 28,33:2
Thurber, James (funl plans, N 4,19:2; funl, N 9,35:5), 1961, N 3,1:3
Thurber, Jeanette Mrs, 1946, Ja 8,23:4
Thurber, John M, 1962, O 4,39:3
Thurber, Orray E, 1941, Ap 24,21:5
Thurber, Samuel, 1943, Je 15,21:2
Thurber, Samuel W Mrs, 1958, My 20,33:1
Thurber, William B, 1937, N 13,19:2
Thureau-Dangin, Paul Marie, 1913, F 25,11:3
Thurlow, Baron (Thos Jno Hevell-Thurlow-Cumming-Bruce), 1916, Mr 15,11:5
Thurlow, Charles Jr, 1922, D 29,13:4
Thurlow, Leon R Mrs, 1956, My 15,31:2
Thurlow, Louis K, 1941, Ja 1,23:2
Thurlow, Nathaniel, 1948, Ja 2,24:1
Thurlow, Thomas Rev, 1874, O 12,4:7
Thurm, Maxwell H, 1957, D 15,86:7
Thurman, A G, 1895, D 13,9:7
Thurman, Albert L Mrs, 1954, Mr 24,27:3
Thurman, Allen G, 1961, N 1,39:1
Thurman, Archie Mrs, 1963, N 4,35:4
Thurman, Bernard, 1914, Ag 12,9:5
Thurman, Beverly R, 1962, N 15,37:3
Thurman, Charles T, 1938, Ja 11,23:4
Thurman, Hal C, 1952, Ag 24,89:1
Thurman, Louis, 1943, D 25,13:2
Thurman, M Burt, 1943, Mr 5,17:3
Thurman, Mary, 1925, D 24,13:4
Thurman, Oliver, 1953, S 11,21:2
Thurman, Richard B, 1943, Ap 30,21:4
Thurmann, Anne Marie, 1904, Mr 5,9:4
Thurmond, Strom Mrs, 1960, Ja 7,29:5
Thurn and Taxis, Beatrice von Princess, 1954, D 14, 38:3
Thurn and Taxis, Dowager Princess Margarete von, 1955, My 3,31:4
Thurn und Taxis, Albert von Prince, 1952, Ja 23,27:2
Thurnauer, Gustav, 1947, Ja 28,23:2
Thurnauer, Helene (will), 1960, Je 4,2:8
Thurnauer, Max H, 1952, Ja 30,25:5
Thurnblad, Arthur J, 1946, S 24,29:5
Thurnheer, Walter, 1945, Ag 8,23:3
Thurrell, George E, 1942, Ap 12,45:2
Thurrott, Jack H, 1954, D 25,17:3
Thursby, Alice Brisbane Mrs, 1953, F 9,27:2
Thursby, E C, 1931, Jl 5,II,6:1
Thursby, Ina L (will, S 19,12:2), 1942, Jl 30,21:5
Thursby, Richard V, 1950, Jl 18,29:3
Thursby, Sidney Mrs, 1944, N 29,23:2
Thursfield, Henry G, 1963, O 24,33:4
Thursh, Joseph J, 1963, O 13,87:1
Thurso, J W, 1922, O 13,17:5
Thurston, Ada, 1944, Je 6,17:4
Thurston, Albert L, 1946, Ja 9,24:2
Thurston, Albert L Mrs, 1962, N 21,30:2
Thurston, Alfred H, 1949, Je 26,60:2
Thurston, Alice M, 1942, Ap 1,21:4
Thurston, Charles E, 1938, Jl 13,21:4
Thurston, Charles Mrs, 1944, Mr 3,16:2
Thurston, Charles S, 1907, Ja 30,9:6
Thurston, Edward D, 1940, Ap 19,21:5
Thurston, Edward H, 1946, Ja 18,19:4
Thurston, Edward S, 1948, F 11,27:4
Thurston, Elbert W, 1957, Ag 3,15:7
Thurston, Eugene Mrs, 1943, O 8,19:3
Thurston, George, 1950, Ja 26,27:5
Thurston, George B, 1952, Je 16,17:2
Thurston, H, 1936, Ap 14,21:3
Thurston, Harry (M Cowan), 1955, S 3,15:4
Thurston, Harry E, 1941, My 8,23:3
Thurston, Henry F, 1948, Ja 1,23:3
Thurston, Henry W, 1946, S 20,32:2
Thurston, Herman S Mrs, 1943, Jl 3,13:6
Thurston, Howard Mrs, 1943, F 11,21:3
Thurston, John A, 1949, N 15,25:5
Thurston, John B, 1951, Mr 26,23:4

Thurston, John L, 1946, Mr 3,44:7
Thurston, John M, 1916, Ag 10,9:4
Thurston, Joseph W, 1947, Mr 25,25:4
Thurston, Katherine Cecil Mrs, 1911, S 7,9:5
Thurston, Lawrence E Mrs, 1958, Ap 20,84:3
Thurston, Lee M, 1953, S 5,16:3
Thurston, M D Wheeler, 1908, Je 27,9:5
Thurston, Nathaniel B Col (funl, Je 18,11:3), 1917, Ja 17,9:1
Thurston, Newman R, 1952, S 8,21:3
Thurston, Richard H Mrs, 1946, Ap 4,25:3
Thurston, Robert H Prof, 1903, O 26,1:6
Thurston, Royal C, 1946, D 6,23:2
Thurston, Royal C Jr, 1959, My 13,37:2
Thurston, W H, 1939, Ja 26,21:4
Thurston, W Harris, 1943, Jl 1,19:3
Thurston, Walter A Maj, 1911, Mr 14,11:4
Thurston-Cotter, 1904, Ap 6,1:2
Thurstone, Louis L, 1955, O 1,19:5
Thurtle, Ernest, 1954, Ag 23,17:3
Thury, Ilona Mrs, 1953, Ap 2,27:2
Thuxton, Olive Mrs, 1942, Mr 5,23:4
Thwaite, Herbert, 1965, My 4,43:1
Thwaite, Milton P, 1951, My 28,21:4
Thwaites, Charles H, 1959, O 25,85:4
Thwaites, Ernest, 1941, Ag 10,37:1
Thwaites, Joseph T, 1953, Ja 17,15:6
Thwaites, Norman G, 1956, Ja 27,23:4
Thwaites, Norman Mrs, 1951, F 25,84:4
Thwaites, Reuben Gold, 1913, O 23,11:6
Thwaites, William, 1947, Je 23,23:5
Thwaits, Frederick C, 1944, My 5,19:5
Thweatt, Alexander S, 1917, D 5,13:4
Thwing, Charles B, 1946, D 13,23:1
Thwing, Charles F Dr (por), 1937, Ag 30,21:3
Thwing, Frederick H, 1943, S 23,21:2
Thwing, Walter E, 1962, Je 30,19:6
Thye, Lilly T C, 1942, O 1,23:5
Thygeson, E Theodore I, 1964, Jl 20,25:5
Thyra, Princess, 1945, N 3,15:2
Thys, Constance, 1910, D 6,13:4
Thyselius, Albert E, 1959, Jl 15,29:2
Thyssen, Aug, 1926, Ap 5,1:2
Thyssen, Fritz, 1951, F 9,25:1
Thyssen, Fritz Mrs, 1965, Ag 27,29:2
Thyssen, Hans, 1943, My 5,27:2
Tibball, Catherine Stone Mrs, 1921, Mr 6,21:3
Tibbals, Charles A, 1948, D 31,15:1
Tibbals, Clarence, 1941, Mr 11,23:1
Tibbals, Edgar R, 1942, My 15,19:2
Tibbals, Edward L Rev, 1937, Ag 16,19:2
Tibbals, George A, 1949, F 21,23:5
Tibbals, Marion H Mrs, 1939, Je 24,17:6
Tibbals, Nathan V (por), 1942, My 1,19:6
Tibbals, Ross H, 1945, Jl 22,38:1
Tibbals, Seymour S, 1949, Ja 10,25:4
Tibbals, Walter A, 1967, Je 4,86:4
Tibbett, Bert M, 1939, Je 10,17:4
Tibbett, Lawrence (mem ser, Jl 19,29:4), 1960, Jl 16, 1:2
Tibbett, Thomas F, 1950, Ag 7,19:5
Tibbetts, Albert P, 1946, F 2,13:2
Tibbetts, Burr L, 1941, S 18,25:5
Tibbetts, Carleton B, 1958, O 29,35:2
Tibbetts, Delbert M, 1952, Je 28,19:2
Tibbetts, Fred E, 1956, Ap 14,17:3
Tibbetts, George A, 1948, F 22,48:2
Tibbetts, Guy D, 1939, Je 3,15:6
Tibbetts, Harland B, 1943, Jl 7,19:1
Tibbetts, Harry E, 1947, Ja 12,59:6
Tibbetts, Howard M, 1922, Ap 13,19:6
Tibbetts, James T Dr, 1937, Ja 17,II,9:2
Tibbetts, Joseph A, 1940, Je 12,25:5
Tibbetts, Mark, 1951, Ja 29,19:3
Tibbetts, Milton, 1959, Ag 30,82:2
Tibbetts, Samuel Dr, 1937, F 21,II,10:3
Tibbetts, Vinal H, 1957, F 2,19:3
Tibbetts, W B Gen, 1880, F 11,5:5
Tibbits, Charles, 1924, Ag 21,11:4
Tibbits, Charles H, 1937, F 2,23:5
Tibbits, Elizabeth B F Mrs, 1940, N 30,17:1
Tibbits, John K, 1955, D 10,21:2
Tibbits, Sarah B, 1947, Ap 21,27:5
Tibbits, William B, 1908, Jl 29,7:4
Tibbitts, Armand R Jr Mrs, 1945, Jl 28,11:6
Tibbitts, Armand R Mrs, 1954, Ag 24,21:3
Tibbitts, Clarkson, 1885, Ap 12,2:5
Tibbitts, Frank B, 1938, Ja 17,19:5
Tibbitts, Frank J, 1947, S 14,60:2
Tibbitts, Frederick R, 1939, Je 9,21:5
Tibbitts, G M, 1878, Jl 20,1:6
Tibbitts, Henry R, 1954, Ag 21,17:4
Tibbott, Everard F, 1941, Ap 15,23:1
Tibbs, John, 1951, Mr 18,47:6
Tibbs, John W, 1943, Ag 31,17:6
Tibbs, Roy W Mrs, 1967, D 9,47:3
Tibby, William, 1903, Jl 21,9:6
Tiberghien, Charles, 1938, My 16,17:1
Tiberini, Silvio, 1955, Jl 26,25:3
Tice, Charles E, 1947, Jl 29,22:3
Tice, David H, 1944, O 26,23:4
Tice, Frederick, 1953, D 19,15:3
Tice, George A, 1941, F 4,21:1
Tice, George H, 1913, N 27,13:6
Tice, Harold Mrs, 1948, My 31,19:5
Tice, Herbert H, 1949, D 22,23:1
Tice, Herman A, 1941, Ap 13,38:3
Tice, J H Prof, 1883, D 1,5:4
Tice, John S, 1950, My 28,44:6
Tice, Marion L, 1945, Mr 1,21:4
Tice, Mary F, 1949, Je 28,27:2
Tice, Sophia Mrs, 1924, O 14,23:3
Tichaz, Bernard, 1968, Ag 23,39:1
Tichborne, Raymond E, 1950, My 14,106:3
Tichenor, Carl M, 1946, O 31,25:2
Tichenor, Frank A, 1950, Mr 5,21:3
Tichenor, Frank D, 1943, Jl 3,13:4
Tichenor, Frederick W, 1950, Mr 8,25:3
Tichenor, G C Col, 1902, Jl 12,7:5
Tichenor, George N, 1959, N 25,29:3
Tichenor, George W, 1911, N 7,13:4
Tichenor, Harvey D, 1960, Je 15,41:4
Tichenor, Harvey D Mrs, 1949, F 26,15:5
Tichenor, Horace V, 1958, Ag 7,25:3
Tichenor, Jay H, 1964, D 20,68:7
Tichenor, Josephine B Mrs, 1942, S 24,27:1
Tichenor, Leslie R Sr, 1961, Ag 10,27:4
Tichenor, Robert M, 1954, Ap 13,31:5
Tichenor, William H, 1944, S 1,13:2
Tichman, Norman, 1967, F 28,37:1
Tichnor, George, 1906, Ja 1,7:5
Tichy, Charles, 1953, O 14,29:4
Tick, Irving, 1951, Ap 14,15:5
Tick, Jacob, 1961, D 31,48:5
Tickell, William J, 1952, S 10,29:5
Tickle, Alfred A, 1955, Ja 5,23:2
Tickle, Howard B, 1967, N 15,47:1
Tickle, Thomas G, 1952, Ap 27,90:3
Tickler, Thomas G, 1938, Ja 20,23:5
Tickner, A E, 1954, Mr 18,31:5
Tickner, Max, 1951, Je 11,25:5
Tickner, Percival C, 1948, D 14,29:2
Ticknor, Benjamin H, 1949, My 29,36:5
Ticknor, Caroline, 1937, My 12,23:2
Ticknor, Celeb, 1921, N 7,15:4
Ticknor, Charles H, 1949, My 18,27:4
Ticknor, Daniel W, 1965, Ja 31,88:6
Ticknor, George, 1871, Ja 27,4:7
Ticknor, Joseph A, 1943, Ap 4,40:3
Ticknor, Thomas Baldwin, 1925, Je 22,15:6
Ticknor, William D, 1864, Ap 11,5:1; 1938, Mr 25,19:5
Ticknor, William D Jr, 1965, Ap 25,88:7
Tidaback, John D, 1956, Ap 13,25:4
Tidaback, John D Mrs, 1962, Jl 4,21:6
Tidaback, John F Sr, 1953, O 20,29:3
Tidball, John Caldwell Brig-Gen, 1906, My 16,9:6
Tidd, Adelbert F, 1942, Mr 28,17:5
Tidd, George N, 1952, Je 19,27:4
Tidd, George N Mrs, 1958, Mr 8,17:5
Tidden, George O, 1913, Jl 1,9:4
Tidden, Paul, 1938, Ag 17,19:6
Tidgewell, Frederick T, 1947, Ap 22,27:2
Tidmarsh, Elmer A, 1965, Ja 27,35:4
Tidwell, Gregory, 1955, Mr 30,29:4
Tidwell, Josiah B, 1946, Mr 19,27:3
Tidyman, Ben C, 1955, Ap 19,31:1
Tiebohl, Frederick, 1951, My 27,69:1
Tiebor, John, 1945, Mr 22,23:1
Tiebout, Cornelius H, 1951, Je 19,29:1
Tiebout, David Crane, 1907, Ap 16,11:6
Tiebout, Frank B, 1959, F 25,31:2
Tiebout, Harry M, 1966, Ap 3,84:7
Tiebout, John, 1955, O 12,29:1
Tiebout, John Sr, 1943, O 16,13:3
Tiebout, William P, 1939, Mr 31,21:2
Tiedeman, C G Dr, 1903, Ag 26,3:4
Tiedeman, Frederick L, 1960, Jl 30,38:4
Tiedeman, Harry F, 1940, Ap 26,21:2
Tiedeman, John C (por), 1942, Jl 13,15:4
Tiedeman, William C, 1950, F 9,29:2
Tiedemann, Henry F, 1962, Mr 5,23:1
Tiedemann, T H A, 1956, Ap 17,31:3
Tiedjen, Richard J, 1950, N 30,33:5
Tief, Francis J (Sept 23), 1965, O 11,61:5
Tief, Sarah, 1938, Mr 27,II,6:5
Tiefenbronner, Alfred, 1948, Mr 5,21:4
Tiefert, Clarence G, 1964, S 23,47:1
Tieger, Max, 1954, O 18,25:3
Tieger, Pincus Mrs, 1951, O 21,93:1
Tiegler, Edward, 1907, N 6,9:2
Tieje, Arthur J, 1944, Ja 26,19:6
Tieke, William H, 1959, Ap 20,31:2
Tiel, Arthur R Mrs, 1953, Ap 15,31:5
Tiel, Henry S, 1964, O 30,38:1
Tiel, William M, 1944, Mr 23,19:5
Tieleman, H W, 1946, D 4,31:3
Tielemans, Frans, 1962, D 22,8:1
Tielsch, William, 1957, Ap 20,7:2
Tiemann, Louis S, 1962, Mr 18,86:5
Tiemer-Wille, Frederick Mrs, 1967, Mr 22,47:2
Tiemeyer, Edwin H, 1955, Ap 23,19:5
Tiemeyer, Rudolph C, 1945, O 29,19:1
Tien, Thomas Cardinal, 1967, Jl 24,28:1
Tienken, Henrietta S M, 1961, Ag 15,29:1
Tienken, John M, 1938, F 3,23:4
Tienken, Louis C Mrs, 1946, S 8,46:5
Tienken, William P Mrs, 1967, Ap 26,47:2
Tiepel, Frederick Mrs, 1947, F 13,24:2
Tier, Walter E, 1947, Jl 25,17:4
Tieran, Thomas J, 1968, D 13,42:3
Tierkel, David B, 1948, My 30,35:1
Tierman, Joseph S, 1939, D 14,27:4
Tiernan, George, 1946, Ag 14,26:3
Tiernan, J Harry Mrs, 1949, Je 21,25:2
Tiernan, J Harry Sr, 1968, O 4,47:1
Tiernan, James J, 1948, D 6,25:1
Tiernan, John, 1948, Ap 20,27:3
Tiernan, L Curtis, 1960, Je 21,33:2
Tiernan, Martin F, 1968, Mr 25,41:4
Tiernan, Martin F Mrs, 1958, Jl 14,21:5
Tiernan, Miles, 1950, Ja 5,40:4
Tiernan, William J, 1938, Ja 7,19:1
Tiernan, William P, 1952, S 5,27:4
Tierney, Agnes M, 1947, My 21,25:3
Tierney, Andrew J, 1962, Ja 31,31:4
Tierney, Charles, 1942, Ag 13,19:3
Tierney, Charles G Mrs, 1968, Ag 24,29:2
Tierney, Charles J, 1952, My 31,14:7
Tierney, Countess (Sayre), 1904, My 13,9:5
Tierney, Daniel M, 1957, D 21,19:4
Tierney, Daniel W, 1938, F 27,II,9:3
Tierney, Dudley R, 1947, Je 26,23:5
Tierney, Edward J, 1946, D 31,17:3; 1963, Jl 19,25:2
Tierney, Edward Joseph Rev, 1918, Jl 31,9:4
Tierney, Eunice K Mrs, 1941, F 27,19:5
Tierney, Eunice S Mrs, 1950, N 7,25:6
Tierney, Evelyn B Mrs, 1945, S 17,19:6
Tierney, Frank, 1949, Ap 19,26:5
Tierney, Frank A, 1923, S 18,21:6
Tierney, Frank A Mrs, 1943, Ap 5,19:4
Tierney, Frank N, 1952, Jl 6,49:2
Tierney, George A, 1955, S 23,25:3
Tierney, J M, 1936, F 21,17:2
Tierney, James A, 1923, Je 10,6:2; 1943, Ja 8,20:3
Tierney, James A (por), 1947, N 18,30:3
Tierney, James A (Cotton), 1953, Ap 19,91:2
Tierney, James A Mrs, 1950, D 28,25:3
Tierney, James E, 1942, Ja 10,15:2
Tierney, James J, 1958, D 31,19:3
Tierney, Jerome E, 1956, O 12,29:3
Tierney, John, 1938, D 5,23:2
Tierney, John A Mrs, 1937, My 8,19:5
Tierney, John J, 1941, My 13,23:1; 1955, S 27,35:1; 1961, Mr 19,89:2
Tierney, John J Mrs, 1945, O 7,44:6
Tierney, John T, 1944, O 26,23:1
Tierney, Joseph F, 1942, Ap 22,24:2
Tierney, Joseph L, 1955, Ja 21,23:2
Tierney, Joseph L Jr, 1951, N 16,25:3
Tierney, Launcelot J, 1904, N 15,7:2
Tierney, Lewis C, 1956, Mr 19,31:3
Tierney, Mary A, 1948, S 6,13:2
Tierney, Mary Mrs, 1941, Ap 14,17:3
Tierney, Matthew J, 1952, Jl 20,53:3
Tierney, Maurice Sr, 1946, My 12,45:3
Tierney, Michael A, 1940, N 15,21:5
Tierney, Michael Bp, 1908, O 6,9:7
Tierney, Michael J, 1960, Jl 17,62:3
Tierney, Michael J Ex-Judge, 1919, S 3,13:5
Tierney, Michael J Mrs, 1946, Ap 17,25:3; 1950, Ja 12,27:3
Tierney, Michael J R, 1959, Ap 7,33:2
Tierney, Michael S, 1953, Ag 24,23:3
Tierney, Myles J, 1951, F 6,27:5
Tierney, Owen S M, 1949, Ag 30,27:3
Tierney, Patrick J, 1952, S 6,17:6
Tierney, Paul A Mrs, 1964, My 3,86:8
Tierney, R H Rev, 1928, F 12,II,7:1
Tierney, Thaddeus W (funl, S 14,23:2), 1956, S 11, 35:2
Tierney, Walter J, 1950, My 13,9:1; 1959, Mr 25,35:4
Tierney, William, 1940, Je 26,23:4; 1948, Je 27,52:6
Tierney, William A, 1938, Ag 23,17:5
Tierney, William J, 1948, N 24,23:3; 1954, Ja 7,31:4; 1959, N 28,21:5
Tierney, William L, 1958, Ap 14,25:4
Tiernon, John L Brig-Gen, 1910, Mr 31,11:4
Tierny, John W, 1914, Jl 14,9:7
Tiers, Cornelius Mrs, 1954, Ja 22,27:4
Tiers, Francis M, 1965, My 25,31:3
Tiesenga, Cornelius, 1942, Ja 19,17:2
Tiesenhausen, Fred P Mrs, 1941, S 19,23:1
Tiesler, Eugene M, 1945, S 21,21:1
Tietgens, Gustav W, 1910, Ap 27,9:4
Tietje, Carl A, 1958, O 15,39:4
Tietje, Christian P, 1942, D 22,25:3
Tietjen, Andrew, 1953, Ap 15,31:6
Tietjen, Charles F, 1961, O 21,21:5
Tietjen, Christian F, 1917, O 26,15:4
Tietjen, Fred W, 1940, My 12,48:4
Tietjen, John F, 1923, Ag 9,13:6
Tietjen, John H, 1954, My 25,27:2
Tietjen, John Mrs, 1946, Ag 17,13:4
Tietjen (Danish Financier), 1901, O 20,7:4
Tietjens, Eunice, 1944, S 7,23:2
Tietjens, Paul, 1943, N 26,23:2
Tietjens, Theresa, 1877, O 4,4:6
Tietz, Carl G, 1950, Ja 14,15:5
Tietz, Herbert D, 1953, O 13,29:3

Tietz, John W, 1964, Ap 25,29:4
Tietz, Max O, 1940, O 22,23:4
Tietze, Erich A J, 1946, Ja 11,21:3
Tietze, Hans, 1954, Ap 13,31:4
Tietze, Henry, 1943, Ag 7,11:5
Tietze, Henry Mrs, 1945, My 22,19:1
Tietze, Walter L E, 1957, D 15,86:6
Tietze, Willy, 1955, Mr 25,21:3
Tiffany, Annie Ward, 1919, Ja 1,17:2
Tiffany, Belmont, 1952, Ja 22,29:4
Tiffany, C J, 1902, F 19,9:4
Tiffany, C L Mrs, 1927, Mr 12,15:5
Tiffany, Cameron Mrs, 1961, S 23,19:1
Tiffany, Charles Comfort Rev, 1907, Ag 21,7:7
Tiffany, Charles H A, 1903, Jl 7,7:6
Tiffany, Charles L, 1947, Ap 4,24:3
Tiffany, Charles L Mrs, 1961, Ag 26,17:3
Tiffany, Dexter O, 1945, D 3,21:4
Tiffany, E J, 1960, D 27,29:1
Tiffany, Ebenezer, 1937, Ja 11,19:2
Tiffany, Eleanor Mrs, 1941, O 12,46:4
Tiffany, Ezra, 1945, D 27,19:4
Tiffany, George, 1946, N 29,26:2
Tiffany, George Mrs (funl, Ja 9,13:6), 1912, Ja 6,13:4
Tiffany, George S, 1938, Je 20,15:5; 1954, Ap 15,29:3
Tiffany, George W, 1938, My 5,23:5
Tiffany, Gilman P, 1954, Jl 30,17:2
Tiffany, Henry Dyer, 1917, Ja 24,9:3
Tiffany, Henry Dyer Mrs, 1906, Mr 15,9:6
Tiffany, Henry L, 1946, Ja 8,24:2
Tiffany, Humphrey C, 1947, S 7,60:8
Tiffany, J Raymond, 1956, Ap 10,31:3
Tiffany, Jane P, 1954, Je 24,27:3
Tiffany, Jesse L, 1947, Ag 30,15:3
Tiffany, John B, 1942, Ag 11,19:3
Tiffany, John F, 1946, Je 14,22:2
Tiffany, John L, 1941, Ja 15,23:1
Tiffany, Joseph Burr, 1917, Ap 4,15:6
Tiffany, Joseph E, 1962, O 17,39:2
Tiffany, L, 1933, Ja 18,19:1
Tiffany, Louis McLane Dr, 1916, O 24,12:6
Tiffany, Louise H (will, F 28,33:6), 1937, F 11,23:4
Tiffany, Lyman, 1912, O 5,13:5
Tiffany, Orrin E, 1950, F 3,23:2
Tiffany, S S Mrs, 1903, My 22,9:4
Tiffany, W G, 1905, Ap 24,1:2
Tiffany, Willard H, 1943, O 11,19:1
Tiffany, William J, 1958, Mr 30,88:8
Tiffany, William Shaw, 1907, S 30,7:6
Tiffer, Alberto, 1942, My 27,23:4
Tiffin, Arthur E, 1955, D 28,24:4
Tifft, Alanson H, 1903, O 7,9:6
Tifft, Charles, 1943, N 17,25:1
Tifft, Charles Jr, 1957, D 27,20:1
Tifft, F L, 1877, S 25,2:4
Tifft, Harold C, 1959, N 9,31:5
Tifft, Harry J, 1965, N 30,41:1
Tifft, Henry N, 1925, Mr 14,13:4
Tifft, Henry Neville, 1925, Mr 12,19:3
Tifft, Thomas D, 1959, My 20,35:3
Tiger, John B, 1945, O 26,19:4
Tiger, Leon V, 1958, S 29,27:3
Tiger, William H Mrs, 1949, Ag 23,23:4
Tigert, Holland M, 1948, N 15,25:2
Tigert, John J, 1965, Ja 22,44:1
Tigert, John J Bp, 1906, N 22,9:6
Tigh, Charles T W, 1965, Jl 22,31:4
Tigh, William F, 1964, My 4,29:3
Tighe, Charles J, 1966, Mr 22,42:1
Tighe, Dixie, 1946, D 31,17:5
Tighe, Ernest W, 1961, Ja 2,25:4
Tighe, Eugene A, 1961, S 1,17:2
Tighe, J G Judge Mrs, 1901, D 13,9:2
Tighe, James, 1948, My 5,25:4
Tighe, James L, 1947, Ap 7,24:2
Tighe, James P, 1963, Je 21,16:4
Tighe, James S (funl), 1911, My 25,11:5
Tighe, Larry, 1965, O 22,43:3
Tighe, Laurence G, 1954, D 4,17:3
Tighe, Leo F, 1961, O 17,39:1
Tighe, Leo R, 1960, Jl 4,15:3
Tighe, Louisa Lady, 1900, Mr 3,6:5
Tighe, Matthew Fitzsimons, 1924, S 18,21:6
Tighe, Michael A, 1943, My 25,23:3; 1947, Ap 9,25:3
Tighe, Michael F (por), 1940, Ag 6,19:4
Tighe, Michael J, 1939, O 31,23:2; 1953, Ap 2,28:3
Tighe, Michael Mrs, 1943, Ag 14,11:6
Tighe, Peter I, 1923, N 28,17:2
Tighe, Richard J, 1937, Ja 22,21:5
Tighe, William A, 1957, Mr 20,37:2
Tighe, William J Sr, 1959, N 7,23:5
Tighe, William P Rev, 1925, My 5,21:4
Tigner, E A, 1948, F 21,13:5
Tigrett, Isaac B, 1954, My 3,25:3
Tikhon, Rev Dr, 1925, Ap 10,19:3
Tikhov, Gavril, 1960, Ja 26,33:5
Tilden, Averill, 1952, Je 27,23:3
Tilden, Beverly Bingham, 1908, O 23,9:4
Tilden, Charles J, 1959, N 17,35:2
Tilden, Charles J Mrs, 1940, Mr 9,15:5
Tilden, Edward, 1915, F 5,11:6
Tilden, Ethel Mrs, 1950, N 1,35:5
Tilden, Frank W, 1940, Mr 30,15:6
Tilden, Frederick R, 1956, Ja 31,29:2
Tilden, George H, 1915, My 15,13:6
Tilden, George W, 1953, Ja 17,15:3
Tilden, H A, 1884, Mr 14,3:3
Tilden, Henry, 1912, N 18,11:4
Tilden, Herbert M, 1915, S 23,13:6
Tilden, John H, 1940, S 3,17:3
Tilden, Linda P T L Mrs, 1949, Mr 22,26:2
Tilden, Louis W, 1949, D 21,29:2
Tilden, M W, 1926, Mr 11,21:1
Tilden, M Y (see also S 10), 1876, S 15,4:7
Tilden, Marmaduke Mrs, 1925, Ja 23,19:4
Tilden, Milano C, 1951, O 2,28:2
Tilden, Paul L (por), 1955, O 18,37:4
Tilden, Phil S, 1957, Mr 20,37:5
Tilden, Russell C, 1950, Je 10,17:2
Tilden, S J, 1886, Ag 5,1:5
Tilden, Samuel Jones, 1914, F 18,9:6
Tilden, Samuel W, 1943, Ja 8,19:2
Tilden, William, 1869, Je 27,4:6
Tilden, William A, 1925, My 2,15:4
Tilden, William Judge, 1873, S 17,5:4
Tilden, William T, 1915, Jl 30,9:7
Tilden, William T (Big Bill), 1953, Je 6,1:2
Tildes, Olga A, 1950, Jl 25,27:5
Tildsley, John L (por), 1948, N 22,21:3
Tildsley, John L Jr, 1943, S 27,19:5
Tildsley, John L Mrs, 1960, Ja 9,21:6
Tildy, Zoltan, 1961, Ag 4,21:4
Tileston, Frederic M, 1945, Mr 29,23:5
Tileston, Thomas, 1864, Mr 6,5:3; 1923, Je 8,19:5
Tiley, Charles A, 1950, Ap 9,85:1
Tiley, Charles B, 1949, Ja 7,21:4
Tiley, Stillman B, 1949, Jl 3,26:5
Tilford, Frank, 1924, Mr 7,15:4
Tilford, Frank Mrs, 1946, Ap 27,17:5
Tilford, Isabelle W Mrs, 1941, Ag 1,15:3
Tilford, Richard Curd, 1912, Mr 7,11:4
Tilford, Wesley Hunt, 1909, Mr 3,9:5
Tilgher, Adriano, 1941, N 4,26:6
Tilghman, Frederick Boyd, 1924, D 23,19:4
Tilghman, Frederick C, 1950, N 14,31:4
Tilghman, Harrison, 1961, O 13,35:1
Tilghman, R C, 1879, Mr 17,5:6
Tilgnman, French Gen, 1874, D 24,5:2
Tilkin, Samuel, 1943, My 11,21:3
Till, George W, 1947, Ja 12,59:2
Till, Mildred, 1940, D 10,25:3
Till, Walter F, 1961, D 16,25:6
Till, William, 1945, My 30,19:3
Till, William D, 1950, Ag 21,19:4
Tillabrowne, Maj, 1871, Ag 23,5:2
Tillard, Aubrey, 1952, D 14,90:3
Tillard, Edward E, 1944, F 3,19:3
Tiller, John, 1925, O 23,23:5
Tilles, C Andrew, 1951, N 23,30:2
Tilles, David Mrs, 1958, Je 19,31:3
Tilles, Herman M, 1950, D 16,17:5
Tilles, Roy E, 1961, D 27,27:2
Tillett, Ben (por), 1943, Ja 28,19:1
Tillett, Duncan P, 1947, F 28,24:3
Tillett, James W, 1941, Ja 14,21:5
Tillett, John, 1943, Jl 4,20:5
Tillett, Paul, 1966, S 27,47:2
Tilley, Albert, 1944, N 4,15:1
Tilley, Arthur, 1950, O 7,19:3
Tilley, Benjamin Rear-Adm, 1907, Mr 19,9:5
Tilley, Earle F, 1957, F 6,25:3
Tilley, Edwin F, 1942, F 22,26:5
Tilley, George, 1948, My 4,25:2
Tilley, George D, 1946, S 17,7:2
Tilley, George Mrs, 1913, D 11,11:4
Tilley, Herbert C Jr, 1956, Mr 29,27:4
Tilley, James N, 1961, My 3,37:4
Tilley, John, 1952, Ap 6,88:1
Tilley, Lydia, 1944, Je 17,13:6
Tilley, Morris P, 1947, Je 27,21:2
Tilley, Richard R Mrs, 1946, Jl 31,27:3
Tilley, Vesta (Lady de Frece), 1952, S 17,31:1
Tilley, W Norman, 1942, Je 11,23:4
Tillich, Paul (funl plans, O 24,86:8; mem ser, N 1,41:2), 1965, O 23,1:7
Tillinger, Eugene, 1966, O 15,29:1
Tillingham, J Charles, 1944, N 20,21:4
Tillinghast, A Roy, 1939, Ap 30,44:8
Tillinghast, Albert W, 1942, My 20,19:3
Tillinghast, Benjamin P Mrs, 1944, S 5,19:5
Tillinghast, Caleb Benjamin, 1909, Ap 29,9:3
Tillinghast, Charles C, 1962, My 1,37:2
Tillinghast, Charles F, 1948, O 4,23:4
Tillinghast, Charles Whitney Gen, 1913, D 28,II,15:5
Tillinghast, Evelyn Mrs, 1953, Ja 20,25:3
Tillinghast, Frank W, 1948, My 2,77:1
Tillinghast, Harry M, 1958, Ap 27,86:4
Tillinghast, Harry S, 1937, Ag 24,21:1
Tillinghast, Henry W, 1922, S 22,15:4
Tillinghast, James, 1957, Ap 15,29:4
Tillinghast, James D Mrs, 1951, F 21,27:2
Tillinghast, John A, 1948, Mr 7,69:1
Tillinghast, Joseph A, 1944, F 26,13:2
Tillinghast, Marion C Mrs, 1938, My 25,23:5
Tillinghast, Mary E, 1912, D 16,13:3
Tillinghast, P E Judge, 1905, F 10,7:4
Tillinghast, Percival P, 1948, O 4,23:5
Tillinghast, Ray C Mrs, 1948, O 4,23:6
Tillinghast, Ruth, 1964, S 12,25:2
Tillinghast, W H, 1902, D 10,9:4
Tillinghast, William Eldridge, 1919, My 19,17:5
Tillion, Clement V, 1947, O 16,27:2
Tillion, Phil G, 1951, Je 4,27:5
Tillion, Philemon Mrs, 1951, N 11,91:2
Tillisch, Jacob, 1940, S 6,21:4
Tillison, David J, 1955, F 24,27:4
Tillitson, Jay H, 1949, S 19,23:5
Tillitt, Malvern H, 1945, Ap 6,15:1
Tillman, Arthur C, 1940, O 26,15:5
Tillman, Benjamin Jr, 1950, My 18,29:2
Tillman, Benjamin R Sen, 1918, Jl 4,13:1
Tillman, Charlie D, 1943, S 4,13:5
Tillman, Edward C, 1956, F 18,19:4
Tillman, Francis, 1921, S 29,17:1; 1965, D 1,47:2
Tillman, Georg, 1941, N 3,19:4
Tillman, George Mrs, 1944, S 19,21:4
Tillman, Harold W, 1964, My 13,47:5
Tillman, James H, 1911, Ap 2,II,13:4
Tillman, John D, 1937, My 27,23:3
Tillman, Lloyd M, 1945, Ap 23,19:5
Tillman, Peter Mrs, 1945, Je 26,19:2
Tillman, Samuel E (por), 1942, Je 25,23:1
Tillman, Walter L, 1964, Je 9,35:5
Tillman, Willard E, 1948, Je 8,25:3
Tillman, William R Jr, 1960, Ja 17,86:2
Tillmann, Alfred J, 1939, My 1,23:6
Tillmanns, Robert, 1955, N 13,87:4
Tillona, Thomas F, 1964, Jl 10,30:1
Tillot, Emanuel, 1948, Ja 31,19:6
Tillotson, Clyde P, 1949, Je 2,27:2
Tillotson, Elbert, 1948, Je 15,27:5
Tillotson, Frederic E T, 1963, N 26,37:2
Tillotson, George D, 1937, D 20,27:4
Tillotson, George G, 1948, My 25,27:1
Tillotson, Gouverneur, 1907, Je 28,7:6
Tillotson, Harry A, 1943, F 15,15:4
Tillotson, Harry C, 1943, S 2,19:4
Tillotson, Harry S, 1955, Je 10,25:4
Tillotson, John B, 1937, Mr 25,25:2
Tillotson, L G, 1885, F 1,7:3
Tillotson, Robert S, 1944, D 5,23:1
Tillotson, W Alfred, 1966, F 6,92:5
Tillotson, W R, 1953, Mr 10,29:3
Tillotson, William M, 1906, D 1,9:6
Tillou, Abijah F, 1904, F 23,7:2
Tillou, Daniel W, 1949, Mr 22,25:3
Tillou, Eldred, 1946, Je 13,27:4
Tillou, F, 1876, Ap 20,8:4
Tillou, Frederick B, 1953, Mr 22,86:7
Tillou, George C, 1938, D 6,23:1
Tillou, Job Brown, 1911, My 3,13:5
Tillou, Samuel B, 1941, S 9,23:5
Tillou, William A, 1948, Ag 31,23:2
Tillson, Benjamin F, 1951, D 5,35:3
Tillson, C Kirk Mrs, 1950, Ja 27,23:3
Tillson, George W, 1940, My 14,23:5
Tillson, Harry L, 1948, Jl 28,23:3
Tillson, Hassie A, 1952, My 28,29:2
Tillson, John C F, 1941, D 17,27:4
Tillson, Lyman, 1951, Ja 19,25:2
Tillson, Ralph, 1950, Jl 30,60:5
Tilly, David L (por), 1949, O 19,29:4
Tilly, Frederick E G, 1952, Je 5,31:4
Tilly, Percy T, 1937, Ap 8,23:1
Tilney, Arthur A (por), 1937, Ag 29,II,7:1
Tilney, Frederick (por), 1938, Ag 8,13:3
Tilney, I Sheldon Mrs, 1959, Ag 4,27:4
Tilney, Norcross S Mrs, 1948, N 1,23:4
Tilney, Robert W, 1954, Ap 22,29:2
Tilp, John, 1949, F 23,27:3
Tilson, James R, 1941, My 12,17:5
Tilson, John Q, 1958, Ag 15,22:3
Tilson, William J, 1949, My 27,21:2
Tilt, Albert, 1946, Je 24,31:4
Tilt, Albert Mrs, 1942, D 11,24:2
Tilt, B B, 1879, O 2,2:3
Tilt, Capel, 1938, Ja 19,23:6
Tilt, Charles A, 1956, S 22,17:5
Tilt, Edgar M, 1943, S 18,17:2
Tilt, Sheldon D, 1946, Ap 9,27:4
Tilton, Abel H, 1948, Mr 8,23:2
Tilton, Andrew I, 1956, S 23,84:5
Tilton, Andrew I Jr, 1946, N 17,68:3
Tilton, Benjamin T, 1945, S 24,19:4
Tilton, Benjamin T Mrs, 1961, Mr 28,35:1
Tilton, C E, 1901, S 29,7:6
Tilton, Charles E, 1940, D 21,17:4
Tilton, Charles P, 1938, My 27,17:5
Tilton, E L, 1933, Ja 6,19:5
Tilton, Edgar Jr, 1954, D 14,33:1
Tilton, Elihu B, 1950, Mr 16,31:3
Tilton, Frank L, 1952, Je 29,58:5
Tilton, Frederic A, 1942, Mr 4,19:4
Tilton, Henry W, 1904, F 13,9:5
Tilton, J Ford (funl, F 12,13:6), 1919, F 10,13:2
Tilton, John P, 1959, Ja 16,28:1
Tilton, L Deming, 1949, O 20,29:3
Tilton, Louis O, 1949, D 1,31:5
Tilton, Mabel F (Countess Stavra), 1910, F 23,9:4

Tilton, Newell W, 1963, Je 28,29:3
Tilton, Perley G, 1940, O 17,25:3
Tilton, Ralph, 1907, F 17,9:6
Tilton, Richard B, 1959, D 1,39:1
Tilton, Roy G, 1939, N 12,49:2
Tilton, Samuel E, 1957, D 24,15:3
Tilton, T Mrs, 1897, Ap 16,7:5
Tilton, Thaddeus F, 1951, Mr 21,33:1
Tilton, Theodore, 1907, My 26,7:1; 1907, My 28,9:5
Tilton, Webster, 1961, Ja 22,85:2
Tilton, Welcome L, 1949, Ag 27,13:6
Tilton, William F, 1948, N 14,76:2
Tilton, William Mrs, 1950, Mr 16,31:1
Tilton, Zebulon, 1952, Mr 1,15:5
Tily, Herbert J (por), 1948, D 29,21:1
Tily, Herbert J Mrs, 1937, N 14,II,11:3
Tily, Stephen B, 1939, D 11,23:3
Tilyou, Edward F (por), 1944, Je 20,19:1
Tilyou, Frank S, 1964, My 9,27:4
Tilyou, George C, 1914, D 1,13:5; 1958, D 27,2:8
Tilyou, George C Mrs (funl, Ag 19,23:5), 1954, Ag 16,17:5
Tilzer, George Mrs, 1965, F 13,21:5
Tilzer, Jacob Mrs, 1946, O 15,26:3
Tim, Louis B, 1954, Ja 11,25:2
Timberg, Herman, 1952, Ap 17,29:3
Timberg, Herman Mrs, 1960, Ag 22,25:5
Timberlake, Baxter H, 1957, S 29,40:4
Timberlake, Charles B (por), 1941, Je 1,41:2
Timberlake, Daniel T, 1938, O 12,27:5
Timberlake, David W, 1956, Jl 23,23:6
Timberlake, David W Mrs, 1939, Ag 15,19:4
Timberlake, Edward J, 1950, N 29,33:3
Timberlake, Edward Mrs, 1940, My 31,19:4
Timberlake, Gideon, 1951, Mr 2,25:2
Timberlake, H G Prof, 1903, Jl 20,7:6
Timberlake, Ralph M, 1949, Ag 28,74:5
Timberman, Harry C, 1943, F 28,49:2
Timberman, William J, 1950, O 2,23:5
Timbers, Harry Dr, 1937, My 17,19:5
Timbie, Burtt N, 1950, Mr 4,17:3
Timbie, Clyde T, 1952, O 16,29:2
Timblin, Louis M (por), 1955, N 22,35:2
Timby, Theodore R, 1909, N 11,9:5
Timiriaseff, K A, 1920, My 2,22:3
Timke, George H Mrs, 1953, Ag 30,88:2
Timken, Henry H, 1940, O 15,23:1
Timken, Henry H Jr, 1968, Mr 17,81:1
Timken, Henry H Mrs, 1948, O 5,26:2
Timken, William R, 1949, Je 13,19:3
Timken, William R Mrs (will, O 27,39:8), 1959, O 25,70:1
Timken, William R Mrs (est tax appr), 1963, Ap 13, 19:3
Timleck, Arthur Mrs, 1955, Mr 20,88:3
Timlin, John, 1937, O 14,25:5
Timlin, John Mrs, 1943, Ap 8,23:2
Timlin, John T, 1940, Ja 31,19:5
Timlin, Miles, 1954, S 3,17:2
Timlin, William H Justice, 1916, Ag 22,9:2
Timm, Carl F, 1948, Ja 30,24:2
Timm, Emanuel A, 1949, Ja 18,23:4
Timm, Eric W, 1962, F 4,82:2
Timm, Fannie E Mrs, 1948, F 27,21:2
Timm, Kenneth B, 1958, N 9,89:1
Timm, Ralph B Mrs, 1951, Ap 3,27:2
Timm, William, 1948, O 17,78:4
Timme, Ernst G Col, 1923, Ap 2,17:4
Timme, Otto, 1937, Ag 10,19:4
Timme, Waldemar F, 1959, D 19,27:3
Timme, Walter, 1956, F 13,27:5
Timme, Walter Mrs, 1940, F 9,19:4
Timmerman, George B Sr, 1966, Ap 23,31:4
Timmerman, Harold Mrs, 1949, My 8,76:8
Timmerman, Karl H, 1951, O 24,31:2
Timmerman, L Stephen, 1944, My 23,23:6
Timmerman, Lucie Mrs, 1950, O 12,31:3
Timmerman, Paul E, 1943, S 29,21:3
Timmerman, Walter R, 1941, Ja 11,17:4
Timmermann, Charles, 1945, Ap 23,19:3
Timmermann, Henry C, 1925, Mr 6,19:5
Timmermann, Louis F, 1921, N 1,19:6
Timmermans, Felix (por), 1947, Ja 26,53:2
Timmins, Edward M, 1944, O 27,23:5; 1948, Mr 17, 25:4
Timmins, James P, 1954, My 4,29:5
Timmins, Patrick J Jr, 1957, Ap 22,25:4
Timmis, Robert J, 1939, Ag 9,17:5
Timmons, Agnes, 1909, Ag 7,9:6
Timmons, Clifford E, 1959, N 9,31:2
Timmons, Edward J, 1938, Ag 2,19:2
Timmons, Edwin S, 1948, N 10,29:3
Timmons, George A, 1941, Je 22,33:1
Timmons, John P, 1948, D 18,19:3
Timmons, John W, 1955, O 16,86:2
Timmons, Mary A (Mrs M J Finneran),(funl, D 15,25:2), 1956, D 12,39:3
Timmons, Nina A Mrs, 1941, S 27,17:5
Timmons, Russell M, 1953, Ag 3,17:5
Timmons, Thomas J, 1942, O 3,15:2
Timmons, William, 1939, Jl 21,19:1
Timmons, William D, 1960, My 31,31:2
Timmons, Wofford C, 1957, Ag 30,19:1
Timms, Harold R, 1958, S 27,21:6
Timms, Raymond J, 1940, Jl 9,21:4
Timofeev, Anatoli L, 1962, N 13,37:3
Timolat, Harry M, 1937, Je 20,II,5:5
Timoldi, Angelo G, 1948, D 27,21:4
Timon, John Rev, 1867, Ap 17,5:3
Timon, Patrick Sr, 1951, Je 28,25:3
Timoney, Francis X, 1967, My 23,47:3
Timoney, John L, 1955, O 24,27:4
Timony, James A, 1954, Ap 6,29:6
Timoshenko, Sergius, 1950, Jl 8,13:6
Timoshenko, Vladimir P, 1965, Ag 18,35:4
Timotheus Themelis, Patriarch of Jerusalem, 1956, Ja 3,31:2
Timothy, Bro (Alexian Bros Congregation), 1956, Je 1,23:4
Timothy, William G, 1947, Ap 28,23:3
Timothy, William G Mrs, 1952, Mr 2,92:1
Timothy Daniel, Bro (Murphy), 1955, D 7,39:1
Timpane, Edward Mrs, 1949, F 7,19:2
Timpanelli, Emilia, 1953, Mr 1,93:1
Timpone, Vincent A, 1947, Ja 24,22:2
Timpson, Alfred, 1944, N 3,21:1
Timpson, George E, 1949, My 27,21:3
Timpson, George T Mrs, 1909, F 19,9:6
Timpson, Gustavus W, 1942, My 8,21:4
Timpson, James Mrs, 1956, O 16,33:3
Timpson, John Sir, 1937, O 20,23:6
Timpson, Thomas W, 1907, Je 21,7:6
Tims, Oliver, 1916, Ap 26,13:5
Tims, Richard W, 1945, D 8,17:4
Tims, Richard W Mrs, 1950, S 3,38:4
Timson, J W Sr, 1879, Ap 9,2:3
Timson, John C, 1962, F 13,35:4
Tinaztepe, Asim, 1951, Je 16,15:4
Tincher, Jasper N (Polly), 1951, N 7,29:6
Tincher, Richard S, 1959, S 7,13:8
Tincter, John L, 1871, D 18,1:4
Tindal, Allen J, 1953, Je 17,27:3
Tindale, Frank C, 1953, Ja 13,27:4
Tindale, John L, 1965, S 5,56:8
Tindall, Jack, 1946, My 4,15:1
Tindall, John W, 1949, Ap 12,29:5
Tindall, Percy A, 1955, My 12,29:5
Tindall, Robert W, 1962, Jl 8,64:3
Tindall, Walter L, 1948, O 9,19:5
Tindall, William J, 1940, Ag 28,19:4
Tindell, Howard Leroy Dr, 1923, Jl 19,15:4
Tinel, Edgar, 1912, O 29,13:5
Tines, George V, 1959, N 19,39:4
Ting Liang, 1913, Je 29,5:5
Ting Wei-fen, 1954, My 14,23:3
Tinghir, Yervan Mrs, 1950, S 23,17:3
Tinghir, Yervent, 1940, Ag 10,13:5
Tingle, E Willard Mrs, 1952, D 18,29:2
Tingle, Harry M, 1951, O 27,19:6
Tingle, Helen N Mrd, 1954, D 9,33:3
Tingle, John L, 1957, Ap 23,31:5
Tingle, Leonard, 1963, S 16,35:4
Tingle, S Murray, 1949, F 9,27:4
Tingler, Lyman T, 1920, Ap 4,22:2
Tingley, Charles D, 1959, Ag 31,21:4
Tingley, Clyde, 1960, D 25,42:1
Tingley, Clyde Mrs, 1961, N 8,35:4
Tingley, H B Dr, 1903, Ja 15,9:7
Tingley, Jennie E, 1942, D 9,27:2
Tingley, K Mrs, 1929, Jl 12,23:3
Tingley, Louisa P, 1952, Jl 17,23:2
Tingley, Philo B, 1939, Jl 2,15:1
Tingue, William J, 1948, O 22,25:4
Tinkelman, Isidore, 1945, Je 28,19:1
Tinken, Henry, 1909, Mr 17,9:3
Tinker, Arthur, 1967, Ag 2,37:2
Tinker, Charles D Mrs, 1949, Ap 26,25:3
Tinker, Charles P, 1942, Ap 29,21:2
Tinker, Charles P Mrs, 1941, N 25,25:4
Tinker, Chauncey B, 1963, Mr 19,7:6
Tinker, Earl W, 1957, S 1,56:3
Tinker, Edward A, 1946, Ag 16,21:4
Tinker, Edward L Mrs, 1958, D 18,2:6
Tinker, Edward Larocque Dr, 1968, Jl 7,53:1
Tinker, Edward R, 1959, Mr 2,27:4
Tinker, George H, 1948, O 22,26:3
Tinker, Giles K, 1938, O 31,15:1
Tinker, Harold L Mrs, 1948, Ag 22,17:2
Tinker, Jackson, 1913, Jl 17,7:5
Tinker, James R, 1955, O 19,33:4
Tinker, Joe, 1948, Jl 28,23:1
Tinker, John F, 1937, S 11,17:2
Tinker, John W Col, 1937, F 28,II,8:6
Tinker, Louis C, 1944, F 9,19:4
Tinker, Wellington H, 1952, F 12,27:3
Tinkham, George H (trb lr, Ag 31,16:6), 1956, Ag 29,29:1
Tinkham, Herbert H, 1940, Jl 21,29:3
Tinkham, Herbert L, 1941, My 26,19:5
Tinkham, Julian R, 1940, O 28,17:4
Tinkham, Thornton W, 1950, S 11,23:1
Tinklepaugh, Frank A, 1966, S 7,41:5
Tinklepaugh, Jacob Mrs, 1952, Je 15,84:3
Tinkler, Loyal G, 1959, My 10,87:2
Tinley, Mathew, 1956, Mr 12,27:5
Tinlot, Gustave, 1942, Mr 3,23:5
Tinlot, Robert (Sept 27), 1965, O 11,61:5
Tinnele, Elizabeth D Mrs, 1939, Ag 6,37:2
Tinnerholm, August F, 1957, Ja 8,31:2
Tinnerholm, Robert F, 1959, My 2,23:5
Tinnerman, Albert H, 1961, S 6,37:4
Tinney, Frank, 1940, N 29,21:3
Tinney, George J, 1945, Ag 30,21:3
Tinney, Mary C, 1941, Jl 4,16:5
Tinney, Roy S, 1957, Ag 6,27:5
Tinnin, Glenna S Mrs, 1945, Mr 25,37:1
Tinning, Louis, 1938, Ap 1,23:4
Tinnon, John B, 1959, D 1,39:5
Tinoco Acero, Jose, 1953, O 10,17:2
Tinsdale, Edmund J, 1937, S 3,17:2
Tinsley, Douglas G, 1958, O 20,29:4
Tinsley, Edward S, 1937, S 12,II,6:6
Tinsley, Frank, 1965, Je 25,33:2
Tinsley, Fred, 1967, Jl 5,41:1
Tinsley, Gervase R, 1945, D 20,23:5
Tinsley, John F, 1952, N 19,29:5
Tinsley, Martin M, 1949, N 7,27:4
Tinsley, Robert J, 1941, My 3,15:3
Tinsley, Thaddeus S, 1942, F 5,22:3
Tinsley, Timothy W, 1943, D 10,27:4
Tinsman, Charles B Mrs, 1951, Ap 1,92:8
Tinsman, Charles P, 1950, Jl 2,24:5
Tinsman, Homer E, 1937, Mr 12,23:4
Tinsman, Jessie Mrs, 1941, S 4,21:2
Tinsman, Robert, 1956, My 13,86:8
Tinsman, William, 1940, Ja 7,48:6
Tinstman, Abraham Overholt, 1915, D 17,11:5
Tintera, William J, 1958, F 6,27:2
Tintner, Benjamin A, 1959, Ja 12,39:3
Tinworth, George, 1913, S 12,11:4
Tiomkin, Dimitri Mrs (A Rasch), 1967, O 6,39:1
Tipaldi, Laura D Mrs, 1938, S 3,13:3
Tiplady, William P, 1953, Ja 26,19:4
Tipling, C A, 1929, Ag 24,13:5
Tiplitz, Hyman, 1955, Ag 9,25:4
Tipper, Harry (por), 1941, My 8,23:4
Tipper, Harry K, 1949, Ag 21,69:1
Tippet, R Jackson, 1949, N 22,29:5
Tippett, Clarence B, 1950, Ja 24,31:4
Tippett, James S, 1958, F 23,92:5
Tippett, John F, 1938, Je 1,23:2
Tippett, Mary A, 1959, Mr 14,23:3
Tippetts, Charles S Dr, 1968, Ag 31,23:4
Tippie, Frank E, 1967, My 25,47:4
Tippie, John W, 1942, Je 28,33:1
Tipping, Kenneth W, 1960, N 26,21:6
Tipple, Adeline M, 1946, F 20,25:2
Tipple, E S, 1936, O 18,II,9:1
Tipple, Edna W Mrs, 1940, Mr 29,21:2
Tippy, Worth M, 1961, O 4,45:2
Tipson, Frederick S, 1964, Ja 4,23:1
Tipton, Arthur C, 1942, Ja 16,21:5
Tipton, Chester H, 1968, Ag 20,41:3
Tipton, Ernest M, 1955, F 26,15:6
Tipton, Harry S, 1945, Ap 11,23:6
Tipton, Jonathan, 1903, Je 16,7:6
Tipton, Reuben E, 1940, N 21,29:5
Tipton, Thomas F Judge, 1904, F 8,5:2
Tirana, Rifat, 1952, Ap 16,27:2
Tirard, Paul, 1945, D 25,23:2
Tirella, Charles, 1945, Ag 18,11:5
Tirella, Edwardo, 1966, O 8,27:1
Tirelli, Charles, 1954, Mr 19,23:2
Tirindelli, Pier A, 1937, F 7,II,9:1
Tirone, Phil Mrs, 1940, F 24,13:2
Tirone, Philip, 1944, O 20,19:5
Tirpitz, A P F von, 1930, Mr 7,9:1
Tirrell, Charles Q, 1910, Ag 1,7:2
Tirrell, Edward L, 1951, Ag 24,15:3
Tirrell, Frank A Jr, 1955, Je 5,84:4
Tirrell, George L, 1949, N 19,17:4
Tirrell, Harry W, 1951, Ja 14,86:2
Tirrell, Henry A, 1952, S 26,21:5
Tirrell, Malcolm C Mrs, 1966, Ap 27,47:1
Tirrell, Mary A Mrs, 1938, Ag 20,15:2
Tirrell, Robert E, 1958, Ja 2,29:4
Tiscar, Fortunato, 1945, F 13,23:3
Tisch, Abraham (Al), 1960, F 3,33:3
Tisch, Alfred F, 1968, S 8,84:5
Tisch, Charles, 1948, Mr 15,23:5
Tisch, Madeline, 1953, My 14,29:4
Tischbein, Carl F, 1950, Ag 20,76:3
Tischendel, Jacob, 1955, O 26,31:4
Tischer, Hans O, 1966, My 26,47:3
Tischer, James W, 1940, Ag 28,19:6
Tischler, Adolph, 1939, Jl 26,19:5
Tischler, Adolph Mrs, 1955, Ag 23,23:3
Tischler, Alexander H, 1968, F 20,47:2
Tischler, Charles W, 1950, D 7,33:2
Tischler, Max, 1943, My 17,15:2
Tischler, Phil, 1949, My 11,29:2
Tischler, Philip Mrs, 1945, F 7,21:1
Tischler, Victor, 1951, F 27,28:2
Tischner, John J Sr, 1962, N 3,25:4
Tiscornia, Manuel, 1949, S 7,30:3
Tisdale, Arthur A, 1939, N 1,23:5
Tisdale, Charles, 1942, O 8,27:4
Tisdale, Charles W, 1941, D 21,41:1
Tisdale, Daniel, 1882, F 19,9:3

Tisdale, E C H (Bud), 1952, N 2,89:1
Tisdale, F G, 1878, D 25,8:2
Tisdale, Frank, 1937, Mr 5,21:4
Tisdale, Glenn A Mrs, 1943, N 19,19:4
Tisdale, John N, 1905, N 30,1:4
Tisdale, Robert B, 1923, Jl 29,6:3
Tisdale, Wesley D, 1944, O 6,23:1
Tisdale, William Mrs, 1951, Jl 13,21:3
Tisdall, Fitz Gerald Prof, 1915, N 12,11:5
Tisdall, Josephine D Mrs, 1941, F 17,15:4
Tisdel, Alton P, 1945, Je 2,15:6
Tisdel, Millard P, 1911, Je 22,11:6
Tishenkel, Samuel, 1945, Ja 11,23:3
Tishman, Charles, 1967, N 13,47:3
Tishman, Charles Mrs, 1960, D 2,29:1
Tishman, Henry Mrs, 1956, Ap 14,17:6
Tishman, Jack A, 1966, Ap 21,40:1
Tishman, Maurice, 1955, Ja 11,25:1
Tismar, Rudolph M (will), 1939, F 19,4:2
Tisne, Jacques T Mrs, 1964, D 30,25:1
Tisne, Marcel E Mrs, 1951, Ja 8,17:4
Tiso, Americo, 1949, My 5,27:4
Tiso, Josephine Mrs, 1961, Jl 10,21:2
Tison, Alex, 1938, Jl 17,26:5
Tison, Alex Mrs, 1952, Jl 10,31:1
Tison, Paul, 1950, My 1,25:4
Tissandier, Albert, 1906, S 6,9:6
Tisse, Eduard K, 1961, N 21,39:4
Tisseyre, Justin Gen, 1937, Mr 28,II,8:7
Tissier, Joseph M, 1948, Ja 10,15:1
Tissier, Pierre, 1955, Ja 20,31:4
Tissot, Artist, 1902, Ag 10,4:1
Tisza, Kolomon, 1902, Mr 24,9:5
Tisza, Stephen, 1925, Mr 18,21:5
Titchener, Charles E, 1953, O 27,27:4
Titchener, Walter E, 1959, My 10,87:1
Titcomb, Harold A, 1953, N 27,27:4
Titcomb, Harvey B, 1954, My 26,29:4
Titcomb, Ledell, 1950, Je 10,17:3
Titcomb, Moses, 1881, Je 27,5:4
Titcomb, William N, 1955, Mr 17,45:1
Titelman, David M (cor, Mr 24,13:4), 1951, Mr 23, 21:4
Titerington, William, 1947, N 14,23:3
Titheradge, Madge, 1961, N 15,43:3
Titherington, Richard H Mrs, 1950, Mr 12,92:6
Titlar, Albert L Mrs, 1949, F 6,76:4
Titlar, Arthur C, 1945, D 19,25:4
Titlar, F Howard Mrs, 1946, Ap 26,21:3
Titlebaum, Emanuel Mrs, 1952, Jl 1,23:3
Titlestad, Nicolay, 1965, Je 8,41:2
Titley, William C, 1947, Je 25,25:6
Titlow, A R, 1923, Ja 7,7:2
Titman, Benjamin, 1960, Ap 10,85:3
Titmus, Joseph A, 1947, Ag 28,23:4
Tito, Thomas, 1942, F 27,17:5
Titsworth, Charles P, 1948, Ja 3,14:2
Titsworth, David E, 1914, Ap 23,13:6
Titsworth, Grant, 1960, My 15,85:3
Titsworth, Henry H, 1943, Je 12,13:4
Titsworth, Jane B Mrs, 1942, Ag 26,19:5
Titsworth, P E, 1933, D 11,22:2
Titsworth, Randolph Mrs, 1922, Ja 2,17:5
Titta, James, 1877, Mr 15,8:2
Tittell, Charlotte W, 1941, D 23,21:5
Tittle, Ernest F (por), 1949, Ag 4,23:1
Tittle, Walter, 1966, Mr 29,41:2
Tittmann, Edward McL Mrs, 1967, S 23,31:4
Tittmann, Otto H, 1938, Ag 22,13:3
Tittoni, Gen, 1922, D 13,21:5
Tittoni, T, 1931, F 8,28:3
Tittoni, Tomaso, 1937, Ja 31,II,9:2
Titulescu, Nicolas, 1941, Mr 18,23:1
Titus, Arthur H, 1943, F 11,19:3
Titus, Arthur H Mrs, 1956, N 17,21:5
Titus, Austin E, 1959, D 22,31:5
Titus, Bennett E, 1913, D 2,11:6
Titus, Calvin, 1925, N 3,25:5
Titus, Calvin P, 1966, My 29,56:3
Titus, Charles T Mrs, 1941, My 8,23:5
Titus, Clifford H, 1951, S 9,90:1
Titus, Constance S, 1967, Ag 25,35:3
Titus, Edmund De Mott, 1924, Ja 21,17:4
Titus, Edward C, 1956, D 16,87:1
Titus, Edward H, 1939, N 4,15:4
Titus, Edward W (trb lr), 1952, F 12,26:6
Titus, Elijah W, 1944, D 12,23:1
Titus, Ellwood V (por), 1944, Ja 24,17:4
Titus, Emily N, 1954, Ag 8,85:1
Titus, Forest M, 1939, Ja 17,22:2
Titus, Frank, 1914, D 14,11:4
Titus, Frederick H, 1953, N 28,15:5
Titus, George F, 1918, My 18,13:6
Titus, George G, 1941, Mr 16,44:7
Titus, Helen, 1952, N 19,33:6
Titus, Henry E Mrs, 1950, F 14,25:3
Titus, Henry W (por), 1949, Mr 18,25:1
Titus, Horace G, 1958, Ap 23,33:3
Titus, Irene C Mrs, 1951, Ja 4,29:4
Titus, John, 1939, N 7,28:5; 1943, Ja 10,48:7
Titus, John H, 1947, O 20,24:2
Titus, John W, 1954, Jl 25,69:1
Titus, Jonathan D, 1955, Jl 9,15:3
Titus, L Parker, 1939, Jl 14,19:5
Titus, Lester F, 1961, Je 13,35:4
Titus, Mary V, 1937, Mr 22,23:4
Titus, Melville Mrs, 1956, My 3,31:1
Titus, Neilson W Mrs, 1952, Mr 29,15:5
Titus, Norman E, 1965, Je 15,41:4
Titus, Norman F, 1939, Ap 20,23:5
Titus, Ormrod, 1960, N 2,39:2
Titus, Paul, 1951, Je 30,15:5
Titus, Raymond, 1960, Ap 22,31:4
Titus, S Champion, 1968, Mr 29,41:2
Titus, Silas Wright, 1922, Ja 10,19:3
Titus, Stanley, 1944, My 28,34:1
Titus, W Frank, 1950, S 12,27:5
Titus, Walter F, 1968, Jl 17,43:1
Titus, Walter L, 1953, D 30,24:3
Titus, William A, 1966, F 25,31:4
Titus, William E, 1950, O 5,31:4
Titus, William H, 1945, Mr 13,23:4
Titus, William S, 1944, N 11,13:6
Titus, William S Mrs, 1950, Mr 18,14:2
Titus (Aunt Sarah), 1902, Ja 3,2:5
Titze, Theodore, 1953, O 4,88:6
Titzel, J M Rev Dr, 1905, Je 17,9:5
Titzell, Frederick C, 1956, Mr 3,19:3
Titzell, Josiah C, 1943, My 16,42:5
Titzell, Josiah C Mrs (A Parrish),(est acctg approved), 1960, Ja 29,50:7
Titzell, Josiah Mrs (Anne Parrish), 1957, S 7,19:3
Tivin, Morris, 1963, D 21,23:4
Tivnan, Edward P Rev Dr (por), 1937, Ap 1,23:1
Tivnen, Richard J, 1946, Ag 30,17:2
Tivnon, Thomas P, 1949, F 1,25:4
Tixier, Adrien (por), 1946, F 19,25:1
Tizard, Henry T, 1959, O 10,21:4
Tjaarda, John, 1962, Mr 21,39:4
Tjader, Charles R Mrs, 1952, F 17,86:4
Tjader, Charles Richard, 1916, D 29,9:5
Tjorn, Curt, 1945, D 14,28:2
Tkach, George J, 1954, My 31,13:4
Tkach, Peter V, 1947, Ap 2,27:5
Tkachenko, Timofey, 1954, Ap 25,87:1
Tntruckova, Magda, 1952, Ap 3,36:3
Toabe, Kiebe, 1948, D 7,32:2
Toadive, John W, 1941, F 2,43:5
Toaff, Sabato A, 1963, N 19,41:2
Toal, Harry A, 1963, Jl 17,31:4
Toal, Helen M Mrs, 1940, N 13,23:5
Toal, John F, 1952, N 20,31:1
Toaz, Robert K, 1938, Ap 17,II,7:1
Tobacco, Anthony, 1941, Ap 13,39:2
Tobacco, Anthony Mrs, 1953, N 27,27:5
Tobani, T M, 1933, D 13,23:3
Tobar y Horgone, Carlos Manuel, 1923, Ja 8,17:6
Tobari, Shinichiro, 1955, Ja 7,21:1
Tobe (Mrs Tobe C Davis),(Dec 25), 1963, Ap 1,35:4
Tobenkin, Elias, 1963, O 21,31:1
Tobenkin, Elias Mrs, 1938, Ap 3,II,7:2
Tobenkin, Paul, 1959, Je 17,35:2
Tober, Charles W, 1953, Jl 25,8:4
Tober, Donald F, 1954, Ja 15,19:3
Tober, Joseph, 1937, D 9,25:1
Tobey, A William, 1953, O 4,88:4
Tobey, Allen, 1959, S 16,39:2
Tobey, B Frank (por), 1938, F 1,21:5
Tobey, Bennett H Lt-Col, 1923, Ap 14,13:5
Tobey, Charles H, 1949, Ja 16,69:2
Tobey, Charles W Mrs, 1947, Ag 31,36:6; 1952, Ja 1, 25:4
Tobey, Ellen H Mrs, 1944, F 17,19:3
Tobey, F W (see also My 8), 1878, My 10,2:5
Tobey, Frank T, 1955, S 12,25:3
Tobey, Guilford, 1950, Mr 14,25:3
Tobey, Harriet B N Mrs, 1937, O 2,21:4
Tobey, Harry G, 1948, Ja 13,26:3
Tobey, Harry W, 1949, Ag 26,19:4
Tobey, Henry E, 1947, Jl 13,44:1
Tobey, Lillian Q, 1962, Ag 5,81:2
Tobey, Rufus B Rev, 1920, Ja 7,19:3
Tobey, Rufus T, 1946, F 25,25:2
Tobey, Waldo F (will, Je 30,20:6), 1949, Je 17,24:4
Tobey, Walter L, 1938, My 14,15:2
Tobi, A C, 1946, Je 2,44:7
Tobias, Alfred J, 1958, O 6,31:2
Tobias, Channing H, 1961, N 6,37:1
Tobias, Channing H Mrs, 1949, My 30,13:2
Tobias, Frank, 1942, Ag 12,19:3
Tobias, Jacob M, 1963, Jl 23,29:4
Tobias, Jacob N, 1959, Mr 7,21:5
Tobias, Jerome J, 1964, My 30,17:2
Tobias, Julius D, 1943, S 17,21:5
Tobias, Margaret (Mrs J Kapros), 1959, Ap 15,33:2
Tobias, Philip, 1913, N 29,13:5
Tobias, Rafael, 1939, Je 20,21:4
Tobias, Raphael (funl, Je 5,13:7), 1922, My 31,15:1
Tobias, Rev Bro, 1919, S 27,13:6
Tobias, Walter S, 1952, Ja 5,11:6
Tobias, William E Jr, 1951, Je 7,33:2
Tobias, Willy E, 1942, My 31,38:1
Tobiasson, Albert M Sr Mrs, 1947, S 6,17:5
Tobie, Edward P, 1952, My 13,30:1
Tobie, Walter E, 1954, Mr 22,27:5
Tobien, Ralph D, 1943, Ag 16,15:5
Tobiessen, Emanuel, 1938, Ag 24,21:1
Tobin, Agnes, 1939, F 22,21:2
Tobin, Andrew J, 1950, Ja 18,31:1
Tobin, Austin J Mrs (funl, Jl 20,41:2), 1966, Jl 17, 68:8
Tobin, C Stuart, 1962, O 30,35:3
Tobin, Charles J, 1954, Ag 21,17:5
Tobin, Christopher E, 1958, Je 25,29:4
Tobin, Clarence J, 1957, Mr 9,19:5
Tobin, Clarence J Jr, 1962, N 15,37:3
Tobin, Clarke W, 1952, Ja 26,13:5
Tobin, Clarke W Mrs, 1950, Jl 6,27:3
Tobin, Claude, 1948, N 17,27:4
Tobin, Daniel A (por), 1942, My 29,17:1
Tobin, Daniel J (funl, N 18,25:1; will, N 20,9:2), 1955, N 15,33:1
Tobin, Daniel J, 1958, My 19,25:1
Tobin, Daniel S, 1951, Ja 12,27:3
Tobin, E W, 1938, Je 25,15:5
Tobin, Edgar, 1954, Ja 11,5:5
Tobin, Edmund J, 1953, O 24,15:6
Tobin, Edward J, 1941, Ap 18,21:5
Tobin, Elise, 1966, Ap 15,39:1
Tobin, Elizabeth M, 1949, D 14,31:4
Tobin, Florence Mrs, 1951, Ap 27,23:4
Tobin, Frank W Sr, 1947, Ap 10,26:2
Tobin, Fred, 1938, My 2,17:6
Tobin, George J, 1939, F 15,23:3
Tobin, George T, 1956, My 7,27:2
Tobin, Harold J, 1942, Je 18,21:5
Tobin, Hugh, 1949, Je 6,19:2
Tobin, James E Dr, 1968, O 31,47:3
Tobin, James Mrs, 1941, O 19,46:4
Tobin, John, 1938, Ap 9,17:4; 1941, My 4,V,8:8; 1951, Je 23,15:6
Tobin, John C, 1949, O 22,17:2
Tobin, John F, 1952, Ja 9,29:3
Tobin, John J, 1940, Je 16,38:6
Tobin, John M, 1938, Ag 19,19:3
Tobin, John N, 1944, F 8,16:3
Tobin, John W, 1957, Ja 10,29:1
Tobin, Joseph J, 1948, Jl 4,26:8
Tobin, Joseph M, 1953, Je 1,23:2
Tobin, Joseph Oliver Mrs, 1968, Mr 1,43:3
Tobin, Laurence H, 1923, Je 7,19:4
Tobin, Lawrence J, 1953, Jl 30,23:6
Tobin, Louis B, 1958, Ag 2,17:4
Tobin, Louis M, 1944, Ja 15,13:5
Tobin, Lyman B, 1961, F 6,21:1
Tobin, M F, 1907, S 14,9:6
Tobin, Mary, 1954, Ap 29,31:4
Tobin, Mary B Mrs, 1942, D 9,28:3
Tobin, Mary W, 1956, Ag 3,19:2
Tobin, Matthew J, 1941, My 4,53:3
Tobin, Maurice J, 1953, Jl 20,17:1
Tobin, Oscar (W Jackson), 1961, N 14,36:1
Tobin, Richard G, 1953, Mr 12,25:2
Tobin, Richard G Mrs, 1967, D 8,42:3
Tobin, Richard M, 1952, Ja 24,27:3
Tobin, Richard M Mrs, 1960, Ja 11,43:1
Tobin, Robert B, 1943, Jl 15,21:4
Tobin, Robert E, 1968, D 11,47:1
Tobin, Robert J, 1943, My 18,23:4
Tobin, Robert P, 1946, S 28,17:5
Tobin, Russell G, 1942, Ap 24,17:4
Tobin, Thomas J, 1953, My 14,29:2; 1967, N 17,47:3
Tobin, Thomas M, 1966, N 17,47:3
Tobin, William H Sr, 1939, My 23,23:5
Tobin, William J, 1963, My 9,37:1
Tobin, William N Mrs, 1947, O 21,24:2
Tobin, William W Mrs, 1949, My 31,23:2
Tobison, Christian A, 1965, Je 11,31:3
Tobler, George H, 1955, Ja 21,23:3
Tobler, Jacob, 1954, Je 30,27:5
Tobler, William A, 1959, Mr 25,35:3
Tobon Uribe, Pablo, 1954, Mr 17,31:5
Toby, Benjamin A, 1951, O 1,23:6
Toby, Harriet (H J Katzman), 1952, Mr 4,1:6
Toby, M P (Sir Hy Lucy), 1924, F 22,15:5
Tobyansen, John R, 1960, Je 22,35:4
Toca, Joaquin S, 1942, Jl 15,19:1
Tocci, Isadore, 1952, Ag 26,25:2
Tocci, Nicholas, 1942, D 12,15:2
Toce, Nicholas, 1951, O 22,23:3
Toch, Dora Mrs, 1937, Mr 28,II,8:7
Toch, Ernst, 1964, O 2,37:1
Toch, H M, 1933, Jl 3,11:1
Toch, Lucas, 1940, N 3,57:2
Toch, Maximilian (por), 1946, My 31,23:3
Tocheff, Andrew, 1944, Ja 15,13:5
Tocher, Charles S, 1954, Mr 7,91:1
Tocks, Lester A, 1954, N 18,33:4
Tocqueville, Alexis Charles Henri Maurice Clerel d 1859, Ap 26,1:3
Tod, A Kinnaird, 1951, S 2,48:5
Tod, David, 1919, My 15,17:6
Tod, David H Ex-Gov, 1868, N 14,4:7
Tod, David M Mrs, 1941, Ap 25,19:2
Tod, George B, 1964, N 10,47:4
Tod, J Kennedy (funl, Je 6,15:6), 1925, Je 3,23:3
Tod, John (will, Ap 10,23:8), 1953, F 15,93:3
Tod, Maria P Mrs, 1939, S 24,43:2
Toda, Josei (funl), 1958, Ap 21,23:4

Todaro, Francesco, 1950, Ja 12,27:4
Todaro, Gaetano, 1954, Ap 23,27:4
Todd, Albert W, 1949, My 27,21:2
Todd, Ambrose G, 1947, Ag 11,23:4
Todd, Ambrose G Mrs, 1953, F 15,93:1
Todd, Andrew L, 1945, Mr 25,38:3
Todd, Archibald L, 1944, F 4,15:6
Todd, Arthur J, 1948, N 24,24:3
Todd, Augustus F, 1939, My 3,23:5
Todd, Barbara S Mrs, 1937, Jl 28,20:1
Todd, Bert L, 1949, Ap 23,13:2
Todd, C E, 1946, Je 25,21:2
Todd, C M, 1885, F 13,2:3
Todd, C O, 1941, My 27,23:2
Todd, Cecil B, 1955, Mr 16,33:5
Todd, Charles A, 1908, Mr 19,7:5
Todd, Charles I, 1968, Mr 29,41:3
Todd, Charles L, 1954, O 2,17:5
Todd, Cliff, 1942, My 17,46:1
Todd, Constance L Mrs, 1944, N 18,14:2
Todd, David (por), 1939, Je 2,23:1
Todd, David H Capt, 1871, Ag 5,2:3
Todd, E H Mrs, 1874, F 21,3:6
Todd, Earle M, 1940, Ja 14,42:8
Todd, Edward, 1907, O 6,11:6; 1937, D 25,15:5
Todd, Edwin S, 1951, Ag 4,15:4
Todd, Elbert Dr, 1902, Ja 9,9:6
Todd, Elizabeth (Mrs L A Kagel), 1965, D 27,25:2
Todd, Elmer E, 1962, S 1,19:2
Todd, Eric Lt, 1917, My 5,13:6
Todd, Ethel, 1907, Ag 17,7:2
Todd, Florence A Mrs, 1937, S 12,II,7:3
Todd, Francis H, 1950, Ja 14,15:5
Todd, Francis H Mrs, 1951, Je 21,27:4
Todd, G Carroll, 1947, D 13,15:1
Todd, George S, 1951, F 3,15:2
Todd, George W, 1938, Mr 20,II,8:1
Todd, George W Mrs, 1943, N 3,25:4
Todd, Gerald B, 1958, D 30,35:3
Todd, Grover C, 1938, O 16,45:4
Todd, Guerin Sr, 1956, Ja 25,31:5
Todd, H B Col, 1882, Ap 9,9:3
Todd, H S, 1941, Ap 22,21:2
Todd, Harry L, 1938, Ja 5,21:2
Todd, Hattie E Mrs, 1941, Ag 28,19:1
Todd, Helen, 1953, Ag 16,77:3; 1963, Ap 29,31:3
Todd, Henry, 1941, My 19,17:4
Todd, Henry A, 1953, N 6,27:4
Todd, Henry A Mrs, 1945, F 1,23:5
Todd, Henry Alfred, 1925, Ja 4,7:2
Todd, Henry B 2d, 1958, O 16,37:1
Todd, Henry D Jr, 1964, Ja 23,31:2
Todd, Henry Davis Prof, 1907, Mr 9,9:6
Todd, Henry H, 1943, S 28,25:5
Todd, Herbert O, 1959, My 9,21:5
Todd, Herbert W, 1946, Mr 22,21:4
Todd, Hiram C, 1965, Ap 8,39:3
Todd, Hiram C Mrs, 1946, Ja 17,23:4
Todd, Hugh A Mrs, 1966, Jl 2,23:3
Todd, J Clinton, 1942, Ja 6,23:4
Todd, Jacob Jr, 1944, S 8,19:4
Todd, James, 1945, O 23,17:2
Todd, James E, 1943, Ap 13,25:4
Todd, James M (por), 1939, Ja 6,21:3
Todd, James M, 1939, Je 4,49:1
Todd, James R, 1952, Jl 21,19:2
Todd, James R Mrs, 1950, My 19,27:2
Todd, Jane E, 1955, My 8,89:1
Todd, Jane H, 1966, N 9,39:1
Todd, John, 1957, Jl 16,26:1
Todd, John B, 1914, Ja 13,9:6
Todd, John F, 1950, Je 28,27:4
Todd, John Gray, 1924, My 27,21:4
Todd, John H L, 1941, Jl 27,31:2
Todd, John R (por), 1945, My 13,20:1
Todd, John R Mrs, 1956, Je 16,19:5
Todd, John Rev, 1873, Ag 25,5:3
Todd, Joseph C, 1905, Ap 18,11:5
Todd, Joseph F, 1962, Je 14,33:6
Todd, Judson S, 1943, S 27,19:4
Todd, Judson S Sr Mrs, 1953, My 19,29:2
Todd, Laird E, 1950, D 17,85:2
Todd, Laurence, 1957, D 1,88:2
Todd, Leon, 1950, O 26,31:4
Todd, Leon E, 1959, F 13,17:1
Todd, Libanus M Mrs, 1948, F 16,22:2
Todd, Louren E, 1942, S 22,21:5
Todd, Luther E Rev Dr, 1937, N 26,21:4
Todd, Manford R Sr, 1955, Ap 12,29:2
Todd, Marjory C, 1953, Mr 16,19:5
Todd, Mary E, 1942, Ag 22,13:3
Todd, Mary J, 1948, Jl 1,23:3
Todd, Michael (Mike),(funl plans, Mr 24,27:4; funl, Mr 26,44:1), 1958, Mr 23,1:6
Todd, Nathan H, 1943, Mr 14,24:6
Todd, Nathaniel W, 1939, My 30,17:3
Todd, Nelson Mrs, 1938, Je 30,23:2
Todd, O A Sgt, 1903, Je 8,7:6
Todd, Paul J, 1939, Ja 17,22:3
Todd, Paul J Mrs, 1949, Jl 29,21:4
Todd, R I, 1928, Jl 13,17:2
Todd, R S, 1874, F 18,1:7
Todd, Ralph, 1949, Ag 17,23:5
Todd, Ralph L, 1949, Je 29,27:3
Todd, Ralph T B, 1960, Jl 10,72:1
Todd, Robert C, 1950, Ja 21,17:5
Todd, Robert R, 1940, My 18,15:2
Todd, Rodwell, 1957, F 2,19:5
Todd, Roosevelt D, 1943, Je 10,21:5
Todd, Stanley W, 1952, N 12,27:4
Todd, T Wingate (por), 1938, D 29,19:1
Todd, Van Winkle, 1959, Ja 17,19:3
Todd, Victor H, 1966, S 13,47:3
Todd, W C, 1903, Je 30,7:5
Todd, William, 1963, Jl 26,25:2
Todd, William A Mrs, 1937, Ja 10,II,9:3
Todd, William B, 1873, Mr 14,1:6
Todd, William C, 1954, Mr 28,89:2
Todd, William E, 1944, N 29,23:4
Todd, William H, 1940, N 24,49:1
Todd, William H Mrs, 1937, Je 25,21:2
Todd, William M Jr, 1960, F 21,92:7
Todd, William Rogers, 1924, My 24,15:3
Todd, William S, 1964, S 25,41:2
Tode, Arthur M, 1966, O 14,40:1
Tode, Walter K Mrs, 1963, Ag 22,27:4
Toder, Emanuel Mrs, 1961, D 4,37:4
Todesco, Joseph, 1946, O 18,24:2
Todieben, F E Gen, 1884, Jl 3,5:1
Todorov, Kosta, 1947, Mr 18,27:5
Todorowski, John J, 1948, Mr 24,25:4
Todorsky, Alexsandr I, 1965, S 1,37:4
Toebe, Charles W, 1956, Ag 21,29:4
Toedt, Ella A Mrs, 1939, Je 14,23:5
Toedtman, William H, 1967, Je 14,47:4
Toegel, Herbert J, 1950, Ap 25,31:3
Toel, Court W, 1947, Mr 22,13:4
Toel, William, 1909, Jl 27,7:3
Toell, Samuel J Sr, 1946, D 7,21:2
Toelle, Hugo W, 1956, Je 2,19:4
Toensfeldt, Hans C T, 1960, Ag 16,29:2
Toensmeier, Emil S, 1957, N 19,33:3
Toepfer, David, 1965, Mr 14,87:1
Toepfer, Solomon Mrs, 1964, Je 24,37:4
Toepfert, Henry J Mrs, 1945, N 4,43:2
Toeplitz, Giuseppe, 1938, Ja 30,II,9:3
Toeplitz, Richard, 1956, O 27,21:3
Toepperwein, Adolph, 1962, Mr 5,23:3
Toepperwein, Lawrence, 1940, O 21,17:5
Toerner, Susie Mrs, 1920, Je 12,13:3
Toerngren, Ralf, 1961, My 17,37:1
Toerring, Christian Mrs, 1949, N 30,27:2
Toerring-Jettenbach, Elizabeth Countess, 1955, Ja 13, 27:1
Toewater, George M, 1949, Ag 28,72:1
Tofel, Jennings, 1959, S 8,35:2
Toffenetti, Dario L, 1962, Ja 17,33:3
Toffenetti, Rudolph, 1961, S 23,19:7
Toffey, Akin Mrs, 1960, Ap 14,31:2
Toffey, Harold J, 1955, D 21,29:2
Toffey, John Col, 1911, Mr 14,11:4
Toffey, William V, 1955, Jl 4,11:4
Tofte, Louis, 1968, N 4,47:3
Toftoy, Holger N, 1967, Ap 20,43:3
Toggenburger, Robert, 1965, O 18,35:2
Togliatti, Palmiro (funl, Ag 26,11:1), 1964, Ag 22,1:4
Togo, H, 1934, My 30,17:1
Togo, Shigenori, 1950, Jl 23,58:1
Toher, James E, 1950, S 18,23:2
Tohn, George, 1961, Je 9,33:1
Toidze, Moisey, 1953, Je 21,84:6
Toivanen, Siiri (S Tovia), 1955, Mr 23,33:4
Toivola, Urho Mrs, 1949, Jl 23,11:4
Tokaji, Bela, 1947, Ag 9,13:5
Tokarev, Nikolai, 1952, F 2,13:3
Tokatyan, Armand, 1960, Je 13,27:4
Toker, Harry, 1952, Ap 10,29:5
Toker, Joseph, 1938, Je 3,21:4
Toker, Moses, 1944, Ap 20,19:5
Toklas, Alice B, 1967, Mr 8,45:1
Tokoi, Oskari, 1963, Ap 5,47:1
Tokschner, Elizabeth Mrs, 1949, My 28,15:3
Tokuda, Kyuichi, 1955, Jl 30,2:4
Tokugawa, Iyesato Prince (por), 1940, Je 5,25:1
Tokugawa, Rairin Marquis, 1925, My 20,23:4
Tokugawa, Yorisada, 1954, Ap 18,88:5
Tokunaga, Sunao, 1958, F 17,23:3
Tokutomi, Iichiro, 1957, N 3,88:5
Tolan, Eddie, 1967, F 1,36:1
Tolan, J Garrett, 1961, Ja 20,29:2
Tolan, J H, 1947, Jl 1,13:3
Tolan, James, 1873, Je 8,8:5
Toland, Clarence G, 1947, O 3,25:4
Toland, Edmund M, 1942, Je 5,17:6
Toland, Edward D, 1964, Ja 7,33:2
Toland, Gregg (por), 1948, S 29,30:2
Toland, Hugh A Sr, 1941, S 5,21:2
Toland, J Hart, 1954, D 12,89:1
Toland, Joseph T, 1959, O 20,39:1
Toland, Robert, 1954, D 11,13:4
Toland, William G, 1950, Ag 21,19:5
Toland, William J Mrs, 1951, S 9,88:4
Toland, William P, 1942, Ag 4,20:3
Tolbert, E B, 1943, Je 18,22:3
Tolbert, Gertrude, 1956, Mr 12,27:1
Tolbert, Ward V (por), 1946, Ap 13,17:5
Tolbert-Hewit, Owen, 1956, F 9,32:1
Tolbukhin, Feodor I, 1949, O 18,27:3
Tolchard, Frederick D, 1958, Je 5,31:4
Tolchinsky, Abraham, 1952, Mr 8,13:2
Tole, James, 1941, Mr 25,23:5
Tole, Vincent E, 1949, My 10,25:3
Tole, William H Rev Father, 1903, D 22,9:5
Toledano, Henry, 1955, My 10,29:3
Toledano, Jacob M, 1960, O 16,89:1
Toledano, Rachel N Mrs, 1937, Ja 16,17:4
Toleman, Nathaniel B, 1949, Ap 15,23:4
Toler, Harriet F Mrs, 1938, Ap 7,23:2
Toler, James M, 1947, Ag 8,17:4
Toler, John T, 1937, Jl 16,19:2
Toler, John Watts de Peyster, 1911, My 28,9:4
Toler, Kenneth, 1966, O 19,47:5
Toler, Sidney, 1947, F 13,23:1
Toler, Sidney Mrs, 1943, O 9,13:7
Tolfree, Edward R Mrs, 1944, Ag 28,11:4
Tolfree, James Rear-Adm, 1920, Ja 11,22:4
Tolibia, Jose R, 1941, S 11,23:3
Tolibia, Jose Ramon Mrs, 1968, Jl 12,31:1
Tolies, C W Col, 1864, N 20,6:1
Tolin, Ernest A, 1961, Je 12,29:2
Tolin, Glen C, 1939, N 14,23:5
Tolins, David B Sr, 1961, My 8,35:1
Tolischus, Edward C, 1949, S 30,23:2
Tolischus, Otto D, 1967, F 25,27:1
Tolk, Herman, 1938, Ja 13,21:2
Toll, Charles H Sr, 1948, Ag 24,23:4
Toll, Harris, 1956, O 21,86:7
Toll, Herman, 1967, Jl 28,31:1
Toll, Irene H Mrs, 1941, D 22,17:5
Toll, Robert M Dr, 1968, O 14,47:3
Toll, William Edward Bp, 1915, Je 28,9:6
Tolle, Ivory C, 1950, D 19,29:1
Tolle, Robert J, 1967, D 29,27:1
Tollefsen, Carl H, 1963, D 11,47:1
Tollefsen, Carl H Mrs, 1955, Ap 10,88:4; 1965, My 19,47:4
Tollemache, Bentley L J Lord, 1955, Ja 14,21:1
Tollen, William B, 1966, My 6,47:3
Tolleris, Charles, 1963, Ap 26,35:2
Tolleris, Harold, 1957, My 30,19:4
Tollerton, Leonard, 1954, S 13,23:3
Tollerton, Levi D, 1949, Ja 28,21:4
Tolles, E Donald, 1962, Jl 3,23:4
Tollet, A Marcus, 1947, S 5,19:1
Tolley, Adelphus C Mrs, 1938, O 16,45:1
Tolley, Adolphus C, 1952, Ja 22,29:3
Tolley, Courtney W, 1943, My 29,13:6
Tolley, Harold S, 1956, My 22,33:2
Tolley, Howard R, 1958, S 20,19:3
Tollfree, Edward R, 1954, Jl 30,17:4
Tolman, A H, 1928, D 26,17:4
Tolman, Albert W, 1965, Mr 7,82:5
Tolman, Charles H, 1956, D 16,87:1
Tolman, Cyrus F, 1942, O 15,24:2
Tolman, Daniel H, 1918, F 14,11:5
Tolman, Edgar B, 1947, N 21,27:1
Tolman, Edward C, 1959, N 21,23:5
Tolman, Frank L, 1957, F 24,84:8
Tolman, Henry L Dr, 1904, Ja 16,9:5
Tolman, Herbert Cushing Dr, 1923, N 25,23:2
Tolman, Herbert E, 1952, S 11,31:3
Tolman, Judson A, 1949, Ja 31,19:5
Tolman, Neil, 1964, Jl 12,68:4
Tolman, Richard C, 1948, S 6,13:3
Tolme, Francis, 1871, Ap 25,1:4
Tolmie, Simon F Dr, 1937, O 14,25:1
Tolna, Festetics de Princess, 1922, My 17,19:5
Tolson, Clara B Mrs (will), 1955, Ja 19,29:7
Tolson, George F, 1954, Mr 23,27:3
Tolson, Harry E Mrs, 1949, Jl 5,23:5
Tolson, T Elliot, 1944, F 15,17:6
Tolson, T Elliott Mrs, 1958, Ja 25,19:3
Tolson, W A, 1903, Ag 15,7:6
Tolstoi, Count Demetrius, 1889, My 8,5:6
Tolstoouhov, Alex V, 1959, Jl 11,19:1
Tolstoy, Alexandre G K Count, 1914, Ag 8,9:6
Tolstoy, Alexei, 1945, F 24,11:1
Tolstoy, I, 1933, D 13,23:1
Tolstoy, Leo Count, 1945, O 21,46:5
Tolstoy, Leo Countess, 1919, N 15,11:3
Tolstoy, Nadine Countess, 1946, Ap 17,25:4
Tolstoy, Serge, 1957, Mr 27,31:5
Tolstoy, Sergei, 1947, D 24,22:2
Tolstoy, Sofia (Mrs S Yesenin), 1957, Ag 2,19:4
Tolstoy, Stanislaus Count, 1949, D 22,23:5
Tolstoy, Tatiana, 1950, S 23,17:4
Toluboff, Alex, 1940, Jl 2,21:4
Tom Thumb (C H Stratton), 1883, Jl 16,8:7
Tomacelli, Countess, 1947, D 28,40:2
Tomack, Sid, 1962, N 14,40:1
Tomaini, Joseph J, 1952, Je 5,31:1
Tomaiuoli, Michael, 1962, Je 14,33:3
Tomaka, Paul J, 1954, My 17,23:3
Tomamoto, Thomas, 1924, S 30,23:4
Toman, Henry C, 1941, S 11,23:3
Toman, John, 1946, D 15,77:5
Toman, Sydney S, 1921, D 16,17:5
Tomanoczy, Paul, 1945, D 20,23:2
Tomars, Semion (por), 1943, Ja 2,11:5

Tomaselli, Cav D A M, 1940, Ap 24,23:3
Tomaselli, Giuseppe, 1949, Je 8,29:5
Tomasetti, Francesco, 1953, My 6,31:6
Tomashevsky, Boris V, 1957, Ag 28,27:4
Tomashevsky, Peter, 1948, N 27,18:2
Tomashoff, Morris B, 1960, Ja 7,29:3
Tomasi, John, 1956, S 9,84:1
Tomaso, A de, 1933, Ag 4,15:4
Tomaso, Alphonse R, 1964, D 17,41:3
Tomasow, Jan, 1961, N 30,34:5
Tomasulo, Anthony, 1955, F 9,27:5
Tomasulo, Giuseppe, 1967, F 23,35:5
Tomasulo, Michael C, 1965, D 25,13:3
Tomasulo, Nicholas A, 1960, O 23,88:4
Tomaszewski, Albert A, 1960, My 5,35:1
Tomaszewyski, Tadeusz, 1950, Ag 12,13:3
Tomb, James H, 1946, S 24,29:1
Tomback, Lewis C, 1964, N 8,88:5
Tombaugh, Paul E, 1954, O 1,23:6
Tombo, Rudolf Jr Prof, 1914, My 22,13:6; 1914, My 25,11:4
Tombo, Rudolph Dr, 1923, Ag 10,11:2
Tombor, Eugen, 1946, Jl 26,21:3
Tomboulian, Diran H, 1964, D 9,50:2
Tombs, Charles M Mrs, 1950, Mr 7,27:5
Tombs, David J Mrs, 1948, Jl 23,19:1
Tome, Peter E, 1939, Ap 20,23:4
Tomec, John, 1939, S 21,23:3
Tomec, Otto C, 1958, Je 15,76:6
Tomecko, Cyprian, 1940, Je 15,15:2
Tomes, William Austin Dr, 1920, Je 29,11:5
Tomey, Mary Mrs, 1938, Ja 5,21:5
Tomhave, William H, 1954, Je 20,85:2
Tomikowski, Joseph M, 1954, N 17,31:1
Tomilty, John L, 1950, Ja 15,85:1
Tomita, Mitsuru, 1961, Ja 16,27:1
Tomitz, Frank, 1950, S 16,19:6
Tomka, Louis A, 1955, Ja 5,23:2
Tomkins, Ambrose, 1951, My 26,17:5
Tomkins, Calvin, 1921, Mr 14,11:5
Tomkins, Calvin Jr, 1958, F 1,19:2
Tomkins, Calvin Mrs, 1947, Je 22,23:3
Tomkins, Calvin T Jr Mrs, 1938, S 19,19:3
Tomkins, Ella C Mrs, 1941, D 29,15:3
Tomkins, F W Rev Dr, 1932, Mr 25,19:1
Tomkins, George W, 1911, My 29,9:6
Tomkins, James Gaston Maj, 1922, N 12,6:4
Tomkins, Robert S, 1959, O 10,21:5
Tomkins, Selah S, 1952, O 30,31:5
Tomkins, Stirling, 1963, N 8,31:2
Tomkins, Watson, 1903, Jl 26,7:6
Tomko, Paul, 1942, My 11,15:2
Tomkpkins, E H, 1883, Ja 1,5:3
Tomlin, Bradley W, 1953, My 13,29:4
Tomlin, Burdette, 1942, My 5,21:2
Tomlin, Charles L, 1942, Ja 26,15:2
Tomlin, Francis H, 1948, O 15,23:3
Tomlin, Franklin M, 1942, O 14,25:3
Tomlin, Maurice Mrs, 1953, Je 3,31:2
Tomlin, Mervin W, 1938, Je 5,45:2
Tomlin, Onis B, 1963, Ap 18,35:4
Tomlin, Robert K, 1950, Jl 6,28:4
Tomlin, William J, 1940, Je 19,23:6
Tomlins, Frank I, 1943, F 4,23:1
Tomlins, Ralph, 1952, Ja 17,27:2
Tomlins, Roy B, 1940, S 5,23:5
Tomlins, William M, 1944, Ag 10,17:6
Tomlinson, A J, 1943, O 3,49:2
Tomlinson, Brian E, 1965, My 26,47:2
Tomlinson, Brian E Mrs, 1960, Ja 1,19:3
Tomlinson, Burt F, 1947, D 8,25:5
Tomlinson, Carl P, 1967, F 24,35:4
Tomlinson, Christian V, 1952, F 7,27:3
Tomlinson, David A, 1944, My 9,19:1
Tomlinson, Devoe, 1947, Ag 27,23:4
Tomlinson, E T, 1931, O 31,17:4
Tomlinson, Edwin A, 1958, Je 1,86:6
Tomlinson, Ernest B, 1953, N 24,29:5
Tomlinson, Ernest H Mrs, 1956, Ja 16,21:2
Tomlinson, Evelyn C, 1947, N 15,17:3
Tomlinson, Everett Mrs, 1944, F 21,15:3
Tomlinson, Everett T, 1953, F 8,91:3
Tomlinson, George, 1952, S 23,33:5
Tomlinson, George A, 1942, Ja 26,15:1
Tomlinson, George A Mrs, 1950, N 12,92:2
Tomlinson, George F, 1950, Ja 4,35:3
Tomlinson, George H, 1953, O 8,29:2
Tomlinson, George M Sr, 1951, O 4,33:5
Tomlinson, H M, 1958, F 6,27:1
Tomlinson, Henry W, 1949, Ja 31,19:5
Tomlinson, Homer A Bp, 1968, D 6,47:2
Tomlinson, Irving C, 1944, O 3,23:5
Tomlinson, J Burleigh, 1948, O 13,25:1
Tomlinson, J Munson, 1919, Je 19,13:4
Tomlinson, John, 1956, My 23,31:2
Tomlinson, John H, 1948, Ag 30,17:1
Tomlinson, John R, 1963, Ag 21,33:3
Tomlinson, John S, 1956, D 13,37:4
Tomlinson, Joseph, 1905, O 2,4:2
Tomlinson, Joseph J, 1965, Ap 27,37:2
Tomlinson, Kenneth K C, 1950, N 15,31:2
Tomlinson, Mildred H Mrs, 1948, Jl 24,15:4
Tomlinson, Paul J, 1966, Ja 7,29:4
Tomlinson, Philip G, 1961, Je 10,23:6
Tomlinson, Robert S, 1959, Jl 12,73:1
Tomlinson, Rolland D, 1965, Ag 2,29:4
Tomlinson, Roy Everett, 1968, Ap 30,47:1
Tomlinson, W P, 1901, Je 14,2:4
Tomlinson, Walter G, 1953, Ag 6,21:3
Tomlinson, Walter W, 1951, F 21,27:4
Tomlinson, Willard P, 1961, O 10,43:5
Tomlinson, William I, 1938, O 15,17:3
Tomlinson, William M (trb, Ap 27,2:5; trb lr, My 14,18:6), 1955, Ap 25,23:4
Tomlinson, William R, 1942, Ap 22,24:2
Tomlinson, William S, 1947, Ap 11,25:5
Tomma, Saul, 1946, Mr 21,25:2
Tommaney, Michael J, 1940, Ja 6,13:3
Tommaseo, Niccolo, 1874, My 2,12:3
Tommasi, Joseph F Mrs, 1943, D 3,24:2
Tommasi, Joseph L, 1949, D 28,32:2
Tommasini, Stauilaus Mother, 1913, S 19,9:4
Tommasini, Vincenzo, 1950, D 25,19:5
Tommers, A E Bernard, 1948, S 17,26:2
Tomney, James M, 1953, S 22,31:4
Tomoike, Maria, 1925, My 12,23:4
Tomon, William J Mrs, 1949, S 23,23:1
Tomoney, Mary E, 1961, Mr 17,31:2
Tomovich, Harold, 1961, Ag 11,24:1
Tompins, Theodore, 1948, Je 29,24:2
Tompkins, Abram H, 1947, S 18,25:3
Tompkins, Albert I, 1939, O 5,23:1
Tompkins, Albert Mrs, 1948, N 6,13:6
Tompkins, Alice M, 1951, D 19,31:4
Tompkins, Allen D, 1949, Ja 17,19:5
Tompkins, Alonzo P, 1945, My 11,19:5
Tompkins, Anna L Mrs, 1937, Jl 21,21:6
Tompkins, Arthur, 1946, D 31,18:3
Tompkins, Arthur S, 1938, Ja 21,19:1
Tompkins, Arthur S Mrs, 1958, N 9,89:1
Tompkins, B Fitch, 1944, My 13,19:2
Tompkins, Bernard, 1965, F 8,25:1
Tompkins, Blanche B Mrs, 1942, N 6,23:2
Tompkins, Briggs C, 1951, O 16,31:1
Tompkins, Burtis, 1953, Mr 3,27:4
Tompkins, C A, 1934, Ag 2,17:4
Tompkins, Carrie, 1938, N 1,23:3
Tompkins, Carrie E, 1940, Ap 5,22:3
Tompkins, Charles H (funl, D 15,25:3), 1956, D 13, 37:3
Tompkins, Charles H Brig-Gen, 1915, Ja 19,9:5
Tompkins, Charles S Mrs, 1945, Ap 3,19:2
Tompkins, Charles Wilson, 1912, N 4,11:6
Tompkins, Chester L, 1950, O 3,31:1
Tompkins, Clarence B, 1953, Ag 2,73:1
Tompkins, Cornelius Jr, 1903, My 25,9:6
Tompkins, Cyrus D, 1946, Ja 31,21:3
Tompkins, D W, 1875, S 4,5:2
Tompkins, Daniel D, 1948, Ja 10,15:4
Tompkins, Daniel F, 1905, D 28,9:6
Tompkins, Daniel J, 1937, Ap 19,21:5
Tompkins, David B, 1941, Jl 15,19:4
Tompkins, Edward B, 1907, My 13,9:6
Tompkins, Eli, 1948, Ag 11,21:4
Tompkins, Elijah E, 1940, O 27,44:3
Tompkins, Elwood B, 1947, Jl 30,21:4
Tompkins, Enoch J, 1947, Mr 8,13:5
Tompkins, Eugene, 1909, F 23,9:2
Tompkins, Francesco B, 1942, Mr 30,17:3
Tompkins, Frank, 1954, D 22,23:3
Tompkins, Frank O, 1941, D 17,27:2
Tompkins, Frank W, 1938, Ag 19,19:2
Tompkins, Franklin J, 1949, S 30,24:2
Tompkins, Fred J Mrs, 1944, Ag 10,17:4
Tompkins, Fred M, 1954, Mr 2,25:5
Tompkins, Frederick C, 1940, N 17,50:5
Tompkins, Frederick E, 1941, Ja 9,21:3
Tompkins, George B, 1962, O 25,39:5
Tompkins, George M Mrs, 1951, N 1,29:4
Tompkins, George Vreeland, 1914, Ag 1,9:5
Tompkins, Gilbert, 1939, My 3,24:2
Tompkins, Grenelle B, 1962, Mr 2,30:5
Tompkins, Gwyn R, 1938, N 27,48:5
Tompkins, Harold D, 1951, N 28,31:2
Tompkins, Harriette W Mrs, 1943, Mr 4,19:2
Tompkins, Harrison, 1951, S 11,29:4
Tompkins, Harry A, 1943, Ap 22,23:2
Tompkins, Harry S Sr, 1956, D 27,25:3
Tompkins, Helen, 1950, O 16,27:4
Tompkins, Helen G, 1940, S 14,17:5
Tompkins, Henry H, 1951, F 3,15:3
Tompkins, Irving N Mrs, 1953, D 29,23:2
Tompkins, J Edward, 1965, Je 12,31:5
Tompkins, J J, 1953, My 6,31:4
Tompkins, J Kirby, 1957, Mr 3,85:2
Tompkins, J Stuart, 1949, My 15,90:6
Tompkins, J Warren, 1874, Ag 25,8:5
Tompkins, Jerome H, 1940, N 2,15:5
Tompkins, Jesse Mrs, 1951, O 21,92:5
Tompkins, John A 2d, 1941, My 23,21:4
Tompkins, John D, 1959, Je 9,37:2
Tompkins, John H, 1966, My 12,45:1
Tompkins, John J Rev, 1937, Ap 7,25:5
Tompkins, John W Mrs, 1943, Ap 30,21:3
Tompkins, L D Mrs, 1941, My 13,23:5
Tompkins, Leon H, 1961, Je 20,33:2
Tompkins, Leslie J, 1952, My 25,94:3
Tompkins, Leslie J Mrs, 1947, Mr 1,15:5
Tompkins, Lloyd L, 1954, Ag 24,21:3
Tompkins, Louis C, 1962, Ag 19,88:2
Tompkins, Lyde Mrs, 1940, Mr 26,21:5
Tompkins, Mary J Mrs, 1937, O 4,21:4
Tompkins, Millard F, 1951, N 25,86:1
Tompkins, Minthorne, 1881, Je 6,5:6
Tompkins, Miriam D, 1954, Mr 4,25:5
Tompkins, Nancy V Mrs, 1942, F 19,19:1
Tompkins, Neal A, 1962, Mr 22,35:4
Tompkins, Nicholas, 1941, D 24,17:4
Tompkins, O, 1884, D 1,2:6
Tompkins, Odell D, 1962, N 10,25:3
Tompkins, Odell D Mrs, 1947, Mr 31,23:3
Tompkins, Otis Mrs, 1949, Ja 25,23:4
Tompkins, Ralph S, 1946, S 28,17:2
Tompkins, Raymond S, 1949, N 23,29:3
Tompkins, Roland Mrs, 1945, Ag 30,21:4
Tompkins, Rowland, 1959, Jl 30,27:3
Tompkins, Sally Louisa Capt, 1916, Jl 26,11:7
Tompkins, Schuyler F, 1959, Ag 27,27:2
Tompkins, Selah R H, 1939, F 7,19:5
Tompkins, Stanley A, 1945, Ja 21,40:2
Tompkins, Theodore Le Baume, 1924, S 7,31:3
Tompkins, Ulysses G, 1948, O 7,29:4
Tompkins, Vinton D, 1961, O 13,35:5
Tompkins, Vreeland, 1956, F 1,31:2
Tompkins, W D, 1938, Ja 5,21:1
Tompkins, W W, 1882, F 8,5:5
Tompkins, W Ward, 1944, Je 19,19:3
Tompkins, Walker, 1903, N 12,9:5
Tompkins, Walter H, 1938, Jl 7,19:5
Tompkins, William C, 1953, S 1,23:3
Tompkins, William C Sr Mrs, 1952, Ap 16,27:3
Tompkins, William H, 1946, O 23,27:4
Tompkins, William J, 1942, Ja 27,21:3
Tompkins, William M Mrs, 1939, O 22,40:7
Tompkinson, Henry A Brig, 1937, Ja 22,21:5
Tompson, George M (por), 1949, Jl 13,27:5
Toms, C W, 1936, Ag 30,II,7:1
Toms, Clifford, 1955, D 8,37:3
Toms, Edgar S, 1952, Mr 24,25:5
Toms, Elizabeth I, 1964, Je 3,43:1
Toms, Eva Mrs, 1908, F 2,9:4
Toms, G Parker, 1937, F 4,21:5
Toms, Grace I, 1939, D 19,26:2
Toms, Harold G Mrs, 1965, F 3,35:4
Toms, James F, 1950, Ag 25,21:3
Toms, Nathan, 1942, Ag 12,19:2
Toms, Robert J, 1937, N 17,23:4
Toms, Robert M, 1960, Ap 8,31:1
Toms, William J, 1954, My 18,29:2
Toms, Zach Sr, 1964, Jl 10,29:1
Tomsak, Valentine J Mrs, 1968, Je 11,44:4
Tomy, Cornelius D, 1942, D 15,27:6
Tondorf, F A, 1929, N 30,19:4
Tondra, John A, 1952, Ja 7,19:3
Tone, Bernard W, 1925, My 15,19:5
Tone, Franchot (will, O 2,44:5), 1968, S 19,58:1
Tone, Frank J (por), 1944, Jl 27,17:3
Tone, Henry A, 1950, Je 30,23:3
Tone, Joseph M, 1962, Mr 2,29:2
Tone, Theobald Wolfe (mem), 1915, Je 21,9:6
Toner, Charles N, 1948, D 30,19:1
Toner, Edmund J, 1951, D 23,22:4
Toner, George E, 1953, Ag 8,11:2
Toner, Harry A, 1940, Ap 2,25:1
Toner, James, 1947, My 30,21:1
Toner, James Mrs, 1938, D 23,19:4
Toner, James V, 1951, O 20,15:2
Toner, John J, 1948, O 16,15:5
Toner, Michael, 1943, My 31,17:4
Toner, Royal, 1959, My 16,23:4
Toner, William M, 1948, Je 24,25:3
Tonery, James A, 1952, Ap 9,31:5
Tonetti, Francois L Mrs, 1945, Mr 15,23:4
Tonetti, Francois M L, 1920, My 3,13:3
Toney, Charles E, 1951, Mr 23,21:6
Toney, Fred, 1953, Mr 12,27:5
Tong, Eddie, 1960, N 28,27:5
Tong, Sammee, 1964, O 28,24:6
Tong King Chong, 1916, Mr 9,13:6
Tongberg, Carl O, 1962, Ag 5,81:1
Tongring, Nils F, 1950, Ap 16,106:3
Tongue, Benjamin S Mrs, 1939, Jl 26,19:4
Tongue, Frank S, 1953, My 30,15:7
Tongue, James, 1939, Ag 25,15:4
Tongue, T H, 1903, Ja 12,9:3
Tongue, Walter B, 1937, S 24,21:4
Tonietti, Alphonse T, 1958, Je 8,89:1
Tonini, Ray R Rev, 1948, Ag 30,25:1
Tonjes, George E, 1951, Jl 7,13:6
Tonjes, John J, 1940, My 29,23:4
Tonkin, Edward, 1951, O 23,29:1
Tonkin, John A, 1952, D 18,29:5
Tonkin, John B, 1940, Ja 27,13:6
Tonkin, Loring L, 1953, D 13,86:6
Tonkin, William J, 1948, Ap 29,24:3
Tonking, James B, 1939, D 8,25:1
Tonking, William H, 1943, Ag 21,11:4
Tonkonow, Benjamin, 1940, Jl 30,19:3
Tonks, Frank Mrs, 1944, Mr 3,15:2

Tonks, Henry Dr, 1937, Ja 9,17:4
Tonks, Oliver S, 1953, D 27,60:4
Tonks, William, 1946, O 31,25:2
Tonne, Herman A, 1937, Ja 7,44:6
Tonnele, John L, 1918, Je 26,13:5
Tonnele, John L (por), 1949, My 25,29:1
Tonnele, Theodore N, 1957, Ag 6,27:5
Tonnelier, J Edmond Mrs, 1950, Je 19,21:4
Tonnell, William Dr, 1915, My 14,13:6
Tonner, Paul, 1943, Mr 10,19:3
Tonner, William T, 1948, Ap 16,23:4
Tonnesen, Martin, 1947, Mr 19,25:3
Tonneson, Birger W Mrs, 1962, Ap 4,43:4
Tonneson, Frank H, 1940, Ja 28,32:3
Tonney, Fred O, 1957, Jl 14,73:3
Tonning, Gerard, 1940, Je 12,25:6
Tonning, Gerard Mrs, 1950, S 27,31:1
Tonry, William P, 1905, O 4,9:6
Tonws, Charles B (por), 1947, F 21,19:3
Toogood, Ernest T Mrs, 1948, F 6,26:8
Toohey, Frank J, 1948, Je 25,23:4
Toohey, James F, 1947, Je 6,23:1
Toohey, John, 1952, Ap 14,19:6
Toohey, John J, 1952, O 13,21:4; 1955, Ap 15,24:2
Toohey, John P, 1946, N 8,23:4
Toohey, John Sr, 1937, Ja 9,17:3
Toohey, Matthew J, 1948, Ap 14,27:2
Toohey, Sarah C, 1947, S 4,25:5
Toohill, Irving E, 1957, S 10,33:2
Toohy, John J, 1967, My 15,43:1
Toohy, John M Prof, 1937, Je 24,25:2
Tooke, Charles W (por), 1943, Mr 3,23:1
Tooker, Benjamin B, 1950, Je 19,21:3
Tooker, C Edward, 1955, O 11,39:4
Tooker, Charles Brush, 1903, N 27,9:5
Tooker, Charles R, 1951, Ap 5,29:4
Tooker, F Westervelt Mrs, 1960, N 3,39:4
Tooker, Frederick J, 1952, D 19,31:3
Tooker, Frederick J Mrs, 1960, Ap 29,31:1
Tooker, Gershom C, 1960, O 18,40:1
Tooker, James L Sr, 1941, Mr 25,23:5
Tooker, John I, 1968, S 16,47:1
Tooker, John N, 1949, My 25,29:5
Tooker, Joseph D (por), 1937, D 29,21:3
Tooker, Joseph D Mrs, 1967, N 26,84:8
Tooker, Joseph H (por), 1949, Je 9,31:5
Tooker, Joseph H Mrs, 1942, Mr 9,19:5
Tooker, L Frank, 1925, S 18,23:6
Tooker, Norman B, 1967, Jl 16,65:2
Tooker, R A, 1882, My 17,5:5
Tooker, Stephen C, 1940, Je 27,23:2
Tooker, Vail G, 1964, S 16,31:6
Tooker, Violette S Mrs, 1940, F 28,21:2
Tooker, William B, 1939, Ap 15,19:5
Tooker, William T, 1957, Ja 13,84:2
Tooker, William Wallace, 1917, Ag 4,7:4
Tool, Lester H, 1949, Je 23,27:4
Tool, Samuel H, 1947, My 20,25:5
Toolan, John Mrs, 1965, Jl 11,68:6
Toolan, Patrick, 1937, D 18,21:5
Toole, Brice, 1949, Ja 6,24:2
Toole, Edward J, 1955, Mr 15,29:3
Toole, F L, 1879, D 22,2:3
Toole, Frank E, 1941, S 25,25:2
Toole, Helan M, 1968, Jl 16,39:3
Toole, Henry M, 1956, N 6,35:1
Toole, J C, 1929, Mr 1,19:2
Toole, J Lawrence, 1940, D 28,15:3
Toole, James F, 1939, Ag 18,19:3
Toole, John E, 1960, Mr 4,25:3
Toole, John K, 1953, Ap 21,27:5
Toole, John Lawrence, 1906, Jl 31,7:6
Toole, Joseph, 1945, Je 6,21:2
Toole, Joseph F, 1953, Je 13,15:6
Toole, Lillian R Mrs, 1939, D 2,17:3
Toole, Patrick J, 1955, Ag 6,15:1
Toolen, Martin J, 1942, Ag 21,19:5
Tooley, Francis L, 1942, My 15,20:3
Tooley, Herbert, 1952, My 27,27:1
Tooley, Howard, 1954, Ag 18,29:2
Tooley, John W, 1947, D 17,29:2
Toolin, John M Mrs, 1952, Mr 1,15:4
Toomath, John, 1876, Mr 19,7:1
Toombs, Elizabeth O, 1923, Je 15,19:6
Toombs, Robert, 1885, D 16,1:5
Toomer, Sydney E, 1954, Mr 24,27:2
Toomey, Bertha H Mrs, 1942, Je 11,23:1
Toomey, Cornelius F Mrs, 1948, O 6,29:5
Toomey, Cornelius P, 1946, Jl 2,25:5
Toomey, D Hubert, 1947, My 5,25:5
Toomey, Daniel F, 1950, Ja 17,27:2
Toomey, Frank, 1951, N 9,27:3
Toomey, George D, 1959, Ja 27,33:4
Toomey, Harold D, 1953, Mr 12,27:3
Toomey, Humphrey J, 1942, Ap 12,45:3
Toomey, Humphrey W Mrs, 1954, Mr 23,27:2
Toomey, James A, 1942, D 3,25:6
Toomey, Jeremiah Mrs, 1949, S 16,27:2
Toomey, Jeremiah T, 1939, Mr 5,48:8
Toomey, John A, 1946, O 30,27:5; 1950, Ja 2,23:6
Toomey, Joseph B, 1958, N 11,29:1
Toomey, Michael J, 1937, Ap 9,21:3
Toomey, Patrick C Rev, 1968, My 27,47:4
Toomey, Richard A, 1925, D 18,23:4
Toomey, Vincent L, 1956, Je 20,31:2
Toomey, Walter J, 1968, Ap 17,32:7
Toomey, William F, 1955, Je 14,29:3
Toone, Bessie, 1910, Ag 14,II,9:4
Tooni, Neal N, 1960, Ag 23,30:1
Toonkel, Joseph M, 1964, S 15,37:4
Toop, George C Sr, 1952, F 10,93:2
Toop, George H, 1942, F 1,43:3
Toor, Frances, 1956, Je 18,25:2
Tooran, Matthew G, 1941, Je 13,19:5
Toorn, Pieter van den, 1956, Ja 15,92:2
Tootell, Frederick D, 1964, O 1,35:5
Tooth, Arthur, 1923, D 9,23:2
Tooth, Arthur Augustus, 1922, D 13,21:5
Toothaker, Charles R, 1952, My 27,27:3
Toothe, Edward S, 1942, N 11,25:3
Toothe, William, 1904, Ja 25,7:7
Toothill, Henry, 1946, Ja 23,27:5
Toothill, John H, 1959, O 5,31:4
Toothill, John W, 1957, Mr 13,31:4
Tootle, Harry K, 1961, Mr 6,25:5
Tootle, Harry M, 1924, Je 10,11:5
Tootle, Mary B Mrs, 1942, Mr 16,15:4
Tootle, Milton Jr, 1946, D 28,15:6
Tooze, Walter L, 1956, D 22,19:6
Topakyan, George H, 1924, N 7,19:3
Topakyan, H H, 1926, O 14,1:4
Topakyan, Mrs, 1907, Mr 5,9:6
Topalian, Asdig M, 1955, Ag 30,27:2
Topalian, Hagop M, 1955, Jl 4,11:4
Topchiev, Aleksandr V, 1962, D 28,8:6
Tope, H W, 1936, Je 5,21:1
Tope, Roy N Mrs, 1961, Ag 23,33:5
Topefert, Henry J, 1953, Mr 10,29:5
Topham, William H, 1952, S 26,21:2
Topkins, Emmett D, 1964, N 28,21:4
Topkis, David L, 1939, N 29,23:5
Topliff, Charles M, 1951, Mr 21,33:2
Topliff, Cyrus Lyman, 1924, D 16,25:4
Toplitz, Alfred J, 1960, Mr 8,33:4
Toplitz, George, 1939, Ag 20,32:6
Toplitz, Melville S, 1921, My 13,15:6
Toplon, Bertha, 1945, Mr 28,23:4
Topmoeller, Godfrey H, 1937, D 2,25:6
Topmoeller, William J, 1947, Mr 12,25:2
Topoleski, Victoria Mrs, 1941, D 25,25:3
Topp, Olaf M, 1945, D 7,21:4
Topp, Roger, 1942, Ap 21,23:3
Toppan, Arthur W, 1939, S 18,19:3
Toppan, Jane, 1938, Ag 18,15:7
Topper, Ettie Mrs, 1925, Ja 12,15:3
Topper, George, 1949, N 4,27:2; 1955, O 28,26:2
Topper, Jack, 1958, Ap 16,33:4
Topper, Ray G, 1947, O 9,25:1
Toppi, Jimmy Sr, 1967, N 17,47:2
Toppin, Frederick, 1941, Ap 24,21:5
Toppin, Henry A, 1965, Ap 9,33:1
Topping, Adelpah Price, 1920, O 28,15:5
Topping, Alfred R, 1948, S 27,23:4
Topping, Allen S, 1962, Ap 19,31:4
Topping, Andrew, 1955, Ag 30,27:5
Topping, Charles H, 1949, Ag 18,21:3
Topping, Charles H Mrs, 1966, Jl 31,72:4
Topping, Edward, 1952, Ag 9,13:3
Topping, Elizabeth, 1940, Jl 28,27:1
Topping, Eugene, 1955, Ag 22,21:6
Topping, Henry J (Bob), 1968, Ap 23,47:2
Topping, Henry J Mrs, 1947, N 3,23:3
Topping, Henry T, 1953, Ap 30,31:2
Topping, J A, 1934, Ag 25,13:4
Topping, James, 1948, Jl 26,17:1
Topping, James Mrs, 1944, S 27,21:3
Topping, John A Mrs, 1951, Je 21,27:6
Topping, Julius, 1955, N 8,31:4
Topping, Julius Mrs, 1955, Ap 13,29:2
Topping, Robert C Mrs, 1950, Ag 2,25:3; 1968, Mr 5, 41:1
Topping, Seymour L, 1959, Ag 21,21:1
Topping, Thomas T, 1947, D 11,33:1
Topping, Victor, 1937, D 29,21:2
Topping, Walter S, 1955, Je 17,23:2
Topping, Wilbur B, 1955, S 30,25:5
Topping, William, 1882, Ja 20,5:6
Torakul, Haji, 1946, Ja 1,27:2
Toraldo, Carlo E, 1956, My 13,86:6
Toranosuke, Onishi, 1945, F 14,20:2
Toranzo, Severo, 1941, O 8,24:2
Torbert, A T A, 1880, S 19,5:4
Torbert, Edward N, 1953, My 8,25:2
Torbert, Willis M, 1961, S 3,60:4
Torbet, Ernest M, 1940, D 3,25:1
Torbett, Granville O, 1872, F 16,1:6
Torbett, Joe H, 1954, D 19,84:3
Torbey, W F, 1879, F 19,1:4
Torborg, Gerald R, 1955, D 26,19:1
Torborg, Gerard R, 1959, Jl 14,29:3
Torborg, Herman H, 1938, N 27,48:5
Torbush, Colden T, 1962, Jl 4,21:4
Torbush, Daniel, 1948, D 7,31:2
Torchiana, H A V C, 1940, Mr 3,45:3
Torchiana, Paul J, 1944, Ja 12,23:3
Torchin, Lilly W, 1954, D 10,42:8
Torchio, Phil (por), 1942, Ja 16,21:3
Torchio, Phil Jr (cor), 1953, Ag 11,16:4
Torchio, Philip Mrs, 1960, D 27,29:2
Torczyner, Numa (por), 1948, O 9,19:1
Tordoff, Thomas R, 1944, D 15,19:3
Tordoff, Thomas R Mrs, 1950, S 16,19:6
Torek, Franz J A, 1938, S 22,23:1
Torelli, Alex L Mrs, 1961, Ap 16,87:1
Toren, Marta, 1957, F 20,33:2
Torgersen, Anton, 1937, F 26,22:1
Torgersen, Harold, 1961, N 6,37:4
Torgerson, Edwin Mrs, 1955, My 14,19:4
Torgerson, Harry L, 1958, Ag 29,23:2
Torgerson, Reinert M (Ray), 1962, S 27,34:5
Torgerson, Thorwald Jr, 1950, Jl 12,29:4
Torgeson, Laverne Mrs, 1953, D 5,2:8
Torgler, Ernst, 1963, Ja 22,15:5
Torian, Oscar N Mrs, 1961, Jl 15,19:4
Torino, David M, 1960, Je 19,88:4
Torkelsen, Hans S, 1959, O 4,86:2
Torlonia, A Prince, 1926, Ap 18,II,11:1
Torlonia, Elsie M Mrs, 1941, D 22,17:4
Torlonia, M (Prince of Civitella Cesi, etc), 1933, Mr 7,18:1
Torlonia, Marina Princess (Mrs E W Slater), 1960, S 16,3:3
Torlonia, Olympia, 1924, N 7,19:3
Torlonia, Prince, 1938, Ap 9,17:5
Torm, D Frederik, 1953, N 6,28:3
Tormann, Bernard, 1950, O 19,31:4
Tormay, John J, 1951, My 18,27:3
Tormey, James A, 1949, D 23,21:4
Tormey, Kathryn A, 1961, Ag 28,25:4
Tormo, Francisco C, 1949, Ap 11,25:4
Tormoen, Clarence O, 1956, My 29,27:3
Tornaquinci, Aldo B M, 1947, Ag 4,17:6
Tornberg, Isador, 1964, Ja 7,33:3
Torney, Henry W, 1942, O 23,21:5
Torney, Kirkham W, 1962, Ag 20,23:4
Tornow, George, 1946, Je 13,27:3
Tornow, Serge, 1964, Ja 13,35:2
Tornquist, Carlos A, 1953, Ap 2,27:3
Tornqvist, Adam R, 1954, F 4,25:4
Tornroth, Jacob G, 1960, N 3,39:3
Tornsey, George F, 1943, Ja 1,23:5
Toro, Guillermo, 1951, N 27,9:4
Toro, Luis, 1941, Ap 19,15:1
Torok, Ervin, 1947, N 5,28:3
Torok, John, 1955, D 12,31:2
Torolo, Gasper, 1950, Je 8,32:3
Torossian, Aram, 1941, D 9,31:4
Torp, Christian, 1947, Ap 24,25:3
Torp, Oscar, 1958, My 2,28:2
Torpey, Harry, 1940, S 9,15:5
Torpey, James J, 1966, Ag 5,31:2
Torpey, John F Mrs, 1951, F 6,27:3
Torpey, Richard F, 1943, D 24,13:3
Torpey, William M, 1955, Ag 27,15:3
Torphichen, Lady, 1948, Ja 5,19:2
Torppey, William F, 1941, Jl 16,17:2
Torpy, Mary E, 1958, Ap 24,31:1
Torpy, Thomas G, 1949, Je 1,31:2
Torr, Cyril J W, 1940, D 9,19:4
Torr, Luella B Mrs, 1963, N 22,37:1
Torr, Raymond O, 1958, Jl 18,21:4
Torrance, Alex, 1950, N 19,92:4
Torrance, Alex Mrs, 1962, N 27,37:4
Torrance, Andrew A, 1943, D 31,15:2
Torrance, Arthur F, 1944, D 13,18:4
Torrance, Bascom H, 1968, Ag 5,39:2
Torrance, Charles E, 1945, Jl 24,23:3
Torrance, Cortis, 1959, F 22,88:3
Torrance, Daniel Mrs, 1912, F 26,11:4
Torrance, David, 1876, F 3,4:7
Torrance, E, 1933, My 16,17:1
Torrance, Francis J, 1919, Ja 9,11:3
Torrance, Henry, 1967, Ja 5,34:1
Torrance, Norman F, 1956, Ag 29,29:5
Torrance, R A Lt-Com, 1921, F 26,11:5
Torrance, Rachel C, 1937, Jl 11,II,4:8
Torrance, William B, 1956, Jl 26,25:6
Torras, Joaquin V Mrs, 1952, D 29,19:5
Torre, Al, 1950, S 22,31:5
Torre, Aloysius M, 1954, Jl 13,23:3
Torre, Anthony, 1951, Ag 21,27:3
Torre, Herbert, 1954, F 27,13:5
Torre e Tasso, Ella della Princess (will, Je 24,16:6), 1959, Je 22,25:1
Torrehermosa, Marquis de (M L Roberts y Terry), 1940, F 19,17:3
Torrence, D L, 1912, O 21,11:6
Torrence, Edward S Mrs, 1943, D 4,13:4
Torrence, John Mrs (Mrs Judah), 1883, Mr 3,5:3
Torrence, Mary M, 1939, Ag 9,17:2
Torrence, Mildred A, 1945, O 10,21:1
Torrence, Olivia H D, 1953, Ja 7,31:2
Torrence, Ridgely, 1950, D 26,23:3
Torrence, Ridgely (trb lr), 1951, Ja 22,16:6
Torrence, W I, 1881, Jl 10,5:6
Torrens, Benjamin, 1943, O 25,15:5
Torrens, James H, 1952, Ap 6,90:3
Torrens, John K Mrs, 1952, Ap 3,35:2
Torrens, R R Sir, 1884, S 3,2:3

Torrens, William Erskine, 1914, Je 21,15:6
Torrente, Henry C de, 1962, Ap 1,86:5
Torres, Carlos A Dr, 1911, Jl 15,7:4
Torres, Endrina Rafael, 1946, Mr 7,25:2
Torres, Ezequiel D, 1939, Ja 8,42:6
Torres, Gumersindo, 1947, Je 19,21:5
Torres, Henry, 1966, Ja 4,31:4
Torres, Isaiah, 1951, Jl 27,21:8
Torres, Jose, 1947, Ja 3,21:2
Torres, Lorenzo Gen, 1912, N 18,11:5
Torres, Manuel, 1952, Ap 11,7:2
Torres, Mohamed, 1920, D 5,22:3
Torres, Rafael A, 1939, F 25,15:6
Torres de Mendoza, Emilio Marquess, 1941, F 20,19:1
Torres Quevedo, Leonardo de Prof, 1937, Ja 10,29:2
Torresoto de Vrivesca, Marques de, 1946, Jl 4,19:3
Torresson, Walter, 1945, My 25,19:1
Torrey, Arthur M, 1949, F 5,15:5
Torrey, Charles C, 1956, N 13,37:5
Torrey, Charles C Mrs, 1946, O 6,58:7
Torrey, Constance L, 1949, Jl 2,15:4
Torrey, Delia Chapin, 1919, F 24,13:3
Torrey, Edwin F, 1944, Je 21,19:4
Torrey, Frank E, 1938, Ja 5,21:3
Torrey, Franklin, 1912, N 18,11:5
Torrey, Frederic C, 1948, Ap 5,21:2
Torrey, George B, 1942, Ap 15,21:3
Torrey, George H, 1939, Ap 29,17:5
Torrey, Henry N, 1945, D 30,14:4
Torrey, Herbert Gray, 1915, Ag 31,9:6
Torrey, Irving Mrs, 1947, D 16,33:2
Torrey, James C, 1948, Ag 1,57:1
Torrey, James E, 1947, Ja 21,23:2
Torrey, James H, 1925, S 29,27:4; 1952, F 29,23:3
Torrey, James H Mrs, 1950, Ja 13,24:3
Torrey, John, 1914, Ap 21,11:5
Torrey, John C, 1946, O 9,27:2
Torrey, John Prof, 1873, Mr 11,5:3
Torrey, Martha M Mrs, 1940, Jl 11,19:2
Torrey, Morris W (por), 1949, Ja 5,25:2
Torrey, Moses E, 1907, Jl 14,7:6
Torrey, Philip H Maj-Gen, 1968, Je 9,84:8
Torrey, Prof, 1867, N 29,3:7
Torrey, R A, 1928, O 27,19:4
Torrey, Ralph M, 1962, Jl 22,64:4
Torrey, Ray E, 1956, Ja 17,33:4
Torrey, Raymond H, 1938, Jl 16,13:2
Torrey, Robert G, 1941, Ja 12,44:4
Torrey, S W, 1903, F 8,7:5
Torrey, W Edward, 1951, D 30,24:1
Torrey, Zerah W Col, 1908, D 8,9:4
Torrie, Alexander, 1947, Ap 13,60:4
Torrie, George, 1964, My 29,29:2
Torriente, Cosme de la, 1956, D 9,88:1
Torrington, Otto M, 1945, O 9,21:5
Torrington, Viscount, 1944, My 26,19:5
Torrington, William J, 1944, Jl 19,19:5
Torrio, Johnny, 1957, My 8,32:2
Torrisi, Samuel S, 1945, My 24,19:4
Torrs, Marino, 1959, Jl 27,25:3
Torry, John C, 1949, Je 8,29:2
Torsch, Edward L, 1940, N 26,23:4
Torsleff, Herbert St J, 1959, D 21,27:4
Torsney, George F, 1942, D 29,22:3
Torsney, George F Mrs, 1938, N 19,17:3
Torsney, James T, 1958, Jl 18,21:3
Torstenson, Frank E, 1953, Mr 2,23:6
Torstenson, Harry E, 1962, O 21,89:2
Tortello, Angelo, 1924, My 4,23:1
Tortolani, Giustino, 1950, Ap 9,87:2
Tortolani, Raffaele E, 1949, F 2,27:3
Tortora, Cyrus E, 1953, My 27,31:3
Tortora, Michael F Mrs, 1947, Mr 11,27:4
Tortora, Robert, 1938, F 17,21:3
Tortorella, Nicholas J, 1958, My 24,14:5
Tory, James C, 1944, Je 27,19:5
Tory, John S D, 1965, Ag 28,21:5
Toscanini, Arturo (funl plans, Ja 19,15:2; funl, Ja 20,92:4), 1957, Ja 17,1:2
Toscanini, Arturo Mrs, 1951, Je 24,72:3
Toscanini Riva, Ada, 1955, Ap 3,86:5
Tose, Frank, 1944, N 17,19:2
Toselli, E, 1926, Ja 16,15:4
Toselli, Pietro, 1948, Jl 25,48:5
Tosh, Joseph N, 1946, N 12,29:1
Tosi, Charles A, 1938, S 1,23:4
Tosi, E, 1929, Ja 8,31:2
Tosick, Andrew S, 1952, D 20,17:5
Tossell, Albert L, 1953, D 16,35:3
Tost, Barnabas, 1951, Jl 21,13:5
Tostes, Miquel, 1948, Jl 24,15:3
Tostevin, Clifford L Mrs, 1942, Jl 19,30:5
Tostevin, Lansing W, 1953, N 24,29:4
Tosti, Francesco Tosti Sir, 1916, D 4,13:5
Tosti, Liberato, 1950, O 21,17:6
Tot Voorst, Voorst van Baron, 1947, Jl 13,44:5
Tota, William, 1949, Jl 29,18:7
Totah, Khalil A, 1955, F 26,15:3
Toth, Benedict, 1945, Ap 4,21:5
Toth, George R Mrs, 1952, My 16,23:2
Toth, John Sr, 1948, Ap 18,68:4
Toth, Lazlo, 1952, S 30,9:3
Tothill, H Sir, 1927, S 27,27:5

Toto (A de Curtis), 1967, Ap 16,83:1
Toto the Clown (A Novello),(por), 1938, D 16,2:3
Totten, Ashley L (Jan 26), 1963, Ap 1,36:7
Totten, B J Commodore, 1877, My 10,1:6
Totten, Bessie L, 1963, S 25,43:2
Totten, Charles A L Lt, 1908, Ap 13,7:4
Totten, Duane R, 1953, O 21,30:7
Totten, E H Lt (see also Je 15), 1878, Je 17,5:5
Totten, Edward, 1946, O 9,27:3
Totten, Edyth, 1953, N 13,28:3
Totten, G M Col, 1884, My 20,5:2
Totten, George D, 1941, S 4,21:4
Totten, George D (will), 1942, S 18,15:2
Totten, George M, 1952, My 8,31:4
Totten, George O Jr (por), 1939, F 3,15:3
Totten, Gilson I, 1916, Mr 7,11:6
Totten, J Charles, 1951, D 25,31:2
Totten, J D Maj-Gen, 1864, Ap 26,4:6
Totten, J Ray, 1949, N 5,13:5
Totten, James Brevet Brig-Gen, 1871, O 4,7:5
Totten, Joe B, 1946, Ap 30,21:3
Totten, Joe B Mrs, 1945, F 8,19:2
Totten, John C, 1903, Jl 18,7:6
Totten, Leonard M, 1953, Mr 5,27:5
Totten, Robert V, 1941, Ag 24,35:3
Totten, William Henry Brackett, 1914, Jl 5,5:6
Totten, William J, 1943, O 11,19:3
Tottenham, Alexander R L, 1946, D 14,15:6
Totterdell, Austin, 1955, O 18,37:1
Tottingham, W E, 1944, Mr 3,15:1
Tottis, Theodore J, 1964, Ag 25,33:4
Totton, Frank M, 1954, N 2,27:1
Totty, Charles H, 1939, D 11,23:6
Totty, Charles H Mrs, 1943, Je 15,21:5
Toub, Martin, 1949, D 4,108:4
Toubin, Isaac Mrs, 1959, D 1,39:4
Touceda, Enrique A, 1943, O 21,27:3
Toucey, Catherine Mrs, 1871, Ag 14,1:3
Toucey, Donald Butler, 1905, Jl 29,1:4
Toucey, Isaac, 1869, Jl 31,5:1
Toucey, John M, 1925, Ag 13,19:5
Touchard, Emeline Holmes Mrs, 1914, My 31,5:6
Touchard, G S Lt, 1918, S 6,13:4
Touchard, P V French Adm, 1879, Ja 21,5:4
Touche, Francis, 1937, Mr 5,21:1
Touchet, A Cardinal, 1926, S 24,23:4
Touchstone, Clay, 1949, Ap 30,13:5
Touchstone, Morris, 1957, N 8,29:3
Toucke, Marion (M Telva), 1962, O 24,39:2
Toudouze, Edouard, 1907, Mr 16,9:5
Touff, G, 1913, O 8,11:5
Tough, Charles C, 1943, D 8,23:5
Touhey, Bridget, 1908, D 24,7:6
Touhey, Charles H Mrs, 1941, D 28,29:1
Touhig, John Mrs, 1945, S 8,15:2
Touhl, Joseph F, 1962, Ap 6,35:4
Toukan, Ninr, 1963, Mr 16,7:2
Toulba, Foad (Ali), 1944, Ap 12,21:4
Toulmin, Harry A Sr, 1942, Mr 27,23:4
Toulmin, Harry Theophilus, 1916, N 13,13:5
Toulmin, J E, 1903, Jl 7,7:6
Toulmin, John E, 1968, Ap 12,35:2
Toulmin, Montell, 1946, My 16,21:1
Toulon, Hope, 1954, D 30,17:4
Toulouse, Edouard, 1947, Ja 30,25:2
Toumanoff, Irakley C Prince, 1947, F 4,25:1
Toumanoff, Leo C, 1948, Jl 29,21:3
Toumanoff, Margaret A Princess, 1945, Ag 19,40:4
Toumey, James W Jr, 1950, O 21,17:3
Toumin, Alfred F, 1905, Ap 12,9:4
Toupin, Felix (Oct 7), 1965, O 11,61:6
Tour, Reuben S, 1952, Ag 2,15:7
Touret, Frank H, 1945, Ag 4,11:2
Touret, Frank H Mrs, 1946, Ja 7,19:4
Tourgee, Albion W, 1905, My 22,7:5
Tourneau, Henry K, 1954, My 25,27:3
Tourner, Frederick M, 1950, O 1,104:5
Tourneur, Maurice, 1961, Ag 5,17:4
Touroff, Nissan, 1953, Mr 31,31:5
Tourscher, Francis E, 1939, Ja 31,21:2
Tourtellot, George P, 1946, O 27,60:6
Tousey, Elizabeth Mrs, 1903, Jl 3,9:6
Tousey, Sinclair, 1887, Je 17,8:4
Tousey, Sinclair Dr, 1937, S 26,II,8:6
Tousey, Thomas S, 1961, Je 29,33:5
Tousey, William, 1913, S 30,13:4
Tousley, Clyde E, 1939, Mr 2,21:6
Tousley, Twining, 1939, Mr 12,19:6
Tousley, Victor H, 1948, Jl 17,16:2
Toussaint, Charles O, 1938, O 26,23:3
Toussaint, Jean J, 1910, My 25,9:4
Toussaint, Winifred H Mrs, 1953, Mr 12,27:1
Toussant, Edward J, 1951, Je 19,29:1
Touton, Charles P, 1942, D 8,25:5
Touzalin, Lida M, 1942, Ap 11,13:5
Touzeau, Henry Mrs, 1939, Mr 19,III,6:6
Tovar, Pedro M A, 1961, N 17,35:2
Tovee, Uncle Bill, 1883, Ag 29,5:4
Tovell, Alfred C, 1944, My 14,46:3
Tovey, David W, 1941, F 13,19:4
Tovey, Donald F (por), 1940, Jl 12,15:6
Tovia, Sigrid (S Toivanen), 1955, Mr 23,33:4
Tow, Harris Mrs, 1945, Ap 17,23:1

Towart, James, 1942, Je 20,13:5
Towart, John Jr, 1939, Jl 9,31:3
Towart, William G, 1949, D 7,31:4
Towberman, Drury L, 1938, O 15,17:5
Towbin, Allen A, 1961, N 11,23:4
Towell, Henry, 1925, N 2,23:5
Towen, William C, 1912, Mr 21,11:4
Towend, Davis S, 1968, Mr 23,28:4
Tower, Albert E, 1941, O 9,23:3
Tower, Augustus Clifford, 1903, D 29,9:5
Tower, Benjamin L M, 1909, Je 16,7:4
Tower, C E, 1929, Ja 22,29:1
Tower, Charlemagne, 1923, F 27,19:4
Tower, Charles Putnam, 1919, Je 2,15:5
Tower, David Horatio, 1907, D 23,9:5
Tower, Edward C M, 1963, D 30,21:2
Tower, Edwin B H Jr, 1948, Mr 29,21:4
Tower, Frank S, 1946, Mr 29,23:2
Tower, Frederick J, 1942, F 25,19:4
Tower, Freeman Pratt Rev Dr, 1911, S 12,11:5
Tower, Geoffrey Mrs, 1959, D 10,39:4
Tower, George Edward, 1914, Je 10,11:6
Tower, George H, 1959, Ap 8,37:2
Tower, George W, 1968, Ag 25,88:4
Tower, George W Jr, 1939, S 17,48:7
Tower, Harry L, 1951, Ag 24,15:5
Tower, Horace L, 1947, F 11,27:3
Tower, James E, 1947, Ja 2,27:4
Tower, James W, 1937, Je 23,25:1
Tower, John B, 1952, My 6,29:5
Tower, John B Mrs, 1939, Ap 27,25:5
Tower, Joseph Tuckerman, 1925, D 19,17:4
Tower, Levi L, 1912, Je 20,11:5
Tower, Lewis C, 1946, Mr 3,46:6
Tower, Margaret, 1942, N 25,23:2
Tower, Morris Mrs, 1941, N 9,55:5
Tower, Olin S, 1945, D 23,18:5
Tower, Oswald, 1968, My 30,25:3
Tower, Peter, 1946, Ag 7,27:2
Tower, Raymond C, 1938, D 18,49:2
Tower, Reginald, 1939, Ja 23,13:5
Tower, W C, 1881, Ap 15,5:2
Tower, W Warren Mrs, 1949, Jl 2,15:3
Tower, Walter L, 1937, N 11,25:5
Tower, Warren M, 1957, D 21,19:4
Tower, William, 1950, D 15,31:4
Tower (Sister Mary James), 1967, O 3,47:1
Towers, Caroline A Mrs, 1942, Je 16,23:4
Towers, David Irving, 1915, My 27,11:6
Towers, Frederic N, 1959, F 17,31:1
Towers, John A, 1956, N 20,37:4
Towers, John H (funl plans, My 2,21:3; funl, My 4,29:5), 1955, My 1,88:3
Towers, Reahome S, 1955, Ag 2,23:3
Towers, Thomas H, 1942, Ag 7,17:6
Towers, Thomas T, 1960, Je 8,39:1
Towey, Eleanor C, 1943, F 9,23:3
Towey, John J, 1954, Ag 27,21:4
Towey, Mary A, 1939, Ja 10,19:5
Towey, Michael J, 1960, S 30,27:4
Towl, Burr A Sr, 1952, N 25,29:4
Towl, Forrest M, 1946, Ja 4,21:4
Towle, Arthur E, 1948, Ag 27,19:3
Towle, Carroll S, 1950, Jl 27,25:2; 1962, S 18,39:2
Towle, Charles H Mrs, 1949, O 3,17:6
Towle, Charlotte (lr on obituary, O 15,28:4), 1966, O 2,86:6
Towle, Felix S, 1938, O 11,25:3; 1957, O 11,27:4
Towle, Frank R, 1949, My 12,31:2
Towle, George W, 1957, Jl 31,23:5
Towle, Harry F, 1913, Ja 2,11:4
Towle, Harvey P Dr, 1937, O 9,19:5
Towle, Henry, 1960, N 12,21:1
Towle, Henry B Mrs, 1949, D 14,31:3
Towle, Herbert L, 1954, Ag 24,21:6
Towle, Howard C Sr, 1961, S 15,33:2
Towle, J Warren, 1903, S 27,7:7
Towle, John F, 1951, Ap 18,31:4
Towle, John R, 1951, D 20,31:5
Towle, John W, 1943, My 1,15:6
Towle, Joseph H, 1951, Jl 14,13:6
Towle, Norman L, 1963, My 17,33:3
Towle, Norman Mrs, 1957, N 15,16:7
Towle, Ralph, 1958, D 11,13:4
Towle, Ralph E Mrs, 1950, S 7,31:3
Towle, Stevenson, 1916, F 15,11:4
Towle, Warren H, 1950, D 25,19:4
Towle, Wilbur H, 1944, Jl 6,15:4
Towle, William F, 1946, My 4,15:2
Towler, Anne Celean Mrs, 1916, F 20,15:4
Towler, Edward T Mrs, 1954, D 31,13:1
Towles, Beverly, 1962, Ap 6,35:5
Towles, Harold R, 1955, Jl 4,11:4
Town, Arno E, 1967, D 13,47:3
Town, Chauncey Warren, 1903, D 24,9:5
Town, Frederic E, 1962, D 1,25:1
Town, Samuel P Col, 1937, Jl 10,16:1
Towne, Arthur E, 1956, D 31,13:1
Towne, Arthur W, 1954, Jl 21,27:4
Towne, C A, 1928, O 23,29:1
Towne, Carroll, 1938, Ap 16,13:5
Towne, Charles H (por), 1949, Mr 1,25:1
Towne, Deidrich E, 1945, Ap 28,15:3

Towne, Edward B, 1942, Mr 19,21:2
Towne, Edward S, 1952, Mr 19,29:2
Towne, Elbert S Mrs, 1954, My 5,31:2
Towne, Floyd S, 1945, Ap 4,21:2
Towne, Frank B, 1946, Ag 15,25:4
Towne, Frederick T, 1906, F 5,9:2
Towne, Frederick W, 1945, O 13,15:4
Towne, G Scott, 1954, Jl 22,23:2
Towne, G Scott Mrs, 1953, Mr 20,23:4
Towne, Harold R, 1952, F 9,13:5
Towne, Henry Robinson (funl, O 19,7:1), 1924, O 16,25:4
Towne, Jane H Mrs, 1962, Je 17,80:7
Towne, John D C Jr, 1959, Ag 4,27:2
Towne, John H (por), 1942, S 30,23:3
Towne, Joseph M, 1958, Ap 13,84:5
Towne, Lucia P, 1942, Ja 16,21:1
Towne, Orville D, 1952, Ja 12,13:5
Towne, Orwell D, 1903, N 8,7:7
Towne, Robert D, 1952, F 25,21:5
Towne, Robert Safford, 1916, Ag 4,9:5
Towne, Salem (cor), 1872, F 22,1:7
Towne, Samuel S, 1953, Ja 14,32:4
Towne, W Marcus, 1941, Ja 31,19:3
Towne, William E Mrs, 1960, Je 2,33:4
Towne, Willis T, 1967, Mr 11,29:4
Towneley, Louis J, 1943, Mr 3,23:1
Townend, William H, 1949, O 10,23:2
Towner, Charles H, 1940, Ag 23,15:5
Towner, Clifford, 1947, N 3,23:5
Towner, Daniel D, 1944, Ja 4,17:1
Towner, Ethel M, 1958, S 14,84:2
Towner, George L, 1963, Ap 15,29:2
Towner, Harry N, 1962, Je 8,31:3
Towner, Horace M Judge, 1937, N 24,23:2
Towner, Horace M Mrs, 1942, N 8,50:6
Towner, Lottie S, 1945, Je 21,19:3
Towner, Merle E, 1956, Ap 14,17:5
Towner, Neile F, 1962, My 25,33:5
Towner, Noble (funl), 1860, My 1,2:2
Towner, Paul D, 1948, Ag 14,13:5
Towner, Reginald F, 1964, Ja 19,77:1
Towner, Rutherford H, 1950, Ja 25,27:3
Towner, William A, 1950, D 14,35:5
Towner, William T, 1950, Ja 30,17:4
Townes, E E, 1962, F 2,30:7
Townes, John C, 1948, F 24,25:4
Townes, John H Dr, 1909, Mr 10,9:3
Townes, Willis Glover, 1922, Mr 18,13:5
Townley, Alfred H, 1954, Ag 1,84:5
Townley, Alfred H Mrs, 1943, O 6,23:1
Townley, Arthur C, 1959, N 8,59:1
Townley, Athol G, 1963, D 25,33:2
Townley, C, 1933, N 28,21:1
Townley, D O'C, 1872, D 29,5:5
Townley, David H, 1939, D 13,27:3
Townley, Dewitt C, 1948, Ag 6,17:4
Townley, Emeline V, 1951, N 6,29:1
Townley, Flora D, 1958, My 2,28:3
Townley, Frank M, 1940, N 2,15:4
Townley, Frank M Mrs, 1959, Mr 13,26:3
Townley, George T, 1960, My 22,86:4
Townley, Grace E, 1946, My 9,21:6
Townley, Helen, 1953, O 1,29:6
Townley, Helen Mrs, 1937, Mr 7,II,8:4
Townley, J, 1880, N 22,5:3
Townley, J Mortimer, 1944, Mr 10,15:4
Townley, James A, 1949, N 15,25:2
Townley, James H, 1939, D 31,18:7
Townley, John B, 1943, My 14,19:3
Townley, John C, 1953, Je 7,84:3
Townley, Lorenzo D, 1947, Ja 14,25:1
Townley, Margaret Mrs, 1947, O 30,25:4
Townley, Moreland T, 1958, Mr 13,29:5
Townley, Moreland T Mrs, 1949, Je 28,27:3
Townley, Richard, 1943, D 11,15:4
Townley, Samuel G Sr, 1949, Jl 24,53:2
Townley, Sidney D, 1946, Mr 17,44:3
Townley, Stephen B, 1945, O 13,15:6
Townley, Walter B, 1945, Ap 8,36:3
Townley, Warren B, 1951, D 17,31:4
Towns, Christine G Mrs, 1939, O 17,25:5
Towns, Delaware L, 1944, Jl 15,13:5
Towns, M L, 1932, N 26,10:1
Towns, Wilson H Mrs, 1962, Ja 6,19:5
Townsend, Alice G Mrs, 1938, Ag 3,19:6
Townsend, Alice M, 1939, Ja 10,19:2
Townsend, Alpheus, 1950, Ag 29,50:3
Townsend, Alva C, 1951, Jl 21,13:6
Townsend, Anna, 1923, S 13,19:3
Townsend, Anne K Mrs, 1940, S 23,17:4
Townsend, Arthur Bronson, 1907, D 14,9:4
Townsend, Arthur C, 1948, Mr 15,23:5
Townsend, Arthur F, 1940, Ja 14,15:3
Townsend, Arthur O, 1940, N 20,21:3
Townsend, Arthur R, 1942, My 15,20:4; 1946, My 29, 23:4
Townsend, Atwood H, 1967, My 29,25:3
Townsend, B Frank, 1942, F 14,15:8
Townsend, Benjamin S, 1941, F 11,23:3
Townsend, Bernard W, 1956, My 17,31:4
Townsend, C C Rev, 1869, F 27,5:3
Townsend, Casper W B, 1946, Ag 27,27:1
Townsend, Charles, 1950, Mr 12,94:6
Townsend, Charles A, 1942, My 5,21:2
Townsend, Charles C, 1965, Ap 22,33:2
Townsend, Charles C Rev, 1915, Je 21,9:6
Townsend, Charles D, 1960, F 6,41:3
Townsend, Charles de Kay, 1922, Mr 3,13:5
Townsend, Charles E, 1924, Ag 4,13:4; 1942, Mr 17, 21:4
Townsend, Charles H, 1944, Ja 29,13:1
Townsend, Charles Mrs, 1921, My 26,13:4
Townsend, Charles Orrin Dr, 1937, Je 3,28:3
Townsend, Charles Rev Dr, 1914, D 15,13:6
Townsend, Charles W, 1948, N 22,21:1; 1950, F 22, 22:7
Townsend, Clara P Mrs, 1937, O 29,22:2
Townsend, Com, 1866, N 15,2:4
Townsend, Dallas S Sr, 1966, My 28,27:5
Townsend, Dallas S Sr Mrs, 1962, Ap 17,35:5
Townsend, Daniel P, 1939, Mr 7,22:2
Townsend, David Mrs, 1962, Jl 5,25:1
Townsend, E Therese F Mrs, 1939, N 12,49:2
Townsend, Edgar J, 1955, Jl 9,15:4
Townsend, Edward (will), 1938, D 8,28:2
Townsend, Edward D, 1954, D 29,23:4
Townsend, Edward H, 1903, N 10,9:5
Townsend, Edward Jr Mrs, 1938, Ja 7,19:3
Townsend, Edward Mitchell, 1904, F 4,9:5
Townsend, Edward N Mrs, 1953, Mr 23,23:2
Townsend, Edward P, 1962, S 24,29:3
Townsend, Edward T, 1950, Mr 10,27:1
Townsend, Edward W, 1942, Mr 17,21:3
Townsend, Edwin F Brig-Gen, 1909, Ag 17,9:5
Townsend, Effingham L, 1942, Je 26,21:6
Townsend, Eli, 1938, Je 3,21:3
Townsend, Emma Dr, 1916, S 14,7:6
Townsend, Ernest N, 1945, O 18,23:2
Townsend, F De Peyster, 1951, My 8,31:5
Townsend, Ferdinand C, 1958, My 28,31:3
Townsend, Ferdinand C Mrs, 1944, F 4,15:4
Townsend, Fitzhugh, 1906, D 12,11:5
Townsend, Francis E, 1960, S 2,1:7
Townsend, Francis E Mrs, 1951, Ag 29,25:4
Townsend, Frank, 1944, D 14,23:4
Townsend, Frank N, 1945, N 10,15:6
Townsend, Frank S, 1954, F 21,68:1
Townsend, Fred B, 1959, S 16,39:2
Townsend, Frederic deP, 1966, Jl 13,43:2
Townsend, Frederick, 1949, D 6,31:5
Townsend, Frederick B, 1938, Ag 19,19:4; 1951, N 9, 27:3
Townsend, Frederick de P, 1961, F 25,21:5
Townsend, Frederick R, 1923, My 19,13:6
Townsend, G A Mrs, 1903, My 31,7:6
Townsend, George, 1954, D 8,35:2
Townsend, George Alfred, 1914, Ap 16,9:3
Townsend, George C, 1944, Mr 19,41:2
Townsend, George E, 1955, F 10,31:3
Townsend, George H (cor, F 23,17:5), 1957, F 20, 33:3
Townsend, George H Mrs, 1912, Mr 1,11:5
Townsend, George P, 1939, Jl 24,13:6
Townsend, Gerald B Mrs, 1967, F 20,37:3
Townsend, Gerard B, 1952, D 13,21:4
Townsend, Grace C Mrs (will), 1940, My 10,20:1
Townsend, Greenough, 1962, O 11,39:3
Townsend, Gustave D Mrs, 1946, Ap 29,21:4
Townsend, H L, 1903, Ja 5,9:5
Townsend, H N, 1927, Jl 22,19:5
Townsend, Hamilton F, 1948, Ag 26,21:3
Townsend, Harold, 1961, Mr 18,23:5
Townsend, Harold O, 1945, D 24,15:3
Townsend, Harriet, 1951, O 18,29:4
Townsend, Harriet F Mrs, 1953, Ap 16,29:3
Townsend, Harry B, 1941, S 19,23:3; 1941, N 2,53:3
Townsend, Harry P, 1942, N 15,56:2
Townsend, Henry, 1955, Jl 3,33:1
Townsend, Henry C Jr, 1952, Ag 8,17:4
Townsend, Henry H Mrs, 1944, F 19,13:3
Townsend, Horace R Mrs, 1950, Ag 9,29:4
Townsend, Hosea Judge, 1909, Mr 6,7:4
Townsend, Howard, 1943, N 25,25:2; 1959, O 24,21:5
Townsend, Howard E, 1941, Jl 5,11:2
Townsend, Howard Mrs, 1912, Ap 7,15:3; 1943, D 1, 21:5
Townsend, Howard R, 1939, Ja 7,15:5
Townsend, Irving, 1951, My 20,89:1
Townsend, Irving J, 1961, S 15,33:2
Townsend, Isaac, 1922, F 22,15:4
Townsend, Israel Leander Rev, 1908, O 11,11:5
Townsend, J L, 1877, O 23,8:3
Townsend, Jackson, 1942, Ag 24,15:5
Townsend, James A, 1947, Je 25,25:2
Townsend, James Bliss, 1921, Mr 11,15:6
Townsend, James J, 1913, Ag 30,7:6
Townsend, James M, 1913, N 1,11:5; 1950, Je 25,68:6
Townsend, James M Mrs, 1943, Mr 28,24:3
Townsend, James Rodman, 1904, Ja 11,7:6
Townsend, James W, 1939, N 20,19:3
Townsend, John, 1952, Ap 1,29:3
Townsend, John B, 1947, D 26,15:4
Townsend, John G Jr, 1964, Ap 11,25:2
Townsend, John Hardenbreck Rev, 1925, Ag 11,21:4
Townsend, John Joseph, 1924, My 27,21:5
Townsend, John M, 1942, N 1,52:5
Townsend, John R, 1923, O 1,7:3; 1940, Ap 6,17:5; 1967, S 21,47:1
Townsend, John Rev, 1905, Je 14,9:6
Townsend, John W, 1939, D 6,25:5
Townsend, Joseph H Dr, 1916, Ja 8,9:5
Townsend, Joseph L Mrs, 1945, N 29,23:5
Townsend, Julius C (por), 1939, D 29,15:1
Townsend, Julius C, 1940, Ja 3,21:3
Townsend, Karel, 1946, Ap 30,21:2
Townsend, Lawrence, 1954, Mr 11,31:1
Townsend, Lee, 1965, Ja 23,25:4
Townsend, Lewis A Sr, 1946, D 29,37:2
Townsend, Louisa D Mrs, 1940, Je 5,25:5
Townsend, M Clifford, 1954, N 12,15:1
Townsend, Margaret O Mrs, 1952, Je 15,84:1
Townsend, Margaret W R Mrs, 1939, Ap 7,21:4
Townsend, Marion E, 1939, D 22,19:4
Townsend, Mark Jr, 1960, Jl 27,29:3
Townsend, Mary A, 1965, Jl 1,28:5
Townsend, Mary E, 1954, My 10,23:3
Townsend, Morris M, 1967, O 29,84:4
Townsend, Mrs, 1876, Ap 4,8:4
Townsend, Myron T, 1952, Je 30,19:2
Townsend, Newman A, 1951, Ap 12,33:3
Townsend, Oliver J, 1942, Ja 31,17:6
Townsend, Pinkney, 1937, D 8,25:3
Townsend, Prescott W, 1961, Ja 6,27:3
Townsend, R A, 1902, N 28,1:4
Townsend, Ray, 1966, D 27,35:3
Townsend, Richard, 1952, Mr 18,27:2
Townsend, Richard S, 1952, D 12,29:5
Townsend, Richard W, 1945, F 13,23:4
Townsend, Robert A, 1949, O 8,13:3
Townsend, Robert Col, 1915, D 29,11:5
Townsend, Royal S, 1940, Mr 18,17:4
Townsend, S, 1881, Ag 2,5:3
Townsend, S Cornelia, 1920, Mr 11,11:6
Townsend, S D Dr, 1869, S 21,5:5
Townsend, Samuel, 1913, S 7,II,13:6
Townsend, Samuel Capt, 1912, Jl 10,9:4
Townsend, Samuel Clinton, 1916, Ap 6,13:6
Townsend, Samuel P, 1956, O 17,35:2
Townsend, Smith D (por), 1944, S 18,19:3
Townsend, Smith D Mrs, 1944, Mr 7,17:5
Townsend, Solomon S, 1910, N 19,11:6
Townsend, Stephen, 1914, My 21,11:5
Townsend, Stephen H, 1943, Ag 9,13:5
Townsend, Stephen S, 1941, Ap 30,19:4
Townsend, Stewart E Jr, 1953, Ja 26,22:7
Townsend, Stockton, 1955, N 10,35:2
Townsend, Sylvester D, 1947, My 14,25:3
Townsend, T C, 1949, N 7,27:3
Townsend, Theodore E, 1944, Je 20,19:5
Townsend, Thomas G, 1949, Ja 13,23:5
Townsend, Tulloch M Mrs, 1951, O 2,15:5
Townsend, W B, 1867, My 21,8:4
Townsend, W C Mrs, 1917, D 18,15:4
Townsend, W Porter Mrs, 1947, My 11,62:4
Townsend, Walter E, 1940, Je 2,44:8
Townsend, Walter P, 1958, Je 3,31:3
Townsend, Walter R, 1951, Jl 31,22:3
Townsend, Willard S, 1957, F 5,23:2
Townsend, William, 1953, F 23,25:2
Townsend, William A, 1946, Je 20,23:3
Townsend, William C Mrs, 1939, N 12,49:1
Townsend, William E, 1945, My 12,13:5
Townsend, William G, 1944, F 13,41:1
Townsend, William H, 1964, Jl 28,29:2
Townsend, William H P, 1968, Mr 4,37:3
Townsend, William Halsey, 1905, Ap 16,9:6
Townsend, William K Judge, 1907, Je 4,7:5
Townsend, William M, 1940, D 4,27:2
Townsend, William S, 1913, My 7,11:6
Townsend, William W, 1958, Mr 25,33:5
Townshend, Charles Mrs, 1965, D 11,33:4
Townshend, Charles V F, 1924, My 19,17:3
Townshend, Dowager Marchioness of, 1959, O 13,39:5
Townshend, Emma S Mrs, 1942, S 12,13:6
Townshend, Henry W, 1953, My 12,27:5
Townshend, John, 1911, Ag 12,9:6
Townshend, Raynham (por), 1940, F 1,21:5
Townsley, C P, 1926, D 29,21:1
Townsley, Fred D, 1940, S 26,23:5
Tows, Cou Downing, 1914, N 1,17:4
Towse, Beachcroft, 1948, Je 22,25:5
Towse, Frank J, 1939, N 24,23:5
Towse, J R, 1933, Ap 13,17:1
Towsend, Terry M, 1942, My 17,45:1
Towsley, Frank R, 1954, Jl 20,19:5
Towsley, William D, 1943, Je 10,21:5
Towson, Charles R, 1949, Ag 23,23:5
Towt, Monroe V, 1960, N 12,21:2
Toy, Calvert R, 1960, F 7,84:8
Toy, Channing R, 1944, Ja 22,13:2
Toy, Harvey M, 1950, Mr 2,27:3
Toy, Thomas D, 1940, Ag 15,19:5
Toy, Walter L, 1940, Ja 26,17:1
Toyama, Mitsuru, 1944, O 6,23:3
Toye, Edward, 1951, Je 17,84:8
Toye, Edward G, 1942, Je 13,15:3
Toye, Geoffrey Mrs, 1948, Ja 29,24:3
Toye, Joe, 1942, Ja 30,19:4

Toye, Mary, 1961, My 22,31:5
Toye, Patrick J, 1944, F 8,15:4
Toye, Robert J, 1951, F 23,27:3
Toyoda, Soemu, 1957, S 23,27:3
Toyoda, Teijiro, 1961, N 23,31:3
Tozer, A W, 1963, My 14,39:3
Tozer, Edwin R, 1951, Ap 16,25:6
Tozer, Horace Sir, 1916, Ag 21,11:6
Tozier, Henry H, 1954, Ag 22,92:4
Tozzer, Alfred M, 1954, O 6,25:4
Tozzer, Arthur C (por), 1942, S 10,27:1
Tozzer, Brent A, 1967, O 31,45:2
Tozzi, Giorgio Mrs, 1963, Je 3,29:4
Tozzi, Nicholas, 1948, O 15,23:2
Trabadelo, Antonio, 1939, Mr 3,23:4
Traband, George L Mrs, 1947, Je 1,60:4
Traband, Harvey, 1959, S 20,86:5
Trabert, Arch W, 1967, F 19,88:8
Trabinger, Herman, 1937, F 11,23:5
Trabue, G W, 1884, My 2,5:2
Trabulsi, John K, 1962, Ag 11,17:4
Trabulsi, Louie, 1955, Ja 9,87:3
Trace, Isadore M, 1955, My 5,33:2
Trace, Margaret A, 1943, Ja 16,13:4
Tracewell, Charles E, 1960, Ag 9,27:3
Tracewell, Robert J Judge, 1922, Jl 30,26:5
Tracey, Andrew, 1903, D 30,7:1
Tracey, Charles Gen, 1905, Mr 25,9:6
Tracey, Christopher, 1913, S 7,II,13:5
Tracey, Edward J, 1948, N 18,27:2; 1954, Jl 23,17:5
Tracey, Edward John Rev, 1918, Jl 6,9:5
Tracey, James F, 1925, S 21,19:5
Tracey, John F, 1938, S 23,27:2
Tracey, Julia E Mrs, 1948, S 8,29:3
Tracey, Mary, 1957, Je 1,17:1
Tracey, Richard Adm, 1907, Mr 9,9:5
Tracey, Robert E, 1942, My 2,13:5
Tracey, Robert J, 1963, O 4,35:4
Tracey, Samuel B, 1951, D 11,33:1
Tracey, Thomas J, 1958, Ag 13,27:2
Tracey, Thomas Mrs, 1961, S 3,61:1
Tracey, William A, 1953, Ja 13,27:5
Tracey, William G, 1957, S 6,21:1
Tracey, William J, 1937, D 25,15:5; 1948, D 18,19:2
Tracht, Roy, 1949, My 31,23:4
Trachtenberg, Alexander, 1966, D 17,33:2
Trachtenberg, Benjamin, 1948, Jl 28,23:4
Trachtenberg, Ely, 1960, Ja 13,48:3
Trachtenberg, Harold B, 1957, O 15,30:2
Trachtenberg, Harry, 1952, Jl 15,21:1
Trachtenberg, Joshua, 1959, S 15,39:5
Track, Antone, 1943, Jl 1,19:2
Tractenberg, George, 1965, Je 6,84:8
Tracy, Agnes Ethel, 1903, My 27,16:3
Tracy, Albion, 1940, O 22,23:3
Tracy, Benjamin Franklin Gen (funl, Ag 10,11:3), 1915, Ag 7,7:5
Tracy, Carrie B Mrs, 1942, Ja 24,17:2
Tracy, Charles, 1885, Mr 15,2:3
Tracy, Charles A, 1951, Ja 10,27:5
Tracy, Charles Chapin, 1917, Ap 21,13:5
Tracy, Charles E, 1949, Ap 6,29:2
Tracy, Charles E Mrs, 1956, Ap 16,27:5
Tracy, Daniel W, 1955, Mr 23,31:2
Tracy, E H, 1875, Ag 29,7:3
Tracy, Edward J, 1945, D 30,14:7; 1947, N 20,29:3; 1953, Ja 14,31:4
Tracy, Edwin S, 1961, Mr 1,33:5
Tracy, Elizabeth Mrs, 1952, D 3,33:5
Tracy, Ellen, 1924, S 6,11:7
Tracy, Elmer C Mrs, 1947, D 10,31:3
Tracy, Ernest B, 1948, Je 26,17:2
Tracy, Evarts, 1922, F 2,17:1
Tracy, Frances B, 1956, My 10,31:4
Tracy, Frank, 1939, D 21,23:4; 1947, Mr 7,25:2
Tracy, Frank H, 1939, O 24,23:3
Tracy, Frank M Mrs, 1942, D 5,15:5
Tracy, Frank W, 1903, N 9,7:6
Tracy, Franklin W, 1959, F 24,30:1
Tracy, George E, 1948, Ja 6,24:2
Tracy, George M, 1874, S 3,4:7
Tracy, George W, 1942, S 28,17:5
Tracy, Harry A, 1958, D 1,29:5
Tracy, Harry J, 1951, D 6,33:2
Tracy, Helen, 1945, My 30,19:2
Tracy, Helen D, 1942, O 13,23:6
Tracy, Henry, 1904, Ja 20,9:7
Tracy, Henry R, 1873, N 6,5:2
Tracy, Henry W, 1948, F 3,25:3; 1951, S 14,26:3
Tracy, Hiram L, 1903, Ag 30,12:7
Tracy, Howard V, 1945, D 24,16:4
Tracy, Isaac R, 1938, D 23,19:5
Tracy, J F, 1878, F 14,1:5
Tracy, J Herbert, 1942, Jl 6,15:6
Tracy, James J, 1950, My 17,29:2
Tracy, Jane W, 1955, O 18,37:3
Tracy, Jeremiah, 1938, Je 28,19:3
Tracy, Jeremiah Evarts, 1923, F 13,21:4
Tracy, John, 1864, Je 26,5:4
Tracy, John A Jr, 1922, N 26,6:2
Tracy, John C, 1944, F 1,19:6; 1952, Ja 18,27:2; 1955, N 3,31:2
Tracy, John C Judge, 1937, Ap 16,23:5
Tracy, John E, 1960, Ja 1,19:1
Tracy, John F, 1944, O 28,15:3
Tracy, John J, 1947, Ag 8,17:6
Tracy, John P, 1915, Mr 22,9:4
Tracy, Joseph, 1959, Mr 21,21:3
Tracy, Joseph F, 1952, My 30,15:2
Tracy, Joseph H, 1949, Mr 17,25:3
Tracy, Joseph N V, 1947, F 13,23:2
Tracy, Joseph P, 1950, My 23,30:3
Tracy, Julia Mrs, 1955, Je 24,21:3
Tracy, Katherine A (will), 1940, Je 18,47:1
Tracy, L, 1928, Ag 14,23:6
Tracy, Lee, 1956, Mr 22,35:3; 1968, O 19,37:1
Tracy, Lee Mrs, 1952, O 10,25:4
Tracy, Lena H Mrs, 1941, Mr 19,21:6
Tracy, Leo J, 1960, Ag 4,25:3
Tracy, Lillian M Mrs, 1949, Ag 30,27:2
Tracy, Lyall, 1959, Je 3,35:2
Tracy, Martha (por), 1942, Mr 23,15:4
Tracy, Martin C, 1963, O 4,35:1
Tracy, Martin C Mrs, 1959, Je 28,69:1
Tracy, Mary E, 1946, D 15,77:2
Tracy, Matthew Mrs, 1952, N 4,29:2
Tracy, Merle E, 1945, Mr 5,19:3
Tracy, Milford E, 1949, Ja 17,19:4
Tracy, Morris de H, 1940, My 13,17:4
Tracy, Olin H, 1944, Ag 8,17:3
Tracy, P L, 1876, O 31,6:7
Tracy, Patrick J, 1921, Ag 25,13:5
Tracy, Ralph W, 1960, My 25,27:1
Tracy, Richard W, 1952, Jl 24,27:1
Tracy, Rose E, 1938, F 1,21:3
Tracy, Rose E Mrs, 1954, S 19,89:1
Tracy, Samuel G, 1942, D 9,27:3
Tracy, Samuel H, 1937, Jl 11,II,4:8
Tracy, Sherman W, 1950, N 2,31:3
Tracy, Spencer (funl, Je 13,47:1), 1967, Je 11,1:2
Tracy, T George, 1965, F 13,21:3
Tracy, Thomas J, 1940, Ja 22,15:5; 1960, O 20,35:2
Tracy, Thomas Rev, 1872, Ag 13,5:6
Tracy, Uriah T, 1917, S 2,13:2
Tracy, Virginia, 1946, Mr 5,25:5
Tracy, W L Mrs, 1952, D 6,21:3
Tracy, W O, 1940, F 9,19:5
Tracy, Wallace B, 1954, D 8,35:3
Tracy, William, 1881, N 3,5:3
Tracy, William B, 1945, N 2,20:3
Tracy, William D Dr, 1937, F 12,23:4
Tracy, William E, 1955, D 8,37:3
Tracy, William Evarts, 1916, F 21,11:4
Tracy, William G, 1924, D 11,23:4
Tracy, William H, 1924, S 1,13:4; 1952, Ja 30,26:3; 1965, Mr 15,31:3
Tracy, William H Judge, 1873, Ja 28,4:7
Tracy, William J, 1937, D 3,23:5; 1945, Ap 17,23:3; 1968, O 27,82:6
Tracy, William J Mrs, 1962, Jl 11,35:2; 1965, Ap 3, 29:5
Tracy, William Rev Dr, 1937, F 15,17:5
Tracy, William W, 1948, Ag 8,57:2
Tradelius, Paul, 1945, O 12,23:3
Trader, Arthur, 1950, D 21,29:4
Trader, Effie C, 1951, D 19,31:4
Trader, George H, 1951, Mr 14,33:2
Trader, Hugh Jr, 1967, N 28,47:4
Trader, William M, 1942, O 13,23:4
Traedal, Nils, 1948, O 13,25:5
Traeger, Cornelius H Dr, 1968, S 25,47:1
Traeger, Frank W, 1957, Ag 17,15:1
Traeger, John E, 1951, F 13,31:5
Traeger, Paul, 1951, Mr 27,29:5
Traendly, Frank H, 1949, F 23,28:2
Traendly, George H, 1948, Mr 12,23:4
Traer, Charles S, 1949, O 26,27:4
Traer, William M, 1961, Ja 6,27:2
Trafford, Abraham T, 1911, Ap 24,9:4
Trafford, B L Col, 1883, D 24,5:4
Trafford, Bernard W (por), 1942, Ja 3,19:1
Trafford, Frederick T Rev, 1953, F 23,25:3
Trafford, Lloyd M, 1966, My 2,37:4
Trafford, Perry D, 1952, D 9,33:5
Traft, Franz, 1913, F 14,15:3
Trafton, Edwin B, 1922, Ag 17,13:4
Trafton, Eliza Y, 1882, My 21,9:1
Trafton, Howard, 1964, S 26,23:4
Trafton, Howard A, 1961, Je 19,27:4
Trager, Benjamin, 1955, Ja 22,11:4
Trager, Beril, 1957, Ja 26,19:6
Trager, Hubert H L, 1948, O 6,29:2
Trager, Newton J Mrs, 1952, Mr 1,15:2
Trager, Sidney C, 1960, Ap 18,29:3
Trageser, Milton E, 1956, Ap 18,31:2
Trageser, Paul A, 1953, F 24,25:1
Trahan, Al (Jas A), 1966, D 15,47:3
Trahan, Arthur, 1950, S 23,17:2
Trahan, Cordelia Mrs, 1940, Mr 6,23:4
Trahan, Mitchell A, 1954, Jl 20,19:5
Trahan, Mitchell A Jr, 1938, Ja 8,15:6
Trahern, Albert L, 1946, Ja 5,14:2
Trahey, James D, 1944, Mr 5,36:2
Trail, Edward, 1941, F 13,19:2
Trail, Ray, 1946, Ag 10,13:2
Traill, Anthony Dr, 1914, O 17,11:4
Train, Arthur C, 1945, D 23,18:1
Train, Arthur C Mrs, 1923, My 17,19:4
Train, Charles Jackson Rear-Adm, 1906, Ag 4,1:5
Train, Charles R, 1967, D 10,87:2
Train, George F, 1968, Ja 31,41:4
Train, John L, 1958, Je 13,23:3
Traina, Anthony, 1966, Ja 3,27:4
Traina, Joseph J, 1959, Je 27,23:4
Traina, S Thomas, 1947, O 20,23:1
Trainer, Camillus R, 1960, Ja 16,21:4
Trainer, David W, 1952, Ja 24,27:2
Trainer, David W Jr, 1965, Jl 12,27:1
Trainer, Frank D, 1955, Je 2,29:5
Trainer, Henry J, 1947, D 29,18:2
Trainer, John N, 1953, D 19,15:1
Trainer, Joseph J, 1952, N 14,23:2
Trainer, Michael J, 1964, Ap 12,87:2
Trainer, William B, 1946, S 20,31:3
Trainin, Aaron N, 1957, F 9,19:3
Trainin, Boruch S, 1946, Mr 21,25:3
Trainor, Alissa K, 1950, O 1,105:1
Trainor, Charles J, 1948, Ja 7,25:2
Trainor, Edward L, 1949, D 8,33:1
Trainor, Francis C, 1955, Je 9,29:3
Trainor, Frank J, 1959, O 20,39:5
Trainor, Frank J Mrs, 1941, Ja 11,17:2
Trainor, Frank P, 1946, Jl 5,19:3
Trainor, James L, 1944, S 6,19:4
Trainor, James Mrs, 1941, S 29,17:3
Trainor, John F, 1948, Jl 1,23:5
Trainor, Joseph F, 1942, Ap 30,19:2
Trainor, Leonard, 1940, Jl 29,13:6
Trainor, Mary A Mrs, 1908, Ap 14,9:6
Trainor, Mary Mrs, 1941, F 27,19:2
Trainor, Owen C, 1956, N 29,35:4
Trainor, P F Sen, 1902, D 26,7:7
Trainor, Peter F, 1946, Je 21,23:5
Trainor, Raymond J, 1949, O 17,23:6
Trainor, Rose E, 1957, Ag 12,19:3
Traise, Earl F, 1950, O 4,31:1
Traitteur, Charles H Col, 1909, Ja 27,9:6
Trajan, Turku, 1959, Mr 17,30:4
Trall, R T Dr, 1877, S 26,4:7
Tralle, Henry E, 1942, Je 10,21:2
Tralow, Johannes, 1968, F 29,37:3
Trambukis, John, 1950, Ja 25,28:3
Tramburg, John W (Jan 14), 1963, Ap 1,36:7
Tramel, George, 1946, Mr 18,21:4
Tramel, William P Mrs, 1953, Ap 10,21:2
Trammell, P, 1936, My 9,15:1
Trammell, Park Mrs, 1922, Mr 15,19:5
Trammell, Pat Dr, 1968, D 11,47:2
Trammell, Walker L (por), 1942, Ag 6,19:2
Trammell, William C, 1951, Ag 9,21:6
Trampler, George M, 1958, Ap 21,23:5
Tran, Irving, 1958, Ap 5,15:5
Tranberg, Louis A, 1915, O 2,11:2
Tranchard, E Paul, 1950, D 22,23:4
Trancuiashi, Grigore, 1940, Ja 9,23:1
Trangmar, Earl R, 1961, O 23,30:1
Tranmael, Martin, 1967, Jl 13,37:4
Tranor, Grover C Sr, 1948, Je 29,23:2
Transeau, Emma L B Mrs, 1937, F 5,21:4
Transeau, T Elmer, 1954, Ap 12,29:3
Transue, Frank, 1950, Ap 1,15:6
Transue, William, 1937, My 17,19:3
Trant, Albert C, 1949, Ag 6,17:2
Trant, Joseph H, 1959, Ja 12,39:2
Tranter, C Edward, 1950, Ap 18,31:1
Tranter, Edith B, 1951, S 6,31:2
Tranter, Edward J, 1938, Je 13,14:2
Tranter, George C, 1925, My 14,19:2
Tranter, John H, 1948, D 16,29:3
Trapani, Ignazio, 1942, Ja 8,21:2
Trapasso, Lewis F, 1955, Ap 10,88:4
Traphagen, C B, 1905, Ap 1,7:3
Traphagen, Frank W, 1941, Ja 22,21:4
Traphagen, Nelson A Mrs, 1948, D 2,29:4
Trapnall, Sallie, 1881, N 7,2:5
Trapp, Albert R, 1939, My 10,23:2
Trapp, Alex O, 1960, Ja 21,31:5
Trapp, Francis H, 1959, F 26,31:4
Trapp, George von, 1947, My 31,13:1
Trapp, M E, 1951, Jl 27,19:1
Trapp, William, 1964, Jl 8,35:3
Traquair, John, 1947, Jl 20,44:3
Trask, Alanson, 1902, Ag 3,7:5
Trask, Birney E, 1949, Jl 16,13:1
Trask, Charles R, 1911, Ja 10,11:5
Trask, Fred L, 1954, Ja 26,27:2
Trask, George F T, 1942, Mr 1,45:2
Trask, Gustavus D S, 1914, Mr 16,9:2
Trask, J D, 1883, S 4,5:2
Trask, J D E, 1926, Ap 17,17:4
Trask, James D, 1942, My 25,15:3
Trask, John E D Mrs, 1955, Ag 8,21:3
Trask, John W, 1951, Ja 7,77:2
Trask, Joseph M, 1947, S 18,25:1
Trask, Katrina (Mrs Geo Foster Peabody),(por), 1922, Ja 9,17:1
Trask, Lillia M D, 1952, F 11,25:5
Trask, Mary G, 1937, D 12,II,9:2
Trask, Paul W, 1954, O 11,27:5

Trask, Robert P, 1950, Ap 16,104:6
Trask, Spencer (funl, Ja 4,13:3), 1910, Ja 2,II,13:4
Trask, Thomas C Q, 1942, Jl 30,21:2
Trask, Wayland, 1905, Ja 29,7:6
Trass, David, 1960, Ap 27,37:3
Tratte, George, 1919, Jl 19,9:7
Trattner, David R, 1961, F 15,35:3
Trattner, George G, 1967, Ap 17,37:3
Trau, Phil A, 1952, Ag 27,27:6
Traub, Edward W, 1955, Ap 9,13:3
Traub, Herbert S, 1949, N 10,31:4
Traub, Herman W, 1956, Je 10,88:3
Traub, Jack, 1960, Jl 15,23:4
Traub, John Mrs, 1946, D 11,31:3
Traub, Michael (por), 1946, Ap 25,21:2
Traub, Nathan, 1943, Jl 4,20:2
Traub, Peter E, 1956, S 28,27:1
Traub, Victor A, 1964, N 26,33:3
Traube, Abraham, 1960, S 25,88:5
Traube, Annette Mrs, 1956, S 16,84:1
Traube, Arthur, 1948, Jl 17,15:5
Traube, Ludwig Frank, 1909, My 29,7:5
Traubman, Emanuel, 1957, Ja 22,29:2
Traubman, Jacob, 1947, Je 16,21:3
Traubman, Michael, 1938, O 8,17:4
Traubman, Morris A, 1950, D 23,16:2
Traubman, Sophie, 1951, Ag 17,17:3
Traubner, Bernard, 1954, S 9,31:3
Traudt, Bernard G, 1945, Jl 25,23:4
Traudt, J Robert, 1955, Mr 1,25:1
Traudt, Louis, 1939, O 1,53:2
Traugott, Albert M, 1954, Ja 2,11:5
Traugott, J Mortimer, 1957, Ja 11,23:4
Traugott, John P, 1948, Ja 16,21:3
Traugut, John S, 1960, Jl 6,33:2
Traum, Arthur A, 1966, Mr 18,39:4
Traung, Charles F, 1940, F 7,21:2
Traung, Louis, 1949, N 16,30:2
Traus, Edouard, 1941, Ap 8,26:2
Trausch, Karl, 1945, F 5,15:4
Trausil, Jessie L Mrs, 1947, Mr 10,21:3
Trausneck, Andrew F, 1943, Ja 31,45:1
Traut, Justus A, 1908, Mr 10,7:5
Traute, Henry C, 1945, S 14,23:5
Trautman, A, 1933, Ag 22,17:1
Trautman, Edward Mrs, 1943, Mr 20,15:1
Trautman, Franklin P, 1937, D 11,19:3
Trautman, George, 1953, Ap 4,13:5
Trautman, George M, 1963, Je 25,33:2
Trautman, George M Mrs, 1940, N 28,23:3
Trautman, Henry A, 1946, D 5,31:2
Trautman, John H Mrs, 1949, Ja 6,23:2
Trautman, Peter, 1937, O 14,25:2
Trautman, William D, 1939, F 22,21:5
Trautmann, August, 1950, Jl 23,56:5
Trautmann, Charles, 1951, O 22,23:4
Trautmann, David, 1939, Ag 31,19:4
Trautmann, Harry Adam, 1968, Je 15,35:2
Trautmann, Mary E Mrs (por), 1941, Ag 19,21:3
Trautmann, Ralph, 1904, N 14,7:4
Trautmann, William F, 1944, O 20,20:2
Trautwein, Frederick H Sr, 1955, Mr 7,27:3
Trautwine, J C, 1883, S 16,2:6
Traux, Caroline S Mrs, 1940, F 2,17:4
Traux, James C Mrs, 1943, N 13,13:5
Traux, Rudd H, 1968, S 21,33:1
Traux, Stephen P Dr, 1904, Ap 1,9:7
Travaille, Forrest C Mrs, 1941, Ap 9,25:4
Travailleur, Maurice, 1950, My 4,27:4
Travaini, Angelo, 1945, Je 24,22:2
Travell, Willard, 1961, Ag 15,29:3
Travell, Willard Mrs, 1950, S 22,31:3
Traver, Alfred D, 1947, My 2,21:2
Traver, Alvah H, 1949, Ja 24,19:3
Traver, Edgar B, 1948, Je 16,29:2
Traver, Frederick G, 1940, My 13,17:5
Traver, George, 1954, Ap 20,29:2
Traver, Harry G, 1961, S 27,42:1
Traver, Harvey S, 1954, My 30,44:8
Traver, Mabel, 1951, Ja 14,85:1
Traver, Nelson, 1940, N 3,57:2
Traver, William A, 1948, Jl 23,20:2
Traver, William E Mrs, 1943, Ap 20,23:1
Traverner, Walter H Mrs, 1946, N 1,23:2
Travers, Aloysius Stanislaus Rev, 1968, Ap 23,44:3
Travers, Arthur H, 1963, Jl 17,31:4
Travers, Arthur M, 1951, D 9,91:2
Travers, Barnard F, 1950, My 24,29:4
Travers, Charles F, 1940, My 15,25:4
Travers, Edna L (Mrs W H Brittingham), 1958, Ap 15,33:4
Travers, Edward J, 1938, Ap 29,21:4
Travers, Edward J Mrs, 1948, My 14,23:1
Travers, Edward S, 1942, Ap 16,21:4
Travers, Eugene J, 1952, Ag 27,27:4
Travers, Frank, 1937, Ag 24,22:2
Travers, Frank C, 1905, Mr 20,6:5
Travers, Gerald F X, 1953, Ja 31,15:3
Travers, J Sr, 1882, My 27,5:3
Travers, J Towsend, 1943, F 22,17:1
Travers, James P, 1921, My 20,15:4
Travers, Jerome D, 1951, Mr 31,15:1
Travers, John J, 1938, D 29,19:4; 1948, S 27,23:6; 1949, Je 25,13:1
Travers, Lawrence J Rev, 1937, Ja 1,23:5
Travers, Paul F, 1943, Je 25,17:4
Travers, Reginald, 1952, Ja 6,92:2
Travers, Susan, 1904, D 8,9:6
Travers, Vincent, 1954, Je 26,13:6
Travers, W R, 1887, Mr 28,2:1
Travers, Walter E, 1957, O 18,23:1
Traversi, Gianniono A, 1939, D 28,21:5
Traversi, Leopold, 1949, Ja 4,19:4
Traverso, Conrado, 1963, My 11,25:2
Traves, J P, 1885, Ap 10,5:5
Travis, Albert C Jr, 1961, O 11,47:5
Travis, Albert D, 1949, N 8,31:1
Travis, Albert K, 1946, Jl 21,40:2
Travis, Arthur B, 1949, Je 30,23:3
Travis, Catherine H, 1948, F 14,13:4
Travis, Charles, 1941, Ag 17,39:3
Travis, Charles B, 1955, Je 25,15:2
Travis, Charles F, 1953, Mr 7,15:3
Travis, Charles M, 1948, Ag 4,21:6
Travis, Clarence M, 1967, Ja 27,45:2
Travis, Clayton V, 1961, Ja 26,29:4
Travis, Cornelius W, 1941, N 26,23:5
Travis, D Murray, 1940, D 15,60:4
Travis, E Baxter, 1949, F 21,23:5
Travis, Earl W, 1948, Mr 26,21:1
Travis, Emmet K, 1938, O 8,17:5
Travis, Eugene M (por), 1940, Jl 27,13:3
Travis, Eugene M Mrs, 1948, O 21,27:5
Travis, Everett H, 1941, Je 7,17:5
Travis, Ezra Johnson, 1919, Jl 13,22:4
Travis, Frank C, 1912, Ag 14,9:5
Travis, Frank H, 1948, Je 21,21:4
Travis, Frank M, 1946, N 26,29:5
Travis, Franklin W (cor, D 10,104:7), 1950, D 9,15:2
Travis, Frederick H, 1960, D 18,84:8
Travis, Frederick M Mrs, 1958, D 7,88:8
Travis, Gasper W, 1912, Je 18,11:5
Travis, George C, 1922, D 17,6:3
Travis, George F Mrs, 1952, Mr 30,92:3
Travis, H Earl Mrs, 1960, Je 27,25:1
Travis, Homer, 1962, Jl 2,29:2
Travis, Horace E, 1962, Je 5,41:1
Travis, Howard M, 1957, Jl 31,23:4
Travis, Ira, 1947, Je 13,23:1
Travis, Jack Mrs, 1944, Je 27,19:3
Travis, James Capt, 1909, Ag 7,9:6
Travis, James I, 1964, My 29,29:2
Travis, James L Rev, 1937, D 16,27:1
Travis, Jasper Mrs, 1952, Ja 31,27:4
Travis, Jeanie A, 1948, O 5,25:4
Travis, John F Mrs, 1951, O 25,29:4
Travis, Lawrence, 1947, O 12,76:5
Travis, Leon E, 1966, Je 18,31:5
Travis, Leonard, 1939, O 19,23:3
Travis, Leonard E, 1946, F 28,23:6
Travis, Lewis N, 1945, Ag 14,21:4
Travis, Lincoln, 1941, Jl 13,23:3
Travis, Marcella, 1957, N 22,26:1
Travis, Martin B, 1967, Ja 28,27:3
Travis, Raymond E, 1956, N 21,27:5
Travis, Robert F, 1950, Ag 7,1:1
Travis, Robert Jr Rev, 1866, O 26,2:6
Travis, Roberta E, 1960, S 17,23:4
Travis, Ruth S Mrs, 1953, My 28,23:6
Travis, S A, 1947, O 16,27:4
Travis, Seward Mrs, 1956, F 19,93:1
Travis, Seward S, 1937, Ja 17,II,8:2
Travis, Sheldon, 1950, N 17,27:4
Travis, Stuart, 1942, D 27,34:7
Travis, Thomas C, 1946, F 4,25:5
Travis, Thomas Mrs, 1957, F 8,23:4
Travis, Vernon W, 1948, Je 9,29:2
Travis, W J, 1927, Ag 1,16:3
Travis, Walter J Mrs, 1946, N 17,68:3
Travis, Walter Mrs, 1948, Mr 26,21:3
Travis, Warren, 1949, S 28,27:5
Travis, Warren L (will), 1941, Ag 7,19:2
Travis, William W, 1940, D 4,27:4
Travisano, Peter F, 1961, Ap 26,39:4
Travo, Nicholas A, 1952, Ag 26,25:4
Trax, Harland A Mrs, 1960, Mr 30,37:4
Trax, Judson D, 1954, Ja 17,92:7
Traxel, Karl E, 1954, S 22,29:5
Traylor, George A, 1914, Je 3,13:6
Traylor, M A, 1934, F 15,1:6
Traylor, Mahlon E, 1942, Mr 6,22:3
Traylor, Mary G, 1946, N 22,23:4
Traylor, Samuel W, 1947, N 13,28:2
Traynor, John H, 1951, D 20,31:4
Traynor, Joseph P, 1944, S 13,19:5
Traynor, Matthew J, 1946, Ja 24,22:3
Traynor, Nora H Mrs, 1941, O 24,23:4
Traynor, Thomas J Jr, 1953, Mr 17,35:5
Traynor, William B, 1968, Ja 9,43:1
Trayser, Donald G, 1955, Ap 16,19:3
Trayser, Lewis W, 1964, F 26,35:2
Treacy, Alfred J M, 1953, Je 8,29:3
Treacy, Benjamin P, 1937, Ap 7,25:4
Treacy, Daniel, 1944, O 7,13:4
Treacy, Daniel P, 1916, Ag 25,7:6
Treacy, Denis J, 1952, Ja 8,27:5
Treacy, Edgar J, 1958, Jl 5,17:6
Treacy, Edgar V, 1955, Ja 27,23:4
Treacy, Edgar V Mrs, 1962, Ja 3,33:3
Treacy, Gerald C, 1965, Ja 1,19:4
Treacy, Hubert J, 1938, Jl 15,17:2
Treacy, James P, 1946, N 25,27:3
Treacy, John, 1949, N 17,29:5
Treacy, John P, 1964, O 12,29:2
Treacy, Patrick, 1947, Jl 19,13:2
Treacy, Patrick S Mrs, 1948, Mr 11,27:4
Treacy, Raymond W, 1938, Mr 1,21:3
Treacy, William J, 1945, Ja 12,15:3
Treadway, Allen T (por), 1947, F 17,19:1
Treadway, Allen T Mrs, 1943, My 23,42:2
Treadway, Charles F, 1946, My 26,32:4
Treadway, Charles T Mrs, 1951, Mr 14,33:5
Treadwell, Aaron L (por), 1947, Je 26,23:5
Treadwell, Aaron L Mrs, 1938, My 26,25:3
Treadwell, Abbot Jr, 1960, N 25,27:4
Treadwell, Abbot Mrs, 1948, O 13,25:5
Treadwell, Alvin H 2d, 1947, Je 13,21:3
Treadwell, C S, 1884, Ja 5,2:4
Treadwell, Cornelius S, 1955, Je 28,27:2
Treadwell, Daniel, 1872, Mr 2,1:6
Treadwell, Eugene, 1937, N 21,II,9:3
Treadwell, Frederick W, 1956, N 24,19:3
Treadwell, G C, 1932, My 17,21:4
Treadwell, George H Maj, 1904, Ja 22,9:5
Treadwell, Harry G, 1948, O 17,76:8
Treadwell, Henry R, 1952, O 28,31:2
Treadwell, J P, 1876, Ap 11,2:2
Treadwell, John C, 1946, Jl 14,38:6
Treadwell, John P Jr, 1945, Je 5,19:4
Treadwell, John W F Brig, 1968, D 11,47:1
Treadwell, Joseph A, 1960, F 9,31:3
Treadwell, Josephine S Mrs (will), 1940, Mr 1,41:1
Treadwell, Louis M (por), 1942, My 5,21:3
Treadwell, Marshall, 1958, Je 13,23:3
Treadwell, Mr, 1879, Ag 10,10:4
Treadwell, Mrs, 1879, Ag 10,10:4
Treadwell, Samuel Dr, 1873, O 1,8:4
Treadwell, T J, 1879, Ag 3,6:6
Treadwell, William A, 1953, Ag 18,23:5
Treadwell, William Beebe, 1919, My 11,22:4
Treanor, Arthur R, 1956, Jl 17,21:1
Treanor, Hugh Father, 1919, D 27,9:4
Treanor, James A Jr, 1964, Ja 24,24:4
Treanor, James B, 1870, Mr 20,5:5
Treanor, John Father, 1880, O 5,5:2
Treanor, Vincent (por), 1941, Ag 9,15:2
Treanor, Walter E (por), 1941, Ap 28,15:5
Treanor, William A, 1946, Ag 31,15:4
Treanor, William C, 1952, Ja 17,27:5
Treat, Alfred B, 1942, Mr 23,15:2
Treat, Charles G (por), 1941, O 12,53:1
Treat, Charles Gould Mrs, 1947, F 9,61:4
Treat, Charles H, 1910, Je 1,6:5; 1947, Ap 20,9:1
Treat, Charles Russell Mrs, 1918, Jl 19,13:6
Treat, Crawford A, 1956, Ag 19,92:5
Treat, Edward Norton, 1922, My 21,30:2
Treat, Edward R, 1950, Jl 13,25:5
Treat, Edwin C, 1957, Ag 12,19:4
Treat, Edwin M Mrs, 1967, Mr 25,23:3
Treat, G Earle, 1945, Jl 26,19:2
Treat, Gail, 1944, S 16,13:4
Treat, George A Sr, 1951, Jl 9,25:2
Treat, Gertrude M, 1943, O 5,25:5
Treat, Herbert A Sr Mrs, 1954, N 22,23:4
Treat, Irving C, 1938, Je 26,27:3
Treat, J Frank, 1922, O 13,17:6
Treat, Jay S, 1912, Jl 4,7:6
Treat, Joshua 2d, 1956, O 14,86:7
Treat, M C, 1925, D 21,21:4
Treat, Mary Mrs, 1923, Ap 13,17:3
Treat, Robert B, 1943, Je 27,32:6
Treat, Robert D, 1964, Ja 4,23:5
Treatman, M David, 1954, D 18,15:4
Treatt, C Court, 1952, Jl 16,25:2
Trebilcock, John T, 1955, Ja 4,21:4
Trebing, Charles J, 1948, N 6,13:2
Trebitsch, Siegfried, 1956, Je 4,29:4
Trebitsch-Lincoln, Ignatius (por), 1943, O 9,13:1
Treble, Arthur L, 1966, S 3,23:1
Trebour, Henry, 1942, N 10,23:6
Treccani Degli Alfieri, Giovanni, 1961, Jl 8,19:7
Treciak, Frank, 1960, Ja 1,19:2
Trecker, Joseph L, 1947, O 8,25:4
Tredegar, Frederic G M Lord, 1954, Ag 22,93:2
Tredegar, Lord (E F Morgan), 1949, Ap 28,31:5
Tredennick, Joseph B, 1953, Mr 20,23:4
Treder, Oscar F R, 1952, My 30,15:1
Tredinick, William T, 1961, O 26,35:2
Tredinnick, Harry G, 1953, D 17,37:1
Tredor, William C Dr, 1948, Jl 22,23:3
Tredway, Floyd W, 1959, S 24,37:4
Tredway, Mary Mrs, 1904, Ja 28,10:5
Tredway, Page, 1968, D 16,47:1
Tredway, Page Mrs, 1958, Ja 18,15:3
Tredwell, Daniel R, 1921, N 12,13:5
Tredwell, Edgar A (por), 1939, S 9,17:4
Tredwell, Edgar A Mrs, 1957, D 5,35:5
Tredwell, Frederick T, 1959, Je 10,37:5
Tredwell, John C, 1952, N 26,23:3

Tredwell, John Sr, 1939, Jl 20,19:3
Tredwell, Roger C, 1961, Jl 13,29:1
Tredwell, Ruth M S Mrs, 1942, S 2,24:3
Tredwell, Sarah Kissam, 1906, O 13,9:1
Tredwell, Warren C, 1905, F 12,7:6
Tredwell, Wesley S Mrs, 1950, D 9,15:5
Tree, Ellen (Mrs Chas Kean), 1880, Ag 22,7:5
Tree, Herbert Beerbohm (por), 1917, Jl 3,9:3
Tree, Lady (por), 1937, Ag 8,II,6:4
Tree, Lambert, 1881, D 21,5:2
Tree, Lambert Ex-Judge, 1910, O 10,9:5
Tree, Lambert Mrs, 1903, O 11,7:6
Tree, O E, 1916, N 25,13:4
Tree, Viola, 1938, N 16,23:6
Treece, Henry, 1966, Je 11,31:1
Treen, Catherine T Mrs, 1921, My 23,13:5
Treen, Charles A, 1951, F 28,27:3
Treene, J Francis, 1953, Ja 31,15:4
Trees, Clifton C, 1949, Ap 27,27:3
Trees, Clyde C, 1960, O 3,31:3
Trees, Clyde C Mrs, 1953, Mr 21,17:6
Trees, Joseph C, 1943, My 20,21:1
Trees, Merle J, 1954, Ag 8,85:1
Trefcer, George F, 1956, Ag 10,17:4
Trefethen, Walter S Jr, 1944, Jl 24,15:6
Trefgarne, G M Lord, 1960, S 8,39:1
Trefz, Edward F, 1941, My 11,44:6
Trefzger, Emil A, 1961, Ap 18,37:4
Treganza, Elbert G, 1955, Je 12,86:4
Tregarthen, James, 1922, Ap 12,21:5
Tregarthen, William J, 1966, F 4,31:1
Tregaskis, Archibald, 1945, Ap 30,19:2
Tregaskis, John, 1919, Mr 27,13:2
Treglown, Edward M Mrs, 1956, Ap 23,27:4
Treglown, Glens, 1937, Jl 15,19:4
Trego, Edward A, 1946, N 27,25:6
Trego, Ralph A, 1955, Je 22,30:2
Trego, William T, 1909, Je 26,7:4
Tregoning, Percy V, 1948, S 12,72:2
Treharne, Bryceson, 1948, F 5,23:5
Treharne, Leonard B, 1904, O 18,9:6
Trehouart, Adm (funl), 1873, D 13,4:7
Treiber, John, 1961, N 16,39:3
Treiber, William J, 1947, O 28,25:2
Treiger, Baruch I, 1954, N 14,89:2
Treinen, Raymond, 1948, Ap 7,25:1
Treitman, Henry, 1965, Ap 1,35:1
Treitschke, H G von, 1896, My 10,5:4
Treitz, Joseph W, 1938, Ja 3,21:1
Trejo, Jesus, 1925, D 27,7:2
Trelawny, E J, 1881, Ag 27,2:7
Trelease, Frank J, 1959, O 4,86:5
Trelease, Sam F, 1958, F 3,23:4
Trelease, William, 1945, Ja 3,17:2
Treloar, Thomas R, 1960, S 13,37:2
Treloar, William P Sir, 1923, S 7,15:4
Trelstad, Anton M, 1938, O 13,23:5
Tremain, Eloise R, 1946, N 16,19:5
Tremain, Grenville, 1878, Mr 16,8:4
Tremain, Grenville Mrs, 1909, F 21,7:6
Tremain, Henry Edwin Gen, 1910, D 10,11:4
Tremain, Hobart L Lt, 1917, Je 30,11:6
Tremain, John F, 1948, F 26,23:5
Tremain, Lyman, 1878, D 1,7:4
Tremaine, Burton G, 1948, F 17,25:2
Tremaine, C Milton Mrs, 1960, Ap 20,39:2
Tremaine, F Orlin, 1956, O 24,37:4
Tremaine, H B, 1932, My 14,15:1
Tremaine, Henry A, 1938, My 14,15:6
Tremaine, Laurence P, 1955, Ja 22,11:6
Tremaine, Lawrence, 1939, D 8,25:5
Tremaine, Lt Col, 1865, F 14,1:5
Tremaine, Lyman L Mrs, 1956, Je 10,89:1
Tremaine, Morris S Mrs (will, Ag 3,19:2), 1938, Jl 27,17:6
Tremaine, Vivien A, 1948, Ja 27,25:2
Treman, C E, 1930, O 17,23:1
Treman, Charles E Mrs, 1956, Jl 28,17:6
Treman, Robert E, 1953, O 19,21:4
Treman, Robert H (por), 1937, Ja 5,23:1
Treman, Robert H Mrs, 1944, My 22,19:6
Trematon, Viscount, 1928, Ap 16,23:4
Tremayne, Charles H, 1951, Ja 10,27:1
Trembath, William C, 1959, N 25,29:1
Trembath, William J, 1942, Je 1,13:4
Tremblay, Eugene, 1947, Ja 3,21:3
Tremblay, Lafayette A, 1961, Mr 10,27:4
Tremblay, Thomas L, 1951, Mr 29,27:6
Tremblay, William H, 1954, Ap 12,29:3
Trembley, Charles C, 1957, O 22,33:3
Trembley, George D, 1944, Mr 3,16:3
Trembley, John T, 1947, Je 24,23:1
Trembley, Maurice, 1942, Jl 23,19:2
Trembly, Harriet A Mrs, 1907, Ja 6,II,9:6
Trembly, John, 1937, Jl 14,21:2
Tremear, Charles H, 1943, Jl 22,19:3
Tremeau, Charles Louis Gen, 1915, Ap 19,9:4
Tremmel, William F Sr, 1956, O 16,33:1
Tremper, Cantine Mrs, 1945, Mr 1,21:2
Tremper, Criss W, 1944, F 13,41:2
Tremper, Harry A, 1948, Je 10,25:4
Tremper, Mary A Mrs, 1937, F 5,21:5
Tremper, William A, 1938, Ag 3,19:3
Tremper, William R, 1937, Mr 6,17:2
Trenary, James M, 1961, D 12,43:3
Trenary, Otis L, 1940, Mr 15,23:3
Trenbath, Robert W Rev, 1937, D 21,23:5
Trench, C S John, 1951, Ag 22,23:4
Trench, Juliet Mrs, 1945, F 27,19:3
Trench, M E, 1927, Ja 7,19:5
Trench, Michael J, 1952, O 20,23:3
Trench, Stewart P, 1953, F 7,15:3
Trench, William P, 1937, D 25,15:6
Trench, William W, 1954, S 23,33:3
Trenchard, Alfred R, 1954, My 15,15:3
Trenchard, Ann B, 1877, Ag 29,4:7
Trenchard, Edward, 1922, Je 22,15:6
Trenchard, Harry E, 1951, My 12,21:5
Trenchard, Henry Mrs, 1951, D 18,31:3
Trenchard, Hugh M, 1956, F 11,17:1
Trenchard, James W, 1938, Ja 5,21:3
Trenchard, S D, 1883, N 16,5:4
Trenchard, Thomas G, 1943, O 19,19:1
Trenchard, Thomas W (por), 1942, Jl 24,19:3
Trenchard, Thomas W, 1942, O 21,42:1
Trenchard, Thomas W Mrs, 1938, F 10,21:5
Trenchard, William A Mrs, 1952, F 18,19:5
Treneer, J Maurice, 1968, Jl 4,19:2
Trengove, Joseph H, 1959, S 11,27:3
Trengrove, Thomas, 1940, F 14,21:1
Trenholm, Derrill De S Mrs, 1959, Ap 19,87:1
Trenholm, G A, 1876, D 11,1:5
Trenholm, Julian T, 1962, S 24,29:3
Trenisidi, Dudley, 1941, D 1,19:4
Trenite, Gerard N, 1946, O 11,23:5
Trenkamp, Henry J, 1964, Ag 18,31:1
Trenkamp, Herman J, 1943, My 29,13:6
Trenkle, Henry L Dr, 1937, D 6,27:5
Trenner, Baron Mrs, 1965, D 17,39:2
Trenor, John H, 1913, Je 18,9:4
Trent, George, 1907, F 17,9:6
Trent, George W, 1939, Mr 4,15:5
Trent, Josiah C, 1948, D 12,92:3
Trent, Lord (J C Boot), 1956, Mr 10,17:4
Trent, Ray S, 1937, F 4,21:5
Trent, Sheila, 1954, My 27,27:2
Trent, Walter E, 1942, Ja 20,19:2
Trent, William P, 1939, D 8,25:1
Trentanove, Michele, 1925, F 17,23:4
Trentinaglia, Erardo, 1950, Je 5,23:2
Trentman, William H Mrs, 1962, Ap 8,86:2
Trentzsch, Phil J, 1958, Je 15,76:5
Trepeklis, Nicholas, 1947, Je 9,21:3
Trepel, Jack, 1965, F 20,25:3
Trepkau, Frederick, 1944, O 15,45:1
Trepoff, Dimitri Fedrovitch Gen, 1915, Ag 15,13:5
Trepov, Dmitri Fedorovich Gen, 1906, S 16,1:1
Trepov, Theodore, 1938, Mr 29,21:2
Trepp, William A, 1954, Mr 8,27:2
Treptow, Bernard, 1940, S 1,21:3
Trerice, Victor, 1948, Mr 25,22:5
Tresca, Ettore, 1942, Ja 16,21:3
Trescott, Boyd Mrs, 1954, D 28,23:4
Trescott, Henry W, 1951, F 28,27:2
Trescott, S Boyd, 1947, Mr 30,56:6
Trescott, Virginia Drew (Mrs Melbourne MacDowell), 1912, Ja 2,11:6
Treseder, Ross C Mrs, 1954, F 7,88:1
Tresh, Mike, 1966, O 5,47:4
Tresidder, Donald B, 1948, Ja 29,19:3
Tresiz, Edward, 1923, F 23,13:5
Treskoff, Olga, 1938, Ap 23,15:5
Tress, John E, 1952, S 16,29:4
Tress, Michael G, 1967, Jl 12,43:3
Tressel, Martin L Mrs, 1966, Ag 10,41:2
Tresselt, Frank, 1952, D 30,19:3
Tressler, Jacob C, 1956, D 26,27:2
Tressler, Otto, 1965, Ap 28,45:4
Trester, Arthur L, 1944, S 19,21:3
Trester, Leonard W, 1957, D 22,40:5
Treston, Frank G, 1953, N 14,17:6
Treston, William C, 1948, S 29,29:2
Trestrail, B A, 1949, D 11,92:6
Tretbar, Charles F, 1909, Je 6,9:5
Treter, Esther L Mrs, 1952, N 26,23:3
Trethaway, Arthur, 1941, Ag 19,21:4
Tretheway, William B, 1938, Ag 25,19:3
Trethewey, Arthur W (por), 1949, Ja 15,17:5
Tretick, Sidney J, 1962, Mr 31,25:4
Trettin, August W, 1947, D 9,76:1
Treuenfels, Hans P, 1965, Jl 28,35:5
Treuer, John G, 1937, D 1,23:6
Treuhaft, Louis J, 1951, My 10,31:4
Treuhaft, Milton A, 1959, Jl 26,68:2
Treuhold, Alvin, 1942, Ja 11,44:1
Treulich, Eric J, 1967, Je 24,29:1
Treusch, Henry, 1948, F 4,23:2
Treutler, Paul T, 1968, S 28,33:2
Treux, Raymond M, 1953, S 14,27:5
Trevail, Silvanus, 1903, N 8,4:1
Trevathan, Charles E, 1907, Mr 18,7:6
Trevelyan, Charles, 1958, Ja 25,19:2
Trevelyan, Francis, 1908, Ja 26,9:3
Trevelyan, George M, 1962, Jl 22,65:1
Trevelyan, Hilda, 1959, N 13,29:1
Trevelyan, Robert C, 1951, Mr 22,31:2
Trevenew, Frederick H, 1946, Ja 5,14:2
Trever, Albert A, 1940, Ap 27,15:1
Treverton, Charles W Dr, 1937, O 19,25:3
Treves, Frederick Sir, 1923, D 10,17:4
Treves, Norman, 1964, My 19,38:1
Treves, Norman Mrs, 1963, S 2,15:3
Trevillian, James T, 1945, My 2,23:4
Trevillian, William J, 1944, Ag 29,17:3
Trevino, Geronimo Gen, 1914, N 14,11:6
Treviranus, Paul C, 1963, F 6,4:8
Trevis, C Merwin, 1953, D 9,11:3
Trevisan, Angelo, 1952, N 4,29:4
Trevisan, Celia M Mrs, 1942, Jl 17,15:5
Trevisan, Vittorio, 1958, Ja 28,27:2
Trevithick, Frederick W, 1954, S 17,27:1
Trevithick, Harry P (por), 1945, Ja 20,11:2
Trevithick, William J, 1947, Je 5,25:5
Trevor, Emily, 1943, D 25,13:5
Trevor, George S, 1951, N 18,90:3
Trevor, George S Mrs, 1967, Je 16,43:1
Trevor, Henry G, 1937, O 21,23:3
Trevor, Henry G Mrs, 1949, Ja 15,17:3
Trevor, John B, 1956, F 21,33:1
Trevor, Joseph E, 1941, My 5,17:6
Trevor, Lord (C E Hill-Trevor), 1950, D 24,34:2
Trevor, N, 1929, N 1,25:3
Trevorrow, Robert J, 1943, F 2,19:4
Trevorrow, Robert J Mrs, 1952, My 11,93:2
Trevvett, Herbert E, 1948, F 6,23:2
Treweeke, Richard L, 1950, Jl 22,15:2
Trewyn, Bryant H, 1942, Je 10,21:5
Trexlar, Edward W, 1940, D 26,19:3
Trexler, H C, 1933, N 18,15:4
Trexler, Samuel G, 1949, My 31,23:1
Trexler, William E, 1939, O 20,23:4
Trexler, Zebulon B, 1961, Je 24,21:7
Trey, Joseph A Mrs, 1949, Ap 9,17:6
Treynor, Albert M, 1948, O 26,31:3
Treyz, Harry A, 1959, My 28,31:4
Trezza, Anthony, 1948, D 23,19:1
Trezzani, Claudio, 1955, S 14,35:4
Triana, Santiago P, 1916, My 26,11:6
Triangali-Casanova, Antonio, 1943, N 3,25:3
Triano, Frank, 1948, F 8,60:1
Triarsi, Anthony J, 1959, O 31,23:4
Tribble, Samuel J, 1916, D 9,11:5
Tribe, Keith W Mrs, 1960, F 4,31:4
Tribe, Noel F, 1937, Je 11,23:2
Tribe, Reginald V, 1956, S 29,19:5
Tribelhorn, Ernest, 1954, Jl 11,73:2
Tribhubana, King of Nepal (cremation ceremony, Mr 18,16:8), 1955, Mr 14,23:1
Tribou, David H Capt, 1922, Je 2,17:6
Tribull, Richard W, 1946, Ag 9,17:5
Tribuno, Mario P, 1954, Je 11,23:2
Tribur, Cyril M, 1962, D 8,27:2
Trick, William C, 1938, My 12,23:3
Tricker, Charles L, 1961, Ap 21,33:4
Tricker, F, 1938, My 6,13:5
Trickett, John, 1947, My 9,21:2
Trickle, Frank, 1938, S 23,27:3
Tricopis, C, 1896, Ap 12,5:1
Tridon, Andre, 1922, N 23,21:5
Triebenbacher, Peter Mrs, 1948, Ap 7,25:3
Trieber, Peter J, 1966, Ja 2,73:1
Triedman, George, 1951, D 16,90:7
Trienens, Joseph, 1953, Ja 28,27:2
Trier, Charles (por), 1949, Ag 17,23:4
Trier, Ralph, 1952, S 26,21:2
Trier, Reuben, 1907, F 19,9:7
Trier, Walter, 1951, Jl 11,23:5
Triest, Karl, 1950, Ja 28,13:2
Triest, Rudolf M, 1954, D 29,29:1
Triest, W Gustav Mrs, 1953, F 11,29:5
Triest, W Gustave, 1946, S 22,60:3
Triester, David E, 1953, Je 29,21:2
Trifari, Gustavo, 1952, O 29,29:6
Trifunovic, Miles, 1957, F 22,21:4
Trigere, Alex Mrs, 1961, N 1,39:4
Trigg, C F, 1880, Ap 29,5:6
Trigg, Charles, 1945, D 31,17:3
Trigg, Ernest T, 1957, Ag 20,27:6
Trigg, Ernest T Mrs, 1943, D 9,27:5
Trigg, George B, 1959, Ag 5,27:5
Trigg, Jean, 1943, My 6,19:4
Trigg, W R, 1903, F 17,1:2
Trigg, William, 1961, My 5,29:4
Trigg, William R Jr, 1940, Ap 25,23:1
Trigger, Raymond, 1962, Jl 29,61:1
Trigger, Raymond Mrs, 1952, Mr 2,93:1
Trigger, Samuel H, 1949, D 19,28:2
Trigger, Samuel H Mrs, 1950, N 16,31:2
Triggs, Clayton E, 1958, D 4,39:4
Triggs, Floyd Wilding, 1919, Ag 26,13:6
Trigler, Louis E, 1957, N 9,27:6
Triglia, Peter Mrs, 1947, Ag 6,23:4
Trigo y Marcos, Dionisio, 1938, O 11,25:6
Trigueros, Luis, 1947, D 22,22:2
Trigueros, Patrocinio G, 1942, Jl 1,25:6
Trihey, John P, 1954, Mr 13,15:6
Trihy, James W, 1938, My 3,23:2
Trilck, John M Lt, 1915, Mr 1,9:5
Triller, A Wesley Mrs, 1943, Ap 9,21:5

Triller, Charles (will, Je 7,42:7), 1951, My 22,31:5
Trilley, Joseph Rear-Adm, 1911, Mr 8,11:4
Trilling, Ilia, 1945, Mr 5,19:5
Trilussa (C A Salustri), 1950, D 22,23:4
Trimakas, Antanas, 1964, F 28,29:4
Trimble, Benjamin, 1961, O 23,30:1
Trimble, Edward G, 1948, Ap 29,23:5
Trimble, Francis C, 1955, Ag 4,25:5
Trimble, Frederick M, 1951, Mr 22,31:5
Trimble, George S, 1872, My 20,5:2; 1925, F 25,19:2
Trimble, Gerald R (por), 1947, Je 23,23:4
Trimble, Henry W, 1964, Ja 23,31:3
Trimble, Henry W Mrs, 1903, D 15,9:5; 1952, Jl 24, 27:4
Trimble, James K, 1949, Mr 9,26:3
Trimble, Jessie, 1957, Ap 17,31:3
Trimble, John B, 1957, My 3,27:1
Trimble, John C, 1967, Mr 23,35:4
Trimble, John M, 1867, Je 9,1:6
Trimble, John R, 1951, My 20,88:4
Trimble, Laurence, 1954, F 10,29:1
Trimble, Paul C, 1948, Ag 3,25:5
Trimble, Richard, 1924, F 19,15:1; 1941, Jl 18,20:2
Trimble, Richard Mrs, 1947, Ja 1,33:5
Trimble, South, 1946, N 24,76:3
Trimble, William, 1941, N 26,23:4
Trimble, William B Dr, 1925, My 26,21:4
Trimble, William J, 1941, S 24,23:2
Trimble, William P, 1943, Mr 21,26:4
Trimboli, Frank M, 1963, O 1,39:3
Trimborn, Karl, 1921, Jl 27,15:5
Trimingham, Eldon H, 1959, D 13,86:6
Trimingham, Thomas D, 1940, My 11,19:5
Trimm, Fred B, 1954, Ap 27,29:1
Trimm, Frederick M Mrs, 1938, Mr 10,21:2
Trimmer, Carmen A, 1948, S 17,26:2
Trimmer, Charles S, 1951, Ap 7,15:6
Trimmer, Fred J, 1956, O 6,21:4
Trimmer, John A Rev Dr, 1914, My 18,9:5
Trimmer, Samuel K, 1958, S 22,31:1
Trimmingham, Ernest, 1942, F 7,17:3
Trimpe, William A, 1955, Mr 17,45:2
Trimpi, Norman W, 1959, O 18,86:3
Trimpi, Richard H, 1967, Mr 23,35:4
Trimpi, William W, 1938, Mr 27,II,7:3
Trimpin, William (cor, Ja 9,29:1), 1951, Ja 8,17:1
Trindade Salgueiro, Manuel, 1965, S 21,6:1
Trinder, Claude E, 1947, Ap 9,25:4
Trine, Ralph W, 1958, F 25,27:3
Triner, Catherine Mrs, 1938, Ja 24,23:3
Trinidad, Totoh, 1946, S 27,23:2
Trinkaus, George J, 1960, My 20,31:3
Trinkaus, Henry D, 1945, Ag 1,19:6
Trinkhaus, Fred C, 1949, Je 22,31:1
Trinkle, E Lee (por), 1939, N 26,42:8
Trinkle, Ray Mrs, 1946, N 30,15:1
Trinkle, William N, 1951, Mr 3,13:4
Trinkle, Wilmer S, 1958, Je 11,35:2
Trinks, Charles, 1950, O 3,31:3
Trinler, Walter A, 1945, Jl 20,19:6
Trip, Leonardus J A, 1947, Mr 6,25:1
Tripler, C S Gen, 1866, O 26,2:6
Tripler, Charles E, 1906, Je 23,7:4
Tripler, Thomas H Dr, 1909, F 27,9:4
Triplett, Clarence P, 1948, D 22,23:4
Triplett, Cleighton A, 1951, Jl 19,23:5
Triplett, James S Sr, 1948, Je 3,25:1
Triplett, John S (Johnny Tripp), 1957, S 13,23:3
Triplett, John W, 1943, Je 1,23:1
Triplett, L Lake, 1953, F 10,27:1
Tripodi, Peter E, 1950, S 8,31:1
Tripp, Arthur F Mrs, 1962, Je 29,27:3
Tripp, Bartlett, 1911, D 9,13:4
Tripp, Benjamin A, 1947, D 17,29:4
Tripp, Bernard E, 1954, F 26,19:1
Tripp, Charles E, 1948, Je 20,62:3
Tripp, David A, 1958, Je 6,23:3
Tripp, Dwight K, 1953, Ap 30,31:2
Tripp, Edwin B, 1940, Ja 11,23:5
Tripp, Edwin F, 1958, Ja 11,17:1
Tripp, Edwin P, 1953, D 12,19:5
Tripp, Eleanor Mrs, 1950, Mr 22,28:4
Tripp, Frank C, 1941, Ja 3,19:1
Tripp, Frank E, 1964, Ap 30,35:1
Tripp, Fred L, 1951, Ap 13,23:2
Tripp, G E, 1927, Je 15,27:1
Tripp, George H, 1943, S 3,19:2
Tripp, Granger Mrs, 1948, D 31,16:4
Tripp, Hiram S, 1937, F 18,21:3
Tripp, Neil E, 1951, N 14,31:2
Tripp, Thomas A, 1954, Jl 3,11:5
Tripp, William H, 1944, Ag 27,33:2; 1959, D 1,39:5
Trippe, Charles, 1910, Je 17,7:5
Trippe, Charles W Mrs, 1947, O 5,68:4
Trippe, Charles White, 1920, Jl 24,9:6
Trippe, Edward, 1953, Jl 23,23:5
Trippe, Harry M, 1939, Ag 2,19:6
Trippe, James, 1955, D 15,39:6
Trippe, Martha G Mrs, 1937, My 2,II,9:1
Trippe, Norman F, 1944, S 19,21:5
Trippet, Oscar A, 1967, N 28,51:7
Trippett, Joseph, 1907, F 28,9:6
Trips, Wolfgang von (funl, S 15,39:1), 1961, S 11,1:3

Trischett, S Seymour, 1944, Mr 23,23:5
Triscott, Samuel P R, 1925, Ap 17,21:5
Triska, Joseph A, 1965, My 28,33:3
Trismen, John H, 1941, F 7,19:3
Tristan, Jane de Countess, 1965, S 5,56:5
Trister, Oscar L, 1959, Mr 20,32:1
Tristram, Katherine A S, 1948, Ag 28,16:3
Tritle, Frederick A, 1906, N 20,9:6
Tritsch, John E, 1956, Ja 6,24:2
Tritsch, John E Mrs, 1960, Ja 9,21:1
Tritschler, Berhold W Mrs, 1951, My 24,35:5
Tritschler, Frank, 1955, Je 17,23:3
Tritt, Olga, 1968, Mr 11,41:4
Tritton, William A, 1946, S 25,27:6
Tritz, Jean-Pierre Mrs, 1968, Ja 9,43:2
Trivanovich, Vaso, 1949, N 7,27:3
Trivelli, Adriaan P H, 1956, Ap 13,25:2
Triver, Annette, 1949, Ja 4,19:4
Trivett, Ethel M, 1961, My 11,37:4
Trivett, George H, 1939, N 23,27:3
Trix, Helen, 1951, N 20,31:2
Troast, Jacob M, 1938, N 30,23:2
Troast, N Lester, 1958, O 11,23:5
Troast, Paul L Mrs, 1965, Je 11,31:2
Trobriand, Countess, 1907, Jl 13,7:6
Trocchi, Tito, 1947, F 13,23:1
Troccoli, Giovanni B, 1940, F 22,23:5
Trochu, L J Gen, 1896, O 8,5:1
Trocki, Josephine Mrs, 1948, Je 5,15:4
Trocola, Paul A, 1961, Jl 22,21:5
Trocquer, Yves Le, 1938, F 22,21:2
Troeber, Joseph W, 1954, Ag 7,13:4
Troeger, Ernst O, 1950, Ja 5,25:4
Troeltsch, Ernst Prof, 1923, F 2,15:5
Troemner, J Louis, 1951, N 29,33:3
Troescher, Albert A (will), 1937, D 28,17:3
Troester, Charles A Dr, 1903, N 22,10:2
Troetschel, Hugo, 1939, S 4,19:5
Trofimenko, Sergei, 1953, O 20,29:2
Trofimov, Sergei, 1950, N 12,93:2
Troger, Henry H 2d, 1950, Mr 28,31:3
Troiano, John, 1958, Ja 8,47:4
Troisi, Fiorentino G, 1950, Ja 25,27:1
Troisier, Jean, 1945, N 4,44:1
Troisio, William F Mrs, 1959, O 10,21:7
Trojan, George J, 1937, Ja 12,23:5
Trojan, Johannes Dr, 1915, N 24,13:6
Troller, Harry, 1961, Ap 12,41:2
Trollope, A, 1882, D 7,4:6
Trollope, Frances Mrs, 1863, O 22,8:1
Trollope, Theodosia, 1865, My 7,3:3
Trombetta, Joseph A, 1942, N 18,26:2
Trombley, Issac J, 1951, D 8,11:4
Tromka, Abram, 1954, Je 22,27:6
Trommer, George F, 1956, N 7,31:4
Trommer, George F (est tax appr), 1958, Mr 19,25:2
Trommer, Lazarus, 1957, Ag 10,15:3
Trompeter, David Mrs, 1965, F 18,33:2
Tronchi, Giovanni, 1952, N 24,23:3
Troncoso, Manuel de J, 1955, Je 1,33:3
Troncoso, Manuel U, 1959, Ja 23,25:1
Trondle, John M, 1967, S 11,45:2
Trook, William H (will), 1940, Ap 13,19:6
Troop, James, 1941, O 16,21:6
Troop, William H Sr, 1956, Mr 16,23:4
Troost, George W, 1956, Ja 25,31:2
Troostwyk, Isidor Mrs, 1948, My 13,25:5
Tropauer, David, 1962, Ja 26,31:2
Trope, Harry G, 1952, O 21,29:3
Troper, Morris C, 1962, N 18,87:1
Troper, Morris C Mrs, 1957, D 13,55:1
Tropin, Bernard, 1940, F 25,39:1
Tropp, Rebecca J, 1954, Mr 28,89:2
Trosk, George Mrs, 1960, Ap 25,29:4
Troskoff, Nicholas I Baron, 1941, S 13,17:5
Trosper, Guy, 1963, D 23,25:1
Trossbach, Herman, 1939, O 2,17:5
Trossett, Roy F, 1952, F 18,19:1
Trossi, Carlo F, 1949, My 11,30:7
Trost, Joseph C, 1940, Mr 9,15:4
Trost, Ralph, 1962, Ja 3,33:3
Trost, Ralph Mrs, 1942, O 28,23:3
Trost, Rudolph A, 1951, N 1,29:2
Trostel, Albert O Jr, 1962, F 3,21:4
Trostle, Edward A, 1948, D 5,92:2
Trostler, Leo L, 1949, F 7,19:4
Trosty, Irving, 1951, Ag 20,19:5
Troth, Edgar A, 1953, S 14,27:4
Troth, Edward E, 1945, Ag 5,38:3
Troth, Emma, 1949, N 3,29:2
Troth, Henry, 1945, Ap 28,15:5
Trotha, Adolph L von (por), 1940, O 12,17:7
Trotman, Edmund B, 1939, Mr 7,22:3
Trotman, Minta B, 1949, My 4,29:2
Trotsky, Leon D Mrs, 1962, Ja 24,33:1
Trott, Frank G, 1949, Ag 26,19:2
Trotta, Dominic A, 1959, Mr 29,81:1
Trotta, Giuseppe, 1957, Ap 24,33:3
Trotter, Clifford S Sr (will, Mr 28,19:1), 1942, Mr 21, 17:6
Trotter, Eugene T, 1943, S 5,29:2
Trotter, Frank B, 1940, Mr 8,22:3
Trotter, Gerald F, 1945, Je 16,13:4

Trotter, James K, 1940, Je 18,23:4
Trotter, James P, 1960, Mr 21,29:5
Trotter, Jonathan, 1865, Ap 8,4:2
Trotter, Joseph W, 1940, Je 18,23:4
Trotter, Massey, 1959, F 9,26:1
Trotter, Melvin E, 1940, S 12,25:2
Trotter, Millard S, 1954, Jl 31,13:4
Trotter, Reginald G, 1951, Ap 8,92:2
Trotter, Spencer L, 1955, Ap 28,29:2
Trotter, Spencer L Mrs (Caroline), 1965, Ap 2,35:2
Trotter, Theodore V Mrs, 1944, My 7,45:1
Trotter, Wilfred, 1939, N 28,26:2
Trotter, William Alexander, 1916, Ag 17,11:3
Trotter, William E, 1937, Ja 2,14:1
Trotter, William R, 1949, Ag 6,17:3
Trotti, Hugh H Sr, 1956, N 20,37:2
Trotti, Lamar, 1952, Ag 29,23:1
Trottier, Dave Mrs, 1940, Ja 1,23:5
Trottier, George A, 1952, Ag 12,19:5
Trottier, Raoul A, 1961, F 19,86:8
Troubetskoi, Daria Princess, 1952, Mr 28,23:1
Troubetskoy, Sergius, 1905, O 13,9:5
Troubetzkoy, Nicholas, 1961, Je 7,41:4
Troubetzkoy, P, 1936, Ag 26,21:5
Troubetzkoy, Paul Prince, 1938, F 14,17:1
Troubetzkoy, Wladimir Prince, 1954, Ap 10,15:3
Troughton, Edward J Sr, 1947, My 11,62:4
Troumaille, Duke de la (Louis Charls), 1911, Jl 5, 11:6
Trouncer, Cecil, 1953, D 16,35:1
Trounstine, Joseph F, 1947, N 21,27:4
Trounstine, Philip J, 1960, Ap 6,41:2
Trounstine, Samuel H, 1937, N 14,II,10:7
Troup, Alexander, 1908, S 6,9:4
Troup, Augusta L Mrs, 1920, S 15,9:1
Troup, Edward, 1941, Jl 10,19:4
Troup, George A, 1941, O 10,23:3
Troup, Jack, 1954, Ap 20,29:4
Troup, James, 1957, Ap 3,31:2
Troup, James Mrs, 1956, Ag 7,27:5
Troup, John A, 1959, Ag 13,27:2
Troup, P, 1936, Ag 31,15:4
Trousdell, Gordon N, 1947, F 18,25:2
Trousdell, John E, 1944, O 11,21:6
Trousdell, Thomas B, 1949, F 4,23:2
Trousdell, Thomas B Jr, 1941, N 3,19:5
Trousdell, Thomas B Mrs, 1947, Ap 7,23:4
Trousedale, William Ex-Gov, 1872, Mr 28,1:4
Trousil, Gerald J, 1952, Mr 8,31:4
Troussoff, Pierre P, 1943, Mr 2,19:3
Trout, Charles E, 1959, Ap 20,31:4
Trout, Clement E, 1960, Jl 18,27:5
Trout, Delmar E, 1938, D 31,15:1
Trout, Francis, 1950, Mr 28,31:2
Trout, Glen H, 1949, Mr 13,76:2
Trout, Harry E, 1947, Ag 8,17:3
Trout, Hugh Sr, 1950, Ja 14,15:6
Trout, John F Maj, 1912, My 24,13:5
Trout, John M, 1939, D 3,61:1
Trout, M C, 1873, Je 26,1:3
Trout, Virgil, 1944, O 12,32:6
Trout, Wetherill P, 1955, Ja 11,25:2
Troutman, George M Mrs, 1938, O 5,23:1
Troutman, Greyson P, 1943, N 26,23:5
Troutman, Howard F, 1959, D 1,39:5
Troutman, Seibert E, 1954, Ja 24,85:2
Troutt, William O, 1948, Ja 30,23:1
Trow, Cecil W, 1944, Je 10,15:5
Trow, Frank H, 1944, D 6,23:4
Trow, J F, 1886, Ag 9,5:5
Trowbridge, A, 1934, Mr 15,26:1
Trowbridge, A H, 1881, Je 27,5:4
Trowbridge, Alex B, 1950, S 28,31:3
Trowbridge, Alexander B Mrs, 1945, O 15,17:4
Trowbridge, Alvah W, 1907, S 19,7:6
Trowbridge, Anna B, 1950, Ja 26,27:2
Trowbridge, Arthur E, 1950, F 11,15:2
Trowbridge, Augustus Mrs, 1948, Ag 13,15:4
Trowbridge, Caroline Hoadley, 1910, D 2,9:5
Trowbridge, Charles Christopher Prof, 1918, Je 3,11:3
Trowbridge, Charles E, 1955, D 2,27:2
Trowbridge, Charles E Mrs, 1942, Ag 27,19:2
Trowbridge, Charles R Mrs, 1947, Ap 26,13:5
Trowbridge, Charles R Rev, 1937, Ja 7,21:4
Trowbridge, Conrad F, 1957, Mr 17,86:2
Trowbridge, Cornelia B, 1958, Mr 4,29:4
Trowbridge, Cornelius H, 1950, Je 25,70:2
Trowbridge, Courtlandt H, 1938, O 19,23:4
Trowbridge, Dorothy Quincy, 1925, Mr 31,19:5
Trowbridge, E L, 1880, Ag 23,5:4
Trowbridge, Edmund Q, 1964, S 4,29:1
Trowbridge, Edward G, 1941, S 29,17:3
Trowbridge, Edwin A, 1948, Je 8,26:2
Trowbridge, Edwin K Mrs, 1937, Ag 20,17:2
Trowbridge, Elizabeth M, 1947, S 2,21:6
Trowbridge, Francis, 1943, D 28,18:2
Trowbridge, Francis E, 1910, S 15,9:6
Trowbridge, Gardiner, 1938, S 15,25:4
Trowbridge, Henry O, 1951, Ja 29,19:5
Trowbridge, James L, 1950, My 21,104:4
Trowbridge, John, 1923, F 20,17:3
Trowbridge, John H, 1946, Jl 9,21:4
Trowbridge, John Townsend, 1916, F 13,15:3

Trowbridge, Lewis H, 1957, N 23,19:4
Trowbridge, Luther S Gen, 1912, F 3,11:4
Trowbridge, Mason, 1962, Mr 11,86:1
Trowbridge, Nettie M, 1939, Ag 25,15:2
Trowbridge, Oliver R, 1937, My 1,19:4
Trowbridge, Phebe, 1947, S 17,25:3
Trowbridge, S Breck Parkman, 1925, Ja 30,17:4
Trowbridge, Spencer L, 1949, Ag 29,17:6
Trowbridge, Stephen, 1941, My 27,23:6
Trowbridge, Walter B Mrs, 1949, Mr 24,28:2
Trowbridge, William D, 1953, Ag 13,25:4
Trowbridge, William R H, 1938, Ag 11,17:6
Trower, John, 1911, Ap 5,9:4
Trown, Francis J, 1938, Mr 1,22:2
Trown, Richard W, 1951, D 17,31:5
Trowt, John A, 1947, F 3,19:4
Troxel, Lynn Sr, 1955, Ja 28,19:1
Troxell, Edgar R Jr, 1963, Ap 3,47:4
Troxell, William S, 1957, Ag 11,81:2
Troxell, Willoughby H, 1945, Jl 13,11:5
Troxler, Emil, 1937, Ag 8,II,7:4
Troxler, Gus, 1945, F 16,23:1
Troy, Bernard J, 1954, Ap 4,87:1
Troy, Carl E Mrs, 1965, Jl 30,25:1
Troy, Edward P, 1946, D 12,29:4
Troy, Elinor, 1949, D 1,31:1
Troy, Garrett F, 1944, N 2,19:2
Troy, Hugh, 1964, Jl 9,33:4
Troy, Hugh C, 1961, Ja 29,85:1
Troy, James J, 1951, Ja 12,27:4
Troy, James S, 1937, S 21,25:4
Troy, John J, 1938, Ap 1,23:5
Troy, John Mrs, 1949, F 9,27:4
Troy, John P, 1939, O 6,25:2
Troy, John U, 1938, F 9,20:3
Troy, John W, 1942, My 3,54:1
Troy, Joseph, 1904, Ja 20,9:6
Troy, Matthew O, 1944, Mr 14,19:3
Troy, Max, 1954, O 21,27:4
Troy, Owen A, 1962, Ja 20,21:4
Troy, Peter H, 1958, Ag 25,21:5
Troy, Peter H Mrs, 1940, Ag 31,13:5
Troy, Richard, 1951, Ap 2,25:5
Troy, Theodore R, 1964, My 6,47:1
Troy, Thomas F, 1937, F 10,23:3
Troy, Thomas F (Oct 3), 1965, O 11,61:6
Troy, William, 1947, O 9,25:2
Troy, William A, 1943, Ap 29,21:2; 1965, Je 6,84:6
Troy, William E, 1961, My 27,23:3
Troy, William W, 1956, Ag 2,25:6
Troy, Zeliaette, 1946, N 3,63:2
Troyan, Mihail P, 1961, Ap 4,37:3
Troyanovsky, Alex A, 1955, Je 24,21:1
Troyanovsky, Boris S, 1951, Jl 8,61:1
Troyon, Painter, 1865, Ap 9,2:5
Truax, Alfred J, 1964, S 1,35:1
Truax, Charles H Ex-Justice, 1910, Ja 15,9:3
Truax, Earle G, 1959, Jl 31,24:1
Truax, Earle G Mrs, 1964, Jl 16,31:1
Truax, Frederick D, 1951, N 16,25:4
Truax, Frederick L, 1941, Jl 25,17:6
Truax, Glenn E, 1965, Je 24,35:2
Truax, Harry, 1958, N 2,88:8
Truax, James, 1903, Je 28,10:3
Truax, Neil, 1953, Je 9,27:2
Truax, Therese, 1944, My 5,21:6
Trube, Carl, 1916, F 4,9:6
Trube, Herbert L, 1959, Jl 15,29:4
Trubee, John H, 1964, Ag 25,33:3
Trubee, William A, 1940, F 8,23:6
Trubek, Morris Mrs, 1948, Ap 12,21:6
Trubenbach, Conrad, 1961, Jl 2,32:1
Trubenbach, Conrad D Mrs, 1949, N 21,25:4
Trubenbecker, Henry, 1914, Jl 6,7:6
Trubitz, Jacob, 1952, Ja 30,25:3
Trubner, N, 1884, Ap 1,5:2
Truby, Albert E, 1954, Mr 5,19:2
Truby, Willard F, 1951, Ag 23,23:6
Truc, Walter, 1950, D 31,42:7
Trucco, Manuel, 1954, O 26,27:2
Trucco, Victor, 1964, My 19,37:1
Truchenburg, M Rev, 1878, F 22,4:6
Truchsess, Rifenback Mrs, 1908, D 15,9:6
Truda, Leonardo, 1942, Jl 19,30:5
Trude, Daniel P, 1946, Jl 25,21:4
Trude, Samuel H, 1940, Jl 7,25:4
Trudeau, Anisis (Mother Saint Damase), 1955, O 3, 27:5
Trudeau, Arthur G Mrs, 1965, Mr 29,36:3
Trudeau, E Carroll, 1949, Ja 17,19:3
Trudeau, E L Jr Dr, 1904, My 4,1:2
Trudeau, Francis B Sr (funl, Jl 24,25:4), 1956, Jl 20, 17:3
Trudeau, Percival W, 1957, Ja 18,21:1
Trudeau, Wilfred, 1948, Mr 1,23:1
Trudell, Harry W, 1964, Ja 28,31:1
Truden, John N, 1939, F 16,21:5
True, C K Rev (see also Je 21), 1878, Je 24,5:3
True, J Rawson, 1945, My 21,19:1
True, Rodney H (por), 1940, Ap 9,24:4
True, Ronald, 1951, Ja 9,7:6
Trueb, Charles C, 1940, Mr 18,17:3
Trueblood, D Elton Mrs, 1955, F 9,25:2
Trueblood, Edwin P, 1951, Ap 6,25:4
Trueblood, Howard, 1953, Ja 1,18:8
Trueblood, Howard M, 1962, F 14,33:1
Trueblood, Ralph W, 1954, My 7,23:4
Trueblood, Thomas C, 1951, Je 5,31:4
Truehaft, Morris, 1949, Jl 26,27:1
Truelle, Jacques, 1945, My 31,15:5
Truelzsch, E Richard, 1952, Mr 18,27:4
Trueman, G Ernest, 1958, Jl 27,61:2
Trueman, George J, 1949, F 19,15:4
Truesdale, George V, 1959, My 14,33:1
Truesdale, Joseph R, 1961, O 2,31:5
Truesdale, Melville D, 1959, O 21,43:2
Truesdale, Philemon E, 1945, Je 13,23:3
Truesdale, William Hayes Mrs, 1923, N 18,23:3
Truesdell, Clara I, 1954, O 15,23:2
Truesdell, Ella Mrs, 1937, S 9,23:4
Truesdell, George E, 1955, N 29,29:2
Truesdell, George W, 1946, D 25,29:4
Truesdell, J A Mrs, 1948, Ap 12,21:4
Truesdell, Julius A, 1952, S 9,31:4
Truesdell, Karl, 1955, Jl 18,21:4
Truesdell, Percy S, 1948, Jl 11,53:2
Truesdell, S E, 1903, O 17,9:6
Truesdell, Waldo B, 1951, Mr 10,13:2
Truesdell, Wallace, 1960, O 14,33:4
Truesdell, Ward N Mrs, 1949, D 13,31:4
Truesdell, William E, 1937, My 4,25:5
Truett, George, 1944, Jl 8,11:4
Truex, Francis S Mrs, 1951, Jl 19,23:6
Truex, Ida M Mrs, 1947, Ag 25,17:5
Truex, Joseph A, 1949, Ja 9,73:1
Truez, Francis S, 1941, Ap 13,39:2
Truffa, Peter E, 1949, Jl 12,27:3
Trugman, Samuel, 1958, N 29,21:3
Truitt, Drexel M, 1946, Ja 1,28:3
Truitt, Frank H, 1955, Ja 21,23:5
Truitt, Max O, 1956, F 3,23:2
Truitt, Samuel H, 1937, S 17,25:1
Truitt, William J B, 1956, F 6,23:3
Trujillo, Anibal, 1948, D 3,25:1
Trujillo-Bravo, Jose L, 1944, Ag 23,19:6
Trull, Elizabeth Mrs, 1938, My 7,15:5
Trull, Frank T, 1961, N 6,37:4
Trull, George, 1879, Ag 16,5:6
Trull, George H, 1964, Je 2,37:3
Trull, Herbert M, 1951, D 22,16:2
Trull, Larkin T, 1941, Ap 3,23:2
Trull, William C, 1915, Je 1,15:7
Trullinger, Ray, 1963, O 30,39:4
Trullinger, Robert W, 1955, N 10,35:4
Trulock, Anna P H Mrs, 1908, Mr 27,9:4
Trulock, Guy P, 1949, Ja 21,22:3
Trulson, Anton H, 1948, Jl 6,23:1
Trulson, Martha F, 1965, Ja 5,30:8
Trum, Walter E, 1963, D 9,35:5
Truman, B H, 1940, O 29,25:3
Truman, C Ray, 1948, S 28,27:1
Truman, David F, 1899, Je 30,7:3
Truman, Harold G, 1954, Ap 24,17:6
Truman, Harry, 1950, Jl 19,31:3
Truman, Helen (Mrs Frank Wynkoop), 1924, My 3, 15:4
Truman, Henry Hertel, 1916, Mr 31,11:6
Truman, James C Mrs, 1951, F 1,25:4
Truman, James Dr, 1914, N 27,11:6
Truman, John V, 1965, Jl 9,26:2
Truman, Lyman, 1881, Mr 26,5:3
Truman, Martha E Mrs, 1947, Jl 27,1:1
Truman, Ralph E, 1962, My 1,37:1
Truman, Robert O, 1961, N 18,23:6
Truman, Stewart W, 1943, Ja 21,21:3
Truman, Whitney R, 1937, O 26,23:6
Trumbauer, Frank, 1956, Je 12,35:4
Trumbauer, Horace, 1938, S 20,23:5
Trumbell, Joseph, 1880, Jl 27,8:4
Trumbitch, Ante (por), 1938, N 19,17:4
Trumble, Frank E, 1943, D 31,16:7
Trumble, Worcester W, 1949, My 9,25:3
Trumbo, George A, 1939, Je 9,21:5
Trumbo, Glenn M, 1965, Je 5,31:5
Trumbo, Isaac Col, 1912, N 9,11:6
Trumbour, Thomas A, 1958, S 4,29:4
Trumbower, William M Mrs, 1925, O 31,17:3
Trumbull, Alice J Mrs, 1940, Ja 29,15:3
Trumbull, Allan T, 1951, Ap 1,92:1
Trumbull, Annie E, 1949, D 24,15:1
Trumbull, Charles G, 1941, Ja 15,23:1
Trumbull, D, 1878, Jl 4,5:4
Trumbull, Daniel F, 1944, D 22,17:4
Trumbull, Edward, 1968, My 28,47:3
Trumbull, Frank (funl, Jl 24,9:7), 1920, Jl 14,9:5
Trumbull, G, 1875, O 10,1:6
Trumbull, Grover C, 1962, My 26,25:6
Trumbull, Gurdon, 1903, D 29,9:5
Trumbull, H Clay Rev Dr, 1903, D 9,9:5
Trumbull, Henry, 1962, Jl 1,56:7
Trumbull, John H, 1961, My 22,31:1
Trumbull, Levi R, 1916, O 25,11:6
Trumbull, Lyman, 1896, Je 26,2:2
Trumbull, Lyman Mrs, 1914, Ap 14,11:6
Trumbull, Roscoe Hale, 1924, Ag 10,24:3
Trumbull, Thomas Col, 1865, Ap 9,8:5
Trumbull, Walter S, 1961, O 19,35:3
Trump, Edward N, 1944, Je 22,19:6
Trump, Robert W, 1950, N 7,27:1
Trumpbour, Edward A, 1963, Jl 15,29:2
Trumpbour, Frederick J Sr, 1953, Jl 14,27:6
Trumper, Jacob, 1954, Mr 11,31:3
Trumpfheller, Herman, 1953, Ja 3,15:3
Trumpler, George H, 1950, N 17,27:2
Trumpoldt, Otto G, 1941, Ja 19,41:2
Trumpy, Donald, 1958, N 24,29:3
Trumpy, Jean Rudolph, 1913, My 23,13:4
Trundy, Victor A, 1949, Je 14,31:4
Truner, Ernest A, 1938, My 2,17:5
Trunk, Anton L, 1968, My 15,47:4
Trunk, J J, 1961, Jl 9,77:1
Trunk, Joseph V, 1940, Jl 11,19:5
Trunk, Otto G, 1941, Ja 9,21:2
Trunk, Robert L, 1941, Ag 25,15:5
Trunz, Maximilian, 1959, Ja 17,19:2
Trupin, Julian C, 1958, My 23,23:4
Trupper, Vincent, 1941, F 24,15:1
Truppo, Vincent J, 1947, Ja 4,15:5
Truran, Ernest A, 1952, F 22,21:3
Truran, Walter W (por), 1947, Mr 9,60:4
Truscott, Barry, 1958, F 6,27:4
Truscott, Lucian K Jr, 1965, S 14,39:4
Truscott, Millwood, 1949, F 3,23:3
Truscott, Starr, 1946, Jl 18,25:3
Truscott, Starr Mrs, 1949, F 4,24:2
Trusdell, John G, 1903, Jl 16,7:6
Trusdell, Richard V Mrs, 1948, O 19,27:4
Truskowski, Robert, 1954, Mr 5,19:3
Trusler, N, 1880, F 2,3:6
Truslow, Francis A (funl, Jl 13,21:4), 1951, Jl 9,10:3
Truslow, Henry A, 1937, Je 2,23:4
Truslow, Henry A Mrs, 1949, Jl 17,56:6
Truslow, John, 1914, D 25,11:4
Truslow, Thomas H Mrs, 1944, Je 21,19:2
Truslow, Walter, 1958, Ag 23,15:5
Truslowe, Edward T, 1962, N 19,31:4
Truss, Cyprian, 1966, N 27,87:1
Truss, Isaac, 1963, D 11,47:2
Truss, William M, 1937, Ap 10,19:1
Trussell, Alva H, 1940, Ja 14,42:8
Trussell, Charles Prescott, 1968, O 3,47:1
Trussell, Percy L (por), 1949, N 3,29:3
Trussell, Verlyn A, 1947, Ap 28,23:5
Trust, Harry K, 1949, Ag 27,13:5
Trust, Harry Mrs, 1946, S 18,31:1
Trustum, Charles P, 1937, Ag 27,19:5
Trusty, William J, 1955, My 14,19:4
Truswell, Charles H, 1952, Je 30,19:2
Trutza, John, 1954, D 12,88:4
Truxal, Jacob Q, 1951, O 3,33:3
Trygger, Ernest (por), 1943, S 25,15:3
Tryggvadottir, Nina, 1968, Je 20,45:3
Trynin, Aaron H, 1967, Ag 23,51:1
Trynin, Max Mrs, 1955, D 15,37:2
Tryon, Dwight W, 1925, Jl 2,19:6
Tryon, Ellen I, 1945, N 4,43:2
Tryon, George H, 1938, O 21,23:2
Tryon, George R, 1925, Jl 27,13:4
Tryon, Gerard E Mrs, 1955, Ap 1,27:5
Tryon, Henry H, 1960, Ja 31,92:5
Tryon, Howard I, 1945, Mr 10,17:2
Tryon, James Rufus Rear-Adm, 1912, Mr 22,9:4
Tryon, Lewis R, 1951, N 24,11:2
Tryon, Lord, 1940, N 25,17:4
Tryon, Maurice F, 1963, Jl 22,23:4
Tryon, Rolla M, 1954, N 12,15:2
Tryon, Thomas L, 1945, D 19,25:2
Tryon, William A, 1943, Je 22,19:3
Tryon, Winifred M Mrs, 1948, F 6,26:6
Tsahai, Princess, 1942, Ag 20,19:3
Tsamis, Spiro G, 1952, Jl 2,25:3
Tsankov, Alex, 1959, Jl 19,68:3
Tsanoff, Stoyan, 1950, D 9,15:6
Tsao, Pao-yi, 1968, N 24,87:1
Tsarong Sawang, 1959, Je 22,7:4
Tschacbasov, Nahum Mrs, 1961, F 22,25:4
Tschaikowsky, P I, 1893, N 7,9:1
Tschakste, J, 1927, Mr 15,25:3
Tschammer und Osten, Hans von, 1943, Mr 26,19:5
Tschan, Francis J, 1957, Jl 25,23:1
Tschenhens, F X Rev, 1877, My 15,5:6
Tschida, Ethel, 1966, D 2,39:4
Tschiffely, A F, 1954, Ja 6,31:5
Tschimoke, Charles Herman, 1916, O 28,13:2
Tschirgi, Anthony, 1948, Mr 30,23:5
Tschirky, August, 1952, S 19,23:2
Tschirky, Leopold, 1960, Ag 8,21:4
Tschirky, Oscar, 1950, N 8,29:1
Tschirky, Oscar Mrs (por), 1939, Ja 12,19:3
Tschirnart, Mary, 1915, S 8,13:4
Tschirsky, Antoinetta Mrs, 1925, Jl 14,21:6
Tschopik, Harry S Jr, 1956, N 13,37:3
Tschorn, Robert H, 1948, Ap 23,23:3
Tschudi, G Von, 1928, O 9,31:3
Tschudi, Samuel W, 1945, S 29,15:2
Tschudl, Rudolph, 1923, Jl 25,11:5
Tschudy, Arnold N, 1955, Mr 14,23:5
Tschudy, Herbert B, 1946, Ap 16,25:1
Tschudy, Jay, 1946, Ja 14,19:2

Tschudy, Jay Mrs, 1954, Je 6,86:4
Tschumi, Jean, 1962, Ja 26,31:1
Tse, Capt, 1915, O 1,11:7
Tselishcheff, M I, 1938, Ap 23,6:7
Tsen, Phil L, 1954, Jl 30,17:2
Tseng, Marquis, 1890, Ap 13,16:4
Tseng Chi, Peter, 1951, My 11,27:1
Tsenoff, Krasto, 1938, N 13,44:7
Tseretelli, Iracli, 1959, My 22,27:1
Tshkakaya, Mikhail G, 1950, Mr 20,21:1
Tsiang, Tingfu F, 1965, O 11,39:4
Tsien, Tai, 1962, Ag 2,25:5
Tsirimokos, Elias, 1968, Jl 14,64:5
Tso-pin, Chiang, 1942, D 26,9:3
Tsolainos, Kyriakos Panyiotis, 1968, Ja 31,38:7
Tsolokoglou, George, 1948, My 23,70:1
Tsou Lu, 1954, F 14,93:1
Tsou Pao-Feng, 1944, S 9,15:4
Tsouderos, Emmanuel, 1956, F 11,17:3
Tsuchlya, Mitsuhard Gen, 1920, N 20,15:4
Tsui Shu-chin, 1957, Jl 18,25:3
Tsuji, Karoku, 1948, D 22,10:3
Tsukamoto, Seiji, 1945, Jl 13,11:6
Tsunehisa, Prince, 1919, Ap 25,15:4
Tsushima, Juichi, 1967, F 8,28:5
Tsutsumi, Yasujiro, 1964, Ap 26,88:2
Tsuzuki, Masao, 1961, Ap 5,37:4
Tsvetayev, Vyacheslav D, 1950, Ag 14,17:5
Tsvetkov, Nikolai I, 1955, Ja 26,25:3
Tsygichko, Patrovich, 1963, Ap 5,47:2
Ttagesser, John, 1948, Je 30,25:5
Tu, Theodoreth, 1939, Mr 21,23:1
Tu Yueh-sen, 1951, Ag 17,18:2
Tua, Angelo, 1955, Ja 22,11:6
Tuan Mao-lan, Mrs, 1956, N 20,37:2
Tuason, Bobby, 1948, Ag 10,22:2
Tubbs, Arthur L, 1946, Ja 29,25:4
Tubbs, Charles C, 1949, D 10,17:1
Tubbs, Edwin C, 1946, S 25,27:5
Tubbs, Frank D, 1939, F 27,15:6
Tubbs, Henry H Mrs, 1964, Ap 12,86:2
Tubbs, James, 1921, My 12,17:5
Tubbs, John L, 1937, O 6,25:4
Tubbs, Robert H, 1942, My 28,17:5
Tubbs, Samuel W, 1903, O 9,7:4
Tubbs, Warren, 1945, Ap 3,19:3
Tubbs, William, 1953, Ja 26,19:5; 1954, Je 30,27:6
Tubby, Josiah T, 1909, D 3,11:4; 1958, Jl 6,56:7
Tubby, William B, 1944, My 10,19:6
Tubelis, Jouzas (por), 1939, O 2,17:5
Tubman, James J, 1955, Jl 16,15:4
Tubridy, James, 1940, Ag 3,15:5
Tubridy, Michael, 1954, Ap 17,13:3
Tubridy, Mortimer B, 1949, My 29,36:5
Tuby, Martin H, 1957, D 28,18:1
Tucares, Alejo, 1956, Mr 28,36:1
Tucci, John D Mrs, 1958, N 20,35:2
Tucci, Michael, 1945, F 17,13:5
Tucciarone, Lodovico, 1953, Ag 22,15:1
Tuch, Herman, 1943, Ja 19,19:3
Tuch, Michael, 1950, S 3,38:6
Tuchapsky, Gregory, 1956, Jl 4,19:2
Tuchet-Jesson, Thomas P G (Baron Audley), 1963, Jl 4,17:3
Tuchmann, Leon (will, Ag 12,17:1), 1938, Ag 5,17:5
Tucich, Serge De, 1940, S 28,17:6
Tuck, Alex J M, 1955, Mr 19,15:3
Tuck, Amos, 1879, D 13,2:6
Tuck, Arthur E, 1940, F 14,21:4
Tuck, Davis H, 1953, Jl 7,27:6
Tuck, Edgar A, 1955, O 9,86:2
Tuck, Edward (will, Ag 16,22:2), 1938, My 1,II,7:1
Tuck, Fred B, 1953, N 4,33:2
Tuck, Gaillard O, 1944, Ja 20,19:1
Tuck, Henry Dr, 1904, S 3,7:6
Tuck, Jenny, 1924, Mr 3,17:4
Tuck, John B Sr, 1955, Je 1,33:4
Tuck, Nat N, 1943, Mr 5,17:5
Tuck, S Pinkney, 1967, Ap 23,94:1
Tuck, Somerville P Mrs, 1940, Ap 15,17:5
Tuck, Somerville Pinkney Judge, 1923, Ap 15,6:3
Tuck, Theodore C, 1953, My 22,27:3
Tuck, Theodore Mrs, 1937, D 9,25:3
Tuck, William H, 1937, Ag 9,20:2; 1966, Ag 31,43:3
Tuck, William W, 1956, Jl 14,15:3
Tucker, Alanson, 1909, My 2,11:5
Tucker, Alfred Robert Rev, 1914, Je 16,9:6
Tucker, Alfred W, 1959, Ap 14,35:2
Tucker, Allen, 1939, Ja 27,19:4
Tucker, Andrew J, 1950, F 15,21:3
Tucker, Anna Mrs, 1938, S 30,21:4
Tucker, Arthur C, 1945, D 16,40:4
Tucker, Arthur L, 1942, Jl 3,17:6
Tucker, Arthur R, 1959, Mr 26,31:2
Tucker, Benjamin R, 1939, Je 23,19:4
Tucker, Bert J, 1953, Ap 22,29:3
Tucker, Beverley R, 1945, Je 20,23:3
Tucker, Carl, 1949, My 1,88:6
Tucker, Carl E, 1944, Mr 19,42:1
Tucker, Carll, 1956, Jl 30,21:3
Tucker, Carll Jr, 1968, F 8,43:3
Tucker, Carlos P Dr, 1912, Mr 12,13:4
Tucker, Carlton E, 1966, Ja 18,34:1
Tucker, Caroline, 1946, O 26,17:5
Tucker, Caroline S, 1939, F 18,15:4
Tucker, Charles A, 1954, D 8,35:1
Tucker, Charles J, 1939, Ja 27,19:5
Tucker, Charles L, 1957, S 30,31:5
Tucker, Charles L Mrs, 1941, F 2,44:2
Tucker, Charles Mrs (V Irwin), 1957, Jl 3,23:3
Tucker, Cissy Mrs (C Fitzgerald), 1941, My 11,44:5
Tucker, Clare de R Mrs, 1939, Mr 17,21:2
Tucker, Clarence A, 1948, Je 30,25:4
Tucker, Clarence J, 1949, Ap 15,23:3
Tucker, Clinton K, 1956, Ag 11,13:4
Tucker, Cummings H Jr, 1938, F 22,21:2
Tucker, David, 1950, D 17,84:5
Tucker, David A, 1958, Je 5,31:4
Tucker, David C, 1907, Ja 25,9:4
Tucker, Edward M, 1939, Ap 23,III,6:8
Tucker, Edward S, 1950, My 26,23:4
Tucker, Edwin A H, 1943, Ap 22,23:5
Tucker, Edwin H, 1939, Ap 27,25:1
Tucker, Edwin W, 1967, D 18,47:2
Tucker, Eli, 1879, Je 15,7:2
Tucker, Elizabeth F Mrs, 1937, Mr 6,17:3
Tucker, Emma C, 1953, Je 6,17:6
Tucker, Enos Houghton, 1907, D 31,7:6
Tucker, Ernest E, 1958, Ja 18,15:5
Tucker, Eugene A, 1942, D 30,23:5
Tucker, Everard K, 1940, N 3,57:3
Tucker, F Elwood, 1949, N 11,25:3
Tucker, Francis F, 1957, D 3,35:6
Tucker, Frank, 1946, My 2,21:4
Tucker, Frank H, 1956, My 28,27:4
Tucker, Frank L, 1944, My 30,21:3
Tucker, Frank P, 1953, Je 12,27:1
Tucker, Frank W, 1943, N 4,23:4
Tucker, Gabriel, 1958, Ap 19,21:4
Tucker, Gardiner C, 1941, N 11,24:2
Tucker, George B, 1943, D 23,19:5
Tucker, George C, 1947, Ag 3,52:8
Tucker, George H, 1952, N 18,31:2
Tucker, George Loane, 1921, Je 22,15:3
Tucker, Gilbert N, 1955, My 25,33:1
Tucker, Gilman Henry, 1913, N 15,11:6
Tucker, H St G, 1932, Jl 24,23:8
Tucker, Harold, 1951, Ap 5,29:1
Tucker, Harrison A, 1943, Je 30,21:4
Tucker, Harrison A Mrs, 1903, Ap 22,9:5
Tucker, Harry, 1944, Mr 18,13:4
Tucker, Helen L, 1949, Ja 1,13:4
Tucker, Henry L, 1949, S 11,95:4
Tucker, Henry O'Reilly, 1910, Jl 17,II,9:4
Tucker, Henry St G (trb lr, Ag 26,28:5), 1959, Ag 9, 88:1
Tucker, Henry St G Mrs, 1962, S 16,86:7
Tucker, Herbert N, 1945, Je 23,13:4
Tucker, Herman F, 1955, F 3,23:1
Tucker, Hibbard A, 1946, S 27,23:6
Tucker, Howard H, 1954, Ap 20,29:1
Tucker, Hugh C, 1956, N 6,35:2
Tucker, Hugh C Mrs, 1953, Ja 13,32:3
Tucker, Irvin B, 1943, D 25,13:4
Tucker, Irving E, 1946, Jl 30,23:3
Tucker, J Driscoll, 1945, Ja 21,40:2
Tucker, J Randolph, 1945, Ap 5,23:3
Tucker, J Robley, 1954, Jl 9,17:4
Tucker, J W, 1878, O 20,7:4
Tucker, J W Jr, 1878, O 20,7:4
Tucker, Jack, 1968, Mr 23,31:4
Tucker, Jacob, 1940, Jl 31,17:2
Tucker, James C Judge, 1923, Jl 31,17:5
Tucker, James W, 1961, N 5,89:1
Tucker, John E, 1949, N 29,29:3
Tucker, John F, 1921, Mr 1,13:4
Tucker, John H, 1946, F 3,40:3
Tucker, John J Mrs, 1956, O 9,35:2
Tucker, John R, 1956, Ja 24,32:6
Tucker, John W, 1942, Ap 4,13:7
Tucker, Joseph, 1867, S 16,5:3
Tucker, Joseph B, 1959, Jl 27,25:4
Tucker, Joseph J, 1962, O 15,29:2
Tucker, Katherine, 1957, Je 7,23:2
Tucker, Kenneth, 1952, N 9,91:2
Tucker, Kenneth J, 1939, Mr 5,49:2
Tucker, Lawrence A, 1944, Mr 22,19:4
Tucker, Lewis P, 1942, Ja 8,21:4
Tucker, Louis, 1952, My 27,27:1
Tucker, Louis A, 1957, N 7,35:5
Tucker, Lucy Sister, 1950, S 16,19:5
Tucker, Luther, 1873, Ja 28,1:6
Tucker, Luther H, 1950, Jl 19,31:4
Tucker, Marshall C, 1949, S 1,21:4
Tucker, Marvin E, 1955, Jl 13,25:5
Tucker, Mary E, 1951, Ap 2,25:4
Tucker, Mary L Mrs, 1940, Mr 18,17:5
Tucker, Meyer, 1956, Je 28,29:2
Tucker, Milton Mrs, 1944, Ap 7,19:4
Tucker, Murray E, 1945, Ja 17,21:2
Tucker, Nelson T, 1942, N 21,13:5
Tucker, Nion R, 1950, Ap 23,92:5
Tucker, Nora, 1939, N 11,15:1
Tucker, Norman M, 1951, F 24,13:3
Tucker, Oliver D, 1940, Jl 14,30:8
Tucker, Oscar G, 1962, Ja 25,31:4
Tucker, P P Mrs, 1941, Ja 14,21:2
Tucker, Preston, 1956, D 27,25:1
Tucker, R Evans Jr, 1954, N 20,17:6
Tucker, Randolph, 1897, F 14,5:4
Tucker, Ray, 1963, My 2,35:5
Tucker, Ray Mrs, 1960, Jl 17,61:2
Tucker, Raymond W, 1937, Je 10,23:6
Tucker, Richard, 1942, D 9,27:3; 1958, Ap 20,85:1
Tucker, Richard B, 1959, N 27,29:3
Tucker, Richard D Mrs, 1956, F 7,31:5
Tucker, Richard H, 1952, Ap 1,29:6
Tucker, Robert B, 1948, D 6,25:2
Tucker, Robert C, 1948, Jl 20,24:3
Tucker, Robert F, 1952, S 13,17:5
Tucker, Robert G, 1941, Jl 19,13:1
Tucker, Robert J, 1949, Ap 11,25:6
Tucker, Ross F Prof, 1937, D 27,16:3
Tucker, Roy E, 1959, Je 22,25:2
Tucker, Ruel E, 1966, Ag 22,29:6
Tucker, Ruth Mrs, 1955, My 2,21:4
Tucker, Samuel A, 1947, F 24,20:2; 1949, O 15,15:3
Tucker, Samuel A Mrs, 1948, O 14,29:2
Tucker, Samuel M, 1962, F 21,45:1
Tucker, Sophie (funl plans, F 11,33:4; mem ser, F 12,27:1), 1966, F 10,1:8
Tucker, Spurgeon, 1968, Je 7,39:1
Tucker, Stanley A Mrs (Dorothy Mae Shackelford), 1968, D 30,31:2
Tucker, Sydnor J, 1944, S 8,19:6
Tucker, Thomas H, 1944, Ap 18,21:5
Tucker, W J Dr, 1926, S 30,25:3
Tucker, Wentworth Capt, 1919, S 14,22:4
Tucker, Wilbur T, 1953, F 12,28:3
Tucker, William, 1875, My 2,6:6
Tucker, William B, 1954, D 27,17:3
Tucker, William C, 1961, Ap 14,29:5
Tucker, William E, 1938, D 4,60:8; 1958, Ja 9,33:4
Tucker, William G, 1942, F 22,26:4
Tucker, William H, 1948, O 4,23:4; 1954, O 8,23:2
Tucker, William J Mrs, 1944, Ap 17,23:5
Tucker, William P, 1959, My 27,35:1
Tucker, Willis G Jr, 1949, S 26,25:4
Tucker, Willis Gaylord Dr, 1922, Ap 23,28:3
Tucker, Wilson H, 1960, Je 6,86:6
Tucker, Winston H, 1958, Ag 4,21:5
Tuckerman, Alfred, 1925, My 26,21:5
Tuckerman, Bayard, 1923, O 21,23:2
Tuckerman, Eliot, 1959, O 30,27:2
Tuckerman, Eliot Mrs, 1955, N 29,29:2
Tuckerman, Emily, 1924, Ap 20,22:2
Tuckerman, Henry T (funl), 1871, D 21,8:2
Tuckerman, Jane F, 1947, O 19,64:3
Tuckerman, Lucius C Mrs, 1961, Je 30,27:4
Tuckerman, Lucius Mrs, 1906, Ag 27,7:7
Tuckerman, Maury, 1966, O 24,39:5
Tuckerman, Paul, 1940, S 10,23:1
Tuckerman, Paul Mrs, 1956, Ja 24,31:6
Tuckerman, Roger, 1967, Ag 15,36:3
Tuckerman, Walter R, 1961, Ja 16,27:4
Tuckerman, Walter R Mrs, 1954, Ja 3,90:5
Tuckley, James H, 1954, O 23,15:5
Tuckley, William H, 1940, Ap 23,23:2
Tucknell, Gertrude, 1951, Ag 7,25:5
Tudhope, Frederic A J, 1951, Mr 26,23:3
Tudisco, Gaetano, 1957, D 3,35:2
Tudor, Charles E, 1952, Mr 18,27:1
Tudor, Frank Gwynne, 1922, Ja 11,21:6
Tudor, Frederic, 1939, Ap 10,17:6
Tudor, Frederick C T, 1946, Ap 15,27:4
Tudor, Harold T, 1956, Mr 24,19:4
Tudor, Isla, 1916, S 25,9:5
Tudor, Jacob, 1945, S 20,23:3
Tudor, Ralph A, 1963, N 14,35:1
Tudor, Robert L (por), 1949, My 15,90:3
Tudor, Rosamund Mrs, 1949, Je 27,27:3
Tuduc, King of Annam, 1883, Ag 4,1:3
Tuechter, August, 1947, My 18,60:7
Tuefel, Fred, 1951, O 11,29:5
Tuel, A Y, 1935, Ag 28,18:1
Tuell, Anne K, 1960, Mr 29,37:2
Tuell, Samuel B, 1942, Jl 4,17:3
Tuensel, Alfred, 1946, S 4,23:5
Tuerk, Fred, 1954, Ap 4,87:1
Tuerk, Jacob, 1940, Ja 29,16:2
Tuerk, Jacob Mrs, 1953, O 5,27:3
Tuerk, John, 1951, My 27,68:4
Tuers, George E, 1942, Ap 22,23:5
Tufaro, Dominick C, 1961, D 3,88:3
Tufflash, Charles, 1945, S 7,23:3
Tuffley, Francis T, 1954, F 4,25:5
Tuffly, Louis F, 1945, N 10,15:4
Tuffy, Patrick J Mrs, 1955, Ag 22,21:6
Tuft, Grover C, 1952, D 3,33:3
Tufts, Bowen Mrs, 1957, Mr 10,88:5
Tufts, Charles Wellington, 1906, Je 29,9:7
Tufts, Edgar H, 1942, Je 16,23:3
Tufts, Fletcher G, 1942, My 15,19:4
Tufts, Irving E, 1953, F 5,23:2
Tufts, James A, 1938, N 22,23:3
Tufts, James H, 1942, Ag 7,17:3
Tufts, Joseph P, 1953, O 14,29:2
Tufts, Leonard (por), 1945, F 20,19:1
Tufts, Leonard Mrs, 1940, Je 15,15:6

Tufts, Nathan A, 1952, N 10,25:1
Tufts, Ray S, 1941, Jl 5,11:4
Tufts, Richard S Mrs, 1961, D 28,27:3
Tufts, S P Maj, 1903, O 22,9:6
Tufts, Timothy, 1910, Ag 8,7:4
Tufts, Walter, 1944, N 7,27:2
Tufts, Warner, 1948, Mr 28,48:3
Tuge of Tonga, Uiliami Prince Consort, 1941, Jl 22, 20:2
Tugliglowicz, Peter, 1947, F 12,25:4
Tugwell, Charles, 1949, Mr 3,25:2
Tugwell, Charles Mrs, 1961, D 6,48:1
Tuigg, Patrick J, 1940, Jl 23,19:5
Tuinen, Christoffel van, 1947, Ja 31,23:4
Tuiney, Thomas B Prof, 1913, S 25,13:6
Tuite, Charles P, 1949, Ap 14,25:5
Tuite, Charles R, 1938, Ja 5,21:3
Tujague, Henry A, 1953, Ap 29,29:5
Tukachinsky, Saul Mrs, 1966, S 26,41:5
Tuke, Fred, 1960, F 18,33:3
Tukey, Adelaide, 1910, F 7,9:5
Tukey, Phil E, 1950, Jl 30,60:2
Tulchin, Simon H Mrs, 1967, F 1,39:3
Tulcin, Henry P, 1946, My 1,26:2
Tulenheimo, Antti, 1952, S 4,27:5
Tules, Phoebe Mrs, 1920, F 28,11:4
Tuley, Murray F, 1905, D 26,8:1
Tulez, Juan, 1948, S 5,40:7
Tulgan, Joseph, 1957, S 17,35:2
Tulian, Gaius D, 1944, Jl 22,15:5
Tulimieri, Angelo, 1962, Jl 1,56:7
Tulin, Mischa, 1957, Mr 21,22:6
Tulipan, Louis, 1963, N 28,39:2
Tulis, Amanda Mrs, 1920, F 20,15:4
Tulis, Jeanne, 1920, F 20,15:4
Tulk, Norman A, 1960, Ap 4,29:4
Tull, Harry C, 1939, Jl 19,19:6
Tull, Herbert H, 1937, My 15,19:5
Tull, John C, 1937, D 9,25:5
Tull, Richard, 1908, F 10,9:4
Tull, Rudulph F, 1958, Jl 23,27:4
Tullar, Charles E, 1949, O 27,27:5
Tullar, Grant C, 1950, My 21,104:5
Tuller, W Lee Mrs (will, My 7,28:4), 1953, Ap 29, 29:5
Tuller, Walter K, 1939, S 28,25:1
Tuller, William L, 1946, My 6,21:2
Tulley, George H, 1966, N 13,88:8
Tulley, Herbert G, 1945, D 15,17:4
Tullgren, Herbert W, 1944, F 24,15:4
Tulling, Frans, 1943, S 2,19:4
Tullis, Don D, 1964, Ja 27,23:4
Tullis, Heber H, 1958, Ap 15,33:2
Tullis, J, 1878, Mr 18,1:4
Tulloch, David J, 1938, S 21,25:4
Tulloch, Donald C, 1949, Ag 29,17:3
Tulloch, John W, 1951, Ja 9,29:2
Tulloch, Marshall E, 1954, N 13,15:2
Tulloch, Marshall Mrs, 1949, O 24,23:5
Tulloch, Thomas G, 1938, Je 10,21:2
Tullock, Gilbert, 1940, Ap 28,36:4
Tullock, Margaret DeW, 1959, O 7,43:4
Tulloss, Rees E, 1959, Je 9,37:3
Tullsen, Stanley A, 1950, N 8,29:5
Tully, Andrew M Dr, 1950, Je 15,14:3
Tully, C Eugene, 1954, Ap 28,31:1
Tully, Charles F, 1940, Je 15,15:5
Tully, Edward A Sr, 1964, Mr 8,87:2
Tully, Eugene P, 1963, S 1,56:4
Tully, Eva M, 1937, Jl 29,19:3
Tully, Francis J, 1940, Ap 11,26:2; 1945, Ap 4,21:3
Tully, Francis W, 1943, Jl 9,17:4
Tully, Francis W Mrs, 1960, F 8,29:2
Tully, Frank P Sr, 1949, My 18,27:6
Tully, Henry J, 1968, Ap 7,92:6
Tully, J H, 1931, Je 9,27:2
Tully, James F Mrs, 1949, Je 7,32:3
Tully, James H, 1964, N 29,87:2
Tully, Jasper, 1938, S 17,17:3
Tully, Jim, 1947, Je 23,23:3
Tully, John G, 1874, Ag 9,8:2
Tully, John J, 1946, Ja 15,23:5
Tully, Joseph E, 1953, My 10,89:1
Tully, Joseph F, 1939, Ja 31,21:5
Tully, Joseph M, 1943, O 16,13:3; 1963, My 2,35:2
Tully, Leo L, 1959, D 5,23:6
Tully, Leo L Mrs, 1953, Jl 20,17:5
Tully, Luke H, 1943, Ja 14,21:2
Tully, May, 1924, Mr 11,19:2
Tully, Michael, 1950, Mr 1,27:4
Tully, Michael J Rev, 1915, O 21,11:6
Tully, Paul B, 1963, Je 6,35:1
Tully, Richard W, 1945, F 2,19:1
Tully, Richard Whitestone, 1913, D 8,11:4
Tully, Thomas A, 1937, Ja 9,17:3; 1950, My 14,106:5
Tully, Thomas De Quincey, 1925, Mr 31,19:4
Tully, Thomas H, 1951, Ap 11,29:2
Tully, Thomas J, 1958, N 5,35:1
Tully, William J Mrs, 1958, Ja 20,23:2
Tully, William Mrs, 1923, Jl 30,13:5
Tulovsky, Joseph, 1949, N 27,104:4
Tuma, Charles, 1954, O 15,23:3
Tuma, Vladimir, 1955, D 15,37:3
Tumbelston, William H, 1955, Jl 19,27:5
Tumber, Percy F, 1950, Ag 29,27:2
Tumbleston, Robert T, 1954, Je 26,13:6
Tumblety, Peter E, 1954, N 5,21:2
Tumbridge, John W, 1945, Mr 18,42:6
Tumbridge, John W Mrs, 1907, Mr 8,9:7
Tumbridge, Judd, 1947, Je 2,25:4
Tumbridge, William Capt, 1921, My 22,22:4
Tumen, Abraham O, 1946, F 15,25:2
Tumen, David, 1953, Ap 28,27:4
Tumen, H Jonas, 1943, Ag 31,17:2
Tummel, Aug H, 1949, D 8,33:5
Tumpane, Frank, 1967, N 25,39:1
Tumulty, Felix E, 1959, Ja 10,17:4
Tumulty, James, 1939, Ag 3,19:3
Tumulty, James Sr Mrs, 1949, Ag 8,15:5
Tumulty, Joseph P, 1954, Ap 9,23:1
Tumulty, Joseph P Mrs, 1952, Ja 4,23:2
Tumulty, Philip (funl, N 23,11:1), 1918, N 21,15:4
Tumulty, Thomas F, 1953, D 29,23:5
Tune, Graham M, 1955, Je 21,2:4
Tune, Lewis J, 1939, Ja 22,34:7
Tunell, George G, 1942, Ap 30,19:4
Tung, Chien-sen, 1950, Jl 2,24:7
Tung Li Yuan, 1965, F 7,92:3
Tung Yiu, 1959, N 29,86:8
Tunglien, Chao, 1950, D 12,33:3
Tunick, Abraham Mrs, 1954, Ja 6,31:4
Tunick, Archibald H Mrs, 1966, My 31,43:1
Tunick, Barney Mrs, 1953, N 24,29:3
Tunick, Benjamin I, 1939, My 16,23:6
Tunick, Harry, 1959, Jl 25,17:3
Tunick, Isidor S, 1949, D 23,22:2
Tunick, Jacques C, 1967, My 18,47:1
Tunick, Louis Mrs, 1957, Ag 19,19:6
Tunick, Michael, 1951, F 21,27:3
Tunick, Richard, 1961, My 12,29:2
Tunick, Walter B, 1952, Ja 30,25:3
Tunicliff, Nelson H (will), 1938, F 19,17:1
Tunik, Joseph Dr, 1968, Je 18,47:4
Tunis, Allyn B, 1948, Ap 29,23:4
Tunis, Annis L, 1951, Ja 8,10:5
Tunis, Bey of (Sidi Ahmed II), 1942, Je 20,13:6
Tunis, Beylof Sidi Mohammed el Sadok, 1882, O 29, 9:2
Tunis, John B, 1953, Mr 4,27:4
Tunis, Robert, 1959, Ja 29,27:1
Tunis, Robert W, 1939, O 29,40:8
Tunison, Florence N L Mrs (will), 1941, Ag 3,28:2
Tunison, George M, 1954, D 5,89:2
Tunison, Joseph S, 1916, O 5,11:4
Tunison, Lester B, 1950, Ap 13,29:4
Tunison, Richard G Dr, 1937, O 13,23:6
Tunison, William F, 1942, N 3,23:1
Tunitsky, Leon J Mrs, 1949, Mr 6,72:1
Tunmore, John S, 1946, Ap 6,17:4
Tunnard, T Edward, 1950, S 26,31:5
Tunnard, William L Mrs, 1951, Je 6,31:4
Tunnecliffe, Thomas, 1948, F 3,25:2
Tunnel, John E, 1944, F 11,19:3
Tunnell, Frederic H, 1956, Mr 29,27:5
Tunnell, George P, 1949, Ag 13,11:2
Tunnell, George P Mrs, 1947, N 12,27:1
Tunner, Etta, 1961, Je 6,37:3
Tunner, Joseph Mrs, 1956, O 24,37:4
Tunner, Joseph R, 1957, Je 2,86:4
Tunner, Ruth, 1958, Mr 21,21:1
Tunney, J Stanley, 1964, Mr 30,29:4
Tunney, Michael J Mrs, 1949, F 6,77:1
Tunney, Thomas J, 1952, Ja 27,76:7
Tunney, Vincent W, 1955, N 23,23:3
Tunnicliff, Ruth, 1946, S 23,23:5
Tunnicliffe, Richard M (will), 1963, Ag 29,29:1
Tunstall, Alfred M Mrs, 1953, Ag 20,27:2
Tunstall, Harry E, 1940, Ap 20,17:3
Tunstall, Richard Baylor, 1919, O 13,13:4
Tunstall, Robert B, 1956, D 31,13:4
Tuohy, James M, 1923, S 8,13:5
Tuohy, John M, 1954, O 10,86:8
Tuohy, Joseph, 1914, My 21,11:5
Tuohy, Matthew Mrs, 1956, Ap 7,19:4
Tuohy, Michael S, 1957, Ap 5,27:4
Tuohy, Payton J, 1947, D 5,26:2
Tuohy, R Joseph, 1942, D 13,72:2
Tuohy, Thomas J, 1956, Ap 8,84:1
Tuohy, Walter J (funl, My 17,47:1), 1966, My 13, 41:1
Tuomey, James W, 1956, Mr 24,19:6
Tuomey, James W Mrs, 1942, Mr 2,19:4
Tuomioja, Sakari S (funl, S 17,43:1), 1964, S 10,35:2
Tuozzo, Anthony F, 1958, O 7,35:2
Tupes, Ernest E, 1941, S 28,48:4
Tupholme, Allen J, 1949, My 5,27:2
Tuppen, Charles F, 1947, O 16,27:5
Tupper, Allen P, 1913, N 15,11:7
Tupper, Charles Mrs, 1912, My 12,II,17:3
Tupper, Charles Sir, 1915, O 31,17:3
Tupper, Edward J, 1922, O 3,21:5
Tupper, Frank E, 1964, Je 28,57:3
Tupper, Frank E Mrs, 1955, D 13,40:1
Tupper, Frederick, 1950, F 13,21:3
Tupper, Frederick M, 1951, My 18,27:2
Tupper, James W, 1953, Je 5,27:3
Tupper, Laura O, 1940, Jl 21,28:8
Tupper, M F, 1889, N 30,5:2
Tupper, Orvis H, 1938, Je 3,21:4
Tupper, Reginald G O, 1945, Mr 7,21:4
Tupper, S G, 1917, Ap 16,13:5
Tupper, Sheridan, 1904, Ap 11,9:5
Tupper, Tristram, 1954, D 31,13:4
Tupper, Valentine R, 1962, Mr 31,25:5
Tupper, Waldo T, 1951, Ja 20,15:3
Tupper, William J, 1947, D 17,29:4
Turano, Charles L, 1942, N 29,65:1
Turbay, Barbara de, 1940, Ja 23,21:4
Turbay, Gabriel, 1947, N 18,29:1
Turbert, Edward J, 1953, Ap 5,77:1
Turbet, Frank A, 1963, Ag 7,33:5
Turbett, Catherine G Mrs, 1948, Mr 17,25:3
Turbett, Frank A, 1944, My 6,15:3
Turbow, Leo, 1956, O 24,37:5
Turbow, Leo Mrs, 1967, Ap 14,39:4
Turbyfill, Charles O, 1966, O 25,48:2
Turbyville, Fred, 1947, Ja 19,53:4
Turcas, Jules, 1917, Mr 17,13:6
Turchin, Ben, 1956, N 27,37:3
Turchin, J B, 1901, Je 20,7:6
Turchin, Meyer V, 1944, My 19,19:2
Turchio, Vincent, 1950, O 1,51:1
Turcios Lima, Luis A, 1966, O 4,18:1
Turck, Dana, 1958, Ja 8,47:4
Turck, F B Dr, 1932, N 17,19:1
Turck, Fenton B Mrs, 1949, Ja 3,23:5
Turck, Harry, 1903, Jl 27,3:3
Turck, Joseph, 1946, D 12,29:5
Turck, Solomon, 1907, F 1,9:4
Turck, William J, 1952, Ag 21,19:6
Turcott, Jack (Jno K), 1965, Je 18,35:1
Turcotte, Edmond E, 1960, N 22,35:2
Turcotte, Frederick A, 1944, My 13,19:2
Turcotte, Joseph L, 1959, Ag 30,82:4
Turczynski, Josef, 1953, D 28,21:1
Turecamo, Bartholdi, 1963, D 30,21:2
Turek, Blaise, 1951, Je 10,92:4
Turek, Charles P Jr, 1956, Mr 23,27:2
Turek, James, 1946, Ag 24,11:3
Turek, Thomas, 1950, My 2,29:1
Turel, Severin, 1958, N 30,86:4
Turell, Neil B, 1961, N 11,23:5
Turetsky, Victor, 1968, Ag 5,39:3
Turetzky, William, 1959, Ja 28,31:3
Turgenieff, Ivan, 1883, S 5,5:1
Turgenieff, Ivan (funl), 1883, O 10,1:4
Turgeon, Onesiphore, 1944, N 19,50:7
Turgeon, Raphael, 1962, Ja 28,76:3
Turiansky, Abraham, 1956, Mr 20,23:4
Turies, Caroline Mrs, 1915, D 25,7:5
Turina y Perez, Joaquin, 1949, Ja 15,17:6
Turinax, C F, 1918, O 22,13:1
Turino, Michael, 1966, Ap 4,24:7
Turitz, Morris, 1957, D 26,19:3
Turk, Edward W, 1950, F 28,29:4
Turk, Harold L, 1968, My 29,39:2
Turk, Herman Mrs, 1945, Mr 20,19:1
Turk, James B, 1954, S 29,31:5
Turk, Louis E Mrs, 1943, Jl 23,17:2
Turk, Milton H, 1949, My 28,15:7
Turk, Milton H Mrs, 1938, Ap 20,23:2
Turk, Morris H, 1939, Mr 4,15:5
Turk, Peter, 1956, Jl 5,25:5
Turk, Richard J Jr, 1961, N 6,37:2
Turk, Robert J, 1950, Ja 12,27:2
Turk-Rohn, Baroness O V, 1940, F 27,21:6
Turkel, Bernard, 1938, Mr 15,23:4
Turkel, Henry L, 1957, O 7,27:3
Turkel, Herman, 1939, My 6,17:3
Turkel, John Mrs (Roma Rudd Turkel), 1968, Mr 8, 39:4
Turkevich, Leonid (Metropolitan Leonty),(funl, My 21,35:1), 1965, My 15,31:1
Turkgeldi, Emin A, 1955, Ap 30,17:4
Turkin, Henry, 1955, Je 25,15:3
Turkington, Andrew J, 1943, D 30,18:2
Turkington, David C, 1953, N 22,88:5
Turkington, Frank H, 1937, O 7,27:1
Turkington, Samuel J, 1955, Ja 14,21:1
Turkish, Harry, 1963, Ap 25,33:5
Turkish, Harry A, 1960, S 20,39:3
Turkish Minister Djemil Mehemed Pasha, 1872, S 25, 1:7
Turkle, Alonso J Rev, 1937, O 16,19:5
Turkow, Jonas Mrs (D Blumenfeld), 1961, S 5,35:2
Turkus, Daniel Mrs, 1953, Mr 7,15:3
Turkus, Samuel, 1946, Jl 18,25:3
Turkus, Seymour H, 1964, Ja 25,23:6
Turl, Joseph Mrs, 1945, Ap 4,21:3
Turletes, Nicholas, 1951, F 26,23:5
Turley, J Frank Sr, 1950, Ap 4,29:4
Turley, John F, 1946, D 11,31:2
Turley, Mary F Mrs, 1950, Mr 29,29:3
Turley, Rocco M, 1942, Jl 10,17:4
Turley, Thomas B Ex-Sen, 1910, Jl 2,7:5
Turlington, Edgar, 1959, S 28,31:1
Turman, Moe, 1957, Je 17,23:4
Turn, John S, 1953, Ap 8,29:5
Turn, John S Mrs, 1953, Ja 23,20:3

Turnage, Needham C, 1949, Je 19,68:8
Turnansky, Phil, 1949, D 1,31:4
Turnau, Josef, 1954, O 3,86:4
Turnblazer, William, 1944, Ap 23,42:7
Turnbull, Alfred C, 1962, S 19,40:1
Turnbull, Alfred C Mrs, 1963, S 28,19:3
Turnbull, Alice, 1938, F 1,21:1
Turnbull, Andrew B, 1960, O 18,39:1
Turnbull, Archibald D, 1958, Ja 5,86:8
Turnbull, Arthur, 1939, D 3,60:4
Turnbull, Barton P (por), 1948, My 12,27:1
Turnbull, Charles N, 1874, D 6,10:4
Turnbull, Charles S Dr, 1918, F 22,11:5
Turnbull, David F, 1946, N 16,19:3
Turnbull, David F Mrs, 1950, Je 14,31:3
Turnbull, Donald R, 1950, Ja 22,78:2
Turnbull, Dora A Mrs (P Wentworth), 1961, F 1,35:2
Turnbull, E Carlton, 1938, N 18,21:2
Turnbull, E Stanley, 1966, S 22,47:1
Turnbull, Edward, 1924, Mr 6,17:3
Turnbull, Ernest H Mrs, 1948, O 7,30:3
Turnbull, Frank Lt-Com, 1903, D 10,9:5
Turnbull, Frank S, 1923, Ja 6,13:6
Turnbull, Frank S Mrs, 1946, Jl 3,25:4
Turnbull, George, 1923, Jl 28,7:6; 1938, Ag 7,33:4
Turnbull, George R, 1909, My 14,9:5
Turnbull, Graeme, 1956, Ag 5,77:1
Turnbull, H, 1934, Ap 9,17:3
Turnbull, Henry P, 1952, Ja 9,29:5
Turnbull, Horatio W, 1940, Ap 30,21:2
Turnbull, J Gordon, 1953, Ap 3,24:5
Turnbull, James A, 1938, F 5,15:3
Turnbull, James L, 1955, D 4,88:3
Turnbull, Jennie, 1912, Je 16,II,17:5
Turnbull, Joel T, 1943, O 1,19:3
Turnbull, John D, 1946, Jl 23,25:5
Turnbull, John L, 1950, Je 22,27:5
Turnbull, Laura S, 1955, D 19,27:6
Turnbull, March, 1943, O 13,23:3
Turnbull, Margaret, 1942, Je 13,15:6
Turnbull, Mary E, 1952, D 30,19:2
Turnbull, N S Jr, 1944, Ap 1,13:6
Turnbull, Ogden P, 1949, D 16,31:2
Turnbull, R Rev, 1877, N 21,4:5
Turnbull, Ramsay, 1924, Ag 6,13:4
Turnbull, Ramsay Mrs, 1957, Mr 11,25:2
Turnbull, Ray W, 1958, N 9,88:4
Turnbull, Robert J, 1951, F 7,29:5
Turnbull, Robert J Mrs, 1953, Ja 7,31:4
Turnbull, W, 1888, S 8,4:7
Turnbull, Wallace R, 1954, N 27,13:5
Turnbull, Werd W, 1951, D 24,13:4
Turnbull, William B Sr, 1946, O 29,25:6
Turnbull, William F, 1937, My 17,19:5
Turnbull, William G, 1944, Mr 12,37:3
Turnbull, William M, 1961, Jl 29,19:5
Turnbull, William Mrs, 1949, D 23,21:4
Turnbull, William W, 1964, Je 15,29:3
Turnbull, Willis A, 1939, O 28,15:4
Turneaure, Frederick E, 1951, Ap 2,25:3
Turner, A B, 1903, Je 10,9:6
Turner, A D, 1919, Ap 9,11:1
Turner, A Murray, 1938, Ap 12,23:6
Turner, Abby H, 1957, N 27,31:3
Turner, Albert, 1916, S 3,19:7
Turner, Albert M, 1944, Je 29,23:4
Turner, Alexander, 1945, Mr 21,23:4
Turner, Alfred, 1961, Jl 4,19:4
Turner, Allan B, 1954, N 20,17:5
Turner, Allan P, 1939, Mr 25,15:2
Turner, Andrew J Mrs, 1940, Jl 20,15:5
Turner, Archelaus E, 1938, Je 25,15:4
Turner, Archibald, 1907, Je 19,7:5
Turner, Archibald A, 1960, Ap 20,39:4
Turner, Arnold K, 1941, Ap 25,19:3
Turner, Arthur B, 1948, F 7,15:4
Turner, Arthur E, 1947, D 14,76:7
Turner, Arthur W, 1943, N 16,23:2; 1951, N 19,23:5
Turner, Beatrice P, 1948, Ag 5,21:3
Turner, Ben (por), 1942, O 2,25:3
Turner, Benjamin F Sr, 1950, My 26,23:3
Turner, Bennett, 1945, Ag 20,19:6
Turner, Bertrand H, 1946, F 26,25:3
Turner, Bryce W, 1942, D 27,34:5
Turner, C Brinkley, 1956, Je 10,88:4
Turner, C Russell Jr, 1964, D 12,31:2
Turner, Carolyn, 1950, Ap 30,102:4
Turner, Carrie S Mrs, 1940, Mr 16,15:6
Turner, Cecelia Mrs, 1924, O 3,21:4
Turner, Charles A, 1951, Ag 15,27:4
Turner, Charles F, 1940, F 2,17:1
Turner, Charles G, 1903, Jl 30,7:6
Turner, Charles H, 1906, F 24,16:3
1938, N 28,15:1; 1946, Jl 4,19:5
Turner, Charles Henry (Turner the Ice Man), 1913, S 1,5:4
Turner, Charles M, 1943, Ag 14,11:5
Turner, Charles Merwin, 1946, Ja 16,24:3
Turner, Charles P, 1943, Ja 15,17:5
Turner, Charles Wesley, 1917, Ap 13,13:5
Turner, Charles William Rev Dr, 1920, S 5,19:5
Turner, Charles Yardley, 1919, Ja 2,9:3
Turner, Clarence W, 1939, Mr 24,21:1
Turner, Claude E, 1960, Ja 14,33:1
Turner, D, 1875, S 3,1:5
Turner, D B, 1878, O 19,8:5
Turner, Daniel L, 1942, Mr 13,20:2
Turner, Dorothy Mrs, 1940, Jl 9,21:1
Turner, Edith L (Mrs J Brazeau), 1966, Ja 15,27:2
Turner, Edward C, 1950, S 14,31:3
Turner, Edward M, 1964, F 1,23:3
Turner, Edward V, 1940, Ap 27,15:4
Turner, Edwin K, 1963, S 10,39:2
Turner, Egbert S, 1956, My 14,25:5
Turner, Elisabeth E, 1961, My 23,39:1
Turner, Ellwood J (por), 1948, Mr 2,23:3
Turner, Emery S Maj, 1921, O 12,15:6
Turner, Ernest J, 1943, F 28,47:5
Turner, Erwin, 1957, Mr 1,23:1
Turner, Ethel, 1958, Ap 9,33:1
Turner, Eugene, 1945, Ja 10,23:2
Turner, Eugene W, 1959, Je 12,27:3
Turner, F J, 1932, Mr 16,21:1
Turner, Farrant L, 1959, Mr 20,31:3
Turner, Florence, 1946, Ag 30,18:3
Turner, Francis ~~M, 1952, Ap 4,33:5~~
Turner, Frank Browne, 1918, F 14,11:5
Turner, Frank E, 1915, O 26,11:5
Turner, Frank I, 1941, F 27,19:4
Turner, Frank Mrs, 1943, O 5,25:2
Turner, Frank R, 1960, O 21,33:2
Turner, Frank T, 1938, Ap 26,21:2; 1951, Ja 3,27:4
Turner, Fred J, 1967, Ap 17,37:2
Turner, Fred Jr, 1964, F 6,30:1
Turner, Frederic R, 1951, S 7,29:1
Turner, Frederick C, 1961, Ja 4,33:1
Turner, George, 1951, Mr 20,29:2; 1968, Jl 31,41:3
Turner, George A, 1941, D 30,19:3; 1945, Jl 18,27:5
Turner, George C (por), 1949, S 23,24:2
Turner, George F, 1925, D 11,23:4
Turner, George G, 1951, Ag 25,11:5
Turner, George H, 1955, My 15,86:6
Turner, George K, 1952, F 16,13:4
Turner, George R, 1946, Ap 20,13:5
Turner, George Sir, 1916, Ag 14,9:6
Turner, George W, 1914, N 18,11:6
Turner, George W Mrs, 1950, Ja 6,21:2
Turner, George W Sr, 1946, Je 21,23:3
Turner, Gilbert H, 1954, O 11,27:4
Turner, Glenn C, 1939, N 5,49:3
Turner, Gordon P, 1939, D 17,49:3
Turner, Grace, 1960, Jl 2,17:5
Turner, Guy, 1967, Je 23,39:3
Turner, H Arthur, 1953, Ap 24,24:4
Turner, H B Capt, 1902, N 15,9:6
Turner, H M, 1951, F 20,25:4
Turner, Harold, 1960, O 26,39:5
Turner, Harold F, 1966, F 15,39:2
Turner, Harold M, 1947, My 6,28:2
Turner, Harold M Mrs, 1945, S 29,15:1
Turner, Harold R, 1960, Ja 3,88:2
Turner, Harold S, 1953, Ag 16,76:8
Turner, Harry B, 1948, N 10,29:3
Turner, Harry C, 1937, Ap 5,20:1; 1956, Jl 26,25:5
Turner, Harry C Mrs, 1955, D 25,48:4
Turner, Has, 1937, S 26,II,8:4
Turner, Helen, 1947, D 1,21:1
Turner, Helen L Mrs, 1941, D 24,17:2
Turner, Helen M, 1958, F 2,86:4
Turner, Henry, 1961, Ap 23,75:7
Turner, Henry C, 1954, Je 6,87:1; 1959, Ja 21,31:1
Turner, Henry C Mrs, 1942, Je 6,13:4
Turner, Henry Ed, 1911, Je 29,11:4
Turner, Henry L Col, 1915, Jl 13,11:5
Turner, Henry Mrs (E A Robertson), 1961, S 24,87:1
Turner, Henry O, 1907, D 22,9:4
Turner, Henry T, 1950, My 7,108:2
Turner, Henry W, 1937, N 27,17:2; 1952, F 26,27:4
Turner, Herbert B, 1937, O 30,19:2
Turner, Herbert Beach, 1903, Jl 9,7:6
Turner, Herbert V Mrs, 1949, D 2,29:1
Turner, Herman S, 1953, N 8,89:2
Turner, Howard S, 1950, Ap 11,31:3
Turner, Howard S Mrs, 1950, Ap 11,31:3
Turner, Hubert M, 1965, F 13,21:2
Turner, Hugh M, 1951, Ag 21,27:5
Turner, Hunt C Sr, 1952, Jl 6,49:1
Turner, Ira D, 1939, Jl 6,23:3
Turner, J Archer (por), 1946, N 2,15:3
Turner, J Charles, 1941, Ja 30,21:2
Turner, J Frank, 1915, D 23,13:4; 1949, Ag 8,15:4
Turner, J Rev Dr, 1877, Jl 22,8:6
Turner, Jacob A, 1957, Jl 13,17:3
Turner, James, 1905, Mr 18,11:5; 1939, My 7,III,6:7
Turner, James J, 1940, My 14,23:5
Turner, Jay H, 1950, Ja 19,27:1
Turner, Jesse, 1959, D 7,31:4
Turner, Joe, 1947, F 19,25:1
Turner, John, 1938, D 7,23:4; 1942, F 8,50:1; 1948, Je 30,25:2
Turner, John B, 1964, My 28,37:1
Turner, John C, 1949, Ja 20,27:5; 1956, Je 17,92:4
Turner, John Charles, 1923, Ap 25,21:4
Turner, John E, 1955, F 22,21:1
Turner, John F, 1940, F 2,17:2
Turner, John M, 1907, S 12,7:6
Turner, John Milton, 1915, N 2,11:4
Turner, John P, 1958, S 16,27:2; 1960, Jl 20,29:4
Turner, John P Mrs, 1967, Jl 11,37:3
Turner, John R, 1958, N 15,23:3; 1960, Mr 25,27:4
Turner, John S, 1922, S 17,30:3; 1942, Ja 17,17:5; 1959, Mr 21,21:4
Turner, John Spencer, 1905, S 20,9:6
Turner, John V, 1945, F 6,19:6; 1947, Mr 11,28:2
Turner, John W, 1941, N 29,17:5
Turner, John W Mrs, 1947, Ag 22,15:1
Turner, Joseph, 1946, F 17,42:5
Turner, Joseph B Jr, 1950, F 11,15:4
Turner, Joseph H, 1909, O 29,9:5
Turner, Joseph L, 1951, Je 13,29:5
Turner, Joseph S, 1940, D 3,25:2
Turner, Julius, 1952, D 25,29:4
Turner, Kate E (por), 1943, My 28,21:1
Turner, Kenneth B, 1955, O 10,27:5
Turner, L C Col, 1867, Mr 15,5:1
Turner, Lambert A, 1959, Je 10,37:4
Turner, Lee, 1953, O 8,29:2
Turner, Lesser, 1940, Ap 1,19:2
Turner, Lewis M, 1938, Ag 24,21:3
Turner, Linton, 1942, Mr 16,15:5
Turner, Luther B, 1959, Mr 7,22:1
Turner, Mabel R Mrs, 1947, My 22,27:5
Turner, Maidel, 1953, Ap 14,27:5
Turner, Marcus W, 1903, D 7,7:3
Turner, Marjorie S, 1963, Jl 13,17:5
Turner, Martha D H Mrs, 1937, O 21,23:3
Turner, Martin, 1958, My 20,33:4
Turner, Marvin T, 1946, My 9,21:2
Turner, Mary M Mrs, 1937, Ja 17,II,8:6
Turner, Maude, 1911, O 13,11:5
Turner, Max, 1940, N 1,25:3
Turner, Mayme D Mrs, 1941, Ap 5,17:4
Turner, Mellony, 1949, N 21,13:3
Turner, Nellie W, 1950, O 22,93:2
Turner, Norman, 1957, Ap 30,29:3
Turner, Olive M (por), 1943, S 11,13:5
Turner, Opie Mrs, 1962, S 8,46:2
Turner, Oren Jack Sr, 1968, My 23,47:3
Turner, Oscar C Mrs, 1967, Ja 16,41:2
Turner, P DeWitt, 1961, Ja 12,29:4
Turner, P W, 1903, Ja 5,9:5
Turner, Paul, 1918, N 15,13:1; 1951, N 2,23:2
Turner, Paul A, 1950, Ap 15,15:3
Turner, Paul Flagler, 1922, Ap 12,21:3
Turner, Paul N, 1950, Ap 10,19:3
Turner, Paul N Mrs, 1959, Jl 28,27:5
Turner, Paul R, 1959, Ag 26,29:2
Turner, R K, 1961, Jl 19,29:2
Turner, R L Mrs, 1948, My 28,23:4
Turner, R R Capt, 1901, D 6,1:6
Turner, Ralph C, 1964, Jl 29,33:3
Turner, Ralph E, 1964, O 6,43:4
Turner, Rear-Adm, 1883, Mr 25,2:2
Turner, Richard, 1940, Ap 1,19:3; 1943, O 1,19:4; 1961, Je 21,37:5
Turner, Richmond K, 1961, F 14,37:1
Turner, Robert A, 1945, Je 14,19:4
Turner, Robert T, 1955, F 5,15:4
Turner, Roscoe W, 1948, Mr 5,22:3
Turner, Roy P, 1955, D 29,23:3
Turner, Samuel G H, 1953, F 28,17:1
Turner, Samuel H, 1951, D 25,31:5
Turner, Samuel S, 1949, My 30,13:3
Turner, Sara C, 1952, N 27,31:4
Turner, Sidney J, 1951, Ag 21,27:1
Turner, Simon, 1941, Ag 13,17:2
Turner, Solon E Mrs (will, Ag 1,17:3), 1944, Jl 29, 13:4
Turner, Stanley F, 1953, Je 4,29:5
Turner, Stephen H, 1939, N 5,49:2
Turner, T C, 1931, O 29,21:2
Turner, Thomas B, 1938, Ap 6,17:4
Turner, Thomas B Jr, 1952, Ag 16,12:6
Turner, Thomas C Mrs, 1957, My 10,27:3
Turner, Thomas Dr, 1865, Mr 23,2:6
Turner, Thomas L, 1962, F 27,33:3
Turner, Thomas L Lt, 1937, Je 26,17:6
Turner, Tracy L, 1942, Jl 7,19:3
Turner, Tracy L Mrs, 1950, Je 5,23:3
Turner, W C B, 1949, N 21,13:3
Turner, W F Mrs, 1907, O 16,9:5; 1948, S 8,29:1
Turner, W T, 1933, Je 24,13:4
Turner, Wallis S, 1947, Je 14,15:3
Turner, Walter E, 1938, Ja 2,40:4
Turner, Walter H, 1946, N 4,25:4
Turner, Wilbur F, 1940, Ap 8,20:4
Turner, Wilfred G, 1957, Je 3,27:5
Turner, William, 1939, Jl 22,15:4; 1940, D 10,25:3
Turner, William A, 1945, Ag 1,19:5; 1953, D 31,19:5
Turner, William D, 1925, N 28,15:4
Turner, William De G, 1961, F 25,21:2
Turner, William E, 1946, D 24,17:6
Turner, William F, 1943, D 31,16:7
Turner, William H, 1942, S 28,17:5
Turner, William Hall, 1906, Mr 20,9:6
Turner, William J, 1943, D 3,24:3
Turner, William L, 1920, O 8,13:2
Turner, William M, 1947, Mr 27,27:1
Turner, William Sir, 1916, F 16,11:4; 1937, Je 14,23:2

Turner, William W Sr, 1963, Je 10,31:5
Turner (Sister Marie Anita), 1964, Jl 14,33:5
Turnery, Harold, 1962, Jl 3,23:2
Turnesa, Frank R (por), 1949, S 13,30:2
Turnesa, Vitale, 1960, Ap 13,39:2
Turnesa, Vitale Mrs, 1957, Mr 30,19:3
Turney, G W, 1884, My 31,2:2
Turney, Hubert J, 1939, Mr 4,15:3
Turney, P W, 1875, O 25,4:6
Turney, Peter, 1903, O 20,9:6
Turney, Theodore L, 1944, D 26,19:4
Turngren, John, 1954, Mr 20,17:5
Turnham, John, 1941, Mr 5,41:1
Turnheim, Edward S, 1952, D 27,9:4
Turnier, Jean, 1923, Ja 9,23:4
Turnier, John F, 1950, Mr 24,26:2
Turnier, John F Mrs, 1958, Ag 8,19:4
Turno, Walter G, 1954, Ja 8,21:2
Turnock, Harry C, 1944, Je 7,19:5
Turnock, Henry M, 1942, O 25,46:2
Turnoff, David, 1953, Je 16,27:5
Turnour, Edward (Earl Winterton), 1962, Ag 28,31:4
Turnquist, Lennart E, 1965, Ap 16,32:8
Turnure, Arthur, 1906, Ap 14,11:2
Turnure, David A, 1959, D 3,37:5
Turnure, Evelyn Mrs, 1948, S 25,17:6
Turnure, George Evans (funl, D 2,11:2), 1920, D 1, 15:5
Turnure, Giles M, 1937, D 3,23:3
Turnure, Harvey A Sr, 1967, D 5,51:4
Turnure, J Harvey, 1955, Jl 9,15:3
Turnure, L, 1899, My 2,2:4
Turnure, Lawrence, 1966, Ap 9,22:8
Turnure, Percy R, 1953, Ja 24,15:6
Turot, Henri, 1920, Je 4,13:4
Turpen, John E, 1945, Ag 26,43:2
Turpie, David Ex-Sen, 1909, Ap 22,9:5
Turpin, Albert E, 1955, F 26,15:4
Turpin, Ben, 1940, Jl 2,21:5
Turpin, Ben Mrs, 1925, O 3,15:4
Turpin, F E, 1927, Ja 25,21:5
Turpin, R E Mrs, 1946, Mr 20,23:2
Turpin, Rufus E, 1950, Mr 30,29:3
Turpin, William, 1940, My 6,17:4
Turpin, William A Maj, 1912, O 3,13:6
Turquand, William G, 1956, F 24,25:1
Turquetil, Arsene, 1955, Je 16,31:4
Turr, Stephen Gen, 1908, My 4,7:4
Turrell, George, 1942, D 6,64:4
Turrell, Guy H, 1956, O 8,27:4
Turrell, Herbert (por), 1947, O 29,27:1
Turrell, Herbert Mrs (will), 1948, Ap 13,31:6
Turrell, Hobert Mrs, 1948, Mr 31,25:1
Turrell, John C, 1956, Mr 18,89:2
Turrell, W J, 1943, Ja 30,15:4
Turrentine, Francis M, 1958, N 19,37:3
Turrentine, James L Mrs, 1967, Ja 19,35:1
Turrentine, John W Mrs, 1950, Ag 19,13:4
Turrill, H S Gen, 1907, My 25,9:4
Turrill, John W, 1918, Mr 12,13:7
Turrill, Julius S, 1943, S 21,23:1
Turroni, Costantino B, 1963, D 9,35:4
Turshen, Abraham, 1955, Ag 6,15:4
Turshen, Max M Mrs, 1966, Ag 31,40:6
Turso, Thomas J, 1956, D 18,31:1
Turteltaub, Abram S, 1961, D 23,23:5
Turteltaub, John J, 1962, My 10,37:2
Turtle, Eugene P, 1961, F 3,25:4
Turtle, John Berry, 1968, Ja 19,44:4
Turtle, M Berry, 1942, N 18,26:2
Turtle, M Berry Mrs, 1964, Ag 2,77:2
Turtletaub, Herman, 1949, Mr 24,28:3
Turton, Charles F, 1948, Mr 1,23:5
Turton, Franklin E, 1952, D 22,25:3
Turton, John K, 1960, O 30,86:5
Turtulli, Vangjel, 1940, Ag 27,21:4
Turtur, Gaspar, 1959, Je 30,31:3
Turtz, Charles A, 1960, F 14,82:4
Turull, Thomas F, 1961, Mr 16,37:1
Tuscany, Arthur J, 1953, Je 7,84:5
Tusch, Cary A Mrs, 1960, Ag 6,19:4
Tushingham, Edward K, 1959, Ag 6,27:2
Tushingham, Walter L, 1957, Mr 14,29:6
Tusini, Giuseppe, 1940, My 24,19:3
Tuska, Morris, 1903, F 4,9:5
Tuska, Samuel A, 1907, N 21,9:6
Tuskin, George E, 1944, D 11,23:3
Tuso, Thomas G, 1945, O 24,21:6
Tussaud, John T, 1943, O 14,21:3
Tussey, C, 1927, D 10,1:7
Tussing, Christian O, 1949, Ag 3,23:4
Tustin, Edward B, 1941, My 15,23:3
Tusting, Robert A, 1952, Ap 12,11:4
Tuston, C B (will), 1939, Jl 19,21:3
Tutchings, Everett, 1963, D 26,28:4
Tutein, E Arthur, 1948, Ag 5,21:6
Tutenberg, Charles H, 1949, S 24,13:3
Tuteur, Julius, 1950, Je 17,15:4
Tuthill, A E, 1903, O 17,9:6
Tuthill, Alex M, 1958, My 27,29:2
Tuthill, Alsop P, 1939, F 19,39:2
Tuthill, Ben, 1937, Mr 6,17:4
Tuthill, C E, 1903, F 27,9:4
Tuthill, Daniel S, 1950, Ap 16,104:6
Tuthill, David W Mrs, 1956, S 19,37:2
Tuthill, Eliza A, 1954, F 9,27:4
Tuthill, Franklin Dr, 1865, Ag 28,5:1
Tuthill, Fred D, 1943, D 24,13:2
Tuthill, Frederic P Prof, 1922, Jl 4,13:6
Tuthill, George G, 1952, D 20,17:4
Tuthill, George I Mrs, 1941, Ag 26,19:5
Tuthill, Harold G, 1950, S 25,23:3
Tuthill, Harry H Mrs, 1955, My 3,31:2
Tuthill, Harry J, 1957, Ja 26,19:6
Tuthill, Henry H, 1960, D 24,13:1
Tuthill, Henry P Mrs, 1957, Ap 24,33:2
Tuthill, Horace S, 1919, S 3,13:4; 1942, Ja 19,20:2
Tuthill, Horace S Jr, 1955, Ja 5,23:4
Tuthill, Howard S, 1939, My 29,15:3
Tuthill, J H, 1877, Jl 29,6:7
Tuthill, Jack, 1952, N 2,88:4
Tuthill, James F, 1954, Jl 14,27:5
Tuthill, Jeremiah G, 1944, Ap 20,19:4
Tuthill, John T Sr, 1944, O 8,44:1
Tuthill, L W C, 1942, O 28,23:6
Tuthill, Lyndon G, 1937, Mr 15,23:4
Tuthill, Mary E, 1951, D 26,25:2
Tuthill, Mott C, 1941, Ja 5,45:2
Tuthill, Nathaniel S, 1939, Ja 17,21:4
Tuthill, Oliver B Mrs, 1950, S 5,27:3
Tuthill, Philip R, 1946, S 21,15:2
Tuthill, Reginald Mrs, 1954, Ap 18,89:1
Tuthill, Richard S Judge, 1920, Ap 11,22:3
Tuthill, Robert K Dr, 1909, Je 10,7:5
Tuthill, Roswell B, 1951, Jl 24,25:2
Tuthill, Royden, 1947, Ja 19,53:1
Tuthill, Selah S Mrs, 1950, Mr 10,27:1
Tuthill, Sherwood E, 1937, My 26,25:5
Tuthill, Terry W, 1963, Je 29,23:3
Tuthill, Theodore R, 1922, D 15,19:5
Tuthill, Walter, 1946, S 7,15:3
Tuthill, Walter Mrs, 1943, D 13,23:5
Tuthill, William D Mrs, 1946, S 9,9:1
Tuthill, Wilmarth J, 1951, O 27,19:5
Tutko, Anthony F, 1952, S 3,30:5
Tutle, Emerson (por), 1946, Mr 9,13:3
Tutt, Charles Leaming, 1909, Ja 22,7:5
Tutt, Myra, 1946, Ja 12,15:5
Tuttie, James M Mrs, 1953, My 1,21:1
Tuttle, Adrianna, 1941, Je 18,21:4
Tuttle, Albert J, 1947, Ap 22,27:4
Tuttle, Albert V, 1945, N 1,23:1
Tuttle, Albert W, 1954, O 26,27:5
Tuttle, Allison E, 1947, O 29,27:5
Tuttle, Arnold D, 1951, O 8,21:3
Tuttle, Arthur B, 1952, D 18,29:6
Tuttle, Arthur B Mrs, 1963, Jl 23,29:5
Tuttle, Arthur E, 1943, Ag 11,19:2
Tuttle, Arthur J (por), 1944, D 4,23:4
Tuttle, Arthur S (por), 1949, My 20,27:1
Tuttle, Arthur S Mrs (cor, O 21,87:2), 1956, O 20, 21:5
Tuttle, Aubrey, 1949, O 22,17:2
Tuttle, Bayard T, 1948, S 13,21:5
Tuttle, Brantley E, 1952, Jl 4,13:3
Tuttle, Bronson B, 1903, S 13,7:5
Tuttle, Bruce M, 1963, My 23,37:6
Tuttle, Bruce R, 1967, F 4,27:3
Tuttle, C E, 1943, My 9,VIII,22:5
Tuttle, Carl, 1949, N 29,29:4
Tuttle, Charles H Mrs (Helene), 1968, O 7,47:2
Tuttle, Charles S, 1938, S 30,21:3
Tuttle, Clarence E, 1962, O 7,82:6
Tuttle, Daniel S, 1923, Ap 21,11:6
Tuttle, Daniel Sylvester (por), 1923, Ap 18,21:3
Tuttle, Donald D, 1945, D 22,19:1
Tuttle, Donald S, 1955, Ja 2,77:2
Tuttle, Earl M, 1947, Jl 7,17:4
Tuttle, Edith M, 1953, F 11,29:4
Tuttle, Edward A, 1939, F 23,23:3
Tuttle, Edward D, 1945, Je 27,19:4
Tuttle, Edward L, 1947, My 20,25:2
Tuttle, Edward W, 1952, Mr 29,15:6
Tuttle, Elizabeth, 1925, Ap 14,23:5
Tuttle, Emmett W, 1949, Ag 20,11:3
Tuttle, Ernest W, 1961, N 21,39:4
Tuttle, Eula K B Mrs, 1940, D 13,26:6
Tuttle, Ezra A Mrs, 1951, D 21,27:3
Tuttle, Frank D Mrs, 1951, Ap 17,29:5
Tuttle, Frank W, 1943, Mr 13,13:1
Tuttle, Franklin E, 1950, Ja 9,25:3
Tuttle, Fred B, 1948, Jl 23,19:4
Tuttle, Frederic B, 1950, Jl 6,27:5
Tuttle, Frederick B (will, N 15,19:2), 1941, N 11,23:2
Tuttle, George A, 1942, My 11,15:2
Tuttle, George B, 1944, My 13,19:2
Tuttle, George H, 1942, Ap 3,21:4
Tuttle, George Montgomery Dr, 1912, O 30,13:5
Tuttle, George R, 1919, Ja 12,22:3
Tuttle, H C, 1882, N 11,5:1
Tuttle, H H Dr, 1901, O 10,9:2
Tuttle, Harlan, 1951, Jl 5,25:4
Tuttle, Harold W, 1950, Je 8,32:2
Tuttle, Harry Mrs, 1948, Ja 28,23:5
Tuttle, Harry W, 1960, F 21,92:7
Tuttle, Henry, 1959, Mr 27,23:1
Tuttle, Henry N Mrs, 1953, N 9,35:4
Tuttle, Henry N Mrs (will), 1954, Ja 9,12:6
Tuttle, Hiram A (por), 1948, My 26,25:3
Tuttle, Hiram A Ex-Gov, 1911, F 11,11:5
Tuttle, Hiram E, 1956, N 13,37:2
Tuttle, Isaac, 1911, Jl 9,11:4
Tuttle, James H Rev Dr, 1903, D 9,9:5
Tuttle, Jay, 1954, N 6,17:5
Tuttle, Jeanette, 1939, Je 8,25:3
Tuttle, Jeannette B Mrs, 1938, Ja 23,II,8:1
Tuttle, John M, 1952, Ja 25,21:3
Tuttle, John M Mrs, 1959, Je 28,69:1
Tuttle, Joseph N, 1948, S 12,72:6
Tuttle, Joseph P Dr, 1913, F 1,13:5
Tuttle, Julius H, 1945, F 12,19:4
Tuttle, Levi, 1921, N 23,15:2
Tuttle, Louis I, 1960, My 15,86:2
Tuttle, Lucius, 1914, D 1,13:5
Tuttle, Mabel A, 1961, Ap 13,35:6
Tuttle, Martin A, 1949, D 11,92:4
Tuttle, Mary E Mrs, 1937, Jl 21,21:4
Tuttle, Miner W, 1957, My 20,25:2
Tuttle, Nathaniel, 1917, My 26,13:4
Tuttle, Peter, 1968, Jl 20,27:4
Tuttle, Pierson M, 1965, S 13,35:3
Tuttle, Robert C, 1941, S 18,25:6
Tuttle, Robert E Mrs, 1966, Jl 20,41:1
Tuttle, Roger W, 1947, Jl 26,13:5
Tuttle, Samuel L Rev, 1866, Ap 17,5:3
Tuttle, Socrates, 1885, F 13,2:2
Tuttle, Stephen D, 1954, Ap 10,15:1
Tuttle, Theodore R, 1941, Jl 11,15:5
Tuttle, Thomas T, 1947, S 20,15:3
Tuttle, Walter H, 1951, Mr 31,15:6
Tuttle, Walter I, 1943, O 15,19:3
Tuttle, Wells D, 1959, D 10,78:8
Tuttle, William, 1938, F 9,20:3
Tuttle, William B, 1957, O 6,85:1
Tuttle, William E, 1923, F 12,13:5
Tuttle, William R, 1941, Jl 17,19:3; 1953, Jl 18,13:4
Tuttle, Wilmer N, 1963, N 20,43:2
Tuttle, Wilson M, 1960, Ja 8,25:3
Tuttle, Winthrop M, 1942, Ap 10,17:6
Tuttle, Winthrop S, 1955, Je 18,17:3
Tuttle, Wylie F, 1939, Jl 18,19:5
Tuttle-Smith, James Rev Dr, 1910, D 20,13:3
Tutty, Charles B Sr, 1945, D 4,29:4
Tutty, Charles H, 1939, D 13,27:6
Tutules, Peter C, 1946, N 30,15:4
Tutwiler, Temple W, 1950, N 10,27:5
Tuve, Rosemond, 1964, D 22,27:5
Tuvim, Abe, 1958, Ja 16,29:2
Tuvim, Joseph, 1967, D 19,47:3
Tuvim, Judith (J Holliday),(funl, Je 10,35:2; will, S 4,21:5), 1965, Je 8,1:7
Tuwim, Julian, 1954, Ja 5,27:4
Tuxbury, Nathaniel C, 1967, F 21,47:1
Tuxen, Erik, 1957, Ag 29,27:4
Tuzeneu, Frederick E, 1961, Jl 26,31:4
Tuzer, Ahmet Fikri Min, 1942, Ag 18,22:2
Tuzo, Paul B, 1953, N 15,88:4
Twachtman, Eric, 1948, Jl 14,23:4
Twachtman, J H, 1902, Ag 9,9:5
Twachtman, Quentin, 1954, F 22,19:4
Twaddell, Horace G, 1941, S 17,23:5
Twaddell, Horace G Mrs, 1958, Mr 18,29:2
Twaddell, John P, 1943, My 9,40:2
Twaddle, Gard W, 1960, Jl 19,29:3
Twain, Mark (Saml L Clemens),(funl), 1910, Ap 25, 9:5
Twaits, Ford J, 1959, Ap 21,35:4
Twaits, Raymond E, 1961, Jl 1,17:4
Twamley, James H, 1948, S 10,23:1
Twamley, William A, 1952, Ja 16,25:4
Twardowski, Mary Mrs, 1946, My 14,27:8
Tweddell, Francis Mrs, 1955, O 23,86:4
Tweddell, Robert, 1945, My 22,19:3
Tweddell, William Hutchinson, 1915, Je 13,15:5
Tweddle, John M, 1949, My 12,31:5
Tweddle, Richard D, 1958, F 2,86:2
Tweed, Charles C, 1907, Mr 22,11:6
Tweed, Charles Harrison, 1917, O 12,11:5
Tweed, Eliza Mrs, 1873, Jl 8,8:5
Tweed, James D, 1945, Mr 21,23:5
Tweed, James D Mrs, 1947, Mr 9,60:5
Tweed, James M, 1938, Mr 12,17:6
Tweed, John H, 1961, Ag 4,21:4
Tweed, Richard, 1884, Ag 28,1:5
Tweed, Samuel Mrs, 1949, Ag 27,13:3
Tweed, Thomas F, 1940, My 1,23:3
Tweed, W M, 1878, Ap 13,1:7
Tweed, W M Mrs, 1880, F 14,8:4
Tweedale, Benjamin A, 1957, Mr 23,19:4
Tweedale, Eliza M Mrs, 1938, Ap 20,23:4
Tweedale, Harry, 1951, My 18,27:1
Tweedale, John F, 1948, D 31,15:2
Tweeddale, Lady, 1944, O 16,19:5
Tweeddale, Marchioness of, 1937, My 19,23:5
Tweeddale, Marquis, 1876, N 8,3:1
Tweeddale, Marquis of, 1878, D 30,5:2
Tweedie, Alex Mrs (por), 1940, Ap 16,23:5
Tweedie, David, 1916, Mr 3,11:5
Tweedmouth, Baron (Edw Marjoribanks), 1909, S 16,9:6

Tweedmouth, Lady, 1904, Ag 6,7:6
Tweedsmuir, Lord, 1940, F 12,1:2
Tweedy, Andrew M, 1949, Ja 7,22:3
Tweedy, Arthur E, 1955, S 14,35:5
Tweedy, Donald N (por), 1948, Jl 23,19:3
Tweedy, E A, 1881, F 25,5:3
Tweedy, Edmund, 1954, Ag 13,15:6
Tweedy, Edmund R, 1962, O 11,39:5
Tweedy, Forrest B, 1961, Ag 14,25:5
Tweedy, Frank, 1937, Jl 2,21:2
Tweedy, George Mrs, 1915, Je 5,9:6
Tweedy, Harry W, 1956, My 26,17:5
Tweedy, Henry H, 1953, S 12,17:3
Tweedy, Isabel, 1941, S 15,19:5
Tweedy, John, 1912, Ag 6,9:6
Tweedy, John E, 1943, F 13,11:4
Tweedy, John E Mrs, 1962, Je 6,41:4
Tweedy, Joseph H, 1953, My 10,89:1
Tweedy, Joseph L, 1940, O 6,49:2
Tweedy, Lawrence L, 1943, Jl 27,17:3
Tweedy, William, 1881, F 13,1:3
Tweh, Didwe, 1961, Mr 21,37:2
Twells, John Steel, 1921, Mr 17,13:4
Twells, Robert, 1966, D 15,47:2
Twelvetrees, Charles, 1948, Ap 7,25:3
Twelvetrees, Helen (Mrs C Payne), 1958, F 14,23:1
Twenhofel, William H, 1957, Ja 8,31:1
Twersky, David M, 1956, S 23,84:4
Twersky, Jacob I, 1945, My 15,19:4
Twersky, Jacob Joseph Grand Rabbi, 1968, Ap 1,45:4
Twesten, John C, 1964, Jl 20,25:3
Twichell, Burton P, 1949, Ag 8,15:4
Twichell, Clara G Mrs, 1937, F 13,13:2
Twichell, Ginery, 1883, Jl 24,5:5
Twichell, Joseph C Mrs, 1910, Ap 25,9:5
Twiddy, Herbert W, 1943, Jl 3,13:3
Twiddy, Norman W, 1946, D 5,31:6
Twiddy, Wesley S, 1960, Ap 22,29:1
Twidy, Charles F, 1949, N 10,31:5
Twigg, Edward P, 1952, My 5,23:4
Twigg, William C, 1961, O 8,87:2
Twiggar, Albert W, 1938, N 2,24:3
Twiggar, Albert W Mrs, 1947, Ap 2,27:5
Twiggar, George E Mrs, 1946, D 22,42:3
Twiggs, Henry C, 1948, Mr 20,13:4
Twiggs, Samuel W, 1948, O 9,19:3
Twinem, Leo Leonard Rev, 1968, O 17,47:4
Twinem, Leonard Mrs, 1954, S 26,86:6
Twinen, James C, 1949, Je 17,23:5
Twing, A T Rev, 1882, N 12,9:2
Twing, Corn L Rev, 1905, F 12,7:6
Twining, Charles, 1941, F 14,17:4
Twining, Edmund S, 1923, Je 26,19:5
Twining, Edward F Lord, 1967, Jl 25,35:2
Twining, Frances S, 1944, Ap 13,19:2
Twining, Frank B, 1945, My 20,32:4
Twining, Harry Mrs, 1945, S 14,23:3
Twining, Kinsley, 1924, Ja 29,19:3
Twining, Laverne, 1942, Mr 27,23:2
Twining, Philip Geoffrey Maj-Gen, 1920, Ja 17,11:4
Twining, W Donald, 1946, Jl 5,19:4
Twining, W J Maj, 1882, My 6,2:5
Twining, William S, 1937, F 10,23:3
Twining, Wilmer A, 1953, Ja 9,21:2
Twiss, C Victor, 1920, O 31,22:3
Twiss, George R, 1944, F 17,19:2
Twiss, J Hayden, 1956, O 6,21:4
Twist, George J, 1943, O 5,25:4
Twist, Ira F, 1937, O 6,25:3
Twitchell, A W, 1904, Ap 27,9:6
Twitchell, Adelbert B, 1961, My 31,33:4
Twitchell, Earl W, 1964, Mr 24,33:3
Twitchell, Emma J, 1938, N 16,23:2
Twitchell, Evans T, 1951, O 31,29:2
Twitchell, H K, 1928, Jl 12,23:5
Twitchell, Henry, 1937, Mr 29,19:5
Twitchell, Herbert K Mrs, 1954, Jl 31,13:6
Twitchell, Karl S, 1968, Ja 10,43:3
Twitchell, Leonard G, 1944, F 8,15:4
Twitchell, Leonard Mrs, 1947, F 23,53:6
Twitchell, Lewis A, 1954, Ag 14,15:3
Twitchell, Lewis A Mrs, 1952, Mr 7,23:2
Twitchell, Marshall C, 1949, Je 16,29:2
Twitchell, Pierrepont E, 1962, Mr 3,21:1
Twitchell, Roger T Mrs, 1956, F 19,92:4
Twitchell, William C, 1953, Mr 26,1:7
Twitmyer, Edward M, 1956, O 8,27:5
Twitmyer, Edwin B, 1943, Mr 4,19:2
Twitmyer, George W Dr, 1914, F 22,IV,5:5
Twitty, Joseph J, 1959, Ag 7,23:3
Two Bears, Earl Chief, 1958, Ja 30,23:5
Twogood, Fred J, 1944, My 2,19:2
Twohey, John J, 1944, Ag 16,19:3
Twohig, James J, 1965, Ap 20,39:3
Twohig, Mark M, 1954, F 10,29:3
Twombley, Eugene, 1968, O 18,47:2
Twombly, A S Dr, 1907, N 20,9:5
Twombly, Arthur Butler, 1917, My 8,11:5
Twombly, Clifford G, 1942, D 30,23:5
Twombly, Frederick W, 1945, Ja 5,15:4
Twombly, George A Mrs, 1955, O 26,31:5
Twombly, H McK Jr (funl, Jl 10,7:1), 1906, Jl 6,1:5
Twombly, Hamilton M Mrs, 1952, Ap 13,76:3
Twombly, Hamilton M Mrs (est tax appr), 1955, F 4,19:3
Twombly, Hamilton McKown (funl, Ja 16,11:4), 1910, Ja 12,9:3
Twombly, Henry B, 1955, Mr 1,25:3
Twombly, Henry B Mrs, 1942, Mr 4,20:3
Twombly, Howland, 1939, Jl 3,13:5
Twombly, Jeannie S Mrs, 1925, D 22,21:4
Twombly, Ruth V (trb lr, S 16,28:6), 1954, S 2,21:4
Twombly, Ruth V (est appr), 1959, Ja 13,21:7
Twomey, Jeremiah, 1947, O 7,27:1
Twomey, Jeremiah F, 1963, O 4,36:6
Twomey, John Joseph, 1968, O 18,53:5
Twomey, M Joseph, 1948, O 31,88:6
Twomey, Patrick A, 1952, Ja 22,29:3
Tworger, Edward, 1949, S 20,29:3
Tworoger, Leo Mrs, 1940, N 10,57:1
Twyeffort, Emile, 1925, My 13,21:5
Twyeffort, Louis V, 1954, D 8,35:2
Twyford, Edward C, 1964, Ap 8,43:4
Twyford, Harry B, 1942, O 15,23:4
Twyford, Harry B Mrs, 1952, My 4,90:3
Twyford, Thomas Sr, 1953, F 10,27:5
Twyford, William J, 1939, Ap 3,15:5
Twyman, Frank, 1959, Mr 10,35:2
Tyack, Thomas, 1943, Ag 10,19:4
Tybaert, Sylvan, 1961, My 17,37:2
Tybus, Gustav, 1951, S 27,31:4
Tychinin, Vladimir A, 1959, Jl 27,25:2
Tydeman, William A, 1947, Ja 16,25:4
Tyden, Emil, 1951, N 25,86:4
Tydings, Millard E (funl plans, F 12,87:1; funl, F 13,27:4), 1961, F 10,27:1
Tydings, Millard F, 1941, S 12,21:4
Tydings, Thomas, 1944, Jl 2,20:1
Tyer, Aaron W, 1952, My 29,3:1
Tyer, Peter J, 1942, My 13,19:4
Tyerech, Michael, 1947, N 7,23:4
Tygel, Zelig (por), 1947, Mr 15,13:4
Tykociner, Joseph T Mrs, 1953, O 7,29:1
Tyldesley, Richard, 1943, S 18,17:2
Tyldsley, John O, 1960, Mr 25,28:2
Tyldsley, William, 1950, My 19,28:3
Tylee, Arthur F Mrs, 1955, S 7,31:1
Tylee, Rebecca Mrs, 1905, Mr 24,9:6
Tyler, Abram R, 1940, Ja 4,23:2
Tyler, Albert C, 1945, Jl 26,19:2
Tyler, Albert F, 1944, F 26,13:2
Tyler, Aldora J, 1941, Je 9,19:2
Tyler, Alfred Lee, 1907, Je 4,7:6; 1907, O 19,9:6
Tyler, Alice (por), 1944, Ap 19,23:4
Tyler, Asher, 1875, Ag 4,4:5
Tyler, Augustus O Col, 1908, N 28,9:5
Tyler, C Boardman, 1955, Mr 23,31:2
Tyler, Charles A, 1952, Ag 3,60:6
Tyler, Charles C, 1908, S 16,9:5; 1937, F 22,17:3
Tyler, Charles H, 1924, Ap 18,19:5
Tyler, Charles R, 1939, N 7,28:4
Tyler, Charles W, 1923, O 6,15:4
Tyler, Chauncey D, 1958, My 12,29:1
Tyler, Clayton W, 1951, N 14,31:5
Tyler, Corydon C, 1939, N 23,27:4
Tyler, Corydon E, 1917, N 25,23:4
Tyler, Daniel Gen, 1882, D 1,4:7
Tyler, E S G, 1901, Ag 21,7:6
Tyler, Edward E, 1960, Ap 8,31:1
Tyler, Edward M, 1945, D 21,21:2
Tyler, Emma A Mrs, 1942, D 29,21:5
Tyler, Ernest F, 1951, Ap 4,29:2
Tyler, Francis, 1941, Mr 7,21:4; 1956, Ap 13,25:4
Tyler, G H, 1884, Ag 18,5:2
Tyler, Gaines A, 1959, Ja 23,25:1
Tyler, George A (Lefty), 1953, S 30,31:6
Tyler, George C, 1946, Mr 15,21:1
Tyler, George F, 1947, Ja 9,23:4
Tyler, George F Mrs (Stella E), 1963, N 5,28:3
Tyler, George G Mrs, 1956, Je 13,37:5
Tyler, George H, 1912, D 24,9:4
Tyler, George M, 1951, D 28,21:1
Tyler, George T, 1940, Mr 21,25:1
Tyler, Harry, 1961, S 16,19:2
Tyler, Harry D, 1951, Ja 23,27:1
Tyler, Harry E Mrs, 1948, Ja 10,15:2
Tyler, Harry W, 1938, F 4,21:2
Tyler, Harvey A, 1943, Jl 4,20:3
Tyler, Helen, 1950, Ag 1,23:4
Tyler, Henry W Sir, 1908, Ja 31,7:5
Tyler, Howard L, 1925, F 16,19:2
Tyler, J Edward, 1938, Ja 23,II,8:1
Tyler, J M Judge, 1926, O 14,25:2
Tyler, J S Gen, 1876, Ja 24,1:3
Tyler, James Hoge Ex-Gov, 1925, Ja 4,7:1
Tyler, James S, 1941, Ap 20,44:1; 1954, O 23,15:3
Tyler, John, 1937, Ag 23,19:3
Tyler, John C, 1948, Ap 14,27:5
Tyler, John ex-Pres, 1862, Ja 22,8:1
Tyler, John Mrs, 1953, Ag 30,88:4; 1958, Jl 15,25:3
Tyler, John R, 1949, O 8,13:6
Tyler, John W, 1947, Ja 19,52:1
Tyler, Joseph B, 1948, S 1,24:3
Tyler, Judy (Mrs G Lafayette),(funl, Jl 10,27:4), 1957, Jl 5,35:1
Tyler, Julia G, 1889, Jl 11,5:2
Tyler, Julian W, 1952, Ag 14,23:3
Tyler, L G, 1935, F 13,19:1
Tyler, Leonard S Mrs, 1951, Ap 23,25:3
Tyler, Leslie H, 1960, F 17,35:1
Tyler, Lester D, 1939, My 13,15:4
Tyler, Lyon G Mrs, 1921, N 3,19:6
Tyler, Margaret Mrs, 1952, My 1,29:5
Tyler, Marshall H, 1942, D 17,29:4
Tyler, Mason Whiting Col, 1907, Jl 3,7:5
Tyler, Maurice L, 1944, F 20,36:2
Tyler, Morris, 1907, D 5,9:4
Tyler, Nathaniel, 1961, S 1,17:2
Tyler, Parker R, 1961, My 25,37:3
Tyler, Parker R Mrs, 1957, S 24,35:4
Tyler, Percy P, 1961, S 20,29:5
Tyler, R Col, 1877, D 5,5:6
Tyler, Ralph S, 1952, Je 28,19:2
Tyler, Raymond J, 1946, Je 21,23:2
Tyler, Robert B, 1963, Mr 28,16:7
Tyler, Robert H Jr, 1949, My 20,27:3
Tyler, Robert O Gen, 1874, D 2,1:6
Tyler, Robert Z, 1950, Mr 22,27:2
Tyler, S, 1877, D 17,1:3
Tyler, S Wyman, 1958, F 8,19:3
Tyler, Samuel, 1946, F 15,25:2
Tyler, Sara M Mrs, 1952, Ag 22,21:2
Tyler, Stanley Beckwith, 1906, Ja 10,9:7
Tyler, Stephen L, 1966, Ap 4,24:8
Tyler, Tazewell Dr, 1874, Ja 26,2:7
Tyler, Thaddeus W, 1910, Ap 10,13:3
Tyler, Tom, 1954, My 3,25:5
Tyler, Victor M, 1959, D 17,37:3
Tyler, W P, 1902, D 29,7:6
Tyler, Walter A Mrs, 1940, Mr 30,15:3
Tyler, Warren Capt, 1903, D 22,9:5
Tyler, Warren J Mrs, 1950, Ag 28,17:5
Tyler, William E, 1939, S 4,19:4
Tyler, William R, 1907, S 26,9:5
Tyler, William S, 1954, Mr 20,15:6
Tyler, William Wellington, 1903, My 6,9:6
Tyler, Winsor M, 1954, Ja 11,25:5
Tylor, E Merrick, 1950, F 24,23:1
Tymeson, Walter R, 1954, S 29,31:2
Tyminski, William B, 1948, My 8,15:3
Tynan, Brandon, 1967, Mr 21,43:1
Tynan, Desmond P, 1961, Je 17,21:4
Tynan, E Capt, 1884, O 9,8:4
Tynan, Edward D, 1949, Ag 14,68:3
Tynan, Frank V, 1955, F 3,23:1
Tynan, Harold V, 1951, D 22,15:4
Tynan, James W, 1943, F 14,48:4
Tynan, John W, 1960, Mr 23,37:3
Tynan, John W Mrs, 1950, Ag 1,23:6
Tynan, Maegt A R Mrs, 1940, S 10,23:3
Tynan, Malachy L, 1955, Ap 21,29:1
Tynan, Murray (por), 1943, Mr 17,21:3
Tynan, Nicholas J, 1937, Jl 10,15:1
Tynan, P J P Mrs, 1925, Jl 21,21:5
Tynan, Patrick J, 1946, Ap 22,21:4
Tynberg, Sigmund Dr, 1915, N 5,13:4
Tyndal, Theodore H, 1917, F 1,11:4
Tyndale, H Gen, 1880, Mr 20,2:7
Tyndale, O S, 1952, O 31,25:1
Tyndall, Evelyn, 1952, F 19,29:5
Tyndall, Henry M, 1943, Ja 20,19:3
Tyndall, Hugh H Mrs, 1952, Ap 19,15:4
Tyndall, John Mrs, 1940, Ag 20,19:5
Tyndall, John Prof, 1893, D 5,1:2
Tyndall, Marian (Mrs D Rogers), 1966, Mr 23,48:1
Tyndall, Martha W, 1957, Je 23,84:6
Tyndall, Mary Sylvester Rev Mother, 1955, N 24,29:2
Tyndall, Robert H, 1947, Jl 10,21:4
Tyndall, Russell M, 1947, S 3,25:6
Tyndall, Stanley G, 1940, D 3,25:2
Tyner, Charles L (por), 1939, Ag 17,21:1
Tyner, Frederick D, 1959, O 11,87:1
Tyner, George N, 1904, F 20,9:5
Tyner, George P, 1957, Mr 21,31:4
Tyner, Gerald K, 1953, Mr 11,29:4
Tyner, James N, 1904, D 6,9:6
Tyner, Ralph T, 1945, S 27,21:3
Tyner, Richard L Mrs, 1965, Ag 23,31:2
Tynes, Achilles Mrs, 1966, Ap 29,47:1
Tynes, Harcourt A Sr, 1958, My 31,15:5
Tyneson, Walter R, 1954, S 28,29:5
Tyng, Alex G, 1919, Je 7,13:6
Tyng, Charles R, 1925, D 31,15:5
Tyng, Harriet M, 1952, N 1,21:4
Tyng, Juliet A (will), 1940, S 6,17:8
Tyng, Juliet A Mrs, 1940, Ag 5,13:4
Tyng, L Mrs, 1933, F 23,17:5
Tyng, Lucien H (por), 1948, Mr 7,69:1
Tyng, Morris Ashhurst, 1915, Ap 5,11:5
Tyng, S H Dr, 1898, N 18,7:5
Tyng, Sewell T, 1946, My 8,25:4
Tyng, Walsworth, 1960, My 29,57:2
Tyno, Stephen Mrs, 1960, Mr 22,37:1
Tyre, Charles A, 1953, Mr 25,31:4
Tyre, Phil S, 1937, Ag 28,15:7
Tyree, Lewis, 1957, Ja 29,31:6
Tyree, William F, 1960, Je 6,29:4
Tyrell, Arthur I, 1958, Ap 30,33:4

Tyrer, Lloyd P, 1965, D 29,29:2
Tyrol, Alfred W, 1949, D 28,25:5
Tyrrel, Elmer B, 1947, Ap 23,25:1
Tyrrell, Edward, 1947, Ap 4,24:2
Tyrrell, Edward T, 1965, Jl 10,25:3
Tyrrell, Florence, 1947, O 17,22:4
Tyrrell, Frank P, 1947, F 13,24:3
Tyrrell, Herbert V, 1942, My 7,19:4
Tyrrell, James, 1960, Ag 21,84:8
Tyrrell, John, 1903, Je 30,7:6; 1955, N 13,88:3
Tyrrell, John H Mrs, 1948, D 17,27:3
Tyrrell, John J Jr Mrs, 1950, Mr 24,25:1
Tyrrell, Joseph B, 1957, Ag 27,29:5
Tyrrell, Leo F, 1962, Ag 7,30:1
Tyrrell, Lord, 1947, Mr 15,13:1
Tyrrell, Patrick D, 1920, Ap 5,15:4
Tyrrell, Robert Y, 1914, S 22,11:5
Tyrrell, Warren A, 1939, Je 30,19:1
Tyrrell-Martin, Eric, 1953, My 12,27:1
Tyrrill, Alfred (por), 1943, Mr 12,17:1
Tyrrill, Arthur E Mrs, 1944, N 12,48:6
Tyrwhitt, Reginald, 1951, My 31,27:1
Tyrwhitt, St John R J, 1961, O 12,29:2
Tysen-Amherst, William Amherst (Baron Amherst), 1909, Ja 18,9:4
Tysinger, Joseph T, 1949, D 11,93:1
Tysliava, Joseph, 1961, N 14,36:1
Tyson, Carroll S Jr, 1956, Mr 20,23:3
Tyson, Carroll S Mrs, 1963, Ag 6,31:2
Tyson, Charles H, 1940, O 8,25:6
Tyson, Edmund H, 1956, D 25,25:3
Tyson, Edward T 3d, 1952, Ja 20,84:4
Tyson, Elizabeth, 1964, S 13,86:8
Tyson, Forrest C, 1953, D 27,61:1
Tyson, Frank L (por), 1946, My 27,27:2
Tyson, Frank M, 1939, Jl 6,24:2
Tyson, Frederick A, 1945, Ap 9,19:3
Tyson, George D, 1904, D 14,9:4; 1959, Mr 29,80:4
Tyson, George G Mrs, 1956, Je 13,37:5
Tyson, George I, 1960, N 25,27:5
Tyson, George I Mrs, 1909, Je 27,7:5
Tyson, George Mrs, 1963, Mr 27,4:6
Tyson, Henry H, 1903, S 10,7:5
Tyson, Hilton Mrs, 1943, Mr 7,39:1
Tyson, Hobart W, 1950, Ja 4,35:5
Tyson, James C, 1944, Mr 23,19:4
Tyson, James C Mrs, 1950, D 6,33:2
Tyson, James Dr, 1919, F 22,9:4
Tyson, James H (will), 1941, N 9,48:1
Tyson, James S Y, 1942, Je 27,13:2
Tyson, James W Jr Mrs, 1939, N 21,23:5
Tyson, John H, 1938, Ja 31,19:6
Tyson, John H Mrs, 1953, S 19,15:7
Tyson, John Russell, 1923, Mr 28,19:4
Tyson, L D, 1929, Ag 25,II,5:1
Tyson, Leonard S, 1958, F 10,23:1
Tyson, Levering, 1966, Je 11,31:3
Tyson, Levering Mrs, 1964, O 17,29:5
Tyson, Marie L, 1954, My 18,29:6
Tyson, Mark, 1967, N 7,39:3
Tyson, Mark Mrs, 1967, D 23,23:4
Tyson, Miriam B Mrs, 1951, Mr 20,29:2
Tyson, Oscar S, 1951, Je 19,30:3
Tyson, Paul, 1950, S 11,23:6
Tyson, Robert A, 1958, F 4,29:4
Tyson, Robert A Mrs, 1962, Mr 30,33:1
Tyson, Russell, 1963, Jl 23,29:4
Tyson, S L, 1932, S 17,18:1
Tyson, Warren A, 1942, Ag 14,17:4
Tyson, William S Mrs, 1961, S 10,87:1
Tyte, Arthur M, 1940, Ja 16,23:2
Tytell, Louis Mrs, 1966, Ap 23,31:1
Tytgat, Edgard, 1957, Ja 12,19:1
Tyther, James D, 1925, Je 20,13:6
Tytheridge, Joseph A, 1952, Je 28,19:3
Tytla, Vladimir W P, 1968, D 31,27:1
Tytler, J Malcolm Mrs, 1948, Jl 19,19:5
Tytus, John B (por), 1944, Je 3,13:3
Tytus, Robb de Peyster, 1913, Ag 16,9:6
Tyven, Gertrude (Mrs E Slavin), 1966, F 15,39:2
Tyyrell, George Father (funl, Jl 22,7:6), 1909, Jl 16, 7:6
Tzara, Tristan, 1963, D 26,27:1
Tziorogh, Elias T, 1942, Mr 30,17:3

U

U So Nyun, 1951, Ja 1,17:4
Uanna, William L, 1961, D 23,23:5
Ubaldi, Ubaldo Rev, 1884, D 15,4:5
Ubbelohde, Francois C, 1955, My 19,29:1
Uber, John, 1955, Mr 12,19:3
Ubico, Jorge (por), 1946, Je 16,40:4
Ubinger, Paul J, 1963, N 5,31:3
Ubrandt, Silas A, 1946, N 1,23:3
Uchida, Ryohei, 1937, Jl 28,19:6
Uchida, Y, 1936, Mr 13,23:4
Uchitel, Samuel R, 1950, Ap 30,102:7
Uchiyama, Kojiro, 1945, F 17,13:4
Uckerman, Frank C, 1963, S 8,86:5
Uckkyum, Yu, 1947, N 14,23:3
Uda, Koichi, 1957, D 31,17:2
Udall, Agnes L Mrs, 1957, Jl 14,72:1
Udall, D H, 1955, S 10,17:5
Udall, Frank O, 1952, Je 2,21:5
Udall, John C, 1953, D 11,34:6
Udall, Levi S, 1960, Je 1,39:3
Udall, Philip A, 1959, O 12,19:6
Udd, John C, 1962, N 13,38:1
Uddo, Giuseppe, 1957, N 2,21:2
Udell, Abraham, 1955, Mr 29,29:1
Udell, Alonzo E, 1960, D 21,31:4
Udell, Foster, 1909, My 3,7:7
Udell, John L, 1949, Mr 20,76:6
Udell, Lester, 1965, F 26,29:3
Udell, Max Mrs, 1949, Ja 27,24:3
Udell, Murray, 1952, Ja 7,19:3
Udell, William D, 1940, Mr 7,23:4
Uderitz, Henry J, 1939, Mr 10,23:2
Udin, Sophie (Mrs P Gingold), 1960, Ap 28,35:4
Udoff, Barney L, 1954, Ap 25,86:1
Udy, Marvin J, 1959, Ap 12,86:4
Uebel, Theodore G, 1959, D 19,27:5
Uebelacker, Armin Dr, 1914, F 7,11:5
Uebelacker, Charles F, 1940, S 18,23:6
Uebelacker, David A, 1964, My 16,25:2
Uechtritz, Charles Edgar von Mrs, 1912, Ag 29,9:5
Uehara, Schichinosuke, 1945, F 8,19:2
Uehling, Edward A, 1952, D 22,25:2
Uehling, F Frederick, 1958, Ja 23,27:3
Uehlinger, Paul M, 1942, Ag 23,42:2
Ueland, Gabriel T, 1945, Ja 25,19:1
Uetz, Paul, 1954, S 29,31:6
Uezzell, William N, 1967, Ag 8,39:4
Ufer, Arthur W, 1903, S 10,14:3
Ufer, Frank B, 1942, Ap 7,22:3
Ufer, Hazel H Mrs, 1940, O 11,21:3
Ufer, Walter Mrs, 1947, Jl 19,13:2
Uffelman, Charles M, 1952, My 7,27:6
Uffenheimer, Albert M, 1941, Ap 10,23:3
Uffert, John F, 1959, D 3,37:1
Uffindell, Benjamin E, 1951, F 16,25:3
Ufford, Frank P, 1954, Ag 19,23:3
Ugaki, Kazunari, 1956, My 2,31:5
Ugarte, Jose G, 1943, Mr 25,21:2
Ugarte, Miguel, 1940, F 18,41:1
Ugarte, Rafael de, 1941, N 8,19:4
Uggla, Bertil, 1945, O 3,19:1
Ughet, Serge A Mrs, 1949, F 23,28:3
Ughetta, Casper Mrs, 1951, F 3,15:5
Ughetta, Henry L, 1967, S 17,84:3
Ughetta, Jerome H L, 1943, Mr 5,17:1
Ugone, Lorenzo, 1952, Mr 21,23:2
Uhde, Herman, 1965, O 15,45:5
Uher, Frank E, 1960, N 13,89:1
Uherka, Frank, 1956, F 6,23:1
Uhl, Byron H, 1944, N 22,19:2
Uhl, Conrad, 1920, F 13,11:3
Uhl, Edward, 1906, Ag 2,7:6
Uhl, Ella A Mrs, 1942, F 13,21:4
Uhl, Frederick, 1966, Jl 7,37:3
Uhl, Frederick Mrs, 1953, Ag 7,19:4
Uhl, George, 1948, Ja 7,25:5
Uhl, Herman, 1881, F 14,8:1
Uhl, James R, 1943, S 17,21:5
Uhl, Jerome P Mrs, 1956, F 5,86:3
Uhl, Kenneth, 1941, Je 4,23:5
Uhl, Lemon L, 1943, Mr 1,19:1
Uhl, Louis F, 1948, O 31,88:6
Uhl, S Jerome Sr, 1916, Ap 13,13:5
Uhl, Willis L, 1940, Mr 1,21:5
Uhland, T Howard, 1944, N 18,13:4
Uhlar, Roman A, 1947, Ag 17,53:1
Uhle, Frederick L, 1952, Jl 16,25:4
Uhlein, William B, 1953, Jl 30,23:2
Uhlemann, William R, 1941, S 17,23:1
Uhlendahl, Heinrich, 1954, D 29,23:3
Uhlenhuth, Edward C A, 1961, My 17,37:4
Uhler, Alfred M, 1963, My 4,25:6
Uhler, Doyle M, 1954, F 6,19:2
Uhler, Edward J, 1956, Je 19,29:5
Uhler, Horace S, 1956, D 8,19:4
Uhler, Joseph M, 1947, Ag 19,23:6
Uhler, Philip Reese Dr, 1913, O 22,9:6
Uhler, Robert D, 1940, N 29,21:5
Uhler, William P, 1939, F 16,21:2

Uhlfelder, Augustus, 1905, Ap 11,1:2
Uhlfelder, Harry H, 1955, N 8,33:7
Uhlhorn, Theodore G, 1911, Ag 3,7:6
Uhlig, Edward C, 1940, Ag 22,19:3
Uhlig, Max E, 1958, My 29,27:4
Uhlig, Paul C Sr, 1946, D 20,24:3
Uhlig, Richard W, 1937, N 2,28:2
Uhlig, William C, 1940, N 30,17:3
Uhlir, Frank G, 1953, S 13,84:8
Uhlmann, Alfred J, 1954, Ap 14,29:2
Uhlmann, Erick, 1964, S 16,31:1
Uhlmann, Ernst, 1922, Ap 29,15:4
Uhlmann, Fred, 1938, O 11,25:4
Uhr, Jacques S, 1953, O 11,89:1
Uhrbrock, Richard S Mrs, 1956, F 13,27:3
Uhrich, J A, 1881, O 25,2:6
Uhrig, Clyde, 1945, Ja 4,19:2
Uhrig, Henry E, 1948, Ja 27,25:1
Uhry, Edmond, 1954, F 26,20:3
Uhry, Edward, 1948, D 30,19:2
Uihlein, Aug E (will, My 30,31:2),(por), 1939, My 23,23:3
Uihlein, Edgar J, 1956, O 3,33:5
Uihlein, Edgar J (est tax appr), 1958, F 1,39:2
Uihlein, Erwin C Jr, 1968, N 14,47:4
Uihlein, Erwin C Sr, 1968, O 21,47:4
Uihlein, Eva C, 1941, Jl 22,19:5
Uihlein, Henry, 1922, Ap 23,28:3
Uihlein, Herbert E, 1947, S 19,23:3
Uihlein, Herbert E Mrs, 1947, D 26,15:3
Uihlein, Joseph E Sr, 1968, Ja 8,39:1
Uihlein, Oscar L, 1942, Je 14,45:1
Uihlein, Paula, 1968, My 18,34:6
Uihlein, Robert A, 1959, My 14,33:3
Ukers, William H, 1954, Ja 21,31:3
Ukers, William H Mrs, 1951, O 30,29:5
Ulanet, Jacob Mrs, 1955, Ap 23,19:5
Ulanoff, Harris, 1963, Ap 7,86:3
Ulanowsky, Paul, 1968, Ag 6,37:1
Ulbrandt, Thomas E, 1949, Ap 13,29:6
Ulbrich, Herman Mrs, 1946, Mr 28,25:5
Ulbricht, R E Col, 1922, My 8,17:4
Uleau, Francis J (por), 1943, Mr 1,19:3
Ulen, Henry C, 1963, My 18,27:3
Ulen, Henry C Mrs, 1951, Mr 18,88:6
Ulery, Ulysses J, 1945, Jl 14,11:3
Uleskes, John, 1949, Ag 19,17:2
Ulianova, Maria I, 1937, Je 13,II,6:8
Ulich, Robert Mrs, 1948, Mr 8,23:5
Ulinski, John A, 1961, Ja 28,19:4
Ulio, James A, 1958, Ag 3,80:4
Ulitzur, Abraham, 1948, Jl 29,21:4
Ulke, Henry, 1910, F 19,11:4
Ulla, Mariano G, 1945, N 26,21:2
Ullah, Najib, 1965, Ag 2,29:3
Ullius, Frederick W, 1938, Ap 30,15:5
Ullman, Adolph, 1957, Ja 3,33:4
Ullman, Albert, 1955, S 22,31:2
Ullman, Albert F, 1942, Ja 23,20:2
Ullman, Alexander F, 1943, S 4,13:2
Ullman, Alice W Mrs (A Woods), 1959, Jl 25,17:3
Ullman, Allen, 1967, Ja 3,37:2
Ullman, Berthold L, 1965, Je 27,64:5
Ullman, Carrie H, 1959, N 24,37:5
Ullman, Edgar S, 1946, Mr 30,15:1
Ullman, Emanuel S, 1943, D 22,23:2
Ullman, Eugene P, 1953, Ap 21,27:5
Ullman, Eugene P Mrs, 1950, Jl 8,13:6
Ullman, Frances Mrs, 1941, Jl 26,15:3
Ullman, Frederic J (por), 1948, D 27,21:3
Ullman, Frederick Sr, 1939, N 12,48:7
Ullman, Harry, 1951, F 9,25:4
Ullman, J Joseph, 1952, F 6,29:4
Ullman, Jerome M, 1964, O 3,29:5
Ullman, Joseph, 1941, F 13,19:3; 1946, F 3,40:3; 1952, Jl 20,52:1
Ullman, Joseph H, 1944, O 12,27:4
Ullman, Julius, 1953, Ag 16,77:3
Ullman, Karl B, 1953, F 8,88:3
Ullman, Lawrence J Mrs, 1958, Mr 25,33:4
Ullman, Leo, 1966, Mr 12,27:4
Ullman, Leo Mrs, 1966, Ja 25,41:1
Ullman, Max G, 1953, Mr 13,27:3
Ullman, Max J Mrs, 1955, Ag 7,73:1
Ullman, Paul I, 1967, N 21,47:2
Ullman, Roland G, 1949, D 3,15:6
Ullman, Samuel, 1949, Ja 23,68:5; 1950, Ag 9,29:4
Ullman, Samuel Mrs, 1937, Ja 1,23:1
Ullman, Sol, 1941, Jl 7,15:3
Ullman, William A, 1938, Mr 5,17:5
Ullman, William S Mrs, 1954, Ap 20,29:2
Ullmann, Frederic, 1942, Ag 24,15:4
Ullmann, Fritz, 1948, My 13,25:3
Ullmann, George Sr, 1961, Mr 22,41:4
Ullmann, Joseph, 1955, Ag 4,25:5
Ullmann, Ludwig, 1959, My 5,33:4
Ullmann, Marcel, 1942, D 8,25:5
Ullmann, Oscar, 1960, Jl 25,23:5
Ullmann, Samuel, 1937, O 31,II,11:2

Ullmann, Siegfried, 1965, D 3,39:1
Ullmer, Edward J, 1957, Ja 1,23:2
Ullo, Lorenzo, 1915, O 15,11:6
Ullo, Monica R Mrs, 1937, S 13,21:4
Ullom, Josephus T, 1965, N 14,88:6
Ullrich, Adelaide W Mrs, 1952, Jl 1,23:4
Ullrich, Albert H, 1951, Ap 27,23:2
Ullrich, Aug C, 1942, Mr 28,17:6
Ullrich, August Mrs, 1947, My 14,25:3
Ullrich, Charles A, 1947, Ap 2,27:4
Ullrich, Ernest R, 1953, Ap 14,27:2
Ullrich, George C, 1954, Mr 30,27:5
Ullrich, William J, 1949, O 11,31:4
Ullstein, H, 1935, My 17,21:4
Ullstein, Herman, 1943, N 24,21:1
Ullstein, Karl H, 1964, Ja 8,34:7
Ullstein, Rudolf, 1964, F 3,27:2
Ulm, Buel F, 1950, D 12,33:5
Ulman, H Charles, 1915, F 25,9:4
Ulman, Joseph N, 1943, Ap 19,19:2
Ulman, Julien Stevens, 1920, My 8,15:3
Ulman, Max, 1946, Je 8,21:6
Ulmann, Albert, 1948, O 9,17:3
Ulmann, Bernard (funl), 1915, D 3,11:6
Ulmann, Emil, 1947, D 10,31:2
Ulmann, Gene (will), 1940, Mr 15,19:4
Ulmar, David, 1967, Ap 24,33:2
Ulmer, Alfred C Sr, 1961, O 10,43:1
Ulmer, Brewer, 1907, D 16,9:4
Ulmer, Frank, 1903, My 24,7:4
Ulmer, Henry C, 1948, F 12,23:4
Ulmer, John C, 1950, Ap 4,29:3
Ulmer, Levi J, 1942, N 26,27:2
Ulmer, Lillie Mrs, 1953, Mr 6,14:4
Ulmer, Samuel, 1944, My 23,23:1
Ulmer, William C, 1943, F 4,23:2
Ulmstead, Charles E, 1956, Mr 14,33:6
Ulp, Clifford M, 1958, Ja 24,23:3
Ulreich, Nora W, 1950, O 27,29:3
Ulrich, Arthur L, 1942, S 12,13:7
Ulrich, Bernard A C, 1946, F 14,26:2
Ulrich, Bernard E, 1948, Je 27,52:4
Ulrich, Bernard Mrs, 1958, Ja 6,39:4
Ulrich, Carl C, 1964, Ja 14,31:1
Ulrich, Carl T, 1960, F 29,27:2
Ulrich, Charles Frederick, 1908, My 21,7:5
Ulrich, Charles K, 1941, Jl 6,27:2
Ulrich, Conrad C, 1953, Mr 17,29:1
Ulrich, Edward Mrs, 1962, Jl 24,27:5
Ulrich, Elmer B, 1955, Ap 26,29:1
Ulrich, Fred S Mrs, 1946, My 18,19:5
Ulrich, Frederick L, 1965, N 11,50:1
Ulrich, Frederick S, 1947, S 9,31:4
Ulrich, G C, 1932, F 18,22:1
Ulrich, George, 1949, O 21,25:5
Ulrich, George A, 1944, Jl 21,19:5
Ulrich, George C, 1961, Ja 21,21:5
Ulrich, George S, 1943, Ap 2,21:3
Ulrich, Henry A, 1946, N 26,29:5
Ulrich, Ida Mrs, 1937, O 26,23:4
Ulrich, J Sewell, 1942, Je 20,13:3
Ulrich, Kurt F, 1953, S 1,23:2
Ulrich, Pauline, 1916, My 27,11:5
Ulrich, Robert, 1952, Ja 29,25:3
Ulrich, Robert C, 1912, Ap 8,11:6
Ulrich, Samuel, 1965, Ag 27,29:5
Ulrich, Vasily V, 1951, My 11,27:3
Ulrich, Walter G, 1955, Ap 23,19:5
Ulrich, William B Dr, 1905, Ap 25,11:6
Ulrych, Julius, 1959, N 7,2:4
Ulsamer, Otto A, 1958, F 15,17:5
Ulsaver, Ervin S, 1956, Mr 22,35:4
Ulsaver, Ervin S Mrs, 1950, Ap 13,29:2
Ulsh, Hollis F, 1944, S 2,11:4
Ulsh, John W, 1950, Mr 12,92:2
Ulshafer, Adam, 1955, O 19,33:4
Ulshafer, Clifford J, 1940, Mr 2,13:5
Ultramachado, Gustavo, 1949, S 26,25:4
Ulyanov, Dmitri, 1943, Jl 18,34:5
Ulyatt, William L, 1951, Ag 11,11:3
Uman, Abraham Mrs, 1949, Ap 8,25:2
Umana, Alvaro, 1953, Mr 23,2:3
Umansky, Harry, 1962, Ja 14,84:3
Umansky, Leonid A, 1957, Ap 5,27:2
Umansky, Samuel, 1952, Ja 5,11:3
Umauer, Sebastian J, 1955, Jl 24,64:6
Umbach, Eckhardt, 1942, Je 3,23:2
Umbach, Edward F, 1937, D 12,II,8:5
Umbach, William J, 1967, Ag 24,37:4
Umber, Franklyn L Mrs, 1953, My 3,88:3
Umber, Louis H, 1947, Jl 24,21:5
Umberger, Harry H, 1967, Ja 28,27:5
Umberger, Robert, 1945, My 14,17:3
Umbreit, Kenneth B, 1962, Mr 30,33:3
Umbreit, Samuel, 1945, Ja 29,13:1
Umbreit, Willard E, 1957, Jl 15,19:4
Umbricht, Jean, 1941, O 28,23:4
Umbricht, Jim (funl, Ap 11,19:3), 1964, Ap 9,31:1
Umbstaetter, Herman D, 1913, N 26,11:6

Umetani, Kaoru, 1963, Jl 13,17:5
Umewake, Manzaburo, 1946, Jl 1,31:2
Umezu, Yoshijiro, 1949, Ja 8,4:7
Umhey, Frederick F (funl, Ja 30,84:5), 1955, Ja 27, 23:3
Umhey, Frederick F Mrs, 1946, N 4,25:4
Umholtz, Ammon M, 1942, N 1,52:3
Uminger, John C, 1957, Jl 13,17:4
Umstadter, Charles F, 1955, D 12,31:2
Umstead, Daniel M, 1958, O 15,39:2
Umstead, Samuel H, 1952, Ja 30,25:3
Umstead, William B, 1954, N 8,21:1
Umsted, John R, 1949, Ja 2,60:4
Unamuno, Miguel de, 1937, Ja 2,11:3
Unangst, Charles Mrs, 1947, Ag 27,23:3
Unangst, Daniel B, 1948, Ja 13,25:6
Unbehend, Warren B, 1953, Je 26,19:4
Unbekant, F E, 1885, My 12,5:4
Uncle Tom (Rev J Henson), 1883, My 6,1:7
Uncles, John F, 1967, Ja 22,77:3
Undeck, John P, 1950, Ag 20,76:1
Underhill, A G, 1881, D 14,5:2
Underhill, A H, 1883, Ap 3,4:7
Underhill, A L, 1902, Mr 11,9:5
Underhill, Abram S, 1942, Ap 11,13:4
Underhill, Alfred Dr, 1873, D 11,3:3
Underhill, Allen B, 1944, Ap 11,19:2
Underhill, Annie E, 1945, S 7,23:4
Underhill, Arthur, 1939, Ja 25,21:4
Underhill, Carl R, 1950, O 5,31:2
Underhill, Charles B Mrs, 1954, F 14,93:1
Underhill, Charles L, 1946, Ja 29,25:6
Underhill, E F, 1898, Je 19,7:4
Underhill, E Milton, 1951, Ag 17,17:5
Underhill, Edward, 1905, Jl 4,1:2
Underhill, Edward A, 1947, Ag 16,13:6
Underhill, Edwin S Jr, 1960, S 1,27:2
Underhill, Elias Hicks, 1905, O 19,9:5
Underhill, Elise T Mrs, 1940, My 15,25:1
Underhill, Elizabeth C, 1947, S 21,60:7
Underhill, Ella, 1909, Ag 19,7:5
Underhill, Elmer, 1942, N 13,23:4
Underhill, Emily, 1944, F 18,17:5
Underhill, Eugene, 1937, Ap 28,23:2; 1938, Ap 6,23:1
Underhill, Eugene B Mrs, 1917, N 6,13:7
Underhill, Francis, 1943, Ja 25,14:2
Underhill, Francis J, 1938, My 22,II,7:3
Underhill, Frederic Edgar, 1925, Ja 17,15:4
Underhill, G E, 1884, Ag 26,5:2
Underhill, Georgia T, 1942, N 3,23:5
Underhill, Gilbert R Rev, 1937, D 28,21:2
Underhill, Henry Clay, 1918, My 2,13:3
Underhill, Henry F, 1948, O 14,29:2
Underhill, Irving, 1960, N 15,39:3
Underhill, Jesse, 1950, S 24,104:3
Underhill, John G, 1946, My 17,22:2
Underhill, John Q, 1907, My 22,9:5
Underhill, Julia S, 1944, Mr 28,19:3
Underhill, L C, 1907, My 15,9:5
Underhill, Lora A Mrs, 1938, Ap 19,21:2
Underhill, Margaret V, 1953, Ag 14,19:3
Underhill, Orra E, 1943, Je 11,19:4
Underhill, R C, 1871, D 22,2:6
Underhill, Reuben L, 1955, Ja 8,13:4
Underhill, Robert W Mrs, 1945, Je 13,23:4
Underhill, Thomas V, 1953, S 4,15:1
Underhill, William A, 1961, O 6,35:1
Underhill, William Anderson, 1917, My 7,9:5
Underhill, William H, 1940, O 30,23:5
Underhill, William J Mrs, 1943, Ja 3,42:3
Underkofler, Leo V, 1957, F 7,27:1
Underndorfer, Leo, 1953, Ag 12,31:6
Underner, John Prof, 1904, Mr 25,2:4
Underriner, Edward A, 1952, F 9,13:5
Underwood, Abby, 1941, Ja 16,21:4
Underwood, Alex, 1948, N 3,27:5
Underwood, Allen C, 1949, My 25,29:3
Underwood, Andrew A, 1952, Jl 8,27:2
Underwood, Bert E (por), 1943, D 29,17:3
Underwood, Bert E Mrs, 1946, Ja 3,20:2
Underwood, Charles P, 1967, Ja 20,43:2
Underwood, Charles W, 1943, Jl 1,19:3; 1948, O 27, 27:2
Underwood, Claude C, 1964, S 17,43:1
Underwood, Cornelius S, 1872, My 1,5:3
Underwood, Drury, 1925, Mr 31,19:6
Underwood, E Marvin, 1960, Ag 30,29:4
Underwood, Edward B (por), 1939, Ap 25,23:1
Underwood, Edward J, 1951, Je 28,25:4
Underwood, Edward L, 1940, Jl 5,13:5
Underwood, Elmer (por), 1947, Ag 19,23:1
Underwood, Enoch W, 1958, O 10,32:1
Underwood, Eric, 1952, Je 15,84:3
Underwood, Frank Livingston, 1918, Mr 18,13:5
Underwood, Franklyn, 1940, D 23,19:3
Underwood, Frederica V Mrs, 1921, D 6,19:6
Underwood, Frederick D, 1942, F 20,17:1
Underwood, G Frank, 1942, Ap 1,21:2
Underwood, George, 1944, N 25,13:2
Underwood, George B, 1938, Je 26,27:3; 1943, Ag 28, 39:3
Underwood, George B Mrs, 1960, Ap 17,92:2
Underwood, George F, 1923, Ag 7,17:2
Underwood, Harrison A, 1949, F 10,27:5
Underwood, Harvey R, 1944, O 12,27:5
Underwood, Herbert M, 1948, Mr 8,23:2
Underwood, Herbert S, 1948, Mr 17,25:3
Underwood, Herbert T, 1950, Ja 8,77:1
Underwood, Horace Grant Dr, 1916, O 13,11:4
Underwood, Horace H (mem ser, Mr 16,31:1), 1951, F 21,27:4
Underwood, J Harris, 1957, N 17,86:2
Underwood, J R, 1876, Ag 25,4:7
Underwood, J S, 1883, D 12,5:3
Underwood, James E, 1952, Ja 18,27:2
Underwood, John, 1951, N 14,31:1
Underwood, John C Judge, 1873, D 9,1:3
Underwood, John Cox Gen, 1913, O 27,9:4
Underwood, John J, 1949, Jl 15,19:2
Underwood, John L, 1937, Ja 3,II,8:5
Underwood, John T (will, Jl 11,4:2),(por), 1937, Jl 3, 15:1
Underwood, Julius E Sr, 1957, N 26,33:2
Underwood, Kennard, 1966, Mr 13,86:6
Underwood, Kenneth Dr, 1968, O 25,47:2
Underwood, Kenneth F H, 1952, F 13,29:4
Underwood, Lawrence S, 1948, Je 27,52:6
Underwood, Loring Mrs, 1961, O 5,37:4
Underwood, Louis E, 1951, Jl 2,23:4
Underwood, O, 1929, Ja 26,1:2
Underwood, Oscar W Jr, 1962, N 13,37:1
Underwood, Oscar W Mrs, 1948, O 27,28:3
Underwood, Paul A, 1968, S 27,47:1
Underwood, Paul M, 1968, Ap 6,39:4
Underwood, Pierson, 1960, Jl 31,69:3
Underwood, Robert, 1952, My 19,17:4
Underwood, Robert H, 1874, D 15,1:7
Underwood, Roy R, 1951, O 17,34:3
Underwood, Thomas R, 1956, Je 30,17:5
Underwood, Valentine X, 1959, Mr 12,31:4
Underwood, Virginia, 1954, F 20,17:5
Underwood, Virginia G D Mrs, 1942, Ag 7,17:5
Underwood, W H, 1914, Mr 26,11:6
Underwood, Walter B, 1942, O 19,19:2
Underwood, William G, 1948, F 19,23:1
Underwood, William J, 1914, D 29,11:6; 1941, F 12, 21:4; 1954, Mr 3,27:1
Undset, Sigrid, 1949, Je 11,17:1
Unfried, Charles J, 1942, Ap 28,21:3
Ungar, Alexander, 1924, Ap 19,13:6
Ungar, Arthur, 1950, Jl 26,25:4
Ungar, Emil, 1919, N 27,15:3
Ungar, Emil Mrs, 1950, F 13,21:4
Ungar, Fritz C H, 1939, S 16,17:6
Ungar, George F, 1917, Je 18,9:6
Ungar, Gustav A, 1950, Ap 1,15:3
Ungar, Harry F, 1940, S 5,23:2
Ungar, Stanley F, 1956, Ap 20,25:2
Ungberg, Warren E Mrs, 1965, Ja 13,25:4
Ungemach, Joseph, 1952, Ap 9,31:5
Unger, Abraham, 1960, S 10,21:3
Unger, Arthur J, 1959, O 27,37:3
Unger, Arthur S, 1967, Jl 23,60:6
Unger, Edward F, 1962, Ag 24,25:1
Unger, Emil, 1904, Ag 21,9:6
Unger, Eugene M Mrs, 1945, S 22,17:2
Unger, Ferdinand, 1917, Mr 11,21:3
Unger, Frances Mrs, 1957, S 25,38:8
Unger, George, 1968, O 1,48:1
Unger, Gladys B (por), 1940, My 26,35:3
Unger, Harry, 1938, N 27,48:7; 1963, Jl 21,64:6
Unger, Heinz, 1965, F 27,25:3
Unger, Henry W, 1942, D 19,19:1
Unger, Henry W Mrs, 1940, D 21,17:2
Unger, Herbert M, 1940, O 6,48:2
Unger, Herman, 1953, O 25,89:2
Unger, Isador, 1953, My 18,21:6
Unger, James S, 1949, Ja 21,21:4
Unger, Jonas J Dr, 1968, Ap 17,47:3
Unger, Joseph L, 1937, Ja 30,17:2
Unger, L Mrs, 1878, Je 24,2:3
Unger, Leonard A, 1960, Mr 27,86:2
Unger, Milton Mrs, 1967, Jl 6,35:1
Unger, Morris, 1952, F 15,26:2
Unger, Nathan, 1941, F 15,15:5
Unger, Richard, 1947, O 7,27:6
Unger, Rudolph Mrs, 1953, Ap 20,25:1
Unger, Samuel, 1940, Je 19,23:5
Unger, Theodore R, 1943, Ag 12,19:1
Unger, W Hudson, 1951, Jl 23,17:4
Unger, William F, 1962, O 29,29:5
Unger-Donaldson, Donald S, 1943, Jl 2,19:5
Ungerathen, George D, 1948, Jl 22,23:5
Ungerer, Frederick H, 1966, Je 12,86:6
Ungerer, Heiby W, 1947, Ja 24,21:2
Ungerer, Jacques C, 1957, N 9,27:2
Ungerfeld, Robert M, 1967, My 5,39:2
Ungerland, Alfred J, 1953, My 5,29:5
Ungnade, Herbert E, 1965, Ag 17,19:2
Ungrich, Martin J, 1946, Jl 26,21:1
Unhoch, Anita (Sister Mray Terence), 1956, O 12, 29:4
Unhoch, Frank Sr, 1952, Ja 25,22:3
Uniac, E H, 1869, O 25,2:2
Uniacke, H, 1934, My 15,21:1
Uniacke, Joseph B, 1949, D 5,23:1
Uniak, Al, 1953, Ja 9,21:3
Uniker, Thomas E, 1961, D 23,23:5
Unkart, Gustava, 1942, Ag 28,19:6
Unkefer, Dudley F, 1965, Ag 10,29:4
Unkelbach, William G, 1950, Mr 9,54:6
Unkles, John, 1943, Mr 4,19:3
Unkles, Stewart, 1952, F 20,29:4
Unlandherm, John H, 1957, Ja 15,29:1
Unmacht, George F, 1954, Ja 11,25:1
Unobskey, Charles, 1958, Mr 9,86:5
Unobskey, William M, 1963, Je 18,37:1
Unruh, Benjamin H, 1959, My 14,33:1
Unruh, Carl F, 1952, D 5,28:3
Unruh, Marilyn, 1950, Mr 18,15:8
Unser, Jerry, 1959, My 18,27:4
Unsworth, Thomas A, 1950, F 15,27:4
Unterberg, David W, 1954, S 21,27:4
Unterberg, I, 1934, My 2,21:5
Untereiner, Harry R, 1942, My 4,19:6
Untermann, Ernest, 1956, Ja 26,29:2
Untermann, William M, 1944, F 9,19:2
Untermeyer, Alvin, 1963, S 21,21:1
Untermeyer, Emanuel, 1918, Mr 28,11:5
Untermeyer, Henry, 1913, N 20,11:4
Untermeyer, Samuel Mrs, 1924, Ag 17,24:3
Untermyer, Alvin Mrs, 1955, My 4,29:6
Untermyer, Eugene, 1959, Je 14,86:4
Untermyer, Irwin Mrs (will, Ap 6,23:2), 1944, Mr 28,19:2
Untermyer, Maurice (funl, Ja 1,11:7), 1908, D 30,9:6
Untermyer, Maurice Mrs, 1915, Je 2,13:5
Untermyer, Samuel, 1940, Mr 17,1:4
Untiedt, Christian A, 1937, S 7,21:2
Unver, Fred J, 1959, O 27,37:4
Unverzagt, Gustav, 1958, Ap 28,23:1
Unverzagt, John L, 1968, F 13,43:2
Unwin, Raymond, 1940, Je 30,33:1
Unwin, Stanley Sir, 1968, O 15,47:2
Unzicker, Willard E, 1968, Ag 10,27:5
Unzicker, Willard E Mrs, 1958, Je 14,21:5
Upatieff, Nicolai N, 1938, Ap 23,6:7
Upcraft, John Capt, 1925, Ag 21,13:6
Updegraff, Allan Mrs (Mrs Dora Loues Miller), 1968, F 17,29:4
Updegraff, Florence Mrs, 1949, Jl 16,13:4
Updegraff, Harlan, 1953, Ap 17,25:2
Updegraff, J T, 1882, D 2,5:1
Updegraff, Laurence V, 1961, Ja 18,30:3
Updegraff, Milton, 1938, S 13,24:2
Updegraff, William B, 1941, F 14,18:2
Updike, D Foster Mrs, 1949, N 25,31:4
Updike, Daniel B, 1941, D 30,19:4
Updike, Donald, 1953, Ja 19,23:3
Updike, Forman A, 1951, My 26,17:6
Updike, Godfrey E, 1966, N 5,31:4
Updike, Harold W, 1959, My 23,25:2
Updike, Ralph E, 1953, S 18,23:3
Updike, Stuart N Mrs, 1942, S 10,27:1
Upfield, Arthur W, 1964, F 14,29:1
Upham, Alfred H (por), 1945, F 18,33:2
Upham, Alfred H Mrs, 1958, Ja 4,15:5
Upham, Alson A, 1949, Ja 11,31:3
Upham, Calvin J, 1955, Ap 20,33:4
Upham, Chester R, 1956, Ag 7,27:1
Upham, Fannie W, 1963, Ag 18,80:1
Upham, Frances L, 1941, My 30,15:5
Upham, Francis B (por), 1941, Mr 20,22:2
Upham, Francis B Jr, 1962, Ag 19,88:3
Upham, Frederick William (por), 1925, F 16,19:3
Upham, George B, 1943, Ja 13,23:5
Upham, George G, 1954, Mr 23,27:2
Upham, Henry Macy Mrs, 1916, Je 18,18:5
Upham, N J, 1942, Ap 23,24:3
Upham, Richard Dana, 1924, O 1,19:3
Upham, Robert B, 1949, D 31,15:5
Upham, Roy, 1956, Ja 6,24:3
Upham, Samuel A, 1956, O 10,39:5
Upham, Samuel F Prof, 1904, O 6,9:6
Upham, Thomas, 1916, Jl 12,11:5
Upham, Thomas C Rev, 1872, Ap 3,8:5
Upham, W H, 1924, Jl 3,15:5
Upham, W R Dr, 1882, My 25,5:4
Upham, William A, 1949, Ap 21,26:6
Upham, William L, 1959, S 17,39:5
Uphills, Joseph Prof, 1911, Ja 3,11:6
Upington, Henry V, 1939, Ja 30,14:1
Upjohn, Charles B, 1953, Ap 14,35:1
Upjohn, Dudley T, 1948, S 29,29:4
Upjohn, Edwin P, 1949, N 15,26:4
Upjohn, Hobart B (por), 1949, Ag 24,26:2
Upjohn, Lawrence N, 1967, Je 3,31:2
Upjohn, R, 1878, Ag 18,7:6
Upjohn, R M, 1903, Mr 4,9:6
Upjohn, Richard R, 1940, S 28,17:6
Upjohn, W E Mrs, 1953, O 22,29:5
Upjohn, William H, 1941, Jl 17,19:3
Uplike, Nelson B, 1948, O 16,15:2
Upp, Susan Mrs, 1947, F 17,19:3
Uppercu, Inglis M (por), 1944, Ap 8,13:3
Upperman, William B Mrs, 1946, Mr 28,25:5
Uppvall, Alex J, 1960, O 27,37:2
Upright, Blanche Mrs, 1948, Ap 5,21:5
Upright, Homer R, 1948, S 11,16:7

Upshaw, Arthur, 1954, F 13,19:8
Upshaw, Arthur Mrs, 1954, F 13,19:8
Upshaw, Ida T Mrs, 1942, Jl 28,17:1
Upshaw, William D, 1952, N 22,23:6
Upshur, Alfred P, 1964, O 7,47:1
Upshur, Amelie M Mrs (will), 1953, Ja 15,29:7
Upshur, Custis Clarke, 1920, O 10,22:3
Upshur, Donald M, 1950, S 16,19:3
Upshur, George L, 1938, Ap 25,15:3
Upshur, George L Mrs, 1959, F 15,86:5
Upshur, John Henry Rear-Adm, 1917, My 31,11:4
Upshur, Stella A Mrs, 1956, D 25,25:5
Upson, Dennis A, 1949, O 7,27:3
Upson, Frederick P, 1952, Ag 20,25:3
Upson, Lent D, 1949, My 11,29:5
Upson, Maxwell M Mrs, 1963, D 15,86:3
Upson, Norton L, 1940, D 31,15:2
Upson, Ralph Hazlett, 1968, Ag 15,37:1
Upson, Uriah L, 1945, N 29,23:4
Upson, William H, 1960, Mr 9,33:1
Upston, John E, 1952, Ag 20,25:4
Uptegrove, Deane, 1968, Ja 11,33:2
Uptegrove, William D, 1944, S 1,13:4
Upthegrove, Daniel (por), 1946, O 23,28:2
Upthegrove, Frank E Mrs, 1946, Ap 13,17:1
Uptigrove, Thalia B F M Mrs, 1963, Jl 3,10:2
Upton, A L Mrs, 1948, S 3,19:4
Upton, C H (see also Jl 6), 1877, Jl 9,2:7
Upton, Clifford B, 1957, S 27,19:4
Upton, Dorothy, 1963, Ja 11,4:5
Upton, E Brig-Gen, 1881, Mr 16,5:1
Upton, Edwin C, 1945, Mr 28,23:2
Upton, Florence K, 1922, O 18,19:4
Upton, Frances May Mrs, 1872, My 12,1:3
Upton, Francis R, 1921, Mr 11,15:6
Upton, Frank J, 1942, My 9,13:2
Upton, Frank M, 1962, Ag 2,25:4
Upton, Frank S, 1943, Ap 21,25:4
Upton, George, 1942, Ap 25,13:6
Upton, George B, 1874, Jl 13,2:6; 1942, O 30,19:2
Upton, George W, 1923, Ap 17,21:5
Upton, George W Mrs, 1945, N 4,44:1
Upton, H Desmond, 1959, F 24,29:2
Upton, J K, 1903, Ja 19,1:2
Upton, James B, 1961, My 24,41:2
Upton, John C S Mrs, 1952, Mr 20,29:1
Upton, John R, 1953, Mr 6,20:5
Upton, Joseph, 1963, Je 21,29:3
Upton, Lawrence M, 1967, S 1,31:3
Upton, Louis C, 1952, O 12,89:2
Upton, Luther J, 1954, Ja 2,11:6
Upton, Thomas R, 1949, Ap 12,29:4
Upton, Winslow Prof, 1914, Ja 9,11:5
Upward, A, 1926, N 18,2:5
Upward, Herbert, 1944, D 2,13:2
Uran, Maurice Dr, 1925, Je 13,15:5
Urbach, Erich, 1946, D 18,29:1
Urbach, Frederick Mrs, 1946, My 9,21:1
Urbach, Louis, 1952, O 6,25:2
Urbain, Georges, 1938, N 6,49:2
Urbain, Louis M, 1945, N 7,23:4
Urban, Albert, 1959, Ap 6,27:5
Urban, Alice, 1923, N 29,21:3
Urban, Arthur A Mrs, 1949, My 25,29:3
Urban, Charles, 1945, Mr 5,19:4
Urban, Emma L Mrs, 1937, Mr 6,17:5
Urban, Henry F, 1924, My 15,19:4
Urban, J, 1933, Jl 11,17:1
Urban, John, 1947, O 1,29:2
Urban, John E, 1949, F 9,27:2
Urban, Otto, 1962, My 5,27:1
Urban, Richard, 1948, F 6,23:4
Urban, Robert, 1947, Mr 8,13:2
Urban, Theodore, 1952, O 3,23:1
Urban, William, 1947, F 23,54:3
Urban, William H, 1950, Ja 28,13:2
Urban, William S, 1960, O 19,45:3
Urbanak, Andrew J, 1941, F 13,19:4
Urband, Edward M Mrs, 1940, Jl 31,17:3
Urbano, Francis G, 1961, My 8,35:2
Urbanowicz, Alex Mrs, 1957, Ap 6,19:6
Urbanowicz, Alphonsus, 1949, O 19,29:2
Urbanowitz, Theodore, 1951, Ja 21,77:1
Urbansky, Yevgeny, 1965, N 7,6:2
Urchenko, Vsevolod P, 1944, D 14,23:4
Urchenko, Vsezold P Mrs, 1956, Ag 1,23:4
Urcuyo, Clodomiro, 1956, F 2,25:4
Urdaneta, Magdalena (funl, S 25,35:7), 1960, S 23, 17:2
Urdang, Bernard, 1957, S 14,19:1
Urdang, George, 1960, Je 28,31:4
Urdang, Harry, 1960, O 31,31:4
Urdang, Peshe Malke Mrs, 1924, O 28,23:3
Urdegongse, Prince, 1909, S 22,9:5
Ure, Herbert, 1948, Jl 9,19:4
Ure, Percy N, 1950, Ap 6,29:4
Ureklyan, Gabriel A, 1945, Jl 31,19:5
Urell, Emmet J, 1954, O 2,17:2
Urell, Michael Emmet Gen, 1910, S 8,9:5
U'Ren, Thomas P Mrs, 1946, Mr 15,21:3
Uren, Tommy, 1954, My 31,13:4
U'Ren, W S, 1949, Mr 10,27:1
Urena, Rafael E, 1945, S 17,19:4
Urevitz, Abraham, 1954, Ja 14,29:2
Urff, C Paul Mrs, 1959, Jl 16,27:4
Urff, Paul W, 1958, Jl 30,29:1
Urguhart, Frank U, 1921, F 26,11:5
Urguhart, Isabelle (funl, F 11,9:4), 1907, F 8,9:5
Urguhart, L, 1933, Mr 15,17:4
Uribe, Antonio J, 1942, Mr 10,19:2
Uribe Piedrahita, Cesar, 1951, D 19,31:3
Uriburu, J F, 1932, Ap 29,17:1
Uriburu, Jose Uriburu Dr, 1914, O 26,9:5
Urice, Jay A, 1957, S 8,84:3
Urich, John P, 1958, My 27,31:2
Urich, Wallace W, 1941, Ja 27,15:1
Urie, Caroline F Mrs, 1955, Ap 7,27:4
Urie, Frank D, 1966, S 12,45:2
Urie, James H, 1950, Je 8,31:2
Urie, John, 1938, My 18,21:5
Urie, John F, 1942, Ja 10,15:3
Urig, Raymond C, 1952, Ja 5,11:3
Urion, Alfred R, 1946, My 28,21:5
Urion, Henry K, 1962, N 16,31:4
Urioste, J Col, 1903, S 5,7:6
Uris, Harris H (will, Ag 29,23:2),(por), 1945, My 8, 19:3
Uris, Harris H Mrs, 1958, Mr 26,37:3
Uris, Michael, 1967, Jl 18,38:1
Uris, Nathan, 1964, Je 2,37:3
Uris, Samuel, 1945, Ap 29,37:1
Uriu, Sotokichi Adm (por), 1937, N 12,21:1
Urling, Wendell, 1943, N 24,21:4
Urmston, Frederic W, 1953, Mr 4,27:4
Urmston, Joseph W, 1958, Ag 13,27:4
Urmy, Louis V, 1953, Mr 11,29:5
Urmy, Ralph B, 1947, F 2,57:2
Urner, Charles A (por), 1938, Je 23,21:4
Urner, Charles A Mrs, 1957, F 19,31:5
Urner, Frank A, 1943, Ja 26,19:4
Urner, Henry, 1949, Ja 14,23:3
Urner, Hermann Mrs, 1948, Je 25,24:3
Urner, Stephen K Sr, 1962, Mr 23,45:3
Urness, Henry L, 1956, Ap 5,29:3
Urquhart, Daniel, 1949, Ja 15,17:5
Urquhart, George W Mrs, 1944, N 1,23:5
Urquhart, James A, 1938, S 6,21:3
Urquhart, John A, 1957, Mr 6,31:4
Urquhart, Kate Mrs, 1903, S 27,7:6
Urquhart, Leonard C, 1960, Mr 5,19:2
Urquhart, Noel, 1949, O 11,31:2
Urquhart, R Glen, 1949, D 10,17:1
Urquhart, Robert Sgt, 1937, Ag 29,II,7:1
Urquhart, Stanley O, 1948, Mr 23,25:4
Urquhart, Ubert, 1941, S 24,23:4
Urquhart, William, 1954, Jl 29,25:7
Urquijo y Ussia, Estanislao de, 1948, Ag 17,21:4
Urraza, Angel, 1946, D 12,29:4
Urriola, Ciro Dr, 1922, Je 28,15:5
Urrutia, Franciso J, 1950, Ag 8,29:4
Urrutia, Ignacio, 1951, F 10,13:4
Urrutibeascoa, Fabian de, 1949, D 19,28:2
Ursaner, Murray A, 1962, My 9,43:4
Urschel, Harold C, 1943, N 12,21:2
Ursel, Duc de, 1903, N 28,9:1
Ursem, Leonard J, 1949, Ap 12,30:3
Ursin, Frederick S, 1955, Ap 5,29:1
Urso, Camilla, 1902, Ja 22,9:3
Ursula, Mary Sister, 1925, Ap 8,21:5
Ursula, Mother, 1946, My 5,46:4
Ursula Marie, Sister (Handwright), 1967, N 2,47:3
Urteaga, Horatio, 1952, Je 12,33:1
Urtecho, Andres, 1938, Ag 3,19:6
Urtecho, Isidro Gen, 1922, Ja 18,17:2
Urueta, Hesus Dr, 1920, D 9,13:3
Ury, Israel B, 1959, Ja 27,33:3
Usay, Luigo, 1911, Ap 10,13:4
Usborne, Cecil V, 1951, F 2,24:3
Usdan, David, 1966, Mr 6,92:5
Usdan, Irving Mrs, 1961, F 24,29:2
Usdan, Morris, 1941, Mr 9,41:2
Usdan, William, 1947, My 19,21:5
Uselaner, Solomon, 1962, Ap 21,20:6
Ushakoff, Ivan J, 1961, N 5,88:7
Ushakov, Georgi A, 1963, D 5,45:1
Ushakov, Sergei N, 1964, S 18,32:6
Usher, Abbott P, 1965, Je 20,73:1
Usher, Edwin F, 1941, F 17,15:4
Usher, Fannie, 1948, Je 20,60:3
Usher, Fred R, 1942, Mr 13,19:4
Usher, George W, 1941, Ag 8,15:4
Usher, Harry, 1950, O 30,27:4
Usher, Leila, 1955, Ag 3,23:5
Usher, N R, 1931, Ja 10,15:1
Usher, Nathaniel Mrs, 1917, Ag 8,7:4
Usher, Roland G, 1957, Mr 23,19:6
Usher, Thomas J, 1938, Mr 26,15:4
Usher, Victor J, 1941, Ap 6,49:2
Ushness, William, 1923, Je 22,17:3
Usigli, Gastone, 1956, Mr 9,23:5
Usilton, Frederick G, 1948, F 8,60:7
Usilton, James A, 1939, Mr 14,21:4
Usina, Clyde Sr, 1952, Jl 21,19:3
Usina, D Anthony, 1937, O 24,II,8:2
Usinger, Robert L Dr, 1968, O 2,39:4
Uskurait, Herbert H, 1943, F 6,13:5
Uspenski, Victor L, 1948, My 12,27:1
Uspensky, Boris G, 1951, Mr 19,27:2
Ussani, Vincenzo, 1952, F 3,84:3
Ussishkin, Menachem M (por), 1941, O 3,23:3
Uster, Rudolph J, 1946, S 1,35:1
Utard, Emile, 1925, Je 7,5:1
Utassy, Joseph, 1944, Je 22,19:6
Utensky, Sylvia, 1962, Ap 21,19:5
Uterhart, Henry A (por), 1946, Ap 13,17:3
Uterhart, Henry A Mrs, 1963, D 1,84:8
Uth, Richard A, 1940, N 20,21:5
Uthe, Edward F N, 1966, F 25,31:3
Uthwatt, Lord, 1949, Ap 25,23:3
Utili, Umberto, 1952, O 28,31:2
Utin, Alex, 1950, Ja 27,23:1
Utley, George B, 1946, O 5,17:6
Utley, Harold H, 1951, Jl 9,25:3
Utley, Harold M, 1961, N 1,39:2
Utley, Lewis S, 1965, F 18,33:4
Utley, Reigh Mrs, 1955, Je 15,31:3
Utley, Wade E, 1947, My 7,27:3
Utrillo, Maurice (funl, N 10,35:5), 1955, N 6,1:8
Utrillo, Maurice Mrs (L Valore), 1965, Ag 20,29:1
Utsinger, Carl H, 1965, Ja 13,25:3
Uttal, David K, 1946, Ap 27,17:2
Uttal, Fred, 1963, N 29,34:3
Utter, Clarence L, 1947, My 1,25:4
Utter, Colleen, 1968, D 4,47:3
Utter, Elizabeth L B Mrs, 1939, S 3,19:1
Utter, George B, 1955, N 13,87:5
Utter, Norwood J, 1959, Jl 21,29:6
Utterback, Hubert (por), 1942, My 14,19:4
Utterback, John G, 1955, Jl 13,25:1
Utterton, J S, 1879, D 22,5:3
Uttley, Joseph, 1941, Jl 2,21:3
Utton, Frederick W, 1939, Ja 24,19:2
Utton, William, 1950, Ap 10,19:3
Utz, George E, 1944, Ag 11,15:2
Utz, J George, 1948, Mr 24,25:1
Utz, Vincent P, 1966, O 29,34:4
Utz, William L, 1938, Mr 19,15:3
Uullenberg, John, 1967, Jl 1,23:6
Uunderdown, Roy H Mrs, 1950, Mr 15,29:2
Uviller, Isidore, 1967, S 30,33:3
Uviller, Max, 1967, Ag 22,34:6
Uzariz, Raul, 1951, S 2,13:1
Uzawa, Somei, 1955, O 22,19:2
Uzes, Dowager Duchess of, 1933, F 4,15:1
Uzes, Duchess d' (Josephine Angela), 1966, S 10,29:4
Uzman, L Lahut, 1962, N 10,25:2
Uzzell, Edwin F, 1956, Ja 22,89:2
Uzzell, Mabel, 1950, D 17,84:4

V

Vacanti, Joseph Rev, 1939, Ag 13,29:3
Vacaresco, Helene, 1947, F 18,26:3
Vacca, Carmi, 1947, S 10,27:4
Vaccaro, Felix P, 1943, O 20,21:6
Vaccaro, Frank, 1951, Je 23,15:5
Vaccaro, John A, 1968, O 7,47:2
Vaccaro, Joseph, 1945, My 1,23:3
Vaccaro, Joseph J, 1944, N 18,13:6
Vaccaro, Luca J, 1950, Ja 29,29:5
Vaccaro, Sebastian P, 1959, O 22,37:5
Vaccaro, Vincent J Mrs, 1951, Ja 2,23:1
Vaccelli, Guido Dr, 1916, Ja 12,13:4
Vacco, Carmen, 1940, N 8,21:2
Vachell, Horace A, 1955, Ja 11,25:3
Vachon, Alexandre, 1953, Mr 31,31:4
Vachon, Andrew, 1951, Ap 1,92:6
Vachon, J P R, 1954, D 18,15:5
Vachris, Anthony, 1944, Ja 7,18:3
Vachris, Domenick, 1909, F 21,7:5
Vacirca, Vincenzo, 1956, D 28,21:2
Vackner, Charles J, 1948, Ag 29,56:6
Vacsey, Imre, 1963, D 24,17:4
Vaczek, Louis Sr, 1962, F 15,29:1
Vadeboncoeur, Antoine F Dr, 1911, N 10,11:4
Vadersen, Herbert, 1954, Je 19,15:4
Vadillo, Marquis del, 1919, N 27,15:3
Vadnay, Emil (por), 1939, Ap 2,III,6:6
Vadurro, Joseph M, 1952, S 16,29:3
Vaeth, George J, 1943, My 15,15:5
Vaeth, Joseph A, 1938, O 4,25:1
Vaganova, Agrippina Y, 1951, N 17,17:4
Vaggiani, Nicolini, 1948, Ap 25,68:6
Vagis, Polygnotis, 1965, Ap 16,29:4
Vagliano, Andre Mrs, 1951, Ja 3,19:3
Vago, Joseph, 1947, Je 17,25:2
Vago, Ricardo A, 1944, Ap 24,19:4
Vahan, Vahan C, 1963, Ag 24,19:4
Vahey, James H, 1949, N 4,27:2
Vahey, Mary Mrs, 1921, F 26,11:5
Vahey, William H, 1949, O 25,28:5
Vahey, William J, 1941, My 6,21:3
Vahlsing, F H Sr Mrs, 1964, Jl 4,13:2
Vaida-Voevod, Alex, 1950, Mr 25,13:4
Vaiden, John L, 1948, Ja 20,24:2
Vaides, Federico P, 1956, Ja 30,27:4
Vail, Archibald E, 1961, Ap 29,23:2
Vail, Arthur H, 1964, Je 20,25:5
Vail, Arthur H Mrs, 1950, Jl 10,21:2
Vail, Bobby, 1957, Ja 28,23:3
Vail, Burr D, 1947, Ag 12,23:5
Vail, Charles E, 1945, Ja 9,19:2
Vail, Charles W Mrs, 1942, Ja 9,21:4
Vail, Chester, 1949, D 16,22:6
Vail, Clarence D Mrs, 1940, S 24,23:2
Vail, Clarence I, 1939, Jl 11,19:3
Vail, Clarence W, 1957, Mr 27,31:5
Vail, Clinton T, 1943, D 27,19:2
Vail, Cyrus H, 1947, Jl 28,15:2
Vail, Cyrus H Mrs, 1952, N 1,21:3
Vail, Daniel, 1938, My 31,19:6
Vail, Davis R, 1906, D 23,4:4
Vail, E Frank, 1952, Ja 13,88:6
Vail, Edgar L, 1955, D 30,19:3
Vail, Edward F R, 1947, Je 7,13:1
Vail, Elias C, 1961, Ap 25,35:3
Vail, Emily, 1948, My 29,15:1
Vail, Ephraim M, 1942, S 22,21:3
Vail, George, 1875, My 26,6:6
Vail, George A, 1908, F 14,7:7
Vail, George M, 1952, N 15,17:3
Vail, George R, 1940, Je 20,23:5
Vail, George W, 1937, S 8,23:5
Vail, H F, 1881, S 23,5:5
Vail, Harry H, 1949, F 10,28:2
Vail, Harry T, 1951, Ap 16,25:4
Vail, Henry Hobart, 1925, S 3,25:5
Vail, Herbert B, 1939, Ap 12,23:2
Vail, Herbert E, 1941, S 25,25:5
Vail, Herman Mrs, 1952, D 23,23:5
Vail, Ida C Mrs, 1955, Ag 4,25:2
Vail, J Dean, 1949, O 11,34:1
Vail, James Cummings, 1918, F 3,15:2
Vail, James D Jr, 1943, O 30,15:4
Vail, James G, 1951, D 12,37:2
Vail, James L, 1941, Mr 14,21:1; 1948, Mr 24,25:2
Vail, James L Mrs, 1947, Je 20,19:2
Vail, John I, 1966, Ja 10,25:1
Vail, Laura A, 1940, F 7,21:1
Vail, Laurence, 1968, My 1,47:2
Vail, Lester, 1959, N 29,86:3
Vail, Louis D, 1948, D 17,27:5
Vail, M H Cash Dr, 1904, My 21,9:6
Vail, Martha C, 1956, F 22,27:3
Vail, May H, 1960, F 14,84:1
Vail, Melissa G Mrs, 1941, Ag 10,23:3
Vail, Melvin L Mrs, 1955, O 6,29:3
Vail, Mott B Mrs, 1945, N 2,19:4
Vail, Oliver B, 1946, D 31,17:5
Vail, Otis F, 1945, Ap 26,23:1
Vail, Philip, 1903, My 15,9:6
Vail, Richard B, 1955, Jl 30,17:3
Vail, Robert H, 1940, Ap 4,23:1
Vail, Robert W G, 1966, Je 23,39:4
Vail, S M Rev, 1880, N 28,2:7
Vail, Samuel E, 1937, N 30,23:3
Vail, Sarah B Mrs, 1940, Mr 1,21:1
Vail, Stephen A, 1937, Mr 27,15:3
Vail, Theodore F, 1903, Jl 17,7:6
Vail, Theodore N, 1920, Ap 17,15:1
Vail, Thomas, 1925, Jl 26,5:3
Vail, Thomas C, 1939, N 4,15:6
Vail, Thomas J, 1945, S 18,23:2
Vail, Thomas Mrs, 1952, S 30,31:4
Vail, Wallace F, 1960, D 14,35:6
Vail, Walter M, 1947, Ja 24,21:3
Vail, Walter N Mrs, 1945, F 28,23:2
Vail, Walter R Mrs, 1951, Ap 4,29:1
Vail, William E, 1947, S 9,31:1
Vail, William F, 1954, Ag 25,27:4
Vail, William H (por), 1944, Ja 1,13:1
Vail, William M, 1904, Ja 6,9:5
Vail, William W, 1951, D 5,35:3
Vaile, Thomas Rev, 1937, Jl 14,22:1
Vaill, Allyn H, 1947, Ja 10,21:2
Vaill, Charles B, 1953, Jl 23,23:4
Vaill, Dudley L Jr, 1960, S 19,31:1
Vaill, Dudley L Mrs, 1948, O 26,32:3
Vaill, Edward W, 1939, D 25,23:2
Vaill, William C, 1938, Je 27,17:4
Vaillancourt, Emile Mrs, 1948, O 29,26:3
Vaillancourt, Francis, 1947, F 5,23:3
Vailland, Roger, 1965, My 13,37:1
Vaillant, Charles (por), 1939, D 5,27:3
Vaillant, Eduoard, 1915, D 19,17:3
Vaillant, Louis D, 1944, F 8,15:6
Vaillant, Marshal, 1872, Je 5,1:6
Vaillant-Couturier, Paul, 1937, O 11,21:6
Vaine, Gerald D, 1951, F 1,25:2
Vainisi, Jack, 1960, N 28,31:4
Vairetta, Domenic, 1947, O 25,19:3
Vairin-Snead, Harry Mrs, 1958, O 9,37:5
Vaisey, Harry, 1965, N 27,31:4
Vaitses, Caliope Mrs, 1950, Je 4,92:2
Vaitses, Stephen, 1941, Jl 14,13:7
Vajda, Albert M, 1966, Je 7,47:1
Vajda, Ernest, 1954, Ap 4,88:3
Vajina, George Dr, 1968, My 23,47:2
Vajs, Albert, 1964, Ap 6,31:4
Vaka, Demetra, 1946, D 19,29:3
Vakhrushev, Vassiliv, 1947, Ja 14,25:3
Vaklyes, John W Sr, 1947, Ap 5,19:6
Vaksdal, Alfred, 1951, O 10,23:7
Val De Camp, William, 1944, Je 17,13:6
Valabregue, Jean, 1962, My 9,43:4
Valadon, Lora, 1946, S 16,5:5
Valadon, Suzanne, 1938, Ap 8,19:4
Valando, Thomas Mrs, 1951, N 14,31:4
Valanti, James A, 1961, D 15,37:2
Valaske, M Thomas, 1958, Mr 31,27:4
Valcarcel, Teodoro, 1942, Mr 21,17:2
Valdagne, Pierre, 1937, F 1,19:3
Valdambrini, Joseph, 1945, Ap 20,19:4
Valdemar, Prince of Denmark, 1939, Ja 14,17:4
Valder, Camille E, 1949, Jl 17,56:1
Valdes, Armando P (por), 1938, F 4,21:1
Valdes, Casimiro H, 1961, O 28,21:2
Valdes, Luis, 1950, S 21,31:2
Valdes, Manuel Mrs, 1948, D 29,21:5
Valdes, Victorio F, 1945, N 29,23:5
Valdez, Ramon, 1918, Je 4,13:3
Valdivia, Rafael, 1949, Ap 20,27:4
Valdiviaso, R F Archbishop, 1878, Jl 28,8:6
Valdrome, J P N E C de, 1878, N 28,5:3
Vale, Alice, 1950, S 8,31:3
Vale, C J Villar, 1948, Ja 12,19:1
Vale, Henry A, 1939, Mr 19,III,6:4
Vale, Robert B, 1957, Ag 25,86:8
Vale, Robert DeB, 1967, Ja 12,39:4
Vale, Ruby R, 1961, Ja 3,29:3
Vale, Thomas E, 1945, Mr 7,21:4
Valen, Karstein, 1952, D 15,25:5
Valencia, Duke of, 1941, Jl 15,19:3
Valencia, Guillermo, 1943, Jl 9,17:5
Valencia, Guillermo L Mrs, 1964, My 20,43:3
Valencia, Manuel, 1951, My 16,35:2
Valens, Ritchie, 1959, F 4,66:3
Valensa, Theodore, 1950, S 2,15:2
Valenstein, Cornelia, 1964, Je 10,45:4
Valenta, Alois, 1957, F 24,31:5
Valenta, Frank L, 1957, S 18,33:5
Valenta, Joseph, 1950, Jl 31,17:5
Valente, Anthony, 1942, Jl 29,17:2
Valente, Ciro, 1949, Ag 12,18:4
Valente, Francis L, 1966, F 13,84:1
Valente, Frank A Mrs, 1964, F 23,84:7
Valente, Louis, 1953, D 22,31:1
Valente, Louis A, 1962, Je 21,31:1
Valenti, Alfredo, 1968, Mr 5,41:2
Valenti, Girolamo, 1958, F 22,17:5
Valenti, John B, 1948, D 21,28:5
Valenti, Santiago, 1949, Ja 16,68:8
Valenti-Mestre, Antonio, 1956, F 25,19:6
Valentia, G G, 1883, My 29,5:4
Valentia, Viscount (C A J Annesley), 1949, O 7,31:2
Valentia, Viscount (W M Annesley), 1951, F 28,28:7
Valentin, Curt (will, S 10,3:1; trb, S 19,II,13:1), 1954, Ag 21,17:3
Valentin, Francois, 1961, S 26,5:4
Valentin, Gustav, 1941, My 29,19:4
Valentin, Herman, 1945, S 20,23:1
Valentin, Hugo, 1963, My 9,37:1
Valentin, Karl, 1948, F 10,23:2
Valentin, Veit, 1947, Ja 13,21:6
Valentine, Alfred J, 1942, Ap 23,23:6
Valentine, Alfred Mrs, 1941, S 22,15:5
Valentine, Andrew E, 1966, Mr 15,39:2
Valentine, Andrew J Mrs, 1943, My 16,43:1
Valentine, Anthony J, 1952, Ag 30,13:4
Valentine, Benjamin P Mrs, 1958, Mr 22,17:4
Valentine, Benk Eyre, 1920, Ag 17,13:5
Valentine, Charles A Mrs, 1948, N 25,31:4
Valentine, Charles C (por), 1940, Ja 16,23:4
Valentine, Charles E, 1944, Mr 15,19:5; 1953, D 21, 31:5
Valentine, Charles F, 1923, F 14,17:5; 1966, Mr 13, 87:1
Valentine, Charles H Capt, 1907, Je 11,7:6
Valentine, Charles W, 1946, Jl 23,25:5
Valentine, Charley, 1947, My 7,27:2
Valentine, Claude H, 1960, Ap 27,37:2
Valentine, Clifford W, 1953, My 10,33:1
Valentine, D M, 1883, O 6,5:2
Valentine, David, 1941, Ja 7,23:3
Valentine, David H, 1910, D 22,13:5
Valentine, David T, 1869, F 26,5:5
Valentine, Dennis, 1903, Jl 23,7:6
Valentine, E V, 1930, O 20,21:4
Valentine, Earl D, 1947, Ag 17,54:3
Valentine, Edward A, 1922, O 16,15:4
Valentine, Edwin F, 1938, N 12,15:2
Valentine, Emma Mrs, 1922, Jl 5,19:3
Valentine, Ferdinand C Dr, 1909, D 14,11:4
Valentine, Francis A, 1957, Jl 21,61:2
Valentine, Frank P, 1948, Mr 30,23:2
Valentine, Frank R, 1942, D 5,15:1
Valentine, Frederick S, 1940, F 4,40:6
Valentine, George, 1952, Ag 29,23:2
Valentine, George B Mrs, 1951, My 29,25:3
Valentine, George J, 1966, Ja 3,27:4
Valentine, George Rockwell, 1916, Ap 4,13:5
Valentine, Gerardus, 1948, Ag 21,15:5
Valentine, Granville, 1943, Je 3,21:4
Valentine, Harry S, 1942, Ja 18,42:2
Valentine, Harvey E (funl plans, S 13,86:6; funl, S 16,31:5), 1964, S 12,25:4
Valentine, Henry C, 1912, Ja 16,13:4
Valentine, Henry C Mrs, 1942, O 16,19:3
Valentine, Henry Jr, 1938, D 6,3:3
Valentine, Ida M (will), 1962, Ag 17,8:6
Valentine, Irving C Mrs, 1956, Je 3,86:8
Valentine, Irving N, 1939, My 12,21:4
Valentine, Isaac R, 1950, My 8,23:3
Valentine, Isidore, 1884, S 7,6:7
Valentine, J Clifford, 1946, Mr 22,22:2
Valentine, Jacob, 1903, Jl 24,7:7
Valentine, Jacob L, 1942, My 1,19:3
Valentine, James O P, 1948, Jl 8,23:2
Valentine, James R, 1942, Ap 28,21:4
Valentine, Janet, 1947, My 25,60:4
Valentine, John, 1942, O 29,23:5
Valentine, John H, 1943, Je 4,21:4; 1951, S 13,31:3
Valentine, John K, 1950, O 13,29:2
Valentine, John O, 1943, D 29,17:2
Valentine, John R Lt-Col, 1921, Jl 10,22:4
Valentine, John W, 1940, S 26,23:3
Valentine, Joseph, 1953, Ag 28,17:4
Valentine, Joseph A, 1949, My 20,27:4
Valentine, Joseph E, 1965, Je 1,39:3
Valentine, Joseph L, 1950, Ja 6,21:3
Valentine, L, 1883, Ag 9,8:6
Valentine, Lewis J Mrs, 1959, Ap 23,31:3
Valentine, Louis L, 1940, Mr 3,44:8
Valentine, Lucinda, 1903, D 19,9:4
Valentine, Lucy W, 1953, O 8,29:2
Valentine, Mary, 1879, Ag 13,8:2
Valentine, Mike, 1938, Je 2,23:2
Valentine, Nathaniel B, 1912, F 13,11:4
Valentine, Norman D, 1966, Mr 3,33:5
Valentine, Patrick A, 1916, Ag 22,9:4
Valentine, Percy O Mrs, 1946, My 23,21:4
Valentine, R B, 1882, Ag 20,7:1
Valentine, R M, 1879, F 16,5:5
Valentine, Rawson J (por), 1946, Je 20,23:3
Valentine, Rene, 1967, D 22,31:3
Valentine, Robert, 1910, Je 24,9:5
Valentine, Robert G, 1916, N 15,11:5
Valentine, Russell D, 1951, My 16,35:4

Valentine, S, 1878, Ap 28,7:2
Valentine, S M Dr, 1884, O 2,2:2
Valentine, S T, 1903, Mr 10,7:6
Valentine, Samuel H, 1916, S 16,11:6
Valentine, Sherwood C, 1966, Je 5,86:5
Valentine, Stephen, 1946, My 24,19:1
Valentine, Stephen F, 1946, F 12,28:1
Valentine, Stephen Jr, 1965, Ja 26,34:1
Valentine, Stephen Mrs, 1939, My 14,III,7:3
Valentine, Sydney, 1919, D 24,13:4
Valentine, Washington S, 1920, Mr 18,11:4
Valentine, Willard L, 1947, Ap 7,23:2
Valentine, William, 1905, My 3,7:1; 1908, S 21,7:7
Valentine, William E, 1940, S 16,19:4; 1948, N 20,13:4
Valentine, William H, 1952, Mr 3,21:3
Valentine, William H Mrs, 1943, O 26,23:1
Valentine, William L Jr, 1948, S 19,78:4
Valentine, William R, 1954, N 3,29:1
Valentine, William R Mrs, 1950, Je 1,27:3
Valentine, William S, 1939, D 16,17:3
Valentine, William T, 1945, D 28,16:3
Valentiner, Clark Mrs, 1942, O 17,15:1
Valentiner, William R, 1958, S 7,86:1
Valentini, Vincent, 1948, Ap 16,23:2
Valentini, von Prof, 1925, D 20,11:2
Valenzio, Vibo Mrs (Billy Callahan), 1964, F 23,85:1
Valenzo, Chevalier, 1940, F 9,19:2
Valenzuela, Ulpiano A de, 1941, Jl 3,19:4
Valera Hernandez, Jose, 1940, My 12,48:2
Valeri, Valerio, 1963, Jl 23,29:4
Valeria, M Sister, 1883, D 27,3:3
Valeria Bielak, Mother, 1950, Mr 25,13:2
Valerie, Olive, 1951, O 29,23:2
Valerio, Albert, 1947, D 5,25:4
Valerio, Alex M, 1953, Jl 18,13:1
Valerio, Alex Mrs, 1961, D 14,43:4
Valery, Paul (por), 1945, Jl 21,11:4
Valesh, Frank S Mrs, 1956, N 9,29:3
Valet, William, 1956, Ap 5,29:4
Valette, Thomas, 1938, O 21,23:4
Valflor, Marqueza de (Dona Mariatt de Carmo Constantino, 1952, F 13,29:3
Valiant, John, 1905, My 22,7:5; 1941, F 9,48:8
Valiant, John W, 1949, Mr 14,19:4
Valiant, Joseph G, 1937, O 23,15:6
Valiant, William E, 1938, S 25,39:2
Valiente, Rafael, 1942, N 17,25:4
Valieri, Count, 1877, D 13,5:3
Valin, Sigmund, 1954, Ap 8,27:3
Valinnotti, Alfred, 1919, My 26,15:5
Valiquette, Alfred H, 1949, Ap 16,15:5
Valk, Allen S, 1966, Ja 9,56:5
Valk, Frederick, 1956, Jl 24,25:1
Valk, John Sr, 1952, My 17,19:6
Valk, Susman J, 1939, N 14,23:4
Valkenburg, Edward S, 1954, O 16,17:3
Valkenburg, Herman J, 1944, Jl 27,17:6
Valkenburgh, Edwin P, 1955, Ap 18,23:2
Vall, Anthony Compton, 1911, Ag 21,9:7
Vall, Charles Delamater, 1921, Jl 26,15:6
Valladares, Frank, 1959, O 7,43:4
Vallance, Harvard F, 1956, O 29,29:5
Vallance, John, 1954, Ja 21,31:3
Vallance, Samuel H Mrs, 1946, O 7,31:5
Vallance, William, 1903, Ap 13,1:7
Vallandigham, Clement L (funl, Je 20,1:3), 1871, Je 18,4:7
Vallandigham, Clement L Mrs, 1871, Ag 14,4:1
Vallar, William H, 1962, Jl 26,27:2
Vallarino, Joaquin Jose, 1968, Ap 14,77:2
Vallas, Nicholas, 1968, Mr 31,81:2
Valldejuli, Jerome K, 1958, O 3,29:1
Valle, Ernest Sen, 1920, Ja 25,22:1
Valle, Jack, 1954, Jl 9,17:4
Valle, Mario, 1951, My 15,31:5
Valle Atiles, Manuel del, 1943, Ap 14,23:3
Vallee, Arthur, 1939, Ja 9,15:5
Vallee, Charles A, 1949, My 13,23:1
Vallee, Henri, 1947, Mr 15,13:6
Vallely, Henry E, 1950, N 26,90:8
Vallely, James Capt, 1937, N 20,17:5
Vallentine, B B, 1926, Mr 31,23:1
Vallentine, Langdon D Mrs, 1946, Ag 28,27:3
Valleria, Alwina, 1925, F 18,19:4
Vallerino, Alberto, 1944, D 21,21:3
Valles, Domingo, 1953, O 25,89:1
Valles, J L J (funl, F 17,1:5), 1885, F 15,2:2
Vallesian, Bro (H J Mallon), 1950, Ap 30,102:7
Vallet, Paul A, 1949, Ap 6,29:1
Valletta, Vittorio, 1967, Ag 11,31:1
Vallette, Alfred Mrs (Rachilde), 1953, Ap 6,19:4
Vallette, Marc F Dr, 1925, N 24,25:5
Valley, John J Sr, 1964, Jl 3,21:1
Valli, Giulio, 1949, N 10,31:5
Valli, Ugo C Mrs, 1949, D 29,25:4
Valli, V, 1927, N 5,19:5
Vallier, M G, 1883, Je 20,4:6
Vallin, Ninon, 1961, N 23,31:4
Vallis, Paul M, 1942, O 31,15:4
Vallon, Edwin E, 1961, O 29,88:5
Vallone, Charles J, 1967, Mr 16,47:2
Vallquette, William H, 1918, Ag 23,9:7
Valminuta, Fulco T Di Count, 1939, N 22,21:1
Valois, Arthur E, 1915, Ap 14,13:4
Valois, J M A, 1941, N 18,25:1
Valore, Lucie (Mrs M Utrillo), 1965, Ag 20,29:1
Valorfe, Samuel, 1943, Jl 18,34:6
Valparaiso y del Merito, Marquesa de (por), 1942, Ja 21,18:3
Valperga, Enrico S de Count, 1947, Jl 16,23:2
Valpey, Harold D, 1946, N 25,27:2
Valstar, Simon M D, 1945, My 7,17:3
Valter, Adrian, 1876, My 31,5:4
Valtin, Jan (R J H Krebs), 1951, Ja 3,27:3
Valtorta, Henry P, 1951, S 4,27:1
Valuchek, Andrew Mrs, 1959, Jl 12,73:1
Value, Beverly Reid, 1920, Je 11,13:3
Value, Burnside R, 1966, S 3,23:5
Valush, Paul J Mrs, 1949, Jl 15,19:2
Valvano, Domenic A, 1959, Jl 13,27:4
Valverde Martinez, Luis, 1942, Je 25,23:4
Valz, Edward V, 1958, My 11,86:6
Vamasescu, Nicholas, 1953, Ap 15,31:2
Vambery, Arminius Prof, 1913, S 16,11:5
Vambery, Rustem, 1948, O 26,31:1
Vames, Chris (Vamvaketis), 1962, S 20,33:3
Vamplew, Paul, 1951, My 24,8:4
Van, Billy (N Gehan), 1949, Ap 8,26:4
Van, Billy B, 1950, N 17,27:3
Van, Ernie, 1946, My 17,21:5
Van, George X, 1950, F 15,27:3
Van, Gus, 1968, Mr 13,47:1
Van, William, 1916, Jl 12,11:4
Van Aalst, C J K, 1939, O 26,23:5
Van Aalten, George, 1959, S 26,23:5
Van Abbe, Solomon, 1955, Mr 1,25:4
Vanabelle, A T De, 1879, Mr 29,2:6
Van Aken, Charles M, 1941, Mr 17,17:5
Van Aken, Elbert W, 1950, Mr 12,94:4
Van Aken, Eugene, 1944, Ja 13,21:4
Van Aken, George T, 1944, Jl 20,19:2
Van Aken, Harry H, 1955, Jl 11,23:3
Van Aken, Neil, 1950, D 5,31:3
Van Aken, William J, 1950, D 29,19:3
Van Akin, A L Jr, 1947, Jl 5,11:4
Vanakin, Edna, 1952, Mr 10,21:4
Van Alen, Benjamin T, 1937, My 14,23:4
Van Alen, George L, 1942, Jl 3,17:5
Van Alen, James J, 1923, Jl 14,11:1; 1923, O 7,6:3
Van Alen, William, 1954, My 25,27:1
Van Allen, Frank H, 1946, O 9,27:5
Van Allen, Fred H, 1953, D 12,19:6
Van Allen, George Mrs, 1956, Je 30,17:7
Van Allen, John W, 1958, Jl 29,23:3
Van Allen, W H, 1931, Ag 24,15:3
Van Alst, Abraham, 1909, O 27,11:3
Van Alst, Edith G Mrs, 1938, Ja 6,19:5
Van Alst, Elizabeth, 1952, Ap 27,91:1
Van Alst, Harry, 1960, Jl 29,25:1
Van Alst, William Mrs, 1947, Je 6,23:4
Van Alstine, Chauncey D, 1955, N 17,35:4
Van Alstine, William N Sr, 1952, D 31,15:5
Van Alstyne, David, 1942, Je 9,23:4
Van Alstyne, David 3d, 1952, Ag 16,11:4
Van Alstyne, Egbert A, 1951, Jl 10,27:5
Van Alstyne, Frank L, 1941, Ag 15,17:5
Van Alstyne, Gansevoort T, 1954, Ap 23,27:3
Vanalstyne, George R, 1944, Mr 13,15:6
Van Alstyne, Henry A, 1947, Ja 24,21:4
Van Alstyne, James H, 1944, D 26,19:3
Van Alstyne, Mabelle C Mrs, 1937, D 6,27:4
Van Alstyne, Pierre L, 1948, Ja 31,19:5
Van Alstyne, T Jeff, 1903, O 27,9:5
Van Alstyne, Thomas B, 1937, Mr 10,23:5
Van Alstyne, Thomas J Mrs, 1939, Jl 14,19:1
Van Alstyne, Ward, 1959, My 27,35:3
Van Alstyne, William B, 1956, Je 22,23:5; 1958, My 3, 19:5
Van Alstyne, William B Mrs, 1951, Je 28,25:6
Van Alstyne, William T, 1965, N 26,37:2
Van Alyea, Thomas S Mrs, 1949, N 15,25:1
Vanaman, Edward W, 1949, Jl 14,27:4
Van Amburgh, Charles J, 1946, Je 27,21:5
Van Amburgh, Everett, 1952, S 14,86:2
Van Amburgh, John D Mrs, 1952, My 27,27:3
Van Amburgh, Lion-Tamer, 1865, D 2,4:2
Vanamee, Grace, 1946, D 11,31:5
Vanamee, William, 1914, My 9,11:6
Van Amringe, Emily B, 1955, Jl 15,21:3
Van Amringe, J Howard Prof (funl, S 14,11:5), 1915, S 11,9:3
Van Amringe, John Howard Mrs, 1914, My 11,11:5
Van Anda, Blanche, 1945, Ja 29,13:5
Van Anda, Carr V, 1945, Ja 29,1:1
Van Anda, Carr V Mrs, 1942, F 18,19:5
Van Anden, Frank, 1952, N 27,31:6
Van Anden, Frederick G, 1947, Je 4,27:2
Van Anden, George W, 1946, F 6,23:4
Van Anden, Isaac, 1875, Ag 5,4:7
Vananden, Norman J, 1947, Jl 18,17:4
Van Anden, William M, 1918, Jl 28,19:3
Van Antwerp, Eugene I, 1962, Ag 7,29:4
Van Antwerp, Francis W, 1951, Je 7,33:2
Van Antwerp, George T, 1966, S 13,47:3
Van Antwerp, John H, 1903, D 15,9:5
Van Antwerp, V S Gen, 1875, D 8,7:1
Van Antwerp, William C, 1938, F 18,19:5
Van Antwerp, William C Mrs, 1949, S 11,92:1
Van Arnam, Hiram L, 1952, O 29,29:5
Van Arnam, John R, 1951, Mr 28,29:2
Van Arsdale, Charles, 1948, N 20,13:5
Van Arsdale, Charles F, 1957, Jl 29,19:5
Van Arsdale, Charles O, 1943, Mr 15,13:5
Van Arsdale, D, 1883, N 15,5:5
Van Arsdale, Elias B Rev, 1937, Ap 17,17:3
Van Arsdale, George D, 1950, Ag 25,21:5
Van Arsdale, George V, 1950, Ap 18,31:1
Van Arsdale, Henry Mrs, 1950, F 12,84:1
Van Arsdale, I Vanderveer, 1954, N 5,15:4
Van Arsdale, J, 1882, Mr 20,5:2
Van Arsdale, James H, 1938, D 19,23:5
Van Arsdale, John, 1873, Jl 29,2:6
Van Arsdale, Lewis H, 1950, Ap 1,15:5
Van Arsdale, May B, 1966, Mr 8,39:2
Van Arsdale, Morris C, 1945, Ag 28,19:4
Van Arsdale, Robert M, 1909, N 24,9:5
Van Arsdale, William E Mrs, 1948, S 16,29:4
Van Arsdale, Wirt (Mrs C B Davis), 1952, Ja 16,25:5
Van Arsdall, Harold P, 1950, Ag 16,29:5
Vanarsdall, John Wesley, 1924, Ag 11,13:6
Vanartsdalen, Joshua P, 1943, Ap 15,25:4
Vanatta, Jacob, 1879, Ap 30,5:6
Van Atta, John W, 1949, D 9,31:3
Van Atten, William T, 1968, N 24,87:1
van Aubel, Jacques J, 1964, N 28,22:2
Van Auken, Charles H, 1944, Ag 28,11:4
Van Auken, Harold K, 1952, N 5,27:1
Van Auken, Harry V, 1948, My 18,23:4
Van Auken, J Lansing Rev Dr, 1915, N 28,17:5
Van Auken, Wilbur R, 1953, Ag 16,76:5
Van Baar, Charles Lawrence, 1913, Ap 27,IV,7:4
Van Beek, Theodore, 1951, S 1,11:6
Van Bemmelen, Henri M, 1959, F 20,25:4
Van Benschoten, A, 1885, My 9,8:2
Van Benschoten, Charles B, 1945, Ap 5,23:3
Van Benschoten, Edward Wilson, 1912, Ap 18,13:5
Van Benschoten, Harry E, 1958, O 11,23:5
van Benschoten, Richard I, 1960, Ja 25,27:4
Van Benschoten, W H, 1928, Ag 12,26:1
van Benschoten, William Henry 2d, 1968, Ap 2,47:2
Van Benthuysen, Alvin S, 1960, N 27,86:4
Van Benthuysen, Barent P, 1937, Ja 22,21:2
Van Benthuysen, C, 1881, O 20,10:1
Vanbenthuysen, Howard D, 1948, Mr 6,13:4
Van Benthuysen, W C, 1903, Je 20,7:6
Van Benthuysen, William, 1906, Ap 8,6:5
van Berg, Salomon, 1964, D 28,29:3
Van Bergen, Harold M, 1939, Ja 6,22:2
Van Bergen, John, 1951, S 30,72:4
Vanbergen, John, 1952, My 17,19:5
Van Berger, Anthony, 1912, F 21,11:4
Van Bergh, J Alvin, 1955, Jl 28,23:3
Van Bergh, Maurice H, 1962, Ap 1,86:7
Van Bergh, Morris, 1942, Ag 6,19:3
Van Berlo, Edward, 1946, N 18,23:1
Van Berschot, Arthur H, 1957, Jl 8,23:4
Van Beuren, Alfred, 1909, Je 23,7:4
Van Beuren, Amedee J, 1938, N 13,45:3
Van Beuren, David, 1882, S 14,5:6
Van Beuren, Elizabeth Spingler, 1908, Jl 23,7:5
Van Beuren, Frederick T Jr (por), 1943, Mr 14,26:3
Van Beuren, Gerardus A C, 1943, S 13,19:5
Van Beuren, Horace A, 1937, N 17,23:4
Van Beuren, M M, 1878, Jl 20,2:4
Van Beuren, Michael M, 1951, Je 8,27:5
Van Beuren, Michael M Mrs (will, Mr 3,15:5), 1951, F 26,24:2
Van Beynum, Clarence W, 1955, Ja 6,27:5
Van Bibber, Arthur E, 1965, Ja 27,35:2
Van Bibber, John, 1956, N 20,37:4
Van Biema, Adolf, 1964, Jl 26,56:6
Van Blarcom, Albert Mrs, 1948, N 18,27:1
Van Blarcom, Harold, 1938, Mr 10,21:3
Van Blarcom, Kenneth M, 1950, F 2,27:3
Van Blarcom, Lewis Capt, 1904, F 22,5:6
Van Blarcom, Mary, 1953, Jl 17,17:3
Van Blarcom, William, 1960, Ag 13,15:5
Van Blaricom, Fred M, 1940, F 6,21:4
Van Blaricom, Ralph S Mrs, 1940, F 6,21:4
Van Bloem, P Schuyler, 1967, Mr 18,29:2
Van Bokkelen, Libertus Mrs, 1946, My 3,21:4
Van Bokkelen, William K, 1907, Mr 27,9:6
Van Bomel, Howard S, 1953, S 6,51:1
Van Bomel, I A, 1928, Ja 26,23:5
Van Bomel, Leroy A, 1966, D 22,33:2
Van Borbstaedt, Col, 1873, Jl 15,4:7
Van Boskerck, Cornelius, 1915, Ja 14,11:4
Van Boskerck, Edith, 1952, N 17,25:5
Van Boskerck, Sarah M, 1942, N 5,26:3
Van Boskerck, Thomas R, 1945, Jl 9,11:6
Van Boskirk, William E Mrs, 1951, F 27,28:5
Van Bourgondien, Peter C, 1966, Jl 7,37:3
Van Boven, John Sr, 1938, Ap 19,21:3
Van Bovene, Gerardus A, 1945, D 18,27:3
Van Breems, Beatrice G Mrs (V Graham), 1964, Jl 26,56:2
Van Brocklin, Ethel Mrs, 1965, Ag 29,84:8
Vanbrugh, Irene, 1949, D 1,31:1
Vanbrugh, Violet (por), 1942, N 12,25:3

Van Brunt, Adele Mrs, 1911, Ja 9,13:5
Van Brunt, Albert, 1922, D 20,19:5
Van Brunt, Arthur H, 1951, My 22,31:2
Van Brunt, Arthur Mrs, 1947, Ap 5,19:6
Van Brunt, Charles C, 1937, Ag 4,19:4
Van Brunt, Charles G, 1951, My 3,29:2
Van Brunt, Charles H, 1905, My 27,9:3
Van Brunt, Cornelius, 1903, O 5,7:6
Van Brunt, Cornelius Bergen, 1921, S 11,21:2
Van Brunt, Frank N, 1960, Ja 11,45:2
VanBrunt, George A, 1966, N 12,29:6
Van Brunt, Henry, 1903, Ap 9,9:5
Van Brunt, Irene S Mrs, 1939, Ja 28,15:4
Van Brunt, Jacques, 1937, Je 13,II,7:1
Van Brunt, Jeremiah R, 1950, Mr 14,25:4
Van Brunt, Jeremiah R Mrs, 1946, O 2,29:5
Van Brunt, Jessie, 1947, Mr 2,60:8
Van Brunt, John Capt, 1914, Ja 31,11:5
Van Brunt, Mervin S, 1955, D 5,31:1
Van Brunt, Nicholas, 1873, My 2,2:2
Van Brunt, Osborn, 1939, Je 9,21:6
Van Brunt, Shirley, 1962, Mr 27,38:1
Van Brunt, William, 1954, D 29,23:4
Van Brunt, Willis D, 1944, Ap 14,19:5
Van Buren, A H, 1869, Ag 1,8:5
Van Buren, A Mrs, 1877, D 31,5:2
Van Buren, Albert W Dr, 1968, F 6,43:1
Van Buren, Alfred D, 1947, D 13,15:4
Van Buren, Alfred V, 1925, Mr 7,13:6
Van Buren, Charles, 1947, My 8,25:4
Van Buren, Charles D, 1954, Je 22,27:1
Van Buren, Charles H, 1941, S 14,51:4
Van Buren, D H, 1883, Mr 26,5:3
Van Buren, David N, 1950, Ap 11,31:4
Van Buren, David T L, 1952, N 21,25:4
Van Buren, David T L Mrs, 1947, Je 24,24:3
Van Buren, De Witt, 1870, O 6,2:7
Van Buren, DeWitt, 1962, Jl 3,23:3
Van Buren, Dewitt Mrs, 1954, Ag 6,17:4
Van Buren, Elmer M, 1948, Mr 23,25:1
Van Buren, Frederick, 1919, S 26,13:4
Van Buren, George F, 1907, Ja 9,9:5
Van Buren, Glenn B, 1955, Je 6,27:5
Van Buren, Harold S, 1907, F 13,9:2
Van Buren, Harold S Mrs, 1950, Mr 25,13:2
Van Buren, J, 1878, S 26,8:5
Van Buren, James Heartt Bp, 1917, Jl 10,13:5
Van Buren, James M, 1965, F 19,36:3
Van Buren, John (funl, Oc 20,2:6), 1866, O 17,4:6
Van Buren, John Dash, 1918, Mr 12,13:7
Van Buren, John M, 1957, Ap 24,33:1
Van Buren, Laurens H Mrs, 1961, Ap 23,86:5
Van Buren, Lawrence Maj, 1868, Jl 4,5:4
Van Buren, Martin, 1942, D 3,29:3
Van Buren, Martin ex-Pres (funl, Jl 29,8:5), 1862, Jl 25,1:2
Van Buren, Peter Dr, 1873, D 9,5:4
Van Buren, Robert S, 1961, Ap 5,37:3
Van Buren, Rosamund, 1951, D 10,29:5
Van Buren, Singleton, 1879, Je 11,8:2
Van Buren, Smith Mrs, 1921, Ap 15,15:4
Van Buren, Thomas Brodhead, 1915, Je 15,13:6
Van Buren, William R, 1964, Jl 29,33:4
Van Buren Effingham, 1913, D 9,11:4
van Burk, John, 1938, Jl 19,22:7
van Burkalow, James T, 1959, S 19,23:3
van Burkalow, James T Mrs, 1959, Ja 21,31:4
Van Buskirk, Andrew, 1942, N 18,25:4
Van Buskirk, Charles G, 1949, D 12,33:1
Van Buskirk, D W, 1933, F 14,15:3
Van Buskirk, De Witt Mrs, 1956, N 19,31:5
Van Buskirk, DeWitt Jr, 1952, My 22,27:5
Van Buskirk, Francis E, 1941, Je 17,21:4
Van Buskirk, George, 1952, Jl 2,25:3
Van Buskirk, Harold J, 1953, Ja 18,93:2
Van Buskirk, Harry C, 1952, N 22,23:4; 1959, Ja 6, 33:2
Van Buskirk, J N, 1883, S 9,2:7
Van Buskirk, John, 1939, Mr 23,23:2
Van Buskirk, L, 1903, Ag 22,9:7
Van Buskirk, Lewis, 1941, Je 17,21:4
van Bylevelt, John S, 1958, Je 27,25:3
Van Camp, Frank, 1937, N 25,31:3
Van Camp, Harry S, 1939, Jl 14,19:5
Van Camp, Harry T, 1937, Je 26,17:5; 1943, F 8,19:4
Van Camp, Oliver F, 1955, Ag 6,15:4
Van Camp, Paul W, 1959, Ag 15,17:3
Van Camp, Samuel Gilbert, 1923, Jl 6,13:6
Van Camp, Walter P, 1958, Ja 24,21:1
Van Camp, William, 1911, N 27,11:6
Van Campen, Isaac Mrs, 1951, Ap 26,29:3
Van Caneghan, Remi R, 1953, N 3,31:5
Van Carpenter, Lewis (por), 1940, My 12,49:1
Vance, Alanson A, 1906, Ja 28,7:7
Vance, Allan S, 1952, N 25,29:1
Vance, Arthur T Mrs, 1943, F 22,17:3
Vance, Benjamin M, 1961, O 30,29:3
Vance, C F, 1940, Je 18,23:5
Vance, Clarence A (Dazzy), 1961, F 17,27:1
Vance, Clyde F, 1953, N 11,31:3
Vance, Earl T, 1944, F 19,13:5
Vance, Harold S, 1959, S 1,29:1
Vance, Harriet S, 1950, F 16,23:5
Vance, Henry T Sr Mrs, 1954, O 19,27:2
Vance, J Nelson, 1939, Ag 7,15:6
Vance, James I, 1939, N 25,17:1
Vance, James M, 1948, Jl 6,23:3
Vance, Jessica S, 1939, Mr 5,49:2
Vance, John, 1875, S 22,5:1
Vance, John F, 1939, My 6,17:6
Vance, John L, 1953, Je 18,32:2
Vance, John T, 1943, Ap 13,25:1
Vance, John W, 1954, N 22,23:3
Vance, Johnstone, 1951, Ap 12,33:4
Vance, Joseph A, 1951, Je 14,27:5
Vance, Joseph A Mrs, 1943, Ag 11,19:5
Vance, Joseph M, 1948, D 15,33:3
Vance, Kenneth W, 1949, F 5,15:5
Vance, L J, 1933, D 17,1:4
Vance, Lee J, 1942, D 10,30:2
Vance, Leland S, 1954, Ap 6,29:4
Vance, Lucie F, 1955, Jl 29,17:2
Vance, Marion R, 1956, Mr 11,88:4
Vance, Mark M, 1939, Ag 23,21:4
Vance, Mathilda O Mrs, 1938, Je 26,27:1
Vance, Nancy, 1942, F 19,19:1
Vance, Raphael, 1958, My 7,35:4
Vance, Ray, 1954, Ag 7,13:7
Vance, Robert C, 1959, N 5,35:4
Vance, Robert J, 1955, D 17,42:4
Vance, Rufus A, 1940, My 31,19:3
Vance, Sam G, 1947, My 18,60:7
Vance, Samuel H, 1955, N 26,19:5
Vance, William B, 1959, Ag 4,27:3
Vance, William C, 1961, D 10,88:8
Vance, William H Mrs, 1944, Jl 1,15:4
Vance, William Mrs (Marguerite), 1965, My 25,41:3
Vance, William R, 1940, O 24,25:5
Vance, Wilson Col, 1911, N 12,II,15:5
Vance, Woodruff M, 1951, Ja 12,27:4
Vance, Z B Mrs, 1878, N 7,2:5
Vance, Z B Sen, 1894, Ap 15,5:3
Vancil, Nicholas W, 1962, Jl 17,25:3
Van Cleaf, George W, 1905, Ja 7,8:2
Van Cleaf, Howard M, 1968, O 22,47:1
Van Cleave, John K, 1910, My 16,9:3
Van Cleef, Catalina, 1944, D 23,13:4
Van Cleef, Edward E, 1949, N 17,29:4
Van Cleef, Frank C Mrs, 1939, F 25,15:1
Van Cleef, Frank L, 1942, Mr 21,17:5
Van Cleef, Garrett W, 1959, Ap 2,31:2
Van Cleef, Isaac A, 1944, Je 20,19:4
Van Cleef, John Schenck, 1916, S 30,11:4
Van Cleef, P Herbert, 1941, D 6,17:1
Van Cleef, Schuyler C, 1964, Je 26,29:3
Van Cleet, Cornelius Dr, 1875, Je 14,5:4
Van Cleft, Joseph, 1914, My 21,11:5
Van Cleve, Edward M Dr (por), 1937, My 22,18:1
Van Cleve, Garret, 1955, Ja 11,25:3
Van Cleve, George B, 1949, Mr 5,17:4
Van Cleve, Herman B, 1939, Ja 7,15:2
Van Cleve, James A, 1915, N 26,13:6
Van Cleve, John H (por), 1940, Je 15,15:2
Van Cleve, Paul L, 1945, Jl 18,27:1
Van Cleve, Seymour, 1914, Mr 21,13:6
Van Cleve, Seymour Mrs, 1917, S 25,11:6
Van Clief, Ray A Mrs, 1948, Ap 5,21:4
Vanclief, William C, 1951, My 28,21:4
Van Clouser, Lionel (L Rand), 1942, O 16,19:5
Van Clute, D, 1933, Mr 7,15:4
Van Coevering, Jay C, 1967, Je 22,39:5
Van Cook, Henry J, 1954, D 10,27:1
Vancor, Chester A, 1960, Je 9,33:4
Van Cortlandt, Anne S, 1940, Je 6,25:5
Van Cortlandt, Augustus, 1912, Je 29,11:5; 1943, Je 9, 22:2
Van Cortlandt, James S, 1917, Ap 29,19:5
Van Cortlandt, P Col, 1884, Jl 13,7:1
Van Cossaboon, Nicholas, 1949, Jl 4,13:5
Van Cott, Bunn J, 1939, Je 7,23:3
Van Cott, Charles, 1962, O 30,22:4
Van Cott, Clifton H Mrs, 1942, Ag 10,19:5
Van Cott, Cornelius, 1904, O 26,1:3
Van Cott, Daniel M, 1903, D 28,2:2
Van Cott, Elbert, 1945, O 30,19:1
Van Cott, Elizabeth J B Mrs, 1940, D 25,27:2
Van Cott, George, 1912, S 6,9:4
Van Cott, John A, 1951, O 31,29:3
Van Cott, Joshua M, 1940, F 10,15:3
Van Cott, Mortimer, 1952, Ag 14,23:5
Van Cott, Richard, 1939, S 9,17:4
Van Cott, Ruskin M, 1958, F 18,27:1
Van Cott, Valentine, 1946, F 7,23:1
Van Cott, William H, 1908, Jl 1,7:5; 1923, Mr 2,15:4
Van Court, De Witt, 1937, O 6,25:2
Vancourt, Will E, 1946, Mr 8,21:3
Van Courtlandt, Robert B, 1918, F 21,11:7
Vand, Vladimir Dr, 1968, Ap 6,39:2
Van Daam, Gerrit, 1949, D 22,23:1
Vandagrift, Emory C, 1940, Ag 13,19:4
Van Dahl, Charles, 1949, Ap 1,25:4
Vandal, Louis Jules, 1910, Ag 31,9:6
Van Dalen, Frank, 1954, N 17,31:3
Van Dalsem, L J, 1940, Ag 11,7:1
Vandam, A D, 1903, O 27,9:4
Vandam, Albert H, 1944, S 9,15:6
Van Dam, Bernard E, 1967, Ja 7,27:5
Van Dam, Emanuel F, 1966, Ja 17,47:1
Van Dam, Emmanuel Mrs, 1948, Ja 9,21:2
Van Dam, Gerard, 1962, Ag 25,19:2
Van Dam, Harry, 1954, Je 23,25:1
Vandam, John, 1922, Ja 15,22:3
Van Dam, Lodewyk, 1951, S 11,29:5
Vandamm, Florence (Mrs Geo R Thomas), 1966, Mr 16,45:1
Vandaworker, J B, 1954, D 24,13:5
Vande Bogart, Mary I, 1950, Ja 11,23:2
Vande Poele, Arthur P, 1950, Mr 1,27:2
Van De Bogart, Geraldine, 1944, Je 28,23:5
Van de Car, Aaron B, 1954, S 9,31:2
Van Decar, Otto C, 1945, Je 11,15:4
Vandecar, Richard H Mrs, 1943, My 21,19:2
Van de Carr, Charles R Jr, 1960, D 30,19:5
Van de Carr, James C, 1949, Jl 4,13:4
Van de Graaff, Robert J, 1967, Ja 17,39:1
Vandegriff, Orian A, 1945, Je 25,17:2
Vandegrift, Alex A Mrs, 1952, Jl 13,60:4
Vandegrift, Rolland A, 1949, D 18,89:1
Van de Kamp, Theodore J, 1956, My 12,19:5
Vandeleur, Edward D, 1943, O 7,23:4
Vandell, Frank L, 1956, Ap 24,31:2
Van Deman, Alfred N, 1944, Je 28,23:2
Van Deman, Esther B Dr, 1937, My 5,25:2
Van Deman, Henry E Prof, 1915, Ap 30,13:4
VanDemark, Alfred, 1946, Jl 30,23:2
Van de Mark, Carleton K, 1956, My 30,21:5
Van De Mark, John, 1939, D 10,68:2
Van Demark, John B, 1949, D 21,29:3
Van DeMark, Loten, 1952, S 5,27:2
Van De Motter, Henry, 1949, F 3,24:2
Van den Berg, Brahm, 1926, Ap 6,29:5
Van Den Berg, Joseph Dr, 1937, Je 23,25:1
Van Den Berg, Lawrence H, 1943, S 28,25:3
Van Den Berg, Lawrence H Mrs, 1943, S 14,23:4
Van den Bogert, Marie, 1953, Ja 10,17:1
Vanden Bulck, Charles, 1962, S 30,86:5
Van Den Deemt, Hedda, 1925, F 16,19:2
van den Elsakker, Rudolf C, 1966, Ja 19,41:3
Van Den Hengel, Walter, 1941, Ag 9,15:6
Van Den Heuvel, Charlotte A, 1910, Ja 13,9:4
Van den Heuvel, Richmond, 1958, O 8,35:4
Van Den Hoek, Aart M, 1950, Ja 5,26:4
Van den Huevel, Peter, 1953, Ag 18,23:5
Vandenberg, Arthur H, 1951, Ap 19,1:1
Vandenberg, Arthur H Jr, 1968, Ja 19,47:1
Vandenberg, Arthur H Mrs, 1950, Je 10,18:2
Vandenberg, Henry, 1922, O 18,19:4
Vandenberg, Hoyt S (funl plans, Ap 4,89:1; funl, Ap 6,29:2), 1954, Ap 3,1:4
Vandenberg, Jacob, 1958, Ja 20,23:4
Vandenberg, Pearl K Mrs, 1950, D 9,15:3
Vandenberg, William C, 1953, D 13,86:1
Vandenbrul, Lambertus, 1950, D 31,43:1
Van Denburg, Joseph K, 1944, Ag 3,19:2
Van Denburgh, James R, 1942, S 18,21:3
Vandenburgh, William T, 1942, Mr 20,19:4
Vandenhof, G Jr, 1884, Ag 13,5:6
Vandenhoff, George Mrs, 1885, Ap 21,5:4
Van Denmark, Benjamin J, 1941, My 25,37:1
Van Denmark, Edward Mrs, 1943, Ag 18,19:2
Van De Pol, Alfons H, 1950, O 25,35:4
Vandeputte, Boniface P, 1947, Ag 22,15:4
Vander Beek, Frank I Sr, 1945, Je 2,15:1
Van der Berg, Jose, 1925, Ja 25,7:2
Van der Beugel, Theodore M, 1953, F 11,29:4
Vander Borgh, Garrit N, 1949, Jl 21,25:5
Vander Borgh, William H, 1957, Ja 22,29:4
Van der Burgcht, Adrien, 1954, D 13,27:5
Vander Clock, Cornelius, 1951, Jl 11,23:2
Vander Clock, Cornelius Mrs, 1960, Jl 8,21:5
Van Der Clock, Jacob, 1947, Mr 13,27:4
Vander Clute, Carl F, 1961, Je 2,31:2
Vander Clute, John J, 1945, Jl 19,23:5
Vander Cook, Hale A, 1949, O 17,23:3
Vander Els, Barth, 1950, My 3,29:2
Van Der Emde, Reinhold, 1909, Je 2,7:5
Van Der Goes, Frank, 1939, Je 6,23:6
Van der Helm, Lion, 1924, Ja 12,13:2
Van der Hoogt, Cornelius Mrs, 1937, O 14,25:6
Vander Horst, Elias, 1937, Je 24,25:2
van der Linde, Victor, 1959, Ap 5,86:7
Van Der Lyke, John, 1944, Je 17,13:6
Vander May, Herman, 1951, F 16,25:3
Vander Meer, Jacob, 1964, Ap 16,37:4
Vander Meer, William, 1945, F 22,27:3
van der Meulen, Peter A, 1967, D 15,47:1
Van der Poel, A Augustus Mrs, 1937, Ap 5,19:5
Van der Poel, John Dr, 1920, F 23,13:6
Vander Poel, Mary L H Mrs, 1941, Ja 9,21:1
Vander Poel, S Oakley, 1947, D 27,14:3
Van der Poel, Samuel Oakley Dr, 1912, Ap 23,13:4
Van der Poel, Washington I Sr, 1960, Ag 26,26:1
Vander Putten, Charles, 1946, D 10,31:5
Vander Roest, Henry C, 1943, N 20,13:5
Vander Roest, Henry Mrs, 1959, O 21,43:2
Van der Smissen, Gilbert J, 1949, Ja 22,14:2
Vander Veer, A, 1929, D 20,29:1
Vander Veer, Albert, 1959, F 1,85:2
Vander Veer, Albert Mrs, 1944, D 3,58:4

Vander Veer, Edgar A, 1953, S 22,31:3
Vander Veer, James N Dr, 1937, My 16,II,8:5
Vander Veer, Jessie, 1950, My 4,27:5
Vander Veer, John H Mrs (Margt), 1965, Ag 1,77:1
Van Der Veer, Nevada Mme, 1958, S 27,21:5
Van der Veer, Norman R, 1966, Jl 28,33:5
Vander Veer, Seely, 1950, D 25,19:6
Van der Veer, Willard, 1963, Je 17,25:2
Van der Voort, John, 1953, O 19,21:5
Vander Waal, John, 1948, S 11,15:4
Van der Waals, Prof, 1923, Mr 9,15:4
Van Der Wart, Andrew L, 1940, F 13,23:2
Vander Wende, Catherine Mrs, 1940, Ag 6,19:4
van der Woude, R Gerrit, 1962, Ag 6,25:2
vander Zee, Abram, 1967, Jl 12,43:2
Van Derau, Clarence L, 1957, D 27,20:1
Vanderbach, Harry W, 1956, Ja 18,31:3
Vanderbeck, Edwin F, 1950, S 12,27:2
Van Derbeck, Frank H, 1966, Je 22,47:3
Vanderbeck, Howard F, 1965, Je 17,33:3
Vanderbeck, William Storms, 1919, Jl 9,13:3
Vanderbeek, Arch Mrs, 1948, F 28,15:3
Vanderbeek, Charles A, 1942, D 17,29:2
Vanderbeek, Edgar, 1943, Ap 8,23:1
Vanderbeek, Francis I, 1909, O 24,13:2
Vanderbeek, James L Dr, 1937, D 24,19:2
Vanderbeek, May B Mrs, 1937, Ap 3,19:4
Vanderbilt, Adriaan J Mrs, 1940, O 1,23:3
Vanderbilt, Anne H Mrs (will, My 4,19:3),(por), 1940, Ap 21,1:4
Vanderbilt, Arthur T (funl plans, Je 17,23:5; funl, Je 19,33:4), 1957, Je 16,1:8
Vanderbilt, Augustus A, 1939, Ap 6,25:3
Vanderbilt, C Sr Mrs, 1934, Ap 23,1:4
Vanderbilt, Charles, 1944, D 28,19:6
Vanderbilt, Charles H, 1951, Ja 22,19:5
Vanderbilt, Chester W, 1941, Ja 18,30:4
Vanderbilt, Clifford M Mrs, 1955, Jl 26,25:3
Vanderbilt, Cornelius, 1877, Ja 5,1:5; 1899, S 13,1:7; 1942, Mr 2,21:1
Vanderbilt, Cornelius Mrs, 1953, Ja 8,1:3
Vanderbilt, Cornelius Mrs (est tax appr), 1955, F 19, 17:4
Vanderbilt, E Louise Mrs, 1961, O 19,35:1
Vanderbilt, E Ward Mrs, 1919, Ap 28,15:3
Vanderbilt, Edmund R, 1965, Ja 22,44:1
Vanderbilt, Effie M Mrs, 1877, N 5,8:4
Vanderbilt, Elizabeth, 1904, F 6,9:5
Vanderbilt, F W Mrs, 1926, Ag 22,27:1
Vanderbilt, Frank A Mrs, 1885, My 5,5:2
Vanderbilt, Frank P, 1941, O 19,45:2
Vanderbilt, Franklin, 1960, N 26,21:6
Vanderbilt, Frederick W (will, Jl 14,23:1),(por), 1938, Je 30,23:3
Vanderbilt, G F Mrs, 1935, Jl 8,15:1
Vanderbilt, George N, 1945, Mr 5,19:2
Vanderbilt, George W, 1914, Mr 11,11:6
Vanderbilt, Gertrude, 1960, F 19,27:1
Vanderbilt, Howard S, 1950, S 15,26:3
Vanderbilt, J, 1877, My 18,4:7
Vanderbilt, J Mortimer, 1947, Jl 22,23:2
Vanderbilt, Jacob, 1925, Jl 13,17:6
Vanderbilt, James Edmond Mrs, 1917, Jl 17,9:4
Vanderbilt, John L, 1952, Ja 20,85:1
Vanderbilt, John Mrs, 1902, Ja 7,7:5
Vanderbilt, Joseph L, 1916, F 21,11:4
Vanderbilt, Lewis Mrs, 1945, Ag 24,19:4
Vanderbilt, Mary, 1878, Ja 23,2:5
Vanderbilt, O de Gray Jr, 1960, Ja 23,21:4
Vanderbilt, R T, 1866, S 16,3:7
Vanderbilt, Reginald C (por),(funl, S 6,7:2), 1925, S 5,13:4
Vanderbilt, Reginald Mrs (Gloria M),(funl plans, F 15,27:1), 1965, F 14,88:1
Vanderbilt, Robert H Mrs, 1949, Je 15,29:3
Vanderbilt, Robert T, 1954, Ag 14,15:7
Vanderbilt, Robert T Mrs, 1950, F 14,25:4
Vanderbilt, Sanderson, 1967, Ja 24,28:7
Vanderbilt, W H (funl), 1885, D 9,1:1
Vanderbilt, W H Mrs, 1896, N 7,1:7
Vanderbilt, Walter S, 1958, My 1,31:5
Vanderbilt, William D, 1945, My 15,19:2
Vanderbilt, William D Mrs, 1954, N 6,17:5
Vanderbilt, William E, 1956, D 4,39:5
Vanderbilt, William E Mrs, 1956, N 29,35:4
Vanderbilt, William K (will, Ja 21,19:4), 1944, Ja 8, 13:4
Vanderbilt, William K Mrs (por), 1947, Ag 29,17:4
Vanderbilt, William Kissam (funl, Ag 27,11:3), 1920, Ag 25,9:2
Vanderblue, Homer B, 1952, Jl 13,60:3
Vanderborgh, Henry, 1952, F 17,84:2
Vanderbreggen, Cornelius Sr, 1951, Ap 19,31:3
Vanderburgh, Ernest D, 1945, Ap 23,19:4
Vanderburgh, Ernest D Mrs, 1949, Ag 1,17:5
Vanderburgh, Frederick A Dr, 1923, O 31,15:3
Vandercar, William H, 1946, Jl 18,25:3
Vandercook, Frank M, 1951, Ja 16,29:3
Vandercook, John, 1908, Ap 12,7:7
Vandercook, John Mrs, 1958, F 9,88:2
Vandercook, John W, 1963, Ja 7,15:1
Vandercook, John W Mrs (funl, S 6,11:1), 1961, S 3, 9:2
Vandercook, Robert O, 1951, Je 9,19:4
Vandercook, Roy C, 1958, Ap 13,83:5
Vanderdrift, Adrian J, 1958, O 13,29:5
Vanderem, Fernand, 1939, Mr 12,III,7:1
Van Deren, Clarence T, 1939, Mr 12,III,6:8
Van de Repe, Abe C, 1938, D 25,14:6
Vandergrift, Hiram, 1949, O 15,15:4
Vandergrift, J Monte, 1939, Jl 31,13:3
Vandergrift, Joseph B, 1915, My 25,15:5
Vandergrift, Nelson M, 1948, Ja 7,25:1
Vanderhauf, Edward Dr, 1903, F 7,6:6
Vanderheim, Leon Mrs, 1949, My 4,29:3
Vanderherchen, Frank Sr, 1912, Jl 14,II,11:5
Vanderheyden, Peter F, 1953, Ap 8,29:3
Vanderheyden, Thomas S, 1954, Jl 14,27:2
Vanderhoef, Francis B, 1964, Je 16,39:4
Vanderhoef, Francis Mrs, 1945, My 19,19:5
Vanderhoef, Frank F, 1947, Ag 22,15:3
Vanderhoef, George W, 1947, Je 8,60:5
Vanderhoef, George W Jr Mrs, 1939, S 10,49:2
Vanderhoef, George W Mrs, 1941, F 24,15:2
Vanderhoef, Harman B, 1941, S 1,15:5
Vanderhoef, Henry C Mrs, 1942, S 15,24:3
Vanderhoef, Marshall, 1953, N 26,31:4
Vanderhoef, N Wyckoff, 1956, N 19,31:5
Vanderhoef, N Wyckoff Mrs, 1944, Ja 18,19:4
Van Derhoes, George, 1943, O 29,19:4
Vanderhoff, Benjamin Mrs, 1938, My 13,19:2
Vanderhoff, Irving M, 1940, My 3,21:5
Vanderhoff, Mable W, 1942, S 29,23:1
Vanderhoof, Charles H, 1937, Jl 10,15:4
Vanderhoof, Edward N, 1945, My 15,19:4
Vanderhoof, Frederick Mrs, 1962, Ag 8,31:4
Vanderhoof, Herbert, 1921, Ag 8,11:7
Vanderhoof, J Curtis Sr, 1956, Ap 28,17:4
Vanderhoof, John H, 1949, Mr 23,27:3
Vanderhoof, Nancy J, 1947, My 8,27:6
Vanderhorst, John F, 1961, Je 6,37:1
Vanderhoven, Clara, 1946, My 1,25:1
Vanderhoven, Halsey, 1949, Ag 21,69:2
Vanderhoven, Jesse, 1951, N 29,33:2
Vanderhoven, Orrin, 1906, D 29,5:3
Van Dering, David B, 1871, Ap 16,1:7
Vanderlaan, W C Mrs, 1924, O 2,23:3
Vanderleck, Carl W, 1961, N 9,35:5
Vanderleck, Jan, 1955, Jl 30,17:2
Vanderlind, Edward, 1951, Mr 25,72:5
Vanderlip, Frank A (por), 1937, Je 30,23:1
Vanderlip, Frank A Mrs, 1966, Mr 6,92:8
Vanderlip, George M Rev, 1903, Ag 3,7:6
Van Derlip, J R, 1935, Mr 24,35:6
Vanderlip, Kelvin C, 1956, Ag 22,29:3
Vanderlipp, William T, 1952, N 1,21:5
Van Derlyn, Alada F, 1954, F 4,25:5
Vanderlyn, Etta, 1951, Jl 12,25:4
Vanderlyn, John H, 1938, My 21,15:3
Van Dermark, Reuben Mrs, 1946, S 27,23:2
Vandermeulen, George T, 1961, D 28,27:3
Vanderminden, Henry J W Sr, 1949, My 21,13:2
Vandermyn, Armand J P, 1941, Ap 5,19:4
Vanderniepen, Pastor, 1925, S 3,25:4
van Dernoot, Emanuel Mrs, 1960, Mr 29,37:3
Vanderoef, John J Mrs, 1944, S 10,46:1
Vanderploeg, Watson H, 1957, My 29,27:2
Vanderpoel, A J, 1887, Ag 23,5:1
Vanderpoel, Aaron J Mrs, 1912, Jl 30,9:6
Vanderpoel, Ambrose E (will, Ap 16,19:4), 1940, Ap 6,17:4
Vanderpoel, Augustus G, 1951, Ap 29,89:2
Vanderpoel, B W, 1878, My 8,5:3
Vanderpoel, Edward (will, S 10,25:1), 1941, Ag 23, 13:7
Vanderpoel, Edward Mrs, 1871, My 6,5:2
Vanderpoel, Emily C N, 1939, F 21,19:4
Vanderpoel, Floyd L, 1948, D 12,93:2
Vanderpoel, George B, 1925, O 17,15:3
Vanderpoel, Harriet G, 1877, My 18,4:7
Vanderpoel, Isaac, 1868, D 30,1:7
Vanderpoel, J, 1884, F 9,5:2
Vanderpoel, John H, 1911, My 3,13:5
Vanderpoel, Mary Van Buren (funl, Ja 4,13:5), 1922, Ja 3,17:3
Vanderpoel, Robert P, 1955, Ja 21,23:2
Vanderpoel, Waldren B Dr, 1915, Mr 11,11:4
Vanderpoel, William K, 1939, O 22,40:4
Vanderpool, Alice D Mrs, 1939, O 5,23:3
Vanderpool, Charles F, 1943, Jl 14,19:2
Vanderpool, Frederick W, 1947, F 15,15:6
Vanderpool, Jacob W, 1871, Ap 23,6:6
Vanderpool, Jesse L, 1944, Ja 5,17:3
Vanderpool, William Eugene, 1903, Jl 13,7:2
Vanderpool, Wynant D (por), 1944, Ag 20,34:1
Vandersall, Stanley B, 1949, Mr 26,17:6
Vanderschaff, John, 1951, Ag 8,25:3
Vanderschmidt, Fred, 1956, N 9,29:2
Vanderslice, Florence L Mrs, 1941, Ag 9,15:6
Vandersloot, John W, 1946, My 14,21:1
Vanderslute, William W Sr, 1960, Je 30,29:6
Vanderstarr, Nelle, 1941, F 17,15:3
Vanderveer, Adrian, 1885, Ap 22,5:5
Vanderveer, E B, 1933, Ag 30,19:3
Van Derveer, Edgar I, 1955, Ag 30,27:5
Vanderveer, Edward B, 1940, Ag 25,35:1
Vanderveer, Edward B Mrs, 1942, S 19,15:4
Vanderveer, George E, 1942, O 23,21:5
Vanderveer, Henry H, 1944, S 6,19:3
Vanderveer, John, 1941, N 26,23:2
Vanderveer, Stephen L, 1960, Ap 11,32:1
Vanderveer, Warren K, 1940, Jl 5,13:4
Vandervelde, Emile (por), 1938, D 28,21:4
Vandervell, Tony, 1967, Mr 11,29:5
Van Derver, Harry C, 1937, Mr 10,23:2
Vanderverg, John E, 1951, N 29,33:4
Vandervliet, John, 1937, S 22,27:3
Vandervoort, Charles, 1874, S 16,4:7
Vandervoort, Cornelius H, 1948, S 5,40:6
Vandervoort, H, 1884, Ap 29,5:4
Vandervoort, John R Mrs, 1948, O 29,25:1
Vandervoort, R J Mrs, 1925, Ag 9,5:2
Vandervoort, Vincent, 1950, Ap 7,25:5
Vandervort, J Scott, 1941, Je 20,21:5
Vanderwalker, Fred N, 1945, N 27,23:5
Vanderwall, John J Jr, 1948, S 17,25:2
Vanderwall, Nicholas H, 1937, S 12,II,6:8
Vanderwart, Herman, 1961, S 21,35:4
Vanderwater, William V, 1942, D 14,28:3
Vanderweg, William G, 1948, O 19,27:2
Vanderwende, John, 1938, Mr 13,II,9:2; 1946, Ja 4, 22:2; 1947, Mr 12,25:3
VanderWende, Tunis, 1947, Ag 10,53:1
Van Derwerker, Earl E, 1947, N 3,23:2
Vanderwerker, Herbert N, 1941, N 12,23:4
Vanderwerker, William R, 1942, S 29,24:2
Vanderwerp, George D, 1941, Ap 1,23:6
Vanderwerp, John, 1939, Ag 13,29:2
Vanderzanden, Henri, 1949, Ap 30,13:2
Vanderzee, Newton B, 1946, Ag 17,13:3
Vanderzee, Ten Eyck B, 1945, Ag 6,15:5
Van Dessel, Joseph, 1951, Ja 3,25:1
Van Deursen, Howard B, 1965, Mr 8,29:3
Van Deusen, Charles A, 1949, Ap 24,76:4
Van Deusen, Charles C, 1938, Je 25,15:5
Van Deusen, Clinton, 1945, Mr 10,17:5
Van Deusen, Edgar, 1950, Je 18,76:8
Van Deusen, Elisha Blackman, 1925, O 28,25:5
Van Deusen, George K, 1937, Mr 16,23:2
Van Deusen, Harold L, 1947, F 2,57:2
Van Deusen, Henry R, 1960, My 5,35:3
Van Deusen, John F, 1960, My 14,23:5
Van Deusen, Lansing Mrs, 1943, N 28,68:2
Vandeusen, Mary Westbrook, 1908, O 17,9:4
Van Deusen, Paul F Mrs, 1948, Mr 5,21:4
Van Deusen, Robert J, 1948, My 26,25:2
Van Deusen, Robert O, 1946, My 13,21:3
Van Deusen, Russell, 1943, Mr 9,23:4
Van Deusen, Wallace J, 1950, O 19,31:3
Van Deusen, Walter M Mrs, 1954, Je 8,27:2
Van Deussen, George W, 1938, Mr 7,17:2
Van Devander, A H Mrs, 1956, Je 30,17:6
Van Devanter, Harry B, 1945, Ja 27,11:6
Van Devanter, Willis, 1941, F 9,47:3
Vandeveer, G Capt, 1865, D 19,5:1
Van Deveer, Henry P, 1907, Ag 30,7:6
Vandeveer, William W Mrs, 1944, S 7,23:3
Van de Velde, H C, 1956, Ja 22,88:4
van de Velde, Robert P, 1957, Ap 25,31:1
Vandeventer, Braden, 1943, S 30,21:2
Van Deventer, Charles, 1954, O 13,31:3
Van de Venter, Charles H, 1905, My 27,9:4
Van Deventer, Elwood, 1950, Ag 31,25:5
Van Deventer, Harry B Mrs, 1946, D 27,20:2
van Deventer, Horace Mrs, 1956, Jl 14,15:4
Vandeventer, James Thayer Col, 1910, S 19,7:6
Van Deventer, John H, 1956, Mr 6,31:3
Vandeventer, Joseph N, 1951, My 17,31:3
Van Deventer, Louis Jacob Gen, 1922, Ag 28,11:6
Van Deventer, Ludlow, 1967, Ag 8,39:3
Van Deventer, Phil, 1955, Ja 24,23:4
Vandeventer, Theodore, 1946, Ap 16,25:6
Van Deventer, William, 1941, F 10,17:6
Vandever, Jacob B, 1941, Jl 31,17:1
Van De Visse, Lewis O, 1948, Mr 29,21:5
Van de Vyver, Augustine Rev, 1911, O 17,11:5
Van de Walker, Hugh, 1943, Ap 9,21:5
Van de Wall, Willem, 1953, Ag 29,17:1
Vandewater, Arthur M, 1951, My 29,25:3
Van De Water, Arthur R, 1968, Ja 11,33:6
Vandewater, Benjamin C, 1955, Jl 16,15:3
Van de Water, Claude, 1951, Ag 17,17:4
Van De Water, Cornelia T Y Mrs, 1937, D 18,21:4
Van de Water, Edward T, 1966, Ap 8,31:2
Van De Water, Edward T Mrs, 1942, N 25,23:6
Vandewater, Edwin, 1953, S 21,25:5
Vandewater, Elmer, 1958, Jl 13,68:7
Van De Water, Frederic F, 1917, D 24,9:5
Van de Water, Frederic F, 1968, S 17,47:1
Van de Water, Frederic F Mrs, 1945, O 18,23:3
Van De Water, George Roe Dr (funl, Mr 19,21:5), 1925, Mr 16,19:1
Van De Water, Isaac N, 1943, D 4,13:4
Van De Water, John H, 1944, Ja 10,17:2
Van De Water, John H Mrs, 1949, F 23,27:3
Van de Water, John Titus, 1924, Ap 7,17:6
Van de Water, Kenneth B Mrs, 1945, My 19,19:2
Van De Water, Lott, 1908, Ja 28,9:5
Van de Water, Lott Mrs, 1952, S 13,17:2

Van de Water, Marjorie, 1962, Ag 4,19:5
Vandewater, Mary I Mrs, 1941, O 31,23:1
Van De Water, William G, 1943, Ap 10,17:4
Vandewater, Winfield S, 1945, D 1,23:5
Van De Watering, Casper D, 1943, Mr 20,15:5
Van De Weyer, M, 1874, Je 12,3:2
van de Woestyne, Royal S, 1967, Ag 6,76:6
Van Di Grisse, Judson C, 1938, Mr 10,21:4
Van Dieren, Bernard, 1937, Ap 25,X,5:5
Vandigriff, Hoke L, 1955, Ja 1,25:2
Van Dike, Roy V, 1951, Je 7,33:4
Van Dillen, David, 1950, Ap 30,102:8
Van Dine, Richard, 1937, Mr 15,23:1
Van Dine, S S (W H Wright),(por), 1939, Ap 13,23:1
Van Dine, Theodore Pell, 1921, My 3,17:4
Vandiver, A, 1931, Je 22,19:4
Vandiver, Eleanor W Mrs, 1938, S 27,21:3
Vandiver, Murray C, 1916, My 24,11:7
Van Diver, Vernon H Mrs, 1960, O 24,29:2
Vandiver, W D, 1932, My 31,17:5
Vandivert, Roderick M, 1948, D 24,18:2
Van Doesburgh, Herman D Mrs, 1946, N 30,15:3
Van Dohlen, William, 1949, Ja 14,23:5
Van Doorn, Russell F, 1940, Ap 2,26:3
van Doorn, William Mrs, 1956, Ag 15,29:5
Van Doorslaer, Hector, 1904, S 25,4:2
Van Dore, Edrie Mrs, 1963, Ap 8,47:3
Van Doren, Abraham E, 1956, N 3,23:5
Van Doren, Carl, 1950, Jl 19,31:1
Van Doren, Charles L Mrs, 1951, N 8,29:6
Van Doren, De Witt T, 1942, My 17,46:2
Van Doren, Earl J, 1967, Ap 18,41:3
Van Doren, George B, 1947, N 30,76:6
Van Doren, George W, 1965, Ap 12,35:1
Van Doren, Harold, 1957, F 4,19:2
Van Doren, Harriet C Mrs, 1939, N 12,49:2
Van Doren, Henry S O, 1953, Jl 2,23:4
Van Doren, Irita Mrs, 1966, D 19,37:1
Van Doren, Louis O, 1938, F 19,15:4
Van Doren, O E, 1951, Jl 19,23:6
Van Doren, Palmer S, 1952, Ag 22,21:2
Van Doren, William, 1951, Ap 23,25:2
Van Dorn, Ferdinand B, 1953, N 23,27:1
Van Dorn, Frank, 1941, Ja 16,21:3
Van Dorn, Thomas B, 1950, My 22,21:4
Van Dorpe, Joseph, 1946, Jl 21,40:2
Van Dover, Frederick W, 1943, F 4,23:3
Van Dresser, Marcia, 1937, Jl 12,18:2
Van Dresser, William, 1950, S 14,31:3
Van Driel, Agnes C, 1951, N 1,29:4
van Druten, John, 1957, D 20,27:1
Van Duesen, Jean, 1939, O 31,18:3
Van Dugteren, Arnold J, 1968, Ja 3,40:1
Van Dulken, Jean T C, 1945, Ja 18,19:2
Van Duren, William L Mrs (Klondike Kate), 1957, F 22,21:1
Van Dusen, Albert E, 1968, O 14,47:2
Van Dusen, Alfred, 1947, Ja 26,53:2
Van Dusen, Bruce B, 1943, F 8,19:3
Van Dusen, Charles B, 1958, Ag 17,86:7
Van Dusen, Charles M, 1947, F 8,17:3
Van Dusen, Charlotte F Mrs, 1938, Ag 30,17:3
Van Dusen, Clarence, 1949, My 19,29:2
Van Dusen, Clyde, 1951, Ja 8,17:4
Van Dusen, Eldon M, 1940, Ja 27,13:5
van Dusen, Frank, 1907, Mr 5,9:6
Van Dusen, Fred Dr, 1922, Ag 21,11:3
Van Dusen, Hannah Mrs, 1914, Ag 16,15:3
Van Dusen, Lewis H, 1948, D 11,15:3
Van Dusen, Lewis H Mrs, 1945, N 21,21:5
Van Dusen, Milton E, 1940, D 25,27:4
Van Dusen, Samuel B Mrs, 1947, D 22,22:2
Van Dusen, Samuel C Mrs, 1953, My 24,89:1
van Duser, H Douglass, 1961, My 4,37:4
Van Duser, Ralph D, 1943, My 7,19:4
Van Duyn, H Norton Mrs, 1952, Ja 18,27:3
Van Duyn, J, 1934, Ja 16,21:1
Van Duyn, James P Mrs, 1949, Jl 26,27:2
Van Duyn, Owen M, 1948, S 7,25:5
Van Duyne, Frederick W, 1958, Ja 19,86:4
Van Duyne, James N Mrs, 1945, Jl 22,37:1
Van Duzee, Harold (por), 1940, Jl 4,15:4
Van Duzer, Adelbert H, 1951, D 12,38:4
Van Duzer, Clarence D, 1947, S 29,21:2
Van Duzer, Edwin Mrs, 1944, Mr 18,13:6
Van Duzer, Ellsworth J, 1940, Je 19,23:4
Van Duzer, Frederick C, 1958, S 22,31:6
Van Duzer, George, 1904, Ja 16,9:3
Van Duzer, Selah Reeve, 1903, D 28,7:4
Van Duzer, William A, 1946, F 24,44:2
Van Duzer, William M, 1949, Jl 17,56:1
Van Duzer, Winifred Mrs, 1951, Mr 7,33:4
Van Dyck, A Van B, 1881, N 4,5:3
Van Dyck, Alex S, 1951, F 21,27:3
Van Dyck, Cassie L, 1945, Ap 15,14:3
Van Dyck, Clinton De Witt Dr, 1916, Ag 12,9:8
Van Dyck, Edwin M, 1953, Ag 16,77:1
Van Dyck, Ernest, 1923, S 10,17:5
Van Dyck, F C, 1927, Ap 13,25:3
Van Dyck, Frank, 1948, F 27,21:4
Van Dyck, Henry A, 1939, S 29,23:4
Van Dyck, Henry H, 1912, Ag 12,9:6
Van Dyck, John W, 1939, S 14,23:3
Van Dyck, Laird S, 1944, Ag 10,17:4
Vandyck, Louis A, 1944, Ag 29,17:2
Van Dyck, Louis B, 1964, Je 15,29:1
Van Dyck, Pierre Mrs, 1945, D 20,23:2
Van Dyck, Richard, 1966, O 7,43:2
Van Dyck, Vedder, 1960, Ag 3,29:1
Van Dyk, Daniel Mrs, 1963, Ag 2,27:4
Van Dyk, Francis C, 1917, My 22,13:4
Van Dyk, Frank Mrs, 1960, Ja 2,13:4
Van Dyk, James J, 1951, D 18,31:4
Van Dyke, Albert Mrs, 1956, D 9,89:2
Van Dyke, Albert Sr, 1957, Je 22,15:4
Van Dyke, Benjamin Lt, 1918, My 14,13:6
Van Dyke, Benjamin S, 1950, Jl 14,21:2
Van Dyke, Carl Chester, 1919, My 21,17:6
Van Dyke, Clifford S, 1942, My 9,13:5
Van Dyke, George B Mrs, 1955, F 2,27:2
van Dyke, H, 1933, Ap 11,19:1
Van Dyke, H J Jr (trb), 1883, F 19,8:3
Van Dyke, Harvey C, 1963, Je 20,33:6
Van Dyke, J C, 1932, D 6,21:1
Van Dyke, J W (will), 1940, F 6,6:3
Vandyke, James C, 1866, Ag 29,3:1
Van Dyke, James E, 1946, Jl 9,21:1
Van Dyke, John, 1878, D 26,5:4
Van Dyke, John E, 1953, My 2,15:4
Van Dyke, John M Prof, 1908, Je 24,7:5
Van Dyke, John R, 1938, F 12,15:4
Van Dyke, Karl S, 1966, O 7,43:4
Van Dyke, Leonard K, 1941, O 23,23:2
Van Dyke, Orson Mrs, 1949, N 22,29:4
Van Dyke, Robert L, 1941, Ap 14,17:5
Van Dyke, Stephen, 1948, My 12,27:5
van Dyke, Tertius, 1958, Mr 1,17:3
Van Dyke, Theodore A, 1952, D 2,31:2
Van Dyke, Thomas N, 1945, N 11,42:6
Van Dyke, Thomas R Sr, 1941, D 30,19:5
Van Dyke, Warren, 1938, Mr 31,23:5
Van Dyke, William D Mrs, 1911, O 9,11:5
Van Dyke, Woodbridge S (por), 1943, F 6,13:1
Van Dyne, Catherine B, 1946, F 10,40:6
Van Dyne, Edward S, 1954, Ap 18,33:1
Van Dyne, Eiza Pope, 1925, S 4,21:6
Van Dyne, George, 1965, N 30,41:4
Van Dyne, Harry J, 1942, F 24,21:2
Van Dyne, Henry B, 1961, N 18,23:5
Vane, August S, 1958, Mr 20,29:1
Vane, Daphne V (Mrs R Day), 1966, D 18,84:8
Vane, Denton, 1940, S 19,23:2
Vane, Robert J, 1952, Mr 12,27:4
Vane, Sutton, 1963, Je 19,37:3
Vane-Tempest, G H R C W Marquis of Londonderry, 1884, N 7,5:6
Vane-Tempest-Stewart, Edward C S R (Marquess of Londonderry), 1955, O 19,33:2
Van Eddie, 1944, Jl 21,19:2
Van Eeghen, Alfred, 1957, F 15,23:3
van Eerden, Albert, 1960, Ja 3,89:1
Van Egri, Edward, 1952, Ag 8,17:2
Van Eizenga, Jacob J, 1940, Jl 13,13:5
Vanek, Joseph F, 1956, Ja 25,31:5
Vaneman Ranck, Than (por), 1947, Jl 31,21:3
Van Emburg, A Col, 1867, Jl 14,3:7
Van Emburgh, David Bosworth, 1916, Mr 17,11:7
Van Emden, Bram, 1953, Je 10,29:5
Van Emden, Eva, 1940, F 11,49:2
Van Emden, Harriet, 1953, D 28,21:2
Van Emden, Henry B, 1923, N 7,17:5
Van Emmerick, Gerrit, 1941, F 3,17:2
Vanenargues, Guy d'Isoard Count, 1916, Ja 21,9:6
Vaneone, Dorothy, 1947, Mr 4,25:4
Van Epps, Guy, 1953, D 11,34:6
Van Epps, John De L, 1960, S 17,23:5
Van Epps, Percy M, 1951, S 2,49:1
Vaneseltine, Glen P, 1938, N 16,23:2
Van Esen, Stephen T, 1948, Mr 18,28:2
Van Ess, Jacob, 1959, D 25,21:6
Van Ess, John, 1949, Ap 27,27:4
Van Ess, John Jr, 1943, Ja 24,38:1
Van Esselstyn, Richard H, 1945, Ap 15,14:7
Van Essendelft, Albert, 1951, Mr 12,25:3
Van Etten, A H, 1940, O 4,23:6
Van Etten, Allie N, 1944, O 20,19:4
Van Etten, Archie, 1944, Je 28,23:6
Van Etten, Charles R, 1951, My 2,31:5
Van Etten, Edwin J, 1956, O 8,27:2
Van Etten, Frank, 1952, Ja 31,28:2
Van Etten, Henry, 1949, Je 19,68:4
Van Etten, John, 1907, F 16,9:6
Van Etten, Lawrence E, 1951, Ja 29,19:5
Van Etten, Lawrence E Mrs, 1943, Mr 20,15:4
Van Etten, Nathan B, 1954, Jl 24,13:3
Van Etten, Phil Mrs, 1948, O 24,76:5
Van Etten, Ralph A, 1950, Ap 30,102:3
Van Etten, Roger, 1950, Ag 19,15:2
Van Etten, William H, 1951, F 15,31:2
Van Ettisch, Raymond, 1951, O 25,29:5
Van Evera, Juliet Potter Mrs, 1905, Ap 29,11:6
Van Evera, Kepler, 1955, My 17,29:2
Vaneveren, Jay, 1948, Ja 1,23:4
Van Every, Ed, 1952, My 31,17:6
Van Every, John Brock, 1920, Ap 28,11:4
Van Every, Leonard H, 1949, My 16,21:1
Van Evra, Cornelius Dr, 1904, My 21,5:4
Van Exem, Arsene J, 1956, Mr 26,29:1
Van Eyck, Alex D, 1961, Jl 7,25:4
Van Eyk, Christiaan J, 1956, Ag 29,29:6
Van Eyndhoven, John W, 1950, F 8,27:5
Vanezia, John, 1948, F 29,61:1
Van Felt, Frank, 1947, Ag 12,23:5
Van Fleet, Charles E, 1949, My 21,13:3
Van Fleet, Charles L, 1948, F 5,23:4
Van Fleet, Dallas, 1954, O 2,17:5
Van Fleet, Emme (will), 1951, Jl 11,23:1
Van Fleet, Frank B, 1944, Je 29,23:5
Van Fleet, Frank Dr, 1919, Ap 6,22:3
Van Fleet, Hart S, 1937, My 10,19:4
Van Fleet, Henry S, 1925, Ap 29,21:6
Van Fleet, Jennie, 1949, Mr 12,17:5
Van Fleet, Ransome, 1947, Ap 25,21:2
Van Fleet, Van Doren, 1946, Ag 22,27:5
Van Fleet, Walter Dr, 1922, Ja 28,13:5
Van Fleet, Wilfred H, 1938, F 7,15:4
Van Fleet, William C Judge, 1923, S 5,15:4
Van Fossen, Charles L, 1943, Ap 12,23:2
Van Gaasbeck, Alexander B, 1911, Ja 16,11:5
Van Gaasbeck, Henry, 1944, Mr 4,13:5
Van Gaasbeek, Helen C Mrs, 1937, Je 20,II,7:2
Van Gaertner, Louis A Mrs, 1924, Mr 5,17:4
Van Galder, Harold C, 1966, N 6,88:4
Van Gasken, Frances C, 1939, O 25,23:4
Van Geisen, Ira Dr, 1913, Mr 25,13:5
Van Gelder, Arthur P, 1947, D 11,34:2
Van Gelder, David, 1938, O 29,19:6
Van Gelder, Eleanor, 1947, Je 17,28:2
Van Gelder, F Harry, 1944, Je 1,19:5
Van Gelder, George S, 1944, D 21,21:3
Van Gelder, Howard M, 1941, N 23,53:3
Van Gelder, John H, 1958, My 9,23:2
Van Gelder, Martinus, 1941, F 27,19:2
Van Gelder, Mary E Mrs, 1938, Ag 2,19:4
Van Gelder, Robert, 1952, Ap 4,25:3
Van Gelder, Samuel, 1947, Ja 29,25:4
Van Gerbig, Howell, 1965, My 14,43:1
Van Gerbig, Howell Mrs, 1945, Jl 29,40:7
Van Gestel, Henry A, 1955, Jl 20,27:1
Van Gieson, G A, 1903, Ap 5,7:5
Van Gieson, Mary C H Mrs, 1942, D 20,45:1
Van Gieson, Ransford Everett Dr, 1921, Ap 2,11:4
Van Gieson, Reynier, 1907, D 19,9:5
Van Gilder, Lincoln, 1946, N 16,19:3
Van Gilluwe, F Louis, 1937, Ap 11,II,8:5
Van Goor, Robert E, 1964, S 23,47:5
Van Gorden, George, 1939, Je 28,21:2
Van Gorden, James G, 1943, Jl 14,19:3
Van Gorder, A H, 1941, D 24,17:5
Van Gorder, Albert H Mrs, 1959, My 30,2:6
Van Gorder, J Rexford, 1957, Jl 29,19:6
Van Gordon, Cyrene (C Pocock), 1964, Ap 6,31:4
Van Gordon, John W, 1941, N 3,19:3
Van Gorp, Leopold Father, 1905, Ap 12,9:4
Van Graflan, Roy, 1953, S 6,50:3
Vangulik, B A Mrs, 1948, Je 13,68:8
Van Gumster, Adela, 1952, Mr 10,21:3
Van Gundy, June, 1963, O 24,30:4
Van Gundy, Lander, 1968, Jl 26,31:4
Van Guysling, Edmund, 1946, Ap 26,21:2
Van Guysling, Walter F, 1944, F 25,17:4
Van Haagen, Henry, 1938, Ap 20,23:4
Van Haagen, Mete R Mrs, 1949, Ja 2,60:4
Van Haagen, Walter K, 1940, My 10,23:5
Van Haeften-Hatch, Baroness, 1939, Ap 23,III,6:8
Van Hagen, Charles A Mrs, 1938, Ja 15,15:2
Van Hagen, George E, 1946, Ap 7,44:2
Van Hagen, George L, 1937, D 1,23:4
Van Hala, Harry H, 1950, Ap 26,31:2
Van Hall, C J, 1947, O 1,29:4
Van Hamm, Amy P Mrs, 1938, D 24,15:2
Van Hamm, Caleb, 1919, D 28,23:2
Van Harlingen, John Dr, 1903, My 19,9:6
Van Hart, Frank S, 1941, Ja 12,46:1
Van Hart, Ralph G, 1953, Mr 6,23:1
Vanhason, Caleb, 1884, Ag 21,2:5
Van Haste, Garry, 1959, My 31,76:3
Van Hausen, G D Rev, 1903, My 10,7:5
Van Hedencamp, Meta, 1925, O 1,27:4
Van Heel, Klaas Mrs, 1925, O 12,21:5
Van Heemst, Nina M, 1937, Jl 8,23:2
Van Hennik, Frank, 1946, Ap 26,21:1
Van Herwerden, Jan, 1944, F 24,15:2
Van Heukelom, Gustave, 1953, Ap 26,85:1
Van Heukelom, Henri W, 1953, Ja 26,19:2
Van Heusen, J M, 1931, D 19,19:3
Van Heusen, Richard Fletcher Dr, 1913, Je 17,11:4
Van Heusen, William P, 1938, O 8,17:5
Van Hise, Charles R Dr, 1918, N 20,15:4
Van Hise, Charles T, 1943, S 30,21:3
Van Hoek, Kees, 1954, D 31,13:1
Van Hoesen, Arthur, 1943, N 11,23:5
Van Hoesen, Ella, 1957, Ja 1,23:2
Van Hoesen, Frank P, 1937, Jl 14,22:3
Van Hoesen, George C Rev, 1916, Jl 6,13:6
Van Hoesen, George M, 1909, Ap 20,9:4
Van Hoesen, Gertrude, 1944, Mr 1,19:1
Van Hoesen, Henry B, 1965, Ja 7,31:2
Van Hoesen, Henry B Mrs, 1955, S 20,31:5

Van Hoesen, Isaac E, 1940, Jl 12,15:5
Van Hoesen, John W, 1908, Mr 1,9:6
Van Hoesen, Stephen G, 1941, Je 11,21:6
Van Hoesen, Stephen G Mrs, 1947, Ag 31,36:5
Van Holland, Henry, 1948, Je 5,15:6
Van Hoogen, Henry Rev, 1907, Ja 6,II,9:6
Van Hook, Carlton R, 1942, Ja 5,20:1
Van Hook, Edmund B (por), 1942, N 28,13:5
Van Hook, La Rue, 1953, S 7,19:4
Van Hoosen, Bertha, 1952, Je 8,86:4
Vanhooser, Hoskins, 1937, Ja 20,21:2
Van Hooser, Ruby, 1957, My 21,35:4
Van Horn, Abraham, 1905, F 8,9:5
Van Horn, Alfred E, 1938, O 2,49:3
Van Horn, Alfred J, 1940, Ja 24,21:5
Van Horn, Amos H, 1908, D 27,9:4
Van Horn, Anna G Mrs, 1941, My 22,21:3
Van Horn, Arthur, 1940, Je 1,15:3
Van Horn, C S, 1953, Ag 8,11:1
Van Horn, Clement J, 1968, Je 23,73:2
Van Horn, Ezra, 1954, O 29,23:2
Van Horn, Frank D, 1961, Ag 21,23:3
Van Horn, Frederick N, 1943, Ja 10,50:3
Van Horn, Garrett, 1872, Ja 26,5:4
Van Horn, John, 1876, Mr 7,4:6
Van Horn, John B, 1941, Ja 12,46:1
Vanhorn, R R, 1953, N 13,27:4
Van Horn, Robert O, 1941, Je 28,15:5
Van Horn, Rollin W, 1964, F 5,35:2
Van Horn, Samuel H, 1938, Je 21,19:3
Van Horn, Walter C, 1954, Ap 10,15:5
Van Horn, William, 1908, Je 29,7:6
Van Horne, Allison, 1943, Je 7,13:2
Van Horne, Ellsworth E, 1940, Ja 19,19:4
Van Horne, Joseph L, 1966, S 2,31:5
Van Horne, O L Mrs, 1960, Ap 26,37:3
Vanhorne, Phillip, 1951, O 14,89:1
Van Horne, Richard Rev, 1903, S 13,7:5
Van Horne, Walter C Mrs, 1943, Ag 12,19:2
Van Horne, Willard, 1953, S 2,25:1
Van Horne, William C Sir, 1915, S 12,17:3
Van Horne, William M Gen, 1923, Ja 20,13:6
Vanhouten, A B, 1914, Ag 26,9:6
Van Houten, Aaron, 1941, My 14,21:4
Van Houten, Albert, 1947, Mr 19,25:5
Van Houten, Albert E, 1943, N 7,57:1
Van Houten, Albert E Mrs, 1955, F 15,27:5
Van Houten, Arthur S, 1956, My 29,27:4
Van Houten, Augustus, 1955, Ap 16,19:4
Van Houten, Charles N, 1953, Ag 15,15:5
Van Houten, Erskine J S, 1925, Mr 7,13:6
Van Houten, Frank, 1952, Ja 8,27:2
Van Houten, James H, 1954, Jl 3,11:6
Van Houten, John M, 1937, N 19,23:1
Van Houten, L Frederick, 1959, Ap 12,86:5
Van Houten, Mortimer T, 1947, My 3,17:6
Van Houten, Richard, 1879, D 10,5:2; 1945, O 2,23:5
Van Houten, Susan, 1951, N 7,29:3
Van Houten, William B, 1938, O 5,23:4
Van Houtin, Hannah E, 1948, N 28,92:5
Van Hove, A, 1947, Jl 19,13:7
Van Hovenburg, Morris J, 1952, F 8,23:4
Van Hovenburgh, George, 1947, Ap 6,60:2
Van Huhl, George H, 1947, Ag 30,15:6
Van Huist, Adrien E Rev, 1909, O 20,9:4
Van Hummel, Quincy Dr, 1924, Ja 14,17:6
Van Iderstine, Ernest, 1959, F 8,86:1
Van Iderstine, Garrett, 1906, My 26,11:6
Van Iderstine, Louis T, 1940, F 24,13:2
Van Iderstine, R, 1933, Ag 8,20:6
Van Iderstine, Robert, 1956, D 31,13:2
Van Iderstine, Willard, 1952, F 24,84:7
Van Iderstine, William P M, 1943, Je 15,21:2
Vanier, Georges P (funl, Mr 9,3:2), 1967, Mr 6,33:1
Vanier, Raymond L, 1965, Ag 26,33:4
Vaniman, Roy L, 1956, F 20,23:4
Vaniman, Vernon V, 1948, D 2,29:5
Van Inden, Bard C, 1952, O 10,25:3
Van Ingen, Alvord L Mrs, 1949, Jl 6,30:5
Van Ingen, Bernard J (por), 1955, Ag 1,19:3
Vaningen, Bessie D, 1944, O 7,13:4
Van Ingen, Edward, 1905, O 28,9:6
Van Ingen, Edward H, 1920, D 25,7:5
Van Ingen, Edward H 2d, 1938, Mr 24,23:5
Van Ingen, Gilbert Prof, 1925, Jl 9,19:4
Van Ingen, H Schuyler, 1962, F 17,19:1
Van Ingen, Harriet Mrs (will), 1939, F 3,17:2
Van Ingen, John, 1949, Ag 12,17:1
Van Ingen, Lawrence B, 1943, N 1,17:6
Van Ingen, McLane, 1938, Mr 24,23:5
Van Ingen, Phil, 1953, Mr 29,92:1
Van Ingen, W Dirk, 1955, Mr 2,27:5
Van Ingen, William B, 1955, F 7,21:6
Van Ingen, William B Mrs, 1945, Mr 2,19:3
Van Ingwegen, Helen H Mrs, 1941, Mr 25,26:1
Vanini, Detti, 1916, Je 3,13:5
Vaninwegan, C J, 1943, Mr 23,19:3
Van Inwegen, Charac J Mrs, 1947, My 6,27:3
Van Inwegen, Willard B, 1939, My 5,23:5
Van Isacker, Phil, 1951, Mr 12,25:2
Van Itallie, Dorus, 1968, Mr 21,47:2
Van Jaeckle, George R, 1952, Je 14,15:5
Van Kampen, Isaac, 1940, Je 27,23:1
Van Kannel, Theophilius Mrs, 1943, N 23,25:1
Van Kannel, Theophilus, 1919, D 25,13:3
Van Karner, Joseph W, 1952, D 26,15:4
Van Keegan, Charles H, 1955, F 6,89:1
Van Kempen, Ambrose, 1947, F 20,25:5
Van Kersen, Henry, 1940, F 8,20:5
Van Keuren, Alexander H, 1966, Jl 7,37:4
Van Keuren, Estella B Mrs, 1940, Je 2,44:6
Van Keuren, Floyd Rev Dr, 1968, O 23,47:3
Van Keuren, J Philip, 1942, S 11,21:6
Van Keuren, James E, 1945, Ja 27,11:6
Van Keuren, Karl, 1945, F 23,18:2
VanKeuren, Laura, 1945, Ap 19,27:2
Van Keuren, Levi, 1938, Ap 9,17:3
Van Keuren, M Mrs, 1941, N 10,17:2
Vankeuren, William S Capt, 1914, Je 16,9:6
Van Keuren, William W, 1938, D 24,15:4
Van Kirk, Agnes E, 1948, Ap 30,23:3
Van Kirk, Charles C, 1937, Ap 19,21:1
Van Kirk, Charles H, 1951, My 30,21:5
Van Kirk, H Thatcher, 1944, Mr 13,15:3
Van Kirk, Herbert, 1954, O 27,29:2
Van Kirk, Hiram Rev, 1920, Ag 15,20:5
Van Kirk, James W, 1946, Je 16,40:5
Van Kirk, Peter A, 1943, Ap 23,17:3
Van Kirk, Russell M, 1947, D 13,15:2
Van Kirk, Walter W, 1956, Jl 8,65:1
Van Kleeck, Barnard D, 1940, N 24,51:1
Van Kleeck, Charles M, 1951, My 19,15:4
Van Kleeck, Edwin, 1965, N 25,35:1
Van Kleeck, Edwin J, 1951, Ap 27,23:3
Van Kleeck, Frederick B Jr, 1949, My 5,27:3
Van Kleeck, Frederick Brinsmald Rev Dr, 1915, Ag 2, 9:4
Van Kleeck, Harold L, 1964, F 24,25:4
Van Kleeck, Harold N, 1952, Je 30,19:1
Van Kleeck, Hewitt, 1948, D 8,32:3
Van Kleeck, Louis A, 1957, My 1,37:4
Vankleeck, Nelson R, 1950, Ja 13,23:4
Van Kleeck, Sarah, 1925, Ja 22,19:4
Vankleeck, William, 1952, Ja 20,84:7
Van Kleeck, William H, 1918, N 2,15:4
Van Kleef, Arie Sr, 1941, D 28,28:7
Van Kol, H H, 1925, Ag 26,19:4
Van Koolen, Jonkheer, 1925, Ag 24,13:6
Van Krimpen, Jan, 1958, O 23,32:1
Van Laar, Harry Mrs, 1954, Mr 1,25:4
Van Ladingham, John H, 1937, My 23,II,10:6
Van Laer, Alexander Theabald, 1920, Mr 24,9:4
Van Laer, Gerrit W A, 1945, D 5,25:3
Van Laeys, L J, 1950, Je 21,27:3
Van Lahr, Leo J Mrs, 1949, Ap 4,23:3
Van Landeghem, Charles, 1952, F 7,27:3
Van Law, Carlos W, 1947, F 27,21:4
Van Lear, Elizabeth, 1949, O 24,23:4
Van Lear, John F, 1942, My 14,19:5
van Lede, William J, 1964, My 3,87:1
Van Leer, Blake R, 1956, Ja 24,32:1
Vanleer, Charles, 1938, Mr 23,23:4
Van Leer, Floris H, 1955, My 18,31:5
Van Leer, Samuel, 1948, F 4,23:4
Van Leer, Sara, 1916, Jl 1,11:6
Van Leeuwen, Peter, 1951, Je 6,31:5
Van Leight, Andrew, 1950, O 12,31:4
Van Leight, Eugene J, 1964, Ja 5,92:3
Van Leight, George P Mrs, 1949, O 31,25:6
Van Lennep, Edward J, 1946, Ap 2,27:2
Van Lennep, Eulalie, 1944, F 16,17:3
Van Lennep, Frederic Mrs, 1938, Mr 17,21:4
Van Lennep, Mary L, 1949, Jl 1,19:5
Van Lennep, W F, 1950, Ap 4,29:4
Van Leusen, Charles M Brig, 1937, Ag 14,13:7
Van Leuvan, Levi, 1949, Mr 15,28:2
Van Leuven, Edgar, 1939, My 9,23:2
Van Leuven, Lewis B, 1955, S 18,86:5
Van Lew, Frederick D, 1956, My 8,33:2
van Lier, Edward, 1967, Mr 6,33:5
Van Lier, Jacques Mrs, 1952, Ap 14,19:5
Van Liew, Alfred B, 1956, O 21,86:3
Van Liew, Alfred B Mrs, 1954, Je 17,29:4
Van Liew, Harry R, 1960, Jl 24,64:4
van Liew, W Randolph Mme, 1961, Ag 2,29:5
Van Liew, Willard R, 1952, Mr 18,27:4
Van Loan, Albert T Sr, 1942, Ag 26,19:3
Van Loan, Charles E, 1919, Mr 3,13:2
Van Loan, Emory C, 1952, N 9,91:2
Van Loan, Harold H, 1958, S 9,35:2
Van Loan, Joseph T, 1937, Mr 16,23:5
Van Loan, Richard, 1939, Ja 28,15:4
Vanloan, Roswell B, 1958, Ja 3,21:5
Van Loan, Samuel D, 1942, F 17,22:2
Van Loan, Seth M, 1945, F 9,15:3
Van Loan, William J (will), 1947, Mr 9,51:4
Van Loan, William S, 1943, F 26,19:4
Van Loan, Zelah J (funl, D 9,27:4), 1925, D 8,25:4
Van Loon, Frank W, 1948, Ag 4,21:4
Van Loon, George A Mrs, 1938, Ap 24,II,7:3
Van Loon, Harry F, 1954, My 22,15:5
Van Loon, Hendrik W, 1944, Mr 12,37:1
van Loon, Hendrik W Mrs, 1958, N 9,89:1
Van Loon, Johannes J, 1968, Ag 23,39:3
Van Loon, Richard Mrs, 1947, D 16,33:4
Vanm, James Nicolas, 1917, Ap 17,11:6
Van Maanen, Adrian (por), 1946, Ja 27,42:2
Van Martar, Charles, 1915, Jl 31,7:4
Van Meer, Hubert, 1947, Ag 6,23:4
Van Meter, Arthur, 1945, Ja 18,19:4
Van Meter, Gregory T, 1950, Je 2,23:2
Van Meter, James W, 1938, Ja 20,23:4
Van Meter, Jesse O, 1954, F 21,68:2
Van Meter, Leslie, 1956, N 19,31:4
Van Meter, Ralph A, 1958, Jl 27,61:3
Van Metre, Thomas E Mrs, 1940, Ap 19,21:6
Van Metre, Thurman W, 1961, Ja 3,29:1
Van Metter, Walter F, 1941, F 17,15:3
Van Millingen, Alexander Prof, 1915, S 18,9:6
Van Moppes, George L, 1966, Ja 26,37:4
Van Muffling, Adrian, 1952, S 8,21:1
Vann, Bert I, 1951, Ja 24,27:5
Vann, Eugene E, 1965, Ja 8,29:4
Vann, Foy, 1958, Mr 17,29:1
Vann, Gerald, 1963, Jl 17,31:4
Vann, Irving Goodwin Ex-Judge, 1921, Mr 23,13:5
Vann, Robert L, 1940, O 25,21:4
Vann, Robert L Mrs, 1967, Je 8,47:4
Vann, Thomas W, 1964, Mr 24,35:1
Vann Etten, Edward D, 1949, O 15,15:3
Vannais, Leon E, 1961, My 7,87:2
Vannaman, Edward C, 1940, Ap 16,23:4
Vannaman, Edward C Mrs, 1957, Ja 3,31:3
Van Name, A Capt, 1882, Jl 20,3:6
Van Name, Addison Prof, 1922, S 30,13:5
Van Name, Calvin D, 1924, S 16,23:4
Van Name, David G, 1914, Je 12,13:6
Van Name, Frederick W Jr, 1967, S 17,84:7
Van Name, George M, 1903, Jl 19,7:6
Van Name, John F, 1946, D 12,29:4
Van Name, Livingston C, 1942, Ja 9,21:3
Van Name, Ralph B Mrs, 1952, S 18,29:1
VanName, Ralph G, 1961, Ja 7,19:4
Van Name, Raymond D, 1959, N 2,31:1
Van Name, Willard G, 1959, Ap 27,27:2
Van Namee, George R, 1949, D 8,33:1
Van Namee, Richard A, 1938, Ag 13,13:4
Van Namen, Theodore, 1953, Jl 22,27:3
Vannatta, Alden M, 1961, Ag 22,29:2
Van Natta, Alden M Mrs, 1955, Jl 27,23:5
Van Natta, Clinton B, 1961, Ap 2,76:1
Van Natta, Franklin P, 1943, Jl 28,15:3
Vannatta, George W, 1953, S 9,29:4
Vanneck, John T Mrs, 1908, D 13,13:5
Vanneman, Charles R, 1959, F 17,31:3
Vanneman, William S Mrs, 1945, N 28,27:3
Van Ness, Andrew J, 1908, N 25,9:5
Van Ness, Anne W Mrs, 1937, S 28,23:2
Van Ness, Archibald O, 1951, Jl 6,23:2
Van Ness, Carroll, 1941, O 18,19:4
Vanness, Cornelius Henry, 1911, Je 26,9:6
Van Ness, Cornelius P, 1953, Ap 21,27:2
Van Ness, Eugene M, 1938, Ja 14,23:2
Vanness, Frank L, 1944, F 6,19:5
Van Ness, Frank O, 1943, S 14,23:3
Van Ness, Fred, 1959, Je 7,86:6
Van Ness, Gardiner B, 1941, Ap 12,15:3
Van Ness, George E Mrs, 1950, My 10,31:3
Van Ness, George W, 1946, S 4,23:3
Van Ness, I J Mrs, 1937, Mr 1,19:5
Van Ness, Isaac J, 1947, F 14,21:1
Van Ness, J Newton, 1909, D 30,9:5
Van Ness, John H, 1937, Jl 27,21:3
Van Ness, Lester H, 1956, O 10,39:4
Van Ness, Norman C, 1941, Ja 20,17:1
Van Ness, Rodney A, 1964, My 14,35:3
Van Ness, Schuyler W, 1956, D 2,86:4
Van Ness, Wallace K, 1943, F 24,21:4
Van Nest, Archibald, 1951, D 8,11:5
Van Nest, Charles B, 1941, My 11,44:6
Vannest, Charles G, 1947, My 25,60:3
Van Nest, George O, 1960, N 16,41:1
Van Nest, George Willett, 1916, My 19,11:6
Van Nest, John S, 1951, O 29,23:3
Van Nest, Lloyd L, 1957, Jl 6,15:3
Vannetta, Howard A, 1954, Jl 31,13:4
Van Nice, Errett, 1938, S 21,25:4
Van Niel, Cornelius J, 1961, My 22,31:5
Vannikov, Boris L, 1962, F 23,29:2
van Noort, Cornelius, 1957, Ag 24,33:3
Van Noort, Frank J, 1954, My 27,27:3
Van Noppen, Leonard C Mrs, 1944, F 25,17:5
Van Norden, Ernest M, 1960, Je 7,35:4
Van Norden, Harry G, 1908, F 15,7:6
Van Norden, John, 1950, Mr 19,94:3
Van Norden, Ottomar H, 1952, Ag 29,23:3
Van Norden, Ottomar H Mrs, 1956, Jl 9,23:3
Van Norden, Peter J, 1955, My 20,25:5
Van Norden, Pierre, 1957, My 20,25:5
Van Norden, Theodore L (por), 1946, D 28,15:5
Van Norden, Warner, 1914, Ja 2,9:5
Van Norden, Warner M, 1959, D 2,43:1
Van Norden, Warner M Mrs, 1957, Mr 7,29:4
Van Norman, Daniel C Rev, 1920, N 9,15:1
Van Norman, Hubert E, 1938, Jl 30,13:4
Van Norstrand, Harold T, 1937, F 18,21:2
Van Nortwick, George, 1953, Ja 20,25:3
Van Nosdall, William H, 1939, Mr 22,23:3
Van Nostrand, Adrian Mrs, 1915, N 21,19:5

Van Nostrand, Benjamin Tredwell Mrs, 1922, Ap 28, 17:6
Van Nostrand, C Richmond, 1950, O 29,92:4
Van Nostrand, David L, 1913, Je 4,11:6
Van Nostrand, Elzaida G, 1937, Jl 28,19:6
Van Nostrand, Franklin L, 1945, Je 15,19:5
Van Nostrand, Harold L, 1938, My 18,21:3
Van Nostrand, Harry, 1943, Ap 16,21:1
Van Nostrand, Harry Mrs, 1950, Ag 15,29:1
Van Nostrand, Henry C, 1913, F 10,11:4
Van Nostrand, J, 1881, D 14,2:6
Van Nostrand, Jacob, 1879, D 1,5:4
Van Nostrand, Morris A, 1950, Ja 6,21:4
Van Nostrand, Norman W, 1952, D 19,31:2
Van Nostrand, Percy E, 1938, O 17,15:6
Van Nostrand, Walter Jr, 1947, Jl 21,17:4
Van Note, Arthur D, 1942, N 25,23:2
Van Note, Frederick, 1943, My 14,19:4
Van Note, G Harry, 1946, Ja 10,23:5
Van Note, George W, 1940, Ap 25,23:4
Van Note, Harry, 1942, My 24,42:8
Vannovski, Gen, 1904, Mr 2,9:7
Van Noz, Lucien, 1938, Ag 9,19:5
Vannucci, Ildebrando, 1955, Ag 24,27:2
Van Nuis, Charles S, 1940, Ap 22,17:4
Vannutelli, Serafino Bp, 1915, Ag 20,11:5
Vannutelli, V, 1930, Jl 10,25:1
Van Nuys, Claude C, 1957, Ag 22,27:5
Van Nuys, Ezra A, 1947, D 3,29:4
Van Nuys, Frederick, 1944, Ja 26,19:1
Van Nuys, Ida T Mrs, 1954, Ja 6,31:1
Van Nuys, J Benton, 1962, S 3,15:5
Van Nuys, Jay C, 1957, O 24,33:4
Vannuys, John D, 1964, F 16,92:7
Van Nuyse, James C C, 1946, N 30,15:2
Vano, Frederick W, 1956, S 9,84:6
Van Ohlen, Henry, 1948, D 15,33:1
Van Olinda, William K, 1943, My 3,17:3
Vanoni, Ezio, 1956, F 17,4:6
Van Ophuijsen, Johan H W, 1950, Je 2,23:1
Van Orden, Charles, 1938, Jl 19,22:2
Van Orden, Clarence S, 1949, S 2,17:1
Van Orden, Cornelia Mrs, 1937, O 8,23:2
Van Orden, Elmer, 1942, F 20,19:8
Van Orden, George A, 1947, Ap 23,25:3
Van Orden, George D, 1940, Ja 16,23:3
Van Orden, George Mrs, 1925, O 24,15:6
Van Orden, George O, 1967, My 15,43:2
Van Orden, Harry, 1943, O 17,48:4
Van Orden, James, 1960, Ag 10,31:3
Van Orden, Louis J Mrs, 1956, F 21,33:3
Van Orden, Ralph P S, 1961, Ap 4,37:4
Van Orden, Sarah Mrs, 1954, Ja 31,88:1
Vanore, Michael, 1955, D 13,39:4
Van Orm, F Harold, 1958, Ja 7,47:2
Van Orman, Frank L, 1961, O 11,47:3
Van Orman, Ray, 1954, My 24,27:6
Van Ormer, A B, 1941, Je 26,23:4
Van Orsdel, Josiah A Justice (por), 1937, Ag 8,II,6:6
Van Oss, Alex, 1957, Ap 7,89:1
Van Ostrand, E S, 1879, Je 22,7:5
Van Ostrand, James, 1905, O 16,9:6
Van Ostrom, Charles R, 1959, S 2,29:4
Vanov, Ivan, 1948, Jl 13,27:1
Vanoy, Martha Mrs, 1961, Mr 30,29:1
Vanozzi, Humbert A, 1937, Je 17,23:5
Van Paassen, Adrian, 1951, Ap 5,29:2
van Paassen, Pierre, 1968, Ja 9,43:1
Van Paddenberg, Alvert, 1917, S 23,23:3
Van Pelt, Alonzo S, 1946, Ja 3,19:2
Van Pelt, Arthur J, 1941, Ag 7,17:2
Van Pelt, Edward C, 1943, Jl 11,34:7
Van Pelt, Eliakim M Sr, 1949, O 30,84:6
Van Pelt, Eliakim Sr Mrs, 1949, Ap 16,15:3
Van Pelt, Fannie Mrs, 1944, F 8,16:3
Van Pelt, George, 1947, N 9,74:5
Van Pelt, Harry Sr Mrs, 1949, Ap 24,76:1
Van Pelt, Henry W, 1947, O 21,23:3
Van Pelt, Herbert, 1968, Mr 19,47:1
Van Pelt, Herbert C, 1941, Ag 11,13:3
Van Pelt, J E, 1902, My 11,9:6
Van Pelt, Jacob E, 1949, Ag 26,19:3
Van Pelt, Jacob Lefferts, 1907, Je 10,7:6
Van Pelt, Jacob Mrs, 1944, Ag 12,11:4
Van Pelt, John H, 1951, Je 18,23:6
Van Pelt, John V, 1962, Je 2,19:1
Van Pelt, Samuel, 1953, N 8,89:3
Van Pelt, Samuel G, 1944, N 25,13:3
Van Pelt, Townsend C, 1910, O 17,9:5
Van Pelt, Townsend Cortelyou Mrs, 1921, Mr 1,13:4
VanPelt, William D, 1964, S 7,19:3
Van Pelt, William F, 1907, O 23,11:6
Van Pelt, William H Sr, 1944, Ag 1,15:2
Van Pelt, William S Mrs, 1943, Mr 7,38:3
Van Peter, Emory, 1944, D 31,26:8
Van Poznak, Aaron Mrs, 1959, Je 25,29:3
Van Praag, Alfred, 1941, D 5,23:3
Van Praag, August M, 1947, S 14,60:3
Van Praag, E William, 1947, Ja 17,23:7
Van Praag, Maurice, 1953, Ag 10,23:3; 1961, My 19, 31:1
Van Prag, A S, 1880, Ja 19,5:6
Van Pragg, Henry, 1939, Je 23,19:6

Van Raalte, Benjamin Mrs, 1956, Je 19,29:3
Van Raalte, Fannie L Mrs, 1940, O 6,48:3
Van Raalte, Morton E, 1954, D 24,13:4
Van Raalte, Zealie, 1921, My 17,17:6
Van Raden, Benjamin, 1964, D 22,27:4
Van Ranst, Mamie, 1905, My 4,2:4
Van Raumer, Frederick Louis George, 1873, Je 15,4:2
Van Reed, David, 1939, Ag 14,15:1
Van Reekum, Johannes, 1953, Ap 22,29:3
Van Rees, Abraham C, 1949, Jl 3,27:2
Van Rees, Abraham C Mrs, 1962, Mr 19,29:1
Van Rees, Richard P, 1948, F 27,21:1
Van Rensselaer, A, 1878, My 12,2:3; 1933, Jl 19,17:4
Van Rensselaer, Adele B Mrs, 1948, Mr 4,25:4
Van Rensselaer, Alex T M, 1962, Ag 22,33:1
Van Rensselaer, Arthur M, 1939, Mr 19,III,7:1
Van Rensselaer, Augustus Cortlandt, 1919, S 4,13:3
Van Rensselaer, Bernard S Mrs, 1945, Jl 23,19:5
Van Rensselaer, C S, 1927, Ja 16,30:3
Van Rensselaer, Catherine, 1960, Ja 17,86:4
Van Rensselaer, Charles A, 1950, Je 24,13:6
Van Rensselaer, Cortlandt S Mrs, 1945, Ag 21,21:2
Van Rensselaer, Eugene, 1925, Ag 6,19:5
Van Rensselaer, Euphemia (Sister Marie Dolores), 1914, My 30,11:6
Van Rensselaer, Florence, 1957, Jl 20,15:5
Van Rensselaer, Fred'k H, 1903, Ag 7,7:6
Van Rensselaer, H Col, 1864, Ap 2,4:6
Van Rensselaer, Harriet Bayard Mrs, 1875, Jl 22,4:7
Van Rensselaer, Henry Rev Father (funl, O 6,11:6), 1907, O 4,11:7
Van Rensselaer, Howard Dr, 1925, Ap 1,23:4
Van Rensselaer, James Fleming Mrs, 1920, D 16,17:4
Van Rensselaer, John King, 1908, O 18,VII,11:5
Van Rensselaer, John King Mrs, 1925, My 12,23:4
Van Rensselaer, John S Gen, 1868, Mr 22,3:7
Van Rensselaer, Kiliaen, 1905, N 27,9:5; 1949, Ag 24, 25:6
Van Rensselaer, Lolita C Mrs, 1947, Ja 11,19:5
Van Rensselaer, Louisa L Mrs, 1937, S 26,II,8:2
Van Rensselaer, M, 1932, My 27,21:2
Van Rensselaer, Maunsell, 1952, Je 19,27:2
Van Rensselaer, P J, 1931, Ag 13,19:1
Van Rensselaer, Peyton J Mrs, 1925, Jl 26,5:4; 1956, F 10,21:1
Van Rensselaer, Stephen, 1904, Ja 22,9:5; 1945, D 20, 23:5
Van Rensselaer, Stephen Mrs, 1915, Jl 12,7:6; 1952, O 3,23:4
Van Rensselaer, William Bayard, 1909, S 26,13:3
Van Reuth, Edward F C, 1925, Mr 16,19:3
Van Reypen, William K Rear-Adm, 1924, D 23,19:5
Van Riper, Andrew, 1941, S 15,17:3
Van Riper, Bert W, 1942, F 20,17:5
Van Riper, Charles, 1916, F 10,11:4
Van Riper, Cornelius Dr, 1919, O 11,9:3
Van Riper, Fred, 1903, My 9,9:6
Van Riper, George B, 1947, F 5,23:4
Van Riper, George S, 1962, Ap 16,29:5
Van Riper, John H, 1939, O 1,53:3
Van Riper, John S, 1951, My 30,22:2
Van Riper, La Motte (por), 1948, D 4,13:4
Van Riper, Richard, 1949, Je 26,60:2
Van Riper, Willard F, 1943, Ap 16,22:3
Van Roden, Frank Sr, 1942, Jl 15,19:5
Van Roden, George C, 1938, S 23,27:2
Van Rosen, Robert E, 1966, N 17,47:5
Van Rosencrance, Joseph, 1953, My 24,88:3
van Saher, Lilla Alexander Mrs, 1968, Jl 19,35:1
Van Sant, Arthur S, 1941, My 16,23:2
Van Sant, Edward A, 1940, Ag 18,37:4
Van Sant, Ernest, 1949, N 16,29:3
Van Sant, George R, 1940, Je 12,25:6
Van Sant, Grant, 1939, N 8,23:2
Van Sant, Grant Jr Mrs, 1961, Je 24,21:2
Van Sant, Harry Cheston, 1903, S 16,9:5
Van Sant, Homer M, 1944, My 27,15:4
Van Sant, Howard D, 1925, S 3,25:6
Van Sant, Nicholas G, 1939, O 13,23:5
Van Sant, S Monroe Mrs, 1940, O 7,17:1
Van Sant, Walter M, 1959, Je 7,86:4
Van Santen, Rient, 1943, Jl 14,19:4
Van Santvoord, Alex S Mrs, 1952, O 30,31:4
Van Santvoord, Anna Townsend, 1919, D 25,13:3
Van Santvoord, Harold, 1913, Ja 14,17:4
van Santvoord, John G (por), 1955, N 23,23:4
Van Santvoord, Richard Dr (funl. S 13,11:3), 1913, S 11,11:6
Van Santvoord, Sarah N, 1914, Ap 15,13:6
Van Santvoord, Seymour, 1938, N 16,23:1
Van Santvoord, Talcott C, 1905, O 22,9:6
Van Saun, Grant W Sr Mrs, 1963, Ag 3,17:5
Van Saun, Joseph P, 1946, S 3,39:1
Van Saun, S A, 1884, Ap 20,2:6
Van Saun, Samuel W, 1946, Jl 22,21:2
Van Saun, Walter, 1950, Jl 27,25:1
Van Sauter, Nannie H Mrs (A Morrisine), 1942, My 15,19:3
Van Schaack, Henry C, 1963, Ag 14,33:4
Van Schaack, Myron B, 1943, Mr 30,26:4
Van Schaack, Raymond, 1953, Ag 25,21:5
Van Schaick, Arthur P, 1938, Je 9,23:5
Van Schaick, Arthur P Mrs, 1943, D 24,13:1

Van Schaick, Benjamin L (por), 1938, F 19,15:3
Van Schaick, Dunnelle, 1923, D 31,13:4
Van Schaick, Edwin J Mrs, 1952, Ja 29,25:4
Van Schaick, Frances C Mrs, 1940, F 21,19:1
Van Schaick, George S, 1968, N 3,89:1
Van Schaick, Henry Mrs, 1912, O 3,13:6
Van Schaick, John, 1949, My 17,25:5
Van Schaick, John B, 1919, F 9,20:5
Van Schaick, John Mrs, 1955, N 4,29:2
Van Schaick, Lemuel W, 1943, D 27,19:4
Van Schaick, Lemuel W Mrs, 1945, Ag 7,23:2
Van Schaick, Louis J, 1945, Mr 10,8:5
Van Schaick, Myndert, 1865, D 3,5:1
Van Schaick, S D (see also Ap 11), 1876, Ap 12,5:4
Van Schaick, Singleton, 1913, Jl 14,7:6
Van Schaick, Stephen, 1920, F 27,13:1
Van Schaick, W, 1927, D 9,25:3
Van Schaick, William H, 1941, N 11,23:2
Van Schaik, William T, 1946, Ag 18,44:4
Van Schassen, Edward, 1943, D 24,13:5
Van Schendel, Arthur, 1946, S 15,9:8
Van Schilgen, Albert Rev, 1901, Je 4,9:6
Van Schlaick, Edwin J, 1949, F 11,24:3
Van Schmus, William G (por), 1942, Ja 15,19:1
Van Schoick, J Albert Mrs, 1949, F 20,60:3
Van Scholck, John Ex-Sen, 1923, Je 10,6:2
Van Schott, Gerard J Mrs, 1954, My 8,17:5
Van Sciver, George D, 1942, Je 2,23:5
Van Sciver, George R, 1948, F 22,48:2
Van Sciver, George R Mrs, 1946, O 29,25:2
Van Sciver, J Howard, 1953, Ja 20,25:3
Van Sciver, Joseph B, 1943, Je 20,34:8
Van Sciver, Joseph B Jr Mrs, 1961, O 29,88:5
Van Scoy, Arthur, 1944, Jl 12,19:4
Van Scriver, Lloyd, 1954, S 12,85:2
Van Seenburgh, Walter J Jr, 1952, O 25,17:5
Vanselow, Otto, 1943, F 19,19:3
Van Shaick, George S Mrs, 1953, S 18,23:3
Van Sickle, Earl R, 1966, Mr 2,41:4
Van Sickle, Earl R Mrs, 1950, Je 19,21:6
Van Sickle, Edward E, 1943, N 17,25:4
Vansickle, Harvey F, 1944, Je 8,21:5
Van Sickle, J H Dr, 1926, F 13,13:5
Van Sickle, Leon H Prof, 1914, D 1,13:6
Van Sickle, Lewis E, 1956, S 13,35:3
Van Sickle, Raymond, 1964, Jl 11,25:1
Van Sicklen, Edgar S Mrs, 1941, Mr 15,17:4
Van Sicklen, Sarah L R Mrs, 1941, My 8,23:6
Van Siclen, Albert H W, 1905, D 28,9:6
Van Siclen, Arthur Mrs, 1944, Ja 8,13:6
Van Siclen, G W, 1903, Ap 21,9:5
Van Siclen, Garrett M, 1955, O 20,35:4
van Siclen, George W, 1958, Mr 24,52:7
Van Siclen, J T, 1903, Ja 6,2:2
Van Siclen, James C, 1963, N 18,33:1
Van Siclen, John R, 1942, Ag 14,17:5
Van Sideren, Henry Brinsmade, 1968, Ja 18,40:1
Van Sighem, J, 1945, Jl 6,11:7
Van Sinderen, Adrian, 1963, O 2,41:1
Van Sinderen, Adrian Mrs, 1968, Ap 30,53:5
Van Sise, Israel W, 1949, Ap 23,13:2
Vansittart, E W Adm, 1904, O 20,7:5
Vansittart, Robert, 1957, F 15,23:1
Vansittart, Robert A, 1938, Ja 10,17:5
Van Sittert, Neola, 1952, Mr 22,13:6
Vansize, William Baldwin, 1922, Je 3,13:5
Van Slyck, Charles B, 1951, Jl 30,17:4
Van Slyck, Charles H, 1945, D 8,17:4
Van Slyck, George W, 1921, Ja 27,13:4; 1959, Jl 25, 17:3
Van Slyke, Charles B, 1940, O 16,23:3
Van Slyke, E J, 1929, F 18,23:3
Van Slyke, E S, 1904, Mr 25,2:5
Van Slyke, Eugene Dr, 1937, N 9,23:2
Van Slyke, Evert Rev Dr, 1909, Mr 11,9:6
Van Slyke, Fred L, 1942, Je 14,46:2
Van Slyke, George M, 1961, Jl 1,17:4
Van Slyke, George W, 1946, Mr 14,25:4
Van Slyke, Horace M Lt, 1925, N 12,25:4
Van Slyke, James Capt, 1907, O 19,9:6
Van Slyke, John J, 1951, Mr 27,31:6
Van Slyke, Ruth C Mrs, 1940, S 1,21:1
Van Slyke, Warren C, 1925, Ap 8,21:4
Van Slyke, Wilberforce, 1938, Mr 28,15:5
Van Slyke, William H, 1939, S 14,23:2
Van Son, Caspert, 1943, My 21,19:4
Van Son, Job C, 1952, My 3,21:3
Van Son, Nicholas A, 1937, Mr 19,23:4
Van Staagen, Harry H, 1937, Mr 30,24:2
Van Steeden, Peter Sr, 1958, S 18,31:3
Van Steeden, Peter Sr Mrs, 1943, N 4,23:5
Van Steenbergh, James T, 1955, Ja 20,31:2
Van Steenbergh, L Ella, 1956, Ag 6,23:4
Van Steenbergh, William A, 1953, Ja 21,31:4
Van Steenbergh, William A Mrs, 1945, F 9,15:2
Van Steenbergh, William H, 1941, D 8,23:5
Van Steenburgh, Kate A, 1947, Jl 31,21:3
Van Steenburgh, Walter M Mrs, 1944, N 1,23:1
Van Steinberg, John, 1903, Mr 7,2:7
Vanston, Anna M, 1943, S 19,48:2
Vanston, William J, 1957, N 29,29:2
Van Stone, Theodore Mrs, 1943, S 15,27:3
Vanstone, Thomas J, 1938, Ja 28,21:4

Van Studdiford, G, 1927, Ja 30,28:1
Van Suetendael, Achille O, 1953, N 20,23:3
Van Surdam, Henderson E Mrs, 1955, Ap 28,29:1
Van Sweringen, Carrie B, 1940, Jl 16,17:3
Van Sweringen, Edith E, 1945, Jl 21,11:3
Van Sweringen, Herbert C, 1942, Ja 6,23:1
Van Sweringen, M J, 1935, D 13,25:1
Van Sweringen, O P, 1936, N 24,1:2
Van Swinderen, D R D, 1943, My 4,23:3
van Swinderen, Gerard R G, 1956, My 6,86:8
Van Swinderen, Jonkheer P J, 1911, D 20,13:5
Van Swinderen, Rene D Mrs, 1950, N 17,27:6
Van Syckel, Bennett Ex-Justice, 1921, D 20,17:5
Van Syckel, Joseph, 1904, F 22,5:6
Van Syckel, Lamar, 1948, Mr 2,23:5
Vanta, Harry, 1940, Ap 3,23:1
Van Tassel, Cameron J, 1943, S 1,19:5
Van Tassel, Carrie A, 1950, N 21,31:3
Van Tassel, Charles C, 1947, Je 12,25:2
Van Tassel, Francis, 1952, Je 9,23:4
Van Tassel, Frank S, 1949, Jl 7,25:1
Van Tassel, George F, 1948, F 8,60:6
Van Tassel, Hannah Mrs, 1911, My 22,11:4
Van Tassel, Howard, 1957, Jl 16,52:1
Van Tassel, Ida, 1944, Ap 13,19:6
Van Tassel, Joseph O M, 1945, O 25,21:1
Van Tassel, Nicholas, 1907, S 2,7:6
Van Tassel, Oscar L, 1952, D 16,31:4
Van Tassel, Sarah Louisa Mrs, 1910, F 24,9:3
Van Tassel, Stephen, 1940, Je 5,25:6
Van Tassel, W Eugene Mrs, 1941, Je 26,23:5
Van Tassel, William H, 1946, Je 1,13:6
Van Tassell, Abel R, 1922, O 25,19:5
Van Tassell, Benjamin A, 1945, D 12,27:3
Van Tassell, Caleb, 1881, O 5,5:6
Van Tassell, Elmer J, 1949, F 1,25:2
Van Tassell, Everett S, 1946, Ja 19,13:4
Van Tassell, Everett S Mrs, 1949, Ja 1,13:1
Van Tassell, Frederick S, 1942, Ja 2,34:3
Van Tassell, Harry Mrs, 1952, Ap 1,29:1
Van Tassell, Herbert, 1947, F 7,23:2
VanTassell, Herbert, 1948, S 28,27:5
Van Tassell, Milton, 1939, O 3,23:6
Van Tassell, Morgan W, 1966, Ap 23,31:5
Van Tassell, Samuel Mrs, 1950, F 5,85:1
Van Tassell, Wilbur F, 1947, O 3,25:3
Van Tassell, Wilbur T Mrs, 1951, O 28,84:7
Van Tassell, William A, 1953, Mr 24,42:2
Van Tassell, William H Mrs, 1948, Jl 19,19:5
Van Thijn, Herman E, 1938, Jl 20,10:2
Van Thoff, William M, 1939, F 3,15:1
Van Tiegham, Philippe Edouard Leon, 1914, Ap 30, 11:6
Van Tine, Addison A, 1953, Ja 14,31:5
Van Tine, Harry Alfred, 1925, Mr 18,21:5
Vantine, Robert T, 1941, O 21,23:1
Van Tine, Ronald, 1960, Ap 26,37:1
Van Toor, James 3d, 1967, Je 30,37:2
Vantra, Dominick, 1957, D 25,32:2
Van Tries, William P, 1957, Jl 11,25:2
Van Trump, Floyd, 1956, Je 26,35:7
Van Tuyl, George C (por), 1938, F 11,23:1
Van Tuyl, George H, 1956, Ap 22,86:6
Van Tuyl, Robert A, 1953, Jl 20,17:2
Van Twisk, Theodore J, 1958, Ag 3,80:8
Van Twistern, Edward, 1921, F 17,11:6
Van Tyne, C H, 1930, Mr 22,19:3
Van Tyne, H Frank, 1945, Ag 7,24:3
Van Urk, Frederick T, 1946, Je 25,21:5
Van Urk, Leontine B Mrs, 1955, D 22,23:3
Van Utt, Arthur G, 1950, F 21,25:3
Van Utt, Arthur G Mrs, 1951, Je 29,22:3
Van Uum, John H, 1948, N 20,13:5
Vanuxem, Louis C, 1903, D 22,9:5
Vanuxem, Mary, 1945, N 7,23:5
Van Valen, Charles B, 1943, S 17,21:3
Van Valen, James M Judge, 1904, My 20,9:6
Van Valen, Ramon S, 1950, Je 19,21:3
Van Valen, William C, 1940, My 1,23:5
Van Valey, Edwin G, 1951, S 3,13:4
Van Valin, William B, 1951, S 28,31:1
Van Valkenberg, Clifford S, 1963, Ap 21,86:8
Van Valkenburg, E A, 1932, N 27,35:1
Van Valkenburg, Frank, 1944, O 30,19:4
Van Valkenburg, Frank D, 1966, F 3,31:3
Van Valkenburg, Harvey, 1952, My 7,27:2
Van Valkenburg, Mary F W Mrs, 1942, N 13,23:5
Van Valkenburg, William, 1947, Mr 25,25:2
Van Valkenburgh, Arba S (por), 1944, N 6,19:5
Van Valkenburgh, Claude E, 1957, S 7,19:1
Van Valkenburgh, Frank J, 1954, Ja 17,92:3
Van Valkenburgh, George B, 1937, My 8,19:6
Van Valkenburgh, J D Mrs, 1956, F 6,23:1
Van Valkenburgh, J W, 1904, Ap 14,9:7
Van Valkenburgh, John, 1945, Ag 17,17:1
Van Valkenburgh, John J, 1938, Ag 5,18:2
Van Valkenburgh, Merritt, 1955, My 26,31:3
Van Valkenburgh, R, 1928, S 8,17:6
Van Valkenburgh, Ralph D, 1950, Ap 15,15:5
Van Valkenburgh, Willard, 1919, Ap 11,11:3
Van Valkenburgh, William A, 1949, N 15,25:1
Van Vechten, Benjamin D, 1946, My 23,21:3
Van Vechten, Carl, 1964, D 22,29:1
Van Vechten, Clarence, 1908, Ag 16,7:7
Van Vechten, Eugene M, 1948, D 15,33:4
Van Vechten, Francis H, 1917, My 26,13:5
Van Vechten, George C, 1946, Mr 21,25:3
Van Vechten, George J Mrs, 1957, F 5,23:3
Van Vechten, George W Jr, 1962, F 4,82:2
Van Vechten, S Rev, 1882, N 4,5:2
Van Vechten, Schuyler L, 1945, Mr 26,19:4
Van Vechten, William M, 1939, Mr 29,23:2
Van Veen, Arthur L, 1964, Jl 27,31:4
Van Veen, Arthur L Mrs, 1963, O 26,27:6
Van Veen, Maurice, 1958, F 12,29:3
Van Veen, Stuyvesant Mrs, 1959, D 25,21:7
Van Velson, William O, 1947, N 13,27:4
Van Velsor, Harry A, 1955, S 1,23:4
Van Velzer, Charles, 1945, N 20,21:2
Van Verwolde, A Baroness, 1948, F 21,13:5
Van Vessem, William, 1944, Jl 2,20:2
Van Vieck, Frederick B, 1915, Je 18,11:4
Van Vieck, John Munroe Prof, 1912, N 5,13:4
Van Vlaanderen, John C, 1953, Mr 5,27:5
Van Vlaaneren, Peter, 1952, Ap 23,29:5
Van Vlack, Howard, 1946, N 1,23:2
Van Vlack, LeRoy, 1950, Ag 27,89:2
Van Vlack, Reuben, 1940, My 5,53:2
Van Vlack, Wagner, 1953, Mr 11,29:1
Van Vleck, Albion N, 1945, Ag 23,23:5
Van Vleck, Charles E, 1950, Ag 28,17:4
Van Vleck, Ernest A, 1956, Ag 9,25:5
Van Vleck, Frank, 1939, F 26,38:8
Van Vleck, George W, 1967, Ja 20,43:2
Van Vleck, H Russ, 1959, Mr 16,31:2
Van Vleck, Jane, 1955, O 29,19:1
Van Vleck, Joseph, 1903, My 26,9:5
Van Vleck, Lt Com, 1869, Jl 1,5:5
Van Vleck, P H, 1865, Ap 21,4:2
Van Vleet, Samuel D, 1943, O 14,21:1
Van Vleit, Granville, 1904, Ja 2,9:4
Van Vlerah, Sylvan, 1954, O 16,17:1
Van Vliet, Abram, 1941, O 9,23:1
Van Vliet, Clinton, 1914, F 7,11:6
Van Vliet, Deuse M, 1939, Ja 2,24:2
Van Vliet, E Rebecca Mrs, 1939, Mr 23,23:6
Van Vliet, Earle R, 1966, My 18,47:4
Van Vliet, George S, 1949, F 1,25:3
Van Vliet, George S Mrs, 1945, Ja 30,19:5
Van Vliet, John J, 1954, Mr 4,25:2
Van Vliet, Morris, 1918, O 4,13:2
Van Vliet, Robert C Brig-Gen, 1943, O 28,23:5
Van Vliet, Robert C Col, 1943, F 17,21:5
Van Vliet, Stewart, 1956, O 31,33:4
Van Vliet, Stuart Jr, 1951, F 8,23:7
Van Vliet, W D, 1942, O 27,25:2
Van Voast, Edward, 1911, Ap 2,II,13:4
Van Voast, Herbert, 1948, O 31,88:3
Van Voast, Phoebe, 1945, Ja 20,11:6
Van Voast, Virginia R, 1947, N 11,27:3
Van Volkenburg, Isaac, 1903, D 4,1:4
Van Volkenburg, John L, 1963, Je 13,33:2
Van Volkenburg, Richard J Rev, 1912, S 10,9:5
Van Volkenburgh, Aaron, 1883, D 13,2:5
Van Volkenburgh, Edward, 1939, Je 2,23:2
Van Volkenburgh, Florence B Mrs (will), 1940, Ja 14,3:3
Van Volkenburgh, Thomas S, 1921, D 27,13:6
Van Voohis, Willis, 1946, D 25,29:3
Van Voollenhoven, Frank C, 1948, D 2,29:3
Vanvoorhees, Colonel, 1944, N 24,23:3
Van Voorhees, Edwin M (por), 1948, Ja 31,19:5
Van Voorhies, Richard C, 1952, Ag 6,21:1
Van Voorhis, Arthur E, 1950, O 3,31:5
Van Voorhis, Belle M Mrs, 1955, My 6,23:3
Van Voorhis, Charles, 1942, Jl 21,19:4
Van Voorhis, Daniel, 1956, Ja 10,34:3
Van Voorhis, Edna, 1950, My 24,30:3
Van Voorhis, Eugene, 1943, D 22,24:2
Van Voorhis, George R, 1956, Je 5,35:3
Van Voorhis, Harry J N, 1940, Ag 21,19:3
Van Voorhis, Quincey, 1923, Mr 18,6:3
Van Voorhis, Richard Mrs (will), 1955, O 1,20:8
Van Voorhis, Robert H, 1962, Ag 11,17:2
Vanvoorhis, Walter F, 1944, F 14,17:4
Van Voorhis, Westbrook, 1968, Jl 15,31:3
Van Vorrhies, Walter F, 1960, Ja 19,35:3
Van Vorst, H C Judge, 1917, D 26,9:3
Van Vorst, M, 1936, D 18,25:5
Van Vranken, A B Mrs, 1944, D 17,38:5
Van Vranken, John K, 1951, My 7,25:4
Van Vranken, Richard, 1948, S 25,17:4
Van Vredenburgh, Lee, 1946, Je 24,31:2
Van Vuren, Clyde A, 1953, F 23,25:2
Van Waganen, W M Rev, 1866, O 16,2:5
Van Wagenan, Albert M, 1941, Ja 5,45:2
Van Wagenen, Albert Mrs, 1946, Jl 18,25:2
Van Wagenen, Bleecker, 1921, N 12,13:5
Van Wagenen, Caroline A, 1939, Mr 9,22:2
Van Wagenen, Chauncey, 1953, S 15,31:4
Van Wagenen, Cornelius D Dr, 1937, Mr 6,17:4
VanWagenen, David T, 1943, My 6,19:3
Van Wagenen, Elizabeth, 1953, Ag 13,25:3
Van Wagenen, Harold S, 1956, S 21,25:2
Van Wagenen, Henry W, 1940, Ap 16,23:3
Van Wagenen, Jacob, 1903, My 6,9:6
van Wagenen, Jared Jr, 1960, Mr 26,21:5
Van Wagenen, R L, 1884, My 6,5:5
Van Wagenen, Reller W Rev, 1937, Ap 28,23:2
Van Wagner, Alfred E, 1949, F 13,77:2
Van Wagner, Asa, 1948, N 26,23:4
Van Wagner, Augustus Mrs, 1945, Ag 10,15:2
Van Wagner, Clarence, 1942, My 14,19:4
Van Wagner, E Walter, 1950, N 28,32:3
Van Wagner, Ernest L, 1947, Ap 19,16:2
Van Wagner, Euphenia D Mrs, 1944, Je 10,15:5
Van Wagner, Jacob H, 1943, O 10,49:2
Van Wagner, Mary Mrs, 1916, Je 19,11:5
Van Wagonen, Frank M, 1941, Mr 25,23:5
Van Wagonen, Maggie D Mrs, 1939, Ap 30,45:3
Van Wagonen, Mary Mrs, 1949, Je 10,27:4
Van Wagonen, Virgil B, 1938, N 9,23:5
Van Wagoner, Alex Sr, 1951, F 10,13:6
Van Wagoner, Cornelius S Mrs, 1903, N 9,7:6
Van Wagoner, Earl, 1957, D 17,35:2
Van Wagoner, John D (por), 1948, Je 25,23:3
Van Wagoner, Lewis M, 1947, O 28,26:2
Van Wakeman, Jeremiah F, 1950, N 23,35:2
Van Walraven, Albert A, 1941, Mr 26,23:3
VanWart, Alfred G, 1953, Jl 13,25:6
Van Wart, Evelyn, 1910, Ap 4,9:5
Van Wart, George C, 1937, My 26,25:2
Van Wart, Harold, 1960, Ap 22,31:2
Van Wart, Hiram T, 1951, N 17,17:4
Van Wart, Isaac F, 1941, Mr 7,21:5
Van Wart, Isaac F Mrs, 1941, Mr 7,21:5
Van Wart, Jennie Mrs, 1940, Je 6,13:2
Van Wart, John S, 1950, Je 11,92:2
Van Wart, L, 1883, O 12,3:2
van Wart, Roy M, 1957, Ap 6,19:3
Van Wart, William, 1946, N 9,17:5
Van Wassenaer, Gotfried H, 1954, D 12,88:8
Van Waters, George B Mrs, 1948, S 26,76:4
van Welie, Anton, 1956, S 27,35:4
Van Wert, Frederick B, 1944, N 19,50:4
Van Wert, Frederick L, 1954, D 19,84:1
Van Wert, John Irving Dr, 1920, Jl 26,11:7
Van Wert, Leland R, 1945, Mr 28,23:4
Van Wert, Susan, 1956, D 26,27:4
Van Werveke, George, 1951, D 29,11:3
van Wesep, Henry B Mrs, 1962, F 23,30:1
Van Westering, Katherine L, 1955, F 14,19:4
Van Westrum, Adriaan Schade, 1917, My 20,23:3
Van Wezel, Andries, 1921, Jl 4,9:6
Van Why, Guy A, 1944, Mr 18,13:6
Van Wickel, Jesse F, 1958, Mr 29,17:3
Vanwickle, Charles E, 1952, Ag 18,17:3
Vanwickle, J C, 1883, N 6,1:2
Van Wicklen, Frederick M, 1947, Je 8,60:6
Van Wie, Bart Mrs, 1954, Jl 15,27:4
Van Wie, Bert, 1937, F 7,II,8:7
Van Wie, Charles H, 1939, D 16,17:4
Van Wie, Frank L, 1941, Ap 11,21:2
Van Wie, Lansing, 1907, Ap 7,9:6
Van Wijk, Fredrik G, 1945, Ja 25,19:1
Van Winckel, Winford H, 1945, N 24,19:3
Van Winckle, P C, 1872, Ap 18,4:6
Van Winkle, Ab Mrs, 1903, My 18,1:3
Van Winkle, Abraham, 1915, O 1,11:5
Van Winkle, Albert, 1942, My 10,43:2
Van Winkle, Anna S Mrs, 1941, Mr 23,45:2
Van Winkle, C T, 1880, My 25,3:3
Van Winkle, Charles, 1948, O 10,76:2
Van Winkle, Charles I, 1963, My 30,17:3
Van Winkle, Clarence E, 1939, Mr 8,21:3
Van Winkle, Clifford S, 1952, F 6,29:6
Van Winkle, Cortlandt, 1939, Ap 5,25:3
Van Winkle, Daniel, 1939, My 26,23:6
Van Winkle, E S, 1882, D 10,2:1
Van Winkle, Edgar Beach Col, 1920, Ap 28,11:4
Van Winkle, Edgar C, 1968, Ja 28,76:3
Van Winkle, Edward H Rev, 1909, Ag 31,7:6
Van Winkle, Frank A, 1950, F 21,25:3
Van Winkle, Howard E, 1951, O 20,15:2
Van Winkle, Isaac H, 1943, D 16,27:5
Van Winkle, Isaac Rev, 1917, N 16,11:5
Van Winkle, J Albert, 1937, F 27,17:4
Vanwinkle, John H, 1948, Je 29,23:2
Van Winkle, Joseph, 1946, D 1,76:4
Van Winkle, Julian, 1965, F 18,33:2
Van Winkle, Marshall, 1957, My 11,21:3
Van Winkle, Marshall Mrs, 1947, My 18,60:1
Van Winkle, Stirling, 1951, D 2,91:2
Van Winkle, Theodore, 1947, Mr 28,24:3
Van Winkle, Thomas E, 1955, Ag 25,23:2
Van Winkle, William J, 1942, N 13,23:4
VanWinkle, William J Mrs, 1948, O 5,25:2
Van Winkle, William M, 1965, N 15,37:4
Van Winkle, Winant (por), 1943, Ja 10,49:1
Van Woert, Henry, 1940, My 9,23:2
Van Woert, William, 1938, Jl 1,19:2
Van Woert, William H, 1951, N 28,31:1
Van Wormer, Augustus B, 1942, Jl 17,15:6
Van Wormer, David C Mrs, 1946, S 5,27:4
Van Wormer, John R, 1909, O 28,9:5
Van Wyck, Augustus, 1922, Je 9,15:4
Van Wyck, Augustus Mrs, 1919, Jl 30,9:3
Van Wyck, Benjamin S, 1951, F 8,33:1
Van Wyck, Charles U, 1948, F 1,60:6

Van Wyck, Charles U Mrs, 1939, Mr 28,23:6
Van Wyck, Cora P, 1941, O 29,23:3
Van Wyck, Ex-Assemblyman, 1871, Ap 12,8:1
Van Wyck, F, 1936, F 17,20:3
Van Wyck, Frederick L, 1951, Ag 7,25:2
Van Wyck, Frederick Mrs, 1947, N 4,25:3
Van Wyck, George E, 1946, Ag 17,13:3
Van Wyck, Halsey A, 1957, Ap 14,86:7
Van Wyck, Harold T, 1952, Jl 31,23:3
Van Wyck, Howard Mrs, 1952, F 15,25:4
Van Wyck, Jacob Southart, 1920, D 14,17:4
Van Wyck, James R Mrs, 1951, N 17,17:5
Van Wyck, Jennie L, 1951, O 31,29:3
Van Wyck, John H Maj, 1906, Ja 30,9:6
Van Wyck, John R Sr, 1953, S 27,87:2
Van Wyck, Katherine V V Mrs, 1939, Mr 1,21:2
Van Wyck, Lawrence, 1905, Ap 5,9:6
Van Wyck, Lillian I, 1938, Ag 8,13:4
Van Wyck, Margaret, 1939, Jl 13,19:3
Van Wyck, P C, 1883, Ap 24,5:1
Van Wyck, Philip V R Mrs, 1951, Ag 15,27:1
Van Wyck, Pierre V C, 1948, Jl 7,46:2
Van Wyck, Richard, 1925, S 9,25:5
Van Wyck, Robert A, 1918, N 16,13:1
Van Wyck, Stephen, 1924, Ja 24,17:4
Van Wyck, William, 1956, D 13,37:4
Van Wyck, William E Col, 1915, Je 4,11:4
Van Wyen, Cornelius, 1942, S 15,24:4
Van Wyen, Herbert, 1945, Mr 1,21:2
Van Wyk, Johann, 1923, Jl 15,24:4
Van Wynen, John A, 1949, F 20,61:1
Van Yorx, Wilfred T, 1939, F 24,19:4
Van Zale, William J, 1941, Ag 16,15:5
Van Zandt, A, 1879, Ja 29,8:4
Van Zandt, A B, 1881, Jl 23,2:6
Van Zandt, C D, 1926, Je 18,23:4
Van Zandt, C L, 1880, Ap 5,5:6
Van Zandt, Carl L, 1941, Mr 23,44:2
Van Zandt, Catherine Mrs, 1956, Ap 15,89:1
Van Zandt, Elliot C, 1959, O 26,29:2
Van Zandt, Francis, 1952, D 26,15:3
Van Zandt, Irving, 1955, Mr 2,27:4
Van Zandt, James R, 1907, D 29,9:5
Van Zandt, M J Dixon, 1948, O 23,15:4
Van Zandt, Milton B, 1914, Jl 8,9:6
Van Zandt, Paul C, 1951, My 28,21:6
Van Zandt, Philip, 1958, F 17,42:4
Van Zandt, Raymond P, 1939, F 20,17:5
Van Zandt, Richard L, 1940, My 1,23:2
Van Zant, Charles B Mrs, 1937, Ja 17,II,8:5
Van Zee, Arthur W, 1943, Ja 12,23:4
Van Zelm, Henri J, 1954, S 27,21:3
Van Zelm, Henri J Mrs, 1942, Jl 31,15:2
Van Zelm, J Louis, 1949, D 12,34:2
Van Zelm, J Louis Mrs, 1947, D 25,21:4
Van Zelm, John A (por), 1937, Ag 1,II,7:2
Van Zelm, John A Mrs, 1948, Je 22,25:2
van Zelm, L Franklin, 1961, Mr 26,92:6
Van Zelm, Zeger W, 1945, F 20,19:2
Van Zile, John C, 1951, N 8,29:1
Van Zile, Philip T Judge, 1917, O 27,17:5
Van Zilen, George Sr, 1940, O 30,23:4
Van Zilen, Howard Sr, 1955, Jl 21,23:1
Van Zuiden, Leopold E, 1955, Je 26,76:2
Vaquerano, Isabel, 1940, D 28,15:5
Vaquero, Eloy, 1960, S 16,28:6
Varady, Anton, 1941, N 24,19:8
Varaklas, Athenagoras, 1952, Ap 25,23:1
Varallo, Domenico, 1961, Jl 30,68:3
Varbalow, Harry, 1940, S 22,49:1
Varbalow, Samuel, 1954, F 2,27:1
Varcoubeil, A E, 1884, N 3,2:6
Vardaman, J K, 1930, Je 26,23:1
Vardell, Charles G, 1958, My 4,89:1
Varden, Evelyn (Mrs W J Quinn),(cor, Jl 14,21:1), 1958, Jl 13,68:6
Vardi, Emil M, 1960, Ja 22,27:3
Vardon, Harry (will, Jl 18,3:2),(por), 1937, Mr 21,II, 9:1
Vardon, Tom, 1938, O 14,23:1
Vare, Daniele, 1956, F 29,28:6
Vare, Edwin H, 1922, O 17,19:4
Vare, Edwin H Mrs, 1962, My 29,31:2
Vare, George, 1908, F 29,7:6
Vare, Ida May (funl, Ag 21,7:5), 1920, Ag 19,9:4
Vare, W S, 1934, Ag 8,1:7
Vare, William S Mrs, 1938, Ap 26,21:4
Varela, Catherine M Mrs, 1939, D 30,15:3
Varela, Jose E, 1951, Mr 25,73:1
Varela, Jose P, 1950, Ap 30,102:4
Varenne, Alexandre, 1947, F 17,19:2
Vares, Johannes Y, 1946, D 1,78:8
Varese, Edgard (ed trb, N 12,46:1), 1965, N 7,89:1
Varet, Eugene E Mrs, 1943, Ap 30,21:1
Varey, Charles, 1949, Mr 2,25:5
Varga, Eugene S, 1964, O 9,39:2
Varga, Jozsef, 1956, D 30,32:2
Vargas, Getulio, 1943, F 3,19:4
Vargas, Luis, 1951, Ag 18,11:6
Vargas, Manoel N, 1943, O 22,17:5
Vargas, Mario, 1949, D 26,29:2
Vargas, Tomas R, 1943, Jl 27,17:4
Vargas Guillemette, Alvaro, 1954, Je 27,68:3
Vargo, John, 1948, Je 16,29:1
Varian, Alfred W, 1950, N 8,29:6
Varian, Alfred W Mrs, 1941, D 11,27:4
Varian, Cabot Mrs, 1944, O 7,13:4
Varian, Chester C, 1946, Mr 10,46:5
Varian, Clarence J, 1946, Je 7,19:2
Varian, Emily C, 1938, D 27,17:2
Varian, Eugene W Mrs, 1955, S 18,86:6
Varian, G W, 1879, F 9,2:5
Varian, George Edmund, 1923, Ap 13,17:3
Varian, Harry E, 1948, Mr 19,23:4
Varian, Henry (por), 1938, D 4,60:6
Varian, Isaac L, 1864, Ag 23,4:6
Varian, J M, 1882, Jl 25,2:4
Varian, Jacob H, 1942, F 12,23:4
Varian, John B, 1950, F 11,15:4
Varian, Joshua M Brig-Gen, 1906, Mr 6,9:6
Varian, Lulu E, 1942, Mr 25,21:6
Varian, Nina, 1880, S 25,5:2
Varian, Russell H, 1959, Jl 30,27:1
Varian, Sarah H, 1947, Ja 21,23:3
Varian, Sigurd F, 1961, O 21,48:6
Varian, Wilbur C, 1960, Ag 12,19:5
Varian, Wilbur L Mrs, 1948, Mr 18,27:5
Varian, William M, 1938, O 28,23:2
Varicie, Anthony Dr, 1907, Jl 28,7:6
Varick, Edgar F R Mrs, 1957, N 2,21:4
Varick, Richard, 1942, S 21,15:5
Varick, Theodore R, 1924, My 20,21:5
Varick, William R Mrs, 1942, N 26,27:1
Variell, Arthur D (por), 1940, Ap 17,23:3
Varkonyi, Bela, 1947, Ja 27,23:5
Varlan, Peter N, 1942, Ap 23,23:5
Varley, Alfred Herbert, 1925, Je 24,17:5
Varley, Arthur, 1945, N 27,23:2
Varley, Ellis C, 1954, Jl 20,19:1
Varley, Hanford, 1949, D 4,108:5
Varley, Harry (cor, Jl 8,19:2), 1949, Jl 7,25:2
Varley, Herbert P, 1950, F 22,30:6
Varley, John F, 1964, Jl 29,33:1
Varley, John F Mrs, 1946, S 20,31:2
Varley, Margaret L, 1960, N 9,35:3
Varley, William (Reddy the Blacksmith),(see also My 11), 1876, My 15,8:3
Varma, Kerala, 1948, Jl 9,19:2
Varma, Ravi, 1946, F 1,23:2
Varma Thampuran, Rama Ex-Maharajah of Cochin, 1964, N 13,35:5
Varmicelli-Casoni, Cardinal, 1874, My 30,1:7
Varn, William O, 1957, F 4,19:3
Varnava, Patriarch, 1937, Jl 24,5:1
Varneau, Alice Mrs, 1939, F 15,23:1
Varnell, George, 1967, F 5,89:2
Varney, Charles W, 1946, Jl 13,15:2
Varney, Floyd W, 1910, Jl 1,7:4
Varney, Frances, 1921, My 11,17:4
Varney, John, 1967, O 1,84:6
Varney, Lindley H, 1948, Ap 30,23:5
Varney, Lucius E, 1955, Jl 6,27:3
Varney, Walter T, 1967, Ja 28,27:2
Varney, William F, 1960, D 15,43:1
Varnum, Amy L, 1964, Ja 28,31:4
Varnum, James M Gen, 1907, Mr 31,9:7
Varnum, Joseph B, 1867, Ja 18,4:6
Varnum, Mary D Mrs, 1941, Je 6,21:3
Varnum, Thaddeus Mrs, 1954, Mr 10,25:6
Varnum, Wayne, 1949, Mr 2,26:3
Varnum, William H, 1946, Jl 5,19:5
Varona, Francisco, 1941, Je 29,32:5
Varona, Ignacio De, 1922, My 13,13:6
Varona y del Castillo, Miguel, 1953, Ja 11,90:6
Varrell, Harry M, 1940, My 28,23:2
Varrier-Jones, Pendrill, 1941, F 1,17:6
Varroy, H A, 1883, Mr 25,2:2
Varry, Edwin, 1907, My 5,9:6
Vars, Jesse, 1940, S 6,21:2
Vartabedian, Armenag, 1951, Je 7,33:5
Vartia, Ilmari, 1951, My 26,13:2
Varty, Leo G, 1958, My 31,15:5
Varvaressos, Kyriakos, 1957, F 26,29:2
Varwig, George B, 1939, Ap 25,23:1
Vary, Alton, 1946, Je 10,21:4
Vary, George W, 1943, D 26,32:6
Varzakakos, Nicholas, 1921, O 4,15:6
Varzos, Edward, 1959, S 30,37:5
Vas, Steven, 1967, Je 6,47:2
Vas Dias, A Arnold, 1966, F 23,39:4
Vasalle, Rudolph A, 1961, Ag 8,29:2
Vasbinder, Lida C, 1942, O 13,23:1
Vasco, Eleonora de, 1943, Ja 22,19:4
Vasco, Filippo, 1952, My 30,15:2
Vasconcelos, Augusto, 1951, S 28,31:2
Vasconcelos, Eduardo, 1953, Ap 28,27:5
Vasconcelos, Jose, 1959, Jl 2,25:5
Vasconcelos Maragliano, Ramon, 1965, Ag 14,23:3
Vasguez, Ignacia Mrs, 1922, My 28,22:3
Vasilakos, Christos, 1949, Ap 4,23:4
Vasilakos, Steve (por), 1943, Mr 1,12:4
Vasilchenko, Aleksandr G, 1960, N 19,4:8
Vasiliev, Alex A, 1953, My 31,74:1
Vasques, Joseph C, 1960, Ap 6,41:4
Vasquez, Alejandro R, 1943, My 8,15:3
Vasquez, Bartolone, 1944, Ap 23,43:3
Vasquez, C, 1879, N 4,2:6
Vasquez, Domingo Gen, 1909, D 14,11:4
Vasquez Treserra, Francisco, 1962, Je 6,41:3
Vass, Edward J, 1937, Ag 11,23:4
Vass, Frederick Mrs, 1916, N 12,23:2
Vass, Siffrein M, 1957, F 16,17:5
Vassallo, Emilio, 1943, Ap 22,23:3
Vassallo, Ernesto, 1940, My 8,23:3
Vassallo, John A Rev, 1905, Je 6,9:5
Vassar, Anne E, 1941, Ag 10,36:8
Vassar, Charles D, 1905, Ja 21,5:2
Vassar, Everett M, 1959, O 23,29:4
Vassar, Frank, 1951, Mr 19,27:1
Vassar, Frank Mrs, 1959, My 18,27:3
Vassar, Helen, 1941, Je 18,21:6
Vassar, Hervey S, 1951, Ag 31,15:1
Vassar, J E, 1878, D 16,5:2
Vassar, John A, 1941, Mr 18,23:3
Vassar, John Guy, 1904, Ja 30,9:5
Vassar, Matthew, 1868, Je 24,4:7; 1881, Ag 11,5:3
Vassar, Matthew Mrs, 1942, D 31,15:5
Vassar, Queenie (Mrs J Cawthorn), 1960, S 13,37:2
Vassar, Thomas E Rev Dr, 1918, Jl 4,13:6
Vassardakis, Cleanthes, 1942, Je 28,33:3
Vassel, Bruno, 1948, Ag 23,17:5
Vassell, Nicholas, 1945, Ag 30,21:3
Vasselli, Anthony J, 1962, O 2,39:1
Vassilenko, Sergei N, 1956, Mr 14,33:4
Vassiliadis, Basil, 1960, Mr 24,33:4
Vassilieff, Dimitry Stepanovitz Gen, 1915, Mr 8,9:5
Vassiliev, Georgy, 1946, Je 21,23:3
Vassiliev, Sergius A, 1962, Mr 13,35:3
Vassilieve, Nicholas B, 1958, O 17,29:2
Vasso, Amerigo, 1963, S 1,56:5
Vassos, John Mrs (Ruth C), 1965, F 21,77:1
Vasta, Joseph, 1943, Jl 8,19:2
Vastine, John H, 1955, Jl 1,21:2
Vaszary, Claudius Cardinal, 1915, S 5,11:4
Vatable, Auguste, 1918, Jl 11,11:5
Vatable, Emile, 1920, Je 12,13:1
Vatable, Jules, 1925, Mr 6,19:5
Vatable, Jules J, 1950, S 28,31:3
Vatalaro, Anthony, 1961, Jl 21,23:4
Vatis, Theofilos, 1960, S 28,39:4
Vatry, Mme de, 1881, Je 5,7:1
Vatter, Emil H Sr, 1956, S 8,17:5
Vatter, Wilbur L, 1957, Ap 27,19:5
Vattier, J L, 1881, Ja 14,1:6
Vattman, Edward J Rev, 1919, S 30,19:2
Vatutin, N F Gen, 1944, Ap 15,3:4
Vaucher, Maurice, 1957, N 3,89:1
Vaucher, Paul, 1959, My 28,31:5
Vauclain, Andrew C, 1938, Ag 20,15:5
Vauclain, Andrew C Mrs, 1961, O 21,21:2
Vauclain, Charles P, 1953, Ja 17,15:5
Vauclain, Samuel M (por), 1940, F 5,17:1
Vauclain, Samuel M Mrs, 1923, Jl 5,15:4
Vaucrosson, A R, 1943, D 30,18:2
Vaudoyer, Jean-Louis, 1963, My 21,37:5
Vaudrin, Phil, 1956, S 4,30:1
Vaughan, Andrew E Sr, 1946, Jl 20,13:4
Vaughan, Arthur S, 1949, O 7,31:2
Vaughan, Bernard Father, 1922, N 1,19:3
Vaughan, Bettie Mrs, 1950, Ag 1,23:4
Vaughan, Blown from train platform, 1879, Ja 26,7:4
Vaughan, C P, 1936, Mr 21,17:3
Vaughan, C Wheaton, 1950, O 16,27:3
Vaughan, Cardinal, 1903, Je 21,4:5
Vaughan, Charles E, 1964, Je 2,37:2
Vaughan, Charles Lincoln, 1920, Ap 14,9:4
Vaughan, Charles P Mrs, 1956, Ja 31,29:3
Vaughan, Chester P, 1952, F 19,29:4
Vaughan, Clement L, 1944, Ja 6,23:3
Vaughan, Dana P Mrs, 1948, N 25,31:3
Vaughan, Daniel J, 1968, Mr 17,80:7
Vaughan, David, 1946, S 28,7:7
Vaughan, Donald C, 1959, O 2,29:2
Vaughan, Dorothy, 1955, Mr 17,45:1
Vaughan, E, 1929, Ja 23,23:3
Vaughan, Edmund G (por), 1940, My 1,23:6
Vaughan, Ernest M, 1954, S 12,84:4
Vaughan, Evan W, 1964, Ap 8,43:3
Vaughan, Frederick, 1942, Ap 15,23:4
Vaughan, Grover C, 1937, D 14,25:5
Vaughan, Guy W, 1966, N 22,41:4
Vaughan, Harold C Mrs, 1962, My 19,27:5
Vaughan, Harry F, 1951, S 8,17:1
Vaughan, Henry Boyd, 1920, S 16,9:2
Vaughan, Henry G, 1938, N 22,23:6
Vaughan, Henry H, 1942, D 13,75:1
Vaughan, Herbert H, 1948, Ja 5,19:4
Vaughan, James E, 1943, Ap 24,13:7
Vaughan, James L, 1963, Je 10,31:5
Vaughan, John A (por), 1940, Je 15,15:5
Vaughan, John Aubrey Dr, 1916, Ja 30,17:4
Vaughan, John C, 1940, Ja 13,16:7
Vaughan, John G (por), 1948, My 19,27:1
Vaughan, John S, 1951, Ja 22,17:2
Vaughan, John W, 1949, Ja 23,70:3
Vaughan, Joseph A, 1961, Jl 17,21:6
Vaughan, Joseph F (Arky),(trbs), 1952, S 1,14:4
Vaughan, Kate, 1903, F 23,7:7
Vaughan, Leonard H, 1943, S 12,52:7

Vaughan, Marceline, 1947, Ap 12,17:4
Vaughan, Margaret L, 1950, Mr 21,32:2
Vaughan, Norman W, 1962, Mr 17,25:2
Vaughan, R B, 1883, Ag 20,5:5
Vaughan, Ralph J, 1952, Ja 14,19:4
Vaughan, Richard M, 1954, D 30,17:2
Vaughan, Richard M Mrs, 1938, Jl 13,21:3
Vaughan, Ridley, 1942, D 8,25:3
Vaughan, Roger T, 1950, N 14,32:2
Vaughan, Thomas W, 1952, Ja 17,28:2
Vaughan, W W, 1902, F 19,9:5
Vaughan, Walter, 1922, Je 17,13:5
Vaughan, Walter L Sr, 1963, O 30,39:3
Vaughan, Warren T, 1944, Ap 3,21:4
Vaughan, Wayland F, 1961, Ja 23,23:4
Vaughan, William, 1902, O 26,7:5; 1940, F 13,23:6
Vaughan, William L, 1949, D 4,109:1
Vaughan, William W, 1938, F 5,15:2; 1939, S 5,23:4; 1946, O 30,27:2
Vaughan, Winfred A, 1957, F 21,27:1
Vaughan-Williams, Arthur H, 1942, Ja 27,21:6
Vaughan Williams, Ralph (burial plans, Ag 29,23:5), 1958, Ag 27,1:3
Vaughen, Frank G, 1951, Mr 2,25:2
Vaughey, James J, 1949, N 14,27:5
Vaughn, Arthur S, 1947, Mr 18,27:4
Vaughn, Charles F, 1953, Ap 3,23:3
Vaughn, David C, 1946, S 3,19:5
Vaughn, Edward W, 1941, N 5,23:4
Vaughn, F Remsen, 1951, D 12,37:1
Vaughn, Floyd (Arky), 1952, Ag 31,47:4
Vaughn, George L, 1949, Ag 18,21:4
Vaughn, Grace A Mrs, 1940, Mr 28,23:4
Vaughn, Grady H Jr, 1967, Ag 11,31:4
Vaughn, Hilda, 1957, D 30,23:2
Vaughn, Howard, 1953, Jl 23,23:2
Vaughn, J Webb, 1946, S 25,28:2
Vaughn, James, 1966, My 30,19:4
Vaughn, John E, 1947, F 24,19:1
Vaughn, John J, 1950, F 8,27:1
Vaughn, Katherine E, 1960, Ja 26,33:4
Vaughn, Miles W, 1949, Ja 31,3:8
Vaughn, S Wilson, 1953, S 10,25:5
Vaughn, Theresa, 1903, O 5,7:7
Vaughn, Wesley E Sr, 1949, My 22,88:1
Vaughn, William T Mrs, 1944, Je 14,19:4
Vaught, Edgar S, 1959, D 6,87:1
Vaught, R S Sr Mrs, 1958, N 21,29:4
Vaugoin, Karl, 1949, Je 12,76:2
Vaun, Calvert, 1895, N 21,1:3
Vaupel, Julia G Mrs, 1952, O 19,89:1
Vaupell, Christina W, 1940, Jl 28,27:3
Vause, Harry R, 1949, Ag 20,11:3
Vause, W Bernard Mrs, 1943, My 6,19:3
Vautel, Clement, 1954, D 27,17:4
Vauthier, Louis, 1954, Mr 18,31:3
Vauthier, Louis Mrs, 1943, O 10,48:5
Vautier, Lillian P, 1942, D 19,19:2
Vaux, Alfred M, 1939, D 7,27:4
Vaux, Baron de (Diable Boiteux), 1915, D 30,13:5
Vaux, George Jr Mrs, 1956, F 17,23:3
Vaux, H G C M, 1935, O 26,15:1
Vaux, Norris W, 1958, Ag 21,25:4
Vaux, Richard, 1895, Mr 22,4:7
Vaux, W S W, 1885, Je 23,5:6
Vaux of Harrowden, Baroness (Mrs W G Gilbey), 1958, My 13,3:6
Vav der Bogert, Frank, 1940, S 25,27:1
Vavasour, James J, 1956, N 5,31:2
Vavbina, Vavclav, 1950, Ja 31,23:4
Vavilov, Sergei I, 1951, Ja 26,23:3
Vavpetich, Rudolph, 1945, Ja 21,39:1
Vavra, A Stephen Mrs, 1956, S 28,27:1
Vavrakin, Alex N, 1953, D 12,19:4
Vawter, Homer T, 1958, S 30,20:8
Vawter, Will, 1941, F 12,21:1
Vaxelaire, Raymond, 1947, Mr 18,27:6
Vayana, Nunzio, 1960, D 14,39:2
Vayhinger, Monroe, 1938, N 2,23:4
Vayson, Paul, 1911, D 14,13:4
Vdofichenko, Gregori, 1952, Je 9,23:3
Veach, Arthur H, 1944, F 2,21:2
Veach, George Mrs, 1946, My 9,21:6
Veach, Robert, 1945, Ag 8,27:5
Veach, Thomas F, 1950, Je 8,31:3
Veach, William W, 1937, N 14,II,11:2
Veakis, Aimilios, 1951, Je 30,15:6
Veale, Frank R, 1943, My 9,40:4
Veale, James J, 1939, Je 20,21:2
Veale, Louis E, 1956, S 30,86:6
Veale, William, 1922, Je 29,15:6
Veasey, William, 1956, N 14,35:3
Veatch, Arthur C, 1938, D 25,14:4
Veatch, Henry C, 1945, S 6,25:4
Veazey, T Stockton, 1944, Ag 9,17:6
Veazie, Joseph A, 1947, O 29,28:2
Veazie, Wildes W, 1959, D 8,45:4
Veber, Daniel, 1951, S 9,90:1
Veblen, Oswald, 1960, Ag 11,27:1
Vecchini, Charles J, 1942, N 11,25:5
Vecchio, Thomas J, 1952, My 11,93:1
Vechsler, Harry, 1949, My 24,27:3
Vecsey, Armand, 1949, Ap 2,15:5
Vedder, A M, 1878, D 30,5:2
Vedder, Albert, 1944, O 1,46:1
Vedder, Byron C Mrs, 1960, D 4,88:4
Vedder, Edward B, 1952, F 2,13:3
Vedder, Elihu, 1923, Ja 30,17:3
Vedder, Elihu Mrs (funl, Je 27,7:5), 1909, Je 26,7:3
Vedder, Estella, 1941, My 18,26:1
Vedder, Harmon A, 1944, Ap 7,19:3
Vedder, Harold L, 1948, N 15,25:3
Vedder, Harry Mrs, 1948, Jl 21,23:5
Vedder, John C (por), 1939, O 14,19:4
Vedder, Maus Rose Vedder Dr, 1914, Je 14,15:5
Vedder, Perry Commodore (funl, D 27,9:4), 1910, D 25,9:2
Vedella, Antonio, 1943, My 12,27:6
Vedeneev, Boris, 1946, S 27,23:5
Vedia, Lautaro D, 1948, N 22,22:3
Vedia y Mitre, Mariano de, 1958, F 20,25:5
Veditz, George W, 1937, Mr 14,II,8:4
Vedova, George C, 1958, S 7,86:2
Vedova, Victor A, 1937, Ja 10,II,10:5
Vedova, Victor A Mrs, 1963, Jl 16,31:5
Vedres, Mark, 1961, Ag 14,25:1
Vedrinskaja-Troubetzkoy, Nadeja V, 1956, Ap 25,35:4
Veeck, Ernest F Mrs, 1944, D 24,26:2
Veeck, W L, 1933, O 6,17:1
Veeck, W L Mrs, 1964, Ag 20,29:2
Veeder, Abram G, 1948, O 15,24:2
Veeder, Albert H, 1914, Jl 15,9:7
Veeder, Curtis H, 1943, D 28,17:2
Veeder, Henry, 1942, Je 10,21:2
Veeder, Paul L, 1942, Mr 11,19:2
Veeder, Ten Eyck De Witt Commodore, 1923, D 3,17:3
Veeder, Van Vechten (por), 1942, D 5,15:1
Veeder, Van Vechten Mrs, 1956, F 24,25:3
Veeneman, Harry, 1950, O 25,35:1
Veer, Imre, 1959, Je 5,27:2
Vees, Frederick W, 1953, Jl 14,27:1
Vega, Fernando de la, 1952, Je 7,19:3
Vega, Josephine, 1950, Jl 13,25:3
Vega, William J, 1946, S 3,19:3
Vega Cascante, Avelina Mrs, 1955, S 29,66:6
Veghte, Charles B Mrs, 1949, F 15,23:3
Veghte, Robert, 1951, D 30,24:6
Veglianette, Jane Mrs, 1947, N 12,27:5
Vegrin, Elia V, 1964, Je 19,31:1
Vehling, Joseph D, 1950, S 22,31:2
Vehon, Michael L, 1945, Ja 22,17:5
Vehring, Charles, 1942, Ja 31,17:2
Vehslage, Henry D, 1946, Ja 4,21:4
Vehslage, John H Mrs, 1959, F 4,23:1
Vehslage, Samuel H, 1938, Je 21,19:2
Veidt, Conrad (por), 1943, Ap 4,40:3
Veil-Picard, Arthur, 1944, N 27,23:4
Veilers, Lazars, 1953, N 13,18:6
Veill, Sylvester J, 1912, Jl 29,9:1
Veiller, Anthony, 1965, Je 29,35:3
Veiller, Bayard (por), 1943, Je 17,21:3
Veiller, Lawrence, 1959, S 1,29:4
Veiller, Philip Bayard, 1906, S 4,9:6
Veintemilla, Ignacio Gen, 1908, Jl 21,7:6
Veit, Benjamin, 1951, S 29,17:2
Veit, Benjamin Mrs, 1956, Ap 17,31:1
Veit, Gustave, 1950, S 7,31:2
Veit, Howard, 1955, Ag 31,25:4
Veit, Howard C, 1960, D 8,35:1
Veit, John, 1939, Ja 21,15:5
Veit, John O, 1956, O 6,21:6
Veit, Louis, 1944, My 20,15:4
Veit, Morris C, 1966, Ap 30,31:2
Veit, P, 1877, D 25,5:6
Veit, Richard Charles, 1919, Ag 31,22:5
Veit, Robert O, 1959, N 7,23:5
Veit, Russell C, 1957, Ja 24,29:5
Veitch, Charles W, 1948, Ja 28,23:4
Veitch, Edwin P, 1939, Ag 21,13:3
Veitch, Johnstone D, 1943, Mr 7,38:5
Veith, George, 1944, N 8,17:4
Veith, George L, 1950, Ag 5,15:3
Veksler, Vladimir I, 1966, S 23,37:1
Vela, Albert H, 1958, Mr 4,29:5
Velander, Edy, 1961, D 2,23:5
Velasquez, Alejandro, 1945, D 15,17:5
Velasquez, Francesco, 1963, Ap 7,V,4:5
Velasquez, Manuel, 1959, Ap 16,33:1
Velasquez, Marcos E, 1944, Ap 12,21:4
Velazco, Filomeno de, 1954, D 30,17:2
Velde, H van de, 1947, Je 10,27:4
Velde, Harold H Mrs, 1952, S 23,33:5
Velde, Harry van de, 1957, O 27,86:7
Velden Vygh, Lillian G van der Mrs (E Russe), 1942, O 7,25:3
Velding, Joseph J H, 1955, O 16,86:3
Velera, Juan, 1905, Ap 20,9:6
Velez, Lucas L, 1940, My 21,23:5
Velez, Lucas L Mrs, 1950, S 28,31:2
Velez-Paiz, Fernando, 1957, Ja 4,23:2
Velez y Lacayo, Cipriano, 1945, Ap 11,23:2
Velichko, Ivan, 1951, Ag 17,17:3
Velie, Charles N, 1948, D 2,29:4
Velie, Chester E, 1954, Ap 22,29:2
Velie, Frank W, 1947, O 23,25:5
Velie, James H, 1947, Ap 3,25:5
Velie, Jesse Mrs, 1948, Ap 26,23:4
Velikanov, Nikolai, 1951, O 25,29:4
Velimirovich, Nicholai, 1956, Mr 21,37:2
Veliz, Claudio R, 1948, Ja 22,27:4
Vella, Ernestina, 1945, Ag 23,23:4
Vella, Mavel, 1943, Ap 16,21:4
Vella, Paul D, 1954, D 29,15:5
Velle, George M, 1943, S 4,13:5
Velle, Josephine de Countess, 1925, O 8,27:4
Velletri, Joseph R, 1950, Ag 3,23:1
Velloso, Enrique G, 1938, Ja 28,21:1
Velloso, Leao, 1923, N 1,21:4
Velloso Netto, Pedro L, 1947, Ja 21,24:2
Velluzzi, Biagio (Murph), 1960, O 7,35:1
Veloni, Artemethius Colo, 1906, D 4,9:5
Veloz, Nicolas, 1957, F 24,84:2
Velpeau, Dr, 1867, Ag 28,4:7
Velsor, Claude, 1954, Jl 10,13:6
Velsor, Eugene, 1938, N 24,27:3
Velsor, Joseph, 1946, Mr 1,2:8
Velte, F Mowbray, 1962, My 23,45:3
Velte, Henry C Mrs, 1945, F 9,15:3
Velte, Henry P, 1952, Ja 25,21:2
Veltfort, Theodore E Mrs, 1945, Ap 1,36:2
Veltri, Frank, 1951, Mr 12,25:1
Velutini, Emilio H, 1946, F 4,25:2
Velzen, N G M Van, 1941, Je 18,21:2
Vena, Joseph, 1949, Je 11,17:4
Vena, Michael J, 1959, O 28,37:3
Vena, Nicholas F, 1951, Ap 5,29:4
Venable, A W, 1876, F 26,5:3
Venable, Bryant, 1956, Ap 1,89:2
Venable, Charles S, 1945, O 3,19:4
Venable, Earl Mrs, 1943, My 24,15:2
Venable, Francis P Mrs, 1948, N 26,23:2
Venable, Reginald S H, 1964, S 29,43:5
Venable, Stella C, 1942, N 8,50:4
Venable, Wade H, 1952, Jl 10,31:3
Venables, A R P, 1876, O 9,2:2
Venables, William F, 1953, My 7,32:3
Venard, Bro (C E Gorman), 1949, D 23,22:5
Venard, Celeste (Celeste Mogador), 1909, F 20,7:4
Venard, Lloyd G Mrs, 1967, Ap 6,39:4
Venator, Louis C, 1955, My 4,29:4
Vendig, Joseph H (funl, Ag 26,19:5), 1925, Ag 24, 13:5
Vending, Lee H, 1939, Ag 1,19:2
Venditto, Dominico G Sr, 1948, Ja 22,27:4
Vendome, Duchess of, 1948, Mr 30,23:2
Vendome, Duke of, 1931, F 2,19:4
Vendrovsky, Isaac Zev Rabbi, 1918, D 18,15:4
Venegas, Benjamin J, 1950, S 11,23:5
Venerable, Sarah A, 1938, Je 4,15:5
Venerasi, Anthony, 1924, My 4,23:1
Veneris, George J, 1954, F 16,25:1
Veneruso, Leonard C, 1953, My 2,15:5
Venezia, Charles C, 1961, Je 9,33:3
Venezia, Joseph, 1948, Jl 21,23:2
Veneziale, Joseph, 1951, My 27,68:4
Veneziani, Carlo, 1950, Ja 19,27:2
Venezio, Frank, 1949, Je 28,27:2
Vengerova, Isabelle, 1956, F 8,33:3
Vengrove, Irving, 1965, Je 23,41:3
Vening Meinesz, Felix A, 1966, Ag 12,31:1
Venini, Antonio, 1941, Mr 1,15:5
Venini, Paolo, 1959, Jl 28,37:5
Venino, Albert F, 1940, S 27,23:4
Venino, Albert W, 1961, Mr 1,33:2
Venino, Aquila N, 1955, D 2,27:1
Venino, Henry, 1942, Ja 15,19:3
Venizelos, E, 1936, Mr 19,12:1
Venizelos, Kyriakos, 1942, Ag 17,15:5
Venizelos, Sophocles (funl, F 10,27:3), 1964, F 7,31:1
Vennard, Iva D, 1945, S 15,15:4
Vennell, Thomas, 1907, N 25,9:7
Vennema, A Whiton, 1940, Mr 24,30:8
Vennema, Ame Rev Dr, 1925, Ap 28,21:5
Venneman, Harry Mrs, 1960, N 17,37:2
Venner, C H, 1933, Je 26,15:1
Venner, Joseph E, 1946, Jl 26,21:5
Vennerbeck, Albert S, 1948, Ap 21,27:4
Venneri, Arthur, 1963, N 23,29:3
Venners, Thomas, 1907, Ap 20,9:6
Venning, Frank L, 1944, F 20,35:1
Venning, Jack, 1944, My 4,19:3
Vennor, H G, 1884, Je 9,1:6
Veno, Joseph (Bro Adelphus Joseph), 1955, Ja 20, 31:5
Venon, Jules H, 1937, Mr 20,19:4
Venson, Russell, 1916, Ag 19,9:4
Venter, Johannes J, 1953, O 6,29:2
Venth, Carl, 1938, Ja 30,II,8:7
Ventiris, Constantine, 1960, D 15,43:2
Ventoura, Anthony, 1967, Ap 14,39:2
Ventres, Charles C Mrs, 1963, Jl 20,19:4
Ventres, Charles Sr, 1947, N 13,27:2
Ventresca, Carmen, 1943, S 10,23:1
Ventsel, Dmitry, 1955, Jl 23,17:5
Ventura, Alfonse, 1960, Ja 9,21:4
Ventura Simo, Juan de Dios, 1960, Mr 18,7:1
Venturi, Adolfo (por), 1941, Je 11,21:4
Venturi, Lionello, 1961, Ag 16,31:1
Venuta, Aloysius Rev, 1876, Ja 28,5:5

Venuti, Giacomo, 1952, F 11,12:6
Veolin, Stephen G, 1939, Ja 2,24:3
Veprek, Charles, 1951, O 7,86:4
Ver Eecke, Harry B, 1942, D 2,25:5
Ver Linden, Edward, 1941, N 10,17:3
Ver Nisie, Thomas C, 1953, Ag 15,17:4
Ver Planck, Helen E, 1959, D 17,37:3
Vera, Tomas, 1941, My 21,23:2
Vera y Zuria, Pedro, 1945, Jl 31,19:4
Veragua, Duke, 1910, O 31,9:5
Verague, Duke of, 1941, Ja 25,15:2
Verbeck, George P, 1941, Jl 2,21:4
Verbeck, Guido F, 1940, Jl 27,13:6
Verbeck, Gustave, 1937, D 6,27:6
Verbeck, Howard Mrs, 1957, Ap 1,25:2
Verbeck, W, 1930, Ag 25,17:4
Verbeck, William Mrs, 1914, Je 28,15:5; 1944, Ag 17, 17:2
Verbeek, Gustave Mrs, 1961, Jl 14,23:1
Verbeet, Gerrit, 1953, Ap 3,23:3
Verber, Blanche A, 1953, F 18,31:2
Verbest, Frank C Mrs, 1948, O 17,76:3
Verboeckhoven, E J, 1881, Ja 24,5:2
Verbrugge, Albert A, 1957, Jl 1,44:8
Verbrugghen, H, 1934, N 13,17:1
Verby, Harry Mrs, 1961, Je 7,41:2
Vercel, Roger, 1957, F 27,27:5
Vercelli, Charles S, 1966, Jl 1,35:4
Verchot, Peter, 1951, Ag 15,27:3
Verchota, J J, 1949, Ja 26,25:5
Vercken de Vreuschmen, Pierre Mrs (D Vernon), 1966, Ap 8,31:3
Verde, Alessandro, 1958, Mr 31,27:3
Verder, William C, 1946, Je 22,19:5
Verderber, William, 1957, O 27,86:7
Verdery, Marion J, 1958, S 19,27:2
Verdery, Marion J Mrs, 1958, S 20,19:6
Verdes, Edward M, 1964, Jl 3,21:2
Verdeschi, Vincent F, 1965, Ag 18,35:5
Verdi, Francis M, 1952, Mr 23,92:1
Verdi, Giuseppe, 1901, Ja 26,1:6
Verdi, Joseph, 1957, D 29,48:4
Verdi, Phil, 1947, F 6,48:6
Verdi, Vincent J, 1950, F 6,25:5
Verdi, William F (will, Ag 1,27:5), 1957, Ap 22,25:5
Verdiani, Ciro, 1952, Mr 5,29:1
Verdier, Gaston Louis, 1915, F 14,3:5
Verdier, Jean (Card), 1940, Ap 9,23:1
Verdin, Eugene R, 1959, D 5,23:3
Verdon, Alex P, 1941, Je 20,21:2
Verdon, Thomas, 1912, My 13,9:6
Verdon-Roe, Alliott, 1958, Ja 6,39:2
Verdumartins, Antonio, 1950, Ja 30,17:1
Verduynen, Michiels van, 1952, My 14,27:3
Vere, Charles, 1937, Ja 17,II,8:7
Vere, Clementine D de (Mrs R Sapio), 1954, Ja 20, 27:5
Vere, Howard, 1921, Ag 17,11:5
Vereen, William J, 1952, O 2,29:3
Vereneault, J Henry, 1968, Ja 4,34:8
Veretennikov, Nikolai I, 1955, Ap 6,29:1
Verga, Eugene F, 1954, D 29,23:1
Verga, Giovanni, 1922, Ja 28,13:4
Verga, Lawrence M, 1948, O 26,31:1
Verga, Mario, 1954, O 10,V,10:4
Vergani, Antonio, 1960, Ap 7,35:4
Vergara, Alejandro, 1944, Ap 13,19:4
Vergara, Joseph, 1949, N 30,27:1
Verge, Edmond, 1938, Jl 11,17:2
Verge, Louis, 1941, N 26,23:4
Verger, A, 1877, D 16,7:2
Vergeri, Amelia, 1950, D 7,33:4
Verges, Henri de, 1944, F 21,15:1
Verhalen, William, 1941, N 9,53:2
Verhaza, Jose I, 1952, Ag 31,44:8
Verhey, Hubert C Jr, 1938, Ag 29,13:6
Verhey, Keith W, 1962, D 4,41:4
Verhoeven, Pauline, 1919, Ja 14,11:3
Verhulst, Jacob P, 1955, My 6,23:3
Verian, Frank, 1965, Ja 4,29:3
Verigen, Peter, 1939, F 12,45:3
Verigin, Evdokia Mrs, 1941, N 20,27:1
Verigin, Michael, 1951, Jl 29,68:6
Verigin, Peter 2d Mrs, 1940, N 23,17:5
Verinder, William J, 1944, Jl 1,15:6
Verity, Ansel P, 1955, Mr 14,23:4
Verity, George M (por), 1942, N 7,15:1
Verity, Georgina Mrs, 1939, Ja 11,19:3
Verity, Laura D Mrs, 1942, S 21,15:6
Verity, Lawrence, 1920, Je 27,18:2
Verity, Russell W Jr, 1946, Ag 19,25:4
Verity, Thomas W, 1944, D 12,23:2
Verkholovich, Pavel, 1952, N 1,21:3
Verkstrom, Alice Mrs, 1950, Je 16,25:4
Verlage, Leander Mrs, 1949, Ap 13,29:5
Verlaine, Paul, 1896, Ja 9,5:1
Verleger, William F Mrs, 1950, S 20,31:2
Verlenden, Joseph S, 1956, Ap 7,19:3
Verlomme, Roger, 1950, Jl 10,21:5
Vermeer, Evert A, 1960, Je 1,39:6
Vermeersch, Adolphe, 1949, Je 4,13:5
Vermeersh, Henry, 1949, My 2,25:3
Vermes, Sigmund Mrs, 1951, Mr 22,31:2
Vermett, John T, 1941, My 28,25:5
Vermeule, John D, 1915, My 21,13:3
Vermilya, Norman L, 1955, Ap 6,29:5
Vermilya, Percy S, 1956, Ja 30,27:4
Vermilya, Percy S Mrs, 1958, Ja 5,87:1
Vermilya, William, 1954, Mr 7,91:2
Vermilye, Anna J, 1953, O 17,15:6
Vermilye, Anna J Mrs, 1940, Je 5,25:2
Vermilye, H Rowland Mrs, 1955, F 24,27:4
Vermilye, Marion H, 1937, N 13,23:4
Vermilye, robt C Rev, 1875, Jl 6,4:5
Vermilye, Ruth M A Mrs, 1963, Ap 5,47:1
Vermilye, T E Rev, 1893, Mr 18,8:2
Vermilye, Theodore C, 1879, N 14,5:2; 1959, D 3,37:5
Vermilye, W M (see also Je 19), 1878, Je 22,8:1
Vermilye, W R, 1876, D 25,8:2
Vermilye, William G, 1942, D 18,27:4
Vermilye, William Gray Dr, 1925, My 3,5:1
Vermilye, William M, 1944, Ag 31,17:1
Vermilyea, Harold, 1958, Ja 9,33:2
Vermilyea, James H, 1943, Ap 20,23:5
Vermont, Boris, 1956, Je 27,31:5
Vermorel, Auguste, 1871, Je 6,1:1
Verna, Ettore, 1962, Ag 7,29:2
Vernam, Clarence C, 1937, Ja 25,19:3
Vernam, Clarence C (will), 1938, O 8,9:2
Vernam, Gilbert S, 1960, F 10,37:2
Vernam, William B, 1938, F 5,15:3
Vernay, Annie, 1941, Ag 20,19:5
Vernay, Arthur S, 1960, O 26,39:3
Verne, Adela, 1952, F 6,29:3
Verne, Henrie, 1949, F 17,23:1
Verne, Jean Jules, 1925, Mr 7,13:6
Verne, Jules, 1905, Mr 25,9:5
Verner, Jules, 1958, Ag 10,93:2
Vernet, Horace, 1863, F 3,5:3
Vernet, Waldemar, 1947, F 25,25:1
Verneuil, De Count, 1873, Je 5,5:6
Verneuil, Louis, 1952, N 4,33:1
Verneuil, Louis Mrs, 1940, D 24,15:1
Verney, Gerald L, 1957, Ap 5,27:2
Verney, Gilbert Mrs, 1955, D 2,27:3
Verney, Harry L, 1950, Mr 3,26:3
Verniaud, Louis Mrs, 1949, My 17,25:5
Vernick, Edward, 1954, S 15,33:5
Vernick, Jack, 1954, O 20,29:1
Vernicos, Basil Mrs, 1966, Ja 5,31:5
Vernoll, Thomas Powell Rev, 1925, S 24,25:4
Vernon, Ambrose W, 1951, Ag 24,15:1
Vernon, Baron, 1915, N 12,11:6
Vernon, Bobby, 1939, Je 29,23:6
Vernon, Charles G, 1948, My 3,21:2
Vernon, Charles H, 1956, Ap 27,27:2
Vernon, Charles W Jr, 1942, Ag 24,15:3
Vernon, Clarence C, 1948, S 22,31:2
Vernon, Dorothy (Mrs P Vercken de Vreuschmen), 1966, Ap 8,31:3
Vernon, E Frank, 1938, F 2,19:6
Vernon, F Joseph, 1914, F 19,9:6
Vernon, Frank, 1940, Mr 19,25:2
Vernon, Frank L, 1944, My 25,21:4
Vernon, Frederick, 1912, O 29,13:5
Vernon, George Edward, 1907, Je 24,7:6
Vernon, George L Mrs, 1915, Jl 23,9:3
Vernon, Grenville, 1941, D 1,19:3
Vernon, Grenville Mrs, 1939, Ap 11,24:4
Vernon, Harold, 1911, O 12,9:4
Vernon, Harry, 1959, Mr 8,86:5
Vernon, Howard A, 1955, Jl 19,27:5
Vernon, Howard W, 1942, N 4,23:2
Vernon, J M F Mrs, 1869, Je 5,5:2
Vernon, John, 1946, D 1,78:7
Vernon, John Murray, 1921, N 21,15:4
Vernon, Joseph A, 1956, S 23,84:2
Vernon, Leroy B, 1945, S 11,23:2
Vernon, Leroy T, 1938, Ja 4,23:1
Vernon, Miles H, 1953, Mr 5,27:2
Vernon, Nell A (Mrs E H Loeffler), 1959, O 20,39:2
Vernon, Paul E, 1957, Je 26,31:4
Vernon, Philip Harwood, 1919, Jl 20,21:3
Vernon, Robert Mrs (N Hawthorne), 1960, Jl 24,65:1
Vernon, Samuel Edward, 1914, O 7,9:6
Vernon, Samuel M Mrs, 1947, S 5,19:2
Vernon, Thomas Alfred, 1904, Je 25,7:6
Vernon, William B Mrs, 1960, Jl 10,72:2
Vernon-Cole, Willis, 1939, Mr 10,23:4
Vernooy, Charles D, 1938, Ja 21,20:3
Vernooy, Simon, 1944, Je 18,35:1
Vernor, James Jr, 1957, Ap 10,33:2
Vernor, Richard E, 1958, Je 4,33:4
Vero, Frank, 1948, My 19,27:1
Veroli, Giorgio di (trb lr), 1952, D 27,8:7
Veron, Louis Desire Dr, 1867, S 10,4:7
Verona, Jane (Mrs J P English), 1941, Jl 23,19:6
Verona, Leonidas, 1949, Ap 13,29:4
Veroni, Dante, 1949, Mr 26,17:1
Veronica Eich, Sister, 1937, Ag 26,21:4
Veronica Mary, Sister (Sisters of Charity), 1959, Ap 25,21:1
Veronis, Nicholas, 1966, Ag 27,29:4
Verplaetse, George W, 1949, Ja 14,24:2
Verplanck, Fred A, 1957, N 11,29:6
Verplanck, Gulian C, 1870, Mr 19,5:1
Verplanck, Gulian Mrs, 1944, Mr 9,17:6
Verplanck, J DeLancey Mrs, 1952, Ap 24,31:2
Verplanck, James D, 1958, Ap 24,31:4
Verplanck, Jessie W Mrs, 1940, Je 13,23:6
Verplanck, John B R, 1955, Ap 8,21:1
VerPlanck, Lewis I, 1941, S 6,15:5
Verplanck, Philip, 1905, N 11,9:6; 1921, My 11,17:5
Verplanck, Samuel, 1911, D 19,13:4
Verplanck, W Harold, 1954, Ag 18,29:4
VerPlanck, William G Mrs, 1947, Ag 18,17:4
Verrall, Edwin H, 1947, Mr 13,27:4
Verrall, Richard P, 1952, D 21,53:1
Verret, Hector, 1943, My 28,21:1
Verrier, Henri, 1940, S 26,23:5
Verriest, Leon, 1953, N 7,17:6
Verrill, A E Prof, 1926, D 12,30:1
Verrill, A Hyatt, 1954, N 16,29:2
Verrill, Albert E, 1955, F 1,29:3
Verro, Charles J, 1945, F 24,11:3
Verro, Frank S, 1957, Ja 6,88:4
Verschleiser, Max, 1957, S 6,21:4
Verschoor, Charles A, 1943, S 4,13:5
Verschoyle, W Denham, 1944, My 27,15:7
Verschuur, T J, 1945, Jl 21,11:2
Versen, Alice von Mrs, 1912, Ag 22,9:6
Versfelt, William H, 1956, S 5,27:5
Vershigora, Pyotr P, 1963, Mr 28,16:4
Vershinin, Boris G, 1953, S 8,31:4
Versluys, Clement J, 1964, Jl 12,68:3
Vertefeuille, Joseph A Mrs, 1951, Ap 10,27:2
Vertes, Marcel, 1961, N 1,39:1
Vertinsky, Alex, 1957, My 28,33:2
Vertner, T Kearney, 1937, Je 1,23:5
Vertrees, John L, 1944, Ja 27,19:1
Vertrees, Joseph H Mrs, 1941, O 15,21:5
Veru, Daniel Mrs, 1968, Ja 21,76:7
Verven, James, 1950, F 1,29:3
Vervena, Mariano, 1955, Jl 27,23:4
Verville, Joseph A, 1937, N 22,19:3
Vervoort, Benjamin F, 1954, Je 8,27:2
Verwayne, Peter C, 1958, Je 7,19:2
Verwilghen, Henry F, 1945, Mr 23,19:3
Verwoerd, Willem J, 1961, Ag 29,31:3
Very, Edward W, 1910, Mr 2,9:4
Very, Samuel Williams Rear-Adm, 1919, Ja 4,11:5
Verzi, Charles, 1941, Ag 1,9:4
Vesce, Gennare Mrs, 1956, Je 3,86:7
Vesce, Joseph V, 1964, Mr 20,33:4
Vescelius, Addison A, 1953, Ag 5,23:6
Vesela-Dewettrova, Anna, 1949, Ap 12,30:4
Vesell, Albert, 1944, Je 3,13:3
Vesell, Morton Dr, 1968, N 12,43:4
Vesell, Myer (will), 1939, Ja 7,13:8
Vesely, John H, 1952, N 1,11:6
Veser, Frederick, 1937, F 3,23:5
Veser, Lucius O, 1960, O 7,35:2
Vesey, W H, 1881, D 21,5:2
Vesnin, Victor A, 1950, S 20,31:4
Vesnitch, Milenko Mrs, 1951, Ja 14,85:2
Vessella, Orestes, 1963, Je 22,23:5
Vesselovsky, Vladimir Mrs, 1945, Ag 20,19:4
Vessey, Joseph, 1947, Ag 12,23:6
Vessy, Sidney C, 1946, F 16,13:1
Vest, G G Sen, 1904, Ag 10,7:5
Vest, George Jr, 1902, N 7,9:6
Vest, Samuel A, 1958, Ap 8,29:2
Vestal, A H, 1932, Ap 2,17:1
Vestal, Edward M, 1946, F 9,13:2
Vestal, Jack, 1938, N 17,32:2
Vestal, Meade, 1954, Ja 9,15:4
Vester, Frederick, 1942, Ja 4,49:3
Vester, Frederick Spafford Mrs, 1968, Je 28,38:2
Vestermark, Seymour D, 1959, F 24,29:5
Vestey, Edmund, 1953, N 20,23:3
Vestey, Lady (por), 1941, My 24,15:5
Vestey, Lord (por), 1940, D 12,27:5
Vestey, Lord (Saml), 1954, My 6,33:4
Vestine, Ernest Harry, 1968, Jl 19,35:2
Vestoff, Valodja, 1947, S 6,17:3
Vestoff, Veronine, 1941, Je 25,21:4
Vetell, Carl W, 1954, N 1,27:3
Vethake, Henry, 1866, D 26,1:6
Vetlesen, George U, 1955, Mr 23,31:1
Vetlesen, George U Mrs, 1958, My 24,21:4
Vetluguin, Voldemar, 1953, My 18,21:2
Vetoyanis, Gust C, 1960, Jl 19,29:2
Vetrano, Michael Mrs, 1950, Ag 15,29:3
Vetsburg, Phil, 1938, D 11,18:1
Vetsera, Marie Baroness, 1925, F 4,21:4
Vetsopoulos, James, 1951, Ja 5,21:2
Vett, Ove, 1948, My 24,20:3
Vetter, Albert A, 1960, F 23,31:2
Vetter, Charles, 1941, Ag 30,13:5
Vetter, Charles T, 1952, Mr 21,23:4
Vetter, Earl R, 1963, D 26,28:3
Vetter, Frank, 1941, N 5,23:3
Vetter, Fred C Sr, 1961, Mr 8,33:1
Vetter, John M, 1962, Ap 19,31:2
Vetter, William L, 1939, Jl 26,19:4; 1940, Jl 3,17:3
Vetter. Jno J, 1946, Je 16,40:5
Vetterlein, Joseph R, 1940, Ap 22,18:2
Vetukhiv, Michael, 1959, Je 12,27:1
Veuillot, L, 1883, Ap 8,2:6

Veuillot, Pierre Cardinal, 1968, F 14,47:2
Vezin, Charles, 1942, Mr 14,15:1; 1965, Ja 18,35:3
Vezin, Hermann, 1910, Je 13,7:6
Vezin, Russell K, 1946, Jl 9,21:1
Vezina, Elie, 1942, Mr 11,19:3
Viafore, Carmine J, 1950, Ap 25,31:4
Viafore, Victor S Mrs, 1958, N 8,21:5
Vialet, Alfredo, 1954, My 12,31:3
Viall, John G Capt, 1913, S 3,9:6
Viall, Nelson Gen, 1903, My 2,9:4
Viall, William A, 1939, O 25,23:3
Vialls, Walter W, 1946, N 3,63:4
Vialonga, Joseph, 1952, F 23,11:6
Vian, Boris, 1959, Je 24,31:5
Vian, Philip Adm Sir, 1968, My 29,39:3
Viana, Maria da Conceicao Pacheco, 1951, Ja 19,25:2
Vianamota, Jose, 1948, Je 2,29:5
Viancour, Richard, 1961, My 10,45:3
Viane, Paul, 1946, Ag 31,15:2
Vianello, Aldo, 1965, D 22,31:1
Vianesi, Auguste, 1908, N 7,7:4
Viarda, Alexandria, 1919, F 8,15:5
Viardot, Louis, 1883, My 7,5:1
Viardot, Paul, 1941, O 16,21:1
Viau, Louise Mrs, 1945, Mr 8,23:2
Viau, Theophile, 1939, Ap 1,19:5
Viaud, Julien Mrs, 1940, Ap 4,23:2
Viault, Max, 1953, Mr 4,10:5
Viaux, Frederic, 1960, S 17,23:5
Viaux, Frederick H, 1940, Mr 5,23:3
Vibbard, C, 1891, Je 6,8:6
Vibbard, Harry L, 1938, Ja 15,15:4
Vibbert, Charles V, 1950, N 21,31:2
Vibbert, Howard C, 1937, O 23,17:2
Vibbert, William H Rev Dr, 1918, Ag 29,7:5
Vibberts, Frank G, 1954, N 10,33:3
Vibberts, Grace C Mrs, 1945, F 5,15:4
Vibert, J G, 1902, Jl 29,9:4
Vibert, James, 1942, My 1,19:2
Vicaji, Dorothy E, 1945, F 22,27:2
Vicario, Giovani, 1945, Jl 6,11:5
Viccaro, Leonard A, 1946, N 13,27:2
Vicellio, Dan, 1955, Ag 13,13:7
Vicentini, Luis, 1938, N 2,23:1
Vicentini, Roberto, 1953, O 14,29:5
Vichert, John F (por), 1948, Ja 18,60:1
Vichi, Ernesto, 1950, O 20,28:2
Vichnin, Willel, 1942, S 14,15:2
Viciano, John Sr Mrs, 1945, Ap 18,23:4
Vicini, Charles P, 1941, N 15,17:5
Vick, Charles H, 1952, F 12,27:2
Vick, Frank H, 1913, O 11,15:3
Vick, George C, 1950, Ja 14,15:5
Vick, Godfrey R, 1958, S 28,88:3
Vick, James, 1882, My 17,5:5
Vicker, Harry W, 1938, Je 14,21:5
Vickerman, Robert E, 1953, Jl 22,27:2
Vickers, Albert, 1919, Jl 13,22:5
Vickers, Alonzo Justice, 1915, Ja 22,11:4
Vickers, Arthur, 1956, Ap 4,29:1
Vickers, Carroll B, 1951, N 9,27:3
Vickers, Douglas, 1937, N 25,31:3
Vickers, George E Mrs, 1947, Je 19,21:2
Vickers, George T, 1945, Ap 17,23:2
Vickers, George T Mrs, 1954, D 27,17:4
Vickers, Harold, 1922, Ja 12,17:6
Vickers, Joseph G, 1945, S 30,46:5
Vickers, M M, 1943, N 4,23:3
Vickers, Squire J, 1947, O 24,23:2
Vickers, Squire J Mrs, 1939, O 8,49:2
Vickers, Thomas Edward Col, 1915, O 20,11:4
Vickers, Walter K, 1944, Je 13,19:4
Vickery, Herman F, 1940, F 23,15:5
Vickery, Howard F, 1951, S 24,28:2
Vickery, Howard L, 1946, Mr 22,21:1
Vickery, James C, 1952, Ag 26,25:5
Vickery, Jess F, 1951, Ja 10,27:5
Vickery, William E, 1961, N 28,37:1
Vickner, Edwin J, 1958, O 1,37:3
Vickrey, Charles V, 1966, S 19,43:3
Vicky (Victor Weisz),(death ruled suicide, Mr 1,2:4), 1966, F 24,37:1
Victor, Abraham W, 1963, S 18,39:1
Victor, Alex F, 1961, Mr 31,27:2
Victor, Alexander, 1966, Jl 13,43:4
Victor, Belle, 1944, Ja 6,23:4
Victor, Carl, 1940, F 5,17:4
Victor, Charles, 1965, D 24,17:2
Victor, Fred A (por), 1938, O 28,23:5
Victor, Fred A Mrs, 1957, F 8,23:1
Victor, Jack, 1958, S 6,17:4
Victor, Jay Mrs, 1961, Ag 31,27:4
Victor, Leon, 1937, F 7,II,8:6
Victor, Leonard B, 1960, Je 30,29:3
Victor, Louis, 1919, Ja 24,11:5
Victor, Metta V, 1885, Je 27,8:2
Victor, O Winthrop, 1957, D 18,35:2
Victor, R, 1926, My 31,1:5
Victor, Royall Mrs, 1965, Je 21,29:1
Victor Emmanuel, former King of Italy, 1947, D 29,1:3
Victor Emmanuel, King of Italy, 1878, Ja 10,5:5
Victori y Domenech, Joseph, 1945, Mr 13,23:2
Victoria, Jose Lopez de Dr, 1908, Ja 12,9:5
Victoria, Mary Louisa Princess of Saxe-Coburg-Gotha, 1861, Ap 1,1:6
Victoria, Princess, 1935, D 3,21:1
Victoria, Queen of England, 1901, Ja 23,1:1
Victoria, Queen of Sweden, 1930, Ap 5,19:1
Victoria, Vesta, 1951, Ap 8,92:1
Victorian, Marguerite Mrs, 1937, Je 2,23:6
Victorine, David, 1945, My 27,25:1
Victorius, Charles G, 1946, D 6,24:2
Victoroff, Irving, 1951, D 6,33:1
Victorson, Adeline A Mrs (A Adler), 1958, Je 5,31:6
Victorson, S Arthur Mrs, 1953, Ap 24,23:3
Victory, Vincent, 1950, O 29,93:2
Vicuna, Manuel R, 1937, Ag 5,23:5
Vida, Stephen, 1944, F 12,28:2
Vidakovich, Aleksander, 1940, F 3,13:4
Vidal, Brig-Gen, 1908, Mr 3,7:5
Vidal, Henri, 1959, D 11,34:1
Vidal, Jean, 1940, Ja 4,23:1
Vidal, U B, 1877, Je 5,1:4
Vidal y Saura, Gines, 1945, Ap 30,19:3
Vidale, Guildo L, 1961, Ap 15,21:6
Vidar, Frede, 1967, Ja 12,39:3
Vidas, Rudolph, 1938, Ag 24,21:5
Vidaver, Falk Rabbi, 1909, O 6,9:2
Videll, Peter, 1967, Mr 11,29:2
Videre, Leontine R (will), 1941, Jl 30,13:5
Vidili, Maria Rota Mrs, 1952, O 13,21:4
Vidler, Sam W, 1942, F 24,21:5
Vidmar, Milan, 1962, O 10,51:3
Vidmer, George, 1952, N 26,23:1
Vidor, Charles (funl, Jl 10,37:3), 1959, Je 5,27:1
Vidsens, George W, 1952, Jl 8,27:3
Vieban, Anthony, 1944, Ja 30,37:2
Viebig, Clara, 1952, Ag 6,21:2
Viedmann, George A, 1918, O 13,23:1
Viedt, Charles, 1953, D 23,25:2
Viehe-Naess, Ivar, 1959, Ja 26,29:5
Vieille, Blanche, 1949, S 27,27:2
Vieira, Antonio C, 1947, Ap 10,25:1
Vieira, Joseph A, 1951, D 4,33:5
Vieira, Raymundo R, 1963, Jl 21,64:4
Viel, Harry B, 1958, Ap 22,33:2
Viele, E L Gen, 1902, Ap 23,9:1
Viele, Helen R Mrs, 1937, Ja 22,21:3
Viele, Herman Mrs, 1946, My 3,22:3
Viele, John J Mrs, 1939, O 21,15:4
Viele, Kathlyne Knickerbocker, 1924, O 3,21:3
Viele-Griffin, Francis, 1937, N 14,II,10:6
Viele-Griffin, Francis Mrs, 1940, Jl 17,21:4
Vienot, Pierre (por), 1944, Jl 21,19:3
Vient, J Virginia, 1968, Jl 27,27:4
Vier, Henry J, 1960, Je 24,27:4
Viera, F, 1927, N 13,29:1
Viereck, George S, 1962, Mr 20,37:2
Viereck, George S Mrs, 1964, F 14,33:5
Viereck, Louis, 1922, S 17,30:3
Vierge, Daniel U, 1904, Je 5,7:2
Viergutz, H A, 1957, S 16,31:1
Vierheller, George P, 1966, S 19,43:2
Vierira, Antonio P, 1964, Mr 28,19:6
Vierling, Charles J, 1951, Ag 21,27:4
Vierne, Louis, 1937, Je 3,25:6
Vierra, Carlos, 1937, D 21,23:3
Viertel, Berthold, 1953, S 26,17:4
Vies, George, 1944, F 7,15:2
Vies, Jen (Sinoel), 1949, S 2,17:4
Viesselman, P W, 1946, Ag 13,27:2
Vietor, Agnes C M, 1951, F 5,23:5
Vietor, Carl L Mrs, 1963, My 13,29:4
Vietor, Clare L Mrs, 1945, Mr 26,19:5
Vietor, Eleanore W Mrs (will), 1938, Ap 13,45:2
Vietor, Ernestine G Mrs, 1937, Jl 14,21:3
Vietor, Frederick A, 1941, Je 19,21:3
Vietor, George F, 1951, Ja 18,27:2
Vietor, George Frederick, 1910, Ja 30,II,11:5
Vietor, John A, 1944, N 1,23:5
Vietor, Karl, 1951, Je 8,27:4
Vietor, Thomas F Mrs, 1957, N 14,33:4
Viets, Paul W, 1937, N 19,23:1
Vieuille, Felix, 1953, Mr 1,92:7
Vieuxtemps, Henri, 1881, Je 7,5:1
Vieweg, Frederic, 1947, Mr 4,25:4
Vieweg, Walter V R, 1960, Mr 21,29:4
Vifquain, Victor Gen, 1904, Ja 8,7:4
Vigara, Rafael M (El Zorro), 1958, My 26,24:3
Vigard, Abel A, 1947, Mr 27,27:4
Vigeant, Joseph E, 1962, N 9,26:1
Vigeant, Napoleon J, 1946, Jl 25,21:5
Vigeland, Arthur, 1965, Ja 11,45:5
Vigeland, Clarence O, 1960, Je 4,23:1
Vigelius, W M, 1919, O 17,17:5
Vigen, Theodore, 1950, F 26,76:6
Viger, George Ernest Rev, 1908, N 12,9:6
Viger, J Arthur, 1963, Ap 1,27:4
Vigeveno, Gabriel, 1952, Ag 27,27:5
Vigeveno, Henri G, 1946, N 27,25:2
Viggiano, Nicholas, 1953, D 21,31:4
Viggo, Princess of Denmark (E M Green),(funl, Jl 9,27:1), 1966, Jl 4,15:1
Vigil, Cesar, 1944, Ap 2,40:2
Vigil, Francisco De Paula Gonzalez Dr, 1875, Jl 11,5:2
Vigler, Vicountess, 1907, N 7,9:6
Viglianti, Dominic, 1943, N 10,23:4
Vignal, Paul Gen, 1920, D 3,15:4
Vignate, Mark J, 1946, D 31,17:3
Vignaud, Henry, 1922, S 19,19:4
Vigneau, Arthur W, 1959, Jl 15,29:4
Vignec, Alfred J, 1962, F 5,31:1
Vignec, Aug Mrs, 1950, Ja 17,27:5
Vigneron, Frank, 1949, Ja 7,21:4
Vigneron, Louis, 1871, S 13,4:7
Vigneron, Pierre Roch, 1872, O 29,1:6
Vigness, L A, 1947, S 23,25:3
Vignola, Pasquale, 1953, D 15,39:4
Vignola, Robert C, 1953, O 26,21:5
Vigo, Sidney G, 1942, O 29,23:1
Vigon, Juan, 1955, My 25,33:2
Vigor, Frank E, 1949, Ap 14,25:3
Vigoroux, Julia L Mrs, 1938, Ap 28,23:2
Vigouroux, George E, 1964, My 1,35:3
Vigouroux, George E Mrs, 1960, Ap 20,39:2
Viguier, Aug C, 1948, Ag 10,22:3
Vigurs, Bernard G, 1964, Mr 12,35:2
Vik, Arvid, 1960, Ja 20,31:3
Vik, Olav R, 1962, Je 30,19:6
Vikentije Prodanov, Patriarch, 1958, Jl 6,56:7
Viker, Guttorm A, 1947, My 8,25:5
Viking, Carl F, 1938, S 12,17:2
Vila, Joseph S, 1965, F 13,21:1
Vilade, Edwin H, 1961, My 10,45:4
Vilain, Viscount, 1878, N 19,5:5
Vilamajo, Julio, 1948, Ap 13,27:4
Vilanch, Bertha Mrs, 1939, Ag 4,13:4
Vilanova Melendez, Santiago, 1953, Ja 19,23:4
Vilas, Albon W Mrs, 1948, D 24,18:3
Vilas, George B, 1944, Ja 15,13:1
Vilas, George H, 1907, N 28,7:5
Vilas, Henry Chapman, 1908, Ja 29,7:5
Vilas, Malcolm G, 1940, N 13,23:6
Vilas, Royal Cooper, 1903, D 31,9:5
Vilas, Royal L Mrs, 1959, D 27,60:8
Vilas, William F (funl, Ag 29,9:4), 1908, Ag 28,7:7
Vilas, William H, 1955, N 6,87:2
Vilate, Edoardo, 1937, D 14,25:1
Vile, Henry J N, 1943, O 18,15:2
Viles, Albert L, 1959, Mr 13,26:2
Viles, Blaine S, 1943, S 10,24:2
Viles, Lawrence M, 1939, Ap 28,25:4
Viles, William P Mrs, 1954, D 16,37:5
Viletteschi, Nobili Cardinal, 1875, O 18,1:3
Vilgrain, Ernest, 1942, Ja 20,19:1
Vilim, Edison T, 1954, Ag 10,19:4
Viljoen, Benjamin J Gen, 1917, Ja 15,9:3
Viljoen, Johannes H, 1957, D 6,29:2
Vilkitski, Boris A, 1961, Ap 5,37:5
Villa, Alfonso P Count, 1968, Mr 7,43:5
Villa, Alfonso P Mrs, 1956, Ag 26,85:1
Villa, Augusto, 1942, Ag 22,13:3
Villa, Guy Sr, 1956, D 26,27:4
Villa, Joseph A, 1949, O 28,23:3
Villa, Joseph Sr, 1944, Ag 13,36:1
Villa, Luigi, 1958, S 11,33:4
Villa, Thomas C, 1957, Ag 30,19:4
Villa-Lobos, Heitor (funl, N 16,39:3; trb, N 29,II,9:3), 1959, N 18,41:1
Villain, Paul, 1941, F 7,19:2
Villaire, John J, 1966, Jl 20,41:3
Villamil, Alberto, 1957, N 19,30:3
Villandre, Abbe James D, 1921, Ag 31,13:5
Villani, Anthony A, 1962, Je 7,35:1
Villani, Mario, 1959, F 18,33:1
Villani, Richard, 1946, Je 19,21:3
Villante, Odoacre B, 1938, Ja 4,23:4
Villanueva, Jose G, 1955, Mr 26,15:5
Villanyi, Emil J, 1944, D 21,21:6
Villaobar, Marquis, 1926, Jl 10,11:4
Villaran, Luis Felipe Dr, 1920, N 6,13:2
Villard, F G Mrs, 1928, Jl 6,21:5
Villard, Harold G, 1952, Jl 21,19:5
Villard, Henry, 1900, N 13,3:3
Villard, Oswald G, 1949, O 2,80:3
Villard, Oswald G Mrs, 1962, Mr 12,31:1
Villareal, Ernest T, 1959, Jl 24,25:5
Villareal, Ernest T Mrs, 1965, Je 14,33:3
Villaret, Gustave E, 1943, F 25,21:5
Villarino, Alvaro S, 1953, Ja 25,86:3
Villars, Arthur, 1946, My 2,21:2
Villaverde, Alberto M, 1960, N 4,33:1
Villazon, Eliodoro, 1939, S 13,25:4
Villegas, Juan A, 1943, Ag 20,15:4
Villegas, Luis C, 1950, Jl 24,17:5
Villegas y Cordero, Jose, 1921, N 12,13:5
Villella, Joseph Mrs, 1968, My 4,39:5
Villelli, Joseph A, 1956, O 26,29:1
Villemero, C, 1871, My 7,1:5
Villemesant, J H L, 1879, Ap 13,2:3
Villeneuve, Camille Guyot de, 1909, My 5,11:6
Villeneuve, Rodrigue, 1947, Ja 18,15:1
Villeon, Voutard de la, 1952, My 14,27:1
Villerabel, Andre du B de la, 1938, Ja 4,23:2
Villie, Frank Mrs, 1945, O 12,23:4
Villiers, C P, 1898, Ja 17,7:2
Villiers, Clementina Lady, 1858, D 29,2:1
Villiers, Edward C, 1939, Ap 18,23:5
Villiers, Edward Hyde (Earl of Clarendon), 1914, O 4,14:4

Villiers, Frederic, 1922, Ap 6,17:5
Villiers, George H H (Earl of Clarendon), 1955, D 14,39:1
Villiers, George Henry Robert Child (Earl of Jersey), 1924, Ja 1,23:2
Villiers, J E R de, 1947, F 6,23:2
Villiers, John Henry de Baron, 1914, S 3,7:7
Villiers, Victor Albert George (Lord Jersey), 1915, Je 1,15:7
Villiger, Father, 1902, N 4,1:2
Villochi, Isabelle Mrs, 1947, Ag 15,17:3
Villon, Jacques (Gaston E Duchamp), 1963, Je 10, 31:1
Vilmar, Frederick, 1880, Je 8,8:4
Vilmorin, Philippe Leveque, 1917, Jl 12,11:6
Vilnitzky, Mrs, 1916, Ja 29,9:4
Vilsack, Carl G Mrs, 1943, Jl 10,13:6
Vilsack, Leopold, 1907, D 27,7:6
Vilter, Emil, 1940, O 31,23:1
Vina, Nestor A, 1953, S 30,31:2
Vinal, Harold, 1965, Mr 10,30:1
Vinal, John P Mrs, 1954, O 17,87:2
Vinal, Le Roy, 1952, Je 13,23:2
Vinal, Walter N Dr, 1909, S 28,9:4
Vinas, Ricardo, 1943, My 1,15:5
Vinassa, Gene, 1949, O 17,23:3
Vinaver, Steven, 1968, Jl 30,39:2
Vince, E Raban, 1955, Je 20,21:1
Vincelette, Alfred L, 1952, N 26,23:2
Vincent, Anna M, 1954, N 3,29:2
Vincent, Arthur S, 1949, D 11,91:4
Vincent, B J, 1931, Jl 19,22:1
Vincent, Bernard J Mrs, 1941, N 25,26:2
Vincent, Bro (por), 1943, Mr 16,19:3
Vincent, Bro (McConville), 1958, F 6,25:1
Vincent, Bro (Barton), 1958, Jl 17,27:4
Vincent, Calvernia W Mrs, 1939, O 30,17:5
Vincent, Calvin L, 1938, F 9,20:3
Vincent, Catherine, 1956, My 23,31:5
Vincent, Charles R, 1937, Ja 27,21:2
Vincent, Charles R Mrs, 1925, Ap 8,21:4
Vincent, Clinton D, 1955, Jl 6,27:1
Vincent, Clovis, 1947, N 15,17:3
Vincent, E Harold, 1957, Ag 14,25:3
Vincent, Edward F, 1940, O 27,45:1
Vincent, Felix A, 1912, Ja 12,13:5
Vincent, Frank, 1916, Je 21,11:5
Vincent, Frank J, 1951, S 14,25:4
Vincent, Frank W, 1946, O 29,26:3
Vincent, Frederick C, 1945, Ap 21,13:2
Vincent, Frederick P, 1940, O 19,17:5
Vincent, Geoffrey Mrs, 1964, Jl 29,33:4
Vincent, George, 1955, S 7,31:1
Vincent, George E (por), 1941, F 2,45:1
Vincent, George E, 1959, Ja 1,31:1
Vincent, George E Mrs, 1953, Ap 9,27:4
Vincent, Gibson N, 1949, F 21,23:3
Vincent, Gillis F, 1948, F 26,23:5
Vincent, Harold, 1968, Jl 11,37:5
Vincent, Harry B, 1942, Ja 23,20:2
Vincent, Hazel, 1947, N 25,31:3
Vincent, Helene, 1949, My 15,90:5
Vincent, Henry B, 1941, Ja 8,19:2
Vincent, Howell S, 1951, S 15,15:3
Vincent, James, 1918, My 12,21:1; 1957, Jl 14,72:5
Vincent, James N, 1952, S 1,17:5
Vincent, Jean-Hyacinthe, 1950, N 24,35:3
Vincent, Jesse G, 1962, Ap 21,19:1
Vincent, John Heyl Rev Dr, 1920, My 10,13:3
Vincent, John M (will), 1939, O 1,51:1
Vincent, John W, 1941, Ja 23,21:2
Vincent, Jonathan G, 1950, O 29,92:6
Vincent, Joseph P, 1950, My 31,29:3
Vincent, Katherine (Mrs H Barnes), 1962, My 28, 29:5
Vincent, Leon H, 1941, F 12,21:5
Vincent, Leon John, 1925, Je 3,23:4
Vincent, Marvin Richardson Rev, 1922, Ag 19,11:7
Vincent, Merle D, 1958, Mr 7,23:4
Vincent, Percy (por), 1943, Ja 24,43:2
Vincent, Peter A, 1915, My 13,15:5; 1950, Je 2,23:2
Vincent, Ralph M, 1947, Jl 28,15:4
Vincent, Ralph W, 1946, Je 23,40:1
Vincent, Ralph W Mrs, 1954, Ap 21,29:2
Vincent, Rev Mother (J Hamilton), 1966, N 30,48:1
Vincent, Robert E, 1967, F 24,35:2
Vincent, Samuel E, 1915, Jl 20,11:4
Vincent, Stanley M, 1954, Jl 29,23:5
Vincent, Stenio, 1959, S 4,21:1
Vincent, Sydney A, 1967, F 11,29:4
Vincent, Thomas, 1904, F 19,9:5
Vincent, Thomas K, 1956, S 12,37:3
Vincent, Thomas McCurdy, 1909, D 2,9:5
Vincent, U Conrad, 1938, D 19,23:2
Vincent, Walter L, 1939, Ap 16,III,6:7
Vincent, Walter Mrs, 1958, Ap 8,29:3
Vincent, Walter W (funl, My 14,33:3), 1959, My 11, 27:3
Vincent, Wesley Grove Dr, 1922, Ja 4,13:5
Vincent, William, 1960, Ag 27,19:5
Vincent, William C, 1956, D 12,39:1
Vincent, William G, 1946, Ja 30,25:4
Vincent, William H H, 1941, Ap 25,19:5
Vincent, William J, 1944, Jl 19,19:4; 1952, N 2,88:1
Vincent, Zola Mrs, 1963, S 15,86:4
Vincent de Paul Mother, 1924, F 15,15:6
Vincenti, G Rudolph, 1944, N 21,25:3
Vincentiis, Cesare di, 1940, Ja 7,48:3
Vincenty, Francisco, 1938, Ap 12,23:3
Vinciguerra, Domenico, 1951, Jl 15,60:6
Vinciguerra, Domenico Mrs, 1943, Ap 6,21:1
Vinciguerra, Michael, 1962, Mr 27,38:1
Vincnet, George E, 1941, My 20,23:6
Vincze, Charles, 1954, F 2,27:3
Vine, Billy, 1958, F 11,31:2
Vine, Dave, 1955, Ap 18,23:4
Vine, Joe, 1946, Ap 26,21:2
Vine, Vernon, 1961, Mr 19,89:1
Vineberg, Abel, 1959, S 10,35:5
Vineberg, Hiram N (por), 1945, My 5,15:1
Vineberg, Shepard, 1943, Jl 13,21:1
Vineburg, Alexander, 1966, F 12,25:4
Vineburg, Sidney, 1959, Ap 7,33:1
Vines, Carol, 1946, Mr 17,45:2
Vines, Edward H 3d, 1958, Jl 28,23:5
Vines, Oscar L, 1963, D 29,43:2
Vinet, Camille, 1956, Ja 27,23:2
Vinet, Camille Mrs, 1955, S 3,15:6
Viney, R M, 1956, Ag 1,12:6
Vingut, George T, 1921, N 17,17:4
Vinicky, Joseph J, 1960, Ja 22,27:2
Vinikas, Matas J, 1961, F 11,23:3
Vining, A J, 1949, Ja 17,19:6
Vining, Albert W, 1952, Jl 14,17:3
Vining, Archie, 1957, D 31,17:4
Vining, Edward Payson, 1921, Ja 1,9:4
Vining, James Parvis, 1924, Mr 23,X,8:2
Vining, L G, 1955, Mr 6,88:1
Vining, Robert E, 1949, O 12,29:3
Vining, Willard C, 1944, D 7,25:2
Vinnedge, Kenneth H, 1959, Mr 6,25:2
Vinnedge, Robert R, 1942, S 3,19:4
Vinnedge, Sydney D, 1946, N 25,27:4
Vinogradof, Valentino, 1949, Je 29,13:6
Vinogradoff, Paul Sir, 1925, D 21,21:3
Vinogradov, Valdmir N, 1964, Jl 31,23:1
Vinokur, Grigory Mrs, 1966, My 26,47:2
Vinoy, Joseph, 1880, Ap 30,2:2
Vinson, Arthur F, 1963, D 7,27:2
Vinson, Carl Mrs, 1950, N 17,27:3
Vinson, Edward S Mrs, 1937, Ag 18,19:2
Vinson, Ernest, 1951, O 14,88:4
Vinson, Frank H Mrs, 1946, Ag 1,23:2
Vinson, Frank O, 1961, Je 23,29:3
Vinson, Fred M, 1953, S 8,1:2
Vinson, George W Mrs, 1943, My 26,23:1
Vinson, Joseph Sanford, 1925, S 1,21:6
Vinson, Lewis A, 1954, Ja 1,23:2
Vinson, Robert E, 1945, S 3,23:4
Vinson, Robert W, 1952, D 30,19:1
Vinson, Thomas M, 1952, N 17,25:4
Vinson, William S, 1948, Ja 20,23:1
Vinsonhaler, Frank, 1942, S 2,23:3
Vinter, Alex V, 1958, Mr 11,29:5
Vinti, Carlo, 1966, Je 21,43:4
Vinton, A H Rev, 1881, Ap 27,5:4
Vinton, Alexander H Bp (funl, Ja 21,13:4), 1911, Ja 18,9:4
Vinton, Alfred, 1949, N 9,27:3
Vinton, Arthur Dudley (funl, S 15,9:7), 1906, S 14,7:5
Vinton, Arthur R, 1963, F 28,4:6
Vinton, David H Brigadier-Gen, 1873, F 22,2:3
Vinton, Elizabeth M, 1878, Je 26,8:3
Vinton, F L, 1879, O 7,2:4
Vinton, Francis Rev Dr, 1872, S 30,1:7
Vinton, Frederic P, 1911, My 21,II,11:4
Vinton, Frederick, 1923, D 31,13:5
Vinton, Guy V, 1942, Je 1,13:1
Vinton, Karl R, 1960, S 14,43:3
Vinton, Lindley, 1944, Mr 16,19:6
Vinton, Stallo, 1946, N 7,31:3
Vintschger, Edward J, 1955, Jl 13,25:5
Viola, Cherubino, 1948, My 7,23:3
Violet, Henry A, 1958, Ap 3,31:1
Violet, Marchioness of Donegall, 1952, O 15,31:4
Violett, Atwood, 1944, Je 1,19:2
Violett, Atwood Mrs, 1944, Ag 7,15:1; 1957, N 24,87:1
Violett, Lanier, 1945, Jl 5,13:4
Violette, Abel J, 1951, My 13,90:1
Violette, Louis, 1950, Ap 15,15:2
Violette, Maurice, 1960, S 10,21:4
Viollet-le-Duc, E E, 1879, S 19,5:6
Viollis, Andree, 1950, Ag 10,25:3
Vion, Charles J Mrs, 1961, N 28,32:7
Vione, Arthur Mrs, 1950, S 2,15:4
Vioni, Alfred, 1945, Ja 10,23:3
Viple, Marius, 1949, N 2,27:4
Vipond, Jonathan, 1954, N 13,15:1
Vipper, Robert G, 1955, Ja 1,13:6
Viquez, Cleto V (por), 1937, S 24,21:1
Vir Den, Ray (funl, D 1,35:4), 1955, N 28,31:5
Virchow, Hans, 1940, Ap 9,23:3
Virden, Clara L, 1948, Ap 11,72:4
Virden, Elizabeth W, 1949, My 11,29:4
Virden, Thomas J, 1955, N 19,19:1
Virden, Thomas J Mrs, 1961, Ja 26,29:1
Virden, William H, 1944, D 13,24:2
Virgien, Carl E, 1920, D 29,11:4
Virgien, Charlotte A Mrs, 1920, D 29,11:4
Virgil, Joseph Mrs, 1949, Ja 18,23:4
Virgin, Edward Warren Rev, 1910, S 19,7:6
Virgin, Herbert W, 1954, O 28,35:3
Virgin, Samuel Henderson Rev Dr, 1911, S 19,13:2
Virginia Siemers, Mother, 1944, N 1,23:4
Virgo, Wilfred, 1951, Mr 6,27:2
Virkus, Frederick A, 1955, Ja 25,25:2
Virta, Arthur F Rev, 1948, Ag 29,59:5
Virtue, John R, 1945, Ja 17,21:2
Virtue, William D, 1958, S 2,25:4
Virtue, William J, 1948, Ap 30,23:3
Visaggio, Prospero Mrs, 1956, N 4,87:2
Visanska, Bertha, 1948, O 26,31:2
Visart, Henry R, 1958, Ag 1,21:4
Visca, Angelo, 1951, Ap 21,17:5
Viscarra, Guillermo, 1942, Ja 6,24:2
Vischer, J D Col, 1864, Jl 15,4:6
Vischer, Peter Mrs, 1950, Je 9,23:4
Visconti, Vincent, 1951, O 23,29:2
Viscount, Sylvester, 1948, O 31,88:8
Visel, Harry A, 1943, My 31,17:2
Visher, John E Mrs, 1947, D 2,29:6
Visher, Stephen S Mrs, 1967, O 26,47:2
Vishinsky, Andrei Y (funl, N 27,4:7), 1954, N 23,1:5
Vishnevsky, A, 1948, N 15,26:2
Vishnevsky, David N, 1951, F 23,27:4
Vishnevsky, Vsevolod, 1951, Mr 2,25:2
Visier, Lodewyk E, 1944, Ap 17,23:4
Visintainer, Alfred A, 1948, S 28,27:2
Visknisskki, Guy T, 1949, S 7,30:6
Vislocky, Alexis G, 1956, O 5,25:4
Visnapuu, Henrik, 1951, Ap 7,15:5
Visone, Frank A, 1962, O 27,25:2
Vissa, Leo, 1924, Jl 18,13:3
Visscher, Henry, 1922, S 22,15:5
Visscher, Hugo, 1947, My 21,25:5
Visscher, William L, 1938, Jl 12,20:1
Vissell, Trester W, 1949, O 7,31:1
Visser, Albert, 1948, Ja 10,15:1
Visser, Cornelia W Mrs, 1944, Ap 19,10:5
Visser, Lodewijk E, 1942, My 3,53:3
Vissering, Gerard, 1937, D 20,27:5
Vissers, Aloysius, 1940, D 21,17:5
Vistreich, Fernand Mrs, 1962, N 5,31:5
Visvesvaraya, Mokshagundam, 1962, Ap 15,81:1
Vita, Vicente, 1942, Ap 22,24:3
Vital, Fezas, 1953, Ja 23,20:3
Vital, Fred, 1954, Ag 9,17:2
Vitale, Albert H, 1949, S 9,26:2
Vitale, Angelo, 1952, D 15,25:5
Vitale, F, 1933, F 27,15:5
Vitale, Giuseppe, 1917, S 18,9:6
Vitale, Michael, 1965, O 26,45:5
Vitale, S George, 1953, My 30,15:5
Vitale, Salvatore, 1947, Ag 24,58:1
Vitale, Vincenzo Mrs, 1951, My 13,88:4
Vitale, William J, 1959, Mr 16,31:3
Vitali, Severino, 1958, Ja 14,33:2
Vitalone, Edward F, 1959, Je 27,23:2
Vitaly Maximenko, Archbishop, 1960, Mr 22,37:1
Vitanza, Joseph, 1965, Je 4,35:4
Vitch, Ludovic, 1873, Je 7,5:4
Vitchestain, Joseph H, 1943, S 21,23:2
Vitek, Ignatius, 1944, S 30,13:5
Vitelli, Francesco Mrs, 1941, D 9,31:2
Vitelli, Salvatore, 1944, Ja 28,17:4
Vitello, Nicholas, 1961, Jl 15,19:2
Viterbo, Dario, 1961, N 12,86:7
Viterbo, Patricia, 1966, N 11,39:1
Viti, Eugenio, 1952, Mr 10,21:6
Viti, Henry A Sr, 1948, D 12,92:3
Viti, Marcel A, 1952, My 7,27:5
Vititoe, David, 1943, Ag 14,11:5
Vito, Stella de Mrs, 1943, Ap 8,23:2
Vitolo, Dominick, 1942, Je 6,13:1
Vitolo, Frank E, 1938, D 18,49:3
Vitolo, Michael J, 1965, Ja 7,31:5
Vitrolles, Regis de Baron, 1940, O 3,12:5
Vitrone, Guido E, 1953, F 24,25:4
Vitry, Ermin, 1960, Jl 11,29:2
Vitt, Bruno C, 1966, F 12,27:3
Vitt, John C, 1942, Ag 8,11:4
Vitt, Oscar, 1963, F 1,10:8
Vittinghoff, Hans, 1943, My 27,28:7
Vittmar, A E F, 1903, S 16,9:6
Vittorini, Domenico, 1958, Mr 11,29:3
Vittorini, Elio, 1966, F 15,36:1
Vittorio, Giuseppe di, 1957, N 4,29:1
Vittorio Emanuel, Prince, 1946, O 17,23:3
Vittum, Harriet E, 1953, D 17,37:2
Vitullo, John C, 1948, O 20,29:2
Vivanti, Annie, 1942, F 26,19:5
Vivarttas, Percie A, 1950, D 25,19:3
Vivash, Ruth A Mrs, 1942, Ja 18,42:1
Vivaudou, Victor, 1954, F 20,17:4
Vivian, Alfred, 1943, O 25,15:4
Vivian, Fred G, 1945, Ap 15,14:3
Vivian, George Sr, 1944, Ja 7,17:4
Vivian, James T, 1937, S 12,II,7:3

Vivian, John C, 1964, F 12,34:1
Vivian, John F I, 1954, Ag 14,15:4
Vivian, John P, 1948, Ag 19,21:3
Vivian, John W, 1953, Jl 21,23:1
Vivian, Leslie L (por), 1943, My 19,25:1
Vivian, Leslie L Mrs, 1940, S 11,25:2; 1967, Ja 23,43:2
Vivian, Lord, 1940, D 30,17:3
Vivian, Percival, 1961, Ja 16,27:1
Vivian, Percival Mrs, 1949, N 20,93:1
Vivian, Robert, 1944, F 1,20:3
Vivian, Ruth, 1949, O 25,27:6
Vivian, Thomas J, 1925, D 16,25:4
Vivian, Thomas J Mrs, 1943, My 4,23:2
Vivian, William J, 1940, Je 14,21:4
Vivian, William O, 1961, N 15,43:4
Viviani, Clito, 1949, Ja 8,15:2
Viviani, Marie V Mrs, 1940, Ja 17,21:5
Viviani, Raffaele, 1950, Mr 23,36:1
Viviani, Rene, 1923, F 17,13:5; 1925, S 11,23:5
Viviano, Anth J, 1948, S 25,17:6
Vivis, Charles F de, 1963, Ap 15,29:3
Vivona, Alex A, 1963, S 11,43:4
Vize, Vladimir, 1954, F 26,19:3
Vizetelly, Bertha M Mrs, 1940, My 1,23:2
Vizetelly, E H, 1903, Ap 26,7:4
Vizetelly, Ernest Alfred, 1922, Mr 27,15:5
Vizetelly, Frank H, 1938, D 22,21:1
Vizzini, Calogero, 1954, Jl 13,12:4
Vlachos, Constantine A, 1948, Ag 28,15:1
Vlachos, Nicholas P, 1943, Ap 16,21:4
Vladeck, B Charney, 1938, O 31,1:4
Vladeck, B Charney Mrs, 1967, Ja 5,34:3
Vladeck, William C, 1958, Mr 21,21:4
Vladimir (Met), 1959, D 19,27:2
Vladimirov, Peter, 1953, S 13,85:1
Vladimirovich, Andrew (mem ser set, N 19,31:1), 1956, N 11,82:4
Vladimirsky, Mikhail F, 1951, Ap 3,27:1
Vlaminck, Maurice de, 1958, O 12,86:1
Vlaming, Julian, 1947, Ag 24,56:3
Vlamynck, Octave, 1958, Ap 17,31:4
Vlas, Bouwe, 1946, Jl 27,17:6
Vlasaty, Stephen Sr, 1951, D 22,15:4
Vlases, George Jr, 1967, S 15,44:4
Vlasov, Aleksandr V, 1962, S 26,39:4
Vlasov, Kuzma A, 1964, O 1,35:5
Vlassov, Alex, 1954, Jl 25,69:4
Vlasto, Demetrius J, 1944, My 19,19:2
Vlchek, Frank J, 1947, Je 11,27:1
Vleit, Harry, 1939, Jl 30,19:5
Vletin, Robert, 1910, Jl 13,7:6
Vliegen, Willem H, 1947, Jl 1,25:2
Vliet, Clarence K (por), 1947, Ap 8,27:5
Vliet, Willard S, 1952, N 9,91:2
Vlugt, Willem de, 1945, Mr 22,23:4
Vlymen, W T, 1934, Ag 17,15:3
Vna Name, Ralph L (Mar 10), 1963, Ap 1,36:3
Vocco, Rocco, 1960, D 7,43:2
Voccoli, Louise, 1953, Ja 27,25:2
Vocke, William, 1907, My 15,9:5
Vockel, Steward M, 1965, Ap 5,31:4
Vockins, Reginald C H Sr, 1949, My 15,90:4
Vockrodt, Frank A, 1943, D 10,27:4
Vodenlitch, Leonidas, 1958, O 21,33:3
Vodge, Allan E, 1909, S 25,11:4
Vodges, Russell T, 1954, D 3,27:1
Vodishka, Emery, 1939, Ja 24,19:5
Vodnay, Matthew, 1939, My 27,15:6
Vodrey, William H, 1954, D 20,29:2
Voecks, Albert, 1940, Je 8,15:5
Voege, Harry W, 1952, Ja 25,21:4
Voege, Walter T, 1940, Ap 17,23:5
Voegel, Carl, 1955, D 10,21:3
Voegele, Walter O, 1959, N 26,37:6
Voegele, William F, 1949, Je 21,25:1
Voegeli, Henry E, 1943, D 29,17:2
Voegelin, Frederick, 1940, Mr 14,23:2
Voegelin, John E, 1937, N 25,31:5
Voegelin, Nettie H Mrs, 1941, N 4,26:3
Voegthen, Henry J, 1952, Jl 21,19:5
Voegtlen, John S, 1945, Ag 22,23:5
Voegtlin, Arthur, 1948, Ja 20,23:3
Voegtlin, Carl, 1960, Ap 11,31:4
Voegtte, Joseph, 1916, My 10,13:7
Voehl, Gustav F, 1949, N 1,27:5
Voehl, Louis, 1951, Jl 27,19:3
Voehl, Philipine E Mrs, 1940, Jl 15,15:5
Voeks, Milton R, 1959, N 3,31:3
Voelbel, Gordon W, 1965, N 20,35:6
Voelbel, Walter H, 1964, Je 15,29:2
Voelchert, Litta, 1940, Ag 24,13:5
Voelcker, Carl, 1952, O 28,31:3
Voelkel, Titus Bernhard Dr, 1916, N 5,23:4
Voelker, Alphonsus F, 1952, Mr 30,92:2
Voelker, Bernard H, 1948, S 15,31:2
Voelker, John P, 1940, My 12,48:1
Voelker, Joseph A, 1952, Jl 14,17:5
Voelker, Otto H, 1946, S 5,27:5
Voelker, Robert, 1966, Ap 14,39:3
Voelker, William C, 1949, Ja 12,28:2
Voelkl, Richard C, 1950, My 23,29:4
Voelkner, George A, 1951, My 27,68:5
Voell, Leo J Sr, 1947, Jl 8,23:2
Voevodsky, George, 1950, Jl 5,31:1
Vogan, Frank M, 1937, S 17,25:1
Vogdes, Judson F Sr, 1947, Mr 27,27:1
Voge, Charlotte, 1943, Ag 16,15:1
Voge, Richard, 1942, Ap 27,15:5
Voge, Richard G (por), 1948, N 18,27:1
Vogel, Albert, 1941, S 5,21:6
Vogel, Albert Rev, 1920, O 3,22:1
Vogel, Andrew Mrs, 1946, N 19,31:1
Vogel, Anna B Mrs, 1960, Jl 12,35:2
Vogel, Benny, 1947, Ag 4,17:5
Vogel, Bernard, 1955, Jl 22,23:5
Vogel, Bernard W, 1960, S 2,23:1
Vogel, Bertram, 1967, O 1,84:2
Vogel, C Herman, 1953, S 5,15:3
Vogel, Charles, 1947, F 7,24:2
Vogel, Charles A, 1955, F 16,29:3
Vogel, Clayton B, 1964, N 28,21:4
Vogel, Cornelius, 1948, N 27,18:2
Vogel, Edna C, 1953, Ap 19,90:4
Vogel, Edward Mrs, 1943, O 19,19:4
Vogel, Edwin C Mrs, 1960, Ag 5,23:3
Vogel, Eugene W, 1957, F 16,17:4
Vogel, Fred, 1953, Ap 3,23:3
Vogel, Frederick C, 1945, Ag 22,23:4
Vogel, Frederick W (funl, Ag 20,9:5), 1917, Ag 17,9:6
Vogel, George G, 1949, N 7,27:2
Vogel, George H, 1943, N 10,23:3
Vogel, George J, 1954, Mr 3,27:2
Vogel, George Mrs, 1962, My 9,43:3
Vogel, Hans, 1945, O 7,44:6
Vogel, Harold, 1952, Jl 10,31:4
Vogel, Harry, 1956, Mr 13,27:5
Vogel, Harry B, 1951, Mr 25,74:2
Vogel, Heinrich, 1939, Jl 21,19:5
Vogel, Henry, 1939, N 9,23:5
Vogel, Henry J, 1907, S 5,9:5
Vogel, Herman, 1917, N 28,13:5
Vogel, Isadore, 1964, D 2,50:7
Vogel, John, 1950, My 21,104:3; 1951, Jl 21,13:5
Vogel, John J, 1941, My 27,23:5; 1941, D 27,19:2
Vogel, John L, 1943, N 30,27:1; 1954, Ag 24,21:4
Vogel, John W, 1951, Ja 3,27:4
Vogel, Joseph, 1958, Jl 22,28:1
Vogel, Joshua F (will, Je 12,III,7:2), 1938, Je 1,23:1
Vogel, Julius, 1957, Mr 17,86:7
Vogel, Kurt R, 1955, Je 8,29:2
Vogel, Les Sr, 1950, Ag 18,21:3
Vogel, Martin, 1938, My 20,19:3
Vogel, Morris A Mrs, 1959, Jl 14,29:3
Vogel, Morris Mrs, 1950, Ja 17,27:5
Vogel, Nathan, 1946, O 17,23:3; 1959, F 5,31:4
Vogel, Oscar, 1952, N 14,1:7
Vogel, Paul, 1951, N 21,25:1
Vogel, Robert A, 1948, Ja 1,23:2
Vogel, Samuel Mrs, 1955, Jl 22,23:2
Vogel, Theodore F, 1947, Ap 11,25:2
Vogel, Theodore F Mrs, 1947, Ag 13,23:2
Vogel, William, 1905, Mr 21,11:5
Vogel, William H, 1939, Jl 2,15:3
Vogel, William M, 1944, O 9,23:4; 1945, Ja 16,19:3
Vogel, William P, 1952, Ag 11,15:5
Vogel, William R Sr, 1944, O 7,13:3
Vogelbach, Oscar, 1959, D 29,26:2
Vogelback, William E, 1960, Ap 18,29:5
Vogeler, Edwin B, 1955, Jl 1,21:3
Vogeler, Henry, 1946, O 16,27:4
Vogeler, Willy R, 1953, D 18,29:3
Vogelgesang, Carl T Mrs, 1949, Ap 27,27:3
Vogelgesang, Heinrich Capt, 1910, Mr 24,9:4
Vogelius, Charles F, 1940, Jl 11,19:5
Vogell, Astraea C, 1949, Ap 12,29:3
Vogelsang, Erwin Mrs, 1946, O 23,27:5
Vogelson, John A, 1942, Ja 18,43:2
Vogelstein, Hans A, 1960, Ag 8,21:3
Vogelstein, Herman, 1942, S 30,23:5
Vogelstein, Hyman, 1962, My 3,33:2
Vogelstein, L, 1934, S 24,17:1
Vogelstein, Theodor M, 1957, My 7,35:3
Vogenitz, Otto C, 1941, Ap 4,21:2
Voges, Alex, 1950, Je 23,25:4
Voges, Herbert, 1952, Je 10,27:3
Voget, Arnold, 1939, N 30,21:5
Voget, William E, 1956, O 15,25:2
Voghera, John B, 1945, F 20,19:4
Vogler, Ernie, 1946, Ag 11,45:2
Vogrich, Max, 1916, Je 11,21:5
Vogt, Adolph W, 1939, N 21,26:4
Vogt, Albert E, 1947, Ag 30,15:5
Vogt, Alfred, 1943, D 11,15:5
Vogt, Arthur C, 1956, F 23,27:2
Vogt, Carl V, 1945, Je 5,19:5
Vogt, Curt G, 1958, Ja 15,39:4
Vogt, Edward Leclerc, 1913, Ap 10,11:6
Vogt, Ernest J, 1951, S 28,31:1
Vogt, Francis C, 1941, N 20,27:4
Vogt, Frederick C, 1950, N 13,27:5
Vogt, Frederick Mrs, 1948, O 7,30:2
Vogt, G S, 1881, Ap 16,5:4
Vogt, George W, 1940, Ag 21,19:2
Vogt, Gustave, 1924, Ag 6,13:3
Vogt, Harold J, 1960, F 26,27:3
Vogt, Harry F, 1951, Ap 4,29:3
Vogt, Harry P, 1949, Ag 5,19:3
Vogt, Henry, 1957, O 31,31:4
Vogt, Henry A (por), 1941, F 7,19:4
Vogt, Henry H, 1948, N 26,23:3
Vogt, John H, 1940, D 31,15:1
Vogt, Joseph, 1938, Ap 20,23:5; 1949, Ja 24,19:5
Vogt, Julie A, 1958, My 17,21:3
Vogt, Leo J Rev, 1953, F 21,13:6
Vogt, Louis A, 1940, Mr 18,18:2
Vogt, Louis F, 1952, S 2,23:5
Vogt, Oskar, 1959, Ag 11,27:2
Vogt, Phil, 1949, Ap 20,27:3
Vogt, William, 1968, Jl 12,31:1
Vogtman, William A Mrs, 1950, F 3,23:4
Vogue, Louis de (por), 1948, Mr 3,23:5
Vohden, John J, 1957, O 6,85:1
Voice, Albert, 1958, Ag 5,27:2
Voiciekawskas, Leo J V, 1963, Ag 19,25:1
Voight, Albert, 1953, O 28,29:5
Voight, Alex F, 1938, S 29,25:4
Voight, Arno C, 1950, S 22,31:1
Voight, Charles A, 1947, F 11,27:5
Voight, Edwin F, 1954, F 16,25:4
Voight, Ernest R, 1943, Ap 1,23:2
Voight, Frank Sr, 1949, F 2,27:4
Voight, Harry A, 1950, N 1,35:3
Voight, Hazel J Mrs, 1958, D 10,5:6
Voight, Henry W, 1947, Ag 15,18:2
Voight, Lewis 3d, 1960, D 31,17:5
Voight, Richard, 1954, Mr 23,27:3
Voight, Tracy, 1943, My 29,22:4
Voight, William Mrs, 1938, Ja 20,23:3; 1963, Jl 30,29:2
Voignier, Gregoire Constant, 1921, Ap 26,15:4
Voigt, Albert, 1941, S 2,17:6
Voigt, E, 1934, Ag 28,21:1
Voigt, Vernon, 1958, D 1,29:5
Voigt, William, 1922, Ja 5,15:4
Voigtlander, Frederick O, 1953, Je 29,21:4
Voiland, Ferdinand B, 1944, Ag 20,34:4
Voinoff, Anatole E, 1965, F 10,41:2
Voislawsky, Antonie P (por), 1939, F 23,23:4
Voislawsky, Antonie P Mrs, 1963, S 30,29:4
Voislawsky, Van Rensselaer S, 1955, Ag 31,25:4
Voison, Rene L, 1952, Ja 18,27:4
Voisson, Anthony S, 1948, Mr 11,27:1
Vojtassak, Jan, 1965, Ag 14,23:5
Vokes, Herbert L, 1952, Ag 23,13:2
Vokes, Jessie, 1884, Ag 8,5:2
Vokes, Margaret Daly, 1908, Ag 28,7:5
Vokes, May (Mrs Robt Lester), 1957, S 14,19:6
Vokes, Rosina, 1894, Ja 30,8:6
Volack, John W, 1950, Mr 5,92:6
Voland, Emil L, 1941, Ja 18,15:5
Volcani, Itzhak, 1955, My 25,33:5
Volck, S Sargeant, 1964, S 2,37:2
Volcker, Paul A, 1960, F 14,84:4
Volckhausen, William C, 1925, Ap 25,15:5
Volckmann, Charles N, 1942, N 2,21:5
Volentine, Thomas J Mrs, 1952, Mr 15,13:3
Voletsky, Harry, 1943, D 5,64:5
Volgenau, Albert F, 1941, My 9,21:3
Volger, Bernard G, 1944, D 28,19:3
Volger, John N, 1941, Ja 21,21:2
Volger, Otto W, 1942, Je 28,32:2
Volgin, Vyacheslav P, 1962, Jl 6,25:1
Volicos, John N, 1944, D 27,20:2
Volin, Lazar, 1966, D 7,47:2
Volini, Camillo, 1948, Je 23,27:2
Volini, Italo F, 1950, Je 25,70:3
Voliva, Wilbur G (por), 1942, O 12,17:3
Volk, Albert A, 1950, S 9,17:3
Volk, Anthony J Sr, 1942, F 20,17:3
Volk, August, 1953, Ag 3,17:7
Volk, Charles, 1949, N 29,29:5
Volk, Eberhardt, 1948, D 28,21:2
Volk, Frederick A, 1953, Ap 14,27:5
Volk, Henry L, 1962, Je 24,68:8
Volk, John H, 1941, My 16,23:1
Volk, John J, 1940, Mr 2,13:6
Volk, Kurt H, 1962, S 4,33:3
Volk, Lester D, 1962, My 1,37:2
Volk, Lester D Mrs, 1945, Ja 27,11:5
Volk, Magnus, 1937, My 21,22:1
Volk, Ricardo, 1943, S 27,19:2
Volk, Robert W, 1946, O 27,63:3
Volk, S A D, 1935, F 8,22:1
Volk, Wilhelm, 1882, Ap 22,5:3
Volk, William, 1937, S 5,II,7:2
Volk, William Mrs, 1945, D 21,22:2
Volk, Winthrop, 1949, D 7,31:5
Volkenau, Denis Mrs, 1958, Ja 28,27:2
Volker, Frank J, 1958, My 2,27:1
Volker, Frank J Mrs, 1956, Je 6,33:6
Volker, William, 1947, N 6,27:5
Volket, Herman, 1951, Ja 14,51:2
Volkhardt, Charles E, 1951, O 26,23:2
Volkhardt, Mary B N Mrs, 1942, Jl 18,13:3
Volkhardt, William, 1939, O 7,17:4
Volkman, Sydney, 1959, Mr 16,31:3
Volkmann, Ludwig, 1947, D 11,33:4
Volkmann, Paul O, 1952, Ap 12,11:6
Volkmann, R, 1883, N 25,14:3
Volkmar, Charles, 1914, F 7,11:6

Volkmar, Leon, 1959, N 6,30:7
Volkoff, Antoine, 1943, Ap 12,23:2
Volkov, Feodor A, 1954, D 29,23:3
Volkov, Galina Tzvetckoff Mrs (Galina Talva), 1968, D 28,27:1
Volkov, Grigori I, 1962, Ag 4,19:4
Volkov, Konstantine, 1953, Ja 28,27:2
Volkwein, Reinhard, 1937, Ap 11,II,8:8
Voll, John A, 1924, Jl 28,11:4
Voll, John E, 1949, Jl 5,23:1
Vollers, Edward L, 1963, D 25,33:3
Vollers, John H, 1942, S 13,52:7
Vollhardt, Charles J, 1965, Mr 23,39:4
Vollherbst, Edward P Sr, 1952, Je 3,29:4
Vollherbst, Edward P Sr Mrs, 1946, Mr 3,46:5
Vollherbst, George C, 1946, Ag 26,25:6
Vollkommer, Martin, 1938, Ja 31,19:4
Vollmann, George Sr, 1951, Ja 3,27:1
Vollmar, August, 1967, My 7,86:4
Vollmar, Edward, 1966, Ap 6,43:1
Vollmar, John Mrs, 1945, O 24,21:1
Vollmar, William G, 1947, Mr 4,25:4
Vollmayer, Edwin J, 1949, Jl 25,15:4
Vollmer, Andreas H, 1945, Mr 8,23:2
Vollmer, Edward R, 1945, Mr 14,19:4
Vollmer, Edward R Mrs, 1949, Mr 24,27:1
Vollmer, Ernest Mrs, 1951, Mr 8,29:5
Vollmer, Fred C, 1951, F 4,76:5
Vollmer, Gustavo, 1954, Ag 31,21:2
Vollmer, H, 1955, My 16,23:4
Vollmer, Harry G, 1956, F 13,27:2
Vollmer, Henry, 1951, Jl 9,25:4
Vollmer, Henry Jr, 1961, F 7,33:1
Vollmer, Herbert E, 1961, N 9,35:4
Vollmer, John Philip, 1917, My 10,13:4
Vollmer, John W, 1952, O 17,27:4
Vollmer, Julius R Mrs, 1945, Jl 8,11:6
Vollmer, Lula (trb lr, My 15,II,3:7), 1955, My 3,31:2
Vollmer, Reinhold, 1942, D 20,44:5
Vollmer, William A, 1944, N 30,23:6
Vollmer, William B, 1953, Je 4,29:2
Vollmer, William S, 1938, Ap 28,23:1
Vollmoeller, Karl, 1948, O 19,27:5
Vollono, Vincent J, 1946, Ja 7,19:1
Vollprecht, Bruno E, 1964, Ag 18,31:4
Vologdin, Valentine, 1953, Ap 25,15:4
Volonte, Anfonso, 1957, Je 7,23:3
Volovic, Anna M Mrs, 1939, Ap 30,28:5
Volovick, Morris, 1951, O 28,85:1
Volpe, Arnold, 1940, F 3,13:5
Volpe, Dominick J, 1950, Jl 12,29:3
Volpe, I James Mrs, 1960, F 17,35:2
Volpe, James, 1967, D 2,39:4
Volpe, Joseph H, 1952, F 12,27:2
Volpe, Joseph Mrs, 1961, N 26,88:2
Volpe, Peter J, 1961, Ap 26,39:2
Volpe, Vito Mrs, 1965, Ag 23,31:4
Volpert, Samuel A, 1948, D 2,29:5
Volpert, Simon J, 1955, S 30,25:3
Volpi, Elia, 1938, N 28,15:2
Volpi, Enrico P, 1951, N 8,29:1
Volpi, Joseph J, 1949, S 3,13:5
Volpini, Msgr, 1903, Jl 10,2:4
Volpp, Hans, 1951, My 27,69:1
Volstead, Andrew J, 1947, Ja 21,23:1
Volta, Luigi, 1952, O 9,31:4
Volterra, Leon, 1949, Je 6,19:2
Volterra, Vito, 1940, O 12,17:6
Voltz, Albert L, 1939, Mr 28,24:3
Voltz, Phil W Mrs, 1956, Je 4,29:5
Volumine, Alex, 1955, Jl 5,29:1
Volz, Frederick J, 1953, Ap 25,15:5
Volz, Hans C, 1945, Ap 27,19:5
Volz, Louis E, 1951, My 28,21:5
vom Baur, Carl H, 1957, My 30,19:6
Vom Baur, Carl H Mrs, 1952, F 1,21:2
von Alvensleben, C Alvo, 1965, O 24,86:5
Von Andre, Adolph, 1911, My 12,11:4
Von Appen, Frederick, 1947, My 19,21:2
Von Bauer, Curt Mrs, 1941, Je 19,21:1
Von Baumann, Cyril, 1953, Ap 11,17:2
von Beckerath, Herbert, 1966, Mr 13,86:7
Von Belsen, Jacobus, 1937, S 29,23:5
Von Bernuth, Anto F (por), 1947, O 1,29:5
von Bernuth, Carl F A, 1959, Jl 20,25:5
von Bernuth, Frederick A Jr Mrs, 1956, Je 16,19:2
Von Bernuth, William S, 1951, Ja 9,20:6
Von Beschwitz, George M, 1945, Mr 9,19:3
Von Bevern, Joseph, 1964, Ja 23,31:4
von Biel, Heinrich, 1958, Ap 19,21:6
Von Blomberg, Adelheid M, 1949, F 3,23:5
von Bonin, Albert, 1966, Ja 5,31:3
Von Bonnewitz, Orlando R Mrs, 1938, Ja 4,23:4
Von Boos, Eugenia F Mrs, 1966, My 18,47:4
Von Borstel, Joseph W, 1956, Mr 13,27:2
Von Briesen, Anna G Mrs, 1938, F 10,21:4
Von Briesen, Arthur, 1920, My 14,11:3
Von Briesen, Fritz, 1941, Mr 8,19:2
Von Briesen, Hans, 1940, S 18,23:5
Von Brincken, Wilhelm, 1946, Ja 20,42:3
von Bruck, Carl P Mrs, 1960, Ap 8,31:4
Von Bruecke, Ernst T, 1941, Je 13,19:6
Von Cabeen, Francis A, 1947, Je 16,21:4
Von Cottendorf, Eleanor Baroness, 1939, My 13,15:3
von Cotzhausen, Frederick Baron, 1924, D 11,23:5
Von Czerny, Vincenz Prof, 1916, O 4,11:6
Von Czoernig, Helene M, 1952, Ag 30,13:7
Von Daacke, James C, 1950, Ag 9,29:5
von Dancz, John O D, 1956, Jl 28,17:4
von dem Bussche, Frederick, 1963, Ap 19,43:1
Von den Busschen, Carl F, 1950, Jl 11,31:3
von der Becke, Otto W, 1957, Ag 17,15:6
Von Der Hayden, Max A, 1947, My 6,27:1
Von der Heid, Henry, 1948, Je 29,25:3
Von der Heid, Henry (will), 1958, S 23,4:5
Von der Heide, Robert D, 1955, O 20,36:1
Von der Heide, Rudolph Mrs, 1952, Je 5,31:5
Von der Heiden, Alex, 1953, F 12,27:2
Von Der Heyt, Baron, 1874, Je 14,1:7
Von der Horst, Harry B, 1905, Jl 29,7:6
Von der Lieth, John D, 1951, S 1,11:2
von der Lieth, John F, 1961, N 29,41:4
von der Lin, Valentine, 1958, S 4,29:4
Von Der Linden, Herman, 1938, Ap 17,II,7:2
Von Der Linden, William Mrs, 1947, D 11,33:4
Von der Lippen, Frederick, 1952, Ap 22,29:2
Von Der Porten, Maximilian, 1955, Je 12,87:2
Vonder Smith, F K, 1948, Ja 23,23:5
Vonderlieth, Henry L, 1968, Ap 6,39:1
Vondermuhll, Alfred E, 1947, Je 6,24:2
VonderMuhll, Alfred Mrs, 1947, Jl 24,21:3
Vondermuhll, George A, 1966, Jl 21,33:4
Vondersmith, Phil G, 1950, My 5,22:3
Von Diosy, Alexander Gen, 1921, N 14,15:1
Von Doenhoff, Albert, 1940, O 4,23:1
von Doenhoff, Albert E, 1962, Mr 25,88:6
von Doenhoff, Helen, 1918, Ag 31,11:5
von Dohln, Henry A, 1938, D 18,49:3
von Domarus, Eilhard, 1958, F 26,27:2
Von Dreele, William H, 1953, Jl 11,11:7
Von Duhn, Edmund, 1949, D 16,31:1
Von Duhn, Gustav A, 1955, Ap 28,29:1
Von Durckheim, Louise, 1945, N 26,21:3
von Dwingelo, Harry, 1957, O 27,85:4
von Dwingelo, Henry L, 1959, F 5,31:4
Von Elm, Christian Mrs, 1944, Jl 23,35:3
Von Elm, George, 1961, My 2,37:1
Von Eltz, Theodore, 1964, O 8,43:4
von Elvers, Walter J Mrs, 1956, Jl 11,29:5
von Engeln, Oskar D, 1965, Ja 29,29:4
von Erdberg, Xever, 1963, Je 10,31:2
Von Erden, Paul, 1947, Ap 8,27:4
Von Euw, Stephen, 1955, Mr 2,27:4
von Ezdorf, Robert (cor, Mr 27,35:4), 1956, Mr 26, 29:2
von Faber du Faur, Curt, 1966, Ja 11,29:4
von Faulhaber, Ernest V, 1967, Ag 22,34:2
Von Fintel, Ernest A, 1952, Jl 26,13:4
Von Frandke, Paul W, 1943, D 22,23:3
von Frankenberg, Herbert T, 1964, Mr 21,26:6
Von Fremd, Charles, 1966, F 26,25:5
von Freytag-Loringhofen, Baron, 1924, O 21,23:4
von Fuehrer, Ottmar F, 1967, My 9,47:2
Von Gablentz, Field-Marshal, 1874, Ja 30,5:3
Von Gaertner, Louis A, 1937, D 17,32:4
von Gebhardt, Eduard, 1925, F 4,21:3
Von Glahn, August Mrs, 1949, Ap 13,29:6
Von Glahn, Henry W, 1921, D 30,15:6
von Glahn, Jack M, 1961, S 10,87:1
Von Glahn, John D Mrs, 1958, Ag 11,21:1
Von Glahn, John L, 1949, O 30,87:4
von Glahn, Theodore A, 1960, My 11,39:4
Von Gogh, Edward P Mrs, 1944, Je 3,13:3
Von Goldberg, Harold G, 1941, My 13,23:5
Von Gontard, Paul C, 1951, D 22,15:4
Von Grabill, S Becker, 1950, Ap 24,25:4
Von Greiff, Edward Sr, 1948, My 12,27:2
Von Greiffenstein, Berta, 1954, N 4,14:7
von Gross, Gustave A, 1959, Ap 22,33:3
Von Hacht, William H, 1952, D 15,25:4
von Hahmann, Ernst H, 1958, N 1,19:2
Von Hahn-Hahn, Countess, 1880, Ja 16,5:6
Von Hake, Herbert, 1941, Ag 17,35:4
Von Hallberg, Sven Jr, 1941, Mr 17,17:4
Von Hann-Kende, Fanny, 1952, Ap 15,27:3
von Hartmann, Max, 1960, D 15,43:2
Von Hartz, August, 1968, Ap 27,39:4
von Hartz, Ernest (funl, Mr 28,29:3; trb lr, Mr 30,-36:6), 1960, Mr 25,27:2
von Hasberg, Edith Baroness, 1916, N 8,13:4
Von Heine, Maximilian, 1879, O 21,5:4
Von Helmolt, Carl W, 1950, D 12,33:5
Von Herman, Edward, 1944, Ag 2,15:2
von Herwath, Hans, 1956, Ag 25,15:4
von Hesse, George L Mrs, 1963, Jl 21,65:1
Von Heydebrand, Ernest, 1924, N 18,25:4
Von Heyking, Elizabeth Baroness, 1925, Ja 6,25:5
Von Hime, Maximilian, 1879, N 20,5:5
Von Hochstetter, F, 1884, Jl 19,4:7
Von Hofe, Edward Charles, 1920, N 28,22:4
Von Hoffmann, Ferdinand A, 1954, S 11,17:5
Von Hohenhausen, Herman, 1919, F 21,13:6
Von Hohenzollern, Leopold Prince, 1905, Je 9,2:4
von Holten-Schmidt, Edward, 1962, Je 18,25:5
Von Hugel, Friedrich Baron, 1925, Ja 28,17:4
Von Humboldt, Wilhelm, 1871, Ag 26,2:5
Von Isakovics, Alois, 1947, F 26,25:2
Von Kahler, Felix, 1951, Ag 20,19:5
Von Kahler, Felix Mrs, 1953, D 18,29:4
von Kahler, Victor, 1963, N 25,19:1
von Karman, Theodore, 1963, My 8,39:1
Von Kaulbach, William, 1874, Ap 9,5:3
Von Kehler, Richard, 1943, Ja 23,13:2
Von Keller, H, 1878, F 5,5:2
von Keller, Nikolai Mrs, 1955, N 25,27:1
Von Kenzie, Guy F, 1950, O 5,31:3
Von Kersburg, Harry E, 1951, Jl 24,26:2
von Kienbusch, C Otto Mrs, 1968, Je 9,85:1
Von Kienlin, Albert, 1940, Ja 12,17:5
von Kleeck, Ernest, 1955, Ja 16,93:1
Von Klein, Carl H Dr, 1913, D 13,13:7
Von Kleinsmid, Bertha, 1945, Ja 29,14:2
von Kleinsmid, Rufus B, 1964, Jl 10,29:1
Von Klenner, Katherine E, 1949, F 6,76:2
Von Kohorn, Henry Mrs, 1954, D 1,31:2
von Kohorn, Oscar, 1963, Jl 1,29:4
Von Kokeritz, Carl O, 1941, N 6,23:3
von Kokeritz, Karl, 1958, Jl 3,25:5
Von Kokeritz, Reinhold G, 1947, Je 19,21:3
Von Kolnitz, Alfred H, 1948, Mr 20,13:6
Von Kreisler, Alex Mrs, 1937, F 24,23:3
Von Krockow, Alida, 1940, Ap 15,17:5
Von Krug, Ferdinand, 1940, My 11,19:4
Von Lambeck, Frederick K, 1950, Mr 28,32:3
Von Lehn, Richard, 1913, N 16,IV,7:5
von Lehn, Russell H, 1958, Ap 11,26:1
Von Lengerke, Carl H, 1954, Ap 5,25:5
von Lengerke, Ernst, 1962, My 29,31:6
Von Lewinski, Karl, 1951, O 30,29:1
Von Lilienthal, Albert W, 1948, F 17,25:3
von Linde, Manfred Mrs, 1962, Mr 24,8:4
Von Lingen, George A, 1907, Je 27,7:6
Von Losberg, Lester W, 1961, Ag 5,17:2
Von Lubken, Phil, 1949, Ap 15,23:1
Von Lucers, Alexander Gen, 1874, F 17,1:7
Von Manteuffel, O T Baron, 1882, N 28,2:3
von Massow, Karl W, 1957, N 19,33:1
Von Matzean, Baron, 1874, Mr 16,5:6
Von Maucher, A C, 1940, Ag 6,22:6
Von Maur, Roland, 1953, Ap 22,29:6
Von Mechow, Adolph, 1924, Ja 14,17:5
Von Meck, Vladimir Mrs, 1954, F 26,20:8
von Meister, Frederick W Mrs, 1955, S 7,31:3
Von Meyer, George L, 1950, Ja 26,27:1
Von Meyer, Johanna Mrs, 1938, Ja 21,40:2
Von Minden, Eraminda Mrs, 1942, Ap 20,21:5
von Minden, Henry, 1918, D 8,22:3
Von Mises, Richard, 1953, Jl 15,25:1
Von Mohl, Robert (see also N 6), 1875, N 7,7:1
Von Moschzisker, Robert, 1939, N 21,23:3
Von Moschzisker, Robert Mrs, 1954, N 23,35:3
Von Nardroff, Ernest R, 1938, N 6,49:2
von Nardroff, Robert, 1966, O 25,48:1
Vonnegut, Franklin, 1952, Ag 15,15:3
Vonnegut, George, 1952, Mr 10,21:6
Vonnegut, Walter, 1940, D 25,27:2
Von Neida, Frederick, 1950, F 18,15:4
von Neumann, John (funl plans;trb, F 10,87:1), 1957, F 9,19:1
Von Nidda, Thassile K, 1949, S 24,13:4
Vonnoh, Edward L Mrs, 1955, Mr 9,27:5
Von Nostitz, Erich, 1950, S 6,30:4
Von Oefele, Felix, 1954, Mr 12,22:3
Von Oehsen, Adolph Mrs, 1949, Ja 24,52:7
Von Ohl, Rudolph, 1946, Jl 17,23:1
Von Ohlen, Adolph Mrs, 1949, S 23,23:4
Von Osten, Frederic, 1952, Ja 3,27:2
Von Palm, Gustave, 1938, Ja 11,23:3
Von Pannwitz, Wolfram (will), 1966, Mr 3,26:2
Von Pein, Henry E, 1952, Mr 12,27:3
Von Phul, William (por), 1949, Ap 18,25:5
Von Pickhardt, Adolf S, 1947, Jl 2,23:6
von Pomer, Alex W, 1956, Ag 21,29:1
Von Pomer, John, 1943, Ap 14,23:5
Von Possart, Ernest, 1921, Ap 9,11:4
Von Poswik, Gisela, 1940, O 3,25:3
Von Redlich, Marcellus D R, 1946, Je 26,25:1
Von Rein, Franz Mrs, 1949, D 31,15:3
von Rhau, Henry Mrs, 1960, Ja 1,19:4
Von Ritter, Heinz F, 1956, O 15,25:4
Von Rogov, Alex O, 1948, Je 30,25:1
Von Rosen, Jonas F C, 1959, Ap 16,33:5
Von Ruck, Carl Dr, 1922, N 7,17:5
Von Rumohr, Christian A, 1964, Jl 30,27:3
Von Rumpf, William L, 1947, N 14,23:4
Von Salis, Emanuel, 1939, Mr 10,23:3
Von Saucken, Emma Mrs, 1921, O 29,13:6
von Saurma, Friedrich G, 1961, D 15,37:1
Von Schlanbush, Ove C, 1940, Jl 18,19:4
Von Schlegell, Arthur, 1953, O 5,27:3
Von Schlegell, William, 1950, Mr 23,29:2
Von Schlichten, A Mrs, 1943, F 18,23:3
von Schlichten, Alex F, 1960, F 22,17:1
Von Schlichten, Alex P, 1951, Ap 8,1:1
von Schlichten, Alexander F Rev Dr, 1968, Mr 17,80:8
Von Schlichten, Erwin, 1956, D 21,23:4
Von Schrenk, Hermann, 1953, Ja 31,15:1
von Schwabach, Paul, 1938, N 18,22:3
von Schwarzenstein, Mumm Baron, 1924, Jl 12,9:7

von Schweinitz, Han Luther Mrs, 1925, Je 20,13:6
von Seekamm, Egon F, 1958, O 22,35:4
Von Seidlitz, Carl G, 1954, Ja 7,31:1
Von Sholly, Anna I, 1964, S 19,27:5
Von Sholly, James I, 1943, O 15,19:4
Von Siemens, J G Dr, 1901, O 24,9:2
Von Sledeneck, Leopold Baron, 1937, My 4,25:3
Von Spreckelsen, Henry Mrs, 1947, N 29,13:2
von Stade, F Skiddy Sr, 1967, F 21,47:1
Von Stahl, Richard Mrs, 1953, S 14,27:3
Von Stamwitz, George C A, 1946, S 25,27:3
Von Steeg, Marcha C Jr Mrs, 1942, Ja 24,15:8
Von Stein, Robert H, 1950, S 29,27:4
von Stephany, Maximilian, 1956, Ja 22,89:1
Von Sternberg, Julius R, 1948, D 11,15:1
Von Storch, Earl Mrs, 1953, Ap 20,25:5
Von Storch, Ernest, 1944, F 28,17:5
Von Stroheim, Agnes Mrs, 1947, F 2,57:3
von Stroheim, Erich, 1957, My 13,31:1
Von Stroheim, Erich Jr, 1968, O 29,47:3
von Struempell, Adolf Dr, 1925, Ja 11,5:1
Von Stuck, F, 1928, S 1,13:3
Von Stumm, Ferdinand Baron, 1925, My 14,19:2
von Tacky, Thomas F, 1966, S 18,84:1
von Thaden, Arthur H, 1959, Jl 28,14:6
von Thaden, Frederick W, 1957, Ag 5,21:4
von Thaden, Harold, 1967, Mr 26,69:1
Von Thaden, Harold Mrs, 1941, N 24,17:3
von Thaden, Harold Mrs, 1966, N 15,41:6
Von Thaden, William, 1947, F 14,21:4
Von Tillenburg, Hugo, 1946, My 19,42:3
Von Tilzer, Albert, 1956, O 2,35:2
Von Tilzer, Harry (por), 1946, Ja 11,23:6
Von Tilzer, Jules, 1954, O 23,15:4
Von Tilzer, Will, 1952, My 15,31:5
von Tish, Joseph A, 1963, My 21,37:5
von Tornow, Georgiana, 1958, Ag 8,19:4
von Tresckon, Udo, 1885, Ja 24,5:4
von Tresckow, Walter, 1958, D 5,31:2
von Twardowski, Hans H, 1958, N 20,35:1
Von Ungern-Sternberg, Baroness, 1949, Ja 23,68:4
Von Unwerth, Frida, 1941, Je 14,17:3
Von Wahl, Constance, 1913, Ap 24,11:4
Von Wedel, Carl, 1953, Ag 29,17:3
von Wedel, Jerrold, 1963, Jl 20,19:2
Von Weise, Charles, 1946, Jl 6,15:3
Von Weise, Louis B, 1941, Mr 13,21:4
Von Weisenstein, Jacob (por), 1946, N 8,23:3
Von Werder, J F, 1879, N 18,5:3
von Wettberg, Niles W, 1965, D 1,47:2
von Wiegand, Karl H, 1961, Je 8,35:2
Von Winden, Frederick R, 1957, Mr 23,19:4
Von Wrangel, T Baron Field Marshall, 1877, N 2,1:3
Von Zastrow, Bertha Mrs, 1938, Mr 8,20:4
Von Zengen, Ernest E, 1937, My 31,16:2
von Zielinski, Carl M, 1955, Je 21,31:1
von Zuleger, Frank G, 1964, D 3,45:4
Von Zweygberg, Lennart, 1960, F 12,28:1
Voor, John B Dr, 1922, F 15,13:2
Voorde, Edward F, 1960, S 3,7:3
Voorhees, Albert V, 1945, Ap 14,15:3
Voorhees, Alex H Mrs, 1963, Jl 30,29:1
Voorhees, Allen R, 1959, Je 1,27:4
Voorhees, Amanda L, 1944, Jl 26,19:4
Voorhees, Anson A, 1940, F 14,21:6
Voorhees, B F, 1876, Ap 11,2:2
Voorhees, Carlton Mrs, 1952, Mr 28,23:1
Voorhees, Charles H, 1937, Ap 9,21:4; 1961, My 29, 19:4
Voorhees, Charles H Mrs, 1951, My 29,25:3
Voorhees, Clark G Mrs, 1947, Jl 29,21:2
Voorhees, Clifford I, 1961, My 7,86:1
Voorhees, D W, 1897, Ap 11,5:4
Voorhees, Dudley A Mrs, 1955, Mr 13,87:2
Voorhees, Dudley A Sr, 1962, Ap 10,39:4
Voorhees, Edward Burnett, 1911, Je 8,11:5
Voorhees, Edward K, 1952, My 23,21:1
Voorhees, F M, 1927, Je 15,27:2
Voorhees, Florence E, 1946, Jl 21,39:2
Voorhees, Frank D, 1956, Je 1,23:1
Voorhees, Frederick, 1951, My 29,25:1
Voorhees, G Coerte, 1964, Ap 5,86:5
Voorhees, George A, 1941, D 31,17:1
Voorhees, George V W, 1939, Ja 30,14:1
Voorhees, H Belin, 1966, D 21,39:2
Voorhees, H Russell (will), 1939, D 4,25:7
Voorhees, Harrison H Ex-Judge, 1917, Je 28,11:4
Voorhees, Harry Mrs, 1951, My 23,35:1
Voorhees, Harvey M, 1938, Jl 31,33:4
Voorhees, Helen G, 1939, D 19,26:3
Voorhees, Herbert R, 1957, F 14,27:5
Voorhees, Herbert W, 1959, Ap 22,21:2
Voorhees, Herman M, 1954, Mr 15,25:3
Voorhees, Howard C, 1949, N 4,27:3
Voorhees, Howard C Mrs, 1945, F 7,21:3
Voorhees, Irving W, 1965, F 5,31:1
Voorhees, Isaac N, 1963, O 6,88:8
Voorhees, J Dayton, 1955, O 1,19:6
Voorhees, J Stanley, 1937, Ag 25,21:4
Voorhees, James D Mrs, 1958, F 2,86:4
Voorhees, James E, 1952, Ap 22,29:4
Voorhees, James M Mrs, 1953, Mr 9,29:1
Voorhees, Jennie T, 1948, Je 30,26:2
Voorhees, John Brownlee, 1919, Ja 9,11:3
Voorhees, John D, 1959, Ag 20,26:2
Voorhees, John H, 1946, S 21,15:6
Voorhees, John J, 1948, D 24,17:2
Voorhees, John S, 1950, D 24,6:4; 1965, Mr 9,35:4
Voorhees, John S Mrs, 1960, Je 17,31:2
Voorhees, Lamar Dr, 1937, N 1,21:2
Voorhees, Louis A, 1945, Ag 16,19:2
Voorhees, Melvin H, 1948, Ap 29,23:1
Voorhees, Nelson A Mrs, 1957, O 17,33:1
Voorhees, Oscar M (por), 1947, Ag 30,15:5
Voorhees, Peter J Mrs, 1924, My 19,17:4
Voorhees, Peter Van D, 1964, My 14,35:5
Voorhees, Ralph, 1907, Ap 5,9:5
Voorhees, Ralph S Sr, 1944, Jl 28,13:4
Voorhees, Raymond B, 1960, Jl 5,31:2
Voorhees, Raymond E, 1959, S 7,13:8
Voorhees, Robert L, 1965, Mr 25,37:3
Voorhees, Shepard Mrs, 1947, Ag 7,21:5
Voorhees, Stephen F, 1965, Ja 25,37:2
Voorhees, Stephen F Mrs, 1958, Mr 26,37:2
Voorhees, Stephen H, 1940, F 12,17:6
Voorhees, Theodore, 1916, Mr 13,9:3
Voorhees, Walter, 1960, Jl 3,32:3
Voorhees, Wheeler N, 1946, Ja 19,14:2
Voorhees, William B, 1950, N 2,31:3
Voorhees, William E, 1952, Ap 4,33:6
Voorhees, William F Jr, 1963, N 27,37:1
Voorhees, William Kouwenhoven, 1921, N 10,19:4
Voorhees, William Penfield, 1914, Je 2,11:7
Voorhees, William S, 1953, My 21,31:5
Voorhees, Willis A, 1959, D 10,39:6
Voorhies, Charles H, 1903, O 13,9:6
Voorhies, Charles S, 1937, Je 22,23:3
Voorhies, George, 1913, D 16,11:5
Voorhies, MacIlburne V, 1961, Je 19,27:2
Voorhies, Peter B, 1962, My 10,37:3
Voorhis, Anna C, 1904, F 5,9:5
Voorhis, Anna H, 1952, Je 11,29:5
Voorhis, Casper J, 1951, My 9,33:3
Voorhis, Clarence G, 1952, D 27,9:1
Voorhis, Demarest, 1949, My 10,25:3
Voorhis, H H, 1885, F 1,7:3
Voorhis, Henry, 1937, Ap 1,24:1
Voorhis, J, 1878, Ja 7,5:3
Voorhis, J R, 1932, F 6,15:1
Voorhis, Jacob, 1921, Ag 4,15:6
Voorhis, John N, 1939, Ap 8,15:3
Voorhis, John W, 1954, D 10,28:3
Voorhis, Ralph N Mrs, 1951, Jl 2,23:5
Voorhis, Thomas G Mrs, 1949, Ap 27,27:5
Voorhis, Warren R, 1953, S 2,25:4
Voorhis, Warren R Mrs, 1944, D 11,23:2
Voorsanger, Elkan C, 1963, My 3,31:3
Voortman, M, 1954, S 27,41:7
Voorwinden, Aire H, 1907, O 9,11:5
Voorzanger, Johan, 1943, N 19,19:2
Voos, Arthur, 1948, Mr 23,25:4
Voos, Frederick J, 1959, Ag 23,93:2
Vopel, Heinz, 1959, Je 23,33:5
Vopicka, C J, 1935, S 5,26:1
Vorbach, George E, 1937, Mr 27,15:1
Vorce, Lafayette D, 1953, F 4,27:1
Vorce, LaFayette D Mrs, 1963, Ap 17,41:5
Vordenberg, Earl, 1948, F 1,60:4
Vordenberg, Elmer G, 1948, Ja 24,16:3
Vorenberg, Felix, 1943, Ag 11,19:3
Vorhaus, David, 1964, F 10,35:2
Vorhaus, Louis J, 1954, D 21,27:4
Vorhaus, Louis J Mrs, 1942, Ag 21,19:3
Vorhaus, Martin G, 1959, Ap 30,31:1
Vorhees, John A, 1942, Je 21,36:1; 1943, O 29,19:2
Vorhees, Ralph S Mrs, 1942, O 5,19:5
Vorhis, Arthur, 1921, Ap 13,15:6
Vorhis, Harry S, 1939, Ap 14,23:2
Vories, Allen L Mrs, 1958, Jl 17,27:1
Voris, John R Dr, 1968, Ja 18,39:1
Voris, Nathaniel H, 1939, D 27,24:5
Vorley, John S Col, 1953, Ja 3,15:5
Vorm, Willem van der, 1957, My 3,27:2
Vorm, William N H van der, 1963, F 21,9:3
Vornkahl, William F Jr, 1961, Mr 19,89:1
Vorobieff, Vladimir P, 1937, N 2,25:5
Voronin, Vladimir, 1952, O 22,27:6
Voronko, Joseph J, 1952, Je 6,23:4
Voronoff, Serge Mrs, 1921, Mr 6,21:3
Voronov, Nikolai Marshal, 1968, Mr 1,43:5
Voronov, Serge, 1951, S 4,27:1
Vorontzoff-Daskoff, Count von, 1916, Ja 29,9:6
Voroshilov, Kliment Mme, 1959, Ap 28,36:1
Vorpe, William G, 1953, O 31,17:6
Vorsanger, Ferdinand, 1946, Ag 29,27:1
Vorse, Albert White, 1910, Je 16,9:4
Vorse, Heaton Mrs, 1938, Ja 9,43:1
Vorse, Mary Heaton Mrs, 1966, Je 15,47:4
Vort, Paul W, 1961, Jl 5,33:5
Vorys, John M, 1968, Ag 27,41:1
Vorzimer, Bertha, 1945, N 5,19:2
Vorzimer, Harold J, 1963, Je 17,25:3
Vos, B Walter, 1949, Jl 27,23:4
Vos, Geerhardus, 1949, Ag 14,68:3
Vos, H, 1935, Ja 9,19:1
Vos, Herman, 1952, My 13,23:2
Vos, Herre de, 1948, F 20,27:4
Vos, Pieter J C, 1953, F 25,27:5
Vos, Simon, 1959, Jl 18,15:5
Vosahlik, Maromir, 1958, N 30,13:1
Vosburg, Alton A, 1944, Ap 29,15:3
Vosburg, Earl J, 1945, F 15,19:2
Vosburg, Edgar G, 1940, My 19,43:1
Vosburg, Nathan Henry, 1903, Jl 26,7:6
Vosburg, Old Bill, 1904, My 1,10:2
Vosburgh, Arthur S Mrs, 1947, Ag 25,17:5
Vosburgh, Carl, 1955, Mr 29,29:3
Vosburgh, Charles D, 1965, Ap 26,31:1
Vosburgh, Charles H, 1967, N 30,47:4
Vosburgh, Charles H Mrs, 1914, Ap 8,13:2
Vosburgh, Charles P, 1938, Ap 30,15:5; 1939, Ag 31, 19:5
Vosburgh, Frank A Jr, 1953, F 8,88:2
Vosburgh, Frederic L Mrs, 1939, S 16,17:2
Vosburgh, James C, 1955, F 5,15:2
Vosburgh, John R Mrs, 1963, Ap 25,33:4
Vosburgh, R, 1931, My 20,25:5
Vosburgh, Royden W Mrs, 1954, Ap 28,31:5
Vosburgh, Walter S (por), 1938, S 12,17:1
Vosburgh, William J Jr, 1962, D 3,31:4
Vosburgh, William R, 1946, Jl 18,25:2
Vose, Alden H, 1939, Ag 16,23:4
Vose, Arthur W, 1941, Mr 13,21:3
Vose, Charles R Mrs, 1954, F 1,25:5
Vose, Chester A, 1960, Je 30,29:4
Vose, George L Prof, 1910, Mr 31,11:4
Vose, Louise Gorham, 1905, S 13,9:4
Vose, Nathaniel M, 1962, Jl 30,23:4
Vose, Richard H Mrs, 1951, O 11,37:2
Vose, Royden M, 1950, D 21,29:2
Voshell, S Howard, 1937, N 11,25:3
Voshell, Samuel S Mrs, 1923, F 2,15:5
Voshell, William J, 1956, Je 27,31:2
Voska, Emanuel V, 1960, Ap 5,37:3
Voskovec, George Mrs (A Gerlette), 1958, My 28, 31:3
Voskuil, Henry J, 1951, O 9,29:4
Vosler, Irving L, 1944, F 6,42:4
Vosler, Jean F, 1959, Je 27,23:3
Vosmik, Joe, 1962, Ja 28,77:1
Vosnjak, Bogumil, 1959, Je 25,29:4
Voss, A George, 1954, S 10,23:3
Voss, Adalbert, 1917, Mr 4,21:2
Voss, Adolph G, 1938, Mr 12,17:5
Voss, Arthur E Mrs, 1959, Mr 28,17:5
Voss, Carl A Mrs, 1961, Ja 10,47:5
Voss, Caroline K N Mrs, 1941, Mr 24,17:5
Voss, Charles, 1943, N 26,23:3
Voss, Charles A, 1955, O 7,25:3
Voss, Clarence T Mrs, 1949, O 7,27:4
Voss, Detlef, 1950, Ja 1,42:4
Voss, Ed, 1953, Mr 25,23:1
Voss, Edna R, 1962, My 12,23:6
Voss, Ernst K J H Prof, 1937, Jl 23,19:7
Voss, Frank S, 1949, Ag 20,11:4
Voss, Frank S Mrs (will), 1955, O 19,28:3
Voss, Fred J, 1961, Jl 4,19:1
Voss, Fred P, 1947, Ag 6,23:5
Voss, Frederick, 1954, Ag 19,23:3
Voss, George A, 1939, S 18,19:4
Voss, Herman F, 1946, Mr 29,24:3
Voss, Jack L, 1961, My 2,37:2
Voss, John C E, 1947, Je 18,25:5
Voss, John M, 1957, Je 16,84:3
Voss, Karl, 1954, Ja 3,90:5
Voss, Otto R, 1940, My 11,19:4
Voss, Robert, 1939, Jl 31,13:5
Voss, Virginia C, 1967, My 31,49:2
Voss, William H N, 1937, Mr 16,23:3
Vossbruch, William, 1955, My 10,29:3
Vosseler, Adolph C, 1941, Jl 17,19:4
Vosseler, Allison J, 1966, Jl 10,69:2
Vosseler, G Henry Rev Dr, 1915, Mr 3,11:5
Vosseler, Jacob J, 1949, Ag 12,17:2
Vosseler, Matthew, 1951, D 29,11:3
Vosseler, Theodore L, 1947, Mr 22,13:5
Vosseler, William F (por), 1945, F 22,28:2
Vosseller, Elizabeth V, 1940, Ja 1,23:2
Vosseller, William F, 1945, Jl 2,15:5
Vossler, George Mrs, 1938, S 1,23:4
Vossler, Karl, 1949, My 21,13:3
Vossler, Lewis S, 1952, Mr 15,13:3
Votaw, Heber H, 1962, O 9,41:3
Votaw, Heber H Mrs, 1951, O 24,31:4
Votee, Milton G, 1961, Ag 10,27:1
Votee, William H, 1939, O 6,25:2
Voter, Perley C, 1953, Je 14,84:1
Votos, Anthony S, 1960, O 2,50:5
Vought, C M, 1930, Jl 26,13:3
Vought, Chance M Jr (will, S 16,33:5), 1964, Ap 4, 27:2
Vought, G Tracy, 1942, S 10,27:6
Vought, George S Sr, 1949, O 18,27:2
Vought, Glen G, 1948, Ap 20,27:5
Vought, Harry H Jr, 1955, D 1,35:3
Vought, Henry J, 1951, F 4,76:4
Vought, J Francis, 1950, Mr 9,29:4
Vought, Kimber R, 1954, N 2,27:6
Vought, Nathan F, 1939, Mr 23,23:5

Vought, Olin F, 1940, Jl 13,13:4
Vought, Theodore H, 1945, F 3,11:2
Vought, Thomas C, 1954, Ap 25,87:3
Vougt, Allen, 1953, Ja 25,86:5
Voules, Horace St George, 1909, My 5,11:7
Voulgaris, Petros, 1957, N 27,31:2
Voutier, Discoverer of the Venus of Milo, 1877, My 20,6:8
Vovsi, Miron S, 1960, Je 8,39:4
Voyevodin, Pyotr I, 1964, N 28,22:1
Voynich, Ethel L Mrs, 1960, Jl 29,25:3
Voynich, W M, 1930, Mr 20,27:3
Voynow, Richard F, 1944, S 18,19:2
Voyse, Mary Mrs, 1937, O 5,25:3
Voziou, James H, 1954, Jl 20,19:3
Vrabcak, Joseph F, 1940, Mr 13,23:5
Vrabek, John S, 1957, Ja 18,21:4
Vradenburg, Irving, 1943, D 8,23:3
Vranian, Margaret Mrs, 1938, Jl 13,21:4
Vranizan, John H, 1963, S 9,27:2
Vraz, Victor E, 1939, S 24,43:4
Vrebenski, Bogoslav, 1944, N 27,23:3
Vredenburg, E H, 1903, My 27,9:3
Vredenburgh, H Kirby, 1950, N 22,25:5
Vredenburgh, John S Mrs, 1946, Ag 1,23:2
Vredenburgh, Peter, 1941, D 19,25:5
Vredenburgh, Peter 3d, 1956, Mr 20,23:4
Vredenburgh, Sally K, 1941, Je 17,21:4
Vredenburgh, William H, 1920, My 16,22:4
Vreeland, Addison G, 1904, S 10,16:3
Vreeland, Albert R, 1964, Mr 9,29:2
Vreeland, Arnold W, 1957, Ag 18,82:8
Vreeland, Asher H, 1909, Je 18,7:3
Vreeland, Charles E Rear-Adm, 1916, S 28,9:5
Vreeland, Charles M, 1924, S 1,13:4
Vreeland, Clarence L, 1941, F 23,40:2
Vreeland, Cornelius D Mrs, 1941, S 19,23:3
Vreeland, Donald R, 1946, Ag 12,21:4
Vreeland, E B, 1936, My 9,15:4
Vreeland, Elizabeth, 1944, F 27,38:2
Vreeland, Elmer C, 1951, Ja 13,15:5
Vreeland, Frank, 1946, Ja 7,19:2
Vreeland, Frank P, 1958, My 20,33:5
Vreeland, Fred B, 1945, F 2,19:4
Vreeland, Frederick D, 1958, Jl 10,27:4
Vreeland, George A, 1943, Mr 23,20:3
Vreeland, George E, 1943, D 31,15:1; 1966, S 24,23:4
Vreeland, George F, 1937, F 17,22:2
Vreeland, Harold W, 1950, N 30,33:4
Vreeland, Henry N, 1954, Ap 30,23:5
Vreeland, Herbert H (por), 1945, F 2,19:3
Vreeland, Herbert H, 1967, Mr 9,39:3
Vreeland, Howard R, 1948, Ja 25,56:3
Vreeland, Jacob M, 1904, Ja 26,9:6
Vreeland, James H, 1940, Jl 2,21:3
Vreeland, James H Mrs, 1949, Je 10,28:3
Vreeland, James P Sr Mrs, 1958, N 11,30:5
Vreeland, Jeannette, 1939, Jl 22,15:5
Vreeland, John Beam, 1923, Jl 3,13:5
Vreeland, John D, 1949, Je 1,31:3
Vreeland, John Van B, 1903, Ag 24,2:4
Vreeland, Kenneth W, 1961, O 29,88:4
Vreeland, Leroy D, 1949, Mr 20,76:6
Vreeland, Louis B, 1966, F 26,25:6
Vreeland, Mary M, 1944, F 22,24:2
Vreeland, Oliver P, 1941, O 27,17:6
Vreeland, Ray A, 1951, Jl 20,21:5
Vreeland, Richard S, 1948, O 4,23:6
Vreeland, Roger S (name cor, N 11,29:2), 1958, N 10,29:3
Vreeland, Stephen B, 1968, S 24,47:1
Vreeland, T Reed, 1966, Ag 5,31:4
Vreeland, Wallace N, 1946, Ja 9,23:2
Vreeland, Walter J, 1939, Ja 17,22:4
Vreeland, William C, 1942, F 10,19:1
Vreeland, William N, 1948, N 8,21:6
Vreeland, Williamson U, 1942, N 7,15:5
Vreeland, Williamson U Mrs, 1947, Mr 8,13:2
Vries, Daniel de Mrs, 1952, S 28,76:8
Vries, Louis de, 1940, Mr 12,23:4
Vries, Maurits de, 1946, D 1,76:3
Vrijenkoek, Machiel, 1947, Mr 20,27:3
Vrionides, Christos, 1962, Ja 1,23:4
Vrionis, James, 1944, Ja 29,13:3
Vroman, Mary E, 1967, Ap 30,86:3
Vroom, C, 1877, Ag 6,8:3
Vroom, Edwin I, 1937, Jl 18,II,7:3
Vroom, Garret Dorset Wall, 1914, Mr 5,9:4
Vroom, George H, 1957, My 3,27:2
Vroom, Lodewick, 1950, Jl 6,27:1
Vroom, Peter D, 1956, Mr 16,23:6
Vroom, Peter D Ex-Gov, 1873, N 19,2:3
Vroom, Robert A, 1962, Mr 28,39:4
Vroom, Robert D H, 1955, N 27,88:5
Vroom, William L, 1966, Ag 2,33:2
Vrooman, Carl, 1966, Ap 10,76:2
Vrooman, Clare M, 1944, F 22,24:2
Vrooman, Fred C, 1903, O 25,7:6
Vrooman, Lucian Mrs, 1911, Je 16,9:3
Vrooman, Morrell Sr, 1959, N 10,47:3
Vrooman, William A, 1949, F 19,15:5
Vrooman, William A Mrs, 1952, F 20,29:5
Vrooman, William B, 1943, N 6,13:6
Vrooman, William H, 1937, Mr 25,25:3
Vroome, Elwood P, 1944, Ap 20,19:6
Vrtiak, Emil G, 1939, Ag 9,17:5
Vu-wei, K, 1927, Ap 2,17:4
Vucassovich, Joseph M, 1952, Ap 19,15:2
Vucetic, Peter P, 1957, N 22,26:1
Vucky, Gustav, 1963, F 21,9:4
Vuedensky, Alexander I, 1946, Jl 27,17:3
Vuida de Barrios, Petra C, 1943, Jl 24,3:6
Vuillard, Edouard, 1940, Jl 12,15:2
Vuillemin, Joseph, 1963, Jl 25,25:2
Vuillemot, Harry L, 1948, Jl 18,52:7
Vuilleumier, Ernest A, 1958, O 7,35:3
Vukcevich, Ivo Mrs, 1965, My 29,27:4
Vukovich, Bill (funl, Je 5,V,10:4), 1955, My 31,1:2
Vulliamy, H F, 1939, Ap 30,45:2
Vunk, John R (por), 1946, Jl 31,27:3
Vurgason, John M Mrs, 1937, S 24,21:1
Vurpillot, Florian C J, 1949, Mr 31,25:4
Vyle, G C, 1933, S 8,19:4
Vynne, Emma Mann Mrs, 1924, D 13,15:3
Vynne, Harold R, 1903, S 15,9:6
Vyse, Arthur J, 1941, S 9,23:2
Vyskogel, Mary Mrs, 1921, O 18,17:3
Vyvyan, R M, 1946, D 19,29:6

W

Wa-Ba, Kosh-a-Na, 1905, Ap 5,1:6
Waack, Gertrude Mrs, 1941, Ag 9,15:2
Waag, Alfred, 1941, O 17,23:6
Wabster, Carl B, 1952, F 20,29:4
Wacaser, Emery E, 1938, S 11,II,11:1
Wace, Alan, 1957, N 11,29:5
Wace, Henry Rev, 1924, Ja 10,21:5
Wach, Joachim, 1955, Ag 30,27:2
Wachaman, Murray, 1955, Jl 16,15:4
Wachek, Louis, 1948, O 31,88:4
Wachenfeld, Elise Mrs, 1940, N 9,17:4
Wachlski, F J (Bro Alphonsus), 1966, D 31,19:1
Wachmeister, Beulah H Countess (Mrs Axel C Wachmeister), 1958, Ja 18,15:4
Wachmeyer, Hazel K, 1940, My 1,23:4
Wachner, Charles S, 1946, Jl 3,25:2
Wachob, Roland, 1952, My 31,17:5
Wachs, Benjamin, 1963, Ap 2,47:3
Wachsman, Alvin L (por), 1948, Jl 15,23:4
Wachsman, Jacob, 1955, F 10,31:1
Wachsman, Max Dr, 1923, Ja 21,6:3
Wachsman, Sallie W Mrs, 1937, S 17,25:3
Wachsman, Zvi H, 1948, S 16,29:6
Wachsmann, Siegfried (por), 1946, F 19,25:3
Wachsner, Leon, 1909, F 22,9:6
Wachstein, Max, 1965, Ja 16,27:5
Wacht, Herman, 1955, Ag 29,19:5
Wacht, William W, 1965, Ap 13,37:2
Wachtel, Charles, 1952, D 2,31:4
Wachtel, David H, 1960, D 11,88:6
Wachtel, Emanuel M, 1954, F 11,30:5
Wachtel, Getzel, 1966, Je 22,47:2
Wachtel, Jacob, 1959, Mr 13,29:2
Wachtel, Sanford H (cor, Mr 31,89:1), 1957, Mr 30, 19:3
Wachtel, William, 1941, Ag 11,13:4; 1952, N 3,27:4
Wachtell, Leon S, 1954, Ag 23,17:5
Wachtell, Samuel R, 1943, S 21,23:5
Wachtell, Theodore, 1966, F 23,39:3
Wachter, Edmund J, 1941, Je 3,21:6
Wachter, Edward A, 1966, Mr 13,86:2
Wachter, Harry P, 1949, Jl 9,13:2; 1951, Jl 22,61:1
Wachter, Harry W, 1941, Ap 20,42:3
Wachter, Peter, 1948, My 27,25:3
Wachter, Theresa Mrs, 1946, D 7,21:3
Wachter, Willard L Dr, 1937, My 19,23:4
Wachtfogel, Moses J, 1951, My 12,21:1
Wachtl, Charles, 1946, Ja 28,19:3
Wachtler, William B, 1958, Jl 8,27:1
Wachtmeister, Constance Countess, 1910, S 25,II,13:5
Wachtmeister, Wanda Countess, 1903, N 22,4:5
Wachuku, Ngwanchiwa Mrs, 1962, O 24,3:4
Wack, Damon D, 1944, F 2,21:1
Wack, Henry W, 1954, D 19,84:4
Wack, Otis, 1951, F 23,27:1
Wack, William H, 1958, Jl 3,25:4
Wackenhut, Frederick, 1941, D 5,23:2
Wackenhuth, Edward, 1961, Je 21,37:2
Wacker, Charles H, 1941, Ja 4,13:3
Wacker, Clarence H, 1964, Ag 1,21:5
Wacker, Edith Mrs, 1950, F 23,21:2
Wacker, Frederick G Sr, 1948, My 19,27:4
Wacker, George G, 1941, Mr 19,21:5
Wacker, Herbert R, 1953, My 21,31:5
Wacker, John H, 1943, Je 12,13:1
Wacker, William F Sr, 1947, D 20,17:3
Wacker, William S, 1938, Mr 5,17:3
Wad, Emanuel, 1940, S 7,15:7
Wada, Hiroo, 1967, Mr 5,86:7
Wadams, William S, 1948, Jl 1,23:5
Waddell, Arch R, 1949, F 1,25:4
Waddell, Benson F, 1940, F 12,17:3
Waddell, Carey Mrs (Louise Forselund), 1910, My 3,13:6
Waddell, Carroll J, 1937, F 26,22:2
Waddell, Charles E, 1945, Ap 21,13:4
Waddell, Charles W, 1943, Mr 30,21:2
Waddell, Chauncey L Mrs, 1961, D 14,43:4
Waddell, George H, 1951, D 13,33:2
Waddell, Harry, 1938, O 11,25:2
Waddell, Helen, 1952, Je 2,21:6
Waddell, James G, 1914, O 17,11:4
Waddell, John A L, 1938, Mr 3,21:3
Waddell, John H 3d, 1966, N 16,29:1
Waddell, Lloyd D Col, 1904, Ja 26,9:6
Waddell, Mary A Mrs, 1924, My 9,19:4
Waddell, Montgomery, 1951, D 22,15:2
Waddell, William A, 1939, F 25,15:3
Waddell, William A Mrs, 1943, F 26,19:4
Waddell, William E, 1940, Ja 30,20:2
Waddell, William S (Doc), 1952, Jl 17,23:1
Wadden, Thomas A, 1957, N 12,34:2
Waddey, D Maxwell Mrs, 1941, My 14,21:1
Waddill, Frank A Dr, 1905, My 23,9:6
Waddingham, Arthur, 1957, Ap 14,86:4
Waddington, John, 1957, Ja 22,29:3
Waddington, Ralph H, 1967, Je 11,87:1
Waddington, Thomas W Mrs, 1955, Ja 5,23:2
Waddy, G A, 1882, Je 8,5:4
Waddy, Percival S Rev Dr, 1937, F 10,23:4
Waddy, Thomas E, 1948, Ag 10,21:2
Wade, Albert G, 1951, O 13,17:2
Wade, Alfred B, 1949, Jl 15,19:3
Wade, Alfred M Mrs, 1946, Je 29,19:5
Wade, Arthur C, 1914, Ag 22,7:4
Wade, B F (see also Mr 3), 1878, Mr 4,5:4
Wade, Billy, 1965, Ja 6,49:1
Wade, Bryan L, 1949, Jl 29,21:1
Wade, C H, 1882, Je 24,5:5
Wade, C Norbert, 1954, S 5,51:2
Wade, Clarence E, 1944, Ap 20,19:6
Wade, Daniel B, 1940, O 8,25:2
Wade, Dudley B, 1941, Ag 21,17:4
Wade, Edward A Mrs, 1949, D 16,31:1
Wade, Edward F, 1953, N 2,25:4
Wade, Edward W, 1950, Mr 20,21:4
Wade, Elizabeth A, 1954, F 21,68:1
Wade, F J, 1927, S 29,27:1
Wade, Florence M, 1960, Ap 27,37:2
Wade, Francis A, 1954, Ap 9,23:5
Wade, Frank B, 1950, O 4,31:5
Wade, Frank H, 1953, Ja 14,31:1
Wade, G F, 1933, F 6,15:3
Wade, George A, 1942, Ap 15,21:2
Wade, George G, 1957, Jl 1,23:3
Wade, George J, 1960, Jl 14,27:5
Wade, George K B, 1938, Ag 30,17:3
Wade, Harold H, 1950, D 4,29:3
Wade, Harriet H W Mrs, 1941, My 13,24:2
Wade, Herbert T, 1955, Mr 20,88:7
Wade, Hugh P Mrs, 1941, S 19,23:4
Wade, J A, 1933, F 17,19:3
Wade, J Floyd, 1960, S 17,23:5
Wade, James, 1950, N 11,15:6
Wade, James D Dr, 1902, O 21,9:4
Wade, James F Maj-Gen, 1921, Ag 26,13:4
Wade, James W Mrs, 1915, D 17,11:5
Wade, John, 1938, Mr 16,23:3; 1945, F 17,13:4
Wade, John E, 1959, N 21,23:6
Wade, John H, 1945, Ap 22,19:5
Wade, John J, 1950, D 27,27:2
Wade, John Leonard Capt, 1922, O 13,17:6
Wade, John T S, 1954, Jl 21,27:2
Wade, Joseph F, 1938, Je 18,15:6
Wade, Lorentz G, 1957, Je 26,31:3
Wade, Louie D Sr, 1943, Ag 4,17:5
Wade, Louis E, 1949, N 9,27:5
Wade, Margaret, 1942, Ag 18,22:3
Wade, Mark, 1968, F 6,43:1
Wade, Michael T, 1959, Je 1,27:5
Wade, Monfort J, 1951, Je 30,15:5
Wade, Newman C, 1952, My 13,30:2
Wade, Oliver E Mrs, 1953, O 2,21:3
Wade, R B, 1884, Ja 12,5:3
Wade, Ralph D, 1949, S 21,32:2
Wade, Raymond F, 1966, Jl 26,32:1
Wade, Robert Bailey, 1907, Ap 7,9:6
Wade, Robert J Sr, 1959, S 4,19:3
Wade, Roy L Mrs, 1954, Jl 31,13:4
Wade, Roy Mrs, 1966, S 10,29:5
Wade, Rufus R, 1904, F 11,9:5
Wade, Russell L, 1958, Ja 4,15:6
Wade, Samuel Mrs, 1949, F 17,23:4
Wade, Simon F, 1950, S 12,27:4
Wade, Simon F Mrs, 1940, Ja 25,21:2
Wade, Stuart A, 1955, N 7,29:3
Wade, Susan E, 1955, N 4,29:4
Wade, Thomas B, 1946, D 20,24:2
Wade, Thomas F, 1945, Jl 29,40:3
Wade, Thomas G, 1942, Ja 5,20:2
Wade, Thomas W, 1943, N 9,21:4
Wade, Truman D, 1952, N 23,89:2
Wade, W H, 1882, Ap 16,2:7
Wade, W N, 1940, Ja 27,13:3
Wade, Wallace Mrs, 1947, Je 4,27:3
Wade, Walter A, 1951, Ja 17,27:1; 1955, Je 25,15:4
Wade, Willard W, 1938, Ap 5,21:5
Wade, William F, 1947, O 22,29:1
Wade, William H, 1945, N 5,19:4
Wadel, Ernest G Mrs, 1949, N 30,1:8
Wadell, A H, 1953, Ag 16,77:2
Wadell, George, 1949, D 18,88:3
Wadell, Robert P, 1951, Ap 20,29:1
Wadelton, Francis B, 1950, Je 29,29:4
Wadenhoff, Peter, 1909, My 23,11:6
Wadeson, Ernest, 1953, N 16,25:5
Wadewitz, Edward H, 1955, Ja 16,92:4
Wadewitz, Robert M, 1954, Jl 25,69:1
Wadham, Harvey N, 1957, Mr 11,25:2
Wadham, Melville S, 1939, Je 28,21:3
Wadhams, A V Rear Adm, 1927, Ja 16,II,9:1
Wadhams, Albion J, 1943, Ag 23,15:5
Wadhams, Cornelia, 1938, F 18,19:1
Wadhams, John M, 1941, S 19,23:4
Wadhams, John M 3d, 1950, Ap 29,15:3
Wadhams, Joseph P, 1944, Ja 18,20:2
Wadhams, Ralph H, 1945, Ap 29,37:1
Wadhams, Robert P (por), 1940, D 18,25:3
Wadhams, Sanford H, 1959, Je 15,27:4
Wadhams, William H, 1952, Je 26,29:4
Wadi, Shakir al, 1957, F 2,19:3
Wadiaeff, Gabriel, 1960, Jl 27,29:1
Wadiak, Steve, 1952, Mr 10,23:7
Wadick, Arthur H, 1910, Mr 18,11:5
Wadin, Ahmed T A K, 1950, Je 5,23:3
Wadkovsky, Basil B Sr, 1941, S 15,17:5
Wadleigh, Francis R (por), 1937, Ja 15,21:1
Wadleigh, George R, 1950, Ja 14,15:6
Wadleigh, George W, 1907, Je 2,7:6
Wadleigh, Henry Rawle Rev, 1937, Je 2,23:5
Wadleigh, John Winthrop Lt-Col, 1923, Ap 5,19:5
Wadler, Arnold D, 1951, S 8,17:6
Wadley, Mary E, 1942, O 9,22:2
Wadley, U Vaugh, 1945, N 18,44:2
Wadlin, Herbert E, 1950, Jl 1,15:4
Wadlin, Horace G, 1925, N 6,23:5
Wadlin, John F, 1953, My 2,15:3
Wadlow, Robert P, 1940, Jl 16,19:1
Wadlund, Arthur P, 1943, S 3,19:4
Wadmond, Louis C, 1958, Mr 6,27:3
Wados, William, 1951, Jl 6,23:1
Wadsten, Sten W, 1950, S 6,30:2
Wadsworth, Adrian R, 1941, My 16,23:4
Wadsworth, Alfred P, 1956, N 5,31:3
Wadsworth, Alvin D, 1941, F 3,20:3
Wadsworth, Arthur H, 1950, S 24,104:3
Wadsworth, Augustus B, 1954, Je 3,27:3
Wadsworth, Augustus B Mrs, 1951, Je 19,29:3
Wadsworth, Burton Mrs, 1951, D 7,27:1
Wadsworth, C Desmond, 1952, Je 29,56:3
Wadsworth, C W Gen, 1872, Ja 4,5:2
Wadsworth, Charles D, 1942, F 18,19:1
Wadsworth, Charles F, 1940, O 25,21:1
Wadsworth, Clarence S, 1941, Ap 8,26:3; 1957, My 1, 37:3
Wadsworth, Clarence S Mrs, 1957, F 15,23:3
Wadsworth, Craig W, 1960, My 21,23:2
Wadsworth, D, 1883, S 13,5:2
Wadsworth, Daniel V Mrs, 1962, Je 6,41:3
Wadsworth, David, 1922, Ag 18,13:3
Wadsworth, David T, 1937, Ja 16,17:4
Wadsworth, Dudley L Mrs, 1962, S 16,86:7
Wadsworth, Edward, 1949, Je 22,31:3
Wadsworth, Edward G, 1937, Mr 2,21:2
Wadsworth, Eliot, 1959, My 30,17:2
Wadsworth, Eliot Mrs, 1958, Ag 7,25:4
Wadsworth, Emory M, 1953, Ap 3,24:4
Wadsworth, Frank, 1940, F 16,19:1; 1955, Ja 13,27:4
Wadsworth, Frank C, 1947, My 4,60:3
Wadsworth, Frank T, 1946, N 23,15:3
Wadsworth, Frederick A, 1958, D 31,19:1
Wadsworth, George, 1958, Mr 6,27:1
Wadsworth, George Mrs, 1946, Ag 2,19:6
Wadsworth, George R, 1937, N 2,25:2
Wadsworth, Guy W, 1951, Jl 9,25:3
Wadsworth, Herbert, 1937, Ag 25,21:6
Wadsworth, Ida C Mrs, 1950, Ja 12,27:2
Wadsworth, J W, 1926, D 25,13:1
Wadsworth, J W Mrs, 1931, My 6,25:3
Wadsworth, James S Gen, 1864, My 10,4:5
Wadsworth, James W, 1952, Je 22,1:2; 1953, My 9, 19:6
Wadsworth, John (funl), 1875, O 15,8:5
Wadsworth, Joseph, 1940, Ap 22,17:5
Wadsworth, Marietta, 1944, Mr 9,17:5
Wadsworth, Phil C, 1952, My 28,29:3
Wadsworth, Philemon T, 1960, D 30,20:1
Wadsworth, Ronald B, 1953, Ag 27,25:4
Wadsworth, Roscoe C, 1962, My 5,27:2
Wadsworth, W Austin Mrs, 1943, D 7,27:5
Wadsworth, Willard, 1959, D 16,41:2
Wadsworth, Willard (est acctg), 1963, N 12,63:8
Wadsworth, William, 1950, Je 7,29:2
Wadsworth, William Austin Maj, 1918, My 4,15:8
Wadsworth, William H, 1942, N 7,15:3
Wadsworth, William M, 1959, Ap 11,21:6
Wadsworth, William P, 1909, Mr 10,9:3
Wadsworth, William P Mrs, 1958, Mr 22,17:2
Wadsworth, William S, 1955, Mr 21,25:3
Waechter, Charles, 1964, D 12,31:5
Waechter, Fred H, 1945, D 7,22:3
Waechter, Henry, 1946, Jl 12,17:4
Waechter, Otto, 1949, S 2,17:2
Waelder, Robert, 1967, S 30,33:2
Waelsch, Heinrich B, 1966, Mr 23,47:2
Waesche, George E, 1957, S 18,33:3
Waesche, Russell R, 1946, O 18,23:1
Waesche, Russell R Mrs, 1947, N 5,27:4
Wafel, Newman D Mrs, 1944, Ja 6,23:1
Wafer, James T, 1905, Je 30,9:4
Wafer, William H, 1951, Jl 24,25:6
Wafford, Rhoda F Mrs, 1947, F 5,23:1
Waful, Edward, 1937, Ja 24,II,8:5
Waganseil, Charles H, 1950, S 26,31:4
Wagar, John E Sr, 1954, Ap 21,29:4
Wagar, Legrand, 1967, N 24,46:3
Wagar, Robert Sr, 1950, My 6,15:4

Wageley, Bernard Mrs, 1949, F 17,23:5
Wagemaker, Isaac, 1940, D 27,14:6
Wagemann, Kurt A Mrs, 1968, S 9,47:1
Wagemans, Henri, 1948, Mr 13,15:3
Wagenblass, John H, 1949, Ag 22,21:4
Wagener, D S, 1875, S 15,4:6
Wagener, George A, 1942, Je 20,13:4
Wagener, H Allen, 1947, Jl 24,21:5
Wagener, John, 1939, Mr 23,23:2
Wagener, Richard E, 1951, My 19,15:4
Wagenhals, L A, 1931, S 12,17:5
Wagenhals, Lincoln A Mrs, 1954, O 20,29:4
Wagenheim, Jack I, 1966, Ap 25,31:4
Wagenheim, Michael L, 1965, O 16,27:5
Wagenhurst, James H, 1958, O 18,21:4
Wagenknecht, Alfred, 1956, Ag 27,19:4
Wagenseil, Oscar, 1962, My 7,31:1
Wager, Ambrose Lee, 1917, N 1,15:1
Wager, Anthony, 1948, Ag 11,21:2
Wager, Burton G, 1953, Jl 4,11:5
Wager, Charles H A, 1939, Jl 2,15:4
Wager, Chester G, 1950, D 24,34:6
Wager, Max L, 1964, S 30,43:4
Wager, Max L Mrs, 1967, D 21,37:1
Wager, Robert H, 1958, Ja 16,29:4
Wager, William T, 1942, Je 3,23:5
Wagg, Kenneth A Mrs (M Sullavan),(funl plans, Ja 3,53:1), 1960, Ja 2,1:2
Waggaman, Thomas E, 1906, Je 28,1:2
Waggener, Thomas R, 1948, S 28,27:3
Waggoner, Chauncey William Dr, 1922, O 27,17:4
Waggoner, Clark, 1903, Jl 3,9:6
Waggoner, Forrest L, 1949, Jl 28,24:2
Waggoner, Guy, 1950, D 12,34:4
Waggoner, Norman L, 1952, Jl 3,25:5
Waggoner, Rod, 1958, Je 1,86:4
Waggoner, William C, 1939, Ja 29,33:2
Waggoner, William T, 1962, Ap 17,35:5
Waghalter, Ignatz, 1949, Ap 8,25:3
Wagley, Carlos W, 1960, My 22,19:6
Wagman, Abe, 1963, O 14,29:5
Wagman, Joel J, 1953, Ja 15,27:3
Wagman, Louis Mrs, 1951, Ap 3,27:3
Wagnalls, Adam Willis, 1924, S 4,19:3
Wagnalls, Adams Willis Mrs, 1914, Ag 18,9:6
Wagner, A, 1944, Ap 18,5:4
Wagner, Adolph Dr, 1917, N 10,13:5
Wagner, Alan C, 1958, Ap 2,31:4
Wagner, Albert H, 1955, Ap 13,29:2
Wagner, Albert J, 1941, Ap 24,21:5
Wagner, Albert Mrs, 1948, N 18,27:4
Wagner, Alfred B, 1947, D 28,40:5
Wagner, Andrew F, 1942, Mr 30,17:2
Wagner, Arthur, 1967, Ap 25,43:5
Wagner, Arthur A, 1937, Ja 15,21:1
Wagner, Arthur Brig Gen, 1905, Je 18,7:5
Wagner, August Mrs, 1952, Mr 27,29:5
Wagner, Bartholomew J, 1965, My 22,31:6
Wagner, Basil, 1937, Jl 22,19:6
Wagner, Boyd D, 1943, Ja 7,11:5
Wagner, Bruno, 1941, S 25,25:3
Wagner, C Alfred, 1944, Mr 31,21:4
Wagner, C Mrs, 1930, Ap 2,29:1
Wagner, Carl, 1965, Ja 18,35:2
Wagner, Carl F, 1957, D 23,23:5
Wagner, Carl P, 1942, Ag 12,19:5
Wagner, Carlie R, 1944, Ap 21,19:5
Wagner, Carlie R Mrs, 1944, Ap 21,19:5
Wagner, Charles, 1918, My 14,13:6; 1943, Mr 21,26:5; 1946, Je 1,13:5
Wagner, Charles A, 1938, My 26,25:5
Wagner, Charles C, 1957, D 20,27:4
Wagner, Charles Gray Dr, 1923, N 7,17:6
Wagner, Charles J, 1951, D 25,31:2; 1956, Jl 4,19:2
Wagner, Charles L, 1943, Je 2,25:1; 1956, F 26,89:1; 1958, Ja 13,29:1
Wagner, Charles P, 1964, Je 3,43:4
Wagner, Charles S, 1956, F 13,27:4
Wagner, Charles S Mrs, 1945, My 28,19:3
Wagner, Charles Valentine Maj, 1915, Ja 29,9:7
Wagner, Chester I, 1942, O 25,44:8
Wagner, Clarence P, 1953, Jl 11,11:4
Wagner, Clinton Dr, 1914, N 26,13:4
Wagner, Constantin Jr, 1956, My 28,27:2
Wagner, Constantin Sr, 1955, O 10,27:4
Wagner, David V H, 1943, Mr 23,19:3
Wagner, Dorothy (Mrs M Neiman), 1967, Jl 25,32:4
Wagner, Douglas G, 1958, N 8,21:5
Wagner, Eddie (Kid), 1956, O 31,33:2
Wagner, Edward, 1940, Je 4,23:3; 1944, F 4,15:4
Wagner, Edward F, 1942, N 26,27:4
Wagner, Edward I Dr, 1968, O 10,47:6
Wagner, Edward L, 1965, My 3,33:4
Wagner, Edward S, 1939, Ag 16,23:3; 1947, Ag 2,13:3
Wagner, Edwin, 1957, Ag 17,15:4
Wagner, Elin, 1949, Ja 12,27:5
Wagner, Elizabeth B Mrs, 1947, Jl 29,21:2
Wagner, Emilio, 1949, S 24,13:4
Wagner, Ernest, 1954, Mr 5,19:2
Wagner, Ernest A, 1953, Mr 26,31:3
Wagner, Ernest C, 1951, Mr 31,15:5; 1952, N 29,17:3
Wagner, Ernest E, 1957, Mr 12,33:4
Wagner, Ethel P Mrs, 1937, Ap 9,21:1
Wagner, Eugene F, 1956, Ja 20,23:2
Wagner, Eugene T, 1939, Jl 11,19:4
Wagner, F Earl, 1958, My 27,31:1
Wagner, Fanie Mrs, 1944, Ja 17,19:4
Wagner, Francis L, 1949, D 11,92:4
Wagner, Frank C, 1951, O 3,33:3
Wagner, Frank D, 1966, Ja 8,25:3
Wagner, Frank H, 1942, Jl 23,19:2
Wagner, Frank J, 1960, My 13,31:1
Wagner, Frank Mrs, 1955, Jl 10,72:1
Wagner, Franklin A, 1937, Mr 24,25:4
Wagner, Franz, 1961, O 29,89:1
Wagner, Fred, 1938, Ap 1,23:5; 1946, N 11,27:3
Wagner, Frederic C, 1914, O 22,11:6
Wagner, Frederick R, 1953, Ja 27,25:1
Wagner, Frederick U Mrs, 1954, My 8,17:1
Wagner, George, 1954, S 1,27:5; 1964, N 23,37:2
Wagner, George F, 1954, My 10,23:5
Wagner, George L Mrs, 1950, O 4,31:3
Wagner, George R (Gorgeous George),(trb, D 28,-23:1), 1963, D 27,25:1
Wagner, George S, 1874, N 13,4:7
Wagner, Gerhard, 1939, Mr 26,III,7:2
Wagner, Gilbert C, 1951, My 12,21:5
Wagner, Guy W, 1939, O 9,19:5
Wagner, Harold C, 1958, O 17,29:4
Wagner, Harold J, 1959, Mr 25,35:4
Wagner, Harry G Jr, 1947, My 15,25:2
Wagner, Henry, 1940, Ja 17,21:1; 1950, S 4,17:6
Wagner, Henry C, 1955, N 9,33:3
Wagner, Henry R, 1957, Mr 29,21:5
Wagner, Herbert A, 1947, D 6,15:1
Wagner, Herbert W, 1948, N 24,23:4
Wagner, Herman C, 1952, Ja 7,19:5
Wagner, Hermann A, 1921, O 31,15:6
Wagner, Hobson C, 1952, Jl 4,13:5
Wagner, Honore, 1965, My 24,43:3
Wagner, Isidor, 1938, D 4,61:1
Wagner, Isidor Mrs, 1964, D 25,29:1
Wagner, J Earl, 1943, N 11,23:4
Wagner, J Earl Mrs, 1946, D 24,17:4
Wagner, Jacob A, 1942, O 22,21:2
Wagner, James G, 1940, D 5,25:4
Wagner, James J, 1940, Je 11,25:2
Wagner, James M, 1950, N 8,29:5
Wagner, Jay, 1968, Ja 16,39:1
Wagner, Jerome, 1955, F 4,21:4
Wagner, Jesse L, 1941, S 5,21:2
Wagner, John, 1940, N 21,29:4; 1942, Ag 6,19:2; 1944, Je 10,15:4; 1951, O 4,33:4; 1956, O 6,21:4
Wagner, John A, 1950, Jl 30,61:1
Wagner, John E, 1938, N 17,25:6
Wagner, John F, 1943, Mr 24,23:1
Wagner, John F Jr, 1937, Ag 17,19:5
Wagner, John H, 1960, D 21,31:4
Wagner, John P (Honus),(funl plans, D 7,39:4; funl, D 10,21:4), 1955, D 6,37:1
Wagner, John R, 1952, Je 12,33:5
Wagner, Joseph, 1946, Ap 23,21:3
Wagner, Joseph E Mrs, 1953, Ag 12,31:4
Wagner, Joseph H Dr, 1937, N 9,23:1
Wagner, Leona J, 1944, S 30,13:6
Wagner, Louis, 1940, Mr 11,15:1
Wagner, Louis Gen, 1914, Ja 16,9:6
Wagner, Louis J Jr, 1943, Jl 6,21:2
Wagner, Louis Sr (por), 1937, Ag 24,21:3
Wagner, Loy A, 1951, Mr 29,27:3
Wagner, Mahlon Manley, 1917, Ag 3,9:2
Wagner, Marcel, 1962, Mr 28,39:3
Wagner, Martin, 1903, D 29,9:6; 1957, My 29,27:5
Wagner, Mary S, 1937, Ag 15,II,7:2
Wagner, Meyer Mrs, 1951, My 21,27:5
Wagner, Morris, 1937, Jl 16,19:2
Wagner, Nathaniel M, 1961, D 19,33:1
Wagner, Oscar, 1955, F 23,27:3
Wagner, Otto, 1924, My 8,19:4; 1946, O 23,27:1
Wagner, Otto Mrs, 1950, S 19,31:1; 1955, N 30,33:1
Wagner, P K, 1864, Ag 5,3:1
Wagner, Ralph Mrs, 1960, N 4,33:1
Wagner, Raymond W, 1952, Je 16,17:3
Wagner, Raymond W Mrs, 1950, N 2,31:4
Wagner, Richard, 1883, F 14,4:6; 1939, Ap 23,III,7:1; 1961, Mr 5,86:7
Wagner, Richard H, 1946, Je 9,40:5
Wagner, Rob, 1942, Jl 21,19:5
Wagner, Robert, 1949, Jl 29,21:1
Wagner, Robert C, 1938, Jl 26,19:2
Wagner, Robert F Mrs, 1919, Jl 31,9:3
Wagner, Robert F Mrs (trb, Mr 3,32:2; funl, Mr 6,1:3), 1964, Mr 3,1:2
Wagner, Robert F Sr, 1953, My 5,1:2
Wagner, Russell H, 1952, Ja 10,32:5
Wagner, S, 1930, Ag 5,23:1
Wagner, Samuel, 1937, My 18,23:2
Wagner, Samuel C Jr, 1940, Ap 1,19:2
Wagner, Samuel Jr, 1939, My 29,16:1
Wagner, Samuel Mrs, 1952, Mr 13,29:2
Wagner, Samuel T, 1951, N 18,91:2
Wagner, Steward, 1958, Je 28,17:6
Wagner, Theodore F, 1963, D 29,42:7
Wagner, Victor, 1939, D 8,25:4
Wagner, Victor Mrs, 1947, D 7,76:2
Wagner, Walter, 1956, S 2,56:7
Wagner, Walter A, 1948, O 20,29:3
Wagner, Walter C, 1958, Ap 25,27:4
Wagner, Webster, 1953, My 1,21:2
Wagner, Webster Sen, 1882, Ja 17,10:3
Wagner, Wieland (trb, O 23,II,17:1), 1966, O 18,45:1
Wagner, William E Dr, 1918, Mr 18,13:5
Wagner, William F Mrs, 1954, Mr 25,29:4
Wagner, William H, 1943, Jl 2,19:2
Wagner, William J, 1951, Ja 12,27:1
Wagner, William Mrs, 1943, Ap 19,19:3
Wagner (Happy Cal), 1916, Ja 28,9:5
Wagner-Jauregg, Julius (por), 1940, O 1,23:4
Wagnitz, William, 1946, Je 17,21:5
Wagon, Edward L, 1955, Ja 15,13:5
Wagoner, Charles E Mrs, 1948, O 19,28:3
Wagoner, Charles P, 1946, Je 7,19:1
Wagoner, Charles S, 1939, My 18,25:4
Wagoner, Clyde D, 1963, N 9,25:2
Wagoner, Ed O, 1954, Je 11,23:6
Wagoner, Edgar L, 1951, Je 14,27:3
Wagoner, Harry B, 1950, Ap 11,31:1
Wagoner, Loren, 1939, My 24,23:6
Wagoner, Phil D Mrs, 1940, O 26,15:3
Wagoner, Philip D, 1962, N 26,29:2
Wagram, Princess de, 1903, O 4,5:2
Wagstaff, Alfred Col, 1921, O 3,13:4
Wagstaff, David, 1951, Je 8,27:4
Wagstaff, David Mrs (cor, Je 21,31:4), 1956, Je 19, 29:5
Wagstaff, George B, 1964, S 5,19:6
Wagstaff, Henry M, 1945, My 29,15:4
Wagstaff, James C Mrs, 1949, D 30,19:1
Wagstaff, Mary A B Mrs, 1938, Je 16,23:6
Wagstaff, Richard A, 1950, Mr 10,27:3
Wagstaff, Samuel Jones, 1920, D 23,11:5
Wagstaff, William, 1951, Mr 29,27:5
Wagsteff, A (see also Ap 28), 1878, My 1,8:2
Wahl, Albert, 1941, Ag 5,19:1
Wahl, Edward G, 1953, Ag 27,25:3
Wahl, Frank A, 1940, Ja 4,24:2
Wahl, Fred A, 1915, F 22,9:3
Wahl, Fred J Mrs, 1938, N 28,15:2; 1941, O 20,17:2
Wahl, Geza, 1946, F 9,13:4
Wahl, Geza Mrs, 1950, S 25,23:1
Wahl, Hans, 1949, F 21,23:5
Wahl, Harry K, 1951, O 7,87:2
Wahl, John O, 1950, Ag 17,27:4
Wahl, L, 1928, D 31,15:3
Wahl, Louis, 1925, Mr 31,19:6
Wahl, Manfred, 1956, Jl 12,23:4
Wahl, Maurice Mrs, 1954, Ag 18,29:1
Wahl, Robert Dr, 1937, Je 13,II,7:1
Wahl, Robert W Jr, 1955, D 1,35:3
Wahl, Spencer A, 1953, My 23,15:4
Wahl, Stephen, 1960, My 2,29:2
Wahl, William Francis Rev, 1925, F 27,17:5
Wahlberg, Carl W, 1947, My 8,25:2
Wahlberg, Harry (H Waldon), 1960, Je 3,31:4
Wahlberg, Oscar, 1945, O 18,23:2
Wahlberg, Victor, 1949, Ap 19,26:4
Wahle, C G F, 1934, O 17,23:4
Wahle, Otto, 1963, Ag 13,31:3
Wahlers, Charles, 1903, Ja 25,10:5
Wahlers, Henry A, 1949, Je 17,23:4
Wahlin, John E, 1948, Ap 9,24:2
Wahlquist, Hugo W, 1959, Jl 10,25:5
Wahls, Henry A, 1945, Ag 19,25:5
Wahlstead, Peter P, 1943, Jl 11,35:1
Wahlstrom, Frederick, 1917, Ag 29,9:4
Wahlstrom, Leonard W, 1944, Mr 26,42:1
Wahn, Henry, 1958, Ja 24,23:1
Wahnon, James M, 1943, N 17,25:2
Wahrburg, Richard G, 1948, Ag 24,23:2
Wahrenberger, J Rev, 1878, Ag 9,2:7
Wahrhaftig, Joseph, 1964, D 12,31:4
Waibel, Gus J, 1938, F 9,19:4
Waibel, Leo, 1951, S 16,85:1
Waibel, Theodore D, 1951, S 17,21:4
Waid, Addison C, 1951, Ja 30,25:1
Waid, C Frank, 1944, Mr 24,19:3
Waid, D Everett (will, N 10,20:4), 1939, N 1,23:4
Waid, Wilfred Philip, 1916, Ap 10,11:5
Waidelich, Luther F, 1951, F 25,84:4
Waidler, George A, 1952, My 30,15:5
Waidner, Charles W Dr, 1922, Mr 12,30:3
Waigli, William, 1876, Ap 30,7:1
Wailes, Annie Mrs, 1903, Jl 28,5:7
Wailes, George H, 1967, Jl 14,31:3
Wailes, Montgomery B, 1938, O 19,23:6
Wain, Louis, 1939, Jl 6,23:2
Wain, Morris Mrs, 1962, S 2,56:8
Wainer, Max R, 1959, Jl 29,29:3
Wainerdi, Harold R, 1965, Ag 19,31:4
Wainess, Emanuel M, 1964, F 16,92:8
Wainewright, Lionel C Mrs, 1943, Ag 27,17:5
Wainger, Morris A, 1956, Ja 7,17:4
Wainhouse, Jonathan, 1953, Ag 16,31:1
Waino, Wild Man of Borneo, 1905, Mr 18,1:4
Wainright, Charles H, 1948, Jl 3,15:1
Wainright, E Z, 1903, D 22,9:5
Wainright, Halsted H, 1937, Je 22,23:4
Wainright, Jesse S, 1958, Je 3,31:4
Wainright, John M, 1938, O 21,23:4

Wainwright, Arnold F, 1914, D 22,13:5
Wainwright, Carroll L, 1967, Jl 7,33:4
Wainwright, Charles S Brig-Gen, 1907, S 15,9:3
Wainwright, Cleveland G, 1949, Ag 23,23:4
Wainwright, Ellis, 1924, N 8,15:5
Wainwright, Elmer C, 1942, Ja 7,19:4
Wainwright, F King Mrs (will), 1956, F 11,9:3
Wainwright, Florence, 1913, Je 29,5:4
Wainwright, Frances M Mrs, 1953, Ja 1,23:1
Wainwright, Francis, 1952, Ja 25,21:3
Wainwright, George W Mrs, 1951, F 25,87:4
Wainwright, Gilbert C S, 1954, Ag 24,21:4
Wainwright, Henry, 1903, S 19,7:6
Wainwright, Henry C Mrs, 1948, O 16,15:6
Wainwright, J Howard, 1871, Ap 7,8:4; 1911, D 30, 11:5
Wainwright, J M Ensign, 1870, Jl 30,2:6
Wainwright, Jeanne A Mrs, 1957, D 6,29:2
Wainwright, Jessie H Mrs, 1950, N 28,31:2
Wainwright, John W, 1940, Ja 19,19:5
Wainwright, Jonathan M (por), 1945, Je 4,19:3
Wainwright, Jonathan M, 1953, S 3,1:4
Wainwright, Jonathan M Mrs, 1946, Ap 7,44:3
Wainwright, Laura S Mrs, 1941, F 4,21:4
Wainwright, Louden S, 1942, Ja 24,17:4
Wainwright, Marie, 1923, Ag 19,26:4; 1923, Ag 21, 17:2
Wainwright, Melvin, 1958, N 6,37:3
Wainwright, R Rear Adm, 1926, Mr 7,30:4
Wainwright, Stuyvesant Mrs, 1961, N 5,88:8
Wainwright, Thomas A, 1955, Ag 19,19:2
Wainwright, Townsend, 1960, D 5,31:5
Wainwright, Walter L, 1961, F 13,27:5
Wainwright, William, 1904, Ag 15,7:7; 1914, My 15, 15:6
Wainwright, William P, 1925, F 6,17:5
Waisman, Morton M, 1963, Ag 23,25:1
Wait, Alfred McLean, 1907, S 22,9:5
Wait, Bertrand H, 1951, Jl 21,13:4
Wait, E D Lt, 1865, S 1,4:5
Wait, Frederick Scott, 1910, Jl 1,7:4
Wait, J W, 1903, Mr 3,3:6
Wait, John Dunning Col, 1903, N 14,9:6
Wait, John V, 1939, N 17,22:2
Wait, Lucien Augustus, 1913, S 7,II,13:6
Wait, Orissa, 1953, Ja 5,21:4
Wait, Phoebe Jane Babcock Dr, 1904, Ja 31,7:6
Wait, Robert E, 1945, Ja 19,19:3
Wait, Robert R, 1938, Ja 6,19:4
Wait, Wesley, 1949, Jl 7,25:2
Wait, William, 1941, Je 26,23:4
Wait, William B, 1949, Je 27,27:4
Wait, William Bell, 1916, O 26,11:5
Wait, William H, 1925, Jl 30,19:5; 1939, Mr 1,21:2
Waite, Abbott L Mrs, 1940, F 12,17:5
Waite, Alice V, 1943, Ap 8,23:3
Waite, Benjamin F, 1941, N 11,24:2
Waite, Brainerd E, 1939, Mr 5,49:3
Waite, C C, 1880, F 4,3:3
Waite, Carl E, 1961, O 15,88:8
Waite, Charles, 1941, F 9,48:6; 1951, S 8,17:1
Waite, Charles B, 1911, Jl 8,9:4
Waite, Charles C, 1961, O 15,88:6
Waite, Charles E Dr, 1923, N 26,17:3
Waite, Clark F, 1958, Ap 8,30:6
Waite, D H ex-Gov, 1901, N 28,7:5
Waite, Edgar A, 1962, Ag 3,23:4
Waite, Edward B Sr, 1947, Je 3,25:1
Waite, Edward F, 1958, Ap 29,29:1
Waite, Frank A, 1964, Je 23,33:3
Waite, Frank L, 1938, S 2,17:4
Waite, George, 1947, D 2,29:2
Waite, George F Mrs, 1944, D 7,25:4
Waite, George L, 1945, Ap 17,23:4
Waite, Guy B Sr, 1943, Je 30,21:2
Waite, Harry F, 1946, Ja 27,41:1
Waite, Harry V, 1951, Ag 16,27:6
Waite, Harvey R, 1955, Je 9,29:5
Waite, Henry, 1940, N 26,23:1
Waite, Henry M (por), 1944, S 2,11:1
Waite, Henry M Mrs, 1963, S 12,37:3
Waite, Henry R Rev, 1909, My 7,9:4
Waite, Herbert E, 1945, Ap 28,15:6
Waite, J H C, 1950, Ja 3,25:1
Waite, James D, 1953, N 8,89:2
Waite, James P, 1938, Mr 19,15:6
Waite, John, 1938, F 6,II,8:7; 1968, My 9,47:2
Waite, Louise, 1944, D 6,23:3
Waite, M B, 1888, Mr 23,1:3
Waite, Mary A Mrs, 1949, D 10,18:3
Waite, Merton B, 1945, Je 7,19:5
Waite, Morison R, 1962, Mr 7,35:4
Waite, Ralph H, 1955, O 4,35:1
Waite, Robert B, 1956, F 14,29:1
Waite, Roy J, 1944, O 24,23:5
Waite, Sumner, 1952, Je 8,86:7
Waite, Walter I, 1967, Jl 28,31:3
Waite, Warren, 1917, Mr 24,11:6
Waite, William J, 1946, Ja 2,19:2
Waite, Winthrop, 1940, My 15,25:5
Waithman, Robert, 1956, My 3,31:2
Waitkevics, Peter J, 1959, Ag 21,21:1
Waits, Edward M, 1949, D 28,32:3
Waitt, Albert H, 1940, N 13,23:6
Waitt, Arthur M, 1920, N 12,15:5
Waitt, Lawrence L, 1944, My 25,21:5
Waitt, Weymer H, 1957, S 15,84:5
Waitz, Henry M Sr, 1941, Jl 30,17:5
Waixel, Lionel David, 1925, Ja 18,7:1
Waizmann, Louis, 1951, Ag 26,77:3
Wajdowicz, George, 1949, Mr 30,25:5
Wakasuigi, Kaname, 1943, D 11,15:1
Wakatsuki, Reijiro, 1949, N 22,29:3
Wake, George H, 1942, F 6,19:2
Wake, Hereward, 1963, Ag 5,29:4
Wake, Thomas J, 1962, Je 27,35:3
Wake-Walker, W Frederick (por), 1945, S 26,23:3
Wakefield, Albert H, 1950, N 29,33:4
Wakefield, Alfred C, 1937, F 7,II,9:1
Wakefield, Arthur W, 1949, F 25,24:2
Wakefield, Bernard, 1967, S 30,33:2
Wakefield, Carl C, 1952, Jl 29,21:3
Wakefield, Cyrus, 1873, O 27,1:6
Wakefield, Douglas, 1951, Ap 16,25:3
Wakefield, Edward W, 1941, Ag 5,20:3
Wakefield, Edwin R, 1943, Ag 28,11:7
Wakefield, Frank W, 1938, Ja 18,23:4
Wakefield, George M, 1903, O 9,7:4
Wakefield, George P (will, Mr 18,25:8), 1947, Mr 6, 25:4
Wakefield, George R, 1963, D 11,47:2
Wakefield, George T Mrs, 1942, N 4,23:2
Wakefield, Harold, 1948, O 12,25:5
Wakefield, Harold F, 1965, N 19,39:2
Wakefield, Homer, 1946, S 2,17:1
Wakefield, Jesse E Mrs, 1948, Ap 18,72:5
Wakefield, John E, 1967, Ja 3,34:1
Wakefield, Lord (por), 1941, Ja 16,21:3
Wakefield, Lyman E, 1945, Jl 26,19:3
Wakefield, Oliver, 1956, Jl 2,21:4
Wakefield, Oscar A, 1945, D 11,25:5
Wakefield, Paul L, 1961, Mr 25,25:5
Wakefield, Paul Mrs, 1957, My 4,21:6
Wakefield, Ralph C, 1966, S 28,47:3
Wakefield, Ruth (Mrs J D McIntosh), 1955, D 25, 48:1
Wakefield, Stanley J Mrs, 1955, S 20,31:4
Wakefield, W Jeffreys, 1954, F 1,23:3
Wakefield, Wallace N, 1954, O 19,53:1
Wakeham, Frederick L Mrs, 1966, Ja 19,41:1
Wakeham, Richard K Rev, 1914, D 29,11:6
Wakeham, William H, 1950, D 22,23:4
Wakelee, Edmund W, 1945, Ap 27,19:1
Wakeler, Murray E, 1964, My 16,25:4
Wakeley, Charles Carmen, 1916, F 5,11:6
Wakeley, Gerald, 1952, Mr 9,92:2
Wakelin, James H, 1941, N 4,26:5
Wakelin, Joseph, 1947, Ag 21,23:5
Wakelin, William B, 1954, D 1,31:3
Wakem, Francis J, 1960, My 31,31:3
Wakeman, A, 1928, Ja 31,3:6
Wakeman, Austin, 1946, O 7,31:3
Wakeman, Bacon, 1954, My 8,17:2
Wakeman, Burr, 1879, Jl 10,3:3
Wakeman, Charles A, 1953, N 19,31:2
Wakeman, Clara, 1924, Ja 21,17:4
Wakeman, David G (por), 1944, Ag 30,17:5
Wakeman, Ebenezer Mrs, 1907, S 29,9:6
Wakeman, Edward A, 1952, O 11,19:6
Wakeman, George, 1870, Mr 20,5:5
Wakeman, H Dr, 1878, Ag 17,5:4
Wakeman, Harwood L, 1937, S 27,21:2
Wakeman, Horace S, 1937, S 27,21:5
Wakeman, Isaac B, 1947, D 14,76:6
Wakeman, James M Mrs, 1944, Ja 14,19:5
Wakeman, R C, 1884, O 1,5:5
Wakeman, Robert C, 1964, D 17,41:1
Wakeman, Samuel W, 1940, My 9,23:3
Wakeman, Sarah J H Mrs, 1942, Ja 6,23:3
Wakeman, Seth Dr, 1968, F 10,34:4
Wakeman, W W, 1881, F 27,7:3
Wakeman, Wesley W, 1946, Ag 6,25:5
Wakim, Francis, 1965, F 20,25:2
Waks, Abram Mrs, 1957, N 30,21:2
Walah, John J, 1940, Ja 20,15:4
Walbank, Rhoda Mrs (will), 1949, Ag 19,20:2
Walber, Harry C, 1949, Ap 2,15:4
Walber, John G, 1953, My 17,88:3
Walbert, Mary E, 1943, Ap 11,48:2
Walbran, Christopher J, 1950, O 15,104:3
Walbridge, Augustus M, 1958, Je 26,27:4
Walbridge, Earle F, 1962, Ja 25,31:3
Walbridge, Ernest A, 1940, O 1,23:3
Walbridge, G H, 1936, Ag 7,19:1
Walbridge, George H Mrs, 1966, O 20,43:5
Walbridge, H S Judge, 1869, Ja 28,8:4
Walbridge, Henry D, 1939, Ap 30,45:2
Walbridge, Henry L, 1941, O 3,23:2
Walbridge, James H Col, 1913, D 16,11:6
Walbridge, John H, 1939, F 17,19:4
Walbridge, William D, 1924, Ag 10,24:3
Walbrodt, chess, 1902, O 4,9:3
Walbrook, Anton, 1967, Ag 10,37:3
Walbrook, Henry M, 1941, F 14,17:4
Walburger, Mother St, 1903, D 22,9:4
Walburn, Virginia, 1925, F 3,13:4
Walby, Thomas F Jr, 1960, F 28,82:8
Walch, Donald E, 1947, S 8,21:3
Walch, Hans G, 1963, D 22,34:4
Walch, Johanes L, 1946, D 14,15:2
Walchek, Louis, 1951, Ja 27,13:6
Walck, Ambroise, 1947, My 7,30:6
Walck, Ambrose Mrs, 1951, O 9,29:5
Walck, Andrew, 1949, Mr 2,26:2
Walck, August J, 1950, My 24,30:3
Walck, Claude, 1962, Mr 16,31:2
Walck, John W Mrs, 1948, Ag 14,13:6
Walcot, Isabella Mrs, 1906, Je 4,9:6
Walcott, A F Col, 1906, F 27,9:5
Walcott, Benjamin Stewart Lt, 1917, D 15,13:4
Walcott, C D, 1927, F 10,23:3
Walcott, Colpoys C, 1961, My 1,29:4
Walcott, Dana Mills Rev, 1919, Jl 6,20:3
Walcott, Edward F, 1938, Ja 12,21:6
Walcott, Frederic C (por), 1949, Ap 28,31:1
Walcott, Harry M, 1944, N 7,27:5
Walcott, Henry J, 1940, Ap 18,23:1
Walcott, Henry R, 1954, Ap 19,23:4
Walcott, M Rev, 1880, D 25,1:2
Walcott, Mary V Mrs, 1940, Ag 25,36:3
Walcutt, Charles C, 1946, D 18,29:4
Walcutt, William (funl), 1882, Ap 27,12:4
Wald, Abraham, 1950, D 20,5:3
Wald, Ben-Zion, 1950, Mr 31,31:3
Wald, Charles, 1940, Je 6,25:2; 1967, Mr 13,37:2
Wald, Charles A, 1952, F 5,29:5
Wald, Flora Mrs, 1940, Jl 17,21:5
Wald, Jacob, 1939, Mr 28,24:4
Wald, Jerry (funl plans, Jl 15,60:2; funl, Jl 17,25:4), 1962, Jl 14,1:5
Wald, Lillian D, 1940, S 2,15:1
Wald, Max Mrs, 1923, D 1,13:4
Wald, Oscar, 1947, Ag 18,17:2
Wald, William Mrs, 1966, D 11,89:1
Waldau, Gustav, 1958, My 27,29:1
Waldbauer, George G Sr, 1939, Ap 9,III,6:6
Waldbauer, Imre (trb), 1952, D 21,II,9:4
Waldbauer, Louis J, 1959, O 21,44:1
Waldeck, E C, 1948, My 19,27:4
Waldeck, George N, 1939, S 26,23:5
Waldeck, Herman, 1960, Mr 23,37:3
Waldeck-Rousseau, M, 1882, F 20,15:4
Waldeck-Rousseau, 1904, Ag 11,7:5
Waldegrave, Countess, 1879, Jl 19,2:3
Waldelton, Thomas D, 1945, Je 1,15:5
Waldemar, Princess, 1909, D 5,13:4
Walden, Arthur T, 1947, Mr 27,4:5
Walden, Austin T (funl, Jl 8,28:3), 1965, Jl 4,37:4
Walden, B H Mrs, 1880, S 21,3:3
Walden, Benjamin H, 1946, Ja 9,23:4
Walden, Charles C Jr, 1962, S 1,19:4
Walden, Charles F, 1956, Mr 31,15:4
Walden, Donald M, 1952, S 17,31:4
Walden, E Beverly, 1922, N 28,21:5
Walden, Elisha Prof, 1909, O 21,9:4
Walden, Erle D, 1942, D 2,25:3
Walden, George Capt, 1925, O 12,21:5
Walden, Harry, 1957, Ja 20,92:5
Walden, Henry W, 1964, S 14,33:3
Walden, Herman N, 1967, Ag 30,43:4
Walden, Howard T, 1957, S 13,23:3
Walden, Howard T Mrs, 1955, S 19,25:2
Walden, James H, 1942, Jl 22,19:2
Walden, John M Bp, 1914, Ja 23,11:5
Walden, Laura J, 1937, My 23,II,11:1
Walden, Lindsey, 1955, Ja 28,19:3
Walden, Lionel A, 1942, N 17,25:5
Walden, Percy T, 1943, Ap 16,21:1
Walden, Percy T Mrs, 1945, Ag 7,23:2
Walden, R W, 1905, Ap 29,11:3
Walden, Reginald P, 1939, Jl 27,19:4
Walden, Reginald P Mrs (A Devoore), 1962, My 26, 25:5
Walden, Robert J, 1951, Je 21,27:4
Walden, Tom Jr, 1961, My 10,45:4
Walden, Van Rensselaer, 1949, Jl 29,21:2
Waldenberger, Emil R, 1948, N 9,27:1
Walder, Abraham, 1964, O 16,39:3
Walder, Bernard, 1949, Je 30,23:2
Walder, John P, 1940, S 21,19:6
Walders, Hugh D, 1954, F 23,27:1
Waldersee, Count von, 1904, Mr 6,4:6
Waldersee, Mary Esther von Countess, 1914, Jl 6,7:6
Waldersee, von Adm, 1903, N 24,9:5
Waldes, Sigmund, 1961, S 20,29:3
Waldeyer, Clara E, 1957, N 30,21:6
Waldhaus, Eleanor E Mrs, 1961, Jl 1,17:4
Waldheim, Aaron, 1938, Mr 8,19:3
Waldheim, Aaron Mrs, 1951, My 24,35:4
Waldheim, Albert P, 1953, F 7,15:4
Waldheim, John, 1958, Ja 30,23:4
Waldheimer, Leo, 1948, Je 4,23:3
Waldheimer, Philip, 1905, Je 30,9:4
Waldhorn, Emil Mrs, 1941, S 7,49:1
Waldie, Thomas E, 1941, S 19,23:4
Waldinger, Emanuel, 1956, Jl 1,56:7
Waldinger, Henry, 1966, O 15,29:4
Waldman, Abraham, 1968, Je 16,68:6
Waldman, Arthur, 1954, Mr 11,31:4

Waldman, David P, 1960, Ap 14,31:3
Waldman, Edward Dr, 1937, Ja 3,II,8:2
Waldman, Henry, 1953, Ag 26,27:1
Waldman, Henry S, 1964, Ag 10,31:4
Waldman, Herman, 1947, F 19,25:3
Waldman, James S, 1952, F 29,23:3
Waldman, Joseph, 1953, D 9,11:5; 1959, O 31,23:4
Waldman, Joseph Mrs, 1967, F 19,89:1
Waldman, Leonard S, 1937, Ap 5,19:4
Waldman, Mark, 1955, S 29,33:1
Waldman, Milton B, 1958, Je 6,23:4
Waldman, Morris, 1945, D 27,19:3; 1956, Je 17,92:3; 1958, Ja 28,27:3
Waldman, Morris D, 1963, S 8,87:1
Waldman, Sol S, 1958, My 21,33:2
Waldman, William M, 1963, O 15,39:1
Waldmann, Louis, 1903, My 24,7:4
Waldmayer, Anna E Mrs, 1942, Je 4,19:3
Waldo, Allan S, 1966, My 18,47:2
Waldo, C G, 1923, Ap 13,17:3
Waldo, Charles M, 1953, Ja 30,22:3
Waldo, Clifford, 1948, D 1,29:2
Waldo, Dorothy, 1960, S 21,37:1
Waldo, Dwight B, 1939, O 30,17:5
Waldo, F L, 1933, O 25,19:5
Waldo, George C, 1942, My 12,19:5
Waldo, George C (funl, O 4,33:1), 1956, O 1,27:6
Waldo, George C Mrs, 1945, S 16,44:4
Waldo, George Curtis Sr, 1921, Ap 3,22:3
Waldo, George E, 1942, Je 17,23:3
Waldo, Gertrude Rhinelander Mrs (funl, My 29,11:3), 1914, My 28,13:6
Waldo, Harold B, 1951, Ap 6,25:4
Waldo, Harold B Mrs, 1947, Je 30,19:3
Waldo, Harry D, 1944, O 23,19:4
Waldo, Helen J, 1937, Ja 26,21:3
Waldo, Henry L Ex-Judge, 1915, Jl 12,7:6
Waldo, Horace, 1914, Jl 24,9:6
Waldo, Howard Lovett, 1914, Ap 20,9:4
Waldo, Ira F, 1948, O 17,76:6
Waldo, Joseph M, 1959, N 13,26:3
Waldo, L P, 1881, S 9,2:1
Waldo, Lewis H, 1952, Je 29,59:3
Waldo, Louis T, 1950, Ja 25,28:2
Waldo, Paul Van W, 1965, My 1,31:6
Waldo, R, 1927, Ag 14,28:3
Waldo, Ralph, 1940, Ag 8,19:5
Waldo, Richard H, 1943, Je 12,13:5
Waldo, Richard H Mrs, 1948, Ag 11,22:3
Waldo, William C, 1949, Je 26,60:6
Waldon, Henry (H Wahlberg), 1960, Je 3,31:4
Waldon, Sidney D (por), 1945, Ja 21,39:1
Waldon, Sidney D Mrs, 1967, S 12,47:4
Waldor, Jack M, 1967, My 27,31:2
Waldorf, Daniel, 1909, Mr 5,9:4
Waldorf, Ernest L, 1943, Jl 28,15:1
Waldorf, Frederick H Mrs, 1949, Ag 2,20:2
Waldorf, George P, 1939, F 22,21:6
Waldorf, Jacob, 1947, My 2,22:3
Waldorf, Louis Rabbi, 1924, Je 21,13:6
Waldorf, Mirl, 1937, D 15,25:3
Waldorf, Wilella, 1946, Mr 13,29:6
Waldridge, Harold, 1957, Je 28,23:4
Waldron, Alfred, 1958, Je 7,19:5
Waldron, Alfred M, 1952, Je 30,19:4
Waldron, Austin J, 1942, Mr 13,19:2
Waldron, Billy, 1924, My 19,17:3
Waldron, Carroll T, 1949, Mr 11,25:3
Waldron, Charles, 1946, Mr 7,25:1; 1951, Jl 25,24:2
Waldron, Charles F, 1916, Je 6,13:6
Waldron, Cornelius A, 1912, Ja 22,9:4
Waldron, Daniel C Mrs, 1939, Jl 20,20:3
Waldron, Earl W, 1956, S 22,17:5
Waldron, Edward A, 1942, Ja 27,21:5; 1964, Ja 25,23:5
Waldron, Edward F, 1940, Ap 30,21:5
Waldron, Edward M, 1942, F 1,43:1
Waldron, Florence, 1946, Je 5,23:5
Waldron, Francis E (E Dennis),(funl plans, F 2,29:1), 1961, F 1,35:1
Waldron, Frederick A, 1939, Jl 14,19:4
Waldron, Frederick A Mrs, 1951, Jl 24,25:2
Waldron, George B Mrs (Isabel Waldron), 1915, Jl 22,9:4
Waldron, Gilbert, 1947, O 20,27:2
Waldron, Gordon, 1939, O 5,23:5
Waldron, H, 1880, S 15,5:4
Waldron, Hampden Maj, 1924, D 7,7:2
Waldron, Harry E Mrs, 1952, My 11,93:1
Waldron, Herbert M, 1941, Ja 22,21:3
Waldron, Irving, 1944, Jl 23,35:2
Waldron, John A Bro, 1937, N 11,25:5
Waldron, John D, 1950, S 11,23:3
Waldron, Laurence A, 1923, D 29,13:5
Waldron, Louis V Dr, 1937, Mr 14,II,8:3
Waldron, Martin Mrs, 1949, D 14,31:4
Waldron, Maurice L, 1955, S 15,33:3
Waldron, Patrick J Mrs, 1947, Ja 11,19:5
Waldron, Ralph, 1957, Jl 26,19:5
Waldron, Ralph I, 1939, F 9,21:5
Waldron, Robert E, 1965, Je 10,35:1
Waldron, Selden F, 1950, N 9,33:5
Waldron, Thomas A, 1950, D 27,27:4
Waldron, Thomas F, 1953, S 14,27:6
Waldron, W H, 1881, Mr 2,3:3
Waldron, Warren H, 1957, Ap 28,87:1
Waldron, Webb, 1945, Ag 6,16:4
Waldron, William, 1945, Mr 11,40:1
Waldron, William D, 1947, Mr 2,61:1
Waldron, William Francis Dr, 1916, Ag 26,7:5
Waldron, William H, 1945, F 2,20:2
Waldron, William H Mrs, 1945, Ap 3,19:1
Waldron, William J, 1954, S 25,15:5
Waldrop, Pike P Mrs, 1947, S 16,23:3
Waldrop, Robert, 1963, S 28,19:5
Waldrop, Uda, 1951, Je 10,48:2
Waldstein, Ernst, 1954, My 16,88:1
Waldstein, Louis Dr, 1915, Ap 13,11:5
Waldteufel, Emile C, 1915, F 17,11:5
Waldteufel, Henri, 1951, My 21,27:5
Waldvogel, Edward N, 1954, My 8,17:5
Waldvogel, Edwin C, 1966, Ap 24,86:6
Waleffe, Maurice de, 1946, Ap 1,27:2
Walenta, Edmund J, 1948, S 20,25:5
Walenta, Edmund J Mrs, 1938, N 17,25:4
Walenta, Max J H, 1958, Jl 29,23:5
Walerstein, Julius, 1964, Mr 29,60:6
Wales, B R, 1929, N 26,31:3
Wales, Charles M Mrs, 1962, N 6,33:5
Wales, Frank J, 1951, D 15,13:4
Wales, George C, 1940, Mr 22,19:3
Wales, Henry, 1960, Ja 30,21:1
Wales, James A Mrs, 1937, Mr 23,23:2
Wales, Leonard E, 1943, Mr 29,15:5
Wales, Philip Skinner Dr, 1906, S 16,7:6
Wales, Prince of (Child of),(funl, Ap 26,5:3), 1871, Ap 8,1:2
Wales, Salem H, 1902, D 3,9:4
Wales, Samuel G, 1966, Ap 11,35:1
Wales, Wellington, 1966, Ap 11,35:1
Wales, Wellington E, 1954, S 30,31:5
Walewski, Count, 1868, S 29,4:7
Walewski, S Colonna, 1955, My 22,89:2
Waley, Arthur D, 1966, Je 28,42:1
Walford, Kenneth C, 1938, Ja 8,15:2
Walger, Louis M, 1967, N 8,47:3
Walgering, Frank J, 1909, My 29,7:5
Walgreen, Charles R (will, D 20,52:1),(por), 1939, D 12,27:1
Walinska, Rosa N Mrs, 1953, My 23,15:5
Walk, Albert Mrs, 1954, My 19,32:5
Walk, Arthur R, 1953, Ap 21,27:4
Walk, George E, 1962, N 8,39:4
Walk, George E Mrs, 1947, My 2,22:2
Walk, Henry W J, 1948, Ap 7,25:3
Walkden, Alex G Lord, 1951, Ap 26,29:2
Walkel, Frederick, 1950, D 13,35:2
Walkem, Joseph B, 1938, My 22,II,6:8
Walker, A (see also S 15), 1875, O 30,6:7
Walker, A, 1934, F 14,19:4
Walker, A B, 1926, O 9,17:5
Walker, A Lucien Jr Mrs, 1947, D 15,25:5
Walker, A Selden, 1950, N 22,25:1
Walker, A Stewart, 1952, Je 11,29:4
Walker, A T, 1927, Ag 9,23:5
Walker, Adalene M, 1949, F 1,25:1
Walker, Adelaide H Mrs, 1924, Jl 21,11:5
Walker, Alanson B, 1947, Ja 23,23:2
Walker, Albert, 1941, F 18,24:2
Walker, Albert B (Ab), 1954, Ag 4,46:6
Walker, Albert H, 1944, F 26,13:2
Walker, Albert Henry, 1915, S 2,9:5
Walker, Albert O, 1951, Mr 10,13:4
Walker, Albert R, 1958, S 18,31:4
Walker, Alex, 1950, My 17,29:4
Walker, Alex D, 1954, S 9,31:2
Walker, Alex E Sr, 1960, Ap 20,39:3
Walker, Alfred, 1947, F 8,17:4
Walker, Alfred (por), 1948, O 18,23:5
Walker, Alfred S, 1958, O 20,29:5
Walker, Alixe, 1961, Ja 4,33:5
Walker, Allyn W, 1921, S 18,22:2
Walker, Amasa, 1939, D 28,22:3
Walker, Andrew M, 1938, My 3,23:4
Walker, Annie (Sister Theresa), 1885, Ja 22,5:3
Walker, Arch F, 1949, My 1,88:6
Walker, Arch F Mrs, 1937, Ag 10,19:4
Walker, Arthur G, 1939, S 15,23:2
Walker, Arthur J, 1953, O 1,29:3
Walker, Arthur L, 1952, O 1,34:3
Walker, Arthur L Jr, 1956, Ag 9,25:3
Walker, Arthur L Mrs, 1952, N 16,88:7
Walker, Arthur T, 1948, S 4,15:4
Walker, Arthur V, 1946, Ap 12,27:4
Walker, Arthur W, 1945, Je 26,19:3
Walker, Asa Rear-Adm, 1916, Mr 8,11:4
Walker, B W Sir, 1876, F 14,4:6
Walker, Barbour Mrs, 1950, Ja 20,26:2
Walker, Bartol, 1944, D 30,11:6
Walker, Belle, 1953, Mr 10,29:3
Walker, Benson, 1943, O 11,19:2
Walker, Bert, 1947, Je 20,19:4; 1952, Mr 8,13:2
Walker, Bert J Sr, 1954, My 30,44:2
Walker, Bertram W, 1941, My 29,19:3
Walker, Bertrand Mrs, 1946, S 3,19:5
Walker, Bill (Wm H), 1966, Je 15,47:2
Walker, Bradford H (will, D 29,16:5), 1949, N 30, 27:4
Walker, Burt C, 1943, My 6,19:5
Walker, Buz M, 1949, Ag 22,21:3
Walker, C C B, 1888, Ja 27,1:6
Walker, C H, 1936, Ap 13,17:3
Walker, C J Mrs, 1919, My 26,15:6
Walker, C S, 1933, Ja 15,25:1
Walker, Calvin Bruce, 1908, Ja 24,7:5
Walker, Carl J, 1943, S 7,23:5
Walker, Cecil, 1950, Ja 22,78:2
Walker, Charles, 1952, Ja 14,19:3
Walker, Charles A Jr, 1943, My 21,19:4
Walker, Charles C, 1919, O 27,11:6; 1950, N 4,17:2
Walker, Charles Clement, 1968, O 2,39:3
Walker, Charles E, 1950, F 24,24:2
Walker, Charles J Mrs, 1964, Mr 29,61:1
Walker, Charles Johnson, 1920, Mr 23,9:6
Walker, Charles M, 1947, S 4,25:6; 1952, S 2,23:3
Walker, Charles T, 1956, Ja 15,92:5
Walker, Charles T Rev, 1921, Jl 30,9:6
Walker, Charles W, 1944, D 2,13:3; 1950, Jl 21,19:4
Walker, Charlotte, 1958, Mr 26,37:1
Walker, Claude F, 1966, N 16,47:4
Walker, Claude F Mrs, 1965, Ja 2,19:1
Walker, Clifford, 1937, Ap 30,21:4
Walker, Clifford B, 1943, Jl 6,21:6
Walker, Clifford M, 1954, N 10,33:5
Walker, Corliss P, 1942, D 24,15:2
Walker, Curtis, 1955, D 11,88:8
Walker, Cyril (por), 1948, Ag 7,1:2
Walker, Cyril C, 1941, My 9,21:3
Walker, D A, 1881, F 5,2:6
Walker, Daniel T, 1956, My 23,31:4
Walker, Danton, 1960, Ag 9,27:1
Walker, David, 1903, Ag 23,7:5; 1941, N 16,56:4
Walker, David B Rev (S J), 1911, D 20,13:5
Walker, David Dr, 1917, My 12,11:4
Walker, David E, 1968, O 26,37:3
Walker, David H Mrs, 1943, S 17,22:3
Walker, David S, 1939, Ap 2,III,6:8
Walker, Delos (Mar 1), 1963, Ap 1,36:7
Walker, Delos Mrs, 1966, Ag 16,39:5
Walker, Dexter H, 1914, F 27,11:4
Walker, Don H, 1943, Je 29,19:5
Walker, Donald H, 1960, My 15,86:8
Walker, Doretta V Mrs, 1945, Jl 12,11:6
Walker, Dudley P, 1962, Ap 30,27:4
Walker, Dugald S, 1937, F 27,17:6
Walker, Duncan S Gen, 1912, Je 6,11:4
Walker, E, 1879, Ja 13,5:4
Walker, E Chandler Mrs, 1937, Ap 4,II,10:6
Walker, E D Rev, 1903, Ap 24,9:6
Walker, E R, 1932, O 15,15:1
Walker, Eadith C Dame, 1937, O 9,19:2
Walker, Eddie (Archie), 1962, Mr 8,31:2
Walker, Edgar S, 1955, Ja 3,27:5
Walker, Edith E, 1954, Mr 11,34:7
Walker, Edmund Sir, 1924, Mr 28,17:3
Walker, Edward, 1905, Ap 4,11:6
Walker, Edward C Sen, 1903, Jl 19,7:6
Walker, Edward T, 1953, Ag 6,21:4
Walker, Edwin, 1910, S 4,9:5
Walker, Edwin K, 1953, S 5,15:6
Walker, Edwin L, 1951, Ja 12,27:4
Walker, Edyth, 1950, F 26,78:1
Walker, Elbridge Jr, 1961, Ja 10,47:4
Walker, Elisha (will, D 13,28:3), 1950, N 10,27:1
Walker, Elisha Mrs, 1961, Ap 17,29:4
Walker, Eliza Blaine, 1885, Mr 4,4:7
Walker, Eliza Harding Mrs, 1906, Ja 17,11:6
Walker, Elton D, 1944, F 25,17:2
Walker, Emma E, 1954, Ap 16,21:1
Walker, Ephraim A, 1917, D 14,13:4
Walker, Ernest A, 1943, Mr 17,21:3
Walker, Ernest G, 1944, F 8,15:3
Walker, Ernest L, 1952, Ja 21,16:3
Walker, Ernest M, 1961, Ag 31,27:1
Walker, Ernest R, 1940, Ja 1,23:4
Walker, Ernest R Mrs, 1956, D 23,30:4
Walker, Ernest T, 1949, Mr 19,15:2; 1965, Ja 11,45:1
Walker, Ethel, 1951, Mr 4,92:3
Walker, Evelyn, 1953, O 30,23:4
Walker, Evelyn T, 1947, Mr 21,22:2
Walker, F A Gen, 1897, Ja 6,9:1
Walker, F Lawrence, 1942, My 17,47:3
Walker, Faye Rev Dr, 1903, Je 10,9:6
Walker, Flora D Mrs, 1955, F 20,89:2
Walker, Florence C Mrs, 1940, D 10,25:6
Walker, Florence L, 1955, F 28,19:5
Walker, Florence M, 1956, My 17,31:3
Walker, Forest A, 1950, S 11,23:4
Walker, Francis, 1881, N 26,4:7; 1950, Ja 16,26:4
Walker, Francis Capt, 1937, Ja 14,22:1
Walker, Francis R Mrs, 1951, My 18,28:3
Walker, Francis S, 1952, Ja 21,15:3
Walker, Frank, 1952, Ag 26,25:1
Walker, Frank B, 1963, O 17,35:2
Walker, Frank C, 1945, N 25,48:4
Walker, Frank C (funl, S 17,39:5), 1959, S 14,29:1
Walker, Frank R, 1949, Jl 10,56:3
Walker, Franklin H, 1916, Je 18,18:5
Walker, Fred A (por), 1947, Mr 26,25:1
Walker, Fred A Mrs (cor, Ja 13,23:4), 1943, Ja 12, 24:2

Walker, Fred C, 1955, Mr 26,15:2
Walker, Fred M, 1958, F 2,86:8
Walker, Frederick J (por), 1944, Jl 11,15:1
Walker, Frederick P, 1960, F 4,31:2
Walker, Frederick W, 1938, F 8,21:5
Walker, G C, 1885, My 12,5:4
Walker, G M Capt, 1903, Ag 1,7:6
Walker, Gale H, 1958, Ap 23,33:3
Walker, Gardner Maj, 1873, O 8,5:4
Walker, Gayle C, 1941, O 11,17:2
Walker, Geoffrey Fritz, 1913, S 9,7:6
Walker, George (funl, Ja 9,13:5), 1911, Ja 8,13:4
Walker, George, 1924, O 16,25:4; 1947, O 30,25:5; 1966, My 4,47:4
Walker, George A, 1955, D 17,23:2; 1959, Je 9,37:6; 1963, Ag 10,17:5
Walker, George B, 1937, Mr 6,17:4; 1943, Jl 4,21:2; 1947, Ag 4,17:4; 1963, Ag 28,33:6
Walker, George C, 1937, Mr 1,19:1
Walker, George Dr, 1937, Ap 1,23:4
Walker, George H, 1906, My 6,9:6; 1949, Mr 22,25:1; 1953, Je 25,27:3; 1959, Mr 14,23:5
Walker, George H Mrs, 1961, Ag 29,31:4
Walker, George L, 1952, Ja 28,17:2
Walker, George R, 1954, F 5,19:1
Walker, George S, 1954, D 5,88:7
Walker, George T, 1944, S 23,13:4; 1952, Mr 21,24:3
Walker, George W, 1914, F 16,7:5; 1943, My 17,15:1; 1946, Je 18,25:2; 1959, F 2,15:5
Walker, Gerald S, 1953, O 15,33:2
Walker, Gerard S, 1945, Jl 7,13:5
Walker, Gertrude D, 1942, D 18,28:2
Walker, Gertrude D (will), 1943, Ja 3,32:8
Walker, Gilbert, 1958, N 6,37:4
Walker, Gordon, 1959, Je 2,35:3
Walker, Gus, 1939, D 14,27:3
Walker, Gus Mrs, 1966, F 27,85:1
Walker, Guy M, 1945, Ag 7,24:3
Walker, Guy W, 1943, Jl 11,35:2
Walker, Gwyn, 1940, Mr 20,27:2
Walker, H C, 1932, N 3,21:1
Walker, H J Ex-Chief-Justice, 1872, Ap 26,1:6
Walker, H Mercer, 1948, Ap 27,25:4
Walker, H Newton, 1946, Jl 9,22:3
Walker, H O, 1929, Ja 15,29:1
Walker, Harlan, 1942, Je 2,23:2
Walker, Harley M, 1937, Je 24,25:4
Walker, Harold, 1938, Jl 9,13:4
Walker, Harold D, 1937, Ap 18,II,8:8
Walker, Harold F, 1957, Je 6,31:5
Walker, Harold Strother, 1919, F 13,15:3
Walker, Harriet G H Mrs, 1917, Ja 14,19:1
Walker, Harrington E, 1958, N 19,37:4
Walker, Harris H Col, 1937, Mr 12,23:1
Walker, Harry B, 1956, Ag 28,27:3
Walker, Harry H Mrs, 1947, Je 8,60:3
Walker, Harry J, 1941, Ag 15,17:3
Walker, Harry L, 1954, Ja 7,31:1
Walker, Harry L Mrs, 1961, N 28,37:4
Walker, Harry W, 1948, N 10,29:3
Walker, Harry W Sr, 1953, Jl 28,19:5
Walker, Harvey J Mrs, 1951, Mr 26,23:2
Walker, Hasseltine S, 1946, O 26,17:4
Walker, Hay 3d, 1925, My 15,19:5
Walker, Helen, 1968, Mr 12,43:2
Walker, Henry A, 1950, S 8,31:2
Walker, Henry B, 1940, Ap 8,19:2
Walker, Henry B Jr, 1965, D 4,31:1
Walker, Henry C, 1939, Mr 27,15:4
Walker, Henry Col, 1914, D 21,9:4
Walker, Henry F Dr, 1917, Ag 17,9:7
Walker, Henry Harrison Gen, 1912, Mr 23,13:5
Walker, Henry L, 1943, Jl 1,19:3; 1946, Mr 3,45:1
Walker, Henry M, 1937, O 22,23:1
Walker, Henry S, 1957, Mr 17,86:5
Walker, Henry W, 1964, Ap 2,33:4
Walker, Henry Y, 1955, Jl 4,11:5
Walker, Herbert, 1952, Je 14,15:5; 1955, Ja 25,25:3
Walker, Herbert A, 1949, S 30,24:2
Walker, Herbert B, 1942, Ag 26,19:6
Walker, Herbert E, 1951, My 25,27:4
Walker, Herbert S, 1944, O 25,21:3
Walker, Herbert W, 1967, Ja 21,31:1
Walker, Herman B, 1959, Ja 12,39:4
Walker, Hervey S, 1958, S 18,31:4
Walker, Hiram A, 1940, O 27,45:2
Walker, Horace A, 1956, Ap 20,25:2
Walker, Horatio (por), 1938, S 28,25:1
Walker, Hosea Ellsworth Dr, 1917, Ag 17,9:5
Walker, Howard A, 1947, My 7,27:2
Walker, Hubert M, 1943, D 1,21:2
Walker, Hugh, 1939, Je 30,19:4; 1942, Ap 26,39:1
Walker, Hugh K, 1949, S 20,29:2
Walker, Hugh K Jr, 1959, F 13,27:5
Walker, I Henry, 1943, Ag 28,11:6
Walker, Irving L, 1938, F 19,15:2
Walker, Isaac P Ex-Sen, 1872, Mr 31,1:6
Walker, Isaac S, 1938, Ja 24,23:5
Walker, Isaac W, 1937, F 2,23:5
Walker, J, 1927, Ap 16,15:5
Walker, J B, 1903, My 21,3:2; 1931, Jl 8,25:1
Walker, J Brandt, 1925, Mr 31,19:5
Walker, J J, 1884, N 5,4:6
Walker, J Townsend, 1966, Mr 6,93:1
Walker, James, 1941, Mr 20,21:3
Walker, James A, 1946, Mr 8,21:4
Walker, James B, 1943, Ja 29,19:3
Walker, James B (por), 1945, Mr 31,19:1
Walker, James B Jr Mrs, 1955, D 26,19:3
Walker, James B Mrs, 1946, Ap 3,25:4
Walker, James D, 1940, Je 11,25:4
Walker, James E (por), 1955, O 16,86:1
Walker, James G, 1948, Jl 13,27:4
Walker, James H, 1939, Mr 11,17:6; 1954, D 3,27:3
Walker, James J, 1946, N 19,1:3
Walker, James P Mrs, 1959, Mr 6,25:3
Walker, James R, 1937, Ag 9,19:2; 1942, D 31,15:5; 1946, Je 17,21:3
Walker, James Rev Dr, 1874, D 25,4:7
Walker, James S, 1940, Ag 1,21:2
Walker, James W, 1943, S 25,15:3
Walker, Jane Gilbert, 1925, Ap 16,21:4
Walker, Jane H, 1938, N 18,22:2
Walker, Janet A Mrs, 1956, O 7,86:6
Walker, Jennie M Mrs, 1943, O 8,19:3
Walker, Jennie Mrs, 1943, Mr 25,21:4
Walker, Jerome Dr, 1924, Je 21,13:6
Walker, Jessie M, 1940, Je 7,23:4
Walker, John, 1859, My 24,2:3; 1943, F 25,21:5; 1950, Ap 3,23:1
Walker, John A, 1947, Ap 19,15:3
Walker, John B, 1937, My 1,19:4; 1939, My 18,25:5
Walker, John B (por), 1942, Ap 14,21:1
Walker, John B Mrs, 1967, Ja 22,76:4
Walker, John C 2d, 1960, N 2,39:3
Walker, John G, 1925, Jl 17,15:5
Walker, John G Mrs, 1949, Ap 9,17:3
Walker, John G Rear-Adm, 1907, S 22,9:6
Walker, John Grimes Rear-Adm, 1907, S 17,11:7
Walker, John H, 1955, Ag 29,19:6; 1960, Jl 3,33:2; 1966, Je 24,37:1
Walker, John H Mrs, 1958, Je 25,29:2
Walker, John Leeming, 1925, Ag 16,5:3
Walker, John M, 1951, Jl 27,17:1
Walker, John Mrs, 1950, D 16,17:5; 1951, Ag 16,27:3
Walker, John R, 1914, Ja 11,15:5
Walker, John S, 1953, N 22,88:3
Walker, John Sr, 1947, Jl 10,21:2
Walker, John T, 1940, N 24,51:2
Walker, John T Jr, 1945, D 17,21:1
Walker, John W, 1945, D 13,29:4; 1950, Ja 17,27:4
Walker, John Y G, 1940, F 18,43:3
Walker, Joseph, 1866, Ap 1,5:5; 1937, Ap 30,4:6; 1940, Je 27,23:6; 1941, N 26,23:5; 1951, Je 29,21:5
Walker, Joseph A, 1953, Ag 28,17:1; 1966, Je 9,1:6
Walker, Joseph G Mrs, 1946, Ja 17,23:3
Walker, Joseph H, 1949, Je 20,19:4; 1958, Ap 5,15:4
Walker, Joseph J, 1944, Jl 27,17:4
Walker, Joseph Mrs, 1960, D 10,23:2
Walker, Joseph R, 1940, Je 22,15:6
Walker, Joseph Sr, 1918, Ag 28,7:2
Walker, Joseph T, 1944, D 1,23:3
Walker, Julian C, 1947, O 28,25:1
Walker, June, 1966, F 5,29:3
Walker, Kendall, 1951, D 26,25:3
Walker, Kenneth M, 1966, Ja 25,41:1
Walker, Kenneth S, 1966, Ap 10,76:5
Walker, Kent, 1949, O 10,23:3
Walker, L Clark, 1937, Je 8,25:5
Walker, Lapsley G (por), 1939, Jl 13,19:1
Walker, Laura B, 1960, F 4,31:3
Walker, Lawis Sr Mrs, 1945, Mr 4,38:6
Walker, Lawrence A, 1951, N 10,17:4
Walker, Lee E Maj, 1937, D 20,27:4
Walker, Legare, 1948, O 1,26:3
Walker, Leona L, 1947, Jl 9,23:3
Walker, Leonard, 1952, Mr 10,21:4
Walker, Leverett H Col, 1907, O 30,9:5
Walker, Lewis, 1938, Ja 25,21:4
Walker, Lewis C, 1947, Je 13,23:4
Walker, Lilian, 1921, Ap 13,15:6
Walker, Louis C, 1963, O 6,88:5
Walker, Louis E, 1960, Ja 22,25:2
Walker, Louis W, 1940, D 16,23:5
Walker, Louisa, 1964, Jl 14,33:2
Walker, Louise, 1946, Jl 6,15:4; 1959, S 7,17:6
Walker, Loulie, 1955, S 7,23:3
Walker, Lula Mrs, 1952, Ap 21,21:4
Walker, Lyman T, 1944, Ag 14,15:5
Walker, M R, 1881, S 24,2:6
Walker, Mannie, 1958, O 2,37:5
Walker, Margaret M (Sister Mary Angela), 1953, D 14,31:3
Walker, Marie W, 1950, N 13,28:3
Walker, Marlborough S (por), 1946, N 10,62:3
Walker, Marshall B, 1956, N 14,35:3
Walker, Martha A, 1951, Jl 28,11:6
Walker, Mary, 1952, Ja 8,27:2
Walker, Mary A Mrs, 1873, Ja 21,5:2
Walker, Mary Dr, 1919, F 23,18:1
Walker, Mary L, 1946, Ja 16,24:2
Walker, Melvin H Jr, 1940, N 22,23:3
Walker, Meriweather L, 1947, Jl 30,21:3
Walker, Michael Mrs, 1954, F 23,27:1
Walker, Milledge P, 1950, Ap 1,15:2
Walker, Milton E, 1941, N 6,23:2
Walker, Nathan, 1925, Jl 15,17:6
Walker, Nathaniel F, 1940, My 20,17:3
Walker, Norbert J, 1953, N 4,33:2
Walker, Norman, 1952, Jl 2,25:6
Walker, Norman L, 1951, Ja 26,24:2
Walker, Norman S, 1944, Jl 24,15:6
Walker, Norman S Mrs, 1951, Ap 6,25:4
Walker, Odie B, 1937, Ja 19,23:2
Walker, Oliver C, 1960, Ap 6,41:3
Walker, Oscar J, 1941, O 17,23:5
Walker, Paul A, 1965, N 4,47:1
Walker, Percy, 1880, D 28,5:4
Walker, Peter, 1960, S 2,23:1
Walker, Peter A, 1952, O 9,31:5
Walker, Peter G, 1912, Ag 22,9:6
Walker, Prescott H, 1954, Ap 30,15:1
Walker, Q Forrest, 1966, Ap 26,45:1
Walker, R, 1926, D 23,19:3
Walker, R Gordon, 1959, Ja 16,27:2
Walker, R J C, 1903, D 20,7:6
Walker, R Murdock Mrs, 1939, My 2,23:5
Walker, Rahno Mrs, 1946, Jl 27,17:3
Walker, Ralph C, 1962, S 29,23:3
Walker, Ralph D, 1947, N 26,23:5
Walker, Ralph E, 1958, Je 11,36:1
Walker, Ralph E Mrs, 1958, N 3,37:4
Walker, Ralph H, 1961, Ap 22,25:6
Walker, Ralph J Mrs, 1949, Je 5,92:3
Walker, Randolph C, 1958, Ja 28,27:1
Walker, Randolph S, 1949, Mr 30,25:4
Walker, Ray (Warren R), 1960, Je 22,35:5
Walker, Reggie, 1951, N 7,29:4
Walker, Reginald, 1949, N 21,25:3
Walker, Reginald E Mrs, 1948, N 8,21:3
Walker, Reuben L, 1950, O 31,27:4
Walker, Richard A, 1951, D 2,91:1
Walker, Richard A Mrs, 1954, Je 24,27:1
Walker, Richard L, 1923, N 26,17:3
Walker, Richard P, 1941, D 10,25:2
Walker, Richard Sr Mrs, 1938, Ap 21,19:2
Walker, Richard W, 1874, Je 18,5:4; 1947, Mr 4,25:2
Walker, Robert, 1951, Ag 29,25:4; 1954, Je 15,29:5
Walker, Robert B, 1956, D 18,31:5
Walker, Robert C, 1954, D 23,19:4
Walker, Robert E, 1945, Ap 13,17:3; 1958, Mr 17,29:3
Walker, Robert F, 1952, Je 15,84:2
Walker, Robert J, 1869, N 12,5:1
Walker, Robert Rev, 1917, Jl 11,9:5
Walker, Robert S, 1950, Ap 8,13:5
Walker, Robert W, 1909, Jl 23,7:4; 1950, O 28,17:6
Walker, Roger A P, 1955, Ja 7,21:2
Walker, Rollin H, 1955, Ag 5,19:5
Walker, Romine, 1937, Jl 6,19:2
Walker, Russell P, 1955, D 12,31:1
Walker, Russell S, 1920, D 26,22:2
Walker, S Wylie, 1946, My 2,21:3
Walker, Samuel, 1911, Ag 14,7:6
Walker, Samuel C, 1907, N 24,9:6
Walker, Samuel D, 1952, N 24,23:5
Walker, Samuel E, 1941, Ap 13,39:1
Walker, Samuel H, 1955, My 28,15:2
Walker, Samuel J Dr, 1919, Mr 16,20:5
Walker, Samuel N, 1947, Jl 31,21:3
Walker, Samuel N Mrs, 1951, Mr 21,33:4
Walker, Samuel P 3d, 1946, Ap 29,21:4
Walker, Sidney J Mrs, 1960, My 2,29:4
Walker, Sophia A, 1943, O 30,15:2
Walker, Stanley E, 1956, D 26,27:3
Walker, Stanley M, 1954, Je 19,15:5
Walker, Stanley Mrs, 1964, Ap 5,87:1
Walker, Stanley R, 1950, D 4,29:5
Walker, Stanley W, 1964, Je 1,29:2
Walker, Stuart (por), 1941, Mr 14,21:1
Walker, Stuart B, 1964, Ag 20,29:3
Walker, Stuart H, 1967, My 24,47:4
Walker, Syd, 1945, Ja 15,19:4
Walker, Sydnor H, 1966, D 14,47:5
Walker, T B, 1928, Jl 29,25:3
Walker, T Dart, 1914, Jl 22,9:4
Walker, T George, 1956, Mr 21,37:1
Walker, Terrell H, 1950, Je 10,17:4
Walker, Theodore F Mrs, 1943, O 27,23:4
Walker, Theodore P, 1951, N 29,33:2
Walker, Theodore V, 1952, Ja 24,27:1
Walker, Thomas, 1863, Je 12,5:3
Walker, Thomas B, 1955, Ap 9,13:3; 1964, Je 4,37:6
Walker, Thomas C, 1943, Mr 24,23:3; 1945, Ag 17, 17:1; 1951, Ap 3,27:3
Walker, Thomas Dixon Capt, 1907, D 1,11:5
Walker, Thomas E, 1944, D 27,19:2; 1951, Je 21,27:2
Walker, Thomas J, 1945, Ja 19,19:3
Walker, Thomas L, 1942, Ag 7,17:6
Walker, Thomas L Mrs, 1949, S 18,94:5
Walker, Tom P, 1961, Ja 11,47:3
Walker, W Frank (por), 1941, S 28,48:2
Walker, W Leslie, 1937, O 17,II,9:3
Walker, W S Commodore, 1863, D 6,2:3
Walker, Waldo C, 1961, S 10,86:3
Walker, Walter, 1947, D 5,26:2; 1956, O 9,35:1; 1962, Jl 1,56:2
Walker, Walter B, 1938, Ap 8,19:3
Walker, Walter M, 1939, Ag 15,19:2

Walker, Walter N Mrs, 1949, F 21,23:5
Walker, Warren, 1955, Ap 28,29:4
Walker, Warren H, 1941, My 10,15:1
Walker, Wesley S, 1961, Ja 19,29:1
Walker, Weyman, 1951, Jl 8,60:4
Walker, Wiley A, 1966, My 19,47:2
Walker, Wilfred, 1912, Ag 31,7:1
Walker, Will A, 1953, O 30,23:3
Walker, Will A Mrs, 1960, Ag 19,23:3
Walker, William, 1903, Jl 29,7:6; 1903, Ag 17,7:5; 1942, F 27,17:3; 1947, Je 27,21:3
Walker, William A, 1957, Je 18,33:3
Walker, William A D Mrs, 1949, Jl 30,15:5
Walker, William Augustus, 1910, Ag 16,7:6
Walker, William D Bp, 1917, My 3,15:4
Walker, William F B Mrs, 1943, Mr 30,21:5
Walker, William G Mrs, 1947, Je 21,17:3
Walker, William H, 1916, My 16,13:4
Walker, William H (por), 1938, Ja 19,23:3
Walker, William H, 1946, Ag 29,27:1
Walker, William Hall, 1917, N 30,13:7
Walker, William Isaac, 1924, Ag 20,13:3
Walker, William J, 1939, S 16,17:6; 1958, My 20,34:3
Walker, William K, 1938, Mr 25,19:2; 1944, Mr 16, 19:5
Walker, William L, 1954, N 13,15:3
Walker, William M, 1939, S 12,25:5; 1947, Ja 13,21:5
Walker, William M T, 1941, My 2,21:4
Walker, William R, 1922, D 22,15:5
Walker, William Rev, 1937, Je 10,23:5
Walker, William W, 1947, Mr 6,25:2
Walker, William W Capt, 1866, N 23,1:7
Walker, William Wallace Dr (funl, Je 16,21:3), 1925, Je 15,15:6
Walker, Williston Prof, 1922, Mr 10,15:4
Walker, Winter B, 1948, Je 12,15:1
Walker-Heneage-Vivian, Algernon, 1952, F 27,27:4
Walkinshaw, Millie F, 1883, Mr 22,8:2
Walkley, Charles T, 1947, Ja 7,27:5
Walkley, Frances S, 1951, Ja 29,19:1
Walkley, Harry T, 1953, Ja 11,90:4
Walkley, Raymond L, 1962, Ap 26,33:4
Walko, Gustav M Mrs, 1949, Mr 13,76:7
Walkonis, Stanley, 1952, Ja 3,27:1
Walkowitz, Abraham, 1965, Ja 28,29:2
Walkup, Thomas, 1942, My 6,19:1
Wall, Albert C, 1945, My 4,19:5
Wall, Albert C Mrs, 1946, Mr 21,25:2
Wall, Albert F, 1959, Ag 11,27:2
Wall, Alex, 1957, Je 26,31:4
Wall, Alexander J (por), 1944, Ap 16,41:1
Wall, Anne M, 1946, F 10,42:5
Wall, Ashbel T, 1949, Mr 13,76:1
Wall, Ashbelt T Mrs, 1965, D 12,86:4
Wall, Bernhardt Mrs, 1938, N 17,25:2
Wall, Celia B Mrs, 1944, My 24,19:3
Wall, Charles A, 1958, D 9,41:1
Wall, Charles S Mrs, 1938, Ap 30,15:5
Wall, Charley, 1879, Je 28,5:4
Wall, Christopher J, 1956, F 13,27:4
Wall, Constant van de, 1945, Ja 10,23:2
Wall, Daniel W (cor, F 3,85:1), 1952, Ja 29,25:2
Wall, David V, 1938, Je 2,23:4
Wall, E Berry (por), 1940, My 6,17:1
Wall, Edward B Mrs, 1952, Ap 8,29:5
Wall, Edward C, 1915, Ap 26,9:5
Wall, Edward Mrs, 1951, N 9,27:3
Wall, Emeline Mrs, 1913, Je 13,9:4
Wall, Enos A Col, 1920, Jl 1,13:3
Wall, Eugene W, 1951, Ja 31,25:3
Wall, Francis, 1947, My 17,15:4
Wall, Francis H Msgr (funl, S 26,17:6), 1925, S 23, 25:3
Wall, Frank D, 1946, S 5,27:4
Wall, Frank E, 1955, Je 8,29:3
Wall, Frank J, 1947, S 22,23:3
Wall, Frank J (por), 1947, N 20,29:1
Wall, Frank T Mrs, 1951, O 2,27:2
Wall, Frederick, 1944, Mr 26,42:2
Wall, Frederick R, 1939, N 17,21:3
Wall, Glenn C, 1953, D 15,39:2
Wall, Henry C, 1963, My 1,39:4
Wall, Henry R, 1956, Je 12,35:5
Wall, Herbert N, 1949, N 8,31:3
Wall, Jacob, 1937, My 20,21:4
Wall, James Col, 1872, Je 11,4:7
Wall, James E, 1959, N 11,35:2
Wall, James J, 1941, My 15,23:2
Wall, Jerry P, 1950, Ag 10,25:5
Wall, Jessie C, 1940, O 12,17:5
Wall, John, 1947, Ja 9,23:2; 1952, Mr 1,15:6
Wall, John B, 1943, D 28,17:4
Wall, John F, 1943, Ap 5,19:5
Wall, John J, 1949, Je 26,60:4
Wall, John M, 1941, Ja 27,15:2; 1963, Jl 24,31:5
Wall, Joseph Mrs, 1952, Ap 13,76:5
Wall, Margaret V, 1958, Jl 7,27:4
Wall, Melvin L, 1967, Mr 25,3:5
Wall, Michael Mrs, 1943, Ap 17,17:3
Wall, Mose M, 1922, D 1,17:4
Wall, Pierce, 1950, Mr 26,92:4
Wall, Pierce E, 1951, Ja 5,21:4
Wall, Robert C, 1939, N 29,23:5
Wall, Robert E, 1946, O 29,25:5
Wall, Robert W, 1939, Jl 10,19:2
Wall, Thomas J, 1948, S 6,13:4
Wall, W H, 1934, Ja 21,29:3
Wall, Walter V, 1952, S 26,21:2
Wall, William, 1872, Ap 24,5:7
Wall, William C, 1948, Ap 4,60:3
Wall, William D, 1948, My 11,25:3
Wall, William F, 1942, N 3,23:3
Wall, William G, 1941, Ja 18,15:2
Wall, William O, 1938, Mr 17,21:5
Wall (Bro Gregory Auxilian), 1958, Ap 20,84:4
Wallace, A Vanduzer Sr, 1943, My 28,21:4
Wallace, Aaron, 1951, Ja 15,17:4
Wallace, Adam Rev, 1903, S 24,9:6
Wallace, Agnes E, 1954, F 4,25:5
Wallace, Agnes I, 1943, Ja 1,23:6
Wallace, Albert, 1882, O 14,3:7
Wallace, Albert H Dr, 1937, D 20,27:2
Wallace, Alexander, 1947, N 30,76:4
Wallace, Alfred Russell Dr, 1913, N 8,13:5
Wallace, Allan, 1945, My 9,23:3
Wallace, Allan B, 1938, O 18,25:5
Wallace, Alta M, 1937, Ag 25,21:4
Wallace, Andrew, 1940, My 9,23:3
Wallace, Andrew B, 1923, D 24,11:6; 1956, Mr 14,33:4
Wallace, Andrew B Mrs, 1951, Mr 19,27:2
Wallace, Ansel E, 1941, D 21,40:7
Wallace, Archer, 1958, Ag 1,21:1
Wallace, Arthur E, 1950, Ap 8,13:4
Wallace, Arthur J, 1954, Jl 11,72:2
Wallace, Arthur N Mrs, 1960, Mr 31,33:4
Wallace, August, 1946, O 8,23:5
Wallace, Benjamin B, 1947, Ja 6,23:1
Wallace, Benjamin D Mrs, 1938, Ag 18,20:5
Wallace, Benjamin E, 1921, Ap 9,11:5
Wallace, Benjamin F, 1908, Jl 4,5:4
Wallace, Benjamin L, 1944, My 26,19:3
Wallace, Bertrand H, 1938, Mr 19,15:4
Wallace, Bodine, 1952, Ap 9,31:3
Wallace, Bruce, 1950, N 18,15:2
Wallace, Bruce H, 1961, Ap 25,35:3
Wallace, C Brook, 1949, Mr 1,25:5
Wallace, C Earl, 1949, Ap 8,26:5
Wallace, C I, 1903, My 24,7:4
Wallace, C W, 1932, Ag 8,15:4
Wallace, C Walter, 1949, S 4,40:4
Wallace, Catherine (Mother Ignatius), 1952, Ag 4, 15:5
Wallace, Charles, 1954, Ap 9,24:6
Wallace, Charles A, 1954, My 15,15:1
Wallace, Charles F, 1964, Je 4,37:5
Wallace, Charles S, 1942, N 16,19:4
Wallace, Charles W, 1949, F 17,23:5
Wallace, Charlton, 1946, Ag 17,13:6
Wallace, Chester, 1966, My 27,46:2
Wallace, Chester M, 1938, D 2,23:5
Wallace, Cuthbert, 1944, Je 1,19:3
Wallace, Dan A, 1954, F 13,13:4
Wallace, Dana, 1951, Je 14,27:3
Wallace, Daniel, 1948, Ap 21,27:5
Wallace, David, 1904, Mr 20,7:3; 1955, Je 17,23:3
Wallace, David F, 1948, S 13,21:5
Wallace, David Mrs (Zelda Seguin Wallace), 1914, F 20,9:4
Wallace, David W Mrs, 1952, D 6,21:1
Wallace, Dillon, 1939, S 29,23:5
Wallace, Don, 1939, F 23,23:4
Wallace, Donald F, 1965, F 27,25:5
Wallace, Donald H, 1953, S 20,87:2
Wallace, E, 1932, F 11,21:1
Wallace, E W, 1941, Je 21,17:6
Wallace, Edgar, 1937, Mr 6,17:4
Wallace, Edward E, 1948, Mr 6,13:3
Wallace, Edward S, 1964, N 15,86:8
Wallace, Edwin F, 1961, Ap 15,21:2
Wallace, Edwin W, 1968, Ag 24,29:2
Wallace, Eleanor B, 1952, O 15,31:2
Wallace, Elizabeth, 1960, Ap 13,40:1
Wallace, Ellerslie Dr, 1885, Mr 10,2:3
Wallace, Ernest C, 1867, Je 4,5:5
Wallace, Estrinna Mrs, 1953, F 4,29:7
Wallace, Euan (por), 1941, F 11,23:4
Wallace, Eugene L, 1950, Ag 22,27:2
Wallace, Eugenia, 1956, My 28,27:4
Wallace, F B, 1883, Je 22,4:7
Wallace, F Ernest, 1940, Jl 6,15:5
Wallace, Faye, 1959, D 11,33:3
Wallace, Fergus F, 1956, F 25,19:4
Wallace, Floyd, 1946, Ag 13,27:4
Wallace, Frank, 1951, Mr 29,27:5; 1962, Jl 12,29:4; 1966, O 17,37:3
Wallace, Frank F, 1916, O 25,11:5; 1948, Ja 11,56:4
Wallace, Frank G, 1960, Ag 13,15:5
Wallace, Frank R, 1954, Ap 20,29:4
Wallace, Frank T, 1956, D 18,31:4
Wallace, Fred, 1957, O 1,34:1
Wallace, Fred G, 1948, N 30,27:1
Wallace, Frederic W Mrs, 1956, O 23,33:2
Wallace, Frederick, 1952, Mr 30,93:1
Wallace, Frederick W, 1948, N 2,25:1; 1958, Jl 16,29:2
Wallace, George, 1938, O 30,41:2; 1940, Ag 5,13:5
Wallace, George B (por), 1948, Ja 16,21:1
Wallace, George D Mrs, 1959, S 21,31:4
Wallace, George K, 1955, Mr 16,33:2
Wallace, George M, 1937, F 13,13:3; 1956, My 18,25:4
Wallace, George Mrs, 1925, Mr 3,23:5; 1952, D 4,35:6
Wallace, George N, 1944, Jl 28,13:5; 1951, Ap 13,23:3
Wallace, George P, 1963, My 26,92:6
Wallace, Gertrude L, 1954, My 8,17:1
Wallace, Grant, 1954, Ag 14,15:6
Wallace, Gustavus Swan, 1916, N 2,13:4
Wallace, Guy C, 1967, Ag 30,43:4
Wallace, H C, 1931, Ja 2,21:1; 1939, N 16,23:1
Wallace, H L, 1926, Ja 10,29:2
Wallace, Harold A, 1958, N 8,21:6
Wallace, Harold D, 1968, Mr 31,81:1
Wallace, Harry, 1921, D 7,17:6
Wallace, Harry A Sr, 1947, O 1,29:3
Wallace, Harry B, 1955, Ag 12,19:5
Wallace, Harry C, 1948, F 27,21:4; 1951, Jl 11,23:4
Wallace, Harry C Dr, 1951, Ap 19,31:3
Wallace, Harry H, 1938, S 24,17:2
Wallace, Henry, 1958, Ap 27,86:7
Wallace, Henry A (funl plans, N 20,18:7), 1965, N 19,1:2
Wallace, Henry C (funl), 1924, O 28,23:1
Wallace, Henry C, 1945, Mr 29,23:3
Wallace, Henry C Mrs, 1948, Ap 13,27:5
Wallace, Henry K, 1956, Je 10,89:1
Wallace, Herbert A, 1942, Ja 7,19:2
Wallace, Herbert K, 1938, Mr 27,II,7:2
Wallace, Herbert M, 1942, S 29,23:2
Wallace, Homer H, 1938, Jl 14,21:4
Wallace, J Col, 1865, F 19,4:6
Wallace, J Harry, 1950, D 24,34:1
Wallace, J W, 1884, Ja 13,2:1
Wallace, Jack N, 1955, My 29,44:5
Wallace, James, 1938, O 27,23:4; 1939, Ag 25,15:6; 1956, D 31,13:2
Wallace, James C, 1916, N 1,11:6; 1942, D 13,74:3
Wallace, James G (funl, D 2,86:3), 1956, N 30,23:1
Wallace, James H, 1943, Mr 19,19:3; 1951, My 31, 27:3
Wallace, James H Mrs, 1938, F 26,15:5
Wallace, James Herbert, 1951, My 27,69:2
Wallace, James N, 1919, O 12,22:3
Wallace, James N Mrs, 1913, Mr 30,IV,7:5
Wallace, James W, 1946, Je 8,21:3
Wallace, James W Mrs, 1951, Jl 29,69:2
Wallace, Jesse R, 1961, Ja 31,29:3
Wallace, John, 1872, Ja 2,5:6; 1909, S 19,11:4; 1943, Ap 13,26:3
Wallace, John A, 1914, Mr 28,13:4
Wallace, John C Dr, 1914, Ap 3,11:6
Wallace, John Calvin, 1944, N 30,23:2
Wallace, John E, 1949, F 16,25:4
Wallace, John E Mrs, 1944, Ap 18,21:5
Wallace, John F, 1921, Jl 4,9:7; 1955, F 15,27:5
Wallace, John J, 1947, Ap 5,19:1
Wallace, John K, 1950, S 27,31:4
Wallace, John L, 1951, O 18,29:3
Wallace, John Mrs, 1949, Ja 12,28:2
Wallace, John P, 1948, Mr 11,27:4
Wallace, John W, 1942, Ag 27,19:1; 1949, S 16,27:1
Wallace, Joseph, 1955, O 18,37:5; 1959, My 25,29:4
Wallace, Joseph (Banjo), 1961, My 20,23:6
Wallace, Joseph A, 1949, Je 18,13:1; 1950, N 13,28:2
Wallace, Joseph F, 1943, F 13,11:6
Wallace, Kenneth V C, 1953, Ag 11,27:1
Wallace, Leroy A, 1950, O 15,104:3
Wallace, Leslie E, 1940, My 10,23:2
Wallace, Lew, 1905, F 16,9:3
Wallace, Lew Jr, 1949, Ap 28,31:5
Wallace, Lew Mrs, 1907, O 3,9:4
Wallace, Lewis, 1905, Je 21,7:7
Wallace, Lewis G, 1965, Ja 21,31:4
Wallace, Lewis G Mrs, 1953, S 19,15:3
Wallace, Lewis R, 1953, Jl 22,27:4
Wallace, Lindsay H, 1938, F 16,21:2
Wallace, Lurleen Burns Gov (funl plans, My 8,44:1), 1968, My 7,1:7
Wallace, M Etta, 1946, Mr 15,21:2
Wallace, Malcolm W, 1960, Ap 10,86:1
Wallace, Mary C Mrs, 1952, N 28,25:2
Wallace, Matthew E, 1950, D 11,25:1
Wallace, May M Mrs, 1938, D 13,26:2
Wallace, Melville W F Mrs, 1944, S 22,19:2
Wallace, Michael, 1940, F 1,21:3
Wallace, Mildred F Mrs (will, Ag 29,4:5), 1937, Jl 11,II,5:1
Wallace, Mildred V, 1960, Jl 29,25:3
Wallace, Mimi Mrs, 1925, F 26,21:3
Wallace, Minott T Sr, 1947, Ja 11,19:3
Wallace, Morgan, 1953, D 15,39:3
Wallace, Nellie, 1948, N 25,31:5
Wallace, Nicholas L, 1967, S 17,84:2
Wallace, Oates C S, 1947, Ag 30,15:2
Wallace, Paris A, 1952, F 23,11:2
Wallace, Peter, 1962, S 1,4:5
Wallace, Ralph C, 1941, S 24,23:4
Wallace, Ralph E Mrs, 1960, N 22,35:3
Wallace, Ralph W Mrs, 1956, D 5,39:4
Wallace, Rhoderick J (Bobby), 1960, N 5,23:4
Wallace, Richard, 1938, Ap 5,21:5; 1951, N 5,31:5
Wallace, Richard F, 1945, O 23,17:6

Wallace, Richard H Jr, 1943, Ap 19,19:1
Wallace, Robert, 1938, Ap 2,15:2; 1939, Ja 18,19:2; 1952, F 12,27:3; 1957, D 9,35:2
Wallace, Robert A, 1941, Ag 27,19:2
Wallace, Robert B, 1949, D 17,17:1; 1963, Ag 28,33:3
Wallace, Robert C, 1955, Ja 30,84:8
Wallace, Robert J, 1945, D 13,29:2
Wallace, Robert L, 1956, Je 27,31:3
Wallace, Robert P, 1957, O 10,33:2
Wallace, Robert Sir, 1939, Mr 21,23:5
Wallace, Robinson C, 1951, Ag 3,21:6
Wallace, Rodney, 1903, F 28,9:6
Wallace, Roy S, 1968, D 20,42:4
Wallace, Ruth T (will), 1967, Ja 12,45:2
Wallace, S, 1934, My 25,24:1
Wallace, Samuel H (por), 1949, O 12,29:1
Wallace, Samuel J, 1956, Mr 25,92:7
Wallace, Stratford C, 1955, Ja 10,23:3
Wallace, T J, 1903, Ag 21,9:6
Wallace, T S Lt, 1879, Ja 14,3:2
Wallace, Thomas, 1916, Ja 3,13:2; 1947, Ja 8,24:3
Wallace, Thomas A, 1941, Ja 4,13:4
Wallace, Thomas B, 1907, D 11,11:4
Wallace, Thomas R Mrs, 1943, Ap 11,49:1
Wallace, Thomas W, 1943, Jl 18,1:2
Wallace, Thomas W Mrs, 1951, O 5,27:3
Wallace, Thomas W Rev, 1913, S 6,7:3; 1915, N 27, 15:4
Wallace, Tom, 1961, Je 6,37:1
Wallace, Tom Mrs, 1961, Mr 31,27:4
Wallace, W A, 1896, My 23,9:5
Wallace, W F, 1912, S 14,13:6
Wallace, W J, 1934, Mr 24,15:5
Wallace, W R, 1881, My 7,5:3; 1960, Je 26,47:4
Wallace, W Vincent, 1865, N 5,1:5
Wallace, Walker J, 1965, Ag 21,21:6
Wallace, Walter D, 1941, Ag 18,13:3
Wallace, Wesley H, 1947, O 15,27:2
Wallace, Wesley H Mrs, 1966, Ja 5,31:4
Wallace, William, 1939, O 27,23:2; 1945, D 13,29:1; 1946, S 9,9:5; 1947, D 3,29:3; 1950, Jl 1,15:5; 1951, Jl 23,17:5
Wallace, William A, 1941, Ja 11,17:5
Wallace, William B, 1944, Mr 19,41:2
Wallace, William B Rev, 1915, Je 27,15:4
Wallace, William C, 1960, F 9,31:4
Wallace, William C Mrs, 1944, Ag 30,17:5
Wallace, William E, 1953, S 20,87:1; 1957, O 17,33:4
Wallace, William H Judge, 1937, O 23,15:8
Wallace, William Henry, 1915, Jl 21,11:5
Wallace, William Henry Jr, 1968, S 7,29:5
Wallace, William J, 1943, Ap 27,23:2; 1950, F 17,24:4; 1953, Ag 26,27:4
Wallace, William J Ex-Judge, 1917, Mr 13,11:5
Wallace, William J Mrs, 1948, Ja 6,23:2
Wallace, William K, 1965, My 29,27:6
Wallace, William L, 1953, D 21,31:5
Wallace, William M, 1949, F 8,25:4
Wallace, William McLean Prof, 1968, N 10,88:8
Wallace, William P, 1947, N 4,26:3
Wallace, William R, 1937, D 16,27:3; 1957, Ja 30,29:5
Wallace, William R J, 1943, Jl 12,15:5
Wallace, William S, 1938, D 10,17:2
Wallace, William Sir, 1916, Jl 12,11:6
Wallace, William T (por), 1941, Ja 21,21:5
Wallace, William T, 1946, D 5,32:2
Wallace, Zelda Seguin Mrs, 1911, Je 23,11:4
Wallach, Carl D Mrs, 1951, S 6,31:5
Wallach, David A, 1954, Ap 10,15:2
Wallach, Edgar, 1953, Ap 11,17:5
Wallach, Ernst G, 1939, Mr 14,21:2
Wallach, Frank, 1964, My 4,29:4
Wallach, Harry K, 1951, Jl 16,21:5
Wallach, Isaac (funl, Mr 18,7:4), 1907, Mr 16,9:5
Wallach, Jacob, 1949, Mr 24,28:4
Wallach, Joseph G, 1943, D 18,16:2
Wallach, K Richard, 1960, N 12,21:1
Wallach, Kaufman, 1966, D 28,43:7
Wallach, Leon, 1963, Je 12,43:5
Wallach, Leonard, 1954, N 12,15:1
Wallach, Leopold (por),(funl, Ja 26,9:5), 1908, Ja 25,9:5
Wallach, Leopold Mrs, 1949, Ja 29,13:3
Wallach, Louis S, 1964, F 11,39:4
Wallach, Maud B Mrs, 1954, Ap 3,15:3
Wallach, Milton, 1963, Je 2,84:2
Wallach, Moritz, 1963, Ap 18,35:2
Wallach, Moses U, 1961, Ja 30,23:5
Wallach, Moshe, 1957, Ap 12,23:1
Wallach, R, 1881, Mr 6,2:2
Wallach, Richard Jr, 1948, O 19,28:3
Wallach, Roger N, 1941, D 8,23:3
Wallach, Sol J, 1948, S 3,19:4
Wallach, Sol J Mrs, 1944, N 30,23:2
Wallach, W D, 1871, D 2,1:4
Wallach, William I Dr, 1937, D 31,15:5
Wallach, Willy, 1882, F 13,5:5
Wallack, Arthur J, 1940, Jl 22,17:5
Wallack, Ben, 1949, O 20,29:6
Wallack, Harold B Mrs, 1943, S 18,17:2
Wallack, J Lester, 1888, S 7,5:1
Wallack, J W Mrs, 1879, F 13,5:4
Wallack, James W, 1873, My 25,5:2
Wallack, James William, 1864, D 27,5:2
Wallack, Joseph F Sr, 1946, Jl 26,21:2
Wallack, Lester Mrs, 1909, Mr 29,7:4
Wallant, Edward L, 1962, D 6,43:5
Wallar, Glen L, 1955, Ja 29,15:2
Wallard, Lee, 1963, N 30,27:4
Wallas, G, 1932, Ag 11,15:1
Wallauer, Clarence R, 1952, Je 24,29:4
Wallberg, Elias, 1965, D 1,47:3
Wallbridge, Hiram Gen, 1870, D 7,1:7
Wallce, Fielding H, 1954, N 16,29:5
Wallce, Kieran A, 1943, Mr 20,15:2
Walle, Alfred W, 1943, O 22,17:4
Walle, Edwin W van de, 1943, S 28,25:6
Wallen, Benjamin, 1951, D 6,33:2
Wallen, Clarence H, 1965, F 22,21:4
Wallen, Francis B, 1949, Ag 11,23:2
Wallen, George G, 1964, F 3,27:4
Wallen, George W, 1941, O 23,23:5
Wallen, T C, 1936, Ja 20,19:3
Wallen, William L, 1952, My 8,31:6
Wallenberg, Adolf, 1949, Ap 13,29:3
Wallenberg, Ernst, 1948, Ag 23,17:3
Wallenberg, Gustav (Gus Wally), 1966, Mr 6,93:1
Wallenberg, Knut, 1938, Je 2,23:1
Wallenberg, Marcus, 1943, Jl 23,17:6
Wallenius, Carl G, 1947, Ja 15,25:4
Wallenrod, Reuben, 1966, D 28,43:2
Wallenstein, Frank Mrs, 1950, Ag 6,72:5
Wallenstein, Jacob J, 1915, Je 3,11:5
Wallenstein, Milton H, 1948, Jl 4,27:1
Wallenstein, Reuben, 1939, Ag 20,32:4
Waller, Albert A, 1942, Mr 16,15:5
Waller, Anna L Mrs, 1944, Jl 24,15:4
Waller, Arthur W C, 1943, F 23,21:5
Waller, C Charles, 1950, F 23,27:2
Waller, C W, 1927, Ja 20,23:1
Waller, Cecile F H Mrs, 1953, Ag 22,15:4
Waller, Charles Christian Sir (Baronet of Newport), 1912, My 29,11:5
Waller, Conrad, 1874, Ja 30,8:2
Waller, D W, 1882, Ja 31,5:4
Waller, David J, 1941, Je 29,33:3
Waller, David M, 1938, F 4,21:1
Waller, Edwin S, 1938, D 24,15:2
Waller, Elwood E, 1944, Ja 18,19:5
Waller, Elwyn Prof, 1919, Jl 7,13:4
Waller, Frank, 1923, Mr 10,13:4
Waller, Frank J, 1937, My 12,23:5
Waller, Frank L, 1941, N 30,69:2
Waller, Fred, 1954, My 19,31:3
Waller, George P Jr, 1962, F 28,33:3
Waller, Gilbert J, 1945, Ja 28,38:3
Waller, Henry D Mrs, 1957, Je 2,87:1
Waller, Henry D Rev (funl, S 17,23:2), 1925, S 15, 25:4
Waller, Herbert, 1947, N 21,27:1
Waller, Howard, 1942, F 3,19:4
Waller, J Cody, 1957, Ja 28,23:4
Waller, J Hammond, 1907, Jl 6,7:6
Waller, J R, 1883, Ap 26,4:7
Waller, Jack, 1957, Jl 29,19:6
Waller, James B, 1949, S 15,27:5
Waller, James H, 1923, N 5,17:5
Waller, James Mrs, 1947, Mr 8,14:2
Waller, Jerome, 1940, Mr 29,21:1
Waller, Johannes O, 1945, F 14,19:4
Waller, L T Maj Gen, 1926, Jl 14,21:5
Waller, Lewis, 1915, N 2,11:4
Waller, Littleton W T Jr Mrs, 1945, Ja 16,19:4
Waller, Marie Hertenstein Mrs (Mrs Adolph Waller), 1968, D 13,47:2
Waller, Mary E, 1938, Je 15,23:6
Waller, Otis L, 1953, Ag 28,17:4
Waller, Owen M Mrs, 1939, F 5,40:4
Waller, Owen M Sr, 1939, O 14,19:2
Waller, Percy G, 1956, Ap 29,86:8
Waller, Raymond, 1956, Ap 18,33:2
Waller, Robert, 1915, F 22,9:4
Waller, Robert Mrs, 1941, Ag 17,39:2
Waller, Roderick G, 1953, S 21,25:4
Waller, Roland E, 1958, My 30,21:4
Waller, Samuel G, 1955, D 3,17:4
Waller, Theodore Mrs, 1946, Ag 16,21:3
Waller, Theodore Mrs (Helen H), 1961, Ag 23,33:2
Waller, Thomas M, 1924, Ja 25,17:5
Waller, Thomas W (Fats), 1943, D 16,27:3
Waller, Tom T, 1944, Ja 17,19:6
Waller, Virgil C, 1946, Mr 27,27:2
Waller, Williard W, 1945, Jl 28,11:5
Waller, Wilmer J Mrs, 1947, O 1,29:4
Wallerich, George W, 1950, Jl 4,17:2
Wallerstein, Abraham, 1948, Ag 10,21:2
Wallerstein, Alfred E, 1964, F 14,29:2
Wallerstein, Joseph, 1910, My 19,9:4
Wallerstein, Leo, 1942, D 12,17:1; 1956, N 7,31:2
Wallerstein, Lothar (por), 1949, N 15,25:5
Wallerstein, Max Dr (por), 1937, Ap 3,19:3
Wallerstein, Max Mrs, 1963, Ag 21,33:4
Wallerstein, Ralph D Mrs, 1945, O 9,21:5
Wallerstein, Rose (Mrs O Ostroff), 1961, Ap 21,33:1
Wallerstein, Samuel Mrs, 1945, Jl 28,11:5
Walley, Abigail B P, 1942, Je 25,23:5
Walley, Edward P, 1950, F 8,27:1
Walley, George P, 1950, Je 20,27:3
Wallfield, Jacob M, 1956, O 27,21:3
Wallgren, A Samuel, 1940, Ag 8,19:5
Wallgren, Abian A, 1948, Mr 25,27:2
Wallgren, Abian L, 1940, Jl 29,13:5
Wallgren, Martha C Mrs, 1949, Jl 24,53:1
Wallgren, Mon C, 1961, S 19,35:1
Wallhauser, H J F Mrs, 1937, Ap 12,17:1
Wallhauser, Henry J F, 1945, My 6,38:2
Wallheinke, Martha Mrs, 1925, Je 17,21:5
Wallian, Samuel S Dr, 1907, Je 15,9:6
Wallick, James H, 1908, My 2,9:5
Wallin, Alfred C, 1941, Mr 12,22:2
Wallin, Arthur P, 1950, Ag 19,13:4
Wallin, Irving, 1954, Je 3,27:4
Wallin, Mathilda K Mrs, 1955, S 20,31:3
Wallin, Walter W, 1956, D 11,39:4
Wallin, William, 1942, Ag 29,15:2
Wallin, William A (cor), 1942, Ja 4,49:2
Wallin, William J, 1963, Jl 8,21:1
Wallin, William J Mrs, 1942, D 3,25:1
Walline, Ralph E, 1952, Ag 23,13:3
Walling, Burns T, 1938, My 14,15:2
Walling, C S, 1953, My 31,73:1
Walling, Everett, 1957, D 21,19:4
Walling, Joel A, 1937, Ap 20,25:6
Walling, Mary C Mrs, 1925, Je 14,5:2
Walling, Mrs, 1874, N 26,8:4
Walling, Oliver S, 1947, Ja 1,33:2
Walling, Percy, 1922, Jl 31,11:7
Walling, R A J (por), 1949, S 18,92:5
Walling, Ralph, 1949, D 3,15:5
Walling, Roy, 1964, My 9,27:6
Walling, Rufus O, 1962, Ag 23,29:1
Walling, W E, 1936, S 13,II,11:1
Walling, William E Mrs (A Strunsky), 1964, F 26, 35:4
Walling, Willoughby G, 1938, F 24,19:5
Wallingford, Buckner A Mrs, 1953, My 19,29:4
Wallingford, George C, 1945, D 30,14:8
Wallingford, J A, 1879, My 24,7:2
Wallingford, John Duvall, 1924, S 22,19:7
Wallington, Hubert J, 1962, Ja 20,21:4
Wallis, A H, 1879, Jl 23,2:6
Wallis, Albert O, 1941, D 28,28:1
Wallis, Allan D Jr, 1963, Je 16,84:3
Wallis, Allan D Mrs, 1956, Ag 14,25:2
Wallis, Allen M, 1924, F 9,13:5
Wallis, Ben, 1947, O 28,25:4
Wallis, Calvin P Mrs, 1945, F 2,19:2
Wallis, Charles B, 1945, Ag 8,23:4
Wallis, Everett S, 1965, Jl 11,68:5
Wallis, Frederick A, 1951, D 23,22:6
Wallis, Guy L, 1942, Jl 26,30:8
Wallis, Hal Mrs (L Fazenda),(funl, Ap 21,19:4), 1962, Ap 18,39:3
Wallis, Herman P, 1940, O 29,25:1
Wallis, James H, 1958, Ja 15,39:2
Wallis, John B Jr, 1943, My 7,19:5
Wallis, Joseph J, 1940, N 30,17:3
Wallis, Lawrence B, 1963, N 27,27:4
Wallis, Nathaniel W, 1940, Ap 5,21:4
Wallis, Philip, 1960, S 16,28:5
Wallis, R, 1878, D 15,8:1
Wallis, Ralph E, 1953, F 21,13:6
Wallis, Richard G, 1964, My 23,23:5
Wallis, Roy R, 1954, O 24,89:2
Wallis, William H, 1948, N 16,29:1
Walliser, William, 1943, D 3,23:4
Wallison, Henry Yernet Dr, 1923, Ja 24,13:5
Wallner, Thomas J, 1942, Ag 19,19:3
Wallock, Anthony M, 1948, D 27,21:4
Wallon, J G, 1882, My 21,9:1
Wallop, Oliver H, 1943, F 11,19:5
Wallop, Oliver M Mrs, 1943, Ap 8,23:6
Wallot, Albert, 1954, D 15,31:1
Wallower, Edgar Z, 1963, S 21,21:5
Wallower, Edgar Z Mrs, 1960, Ap 28,35:4
Wallower, Elias Z (por), 1941, S 11,23:2
Wallowick, Jacob, 1955, F 27,87:1
Wallrath, William B, 1943, N 17,25:2
Wallrich, Matthew, 1950, O 4,31:1
Walls, Alexander, 1918, N 15,13:1
Walls, Alexander L, 1947, F 7,23:1
Walls, Annie (Sister Cecilia Clare), 1942, Ap 5,41:2
Walls, Charles S Sr, 1943, S 23,21:2
Walls, Elwood G, 1956, O 25,33:4
Walls, Ewart G, 1960, Je 21,33:4
Walls, Frank X, 1946, Ja 16,23:4
Walls, Gordon L, 1962, Ag 24,25:4
Walls, Raymund Sr, 1957, N 17,86:5
Walls, Tom, 1949, N 29,29:1
Walls, Tom (will), 1950, Mr 25,8:1
Walls, Walter, 1938, O 27,23:4
Walls, William A, 1937, Ag 22,II,7:2
Walls, William C, 1941, O 13,17:5
Wallschlaeger, Walter G, 1938, D 2,24:2
Wallstein, Leonard M, 1968, Ag 7,43:2
Wallstein, Leonard M Jr Mrs, 1968, Je 30,52:5
Walltearss, Solomon de, 1923, Ja 25,19:6
Wallum, Charlotte K, 1960, Ja 10,87:2
Wallum, George, 1953, Ap 9,27:1

Wallwork, Howard L, 1949, Jl 31,60:8
Wallwork, Joseph, 1942, S 9,23:2
Wallworth, Chancellor, 1867, D 8,8:2
Wallworth, Joseph F Mrs, 1953, F 24,25:2
Wally, Gus (Gustav Wallenberg), 1966, Mr 6,93:1
Walmisley, Arthur L, 1956, Ap 29,86:1
Walmsley, Carl R, 1939, My 31,23:1
Walmsley, Frank, 1957, Ja 1,23:5
Walmsley, Hardie B, 1939, Jl 15,15:5
Walmsley, Mary M Mrs, 1939, S 17,49:1
Walmsley, R P, 1953, Ja 21,31:5
Walmsley, Sidney C Mrs, 1960, Mr 20,86:5
Walmsley, T Semmes (por), 1942, Je 18,21:4
Waln, Nora, 1964, S 28,29:4
Waln, William H, 1951, Jl 24,25:2
Waloszec, Phil (Bro Philip), 1953, Ap 11,17:6
Walp, Henry, 1948, O 27,27:1
Walp, Wilbur M, 1946, D 6,23:3
Walper, Louis P, 1950, N 1,35:1
Walpole, Clare H Mrs, 1944, My 22,19:6
Walpole, Gordon A, 1948, Jl 10,15:4
Walpole, Hugh, 1941, Je 2,17:1
Walquist, John A, 1965, Jl 30,22:5
Walrad, James H, 1943, Mr 12,17:6
Walrad, John R, 1952, Ag 6,21:4
Walrad, William J, 1947, N 16,76:4
Walradt, Henry F, 1942, N 13,23:2
Walrath, Alton A, 1951, F 15,31:1
Walrath, Edson J, 1949, My 3,25:1
Walrath, George, 1941, D 22,17:2
Walrath, George B, 1949, My 10,26:3
Walrath, John C, 1946, Mr 8,21:3
Walrath, John H, 1948, Je 25,23:2
Walrath, Otto J, 1949, Jl 10,57:3
Walrath, Russell J (funl, Je 11,15:6), 1955, Je 8,29:1
Walrath, William B Mrs, 1958, N 9,88:8
Walrod, Raymond J, 1962, Jl 9,31:5
Walrond, Lionel, 1915, N 3,13:5
Walscheid, Arthur J (por), 1947, Je 15,60:4
Walscheid, Arthur J Mrs, 1947, N 20,30:2
Walscheid, J Emil, 1945, My 1,23:5
Walser, Arthur C, 1946, O 19,21:3
Walser, Fred, 1942, Je 11,23:2
Walser, Guy O, 1958, My 13,29:5
Walser, Havelock, 1949, Ap 25,23:5
Walser, Henry J Mrs, 1952, Mr 5,29:1
Walser, Henry Mrs, 1939, Jl 26,19:2
Walser, Kenneth E, 1942, Jl 28,17:3
Walser, Theodore D, 1949, Ag 15,17:4
Walser, Theodore Dr, 1902, Ap 24,9:5
Walser, William Dr, 1917, My 22,13:4
Walsh, Agnes E, 1948, Ag 1,57:2
Walsh, Albert A, 1949, Jl 11,17:3
Walsh, Albert Mrs, 1965, My 17,35:3
Walsh, Albert S, 1952, S 19,23:3
Walsh, Alice M Mrs, 1938, Ap 26,15:4
Walsh, Anna, 1920, S 20,15:5
Walsh, Anthony, 1916, Ag 29,9:5
Walsh, Anthony R, 1874, My 7,5:5
Walsh, Arthur, 1947, D 15,28:2
Walsh, Arthur G, 1960, F 9,31:1
Walsh, Basil S, 1943, O 12,27:2
Walsh, Bernard H, 1960, Ja 2,13:5
Walsh, Bernard J, 1942, Ja 10,15:4
Walsh, Bertram E, 1946, Jl 29,21:5
Walsh, Blanche (funl, N 3,13:5), 1915, N 1,11:5
Walsh, Bridget J Mrs, 1938, F 5,15:3
Walsh, C K Dickson Mrs, 1952, Je 1,84:4
Walsh, Catherine I, 1940, F 29,19:5
Walsh, Charles A, 1951, O 2,27:3
Walsh, Charles E, 1942, Jl 13,15:1; 1956, Jl 28,17:6; 1958, S 28,88:2
Walsh, Charles J, 1952, Ap 12,11:4; 1967, S 8,40:2
Walsh, Charles J Mrs, 1959, Ja 17,19:3
Walsh, Charles Mrs, 1950, N 12,93:2
Walsh, Charles S (Buck), 1950, N 22,25:1
Walsh, Charles V A, 1943, S 11,13:5
Walsh, Christy, 1955, D 30,20:1
Walsh, Clara D D B Mrs (Mrs J S Walsh Jr), 1957, Ag 14,25:2
Walsh, Clarence A, 1938, D 4,61:2
Walsh, Clifford S, 1954, F 16,25:4
Walsh, Cornelius, 1879, S 21,7:1
Walsh, Cornelius A, 1955, Mr 21,25:1
Walsh, Cornelius J, 1939, D 29,15:1
Walsh, Cornelius Mrs, 1872, F 7,8:6
Walsh, Daniel J, 1959, Mr 13,37:2
Walsh, Daniel R, 1958, Ja 23,21:4
Walsh, David I, 1947, Je 12,25:1
Walsh, David J, 1966, Ag 26,33:4
Walsh, David L, 1943, F 15,15:4
Walsh, De Witt Mrs, 1950, N 13,27:2
Walsh, Dominic, 1943, F 26,19:2
Walsh, Donald J, 1965, Ag 13,26:8
Walsh, E, 1881, D 6,2:2
Walsh, E J, 1934, O 16,23:3
Walsh, Earl, 1961, Je 29,33:6
Walsh, Edmund A, 1956, N 1,39:5
Walsh, Edmund J, 1944, Ja 12,23:4
Walsh, Edward, 1946, Jl 10,23:6; 1947, D 25,4:6; 1948, F 14,13:1
Walsh, Edward A (Big Ed), 1959, My 27,35:4
Walsh, Edward A Jr, 1937, N 1,21:6
Walsh, Edward D, 1957, Je 12,19:4
Walsh, Edward G, 1957, Je 16,84:1; 1960, F 24,37:4
Walsh, Edward H, 1944, Ag 9,17:6
Walsh, Edward I, 1943, F 10,25:5
Walsh, Edward J, 1940, Ap 9,23:2; 1942, Ap 17,17:5
Walsh, Edward J (por), 1942, N 7,15:6
Walsh, Edward J, 1946, Mr 21,25:3
Walsh, Edward J (por), 1947, Mr 23,60:1
Walsh, Edward J, 1947, Ap 23,25:3; 1949, D 17,17:6; 1953, F 5,23:2; 1955, Ja 19,27:2
Walsh, Edward J Mrs, 1959, F 28,19:5
Walsh, Edward M, 1944, Mr 3,15:3
Walsh, Edward P, 1941, Jl 12,13:2
Walsh, Elizabeth A (por), 1940, Ap 16,23:1
Walsh, Elizabeth P, 1955, Ag 19,19:4
Walsh, Elizabeth V, 1944, Ap 28,19:2
Walsh, Ellen M, 1937, Jl 2,21:2
Walsh, Emma L, 1940, Mr 31,44:3
Walsh, Emmet Michael Bp, 1968, Mr 17,80:7
Walsh, Ernest, 1937, Mr 22,23:1
Walsh, Eugene A, 1968, Ag 16,33:2
Walsh, Eugene F, 1966, Ja 13,25:3
Walsh, Eugene F Mrs, 1965, O 30,35:5
Walsh, Eugene J, 1946, Je 9,40:5
Walsh, Evelyn M, 1951, Mr 9,25:3
Walsh, F Irving, 1948, F 14,13:6
Walsh, Frances T Mrs, 1957, Mr 31,88:6
Walsh, Francis A, 1938, Ag 14,33:5
Walsh, Francis D, 1963, Jl 5,19:3
Walsh, Francis H, 1938, N 5,19:4
Walsh, Francis J, 1959, My 12,35:5
Walsh, Francis K, 1949, Ja 4,19:2
Walsh, Frank, 1937, S 17,25:4
Walsh, Frank A, 1950, D 4,29:3
Walsh, Frank J, 1940, F 13,23:3; 1942, Mr 21,17:5
Walsh, Frank J Mrs, 1956, D 5,39:5
Walsh, Frank M, 1940, Jl 17,21:2
Walsh, Frank P, 1939, My 3,23:1
Walsh, Frank P Jr, 1925, Mr 6,19:4
Walsh, Frank V, 1943, O 23,13:5
Walsh, Franklin D, 1949, D 25,26:4
Walsh, Fred H, 1964, F 21,29:4
Walsh, George, 1953, My 28,23:5
Walsh, George C Mrs, 1947, Ag 4,17:4
Walsh, George D, 1944, Mr 9,17:4
Walsh, George E, 1941, F 10,17:5
Walsh, George N, 1952, My 6,29:6
Walsh, George P, 1954, F 2,27:5
Walsh, Gerald G, 1951, D 18,31:3
Walsh, Groebeck, 1944, S 2,11:4
Walsh, H C, 1927, Ap 30,19:5
Walsh, Hannah M, 1946, S 19,31:2
Walsh, Harold W, 1955, Ja 26,25:3
Walsh, Harry C H, 1939, Ja 18,19:2
Walsh, Harry F, 1951, Ap 8,92:2
Walsh, Harry H, 1947, D 18,29:3
Walsh, Harry J, 1963, O 15,39:2
Walsh, Harry N, 1967, D 20,49:1
Walsh, Harry W, 1967, Ap 1,31:6
Walsh, Henry J (por), 1949, Ap 17,76:3
Walsh, Henry V, 1950, Je 10,17:6
Walsh, Herbert F, 1966, Ag 18,32:5
Walsh, Herbert S, 1953, Ap 12,88:4
Walsh, Hilary Rev, 1921, Mr 9,13:4
Walsh, Homer V, 1947, My 25,60:2
Walsh, Howard V, 1952, Ja 1,25:1
Walsh, Irene, 1956, My 29,27:4
Walsh, J A, 1936, Ap 15,21:1
Walsh, J Brandon, 1955, Ja 14,19:7
Walsh, J J, 1934, F 28,19:4
Walsh, J J Rev, 1884, F 9,5:3
Walsh, James, 1943, Ag 1,39:1
Walsh, James A, 1937, Ap 1,24:2; 1940, Je 12,25:5; 1942, F 23,21:5; 1956, F 16,29:1; 1960, My 31,31:4; 1963, S 9,27:1
Walsh, James B, 1944, D 22,17:4
Walsh, James D, 1940, F 16,19:2
Walsh, James E, 1953, Ja 21,31:3
Walsh, James F, 1939, N 5,49:3; 1944, Mr 12,38:2
Walsh, James F (por), 1944, N 2,19:1
Walsh, James F, 1947, Je 12,25:3; 1955, Ja 7,21:1
Walsh, James F Mrs, 1966, Jl 30,25:3
Walsh, James H, 1958, N 21,29:1
Walsh, James J, 1909, My 9,11:6; 1922, Ap 4,17:5; 1941, O 21,23:4; 1942, Mr 1,44:1; 1943, S 12,53:2; 1947, Je 12,25:3; 1948, F 4,23:4
Walsh, James J S, 1942, Ap 6,15:3
Walsh, James L, 1952, Je 12,33:3; 1955, Ja 10,23:5
Walsh, James P, 1939, N 7,28:2
Walsh, James S, 1955, F 26,15:2
Walsh, James T Msgr, 1925, N 21,17:5
Walsh, James V, 1947, N 7,23:2
Walsh, James W, 1908, Je 5,7:4; 1943, Je 25,17:3
Walsh, Jeremiah A, 1940, F 19,17:4
Walsh, Jeremiah H, 1956, O 14,87:1
Walsh, Jerome, 1945, F 8,19:5
Walsh, John, 1939, D 11,23:4; 1941, Ag 26,19:1; 1954, Ja 21,31:4
Walsh, John A, 1951, Ja 14,84:6; 1954, Ja 7,31:5; 1960, Ap 17,92:8
Walsh, John A Judge, 1937, S 21,35:5
Walsh, John A Mrs, 1957, Jl 21,60:3
Walsh, John B, 1963, Ag 24,19:5
Walsh, John B Rev, 1968, O 21,47:1
Walsh, John D, 1951, S 1,11:6
Walsh, John E, 1939, N 14,23:3; 1946, Ag 7,27:3
Walsh, John E J, 1966, O 13,45:1
Walsh, John F, 1919, D 10,13:1; 1939, D 30,15:6; 1940, Ja 3,21:4; 1943, My 19,25:3; 1947, S 21,60:4; 1948, My 25,27:1; 1951, S 6,31:1; 1966, F 1,31:2
Walsh, John F Sr, 1951, My 19,15:3
Walsh, John F X Rev, 1937, D 11,19:2
Walsh, John G, 1953, Ag 29,17:2; 1961, Ap 2,76:3
Walsh, John H, 1941, Ap 23,21:4
Walsh, John H A, 1946, Ag 11,45:1
Walsh, John H Dr, 1924, D 14,7:2
Walsh, John J, 1924, My 28,23:4; 1940, Ap 5,21:4; 1940, N 5,25:2; 1942, O 28,23:3; 1942, D 4,25:5; 1944, My 26,19:4; 1946, D 18,29:6; 1947, Ja 28,24:2; 1949, S 21,31:5; 1950, Ag 15,29:2; 1954, Ag 27,21:5; 1955, O 17,27:4; 1961, O 19,35:3
Walsh, John J Mrs, 1943, O 3,48:4
Walsh, John L, 1943, D 15,27:1
Walsh, John M, 1943, My 31,17:3; 1954, F 5,19:3
Walsh, John Mrs, 1948, S 30,27:3
Walsh, John P, 1942, Ag 31,17:3
Walsh, John R Mrs, 1966, Je 4,29:4
Walsh, John Rev, 1919, N 20,13:3
Walsh, John T, 1939, O 8,49:1; 1944, O 19,23:6; 1950, S 18,23:5
Walsh, John V, 1952, F 13,29:5; 1967, Je 6,44:3
Walsh, Joseph, 1946, Ja 14,19:5; 1946, O 24,27:2; 1962, Je 12,37:1
Walsh, Joseph A, 1964, Mr 5,33:1
Walsh, Joseph A Dr, 1968, S 26,55:1
Walsh, Joseph A Mrs, 1952, My 16,23:1
Walsh, Joseph B, 1950, N 1,35:6
Walsh, Joseph C, 1955, Ag 6,15:4
Walsh, Joseph C Mrs, 1947, Ap 4,23:3
Walsh, Joseph E, 1962, S 11,33:5; 1968, Je 20,45:4
Walsh, Joseph F, 1956, F 28,31:2
Walsh, Joseph H Mrs, 1945, S 19,25:5
Walsh, Joseph J, 1952, S 22,23:3
Walsh, Joseph M, 1939, Je 3,15:6
Walsh, Joseph Mrs, 1949, S 2,17:1
Walsh, Joseph O, 1951, F 10,13:2
Walsh, Joseph R, 1955, N 26,19:1
Walsh, Julia, 1938, Ag 2,19:5; 1947, Ag 16,13:5
Walsh, Karin J (more details, Ag 29,85:1), 1965, Ag 28,4:5
Walsh, Katherine, 1937, N 11,25:3
Walsh, Lassen L, 1966, N 24,35:3
Walsh, Laurence A, 1953, Jl 27,19:5
Walsh, Lawrence A Rev, 1968, Je 4,44:3
Walsh, Lawrence E Mrs, 1964, My 13,47:5
Walsh, Lawrence J, 1947, S 2,21:3
Walsh, Leo E, 1941, Jl 19,13:3
Walsh, Leonard T, 1954, O 17,87:2
Walsh, Lillie A Mrs, 1942, Ap 3,21:1
Walsh, Lionel Maj, 1916, Jl 6,13:5
Walsh, Louis J, 1942, D 27,34:3
Walsh, Louis Sebastian Bp, 1924, My 13,21:3
Walsh, M J, 1935, N 25,19:3
Walsh, Margaret A, 1938, Mr 23,23:4
Walsh, Maria Mrs, 1925, Jl 22,19:5
Walsh, Marie C, 1954, S 27,21:3
Walsh, Marie L Mrs, 1946, S 30,25:3
Walsh, Marie Mrs, 1910, My 9,7:4
Walsh, Mark A, 1950, O 27,29:5
Walsh, Martin, 1878, Ag 6,8:2
Walsh, Martin J, 1961, F 22,25:3; 1966, F 23,27:4
Walsh, Martin P, 1951, Ap 1,92:3
Walsh, Martin W, 1968, Ag 24,29:4
Walsh, Mary (Sister Mary Angelica), 1953, My 26, 29:6
Walsh, Mary A, 1947, Mr 16,61:1
Walsh, Mary E, 1954, Ag 3,19:2
Walsh, Mary F Mother, 1951, O 16,31:4
Walsh, Mary G, 1957, N 20,32:2
Walsh, Mary G Mrs, 1941, S 1,15:4
Walsh, Mary M, 1952, Mr 25,27:1
Walsh, Matthew, 1949, My 1,88:7
Walsh, Matthew J (Jan 19), 1963, Ap 1,36:7
Walsh, Maurice, 1944, Ag 11,15:4; 1946, N 28,27:4; 1947, Mr 2,60:1
Walsh, Michael, 1910, Ag 6,7:5; 1910, O 9,II,13:3; 1956, S 30,87:1; 1958, Je 26,27:6
Walsh, Michael A, 1958, Ag 9,13:2
Walsh, Michael E, 1939, Jl 1,17:4
Walsh, Michael F (Bro Castoris), 1924, My 30,15:6
Walsh, Michael F (funl, Jl 27,21:6), 1956, Jl 24,25:1
Walsh, Michael J, 1939, My 7,III,7:2; 1944, N 22,19:2
Walsh, Michael J Mrs, 1960, Ja 11,45:4
Walsh, Michael J Rev, 1937, Ja 24,II,8:8
Walsh, Michael Justice, 1867, Mr 20,8:4
Walsh, Michael L, 1937, Mr 27,15:5
Walsh, Michael N, 1961, O 12,29:5
Walsh, Michael P, 1921, N 22,19:5
Walsh, Mike (funl, Mr 21:5:2), 1859, Mr 18,1:3
Walsh, Nicholas F, 1949, Ag 28,72:2
Walsh, Noble L, 1955, F 17,27:4
Walsh, Patrick E, 1957, Ja 8,31:2
Walsh, Patrick J, 1946, S 22,62:3; 1946, O 16,27:3; 1948, Ja 30,24:3; 1960, D 20,33:3
Walsh, Patrick J Mrs, 1952, O 16,29:3
Walsh, Patrick S, 1943, My 19,25:4

Walsh, Peter J, 1953, O 20,29:2; 1964, Ag 26,39:5
Walsh, Philip X, 1966, My 30,19:5
Walsh, Phillip Rev Dr, 1909, Ja 8,9:5
Walsh, Raycroft, 1952, Ag 19,23:1
Walsh, Raymond A, 1939, Je 8,25:4
Walsh, Raymond J, 1960, D 17,12:2
Walsh, Raymond L, 1956, F 24,25:4
Walsh, Redmond, 1945, D 30,14:7
Walsh, Redmond J Rev, 1921, Ja 22,11:4
Walsh, Richard, 1918, My 16,13:6; 1925, My 30,9:4
Walsh, Richard B, 1948, Ap 26,23:3
Walsh, Richard J, 1944, F 4,15:3
Walsh, Richard M L, 1908, O 30,9:6
Walsh, Richard P Mrs, 1923, N 6,19:4
Walsh, Richard W, 1943, Mr 24,23:3; 1951, Jl 29,69:3
Walsh, Robert, 1859, Mr 1,4:5
Walsh, Robert E Mrs, 1949, N 24,31:4
Walsh, Robert H, 1940, Ja 3,22:2; 1952, Jl 10,31:1
Walsh, Robert J, 1939, My 6,17:4; 1943, O 28,23:3; 1949, Ap 24,76:3
Walsh, Robert J Mrs, 1951, O 17,31:2
Walsh, Robert Jay Judge, 1917, D 8,15:7
Walsh, Robert M, 1947, O 26,68:6
Walsh, Roger K, 1921, Ag 26,13:4
Walsh, Roland, 1956, Ag 13,19:2
Walsh, Samuel A, 1937, D 8,25:2
Walsh, Stephan A, 1950, N 19,93:1
Walsh, T F Mrs, 1932, F 26,19:1
Walsh, T J, 1933, Mr 3,1:3
Walsh, Thomas, 1883, Jl 3,1:4; 1956, Jl 16,21:5; 1964, Mr 16,31:1
Walsh, Thomas A, 1948, Mr 21,60:3; 1952, Jl 30,23:3
Walsh, Thomas D, 1914, S 29,11:5
Walsh, Thomas E, 1947, F 5,23:3; 1950, Ja 25,27:3
Walsh, Thomas E Mrs, 1960, My 3,39:1
Walsh, Thomas F, 1910, Ap 9,11:1; 1941, O 5,49:3; 1943, Ag 13,17:3; 1945, Ja 29,13:1; 1945, Ag 8,23:3; 1945, D 14,27:1; 1948, Je 13,44:4; 1948, Ag 3,25:4; 1950, Je 1,27:4; 1958, Jl 1,31:3
Walsh, Thomas F Mrs, 1964, Je 21,84:8
Walsh, Thomas G, 1946, N 5,25:1; 1962, Ap 25,39:3
Walsh, Thomas H, 1925, Ap 26,7:1
Walsh, Thomas J, 1865, N 17,2:3; 1937, S 16,25:3; 1939, N 11,15:1; 1947, Jl 3,21:6; 1947, D 3,29:1; 1950, My 20,15:3; 1950, O 4,31:1
Walsh, Thomas J (will, S 30,31:1), 1952, Je 7,19:1
Walsh, Thomas J, 1955, O 10,27:6; 1956, S 12,37:5; 1959, O 3,19:5; 1963, Ag 26,27:3
Walsh, Thomas J C, 1953, S 21,25:6
Walsh, Thomas J Dr, 1955, My 17,29:1
Walsh, Thomas J Mrs, 1949, Jl 30,15:4; 1950, Je 16, 25:2
Walsh, Thomas J Sr, 1953, F 11,29:3
Walsh, Thomas J Sr (Mar 16), 1963, Ap 1,36:7
Walsh, Thomas M, 1944, Ja 29,13:5; 1953, Mr 16,19:3
Walsh, Thomas Mrs, 1961, My 24,41:3
Walsh, Thomas Sr Mrs, 1948, F 3,26:1
Walsh, Thomas W, 1937, S 18,19:3
Walsh, Timothy F, 1937, Jl 23,19:4
Walsh, Townsend, 1941, Ag 5,19:2
Walsh, W (see also Mr 8), 1878, Mr 12,8:6
Walsh, W, 1882, Je 12,5:4
Walsh, W J, 1948, O 20,29:3
Walsh, Walter A, 1952, O 10,25:3
Walsh, Walter B, 1949, D 13,38:3
Walsh, William, 1939, D 19,23:3; 1941, Mr 28,23:3; 1949, N 9,27:4
Walsh, William A, 1967, Mr 19,92:5
Walsh, William A Jr, 1964, Je 10,45:4
Walsh, William A Mrs, 1952, Mr 20,29:3; 1957, D 23, 23:3
Walsh, William A Sr, 1949, S 22,31:5
Walsh, William A Sr Mrs, 1944, Ap 9,34:4
Walsh, William C Mrs, 1948, O 12,25:5
Walsh, William E, 1952, Je 8,86:5
Walsh, William F, 1946, S 17,7:4; 1957, D 24,15:1
Walsh, William G, 1955, S 14,35:4
Walsh, William H (por), 1941, Mr 29,15:1
Walsh, William H, 1945, Ap 10,19:3
Walsh, William H Mrs, 1949, Ja 13,23:2; 1956, N 20, 37:5
Walsh, William J, 1940, My 17,19:4; 1944, Je 10,15:6; 1948, N 8,31:5; 1959, Ap 19,86:1; 1964, O 3,29:3
Walsh, William J Archbishop, 1921, Ap 9,11:3
Walsh, William K, 1956, D 28,21:3
Walsh, William L, 1938, Ja 14,23:5
Walsh, William Mrs, 1962, Je 30,19:4
Walsh, William Mrs (Bernadette), 1965, Mr 22,33:2
Walsh, William P, 1949, Ap 21,26:4
Walsh, William P Mrs, 1949, N 19,17:5
Walsh, William S, 1941, Ap 2,23:1; 1951, Ap 29,88:8
Walsh, William Shepard, 1919, D 10,13:4
Walsh, William T (por), 1949, F 23,27:3
Walsh, William T, 1957, Jl 19,19:2
Walsh, William T (funl plans, Je 21,37:2), 1961, Je 20,33:6
Walsh, William T Mrs, 1967, Ja 2,19:3
Walsh, William V, 1954, Ag 31,21:3
Walshaw, Robert, 1958, My 24,21:6
Walshe, Jane D Mrs, 1941, O 10,23:2
Walshot, Fred, 1939, Ap 11,46:1
Walsingham, Frances, 1941, Ag 24,36:2
Walsky, Philip R, 1959, My 28,31:4
Walsman, Everett C, 1959, O 11,86:8
Walson, Charles M, 1959, My 19,33:1
Walster, H L, 1957, O 8,35:4
Walstrom, John A Mrs, 1960, S 13,37:5
Walstrum, John A, 1940, N 26,23:2
Walstrum, Samuel S, 1961, O 1,86:2
Walt, Abraham, 1938, N 6,49:3
Walt, Edward J, 1951, F 28,27:2
Walte, Charles B, 1909, Mr 27,9:4
Waltemade, Henry Sr, 1938, Ag 28,33:4
Walter, Adolph J, 1953, My 2,15:2
Walter, Alex A, 1940, My 5,52:1
Walter, Alfred, 1907, F 13,9:2
Walter, Alfred A, 1950, Je 4,92:5
Walter, Alfred G, 1937, D 22,25:6
Walter, Anton, 1964, Ja 6,47:3
Walter, Anton W, 1947, Ap 28,23:5
Walter, Arthur, 1921, Ja 28,11:4
Walter, Arthur Fraser, 1910, F 23,9:4
Walter, Arthur G, 1960, D 30,19:4
Walter, Beverly, 1940, Ap 4,23:6
Walter, Bro, 1939, Ag 17,21:3
Walter, Bruno (funl, F 21,41:3; will, Mr 9,26:2), 1962, F 18,1:4
Walter, Bruno H, 1962, N 29,37:2
Walter, Bruno Mrs, 1945, Mr 27,19:5
Walter, C Wood, 1939, Ja 18,19:1
Walter, Carroll G, 1965, Ja 6,39:4
Walter, Charles, 1925, S 9,25:6
Walter, Charles A, 1943, D 30,17:5
Walter, Charles H, 1941, N 25,25:5
Walter, Charles J (will), 1950, O 8,89:4
Walter, Charles M, 1946, D 9,25:2
Walter, Charles W, 1946, Ap 9,27:3
Walter, Claude H, 1942, Jl 3,17:5
Walter, Cornelius J, 1955, Mr 11,25:2
Walter, Cy (Cyril F Walter), 1968, Ag 20,41:1
Walter, David S, 1946, Ja 27,42:2
Walter, Ebe, 1962, Ag 11,17:3
Walter, Edward C, 1943, F 23,21:2
Walter, Edwin, 1953, N 24,29:5
Walter, Elizabeth, 1951, N 18,91:2
Walter, Ernest, 1964, Ja 29,30:3
Walter, Eugene, 1941, S 27,17:4; 1953, Ag 10,23:6
Walter, Ferdinand, 1951, Mr 7,33:5
Walter, Franc, 1959, Jl 30,27:2
Walter, Francis E (funl, Je 5,41:5; will, Je 18,31:4), 1963, Je 1,21:1
Walter, Frank, 1952, Mr 2,92:2
Walter, Franz C, 1945, F 3,11:4
Walter, Fred J, 1943, Ja 28,20:2
Walter, Fred S, 1968, Ja 31,41:4
Walter, Frederick, 1965, My 11,39:3
Walter, Frederick P, 1950, Ap 1,15:6
Walter, George, 1952, N 23,88:4
Walter, George F, 1952, Ap 22,29:2
Walter, Gordon, 1960, D 28,27:3
Walter, Gustave E, 1950, Ap 6,29:1
Walter, H Dixon, 1947, D 21,54:1
Walter, Harold J, 1962, Je 26,33:2
Walter, Henry, 1903, D 1,9:3
Walter, Henry M, 1959, Ja 28,31:5
Walter, Herbert E, 1945, O 2,23:5
Walter, Herbert J, 1958, Jl 18,21:2
Walter, Herbert T, 1948, N 2,25:2
Walter, Herman, 1943, F 26,19:3
Walter, Ida Mrs, 1951, N 15,29:1
Walter, Isidor Mrs, 1961, O 3,36:6
Walter, Jacob, 1952, My 25,92:6
Walter, John, 1894, N 4,5:4; 1968, Ag 12,35:3
Walter, John E, 1946, S 24,29:4
Walter, John F, 1940, N 9,17:3
Walter, John Mrs, 1937, Ap 5,19:4
Walter, Joseph C, 1950, Jl 14,21:3
Walter, Karl O, 1939, O 18,26:3
Walter, L Rohe, 1966, Ap 24,86:3
Walter, Lewis L, 1953, Je 7,84:5
Walter, Louis J, 1955, Ag 11,21:5
Walter, Luther M, 1947, Jl 2,23:4
Walter, Madison M, 1960, D 10,23:5
Walter, Martin, 1942, N 12,25:3; 1949, Je 14,31:4
Walter, Martin Mrs, 1942, S 3,19:2; 1942, N 12,25:3
Walter, Mason A, 1917, My 22,13:4
Walter, Maurice Mrs, 1956, Ag 18,17:2
Walter, Moses R, 1916, D 29,9:5
Walter, Otis L, 1966, D 12,47:2
Walter, Otis W, 1955, N 9,33:3
Walter, Otto, 1955, Ag 18,23:4
Walter, Otto M, 1949, D 14,31:5
Walter, Ralph, 1937, F 24,23:2
Walter, Rev Dr, 1869, O 3,3:7
Walter, Robert H, 1953, O 29,31:1
Walter, Simon, 1945, D 28,15:3
Walter, T Henry, 1925, D 30,17:5
Walter, Theodore C, 1959, Je 13,21:4
Walter, Thomas C, 1965, Jl 31,21:2
Walter, W, 1882, Je 19,7:2
Walter, Wilfrid, 1958, Jl 10,27:6
Walter, William, 1945, Je 25,17:5
Walter, William E, 1942, F 23,21:5; 1945, F 24,11:2
Walter, William H, 1937, Ag 12,19:5
Walter, William I, 1944, N 5,54:3
Walter, William M, 1941, N 12,5:3
Walter, William O, 1959, O 25,85:4; 1961, D 4,37:1
Walter, Wilmer, 1941, Ag 25,15:1
Walter, Z M, 1952, O 23,31:4
Walter-Zucker, Paul Mrs, 1962, O 25,39:3
Walters, A Edward, 1965, Ag 19,31:5
Walters, Albert B, 1945, S 27,21:3
Walters, Alex Mrs, 1949, Mr 18,25:4
Walters, Alexander Rev, 1917, F 3,13:5
Walters, Alexander W, 1919, Jl 4,9:5
Walters, Anderson H Mrs, 1949, Mr 12,17:4
Walters, Angus Capt, 1968, Ag 13,36:1
Walters, Arthur L, 1961, Ja 29,85:1
Walters, Augustus J, 1925, My 9,15:5
Walters, Benjamin, 1956, N 25,88:4
Walters, Carl, 1955, N 13,89:3
Walters, Charles E, 1938, D 18,49:1
Walters, Chester, 1958, D 11,13:2
Walters, Clarence, 1947, S 21,60:5
Walters, Curtis, 1960, N 27,86:5
Walters, Edward, 1962, My 17,37:5
Walters, Edward B Mrs, 1938, Ja 13,21:5
Walters, Edward W, 1948, Ag 21,15:1
Walters, Evan W Sr, 1959, N 18,41:4
Walters, Frank R, 1954, Ap 25,87:3
Walters, Fred, 1923, Ag 24,11:6
Walters, Frederick, 1960, My 4,45:1
Walters, Frederick A Mrs, 1962, Ja 17,33:6
Walters, Frederick J Mrs, 1964, Ag 21,30:8
Walters, George, 1944, O 13,19:4
Walters, George A, 1960, Ja 3,89:1
Walters, George L, 1943, Ja 12,23:4
Walters, H, 1931, D 1,27:1
Walters, Hannah B Mrs, 1943, Mr 21,27:1
Walters, Harold C, 1958, F 25,27:1
Walters, Harry J, 1956, Ja 22,89:2
Walters, Harry L, 1941, Ag 19,21:5
Walters, Henry Mrs, 1941, Ja 10,19:3; 1943, Je 17,21:2
Walters, J Henry, 1952, Ja 29,25:1
Walters, Jacob C, 1925, D 14,21:4
Walters, James, 1944, Je 27,19:5
Walters, James D, 1949, S 29,29:4
Walters, John M, 1956, Ap 18,31:4
Walters, John N, 1951, Ap 2,25:4
Walters, Joseph, 1952, D 16,36:6
Walters, Otto C, 1952, N 14,23:4
Walters, Otto C Mrs, 1952, N 14,23:4
Walters, Raymond Mrs, 1956, My 21,25:3
Walters, Samuel, 1951, Ag 9,21:5
Walters, Stanley C, 1962, S 23,87:1
Walters, Theodore A, 1937, N 28,II,9:1
Walters, W Harry, 1949, S 15,27:2
Walters, W J, 1952, Mr 4,27:1
Walters, W T, 1894, N 23,9:4
Walters, William, 1939, Ja 27,20:2
Walters, William B Jr, 1948, D 26,52:4
Walters, William B Sr, 1943, O 29,19:1
Walters, William H, 1940, Ag 11,31:4; 1956, Je 19,29:4
Walters, William H Mrs, 1950, Jl 10,21:5
Walthall, E C Gen, 1898, Ap 21,7:5
Walthall, H B, 1936, Je 18,23:3
Walthall, Isabel Mrs, 1937, D 1,23:6
Walthall, Walter, 1937, Ap 21,23:5
Waltham, Owen J, 1949, Ja 2,63:2
Walthausen, Herman, 1962, S 23,86:2
Walther, Arnold, 1938, My 21,15:4
Walther, Charles H, 1938, My 8,II,7:2
Walther, Frederick P, 1966, S 21,47:1
Walther, George, 1961, Ap 11,37:3
Walther, George W, 1925, Mr 30,17:5
Walther, Henry W, 1941, N 13,28:2
Walther, John, 1937, N 23,23:3
Walther, John L, 1948, Ja 7,25:3
Walther, Jules B Mrs, 1958, Mr 13,29:3
Walther, Paul Sr Mrs, 1951, Je 13,29:5
Walthew, Francis G, 1937, F 3,24:2
Waltho, David, 1937, N 11,25:1
Walthour, Bobby, 1949, S 3,13:5
Walthour, John B, 1952, O 31,25:5
Walthour, Leroy, 1950, D 24,22:2
Walthour, Robert, 1917, D 10,15:5
Waltman, Cloyd F, 1940, O 13,49:3
Waltman, Edwin G Mrs, 1948, S 28,28:3
Waltman, Harry, 1951, Ja 25,25:3
Waltner, Henry Mrs, 1939, Ja 4,21:1
Walton, Alfred Dr, 1920, F 25,11:5
Walton, Alice, 1954, Ja 27,27:3
Walton, Arthur G, 1937, Ag 7,15:3
Walton, Beekman S, 1938, Ag 23,17:5
Walton, Beekman S Mrs, 1945, Ja 27,11:6
Walton, Charles, 1955, N 21,29:4
Walton, Charles D, 1952, Jl 27,57:2
Walton, Charles Ellis Rev, 1905, Ap 19,11:4
Walton, Charles M Jr, 1968, Je 7,36:3
Walton, Charles S, 1945, Ja 30,19:3
Walton, Charles W, 1942, Je 15,19:5; 1945, Mr 21,23:5
Walton, Clifford S, 1912, My 16,11:4
Walton, Daniel D, 1948, S 20,25:4
Walton, Daniel J Mrs, 1962, O 5,33:4
Walton, David S Jr, 1938, Mr 19,15:5
Walton, Donald, 1961, My 3,37:1
Walton, Donald F, 1958, Jl 4,19:2
Walton, Duncan C, 1942, Mr 8,43:3
Walton, Duncan Mrs, 1967, My 29,25:4

Walton, E Clayton, 1952, S 4,27:6
Walton, Eben N, 1907, N 23,9:5
Walton, Edward, 1959, My 17,83:2
Walton, Edward Arthur, 1922, Mr 21,19:6
Walton, Edward L, 1925, My 2,15:5
Walton, Ellsworth J, 1939, O 2,17:5
Walton, Emma, 1951, Ja 24,27:1
Walton, Eri B Mrs, 1959, Mr 17,30:4
Walton, Ernest F Mrs, 1963, Jl 18,27:5
Walton, Frank, 1953, S 23,31:3
Walton, Frank L, 1947, Jl 12,13:4
Walton, Frank W, 1945, My 21,19:4
Walton, Fred, 1942, Jl 10,17:4
Walton, George, 1962, Mr 11,76:8
Walton, George L, 1941, Ja 19,40:3
Walton, Harold, 1942, D 25,17:3
Walton, Harry, 1968, O 27,82:5
Walton, Harry G, 1945, N 25,48:5
Walton, Helen M Mrs, 1905, Mr 17,9:4
Walton, Henry, 1948, Ag 14,13:4
Walton, Horace A, 1942, N 16,19:3
Walton, Hugh G, 1962, My 9,43:4
Walton, Isaac, 1884, Ap 16,4:6
Walton, J C, 1949, N 26,15:3
Walton, J Francis, 1865, Ja 7,4:6
Walton, J L, 1924, Je 3,17:3
Walton, J T, 1883, Je 7,5:2
Walton, James, 1955, Ag 29,19:4
Walton, James A, 1945, Ja 27,11:3
Walton, James McLean, 1923, S 1,11:6
Walton, Jane Mrs, 1923, O 3,15:3
Walton, John, 1907, Ap 1,9:7
Walton, John C, 1957, Ag 3,15:7
Walton, John D Mrs, 1947, Ag 24,56:4
Walton, John F, 1908, F 3,9:4
Walton, John Lawson Sir, 1908, Ja 19,11:4
Walton, Joseph, 1954, Ap 15,29:5
Walton, Joseph F, 1951, Ag 16,27:5
Walton, Kate, 1937, Jl 28,20:1
Walton, Kenneth Mrs, 1957, Ja 23,29:5
Walton, Leo, 1961, S 9,19:5
Walton, Lester A, 1965, O 19,43:1
Walton, Levi S, 1938, Je 9,23:6
Walton, Lewis, 1939, O 22,40:4
Walton, Louis C, 1952, Mr 17,21:5
Walton, Mary I Mrs, 1949, Ag 9,25:4
Walton, Norman B, 1950, Ja 22,76:6
Walton, Otto F, 1949, O 13,27:5
Walton, Phil S, 1956, Ag 4,15:5
Walton, R Foster Lt-Col, 1915, Ja 16,9:4
Walton, Ralph W, 1961, Ap 23,86:5
Walton, Richard, 1941, Mr 29,15:3
Walton, Rudolph L, 1962, Je 20,32:6
Walton, Samuel F, 1955, Ja 22,11:5
Walton, Sarah Mrs, 1873, Jl 2,8:4
Walton, Sydney W, 1940, D 31,15:3
Walton, T C Dr, 1909, Mr 3,9:5
Walton, Thomas B Jr, 1951, D 17,19:7
Walton, Thomas C Dr, 1909, Mr 5,9:4
Walton, Thomas E Jr, 1964, Jl 22,33:1
Walton, Thomas O, 1961, F 19,86:4
Walton, Wellington, 1945, Je 28,19:5
Walton, William, 1915, N 27,15:6; 1921, D 18,22:3
Walton, William B, 1939, Ap 15,19:3
Walton, William C, 1941, Ap 28,15:4
Walton, William E, 1947, Ag 6,23:5
Walton, William E Mrs, 1955, D 14,39:1
Walton, William G Sr, 1956, Jl 26,25:5
Walton, William M, 1950, Mr 3,26:4
Walton, William Ponsonby Col, 1912, O 5,13:6
Walts, Charles C, 1943, O 6,23:2
Walty, Otto A, 1957, O 6,84:6
Walty, Percival D, 1946, S 27,23:4
Waltz, Benjamin F, 1958, N 23,88:7
Waltz, Elizabeth Cherry Mrs, 1903, S 20,7:6
Waltz, George E Mrs, 1946, Ag 20,27:4
Waltz, George H Jr, 1961, O 1,86:1
Waltz, J J (Hansi), 1951, Je 11,25:4
Waltzer, Isidore, 1953, S 25,21:1
Waltzer, Samuel, 1964, Je 14,84:5
Waltzinger, Frederick J, 1957, F 5,23:4
Walvisch, Jonas, 1960, My 17,37:3
Walworth, C W, 1928, Ap 8,II,7:1
Walworth, Chancellor Mrs, 1874, Jl 16,4:6
Walworth, Corinne B Mrs, 1937, Ap 27,23:4
Walworth, De Zosier, 1940, Ja 24,21:2
Walworth, Dorothy (Mrs M Cromwell), 1953, N 7, 17:4
Walworth, Ellen Hardin, 1915, Je 24,11:5
Walworth, Gardner C, 1940, Jl 22,17:3
Walworth, John C, 1949, D 15,35:3
Walworth, Joseph, 1941, Ag 14,17:6
Walworth, William J, 1943, My 20,21:2
Walworth, William J Mrs, 1951, My 23,35:5
Walwyn, Humphrey T, 1957, D 30,23:2
Walz, Aug, 1940, Ap 18,48:3
Walz, E Louis, 1948, N 3,27:4
Walz, Fred, 1953, F 13,21:2
Walz, Frederick W, 1944, Jl 25,19:4
Walz, Jack S, 1956, Ja 13,23:3
Walz, Jacob M, 1950, Jl 27,25:5
Walz, John A, 1954, Ap 17,13:6
Walz, Paul C H, 1937, Ap 30,22:3
Walz, Thomas C, 1961, S 20,29:4
Walz, William L, 1941, Ag 31,22:7
Walz, William L Mrs, 1941, S 2,17:4
Walzer, Abraham, 1965, Ja 28,29:3
Walzer, Harry, 1960, Je 16,33:5
Walzer, John J, 1939, My 4,6:6
Walzer, Morris, 1951, O 5,27:3
Walzer, Samuel J, 1951, Ja 1,17:5
Walzogen, Baron, 1883, Ja 16,5:5
Wambach, Kathryn M, 1939, Mr 16,23:5
Wambach, Thomas C Jr, 1957, F 27,27:6
Wambaugh, Cyrene J, 1941, My 3,15:6
Wambaugh, Eugene, 1940, Ag 7,19:6
Wambaugh, Eugene Mrs, 1938, My 4,23:5
Wambaugh, Sarah, 1955, N 13,88:4
Wambold, Jacob, 1903, Jl 22,7:6
Wambold, James K, 1952, S 12,21:1
Wamester, Raymond J, 1957, Je 8,19:5
Wampler, William M (por), 1946, Ag 19,25:2
Wampole, Henry K Dr, 1906, S 15,4:5
Wamsley, Frederic Mrs, 1951, S 9,88:4
Wamsley, Paul, 1956, F 17,21:1
Wamsley, Richard W, 1953, Jl 6,17:6
Wan Fu-lin, 1951, Jl 19,23:5
Wanamaker, Allison, 1944, Je 22,19:5
Wanamaker, Charles C, 1948, Jl 23,19:2
Wanamaker, Edmund E, 1949, Je 14,31:4
Wanamaker, Elizabeth Mrs, 1925, My 3,5:1
Wanamaker, Francis Marion, 1916, Ag 24,9:4
Wanamaker, Horace Sr, 1947, O 11,17:5
Wanamaker, J Jr, 1934, N 30,19:3
Wanamaker, John Dr, 1923, N 18,23:3
Wanamaker, John Mrs (funl, Ag 24,9:4), 1920, Ag 21,7:6
Wanamaker, Lewis Cass, 1917, F 8,13:6
Wanamaker, Pauline D Mrs, 1956, F 2,25:4
Wanamaker, R, 1928, Mr 10,1:3
Wanamaker, Thomas B, 1908, Mr 3,7:4
Wanamaker, Thomas B (funl, Mr 29,9:5), 1908, Mr 26,7:4
Wanamaker, Walter B, 1965, My 27,37:4
Wanamaker, William H, 1905, O 21,1:6
Wanamaker, William H Jr, 1956, O 23,33:2
Wanamaker, William W Mrs, 1962, Je 24,69:1
Wanat, John, 1948, Ja 25,56:4
Wand, Elmer W, 1955, Ap 19,31:2
Wand, Fred Mrs, 1968, F 28,47:3
Wandall, Francis S, 1948, D 17,27:1
Wandel, Blanche E G Mrs, 1940, Ag 21,19:5
Wandel, Elliott H, 1956, Je 18,25:4
Wandell, Francis Livingston, 1918, My 9,13:5
Wandell, Mortimer D, 1952, Je 29,56:2
Wandell, Samuel, 1943, S 27,19:5
Wandelt, Frederick H, 1952, F 21,27:2
Wandelt, Samuel Capt, 1907, Ag 3,7:6
Wander, Fred, 1939, Jl 4,13:3
Wander, Harry, 1951, S 12,31:1
Wander, Maurice C, 1965, Je 14,33:2
Wander, Sol, 1937, Ag 16,19:3
Wander, William, 1905, Mr 5,9:3
Wanderman, Charles, 1961, My 28,64:3
Wanderman, Daniel N, 1956, Mr 9,23:1
Wanderman, Herman P, 1944, My 15,19:5
Wanders, George, 1961, Ja 9,39:5
Wandewalker, Hannibal, 1947, Ap 1,27:5
Wandling, George H, 1953, Ag 8,11:5
Wandling, George S V, 1950, Je 28,27:5
Wandling, James L, 1919, Ap 19,17:4
Wandling, William J, 1945, Mr 29,23:4
Wandras, William G, 1964, S 28,29:5
Wands, T Edward Mrs, 1961, Ap 30,87:1
Wands, T Edward Sr, 1953, F 14,17:3
Waner, O L, 1948, D 17,27:4
Waner, Paul G, 1965, Ag 30,25:1
Wang, A R William, 1959, Mr 27,23:2
Wang, C T Mrs, 1945, Ja 24,21:2
Wang, Cheng-t'ing, 1961, My 22,31:3
Wang, Chung Yu, 1958, S 1,13:5
Wang, Francis X, 1957, Ap 19,10:5
Wang, S T, 1946, Je 28,22:3
Wang, Sigmund, 1964, Ap 5,86:5
Wang, Sih T Mrs, 1961, My 27,23:4
Wang Chi-teh, 1955, Ap 23,19:2
Wang Ching-wei, Mme, 1959, Je 27,2:7
Wang Ching-wei, 1944, N 13,11:3
Wang Chung-hui, 1958, Mr 16,87:1
Wang I-Ting, 1938, N 14,19:3
Wang Keh-Min, 1945, D 28,15:3
Wang Mu-to, 1959, O 6,10:4
Wang Po-chun, 1944, D 22,17:5
Wang Wen-cheng, Paul, 1961, My 1,29:4
Wangchuk, Jigmey, 1952, Mr 30,93:1
Wangel, Hedwig, 1961, Mr 14,35:4
Wangenheim, Hans von Baron, 1915, O 26,11:5
Wangenstein, Frederick Mrs, 1951, Ja 1,17:4
Wanger, Beatrice, 1945, Mr 15,23:3
Wanger, Henry F, 1964, S 21,31:2
Wanger, Ruth, 1943, Ag 19,19:3
Wanger, Walter, 1968, N 19,41:1
Wangerin, Albert W, 1940, My 18,15:2
Wangler, Joseph A, 1951, Ap 8,92:7
Wanglin, Byron C Mrs, 1949, Ag 30,27:2
Wangner, Henry Mrs, 1944, My 31,19:2
Wanhope, John, 1946, D 9,25:2
Wankel, Bernhard Jr, 1952, Ja 19,15:5
Wanko, Charles G, 1953, O 11,89:2
Wanlass, Stanley A, 1959, Jl 13,27:4
Wanless, W G Dr, 1922, Jl 8,11:7
Wanliss, David S, 1943, S 27,19:4
Wanmaker, George W, 1917, D 10,15:5
Wann, Louis, 1956, Ap 23,27:2
Wannamaker, William H, 1958, Ag 5,27:2
Wannemacher, Edward H, 1957, Jl 6,15:5
Wanner, Frank A, 1958, O 14,37:1
Wanner, Nevin M, 1943, Ap 24,13:3
Wanninger, Sophie B Mrs, 1940, My 21,23:6
Wansbrough, Robert M, 1956, My 26,17:4
Wanser, Frank, 1942, F 3,19:4
Wanser, Latou, 1950, N 28,31:1
Wanser, William H, 1942, S 9,23:3
Wansor, Edward, 1949, O 12,29:4
Wanstall, Fred E, 1950, Mr 14,25:2
Wantage, R J L Baron, 1901, Je 11,9:6
Wanting, Emma N, 1945, S 24,19:3
Wantoch, Joseph, 1957, Ap 20,17:3
Wantz, Dick, 1965, My 15,23:7
Wantz, Julius B, 1952, Ap 8,29:3
Wanvig, Harry F, 1957, Mr 28,31:4
Wanvig, Jonas, 1944, F 16,17:2
Wanzer, Charles H, 1941, N 18,25:3; 1948, D 6,25:3
Wanzer, George M, 1937, D 30,19:3
Wanzer, James H, 1939, Je 7,23:4
Wanzor, Daniel P, 1948, My 27,25:1
Waples, Charles J Mrs, 1949, Je 29,28:2
Waples, Harold J, 1955, Jl 4,11:5
Waples, James E, 1938, D 31,15:6
Waples, Joseph B, 1960, S 25,88:4
Waples, Rufus, 1940, Ja 31,19:2
Wappler, Frederick C, 1944, N 27,23:3
Wappler, Frederick H, 1955, Jl 17,60:6
Waram, Percy C, 1961, O 7,23:3
Waram, Percy C Mrs, 1961, Mr 12,86:2
Warbasse, Charles N, 1959, Ap 5,87:1
Warbasse, James D Mrs, 1945, F 4,38:4
Warbasse, James P, 1957, F 24,85:1
Warbasse, Justin, 1953, Ap 19,91:1
Warbeke, John M, 1950, My 22,21:3
Warburg, Felix M, 1937, O 21,1:3
Warburg, Felix M Mrs (will, S 23,30:3), 1958, S 15, 21:3
Warburg, Fritz M, 1964, O 15,39:2
Warburg, Julius, 1938, N 27,49:1
Warburg, Max M, 1946, D 28,15:1
Warburg, Max M Mrs, 1960, D 9,31:4
Warburg, Moritz Mrs, 1921, O 20,17:5
Warburg, Otto, 1938, Ja 12,21:2
Warburg, Otto C, 1947, Je 14,15:6
Warburg, P M, 1932, Ja 25,1:2
Warburg, Paul F, 1965, O 11,39:1
Warburg, Paul M Mrs (will, Ja 25,20:4), 1946, Ja 22,27:5
Warburg, Theresa B Mrs, 1940, F 23,15:4
Warburton, Barclay H Mrs, 1954, N 18,33:4
Warburton, Barday H, 1954, D 6,27:3
Warburton, Benjamin J, 1962, N 10,25:1
Warburton, Cecil, 1958, O 9,37:5
Warburton, Charles, 1952, Jl 20,53:3
Warburton, Eliot Mrs, 1954, D 3,27:2
Warburton, Frank T (por), 1938, N 16,23:3
Warburton, Frank W, 1961, D 24,36:4
Warburton, Frederick John, 1917, N 3,15:4
Warburton, George, 1948, D 8,31:5
Warburton, George A, 1955, Ag 10,25:5
Warburton, Harry A, 1952, My 17,19:5
Warburton, Mary B, 1937, S 15,7:3
Warburton, P G Eliot, 1961, O 6,35:3
Warburton, Ruth Mrs, 1954, D 15,31:4
Warchal, John, 1949, Je 12,76:1
Warchauer, David, 1947, D 29,18:3
Ward, A H Dr, 1917, O 29,13:2
Ward, A Lynch, 1944, My 4,19:3
Ward, A M Mrs, 1926, Jl 27,17:4
Ward, A Montgomery, 1913, D 8,11:4
Ward, Aaron Condit, 1909, Jl 21,7:6
Ward, Aaron L, 1961, Ja 31,29:4
Ward, Adron, 1918, Jl 6,9:6
Ward, Agnes S, 1938, N 30,23:4
Ward, Albert, 1952, N 1,21:2
Ward, Albert N Mrs, 1938, Jl 14,21:2
Ward, Alexander S, 1923, Ap 8,6:2
Ward, Alfred, 1916, S 26,11:2
Ward, Alfred J, 1957, Ja 29,31:1
Ward, Alfred W, 1941, F 9,48:2
Ward, Alice G B, 1948, D 6,25:3
Ward, Alice L, 1947, F 10,29:5
Ward, Alonzo H Capt, 1903, D 12,7:6
Ward, Amelia Duncan Mrs, 1925, My 22,19:6
Ward, Andrew, 1942, Ag 24,15:5; 1947, S 5,19:2
Ward, Andrew J, 1939, Ag 25,15:6
Ward, Anne C, 1949, S 10,17:3
Ward, Annie Mrs, 1938, Ap 7,23:2
Ward, Arch (funl, Jl 13,25:5), 1955, Jl 10,73:1
Ward, Artemas (funl, Mr 18,21:1), 1925, Mr 15,26:
Ward, Artemas Jr, 1946, Ap 30,21:5
Ward, Arthur, 1951, My 18,27:5
Ward, Arthur B, 1947, Je 25,25:4

Ward, Arthur S (S Rohmer), 1959, Je 3,35:1
Ward, Baron, 1858, O 25,4:6
Ward, Benjamin I, 1954, Jl 23,17:4
Ward, Bernard, 1940, Jl 25,17:6
Ward, Bertha, 1952, Jl 28,15:3
Ward, Beverley, 1915, Jl 17,7:5
Ward, Bud (Marvin Ward), 1968, Ja 3,40:2
Ward, C, 1936, My 14,25:3
Ward, C C, 1939, My 28,III,7:1
Ward, C Jack Mrs, 1949, N 21,25:3
Ward, C O, 1902, Mr 21,9:6
Ward, Caroline C, 1942, Je 24,19:4
Ward, Caroline E, 1961, F 18,19:1
Ward, Carrie C Mrs, 1940, Ap 12,23:1
Ward, Carrie W Mrs, 1946, My 16,21:1
Ward, Channing M, 1945, D 20,23:3
Ward, Channing M Mrs (H de Motte), 1955, Jl 10, 72:3
Ward, Charles, 1907, D 28,7:6; 1944, My 13,19:4; 1946, Jl 21,40:1; 1947, Je 2,25:4
Ward, Charles A, 1951, Ja 13,15:4; 1959, My 27,35:1
Ward, Charles B, 1917, Mr 23,9:4; 1946, My 28,21:1; 1956, Mr 29,27:4
Ward, Charles C, 1952, F 29,23:5; 1957, Mr 16,19:2
Ward, Charles Dod, 1915, Ag 1,15:6
Ward, Charles E, 1944, O 6,23:2
Ward, Charles F Mrs (will), 1960, Jl 23,11:2
Ward, Charles F Sr, 1950, My 9,30:2
Ward, Charles G, 1960, Ja 1,19:5
Ward, Charles H (por), 1943, Ja 19,19:3
Ward, Charles H, 1955, F 5,15:3
Ward, Charles J, 1956, Jl 8,65:1
Ward, Charles L Mrs, 1947, O 2,27:5
Ward, Charles M, 1950, Ag 8,29:1
Ward, Charles M Mrs, 1953, N 16,25:5
Ward, Charles P, 1940, Ap 30,21:3; 1960, Ag 4,29:6
Ward, Charles R, 1945, Ja 16,19:3
Ward, Charles S, 1943, My 19,25:1
Ward, Charles S Mrs, 1955, Ag 22,21:5
Ward, Charles T, 1937, S 8,23:1
Ward, Charles W, 1946, Ap 13,17:1
Ward, Charles W Mrs, 1956, O 9,35:1
Ward, Chauncey I, 1944, Ja 22,13:2
Ward, Christopher L, 1943, F 23,21:3
Ward, Clara, 1916, D 20,13:4
Ward, Clarence D Mrs, 1950, Mr 14,25:1
Ward, Cleland A, 1947, O 28,27:4
Ward, Clement E B Mrs, 1957, Mr 15,26:1
Ward, Clifford C, 1949, Je 18,13:4
Ward, Clifford E, 1943, S 29,21:4
Ward, Clifford T, 1946, Mr 13,29:1
Ward, Clyde E, 1943, S 4,13:3
Ward, Daniel, 1941, Ap 1,23:5; 1960, My 24,37:1
Ward, David B, 1956, Mr 16,23:5
Ward, De Wit C, 1907, Ja 26,9:5
Ward, De Witt, 1937, S 8,23:2
Ward, Delos E, 1946, Mr 27,27:1
Ward, Duren J H, 1942, Ja 25,41:3
Ward, E M, 1879, Ja 17,2:4
Ward, E Mortimer Mrs, 1956, N 27,38:1
Ward, E P, 1942, Ap 22,20:3
Ward, Earl F, 1949, Je 1,31:5
Ward, Edgar M 2d, 1943, Ap 5,19:1
Ward, Edgar Melville, 1915, My 17,9:3
Ward, Edmond A, 1951, D 17,32:2
Ward, Edmund, 1909, My 17,9:6
Ward, Edmund F, 1943, Mr 27,14:7
Ward, Edward E, 1945, F 17,13:5
Ward, Edward H, 1944, Mr 24,19:5
Ward, Edward M, 1947, Mr 24,25:4
Ward, Edward M Jr, 1964, F 17,31:1
Ward, Edwin C Mrs, 1943, Mr 20,15:4
Ward, Edwin F Dr, 1912, N 24,II,17:4
Ward, Edwin K Sr, 1948, Ja 19,23:1
Ward, Edwin S, 1951, Ag 2,21:3
Ward, Eliab Dr, 1871, Ap 17,5:3
Ward, Elijah, 1882, F 8,5:5
Ward, Eliot L, 1962, Jl 27,25:5
Ward, Elizabeth S Mrs, 1941, O 11,17:2
Ward, Elizabeth Stuart Phelps Mrs (funl, F 2,11:4), 1911, Ja 29,II,11:1
Ward, Ellis, 1922, Ag 26,11:7
Ward, Elroy H, 1947, Jl 10,21:3
Ward, Emily J Mrs, 1948, N 6,13:6
Ward, Emma F, 1956, D 8,19:4
Ward, Eoghan R, 1947, Ja 23,26:1
Ward, Ephraim Mrs, 1946, O 27,62:3
Ward, Estelle F, 1941, Ap 21,19:5
Ward, Eugene B, 1956, N 3,23:4
Ward, Eugene C, 1948, S 14,30:3
Ward, Eugene J, 1961, D 16,25:6
Ward, Eugene L Mrs, 1956, Je 8,25:2
Ward, Evans, 1963, Jl 2,30:1
Ward, Evelyn Lady, 1955, My 6,23:3
Ward, F, 1927, Je 10,23:5
Ward, F A Judge, 1903, Ap 30,2:5
Ward, F C Mrs, 1937, Je 2,23:4
Ward, Fanny (left no will, F 5,23:8), 1952, Ja 28,17:3
Ward, Fanny C Mrs, 1947, D 21,52:4
Ward, Fleming, 1962, Ag 3,23:4
Ward, Florence A, 1948, Ap 2,24:2
Ward, Florence Nightingale Dr, 1919, D 17,17:2
Ward, Florence S, 1945, O 25,21:5
Ward, Francis E, 1917, Mr 13,11:4
Ward, Francis R, 1944, D 20,23:3
Ward, Francis R Mrs, 1944, D 20,23:3
Ward, Francis T, 1939, F 20,17:3
Ward, Frank B, 1952, F 3,85:1
Ward, Frank E, 1953, S 17,29:5
Ward, Frank E Mrs, 1953, Jl 12,65:1
Ward, Frank H, 1944, My 25,21:4; 1958, Je 17,29:6
Ward, Frank J, 1948, Je 14,23:2
Ward, Frank L, 1942, O 30,19:4
Ward, Frank M, 1948, F 22,48:3
Ward, Frank R, 1945, S 27,21:4
Ward, Frank T, 1921, My 2,15:5
Ward, Franklin W (por), 1938, Mr 18,19:1
Ward, Fred E, 1949, My 5,27:2
Ward, Fred K, 1959, Ja 17,19:5
Ward, Frederick F, 1943, Jl 7,19:5
Ward, Freeman, 1943, S 15,27:5
Ward, Freeman A Capt, 1910, D 14,13:4
Ward, G A Dr, 1882, O 3,5:6
Ward, G Howard, 1939, My 31,23:4
Ward, G R, 1880, Ja 30,2:7
Ward, Genevieve, 1922, Ag 19,11:6
Ward, George A, 1947, Ap 23,25:2
Ward, George C, 1964, Mr 31,35:4
Ward, George F, 1954, Mr 19,23:2
Ward, George G, 1950, D 21,29:1
Ward, George Gray, 1922, Je 16,17:5
Ward, George H, 1943, Jl 17,13:5
Ward, George K Mrs, 1939, Mr 16,23:2
Ward, George K Rev, 1937, Jl 20,23:3
Ward, George M, 1903, D 16,9:5
Ward, George N, 1951, Ja 11,26:3
Ward, George S (por), 1940, S 4,23:1
Ward, George W, 1955, Ag 24,27:3
Ward, George W Ex-Judge, 1918, O 4,13:2
Ward, George W Mrs, 1949, Ap 6,29:3
Ward, Gertrude, 1956, My 23,31:5
Ward, Gilbert, 1920, Mr 28,22:3
Ward, Gilbert D, 1953, Mr 9,29:3
Ward, Grant E, 1958, F 17,23:2
Ward, Grant P, 1941, D 6,17:1
Ward, Granville D Sr, 1940, Jl 14,31:2
Ward, Guy A, 1940, Mr 4,15:5
Ward, H, 1932, O 9,32:1
Ward, H G, 1933, Ag 25,15:2
Ward, H M, 1916, Ja 6,13:3
Ward, H Nelson Mrs, 1881, Mr 28,8:4
Ward, Hallet S, 1956, Ap 2,23:5
Ward, Hamilton Sr Mrs, 1946, Jl 22,21:4
Ward, Hap Mrs, 1951, My 3,29:4
Ward, Harold B, 1951, Ag 22,23:1
Ward, Harriet, 1909, Jl 30,7:6
Ward, Harry, 1952, Ja 7,19:3
Ward, Harry C, 1948, Mr 16,27:4
Ward, Harry E, 1960, S 24,23:3
Ward, Harry F, 1966, D 10,37:1
Ward, Harry G, 1941, F 2,43:5
Ward, Heber Mrs (L Levine), 1966, My 5,47:2
Ward, Helen J, 1951, S 2,48:8
Ward, Henry A Dr (burial plans, Jl 7,1:6), 1906, Jl 5,1:4
Ward, Henry B, 1945, D 1,23:2
Ward, Henry C, 1912, My 3,11:4
Ward, Henry Capt, 1904, D 24,7:6
Ward, Henry Clay Gen, 1925, N 17,25:4
Ward, Henry Heman, 1916, Jl 19,9:6
Ward, Henry L, 1943, D 18,15:2
Ward, Henry M, 1939, N 15,23:4; 1949, F 10,27:4
Ward, Henry M Mrs, 1951, Je 13,29:4
Ward, Henry S, 1937, N 30,23:5
Ward, Henry Sanford Mrs, 1907, S 11,9:6
Ward, Herbert L Sr, 1945, Je 9,13:5
Ward, Holcombe, 1967, Ja 24,37:1
Ward, Holcome Mrs, 1956, S 25,33:3
Ward, Hugh B Rev Father, 1908, Ja 20,9:4
Ward, Hugh Campbell, 1909, Ag 17,9:6
Ward, Humphrey Mrs, 1920, Mr 25,11:5
Ward, Irving, 1924, Ap 18,19:5
Ward, Irving A, 1943, N 30,27:1
Ward, Irving K, 1948, F 17,25:5
Ward, Isaac, 1952, Ag 31,45:2
Ward, J E, 1902, D 1,9:5
Ward, J Francis, 1939, Ag 12,13:7
Ward, J G T Mrs, 1882, Ag 11,8:3
Ward, J H, 1926, D 17,23:5
Ward, J H Hobart Gen, 1903, Jl 25,7:6
Ward, J Harry Mrs, 1951, O 2,27:1
Ward, J Langdon, 1915, Jl 19,9:4
Ward, J Pearson, 1937, My 14,23:2
Ward, J R W, 1929, S 28,19:1
Ward, J Rigney, 1952, S 21,89:2
Ward, J Sir, 1930, Jl 8,23:1
Ward, Jacob Ewing, 1913, Jl 31,7:4
Ward, James, 1924, Je 2,17:6
Ward, James A, 1954, F 4,25:5; 1955, Mr 6,88:6
Ward, James A 3d, 1968, Ap 13,25:5
Ward, James B, 1952, Jl 11,17:4; 1954, O 19,27:3
Ward, James E, 1951, Ap 5,29:2; 1954, Ap 24,17:5
Ward, James F, 1947, My 18,61:1
Ward, James H, 1958, Jl 13,68:5
Ward, James J, 1963, Je 12,43:4
Ward, James L (por), 1945, N 25,50:2
Ward, James Prof, 1925, Mr 5,19:6
Ward, James W, 1938, My 31,2:3; 1952, Ja 10,29:3; 1954, Ap 21,29:5
Ward, Jane K, 1951, Ja 2,23:3
Ward, Jean T Lady, 1962, My 3,33:5
Ward, Jem, 1884, Ap 7,5:2
Ward, John, 1866, Ap 4,4:7; 1904, My 17,9:6; 1911, Mr 20,9:5; 1939, Mr 2,21:5; 1944, Ja 4,17:4; 1956, My 14,25:5; 1964, D 12,31:2
Ward, John A, 1956, Mr 28,31:3
Ward, John C, 1949, F 16,25:1
Ward, John E, 1951, My 8,31:4; 1953, D 27,60:2
Ward, John Gilbert, 1923, Ap 24,21:5
Ward, John H (por), 1938, D 3,19:1
Ward, John J, 1947, Mr 28,23:2
Ward, John L, 1906, Ag 27,7:7; 1967, Ja 3,37:2
Ward, John M E, 1940, S 1,20:8
Ward, John Q A, 1910, My 2,9:1
Ward, John R, 1944, D 21,22:2
Ward, John T, 1949, My 3,25:4
Ward, John T Jr, 1951, Ja 22,26:5
Ward, John Wesley Dr, 1916, Ag 25,7:6
Ward, Joseph, 1946, My 10,19:2
Ward, Joseph A, 1941, Jl 17,19:4
Ward, Joseph H, 1946, Ap 17,25:1
Ward, Joseph J, 1949, N 6,92:3
Ward, Joseph L, 1941, D 14,68:6; 1948, F 22,48:3
Ward, Joseph P, 1946, D 28,15:3
Ward, Joseph S, 1952, Je 1,85:1
Ward, Joshua, 1903, D 3,9:4
Ward, Josiah O, 1938, Mr 16,23:6
Ward, Julia F Mrs, 1940, S 10,23:3
Ward, Kenneth H Mrs, 1958, Ap 10,29:3
Ward, Kenneth K, 1939, Ap 4,25:1
Ward, L B, 1885, Je 16,5:1
Ward, Laura P, 1937, Ja 3,II,8:4
Ward, Laurence C Mrs, 1941, My 17,15:6
Ward, Lauriston, 1960, F 3,33:1
Ward, Lawrence S, 1948, D 17,27:2
Ward, Lem (por), 1942, N 25,23:3
Ward, Leo L, 1953, Ja 23,19:3
Ward, Leslie A, 1959, Ag 18,29:1
Ward, Leslie Dodd Dr (funl, Jl 20,9:5), 1910, Jl 14, 7:2
Ward, Lester W, 1944, D 3,57:2
Ward, Levi A, 1944, Jl 15,13:5
Ward, Lillian E Mrs, 1937, F 13,13:6
Ward, Lot R, 1946, Ag 6,25:1
Ward, Lot R Jr, 1953, Ap 3,23:2
Ward, Louis B, 1942, Ap 21,23:2
Ward, Louis F, 1953, F 3,25:3
Ward, Louis H, 1950, F 14,25:4
Ward, Louis S, 1941, Ja 4,13:1
Ward, Lucille, 1952, Ag 10,61:2
Ward, M, 1884, Ag 19,5:2
Ward, M L, 1884, Ap 26,5:2
Ward, Marcus L, 1920, My 29,15:5
Ward, Maria E M, 1941, S 11,23:1
Ward, Marion M Mrs, 1940, Jl 22,17:4
Ward, Mark H, 1952, D 23,23:2
Ward, Mark H Mrs, 1950, Ja 24,31:3
Ward, Martha C Mrs, 1941, F 15,15:3
Ward, Martin P, 1949, D 10,18:3
Ward, Mary (Mrs J S Crawley), 1966, My 4,47:4
Ward, Mary Mrs, 1922, O 31,15:4
Ward, Michael J, 1946, Je 6,21:2
Ward, Milton S, 1957, Jl 22,19:2
Ward, Montague R, 1949, My 6,25:3
Ward, Morris Mrs, 1945, Je 25,17:3
Ward, Moses, 1866, My 6,4:5
Ward, Newell J Mrs, 1952, My 28,29:3
Ward, Norman W, 1963, F 2,8:8
Ward, Paul B, 1951, Ap 20,29:4
Ward, Paul W, 1947, Ap 15,25:4
Ward, Perley E, 1939, Ja 23,13:2
Ward, Peter, 1908, Mr 16,7:4
Ward, Phil D, 1941, Ap 18,21:2
Ward, Philip A, 1944, S 29,21:1
Ward, Philip H Jr, 1963, Ag 25,82:8
Ward, R De C, 1931, N 13,23:1
Ward, R F Capt, 1884, Je 9,5:5
Ward, Ralph A, 1958, D 29,15:6
Ward, Ralph A Mrs, 1947, F 9,62:6
Ward, Ralph D, 1953, Ja 18,92:2
Ward, Ralph M Mrs, 1947, O 7,27:2
Ward, Raymond L, 1949, Jl 30,15:4
Ward, Reginald A, 1953, Jl 28,19:3
Ward, Reginald H, 1925, N 21,17:5
Ward, Rhoda E, 1954, F 23,27:4
Ward, Richard, 1920, Mr 10,11:4
Ward, Richard P, 1951, D 30,25:1
Ward, Robert, 1950, N 7,27:3
Ward, Robert A, 1942, Je 16,23:3
Ward, Robert B L, 1937, Jl 17,15:1
Ward, Robert B Mrs, 1951, Mr 14,33:5
Ward, Robert Boyd, 1915, O 19,11:5
Ward, Robert G Mrs, 1956, Je 4,29:6
Ward, Robert L, 1948, Ja 29,23:4
Ward, Robert M C, 1955, F 18,22:1
Ward, Robertson Mrs, 1961, Ja 11,47:3
Ward, Roger J Mrs, 1952, Je 18,27:2
Ward, Rowland, 1912, D 30,7:4
Ward, Ruth H, 1940, Ja 16,23:5

Ward, S Lawrence, 1944, Ja 4,17:3
Ward, S Mortimer Jr, 1955, My 26,31:3
Ward, S W H, 1871, D 31,6:2
Ward, Sam, 1884, My 20,5:1; 1960, My 7,23:6
Ward, Sampson L, 1965, Ap 7,43:1
Ward, Samuel Baldwin Dr, 1915, Je 4,11:5
Ward, Samuel Dexter, 1905, Mr 6,7:5
Ward, Samuel P Mrs, 1950, F 4,15:6
Ward, Seth Bp, 1909, S 21,9:6
Ward, Sherman B, 1942, Jl 4,17:6
Ward, Sidney F, 1951, Ja 23,27:3
Ward, Solly, 1942, My 26,21:2
Ward, Stanley, 1914, Je 28,15:4
Ward, Stephen, 1954, Mr 10,25:5
Ward, Susanne W Mrs, 1938, Ap 14,23:1
Ward, Sylvanus D Mrs, 1964, Je 24,37:2
Ward, Sylvester L, 1960, My 24,37:5
Ward, Sylvester L H, 1910, O 26,9:5
Ward, Sylvester L H Mrs, 1947, S 24,23:6
Ward, T Arnold, 1958, O 6,31:5
Ward, T Arnold Mrs, 1958, O 6,31:5
Ward, Theodore G Mrs, 1939, Ap 6,25:4
Ward, Thomas B, 1953, Jl 19,57:1
Ward, Thomas F Jr (por), 1943, Jl 24,13:1
Ward, Thomas F Mrs, 1943, F 19,20:2
Ward, Thomas G, 1944, Ap 23,43:3
Ward, Thomas J, 1959, Ja 17,19:5
Ward, Thomas L, 1950, Ap 8,13:6
Ward, Thomas P, 1963, O 19,25:2
Ward, Thomas W, 1940, Jl 19,19:3
Ward, Tom S Mrs, 1963, Ag 19,25:5
Ward, Union S, 1943, My 2,45:1
Ward, Vanderbilt B Jr, 1957, Mr 20,37:4
Ward, Varney S, 1964, S 13,86:7
Ward, Vincent B, 1940, Ag 12,15:2
Ward, W B, 1929, F 7,27:1
Ward, W C, 1903, Ja 21,1:5
Ward, W C Mrs, 1903, Ja 21,1:5
Ward, W L, 1933, Jl 17,1:7
Ward, W P, 1928, Ja 18,25:5
Ward, Waldron M, 1968, N 9,33:5
Ward, Walter C, 1942, F 21,19:5
Ward, Walter D (Dad), 1955, Mr 10,18:4
Ward, Walter S, 1946, My 24,19:5
Ward, Warren L, 1952, Ap 30,27:1
Ward, Warren R, 1940, F 20,21:3
Ward, Wilbert, 1959, Ja 16,27:3
Ward, Wilbert Mrs, 1942, Ap 19,43:1; 1950, F 21,26:2
Ward, Wilbur, 1954, S 21,27:6
Ward, Will D, 1940, D 24,15:4
Ward, William, 1916, O 26,11:5; 1952, Ja 6,95:3; 1958, Ag 8,17:8
Ward, William B Mrs, 1965, Ap 25,88:6
Ward, William C, 1952, Ag 6,21:2
Ward, William E, 1945, Je 21,19:5
Ward, William F, 1953, Ja 19,23:2; 1953, Mr 30,21:5
Ward, William F Sr, 1952, O 21,29:5
Ward, William G Prof, 1923, N 4,23:2
Ward, William H, 1942, Je 23,19:5; 1943, Je 7,13:3; 1945, S 25,25:3; 1961, Mr 2,27:1
Ward, William Hayes Rev Dr, 1916, Ag 29,9:4
Ward, William I, 1956, S 8,17:2
Ward, William J, 1937, S 8,23:2; 1942, S 16,23:5; 1949, Jl 23,11:3; 1959, Mr 30,31:4
Ward, William J Sr, 1949, Ja 9,72:2
Ward, William L, 1938, N 30,23:3
Ward, William Mrs, 1947, O 10,25:3
Ward, William P, 1955, F 2,27:4; 1966, Ja 23,88:6
Ward, William R, 1955, F 11,23:3
Ward, William 3d, 1949, My 11,30:8
Ward, Willis B, 1943, Ag 9,13:6
Ward (Mother M Dominic), 1959, Ja 12,39:4
Ward-Smith, Kenneth, 1940, Ja 17,21:5
Wardall, William J Mrs, 1942, Ja 18,42:4
Wardburgh, Russell L, 1961, Jl 5,33:1
Warde, Arthur F, 1938, Jl 16,13:4
Warde, Charles Mrs, 1950, Je 13,27:2
Warde, F, 1935, F 9,15:1
Warde, Frederick, 1939, Ag 1,19:4
Warde, George N, 1937, Ap 30,22:2
Wardell, Asher, 1905, Je 13,9:6
Wardell, Charles L, 1937, N 3,23:2
Wardell, Charles W B, 1955, Je 7,33:3
Wardell, Daniel, 1952, My 20,25:4
Wardell, Daniel E, 1912, Ap 1,13:5
Wardell, Edwin F, 1941, F 22,15:3
Wardell, Frank C, 1939, S 1,17:6
Wardell, Frederick A, 1942, N 10,28:2
Wardell, Frederick K, 1938, My 14,15:3
Wardell, Harry, 1948, S 18,17:3
Wardell, Jane, 1950, Ja 15,84:5
Wardell, John A, 1955, F 24,27:4
Wardell, Percy J, 1963, O 6,88:7
Wardell, William J, 1952, Je 12,34:5
Warden, Carl A, 1960, Ag 22,25:2
Warden, Carl J, 1961, Mr 1,33:1
Warden, Carl J Mrs, 1944, Je 16,19:3
Warden, Clarence A, 1951, My 7,25:4
Warden, Clarence Mrs (see also S 11), 1903, S 13,7:5
Warden, Dave, 1942, Ag 22,13:4
Warden, David T, 1938, Mr 28,15:3
Warden, Elizabeth B Mrs, 1938, S 10,17:4
Warden, Frank R, 1947, My 29,21:1
Warden, Frederick A, 1945, S 15,15:3
Warden, Oliver S, 1951, Mr 13,31:3
Warden, Paul S, 1955, Je 26,77:1
Warden, Randall D, 1967, S 18,47:2
Warden, William G, 1941, F 24,15:3
Warden, William G Mrs, 1940, Jl 12,15:5
Wardenburg, Frederic A, 1966, Ja 28,47:4
Wardener, Gabrielle Baroness, 1921, O 18,17:4
Warder, Frank H, 1955, Mr 3,27:5
Warder, Frederick W, 1954, N 19,23:4
Wardhaugh, William T, 1938, Ag 6,13:5
Wardi, Louis H, 1952, Mr 9,93:1
Wardington, Lord (J W B Pease), 1950, Ag 8,29:3
Wardlaw, Charles D, 1960, O 4,43:5
Wardlaw, John B, 1957, My 25,21:3
Wardlaw, John B Mrs, 1947, D 5,25:1
Wardlaw, John G, 1943, Ag 27,17:3
Wardlaw, Patterson, 1948, Ja 19,23:1
Wardlaw, William Mrs (mem ser set), 1963, Ap 26, 35:2
Wardle, Edward, 1951, Jl 12,25:2
Wardle, G J, 1947, Je 19,21:4
Wardle, Thomas E, 1944, My 12,19:2
Wardle, Thomas L, 1951, Je 27,29:5
Wardle, Warren H, 1960, My 31,31:1
Wardle, William R, 1943, Je 27,32:2
Wardley, George P, 1946, O 7,31:3
Wardman, Ervin (funl, Ja 15,15:5), 1923, Ja 14,6:3
Wardman, Harry, 1938, Mr 19,15:3
Wardner, Allen, 1877, S 1,4:7
Wardner, Drew M, 1954, Mr 5,20:4
Wardner, G Philip, 1963, S 11,43:4
Wardner, James F, 1905, Mr 31,9:3
Wardner, William, 1943, Ap 19,19:4
Wardrop, Edmund D, 1963, Ap 25,33:5
Wardrop, John, 1951, F 11,88:1
Wardrop, Robert, 1937, S 29,23:4
Wardrop, William W, 1954, O 14,29:4
Wardwell, Allen, 1910, Ap 30,9:6
Wardwell, Allen (trb lr, D 21,30:7), 1953, D 9,11:2
Wardwell, Claison S Mrs, 1951, F 19,23:3
Wardwell, D Judge, 1878, Mr 29,4:7
Wardwell, Florence, 1959, F 13,27:1
Wardwell, Henry L, 1923, N 10,13:4
Wardwell, Ida L, 1941, Ja 14,21:4
Wardwell, J Otis, 1940, S 11,25:2
Wardwell, John J, 1943, O 9,13:6
Wardwell, Sheldon E, 1961, Je 9,33:4
Wardwell, Walter C, 1940, S 30,17:4
Wardwell, William T, 1911, Ja 4,9:3
Wardwell, William T Mrs, 1913, F 24,11:5
Ware, Addison H, 1940, Ja 9,23:5
Ware, Alice H Mrs, 1937, Ap 2,23:1
Ware, Arthur, 1939, F 20,17:2
Ware, Ashur, 1873, S 11,5:6
Ware, Bruce R 2d, 1938, Ja 18,23:1
Ware, Charles, 1940, Ag 31,13:2
Ware, Charles E, 1939, Ja 11,19:6
Ware, Charles S, 1952, Ap 8,29:4
Ware, Darrell, 1944, My 27,15:5
Ware, Dewitt T, 1957, Jl 18,25:5
Ware, E E, 1951, Jl 10,27:4
Ware, Edgar L Mrs, 1947, O 16,28:3
Ware, Edward J Dr, 1918, S 30,9:8
Ware, Edward N, 1941, Ag 21,17:4
Ware, Eugene F, 1911, Jl 3,7:4
Ware, F, 1931, Ag 30,II,6:3
Ware, Fabian, 1949, Ap 29,23:5
Ware, Franklin B, 1945, My 4,19:2
Ware, Frederick A, 1921, Je 1,17:4
Ware, George A, 1948, Ap 14,27:1
Ware, George H, 1945, Mr 14,20:2
Ware, Gilbert L, 1945, N 10,15:5
Ware, Hamilton R, 1938, Je 27,10:6
Ware, Harlan, 1967, My 8,41:3
Ware, Harriet, 1962, F 11,86:7
Ware, Helen (por), 1939, Ja 26,21:1
Ware, Henry, 1956, S 23,84:1
Ware, Henry B, 1940, Jl 23,19:5
Ware, Henry C, 1948, Ja 3,13:2
Ware, Henry C Mrs, 1937, O 5,25:4
Ware, Herbert L, 1949, S 8,29:3
Ware, Howard R, 1944, Je 6,17:3
Ware, J F W Rev, 1881, F 28,5:6
Ware, J Stratton, 1942, Mr 7,17:2
Ware, James Edward, 1918, Ap 15,15:6
Ware, James G, 1954, N 10,33:3
Ware, John D Mrs, 1944, F 6,42:3
Ware, John Dr, 1864, My 7,2:2
Ware, John S, 1949, Ap 25,23:5
Ware, John S Sr, 1937, F 24,24:2
Ware, Katherine E Mrs (cor, Jl 10,25:4), 1959, Jl 9, 27:4
Ware, Keith L Maj-Gen (funl, S 18,10:1), 1968, S 14, 3:5
Ware, Kenody R Mrs, 1960, Ap 23,23:4
Ware, Leonard E, 1914, D 29,11:6
Ware, Norman J, 1949, D 29,25:2
Ware, Paul B, 1957, Ap 21,89:2
Ware, Richmond A, 1941, F 3,17:4
Ware, Richmond A Mrs, 1955, F 18,21:2
Ware, Robert A Mrs, 1945, Ap 16,23:2
Ware, Sara J, 1952, F 12,27:3
Ware, Thomas M, 1943, O 23,13:3
Ware, W Fred, 1940, O 26,15:1
Ware, Willard, 1903, S 11,7:7
Ware, William B, 1946, Je 6,21:4
Ware, William E, 1953, Ag 22,15:1
Ware, William J, 1950, Ja 17,28:3
Ware, William L Mrs, 1954, Mr 15,25:5
Wareham, Harry P, 1951, Je 12,29:3
Wareing, Ernest C, 1944, F 6,42:2
Wareing, Robert, 1943, N 2,25:3
Wareing, William D, 1954, Jl 16,21:5
Warendorff, Alexander, 1943, S 7,23:4
Warendorff, Edward, 1944, Je 18,35:1
Warendorff, Walter P, 1961, N 2,37:1
Warenoff, Leon Mrs (Bert), 1966, Mr 21,33:2
Warenskjold, William, 1953, O 12,27:5
Wares, Buzzy (Clyde Wares), 1964, My 28,37:1
Warfield, Benjamin Breckenridge, 1921, F 18,11:5
Warfield, Charles H, 1948, O 28,29:4
Warfield, David, 1951, Je 28,25:1
Warfield, David A, 1961, N 13,29:5
Warfield, Douglas R, 1956, D 9,89:1
Warfield, E D, 1936, Jl 7,19:1
Warfield, Edwin Ex-Gov, 1920, Ap 1,11:6
Warfield, Edwin Jr, 1952, N 20,31:3
Warfield, Eleanor F, 1946, Ap 6,17:3
Warfield, Elisha G, 1953, Mr 20,23:4
Warfield, Estelle, 1958, Jl 10,27:5
Warfield, Frances (Mrs F R Marindin), 1964, S 20, 88:4
Warfield, Frederic P, 1957, N 18,31:4
Warfield, G Harold, 1952, Ag 9,13:2
Warfield, George, 1924, Ag 22,13:3
Warfield, George R, 1941, Je 28,15:4
Warfield, Guy T, 1937, Ap 15,23:4
Warfield, H M, 1885, Ja 19,2:5
Warfield, Harry H, 1944, F 6,41:2
Warfield, Henry M, 1947, O 11,17:7
Warfield, Jennie Frances Mrs, 1924, Ag 22,13:3
Warfield, John Mrs, 1947, O 20,23:2
Warfield, John O, 1950, Mr 17,23:2
Warfield, Marguerite D, 1956, My 18,25:4
Warfield, Mary C B Mrs, 1902, Ja 14,9:5
Warfield, Mervine, 1939, Mr 22,12:7
Warfield, Nellie F Mrs, 1941, Ag 23,13:6
Warfield, R H Gen, 1906, Jl 17,1:6
Warfield, Ralph M, 1939, Mr 23,23:2
Warfield, Richard, 1924, F 28,19:5
Warfield, Ridgely B Dr, 1920, F 5,9:4
Warfield, Ruth M, 1941, Ap 13,39:3
Warfield, William, 1947, Mr 17,23:3
Warfield, William Capt, 1907, Ja 22,9:6
Warford, Claude, 1950, Mr 12,92:6
Warford, Mary M Mrs, 1938, Ag 19,19:2
Warga, John J, 1953, N 8,88:5
Wargo, John, 1951, Jl 27,19:3
Warhaftig, Morris, 1952, F 4,17:2
Warhaftig, Morris Mrs, 1952, Mr 12,27:2
Warhatig, Nathan, 1950, Ja 27,23:2
Warhol, John Sr Mrs, 1964, O 19,33:3
Warhop, Jack, 1960, O 5,41:4
Waring, Angrum Jr, 1949, Mr 9,25:4
Waring, Bernard G, 1959, D 4,31:3
Waring, Burt Mrs, 1949, F 25,23:4
Waring, Charles Edwin, 1907, Mr 20,9:6
Waring, Charles J F, 1955, D 29,23:3
Waring, David C, 1962, F 6,32:5
Waring, David L, 1945, N 2,11:3
Waring, Edmund, 1937, S 17,25:2
Waring, Eleanor C Lady, 1941, My 2,21:6
Waring, Frank M, 1939, N 5,49:3
Waring, Frank M Mrs, 1948, Ag 2,21:2
Waring, G E Col, 1898, O 30,1:7
Waring, George H, 1947, F 10,29:5
Waring, George J (por), 1943, F 25,21:3
Waring, Holburt J, 1953, F 11,29:5
Waring, Howard Mrs, 1953, N 6,27:3
Waring, J Waties (name spelling cor, Ja 13,31:3), 1968, Ja 12,27:2
Waring, J Waties Mrs, 1968, N 1,47:3
Waring, James H, 1959, Ap 19,87:2
Waring, James J, 1962, Je 4,29:4
Waring, James M S, 1946, O 24,28:2
Waring, Janet, 1941, Ja 19,41:2
Waring, John A, 1957, F 19,31:4
Waring, John L, 1942, D 7,27:4
Waring, John P Maj, 1911, O 31,9:5
Waring, Laura W, 1948, F 5,24:3
Waring, Lewis E, 1949, My 21,13:4
Waring, Lewis E Mrs, 1939, Jl 8,15:5; 1953, F 3,25:3
Waring, Lord, 1940, Ja 10,21:4
Waring, Mary Mrs, 1964, Ja 12,92:4
Waring, Olaf (por), 1948, Ag 12,21:4
Waring, Orville G, 1950, Ja 11,23:3
Waring, Orville T (funl, My 19,13:6), 1923, My 19, 13:6
Waring, Oscar B, 1952, Jl 2,25:4
Waring, Roane, 1958, S 11,33:3
Waring, Samuel C, 1942, My 22,21:3
Waring, Stanley B, 1949, My 12,31:5
Waring, Stewart, 1953, F 19,23:1
Waring, Susan B, 1953, S 5,15:3
Waring, Thomas L, 1960, D 30,19:4

Waring, Tracey D, 1947, Ap 28,23:4
Waring, W E, 1882, O 7,5:4
Warinner, Algernon S, 1953, Jl 12,65:2
Wark, Charles F, 1956, Ja 5,33:4
Wark, David A, 1941, Ja 11,17:5
Wark, George K, 1922, Ap 26,19:4
Wark, John F, 1958, My 18,87:2
Wark, Thomas J, 1945, Je 30,17:4
Wark, William E, 1941, N 5,23:3
Warkins, Harvey M, 1962, My 3,33:1
Warland, Henry G, 1945, Ag 18,11:7
Warland, John H, 1872, Jl 11,1:6
Warley, Harry W, 1959, D 17,37:2
Warlich, Reinhold, 1939, N 13,19:3
Warlow, A Judson, 1959, Jl 14,29:4
Warm, William, 1917, Je 12,13:4
Warmack, Janie Mrs, 1948, N 2,25:5
Warmack, Robert N Mrs, 1956, Mr 19,31:2
Warman, A B, 1951, Ag 31,15:5
Warman, Cy, 1914, Ap 8,13:6
Warman, Frederic S G, 1953, F 15,92:2
Warman, Irving G, 1951, D 20,31:4
Warman, Olive P, 1946, My 26,32:3
Warmbier, Marie, 1937, N 11,25:3
Warmer, George A Sr, 1957, Jl 19,19:3
Warmers, Louis, 1937, O 1,21:1
Warmflash, Leo M, 1962, F 2,29:3
Warmingham, George H, 1949, S 6,27:2
Warmington, Richard G, 1964, My 15,36:1
Warms, Edwin H, 1950, Ap 12,27:3
Warms, William F, 1953, My 16,19:1
Warmuth, Mitchell P Dr, 1937, Je 16,23:6
Warn, W Axel, 1947, D 8,25:1
Warn, W Axel Mrs, 1953, F 4,27:4
Warn, William H, 1955, Jl 28,23:2
Warnack, James H, 1958, Ja 2,27:1
Warnas, Stanley, 1946, O 2,29:5
Warncke, Frank H, 1940, D 27,20:2
Warncke, George L, 1954, O 8,23:5
Warncke, Henry A Mrs, 1952, Ag 14,23:5
Warncke, Henry E, 1950, D 15,31:2
Warndof, Fred, 1939, Ag 10,19:4
Warne, Charles C, 1940, Jl 7,25:2
Warne, F W, 1932, Mr 2,19:3
Warne, Frank V, 1940, Jl 3,17:6
Warne, Hezekiah Jr, 1957, D 20,27:4
Warne, Joseph B, 1961, Mr 24,31:3
Warne, Joseph B Mrs, 1957, F 1,25:3
Warne, Louis A, 1940, Ap 24,23:1
Warne, W R, 1947, S 27,15:1
Warnecke, Charles Mrs, 1955, S 28,35:1
Warnecke, Charles W, 1945, My 9,23:3
Warnecke, George W Mrs, 1954, Jl 28,23:1
Warnecke, Rudolph E, 1967, O 2,47:4
Warnecke, William F, 1939, My 27,15:3
Warnefeld, William F, 1943, Ap 30,21:5
Warneford, Robert L, 1938, Ap 20,23:4
Warner, A J Gen, 1910, Ag 14,II,9:4
Warner, A P, 1957, Mr 23,19:5
Warner, Addison R, 1940, Je 18,23:4
Warner, Albert (funl plans, N 28,51:6), 1967, N 27, 47:1
Warner, Alexander Col, 1914, S 8,11:7
Warner, Alfred D, 1950, N 27,25:2
Warner, Allen E, 1960, Ap 29,31:1
Warner, Alton G, 1943, D 28,18:3
Warner, Anna Bartlett, 1915, Ja 23,11:4
Warner, Anne P Mrs, 1953, N 27,27:5
Warner, Arnold P, 1953, N 22,88:5
Warner, Arthur D, 1959, My 15,29:4
Warner, Arthur G, 1958, My 20,33:4
Warner, Arthur Mrs, 1950, Ja 5,25:3
Warner, Arthur T, 1960, S 24,23:5
Warner, Arthur W, 1957, S 26,25:5
Warner, Austin G, 1942, Ap 27,15:6
Warner, C A, 1907, My 8,7:6
Warner, Capt, 1871, N 28,5:6
Warner, Carl E, 1942, Ja 2,23:4
Warner, Charles, 1956, D 12,39:2
Warner, Charles Blaine, 1923, Ag 13,13:4
Warner, Charles Douglas, 1916, Jl 16,17:7
Warner, Charles Dudley, 1900, O 21,1:3
Warner, Charles Dudley Mrs, 1921, Ja 14,11:3
Warner, Charles E, 1941, N 13,28:3; 1942, My 8,21:3
Warner, Charles H (por), 1943, Ap 4,40:5
Warner, Charles H, 1944, Ja 9,42:6
Warner, Charles H Mrs, 1949, D 8,33:5
Warner, Charles J, 1955, S 26,23:5
Warner, Charles L, 1948, Ja 13,25:3
Warner, Charles M, 1923, D 2,23:2; 1938, Je 18,15:3
Warner, Charles N, 1946, Ja 28,19:3
Warner, Charles S, 1943, D 29,17:1
Warner, Charles T, 1949, Ja 19,28:3
Warner, Charles W, 1940, Ap 24,23:2
Warner, Charles W Mrs, 1950, Jl 18,29:3
Warner, Clarence W, 1945, F 5,15:4
Warner, Cora Mrs, 1946, Ag 17,13:4
Warner, D B, 1881, Mr 13,5:4
Warner, D V H, 1934, S 24,17:3
Warner, David, 1939, Mr 8,21:3
Warner, David C, 1956, My 8,33:3
Warner, David S, 1949, N 15,25:4
Warner, Donald F, 1952, F 13,29:2
Warner, Donald J, 1956, Je 22,23:5
Warner, E Carl, 1946, Mr 11,25:4
Warner, Edmund L, 1949, F 12,17:4
Warner, Edward E, 1954, F 6,19:4
Warner, Edward P, 1958, Jl 13,68:4
Warner, Edward R Gen, 1905, Ja 3,9:7
Warner, Edward W, 1952, Mr 20,29:1
Warner, Edwin G, 1953, Jl 8,27:2
Warner, Elbridge S, 1958, S 30,31:4
Warner, Elizabeth, 1949, Ag 11,24:5
Warner, Elizabeth A Mrs, 1937, N 12,21:4
Warner, Ellsworth C, 1942, Ja 6,24:2
Warner, Eltinge F, 1965, Mr 1,27:5
Warner, Elton D, 1937, N 17,II,9:2
Warner, Emalea P Mrs, 1948, Ap 14,27:4
Warner, Eugene, 1943, D 31,15:5
Warner, Eugene T, 1937, Mr 18,25:2
Warner, Everett L, 1963, O 21,31:2
Warner, F Richard, 1959, N 12,35:6
Warner, Frank, 1959, Ag 13,27:3
Warner, Frank A, 1959, Je 28,69:1
Warner, Frank C, 1939, Ag 20,33:4
Warner, Frank D, 1952, S 18,29:4
Warner, Frank E, 1941, O 25,17:4
Warner, Frank H, 1941, D 15,19:6
Warner, Frank R, 1944, Ag 6,37:3
Warner, Franklin M, 1948, Ja 30,24:2
Warner, Fred M, 1923, Ap 18,21:5
Warner, G E, 1933, D 3,39:1
Warner, George, 1914, Ag 20,11:4
Warner, George E, 1937, Je 12,15:2
Warner, George H, 1960, Je 29,33:3
Warner, George K Sr, 1949, My 10,25:5
Warner, George V, 1944, O 10,23:1
Warner, Glenn Mrs, 1961, N 5,88:1
Warner, Glenn S (Pop),(funl, S 10,23:5; burial, S 13,23:5), 1954, S 8,31:1
Warner, Grace M, 1939, Jl 15,15:1
Warner, Grove E Mrs, 1949, N 25,31:3
Warner, H B, 1958, D 23,2:6
Warner, H H, 1923, Ja 28,6:2
Warner, Harold, 1948, Ap 21,27:3
Warner, Harold L, 1963, Ag 12,21:4
Warner, Harold R, 1938, N 21,19:3; 1952, My 12,25:5
Warner, Harry B, 1909, Ag 29,9:6
Warner, Harry C V, 1941, My 5,17:4
Warner, Harry M (funl plans, Jl 27,60:7; funl, Jl 28,23:4), 1958, Jl 26,15:3
Warner, Harry O, 1950, S 17,105:2
Warner, Hazel E, 1945, Je 5,19:4
Warner, Henry B, 1909, S 3,9:2
Warner, Henry C, 1960, Ap 14,31:2
Warner, Henry E, 1941, Ap 12,15:4; 1953, S 14,27:3
Warner, Henry S Mrs, 1919, S 5,11:1
Warner, Hugh C, 1955, Jl 3,33:1
Warner, Hugh L, 1939, D 29,15:2
Warner, I De Ver, 1913, Ja 12,II,17:1
Warner, Irving, 1964, Je 5,31:5
Warner, J Capt, 1877, Jl 13,4:6
Warner, J D, 1951, N 18,90:1
Warner, J E, 1933, S 18,19:3
Warner, J Foster (por), 1937, Ap 21,23:4
Warner, J Foster Mrs, 1943, F 27,14:8
Warner, Jacob W, 1949, Ja 23,68:8
Warner, James, 1939, Ja 31,21:3
Warner, James D, 1944, Jl 20,19:3
Warner, James Douglas, 1911, Mr 14,11:4
Warner, John A, 1963, Ag 20,33:1
Warner, John C, 1938, Jl 24,29:3; 1945, D 14,27:5; 1959, Jl 23,27:3
Warner, John De Witt, 1925, My 28,21:5
Warner, John F, 1962, Ja 20,21:6
Warner, John L, 1939, Ja 4,21:4
Warner, John L Mrs, 1951, Mr 18,89:1
Warner, John McMurdrie, 1911, N 12,II,15:5
Warner, John W, 1946, O 30,27:5
Warner, Joseph E, 1958, Je 1,86:4
Warner, Joseph R Jr, 1940, Je 9,44:3
Warner, Julius, 1924, Mr 6,17:4
Warner, Keith, 1959, S 8,32:8
Warner, Kenneth B, 1948, S 3,19:1
Warner, L T, 1883, O 2,5:5
Warner, Langdon, 1955, Je 10,25:1
Warner, Langdon P Mrs, 1965, Je 27,64:8
Warner, Lansing B, 1941, D 14,69:3
Warner, Laurence M Mrs, 1950, O 31,27:5
Warner, Lee C, 1945, O 13,15:3
Warner, Lee R, 1947, D 5,25:1
Warner, Lena A Mrs, 1948, Ag 20,17:6
Warner, Leon, 1957, Ja 16,35:1
Warner, Levi, 1911, Ap 14,11:4
Warner, Levi Francis Dr, 1915, Ja 21,9:4
Warner, Lewis, 1915, Ag 12,9:6
Warner, Louis (por), 1949, My 4,29:3
Warner, Louis H, 1950, Ag 30,32:3
Warner, Louis J Mrs, 1953, Ap 28,27:1
Warner, Lucien C Dr (funl, Ag 3,15:6), 1925, Jl 31, 15:6
Warner, Lucien T, 1950, Mr 7,28:2
Warner, Luther C Mrs, 1947, O 31,23:4
Warner, MacDonald S, 1961, D 29,24:7
Warner, Marie L, 1940, O 31,23:2
Warner, Martin J, 1945, Mr 14,19:3
Warner, Mary A Mrs, 1939, O 23,19:4
Warner, Mary E Mrs, 1941, Ap 24,21:5
Warner, Mary Mrs, 1961, Ap 13,35:3
Warner, Milo J, 1968, Ja 5,24:2
Warner, Milton B, 1944, N 13,19:3
Warner, Milton J, 1952, Jl 10,31:4
Warner, Mony J, 1941, Mr 29,15:5
Warner, Neil (W B Lockwood), 1901, Je 16,7:6
Warner, Nelson D, 1945, F 1,23:6
Warner, Oliver L, 1942, O 5,19:5
Warner, Paul C, 1955, Ag 2,23:5
Warner, Pelham, 1963, Ja 31,7:1
Warner, Perry B, 1903, N 5,9:6
Warner, Phil, 1938, Ja 21,20:3
Warner, Phil A, 1949, My 25,29:6
Warner, Phillips B, 1963, S 12,37:2
Warner, R Dean, 1940, My 10,23:3
Warner, R I, 1945, My 19,19:5
Warner, Reuben, 1951, F 15,31:1; 1966, Je 2,43:2
Warner, Richard F, 1951, Jl 22,61:1; 1957, O 5,17:6
Warner, Rita S Mrs, 1961, N 18,23:4
Warner, Robert, 1950, Ja 25,28:2; 1951, Jl 10,27:4
Warner, Robert A, 1939, Je 8,25:5
Warner, Roger, 1952, D 2,31:5
Warner, Roger S, 1940, N 9,17:3
Warner, S L, 1927, O 6,25:3
Warner, Sarah A Mrs, 1944, My 27,15:5
Warner, Selden G, 1952, F 29,23:3
Warner, Stuart D, 1965, Ap 20,39:2
Warner, Susan, 1885, Mr 19,5:4
Warner, Theodore J, 1940, My 5,53:3
Warner, Thomas H, 1950, Ag 25,21:2
Warner, Thomas W Jr (will, My 19,60:1), 1955, My 14,37:2
Warner, Thomas W Sr, 1947, D 3,29:2
Warner, Truly, 1948, Mr 29,21:3
Warner, Verner J, 1954, Ap 9,24:3
Warner, Vespasian Col, 1925, Ap 2,21:4
Warner, W Arthur, 1949, My 17,25:2
Warner, W P, 1955, D 4,88:5
Warner, Walter, 1941, Mr 16,44:7
Warner, Walter E, 1944, Jl 5,11:2
Warner, Walter E Mrs, 1961, Je 6,37:5
Warner, Warren W, 1950, N 20,25:2
Warner, Westford E, 1947, D 19,25:2
Warner, Willard Gen, 1906, N 24,11:6
Warner, William, 1920, D 29,11:4; 1922, Ap 9,28:3; 1957, S 9,25:2
Warner, William B (por), 1946, My 5,44:1
Warner, William B Mrs, 1963, Je 27,33:3
Warner, William E, 1967, N 19,84:8
Warner, William H A, 1950, My 14,106:4
Warner, William J, 1944, F 13,41:2; 1952, Mr 27,29:4
Warner, William Maj, 1916, O 5,11:5
Warner, William Mrs, 1903, Jl 8,9:7
Warner, William R Jr, 1942, My 4,19:4
Warner, Worcester R Mrs (will, Mr 26,30:3), 1947, Mr 23,61:1
Warner, Wyllis, 1869, N 15,2:1
Warnick, Henry C, 1964, S 9,43:2
Warnick, Spencer K, 1954, My 19,31:4
Warnke, Fred W, 1938, O 12,27:4
Warnke, Fred W Mrs, 1949, Ap 1,25:4
Warnke, Phil W, 1951, N 19,23:3
Warnken, August J L, 1951, Jl 20,21:2
Warnken, Henry, 1940, F 12,17:4
Warnock, A Dewgrauw Sr, 1951, Mr 28,29:4
Warnock, Andrew R, 1944, S 30,13:6
Warnock, Annie E, 1944, Mr 3,15:1
Warnock, Arthur R, 1951, N 5,31:6
Warnock, Charlotte, 1941, O 10,23:6
Warnock, George F, 1949, Je 24,23:3
Warnock, James Jr, 1954, Jl 22,23:1
Warnock, John B, 1949, Je 11,17:5
Warnock, Milton C, 1956, D 27,25:4
Warnock, Robert, 1947, Je 22,52:4
Warnock, Robert T, 1955, N 1,31:1
Warnock, Thomas H, 1952, N 29,17:4
Warnock, Thomas H Mrs, 1952, Ag 13,21:5
Warnock, Thomas M, 1942, F 3,19:5
Warnock, Wallace S, 1950, Ja 23,23:3
Warnock, William A, 1917, F 3,13:4
Warnock, William J, 1958, F 22,17:5
Warnock, William K, 1938, O 18,25:5
Warnoff, Albert, 1962, Ag 16,27:1
Warnow, Mark (por), 1949, O 18,27:4
Warnow, Mark Mrs, 1939, Ja 15,38:8
Warnshuis, A L Mrs, 1941, O 27,17:4
Warnshuis, A Livingston, 1958, Mr 18,29:3
Warnurst, James C, 1942, F 12,23:5
Warr, Earl de la (Gilbert Geo Reginald Sackville), 1915, D 18,11:5
Warr, F Louise, 1958, Mr 8,17:6
Warr, Walter H, 1948, Je 30,25:1
Warr, Wilbur F, 1942, N 9,23:3
Warren, A E, 1939, O 17,25:2
Warren, A F, 1934, F 19,15:1
Warren, A K, 1883, Je 11,5:1
Warren, Abraham F, 1961, F 4,19:4
Warren, Adelbert, 1946, Ja 5,13:2
Warren, Aldred E, 1948, N 22,21:5
Warren, Aldred K Mrs, 1941, Ag 28,19:3
Warren, Alex G, 1938, My 24,17:2

Warren, Alfred I, 1952, S 3,30:3
Warren, Alice F, 1962, Ja 26,31:1
Warren, Allene, 1948, Ag 28,16:3
Warren, Arthur S, 1963, Ap 16,35:3
Warren, Arthur W, 1953, Ap 30,31:4
Warren, Avra M, 1957, Ja 24,29:1
Warren, B H Mrs, 1909, Ap 16,9:4
Warren, Barnett M, 1953, My 18,21:6
Warren, Barney E, 1951, Ap 23,25:3
Warren, Benjamin C, 1952, F 3,84:2
Warren, Benjamin C Mrs, 1937, Ja 27,21:4
Warren, Benjamin O, 1949, D 4,108:8
Warren, Bentley W, 1947, F 28,23:4
Warren, Bentley W Mrs, 1941, N 21,17:4
Warren, Benton E, 1958, N 12,27:3
Warren, Burtt E, 1950, N 28,31:2
Warren, C B, 1936, F 4,21:1
Warren, C C, 1884, My 14,2:6
Warren, C J Rev, 1883, Mr 15,2:7
Warren, Carl N, 1966, Ja 11,29:4
Warren, Catherine C Mrs, 1941, D 31,18:2
Warren, Charles, 1927, Ja 23,24:2; 1954, Ag 17,21:1
Warren, Charles B, 1957, Je 27,25:2
Warren, Charles B Mrs, 1941, Ap 14,17:1
Warren, Charles E, 1945, D 26,19:3; 1950, Jl 1,15:6
Warren, Charles E Jr Mrs, 1962, My 3,33:1
Warren, Charles H, 1950, Ag 17,27:4; 1955, My 22, 89:1
Warren, Charles H Mrs, 1951, O 29,23:4
Warren, Charles J, 1951, Ja 6,15:2
Warren, Charles M, 1951, N 28,31:5
Warren, Charles O, 1963, Jl 26,25:2
Warren, Charles Peck Prof, 1918, O 18,13:1
Warren, Charles W, 1937, Jl 23,19:6
Warren, Clarence N Jr Mrs, 1961, My 27,10:6
Warren, Claude C, 1945, Ja 31,21:3
Warren, Clifford P, 1939, Jl 8,15:5
Warren, Clinton J, 1938, Mr 18,19:2
Warren, Cora K Mrs, 1954, S 12,85:1
Warren, Daniel J, 1960, F 6,19:3
Warren, David H, 1966, N 3,39:2
Warren, Donald G, 1946, Jl 12,17:2
Warren, E, 1929, N 25,1:7
Warren, E Alyn, 1940, Ja 24,21:3
Warren, E E S, 1880, Jl 27,5:3
Warren, E Walpole Rev, 1925, F 25,19:2
Warren, Ed A, 1875, Jl 9,4:6
Warren, Ed J, 1872, Ap 28,4:4
Warren, Edgar C, 1948, Ja 1,23:5
Warren, Edward, 1940, Mr 11,15:2
Warren, Edward B, 1945, Je 28,19:4
Warren, Edward H, 1945, Jl 26,19:3
Warren, Edward K, 1919, Ja 17,13:5; 1965, Ag 2,29:2
Warren, Edward P, 1937, N 24,23:2
Warren, Edward R, 1942, Ap 22,23:2
Warren, Edward Walpole Rev, 1903, Jl 25,7:6
Warren, Eliza H, 1961, Je 6,37:1
Warren, Eugene, 1958, Je 5,31:5
Warren, Everett Mrs, 1949, Mr 9,26:3
Warren, Fiske, 1938, F 2,19:3
Warren, Forrest (por), 1949, Jl 5,24:2
Warren, Frances K Mrs, 1953, O 27,27:3
Warren, Frank B (por), 1945, Je 26,19:3
Warren, Frank Dale, 1925, O 7,27:4
Warren, Frank E, 1939, Ap 21,23:6; 1940, My 8,23:4
Warren, Frank E Mrs, 1945, Ag 26,43:2
Warren, Frank H, 1948, Jl 31,15:2
Warren, Frank K, 1956, Ag 3,19:1
Warren, Frank W, 1948, Mr 27,13:4
Warren, Frank X, 1948, O 3,64:3
Warren, Franklin D, 1952, Mr 4,28:4
Warren, Fred R, 1953, Mr 31,31:5
Warren, Frederic, 1944, Ja 31,17:2
Warren, Frederick B, 1950, Je 5,23:1
Warren, Frederick C Mrs, 1944, Ap 4,21:5
Warren, G K Gen, 1882, Ag 9,5:2
Warren, G W, 1883, Mr 14,4:7
Warren, G W Dr, 1902, Mr 17,9:5
Warren, Garnet, 1937, My 29,17:6
Warren, George, 1942, S 6,34:2
Warren, George A, 1938, Jl 2,13:7
Warren, George C, 1913, Mr 11,11:5; 1940, Ag 1,21:3
Warren, George C (por), 1949, My 3,25:3
Warren, George E Mrs, 1961, N 28,37:3
Warren, George F (por), 1938, My 25,23:3
Warren, George F Jr, 1957, Ag 17,15:6
Warren, George H, 1943, Je 4,21:3
Warren, George H Mrs (will), 1937, Ag 21,16:2
Warren, George Jr, 1905, Ap 15,8:2
Warren, George L Dr, 1925, My 21,23:5
Warren, George S, 1943, D 2,27:1; 1951, Mr 14,33:2
Warren, Gertrude M Mrs, 1941, Mr 15,17:5
Warren, Griffith J, 1953, O 22,29:2
Warren, H, 1930, Je 10,27:3
Warren, H C, 1934, Ja 5,21:3
Warren, H Ernest, 1955, F 18,21:3
Warren, Harold F Mrs, 1949, Ap 11,25:2
Warren, Harrington L, 1948, Ag 1,57:1
Warren, Harry C, 1949, Jl 31,60:7
Warren, Harry D Mrs, 1952, Ja 9,29:5
Warren, Harry M, 1940, D 23,19:3; 1950, O 1,104:1
Warren, Hector, 1949, Ja 11,31:4
Warren, Henry E, 1957, S 22,86:1
Warren, Henry E Jr, 1955, S 18,87:1
Warren, Henry M, 1942, D 12,15:3
Warren, Henry P Jr, 1950, My 23,60:3
Warren, Henry Pitt Dr, 1919, My 28,15:2
Warren, Henry W Bp, 1912, Jl 25,9:5
Warren, Herbert L Prof, 1917, Je 28,11:5
Warren, Herbert S, 1944, O 21,17:5
Warren, Herman T, 1948, Jl 23,19:2
Warren, Hobart E, 1949, Mr 18,25:4
Warren, Homer S, 1941, Ja 20,17:2
Warren, Howard B Mrs, 1955, Ap 28,29:4
Warren, Howard R, 1945, Ag 6,15:5
Warren, Howard S, 1960, F 24,37:3
Warren, Huell Jr Mrs, 1955, S 10,17:4
Warren, Ida S, 1943, N 6,13:4
Warren, Ina R, 1951, Ap 19,31:4
Warren, Ira De Forest, 1907, Ag 8,7:6
Warren, Isabel R Mrs, 1940, My 18,15:5
Warren, J, 1878, Jl 20,2:4
Warren, J C, 1927, N 4,21:3
Warren, J Henry, 1961, S 28,41:5
Warren, J M Dr, 1867, Ag 23,2:7
Warren, James C, 1959, Jl 7,33:3
Warren, James G, 1949, F 13,76:1
Warren, James G Col, 1937, N 3,24:2
Warren, James J, 1939, Ja 30,13:3; 1958, F 19,27:4
Warren, James L, 1940, Ja 17,21:3
Warren, James P, 1954, Jl 11,73:2
Warren, James S, 1955, Mr 30,13:5
Warren, James T, 1948, Ja 17,17:2
Warren, James W, 1946, O 9,27:4
Warren, John, 1943, Jl 20,19:3; 1945, D 1,23:5; 1953, Je 10,29:4
Warren, John A, 1938, F 11,23:4
Warren, John B, 1940, Ag 21,15:1; 1957, Ag 17,15:2
Warren, John D Mrs, 1940, O 24,25:5
Warren, John J, 1946, Jl 16,23:2; 1966, Mr 20,87:2
Warren, John L, 1939, F 1,21:4
Warren, John N, 1955, Ap 20,33:5
Warren, John N Mrs, 1958, Mr 19,31:3
Warren, John R, 1937, Ja 16,15:3
Warren, John S, 1940, D 28,15:5
Warren, John S Mrs, 1950, Ag 9,29:3
Warren, John T, 1958, Ja 29,27:3
Warren, Joseph (see also O 1), 1876, O 2,7:2
Warren, Joseph, 1945, N 29,23:3
Warren, Joseph A, 1929, Ag 14,1:3
Warren, Joseph H, 1939, Ja 15,39:2
Warren, Joseph Prof, 1909, D 6,9:4
Warren, Julius E, 1963, S 1,56:4
Warren, Langford, 1954, Ja 23,13:6
Warren, Lansing, 1901, O 14,7:4
Warren, Lawrence E, 1945, Ja 18,19:5
Warren, Leander, 1881, Je 25,2:5
Warren, Leander H, 1937, D 6,27:4
Warren, Leonard (trb, Mr 6,86:1; funl, Mr 8,33:1), 1960, Mr 5,1:2
Warren, Leonard A, 1943, Jl 28,15:4
Warren, Leroy W, 1938, Je 8,23:3
Warren, Lewis L, 1937, Jl 20,3:5
Warren, Lucius Henry Gen, 1924, My 16,19:2
Warren, Luther F Dr, 1937, Ja 19,24:3
Warren, Luther F Mrs, 1958, Ja 30,23:1
Warren, Mabel Mrs, 1949, Ja 7,21:2
Warren, Marshall R, 1961, Ap 18,37:4
Warren, Mary C, 1941, My 19,17:2
Warren, Mary H, 1958, Mr 28,25:5
Warren, Minnie, 1878, Jl 24,5:3
Warren, Minton M, 1947, N 5,27:5
Warren, Minton Prof, 1907, N 27,7:6
Warren, Moses A, 1942, Mr 5,23:2
Warren, Nathan A, 1944, Ag 15,17:5
Warren, Nellie T, 1949, O 9,94:4
Warren, Norcot H, 1947, Ap 25,21:3
Warren, Northam, 1962, My 15,39:1
Warren, O H Rev, 1901, N 24,7:6
Warren, Otey Y, 1955, My 8,89:2
Warren, Pauline G Mrs, 1950, Ap 17,23:2
Warren, R H, 1933, D 4,17:1
Warren, R P, 1876, F 4,4:6
Warren, Ralph L, 1944, O 30,19:5
Warren, Rawson, 1942, Ag 11,19:6
Warren, Richard F Jr, 1951, F 18,78:4
Warren, Richard H, 1968, Je 28,41:1
Warren, Robert B, 1950, Mr 25,13:6
Warren, Robert D Mrs, 1957, D 13,27:1
Warren, Robert F, 1952, Ja 19,15:5
Warren, Robert H, 1938, S 8,23:1
Warren, S, 1931, S 18,23:3
Warren, S N, 1933, F 18,16:3
Warren, Sallie A, 1953, S 21,25:5
Warren, Samuel, 1877, Ag 1,4:7
Warren, Samuel Dennis, 1910, F 21,9:5
Warren, Samuel P, 1915, O 8,11:5
Warren, Sarah M Mrs, 1937, My 23,II,11:1
Warren, Sargie L, 1948, O 20,29:1
Warren, Schuyler Mrs, 1950, O 13,29:2
Warren, Spencer S, 1949, Ag 17,23:3
Warren, T Robinson, 1915, Je 26,9:6
Warren, Theodore D, 1914, D 7,11:6
Warren, Tracy B Col, 1937, My 11,25:4
Warren, Ulysses G, 1943, Je 12,13:6
Warren, Vera, 1951, Jl 1,50:8
Warren, Virginia H Mrs, 1938, Ap 28,23:1
Warren, W E, 1877, Ja 16,5:1
Warren, W W, 1880, My 3,2:1
Warren, Walter P, 1944, F 24,15:3
Warren, Walter Phelps Col, 1914, Ag 9,15:5
Warren, Whitney (por), 1943, Ja 25,13:1
Warren, Whitney Mrs, 1951, S 13,31:1
Warren, Willard C Mrs, 1957, My 29,27:4
Warren, William, 1888, S 22,8:1
Warren, William E, 1942, Jl 12,36:5
Warren, William Fairfield Dr, 1925, Mr 14,13:3
Warren, William H, 1941, Mr 1,15:3; 1950, Ap 5,31:4; 1951, D 19,31:3
Warren, William J Sr, 1964, My 30,17:4
Warren, William L, 1961, Je 28,35:3
Warren, William L Mrs, 1945, My 3,23:4
Warren, William M, 1953, Ap 18,19:6
Warren, William Mrs, 1950, My 1,25:4
Warren, William R, 1918, Ap 4,13:4; 1947, S 16,23:4
Warren, William S, 1965, N 21,87:1
Warrender, George John Scott Vice-Adm, 1917, Ja 9, 13:3
Warrender, Harold, 1953, My 7,31:5
Warrender, James, 1952, Ja 22,29:4
Warrender, Maud Lady, 1945, S 5,23:2
Warrick, Harold D, 1945, Jl 15,15:6
Warrick, William H, 1940, D 9,19:4
Warrin, Edmondson Mrs, 1951, Ja 17,27:4
Warrin, Marshall L Mrs, 1956, S 21,25:1
Warriner, Eugene C, 1945, Jl 22,37:2
Warriner, Gerard Mrs, 1904, F 22,5:6
Warriner, Henry B, 1937, My 14,23:4
Warriner, Kate, 1960, S 16,28:6
Warriner, Lew H, 1909, Jl 6,7:4
Warriner, Myron A, 1943, D 20,23:4
Warriner, Samuel D, 1942, Ap 4,13:1
Warriner, Virgil C, 1941, D 18,27:1
Warriner, Willard I, 1943, Jl 7,19:2
Warring, Charles Hartlett, 1907, Jl 5,7:4
Warring, Francis B Maj, 1937, Je 13,II,7:1
Warrington, Albert P, 1939, Je 17,15:6
Warrington, Charles W R, 1957, F 18,27:1
Warrington, George H, 1940, D 1,60:2
Warrington, John W Judge, 1921, My 27,17:6
Warrington, Ralph M Sr, 1948, Ap 19,23:3
Warrington, W F, 1943, My 19,25:1
Warrington, W Othniel, 1960, O 21,33:2
Warrington, William J, 1941, Ja 24,38:3
Warrington of Clyffe, Lord, 1937, O 27,31:5
Warrum, Henry, 1939, Ap 19,23:4
Warrum, Noble Sr, 1951, N 4,87:2
Warsaw, Isidor, 1953, D 23,25:2
Warsaw, M Claudius (por), 1944, D 31,26:5
Warsawer, Lillian Z Mrs, 1942, N 30,23:6
Warsawer, Sidney L, 1942, Ap 9,19:3
Warshauer, Jack, 1956, F 4,19:4
Warshauer, Joseph, 1949, O 28,23:4
Warshaw, Abraham, 1955, Mr 24,31:2
Warshaw, David, 1960, My 28,21:6
Warshaw, Irving, 1963, My 22,41:5
Warshaw, Irving G, 1938, Je 18,15:5
Warshaw, Jack F, 1962, Ja 11,33:4
Warshaw, Phil, 1939, Ag 20,22:3
Warshaw, Samuel, 1954, Ja 21,31:2
Warshaw, Samuel M, 1956, My 27,88:7
Warshawsky, Abel G, 1962, Je 1,28:1
Warshawsky, Irving, 1965, Jl 5,17:3
Warshow, Adolph (por), 1948, N 30,27:3
Warshow, Robert, 1955, Mr 19,15:5
Warshow, Robert I (por), 1938, N 8,23:5
Warsinski, Erwin H Mrs, 1952, F 25,21:1
Warsoff, Abraham Mrs, 1950, Ap 23,94:4
Warsoff, Louis A, 1959, Ja 18,89:1
Warstler, Harold, 1964, Je 2,37:2
Wartels, Aaron, 1953, O 21,29:4
Wartenberg, Robert, 1956, N 17,21:5
Warter, Emile, 1950, Jl 13,25:4
Warth, Henry J, 1947, N 26,23:1
Warthburgh, Albert O Von, 1914, My 10,IV,7:4
Warthen, George S, 1954, F 8,23:2
Warther, William, 1945, F 7,22:2
Wartherton, Charles F, 1941, Ja 2,23:5
Warthman, J Harris, 1959, S 5,15:6
Wartman, Ira J, 1941, Ag 20,19:2
Wartman, William B, 1939, Je 14,23:5
Warton, Frank R, 1959, O 23,17:6
Wartur, Samuel, 1950, Ag 17,27:2
Wartur, Samuel Mrs, 1951, N 10,17:5
Warvelle, George W, 1940, N 13,23:1
Warwick, Arthur D, 1949, Mr 17,25:3
Warwick, C Laurence, 1952, Ap 25,23:3
Warwick, Charles J, 1949, D 9,32:2
Warwick, D Branch (will, Je 25,4:1), 1939, Je 6,23:3
Warwick, Earl of, 1924, Ja 16,19:5; 1928, F 1,27:2
Warwick, Frank M, 1947, Ja 13,21:4
Warwick, Harold L, 1941, Ap 29,19:4
Warwick, Harry A Dr, 1968, D 17,47:2
Warwick, J Chalmers, 1950, F 9,29:4
Warwick, Lady (por), 1938, Jl 27,17:5
Warwick, Leo J, 1959, O 20,39:1
Warwick, Marjorie (por), 1943, F 11,19:4
Warwick, Paul R Sr, 1953, Jl 18,13:4
Warwick, Richard C, 1947, Ja 25,17:1

Warwick, Robert Mrs (S Larrimore), 1960, D 2,29:1
Warwick, Robert R T Bien, 1964, Je 7,86:4
Warzala, Stanley, 1941, Je 10,23:2
Wasasieri, Harry A Mrs, 1962, O 8,23:4
Wasch, Milton G, 1957, F 23,17:2
Waschen, John G, 1938, F 15,26:8
Wascher, Howard G, 1964, O 24,29:2
Waschinsky, Michael Prince, 1965, F 22,21:3
Wasdin, Eugene Dr, 1911, N 18,13:6
Waser, Gus, 1949, O 21,26:2
Wasey, Louis R, 1961, Ag 27,84:6
Wasgatt, Asa, 1950, D 3,89:2
Washabaugh, George, 1949, Mr 19,15:3
Washabaugh, Jacob E, 1965, D 18,29:1
Washbourne, Forde, 1949, N 24,31:5
Washbourne, William L, 1941, Jl 27,30:3
Washburn, A H, 1930, Ap 3,29:1
Washburn, Abel, 1903, O 4,7:6
Washburn, Abram C Mrs, 1948, Ag 30,18:2
Washburn, Adolphus D, 1955, Ja 3,27:1
Washburn, Albert H Mrs, 1953, Ja 12,27:1
Washburn, Albert S, 1919, Mr 20,13:3
Washburn, Arthur L, 1964, Ja 19,76:6; 1965, Ja 8,29:2
Washburn, Benjamin M, 1966, O 17,37:4
Washburn, Bryant, 1963, My 3,32:2
Washburn, C C, 1926, Ag 12,19:5
Washburn, C C Ex-Gov, 1882, My 15,5:6
Washburn, Cadwallader L, 1965, D 22,31:2
Washburn, Caroline V S Mrs, 1941, Mr 4,23:5
Washburn, Charles M, 1943, Ap 13,25:3
Washburn, Chester C, 1937, Jl 20,23:3
Washburn, Clinton M, 1959, S 16,39:2
Washburn, E A Rev Dr, 1881, F 3,2:6
Washburn, Edwin C, 1937, Ag 11,23:1
Washburn, Emory (see also Mr 20), 1877, Mr 22,8:2
Washburn, Fay B, 1943, Jl 4,20:5
Washburn, Francis R, 1951, My 22,31:2
Washburn, Francis Rev, 1914, D 7,11:6
Washburn, Frank B, 1940, F 12,17:3
Washburn, Frank D, 1949, F 13,76:1
Washburn, Frank H, 1943, N 11,23:3
Washburn, Frank S, 1922, O 10,21:3; 1922, O 12,19:5; 1963, Ap 8,47:2
Washburn, Frank S Mrs, 1957, Ja 19,15:4
Washburn, Frederic A (por), 1949, Ag 22,21:4
Washburn, Frederick B, 1944, O 24,23:5
Washburn, Frederick E, 1945, Ja 18,19:3
Washburn, George Capt, 1903, Ja 12,9:7
Washburn, George Rev, 1915, F 16,9:3
Washburn, Harold C, 1952, Ap 27,90:6
Washburn, Harold E, 1964, Mr 31,35:5
Washburn, Henry B, 1962, Ap 26,33:2
Washburn, Henry D Gen, 1871, F 2,5:4
Washburn, Henry L, 1920, Ja 25,22:1
Washburn, Henry S, 1919, S 27,13:6; 1955, Ap 2,17:5
Washburn, Howard R, 1955, O 30,88:8
Washburn, Howard R Mrs, 1946, My 8,25:4
Washburn, I B Dr, 1903, D 13,1:6
Washburn, Irving, 1954, N 11,31:2
Washburn, Israel, 1876, S 8,4:7
Washburn, Israel Jr, 1883, My 13,9:2
Washburn, Ives (por), 1947, F 6,23:1
Washburn, J D, 1903, Ap 5,7:6
Washburn, J H, 1932, Ag 4,19:5
Washburn, Jacob, 1939, My 28,III,7:3
Washburn, James M, 1949, Ja 17,19:3
Washburn, John W, 1909, D 24,9:5
Washburn, Joseph S, 1949, N 2,27:2
Washburn, Joshua, 1905, Ap 26,11:5
Washburn, Joshua J, 1943, O 11,19:4
Washburn, Julia, 1949, Ag 15,17:4
Washburn, Kendrick H, 1954, My 26,29:4
Washburn, Lester H, 1961, S 17,86:8
Washburn, Louis, 1920, Ja 2,11:3
Washburn, Louis C, 1938, Je 16,23:4
Washburn, Louisa G Mrs, 1942, S 29,24:2
Washburn, Margaret F, 1939, O 30,17:4
Washburn, Margaret P Mrs, 1945, S 14,23:2
Washburn, Mary Maud, 1873, Jl 23,3:2
Washburn, Morgan, 1939, My 6,17:3
Washburn, N P Dr, 1903, Je 24,9:6
Washburn, Paul, 1942, O 8,27:2
Washburn, Ralph B, 1937, Ag 17,19:2
Washburn, Robert M (por), 1946, F 27,25:3
Washburn, S H, 1901, O 19,1:4
Washburn, Seth M, 1942, Je 12,21:3
Washburn, Slater, 1941, Jl 14,13:5
Washburn, Stanley, 1950, D 15,31:3
Washburn, Uriah, 1914, Ag 8,9:7
Washburn, W I, 1933, Jl 31,13:4
Washburn, Walter A, 1942, Mr 22,48:8
Washburn, Wendell J, 1966, Jl 9,27:3
Washburn, Wesley W Mrs, 1967, F 3,31:2
Washburn, William D Ex-Sen, 1912, Jl 30,9:5
Washburn, William D Mrs, 1950, N 9,33:4
Washburn, William H, 1939, O 5,23:3
Washburn, William K, 1950, S 20,31:2
Washburne, A S, 1879, O 2,2:3
Washburne, Carleton W Dr, 1968, N 28,37:4
Washburne, Conway M, 1942, S 8,24:3
Washburne, E B, 1887, O 23,3:4
Washburne, Edward G, 1943, My 18,23:2
Washburne, Frank L, 1945, N 15,19:2
Washburne, George A, 1948, My 12,27:4
Washburne, Hempstead, 1918, Ap 15,15:6
Washburne, Israel A, 1938, Jl 1,19:6
Washburne, James M (por), 1942, D 26,9:1
Washburne, John N, 1941, Je 28,15:3
Washburne, Rutherford B, 1949, Mr 4,21:4
Washburne, W B, 1887, O 6,5:4
Washburne, Walter A, 1937, Je 4,23:6
Washeim, Henry Jr, 1948, O 22,26:3
Washer, Benjamin S Mrs, 1946, Ja 13,44:2
Washer, Herbert A, 1966, D 13,47:2
Washer, Monroe, 1940, O 17,25:4
Washer, Ross, 1959, F 7,19:2
Washer, Theodore F, 1963, My 19,86:7
Washer, William W, 1940, Ap 4,23:3
Washienko, Alex Mrs, 1948, O 19,28:3
Washington, Allen Cooper (funl), 1907, Ag 10,7:5
Washington, B F, 1872, F 18,5:2
Washington, Basil G, 1940, S 20,23:5
Washington, Booker T Jr, 1945, F 6,19:4
Washington, Daniel, 1958, F 26,27:3
Washington, Dinah (Mrs Dick Lane),(funl, D 19,-28:6), 1963, D 15,79:1
Washington, Elizabeth Codwise, 1921, F 21,11:5
Washington, Elizabeth F, 1953, S 1,24:3
Washington, Ferdinand L, 1945, S 28,21:3
Washington, Forrester B, 1963, Ag 27,31:2
Washington, Frances H Mrs, 1920, My 31,11:4
Washington, Francis J Sr Mrs, 1952, My 15,31:4
Washington, George, 1946, Mr 30,15:6
Washington, George Col, 1916, N 30,13:3
Washington, George Jr, 1966, D 27,32:4
Washington, George Lafayette, 1968, F 13,43:2
Washington, George S, 1943, Je 19,13:2
Washington, Helen W Mrs, 1940, F 24,13:4
Washington, Horace L (por), 1938, Ag 28,33:3
Washington, James V, 1949, Ja 20,27:4
Washington, Joe E, 1915, Ag 29,15:6
Washington, John Augustin, 1923, Ag 13,13:5
Washington, John Dr, 1874, Jl 27,8:6
Washington, Joseph E Mrs, 1946, Mr 25,25:2
Washington, L Q Col, 1902, N 5,9:6
Washington, Lamont, 1968, Ag 26,39:1
Washington, Lawrence, 1920, Ja 29,9:3
Washington, Lewis William, 1906, My 16,9:6
Washington, M von, 1933, Ap 13,18:1
Washington, Martha, 1956, Ag 15,29:5
Washington, Mary Mrs, 1901, N 3,4:6
Washington, Max Baron, 1903, Jl 4,7:6
Washington, Minnie, 1948, Jl 19,19:4
Washington, Richard B Jr, 1922, O 14,13:5
Washington, Roebuck Mrs, 1939, N 26,42:6
Washington, S S H Mrs, 1949, Mr 19,15:3
Washington, Samuel Walter, 1923, Jl 17,19:5
Washington, Thomas, 1954, D 16,37:4
Washington, W L, 1933, S 12,23:1
Washington, Walker, 1939, D 12,27:2
Washington, William de Hertburn (funl, S 3,7:5), 1914, Ag 31,7:6
Washington, William E Jr, 1951, My 12,21:2
Washington, William M, 1942, F 8,48:8
Washington, Winston Lanier, 1921, S 20,17:5
Washkansky, Louis, 1967, D 21,1:2
Washkewich, George, 1947, O 27,21:5
Washor, Maxwell B, 1964, Jl 6,29:3
Washow, Adolph Mrs, 1964, O 14,45:4
Washton, Jacob, 1939, Mr 19,III,7:1
Washton, Samuel, 1953, Jl 22,27:5
Wasielewski, Benjamin J, 1966, Ag 6,23:2
Wasil, J Edward, 1951, Ag 21,27:5
Wasilewska, Wanda (Mrs A Y Korniechuk), 1964, Jl 30,27:4
Wasilewski, Joseph, 1954, S 18,15:5
Wasilewski, Peter, 1952, My 27,29:1
Waskey, Frank H, 1964, Ja 27,23:5
Wasley, Thomas R, 1959, O 13,39:4
Wasmund, Henry C, 1953, Ja 31,15:4
Wasmund, Paul H Mrs, 1961, My 11,37:3
Wasney, Joseph S, 1942, Ja 26,15:3
Wason, Dorothy Ruth, 1922, F 7,17:3
Wason, Edward H, 1941, F 7,19:3
Wason, Robert A, 1955, My 13,25:3
Wason, Robert R, 1950, Jl 8,13:3
Wason, William J Jr, 1958, F 3,23:5
Wass, Arthur, 1941, Ag 25,15:4
Wass, Harold S Mrs, 1952, O 28,31:2
Wassa, Mihill Selim Capt, 1920, Ja 29,9:5
Wassell, Corydon M, 1958, My 13,29:1
Wassell, Harry B, 1943, Mr 15,13:3
Wassell, Leona Mrs, 1945, Jl 16,11:6
Wassenmuller, Richard E, 1943, F 28,47:5
Wasser, Charles, 1953, Ag 11,27:1
Wasser, George N, 1951, N 11,91:4
Wasser, Louis K, 1959, Ja 17,19:2
Wasserback, Hyman, 1947, My 3,19:6
Wasserberger, Oscar, 1949, Ag 25,23:1
Wasserman, A Alfred, 1946, D 2,25:3
Wasserman, Albert, 1942, N 20,24:3
Wasserman, Albert S, 1959, Ap 29,33:4
Wasserman, August von Prof, 1925, Mr 17,21:1
Wasserman, Augusta P Mrs, 1939, Ja 27,19:4
Wasserman, Bernard, 1949, N 27,104:3
Wasserman, David, 1953, F 8,88:3
Wasserman, Flora K Mrs, 1940, D 15,61:2
Wasserman, Jean P (por), 1955, N 22,35:2
Wasserman, Joseph, 1937, S 10,23:5; 1954, My 22,15:3
Wasserman, Joseph H, 1966, D 21,32:8
Wasserman, Joseph Rev Dr, 1921, O 9,22:4
Wasserman, Leon, 1948, Ja 20,24:3
Wasserman, Lucius P, 1962, S 24,29:5
Wasserman, Morris J, 1949, Ja 16,68:1
Wasserman, Olga L, 1944, Ap 10,19:5
Wasserman, Rene D Mrs, 1958, Mr 17,29:1
Wasserman, Samuel, 1954, Ja 10,87:1
Wasserman, Sol, 1955, Ja 5,15:2
Wasserman, Solomon Prof, 1873, My 24,5:2
Wassermann, Edward, 1914, F 2,7:5
Wassermann, J, 1934, Ja 2,25:1
Wassermann, Michael M, 1956, F 22,27:2
Wasserscheid, Aug A, 1954, S 29,31:2
Wasserstrom, Benjamin, 1957, Je 15,17:3
Wasserstrom, William, 1956, Jl 20,17:5
Wasservogel, Isidor, 1962, F 9,29:1
Wasservogel, Isidor Mrs, 1950, Ap 3,23:4
Wassing, Hans, 1962, Ap 30,27:4
Wassler, George, 1951, S 18,32:3
Wassman, Edward J, 1941, Mr 4,23:5
Wassman, Emil, 1924, D 22,17:2
Wassman, James, 1960, Je 9,33:5
Wassman, Norman W, 1952, Ja 9,29:4
Wassmuth, August C, 1946, S 26,25:2
Wassner, Erwin Rear-Adm (por), 1937, Ag 25,21:3
Wasson, Charles M, 1945, Je 1,15:4
Wasson, Dav A Dr, 1915, Ag 10,11:6
Wasson, Edmund A, 1949, Je 12,79:4
Wasson, Edmund A Mrs, 1953, Je 4,29:4
Wasson, H Cecil, 1942, Je 8,15:1
Wasson, Harry E, 1953, Ag 1,11:5
Wasson, J B Rev, 1927, N 15,29:3
Wasson, John L, 1954, F 14,92:4
Wasson, Pearl Randall Mrs, 1922, S 12,21:5
Wasson, R Gordon Mrs, 1959, Ja 2,25:3
Wasson, Richard B, 1942, Ja 27,22:3
Wasson, Robert B, 1951, Je 1,23:3
Wasson, Robert Q, 1961, O 4,45:4
Wasson, Samuel A Sr Mrs, 1957, S 20,25:4
Wasson, William A Mrs, 1956, D 22,19:6
Wasson, William H, 1961, N 23,31:3
Wasson, William W, 1948, Ja 16,21:1
Wassung, Frank R, 1964, F 4,33:4
Wassuta, Walter Mrs, 1953, Jl 28,19:3
Wassweiler, Gustave F, 1949, Je 30,23:4
Wastcoat, Carleton L, 1958, N 12,37:4
Waste, William H, 1940, Je 7,23:3
Wastl, Francis X, 1943, Ap 12,23:3
Wasum, Ludwig W, 1957, S 18,33:4
Wasylenko, Alex Mrs, 1950, O 17,31:5
Waszeski, Frank S, 1945, D 22,19:5
Waszink, Marius A M, 1943, O 27,23:5
Watanabe, Chifuyu Viscount, 1940, Ap 18,23:2
Watanabe, Toshihide, 1966, Ap 16,33:5
Watchorn, John, 1949, Je 29,28:4
Watchorn, John A, 1938, S 27,21:4
Watchorn, Robert (por), 1944, Ap 15,11:3
Water, Walter N, 1945, Ja 24,21:4
Waterbor, Melvin M, 1966, Je 2,43:4
Waterbury, Abigail W Mrs, 1905, Ap 21,9:5
Waterbury, Angus M, 1949, Ag 3,23:2
Waterbury, Arthur E, 1945, Je 6,21:2
Waterbury, Bayard H, 1949, D 17,17:3
Waterbury, C A Mrs, 1903, Ja 24,9:5
Waterbury, C Russell, 1955, My 13,25:5
Waterbury, Charles S, 1941, My 11,45:2
Waterbury, Clarence M, 1939, O 12,25:3
Waterbury, Cornelius Read, 1914, Ag 20,11:7
Waterbury, David H, 1923, D 2,23:2
Waterbury, David Mrs, 1961, Ag 17,27:6
Waterbury, Earl C Mrs, 1951, O 25,29:3
Waterbury, Edwin M, 1952, D 31,15:3
Waterbury, Eugene W, 1958, Mr 23,89:1
Waterbury, Ezra K, 1946, Ap 19,29:2
Waterbury, Ezra K Mrs, 1945, S 18,23:5
Waterbury, Florance, 1968, Mr 3,88:7
Waterbury, Florence D Mrs, 1953, Mr 3,27:3
Waterbury, Frederic M, 1939, My 11,25:5
Waterbury, Frederick M, 1960, Je 9,33:2
Waterbury, Grenville F, 1968, F 9,27:2
Waterbury, Harry, 1946, Ap 2,27:3
Waterbury, Henri S Mrs, 1952, Ap 2,33:4
Waterbury, Henry S, 1953, Mr 3,27:3
Waterbury, J I, 1929, Mr 5,33:2
Waterbury, James E, 1944, D 13,23:2
Waterbury, James R, 1903, O 8,9:5
Waterbury, Josie M Mrs, 1871, S 22,2:4
Waterbury, Lawrence, 1879, S 6,5:4
Waterbury, Lawrence (por), 1943, My 27,28:8
Waterbury, Louisa M Mrs, 1945, Je 11,15:4
Waterbury, Margaret E Mrs, 1943, N 5,19:2
Waterbury, Milton C, 1914, N 16,9:5
Waterbury, Monte, 1920, Ag 29,20:5
Waterbury, Nelson J, 1943, D 15,27:3
Waterbury, Rodney A, 1953, Mr 12,25:2
Waterbury, Stephen W, 1964, Ja 28,31:1
Waterbury, Warren H, 1961, Jl 28,21:4
Waterbury, William H, 1951, O 13,17:2
Waterbury, William H Mrs, 1942, O 21,21:2

Waterfall, Arthur T, 1949, Ja 29,13:5
Waterfield, Anne A Mrs, 1940, S 25,27:4
Waterfield, Charles, 1953, Mr 11,29:4
Waterfield, Hanford, 1948, Ag 21,15:5
Waterford, Marquis of, 1859, Ap 13,1:1
Waterhouse, Alfred, 1905, Ag 23,7:6
Waterhouse, Charles R, 1940, S 17,23:3
Waterhouse, George B, 1952, My 11,93:1
Waterhouse, Homer T, 1948, Je 28,19:2
Waterhouse, J H, 1879, Jl 7,8:4
Waterhouse, James, 1881, O 18,5:1
Waterhouse, John, 1945, O 12,23:4
Waterhouse, John H, 1948, Ap 30,23:3
Waterhouse, Joseph R, 1967, N 27,47:5
Waterhouse, Kingman H, 1942, N 30,23:4
Waterhouse, Margaret M Mrs, 1949, D 28,32:4
Waterhouse, Miles, 1884, Mr 7,5:2
Waterhouse, Paul, 1924, D 20,15:5
Waterhouse, Ronald, 1942, N 29,64:8
Waterkotte, Raymond J, 1966, F 10,37:2
Waterloo, Stanley, 1913, O 12,15:2
Waterlow, Edgar, 1954, Ja 14,29:3
Waterlow, Ernest Albert Sir, 1919, O 27,11:5
Waterlow, Sidney Sir, 1906, Ag 4,7:5
Waterlow, Sydney (por), 1944, D 7,25:5
Waterman, Alan T, 1967, D 2,39:2
Waterman, Albert P, 1949, S 15,27:5
Waterman, Arthur A, 1939, Mr 12,III,7:3
Waterman, Arthur C, 1958, N 27,29:1
Waterman, Arthur C Mrs, 1958, Mr 17,29:4
Waterman, Bertha Mrs, 1951, Jl 5,34:3
Waterman, Burleigh K, 1966, N 14,41:5
Waterman, C Herbert, 1947, O 2,27:5
Waterman, C W Sen, 1932, Ag 28,24:1
Waterman, Cameron B, 1955, Ap 20,33:3
Waterman, Charles C, 1958, Je 28,17:5
Waterman, Charles N, 1949, N 29,29:1
Waterman, Edmund, 1956, F 17,23:1
Waterman, Elisha H, 1954, Ag 17,21:2
Waterman, Frances I, 1950, My 11,29:2
Waterman, Francis E, 1947, Ag 11,23:4
Waterman, Frank A, 1958, N 18,37:5
Waterman, Frank D (will, My 15,40:3),(por), 1938, My 7,15:1
Waterman, Frank E, 1949, Je 30,23:2
Waterman, Frank N, 1948, Ja 20,23:3
Waterman, Frank N Mrs, 1948, Mr 26,21:4
Waterman, Fred W, 1945, N 22,35:4
Waterman, George A, 1925, Ja 25,7:2
Waterman, George B, 1951, O 24,31:1
Waterman, George H, 1941, F 10,17:5
Waterman, Grace E V Mrs, 1938, Ag 18,20:5
Waterman, Helen L H Mrs, 1939, Ja 13,19:2
Waterman, Henry A, 1955, O 28,25:3
Waterman, Henry L, 1947, Je 20,19:2
Waterman, Herbert, 1947, Ag 3,52:2
Waterman, Herman, 1903, Jl 16,7:6
Waterman, I, 1883, Mr 11,9:4
Waterman, J Hilton Dr, 1912, Je 10,9:6
Waterman, J L Mrs, 1948, F 3,25:3
Waterman, Jane, 1952, F 15,25:2
Waterman, Joe, 1949, My 6,25:2
Waterman, John B, 1937, My 1,19:5
Waterman, John B Mrs, 1953, Ag 24,23:3
Waterman, John S, 1946, Ap 28,42:2
Waterman, Julian S, 1943, S 19,48:7
Waterman, Lewis E Jr, 1945, N 19,21:4
Waterman, Louis E Mrs, 1941, My 31,11:3
Waterman, Max, 1961, O 11,47:4
Waterman, Nixon, 1944, S 2,11:6
Waterman, R H Capt, 1884, Ag 15,4:7
Waterman, Ralph D, 1962, Ap 3,39:2
Waterman, Roy E, 1949, Ag 9,25:3
Waterman, S K Mrs, 1910, F 16,9:4
Waterman, Samuel A, 1950, F 19,76:1
Waterman, Stephen, 1944, O 5,23:2
Waterman, Theodore H, 1913, S 12,11:4
Waterman, Thomas T, 1951, Ja 23,27:3
Waterman, Thomas W Mrs, 1949, My 15,90:8
Waterman, Walter A, 1948, S 21,28:2
Waterman, Warren G, 1952, N 18,31:1
Waterman, Whitney, 1940, D 11,27:6
Waterman, William E, 1943, S 14,23:3
Waterman, William K, 1953, S 29,29:2
Watermann, J Henry, 1964, My 30,17:3
Watermen, F M, 1927, My 22,28:3
Watermulder, Gustavus A, 1946, O 4,24:2
Waterous, Allen H, 1965, Ag 6,27:4
Waterous, Donald J, 1958, Jl 23,27:3
Waterous, Herbert L (por), 1947, Ag 30,15:3
Waters, Anne E, 1884, Mr 22,3:2
Waters, Arthur G, 1953, N 18,31:1
Waters, Caroline E, 1938, S 1,23:2
Waters, Cary D (por), 1942, My 10,42:8
Waters, Cary D Mrs, 1958, D 11,13:4
Waters, Charles A, 1956, Ag 28,27:6
Waters, Charles C, 1952, Ja 7,19:5
Waters, Chester A, 1941, Ja 8,19:3
Waters, Clarence Mrs, 1947, Ag 5,23:2
Waters, Clyde, 1944, My 12,19:1
Waters, Daniel F, 1953, O 13,29:1
Waters, Francis V, 1946, S 3,19:2
Waters, Frank A, 1938, Ag 26,17:6
Waters, Frank A Mrs, 1948, Ag 17,21:4
Waters, Frank H, 1954, O 19,27:4
Waters, Frank R Judge, 1907, O 2,11:7
Waters, Frank T Mrs, 1966, Ja 15,27:1
Waters, George, 1961, D 31,48:3
Waters, George E, 1938, Ap 2,15:4
Waters, George F, 1961, D 17,83:1
Waters, George S, 1938, Je 20,3:5
Waters, Harold L, 1954, Ja 22,27:3
Waters, Harry F, 1962, Ap 7,25:1
Waters, Henry H, 1940, D 5,25:3
Waters, Henry Jackson, 1925, O 27,23:4
Waters, Henry Mrs, 1943, Je 2,25:4
Waters, Herbert S (por), 1955, D 7,39:1
Waters, I Ward, 1938, Jl 2,13:5
Waters, J Berrens, 1968, Jl 25,33:3
Waters, J Frederic, 1945, Ap 20,19:3
Waters, J H, 1933, Ag 15,17:4
Waters, James F, 1954, Ap 1,31:3
Waters, James J, 1958, Jl 18,46:3
Waters, James M, 1959, F 17,32:1
Waters, James R (por), 1945, N 21,21:1
Waters, Jason, 1923, F 16,13:5
Waters, Jesse H Mrs, 1950, Ja 17,27:4
Waters, John, 1940, Ja 23,21:4
Waters, John C, 1945, Je 22,15:5
Waters, John Jr, 1964, Ja 28,31:4
Waters, John K Mrs, 1952, O 25,19:3
Waters, John S, 1965, My 8,31:3
Waters, Joseph, 1950, N 25,13:6
Waters, Joseph A (por), 1942, Ja 14,21:5
Waters, Joseph J, 1951, Ja 16,29:2
Waters, Joseph S, 1968, N 19,47:1
Waters, Laverne F, 1954, Ja 16,15:6
Waters, Lewis W, 1944, Ap 1,13:3
Waters, Lyman S, 1924, Ap 10,23:4
Waters, Michael, 1951, Ja 8,17:5
Waters, Nacy McGee Rev Dr, 1916, My 15,9:8
Waters, Patrick Mrs, 1955, Ap 3,86:6
Waters, Percival L, 1942, F 2,15:4
Waters, Peter, 1949, Je 4,13:6
Waters, Peter L Sr, 1962, Ja 27,21:6
Waters, Robert, 1956, N 5,31:4
Waters, Robert A Sr, 1955, Jl 11,23:4
Waters, Roger J, 1964, My 16,25:2
Waters, Samuel J, 1954, S 5,50:2
Waters, Silas B Mrs, 1951, Mr 25,74:7
Waters, T Hadley, 1964, N 14,29:5
Waters, Thomas A Mrs, 1937, Ag 12,19:4
Waters, Thomas J, 1947, Ag 28,23:3
Waters, Tom, 1953, Jl 12,65:3
Waters, W S, 1873, S 9,5:5
Waters, Walter Mrs, 1953, O 13,29:2
Waters, William A, 1939, N 25,17:1
Waters, William D I, 1940, D 12,27:5
Waters, William E, 1948, S 23,29:5
Waters, William E Lt-Col, 1903, O 28,9:6
Waters, William H, 1943, O 24,45:1; 1953, D 23,25:4
Waters, William L, 1956, Mr 13,27:4
Waters, William Mrs, 1965, Ap 20,39:2
Waters, William O, 1940, My 2,23:2
Waters, William P, 1957, My 8,37:3
Waters, William S, 1943, Je 4,21:2
Waters, Yssabella G, 1938, Ag 17,19:2
Waterstone, Satella S, 1938, Je 17,21:5
Waterworth, Kenneth F, 1957, Je 4,35:5
Waterworth, Samuel J, 1940, Je 7,23:3
Waterworth, Samuel J Mrs, 1939, N 20,19:3
Wathall, Alfred G, 1938, N 16,23:6
Wathen, Albert L, 1950, N 4,17:3
Wathen, George Mrs, 1950, My 6,15:5
Wathen, Hugh L, 1963, D 17,39:1
Wathen, J Bernard Jr, 1942, Jl 15,19:4
Wathen, Richard E, 1946, S 18,31:5
Wathen, Stanley A, 1955, D 30,20:1
Wathey, Manful J, 1941, O 20,17:2
Wathon, Stanley W, 1960, Ja 10,86:4
Watie, Arthur E, 1942, My 21,19:5
Watiz-Felder, Florence C (will), 1939, N 2,19:8
Watjen, Louis, 1955, F 26,15:2
Watjen, Louis Mrs, 1951, Jl 17,27:4
Watkeys, Dean H, 1953, N 27,27:1
Watkin, Adelaide V, 1942, N 8,50:4
Watkin, William W, 1952, Je 26,29:2
Watkin-Jones, Howard, 1953, O 24,15:2
Watkins, Aaron D, 1941, F 11,24:3
Watkins, Abiathar Hubbard, 1903, Jl 26,7:6
Watkins, Andrew, 1967, Ja 23,33:1
Watkins, Arthur A (A Watkyn), 1965, Ag 2,29:5
Watkins, Catherine R, 1948, Jl 17,15:6
Watkins, Charles D, 1962, My 25,33:4
Watkins, Charles H, 1939, Ag 31,19:5; 1942, My 14, 19:3; 1957, F 20,33:5
Watkins, Charles L, 1966, Ag 31,40:4
Watkins, Charles M, 1945, My 15,19:3
Watkins, Charles P Mrs, 1967, My 17,47:2
Watkins, Charlotte Mrs, 1942, F 5,21:4
Watkins, Clarence E, 1944, N 14,23:4
Watkins, David G, 1940, Ag 2,15:6
Watkins, Dora Mrs, 1909, My 30,9:5
Watkins, Dudley W Mrs, 1965, Jl 18,68:6
Watkins, E W, 1941, N 15,17:6
Watkins, Edgar, 1945, Ag 23,23:4
Watkins, Edna, 1950, Mr 22,27:3
Watkins, Edward G, 1942, D 16,25:4
Watkins, Edwin D, 1945, My 28,19:5
Watkins, Everett C, 1955, N 7,29:2
Watkins, F Ernest, 1942, F 12,23:5
Watkins, Frank B, 1944, Je 28,23:5
Watkins, Fred, 1954, F 2,27:3
Watkins, Fred E, 1948, Ag 24,23:5
Watkins, Frederick William Maj, 1918, Ag 22,11:3
Watkins, G Law, 1945, Mr 4,36:1
Watkins, G R S, 1950, Ag 1,23:5
Watkins, George C, 1872, D 8,1:7
Watkins, George T, 1943, O 7,23:1
Watkins, Gertrude, 1938, Jl 18,13:5
Watkins, Harriet Titus, 1906, Ja 29,9:4
Watkins, Harry E, 1947, Jl 3,21:3
Watkins, Harvey H, 1958, My 14,33:2
Watkins, Horton, 1949, Jl 7,25:3
Watkins, Howard S, 1952, Ag 26,25:2
Watkins, Hunter, 1952, Ap 6,88:1
Watkins, J Raiford, 1942, Je 17,23:6
Watkins, J Y, 1883, O 28,8:7
Watkins, James, 1940, Mr 4,15:5
Watkins, James R, 1938, O 24,17:5
Watkins, James T Commodore, 1868, F 24,2:6
Watkins, John E, 1946, F 15,26:3
Watkins, John H, 1948, S 27,23:4
Watkins, John T, 1943, My 10,19:2
Watkins, Joseph Bookhout, 1919, Jl 7,13:4
Watkins, Joseph O Mrs, 1942, Ap 3,21:5
Watkins, Julia C, 1961, Ap 20,33:2
Watkins, Louis D Gen, 1868, Ap 12,3:7
Watkins, Louis H, 1925, Mr 7,13:6
Watkins, Malvin D, 1940, O 9,25:1
Watkins, Mary Mrs, 1909, Ap 18,11:4
Watkins, Mary W Mrs, 1937, F 16,24:1
Watkins, Milton, 1959, Mr 24,39:3
Watkins, Nelson J, 1961, O 11,47:2
Watkins, Paul F, 1951, D 15,13:6
Watkins, Robert M, 1953, My 31,54:1
Watkins, Samuel A, 1954, N 25,29:2
Watkins, Samuel C G, 1942, Mr 12,19:5
Watkins, Samuel S, 1959, S 25,29:3
Watkins, Schurmann H Rev Dr, 1937, My 29,17:3
Watkins, Thomas C, 1949, Je 5,92:5
Watkins, Thomas D Mrs, 1947, Ap 28,23:5
Watkins, Thomas F, 1938, F 3,23:3
Watkins, Thomas H (por), 1947, Je 26,23:3
Watkins, Thomas J Dr, 1925, Ap 2,21:4
Watkins, Thomas R (Tradin' Tom), 1954, My 18,30:3
Watkins, W G Capt, 1912, N 24,II,17:5
Watkins, Walter, 1937, Ap 17,17:2; 1955, F 6,88:5
Watkins, William H, 1937, Je 11,23:3; 1951, D 25,31:4
Watkins, William R, 1945, D 11,25:3
Watkins, William T, 1961, F 8,31:2
Watkis, James E, 1945, F 6,19:4
Watlington, B T, 1884, Ja 5,3:2
Watlington, Francis W W, 1941, S 10,23:2
Watlington, Henry, 1942, D 16,25:3
Watmough, James H Adm, 1917, Ja 19,7:3
Watmough, John G, 1913, O 12,15:3
Watmough, Richard L, 1944, F 1,19:1
Watmough, William N, 1949, D 27,23:2
Watner, Abraham, 1961, Je 20,33:4
Watney, Mark, 1965, D 8,7:6
Watney, Ralph R, 1945, My 19,19:6
Watral, John, 1951, Ag 23,23:3
Watres, Laurence H, 1964, F 9,88:6
Watres, Louis A Col, 1937, Je 29,21:5
Watriss, Frederick N, 1938, Ap 11,15:5
Watriss, Frederick N Mrs, 1922, D 7,19:6
Watrous, A E, 1902, Mr 14,9:5
Watrous, Benjamin A, 1957, Ag 12,19:5
Watrous, Carlisle B, 1947, Ja 27,23:1
Watrous, Clarence H Mrs, 1962, F 25,88:7
Watrous, George D, 1940, N 15,21:1
Watrous, George H, 1938, Jl 29,17:3
Watrous, George R, 1952, F 26,27:1
Watrous, Harry W, 1940, My 10,23:1
Watrous, Ralph C Mrs, 1947, Ag 1,17:3
Watrous, Richard D, 1945, O 21,46:2
Watrous, Ruth A (will), 1914, O 30,9:5
Watrous, Ward W, 1946, My 6,21:3
Watry, Joseph, 1942, Ja 24,17:4
Watson, A A Rev, 1905, Ap 22,11:5
Watson, A L, 1882, Jl 1,2:7
Watson, Adele, 1947, Mr 24,25:1
Watson, Adolphus E, 1949, O 5,29:2
Watson, Albert L, 1960, D 21,31:2
Watson, Albert P, 1909, Je 23,7:4
Watson, Alex, 1937, S 16,25:4; 1963, Ap 16,35:4
Watson, Alex G, 1949, My 18,27:5
Watson, Alfred, 1960, O 2,84:7
Watson, Alfred C, 1938, Ja 24,23:2
Watson, Alfred J, 1947, Ap 29,27:3
Watson, Alwin K, 1964, Ag 31,25:1
Watson, Amos C, 1945, Ag 7,23:6
Watson, Annie C, 1960, Ja 9,21:3
Watson, Annie Duncan Mrs (est), 1914, D 8,11:5
Watson, Archibald R Mrs, 1960, S 8,35:4
Watson, Archiblad R, 1957, O 27,86:4
Watson, Arthur, 1950, D 29,19:1
Watson, Arthur A, 1960, Je 26,73:1

Watson, Arthur C, 1940, S 24,23:5
Watson, Arthur E, 1956, O 30,34:2
Watson, Arthur H, 1941, Je 30,17:1
Watson, Arthur K L (will), 1938, Jl 19,19:6
Watson, Arthur Mrs, 1954, D 1,36:1
Watson, Arthur N Mrs, 1943, Je 23,21:3
Watson, Arthur S, 1962, Ag 15,31:2
Watson, Benjamin, 1923, Jl 16,11:6
Watson, Benjamin Mrs, 1959, D 1,39:3
Watson, Bertrand, 1948, F 17,25:5
Watson, Beulah, 1917, My 29,13:4
Watson, Billy, 1945, Ja 15,19:5
Watson, Bruce M, 1943, Ja 28,19:4
Watson, Bryon S, 1947, S 10,27:6
Watson, Carl H (cor, D 1,31:4), 1954, N 30,29:2
Watson, Carl H Sr Mrs, 1955, O 14,27:3
Watson, Cassius H, 1959, Je 2,35:3
Watson, Cedric S, 1951, Je 16,15:4
Watson, Charles A, 1937, My 16,II,8:5
Watson, Charles E, 1948, Ap 13,27:3
Watson, Charles F Jr, 1954, Ap 20,29:5
Watson, Charles F Jr Mrs, 1957, My 29,27:4
Watson, Charles L, 1952, N 17,25:5
Watson, Charles Moore Col, 1916, Mr 16,13:6
Watson, Charles Mrs, 1945, My 14,17:4
Watson, Charles P, 1953, My 17,88:2
Watson, Charles R (por), 1948, Ja 12,19:3
Watson, Charles White, 1917, Ag 19,15:1
Watson, Clara, 1940, Jl 27,13:2
Watson, Clarence W, 1940, My 25,17:2
Watson, Claude C, 1945, O 9,21:6
Watson, Cole W Sr, 1952, Mr 14,23:2
Watson, Cornelius B, 1950, N 3,27:3
Watson, Curry, 1944, Jl 1,15:3
Watson, Daniel Dr, 1871, My 18,1:5
Watson, Daniel H, 1903, S 27,7:6
Watson, David E, 1956, N 25,88:8
Watson, David Sir, 1922, F 20,11:4
Watson, David T, 1916, F 26,9:4
Watson, Donald C, 1951, Je 26,29:1
Watson, Douglas S, 1948, D 19,76:6
Watson, Drake, 1951, D 27,21:2
Watson, Dudley M, 1909, N 25,11:6
Watson, Dwight L, 1953, F 26,25:5
Watson, E, 1941, Mr 16,45:2
Watson, E Bradlee, 1961, D 8,42:6
Watson, E M, 1937, D 1,23:5; 1945, F 28,23:1
Watson, E S, 1902, My 8,9:5
Watson, Earl F, 1948, F 23,25:2
Watson, Edgar Mrs, 1940, Mr 15,23:5
Watson, Edith M, 1953, O 16,27:5
Watson, Edward, 1941, N 18,25:3
Watson, Edward A, 1941, S 23,23:3
Watson, Edward B, 1960, Je 22,35:5
Watson, Edward F, 1959, Jl 25,17:4
Watson, Edward H, 1942, Ja 8,21:2
Watson, Edward J, 1939, Ja 18,20:2
Watson, Edward P, 1947, O 11,17:5
Watson, Edwin A, 1912, Ap 12,13:4
Watson, Edwin G, 1951, Mr 3,13:2
Watson, Edwin H, 1939, S 25,20:1
Watson, Elizabeth, 1938, F 14,17:2
Watson, Elizabeth C, 1951, S 2,48:7
Watson, Ella B Mrs, 1937, Jl 17,15:3
Watson, Ella M, 1940, Ap 27,15:4
Watson, Elmo S, 1951, My 6,93:1
Watson, Emily T Mrs, 1941, S 27,17:3
Watson, Ernest C, 1957, N 28,31:3
Watson, Ernest H, 1956, Ag 25,15:4
Watson, Ernest L, 1942, S 20,41:1
Watson, Ernest M, 1948, D 6,25:2
Watson, Ernest S, 1957, N 29,29:3
Watson, Ernest W Mrs, 1948, D 18,19:5
Watson, Eugene H B, 1955, My 17,29:2
Watson, Eugene H B Mrs, 1955, F 7,21:1
Watson, Everett I, 1960, Ja 20,16:3
Watson, Forbes, 1960, Je 1,39:1
Watson, Forbes Mrs, 1966, S 28,47:3
Watson, Forrest E, 1949, Ap 18,25:3
Watson, Francis A, 1910, F 23,9:5
Watson, Frank A Mrs, 1952, My 12,25:5
Watson, Frank B, 1955, Jl 26,25:5
Watson, Frank D, 1959, F 23,23:3
Watson, Frank D Mrs, 1961, My 19,31:2
Watson, Frank J, 1949, N 23,29:2
Watson, Frank R, 1940, O 31,23:2
Watson, Frank S, 1949, Ap 22,23:2
Watson, Frasier J, 1966, My 4,47:2
Watson, Frederick, 1947, S 16,23:2
Watson, Frederick A, 1937, F 25,23:5
Watson, Frederick G, 1955, F 9,27:1
Watson, Frederick Mrs, 1944, D 8,21:3
Watson, Frederick V, 1939, Mr 14,21:3
Watson, Fredric, 1953, Mr 19,29:2
Watson, Fulton, 1942, N 29,65:1
Watson, G Clarke, 1966, F 20,88:4
Watson, Garrett F Mrs, 1957, Mr 4,27:4
Watson, George, 1939, O 13,23:4
Watson, George A, 1943, Ja 15,17:4
Watson, George C, 1941, N 10,17:4; 1948, Jl 17,15:4
Watson, George E, 1953, Ja 30,21:2; 1953, O 17,15:4
Watson, George E Jr, 1957, My 9,31:6
Watson, George E Mrs, 1959, Ja 1,31:3
Watson, George H, 1944, O 9,23:5
Watson, George Jr (funl, Jl 24,7:5), 1910, Jl 22,7:6
Watson, George L, 1904, N 13,7:6
Watson, George Mrs, 1953, N 17,31:3
Watson, Geraldine E, 1965, Mr 11,33:4
Watson, Gertrude, 1938, Ja 17,19:4
Watson, H W, 1933, Ag 28,13:4
Watson, Harley A, 1967, Ag 28,31:4
Watson, Harold D, 1965, F 9,37:4
Watson, Harry A, 1940, S 15,48:6
Watson, Harry G, 1945, O 3,19:1
Watson, Harry G Mrs, 1942, D 4,25:1
Watson, Harry L, 1956, N 7,31:2
Watson, Harry R, 1945, F 1,23:2
Watson, Harry R Mrs, 1944, S 18,19:5
Watson, Helen, 1943, D 21,27:1
Watson, Henrietta M, 1947, O 29,27:2
Watson, Henry Brereton M, 1921, O 31,15:5
Watson, Henry D, 1950, Je 21,27:4; 1955, My 25,33:2
Watson, Henry R C, 1921, Ap 28,13:3
Watson, Herbert H, 1948, Je 7,19:2
Watson, Herbert W Mrs, 1946, D 2,25:3
Watson, Howard E Mrs, 1956, Mr 15,31:3
Watson, Hugh, 1951, Je 1,23:2
Watson, Hugh H, 1947, My 25,62:3
Watson, Hugh S, 1950, S 10,94:1
Watson, Irving Allison Dr, 1918, Ap 4,13:4
Watson, Isabelle, 1941, F 13,19:4
Watson, J C, 1880, N 24,5:2
Watson, J Capt, 1877, S 27,5:6
Watson, J Curry, 1925, Ja 20,21:4
Watson, J Henry Rev, 1913, N 1,11:4
Watson, J J, 1902, Ag 7,9:6; 1940, Ja 17,21:2
Watson, J Kenneth, 1937, D 14,25:2
Watson, James, 1871, Ja 31,8:2; 1952, Ap 30,27:2
Watson, James A, 1941, D 6,17:5; 1959, Ja 29,27:4
Watson, James B, 1960, F 20,13:4
Watson, James C, 1944, S 24,46:2
Watson, James E, 1938, Je 18,15:4
Watson, James E (por), 1948, Jl 30,17:1
Watson, James E Mrs, 1949, My 23,23:1
Watson, James F, 1954, Ja 26,27:5; 1955, S 13,31:4
Watson, James G, 1956, Ag 10,17:3
Watson, James L, 1959, Mr 13,29:2
Watson, James M, 1955, N 3,31:2
Watson, James S, 1951, My 5,17:5; 1952, My 10,21:2; 1960, Ag 1,23:4
Watson, James S Mrs, 1945, F 9,15:4
Watson, James V, 1937, Ag 6,17:3
Watson, Jean M, 1960, My 1,87:2
Watson, Jesse, 1950, Ap 15,15:2
Watson, John, 1910, S 26,13:5; 1919, O 28,13:2; 1939, Ja 28,15:1; 1943, Je 9,21:6; 1945, Je 9,13:5; 1946, S 19,33:4
Watson, John A, 1944, Je 13,19:3
Watson, John B, 1942, D 8,26:3; 1958, S 26,27:1
Watson, John C, 1941, N 19,23:2; 1944, F 10,15:3; 1949, Ag 3,23:5; 1953, O 28,29:3
Watson, John Crittenden Rear-Adm, 1923, D 17,17:4
Watson, John D, 1953, Jl 16,21:3
Watson, John E, 1951, Je 19,29:1; 1954, Jl 10,13:4
Watson, John F Mrs, 1953, Mr 28,17:5
Watson, John F Sir, 1952, Ag 26,25:3
Watson, John H, 1938, Ag 3,19:4
Watson, John J (por), 1939, Mr 31,21:3
Watson, John J, 1950, O 26,31:4; 1955, Je 4,15:6
Watson, John J Mrs (est acctg, O 18,24:1), 1957, S 13,23:1
Watson, John J Mrs, 1960, Ap 20,39:4
Watson, John L Mrs, 1949, S 26,25:2; 1951, D 28,21:4
Watson, John M, 1942, F 15,44:2; 1943, S 22,24:3
Watson, John O, 1966, Ag 12,31:3
Watson, John R, 1949, Jl 21,25:2; 1960, Mr 31,33:3; 1965, Ag 6,27:3
Watson, John Rev Dr (Ian Maclaren), 1907, My 7, 9:5
Watson, John W, 1939, F 11,15:5; 1954, Mr 5,19:3; 1954, N 11,31:3; 1959, Je 19,25:1; 1961, S 10,86:4
Watson, Johnny, 1942, D 29,22:3
Watson, Joseph C, 1950, Mr 27,23:5
Watson, Joseph J, 1915, My 28,13:5
Watson, Kenneth B, 1948, D 11,15:5
Watson, Kenneth N Mrs, 1949, Mr 5,18:2
Watson, Leon A Sr, 1960, Ap 2,23:5
Watson, Leonard A, 1960, F 4,31:2
Watson, Leonard C, 1937, My 1,19:2
Watson, Leroy Mrs, 1949, Mr 23,27:5
Watson, Lester, 1949, Mr 7,21:5
Watson, Lewis H, 1943, D 7,27:1
Watson, Lewis M, 1961, Mr 14,35:2
Watson, Lillian Mrs, 1940, Ap 3,23:4
Watson, Lloyd R, 1948, F 27,21:2
Watson, Lorenzo D Rev Dr, 1915, O 8,11:4
Watson, Lucile, 1962, Je 25,29:2
Watson, Lucy C, 1938, D 13,25:2
Watson, Lucy L, 1939, Ag 7,15:5
Watson, Malcolm, 1955, D 29,23:5
Watson, Malcolm D, 1950, S 19,29:5
Watson, Margaret, 1949, D 31,15:2
Watson, Mark S, 1966, Mr 26,29:1
Watson, Mary A, 1961, N 17,35:4
Watson, Matthew H, 1942, Ja 16,21:3
Watson, Maud, 1946, Je 7,19:5
Watson, Maud E, 1945, F 2,19:4
Watson, Merrill, 1923, F 23,13:4
Watson, Minor, 1965, Jl 30,25:3
Watson, Murray D, 1941, S 12,22:2
Watson, Nathan, 1925, Je 18,21:5
Watson, Orville E, 1951, My 19,15:3
Watson, Oscar, 1941, Jl 11,15:5
Watson, Paul B, 1948, Mr 20,13:2
Watson, Paul E, 1943, S 19,48:4; 1952, Mr 18,27:5
Watson, Pauline E Mrs, 1942, F 10,19:2
Watson, Percy A, 1953, S 2,19:5
Watson, Phil M, 1938, Ag 10,19:2
Watson, Philip B, 1960, S 12,29:4
Watson, Rachel, 1949, S 23,23:3
Watson, Ralph H, 1961, Ja 30,23:2
Watson, Ralph J, 1956, S 17,27:2
Watson, Richard, 1873, Ag 20,4:7
Watson, Ripley, 1962, F 18,92:5
Watson, Robert, 1952, Ja 12,13:4
Watson, Robert A, 1944, Ja 1,13:3; 1944, My 31,19:3; 1956, S 22,17:6
Watson, Robert C, 1925, My 22,19:6
Watson, Robert E, 1952, D 29,19:2
Watson, Robert H, 1950, D 21,29:4
Watson, Robert I, 1948, Ja 28,23:3
Watson, Robert R, 1948, Ap 23,23:5
Watson, Robert S, 1943, Ja 20,20:3
Watson, Robert W (por), 1944, D 2,13:4
Watson, Robert W Mrs, 1941, Ja 30,21:4
Watson, Rollo B, 1924, F 1,17:4
Watson, Roy R, 1943, Jl 20,19:4
Watson, Rupert D, 1940, O 6,49:3
Watson, Sam, 1967, My 9,47:2
Watson, Samuel, 1937, F 5,21:1
Watson, Samuel C, 1942, Ja 26,15:2
Watson, Samuel J, 1915, Ap 15,13:5
Watson, Samuel N, 1942, Mr 29,45:3
Watson, Sarah S Mrs, 1938, S 21,25:5
Watson, Susan M H Mrs (will, Ap 7,13:2), 1937, Ap 1,24:2
Watson, Susan M Mrs (will), 1938, Ap 30,15:1
Watson, T A, 1934, D 15,14:1
Watson, T Harold, 1946, My 18,19:5
Watson, T Sir, 1882, D 13,5:1
Watson, Thomas, 1904, Ja 23,1:7
Watson, Thomas A Mrs, 1948, Ap 25,68:6
Watson, Thomas E Mrs, 1923, My 16,19:5
Watson, Thomas E Sen (por), 1922, S 27,19:1
Watson, Thomas J Sr (funl plans, Je 21,31:4; funl, Je 22,23:1), 1956, Je 20,1:4
Watson, Thomas J Sr (est acctg), 1957, N 14,27:4
Watson, Thomas J Sr Mrs, 1966, F 12,27:1
Watson, Thomas Lansdell Gen, 1919, D 12,17:3
Watson, Victor, 1938, N 7,19:3
Watson, Vincent C, 1962, Ap 4,43:1
Watson, W, 1877, O 2,8:1; 1935, Ag 14,19:3
Watson, W Rear-Adm, 1914, D 12,15:7
Watson, Walter, 1963, D 26,28:3
Watson, Walter A, 1919, D 25,13:4
Watson, Walter Dr, 1922, Ja 9,17:4
Watson, Walter J, 1964, Jl 8,35:1
Watson, Walter S, 1941, S 26,23:2
Watson, Walter W, 1951, Mr 14,33:4
Watson, Wesley, 1944, My 2,19:3
Watson, Wesley Mrs, 1963, Je 18,41:6
Watson, Wilbur J, 1939, My 21,III,7:2
Watson, William, 1909, F 27,9:4; 1909, O 5,9:5; 1915, O 1,11:5; 1925, Je 16,21:6; 1938, Ja 7,20:1
Watson, William A, 1941, O 10,23:3
Watson, William A Mrs, 1952, Je 2,22:3
Watson, William F, 1947, Ag 5,23:5
Watson, William F A, 1954, Mr 14,89:2
Watson, William G, 1947, N 27,31:3; 1962, My 27,92:7
Watson, William Henry Dr, 1913, Ja 3,9:5
Watson, William J Mrs, 1945, Je 12,19:4
Watson, William Mrs, 1940, D 1,62:8; 1955, My 27, 23:4
Watson, William P, 1941, Jl 10,19:2
Watson, William Perry Dr (funl, Jl 20,15:6), 1925, Jl 18,13:6
Watson, William R, 1960, Ag 13,15:6
Watson, William R Dr, 1937, O 27,31:6
Watson, William S, 1943, Jl 30,15:2; 1944, Je 18,36:2
Watson, William Sr Mrs, 1950, D 16,17:4
Watson, William T, 1961, S 10,86:3
Watson, William W, 1962, Ja 30,29:3
Watson, William W Jr, 1952, Mr 4,27:4
Watson, William W Mrs, 1964, Ja 26,80:8
Watson, Winfred, 1949, O 15,15:6
Watson-Williams, Patrick, 1938, N 26,16:3
Watt, Alex, 1940, Jl 27,13:6
Watt, Alfred Mrs, 1948, N 30,27:5
Watt, Archibald (will, Jl 4,7:4), 1906, Je 20,7:6
Watt, Archibald H, 1959, F 24,29:4
Watt, Arthur C, 1948, N 22,21:2
Watt, Charles C, 1941, My 27,23:3
Watt, Charles C Jr, 1953, Mr 19,29:5
Watt, Charles F, 1950, Mr 28,31:2
Watt, Charles M, 1941, N 26,23:1
Watt, David A, 1948, Mr 16,27:2; 1960, Je 4,23:5
Watt, Duncan, 1946, Je 19,21:2
Watt, Edward W B, 1948, Je 2,29:2
Watt, Emma W Mrs, 1941, Ap 6,48:5

Watt, G Fiddes, 1960, N 23,29:1
Watt, G Howard, 1940, Ap 24,23:3
Watt, George W, 1940, N 8,21:3; 1947, N 21,27:4
Watt, Harry B, 1944, Mr 31,21:6
Watt, Henry C, 1963, Je 4,39:2
Watt, Henry R, 1964, S 12,25:4
Watt, Hiram, 1946, My 8,25:1
Watt, Homer A (por), 1948, O 5,26:3
Watt, Homer A Mrs, 1950, D 20,31:2
Watt, James, 1941, Je 21,17:1; 1945, Ag 18,11:4
Watt, James Birnie, 1920, Je 20,18:4
Watt, James H Mrs, 1952, D 6,21:6
Watt, James R (por), 1941, S 21,45:1
Watt, James T, 1964, Ap 25,29:3
Watt, John, 1939, Jl 31,13:3; 1950, F 8,27:4
Watt, John H, 1909, Je 19,7:5
Watt, Lauchlan MacL, 1957, S 12,31:3
Watt, Marie E Mrs, 1941, D 20,19:5
Watt, Percy D, 1958, Ag 26,29:4
Watt, R R G, 1952, My 19,17:5
Watt, Richard M, 1938, My 17,23:3
Watt, Robert J, 1947, Jl 26,13:1; 1967, Mr 14,22:4
Watt, Robert M, 1963, Jl 24,31:5
Watt, Robert W, 1940, My 2,23:1
Watt, Thomas L, 1910, Ap 12,11:5
Watt, William, 1951, F 28,27:1; 1952, Je 2,22:4
Watt, William A, 1946, S 14,7:6
Watt, William C, 1944, D 1,24:2
Watt, William H, 1947, Ap 8,27:2
Watt, William J, 1948, Mr 4,25:2; 1948, Jl 19,19:2
Watteau, Andre, 1946, Ja 12,15:3
Wattenberg, Abraham, 1954, O 8,23:2
Wattenberg, Alfred W, 1938, Ja 21,20:5
Wattenberg, John, 1954, My 3,25:5
Wattenberg, Joseph, 1951, F 18,77:1
Wattenberg, Sidney W, 1958, Ja 17,30:1
Watters, Ada S Mrs, 1939, Ag 13,29:2
Watters, Arthur C, 1944, Je 20,19:2
Watters, Charles J, 1943, Mr 24,23:5
Watters, E McLain, 1962, S 25,37:5
Watters, Edwin L, 1943, Ap 1,23:4
Watters, George M, 1943, Mr 17,21:4
Watters, Harrison H, 1938, O 19,23:5
Watters, J Howard, 1960, O 21,33:3
Watters, James D Judge, 1908, Mr 30,7:5
Watters, John G, 1965, D 26,68:8
Watters, Leon L, 1967, Ap 19,45:1
Watters, Margaret E, 1950, Mr 30,18:2
Watters, Samuel, 1950, Ag 31,26:2
Watters, William, 1956, My 26,17:3
Watters, William F, 1963, D 18,41:4
Watters, William G, 1959, Jl 26,69:2
Watters, William H, 1924, Je 14,11:6; 1949, O 12,29:3
Watterson, Henry (por), 1921, D 23,13:1
Watterson, Henry Jr, 1959, My 8,27:3
Watterson, Irving, 1955, Ag 9,26:4
Watterson, Peter F, 1951, Mr 22,31:4
Watterson, Richard Mrs, 1964, O 28,45:4
Watterson, Walter, 1947, Je 18,25:5
Watteville, W A de, 1927, Mr 28,21:5
Wattis, Edmond O, 1944, Ja 6,23:4
Wattles, Willard, 1950, S 26,31:2
Wattles, William, 1882, S 1,8:2
Wattley, George, 1950, Ag 31,25:3
Wattley, Harold, 1964, N 19,39:6
Watts, Alfred, 1951, Je 11,25:5
Watts, Alfred A, 1946, Ja 10,23:2
Watts, Arthur P, 1959, S 1,30:2
Watts, Benton C Mrs, 1947, Mr 14,23:3
Watts, Bigelow, 1967, D 1,47:4
Watts, Charles, 1966, D 16,47:3
Watts, Charles A, 1946, My 16,21:4
Watts, Charles H, 1955, Ag 19,19:2; 1967, Je 9,45:1
Watts, Claude D, 1966, Ag 31,40:4
Watts, David, 1882, N 17,5:4
Watts, Diana Mrs, 1968, My 15,47:1
Watts, Edward C, 1958, Jl 27,60:8
Watts, Edward E, 1946, S 10,7:3
Watts, Edward E Mrs, 1960, D 13,31:3
Watts, Elizabeth, 1967, Jl 27,35:2
Watts, Erwin H, 1964, Ap 11,25:2
Watts, Ethelbert, 1919, Jl 14,11:3
Watts, Euclid V, 1966, D 28,27:4
Watts, F Kenneth, 1954, S 29,31:5
Watts, Frank A, 1956, My 21,25:4
Watts, Frank O, 1946, N 7,31:6
Watts, Franklin, 1945, N 16,19:3
Watts, Frederick N, 1940, Ja 20,15:3
Watts, George, 1949, D 11,92:8
Watts, George B, 1912, N 26,15:6
Watts, George E, 1958, D 7,89:1
Watts, George F, 1947, Je 17,28:1
Watts, George Fred, 1904, Jl 2,7:6
Watts, George Livingston, 1921, Mr 9,13:4
Watts, George M, 1955, My 5,33:4
Watts, H Bascom, 1959, N 4,35:2
Watts, H D, 1952, Jl 28,15:1
Watts, Harry, 1962, Ja 7,88:5
Watts, Harry D Mrs, 1943, S 21,23:3
Watts, Harry J, 1945, D 3,21:5
Watts, Harry S, 1938, Ap 19,21:6
Watts, Harvey M, 1939, Ag 13,29:3
Watts, Henry F, 1950, Ag 4,21:6
Watts, Henry F R, 1957, Ap 16,33:1
Watts, Henry M, 1959, Jl 14,29:3
Watts, J Allen, 1904, Ja 6,9:5
Watts, J Elmer, 1944, Ja 25,19:6
Watts, James B, 1942, Ag 6,19:2
Watts, James S, 1938, D 18,49:1
Watts, James W, 1940, O 11,21:3; 1948, O 16,15:1; 1952, N 7,23:1
Watts, James W Mrs, 1952, Jl 16,25:1
Watts, John A, 1949, Ja 16,68:2
Watts, John C, 1948, My 30,34:4
Watts, John J, 1947, D 30,24:3
Watts, John Mrs, 1876, F 19,4:6
Watts, John R Jr, 1963, O 4,35:3
Watts, Joseph C, 1965, Je 5,31:4
Watts, Joseph W, 1953, Ja 24,15:4
Watts, Laurence Mrs, 1937, Je 4,23:3
Watts, Llewellyn, 1954, N 29,25:3
Watts, Llewellyn Sr Mrs, 1952, D 29,19:5
Watts, Lyle F, 1962, Je 17,81:1
Watts, Malcolm S, 1939, Ja 10,19:6
Watts, Marjorie S, 1966, My 3,44:8
Watts, Martin S, 1949, Ap 29,23:2
Watts, Mary E, 1961, Je 11,86:3
Watts, Mary Mrs, 1938, S 7,36:5; 1959, Je 19,52:1
Watts, Mary S Mrs, 1958, My 23,23:1
Watts, Morey S, 1954, Ap 7,31:1
Watts, Oliver, 1953, F 7,15:6
Watts, Ralph J, 1954, My 24,27:5
Watts, Ralph L (por), 1949, Jl 4,13:3
Watts, Richard Sr, 1952, Mr 23,92:4
Watts, Richard Sr Mrs, 1946, Ag 26,23:5
Watts, Robert Dr, 1917, O 17,13:2
Watts, Robert S Jr, 1967, My 15,43:4
Watts, Roderick J, 1959, S 17,39:3
Watts, Samuel H, 1953, My 27,31:2
Watts, Stephen H, 1953, Je 9,27:3
Watts, Steve L, 1966, Je 1,44:1
Watts, Thomas, 1869, S 29,4:6
Watts, Warren S, 1967, Je 25,69:1
Watts, William, 1941, N 4,19:6
Watts, William C, 1956, Ja 6,24:1
Watts, William H, 1955, D 8,37:5
Watts, William Lt-Com, 1914, Ja 2,9:6
Watts, William P, 1948, Ja 6,24:2
Watts, William W, 1947, Ag 1,17:4
Watts, Wintter, 1962, N 2,31:1
Watts-Dunton, Clara Mrs, 1938, S 16,21:5
Watts-Dunton, Walter Theodore, 1914, Je 8,7:6
Wattson, James, 1937, Jl 26,3:2
Watumull, Gobindram J, 1959, Ag 14,21:1
Watzka, Adolph, 1956, Ap 16,27:5
Watzka, John A Sr, 1950, Ap 18,32:2
Wauchope, Arthur G (por), 1947, S 15,17:3
Wauchope, George A, 1943, Je 11,19:5
Wauchope, Joshua, 1945, Ag 1,19:3
Waugh, Arthur, 1943, Je 28,21:4
Waugh, Catherine Mrs, 1954, D 9,33:4
Waugh, Coulton Mrs, 1944, Mr 21,20:2
Waugh, Dan F, 1956, F 9,32:1
Waugh, Daniel D Dr, 1924, Ag 11,13:5
Waugh, Donald B, 1962, My 24,35:5
Waugh, Evelyn A St J (est acctg, Jl 21,11:1), 1966, Ap 11,1:2
Waugh, Frank A Mrs, 1947, D 7,77:2
Waugh, Frederick J (por), 1940, S 11,25:1
Waugh, H P Mrs, 1924, O 15,23:4
Waugh, Harry, 1951, Ja 23,27:5
Waugh, Henry Proctor, 1924, N 13,21:4
Waugh, Howard R, 1946, Ap 18,27:4
Waugh, Ida, 1919, Ja 27,13:4
Waugh, John L, 1945, Je 10,32:6
Waugh, John M (funl), 1962, Ag 15,31:2
Waugh, Julia N, 1958, Ja 20,23:5
Waugh, Leuman M Mrs, 1941, D 16,27:1
Waugh, Richard D, 1938, My 21,15:4
Waugh, Richey L, 1959, N 28,21:5
Waugh, Samuel C Mrs, 1967, Jl 13,37:5
Waugh, Sidney B, 1963, Jl 1,29:1
Waugh, Thomas, 1949, My 10,25:6
Waugh, Tom, 1946, My 23,21:4
Waugh, William F Judge, 1953, Mr 7,15:4
Waugh, William L, 1916, Jl 22,9:7
Wauseka (E Hauser), 1941, My 21,23:4
Wauters, William M, 1939, Je 11,45:2
Wavell, Archibald J A)arl (est acctg), 1954, Ap 4, 2:4
Wavell, Archibald P (Field Marshal Earl), 1950, Mr 25,29:1
Waverly, Jack, 1951, Ja 31,25:3
Waverly, Viscount (Jno Anderson), 1958, Ja 5,86:1
Wavertree, Lord, 1933, F 3,20:1
Wavertree, Sophie F, 1952, N 28,25:3
Wavle, James H, 1947, S 9,32:2
Wavrinsky, Edward, 1924, Ja 7,19:4
Wax, Benjamin M, 1961, Ag 9,33:1
Wax, Benjamin Mrs, 1962, O 20,25:5
Waxberg, Herman Mrs, 1962, O 4,39:4
Waxman, Abraham P, 1962, Jl 21,19:4
Waxman, Benjamin, 1944, D 28,20:2
Waxman, David, 1944, Ag 31,17:3
Waxman, Franz, 1967, F 26,84:1
Waxman, Hyman, 1956, My 2,31:4
Waxman, Julius Z, 1966, Je 4,29:4
Waxman, Marvin, 1965, Je 15,38:1
Waxman, Max, 1957, Ag 8,23:1
Waxman, Max M, 1959, Ap 3,27:4
Waxman, Percy (por), 1948, Ja 13,26:3
Waxman, Peter J, 1954, My 9,88:6
Waxman, Sydney W, 1967, Jl 25,32:6
Waxter, Thomas J S, 1962, N 12,29:4
Way, Adelaide Mrs, 1937, Ag 27,19:5
Way, Alva O, 1950, D 27,27:2
Way, Arthur C, 1962, D 8,27:2
Way, Channing Sr, 1954, F 1,23:4
Way, Charles A, 1942, Ag 28,19:4
Way, Clarence E, 1937, My 16,II,8:6
Way, Clarence W, 1956, Ag 2,25:5
Way, Clyde C, 1952, Mr 15,13:4
Way, Ernest N, 1939, Je 20,21:5
Way, George A, 1942, Jl 12,36:2
Way, George E, 1950, Jl 11,31:1
Way, George H, 1913, Jl 8,7:6
Way, H Bert, 1963, Ag 13,31:3
Way, Harold D, 1959, D 17,37:2
Way, Harry A, 1950, Mr 23,36:4
Way, Herbert C, 1941, N 3,19:6
Way, Howard M, 1956, Je 16,19:3
Way, J M, 1941, O 28,23:3
Way, James B, 1939, Jl 5,17:6
Way, Lewis T, 1940, Ap 2,25:4
Way, Louis F, 1946, Je 11,23:3
Way, Luther, 1943, O 24,44:6
Way, Palmer M, 1944, Ja 30,37:1
Way, Royal B Prof, 1937, N 30,23:3
Way, Samuel A, 1872, Je 6,8:2
Way, Walker Mrs, 1958, O 26,88:8
Way, Warren W, 1943, Je 12,13:4
Way, William A, 1948, O 5,25:3
Way, William E, 1949, N 22,29:2
Way, William G, 1903, S 22,7:4
Way, William S, 1955, S 29,66:6
Waybrant, Alex, 1952, My 30,15:2
Waybrant, Alex Mrs, 1952, Ja 18,27:3
Wayburn, Ned, 1942, S 3,19:5
Waycie, John Mrs, 1950, D 26,23:2
Waye, Lee J (S Lee), 1955, Mr 16,33:3
Waye, Raymond T, 1952, Jl 11,17:3
Waygood, James J, 1965, N 20,35:4
Waygood, Walter H, 1939, S 3,19:1
Wayland, Chanler N, 1922, O 24,17:4
Wayland, Charles A Mrs, 1946, Mr 13,29:1
Wayland, Francis, 1904, Ja 10,7:5
Wayland, Francis Dr, 1865, O 2,5:3
Wayland, John, 1938, F 21,19:5
Wayland-Smith, Robert, 1961, D 24,36:8
Wayling, Thomas, 1949, Je 6,19:3
Waymaker, Michael R, 1937, N 30,23:1
Wayman, Christina W, 1941, Ja 30,21:4
Wayman, Edmund F, 1957, Ja 4,23:2
Wayman, Edwin L, 1960, S 7,41:2
Waymer, Sam S, 1959, Ja 15,33:4
Wayne, Albert F, 1946, D 28,15:4
Wayne, Arnold B, 1958, N 3,37:5
Wayne, Elmer C, 1942, D 26,11:1
Wayne, James M, 1867, Jl 6,5:2
Wayne, Joseph B Jr (por), 1942, My 27,23:3
Wayne, Joseph H, 1954, D 18,15:4
Wayne, Justine, 1951, D 3,31:6
Wayne, Malcolm, 1940, Ag 6,19:4
Wayne, Mullin H, 1956, Ap 19,31:3
Wayne, Rollo L, 1954, Mr 20,15:6
Wayne, William Maj, 1901, N 21,9:5
Wayo, Alex, 1955, Ap 28,29:2
Wayrick, Fred William Rev, 1907, Mr 10,9:6
Wazeter, Francis X, 1954, Ja 22,27:2
Wazeter, Leon F, 1957, F 3,76:1
Wazeter, Leon Mrs, 1957, Jl 17,27:4
Wazewski, Peter, 1949, Mr 4,21:4
Wazir Ali, Syed, 1950, Je 18,77:1
Wead, F F Col, 1864, Je 18,2:2
Wead, Frank, 1947, N 18,30:2
Wead, Margaret, 1946, Jl 16,23:4
Weadlick, Guy, 1953, D 17,37:3
Weadock, Bernard F (por), 1947, O 28,25:4
Weadock, Thomas A E, 1938, N 19,17:6
Weadon, Charles H, 1947, D 17,30:2
Weadon, Emile, 1960, My 1,86:4
Weadon, Frank P, 1939, Je 1,25:4
Weadon, Paul A, 1939, Mr 14,21:3
Weagant, Herman, 1947, Ag 24,57:2
Weagant, Roy A, 1942, Ag 24,15:1
Weagle, J Albert, 1938, Je 19,29:2
Weakland, Charles H, 1946, O 7,31:2
Wealch, John E, 1938, N 7,19:5
Weale, Fred E, 1947, Jl 4,13:5
Weale, Gilbert H, 1968, O 26,37:2
Wealty, Henry, 1943, Jl 25,31:1
Wean, Corinthia E Mrs, 1952, Ap 4,27:3
Weaning, Lawrence D Mrs, 1949, My 5,27:4
Wear, Joseph W (por), 1941, Je 5,23:3
Wear, Mike P Mrs, 1956, S 5,27:4
Wear, Walker, 1960, N 4,33:1
Wear, Walter Sr, 1948, Mr 28,48:6
Weare, Portius B, 1909, F 27,9:4
Wearn, George E, 1954, F 6,19:4

Wearne, Raymond G, 1965, Ag 20,29:1
Weart, James T, 1958, N 10,29:1
Weart, William G, 1917, D 8,15:6
Weary, Frederick R Mrs, 1956, O 18,33:1
Weastell, John H, 1914, F 12,9:4
Weatherbee, Edwin H, 1912, F 12,11:5
Weatherbee, Edwin H Mrs (will, Ag 2,19:2), 1945, Jl 14,11:7
Weatherbee, Hicks A (will, S 13,21:6), 1940, Ag 24, 13:2
Weatherby, Charles A, 1949, Je 22,31:3
Weatherby, Edward, 1903, Ja 1,9:5
Weatherby, Harry, 1939, Jl 23,29:3
Weatherby, Howard, 1925, N 8,5:2
Weatherby, Jeremiah L, 1938, Je 20,15:4
Weathered, Thomas W, 1903, D 6,7:6
Weatherell, Albert, 1952, O 27,27:2
Weatherell, Thomas A, 1947, S 9,31:5
Weatherford, Harold L, 1948, Jl 8,23:4
Weatherhalt, Marion Mrs, 1945, D 23,18:6
Weatherly, Fred, 1958, Ja 5,86:2
Weatherly, Goodhue, 1953, Mr 21,17:2
Weatherly, Joe, 1964, Ja 20,26:6
Weatherly, Robert H, 1942, D 2,25:2
Weatherly, Ulysses G, 1940, Jl 19,19:2
Weathers, Charles C, 1942, Je 10,21:3
Weathers, Curtis L, 1954, F 9,27:1
Weathers, Lee B, 1958, Ja 13,29:5
Weathers, N A, 1932, Ja 14,21:5
Weathers, Neil A Mrs, 1962, My 31,27:2
Weathersby, Emie, 1884, Mr 16,2:4
Weathersby, Helen, 1943, N 27,13:3
Weatherwax, Albert E, 1951, F 23,22:4
Weatherwax, Harry B, 1939, Jl 2,15:3
Weatherwax, Harry B Mrs, 1943, Mr 21,26:6
Weatherwax, Paul J, 1960, S 15,37:1
Weaver, Affie (Mrs H McVicker), 1940, N 19,24:3
Weaver, Albert, 1941, Mr 22,17:7; 1941, N 26,23:2
Weaver, Albert Mrs, 1941, Mr 22,17:7
Weaver, Andrew T, 1965, My 20,43:3
Weaver, Andrew T Mrs, 1965, My 20,43:3
Weaver, Arthur, 1907, F 27,9:5
Weaver, Arthur J (por), 1945, O 19,23:3
Weaver, Ben J (Buck),(por), 1949, Je 5,92:3
Weaver, Benjamin, 1915, N 10,13:2
Weaver, Benjamin B, 1953, N 5,31:4
Weaver, Bruce S, 1948, Ja 10,15:4
Weaver, C E, 1938, N 28,15:2
Weaver, Caius E, 1953, Ja 18,92:4
Weaver, Charles J, 1937, Ap 1,23:2
Weaver, Charles P, 1945, F 13,23:1
Weaver, Charles W Jr, 1953, My 24,89:2
Weaver, Cristian, 1962, F 23,29:2
Weaver, David, 1943, O 25,15:3
Weaver, David B, 1925, Ap 9,23:4
Weaver, David S, 1966, N 13,88:6
Weaver, Edwin O, 1960, F 5,3:1
Weaver, Eli Witiver, 1922, N 3,17:6
Weaver, Elvin D, 1951, D 13,33:2
Weaver, Emily P, 1943, Mr 12,17:5
Weaver, Ernest, 1953, Ag 14,19:3
Weaver, F Bayzer, 1960, Ja 2,13:3
Weaver, F Joseph, 1953, My 30,15:5
Weaver, Findlay I, 1967, Jl 3,17:3
Weaver, Fisher P, 1955, Mr 6,88:6
Weaver, Francis D, 1938, Ja 29,15:4
Weaver, Frank (Buck), 1952, Jl 11,17:3
Weaver, Frank M, 1958, Jl 10,27:2
Weaver, Frederick, 1941, D 10,25:6
Weaver, Frederick P, 1940, S 7,15:3
Weaver, Galen R, 1965, S 6,15:5
Weaver, Galen R Mrs, 1968, S 26,55:1
Weaver, George (Buck), 1924, Jl 30,13:4
Weaver, George (Buck), 1956, F 1,31:2
Weaver, George C, 1960, Mr 5,6:6
Weaver, George J, 1905, Ap 25,11:6; 1962, O 29,29:1
Weaver, George M, 1949, Ap 9,17:6
Weaver, George Mrs, 1953, N 12,31:1
Weaver, George S, 1949, Mr 6,73:2
Weaver, George W, 1940, Mr 3,45:3
Weaver, Gilbert G, 1968, D 22,52:4
Weaver, H A Sr, 1903, F 27,9:5
Weaver, Harold B, 1956, N 6,35:4
Weaver, Harrison R, 1968, Ag 17,27:3
Weaver, Harry R, 1943, F 20,13:2
Weaver, Harry S, 1938, Jl 8,17:4
Weaver, Harvey C, 1943, N 5,19:3
Weaver, Henry G (por), 1949, Ja 4,19:4
Weaver, Herbert A, 1943, S 17,21:2
Weaver, Herbert R, 1939, N 19,39:2
Weaver, Herbert S, 1937, Ja 24,II,9:1
Weaver, J B, 1882, Ap 10,5:5
Weaver, J Ward Sr, 1956, Mr 26,29:3
Weaver, J Wells, 1948, S 12,72:2
Weaver, Jack J, 1957, Ap 14,86:6
Weaver, Jacob E, 1945, O 23,17:5
Weaver, James B Gen, 1912, F 7,11:4
Weaver, James B Mrs, 1913, Jl 8,7:6
Weaver, John E A, 1960, O 20,35:2
Weaver, John H, 1943, Ja 21,21:4
Weaver, John H Lt, 1920, Ag 28,7:5
Weaver, John Mrs, 1949, F 24,23:5
Weaver, John R H, 1965, Mr 23,39:1
Weaver, John T, 1949, Mr 23,27:1
Weaver, John V A, 1938, Je 16,23:3
Weaver, John W, 1938, Jl 7,19:2; 1950, My 4,27:1
Weaver, Joseph C, 1961, Mr 21,37:1
Weaver, Joseph E, 1944, Jl 29,13:5
Weaver, Joseph Jr Mrs, 1950, Ja 28,13:6
Weaver, Joseph M, 1907, Mr 9,9:5
Weaver, L Sir, 1930, Ja 11,17:3
Weaver, Laurence A, 1953, O 2,21:5
Weaver, Leon (Abner), 1950, Mr 28,44:3
Weaver, Lydia S Mrs, 1947, Ap 3,25:3
Weaver, Martha Mrs, 1944, Ja 20,19:4
Weaver, Mary A, 1957, Ap 14,87:1
Weaver, Mary Jane Mrs, 1924, S 19,23:5
Weaver, Myron M, 1963, D 26,27:2
Weaver, Peter Lyle Capt, 1914, Jl 22,9:4
Weaver, Powell, 1951, D 23,22:3
Weaver, Ralph (Buck), 1956, Jl 30,21:5
Weaver, Ralph A, 1950, F 20,25:1
Weaver, Ralph S, 1939, O 28,15:3
Weaver, Raymond M (por), 1948, Ap 5,21:1
Weaver, Richard A, 1951, Ag 14,23:5
Weaver, Richard G, 1962, Ag 8,32:1
Weaver, Richard L, 1964, O 17,29:6
Weaver, Robert C Jr, 1962, N 7,80:1
Weaver, Robert E, 1947, My 10,13:5
Weaver, Robert S, 1949, D 9,31:5
Weaver, Rufus L, 1951, My 9,33:3
Weaver, Rufus W (por), 1947, F 1,15:4
Weaver, S Fullerton, 1939, Ja 2,23:1
Weaver, S Fullerton Mrs, 1959, Ja 24,19:5
Weaver, S Marshall, 1956, F 14,29:3
Weaver, Sam, 1941, Ja 14,21:6
Weaver, Stephen G, 1937, F 1,19:3
Weaver, Sylvester L, 1958, S 13,19:5
Weaver, T A D, 1958, Mr 2,89:1
Weaver, Walter A, 1951, Ag 12,78:5
Weaver, Walter B, 1938, D 16,25:2
Weaver, Walter D, 1967, Ja 31,31:3
Weaver, Walter R (por), 1944, O 28,15:1
Weaver, Walter S, 1952, O 11,19:2
Weaver, Washington A Mrs, 1961, My 30,17:5
Weaver, William, 1937, Ag 15,II,7:1
Weaver, William A, 1942, My 20,19:5
Weaver, William E, 1956, Ag 22,29:4
Weaver, William G, 1939, Ap 19,23:2
Weaver, William J (por), 1948, Je 6,72:6
Weaver, William J, 1949, S 8,29:2; 1956, My 23,31:4
Weaver, William M, 1946, Mr 11,25:3
Weaver, Willis E, 1947, D 6,15:6
Weaver, Zebulon (por), 1948, O 30,15:5
Weavers, Horace, 1951, N 5,31:1
Webb, A H, 1939, D 26,19:4
Webb, Albert C, 1946, Je 16,40:7
Webb, Albert T, 1941, My 1,23:2
Webb, Alec D, 1948, N 10,29:3
Webb, Alex S (por), 1948, Ja 24,15:4
Webb, Alex S Mrs, 1912, N 16,15:6; 1941, S 11,23:6
Webb, Alexander H, 1916, O 3,11:4
Webb, Alexander Stuart Gen (funl, F 16,11:6), 1911, F 15,9:4
Webb, Alfred L, 1925, O 20,25:4
Webb, Alice, 1947, N 7,23:1
Webb, Alonzo G, 1939, Je 13,23:5
Webb, Anne R, 1943, Jl 13,21:2
Webb, Aquilla, 1938, Jl 2,13:5
Webb, Arthur C, 1946, N 30,15:2
Webb, Arthur L, 1943, Ap 15,25:2; 1957, N 29,29:3
Webb, Austin, 1937, D 10,25:2
Webb, Barbara (Mrs B W Larkin), 1964, S 12,25:6
Webb, Bayard B, 1960, Jl 14,27:5
Webb, Benjamin L, 1945, Jl 1,17:2
Webb, C Edwin, 1950, F 20,25:4
Webb, Carl N, 1951, D 16,91:1
Webb, Catherine, 1952, S 11,31:1
Webb, Charles, 1949, Ag 12,17:5
Webb, Charles A, 1949, D 12,33:3
Webb, Charles H, 1963, My 8,36:2
Webb, Charles L, 1945, Ag 2,19:5
Webb, Charles Mrs, 1949, Je 2,28:3
Webb, Charles R, 1942, Mr 23,15:2
Webb, Charles S, 1957, N 14,33:4
Webb, Charles V, 1959, Ja 21,22:5
Webb, Charles W, 1949, Jl 8,19:4
Webb, Chick, 1939, Je 17,15:2
Webb, Claude A, 1940, Ag 8,19:3
Webb, Clifton (futher destails, O 15,29:1), 1966, O 14,40:1
Webb, David T, 1952, N 3,27:4
Webb, David W, 1943, N 14,57:1
Webb, E Yates, 1955, F 8,28:3
Webb, Earle W, 1965, Jl 8,28:1
Webb, Earle W Mrs, 1941, O 17,23:2
Webb, Elisabeth H, 1942, Ag 16,45:3
Webb, Elisha Jr, 1942, Ja 14,21:5
Webb, Elisha Jr Mrs, 1957, My 12,87:1
Webb, Elizabeth L Mrs, 1938, Ag 20,15:2
Webb, Elizabeth S, 1949, O 13,27:2
Webb, Ernest, 1955, Ag 20,17:4
Webb, Ernest G (Griff), 1954, Je 20,84:6
Webb, F Egerton, 1942, F 27,18:2
Webb, Frank C, 1949, N 29,29:3
Webb, Frank E, 1949, Je 17,23:6
Webb, Frank G, 1951, O 23,29:3
Webb, Frank J, 1940, Ap 24,23:2
Webb, G Creighton (por), 1948, Mr 20,13:3
Webb, George F, 1949, Je 11,17:2
Webb, George H, 1941, F 7,19:2
Webb, George M, 1909, Jl 24,7:4
Webb, George R, 1919, Jl 8,11:4
Webb, Gregory B, 1948, D 13,23:2
Webb, H Doyle, 1952, Ap 3,35:2
Webb, H L, 1876, O 12,4:7
Webb, Harold, 1938, N 7,19:6
Webb, Harold G, 1946, Ja 16,23:2
Webb, Harriet Mrs, 1904, O 17,9:5
Webb, Harrison E, 1951, Ap 19,31:5
Webb, Harry H, 1939, Je 4,48:7
Webb, Helen I Mrs, 1939, O 3,23:3
Webb, Henry, 1940, O 31,23:4
Webb, Henry Walter, 1919, Ja 20,15:4
Webb, Herbert Mrs, 1958, N 21,29:2
Webb, J Alex, 1959, Jl 4,15:4
Webb, J Alfred, 1941, Jl 13,28:8
Webb, J F, 1943, D 30,17:2
Webb, J F Mrs, 1956, O 10,39:4
Webb, J G, 1934, My 6,31:1
Webb, J H, 1938, O 7,23:3
Webb, J M, 1885, Ja 29,4:7
Webb, J T, 1880, My 3,4:7
Webb, J W Gen (funl), 1884, Je 8,3:1
Webb, J Watson, 1960, Mr 5,19:3
Webb, J Watson Mrs (will, D 2,33:4), 1960, N 20, 86:2
Webb, Jack D, 1954, Ja 4,19:2
Webb, James, 1874, D 29,5:1
Webb, James A, 1953, Ag 29,17:5
Webb, James D, 1960, S 16,31:1
Webb, James Henry Judge, 1924, Ap 20,22:2
Webb, James M, 1946, Ja 31,21:2
Webb, James R Mrs, 1946, Mr 21,25:1
Webb, Jervis B, 1952, D 22,25:6
Webb, John B, 1942, Je 19,23:5
Webb, John H, 1909, Je 12,7:3
Webb, John L, 1946, Ag 31,15:5; 1957, Ap 8,23:5
Webb, John O, 1968, F 17,29:4
Webb, Johnny, 1938, Jl 20,19:5
Webb, Joseph F Sr, 1957, Ja 30,29:2
Webb, Josephine W Mrs, 1937, N 13,19:4
Webb, Leonard S, 1946, My 17,22:2
Webb, Louis, 1941, O 1,21:2; 1951, Ag 22,23:1
Webb, Louis H, 1940, N 14,23:5
Webb, Marion E, 1961, Jl 20,27:3
Webb, Martin L, 1964, O 3,29:2
Webb, Mary Ann Mrs, 1874, N 24,5:6
Webb, Mary E Mrs, 1944, Jl 30,36:1
Webb, Mary G, 1938, Ja 6,19:4
Webb, Mary Mrs, 1955, Je 2,29:3
Webb, Maurice, 1956, Je 11,31:2
Webb, Maybelle Mrs, 1960, O 19,45:4
Webb, Melville E, 1961, O 24,37:4
Webb, Melvin C Mrs, 1947, Je 16,21:5
Webb, Montagu, 1938, My 7,15:3
Webb, N Conant, 1964, S 19,27:4
Webb, Nathaniel L, 1956, Ja 13,23:3
Webb, Nellie P Mrs, 1938, D 30,16:1
Webb, Oliver B, 1941, S 25,25:2
Webb, Paul R, 1959, O 4,86:1
Webb, Percy A, 1945, My 5,15:5
Webb, Ralph H, 1945, Je 2,15:2
Webb, Richard R, 1954, O 9,17:3
Webb, Robert A Dr, 1919, My 24,13:3
Webb, Robert H, 1952, N 3,27:3
Webb, Robert L, 1943, O 5,25:5
Webb, Robert L Mrs, 1943, Jl 6,21:2
Webb, Samuel G Mrs, 1952, F 26,27:4
Webb, Sidney Mrs (por), 1943, My 1,15:1
Webb, Sim, 1957, Jl 15,19:4
Webb, Spencer Mrs, 1944, Je 1,19:3
Webb, Spike (Hamilton M), 1963, Jl 4,17:3
Webb, Stuart Weston, 1968, Ag 8,33:2
Webb, Thomas H, 1939, Ap 11,23:5
Webb, Ulysses S (por), 1947, Ag 1,17:3
Webb, Vanderbilt, 1956, Je 18,25:3
Webb, W Carson, 1952, My 16,23:3
Webb, W S Dr, 1926, O 30,17:3
Webb, W S Mrs, 1936, Jl 11,15:3
Webb, W Seward, 1956, Ja 21,21:2
Webb, W T Mrs, 1954, S 30,31:4
Webb, Walter, 1961, My 31,33:1
Webb, Walter F, 1957, Je 20,29:4
Webb, Walter L, 1941, Ja 26,36:3
Webb, Walter P, 1963, Mr 11,9:4
Webb, William E, 1915, Ag 20,11:6
Webb, William H, 1963, Je 4,39:4
Webb, William J, 1943, Ja 13,23:2; 1952, Ag 15,16:5
Webb, William R, 1943, Ap 20,23:5
Webb, William S, 1964, F 17,31:4; 1965, N 11,47:1
Webb, William W Mrs, 1946, D 5,31:3
Webb, Willoughby L, 1937, Ag 12,19:4
Webb, Wilson D, 1947, Ag 8,17:5
Webb, Z S Dr, 1916, Ja 20,9:4
Webb-Johnson, Alfred E Lord, 1958, My 29,27:5
Webbe, Ted, 1967, Ag 17,37:5
Webbe, William Y, 1957, Ja 26,19:4
Webber, Albert W Mrs, 1915, O 30,13:4

Webber, Amherst, 1946, Jl 27,17:6
Webber, Charles, 1954, Jl 29,23:5
Webber, Charles A, 1937, F 11,23:2
Webber, Charles G Mrs, 1951, F 12,23:2
Webber, Florence, 1948, Je 4,23:3
Webber, Frederick R, 1963, D 29,42:5
Webber, Frederick S, 1944, N 19,49:1; 1952, D 2,31:6
Webber, George H Mrs, 1954, D 24,13:3
Webber, George Nelson Rev Dr, 1907, D 21,9:6
Webber, George R, 1941, N 4,23:4
Webber, Harry C, 1955, Ja 8,13:4
Webber, Herbert J, 1946, Ja 20,43:1
Webber, Herman J, 1946, My 29,23:4
Webber, Jacques, 1967, Ap 9,V,1:5
Webber, James B Jr, 1956, Ag 29,29:5
Webber, James Sr, 1960, Je 12,86:8
Webber, John, 1909, Je 16,7:4; 1940, D 6,27:2
Webber, John E, 1948, My 22,15:2
Webber, John F, 1943, N 26,23:1
Webber, John Joshua Nathaniel Capt, 1909, O 10,13:4
Webber, Louis C Gen, 1872, Ja 14,1:6
Webber, Louis P, 1904, F 14,7:6
Webber, Marvelle C, 1938, Ag 11,17:3
Webber, Norman W, 1950, Ap 21,23:2
Webber, Oscar, 1967, My 25,47:1
Webber, Oscar Mrs, 1941, N 18,25:4
Webber, Phineas L, 1952, F 7,27:2
Webber, Phineas Mrs, 1954, Ja 1,23:3
Webber, Richard, 1908, O 10,9:5
Webber, Richard H, 1967, F 23,35:4
Webber, Richard Mrs, 1946, Mr 23,13:2
Webber, Stephen J, 1955, Mr 5,17:3
Webber, Thomas F, 1956, D 25,25:3
Webber, Wentworth A, 1944, Jl 14,13:6
Webber, William V, 1939, S 27,25:1
Webber, Wolfert G, 1954, D 10,27:2
Webbert, Charles, 1939, Ag 3,19:5
Webbon, Ernest, 1943, N 27,13:3
Webel, Richard K Mrs, 1966, S 12,45:4
Webendorfer, John, 1964, Ag 17,25:3
Webendorfer, John F Mrs, 1960, My 11,39:4
Weber, A, 1879, Je 26,5:2
Weber, Abraham S (por), 1946, Ap 30,22:3
Weber, Adam, 1906, D 23,7:6
Weber, Adna F Dr, 1968, F 29,37:5
Weber, Adna F Mrs, 1963, My 31,23:6
Weber, Albert, 1941, D 14,69:1; 1952, N 7,23:5; 1965, Je 24,35:4
Weber, Albert F, 1956, Ap 24,31:1
Weber, Albrecht Prof, 1901, D 2,7:2
Weber, Alfred, 1943, Ja 25,13:4; 1958, My 3,19:3
Weber, Anton, 1915, My 6,13:5; 1941, Ap 6,49:1
Weber, Arthur B, 1938, My 6,21:3
Weber, Arthur W, 1968, S 16,47:2
Weber, Aug C, 1940, Ap 7,44:7
Weber, August, 1907, Jl 3,7:5
Weber, August Jr, 1946, Jl 30,23:3
Weber, Augustus J, 1959, Ja 4,88:3
Weber, Benjamin S, 1949, D 22,23:3
Weber, Bertrand S, 1954, Jl 14,27:2
Weber, Blanchard B, 1943, Jl 16,17:4
Weber, Bonnie, 1953, Je 24,25:3
Weber, Carl A, 1946, My 3,21:4
Weber, Carl J, 1966, D 21,39:1
Weber, Charles, 1940, O 24,25:3; 1956, D 19,31:4
Weber, Charles A, 1947, Ap 9,25:4
Weber, Charles Dr, 1937, Ja 29,19:4
Weber, Charles F, 1951, S 30,73:1
Weber, Charles G, 1949, Ja 19,27:5; 1960, O 2,85:1
Weber, Charles H, 1939, O 20,23:3; 1947, O 2,27:2; 1947, D 19,25:1; 1951, S 11,29:4; 1960, Ag 17,29:6
Weber, Charles H Mrs, 1960, Ag 17,29:6
Weber, Charles J, 1940, Jl 19,19:6; 1949, F 20,61:1
Weber, Charles L, 1944, Ja 4,17:3
Weber, Christian A, 1954, Ja 13,31:4
Weber, David, 1956, Je 30,17:4
Weber, Edward, 1941, My 22,21:5
Weber, Edward A Mrs, 1947, Je 9,21:2
Weber, Edward M Mrs, 1959, N 20,31:3
Weber, Edward W Mrs, 1954, Ag 22,92:1
Weber, Edwin J, 1968, Ag 27,41:1
Weber, Eleanor, 1951, Jl 24,49:5
Weber, Elizabeth L Mrs, 1943, O 24,44:2
Weber, Elliott R, 1950, Jl 4,17:5
Weber, Emma Mrs, 1940, F 23,15:3
Weber, Ernest, 1950, My 14,106:7
Weber, Ernst Mrs, 1951, Jl 9,25:5
Weber, Ferdinand, 1957, D 25,32:2
Weber, Frank A, 1941, N 3,19:4
Weber, Frederic L, 1961, D 28,27:1
Weber, Frederick C, 1937, My 2,II,9:1
Weber, Frederick C Mrs, 1945, Jl 25,23:5
Weber, Frederick J, 1937, Jl 9,21:5
Weber, Frederick T, 1956, Ja 2,21:4
Weber, Frederick W, 1944, Mr 25,15:4
Weber, George, 1964, Ja 16,25:1
Weber, George Adam, 1923, Mr 30,17:5
Weber, George B, 1953, O 16,27:2
Weber, George C, 1949, O 28,23:2
Weber, George G, 1941, N 27,23:3
Weber, George R, 1953, Ja 16,23:1
Weber, George T, 1941, D 28,28:1
Weber, Gerhardt E (por), 1937, N 8,23:6
Weber, Gustave C E Dr, 1912, Mr 22,9:4
Weber, Hans, 1954, Mr 13,15:4
Weber, Harry, 1939, Mr 9,21:2
Weber, Harry L, 1961, Jl 9,77:1
Weber, Harvey H, 1943, Mr 28,24:1
Weber, Helen E, 1938, Ja 14,23:2
Weber, Henry D, 1938, S 23,23:4
Weber, Henry T, 1962, Ja 20,21:6
Weber, Herbert J, 1961, F 20,27:2
Weber, Herbert S, 1950, Je 1,27:3
Weber, Herman A, 1964, D 17,41:4
Weber, Herman C (por), 1939, Jl 26,19:3
Weber, Isaac N, 1943, Je 5,15:2
Weber, Isidore H, 1938, Je 14,21:5
Weber, J B Col, 1926, D 19,II,11:1
Weber, J Henry Mrs, 1951, S 20,31:5
Weber, Jacob (Jake), 1950, N 12,92:1
Weber, Jacob Mrs, 1943, Je 17,21:1
Weber, James J, 1962, Je 7,35:2
Weber, Joe Mrs, 1951, N 12,25:2
Weber, Joe N, 1950, D 13,35:3
Weber, John A, 1947, Mr 8,13:3; 1966, O 27,47:2
Weber, John A Mrs, 1946, My 16,21:1
Weber, John B, 1944, F 6,42:4
Weber, John C, 1938, S 9,21:3
Weber, John J, 1947, S 13,11:1; 1964, Jl 8,35:1
Weber, Johnny, 1957, Ag 7,54:7
Weber, Josef, 1946, Je 7,19:6
Weber, Joseph, 1944, Ap 1,13:2; 1961, Je 18,88:4
Weber, Joseph H, 1962, Jl 11,35:1
Weber, Joseph M (por), 1942, My 11,15:1
Weber, Jules, 1940, My 26,34:4
Weber, Julia, 1903, Ag 21,9:6; 1963, O 26,27:4
Weber, Julius C, 1950, O 24,29:2
Weber, L Lawrence (por), 1940, F 23,15:3
Weber, Leo F, 1952, Ag 10,60:5
Weber, Leo M, 1952, Jl 20,52:2
Weber, Leonard G, 1947, D 3,29:4
Weber, Leonard Prof, 1912, Mr 2,13:4
Weber, Leroy S, 1967, Je 7,47:1
Weber, Lewis F, 1941, Jl 13,29:3
Weber, Lina A, 1949, My 26,29:4
Weber, Lloyd, 1956, Ag 23,27:4
Weber, Lois, 1939, N 14,23:2
Weber, Lothar Mrs, 1957, Ag 3,15:7
Weber, Lou K, 1947, My 21,25:3
Weber, Louis G Mrs, 1951, O 26,23:3
Weber, Mager K, 1961, Ja 16,27:2
Weber, Marie T Mrs, 1947, N 14,23:4
Weber, Matthew Mrs, 1957, Mr 4,27:5
Weber, Max, 1920, Je 17,11:4; 1944, F 10,15:5
Weber, Max (M Cossman), 1960, Ag 21,80:6
Weber, Max, 1961, O 5,37:1
Weber, Max Gen, 1901, Je 16,7:6
Weber, Michael Sr, 1950, Ap 12,27:2
Weber, Morris L, 1942, My 16,13:5
Weber, Neal Mrs, 1963, Ap 9,32:1
Weber, Nicholas, 1951, Ag 4,15:7
Weber, Norton H (por), 1948, Ap 6,23:5
Weber, Oliver A, 1951, D 18,31:2
Weber, Orlando F, 1945, S 7,23:5
Weber, Otto G, 1949, O 30,84:3
Weber, Paul A, 1961, My 3,37:4
Weber, R Dale Jr, 1955, Ap 7,27:4
Weber, Ralph E Mrs, 1957, Mr 30,19:5
Weber, Randall J, 1942, S 7,19:3
Weber, Richard E, 1937, S 1,19:4
Weber, Richard P, 1956, My 11,27:3
Weber, Robert, 1959, S 14,29:6; 1960, Mr 9,33:4
Weber, Robert J, 1949, Ja 7,21:4; 1954, Je 8,27:4
Weber, Rudolf H Mrs, 1939, My 13,15:6
Weber, Russell, 1951, Ap 13,24:2
Weber, Salo N, 1949, Ag 3,23:4
Weber, Sam, 1937, N 7,II,9:4
Weber, Samuel E, 1961, My 30,17:3
Weber, Sarah S S, 1939, Ap 6,25:2
Weber, Solomon Mrs, 1958, Ap 2,31:3
Weber, Walter C, 1962, F 2,29:3
Weber, William A, 1955, F 9,25:2
Weber, William A Mrs, 1946, O 27,63:4
Weber, William A Rev Dr, 1968, Ja 19,47:1
Weber, William C, 1966, N 23,39:2
Weber, William C Mrs, 1963, Ap 27,25:1
Weber, William Edmund Dr, 1914, My 8,13:6
Weber, William F, 1942, Je 30,21:1
Weber, William J, 1962, Ag 8,32:1
Weber, William J Mrs, 1962, Ag 25,19:5
Weber, William L, 1958, Je 21,19:4
Weber, William R, 1954, My 28,23:2; 1958, Ag 4,21:4
Weber, Wolf, 1961, Ja 18,33:2
Weberbauer, Arthur, 1943, Ag 4,17:3
Weberbauer, Augusto, 1948, Ja 18,60:2
Weberman, Abraham, 1951, D 30,24:6
Weberman, Abraham Mrs, 1965, Ap 29,35:2
Weberman, Celia B Mrs, 1939, S 3,19:1
Weberman, Herman, 1959, O 31,23:3
Weberman, Samuel L Mrs, 1959, D 23,27:3
Weberman, Samuel W Mrs, 1963, Jl 28,64:8
Webler, Paul, 1952, My 19,17:5
Weborg, Mary A, 1951, O 22,23:1
Webster, A F, 1877, F 10,5:4
Webster, A Lincoln, 1945, Jl 10,11:6
Webster, Alan de F, 1965, Je 20,72:6
Webster, Albert L Mrs, 1944, F 1,19:3
Webster, Alfred A, 1947, O 13,23:3
Webster, Alice I, 1960, F 24,37:4
Webster, Alvah J, 1954, My 9,88:4
Webster, Arthur E Sr, 1954, D 3,27:2
Webster, Arthur L, 1951, Jl 10,27:4
Webster, Aubrey B, 1943, O 11,19:4
Webster, Barbara, 1946, N 3,63:1
Webster, Benjamin, 1874, Mr 8,5:2; 1882, Jl 10,5:6
Webster, Benjamin (por), 1947, F 27,21:1
Webster, Bernard, 1950, Mr 28,32:2
Webster, Bethuel M Mrs, 1967, Je 30,37:3
Webster, Blakely R, 1946, My 11,27:1
Webster, Byron, 1907, F 1,9:4
Webster, C Percy, 1953, F 13,21:3
Webster, Carl S, 1943, Ap 16,21:2
Webster, Carlos G, 1947, O 31,23:3
Webster, Charles, 1944, S 27,21:6
Webster, Charles A, 1941, N 24,17:1
Webster, Charles Bertram, 1916, Mr 18,11:5
Webster, Charles K, 1961, Ag 23,33:3
Webster, Charles R Mrs, 1942, N 18,26:3
Webster, Chester A, 1957, Mr 22,23:1
Webster, Clarence W, 1966, My 8,82:1
Webster, Clement B, 1954, Ja 11,25:5
Webster, Clifford O Lt, 1922, O 19,21:6
Webster, Clyde C, 1938, Jl 3,12:8
Webster, Cornelius C, 1947, Ja 8,24:3
Webster, Daniel Mrs, 1882, F 28,2:7; 1950, Ja 27,24:3
Webster, Daniel T, 1939, S 24,44:4
Webster, David, 1884, Je 17,5:3
Webster, David F, 1960, My 26,33:1
Webster, David H, 1967, Ag 4,29:1
Webster, David L, 1903, Ap 29,9:6
Webster, Dick (Lord Alverstone), 1915, D 16,15:5
Webster, Douglas, 1958, Ag 21,49:1
Webster, Dudley L, 1947, Jl 24,21:2
Webster, Earl C, 1947, Ja 14,25:6
Webster, Earl P, 1950, Mr 11,15:5
Webster, Edward H Prof, 1937, N 15,23:3
Webster, Edwin S, 1950, My 11,29:1
Webster, Eugene C, 1939, O 13,23:4
Webster, Everett B, 1907, N 30,7:5
Webster, Felix P, 1914, Ag 20,11:6
Webster, Francis E, 1941, S 19,23:4
Webster, Francis Marion, 1916, Ja 4,13:7
Webster, Frank B, 1947, Ap 2,27:2
Webster, Frank D Maj, 1909, N 1,11:4
Webster, Fred B, 1962, Ap 3,39:2
Webster, George B, 1945, Ja 13,11:6; 1948, Mr 1,23:2
Webster, George C, 1954, Ja 19,26:3
Webster, George S Rev Dr, 1937, O 28,25:2
Webster, Gilbert E, 1958, Mr 4,29:5
Webster, H C, 1941, Ag 29,17:4
Webster, H K, 1932, D 10,15:1
Webster, Hamilton F, 1939, S 27,25:1
Webster, Hamilton F Mrs, 1951, My 11,28:2
Webster, Harold M, 1956, N 13,37:4
Webster, Harold T (will, O 4,36:3), 1952, S 23,33:1
Webster, Harrison Edwin, 1906, Je 17,9:6
Webster, Harry, 1950, N 10,27:4
Webster, Harry S, 1948, Mr 30,23:2
Webster, Hedley, 1954, Je 30,27:2
Webster, Hollis, 1943, N 9,21:6
Webster, Horace Prof, 1871, Jl 14,2:5
Webster, Hosea, 1939, Ja 4,21:4
Webster, Howard J, 1942, S 6,31:2
Webster, Hutton, 1955, My 21,15:5
Webster, Hutton Jr, 1956, F 1,31:5
Webster, J A (see also Jl 5), 1877, Jl 12,2:7
Webster, J B Dr, 1916, Ag 11,9:6
Webster, J D, 1876, Mr 13,5:4
Webster, J F, 1939, F 22,21:4
Webster, James, 1948, Ag 30,17:2
Webster, James C, 1948, Ag 11,21:2
Webster, James L, 1937, My 21,22:1; 1955, S 20,31:2
Webster, James Mrs, 1949, Ja 21,22:2
Webster, James R, 1958, Mr 1,17:5
Webster, Jean, 1916, Je 12,11:4
Webster, Jerome P Mrs (por), 1938, O 31,15:5
Webster, Jerome P Mrs, 1965, D 12,87:2
Webster, Jessie T Mrs, 1940, F 13,23:2
Webster, John, 1925, My 14,19:2
Webster, John B, 1955, Jl 2,15:6
Webster, John C, 1950, Mr 17,23:2
Webster, John H Sr, 1951, N 13,29:4
Webster, John S, 1962, Ag 20,23:5
Webster, Joseph Outen Bogart, 1919, Je 1,22:3
Webster, Josiah L (will), 1942, Mr 25,21:1
Webster, Judson H, 1945, Ag 17,17:2
Webster, K Kenly, 1961, Ag 12,17:1
Webster, Kenneth G T, 1942, N 2,21:3
Webster, Leslie T, 1943, Jl 13,21:3
Webster, Lorin Rev Dr, 1923, Jl 14,11:4
Webster, Lorne C, 1941, S 29,17:1
Webster, Margaret B, 1953, O 20,29:2
Webster, Marjorie F, 1963, Je 20,33:3
Webster, Martha Evans Mrs, 1908, D 16,11:5
Webster, Merton W, 1956, Je 1,23:3
Webster, Milton P, 1965, F 26,29:4
Webster, Norman E, 1956, Jl 17,23:2
Webster, Oliver C Mrs, 1942, D 19,19:1
Webster, Ora S, 1962, O 16,39:2

Webster, Ozro C, 1944, F 24,15:3
Webster, Paul A, 1955, Ap 24,86:5
Webster, Paul K, 1957, Jl 1,23:2
Webster, Raymond K, 1946, F 1,24:2
Webster, Richard Dr, 1925, D 21,21:2
Webster, Richard F, 1961, My 23,39:4
Webster, Robert C, 1941, D 4,25:4
Webster, Robert J, 1962, Mr 17,25:5
Webster, Rome M, 1947, N 26,23:5
Webster, Ronald, 1959, Je 24,31:3
Webster, Rose V Mrs, 1938, D 27,17:1
Webster, Roy C, 1943, S 6,17:5
Webster, Royal D, 1949, My 13,23:2
Webster, Rufus P S, 1925, Ap 18,15:5
Webster, Samuel C, 1962, Mr 26,31:1
Webster, Sarah Mrs, 1967, Mr 4,22:3
Webster, Sidney, 1910, My 31,9:5; 1923, F 17,13:4
Webster, Thomas E, 1960, Ap 3,86:7
Webster, Thomas W, 1943, Ag 22,36:6
Webster, W A, 1903, Mr 18,2:4
Webster, W P, 1877, Mr 1,5:6
Webster, W P Mrs, 1937, Ag 24,22:2
Webster, W V, 1883, Je 29,5:3
Webster, Warren, 1938, D 22,21:5
Webster, Wilbur E, 1942, N 5,25:5
Webster, William, 1944, N 11,13:5; 1954, O 22,27:2
Webster, William H, 1950, N 24,35:2; 1951, O 2,27:4
Webster, William J, 1946, D 18,29:3
Webster, William R, 1945, Ap 30,19:4
Webster, Wooster C, 1958, O 6,31:5
Webt, Catharine J Mrs, 1872, Jl 22,8:3
Wechaler, Barbara Mrs, 1906, Ja 30,9:6
Wechesler, Magdalena B, 1967, F 11,29:3
Wechsler, Abraham, 1909, Ap 16,9:1
Wechsler, Benjamin, 1914, Ag 17,7:4
Wechsler, David, 1954, Ap 11,86:3
Wechsler, Edward I, 1947, O 28,25:5
Wechsler, Edward S, 1955, My 6,23:4
Wechsler, Isaac, 1960, Jl 11,29:2
Wechsler, Israel S, 1962, D 7,39:1
Wechsler, Jacob, 1947, Ja 4,15:2
Wechsler, Lawrence A Jr, 1964, Ap 18,29:3
Wechsler, Lawrence Mrs, 1953, Je 25,27:1
Wechsler, Leo, 1953, Mr 28,9:8
Wechsler, Martin, 1942, Jl 20,13:5
Wechsler, Martin Mrs, 1940, Ag 29,19:5
Wechsler, Morris, 1919, F 24,13:3
Wechsler, Phil, 1954, Mr 1,25:3
Wechsler, Phil Mrs, 1957, Ja 17,29:1
Wechsler, Philip, 1960, O 25,35:4
Wechsler, Ralph V, 1938, Je 17,21:6
Wechsler, Richard S, 1966, Ap 26,45:3
Wechsler, Robert M, 1944, F 23,19:4
Wechsler, Sam, 1904, F 6,9:5
Wechsler, Samuel, 1965, N 2,33:4
Wechsler, Samuel Mrs, 1947, Mr 1,15:1
Wecht, Milton M, 1965, Ap 11,92:4
Wecht, Milton M Mrs, 1964, Ag 27,33:3
Wechter, Joseph, 1951, S 12,31:5
Wechter, Pinchos, 1952, Jl 2,25:5
Weck, Albert H, 1957, Mr 17,87:2
Weck, Charles W, 1950, F 18,15:5
Weck, Edward G, 1952, N 13,31:3
Weckbach, George, 1937, Ja 4,29:3
Weckel, A te, 1948, Mr 30,23:4
Weckel, Ada L, 1945, Jl 11,11:7
Weckel, John H, 1941, Jl 1,23:1
Wecker, Charles, 1962, N 26,29:4
Weckesser, Frederick J, 1953, S 30,31:3
Weckley, Ronnie, 1954, Ja 24,84:3
Weckman, Robert L, 1951, N 24,13:2
Weckstein, Abraham M Dr, 1968, F 20,44:1
Weckstein, Harris, 1939, Mr 12,III,7:2
Weckstein, Isidore, 1956, F 23,27:3
Weckstein, Ronia Mrs, 1941, D 3,25:2
Wecter, Dixon, 1950, Je 26,27:3
Wedd, Benjamin C, 1943, D 12,68:2
Wedda, Joseph A, 1947, Jl 31,21:2
Weddell, Fitz-John, 1949, F 18,23:4
Weddell, Reid, 1949, Jl 2,15:1
Weddendorf, Henry C, 1951, N 28,31:2
Wedderburn, Joseph H M, 1948, O 11,23:6
Wedding, Charles C, 1942, Jl 2,21:6
Weddle, Chandos Mrs, 1949, S 30,23:2
Weddle, Charles Mrs, 1966, S 24,23:4
Wedeen, William E Mrs (cor, Jl 23,17:1), 1954, Jl 20,19:2
Wedegartner, Herman C, 1944, D 11,23:2
Wedekind, Frank, 1918, Ap 4,13:4
Wedekind, Gerhard Georg, 1968, My 9,47:4
Wedel, Walter, 1955, S 13,31:2
Wedel-Jarlsberg, Baroness de, 1941, Ag 15,17:2
Wedel-Piesdorf, Wilhelm von, 1915, Jl 13,11:6
Wedell, A L, 1940, N 24,48:3
Wedell, J R, 1934, Je 25,1:2
Wedell, Max, 1948, F 13,21:1
Wedemeyer, Arnold J B, 1963, D 27,23:3
Wedemeyer, Margaret Mrs, 1958, N 21,29:3
Wedemeyer, William A, 1963, My 22,41:5
Weden, David B, 1941, Je 14,17:6
Weden, Howard G, 1947, Ag 30,15:4
Weder, Emily H, 1943, S 11,13:3
Wederkinch, Holger, 1959, D 26,13:5
Wedge, Charles, 1947, O 15,27:3
Wedge, Daniel A, 1947, O 27,21:1
Wedge, George A, 1964, N 4,39:4
Wedge, Will, 1951, S 9,90:4
Wedgewood, Josiah C, 1943, Jl 27,17:1
Wedgwood, Annie Reese Mrs, 1968, Je 22,33:3
Wedgwood, Josiah, 1968, My 7,47:1
Wedgwood, Kennard L, 1950, Ja 21,17:3
Wedgwood, Lawrence, 1913, My 8,11:5
Wedinger, Frederick, 1949, Ag 30,27:2
Wedlake, Edwin C, 1945, D 15,17:3
Wedmore, Charles K, 1946, O 24,27:2
Wedmore, Frederick Sir, 1921, F 27,22:3
Wee, Oscar E, 1941, D 11,27:5
Weed, Adelaide M, 1939, Jl 28,17:3
Weed, Alice B Mrs (will), 1942, F 16,10:3
Weed, Alonzo F, 1958, Jl 9,27:2
Weed, Arthur R Dr, 1937, F 9,23:1
Weed, B Rev, 1879, Je 7,5:4
Weed, Benjamin, 1909, Jl 14,7:5
Weed, Bradley T Mrs, 1947, O 18,15:1
Weed, C, 1936, D 28,17:4
Weed, Charles C, 1959, Ap 21,38:1
Weed, Charles F (por), 1940, Je 1,15:3
Weed, Charley Capt, 1871, Ap 11,1:6
Weed, Clara A, 1950, Je 19,21:5
Weed, Clarence E, 1948, Je 9,29:6
Weed, Clarence M, 1947, Jl 20,45:3
Weed, Edward F Mrs, 1950, F 17,23:2
Weed, Edward G (por), 1945, Ap 25,23:5
Weed, Edward W, 1942, My 26,21:2
Weed, Edwin D, 1947, Je 24,23:2
Weed, Elliott, 1939, My 23,23:4
Weed, Eugene P, 1940, D 7,17:2
Weed, Frank W, 1945, O 1,19:2
Weed, Garner R, 1938, F 19,15:3
Weed, George S, 1920, Ja 20,7:2
Weed, George W, 1917, Ap 9,13:7
Weed, Gretchen Mrs, 1942, Je 30,21:2
Weed, Harold (Tony), 1956, Ag 22,29:5
Weed, Harold D, 1961, N 9,31:6
Weed, Harry S, 1952, Jl 29,21:5
Weed, Helen, 1955, My 19,29:1
Weed, Herman H, 1951, Je 16,15:4
Weed, Jarvis, 1920, Je 29,11:5
Weed, Jefferson, 1963, My 23,37:6
Weed, John Rye, 1904, Jl 28,1:2
Weed, John W, 1915, N 8,13:5
Weed, Joseph Bartholomew, 1903, Jl 6,2:3
Weed, Joseph T, 1946, S 26,25:2
Weed, L S, 1882, Je 15,3:4
Weed, LeRoy J, 1961, Je 10,23:6
Weed, Lewis H, 1952, D 22,25:4
Weed, Louis E, 1966, N 29,43:2
Weed, Margaret B, 1943, D 8,23:2
Weed, Marion, 1947, Je 23,23:5
Weed, Melrose Mrs, 1956, S 7,23:1
Weed, Newell P, 1957, O 31,31:2
Weed, Oliver D, 1939, Je 1,25:1
Weed, Paul C Mrs, 1963, Jl 31,29:4
Weed, Randolph W, 1964, F 3,27:4
Weed, Randolph W Mrs, 1957, Ja 31,27:3
Weed, Raymond H, 1943, Jl 21,15:1
Weed, Richmond, 1950, D 27,27:5
Weed, Robert L, 1961, O 10,43:5
Weed, Robert M Dr, 1904, Ja 28,9:7
Weed, Shelton, 1946, F 2,13:5
Weed, T, 1882, N 23,2:1
Weed, Ver Nooy Wayland Dr, 1920, F 28,11:4
Weed, W H, 1879, Mr 18,5:4
Weed, W Myron, 1961, D 22,24:1
Weed, Walker (funl, Mr 2,13:2), 1918, Mr 1,11:5
Weed, Walter H, 1944, S 8,19:6
Weed, Walter H Mrs, 1958, Ap 26,19:2
Weed, William A Mrs, 1965, F 7,92:4
Weed, William E, 1924, Je 9,17:5
Weed, William F, 1964, F 11,39:1
Weed, William L, 1953, My 1,21:1
Weed, William W Mrs, 1950, Ap 9,85:1
Weed, William X Mrs, 1943, Ag 5,15:4
Weeden, Albert, 1939, Ja 8,42:5
Weeden, Alger E, 1940, N 7,25:5
Weeden, G O, 1933, Ag 12,11:4
Weeden, Howard, 1905, Ap 13,11:5
Weeden, William B Mrs, 1940, O 1,23:6
Weedon, Clarence D, 1942, N 21,11:5
Weedon, Frank W, 1950, Ag 20,76:1
Weedon, George S, 1943, O 30,15:5
Weedon, John F, 1939, Je 6,23:5
Weedon, Leslie Dr, 1937, N 13,19:6
Weedon, Winfield Scott Mrs, 1916, My 29,11:6
Weeghman, Charles H (por), 1938, N 3,23:3
Week, Cora A, 1951, O 25,29:4
Week, Perry P, 1941, Ap 27,38:2
Weeker, Samuel, 1941, My 8,23:4
Weekes, Arthur D, 1952, Jl 22,25:5
Weekes, Arthur D Jr Mrs, 1952, O 25,17:6
Weekes, Clarence R J, 1965, F 16,35:4
Weekes, Francis (por), 1948, F 7,15:4
Weekes, Frederic R, 1959, S 4,21:4
Weekes, H Hobart, 1950, D 15,32:3
Weekes, Harold H, 1950, Jl 26,25:5
Weekes, John A, 1939, My 5,42:6
Weekes, John A Mrs, 1917, N 1,15:3
Weekes, Walter W, 1960, D 16,38:3
Weekes, William A, 1953, Ag 14,19:5
Weeks, Alanson, 1947, N 27,31:1
Weeks, Albert L, 1963, Ag 26,27:2
Weeks, Alfred C, 1945, Ap 13,17:5
Weeks, Alice S Mrs, 1940, D 13,23:1
Weeks, Amanda Mrs, 1914, S 10,9:5
Weeks, Andrew G, 1903, Je 27,9:6
Weeks, Ann Mrs, 1903, N 28,9:5
Weeks, Anna R Mrs, 1941, Ja 30,21:5
Weeks, Arthur Delano, 1925, My 7,19:5
Weeks, Augustus, 1907, My 15,9:4
Weeks, Bartow S, 1922, F 9,17:4
Weeks, Bartow S Mrs, 1917, Ag 1,9:6
Weeks, Carnes Dr, 1968, S 19,47:2
Weeks, Charles A, 1950, N 2,31:1
Weeks, Charles H, 1938, F 24,19:5; 1943, Ag 27,17:5
Weeks, Charles R (por), 1948, Jl 6,23:1
Weeks, Clinton B, 1950, S 22,31:2
Weeks, Clinton M, 1951, Jl 19,23:2
Weeks, Cyrus Dr, 1875, S 22,4:7
Weeks, Daniel W, 1939, N 26,42:6
Weeks, Dewitt C, 1948, Ag 17,21:2
Weeks, Edson J, 1951, Mr 27,29:3
Weeks, Edward A, 1950, Mr 14,25:4
Weeks, Edward A Mrs, 1960, Ja 19,35:3
Weeks, Edward Lord, 1903, N 18,1:4
Weeks, Edward M, 1959, F 23,23:2
Weeks, Edwin C, 1937, Je 6,II,8:8; 1943, Ap 5,19:2
Weeks, Edwin R, 1940, Jl 1,19:4
Weeks, Ella C M Mrs, 1940, Ja 12,17:3
Weeks, Emily Mrs, 1903, Ag 23,7:5
Weeks, Emyrus R, 1947, F 5,23:4
Weeks, Ernest F, 1963, Ap 19,43:3
Weeks, Ernest H, 1942, Ag 22,13:6
Weeks, Eva L Mrs, 1959, N 16,31:2
Weeks, F J, 1879, Mr 8,3:7
Weeks, Florence B Mrs, 1942, Ap 21,23:5
Weeks, Floyd, 1946, O 7,31:4
Weeks, Francis H, 1940, Ag 27,21:3
Weeks, Frank M, 1939, My 21,III,7:3
Weeks, Frederick E (por), 1946, S 28,17:1
Weeks, Frederick E Jr, 1966, N 4,39:4
Weeks, Frederick E Mrs, 1959, F 4,26:2
Weeks, Frederick W (por), 1940, D 26,19:2
Weeks, George F, 1961, Mr 4,23:2
Weeks, George K, 1953, Je 19,21:3
Weeks, George K Mrs, 1955, Ag 26,19:3
Weeks, George W Jr, 1956, My 16,35:1
Weeks, H, 1877, My 30,5:1
Weeks, Harold E, 1960, Jl 1,25:2
Weeks, Harold M, 1962, O 16,39:3
Weeks, Harry F Mrs, 1951, My 15,31:2
Weeks, Harry T, 1952, Je 3,29:4
Weeks, Harvey, 1958, F 15,17:1
Weeks, Henry Clay, 1910, Jl 2,7:6
Weeks, Henry de Forest, 1921, F 24,13:4
Weeks, Herbert A (por), 1941, Je 18,21:5
Weeks, Howard W, 1949, Jl 3,26:8
Weeks, J Borton, 1940, N 15,21:2
Weeks, J R, 1879, S 8,5:2
Weeks, J W, 1926, Jl 13,21:1
Weeks, James H, 1942, Mr 11,19:5
Weeks, James N, 1962, S 29,23:6
Weeks, John E (por), 1949, F 4,23:3
Weeks, John H Mrs, 1947, Je 11,27:2
Weeks, John L, 1951, D 19,31:1
Weeks, John L Lt, 1920, N 7,22:3
Weeks, John R, 1938, F 8,22:2; 1944, Mr 25,15:3
Weeks, Joseph H, 1948, Jl 7,23:2
Weeks, Joseph W, 1953, F 21,13:6
Weeks, Josephine D de M Mrs, 1939, Je 21,23:3
Weeks, Joshua H, 1956, Ja 6,24:6
Weeks, Kenneth E, 1955, D 5,31:3
Weeks, Lawrence B, 1959, D 1,39:4
Weeks, Lewis G Mrs, 1956, My 14,25:4
Weeks, Lysander S, 1903, My 15,9:6
Weeks, Mabel F, 1964, Ag 23,87:1
Weeks, Marion (Mrs Henri Barron), 1968, Ap 22, 47:4
Weeks, Percy, 1948, N 2,25:4
Weeks, Percy S, 1965, F 5,31:3
Weeks, Phil H, 1959, Jl 30,27:4
Weeks, R K, 1876, Ap 14,7:2
Weeks, Ralph E, 1950, S 29,27:3
Weeks, Ralph Mrs, 1940, My 6,17:5
Weeks, Raymond, 1950, O 7,19:1; 1954, F 18,31:3
Weeks, Richard E, 1947, Jl 12,13:3
Weeks, Robert S, 1953, O 14,29:4
Weeks, Ronald M, 1960, Ag 20,19:2
Weeks, Rufus K, 1952, Ag 18,17:5
Weeks, Sinclaid Mrs, 1945, Jl 11,11:8
Weeks, Smith W, 1939, N 14,23:3
Weeks, Stephen H Dr, 1909, S 2,9:5
Weeks, Susan J Mrs, 1904, Ja 5,9:7
Weeks, Theodore, 1937, S 13,21:2
Weeks, Thomas S Rev Dr, 1912, F 16,9:5
Weeks, Victor O, 1948, N 25,32:3
Weeks, W Holden, 1916, My 13,9:5
Weeks, Walter F, 1963, O 23,41:2
Weeks, Warren B P, 1943, O 8,19:4
Weeks, Webb W (por), 1940, Ja 11,23:3

Weeks, William A, 1958, Je 9,23:6
Weeks, William B Mrs, 1945, O 13,15:5
Weeks, William F Mrs, 1945, S 2,32:1
Weeks, William Farrar Rev, 1914, O 24,13:7
Weeks, William H, 1939, Mr 2,21:4
Weeks, William H Rev, 1920, My 29,15:4
Weeks, William Raymond, 1919, O 31,13:6
Weeks, William S, 1956, My 26,17:2
Weeks, Wilson H, 1946, D 12,29:5
Weeks, Wilson H Mrs, 1948, My 26,25:4
Weeman, Gerald, 1937, My 20,21:2
Weems, Arthur C, 1960, Ja 4,29:1
Weems, F Carrington, 1966, Ag 3,37:2
Weems, Ted (Wilfred T), 1963, My 7,43:1
Weeper, William J, 1953, Ap 12,89:1
Weer, John H, 1942, Ja 21,17:2
Weer, Paul W, 1956, O 25,33:5
Weerth, Ernest de, 1967, Mr 31,37:5
Wees, William T Rev, 1937, O 11,21:4
Weese, Arthur H, 1955, Je 11,15:6
Weet, Herbert S, 1953, Ag 31,18:4
Weeter, Harry M, 1951, F 26,23:1
Wefel, Elmer T, 1952, Jl 10,31:2
Wefer, F H, 1936, Ag 7,19:4
Wefers, Bernard J Jr, 1962, Je 24,68:7
Wefers, Bernard J Sr, 1957, Ap 19,21:1
Wefferling, William H, 1962, Ja 13,21:4
Wege, Walter R, 1949, Jl 22,19:4
Wegefarth, Gustavus A, 1907, N 7,9:7
Wegelin, George H, 1965, F 13,49:3
Wegeman, Charles, 1952, Ja 22,29:1
Wegener, Albert B, 1953, S 15,31:2
Wegener, Hugo R F Mrs, 1943, Ja 22,19:3
Wegener, Paul, 1948, S 14,29:2
Wegener, Theodore H, 1958, N 20,35:4
Wegerowicz, Stanislaus Rev, 1922, Ag 4,15:5
Wegge, Camiel, 1941, My 3,15:5
Wegle, John C, 1958, O 28,35:5
Weglein, David E, 1950, O 11,33:2
Weglein, Emma (will), 1937, D 28,17:3
Weglein, Richard, 1941, Ap 30,19:2
Wegman, Charley, 1911, Jl 5,11:4
Wegman, John F, 1950, S 29,27:2
Wegman, Max, 1942, F 5,21:1
Wegmann, Earl F, 1959, O 22,37:5
Wegmann, Ludwig, 1950, Mr 1,27:2
Wegner, Julius, 1961, Je 29,33:1
Wegner, Tine, 1883, D 2,4:4
Wegryn, Joseph, 1953, D 22,31:3
Wegryn, Joseph Mrs, 1944, Mr 18,13:4
Wegrzynek, Maximilian F, 1944, N 9,27:6
Wegscheider, Hildegard, 1953, Ap 6,19:5
Wehbring, Leon J, 1949, D 12,34:3
Wehle, Elizabeth Mrs, 1955, My 15,86:5
Wehle, Frank A, 1944, Je 3,13:4
Wehle, Louis A, 1964, N 22,86:3
Wehle, Louis B, 1959, F 14,21:1
Wehle, Theodore, 1921, Ap 23,11:5
Wehman, Frederick C, 1962, S 12,39:4
Wehman, John H, 1962, Je 19,35:1
Wehman, William T, 1948, F 5,24:2
Wehmann, Herman, 1945, Ap 18,23:4
Wehmer, Harry, 1949, Mr 22,25:5
Wehn, Josephine Mrs, 1939, Jl 20,19:2
Wehn, Louis W, 1942, My 1,19:2
Wehner, Clyde, 1948, My 18,24:2
Wehner, Karl, 1957, Jl 13,17:4
Wehner, Walter, 1951, D 21,27:2
Wehr, C Frederick (Sept 28), 1965, O 11,61:6
Wehr, Nicholas J, 1959, Jl 14,29:4
Wehrbein, Heinrich L, 1951, Ja 10,27:1
Wehrenberg, Fred, 1949, My 8,76:4
Wehrhane, Henry H, 1950, F 16,23:1
Wehrheim, Henry L, 1948, Ag 23,17:4
Wehrie, Celestin S, 1916, Ap 23,19:5
Wehrle, Joseph, 1950, D 5,31:1
Wehrlin, Max, 1956, Je 6,33:5
Wehrman, Harry Mrs (Billie Leigh), 1963, Ag 24, 19:3
Wehrmann, Charles, 1943, Jl 25,30:8
Wehrstein, Joseph S, 1942, Jl 7,19:3
Wehrum, Charles C, 1908, Mr 12,7:6
Wehrwein, George S (por), 1945, Ja 12,15:4
Wehser, William E, 1954, Ap 18,88:4
Wei-fan Chen, 1911, D 30,11:4
Wei Li-huang, 1960, Ja 18,27:3
Wei Tao Ming, Mme, 1959, D 17,37:5
Weiant, Charles A, 1957, F 21,27:2
Weiant, William M Mrs, 1958, My 23,23:4
Weibel, Joseph A, 1963, Jl 23,29:1
Weibel, Mary M Mrs, 1905, Je 18,7:6
Weibly, Israel L, 1951, Mr 8,29:5
Weichec, Leon, 1952, D 14,90:8
Weichel, Alvin F, 1956, N 29,35:3
Weichs, Maximilian von, 1954, S 29,31:4
Weichsel, Herbert S, 1965, Ap 22,33:4
Weick, Carl A, 1948, Mr 9,23:3
Weick, John S, 1941, Ap 20,43:2
Weicker, Herman G, 1955, O 15,15:2
Weicker, Theodore (will, Ag 23,17:8),(por), 1940, Ag 8,19:3
Weicker, Theodore, 1968, Mr 20,47:2
Weicker, Theodore Mrs, 1949, Ag 23,23:3
Weickert, Frederick W Mrs, 1954, Ja 13,31:2
Weickert, Stephen, 1952, Mr 17,21:4
Weidel, Gustaf, 1959, D 12,23:4
Weidely, George, 1948, S 1,48:4
Weidemann, Oscar H, 1940, S 16,19:5
Weidemann, Walter, 1948, S 30,27:3
Weiden, Charles R, 1937, Ag 20,17:2
Weiden, Robert H, 1965, Je 28,29:3
Weidenbaum, Jacob, 1965, Mr 27,27:2
Weidenfeld, Helen T Mrs, 1940, Jl 18,19:5
Weidenfeld, Sidney, 1941, My 28,25:2
Weidenhammer, Philip, 1960, My 2,29:1
Weidenmann, Charles, 1952, My 28,29:3
Weidenmiller, Carl R, 1961, N 18,23:5
Weidenreich, Franz, 1948, Jl 13,28:2
Weidenthal, Henry J, 1940, Jl 10,19:1
Weider, Frederick J, 1948, N 7,88:8
Weider, John Mrs, 1960, N 6,87:4
Weiderowitz, Jacob Rabbi, 1911, My 11,11:5
Weidersheim, Theodore E Gen, 1916, F 11,11:5
Weidhaas, Arthur E Mrs, 1959, Ag 29,17:5
Weidhaas, Gustav A, 1938, Ag 23,17:4
Weidig, W John, 1954, N 11,31:2
Weidler, Eric, 1951, O 16,31:5
Weidler, Harry M, 1945, Ap 29,37:2
Weidlich, Louis, 1950, Jl 23,56:1
Weidling, Charles G, 1946, F 27,25:3
Weidman, Claire O Mrs, 1959, S 26,23:4
Weidman, Frederick D, 1956, S 2,56:6
Weidman, Roy W, 1948, Ja 30,23:3
Weidmann, Frederick W, 1951, D 10,29:4
Weidmann, Jacob, 1911, Jl 5,11:5
Weidmann, John, 1958, Je 22,77:1
Weidner, Annie Mrs, 1957, Ap 23,31:3
Weidner, David C, 1955, My 7,17:6
Weidner, Edward J, 1951, Je 27,29:4
Weidner, Fred L, 1948, My 2,76:4
Weidner, Frederick, 1939, F 11,15:6
Weidner, George H, 1937, Jl 2,21:2
Weidner, George S, 1947, F 10,29:2
Weidner, Walter F, 1959, My 3,87:1
Weidner, William E, 1941, F 3,17:4
Weidowke, William, 1955, O 29,19:4
Weidt, Hugo Mrs, 1950, Ja 2,23:3
Weier, John Edward, 1925, Jl 18,13:5
Weierstall, Edward J, 1956, O 22,33:3
Weigall, A E P B, 1934, Ja 3,20:1
Weigall, Archibald, 1952, Je 4,27:1
Weigand, Aug L, 1941, Ap 29,19:4
Weigand, Chev August, 1904, My 27,9:6
Weigand, Henry, 1942, N 17,25:5
Weigand, John F, 1959, O 27,37:4
Weigand, Louis, 1912, Ja 3,13:4
Weigand, Michael, 1947, Jl 22,23:4
Weiged, Louis A Dr, 1906, Je 1,1:4
Weigel, Alfred P, 1952, O 4,17:4
Weigel, Edgar W, 1963, N 5,31:1
Weigel, Edward M Rev, 1937, Ja 30,17:4
Weigel, Elmer P, 1966, N 10,47:1
Weigel, George A, 1943, Ap 29,21:4
Weigel, Gustave A (trb lr, Ja 14,30:6), 1964, Ja 4,1:6
Weigel, Louis, 1925, O 6,27:5
Weigel, W, 1936, Mr 5,21:1
Weigele, Carl E, 1958, F 11,31:2
Weigelt, F Carl, 1958, F 5,27:1
Weigelt, Kurt, 1968, Ag 6,37:4
Weigert, Hermann, 1955, Ap 13,29:2
Weigert, Louis, 1955, Ap 6,29:4
Weigert, Mabel, 1949, S 18,92:2
Weigert, Oscar Dr, 1968, Ja 14,84:5
Weigester, Robert G Mrs, 1958, Mr 12,31:3
Weightman, Aubrey Mrs, 1908, O 3,9:3
Weightman, Richard Coxe, 1914, F 19,9:5
Weightman, William, 1904, Ag 26,1:4
Weigl, Karl, 1949, Ag 12,17:3
Weigl, Rudolf, 1957, Ag 13,27:4
Weigle, Luther H Mrs, 1964, S 7,19:1
Weigle, Minnie R Mrs, 1946, Ag 20,17:1
Weigner, Walter C, 1948, O 7,29:4
Weigt, John W, 1965, My 8,31:4
Weihenmayer, Frederick C, 1947, Jl 20,44:2
Weiher, Charles L, 1940, N 20,21:3
Weihman, Clifford T Mrs, 1940, Ag 15,19:3
Weihs, Joseph S, 1949, O 27,27:4
Weijne, Josef, 1951, Mr 9,25:2
Weikel, Charles Henry Harrison, 1968, S 15,85:1
Weikert, Constantine (por), 1949, Ja 13,23:4
Weikert, Samuel A, 1938, Ap 14,23:4
Weikmann, Albert M, 1942, Ja 13,19:1
Weil, A G Mrs, 1945, N 16,19:3
Weil, A Leo, 1938, S 18,44:7
Weil, Aaron, 1964, Ja 1,25:3
Weil, Abraham L, 1942, Jl 7,19:3
Weil, Adolph L, 1952, F 26,28:4
Weil, Adolph Sr, 1968, Ja 5,24:6
Weil, Alfred, 1948, N 5,25:2; 1949, My 2,25:5
Weil, Arthur, 1957, My 6,29:3; 1962, My 17,37:4
Weil, Arthur W (por), 1940, Ap 30,21:5
Weil, Benjamin, 1941, S 18,25:2; 1956, D 20,29:5
Weil, Benjamin J, 1963, Jl 10,35:3
Weil, Benjamin Mrs, 1940, Ag 22,19:3
Weil, Bert, 1965, F 4,31:4
Weil, Bruno, 1961, N 13,31:2
Weil, Carl, 1950, O 31,27:4
Weil, Charles, 1939, S 8,23:6
Weil, Charles Mrs, 1907, N 30,7:5
Weil, David L, 1956, Ja 24,32:1
Weil, E, 1932, Mr 5,15:1
Weil, Earl D, 1945, S 28,21:6
Weil, Edwin H, 1949, My 3,25:5
Weil, Elisabeth, 1952, Jl 10,31:4
Weil, Emil, 1954, N 3,29:3
Weil, Felix, 1958, Jl 5,17:6
Weil, Frank P, 1962, S 24,29:4
Weil, Frederick S (cor, N 8,88:2), 1959, N 7,23:3
Weil, G Lloyd, 1948, Ag 19,21:5
Weil, Gustave M, 1953, My 8,25:1
Weil, Harry D, 1955, D 1,35:3
Weil, Harry E, 1940, Ja 9,24:2; 1952, My 14,28:3
Weil, Harry G, 1922, F 16,15:5
Weil, Henri, 1949, Jl 28,23:5
Weil, Henry V, 1943, Ja 18,15:5
Weil, Herbert, 1946, O 3,27:3
Weil, Isaac Mrs, 1952, D 18,29:3
Weil, Isidor, 1944, Ap 12,21:4; 1946, Mr 31,46:5
Weil, J, 1883, D 18,5:2
Weil, Jacob, 1944, N 24,23:2
Weil, Jacob H, 1940, Ap 24,23:3
Weil, Jacob Mrs, 1961, Mr 25,25:3
Weil, James M, 1965, Mr 12,33:3
Weil, Janet K, 1966, Mr 21,33:4
Weil, Jerome L, 1943, N 6,13:1
Weil, Jonas, 1917, Ap 12,11:6
Weil, Joseph, 1903, Ag 31,7:6; 1949, Mr 13,76:8
Weil, Joseph A, 1948, N 14,76:2; 1952, My 16,23:2
Weil, Joseph C, 1956, S 22,17:5
Weil, Jules, 1943, Ag 24,19:1
Weil, Julius, 1956, Je 4,29:4
Weil, Kurt, 1963, D 18,37:8
Weil, L Victor, 1958, F 8,19:3
Weil, L Victor Mrs, 1945, Je 28,19:2
Weil, Leon Mrs, 1949, Ja 27,24:2
Weil, Leonard D Mrs, 1963, Ag 31,17:6
Weil, Leopold (will), 1914, Je 17,11:5
Weil, Lionel, 1948, F 12,23:3
Weil, Louis, 1954, Ap 12,29:4
Weil, Louis A, 1959, D 11,34:1
Weil, Louis Mrs, 1945, S 18,24:2
Weil, Mathilde C Mrs, 1903, Jl 28,7:5
Weil, Maurice, 1945, F 15,19:4
Weil, Milton, 1937, D 31,15:1; 1938, D 25,15:1
Weil, Nathan H, 1938, Mr 30,21:2
Weil, Norman O, 1963, Jl 11,29:2
Weil, Norton, 1958, O 16,37:5
Weil, Norton Mrs (Alice), 1968, Jl 16,39:1
Weil, Rica Mrs, 1942, My 5,21:2
Weil, Richard C, 1961, D 19,33:1
Weil, Richard Jr, 1958, My 12,29:1
Weil, Richard Maj (funl, N 24,13:5), 1917, N 20,13:4
Weil, Robert K, 1960, D 7,43:2
Weil, Robert Mrs, 1956, N 25,89:1; 1959, My 30,17:5
Weil, Sam M, 1943, Ja 24,42:3
Weil, Samuel, 1920, S 17,11:5; 1925, F 16,19:4; 1940, Mr 10,51:4
Weil, Sarah, 1940, Ja 21,34:4
Weil, Saul J, 1957, S 24,35:4
Weil, Sidney, 1966, Ja 15,27:5
Weil, Simon S, 1944, Je 1,19:3
Weil, Sumner S (cor, My 24,31:5), 1965, My 23,85:1
Weil, Sylvan E, 1952, Mr 26,29:4
Weil, V Mason, 1942, D 2,25:1
Weil, Walter, 1956, D 14,29:3
Weil, Walter L, 1964, Jl 27,31:1
Weil, William, 1947, Ap 8,27:2
Weil, William (por), 1955, My 27,23:4
Weil, Winnie S Mrs, 1940, S 15,48:3
Weiland, Arthur J, 1957, Mr 22,23:1
Weiland, Christian Frederick van Leeuwen, 1953, Ja 14,31:2
Weiland, George W, 1957, Ag 4,81:3
Weiland, Henry, 1956, F 19,92:4
Weiland, Jonas, 1951, Ag 23,15:1
Weiland, Michael, 1919, My 14,17:6
Weiland, Stanley M, 1958, Mr 20,29:4
Weilbacher, Frank, 1951, Ap 11,29:2
Weiler, Albert Mrs, 1962, My 5,27:4
Weiler, Alfons E, 1961, Jl 6,29:2
Weiler, Carrie W Mrs, 1955, Ja 30,84:7
Weiler, Emil, 1965, F 18,33:5
Weiler, Fred W, 1951, O 3,36:4
Weiler, Frederick, 1908, F 16,11:5
Weiler, George H, 1967, Ap 12,47:3
Weiler, Henry, 1951, Ja 22,17:2
Weiler, Jacob L W C von, 1942, Ag 29,15:6
Weiler, Josephine (Mother Bernarda), 1940, Je 26, 23:4
Weiler, Matthew A, 1950, O 24,29:2
Weiler, Merrill Jr, 1945, F 27,19:5
Weiler, Royal W, 1948, S 14,30:2
Weilerstein, B Reuben, 1963, My 22,41:5
Weilert, Henry G, 1954, My 1,15:7
Weilheimer, Martin, 1961, D 28,27:1
Weill, Alex J, 1949, S 28,27:5
Weill, Alexandre, 1906, Je 25,7:6
Weill, Alfred S, 1941, D 1,19:2
Weill, Charles, 1953, Ja 1,23:2; 1957, N 13,35:1

Weill, Claire H, 1946, Ag 20,27:2
Weill, Clarence A, 1945, N 8,19:5
Weill, David, 1956, N 16,27:2
Weill, Felix (por), 1948, D 22,23:5
Weill, Jacob, 1950, Je 26,27:3
Weill, Julien, 1950, Ap 26,29:5
Weill, Julius, 1944, O 25,21:6
Weill, Kurt, 1950, Ap 4,29:1
Weill, Max, 1955, Mr 31,27:2
Weill, Max Mrs, 1946, N 18,23:5
Weill, Raymond, 1950, Jl 14,21:1
Weiller, Clarence A, 1958, Mr 8,17:4
Weiller, Edwin A, 1952, Mr 31,19:1
Weiller, Louis M, 1939, Ag 7,15:4
Weiller, Rene, 1942, S 7,19:4
Weiller, Suzanne E, 1941, Ja 22,21:1
Weilman, Marlin H, 1964, Ag 21,29:2
Weiman, Rita, 1954, Je 25,21:5
Weimann, John, 1912, D 28,7:4
Weimar, Edward W Sr, 1944, D 2,13:1
Weimar, Elsie D, 1959, Mr 22,86:8
Weimar, George, 1952, Ja 3,29:2
Weimar, George Martin, 1948, Jl 29,21:6
Weimar, Henry, 1942, Jl 28,17:5
Weimar, Marcus C, 1953, Ag 2,72:6
Weimer, Annie Mrs, 1903, D 26,1:6
Weimer, Claud F, 1955, Jl 22,23:5
Weimer, Frederick C, 1945, S 29,15:5
Weimer, George V, 1948, S 2,23:3
Weimer, Henry L, 1954, Ag 21,17:4
Weimer, Herman H, 1955, Ap 18,23:5
Weimer, Peter L, 1942, Ja 29,19:3
Wein, Alex, 1952, Ja 9,29:2
Wein, David, 1955, O 29,19:1
Wein, Isaac, 1951, Ja 30,25:4
Wein, Isaac Mrs, 1941, S 25,25:7
Wein, Jens D, 1942, O 1,23:3
Wein, Sidney, 1960, N 11,31:3
Weinacht, Rudolph, 1925, N 3,25:6
Weinacker, Herman, 1958, O 13,29:4
Weinar, Louis C Mrs, 1954, Je 10,31:2
Weinbaum, Ralph, 1945, F 24,11:2
Weinberg, Aaron, 1940, N 12,23:2
Weinberg, Aaron O, 1954, My 5,31:2
Weinberg, Akiba Mrs, 1948, N 5,25:4
Weinberg, Arthur M, 1964, Ja 27,23:2
Weinberg, Benjamin, 1965, Ap 7,43:4
Weinberg, Benjamin J, 1949, N 11,25:3
Weinberg, Benjamin M, 1951, Je 20,27:6
Weinberg, C Berenda, 1959, Je 11,33:2
Weinberg, Daniel A, 1949, My 7,13:4
Weinberg, Emil Z, 1962, Je 25,29:1
Weinberg, Frank G, 1952, S 24,33:6
Weinberg, Gus, 1952, Ag 13,21:5
Weinberg, Haim J Mrs, 1967, F 6,29:3
Weinberg, Harry, 1948, Ja 12,19:3; 1964, F 16,93:2
Weinberg, Herman, 1943, Je 14,17:4
Weinberg, Irving J, 1959, Ja 16,27:1
Weinberg, Irving R, 1958, S 3,33:3
Weinberg, Jacob, 1946, O 20,60:7; 1956, N 3,23:7
Weinberg, Jacob H, 1945, S 7,23:4; 1948, N 18,27:3; 1955, Ap 7,27:3
Weinberg, Jacob L, 1946, Je 8,21:2
Weinberg, Joseph, 1950, Ag 5,15:5; 1955, F 14,19:5; 1959, D 29,25:4
Weinberg, Joseph H, 1941, Ja 3,21:3
Weinberg, Julius, 1944, My 9,19:6
Weinberg, Kurt, 1966, S 13,47:2
Weinberg, Kurt Mrs, 1963, N 13,41:5
Weinberg, Leonard D, 1950, My 16,31:4
Weinberg, Louis, 1954, Ag 29,89:2; 1964, N 11,43:2
Weinberg, Maurice G, 1962, Ap 27,35:3
Weinberg, Max, 1947, O 8,25:4; 1956, My 18,25:3
Weinberg, Milton, 1968, Mr 10,92:6
Weinberg, Milton D, 1957, Jl 9,29:1
Weinberg, Morris, 1968, D 22,52:5
Weinberg, Mortimer, 1956, Je 24,77:1
Weinberg, Moses, 1968, F 7,47:4
Weinberg, Nat, 1957, Ag 18,82:1
Weinberg, Nathan, 1954, D 14,33:4
Weinberg, Ruth F, 1958, D 7,88:4
Weinberg, Samuel D, 1943, Ap 17,17:3
Weinberg, Sidney, 1958, Ag 8,19:2
Weinberg, Sidney J Mrs, 1967, F 4,27:2
Weinberg, Simon C, 1917, Ap 5,13:6
Weinberg, Wilhelm, 1957, F 15,23:1
Weinberg, William, 1962, Ap 16,29:5; 1967, D 20,45:4
Weinberger, Aaron V, 1958, Je 4,33:4
Weinberger, Adolf S, 1967, D 14,47:1
Weinberger, Alfred, 1946, Ag 17,13:5
Weinberger, Amelia, 1963, Ap 26,36:5
Weinberger, Bernard W, 1960, My 9,29:5
Weinberger, Carrie B Mrs, 1939, O 11,30:2
Weinberger, Eric M, 1957, Ag 3,15:6
Weinberger, Harry (por), 1944, Mr 6,19:4
Weinberger, Harry H, 1938, Mr 14,15:4
Weinberger, Ignatz, 1945, Ap 9,19:5
Weinberger, Jaromir, 1967, Ag 11,21:4
Weinberger, Joseph J (cor, Jl 24,15:2), 1948, Jl 23, 19:3
Weinberger, Louis I, 1943, Je 26,13:4
Weinberger, Martin, 1965, S 8,47:2
Weinberger, Martin Mrs, 1967, O 21,31:4
Weinberger, Maurice X C, 1961, F 2,29:3
Weinberger, Morris, 1958, Jl 8,27:4
Weinberger, Morris Mrs, 1951, Jl 25,23:4
Weinberger, Moses, 1940, Je 14,21:1
Weinberger, William, 1958, Ag 16,17:5
Weinberger, William D, 1961, O 2,31:4
Weinberger, William Mrs, 1953, Jl 17,17:4
Weinblatt, Charles, 1937, Mr 24,25:2
Weinbrenner, Albert H, 1949, Jl 6,27:2
Weinbrenner, George P, 1949, O 4,27:4
Weiner, Albert B, 1938, N 14,19:5
Weiner, Alfred, 1948, Jl 23,19:4
Weiner, Alphonse, 1912, Jl 25,9:6
Weiner, Annie Mrs, 1938, Ap 13,25:5
Weiner, Arthur R, 1962, O 17,39:5
Weiner, August, 1951, Ja 26,23:1
Weiner, Benjamin, 1944, D 2,13:4
Weiner, Chaim, 1952, Mr 21,24:4
Weiner, Charles, 1948, Ap 11,72:5
Weiner, David, 1952, Je 7,19:3
Weiner, Elias, 1951, Mr 14,33:5
Weiner, Frank S, 1964, Ag 17,25:5
Weiner, Harry, 1947, Mr 3,21:4; 1952, Ja 4,23:1
Weiner, Harry A, 1957, Ap 11,31:1
Weiner, Harry J, 1966, Ja 11,29:1
Weiner, Hyman, 1950, Ag 11,19:3
Weiner, Irving, 1950, N 7,27:4
Weiner, Irving N, 1960, N 26,21:5
Weiner, Jacob, 1941, My 29,19:5
Weiner, Jess J, 1966, Ag 7,81:1
Weiner, John, 1952, My 7,27:4
Weiner, Joseph Mrs, 1950, Jl 20,25:5
Weiner, Lawrence A, 1961, N 17,35:3
Weiner, Leo, 1960, S 15,37:2
Weiner, Louis, 1959, Jl 3,17:5
Weiner, M A, 1965, My 30,51:1
Weiner, Manuel, 1964, N 4,39:3
Weiner, Max, 1944, Mr 11,13:2
Weiner, Max Mrs, 1957, D 10,35:5
Weiner, Meyer, 1965, Ag 1,77:3
Weiner, Meyer Mrs, 1954, Mr 4,25:4; 1956, Mr 12,27:5
Weiner, Morris, 1948, Jl 4,26:7
Weiner, Nathan, 1966, D 3,39:5
Weiner, Robert W, 1946, Je 2,44:4
Weiner, Samuel, 1950, Ja 14,15:7; 1968, D 15,86:1
Weiner, Samuel A Mrs, 1965, Jl 31,21:3
Weiner, Samuel N, 1947, Mr 11,27:3
Weiner, Sigmund E, 1962, Ap 7,25:2
Weinert, Albert, 1947, D 1,22:2
Weinert, George G, 1952, Mr 24,25:4
Weinert, Henry, 1956, My 1,33:1
Weinert, Joseph L, 1965, O 19,43:4
Weinert, Oswald H, 1954, Mr 5,19:3
Weinfeld, Charles Mrs, 1950, N 9,33:3
Weinfeld, Morris Mrs, 1967, O 26,47:1
Weinfurtner, Edward W, 1955, Ap 17,86:2
Weingart, Andrew M, 1952, Ap 11,23:5
Weingart, Irving, 1956, Ap 20,25:4
Weingart, Isaac, 1913, N 9,IV,7:5
Weingart, Jennie Mrs, 1952, Ja 30,25:3
Weingart, John A, 1951, F 11,88:2
Weingart, Robert A, 1963, Ag 10,17:2
Weingart, Samuel Mrs, 1923, Je 14,19:5
Weingart, Samuel Prof, 1914, Ag 15,9:7
Weingarten, Aaron, 1945, Ja 17,21:5
Weingarten, Adolph Mrs, 1965, Je 21,29:4
Weingarten, Charles, 1966, Jl 28,33:3
Weingarten, Edward A, 1963, My 7,43:1
Weingarten, Herman, 1943, My 3,17:3
Weingarten, Joe, 1967, F 27,29:2
Weingarten, Markus, 1944, S 17,42:1
Weingarten, Melville D, 1954, Ja 5,27:1
Weingarten, Milton O, 1953, N 19,31:2
Weingarten, Myron, 1955, N 3,31:5
Weingarten, Oscar L, 1942, Ap 15,21:5
Weingarth, Frank, 1955, N 17,35:4
Weingartner, Felix (por), 1942, My 8,21:1
Weingartner, Felix Mrs (Lucille Marcel), 1921, Je 24,15:6
Weingast, Louis, 1963, Ag 6,31:3
Weingates, Charles A, 1949, N 30,27:4
Weingort, Nahum, 1937, Jl 29,19:3
Weinhardt, Robert A, 1949, S 27,27:3
Weinhart, Howard W Mrs, 1957, D 28,17:2
Weinhausen, Max, 1961, O 25,37:2
Weinheimer, John H, 1945, D 23,18:7
Weinheimer, John J, 1951, D 19,31:1
Weinhouse, Sam Mrs, 1951, S 1,11:2
Weinig, Margaret, 1964, Ag 14,27:5
Weinman, Abraham, 1968, Ag 15,37:3
Weinman, Adolph A (trb lr, Ag 15,14:6), 1952, Ag 10,61:1
Weinman, Isak Mrs, 1948, Ag 29,56:6
Weinman, Isak W, 1951, F 27,27:3
Weinman, Max S, 1965, My 10,33:2
Weinman, Moses, 1912, Ap 14,II,17:2
Weinmann, Isadore, 1957, F 20,33:4
Weinmann, John F Mrs, 1962, Ag 8,31:4
Weinmann, Joseph P, 1960, My 19,37:5
Weinper, Zishe, 1957, Ja 28,23:4
Weinperl, Ignatz, 1950, Ja 24,31:3
Weinrach, Benjamin, 1952, Jl 18,19:2
Weinreich, Bernard, 1954, My 26,29:4
Weinreich, Uriel, 1967, Ap 1,32:3
Weinrich, Arthur J, 1944, N 28,23:4
Weinrich, Ernest F, 1967, S 10,82:6
Weinrich, Herman J Sr, 1946, Ja 22,27:1
Weinrich, Morris F, 1960, O 13,37:3
Weinrich, Rudolph A, 1956, Je 5,35:4
Weinroth, James, 1957, Mr 24,86:1
Weinschel, Oskar, 1949, Mr 1,25:4
Weinschenk, Harvey, 1949, Jl 6,27:3
Weinschenker, Irwin, 1946, Ja 30,25:1
Weinshenker, Pincus, 1955, F 4,21:1
Weinsier, Michael, 1954, Ap 16,21:2
Weinstein, Aaron H, 1949, Ja 6,24:3
Weinstein, Aaron L, 1947, Ap 30,25:5
Weinstein, Abraham J, 1965, D 30,23:4
Weinstein, Albert A Mrs, 1961, Ag 16,31:2
Weinstein, Alex J Mrs, 1958, Ap 9,33:1
Weinstein, Alexander, 1947, F 20,26:2
Weinstein, Allen Mrs, 1964, Ap 25,29:4
Weinstein, Barnet, 1968, S 30,47:1
Weinstein, Bernard (por), 1946, Ap 26,21:5
Weinstein, Bernard Mrs, 1951, Ag 19,84:6
Weinstein, Charles, 1959, Mr 10,35:4
Weinstein, Charles C, 1958, Ja 23,21:4
Weinstein, David, 1946, Ja 11,22:3
Weinstein, Edward, 1947, N 2,73:1
Weinstein, Edward Mrs, 1966, N 16,47:1
Weinstein, Gertrude Mrs (G Frank), 1963, Ag 18, 80:2
Weinstein, Godfrey M, 1967, D 4,47:1
Weinstein, Grace L Mrs, 1962, S 6,31:1
Weinstein, Gregory, 1953, S 23,31:3
Weinstein, H Lou, 1951, S 13,31:3
Weinstein, Henry, 1944, Jl 14,13:5; 1967, O 15,85:3
Weinstein, Herman, 1937, Je 30,23:3
Weinstein, Hyman, 1968, Je 10,45:1
Weinstein, Irving, 1965, D 17,39:1; 1968, Ja 9,32:4
Weinstein, Isaac E, 1964, Ag 29,21:5
Weinstein, Isidor, 1943, My 2,45:2
Weinstein, Isidor (will), 1956, Ap 21,38:6
Weinstein, Isidor, 1959, Ja 18,88:1
Weinstein, Isidore M, 1954, F 14,92:8
Weinstein, Jack, 1952, S 28,78:8
Weinstein, Jacob I, 1957, D 10,35:3
Weinstein, Jerome, 1960, N 23,29:2
Weinstein, Joe, 1963, Je 14,31:1
Weinstein, Joseph, 1947, S 7,60:8; 1966, O 12,43:3
Weinstein, Joseph Dr, 1917, My 16,13:6
Weinstein, Joseph Mrs, 1955, F 4,19:8
Weinstein, Jules, 1954, Jl 28,23:4
Weinstein, Louis, 1966, F 12,27:4
Weinstein, Marcia, 1951, D 4,41:3
Weinstein, Max, 1950, F 1,29:1
Weinstein, Max Mrs, 1958, Ap 13,83:5
Weinstein, Meyer, 1961, Ag 21,23:5
Weinstein, Michael J, 1967, D 4,47:2
Weinstein, Morris, 1925, Je 6,15:6
Weinstein, Morris A, 1962, F 27,34:1
Weinstein, Morris J Mrs, 1955, Ja 20,31:5
Weinstein, Mortimer S, 1964, Jl 30,27:4
Weinstein, Murray, 1958, Jl 1,31:2
Weinstein, Nathan, 1959, Mr 24,39:3
Weinstein, Phil, 1938, Ja 19,23:4
Weinstein, Phil Mrs, 1938, O 10,19:5
Weinstein, Robert M, 1968, My 7,41:6
Weinstein, Samuel, 1939, S 7,25:3
Weinstein, Samuel R, 1923, Ag 7,17:3
Weinstein, Sarah M Mrs, 1948, S 15,31:3
Weinstein, William, 1952, N 25,29:2; 1959, S 5,15:5
Weinstock, Abraham L, 1940, D 26,19:5
Weinstock, Alexander, 1968, S 2,19:1
Weinstock, Bernard, 1958, Je 12,31:1
Weinstock, Cantor U H (por), 1937, D 11,19:2
Weinstock, David, 1952, S 29,23:5
Weinstock, Elias, 1952, Jl 30,23:5
Weinstock, Harold, 1948, My 18,23:2
Weinstock, Harry, 1958, Mr 26,37:2
Weinstock, Harry H, 1960, D 12,29:3
Weinstock, Harry H Mrs, 1957, Ag 6,27:1
Weinstock, Isaac J, 1957, My 1,37:4
Weinstock, Louis, 1953, Mr 20,23:3
Weinstock, Michael B, 1951, Je 29,21:2
Weinstock, Natt, 1951, Jl 23,17:2
Weinstock, Simon, 1946, Ag 27,27:1
Weinthal, Louis S, 1938, Mr 27,II,7:2
Weintraub, Abe, 1953, N 17,31:4
Weintraub, Abraham J, 1968, D 17,50:1
Weintraub, Benjamin Mrs, 1960, My 31,31:4
Weintraub, George R, 1937, N 26,21:3
Weintraub, Harold, 1954, N 9,27:1
Weintraub, Harry H, 1940, My 25,17:4
Weintraub, Joseph H, 1953, N 26,31:5
Weintraub, Louis M, 1960, S 17,23:3
Weintraub, Milton, 1968, N 18,47:4
Weintraub, Rebecca, 1952, Jl 31,23:2
Weintraub, Samuel, 1948, Ag 1,59:3
Weintraub, Sigmund, 1939, O 27,23:5
Weintraub, Sydney, 1956, Mr 25,93:1
Weintrob, Joseph R, 1957, Ja 30,29:1
Weintrob, Morris, 1953, Ap 9,27:1
Weintz, Jacob F, 1962, N 9,35:1
Weintz, Jacob F Mrs, 1968, Je 17,39:2
Weinzweig, Irving, 1955, Ag 31,25:3

Weir, A D Mrs, 1945, O 30,19:4
Weir, Andrew K (Lord Inverforth), 1955, S 18,87:1
Weir, Cecil M, 1960, O 31,31:2
Weir, Cecil T, 1965, Ag 6,27:1
Weir, Daniel J, 1951, Mr 25,72:5
Weir, David, 1955, F 6,89:2
Weir, David A, 1965, Ap 18,80:8
Weir, Dwight A, 1950, F 16,23:1
Weir, Emma Mrs, 1922, My 24,19:5
Weir, Ensley A, 1941, N 5,23:3
Weir, Ernest T (funl plans, Je 28,23:5; funl, Je 29,-17:7), 1957, Je 27,25:1
Weir, Ernest T (est acctg), 1958, F 18,11:6
Weir, Ernst A, 1925, Ag 25,17:4
Weir, Frank H, 1966, S 4,64:8
Weir, Gavin, 1947, O 7,27:4
Weir, George C, 1950, Ja 20,25:2
Weir, George M, 1949, D 6,31:2
Weir, Gulian V, 1953, My 17,89:2
Weir, H C, 1934, Mr 18,35:3
Weir, Harrison W, 1906, Ja 5,11:4
Weir, Harry E, 1947, Ja 16,25:4
Weir, Howard R Rev, 1937, S 2,21:4
Weir, Irene, 1944, Mr 23,19:2
Weir, J F, 1926, Ap 9,19:5
Weir, J Frank Mrs, 1957, N 16,19:2
Weir, James Mrs (Madelyn), 1966, My 8,82:3
Weir, James W, 1954, F 19,27:2
Weir, John, 1907, Ag 12,7:3; 1953, Ja 20,25:2
Weir, John A, 1938, N 18,21:2; 1942, Je 5,17:6
Weir, John C, 1948, N 5,26:2
Weir, John F, 1961, D 25,23:3
Weir, John M (por), 1948, N 23,29:1
Weir, John Marshall, 1907, Mr 9,9:5
Weir, John T, 1867, D 21,1:6
Weir, John W Mrs, 1947, Ap 29,27:4
Weir, Julian Alden (funl, D 11,13:3), 1919, D 9,17:3
Weir, Julian F, 1943, Ag 2,15:3
Weir, Lebert H, 1949, N 15,26:3
Weir, Levi C Col (funl, Mr 31,11:4), 1910, Mr 29,11:3
Weir, MacNeill, 1939, Ag 19,15:6
Weir, Paul, 1952, D 3,33:3
Weir, R F, 1927, Ap 7,25:4
Weir, Robert, 1905, Ja 18,9:3
Weir, Robert A, 1945, Ja 11,23:5
Weir, Rudolph E, 1945, Ja 24,21:2
Weir, Saidee G Mrs, 1950, Ag 29,27:5
Weir, T B, 1876, D 10,1:6
Weir, W B Lt, 1879, O 23,1:5
Weir, Walter Mrs, 1964, Jl 26,56:4
Weir, William D Viscount, 1959, Jl 3,17:2
Weir, William F, 1949, Mr 3,25:3
Weir, William H, 1942, Je 10,21:6
Weir, William M, 1956, Jl 18,27:4
Weirbach, John A, 1948, Ap 20,27:3
Weirich, Charles D, 1941, Ap 7,17:5
Weirman, A H, 1884, Ap 18,1:7
Weis, Albert Col, 1918, My 3,15:4
Weis, Arthur H, 1947, N 12,27:2
Weis, Charles L Jr, 1942, Ap 14,21:4
Weis, Charles W Jr, 1958, Jl 20,65:2
Weis, Clarence, 1918, O 12,13:3
Weis, Ezra H F, 1948, D 31,16:3
Weis, Frank W, 1949, Jl 12,27:2
Weis, Gerald F, 1959, N 5,35:2
Weis, Henry, 1948, My 14,23:2
Weis, Herman K, 1955, Jl 13,25:1
Weis, Herman K Mrs, 1937, S 22,27:5
Weis, J Max, 1968, Ja 4,34:4
Weis, Jacob, 1959, Je 14,86:3
Weis, Jessica M (Mrs Chas W Jr), 1963, My 2,35:1
Weis, John A, 1941, Ag 25,17:6
Weis, John P, 1954, N 15,27:5
Weis, Joseph B, 1948, O 1,26:3
Weis, Joseph H, 1937, Ag 12,19:2
Weis, Minnie, 1948, O 26,31:1
Weis, Viola I, 1952, Mr 7,24:3
Weis, William D, 1954, Ap 20,29:3
Weisbach, Harry, 1946, F 24,44:4
Weisbart, David, 1967, Jl 22,26:2
Weisbart, Morris, 1957, Jl 10,27:5
Weisbaum, Edward J, 1960, Ap 15,23:1
Weisbaum, Samuel, 1966, Ja 16,82:8
Weisbecker, Charles, 1947, F 6,23:2
Weisbecker, Fred F, 1957, S 3,27:4
Weisbecker, Harry A, 1951, N 18,91:1
Weisbecker, Willie, 1955, D 4,88:5
Weisberg, Aaron, 1966, My 19,47:4
Weisberg, Bernard Mrs, 1953, O 25,88:6
Weisberg, Frank H, 1952, D 25,29:4
Weisberg, Frederick H, 1954, Je 5,17:4
Weisberg, Herman, 1954, Jl 1,25:2
Weisberg, Jacob M, 1941, O 10,23:3
Weisberg, Julius, 1948, S 10,23:1
Weisberg, Mandel, 1948, Je 27,52:4
Weisberg, Max Mrs, 1950, Je 20,27:2
Weisberg, Milton (funl), 1958, Ja 20,23:5
Weisberger, Adolph, 1950, Ag 25,21:4
Weisberger, Irving, 1955, F 6,89:1
Weisberger, Martin J, 1957, Ag 7,27:5
Weisberger, Moritz, 1942, F 9,15:2
Weisbrod, August, 1952, Je 17,27:1
Weisbrod, Frederick, 1967, F 17,37:3
Weisbrod, Yetta Mrs, 1943, Je 15,23:3
Weisbrot, Michael Mrs, 1967, D 5,50:2
Weisbrot, Samuel, 1954, S 12,84:8
Weisburd, Israel, 1952, Ap 18,25:4
Weise, Saxton A, 1941, Jl 20,31:2
Weise, William J Mrs, 1955, O 25,33:2
Weisel, Otto K, 1946, N 7,31:4
Weiseman, Albert, 1957, N 22,25:3
Weisenbach, Robert C, 1941, Mr 11,24:2
Weisenberg, Morris, 1965, Ja 19,33:5
Weisenberg, William, 1940, O 2,23:6
Weisenberger, Harry, 1951, D 31,13:4
Weisenburg, Leslie A, 1956, S 1,15:6
Weisenburger, Rex M, 1955, S 16,23:1
Weisenburger, Walter B, 1947, Je 24,23:3
Weisenfeld, Joseph, 1954, Ja 11,25:2
Weiser, Adolph, 1952, O 29,29:5
Weiser, Budd S, 1942, Jl 15,19:4
Weiser, Charles, 1939, S 28,25:2
Weiser, Felix, 1944, Mr 11,13:6
Weiser, Frank E, 1965, Jl 12,27:5
Weiser, Gustave B, 1968, D 9,47:3
Weiser, Harry B, 1950, S 29,27:1
Weiser, Herbert D, 1955, Ap 12,29:2
Weiser, Irving L, 1958, Ag 24,86:4
Weiser, Joseph G, 1949, Ag 23,23:3
Weiser, Ralph, 1954, D 12,V,1:4
Weiser, Samuel, 1958, My 3,19:1
Weiser, Samuel Mrs, 1958, My 3,19:1
Weiser, Walter R Dr, 1937, Ap 14,26:1
Weisfeldt, Max J, 1965, O 13,47:2
Weisgerber, Harry E, 1937, Ag 20,17:3
Weisgerber, Vexil D, 1959, My 30,17:3
Weisglass, Samuel, 1938, My 9,17:6
Weishaar, Aug, 1942, Ja 6,23:4
Weishaar, Christian, 1949, Mr 13,76:6
Weishaar, Wayne M, 1956, S 26,33:3
Weishar, Louis E, 1957, N 17,87:1
Weishaupt, Richard G, 1945, F 11,38:3
Weisheit, Karl Mrs, 1952, N 17,25:5
Weishoff, Samuel, 1956, Ja 13,23:2
Weisinger, Morris, 1949, Mr 21,23:5
Weiskopf, Daniel K, 1948, Mr 24,25:3
Weiskopf, Edward A, 1950, My 9,30:2
Weiskopf, Edwin C, 1968, F 9,27:1
Weiskopf, Emil B Mrs (R Ducker), 1961, Mr 8,33:2
Weiskopf, Samuel Dr, 1968, Je 30,52:7
Weiskopf, Walter H, 1958, F 26,27:1
Weiskotten, Ernest E, 1925, Ap 2,21:4
Weiskotten, Herbert T, 1955, Ja 13,27:2
Weisl, Carl, 1961, S 11,27:5
Weisl, Edwin, 1949, Ja 15,17:3
Weisl, Henry, 1919, Mr 26,15:4
Weisl, Walter M Mrs, 1963, N 26,38:4
Weisler, Herman L, 1964, Mr 19,33:2
Weislogel, Louis F, 1940, Je 25,23:4
Weisman, A Henry, 1962, F 27,33:3
Weisman, Abraham, 1947, Ap 29,27:4
Weisman, Donald, 1961, Jl 19,29:4
Weisman, Henry M, 1948, Mr 17,25:3
Weisman, Herman J, 1961, Mr 24,31:4
Weisman, Lawrence A, 1947, F 16,57:1
Weisman, Max, 1949, N 5,13:3
Weisman, Robert R, 1947, N 8,17:5
Weisman, Russell, 1949, N 9,28:2
Weisman, Samuel G Mrs, 1956, Mr 19,31:4
Weisman, Samuel Mrs, 1945, Mr 17,13:3
Weisman, Sarah Mrs, 1942, Ap 28,21:5
Weismann, A, 1884, Mr 4,5:3
Weismann, Albert, 1960, Ja 28,31:4
Weismann, August Prof, 1914, N 8,9:6
Weismann, H, 1935, Ap 18,23:4
Weismann, Robert, 1942, F 4,19:1
Weismantel, John, 1938, D 12,19:5
Weismantel, Lawrence W, 1950, My 27,17:1
Weismeyer, Charles, 1951, Ja 24,27:5
Weisner, Herman Mrs, 1957, S 23,27:2
Weiss, Abner A, 1963, D 6,35:3
Weiss, Abraham Mrs, 1952, Mr 6,31:4
Weiss, Adele L, 1955, F 11,23:1
Weiss, Adolph, 1959, Je 1,27:3
Weiss, Albert, 1943, Ap 1,23:3; 1947, My 2,21:2
Weiss, Albert C, 1963, Ap 26,35:4
Weiss, Albert C Mrs, 1956, D 13,37:5
Weiss, Albert L, 1959, Ja 21,31:1
Weiss, Albert Mrs, 1946, F 24,43:1
Weiss, Alfred, 1940, N 21,29:5
Weiss, Andrew, 1939, Je 17,15:4
Weiss, Anna Mrs, 1937, Je 14,23:5
Weiss, Anton C, 1938, N 28,15:5
Weiss, Arnold, 1968, O 30,47:4
Weiss, Arthur, 1954, Mr 7,91:2
Weiss, Benjamin, 1947, Ja 2,28:2
Weiss, Benjamin P, 1957, F 21,27:5
Weiss, Benjamin S, 1941, O 29,25:4
Weiss, Bernard, 1942, D 31,15:6; 1965, Mr 14,87:1
Weiss, Carl A Sr, 1949, N 22,29:5
Weiss, Carolyn J, 1965, Mr 13,25:1
Weiss, Charles, 1907, Jl 25,7:5; 1953, S 10,25:2; 1956, F 15,31:2
Weiss, Charles K, 1938, F 10,21:3
Weiss, Charles S, 1950, Mr 27,23:3
Weiss, Cyrus S, 1955, Ja 18,27:2
Weiss, Dan, 1955, S 11,84:4
Weiss, David, 1946, Mr 12,25:1; 1952, Ja 6,92:4
Weiss, E Bernard, 1954, Ja 11,5:5
Weiss, Earle A, 1953, Je 2,29:4
Weiss, Edward, 1960, Ja 15,31:1; 1962, N 19,31:5
Weiss, Ervin J, 1950, Jl 22,15:3
Weiss, Eugene Mrs, 1961, O 1,86:4
Weiss, F Paul, 1966, Ap 1,35:3
Weiss, Fernand C, 1959, My 30,17:3
Weiss, Francis, 1958, Ap 4,21:3
Weiss, Francis Col, 1915, Ap 26,9:5
Weiss, Frank A, 1959, Ap 27,27:3
Weiss, Fred E, 1941, Ag 30,13:7
Weiss, Fred M, 1939, S 28,25:4
Weiss, Fred W, 1945, My 30,19:3
Weiss, Frederick A, 1967, F 19,89:1
Weiss, Frederick B, 1942, O 16,19:5
Weiss, G D, 1903, Ag 25,7:6
Weiss, George, 1952, N 8,17:3
Weiss, George A, 1963, Ap 27,25:4
Weiss, George C, 1939, Je 1,25:1
Weiss, Gus W, 1955, S 8,31:4
Weiss, Harriett J Mrs, 1940, Mr 17,51:4
Weiss, Harry, 1943, Ag 18,19:3; 1952, Mr 6,31:4; 1955, Ap 22,25:3; 1966, Jl 25,27:5
Weiss, Harry B, 1962, My 24,35:4
Weiss, Harry Mrs, 1966, O 6,47:3
Weiss, Henrietta Mrs, 1921, Jl 8,9:4
Weiss, Henry, 1961, O 7,23:2
Weiss, Henry A, 1964, D 5,31:3
Weiss, Heraldo, 1952, S 1,17:3
Weiss, Herbert A, 1948, Mr 17,25:2
Weiss, Howard F, 1940, Jl 9,21:3
Weiss, Hugo L Mrs, 1959, O 22,37:2
Weiss, Ida Mrs, 1942, My 26,21:5
Weiss, Ignatz, 1947, F 7,23:2
Weiss, Isidor, 1958, Ja 7,47:1
Weiss, Isidore E, 1939, Ap 28,25:4
Weiss, J Purdy, 1949, O 19,29:1
Weiss, James M, 1958, Jl 6,56:4
Weiss, Jerome, 1962, My 2,37:4
Weiss, Jerome Mrs, 1966, N 16,38:2
Weiss, John K (trb lr, Ap 17,30:6), 1958, Ap 8,20:1
Weiss, John M, 1963, Je 7,31:1
Weiss, Joseph, 1941, D 26,13:2
Weiss, Joseph (Feb 5), 1963, Ap 1,36:8
Weiss, Joseph Mrs (E W Gruenberg), 1965, Ap 1, 35:4
Weiss, Jules C, 1940, Ja 21,34:7
Weiss, Julius, 1939, Ap 12,24:4; 1954, Ag 31,21:3
Weiss, Julius Mrs, 1965, Ap 24,29:3
Weiss, Leon, 1941, Ja 25,15:4
Weiss, Leon J, 1954, F 18,31:3
Weiss, Leon M, 1939, N 12,48:8
Weiss, Leonard Mrs, 1964, Je 19,31:4
Weiss, Leopold D, 1962, O 7,30:7
Weiss, Leopold Mrs (por), 1940, Ap 29,15:6
Weiss, Louis, 1925, Je 2,23:2; 1939, Je 16,23:6; 1959, Mr 23,31:2
Weiss, Louis S (trb lr, N 21,30:6), 1950, N 15,31:3
Weiss, Martha, 1951, O 4,33:3
Weiss, Martin G, 1954, F 23,27:1
Weiss, Mary A Mrs, 1949, O 18,27:3
Weiss, Maurice, 1957, F 14,27:3
Weiss, Maurice H, 1942, D 14,28:1
Weiss, Max, 1937, N 20,17:1
Weiss, Micajah, 1914, S 26,11:7
Weiss, Michael M, 1956, My 21,25:3
Weiss, Milton, 1954, Ja 11,5:5
Weiss, Milton M, 1961, O 10,43:1
Weiss, Morris, 1939, Jl 22,15:1
Weiss, Morris J, 1960, My 17,37:1
Weiss, Mortimer, 1948, Ag 8,56:6; 1950, Ag 14,17:4
Weiss, Moses, 1943, Ag 9,13:6
Weiss, Moses L Mrs, 1957, N 15,27:2
Weiss, Murray, 1968, D 11,41:1
Weiss, Otto, 1946, O 15,26:3
Weiss, Paul, 1941, Ap 21,19:4
Weiss, Paul Mrs, 1954, Ja 1,23:5
Weiss, Philip J, 1966, N 26,35:2
Weiss, Ray M, 1951, Mr 7,33:2
Weiss, Remigius B, 1941, S 4,21:3
Weiss, Roscoe, 1948, S 13,21:3
Weiss, Rudolph A, 1955, O 19,33:4
Weiss, Sam Z, 1965, Mr 16,39:3
Weiss, Samuel, 1947, Jl 23,23:4; 1950, Ja 4,35:5; 1955 Jl 25,19:2; 1966, Ap 6,43:4
Weiss, Samuel L, 1940, Je 20,23:6
Weiss, Samuel W Mrs, 1938, F 3,23:2
Weiss, Selma, 1960, Ja 19,35:2
Weiss, Solomon, 1960, Jl 5,31:5
Weiss, Soma, 1942, F 1,42:3
Weiss, Stanley, 1966, D 1,47:5
Weiss, Walter S, 1954, O 26,27:3
Weiss, William, 1958, My 11,87:1
Weiss, William E Jr Mrs, 1958, N 23,88:5
Weiss, William F (por), 1939, Ap 18,23:4
Weiss, William Mrs, 1955, Ja 24,23:2
Weiss, William S (trb, S 30,24:7), 1946, S 24,29:5
Weiss, William S Mrs, 1964, O 17,29:6
Weiss, William W, 1947, O 18,15:1
Weissberg, Isadore Mrs, 1958, Ja 17,25:1
Weissberg, Jonas, 1965, O 22,43:2

Weissberg, Leon, 1953, Mr 29,92:1
Weissberg, Morris, 1945, Mr 19,19:5
Weissberg, Morris S, 1951, Je 16,15:6
Weissberg, Phylipp, 1961, Jl 9,77:2
Weissberg, Will, 1966, Jl 16,25:2
Weissberger, Arnold Mrs, 1962, S 6,31:3
Weissberger, Harry, 1958, Ja 18,15:1
Weissberger, Jose A, 1954, N 11,31:4
Weissblatt, Franz, 1961, S 13,45:2
Weisse, Augustus T, 1946, D 10,31:3
Weisse, Faneuil S, 1940, F 26,15:2
Weisse, Fanueil Dunkin, 1915, Je 23,11:6
Weisse, Hans, 1940, F 11,48:2
Weisse, Jack, 1947, D 16,33:4
Weisselberg, Arnold, 1965, Jl 8,28:3
Weissenborn, Albert B, 1938, Je 3,21:2
Weissenborn, Leo J, 1967, Ag 14,31:3
Weisser, Frederick G, 1966, Ap 21,40:1
Weissert, John F, 1958, Je 18,33:5
Weissfield, Hyman M, 1941, D 17,27:6
Weissgatterer, Alfons, 1951, F 1,25:2
Weissglass, Julius, 1946, Ap 2,27:2
Weissinger, Muir, 1952, Ag 3,61:2
Weissleder, Anton, 1950, S 23,17:5
Weissleder, Mary Mrs, 1937, Ja 12,23:4
Weissman, Adolph, 1958, F 20,25:2
Weissman, Bernard Mrs, 1953, Ap 4,18:8
Weissman, Charles, 1961, N 8,35:2
Weissman, Fred S Dr, 1968, Jl 27,27:5
Weissman, Harry, 1957, N 23,19:1
Weissman, Harry Mrs, 1957, N 23,19:1
Weissman, Herman Mrs, 1955, Je 4,15:5
Weissman, Max, 1957, Ag 26,23:4
Weissman, Max S, 1940, My 13,17:6
Weissman, Morris, 1915, S 7,13:6
Weissman, R, 1936, F 25,20:3
Weissman, Samuel, 1958, Jl 27,61:3
Weissman, Samuel A, 1967, Je 22,39:2
Weissman, Samuel Mrs, 1967, Mr 3,35:2
Weissman, Walter J, 1951, Jl 4,35:2
Weissmandl, Michael B, 1957, N 30,21:5
Weissmann, Henry, 1960, Mr 16,37:5
Weissner, Charles H Sr, 1966, Ag 23,39:2
Weist, Dwight W Sr, 1953, My 13,29:2
Weist, Milton W, 1953, Mr 7,15:4
Weiswasser, Abraham H, 1955, Je 9,29:5
Weisz, Jacob J, 1948, Ag 18,25:3
Weisz, Victor (Vicky),(death ruled suicide, Mr 1,2:4), 1966, F 24,37:1
Weiszmiller, Anton, 1954, Mr 21,88:5
Weitekamp, Francis J, 1948, Ja 15,23:3
Weitekamp, Mary F D Mrs, 1941, F 13,19:5
Weitenkampf, Frank, 1962, Ag 24,25:1
Weith, Archie James Jr, 1968, My 2,48:1
Weith, John, 1943, N 29,19:4
Weitschell, F A, 1871, My 23,2:5
Weitz, Abraham, 1967, Ja 25,43:4
Weitz, Charles K, 1937, Ja 12,24:2
Weitz, Emanuel, 1938, Jl 22,17:4
Weitz, George L, 1941, Ja 4,13:5
Weitz, Heinrich, 1962, O 31,37:5
Weitz, Jeremiah, 1945, O 16,23:4
Weitze, Henry, 1951, D 19,31:2
Weitzel, Charles, 1938, My 23,17:4
Weitzel, G Gen, 1884, Mr 20,5:4
Weitzel, Johnny, 1956, S 19,37:3
Weitzel, William F, 1964, N 14,29:2
Weitzell, William S, 1937, Jl 19,16:2
Weitzenkorn, Joseph K, 1938, N 21,19:4
Weitzer, Bernard, 1960, My 2,29:4
Weitzman, E J, 1947, Ja 1,34:2
Weitzman, Francis, 1941, Ap 9,25:5
Weitzman, Joseph, 1952, Mr 25,27:2
Weitzman, Seymour, 1965, S 10,32:5
Weitzner, Emil, 1965, My 27,37:3
Weitzner, Henry M, 1954, My 20,31:3
Weitzner, William, 1955, Jl 8,23:4
Weixelbaum, Moses, 1956, S 5,27:2
Weizmann, Chaim, 1952, N 9,1:7
Weizmann, Chaim Mrs (funl plans, S 26,41:2; funl, S 28,47:2), 1966, S 25,85:1
Weizmann, Moshe, 1957, Je 25,29:4
Weizmann, Rachel Mrs, 1939, Jl 31,13:3
Weizmann, Yehiel, 1957, Jl 5,17:4
Weizsaecker, Ernst von, 1951, Ag 7,25:1
Wekerle, Alexander Dr, 1921, Ag 28,22:5
Wekerle, Frank P, 1953, N 3,31:1
Wekstein, Jacob, 1950, Jl 4,17:7
Weland, John A Rev, 1937, Mr 26,21:3
Welanetz, Ludolph P, 1949, Ap 27,27:6
Welansky, Barnett, 1947, Ja 28,10:4
Welber, Will, 1946, Ap 28,44:2
Welborn, Earle, 1938, O 8,17:4
Welby, Alfred Sir, 1937, My 20,21:5
Welby, Bertha, 1917, F 23,11:6
Welby, Reginald Earle, 1915, O 31,7:4
Welch, Adelaide D Mrs, 1943, O 25,15:4
Welch, Albert E Sr Mrs, 1955, Ja 27,23:1
Welch, Alberta M, 1965, My 3,33:4
Welch, Alden W, 1961, O 31,31:1
Welch, Alex M Mrs, 1951, Ag 1,23:1
Welch, Alexander M, 1943, S 25,15:5
Welch, Arthur D (will, Mr 20,34:3), 1953, F 23,25:5
Welch, Arthur W, 1946, N 18,23:2
Welch, B, 1926, S 3,17:6
Welch, Benjamin, 1863, Ap 15,1:6
Welch, C E, 1926, Ja 7,25:3
Welch, C Stuart Mrs, 1951, Je 3,92:4
Welch, Charles A, 1945, Ja 3,17:5
Welch, Charles E, 1944, Ja 11,19:2
Welch, Charles J, 1959, D 10,39:4
Welch, Charles J Mrs, 1942, Ja 20,19:5
Welch, Charles S, 1942, Ap 27,15:4
Welch, Clarence J, 1951, S 14,25:2
Welch, David A, 1924, N 27,19:3
Welch, Deshler, 1920, Ja 8,17:3
Welch, Donald D, 1957, Mr 3,85:2
Welch, Doug (C Douglas Welch), 1968, My 27,47:4
Welch, E Bostwick, 1950, My 9,29:1
Welch, Earle S Sr, 1948, O 17,76:4
Welch, Eddie, 1952, F 29,23:4
Welch, Edgar T, 1963, Je 27,33:4
Welch, Edward, 1946, D 7,21:4; 1964, Mr 26,35:4
Welch, Edward S, 1944, F 1,19:5; 1948, Je 28,19:3; 1951, S 24,27:4
Welch, Ella Lindsay Mrs, 1908, Ap 2,7:3
Welch, Ernest F, 1949, Je 18,13:3
Welch, F Ambler, 1945, My 26,15:2
Welch, Fanny D Mrs (por), 1947, Ap 25,22:2
Welch, Frances E Mrs, 1948, Mr 25,27:4
Welch, Francis J, 1955, F 12,15:1
Welch, Francis W, 1953, Ja 15,27:6
Welch, Frank, 1941, O 14,23:6; 1957, Jl 27,17:2
Welch, Frank P, 1941, Ag 24,35:2
Welch, Fred S, 1948, D 3,25:3
Welch, Galen, 1941, Jl 27,31:2
Welch, George, 1943, Ja 15,17:5
Welch, George L, 1952, F 12,29:4
Welch, George M, 1955, Mr 17,45:1; 1957, Jl 5,17:4
Welch, George P, 1944, O 2,19:5
Welch, Harold F, 1950, My 9,29:4
Welch, Harry C, 1949, Mr 30,25:6
Welch, Harry V Mrs, 1949, D 7,31:4
Welch, Helen, 1948, D 15,33:3
Welch, Henry K W, 1948, S 25,17:4
Welch, Herbert L, 1960, My 21,23:5
Welch, Herbert Mrs, 1958, S 17,37:2
Welch, Herbert R, 1946, D 24,17:2
Welch, Herbert S, 1953, O 11,89:2
Welch, Huldah Mrs, 1951, Ag 11,11:2
Welch, Jacob G, 1958, Ag 13,27:4
Welch, James, 1917, Ap 12,11:7
Welch, James A, 1960, Ja 22,25:4
Welch, James A Mrs, 1944, Ja 15,13:2
Welch, James B, 1965, N 24,39:5
Welch, James E, 1944, S 5,19:4; 1951, Mr 23,21:5
Welch, James H, 1915, N 23,13:4
Welch, James J (por), 1938, N 10,27:1
Welch, James J, 1945, F 3,11:3
Welch, Jennie B Mrs, 1948, O 1,25:4
Welch, Jeremiah, 1958, N 5,35:2
Welch, Jeremiah Mrs, 1938, O 5,23:2
Welch, Jesse D, 1938, Ja 27,21:5
Welch, Joe (funl, Jl 18,9:6), 1918, Jl 16,13:5
Welch, John, 1951, Mr 19,27:5
Welch, John C, 1941, O 17,23:2
Welch, John Carrington, 1922, D 12,19:4
Welch, John D, 1948, Je 30,25:1
Welch, John E, 1956, Mr 28,31:5
Welch, John F, 1962, F 26,27:3
Welch, Johnny V, 1940, S 4,23:1
Welch, Joseph N (private funl planned, O 8,23:5), 1960, O 7,1:6
Welch, Joseph N Mrs, 1956, D 22,19:5
Welch, Joseph P, 1948, N 17,27:4
Welch, Joseph T Sr, 1939, Jl 24,13:6
Welch, Julia Mrs, 1939, N 12,49:3
Welch, Leo R, 1968, D 21,37:4
Welch, Lew, 1952, Je 24,29:5
Welch, Lewis A, 1940, Mr 30,15:2
Welch, Mabel R, 1959, Ja 3,17:4
Welch, Madeline M, 1958, Ap 6,88:4
Welch, Martin Mrs, 1950, F 15,27:2
Welch, Mary (Mrs D White), 1958, Je 2,27:3
Welch, Mary S W Mrs, 1940, Ag 29,19:4
Welch, Matthew W, 1965, Je 13,84:5
Welch, Michael, 1941, Jl 31,17:4
Welch, Nathaniel V, 1944, Mr 8,19:5
Welch, Ninian H, 1939, Ap 22,17:2
Welch, Norman A, 1964, S 4,27:1
Welch, Otis Z, 1948, F 13,21:1
Welch, Paul R, 1952, N 23,88:2
Welch, Paul S, 1959, O 3,19:6
Welch, Peter A, 1907, Ag 23,7:5
Welch, Phil P, 1952, Ja 4,40:4
Welch, Philip H Mrs, 1904, Jl 13,7:7
Welch, Pierce N, 1909, O 28,9:4
Welch, R A, 1952, D 28,49:1
Welch, R W, 1933, N 29,19:3
Welch, Richard A Jr, 1941, Ja 19,41:1
Welch, Richard J (por), 1949, S 11,92:2
Welch, Robert A (will), 1953, Ja 1,40:4
Welch, Robert E, 1951, Mr 24,13:2
Welch, Robert Mrs (por), 1943, Ap 12,24:2
Welch, Robert O, 1959, D 22,31:6
Welch, Robert W Mrs, 1944, D 22,17:3
Welch, Robert William, 1924, O 26,7:1
Welch, Ross, 1953, Ag 13,25:1
Welch, Roy D, 1951, Ja 9,29:4
Welch, Roy M, 1951, N 18,90:4
Welch, S W, 1928, Ag 23,21:5
Welch, Samuel M Gen, 1919, N 24,15:3
Welch, Sherman E, 1945, Jl 31,19:1
Welch, Stephen A, 1949, S 9,25:4
Welch, Stephen E, 1938, D 20,26:2
Welch, Stuart C, 1959, O 22,37:5
Welch, Stuart C Mrs, 1952, Mr 29,15:2
Welch, T, 1878, S 14,2:7
Welch, Thomas F, 1942, Ag 8,11:4
Welch, Thomas P, 1946, D 3,31:3
Welch, Thomas R, 1947, Mr 11,27:3
Welch, Thomas Vincent, 1903, O 21,9:6
Welch, V, 1878, Mr 22,2:2
Welch, Vincent S, 1951, Ag 4,15:5
Welch, W H, 1934, My 1,23:4
Welch, Walter J, 1954, Jl 16,21:2
Welch, Walter P, 1953, D 19,15:2
Welch, William, 1911, O 9,11:4
Welch, William A (por), 1941, My 5,17:1
Welch, William D, 1945, D 17,21:2
Welch, William F, 1949, D 4,108:7
Welch, William Jr, 1961, Je 24,21:3
Welch, William M, 1921, F 9,9:4
Welch, William S, 1952, Mr 9,93:2
Welch, William T, 1961, Mr 13,29:3
Welch, William W, 1960, Jl 29,25:5
Welch, William Walton, 1925, Jl 5,3:4
Welcher, Thomas W, 1953, Je 27,15:5
Welcke, Adelheid T Mrs, 1941, Ap 17,23:5
Welcke, William A R, 1945, Jl 14,11:6
Welcome, Carl E W, 1951, O 26,23:2
Welcome, Ernest H, 1952, Ag 8,17:5
Weld, A Winsor, 1956, O 8,27:3
Weld, Alfred W, 1957, S 9,25:5
Weld, Arthur (funl, O 15,13:6), 1914, O 12,9:4
Weld, Bernard C, 1940, Ag 22,19:4
Weld, Christopher Minot, 1918, Ag 28,7:2
Weld, DeWitt C Brig-Gen, 1937, S 12,II,7:1
Weld, Edward M Mrs, 1959, Mr 22,86:7
Weld, Eloise M, 1908, Ja 7,7:6
Weld, Francis M, 1949, N 2,12:1
Weld, J Linzee, 1956, F 20,23:3
Weld, James Gould, 1904, F 25,9:5
Weld, James W, 1943, F 17,21:4
Weld, Lathrop M, 1947, Je 7,13:3
Weld, Louis D H, 1946, Jl 8,29:1
Weld, Philip B, 1964, My 15,35:2
Weld, Stephen Minot Gen, 1920, Mr 17,11:4
Weld, William E, 1964, Ja 24,24:3
Weld, William E Mrs, 1954, S 14,27:1
Welday, William W Mrs, 1949, Ag 24,26:3
Welde, Charles, 1907, Ap 7,9:5
Welden, Henry F Mrs, 1947, Ag 17,54:3
Welderen, A J Van, 1947, F 26,25:3
Weldgen, Nicholas J, 1947, Ja 6,23:4
Weldin, Winifred, 1954, Ja 4,19:4
Welding, James T, 1942, Mr 11,19:4
Weldon, Edwin B, 1945, Ag 13,19:4
Weldon, Edwin C, 1950, N 7,27:3
Weldon, Elizabeth (E Martin), 1941, Ag 23,13:2
Weldon, Frank E, 1961, O 25,37:1; 1964, O 13,43:4
Weldon, James J, 1915, Ja 23,11:6
Weldon, John L Sr, 1957, Je 13,31:4
Weldon, Lawrence Judge, 1905, Ap 11,11:6
Weldon, Martin, 1966, N 2,30:1
Weldon, Mary D Mrs, 1956, Ap 18,31:5
Weldon, Oscar J, 1961, Ag 13,88:3
Weldon, Richard Chapman, 1925, N 28,15:4
Weldon, Richard E, 1947, Ag 23,13:7
Weldon, Robert F Jr, 1961, Ag 25,25:3
Weldon, Thomas H, 1942, Jl 1,25:7
Weldon, Thomas W, 1950, N 12,92:3
Weldon, Timothy J, 1945, Jl 17,13:3
Weldon, Urban Mrs, 1948, Jl 7,46:8
Weldon, W R H, 1947, Ap 17,27:1
Weldon, Willard, 1945, F 25,37:2
Weldon, William A Mrs, 1955, S 5,11:4
Weldon, William H, 1955, D 23,18:2
Weldon, William J, 1964, N 25,37:4
Weldy, Bernard B, 1947, Mr 25,26:2
Weldy, Jacob E Mrs, 1946, Ap 13,17:5
Welfare, Fulton, 1952, Jl 5,15:2
Welfle, Frederick E, 1956, Ag 18,17:3
Welford, Charles, 1885, My 20,5:4
Welge, Charles H Mrs, 1952, Jl 19,15:6
Welham, John C, 1952, Je 10,27:4
Welhaven, Sven, 1955, Je 14,29:5
Welinsky, Jacob Mrs, 1946, F 26,25:3
Welk, Don, 1949, O 30,66:5
Welker, Frederick R, 1937, Ag 29,II,7:4
Welker, George E, 1942, Ag 25,23:5
Welker, Herman (funl, N 2,21:5), 1957, O 31,31:1
Welker, Oscar B, 1940, S 22,48:1
Welker, P A, 1926, D 25,13:5
Welker, Roy A, 1950, My 18,29:5
Welker, William H, 1956, Jl 8,64:3; 1964, Ag 8,19:6
Well, Jean, 1915, Ap 20,15:4
Wellar, Arthur B, 1949, F 16,25:5
Wellbaum, George B, 1965, Ja 17,89:1

Wellbery, Edward M, 1953, O 13,29:4
Wellborn, Charles, 1945, Mr 24,17:3
Wellbrock, Walter B, 1943, F 4,23:2
Wellcome, H S, 1936, Jl 26,II,7:1
Welldon, James Bp (por), 1937, Je 19,17:4
Welldon, Samuel A, 1962, Ap 14,25:4
Welle, Francis F, 1959, D 11,34:5
Welle, George M Jr, 1956, Ja 15,92:1
Welleck, Ernest, 1941, Ap 20,44:1
Wellemeyer, Elmer H, 1963, My 28,28:4
Wellemeyer, Elmer H Mrs, 1957, Ap 7,89:1
Welleminsky, Ignaz M, 1942, Jl 18,13:4
Wellenbrink, Herman H, 1953, Jl 8,27:3
Wellenbusher, August, 1944, Jl 18,19:4
Wellens, Adrien S, 1940, Ap 22,18:2
Weller, A N Judge, 1901, S 19,7:5
Weller, Albert H, 1958, Ag 20,27:1
Weller, Arthur, 1961, F 24,21:4
Weller, Arthur A, 1962, My 16,41:2
Weller, Carl V, 1956, D 11,39:4
Weller, Carrie, 1954, Je 7,23:4
Weller, Cedric, 1939, F 28,19:3
Weller, Charles, 1939, F 27,15:5; 1957, S 20,25:2
Weller, Charles B, 1953, D 22,31:2
Weller, Charles C, 1961, Ag 7,23:5
Weller, Charles F, 1957, My 18,19:4
Weller, Daniel, 1962, N 27,38:1
Weller, David, 1946, My 27,23:1
Weller, Emory J, 1948, Ap 6,23:3
Weller, Frank I, 1951, Ap 21,17:6
Weller, Fred W Col, 1937, D 3,23:5
Weller, George J, 1954, Mr 25,29:2
Weller, Harold R, 1949, O 23,86:3
Weller, Harry C, 1944, Ag 29,17:5
Weller, Hayden, 1954, Je 14,21:2
Weller, Henry J, 1964, Je 2,37:3
Weller, Hubert R, 1943, O 11,19:3
Weller, John F, 1939, Jl 13,19:2
Weller, John H, 1948, N 20,13:5; 1952, S 30,31:5
Weller, Joseph W, 1955, F 10,31:4
Weller, Lester R Sr, 1945, Ja 30,19:1
Weller, Margareta Sister, 1954, N 7,87:5
Weller, Matilda Mrs, 1953, Ja 20,25:2
Weller, Ovington E (por), 1947, Ja 7,27:1
Weller, R H, 1929, Mr 2,17:3
Weller, Samuel M, 1957, S 23,27:4
Weller, Walter F, 1924, Je 26,23:5
Weller, William C Mrs, 1953, D 30,24:3
Weller, William H, 1945, Mr 18,42:1
Weller, William J (por), 1948, My 21,23:2
Weller, William J Mrs, 1939, My 23,23:4
Weller, William W, 1945, N 13,21:1
Wellerson, Monroe, 1954, Ag 21,17:6
Welles, Anna F T Mrs, 1937, My 13,25:5
Welles, Benjamin S, 1904, Mr 13,7:5
Welles, C S, 1927, F 7,19:5
Welles, Charles E Mrs, 1949, Ja 19,27:1
Welles, E R, 1928, D 16,II,8:1
Welles, Edgar T, 1914, Ag 23,13:5
Welles, Edward M Jr, 1950, Ja 3,25:6
Welles, Edward P, 1946, Ag 26,23:1
Welles, Frank M, 1942, My 2,13:5
Welles, Frank Mrs, 1944, N 6,19:5
Welles, Georgia, 1906, Mr 31,9:5
Welles, Gideon (see also F 12), 1878, F 15,5:2
Welles, Harriet K, 1959, Mr 2,27:5
Welles, Harry L, 1952, F 28,27:5
Welles, Henry H, 1963, Je 25,33:4
Welles, Henry H Jr, 1943, Ja 8,19:5
Welles, Henry H Jr Mrs, 1942, D 1,25:4
Welles, James B Mrs, 1940, My 31,19:5
Welles, Kenneth B, 1953, Ag 23,88:5
Welles, Lemuel A, 1953, F 17,27:4
Welles, Lucinda A Tenney Mrs, 1904, F 4,9:6
Welles, Mary S, 1960, Mr 26,21:4
Welles, Merrill C, 1954, Jl 17,13:2
Welles, R, 1932, Ap 27,17:3
Welles, Roger Mrs, 1947, Jl 10,21:5
Welles, Samuel E Mrs, 1950, D 20,32:2
Welles, Samuel G, 1940, D 12,27:1
Welles, Sarah, 1878, Ja 6,7:2
Welles, Sumner (trb, S 26,5:3; mem ser, S 30,25:6), 1961, S 25,1:6
Welles, Sumner Mrs, 1949, Ag 9,25:1
Welles, Theodore L Jr, 1953, Ag 11,27:1
Welles, Thomas, 1947, S 2,21:2
Wellesley, Arthur C, 1941, D 12,26:2
Wellesley, Arthur R (Duke of Wellington), 1884, Ag 14,5:3
Wellesley, Charles, 1946, Jl 25,21:3
Wellesley, Charles Mrs, 1944, Ap 25,23:4
Wellesley, Edward C, 1943, D 29,18:3
Wellesley, G V, 1882, S 19,2:3
Wellesley, Henry Arthur Mornington (Lord Cowley), 1919, Ja 16,13:3
Wellever, David S, 1922, My 20,15:6
Wellhofer, William G, 1944, Je 1,19:4
Welli, Raphall, 1920, D 11,13:4
Welling, Charles Hunt Mrs, 1908, D 4,11:4
Welling, George B, 1950, Ja 1,42:4
Welling, Gertrude L Mrs, 1941, Je 27,17:4
Welling, John Calvin, 1906, N 10,1:1
Welling, Leonard C, 1950, Mr 1,27:2
Welling, Lindsay H Mrs, 1957, Je 21,28:8
Welling, Richard W G (trb, D 30,18:6),(por), 1946, D 18,29:1
Welling, Samuel G Mrs, 1916, My 16,13:5
Welling, William C, 1946, Ag 20,27:2
Welling, William Randolph, 1925, My 14,19:2
Wellinger, Carl L, 1949, O 12,30:3
Wellinghausen, Edward G, 1958, Ja 19,86:4
Wellinghoff, Thomas F, 1949, N 22,29:5
Wellings, Augustus J, 1956, N 30,23:5
Wellington, Amy, 1948, Mr 7,68:3
Wellington, Arthur J, 1942, Ap 4,13:6
Wellington, Arthur W, 1938, Ap 13,25:4
Wellington, Barrett R, 1941, Ja 15,23:5
Wellington, Benjamin W, 1946, S 8,44:3
Wellington, C H, 1942, Ap 2,21:7
Wellington, C Oliver, 1959, F 7,19:1
Wellington, Clarence G (funl plans, Ja 25,27:4), 1960, Ja 21,31:1
Wellington, Cornie O, 1943, O 30,15:3
Wellington, Duke of (Arth R Wellesley), 1884, Ag 14,5:3
Wellington, Duke of, 1934, Je 18,17:4
Wellington, Edmund S, 1943, D 30,17:1
Wellington, Elizabeth R, 1940, Mr 22,19:4
Wellington, G L, 1927, Mr 21,19:4
Wellington, George, 1904, Ja 12,7:5
Wellington, George B Mrs, 1940, S 5,23:3
Wellington, Herbert, 1937, F 17,22:2
Wellington, Herbert G, 1965, Jl 25,68:6
Wellington, Jack, 1958, Mr 13,29:5
Wellington, James H, 1944, D 12,23:1
Wellington, James Lloyd Dr, 1916, F 12,11:5
Wellington, Sarah Etz, 1952, Jl 20,52:5
Wellington, Stanwood Mrs, 1953, My 29,25:3
Wellington, Walter J, 1940, N 30,17:3
Wellington, Walter L, 1914, Jl 16,9:6
Welliver, Anna K Mrs, 1940, N 19,23:4
Welliver, Judson C, 1943, Ap 15,25:3
Wellman, A Minor, 1937, O 22,24:2
Wellman, Allen Gouverneur, 1968, My 6,47:2
Wellman, Arthur H, 1948, Ag 25,25:1
Wellman, Charles H, 1905, Je 23,2:2
Wellman, Elias, 1950, My 4,27:1
Wellman, Elmer G, 1953, Mr 20,23:4
Wellman, Emily A, 1946, Mr 20,23:5
Wellman, Emma A J J Mrs (por), 1939, Mr 7,21:5
Wellman, Francis L (por), 1942, Je 8,15:3
Wellman, Frank A, 1950, F 19,78:1
Wellman, Frederick C, 1960, S 5,15:5
Wellman, Gordon B, 1942, Mr 31,21:5
Wellman, Guy, 1941, Jl 27,31:3
Wellman, H Homer Mrs, 1903, Je 16,7:6
Wellman, Harry R, 1956, D 20,29:3
Wellman, Harvey E Dr, 1937, O 22,19:4
Wellman, Henry C, 1951, My 5,17:5
Wellman, Hiller C, 1956, F 4,19:6
Wellman, Howard C, 1954, O 17,87:2
Wellman, James A, 1944, N 4,15:3
Wellman, John H, 1952, O 8,31:2
Wellman, Katherine F, 1955, N 20,60:5
Wellman, Lynn E, 1959, O 3,19:6
Wellman, Margaret, 1956, Ag 19,92:4
Wellman, Paul I, 1966, S 18,84:2
Wellman, Phil M, 1957, F 3,77:2
Wellman, Prescott H, 1951, Ja 8,17:3
Wellman, Robert L Mrs, 1949, O 11,31:5
Wellman, Roderic, 1948, My 9,70:2
Wellman, Roderic Mrs, 1941, D 4,25:3
Wellman, Ruth, 1939, O 26,23:5
Wellman, Victor E, 1964, F 2,88:6
Wellman, W, 1934, F 1,19:1
Wellmann, James M, 1942, Je 27,13:6
Wellmona, Jose, 1872, S 16,2:5
Wellner, Emil, 1963, N 28,39:4
Wellner, Louis R, 1938, F 6,II,9:2
Wells, Agnes E, 1959, Jl 8,29:2
Wells, Alan B, 1952, Je 22,68:8
Wells, Albert B, 1953, Mr 11,29:3
Wells, Albert B Mrs, 1949, Ap 2,15:6
Wells, Albert C S, 1950, N 15,31:1
Wells, Albert P, 1903, D 13,7:5
Wells, Alden, 1954, Ja 15,19:1
Wells, Alex T, 1954, Ap 10,15:6
Wells, Alfred S, 1946, Je 5,23:1
Wells, Almond Brown Brig-Gen, 1912, S 8,II,13:4
Wells, Amelia E, 1937, F 24,23:2
Wells, Anna Maria Mrs, 1868, D 25,7:4
Wells, Arthur, 1950, N 30,33:5
Wells, Arthur C, 1938, My 7,15:1
Wells, Arthur E, 1922, Ap 16,28:3; 1939, My 26,23:6
Wells, Belle P Mrs, 1939, D 9,15:4
Wells, Benjamin B Mrs, 1940, My 6,17:5
Wells, Benjamin Warner Com, 1917, Je 14,11:5
Wells, Bradford, 1941, O 7,23:5
Wells, Briant H, 1949, Je 11,18:4; 1949, Je 18,13:4
Wells, Brooks Hughes Dr, 1917, Jl 7,9:5
Wells, C E, 1942, Mr 17,22:3
Wells, C Raymond, 1966, D 10,37:3
Wells, Calvin, 1909, Ag 3,7:5
Wells, Carlton, 1952, Je 12,33:2
Wells, Caroline C Mrs, 1939, Je 25,37:2
Wells, Caroline T, 1939, My 2,24:3
Wells, Carolyn (por), 1942, Mr 27,23:1
Wells, Carveth, 1957, F 17,92:1
Wells, Channing M, 1959, F 2,25:3
Wells, Channing M Jr, 1949, Je 10,27:2
Wells, Charles B, 1924, O 15,23:4
Wells, Charles Dr, 1917, O 26,15:4
Wells, Charles E, 1940, Ag 6,19:5
Wells, Charles J, 1954, O 24,88:5
Wells, Charles L, 1924, Je 1,8:1; 1938, Ap 19,21:2
Wells, Charles Mrs, 1955, Mr 19,15:2
Wells, Charles P, 1937, Je 5,17:5
Wells, Christina H Mrs, 1945, Je 26,19:2
Wells, Clarence, 1953, Ap 12,80:3
Wells, Clarence D, 1964, Ja 10,43:2
Wells, Clement C, 1948, N 15,25:4
Wells, Clifford H, 1952, Mr 18,27:1
Wells, Clifton K Sr, 1948, Jl 2,21:5
Wells, Cornelius L Rev, 1904, D 13,9:2
Wells, D A, 1898, N 6,6:1
Wells, D L, 1884, N 25,2:6
Wells, Daniel R, 1948, D 31,15:3
Wells, David T, 1942, O 10,15:6
Wells, David T Mrs, 1954, Ag 2,17:4
Wells, Donald B, 1953, D 23,25:2
Wells, Dora, 1948, Ap 7,25:2
Wells, Dorothy, 1946, N 30,15:4
Wells, Eben F, 1915, D 20,11:4
Wells, Edgar H, 1938, Jl 3,13:4
Wells, Edward A, 1941, D 23,21:6; 1942, Jl 9,21:2
Wells, Edward D, 1962, S 25,37:2
Wells, Edward L (will, F 5,16:4), 1941, Ja 10,19:4
Wells, Edward W, 1947, F 1,15:4
Wells, Edwin B, 1943, O 5,25:2
Wells, Edwin L, 1952, N 10,25:3
Wells, Emmeline B Mrs, 1921, Ap 27,17:5
Wells, Ernest H, 1939, S 5,23:6
Wells, Eugene L, 1966, Ja 28,47:2
Wells, Frances Estelle Mrs, 1916, Ja 11,11:5
Wells, Francis, 1961, Je 11,86:3
Wells, Francis C, 1941, F 1,17:2
Wells, Francis Marion, 1903, Jl 23,7:6
Wells, Frank A, 1938, My 24,19:4
Wells, Frank C Mrs, 1948, My 16,68:4
Wells, Frank H, 1953, Jl 1,29:2; 1959, Mr 27,24:8
Wells, Frank M, 1944, My 1,15:6
Wells, Franklin, 1903, Jl 4,7:6
Wells, Franklin C Mrs, 1955, Ag 9,25:5
Wells, Fred, 1956, N 27,38:1
Wells, Fred M, 1956, S 3,13:6
Wells, Frederic L, 1964, Je 6,23:2
Wells, Frederick, 1915, S 5,11:6
Wells, Frederick B, 1953, Ag 5,23:3
Wells, Frederick Mrs, 1960, S 4,68:6
Wells, Fullerton, 1959, O 18,87:1
Wells, Gabriel (por), 1946, N 7,31:1
Wells, George A, 1941, Ja 16,23:2
Wells, George A Mrs, 1945, Ag 14,21:3
Wells, George A Sr Mrs, 1949, Ap 27,27:3
Wells, George B, 1967, Ag 22,39:1
Wells, George E T, 1947, S 27,15:5
Wells, George F, 1940, F 13,23:5
Wells, George H, 1957, Jl 15,19:5
Wells, George M, 1957, My 4,21:3
Wells, George M Mrs, 1960, Ap 9,23:6
Wells, George P, 1938, D 1,23:2
Wells, George Washington, 1912, O 1,13:6
Wells, George Y, 1963, Jl 25,25:1
Wells, Gordon, 1964, Jl 24,27:1
Wells, Grace H, 1953, Jl 26,69:3
Wells, Graham C, 1953, F 8,88:1
Wells, Guiford Wiley Col, 1909, Mr 23,9:5
Wells, Guy E, 1941, F 11,23:3
Wells, Guy Mrs, 1954, Ag 29,88:5
Wells, Guy W, 1948, Je 16,29:1
Wells, H, 1878, D 11,5:4
Wells, H (funl), 1879, Ja 3,8:3
Wells, H Cady, 1954, N 6,17:2
Wells, H Edward, 1947, My 26,22:2
Wells, H G, 1885, Ap 5,9:3; 1946, Ag 14,1:6
Wells, H Gideon, 1943, Ap 27,24:2
Wells, H M, 1878, Ap 23,5:4
Wells, H M Dr, 1905, Ja 13,9:4
Wells, H T, 1903, Je 17,9:4
Wells, Hannah, 1954, Je 29,27:3
Wells, Harold B Sr, 1961, Jl 30,68:1
Wells, Harold M, 1967, D 11,47:2
Wells, Harold M Mrs, 1967, Ag 8,39:4
Wells, Harold S, 1937, Mr 14,II,8:5
Wells, Harry, 1917, Ag 7,9:5; 1949, D 30,19:2
Wells, Harry L, 1953, Ag 21,17:2
Wells, Heber M, 1938, Mr 13,II,9:3
Wells, Henry C Mrs, 1943, S 17,21:2
Wells, Henry M, 1957, D 2,27:6
Wells, Herman S, 1942, N 17,25:4
Wells, Hermon J, 1950, D 18,31:2
Wells, Heustis I, 1964, Mr 18,41:4
Wells, Holliday, 1925, Ag 15,11:6
Wells, Horace L, 1924, D 20,15:5
Wells, Howard, 1951, N 21,25:1
Wells, Howard (Babe), 1955, S 11,84:8
Wells, Isabelle Mrs, 1941, Mr 29,15:4
Wells, J Donoven, 1964, D 27.64:2
Wells, J Godfrey (por), 1949, S 4,40:7

Wells, J L, 1928, S 6,25:4
Wells, J Walter Mrs, 1937, O 19,26:1
Wells, Jackson B, 1940, Ap 16,23:1
Wells, James, 1961, F 19,86:7
Wells, James F, 1957, F 8,23:2
Wells, James H, 1873, Ja 10,8:3
Wells, James L Jr, 1941, F 21,19:2
Wells, Jere A, 1947, Ag 8,17:6
Wells, Joel C, 1960, Ja 7,29:3
Wells, Joel C Mrs, 1955, F 19,15:6
Wells, John (funl, N 27,8:2), 1875, N 24,5:2
Wells, John, 1925, Jl 12,7:4; 1939, Ag 13,29:2
Wells, John A, 1941, Ag 27,19:3
Wells, John A Mrs, 1943, Ap 6,21:2
Wells, John B, 1950, F 13,21:2
Wells, John C, 1946, My 25,15:2
Wells, John D Rev, 1903, N 1,8:2
Wells, John E (will, Jl 7,14:4), 1943, Je 24,21:3
Wells, John H, 1962, Ja 29,25:2
Wells, John L, 1953, Je 1,23:5
Wells, John L Capt, 1907, O 15,9:4
Wells, Joseph A, 1956, Ag 2,25:4
Wells, Josephine L Mrs, 1942, Ag 15,11:5
Wells, Joshua R, 1908, Ja 28,9:5
Wells, Judd S, 1946, Ag 14,25:1
Wells, Julian L, 1917, O 27,17:5
Wells, Karl S, 1953, N 18,31:2
Wells, Kate Gannett, 1911, D 14,13:5
Wells, Katherine A Mrs, 1942, N 16,20:3
Wells, Kenneth R, 1958, Je 9,23:5
Wells, King William, 1916, Ag 24,9:2
Wells, L Nathaniel D, 1963, S 12,37:4
Wells, L Stewart, 1939, D 23,15:2
Wells, L W, 1884, D 19,8:2
Wells, Lansing S, 1954, Ag 10,19:1
Wells, Laura P J Mrs, 1938, Je 22,23:2
Wells, Laurence, 1911, Je 1,11:5
Wells, Lee, 1941, F 26,22:2
Wells, Lemuel E, 1908, Mr 20,7:5
Wells, LeRoy S, 1963, My 2,13:1
Wells, Levi Maj, 1912, S 18,11:4
Wells, Lewis P, 1959, N 23,31:3
Wells, Lizzie R, 1939, O 19,23:4
Wells, Loren S, 1957, O 7,27:5
Wells, Louis H, 1938, Ag 4,17:3
Wells, Mackey, 1946, Mr 23,13:3
Wells, Margaret E, 1952, Ag 27,27:1
Wells, Maria L, 1883, F 8,5:1
Wells, Mary (Mrs Staples) (see also Jl 17), 1878, Jl 20,5:2
Wells, Mary A, 1951, Ag 2,21:4; 1960, F 5,27:1
Wells, Mary B, 1946, D 7,21:2
Wells, Mary E (Oct 7), 1965, O 11,61:6
Wells, Melville B, 1956, D 2,86:3
Wells, Norman F, 1939, F 16,21:3
Wells, Oliver J, 1925, Mr 26,23:5
Wells, Orange E, 1949, Jl 31,60:3
Wells, Orlando W, 1956, Ja 20,23:3
Wells, Orson C (will, D 29,13:3), 1939, D 11,23:2
Wells, Oscar, 1953, My 31,73:2
Wells, Oscar M, 1947, Jl 19,13:5
Wells, Oscar M Mrs, 1944, Ja 18,19:3
Wells, Percy L, 1964, Ap 5,87:1
Wells, Rainey T, 1958, Je 18,33:5
Wells, Ralph C, 1955, Jl 6,28:1
Wells, Ralph C Mrs, 1952, N 14,24:5
Wells, Ralph G, 1958, Ap 30,33:2
Wells, Ralph O, 1946, D 18,29:2
Wells, Rex W, 1954, My 11,29:1
Wells, Richard H (por), 1947, Ja 7,27:5
Wells, Richard H, 1947, Ja 22,23:2
Wells, Richard J, 1863, Mr 22,6:1
Wells, Robert A, 1962, F 24,27:5
Wells, Robert C, 1952, Jl 30,24:6
Wells, Robert F, 1962, Ja 23,33:4
Wells, Robert H, 1966, Mr 23,47:4
Wells, Roe Mrs, 1941, S 6,16:5
Wells, Roger C, 1944, Ap 21,19:4
Wells, Rolla W, 1944, D 1,23:4
Wells, Rulon S, 1941, My 8,23:6
Wells, Russell D, 1937, Ap 9,21:4
Wells, Samuel, 1903, O 4,7:6
Wells, Stanley P, 1944, S 11,17:4
Wells, Stephen W, 1948, My 22,15:5
Wells, Stuart W Jr, 1967, D 18,47:1
Wells, T Tileston (por), 1946, Ap 24,25:1
Wells, T Tileston Mrs, 1956, Je 22,23:5
Wells, Thomas B (por), 1944, S 29,21:1
Wells, Thomas B Mrs, 1961, F 10,27:4
Wells, Thomas Miller, 1908, Mr 11,7:5
Wells, Travis D, 1939, Jl 2,15:4
Wells, Travis De S, 1960, Ag 23,30:1
Wells, W A (Archie), 1950, F 24,23:1
Wells, W B, 1930, Mr 12,29:3
Wells, W H, 1885, Ja 23,5:2
Wells, Walter F, 1958, S 2,25:2
Wells, Walter H, 1959, O 29,33:1
Wells, Walter H Mrs (J Dixon), 1960, O 23,88:7
Wells, Walter M, 1957, My 6,29:2
Wells, Walter P Mrs, 1953, S 12,17:6
Wells, Warrington W, 1951, S 8,17:2
Wells, Wayne B, 1941, My 16,23:2
Wells, Wellington, 1954, Ap 24,17:7
Wells, Will N, 1950, D 21,29:5
Wells, Willard, 1947, D 6,15:4
Wells, Willard Mrs, 1948, D 26,52:6
Wells, William, 1949, Mr 21,23:5
Wells, William B, 1942, Mr 8,IX,4:8
Wells, William C, 1938, Je 11,15:6
Wells, William H, 1958, F 9,88:8
Wells, William J (por), 1940, Mr 23,13:1
Wells, William K (Billy), 1956, Ap 18,31:3
Wells, William Lowndes Dr, 1917, Ag 19,15:2
Wells, William W, 1953, F 4,27:5
Wells, Willis, 1949, My 7,13:3
Wells-Cole, J H, 1952, S 23,33:2
Wellsted, T C Mrs, 1950, Ap 13,29:4
Wellwood, Arthur R, 1947, Mr 7,25:1
Wellwood, Frances L, 1951, N 3,17:5
Wellwood, Robert M, 1954, Ap 3,15:2
Weloff, Max, 1938, S 29,25:2
Welp, George L, 1951, N 30,23:2
Wels, Isidor, 1963, S 7,19:1
Wels, Otto, 1939, S 18,19:5
Welsch, James M, 1965, F 20,25:4
Welsch, Roy J, 1945, Ja 31,21:1
Welsford, Cyril, 1953, Ap 14,27:2
Welsford, Harry M, 1957, Ap 18,29:4
Welsh, Alfred W, 1914, Jl 5,5:6
Welsh, Alice R Mrs, 1939, My 12,21:4
Welsh, Alma S Mrs, 1939, F 10,23:5
Welsh, Andrew A, 1944, Ja 26,19:3
Welsh, Charles S, 1947, F 19,25:3
Welsh, Charles W (por), 1949, N 14,27:5
Welsh, Devitt, 1942, Jl 12,36:4
Welsh, Edwards, 1883, N 9,8:3
Welsh, Elizabeth, 1951, N 8,29:3
Welsh, Emilie B, 1938, Mr 20,II,8:6
Welsh, Emory H, 1956, Jl 25,29:2
Welsh, F, 1927, Jl 29,9:1
Welsh, Francis J, 1940, N 17,50:7
Welsh, Francis R, 1938, Ap 6,23:4
Welsh, Francis X, 1951, Mr 14,33:2
Welsh, Frederick H, 1949, Jl 9,13:3
Welsh, George, 1943, Ja 30,15:5; 1944, D 18,19:4
Welsh, George A, 1956, N 28,35:3
Welsh, George W, 1946, N 28,27:3
Welsh, George W Mrs, 1952, My 10,21:2
Welsh, Guard C Sr, 1954, Jl 8,23:2
Welsh, Harold W, 1954, Ag 24,21:3
Welsh, Harriet de B K Mrs, 1941, F 17,15:1
Welsh, Harry L, 1949, N 8,31:5
Welsh, Henry E, 1944, Je 3,13:4
Welsh, Henry J, 1956, S 9,84:5
Welsh, Herbert, 1941, Je 30,17:4
Welsh, Herbert S, 1950, N 6,27:2
Welsh, Hubert H, 1954, Ja 16,15:2
Welsh, Isaac, 1875, N 30,5:2
Welsh, J Gilbert, 1953, Ja 21,31:2
Welsh, J Miller, 1949, My 31,23:2
Welsh, James, 1880, D 1,3:7; 1922, O 2,17:6
Welsh, James J, 1957, Ja 1,23:2; 1966, N 29,32:3
Welsh, James P, 1950, O 18,33:4
Welsh, James W, 1949, Ag 25,23:3
Welsh, Jay C, 1943, N 5,19:2
Welsh, John D, 1947, S 12,21:5
Welsh, John J, 1942, Ap 7,21:3
Welsh, John Lowber, 1904, Ag 23,7:6
Welsh, John P, 1941, Ja 10,19:3
Welsh, Joseph H, 1954, Ag 31,21:3
Welsh, Joseph Mrs, 1921, Jl 15,11:5
Welsh, Leo, 1950, Ap 13,29:3
Welsh, Lillian, 1938, F 25,17:6
Welsh, Margaret Mrs, 1909, Mr 1,9:2
Welsh, Martin S, 1961, Je 24,21:5
Welsh, Mary E, 1937, O 16,19:5
Welsh, Mary M, 1950, O 30,27:5
Welsh, Morgan E, 1950, F 22,29:1
Welsh, Oliver W, 1959, O 1,35:3
Welsh, Orville A, 1939, Mr 18,17:2
Welsh, R K, 1942, Ag 4,19:3
Welsh, Rebecca, 1959, N 2,31:3
Welsh, Regis M, 1963, My 18,27:5
Welsh, Richard, 1951, Je 12,29:2
Welsh, Richard H, 1963, Ap 15,29:3
Welsh, Robert G (funl, Jl 30,13:5), 1924, Jl 25,13:5
Welsh, Robert G, 1924, Jl 28,11:4
Welsh, Samuel, 1907, Ag 11,7:6
Welsh, St Clair D, 1951, Ap 21,17:2
Welsh, Thomas Brig-Gen, 1863, Ag 23,6:4
Welsh, Thomas P Mrs, 1947, D 24,22:2
Welsh, Thomas W, 1939, Mr 17,21:4
Welsh, Ulysses S G, 1954, My 1,15:1
Welsh, W, 1878, F 12,1:6
Welsh, William, 1907, Mr 1,9:6
Welsh, William G, 1964, Ja 11,23:5
Welsh, William H, 1951, Jl 22,61:1; 1960, Jl 15,23:5
Welsh, William Henry, 1903, D 5,9:4
Welsh, William J Jr, 1939, Ja 24,19:3
Welsh, William L, 1962, Ja 3,33:2
Welsh, William M, 1960, Jl 31,69:2
Welsh, William W, 1940, D 29,24:5
Welsher, John, 1910, Ag 16,7:6
Welshimer, Helen, 1954, D 23,19:2
Welsker, Charles F, 1919, S 8,13:2
Welskotten, S G Rev, 1924, Je 19,21:4
Welsman, Frank S, 1952, Jl 5,15:5
Welstead, Edward J Rev, 1918, D 30,9:5
Welstead, Richard J, 1946, Je 15,21:4
Welt, Deborah L, 1957, O 31,31:3
Welt, Isidor Mrs, 1937, Ap 21,23:4
Welt, M Albert, 1953, F 25,27:2
Welt, Sara, 1943, D 28,18:3
Welt, Sigmund, 1954, S 2,21:5
Weltchek, Abraham, 1948, F 20,28:2
Weltchek, Lawrence L, 1967, N 3,48:4
Weltchek, Morris, 1939, My 3,23:2
Weltewitse, William, 1903, S 5,14:2
Welti, Andrew E, 1939, Jl 29,15:3
Weltman, Edward, 1948, Ja 14,25:5
Weltman, George, 1956, Ap 14,17:3
Welton, Alton R, 1958, N 11,29:3
Welton, Arch J, 1942, O 27,25:2
Welton, Arthur D, 1940, O 30,23:3
Welton, Ralph P, 1955, D 1,35:4
Welton, Robert Bradice Dr, 1913, Ja 10,11:4
Welton, Spencer, 1948, Ag 9,19:2
Welton, Thurston S, 1961, Mr 16,37:3
Welty, Alice E, 1949, Jl 26,27:3
Welty, George M, 1918, O 14,11:7
Welty, George Washington Dr, 1915, D 3,11:6
Welty, Harry T Mrs, 1958, Ja 1,25:3
Weltzien, Julius C, 1954, My 17,23:4
Weltzin, Christian F, 1938, N 28,15:3
Welwood, J Foster, 1953, O 13,29:1
Welwood, John C, 1940, S 15,48:8
Welwood, Robert, 1939, Jl 26,19:5
Welz, Ida Mrs (will), 1940, Ag 23,12:5
Wemett, Arthur, 1947, Je 2,25:2
Wemett, Harrison E, 1962, Mr 30,33:5
Wemmer, William H, 1949, F 23,27:4
Wemple, Alonzo E, 1904, Mr 18,1:6
Wemple, Caroline J Mrs, 1942, Jl 6,15:4
Wemple, Ernest, 1947, O 3,25:3
Wemple, Flint L, 1945, Jl 16,11:7
Wemple, Holland R, 1959, D 29,26:1
Wemple, John P, 1945, D 26,19:2
Wemple, Leland E, 1947, Ja 4,15:6
Wemple, Raymond V, 1957, Jl 17,27:2
Wemyss, Colville, 1959, Ap 5,86:5
Wemyss, Earl of, 1937, Jl 13,19:2
Wemyss, James Mrs, 1952, Je 14,15:6
Wemyss, James S, 1946, Ap 13,17:4
Wemyss, Lord, 1914, Jl 1,11:5
Wemyss, Robert H, 1919, Ag 19,13:4
Wen, Ying H Lt-Gen, 1968, Je 2,89:2
Wen Siang, 1876, Jl 19,4:7
Wenaman, James W, 1943, F 9,23:3
Wenban, Sion W, 1951, D 9,90:6
Wenberg, B J, 1885, Je 15,5:5
Wenberg, L C, 1885, Je 15,5:5
Wenchel, John P, 1962, Mr 27,38:1
Wenck, Fred A, 1946, Jl 27,17:2
Wenckebach, Karel F, 1940, N 15,21:2
Wenckeback, Carla, 1902, D 30,2:2
Wend, Charles F, 1950, Je 4,92:2
Wendbridge, Eleanor R, 1944, F 21,15:1
Wendehack, Clifford C, 1948, My 16,68:8
Wendel, Albert, 1960, Ja 23,21:2
Wendel, Charles L, 1947, Je 30,19:3
Wendel, Daniel C, 1965, N 4,41:4
Wendel, E, 1931, Mr 15,1:5
Wendel, F Williams Mrs, 1943, Jl 27,17:4
Wendel, Francois de, 1949, Ja 13,24:2
Wendel, G von, 1929, F 24,II,1:7
Wendel, Guy de, 1955, Ap 8,21:3
Wendel, Hugo C M, 1949, Ja 17,19:5
Wendel, Humbert de, 1954, N 15,27:2
Wendel, Josef Cardinal (funl, Ja 6,27:2), 1961, Ja 1, 48:4
Wendel, Louis, 1947, S 7,60:7
Wendel, Louis Capt, 1914, Ap 6,9:6
Wendel, Louis Mrs (will, F 28,25:1), 1945, F 13,23:3
Wendel, Maurice de, 1961, Mr 21,37:3
Wendel, Rudolf P, 1955, My 2,28:4
Wendelbo, Per, 1937, F 27,17:3
Wendelken, John H, 1959, D 14,31:1
Wendell, Arthur R, 1952, Je 1,84:6
Wendell, B Rush, 1937, Je 1,23:5
Wendell, Barrett, 1921, F 9,9:3
Wendell, Charles K, 1956, O 14,86:7
Wendell, Cornelius, 1870, O 11,2:4
Wendell, Edith G Mrs (will, O 12,29:2), 1938, O 4, 25:5
Wendell, Edward N, 1967, S 26,47:4
Wendell, Evert Jansen, 1917, Ag 29,9:5
Wendell, Evert Jansen (funl, O 2,15:6), 1917, O 28, 21:2
Wendell, Frederick Clow, 1912, D 11,13:4
Wendell, G B, 1881, S 26,5:6
Wendell, George, 1915, Je 20,15:6
Wendell, George B, 1939, Jl 3,13:6
Wendell, George B Mrs, 1943, Ap 22,23:4
Wendell, George K, 1938, S 30,21:5
Wendell, George S, 1943, Mr 15,13:3
Wendell, George Vincent (funl, Mr 18,13:4), 1922, Mr 16,17:5
Wendell, Gordon, 1910, F 2,9:4
Wendell, Jacob Jr, 1911, Ap 23,11:1

Wendell, Jacob Mrs, 1912, D 21,13:4
Wendell, James, 1958, N 23,89:2
Wendell, James Augustus, 1922, My 11,17:3
Wendell, Jessie, 1957, D 20,24:2
Wendell, Lorenz A, 1957, F 23,17:4
Wendell, Sarah S Mrs, 1937, D 5,II,8:6
Wendell, Ten Eyck Mrs, 1944, My 10,19:2
Wendell, William G, 1967, D 27,37:1
Wender, Harold H, 1965, D 19,84:8
Wender, Louis, 1966, F 9,36:1
Wender, Max, 1956, Ag 6,23:5
Wenderoth, Oscar, 1938, Ap 16,13:6
Wendle, William D, 1949, S 7,30:7
Wendler, John, 1952, D 15,25:2
Wendler, John H, 1945, F 2,19:2
Wendling, Charles C, 1942, N 8,51:4
Wendling, George R, 1960, F 20,23:2
Wendling, George Reuben, 1915, S 15,9:4
Wendling, Irving A E, 1961, Ja 14,23:2
Wendrem, James R, 1946, Ag 23,19:4
Wendroff, Isaac Mrs, 1959, Ja 30,27:1
Wendt, Anne M Mrs, 1951, Ja 18,27:5
Wendt, Benjamin T, 1944, F 6,42:1
Wendt, Carl F A, 1950, Ag 13,76:2
Wendt, E C Dr, 1903, My 26,2:2
Wendt, Edward G, 1958, Jl 18,21:1
Wendt, Edwin F, 1952, O 2,29:4
Wendt, Erich, 1965, My 9,87:2
Wendt, Fred J, 1954, My 16,88:1
Wendt, George, 1954, F 16,25:2
Wendt, George E, 1942, Je 24,19:1
Wendt, Herman, 1954, D 24,13:4; 1959, Mr 10,35:4
Wendt, John A F, 1945, O 21,46:1
Wendt, Julia B Mrs, 1942, Je 23,20:2
Wendt, Samuel J, 1952, Jl 5,15:4
Wendt, Theophil, 1951, F 6,27:4
Wendt, William, 1946, D 30,19:4; 1965, N 25,35:5
Wendt, William H, 1949, Ap 6,29:5
Wendt-zu-Eulenburg, Count, 1875, D 6,5:3
Wene, Elmer H, 1957, Ja 27,85:1
Wener, Harry Mrs, 1951, S 7,29:2
Wengen, Henry Mrs, 1945, O 21,46:3
Wenholt, John Mrs, 1939, N 11,15:3
Wenig, Frank E, 1950, S 15,25:6
Wenig, Hyman L, 1967, D 15,47:2
Wenig, Irving, 1961, Je 1,35:2
Weniger, F W Mrs, 1953, O 8,29:5
Wening, Frederick J Mrs, 1949, Je 26,60:2
Wenis, Edwin S, 1946, Je 3,21:2
Wenisch, Walter F, 1948, F 7,15:2
Wenk, Charles S, 1962, O 3,41:1
Wenk, Jacob, 1944, S 4,19:2
Wenke, Adolph, 1961, Mr 4,23:4
Wenke, William F, 1943, S 28,25:3
Wenkenbach, H Albert, 1949, Jl 19,29:1
Wenker, Frederick O Mrs, 1943, S 30,21:4
Wenker, William G, 1942, Ag 4,20:2
Wenley, Archibald D, 1962, F 20,35:2
Wenman, Byrd W, 1957, Jl 11,25:4
Wenman, Byrd W Mrs, 1967, My 20,35:2
Wenman, Charles W, 1957, Je 18,33:1
Wenman, James Fowler, 1919, My 31,13:3
Wenman, Louis P, 1948, Mr 9,23:2
Wenn, Julius F, 1942, S 5,13:5
Wennemer, Frank, 1925, O 9,23:4
Wenner, Frank, 1954, F 8,23:4
Wenner, Fred L, 1956, Ag 19,92:2
Wenner, G U, 1934, N 2,23:1
Wenner, Peter, 1941, O 4,15:5
Wenner, T J, 1942, Je 18,21:5
Wenner-Gren, Axel (funl, D 2,23:5), 1961, N 25,1:3
Wennerberg, Gunnar, 1901, Ag 24,7:6
Wennerberger, Henry P, 1960, Je 9,33:3
Wennerholm, Frank, 1948, Ag 24,23:3
Wennerlund, E Karl, 1957, Jl 21,61:2
Wenning, Arthur H, 1946, Jl 7,35:1
Wenning, Thomas H, 1962, D 3,31:1
Wenninger, Francis T, 1940, F 13,23:6
Wennstrom, John M, 1956, F 4,19:1
Wenrich, Paul A, 1953, Ja 24,15:5
Wenrich, Percy, 1952, Mr 19,29:1
Wenrick, John C, 1955, N 2,35:2
Wenroth, Sol, 1949, Ja 7,21:2
Wensinger, Carl F, 1967, My 21,86:8
Wensley, Frederick, 1949, D 5,23:1
Wensley, Roger L, 1967, O 22,84:7
Wenstrand, David E W, 1953, Je 6,17:6
Went, Harvey C, 1937, Ja 12,24:2
Went, Stanley, 1956, Ag 21,29:2
Wente, Herman L, 1961, Ap 18,37:2
Wentholt, Alexis D Mrs, 1961, F 13,27:4
Wentink, Leonard, 1943, Ja 26,19:4
Wentworth, Arioch, 1903, Mr 14,9:5
Wentworth, Arthur C, 1953, Je 29,21:5
Wentworth, Baroness (Lady Anne Blunt), 1918, Ja 22,11:5
Wentworth, Baroness (J A D Blunt-Lytton), 1957, Ag 10,15:3
Wentworth, Bert, 1938, Ag 15,15:5
Wentworth, Carl M, 1962, Ag 17,23:5
Wentworth, Catherine D Mrs, 1948, Mr 5,22:3
Wentworth, Charles H, 1953, My 18,21:6
Wentworth, Charles S Col, 1937, Jl 11,II,4:8
Wentworth, D F, 1876, Ag 3,5:2
Wentworth, Edward N, 1959, Ap 22,33:1
Wentworth, Elmer E, 1937, O 29,21:2
Wentworth, Frank T, 1945, Ja 25,19:5
Wentworth, Frank T Mrs, 1940, Mr 19,25:5
Wentworth, Fred Mrs, 1941, My 14,21:4
Wentworth, Fred W, 1943, O 5,25:3
Wentworth, Gene S Mrs, 1953, N 12,43:4
Wentworth, George A, 1947, D 2,29:2
Wentworth, George L, 1957, O 27,86:8
Wentworth, George O Mrs, 1944, D 1,23:4
Wentworth, Harold G, 1960, Mr 5,19:1
Wentworth, Isaac B Mrs, 1915, D 23,13:3
Wentworth, John A, 1951, S 18,31:5
Wentworth, Joseph, 1944, Ap 9,33:2
Wentworth, Mark H, 1944, My 17,19:6
Wentworth, Patricia (Mrs D A Turnbull), 1961, F 1, 35:2
Wentworth, Phil M, 1949, F 19,15:5
Wentworth, Ralph, 1949, F 2,27:4
Wentworth, Ralph C, 1954, Mr 19,23:6
Wentworth, Ralph P, 1957, F 5,23:4
Wentworth, Sidney D, 1942, Ag 28,19:1
Wentworth, Thomas, 1907, N 12,9:5
Wentworth, Thomas Foote, 1968, Je 21,41:4
Wentworth, Walter V, 1958, Mr 10,23:2
Wentworth, William C, 1956, Mr 11,89:1
Wentworth, William O, 1945, Ag 26,43:2
Wentworth, Zenas O Mrs, 1960, F 12,28:1
Wentz, Charles F, 1943, Ja 7,19:4
Wentz, Charles R, 1949, N 30,27:2
Wentz, Daniel B Jr, 1940, Mr 10,51:6
Wentz, George E, 1961, Ja 5,31:6
Wentz, James G Mrs, 1945, Jl 29,39:3
Wentz, Jere L Mrs, 1958, Jl 27,61:4
Wentz, Lew H (por), 1949, Je 10,27:1
Wentz, Oscar W, 1942, Je 23,20:2
Wentz, Robert C, 1967, Ag 11,31:3
Wentz, Stanley B, 1957, Je 1,17:2
Wentz, Theodore, 1939, Ap 21,23:3
Wentz, Willard W, 1956, Je 10,89:1
Wentz, William, 1913, My 21,11:6
Wentz, William F, 1943, F 14,48:8
Wentz, William M, 1942, N 18,25:2
Wentzel, Henry H, 1952, O 3,23:5
Wentzel, Laurene Mrs, 1952, Je 23,19:5
Wentzel, Paul F, 1950, Ap 25,31:5
Wentzell, John F, 1942, N 25,23:3
Wenyon, C M, 1948, O 26,31:2
Wenz, Aug, 1942, Ap 19,44:8
Wenz, Frank T, 1952, Mr 19,29:2
Wenz, Harold A, 1958, N 12,37:4
Wenz, Phil N, 1948, Mr 20,13:4
Wenz, Rudolph B, 1942, F 12,23:4
Wenzel, A E, 1880, Jl 28,5:5
Wenzel, Albert W, 1937, Ag 13,18:2
Wenzel, Carl R, 1950, Je 2,24:2
Wenzel, Caroline, 1959, Mr 28,17:5
Wenzel, Clifford C, 1953, Je 16,27:1
Wenzel, Frank, 1950, O 27,30:5
Wenzel, Fred W, 1941, S 11,23:3
Wenzel, Gustav M, 1944, Jl 30,35:3
Wenzel, Henry G Jr (mem ser, S 8,22:4), 1960, Ag 31,29:1
Wenzel, John, 1950, S 15,25:4
Wenzel, Joseph E, 1956, O 29,29:5
Wenzel, Louis, 1960, Je 6,29:3
Wenzel, Paul, 1938, My 31,19:4
Wenzel, Paul A Rev, 1907, O 3,9:4
Wenzel, Theodore H, 1955, Ag 30,27:3
Wenzel, Wilfred H, 1944, Ag 2,15:4
Wenzel, William C, 1959, Ap 15,33:3
Wenzel, William J, 1963, My 1,39:1
Wenzelberger, Henry J, 1938, F 15,25:3
Wenzell, Albert Beck, 1917, Mr 6,11:5
Wenzell, Louis P, 1955, Ag 15,15:4
Wenzell, William W, 1940, Ap 8,19:2
Wenzer, William J, 1952, F 7,27:5
Weper, Frederick G, 1945, N 3,15:6
Weppler, Frederick J, 1939, My 6,17:5
Werb, Samuel, 1951, O 14,89:1
Werba, Louis F, 1942, N 17,25:3
Werbel, David Mrs, 1953, O 3,17:5
Werbel, Leonard Dr, 1968, Ap 4,47:3
Werbelovsky, Abraham Mrs, 1957, F 5,23:4
Werbelowsky, David (por), 1937, S 18,19:2
Werbelowsky, Joseph L, 1919, Je 12,15:6
Werber, Charles H Jr Mrs, 1957, Ja 3,33:2
Werbezirk-Piffl, Gisela, 1956, Ag 25,35:1
Werblin, Irving I, 1952, Ap 13,77:2
Werblow, Robert M, 1959, Ja 7,33:2
Werckle, Marie J, 1948, Jl 15,23:3
Werda, Joel, 1941, D 7,76:1
Werde, A Kenneth, 1953, S 1,23:3
Werden, David, 1942, Je 19.23:3
Werden, David Mrs, 1950, Jl 29,13:6
Werden, Henrietta T Mrs, 1941, Je 11,21:7
Werden, Reed Rear Adm, 1886, Jl 13,5:3
Werdenschlag, Sylvian, 1951, Mr 12,25:4
Werder, Frederick C Sr, 1955, Ja 11,25:1
Werdermann, John H, 1945, D 15,17:1
Werfel, Albine Mrs, 1953, Ag 23,89:2
Werfel, Franz, 1945, Ag 27,19:1
Werfel, Franz Mrs (Alma M), 1964, D 12,31:3
Werher, Albert J, 1944, Ag 6,37:3
Werk, Julius N, 1968, Ag 1,31:2
Werk, Sigmund Mrs, 1952, Ap 20,92:6
Werkau, Carlton W, 1955, Jl 6,27:2
Werkheiser, George, 1953, Jl 26,69:3
Werking, Edward, 1957, S 4,34:3
Werkley, John, 1949, Jl 13,1:8
Werle, Alfred Count, 1907, My 28,9:6
Werle, Edward C (mem ser, Ja 23,33:5), 1962, Ja 8, 39:3
Werle, William P Mrs, 1949, S 3,13:6
Werlock, Stephen K, 1960, Jl 6,33:3
Werman, Abraham, 1955, Jl 28,23:6
Werman, Jacob I, 1942, O 6,23:4
Werman, Meyer E, 1958, D 6,23:3
Wermath, Oscar W, 1948, Mr 22,23:4
Werme, William, 1946, D 1,78:4
Wermer, Henry Dr, 1968, N 8,47:4
Wernaer, Robert M, 1951, Ag 15,27:4
Werndel, William H G, 1945, Mr 9,19:4
Werndorff, Karl R, 1944, My 29,15:4
Werne, Isaac, 1940, Mr 12,23:4
Werne, Joseph A, 1939, S 3,19:3
Werne, Peter T, 1951, Ja 17,28:3
Werneck, Francis J Capt, 1910, S 28,11:5
Werneke, A F, 1884, D 5,5:6
Werneke, Raymond A, 1950, Ja 3,25:5
Werneke, Richard A, 1938, Ag 9,19:4
Wernel, Michael T, 1962, F 8,32:1
Werner, Adolph, 1919, Ag 27,11:4
Werner, Alfred C, 1953, Ap 28,27:4
Werner, Alfred T, 1950, D 13,35:5
Werner, Andrew M, 1956, Je 2,19:2
Werner, Anton von, 1915, Ja 6,13:4
Werner, Benjamin F, 1946, My 15,21:2
Werner, Bud (Wallace),(funl, Ap 18,23:2), 1964, Ap 13,3:2
Werner, C George Mrs, 1945, S 15,15:4
Werner, Carl A, 1945, F 20,19:5
Werner, Chris H, 1948, Mr 11,27:4
Werner, Christopher C, 1943, Ag 13,17:5
Werner, Clarence E, 1938, Ap 28,23:4
Werner, David C, 1941, Ag 20,19:1
Werner, Edward, 1945, N 17,17:5
Werner, Edward E Mrs, 1953, F 24,25:2
Werner, Edwin, 1951, O 6,19:4
Werner, Eugene P Sr, 1950, Mr 26,92:5
Werner, Florence C, 1954, Ag 31,21:4
Werner, Florence E Mrs, 1949, Jl 15,22:5
Werner, Frank, 1945, N 23,23:2
Werner, Frank A, 1953, Jl 7,27:3
Werner, Frank E, 1950, O 3,31:5
Werner, Fred Mrs, 1953, F 23,11:3
Werner, Frederick W, 1941, S 30,23:5
Werner, Frederick W Mrs, 1908, Je 17,9:5
Werner, G J, 1931, O 24,17:3
Werner, George C Jr, 1958, O 6,31:6
Werner, George H, 1948, S 9,27:5
Werner, George J, 1963, D 1,84:5
Werner, Gerard, 1963, Je 23,85:2
Werner, Gertraud, 1952, N 1,21:6
Werner, Gustav R, 1950, D 29,19:2
Werner, Harold H, 1955, O 1,19:5
Werner, Heinz, 1964, My 16,25:6
Werner, Henry, 1922, Jl 6,19:6
Werner, Henry C, 1945, F 7,21:4
Werner, Henry E, 1947, D 4,31:5
Werner, Henry P, 1955, O 25,33:4
Werner, J Benton, 1942, Ap 28,21:3
Werner, John, 1963, Je 28,29:2
Werner, John A, 1960, Ag 29,25:4
Werner, John C, 1954, Ja 3,89:2
Werner, John F, 1947, D 13,15:2
Werner, John F Sr, 1962, My 27,93:2
Werner, John M, 1941, O 16,21:4
Werner, John Mrs, 1943, F 8,19:2
Werner, Joseph C, 1964, D 7,35:2
Werner, Josephine Mrs, 1963, S 8,86:5
Werner, Jules J Mrs, 1958, Mr 8,17:2
Werner, Julius L, 1949, D 13,31:3
Werner, K A, 1936, O 13,27:5
Werner, Kurt, 1963, My 15,39:4
Werner, Leo S, 1938, Mr 15,23:2
Werner, Lewis A, 1953, Mr 10,29:1
Werner, Lewis 2d, 1966, S 25,1:3
Werner, Louis F, 1956, My 8,33:2
Werner, Louis L, 1950, N 29,33:1
Werner, Ludlow W, 1967, F 5,88:8
Werner, Luther M Mrs, 1948, Ja 27,25:1
Werner, Max, 1951, Ja 9,29:1
Werner, Morris Mrs, 1943, N 28,68:5
Werner, Mortiz Mrs, 1964, F 2,89:2
Werner, Pierre R, 1960, My 22,86:5
Werner, Ralph L, 1965, D 17,39:1
Werner, Richard C Sr, 1967, Ap 18,41:3
Werner, Rose M, 1944, Mr 18,13:7
Werner, Rose Mrs, 1941, Je 3,21:3
Werner, Samuel E Mrs, 1950, F 28,29:3
Werner, Siegmund, 1968, Mr 30,33:3
Werner, Victor Mrs, 1956, S 21,25:2
Werner, Wade, 1953, D 30,24:3
Werner, William, 1939, Jl 21,19:5

Werner, William E Judge (funl, Mr 4,11:7), 1916, Mr 2,11:5
Werner, William E Mrs, 1949, D 8,33:3
Werner, William F, 1957, D 28,17:6
Werner, William H, 1959, S 16,39:3
Werner, William L, 1965, Ap 3,29:5
Werner, William O, 1954, D 30,17:1
Werner, William V, 1960, D 15,44:1
Wernher, Hilda Mrs, 1956, Mr 1,33:3
Wernher, Julius Charles Sir, 1912, My 22,13:6
Wernick, Abraham, 1956, N 23,27:2
Wernick, Harry Mrs, 1961, F 28,33:2
Wernick, Hyman, 1955, S 28,35:1
Wernig, Charles M, 1947, Jl 28,15:1
Wernig, Charles W, 1907, Mr 9,9:6
Wernimont, Eleanor Mrs, 1952, F 20,12:2
Werno, Charles, 1946, Mr 17,43:1
Wernow, Abraham, 1961, N 4,19:5
Wernsdorf, O F, 1938, N 8,23:5
Werntz, Carl N (por), 1944, O 28,15:5
Werntz, Hayes L, 1946, Je 4,23:2
Werntz, William W, 1964, N 21,29:5
Werrenrath, Reinald, 1953, S 13,85:1
Werry, J Wilbur, 1949, Ap 26,25:4
Werschinger, Carl, 1959, F 28,19:4
Werschinger, John, 1940, Mr 17,48:6
Wersebe, Frederic W, 1954, My 10,23:6
Wershaw, Irving B, 1963, My 3,32:1
Wert, James A, 1948, Jl 23,19:2
Wertenbaker, Charles, 1955, Ja 9,87:1
Wertenbaker, Clark Mrs, 1959, D 19,27:5
Wertenbaker, George L, 1941, My 27,23:2
Wertenbaker, Thomas J, 1966, Ap 23,31:4
Wertenbaker, William, 1882, Ap 8,5:4
Werth, Alex, 1942, Ap 23,23:3
Werth, Andrew B, 1960, O 28,31:3
Werth, Jean F, 1953, Ja 23,19:3
Werth, Julia Mrs, 1922, Ag 23,13:6
Wertheim, Albert (por), 1943, Ag 22,36:3
Wertheim, Alfred H, 1947, Jl 31,21:5
Wertheim, Benjamin, 1951, My 16,35:5
Wertheim, Clara, 1903, Ag 17,7:5
Wertheim, David, 1953, Ap 11,17:4
Wertheim, Edes L Mrs (M Geo), 1960, Ap 6,41:5
Wertheim, Edward L, 1965, My 22,32:4
Wertheim, Edward Mrs, 1947, S 12,22:2
Wertheim, Emma S Mrs, 1937, O 22,23:2
Wertheim, Henri Mrs, 1903, Ag 16,7:6
Wertheim, Hippolyte (por), 1948, N 9,27:1
Wertheim, Jacob (funl, N 17,13:1), 1920, N 15,15:1
Wertheim, Joseph, 1924, D 18,21:4
Wertheim, Maurice (will, Je 8,62:1), 1950, My 28, 44:3
Wertheim, Sanders A Sr, 1952, S 12,21:2
Wertheim, Solomon, 1939, O 28,15:3
Wertheim, William, 1961, S 7,35:2
Wertheimer, Asher, 1918, S 11,13:4
Wertheimer, Charles, 1911, Ap 26,15:4
Wertheimer, Edward H, 1942, N 13,23:2
Wertheimer, Elsie, 1922, S 5,17:5
Wertheimer, Emile (will), 1953, Ap 24,28:8
Wertheimer, Ernest, 1964, S 2,37:3
Wertheimer, Henry W, 1959, S 20,86:5
Wertheimer, Isaac, 1942, Ap 16,21:5
Wertheimer, John F, 1949, Ap 17,76:3
Wertheimer, Leon G, 1944, F 26,13:5
Wertheimer, Lou, 1958, My 20,33:5
Wertheimer, Mathilde Mrs, 1946, Ag 7,27:5
Wertheimer, Max, 1943, O 13,23:5
Wertheimer, Mert, 1958, Jl 21,21:2
Wertheimer, Mildred S Dr (por), 1937, My 7,30:3
Wertheimer, Monroe A, 1939, Mr 2,21:1
Wertheimer, Moses, 1943, Ja 7,19:4
Wertheimer, Nathan, 1952, Ag 1,17:3
Wertheimer, Paul, 1948, D 30,19:4
Wertheimer, Samuel, 1907, Jl 26,7:6; 1943, S 26,49:1
Wertheimer, Sydney B, 1937, My 20,21:4
Werthmann, Mark Mrs, 1945, Mr 2,19:2
Werthner, Phil Mrs, 1948, S 19,76:4
Wertime, Walter H Sr, 1953, Jl 17,17:5
Wertimer, Sidney, 1951, N 12,25:3
Wertman, F R, 1947, My 14,25:2
Werts, Charles L, 1965, Jl 25,68:5
Werts, George T Ex-Gov, 1910, Ja 18,11:3
Werts, George T Mrs, 1925, F 8,7:1
Wertsch, Charles W, 1950, S 27,32:2
Wertsner, George S, 1938, Jl 10,29:2
Wertz, D Maurice, 1940, Mr 20,27:5
Wertz, Edwin S, 1943, N 9,21:6
Wertz, Frederick L, 1956, Je 29,21:5
Wertz, Frederick L Mrs, 1959, Ag 14,21:2
Wertz, H Ray, 1942, F 28,17:2
Wertz, Irvin M Dr, 1937, F 24,23:3
Wertz, Marcus E, 1951, Jl 19,23:2
Wertz, Mary A, 1947, Jl 28,15:4
Wertzberger, Susan Mrs, 1937, Ja 28,25:4
Weschler, F J, 1942, D 10,42:4
Weschler, George A, 1954, D 29,23:4
Weschler, Henry Mrs, 1961, Mr 25,25:4
Weschler, J Charles, 1959, Ap 9,31:4
Wescoat, Absalom S, 1955, N 22,35:4
Wescoat, Albert C Capt, 1937, F 21,II,11:1
Wescoat, Philip, 1947, My 16,23:2
Wescott, A Lincoln, 1956, Ja 12,27:3
Wescott, Bruce P Mrs, 1960, Ja 6,35:3
Wescott, Cassius D, 1946, My 7,21:1
Wescott, Charles G, 1940, O 22,23:5
Wescott, Charles L, 1940, Jl 1,19:5
Wescott, Clarence Lincoln, 1925, D 8,25:4
Wescott, Donald A, 1960, Ja 9,21:4
Wescott, E Keats Mrs, 1925, Ag 25,17:6
Wescott, Ernest W, 1950, Ja 16,25:6
Wescott, J D, 1880, Ja 21,2:7
Wescott, J W, 1927, Je 12,25:3
Wescott, Myron N, 1938, S 26,17:2
Wescott, Ralph W, 1955, O 5,35:4
Wescott, Walter J, 1953, Je 28,61:1
Wescott, William B, 1952, Je 20,84:5
Wescott, William C, 1941, Jl 27,30:6
Wescott, William C Mrs, 1951, N 15,29:5
Weseen, Maurice H, 1941, Ap 15,23:1
Wesel, Ferdinand Mrs, 1912, D 6,15:5
Weselak, William T, 1938, F 16,21:5
Weseman, John W, 1946, N 23,15:6
Weser, Nicholas W, 1966, My 12,45:1
Wesighan, Charles, 1950, O 13,29:1
Weskamm, Wilhelm, 1956, Ag 22,29:2
Wesle, Carl, 1950, O 28,17:4
Wesler, Raymond D, 1956, N 18,89:2
Wesley, Arthur F Mrs, 1944, Mr 3,15:4
Wesley, Charles S, 1939, O 30,17:2
Wesley, Edward B, 1906, O 4,9:3
Wesley, Frank B, 1949, Ja 11,27:4
Wesley, Frank J, 1949, My 6,25:2
Wesley, Harold G, 1951, S 10,21:5
Wesley, Harry P Mrs, 1955, Ag 18,23:3
Wesley, Henry B, 1948, Mr 19,23:1
Wesley, Herman H, 1941, Ap 29,19:2
Wesley, James K, 1958, S 3,33:5
Wesley, Joseph J, 1965, Jl 4,37:2
Wesley, Joseph J Mrs, 1964, My 10,83:2
Wesley, Leland G, 1962, Ag 19,88:3
Wesley, Phil G, 1950, Ag 23,29:4
Weslow, Harry Mrs, 1948, Mr 6,13:2
Weslyn, Louis, 1937, Ja 2,14:2
Wesner, Ella (funl, N 14,15:3), 1917, N 12,13:6
Wesolowski, Stanley, 1952, N 19,29:3
Wesp, Edward, 1950, O 10,31:5
Wesp, Frank C, 1952, Je 29,56:6
Wesp, George, 1958, N 28,27:2
Wessa, Ida, 1954, Ap 4,43:2
Wessel, Albert A, 1947, Mr 28,23:3
Wessel, Albert H, 1954, Ja 25,13:8
Wessel, Charles, 1902, D 31,1:3
Wessel, Dick, 1965, Ap 23,35:4
Wessel, George H Sr, 1962, Je 30,19:5
Wessel, Harry N, 1958, Jl 11,23:5
Wessel, Henry Jr, 1951, S 9,90:1
Wessel, John F, 1949, D 9,31:2
Wessel, Lewis, 1959, D 6,87:1
Wessel, Maude Mrs, 1956, N 9,25:2
Wessel, Otto E, 1944, O 5,23:4
Wessel, Theodore W, 1948, S 1,24:3
Wessel, William C (por), 1949, S 15,27:3
Wesselhoeft, William F, 1943, Je 28,21:5
Wessell, Arthur L, 1959, Ja 20,35:1
Wessell, Charles A Mrs, 1945, My 14,17:5
Wessell, Francis, 1960, F 8,29:4
Wessell, Francis Mrs, 1960, F 8,29:4
Wessell, Nils J, 1946, F 5,23:2
Wessells, C B, 1881, Ap 12,3:1
Wessells, Emily M (will), 1940, Ja 10,23:2
Wessells, F Col, 1881, F 19,5:3
Wessells, Henry W Jr, 1959, Je 27,23:4
Wessells, Theodore D, 1947, N 10,29:5
Wesselman, Henry B, 1923, Mr 14,19:4
Wesselman, Henry B Mrs, 1940, Ap 8,19:1
Wessels, Claus, 1903, N 28,2:1
Wessels, Emily M, 1939, D 23,15:6
Wessels, Emrich R, 1922, S 5,17:5
Wessels, Frederick J, 1948, N 4,29:1
Wessels, George W, 1908, F 22,7:5
Wessels, John L, 1923, Mr 6,21:3
Wessels, Lewis C, 1942, S 6,31:2
Wessels, Louis Mrs, 1948, Jl 23,19:1
Wessels, Lynn D, 1942, Jl 4,17:5
Wessels, Margaret, 1937, S 26,II,8:7
Wessels, W H Col, 1909, S 28,9:4
Wessels, Walther J, 1945, O 30,19:4
Wessinger, John A, 1954, N 13,15:3
Wessler, Harry, 1966, Ja 2,72:3
Wessman, John, 1946, Jl 2,25:5
Wessmann, Alfred Charlton (funl, D 2,13:5), 1922, D 1,17:4
Wessner, Albert, 1959, My 11,27:1
Wessolock, Louise Mrs, 1940, Ag 24,13:6
Wessolowski, Hans, 1948, My 14,23:4
Wesson, Charles M, 1956, N 25,88:5
Wesson, D, 1934, My 23,19:5
Wesson, Daniel B (will, Ag 23,1:6), 1906, Ag 5,1:2
Wesson, David J, 1938, Mr 2,19:6
Wesson, Douglas B, 1956, Mr 20,23:2
Wesson, Elizabeth H, 1949, Jl 29,21:5
Wesson, Frank H, 1962, Ja 11,33:4
Wesson, Frank H Mrs, 1952, Ag 29,23:2
Wesson, Harold, 1946, Ag 31,15:4
Wesson, Harry B, 1941, Je 27,17:4
Wesson, James H, 1920, My 1,15:4
Wesson, Leonard, 1942, Ag 17,15:5
Wesson, Peter Mrs, 1944, Mr 17,17:5
Wesson, Victor H, 1945, My 29,15:5
Wesson, Walter H, 1921, N 30,17:4
West, Al (Sonny Boy), 1950, D 22,29:1
West, Alden B, 1952, Je 7,19:4
West, Algernon Sir, 1921, Mr 22,17:4
West, Allen L Jr, 1943, F 3,19:3
West, Amelia G, 1947, Ja 13,59:3
West, Andrew F (por), 1943, D 28,17:1
West, Annie B, 1941, Mr 16,44:6
West, Arthur P, 1944, Ap 11,19:3
West, Austin, 1921, My 21,13:5
West, Barzillia R, 1951, My 18,27:3
West, Benjamin T, 1965, Ja 9,25:1
West, Buster, 1966, Mr 20,86:6
West, Camden H, 1949, Ja 20,27:5
West, Carl J, 1940, Ja 16,23:3
West, Carl W, 1963, Ag 2,27:4
West, Charles C, 1952, Ja 26,13:4
West, Charles C Mrs, 1955, Ag 5,19:3
West, Charles E, 1953, My 13,29:2
West, Charles F, 1955, D 30,19:3
West, Charles G, 1962, F 4,82:5
West, Charles Gifford Maj, 1924, O 11,15:5
West, Charles H, 1940, Je 3,15:2
West, Charles J, 1951, N 3,17:4
West, Charles R, 1943, Je 28,21:4
West, Chester A, 1949, S 24,13:5
West, Christopher, 1967, O 29,84:4
West, Christopher H Mrs, 1938, My 20,19:2
West, Clara Linforth, 1923, My 14,15:5
West, Clarence E, 1949, F 6,76:1
West, Clarence J, 1953, Ja 30,22:6
West, Claudine, 1943, Ap 13,25:3
West, Clifford Hardy Rear-Adm, 1911, N 3,11:4
West, Clyde B, 1942, S 15,23:4
West, Davenport, 1960, Mr 31,33:5
West, De W C, 1880, Ag 28,2:1
West, Don L, 1954, N 25,29:6
West, Douglas H, 1965, O 16,27:5
West, Duval, 1949, My 15,91:1
West, E Borden, 1961, Ja 8,86:1
West, E E Capt, 1914, Jl 18,7:6
West, E Lovette, 1944, Mr 8,19:1
West, E Lovette Mrs, 1962, Ap 23,29:3
West, Earle E, 1953, N 1,87:2
West, Edgar F, 1956, Ja 13,23:3
West, Edgar L, 1947, F 8,17:2
West, Edmond Abbott, 1922, My 1,17:2
West, Edward A, 1939, N 10,23:3
West, Edward J, 1964, Ag 31,25:2
West, Edward M, 1938, Mr 9,23:4; 1954, Ap 3,15:2
West, Edward M Mrs, 1953, Mr 22,86:1
West, Edward Mrs, 1937, F 20,17:4
West, Egbert W, 1944, Ag 14,15:5
West, Egbert W Mrs, 1953, F 3,25:5
West, Elliott M, 1944, My 23,23:2
West, Elliott M Mrs, 1940, Ag 18,37:3
West, Ellsworth L, 1949, Ap 12,30:4
West, Elsie M (por), 1943, My 14,19:3
West, Emil Mrs, 1946, F 6,23:5
West, Emma F Mrs, 1942, Jl 9,21:3
West, Ernest H, 1950, Ja 4,35:4
West, Everett Martin, 1968, Mr 23,25:1
West, Francis D, 1958, Mr 22,17:5
West, Frank C, 1942, Ag 9,42:6
West, Frank E, 1940, N 22,23:3
West, Frank E Mrs, 1966, F 16,43:4
West, Frederick, 1964, Mr 31,35:1
West, G Bernard, 1925, N 4,23:4
West, G Leroy, 1954, D 7,33:2
West, George, 1943, Mr 8,15:2
West, George F, 1943, Jl 13,22:2
West, George Mrs, 1947, Ag 19,23:5
West, George S, 1959, O 31,23:6
West, Gerald B, 1960, Ap 23,23:4
West, Gordon F, 1945, Jl 27,15:3
West, Graham W, 1955, S 1,23:4
West, Hamilton A Dr, 1904, Ja 1,7:5
West, Harmon, 1953, Ag 20,27:2
West, Harold, 1951, My 6,93:1
West, Harold B, 1945, Je 23,13:5
West, Harold E, 1948, Jl 25,48:6
West, Harold W Mrs, 1953, Jl 15,25:3
West, Harry F, 1906, Jl 4,7:6
West, Harry G, 1942, F 19,19:3
West, Hartland St C, 1967, S 16,33:4
West, Henry E, 1956, F 12,88:4
West, Henry L, 1940, S 4,23:2
West, Herbert C Mrs, 1968, Mr 7,43:3
West, Herbert J, 1939, Je 1,25:3
West, Herman O, 1965, Jl 15,29:4
West, Heston R, 1953, Ja 11,91:2
West, Hewitt S (por), 1955, S 4,58:1
West, Howard, 1966, S 17,29:3
West, Howard L, 1955, Jl 11,23:5
West, Howard S, 1967, Mr 1,43:1
West, Hugh H, 1954, S 1,27:4
West, J Roy, 1941, N 26,23:5
West, J Royer Mrs, 1942, Je 30,21:4

West, J T, 1876, Jl 10,4:6
West, J Terry, 1945, D 28,15:2
West, J Terry Mrs, 1953, Mr 4,27:1
West, Jack, 1941, My 24,15:4
West, James E, 1948, My 16,68:2
West, James F, 1903, N 17,9:6; 1947, F 20,25:1
West, James H, 1942, F 6,19:6
West, James M, 1941, Ag 25,15:4
West, James M Jr, 1957, D 19,31:3
West, James S, 1959, Ag 8,17:4
West, James W, 1943, Mr 18,20:2; 1959, D 19,27:3
West, Jane L Mrs, 1940, Ag 1,21:4
West, Jere, 1937, Ap 1,23:1
West, Joe Y, 1955, Ap 30,17:2
West, John, 1950, Ag 3,23:5
West, John A, 1951, Jl 14,13:6
West, John C (por), 1946, F 15,25:4
West, John C, 1961, Jl 23,68:4
West, John E Dr, 1908, O 15,9:5
West, John M, 1947, Jl 10,21:1
West, John Mrs, 1954, Ap 13,31:4
West, John R 3d, 1954, Jl 1,25:4
West, John T, 1956, Jl 20,17:1
West, John W, 1952, Ja 6,92:6
West, John W Sr, 1949, Ap 22,23:1
West, Joseph H, 1948, Mr 8,23:4
West, Joseph P, 1950, F 4,15:6
West, Junius E, 1947, Ja 2,27:2
West, Kensey S, 1948, Ap 24,15:2
West, Lavinia J Mrs, 1942, D 3,25:1
West, Leon O, 1950, Jl 23,58:1
West, Levon (Ivan Dmitri), 1968, Ap 26,47:3
West, Lewis E, 1964, Ag 2,77:1
West, Lewis S, 1938, D 4,60:7
West, Louis, 1955, Ag 13,13:2
West, Lyman C, 1950, S 20,31:3
West, Marshall B, 1939, Je 11,44:4
West, Max A, 1960, My 10,37:5
West, Mercer E, 1951, Je 7,33:6
West, Mercy A Mrs, 1950, Ja 26,27:1
West, Merle Mrs, 1948, Ag 19,21:1
West, Milton H, 1948, O 29,25:3
West, Myron A Mrs, 1946, Ap 30,21:5
West, Nathan M, 1954, My 12,31:2
West, Nelson W, 1948, Ag 10,21:3
West, Olin, 1952, Je 21,15:3
West, Orman M, 1944, O 5,23:4
West, Ortello W, 1950, D 27,27:1
West, Orville E, 1943, O 21,27:2
West, P E, 1954, Ja 26,27:3
West, Paul B, 1960, My 6,31:3
West, Paul Mrs, 1954, F 15,23:3
West, Pauline Mrs, 1940, Mr 24,31:1
West, Pennerton (Mrs J L Herma), 1965, Jl 1,31:4
West, Percy, 1942, Je 26,21:7; 1947, Ap 14,27:4
West, Phillip L Mrs, 1955, F 28,19:5
West, Preston C, 1949, S 10,17:3
West, R K Mrs, 1951, S 14,25:3
West, Radford C, 1951, F 25,7:2
West, Randolph, 1949, My 21,13:3
West, Randolph Mrs, 1945, D 15,17:1
West, Ray A, 1946, Mr 17,44:5
West, Reginald G, 1949, N 4,27:2
West, Richard S Jr, 1968, F 15,43:3
West, Robert A, 1966, Ag 15,27:5
West, Robert Athol, 1865, F 3,5:4
West, Robert H Jr, 1942, Ap 11,13:2
West, Robert R, 1962, O 21,89:2
West, Rodney M, 1941, Mr 6,21:3
West, Roland, 1952, Ap 1,29:3
West, Roy A, 1941, Mr 21,21:4; 1945, F 8,19:2
West, Roy O, 1958, D 1,29:5
West, S W, 1876, Mr 9,4:7
West, Samuel A, 1952, Ag 8,17:4
West, Samuel H, 1938, O 21,23:3
West, Samuel P, 1946, S 24,29:1
West, Stanley Q, 1952, D 11,33:4
West, Stephen C, 1948, Ap 10,13:4
West, Stuart P Mrs, 1925, D 13,13:1
West, Theodore S, 1957, Ja 6,88:2
West, Thomas H Mrs, 1945, N 30,23:4
West, Thomas J, 1922, My 30,13:6; 1953, S 22,31:4; 1963, O 3,35:5
West, W H, 1902, F 16,7:7
West, W Nelson L, 1954, O 21,27:3
West, Walter H, 1951, N 9,27:3
West, Walter J, 1951, F 19,23:2
West, Walter M, 1960, O 8,23:4
West, William, 1961, Jl 6,29:5
West, William A, 1951, D 14,31:4
West, William B, 1950, O 24,29:2; 1953, Mr 19,29:5
West, William C, 1923, Je 18,13:6; 1952, D 26,15:4
West, William E, 1951, F 9,25:5
West, William G, 1955, Ap 26,29:4
West, William H, 1946, N 13,28:3; 1948, Mr 18,27:4
West, William Judge, 1911, Mr 15,13:5
West, William Mrs, 1908, F 28,7:5
West, William Stanley Ex-Sen, 1914, D 23,13:4
West-Watson, Campbell, 1953, My 20,29:5
Westacott, Richard, 1922, Ja 29,22:2
Westad, Rolf (mem ser), 1967, Jl 26,36:1
Westall, Charles, 1955, N 19,19:6
Westall, Henry A, 1947, Ag 14,23:3
Westall, John, 1945, Mr 17,13:5
Westall, John W, 1944, Mr 1,19:3
Westall, Walter W, 1968, Je 6,47:1
Westall, Walter W Mrs, 1966, My 26,47:2
Westarp, Kuno F von, 1945, Ag 6,15:5
Westberg, Carl A, 1953, Jl 10,19:1
Westberg, Frank G, 1954, D 5,88:5
Westberg, William J, 1947, Ap 30,25:4
Westbrook, Daniel P, 1951, Ag 5,73:2
Westbrook, E, 1933, Ja 6,19:1
Westbrook, Edward S W, 1941, Ap 22,21:5
Westbrook, Elroy D, 1943, F 16,20:3
Westbrook, Eugene, 1947, D 23,23:3
Westbrook, H Theodric, 1944, Jl 22,15:3
Westbrook, Harry L, 1942, Je 5,17:5
Westbrook, Henrietta Dr, 1909, O 17,13:4
Westbrook, James S, 1967, F 20,37:3
Westbrook, Joseph W, 1941, D 5,23:5
Westbrook, Kate E, 1943, D 6,23:4
Westbrook, Lawrence, 1964, Ja 26,81:2
Westbrook, Marie M Mrs (will), 1952, S 12,23:6
Westbrook, Ralph E, 1967, S 8,40:1
Westbrook, Richard W Mrs, 1948, Jl 14,23:3
Westbrook, Stillman F, 1943, Ap 29,21:5
Westbrook, T B, 1903, Ag 21,9:6
Westbrook, T R Judge, 1885, O 7,1:7
Westbrook, William E, 1937, Jl 26,19:5
Westbrook, Zerah D, 1953, Jl 5,49:2
Westbury, Harry, 1940, O 11,21:6
Westbury, Lady, 1941, Ja 10,19:2
Westbury, Lord (Richard Bethell), 1873, Jl 21,5:4
Westbury, Lord (R M T Bethell), 1961, Je 30,27:3
Westbury, William, 1942, D 3,25:2
Westby, Cleve O Dr, 1968, Jl 10,39:2
Westby, Edwin Lt, 1919, Ja 10,13:4
Westby-Gibson, Harry, 1950, Jl 15,13:2
Westchiloff, Constantin, 1945, Ap 24,19:3
Westcot, Warren, 1948, My 29,15:5
Westcott, A L, 1949, Je 14,31:4
Westcott, Bishop of Durham, 1901, Jl 29,7:6
Westcott, Boyce N, 1916, D 5,11:3
Westcott, Clinton S, 1951, Ja 9,29:4
Westcott, E J Brig Gen, 1926, F 10,23:3
Westcott, Earle H, 1959, My 28,31:4
Westcott, F Howard Mrs, 1957, D 4,39:4
Westcott, Foss, 1949, O 21,25:1
Westcott, Frank W Dr, 1924, Je 25,23:5
Westcott, George E, 1955, My 26,31:4
Westcott, George H, 1951, O 30,29:1
Westcott, Harold F, 1942, Je 27,13:2
Westcott, James H, 1938, My 4,23:5
Westcott, James W, 1941, Jl 4,13:2
Westcott, John H, 1942, My 20,19:6
Westcott, John W, 1950, Ap 26,29:1
Westcott, L Rev, 1879, Je 6,1:7
Westcott, Nelson S Dr, 1922, D 5,19:5
Westcott, Robert Estling, 1907, Ap 25,9:5
Westcott, Wilbert, 1950, Mr 14,25:5
Westcott, William W, 1951, S 17,21:6
Westdahl, Lawrence H, 1942, O 29,23:1
Westdyke, Henry, 1945, Ja 6,11:4
Westendorf, August, 1953, Jl 16,21:1
Westenhaver, D C, 1928, Jl 31,21:5
Wester, Charles, 1950, Ap 26,29:2
Wester Wemyss, Lord, 1933, My 25,19:1
Westerbeke, John, 1941, D 9,31:4
Westerberg, Charles H, 1957, My 1,37:1
Westerdahl, Axel, 1965, Mr 31,39:4
Westerdahl, Carl G, 1949, D 14,31:1
Westerdahl, Clifford A, 1944, O 3,23:1
Westerfeld, Sol, 1942, O 9,21:2
Westerfield, Arthur F, 1953, Je 17,27:3
Westerfield, Jason R, 1959, Ag 31,21:3
Westerfield, Milo H, 1961, N 27,29:3
Westerfield, Randolph F, 1946, Jl 5,19:5
Westerfield, Ray B, 1961, Ag 22,29:3
Westergaard, Harald M, 1950, Je 24,13:6
Westergren, Mouritz F, 1959, Ja 24,19:4
Westerhoff, Garret P, 1951, Mr 29,27:4
Westerhoff, Harrison J, 1949, F 11,23:5
Westerhoff, Peter D, 1957, Je 23,84:3
Westerlin, John M, 1939, Je 13,23:6
Westerlund, John S, 1953, O 15,33:2
Westerlund, Minnie Mrs, 1942, Je 6,13:3
Westerlund, William N Jr, 1966, Ja 2,72:4
Westerman, Frederick G, 1955, Je 15,31:5
Westerman, Gerhardt von, 1963, F 15,9:7
Westerman, Harry J, 1945, Je 28,19:6
Westerman, John H, 1942, D 19,19:2
Westermann, August H Mrs, 1962, Je 2,19:3
Westermann, H Theodore, 1948, Ap 7,25:4
Westermann, H Theodore Mrs, 1948, Mr 23,25:3
Westermann, John J, 1950, Ja 29,44:2
Westermann, John J Jr, 1968, F 9,27:3
Westermann, William L, 1954, O 5,27:1
Westermann, William L Mrs, 1960, D 22,23:1
Westermarck, Edward A, 1939, S 5,23:5
Western, Helen, 1868, D 12,4:6
Western, Lucille (see also Ja 12), 1877, Ja 16,5:3
Westervelt, A J, 1879, Mr 11,2:2
Westervelt, Abram, 1962, O 1,31:4
Westervelt, Andrew B, 1948, S 4,15:6
Westervelt, Arthur B (por), 1945, D 5,25:5
Westervelt, Arthur F, 1946, S 17,7:4
Westervelt, Charles E, 1940, O 14,19:4
Westervelt, Charles E Mrs, 1940, Mr 28,23:2
Westervelt, Cornelius J, 1946, Mr 5,25:2
Westervelt, David Z, 1954, Jl 1,25:4
Westervelt, Edward G, 1953, Ja 3,15:5
Westervelt, Edwin A, 1961, F 20,27:5
Westervelt, Elmer, 1950, Ag 10,25:4
Westervelt, Frances A Mrs, 1942, My 5,21:5
Westervelt, Frederick, 1952, Ja 17,28:2
Westervelt, Frederick V, 1955, My 6,23:1
Westervelt, George C, 1956, Mr 16,23:5
Westervelt, George N, 1947, O 27,21:3
Westervelt, Herbert E, 1938, S 4,17:2
Westervelt, Horace, 1945, Ja 25,19:2
Westervelt, J, 1877, Mr 29,2:2
Westervelt, J A, 1879, F 22,2:2
Westervelt, J C, 1955, O 31,25:5
Westervelt, J J V, 1866, F 7,5:3
Westervelt, J L, 1880, N 17,4:7
Westervelt, James D, 1941, Mr 20,21:2
Westervelt, James Mrs, 1956, Jl 18,27:3
Westervelt, John W (por), 1946, O 21,31:4
Westervelt, Josiah H, 1924, N 4,21:1
Westervelt, Leonidas, 1952, Ag 18,17:5
Westervelt, Peter Mrs, 1915, F 6,11:6
Westervelt, Tompkins, 1882, Ap 21,5:2
Westervelt, Warner W Mrs, 1914, Ag 2,15:6
Westervelt, William H, 1951, Jl 20,21:5
Westervelt, William I, 1960, Mr 3,29:2
Westervelt, William S, 1950, Ap 22,19:3
Westervelt, Zenas F, 1918, F 19,13:5
Westfall, Charles, 1942, O 3,15:4
Westfall, Curtis C, 1947, Jl 25,18:2
Westfall, Edward A, 1958, N 10,29:4
Westfall, John G, 1903, Ap 29,9:6
Westfall, John L, 1946, Ja 15,23:1
Westfall, John V, 1944, F 21,15:3
Westfall, Martha, 1952, Je 3,29:2
Westfall, Mary H, 1940, Ag 5,13:3
Westfall, Oliver A Mrs, 1945, Jl 11,11:6
Westfall, William R, 1956, Ja 28,17:5
Westfehling, Henry Mrs, 1943, D 10,27:2
Westfeldt, George, 1961, D 24,36:2
Westfelt, Pamela, 1960, Ag 19,46:4
Westgard, A L Mrs, 1946, F 8,19:1
Westgarth, George W, 1956, Je 6,33:6
Westgarth, Thomas H, 1950, Mr 22,27:3
Westgate, Harvey E, 1940, Mr 19,26:2
Westgate, Ralph S, 1946, N 30,15:1
Westheim, Aaron, 1920, Mr 9,11:1
Westheimer, Eugene F, 1957, F 23,17:4
Westheimer, Henry G B, 1947, My 17,15:1
Westigate, Frank N, 1947, Ap 10,25:2
Westing, Charles, 1942, Ja 29,19:5
Westinghouse, George Mrs, 1914, Je 24,11:5
Westinghouse, H H, 1933, N 19,34:1
Westlake, Albert J, 1951, Ag 12,78:5
Westlake, Edward T, 1945, Mr 1,21:2
Westlake, Emory H, 1967, Ja 26,33:5
Westlake, Emory Mrs, 1961, My 21,87:2
Westley, Helen (por), 1942, D 13,74:1
Westley, John, 1915, Ag 20,11:6; 1948, D 28,21:5
Westley, John Mrs, 1952, Jl 12,13:2
Westling, Charles Mrs, 1951, Ap 30,21:2
Westling, Edward R Sr, 1952, Ap 4,33:5
Westlink, Hugh, 1951, Ja 16,29:4
Westlund, Signe, 1953, Ap 20,25:1
Westman, Eric E, 1945, Ap 27,19:2
Westman, Gustav Marvitz, 1908, Mr 7,7:6
Westman, Karl G, 1944, Ja 26,19:5
Westman, Leroy E, 1945, Jl 3,13:4
Westman, Lolita A (Mrs C Murray), 1965, N 15,37:3
Westmeath, Marquis of, 1871, My 20,2:4
Westmeyer, Edward E, 1951, My 27,68:4
Westminster, Duchess of, 1880, D 20,5:4
Westminster, Duke of, 1899, D 23,7:1
Westminster, Duke of (H R A Grosvenor), 1953, Jl 21,23:3
Westminster, Duke of (Wm Grosvenor 3d),(Feb 22), 1963, Ap 1,36:8
Westmore, Alan Mrs, 1953, Ag 16,76:5
Westmore, Ernest, 1967, F 2,35:3
Westmore, Montague, 1940, Mr 31,46:3
Westmoreland, James R Mrs, 1967, Jl 16,28:6
Westmoreland, Vernon, 1961, Ja 18,30:3
Westmorland, Lord, 1948, My 13,26:3
Westney, Alfred W, 1942, O 13,23:3
Westney, Harry L, 1940, Mr 21,26:4
Westoff, A W F Mrs, 1940, Je 9,45:2
Weston, Aileen, 1942, N 19,25:1
Weston, Al G, 1941, Mr 22,15:3
Weston, Andrew, 1947, My 6,27:1
Weston, Arthur F, 1945, Mr 24,17:6
Weston, Arthur J, 1966, O 6,47:5
Weston, Catherine B Mrs, 1942, D 7,27:5
Weston, Cecilia, 1945, N 17,17:2
Weston, Charles, 1943, N 30,27:5; 1955, Jl 20,27:3
Weston, Charles J, 1950, Ap 8,13:3
Weston, Charles S (will, O 21,19:6), 1947, O 15,27:6
Weston, Charles S Mrs, 1946, Mr 21,25:1
Weston, Charles W, 1938, Ag 5,17:4
Weston, Chester E, 1953, O 10,17:6

Weston, Clifford G, 1967, D 23,23:4
Weston, D C Rev, 1903, Mr 21,9:5
Weston, Dacre L, 1955, F 9,25:3
Weston, Donald M, 1939, S 10,49:3
Weston, Doris (Mrs M L Borden), 1960, Jl 29,25:2
Weston, E, 1936, Ag 21,15:1
Weston, E G, 1952, Je 28,19:1
Weston, E P, 1929, My 14,18:2
Weston, Edith B Mrs, 1939, Ja 28,15:2
Weston, Edmund L, 1942, Ap 7,21:4
Weston, Edward, 1903, N 27,9:5; 1958, Ja 2,29:1
Weston, Edward F Mrs, 1954, S 22,29:3
Weston, Edwin H, 1940, Ap 5,21:3
Weston, Ehren F, 1965, Je 3,35:3
Weston, Ephraim J, 1968, My 16,47:2
Weston, Everett L, 1924, F 9,13:5
Weston, Frank, 1922, Ja 29,22:3
Weston, Frank M, 1956, O 6,21:6
Weston, Franklin, 1920, S 26,22:4
Weston, Fred B, 1938, N 22,23:4
Weston, Frederick H, 1903, Ag 7,7:7
Weston, Frederick P, 1943, Je 25,17:6
Weston, George B, 1959, D 21,27:2
Weston, George F, 1951, Ap 10,27:3
Weston, George K, 1942, Ap 27,15:4; 1953, N 4,33:4
Weston, George S, 1951, Ap 9,25:4; 1957, D 8,88:2
Weston, Gerritt Mrs, 1956, Mr 19,31:5
Weston, Gerritt Van Ingen, 1968, Je 29,29:4
Weston, Harold M Mrs, 1944, Jl 8,11:3
Weston, Henry Griggs Rev Dr, 1909, F 7,11:4
Weston, Herbert, 1964, Je 3,43:1
Weston, Herbert Mrs, 1965, S 8,47:1
Weston, J L, 1928, O 1,23:5
Weston, James F, 1950, Ag 4,21:5
Weston, John Francis Maj-Gen, 1917, Ag 4,7:4
Weston, John H, 1956, S 13,35:1
Weston, John W, 1961, Mr 19,89:2
Weston, Karl E, 1956, My 6,86:7
Weston, Karl E Mrs, 1951, F 21,27:5
Weston, Leo F, 1956, Ja 5,33:4
Weston, Lydia A, 1939, Mr 4,15:3
Weston, Milton, 1902, F 26,9:6
Weston, Paul G, 1939, D 20,25:4
Weston, R Warren, 1873, My 10,2:6
Weston, Ray (R Dunaeff), 1967, Ag 25,43:1
Weston, Rensselaer, 1920, F 29,22:5
Weston, Robert S, 1943, Jl 30,15:3
Weston, Robert W, 1951, My 17,31:3
Weston, Roy F, 1959, Mr 14,23:4
Weston, Ruby F Mrs, 1942, Ag 29,15:5
Weston, Ruth, 1955, N 7,29:5
Weston, Samuel P (por), 1938, N 24,27:1
Weston, Stanley H, 1966, My 14,31:2
Weston, Theodore, 1919, My 7,15:4
Weston, Theodore A, 1964, O 10,29:2
Weston, Thomas A (por), 1946, My 7,21:3
Weston, Thomas A Mrs, 1946, F 8,19:4
Weston, Walter L, 1943, Ag 24,19:4
Weston, William B, 1938, Ag 1,13:6
Weston, William H Dr, 1937, Ag 1,II,6:3
Weston, Willie, 1919, N 12,13:2
Weston, Willoughby Mrs, 1923, Ja 24,13:6
Weston, Zaccheus Mrs, 1949, S 21,31:5
Westover, Fred C, 1940, O 22,23:2
Westover, Harvey L, 1943, Ja 3,42:4
Westover, John, 1942, Ja 30,19:4
Westover, Myron, 1952, Ja 16,25:4
Westover, Robert R, 1942, Ja 14,21:2
Westover, Russ, 1966, Mr 7,27:3
Westover, Wendell, 1960, S 26,33:1
Westphal, Arthur W, 1939, Jl 6,24:2
Westphal, Augustus, 1939, N 27,17:5
Westphal, Emil C, 1951, My 27,68:3
Westphal, Frank C, 1948, N 26,23:2
Westphal, Frederick, 1951, N 5,31:3
Westphal, Frederick N, 1958, S 15,21:4
Westphal, George, 1922, Ag 19,11:5
Westphal, Henry E, 1954, S 3,17:5
Westphal, Julius W (por), 1941, Ag 5,19:4
Westphal, Oscar, 1962, O 29,29:2
Westphal, Roland G, 1949, Mr 10,27:4
Westphal, William H, 1964, My 20,43:5
Westphal, William J, 1942, S 26,15:5
Westpheily, 1913, Jl 19,7:7
Westreich, Alex Mrs, 1963, Jl 28,65:1
Westrope, Jackie (funl, Je 24,40:4), 1958, Je 20,19:1
Westwood, Frederick F, 1942, Mr 3,24:2
Westwood, Guy B, 1950, Jl 10,21:6
Westwood, Horace, 1956, D 25,25:6
Westwood, Lord (Wm), 1953, S 14,27:5
Westwood, Walter H, 1946, Ag 30,17:3
Wetchler, Benjamin B Mrs, 1960, N 29,37:5
Weth, Martin W, 1949, Je 11,17:5
Wetheral, William P, 1944, My 13,19:2
Wetherald, Agnes E, 1940, Mr 11,15:2
Wetherald, Harry H, 1955, Je 5,84:5
Wetherald, J Stanley, 1954, F 27,13:3
Wetherbee, C L, 1933, Je 25,22:3
Wetherbee, Charles, 1938, Ag 10,19:2
Wetherbee, Gardner (funl, Mr 28,13:4), 1916, Mr 25, 13:3
Wetherbee, Gardner G Mrs, 1909, D 31,9:6
Wetherby, Burton H, 1950, F 1,29:2
Wetherby, Charles B, 1942, O 15,23:3
Wetherby, Charles E, 1955, My 21,17:5
Wetherby, George E, 1945, Ag 3,17:4
Wetherell, Albert Laurence Col, 1908, Jl 14,5:4
Wetherell, Carl B, 1944, My 25,21:6
Wetherell, Harry C Mrs, 1951, Jl 18,29:3
Wetherill, Abel P, 1949, Mr 24,28:6
Wetherill, Alexander Stewart, 1914, S 3,7:6
Wetherill, Edith B Mrs, 1944, O 17,23:4
Wetherill, Frederic V, 1957, Mr 19,37:4
Wetherill, Frederick, 1944, D 18,19:2
Wetherill, Henry E, 1946, Mr 9,13:4
Wetherill, Herbert J, 1955, Jl 19,27:4
Wetherill, J L, 1941, Mr 2,42:8
Wetherill, John, 1944, D 1,24:2
Wetherill, John P Jr, 1940, Jl 17,21:2
Wetherill, Katherine L, 1938, Mr 20,II,8:3
Wetherill, Samuel, 1951, O 16,63:5
Wetherill, W Chattin Mrs, 1958, Jl 22,27:3
Wetherington, John M, 1952, Jl 10,31:1
Wetherton, Bertha Mrs, 1941, S 18,25:5
Wetherwax, John E, 1948, S 12,72:1
Wethling, Harry D, 1948, D 12,92:3
Wetjen, Albert R, 1948, Mr 10,27:5
Wetjen, Henry W, 1968, Je 1,27:3
Wetlesen, Thorvald, 1952, Jl 17,23:6
Wetmore, A R, 1881, Ja 22,8:4
Wetmore, Annie, 1880, Jl 27,1:7
Wetmore, Burton O, 1942, S 26,15:4
Wetmore, C F, 1880, My 16,2:3
Wetmore, Charles D (cor, My 10,15:1), 1941, My 9, 21:4
Wetmore, Charles Whitman, 1919, Je 3,13:3
Wetmore, David Mrs, 1914, Mr 9,9:3
Wetmore, Dwight S, 1948, N 19,27:2
Wetmore, Edith M K, 1966, Mr 11,34:1
Wetmore, Edmund, 1918, Jl 9,13:6
Wetmore, Edward W Dr, 1911, Mr 24,11:4
Wetmore, Florence Mrs, 1949, Ja 26,25:4
Wetmore, Fred G, 1943, D 30,17:2
Wetmore, George F, 1941, My 27,23:4
Wetmore, George P Ex-Sen, 1921, S 12,13:3
Wetmore, George W, 1923, Je 11,13:4
Wetmore, Horace O Mrs, 1944, Je 26,15:3
Wetmore, James A, 1940, Mr 15,23:3
Wetmore, John McEwen Dr, 1908, Jl 22,5:6
Wetmore, John W, 1940, O 10,25:1
Wetmore, Maude E K (will, N 24,12:4), 1951, N 4, 85:1
Wetmore, Monroe N, 1954, N 20,17:6
Wetmore, Moses C Col (funl, N 30,11:4), 1910, N 27,II,13:4
Wetmore, P D K, 1917, Ap 27,11:4
Wetmore, P M (see also Mr 17), 1876, Mr 19,12:2
Wetmore, Richard C Sr, 1951, Jl 1,50:8
Wetmore, Samuel, 1885, Mr 28,3:4
Wetmore, Stephen S, 1950, D 20,32:5
Wetmore, V C Bruce, 1953, Ap 13,27:4
Wetmore, W C, 1880, Mr 24,8:3
Wetmore, W J, 1880, N 28,2:7
Wetmore, Warren G, 1943, Jl 10,13:4
Wetmore, Willett A, 1945, Mr 25,38:4
Wetmore, William S K, 1925, Ja 31,13:5
Wetmore, Wing T, 1944, Je 20,19:5
Wetroba, Peter, 1911, Ag 14,7:5
Wetsel, Bill, 1951, Ja 15,17:1
Wettach, Adrian (Grock), 1959, Jl 15,29:1
Wettach, Robert H, 1964, Ag 30,93:2
Wettel, William A, 1951, S 27,31:4
Wettels, Louis S, 1944, Mr 4,13:4
Wetten, Albert H, 1953, S 5,15:3
Wetten, Emil C, 1947, Mr 12,25:4
Wettengel, Walter, 1962, Je 4,29:4
Wetter, Charles G, 1939, Je 25,36:5
Wetter, Pierce T, 1963, My 12,86:1
Wetterau, Charles A, 1957, Ap 30,29:1
Wetterau, Garret, 1958, Jl 22,28:6
Wetterau, Rudolf, 1953, My 18,21:3
Wetterau, Stanley D, 1953, Ja 9,21:1
Wetterberg, Ferdinand, 1957, Ja 24,29:1
Wettereau, James O, 1961, N 10,35:5
Wetterer, Charles F, 1939, Ja 26,21:5
Wettergren, Erik, 1961, Jl 19,29:5
Wettje, Robert A H, 1945, Ag 30,21:2
Wettlaufer, Andrew C, 1957, My 24,25:4
Wettlaufer, Conrad E, 1959, Ap 9,31:4
Wettlaufer, George, 1941, Ap 28,15:5
Wettlaufer, William O, 1938, Je 23,21:5
Wettleson, J W T Mrs, 1958, Je 13,23:4
Wettleson, John W T, 1955, Ja 18,27:1
Wettling, George, 1968, Je 8,27:2
Wetton, Walter H, 1937, D 25,15:3
Wetton, Walter H Mrs, 1963, Jl 24,31:4
Wettrick, Samuel J, 1954, Mr 11,34:4
Wettstein, John R, 1939, F 12,45:2
Wettyen, Harold E, 1938, Jl 30,13:5
Wetz, Homer F, 1952, D 21,52:6
Wetzel, Arthur M, 1946, Ag 20,28:3
Wetzel, Charles F, 1943, F 28,47:4
Wetzel, Daniel J, 1959, D 31,21:3
Wetzel, Frank J, 1940, D 21,17:6
Wetzel, Fred C, 1952, D 24,17:5
Wetzel, Frederick W, 1949, Mr 27,76:1
Wetzel, Harry H (por), 1938, Jl 6,23:3
Wetzel, Harry T, 1954, My 5,31:3
Wetzel, John, 1944, F 22,23:3
Wetzel, John W, 1945, O 29,19:4
Wetzel, John W Mrs, 1949, S 15,27:5
Wetzel, Otto, 1949, Ap 24,76:2
Wetzel, Ray, 1951, Ag 19,43:5
Wetzel, Reinhard A, 1953, D 25,17:4
Wetzel, Robert, 1956, Ap 10,31:2
Wetzel, Robert J, 1944, S 14,23:4
Wetzel, William, 1947, Ap 17,27:1
Wetzels, Joseph, 1953, D 17,37:4
Wetzler, Charles M, 1937, Ap 24,19:5
Wetzler, Charles N, 1951, Je 20,29:3
Wetzler, Herman H, 1943, My 30,26:3
Wetzler, Raymond A, 1955, Mr 28,27:5
Wetzler, Samuel G, 1958, D 3,37:5
Wetzler, Sol Mrs, 1951, Ap 19,31:3
Weust, Christopher, 1937, D 2,25:5
Weve, Henricus J, 1962, Ja 5,29:1
Wever, B F, 1948, Ja 13,25:4
Wever, John M, 1914, S 28,9:2
Wexberg, Leopold E, 1957, Ja 12,19:2
Wexelblatt, Abraham S, 1953, F 5,23:5
Wexler, Harry, 1962, Ag 12,80:1
Wexler, Harry Mrs, 1962, S 6,31:3
Wexler, Jacob, 1941, Ja 17,17:5
Wexler, Milton R (por), 1949, Ag 13,11:4
Wexler, Robert, 1951, Ja 14,84:4
Wexler, Solomon, 1921, Ap 23,11:6
Wexley, George J, 1951, D 6,33:5
Wexley, Irving, 1952, My 27,27:3
Wexman, Oscar, 1940, Ja 31,13:2
Wexner, Philip F Mrs, 1963, Jl 21,64:7
Wey, Henry F G, 1940, Ja 27,13:2
Weyand, Alfred E, 1957, Ag 31,15:4
Weyand, Edmund, 1946, D 4,48:1
Weyand, Henry A, 1951, Ap 24,29:3
Weyant, Andrew Mrs, 1948, S 30,27:2
Weyant, Charles C Mrs, 1943, N 20,13:5
Weyant, Charles W, 1940, My 19,42:3
Weyant, Clarence J, 1950, Jl 12,29:4
Weyant, David H Jr, 1960, S 2,23:3
Weyant, Isaac, 1955, Je 10,25:2
Weyant, Peter C, 1949, Mr 21,23:5
Weyant, Peter C Mrs, 1941, Ag 14,17:5
Weybret, Fred, 1955, F 1,29:5
Weyburn, Samuel F, 1941, F 23,41:2
Weydemeyer, Joseph Col, 1866, Ag 27,5:5
Weydig, George A, 1948, D 6,25:3
Weydman, Charles B, 1948, Ja 11,56:2
Weyer, Eugene, 1907, Mr 2,9:6
Weyer, Kenneth W, 1958, Ag 13,27:4
Weyer, Robert A, 1948, Ja 19,23:4
Weyerhaeuser, Frederick, 1914, Ap 5,15:1; 1961, F 2, 29:3
Weyerhaeuser, Frederick E, 1945, O 19,23:1
Weyerhaeuser, John P Jr, 1956, D 9,87:5
Weyerhaeuser, Rudolph M, 1946, Jl 13,15:6
Weyers, Arthur W Mrs, 1948, S 14,29:4
Weyers, Bruno, 1952, Ap 18,25:4
Weyforth, B Stuart Jr, 1966, Jl 5,27:2
Weygand, Maxime (funl plans, Ja 30,1:1; funl, F 3,14:5), 1965, Ja 29,29:1
Weygandt, Carl V, 1964, S 5,19:3
Weygandt, Cornelius, 1957, Ag 2,19:2
Weygandt, Cornelius Nolan, 1907, F 18,9:6
Weygandt, John H, 1951, Jl 31,21:1
Weygandt, Lillian J, 1938, Jl 26,19:4
Weygandt, Louisa E Mrs, 1921, F 21,11:6
Weygandt, William H, 1942, N 10,27:6
Weygant, Charles H Col, 1909, Mr 11,9:6
Weygant, Charles H Sr, 1943, Jl 5,15:2
Weygant, William M, 1938, S 15,25:3
Weygold, Frederick P, 1941, Ag 18,13:6
Weyh, Robert G, 1953, Mr 6,23:1
Weyhing, Augustus (Gus), 1955, S 5,11:4
Weyl, Adolph, 1937, D 24,17:3
Weyl, Hermann, 1955, D 10,21:3
Weyl, Hermann Mrs, 1948, S 7,26:3
Weyl, Max, 1914, Jl 7,9:6
Weyl, Thomas J, 1952, My 10,21:5
Weyl, Walter Edward, 1919, N 11,13:3
Weyland, Grover C, 1953, N 26,31:2
Weyler, Jacob, 1944, Je 20,19:2
Weyler, V, 1930, O 21,27:1
Weyler, Valeriano Mrs, 1920, My 4,11:1
Weyman, Edward A Dr, 1906, N 6,9:6
Weymann, Albert C, 1953, Jl 27,19:2
Weymann, Arthur C, 1951, Ja 6,15:2
Weymer, Bertine D, 1937, Je 12,15:4
Weymouth, Aubrey, 1939, Jl 28,17:2
Weymouth, Aubrey Mrs, 1959, Ag 27,27:3
Weymouth, Clarence A, 1958, Ja 30,23:1
Weymouth, Frank E, 1941, Jl 23,19:3
Weymouth, Fred A, 1964, Mr 27,27:1
Weymouth, Frederick A, 1955, F 2,27:2
Weymouth, George, 1950, F 1,29:1
Weymouth, Lucius P, 1961, My 24,41:2
Weymouth, Thomas R, 1958, S 24,27:1
Weymuller, Charles F Mrs, 1949, My 14,13:2
Weyner, Hannah E Mrs, 1955, D 17,23:2
Weyrauch, Henry M, 1940, Ap 15,17:4

Weyrauch, Henry W Mrs, 1943, Ag 11,19:3
Weyrauch, Martin H, 1958, F 2,86:7
Weyrauch, Paul H Gen, 1937, O 13,23:4
Wezenaar, Leonard J M, 1968, Ap 13,25:2
Whadcook, Russell, 1956, Je 26,29:4
Whaland, Charles W Dr, 1937, My 8,19:6
Whale, George, 1925, My 5,21:4
Whale, James, 1957, My 30,23:1
Whalen, Charles H, 1945, Ag 9,21:3
Whalen, Charles J, 1941, Ap 8,25:4
Whalen, Charles J Mrs, 1950, Ag 14,17:4
Whalen, Daniel F, 1959, Jl 2,26:1
Whalen, Edgar C, 1953, O 15,33:5
Whalen, Edward J, 1944, Ag 19,11:1
Whalen, Ella F, 1912, Ja 3,13:4
Whalen, Elmer O, 1949, Je 20,19:3
Whalen, Elwell, 1957, S 3,27:4
Whalen, Frank D, 1953, N 21,13:3
Whalen, Grover A (funl, Ap 25,39:2; will, My 8,35:7), 1962, Ap 21,1:4
Whalen, Grover A Mrs, 1968, D 8,86:6
Whalen, H Stevenson Lt, 1916, Jl 28,11:6
Whalen, Harold, 1940, Ja 18,23:4
Whalen, J, 1927, Ja 1,13:3
Whalen, James E (cor, N 25,29:1), 1959, N 24,34:1
Whalen, James F, 1942, Ap 10,17:1; 1953, Ja 22,23:1
Whalen, James M, 1954, D 18,15:6
Whalen, John, 1941, S 16,23:3
Whalen, John E, 1953, Jl 17,17:6
Whalen, John J, 1948, O 26,31:2; 1951, O 6,19:5; 1955, My 21,17:4; 1958, N 24,29:2
Whalen, John J Mrs, 1946, Mr 29,23:4
Whalen, John K, 1942, D 10,25:2
Whalen, John N, 1925, N 17,25:5
Whalen, John P, 1951, D 31,13:3; 1954, O 21,27:2
Whalen, John T, 1960, Ja 29,25:1
Whalen, Joseph A, 1956, O 7,87:1
Whalen, Joseph M, 1957, N 28,31:4
Whalen, Louis A, 1946, Ja 15,23:2
Whalen, Martin J, 1949, N 24,31:2
Whalen, Michael J, 1943, Ap 28,39:3
Whalen, Michael J Msgr, 1937, F 5,21:5
Whalen, Peter F, 1952, Je 10,27:4
Whalen, Peter R, 1944, Je 10,15:3
Whalen, Richard, 1945, O 14,42:6
Whalen, Robert A, 1951, F 1,25:2
Whalen, Robert E, 1951, Ag 13,17:6
Whalen, Rose, 1869, Jl 28,2:7
Whalen, S C Jr, 1904, F 7,7:6
Whalen, Thomas F, 1944, Ja 7,17:3
Whalen, Thomas J, 1968, Ag 24,29:4
Whalen, Thomas P, 1949, F 11,24:3
Whalen, Will W Rev, 1949, Jl 4,26:8
Whalen, William A, 1948, Ap 14,28:3
Whalen, William F, 1957, Jl 29,19:2
Whalen, William H, 1950, D 15,31:2
Whalen, William L, 1957, O 10,33:2
Whalen, William P, 1961, Ja 30,23:3
Whalen, William T, 1957, My 29,27:4
Whaley, A R, 1934, Ap 20,21:1
Whaley, Davis H, 1954, Ja 2,11:2
Whaley, E A Dr, 1885, My 15,2:2
Whaley, Eddie, 1960, N 15,39:4
Whaley, Frank J, 1965, F 7,92:2
Whaley, George P, 1949, Jl 11,17:2
Whaley, Herman S, 1945, O 13,15:4
Whaley, James, 1937, N 7,II,9:2
Whaley, James H Jr, 1949, O 13,27:5
Whaley, John R, 1949, Mr 17,25:2
Whaley, Mark L Sr, 1949, O 1,13:2
Whaley, Percival H, 1963, Ap 3,47:1
Whaley, Richard S, 1951, N 9,27:5
Whaling, Henry M, 1944, N 19,49:2
Whaling, Joshua B, 1943, N 9,21:4
Whalley, A F Cecil, 1942, Je 25,23:4
Whalley, Mr, 1878, O 25,5:2
Whallon, Albert K, 1940, Ap 18,23:5
Whallon, Edward P, 1939, Je 4,49:1
Whallon, Walter L, 1960, Ag 27,19:2
Wham, Fred L, 1967, F 4,27:3
Wham, Joseph W Maj, 1908, D 22,9:2
Whamond, Reginald Mrs, 1952, Mr 22,13:4
Whan, Samuel W, 1939, F 24,19:2
Wharff, Justin W, 1915, N 15,11:6
Wharry, Grace A Mrs, 1915, D 27,9:4
Wharton, A H, 1928, Jl 30,17:5
Wharton, Albert E Mrs, 1956, Ja 8,86:2
Wharton, Bromley, 1938, Jl 23,13:6
Wharton, Charles M, 1949, N 16,30:5
Wharton, Charles M Mrs, 1947, D 9,29:3
Wharton, Charles S, 1939, S 5,23:5
Wharton, D D, 1948, S 10,23:5
Wharton, Edith (por), 1937, Ag 13,17:1
Wharton, Edward L, 1956, Je 18,25:3
Wharton, F, 1889, F 22,5:2
Wharton, Francis A, 1963, D 16,33:4
Wharton, George Mifflin, 1924, Ja 21,17:5
Wharton, Harry J Sr, 1949, Je 6,19:2
Wharton, Henry R, 1957, My 21,35:3
Wharton, Irvine N, 1948, O 15,24:3
Wharton, Jack Marshal, 1882, Ap 8,5:4
Wharton, Joseph, 1909, Ja 12,9:5
Wharton, Philip G, 1964, My 30,17:6
Wharton, R, 1933, Jl 17,13:4
Wharton, Thelma, 1938, N 25,23:2
Wharton, William B, 1939, Je 25,36:8
Wharton, William R M, 1949, S 10,17:4
Whately, Richard Archbishop, 1863, O 22,8:1
Whatham, Richard, 1964, Je 14,85:1
Whatley, Seaborn T, 1944, D 3,58:7
Whatmore, Hugh, 1939, Mr 30,23:5
Whatmough, Joshua, 1964, Ag 28,37:1
Whatnall, George E, 1944, S 25,17:6
Whealan, Emmett, 1950, F 19,77:1
Wheary, George, 1942, Ap 24,17:4
Wheat, A Leonard, 1941, Ja 11,17:3
Wheat, Alfred A (por), 1943, Mr 13,13:1
Wheat, Alice C Mrs, 1941, Je 28,15:3
Wheat, Charles, 1946, Ag 30,17:4
Wheat, Corydon, 1943, F 23,21:4
Wheat, David H Mrs, 1951, Je 28,25:5
Wheat, Frank M, 1955, Ag 4,25:3
Wheat, George S (por), 1937, D 27,15:3
Wheat, George S Mrs, 1954, S 2,21:4
Wheat, Henry A, 1939, Mr 22,23:2
Wheat, Roscoe M, 1954, N 24,23:4
Wheat, Silas C, 1922, S 4,13:6
Wheat, William H (por), 1944, Ja 17,19:1
Wheatcroft, Harry R, 1967, Je 1,44:1
Wheatcroft, Irving H, 1967, F 18,29:3
Wheatcroft, N, 1897, Mr 4,7:5
Wheater, Frank B, 1940, Ja 27,13:4
Wheatland, Clifford J, 1944, My 2,19:3
Wheatland, Frank L, 1940, Ag 1,21:6
Wheatland, Richard, 1944, Mr 30,21:3
Wheatley, Abram C, 1954, N 5,15:4
Wheatley, Henry Benjamin, 1917, My 2,11:3
Wheatley, John, 1957, Jl 9,29:1
Wheatley, John N, 1940, N 11,19:4
Wheatley, Leon F, 1944, D 20,23:5
Wheatley, Lucille, 1952, O 13,21:3
Wheatley, Richard Rev Dr, 1909, Je 12,7:4
Wheatley, William J, 1953, My 7,31:2
Wheatley, William Sr, 1946, Mr 15,22:3
Wheatly, W (see also N 4), 1876, N 7,2:3
Wheaton, A Warren, 1955, Ap 20,33:4
Wheaton, Anna (Mrs W T Collins), 1961, D 27,27:4
Wheaton, Charles F, 1955, Mr 11,25:3
Wheaton, Charles W, 1943, Ag 26,17:3
Wheaton, Francis, 1942, Je 24,19:4
Wheaton, Frank, 1937, F 5,21:1
Wheaton, Frank Gen, 1903, Je 19,9:5
Wheaton, Henry G, 1865, Ag 28,8:4
Wheaton, Isaac S, 1947, S 19,23:2
Wheaton, James L, 1950, S 20,31:3
Wheaton, Loyd Gen, 1918, S 19,13:2
Wheaton, Minor L, 1959, Mr 11,35:2
Wheaton, Olive, 1940, Mr 4,15:5
Wheaton, Oliver, 1940, My 16,23:2
Wheaton, Ralph H Mrs, 1958, S 30,31:3
Wheatstone, Charles F R S Sir, 1875, O 21,5:5
Whedon, Burt D, 1947, Mr 27,27:4
Whedon, D D, 1884, Ag 20,3:4; 1885, Je 9,5:4
Whedon, Legrand S, 1939, D 7,27:4
Whedon, Milton J, 1944, Ja 9,42:2
Wheelan, Albertine R Mrs, 1954, Ja 10,87:2
Wheelan, Frank M, 1938, N 1,24:4
Wheelan, James Nicholas Gen, 1922, D 1,17:5
Wheelan, Raymond A, 1962, My 25,33:6
Wheelan, Robert B, 1964, Ja 20,43:1
Wheeler, A C, 1903, My 11,9:5
Wheeler, Alan R, 1956, Jl 19,27:1
Wheeler, Albert G, 1937, F 6,17:3
Wheeler, Albert Gallatin, 1917, S 25,11:6
Wheeler, Alfred E, 1938, O 27,23:5
Wheeler, Alfred N, 1937, Ap 15,23:3
Wheeler, Alonzo Ex-Judge, 1913, O 12,15:3
Wheeler, Alvin S, 1940, My 13,17:5
Wheeler, Andrew, 1903, N 22,7:5
Wheeler, Andrew T, 1938, Mr 12,17:1
Wheeler, Anna M Mrs, 1937, Ja 5,23:2
Wheeler, Anna S Mrs, 1943, D 20,23:1
Wheeler, Annie E, 1955, Ap 12,29:1
Wheeler, Archer C, 1956, S 5,27:4
Wheeler, Archer E, 1956, Mr 9,23:4
Wheeler, Archer E Mrs, 1956, Mr 16,23:2
Wheeler, Arthur, 1941, O 7,24:4
Wheeler, Arthur D, 1940, Ja 11,23:3
Wheeler, Arthur E, 1966, N 23,39:3
Wheeler, Arthur L Mrs, 1966, Ap 1,35:1
Wheeler, Arthur Martin Prof, 1918, Jl 18,9:6
Wheeler, Augustus B Mrs, 1941, Mr 17,17:3
Wheeler, B I, 1927, My 4,25:3
Wheeler, Bert, 1955, N 3,31:4; 1968, Ja 19,44:2
Wheeler, Bleecker L, 1959, Ja 6,33:4
Wheeler, Burr, 1964, Jl 31,23:5
Wheeler, Burton K Mrs, 1962, S 7,29:5
Wheeler, C Albert, 1937, D 1,23:2
Wheeler, C E Dr, 1935, Ag 6,6:2
Wheeler, C H, 1883, Ag 17,8:3
Wheeler, Charles, 1945, N 9,19:3
Wheeler, Charles A, 1944, F 25,17:4; 1949, O 24,23:3; 1957, D 30,23:4
Wheeler, Charles A Dr, 1904, F 13,9:5
Wheeler, Charles B, 1946, Ap 12,27:2; 1950, Jl 21,19:6
Wheeler, Charles C, 1939, Ap 18,23:1
Wheeler, Charles E (por), 1949, Mr 20,76:4
Wheeler, Charles E, 1949, N 26,15:6
Wheeler, Charles Gilbert, 1912, F 1,13:4
Wheeler, Charles Mrs, 1947, Je 5,25:2
Wheeler, Charles N, 1949, D 4,108:4
Wheeler, Charles S Mrs, 1952, Ap 6,88:1
Wheeler, Charles W Mrs, 1943, N 30,27:5
Wheeler, Charlotte A Mrs, 1940, Je 9,44:3
Wheeler, Chauncey E, 1948, O 14,29:3
Wheeler, Chester E, 1951, Ja 30,25:3
Wheeler, Clarence, 1966, Ap 30,31:5
Wheeler, Clarence J, 1943, Ja 1,23:5
Wheeler, Clayton L, 1950, D 28,25:4
Wheeler, Clifton, 1953, My 12,27:2
Wheeler, Corbin, 1950, Ag 15,30:3
Wheeler, Cortlandt S, 1943, Mr 23,19:4
Wheeler, Cottrell C, 1963, Jl 3,25:3
Wheeler, D M, 1879, My 29,5:5
Wheeler, Daniel E Mrs, 1963, O 3,35:6
Wheeler, Daniel M, 1943, S 30,21:4
Wheeler, DeLoyd H, 1965, Ag 12,27:4
Wheeler, Donald Dr, 1968, Ap 7,92:8
Wheeler, Dunham, 1938, Mr 4,23:3
Wheeler, E A Mrs, 1921, D 12,15:1
Wheeler, E P, 1876, Ap 1,1:6
Wheeler, E P Mrs, 1902, Ja 19,9:1
Wheeler, Edward Jewitt Dr (funl, Jl 17,13:5), 1922, Jl 16,26:5
Wheeler, Edward Pepperell (por), 1925, F 10,23:1
Wheeler, Edward W, 1963, N 2,25:1
Wheeler, Edwin B, 1944, Jl 15,13:7
Wheeler, Elmer, 1968, O 3,47:2
Wheeler, Emma G, 1942, D 30,23:2
Wheeler, Ernest B, 1959, Jl 12,73:1
Wheeler, Ernest E, 1955, F 23,27:4
Wheeler, Ernest H, 1950, Ag 31,25:4
Wheeler, Evan R, 1954, N 16,27:2
Wheeler, Evan R Mrs, 1957, D 20,24:2
Wheeler, Everett P Mrs, 1945, Mr 21,23:3
Wheeler, Ezra, 1871, S 24,1:6
Wheeler, Ferdinand C, 1944, Ag 25,13:4
Wheeler, Frances E, 1955, D 24,13:6
Wheeler, Francis Q, 1952, Mr 28,23:2
Wheeler, Frank E, 1925, Mr 17,21:5; 1938, Ap 12,23:5
Wheeler, Frank L, 1940, O 26,15:2
Wheeler, Frank M, 1919, D 30,13:3
Wheeler, Frank Mrs, 1949, F 13,76:1
Wheeler, Frank Q Mrs, 1950, N 2,31:2
Wheeler, Frank T, 1951, Ja 5,21:1
Wheeler, Frank W, 1941, S 1,15:4
Wheeler, Frank W Mrs (W Lenihan), 1964, Jl 30,27:1
Wheeler, Fred Y, 1949, Mr 3,25:3
Wheeler, Frederick, 1947, D 23,23:5
Wheeler, Frederick J, 1951, Ag 8,25:5
Wheeler, Frederick Maj, 1920, Ja 14,9:1
Wheeler, G W, 1932, Jl 28,17:1
Wheeler, George, 1941, Ap 2,23:2; 1945, S 26,23:5
Wheeler, George A Mrs, 1909, Mr 22,7:5
Wheeler, George B, 1943, Ja 24,42:4; 1955, My 2,21:5
Wheeler, George B Mrs, 1945, Mr 4,36:4; 1947, O 5, 71:2
Wheeler, George C, 1959, Jl 1,25:4; 1966, S 29,47:4
Wheeler, George C Mrs, 1951, My 19,15:5
Wheeler, George M, 1953, Mr 4,27:4
Wheeler, George Montague Maj, 1905, My 5,9:4
Wheeler, George R, 1938, N 17,25:5
Wheeler, George W, 1948, S 14,29:5; 1960, Ja 20,31:4
Wheeler, George Wakeman Ex-Judge, 1917, S 21,9:6
Wheeler, H Ambrose, 1942, Je 7,42:1
Wheeler, H Condit, 1914, O 30,9:6
Wheeler, Harold F, 1956, F 17,23:3
Wheeler, Harriet, 1924, Ap 10,23:4
Wheeler, Harriet W, 1942, Jl 29,17:2
Wheeler, Harry A, 1960, Ja 25,27:4
Wheeler, Harry T, 1948, Ja 21,25:4
Wheeler, Hayden W, 1904, O 29,9:4
Wheeler, Henry, 1945, Je 21,19:1
Wheeler, Henry A (est), 1914, Je 17,11:6
Wheeler, Henry H, 1955, D 17,23:4
Wheeler, Henry Holt, 1917, D 19,11:7
Wheeler, Henry L, 1945, Ag 9,21:4; 1947, F 23,53:3
Wheeler, Henry Lord Mrs, 1921, O 10,13:5
Wheeler, Herbert, 1942, Ja 13,19:5
Wheeler, Herbert B, 1960, Ja 15,31:4
Wheeler, Herbert Mrs, 1953, S 10,25:2
Wheeler, Hiland H, 1952, Ap 1,29:4
Wheeler, Homer J, 1945, N 19,21:5
Wheeler, Howard D, 1958, F 27,27:2
Wheeler, Howard E, 1961, Mr 24,31:1
Wheeler, Hoyt H Judge, 1906, N 20,9:6
Wheeler, Imogene H, 1945, N 9,19:3
Wheeler, Isaac M Mrs (Eliz), 1966, N 23,39:4
Wheeler, J Donovan, 1903, Jl 17,7:6
Wheeler, J Harmon, 1953, Je 30,23:3
Wheeler, J J Mrs, 1942, O 7,25:6
Wheeler, J W, 1882, Mr 19,2:2; 1923, Jl 29,6:5
Wheeler, James, 1904, F 5,9:4
Wheeler, James Cooper, 1912, S 25,13:2
Wheeler, James E, 1954, F 17,31:4
Wheeler, James R, 1925, Ja 25,7:2
Wheeler, James Rignall Prof, 1918, F 10,17:1
Wheeler, James Sr, 1950, My 6,15:2
Wheeler, Jane H P Mrs, 1942, Ap 27,15:5

Wheeler, Janet, 1945, O 26,19:1
Wheeler, Jennie P Mrs, 1941, S 26,23:4
Wheeler, Jessie L, 1949, Mr 2,25:4
Wheeler, John A, 1953, Ap 20,25:5
Wheeler, John B, 1942, My 2,13:3; 1943, D 3,23:1
Wheeler, John C, 1949, Ap 29,23:1; 1949, Jl 6,27:3
Wheeler, John C Mrs, 1956, O 12,29:2
Wheeler, John H, 1940, Ap 4,23:4
Wheeler, John M (por), 1938, Ag 23,17:3
Wheeler, John M Mrs, 1952, Ja 30,26:3
Wheeler, John P, 1964, D 1,41:1
Wheeler, John T, 1947, S 14,60:2
Wheeler, Joseph A, 1957, Je 18,33:3
Wheeler, Joseph Brig-Gen, 1906, Ja 26,2:4
Wheeler, Joseph E, 1966, Ap 8,31:3
Wheeler, Joseph Jr, 1938, Ag 7,32:8
Wheeler, Joseph L Mrs, 1960, D 21,31:2
Wheeler, Joseph R, 1944, Jl 11,15:1
Wheeler, K M, 1947, D 21,55:8
Wheeler, Karl V, 1956, S 21,25:4
Wheeler, Lawrence, 1952, N 11,30:3
Wheeler, Lee C, 1949, Je 28,27:3
Wheeler, Leon, 1941, N 21,17:2
Wheeler, Leonard Mrs, 1947, Jl 13,44:6
Wheeler, Lewis H, 1957, Ag 30,19:5
Wheeler, Lilla C, 1951, O 2,27:4
Wheeler, Louis H, 1940, My 17,19:4
Wheeler, Lucia, 1952, N 26,23:3
Wheeler, Lucien C, 1950, Jl 24,17:6
Wheeler, Lucylle, 1924, D 26,15:6
Wheeler, Margaret M Mrs, 1948, F 22,48:8
Wheeler, Margaret V Mrs, 1937, Ja 29,19:4
Wheeler, Marguerite F, 1951, Ja 31,25:4
Wheeler, Mary Mrs, 1925, Ag 20,19:6
Wheeler, Maxwell S, 1956, Mr 18,88:1
Wheeler, Minnie, 1906, Je 4,1:5
Wheeler, Mrs (Belle Palmer), 1874, Ap 24,2:3
Wheeler, N K, 1880, S 23,8:3
Wheeler, Nathaniel, 1960, Jl 15,23:4
Wheeler, Nelson P, 1961, Mr 28,29:6
Wheeler, Nelson P Jr, 1939, Ap 28,25:2
Wheeler, Nelson P Mrs, 1961, Mr 28,29:6
Wheeler, Ogden H Sgt-Maj, 1864, Mr 21,5:1
Wheeler, Oscar L, 1937, N 28,II,9:2
Wheeler, Paul, 1949, O 2,80:7
Wheeler, Perry M, 1954, O 25,27:2
Wheeler, Plumer, 1954, D 14,33:3
Wheeler, Post, 1956, D 24,13:5
Wheeler, Post Mrs, 1956, Ag 18,17:3
Wheeler, R C Mrs, 1916, F 9,11:5
Wheeler, Ralph A, 1949, O 4,27:3
Wheeler, Ralph B, 1942, My 28,17:2
Wheeler, Ralph H, 1950, Mr 11,15:4; 1962, Mr 22,35:5
Wheeler, Ralph N, 1938, My 12,23:5
Wheeler, Ralph N Mrs, 1949, N 28,27:6
Wheeler, Ralph R, 1945, Ag 13,19:3
Wheeler, Reginald T, 1954, O 16,17:6
Wheeler, Richard E, 1952, Je 16,17:5
Wheeler, Robert A, 1962, My 27,92:7
Wheeler, Robert A Mrs, 1953, Mr 26,31:2
Wheeler, Robert T, 1945, Je 6,21:2
Wheeler, Roger W, 1947, S 21,60:6
Wheeler, Rufus, 1865, My 17,4:1
Wheeler, Russell Jr, 1951, Ap 17,29:4
Wheeler, Ruth, 1948, O 1,25:5
Wheeler, Samuel, 1875, O 29,5:2
Wheeler, Samuel H, 1920, N 15,15:4
Wheeler, Samuel Mrs, 1955, My 21,17:6
Wheeler, Schuyler Skaats Dr (funl, Ap 24,21:4), 1923, Ap 21,11:3
Wheeler, Seth Jr, 1941, Ap 29,19:2
Wheeler, Sidney Mrs, 1949, D 31,15:6
Wheeler, Sylvia, 1937, Mr 11,24:1
Wheeler, T H, 1926, S 16,27:3
Wheeler, Theodore, 1922, N 1,19:6
Wheeler, Thomas B, 1957, F 10,86:2
Wheeler, Thomas B Mrs, 1949, D 3,15:2
Wheeler, Thomas F Mrs, 1923, Ag 6,11:2
Wheeler, Thomas J, 1942, Ap 10,17:3
Wheeler, Tom L, 1951, Ja 19,25:3
Wheeler, Victor W, 1952, Je 20,23:6
Wheeler, W A, 1874, O 31,12:3; 1887, Je 5,5:1
Wheeler, W A Mrs, 1876, Mr 4,5:2
Wheeler, W B, 1927, S 6,1:4
Wheeler, W Kenneth, 1963, Ap 29,31:2
Wheeler, W Reginald, 1963, Ag 21,33:2
Wheeler, W Ridley, 1959, Je 2,35:5
Wheeler, Walter H, 1938, S 28,25:3
Wheeler, Walter H Jr Mrs, 1967, S 26,47:3
Wheeler, Walter R, 1951, My 10,31:3
Wheeler, Wilfrid, 1961, D 26,25:3
Wheeler, Willard C, 1950, D 26,23:1
Wheeler, William B, 1941, S 7,51:4
Wheeler, William B (por), 1947, F 22,13:4
Wheeler, William E 2d, 1938, Mr 11,19:1
Wheeler, William G, 1950, F 22,30:4
Wheeler, William H, 1941, N 16,57:3; 1960, Jl 24,64:4
Wheeler, William I D, 1943, S 14,23:4
Wheeler, William J, 1938, Je 24,19:5
Wheeler, William M, 1937, Ap 20,26:1
Wheeler, William M Mrs, 1947, S 7,60:3
Wheeler, William N, 1945, Mr 24,17:4
Wheeler, William O, 1947, Mr 3,21:4
Wheeler, William O Mrs, 1955, Ap 3,86:3
Wheeler, William R, 1963, N 14,35:1
Wheeler, Wilmot F, 1963, My 21,37:5
Wheeler, Xenophon Gen, 1914, F 1,5:5
Wheeless, Grace, 1950, Ja 31,23:1
Wheelhouse, Wilfrid N, 1941, My 17,15:5
Wheelihan, Charles A, 1946, F 22,25:4
Wheelihan, John J, 1947, S 25,29:5
Wheelin, James E, 1951, Ap 6,25:2
Wheelock, Albert A, 1949, Je 22,31:1
Wheelock, Albert H, 1947, My 7,27:2
Wheelock, Austin W, 1953, D 11,34:2
Wheelock, Carrie M, 1944, S 7,23:5
Wheelock, Charles H, 1960, Je 6,29:4
Wheelock, Edward J, 1945, O 29,19:3
Wheelock, F R, 1948, My 14,23:3
Wheelock, G H, 1882, Ja 24,2:5
Wheelock, Gen, 1865, Ja 29,4:6
Wheelock, George Alexander, 1922, N 12,6:4
Wheelock, George G Dr, 1907, Mr 23,9:5
Wheelock, George L Mrs, 1943, O 1,19:5
Wheelock, Harvey L, 1958, S 5,27:2
Wheelock, Henry A, 1954, Jl 14,27:5
Wheelock, James R, 1941, Ja 14,21:5
Wheelock, Joseph (Cor, O 19,9:4), 1909, O 18,7:2
Wheelock, Joseph A, 1906, My 10,9:4
Wheelock, Joseph Jr, 1910, Ja 26,9:5
Wheelock, Joseph Sr, 1908, S 29,9:5
Wheelock, Kate, 1951, Jl 20,21:2
Wheelock, Louis W, 1950, Ja 11,23:3
Wheelock, Lucy, 1946, O 3,27:2
Wheelock, R L, 1962, Ag 25,22:1
Wheelock, Samuel W, 1937, Mr 16,23:2
Wheelock, Silas M, 1937, Je 25,21:3
Wheelock, W A (see also Je 24,25), 1878, Je 26,8:3
Wheelock, W W, 1940, D 5,25:1
Wheelock, Warren, 1960, Jl 9,19:1
Wheelock, William A, 1951, N 26,25:1
Wheelock, William E Mrs, 1950, Ja 29,68:4
Wheelock, William H (por), 1942, F 17,21:1
Wheelock, William H Mrs, 1960, Ja 16,21:5
Wheelock, William Jr, 1875, Jl 13,4:6
Wheelock, William Mrs, 1952, O 23,31:4
Wheelright, William, 1873, S 27,1:7
Wheelwright, B F (funl, O 11,8:2), 1875, O 9,2:3
Wheelwright, C Edward, 1954, Ap 16,21:4
Wheelwright, C T Mrs, 1932, Je 13,15:3
Wheelwright, Edmund M, 1912, Ag 16,9:5
Wheelwright, Farley Mrs, 1941, S 12,21:4
Wheelwright, James M, 1940, O 19,17:2
Wheelwright, Jere H, 1920, Ja 8,17:1
Wheelwright, Jere H Jr, 1961, Ja 23,23:4
Wheelwright, John Tyler, 1925, D 24,13:4
Wheelwright, Joseph S (por), 1941, O 11,17:1
Wheelwright, Margaret C, 1952, Ja 21,15:1
Wheelwright, Robert, 1965, N 3,35:6
Wheelwright, Thomas J, 1946, Jl 23,25:3
Wheelwright, Thomas S, 1937, Ja 1,23:5
Whelan, Albert, 1961, F 20,27:1
Whelan, Albert I, 1941, Ja 11,17:5
Whelan, Bp, 1874, Jl 8,4:7
Whelan, Charles, 1918, D 2,13:7; 1939, Ja 29,33:2
Whelan, Charles A, 1941, D 10,25:1
Whelan, Charles H, 1945, My 30,19:1
Whelan, Charles J Mrs, 1963, S 14,25:6
Whelan, Charles S, 1910, Je 11,11:5
Whelan, Charles T, 1950, S 16,19:3
Whelan, Daniel A, 1967, Ap 2,92:8
Whelan, David, 1922, Ja 15,22:3
Whelan, Edward F, 1953, O 16,27:4
Whelan, Frederick A, 1913, Jl 28,7:6
Whelan, Frederick D, 1942, O 16,19:2
Whelan, George J (por), 1945, D 30,14:8
Whelan, George M, 1958, Mr 21,21:2
Whelan, Harriet (Sister M Margarita), 1959, Je 3, 35:2
Whelan, Harriette, 1946, Jl 15,25:5
Whelan, Harry G Sr, 1948, Mr 17,25:2
Whelan, Helen L, 1942, F 6,19:1
Whelan, Herbert F, 1948, Je 24,26:3
Whelan, Howard J, 1951, Ap 1,93:2
Whelan, Isaac P Msgr, 1918, D 15,22:3
Whelan, James, 1948, Ag 14,13:1
Whelan, James C, 1964, S 18,32:5
Whelan, James J, 1961, Ja 11,47:5
Whelan, James J Jr, 1945, Mr 13,23:4
Whelan, James P, 1950, F 13,21:3
Whelan, John A, 1939, Ap 13,23:5; 1953, Ap 14,27:4
Whelan, John C, 1950, D 20,31:2
Whelan, John F Mrs, 1948, S 21,27:2
Whelan, John J, 1951, S 17,21:5; 1953, Mr 3,27:5
Whelan, Joseph, 1925, Je 20,13:6
Whelan, Joseph A, 1955, My 7,17:5
Whelan, Joseph A Mrs, 1939, Ja 4,21:5
Whelan, Joseph B, 1961, Jl 25,27:1
Whelan, Joseph F, 1958, S 18,31:2
Whelan, Joseph F Mrs, 1945, Je 29,15:2
Whelan, Joseph Mrs, 1966, Ap 12,39:1
Whelan, Joseph T, 1944, N 7,27:2
Whelan, Joseph W, 1945, My 25,19:4
Whelan, Martin J Sr, 1945, S 8,15:4
Whelan, Mary A, 1954, Je 9,31:3
Whelan, Mary C, 1939, Jl 4,13:3
Whelan, Patrick A, 1943, Je 23,21:4; 1947, Mr 11,27:1
Whelan, Patrick J, 1942, D 31,16:2; 1943, Ja 3,42:3; 1952, My 20,25:5; 1968, My 4,39:4
Whelan, Philip J Rev, 1916, Ja 25,9:4
Whelan, Richard G, 1946, Jl 2,25:5
Whelan, Robert J, 1952, D 12,29:3
Whelan, Robert T, 1967, Ja 30,29:1
Whelan, Russell, 1946, S 16,5:5
Whelan, Sidney S, 1959, N 6,29:4
Whelan, Thomas A, 1924, Mr 5,17:5
Whelan, Tim, 1957, Ag 13,27:2
Whelan, Walter A, 1951, S 14,25:1
Whelan, Walter A Mrs, 1950, Ja 10,29:1
Whelan, William, 1943, N 10,23:3
Whelan, William P, 1947, Je 11,27:5
Whelan, William T, 1952, Mr 11,27:3
Wheland, Zenas W, 1958, Ja 1,25:1
Whelchel, B Frank, 1954, My 12,31:3
Whelden, Chester H Jr, 1961, N 15,43:4
Wheldon, R W, 1954, Ja 16,15:2
Whelen, Alfred, 1907, N 20,9:7
Whelen, Charles S Mrs, 1910, Je 20,7:2
Whelen, Henry, 1907, My 18,7:3
Whelen, John H, 1967, O 4,51:2
Whelen, Townsend, 1961, D 25,23:6
Wheless, Joseph, 1950, S 21,31:3
Whelihan, John, 1905, Mr 10,9:7
Wheller, Alfred, 1945, S 5,23:5
Whelpley, Chief Justice, 1864, F 28,4:6
Whelpley, Clare, 1957, D 31,17:2
Whelpley, Edgar J, 1948, S 14,29:4
Whelpley, Gordon B, 1965, Ag 7,21:2
Whelpley, Medley G B, 1968, Mr 25,41:2
Whelpley, Phil B Mrs, 1940, N 14,23:3
Whelpley, Richard H Dr, 1937, D 10,25:5
Whelpton, P K, 1964, Ap 7,35:3
Wheltle, John B A, 1942, S 2,24:3
Whelton, Aldred D, 1964, Ja 6,47:2
Whelton, Francis R, 1946, Mr 7,25:1
Whelton, Paul, 1953, Ap 24,23:2
Wherrett, Harry S, 1944, Ag 15,17:6
Wherrett, Harry S Mrs, 1946, Mr 30,15:2
Wherry, Arthur C, 1944, D 27,20:3
Wherry, D E, 1947, D 12,27:2
Wherry, Elmer G, 1944, Je 25,30:1
Wherry, John B, 1965, My 7,41:1
Wherry, John Dr, 1919, Ja 6,13:1
Wherry, Kenneth S, 1951, N 30,1:2
Wherry, Nellie B, 1949, F 10,27:2
Wherry, W P, 1942, Je 15,19:4
Wherry, William M, 1960, My 8,88:1
Wherry, William M Gen, 1918, N 4,13:4
Whetro, William H, 1944, Mr 24,19:2
Whetsel, Raymond V, 1960, Ja 16,21:5
Whetstone, Lambert F, 1960, D 2,29:1
Whetstone, Stanley L, 1964, S 2,37:1
Whetstone, Walter, 1940, My 3,21:3
Whettnall, Baron, 1903, Mr 29,7:6
Whetzel, Herbert H, 1944, D 1,24:2
Whewell, Prof, 1866, Mr 19,4:7
Whichcote, Hugh C, 1949, My 10,25:2
Whicher, George F, 1954, Mr 8,27:3
Whicher, George F Mrs (Harriet), 1966, N 8,39:3
Whicher, George M Dr, 1937, N 3,23:1
Whicher, George M Mrs, 1946, Ja 28,19:2
Whicher, Louis E, 1958, O 24,33:2
Whidden, C K, 1946, D 7,21:2
Whidden, Charles W, 1955, My 8,88:5
Whidden, Frank Mrs, 1903, My 15,2:6
Whidden, Rae W Capt, 1918, S 26,13:6
Whidden, Ray A, 1949, O 13,27:3
Whiffen, George S, 1961, S 16,19:4
Whiffen, Percy E, 1942, O 7,25:4
Whiffen, T Mrs, 1936, N 27,21:1
Whiffen, Thomas, 1897, O 12,7:5
Whiffen, Walter W Mrs, 1956, N 5,31:3
Whigam, Edgeworth L, 1940, Ag 31,13:4
Whigam, Margaret F Mrs, 1938, Ap 3,II,7:2
Whigan, Edgarita, 1949, Jl 8,19:4
Whigelt, George, 1950, F 22,29:5
Whigham, George H, 1960, N 8,29:5
Whigham, Henry J, 1954, Mr 18,31:1
Whigham, Walter K, 1948, Ag 16,19:4
Whilden, Charles S, 1968, Jl 6,21:2
Whildin, Oliver J, 1943, Mr 9,23:3
Whimpleberg, Samuel Dr, 1907, Jl 13,7:6
Whinery, Andrew J, 1939, Ap 24,17:3
Whinery, Charles C, 1950, S 2,15:5
Whinery, Samuel, 1925, Ja 16,17:4
Whinfrey, Charles G, 1961, Ap 10,31:4
Whinny, Robert N, 1953, Ag 11,27:4
Whinston, Benjamin H, 1964, Ja 22,37:3
Whinston, Charles N, 1964, My 28,37:2
Whinston, Louis Mrs, 1948, Mr 15,23:4
Whinston, Morris, 1951, Ja 30,25:3
Whipp, Hartridge, 1918, D 28,11:5
Whipp, Paul C, 1966, F 27,84:8
Whipple, A W Gen, 1863, My 30,2:4
Whipple, Abram L, 1940, Ag 11,31:4
Whipple, Alfred Jr, 1959, Ag 25,1:2
Whipple, Allen O, 1963, Ap 17,41:1
Whipple, Allen O Jr, 1963, Ap 9,31:2
Whipple, Allen O Mrs, 1959, F 25,31:1

Whipple, C H, 1932, N 7,17:1
Whipple, Charles J, 1958, O 30,31:3
Whipple, Clinton C, 1951, My 20,88:2
Whipple, Clyde C, 1967, Mr 24,31:2
Whipple, Clyde C Mrs, 1953, S 4,34:3
Whipple, Dana de P, 1958, N 19,37:1
Whipple, Eliza B, 1906, Je 27,7:6
Whipple, Frank H, 1944, Jl 2,20:1
Whipple, Fred M, 1958, Je 15,77:1
Whipple, Frederick E, 1952, My 27,27:4
Whipple, George, 1876, O 8,6:7
Whipple, George Chandler, 1924, N 29,13:4
Whipple, George H, 1915, F 6,11:6
Whipple, Gurth A, 1952, S 12,21:2
Whipple, Guy M, 1941, Ag 3,35:4
Whipple, H B Bishop (funl, S 20,1:2), 1901, S 17,7:5
Whipple, Harry V, 1949, Je 8,30:7
Whipple, Henry W Mrs, 1950, Je 23,25:5
Whipple, Herbert Sydney Maj, 1923, Je 14,19:4
Whipple, Howard Thompson, 1968, F 6,44:1
Whipple, J Dana, 1942, Ja 23,20:2
Whipple, James S, 1941, Ap 2,23:1
Whipple, John J, 1948, S 4,15:5
Whipple, John Jay, 1921, N 15,19:4
Whipple, Julian Van N Mrs, 1962, Je 18,25:4
Whipple, Katherine J Mrs, 1937, D 28,22:4
Whipple, Leon R, 1964, O 3,29:3
Whipple, Lucius A, 1952, Ap 22,29:4
Whipple, Lynn M, 1939, Ap 28,25:3
Whipple, Melville C, 1966, Ja 16,82:6
Whipple, Nella, 1910, Ag 16,7:6
Whipple, Nelson M, 1903, S 19,7:6
Whipple, Oliver M, 1959, Ap 28,36:1
Whipple, Reed, 1912, Je 16,II,17:5
Whipple, S L, 1930, O 21,27:3
Whipple, Sherman L Jr, 1967, My 17,47:3
Whipple, W D Gen, 1902, Ap 3,9:5
Whipple, W W, 1954, Ap 19,23:3
Whipple, William C, 1947, D 17,30:2; 1948, Ap 20,27:4
Whipple, William H, 1948, D 8,31:5
Whipple, William Mrs, 1954, Je 19,15:2
Whipple, William W, 1945, Mr 23,19:3
Whipple, Z C, 1879, S 16,5:3
Whippler, Joseph F, 1958, F 12,29:2
Whippler, William F, 1952, Ap 4,33:5
Whisenand, James F, 1967, My 1,37:5
Whisenand, John W, 1940, My 22,23:4
Whisenant, John C, 1956, Ap 17,31:3
Whisnant, Lucille D, 1951, Jl 1,50:6
Whispell, Irving M, 1943, N 18,23:3
Whisple, Neil K, 1949, Je 30,23:5
Whistler, Garland N Gen, 1914, Je 27,7:6
Whistler, Garland N Mrs, 1914, S 2,9:6
Whistler, James McNeil, 1903, Jl 18,1:5
Whistler, Joseph Swift, 1905, N 29,9:3
Whistler, Lashmer, 1963, Jl 7,52:6
Whistler, R W, 1927, F 14,17:6
Whistler, Ross, 1963, Jl 25,25:5
Whiston, Raleigh W, 1959, Ag 9,88:5
Whit, Edwin S, 1938, F 16,21:3
Whitacre, Hume T, 1947, Ag 19,23:2
Whitacre, Rolland J, 1956, F 18,19:5
Whitaker, Alma Mrs, 1956, N 25,88:3
Whitaker, Arthur C, 1937, Ja 29,19:5
Whitaker, Arthur T, 1954, F 17,31:3
Whitaker, Ben F, 1954, Ap 21,29:3
Whitaker, Charles F Mrs, 1950, Ag 1,23:2
Whitaker, Charles H, 1938, Ag 13,13:1
Whitaker, Christopher J, 1922, F 9,17:3
Whitaker, Clem Sr, 1961, N 4,19:4
Whitaker, Cuthbert, 1950, Ap 6,29:1
Whitaker, De Berniere, 1922, Ja 2,17:5
Whitaker, Edward K, 1949, Jl 23,11:6
Whitaker, Emily S Mrs, 1948, Mr 14,73:1
Whitaker, Epher Rev Dr, 1916, S 3,19:6
Whitaker, Ernest T, 1960, Ag 23,29:5
Whitaker, Ezra D Mrs, 1945, D 27,19:3
Whitaker, Florence G Mrs, 1942, Mr 2,19:1
Whitaker, Frank M, 1939, O 26,23:4
Whitaker, Frederick A, 1963, My 27,29:3
Whitaker, George E Mrs, 1963, My 28,28:7
Whitaker, George W, 1958, Jl 23,27:2
Whitaker, H, 1942, Mr 18,23:2
Whitaker, Harry P, 1910, Mr 10,9:4
Whitaker, James, 1949, My 26,29:1
Whitaker, James L, 1953, My 24,89:2
Whitaker, Jesse Mrs, 1952, N 15,17:4
Whitaker, John A, 1951, D 16,91:2
Whitaker, John K, 1948, Ag 27,19:2
Whitaker, Joseph A, 1947, Ap 29,27:1
Whitaker, Lester R, 1961, Ja 10,47:4
Whitaker, Louis P, 1944, Ja 1,13:2
Whitaker, Lyndon C, 1946, N 29,25:2
Whitaker, Lynn S, 1945, O 14,44:4
Whitaker, Martin D, 1960, S 1,27:2
Whitaker, Milton C, 1963, Ap 4,47:4
Whitaker, Nelson L, 1958, Je 11,35:1
Whitaker, Omar B, 1951, Ag 2,21:1
Whitaker, Ozi Bp (funl, F 14,11:5), 1911, F 10,9:5
Whitaker, Ridley, 1954, My 6,33:6
Whitaker, Robert, 1944, Jl 2,19:1
Whitaker, Robert L, 1964, Jl 25,19:4
Whitaker, Spier, 1948, Ja 5,19:5
Whitaker, Thomas Jefferson Rev Dr, 1921, N 2,17:5
Whitaker, Tommy, 1951, Ag 5,V,1:3
Whitaker, Wayne L, 1957, O 2,33:4
Whitaker, William A, 1960, F 29,27:2
Whitaker, William Force Rev Dr, 1916, Jl 10,11:5
Whitaker, William J, 1922, F 9,17:3
Whitall, James, 1954, Mr 25,29:1
Whitall, Sam, 1882, F 19,9:3
Whitall, William H B, 1947, N 7,23:1
Whitam, William J, 1947, Ap 10,25:4
Whitbeck, Brainerd H Mrs, 1943, Je 16,21:2
Whitbeck, Harman B, 1903, D 19,1:4
Whitbeck, Henry W, 1938, Jl 12,19:5
Whitbeck, Leonard F, 1925, F 22,19:3
Whitbeck, Lott Z, 1960, Je 3,31:3
Whitbeck, Mervin P, 1961, Ap 19,39:1
Whitbeck, Theodore H, 1947, Ja 11,19:2
Whitbeck, Tunis, 1908, Ap 21,9:5
Whitbeck, William A (mem ser, Je 24,2:4), 1872, Je 12,8:2
Whitbeck, William F, 1952, Je 13,23:2
Whitbread, George W Mrs, 1961, My 28,64:3
Whitbread, John D, 1954, My 23,89:1
Whitbred, Thomas E, 1964, O 2,37:3
Whitby, Lionel, 1956, N 26,27:2
Whitcher, Frank, 1940, F 22,23:4
Whitcher, Lamar C (por), 1945, Ag 2,19:4
Whitcher, Scott, 1960, Je 27,25:5
Whitcomb, Anna W Mrs (will), 1945, Ja 28,36:2
Whitcomb, Charles F, 1953, Ap 15,31:4
Whitcomb, Edgar B, 1953, O 14,29:2
Whitcomb, Frank G, 1948, Ag 22,V,8:2
Whitcomb, Franklin L, 1949, Jl 27,23:4
Whitcomb, Fred C, 1946, D 21,19:6
Whitcomb, G Henry, 1916, F 14,13:4
Whitcomb, Harold D, 1950, S 27,31:4
Whitcomb, Harriet M Mrs, 1941, Ja 27,15:5
Whitcomb, Jean Mrs, 1912, My 29,11:4
Whitcomb, Kenneth F, 1949, Ja 18,23:3
Whitcomb, Leslie S, 1946, O 26,17:4
Whitcomb, Merrick Prof, 1923, O 14,6:2
Whitcomb, Myron L, 1937, D 6,27:5
Whitcomb, Newell Bryant, 1924, My 11,7:1
Whitcomb, Royden P, 1946, S 15,9:7
Whitcomb, Russell E, 1947, My 27,25:3
Whitcomb, William C, 1939, Ag 7,15:5
Whitcomb, Winfred F, 1955, S 14,35:5
Whitcombe, Reginald A, 1957, Ja 13,84:2
Whitcombe, Susan L, 1951, S 6,31:5
Whitcombe, William W, 1948, F 22,48:6
Whitcraft, Harry R, 1938, Ja 20,23:1
Whitcup, Henry, 1948, Ja 9,22:2
White, A Ludlow, 1925, My 30,9:4
White, A M, 1929, S 22,29:3
White, A S, 1864, S 11,8:2
White, A Stewart, 1946, Ag 28,27:4
White, Adolph, 1965, Je 21,29:4
White, Alain C, 1951, Ap 25,29:5
White, Alan, 1955, F 3,23:3
White, Albert B, 1941, Jl 4,13:6; 1952, My 13,30:2
White, Albert C, 1947, N 17,21:1
White, Albert E, 1956, D 19,31:2
White, Albert L, 1938, Ag 2,19:5
White, Albert Mrs, 1953, Ap 27,23:3
White, Alex, 1939, F 7,20:1; 1950, Mr 14,25:1
White, Alex D Mrs, 1937, Mr 18,25:6
White, Alex M Mrs, 1953, D 28,21:4
White, Alex P, 1940, Ap 30,21:1
White, Alexander, 1944, Jl 6,15:6
White, Alexander Moss, 1906, N 1,9:5; 1968, N 29, 45:2
White, Alexander S, 1947, O 20,23:4
White, Alfred G H, 1945, Jl 11,11:6
White, Alfred H, 1953, Ag 26,27:3
White, Alfred Livingston, 1914, F 18,9:4
White, Alfred W, 1941, S 10,23:5
White, Alice J, 1948, F 10,23:2
White, Alice L M Mrs, 1942, F 14,15:7
White, Allan T, 1945, O 25,21:5
White, Allen A, 1959, D 22,31:4
White, Alma (por), 1946, Je 27,21:4
White, Alverse L, 1955, Je 28,27:1
White, Alvin E Mrs, 1954, S 16,29:4
White, Alwilda L Mrs, 1937, F 5,21:5
White, Ambrose H Mrs, 1949, O 5,29:2
White, Andrew, 1948, Ag 10,21:4
White, Andrew D Dr, 1918, N 5,13:1
White, Andrew D Mrs, 1944, O 30,19:5
White, Andrew Mrs, 1940, D 10,25:4
White, Anna, 1910, D 17,13:4
White, Anna Mrs, 1954, Jl 19,19:5
White, Annie H M Mrs, 1938, My 16,7:2
White, Annie J, 1938, O 10,19:5
White, Antoinette, 1961, Ja 21,21:3
White, Archibald S, 1924, O 1,19:2
White, Arnold, 1925, F 6,17:5
White, Arthur, 1951, S 26,31:3
White, Arthur O, 1953, S 4,34:4
White, Arthur R, 1948, S 8,29:1
White, Arthur W, 1941, N 20,27:6; 1944, S 29,21:2
White, Augustine Dr, 1925, Jl 10,17:6
White, Austin J, 1949, Ja 14,23:3
White, Barclay, 1906, N 24,11:6
White, Ben, 1958, My 21,33:1; 1963, S 14,25:3
White, Benjamin (will, Ap 12,24:3), 1938, Mr 29,21:3
White, Benjamin D, 1951, Jl 8,61:1
White, Benjamin S, 1948, My 25,27:3
White, Benjamin V Sr Mrs, 1954, D 18,15:5
White, Bernard, 1940, N 16,17:3
White, Bert H, 1951, Jl 31,21:5
White, Beverly T, 1940, O 26,15:1
White, Blanchard H, 1940, F 25,39:2
White, Bouck, 1951, Ja 9,30:2
White, Burt W, 1940, Ja 3,22:4
White, Burton F, 1942, Mr 8,42:2
White, Bushnell, 1885, Ap 25,2:2
White, Byron E, 1950, Ap 4,29:5
White, C Arthur, 1940, Mr 3,44:1
White, C B, 1882, Ap 18,5:4
White, C D Mrs, 1951, Jl 29,69:2
White, C N, 1903, My 4,7:6
White, C R, 1934, Ag 29,17:3
White, Carlton, 1919, Jl 5,17:6
White, Carolina Mrs, 1913, F 27,13:3
White, Caroline (will), 1941, F 12,18:5
White, Carr B, 1871, O 7,3:6
White, Charles, 1917, D 6,13:5; 1937, Mr 16,23:1; 1937, Ap 22,23:5
White, Charles A, 1947, Jl 13,44:6
White, Charles D, 1947, F 13,23:1; 1955, S 26,23:3; 1957, Ap 9,33:2; 1962, O 28,88:2
White, Charles D Mrs, 1951, Ag 17,17:5
White, Charles E, 1946, Mr 1,21:4
White, Charles F, 1905, Mr 9,7:6; 1944, Mr 29,21:5; 1955, Ja 2,77:2
White, Charles H Mrs, 1958, N 16,88:3
White, Charles J Prof, 1917, F 13,11:4
White, Charles L, 1941, Ap 21,19:3; 1959, My 11,27:1
White, Charles N, 1944, S 25,17:2; 1952, O 27,27:5
White, Charles P, 1938, Ap 15,19:2; 1942, Ap 8,19:6; 1957, Jl 21,61:2
White, Charles R, 1950, O 29,95:2
White, Charles S (por), 1944, N 5,53:2
White, Charles S, 1949, Ja 27,23:2
White, Charles S Mrs, 1952, My 17,19:4
White, Charles T, 1941, D 19,25:2; 1954, Ja 27,27:4
White, Charles V Sr, 1958, Ag 26,29:4
White, Charles W, 1954, Ag 27,21:2; 1962, Jl 26,27:2
White, Christopher, 1966, N 29,39:3
White, Clara P, 1951, S 27,31:5
White, Clara W, 1959, Ap 12,86:6
White, Clarence B, 1950, Ja 22,76:3
White, Clarence C, 1960, Jl 2,17:5
White, Clarence C Mrs, 1942, O 29,23:4
White, Clarence E, 1942, Je 3,23:4
White, Clarence H, 1925, Jl 9,19:4
White, Clarence H Mrs, 1943, Ap 20,23:6
White, Clarence W, 1953, D 30,23:4
White, Clarence W Mrs, 1953, Jl 1,29:3
White, Claude, 1945, Jl 11,11:5
White, Clement J, 1944, Mr 12,38:4
White, Clifton B, 1955, Mr 17,45:4
White, Clinton C, 1950, Ag 12,13:3
White, Clinton R, 1959, N 24,37:3
White, Compton I, 1956, Ap 2,23:5
White, Conrad R, 1962, F 7,37:3
White, Cornelius Capt, 1903, Ag 31,7:6
White, Cornelius J, 1962, Je 24,68:6
White, Courtland Y, 1938, Ja 16,II,9:2
White, Courtland Y 3d, 1950, Ja 27,23:3
White, Courtney, 1940, F 12,17:4
White, Curtis, 1951, F 23,27:4
White, Cyril J, 1963, N 16,27:4
White, D Charles, 1950, Ja 19,27:2
White, D Charles Mrs, 1959, Mr 8,86:6
White, D McCall, 1950, Ja 31,24:3
White, Daniel D, 1939, Mr 28,23:5
White, Daniel D F, 1950, N 22,25:2
White, Daniel F, 1942, Ag 30,42:3
White, Daniel M Brig-Gen, 1909, My 2,11:5
White, David, 1947, Jl 3,21:3
White, David A, 1958, Mr 20,29:5
White, David C, 1960, S 12,29:3
White, David M, 1945, Ag 2,19:6
White, David Mrs (M Welch), 1958, Je 2,27:3
White, De Gray, 1967, Ap 15,31:4
White, De La Pierre, 1948, Mr 31,25:2
White, Delancey P, 1948, D 9,33:1
White, Dexter, 1939, My 4,23:2
White, Donald M Mrs, 1958, Mr 26,37:2
White, Dudley A, 1957, O 15,30:5
White, E, 1877, Je 9,4:7
White, E B Col, 1882, My 11,2:4
White, E L C, 1950, F 24,23:3
White, E Laurence, 1968, My 14,47:1
White, Earl A, 1958, Jl 2,29:1
White, Earl D, 1937, My 18,23:4
White, Ed, 1955, Ag 7,72:6
White, Edna, 1965, Mr 24,43:4
White, Edson Jr, 1923, S 8,13:3
White, Edward, 1914, Ap 13,11:4
White, Edward A, 1939, S 18,19:4; 1943, My 14,20:2; 1945, N 16,19:3
White, Edward C, 1939, Je 7,23:3
White, Edward C Mrs (por), 1944, Ja 29,13:2
White, Edward D, 1915, O 15,11:6

White, Edward F, 1940, Ap 23,23:3
White, Edward G, 1940, Mr 23,13:2
White, Edward H, 1939, My 19,21:4; 1940, Mr 1,21:4; 1940, Jl 15,15:4
White, Edward H Mrs, 1917, N 14,15:3
White, Edward H 2d (funl and burial plans, Ja 29,-49:2), 1967, Ja 28,1:8
White, Edward J, 1959, Ag 28,23:4
White, Edward L Sr, 1948, Jl 23,20:2
White, Edward P, 1938, S 3,13:1
White, Edward R, 1953, My 24,89:1
White, Edward S, 1947, S 24,23:6
White, Edward S Mrs, 1943, Jl 15,21:4
White, Edward T, 1939, N 6,23:5
White, Edwin A Rev Dr, 1925, Jl 7,19:4
White, Edwin Adm, 1903, D 24,9:5
White, Edwin C, 1957, My 20,25:4
White, Edwin G Rev, 1937, Ag 25,21:3
White, Edwin J, 1953, Ap 7,29:4
White, Eli, 1873, D 5,8:5
White, Eliot, 1967, Ja 24,28:6
White, Elizabeth Colemane Mrs, 1906, N 25,9:6
White, Elizabeth W, 1944, O 11,21:4
White, Ella M, 1950, F 27,19:4
White, Elmer S, 1912, Ja 1,13:3
White, Elwood S (por), 1942, My 28,17:3
White, Ernest B, 1965, S 6,15:5
White, Ernest C, 1955, Ap 16,19:4
White, Ernest H, 1952, Ap 19,15:4; 1955, F 22,21:6
White, Ernest I, 1957, O 21,25:3
White, Estelle L Mrs, 1940, Je 2,44:5
White, Eugene F, 1942, Ap 15,21:1
White, Eugene L, 1951, Ja 12,27:3
White, Everett A (will), 1944, F 25,11:1
White, Ewart J, 1945, Jl 14,11:2
White, F Ambrose, 1943, F 8,20:3
White, F D Mrs, 1941, N 18,25:2
White, F Winthrop Mrs, 1953, S 9,29:4
White, Fannie, 1917, Ap 7,13:5
White, Fannie S Mrs, 1944, Ap 17,23:4
White, Florence D (cor, D 17,85:1), 1950, D 16,17:4
White, Florence D, 1956, S 16,84:3
White, Frances E, 1937, Mr 12,24:1
White, Frances E Prof, 1903, D 30,7:2
White, Frances H, 1943, Ja 5,19:2
White, Frances M, 1958, Ap 13,83:4
White, Francis, 1914, Ap 20,9:4; 1945, D 18,27:4; 1961, F 24,21:1
White, Francis B, 1948, Ja 19,23:3
White, Francis D, 1941, Ap 25,19:3
White, Francis J, 1947, O 7,27:3
White, Francis J Mrs, 1945, N 30,23:1
White, Francis L, 1957, Ap 30,30:1
White, Francis O Jr, 1946, My 5,46:3
White, Francis R, 1950, Ap 7,25:5
White, Francis S, 1962, Ap 7,25:4
White, Francis T, 1907, Je 19,7:5; 1954, D 13,27:4
White, Francis W, 1943, F 15,15:6; 1962, Mr 30,33:4
White, Frank, 1939, Je 13,23:3
White, Frank (por), 1940, Mr 24,31:1
White, Frank, 1940, O 12,17:5; 1947, S 12,21:4; 1950, Mr 4,17:1
White, Frank D Mrs, 1947, O 8,25:2
White, Frank E, 1939, Mr 4,15:3
White, Frank H, 1943, D 25,13:6
White, Frank H Mrs, 1958, O 24,33:1
White, Frank L, 1940, S 6,21:1; 1949, Ja 5,26:3
White, Frank M Capt, 1920, N 6,13:2
White, Frank Marshall, 1919, D 30,13:3
White, Frank Mrs, 1925, Jl 15,17:6
White, Frank R, 1963, Ap 16,35:4
White, Frank R Dr, 1913, Ag 20,9:6
White, Frank S Ex-Sen, 1922, Ag 3,13:7
White, Frank W, 1950, D 20,31:4
White, Frank X, 1940, N 28,23:5
White, Frederic F, 1949, O 4,27:5
White, Frederick, 1944, S 4,19:3
White, Frederick C, 1939, F 1,21:4; 1962, Ap 13,35:1
White, Frederick G, 1948, N 1,23:3
White, Frederick R, 1963, O 25,31:5
White, Frederick W, 1937, My 4,25:6
White, Fredus A, 1958, Ja 30,23:2
White, Frida G Mrs (will), 1940, N 26,25:2
White, G Derby, 1939, Mr 15,23:6
White, G S, 1931, N 26,27:1
White, G W Blunt, 1962, Ap 19,31:1
White, Gardiner W Sr Mrs, 1961, D 23,23:3
White, Gaylord, 1954, Mr 16,29:4
White, George, 1939, My 9,23:2; 1939, N 18,17:6; 1951, F 27,27:1; 1953, N 10,31:4; 1968, O 12,37:1
White, George A, 1941, N 24,17:4; 1951, S 13,31:3
White, George A Capt, 1917, Mr 10,11:6
White, George B, 1944, Ja 10,17:2
White, George B Judge, 1937, D 27,16:2
White, George C, 1937, Jl 31,15:6; 1943, S 6,18:2
White, George D, 1953, D 29,23:2
White, George E, 1942, Jl 3,17:2; 1946, My 4,15:5
White, George E Mrs, 1943, My 27,25:3
White, George Emmons, 1907, O 19,9:6
White, George Ex-Gov, 1953, D 16,35:3
White, George F, 1947, D 9,29:4
White, George F Jr, 1950, My 24,30:3
White, George H, 1903, D 4,9:5
White, George K, 1938, My 10,21:3
White, George L, 1949, My 16,21:3
White, George Mrs, 1951, Mr 9,25:2
White, George N, 1938, Ag 2,19:6; 1945, Mr 15,23:5
White, George Sir, 1916, N 24,13:4
White, George T, 1940, O 6,49:1; 1952, O 15,31:3
White, George W, 1938, O 28,23:3; 1940, D 2,23:4; 1941, Ap 29,19:5; 1943, Je 1,17:7; 1948, F 25,23:3
White, Georgia A Mrs, 1957, S 14,19:3
White, Gershom F Dr, 1937, Ap 30,22:3
White, Gilbert H, 1925, S 24,25:3
White, Glenn H, 1945, Ag 2,19:4
White, Glenn W, 1952, O 12,88:3
White, Grace B, 1959, Mr 19,33:4
White, Grace E, 1938, Jl 7,19:3
White, Grace H Mrs, 1937, Jl 19,15:4
White, Grace M, 1965, D 22,31:1
White, Graham H Mrs, 1954, Ja 9,15:4
White, Graham Mrs, 1950, N 12,93:2
White, Grosvenor, 1952, Je 7,19:4
White, Gustave J S, 1963, O 22,37:5
White, Gwo Sir, 1912, Je 25,11:6
White, H, 1927, Jl 16,11:3
White, H Edith, 1944, Jl 3,12:6
White, H G Evelyn, 1924, S 12,21:5
White, H H Prof, 1903, D 10,9:5
White, H Kirke, 1937, O 22,19:5
White, Haines D, 1947, Ag 20,21:2
White, Hal S, 1962, Jl 13,23:1
White, Harold, 1963, N 16,27:4
White, Harold B Mrs, 1959, Jl 30,27:4
White, Harold E, 1938, N 5,19:5; 1953, S 11,21:3; 1955, Je 1,33:4
White, Harold T Mrs, 1944, Ag 11,15:4
White, Harold T Sr, 1960, Ag 13,15:4
White, Harrie C, 1954, O 1,23:4
White, Harriet H, 1947, F 11,27:3
White, Harry, 1940, F 22,23:3
White, Harry B, 1960, Ap 1,33:4
White, Harry C, 1954, Je 18,23:6
White, Harry C Mrs (Clemme E), 1960, Ja 12,47:2
White, Harry D, 1948, Ag 18,1:2
White, Harry E, 1955, Ja 19,27:4
White, Harry F, 1946, Je 29,19:2
White, Harry H Mrs, 1952, Ag 4,15:6
White, Harry J, 1951, S 22,17:3
White, Harry K, 1966, Je 10,45:1
White, Harry K Mrs, 1960, My 7,23:3
White, Harry M, 1946, Ag 6,25:4
White, Harry N, 1966, Mr 11,33:2
White, Harvey, 1905, Ap 27,5:1; 1951, S 28,31:1
White, Harvey T, 1943, Je 29,19:5
White, Harwood A, 1954, Ja 17,92:4
White, Hawley C, 1925, Ja 31,13:5
White, Helen C Mrs, 1938, D 10,17:3
White, Helena, 1946, O 9,27:2
White, Henderson N, 1940, Mr 27,21:2
White, Henry A, 1951, N 26,25:1
White, Henry B, 1955, N 12,19:6
White, Henry C, 1914, F 8,15:5
White, Henry C Mrs, 1951, Ag 11,11:3
White, Henry F, 1955, Je 21,31:1
White, Henry M, 1948, N 17,27:3
White, Henry Mrs, 1916, S 3,19:7; 1946, Jl 29,21:3; 1946, Ag 1,23:6
White, Henry S, 1943, My 21,19:4
White, Henry S Sr, 1946, O 26,17:6
White, Henry S T Jr, 1944, Ag 16,19:5
White, Henry T E, 1942, S 2,23:6
White, Herbert H, 1963, N 6,41:2
White, Herbert K (trb, Ag 14,23:4), 1951, Ag 12,76:4
White, Herbert L Mrs, 1947, Mr 13,27:2
White, Herman C, 1922, O 14,13:6
White, Hervey, 1944, O 21,17:5
White, Holman, 1945, D 10,21:3
White, Horace (funl, S 18,13:4), 1916, S 17,19:3
White, Horace (will, D 3,25:3),(por), 1943, N 29,19:3
White, Horace Keep, 1915, Mr 24,11:4
White, Horace Mrs, 1873, Ja 15,5:5; 1937, S 30,23:2
White, Howard, 1919, Ja 24,11:4; 1937, Ja 18,17:2; 1937, O 22,17:6
White, Howard H, 1944, Ag 22,17:6
White, Howard L, 1957, Ja 4,23:1
White, Howard L Mrs, 1947, Ja 11,19:5
White, Hugh L (Sept 20), 1965, O 11,61:6
White, Hugh Sr, 1940, O 15,23:6
White, Huntington (will), 1953, Ja 17,12:2
White, I C, 1927, N 26,15:5
White, Isaac, 1942, Jl 8,23:2
White, Isaac D, 1943, S 25,15:1
White, J, 1927, Je 30,27:4
White, J B, 1883, Mr 25,2:2; 1945, Je 1,15:5
White, J Campbell, 1962, Mr 25,88:8
White, J Clinton, 1938, N 9,23:3
White, J Courtney, 1945, Ja 6,11:5
White, J Du Pratt Mrs, 1955, Mr 13,87:1
White, J DuPratt, 1939, Jl 15,15:3
White, J Frank, 1954, Jl 20,19:5
White, J H (see also Mr 1), 1877, Mr 2,8:4
White, J H Dr, 1873, Je 23,1:6
White, J Irving, 1944, Ap 19,23:6
White, J Leslie, 1968, N 22,47:2
White, J P, 1881, S 30,5:2
White, J P P, 1882, D 4,5:2
White, J Roger, 1951, Mr 20,29:2
White, J Sloane, 1953, Ap 2,28:3
White, J W Huyler, 1961, Ja 10,47:4
White, J W Mrs, 1944, F 3,19:2
White, J Warren, 1959, S 14,29:5
White, J William Dr, 1916, Ap 25,11:5
White, Jack (por), 1942, Jl 14,20:2
White, Jack, 1949, Mr 25,23:4
White, James, 1881, Ag 9,5:2; 1939, Jl 8,15:2
White, James A, 1947, N 27,32:3
White, James B, 1964, Je 11,33:5
White, James D, 1945, Jl 24,23:4
White, James E, 1940, Ag 6,20:4
White, James F, 1965, Jl 15,29:4
White, James G (por), 1942, Je 3,23:1
White, James J, 1941, Ja 13,15:5
White, James J (death ruled suicide, O 23,15:1), 1968, S 28,66:6
White, James J Jr, 1949, S 22,31:2
White, James L, 1946, Ap 30,22:3
White, James Leigh, 1968, My 22,47:2
White, James M, 1951, F 11,89:1
White, James Mrs (Ellen G White), 1915, Jl 17,7:7
White, James Mrs, 1951, Mr 27,29:5
White, James O, 1952, F 14,27:5
White, James S (Marrying Justice), 1910, F 13,II,11:4
White, James S Sr, 1950, Jl 11,31:5
White, James Sr, 1945, Ag 24,19:1
White, James T, 1962, My 19,27:6
White, James Terry, 1920, Ap 6,11:6
White, James W, 1867, Je 16,5:5; 1945, Ja 21,40:5
White, James W (por), 1946, My 16,21:3
White, James W, 1961, Mr 15,39:4
White, Jay, 1918, My 25,13:4
White, Jennie S Mrs, 1940, Ja 29,15:5
White, Jesse E, 1959, Ja 6,33:1
White, Jesse M, 1948, Ja 11,58:5
White, Jesse S, 1948, O 19,28:2
White, Joe K, 1967, Je 20,39:3
White, Joel G, 1938, S 9,21:1
White, Joel L, 1966, F 1,31:2
White, John, 1882, S 20,2:4; 1940, F 7,21:2; 1951, Ag 22,23:6; 1952, N 13,31:5
White, John (funl), 1959, Mr 31,30:4
White, John A, 1945, Ja 1,22:2; 1950, Ja 29,68:4; 1952, Je 13,23:4
White, John A Mrs, 1947, Je 14,15:6
White, John A 2d, 1945, N 24,20:2
White, John B, 1940, Je 14,21:3; 1946, Ap 26,21:3; 1949, Ap 13,29:3; 1963, N 26,37:1
White, John B Mrs, 1961, F 9,31:2
White, John C, 1942, D 18,28:3; 1956, F 12,88:7; 1967, Je 12,45:1
White, John C Mrs, 1948, S 15,31:2
White, John D, 1938, D 3,20:1; 1947, Ag 29,17:1; 1956, Ja 3,31:1
White, John E, 1943, S 23,21:2; 1944, N 17,19:1; 1949, Jl 13,28:4
White, John F, 1943, Ap 3,15:3
White, John G, 1964, O 18,89:2
White, John H, 1946, N 1,23:4; 1952, My 5,23:4
White, John J, 1920, Ja 16,9:5; 1939, N 8,23:5; 1942, Jl 24,20:3; 1952, My 17,19:5; 1968, Mr 20,47:3
White, John P, 1943, O 3,48:3; 1944, Ag 27,33:2; 1948, Je 9,29:5
White, John R, 1961, D 11,31:5
White, John S, 1961, Jl 6,29:5
White, John S Dr, 1922, O 6,23:4
White, John V Col, 1915, Ag 25,11:4
White, John W, 1944, D 24,25:1; 1946, D 19,30:2; 1949, Ag 4,23:1; 1952, Mr 26,29:3
White, John W Mrs, 1958, Mr 9,86:3
White, John Williams, 1917, My 10,13:6
White, Jonah H, 1907, Ja 1,9:5
White, Jonathan, 1912, Jl 26,9:6
White, Joseph A, 1941, F 17,15:1; 1948, Je 20,60:3
White, Joseph B, 1904, Ja 15,9:6; 1924, My 5,15:4; 1958, Mr 12,32:1; 1961, My 8,35:4
White, Joseph C, 1961, Jl 7,6:4
White, Joseph E, 1945, S 4,23:6; 1948, Ap 8,25:3
White, Joseph F, 1965, Ap 19,29:3
White, Joseph M, 1959, Mr 1,86:4
White, Joseph M Mrs, 1967, D 18,47:1
White, Joseph N Jr, 1939, Mr 9,21:4
White, Joseph P, 1964, O 24,29:4
White, Joseph R, 1952, Ag 4,15:5
White, Josephine M Mrs, 1946, Ag 9,19:6
White, Josephine S Mrs, 1948, Ja 14,25:3
White, Josiah, 1914, S 19,11:3
White, Josiah D Mrs, 1948, D 14,29:4
White, Josiah Mrs, 1923, F 5,15:6
White, Julian Leroy, 1923, F 15,19:4
White, Kemble Mrs, 1941, Mr 21,21:3
White, Kenneth, 1953, N 22,88:6
White, Kenneth G, 1920, Ag 19,9:4
White, Kenneth P Mrs, 1962, F 18,92:7
White, Kirby, 1943, Ap 23,17:5
White, L Mitchell, 1965, Mr 18,5:5
White, Laura M, 1937, Ja 26,21:1
White, Laura S Mrs, 1942, D 22,25:5
White, Lawrence (funl, Jl 29,23:1), 1958, Jl 28,23:5
White, Lawrence G (trb lr, O 4,32:6), 1956, S 9,84:3

White, Lazarus, 1953, Jl 31,19:1
White, Lee A Mrs, 1960, Je 16,33:2
White, Lee H, 1949, N 10,31:4
White, Lee Mrs, 1941, Mr 14,21:1
White, Lee R, 1949, D 17,17:2
White, Leland O, 1954, F 11,29:4
White, Lena Mrs, 1938, Je 7,23:4
White, Leo, 1948, S 22,32:3
White, Leo W, 1953, N 24,29:1
White, Leonard C, 1955, My 12,29:3
White, Leonard D, 1942, Ag 17,15:3; 1958, F 24,19:3; 1963, D 27,25:2
White, Leslie, 1952, D 11,33:4
White, Levi Mrs, 1937, Ja 14,21:4
White, Lew, 1955, Mr 4,21:1
White, Lewis F, 1967, Ja 13,23:3
White, Linden H, 1950, Ap 12,28:2
White, Linn, 1949, Ja 14,24:2
White, Llewellyn B, 1959, My 16,23:1
White, Llewellyn O, 1953, Jl 23,23:5
White, Lloyd A, 1954, Mr 29,19:6
White, Loomis L, 1948, Mr 10,27:2
White, Louis P, 1948, Jl 2,21:3
White, Lucy Mrs, 1952, Ja 29,25:3
White, Luke A Sr, 1957, Je 15,17:4
White, Luke M, 1955, O 3,27:4
White, Luke M Jr, 1956, Jl 22,61:3
White, Luke M Mrs, 1953, Ag 4,21:2; 1959, Ja 29,27:2
White, Luke S, 1948, Je 27,52:8
White, Lynne L, 1964, My 30,17:1
White, M F, 1876, N 30,4:7
White, Margaret (Sister R Alice), 1942, Ag 18,21:5
White, Margot (Mrs A U Newton), 1960, D 27,29:5
White, Marshall D, 1951, F 6,27:3
White, Marshall W, 1957, F 7,27:6
White, Martha R, 1937, My 31,15:3
White, Martin A, 1946, My 1,25:1
White, Martin A Mrs, 1956, D 4,39:2
White, Martin J, 1921, S 6,15:5
White, Mary A Mrs, 1942, Je 9,23:5
White, Mary E Mrs, 1951, F 25,84:6
White, Mary O, 1938, Je 1,23:4
White, Mary P, 1947, O 30,25:4
White, Mary T, 1964, Ja 22,37:3
White, Matthew Jr, 1940, S 18,23:2
White, Maude V, 1937, N 3,24:1
White, Maunsel, 1912, O 24,11:6
White, Maurice, 1952, Mr 3,21:2
White, Mercer V Sr, 1941, O 16,21:5
White, Merion T Mrs, 1950, Ag 10,25:1
White, Merle H, 1956, My 8,33:4
White, Merle L, 1949, Je 12,76:1
White, Merrill G, 1959, Mr 25,35:1
White, Michael, 1908, Mr 2,9:4; 1939, Jl 26,3:7; 1942, Je 28,32:3
White, Michael H, 1944, S 2,11:4
White, Michael J, 1944, Ja 21,17:4
White, Michael J Msgr (por), 1940, My 21,23:1
White, Miles, 1876, Mr 14,7:4
White, Miles Jr, 1938, Jl 7,19:5
White, Montagne Prof, 1905, Ap 1,5:4
White, Morris, 1962, O 7,82:1
White, Nathan L, 1955, S 25,92:6
White, Nathaniel Mrs (Dupree C), 1965, Mr 18,33:4
White, Neville W, 1953, N 15,89:2
White, Newman I (por), 1948, D 7,31:5
White, Newton H Jr, 1958, N 30,86:5
White, Nicholas V, 1939, Ja 31,21:4
White, Norman, 1883, Je 14,4:7
White, Norman Mrs, 1946, O 7,31:1
White, O A Dr, 1903, My 26,9:4
White, Octavius A Mrs, 1904, Ja 5,9:5
White, Oliver Dr, 1879, N 9,6:7
White, Oliver W, 1939, Jl 28,17:6
White, Owen P, 1946, D 8,79:3
White, Owen W, 1944, F 21,15:2
White, Pat, 1943, Ag 7,11:6
White, Patience, 1938, S 14,23:3
White, Patrick, 1906, My 6,9:6
White, Patrick J, 1941, Ja 28,19:4
White, Patrick J Mrs, 1946, Ap 5,25:3; 1951, Jl 29,68:3
White, Patrick Mrs, 1947, Ag 3,53:2
White, Paul C, 1946, Ap 10,27:4
White, Paul M, 1944, Ap 8,13:6
White, Paul Mrs, 1960, N 25,27:3
White, Paul W, 1955, Jl 10,72:1
White, Pauline S Mrs, 1942, D 21,23:4
White, Pearl, 1938, Ag 5,17:1
White, Percival G, 1942, Ap 29,21:4
White, Percy, 1938, Jl 4,13:6
White, Peter D, 1948, My 7,23:2
White, Peter G, 1968, D 27,33:2
White, Peter J, 1954, N 27,13:4
White, Phil B, 1949, Mr 20,76:7
White, Philip R Dr, 1968, Mr 26,45:3
White, Philip R Mrs, 1968, N 29,45:4
White, Pierre A, 1950, S 16,19:6
White, Pilot, 1880, Ja 15,1:4
White, R, 1880, F 26,4:6
White, R C, 1884, Ag 30,5:6
White, R G, 1885, Ap 9,5:3
White, R Rostin, 1959, S 6,72:6
White, R S, 1936, D 18,25:1
White, Ralph A, 1958, My 21,33:4
White, Ralph E, 1951, S 23,86:1
White, Ralph L Mrs, 1957, Je 13,31:2
White, Ray B, 1946, N 6,23:3
White, Raymond A, 1941, Mr 26,23:2
White, Raymond C, 1941, O 12,53:2
White, Raymond H, 1957, Ap 5,27:4
White, Raymond J, 1954, My 13,29:4
White, Raymond J Mrs, 1941, Ap 20,43:1
White, Raymond M, 1955, S 16,23:3
White, Raymond S, 1903, D 22,9:5
White, Raymond T, 1956, F 16,29:4
White, Reid, 1952, D 6,21:3
White, Rex G, 1951, Jl 20,21:6
White, Richard, 1910, Je 22,9:4
White, Richard D, 1953, N 21,13:6
White, Richard L, 1966, Mr 14,31:3
White, Richard Mrs, 1946, Ap 20,23:6
White, Richard P, 1905, My 24,9:5
White, Richard S, 1959, Jl 19,68:3
White, Robe C, 1951, Ja 8,17:5
White, Robert, 1884, Jl 6,3:2; 1959, Jl 16,27:5
White, Robert B, 1961, Jl 20,55:5
White, Robert D, 1943, My 17,15:4
White, Robert F Jr, 1964, My 27,39:3
White, Robert G, 1951, My 31,27:5
White, Robert H, 1952, S 24,33:6
White, Robert I Sr, 1966, S 3,23:3
White, Robert J, 1948, My 8,15:5; 1951, Jl 18,29:4; 1952, Je 7,19:3
White, Robert K, 1915, My 9,18:4
White, Robert L, 1960, Ag 3,29:3
White, Robert M, 1958, Ap 1,31:5
White, Robert M Mrs, 1953, Ap 22,29:4
White, Robert Mrs, 1948, N 11,27:1
White, Robert S, 1944, D 6,23:6; 1950, F 16,20:5
White, Robert V, 1960, Je 22,35:1
White, Roderick, 1945, Mr 1,21:5
White, Roland A, 1956, S 19,37:4
White, Roland W, 1953, D 30,24:4
White, Rollin H, 1962, S 12,39:3
White, Rollin H Mrs, 1949, My 16,21:4
White, Ross, 1916, S 9,11:6
White, Ross Jr, 1952, My 20,25:1
White, Roy, 1965, My 24,31:4
White, Roy B, 1961, Je 5,31:1
White, Roy B Mrs, 1964, Mr 25,41:4
White, Ruby, 1957, My 16,31:5
White, Rufus A Dr, 1937, Jl 26,19:5
White, Russel H, 1949, F 20,60:5
White, Russell, 1952, Mr 1,15:6
White, Russell S, 1946, N 8,23:2
White, Ruth M, 1959, S 20,86:4
White, S Harrison, 1945, D 23,18:3
White, S Marx, 1966, Ag 31,43:2
White, Sallie Joy Mrs, 1909, Mr 26,9:5
White, Sammy, 1960, Mr 7,29:2
White, Samuel J, 1945, Je 27,19:1
White, Samuel K, 1939, Ja 15,38:7
White, Samuel S Mrs, 1947, N 29,13:5
White, Samuel S 3d, 1952, N 3,27:3
White, Sarah P E Mrs, 1938, Mr 17,21:4
White, Saul J, 1968, Je 21,41:2
White, Sidney J, 1937, Ag 10,19:4
White, Sidney T, 1912, Je 12,13:6
White, Sidney Y, 1957, Ja 25,21:5
White, Stanford Mrs, 1950, Jl 5,32:4
White, Stanley Mrs, 1950, F 2,27:5
White, Stephen V Mrs, 1907, Je 3,7:6
White, Stewart E, 1946, S 19,31:1
White, Sue S (por), 1943, My 8,15:3
White, Susan P, 1911, Ag 2,7:6
White, Sydney, 1958, Mr 10,23:4
White, T Gilbert (por), 1939, F 18,15:1
White, Terence H, 1964, Ja 18,21:4
White, Theodore K, 1953, O 17,15:2
White, Theodore L, 1960, Ag 4,25:5
White, Thomas, 1938, Ja 26,23:2; 1944, Je 17,13:4; 1947, Mr 25,25:1; 1955, F 13,87:1
White, Thomas A, 1951, Ja 26,23:1; 1954, O 2,17:4
White, Thomas C Mrs, 1950, N 9,33:2
White, Thomas D, 1951, Mr 29,27:5
White, Thomas D (funl, D 29,29:4), 1965, D 23,27:1
White, Thomas E, 1948, F 2,20:2; 1958, Ja 29,27:4
White, Thomas Earle, 1916, O 9,11:5
White, Thomas F, 1904, Ap 12,9:6; 1941, My 18,44:1; 1947, Mr 26,25:5
White, Thomas F X, 1951, Ja 28,76:4
White, Thomas H, 1914, Je 23,11:5
White, Thomas J (por), 1948, Jl 10,15:1
White, Thomas J, 1949, Jl 26,27:4
White, Thomas M Mrs, 1945, S 13,23:5
White, Thomas Mrs, 1945, Ap 1,36:3
White, Thomas R, 1942, D 20,45:2; 1959, D 18,30:1
White, Thomas W, 1950, O 16,27:6
White, Trentwell M (cor, S 21,31:3), 1959, S 20,86:3
White, Trueworthy Mrs, 1944, N 11,13:5
White, Truman C Ex-Justice, 1912, F 8,11:4
White, Trumbull, 1941, D 14,69:1
White, Val, 1953, Ap 21,27:1
White, Verne S Sr, 1955, F 23,27:4
White, Victor G, 1954, Ap 24,17:6
White, Victoria, 1942, N 15,58:1
White, Virgil, 1905, Je 20,4:4
White, W A, 1881, Je 23,5:5; 1927, My 7,17:5
White, W Culver, 1948, Ja 31,19:2
White, W H, 1903, N 13,9:6
White, W H Capt, 1904, Jl 4,5:6
White, W Hughes, 1957, Ja 22,29:3
White, W Judge, 1883, Mr 14,2:4
White, W Lee Dr, 1909, Ja 3,11:5
White, W P (por), 1947, Ja 23,23:3
White, W W, 1927, D 24,15:5
White, W Wilson, 1964, N 12,37:1
White, Walker G, 1956, My 15,31:3
White, Wallace D, 1954, N 20,17:4
White, Wallace H Jr, 1952, Ap 1,29:3
White, Wallace H Sr, 1920, S 20,15:5
White, Walter, 1951, F 16,25:4; 1965, Ag 1,77:2
White, Walter C Mrs, 1959, Ap 25,21:3
White, Walter F (funl plans, Mr 23,31:3; funl, Mr 25,21:3), 1955, Mr 22,31:1
White, Walter M, 1947, Jl 17,19:5
White, Walter R, 1952, Ag 5,19:4
White, Walter W, 1947, Je 21,17:6
White, Walter W Mrs, 1945, My 29,15:4
White, Walton W Jr, 1943, Ja 3,42:4
White, Ward B, 1951, F 25,87:2
White, Wellington M Capt, 1937, Mr 11,23:2
White, Whitman Vassel Dr, 1917, F 23,11:6
White, Wilbert W (por), 1944, Ag 13,35:1
White, Wilbert W Mrs, 1943, My 18,23:3
White, Wilbur E, 1939, S 10,48:8
White, Wilbur W, 1950, N 16,31:2
White, Wilfred B, 1948, D 3,26:2
White, Wilfrid O, 1955, Ag 14,80:5
White, Willard A, 1959, F 12,27:4
White, Willard C, 1949, S 17,17:1
White, William, 1873, Ap 29,1:6; 1956, F 19,93:2
White, William (funl plans, Ap 8,37:8), 1967, Ap 7, 34:3
White, William A, 1939, F 7,20:1; 1940, Je 11,25:6; 1943, D 3,23:3; 1945, Ja 30,38:1; 1946, Mr 26,29:1; 1946, Jl 26,21:2; 1955, F 20,89:1; 1958, Je 30,19:4
White, William A Dr (por), 1937, Mr 8,19:3
White, William A Mrs, 1950, D 20,32:2
White, William Anthony Parker (Anthony Boucher), 1968, My 1,47:1
White, William B, 1959, Je 5,27:2
White, William C, 1947, Ag 12,24:2; 1949, My 23, 23:3; 1955, N 29,29:2; 1960, Ja 26,33:4; 1962, N 23, 29:3; 1964, O 1,35:4; 1965, Ja 30,27:2
White, William D, 1952, Ag 23,13:4
White, William F, 1943, Je 18,22:2; 1955, Ag 5,19:3; 1964, Ja 26,81:1
White, William G, 1939, D 17,49:2
White, William G Mrs, 1949, Ja 23,68:3
White, William H, 1939, S 9,17:6; 1942, My 24,43:2; 1951, Mr 15,29:4; 1952, Ag 20,25:5
White, William Hale (Mark Rutherford), 1913, Mr 16,IV,7:4
White, William Henry, 1916, S 8,29:4
White, William Hubbard, 1917, O 27,17:4
White, William J, 1923, F 17,13:5; 1939, Ap 1,19:3; 1939, Ap 4,25:3; 1940, Je 25,23:1; 1944, S 20,23:6; 1948, Je 27,52:6; 1949, F 17,23:3; 1950, Jl 15,14:7; 1952, D 15,25:4
White, William J Msgr, 1911, Ag 30,7:5
White, William L, 1944, Je 3,13:1; 1952, Ag 1,17:5
White, William L Col, 1910, N 17,9:5
White, William M, 1946, Ap 26,21:2; 1949, F 11,24:3
White, William Mrs, 1947, Ag 11,23:3
White, William O, 1937, O 21,24:3
White, William P, 1938, Jl 10,31:3; 1938, N 29,23:6
White, William R, 1939, Ap 23,III,6:7; 1941, Ja 28,19:5
White, William S, 1939, F 7,20:1; 1943, F 25,21:1
White, William Thomas, 1957, Ag 19,19:4
White, William Townsend, 1957, My 24,25:1
White, William W, 1942, S 17,25:5; 1944, N 30,23:4
White, William W Mrs, 1937, Jl 15,19:2; 1944, O 10, 23:5
White, Wilson H, 1948, D 21,25:6
White, Wilton P, 1949, Jl 19,29:3
White, Windsor T, 1958, Ap 10,29:2
White, Winsor T Mrs, 1947, My 16,23:4
White, Winthrop T, 1949, N 5,14:2
White Cloud, Chief, 1947, Ap 24,25:3
White Horse Eagle, Chief, 1937, Je 16,24:2
Whiteaves, Joseph F Dr, 1909, Ag 9,7:5
Whitebread, Edward C, 1944, Mr 2,17:5
Whitebrook, Lloyd G, 1962, Jl 23,21:2
Whitecar, Fred C, 1943, Ap 15,25:1
Whitechurch, Ernest V L, 1954, D 30,17:4
Whitecotton, Jay A, 1963, Ag 9,23:1
Whited, Ambrose B Mrs, 1950, Ap 21,24:3
Whited, Frank Thayer E, 1925, Ag 12,21:5
Whitefield, Richard A, 1947, Je 13,23:5
Whiteford, Alex W, 1957, Ja 24,29:5
Whiteford, Alexander W Mrs, 1964, Mr 29,60:7
Whiteford, Andrew, 1944, S 28,19:3
Whiteford, James A, 1949, Ap 9,17:5
Whiteford, William K, 1968, S 12,47:2
Whitehall, Frank M, 1939, Ag 28,19:4
Whitehall, William C, 1953, Ja 12,27:3
Whitehead, Albert, 1951, My 12,21:4
Whitehead, Alfred N, 1947, D 31,15:1

Whitehead, Alfred W, 1943, N 4,23:5
Whitehead, Annie L, 1951, Ag 17,17:3
Whitehead, Benjamin S (por), 1940, Ap 18,23:6
Whitehead, C Campbell, 1955, Je 21,31:5
Whitehead, C Kyle, 1957, Ag 13,27:5
Whitehead, C N, 1926, D 11,17:5
Whitehead, Carle, 1955, Ja 4,21:5
Whitehead, Charles B, 1961, F 18,19:2
Whitehead, Conkey P, 1940, N 3,56:5
Whitehead, Cortlandt Rev, 1922, S 19,19:4
Whitehead, E Winston, 1951, Ja 24,20:4
Whitehead, Edward, 1941, O 19,44:7
Whitehead, Edward J, 1924, Mr 26,19:4; 1966, My 24, 43:7
Whitehead, Edward T, 1958, Je 21,19:2
Whitehead, Elizabeth Mrs, 1953, Mr 6,23:1
Whitehead, Ennis C, 1964, O 13,39:4
Whitehead, Ernest C, 1961, Jl 6,29:5
Whitehead, Frank, 1950, Jl 23,56:1; 1955, F 6,88:2
Whitehead, George A, 1941, Ja 19,40:5; 1953, Ja 25, 86:3
Whitehead, George B, 1950, Jl 18,29:4
Whitehead, George G, 1940, O 7,17:4
Whitehead, George Sr, 1950, My 23,29:2
Whitehead, H F Mrs, 1947, Je 20,19:1
Whitehead, Harold, 1958, F 13,29:3
Whitehead, Harry, 1946, D 8,77:7
Whitehead, Harry B, 1956, Ja 8,87:1
Whitehead, Harry F, 1954, F 2,27:5
Whitehead, Henry C, 1958, D 28,2:8
Whitehead, Henry W, 1937, Ag 9,20:1
Whitehead, Herbert Mrs, 1943, Jl 10,13:5
Whitehead, Howard R, 1950, Je 14,31:5
Whitehead, J C Judge, 1867, Ag 28,1:5
Whitehead, James H, 1942, Je 6,13:2
Whitehead, James J, 1967, O 19,47:2
Whitehead, James L, 1943, Ap 11,49:1
Whitehead, John, 1950, Jl 17,21:6; 1962, Mr 24,25:2
Whitehead, John B, 1954, N 17,31:1
Whitehead, John H C, 1960, My 9,29:2
Whitehead, John W (por), 1949, My 28,15:3
Whitehead, Joseph A, 1953, O 2,21:4
Whitehead, Joseph E, 1950, Ja 4,35:2
Whitehead, Joseph Rev, 1920, O 22,15:6
Whitehead, Judson J, 1939, Mr 2,21:5
Whitehead, Lizzie B Mrs, 1941, My 3,15:4
Whitehead, Lyman T, 1958, O 21,33:2
Whitehead, Marcus Mrs, 1949, My 30,13:1
Whitehead, Margaret V, 1950, O 17,31:5
Whitehead, R R, 1902, Jl 27,7:6
Whitehead, Ralph C, 1960, N 12,21:4
Whitehead, Ray B, 1955, Jl 25,19:5
Whitehead, Robert, 1905, N 15,13:6; 1960, Je 9,33:2
Whitehead, Robert H, 1956, F 26,89:2
Whitehead, Robert L W Mrs, 1965, O 12,48:1
Whitehead, Robert S, 1946, My 29,23:4
Whitehead, Robert V, 1937, Ap 15,23:2
Whitehead, Russell F, 1954, D 5,88:5
Whitehead, Samuel G, 1943, Ja 6,27:3
Whitehead, Samuel J, 1945, Ag 21,21:4
Whitehead, Sydney G, 1941, Mr 17,17:5
Whitehead, Virginia, 1965, F 11,39:4
Whitehead, W A, 1884, Ag 9,4:7
Whitehead, W C, 1931, Je 28,27:8
Whitehead, William H, 1953, Jl 26,68:6
Whiteheart, James A, 1946, N 19,31:4
Whitehill, Arthur M Sr, 1945, Ag 4,11:6
Whitehill, C E, 1932, D 20,19:1
Whitehill, C Guy, 1951, F 28,28:6
Whitehill, Clarence K, 1958, D 11,13:5
Whitehill, Clyde E, 1952, O 22,27:3
Whitehill, Earl, 1954, O 23,15:4
Whitehill, Laura Mrs, 1965, N 20,10:4
Whitehill, Robert, 1903, N 24,9:5; 1943, O 22,17:5
Whitehill, Walter H, 1938, N 7,19:4
Whitehill, Walter H Mrs, 1954, Ap 28,31:3
Whitehill, William Mrs, 1949, D 7,31:5
Whitehorn, Homer A, 1943, Ap 23,17:5
Whitehorn, Max, 1959, F 23,23:4
Whitehorne, Earl, 1941, O 24,23:3
Whitehorne, Frederick N, 1940, Ap 8,20:4
Whitehorne, George F, 1960, Je 16,33:3
Whitehouse, Bp, 1874, Ag 11,4:6
Whitehouse, C Austen Mrs, 1937, D 23,22:3
Whitehouse, Carolyn B, 1950, S 24,104:4
Whitehouse, E N Capt, 1904, O 21,6:4
Whitehouse, Fitz H Mrs, 1944, Mr 8,19:5
Whitehouse, Fitzhugh, 1909, Ap 10,9:4
Whitehouse, Florence B Mrs, 1945, Ja 23,19:1
Whitehouse, Francis M, 1938, Mr 10,21:6
Whitehouse, Franklin S, 1952, My 21,27:3
Whitehouse, Frederick Cope (funl, N 19,15:5), 1911, N 17,13:3
Whitehouse, G Norman, 1960, Je 10,31:3
Whitehouse, Guill S, 1957, My 5,88:5
Whitehouse, Harold B, 1943, Jl 30,15:1
Whitehouse, Harold N, 1955, S 29,33:4
Whitehouse, Henry, 1941, Jl 25,15:5
Whitehouse, Henry H (por), 1938, Ag 25,19:1
Whitehouse, Henry J, 1965, D 26,69:2
Whitehouse, Henry J Mrs, 1940, Jl 17,21:2
Whitehouse, Horace, 1958, Jl 29,23:4
Whitehouse, Howard D, 1946, N 26,29:5
Whitehouse, J Norman, 1949, O 8,13:3
Whitehouse, J O, 1881, Ag 25,5:1
Whitehouse, James, 1937, Jl 7,24:3
Whitehouse, James Henry, 1924, My 12,17:3
Whitehouse, Jasper H, 1951, S 16,84:4
Whitehouse, Joseph, 1952, N 7,23:2
Whitehouse, Julius, 1917, Ag 20,9:4
Whitehouse, Norman de R (trb lr, Ap 16,37:7), 1957, Ap 12,25:4
Whitehouse, Richard, 1912, Ag 8,9:3
Whitehouse, Richard M, 1945, Mr 29,23:4
Whitehouse, Samuel S Mrs, 1950, D 5,31:3
Whitehouse, Sheldon, 1965, Ag 7,21:4
Whitehouse, William F, 1955, My 28,15:3
Whitehouse, William F Mrs, 1950, N 11,15:2
Whitehurst, Charles E, 1924, Ja 31,15:4
Whitehurst, Jacob Rev, 1917, O 30,15:5
Whitehurst, James T Sr, 1955, Je 24,19:1
Whitehurst, John F, 1947, Ja 15,25:2
Whitehurst, William, 1953, Ap 16,31:3
Whitelam, George E, 1950, Jl 1,15:1
Whitelaw, Donald W, 1941, N 6,23:5
Whitelaw, Edward A (por), 1945, D 6,27:6
Whitelaw, Eric, 1953, N 1,87:1
Whitelaw, George P Sr Dr, 1968, My 6,47:1
Whitelaw, James G, 1958, F 18,27:3
Whitelaw, Louis, 1954, N 5,21:5
Whitelaw, Robert H, 1937, Jl 29,19:6
Whiteleather, Eleanor L Mrs, 1957, F 4,19:4
Whiteley, Amos Nelson, 1925, Ag 4,19:5
Whiteley, Benjamin, 1938, D 21,23:5
Whiteley, Cecil, 1942, O 17,15:7
Whiteley, James, 1950, D 12,33:2
Whiteley, James G, 1947, Je 18,25:6
Whiteley, James G Mrs, 1939, S 4,19:6
Whiteley, John, 1963, D 27,25:3
Whiteley, John W, 1938, N 21,19:1; 1949, My 16,21:2
Whiteley, William, 1955, N 4,29:5
Whiteley, William G, 1949, Ja 21,21:3
Whiteling, Harry C, 1946, Ja 16,24:2
Whitelock, Frank L, 1962, Mr 1,31:1
Whitelock, Herbert R Mrs, 1950, N 19,93:3
Whitelock, William W, 1940, Ja 29,16:2
Whitelock, William W Mrs (por), 1949, Je 26,60:3
Whitely, L A Col, 1869, Jl 21,5:2
Whitely, Philetus Mrs, 1947, O 13,23:2
Whiteman, Daniel S, 1952, Je 1,84:5
Whiteman, Harry A, 1937, Jl 4,II,7:2
Whiteman, John Mrs, 1952, N 19,29:1
Whiteman, Kalman, 1946, S 25,28:2
Whiteman, Paul, 1967, D 30,1:5
Whiteman, Richard, 1941, Jl 3,19:6
Whiteman, Robert D Sr Mrs, 1960, O 16,88:8
Whiteman, Sidney, 1948, F 23,25:5
Whiteman, Simon H, 1943, Jl 7,19:5
Whiteman, Thomas M, 1940, Ag 22,19:1
Whiteman, Wilberforce J, 1939, D 18,23:4
Whitemore, Brewer G, 1943, Jl 23,17:4
Whitenack, George M Jr, 1949, D 11,92:4
Whitenack, Jacob M, 1940, Ap 22,17:2
Whitenack, Miller Royal Dr, 1922, D 13,21:3
Whitenack, William, 1945, Ap 2,19:5
Whitenack, William G, 1965, My 6,39:5
Whitenecht, W H, 1881, N 30,5:4
Whitener, Will L Mrs, 1964, Je 3,43:5
Whiter, E T, 1947, Je 1,60:6
Whitesell, George P Sr, 1953, Ag 11,27:5
Whitesell, Joseph W, 1958, F 20,25:5
Whitesell, M Jean Dr, 1937, My 7,30:2
Whitesell, Richard S, 1955, Ag 13,13:2
Whiteside, Abby, 1956, D 12,39:3
Whiteside, Alexander, 1966, Mr 7,27:1
Whiteside, Arthur D, 1960, Je 18,23:2
Whiteside, Arthur D Mrs, 1938, Ja 9,42:6
Whiteside, Fred W, 1937, O 26,23:1
Whiteside, George, 1941, O 5,49:3
Whiteside, George S, 1940, Ja 30,19:3
Whiteside, George S Mrs, 1964, Ja 24,27:2
Whiteside, George W, 1962, O 31,37:2
Whiteside, George W Mrs, 1957, Je 17,23:2
Whiteside, Harry Capt, 1905, Ap 18,5:4
Whiteside, Horace E, 1956, Je 11,31:5
Whiteside, J (see also N 27), 1876, D 25,5:1
Whiteside, John G (por), 1947, Jl 4,13:3
Whiteside, Joseph S Mrs, 1949, N 18,29:2
Whiteside, Mary B, 1962, Jl 20,25:4
Whiteside, Nicholas (Bro Nicholas Mary), 1957, O 21,25:2
Whiteside, Thomas Dr, 1921, Ja 29,11:5
Whiteside, Walker (por), 1942, Ag 18,21:5
Whiteside, Walker Mrs, 1944, Ja 5,17:2
Whiteside, William, 1882, O 2,5:4
Whiteside, William J, 1937, S 20,23:4
Whiteson, Isadore, 1957, F 1,25:3
Whiteson, Isadore Mrs, 1948, Ja 1,23:2
Whitestone, Dorsey, 1965, Je 9,47:2
Whitestone, Henry A Mrs, 1955, Ja 7,22:3
Whitestone, Jerome, 1956, S 3,13:6
Whitestone, Louis J, 1953, S 5,15:2
Whitestone, Samuel L, 1945, Jl 2,15:5
Whitestone, Trygve R, 1959, Je 17,35:1
Whitesy, Mr, 1872, S 18,1:6
Whiteway, William Sir, 1908, Je 25,9:5
Whitfiel, James B, 1948, Ag 21,15:4
Whitfield, Arthur, 1947, F 5,23:1
Whitfield, B W Sr, 1949, Ja 6,23:1
Whitfield, Frederick E B, 1940, O 16,23:5
Whitfield, Harold B, 1965, S 8,47:4
Whitfield, Henry D, 1949, F 14,19:3
Whitfield, Howard, 1938, S 22,23:3
Whitfield, Inez, 1951, Je 28,25:2
Whitfield, J Randolph, 1939, My 11,25:5
Whitfield, Jacob H, 1944, D 14,23:5
Whitfield, James A (Bill Lewis), 1961, Ap 2,76:1
Whitfield, James P, 1905, Jl 28,7:1; 1953, Jl 18,14:8
Whitfield, Owen H, 1965, Ag 13,26:8
Whitfield, Paul O Mrs, 1962, My 6,88:4
Whitfield, Robert, 1951, Mr 15,29:5
Whitfield, Susan B, 1946, O 20,60:4
Whitfield, William L, 1955, Ag 13,13:7
Whitfield, William Mrs, 1956, D 15,25:1
Whitford, Alfred H, 1940, Jl 18,19:5
Whitford, Daniel E, 1961, My 23,39:1
Whitford, Ella Mrs, 1952, Jl 9,27:4
Whitford, Frances, 1954, Jl 1,25:3
Whitford, George, 1940, Je 8,15:7
Whitford, Greeley W, 1940, My 7,25:4
Whitford, Harold C, 1953, My 21,31:2
Whitford, Harold K, 1964, F 28,29:4
Whitford, Harry N, 1941, My 18,44:2
Whitford, Henry, 1948, Ap 27,25:2
Whitford, James Sr, 1947, S 11,27:5
Whitford, James Sr Mrs, 1946, D 10,32:3
Whitford, Langford C, 1937, O 14,25:2
Whitford, Morton D, 1937, Mr 7,II,8:3
Whitford, Noble E, 1956, My 9,33:1
Whitford, Otis B, 1942, Je 21,37:2
Whitford, William C Prof, 1925, Ag 15,11:5
Whitham, Douglas K, 1952, Mr 18,27:3
Whitham, Edmund S, 1944, N 1,23:4
Whitham, Jay M, 1951, F 27,27:4
Whitin, Ernest S, 1946, F 12,28:2
Whitin, Isabelle Stagg Mrs, 1921, F 25,11:7
Whitin, James E, 1941, Je 1,41:2
Whiting, A, 1936, Jl 22,19:6
Whiting, Ada S Mrs, 1942, Ja 14,21:4
Whiting, Allen E, 1955, Jl 1,21:5
Whiting, Arthur C, 1951, Je 18,23:5
Whiting, Benjamin C, 1945, Ap 14,15:4
Whiting, Borden D, 1961, N 4,19:6
Whiting, Borden D Mrs, 1959, My 30,17:5
Whiting, Boyd S, 1948, D 6,25:5
Whiting, Butler, 1948, Ja 9,21:4
Whiting, Charles A, 1940, Ag 10,13:6
Whiting, Charles B, 1908, Ap 13,7:4
Whiting, Charles R Mrs, 1947, My 20,25:4
Whiting, Charles W, 1921, My 14,9:4
Whiting, Clarence C, 1939, Mr 2,21:1
Whiting, David, 1881, Mr 3,5:3
Whiting, Donald N, 1954, Ja 31,88:3
Whiting, E K, 1940, Ap 16,23:4
Whiting, Edward D, 1962, F 3,21:4
Whiting, Edward E, 1956, D 25,25:3
Whiting, Edward M Mrs, 1943, Mr 18,19:1
Whiting, Edward McKinstry, 1923, Ag 14,15:4
Whiting, Eliot B Mrs, 1953, Mr 1,93:2
Whiting, Florence S, 1947, F 8,17:5
Whiting, Frank B, 1952, Ap 1,29:5
Whiting, Frank P, 1952, Ja 27,77:2
Whiting, Frank V, 1940, N 16,17:5
Whiting, Frank V Mrs, 1945, D 12,27:2
Whiting, Fred T, 1953, Ag 24,23:1
Whiting, Frederic A, 1959, D 23,27:1
Whiting, Frederick, 1946, Mr 13,29:2
Whiting, Frederick G, 1939, O 25,23:6
Whiting, Frederick Mrs, 1949, F 15,23:2
Whiting, George, 1943, D 20,23:1
Whiting, Gertrude, 1951, Ap 16,25:4
Whiting, Giles, 1937, Ap 28,23:4
Whiting, H A, 1903, My 31,7:6
Whiting, H Kneeland, 1947, O 19,66:3
Whiting, Herbert Mrs, 1943, N 3,25:3
Whiting, Howard M, 1946, N 15,23:4
Whiting, Irving B, 1943, F 9,23:1
Whiting, Irving S, 1951, Mr 2,26:2
Whiting, J Hill Mrs, 1943, D 24,13:4
Whiting, J R, 1903, F 1,7:5
Whiting, Jack, 1954, Je 27,68:4; 1961, F 16,31:1
Whiting, Jack Mrs, 1967, Ag 7,29:2
Whiting, James A, 1937, Mr 8,19:2
Whiting, James R, 1908, F 4,7:5
Whiting, Jasper, 1941, Ag 19,21:2
Whiting, John, 1963, Je 17,25:3
Whiting, John C, 1951, O 21,92:4
Whiting, John D Mrs, 1946, Ag 27,27:1
Whiting, John T, 1965, Ap 18,80:7
Whiting, Joseph E, 1910, Ja 25,9:6
Whiting, Justin R, 1965, Mr 2,35:3
Whiting, Kenneth, 1943, Ap 25,34:5
Whiting, L E Dr, 1882, Ag 3,2:4
Whiting, Lewis B, 1950, Ja 28,13:5
Whiting, Lilian, 1942, My 1,19:2
Whiting, Margery, 1943, Mr 13,13:4
Whiting, Max O, 1957, N 17,87:1
Whiting, Merl J, 1941, Ja 12,44:2
Whiting, N F, 1882, N 28,2:2

Whiting, Percy H, 1967, Ag 9,39:2
Whiting, Ralph D, 1958, My 12,29:3
Whiting, Raymond H, 1950, O 14,19:1
Whiting, Raymond Mrs, 1951, Ja 24,27:2
Whiting, Richard, 1938, F 20,II,8:5
Whiting, Robert C (por), 1944, My 12,19:5
Whiting, Robert R Mrs, 1947, My 16,23:4
Whiting, Robert Rudd, 1918, O 16,15:2
Whiting, Romeo H, 1940, My 11,19:6
Whiting, Sidney E Sr Mrs, 1955, N 20,89:2
Whiting, Thomas Mrs, 1949, Ag 21,69:2
Whiting, Virginia Loring, 1865, Mr 15,8:3
Whiting, W D Commodore, 1894, Mr 19,1:4
Whiting, W H C Gen (funl, Mr 12,4:6), 1865, Mr 11, 5:2
Whiting, Walter R, 1957, N 24,86:5
Whiting, Wilfred B, 1946, Ag 31,15:6
Whiting, William, 1873, Je 30,5:6; 1911, Ja 10,11:3
Whiting, William E, 1948, N 9,28:2
Whiting, William Henry Rear-Adm, 1925, Jl 28,13:6
Whiting, William M, 1943, Ag 26,17:6
Whiting, William S Mrs, 1943, Ag 20,15:6
Whiting, Winifred H Judge, 1937, D 7,25:3
Whitings, Charles S Justice, 1922, Mr 26,27:2
Whitington, Albert H, 1958, Ag 6,25:2
Whitis, Charles W, 1946, O 29,25:5
Whitken, Emanuel, 1950, D 17,84:5
Whitla, Valentine A, 1965, D 11,33:5
Whitla, W Sir, 1933, D 12,24:3
Whitley, Charles W, 1921, O 10,13:5
Whitley, Elizabeth Mrs, 1938, Ap 21,19:3
Whitley, Ennis P, 1964, F 16,93:1
Whitley, Frederick E, 1949, Mr 17,25:3
Whitley, Harvey, 1950, D 12,34:4
Whitley, James L, 1959, My 18,27:4
Whitley, Mary T, 1956, Mr 17,19:3
Whitley, Robert J Sr, 1950, N 9,33:4
Whitley, Roland B, 1949, Ag 15,17:4
Whitley, Sam H, 1946, O 3,27:3
Whitley, W Raymond, 1950, Je 9,23:5
Whitley, Walter, 1941, S 29,17:5
Whitlock, Abraham H, 1953, F 16,21:5
Whitlock, B, 1934, My 25,21:1
Whitlock, Bache E, 1948, Ja 9,22:2
Whitlock, Bache M Mrs, 1947, D 25,21:3
Whitlock, Bernard Mrs, 1955, My 23,23:4
Whitlock, Charles Mrs, 1960, F 27,19:6
Whitlock, Charles W, 1941, Mr 30,48:6
Whitlock, Charles W Mrs, 1961, Je 6,37:1
Whitlock, Claude R, 1952, My 27,27:5
Whitlock, Donald W, 1955, Ap 22,25:2
Whitlock, Dora F Mrs, 1948, D 4,19:2
Whitlock, E J, 1881, Jl 1,5:4
Whitlock, Elias D Rev Dr, 1913, D 24,11:6
Whitlock, Ella B Mrs (will, Jl 31,12:2), 1942, Jl 12, 36:8
Whitlock, Frederick S, 1948, Je 28,20:3
Whitlock, George, 1964, O 28,45:3
Whitlock, Harold A, 1957, D 8,88:7
Whitlock, Harry A, 1942, Ag 12,19:4
Whitlock, Herbert P, 1948, F 24,25:3
Whitlock, Herbert Percy Mrs, 1919, O 13,13:4
Whitlock, Lester J Mrs, 1947, Je 10,27:4
Whitlock, Louis I Mrs, 1945, O 10,36:3
Whitlock, Silas J, 1956, S 28,27:2
Whitlock, Victor, 1965, Mr 18,30:3
Whitlock, W S, 1903, Ap 1,9:6
Whitlock, Willard P Jr, 1961, S 11,27:6
Whitlow, Benjamin G, 1943, Jl 26,19:5
Whitlow, Rolfe, 1941, Ap 2,23:5
Whitlow, William V, 1958, Ja 2,29:2
Whitman, Albert H, 1940, Ja 7,48:7
Whitman, Alfred, 1907, N 5,9:5
Whitman, Alfred A Mrs, 1954, Mr 18,31:1
Whitman, Alfred F, 1951, F 28,28:2
Whitman, Armitage, 1962, S 18,39:3
Whitman, Arthur D, 1957, F 19,31:2
Whitman, B L Rev, 1911, N 28,13:5
Whitman, Bert H, 1938, Jl 11,17:4
Whitman, Bradley, 1964, Mr 11,39:3
Whitman, Charles H Dr (por), 1937, D 28,22:1
Whitman, Charles Otis Prof, 1910, D 7,13:4
Whitman, Charles S, 1947, Mr 30,1:7
Whitman, Charles S Mrs, 1926, My 30,14:5
Whitman, Ernest, 1954, Ag 10,19:5
Whitman, Ezekiel, 1866, Ag 5,5:4
Whitman, Frank B, 1949, My 9,25:2
Whitman, Frank E, 1946, Jl 17,23:2
Whitman, Frank J, 1960, F 21,92:7
Whitman, Frank N Mrs, 1947, F 4,19:4
Whitman, Frank S, 1940, N 22,23:6; 1968, Ja 30,38:4
Whitman, Frank S Mrs, 1965, O 30,35:2
Whitman, Frederick R, 1957, N 30,21:4
Whitman, G S, 1903, Ag 17,7:5
Whitman, Gayne, 1958, S 4,29:1
Whitman, H Harold, 1963, Je 9,86:5
Whitman, Hamilton, 1952, N 26,23:3
Whitman, Harold C, 1966, O 30,89:2
Whitman, Helen K Mrs, 1962, O 19,31:2
Whitman, Hendricks H, 1950, Mr 19,94:5
Whitman, Henry Hyde, 1917, N 30,13:7
Whitman, Herbert S Mrs, 1939, Mr 31,21:5
Whitman, Herman, 1938, Ap 6,23:1
Whitman, Homer J, 1937, Ja 3,II,8:8
Whitman, Irving, 1958, F 22,17:4
Whitman, J L, 1926, D 14,27:3
Whitman, J M Judge, 1903, Je 16,7:6
Whitman, John, 1911, N 15,11:5; 1952, Ap 25,23:4
Whitman, John Munro, 1912, O 30,13:5
Whitman, John P Mrs, 1948, D 27,21:5
Whitman, Lauris B Mrs, 1966, Jl 27,39:2
Whitman, LeRoy, 1968, O 19,37:1
Whitman, Malcolm Mrs, 1909, D 19,11:5
Whitman, Meyer, 1942, S 1,19:4
Whitman, Nathaniel, 1919, Ja 8,11:2
Whitman, Peter Mrs, 1962, Ja 5,29:1
Whitman, Philip G, 1965, My 8,31:3
Whitman, Ralph, 1946, F 5,23:5
Whitman, Ray B, 1946, N 24,78:6
Whitman, Roger B, 1942, Jl 22,19:5
Whitman, Roger W, 1961, D 16,25:4
Whitman, Roscoe L, 1955, S 4,56:1
Whitman, Roswell H, 1962, N 29,38:2
Whitman, Royal, 1946, Ag 20,27:5
Whitman, Royal 2d, 1961, Je 28,35:2
Whitman, Russell, 1949, D 24,16:2
Whitman, Russell R, 1939, O 13,23:6
Whitman, Russell W, 1947, Jl 13,44:1
Whitman, S H, 1878, Je 28,5:4
Whitman, Samuel, 1965, D 22,31:4
Whitman, Sarah H, 1878, Jl 1,5:5
Whitman, W, 1928, S 21,29:5
Whitman, W E S (Toby Candor), 1901, O 8,7:7
Whitman, Walt, 1892, Mr 27,4:7
Whitman, Walter B, 1953, N 3,31:2
Whitman, Walter L, 1959, F 9,26:1
Whitman, Walter M, 1948, N 23,29:3
Whitman, William 3d Mrs, 1955, Ja 3,27:1
Whitmarsh, Henry A, 1939, D 3,60:4
Whitmarsh, John H, 1953, Mr 7,15:5
Whitmarsh, T F, 1936, My 13,23:3
Whitmarsh y Garcia, Calixto Dr, 1943, Je 30,21:2
Whitmer, Buck, 1949, My 23,31:2
Whitmeyer, George A, 1952, My 9,23:1
Whitmeyer, John H Sr, 1956, N 27,38:6
Whitmeyer, John H Sr Mrs, 1956, Jl 4,19:2
Whitmore, Bez H, 1953, S 15,31:3
Whitmore, Carl, 1958, O 14,37:1
Whitmore, Daniel W Jr, 1940, O 3,25:3
Whitmore, Edgar, 1941, Ja 30,21:2
Whitmore, Eva B, 1946, S 26,25:1
Whitmore, Frank C, 1947, Je 25,25:5
Whitmore, Fred G, 1956, Ag 13,19:6
Whitmore, Frederic, 1954, S 21,27:5
Whitmore, Gayton, 1942, Ap 6,15:4
Whitmore, Henry, 1940, N 15,21:1
Whitmore, James A, 1962, Ag 3,23:3
Whitmore, James B, 1959, D 19,27:2
Whitmore, Raymond D, 1945, F 8,19:3
Whitmore, Sam A, 1944, Jl 23,36:1
Whitmore, Tyler, 1947, Jl 4,13:5
Whitmore, Walter F, 1937, D 24,20:2
Whitmore, Will, 1959, O 22,37:4
Whitmore, Willet F, 1950, Mr 21,29:3
Whitmyer, John Franklin Dr, 1911, Je 24,9:6
Whitnall, Harold O, 1945, My 19,19:3
Whitner, W C, 1940, My 13,17:3
Whitner, William M, 1945, Ag 12,40:4
Whitney, A D T Mrs, 1906, Mr 22,9:5
Whitney, A F, 1949, Jl 17,57:1
Whitney, Abijah, 1903, S 21,7:6
Whitney, Albert Beach Dr, 1909, Ag 31,7:6
Whitney, Albert W (por), 1943, Jl 29,19:1
Whitney, Albert W Mrs, 1959, My 22,27:2
Whitney, Alfred R, 1946, O 8,23:4
Whitney, Alfred Rutgers, 1909, O 23,11:1
Whitney, Allan B, 1942, D 26,11:5
Whitney, Allan S, 1962, S 27,37:2
Whitney, Allen S, 1944, S 12,19:2
Whitney, Amos, 1920, Ag 7,5:6
Whitney, Arthur (por), 1942, N 20,23:4
Whitney, Arthur E, 1966, Ag 15,27:5
Whitney, Arthur Mrs (will), 1960, Ap 9,1:3
Whitney, Arthur S, 1950, N 13,27:5
Whitney, Arthur T Mrs, 1937, D 7,25:3
Whitney, Arthur W, 1943, Ag 17,17:4
Whitney, C (por), 1929, Ja 19,17:3
Whitney, C M, 1932, Ag 1,15:3
Whitney, Carl E, 1940, O 30,23:2
Whitney, Carl E Mrs, 1951, N 23,29:3
Whitney, Caroline Mrs (por), 1938, N 21,19:1
Whitney, Casper L, 1948, Mr 25,27:3
Whitney, Charles A, 1951, F 7,29:1
Whitney, Charles C, 1904, Mr 5,1:3
Whitney, Charles F, 1954, N 1,27:5
Whitney, Charles L A, 1944, O 12,27:6
Whitney, Charles M, 1913, N 16,IV,7:6
Whitney, Charles M (will), 1954, Mr 29,90:4
Whitney, Charles M Jr, 1943, Jl 9,17:1
Whitney, Charles S, 1939, Ag 10,19:5; 1959, O 27,37:1
Whitney, Charles Sumner, 1918, Ja 26,13:8
Whitney, Charles W, 1908, D 27,9:4
Whitney, Charlotte A, 1955, F 5,15:2
Whitney, Chester F S, 1960, Ap 15,23:3
Whitney, Corydon E, 1905, Mr 16,9:6
Whitney, Daniel D, 1914, N 11,13:6
Whitney, David C, 1942, Ap 26,40:1
Whitney, Douglas M, 1951, Mr 19,27:1
Whitney, E R, 1905, S 10,7:6
Whitney, Eddy R Mrs, 1961, Je 24,21:6
Whitney, Edward A, 1962, Je 28,31:5
Whitney, Edward Baldwin Justice (funl, Ja 8,13:5), 1911, Ja 6,9:3
Whitney, Edward P, 1938, N 22,23:2
Whitney, Edward S, 1951, F 13,31:5
Whitney, Edward S Mrs, 1948, O 21,27:4
Whitney, Edwin M, 1957, Je 6,31:5
Whitney, Eli, 1924, Je 13,19:6
Whitney, Eli Mrs, 1909, Ja 13,9:5
Whitney, Ernest E, 1947, Ja 3,21:4
Whitney, Ex-Judge, 1872, Mr 19,2:1
Whitney, F A Russell, 1921, Ag 5,13:5
Whitney, Flora A Mrs, 1948, Ja 25,56:4
Whitney, Francis H, 1944, Ja 18,20:2
Whitney, Frank G, 1940, My 28,23:4
Whitney, Frank L, 1940, S 24,23:4
Whitney, Franklin, 1943, F 12,19:2
Whitney, Frederick A Prof, 1968, Jl 23,39:2
Whitney, Frederick M, 1942, O 12,34:3
Whitney, G J, 1879, Ja 1,4:7
Whitney, G W S, 1926, D 18,17:4
Whitney, Gail (Mrs L S Stur), 1963, S 14,25:2
Whitney, Geoffrey G, 1953, Jl 26,69:2
Whitney, Geoffrey G Mrs (will, Jl 6,19:2; est appr, N 5,21:5), 1955, My 10,29:3
Whitney, George (Racetrack Geo), 1906, My 30,2:5
Whitney, George, 1963, Jl 23,29:1
Whitney, George A, 1948, S 8,29:5
Whitney, George E, 1963, D 6,36:2
Whitney, George H Dr, 1913, Je 7,11:4
Whitney, George J, 1938, Ap 2,15:1
Whitney, George K, 1958, Ja 18,15:6
Whitney, George Mrs, 1915, Ja 18,9:3; 1967, O 16,45:1
Whitney, George Q Maj, 1925, Ag 5,17:5
Whitney, George T, 1938, My 30,11:3
Whitney, Gertrude C Mrs, 1941, My 23,21:4
Whitney, Gilbert C Sr, 1958, F 24,19:2
Whitney, Gordon B, 1956, D 17,31:5
Whitney, Gorham H, 1948, D 19,76:6
Whitney, Gwin A, 1939, F 13,15:5
Whitney, H, 1936, My 21,23:1
Whitney, H F, 1927, Jl 1,21:4
Whitney, H LeRoy, 1965, N 1,41:1
Whitney, H P, 1930, O 27,1:3
Whitney, Harold E, 1939, Je 11,44:8
Whitney, Harold S, 1953, Ja 29,27:1
Whitney, Harold W, 1949, Mr 28,21:4
Whitney, Harry G, 1956, Jl 31,23:3
Whitney, Harry Mrs, 1960, Jl 2,17:1
Whitney, Harry P, 1963, Ap 10,39:4; 1966, My 22,85:4
Whitney, Harry P Mrs, 1942, Ap 18,15:1
Whitney, Harry S, 1945, Ja 26,21:2
Whitney, Harvey E, 1951, My 9,33:2
Whitney, Helen M, 1906, N 29,9:4
Whitney, Henry C, 1957, F 14,27:4
Whitney, Henry H, 1949, Ap 4,23:2
Whitney, Henry Melville, 1923, Ja 26,17:4
Whitney, Henry Mitchell Prof, 1911, Mr 27,11:4
Whitney, Henry N, 1920, Ja 22,17:2
Whitney, Herbert Mrs, 1957, Jl 31,23:4
Whitney, Herbert P, 1957, Mr 23,19:5
Whitney, Howard F (por), 1947, Mr 26,25:3
Whitney, Howard F, 1954, F 5,19:2
Whitney, Howard F Mrs, 1958, Jl 22,27:1
Whitney, Hurd, 1967, My 3,42:4
Whitney, Isabel L, 1962, F 4,83:1
Whitney, J F, 1902, Ap 20,8:6
Whitney, J N, 1885, Ap 21,5:4
Whitney, J S, 1878, O 25,1:6
Whitney, J Theodore, 1951, N 29,33:5
Whitney, James L, 1910, S 26,13:6
Whitney, James P, 1914, S 26,11:5; 1939, Je 19,15:6
Whitney, James S Mrs, 1904, F 8,9:6
Whitney, Jessamine S, 1941, Mr 12,21:3
Whitney, John, 1955, Jl 12,25:2
Whitney, John B, 1958, Mr 13,29:5
Whitney, John D Rev Dr, 1917, N 28,13:5
Whitney, John H, 1944, Ja 4,18:2; 1958, S 29,27:3
Whitney, Jophanus H Gen, 1915, Mr 29,9:4
Whitney, Josephine Mrs, 1948, F 15,60:6
Whitney, Kathryn F Mrs, 1961, Je 22,31:5
Whitney, King, 1964, Ja 21,29:4
Whitney, Klee A, 1948, F 16,22:2
Whitney, L Annie, 1937, D 9,25:2
Whitney, L Starkey, 1953, My 10,88:5
Whitney, Larned S Mrs, 1957, Je 25,29:1
Whitney, Leon R, 1951, Ja 27,13:5
Whitney, Livingston, 1949, Jl 28,23:2
Whitney, Lucian J Prof, 1925, F 4,21:4
Whitney, Margaret D, 1945, O 13,15:5
Whitney, Maria, 1910, Ja 21,11:5
Whitney, Mary Watson Prof, 1921, Ja 22,11:4
Whitney, Miriam P, 1946, Je 17,21:3
Whitney, Myron W, 1910, S 20,11:4; 1954, Je 4,23:1
Whitney, Myron W Mrs, 1952, S 7,87:1
Whitney, Nelson J Mrs, 1950, Ap 17,23:2
Whitney, Olive Buckley, 1904, Ag 21,2:2
Whitney, P, 1927, My 26,1:3
Whitney, Parkhurst L, 1957, F 7,27:4

Whitney, Paul C, 1954, Je 10,31:2
Whitney, Paul L B Mrs, 1957, S 19,29:5
Whitney, Payne Mrs, 1944, S 25,17:1
Whitney, Phoebe T, 1937, Je 2,23:4
Whitney, R W, 1938, My 4,23:5
Whitney, Richard E, 1938, Ap 7,23:3
Whitney, Richard Merrill, 1924, Ag 17,24:4
Whitney, Robert B, 1952, D 26,16:3
Whitney, Robert E, 1948, O 9,19:5
Whitney, Robert L, 1925, O 21,23:3
Whitney, Robert P, 1955, Mr 20,88:8
Whitney, Roger, 1965, Jl 24,3:5
Whitney, Rosalie L Mrs, 1939, S 4,19:3
Whitney, Russell, 1944, Jl 11,15:3
Whitney, Russell W, 1950, Mr 10,28:2
Whitney, S T, 1934, F 14,22:4
Whitney, Scudder V, 1907, Ja 13,9:5
Whitney, Stephen, 1924, Ja 22,17:4
Whitney, Stephen Whitney Mrs, 1925, N 21,17:5
Whitney, Stuart H, 1939, N 4,15:5
Whitney, T H, 1934, Ja 9,1:5
Whitney, Thomas H, 1958, N 30,86:5
Whitney, Thomas Henry, 1907, F 27,9:6
Whitney, Thomas P Mrs (Julia), 1965, Ag 14,23:1
Whitney, Travis H Jr, 1955, Ap 28,29:4
Whitney, Vernon L, 1957, Je 4,35:4
Whitney, W C Mrs, 1899, My 7,1:5
Whitney, W D Prof, 1894, Je 8,5:3
Whitney, Walter L, 1958, Ag 6,25:4
Whitney, Warren A, 1944, Mr 30,21:3
Whitney, Warren Webster, 1905, Mr 7,9:6
Whitney, Will A, 1955, O 4,35:4
Whitney, William A Col, 1906, N 20,9:6
Whitney, William C, 1904, F 3,1:7; 1939, Mr 7,21:5
Whitney, William F, 1945, My 31,15:5
Whitney, William F Dr, 1921, Mr 5,13:6
Whitney, William L, 1949, D 28,32:2
Whitney, Willis R, 1958, Ja 10,23:1
Whitney, Wilmer B, 1937, O 25,19:3
Whitney-Smith, Emma Mrs, 1941, D 26,13:3
Whiton, A Sherrill, 1961, Je 16,33:6
Whiton, Alpha R, 1963, D 22,35:1
Whiton, Frederic J, 1959, Mr 28,17:2
Whiton, Herman F, 1967, S 7,45:3
Whiton, James M Rev Dr, 1920, Ja 28,11:4
Whiton, Juliet, 1947, F 4,25:5
Whiton, Louis C (por), 1944, N 15,27:5
Whiton, Lucius E, 1949, N 12,15:4
Whiton, Mary C Mrs, 1906, Mr 30,9:4
Whiton, Sylvester G, 1946, Ap 24,25:2
Whiton, Walter H Mrs, 1960, Ag 19,23:1
Whiton, Wilson, 1873, Je 7,5:4
Whiton-Stuart, Jesse P, 1950, S 19,29:4
Whitridge, J Dr, 1878, Jl 25,3:4
Whitridge, John A, 1907, My 25,9:3
Whitridge, Thomas Jr, 1948, Ja 22,27:4
Whitsett, Joseph H, 1951, Ag 16,27:3
Whitsett, William B Rev, 1911, Ja 21,13:4
Whitsitt, Joseph M, 1941, Ap 29,19:4
Whitsitt, Vincent P, 1945, Mr 30,15:1
Whitson, George W, 1948, Mr 8,23:5
Whitson, Gilson S, 1907, N 25,9:4
Whitson, Milton J, 1955, D 16,29:3
Whitson, Samuel W, 1938, N 27,48:4
Whitson, T Barclay, 1954, Ja 24,85:1
Whitson, Thomas, 1948, O 2,15:3
Whitt, Hugh, 1955, F 3,23:2
Whittaker, A L, 1925, Mr 4,19:5
Whittaker, Albert L, 1938, Mr 15,23:5
Whittaker, Alice J Mrs, 1941, Mr 27,23:4
Whittaker, Benjamin, 1949, My 19,29:4
Whittaker, Catherine G (Sister Cath), 1941, Jl 10, 19:3
Whittaker, Edmund B, 1958, Mr 12,31:3
Whittaker, Edmund T, 1956, Mr 25,92:4
Whittaker, Frank, 1954, My 9,89:1
Whittaker, Fred, 1953, Ag 13,25:6
Whittaker, Guerdon W, 1945, Ag 25,11:2
Whittaker, J E, 1945, D 10,21:2
Whittaker, James, 1964, Mr 21,26:6
Whittaker, James M, 1881, Mr 12,2:7
Whittaker, Johanna H, 1884, S 16,2:2
Whittaker, John D, 1941, S 2,18:2
Whittaker, Joseph S, 1958, Mr 16,86:5
Whittaker, Lincoln T, 1959, Ja 17,19:5
Whittaker, Lloyd Mrs, 1949, Ag 17,23:4
Whittaker, Milo W, 1954, S 20,23:3
Whittaker, Percival J H, 1945, Ag 28,19:2
Whittaker, Robert, 1925, My 30,9:5
Whittaker, Thomas, 1914, D 27,3:6
Whittaker, William, 1937, Ap 7,25:2; 1942, S 13,52:7; 1944, Mr 15,19:3
Whittaker, William A, 1960, Ap 27,37:4
Whittall, Frank A, 1961, My 7,86:2
Whittall, M Whitin, 1948, S 15,31:4
Whittall, Matthew J, 1922, N 1,19:5
Whittall, Matthew J Mrs, 1965, Je 30,37:4
Whittam, Jemima C Mrs, 1946, Ja 4,22:2
Whitteaker, William J, 1961, N 4,19:2
Whitteley, Aubrey S, 1965, My 22,31:5
Whittelsey, Edward L Judge, 1920, Ja 29,9:5
Whittelsey, Harriet S A Mrs, 1941, F 27,19:5
Whittelsey, Henry N (por), 1945, N 27,23:4
Whittelsey, Theodore Sr, 1953, Je 29,21:6
Whittelsey, Thomas D, 1946, S 6,21:4
Whittelsy, Joseph T, 1903, Je 18,9:6
Whittem, Arthur F, 1958, F 15,17:3
Whittem, William A, 1940, Ap 6,17:7
Whittemore, A H, 1938, Ag 26,17:4
Whittemore, Abby R, 1940, N 23,17:4
Whittemore, Alan G, 1960, S 26,33:3
Whittemore, Audenried, 1968, Mr 12,43:2
Whittemore, Charles B, 1937, Ag 25,21:2
Whittemore, Clark M, 1953, My 19,29:3
Whittemore, Clarke M Mrs, 1949, Ja 1,13:6
Whittemore, Courtney, 1954, Jl 16,21:2
Whittemore, Don Juan, 1916, Jl 19,9:7
Whittemore, E A, 1881, Ap 16,5:4
Whittemore, Edward H, 1948, F 17,25:2
Whittemore, F W, 1884, F 2,5:4
Whittemore, Floyd, 1939, My 7,III,6:8
Whittemore, Frederick O Mrs, 1954, Jl 27,21:3
Whittemore, George H, 1940, Ag 23,15:2
Whittemore, Gertrude B (will, S 27,19:6), 1941, Ap 15,15:6
Whittemore, Herbert L, 1954, Jl 13,23:5
Whittemore, Howard, 1948, S 20,25:5
Whittemore, Ira M, 1944, Ap 12,21:2
Whittemore, J M, 1883, O 16,4:7
Whittemore, James, 1941, Ag 3,35:2
Whittemore, James K, 1948, Mr 23,25:4
Whittemore, James M Brig-Gen, 1916, S 7,9:4
Whittemore, Jane, 1961, F 4,19:4
Whittemore, John, 1963, Ap 14,92:7
Whittemore, Joseph, 1946, Jl 7,36:1
Whittemore, Laurence F, 1960, Ag 11,27:2
Whittemore, Lewis B, 1965, D 7,47:4
Whittemore, Manvel, 1961, Ag 17,27:3
Whittemore, Margaret, 1937, D 3,23:2
Whittemore, Martha A R Mrs, 1938, Ja 23,II,8:7
Whittemore, Norman C, 1952, My 19,17:5
Whittemore, Robert D Mrs, 1962, Mr 29,33:5
Whittemore, Robert J, 1908, Mr 26,7:7
Whittemore, Robert M, 1937, N 24,23:2
Whittemore, Sidney Varnum Rev, 1909, S 17,9:4
Whittemore, Theodore B, 1964, My 23,23:3
Whittemore, Thomas, 1950, Je 9,23:3
Whittemore, Timothy, 1873, F 26,6:2
Whittemore, Walter F, 1944, O 28,15:5
Whittemore, Wilfred D, 1964, Je 6,23:3
Whittemore, William, 1942, S 30,23:2
Whittemore, William G, 1948, My 10,21:6
Whittemore, William J, 1955, F 8,27:1
Whittemore, Wyman, 1957, Ja 26,19:2
Whitten, Alice L Mrs, 1941, Ja 21,21:3
Whitten, Charles E, 1951, Ap 22,89:2
Whitten, Francis S, 1950, My 13,17:4
Whitten, Frank L, 1940, Jl 9,21:3
Whitten, Harold W, 1941, F 6,21:4
Whitten, Harvey B (will), 1949, D 8,36:5
Whitten, Philip F, 1947, Mr 22,13:3
Whitten, Sumner H, 1940, Mr 31,45:2
Whitten, Wilfred, 1942, D 23,19:3; 1943, Ja 2,11:2
Whitten, William M, 1951, Ap 11,29:4
Whitten-Brown, Arthur, 1948, O 5,4:4
Whitten-Brown, Arthur Mrs Lady, 1952, My 3,21:2
Whittenberger, Herbert E, 1951, F 23,27:5
Whittet, Marjorie M Mrs, 1942, Jl 18,13:5
Whittier, Allen W, 1945, S 3,23:6
Whittier, Amy I Mrs, 1940, Ag 28,19:4
Whittier, Arthur H, 1954, Je 1,27:1
Whittier, Cahs A Brig-Gen, 1908, My 20,7:5
Whittier, Charles Albert, 1908, My 15,9:5
Whittier, Charles R (por), 1945, Je 7,19:2
Whittier, Charles R Mrs, 1954, Ag 6,17:5
Whittier, Charles W, 1949, Ap 14,25:3
Whittier, Edward, 1942, Mr 10,20:2
Whittier, Ethel, 1942, Je 18,21:6
Whittier, Frank N Dr, 1924, D 24,15:3
Whittier, G F, 1940, O 8,25:4
Whittier, Harriet S, 1957, F 16,17:6
Whittier, J G, 1892, S 8,8:1
Whittier, John G, 1948, Ag 7,15:7
Whittier, M F, 1883, Ja 9,5:4
Whittier, Rufus Mrs, 1951, D 9,91:1
Whittier, Stephen T, 1948, S 20,25:4
Whitting, Edward L, 1941, Mr 19,21:3
Whittingham, W R Bp, 1879, O 18,5:5
Whittingham, Walter G, 1941, Je 18,21:4
Whittingham, William, 1940, O 2,23:2
Whittingham, William R, 1937, Je 25,21:2
Whittinghill, Dexter G, 1956, Je 5,35:4
Whittinghill, W E, 1949, Ja 3,23:1
Whittington, Alex M, 1940, Mr 25,15:4
Whittington, Samuel Dr, 1921, Ag 18,11:6
Whittington, William E, 1966, Jl 4,15:3
Whittington, William E Mrs, 1959, S 6,73:2
Whittington, William M, 1962, Ag 21,33:1
Whittkin, William H, 1954, Ap 11,87:1
Whittle, Charles R, 1947, N 28,27:3
Whittle, Daniel, 1939, F 4,15:3
Whittle, F M Bp, 1902, Je 19,9:6
Whittle, Harry D, 1944, Ja 13,21:2
Whittle, Henry D Mrs, 1949, Jl 11,17:4
Whittle, Horace, 1942, F 20,17:2
Whittle, John M, 1949, My 19,29:4
Whittle, Thomas A, 1938, Je 12,38:7
Whittle, Thomas W, 1951, Ap 29,89:3
Whittle, Wilbur F, 1944, My 26,19:5
Whittlesey, Charles B, 1949, O 18,27:1
Whittlesey, Charles F, 1941, Ja 2,23:2
Whittlesey, Charles W, 1940, D 7,17:2
Whittlesey, Clyde W, 1949, Jl 3,26:8
Whittlesey, Derwent S, 1956, N 26,27:1
Whittlesey, Eliphalet Gen, 1909, O 2,9:4
Whittlesey, Elisha, 1922, Mr 5,26:4
Whittlesey, George N, 1957, My 16,31:5
Whittlesey, George N Mrs, 1957, S 9,25:4
Whittlesey, Henry M Gen, 1873, Ag 16,3:1
Whittlesey, Isaac, 1863, Ja 9,1:4
Whittlesey, Roger Mrs, 1943, Ja 7,19:5
Whittlesey, Walter L, 1961, O 7,23:6
Whittlesey, Walter L Mrs, 1948, N 30,27:2
Whittlesly, Curtis E, 1914, O 10,11:6
Whittlessey, Edward B, 1945, Ag 4,11:6
Whittley, John P, 1953, Je 19,21:2
Whittmore, Edward R, 1945, N 13,21:4
Whittmore, George E, 1955, S 17,15:4
Whittmore, Irene K, 1946, O 24,27:2
Whittmore, William J Mrs, 1955, Jl 12,25:4
Whitton, Charles D, 1946, Jl 26,21:3
Whitton, Edward R, 1960, Jl 29,25:3
Whitton, John R Mrs, 1958, S 22,31:5
Whitton, William H, 1951, O 3,33:1
Whittredge, Euphemia, 1940, Ap 26,21:4
Whittridge, T, 1883, O 28,8:7
Whitty, James H, 1937, Je 4,23:5
Whitty, James S, 1938, S 25,39:1
Whitty, John T, 1948, My 11,26:2
Whitty, Joseph B, 1963, O 17,35:1
Whitty, M J Mrs, 1864, N 22,2:2
Whitty, Mary J, 1944, Je 12,19:3
Whitty, May Dame, 1948, My 30,34:1
Whitty, Michael J Mrs, 1952, O 25,17:2
Whitty, Thomas F, 1952, My 26,23:4
Whitwell, Frederick S, 1941, My 22,21:4
Whitwell, George E, 1967, Jl 6,35:2
Whitwell, Livingston M, 1951, My 30,21:4
Whitworth, Geoffrey, 1951, S 11,29:5
Whitworth, J B, 1960, Mr 8,33:3
Whitworth, Stanley, 1957, O 17,33:2
Wholean, William J, 1952, S 7,87:1
Wholey, John F, 1961, Mr 3,27:1
Wholihan, Terence, 1955, F 15,27:2
Wholley, Francis R (cor, Mr 25,21:6), 1942, Mr 24, 19:5
Whomsley, John A, 1957, F 8,23:4
Whorf, Benjamin L, 1941, Jl 28,13:6
Whorf, John, 1959, F 14,21:4
Whorf, Richard, 1966, D 15,47:1
Whote, Harvey T Mrs, 1943, Je 22,19:5
Whowell, Charles E (por), 1945, Je 13,23:4
Whritenour, Charles A, 1953, Ag 9,77:3
Whyard, Charles E, 1940, F 28,21:2
Whyland, A E, 1902, F 21,9:6
Whyman, Albert E (por), 1955, N 10,35:4
Whyman, Henry L, 1949, N 26,15:6
Whymper, Edward, 1911, S 17,II,11:5
Whymper, J W, 1903, Ap 8,9:2
Whyte, Archibald Sr, 1947, F 6,23:3
Whyte, Arthur K, 1950, Mr 8,25:1
Whyte, Charles G, 1943, Ap 6,21:5
Whyte, Chesterfield, 1949, Je 30,23:3
Whyte, Clarence R Sr, 1950, D 27,28:2
Whyte, Frank D, 1942, Jl 10,17:5
Whyte, Fred, 1952, Ag 19,23:4
Whyte, George S, 1944, D 18,19:4
Whyte, Gordon R, 1946, Ag 21,28:2
Whyte, Hilson H, 1953, O 7,29:4
Whyte, Ira E, 1940, Ap 10,25:4
Whyte, James J, 1958, Mr 1,17:4
Whyte, James P, 1937, Ap 19,21:3
Whyte, Jessel S, 1952, My 29,27:5
Whyte, John, 1952, Mr 31,19:2
Whyte, Malcolm K, 1967, N 11,33:5
Whyte, Matthew A, 1959, Mr 6,25:4
Whyte, Robert, 1950, Je 7,29:6
Whyte, Thomas Jr Mrs, 1951, Ap 25,29:3
Whyte, William, 1945, Ap 23,19:5
Whyte, William H, 1958, Ag 10,92:1
Whyte, William Pinkney Sen, 1908, Mr 21,9:6
Whyte, William R, 1946, N 14,29:5
Whyte, William Sir, 1914, Ap 15,13:7
Wiand, William H, 1948, Ja 27,25:2
Wiant, James S, 1952, Mr 16,91:1
Wiant, Thoburn H, 1963, F 7,7:6
Wiard, William W, 1945, O 24,21:5
Wiarda, William M Mrs, 1966, O 22,31:4
Wiart, Henri C de Count, 1951, My 7,25:3
Wibecan, George E (por), 1946, S 9,9:5
Wibecan, George E Jr, 1964, N 25,37:3
Wiberg, Peter E, 1954, D 15,31:4
Wiberg, Sven, 1947, O 30,25:3
Wiberley, Ella, 1949, Mr 28,21:5
Wiberly, William J, 1945, D 13,29:3
Wiborg, Charles H, 1944, Ap 12,21:5
Wiborg, F B, 1930, My 13,29:1
Wiborg, Frank B Mrs, 1917, Ja 4,11:5
Wiborg, Mary H, 1964, Mr 28,19:2

Wich, Ferdinand K, 1938, D 6,23:4
Wichern, Charles F W, 1941, Ag 13,17:5
Wichers, Gerard G V, 1945, N 20,21:2
Wichert, Ernest L, 1937, N 10,25:2
Wichfeld, Ivan H, 1959, Ja 3,17:1
Wichfield, Aksel C P, 1956, S 12,37:2
Wichin, Ernest A, 1957, Ag 15,21:1
Wichner, Adam, 1952, Ja 25,21:2
Wicht, Henry C, 1943, Ja 29,19:3
Wichum, George H, 1953, Ja 12,27:1
Wick, Elizabeth B Mrs, 1938, My 27,17:3
Wick, Frances G, 1941, Je 16,15:6; 1942, Ja 22,17:4
Wick, Frederick H, 1921, Ja 20,9:4
Wick, George D, 1950, D 19,29:2
Wick, Gustav A, 1940, N 12,23:3
Wick, Henry C, 1940, Mr 10,51:3
Wick, Hermon, 1953, O 5,27:6
Wick, James A, 1947, S 20,15:4
Wick, James L, 1964, N 8,89:1
Wick, Jean, 1939, F 4,15:6
Wick, Louise C, 1941, S 12,22:3
Wick, Otto, 1957, N 20,35:2
Wick, Samuel I, 1960, Jl 6,33:4
Wick, Waldemar J, 1962, Je 16,19:6
Wick, William, 1957, Mr 5,31:1
Wick, William A, 1939, Mr 1,21:2
Wick, William L, 1958, F 11,31:4
Wickard, Andrew J, 1943, D 17,27:2
Wickard, Andrew J Mrs, 1945, Ja 5,15:3
Wickard, Claude Mrs, 1966, O 11,47:1
Wickard, Claude R, 1967, Ap 30,87:1
Wicke, Charles E, 1948, N 11,27:3
Wicke, Charles E Mrs, 1941, F 27,19:2
Wicke, Otto, 1922, Mr 30,17:3
Wickenden, Arthur C, 1967, Je 8,47:2
Wickenden, Charles R F, 1962, O 20,25:2
Wickenden, Homer E, 1966, Ja 11,29:2
Wickenden, Leonard, 1959, Ap 22,33:4
Wickenden, William E (por), 1947, S 2,21:3
Wickenden, William E Mrs, 1961, Ag 27,85:1
Wickenheiser, Walter Mrs, 1951, N 29,35:4
Wicker, Charles M, 1941, Je 25,21:4
Wicker, Ernest Mrs, 1952, F 9,13:3
Wicker, George Ray Prof, 1917, N 26,13:7
Wicker, John J, 1958, Mr 18,29:5
Wicker, Robert W, 1955, Ja 26,25:4
Wickers, Charles E, 1949, Ja 11,31:2
Wickersham, Cornelius W Jr, 1966, O 12,43:1
Wickersham, Cornelius Wendell Sr, 1968, F 1,37:1
Wickersham, G W, 1936, Ja 26,1:6
Wickersham, George W Mrs (will, Jl 9,36:8), 1944, My 29,15:4
Wickersham, Iva K Mrs, 1941, F 8,15:3
Wickersham, James, 1939, O 25,23:4
Wickersham, John T, 1944, Je 16,19:4
Wickersham, Marguerite H, 1956, Ja 22,89:2
Wickersham, Morris D, 1904, Ja 2,9:4
Wickersham, Nathan R, 1954, S 14,27:2
Wickersham, Nathaniel, 1953, Jl 29,23:4
Wickersham, Rowland deB, 1960, Mr 26,21:2
Wickes, Edward A, 1918, D 7,15:5
Wickes, Forsyth, 1964, D 21,29:3
Wickes, Isaac C Capt, 1912, Ag 11,II,11:5
Wickes, James C, 1945, Ag 3,17:6
Wickes, Joseph E, 1960, My 23,29:5
Wickes, Robert A, 1944, D 6,23:5
Wickes, Sheldon F Mrs, 1960, My 31,31:2
Wickes, T H, 1905, Mr 29,6:1
Wickes, Thomas Mrs, 1967, My 7,86:5
Wickes, W Wirt, 1939, Je 10,17:3
Wickes, W Wirt Mrs, 1938, Ja 14,23:3
Wickes, Walter F Mrs, 1942, Ap 22,23:5
Wickett, R Morley, 1963, Je 15,23:3
Wickey, Clark C, 1945, Mr 30,15:4
Wickey, Harry H, 1968, Ap 3,51:1
Wickey, Harry Mrs, 1955, O 2,87:3
Wickfors, G Edward, 1960, F 23,31:1
Wickham, Ben B, 1949, Mr 9,26:3
Wickham, D O, 1914, D 31,9:6
Wickham, Ellen S Mrs, 1942, My 20,19:3
Wickham, Ernest W, 1948, Je 4,23:2
Wickham, Eugene, 1947, O 3,25:2
Wickham, Farington, 1941, My 5,17:3
Wickham, Florence (Mrs E Lueder), 1962, O 21,89:1
Wickham, George, 1905, Mr 6,3:1
Wickham, George Stevens, 1921, O 14,17:4
Wickham, Harry E, 1943, Ja 24,42:4
Wickham, Henry T, 1943, Mr 6,13:1
Wickham, John C, 1958, Mr 2,89:3
Wickham, John D, 1949, Je 20,19:3
Wickham, John E (por), 1938, Ja 13,21:3
Wickham, John W, 1944, My 14,46:3
Wickham, Joseph F, 1950, Je 23,25:2
Wickham, Joseph N, 1946, Ap 8,27:3
Wickham, Mark E, 1954, My 3,25:1
Wickham, Samuel W, 1940, D 29,24:8
Wickham, Stephen H, 1918, Ja 27,17:3
Wickham, Vincent S, 1968, D 10,77:5
Wickham, Vincent S Mrs, 1948, D 9,33:5
Wickham, William, 1881, Mr 1,8:5
Wickham, William H Mrs, 1943, D 11,15:3
Wickham, William Hull, 1925, N 22,9:1
Wicklein, Louis M, 1951, Ap 28,15:5
Wicklein, Raymond R, 1960, F 20,23:2
Wickliff, Harvey V, 1948, D 27,21:4
Wickliffe, Charles A, 1944, My 2,19:4
Wicklow, Earl of, 1946, O 13,59:4
Wickman, August, 1937, O 5,13:4
Wickman, Carl E, 1954, F 6,19:3
Wickman, Louis, 1947, Ja 25,17:3
Wickoff, Charles M, 1953, Je 21,84:6
Wicks, Alfred, 1873, My 1,5:5
Wicks, Archie B, 1948, N 9,27:3
Wicks, Charles F Sr, 1950, Ja 4,46:2
Wicks, Correlia G, 1943, Jl 12,15:6
Wicks, David I Mrs, 1945, F 13,23:3
Wicks, Elverton H, 1942, My 12,19:2
Wicks, Frank S C, 1952, D 23,23:2
Wicks, Lily D Mrs, 1937, My 5,25:3
Wicks, Robert R, 1963, Ap 22,27:3
Wicks, S Clayton, 1938, Je 24,19:6
Wickser, John G Mrs, 1943, S 11,13:4
Wickser, Phil J (por), 1949, Ag 15,17:1
Wickstrom, John H, 1962, My 7,31:3
Wickware, Francis G, 1940, O 13,49:2
Wickware, Francis S, 1951, Ag 26,51:4
Wickware, M S, 1875, My 18,1:6
Wickwire, Arthur M, 1937, Ap 12,17:4
Wickwire, Arthur M Jr, 1955, Ag 29,19:4
Wickwire, Byron F, 1943, Mr 26,19:2
Wickwire, Charles C, 1956, Ag 21,29:5
Wickwire, Chester F, 1910, S 15,9:6
Wickwire, Louise D Mrs, 1942, Mr 3,23:2
Wickwire, Myra G Mrs, 1937, Ap 15,23:2
Wickwire, Theodore H Jr, 1960, O 30,86:7
Wicoff, C Raymond, 1957, My 7,35:2
Wicoff, John V B, 1952, F 27,27:5
Widdecombe, John, 1917, F 2,11:5
Widdemer, Howard T Mrs, 1944, F 22,23:3
Widdemer, Kenneth De W Mrs (M Cleland), 1964, Ag 6,29:4
Widdemer, Kenneth DeW, 1963, S 16,35:4
Widdemer, William L, 1938, N 10,27:3
Widder, Harry H, 1953, S 26,19:7
Widder, Jacob, 1968, Mr 22,47:4
Widdi, Daniel, 1941, O 29,17:2
Widdicombe, Ralph H, 1959, N 21,23:7
Widdis, Henry J, 1940, Mr 5,23:4
Widdleton, W J, 1882, My 3,5:2
Widdop, Walter, 1949, S 7,29:1
Wideman, Frank J, 1952, S 30,31:4
Wideman, Melcher, 1906, Ag 2,7:5
Widener, Alton, 1968, Ap 25,47:3
Widener, George D Mrs, 1968, Mr 12,43:3
Widener, Joseph E (will, No 9,23:3),(por), 1943, O 27,23:1
Widener, Peter A B 2d (por), 1948, Ap 21,27:1
Widener, Peter A B 3d Mrs, 1963, F 5,4:7
Widener, Peter A H (funl, N 9,13:4), 1915, N 8,13:6
Widenmann, Hans Mrs, 1949, Ap 5,29:2
Widgery, John, 1873, Ag 3,1:6
Widin, Peter W, 1950, S 6,29:1
Widing, Herbert Z, 1953, Je 2,29:5
Widli, August E (por), 1937, Jl 7,23:5
Widmaier, Frederick G, 1954, Ap 12,29:5
Widman, Benjamin, 1952, My 31,12:2
Widmann, Carl, 1946, Mr 7,25:1
Widmann, Eugene A, 1938, F 4,21:5
Widmann, Henry P, 1956, D 15,25:2
Widmann, Oscar O, 1961, Je 3,23:3
Widmann, William, 1938, Mr 27,II,7:2
Widmark, Bror T, 1961, Ja 21,21:4
Widmayer, C William, 1949, Ag 29,18:2
Widmayer, George A, 1916, Ja 24,11:2
Widmer, Carl, 1944, F 12,13:1
Widmer, George, 1962, Ja 29,25:2
Widmer, Harry K, 1953, Jl 21,23:1
Widmer, Henry R Mrs, 1947, Jl 15,23:4
Widmer, Louis C, 1951, Ag 28,23:5
Widmer, Robert, 1956, F 12,89:1
Widnall, Edith A Mrs, 1957, Jl 25,23:5
Widney, Erwin W, 1949, O 12,29:2
Widney, Joseph P, 1938, Jl 5,17:2
Widoff, Gustav B, 1955, Ag 30,27:4
Widor, Charles M, 1937, Mr 13,19:1
Widra, Waclav, 1953, Ap 9,27:1
Widre, Harry Mrs, 1956, Mr 3,19:1
Widtsoe, John A, 1952, N 30,86:3
Wieand, Albert C, 1954, Jl 25,69:3
Wieand, Henry D, 1947, N 19,27:4
Wieand, Irma C, 1951, Mr 5,21:2
Wiebe, Albert C, 1955, Ja 18,27:6
Wiebe, William Sr, 1951, Ja 13,15:2
Wiebesiek, Fred H, 1964, Ap 16,37:4
Wiebke, Herman, 1952, F 22,22:2
Wieboldt, William A, 1954, D 11,13:4
Wieboldt, William A Mrs, 1958, F 25,27:4
Wieboldt, William H, 1950, N 8,29:6
Wieche, Robert H, 1966, Je 18,31:4
Wiechert, Ernst, 1950, Ag 26,13:6
Wiechmann, Marie D Mrs, 1937, D 29,21:4
Wiechmann, Walter G, 1964, O 14,45:2
Wieck, William, 1941, My 24,15:5
Wieczorek, Peter, 1957, Mr 14,29:5
Wiedemann, Francis J, 1946, F 15,26:2
Wiedemann, Theodore, 1939, F 3,15:5
Wiedenmann, Andrew J, 1946, My 25,15:6
Wiedenmayer, George W, 1909, S 7,9:6
Wieder, Franklin E Rev, 1937, O 28,23:3
Wieder, Samuel Mrs (Gertrude), 1968, N 5,44:4
Wieder, Walter Mrs (cor, Jl 24,21:2), 1940, Jl 21,28:8
Wiederhold, Antoinette, 1945, Jl 29,40:3
Wiederhold, Oscar, 1951, My 29,25:4
Wiederhold, Rudolph, 1940, D 8,69:3
Wiederkehr, John, 1966, Ja 6,27:1
Wiedermann, Carl, 1962, Je 21,13:4
Wiedersheim, William A, 1953, Je 28,61:2
Wiedfeldt, O Dr, 1926, Jl 6,21:3
Wiedman, Joseph E, 1937, Jl 14,22:1
Wiedman, Oliver T, 1941, Ja 2,23:3
Wiedmann, Carl, 1958, D 30,32:2
Wiedmann, G Adolphe, 1944, D 6,23:6
Wiedmann, John A, 1951, O 20,15:2
Wiedoeft, Anna Mrs, 1940, F 22,23:5
Wiedoeft, Rudy (por), 1940, F 19,17:3
Wiegand, Anna L Mrs, 1940, Jl 8,17:5
Wiegand, Charles A, 1953, Je 3,31:4
Wiegand, Florence Mrs, 1937, Ag 29,II,7:1
Wiegand, George G, 1949, Jl 23,11:3
Wiegand, Gustave, 1957, N 6,35:2
Wiegand, H Frank, 1944, My 30,21:2
Wiegand, Harold J Mrs, 1943, O 27,23:4
Wiegand, Heinrich, 1909, Mr 30,9:7
Wiegand, Henry H, 1943, N 18,23:5
Wiegand, John A, 1941, O 9,23:5
Wiegand, Karl M, 1942, Mr 14,15:4
Wiegand, Mary R Mrs, 1948, F 4,23:3
Wiegand, Peter C, 1957, Jl 12,21:5
Wiegand, William, 1951, F 10,13:2
Wiegand, William B, 1942, Ap 6,15:6
Wiegel, Julius A, 1940, D 24,15:2
Wiegel, Martin Min, 1949, My 9,2:3
Wiegers, Jan, 1959, D 2,43:1
Wiegers, Lester B, 1945, Ja 9,19:5
Wiegler, Max, 1956, Je 12,35:1
Wiegman, Fred C, 1957, D 4,26:6
Wiegman, George J, 1953, F 1,88:3
Wiegman, Ralph G, 1951, D 12,37:1
Wiegman, W Ross, 1911, Ag 5,7:6
Wiehe, William H, 1942, My 22,21:6
Wieland, Albert, 1958, O 4,21:5
Wieland, Arthur, 1945, My 19,19:1
Wieland, Charles, 1944, Mr 2,17:2
Wieland, Charles E, 1952, Mr 27,29:3
Wieland, Charles Mrs, 1954, Ap 6,29:5
Wieland, Frederick, 1950, Ja 26,27:3
Wieland, George A, 1955, O 7,25:3
Wieland, George C, 1938, Jl 30,13:4
Wieland, George R, 1953, Ja 20,25:1
Wieland, Heinrich, 1957, Ag 7,27:2
Wieland, Herman J Mrs, 1944, F 8,15:1
Wieland, John C, 1961, Ja 27,23:4
Wieland, William (trb, Ag 9,15:1; funl, Ag 10,15:3), 1954, Ag 4,1:4
Wieland, William G, 1905, Ap 26,1:1
Wielandy, Paul J, 1953, Mr 6,20:6
Wielawski, Joseph S L Dr, 1968, Je 14,47:2
Wielenga, Andrew H, 1954, Jl 10,13:6
Wieler, Frances M Mrs, 1938, Je 7,23:5
Wieler, Joseph F, 1949, Jl 6,27:4
Wielich, Albert, 1942, O 8,27:2
Wielich, Ludwig, 1951, My 5,17:2
Wielland, George F, 1948, My 5,25:5
Wielopolski, Count Alfred, 1955, My 17,29:2
Wieman, Elton E Mrs, 1962, Ap 23,29:4
Wieman, J L, 1902, N 1,9:4
Wiemann, Albert B, 1958, Ap 5,15:6
Wiemann, George F, 1952, Mr 1,15:2
Wiemann, William, 1952, My 16,24:3
Wiemeler, Ignatz, 1952, Je 5,31:4
Wiemer, Martin J, 1953, Je 4,29:3
Wiemer, Martin J Mrs, 1942, S 9,23:4
Wiemer, Otto E, 1965, O 29,43:1
Wien, Joseph, 1939, Ag 3,19:6
Wien, Joseph Mrs, 1967, Ap 11,47:2
Wien, Max S, 1942, Je 24,19:1
Wien, Morris W, 1961, Ap 18,37:1
Wienandt, Roderick G, 1951, My 18,27:3
Wiencrot, Harold E, 1959, Jl 16,27:5
Wiendreck, August, 1921, O 11,19:5
Wiener, Abraham, 1955, Jl 29,17:1
Wiener, Abraham A, 1937, Ag 10,19:2; 1960, D 4,88:6
Wiener, Alfred, 1964, F 6,29:5
Wiener, Benjamin, 1958, Jl 24,25:5
Wiener, Cecil B, 1960, S 4,69:1
Wiener, Charles A, 1939, F 15,23:3
Wiener, David, 1944, Jl 21,19:5
Wiener, Edward, 1961, S 13,45:2
Wiener, Edward Mrs, 1943, D 9,27:4
Wiener, Elmer A, 1966, Ag 31,43:2
Wiener, Ernest H, 1960, Ag 6,19:6
Wiener, Ernst, 1967, Ap 22,29:8
Wiener, Henry Jr, 1952, O 7,29:5
Wiener, Herbert J Mrs, 1942, F 17,22:2
Wiener, Joseph, 1938, Ja 6,19:3; 1938, Ag 30,17:2; 1941, S 9,23:4
Wiener, Joseph Dr, 1904, Ag 12,7:5
Wiener, Joseph M Mrs, 1945, Je 24,22:3
Wiener, L J, 1939, Ja 20,21:2

Wiener, Leo, 1939, D 14,27:5
Wiener, Ludwig, 1921, N 15,19:4
Wiener, Max, 1950, Jl 2,24:8
Wiener, Morris Mrs, 1954, Mr 8,27:1
Wiener, Norbert, 1964, Mr 19,1:3
Wiener, Paul L, 1967, N 18,37:1
Wiener, Philip, 1959, Jl 11,19:6
Wiener, Richard G Dr, 1937, F 9,23:2
Wiener, Robert L Mrs, 1959, Mr 7,21:3
Wiener, Robert W, 1954, F 22,19:4
Wiener, Samuel, 1964, Ap 7,32:3
Wiener, Sumner C, 1953, Ap 1,29:4
Wiener, William, 1948, Ag 1,56:3
Wiener, William P, 1957, Ja 2,27:3
Wiener, Zachary, 1952, N 19,29:2
Wieners, Frederica Mrs, 1945, Ja 16,19:2
Wieners, Godfrey A S, 1948, Ja 15,23:1
Wieniawa-D'Lugoszewski, Bolwslaw, 1942, Jl 2,6:5
Wieniawski, Adam, 1950, Ap 28,21:2
Wieniawski, H, 1880, Ap 6,5:4
Wienken, Heinrich, 1961, Ja 23,23:1
Wiens, A F Rev, 1937, Ja 11,20:1
Wiepert, George F, 1947, N 26,23:4
Wieprecht, Bernardine, 1940, Mr 24,30:8
Wier, Albert E, 1945, S 10,19:5
Wier, Hiram, 1940, O 15,23:1
Wier, Jeanne E, 1950, Ap 16,104:5
Wier, Marion C, 1962, Je 19,35:1
Wier, Roy M, 1963, Je 30,56:3
Wierdsma, Johan R, 1948, Ap 30,24:3
Wierk, Frederick, 1958, Jl 10,27:5
Wierman, George E, 1950, Mr 26,92:6
Wiernik, P, 1936, F 13,19:4
Wiers, E S, 1931, Jl 1,25:3
Wierum, Howard F, 1946, Ja 2,19:2
Wierum, Otto C, 1950, O 10,31:4
Wiesbader, Hans, 1959, N 5,35:1
Wieschhoff, Heinrich A, 1961, S 19,14:2
Wiese, Victor H, 1945, Je 14,19:4
Wiese, William, 1951, D 7,27:2
Wiese, William F, 1961, Jl 16,69:1
Wiesel, Ernest K, 1944, S 20,23:2
Wiesel, Ernst K Mrs, 1949, Je 21,25:3
Wieselthier, Vally, 1945, S 3,23:6
Wiesemann, Carl R, 1954, Je 1,27:4
Wiesemann, John, 1942, Je 5,17:3
Wiesen, Bessie Mrs, 1938, N 18,21:5
Wiesen, Max, 1943, Je 24,21:3
Wiesendanger, Charles H, 1939, Je 28,21:5
Wiesendanger, Grace L, 1958, Je 26,27:6
Wiesendanger, Ulrich, 1949, S 9,25:3
Wiesendanger, Ulrich Mrs, 1949, My 27,22:2
Wiesenfeld, Paul C, 1958, Ag 10,93:3
Wiesenfelder, Max, 1955, My 10,29:2
Wiesenthal, Alfred V, 1961, Ag 15,29:1
Wiesenthal, Samuel, 1949, Ja 7,21:1
Wieser, Charles E, 1948, O 20,29:5
Wieser, Thomas J, 1957, N 18,31:4
Wieser, Thomas J Mrs, 1954, Jl 26,17:1
Wieser, Thomas Sr, 1949, Je 14,31:1
Wiesike, Lillian Mme (Mrs L A Flickinger), 1960, Ja 13,92:5
Wiesing, John A, 1955, N 1,31:5
Wiesner, August H, 1949, Mr 13,76:3
Wiesner, Daniel H, 1950, Ja 27,23:2
Wiesner, John M, 1939, Mr 4,15:2
Wiess, Harry C (por), 1948, Ag 27,19:5
Wiess, John Rev, 1879, Mr 10,1:4
Wiess, Robert, 1925, Jl 14,21:5
Wiest, Albert F, 1959, S 2,29:2
Wiest, Allen C, 1948, Ap 7,25:2
Wiest, Harry B, 1949, D 19,27:5
Wiest, Howard, 1945, S 18,23:5
Wieters, Edward O, 1953, N 27,27:4
Wieters, Edward O Mrs, 1945, S 12,25:2
Wieth, John C, 1950, O 28,17:6
Wietzman, Nathan, 1944, N 28,23:5
Wiffler, May F, 1952, My 19,17:4
Wiften, Louis A, 1967, D 9,47:3
Wigan, A, 1878, D 2,1:6
Wigand, Adeline A, 1944, Ap 1,13:7
Wigand, Otto C, 1944, Jl 19,19:5
Wigg, Arthur S, 1939, N 11,15:4
Wigg, Marcus D, 1950, Je 11,92:8
Wiggam, Albert E, 1957, Ap 27,19:6
Wiggam, Albert E Mrs, 1943, Ja 27,21:5
Wiggeringloh, William J, 1956, Ja 26,29:1
Wiggers, Carl J (trb lr, My 6,28:5), 1963, Ap 30,35:2
Wiggers, H H, 1953, D 26,13:2
Wiggers, Herbert A, 1953, Je 23,29:3
Wiggin, Albert E, 1941, Ap 19,15:3
Wiggin, Albert H (will, My 26,17:2), 1951, My 22, 31:1
Wiggin, Albert H (est tax appr), 1955, F 5,16:5
Wiggin, Albert H Mrs (est tax appr), 1958, N 19,24:6
Wiggin, Augustus, 1908, N 27,9:3
Wiggin, Charles B Mrs, 1968, F 19,39:3
Wiggin, Ernest W, 1941, S 6,15:6
Wiggin, Frederick A, 1940, Jl 27,13:2
Wiggin, Frederick Holme Dr, 1910, O 29,11:6
Wiggin, Henry D, 1957, S 7,19:5
Wiggin, John D, 1958, O 16,37:4
Wiggin, Joseph, 1948, My 2,76:4
Wiggin, Joseph A, 1956, Ag 16,25:2
Wiggin, Kate Douglas, 1923, Ag 25,7:5
Wiggin, Lewis Mrs, 1952, F 13,29:4
Wiggin, Parry G, 1949, Ag 14,69:1
Wiggin, Paul F, 1958, D 3,37:1
Wiggin, Thomas H, 1964, Ja 18,23:1
Wiggin, William I, 1945, Ja 4,19:2
Wiggins, Albert H Mrs, 1954, D 17,31:6
Wiggins, Alice S Mrs, 1941, Ja 19,40:3
Wiggins, Charles F, 1942, My 19,19:4
Wiggins, Charles 2d, 1943, N 27,13:6
Wiggins, Dean C, 1953, S 14,27:3
Wiggins, Edward H, 1956, D 30,32:6
Wiggins, Ella L Mrs, 1942, O 19,19:5
Wiggins, Elmer W, 1944, O 20,19:1
Wiggins, Frank H, 1943, Ap 18,49:1
Wiggins, Frank Mrs, 1949, Ap 5,29:2
Wiggins, Frank W, 1948, D 29,21:5
Wiggins, Frederick H, 1963, My 24,31:1
Wiggins, Guy, 1962, Ap 26,33:3
Wiggins, H L, 1933, F 26,27:1
Wiggins, John A, 1941, Mr 9,40:5
Wiggins, John G, 1956, N 25,88:3
Wiggins, John H, 1968, O 18,47:4
Wiggins, John Judge, 1904, Ja 10,7:6
Wiggins, John W, 1948, My 26,25:1
Wiggins, Joseph S, 1954, S 28,29:2
Wiggins, Kate D, 1923, S 13,19:3
Wiggins, Leslie A (por), 1948, Mr 6,13:6
Wiggins, May, 1958, My 1,31:1
Wiggins, Norman E, 1939, Mr 9,21:4
Wiggins, Russell, 1941, Jl 26,15:6
Wiggins, Sidney M, 1940, Ap 30,21:4
Wiggins, Thomas, 1908, Je 15,7:5
Wiggins, Thomas J, 1958, O 17,29:3
Wiggins, W J, 1872, N 25,1:6
Wiggins, William D, 1949, Je 14,32:2
Wiggins, William H, 1951, My 9,33:2
Wiggins, William T, 1949, Ag 2,19:2
Wigginton, George, 1942, N 27,23:2
Wigglesworth, Albert W, 1950, Ap 2,92:3
Wigglesworth, Edward, 1945, My 7,17:4
Wigglesworth, G, 1930, N 28,19:6
Wigglesworth, Henry, 1945, Mr 23,19:3
Wigglesworth, Mary Mrs, 1951, Ja 24,27:5
Wigglesworth, Richard B (funl plans, O 24,29:4; mem ser, N 2,39:1), 1960, O 23,88:2
Wigglesworth, Thomas, 1907, Mr 22,11:6
Wigglesworth, Virginia Mrs, 1950, Mr 30,25:6
Wiggs, George W, 1938, Mr 29,21:5
Wiggs, Harvey A Dr, 1968, Ap 13,25:2
Wighall, Lewis T Ex-Sen, 1874, F 21,1:7
Wigham, Edward H, 1951, N 22,31:4
Wight, Claire D, 1940, Mr 30,15:5
Wight, David, 1906, D 4,9:5
Wight, E M, 1881, Ja 7,5:4
Wight, E Van Dyke, 1957, D 16,29:1
Wight, Edwin M, 1914, D 14,11:4
Wight, Frank Jr, 1948, Mr 10,27:3
Wight, Frank L, 1958, Je 30,19:4
Wight, Fred W, 1940, N 27,23:3
Wight, George T, 1950, O 27,29:5
Wight, Goulding K, 1958, N 7,27:3
Wight, James E, 1939, Mr 8,21:4
Wight, James S, 1949, Jl 16,13:6
Wight, John, 1944, Ap 7,19:3
Wight, John C, 1958, My 2,27:2
Wight, John M, 1938, D 17,15:4
Wight, Lawrence H, 1958, O 17,29:3
Wight, Malcolm G, 1956, My 2,31:5
Wight, Mary Mrs, 1940, O 17,25:4
Wight, Percy L, 1961, Mr 2,27:4
Wight, Ray, 1952, O 29,29:6
Wight, Sydney B Jr, 1948, Ap 9,24:3
Wight, William W, 1958, Je 18,33:2
Wightman, Alfred R, 1951, D 27,21:3
Wightman, C S, 1934, Mr 22,22:1
Wightman, E K Lt, 1865, F 12,2:5
Wightman, Frederick C, 1956, N 2,27:3
Wightman, George B, 1937, Mr 19,24:2
Wightman, George H, 1937, Ap 21,23:2
Wightman, Harold W, 1947, Je 7,13:5
Wightman, Henry N, 1941, Je 17,21:6
Wightman, Mary Utley Mrs, 1924, F 17,23:1
Wightman, Matilda Mrs, 1910, D 9,11:4
Wightman, McQueen S, 1947, D 15,25:4
Wightman, Orrin S, 1965, Jl 1,31:5
Wightman, Percy B, 1958, Mr 11,29:2
Wightman, Roberts, 1944, My 1,15:6
Wightman, Thomas, 1908, S 3,7:5
Wightman, W M, 1882, F 16,2:4
Wightman, William D, 1949, S 18,92:2
Wightman, William Dr, 1909, My 18,9:4
Wiginton, Marquis C, 1959, N 27,31:7
Wigle, Jack, 1962, Mr 21,39:4
Wigley, Herbert, 1939, Ap 9,28:6
Wigley, Margaret G Mrs, 1939, Je 23,19:6
Wiglus, Peter, 1909, My 16,9:7
Wigmore, George H, 1944, F 12,13:4
Wigmore, Herbert L Maj, 1913, S 3,9:4
Wigmore, Joseph Jr, 1959, Je 16,35:4
Wigmore, Rupert W, 1939, Ap 4,25:5
Wigmore, Thomas A, 1953, O 8,29:5
Wigmore, William F, 1950, S 21,31:3
Wignall, James, 1925, Je 11,19:4
Wigne, Ferdinand de, 1904, Ja 31,7:6
Wigny, Henri, 1947, My 8,25:3
Wigod, Jacob, 1946, Ap 3,25:4
Wigod, Nathan, 1968, D 24,20:8
Wigram, Clive Lord, 1960, S 4,69:1
Wigren, James T Mrs, 1950, N 18,15:5
Wigsten, Hjalmar G, 1958, Mr 6,27:1
Wigton, Charles B, 1961, My 9,39:1
Wigton, Juanna J Mrs, 1939, My 4,23:6
Wigton, Nutting, 1937, Ja 21,23:6
Wihuri, Antti T, 1962, D 29,4:5
Wiig, Olaf H, 1949, Jl 15,19:2
Wijeyekoon, Gerard, 1952, S 19,24:3
Wijk, Jonkheer H A M van, 1947, Mr 11,27:4
Wikander, Oscar R, 1956, Ag 13,19:4
Wikdall, Edgar C, 1945, N 22,35:4
Wikel, Henry H, 1945, Ap 11,23:6
Wikle, Douglas, 1938, N 10,27:1
Wikle, Herbert T, 1947, Je 27,22:3
Wikler, Julius S, 1963, Jl 3,25:1
Wikoff, Alan G, 1942, F 13,21:3
Wikoff, Anna T, 1938, N 8,23:1
Wikoff, Fred D, 1957, D 6,29:4
Wikoff, Fred D Mrs, 1950, N 3,27:5
Wikoff, Henry, 1884, My 3,5:1
Wiland, Jesse Dr, 1968, Jl 17,43:4
Wilber, Charles P, 1954, Ap 6,29:4
Wilber, Charles Seymour, 1925, Jl 22,19:5
Wilber, Cortland A (por), 1946, Ag 1,23:5
Wilber, D F, 1928, Ag 15,21:3
Wilber, David N, 1941, S 17,23:4
Wilber, Edward B, 1956, Ja 4,27:1
Wilber, Henry R, 1940, Je 28,19:1
Wilber, Joshua F, 1947, D 21,54:1
Wilber, Willis C, 1951, Jl 14,13:6
Wilberding, Joseph C, 1939, Jl 28,17:3
Wilberforce, Basil Orme, 1916, My 15,9:5
Wilberforce, Bishop of Winchester, 1873, Jl 21,1:7
Wilberforce, Ernest Roland (Bp of Chichester), 1907, S 10,7:4
Wilberforce, Henry E, 1938, Ag 31,15:4
Wilberforce, William W W, 1941, Mr 29,15:5
Wilbern, Edward V, 1950, My 13,17:6
Wilbour, Charlotte Beeber Mrs, 1914, D 26,7:4
Wilbraham, Hazel J, 1957, Je 8,19:4
Wilbur, Albert L, 1917, Mr 24,11:6
Wilbur, Arthur T, 1947, D 13,15:3
Wilbur, Bertha, 1956, Je 6,33:4
Wilbur, Bertha M Mrs, 1951, Mr 7,33:5
Wilbur, Bertrand K, 1945, Ja 8,17:3
Wilbur, Curtis D, 1954, S 9,31:1
Wilbur, Delbert S, 1941, Ap 20,44:2
Wilbur, Edward, 1949, O 3,17:4
Wilbur, Edward P, 1939, Jl 26,19:5
Wilbur, Francis C, 1944, D 30,11:5
Wilbur, Harold R, 1952, F 14,27:3
Wilbur, Harry P, 1951, Ag 3,21:3
Wilbur, Hollis A, 1964, Ag 20,29:3
Wilbur, Howard C, 1951, F 13,31:2
Wilbur, J B, 1929, Ap 29,23:3
Wilbur, J Minor Mrs, 1945, O 24,21:3
Wilbur, John A, 1955, Ag 22,21:5
Wilbur, John M, 1947, O 3,25:4
Wilbur, Leonard F, 1940, Mr 28,23:5
Wilbur, Louis A, 1957, Jl 19,19:5
Wilbur, Louis J, 1953, Ja 1,23:6
Wilbur, Nancy L Mrs, 1941, O 17,23:3
Wilbur, Nehmiah C, 1937, S 23,27:1
Wilbur, Oscar, 1939, My 4,23:2
Wilbur, Prof, 1871, O 3,8:2
Wilbur, Ray L, 1949, Je 27,27:1
Wilbur, Ray L Mrs, 1946, D 25,29:4
Wilbur, Rollin A (por), 1937, O 22,19:5
Wilbur, Rollin H, 1938, S 7,25:1
Wilbur, Thomas Mrs, 1924, Ag 13,15:3
Wilbur, W, 1932, Ja 16,15:5
Wilbur, William L, 1939, Je 12,17:3
Wilbushewitz, Moshe, 1952, Jl 16,25:5
Wilby, Arthur C, 1963, D 1,84:8
Wilby, Ernest, 1957, D 13,27:2
Wilby, Francis B, 1965, N 21,86:7
Wilby, Francis B Mrs, 1948, Ja 27,25:2
Wilby, Margaret C, 1968, Jl 26,33:1
Wilce, John W, 1963, My 18,27:2
Wilckens, William J, 1965, N 28,88:7
Wilckes, Ferdinand, 1941, Jl 16,17:2
Wilckes, Ferdinand Mrs, 1954, Mr 5,19:4
Wilcox, Albert A, 1916, Je 6,13:6
Wilcox, Albert C Mrs, 1955, O 28,26:2
Wilcox, Albert E, 1959, N 16,31:2
Wilcox, Albert H, 1943, Ja 7,19:4
Wilcox, Albert J, 1952, D 16,31:6
Wilcox, Alfred C, 1953, Mr 2,23:3
Wilcox, Alfred M, 1960, Mr 19,21:5
Wilcox, Algernon H, 1909, Ag 11,7:4
Wilcox, Alva M, 1952, Ag 27,27:1
Wilcox, Arthur L, 1955, My 24,31:4
Wilcox, Arthur R, 1947, Je 4,27:4
Wilcox, B M Mrs, 1904, F 23,7:6
Wilcox, Benjamin Martin, 1912, Ag 28,9:5
Wilcox, Burton B, 1948, Ag 18,25:2

Wilcox, C B, 1939, F 21,19:1
Wilcox, C G, 1925, S 14,19:5
Wilcox, C Lorrin, 1923, Ag 26,26:4
Wilcox, Calvin E, 1953, O 5,27:1
Wilcox, Carra E, 1948, Ap 29,23:3
Wilcox, Charles H, 1943, Jl 6,21:6
Wilcox, Charles L, 1937, S 24,21:3
Wilcox, Charles S, 1938, Je 7,23:1
Wilcox, Charles W, 1955, Ap 23,19:4
Wilcox, Charles W Mrs, 1953, Jl 8,27:4
Wilcox, Chester M, 1958, Mr 10,23:1
Wilcox, Clark R, 1967, Ap 25,43:2
Wilcox, Cornelia C Mrs, 1940, Mr 7,23:5
Wilcox, Daniel A, 1952, Je 14,15:6
Wilcox, De Witt G, 1951, S 27,31:4
Wilcox, Donald C, 1959, F 2,26:7
Wilcox, Edith F, 1947, S 3,25:2
Wilcox, Edwin, 1941, S 22,15:5
Wilcox, Elias B, 1942, O 29,23:1
Wilcox, Ella Wheeler, 1919, O 31,13:3
Wilcox, Elon Farnsworth Maj, 1910, Jl 14,7:4
Wilcox, Elva W, 1951, F 20,25:5
Wilcox, Ernest, 1941, Ap 21,19:4
Wilcox, Ernest H, 1958, Ag 15,22:1
Wilcox, Ernest N, 1960, O 22,23:6
Wilcox, Frances W Mrs, 1941, Je 29,32:4
Wilcox, Frank, 1944, S 29,21:2
Wilcox, Frank A Col, 1918, F 13,13:4
Wilcox, Frank S, 1942, D 29,21:3
Wilcox, Frank W, 1950, Ag 9,29:4
Wilcox, Franklin A, 1908, Ag 27,7:6
Wilcox, Fred C, 1955, F 9,27:4
Wilcox, Fred C Mrs, 1951, My 24,35:2
Wilcox, Fred M, 1944, Ja 16,43:2; 1964, S 25,41:3
Wilcox, Fred W, 1951, Ja 1,17:1
Wilcox, Frederick, 1942, Ag 5,19:2
Wilcox, Frederick B, 1965, F 17,43:3
Wilcox, George, 1907, Mr 21,9:6
Wilcox, George A Mrs, 1943, N 30,27:3
Wilcox, George D, 1941, My 8,23:2
Wilcox, George E, 1903, S 23,7:6
Wilcox, George H, 1940, N 27,23:4
Wilcox, George L, 1938, Ap 16,13:4
Wilcox, Giles Buckingham, 1922, Jl 24,15:5
Wilcox, Grafton S, 1964, F 17,31:1
Wilcox, Grafton S Mrs, 1947, My 5,23:4
Wilcox, H P, 1912, Mr 14,11:4
Wilcox, H R, 1882, D 14,5:2
Wilcox, Harley H, 1937, Ja 29,19:3
Wilcox, Harlow, 1960, S 25,86:3
Wilcox, Harold H, 1954, Ap 4,88:3
Wilcox, Harry L, 1946, D 30,22:2
Wilcox, Harry M, 1948, My 20,29:5
Wilcox, Helen B Mrs, 1941, O 7,23:2
Wilcox, Henry, 1953, Ag 27,25:4
Wilcox, Henry B, 1949, F 11,23:1
Wilcox, Henry T, 1925, Je 23,19:4
Wilcox, Herbert, 1938, N 9,23:2
Wilcox, Herbert B, 1955, F 2,27:1
Wilcox, Herbert B Mrs, 1961, N 26,88:1
Wilcox, Herbert M, 1938, Jl 29,17:2
Wilcox, Hettie, 1947, S 9,31:3
Wilcox, Homer B Sr, 1950, Ja 10,29:5
Wilcox, Homer F, 1946, D 28,15:2
Wilcox, Horace N Mrs, 1956, F 7,31:2
Wilcox, Howard, 1937, S 3,13:1
Wilcox, Howard E, 1946, Ap 18,27:5
Wilcox, Howard N, 1944, D 22,17:3
Wilcox, J Foster, 1943, Ag 5,15:4
Wilcox, J Mark, 1956, F 4,19:2
Wilcox, J Thomas, 1955, F 7,21:1
Wilcox, Jerome K, 1961, O 5,37:3
Wilcox, John C, 1947, N 21,28:2
Wilcox, Josiah North, 1925, Ag 13,19:7
Wilcox, Josiah T, 1943, My 5,27:6
Wilcox, Katherine V, 1945, O 6,13:1
Wilcox, Lansing, 1956, N 12,29:5
Wilcox, Lansing A, 1951, S 30,74:5
Wilcox, Laura E, 1949, Ja 12,27:2
Wilcox, Leroy H, 1941, D 27,19:4
Wilcox, Leroy H Mrs, 1957, Mr 1,23:1
Wilcox, Linda Mrs, 1948, D 15,33:5
Wilcox, Louis N, 1937, Ag 24,21:3
Wilcox, Louise, 1903, O 17,9:6
Wilcox, M, 1883, Ap 18,4:7
Wilcox, Melvin L, 1940, Mr 15,23:3
Wilcox, Miner W, 1943, S 14,23:4
Wilcox, Morgan A, 1944, S 17,42:3
Wilcox, Nelson J, 1949, My 22,88:7
Wilcox, Norris, 1946, O 23,27:2
Wilcox, P Ferdinand Mrs, 1961, N 2,37:4
Wilcox, Paul, 1912, N 25,13:6
Wilcox, Perley S, 1953, My 18,21:3
Wilcox, R W, 1931, Je 7,30:3
Wilcox, Ralph B Mrs, 1949, Ja 8,15:6
Wilcox, Ransom E Mrs, 1945, Ja 13,11:3
Wilcox, Ray, 1959, Ag 14,21:3
Wilcox, Raymond B, 1949, O 23,87:3
Wilcox, Raymond H, 1959, Je 19,25:5
Wilcox, Richard W, 1961, F 8,28:1
Wilcox, Robert, 1951, Jl 20,21:3; 1955, Je 12,86:4
Wilcox, Robert L, 1943, O 4,17:2
Wilcox, Robert M, 1943, Mr 20,15:2; 1951, N 12,25:4
Wilcox, Rowse B, 1956, D 25,25:6
Wilcox, Roy P, 1946, My 22,21:2
Wilcox, Sidney F Dr, 1920, Ap 21,9:4
Wilcox, Thomas F, 1958, D 28,2:5
Wilcox, U V, 1965, Mr 15,31:4
Wilcox, Urquhart, 1941, My 18,45:2
Wilcox, W J, 1874, Ja 25,8:4
Wilcox, Washington F, 1909, Mr 9,9:7
Wilcox, Wayland D, 1954, Mr 11,31:2
Wilcox, William F, 1950, Je 4,92:2
Wilcox, William F Sr, 1945, Ja 6,11:3
Wilcox, William H, 1943, D 24,13:1
Wilcox, William H Mrs, 1951, My 24,35:2
Wilcox, William S, 1951, Ja 23,27:5
Wilcox, William T, 1939, My 18,25:3
Wilcox, William W, 1941, Je 13,19:3
Wilcox, William W Jr, 1940, Ap 3,23:2
Wilcox, William W Mrs, 1946, Ag 20,27:3
Wilcox, Willis H, 1916, S 14,7:5
Wilcoxon, Frank, 1965, N 19,39:2
Wilcoxon, Lloyd T, 1948, Ap 7,25:5
Wilczek, Mary Mrs, 1940, O 15,23:3
Wilczynska, Antonina Mrs, 1925, Mr 20,19:5
Wild, A Clement, 1950, Ap 13,29:5
Wild, E, 1934, S 14,27:4
Wild, F Percy, 1950, Ap 15,15:5
Wild, Frank, 1939, Ag 21,13:3
Wild, Frank G, 1941, S 30,23:2
Wild, Frederick A, 1942, Jl 16,19:2
Wild, Frederick H, 1950, Ag 17,27:2
Wild, Horace B (por), 1940, Jl 25,17:1
Wild, Isaac J, 1938, F 5,15:5
Wild, John J, 1937, O 20,23:5
Wild, Joseph G, 1950, Ag 2,25:1
Wild, Joseph Rev Dr, 1908, Ag 21,7:5
Wild, Michael B, 1940, Jl 20,15:4
Wild, Morton, 1954, Ap 16,21:2
Wild, Payson S Sr, 1951, F 8,33:3
Wild, Rudolf, 1952, Ja 3,27:3
Wild, W H, 1903, Ap 28,9:5
Wild, William F, 1944, N 15,27:5
Wild, Willis T, 1946, Mr 30,15:3
Wilday, David H, 1912, My 4,13:6
Wilday, Edwin C, 1962, S 5,39:1
Wilday, John H, 1938, F 28,15:4
Wildberg, Joan S Mrs, 1937, Ja 1,23:3
Wildberg, John, 1959, F 9,26:2
Wildblood, Arthur F Sr, 1941, Ag 24,34:8
Wilde, Arthur, 1952, D 10,35:5
Wilde, Arthur H, 1944, Ja 5,18:2
Wilde, Arthur Mrs, 1958, Mr 20,29:4
Wilde, Charles L, 1948, Je 11,23:4
Wilde, Elton S, 1948, F 8,60:5
Wilde, Francis E J, 1940, O 10,25:6
Wilde, George H H Rear-Adm, 1911, D 4,13:5
Wilde, George H Mrs, 1951, Ag 21,27:2
Wilde, H Judson, 1952, Ja 2,25:5
Wilde, H Wickham Mrs, 1953, Ap 30,31:3
Wilde, Harold R, 1962, Jl 15,60:3
Wilde, J, 1878, Ja 4,8:2; 1879, O 5,5:4
Wilde, J Warren Mrs, 1956, Mr 28,31:4
Wilde, John P, 1953, S 3,22:5
Wilde, Louis B, 1958, Jl 24,25:4
Wilde, Marie V, 1938, Jl 6,23:2
Wilde, Maurice H, 1947, O 13,23:2
Wilde, Oscar, 1900, D 1,1:5
Wilde, Percival, 1953, S 20,86:3
Wilde, Samuel H, 1958, Ja 28,27:4
Wilde, Theodore L H, 1956, My 25,23:4
Wilde, William H 2d, 1942, D 11,23:6
Wildemore, John K, 1947, Je 19,21:4
Wildenberg, Thomas Mrs, 1939, Jl 1,17:5
Wildenbruch, Ernst von, 1909, Ja 16,11:6
Wildenstein, Felix, 1952, Je 12,33:5
Wildenstein, Georges, 1963, Je 12,43:2
Wildenstein, Laure Mrs, 1937, F 7,II,8:7
Wildenstein, N, 1934, Ap 25,21:3
Wilder, A C, 1875, D 25,4:7
Wilder, A P, 1936, Jl 3,19:3
Wilder, Alexander Dr, 1908, S 20,9:5
Wilder, Alvin D, 1942, S 20,41:3
Wilder, Amos P Mrs, 1946, Je 30,38:5
Wilder, Arthur B, 1949, F 16,25:1
Wilder, Betty H Mrs, 1942, S 23,25:2
Wilder, Burt Green Dr, 1925, F 3,13:3
Wilder, Charles A, 1957, Jl 24,25:2
Wilder, Charles E, 1950, F 10,23:3
Wilder, Charles R, 1942, Ja 30,19:3
Wilder, Clinton E, 1940, My 24,19:3
Wilder, E M, 1952, My 30,15:5
Wilder, Edward W, 1965, D 29,29:4
Wilder, Edwin F, 1940, F 21,19:5
Wilder, Enos, 1915, F 6,11:5
Wilder, Francis A, 1949, Mr 31,25:1
Wilder, Francis S, 1952, D 21,52:7
Wilder, George D, 1946, My 8,25:6
Wilder, George F, 1937, Ap 9,21:4
Wilder, Gerald C, 1944, Je 29,23:2
Wilder, Grace E, 1911, Ap 22,13:6
Wilder, Guert E Mrs, 1940, O 3,25:5
Wilder, Harry A, 1967, Mr 9,39:1
Wilder, Henry, 1949, My 26,29:2
Wilder, Henry L Mrs, 1951, O 18,29:5
Wilder, Herman, 1966, Ag 10,41:3
Wilder, Laura I Mrs, 1957, F 12,27:1
Wilder, Laurence R, 1937, N 8,23:4
Wilder, Loren, 1939, Ag 20,32:5
Wilder, Louise B Mrs, 1938, Ap 22,19:3
Wilder, Magel C, 1947, S 9,31:6
Wilder, Mark S, 1948, Ag 19,21:3
Wilder, Marshall P (funl, Ja 12,9:4), 1915, Ja 11,9:5
Wilder, Marshall P Mrs, 1913, D 22,9:5
Wilder, Milo W Jr Mrs, 1958, N 13,33:1
Wilder, Percy J, 1937, Ja 19,17:4
Wilder, Richard E, 1945, Ag 25,11:2
Wilder, Robert, 1953, My 23,11:8
Wilder, Robert H, 1948, S 12,72:1
Wilder, Robert P, 1938, Mr 29,21:2
Wilder, Royal G Mrs, 1910, My 12,11:4
Wilder, Russell M, 1959, D 18,29:1
Wilder, Stephen W, 1955, Mr 27,86:3
Wilder, Stuart, 1963, Jl 20,19:2
Wilder, Thomas Edward, 1919, Ag 23,7:7
Wilder, Throop M, 1956, N 22,33:5
Wilder, W H, 1882, Ag 9,8:4
Wilder, Wilbur E, 1952, Ja 31,27:1
Wilder, William F, 1940, O 17,25:2
Wilder, William Henry, 1913, S 12,11:6
Wilder, William Royal, 1925, Ap 20,17:4; 1925, Ap 22,23:5
Wilder, Winford O, 1950, S 18,23:2
Wildermann, Paul J, 1940, O 20,49:2
Wildermuth, Eberhard, 1952, Mr 10,21:4
Wildermuth, Henry, 1952, Mr 19,29:4
Wildermuth, Ora L Mrs, 1952, Mr 24,25:4
Wilderotter, Frederick W, 1945, N 22,36:3
Wilderotter, Phil J Sr, 1955, My 10,29:2
Wildes, Frank Adm, 1903, F 8,7:5
Wildes, Julia Mrs, 1947, Ja 10,21:4
Wildes, Lucy A Mrs, 1942, Ag 8,11:2
Wildes, Thomas Dr, 1907, N 29,9:6
Wildey, Charles F, 1914, Mr 2,9:4
Wildey, Frank, 1941, Jl 30,17:4
Wildey, Otto G, 1942, N 10,28:2
Wildey, Spence, 1945, N 1,23:4
Wildey, William H, 1938, Ag 23,17:1; 1941, O 24,23:2
Wildey, William L, 1952, S 28,77:2
Wildhaber, Eugene H, 1944, S 27,21:5
Wildhack, Henry J, 1951, N 8,29:2
Wildhack, Robert, 1940, Je 21,21:2
Wildin, George W, 1939, Mr 1,21:2
Wilding, Frederick, 1945, Jl 12,11:5
Wilding, Lewis, 1956, My 11,27:4
Wilding, Wilbur S, 1951, O 2,27:1
Wilding, William A, 1940, Mr 15,23:5
Wildman, Bertha E, 1952, S 14,86:1
Wildman, Clyde E, 1955, N 2,35:2
Wildman, Edward E, 1956, My 8,33:2
Wildman, Henry Valentine Dr, 1968, Ap 25,47:2
Wildman, Ira R, 1939, F 1,21:3
Wildman, John R, 1938, S 22,23:3
Wildman, Roy S, 1947, Je 9,21:2
Wildmann, Karl, 1956, Ap 1,88:5
Wildnauer, Frederick A, 1960, O 27,37:3
Wildner, Harry C, 1966, Ap 20,47:2
Wildrick, Charles D, 1968, Mr 6,47:3
Wildrick, Edward W (por), 1945, F 23,17:3
Wildrick, Exa J, 1950, N 25,13:3
Wildrick, George A, 1954, Ap 20,29:5
Wildrick, Meade, 1959, Jl 26,68:4
Wilds, Abbie J, 1941, F 20,19:4
Wilds, J T, 1933, O 29,30:1
Wilds, Marion W Mrs, 1948, Jl 24,15:5
Wilds, Percival (por), 1942, Je 15,19:3
Wilds, Robert H, 1949, N 2,27:4
Wilds, Z P, 1883, My 23,4:7
Wildwood, Will (Fredk Eug Pond), 1925, N 2,23:5
Wile, Alfons, 1945, Jl 31,19:2
Wile, Edwin, 1957, S 17,35:4
Wile, Ernest J, 1951, F 18,77:2
Wile, Frederic Jr Mrs, 1952, F 21,27:2
Wile, Frederic W Jr, 1961, D 18,35:5
Wile, Frederick W (por), 1941, Ap 8,25:3
Wile, Herman, 1958, D 30,35:4
Wile, Ira S, 1943, O 10,49:1
Wile, Irwin (por), 1955, N 18,25:1
Wile, Julius M, 1937, Ap 22,23:1
Wile, Oscar J, 1959, F 21,21:7
Wile, Udo J, 1965, Je 8,41:3
Wilen, Areese M Mrs, 1920, F 9,9:4
Wilen, Benjamin Mrs, 1965, Mr 2,35:2
Wilen, Jesse D Mrs, 1956, N 16,27:1
Wilen, Morris, 1957, My 16,31:5
Wilenchick, Clement, 1957, Mr 3,84:6
Wilenchik, Israel W, 1961, Ja 21,21:5
Wilensky, Abraham O (por), 1949, F 5,15:4
Wilensky, Abraham O Mrs, 1968, Jl 30,39:2
Wilensky, Mary, 1953, S 6,50:2
Wilensky, Michael, 1955, Je 23,29:4
Wilensky, Nathan D, 1954, Ag 31,21:3
Wilensky, Ossip Mrs, 1953, My 23,15:5
Wilentz, Bertha Mrs, 1944, F 18,17:3
Wiler, Lester O, 1968, N 27,47:4
Wiles, Ben, 1948, D 23,20:2
Wiles, Charles P, 1944, O 7,13:2
Wiles, Howard R, 1942, F 8,49:2

Wiles, Irving R Mrs, 1939, Jl 17,19:4
Wiles, John H, 1941, Je 24,19:4
Wiles, Kimball, 1968, F 3,23:2
Wiles, Ted Mrs, 1960, Jl 13,35:2
Wiles, Thomas, 1951, My 19,15:5
Wiley, A A, 1908, Je 18,9:4
Wiley, Adaline K Mrs, 1946, F 13,23:2
Wiley, Alex, 1955, O 31,25:3; 1967, O 27,45:1
Wiley, Alex Mrs, 1948, Ag 20,17:5
Wiley, Alexander C, 1920, D 1,15:4
Wiley, Andrew T, 1940, D 27,20:2
Wiley, Arthur G, 1953, Ap 30,31:5
Wiley, Bradford K Mrs, 1956, Ap 26,33:4
Wiley, Carl D, 1941, Ag 20,19:3
Wiley, Charles E, 1943, Mr 1,19:5
Wiley, Charles M, 1939, F 16,21:3
Wiley, Charles S, 1938, Ap 27,23:3
Wiley, Clarence H, 1947, D 4,31:4
Wiley, Don C, 1962, Mr 8,31:4
Wiley, Dora, 1924, N 3,17:4
Wiley, Dwight M, 1949, Ap 6,29:4
Wiley, E, 1946, Mr 1,22:3
Wiley, Edward C, 1958, S 24,27:1
Wiley, Edward M, 1942, D 28,20:1
Wiley, Edward R, 1947, Ja 6,23:4
Wiley, Edwin C Dr, 1924, O 21,23:4
Wiley, Ella M G Mrs, 1937, O 23,15:6
Wiley, Fletcher, 1966, Ja 27,33:3
Wiley, Forbes B, 1956, D 15,25:3
Wiley, Frances, 1945, Ja 5,15:4
Wiley, Franklin, 1904, Ap 24,7:6
Wiley, Fred W, 1948, N 13,15:5
Wiley, George, 1940, S 18,23:5; 1940, N 30,17:2; 1945, D 3,21:4
Wiley, George E, 1954, Mr 4,25:1
Wiley, George L, 1924, Ap 17,19:4
Wiley, George Mrs, 1947, F 2,57:5
Wiley, George Washington, 1920, D 1,15:4
Wiley, H W, 1930, Jl 1,29:1
Wiley, Harry D, 1940, Ag 6,20:3
Wiley, Harvey W Jr, 1951, Ap 25,29:2
Wiley, Harvey W Mrs, 1964, Ja 7,33:1
Wiley, Henry A (por), 1943, My 21,19:1
Wiley, Henry A Mrs, 1945, O 14,44:4
Wiley, Henry W, 1948, F 26,23:4
Wiley, Herbert E, 1962, Ja 1,23:6
Wiley, Herbert V, 1954, Ap 30,23:2
Wiley, I W Bp, 1884, N 23,2:2
Wiley, J Allen, 1945, Ja 22,17:3
Wiley, J F, 1877, N 19,5:3
Wiley, J William, 1960, Ja 17,86:2
Wiley, Jacob S, 1947, Ag 31,36:8
Wiley, James A, 1949, O 6,31:2
Wiley, James H, 1924, Ag 7,15:5
Wiley, James S, 1940, Mr 26,21:5
Wiley, James S Mrs, 1966, N 28,39:2
Wiley, John, 1954, Jl 2,19:2
Wiley, John A Gen, 1909, D 29,9:6
Wiley, John A Mrs, 1958, Je 8,88:5
Wiley, John C, 1967, F 4,27:1
Wiley, John H Mrs, 1952, Jl 2,25:4
Wiley, John McClure, 1912, Ag 14,9:4
Wiley, Julian Mrs, 1944, Mr 17,17:2
Wiley, L, 1935, Mr 21,1:4
Wiley, Martha L Mrs, 1940, S 28,17:5
Wiley, Martin B, 1951, D 5,35:2
Wiley, Melvin C, 1948, S 27,23:5
Wiley, Octavius G, 1952, Jl 13,61:1
Wiley, Osgood S, 1903, D 21,9:5
Wiley, Ralph W, 1948, F 8,60:3
Wiley, Richard T, 1955, Ja 13,27:5
Wiley, Robert H, 1952, Ja 31,27:3
Wiley, Roger M, 1941, Jl 5,11:7
Wiley, Samuel D, 1952, Mr 13,29:2
Wiley, Seabury Brewster, 1905, Mr 13,7:5
Wiley, Wabishaw S, 1944, N 5,54:3
Wiley, William E (por), 1944, Ag 25,13:3
Wiley, William F Mrs, 1953, My 11,27:2
Wiley, William G, 1915, Jl 3,7:7
Wiley, William J, 1949, Je 9,31:2
Wiley, William O, 1958, Ja 16,29:5
Wiley, William O Mrs, 1962, N 27,38:1
Wiley, William U, 1946, O 31,25:2
Wilf, Marcus, 1949, Je 5,94:3
Wilf, Oscar, 1954, Je 22,27:1
Wilfley, L R, 1926, My 27,25:5
Wilfong, John E Mrs, 1953, Ap 20,25:3
Wilford, George B, 1903, N 7,1:3
Wilford, James W, 1941, Ap 8,25:4
Wilfred, Thomas, 1968, Ag 16,33:2
Wilfreda, Mary Mother, 1940, Ja 28,32:1
Wilfrid, Adolf A, 1941, Ja 10,19:4
Wilfrid, Lynn J W, 1960, D 23,19:4
Wilgress, Helene M Mrs, 1943, Mr 15,14:2
Wilgus, George, 1964, D 15,44:1
Wilgus, Herbt S Col, 1937, Jl 8,23:2
Wilgus, James A, 1939, Jl 25,19:6
Wilgus, Sidney D, 1940, F 24,13:5
Wilgus, William J (por), 1949, O 25,27:1
Wilgus, William J, 1961, O 30,29:4
Wilgus, William J Lt-Col, 1937, Jl 7,23:5
Wilheim, Paul G, 1964, Ja 1,25:5
Wilheim, Paul G Mrs, 1964, Ja 1,25:5

Wilhelm, Alfred J, 1938, Mr 25,19:3
Wilhelm, Arthur, 1962, F 6,35:1
Wilhelm, Arthur F, 1950, Ap 11,31:4
Wilhelm, Aug H (est acctg), 1959, Ag 27,25:4
Wilhelm, Carl, 1873, Ag 27,1:2
Wilhelm, Donald, 1945, F 7,19:2
Wilhelm, Edward, 1914, S 24,11:6
Wilhelm, Emil, 1938, Ap 12,23:5; 1942, N 13,23:3
Wilhelm, Ernest R Mrs, 1954, Je 14,21:2
Wilhelm, Frank E, 1944, Ag 30,17:1
Wilhelm, Glenn P, 1941, Je 12,23:3
Wilhelm, Harry L, 1944, F 21,15:2
Wilhelm, Henry T Mrs, 1948, Ja 18,60:6
Wilhelm, Ira R, 1945, F 1,23:1
Wilhelm, Jack, 1945, Ap 26,23:5
Wilhelm, Kurt, 1965, My 20,43:1
Wilhelm, Laurie C Mrs, 1937, Ja 28,25:2
Wilhelm, Prince of Sweden, 1965, Je 6,85:1
Wilhelm, Richard (will, S 5,25:4), 1940, Ag 6,20:4
Wilhlem, Richard H Dr, 1968, Ag 7,43:1
Wilhelm, Richard H Mrs, 1964, S 13,86:4
Wilhelm, Robert P, 1958, S 12,25:2
Wilhelm, Roy C, 1951, D 21,27:5
Wilhelm, Seymour F, 1958, F 16,86:8
Wilhelm, Thomas, 1953, Ap 16,29:6
Wilhelm, Victor H, 1949, Jl 8,19:1
Wilhelm, William, 1951, Ap 6,25:3
Wilhelm II, former German Emperor, 1941, Je 5,1:4
Wilhelme, Ernst August (Duke of Brunswick-Luneberg), 1923, N 15,19:4
Wilhelmi, Alfred E Mrs (J A Russell), 1967, Mr 14, 47:1
Wilhelmi, Frank A, 1943, Ag 12,19:4
Wilhelmi, Paul, 1943, My 29,13:4
Wilhelmina, Dowager Princess of Netherlands, 1962, N 28,1:4
Wilhelmj, Auguste, 1908, Ja 25,9:4
Wilhelms, Carl G, 1953, Ap 2,27:4
Wilhelms, Charles, 1949, Je 14,32:3
Wilhelms, Frederick Sr, 1948, Ap 28,27:3
Wilhelmson, Halfdan, 1923, N 19,15:3
Wilher, Jerome L, 1951, S 10,21:4
Wilhlem, Rutledge P Mrs, 1959, Ap 25,21:4
Wilhoft, Charles A, 1937, S 2,21:5
Wilhoit, Walter W, 1940, Ap 8,19:5
Wilie, Porter, 1962, D 27,7:3
Wilierstorf-Urbair, Bernard Von, 1883, Ag 18,4:7
Wilins, John J Jr, 1954, Ag 17,21:1
Wilk, Benjamin, 1949, F 10,27:2
Wilk, Jacob, 1956, N 13,37:1
Wilk, Phil Mrs, 1943, Jl 30,15:2
Wilk, William F, 1939, O 23,16:5
Wilkaira, Maria Mrs, 1946, S 29,62:2
Wilke, Daniel R, 1914, N 18,11:6
Wilke, Edward A, 1948, My 7,23:1
Wilke, H Wickham Mrs, 1953, Ap 28,27:3
Wilke, Hubert, 1940, O 23,23:5
Wilke, Hubert Mrs, 1939, Ja 10,19:6
Wilke, Louis G, 1962, Mr 1,31:5
Wilke, Russell B, 1942, Ag 11,19:5
Wilke, Wesley T, 1946, Je 11,23:2
Wilke, William F, 1949, O 2,80:7
Wilken, August G, 1952, S 14,86:1
Wilken, Martin S, 1942, Ja 17,17:5
Wilken, Ray T (por), 1939, D 15,25:3
Wilken, William E, 1947, Ag 8,17:2
Wilkening, Carl F, 1948, Jl 30,17:2
Wilkening, F W, 1954, Ap 24,17:5
Wilkening, Henry F, 1948, Je 19,15:6
Wilkening, William E, 1964, My 19,37:2
Wilkens, Albert, 1943, Mr 23,19:2
Wilkens, Bernard, 1966, Jl 29,31:2
Wilkens, Frederick H, 1939, Ag 2,19:5
Wilkens, Henry, 1944, N 21,25:2
Wilkens, Henry G, 1948, F 4,23:3
Wilkens, Henry R A, 1944, Ja 26,19:4
Wilkens, William, 1879, Jl 18,3:5
Wilkenshaw, Mary, 1948, Jl 13,27:1
Wilker, Arthur V, 1960, F 9,31:2
Wilkerson, James H (cor, O 8,25:3), 1948, O 1,26:2
Wilkerson, Marcus M, 1953, Mr 15,93:1
Wilkerson, Oscar A Sr, 1956, Jl 9,23:3
Wilkerson, T Leland, 1958, Mr 12,31:3
Wilkerson, Thomas J, 1949, S 4,41:2
Wilkerson, William R (Billy), 1962, S 3,15:6
Wilkes, Abraham P, 1943, Ja 28,19:1
Wilkes, Albert, 1951, My 6,92:2
Wilkes, Bertram A, 1964, N 10,47:4
Wilkes, Charles, 1877, F 9,4:6
Wilkes, E Willington Col, 1909, F 28,11:4
Wilkes, Ernest H (por), 1941, Ag 1,15:1
Wilkes, F G Dr, 1882, S 6,8:2
Wilkes, Francis G, 1951, Mr 22,31:4
Wilkes, Frank M, 1958, My 30,22:2
Wilkes, Fred M, 1938, F 10,22:4
Wilkes, James R, 1939, Ap 20,23:5
Wilkes, James S, 1954, Mr 20,15:4
Wilkes, John, 1957, Jl 24,25:2
Wilkes, Kneeland B, 1949, Ap 7,29:2
Wilkes, Leroy A (por), 1942, D 1,25:3
Wilkes, Marion R, 1951, D 31,13:6
Wilkes, Michael H, 1940, F 16,19:4
Wilkes, Nathaniel R, 1960, D 7,44:5

Wilkes, Paul Tupper, 1911, N 1,11:5
Wilkes, Robert R, 1942, Ag 28,19:2
Wilkes, Robert R Mrs, 1940, Ag 30,19:5
Wilkes, W Ben, 1949, Ag 2,19:5
Wilkes, Willamene, 1925, My 28,21:5
Wilkes, William C, 1957, Ap 3,31:3
Wilkes, William D, 1949, N 13,92:5
Wilkes, William G, 1950, D 2,13:3
Wilkey, Frederick, 1943, N 13,13:3
Wilkey, Gene, 1968, Jl 16,39:2
Wilkie, Al, 1955, O 28,25:3
Wilkie, Boyd Mrs, 1948, Jl 22,23:1
Wilkie, David, 1938, Ag 30,17:4
Wilkie, David (will, Mr 9,34:3), 1944, Ja 17,19:3
Wilkie, David J, 1963, N 19,42:1
Wilkie, Francis X, 1960, Mr 9,33:4
Wilkie, Harold M, 1950, My 5,22:2
Wilkie, J J, 1878, F 3,6:7
Wilkie, James W, 1948, Ap 13,27:5
Wilkie, Magdalen S Mrs, 1950, Ja 30,17:2
Wilkie, Robert R, 1955, S 28,35:1
Wilkie, William, 1942, Mr 13,19:4
Wilkie, William J, 1949, My 5,27:2
Wilkin, Frank J, 1952, My 2,25:2
Wilkin, J Foster Justice, 1914, D 5,13:6
Wilkin, John C Jr, 1958, Jl 29,23:5
Wilkin, Joseph D, 1951, My 20,89:1
Wilkin, Melvin R Mrs, 1941, Ag 28,19:4
Wilkin, Phil, 1955, Jl 5,29:2
Wilkin, R J, 1927, D 4,31:5
Wilkin, Warren D, 1958, Je 22,76:4
Wilkins, Albert W, 1942, O 18,52:3
Wilkins, Aloyn, 1903, Je 18,9:6
Wilkins, Beriah, 1905, Je 8,9:7
Wilkins, Charles, 1951, N 19,23:3
Wilkins, Charles H, 1948, My 19,27:2
Wilkins, Donald J, 1968, Ap 5,47:1
Wilkins, E Col, 1878, D 29,7:4
Wilkins, E Percival, 1949, Mr 12,17:5
Wilkins, Elbert J, 1948, Ap 11,72:5
Wilkins, Ernest H, 1966, Ja 4,27:4
Wilkins, Ernest J Mrs, 1964, N 15,86:7
Wilkins, Ezra M (funl), 1919, Ag 27,11:4
Wilkins, Ezra Mandeville, 1919, Ag 25,11:4
Wilkins, F K, 1905, Ap 6,8:7
Wilkins, Fred A, 1947, O 16,27:2
Wilkins, Frederick, 1945, Ag 6,15:1
Wilkins, Frederick Rapelje, 1968, Ap 18,47:3
Wilkins, Georgia M, 1959, Je 22,25:3
Wilkins, Gordon A, 1966, Ja 11,29:2
Wilkins, H Percy, 1960, Ja 24,88:1
Wilkins, Harold A, 1940, My 13,17:3
Wilkins, Harold J Mrs, 1955, N 24,29:4
Wilkins, Harold S, 1946, Je 17,21:4
Wilkins, Harry E, 1941, Ag 17,39:3
Wilkins, Henry J, 1939, Ap 5,25:3
Wilkins, Henry J Sr, 1950, Je 22,27:3
Wilkins, Henry W, 1921, Ja 28,11:2
Wilkins, Horace M, 1953, S 15,31:1
Wilkins, Hubert (funl plans, D 3,37:3; funl, D 5,32:2), 1958, D 2,1:3
Wilkins, J Ernest, 1959, Ja 20,35:1
Wilkins, James P, 1946, Ag 13,27:3
Wilkins, John F, 1941, D 16,28:2
Wilkins, John F Mrs, 1957, F 27,27:1
Wilkins, John H Jr, 1967, Ap 2,93:2
Wilkins, John J, 1940, My 18,15:2
Wilkins, Lawrence A, 1945, D 25,23:5
Wilkins, Lawson, 1963, S 29,86:7
Wilkins, Lyle L, 1953, F 20,19:1
Wilkins, Mervyn, 1956, My 23,28:3
Wilkins, Peter N, 1955, My 19,29:5
Wilkins, Ross Judge, 1872, My 18,1:4
Wilkins, S Rev, 1878, F 12,5:3
Wilkins, T Russell (por), 1940, D 11,27:1
Wilkins, W Nelson, 1958, O 30,31:4
Wilkins, Wellington Jr, 1951, D 11,33:2
Wilkins, William, 1865, Je 24,1:3
Wilkins, William C Rev, 1937, D 21,23:2
Wilkins, William E, 1942, My 18,15:5
Wilkins, William J, 1950, D 31,42:6; 1964, Je 30,33:3
Wilkins, William T Sr, 1952, N 20,31:2
Wilkinson, Ada M L Mrs, 1941, Mr 7,21:5
Wilkinson, Alan J, 1952, My 5,23:4
Wilkinson, Albert E, 1947, My 24,15:6
Wilkinson, Albert J Capt, 1915, F 5,11:5
Wilkinson, Albert T, 1948, Mr 23,25:3
Wilkinson, Alex K, 1953, Ja 30,21:1
Wilkinson, Alfred Mrs, 1909, Ag 6,7:6
Wilkinson, Allen L, 1951, Ag 9,21:2
Wilkinson, Arthur M, 1949, Mr 6,72:4
Wilkinson, Arthur Mrs (P Dudley), 1950, D 7,33:4
Wilkinson, Arthur W, 1945, Jl 30,19:4
Wilkinson, Asa Dr, 1908, Ja 27,7:6
Wilkinson, Boyd E, 1939, Ap 12,23:5
Wilkinson, Cecil J, 1961, My 21,87:2
Wilkinson, Charles H, 1962, My 7,31:4
Wilkinson, Charles N, 1938, Mr 2,19:3
Wilkinson, Charles P, 1960, Mr 31,33:5
Wilkinson, Clifford H, 1941, Mr 10,17:6
Wilkinson, Clyde H, 1963, N 28,39:1
Wilkinson, Edward S, 1939, Je 13,23:5
Wilkinson, Ellen, 1947, F 7,23:1

Wilkinson, Ellen S, 1951, O 22,23:5
Wilkinson, Emma L Mrs, 1942, D 4,25:6
Wilkinson, Eric, 1964, F 19,39:2
Wilkinson, F W Mrs, 1942, Mr 14,15:6
Wilkinson, Florence M Mrs, 1954, S 8,32:7
Wilkinson, Ford L, 1958, S 2,25:3
Wilkinson, Frank E Mrs, 1949, O 31,25:5
Wilkinson, Fred H, 1958, Ag 6,25:1
Wilkinson, Fritz, 1966, S 26,41:2
Wilkinson, George E, 1950, D 10,104:6
Wilkinson, George L, 1958, O 27,27:2
Wilkinson, Harry, 1949, Mr 19,15:5
Wilkinson, Henry Mrs, 1966, D 10,38:5
Wilkinson, Herbert W, 1948, O 10,76:3
Wilkinson, Horace C, 1957, Mr 31,88:5
Wilkinson, Horace R, 1957, Ap 14,86:7
Wilkinson, Horace S (will, Jl 3,28:4),(por), 1937, Ap 12,17:1
Wilkinson, Horatio L, 1962, Ap 25,39:4
Wilkinson, Howard S (por), 1948, Ag 2,21:2
Wilkinson, Hugh P, 1943, Mr 8,15:4
Wilkinson, Ignatius M, 1953, Je 23,29:1
Wilkinson, Ignatius M (est tax appr), 1954, D 17, 20:7
Wilkinson, Ignatius M Mrs, 1944, F 17,19:3
Wilkinson, Iris, 1939, Ag 24,19:1
Wilkinson, J B, 1915, O 24,17:6
Wilkinson, J G Sir, 1875, N 3,4:5
Wilkinson, J L, 1964, Ag 22,21:5
Wilkinson, Jack H, 1952, Je 3,29:3
Wilkinson, James, 1949, Mr 22,25:5
Wilkinson, James E (por), 1943, Ag 12,19:4
Wilkinson, John, 1951, Je 27,29:6
Wilkinson, John G, 1937, Mr 2,21:4
Wilkinson, John H, 1941, Ag 8,15:2; 1942, Ja 11,45:1
Wilkinson, Joseph P Sr, 1947, F 16,57:4
Wilkinson, Joseph R, 1948, Jl 13,27:3
Wilkinson, Julia, 1943, Ag 11,19:2
Wilkinson, Kenneth A, 1943, Mr 21,26:6
Wilkinson, Kenneth L Mrs, 1941, Ja 12,44:1
Wilkinson, Lillie E Mrs, 1920, Ap 11,22:3
Wilkinson, Lyman M, 1955, Ja 19,27:2
Wilkinson, Nevile (por), 1940, D 25,27:3
Wilkinson, Ogden, 1938, My 25,23:4
Wilkinson, R B, 1912, Jl 14,II,11:6
Wilkinson, R F Col, 1903, Jl 1,9:5
Wilkinson, Ralph R, 1966, Ag 27,29:5
Wilkinson, Richard R, 1958, Mr 31,27:3
Wilkinson, Robert, 1941, S 24,23:2
Wilkinson, Robert Mrs, 1949, Ap 7,29:6
Wilkinson, Samuel, 1941, N 26,23:3
Wilkinson, Samuel I, 1939, F 2,19:1
Wilkinson, Samuel O, 1942, O 25,46:2
Wilkinson, Smith Mrs, 1924, D 4,21:4
Wilkinson, Spenser, 1937, F 1,19:5
Wilkinson, Stanley L, 1939, F 14,19:2
Wilkinson, Theodore S, 1955, S 19,25:2
Wilkinson, Thomas, 1955, Ag 3,23:5
Wilkinson, V Parker, 1954, D 22,23:2
Wilkinson, W A, 1942, D 5,15:5
Wilkinson, Wilbur N, 1951, D 13,33:5
Wilkinson, William, 1952, S 12,21:4
Wilkinson, William Cleaver Dr, 1920, Ap 27,9:3
Wilkinson, William E, 1914, N 1,17:4
Wilkinson, William H, 1907, Mr 6,9:6; 1948, Jl 8,23:1
Wilkinson, William Rev (por), 1925, D 8,25:3
Wilkinson, William Rev, 1925, D 11,23:3
Wilkinson, William Rev Dr, 1921, O 16,22:4
Wilkinson, William S, 1944, N 23,31:3
Wilkisson, Frank W, 1941, N 13,27:5
Wilklow, Ward, 1958, S 30,31:3
Wilko, Anthony, 1960, O 28,31:2
Wilkoff, Samuel, 1937, D 22,25:5
Wilkonska, Antonina P Mrs, 1941, O 7,23:3
Wilks, Maria B Mrs, 1904, N 26,9:7
Wilks, Matthew A Mrs, 1951, F 6,27:1
Wilks, Maurice C, 1963, S 19,39:1
Wilks, Samuel S, 1964, Mr 9,29:1
Wilks, Washington, 1864, Ag 8,2:5
Will, A S, 1934, Mr 11,30:1
Will, Albert, 1942, My 15,20:2
Will, Andrew, 1940, O 21,17:5
Will, Anthony, 1922, S 18,13:5
Will, Augusta, 1952, N 7,23:4
Will, Carl F, 1960, Ag 16,29:4
Will, Carl R L, 1952, Je 6,23:2
Will, Casper M, 1942, Ag 5,19:1
Will, David C, 1944, Ap 1,13:1
Will, Edward J, 1950, Je 6,29:2
Will, Frank P, 1960, Ag 11,27:5
Will, George W, 1959, Mr 16,31:6
Will, Harold H, 1963, Ap 7,86:2
Will, John A, 1947, Je 27,21:5
Will, John D, 1951, Jl 17,27:1
Will, John M Mrs, 1968, Ap 2,47:2
Will, Otto G, 1947, F 24,19:1
Will, Shirley, 1954, Ja 8,19:3
Will, T Marion, 1967, Ja 18,43:1
Will, Theodore S, 1944, O 12,27:2
Will, Walter, 1945, Mr 22,23:6
Will, William, 1958, F 5,27:1; 1961, Ja 10,47:2
Willaims, Edward T, 1944, Ja 29,13:3
Willaims, Fred D, 1947, Ap 1,28:2
Willaims, Robert J, 1964, N 4,39:4
Willaims, Valentine (por), 1946, N 21,31:1
Willan, Healey, 1968, F 17,26:1
Willans, Frederic J, 1949, Ja 28,21:4
Willard, Alfred E, 1945, O 17,19:3
Willard, Alfred E Mrs, 1949, Mr 20,76:8
Willard, Alfred S, 1949, F 3,23:3
Willard, Arthur C, 1960, S 13,37:1
Willard, Ben, 1940, Jl 31,17:2
Willard, Ben C, 1963, Jl 10,35:4
Willard, Bessie H, 1953, Ja 6,29:3
Willard, Bryan, 1913, Ja 1,17:4
Willard, C A Judge, 1914, Mr 15,7:4
Willard, Catherine (Mrs C W Bellamy), 1954, N 5, 21:4
Willard, Charles Mrs, 1945, Ja 14,40:3
Willard, Charles T Mrs, 1951, Je 12,29:4
Willard, Clarence G, 1947, Mr 14,23:2
Willard, Clarke L, 1952, O 14,31:3
Willard, Cyrus F, 1942, Ja 19,17:4
Willard, Daniel (por), 1942, Jl 7,19:1
Willard, Daniel Jr (por), 1940, My 18,15:6
Willard, Daniel Mrs, 1956, Ja 23,25:3
Willard, De Forest P, 1957, O 5,17:5
Willard, Donald, 1949, S 28,27:3
Willard, E S, 1915, N 10,13:2
Willard, Edward Kirk, 1921, Ag 31,13:4
Willard, Emma Mrs, 1870, Ap 19,8:3
Willard, Ernest R, 1937, My 7,30:2
Willard, Eugene S, 1946, D 28,15:3
Willard, Everett C, 1912, Ag 21,9:6
Willard, F E, 1898, F 18,1:2
Willard, Faith, 1921, O 12,15:6
Willard, Frank, 1958, Ja 13,29:3
Willard, Frank E, 1949, Ag 16,23:1
Willard, Frank G Mrs, 1945, S 8,15:3
Willard, Frank J, 1942, Je 28,32:3
Willard, Frederic W (por), 1947, Ag 12,23:1
Willard, Frederick R, 1948, Ja 13,26:2
Willard, Frederick W, 1952, Ap 11,23:4
Willard, Gale, 1968, Je 15,35:3
Willard, Gerald W, 1955, N 19,19:1
Willard, Harley R, 1946, Mr 28,25:4
Willard, Harry S, 1938, D 12,19:5
Willard, Harvey L Mrs, 1955, Je 3,23:6
Willard, Henry Augustus, 1909, D 6,9:4
Willard, Horace Mann Dr, 1907, Ag 25,7:5
Willard, Howard W, 1960, O 25,35:5
Willard, Hudson E, 1948, Ap 24,15:4
Willard, J Harold, 1937, N 20,17:5
Willard, J M, 1940, Ap 20,17:1
Willard, James A, 1941, Mr 28,23:4
Willard, James Le Baron, 1915, D 24,9:4
Willard, Jess, 1968, D 16,47:2
Willard, John, 1942, S 1,20:2
Willard, John D Mrs, 1952, Ja 6,92:4
Willard, John M, 1952, D 20,17:3
Willard, Joseph E Mrs, 1954, Ja 29,19:4
Willard, Joseph Edward (funl, Ap 7,17:6), 1924, Ap 5,15:5
Willard, Joseph H Mrs, 1925, N 29,13:1
Willard, Joseph S, 1949, My 5,27:3
Willard, Josiah Flynt, 1907, Ja 22,9:5
Willard, L Leigh, 1951, D 6,33:1
Willard, Lavia M, 1950, Mr 9,30:3
Willard, LeBaron S, 1964, Jl 17,27:4
Willard, Marcel, 1956, F 18,19:5
Willard, Mary Mrs, 1926, Mr 30,25:3
Willard, Percy W, 1953, O 6,29:4
Willard, Ray F, 1952, S 20,15:6
Willard, S Adams Mrs, 1913, Ja 16,17:5
Willard, Samuel L, 1958, F 11,31:3
Willard, Samuel Rev, 1859, O 15,8:1
Willard, Sumner P, 1948, Ja 7,25:4
Willard, Theodore A (por), 1943, F 4,23:5
Willard, Walter, 1950, Ap 27,29:4
Willard, Walter Mrs, 1945, N 23,23:3
Willard, Willis R, 1940, O 15,23:1
Willard, X A Prof, 1882, O 27,5:4
Willat, C A, 1937, Ag 8,II,7:3
Willats, Marietta Mrs, 1950, N 18,15:3
Willauer, Whiting W, 1962, Ag 7,29:2
Willbur, Fred S, 1952, N 20,31:4
Willcock, Clarence H, 1952, D 13,5:5
Willcocks, James Gen Sir, 1926, D 20,21:3
Willcocks, W Sir, 1932, Jl 29,15:5
Willcomb, George E, 1941, Je 2,17:2
Willcomb, J W, 1883, O 5,5:2
Willcox, Albert S Mrs, 1945, My 26,15:6
Willcox, Byron C, 1964, Ja 18,23:4
Willcox, Clairborne, 1945, D 31,17:2
Willcox, Cornelis de W, 1938, Ja 20,24:4
Willcox, Donald D, 1957, D 11,32:1
Willcox, Dudley, 1940, Je 15,15:6
Willcox, Ellery I, 1948, My 16,68:5
Willcox, Faith E, 1967, F 20,37:4
Willcox, Frank G, 1955, S 23,26:3
Willcox, George E Mrs, 1956, My 9,33:2
Willcox, George W, 1938, Ja 28,21:3
Willcox, H C, 1927, F 27,30:6
Willcox, H Case, 1953, S 19,15:5
Willcox, Harriett M Mrs, 1938, D 8,28:1
Willcox, Harry P, 1955, Ja 18,27:3
Willcox, Harry P Mrs, 1949, Jl 14,27:2
Willcox, J Taney, 1960, N 18,31:1
Willcox, John Mrs, 1952, Mr 21,23:4
Willcox, Julius A Mrs, 1948, N 30,27:2
Willcox, Kate T Mrs, 1948, N 19,28:3
Willcox, Mary A, 1953, Je 7,84:5
Willcox, O Blake, 1959, Je 20,35:2
Willcox, Orlando B, 1952, F 24,84:5
Willcox, Orlando Bolivar Brig-Gen, 1907, My 11,7:4
Willcox, Roland C, 1954, Ja 7,31:2
Willcox, Sidney G, 1950, My 29,17:4
Willcox, Thomas C, 1947, N 7,23:3
Willcox, Thomas C Mrs, 1940, Ja 7,48:1
Willcox, Walter F, 1964, O 31,29:3
Willcox, William G, 1923, S 20,4:7
Willcox, William G 2d, 1946, Ag 6,25:3
Willcox, William H, 1941, Jl 10,19:2
Willcox, William R (por), 1940, Ap 11,25:5
Willcox, William R Mrs, 1939, Mr 14,21:5
Wille, Carl I, 1949, D 14,31:1
Wille, Charles J, 1949, D 11,92:7
Wille, Ernest, 1954, Ja 25,19:3
Wille, Frank J, 1966, Mr 9,41:3
Wille, Frank J Mrs, 1946, Jl 21,40:3
Wille, Frederick B, 1953, My 8,25:2
Wille, Herman H, 1964, My 6,47:4
Willebrandt, Mabel W Mrs, 1963, Ap 9,31:3
Willedsen, John R, 1939, F 2,19:3
Willeke, Willem, 1950, N 27,26:2
Willemetz, Albert, 1964, O 8,43:1
Willemse, Cornelius W (por), 1942, Jl 12,35:1
Willen, Alan J, 1966, N 13,88:7
Willen, Joseph Mrs (Pearl),(funl plans, Mr 21,47:3), 1968, Mr 18,45:1
Willenberg, Charles C, 1872, Mr 26,1:4
Willenberg, Herbert C Rev, 1968, Ag 12,35:3
Willenborg, Walter J, 1962, My 10,37:2
Willenbrock, August W, 1947, N 22,15:2
Willenbrok, John, 1952, Ap 18,25:3
Willens, David, 1953, Mr 6,23:2
Willens, George, 1947, N 23,74:6
Willer, Bert M, 1955, Ja 31,19:4
Willerman, Ben, 1965, Je 22,35:2
Willers, Charles, 1951, Je 6,31:2
Willers, Diedrich, 1908, Je 26,7:4
Willert, Florence McKay Lady, 1955, Ap 5,29:4
Willerton, Taylor P, 1947, D 6,15:2
Willes, Sylvia (Midget Melba), 1917, Ap 26,13:6
Willet, Anne L, 1943, Ja 19,19:5
Willet, Carrie N Mrs, 1950, Je 19,21:5
Willet, Fernando C, 1875, Jl 8,1:2
Willet, Hugh M, 1944, N 17,20:3
Willet, John H, 1940, S 14,17:2
Willet, Wallace R, 1955, Je 7,8:6
Willets, A A Mrs, 1912, Ag 17,9:6
Willets, A A Rev, 1913, Mr 22,13:5
Willets, Amy, 1937, Ag 18,19:4
Willets, David Gifford Dr, 1922, Mr 27,15:5
Willets, Edward B, 1950, O 10,31:2
Willets, Eliza L, 1956, Ja 20,23:1
Willets, Elmore A, 1949, D 13,38:4
Willets, Emma, 1941, Ja 4,30:2
Willets, Frank, 1947, O 22,29:2
Willets, Frank P, 1923, Jl 31,17:5
Willets, Frederick, 1941, Ja 7,23:3
Willets, Howard, 1938, Ap 11,15:4
Willets, Isaac U Mrs, 1908, O 19,9:7
Willets, J Frederick, 1955, Ja 25,25:3
Willets, John Titus, 1912, N 14,11:4
Willets, Maria, 1937, Ap 28,23:3
Willets, Morris L, 1956, Ag 24,19:4
Willets, Morris L Mrs, 1941, Ag 22,15:2
Willets, Robert T, 1957, Mr 26,33:1
Willets, Samuel, 1883, F 7,5:5
Willets, Sarah P T Mrs, 1937, Ap 12,17:4
Willets, William D, 1948, O 8,5:3
Willets, William D Mrs, 1948, O 8,5:3
Willets, William E, 1940, O 30,23:4
Willett, Charles, 1939, N 14,23:5
Willett, Edward C, 1940, Mr 12,23:4
Willett, Frederic, 1939, Je 6,23:4
Willett, Herbert L (por), 1944, Mr 29,21:3
Willett, J, 1881, S 18,7:5
Willett, Jacques I, 1958, My 21,33:4
Willett, James W, 1940, My 14,23:3
Willett, John Allen, 1904, Jl 31,5:6
Willett, M Rev, 1881, F 26,5:5
Willett, Mary J, 1967, Jl 26,36:2
Willett, Norman C (por), 1941, Jl 8,19:5
Willett, Oscar L, 1945, Ap 26,23:2
Willett, William, 1915, Mr 5,9:2; 1938, F 13,II,6:6
Willett, William M Sr, 1946, Ja 30,25:5
Willett, William W, 1938, My 18,21:4
Willetts, Annie C Mrs, 1940, Ag 28,19:6
Willetts, Henry N, 1964, O 28,45:2
Willetts, Herbert, 1968, Jl 6,21:1
Willetts, Joseph F, 1938, S 17,17:3
Willetts, Robert R, 1903, Ag 23,7:5
Willetts, Willard P, 1939, Ja 25,21:1
Willetts, William P, 1964, N 7,27:3
Willever, Charles W Sr, 1950, Mr 21,32:4
Willever, John C, 1951, Je 26,29:1
Willever, Milton A, 1956, D 24,13:2

Willey, Albert G, 1943, D 13,23:4
Willey, Arthur, 1942, D 28,19:5
Willey, Charles, 1959, Ap 1,37:1
Willey, Dean F, 1948, Ja 24,16:3
Willey, Earle D, 1950, Mr 19,92:8
Willey, Edward G, 1937, My 11,25:1
Willey, George E, 1939, O 14,19:5
Willey, Guy L, 1950, Mr 1,27:5
Willey, J Ronald R Sr, 1963, S 27,29:2
Willey, Jacob, 1939, Jl 27,19:2
Willey, James R, 1949, Jl 3,27:2
Willey, John E, 1968, Ap 23,47:3
Willey, John H (por), 1942, N 9,23:1
Willey, John S, 1958, N 30,86:8
Willey, O G, 1952, Jl 13,3:3
Willey, Ralph T, 1949, Ag 12,17:3
Willey, Raymond Mrs, 1943, D 21,27:3
Willey, Richard R, 1941, O 5,49:1
Willey, Roland E, 1952, D 14,90:4
Willey, Sallie R Mrs, 1950, Jl 16,68:4
Willey, Samuel H, 1945, Ja 21,39:2
Willey, Samuel H Mrs, 1938, Ag 17,19:4
Willey, Stewart, 1958, O 29,35:6
Willey, Walter J, 1947, O 1,29:3
Willging, Joseph C, 1959, Mr 5,31:2
Willgohs, Herbert, 1957, Mr 31,31:5
Willgoos, Andrew V D (por), 1949, Mr 2,25:5
Willgus, Ralph O Mrs, 1950, Je 6,29:6
Willguss, Frank O, 1952, O 28,31:4
William, Bro (J T Strichter), 1963, N 21,39:4
William, Emperor of Germany, 1888, Mr 10,1:1
William, George A, 1946, Jl 6,21:2
William, George G, 1943, Je 7,13:2
William, Hugh (Earl Fortescue), 1958, Je 16,23:5
William, John Bishop, 1899, F 8,7:4
William, Norman F, 1947, Mr 16,60:1
William, Rev Bro, 1921, Jl 8,9:4
William, Seymour Mrs, 1941, O 21,23:3
William, Silas, 1944, D 9,15:5
William, Warren (por), 1948, S 25,17:1
William I I I, King of Holland, 1890, N 24,1:1
William II, Ex-King of Wurttemberg (funl, O 8,13:5), 1921, O 3,13:4
William Nicholas, Prince of Orange, 1879, Je 12,2:2
Williams, A B, 1873, Ap 7,9:3
Williams, A G, 1880, F 7,3:2
Williams, A J, 1933, D 12,23:1
Williams, A S, 1878, D 22,2:2
Williams, A W Mrs, 1946, Jl 24,27:3
Williams, A Winthrop, 1949, Jl 2,15:6
Williams, Aaron F, 1946, Ja 16,23:4
Williams, Aaron J, 1953, N 3,31:2
Williams, Abram L Mrs, 1944, N 28,23:3
Williams, Abram Pease Ex-Sen, 1911, O 19,13:5
Williams, Ada J Mrs, 1957, Jl 15,19:2
Williams, Addie (Mrs Geo Greenberg), 1968, Jl 26, 33:4
Williams, Adelaide G Mrs, 1942, My 13,19:4
Williams, Adelbert F, 1943, Mr 13,13:1
Williams, Adele F Mrs, 1937, Ag 19,20:1
Williams, Adriana D Mrs, 1939, O 24,23:6
Williams, Alan, 1942, My 13,19:5; 1945, N 6,20:3
Williams, Albern W, 1950, Ja 13,23:2
Williams, Albert, 1941, N 6,23:3
Williams, Albert J, 1945, S 18,23:4; 1945, O 19,23:1
Williams, Albert J (Pat), 1957, Ja 2,27:4
Williams, Albert L Mrs, 1964, N 27,35:2
Williams, Albert N, 1961, O 4,45:1
Williams, Albert R, 1962, F 28,33:2
Williams, Alex, 1956, Ag 1,23:1
Williams, Alex H, 1952, D 12,29:4
Williams, Alex J, 1942, My 18,15:5
Williams, Alex T, 1956, Je 1,23:1
Williams, Alexander Mrs, 1917, Mr 27,11:5
Williams, Alexander P, 1967, N 28,51:7
Williams, Alexander S, 1917, Mr 26,11:3
Williams, Alford, 1958, Je 16,23:5
Williams, Alfred, 1881, Mr 31,8:3
Williams, Alfred A, 1943, F 24,21:4
Williams, Alfred D, 1949, Ag 8,15:4
Williams, Alfred G, 1937, F 24,23:5
Williams, Alfred H, 1960, F 17,35:3
Williams, Alfred N, 1904, Ja 2,9:4; 1945, My 5,15:3
Williams, Alice P, 1963, S 11,43:5
Williams, Alice V Mrs, 1947, Ag 16,13:5
Williams, Allen M, 1924, O 2,23:3
Williams, Allen S, 1922, F 6,13:3
Williams, Alonzo R, 1907, S 3,9:5; 1948, Mr 15,23:3
Williams, Alpheus F, 1953, Ja 7,31:4
Williams, Alvin J, 1946, O 8,23:5; 1949, Ag 28,72:1
Williams, Alvin P Sr, 1954, F 13,13:5
Williams, Americus A, 1940, Ag 11,30:7
Williams, Andrew, 1907, O 7,9:6; 1963, My 3,31:2
Williams, Andrew M, 1948, Ja 10,15:1
Williams, Aneurin R, 1950, Ag 19,13:4
Williams, Anna Mrs, 1951, F 28,27:2
Williams, Anna W, 1937, D 2,25:4; 1954, N 21,86:6
Williams, Anne K, 1944, My 9,19:5
Williams, Anne S, 1948, F 17,25:4
Williams, Annie B Mrs, 1957, Ja 10,12:4
Williams, Annie W C Mrs, 1939, O 5,23:2
Williams, Aras J, 1939, Ag 18,19:2
Williams, Archibald D, 1959, O 19,29:1
Williams, Arthur, 1915, S 16,11:4; 1937, Ap 15,23:1; 1937, Jl 29,19:6
Williams, Arthur B, 1951, Ag 20,19:6
Williams, Arthur C, 1948, N 19,27:4
Williams, Arthur D, 1947, Jl 8,23:4; 1958, F 23,92:7
Williams, Arthur G, 1937, My 10,19:2; 1937, N 28,II, 9:1
Williams, Arthur H Mrs, 1956, Ap 19,31:4
Williams, Arthur J, 1956, N 23,27:1
Williams, Arthur K, 1953, F 2,21:3
Williams, Arthur K Mrs, 1951, D 11,33:5
Williams, Arthur L, 1955, O 22,19:4
Williams, Arthur L Bp, 1919, Ja 30,13:3
Williams, Arthur M, 1953, N 19,31:5; 1957, Je 29,17:7
Williams, Arthur P, 1943, O 15,19:5
Williams, Arthur S, 1952, Ag 20,25:6; 1962, Ap 5,33:3
Williams, Arthur W, 1957, Mr 9,19:2
Williams, Ashton H, 1962, F 27,34:1
Williams, Aubrey, 1965, Mr 5,33:2
Williams, Austin B, 1864, F 22,1:5
Williams, B B Mrs, 1952, D 2,36:5
Williams, B Y Mrs, 1951, F 17,15:2
Williams, Barney, 1876, Ap 26,5:1
Williams, Barney Mrs (Maria Pray), 1911, My 7,II, 11:4
Williams, Ben, 1946, F 12,25:5
Williams, Ben A, 1953, F 5,23:1
Williams, Ben J, 1956, My 21,25:3
Williams, Benjamin, 1957, F 13,35:4
Williams, Benjamin F, 1937, Mr 31,23:5; 1954, Je 14, 21:3
Williams, Benjamin L, 1945, N 27,23:2
Williams, Benjamin Mrs, 1952, N 17,25:5
Williams, Bertha, 1944, O 7,13:4
Williams, Bertha Mrs, 1948, Ag 14,13:1
Williams, Betsey K, 1941, D 9,31:4
Williams, Bill, 1947, Ja 20,25:2; 1964, N 14,29:6
Williams, Blair S, 1953, D 12,19:6
Williams, Blair S 2d, 1953, Je 23,22:7
Williams, Blanche C (por), 1944, Ag 10,17:3
Williams, Boston Billy (J F Monahan), 1960, O 25, 18:5
Williams, Boylston L, 1943, O 24,44:2
Williams, Bradford, 1960, Mr 24,33:2
Williams, Bradford G, 1948, F 18,27:1
Williams, Bransby, 1961, D 4,37:4
Williams, Bud Mrs, 1959, O 26,29:2
Williams, Burdett S, 1945, O 3,19:4
Williams, Burt, 1954, My 2,89:2
Williams, Byron G, 1937, Je 4,23:3
Williams, C B, 1956, Ag 6,23:5
Williams, C Dr, 1879, Ag 11,2:7
Williams, C H Gen, 1867, Ja 7,5:3
Williams, C Jay, 1945, Ja 27,11:4
Williams, C P, 1879, O 29,5:5
Williams, C S, 1936, S 5,15:3
Williams, Carl, 1915, Ag 3,9:5; 1953, Je 8,29:2; 1965, My 30,51:2
Williams, Carl Mrs, 1949, Je 22,31:1
Williams, Carl S, 1939, Mr 12,III,7:1; 1960, N 10,47:4
Williams, Carl S Mrs, 1952, Ap 19,15:5
Williams, Caroline A Mrs, 1940, Mr 28,24:3
Williams, Caroline Mrs, 1942, D 30,23:4
Williams, Channing Moore Rev, 1910, D 3,11:4
Williams, Charles, 1925, Mr 14,13:5
Williams, Charles A, 1911, Ap 11,11:4; 1937, My 6, 25:1; 1952, Mr 26,29:3
Williams, Charles B, 1942, O 7,25:5; 1943, Ja 7,15:6
Williams, Charles D, 1954, Ja 11,25:4
Williams, Charles David Bp (funl, F 16,13:4), 1923, F 15,19:5
Williams, Charles E Sr, 1955, F 21,21:3
Williams, Charles F, 1921, Ag 12,13:6
Williams, Charles F (will, D 10,31:6), 1952, S 12,21:1
Williams, Charles G, 1917, Ja 23,9:5; 1947, Ap 23,25:2
Williams, Charles H, 1949, O 8,13:5
Williams, Charles I, 1968, N 30,39:3
Williams, Charles J, 1952, Je 30,19:3; 1956, Ja 3,31:2; 1957, Ja 29,31:2
Williams, Charles K, 1944, O 13,19:3
Williams, Charles K Mrs, 1940, D 30,17:3
Williams, Charles L, 1945, O 13,15:3
Williams, Charles M, 1951, N 13,30:2
Williams, Charles Mrs, 1953, Ja 16,24:3; 1964, Mr 17, 35:4
Williams, Charles P, 1944, Je 5,19:4
Williams, Charles Richard, 1917, D 23,15:4
Williams, Charles S, 1922, Ja 22,22:1; 1952, My 24, 19:1
Williams, Charles S Mrs, 1955, Ap 5,26:6
Williams, Charles T, 1965, Ag 7,21:1
Williams, Charles U, 1953, O 31,17:2
Williams, Charles W, 1925, Ag 11,21:3; 1962, Ja 1,23:3
Williams, Charles W Mrs, 1951, F 17,15:4
Williams, Charles W S, 1945, My 17,19:5
Williams, Chauncey, 1943, Ap 30,21:1
Williams, Chauncey J, 1944, Ap 18,21:4
Williams, Chauncey L, 1964, N 24,39:1
Williams, Chester M, 1953, Ap 22,29:3
Williams, Chester T, 1946, My 7,21:4
Williams, Christopher H, 1962, Ja 9,47:4
Williams, Clarence, 1965, N 9,43:3
Williams, Clarence C Mrs (will, Jl 4,26:2), 1948, Je 28,19:3
Williams, Clarence E, 1924, Mr 20,19:6; 1952, Jl 23, 23:3
Williams, Clarence L, 1943, Ja 10,50:1
Williams, Clarence R, 1948, D 5,92:5
Williams, Clarence S, 1951, O 25,29:4
Williams, Clarence V, 1937, O 10,II,8:4
Williams, Clark (por), 1946, D 19,29:1
Williams, Clark Mrs, 1968, Mr 13,47:1
Williams, Claude P, 1959, N 7,23:3
Williams, Clement C, 1947, F 21,20:2
Williams, Clifford E, 1946, N 13,27:4
Williams, Clifford H, 1961, Ag 27,84:2
Williams, Clifford V, 1948, D 18,19:5
Williams, Clinton E Mrs, 1946, N 11,27:5
Williams, Clinton R, 1955, F 3,23:2
Williams, Clyde, 1954, N 13,15:5
Williams, Cora M, 1946, Mr 12,25:1
Williams, Cordella Dr, 1921, My 1,22:4
Williams, Cornelius C, 1957, Mr 28,31:5
Williams, Craig, 1941, Jl 6,27:4
Williams, Curtis L, 1961, S 18,29:3
Williams, Cy, 1956, D 25,25:3
Williams, D Gene, 1964, D 26,17:5
Williams, D M, 1902, Je 17,9:5
Williams, Dan D, 1950, D 20,31:4
Williams, Dana S, 1940, O 22,23:5
Williams, Daniel, 1944, S 20,23:2
Williams, Daniel R, 1941, Ap 20,43:2
Williams, David, 1879, Jl 23,2:6; 1941, Ja 23,22:2
Williams, David A Sr, 1953, Ag 19,29:4
Williams, David D Mrs, 1939, Mr 10,23:3
Williams, David E, 1940, D 29,24:7; 1953, S 3,21:3; 1961, Ag 11,23:3
Williams, David L, 1942, Je 8,15:5; 1962, F 5,31:5
Williams, David L Mrs, 1947, S 16,24:3
Williams, David M, 1945, Ag 1,19:2; 1948, Ap 13,28:3
Williams, David Mrs, 1916, Ap 12,13:5; 1966, O 8,31:3
Williams, David T, 1949, Mr 24,27:3
Williams, David V P, 1965, Ap 16,26:4
Williams, De D, 1946, Ja 26,13:5
Williams, Dean, 1955, Ag 16,23:2
Williams, Dion, 1952, D 12,29:5
Williams, Donald A, 1948, D 13,23:5
Williams, Donald S, 1951, Je 9,19:4
Williams, Douglas, 1945, N 7,23:3
Williams, Dwight S Jr, 1949, N 6,92:1
Williams, E G Harcourt, 1957, D 14,21:2
Williams, E P, 1903, My 5,9:6
Williams, E Reginald, 1951, O 19,27:2
Williams, E Roderick, 1959, Ap 3,27:2
Williams, E Victor, 1938, F 1,21:2
Williams, Edgar, 1956, O 27,21:5
Williams, Edgar J, 1938, F 16,21:4; 1946, F 26,25:3
Williams, Edgar Sr, 1942, Jl 24,19:2; 1953, Je 9,27:5
Williams, Edison G, 1950, Ja 10,29:3
Williams, Edmonia, 1951, Mr 27,29:4
Williams, Edmund, 1949, D 8,33:3
Williams, Edmund R, 1952, Je 11,29:5
Williams, Ednyfed H, 1958, S 22,31:5
Williams, Edward B Mrs, 1949, My 31,23:4; 1959, My 11,27:5
Williams, Edward D Mrs, 1960, Jl 23,19:5
Williams, Edward F, 1946, Mr 2,13:3
Williams, Edward G (por), 1942, O 23,21:3
Williams, Edward H, 1944, Je 18,36:3
Williams, Edward H (por), 1944, Je 25,30:1
Williams, Edward H, 1956, Mr 5,23:4
Williams, Edward H Mrs, 1938, Mr 24,23:3
Williams, Edward J, 1921, Ap 15,15:4
Williams, Edward L, 1919, Mr 31,13:4; 1957, Ja 20, 92:3
Williams, Edward S, 1941, Ag 20,19:5
Williams, Edward T, 1949, F 21,23:3; 1952, Je 16,17:3
Williams, Edward T Mrs, 1945, My 20,32:4
Williams, Edward T T, 1968, Ja 8,39:2
Williams, Edwin M, 1945, Mr 28,23:5
Williams, Edwin S, 1940, S 6,21:2
Williams, Egbert Austin, 1922, Mr 6,13:5
Williams, Elbert T Mrs, 1949, Ag 31,23:5
Williams, Elihu S Capt, 1903, D 2,9:5
Williams, Eliphalet, 1874, Mr 16,5:6
Williams, Elisha A, 1939, O 23,19:5
Williams, Elizabeth B Mrs (will, Ap 10,27:8), 1940, Mr 31,46:3
Williams, Elizabeth J, 1944, Ag 20,34:3
Williams, Elmer L, 1947, Mr 11,27:4
Williams, Elwood, 1952, My 24,19:5
Williams, Emil C Mrs, 1937, Ap 26,21:3
Williams, Emily, 1910, D 6,13:4
Williams, Emmett A, 1953, Ap 15,31:1
Williams, Emmons L, 1921, Je 26,22:3
Williams, Ephie E Mrs, 1940, Jl 23,19:4
Williams, Ernest, 1946, D 24,17:3; 1961, Ag 24,29:3
Williams, Ernest S, 1947, F 9,62:5; 1961, Jl 26,31:2
Williams, Eugene F, 1950, O 23,23:1
Williams, Eugene J, 1943, Ag 21,11:5
Williams, Evan, 1918, My 25,13:5
Williams, Evan J, 1937, Ja 23,18:2
Williams, Everett C, 1962, F 5,31:2
Williams, Ezekiel C, 1917, D 27,11:6
Williams, F, 1930, Ap 2,29:3
Williams, F B Dr, 1903, Ap 21,9:5

Williams, F E, 1936, S 26,15:5
Williams, F S, 1882, S 23,2:4
Williams, Faith M (Mrs F Lorimer), 1958, S 22,31:3
Williams, Fannie B Mrs, 1944, Mr 8,19:1
Williams, Fanny R Mrs, 1942, D 15,27:4
Williams, Ferdinand N, 1964, Ap 16,37:3
Williams, Fero, 1956, D 25,25:5
Williams, Floyd E, 1949, My 21,13:5
Williams, Floyd E Sr, 1951, Ja 15,17:5
Williams, Foster J, 1948, My 15,15:4
Williams, Frances (F Jellinek),(cor, Ja 29,27:4), 1959, Ja 28,31:4
Williams, Francis A, 1965, F 2,33:3
Williams, Francis C, 1945, Ap 12,23:5
Williams, Francis F, 1925, Mr 10,21:4
Williams, Francis Howard, 1922, Je 19,15:6
Williams, Francis J, 1967, S 12,47:1
Williams, Francis K, 1940, Ag 13,19:4
Williams, Frank, 1940, Ja 19,19:1; 1941, Ap 12,15:6
Williams, Frank A, 1940, Jl 9,21:2; 1966, N 6,88:5
Williams, Frank B, 1954, D 7,33:5
Williams, Frank C, 1947, F 6,15:2
Williams, Frank D, 1940, Ja 12,17:1
Williams, Frank E, 1957, F 14,27:3; 1960, Jl 14,27:6
Williams, Frank F, 1949, Mr 14,21:5
Williams, Frank G H, 1960, Ag 10,31:4
Williams, Frank J, 1941, D 5,23:2; 1955, F 8,27:5
Williams, Frank L, 1943, O 26,23:5; 1945, Ap 12,23:3
Williams, Frank M, 1956, Je 25,23:5
Williams, Frank O, 1953, N 8,89:2
Williams, Frank S, 1919, Ap 14,13:4
Williams, Frank W Sr, 1953, Je 4,29:3
Williams, Franklin G, 1963, My 22,41:6
Williams, Fred B, 1954, F 6,19:5
Williams, Fred C, 1920, My 16,22:4
Williams, Fred Col, 1924, Ag 5,17:4
Williams, Fred L, 1942, Ap 5,41:2
Williams, Fred O, 1946, Je 17,21:2
Williams, Fred R, 1950, F 21,25:2
Williams, Fred W, 1960, Ap 3,86:7
Williams, Frederic A, 1953, My 25,25:4
Williams, Frederic A Dr, 1919, My 4,22:5
Williams, Frederic A Mrs, 1949, F 9,27:2
Williams, Frederic H, 1961, My 6,31:4
Williams, Frederick, 1946, Ag 9,17:6; 1958, Jl 14,21:3
Williams, Frederick A, 1958, D 8,31:1
Williams, Frederick B, 1950, F 24,23:1; 1956, D 12, 39:5
Williams, Frederick B Mrs, 1961, F 20,27:1
Williams, Frederick G H, 1944, Je 17,13:1
Williams, Frederick H, 1940, D 8,71:3; 1943, O 9,13:6; 1946, O 2,29:5
Williams, Frederick J, 1937, Je 7,19:3
Williams, Frederick J Maj, 1920, Mr 23,9:6
Williams, Frederick K, 1948, N 10,29:4
Williams, Frederick M, 1937, Ag 18,19:3; 1941, Mr 16,45:3
Williams, Frederick Mrs, 1949, N 30,27:2
Williams, Frederick N, 1954, N 24,23:4
Williams, Frederick S, 1940, Ap 16,23:1; 1953, Je 19, 21:3
Williams, Freeman L, 1950, Ap 23,92:8
Williams, Fritz Mrs, 1952, O 25,17:6
Williams, G C F Dr, 1933, N 16,23:1
Williams, G F, 1932, Jl 12,17:1
Williams, G Ferris, 1961, Jl 29,19:5
Williams, G Kelly, 1953, N 21,13:3
Williams, G Walter, 1946, Jl 22,21:3
Williams, G Walter Mrs, 1948, F 24,25:4
Williams, Gardner F, 1922, Ag 24,15:5
Williams, Gary, 1950, Ag 7,36:3
Williams, George (mem ser, N 20,6:4), 1905, N 7,9:5
Williams, George, 1912, S 27,13:5; 1939, Jl 1,17:4; 1955, F 25,21:3
Williams, George A, 1938, N 3,23:5
Williams, George A Mrs, 1952, D 29,19:2
Williams, George Albert Dr, 1918, My 12,21:1
Williams, George B, 1946, Je 19,21:4; 1966, S 20,47:4
Williams, George B Mrs, 1958, Jl 31,23:5
Williams, George C, 1941, Ja 9,21:3; 1951, Ja 4,29:3; 1955, D 22,23:1
Williams, George Capt (por), 1937, S 24,3:2
Williams, George F, 1946, N 14,29:5
Williams, George F Sr, 1942, Jl 7,20:3
Williams, George Forrester Maj, 1921, Ja 1,9:5
Williams, George G, 1940, Ap 8,19:2; 1944, My 19, 19:4
Williams, George H, 1937, Mr 14,II,8:8; 1942, Ap 30, 19:2; 1945, S 13,23:3
Williams, George H Dr, 1937, O 8,23:5
Williams, George H Judge, 1910, Ap 5,11:4
Williams, George Haskell, 1908, Ag 22,7:5
Williams, George L, 1940, F 11,48:1; 1957, O 28,27:1
Williams, George L Mrs, 1952, Ja 14,19:6
Williams, George N Jr, 1940, Mr 27,21:2
Williams, George O, 1952, N 9,89:4
Williams, George P, 1940, Ap 9,24:3; 1944, S 26,23:3; 1952, N 2,88:1
Williams, George R Mrs, 1944, Ja 6,23:2
Williams, George V, 1942, Ap 13,15:5
Williams, George W, 1937, Je 25,22:1; 1943, Je 21, 17:5; 1947, Mr 8,13:4
Williams, George W Jr Mrs, 1964, D 30,25:1
Williams, George W Rear-Adm, 1925, Jl 18,13:5
Williams, Gerald B, 1952, Mr 4,27:3
Williams, Gerard R, 1958, Je 28,17:5
Williams, Gertrude K Mrs, 1939, Jl 25,19:1
Williams, Gilman, 1956, S 26,33:4
Williams, Gladstone, 1968, Ja 24,42:2
Williams, Godfrey, 1940, S 4,23:5
Williams, Gordon, 1948, N 6,13:5
Williams, Gowan H, 1962, N 28,39:4
Williams, Grace, 1953, Jl 30,23:3
Williams, Grant Lt, 1937, Je 3,25:5
Williams, Granville, 1947, Je 11,27:5
Williams, Griffith C, 1966, Ag 19,33:2
Williams, Griffith E 3d, 1959, F 25,31:3
Williams, Gross T, 1944, F 21,15:1
Williams, Guinn, 1948, Ja 10,15:1
Williams, Guinn (Big Boy), 1962, Je 7,35:2
Williams, Gurney, 1965, Ag 26,33:4
Williams, Gus, 1915, Ja 19,9:5
Williams, Gustave, 1951, Ag 3,21:6
Williams, Guy B W Mrs, 1954, Ag 27,21:3
Williams, Guy R, 1940, F 9,19:4
Williams, H, 1936, O 2,25:5
Williams, H I, 1965, Mr 17,45:3
Williams, H J Mrs, 1944, Jl 11,15:4
Williams, H L, 1931, Jl 15,19:1
Williams, H Lewis, 1959, S 4,21:3
Williams, Hamilton Dr, 1925, Je 23,19:4
Williams, Hank, 1953, Ja 2,4:4
Williams, Harold, 1949, Ag 28,72:2; 1950, S 23,17:4
Williams, Harold A, 1958, My 2,27:1
Williams, Harold E, 1955, D 4,88:8
Williams, Harold G, 1962, Mr 9,19:2; 1964, N 5,45:4
Williams, Harold M (Josh), 1958, Ag 14,29:5
Williams, Harold P, 1965, Ag 7,21:5
Williams, Harriet F, 1937, Ap 8,23:4
Williams, Harris F, 1944, F 18,17:6
Williams, Harrison, 1946, Je 9,40:4; 1953, N 11,31:1
Williams, Harrison Mrs, 1915, Jl 21,11:5
Williams, Harry, 1907, D 28,7:7; 1941, S 9,23:3; 1943, My 29,13:3; 1946, Je 11,23:2; 1947, O 2,27:4; 1953, F 1,89:2
Williams, Harry A, 1953, Je 15,29:6
Williams, Harry B, 1950, Je 5,23:5; 1955, D 21,29:5
Williams, Harry C, 1959, F 2,25:5
Williams, Harry C R, 1950, Ja 15,85:1
Williams, Harry D, 1947, Je 22,52:2
Williams, Harry E, 1948, D 7,32:3
Williams, Harry H, 1922, My 17,19:4
Williams, Harry H Mrs, 1955, O 15,15:4
Williams, Harry J, 1951, O 2,28:2
Williams, Harry L (por), 1943, N 6,13:6
Williams, Harry M, 1942, Je 3,24:3; 1945, Mr 3,13:2
Williams, Harry Mrs, 1945, Mr 15,25:6
Williams, Harry P, 1941, Mr 15,32:5
Williams, Harry R, 1940, Jl 9,21:2; 1958, O 14,37:4
Williams, Harry S, 1949, D 12,33:3
Williams, Harry W, 1943, Ap 24,13:6
Williams, Hartley, 1882, Ag 18,5:5
Williams, Hattie, 1942, Ag 18,21:6
Williams, Helen I (Mrs C E Lindsley), 1961, My 8, 35:4
Williams, Henrietta, 1920, F 19,11:4
Williams, Henry A, 1958, Mr 24,27:3; 1962, Ja 29,25:4
Williams, Henry B, 1955, S 5,11:4
Williams, Henry C, 1943, S 16,21:2
Williams, Henry D (por), 1945, O 16,23:1
Williams, Henry D, 1952, Je 25,29:3
Williams, Henry de V, 1942, S 20,41:3
Williams, Henry Dudley, 1907, Ja 4,7:5
Williams, Henry E, 1946, O 26,17:4
Williams, Henry H, 1940, D 27,19:4; 1952, D 23,23:3
Williams, Henry K, 1944, Ap 1,13:5; 1954, F 20,17:5
Williams, Henry K S, 1944, My 18,19:6
Williams, Henry K S Mrs, 1939, S 1,17:5
Williams, Henry Mrs, 1947, Jl 12,13:5
Williams, Henry O, 1939, D 29,15:4
Williams, Henry P Mrs, 1963, N 17,86:4
Williams, Henry Phillips Jr, 1968, Mr 29,41:3
Williams, Henry S, 1943, Jl 5,15:3
Williams, Henry Shaler, 1918, Ag 1,11:5
Williams, Henry T, 1948, Ag 3,26:2
Williams, Henry W, 1940, Mr 2,13:4
Williams, Herbert D, 1960, My 29,57:2
Williams, Herbert E, 1964, Ag 24,27:3
Williams, Herbert G, 1937, Ja 9,17:2; 1941, Ag 16,15:2
Williams, Herbert J, 1961, My 3,37:4
Williams, Herbert L, 1942, Ja 11,46:2
Williams, Herbert Mrs, 1958, Ap 30,33:2
Williams, Herbert O, 1939, Ag 18,19:4
Williams, Herbert Sir, 1954, Jl 26,17:6
Williams, Herbert U, 1938, D 10,17:1
Williams, Herberton L, 1951, N 27,31:3
Williams, Herman E, 1965, O 14,47:2
Williams, Herschel V, 1948, F 18,27:1
Williams, Hobart, 1921, N 4,17:6
Williams, Holman, 1967, Jl 16,50:5
Williams, Homer D, 1937, N 14,II,10:1
Williams, Homer R Mrs, 1944, Jl 10,15:5
Williams, Horatio B, 1955, N 2,35:2
Williams, Howard C, 1949, Jl 16,13:4
Williams, Howard F, 1950, Jl 13,25:2
Williams, Howard H Mrs, 1958, F 25,27:3
Williams, Howard R, 1963, My 24,31:4
Williams, Howe, 1955, N 23,23:3
Williams, Hubert W, 1961, D 11,31:5
Williams, Hugh, 1942, O 13,23:3
Williams, Hugh G Sr, 1951, Ap 27,23:3
Williams, Hugh T, 1960, D 24,15:2
Williams, Hugo H Mrs, 1948, My 1,15:4
Williams, I D, 1933, Ap 8,13:1
Williams, I Newton, 1955, O 18,37:1
Williams, I Newton Mrs, 1940, My 15,25:1
Williams, I Stuart, 1942, Ap 30,19:3
Williams, Idras R, 1942, F 4,19:5
Williams, Ira, 1958, Mr 4,29:1
Williams, Ira C, 1949, D 27,23:1
Williams, Ira W, 1955, F 19,15:4
Williams, Irving G, 1966, My 20,47:4
Williams, Isaac N, 1874, F 26,4:6
Williams, Isidor, 1948, O 30,15:5
Williams, J (Prof Jim), 1878, My 21,5:1
Williams, J A Rev Dr, 1883, S 3,2:4
Williams, J B, 1883, S 28,5:2
Williams, J C, 1936, Je 2,27:1
Williams, J D, 1880, N 21,1:2
Williams, J E (see also S 27), 1877, S 23,8:6
Williams, J Eugene, 1939, Jl 16,31:4
Williams, J Grenfell, 1954, D 29,23:3
Williams, J Henry Heard, 1915, Ag 16,9:5
Williams, J Henry Judge, 1919, O 25,11:4
Williams, J Herbert, 1947, N 3,23:4
Williams, J Howard, 1958, Ap 21,23:4
Williams, J L, 1883, S 25,1:6
Williams, J Nelson, 1962, S 28,25:4
Williams, J Oliver, 1943, Ja 3,42:3
Williams, J Oscar, 1943, Ja 7,19:3
Williams, J Peter Jr, 1964, Mr 3,36:1
Williams, J Randall, 1953, D 18,29:1
Williams, J Rev, 1926, O 26,27:3
Williams, J S (see also N 15,17), 1876, N 18,10:1
Williams, J S, 1926, N 5,21:4; 1932, S 28,19:1
Williams, J T, 1879, Ja 25,5:5
Williams, Jack, 1958, F 12,29:3
Williams, Jack Mrs, 1951, Je 20,27:5
Williams, James, 1951, S 14,26:3; 1952, Mr 7,23:4
Williams, James A, 1951, Ag 28,8:5; 1953, Mr 24,31:5
Williams, James B, 1941, Ja 19,40:1
Williams, James C Mrs, 1959, D 8,45:1
Williams, James D, 1938, S 2,17:5
Williams, James F Mrs, 1947, Ag 17,52:4
Williams, James H, 1904, D 6,9:3
Williams, James H (por), 1942, F 24,21:5
Williams, James H (por), 1948, My 5,25:6
Williams, James H, 1952, Mr 12,27:2; 1958, Jl 31,23:4
Williams, James M, 1944, Ag 29,17:4
Williams, James M Gen, 1907, F 16,9:6
Williams, James Philip, 1903, S 29,9:5
Williams, James R, 1957, Je 19,35:1
Williams, James R Mrs, 1945, O 4,23:5
Williams, James Rev, 1951, F 22,31:2
Williams, James T, 1942, O 1,23:2
Williams, James T 2d, 1954, O 9,17:2
Williams, Jane H, 1950, S 3,39:1
Williams, Jay J, 1961, My 31,33:5
Williams, Jeffrey, 1938, D 29,20:3
Williams, Jennie Mrs, 1950, D 21,29:6
Williams, Jere Col, 1915, My 12,13:4
Williams, Jeremiah, 1916, Je 24,11:7
Williams, Jesse F, 1942, Mr 21,17:3; 1966, Ag 7,80:7
Williams, Jessie R Mrs, 1943, Ja 14,21:1
Williams, Joe C, 1950, My 27,17:4
Williams, John, 1938, My 28,15:4; 1944, Mr 6,19:5; 1945, F 4,38:3
Williams, John A, 1941, D 27,19:4; 1946, S 21,15:6; 1951, D 2,91:3
Williams, John B, 1907, Mr 4,9:5; 1941, Mr 22,15:6; 1948, N 24,24:3
Williams, John B Mrs, 1910, F 22,9:3
Williams, John C, 1943, Je 7,13:4; 1947, S 9,31:1; 1960, Mr 31,33:3
Williams, John C Mrs, 1950, Ag 26,13:1
Williams, John Capt, 1903, My 16,9:6
Williams, John D, 1941, Mr 25,23:1; 1964, N 22,86:1
Williams, John E, 1943, Ap 21,25:4; 1958, Mr 1,17:4; 1964, N 27,35:3
Williams, John F, 1947, My 19,21:5; 1950, Ap 9,85:1; 1950, S 22,31:3; 1953, My 31,74:2
Williams, John G, 1941, N 11,23:3; 1950, Mr 29,29:1
Williams, John H, 1904, Mr 27,7:4; 1939, Ag 27,35:2; 1966, Ap 19,41:3
Williams, John H B, 1954, D 26,61:1
Williams, John H C Mrs, 1944, O 25,21:6
Williams, John H Judge, 1875, Jl 19,5:4
Williams, John H Mrs, 1949, Ja 13,23:3; 1960, Ap 3, 87:1
Williams, John J, 1956, Ap 26,33:4
Williams, John Jabez, 1922, S 7,17:5
Williams, John Joseph Archbishop (funl, S 1,7:6), 1907, Ag 31,7:6
Williams, John Jr, 1944, My 21,44:2
Williams, John L, 1961, Mr 19,88:3; 1968, Jl 1,33:2
Williams, John L B, 1963, Ag 12,21:4
Williams, John M, 1907, D 18,9:5; 1939, F 18,15:2; 1950, Je 18,76:6; 1953, Ag 22,15:4
Williams, John M Sr, 1951, Mr 24,13:2

Williams, John Mrs, 1951, My 8,31:2
Williams, John O, 1950, S 26,31:2
Williams, John P Sr, 1952, Ap 11,23:1
Williams, John R, 1944, Je 4,42:2; 1964, Jl 21,33:3; 1965, D 28,27:2
Williams, John S, 1940, O 14,19:5; 1944, Ja 3,21:5
Williams, John S Mrs, 1946, N 29,25:1
Williams, John T, 1949, Ja 4,19:3
Williams, John V, 1963, Ag 29,29:2
Williams, John W, 1945, My 15,19:2; 1946, Ap 4,25:5; 1965, F 8,25:2
Williams, John W Mrs, 1950, O 27,29:1; 1952, My 16, 23:4
Williams, Johnston, 1957, D 3,35:4
Williams, Joseph, 1919, Jl 26,9:7; 1952, My 31,17:5
Williams, Joseph D (will, Ap 18,9:2), 1940, F 3,13:3
Williams, Joseph E, 1943, My 29,13:3
Williams, Joseph H, 1948, S 7,25:3
Williams, Joseph J (por), 1940, O 30,23:5
Williams, Joseph M, 1941, Ap 30,19:6; 1945, Mr 10, 17:2
Williams, Joseph R, 1954, Mr 18,31:1
Williams, Joseph Sr, 1946, O 11,23:2
Williams, Josephine, 1937, Je 15,23:6
Williams, Joshua O, 1963, O 4,35:1
Williams, Judith B, 1956, O 17,41:1
Williams, Julian Tainter Dr, 1905, Ap 11,11:6
Williams, Julius, 1952, Ag 7,21:2
Williams, Junius E, 1937, Jl 24,15:6
Williams, Justin, 1962, Ag 14,32:1
Williams, Kate A, 1939, Ag 9,17:2
Williams, Kate Mrs, 1951, Ap 6,25:4
Williams, Katherine R, 1942, Je 25,23:2
Williams, Kathlyn, 1960, S 25,86:4
Williams, Kathryn D Mrs, 1937, Je 23,25:3
Williams, Keith S, 1951, F 14,29:4
Williams, Kenneth, 1945, Ag 22,23:5
Williams, Kenneth P, 1958, S 26,27:2
Williams, Kenneth R, 1959, Ja 23,26:1
Williams, Kiaulani S Mrs, 1949, My 26,29:2
Williams, Kid (J Gutenko), 1963, O 20,88:7
Williams, Kimball M, 1953, Ja 25,85:1
Williams, Kinne F, 1956, Je 19,29:3
Williams, L A, 1944, Jl 13,17:4
Williams, L Chandler Mrs, 1940, O 19,17:2
Williams, L M, 1931, Ap 3,25:1
Williams, Langbourne Mrs, 1956, N 27,37:1
Williams, Laura H Mrs, 1942, N 23,23:2
Williams, Laurence Mrs, 1912, Je 3,9:6
Williams, Lawrence, 1945, Ag 14,21:3
Williams, Lawrence G Mrs, 1956, O 20,21:6
Williams, Lawrence S, 1949, O 8,13:5
Williams, Leander P Maj, 1914, My 19,9:5
Williams, Leo E, 1967, Ja 30,29:2
Williams, Leola M, 1958, My 6,35:2
Williams, Leon, 1947, Mr 2,60:2
Williams, Leon (will), 1958, Je 24,25:6
Williams, Leonard G, 1952, S 23,33:3
Williams, Leonard L B, 1939, Ag 21,13:5
Williams, Leonard W Dr, 1912, S 27,13:5
Williams, Leroy B, 1945, Ag 14,21:4
Williams, Leroy B (will), 1946, S 5,30:3
Williams, Leslie H, 1954, My 23,90:1
Williams, Lewis, 1907, S 8,7:5
Williams, Lewis A, 1924, My 20,21:5
Williams, Lewis C, 1952, Mr 23,92:1
Williams, Lewis C Mrs, 1949, D 24,15:3
Williams, Lewis D Sr, 1950, S 13,27:5
Williams, Lewis W, 1950, My 16,31:2
Williams, Linsly R Mrs, 1959, Ap 16,33:3
Williams, Lola M, 1956, D 24,13:1
Williams, Louis E, 1949, O 23,87:3
Williams, Louis L, 1939, S 18,19:2
Williams, Louis N D, 1942, S 2,23:2
Williams, Louise S, 1947, My 23,23:4
Williams, Lucien E, 1941, Ja 13,15:4
Williams, Lucy A, 1960, D 1,35:1
Williams, Lucy A Mrs, 1959, Jl 24,8:3
Williams, Lynn A, 1944, Ap 17,23:2
Williams, M J, 1952, F 3,85:1
Williams, M J Col, 1872, Ag 30,1:6
Williams, M Mrs, 1939, N 28,17:5
Williams, MaBelle W Mrs, 1965, D 23,27:2
Williams, Madaline A Mrs (Mrs Saml A Williams), 1968, D 15,86:1
Williams, Malcolm, 1937, Je 11,23:4
Williams, Margaret L, 1960, Je 6,29:5
Williams, Marion E Mrs, 1941, Jl 2,21:5
Williams, Marion S Mrs, 1940, D 21,17:4
Williams, Marion T Mrs, 1960, Je 8,39:1
Williams, Mark W, 1960, Mr 18,26:4
Williams, Marshall C, 1954, My 22,15:2
Williams, Martha J Mrs, 1939, O 8,48:8
Williams, Martin R, 1939, Ja 9,15:3
Williams, Martin T, 1959, F 3,31:3
Williams, Marvin W, 1951, Ag 20,19:5
Williams, Mary A Mrs, 1943, Ja 3,42:1
Williams, Mary G, 1938, Je 1,23:2
Williams, Mary L, 1943, Ag 14,11:6
Williams, Mary L Mrs, 1939, Ag 20,33:3
Williams, Mary M Mrs, 1938, Ap 3,II,7:1
Williams, Mary S B Mrs, 1941, N 25,26:3
Williams, Mary V M Mrs, 1940, Mr 29,21:2
Williams, Mary W, 1944, Mr 13,15:4
Williams, Matthew, 1950, My 27,17:3
Williams, Maud D Mrs, 1943, Je 7,13:4
Williams, Maurice S, 1955, N 27,89:1
Williams, Max W, 1951, N 29,33:3
Williams, May Mrs, 1961, Ag 29,31:3
Williams, Maynard O, 1963, Je 28,29:3
Williams, Meredith C, 1953, My 29,25:3
Williams, Meredith N, 1950, S 12,27:2
Williams, Meritt R, 1948, D 24,17:1
Williams, Michael, 1950, O 13,29:1
Williams, Mildred A Mrs (will), 1939, O 12,25:1
Williams, Millard A Sr, 1954, Jl 29,23:2
Williams, Miller, 1939, N 8,20:4
Williams, Milton H, 1953, Ap 25,15:4
Williams, Milton I, 1957, Jl 25,23:4
Williams, Morgan B, 1903, O 14,9:6
Williams, Morgan Bransby, 1914, Je 23,11:4
Williams, Mornay, 1926, Je 19,15:3
Williams, Morris, 1957, N 27,31:5
Williams, Mosely H Rev Dr, 1917, N 10,13:7
Williams, Moses H, 1961, Ap 1,17:1
Williams, Murray, 1922, Ja 9,17:4
Williams, Myron P, 1961, Ap 28,31:2
Williams, N Russell, 1961, D 11,31:3
Williams, N Winslow, 1924, D 30,17:5
Williams, Nat, 1957, N 16,19:6
Williams, Nathan B, 1951, D 30,24:2
Williams, Nathan W, 1940, Ja 15,15:4
Williams, Nellie C, 1944, My 30,21:4
Williams, Nelson B, 1945, Mr 22,23:5
Williams, Nelson B Mrs, 1958, Ap 26,19:4
Williams, Newton A, 1940, S 18,23:3
Williams, Norman C, 1968, Ja 10,43:1
Williams, O B, 1959, S 24,37:1
Williams, Odell, 1902, Je 10,9:5
Williams, Oliver E, 1947, S 24,23:6
Williams, Oscar, 1964, O 11,88:1
Williams, Oscar H, 1954, S 9,31:2
Williams, Oscar Jr, 1954, F 21,68:1
Williams, Othneil G, 1960, Ja 20,31:2
Williams, Otto, 1937, Mr 20,19:1
Williams, Otto A, 1956, O 5,25:4
Williams, P Whitcomb, 1949, Ja 7,4:7
Williams, Pardon C Ex-Justice, 1925, Ja 19,17:4
Williams, Parker S, 1942, F 22,26:6
Williams, Pascoe W, 1945, Ja 21,40:5
Williams, Paul A, 1953, Je 26,19:4
Williams, Paul B, 1957, D 13,27:1; 1960, My 24,37:2
Williams, Paul F, 1937, F 17,21:1
Williams, Paul N, 1949, Jl 16,13:5
Williams, Paul P Mrs, 1961, S 8,31:1
Williams, Pearce Mrs, 1944, Je 27,21:6
Williams, Pearce P, 1942, N 25,23:6
Williams, Pearl, 1950, Mr 15,29:1
Williams, Percival A, 1958, Ja 12,86:6
Williams, Percy C, 1961, My 23,39:4
Williams, Percy G (funl, Jl 25,11:6), 1923, Jl 22,24:5
Williams, Percy H, 1959, Ja 1,31:2
Williams, Percy M, 1946, N 6,23:2
Williams, Percy N Dr, 1937, F 10,23:2
Williams, Perry P, 1912, O 20,II,15:4
Williams, Phil, 1942, N 4,23:6
Williams, Phil T, 1945, Je 14,19:4
Williams, Philip T, 1916, F 12,11:6
Williams, Pierce, 1952, Ap 26,23:4
Williams, R Clyde, 1954, D 30,7:1
Williams, R Marvin Mrs, 1953, Ja 14,31:1
Williams, R Morris, 1950, S 13,27:1
Williams, R Neil, 1945, D 6,27:4
Williams, R Norris 2d, 1968, Je 4,44:2
Williams, R Roy, 1956, F 27,23:6
Williams, Ralph, 1967, Ja 6,35:2
Williams, Ralph C, 1940, S 4,23:4
Williams, Ralph D, 1955, Mr 17,45:2
Williams, Ralph E (por), 1940, My 17,19:1
Williams, Ralph H, 1948, F 29,60:6
Williams, Ralph J, 1949, Ag 26,20:2
Williams, Ralph O, 1966, Mr 27,86:4
Williams, Ralph V Mrs, 1951, My 13,88:6
Williams, Ralph W, 1951, N 22,31:5
Williams, Ramon O, 1913, O 3,11:5
Williams, Randolph Mrs, 1937, Ja 4,29:1
Williams, Raymond B, 1967, Ap 12,47:3
Williams, Raymond E, 1952, N 8,17:5
Williams, Raymond S, 1944, F 15,17:3
Williams, Reese, 1965, Jl 13,33:5
Williams, Remsen T, 1937, F 23,27:3
Williams, Rene Lois, 1916, Ja 21,9:6
Williams, Rhys R Lady, 1964, S 19,27:4
Williams, Richard, 1959, F 19,63:5
Williams, Richard H, 1938, Ja 13,21:5
Williams, Richard L, 1941, Je 3,21:2
Williams, Richard P, 1950, Mr 15,29:1; 1965, Ap 3, 29:6
Williams, Richard R Rev, 1915, O 1,11:7
Williams, Richard T B, 1956, Ja 7,1:2
Williams, Robert, 1938, Ap 26,21:5; 1939, O 12,25:3
Williams, Robert D, 1950, Jl 12,29:3; 1957, Ap 13,19:5
Williams, Robert E, 1940, Je 18,23:3; 1959, Ap 12,86:8
Williams, Robert Gen, 1901, Ag 26,7:6
Williams, Robert H, 1953, Ja 4,76:4
Williams, Robert H (Oct 2), 1965, O 11,61:5
Williams, Robert Jr, 1953, Ja 2,16:4
Williams, Robert Jr Col, 1914, D 11,13:5
Williams, Robert Judge, 1923, F 20,17:2
Williams, Robert L, 1948, Ap 11,72:1; 1949, O 27,29:4
Williams, Robert M Jr, 1953, Ja 24,15:2
Williams, Robert Mrs, 1959, Jl 11,19:6
Williams, Robert O, 1944, Je 20,19:4
Williams, Robert S, 1950, F 21,25:1
Williams, Robert V, 1959, N 20,31:2
Williams, Rodney R, 1951, Ap 16,25:5
Williams, Roger, 1939, Ja 4,21:2; 1942, D 15,28:3; 1945, Ag 12,40:5; 1952, My 26,23:3; 1959, N 29,87:1; 1960, My 27,86:2
Williams, Roger B 2d, 1938, D 6,23:1
Williams, Roger C, 1940, Ag 7,19:3
Williams, Roger H, 1950, O 27,29:3
Williams, Roger H Mrs, 1958, F 26,27:4
Williams, Roger J Mrs, 1952, F 17,14:1
Williams, Roger Mrs, 1954, D 12,88:4; 1965, My 27, 37:4
Williams, Roger P, 1946, Je 4,23:2
Williams, Roger W, 1954, D 14,33:1
Williams, Roland B, 1941, Ja 15,23:5
Williams, Rolland, 1968, Ap 6,39:1
Williams, Romine, 1939, Jl 26,19:2
Williams, Ronald W, 1958, Mr 16,86:4
Williams, Rose, 1950, N 14,32:3
Williams, Roy F, 1968, D 31,27:1
Williams, Roy H, 1946, D 19,30:2
Williams, Roy L, 1938, O 19,23:2
Williams, Russell B, 1948, F 13,21:4
Williams, Russell R Jr, 1961, Jl 7,25:4
Williams, Ruth M, 1967, Mr 11,29:5
Williams, S, 1878, Je 17,1:2
Williams, S Clay, 1949, F 26,15:1
Williams, S Herbert, 1943, Ap 24,13:4
Williams, S Norman, 1962, Jl 12,29:4
Williams, S Thomson, 1903, Je 26,9:6
Williams, S W Prof, 1884, F 17,2:5
Williams, Samuel A, 1950, Ag 15,30:2
Williams, Samuel B, 1966, F 2,35:1
Williams, Samuel C, 1947, D 15,25:2; 1968, N 12,47:2
Williams, Samuel D, 1952, N 10,25:3
Williams, Samuel H, 1951, F 19,23:4
Williams, Samuel L, 1912, Ag 16,9:5
Williams, Samuel M, 1959, My 12,35:2
Williams, Samuel Mrs, 1950, F 15,27:2
Williams, Samuel P, 1943, My 2,45:1; 1964, Mr 20, 33:1
Williams, Samuel P Jr, 1942, Ja 24,17:4
Williams, Samuel S, 1952, N 18,31:5
Williams, Samuel W, 1913, Ag 6,7:4
Williams, Sarah B Mrs, 1951, O 13,17:3
Williams, Sarah L Mrs, 1938, N 12,15:1
Williams, Seth, 1963, Jl 30,29:5
Williams, Seth Gen, 1866, Mr 26,5:3
Williams, Seymour, 1967, Jl 2,35:1
Williams, Shelby, 1965, Je 3,35:4
Williams, Sherman, 1920, Ap 27,9:3
Williams, Sherman Dr, 1923, D 13,21:5
Williams, Sidney C, 1949, My 25,30:2
Williams, Sidney F Mrs, 1952, S 30,31:2
Williams, Sidney J, 1943, S 27,19:2; 1956, Ag 7,27:1
Williams, Sidney M, 1922, Jl 7,17:5
Williams, Sidney Sr, 1951, My 11,27:3
Williams, Sidney T, 1960, F 17,35:2
Williams, Spencer, 1964, O 25,88:1; 1965, Jl 17,25:2
Williams, Stacy Mrs, 1938, My 24,17:2
Williams, Stalham L, 1955, My 1,88:5
Williams, Stanley A Mrs, 1961, O 5,37:4
Williams, Stanley T, 1956, F 6,23:3
Williams, Stephen, 1957, Jl 14,72:4
Williams, Stephen G, 1938, N 23,21:4
Williams, Stephen G Mrs, 1955, O 29,19:1
Williams, Stephen K, 1916, Mr 30,13:6
Williams, Steven C, 1954, F 16,25:4
Williams, Stuart C, 1953, Ja 27,25:1
Williams, Stuart L, 1949, Ap 29,23:3
Williams, Stuart R, 1953, N 5,31:5
Williams, Sylvester P, 1947, Jl 21,17:3
Williams, T, 1928, Ja 25,23:1
Williams, T A, 1926, N 25,25:3
Williams, T J, 1927, Mr 10,25:6
Williams, T Morgan Mrs, 1959, F 19,63:5
Williams, T S, 1930, Je 4,27:4
Williams, T Walter (por), 1942, N 10,27:1
Williams, T Walter Mrs, 1960, Ja 5,31:3
Williams, Teraceda V, 1956, Je 13,37:4
Williams, Th Col, 1903, Ap 14,9:6
Williams, Theophilus G, 1959, Ag 27,27:4
Williams, Thomas, 1872, Ap 1,1:3; 1876, O 1,2:4; 1939, F 10,23:5; 1939, Je 8,25:5; 1943, D 21,27:4; 1956, Ag 27,19:6
Williams, Thomas B, 1942, N 18,25:2
Williams, Thomas C, 1940, D 6,23:2; 1950, S 26,31:5
Williams, Thomas D Dr, 1911, Ag 6,II,9:5
Williams, Thomas E Mrs, 1967, Jl 25,32:6
Williams, Thomas H, 1943, F 20,13:5; 1944, Mr 11, 13:4
Williams, Thomas H Mrs, 1940, D 9,19:5
Williams, Thomas Hilton Sr, 1907, O 21,7:5
Williams, Thomas J, 1945, Ag 11,13:7; 1948, Ja 28, 23:6; 1954, Je 6,86:4; 1957, Jl 7,60:7

Williams, Thomas L, 1946, Ap 2,27:2; 1965, D 3,35:8
Williams, Thomas M, 1947, Mr 28,23:1
Williams, Thomas Mrs, 1872, Ap 1,1:3; 1962, Je 11, 31:6
Williams, Thomas R, 1937, O 23,15:5
Williams, Thomas S (por), 1940, Ap 6,17:4
Williams, Thomas T (trb, Mr 24,11:4), 1911, Mr 23, 9:5
Williams, Thomas W (por), 1946, Mr 30,15:1
Williams, Thomas W, 1956, My 5,19:7
Williams, Thomas W Jr, 1963, Ap 3,47:2
Williams, Thomas Y, 1946, D 20,23:3
Williams, Thornton R, 1939, Je 25,36:7
Williams, Tiffany J, 1947, Ag 21,23:4
Williams, Tom, 1939, Ja 16,15:3; 1953, Mr 12,27:5
Williams, Tom E Mrs (M Selee), 1961, S 19,35:3
Williams, U B, 1943, Jl 18,34:7
Williams, Van Zandt, 1966, My 14,31:4
Williams, Vasily R, 1939, N 13,19:5
Williams, Vaughan E, 1962, Je 20,25:2
Williams, Vernal J, 1952, F 9,13:2
Williams, Vernon, 1955, My 27,23:2
Williams, Victor W Mrs, 1955, Ag 2,23:4
Williams, Vincent D, 1952, Mr 1,15:5
Williams, W, 1935, Jl 30,19:1
Williams, W Edwin, 1961, S 17,86:4
Williams, W Ellis Dr, 1925, N 8,5:2
Williams, W Emerson, 1940, N 1,25:1
Williams, W Fischer Mrs (Peggy Read), 1968, Jl 3, 32:1
Williams, W H, 1931, O 15,23:1
Williams, W R Rev, 1885, Ap 2,2:1
Williams, W T B, 1941, Mr 27,23:5
Williams, W T Mrs, 1949, Mr 29,26:2
Williams, W Theodore Mrs, 1959, D 13,86:3
Williams, W W, 1903, Jl 30,7:6
Williams, Wade, 1948, D 5,92:3
Williams, Waldron, 1917, Jl 20,9:7
Williams, Walter, 1939, D 16,17:5; 1947, Je 20,19:2; 1950, O 14,19:4; 1952, S 8,21:4; 1960, F 13,19:4
Williams, Walter C, 1953, My 7,31:3
Williams, Walter D, 1961, Mr 8,33:5
Williams, Walter E, 1942, Ja 1,25:6; 1946, Jl 23,25:4
Williams, Walter H, 1951, N 2,23:4
Williams, Walter L, 1945, O 24,21:4
Williams, Walter Mrs, 1942, N 7,15:3; 1954, Ap 21, 29:3; 1957, N 3,89:1; 1961, Jl 7,25:1
Williams, Walter W (trb; funl plans, D 21,27:1;funl, D 24,20:1), 1959, D 20,1:3
Williams, Ward B, 1950, Ag 12,13:5
Williams, Warren, 1954, O 22,27:1
Williams, Watkin, 1944, N 20,21:6
Williams, Wayland W, 1945, My 8,19:3
Williams, Webster F Mrs, 1950, Ap 8,13:5
Williams, Wilfred W, 1960, S 7,42:1
Williams, Willard W, 1948, N 22,22:3
Williams, Willard W Mrs, 1960, S 27,37:3
Williams, William, 1907, Mr 23,9:6; 1923, Ag 21,17:3; 1943, F 4,23:4; 1946, N 30,15:5; 1947, F 9,63:3; 1951, Ap 15,92:2
Williams, William A, 1938, My 8,II,6:2
Williams, William A (Al), 1960, My 30,17:3
Williams, William B, 1944, Mr 24,19:4
Williams, William Biddle, 1908, F 9,11:5
Williams, William C, 1950, F 18,15:3; 1963, Mr 5,1:3
Williams, William C Jr (por), 1945, N 3,15:6
Williams, William E, 1952, Mr 20,29:1
Williams, William Elza, 1921, S 14,19:4
Williams, William F, 1939, N 18,17:5; 1941, My 25, 36:6; 1943, Ap 1,23:3
Williams, William F Mrs, 1953, Jl 1,29:3
Williams, William H, 1909, My 30,9:5; 1916, N 18, 11:4; 1940, Mr 15,23:4
Williams, William H (por), 1943, F 16,19:1
Williams, William H (will, Jl 14,21:7), 1943, Je 20, 34:6
Williams, William H Capt, 1922, My 6,11:5
Williams, William H Mrs, 1948, O 30,15:2; 1952, Ap 9,13:1
Williams, William Henry Harrison, 1909, D 10,11:5
Williams, William K Mrs, 1959, F 19,31:5
Williams, William L, 1952, N 14,23:1
Williams, William M, 1949, Ap 2,15:5; 1950, Ag 12, 13:2
Williams, William M Mrs, 1951, Je 21,27:6
Williams, William Mrs, 1956, Jl 31,23:1
Williams, William R, 1937, Je 29,21:4
Williams, William R (por), 1940, N 18,19:3
Williams, William R, 1951, D 9,90:7
Williams, William R Dr, 1937, Mr 6,17:4
Williams, William R Mrs (Flora N), 1958, Ja 12,86:6
Williams, William R Mrs (Bertha), 1958, Je 22,76:8
Williams, William S, 1949, N 7,27:3
Williams, William T, 1950, Je 2,23:1
Williams, William W, 1941, Je 29,32:4
Williams, Willoughby H, 1944, O 27,23:3
Williams, Winslow T Mrs, 1952, D 9,33:4
Williams, Wirt A, 1960, Ja 4,29:5
Williams, Wister C, 1952, Ag 8,17:2
Williams, Wynant J, 1950, Mr 2,29:4
Williams, Wythe (funl plans, Jl 15,60:8; funl, Jl 18,-27:4), 1956, Jl 14,15:4
Williams, Yancey S (por), 1938, N 2,23:3
Williams, Zella M, 1953, D 28,21:2
Williams-Bulkeley, Richard, 1942, Jl 9,21:3
Williams-Hunt, P D R, 1953, Je 13,15:6
Williams of Banburgh, Lord (Tom Williams), 1967, Mr 31,37:4
Williams-Taylor, Frederick, 1945, Ag 2,19:5
Williams-Taylor, Jane Lady (cor, D 8,29:1), 1950, D 7,33:2
Williams-Wynn, Watkin, 1949, My 10,25:4
Williams-Wynn, Watkin Sir, 1885, My 31,10:2
Williamson, Adrian M, 1940, S 2,15:4
Williamson, Alan H, 1961, Jl 3,15:5
Williamson, Alex, 1903, Je 4,9:6
Williamson, Alex H, 1961, O 12,29:2
Williamson, Amor J, 1867, Mr 2,3:2
Williamson, Anna W, 1944, Mr 20,17:2
Williamson, Anne, 1938, Je 14,21:5
Williamson, Anne A, 1955, Ag 13,13:2
Williamson, Arthur, 1940, Ap 20,17:6
Williamson, Arthur M, 1953, Ap 18,19:2
Williamson, Arthur T, 1953, My 31,72:4
Williamson, Ben, 1941, Je 25,21:3
Williamson, Butler Mrs, 1952, Ap 30,27:1
Williamson, Charles C, 1965, Ja 13,25:3
Williamson, Charles E, 1963, Ap 6,19:3
Williamson, Charles E Mrs, 1956, Ap 8,84:2
Williamson, Charles H, 1948, N 13,15:5
Williamson, Charles Norris, 1920, O 6,15:5
Williamson, Clarence W Sr, 1958, O 13,29:5
Williamson, Clifton P, 1968, D 24,20:5
Williamson, Cobert P, 1944, F 10,15:5
Williamson, Cornelius T, 1950, Ag 29,27:5
Williamson, Daisy D, 1942, O 26,15:6
Williamson, Donald V, 1949, Ja 1,13:3
Williamson, Dudley, 1948, My 4,26:2
Williamson, E E, 1903, F 25,9:7
Williamson, E F, 1880, D 24,8:1
Williamson, Earl C, 1952, My 30,15:5
Williamson, Earl W, 1948, My 12,27:5
Williamson, Edgar M, 1944, Mr 13,15:2
Williamson, Edison, 1947, Jl 20,44:1
Williamson, Edward J, 1944, Mr 23,19:4
Williamson, Edward Mrs, 1923, Ja 15,15:5
Williamson, Ellen E Mrs, 1940, Ja 5,20:4
Williamson, Emily E Mrs, 1909, Jl 14,7:6
Williamson, Eric de Visme, 1968, My 7,47:2
Williamson, Ezra E, 1945, N 30,23:3
Williamson, Florence Mrs, 1943, Ja 3,42:4
Williamson, Francis John, 1920, Mr 13,9:6
Williamson, Francis S, 1952, O 3,23:4
Williamson, Francis T, 1964, F 8,23:2
Williamson, Frank, 1953, Ja 25,85:2
Williamson, Frank Mrs, 1945, Jl 9,11:6
Williamson, Frederic, 1939, F 28,19:5
Williamson, Frederic E, 1944, S 30,13:1
Williamson, Frederick B Jr, 1957, Jl 29,19:5
Williamson, Frederick B Sr Mrs, 1945, S 8,15:2
Williamson, Frederick E, 1951, N 12,25:4
Williamson, Frederick R (por), 1948, Ja 15,23:2
Williamson, Frederick W, 1942, Jl 15,19:6
Williamson, Garfield, 1945, My 19,19:4
Williamson, George, 1915, Ag 9,7:5; 1950, Mr 2,27:1; 1951, Jl 4,17:4
Williamson, George H, 1938, Mr 19,15:3
Williamson, George M, 1956, My 24,31:4
Williamson, George N, 1905, Ap 29,11:6
Williamson, George P, 1940, Je 23,31:4; 1957, Jl 10, 27:2
Williamson, George Prof, 1968, S 11,47:1
Williamson, George R, 1951, S 7,29:2
Williamson, George S, 1952, Je 18,27:6
Williamson, Gilbert R, 1943, Ja 14,21:2
Williamson, Hale, 1956, Mr 20,23:2
Williamson, Hannah B Mrs, 1941, D 2,24:3
Williamson, Harold L, 1953, Ja 21,31:2
Williamson, Harry, 1953, Ja 25,86:4
Williamson, Harry A, 1946, Ag 30,17:4
Williamson, Helen L, 1959, D 31,21:5
Williamson, Helen M, 1957, Je 11,35:4
Williamson, Hervey C, 1951, F 2,23:3
Williamson, Hervey C Mrs, 1956, O 31,33:5
Williamson, Hugh S, 1965, My 13,37:4
Williamson, I V, 1889, Mr 8,5:2
Williamson, Ira M, 1942, S 5,13:5
Williamson, J C Capt (funl), 1871, Jl 28,5:6
Williamson, J F Rev, 1903, D 6,7:6
Williamson, J Gen, 1883, My 25,5:4
Williamson, J Maynard, 1954, Ap 2,27:2
Williamson, J Robert, 1944, Ja 20,19:2
Williamson, J S, 1932, D 3,20:1
Williamson, Jacob, 1956, Ap 25,35:4
Williamson, Jacob Mrs, 1950, O 26,31:5
Williamson, James E Sr, 1937, Mr 10,23:4
Williamson, James J, 1915, D 16,15:5; 1945, Je 2,15:2
Williamson, James R, 1955, N 19,19:4
Williamson, James T (will), 1958, Mr 19,17:4
Williamson, Jervis C, 1952, Ja 1,25:4
Williamson, Jesse B, 1940, My 2,23:6
Williamson, John, 1885, My 30,5:6; 1941, F 8,15:4; 1943, F 6,13:2; 1949, F 11,23:4
Williamson, John D Jr, 1942, D 27,34:7
Williamson, John E, 1966, Jl 17,68:4
Williamson, John F, 1964, My 29,29:2
Williamson, John G, 1942, Ja 27,21:4
Williamson, John H, 1957, Mr 14,29:2
Williamson, John S, 1953, Je 14,84:2
Williamson, John T, 1958, Ja 9,33:3
Williamson, Linn R, 1944, Je 7,19:3
Williamson, Louis E, 1948, D 1,29:3
Williamson, Louis K Mrs, 1961, Ag 14,25:1
Williamson, Loyal A, 1956, N 2,27:4
Williamson, Luther M Mrs, 1948, Jl 23,19:1
Williamson, Nicholas, 1944, F 24,15:2
Williamson, Otto J, 1947, Ja 7,27:4
Williamson, Paul B, 1955, Ap 14,29:4
Williamson, Percy E, 1943, Ap 14,23:1; 1954, Ja 31, 89:2
Williamson, Percy E Jr, 1961, Ja 31,29:2
Williamson, Percy E Sr Mrs, 1949, N 24,31:6
Williamson, Phoebe E Mrs, 1937, O 9,19:4
Williamson, Pliny W (funl, O 25,16:3), 1958, O 22, 35:3
Williamson, Pliny W Mrs, 1941, Ap 29,19:6
Williamson, R B, 1932, D 11,34:4
Williamson, R S Col, 1882, N 12,9:2
Williamson, Reginald C, 1963, S 17,35:1
Williamson, Richard W, 1955, My 25,33:4
Williamson, Robert, 1949, Mr 15,27:3; 1960, My 17, 37:2
Williamson, Robert D, 1946, Mr 4,23:4; 1963, Ap 14, 92:8
Williamson, Robert G, 1948, My 3,21:2
Williamson, Robert W, 1919, Je 27,15:4
Williamson, Roy E, 1944, D 24,26:3
Williamson, Russell B, 1964, O 4,88:8
Williamson, Samuel T, 1962, Je 19,32:2
Williamson, Sarah F, 1940, Je 11,25:5
Williamson, Stanley, 1955, Je 14,29:5
Williamson, Stanley L, 1965, Ag 18,35:6
Williamson, Susan M, 1949, My 3,25:3
Williamson, Sven J Mrs, 1959, Ja 9,27:2
Williamson, Sydney B, 1939, Ja 14,17:1
Williamson, T G, 1903, Ap 26,3:5
Williamson, Thomas, 1942, Mr 8,42:4
Williamson, Thomas L, 1963, Je 13,33:1
Williamson, Thomas W, 1955, Mr 5,17:5
Williamson, Victor W Mrs, 1963, My 2,35:4
Williamson, W C, 1903, Je 14,7:5
Williamson, W J Rev Dr, 1918, Ag 19,9:8
Williamson, Walter, 1941, Jl 29,15:3
Williamson, Walter H, 1955, Ja 30,84:3
Williamson, William A, 1948, Je 30,25:5
Williamson, William F, 1965, F 10,41:1
Williamson, William H Mrs, 1956, My 10,31:3
Williamson, William H Rev, 1905, Ap 23,9:6
Williamson, William L, 1944, D 29,15:3
Williamson, William T, 1942, D 8,25:5
Williamson, William W, 1938, N 8,23:2
Willians, Roy C, 1958, Ag 17,86:1
Willianson, G DeWitt Mrs, 1950, My 25,29:3
Williard, Harry C, 1939, Ap 27,25:4
Williard, John H, 1943, My 2,45:2
Williard, Lester R, 1966, N 4,39:2
Williasm, Edwin R, 1961, Jl 17,21:4
Williasm, W H, 1947, Ag 27,23:4
Willich, A Maj-Gen, 1878, Ja 24,5:5
Willich, Carl Dr, 1913, S 25,13:6
Willich, Norman A, 1953, Ap 30,34:4
Willich, Theodore, 1964, N 6,38:1
Willicombe, Joseph Sr, 1948, Jl 31,15:6
Willie, Burdell A, 1940, S 1,20:7
Willig, Frederick W, 1947, Je 20,19:3
Willig, Laurent, 1947, Ja 16,25:4
Willig, Lawrence H, 1948, Je 24,25:2
Willig, Louis, 1958, N 23,88:4
Willigerod, Alice, 1951, Mr 6,27:2
Willigerod, William D, 1960, Mr 6,84:4
Willimas, Harley L, 1956, My 5,19:5
Willing, Charles Mrs, 1948, N 9,27:5
Willing, E S Mrs, 1903, Ap 18,9:4
Willing, Edward Shippen, 1906, Ap 11,1:4
Willing, H J, 1903, S 30,9:6
Willing, J Edgar Mrs, 1943, Ag 16,15:4
Willing, J Kent, 1945, Ap 10,19:4
Willing, John T, 1947, Jl 9,23:1
Willing, Joseph K, 1938, Je 5,46:3
Willing, Lionel, 1938, D 4,60:4
Willing, Thomas G, 1946, D 10,31:3
Willingale, William E, 1950, Ap 19,29:5
Willingdon, Marquess of, 1941, Ag 13,17:3
Willingham, Broadus E, 1937, N 28,II,9:1
Willingham, Carl H, 1961, Jl 4,19:4
Willingham, Henry J, 1948, D 5,92:5
Willingham, Joseph H Jr, 1948, D 31,15:2
Willingham, William A, 1945, My 30,19:5
Willinghurst, Charles, 1949, D 15,35:5
Willingmyre, George, 1943, My 10,19:3
Willings, Frederick H, 1953, N 17,31:2
Willings, George C, 1941, F 9,47:6
Willins, Irwin, 1951, Ag 21,4:7
Willinsky, Joyce, 1963, Jl 30,1:2
Willis, A S, 1897, Ja 16,3:1
Willis, Alfred F, 1952, S 21,88:2
Willis, Alonzo, 1959, Jl 3,17:4
Willis, Amelia K Mrs, 1909, F 3,9:4
Willis, Arthur H, 1948, Ag 9,19:1

Willis, Arthur L, 1963, S 27,29:3
Willis, Arthur W, 1941, Ap 8,26:2; 1953, S 24,33:4
Willis, Aylburton T, 1941, Jl 26,15:3
Willis, B Marshall, 1968, Je 1,27:4
Willis, Bailey, 1949, F 21,23:1
Willis, Benedict P, 1960, F 1,27:1
Willis, Charles H, 1951, Ja 29,19:5
Willis, Charles L, 1949, D 7,31:3
Willis, Charlotte, 1960, S 4,68:7
Willis, Clarence A, 1944, My 5,19:5
Willis, Clarence D, 1937, Je 26,17:5
Willis, Clayton E, 1943, Je 15,21:1
Willis, Clodius H, 1964, D 16,44:5
Willis, Don J, 1954, Ag 25,27:4
Willis, Douglas, 1963, Jl 24,31:2
Willis, Edward J, 1941, Jl 12,13:3
Willis, Edward T, 1958, My 5,29:3
Willis, Edwin F, 1939, F 3,15:2
Willis, Ella L Mrs, 1953, Je 28,60:6
Willis, Elvira, 1945, O 26,19:4
Willis, F B, 1928, Mr 31,1:7
Willis, Frank G, 1942, N 12,25:3
Willis, Frank L Mrs, 1959, Je 30,31:2
Willis, Frederick, 1946, Je 20,23:4
Willis, Frederick Llewellyn Hovel Dr, 1914, Ap 14, 11:6
Willis, Frederick M, 1942, S 11,21:6
Willis, George, 1952, Ja 6,92:5
Willis, George Dr, 1924, Mr 26,19:4
Willis, George E, 1948, Mr 27,13:4
Willis, George S Mrs, 1961, F 26,92:2
Willis, Gilbert A, 1941, Ja 18,15:5
Willis, H E Mrs, 1876, Jl 14,1:4
Willis, H Parker Dr (por), 1937, Jl 19,15:1
Willis, Harold B, 1962, Ap 19,31:2
Willis, Harold S, 1958, N 11,29:1
Willis, Harry A, 1948, O 23,15:6
Willis, Harry K, 1939, Ja 3,18:2
Willis, Henry B, 1925, Ag 27,19:5
Willis, Herbert, 1941, Ap 10,23:3
Willis, Humphrey W, 1949, Jl 31,60:3
Willis, J C Dr, 1922, Ap 13,19:5
Willis, J Wirt, 1946, D 28,15:4
Willis, James, 1953, D 15,44:7
Willis, James F, 1952, O 10,25:2
Willis, James H, 1942, My 21,19:6
Willis, Jay B, 1920, D 15,15:4
Willis, John, 1943, F 19,19:3
Willis, John J, 1952, My 7,27:5
Willis, John M, 1961, O 7,48:2; 1962, Jl 24,27:3
Willis, John W, 1925, O 17,15:4
Willis, Jonathan S Rev, 1903, N 25,9:5
Willis, Joseph E, 1951, N 29,33:3
Willis, Joseph Grinnell, 1919, Je 24,13:3
Willis, Josephine (will), 1938, N 1,26:8
Willis, Kirk, 1966, N 18,43:2
Willis, Letitia S, 1924, My 8,19:4
Willis, Loring S, 1949, F 6,76:1
Willis, Mary J Mrs, 1937, Ja 18,17:3
Willis, Merton L, 1945, N 23,23:4
Willis, Morris Mrs, 1949, My 16,21:2
Willis, Morton W, 1953, My 25,25:5
Willis, N E Rev, 1874, S 26,1:5
Willis, N P Mrs, 1904, Mr 27,7:4
Willis, Nathaniel, 1870, My 28,1:3
Willis, Nathaniel Parker, 1867, Ja 22,4:5
Willis, Newell A, 1955, Mr 24,31:4
Willis, O B Rev, 1926, O 24,II,6:7
Willis, Paul H, 1939, S 6,23:5
Willis, R H Mrs, 1945, O 25,21:5
Willis, Raymond E, 1956, Mr 22,35:5
Willis, Raymond S, 1944, Jl 3,11:4
Willis, Richard, 1964, S 6,56:7
Willis, Richard L, 1961, Jl 15,19:5; 1964, S 2,35:1
Willis, Robert A, 1944, N 18,13:2
Willis, Robert E, 1943, N 22,19:5
Willis, Robert M, 1945, Jl 22,37:1
Willis, Roy, 1949, Mr 9,26:3
Willis, S Vincent, 1957, F 24,85:3
Willis, Samuel J, 1947, Ap 25,21:4
Willis, Samuel W W, 1948, Mr 4,25:4
Willis, Simeon S, 1965, Ap 3,29:4
Willis, Theodore B, 1913, My 18,IV,7:6
Willis, Thomas E, 1961, Jl 8,19:5
Willis, Thomas J, 1963, D 14,27:3
Willis, Victor G, 1947, Ag 5,23:5
Willis, W Charles Dr, 1913, Jl 17,7:5
Willis, W E Mrs, 1944, F 19,13:6
Willis, W Spader, 1939, Jl 6,23:2
Willis, Walter I, 1937, D 22,25:2
Willis, Walter J, 1947, Je 29,48:4
Willis, Walter R, 1953, My 30,15:5
Willis, Warren J, 1941, Ap 17,23:3
Willis, Wilfred E, 1950, D 16,30:7
Willis, William, 1950, Ag 11,19:4
Willis, William A, 1945, F 8,19:4
Willis, William A Mrs, 1957, S 1,57:1
Willis, William H, 1962, Ja 25,31:3
Willis, William Henry, 1918, My 7,13:6
Willis, William Henry Sir (Baron Winterstoke), 1911, Ja 30,9:4
Willis-Frost, Lillie E Mrs, 1923, Ag 24,11:5
Willis-O'Connor, H, 1957, Ap 27,19:1
Willison, Charles C, 1943, Ap 1,23:4
Willison, Frank M, 1948, My 21,23:2
Willison, J S Sir, 1927, My 28,17:3
Willison, Lady, 1938, D 16,26:1
Willison, Louis G, 1951, F 10,13:5
Willison, T Blair, 1946, Jl 27,17:1
Willison, Walter A, 1946, S 15,9:7
Williston, Charles S, 1941, N 23,51:6
Williston, Emily G, 1885, Ap 13,5:2
Williston, George A, 1955, S 6,25:2
Williston, Harry S, 1942, Mr 10,19:4
Williston, Samuel, 1874, Jl 20,4:7; 1963, F 19,8:7
Williston, Samuel Wendell, 1918, Ag 31,11:3
Williston, William, 1959, Ag 5,27:4
Willits, A B Rear Adm, 1926, Ja 8,19:5
Willits, Alfred S, 1959, Jl 30,27:5
Willits, Cecelia B Mrs (est acctg), 1965, F 3,9:5
Willits, Charles H, 1942, Ja 5,17:4
Willits, Charles M, 1956, Mr 6,31:4
Willits, Clement, 1941, O 22,23:6
Willits, Frank P, 1945, Jl 14,11:8
Willits, Frank P Mrs, 1947, D 22,21:1
Willits, George Sidney Rear-Adm, 1917, My 5,13:6
Willits, Henry M, 1950, Mr 4,17:4
Willits, Sanford, 1948, S 16,29:1
Willits, Sylvia B Mrs, 1939, Je 2,23:1
Willkie, Edward E, 1956, O 16,33:3
Willkie, H Frederick, 1959, D 29,25:4
Willkie, Henrietta Mrs, 1940, Mr 11,15:3
Willkie, Julia E, 1943, O 8,19:5
Willkie, Wendell L, 1944, O 8,1:1
Willkins, W T, 1903, S 20,7:6
Willman, James Q, 1903, Jl 26,7:6
Willman, Leon K Rev Dr, 1937, Je 12,15:6
Willman, Walter J, 1958, S 9,35:5
Willmann, A, 1878, Mr 5,4:6
Willmann, Florence L E, 1939, Mr 26,III,7:2
Willmann, Lillian M, 1946, Ja 16,23:3
Willmann, William G, 1938, Mr 6,II,8:5
Willment, Milton A, 1956, S 22,17:5
Willmer, David, 1958, Jl 20,67:3
Willmont, Robert H, 1937, S 5,II,7:1
Willmore, Arthur, 1945, F 24,11:4
Willmore, Cyrus C, 1949, Ap 11,25:4
Willmore, Lizzie, 1877, Je 14,4:6
Willmot, Clarence, 1948, Ag 21,15:4
Willmot, Laura V, 1943, O 13,23:1
Willmot, Walter A, 1947, O 10,25:3
Willmott, Thomas E, 1943, Ap 29,21:4
Willmsen, Carl, 1944, S 1,13:5
Willner, Abraham J Mrs, 1951, S 23,85:4
Willner, Benjamin, 1956, My 25,23:2
Willner, David C, 1959, F 28,19:5
Willner, Joseph M Mrs, 1964, Ag 9,76:1
Willner, Leon L, 1960, S 13,37:4
Willner, Louis, 1944, Ja 30,38:4
Willner, Samuel J, 1964, Ag 27,33:3
Willner, Victor, 1960, Mr 14,29:2
Willock, Alice J Mrs, 1939, Je 1,25:2
Willock, Franklin J, 1952, Je 28,20:6
Willock, Frederick J, 1941, Ag 5,19:5
Willock, Michael, 1963, Jl 26,54:1
Willock, William W, 1939, Mr 9,21:4
Willon, Joseph (por), 1944, My 12,19:3
Willoughby, Barrett (Mrs R Prosser), 1959, Jl 31,24:4
Willoughby, Benjamin M, 1940, Je 30,33:3
Willoughby, C H, 1880, F 5,5:4
Willoughby, Charles C, 1943, Ap 22,23:5
Willoughby, Charles G, 1951, Je 9,19:5
Willoughby, Charles H, 1951, Je 13,29:6
Willoughby, Clifford P, 1956, Ap 22,85:3
Willoughby, Edward, 1948, My 13,25:4
Willoughby, Edward Mrs, 1947, S 24,23:3
Willoughby, Edwin E, 1959, O 4,86:6
Willoughby, Francis C, 1955, Ag 14,81:1
Willoughby, Frank N, 1960, Mr 2,37:2
Willoughby, Frederick J Mrs, 1948, F 17,26:2
Willoughby, H Hamilton, 1939, N 12,48:8
Willoughby, Harold R, 1962, F 3,21:4
Willoughby, Hugh L, 1939, Ap 5,25:3
Willoughby, John B, 1943, F 21,32:8
Willoughby, John T, 1914, Ja 3,11:5
Willoughby, Philip A, 1962, Mr 2,30:4
Willoughby, Raymond C, 1946, F 19,25:4
Willoughby, Westel W, 1945, Mr 27,19:4
Willoughby, William F, 1945, Mr 2,19:4
Willoughby, William G, 1949, Ag 17,23:2
Willoughby, William H, 1946, O 22,25:2
Willoughby, Woodbury, 1964, Mr 19,33:4
Willox, Alexander, 1947, F 27,21:4
Willrath, Theodore F (por), 1946, My 25,15:5
Willridge, Edwin, 1951, Ja 7,77:2
Wills, Albert P Dr, 1937, Ap 18,II,8:4
Wills, Arthur L, 1946, S 14,7:5
Wills, C Harold, 1940, D 31,15:6
Wills, Charles J, 1914, Jl 2,9:6
Wills, Charles R, 1951, N 17,17:4
Wills, Charles S, 1959, D 22,31:4
Wills, Charles T, 1915, S 1,9:6
Wills, Charles T Mrs, 1949, Mr 13,23:4
Wills, D H, 1880, S 4,5:2
Wills, David, 1922, N 23,21:6
Wills, David C, 1925, O 22,25:3
Wills, David Crawford, 1925, O 23,23:4
Wills, Drusilla, 1951, Ag 12,77:3
Wills, Ell N, 1947, O 5,68:2
Wills, Ernest C, 1951, Ja 28,76:5
Wills, Ernest E D Mrs, 1946, F 5,23:3
Wills, Ernest S, 1958, Ja 15,29:3
Wills, Ernest Salter Sir, 1925, F 13,17:5
Wills, F M, 1903, My 7,9:6
Wills, Floyd M, 1944, Ap 30,46:2
Wills, Francis R, 1966, My 23,41:3
Wills, Frank A, 1941, Je 21,17:2
Wills, Frederick Mrs (G Tiemer-Willie), 1967, Mr 22,47:2
Wills, Frederick Sir, 1909, F 19,9:5
Wills, Furman R, 1937, Mr 1,19:2
Wills, George B Mrs, 1944, Ap 19,23:1
Wills, George E Mrs, 1939, S 25,19:5
Wills, George J Mrs, 1948, N 10,29:4
Wills, George S, 1956, F 29,31:2
Wills, Gilbert A H (Lord Dulverton), 1956, D 2,86:2
Wills, Guy O, 1964, Mr 11,39:2
Wills, H E, 1932, Mr 27,II,5:5
Wills, Harry, 1958, D 22,2:5
Wills, Henry T Mrs, 1963, S 27,29:1
Wills, Henry Tarleton, 1914, Ap 27,11:6
Wills, Henry W, 1961, D 6,47:3
Wills, Joseph J, 1939, S 27,25:1
Wills, L Clifford, 1940, N 12,23:3
Wills, Louis A, 1954, F 20,17:6
Wills, N K, 1951, D 11,33:3
Wills, Nat M (funl, D 12,15:5), 1917, D 10,15:5
Wills, R Reed, 1938, Ja 22,18:1
Wills, Royal B, 1962, Ja 11,33:4
Wills, Vanleer, 1947, Mr 20,27:3
Wills, W G, 1891, D 15,2:6
Wills, William A Maj, 1937, Ap 3,19:4
Wills, William H, 1946, Mr 6,28:2
Willsea, Louis P, 1940, D 1,62:5
Willsea, Morgan L, 1940, F 13,23:3
Willsey, William J, 1960, D 25,42:2
Willshaw, Arthur, 1952, Ja 29,25:2
Willshaw, Thomas H, 1918, Jl 27,9:5
Willsie, Luther B, 1938, F 26,15:4
Willson, A E, 1931, Ag 25,21:1
Willson, Albert C, 1944, O 27,23:2
Willson, Albert Daniels Rev, 1920, Ag 22,20:5
Willson, Beckles (por), 1942, S 22,21:3
Willson, Edward T, 1940, Ja 15,15:3
Willson, Frances H Mrs (Peaches Browning),(will, S 22,7:1), 1956, Ag 24,19:2
Willson, Francis A, 1937, D 27,15:2
Willson, Frank A, 1949, My 6,25:5
Willson, Frank C, 1960, Mr 7,29:4
Willson, George L, 1948, My 11,25:2
Willson, George L Mrs, 1919, S 15,11:6
Willson, George T, 1950, Je 19,21:5
Willson, Harry G, 1949, Ja 15,17:6
Willson, Hubert E, 1961, Je 2,31:1
Willson, James C (por), 1948, My 3,21:5
Willson, John G, 1925, S 21,19:7
Willson, John G Mrs, 1940, Ja 3,22:2
Willson, Joseph H, 1950, Ap 4,29:3
Willson, Julia C, 1942, Jl 19,31:3
Willson, Lillian A, 1954, D 16,37:3
Willson, Meredity Mrs, 1966, D 7,47:4
Willson, Nettie E Mrs, 1940, Ja 2,19:4
Willson, Osborn, 1961, Ja 21,21:2
Willson, Paul B, 1962, Ja 4,33:2
Willson, Paul W, 1960, Ap 9,23:4
Willson, Pierpont Mrs, 1943, N 29,19:5
Willson, Robert, 1948, O 22,25:2
Willson, Robert H, 1955, D 13,39:5
Willson, Robert Mrs, 1942, Ag 22,13:2
Willson, Robert Z Mrs, 1953, Ag 29,17:5
Willson, Russell (por), 1948, Jl 7,23:1
Willson, Samuel H, 1940, D 29,24:6
Willson, Sidney L, 1944, O 11,21:4
Willson, Wallace C, 1946, D 15,77:1
Willstaetter, Richard (por), 1942, Ag 4,20:2
Willumsen, Jens F, 1958, Ap 6,88:7
Willvonseder, Ernest, 1956, F 1,31:5
Willy, George Sr, 1959, Ja 29,27:4
Willy, John, 1944, D 25,19:4
Willyoung, Arthur K, 1945, Je 8,19:4
Willys, J N, 1935, Ag 26,15:1
Willys, John N Mrs, 1945, Ja 19,19:4
Wilm, Alfred Prof, 1937, Ag 12,19:3
Wilmann, Edward, 1937, My 3,19:4
Wilmarth, Agnes Mrs, 1919, Mr 25,13:4
Wilmarth, Mark, 1941, My 7,25:4
Wilmarth, Martin L C, 1953, Je 15,29:5
Wilmer, Antoninus Rev, 1915, N 19,11:6
Wilmer, Edward G, 1962, Ag 25,19:1
Wilmer, Eric G, 1958, My 26,29:4
Wilmer, Harry B, 1943, Ja 17,44:4
Wilmer, J B P Bp, 1878, D 3,4:7
Wilmer, Sidney, 1941, Je 26,23:2
Wilmer, W H, 1936, Mr 13,23:1
Wilmer, William N, 1907, O 15,9:4
Wilmerding, A Clinton, 1953, D 14,31:4
Wilmerding, Anne C Mrs, 1954, My 1,15:3
Wilmerding, Charles H, 1940, Ap 27,15:1
Wilmerding, Charles Henry, 1917, N 29,13:5

Wilmerding, E Coster, 1950, Jl 26,25:5
Wilmerding, F S, 1877, My 19,10:5
Wilmerding, Gustave Larmann, 1909, Ag 12,7:5
Wilmerding, Henry A, 1945, Ap 1,36:4
Wilmerding, John C, 1903, D 12,9:5; 1911, S 11,9:4; 1965, Ag 11,35:2
Wilmerding, John Currie, 1923, O 1,7:3
Wilmerding, Louise Canning, 1917, S 27,13:6
Wilmerding, Lucius, 1949, Jl 16,13:4
Wilmerding, Lucius K, 1922, D 9,13:4
Wilmerding, T T, 1885, Ja 6,5:3
Wilmerding, Thomas A Mrs, 1914, Mr 9,9:2
Wilmerding, William E, 1948, My 11,25:3
Wilmes, Joseph, 1941, N 19,23:3
Wilmeth, James L, 1959, Ap 25,21:6
Wilmington, Martin W, 1964, My 2,27:4
Wilmont, Alden, 1942, Ap 13,16:2
Wilmont, Aug, 1939, Jl 24,15:5
Wilmot, Alfred J Mrs, 1947, N 1,15:5
Wilmot, Charles E, 1903, S 28,5:3
Wilmot, Charles R, 1945, O 16,23:1
Wilmot, Chester, 1954, Ja 11,1:6
Wilmot, Clifford R, 1963, S 24,29:1
Wilmot, David, 1868, Mr 20,2:2
Wilmot, E P Dr, 1923, Jl 25,11:6
Wilmot, Elizabeth B, 1937, N 4,25:5
Wilmot, Frank, 1944, D 28,19:2
Wilmot, Frederick G, 1949, Ap 27,27:1
Wilmot, Harrison F, 1938, My 25,23:4
Wilmot, Irving R, 1963, Jl 26,25:4
Wilmot, James E, 1947, Ja 26,53:3
Wilmot, John H, 1945, N 10,17:5
Wilmot, John T, 1952, Ap 3,35:2
Wilmot, L Howard, 1940, Ap 24,23:5
Wilmot, Mary V Mrs, 1938, S 7,36:4
Wilmot, Nellie M, 1943, Mr 13,13:2
Wilmot, William A, 1944, N 11,13:3
Wilmot of Selmeston, John, 1964, Jl 24,27:1
Wilmoth, Grover C, 1951, F 2,24:2
Wilmott, Alfred J, 1950, Ja 29,68:5
Wilmott, George V Sr, 1951, F 27,27:4
Wilms, John H, 1938, N 28,15:4
Wilner, Anna, 1940, F 11,48:2
Wilner, Bernard, 1941, S 20,17:6
Wilner, Ellis H, 1963, Je 21,29:2
Wilner, Isidore, 1955, Je 23,29:1
Wilner, Max (por), 1946, My 13,21:2
Wilner, Max, 1956, Ap 16,27:3
Wilner, Max R, 1958, Ja 11,17:1
Wilner, Robert F, 1960, Mr 25,27:1
Wilpon, Julius T, 1960, Ap 17,92:5
Wilputte, Louis N Mrs, 1939, D 5,27:2
Wilsdorf, Hans, 1960, Jl 8,21:2
Wilsea, Eugene, 1951, Ag 3,21:4
Wilser, Bernhardt, 1948, N 15,25:6
Wilsey, Edmund, 1903, Ap 1,9:5
Wilsey, Edwin S, 1952, S 20,15:2
Wilsey, Frank D, 1941, My 28,25:3
Wilsey, Fred H, 1948, Ap 7,25:2
Wilsey, George O, 1943, Ap 14,23:3
Wilsey, Irvin H, 1943, Jl 25,31:2
Wilsey, J L Capt, 1903, Je 29,7:6
Wilsey, James, 1959, F 10,33:2
Wilshaw, Edward Sir, 1968, Mr 4,37:4
Wilshire, Frank W, 1949, Mr 19,15:2
Wilshire, George, 1944, Je 24,13:4
Wilshire, Joseph, 1951, N 18,90:1
Wilsnack, Theodore P, 1941, F 1,17:5
Wilson, A B, 1903, Ap 21,9:5
Wilson, A Hughes Jr, 1962, S 4,31:6
Wilson, A Peter, 1957, Je 6,31:3
Wilson, Agnes Williamson, 1920, O 14,13:1
Wilson, Alan, 1908, Jl 8,7:3
Wilson, Albert A, 1907, O 22,9:4
Wilson, Albert D, 1951, Ja 19,25:4
Wilson, Albert E, 1955, Je 18,17:4
Wilson, Albert F, 1940, Je 27,23:6
Wilson, Albert H, 1942, F 24,21:4; 1958, F 13,29:2
Wilson, Albert J M, 1959, Ag 21,21:5
Wilson, Albert J Sr, 1953, N 7,17:4
Wilson, Alberta Mrs, 1948, N 25,31:4
Wilson, Alex R, 1941, Ag 20,19:4; 1941, O 13,17:4
Wilson, Alex S, 1954, D 29,29:1
Wilson, Alexander, 1964, Ja 4,23:2
Wilson, Alexander M Jr, 1943, Je 16,21:3
Wilson, Alexander Mrs, 1945, Ag 6,15:5
Wilson, Alfred B, 1945, Mr 22,23:1
Wilson, Alfred G, 1962, Ag 8,87:2
Wilson, Alfred G Mrs, 1967, S 20,47:1
Wilson, Algot, 1945, S 24,19:2
Wilson, Alice R, 1940, Ja 28,33:1
Wilson, Alonzo E, 1949, Je 19,68:1
Wilson, Alphesus W, 1916, N 22,13:6
Wilson, Alvin, 1938, Je 2,23:2
Wilson, Amelia E, 1939, Mr 15,23:4
Wilson, Andrew, 1941, N 11,23:3; 1952, S 11,31:4; 1965, Ap 23,36:1
Wilson, Andrew C, 1952, My 29,27:2
Wilson, Andrew F, 1938, F 5,15:4
Wilson, Andrew Jr Mrs, 1946, Mr 17,45:1
Wilson, Andrew K, 1940, Ja 15,15:5
Wilson, Andrew Mrs, 1947, Mr 19,25:4; 1951, Ja 12, 27:2
Wilson, Anna D Mrs, 1948, D 12,93:1
Wilson, Anna F, 1943, S 14,23:5
Wilson, Anna M Mrs, 1944, Je 14,19:5
Wilson, Archdale Gen Sir, 1874, My 11,1:7
Wilson, Archibald S Mrs, 1952, Ja 19,15:3
Wilson, Archie F, 1960, Ag 24,29:1
Wilson, Arminet T, 1964, D 9,50:6
Wilson, Arnold, 1952, Ja 5,11:3
Wilson, Arthur, 1909, O 22,7:5; 1949, Ap 14,25:2; 1951, D 8,11:4; 1954, Mr 27,17:2
Wilson, Arthur A, 1960, Ja 30,21:3
Wilson, Arthur B, 1938, Je 7,23:4
Wilson, Arthur C, 1957, D 31,17:5
Wilson, Arthur D, 1947, Ja 30,25:3
Wilson, Arthur E, 1955, Ja 14,21:3
Wilson, Arthur H, 1963, My 11,25:5
Wilson, Arthur J, 1948, N 12,24:2
Wilson, Arthur Knyvet Sir, 1921, My 26,13:4
Wilson, Arthur M, 1951, Jl 25,23:2
Wilson, Arthur P, 1965, Ag 14,23:4
Wilson, Arthur R, 1956, Ag 12,85:1
Wilson, Arthur S, 1938, Ap 13,25:6
Wilson, Arthur W, 1942, Ja 23,19:4
Wilson, Ashton F, 1952, Mr 16,91:1
Wilson, Augusta Evans Mrs, 1909, My 10,9:3
Wilson, B A, 1950, N 25,13:6
Wilson, B Brittain, 1965, Je 9,47:4
Wilson, Barnett, 1907, Ag 15,7:6
Wilson, Barton T, 1948, S 9,27:2
Wilson, Benjamin, 1939, Ag 17,21:4
Wilson, Benjamin Lee, 1911, Je 24,9:3
Wilson, Benjamin W, 1910, Ag 14,II,9:5
Wilson, Bennett A Mrs, 1938, N 29,23:2
Wilson, Bernard R Mrs, 1963, Ag 11,84:8
Wilson, Bert, 1943, Mr 15,13:4; 1955, N 6,86:7
Wilson, Bertram E, 1940, Ap 26,21:4
Wilson, Billy Col, 1874, N 16,5:2
Wilson, Bina J Mrs, 1950, Ja 31,23:4
Wilson, Bingham T, 1937, S 25,17:3
Wilson, Blanche L Mrs, 1945, F 27,19:1
Wilson, Bob, 1958, Mr 9,86:5
Wilson, Boyd, 1959, Mr 2,27:1
Wilson, Brayton F, 1940, Jl 28,27:1
Wilson, Brewer, 1952, N 20,31:5
Wilson, Bruno, 1951, F 22,31:5
Wilson, Bryce, 1945, D 7,21:1
Wilson, Burriss G, 1962, D 6,43:2
Wilson, C C, 1944, Je 28,12:8
Wilson, C Haines, 1942, O 18,53:1
Wilson, C L, 1878, Mr 13,4:7
Wilson, Calvin M, 1939, N 7,28:6
Wilson, Carey, 1962, F 2,30:4
Wilson, Carey Mrs (C Geraghty), 1966, Jl 8,35:4
Wilson, Carl H, 1940, S 15,48:7
Wilson, Carl S, 1965, Mr 11,33:4
Wilson, Carolyn, 1961, N 13,31:4
Wilson, Carroll A, 1947, Je 28,13:6
Wilson, Catherine M, 1957, Ja 5,17:4
Wilson, Cecil, 1955, Mr 11,25:1
Wilson, Cecil W, 1937, Jl 27,21:4
Wilson, Cecil W Bp, 1937, Ag 19,20:1
Wilson, Charles, 1909, Jl 26,7:5; 1943, F 17,21:2; 1946, Ap 14,46:1; 1964, Ag 13,32:5
Wilson, Charles A, 1907, O 8,11:6; 1941, D 19,25:1; 1942, S 21,15:3; 1955, My 11,31:4
Wilson, Charles A Gen, 1913, S 23,11:7
Wilson, Charles A Mrs, 1948, Ap 23,23:4; 1948, Je 24, 26:2
Wilson, Charles B, 1937, Jl 24,15:4; 1938, F 22,21:4; 1941, Ag 19,21:3
Wilson, Charles C, 1938, Ag 22,13:3; 1944, D 16,15:4; 1948, Ag 14,13:5
Wilson, Charles Capt, 1915, S 9,11:6
Wilson, Charles D, 1952, F 6,29:2
Wilson, Charles E, 1949, Ja 26,25:3
Wilson, Charles E (est acctg), 1962, Je 9,26:2
Wilson, Charles Erwin (trbs, S 27,37:1; funl, S 30,-25:1), 1961, S 27,1:1
Wilson, Charles George, 1906, My 19,11:6
Wilson, Charles H, 1937, Ag 9,19:4; 1943, Mr 3,23:2; 1948, My 14,23:3; 1949, Mr 11,26:2
Wilson, Charles H Mrs, 1949, Ag 6,17:5; 1955, S 6, 25:1
Wilson, Charles Henry (Lord Nunburnholme), 1907, O 28,9:5
Wilson, Charles J, 1967, Ag 8,39:3
Wilson, Charles L, 1952, Mr 12,27:1
Wilson, Charles O, 1955, N 2,35:5
Wilson, Charles P Sr, 1950, Ag 10,25:3
Wilson, Charles R, 1940, Jl 25,17:5; 1942, Ja 30,19:6; 1951, Mr 15,29:2; 1955, My 10,29:4
Wilson, Charles R Mrs, 1951, Je 29,21:5
Wilson, Charles S, 1954, Ja 25,19:1
Wilson, Charles T R, 1959, N 16,31:5
Wilson, Charles W, 1939, Mr 16,23:1; 1945, Ja 21, 39:2; 1951, Ap 10,27:4
Wilson, Charles W Capt, 1912, Ja 8,13:5
Wilson, Charles W S, 1948, Ag 7,15:4
Wilson, Christian, 1947, Mr 12,25:3
Wilson, Christopher W Maj, 1916, S 14,7:7
Wilson, Claggett, 1952, My 21,27:1
Wilson, Clare, 1964, Ap 7,35:2
Wilson, Clarence, 1958, Mr 29,17:2
Wilson, Clarence D, 1945, F 3,11:1
Wilson, Clarence E, 1949, Ap 26,25:3
Wilson, Clarence H, 1952, Ap 3,35:5
Wilson, Clarence Mrs, 1956, Ja 6,23:2
Wilson, Clarence T (por), 1939, F 17,19:1
Wilson, Clarke L, 1957, D 31,17:1
Wilson, Clifford B (por), 1943, Ja 3,42:3
Wilson, Clifford C Mrs, 1955, D 2,27:1
Wilson, Clifton W, 1959, F 15,86:5
Wilson, Comar, 1961, F 16,31:2
Wilson, Cornelius, 1918, F 11,9:4
Wilson, Curtiss A, 1943, Jl 27,17:4
Wilson, Cuthbert E, 1944, Ja 5,17:5
Wilson, Cyrus J Mrs, 1947, Mr 16,60:5
Wilson, D Palmer, 1943, Mr 29,16:2
Wilson, D Wright, 1965, Jl 15,29:2
Wilson, Daniel Leet, 1916, N 11,9:1
Wilson, Daniel S, 1945, Ag 15,19:2
Wilson, Daniel T, 1937, Ag 8,II,6:8
Wilson, David, 1923, My 13,8:2; 1925, Ja 21,21:3; 1946, Ap 12,27:3
Wilson, David A, 1966, Jl 9,27:4
Wilson, David C, 1958, Jl 18,21:4
Wilson, David H, 1955, S 28,35:5
Wilson, David H Mrs, 1920, Mr 19,13:4
Wilson, David L, 1965, My 20,43:1
Wilson, David M, 1946, Ap 23,21:3; 1958, D 8,31:4; 1961, D 5,43:1
Wilson, David Maj, 1911, O 8,II,13:5
Wilson, David R (por), 1949, Mr 13,76:1
Wilson, Diana, 1937, O 29,21:3
Wilson, Don, 1966, Je 20,45:1
Wilson, Donald, 1951, Mr 22,31:4
Wilson, Donald B, 1954, Ap 15,29:3
Wilson, Dorothy E, 1956, Je 28,18:6
Wilson, Douglas E, 1951, S 18,32:4
Wilson, Douglas H, 1957, S 21,19:4
Wilson, Drayton E, 1943, D 6,23:3
Wilson, Dudley A, 1953, My 15,23:2
Wilson, Dwight R Mrs, 1967, Ja 17,39:4
Wilson, Dwight R Sr, 1966, N 20,88:5
Wilson, E W, 1927, F 7,1:4; 1940, F 3,13:6
Wilson, E Waring, 1939, Ja 13,19:4
Wilson, Earl B, 1954, D 5,88:6
Wilson, Earl H, 1939, N 19,38:6
Wilson, Earl M, 1948, Ag 19,21:2
Wilson, Earle E, 1946, Je 28,21:2
Wilson, Ebin, 1948, D 19,76:5
Wilson, Edgar, 1938, Ap 7,23:5
Wilson, Edgar H, 1956, D 11,39:3
Wilson, Edgar M Mrs, 1946, Jl 4,19:6
Wilson, Edgar P Mrs, 1948, Ag 13,15:3
Wilson, Edith H M Mrs, 1939, Je 23,19:4
Wilson, Edmund, 1923, My 16,19:5
Wilson, Edmund B (por), 1939, Mr 4,15:1
Wilson, Edmund LeRoy, 1968, N 15,47:1
Wilson, Edmund Mrs, 1951, F 4,76:3
Wilson, Edmund W, 1955, Ag 16,49:3
Wilson, Edward, 1946, D 18,30:2
Wilson, Edward A, 1924, D 26,15:5
Wilson, Edward A Sr, 1952, Ap 26,23:5
Wilson, Edward B, 1939, My 9,23:4
Wilson, Edward Bp, 1908, Je 4,7:7
Wilson, Edward F, 1939, My 6,17:2
Wilson, Edward H (por), 1942, N 27,24:3
Wilson, Edward H, 1950, Ag 28,17:4; 1952, D 16,31:5
Wilson, Edward J, 1949, Jl 21,26:2; 1958, Mr 7,23:5
Wilson, Edward L, 1903, Je 25,7:6
Wilson, Edward R, 1939, O 27,23:2
Wilson, Edward T, 1957, D 29,48:7
Wilson, Edwin B, 1950, Ja 22,78:2; 1953, Ag 4,21:5; 1964, D 29,27:2
Wilson, Eileen, 1942, S 13,53:1
Wilson, Elbert A, 1954, Jl 21,27:5
Wilson, Eleanor V, 1951, D 3,31:4
Wilson, Elias, 1909, S 10,9:5
Wilson, Elisa E Mrs, 1967, Jl 10,28:8
Wilson, Eliza Anna, 1925, Ap 16,21:5
Wilson, Elizabeth, 1957, Ag 18,82:1
Wilson, Elizabeth C Mrs, 1942, Mr 3,23:5
Wilson, Elizabeth L Mrs, 1946, My 26,32:7
Wilson, Elizabeth Mrs, 1941, My 17,17:1
Wilson, Elkin C Mrs (M Matyas), 1963, Ap 21,86:6
Wilson, Ellen A Mrs, 1939, Ja 28,15:3
Wilson, Ellery L, 1938, Je 27,17:3
Wilson, Elliott, 1962, Jl 15,60:3
Wilson, Elmo C, 1968, Mr 11,37:1
Wilson, Emily R A Mrs, 1942, Jl 10,17:2
Wilson, Emily S, 1941, Ja 26,37:1
Wilson, Emmet H, 1951, D 20,31:4
Wilson, Enus, 1937, My 30,18:3
Wilson, Epiphanius Rev, 1916, My 17,11:5
Wilson, Erasmus Sir, 1884, Ag 15,5:3
Wilson, Erastus William Maj-Gen, 1922, My 16,19:5
Wilson, Eric M, 1960, Jl 6,33:2
Wilson, Erle N, 1950, S 18,23:4
Wilson, Ernest D, 1958, O 20,29:5
Wilson, Ernest E, 1947, Mr 16,60:2
Wilson, Errett I, 1951, Mr 19,27:2
Wilson, Ethel Mrs, 1937, S 9,12:5
Wilson, Ethelbert, 1903, My 17,7:6
Wilson, Eugene, 1949, Ja 22,13:3
Wilson, Eugene A, 1939, N 28,26:2

Wilson, Eugene S, 1937, D 20,27:3
Wilson, Eva, 1956, Je 4,29:5
Wilson, Evan M Jr, 1964, Jl 2,31:4
Wilson, Everett, 1921, Je 1,17:4
Wilson, Everett R, 1947, O 14,28:3
Wilson, Everett W, 1938, Ap 26,21:1
Wilson, Everitt W, 1958, My 18,87:1
Wilson, F, 1935, O 8,23:1
Wilson, F M, 1932, O 13,19:4
Wilson, F M Lt-Col, 1875, S 7,1:4
Wilson, Fay (Mule), 1937, Jl 19,15:4
Wilson, Ferdinand S, 1940, My 18,15:4
Wilson, Ferman, 1961, Ja 30,23:4
Wilson, Findley M, 1958, Mr 3,27:2
Wilson, Florence Mary (Florence Mary Austral), 1968, My 17,44:1
Wilson, Forest B, 1950, My 2,29:2
Wilson, Forrest, 1942, My 11,15:5
Wilson, Frances M, 1959, Ja 7,33:2
Wilson, Francis C, 1952, Ja 18,27:3
Wilson, Francis D, 1939, O 26,23:3; 1963, S 17,35:4
Wilson, Francis French, 1915, Ap 7,13:3
Wilson, Francis Henry, 1910, S 26,13:6
Wilson, Francis M, 1947, Ja 1,34:2
Wilson, Francis Mrs, 1915, N 19,11:5; 1960, Jl 25,23:3
Wilson, Francis S, 1951, Mr 15,29:4
Wilson, Francis V, 1938, Ap 19,21:4
Wilson, Frank, 1952, Jl 28,15:4
Wilson, Frank B, 1946, F 1,24:3
Wilson, Frank C Sr, 1959, Ag 15,17:2
Wilson, Frank E, 1944, F 17,19:2
Wilson, Frank H, 1940, Ja 26,17:5; 1949, Ap 3,76:3; 1956, F 17,23:1
Wilson, Frank L Rev Dr, 1922, F 28,19:3
Wilson, Frank Mrs, 1956, Jl 17,21:1
Wilson, Frank N, 1952, S 12,21:5
Wilson, Frank P, 1950, Mr 9,29:4; 1961, D 27,25:7; 1963, My 31,25:2
Wilson, Frank P Mrs, 1960, O 6,41:5
Wilson, Frank R, 1960, D 6,37:2
Wilson, Frank R Mrs, 1955, N 9,33:1
Wilson, Frank W, 1940, Ap 3,23:2
Wilson, Frank W Mrs, 1946, D 10,32:2
Wilson, Franklin B, 1949, My 12,31:3
Wilson, Franklin H Sr, 1952, Je 16,17:4
Wilson, Franklin S, 1905, My 7,7:3
Wilson, Fred, 1951, Jl 13,21:3
Wilson, Fred C, 1949, N 27,105:1
Wilson, Fred L, 1937, N 27,17:4
Wilson, Frederic N Mrs, 1940, My 31,19:4
Wilson, Frederick, 1949, Je 14,31:1
Wilson, Frederick A Mrs, 1952, Je 16,17:4
Wilson, Frederick J, 1946, My 21,24:2
Wilson, Frederick N, 1939, N 16,24:2
Wilson, Frederick V Z, 1945, N 2,19:1
Wilson, G Howard, 1958, D 8,31:5
Wilson, G Lloyd, 1956, Ap 12,31:1
Wilson, G Searing, 1940, O 7,18:2
Wilson, G T, 1933, S 30,15:1
Wilson, G W, 1931, D 25,21:5
Wilson, Garret H Mrs, 1959, S 19,23:5
Wilson, George, 1872, Ap 17,8:4; 1908, O 9,9:4; 1940, Je 7,23:1
Wilson, George (A Ensom), 1954, Ag 4,21:3
Wilson, George, 1959, Mr 24,39:1
Wilson, George A, 1937, F 1,19:2; 1941, O 6,17:6; 1947, D 3,29:3; 1950, Ja 6,22:4; 1953, S 9,29:2; 1964, My 13,47:6; 1967, D 19,47:1
Wilson, George B, 1949, D 5,23:5
Wilson, George Baird, 1909, Ja 18,9:4
Wilson, George C Prof, 1925, Ja 13,19:5
Wilson, George D, 1963, Ag 6,31:3
Wilson, George E, 1961, O 11,47:4
Wilson, George E Jr, 1947, Jl 12,13:6
Wilson, George F, 1942, F 16,17:4
Wilson, George G, 1951, My 2,31:5
Wilson, George H, 1948, D 29,21:3; 1950, My 15,21:3
Wilson, George H Mrs, 1967, S 1,31:3
Wilson, George J, 1967, Mr 8,46:1
Wilson, George L, 1944, F 1,19:4
Wilson, George P Mrs, 1950, F 3,24:2
Wilson, George R, 1951, Jl 30,17:4; 1957, S 10,33:4
Wilson, George R Mrs, 1966, D 24,19:6
Wilson, George R Sr, 1958, N 3,37:5
Wilson, George S, 1942, Ag 22,13:5; 1954, Jl 16,21:2
Wilson, George W, 1909, N 27,9:4; 1945, Je 6,21:2; 1947, N 12,27:3; 1958, Je 21,19:6; 1967, S 26,47:2
Wilson, George Wesley, 1925, Ap 23,21:1
Wilson, Georgeanna Mrs, 1941, Jl 20,31:1
Wilson, Gerald W, 1959, N 24,37:4
Wilson, Gill R, 1966, S 9,45:4
Wilson, Grafton Lee, 1968, D 20,42:5
Wilson, Graham L, 1937, Mr 22,23:2
Wilson, Grove, 1954, O 12,27:2
Wilson, Gus, 1951, Jl 28,11:5
Wilson, Guy F, 1940, D 29,24:6
Wilson, H, 1929, Ap 17,27:3
Wilson, H Augustus Dr, 1919, Ap 17,11:5
Wilson, H Bryan Mrs, 1949, Ja 24,19:5
Wilson, H Cornwell, 1916, Je 16,13:5
Wilson, H H, 1966, D 31,19:5
Wilson, H L, 1932, D 23,17:1
Wilson, Halsey W, 1954, Mr 2,25:1
Wilson, Halsey W Mrs, 1955, S 10,17:3
Wilson, Hamilton M, 1955, F 25,21:5
Wilson, Hannah Mrs, 1940, My 1,23:2
Wilson, Harold, 1954, O 26,27:1
Wilson, Harold A, 1964, O 16,39:2
Wilson, Harold C, 1950, N 26,90:4
Wilson, Harold K, 1958, N 29,21:4
Wilson, Harold M, 1960, N 29,37:1
Wilson, Harold R, 1959, F 26,31:4
Wilson, Harold S, 1955, Je 22,30:1
Wilson, Harold V, 1951, My 19,15:5
Wilson, Harriette S Mrs, 1948, Mr 24,25:5
Wilson, Harris, 1925, Ap 1,23:4
Wilson, Harrison, 1948, F 7,15:4
Wilson, Harry A Sr, 1957, S 10,33:4
Wilson, Harry B, 1956, F 18,19:4
Wilson, Harry D, 1948, Ja 8,25:3
Wilson, Harry E, 1948, S 11,15:5
Wilson, Harry E S, 1943, Je 6,42:5
Wilson, Harry F, 1950, My 30,17:2
Wilson, Harry L (por), 1939, Je 30,19:3
Wilson, Harry L Prof, 1913, F 25,11:3
Wilson, Harry M, 1951, Je 10,93:2
Wilson, Harry R Dr, 1968, S 25,43:1
Wilson, Harry T, 1952, D 26,15:3
Wilson, Harvey C, 1940, My 28,23:3
Wilson, Harvey S, 1950, D 14,35:4
Wilson, Hattie B Mrs, 1949, Jl 16,13:2
Wilson, Helen G, 1951, Jl 18,29:4
Wilson, Helen G Mrs, 1937, Ag 21,15:1
Wilson, Helen Mrs, 1945, N 20,21:3
Wilson, Helen R, 1946, N 12,29:1
Wilson, Helyn R Mrs, 1938, Jl 8,17:3
Wilson, Henrietta Mrs, 1940, F 7,21:2
Wilson, Henry, 1875, N 23,1:4
Wilson, Henry A, 1949, Jl 21,25:2; 1961, Jl 17,21:6
Wilson, Henry B (ed trb, Mr 17,30:3), 1954, Ja 31, 89:1
Wilson, Henry B Mrs, 1924, N 10,17:2
Wilson, Henry Bramble, 1909, Mr 8,7:4
Wilson, Henry D, 1946, Jl 24,27:4
Wilson, Henry D Mrs, 1957, D 19,31:1
Wilson, Henry E, 1946, S 18,31:4
Wilson, Henry F Jr, 1947, D 24,21:2
Wilson, Henry F Jr Mrs, 1937, Je 11,23:4
Wilson, Henry F M, 1941, N 17,19:1
Wilson, Henry F Sir, 1937, My 7,30:2
Wilson, Henry I, 1948, Ag 15,61:2
Wilson, Henry L, 1944, O 27,23:5; 1958, My 8,27:5
Wilson, Henry M, 1965, Ja 1,19:1
Wilson, Henry M Mrs, 1953, Je 24,25:4
Wilson, Henry Merryman Dr, 1918, My 9,13:5
Wilson, Henry Rev, 1908, F 16,11:5
Wilson, Henry Rev Dr, 1908, F 14,7:4
Wilson, Henry Suydam, 1908, S 24,9:4
Wilson, Henry V, 1939, Ja 5,23:6; 1954, Ja 7,31:2
Wilson, Henry W, 1945, Jl 20,19:6; 1945, Ag 22,23:5
Wilson, Herbert, 1965, Ag 21,21:5
Wilson, Herbert M Jr, 1954, O 28,35:1
Wilson, Herbert W, 1940, Jl 13,13:2
Wilson, Herman Lesley, 1918, My 16,13:5
Wilson, Homer W, 1943, Ja 29,19:6
Wilson, Horace, 1938, S 30,21:5
Wilson, Horace Hayman, 1860, My 25,8:4
Wilson, Howard Brewster, 1907, Je 24,7:6
Wilson, Howard C, 1959, Ap 8,37:1
Wilson, Howard E, 1966, Ag 13,25:3
Wilson, Howard H, 1945, Jl 25,23:6
Wilson, Howard R, 1949, Ap 19,25:3
Wilson, Hugh C, 1949, My 1,88:3
Wilson, Hugh D Rev, 1921, Jl 1,13:6
Wilson, Hugh Irvine, 1925, F 4,21:4
Wilson, Hugh R, 1946, D 30,19:1
Wilson, Hugh R Mrs, 1957, D 23,23:4
Wilson, Hugh T, 1955, Ap 7,27:2
Wilson, Ira B, 1950, Ap 5,31:3
Wilson, Irving L, 1946, Mr 22,22:2
Wilson, Isabel Lady, 1905, O 13,9:4
Wilson, Ivan O, 1946, Ap 4,25:2
Wilson, J, 1877, F 11,8:2
Wilson, J Byron, 1965, F 25,31:2
Wilson, J Cameron, 1958, S 5,27:1
Wilson, J E Jr, 1903, Jl 12,7:6
Wilson, J Finley, 1952, F 21,27:3
Wilson, J Frank, 1951, Mr 11,93:1
Wilson, J Grant Mrs, 1904, Ap 11,9:5
Wilson, J Harmon, 1940, N 5,34:1
Wilson, J K, 1949, Ag 20,11:6
Wilson, J Marcelin Mrs, 1954, S 12,85:1
Wilson, J Otis Mrs, 1948, N 13,15:4
Wilson, J R, 1927, F 27,30:3
Wilson, J Rev, 1903, Jl 11,3:1
Wilson, J Stitt, 1942, Ag 29,15:5
Wilson, J Walter, 1957, Jl 16,25:3
Wilson, Jackie, 1956, Mr 11,88:5; 1966, D 5,45:1
Wilson, Jacob D Jr, 1957, Ag 26,23:5
Wilson, Jade C, 1943, Ap 26,19:2
Wilson, James, 1906, D 21,9:4
Wilson, James (funl, Ag 28,7:7), 1920, Ag 27,11:5
Wilson, James, 1953, Mr 24,31:3
Wilson, James A, 1871, Je 11,8:5; 1903, Ag 7,7:3; 1941, F 17,15:3; 1942, Mr 30,17:1; 1945, S 4,23:4; 1951, Ja 25,25:3; 1954, S 14,27:5
Wilson, James C, 1958, O 20,29:3; 1959, Ag 25,31:5; 1967, N 29,47:2
Wilson, James C Mrs, 1949, Ja 19,27:5
Wilson, James D, 1941, Mr 21,21:3; 1961, O 26,35:5
Wilson, James E, 1912, Mr 20,13:4; 1944, Ja 8,13:5; 1947, S 1,19:3; 1950, S 18,23:4
Wilson, James F Maj-Gen, 1911, Ap 13,13:4
Wilson, James Fyffe, 1919, S 26,13:4
Wilson, James G, 1940, S 25,27:5
Wilson, James Gen, 1914, F 2,7:3
Wilson, James H, 1915, My 16,16:6; 1943, Je 8,21:1; 1945, My 31,15:4
Wilson, James Harrison Maj-Gen, 1925, F 24,19:4
Wilson, James I, 1942, Ag 4,19:4
Wilson, James I Mrs, 1963, Jl 14,61:2
Wilson, James J, 1937, Je 1,19:4; 1941, My 14,21:2
Wilson, James M, 1943, O 9,13:5
Wilson, James Mrs, 1956, O 18,33:2
Wilson, James O, 1950, Ap 5,32:2
Wilson, James Oliver, 1908, Je 14,11:5
Wilson, James P, 1933, D 11,19:4; 1938, Ap 21,19:5
Wilson, James R, 1946, O 14,29:5
Wilson, James S, 1958, N 25,33:3; 1963, Je 28,30:1
Wilson, James T, 1945, S 5,23:5; 1946, Ja 18,19:2
Wilson, James T Mrs, 1916, Ja 3,13:3
Wilson, James W, 1954, Ap 16,21:1
Wilson, Jarvis M, 1967, Ag 21,31:3
Wilson, Jay, 1940, Jl 30,19:5
Wilson, Jere M Judge, 1901, S 25,5:1
Wilson, Jerome, 1943, Je 2,25:5
Wilson, Jesse E, 1945, My 23,19:3
Wilson, Jimmy, 1947, Je 2,25:3
Wilson, Joe, 1963, Je 26,39:4
Wilson, Johanna, 1946, F 19,25:5
Wilson, John, 1868, Ag 6,4:1; 1882, F 11,8:3; 1903, My 13,9:5; 1903, O 15,9:7; 1915, Mr 25,11:6; 1939, Ja 9,15:3; 1951, Je 2,19:2; 1953, N 3,31:3
Wilson, John A, 1938, D 3,20:1
Wilson, John A (por), 1942, S 11,21:3
Wilson, John A, 1947, D 5,25:3; 1952, Jl 25,17:3; 1954, D 10,28:5; 1957, Ap 21,88:4; 1967, Ja 17,39:1
Wilson, John B, 1943, Mr 14,25:2; 1946, F 23,13:2; 1948, N 22,21:6
Wilson, John C, 1923, My 15,19:5; 1941, D 7,79:3; 1958, N 13,33:1
Wilson, John C (funl plans, O 31,31:3), 1961, O 30, 29:1
Wilson, John Cook Prof, 1915, Ag 13,9:6
Wilson, John D, 1937, Ja 21,23:5
Wilson, John Delameter, 1903, Ap 23,9:5
Wilson, John E, 1942, Jl 23,19:2
Wilson, John F, 1937, Ap 27,23:1
Wilson, John Farmer, 1909, O 11,9:5
Wilson, John G, 1948, Ag 14,13:5; 1950, Je 3,15:3; 1963, S 8,86:6
Wilson, John H, 1944, O 17,23:5; 1956, Jl 4,19:1
Wilson, John I, 1937, Ag 11,23:3
Wilson, John J, 1960, Ag 5,23:3
Wilson, John J Mrs, 1960, Ag 5,23:3
Wilson, John Jr Mrs, 1950, Ag 13,77:2
Wilson, John L, 1956, F 2,25:2
Wilson, John L Ex-Sen, 1912, N 7,13:5
Wilson, John L Mrs, 1951, My 17,31:3
Wilson, John M, 1940, S 7,15:5; 1941, S 15,17:5; 1955, Ap 30,7:1; 1967, Ja 12,39:5
Wilson, John M Gen, 1919, F 3,15:2
Wilson, John Mrs (Kate Denin), 1907, F 6,9:6
Wilson, John N, 1954, S 25,15:5
Wilson, John O, 1940, Ag 16,15:3
Wilson, John P, 1922, O 4,23:5; 1937, Jl 13,20:2; 1959, Jl 27,25:4
Wilson, John R, 1946, My 25,15:2
Wilson, John R Mrs, 1939, F 27,15:2
Wilson, John S, 1946, Ja 3,19:5; 1948, N 19,27:3
Wilson, John S Jr, 1966, Ag 11,33:1
Wilson, John S Mrs, 1948, N 30,28:2
Wilson, John T, 1947, Ap 17,27:6
Wilson, John T Sr, 1959, Mr 3,33:2
Wilson, John W, 1904, O 4,9:6; 1942, Jl 16,19:5; 1947, Ap 5,19:2
Wilson, Jonathan D Jr, 1941, Ap 5,17:3
Wilson, Joseph, 1946, Je 18,25:5; 1948, Jl 13,27:4
Wilson, Joseph A, 1939, Mr 16,23:4
Wilson, Joseph D Rev Dr, 1925, Ja 23,19:5
Wilson, Joseph G Mrs, 1948, F 20,27:3
Wilson, Joseph H, 1951, D 13,33:3; 1958, Ja 24,21:5
Wilson, Joseph Hunt Dr, 1915, Ja 5,15:4
Wilson, Joseph J, 1873, Jl 3,5:4; 1943, Ag 11,19:3
Wilson, Joseph M, 1940, S 11,25:4
Wilson, Joseph R, 1941, Jl 30,17:5; 1957, F 2,19:6; 1961, F 20,27:4
Wilson, Joseph R Mrs, 1951, Ap 10,27:2
Wilson, Joseph T, 1965, Je 25,33:3
Wilson, Joseph W, 1941, Ja 14,21:3
Wilson, Joshua P, 1958, S 9,35:2
Wilson, Julian D, 1958, S 3,33:3
Wilson, Julius G, 1950, Mr 21,29:1
Wilson, Julius H Mrs, 1949, Je 28,27:5
Wilson, Karl L, 1957, Jl 30,23:4
Wilson, Karl P H, 1943, D 25,13:4
Wilson, Kendrick R, 1952, Ja 1,25:2
Wilson, Kenneth, 1966, Mr 5,27:3
Wilson, Kenneth C, 1953, F 4,27:3

Wilson, Kenneth L, 1947, S 3,25:4
Wilson, Kenneth M, 1949, Jl 10,57:2
Wilson, Kirke R (will), 1948, O 1,28:1
Wilson, L Alex, 1960, O 12,39:1
Wilson, L B (will, N 7,7:1), 1954, O 30,17:2
Wilson, L B Bishop, 1928, Je 5,29:3
Wilson, L D Mifflin, 1948, F 15,60:3
Wilson, Lachlan C, 1947, Ap 10,25:2
Wilson, Lawrence G, 1954, D 18,15:2
Wilson, Lawton H, 1950, My 6,15:6
Wilson, Leah D Mrs, 1950, S 6,29:3
Wilson, Lee R, 1951, Ja 13,15:5
Wilson, Leo, 1953, O 8,29:3
Wilson, Leo E, 1940, O 14,19:4
Wilson, Leonard G, 1937, Ag 25,21:2
Wilson, Leonard M, 1953, N 19,31:5
Wilson, Leroy A, 1951, Je 29,21:1
Wilson, Lester M Prof, 1937, My 27,23:5
Wilson, Lester T, 1938, N 7,19:4
Wilson, Lewis G, 1951, N 14,31:5
Wilson, Lewis R (Hack; por), 1948, N 24,23:1
Wilson, Lilian B Mrs, 1940, Jl 10,19:4
Wilson, Lilith M Mrs, 1937, Jl 9,21:2
Wilson, Louis B, 1943, O 6,23:6
Wilson, Louis E, 1944, N 25,13:2
Wilson, Louis R Mrs, 1949, Jl 20,25:2
Wilson, Louis V P, 1955, F 15,27:3
Wilson, Lucian S, 1947, D 18,29:3
Wilson, Lucy Dr (por), 1937, S 4,15:6
Wilson, Lucy Mrs, 1952, N 26,23:1
Wilson, Ludwig Mrs, 1955, Jl 9,32:3
Wilson, Luke S, 1917, Mr 11,21:3
Wilson, Lyle C Mrs, 1952, O 9,31:5
Wilson, Lyman A, 1954, Jl 22,23:5
Wilson, Lyman P, 1951, Ap 21,17:5
Wilson, Lynn W, 1941, O 9,23:6
Wilson, M, 1932, Ja 28,21:3
Wilson, M Ernest, 1952, Ap 3,35:4
Wilson, M Orme Mrs, 1948, S 14,29:1
Wilson, Mabel C, 1950, D 20,31:3
Wilson, Madele, 1942, O 13,23:4
Wilson, Margaret, 1937, Ap 4,26:4
Wilson, Margaret B (por), 1945, O 10,21:1
Wilson, Margaret S, 1943, Mr 23,19:3
Wilson, Margaret W, 1944, F 14,1:2
Wilson, Marian F, 1949, N 23,29:4
Wilson, Marie L Mrs, 1955, My 27,23:1
Wilson, Mark, 1950, Mr 9,29:3
Wilson, Mark Mrs, 1960, N 23,29:1
Wilson, Martin L, 1958, Ap 13,84:4
Wilson, Mary E, 1949, Mr 7,21:5; 1962, O 14,85:5
Wilson, Mary J Mrs (will), 1941, Ag 21,14:2
Wilson, Mary L Mrs, 1939, D 11,23:1
Wilson, Mary M, 1943, Ag 21,11:6
Wilson, Mary R, 1951, D 22,15:5
Wilson, Matthew L, 1966, Ja 24,35:1
Wilson, Michael, 1943, D 6,23:3; 1952, Ap 15,27:1
Wilson, Michael L, 1950, Mr 29,2:5
Wilson, Millard T, 1960, O 24,29:5
Wilson, Minnie E Mrs, 1941, Je 11,21:6
Wilson, Minnie I, 1949, O 6,31:3
Wilson, Mira B, 1953, Ap 6,19:6
Wilson, Mizell, 1968, Jl 19,35:3
Wilson, Mollie E, 1955, N 30,33:4
Wilson, Monmouth B, 1910, Mr 15,7:4
Wilson, Morris W, 1946, My 15,21:5
Wilson, Mortimer Mrs, 1948, S 19,76:6
Wilson, Murray S (por), 1946, Ag 15,25:5
Wilson, Myron, 1962, Ag 20,23:4
Wilson, Myron H, 1951, S 5,31:2
Wilson, N L, 1931, N 14,17:5
Wilson, Nathan, 1955, Ap 14,29:3
Wilson, Norman F Mrs, 1962, Mr 4,86:5
Wilson, Norton L Mrs, 1945, Mr 13,23:6
Wilson, O G, 1959, Je 29,29:2
Wilson, Odbert P, 1958, S 23,33:4
Wilson, Olive T Mrs, 1938, Ja 15,15:5
Wilson, Oren Elbridge, 1917, Mr 3,9:2
Wilson, Orme, 1966, F 14,29:2
Wilson, Oscar S, 1944, D 12,23:2
Wilson, P W Mrs, 1951, Ja 3,25:2
Wilson, Pamela L, 1945, N 30,23:4
Wilson, Paul C, 1953, Ja 1,23:1
Wilson, Paul K, 1958, Mr 5,31:2
Wilson, Paul S, 1941, D 20,20:3
Wilson, Pauline L Mrs, 1937, D 17,25:1
Wilson, Percy, 1950, Mr 25,11:7
Wilson, Percy R, 1943, S 3,19:2
Wilson, Perry M, 1942, Jl 21,19:3
Wilson, Peter Dr, 1872, Ap 5,1:3
Wilson, Peter K, 1913, D 10,13:5
Wilson, Peter M, 1939, Je 25,36:6
Wilson, Peter W, 1950, Ag 14,17:2
Wilson, Phil, 1949, N 16,29:5
Wilson, Phil W, 1956, Je 7,31:2
Wilson, Phil W Mrs, 1939, F 1,21:5
Wilson, Pliny J, 1960, Jl 16,19:2
Wilson, Porter A, 1943, D 30,18:3
Wilson, R, 1926, F 13,13:4
Wilson, R Edward, 1953, Ag 18,23:1
Wilson, R H, 1934, Jl 4,15:4
Wilson, R T, 1929, D 30,19:1
Wilson, R Thornton Mrs, 1943, Ap 24,13:5
Wilson, Ralph B, 1950, Je 16,25:3; 1961, Ag 15,29:2
Wilson, Ralph L, 1960, Jl 19,29:5
Wilson, Randall, 1939, Ag 19,15:6
Wilson, Randolph C, 1941, Je 17,21:2
Wilson, Ray, 1963, Ja 19,7:4
Wilson, Raymond P, 1957, F 12,27:2
Wilson, Richard, 1944, S 23,13:5
Wilson, Richard B, 1947, Ap 22,27:3
Wilson, Richard B Mrs, 1948, D 7,32:2
Wilson, Richard H, 1948, My 23,68:4
Wilson, Richard T Mrs, 1908, My 31,9:3; 1947, Jl 6, 40:5
Wilson, Richard W Mrs, 1943, N 8,19:6
Wilson, Riley J, 1947, F 25,25:5
Wilson, Ripley, 1917, O 3,13:5
Wilson, Robert, 1937, Ag 7,15:3; 1946, My 21,23:4; 1948, Ap 12,21:5; 1954, Jl 18,56:8
Wilson, Robert (NJ), 1964, Mr 2,27:2
Wilson, Robert (GB), 1964, S 26,23:4
Wilson, Robert A, 1960, Je 28,31:5
Wilson, Robert Burns (funl, Ap 3,13:4), 1916, Ap 1, 13:6
Wilson, Robert C, 1952, D 15,25:3; 1954, D 11,13:1; 1958, Jl 2,29:1
Wilson, Robert C Jr, 1966, Jl 16,25:2
Wilson, Robert E, 1960, D 4,88:7; 1964, S 2,37:1
Wilson, Robert G, 1942, S 9,23:1; 1943, Ja 20,19:5; 1949, S 27,27:2
Wilson, Robert Gen, 1870, My 18,2:3
Wilson, Robert H, 1937, O 6,25:1
Wilson, Robert L Jr, 1968, Mr 23,31:3
Wilson, Robert L Mrs, 1946, Ap 4,25:4
Wilson, Robert M, 1948, N 16,30:2
Wilson, Robert Mrs, 1945, My 20,32:3
Wilson, Robert N, 1959, Ag 10,27:5; 1960, N 22,35:1
Wilson, Robert P, 1951, F 20,25:2
Wilson, Robert S, 1954, O 5,27:4; 1967, Jl 11,37:3
Wilson, Robert T, 1947, F 22,13:1
Wilson, Robert W Mrs, 1952, Je 29,59:6
Wilson, Robert Wheeler Prof, 1922, N 2,19:5
Wilson, Rollin C Mrs, 1950, Ja 20,25:2
Wilson, Ronnie, 1955, F 1,55:3
Wilson, Ross M, 1961, D 12,43:2
Wilson, Roy H, 1952, Ap 5,15:3
Wilson, Rufus R, 1949, D 15,35:1
Wilson, Rush, 1956, F 12,88:8
Wilson, S, 1927, O 18,29:4
Wilson, S B, 1937, Ja 21,23:5
Wilson, S Davis, 1939, Ag 20,33:1
Wilson, S Taylor, 1944, S 4,19:6
Wilson, Sallett H, 1937, N 28,II,8:4
Wilson, Sam E Jr, 1957, F 19,31:3
Wilson, Sammy L Mrs, 1955, F 12,15:2
Wilson, Sampson J, 1961, S 15,33:3
Wilson, Samuel A, 1946, D 17,31:4
Wilson, Samuel A Dr, 1937, My 13,25:6
Wilson, Samuel B, 1946, D 14,15:1
Wilson, Samuel G, 1916, Jl 4,11:3
Wilson, Samuel G Mrs, 1945, O 7,45:2; 1952, F 2,13:6
Wilson, Samuel H, 1950, Ag 7,19:4
Wilson, Samuel J, 1960, F 8,29:2
Wilson, Samuel K, 1959, Ap 3,27:2
Wilson, Samuel Mrs, 1950, Mr 14,25:3
Wilson, Samuel N, 1948, Je 5,15:5
Wilson, Scott (por), 1942, O 23,22:2
Wilson, Scott, 1961, My 3,75:2
Wilson, Sinclair J (por), 1943, Mr 21,26:6
Wilson, Stacey B, 1950, S 27,31:3
Wilson, Stanley, 1946, S 29,62:2; 1954, Mr 4,25:1
Wilson, Stanley C, 1967, O 7,29:2
Wilson, Stanley E, 1951, D 10,29:5
Wilson, Stanley K, 1944, N 17,19:2
Wilson, Stanley L, 1948, D 12,92:8
Wilson, Stanley M, 1950, Ja 22,76:5
Wilson, Stephen, 1963, D 19,33:4
Wilson, Stephen A Mrs, 1957, N 2,21:1
Wilson, Stephen H, 1953, Ja 2,15:2
Wilson, Stuart, 1937, Ja 21,24:1
Wilson, Stuart S, 1949, Je 3,25:1
Wilson, Susan C M Mrs, 1937, Mr 25,25:5
Wilson, Susan Mrs, 1947, My 1,25:5
Wilson, Susan P Mrs, 1939, Mr 10,23:3
Wilson, T Bert, 1957, My 25,21:5
Wilson, T Hubert, 1941, D 2,23:5
Wilson, T W, 1880, My 21,5:4
Wilson, T Webber, 1948, F 1,60:8
Wilson, Theodore P, 1954, Jl 1,25:5
Wilson, Thomas, 1943, Ja 17,44:3; 1946, My 6,21:3; 1956, D 9,88:7
Wilson, Thomas A, 1955, N 15,33:4
Wilson, Thomas B, 1963, My 8,36:2
Wilson, Thomas Dr, 1902, My 5,9:6
Wilson, Thomas E, 1949, F 10,28:3; 1957, F 13,35:2; 1958, Ap 5,27:1
Wilson, Thomas H (por), 1943, Mr 31,19:3
Wilson, Thomas H, 1954, D 3,27:2
Wilson, Thomas J, 1937, O 11,27:3
Wilson, Thomas J Jr, 1945, O 26,19:4
Wilson, Thomas J Jr Mrs, 1940, Mr 3,45:2
Wilson, Thomas Mrs, 1967, O 23,45:2
Wilson, Thomas Padon Dr, 1909, Je 24,7:4
Wilson, Thomas Sheldon, 1913, N 2,IV,7:6
Wilson, Thomas T, 1945, Ja 16,19:2; 1951, Ap 4,29:5
Wilson, Thomas W, 1939, Ag 1,19:3; 1948, Je 17,25:4
Wilson, Tom, 1908, F 6,7:5; 1945, S 25,23:2
Wilson, Townsend, 1950, Mr 25,11:7
Wilson, V Palmer, 1955, Je 20,21:3
Wilson, Val H, 1964, Ap 25,29:4
Wilson, Verne J, 1951, Ja 31,25:2
Wilson, W A, 1939, Mr 16,23:5
Wilson, W Addison, 1948, Ap 17,15:4
Wilson, W B, 1934, My 26,17:1
Wilson, W C, 1882, Ap 18,2:5
Wilson, W E Mrs, 1951, Jl 27,19:6
Wilson, W Hamilton, 1940, Mr 13,23:3
Wilson, W Henry, 1941, My 17,15:4
Wilson, W L, 1900, O 18,7:3
Wilson, W Llewellyn, 1950, S 27,31:2
Wilson, W S Mrs, 1952, N 7,23:4
Wilson, W T Gen, 1905, Je 6,9:5
Wilson, Wallace, 1948, S 22,31:3
Wilson, Walter G, 1950, F 28,29:4; 1957, Jl 2,27:2
Wilson, Walter K, 1954, Ja 21,31:2
Wilson, Walter M, 1945, Ja 20,11:5
Wilson, Walter R, 1942, N 9,25:6
Wilson, Walter Sibbald, 1917, Jl 5,9:6
Wilson, Walter V, 1950, My 2,29:1
Wilson, Walter W, 1948, Mr 31,26:2; 1965, My 9,86:4
Wilson, Warren C Mrs, 1952, Ja 4,23:4
Wilson, Warren H Rev Dr (por), 1937, Mr 3,23:1
Wilson, Warren W, 1947, Jl 13,44:7
Wilson, Wendell J, 1938, F 28,15:3
Wilson, Wesley R, 1956, N 12,29:3
Wilson, Wiley M, 1962, N 9,35:2
Wilson, Willard, 1938, Ag 2,19:1
Wilson, William, 1864, Ag 11,5:3; 1903, N 15,7:6; 1938, N 23,21:2; 1943, Ag 9,15:3
Wilson, William (por), 1948, My 7,23:3
Wilson, William, 1951, Ja 30,25:5; 1965, O 11,39:6
Wilson, William A, 1941, N 18,25:1; 1942, Mr 8,43:1; 1947, O 3,25:1; 1953, S 29,29:1; 1960, N 14,31:3
Wilson, William B, 1955, Jl 23,17:2
Wilson, William Brig-Gen, 1937, Ja 7,21:3
Wilson, William C, 1937, Ja 13,24:3; 1943, N 30,27:2; 1950, O 17,31:5; 1951, Ja 15,17:3
Wilson, William E, 1952, O 7,29:4
Wilson, William E Sr, 1948, S 30,27:4
Wilson, William G, 1917, O 21,23:2; 1945, Mr 23,19:4; 1952, Jl 27,57:2; 1953, Ja 25,86:4
Wilson, William H, 1924, S 17,23:3; 1937, Ag 13,17:5; 1939, Je 1,25:2; 1941, F 28,19:6; 1948, Ja 14,25:4; 1958, Ag 1,21:2
Wilson, William J, 1937, Mr 23,23:3; 1939, Jl 2,15:3; 1945, Jl 6,11:4; 1947, D 19,25:2; 1954, My 20,31:3; 1955, Jl 5,29:3; 1963, O 16,45:3
Wilson, William J Mrs, 1960, S 21,37:1
Wilson, William James, 1920, Ag 24,9:4
Wilson, William Jr Capt, 1914, My 14,11:4
Wilson, William K, 1950, Ag 4,21:5
Wilson, William L, 1939, Ag 13,29:1
Wilson, William L Mrs, 1962, Ap 5,33:4
Wilson, William M, 1945, D 22,19:1
Wilson, William Mrs, 1939, My 12,21:4; 1950, S 22, 31:4
Wilson, William P, 1960, Ap 8,31:2
Wilson, William R, 1939, My 7,III,6:8
Wilson, William R (por), 1945, F 22,27:3
Wilson, William R, 1958, Je 7,19:5
Wilson, William Robert Anthony Dr, 1911, My 15,11:6
Wilson, William S, 1952, O 6,25:4
Wilson, William S Jr, 1957, S 17,35:3
Wilson, William Stockton Dr, 1914, Ap 11,11:5
Wilson, William T, 1941, Jl 4,13:4
Wilson, William Tyson, 1921, Ag 16,15:4
Wilson, William W, 1940, Je 1,15:6; 1942, Jl 23,19:2
Wilson, William W W (por), 1947, My 1,25:4
Wilson, Willis R, 1948, O 23,15:3
Wilson, Woodrow (trb), 1924, D 7,7:2
Wilson, Woodrow Mrs (funl; trb, Ag 11,9:1), 1914, Ag 8,9:1
Wilson, Woodrow Mrs (funl plans, D 30,19:5), 1961, D 29,1:4
Wilson, Woodrow Mrs (funl, Ja 2,29:3; will), 1962, Ja 4,31:3
Wilson, Wylie G, 1948, S 28,27:4
Wilson, Zebulon, 1937, F 1,19:5
Wilson-Young, Ian A D, 1948, My 22,15:2
Wilstach, Claxton, 1915, Ap 27,13:4
Wilstach, Paul, 1952, F 10,92:5
Wilt, A H, 1941, Ag 12,12:6
Wilt, Elmer E, 1953, Ja 17,15:5
Wilt, Robert L, 1951, Ag 1,23:3
Wiltbank, Henry C, 1951, D 4,33:3
Wiltbank, William W Judge, 1914, Ja 24,9:4
Wiltenburg, William J, 1952, Mr 28,24:5
Wilton, Alfred T, 1946, F 20,25:4
Wilton, Herbert E, 1937, F 2,23:5
Wilton, Stanley M, 1964, Ag 25,33:2
Wiltse, Charles E, 1953, Je 20,17:5
Wiltse, George (Hooks), 1959, Ja 22,31:5
Wiltse, John M, 1939, Ap 4,25:4
Wiltse, Lloyd J Mrs, 1959, F 23,23:2
Wiltse, Sara T Mrs, 1939, D 7,27:3
Wiltsey, Ephriam, 1965, F 9,37:4
Wiltshire, George, 1950, S 22,31:3
Wiltsie, Egbert Mrs, 1948, Jl 14,23:6

Wiltz, Arnold, 1937, Mr 15,23:4
Wiltz, L A, 1881, O 17,1:4
Wiltzius, Michael H, 1950, Ja 31,24:3
Wilus, Alphonse, 1958, Jl 16,29:4
Wilusz, Stanley, 1946, Je 26,25:5
Wiman, Anna D, 1963, Mr 25,7:7
Wiman, Charles D, 1955, My 13,25:1
Wiman, Dwight D, 1951, Ja 21,76:3
Wiman, Erastus, 1904, F 10,7:3
Wiman, Erastus Mrs, 1907, N 1,9:5
Wimberly, Byron, 1956, My 13,86:7
Wimberly, Lowry C, 1959, Jl 10,25:5
Wimborne, Baron (Ivor Bertie Guest), 1914, F 23,9:5
Wimborne, Viscount (por), 1939, Je 15,23:5
Wimer, Florence E, 1956, Mr 22,35:4
Wimer, William, 1952, Ag 31,47:4
Wimille, Jean P, 1949, Ja 29,18:1
Wimmer, August A, 1952, Je 29,56:2
Wimmer, Curt P, 1951, S 11,29:2
Wimmer, Frank L, 1945, Ag 9,21:5
Wimmer, James, 1946, Mr 30,15:1
Wimmer, Louis Mrs, 1947, Je 22,52:5; 1967, F 4,27:1
Wimmer, Robert J Sr, 1949, D 29,25:5
Wimmer, Rudolph A, 1941, Ag 12,19:2
Wimpenny, Capt, 1866, Ja 27,4:2
Wimperis, Archibald E, 1948, Jl 13,27:4
Wimperis, Arthur H, 1953, O 15,33:3
Wimpffen, E F de Gen, 1884, F 27,5:2
Wimpfheimer, A, 1931, Ag 4,21:1
Wimpfheimer, Charles A Mrs, 1953, Ag 8,11:2
Wimpfheimer, Clarence A, 1962, Ag 18,19:5
Wimpfheimer, Freida Mrs, 1945, Ap 13,17:4
Wimpfheimer, Henrietta Mrs, 1939, S 17,49:1
Wimpress, Abram D, 1938, D 28,21:2
Winans, Charles A, 1966, Ag 27,29:5
Winans, Charles I, 1952, Ja 25,21:1
Winans, Clarence F Mrs, 1945, F 16,23:2
Winans, Clarence H, 1942, S 23,25:3
Winans, Edward R, 1942, S 15,23:5
Winans, Edwin B, 1948, Ja 1,23:1
Winans, Ellen F Mrs, 1942, Ja 31,17:1
Winans, Frank F Mrs, 1955, N 26,19:5
Winans, Henry D, 1924, F 10,23:2
Winans, J J, 1879, My 3,5:5
Winans, James A, 1956, N 22,33:4
Winans, James M, 1955, Jl 28,23:2
Winans, John E, 1957, Ja 12,19:1
Winans, John H, 1959, D 4,31:3
Winans, John R, 1957, Ag 9,19:4
Winans, Joseph P Mrs, 1951, Je 14,27:2
Winans, Laurence C, 1956, My 1,25:5
Winans, M H, 1903, O 10,9:6
Winans, Mark E, 1946, Ja 19,13:2
Winans, Raymond F, 1949, Je 26,1:4
Winans, Raymond W, 1944, F 11,19:4
Winans, Ross, 1877, Ap 12,1:6
Winans, Ross R, 1912, Ap 26,11:5
Winans, Ross R Mrs, 1907, Ap 30,9:6
Winans, Roswell Brig-Gen, 1968, Ag 9,48:1
Winans, Samuel Ross, 1910, Jl 27,9:5
Winans, Thomas (see also Je 11), 1878, Je 12,5:5
Winans, Wallace, 1920, Ag 14,7:5
Winans, Walter, 1920, Ag 13,9:5
Winans, William, 1949, F 4,23:1
Winans, William W, 1938, S 26,17:1
Winant, B Heywood, 1949, O 13,27:5
Winant, C E Mrs, 1880, S 18,6:3
Winant, Charles Mrs, 1950, N 7,27:6
Winant, Emily, 1907, Je 28,7:6
Winant, Frederick, 1939, F 16,21:4
Winant, Gilbert S, 1948, Ag 11,21:2
Winant, Henry B, 1953, Ja 5,21:4
Winant, William A, 1953, N 24,29:3
Winant, William A Mrs, 1948, Jl 13,27:2
Winant, William E Lt, 1916, Jl 17,11:7
Winarick, Arthur (biog;por, N 22,86:4), 1964, N 21, 29:6
Winarick, Arthur Mrs, 1960, Ag 15,23:4
Winas, William B, 1962, O 22,29:3
Winborne, Alice, 1948, Ap 18,68:5
Winborne, Charles A Mrs, 1944, Ja 23,38:3
Winburn, Abel M, 1942, Je 22,15:3
Winburn, Jay T, 1963, O 13,86:4
Winburn, W A, 1924, Ja 9,21:5
Winch, Howard A, 1943, N 29,19:1
Winch, J Russell, 1951, Mr 16,31:4
Winch, Simeon R, 1946, Ag 25,46:2
Winchcombe-Taylor, Robert, 1953, S 2,25:1
Winchell, A Prof, 1891, F 20,5:3
Winchell, Alex N, 1958, Je 10,33:5
Winchell, Benjamin (por), 1942, Mr 18,23:1
Winchell, J M, 1877, F 7,4:7
Winchell, J Rice, 1916, S 15,11:4
Winchell, Jacob, 1940, Ag 19,17:5
Winchell, Lucy B S Mrs, 1942, Ja 15,19:4
Winchell, Newton Horace, 1914, My 3,13:4
Winchell, Simon K, 1943, F 27,13:2
Winchell, Sylvester, 1938, N 3,23:5
Winchell, Virgil Mrs, 1946, O 20,60:2
Winchell, W W, 1934, O 7,34:1
Winchester, Alexander B, 1943, S 7,23:4
Winchester, Arthur S, 1925, Ja 13,19:5
Winchester, Benjamin S, 1955, Ap 30,17:4
Winchester, Caleb Thomas Prof, 1920, Mr 25,11:5
Winchester, Charles M Sr, 1949, Mr 20,76:7
Winchester, Edgar C, 1941, F 1,17:1
Winchester, Edmund, 1937, Ap 29,21:2
Winchester, George, 1960, F 16,37:1
Winchester, Harold P, 1966, Ap 29,47:2
Winchester, Henry M, 1967, My 17,47:2
Winchester, James P Mrs, 1939, Ap 2,III,7:2
Winchester, James R, 1941, O 28,23:4
Winchester, Mamie V Mrs, 1938, Ap 28,23:3
Winchester, Marchioness Caroline of, 1949, F 12,17:2
Winchester, Marquess of (H W M Paulet), 1962, Je 29,27:5
Winchester, Maud W Mrs, 1953, Ja 7,31:3
Winchester, Milo, 1909, My 25,9:6
Winchester, Phil H, 1957, D 24,15:3
Winchester, Tarleton, 1967, Je 23,39:2
Winchester, W H, 1903, Ag 26,7:6
Winchester, W W, 1881, Mr 9,2:3
Winchester, Wilfred S, 1943, S 15,27:4
Winchester, William E (por), 1943, Ja 16,13:4
Winchester, William J, 1952, Ja 4,23:4
Winchester, William T, 1963, D 17,39:4
Winchester, William Wirt Mrs, 1922, S 8,13:4
Winchilsea and Nottingham, Countess of (Agnes), 1964, Je 24,37:4
Winchilsea and Nottingham, Earl of, 1939, F 11,15:5
Winckelmann, A, 1947, F 2,17:4
Winckelmann, Leo William, 1916, Ag 20,15:5
Winckelmann, William C T (cor, S 16,37:2), 1966, S 14,43:6
Winckler, Dyckman W, 1949, Ap 17,76:5
Winckler, Fred J, 1955, Jl 28,23:6
Winckler, Frederick E C Mrs, 1947, Ja 14,25:3
Winckler, Gustav A, 1948, Jl 8,23:3
Wincoop, Henry M, 1918, Ag 9,11:5
Wincor, Henry G, 1960, Jl 18,27:3
Wincott, Harry, 1947, Ap 22,27:1
Wind, Edward J, 1943, N 6,13:2
Wind, Ferdinand Mrs, 1946, Mr 8,21:3
Wind, George J, 1944, Ap 5,19:1
Wind, Mary E, 1950, N 22,25:4
Wind, Rose L Mrs, 1939, Jl 9,30:4
Wind, Solomon, 1966, D 17,33:6
Windaus, Adolf, 1959, Je 13,21:4
Windbolz, Hans, 1940, D 17,25:4
Windecker, C N, 1938, Je 3,21:3
Windecker, Charles E, 1967, Je 21,47:2
Windecker, Sidney, 1921, Ap 15,15:4
Windecker, William, 1943, D 1,21:5
Windeknecht, Henry C, 1937, D 28,22:1
Windelband, Wilhelm Prof, 1915, O 26,11:5
Windeler, G Herbert, 1937, D 16,27:1
Windell, Frank D, 1958, Ap 9,33:3
Windels, Arthur, 1953, N 12,43:7
Windels, Paul, 1967, D 16,41:1
Windels, Paul Mrs, 1960, Mr 5,19:2
Windels, Pauline Mrs, 1941, Ap 3,23:5
Winder, Clarence A, 1959, Jl 23,27:3
Winder, G Norman, 1961, F 22,25:1
Winder, Isaac, 1944, My 14,45:2
Winder, J Russell, 1957, Je 2,86:8
Winder, John H, 1953, Jl 25,11:3
Winder, John R, 1910, Mr 28,9:4
Winder, Ray, 1967, Jl 16,64:7
Winder, William D, 1939, S 1,17:6
Winderl, Otto A, 1959, My 12,35:1
Windesheim, Karl A, 1966, N 21,35:5
Windham, Charles F, 1957, Ja 6,89:2
Windham, Walter G (por), 1942, Jl 7,19:3
Windheim, Marek, 1960, D 2,29:1
Windholz, Frank, 1950, My 1,25:5
Windholz, Frank Mrs, 1959, F 26,31:4
Windholz, Louis, 1942, Jl 25,13:4
Windhorst, Anna, 1940, Mr 21,25:5
Windhorst, Henry George, 1922, Je 15,19:6
Windhorst, William F, 1940, Ag 30,19:5
Windingstad, Ole, 1959, Je 5,27:4
Windisch, Charles F, 1939, Je 24,17:5
Windisch, Frederick J, 1951, Ag 10,15:6
Windisch-Graetz, Alfred Candidus Ferdinand zu Prince, 1862, Ap 8,4:6
Windischgraetz, Leontina de Princess, 1962, Jl 14,21:3
Windish, Charles, 1955, Jl 7,27:4
Windle, Edwin H, 1950, Je 24,13:4
Windle, R T, 1951, S 4,27:3
Windle, V Dewey, 1960, F 21,92:1
Windlesham, James B G Baron, 1962, N 17,28:2
Windlesham, Lord (G R J Hennessy), 1953, O 10, 17:6
Windmann, Harold F, 1959, O 11,86:4
Windmuller, Adolf C E Mrs, 1954, Jl 19,19:6
Windmuller, Louis, 1913, O 2,11:1
Windnagle, T Warner, 1941, Ag 16,15:3
Windner, Julius, 1957, My 7,29:1
Windolph, John P, 1924, Ap 19,13:6
Windom, Paul, 1955, Jl 6,27:2
Windom, W, 1891, Ja 30,1:7
Windrim, J T, 1934, Je 28,23:3
Windship, G B, 1876, S 18,5:3
Windsor, Charles, 1950, Mr 31,31:3
Windsor, Charles C Mrs, 1950, O 31,27:5
Windsor, Harold R, 1955, Je 26,76:3
Windsor, Harry E, 1941, My 10,15:6
Windsor, Helen J Mrs, 1967, Ag 15,39:1
Windsor, Henry H Jr, 1965, F 28,88:5
Windsor, Henry Haven, 1924, My 13,21:5
Windsor, Henry J, 1941, N 26,23:4
Windsor, Janette B, 1940, D 19,25:5
Windsor, John, 1951, Ja 7,76:7
Windsor, Leland W, 1942, Ag 16,44:7
Windsor, Lina J Mrs, 1939, My 29,15:5
Windsor, Thomas P, 1959, Ag 7,23:4
Windsor, Thomas T, 1950, F 18,15:3
Windsor, W Percy, 1947, N 2,72:6
Windsor, William Augustus Rear-Adm, 1907, Ag 31, 7:6
Windt, Valentine B, 1956, Ja 18,31:5
Windthorst, L Dr, 1891, Mr 15,9:7
Windus, Michael, 1955, O 9,87:2
Windust, Bretaigne, 1960, Mr 19,21:4
Windust, E (see also Mr 13), 1877, Mr 15,8:2
Windwer, Charles, 1962, My 11,31:3
Wine, John B, 1948, D 15,33:5
Wineberg, Samuel, 1943, S 27,19:3
Winebrenner, David C 3d, 1940, Mr 28,23:4
Wineburgh, Abraham, 1951, S 15,15:6
Wineburgh, Henry, 1937, F 25,23:4
Winegar, Charles T, 1945, Ja 15,19:3
Winegar, Oscar, 1968, F 22,32:8
Winegard, Oscar Mrs, 1951, N 5,31:1
Winegarden, David, 1952, S 21,89:1
Winehouse, Benjamin, 1947, Mr 17,23:4
Winehouse, Irwin, 1966, N 27,86:8
Wineman, Henry, 1957, F 11,29:3
Wineman, Joseph M, 1957, S 28,17:3
Winemiller, George M, 1941, My 16,23:2
Winemiller, James L, 1944, O 2,19:2
Winer, Elias, 1956, Mr 24,19:2
Winer, Elias W Mrs, 1955, Jl 5,29:4
Winer, Henry, 1961, O 17,39:3
Winer, Jack M, 1960, Ag 31,29:5
Winer, Leonard, 1955, F 25,21:2
Winer, Norman Mrs, 1967, F 24,35:4
Winer, P Wolf, 1962, My 19,27:5
Wines, david Mrs, 1952, Jl 9,27:3
Wines, E C, 1879, D 11,5:2
Wines, Gustave, 1942, O 4,52:7
Wines, Levy D, 1938, Ag 7,33:4
Wines, Walter E, 1960, F 13,19:2
Winetzkaja, Maria Mrs, 1956, My 23,31:4
Winfield, Charles R, 1952, Ag 21,19:7
Winfield, George W Lt, 1920, Ap 14,9:4
Winfield, Harold J, 1949, Mr 22,25:1
Winfield, James M, 1964, D 1,41:3
Winfield, James Macfarlane Dr, 1923, Ap 25,21:5
Winfield, Richard M, 1957, Ap 2,31:1
Winfield, Richard M Mrs, 1941, Je 9,19:3
Winfield, Samuel A, 1953, Je 23,30:6
Winfield, Sydney J, 1958, Ag 7,25:1
Winfield, Thomas F Mrs, 1961, N 7,33:4
Winfield, Victor J, 1943, Ja 28,19:2
Winfield, W A, 1953, D 9,11:2
Winfield, Ward Mrs, 1954, D 3,27:2
Winfield, William A, 1950, Ja 10,29:3
Winfield, William H Mrs, 1951, S 10,21:3
Winfield, William N, 1954, My 13,29:4
Winfrey, G Carey, 1962, N 14,39:3
Winfrey, Richard, 1944, Ap 19,23:4
Wing, Albert Mrs, 1947, Je 4,27:3
Wing, Alfred T, 1937, D 29,21:4
Wing, Arthur K, 1945, My 4,19:2
Wing, C R, 1954, Ag 28,89:2
Wing, Charles B, 1945, Ag 24,19:1
Wing, Charles Jr, 1948, O 1,25:2
Wing, Charles S Rev Dr, 1911, Ja 25,9:5
Wing, Daniel G Mrs, 1949, D 31,15:2
Wing, David L Mrs (L Madeira), 1960, Je 30,29:4
Wing, E D, 1939, F 2,19:1
Wing, E R, 1874, N 3,1:6
Wing, Emery L, 1938, Jl 7,19:4
Wing, Francis J Ex-Judge, 1918, F 3,15:2
Wing, George B, 1941, Jl 8,19:4
Wing, George C Jr, 1951, Mr 20,29:3
Wing, George Mrs, 1945, D 21,21:3
Wing, Gordon F, 1965, Ap 8,39:5
Wing, Henry A, 1962, Jl 26,27:4
Wing, Henry A Col, 1912, F 11,II,13:2
Wing, Henry A Mrs, 1945, Jl 10,11:3
Wing, Henry T, 1924, Ag 18,13:5
Wing, Herbert, 1950, N 23,35:2
Wing, Herbert C, 1960, S 7,37:6
Wing, Herbert Jr Mrs, 1952, N 30,86:3
Wing, Herbert S, 1956, D 25,25:1
Wing, Isaac Col, 1907, Ag 28,7:6
Wing, John D, 1910, Ja 2,II,13:5; 1960, Mr 1,33:1; 1964, Ja 8,37:2
Wing, L Stuart, 1916, Mr 2,11:7; 1962, S 15,25:6
Wing, L Stuart Mrs, 1947, Je 29,48:8; 1961, My 11, 37:3
Wing, Leonard F, 1945, D 20,23:1
Wing, Leroy C, 1948, O 8,25:3
Wing, Lucius A, 1946, F 18,21:2
Wing, Morgan, 1957, S 15,84:6
Wing, Morgan Mrs, 1942, D 25,17:6
Wing, Paul R, 1957, My 31,19:3

Wing, Raymond Mrs, 1951, My 31,27:4
Wing, Richard D, 1951, My 17,31:3
Wing, S Bryce Mrs, 1937, N 16,23:5
Wing, Simon, 1911, F 2,11:4
Wing, Sumner P, 1951, Mr 23,21:1
Wing, Thomas, 1950, My 16,38:5
Wing, Walter S, 1952, My 25,92:5
Wing, Walter S Mrs, 1941, Ap 30,19:3
Wing, William A, 1950, D 23,15:5
Wing, Wilson G (por), 1944, F 4,15:2
Wing, Wilson G Mrs, 1949, D 22,23:2
Wingard, Robert F, 1951, Ap 14,15:1
Wingate, Charles, 1903, Mr 3,9:5
Wingate, Charles E L, 1944, My 16,21:2
Wingate, Francis R, 1953, Ja 29,27:1
Wingate, G W, 1928, Mr 23,21:1
Wingate, George A, 1955, Ap 3,86:5
Wingate, George W Mrs, 1915, S 1,9:5
Wingate, Henry C, 1949, D 20,31:3
Wingate, Henry K Mrs, 1952, Ap 24,31:2
Wingate, J C A, 1905, Mr 12,9:4
Wingate, James P D, 1937, Ja 12,23:4
Wingate, John S, 1950, F 9,29:5
Wingate, Julia C Mrs, 1867, F 26,5:6
Wingate, Moses, 1870, Je 7,5:2
Wingate, Rachel, 1953, Je 14,86:1
Wingate, Robert, 1952, F 8,23:1
Wingate, Roy, 1959, Jl 4,15:4
Wingate, Roy W Mrs, 1940, S 7,15:3
Wingate, William W, 1939, Ag 18,19:3
Winge, Frank, 1958, Ja 3,23:1
Winger, G Glenn, 1954, My 1,15:4
Winger, Otho, 1946, Ag 15,25:6
Wingert, Bertha C, 1945, My 12,13:6
Wingert, Frank B Sr, 1955, S 15,33:4
Wingert, Howard P, 1940, O 28,17:3; 1956, D 26,27:2
Wingert, J Albert, 1945, Jl 12,11:7
Wingert, Mary C, 1944, Ja 5,17:4
Wingert, P Carroll Mrs, 1948, F 19,23:2
Wingert, William B, 1956, N 16,27:3
Wingerter, Emery G Dr, 1968, F 21,47:3
Wingerter, John J, 1966, Mr 10,33:4
Winget, C Nelson, 1944, O 16,19:6
Winget, Rader W W (funl plans, Je 18,25:1), 1956, Je 17,92:6
Wingfield, Anthony, 1952, S 21,89:2
Wingfield, Conway, 1948, F 10,23:4
Wingfield, George, 1959, D 27,60:4
Wingfield, Portia J, 1951, S 26,31:3
Wingfield, Samuel G, 1957, N 24,86:8
Wingfield-Stratford, Cecil V, 1939, F 6,13:4
Wingo, Absalom H (Red), 1964, O 10,25:1
Wingo, Ivy, 1941, Mr 2,42:2
Wingo, Richard T, 1941, D 16,28:2
Wingo, Wade B, 1950, Ap 27,29:2
Wingquist, Sven G, 1953, Ap 19,90:3
Wingrade, Sidney L, 1963, Jl 13,17:4
Wingrave, John O, 1954, D 13,27:5
Winham, B H, 1957, Ap 17,31:1
Winick, Ben R, 1965, Ja 1,19:4
Winik, Leon, 1954, F 4,26:3
Wink, Earl B, 1954, Mr 5,19:1
Winkel, Capt, 1880, Ja 15,8:3
Winkel, Gustaaf A, 1945, S 4,23:4
Winkel, Leon, 1940, Ja 31,19:1
Winkel, Mel, 1964, Je 24,37:3
Winkel, Simon, 1917, Ja 5,9:4
Winkel, W H, 1943, O 3,48:4
Winkel, Walter L, 1950, My 30,17:3
Winkelkemper, Peter, 1944, Je 22,19:5
Winkelman, Charles, 1951, N 10,17:6
Winkelman, Frank N, 1952, Ja 20,85:2
Winkelman, Henri-Gerard, 1952, D 29,19:4
Winkelman, Louis, 1948, Ja 1,23:3
Winkelman, Max C, 1947, Ja 19,53:4
Winkelman, Moses P, 1940, Mr 15,23:5
Winkelman, Nathaniel W Sr, 1956, F 15,31:4
Winkelmann, Hermann, 1912, Ja 20,13:6
Winkelstein, Lawrence B, 1966, S 3,23:5
Winkelstein, Meyer Mrs, 1949, My 5,27:5
Winker, Ernest Mrs, 1945, Ap 7,15:4
Winkert, Theodore H, 1953, O 25,88:6
Winkhaus, Augusta C Mrs, 1937, Jl 16,19:4
Winkhaus, Frederick, 1951, Jl 10,27:5
Winkhaus, John T Sr, 1950, Ap 11,31:2
Winkle, James P, 1941, My 5,17:5
Winkle, James P Sr Mrs, 1951, N 11,90:3
Winkle, William E, 1946, Je 5,23:1
Winklebleck, Samuel H, 1942, N 21,13:5
Winkleman, Arthur E, 1952, Je 29,56:7
Winkleman, Greenleaf, 1944, Ja 7,17:2
Winklepleck, Roy R, 1965, Ag 19,31:4
Winkler, Albin, 1956, F 26,89:2
Winkler, Alexander W, 1947, Je 27,21:6
Winkler, Charles F, 1941, D 21,40:6
Winkler, Charles M, 1953, Ap 30,31:3
Winkler, Edward, 1955, Je 12,86:4
Winkler, Eli (por), 1949, N 11,25:5
Winkler, Ferdinand H, 1943, Jl 18,35:3
Winkler, Frank P, 1944, My 11,19:6
Winkler, George N Sr, 1957, O 10,33:4
Winkler, Guenther E, 1965, D 7,47:3
Winkler, Hans, 1964, Mr 10,37:4
Winkler, Harold L, 1956, My 31,27:3
Winkler, Heinz, 1958, Je 26,3:2
Winkler, Helen (por), 1947, N 25,32:4
Winkler, Henry A, 1954, Je 5,17:6
Winkler, John J, 1953, Mr 11,29:2
Winkler, John K, 1958, Ag 1,21:1
Winkler, Leland E, 1946, N 15,23:1
Winkler, Leopold, 1924, D 23,19:4
Winkler, Louis, 1966, N 19,33:2
Winkler, Max, 1952, My 25,94:5; 1953, S 6,50:5
Winkler, Max (Oct 5), 1965, O 11,61:7
Winkler, Oto W, 1950, O 31,27:2
Winkler, Paul E, 1949, O 31,25:1
Winkler, Robert, 1941, Mr 4,23:4
Winkler, Rudolph Prof, 1937, Ap 15,23:1
Winkley, Frank H, 1947, My 2,21:1
Winkopp, H Adolph, 1960, D 7,43:1
Winkopp, H Adolph Mrs, 1942, N 11,25:5
Winkworth, Edwin D, 1955, N 16,35:1
Winlock, George L, 1948, Ap 11,73:1
Winlock, George L Jr, 1950, Mr 8,25:2
Winlock, Herbert E, 1950, Ja 27,23:1
Winlock, Isabel, 1953, O 11,89:1
Winlock, Joseph Prof, 1875, Je 12,6:5
Winlock, Sara M Mrs, 1942, D 3,25:3
Winmill, Robert C, 1957, F 1,25:2
Winmill, Thomas F, 1953, N 21,13:3
Winn, Arthur H, 1949, D 23,22:3
Winn, Carona, 1940, Mr 29,21:4
Winn, Charles D, 1942, Ag 2,39:2
Winn, Charles J F, 1968, My 3,54:5
Winn, Cooper D, 1963, O 27,89:1
Winn, Dennis, 1940, N 22,23:4
Winn, Edward B, 1943, Ja 13,24:3
Winn, Erwin L, 1937, My 6,25:2
Winn, Frank L (por), 1941, F 25,23:3
Winn, George H Sr, 1963, Je 21,29:2
Winn, George H Sr Mrs, 1955, Ja 26,25:2
Winn, George P, 1938, D 30,16:2
Winn, Herbert J, 1945, Je 28,19:5
Winn, Herbert S, 1958, Ja 30,23:2
Winn, James S, 1938, Je 2,23:3
Winn, John B, 1955, Je 10,25:4
Winn, John S, 1940, Ja 27,13:3
Winn, Joshua H, 1938, Jl 13,21:5
Winn, Margaret Sumner, 1920, O 12,15:2
Winn, Mary D (Oct 1), 1965, O 11,61:7
Winn, Matt J, 1949, O 7,28:2
Winn, Michael H, 1959, D 3,37:4
Winn, Milton (ashes scattered in Bosporus strait, S 23,37:2), 1966, Mr 2,41:1
Winn, Murray, 1950, Jl 27,25:1
Winn, Robert N Maj, 1916, Ag 13,15:6
Winn, Walter, 1953, Mr 6,20:5
Winn, William J, 1950, S 1,21:2
Winn, William J Mrs, 1941, My 9,21:2
Winn, Willis H, 1940, Mr 18,17:2
Winne, A L I, 1950, F 4,15:5
Winne, Charles E Jr, 1964, O 7,47:3
Winne, David C, 1961, Je 23,29:4
Winne, F P Rev, 1904, F 2,9:6
Winne, Frank D, 1950, Mr 27,23:2
Winne, George T, 1945, Jl 24,23:3
Winne, Horace W, 1937, Ap 27,23:5
Winne, Isaiah D, 1938, Mr 31,23:2
Winne, John, 1925, My 22,19:6
Winne, Worden E Sr, 1952, My 29,27:5
Winnek, Phil, 1948, D 19,76:5
Winner, Charles (Doc), 1956, Ag 12,84:7
Winner, Elmer, 1923, F 26,13:5
Winner, Frank C, 1952, My 22,27:3
Winner, Harry L, 1940, Je 6,25:2
Winner, Herman (funl, N 23,29:2), 1960, N 21,29:1
Winner, James M, 1939, Je 19,15:3
Winner, James R, 1954, O 31,89:2
Winner, Lt, 1871, Ap 11,1:4
Winner, Margaret F, 1937, D 22,25:2
Winner, Stephen D, 1903, N 5,9:7
Winnett, P G Mrs, 1949, F 20,60:6
Winnick, Maurice, 1962, My 30,19:5
Winnicki, Stanislaus, 1951, N 18,91:2
Winnie, Russell, 1956, Ap 1,88:8
Winning, W Carl, 1964, Ap 5,86:8
Winningham, Charles C, 1954, O 4,27:4
Winnings, W C, 1947, My 13,25:4
Winnington-Ingram, Arthur F (por), 1946, My 27,23:4
Winocour, Wolf, 1955, Ja 11,25:3
Winokur, Joseph B, 1958, Je 4,33:2
Winokur, Max, 1924, Ag 4,13:5
Winpenny, Bolton S, 1945, D 3,21:3
Winquist, Eric E, 1947, My 27,26:3
Winrod, Gerald B, 1957, N 13,35:3
Winsch, Frederick, 1908, F 20,7:6
Winsche, John W, 1941, D 12,25:2
Winser, Beatrice, 1947, S 16,23:5
Winser, Gerald C, 1957, Jl 10,27:5
Winser, Lindley, 1947, Je 28,14:3
Winship, A E, 1933, F 18,15:4
Winship, Amy Davis Mrs, 1923, F 20,17:3
Winship, Blanton, 1947, O 10,25:1
Winship, Charles Allen, 1925, Jl 20,15:6
Winship, Charles N, 1946, Mr 5,26:3
Winship, Charles O, 1954, S 27,21:2
Winship, Edith A, 1938, S 2,17:6
Winship, Emma H Mrs, 1942, S 10,27:3
Winship, Frank A, 1945, D 4,29:2
Winship, Gardiner G, 1938, D 7,23:3
Winship, George P, 1952, Je 24,29:2
Winship, Glen B, 1966, N 22,41:3
Winship, Harry E (por), 1947, Ja 8,24:2
Winship, Leslie M, 1957, My 27,31:4
Winship, S Davis, 1947, D 29,17:4
Winsko, Joseph, 1968, D 31,27:3
Winslow, A, 1933, Ag 16,17:1
Winslow, Archibald S, 1944, D 13,23:1
Winslow, Arthur, 1938, Mr 29,21:5
Winslow, Arthur E, 1950, O 18,33:2
Winslow, Austin S, 1939, My 17,23:3
Winslow, Barbara, 1942, My 10,42:8
Winslow, Benjamin, 1951, N 3,17:4
Winslow, Betsy Baldwin, 1925, Ap 2,21:3
Winslow, C D, 1932, D 28,17:3
Winslow, C McR, 1932, Ja 3,30:3
Winslow, Cameron M Mrs, 1945, Je 10,31:1
Winslow, Capt, 1864, Ag 21,5:3
Winslow, Carleton M, 1946, O 17,23:4
Winslow, Carlile P, 1960, S 26,33:5
Winslow, Charles, 1956, F 26,89:1
Winslow, Charles E Mrs, 1963, N 24,22:2
Winslow, Charles H, 1938, F 6,II,8:8
Winslow, Charles H Dr, 1908, Je 18,9:4
Winslow, Charles H Mrs, 1946, F 3,40:3
Winslow, Charles J Mrs, 1949, Ja 18,24:3
Winslow, Charlotte H Mrs (por), 1941, My 4,53:1
Winslow, Chas-Edward A (trb lr, Ja 12,18:6), 1957, Ja 9,31:3
Winslow, Clarion B (will, N 1,19:6),(por), 1943, O 27,23:3
Winslow, Clarion B Mrs (will, N 28,14:7), 1942, Ap 9,19:3
Winslow, Cleveland Col, 1864, Jl 12,5:2
Winslow, Dallas E, 1961, My 10,45:3
Winslow, Edward, 1905, F 12,7:6; 1948, D 21,25:3
Winslow, Edward D, 1941, Ja 23,21:5
Winslow, Edward F Gen, 1914, O 24,13:6
Winslow, Edward W (will), 1966, Mr 9,24:3
Winslow, Ellen A, 1952, Ag 15,16:4
Winslow, Emma A, 1943, Ap 11,48:5
Winslow, Erving, 1922, Mr 11,13:6
Winslow, Eveleth Mrs, 1959, N 26,38:1
Winslow, F A, 1932, Mr 30,19:1
Winslow, F Gordon, 1966, Ag 15,27:5
Winslow, Floyd S, 1958, F 19,27:3
Winslow, Forbes Dr, 1874, Mr 5,5:3
Winslow, Francis, 1923, Je 30,11:4; 1948, S 28,28:2
Winslow, Francis D, 1937, F 23,27:5; 1956, O 10,39:2
Winslow, Fred G, 1946, Ag 20,27:3
Winslow, Frederic J, 1941, Je 19,21:5
Winslow, Frederick Dr, 1937, N 27,17:5
Winslow, George J, 1949, Je 20,19:5
Winslow, George Scott Mrs, 1925, O 13,23:4
Winslow, Gordon Rev Dr, 1864, Je 9,2:4
Winslow, Graven F, 1946, N 14,29:5
Winslow, H Allen, 1942, D 6,76:8
Winslow, Harry F, 1959, F 13,27:4
Winslow, Harvey L, 1937, F 9,23:3
Winslow, Helen M, 1938, Mr 28,15:3
Winslow, Herbert F, 1941, My 13,23:1
Winslow, Herbert Rear-Adm, 1914, S 26,11:6; 1914, O 29,11:4
Winslow, Hubbard Dr, 1864, Ag 19,5:3
Winslow, Isaac O, 1949, Ja 17,19:3
Winslow, Isaac Staynor, 1903, D 27,7:6
Winslow, James, 1874, Jl 19,4:7
Winslow, James North, 1923, Ap 3,23:5
Winslow, Jasper Andrew Capt, 1917, Mr 30,11:7
Winslow, John R Dr, 1937, Je 27,II,7:1
Winslow, John W S, 1954, Ja 5,27:3
Winslow, John W S Mrs (Elsie L G), 1965, Mr 19, 35:4
Winslow, Julius M, 1939, Jl 6,24:2
Winslow, Lawrence L Mrs, 1951, Ag 7,25:4
Winslow, Mary B, 1957, Mr 12,33:2
Winslow, Max, 1942, Je 9,24:3
Winslow, May N, 1952, My 3,21:6
Winslow, Myron Dr, 1864, D 19,4:5
Winslow, Park T, 1938, Jl 27,17:2
Winslow, Park T Mrs, 1965, My 10,33:1
Winslow, Paul T, 1963, Ag 14,33:3
Winslow, Paul V, 1943, Mr 13,13:3
Winslow, Pearson, 1950, D 14,35:3
Winslow, Ralph G Mrs, 1947, Mr 10,21:4
Winslow, Randolph Dr, 1937, F 28,II,8:6
Winslow, Richard H, 1861, Mr 9,2:6
Winslow, Samuel E, 1940, Jl 12,15:3
Winslow, Samuel E Mrs, 1947, F 16,57:1
Winslow, Sidney Jr Mrs, 1955, Jl 25,19:4
Winslow, Sidney W, 1917, Je 19,13:4
Winslow, Sidney W Jr, 1963, Jl 15,29:4
Winslow, Stephen W, 1907, F 22,9:5
Winslow, Thacher (trb lr, F 4,20:7), 1955, Ja 10,23:2
Winslow, Thomas N, 1942, D 12,17:2
Winslow, Thomas S, 1941, Ap 5,17:1
Winslow, Thomas S Mrs, 1956, My 30,21:6
Winslow, Thyra S Mrs, 1961, D 3,88:4
Winslow, Walker W, 1958, O 27,27:4

Winslow, Wentworth, 1938, Ag 17,19:5
Winslow, William B, 1944, F 9,19:3
Winslow, William Copley Rev, 1925, F 3,13:4
Winslow, Williamson R, 1945, Mr 14,19:3
Winslow-Spragge, Edward, 1953, F 24,25:2
Winsmore, Robert J, 1949, Je 12,76:8
Winsmore, Robert Mrs, 1954, Ag 17,21:1
Winsmore, Robert S, 1937, N 10,25:6
Winsor, Bancroft, 1939, Ap 9,II,6:7
Winsor, Charles P, 1951, Ap 7,15:4
Winsor, Frank E (por), 1939, F 1,21:1
Winsor, Frederick, 1940, N 27,23:2
Winsor, Frederick Jr, 1958, N 27,29:4
Winsor, George A, 1944, S 27,21:5
Winsor, Harry O Mrs, 1949, S 2,17:4
Winsor, Henry, 1949, Jl 28,23:2
Winsor, James D Jr, 1957, Ja 12,19:5
Winsor, Justin, 1897, O 23,7:3
Winsor, Mary, 1956, S 11,35:2
Winsor, Mary P, 1950, S 4,17:6
Winsor, Max, 1945, My 5,16:2
Winsor, Robert Jr, 1944, Ap 18,21:4
Winsor, Thomas K, 1949, D 16,31:4
Winspear, Harvey F, 1949, Ap 4,23:3
Winspeare, Francesco Mrs, 1954, Mr 5,19:2
Winspeare, Onorato, 1939, D 23,15:5
Winsper, I R, 1950, O 19,31:3
Winstanley, James, 1948, F 28,15:2
Winstanley, Oliver J, 1951, Ag 10,14:5
Winstead, Ralph, 1957, D 23,29:1
Winsten, Albert, 1952, S 1,17:6
Winsten, Harry, 1949, Mr 12,17:3
Winsten, Harry J, 1960, Je 19,88:5
Winster, Lord (R T H Fletcher), 1961, Je 9,33:3
Winstian, Louis Mrs, 1946, Ja 31,21:4
Winstock, Walter B, 1940, O 15,23:2
Winston, Andrew, 1951, S 28,31:1
Winston, Bruce, 1946, S 28,17:3
Winston, Charles A, 1954, Ja 25,19:3
Winston, Charles M, 1964, O 15,39:2
Winston, Charles S Sr, 1944, N 12,49:3
Winston, E W Mrs, 1952, N 17,25:5
Winston, Esther Mrs, 1940, Mr 27,21:3
Winston, F S, 1885, Mr 29,3:3
Winston, Francis D, 1941, Ja 30,21:2
Winston, Fred H, 1904, F 20,9:4
Winston, Frederick J, 1940, D 10,26:2
Winston, Garrard B (est acctg), 1957, Jl 27,19:3
Winston, Gerrard B, 1955, Jl 29,17:2
Winston, Isaac, 1923, D 9,23:2
Winston, James Mrs, 1947, Ag 27,23:4
Winston, James O, 1947, Mr 14,24:2
Winston, James O Mrs, 1956, N 15,35:4
Winston, John A Rear-Adm, 1873, O 1,2:1
Winston, John C, 1920, My 7,11:2
Winston, Joseph, 1959, Jl 25,17:2
Winston, Louis P, 1954, Jl 4,31:3
Winston, Mayer J, 1950, Jl 26,25:2
Winston, Owen, 1950, D 23,15:6
Winston, Perry, 1959, My 21,31:2
Winston, Robert W (por), 1944, O 15,45:1
Winston, Samuel, 1907, N 25,9:4
Winston, Sidney S, 1965, My 1,31:4
Winston, William A (por), 1948, Ag 26,22:2
Wint, Dunbar T, 1938, Jl 11,17:5
Wint, Theodore J (funl, Mr 26,9:6), 1907, Mr 22,11:5
Winter, Albert, 1944, Mr 28,19:4
Winter, Alpheus Sr, 1948, O 18,23:4
Winter, Andrew, 1958, O 28,35:1
Winter, Arthur E, 1945, S 12,25:5
Winter, Arthur W Mrs, 1957, Je 8,19:4
Winter, Benjamin, 1944, Je 17,13:1
Winter, Charles A, 1939, My 2,23:2; 1942, S 24,27:2
Winter, Charles R, 1952, Je 30,19:3
Winter, Chester J, 1952, N 7,23:1
Winter, Christian Mrs, 1965, Ag 20,29:2
Winter, Clara M, 1948, Ag 6,17:1
Winter, Clarence F, 1950, O 2,23:6
Winter, David H, 1938, Ag 21,32:5
Winter, Dwight R, 1943, F 24,21:2
Winter, Edson P, 1952, S 30,31:3
Winter, Edward C, 1950, Ap 10,19:4
Winter, Edward C Mrs, 1946, Jl 11,23:2
Winter, Edward H, 1941, Je 30,17:1
Winter, Egbert, 1949, F 8,26:3
Winter, Emil, 1941, Jl 5,11:3
Winter, Ernest Jerome, 1924, N 26,19:5
Winter, Ernst K, 1959, F 22,88:5
Winter, Frank, 1965, F 1,23:4
Winter, Fred, 1915, Ja 13,9:3
Winter, Fred Mrs, 1962, Mr 5,23:1
Winter, Frederick C, 1966, O 25,45:1
Winter, George B, 1940, Mr 30,15:4
Winter, George J, 1954, Je 29,27:3
Winter, Gordon R, 1951, Jl 31,21:5
Winter, Gustave E, 1946, F 12,25:4
Winter, H, 1926, D 18,17:5
Winter, H Lyle, 1955, My 5,33:2
Winter, Harry, 1964, Ja 23,31:3
Winter, Henry, 1882, F 28,3:4
Winter, Henry J Mrs, 1947, O 4,17:2
Winter, Herman, 1937, F 1,19:3
Winter, Howard, 1961, N 23,31:5
Winter, Hugo, 1943, Mr 2,19:2
Winter, Irving, 1944, O 21,17:5
Winter, Irving A, 1952, My 13,23:4
Winter, Jacob C, 1955, N 18,25:2
Winter, John, 1959, N 29,63:1
Winter, John H, 1940, Ja 3,21:4
Winter, John J, 1959, Ja 9,27:3
Winter, John Strange, 1911, D 15,13:5
Winter, Joseph A, 1955, Je 10,25:3
Winter, Joseph Mrs, 1954, Mr 6,17:3
Winter, Joseph Prof, 1915, Je 9,13:4
Winter, Keyes, 1960, My 14,23:3
Winter, Keyes Mrs, 1957, Je 10,27:4
Winter, Leo, 1948, Jl 8,23:3
Winter, Louis R Jr, 1965, Ag 27,29:3
Winter, Maurice Mrs, 1964, D 17,41:1
Winter, Milo K, 1956, Ag 17,19:6
Winter, Newrie D, 1947, Ag 21,23:3
Winter, Norman, 1959, Ja 25,93:1
Winter, Olice, 1948, Mr 24,25:5
Winter, Paul Mrs, 1955, My 8,57:3
Winter, Sidney C, 1967, My 11,54:6
Winter, Susan C, 1964, D 12,31:5
Winter, Thomas G Mrs, 1944, Ap 6,23:3
Winter, W Rodgers, 1942, S 20,40:5
Winter, W Roland Mrs, 1939, O 17,25:2
Winter, Wallace C, 1947, My 12,21:5
Winter, William (funl, Jl 3,9:5), 1917, Jl 1,19:3
Winter, William, 1940, My 19,43:3; 1950, Ag 23,29:4; 1955, D 19,27:3
Winter, William D, 1955, Mr 9,27:1
Winter, William Mrs, 1922, Ap 9,28:4
Winterbalter, Frederick, 1873, Jl 11,1:7
Winterble, Margaret M Mrs, 1959, O 22,37:3
Winterbotham, Amelia E Mrs, 1938, Ja 9,43:2
Winterbotham, H S P, 1873, D 16,1:7
Winterbotham, Joseph, 1954, Ap 20,29:2
Winterbottom, Charles W E Mrs, 1950, F 7,27:1
Winterbottom, Robert J, 1941, Ag 27,19:5
Winterbottom, W Grayson, 1952, F 14,27:4
Winterbottom, William A (por), 1944, Jl 9,35:1
Winterbury, John A, 1946, D 27,20:2
Winterfeldt, Hans K von (por), 1940, Jl 4,15:6
Winterhalter, Albert Gustavus Rear-Adm, 1920, Je 6, 22:4
Winterhalter, Albert Mrs (Helen Dauvray), 1923, D 7,21:5
Winterhalter, Emil, 1954, Mr 5,19:4
Winterhalter, Leroy F, 1965, S 4,21:4
Winterich, Christ, 1944, Jl 29,13:3
Wintermute, Milton W, 1945, N 9,19:2
Winternitz, Felix (por), 1948, Ag 21,15:1
Winternitz, Milton C, 1959, O 4,86:3
Winternitz, Moritz, 1937, Ja 10,II,9:4
Winternitz, Paul, 1956, Ja 9,25:2
Winterroth, Emil J Mrs, 1954, D 4,17:4
Winters, Andrew, 1940, Je 17,15:5
Winters, Anna Maria Mrs, 1915, S 4,7:6
Winters, Benjamin J, 1948, F 3,25:1
Winters, Blanche Mrs, 1957, Mr 10,89:2
Winters, Charles S, 1948, Mr 21,60:6
Winters, Edward K, 1946, Ja 2,19:4
Winters, Francis, 1944, N 19,50:1
Winters, Fred, 1954, F 25,53:1
Winters, Fred Mrs, 1954, F 25,53:1
Winters, George, 1949, Ja 23,68:7
Winters, George A, 1949, N 22,29:2
Winters, George W, 1943, Jl 31,13:4
Winters, Grance Mrs, 1949, Jl 8,19:5
Winters, Guy H, 1952, Ap 16,27:2
Winters, Henry A, 1949, Je 15,29:3
Winters, Henry C, 1940, N 4,19:3
Winters, Henry M, 1960, O 5,41:3
Winters, Herbert D, 1944, Je 23,19:3
Winters, Irving J, 1958, Ja 21,26:6
Winters, J Calvin, 1944, Je 25,29:2
Winters, James J, 1950, Mr 9,29:3
Winters, James M, 1959, F 18,33:4
Winters, John C, 1948, Jl 28,23:2
Winters, John F, 1955, Jl 28,23:1; 1959, My 2,23:3
Winters, John W, 1948, My 23,69:1
Winters, Joseph E Dr, 1922, O 6,23:5
Winters, Laurence, 1913, Je 6,11:5
Winters, Owen B, 1940, N 13,23:4
Winters, Paul E Mrs, 1944, Ja 8,13:3
Winters, Richard, 1956, Mr 19,12:4
Winters, Robert A, 1950, Jl 29,13:3
Winters, W A, 1940, Ag 20,19:2
Winters, William B, 1948, Ag 25,25:1
Winters, William E, 1937, Ag 17,19:2
Winters, William Huffman, 1917, F 1,11:4
Winters, Yvor, 1968, Ja 27,29:1
Winters (Sister Grace Miriam), 1965, Mr 4,31:4
Wintersteen, A H, 1944, N 9,27:6
Wintersteen, A H Mrs, 1939, Ap 30,44:8
Winterstella, Frederick J, 1948, O 4,23:5
Winterstoke, Baron (Sir Wm Henry Willis), 1911, Ja 30,9:4
Winterton, Earl (E Turnour), 1962, Ag 28,31:4
Winther, Albert W, 1940, Ap 6,17:6
Winther, R V C A, 1877, Ja 7,7:2
Winthrop, B R, 1879, Ag 21,8:3
Winthrop, Beekman (por), 1940, N 11,19:3
Winthrop, Bertram, 1940, N 10,57:2
Winthrop, Brig-Gen (funl), 1865, Ap 13,8:1
Winthrop, Bronson, 1944, Jl 15,13:3
Winthrop, Egerton L Jr Mrs, 1948, Mr 4,25:1
Winthrop, Egerton Leigh (funl, Ap 11,13:4), 1916, Ap 7,11:7
Winthrop, Grenville L, 1943, Ja 20,20:2
Winthrop, Henry R, 1958, N 15,23:4
Winthrop, Henry R Mrs, 1941, Ag 26,19:1
Winthrop, Robert (Bud Flanagan), 1968, O 21,47:1
Winthrop, Robert C, 1894, N 17,8:1
Winthrop, Robert D, 1912, Ap 17,13:5
Winthrop, Robert M, 1938, My 7,15:6
Winthrop, Robert Mrs, 1925, Je 8,15:5
Winthrop, Rudolph J, 1959, Jl 3,17:4
Winthrop, William D, 1938, Ag 7,32:8
Winthrop-Young, Geoffrey, 1958, S 8,29:3
Wintjen, John G, 1953, Ag 17,15:5
Wintjen, John G Mrs, 1941, Mr 1,15:4
Wintle, Alfred D, 1966, My 12,45:1
Wintle, Harry D, 1940, Ap 3,23:2
Wintle, William H, 1949, Ap 13,29:5
Wintner, Aurel, 1958, Ja 16,30:1
Wintner, Elvia S Mrs, 1956, Ap 28,86:1
Wintner, George, 1960, Ja 8,25:4
Winton, A, 1932, Je 23,21:1
Winton, Andrew L, 1946, O 18,23:4
Winton, Arthur S, 1942, My 27,23:4
Winton, Jane, 1959, S 23,35:6
Winton, Thomas, 1944, My 2,19:4
Winton, W Brewster Mrs, 1955, My 12,29:3
Winton, Zerling Mrs, 1954, Ag 7,13:5
Wintrab, Oscar, 1961, My 30,17:5
Wintres, Mary, 1943, O 29,19:1
Wintress, David H, 1908, Jl 2,9:7
Wintrich, Josef, 1958, O 20,29:5
Wintringer, George C, 1957, N 24,86:1
Wintringham, Sidney, 1908, Ja 17,9:6
Wintringham, Thomas H, 1949, Ag 19,17:3
Wintringham, Tom, 1921, Ag 9,9:5
Wintrup, William, 1946, Ap 19,29:2
Winwart, H, 1881, Mr 31,8:3
Winzeler, Natalie, 1950, O 7,19:4
Wipf, Walter W, 1939, F 10,23:3
Wipperman, W Kendell Mrs, 1949, Ja 11,27:5
Wipple, William J, 1943, Je 13,45:1
Wipplinger, Natalie, 1950, F 21,26:2
Wire, George L, 1940, Ja 17,21:5
Wire, George W, 1940, My 15,23:5
Wire, George W Sr Mrs, 1947, Ap 22,27:4
Wire, Samuel, 1874, My 4,1:7
Wireback, Artemus A, 1941, O 22,23:3
Wireback, Joseph F, 1951, F 23,27:3
Wireback, Walter E, 1945, Jl 6,11:6
Wirfel, Samuel, 1953, D 14,31:4
Wirjopranoto, Sukardjo, 1962, O 24,39:4
Wirkus, Edward F, 1952, O 30,31:3
Wirkus, Faustin E (por), 1945, O 9,23:7
Wirsching, Alola, 1910, Jl 16,7:7
Wirt, Charles Summer, 1924, Ap 15,21:2
Wirt, Loyal L, 1961, Ap 29,23:3
Wirt, Lucius A, 1946, Ag 25,46:4
Wirt, William A (por), 1938, Mr 12,17:3
Wirt, William T, 1955, F 13,86:2
Wirtenberg, Abraham, 1939, Ja 7,15:2
Wirth, Albert E, 1949, Ja 15,17:1; 1951, Ag 4,15:5
Wirth, Augustine, 1960, S 21,32:4
Wirth, Ben, 1957, Je 13,31:3
Wirth, Charles, 1954, N 28,87:1
Wirth, Charles L, 1950, My 22,21:4
Wirth, Elmer H, 1947, S 28,60:7
Wirth, Frederick, 1941, O 8,23:5
Wirth, Fremont P, 1960, Ag 7,85:1
Wirth, George, 1941, O 18,19:2
Wirth, Irvin, 1951, Ja 11,25:4
Wirth, Jacob A Mrs, 1947, Ja 6,23:4
Wirth, John, 1941, My 10,15:2
Wirth, John Mrs, 1948, Ap 1,25:2
Wirth, John W Mrs, 1940, D 31,15:3
Wirth, John W Sr, 1952, N 6,29:5
Wirth, Josef, 1956, Ja 4,27:1
Wirth, Louis, 1952, My 4,90:5
Wirth, Mary H Mrs, 1949, Ja 18,23:1
Wirth, Phil, 1958, Je 24,31:5
Wirth, Theodore, 1949, Ja 30,60:7
Wirth, Walter F, 1952, Je 22,70:4
Wirth, William, 1948, Ja 16,21:3; 1959, S 5,15:2
Wirtner, Modestus A, 1948, S 1,48:4
Wirtschafter, Burton S, 1966, O 18,45:3
Wirtz, Alvin J, 1951, O 28,84:4
Wirtz, Aurella F, 1939, Ja 21,15:3
Wirtz, Oscar, 1954, Je 14,21:1
Wisa, Louis, 1953, Ja 20,25:2
Wisan, Jacob M, 1958, O 6,31:2
Wisan, Julian, 1958, Ap 27,86:7
Wischnitzer, Mark, 1955, O 18,37:5
Wisdom, Edmund A, 1941, Ag 10,37:3
Wisdom, John, 1940, Jl 10,19:1
Wise, A C Rear-Adm, 1923, N 24,13:3
Wise, Aaron Rabbi, 1917, N 29,13:5
Wise, Albert G, 1960, Ag 21,84:4
Wise, Albert J, 1903, D 11,9:5; 1942, F 5,21:2
Wise, Alfred L, 1947, Ag 11,23:3

Wise, Alfred M, 1952, D 30,19:1
Wise, Arthur J, 1955, Mr 13,86:6
Wise, Benedict S, 1939, F 10,23:3
Wise, Charles C, 1915, S 9,11:6
Wise, Charles F, 1938, S 30,21:2
Wise, Charles S, 1967, N 24,46:7
Wise, Clarence R, 1938, Ja 23,II,8:7
Wise, E F, 1933, N 6,19:4
Wise, Edward (por), 1939, Je 20,21:1
Wise, Edward H, 1923, Jl 17,19:6
Wise, Edward W Sr, 1962, O 7,82:7
Wise, Eliphalet C, 1943, N 28,68:2
Wise, Esther F Mrs, 1939, Ag 18,19:2
Wise, F M Com, 1901, Ag 15,7:6
Wise, Frank L, 1950, Mr 4,17:4
Wise, Frank W, 1940, Ja 29,15:4
Wise, Franklyn M, 1953, Ag 2,73:1
Wise, Fred, 1950, Jl 28,31:3; 1966, Ja 19,21:1
Wise, Frederic M (por), 1940, Jl 25,17:4
Wise, G Stewart, 1950, F 26,78:2
Wise, George, 1948, Je 26,18:2
Wise, George D, 1908, F 5,7:5
Wise, George J, 1957, O 26,21:6
Wise, H A, 1876, S 13,4:7
Wise, H A Capt, 1869, Je 23,5:4
Wise, Harold, 1954, D 22,48:1
Wise, Harry Jr, 1962, Je 10,86:4
Wise, Harry Sr, 1954, Ja 9,15:3
Wise, Helen G, 1952, F 10,93:1
Wise, Henry M Mrs, 1925, My 18,15:4; 1925, My 23, 15:6
Wise, Henry W, 1965, Jl 10,25:6
Wise, Herbert A, 1961, O 4,45:2
Wise, Herbert C, 1945, Je 12,19:3
Wise, Hugh D, 1942, My 29,17:3
Wise, Hugh D Mrs, 1956, O 28,88:1
Wise, Isaac M, 1955, Jl 12,25:1
Wise, Isaac M Dr, 1900, Mr 27,1:7
Wise, Isidore, 1956, Ja 26,29:5
Wise, J Robert Mrs, 1953, Jl 1,29:3
Wise, Jacob M, 1965, Je 28,29:3
Wise, James, 1939, Jl 9,31:1
Wise, James B, 1916, Je 8,13:6
Wise, James D Mrs, 1952, N 29,17:4
Wise, James W, 1939, D 7,27:5
Wise, Joanna D, 1958, Ag 23,15:2
Wise, John S, 1913, My 13,11:7
Wise, John S Jr, 1951, Mr 16,31:2
Wise, John S Jr Mrs, 1919, My 12,13:4
Wise, John S Mrs, 1925, Ap 14,23:4
Wise, Jonah B (trb, F 3,31:2; funl, F 4,33:2), 1959, F 2,25:1
Wise, Jonah B Mrs, 1950, My 9,30:3
Wise, Julius Dr, 1902, Ap 20,7:5
Wise, Leo A, 1950, N 26,90:5
Wise, Levi M Mrs, 1952, D 15,25:3
Wise, Lillian Mrs, 1907, F 18,9:5
Wise, Lorilard, 1947, S 25,29:4
Wise, Louis, 1956, Je 2,19:3
Wise, Marion J, 1950, Ap 27,29:4
Wise, Michael, 1942, N 30,23:5
Wise, Michael Mrs, 1952, Ja 27,76:3
Wise, Murray M, 1966, N 3,39:1
Wise, Nellie R Mrs, 1938, Jl 18,13:3
Wise, Otto Irving (funl, F 3,15:2), 1919, Ja 24,11:4
Wise, Roger M, 1950, F 6,25:4
Wise, Russell S, 1958, S 18,31:1
Wise, Sidney L, 1959, Mr 1,86:2
Wise, Sigmund Mrs, 1961, Jl 4,19:1
Wise, Stephen S, 1949, Ap 20,1:4
Wise, Stephen S Mrs, 1947, D 11,33:1
Wise, T A, 1928, Mr 22,25:3
Wise, Thomas J, 1937, My 14,23:3
Wise, Willard K Sr, 1963, Ag 14,33:5
Wise, William, 1903, D 11,9:5
Wise, William B Mrs, 1951, D 11,33:1
Wise, William C Jr, 1955, My 7,17:5
Wise, William H, 1954, O 27,29:4
Wisedell, John E, 1953, Mr 5,27:5
Wisedell, T, 1884, Ag 2,4:6
Wiseley, Clarence H, 1958, Je 23,23:4
Wiseltier, Henry Mrs, 1954, F 9,27:2
Wisely, Edward D, 1954, Je 3,27:4
Wisely, James, 1943, O 23,13:2
Wisely, James A, 1942, F 27,18:3
Wiseman, A M, 1948, Ap 7,25:3
Wiseman, Bruce K, 1960, Mr 16,37:2
Wiseman, Cardinal (funl, Mr 10,5:2), 1865, Mr 2,5:1
Wiseman, Eugene R, 1954, Je 15,29:3
Wiseman, Frederick A, 1952, Mr 3,21:4
Wiseman, Frederick J, 1961, O 6,35:3
Wiseman, Frederick L, 1944, Ja 17,19:5
Wiseman, George A, 1940, Mr 23,13:5
Wiseman, Guy E (will), 1939, Ap 9,III,2:4
Wiseman, Harrison G, 1945, Ja 14,40:4
Wiseman, John W, 1947, Je 10,27:4
Wiseman, Lloyd, 1952, O 6,33:6
Wiseman, Mark H Mrs, 1962, O 30,35:2
Wiseman, Philip, 1945, O 4,23:2
Wiseman, Robert Cummings Mrs (Ruth), 1968, Ap 29,43:5
Wiseman, Sam, 1950, F 20,25:4
Wiseman, W Wesley, 1943, Ag 13,17:4
Wiseman, William, 1962, Je 18,25:1
Wiseman, William Adm Sir, 1874, Jl 28,3:1
Wiseman, William H, 1951, D 21,27:3
Wisemiller, Bertha, 1940, N 13,23:3
Wiser, Isaac P Mrs, 1956, Jl 17,23:3
Wiser, William H, 1961, F 22,25:1
Wiser, Willis G, 1923, Ap 21,11:6
Wish, Merrill D, 1943, O 24,44:3
Wish, P Edward, 1948, Je 11,23:4
Wishard, Albert W, 1917, Jl 13,9:5
Wishard, Glenn P Mrs, 1939, Mr 13,17:4
Wishard, Luther D, 1925, Ag 7,15:6
Wishard, Luther D Mrs, 1947, Mr 9,60:8
Wishard, William N, 1941, Ja 23,22:2
Wishart, Charles F, 1960, Ap 12,33:3
Wishart, Charles F Rev Dr, 1924, Ap 5,15:5
Wishart, Clifton A, 1962, My 26,25:3
Wishart, James, 1943, Jl 22,19:1
Wishart, John, 1951, Jl 18,29:2
Wishart, Joseph, 1914, Ap 25,15:6
Wishart, William C, 1965, N 2,33:1
Wishart, William C Mrs, 1961, S 7,35:2
Wishengrad, I Bernard, 1959, Jl 19,69:1
Wishengrad, Morton, 1963, F 15,9:7
Wishengrad, Morton Mrs, 1951, Ja 10,27:4
Wishnack, Carl, 1957, Ag 6,27:2
Wishnevitz, Jacob Mrs, 1964, Ap 17,32:5
Wishon, Emory, 1948, Ja 5,19:5
Wiske, Prescott B, 1944, Je 6,17:2
Wisker, Thomas C, 1915, O 14,11:5
Wiskirchen, Rome Mrs, 1943, Ap 7,25:3
Wiskosky, Frank, 1951, Je 13,31:8
Wisler, Abe L, 1947, S 3,25:2
Wisler, Frank, 1955, Jl 23,32:3
Wislocki, George B, 1956, O 23,33:1
Wislon, Lyle C, 1967, My 24,47:2
Wisman, Walter, 1950, S 16,19:6
Wismar, William F Mrs, 1950, N 17,27:5
Wismer, Ernest L, 1940, Ap 23,23:3
Wismer, Harry, 1967, D 5,47:1
Wismer, Henry R, 1965, O 23,7:1
Wismer, Walter R, 1950, N 7,27:5
Wisner, Arthur, 1954, O 19,27:2
Wisner, Arthur Prof, 1903, Ja 19,1:4
Wisner, Charles K, 1942, Jl 7,20:5
Wisner, Ferdinand W, 1950, Ja 5,25:3
Wisner, Frank, 1947, Mr 20,27:2
Wisner, Frank G, 1938, Ap 25,15:2
Wisner, Frank P, 1944, S 6,19:4
Wisner, G Franklin, 1940, Jl 26,17:2
Wisner, George Y, 1906, Jl 4,7:6
Wisner, Herbert L, 1955, Je 14,29:2
Wisner, James Gov, 1867, Jl 14,3:7
Wisner, Jeffrey Amherst, 1908, Mr 24,7:5
Wisner, John H, 1906, Ja 14,9:6
Wisner, Louis L, 1937, Ja 19,24:2
Wisner, Paul, 1964, O 5,33:2
Wisner, Roger, 1946, Mr 2,13:3
Wisner, Samuel E, 1954, Je 11,23:5
Wisner, William D Sr, 1942, Ag 4,19:5
Wisner, William H, 1963, D 13,36:7
Wisniewski, Joseph, 1949, F 20,61:1
Wisotski, Felix, 1958, Ja 11,17:6
Wisotzkey, Harry A, 1946, Ja 26,13:6
Wisotzkey, Harry A Mrs, 1966, Je 12,86:5
Wiss, Frederick C J Mrs, 1959, Mr 7,22:1
Wiss, J Robert, 1955, Mr 9,27:3
Wiss, Jerome B, 1960, S 12,29:2
Wiss, Norman F, 1954, S 17,27:4
Wiss, Thomas H, 1947, Ag 6,23:6
Wiss, Thomas H Mrs, 1968, Ag 9,35:2
Wissel, Henry, 1959, N 26,37:3
Wissinger, Spencer V, 1963, Jl 11,29:1
Wissler, Clark, 1947, Ag 26,23:1
Wissler, Susan B Mrs, 1938, F 11,24:4
Wissman, Charles, 1951, N 20,31:5
Wissman, Leonard, 1957, Jl 26,19:1
Wissmann, Francis D Mrs, 1949, D 28,25:4
Wissmann, von Col, 1905, Je 17,2:5
Wissner, Charles E, 1938, O 9,45:3
Wissotzky, Abraham, 1949, Mr 8,25:2
Wistar, Dillwyn, 1916, F 13,15:4
Wistar, Edward M, 1941, Ja 23,21:3
Wistar, Isaac J Gen (will, S 22,6:4), 1905, S 19,9:6
Wistar, J Morris, 1958, Mr 22,17:4
Wister, Annis Lee Mrs, 1908, N 16,9:5
Wister, Charles J, 1954, Jl 4,31:2
Wister, Daniel W, 1938, Ag 6,13:3
Wister, Frances A (will, Mr 24,21:5), 1956, Mr 19, 31:5
Wister, James W, 1955, N 15,33:2
Wister, Owen (por), 1938, Jl 22,17:1
Wister, Owen J, 1968, Jl 6,21:4
Wister, Owen Jones Mrs, 1908, Je 10,7:5
Wister, Owen Mrs, 1913, Ag 25,5:4
Wister, Rodman Mifflin, 1922, D 24,20:3
Wister, William R, 1911, Ag 24,7:6
Wister, William R Mrs, 1944, Mr 2,17:2
Wister, William W, 1947, Ja 5,53:5
Wisting, O, 1936, D 5,19:3
Wiswall, Clarence A, 1942, Jl 22,19:3
Wiswall, Thomas C Mrs, 1949, Ap 15,23:1
Wiswell, Andrew P, 1906, D 5,11:5
Wiswell, George, 1963, My 21,37:4
Wiswell, George C, 1960, Ag 22,25:3
Wiswell, Robert I, 1951, My 24,35:4
Witaskin, Benjamin, 1924, D 30,17:5
Witbeck, Benjamin F, 1942, N 23,23:4
Witbeck, Clark, 1937, Ag 24,21:2
Witbeck, George H, 1941, F 27,19:2
Witchey, Frank, 1945, O 2,23:3
Witenberg, Joseph C, 1966, Ag 10,41:1
With, Hendrik M V De, 1945, S 12,25:2
Witham, Carlton C, 1949, Ag 13,12:2
Witham, Carlton Lee, 1968, Ag 17,27:5
Witham, Ernest C, 1958, F 22,17:1
Witham, George S, 1939, Je 8,25:4
Witham, George S Jr, 1953, Mr 25,31:4
Witham, Guy C, 1963, O 22,37:4
Withee, Mabel (Mrs L Puck), 1952, N 4,29:2
Witherbee, Barrett, 1914, Ag 26,9:6
Witherbee, Frank D, 1955, Ag 12,19:1
Witherbee, Frank Spencer, 1917, Ap 14,13:5
Witherbee, J G, 1875, Ag 27,4:5
Witherbee, Lispenard S, 1907, F 9,9:6
Witherbee, Walter T, 1922, S 29,19:6
Witherell, Alphonse, 1944, F 8,15:3
Witherell, Charles S, 1941, D 26,13:2
Witherell, Richard A, 1964, D 27,64:2
Witherell, Robert L, 1945, N 26,34:6
Witherill, Harriette E Mrs, 1941, F 15,15:2
Witherill, Nathaniel, 1906, My 24,9:5
Witherington, Horace V, 1960, N 23,29:1
Witherow, Kenneth C, 1946, My 10,19:4
Witherow, William P Sr, 1960, Ja 8,25:2
Withers, Carl K, 1961, F 5,81:1
Withers, Charles, 1947, Jl 11,15:2
Withers, Charles A, 1939, N 2,23:6
Withers, D D, 1892, F 19,8:3
Withers, Garrett L, 1953, My 1,21:2
Withers, George K, 1959, F 10,33:3
Withers, Glenn S, 1960, Jl 24,64:5
Withers, Grant, 1959, Mr 28,8:3
Withers, Granville G, 1941, Ja 24,17:2
Withers, Hector M, 1950, Ja 6,22:3
Withers, John J Sir, 1939, D 30,15:2
Withers, John W, 1961, F 7,33:4
Withers, Mary S, 1950, N 25,13:4
Withers, Pierce, 1948, S 14,30:2
Withers, Robert E, 1952, D 30,19:5
Withers, Robert E (will), 1953, Je 21,33:6
Withers, Sanford M, 1938, Mr 10,21:3
Withers, Sarah, 1955, Ja 4,21:1
Withers, Thomas Mrs, 1937, Ja 4,29:2
Withers, Walter E, 1948, Ja 28,23:4
Withers, Walter H, 1946, D 5,32:3
Withers, William G, 1953, Jl 26,69:3
Withers, William S, 1905, Jl 16,12:5
Witherspoon, Alex M, 1964, Mr 5,33:3
Witherspoon, Charles G, 1962, Jl 28,19:6
Witherspoon, Charles S Mrs, 1938, Jl 1,19:6
Witherspoon, Cora, 1957, N 19,33:2
Witherspoon, Cora Victoria Mrs, 1925, Jl 24,13:6
Witherspoon, H, 1935, My 11,1:1
Witherspoon, Preston, 1947, D 12,27:2
Witherspoon, Robert A, 1953, O 27,27:4
Witherspoon, Samuel A, 1915, N 25,13:5
Witherwax, Trueman, 1946, Ap 10,27:4
Withey, Frederic N, 1945, F 20,19:6
Withey, Herbert C Rev, 1937, F 12,23:3
Withey, Morton O, 1961, D 13,43:1
Withey, Newell E, 1948, Mr 23,25:5
Withington, Alfreda B, 1951, O 2,27:5
Withington, Alonzo O, 1949, Ag 8,15:1
Withington, Frederic S, 1939, F 5,40:4
Withington, Frederick B, 1943, Jl 8,19:5
Withington, Henry Jr, 1958, My 22,29:4
Withington, I C, 1881, N 23,2:5
Withington, L Rev, 1885, Ap 23,5:6
Withington, Paul C, 1966, Ap 3,85:3
Withington, Robert, 1957, S 2,13:5
Withington, Robert W, 1940, Ja 6,13:4
Withington, Sidney, 1962, F 14,33:1
Withorne, Emerson, 1958, Mr 27,33:2
Withrow, Atkinson R, 1941, Ag 10,37:2
Withrow, Gardner R, 1964, S 24,41:4
Withrow, John G, 1942, N 27,23:5
Withrow, John W, 1955, D 24,13:2
Withrow, Robert B, 1958, Ap 9,33:2
Withrow, William J, 1953, S 8,31:1
Withstandley, Victor D, 1955, Ag 28,85:2
Withstandley, Victor D Mrs, 1954, Ja 29,19:1
Withycomb, Donald, 1960, O 14,33:2
Witkiewicz, John P, 1954, Je 21,27:4
Witkin, Morton Mrs, 1950, O 26,31:5
Witkoski, Felix M, 1952, F 6,29:5
Witkowsky, James, 1950, F 10,23:4
Witlin, William G, 1951, Ag 16,27:4
Witman, Charles B Judge, 1925, Ap 8,21:5
Witman, John C, 1951, D 18,32:3
Witman, Walter F, 1943, S 17,21:3
Witmans, A J, 1944, O 18,21:1
Witmark, Frank, 1948, Ag 6,17:6
Witmark, Isidore (por), 1941, Ap 10,23:5
Witmark, Jay, 1950, F 18,15:5
Witmark, Marcus, 1910, Mr 30,12:1

Witmer, Adelaide C Mrs, 1942, D 30,23:3
Witmer, Francis Sr, 1954, O 29,23:4
Witmer, Lightner, 1956, Jl 21,15:5
Witmer, Martin W, 1956, O 11,39:2
Witmer, Roy C, 1950, Ap 2,92:3
Witmond, Albert, 1957, Ap 7,88:8
Witney, Frank E, 1940, O 23,23:4
Witney, Richard A, 1950, N 2,31:3
Witruk, John, 1950, Je 18,76:6
Witry, Louis A (will, Ap 22,21:5), 1939, Ap 20,23:2
Witschey, Robert E, 1966, D 26,21:1
Witschger, Eugene O, 1948, My 28,23:2
Witschieben, A H, 1965, O 24,86:7
Witschieben, Frederick, 1944, D 4,23:1
Witschief, Graham (por), 1945, Ja 12,15:1
Witsenhuysen, Hartog, 1961, Jl 12,31:2
Witt, Charles E, 1947, N 28,27:1
Witt, Dan H (por), 1942, F 16,17:4
Witt, Eli, 1947, F 1,15:6
Witt, Emil E, 1948, Ap 6,23:3
Witt, Erwin, 1965, Mr 28,93:1
Witt, Erwin Mrs, 1964, Mr 24,33:1
Witt, Frank E, 1951, N 17,17:3
Witt, George F, 1940, Mr 4,15:2
Witt, Gustave Mrs, 1959, Je 10,37:3
Witt, Herman H, 1953, D 27,60:4
Witt, Isaac M, 1942, My 27,23:3
Witt, J Henry, 1960, Je 3,31:4
Witt, John H Mrs, 1952, O 17,27:1
Witt, Joseph T Mrs, 1950, Mr 2,27:5
Witt, Julius, 1879, D 22,2:4
Witt, Louis, 1950, N 18,15:6
Witt, Natalie Mrs, 1950, N 19,55:2
Witt, Peter, 1948, O 21,27:1
Witt, Robert, 1952, Mr 28,24:4
Witt, Robert H, 1967, Jl 11,37:1
Witt, Stillman, 1875, My 4,6:7
Witt, T Foster, 1939, O 29,40:8
Witt, Walter W, 1959, F 28,19:6
Witt, Webster W, 1949, S 15,27:3
Witt, William, 1949, O 24,25:4
Witt, William N, 1948, S 14,29:3
Wittal, Julian J, 1952, Ja 15,27:3
Wittcoff, Harold, 1962, N 1,31:4
Wittcoff, Isaak, 1952, Ja 11,22:2
Witte, B Victor Mrs, 1943, O 12,27:5
Witte, C, 1883, Mr 18,9:2
Witte, Edwin E, 1960, My 22,86:3
Witte, Fred C Mrs, 1952, Ap 15,27:1
Witte, Fred J, 1943, Ap 30,21:5
Witte, Harry S Sr, 1952, Ag 1,17:4
Witte, Henry J, 1952, N 7,23:4
Witte, Lawrence E, 1965, F 22,21:4
Witte, Otto, 1958, Ag 14,29:4
Witte, Paul J, 1960, Ap 9,23:4
Witte, Sergius Julievitch Count, 1915, Mr 14,3:5
Witte, Theodore, 1937, N 18,23:5
Witte, William C F, 1947, O 13,23:2
Witte, William J, 1945, O 20,11:2
Witte, William J Mrs, 1962, Jl 26,27:5
Wittegren, Charles J (will), 1938, D 7,2:2
Wittell, William F, 1954, N 3,29:1
Wittels, Fritz, 1950, O 17,31:3
Wittels, Ludwig, 1956, D 15,25:3
Witteman, Anna M, 1952, Jl 1,23:2
Wittemann, Char R (cor, Jl 11,37:4), 1967, Jl 9,60:6
Wittemann, Herman L, 1952, D 16,31:2
Wittemore, Charles H, 1946, S 15,9:8
Wittemore, John H, 1910, My 29,II,7:5
Witten, Henry A, 1937, D 18,21:5
Witten, Jack W, 1959, N 1,85:5
Witten, John D, 1948, F 19,23:3
Wittenberg, Albert M, 1941, Ja 31,19:5
Wittenberg, Charles J, 1919, Mr 20,13:3
Wittenberg, Charles J Mrs, 1919, Ap 8,11:4
Wittenberg, George, 1953, Ja 30,21:2
Wittenberg, Joseph, 1949, Ja 13,24:2
Wittenberg, Lester, 1937, Ja 19,24:3
Wittenberg, Max, 1956, Ja 23,25:4
Wittenberg, Robert B, 1964, Ja 2,27:2
Wittenberg, Robert B Mrs, 1965, Mr 23,39:1
Wittenham, Lord, 1931, F 2,19:1
Wittenmyer, Edmund Maj-Gen, 1937, Jl 6,19:5
Wittenstein, Martin, 1959, My 30,17:3
Witter, William Clitus, 1914, Mr 29,5:5
Wittershagen, Gerhard, 1946, F 17,42:5
Wittes, Saul A Mrs, 1946, D 10,31:4
Wittgenstein, Paul, 1961, Mr 4,23:4
Wittgenstein, Victor, 1961, Jl 26,16:3
Witthack, Henry, 1938, Ag 19,19:2
Witthaus, Rudolph August Dr, 1915, D 21,13:4
Witthohn, Adolph H, 1945, S 6,25:5
Witthuhn, Fred G, 1948, O 5,25:4
Wittich, George, 1943, Ap 15,25:4
Wittich, Wilbur R, 1964, Ja 15,31:4
Wittig, Edward, 1941, N 29,17:2
Wittig, Isaac P, 1937, Mr 8,19:3
Wittig, Robert V, 1945, N 8,19:1
Witting, Richard, 1923, D 26,15:5
Witting, Rolf J, 1944, O 13,19:3
Wittke, Paul A, 1946, D 3,31:3
Wittke, Richard O, 1938, D 3,20:1
Wittke, Wellington C Mrs, 1955, Ja 20,31:3
Wittkop, Joseph, 1951, F 24,13:3
Wittland, Frank, 1959, F 24,29:3
Wittler, Lelia, 1960, F 28,82:2
Wittlin, Louis Mrs, 1961, D 30,19:2
Wittmack, E Franklin, 1956, Ap 29,87:1
Wittman, Chris Mrs, 1948, Ap 30,23:1
Wittman, Frank, 1967, D 31,44:4
Wittman, Harry L, 1948, Je 6,72:5
Wittman, Joseph, 1940, S 29,44:1
Wittman, Joseph J, 1948, D 29,22:3
Wittmann, Catherine T Mrs, 1942, Jl 11,13:4
Wittmann, Christoph, 1956, Je 15,25:4
Wittmann, George J, 1944, Ja 15,13:4
Wittmann, Konrad F, 1951, Ap 18,31:4
Wittmann, Leonard, 1949, O 11,34:4
Wittmann, Leonard W Mrs, 1952, My 8,31:4
Wittmann, William Mrs, 1958, Jl 19,15:5
Wittmer, Albert, 1950, Mr 11,15:6
Wittmer, August, 1951, Ag 20,19:4
Wittmer, George Jr, 1945, Mr 2,19:4
Wittmer, John J, 1951, My 21,27:3
Wittmer, Thomas, 1939, Ag 16,23:4
Wittmeyer, A V Rev, 1926, N 13,17:5
Wittnauer, Albert C, 1908, Mr 27,9:6
Wittnauer, Emile J, 1916, Je 16,13:6
Wittnauer, Martha S, 1951, Je 25,19:3
Wittnebert, Lester V, 1949, Jl 28,23:3
Witton, Thomas, 1903, D 22,9:5
Wittpen, John N, 1940, Je 8,15:3
Wittpen, Russell, 1965, Mr 9,35:2
Wittpenn, C S Mrs, 1932, D 5,17:1
Wittrisch, Marcel, 1955, Je 4,15:5
Witts, Frank H, 1941, My 13,23:3
Wittschen, Harry J, 1955, Mr 18,27:3
Wittschen, Harry J Mrs, 1965, N 6,29:4
Wittschen, John G Jr, 1949, S 23,23:4
Wittson, Clara B Mrs, 1942, My 29,17:1
Wittson, Girard S, 1940, Ap 11,25:4
Wittstein, Reuben J, 1966, Je 12,87:1
Wittwer, George G Mrs, 1951, Je 21,27:5
Witty, Henry, 1937, My 24,19:4
Witty, Irving, 1960, Jl 30,17:5
Witty, Noah, 1957, F 25,25:1
Witty, Samuel (por), 1943, S 19,49:1
Witwer, Albert M, 1951, Mr 2,25:3
Witwer, George M, 1942, My 29,17:2
Witz, Albert A, 1953, My 24,88:4
Witz, Garfield T, 1953, Ag 21,17:1
Witz, Warren R, 1951, N 12,25:3
Witzel, August E, 1944, My 16,21:5
Witzel, Emil, 1952, Je 13,23:5
Witzel, Joseph, 1913, O 26,15:6
Witzel, Theodore, 1923, D 31,13:4
Witzell, Paul J Mrs, 1956, F 14,29:5
Witzendorff, Bodo von, 1943, Ag 13,4:4
Witzig, Herman J, 1944, N 29,23:2
Witzork, Bernard J, 1952, Ap 12,11:3
Wixson, John H, 1937, F 27,17:5
Wixted, Joseph F, 1948, Ja 30,24:3; 1953, Ag 16,76:5
Wizla, Piotr, 1955, Mr 25,23:2
Wlach, Oskar, 1963, Ag 20,33:3
Wladasz, Francis M Msgr, 1959, Jl 27,25:5
Wladaver, Monte M, 1954, O 6,25:1
Wlecke, Bernard, 1947, N 1,15:3
Wobber, Edward H, 1961, Je 4,86:3
Wobber, Edward H Mrs, 1964, O 13,43:2
Wobensmith, George H, 1938, Je 4,15:4
Wobensmith, Z Taylor, 1937, N 5,23:4
Wochinski, Aloysius J, 1944, My 31,19:1
Wode, George V, 1950, D 3,89:1
Wodehouse, Eleanor Mrs, 1941, F 22,15:3
Wodell, Frederick W, 1938, F 15,25:3
Wodey, Augustus, 1951, Jl 18,29:3
Wodey, Richard J, 1950, Ag 15,29:4
Wodey, Walter H, 1937, Ap 15,23:5
Wodiska, Edward, 1938, Mr 10,21:3
Wodiska, Julius, 1925, F 8,7:2
Wodon, Louis, 1946, D 28,15:5
Wodtke, Hans V, 1950, Ap 1,15:6
Wodzicki, Edward P, 1964, Je 23,33:4
Wodzicki, Stanley Mrs, 1959, Ap 2,31:4
Woebse, Henry R, 1937, F 18,21:4
Woebse, Theodore H, 1940, My 21,23:3
Woehl, Arthur L, 1967, Mr 19,92:7
Woehler, Conrad W, 1947, N 28,27:2
Woehler, F, 1882, S 26,5:3
Woehning, Paula, 1910, N 29,11:4
Woehr, Edward P, 1943, Ja 18,15:1
Woehr, J A Rudolph, 1950, Ag 2,25:4
Woehrle, Otto A E, 1947, N 19,27:1
Woelfel, George, 1950, Mr 17,24:3; 1951, S 20,31:1
Woelfel, Herbert E, 1949, F 14,19:5
Woelfert, Ludwig P O, 1946, Jl 4,19:6
Woelfflin, Heinrich, 1946, Ja 15,23:1
Woelfkin, C, 1928, Ja 7,17:1
Woelfkin, L D Mrs, 1932, D 9,21:1
Woelfle, John J, 1961, N 16,39:3
Woelfling, Leopold former Archduke of Austria, 1935, Jl 5,13:1
Woeltge, Albert Prof, 1910, S 13,9:6
Woerishoffer, C F, 1886, My 11,1:7
Woerishoffer, Emma Carola (est), 1912, Jl 17,9:5
Woermann, Adolph, 1911, My 5,11:4
Woermann, Eduard, 1920, My 28,13:4
Woerner, Carl G, 1950, Ag 1,23:4
Woerner, Kurt, 1957, My 4,21:5
Woerner, William M, 1950, S 27,31:1
Woertendyke, Harold P, 1957, D 28,18:1
Woerter, Otto C, 1943, Ag 19,19:6
Woerz, Charles H, 1923, Ag 27,11:3
Woerz, Ernest G W, 1916, My 10,13:7
Woerz, Frederic, 1947, F 15,15:5
Woerz, Frederick, 1949, My 11,29:4
Woessner, Anna F, 1967, My 20,35:5
Woessner, J Frederick Sr, 1955, D 7,39:1
Woeste, Baron, 1922, Ap 6,17:5
Woeste, Joseph H, 1958, N 5,35:3
Woesthoff, William H, 1945, Ag 27,19:5
Woestijne, Gustaaf van de, 1947, Ap 22,28:3
Woffindin, Reginald V, 1948, F 21,13:5
Wofford, Harris Mrs, 1961, Jl 1,17:1
Wofford, John W, 1955, Mr 1,25:4
Wofford, Kate V, 1954, N 1,27:6
Wofsey, Abraham, 1944, D 28,19:5
Wofsey, Michael, 1951, N 6,29:6
Wofsy, Nathan, 1961, Je 9,33:2
Wogan, Thomas F (por), 1949, Je 16,30:3
Woggon, Arthur C, 1949, Mr 18,25:1
Woglom, Russell S, 1949, Ap 28,31:3
Woglom, Theodore, 1953, F 8,88:2
Woglom, William H, 1953, Ag 9,77:3
Wohl, Abraham, 1948, Ag 19,21:3
Wohl, David P, 1960, Mr 4,25:5
Wohl, Fannie Mrs, 1942, My 13,19:5
Wohl, George W, 1967, Je 5,43:4
Wohl, Hyman, 1940, O 7,18:2
Wohl, Ignatz, 1958, F 4,29:1
Wohl, Maurice J, 1947, S 6,18:2
Wohl, Mordecai, 1948, N 5,25:3
Wohl, R Richard, 1957, N 16,19:1
Wohlauer, Leopold, 1956, Mr 3,19:4
Wohlenberg, Charlotte A Mrs, 1949, S 21,24:3
Wohlenberg, Walter J, 1956, Ag 9,25:1
Wohlers, C William, 1940, Je 22,15:2
Wohlers, Charles, 1944, F 5,15:3
Wohlfahrt, Karl K, 1957, N 28,31:3
Wohlfarth, Conrad R, 1942, D 28,19:4
Wohlfarth, Julia H, 1945, Mr 22,23:3
Wohlfarth, Rudolph Mrs, 1942, S 1,20:2
Wohlfarth, William C, 1946, Jl 12,17:2
Wohlforth, Martin, 1948, Ap 20,27:2
Wohlgelernter, Jacob I, 1966, My 30,19:4
Wohlleb, Charles, 1955, Je 1,33:3
Wohlman, Irving, 1949, Je 25,13:6
Wohlman, William, 1964, D 23,27:3
Wohlmuth, Louis, 1939, F 15,23:2
Wohlmuth, Samuel, 1959, S 23,35:3
Wohlrab, Leonard L, 1952, Mr 10,21:4
Wohlstetter, Isidor, 1959, Je 3,35:1
Wohlwender, Fred, 1946, Ap 6,17:4
Wohnsiedler, Jacob (por), 1946, N 29,25:2
Wohnsiedler, John, 1945, S 18,23:5
Woiceske, Ronau W, 1953, Jl 22,27:5
Wojack, Frank, 1943, O 12,33:1
Wojahn, Max, 1951, Je 22,31:3
Wojcicki, Michael, 1953, O 22,29:4
Wojciechowski, Bogumil M, 1960, Ap 19,37:1
Wojcik, Marion, 1956, Ag 29,29:2
Wojczynski, Leo J, 1950, Ap 20,29:4
Wojewodski, Serge S, 1961, N 4,19:4
Wojtech, Joseph, 1952, F 5,29:5
Wojtkowiak, Stephen J, 1945, Ap 7,15:6
Wojtkowski, Adam F, 1954, Je 27,68:2
Wojtkowski, Chester, 1952, My 30,15:3
Wojtul, Peter P Mrs, 1968, D 5,47:4
Wokes, Zaidie, 1952, Mr 10,21:6
Woladorsky, Julius, 1939, Mr 19,III,6:3
Wolaver, Earl S, 1950, Jl 1,15:6
Wolbach, Robert, 1967, Mr 14,47:4
Wolbach, S Burt, 1954, Mr 20,15:3
Wolbarst, Abraham L, 1952, Je 4,27:5
Wolbarst, Abraham L Mrs, 1938, Ap 14,23:3
Wolbarst, Bernard Mrs, 1904, S 20,9:6
Wolbarst, Eli S, 1952, D 5,27:4
Wolber, Gustave C, 1949, N 15,25:1
Wolber, Joseph G, 1947, Ap 9,25:1
Wolber, Joseph W Mrs, 1940, F 22,23:2
Wolbert, Howard E, 1947, O 16,28:3
Wolbert, Sue B Mrs, 1940, Ap 27,15:4
Wolburg, Morris, 1944, Ja 13,21:3
Wolcott, Allen J, 1922, Mr 16,17:5
Wolcott, Caroline Mrs, 1925, S 17,23:4
Wolcott, Clarence, 1950, N 6,27:2
Wolcott, Clarence E, 1937, Mr 30,23:6
Wolcott, Clarence M, 1948, Ap 18,68:4
Wolcott, D Oliver, 1949, Jl 30,15:5
Wolcott, Edgar C, 1943, Ag 27,17:5
Wolcott, Edward O ex-Sen, 1905, Mr 2,1:3
Wolcott, F H, 1883, Ap 15,13:2
Wolcott, Frank B, 1964, Je 13,23:3
Wolcott, Frederick F, 1937, My 25,27:2
Wolcott, George N, 1965, O 22,43:1
Wolcott, George R, 1948, My 27,25:4
Wolcott, George R Mrs, 1949, Ja 27,23:2
Wolcott, Harry E, 1941, My 30,15:2
Wolcott, Helen B, 1956, D 10,31:5

Wolcott, Henry Roger, 1921, Je 8,17:6
Wolcott, Herbert R, 1951, D 29,11:5
Wolcott, Herman F, 1941, S 6,15:5
Wolcott, Ira E Mrs, 1948, Ag 31,23:1
Wolcott, John D, 1945, N 25,49:1
Wolcott, Joseph, 1940, Ja 5,10:6
Wolcott, Josiah O (por), 1938, N 12,15:1
Wolcott, Katherine, 1944, Ag 26,11:6
Wolcott, Kenneth W, 1959, Je 30,31:3
Wolcott, Maurice R Mrs, 1963, Jl 18,27:5
Wolcott, Roger G, 1958, N 2,40:4
Wolcott, Roger Mrs (Delphine W), 1964, S 26,23:2
Wolcott, Wallace Mrs, 1951, N 27,31:5
Wolcott, William E, 1937, S 18,19:3; 1942, Ja 13,22:5
Wolcoxen, Fred S, 1948, Jl 30,18:2
Wold, Emma, 1950, Jl 22,15:4
Wold, Paul, 1965, Ag 6,27:3
Wold, Peter H, 1959, D 13,86:5
Wold, Peter I, 1945, Je 18,19:4
Woldike, Aage, 1958, S 11,33:4
Wolf, Abraham, 1951, Mr 1,27:4
Wolf, Adam, 1951, Ap 1,93:1
Wolf, Adolph E, 1949, D 11,92:8
Wolf, Albert, 1943, Ag 14,11:4
Wolf, Alexander, 1966, Ag 11,33:5
Wolf, Alfred M, 1955, Je 14,29:5
Wolf, Arthur P, 1946, D 4,31:1
Wolf, August, 1920, Jl 26,11:7
Wolf, Austin M, 1949, Ag 24,25:1
Wolf, Benjamin, 1966, F 20,88:5
Wolf, Benjamin H, 1962, Ag 17,23:5
Wolf, Benjamin Mrs, 1954, Ja 27,27:1
Wolf, Bernard J Mrs, 1942, Je 18,21:1; 1948, Ja 30, 24:2
Wolf, Charles, 1968, O 17,47:3
Wolf, Charles B, 1951, Ja 9,30:3
Wolf, Charles J, 1939, D 6,25:2; 1946, S 2,17:5
Wolf, Charles K, 1908, Ja 13,7:4
Wolf, Charlie (One Arm), 1959, Je 27,24:2
Wolf, Clarence, 1937, Jl 24,15:2
Wolf, Clifford A, 1952, F 6,29:2
Wolf, Clifford C Mrs, 1959, Jl 21,30:7
Wolf, Daniel, 1962, Mr 9,19:4
Wolf, David J, 1950, O 14,19:4
Wolf, David R, 1937, Mr 14,25:2
Wolf, E L, 1881, Ag 21,7:3
Wolf, Edith T, 1948, F 12,23:1
Wolf, Edwin H, 1937, S 26,II,9:3
Wolf, Emanuel M, 1968, S 11,47:2
Wolf, Erich, 1913, Mr 20,11:4
Wolf, Everett D, 1960, My 15,86:2
Wolf, Frank, 1948, Ja 18,60:4; 1952, Mr 24,25:5
Wolf, Frank E, 1951, D 20,31:3
Wolf, Frank N, 1949, Ap 4,23:4
Wolf, Frank W, 1939, My 8,17:3
Wolf, Franklin W, 1946, Ja 4,22:3
Wolf, Fred L, 1957, O 31,31:4
Wolf, Frederic L, 1942, O 22,21:5
Wolf, Frederic L Jr, 1961, Ja 25,33:4
Wolf, Frederick, 1960, Mr 28,29:4
Wolf, Frederick C, 1949, D 23,21:3
Wolf, Frederick M, 1956, Ap 3,35:1
Wolf, Friedrich, 1953, O 6,29:5
Wolf, George, 1947, Jl 19,13:2; 1949, O 25,27:2
Wolf, George A, 1958, O 20,29:1
Wolf, George D, 1954, Ap 14,29:4
Wolf, George H, 1942, D 20,44:5
Wolf, George J Mrs, 1960, F 25,29:2
Wolf, George W, 1962, Je 7,35:1
Wolf, George W Mrs, 1954, Je 17,29:4
Wolf, Gustav, 1947, D 19,25:4
Wolf, H J Rabbi, 1927, F 18,21:6
Wolf, Harry, 1960, Ja 10,86:8
Wolf, Harry B, 1944, F 18,17:4
Wolf, Harry F, 1966, S 24,23:4
Wolf, Harry G, 1939, Ag 8,17:2
Wolf, Harry J, 1961, D 26,25:2
Wolf, Harry S, 1960, Ja 24,88:4
Wolf, Heinrich F, 1959, My 13,37:2
Wolf, Henry, 1916, Mr 20,11:4; 1943, Ag 23,15:5; 1962, S 29,23:6
Wolf, Henry F A, 1947, O 24,23:5
Wolf, Henry J Dr (por), 1937, Mr 23,24:2
Wolf, Henry J Mrs, 1955, F 21,21:1
Wolf, Herman Mrs, 1943, S 18,17:1; 1954, N 6,17:3
Wolf, Irwin D, 1956, Ap 19,31:3
Wolf, Isaac W, 1951, N 8,29:5
Wolf, Jack Dr, 1968, Jl 9,35:4
Wolf, Jacob, 1950, Ap 11,31:4
Wolf, Jacques P, 1954, Ja 27,27:3
Wolf, James J Mrs, 1950, Je 24,13:4
Wolf, James M, 1962, Jl 24,27:2
Wolf, John, 1962, N 29,37:5
Wolf, John C, 1942, Ag 25,23:5
Wolf, John E Sr, 1946, O 8,24:2
Wolf, John M, 1941, F 28,19:4
Wolf, John N, 1938, Ag 5,18:4
Wolf, John R, 1938, My 25,23:4
Wolf, Joseph F Mrs, 1958, Ap 25,27:3
Wolf, Joseph J, 1955, F 3,23:4
Wolf, Julius, 1944, Ja 21,17:5
Wolf, Julius Mrs, 1962, S 28,33:2
Wolf, Jutta (Mrs D S Broun), 1958, F 25,55:5
Wolf, Kilian Mrs, 1950, S 9,17:4
Wolf, L J Mrs, 1947, Je 12,25:3
Wolf, Leonard J, 1965, Ja 20,39:1
Wolf, Leopold J, 1947, D 2,30:2
Wolf, Leroy J Mrs, 1967, F 8,28:6
Wolf, Louis, 1937, Ap 15,23:2; 1945, Jl 6,11:6; 1949, Ap 6,29:4; 1955, F 16,29:1
Wolf, Louis E, 1955, My 30,13:5
Wolf, Luther B, 1939, N 26,42:6
Wolf, Manny, 1940, D 14,17:3
Wolf, Margaret R Mrs, 1941, O 30,23:1
Wolf, Marguerite L, 1951, Ap 11,29:5
Wolf, Mary J, 1941, Je 1,35:3
Wolf, Milton, 1955, S 17,15:2
Wolf, Milton Mrs, 1951, N 25,87:2
Wolf, Morris Dr, 1914, Ap 19,IV,7:5
Wolf, Otto, 1959, Mr 1,86:1
Wolf, Paul O, 1958, Mr 3,27:1
Wolf, Paula, 1960, Je 3,31:3
Wolf, Philip, 1908, My 9,7:5
Wolf, Phillip M, 1944, S 24,46:3
Wolf, Ralph, 1951, O 27,19:3
Wolf, Ralph W, 1967, Jl 20,37:5
Wolf, Raymond J, 1948, Ag 15,60:5
Wolf, Rennold, 1922, Ja 3,17:3
Wolf, Robert B, 1954, N 12,21:2
Wolf, Robert O, 1966, Mr 2,41:4
Wolf, Rudolph, 1948, Je 17,25:2
Wolf, Sadie Mrs, 1949, S 30,23:3
Wolf, Samuel D, 1967, Mr 6,28:8
Wolf, Sandor, 1946, F 19,25:5
Wolf, Silas A Mrs, 1944, Ap 3,21:6
Wolf, Simon (funl, Je 6,21:4), 1923, Je 5,21:3
Wolf, Solomon B, 1917, Mr 6,11:5
Wolf, T Martin, 1957, My 9,31:4
Wolf, Theodore B, 1959, Ag 18,30:3
Wolf, Theodore G, 1960, S 12,29:6
Wolf, Victor Capt, 1910, Ja 22,9:4
Wolf, Walter B, 1961, Jl 1,17:2
Wolf, Walter I Mrs, 1950, My 1,25:5
Wolf, Walter R, 1963, My 19,86:2
Wolf, William B, 1960, Ja 25,27:3
Wolf, William C, 1962, O 17,39:4
Wolf, William E, 1958, Jl 28,23:5
Wolf, William F Mrs, 1967, Mr 7,41:1
Wolf, William J, 1940, N 26,23:2; 1952, D 2,36:5
Wolf, William M, 1965, N 22,37:1
Wolf, William Mrs, 1952, N 20,31:2
Wolf-Andrews, Eva Mrs, 1955, O 6,29:2
Wolf-Ferrari, Ermanno, 1948, Ja 22,27:1
Wolfe, Abraham M Mrs, 1950, Mr 24,25:2
Wolfe, Albert, 1944, Mr 14,19:5
Wolfe, Allan Mrs, 1963, N 8,32:1
Wolfe, Allen S, 1945, S 27,21:5
Wolfe, Archie R, 1958, Ja 4,15:3
Wolfe, Arthur L Mrs, 1964, Mr 29,61:1
Wolfe, Arthur W, 1953, Ja 21,31:2
Wolfe, Carver W, 1948, Ap 18,71:3
Wolfe, Catharine L, 1887, Ap 5,8:1
Wolfe, Charlemagne T, 1948, F 24,25:4
Wolfe, Charles, 1954, N 11,31:1
Wolfe, Charles A, 1956, Ag 24,19:4
Wolfe, Charles H, 1951, N 29,33:6
Wolfe, Chris, 1901, Je 15,9:6
Wolfe, Christian F, 1962, Ap 18,39:3
Wolfe, Claire, 1952, My 14,28:3
Wolfe, Clifford M, 1947, My 9,22:2
Wolfe, De Forrest, 1943, Je 5,15:5
Wolfe, Earl Mrs, 1963, N 14,35:4
Wolfe, Edgar B, 1949, O 19,29:3
Wolfe, Edgar F (Jim Nasium), 1958, Ag 10,93:2
Wolfe, Edgar T Sr, 1957, F 3,76:8
Wolfe, Edward I Jr, 1951, F 17,15:1
Wolfe, Emil E, 1952, Ap 22,29:2
Wolfe, Emilie E Mrs, 1949, Je 15,29:4
Wolfe, Emma J Mrs, 1944, F 12,13:6
Wolfe, Ernest H Mrs, 1947, Ja 1,33:4
Wolfe, Frank, 1961, Jl 16,69:2
Wolfe, Frank E, 1948, Jl 9,19:4
Wolfe, Frank J, 1953, Jl 6,17:5
Wolfe, Frederick Fay, 1925, Ja 14,21:4
Wolfe, Frederick J, 1953, Ag 18,23:3
Wolfe, George C, 1951, Ja 18,27:2
Wolfe, George O, 1942, N 28,13:5
Wolfe, Gordon W, 1943, F 28,48:1
Wolfe, H Carl (por), 1955, Je 27,21:2
Wolfe, H Rev, 1884, Jl 14,5:2
Wolfe, Harry D Mrs, 1957, Mr 8,25:2
Wolfe, Harry G, 1968, O 8,47:1
Wolfe, Harry P (por), 1946, Ja 11,22:2
Wolfe, Harry P Mrs, 1941, S 23,23:3
Wolfe, Henderson M, 1951, Ag 25,11:6
Wolfe, Herbert O, 1964, D 23,30:3
Wolfe, Herman, 1966, F 19,27:1
Wolfe, Horace G, 1938, F 3,23:2
Wolfe, Howard D, 1945, N 29,23:3
Wolfe, Humbert (por), 1940, Ja 6,13:4
Wolfe, I Erlich, 1955, Mr 28,27:1
Wolfe, Isaac, 1938, Ap 29,21:4
Wolfe, J Theodore, 1963, My 5,86:4
Wolfe, James C, 1938, My 24,19:5
Wolfe, James E Mrs, 1950, Ap 1,15:3
Wolfe, James H, 1958, Mr 29,17:2
Wolfe, James Mrs (L Lauferty), 1958, F 20,25:4
Wolfe, Jeannette, 1951, Jl 29,44:7
Wolfe, John C Mrs (Helen Worth), 1957, Jl 24,25:2
Wolfe, John David, 1872, My 20,5:2
Wolfe, John J, 1954, Ag 2,17:3
Wolfe, John M, 1958, O 5,86:8
Wolfe, John Mrs, 1913, Ja 12,II,17:1; 1917, Ag 25,7:5
Wolfe, John W, 1939, Je 5,17:4
Wolfe, Jonas T, 1948, Mr 9,23:4
Wolfe, Joseph E, 1960, Ja 16,21:4
Wolfe, Joseph L N, 1949, Je 29,28:2
Wolfe, Kate Mrs, 1937, Jl 13,19:2
Wolfe, LeRoy E, 1946, S 15,9:6
Wolfe, Louis J, 1944, Mr 23,3:1; 1947, S 20,15:2
Wolfe, M Goode, 1945, Ja 31,21:2
Wolfe, Manny, 1952, O 22,27:4
Wolfe, Marcella G Mrs, 1939, Ja 28,15:3
Wolfe, Mary M, 1962, O 19,31:4
Wolfe, Nat H, 1873, Ja 9,4:7
Wolfe, Oliver T, 1946, Ag 9,17:4
Wolfe, Otis R, 1954, S 12,85:1
Wolfe, Otto, 1940, Ja 23,21:2
Wolfe, Paul A, 1964, O 31,29:4
Wolfe, R F, 1927, Ja 14,19:6
Wolfe, Ralph, 1950, Mr 15,29:4
Wolfe, Ralph R, 1947, Ag 11,23:2
Wolfe, Raymond, 1952, D 29,19:2
Wolfe, Richard S, 1953, D 28,22:3
Wolfe, Richard W, 1951, Mr 31,15:3
Wolfe, Robert N, 1903, Ag 9,7:6
Wolfe, Roscoe, 1961, Ag 26,17:4
Wolfe, Roscoe V Mrs, 1950, Ap 1,15:1
Wolfe, S H, 1928, Ja 1,19:3
Wolfe, Samuel, 1937, Ja 24,II,8:6
Wolfe, Samuel Dr, 1937, Ap 29,21:2
Wolfe, Theodore F Dr, 1915, Je 16,11:5
Wolfe, Theodore P, 1954, Ag 1,84:3
Wolfe, Thomas, 1938, S 16,21:1
Wolfe, Thomas (will), 1940, Ja 26,9:2
Wolfe, Thomas J Comr, 1937, My 1,19:2
Wolfe, W B Dr, 1935, Ag 17,2:4
Wolfe, Walter A, 1955, Mr 5,17:2
Wolfe, Walter G, 1938, Ja 11,23:2
Wolfe, Walter M Col, 1937, My 12,23:3
Wolfe, William B, 1948, N 17,27:3
Wolfe, William D, 1941, N 27,23:5
Wolfe, William J, 1963, S 21,21:6
Wolfe, William Mrs, 1945, D 8,17:5
Wolfe, William W Mrs, 1953, Ag 3,17:5
Wolfe-Murray, J Gen, 1919, O 19,22:2
Wolfel, Harry G, 1955, Ag 24,27:4
Wolfenden, James, 1949, Ap 9,17:5
Wolfenden, Jeremy, 1965, D 29,26:7
Wolfenden, Samuel, 1947, My 31,13:3
Wolfer, Henry P, 1959, My 24,89:2
Wolfers, Arnold Oscar, 1968, Jl 17,43:1
Wolfert, Jerome N, 1966, Ja 15,27:2
Wolferth, Charles C, 1965, D 28,27:4
Wolferz, Frederick W, 1949, F 19,15:6
Wolff, A, 1891, D 24,5:2
Wolff, Aaron Jr, 1920, Ja 6,15:2
Wolff, Adolph L, 1921, Je 5,22:3
Wolff, Alfred D Jr, 1959, My 26,35:3
Wolff, Alfred R, 1909, Ja 8,9:5
Wolff, Arthur, 1968, My 14,47:2
Wolff, Arthur M, 1964, Mr 26,35:1
Wolff, Arthur M Mrs, 1958, Je 1,86:5
Wolff, Arthur Mrs, 1957, My 2,31:1
Wolff, Barnet, 1944, Ag 16,19:4
Wolff, Bernard, 1925, My 17,6:1
Wolff, Bertha A Mrs, 1940, S 14,17:2
Wolff, Bertram, 1963, Ap 3,47:5
Wolff, Carl F Mrs, 1960, Mr 14,29:4
Wolff, Charles E, 1946, Jl 18,25:6
Wolff, Clara F Mrs, 1940, Ap 13,17:6
Wolff, Clarence L, 1944, Ag 21,15:4
Wolff, Clarence Mrs (F L La Boschin), 1962, N 11, 88:5
Wolff, David M, 1956, Ap 7,19:4
Wolff, David Mrs, 1944, Ag 8,17:2
Wolff, Dietrich C H, 1948, D 28,21:2
Wolff, Edward J Sr, 1941, Ag 28,19:5
Wolff, Eleanore M Mrs, 1963, S 21,21:4
Wolff, Elsie M, 1948, F 9,21:2
Wolff, Emnad, 1872, Je 4,8:4
Wolff, Ernest V, 1960, Ag 23,29:4
Wolff, Ernst, 1959, O 13,39:1
Wolff, Esther Mrs, 1937, Mr 5,25:2
Wolff, Fanny (Mrs F W Arvintz), 1961, N 29,41:1
Wolff, Frank A, 1946, Mr 29,23:4
Wolff, Frank H, 1952, Ap 5,15:3
Wolff, Frederic O, 1962, N 14,39:3
Wolff, Frederick, 1942, Mr 17,21:4
Wolff, George, 1955, D 22,23:1
Wolff, H Edward, 1954, Jl 17,13:4
Wolff, H F, 1935, Jl 29,15:5
Wolff, Harold G, 1962, F 22,25:2
Wolff, Harry W Mrs, 1945, Ag 2,19:5
Wolff, Henry C, 1951, O 31,29:5
Wolff, Henry F Jr, 1965, My 11,39:4
Wolff, Henry L, 1952, Mr 23,92:4
Wolff, Henry Mrs, 1963, Ap 22,27:2
Wolff, Herbert W, 1940, Jl 28,26:7

Wolff, Hermann, 1902, F 5,7:3
Wolff, Howard Mrs, 1957, Je 6,31:5
Wolff, J, 1934, Ap 21,15:1
Wolff, Jacob Jr, 1937, Ja 17,II,8:5
Wolff, Jacob L, 1949, Jl 11,17:6
Wolff, John E, 1940, Ag 13,21:4
Wolff, John F Jr, 1956, Ag 4,15:4
Wolff, John Mrs, 1949, Je 10,27:3
Wolff, Joseph Mrs, 1956, S 23,84:6
Wolff, Josephine B Mrs, 1941, Ja 28,19:2
Wolff, Julius, 1942, Ja 27,21:5
Wolff, Julius Mrs, 1966, Mr 9,41:2
Wolff, Julius R Mrs, 1949, Je 6,19:6
Wolff, Kurt, 1963, O 23,41:1
Wolff, Lawrence, 1964, F 15,23:4
Wolff, Leo, 1952, Mr 3,21:4; 1958, N 12,37:1
Wolff, Leopold S, 1952, O 13,21:3
Wolff, Louis, 1940, Ag 17,15:3; 1955, D 3,17:2
Wolff, Ludwig, 1950, S 12,27:3
Wolff, M, 1927, D 26,23:1
Wolff, Marcus A, 1961, Mr 28,35:4
Wolff, Martin E, 1920, D 26,22:2
Wolff, Martin Mrs, 1964, My 22,35:3
Wolff, Maty E (Sister Mary Madeleva), 1964, Jl 26, 57:2
Wolff, Max, 1939, Jl 11,19:3; 1962, O 14,87:1
Wolff, Max E, 1946, Je 19,21:4
Wolff, Max F, 1951, Mr 9,25:1
Wolff, Max J, 1963, O 21,31:3
Wolff, Mervyn, 1958, Mr 5,31:2
Wolff, Milton B, 1961, D 30,19:5
Wolff, Nat, 1959, Mr 5,31:5
Wolff, Otto, 1937, Ag 22,II,7:2
Wolff, Otto Jr, 1957, My 3,27:3
Wolff, Paul, 1951, Ap 12,33:4
Wolff, Paul C, 1952, Mr 24,25:1
Wolff, Peter A, 1948, My 16,68:6
Wolff, Reuben Mrs, 1938, Ag 14,32:7
Wolff, Sam, 1961, O 23,29:2
Wolff, Samuel L, 1941, Ag 17,38:2
Wolff, Sidney E, 1951, Mr 27,29:5
Wolff, Sol M, 1961, N 30,37:3
Wolff, Stanley L, 1960, S 24,23:2
Wolff, Theodore, 1944, F 29,17:2
Wolff, Theodore W, 1947, S 7,63:3
Wolff, W A, 1941, Jl 26,15:4
Wolff, Werner, 1957, My 19,88:1; 1961, N 25,23:5
Wolff, Werner Mrs, 1955, N 20,88:6
Wolff, William Almon, 1909, Ap 21,7:5
Wolff, William F, 1954, D 28,23:3
Wolff, William F Jr, 1967, Ja 18,43:2
Wolff, William M, 1947, N 20,29:2
Wolff, Winifred K, 1956, My 14,25:4
Wolffe, Findley P, 1967, Ja 4,41:4
Wolffe, Jabez, 1943, O 23,13:4
Wolffe, Joseph B, 1966, N 12,29:3
Wolffe, Murry (cor, S 19,29:1), 1957, S 18,33:2
Wolffe, William B, 1942, D 14,23:4
Wolfford, Luke P, 1944, Ag 22,17:4
Wolffram, Charles B, 1916, Ap 4,13:7
Wolffsohn, John F Mrs, 1963, My 18,27:5
Wolfgang, Joseph, 1957, F 17,92:3
Wolfgang, Max, 1943, Ap 2,21:3
Wolfgang, Meldon, 1947, Jl 2,23:4
Wolfgram, Irving F, 1953, F 3,25:4
Wolfington, Harry J, 1960, Mr 29,37:2
Wolfington, Harry J Mrs, 1961, O 9,35:3
Wolfington, J Eustace, 1955, N 27,88:5
Wolfit, Donald Sir, 1968, F 18,80:3
Wolfner, I Benedict (por), 1949, Ap 5,29:2
Wolfner, Rudolph, 1938, Mr 23,23:2
Wolford, Aubrey S, 1962, Ag 28,31:4
Wolford, John J, 1952, F 20,29:2
Wolford, Lewis C, 1941, S 5,22:3
Wolfort, Benjamin E, 1950, S 19,32:3
Wolfram, Charles J, 1951, Je 9,19:5
Wolfrom, Carl E, 1960, Ja 23,21:3
Wolfskeil, William D, 1943, Jl 16,17:1
Wolfskeil, William D Mrs, 1937, Ap 26,19:4
Wolfsohn, David, 1914, S 17,9:6
Wolfsohn, Henry, 1909, Je 2,7:5
Wolfsohn, Joel D, 1961, Jl 10,21:3
Wolfsohn, Leo A, 1956, My 26,17:4
Wolfsohn, Nat N (est inventory filed), 1957, Jl 31, 23:1
Wolfsohn, Raymond J, 1941, S 27,17:2
Wolfson, Abraham, 1952, Jl 20,52:7
Wolfson, Albert L, 1937, Je 18,21:2
Wolfson, David S, 1953, D 31,19:6
Wolfson, Erwin S (will, Jl 7,17:1), 1962, Je 27,35:1
Wolfson, George, 1959, Ja 23,25:2
Wolfson, Herman, 1960, Je 2,33:3
Wolfson, Irving T, 1960, Mr 1,33:5
Wolfson, Lena Mrs, 1948, S 20,25:2
Wolfson, Leo, 1946, Mr 17,44:2; 1959, Je 4,31:5
Wolfson, Louis, 1949, Ag 12,17:3
Wolfson, Max, 1949, F 23,27:3
Wolfson, Max S, 1957, N 14,33:3
Wolfson, Nathan, 1953, S 13,84:5
Wolfson, Samuel, 1946, N 7,31:6
Wolfson, Samuel Mrs, 1943, F 21,32:4
Wolfson, Samuel W, 1963, Ag 17,19:5
Wolfson, William L, 1955, My 23,23:3
Wolfstein, David I Mrs, 1954, S 30,31:3
Wolfstein, James S, 1945, Jl 29,40:3
Wolfsten, George W, 1949, N 16,29:2
Wolgast, Ad (funl plans, Ap 16,19:1), 1955, Ap 15, 23:1
Wolgast, Midget (por), 1955, O 21,27:3
Wolgin, Israel, 1961, N 24,28:3
Wolgin, Nathan, 1960, F 12,27:3
Wolgin, Nathan Mrs, 1944, N 28,23:3
Wolhaupter, Frances E N W Mrs, 1957, My 11,21:5
Wolheim, L, 1931, F 19,23:1
Wolin, Donald M, 1959, Ag 22,17:2
Wolin, Martin E, 1955, Ap 9,18:6
Wolins, William, 1962, Jl 17,25:4
Wolinsky, Barnett Rabbi, 1917, S 27,13:6
Wolinsky, Jacob, 1943, Mr 5,17:2
Wolk, Frank Mrs, 1957, D 8,88:4
Wolk, Harold, 1962, Ag 19,89:2
Wolk, Henry, 1944, Mr 14,19:4
Wolk, Julius, 1944, My 10,19:4
Wolk, Peisach, 1959, Ap 9,31:4
Wolk, Samuel, 1942, O 29,23:5; 1957, My 30,19:5
Wolk, Samuel J B, 1962, Ja 12,23:6
Wolke, John C, 1937, O 19,25:3
Wolke, Karel A, 1965, Je 12,31:6
Wolken, Rudolph, 1956, Ja 11,29:1
Wolkenberg, Alfred Mrs, 1967, S 14,47:3
Wolkiser, Malwina M Mrs, 1939, O 10,23:4
Wolkoff, Daniel, 1950, Jl 24,17:3
Wolkoff, Daniel Mrs, 1952, F 24,84:4
Wolkoff, Nicholas, 1954, Mr 11,31:2
Wolkonsky, Serge Pronce, 1937, O 26,23:1
Wolkowski, Tadeusz S, 1965, My 5,47:3
Wolkstein, Harry W, 1968, Jl 14,64:6
Woll, Arne, 1951, N 10,19:6
Woll, Frederic A, 1955, F 7,21:1
Woll, Frederic A Mrs, 1941, O 11,17:6
Woll, Frederick P, 1949, My 8,78:1
Woll, Lazar B, 1967, Mr 14,47:3
Woll, Matthew (funl plans, Je 3,85:1), 1956, Je 2,19:1
Woll, Matthew Mrs, 1946, Jl 13,15:5
Wollam, Arthur B, 1958, S 10,33:1
Wollard, Jacques, 1954, My 6,33:2
Wollaston, Gerald W, 1957, Mr 5,31:2
Wolle, J F, 1933, Ja 13,15:3
Wollebaek, Johan H, 1940, O 25,21:5
Wollen, Evans (por), 1942, My 21,19:1
Wollenhaupt, Bruno, 1903, Jl 21,9:7
Wollenhaupt, Herman J, 1863, S 26,4:6
Wollensak, Frank J, 1949, N 20,92:6
Wollentin, Otto R, 1953, Ag 21,17:3
Wollenweber, Hans, 1949, F 5,15:1
Wollenweber, Henry, 1941, S 8,15:5
Wollenweber, Henry Mrs, 1966, F 2,35:5
Woller, J B, 1903, Ja 12,9:5
Woller, William, 1954, D 12,89:1
Wollerstein, Emanuel, 1941, Je 19,21:5
Wollerton, Frederick W, 1942, N 28,13:2
Wollery, Robert D, 1946, My 16,21:2
Wolleson, H Dean, 1960, F 7,84:1
Wolley, Frederick M, 1952, Ja 29,25:4
Wollf, Henry Drummond Sir, 1908, O 13,9:4
Wollf, Nathaniel S, 1959, D 25,21:3
Wollheim, Albert P, 1948, Mr 9,24:3
Wollheim, Jacob L, 1963, S 3,33:3
Wollman, B F, 1934, My 2,21:1
Wollman, Bernard, 1937, S 21,25:3
Wollman, Bernard Mrs, 1950, Ap 30,102:3
Wollman, Charles E, 1946, F 13,23:3
Wollman, H, 1936, Mr 14,15:1
Wollman, Henry N Mrs, 1940, Je 26,23:1
Wollman, Jack A, 1958, Ap 6,88:6
Wollman, Kate (funl, O 19,33:3), 1955, O 16,87:1
Wollman, Kate (est tax appr), 1957, Ag 30,17:5
Wollman, Morton, 1924, Jl 12,9:6
Wollman, William J (will, Ap 14,30:2), 1937, Mr 27, 15:3
Wollmuth, Edmund W, 1964, Ag 17,25:4
Wollner, Henry, 1955, N 11,25:4
Wollny, Henry, 1963, Ap 6,19:2
Wollschlager, Alex C, 1952, N 14,23:4
Wollstein, Louis, 1914, O 6,11:5
Wollstein, Martha, 1939, O 1,53:2
Wollweber, Ernst F, 1967, My 11,47:3
Wolman, Benjamin, 1944, O 5,23:2
Wolman, Leo, 1961, O 3,39:1
Wolmarans, Jan B, 1948, Ap 22,27:4
Wolmark, Alfred, 1961, Ja 7,19:5
Woloch, George, 1964, O 6,39:3
Wolohan, Thomas J, 1946, S 11,7:2
Wolohon, Grace, 1915, Jl 17,7:4
Wolohon, Harry H, 1947, Ja 1,33:5
Wolohon, Katherine, 1915, Jl 17,7:4
Woloshin, Benjamin, 1942, My 27,23:1
Wolosoff, Leon, 1949, Je 8,30:2
Wolowitz, Isidor Mrs, 1961, Jl 29,19:5
Wolowski, Louis (see also Ag 5), 1876, Ag 31,2:7
Wolozin, Meyer, 1948, F 6,26:6
Wolper, Harry, 1951, N 13,29:2
Wolper, Max, 1949, Je 23,27:5
Wolpers, John H, 1951, My 21,27:3
Wolpert, George Mrs, 1964, Ag 19,37:4
Wolpert, Harry L, 1949, N 4,27:1
Wolpert, Meyer G, 1954, D 9,33:4
Wolpert, Richard K, 1958, O 7,35:3
Wolpert, Wallace I, 1953, Ja 30,21:3
Wolpert, William Mrs, 1949, Jl 25,15:3
Wolrich, Irving, 1957, D 16,29:4
Wolse, Bernard, 1874, Je 14,6:7
Wolseley, Dowager Viscountess, 1920, Ap 13,9:3
Wolsey, Charles J, 1948, Ja 6,23:5
Wolsey, George B, 1957, Ap 25,31:4
Wolsey, Louis, 1953, Mr 5,27:1
Wolsieffer, Frederick Rear-Adm, 1968, D 29,52:3
Wolski, Julian, 1950, My 24,29:4
Wolstenholme, Alfred, 1941, Ap 13,39:2
Wolter, Frank, 1945, My 31,15:5
Wolter, Frank Mrs, 1950, Jl 29,13:4
Woltersdorf, Arthur F, 1948, Mr 6,13:4
Woltersom, Herman L, 1960, Ag 11,27:3
Wolthoff, Margaret Mrs, 1946, Mr 5,25:2
Wolthuis, Anna Mrs, 1939, D 6,25:4
Woltjen, John G, 1945, N 12,22:3
Woltman, Frederick E Mrs, 1952, Ag 5,19:4
Woltman, Henry A, 1964, N 29,87:1
Woltmann, Ernst, 1940, My 12,48:1
Woltner, Henri Mrs, 1940, S 7,15:3
Wolton, J A Capt, 1885, Ap 24,2:1
Woltz, Albert, 1940, F 1,15:1
Woltz, George W, 1940, F 7,21:4
Woltz, Lawrence H, 1946, D 11,31:5
Woltz, William H, 1954, N 4,31:4
Wolverhampton, Viscount (Hy Hartley Fowler), 1911, F 26,II,11:4
Wolverton, Baron, 1873, Jl 25,4:6
Wolverton, Job A, 1945, D 12,27:4
Wolverton, Sara D, 1938, S 19,19:5
Wolvin, Roy M (por), 1945, Ap 8,36:1
Wolzogen, E L von, 1934, Jl 31,24:6
Wolzogen, Hans P von, 1938, Je 3,21:3
Womack, Bannister L, 1954, Ag 1,85:1
Womack, Edward, 1940, Jl 4,15:3
Womack, Robert, 1909, Ag 11,7:6
Womack, William T, 1949, Ap 25,23:2
Wombacher, John D, 1953, Ap 2,27:5
Womble, John P Jr, 1956, O 7,86:1
Wombwell, Charles H, 1941, Ja 26,36:5
Wombwell, Charles H Mrs, 1956, Ja 23,25:5
Wombwell, Frederick C, 1943, Ap 6,21:1
Wombwell, George Orby Sir, 1913, O 18,13:2
Womersley, Walter, 1961, Mr 17,24:1
Womrath, Arthur R, 1945, N 19,21:4
Wonderly, Otto, 1905, Ap 3,7:4
Wonders, Homer F, 1943, Ag 30,15:6
Wong, Anna M, 1961, F 4,19:3
Wong, Haig Son, 1871, D 27,1:7
Wong, Jennings L, 1965, S 5,57:3
Wong Dah Ding, 1959, Jl 17,21:4
Wong Tong, 1952, Ja 7,19:5
Wonham, Frederick S, 1952, N 6,29:5
Wonham, Frederick S Mrs, 1941, D 9,31:2
Wonn, Christian G, 1937, O 17,II,8:7
Wonson, Harold S, 1949, Jl 23,11:3
Wonson, Leroy W, 1942, O 12,17:5
Wontner, Arthur, 1960, Jl 12,35:2
Wontz, Wincenty, 1952, My 23,21:2
Wood, A J, 1882, S 21,4:7
Wood, Adeline Mrs, 1955, F 4,21:3
Wood, Adeline S Mrs, 1946, D 28,15:3
Wood, Alan A, 1955, Ja 30,85:2
Wood, Alan W (funl, Ag 16,7:2), 1905, Ag 14,7:6
Wood, Albert C, 1949, Mr 15,27:4
Wood, Albert E, 1951, My 31,27:5
Wood, Albert E Mrs, 1960, Mr 9,33:3
Wood, Albert N Mrs (lr, My 2,22:7; trb, My 10,18:4), 1945, My 1,23:3
Wood, Alex C Jr, 1959, Ag 12,29:3
Wood, Alex P, 1950, Ag 24,27:5
Wood, Alex T Mrs, 1955, Ja 18,27:2
Wood, Alexander George, 1909, Jl 3,7:4
Wood, Alfred, 1943, Jl 19,15:3
Wood, Alfred L S, 1946, Ap 30,21:4
Wood, Alfred S, 1953, Je 9,27:3
Wood, Alfred W, 1941, S 13,17:1
Wood, Alton C, 1951, N 15,29:3
Wood, Alvena H, 1968, My 7,41:6
Wood, Anna P Mrs (will), 1958, Ap 14,20:3
Wood, Anson Col, 1904, Ag 22,7:3
Wood, Arch P, 1939, Mr 27,15:5
Wood, Archibald O M, 1963, D 19,33:1
Wood, Arnold, 1942, Je 22,15:1
Wood, Arnold Mrs, 1958, Je 30,19:5
Wood, Arthur, 1953, Ja 19,23:2
Wood, Arthur B, 1952, Je 16,17:3
Wood, Arthur D, 1958, Ap 10,29:3
Wood, Arthur E, 1960, Ag 23,29:3
Wood, Arthur H, 1945, Ja 7,37:1
Wood, Arthur K, 1938, O 6,23:4
Wood, Arthur M, 1947, Ag 27,23:5
Wood, Arthur S Mrs, 1949, Ja 17,19:3
Wood, Asa B, 1945, My 9,23:1
Wood, B, 1934, Mr 16,21:1
Wood, B Frank, 1912, S 3,11:4
Wood, Benjamin, 1875, O 10,1:6; 1948, D 28,21:4; 1958, My 22,24:6
Wood, Benjamin F, 1949, Ja 12,27:5; 1960, Mr 31,33:5

Wood, Benjamin F Com, 1910, Jl 5,13:6
Wood, Benjamin F Jr, 1947, Ap 5,19:2
Wood, Bernard H 3d, 1952, Ja 20,84:4
Wood, Brison, 1966, Jl 27,39:1
Wood, Burt L, 1941, Ap 12,15:4
Wood, C S, 1931, S 9,27:1
Wood, C Wilson Mrs, 1950, Mr 19,95:6
Wood, Caroline A Mrs, 1940, Jl 24,21:3
Wood, Casey A, 1942, Ja 27,22:3
Wood, Cecil R Sr, 1955, D 13,39:2
Wood, Chalmers, 1952, Jl 24,27:5
Wood, Chandler M, 1938, D 13,26:1
Wood, Charles, 1945, Je 3,31:1
Wood, Charles A, 1944, Je 5,19:5
Wood, Charles A Mrs, 1944, Ap 28,19:2
Wood, Charles B D, 1939, My 28,III,7:2
Wood, Charles B Mrs, 1953, N 21,13:5
Wood, Charles C, 1938, Ja 2,40:3
Wood, Charles D, 1944, Ja 4,17:3
Wood, Charles E, 1908, F 19,7:7; 1940, Ja 9,23:5
Wood, Charles E S, 1944, Ja 24,17:6
Wood, Charles F, 1942, F 27,17:3; 1944, O 2,19:6; 1949, O 26,27:4
Wood, Charles G, 1952, F 21,27:1
Wood, Charles Greenleaf, 1913, Mr 3,9:4
Wood, Charles H, 1946, O 17,23:1
Wood, Charles H Mrs, 1938, Ja 9,42:7; 1950, Ap 2, 92:4
Wood, Charles I, 1947, S 26,23:3
Wood, Charles P, 1968, Jl 2,26:5
Wood, Charles P Mrs, 1960, O 8,23:5
Wood, Charles S, 1940, O 25,21:4; 1955, F 27,87:1
Wood, Charles T, 1956, N 29,35:1
Wood, Charles W, 1953, Je 11,29:1; 1954, N 17,31:1
Wood, Charles Watson, 1925, My 15,19:5
Wood, Chester C, 1951, Je 13,29:3; 1965, Jl 27,33:1
Wood, Clarence S, 1946, Ap 6,17:5
Wood, Clark V, 1940, O 29,25:6
Wood, Clement, 1950, O 27,29:2
Wood, Clement B, 1940, O 6,48:3
Wood, Cleora (Mrs O Adams Jr), 1961, My 24,41:4
Wood, Clotilde Baroness, 1951, Je 10,93:2
Wood, Cornelius Delano, 1906, Je 12,9:5
Wood, Craig, 1968, My 9,47:3
Wood, Cyril W, 1955, Je 8,29:6
Wood, D S, 1881, F 17,2:1
Wood, Daniel B, 1944, S 13,19:5
Wood, Daniel P Mrs, 1943, Jl 21,15:3
Wood, David D Dr, 1910, Mr 28,9:5
Wood, David D Mrs, 1948, O 8,26:2
Wood, David Kimble, 1968, N 19,40:1
Wood, David M, 1960, Mr 10,31:1
Wood, Dennistoun, 1944, Jl 15,13:4
Wood, Donna, 1947, Ap 10,25:1
Wood, Douglas F, 1966, D 28,43:6
Wood, E Frederick, 1920, Ja 6,15:3
Wood, Earl F, 1960, Jl 7,31:4
Wood, Eben A, 1955, Ag 15,15:5
Wood, Edgar, 1952, F 24,84:5
Wood, Edith M, 1954, My 22,15:4
Wood, Edmund B, 1952, Je 28,19:4
Wood, Edward A, 1937, Ap 18,II,9:3
Wood, Edward B, 1947, Jl 11,15:2
Wood, Edward C, 1951, My 31,27:3
Wood, Edward F L (Earl of Halifax),(trb lr, D 29,-24:6), 1959, D 24,1:3
Wood, Edward R, 1941, Je 17,21:5; 1946, D 30,19:3
Wood, Edward R Mrs, 1944, Je 15,19:4
Wood, Edward S, 1943, Mr 24,23:5
Wood, Edwin E, 1940, Ja 24,21:5
Wood, Edwin O, 1918, Ap 24,13:5
Wood, Edwin T, 1941, F 16,41:3
Wood, Edwin T Mrs, 1951, N 21,25:3
Wood, Elbert M, 1965, Mr 13,25:5
Wood, Elizabeth C, 1947, D 19,25:2
Wood, Elizabeth Mrs, 1941, N 17,12:4
Wood, Elizabeth O Mrs (por), 1940, Ja 4,23:3
Wood, Elmer E, 1939, Ja 6,21:4
Wood, Emily S, 1940, Mr 27,21:5
Wood, Emma A, 1949, Mr 17,25:4
Wood, Ennis A, 1948, N 19,27:1
Wood, Ephraim L, 1944, Ja 2,38:4
Wood, Erborn W, 1943, Ja 31,46:3
Wood, Eric F, 1962, O 5,36:3
Wood, Ernest D, 1942, Jl 15,19:1
Wood, Ernest N, 1956, Je 8,25:3
Wood, Eugene, 1923, F 26,13:4
Wood, Eugene V, 1924, Ap 19,13:6; 1951, Ja 5,21:3
Wood, Eugene W, 1941, Ap 24,21:5
Wood, Eva C, 1939, Ag 30,17:4
Wood, Evelyn Sir, 1919, D 3,15:2
Wood, Everett J, 1959, Je 25,29:2
Wood, Ezra B, 1945, My 15,19:3
Wood, F Archbishop (see also, Je 20), 1883, Je 27, 4:7
Wood, F D, 1926, F 20,15:3
Wood, Fannie A, 1946, S 16,5:3
Wood, Fernando (funl, Fe 20,2:6), 1881, F 15,2:4
Wood, Fernando Mrs (funl, D 13,5:3), 1859, D 10,1:5
Wood, Fiske, 1943, My 4,23:5
Wood, Fiske Mrs, 1943, N 9,21:5
Wood, Forest B, 1954, D 31,13:4
Wood, Frances F Mrs, 1938, Ag 31,15:1
Wood, Francis C, 1951, Ja 7,77:1
Wood, Francis C Mrs, 1944, Ap 22,15:5
Wood, Francis E, 1950, Ag 25,21:6
Wood, Francis G, 1922, My 11,17:4
Wood, Francis G Mrs, 1944, D 22,17:2
Wood, Francis M, 1943, My 9,40:8
Wood, Francis Mrs, 1903, Ap 21,9:5
Wood, Frank, 1948, Jl 1,23:1; 1953, Mr 24,31:4
Wood, Frank E, 1944, Mr 25,15:5; 1952, Ja 11,22:2
Wood, Frank E Sr Mrs, 1959, Je 4,31:5
Wood, Frank G, 1950, Je 25,68:2
Wood, Frank G Jr, 1951, Ag 2,21:2
Wood, Frank H, 1941, Mr 21,21:5
Wood, Frank L, 1945, F 9,15:1
Wood, Frank P, 1955, Mr 22,31:3
Wood, Franklin P, 1952, Jl 20,52:2
Wood, Franklin T, 1945, My 23,19:4
Wood, Franz J, 1956, Ap 15,89:2
Wood, Fred B Mrs, 1950, Mr 29,29:2
Wood, Fred M, 1962, D 6,43:5
Wood, Fred M Mrs, 1945, Ja 18,19:6
Wood, Fred P, 1949, Je 30,23:4
Wood, Frederic D, 1951, Je 27,29:4
Wood, Frederic T, 1955, S 30,25:1
Wood, Frederic T Mrs, 1956, D 7,27:1
Wood, Frederick A, 1942, Ja 6,23:2
Wood, Frederick E, 1945, N 12,21:3; 1951, N 13,29:2
Wood, Frederick H (por), 1943, D 29,17:1
Wood, Frederick H Mrs, 1945, Mr 20,19:2
Wood, Frederick J, 1955, Je 29,29:5
Wood, Frederick M, 1941, S 8,15:3
Wood, Frederick W, 1943, D 24,13:4
Wood, Fremont, 1940, D 23,19:2
Wood, G T, 1876, F 28,5:2
Wood, Gar Mrs, 1948, Ag 25,25:4
Wood, Gardner W, 1958, F 11,31:1
Wood, George (funl, Mr 23,8:4), 1860, Mr 20,5:1
Wood, George, 1942, Ap 7,21:3; 1963, N 11,31:5
Wood, George A Mrs, 1945, Ap 26,23:2
Wood, George B, 1954, N 4,31:5
Wood, George B Mrs, 1940, O 4,23:3
Wood, George B Sr, 1949, Ja 27,23:2
Wood, George C, 1964, Ap 16,37:2
Wood, George D, 1948, Ag 3,26:2
Wood, George E Mrs, 1942, My 30,15:5
Wood, George G Mrs, 1950, Ag 12,13:2
Wood, George L, 1940, D 11,27:4
Wood, George L Mrs, 1953, F 16,21:3
Wood, George M, 1957, Ja 21,25:5
Wood, George Mrs, 1872, Ja 16,5:2
Wood, George P, 1940, O 17,25:3
Wood, George R (will, Ag 5,13:1), 1943, Ap 28,23:3
Wood, George R, 1951, F 6,27:3
Wood, George T, 1954, O 12,27:3
Wood, George W, 1941, N 13,27:5; 1944, Ap 14,19:4; 1945, N 21,21:1; 1948, Ja 29,23:4
Wood, Glen E, 1956, My 15,31:2
Wood, Gordon L, 1953, Je 30,23:3
Wood, Grahame, 1954, O 26,27:5
Wood, Grant, 1942, F 13,21:1
Wood, H, 1933, Mr 21,17:5
Wood, H A Prof, 1903, S 30,9:6
Wood, H F, 1938, N 24,27:1
Wood, H P, 1951, Mr 20,29:2
Wood, Hamilton B, 1962, S 30,86:3
Wood, Harlan N, 1945, Ja 11,23:1
Wood, Harley W, 1949, Jl 25,17:7
Wood, Harold E, 1961, O 9,69:5
Wood, Harold P Mrs, 1951, My 19,15:5
Wood, Harold S, 1950, Ap 24,25:6
Wood, Harrison, 1938, S 3,13:5
Wood, Harrison E, 1942, D 7,27:1
Wood, Harry, 1943, My 15,15:2
Wood, Harry B, 1952, Ap 15,27:3
Wood, Harry D, 1947, Mr 31,23:4
Wood, Harry G, 1944, Ap 6,23:3
Wood, Harry H, 1948, O 14,29:1; 1951, Mr 19,28:4
Wood, Harry J, 1940, Ja 21,34:7
Wood, Harry M, 1938, Ag 4,17:2
Wood, Harry R, 1947, Je 9,21:2
Wood, Harry W, 1954, S 23,33:4
Wood, Harry W Mrs, 1954, O 6,25:2
Wood, Harvey C Sr, 1964, D 24,19:4
Wood, Harvey D, 1938, My 14,15:3
Wood, Harvey E, 1947, Jl 22,24:3
Wood, Haydn, 1959, Mr 13,26:3
Wood, Helen A, 1964, N 21,29:5
Wood, Helen P, 1946, Ag 11,45:2
Wood, Henry, 1909, Mr 30,9:6; 1946, Ag 28,27:5
Wood, Henry A, 1942, F 23,21:3
Wood, Henry A W (will, My 10,26:7),(por), 1939, Ap 10,17:1
Wood, Henry B Col, 1907, Ap 1,9:7
Wood, Henry Bayles Col, 1907, Ap 3,9:7
Wood, Henry Clay, 1912, Je 21,13:4
Wood, Henry E Mrs, 1946, D 23,23:4
Wood, Henry J (por), 1944, Ag 20,33:1
Wood, Henry L, 1938, Ja 11,28:5
Wood, Henry Mrs, 1887, F 11,5:5
Wood, Henry Prof, 1925, Ag 21,13:5
Wood, Henry Rev, 1873, O 10,1:2
Wood, Henry W, 1941, Je 11,21:4
Wood, Herbert A, 1946, F 24,43:1
Wood, Hiram T, 1949, Jl 31,60:2
Wood, Horatio C, 1943, O 9,13:4
Wood, Horatio C Jr, 1958, Ap 2,31:2
Wood, Howard, 1911, Jl 3,7:5; 1949, F 22,23:1
Wood, Howard E, 1939, N 29,23:2
Wood, Howard Jr, 1956, Ja 19,33:5
Wood, Howard O, 1940, Je 17,15:4
Wood, Howell R, 1958, My 5,29:3
Wood, Howland (por), 1938, Ja 5,21:3
Wood, Hubert S, 1953, Ap 3,23:3
Wood, Hugh J, 1954, Jl 6,23:6
Wood, Hugh M, 1955, F 25,21:3
Wood, Hulda E, 1950, Jl 26,25:5
Wood, I E Mrs, 1932, Mr 13,1:4
Wood, I Lester, 1950, Ap 30,102:5
Wood, Irving H, 1949, D 18,90:2
Wood, Irwin D, 1939, N 12,48:6
Wood, Isaac H Capt, 1904, Ja 24,5:6
Wood, J B Dr, 1884, Ja 28,8:1
Wood, J D, 1901, O 22,13:6
Wood, J F, 1883, Je 21,4:7
Wood, J H Gen, 1884, Jl 12,5:1
Wood, J J, 1928, Ap 21,17:3
Wood, J M, 1864, D 25,8:3
Wood, J Noble, 1950, Ag 30,31:1
Wood, J P, 1927, Je 25,17:5
Wood, J Walter, 1905, Je 30,9:4
Wood, J Walter Mrs, 1943, Jl 20,19:1
Wood, James, 1925, D 20,11:1
Wood, James A, 1947, F 12,25:4
Wood, James C, 1948, Ag 31,26:1
Wood, James D I, 1956, Je 26,35:5
Wood, James E, 1965, Ag 25,39:5
Wood, James F, 1961, O 28,21:1
Wood, James F Mrs, 1962, N 9,26:2
Wood, James H, 1943, My 27,25:6; 1946, My 2,21:1; 1951, My 12,21:4
Wood, James J, 1952, N 17,25:6
Wood, James M, 1958, S 29,27:3
Wood, James P, 1938, Jl 18,13:2
Wood, James R, 1917, My 4,11:5
Wood, James R Dr, 1882, My 5,5:5
Wood, James R Dr (funl, Ag 17,7:6), 1914, Ag 16, 15:6
Wood, James T Mrs, 1952, Mr 1,15:4
Wood, James Tuthill, 1917, F 7,13:5
Wood, James W, 1950, N 8,29:5
Wood, James W Jr, 1952, S 18,29:1
Wood, Jarvis A, 1925, Ap 10,19:4
Wood, Jeremiah, 1962, Je 18,29:3
Wood, John, 1940, My 26,34:1
Wood, John A, 1947, O 26,70:4
Wood, John A Mrs, 1941, Jl 20,31:1
Wood, John B, 1949, Ja 6,23:5; 1951, Ja 22,23:1
Wood, John C, 1950, N 29,36:4
Wood, John E, 1964, F 11,39:2
Wood, John Ex-Gov. 1880, Je 5,5:6
Wood, John F, 1944, F 29,17:6
Wood, John H, 1943, N 25,25:1; 1954, Jl 28,23:1
Wood, John H Capt, 1905, Ap 16,9:6
Wood, John J, 1948, Ja 3,13:3
Wood, John M, 1955, S 17,15:2
Wood, John Mrs, 1915, Ja 13,9:3; 1948, S 22,31:4
Wood, John R, 1938, D 8,27:3; 1944, Mr 24,19:5; 1950, Jl 17,21:5; 1963, My 23,37:5; 1965, Ag 24,36:1
Wood, John S, 1959, Ap 16,33:4; 1966, Jl 4,15:4; 1968, S 14,31:4
Wood, John W, 1944, My 11,19:3
Wood, John W (por), 1947, Ag 8,17:3
Wood, John W, 1958, N 27,29:2
Wood, Jonathan E, 1950, S 19,31:3
Wood, Joseph, 1922, Mr 5,26:4
Wood, Joseph B, 1966, Mr 28,33:5
Wood, Joseph C, 1942, My 19,19:2
Wood, Joseph H, 1946, O 5,17:3
Wood, Joseph K, 1960, Mr 1,33:4
Wood, Joseph L R, 1917, F 9,11:5
Wood, Joseph Mrs, 1913, D 15,9:4
Wood, Joseph R, 1952, Jl 2,25:6; 1954, Ja 22,27:4
Wood, Joseph S, 1922, Ja 7,13:5
Wood, Josephine Downs Mrs, 1908, Ja 20,9:4
Wood, Josiah L, 1954, S 3,17:4
Wood, Julian, 1946, Je 6,21:3
Wood, Juliana, 1941, Ja 1,23:4
Wood, Junius B, 1957, Ap 4,33:4
Wood, Kate D Mrs (will, N 19,21:2), 1940, N 2,15:4
Wood, Katherine B, 1913, Je 15,IV,5:5
Wood, Keith, 1955, Ap 18,23:3
Wood, Kenneth A, 1967, O 27,45:3
Wood, Kenneth F, 1925, S 23,25:3
Wood, Kenneth F Mrs, 1948, D 24,17:1
Wood, Kenneth R, 1944, N 8,17:3
Wood, Kingsley, 1943, S 22,23:1
Wood, L, 1927, Ag 7,1:1; 1931, Ag 28,9:6
Wood, L A S, 1942, My 8,21:3
Wood, L Elmer, 1937, Ja 6,23:4
Wood, L Hollingsworth, 1956, Jl 23,23:3
Wood, Lainson, 1957, S 25,29:1
Wood, Langdon B, 1941, Je 16,15:3
Wood, Leland N, 1946, N 5,25:2
Wood, Leonard E, 1954, Ja 2,11:5
Wood, Leonard P, 1962, F 3,21:6
Wood, Leslie S, 1950, Ap 7,25:3

Wood, Lewis G, 1953, Je 8,29:1
Wood, Lewis M, 1915, My 15,13:6
Wood, Lewis N, 1944, Jl 13,17:3
Wood, Lewis R, 1946, O 12,19:4
Wood, Linden D, 1948, Ap 26,23:2
Wood, Lionel C K, 1941, Ja 1,23:2
Wood, Lloyd H, 1964, F 16,92:8
Wood, Logan, 1938, Mr 29,21:6
Wood, Loraine M Mrs, 1964, Ja 7,33:3
Wood, Loren N, 1960, O 30,87:1
Wood, Louise B, 1960, N 28,31:3
Wood, Luther E, 1946, Ap 10,27:4
Wood, Luther M, 1944, Ja 25,19:4
Wood, Lydia J Mrs, 1942, S 6,30:7
Wood, Lynn K, 1951, O 4,33:3
Wood, Margaret M Mrs, 1948, Ja 13,25:5
Wood, Marion A Mrs, 1957, O 19,21:4
Wood, Martha, 1948, S 29,29:5
Wood, Mary E, 1939, Ap 17,17:3
Wood, Mary J, 1951, My 6,92:3
Wood, Mary L, 1944, Ja 13,21:5
Wood, Mary L Mrs, 1922, Jl 25,11:6
Wood, Mary M Mrs (will), 1940, Mr 28,25:7
Wood, May L, 1957, Ap 10,33:2
Wood, Minot C, 1952, Ag 17,77:2
Wood, Monte H, 1952, S 29,23:6
Wood, Morgan L, 1951, Ag 16,27:6
Wood, Morris, 1967, My 20,35:5
Wood, Myron E, 1942, S 2,23:5
Wood, Myron R, 1946, O 31,25:1
Wood, Nathan E Rev, 1937, Jl 9,21:4
Wood, Noble F, 1940, F 3,13:4
Wood, Norman S Mrs, 1954, S 21,27:4
Wood, Norris G, 1948, My 27,25:5
Wood, O E, 1883, D 20,4:7
Wood, Oakley Mrs, 1937, S 9,23:4
Wood, Oliver E Brig-Gen, 1910, D 5,13:4
Wood, Oliver W, 1949, Mr 30,30:2
Wood, Orien, 1952, Ja 12,13:4
Wood, Osborne C, 1950, F 2,23:4
Wood, Otis F, 1939, My 2,23:4
Wood, Palmer Gaylor Gen, 1915, Jl 20,11:6
Wood, Pat O, 1961, D 4,37:1
Wood, Paul H, 1962, Jl 16,23:4
Wood, Paul M, 1963, My 31,25:1
Wood, Paul Mrs, 1967, S 1,31:3
Wood, Paul S, 1955, Ja 12,27:1
Wood, Pauline, 1956, S 21,25:3
Wood, Percival, 1945, D 26,19:3
Wood, Percival J, 1963, N 7,37:3
Wood, Phil, 1940, Mr 5,24:4
Wood, Philip M Mrs, 1945, Ap 4,21:6
Wood, Philo C, 1950, Mr 26,92:4
Wood, Prescott E, 1955, Mr 6,88:1
Wood, R B, 1926, Ap 29,23:5
Wood, R Preston H, 1945, My 4,19:2
Wood, R W, 1880, Ap 13,2:4
Wood, Ralph E, 1951, D 9,90:3
Wood, Ralph J Mrs, 1949, Ap 4,23:1
Wood, Raymond J, 1961, Jl 31,19:5
Wood, Raymond P, 1955, S 2,17:6
Wood, Richard D, 1869, Ap 4,3:5
Wood, Richard D Sr, 1948, O 2,15:4
Wood, Richmond, 1945, F 18,34:4
Wood, Robert B, 1967, F 2,35:1
Wood, Robert C, 1956, D 20,29:1; 1963, Je 2,84:6
Wood, Robert E, 1952, N 11,29:3
Wood, Robert E Mrs, 1960, Mr 11,25:1
Wood, Robert J Mrs, 1950, My 13,17:5
Wood, Robert M, 1957, Ja 11,24:1
Wood, Robert N, 1915, O 1,11:5
Wood, Robert N Mrs, 1944, My 27,15:5
Wood, Robert S, 1949, Ap 21,26:2
Wood, Robert S W Rev Dr, 1937, My 24,19:2
Wood, Robert T Sr, 1952, N 18,31:5
Wood, Robert W, 1955, Ag 12,19:3; 1958, N 28,30:5; 1961, F 28,33:3
Wood, Robert W Mrs, 1942, Je 21,36:8
Wood, Rodman H Capt, 1937, N 4,25:5
Wood, Roland, 1967, F 6,29:2
Wood, Rowland, 1954, F 25,31:2
Wood, Roy I, 1959, Ja 17,19:5
Wood, Ruby R, 1950, F 19,79:3
Wood, Rufus Henry, 1905, Je 25,7:2
Wood, Russell A, 1952, S 21,88:2
Wood, Russell W, 1948, D 10,25:2
Wood, Ruth K, 1950, Ag 12,13:5
Wood, S (see also Mr 22), 1878, Mr 23,8:4
Wood, S A, 1930, F 5,23:5
Wood, Sadie M, 1959, N 16,31:1
Wood, Sallie, 1954, D 15,63:2
Wood, Sam, 1949, S 23,23:1
Wood, Samuel, 1952, S 14,87:1
Wood, Samuel A, 1904, Ap 8,9:6; 1952, Ag 17,77:2
Wood, Samuel H Mrs, 1954, F 25,31:5
Wood, Samuel J, 1958, Je 10,33:1
Wood, Samuel J Mrs, 1968, Ap 14,76:4
Wood, Samuel Mrs, 1951, Ag 7,25:5
Wood, Samuel S Mrs, 1938, F 7,15:2
Wood, Seth Stoddard, 1904, D 22,9:4
Wood, Sheldon V, 1959, Je 1,27:1
Wood, Sidney B (por), 1947, Ja 28,23:5
Wood, Sidney B Mrs, 1954, Mr 25,29:3
Wood, Sidney B 3d, 1961, Mr 23,13:1
Wood, Smith M, 1920, Je 8,11:3
Wood, Smith W, 1920, Je 8,11:3
Wood, Spencer S, 1940, Jl 31,17:4
Wood, Spencer S Mrs, 1938, F 9,19:2
Wood, Stacy H, 1942, Je 9,23:2
Wood, Stanley B, 1953, F 10,27:2
Wood, Starr, 1944, S 4,19:3
Wood, Susan M, 1966, Je 9,47:5
Wood, T, 1903, Ap 15,9:6
Wood, Theodore, 1949, Ja 25,24:2; 1963, Je 11,37:5
Wood, Theodore F, 1947, Jl 14,21:5
Wood, Theodore M, 1946, O 26,17:1
Wood, Theodore V, 1958, Jl 5,17:5
Wood, Theresa, 1960, My 7,23:4
Wood, Thomas, 1950, N 20,25:5
Wood, Thomas (will), 1951, Ap 24,16:5
Wood, Thomas B, 1950, S 19,29:3
Wood, Thomas Capt, 1908, N 29,11:5
Wood, Thomas D, 1951, Mr 21,33:4
Wood, Thomas D Mrs, 1947, Ap 29,27:3
Wood, Thomas E Mrs, 1957, F 25,25:1
Wood, Thomas E Sr (will, My 3,39:6), 1961, Ap 25, 35:4
Wood, Townsend D Mrs, 1946, D 25,29:2
Wood, Turnbull Mrs, 1949, N 4,28:6
Wood, Vesta Mrs, 1948, S 9,27:6
Wood, W, 1877, Ap 10,4:7
Wood, W A, 1884, N 20,5:3
Wood, W Clifford, 1939, F 18,15:4
Wood, W Donald, 1966, S 21,47:2
Wood, W H, 1884, Ap 16,4:6
Wood, W M, 1880, Mr 3,5:4; 1926, F 3,1:8; 1956, Jl 29,65:1
Wood, W P Col, 1903, Mr 21,2:2
Wood, W R, 1933, Mr 8,13:3
Wood, W W, 1882, S 2,1:6
Wood, Waddy B, 1944, Ja 27,19:3
Wood, Wallace A, 1915, O 9,9:3
Wood, Wallace Dr, 1916, D 17,19:3
Wood, Walter A, 1937, D 23,22:4; 1948, N 20,13:6
Wood, Walter A Jr, 1957, Je 29,17:3
Wood, Walter C, 1953, N 24,29:1
Wood, Walter E, 1939, S 15,23:4
Wood, Walter H, 1945, Mr 23,19:4
Wood, Walter M, 1941, My 24,15:3
Wood, Walter S, 1951, O 31,29:4
Wood, Walton J, 1945, S 3,23:2
Wood, Warren E, 1947, Ap 15,25:5
Wood, Washington F, 1940, Ag 6,19:6
Wood, Wee W, 1941, My 28,25:4
Wood, Wilbur, 1968, Mr 20,47:1
Wood, Wilbur F, 1940, O 1,23:1
Wood, Wilfred R, 1939, Jl 15,15:2
Wood, Wilfrid, 1960, N 19,21:5
Wood, Will R Mrs, 1924, O 9,23:5
Wood, Willard B Sr, 1953, S 18,24:3
Wood, William, 1872, F 29,5:5
Wood, William A, 1941, Mr 21,23:6; 1946, N 3,62:7; 1951, F 8,33:4
Wood, William A Mrs, 1944, Ag 25,13:3
Wood, William C, 1956, Je 6,33:4
Wood, William E, 1957, F 3,77:2
Wood, William G, 1951, Ja 10,27:5
Wood, William H, 1903, Ag 17,7:5
Wood, William H (funl, Jl 23,17:5), 1916, Jl 21,9:7
Wood, William H, 1952, Je 26,29:4; 1953, S 2,25:2; 1960, Ag 28,82:8; 1960, D 16,38:4
Wood, William H Mrs, 1950, Ja 25,27:2
Wood, William H S, 1907, D 13,11:3
Wood, William J, 1917, O 4,13:5; 1941, Mr 11,24:2; 1954, S 30,31:5
Wood, William J Mrs, 1939, N 29,23:2
Wood, William K, 1962, Mr 18,86:8
Wood, William L, 1938, O 10,37:8
Wood, William M, 1943, Mr 4,20:1
Wood, William M Jr (funl), 1922, Ag 21,11:4
Wood, William M Mrs, 1951, Jl 7,13:3
Wood, William Macdonald, 1919, F 16,20:4
Wood, William P, 1938, Ja 15,15:3
Wood, William P Mrs, 1943, N 7,57:2
Wood, William R, 1946, Ja 25,24:2; 1960, D 10,23:4
Wood, William T, 1959, Ap 8,37:3
Wood, William W, 1938, D 25,15:1
Wood, Willis D, 1957, My 7,35:5
Wood, Wilson G, 1957, Je 18,29:4
Wood, Wilson G Mrs, 1941, My 7,25:5
Wood, Winthrop A, 1949, S 3,13:6
Wood, Winthrop S Brig-Gen, 1937, Ap 13,25:4
Wood, Word H, 1951, D 27,21:5
Wood-Billetdoux, Marc R, 1959, Ag 26,29:3
Wood-Hill, M Mrs, 1954, Mr 3,27:2
Woodall, Charles A Jr, 1944, N 10,19:2
Woodall, Charles S, 1939, Mr 27,15:6
Woodall, Corbet Sir, 1916, My 19,11:7
Woodall, David L, 1938, My 21,15:3
Woodall, Doris Mrs, 1954, F 9,27:1
Woodall, Harding C, 1967, Ja 30,26:4
Woodall, Inez J Mrs, 1940, Mr 5,24:4
Woodall, John E Mrs (ZaSu Pitts), 1963, Je 8,25:2
Woodall, Stanley F Mrs, 1959, My 17,83:3
Woodard, Allan J, 1949, Jl 5,23:2
Woodard, Clement M, 1955, D 26,19:1
Woodard, Emma W Mrs, 1939, Mr 12,III,6:7
Woodard, Francis C, 1939, Jl 17,19:6
Woodard, John S, 1943, Je 29,19:5
Woodard, Lawrence, 1957, My 22,33:4
Woodard, Myron C, 1946, Ap 21,47:1
Woodard, Sara J Mrs, 1940, Ja 10,21:3
Woodard, Stacy, 1942, Ja 28,19:6
Woodard, Tedford, 1958, My 27,26:6
Woodard, Zebulon V Mrs, 1948, Ag 28,15:4
Woodason, Henry, 1880, My 13,8:3
Woodberry, Horace W, 1939, D 17,48:8
Woodbine, George E, 1953, Ag 21,18:3
Woodbridge, Arthur, 1952, Je 21,15:5
Woodbridge, C N, 1903, Jl 12,11:1
Woodbridge, Charles E, 1943, My 18,23:4
Woodbridge, Charles K, 1960, O 17,29:4
Woodbridge, Charles K Mrs, 1964, Ap 26,89:3
Woodbridge, Frederick J, 1940, Je 2,45:1
Woodbridge, Freeman, 1947, O 20,23:6
Woodbridge, Homer E, 1958, Ja 23,21:6
Woodbridge, J E Rev, 1877, N 19,5:3
Woodbridge, Jahleel D Mrs, 1962, N 17,25:5
Woodbridge, Lord (A Churchman), 1949, F 4,23:2
Woodbridge, Richard G Mrs, 1943, Je 8,22:2
Woodbridge, Richard G Rev Dr, 1921, Jl 7,11:4
Woodbridge, Sumner, 1959, Mr 1,86:5
Woodburn, Caroline Mrs, 1923, F 24,11:4
Woodburn, Helen T, 1944, N 1,23:2
Woodburn, Hervey E, 1962, Mr 5,23:3
Woodburn, James A, 1943, D 13,23:4
Woodburn, John M, 1952, O 25,17:6
Woodburn, Joseph D, 1954, F 21,68:1
Woodburn, Joseph J, 1948, O 31,88:6
Woodburn, Robert, 1955, My 25,9:3
Woodburne, Angus S, 1938, F 15,26:8
Woodbury, Adin Mrs, 1947, Ja 12,59:4
Woodbury, Carl V, 1948, D 14,29:4
Woodbury, Charles H, 1940, Ja 22,15:5
Woodbury, Chester T, 1945, Ja 30,20:3
Woodbury, Clare, 1949, Mr 15,27:5
Woodbury, Clark Mrs, 1943, D 15,27:2
Woodbury, E Walter, 1959, Ja 11,88:2
Woodbury, Egbert E, 1920, Mr 14,22:4
Woodbury, Ellen C Dequincy, 1909, S 23,11:2
Woodbury, F W, 1927, My 25,23:3
Woodbury, Frances, 1956, Jl 29,65:1
Woodbury, Frank Sr Mrs, 1953, Ja 16,24:3
Woodbury, Frank T, 1954, D 21,27:2
Woodbury, Freeman P Mrs, 1907, O 2,11:6
Woodbury, Gordon, 1924, Je 18,19:6
Woodbury, Hulda Mrs, 1940, Ja 16,23:3
Woodbury, Jesse, 1950, Mr 7,27:2
Woodbury, Jesse S Mrs, 1944, My 9,19:6
Woodbury, John, 1940, Ja 5,20:4
Woodbury, John E, 1949, Jl 29,21:2
Woodbury, John McGaw Dr, 1914, S 25,11:7
Woodbury, John Page, 1910, Je 19,II,11:4
Woodbury, Lawrence D, 1955, Je 15,31:4
Woodbury, Margaret, 1924, Ag 21,11:4
Woodbury, Miriam L, 1949, F 15,23:1
Woodbury, Nancy M, 1961, My 3,37:2
Woodbury, Orsen E, 1904, D 11,7:6
Woodbury, Peter T, 1862, Mr 29,6:2
Woodbury, Roger W, 1903, Jl 13,2:2; 1959, Je 9,37:1
Woodbury, Roliston G, 1968, S 24,47:3
Woodbury, Thomas C, 1944, My 6,15:2
Woodbury, Urban A Ex-Gov, 1915, Ap 16,13:4
Woodbury, Walter E, 1964, O 23,39:4
Woodbury, Webster Rev, 1909, Ag 26,9:6
Woodbury, William A, 1957, Ag 7,27:6
Woodbury, William B Mrs, 1950, My 10,31:4
Woodbury, William B 2d, 1951, Ja 20,15:2
Woodcock, Amos W W, 1964, Ja 18,23:2
Woodcock, Charles, 1946, D 10,31:2
Woodcock, Charles E, 1940, Mr 13,23:5
Woodcock, Fred W, 1943, Ag 12,19:2
Woodcock, Harold F, 1961, O 2,31:2
Woodcock, Hazel M, 1946, S 20,31:2
Woodcock, James F, 1947, Ap 9,25:3
Woodcock, John L, 1943, Jl 14,19:3
Woodcock, John L Mrs, 1940, N 6,23:3
Woodcock, Joseph C, 1966, Ap 10,76:7
Woodcock, Leslie E Mrs, 1957, Mr 10,88:8
Woodcock, Mary C Mrs, 1943, Ja 23,13:6
Woodcock, William W Mrs, 1947, S 1,19:4
Woodd-Cahusac, Kenneth A, 1953, Ag 24,23:4
Woodell, Alex, 1942, Ag 26,19:6
Wooden, Alex, 1952, Jl 8,27:5
Wooden, Walter B, 1949, D 6,32:2
Woodend, Jane H Mrs, 1938, Mr 29,21:4
Woodfield, Albert W, 1946, O 8,24:2
Woodfield, Arthur G Mrs, 1948, Mr 5,21:5
Woodfield, Catherine Mrs, 1941, Ja 19,40:1
Woodfield, Harry T, 1950, D 7,33:5
Woodfield, Leonard B, 1961, S 26,39:1
Woodfill, Samuel, 1951, Ag 14,23:2
Woodfin, William M, 1943, Je 12,13:3
Woodford, C Willis, 1946, Ja 27,42:2
Woodford, Charles F Mrs (D Humphrey), 1958, D 30,32:1
Woodford, Chester Randolph, 1921, D 11,22:2
Woodford, Clinton M, 1942, Mr 10,20:2
Woodford, Ethelbert G, 1923, N 11,23:3

Woodford, Frank B, 1967, Je 20,39:1
Woodford, Frank E, 1905, Ja 12,5:4
Woodford, George E, 1954, My 25,27:4
Woodford, Harry E, 1954, Mr 28,23:1
Woodford, Harry E Mrs, 1954, O 21,27:4
Woodford, J Wallace, 1957, Ag 6,27:5
Woodford, Laurance G Mrs, 1944, Mr 10,15:4
Woodford, M De Witt, 1907, S 17,11:6
Woodford, Stewart Lyndon (por),(funl, F 17,11:4), 1913, F 15,15:4
Woodford, Stewart Lyndon Gen (est appr), 1914, My 28,13:5
Woodger, Herbert, 1949, Ag 21,69:3
Woodger, William G, 1952, Ja 1,25:3
Woodhall, Charles H, 1950, Jl 26,25:4
Woodhall, Solomon, 1938, O 29,19:2
Woodhead, Alfred W, 1954, Je 30,27:3
Woodhead, Ben S, 1939, Jl 5,17:6
Woodhead, Charles Mrs, 1947, O 29,27:5
Woodhead, Daniel, 1953, O 13,29:6
Woodhead, Frank A, 1950, Ja 28,13:3
Woodhead, George R, 1962, Ag 14,25:1
Woodhead, Harry, 1961, N 1,39:5
Woodhead, Henry G, 1959, O 3,19:4
Woodhead, Ruthford W, 1945, Jl 13,11:7
Woodhead, William, 1920, Ja 28,11:4
Woodhouse, Adelaide M Mrs, 1956, O 15,25:6
Woodhouse, Arthur S P, 1964, N 3,31:2
Woodhouse, Charles L Lt, 1905, My 5,1:4
Woodhouse, Daniel A, 1942, Ag 7,17:2
Woodhouse, George, 1954, Ja 8,21:2
Woodhouse, George E, 1909, N 22,9:7
Woodhouse, Horace M (Lord Terrington), 1961, Ja 8,86:2
Woodhouse, Irving, 1953, Mr 31,31:3
Woodhouse, James M Jr, 1961, Jl 19,29:5
Woodhouse, Joseph Stuyvesant, 1912, Je 28,13:6
Woodhouse, L E, 1935, Ja 24,19:6
Woodhouse, Lorenzo E Mrs, 1961, D 5,43:1
Woodhouse, Lorenzo Guernsey, 1903, S 6,7:6
Woodhouse, Samuel W J Jr, 1943, F 3,19:6
Woodhull, Alfred A Gen, 1921, O 19,19:4
Woodhull, Anna Mrs, 1939, S 20,28:4
Woodhull, C H, 1879, F 8,3:1
Woodhull, Daniel E, 1942, O 9,21:5
Woodhull, Daniel E Jr, 1956, N 7,31:3
Woodhull, Daniel E Mrs, 1946, N 28,27:4
Woodhull, George Maxwell Van Zant Gen, 1921, Jl 27,15:7
Woodhull, George S Rev Dr, 1912, S 10,9:5
Woodhull, George Spofford, 1907, Je 20,7:5
Woodhull, Gilbert P, 1949, Jl 2,15:2
Woodhull, J Clifford Sr, 1942, Ag 27,19:4
Woodhull, Jerry (Jerry Cuffy), 1910, Ja 21,11:5
Woodhull, John B, 1951, Ap 3,27:5
Woodhull, John F, 1941, Jl 28,13:3
Woodhull, John R, 1950, Ja 22,76:4
Woodhull, Minerva, 1943, F 28,48:2
Woodhull, Ross A, 1944, My 27,15:3
Woodhull, Sylvester H, 1939, S 16,17:6
Woodhull, William A, 1904, Ja 12,7:5
Woodhull, William J, 1957, O 5,17:2
Woodin, Anne J Mrs (por), 1941, My 18,43:5
Woodin, Harolk P, 1951, Jl 24,25:5
Woodin, Lee D, 1953, Ag 30,88:6
Woodin, Mary B, 1881, Ag 13,5:6
Woodin, Raye P, 1944, F 20,35:2
Woodin, W H, 1934, My 4,1:1
Woodin, W R Capt, 1903, My 30,7:5
Wooding, Frances P, 1958, Je 18,33:1
Wooding, Harry (por), 1938, N 17,25:2
Wooding, Mary E P Mrs, 1944, Ag 22,17:5
Wooding, W Crews, 1937, Ja 1,23:2
Wooding, William A, 1960, F 19,28:1
Woodland, Edward S Mrs, 1953, F 6,20:6
Woodland, Frank D, 1951, S 10,21:3
Woodland, J Ernest Prof, 1921, O 18,17:2
Woodle, Bernon T, 1957, My 4,21:4
Woodley, Charles C, 1949, D 8,33:4
Woodley, Frederick D, 1942, O 12,34:6
Woodley, T Fred, 1951, S 8,17:2
Woodling, Bertha D Mrs, 1937, O 22,24:2
Woodling, Charles F Sr, 1940, Ja 15,15:3
Woodlinger, Harry M, 1956, Ja 17,33:4
Woodlock, Francis, 1940, Ap 12,23:4
Woodlock, Henry J, 1941, Je 16,15:5
Woodlock, Joseph P, 1959, Jl 1,25:6
Woodlock, Thomas F, 1945, Ag 26,44:3
Woodman, Aaron H, 1959, My 20,35:2
Woodman, Charles H, 1911, Ja 3,11:5; 1940, Jl 30,19:2
Woodman, Clarence E Rev, 1924, D 7,7:3
Woodman, Clarence L, 1941, D 30,19:5
Woodman, Edward W, 1939, O 31,23:3
Woodman, Francis C, 1959, S 6,73:2
Woodman, Frederic T, 1949, Mr 26,17:3
Woodman, George D, 1940, Ap 20,17:5
Woodman, H Staunton, 1964, Je 27,25:6
Woodman, Hannah R, 1951, My 15,31:3
Woodman, Harold J, 1942, D 14,28:1
Woodman, Harry C, 1950, Jl 14,21:5
Woodman, Howard H, 1938, Mr 29,21:5
Woodman, J Edmund (por), 1939, My 20,15:1
Woodman, John L, 1944, N 7,27:1
Woodman, John S Prof, 1871, My 10,1:3
Woodman, Lucy J Mrs, 1951, Ap 30,21:4
Woodman, R Huntington (por), 1943, D 26,32:1
Woodman, Walter, 1955, Mr 3,27:1
Woodmancy, L D, 1942, F 11,21:2
Woodmansee, James A, 1955, Ap 20,33:5
Woodmansee, Robert E, 1952, N 24,23:2
Woodring, Frederick K, 1953, D 23,26:3
Woodring, Harry H, 1967, S 10,82:1
Woodring, J R, 1946, Ap 5,25:2
Woodring, John J, 1937, F 25,23:3
Woodring, Lida C, 1938, F 10,21:6
Woodring, Marcus C, 1946, Jl 20,14:2
Woodroofe, Robert W Rev Dr, 1953, F 21,13:2
Woodrow, Harry R (por), 1940, Ag 14,19:3
Woodrow, Helen Sill Mrs, 1919, Ja 25,11:5
Woodrow, Henry W, 1913, D 27,9:6
Woodrow, John F Mrs, 1945, N 25,49:1
Woodrow, John Mrs, 1913, My 20,11:6
Woodrow, Mary S Mrs, 1916, Mr 24,11:5
Woodrow, N M W Mrs, 1935, S 8,38:1
Woodrow, Samuel H, 1943, S 7,23:4
Woodrow, Samuel Jr, 1950, Je 20,27:4
Woodruff, A Allen, 1949, Jl 23,11:2
Woodruff, Albert C, 1920, F 27,13:4; 1938, Ja 21,19:5
Woodruff, Albert M, 1948, F 27,21:1
Woodruff, Albert S, 1948, Ag 30,17:4
Woodruff, Alfred Mrs, 1952, Jl 4,13:5
Woodruff, Amos, 1884, Jl 1,5:2
Woodruff, Amos Mrs, 1884, Jl 1,5:2
Woodruff, Amy L, 1957, N 15,27:1
Woodruff, Ann E, 1884, Jl 8,2:2
Woodruff, Arch M, 1940, F 15,19:5
Woodruff, Arthur E, 1939, F 22,21:4
Woodruff, Arthur Mrs, 1944, F 26,13:6
Woodruff, Arthur S Mrs, 1959, D 26,13:6
Woodruff, Austin E, 1949, Ag 9,25:1
Woodruff, Benjamin M Mrs, 1964, D 24,19:4
Woodruff, C Rogers, 1945, My 1,23:2
Woodruff, Caroline S, 1949, Jl 16,13:2
Woodruff, Charles, 1949, N 27,105:1
Woodruff, Charles C, 1941, O 21,23:3
Woodruff, Charles Mrs, 1948, F 18,27:5
Woodruff, Charles S, 1940, Ja 8,15:5
Woodruff, Charles T, 1939, Ja 15,38:7
Woodruff, Charles W, 1943, Ag 13,17:3
Woodruff, Christian Ex-Sen, 1871, N 25,8:3
Woodruff, Clarence C, 1945, Ag 28,19:4
Woodruff, Clarence Mrs, 1957, D 21,19:2
Woodruff, Claude A, 1941, Ap 19,15:4
Woodruff, Clinton R, 1948, Ja 25,56:4
Woodruff, David H, 1955, Ap 28,29:2
Woodruff, Deline Mrs, 1949, F 9,27:5
Woodruff, Douglas, 1957, Ap 10,33:4
Woodruff, E A Lt (trb), 1873, O 26,1:6
Woodruff, Edith S, 1950, Mr 26,92:4
Woodruff, Edward Col, 1920, Jl 9,13:5
Woodruff, Edward J Sr, 1951, Mr 6,27:2
Woodruff, Edward Mrs, 1949, Je 1,31:2
Woodruff, Edward Seymour, 1909, Ja 17,11:5
Woodruff, Edwin H, 1941, Jl 9,21:5
Woodruff, Emily Mrs (will), 1939, O 2,18:2
Woodruff, Ernest, 1944, Je 6,17:3
Woodruff, Ernest Mrs, 1939, Ag 20,32:6
Woodruff, F M, 1926, Jl 22,19:4
Woodruff, Francis Eben, 1914, Je 5,11:5
Woodruff, Frank, 1950, D 20,32:2
Woodruff, Frank C, 1944, S 8,19:5
Woodruff, Frank D, 1947, Je 7,13:4
Woodruff, Frank H, 1938, D 8,27:5
Woodruff, Frank H Mrs, 1950, N 4,17:2
Woodruff, Frank T, 1958, Je 27,25:3
Woodruff, Franklin, 1920, My 27,11:3
Woodruff, Franklin E, 1939, My 31,23:2
Woodruff, Frederick Jr, 1946, D 27,19:2
Woodruff, Frederick Mrs, 1923, S 23,7:5
Woodruff, Frederick P Sr, 1948, Ja 23,24:2
Woodruff, Frederick Sanford, 1917, Je 13,13:4
Woodruff, Frederick W, 1959, My 22,27:3
Woodruff, G Bartram Mrs (Helen), 1965, Ap 26,31:4
Woodruff, G W, 1882, Mr 22,5:5; 1934, Mr 24,16:1
Woodruff, George (por), 1946, Jl 27,17:3
Woodruff, George C Mrs, 1944, Ja 8,13:2
Woodruff, George Cecil, 1968, N 18,47:1
Woodruff, George L, 1950, Ag 29,27:2
Woodruff, George W Mrs, 1956, Jl 27,21:3
Woodruff, Graham C, 1960, S 21,32:4
Woodruff, Hannah Mrs, 1938, My 4,23:4
Woodruff, Harriett Mrs, 1951, Mr 29,27:5
Woodruff, Harry L Sr, 1924, My 8,19:5
Woodruff, Harry W, 1947, Je 21,17:3
Woodruff, Harvey T (por), 1937, Je 3,25:5
Woodruff, Hattie C Mrs, 1941, S 16,23:2
Woodruff, Henrietta C S Mrs, 1942, Ja 22,18:2
Woodruff, Henry, 1916, O 7,11:4
Woodruff, Hiram, 1867, Mr 16,5:3
Woodruff, I C Brig-Gen, 1878, D 13,5:4
Woodruff, I Carle, 1909, Mr 9,9:6
Woodruff, J Eugene, 1952, Ap 22,29:2
Woodruff, J O, 1879, Je 5,2:6
Woodruff, J S, 1929, Ja 14,23:5
Woodruff, J W, 1877, Jl 10,4:6
Woodruff, James W Sr, 1963, F 5,4:8
Woodruff, Jay M, 1958, S 27,21:2
Woodruff, Joe E Mrs, 1948, Jl 14,24:2
Woodruff, John, 1941, Je 3,21:4
Woodruff, John E, 1945, Mr 9,19:4
Woodruff, John K, 1956, Je 16,19:3
Woodruff, John S, 1939, Mr 13,17:4
Woodruff, John T, 1904, Mr 3,9:6
Woodruff, Joseph E, 1949, Ap 7,29:2
Woodruff, Joseph W, 1950, N 1,35:1
Woodruff, L De F, 1876, Jl 12,8:3
Woodruff, Lewis B, 1925, N 28,15:5
Woodruff, Lewis B Judge, 1875, S 11,4:7
Woodruff, Lorande L, 1947, Je 24,23:1
Woodruff, Lyle D Mrs, 1954, Mr 25,29:3
Woodruff, M Dorothy, 1964, Ag 22,21:5
Woodruff, Malcolm B, 1939, N 17,21:5
Woodruff, Melbern J, 1946, Mr 12,25:1
Woodruff, Mormon, 1898, S 3,12:6
Woodruff, Noah O, 1940, D 21,17:6
Woodruff, Oscar A, 1951, Je 13,29:4
Woodruff, Oscar A Mrs, 1947, My 14,25:1
Woodruff, Robert F, 1967, S 22,47:2
Woodruff, Rollin S, 1925, Jl 1,23:4
Woodruff, Roy L, 1939, O 31,46:1
Woodruff, Roy O, 1953, F 13,22:3
Woodruff, Stanley R, 1945, O 14,44:6
Woodruff, Susan H Mrs, 1953, Ja 28,27:6
Woodruff, Thomas A, 1941, Ap 16,23:3
Woodruff, Tim L Mrs, 1904, Mr 29,9:5
Woodruff, Timothy, 1913, O 16,11:5
Woodruff, W Stanley, 1956, N 21,27:6
Woodruff, W Stuart, 1941, Ag 20,19:3
Woodruff, Walter G, 1944, Ag 29,17:1
Woodruff, Warren Mrs, 1947, S 26,23:5
Woodruff, Wesley E, 1949, D 24,15:6
Woodruff, William, 1947, N 15,17:2; 1948, Jl 4,21:5
Woodruff, William S, 1953, N 28,15:5
Woodrug, John, 1868, My 24,1:6
Woodrum, Clifton A, 1950, O 7,19:1
Woods, A H, 1951, Ap 25,29:1
Woods, Alan C (Feb 15), 1963, Ap 1,36:8
Woods, Alan 3d, 1955, D 7,39:2
Woods, Albert F, 1948, Ap 13,27:2
Woods, Albert W Sir, 1904, Ja 8,7:4
Woods, Alex R, 1954, N 2,27:2
Woods, Alfred S, 1942, D 30,23:2
Woods, Alice (Mrs A W Ullman), 1959, Jl 25,17:3
Woods, Ambrose, 1950, Mr 22,27:4
Woods, Anthony J, 1921, Ap 22,13:6
Woods, Anthony S, 1965, O 18,35:5
Woods, Anthony S Lt-Col, 1916, D 21,11:3
Woods, Arch J, 1961, D 30,19:4
Woods, Archie C, 1944, Ap 26,19:4
Woods, Arthur (por), 1942, My 13,19:1
Woods, Arthur L, 1951, F 19,23:4
Woods, Baldwin M, 1956, S 8,17:4
Woods, Bernard, 1906, Mr 21,9:5
Woods, Billy, 1957, Ap 27,10:7
Woods, C R Maj-Gen, 1885, F 28,4:7
Woods, Charles, 1909, Ag 7,9:2; 1943, Ja 29,38:4
Woods, Charles A Judge, 1925, Je 22,15:5
Woods, Charles B, 1965, F 23,33:3
Woods, Charles E, 1946, Ag 15,25:6
Woods, Charles H, 1962, Jl 19,27:2
Woods, Charlotte, 1947, O 7,27:1
Woods, Cyrus E (por), 1938, D 9,25:1
Woods, Cyrus E Mrs, 1953, Ja 29,27:2
Woods, D J, 1951, Jl 2,23:5
Woods, Damon C, 1938, D 4,61:2
Woods, David S, 1939, N 2,23:6
Woods, Edward F, 1964, Ag 1,21:4
Woods, Edward G (por), 1942, O 27,25:3
Woods, Edward Hutton Col, 1910, O 12,9:4
Woods, Edward S, 1953, Ja 12,27:3
Woods, Eliza, 1960, N 22,15:3
Woods, Elliott, 1923, My 23,21:5
Woods, Elmer B, 1955, N 8,31:5
Woods, Erville B, 1959, My 31,76:5
Woods, Everett T, 1959, F 22,88:5
Woods, Francis F, 1964, F 21,27:1
Woods, Francis L Mrs, 1959, Ap 11,21:6
Woods, Frank, 1959, F 28,19:3
Woods, Frank C, 1943, Jl 11,34:7
Woods, Frank E, 1939, My 2,23:2
Woods, Frank H, 1952, Ap 2,20:8
Woods, Frank P, 1944, Ap 26,19:5
Woods, Frederick A, 1939, N 7,25:5
Woods, George, 1955, S 10,17:3
Woods, George A, 1937, Ja 20,22:1
Woods, George B, 1871, Ap 30,1:3; 1871, My 1,4:6; 1954, Mr 5,19:4; 1958, O 9,37:4
Woods, George M, 1944, F 26,13:1
Woods, George R, 1951, Mr 22,31:6
Woods, George S, 1951, Jl 10,3:6
Woods, Gilbert E, 1938, O 13,23:2
Woods, H C Mrs, 1925, Je 10,23:5
Woods, H Charles, 1939, Ja 5,23:2
Woods, Harry F Mrs, 1938, Mr 24,23:5
Woods, Harry L, 1950, F 14,26:5
Woods, Henry J B, 1916, S 2,7:3
Woods, Henry M, 1943, D 3,24:3
Woods, Ida E, 1940, O 6,48:2
Woods, Ida Mrs, 1939, F 5,40:5

Woods, J A, 1879, Mr 22,5:2
Woods, J Albert, 1964, Je 22,27:2
Woods, J Arthur Sr, 1951, Ag 10,15:5
Woods, J B C Mrs, 1964, Ag 12,35:2
Woods, J Edward, 1961, Ag 15,29:4
Woods, James, 1940, Mr 22,20:2; 1941, Ap 26,15:3; 1947, N 7,23:1
Woods, James E, 1937, D 19,II,9:1
Woods, James E Mrs, 1938, O 31,15:3
Woods, James H, 1941, My 22,21:6; 1942, My 23,13:1
Woods, James M, 1950, D 4,29:2
Woods, James M Mrs, 1947, D 1,21:4
Woods, Jesse W, 1950, S 26,31:3
Woods, John Capt, 1924, S 22,19:5
Woods, John F, 1947, D 6,15:6
Woods, John F Sr, 1965, O 17,86:4
Woods, John J, 1949, O 26,27:3; 1954, Ja 3,88:5
Woods, John L, 1941, My 20,23:3
Woods, John S Mrs, 1954, S 25,15:4
Woods, John Stillman, 1911, S 2,7:4
Woods, John T Msgr, 1924, My 9,19:5
Woods, John W, 1966, My 29,56:5
Woods, Joseph F, 1948, Je 27,52:4
Woods, Joseph F Mrs, 1944, D 25,19:4
Woods, Joseph M Rev, 1925, My 8,19:5
Woods, Joseph R, 1947, Ag 1,17:6
Woods, Julia Mrs, 1942, Je 1,13:2
Woods, Katharine Pearson, 1923, F 20,17:3
Woods, Katherine Irvin, 1968, F 7,47:3
Woods, Lady, 1942, S 14,15:4
Woods, Lawrence J, 1947, O 2,27:2
Woods, Leonard, 1878, D 27,5:2; 1947, Ag 20,21:6
Woods, Leonard Mrs, 1943, Ja 30,15:1
Woods, Love B, 1967, My 30,19:4
Woods, Margaret L Mrs, 1945, D 2,46:4
Woods, Mark W, 1956, Je 30,17:5
Woods, Matthew Dr, 1916, O 14,11:2
Woods, N Montgomery, 1956, Je 7,31:2
Woods, Owen F, 1925, Ap 21,21:6
Woods, Patrick M, 1938, Ja 9,42:2
Woods, Paul C, 1956, Ag 14,25:5
Woods, Ralph H, 1951, O 17,31:4
Woods, Reginald F, 1955, F 20,88:8
Woods, Richard C, 1950, O 26,31:4
Woods, Richard H, 1938, Mr 2,19:4
Woods, Robert A, 1953, Je 24,25:3
Woods, Robert Archey, 1925, F 19,19:5
Woods, Robert E, 1954, Ap 10,15:1
Woods, Robert F, 1943, N 22,19:4
Woods, Robert H, 1964, My 14,35:4
Woods, Robert J, 1956, N 6,35:1
Woods, Robert S, 1954, N 21,86:7
Woods, Rogers H, 1955, Ja 15,13:5; 1964, N 30,33:3
Woods, Roscoe, 1951, My 31,27:5
Woods, Rufus, 1950, My 30,17:4
Woods, Sam E (will, Je 14,47:5), 1953, My 23,15:3
Woods, Sam E Mrs, 1952, N 24,23:5
Woods, Sam E Mrs (will), 1953, Ja 23,21:1
Woods, Samuel Baker Jr, 1923, F 22,15:4
Woods, Shirley E, 1954, D 13,27:3
Woods, Thomas, 1961, Ap 18,37:2
Woods, Thomas A, 1945, N 26,21:6
Woods, Thomas C, 1958, Mr 23,88:4
Woods, Thomas F, 1949, D 19,27:1
Woods, Thomas H Sr Mrs, 1953, Ja 15,27:2
Woods, Virna, 1903, Mr 7,9:5
Woods, W A Judge, 1901, Je 29,2:5
Woods, W B Justice, 1887, My 15,1:6
Woods, W H, 1942, Jl 13,16:4
Woods, Walter O, 1951, Je 9,19:2
Woods, William, 1942, Je 4,19:2
Woods, William C, 1961, O 11,47:2
Woods, William F, 1942, Je 10,21:5
Woods, William J, 1954, N 16,29:1
Woods, William S, 1945, My 14,17:4; 1962, D 4,41:4
Woods, William T, 1904, F 20,9:5
Woods, William W, 1939, Ja 21,15:6
Woods, William W Sr, 1960, Ap 20,39:1
Woodsend, Henry E (por), 1939, Ja 10,19:4
Woodside, Grace O, 1946, F 22,25:3
Woodside, James, 1945, Mr 19,19:5
Woodside, John H, 1940, N 6,23:5
Woodside, John T, 1956, Ja 31,29:1
Woodside, John W, 1957, Ja 11,23:3
Woodside, Robert G, 1964, Jl 19,64:7
Woodside, William G, 1951, S 2,48:6
Woodside, William L, 1925, S 30,23:4
Woodside, William P, 1956, D 7,27:3
Woodsmall, Ruth F, 1963, My 27,29:3
Woodson, Albert E Col, 1903, Ag 8,7:6
Woodson, Carter G, 1950, Ap 5,31:5
Woodson, Charles R, 1953, S 5,15:2
Woodson, Lewis B, 1949, Je 1,31:6
Woodson, S H, 1881, Je 27,5:4
Woodson, Urey (por), 1939, Ag 8,17:4
Woodson, W, 1878, Jl 6,1:2
Woodson, Walter B (por), 1948, Ap 24,15:5
Woodstein, Hyman Mrs, 1949, S 30,23:2
Woodston, F Payton, 1952, D 23,23:4
Woodsworth, J S, 1942, Mr 23,15:3
Woodward, A H (Rick), 1950, N 24,35:3
Woodward, Adele Mortimer, 1921, Je 11,13:5
Woodward, Anthony Dr, 1915, F 5,11:5
Woodward, Arthur H, 1953, S 14,27:3
Woodward, Arthur Mrs (Alma N), 1965, Jl 11,68:7
Woodward, Arthur S, 1944, S 4,19:3
Woodward, Benjamin D, 1948, Ap 18,68:6
Woodward, Brady E Mrs, 1955, Jl 14,23:4
Woodward, Burton K, 1942, My 29,17:2
Woodward, C, 1883, Ag 7,5:3
Woodward, C H, 1927, S 8,29:8
Woodward, C W, 1944, D 17,38:5
Woodward, Charles E (por), 1942, My 16,13:1
Woodward, Charles E, 1955, Ja 20,31:1
Woodward, Charles Fuller Justice, 1907, Je 18,7:5
Woodward, Charles G (will, My 30,32:7), 1950, F 2, 28:2
Woodward, Charles K, 1938, My 28,15:5
Woodward, Clark H, 1967, My 30,21:3
Woodward, Clark H Mrs, 1957, Ja 20,93:1
Woodward, Clifford B, 1954, O 26,27:1
Woodward, Clifford D, 1949, O 28,23:3
Woodward, Cornelius W, 1949, F 13,76:3
Woodward, Dave, 1940, F 11,48:2
Woodward, Donald, 1942, F 28,17:2; 1959, Ja 11,88:4
Woodward, E Frances, 1951, My 12,21:5
Woodward, Edgar J, 1944, Ag 7,15:2
Woodward, Edward M, 1943, Mr 24,23:2
Woodward, Elijah, 1949, F 3,23:5
Woodward, Elizabeth Mrs, 1952, Jl 7,21:3
Woodward, Ellsworth, 1939, Mr 1,21:6
Woodward, Elmer E, 1941, Ja 2,23:5
Woodward, Ernest L (will, Ap 23,7:2), 1948, Ap 18, 68:5
Woodward, Eugenie L Mrs, 1947, Mr 30,56:7
Woodward, Frank J, 1951, S 21,23:3
Woodward, Franklin T, 1945, S 18,23:3
Woodward, Frederic C, 1956, Ja 18,31:5
Woodward, George, 1952, My 26,23:3
Woodward, George A Brig-Gen, 1916, D 23,9:6
Woodward, George B, 1923, Jl 10,19:6
Woodward, George H Mrs, 1945, Mr 25,38:3
Woodward, George L, 1954, D 12,89:1
Woodward, George L Mrs, 1947, Mr 20,27:3
Woodward, George M, 1943, Ap 26,19:4
Woodward, George W Judge (funl, Jl 11,1:6), 1875, My 11,6:6
Woodward, Graham C, 1946, F 16,13:3
Woodward, Harold, 1941, N 1,15:4
Woodward, Harold C, 1964, Ag 5,33:3
Woodward, Harry J, 1944, Ap 6,23:5; 1957, Mr 21,31:3
Woodward, Harry J Mrs, 1944, Ap 6,23:5
Woodward, Harry S, 1949, Ja 29,13:3
Woodward, Hedley Mrs, 1945, O 18,23:2
Woodward, Helen, 1941, O 29,23:2
Woodward, Henry J, 1951, Ap 15,93:1
Woodward, Herbert Preston Dr, 1968, Je 4,44:1
Woodward, Hiram C, 1943, S 7,23:4
Woodward, Horace A, 1941, Jl 6,26:3
Woodward, Hu, 1950, Ap 11,31:4
Woodward, J J, 1884, Ag 19,5:2
Woodward, J K, 1915, S 28,11:3
Woodward, J M Surgeon-Gen, 1879, Mr 15,5:2
Woodward, J Taylor, 1968, O 2,39:3
Woodward, James Bingham, 1914, S 3,7:7
Woodward, James E, 1947, Jl 24,21:4
Woodward, James T, 1955, Je 7,33:5
Woodward, James W, 1960, Ag 16,29:3
Woodward, John B, 1953, D 28,21:3
Woodward, John C, 1939, Ag 28,19:3
Woodward, John E, 1944, Ag 5,11:3
Woodward, John Justice, 1923, Je 2,11:6
Woodward, John S, 1943, Ag 11,19:4
Woodward, John W, 1947, Ag 15,17:2
Woodward, Joseph J, 1906, Jl 8,9:6
Woodward, Julian L, 1952, N 5,27:3
Woodward, Julius Hayden Dr, 1916, Jl 3,9:6
Woodward, Katherine S, 1945, O 28,44:3
Woodward, Lamo H, 1951, Ap 25,29:3
Woodward, Leonard, 1950, Jl 21,19:5
Woodward, Lorenzo D C, 1939, Ja 27,20:3
Woodward, Luke Rev, 1925, Ja 11,5:2
Woodward, Luther E, 1961, N 9,35:3
Woodward, Mark, 1947, Ag 24,56:5
Woodward, Mary B, 1943, Mr 1,19:4
Woodward, Mary B Mrs, 1942, Ag 8,11:1
Woodward, Mary S Mrs, 1940, Ap 18,23:4
Woodward, Morgan, 1903, My 20,9:5
Woodward, Orville D, 1946, Ja 10,23:4
Woodward, Parke L, 1942, My 31,38:8
Woodward, Parker G, 1952, Jl 16,25:3
Woodward, Percy E, 1952, Ag 13,21:4
Woodward, Peter H (por), 1939, S 30,17:4
Woodward, Peter H Mrs, 1937, O 29,22:3
Woodward, R B, 1879, Ag 23,4:7
Woodward, Ray L, 1953, Jl 2,23:3
Woodward, Richard H, 1907, N 23,9:5
Woodward, Rignal T, 1904, Mr 30,9:5
Woodward, Robert, 1879, Mr 20,4:7
Woodward, Robert B Col, 1915, S 3,9:5
Woodward, Robert S Jr (por), 1949, N 10,31:1
Woodward, Robins B, 1904, My 24,1:2
Woodward, Roland B, 1946, D 28,16:3
Woodward, Rowland B Mrs, 1959, Jl 8,29:4
Woodward, Russel Williams, 1921, Ap 14,13:5
Woodward, Samuel, 1945, D 9,44:5
Woodward, Sherman M, 1953, S 9,29:2
Woodward, Silas H, 1961, D 9,27:5
Woodward, Stanley, 1963, S 4,39:3; 1965, N 30,41:2
Woodward, Stanley H, 1949, Ag 28,73:1
Woodward, Stewart M, 1941, My 20,23:4
Woodward, Talmadge (will, N 22,31:3), 1955, N 16, 33:2
Woodward, Thomas C, 1942, Ja 6,23:6
Woodward, Thomas Jr Mrs, 1952, Je 16,17:5
Woodward, Van Lear, 1951, Jl 20,21:2
Woodward, Van Lear Jr, 1962, Ag 17,23:4
Woodward, Vivian E, 1954, N 18,33:5
Woodward, Vivian J, 1954, F 2,27:5
Woodward, Walter B Jr, 1966, D 22,33:2
Woodward, Walter C, 1942, Ap 15,21:6
Woodward, Walter C (por), 1947, My 4,60:3
Woodward, Walter D, 1960, O 9,86:4
Woodward, Walter M, 1943, S 29,21:4
Woodward, Walter R, 1944, S 29,21:1
Woodward, Warren M Capt, 1937, O 19,26:1
Woodward, Willard F, 1946, S 14,7:4
Woodward, William, 1947, S 7,60:3; 1953, S 27,87:1
Woodward, William C, 1949, D 23,22:3; 1957, F 25, 25:2
Woodward, William E (por), 1942, Mr 25,21:4
Woodward, William E, 1950, S 30,17:1
Woodward, William E Mrs, 1961, Mr 25,25:3
Woodward, William G, 1947, S 9,31:4
Woodward, William H, 1938, S 6,21:4
Woodward, William Henry, 1909, Ag 31,7:7
Woodward, William Jr (funl, N 3,23:1; will, N 10,-36:1), 1955, O 31,1:2
Woodward, William Jr (est tax appr), 1960, Je 1,37:3
Woodward, William Mrs (est), 1914, Ag 7,11:3
Woodward, William R, 1952, N 1,21:6
Woodward, William Sr (est tax appr), 1957, N 30, 10:1
Woodward, William W, 1939, N 18,17:4; 1946, Ja 8, 24:3
Woodwark, Stanley, 1945, My 14,17:5
Woodwell, C H, 1871, F 3,5:3
Woodwork, George G, 1938, D 28,26:3
Woodworth, Albert L, 1953, My 18,21:4
Woodworth, Albert M, 1948, N 19,28:2
Woodworth, Alden J, 1950, Mr 18,13:4
Woodworth, Arthur H, 1945, O 17,19:4
Woodworth, Arthur V, 1950, Je 16,25:6
Woodworth, Carlos A, 1945, F 22,27:2
Woodworth, Charles A, 1943, My 2,45:1
Woodworth, Charles W, 1940, N 21,29:4
Woodworth, Chauncey C, 1937, Jl 16,20:1
Woodworth, Dorothea Mrs, 1944, Ag 11,15:3
Woodworth, E D, 1940, Jl 27,13:5
Woodworth, E Huling, 1964, D 22,29:4
Woodworth, Edward K, 1938, S 29,25:5
Woodworth, Eleanor, 1942, N 17,26:3
Woodworth, Emmett J Mrs, 1943, Mr 21,27:1
Woodworth, Harry C, 1953, S 20,87:1
Woodworth, Jay Backus, 1925, Ag 6,19:6
Woodworth, Laura E, 1955, Mr 23,31:4
Woodworth, Mary Parket Mrs, 1919, Je 15,22:5
Woodworth, Newell, 1925, Ja 13,19:6
Woodworth, Newton A, 1950, D 29,19:3
Woodworth, Phil B Dr, 1937, Je 8,25:6
Woodworth, Robert S, 1962, Jl 5,25:1
Woodworth, Robert S Mrs, 1960, N 28,31:5
Woodworth, S E Com, 1871, F 9,1:4
Woodworth, Samuel, 1954, O 24,88:7
Woodworth, Susan Mrs, 1921, F 15,9:5
Woodworth, Willard H, 1923, D 8,13:5
Woodworth, William A, 1922, O 28,13:6
Woody, Charles L, 1956, Je 14,33:3
Woody, Charles L Jr Mrs, 1963, Jl 4,17:4
Woody, Clifford, 1948, N 21,88:3
Woody, Frederick W, 1949, Mr 6,72:1
Woody, Howard L, 1916, S 19,11:6
Woody, Kennerly Mrs, 1959, Je 5,27:3
Woody, Robert L, 1937, Ag 14,13:1
Woody, Thomas, 1960, S 13,37:3
Woodyard, Edward D, 1942, O 15,23:4
Woodyatt, Clara B Mrs, 1939, Jl 24,13:6
Woodyatt, Philip C, 1965, Ap 16,29:2
Woodyatt, Rollin T, 1953, D 19,15:6
Woofruff, George P, 1959, O 15,39:5
Woog, Henry, 1959, Mr 6,25:2
Woog, Henry Mrs, 1957, Ap 20,17:3
Wooge, Caroline, 1966, O 31,35:2
Wooge, Thomas, 1968, O 18,6:2
Wool, Gen Mrs, 1873, My 8,5:2
Wool, John E, 1953, N 23,27:2
Wool, John E Gen, 1869, N 11,5:3
Woolard, Clarence C, 1923, D 24,11:6
Woolard, Warden, 1965, F 18,33:4
Woolatt, William R, 1938, Mr 14,16:2
Woolavington, Lord, 1935, Ag 10,13:3
Woolcock, Cyril W, 1964, Jl 6,29:2
Wooldridge, Edmund T Adm, 1968, D 17,47:1
Wooldridge, John M, 1947, Je 11,27:4
Wooldridge, N B, 1873, Ap 27,8:1
Wooldridge, Norman S Mrs, 1960, O 29,23:6
Wooldridge, Powhattan, 1940, S 22,49:3
Wooler, Alfred, 1937, Ag 9,20:1
Woolever, Francis R, 1965, My 18,39:3

Woolever, Harry, 1940, Jl 8,17:5
Woolever, Samuel S, 1943, O 29,19:4
Wooley, Clarence H Mrs, 1945, Ap 29,38:1
Wooley, Edward B, 1949, Je 7,31:2
Wooley, George, 1944, Ag 14,15:4
Wooley, J (see also Feb 11), 1879, F 13,1:5
Wooley, J Herbert, 1962, My 29,31:5
Wooley, John, 1951, D 12,37:1
Wooley, Scudder J Mrs, 1948, Ja 12,19:3
Wooley, Thomas R, 1917, Jl 29,15:2
Wooley, Walter B, 1949, Je 26,60:8
Wooley, William P, 1945, F 8,19:1
Woolf, Albert, 1925, Ag 24,13:6
Woolf, Charles M, 1943, Ja 2,11:2
Woolf, Edgar A, 1943, D 10,27:5
Woolf, Edward, 1882, Mr 17,8:4
Woolf, George, 1958, S 1,13:5
Woolf, George C, 1948, Ap 20,27:4
Woolf, Harold, 1953, My 28,23:5
Woolf, James, 1966, My 31,43:2
Woolf, Jesse, 1949, Ag 31,23:3
Woolf, Lawrence E, 1951, D 29,11:2
Woolf, Mollie B Mrs, 1941, Ap 6,49:2
Woolf, Philip Dr, 1903, S 1,7:6
Woolf, S J, 1948, D 4,13:1
Woolf, Samuel, 1940, F 15,19:3; 1952, Mr 28,24:3
Woolf, Samuel J Mrs, 1956, Je 20,31:3
Woolf, Solomon, 1911, My 28,9:4
Woolf, Stanley, 1959, Mr 5,31:4
Woolf, Stanley Mrs, 1967, D 12,47:4
Woolfall, F Hartley, 1942, F 1,43:1
Woolfenden, L Theodore, 1958, Ap 22,33:4
Woolfolk, Joseph W Capt, 1915, N 2,11:4
Woolfolk, Robert B, 1939, F 25,15:4
Woolfolk, William G, 1954, Ap 22,30:4
Woolford, John R Mrs, 1952, Ja 17,27:3
Woolford, John Roger, 1968, D 22,52:4
Woolford, T Guy, 1952, My 21,27:5
Woolford, Theodore F, 1947, N 24,23:5
Woolheater, Benjamin, 1952, My 22,27:5
Woollard, Herbert H, 1939, Ja 19,19:3
Woollard, William E, 1940, S 2,15:6
Woollaston, Ronald E, 1964, D 29,27:3
Woollcott, William W, 1949, Mr 2,25:4
Woollen, Charles T, 1938, S 22,23:4
Woollen, Evans Jr, 1959, Ja 26,29:3
Woolley, Alice S, 1946, N 18,23:1
Woolley, Allan R, 1961, N 10,35:2
Woolley, Alvah, 1959, O 4,86:2
Woolley, B Drummond, 1957, Je 1,17:5
Woolley, Charles H, 1950, N 12,94:6
Woolley, Clarence M, 1956, Jl 20,17:1
Woolley, Cornell, 1916, S 25,9:3
Woolley, D Wayne, 1966, Jl 26,35:1
Woolley, Daniel P (cor, Ag 20,19:5), 1960, Ag 15, 23:3
Woolley, Daniel S, 1949, Ja 5,26:3
Woolley, Daniel W Mrs, 1951, My 4,27:4
Woolley, David R, 1937, Mr 9,23:2
Woolley, Earl L, 1963, Ag 3,17:5
Woolley, Edward M, 1947, Ap 2,27:4
Woolley, Edward M Mrs, 1966, Ap 1,35:5
Woolley, Edward W, 1941, Ap 21,19:3
Woolley, Eugene, 1949, D 13,31:2
Woolley, Frank, 1958, S 13,19:3
Woolley, Frank F, 1941, F 18,23:4
Woolley, George, 1937, D 9,25:3; 1938, O 25,23:2
Woolley, George C, 1948, Je 6,72:2
Woolley, George H, 1942, D 16,25:5
Woolley, George I, 1951, F 3,15:4
Woolley, Harriet E, 1944, Ag 19,11:3
Woolley, Harry G, 1939, F 19,39:1
Woolley, Herbert C, 1954, Ag 29,88:5
Woolley, Isaac, 1945, My 6,38:3
Woolley, James H, 1941, D 5,23:3
Woolley, James S, 1958, N 9,88:4; 1962, N 15,37:5
Woolley, John E, 1966, Je 28,42:1
Woolley, John G, 1922, Ag 14,11:7
Woolley, Knight Mrs, 1954, Ag 3,19:3
Woolley, Lady, 1945, N 10,15:2
Woolley, Le Roy E, 1946, Ap 9,27:3
Woolley, Leonard (Chas), 1960, F 21,92:2
Woolley, Mary E, 1947, S 6,17:1
Woolley, Minnie K T Mrs, 1942, F 14,15:2
Woolley, Monty (Edgar M),(funl, My 9,37:2; will, My 11,25:1), 1963, My 7,43:3
Woolley, Nephi S, 1949, F 12,18:2
Woolley, Percy R, 1949, N 11,25:3
Woolley, Robert W, 1958, D 16,2:4
Woolley, Samuel G, 1943, Ag 11,19:3
Woolley, Scudder J, 1946, Ja 20,43:1
Woolley, Vern C, 1946, O 29,25:4
Woolley, Victor B, 1945, F 23,17:3
Woolley, Walter R, 1962, Je 20,35:1
Woolley, Wayne W, 1944, F 8,15:5
Woolley, William H, 1939, Ap 9,III,7:2; 1964, Je 3,43:3
Woolley-Hart, Arthur, 1941, N 27,23:3
Woollom, Inez, 1951, Mr 11,6:1
Woolman, Collett E, 1966, S 12,45:1
Woolman, Henry N, 1953, D 29,23:4
Woolman, Josephine T, 1944, My 5,19:5
Woolman, Walter K, 1955, N 21,29:5
Woolner, Adolph M, 1963, N 15,35:2
Woolner, Adolph Mrs, 1960, Je 19,88:3
Woolner, Alfred C, 1968, Ap 17,32:6
Woolner, S, 1931, Ap 14,27:3
Woolner, Samuel Jr Mrs, 1947, My 28,25:3
Woolnough, Howard V, 1953, F 27,21:3
Woolrich, Cornell (will, D 12,29:3), 1968, S 26,47:2
Woolridge, Mary Mrs, 1938, My 25,23:2
Woolrynch, F Humphrey, 1941, N 19,23:4
Woolsey, C A Capt, 1877, S 22,8:4
Woolsey, Charles W Col, 1907, Ja 7,7:4
Woolsey, Edward W, 1944, Mr 27,19:5
Woolsey, Frank, 1937, Ja 13,23:3
Woolsey, Frank Mrs, 1945, Je 15,19:4
Woolsey, Franklin E, 1944, Jl 21,19:5
Woolsey, Frederick W, 1946, Ag 2,19:2
Woolsey, George, 1950, Jl 2,25:1
Woolsey, George M (por), 1937, Ap 23,21:1
Woolsey, Heathcote M, 1957, F 8,23:3
Woolsey, Heathcote M Mrs, 1965, Je 20,72:6
Woolsey, Jerome K, 1951, O 2,27:2
Woolsey, John Brodehead, 1919, Ag 21,11:5
Woolsey, John M (por), 1945, My 5,15:5
Woolsey, Lee A, 1949, Je 28,28:2
Woolsey, Lester H, 1961, Je 21,37:6
Woolsey, Louis, 1948, Ag 25,25:2
Woolsey, Mabel F, 1953, Ja 10,17:5
Woolsey, Melanchthon B Capt, 1874, O 3,6:7
Woolsey, Orson, 1937, Je 1,23:5
Woolsey, Robert (por), 1938, N 1,24:4
Woolsey, Robert L, 1953, N 8,88:6
Woolsey, Ross A, 1942, F 25,19:3
Woolsey, Sarah Chauncey (Susan Coolidge), 1905, Ap 10,9:5
Woolsey, T D, 1889, Jl 2,4:7
Woolsey, T S, 1929, Ap 25,29:5
Woolsey, Walter, 1955, F 12,15:3
Woolsey, Walter Mrs, 1950, Ja 26,27:1
Woolsey, William B, 1945, D 22,19:2
Woolsey, William C Dr, 1919, Je 25,19:5
Woolsey, William H, 1942, S 19,15:4
Woolsey, William W Mrs, 1954, Ap 6,17:4
Woolson, Albert (funl plans, Ag 4,15:5; funl, Ag 7,27:2), 1956, Ag 3,1:5
Woolson, Clyde A, 1938, Jl 29,17:6
Woolson, George B Mrs, 1949, Je 19,68:3
Woolson, I, 1927, My 11,25:3
Woolson, I T, 1941, Mr 30,48:3
Woolson, Ira H Mrs, 1957, Mr 7,29:1
Woolson, James A, 1904, Ja 27,9:7
Woolson, Lawrence I, 1966, Mr 6,93:1
Woolson, Richard H, 1955, Jl 27,23:2
Woolson, Sarah A, 1947, O 4,17:3
Woolson, William D, 1945, D 11,25:3
Woolston, Clarence Mrs, 1951, Ja 5,21:4
Woolston, H Jackson, 1953, Ag 15,15:4
Woolston, Robert W, 1947, O 17,22:3
Woolston, Sarah, 1910, Je 14,11:5
Woolton, Lord (Fredk J Marquis), 1964, D 15,43:3
Woolverton, Ernest E, 1951, Ja 9,30:2
Woolverton, Samuel, 1952, Ja 29,25:1
Woolverton, Samuel Mrs, 1960, Ja 8,23:1
Woolverton, Thomas Henderson, 1914, Ja 23,11:6
Woolverton, William H, 1946, Ag 31,15:5
Woolwine, Thomas Lee, 1925, Jl 9,19:5
Woolworth, Calvin C, 1925, Mr 10,21:3
Woolworth, Charles S, 1947, Ja 8,23:1
Woolworth, Charles S 2d, 1949, S 6,29:5
Woolworth, Chester M Mrs, 1960, My 3,39:3
Woolworth, Clara B, 1944, D 6,23:4
Woolworth, Eugene B, 1917, N 9,13:6
Woolworth, Frank Winfield, 1919, Ap 9,11:2
Woolworth, Fred M, 1923, Ja 28,6:3
Woolworth, Gilbert S, 1954, F 20,17:4
Woolworth, Helen S (will), 1939, D 10,62:3
Woolworth, Ida L, 1944, Jl 22,15:3
Woolworth, James Mills, 1906, Je 17,9:6
Woolworth, Jennie, 1924, My 22,17:5
Woolworth, Norman B (will, Jl 24,17:4), 1962, Je 21, 31:2
Woolworth, Richard W, 1959, Ap 13,31:2
Woolworth, William S, 1947, Ja 11,19:2
Woolworth, William S Mrs, 1947, Ag 26,23:6
Woone, John R, 1951, F 20,25:3
Woosley, Cecil G, 1956, Mr 18,89:2
Wooster, Albert M, 1945, N 27,23:1
Wooster, Edward B, 1944, F 11,19:1
Wooster, Len F, 1958, My 27,31:4
Wooster, Samuel C, 1955, F 28,19:3
Wooster, William H, 1960, S 20,39:4
Wooten, Benjamin A, 1947, Jl 10,21:1
Wooten, Harry A, 1951, N 7,29:4
Wooten, Jack D, 1948, O 11,23:6
Wooten, Leland A, 1952, D 30,19:3
Wooten, Lewis, 1955, F 15,27:2
Wooten, William P, 1950, D 13,35:5
Wooters, J Dukes, 1952, My 30,15:1
Wooton, Gertrude Mrs, 1942, F 22,26:2
Wooton, Paul, 1961, F 17,28:1
Wooton, Paul Mrs, 1946, My 4,15:2
Wooton, Thomas B, 1957, S 2,13:3
Wooton, Thomas L Sr, 1950, F 22,29:4
Wootten, William, 1943, D 7,27:3
Wootton, Bailey P (por), 1949, Ap 17,76:6
Wootton, Henry E, 1950, Ap 10,19:3
Wootton, Henry T, 1956, D 28,21:1
Wootton, Herbert W, 1941, Mr 1,15:4
Wootton, Philip W, 1959, Je 15,27:2
Wootton, Ray B, 1939, O 27,23:5
Wootton, William T, 1944, My 4,19:6
Worby, John, 1950, Ja 16,26:3
Worcester, Alfred, 1951, Ag 29,25:5
Worcester, Charles H (will, Mr 30,17:5), 1956, Mr 25,92:2
Worcester, Charles Mrs, 1954, Je 21,23:2
Worcester, Daniel, 1915, D 17,11:5
Worcester, David, 1947, Je 21,17:4
Worcester, Dean C, 1924, My 3,15:3
Worcester, Edward S Rev, 1937, Je 26,17:7
Worcester, Edwin Dean, 1904, Je 14,7:2
Worcester, Elizabeth, 1881, Ag 14,7:6
Worcester, Elwood (por), 1940, Jl 20,15:3
Worcester, Franklin, 1916, My 3,13:5
Worcester, George, 1958, My 17,19:2
Worcester, George W, 1938, Ap 10,II,6:8
Worcester, Gurdon S Mrs (N Shipman), 1967, My 15,43:4
Worcester, Harry A, 1938, S 19,19:5
Worcester, Henry E, 1954, Ap 11,86:2
Worcester, Joseph E Dr, 1865, O 30,8:5
Worcester, Joseph R (por), 1943, My 10,19:1
Worcester, S T, 1882, D 7,5:1
Worcester, T Rev, 1878, Ag 16,5:4
Worcester, Wakefield Mrs, 1966, O 27,47:2
Worcester, Wilfred J, 1953, Ja 11,90:4
Worcester, William J, 1943, Ja 31,44:8
Word, Edward, 1950, Ag 13,77:2
Worden, Albert W Sr, 1946, F 15,25:1
Worden, Charles B, 1954, N 16,29:1
Worden, Charles B Mrs, 1965, My 2,89:1
Worden, Charles Mrs, 1948, N 4,30:2
Worden, Clarence C, 1961, Ap 5,37:1
Worden, Daniel T, 1914, Jl 10,9:4
Worden, Edward C, 1940, S 23,17:4
Worden, Eugene C, 1963, My 1,39:5
Worden, Floyd, 1946, Ag 26,23:1
Worden, Fred E, 1948, O 31,88:3
Worden, J L, 1897, O 19,7:4
Worden, J Lorimer Mrs, 1946, Jl 25,21:5
Worden, James A Rev, 1917, O 25,15:5
Worden, Jarvis C Sr, 1949, S 1,21:5
Worden, Joel H Sr, 1943, D 20,23:2
Worden, John H, 1950, Mr 26,92:7
Worden, John L Lt, 1873, My 6,4:7
Worden, Mary E Mrs, 1937, My 27,23:5
Worden, R J, 1946, D 27,20:2
Worden, Robert W, 1938, Ap 19,21:2
Worden, Scott B, 1943, Ap 24,13:1
Worden, Thomas C, 1943, S 4,13:3
Worden, Walter G, 1946, Ap 21,47:1
Worden, Wilbertine T Mrs, 1949, Ap 27,27:5
Worden, William W, 1915, My 29,11:7
Worden, Wirt, 1943, Ja 4,15:3
Wordhoff, William H, 1940, N 19,27:3
Wordie, James M, 1962, Ja 17,33:5
Wordin, Thomas Cook, 1905, Ap 8,9:5
Wordley, James E, 1962, Jl 11,35:1
Wordsman, John P, 1955, Ja 27,23:1
Wordsworth, Christopher, 1938, Ja 31,19:4
Wordsworth, John Bp of Salisbury, 1911, Ag 17,7:6
Wordsworth, W, 1883, F 11,7:3
Wordsworth, William Mrs, 1859, F 8,1:1
Work, Alanson, 1879, Jl 8,2:4
Work, B G, 1927, Ag 31,21:5
Work, E W, 1934, Ap 18,22:1
Work, Effie Abell Mrs, 1941, Ap 6,49:3
Work, Ellen W Mrs, 1942, N 4,23:6
Work, Frank (funl, Mr 19,11:2), 1911, Mr 17,9:5
Work, Frederick, 1945, Ag 30,21:4
Work, Frederick J, 1942, Ja 21,18:3
Work, Harry W, 1941, O 8,24:3
Work, Hubert (por), 1942, D 15,27:1
Work, Hubert Mrs (funl, My 11,7:2), 1924, My 10, 13:5
Work, James A, 1961, Ja 24,29:4
Work, James H Jr, 1954, Je 1,27:4
Work, James Henry, 1916, O 24,12:6
Work, John C, 1959, My 5,33:3
Work, John M, 1961, Ja 11,47:5
Work, John W, 1967, My 19,39:1
Work, Lincoln T Dr, 1968, N 5,44:4
Work, Lincoln T Mrs, 1968, O 15,47:2
Work, M C, 1934, Je 27,19:4
Work, Norman P Mrs, 1949, Je 15,29:4
Work, Robert D, 1940, F 21,19:2
Work, Robert Dixon, 1968, Mr 4,37:2
Work, Ruth A, 1953, N 22,88:2
Work, William R, 1948, O 4,23:4
Working, Daniel W, 1944, Ap 9,34:4
Workman, Charles T, 1953, Ja 5,21:1
Workman, Espy A, 1951, My 12,21:4
Workman, Frederick W, 1945, Je 8,19:1
Workman, George R, 1960, D 5,31:5
Workman, Grover W, 1939, Mr 10,23:1
Workman, Herbert B, 1951, Ag 27,19:5
Workman, Jacob S, 1943, My 18,23:3
Workman, James C, 1945, Ja 25,19:5

Workman, Joseph M, 1947, F 7,24:2
Workman, Lee W, 1952, S 12,21:1
Workman, Robert C, 1954, N 26,29:3
Workman, Samuel H, 1949, N 25,16:4
Workman, Sonny (Raymond), 1966, Ag 22,33:4
Workman, William H Dr, 1937, O 10,II,9:3
Workman, William Hunter Mrs (Fannie Bullock Workman), 1925, Ja 27,13:2
Works, J D, 1928, Je 7,27:5
Works, Samuel, 1868, Ja 6,5:5
Works, Samuel D, 1956, Jl 23,23:4
Workum, Julius F, 1924, S 2,19:4
Workum, Julius F Mrs, 1963, Je 27,33:1
Worl, Edward E, 1942, O 31,15:3
Worley, Alfred C, 1947, My 24,15:5
Worley, Alice, 1951, Ap 26,32:3
Worley, H F, 1948, O 7,29:1
Worley, Harry W, 1948, F 18,27:3
Worley, John S, 1956, My 26,17:5
Worley, Joseph, 1871, Je 3,2:4
Worley, Lee, 1958, Ap 16,33:4
Worley, Leonard G, 1960, N 9,35:2
Worley, Loyd F, 1966, Jl 12,43:5
Worley, Robert W, 1962, Jl 18,29:4
Worley, Thomas W, 1948, Mr 7,69:1
Worm, A Toxen, 1922, Ja 15,22:3
Worm, Erik J-L, 1962, O 18,39:2
Wormall, Arthur, 1964, My 12,37:5
Worman, Caroline, 1902, D 17,3:4
Worman, Cyrene Mrs, 1945, My 8,19:2
Worman, Floyd, 1959, D 20,60:7
Worman, H L, 1946, N 10,63:3
Wormeley, Carter W, 1938, Ag 25,19:3
Wormeley, Katherine Prescott, 1908, Ag 6,5:4
Wormer, Parley P, 1957, O 18,23:3
Wormley, James, 1884, O 19,9:4
Worms, Anthony D De, 1938, Ja 12,21:4
Worms, Blanche B Mrs, 1939, Ja 3,17:3
Worms, Conrad, 1943, My 22,13:3
Worms, Ferdinand, 1939, S 17,49:2
Worms, Leon, 1949, O 2,80:8
Worms, Percy de, 1941, Ap 13,X,6:8
Worms, Samuel E, 1957, Jl 1,23:5
Worms, Sidney A, 1949, O 14,27:1
Wormser, C W, 1946, Ag 10,13:5
Wormser, I Maurice (cor, O 25,33:4), 1955, O 23, 86:1
Wormser, Isidor (funl), 1907, Je 25,7:6
Wormser, Isidor, 1914, Je 25,9:6
Wormser, Isidor Mrs, 1917, F 3,13:5
Wormser, Leon, 1950, D 10,105:1; 1962, O 1,31:1
Wormser, Louis, 1903, D 7,2:4
Wormser, Louis W, 1918, O 17,15:2
Wormser, Maurice S, 1909, O 1,9:4
Wormser, Moritz, 1940, My 23,23:2
Wormser, Otto D, 1951, Jl 30,17:6
Wormser, Robert S, 1943, D 8,23:5
Wormser, Sidney L, 1940, Mr 31,45:2
Wormsham, George W Jr, 1937, Mr 22,23:2
Wormuth, William H, 1960, Je 9,33:5
Wormwood, Archie H, 1953, D 24,15:2
Wormwood, Robert F, 1942, F 1,43:3
Wornham, Charles, 1947, Je 29,48:2
Wornow, Edward, 1954, Jl 25,69:3
Woronock, Morris, 1947, Je 25,25:2
Woronock, Morris Mrs, 1958, Ja 27,27:1
Woronoff, Samuel M, 1962, Jl 8,65:1
Woronov, Nathan, 1951, Ap 14,15:3
Worrall, Charlotte, 1949, Mr 29,26:2
Worrall, David E, 1944, F 8,15:4
Worrall, Douglas H, 1956, Ja 22,88:8
Worrall, George Mrs, 1944, F 1,19:1
Worrall, Georgia M Mrs, 1941, Mr 20,21:3
Worrall, Jack, 1937, N 18,23:3
Worrall, Jane M Mrs, 1905, Je 9,9:5
Worrall, Petera B, 1916, F 18,11:5
Worrall, Richard P, 1953, Ap 5,76:3
Worrall, Thomas, 1955, D 4,89:1
Worrall, William H, 1939, O 8,49:1
Worrell, C F, 1881, F 1,5:2
Worrell, C L, 1934, Ag 11,13:3
Worrell, C T W E, 1953, Mr 11,29:1
Worrell, Edna R, 1961, N 11,23:5
Worrell, Everett E, 1938, N 20,39:2
Worrell, Frank, 1967, Mr 14,47:4
Worrell, Frank I, 1920, Mr 25,11:6
Worrell, George D, 1965, Ag 18,35:3
Worrell, John W, 1939, Je 12,17:6
Worrell, Rufus Mrs, 1953, Je 6,17:1
Worrell, William H, 1952, D 4,35:2
Worrick, Elmero, 1940, F 25,38:7
Worron, Herbert B, 1943, D 20,23:5
Worsley, Francis, 1949, S 16,28:2
Worsley, Frank A, 1943, F 2,20:2
Worsoe, Hercules, 1954, D 29,23:3
Worst, Charles A, 1943, D 18,15:3
Worst, Harold, 1966, Je 17,45:1
Worstall, Edward, 1947, Ag 14,23:3
Worster, Eldridge G, 1907, Mr 16,9:5
Worster, Harry P, 1939, O 13,23:2
Worster, J Dr (see also Ap 9), 1877, Ag 12,12:4
Worster, Philip Sr, 1946, O 18,24:2
Worster, Stephen C, 1966, O 7,43:3

Worsthorn, Louise E, 1958, Ap 9,33:2
Wort, Frederick J, 1949, Jl 30,15:6
Wort, Robert J, 1942, N 12,25:1
Wort, Robert J Mrs, 1958, Ag 11,21:1
Wortche, Henry W, 1941, Je 10,23:3
Wortendyke, A C, 1884, D 2,5:2
Wortendyke, Jacob R, 1943, Jl 4,20:2
Wortendyke, Nicholas D, 1942, Ag 8,11:1
Wortendyke, Reynier J Mrs, 1945, S 27,21:6; 1965, Jl 19,27:3
Wortendyke, Reynier J Sr, 1952, Ag 26,25:2
Worters, Roy, 1957, N 8,29:4
Worth, Adam, 1902, F 7,2:5
Worth, C F, 1895, Mr 12,5:2
Worth, Charles C, 1943, D 31,15:4
Worth, Clifford, 1945, My 26,15:4
Worth, Clifford I Mrs, 1951, O 28,84:5
Worth, Daniel F Jr, 1955, Jl 1,21:2
Worth, Edward H, 1952, Jl 9,27:4
Worth, Edwin F Sr, 1939, Mr 14,21:3
Worth, Ernest, 1950, O 18,33:5
Worth, Francis J, 1873, S 27,8:5
Worth, Frederick, 1909, O 27,11:3
Worth, George C, 1941, Ap 2,23:1
Worth, George C Jr, 1953, N 7,17:2
Worth, Gracia A, 1951, S 8,17:2
Worth, Harold G, 1955, N 29,29:5
Worth, Helen (Mrs J C Wolfe), 1957, Jl 24,25:2
Worth, Huntting C, 1959, My 1,29:4
Worth, J L, 1879, Ag 30,2:4
Worth, Jacob, 1905, F 22,2:5
Worth, Jacques, 1941, Ja 29,17:5
Worth, John G, 1941, My 22,21:4
Worth, John W, 1938, Ja 19,23:3
Worth, Jonathan Ex-Gov, 1869, S 7,1:7
Worth, Lewis R, 1939, Ap 27,25:2
Worth, Lon B, 1952, O 18,19:4
Worth, Paul S, 1943, F 4,23:1
Worth, Peggy, 1956, Mr 25,92:8
Worth, Ruth A, 1945, S 22,17:1
Worth, William A, 1940, Jl 3,17:2
Worth, William E, 1948, D 5,92:2; 1953, Je 25,27:3
Worth, William Mrs, 1954, D 22,23:2
Worth, William P, 1939, My 1,23:3
Worth, William Penn, 1923, F 15,19:4
Worth, William Scott Gen, 1904, O 17,9:3
Wortham, Arthur M, 1942, Jl 30,21:2
Wortham, Hugh E, 1959, Jl 10,25:3
Wortham, Richard J, 1938, F 11,24:2
Worthen, Albert L, 1968, Mr 9,29:4
Worthen, C Nathaniel, 1944, Jl 4,19:3
Worthen, Clarence E, 1941, Ag 25,15:1
Worthen, Samuel C, 1948, N 22,21:4
Worthing, Archie G, 1949, Ag 1,17:3
Worthing, Harry J, 1958, Jl 24,25:2
Worthing, Helen L (will, S 23,37:1), 1948, Ag 27,21:6
Worthington, Arthur Rev (Saml Oakley Crawford), 1917, D 14,13:4
Worthington, Arthur W Sr, 1953, D 22,31:4
Worthington, Augustus S, 1922, Ap 10,15:2
Worthington, Charles C, 1944, O 22,45:1
Worthington, Charles V Mrs, 1942, Ag 3,15:6
Worthington, Dorothy, 1962, S 13,37:1
Worthington, Edward H, 1966, Ap 14,39:3
Worthington, Everett, 1938, Ag 5,17:5
Worthington, Frank F, 1967, D 9,47:4
Worthington, George, 1948, Ag 4,21:3; 1964, D 9,50:8
Worthington, George Bp, 1908, Ja 9,9:5
Worthington, George C, 1942, Ap 6,15:4
Worthington, George H, 1924, Ja 11,17:3
Worthington, Glenn Mrs, 1949, Je 4,13:3
Worthington, H R, 1880, D 18,2:5
Worthington, Harry J, 1943, N 8,19:4
Worthington, Henry C Gen, 1909, Jl 30,7:6
Worthington, Irvin R, 1957, Ja 9,31:1
Worthington, J Kent, 1923, D 17,17:4
Worthington, John, 1912, My 21,13:5; 1918, My 12, 21:2
Worthington, John F, 1942, N 6,23:2
Worthington, Joseph A, 1960, O 2,84:1
Worthington, Joseph E Jr, 1949, F 15,23:5
Worthington, Julia H Mrs, 1913, Je 9,9:4
Worthington, Katherine S, 1960, S 3,17:6
Worthington, Leslie B Mrs, 1968, Ag 16,33:4
Worthington, Louise, 1946, N 22,23:2
Worthington, M H, 1944, F 29,17:1
Worthington, Mary G Mrs, 1937, D 11,19:1
Worthington, Percy Sir, 1939, Jl 17,19:4
Worthington, Ralph A, 1951, Ap 27,23:1
Worthington, Ralph E, 1939, F 1,21:4
Worthington, Stephen P, 1938, O 27,23:5
Worthington, W Alfred, 1945, D 26,19:4
Worthington, W W, 1912, Ja 31,11:4
Worthington, Walter F Adm, 1937, Ag 3,23:4
Worthington, William, 1966, Mr 10,33:3
Worthington, William J, 1941, Ap 11,22:3
Worthington, Willis C, 1943, F 28,47:5
Worthington-Evans, L Sir, 1931, F 15,12:1
Worthley, Abigail P Mrs, 1938, F 5,15:5
Worthley, George C Sr, 1950, My 12,27:2
Worthley, Leon H, 1937, O 10,II,9:2
Worthley, Montague W, 1939, F 22,21:3
Worths, Herbert N, 1942, Je 21,22:3

Worthy, Roy B, 1959, Jl 28,27:4
Wortley, A Stuart, 1905, O 12,9:5
Wortley, J A S, 1870, N 29,5:6
Wortley, J S, 1881, S 5,2:1
Wortman, Denys, 1958, S 21,86:4
Wortman, Edward J, 1944, Mr 27,19:6
Wortman, Elbert E M Mrs, 1967, Je 9,45:2
Wortman, Fred Y, 1949, F 3,24:3
Wortman, Irving, 1957, Je 15,17:5
Wortman, Irving W, 1944, F 29,17:5
Wortman, William C, 1937, S 7,21:2
Wortmann, Dietrich, 1952, S 22,23:5
Wortmann, Herbert D, 1955, N 4,29:2
Wortmann, Martin, 1939, Ja 28,15:6
Wortsman, Charles, 1938, My 17,23:5
Wortsmann, Max, 1912, O 19,11:5
Wortzel, Samuel J, 1967, Ja 4,43:1
Wose, Alfred M, 1946, F 15,25:2
Wose, Frederick, 1946, Ag 7,27:2
Wose, Frederick W Mrs, 1946, Ap 2,27:5
Wosniak, Bernard, 1960, Ja 3,88:2
Wosnitzer, Abraham, 1968, Jl 9,35:7
Wostbrock, Henry J, 1953, Mr 9,29:2
Wostbrock, Marie Mrs, 1937, Mr 24,25:3
Wotawa, Edward J, 1963, Ag 24,19:6
Wotherspoon, George, 1949, O 9,92:3
Wotherspoon, Henry H, 1914, F 17,11:5; 1949, Ap 7, 30:3
Wotherspoon, William W Mrs, 1953, D 18,29:2
Wotherspoon, William Wallace Gen, 1921, O 22,13:6
Wotiz, Mark H, 1958, N 24,29:2
Wotterbeek, Daniel R, 1920, My 28,13:3
Wotton, Pierce O, 1959, My 14,33:1
Wottrich, Wilfred, 1963, S 2,15:3
Woud, Victor C Vant, 1905, Mr 26,9:5
Wouk, Abraham I, 1942, Jl 23,19:2
Woulfe, John C, 1958, Ja 27,27:2
Wounderly, William E, 1949, Ag 6,17:1
Woursell, Abraham, 1957, S 29,86:8
Wovschin, William A, 1938, Ap 16,13:4
Woycik, D A, 1947, Ap 16,25:4
Woytinsky, Wladimir S, 1960, Je 13,27:3
Woytinsky, Wladimir S Mrs (Emma), 1968, Ap 14, 77:1
Woywod, Stanislaus, 1941, S 21,44:2
Wozencraft, Frank W, 1966, S 6,47:1
Wozniak, E, 1937, D 22,32:4
Woznick, Michael J, 1946, Jl 17,23:1
Wraga, Richard, 1968, F 1,37:3
Wrage, Ernest J, 1965, My 5,47:4
Wragg, Samuel A, 1953, D 22,31:4
Wragge, Bernard, 1954, Ja 12,23:2
Wragge, Clement Lindley, 1922, D 11,17:5
Wraight, Raymond, 1954, My 2,89:2
Wraith, William, 1956, O 13,19:2
Wrangel, Olga Baroness, 1968, S 10,47:1
Wrangel, P, 1928, Ap 26,27:3
Wrase, Alfred F, 1962, F 25,88:8
Wrather, William E, 1963, N 30,27:1
Wratten, Stanley T, 1950, O 2,23:5
Wraxall, H H, 1882, Ap 25,4:7
Wray, A H, 1931, F 2,19:3
Wray, C C, 1919, O 18,13:4
Wray, Clive E, 1940, Ap 4,23:6
Wray, Daniel J, 1951, O 24,31:5
Wray, Henry, 1950, Ja 1,42:7
Wray, J L Lt, 1918, F 14,11:5
Wray, J R Ludlow, 1967, Jl 26,36:2
Wray, J R Ludlow Mrs, 1950, D 8,30:3
Wray, James, 1954, D 28,23:3
Wray, James M, 1955, Jl 8,23:4
Wray, John (por), 1940, Ap 7,44:8
Wray, Mary E Mrs, 1950, Ja 20,25:1
Wray, Robert, 1944, D 2,13:2
Wray, Sara, 1952, My 5,23:4
Wray, Stephen, 1958, Je 1,86:7
Wray, Stephen G, 1960, O 2,85:1
Wray, William, 1956, S 5,27:2
Wrede, Frank C, 1967, Jl 10,31:4
Wrede, John A, 1923, Je 1,19:5
Wreden, Carl V, 1943, F 1,15:1
Wreden, Nicholas, 1955, Ag 8,21:4
Wregg, W P Burns, 1961, Je 15,43:5
Wrelius, Axel F, 1957, Ag 10,15:1
Wren, Alphonse A, 1953, N 24,29:3
Wren, Amy, 1958, Mr 24,27:3
Wren, Arthur, 1959, O 17,23:6
Wren, Baden P, 1951, Ap 17,29:2
Wren, Charles F, 1944, O 7,13:4
Wren, Edward C, 1962, Ja 26,16:3
Wren, Edward Mrs, 1949, S 5,17:5
Wren, Frank G (por), 1940, Jl 18,19:4
Wren, John, 1953, O 28,29:4
Wren, John E Mrs, 1950, N 23,38:2
Wren, Joseph Mrs, 1947, S 23,25:4
Wren, Mary I Mrs, 1941, Je 15,36:7
Wren, Mathilde F P Mrs, 1953, O 15,33:3
Wren, Percival C (por), 1941, N 24,17:3
Wren, Rosaline C, 1940, O 22,23:3
Wren, Sam, 1962, Mr 17,25:4
Wren, Thomas J, 1949, My 17,25:4
Wren, William C, 1956, Ag 12,84:8
Wren, William P, 1948, Jl 27,25:4

Wrench, Evelyn, 1966, N 12,29:1
Wrench, George P, 1952, S 5,27:3
Wrenn, Allen S, 1942, Ja 18,42:3
Wrenn, Beverly Col, 1912, F 7,11:4
Wrenn, Charles L, 1952, O 30,19:5
Wrenn, George L, 1948, Jl 31,15:5
Wrenn, Henry, 1958, Je 10,33:4
Wrenn, John H, 1911, My 14,13:4
Wrenn, McDonald E, 1949, Mr 3,25:4
Wrenn, Philip W, 1954, O 21,27:2
Wrenn, Robert D, 1925, N 13,19:6
Wrenn, Thomas J, 1951, Ap 30,21:4
Wrensch, Carl H, 1956, Ap 25,35:3
Wrenshall, John C Jr, 1942, Mr 3,24:3
Wresley, Fred, 1872, Ag 9,5:5
Wreszin, Henry M, 1958, Ag 4,21:2
Wrhel, Rudolph, 1960, O 1,19:2
Wriedt, Hans F, 1962, Jl 20,25:5
Wriedt, Henrietta Mrs, 1942, S 16,23:2
Wriggins, Thomas Sr, 1958, S 7,86:5
Wriggins, Wilbur F, 1945, My 22,19:1
Wrighley, Charles W, 1957, D 5,35:5
Wrighley, Rogers, 1947, Ap 10,25:4
Wright, A Adair, 1959, S 26,23:2
Wright, A C, 1952, D 20,17:5
Wright, A H, 1881, N 6,7:4
Wright, Abigail, 1879, O 18,2:4
Wright, Abigail H Mrs, 1953, Ja 8,27:5
Wright, Abner K, 1954, Ja 4,19:2
Wright, Abram K (will), 1951, O 28,1:6
Wright, Adelaide, 1944, Je 6,17:5
Wright, Agnes S, 1962, O 18,39:2
Wright, Albert (Chalky), 1957, Ag 13,52:6
Wright, Albert, 1960, My 18,41:4
Wright, Albert A Prof, 1905, Ap 3,9:4
Wright, Albert B, 1942, Je 24,19:6
Wright, Albert J, 1940, Jl 3,17:3
Wright, Albert W, 1948, Ja 27,25:1
Wright, Alfred, 1952, O 1,33:3
Wright, Alfred H Mrs, 1954, S 6,15:2
Wright, Alfred R L, 1939, Ap 26,23:4
Wright, Alfred V, 1953, S 1,23:2
Wright, Alfred W, 1952, Jl 14,17:3
Wright, Alice, 1882, Mr 7,1:4
Wright, Allen Henry, 1943, Je 19,13:3
Wright, Almroth, 1947, My 1,25:3
Wright, Ann, 1962, Ag 9,25:3
Wright, Anne, 1958, O 4,21:3
Wright, Anne R Mrs, 1953, O 10,17:6
Wright, Annie F Mrs, 1924, Ap 9,21:2
Wright, Annie V Mrs, 1949, Mr 17,25:1
Wright, Archibald, 1921, N 20,22:3
Wright, Arthur, 1939, O 1,53:2; 1956, Ag 2,25:6
Wright, Arthur C, 1956, Jl 10,31:1
Wright, Arthur D, 1947, My 11,62:2
Wright, Arthur E, 1917, F 8,13:5; 1947, Ja 9,24:3
Wright, Arthur G, 1961, S 8,17:7
Wright, Arthur J, 1954, Je 26,13:5
Wright, Arthur M, 1948, Je 25,23:2
Wright, Arthur M Mrs, 1941, Jl 31,17:2
Wright, Arthur Mrs (Anna Perrot Rose), 1968, S 5, 47:2
Wright, Arthur W, 1953, Jl 15,25:3
Wright, Arthur Williams Prof, 1915, D 20,11:4
Wright, B Dunbar, 1937, D 17,32:2
Wright, Beals C, 1961, Ag 24,29:5
Wright, Benjamin S, 1942, Ag 15,11:3
Wright, Berlin H, 1940, N 28,23:5
Wright, Bert R, 1948, Ag 29,60:1
Wright, Berton L, 1940, Jl 12,15:3
Wright, Boardman, 1950, D 18,31:3
Wright, Boucher R, 1958, S 22,31:5
Wright, Boykin C (funl, N 13,37:4), 1956, N 10,19:4
Wright, Boykin C Mrs, 1947, D 13,15:3
Wright, Burchard U, 1945, Ja 27,11:3
Wright, C Bagley, 1963, Ag 11,85:1
Wright, C Dr, 1883, S 4,5:2
Wright, C Fred, 1925, N 12,25:5
Wright, C Howard, 1954, Ap 9,23:2
Wright, C Melville, 1946, S 29,60:6
Wright, Calvert C, 1954, F 3,23:5
Wright, Carl P Jr Mrs, 1948, O 26,31:4
Wright, Carroll D (funl, F 25,9:4), 1909, F 21,7:5
Wright, Carroll Q, 1924, Ap 5,15:5
Wright, Charles, 1942, N 20,23:5
Wright, Charles B, 1942, Ap 26,40:3; 1944, Ja 7,18:3
Wright, Charles C, 1954, Mr 12,22:3; 1958, Ag 21,25:3
Wright, Charles D, 1952, Je 23,19:3
Wright, Charles E, 1950, Ja 2,23:5
Wright, Charles G, 1950, Ap 16,107:3
Wright, Charles H, 1939, Ap 4,25:1
Wright, Charles H C, 1957, My 17,25:2
Wright, Charles J Mrs, 1948, Je 10,25:3
Wright, Charles K, 1957, Jl 28,60:8
Wright, Charles O, 1954, F 2,27:5
Wright, Charles S, 1945, O 31,23:5
Wright, Charles T Col, 1910, N 8,9:4
Wright, Charles Will, 1968, S 26,55:1
Wright, Clarence B, 1954, N 11,31:5
Wright, Clarence M, 1967, D 20,45:2
Wright, Clark C, 1948, O 13,25:4
Wright, Claude E, 1956, Mr 26,29:2
Wright, Claude F, 1923, Ja 13,13:5
Wright, Clement H, 1966, S 12,45:4
Wright, Clifford A, 1961, Ap 30,86:7
Wright, Clifford C, 1953, O 27,27:4
Wright, Clifford R, 1947, F 16,57:4; 1956, Ag 8,25:3
Wright, Clinton H, 1951, My 8,31:2
Wright, Clyde J, 1953, F 8,88:2
Wright, Coley P, 1941, Ap 12,15:4
Wright, Constance C Mrs, 1942, S 7,19:4
Wright, Cora A, 1955, S 25,92:6
Wright, Cora C Mrs, 1951, Ap 30,21:5
Wright, Cora E Mrs, 1940, D 31,15:3
Wright, Courtney, 1961, S 5,32:4
Wright, Cuthbert, 1948, N 30,27:2
Wright, D Wentworth, 1955, Ap 3,87:1
Wright, Daniel L, 1962, N 13,37:1
Wright, Daniel T, 1943, N 19,19:3
Wright, Daniel Thew Judge, 1912, S 12,11:4
Wright, David, 1869, Ag 2,3:2
Wright, David McCord Dr, 1968, Ja 8,39:2
Wright, David S, 1954, S 18,15:4
Wright, David W, 1966, Je 25,31:4
Wright, Dawson Mrs, 1950, D 31,43:1
Wright, Deborah A, 1944, Ja 19,19:2
Wright, Deodatus Judge, 1875, Ag 15,6:7
Wright, Dilapalain H, 1945, My 3,23:2
Wright, Donald M Mrs (E L Meadowcroft), 1966, N 24,35:5
Wright, E Delafield, 1947, My 7,27:3
Wright, E Stanley, 1959, S 8,35:3
Wright, E V R Gen, 1871, Ja 20,6:2
Wright, E W Rev, 1866, O 1,2:4
Wright, Earle E, 1953, Ag 10,23:4
Wright, Edgar B Sr, 1957, Mr 17,86:7
Wright, Edmund, 1964, F 13,31:5
Wright, Edmund S, 1946, Ap 16,25:4
Wright, Edna, 1948, Jl 7,23:1
Wright, Edward B, 1959, O 18,86:7
Wright, Edward col, 1913, S 18,11:2
Wright, Edward F, 1925, Ja 12,15:3
Wright, Edward G, 1945, Mr 30,15:3
Wright, Edward H, 1960, Jl 26,29:4
Wright, Edward H 3d, 1952, Je 5,31:2
Wright, Edward Maj, 1873, D 26,1:6
Wright, Edward N, 1951, Mr 6,27:3
Wright, Edward R, 1941, F 16,41:2; 1947, Ja 2,27:3
Wright, Edward S, 1910, Ag 17,7:5
Wright, Edward T, 1948, S 1,23:3
Wright, Edwin M, 1961, S 21,35:4
Wright, Edwin P, 1947, Jl 21,17:4
Wright, Edwin Vorras Prof, 1913, F 20,11:3
Wright, Eleanor, 1939, O 27,23:4
Wright, Elizabeth T Dr, 1937, Mr 19,24:2
Wright, Elizabeth W, 1945, Jl 15,13:6
Wright, Ellphalet Dr, 1907, Ag 23,7:5
Wright, Emile B, 1947, S 9,31:3
Wright, Emma, 1921, S 13,17:4
Wright, Eric E, 1943, Ap 27,23:3
Wright, Ernest, 1953, F 10,27:4
Wright, Ernest B, 1952, Ag 12,19:6
Wright, Ernest H, 1950, Ap 6,29:3
Wright, Ernest Hunter Dr, 1968, D 23,39:1
Wright, Ernest T, 1956, S 19,37:4
Wright, Eugene, 1958, Ag 18,19:4
Wright, Everett S, 1967, O 2,47:4
Wright, Evia A, 1950, Jl 20,25:6
Wright, F, 1928, D 13,29:2
Wright, F C, 1927, S 19,25:6
Wright, F Walden, 1949, F 24,24:3
Wright, Fatima Mrs, 1938, O 25,23:4
Wright, Fielding L (funl, My 8,33:1), 1956, My 5,19:4
Wright, Florence, 1911, F 3,9:5
Wright, Florence D, 1939, D 28,21:1
Wright, Frank, 1939, Ja 3,17:3; 1941, My 9,21:5; 1942, Ja 20,19:2
Wright, Frank C (por), 1946, My 30,21:1
Wright, Frank C, 1952, N 18,31:2
Wright, Frank C Mrs, 1948, Je 22,25:1
Wright, Frank E, 1940, My 2,23:4; 1945, F 7,21:2
Wright, Frank G, 1960, Je 20,31:3
Wright, Frank H, 1947, S 11,27:4
Wright, Frank J, 1954, S 7,26:2
Wright, Frank L, 1942, Ap 11,13:6; 1953, N 12,31:4
Wright, Frank L (funl plans, Ap 11,21:2; funl, Ap 13,31:4), 1959, Ap 10,1:2
Wright, Frank Mrs (Rosa Lind), 1921, S 4,18:3
Wright, Frank R, 1943, Ja 30,15:3
Wright, Frank S, 1938, D 10,17:5
Wright, Frank Walden Dr, 1923, Ap 3,23:4
Wright, Franklin O, 1947, Ap 26,13:4
Wright, Fred A, 1949, Je 5,92:3
Wright, Fred B, 1963, D 23,25:1
Wright, Fred D, 1958, Ap 13,84:4
Wright, Fred E Mrs, 1948, Je 14,23:2; 1962, Ap 25,39:3
Wright, Fred O, 1903, S 12,9:6
Wright, Frederic J, 1941, Ag 19,21:5
Wright, Frederick, 1952, Ja 26,13:5
Wright, Frederick A, 1950, O 30,27:2
Wright, Frederick B, 1951, Mr 24,13:4
Wright, Frederick C E Mrs, 1954, F 24,25:3
Wright, Frederick E, 1953, Ag 26,27:1
Wright, Frederick F Jr, 1942, Ja 15,19:4
Wright, Frederick J, 1958, Ag 27,29:2
Wright, Frederick L, 1956, Ja 20,14:3
Wright, Frederick Mrs, 1956, O 12,29:1
Wright, Frederick W, 1940, Ja 7,48:5
Wright, G M, 1885, Ja 9,5:6
Wright, G Otis, 1949, Mr 26,17:5
Wright, G Wilfred, 1967, Ag 3,33:4
Wright, George, 1911, O 20,13:4; 1937, Ag 22,II,6:6; 1942, Ja 8,21:3; 1949, F 25,23:3; 1968, Mr 25,41:4
Wright, George B, 1958, Ag 3,81:2
Wright, George B Gen, 1903, S 2,7:6
Wright, George B Sr, 1947, Je 17,25:4
Wright, George Brig-Gen, 1865, S 7,4:5
Wright, George C, 1944, Ag 7,15:6
Wright, George Capt, 1872, My 20,2:1
Wright, George D, 1941, N 23,53:2; 1954, O 13,31:4
Wright, George E, 1940, D 31,15:1; 1946, F 7,23:3; 1965, Jl 16,27:2
Wright, George F, 1967, Ap 21,39:4
Wright, George F Mrs, 1950, Ja 4,35:1
Wright, George Frederick Prof, 1921, Ap 21,13:5
Wright, George H, 1951, Mr 15,29:3
Wright, George H Mrs, 1957, Ag 27,29:4
Wright, George L, 1909, S 25,11:4; 1951, Jl 5,34:3
Wright, George M, 1917, S 18,9:6
Wright, George S, 1945, O 6,13:5
Wright, George T, 1945, Ja 27,11:5; 1964, Ag 22,21:5
Wright, George W, 1940, Mr 27,21:4
Wright, George W Mrs, 1955, F 27,86:5
Wright, Gifford K, 1949, Ag 14,69:2
Wright, Glen, 1941, Ag 21,19:3
Wright, Graham A, 1948, Je 6,72:6
Wright, Grant, 1952, D 17,33:2
Wright, Granville, 1903, Jl 23,7:6
Wright, Grosvenor, 1944, S 21,19:4
Wright, Grove M Mrs, 1949, Ja 7,21:1
Wright, Guire S, 1952, F 13,29:3
Wright, H Amelia Dr, 1924, O 11,15:5
Wright, H B, 1881, S 3,5:5
Wright, H G, 1880, F 23,4:7
Wright, H H Gen, 1905, Ap 29,11:6
Wright, Haidee, 1943, Ja 30,15:6
Wright, Hal F, 1951, Ag 28,23:5
Wright, Hamilton M, 1954, Ap 11,86:1
Wright, Hamilton Mrs, 1952, F 14,27:3
Wright, Harold B, 1944, My 25,21:1
Wright, Harold B Sr, 1953, Ja 7,31:2
Wright, Harold W, 1939, My 11,25:5
Wright, Harriet S, 1960, Je 10,31:2
Wright, Harrison, 1966, My 26,47:3
Wright, Harrison B, 1941, F 2,45:2
Wright, Harrison B Mrs, 1958, Jl 10,27:5
Wright, Harry, 1953, Ja 8,27:1; 1954, Ag 17,21:3
Wright, Harry B, 1958, My 23,23:4
Wright, Harry E, 1944, Ja 15,13:4
Wright, Harry F, 1944, Ap 16,42:1
Wright, Harry G, 1940, Ap 18,23:1
Wright, Harter F, 1958, F 20,25:1
Wright, Helen M, 1951, F 28,27:3
Wright, Henry A, 1941, O 30,23:5
Wright, Henry B Dr, 1923, D 28,15:6
Wright, Henry C Mrs, 1954, Ap 8,27:6
Wright, Henry C Prof, 1909, Ap 13,9:5
Wright, Henry J, 1949, My 5,27:4
Wright, Henry L, 1943, F 22,17:4
Wright, Henry P Sr, 1940, D 22,30:7
Wright, Henry Parkes, 1918, Mr 18,13:5
Wright, Herbert, 1940, O 29,25:4; 1959, Jl 27,25:4
Wright, Herbert Carleton, 1923, Ap 27,17:4
Wright, Herbert E, 1943, Mr 25,21:5
Wright, Hinton P Mrs (Marie R Wright), 1914, F 3, 11:6
Wright, Horace, 1939, Mr 29,23:6
Wright, Howard E, 1947, F 19,25:5
Wright, Howard L, 1948, Mr 1,23:4
Wright, Hubert J, 1942, F 22,26:5
Wright, Hugh E, 1940, F 14,21:6
Wright, Hugh Mrs, 1947, S 28,60:7
Wright, Huntley, 1941, Jl 12,13:3
Wright, Irving C, 1953, Je 24,25:3
Wright, Irving Mrs, 1946, O 12,19:6
Wright, Isaac M, 1948, Ja 16,21:4
Wright, Isaac Merritt, 1907, Ja 30,9:6
Wright, J A Ex-Gov, 1867, My 12,1:1
Wright, J Bidmead, 1944, Ja 10,17:3
Wright, J Butler, 1939, D 5,27:5
Wright, J Butler Mrs, 1958, My 16,25:4
Wright, J Capt, 1880, S 21,3:2
Wright, J D, 1879, Ag 22,5:3
Wright, J Dr, 1883, S 26,4:6
Wright, J Ernest, 1958, My 11,86:5
Wright, J Franklin, 1940, S 9,15:4
Wright, J Hood Mrs, 1924, Ag 1,11:5
Wright, J Howard, 1914, N 20,9:5
Wright, J Joseph, 1949, S 8,29:4
Wright, J Marshall, 1905, Ap 4,11:5
Wright, J Marvin, 1947, O 6,21:5
Wright, J Merrill, 1949, Jl 5,24:4
Wright, J S, 1883, Ja 25,5:6
Wright, James, 1943, Ja 5,19:2
Wright, James C, 1955, D 12,31:4
Wright, James E, 1944, My 18,19:3
Wright, James F Sr, 1954, Ap 23,27:3
Wright, James H, 1947, S 29,21:2; 1948, Mr 22,23:3; 1954, S 14,27:2; 1957, D 10,35:4

Wright, James J Mrs, 1952, Je 3,29:5
Wright, James L, 1952, D 8,41:3
Wright, James R, 1937, N 26,21:1
Wright, James W, 1949, O 19,29:1; 1954, Ja 2,11:3
Wright, Jane C Mrs (will), 1939, Jl 22,17:1
Wright, Joe Sr, 1950, O 19,31:5
Wright, John, 1950, Mr 29,29:1
Wright, John D, 1938, Jl 15,17:4; 1946, S 25,27:2; 1952, Ja 20,84:1
Wright, John E, 1924, O 25,15:6
Wright, John F, 1944, Jl 24,15:6
Wright, John G, 1954, N 18,33:5
Wright, John H, 1939, N 13,19:6; 1951, F 17,15:5
Wright, John H Prof, 1908, N 26,9:6
Wright, John J, 1952, Jl 24,27:5
Wright, John M Mrs, 1948, Ag 8,57:1
Wright, John Montgomery, 1925, S 18,23:5
Wright, John P, 1947, Ap 19,15:5
Wright, John Rev Dr, 1919, D 25,13:4
Wright, John S, 1874, Jl 2,4:7; 1958, S 16,27:4; 1965, F 21,77:2
Wright, John Sr, 1964, My 16,25:5
Wright, John Vines, 1908, Je 13,7:5
Wright, John W, 1953, S 30,31:1
Wright, Joseph B Mrs, 1958, Mr 14,25:3
Wright, Joseph Mrs, 1965, F 1,23:3
Wright, Joseph T, 1950, Ja 12,27:4
Wright, Joseph V Mrs, 1956, My 5,19:4
Wright, Josephine L, 1966, Je 1,47:2
Wright, Judson D, 1948, My 14,23:1
Wright, Julia S Mrs, 1940, Ja 21,35:2
Wright, Julian, 1945, Ap 6,15:2
Wright, Julian M (por), 1938, O 7,23:2
Wright, Kate S Mrs, 1937, Ja 2,14:2
Wright, Katherine O, 1958, Jl 4,19:5
Wright, Laura M Dr, 1922, O 31,15:4
Wright, Laura R Mrs, 1939, Je 11,44:7
Wright, Lawrence, 1964, My 17,87:1
Wright, Leonard C, 1967, Mr 11,29:4
Wright, Leonard S, 1944, Je 22,19:6
Wright, LeRoy E, 1964, Ag 15,21:4
Wright, Leslie Mrs, 1951, S 29,17:3
Wright, Lewis C, 1940, S 11,25:4
Wright, Lewis T, 1953, N 6,27:4
Wright, Lillian, 1941, My 20,23:6
Wright, Lloyd D, 1956, Mr 17,19:6
Wright, Lorin, 1939, D 2,17:3
Wright, Louis C, 1953, F 12,28:3
Wright, Louis T, 1952, O 9,31:4
Wright, Lucien B, 1919, D 17,17:2
Wright, Lucy C (will), 1939, Je 7,10:5
Wright, Lucy S (will), 1940, Mr 1,41:1
Wright, Luessa, 1952, D 2,36:4
Wright, Luke E, 1912, Jl 4,7:5
Wright, Luke E Gen, 1922, N 18,15:6
Wright, Lynn G, 1919, Ap 14,13:4
Wright, M A Mrs, 1967, N 10,47:2
Wright, Malcolm M, 1958, Ap 7,21:4
Wright, Malcolm Prof, 1937, Jl 2,21:5
Wright, Marcus Joseph, 1922, D 28,17:5
Wright, Margaret, 1948, Ap 10,13:5
Wright, Margaret I Mrs, 1942, N 7,15:2
Wright, Marmaduke B, 1938, Ja 16,II,8:7
Wright, Marmaduke B 3d, 1955, Ja 17,23:4
Wright, Mary, 1951, Ap 3,27:2
Wright, Mary W N Mrs, 1937, O 9,19:5
Wright, Maurice L Ex-Justice, 1911, O 15,II,15:4
Wright, Melvin B, 1958, O 19,87:1
Wright, Merle St Croix Rev Dr, 1925, Ap 27,17:5
Wright, Milton, 1941, D 30,19:4
Wright, Milton H, 1949, Mr 22,25:3
Wright, Monroe H, 1945, Ag 26,43:1
Wright, Montgomery, 1958, Mr 20,29:2
Wright, Montserrat J, 1937, Ja 17,II,8:4
Wright, Moorhead, 1962, S 5,39:4
Wright, Mortimer W Mrs, 1948, Ja 24,16:2
Wright, Nathaniel Curwin, 1923, My 14,15:5
Wright, Nathaniel V Dr, 1937, Je 20,II,6:5
Wright, Nora G, 1948, Je 10,25:3
Wright, Norris D, 1957, F 16,17:4
Wright, Norris N, 1951, Mr 29,27:5
Wright, Northam L, 1952, F 29,23:3
Wright, Oliver M, 1966, D 14,47:4
Wright, Omar H, 1941, Ag 29,17:5
Wright, Orville, 1948, Ja 31,1:2
Wright, Otis Mrs, 1937, Jl 16,19:5
Wright, Peter C, 1947, My 6,27:6
Wright, Prescott J, 1940, Ja 3,21:5
Wright, Ralph E, 1955, Jl 4,11:4
Wright, Ralph G, 1954, Je 23,25:1
Wright, Ralph G Mrs, 1958, My 29,27:3
Wright, Raymond D B, 1957, Jl 3,23:4
Wright, Rebekah, 1945, Mr 30,15:5
Wright, Reginald, 1949, Jl 28,23:5
Wright, Richard, 1960, N 30,37:1
Wright, Richard C Mrs, 1953, Je 3,31:1
Wright, Richard R, 1947, Jl 3,21:3
Wright, Richard R Jr, 1967, D 14,47:2
Wright, Richard W, 1948, O 28,29:3
Wright, Richardson L, 1961, Ag 7,23:5
Wright, Richardson L Mrs, 1939, My 11,25:4
Wright, Robert, 1938, Mr 2,19:4; 1960, Ap 20,39:5
Wright, Robert A, 1958, Jl 7,27:5; 1964, Je 28,56:7
Wright, Robert A Jr, 1958, Ag 14,29:5
Wright, Robert A Mrs, 1949, D 29,25:2
Wright, Robert C, 1924, D 7,7:2; 1946, O 7,31:4; 1951, F 12,23:3
Wright, Robert F, 1922, Ap 1,15:4
Wright, Robert Jefferson, 1909, Jl 4,7:6
Wright, Robert M, 1955, Je 29,29:3
Wright, Robert P, 1957, N 13,32:3
Wright, Roscoe, 1943, Ag 17,17:6
Wright, Roy, 1949, Mr 4,21:3
Wright, Roy A, 1959, Mr 17,30:5
Wright, Roy V (por), 1948, Jl 10,15:3
Wright, Roy V Mrs, 1962, F 9,29:2
Wright, Royce E, 1938, D 11,60:6
Wright, Russell Mrs, 1952, Ag 17,76:5
Wright, S Dickinson, 1940, S 2,15:5
Wright, S J Mrs, 1913, Ag 21,9:7
Wright, Sallie M S Mrs, 1937, F 10,23:3
Wright, Samuel, 1941, O 1,21:3; 1951, N 3,17:6
Wright, Saunders, 1944, O 17,23:4
Wright, Seaman L, 1953, My 30,15:6
Wright, Solomon, 1952, D 14,91:1
Wright, Sophie B, 1912, Je 11,9:6
Wright, Stafford, 1940, Mr 22,19:3
Wright, Stanley Jr, 1954, S 11,17:6
Wright, Stanley V, 1956, Ja 15,93:1
Wright, Stephen A Mrs, 1960, My 28,21:7
Wright, Stuart M, 1946, Ag 31,15:5
Wright, Stuyvesant B, 1956, Ap 16,28:1
Wright, Sumner B, 1958, Ap 30,33:4
Wright, T M, 1946, Ap 16,25:2
Wright, Theodore, 1924, Ag 18,13:5
Wright, Theodore F Rev, 1907, N 20,9:5
Wright, Thomas, 1947, Je 14,15:2
Wright, Thomas A, 1945, My 26,15:2
Wright, Thomas B, 1950, F 27,19:5
Wright, Thomas C Sr, 1942, O 13,23:5
Wright, Thomas H, 1952, Je 19,27:1; 1961, My 17,38:1
Wright, Thomas J J, 1954, Mr 31,27:2
Wright, Thurston, 1950, N 28,31:3
Wright, V Murray, 1947, My 17,15:2
Wright, Vester R T, 1966, Jl 26,32:1
Wright, W Charles, 1950, Ag 17,28:5
Wright, W DeForest, 1953, Ag 31,17:2
Wright, W H De Courcy, 1951, Ja 25,25:4
Wright, W J Mrs, 1923, Mr 30,17:5
Wright, W P, 1880, Jl 8,5:4
Wright, W S, 1878, Jl 9,2:5
Wright, W W, 1882, Mr 11,2:4
Wright, Walter, 1961, S 19,35:2
Wright, Walter C, 1937, Ja 6,23:4
Wright, Walter H, 1952, Ja 1,25:1
Wright, Walter L, 1946, Ja 18,19:1
Wright, Walter L Jr (por), 1949, My 17,25:1
Wright, Walter Mrs, 1946, Mr 5,25:1
Wright, Walton O, 1937, F 17,22:2
Wright, Warren, 1950, D 29,19:1
Wright, Warren (will), 1951, Ja 9,17:5
Wright, Warren, 1962, Mr 30,33:2
Wright, Washington, 1866, S 12,2:4
Wright, Watkins E, 1967, Jl 26,39:2
Wright, Wendell J, 1948, Ap 22,27:2
Wright, Wendell W, 1961, O 17,39:1
Wright, Wilbur (funl), 1912, Je 2,II,13:4
Wright, Wilbur S, 1937, D 8,25:2
Wright, Wilfred H, 1956, S 25,33:5
Wright, Wilfred L, 1947, N 11,27:6
Wright, Will, 1962, Je 21,31:3
Wright, Willard H (S S Van Dine),(por), 1939, Ap 13,23:1
Wright, Willard H Mrs, 1956, My 23,31:4
Wright, William, 1866, Mr 15,5:4; 1866, N 2,4:6; 1938, F 20,II,9:1; 1941, Jl 8,19:4; 1946, Ap 15,27:1; 1950, D 10,104:3; 1959, My 7,33:5
Wright, William Aldis, 1914, My 21,11:5
Wright, William B Rev, 1924, Ag 4,13:4
Wright, William Bennett, 1919, Jl 16,13:2
Wright, William C, 1938, My 6,21:5; 1951, S 17,21:6
Wright, William E, 1942, S 24,27:5
Wright, William F, 1942, Ja 21,18:2
Wright, William G, 1956, F 1,31:3
Wright, William H, 1937, Ag 17,19:5; 1938, O 15,17:5; 1940, F 25,38:2; 1944, N 2,19:3; 1951, S 21,23:3; 1954, My 4,29:2; 1959, My 19,33:2
Wright, William H Mrs, 1956, Ag 21,17:5
Wright, William J, 1915, Ap 22,13:4; 1938, F 1,21:4; 1940, Ja 8,15:4; 1945, S 10,19:5; 1954, F 17,31:1
Wright, William J Mrs, 1903, S 4,7:7
Wright, William K, 1956, Mr 30,19:5
Wright, William L D, 1938, D 22,22:1
Wright, William M (por), 1943, Ag 18,19:1
Wright, William M Mrs, 1954, Ag 8,85:2
Wright, William Prof, 1937, O 22,19:5
Wright, William R, 1951, Ap 30,21:4
Wright, William T, 1937, F 6,17:4
Wright, William W, 1944, O 29,44:2
Wright, Wilmer C, 1951, N 17,17:4
Wright, Witney, 1948, F 18,28:2
Wright, Wynn, 1965, Mr 24,43:3
Wright, Zillian C Mrs, 1954, Jl 4,1:1
Wrightington, Dana C, 1955, O 14,36:7
Wrightington, Edgar N, 1945, N 2,20:2
Wrightman, R C, 1876, F 3,1:2
Wrightsman, Charles J, 1959, Je 1,27:4
Wrightson, Francis G 3d, 1955, N 23,23:6
Wrightson, Francis G 3d Mrs, 1940, Ag 10,13:1
Wrightson, G D, 1965, My 1,31:6
Wrightson, Sidney, 1922, Mr 28,17:4
Wrightson, Sydney M, 1958, Ja 2,29:1
Wrightson, William G (por), 1942, Mr 10,19:1
Wrightson, William G Mrs, 1939, Mr 4,15:6
Wrigley, Arthur, 1942, N 5,25:4
Wrigley, Arthur B, 1966, O 7,43:2
Wrigley, Edward, 1948, Mr 5,21:3
Wrigley, Richard D, 1944, Mr 3,15:4
Wrigley, W Jr, 1932, Ja 27,21:1
Wrigley, William Jr Mrs, 1958, D 17,2:6
Wrigley, William Mrs (est appr), 1959, S 30,29:3
Wrigley, William 3d, 1939, S 15,23:3
Wrihgt, Henry B Mrs, 1949, Ja 22,13:5
Wrihgt, Howard E, 1953, N 8,88:5
Wrinn, William J, 1944, Ag 5,11:7
Wrisley, Frank Col, 1884, Mr 13,4:7
Wriston, Henry L, 1955, Ag 2,23:4
Wriston, Henry L Mrs, 1944, D 26,19:4
Wriston, Henry M Mrs, 1946, My 13,21:3
Wriston, Walter B Mrs, 1966, Je 19,85:2
Writer, James H, 1957, D 20,27:4
Wrong, George M, 1948, Je 30,26:2
Wrong, Humphrey H, 1954, Ja 25,19:1
Wrong, Louisa, 1952, D 24,17:3
Wrong, Margaret, 1948, Ap 17,15:6
Wroth, James S, 1964, Ag 13,29:5
Wrothe, Edward Lee, 1922, Ag 7,13:5
Wrottesley, Frederic J, 1948, N 16,29:4
Wrtalik, Harry J, 1951, Ag 9,21:4
Wrubel, Arthur M, 1964, Ja 9,31:4
Wrubel, Isaac Mrs, 1952, Ap 6,88:4
Wrubel, Marshal H Dr, 1968, O 28,47:4
Wrubel, Robert H, 1964, Ag 31,25:3
Wrubel, Robert H Mrs, 1944, Je 22,19:6
Wry, Patricia A, 1945, Ag 31,19:1
Wszelaki, Jan, 1965, Jl 3,19:1
Wu, C C, 1934, Ja 3,19:1
Wu, Chuck Sun, 1954, Ja 28,17:5
Wu, Hsien, 1959, Ag 10,27:6
Wu, John C H Mrs, 1959, D 1,39:5
Wu, P C, 1953, O 20,29:3
Wu Chih-hui, 1953, O 31,17:2
Wu Lien-teh, 1960, Ja 22,27:1
Wu Pei-fu, Marshal, 1939, D 5,25:2
Wu Ting-Fang, 1922, Je 24,13:4
Wu Yu-chang, 1966, D 16,47:2
Wubbels, Heinrich G, 1944, O 10,23:2
Wucher, T, 1933, My 4,17:6
Wucherer, Christian G, 1940, O 22,23:2
Wuchter, M Leroy, 1949, F 28,19:5
Wuebbens, Everett P, 1949, Ja 29,13:4
Wuellner, Ludwig, 1938, Mr 23,23:1
Wuensch, Charles E (por), 1943, Ja 24,42:2
Wuensch, Charles E, 1949, Ag 29,17:4
Wuensch, John, 1925, Mr 21,13:3
Wuensch, Robert H, 1964, O 6,43:7
Wuenschel, Edward A, 1964, Ja 7,33:4
Wuenschel, Frank X, 1949, F 23,27:4
Wuenz, Alfred, 1921, Ag 1,11:3
Wuerdeman, Emil K, 1950, D 23,15:3
Wuersch, Daniel G, 1939, N 19,39:1
Wuerth, Louis A, 1950, My 10,27:3
Wuerttemberg, Albrecht von Duke, 1939, O 30,17:6
Wuest, Carl Dr, 1908, Ap 7,9:4
Wuest, Charles Sr, 1947, D 10,31:2
Wuest, Richard W, 1957, Ja 27,84:2
Wuest, William Peter, 1917, Mr 29,13:5
Wuestefeld, George B, 1938, N 11,25:6
Wuestehube, Wal, 1965, My 7,41:3
Wuestenhoefer, Carl Mrs, 1949, Ja 27,24:3
Wuestenhoefer, Frances M Mrs, 1943, D 7,27:2
Wuestner, Clarence J Mrs, 1952, Jl 16,25:5
Wugen, William (funl, D 14,46:7), 1960, D 11,88:7
Wulbern, Edward B, 1963, Je 26,39:5
Wulbern, Edward N, 1952, Ap 13,77:1
Wulf, Henry A, 1948, Ap 14,27:1
Wulff, Carl, 1954, Je 27,69:1
Wulff, Herbert, 1967, Ap 11,47:1
Wulff, John F, 1938, Jl 24,28:7
Wulff, Richard J, 1940, Mr 19,25:5
Wulff, Richard Mrs, 1948, Ja 23,23:4
Wulff, Timothy M, 1960, S 26,33:3
Wulfing, Frederick W, 1960, Jl 15,23:2
Wulfsohn, Louis, 1959, N 8,88:3
Wullner, Walter U, 1956, Mr 26,29:2
Wullschleger, Gerret V Mrs, 1946, D 23,23:4
Wulsin, Frederick R, 1946, Je 10,21:4
Wulsin, Lucien, 1964, Ja 15,31:3
Wulsin, Lucien Mrs, 1948, Ap 19,23:3
Wund, William F, 1956, My 25,23:3
Wunder, Berthold H, 1940, O 12,17:3
Wunder, Charles, 1944, S 23,13:6
Wunder, Clarence E, 1940, O 20,49:1
Wunder, Clarence E Mrs, 1961, Ag 6,85:2
Wunder, Suzanne A, 1946, Jl 19,19:4
Wunderle, Horace Mrs, 1954, S 10,23:1
Wunderle, Phil J Sr, 1955, Je 10,25:1
Wunderley, Charles A, 1937, Ja 27,3:4
Wunderlich, Ernest H, 1948, Ap 12,21:4

Wunderlich, Eva C, 1968, Ja 10,43:1
Wunderlich, Frank W, 1948, Je 29,23:4
Wunderlich, Frederick W Dr, 1921, My 17,17:5
Wunderlich, Frieda, 1965, D 31,21:4
Wunderlich, Fritz, 1966, S 18,84:6
Wunderlich, Hermann, 1951, S 29,17:6
Wunderlich, Jake, 1906, Mr 11,9:5
Wundt, Wilhelm Prof, 1920, S 2,9:2
Wunner, John K, 1968, Ja 16,39:3
Wunsch, Francis X, 1956, S 29,19:3
Wunsch, Harold C, 1952, Je 28,19:4
Wunsch, William J, 1945, My 16,19:3
Wunsche, Hugo O, 1956, Mr 1,33:4
Wupperman, A Edward Mrs, 1946, Je 7,19:5
Wupperman, George, 1915, Je 13,15:5
Wuppermann, Adolph E (will, Ag 13,15:5), 1937, Ag 1,II,7:4
Wuppermann, J W Mrs, 1936, S 18,23:1
Wurdeman, Walter, 1949, S 19,23:3
Wurdemann, Audrey (Mrs J Auslander), 1960, My 20,31:3
Wurdemann, Harry V, 1938, F 1,21:1
Wurfel, Lester E Sr, 1937, Ag 18,19:1
Wurlitzer, Howard E Mrs, 1963, D 25,33:5
Wurlitzer, Rembert R, 1963, O 22,37:1
Wurlitzer, Rudolph, 1914, Ja 17,9:5
Wurlitzer, Rudolph H, 1948, My 28,23:5
Wurlitzer, Rudolph Mrs, 1957, S 18,33:2
Wurm, Carl, 1938, N 2,23:2
Wurm, Theopil, 1953, Ja 29,28:3
Wurman, Harry P, 1960, O 1,19:5
Wurmbrand, Michael, 1952, Mr 20,29:3
Wurmfeld, Armin, 1956, F 3,23:2
Wurst, Perry E, 1943, S 6,17:5
Wurster, Annie D Mrs, 1937, Je 20,II,7:1
Wurster, Catherine B Mrs, 1964, N 24,40:1
Wurster, Eugene A, 1966, Ja 17,47:2
Wurster, Frederick W, 1917, Je 26,13:6; 1947, Mr 20, 28:2
Wurster, John J, 1948, Ap 1,25:5
Wurster, Joseph A Sr, 1941, Ja 17,17:1
Wurster, Oscar H, 1946, Ja 27,42:5
Wurtbach, Carl, 1947, Ag 31,36:7
Wurtele, Allan R, 1947, D 5,26:2
Wurtele, Arthur H, 1946, Ag 2,19:3
Wurtele, Lester, 1961, D 7,43:2
Wurtemburg, King of, 1864, Jl 7,4:5
Wurtenberg, William C, 1957, Mr 28,31:2
Wurth, Walter A Mrs, 1959, S 6,73:1
Wurthman, Charles M, 1938, N 20,39:2
Wurthman, John H Mrs, 1952, D 3,33:4
Wurthmann, John H, 1949, D 22,23:3
Wurtmann, Ben E, 1968, F 3,29:4
Wurts, Charles S Mrs, 1953, O 25,89:2
Wurts, John H, 1966, Ja 24,35:2
Wurts, John S, 1958, D 30,35:4
Wurts, Lionel, 1957, O 2,33:2
Wurts, Lionel Mrs, 1961, F 20,27:5
Wurts, Norman, 1944, F 24,15:4
Wurts, Pierre J, 1953, O 29,31:5
Wurts, Robert K, 1944, Jl 31,13:4
Wurts, William H, 1955, O 14,27:2
Wurts, William H Mrs, 1959, D 29,25:3
Wurts, William L R, 1948, Ap 11,72:6
Wurtz, Fred C, 1951, Ja 9,30:5
Wurtz, Henry Dr, 1910, N 11,9:5
Wurtz, John C, 1948, Ja 17,17:3
Wurtzburg, Charles E, 1952, My 1,29:4
Wurtzel, George L, 1945, Je 29,15:3
Wurtzel, Harry, 1945, Ja 17,21:5
Wurtzel, Sol M, 1958, Ap 10,29:4
Wurz, John, 1965, S 4,21:5
Wurzbach, Frederick A, 1950, S 30,17:5
Wurzbach, James A, 1944, Ag 28,11:5
Wurzbach-Tannenberg, Wolfgang, 1957, F 26,29:2
Wurzberg, Francis L, 1954, Ap 25,86:6
Wurzburg, Francis L Mrs, 1964, Ap 30,35:4
Wurzburger, G Walter, 1965, F 14,88:3
Wurzburger, Hugo, 1952, Ag 26,25:3
Wurzburger, Julius, 1876, S 18,8:4; 1950, S 19,29:6
Wurzburger, Sigfried A Mrs, 1967, Mr 21,43:1
Wurzel, Maurice L, 1949, My 15,90:7
Wurzer, Anton W, 1958, Je 13,23:4
Wurzer, Joseph, 1943, Jl 29,19:5
Wurzweiler, Gustav (will filed, Ap 7,37:5), 1954, Mr 4,25:2
Wustl, Frederick J, 1941, O 13,17:6
Wustner, George, 1952, N 1,21:6
Wyant, Andrew R E, 1964, Je 18,35:3
Wyant, Corbin W, 1961, F 24,21:6
Wyant, Ira A, 1968, Jl 3,35:1
Wyant, Paul B, 1958, Je 15,76:7
Wyant, William, 1949, Ag 20,11:4
Wyatt, Albert H Rev Dr, 1909, Ap 30,9:5
Wyatt, Alice B, 1955, Ja 26,25:2
Wyatt, Ben Harrison Commodore, 1968, S 16,47:3
Wyatt, Ernest Mayo, 1913, Ag 14,9:2
Wyatt, Eugene C, 1958, F 14,24:1
Wyatt, Francis Dr, 1916, F 29,11:4
Wyatt, George C Jr, 1966, Jl 2,23:6
Wyatt, George C Jr Mrs, 1960, Ja 23,21:3
Wyatt, Harrison F, 1954, Je 17,29:5
Wyatt, Henry J, 1958, F 11,31:3
Wyatt, James R, 1951, D 5,35:4
Wyatt, Jay, 1959, Je 6,21:4
Wyatt, Kenneth S, 1967, Ja 15,84:6
Wyatt, Lee B, 1960, F 7,84:1
Wyatt, Louis J, 1955, My 1,88:2
Wyatt, M D Sir, 1877, My 23,5:6
Wyatt, Myles Sir, 1968, Ap 16,47:4
Wyatt, Richard H, 1947, My 11,60:6
Wyatt, Roscoe B, 1948, Ap 5,21:3
Wyatt, W E, 1932, Ap 19,21:5
Wyatt, William E, 1937, D 10,26:4
Wyatt, William W, 1939, O 24,23:4
Wyatt-Brown, Hunter, 1952, Ap 25,23:2
Wyatt-Hannath, William Henry, 1907, F 3,7:6
Wybrants, Wade M, 1962, O 15,29:3
Wyburn, John H Mrs, 1958, Jl 1,31:2
Wyche, Charles C, 1966, S 18,84:1
Wyche, Cyril J, 1945, Ja 25,19:2
Wycherly, Margaret, 1956, Je 7,31:5
Wyckoff, Albert C, 1953, Ja 13,27:5; 1960, Ja 11,45:4
Wyckoff, Albert Dr, 1903, Ap 15,9:6
Wyckoff, Alice R, 1948, N 21,88:4
Wyckoff, Anna A, 1958, O 22,35:5
Wyckoff, Cecelia S Mrs, 1966, O 31,35:3
Wyckoff, Charles R Mrs, 1943, D 25,13:3
Wyckoff, Charlotte, 1966, Jl 23,32:1
Wyckoff, Clarence C, 1958, Ja 7,47:4
Wyckoff, Clinton R, 1947, Ag 18,17:6
Wyckoff, David T, 1948, S 29,29:2
Wyckoff, De Witte, 1957, Ag 2,19:6
Wyckoff, Edward, 1960, My 22,86:6
Wyckoff, Elizabeth D Mrs, 1942, O 8,27:5
Wyckoff, Frederick A (por), 1943, My 24,15:3
Wyckoff, Frederick A Mrs, 1952, Mr 31,19:1
Wyckoff, Garrett P, 1951, N 1,29:4
Wyckoff, George H, 1948, S 15,31:2
Wyckoff, Harvey, 1939, N 11,15:7
Wyckoff, Henry Lott Mrs, 1915, O 16,11:5
Wyckoff, J Edwards, 1951, Jl 8,61:1
Wyckoff, Jacob, 1963, Jl 4,17:1
Wyckoff, Jacob V D, 1916, My 23,11:5
Wyckoff, John B, 1959, Mr 9,29:5
Wyckoff, John Dr (por), 1937, Je 1,1:4
Wyckoff, John H Mrs, 1956, S 19,37:3
Wyckoff, John Henry Dr, 1915, My 1,13:7
Wyckoff, John L, 1911, My 14,13:4
Wyckoff, Maxwell, 1959, Jl 8,29:3
Wyckoff, Nathaniel C, 1959, D 7,31:4
Wyckoff, P Finley, 1939, O 9,19:6
Wyckoff, Peter, 1910, F 10,7:5
Wyckoff, Peter Mrs, 1940, Ja 10,21:1
Wyckoff, Rachel S Mrs, 1946, N 27,25:4
Wyckoff, Ralph S, 1939, D 26,19:2
Wyckoff, Raymond L, 1939, My 26,23:3
Wyckoff, Richard Morris Dr, 1911, N 13,9:5
Wyckoff, Samuel S, 1872, Ap 4,8:4
Wyckoff, Stephen N, 1959, S 2,29:5
Wyckoff, W H Rev, 1877, N 3,8:6
Wyckoff, William F Mrs, 1916, Ja 22,9:3
Wyckoff, William Le R, 1966, Ja 31,39:2
Wyckoff, William S, 1909, Ap 25,11:5
Wyckoff, William T Dr, 1937, Ag 1,II,7:2
Wyckoff, William W W (por), 1947, D 18,29:4
Wyckoff, Wilson H, 1951, Ag 20,19:6
Wyer, Arthur C, 1950, F 16,24:2
Wyer, James I, 1955, N 4,30:1
Wyers, Renier, 1950, F 21,26:2
Wyeth, George A, 1964, F 21,27:1
Wyeth, George A Mrs, 1958, N 6,37:2
Wyeth, John, 1907, Ap 1,9:7
Wyeth, John A Dr (funl, My 31,15:2), 1922, My 29, 11:4
Wyeth, Marlborough Churchill Col, 1924, My 16,9:3
Wyeth, Nathan C, 1963, S 3,33:2
Wyfold, Lord, 1937, Je 5,17:6
Wygant, George P, 1940, N 29,21:6
Wygant, Henry Col, 1918, Ag 7,9:8
Wygant, John C Sr, 1948, My 19,27:3
Wygant, Leo, 1945, D 10,21:4
Wygant, S T, 1883, Mr 27,5:4
Wygant, Samuel, 1938, My 15,II,6:2
Wygod, Max N, 1954, F 19,27:1
Wyker, Arthur W, 1959, Je 23,33:5
Wykes, Adeline G, 1955, Ja 22,11:5
Wyldbore-Smith, Edmund, 1938, O 19,23:3
Wylde, Edward, 1920, Je 21,13:5
Wylde, John, 1941, D 29,15:4
Wyle, Armand, 1959, Je 2,35:5
Wyle, Milton, 1954, Je 30,27:5
Wyle, Milton Mrs, 1946, F 13,23:3
Wylegala, Victor B, 1959, Ag 26,29:1
Wyler, Elmer R, 1962, S 25,37:1
Wyler, Julius, 1959, Ja 15,33:4
Wyler, Sigmund (por), 1945, My 21,19:2
Wyler, Sigmund Mrs, 1944, Jl 6,15:4
Wyler, Sue, 1951, Ag 25,17:8
Wyles, Tom R, 1959, Je 18,31:3
Wyles, William, 1946, Ja 25,24:3
Wylie, Alfred S Mrs, 1939, N 30,21:3
Wylie, Arthur J, 1937, Ap 22,23:5
Wylie, Austin, 1947, D 7,76:2
Wylie, Calvin Mrs, 1951, Ja 3,27:1
Wylie, D G, 1930, Ag 27,21:1
Wylie, Daniel D Gen, 1923, Ja 27,13:4
Wylie, Daniel R, 1950, My 30,17:1
Wylie, Daniel R Mrs, 1959, Jl 4,15:6
Wylie, David R, 1958, D 17,2:6
Wylie, David R Mrs, 1945, Je 22,15:2
Wylie, Dwight, 1941, Ja 3,19:2
Wylie, Dwight W (por), 1940, D 31,15:1
Wylie, Dwight W Mrs, 1958, Ag 3,81:1
Wylie, Edmond M, 1955, D 13,39:5
Wylie, Edmund M Mrs, 1953, My 21,31:4
Wylie, Edward A G, 1938, Jl 30,13:5
Wylie, Eugene C, 1943, S 18,17:1
Wylie, Francis J, 1952, O 30,31:1
Wylie, George A, 1951, O 28,84:5
Wylie, Herbert C, 1956, Ja 5,34:1
Wylie, Howard M, 1944, D 28,19:4
Wylie, Ida A R (will, N 21,47:2), 1959, N 5,35:1
Wylie, J Caldwell, 1958, Ja 16,29:4
Wylie, J Herman, 1940, My 11,19:6
Wylie, James A, 1938, F 20,II,8:7
Wylie, John, 1939, Je 1,25:5
Wylie, L J, 1942, Jl 14,19:4
Wylie, Matthew A, 1952, Ap 9,31:2
Wylie, Newton, 1938, F 16,21:6
Wylie, R T Rev, 1903, Ap 28,9:6
Wylie, Richard G, 1953, N 23,27:4
Wylie, Robert B, 1959, Je 10,37:1
Wylie, Robert H, 1964, Ja 4,23:5
Wylie, Sims G, 1925, Mr 24,23:2
Wylie, Thomas G, 1954, Jl 7,31:5
Wylie, Thomas W, 1940, Mr 24,30:7
Wylie, W G Judge, 1903, S 27,7:7
Wylie, Walker Gill Dr, 1923, Mr 14,19:5
Wylie, Willard O, 1944, D 1,23:4
Wylie, William A, 1938, My 20,19:4
Wylie, William D, 1963, D 18,41:3
Wylie, William N, 1960, My 13,31:3
Wyllie, Alfred S, 1944, Jl 13,17:5; 1958, O 20,29:2
Wyllie, John Cook, 1968, Ap 19,47:1
Wyllie, Thomas D, 1955, Jl 31,69:3
Wylly, Martin Dasher, 1916, F 2,11:4
Wylly, Thomas S, 1938, F 4,21:5
Wylucki, Konstanty, 1940, Ag 8,19:5
Wyman, A Lee, 1953, D 17,37:4
Wyman, Albert R, 1939, D 26,19:2
Wyman, Albert U, 1915, Mr 5,9:4
Wyman, Alfred M, 1956, F 16,29:1
Wyman, Arthur H, 1948, O 7,29:4
Wyman, B, 1926, Je 22,23:3
Wyman, Bates, 1946, Ap 3,25:2
Wyman, Bates Mrs, 1956, Ag 1,23:5
Wyman, Belorus, 1940, S 13,23:5
Wyman, Benjamin F, 1954, Je 19,15:6
Wyman, C D, 1907, N 12,9:7
Wyman, Carl O Mrs, 1965, D 31,21:1
Wyman, Charles Francis, 1906, D 1,9:6
Wyman, Charles S Mrs, 1947, Mr 14,23:2
Wyman, Clifton E, 1952, My 30,15:1
Wyman, D W (funl), 1877, F 23,8:4
Wyman, Dwight M, 1948, Jl 20,23:4
Wyman, Elizabeth H, 1953, Ag 31,17:3
Wyman, Everett L, 1952, Jl 20,53:2
Wyman, Frederick, 1953, Ja 1,23:4
Wyman, George F Mrs, 1960, Je 6,29:3
Wyman, Hans, 1960, Je 11,21:3
Wyman, Hans Mrs, 1951, S 5,31:4
Wyman, Harold L Mrs, 1953, Ap 15,31:5
Wyman, Herbert C, 1966, N 23,39:3
Wyman, Hollis J Jr, 1968, N 1,47:2
Wyman, Hugh E, 1951, S 2,48:6
Wyman, J Prof, 1881, Ag 2,5:3
Wyman, Jeffries Dr, 1874, S 10,3:6
Wyman, Julia E Mrs, 1950, My 7,108:4
Wyman, L B, 1879, Jl 29,5:2
Wyman, L B Mrs, 1929, Ja 11,23:4
Wyman, Lemuel A, 1957, S 9,25:4
Wyman, Levi P, 1950, Ap 18,31:5
Wyman, Louis E, 1957, My 1,37:3
Wyman, Morrill Dr, 1903, Ja 31,9:6
Wyman, Phelps, 1947, N 17,21:2
Wyman, Phillips, 1955, My 29,44:1
Wyman, R H, 1882, D 3,2:4
Wyman, Walter, 1911, N 21,9:2
Wyman, Walter F, 1940, N 22,23:4
Wyman, Walter S, 1942, N 16,20:2
Wyman, William, 1903, N 27,1:4; 1963, S 13,30:1
Wyman, William B, 1940, Ja 7,48:7
Wyman, William G, 1923, Ag 21,17:3
Wymental, Wilhlem von Baron, 1937, N 11,25:2
Wyn, Aaron, 1967, N 5,86:2
Wynant, Wilbur, 1939, My 9,23:4
Wynd, William, 1941, F 15,15:2
Wyndam, Charles Lady, 1916, Ja 13,11:3
Wyndam, Hugh Sir, 1916, F 12,11:5
Wyndham, Charles, 1919, Ja 13,11:3
Wyndham, George, 1913, Je 10,11:4
Wyndham, Howard, 1947, Mr 17,23:6
Wyndham, Lady, 1931, Ap 7,27:5
Wyndham, Percy, 1943, O 7,23:3
Wynegar, Howard L, 1957, Ap 14,87:1
Wynell, Henry, 1938, Ap 19,21:5
Wyner, Edward N, 1961, D 6,48:1
Wyner, George, 1943, Ja 3,42:5

Wyner, George Mrs, 1949, Ap 19,25:2
Wyner, I A Mrs, 1962, Ap 21,20:5
Wyner, Maurice E, 1962, My 13,88:7
Wynhoven, Peter M H, 1944, S 15,19:1
Wynkook, David W Mrs, 1904, Mr 25,9:2
Wynkook, Thomas P Mrs, 1949, D 17,17:2
Wynkoop, Asa, 1942, O 24,15:5
Wynkoop, Bion, 1950, O 24,29:1
Wynkoop, Brooke L, 1962, Ja 2,29:2
Wynkoop, C Barton, 1943, F 22,17:3
Wynkoop, Francis J Mrs, 1951, Jl 1,51:2
Wynkoop, Francis Silvester, 1903, O 16,7:6
Wynkoop, Frank M, 1954, Ap 10,15:2
Wynkoop, Frank Mrs (Helen Truman), 1924, My 3, 15:4
Wynkoop, George C Jr, 1943, S 30,21:5
Wynkoop, Gerardus Hilles Dr, 1909, My 17,9:5
Wynkoop, Gerardus M, 1945, N 21,21:4
Wynkoop, John, 1922, D 14,21:2
Wynkoop, Matilda, 1924, D 15,17:1
Wynkoop, Matilda Z Mrs, 1940, Ap 28,37:2
Wynkoop, Rossman H, 1958, Ap 26,19:3
Wynn, Chestien, 1955, Je 7,33:4
Wynn, Daniel A, 1949, My 28,15:2
Wynn, Ed (I E Leopold),(funl plans, Je 21,43:2), 1966, Je 20,1:2
Wynn, Edward, 1943, My 11,21:3
Wynn, Frank D Mrs, 1952, S 17,31:3
Wynn, Harold E, 1956, Ag 13,19:4
Wynn, Harry, 1939, S 11,19:5
Wynn, Hilda Mrs, 1923, F 1,11:4
Wynn, J Maurice, 1947, S 13,11:3
Wynn, James H, 1945, My 20,32:2
Wynn, Michael J, 1955, Jl 15,21:2
Wynn, Thomas G (funl), 1914, Ap 3,11:5
Wynn, Thomas J (Lord Newborough), 1957, Ap 29, 25:1
Wynn, William Charles (Lord Newborough), 1916, Jl 20,11:5
Wynn, William T, 1959, F 22,88:4
Wynn-Wynne, Gerald A, 1960, Je 29,33:6
Wynne, Arthur, 1945, Ja 16,19:6
Wynne, Carl M, 1950, F 3,23:3
Wynne, Charles E, 1956, N 12,29:6
Wynne, Charles J, 1923, Mr 1,15:2
Wynne, Edward A, 1953, Mr 11,29:4
Wynne, Edwin Alvin, 1968, Je 15,35:4
Wynne, Henry A, 1943, Ag 22,36:7
Wynne, J Edward, 1951, Jl 29,69:1
Wynne, John J, 1948, D 2,29:6
Wynne, John P, 1918, S 25,13:4
Wynne, John S, 1946, Jl 20,13:1
Wynne, Margaret Mrs, 1948, F 16,22:3
Wynne, Michael E, 1960, F 10,38:1
Wynne, Michael M, 1950, N 25,13:4
Wynne, Patrick H, 1942, N 21,13:3
Wynne, Peter, 1963, Ap 14,92:5
Wynne, Prentiss D, 1940, S 5,23:4
Wynne, Robert F, 1912, Mr 25,11:4
Wynne, Robert J Mrs, 1915, O 15,11:4
Wynne, Robert John, 1922, Mr 12,30:3
Wynne, Samuel O, 1945, N 6,19:3
Wynne, Shirley W (por), 1942, Ap 20,21:3
Wynne, Thomas W, 1962, Mr 17,25:1
Wynne-Jones, G V, 1957, S 7,19:5
Wynne-Jones, John, 1938, F 19,15:4
Wynne-Roberts, Robert I, 1953, Ag 7,19:2
Wynns, Charles M, 1945, Jl 11,11:4
Wynter, Henry D (por), 1945, F 8,19:2
Wynyard, Diana (cor, My 15,36:8), 1964, My 14, 35:1
Wyon, Albert Sir, 1937, D 3,23:6
Wyper, James, 1945, Je 26,19:4
Wyre, Frank, 1953, Je 10,29:1
Wyrtzen, Harry M Mrs, 1951, Ja 15,17:3
Wyse, Lucien Bonaparte, 1909, Je 16,7:5
Wysocke, Stanley Sr, 1946, O 10,27:4
Wysong, Charles N, 1954, Ja 29,19:5
Wysong, D Preston Mrs, 1948, Ja 16,21:2
Wysong, Donald D Mrs, 1940, Ja 14,42:4
Wysong, Harlan, 1951, Ag 9,21:6
Wysong, John J, 1910, D 22,13:4
Wysong, John J Mrs, 1925, Mr 31,19:4
Wysor, Rufus J, 1967, Je 12,45:2
Wyss, Clement Jr Mrs, 1945, Ap 17,23:4
Wyszatycki, Leon, 1967, Ja 16,41:2
Wyten, John J, 1952, D 19,19:4
Wythes, William H, 1951, Ag 24,15:4
Wytwytsky, Stephen, 1965, O 20,47:4
Wyville, George A, 1949, Mr 10,27:4

X

Xander, E Clyde, 1952, Ja 3,27:4
Xanrof, Leon, 1953, My 18,21:5
Xanthaky, George, 1956, D 27,25:2
Xavier, Frank E, 1946, O 27,63:4; 1954, F 4,25:4
Xavier, Henry, 1901, Je 20,7:6
Xceron, Jean, 1967, Mr 30,45:2
Xenia, Archduchess of Habsburg, 1968, S 27,47:3
Xenia Alexandrovna, Grand Duchess of Russia (funl, Ap 24,88:4), 1960, Ap 21,31:2
Xenides, John P, 1945, Je 8,19:3
Xenopoulo, Gregoire, 1951, Ja 16,29:4
Xydias, Anthony J, 1952, O 29,29:4
Xylander, Oskar R von, 1940, My 23,23:4

Y

Yablochkina, Aleksandra, 1964, Mr 22,77:2
Yablon, Joseph, 1953, Jl 10,19:4
Yacenda, Andrew B, 1939, Mr 23,23:3
Yacenda, Anthony F, 1945, O 27,15:5
Yacenda, Athony F Jr, 1946, F 12,25:3
Yachelson, Max Mrs, 1945, My 30,19:1
Yachnin, Murray H, 1965, D 5,89:2
Yadarola, Mauricio, 1960, Mr 17,33:3
Yadlowsky, Michael, 1952, Jl 11,17:4
Yadoff, Oleg, 1961, Mr 19,88:1
Yadwin, Louis E, 1943, Ag 5,15:2
Yaeger, Christian C, 1949, My 8,76:4
Yaeger, Irving L, 1953, Mr 19,26:5
Yaeger, Irving L Mrs, 1953, Mr 19,26:5
Yaeger, John, 1948, My 13,25:4
Yaeger, Michael, 1949, N 30,27:1
Yaegle, Charles J Mrs (M T Philips), 1962, Je 6,41:5
Yaffa, David, 1947, Ag 14,23:5
Yaffa, David B, 1965, Ag 25,39:2
Yaffe, Louis, 1953, Ap 21,27:5
Yagel, Emile A, 1946, Jl 27,17:5
Yagel, Frank J Mrs, 1947, My 8,25:4
Yagel, Frank X, 1943, Je 6,42:7
Yager, Arthur, 1941, D 25,25:3
Yager, Charles, 1955, F 19,15:4
Yager, Frank, 1948, Jl 24,15:5
Yager, George L, 1939, S 13,25:5
Yager, Louis E Mrs, 1945, S 10,19:3
Yager, William A, 1939, F 12,44:7
Yaghjian, Haig, 1965, Mr 26,35:3
Yagitch, Vatroslav Dr, 1923, Ag 8,15:4
Yaglou, Constantin P, 1960, Je 4,23:3
Yagoda, Herman, 1964, Je 30,33:1
Yaguda, Frank A, 1954, Je 16,31:3
Yaguda, Louis R, 1952, D 15,25:4
Yague, Juan, 1952, O 22,27:4
Yahn, Charles, 1945, N 3,15:5
Yahn, Robert M Mrs, 1951, N 18,90:4
Yahnel, Henry W, 1964, Ap 18,29:5
Yahr, Fred E, 1947, N 15,17:6
Yahr, Harry, 1963, Jl 21,65:1
Yahuda, Abraham S E, 1951, Ag 14,23:3
Yajima, Kajiko, 1925, Je 16,21:3
Yakoob Beg, Ruler of Turkistan, 1877, Jl 17,4:7
Yakovlev, Eugene, 1951, Mr 5,21:4
Yakushkin, Ivan, 1960, Jl 21,27:2
Yalchin, Husseyin J, 1957, O 19,21:5
Yaldcn, James, 1905, Mr 10,9:7
Yalden, James E G, 1937, F 23,27:5
Yalden, James E G Mrs, 1953, My 3,88:1
Yale, Amerton (see also Je 14), 1876, Je 15,3:4
Yale, Carolyn D Mrs, 1938, Ag 16,19:4
Yale, Charles H, 1920, Mr 24,9:5
Yale, Charles M, 1946, D 9,25:4
Yale, E D, 1883, D 31,5:2
Yale, Edson E, 1942, Jl 19,30:7
Yale, F W, 1957, O 2,33:2
Yale, George A, 1937, Je 12,15:4
Yale, John N, 1954, F 25,31:3
Yale, John R (por),(funl, Je 21,21:6), 1925, Jl 18,13:4
Yale, John R Mrs, 1921, Mr 3,13:6
Yale, L M, 1903, Ag 1,7:6
Yale, Lucius P, 1944, Ap 17,23:2
Yale, Milton, 1966, Ag 14,89:1
Yale, William, 1948, Ap 29,24:2
Yale, William T (por), 1943, N 27,13:3
Yale, William W, 1944, Ja 21,17:2
Yales, Charles L, 1912, S 5,9:5
Yamabe, Hidehiko, 1960, N 22,35:4
Yamada, Koji, 1941, S 19,23:3
Yamada, Kosaku, 1966, Ja 1,17:6
Yamada, Otozo, 1965, Jl 19,27:4
Yamada, Tadao, 1954, F 23,9:5
Yamagata, Anitoma, 1919, F 18,11:5
Yamagata, Aritomo Prince, 1922, F 2,17:3
Yamagata, Paul O, 1941, Jl 3,19:4
Yamaguchi, Yoshitada, 1947, N 6,7:4
Yamakawa, Hitoshi, 1958, Mr 24,27:6
Yamamoto, Eisuke, 1962, Jl 28,19:5
Yamamoto, G Count, 1933, D 9,15:3
Yamamoto, Shinjiro, 1942, Mr 3,23:2
Yamamoto, Tadaoki, 1951, Ap 22,88:1
Yamamuro, Gunpei, 1940, Mr 14,23:5
Yamanashi, Hanzo, 1944, Jl 4,19:2
Yamashita, Taro, 1967, Je 10,33:4
Yamaya, Tanin, 1940, S 11,25:2
Yamaza, E, 1914, My 30,11:4
Yamazaki, Takeshi, 1957, D 28,17:3
Yamin, Muhammad, 1962, O 19,20:8
Yampolsky, Cecil Mrs, 1963, D 22,35:1
Yampolsky, Oscar, 1944, Mr 19,42:1
Yamut, Nuri, 1961, Je 6,37:2
Yan-Lai, Dorothy, 1923, Jl 8,27:5
Yanaihara, Tadao, 1961, D 26,25:3
Yancey, Edward B, 1948, O 25,24:2
Yancey, Goodloe H Capt, 1924, Ag 5,17:4
Yancey, Jimmy, 1951, S 19,31:4
Yancey, Lewis A (por), 1940, Mr 4,15:1
Yancey, Perry, 1939, Jl 11,19:5
Yancey, Philo B, 1942, Ap 23,23:6
Yancey, Sterling R, 1942, Jl 22,19:2
Yancey, William Lowndes, 1863, Ag 5,4:6
Yandell, E, 1934, Je 13,23:5
Yandell, L P, 1927, Ag 12,17:5
Yanes, Francisco G, 1946, Ag 5,21:5
Yanes, Francisco J, 1924, F 26,17:2
Yang, Chih-cheng, 1967, F 7,7:1
Yang, Grace, 1956, Mr 11,88:6
Yang, Nick, 1961, Ap 22,25:2
Yang Li-shan, 1954, D 1,31:3
Yang Yung-ching, 1956, Mr 28,31:3
Yangco, Theodore, 1939, Ap 21,23:5
Yaniaji, Joui, 1941, My 13,23:5
Yankauer, David S, 1964, Ja 15,32:1
Yankauer, Max, 1948, Jl 5,15:4
Yankelevich, Jaime, 1952, F 26,27:5
Yanks, Isaac, 1952, F 21,27:3
Yannantuono, Fred, 1943, Ag 25,19:5
Yannella, Donald J, 1967, My 2,47:3
Yanney, Levy, 1905, Ap 13,8:1
Yano, Shotaro, 1949, Je 23,27:2
Yanoff, William, 1960, Mr 7,29:4
Yanofsky, Frank, 1955, Mr 1,25:2
Yanofsky, Saul, 1939, F 2,19:6
Yanosik, Ethel M, 1950, N 1,35:5
Yanosik, John Mrs, 1951, S 25,29:2
Yanotta, Elpidio A, 1937, Ap 29,21:4
Yanovsky, Yuri, 1954, F 28,92:4
Yanowitz, Herman, 1949, Ap 6,29:5
Yanowski, Felix (est appr), 1959, Jl 10,11:1
Yanson, C Roland, 1939, O 19,23:4
Yant, Charles W, 1955, Mr 2,27:4
Yantis, William L Mrs, 1955, Ap 9,13:3
Yantorny, P, 1936, D 15,25:1
Yanush, Charles Mrs, 1950, Ag 8,29:1
Yaple, George L, 1939, D 17,49:2
Yaple, Jerry, 1938, S 25,38:8
Yarborough, Bertram, 1962, D 4,41:2
Yarborough, C R, 1964, O 25,88:7
Yarborough, Earl of, 1948, F 8,60:6
Yarborough, Minnie C, 1941, Mr 5,21:6
Yarcheski, Michael A, 1964, N 27,35:1
Yard, Elisabeth, 1952, O 30,31:3
Yard, George Holt, 1915, Mr 22,9:5
Yard, George W, 1949, O 12,29:2
Yard, Harry, 1943, D 6,15:3
Yard, Hobart, 1953, S 13,84:5
Yard, James M, 1950, Ag 4,21:1
Yard, Joseph A, 1939, N 28,25:2
Yard, Joseph W, 1941, O 28,23:4
Yard, Nicholas, 1958, F 3,23:5
Yard, Nicholas Mrs, 1963, My 17,33:3
Yard, Raymond C, 1964, Je 2,37:4
Yard, Robert B Rev Dr, 1875, Jl 18,7:6
Yard, Robert S, 1945, My 19,19:4
Yard, Wilson R, 1944, Je 4,42:3
Yard, Wilson R Mrs, 1953, Mr 5,27:2
Yarde-Buller, Lady, 1904, N 16,1:3
Yardley, Edwin W, 1952, Jl 3,25:5
Yardley, Farnham, 1956, D 31,13:3
Yardley, George W (por), 1938, Je 1,23:1
Yardley, Herbert O, 1958, Ag 8,17:5
Yardley, John L Sr Mrs, 1949, Ap 15,23:3
Yardley, Samuel Swan, 1914, Mr 12,9:4
Yare, John F, 1949, Ja 6,23:3
Yarger, John H, 1950, S 17,104:5
Yarian, Norman C, 1955, Jl 30,17:5
Yarletts, Emerson E, 1955, Ap 15,23:2
Yarm, William, 1946, Ap 4,25:5
Yarmark, Abraham, 1963, My 14,39:2
Yarnall, Alex C, 1960, O 2,84:5
Yarnall, Alfred R Capt, 1925, S 19,15:3
Yarnall, Chandler P, 1946, My 28,21:1
Yarnall, Charlton C Mrs, 1944, D 19,21:3
Yarnall, D Robert, 1967, S 13,47:3
Yarnall, David G, 1942, My 28,17:3
Yarnall, Edwin A, 1939, F 25,15:4
Yarnall, Harold E Mrs, 1948, Ja 25,56:4
Yarnall, Irvin S, 1943, S 17,21:5
Yarnall, Leon H, 1953, Ap 28,27:1
Yarnall, Mildred Mrs, 1955, Ja 9,87:1
Yarnall, Robert, 1918, Jl 22,11:6
Yarnall, Sarah Gifford Mrs, 1925, S 2,23:4
Yarnall, William K, 1950, My 18,29:5
Yarnborough, Barton, 1951, D 21,27:4
Yarnell, Ellis, 1905, S 20,9:6
Yarnell, Harry E, 1959, Jl 8,29:1
Yarnell, Harry E Mrs, 1965, Ja 4,29:3
Yarnell, Helen, 1956, S 10,27:5
Yarnell, John T, 1945, D 20,23:3
Yaroslavsky, Emelyan, 1943, D 5,64:4
Yarow, Fannie H, 1952, My 11,92:8
Yarr, Thomas C, 1941, D 25,25:3
Yarr, Thomas Gen, 1937, Ap 26,19:4
Yarrick, John, 1941, N 17,19:4
Yarrington, Mary A H Mrs, 1940, F 24,13:3
Yarros, Victor S, 1956, N 2,27:4
Yarrow, A Sir, 1932, Ja 25,17:3
Yarrow, Ernest A, 1939, O 27,23:5
Yarrow, George G, 1954, Ja 11,25:5
Yarrow, George G Mrs, 1943, Ag 20,15:5
Yarrow, Harry C, 1950, My 7,108:1
Yarrow, Phil, 1954, Je 16,31:3
Yarrow, Walter T, 1943, Je 19,13:6
Yarrow, William, 1941, Ap 22,21:5; 1942, N 15,57:1
Yarus, Sidney B, 1954, N 6,17:4
Yarvis, Jacob J, 1967, Ag 9,39:1
Yashin, Aleksandr, 1968, Jl 13,27:4
Yaskin, Joseph C, 1955, Ag 12,19:5
Yassin, Ivor B, 1963, O 16,45:5
Yassin, Youssef, 1962, Ag 21,19:5
Yassin Al Hashimi, Pasha, 1937, Ja 22,22:2
Yassky, Samuel A, 1960, D 10,23:3
Yassukovich, Michael S, 1941, O 25,17:2
Yasuda, Zenshiro, 1937, O 9,19:7
Yasui, Seiichiro, 1962, Ja 19,31:1
Yasui, Tetsu, 1945, D 5,25:6
Yasuna, Isidore Dr, 1968, S 25,47:2
Yatchmeneff, Alexis M, 1937, O 24,II,8:3
Yater, Phil E, 1948, Ag 20,17:4
Yates, Albert E, 1959, Jl 4,15:5
Yates, Arthur, 1957, Jl 23,25:1
Yates, Arthur B, 1949, My 11,30:2; 1967, Ja 14,31:5
Yates, Arthur Gould, 1909, F 10,9:5
Yates, Arthur P, 1924, My 9,19:5
Yates, Charles G, 1945, Mr 9,19:4
Yates, Charles V, 1955, Ja 11,25:2
Yates, David Gilbert Dr, 1918, My 10,11:5
Yates, David M, 1947, Ag 26,23:5
Yates, Dornford (C W Mercer), 1960, Mr 6,84:4
Yates, E H, 1894, My 21,5:1
Yates, Edmund H, 1948, Ag 10,21:2
Yates, Elizabeth U, 1942, D 25,18:2
Yates, Emerin C Mrs, 1946, Je 13,27:2
Yates, Esther, 1880, F 19,2:4
Yates, Eugene A, 1957, O 6,83:3
Yates, Frank L, 1953, Jl 1,29:4
Yates, G W, 1952, Ap 17,29:2
Yates, Gilbert, 1954, Je 18,47:7
Yates, Harry, 1951, S 6,31:5; 1956, F 12,88:6
Yates, Harry (est tax appr), 1957, Ag 22,27:1
Yates, Haydie Mrs, 1950, Jl 2,24:7
Yates, Henry, 1865, S 18,4:1; 1903, My 2,9:5
Yates, Henry A, 1960, D 20,33:1
Yates, Henry R, 1924, S 1,13:5
Yates, Herbert J, 1966, F 4,31:4
Yates, Herbert J Jr, 1959, F 8,86:3
Yates, Ira, 1939, Ap 13,23:6
Yates, James H, 1952, Ap 6,88:1
Yates, John B, 1943, My 1,15:2
Yates, John B Mrs, 1954, N 27,13:2
Yates, John C, 1951, Ag 4,15:2
Yates, John L, 1938, N 4,23:2
Yates, John T, 1939, F 17,20:2
Yates, Joseph J, 1960, Mr 9,33:2
Yates, Joseph T, 1943, Mr 26,19:1
Yates, Junius P, 1941, D 5,23:1
Yates, Liberty L, 1958, F 9,88:5
Yates, M G, 1877, Mr 14,8:2
Yates, Mary C, 1961, O 8,87:2
Yates, Miles L, 1956, Ap 6,25:1
Yates, Norman S, 1943, Ap 4,41:2
Yates, Paul C, 1965, Je 19,29:2
Yates, Richard Ex-Sen, 1873, N 28,5:2
Yates, Richard H, 1940, D 11,27:2
Yates, Richard Mrs, 1943, Mr 14,26:3
Yates, Robert C, 1963, D 20,29:3
Yates, Robert R Mrs, 1952, Mr 21,23:2
Yates, Roy T, 1960, Mr 10,31:2
Yates, Samuel M, 1954, Mr 12,22:4
Yates, Sheldon S, 1967, S 12,47:3
Yates, Ted, 1967, Je 7,21:2
Yates, Thomas W, 1940, Mr 9,15:3; 1950, N 23,35:4
Yates, William C, 1950, Je 25,68:8
Yates, William F, 1947, S 25,29:6; 1953, F 26,25:4
Yates, William H, 1950, Ja 22,76:3
Yates, William J, 1943, Jl 23,17:5
Yates, William W, 1960, O 19,45:2
Yates-Smith, Hilary S, 1941, D 2,23:4
Yatman, C B, 1903, Ag 23,7:5
Yatman, Marion F Mrs, 1960, Ja 25,27:2
Yatsevitch, Michael G, 1951, My 11,27:5
Yatsko, Frank, 1947, Ja 5,53:3
Yavanovitch, Slobodan, 1958, D 29,15:6
Yavelow, Max, 1941, Mr 29,15:2
Yavis, Constantine G, 1957, Ag 25,86:4
Yavlinsky, Nathan A, 1962, Ag 5,5:1
Yavner, William, 1950, S 22,31:1
Yavorska, Lydia, 1921, S 5,11:6
Yaw, Arthur J, 1951, Je 23,15:2
Yaw, Ellen B, 1947, S 10,27:4
Yaw, Myron B, 1939, F 19,39:1
Yawger, Eliza, 1949, F 25,24:2
Yawger, John F Mrs, 1923, Ag 22,15:6
Yawger, John Francis, 1921, Ja 14,11:4
Yawger, Raymond F, 1953, F 10,27:4
Yawger, Roy W, 1945, S 24,19:2

Yawman, Cecilia, 1951, Ja 2,23:2
Yawman, Francis J, 1941, My 3,15:3
Ybarnegaray, Jean, 1956, Ap 27,27:4
Ybarra, Alexander Gen, 1919, D 8,15:4
Ycas, Martynas, 1941, Ap 6,49:1
Ye Ho No La, Empress Dowager of China, 1913, F 22,11:5
Yeager, Albert F, 1961, N 6,37:3
Yeager, Andrew J, 1942, D 10,30:1
Yeager, Edith (Mrs W A Fairservis Sr), 1959, S 5, 15:6
Yeager, Emer, 1956, N 25,88:4
Yeager, Everett E Mrs, 1945, My 12,13:5
Yeager, Fred A, 1956, My 12,19:1
Yeager, Fred A Mrs, 1958, Jl 9,27:2
Yeager, George C, 1952, Jl 9,27:2
Yeager, George E Mrs, 1962, My 16,41:4
Yeager, Harold C, 1960, N 26,21:5
Yeager, Harry H, 1944, Je 29,23:3
Yeager, Howard A, 1967, Mr 12,31:1
Yeager, Howard A Mrs, 1967, Mr 17,41:2
Yeager, John L, 1959, F 19,31:2
Yeager, Lee G, 1949, Mr 5,17:5
Yeager, Louis E, 1938, Ap 19,21:2
Yeager, Norman W, 1966, F 9,39:1
Yeager, Robert N, 1953, Ap 12,89:1
Yeager, William A, 1959, Mr 3,33:4
Yeager, William H, 1950, Jl 23,56:2
Yeagman, Charles A, 1954, Mr 26,21:2
Yeaman, George Helm, 1908, F 24,7:5
Yeaman, Stephen Minor, 1912, N 18,11:4
Yeaman, W Pope Rev, 1904, F 20,9:5
Yeamans, Annie, 1912, Mr 4,11:5
Yeamans, Annie Mrs, 1912, Mr 5,11:4
Yeamans, Jennie, 1906, N 29,6:3
Yeandle, Celeste (Mrs E Delkin), 1916, Ap 21,11:6
Yeandle, Stephen S (por), 1943, D 1,21:1
Yeaple, Abram Mrs, 1950, My 5,22:2
Yeaple, Fred, 1965, Ap 26,63:3
Yeaple, Fred Mrs, 1965, Ap 26,63:3
Yeargain, George W, 1945, N 15,19:5
Yeargin, James A, 1937, My 9,II,11:1
Yearick, Henry C, 1948, D 2,29:3
Yearick, Zwingli A, 1940, S 19,23:4
Yearicks, Freeman, 1954, Je 5,17:5
Yearly, Thomas B C Mrs, 1953, Ja 21,31:4
Yearwood, Arthur C, 1945, O 31,23:3
Yeates, Douglas R, 1943, F 22,17:1
Yeatman, George C W Mrs, 1941, Ja 24,17:3
Yeatman, Guy C, 1950, Jl 26,25:2
Yeatman, Pope, 1953, D 7,2:8
Yeatman, Pope Jr, 1958, Ja 30,24:1
Yeatman, Richard P, 1952, S 22,23:4
Yeatman, Walker N, 1941, O 3,23:5
Yeaton, Bertrand J, 1950, Ag 3,23:2
Yeats, Elizabeth C, 1940, F 13,23:2
Yeats, Jack B, 1957, Mr 29,21:4
Yeats, John Butler, 1922, F 4,13:4
Yeats, William B, 1939, Ja 30,13:1
Yeats, William Butler Mrs, 1968, Ag 25,88:5
Yeats-Brown, Francis (por), 1944, D 21,21:4
Yeatts, Walter S, 1944, N 21,25:4
Yeaw, Everett, 1922, Ja 18,17:4
Yeblon, Benjamin, 1939, O 6,25:1
Yecies, Sidney, 1958, Ag 1,21:1
Yeckel, Herbert C, 1954, N 26,29:5
Yefremov, Alex I, 1951, N 24,11:4
Yefroiken, Salman, 1966, O 2,86:5
Yeh, Francis, 1948, Mr 3,23:3
Yeh Chi-chuang, 1967, Jl 2,35:3
Yehia Pasha, Abdel Fattah, 1951, S 28,31:3
Yelansky, Nikolai N, 1964, S 2,37:5
Yeldell, J Carlton, 1961, Je 30,27:4
Yeldell, James W, 1951, My 22,20:6
Yellen, Max L, 1964, Ap 13,29:5
Yellen, Pesach, 1944, Ap 9,32:1
Yellen, Samuel Mrs, 1965, D 19,84:1
Yellen, Sidney, 1943, Ag 26,17:3
Yellin, Charles, 1966, Ag 26,33:5
Yellin, Samuel, 1940, O 4,23:3
Yellow Thunder, Albert, 1951, O 6,19:3
Yellowley, Edward C, 1962, F 9,29:1
Yells, Gordon W, 1950, F 23,27:2
Yells, Herbert P, 1953, Jl 31,19:1
Yelusich, Joseph Mrs, 1960, N 14,31:3
Yelverton, H R Adm Sir, 1878, Jl 25,5:5
Yelverton, James W, 1949, Je 22,31:4
Yelverton, James W Mrs, 1938, N 1,24:4
Yem, E, 1944, Je 23,20:3
Yen, Hawkling Dr, 1937, Ap 14,25:2
Yen, W W, 1950, My 26,23:1
Yen Hsi-shan, 1960, My 24,37:3
Yenalwicz, Frank, 1949, S 15,27:3
Yendes, Seymour E, 1949, N 28,27:5
Yennie, William J, 1939, O 6,25:2
Yenowine, G H, 1901, Jl 30,2:5
Yensar, Harry J, 1947, Je 1,62:6
Yensen, Trygve D, 1950, Jl 4,17:2
Yenser, Thomas, 1949, S 15,27:3
Yeo, Samuel P, 1956, D 23,30:5
Yeo-Thomas, Forest, 1964, F 27,31:4
Yeolyan, Amo S, 1965, Ja 22,43:1
Yeomans, Andrew, 1953, Ap 19,90:2
Yeomans, Charles W, 1937, My 18,23:5
Yeomans, Claude J, 1940, N 28,23:5
Yeomans, Edwin J, 1947, D 11,34:3
Yeomans, Francis Mrs, 1951, Je 1,23:4
Yeomans, George D (por), 1939, Mr 29,23:1
Yeomans, George D Mrs, 1947, S 8,21:4
Yeomans, Lydia, 1938, My 7,15:4
Yeomans, Manning J, 1939, Ap 11,23:2
Yeomans, Susan C Mrs (por), 1938, N 5,19:3
Yeomans, William M, 1944, F 27,38:1
Yeos, John, 1940, Ap 6,17:6
Yeosock, Michael A, 1953, Ja 21,31:2
Yepsen, Lloyd N, 1955, Ag 3,23:2
Yerance, William, 1917, D 22,11:5
Yerbury, Charles S, 1940, Mr 8,21:5
Yerbury, Edgar C, 1964, Ja 27,23:5
Yerby, Rufus G, 1962, S 2,56:6
Yerby, William J, 1950, Jl 4,17:6
Yerbysmith, Ernest A, 1952, Je 12,33:1
Yereance, Abram, 1947, Ag 4,17:6
Yereance, Irving, 1937, N 7,II,9:3
Yereance, James (funl, Ap 7,17:6), 1924, Ap 5,15:3
Yereance, Jessie A Mrs, 1937, N 27,17:4
Yereance, William B, 1957, Ag 10,15:2
Yereance, William B Mrs, 1945, My 11,19:5
Yerg, Lindley H Mrs, 1952, Ag 17,77:2
Yergason, Edgar Smith, 1920, My 16,22:4
Yergason, William D, 1947, My 12,21:5
Yergens, Henry (Bro Denis Edw), 1961, Ja 9,39:3
Yerger, Rolf, 1957, O 20,86:7
Yerger, Thomas E, 1944, My 13,19:5
Yerger, Wilson S, 1942, N 23,23:5
Yergin, Howard V, 1951, Jl 30,17:1
Yergin, Howard V Mrs, 1950, S 3,39:2
Yerick, Charles A Mrs, 1947, F 7,23:2
Yerick, Paul A, 1965, N 14,88:7
Yerk, John J, 1944, O 29,43:1
Yerke, Abel K, 1940, S 27,23:3
Yerkes, C Carroll, 1950, D 21,29:3
Yerkes, Charles E, 1925, D 21,21:5
Yerkes, Charles T, 1905, D 30,4:1
Yerkes, Charles Tyson (will, Ja 3,1:3; funl), 1906, Ja 2,1:5
Yerkes, Clarence T, 1950, Ja 3,25:4
Yerkes, D Clifford, 1958, Mr 8,17:5
Yerkes, David Joseph Rev Dr, 1905, Mr 12,9:5
Yerkes, Dawson M Mrs, 1954, S 21,27:5
Yerkes, Eliza, 1954, F 9,27:5
Yerkes, Ida K, 1939, O 11,30:2
Yerkes, John W, 1922, Je 24,13:5
Yerkes, Leonard A, 1967, Mr 7,41:2
Yerkes, Leonard A Mrs, 1955, D 4,88:7
Yerkes, Richard W, 1954, Ja 22,27:2
Yerkes, Robert M (cor, F 12,88:8), 1956, F 5,86:1
Yerkes, William S, 1944, N 10,19:4
Yerks, Austin J, 1951, Je 29,21:4
Yerks, Clarence W, 1952, My 7,27:4
Yerks, Elijah M, 1941, D 7,77:1
Yerks, Robert A, 1963, Je 27,33:2
Yerks, William E, 1938, Ap 18,15:6
Yerks, Worrell, 1966, D 18,84:6
Yermakovich, Lavrenty P, 1956, Ja 14,5:1
Yermilov, Vladimir V, 1965, N 20,35:5
Yermolaieff, Vladimir, 1945, Ja 6,11:1
Yero, Juan Eduardo, 1947, F 18,25:3
Yerrington, H M, 1910, N 27,II,13:4
Yerxa, Dwight K Mrs, 1962, Ja 20,21:3
Yerxa, Herbert E, 1941, N 6,23:2
Yerxa, Partlow A, 1941, My 25,36:5
Yesenin, Sergei Mrs (Sofia Tolstoy), 1957, Ag 2,19:4
Yeshukov, I B, 1958, N 27,29:4
Yeska, Joseph, 1920, S 4,9:4
Yeskel, William, 1960, Mr 29,37:3
Yeslin, William F, 1945, N 27,23:5
Yetman, Charles E, 1949, My 18,27:2
Yetman, Harry Mrs, 1959, S 16,39:4
Yetter, Harry A, 1946, Ag 21,27:5
Yetter, John C, 1947, Ap 25,21:2
Yetter, John M, 1954, S 17,27:1
Yetter, Louis N, 1955, Ja 21,23:3
Yettra, Harry, 1948, F 11,27:3
Yeuell, Donovan P, 1953, S 17,29:3
Yeung, Kai C, 1958, Ap 18,23:2
Yevtitch, Bogolyub, 1960, Je 8,39:4
Yew Yanothai (Sup Patriarch), 1965, My 16,27:1
Yewdell, Joseph S, 1946, Ag 28,27:4
Yewell, George Henry, 1923, S 27,7:3
Yewell, John F, 1963, N 15,24:3
Yewell, Noble B, 1940, D 14,17:6
Yezek, Charles, 1941, F 24,15:6
Yi Hiung, 1919, Ja 23,13:3
Yi-Peng, Chang, 1944, Jl 17,15:4
Yin, K Y, 1963, Ja 25,11:4
Ylla (C Koffler),(funl, Ap 1,2:6), 1955, Mr 31,2:3
Yllescas, Francisco, 1963, Jl 14,61:3
Ylvisaker, Lauritz S, 1962, Jl 17,25:4
Yntema, Hessel E, 1966, F 22,23:5
Yoakum, B F, 1929, N 28,27:1
Yoakum, Clarence S, 1945, N 22,35:5
Yoakum, Guy D, 1957, Jl 31,23:5
Yocis, Anthony J, 1950, Ag 2,25:5
Yockel, Frederick C, 1950, Jl 20,25:6
Yocom, Isaac Jr, 1946, S 20,31:3
Yocom, Rutherford B H, 1948, O 7,29:5
Yocom, Stanley, 1954, S 21,27:3
Yocum, Herbert A, 1957, Ag 24,15:4
Yocum, Horatio L, 1957, Mr 22,23:4
Yocum, Howard W, 1941, Mr 2,42:3
Yocum, Reuben E, 1947, F 12,25:2
Yocum, Trell W, 1956, Je 1,23:1
Yocum. Thos S Rev, 1904, Jl 28,7:6
Yoder, A C Sr, 1962, O 5,36:4
Yoder, Albert H, 1940, S 24,23:4
Yoder, Arthur L, 1952, Ag 28,23:6
Yoder, Jocelyn P, 1950, O 1,104:7
Yoder, Lloyd E, 1967, D 2,39:4
Yoder, Nelson B, 1952, N 7,23:3
Yoder, Paul A, 1951, F 14,29:2
Yoder, Robert M, 1959, N 7,23:5
Yodice, Lorenzo, 1946, D 24,17:1
Yoelson, Ida Mrs, 1951, Ja 9,21:1
Yoelson, Meyer (Mike), 1953, S 5,15:4
Yoelson, Moses R, 1945, D 24,15:1
Yoeman, Theron G, 1950, D 29,19:2
Yoemans, Lucien I, 1954, Ag 17,21:3
Yoemans, Orion L, 1941, Mr 17,17:4
Yoerg, Aug Mrs, 1948, O 28,30:3
Yoerg, Leon M, 1947, Mr 8,14:2
Yogananda, Paramhansa, 1952, Mr 9,92:6
Yogg, Albert W, 1950, Ag 31,25:2
Yoh, Harold L Mrs, 1955, Je 5,84:6
Yohanan, Yoel Sr Mrs, 1949, Jl 12,27:2
Yohannan, Abraham Rev Dr, 1925, N 10,25:4
Yohannan, Joseph, 1950, Ja 28,13:4
Yohe, Curtis M, 1967, N 3,45:3
Yohe, John W Mrs, 1937, My 22,15:3
Yohe, May, 1938, Ag 28,32:3
Yohei, Suzuki, 1940, My 3,21:3
Yohn, Fred C Mrs, 1955, F 21,21:2
Yoichl, Honda Bp, 1912, Mr 27,13:4
Yokel, Alex (por), 1947, N 29,13:1
Yokel, Arthur, 1961, Ag 13,89:1
Yokoto, Sonnosuke, 1925, F 5,19:4
Yokoyama, Isamu, 1952, Ap 23,3:1
Yokoyama, Taikwan, 1958, F 26,27:2
Yoldi, Orgaz, 1946, F 1,23:5
Yole, Harry, 1959, Ja 22,31:4
Yole, Joseph R, 1968, Ja 4,34:4
Yolland, Arthur, 1956, N 19,31:1
Yolles, Peter P, 1958, Ag 28,27:2
Yon, Jessie L Mrs, 1942, My 4,19:3
Yon, Lina, 1943, Ap 10,17:5
Yon, Pietro (por), 1943, N 23,25:1
Yon, S Constantino, 1956, Ja 31,29:4
Yon Antonio, 1937, S 26,II,8:8
Yonai, Itsumasa, 1948, Ap 21,28:2
Yonan, Jesse M, 1941, Mr 15,17:5
Yonan, John, 1950, F 10,24:3
Yonce, Stanley L, 1944, O 27,23:6
Yondorf, Milton S, 1949, Je 27,27:2
Yonge, George, 1881, O 31,5:5
Yonge, Guy L, 1965, F 28,89:1
Yonge, Henry, 1883, Jl 3,4:7; 1914, O 8,11:5
Yonkers, Abram L, 1953, F 26,25:4
Yonkers, George H, 1938, My 5,23:4
Yonko, Anna, 1948, O 7,33:6
Yook, Rudolph, 1955, Mr 17,45:5
Yoost, William, 1940, Mr 8,21:4
Yoosuf, Arthur K Dr, 1924, D 27,9:4
Yora, Aichi, 1968, Ap 12,35:4
Yorck, Ruth, 1966, Ja 20,35:3
Yordon, Wesley Mrs, 1956, S 8,17:1
Yordt, Harry G, 1961, F 5,80:2
Yori, Frank Sr, 1952, N 21,25:4
York, A Chesley, 1952, Ja 11,21:1
York, Albert M, 1920, S 7,15:2
York, Albert M Mrs, 1952, Ag 15,15:3
York, Alfred G, 1951, Jl 23,17:6
York, Alvin C (funl, S 6,57:1), 1964, S 3,1:6
York, Arthur N, 1946, S 8,46:3
York, Benjamin H Mrs, 1962, F 25,88:6
York, Bernard J, 1925, Ap 15,19:3
York, Byron J, 1959, F 26,31:4
York, Carl P, 1960, F 25,29:4
York, Clara M, 1950, N 4,17:6
York, Clarence M, 1906, Je 21,1:2
York, E P, 1928, D 31,15:5
York, Edward H Jr, 1966, My 26,47:2
York, Eleanor G, 1937, D 1,23:5
York, Ella M, 1947, S 7,60:4
York, Francis L, 1955, Ja 16,93:3
York, Frank B, 1937, F 4,21:2
York, Frank B Mrs, 1957, Mr 25,25:4
York, Frank L (Sept 24), 1965, O 11,61:7
York, George W, 1915, Je 21,9:5
York, Gertrude, 1965, Ap 22,33:5
York, James L, 1942, O 5,19:5
York, James R, 1956, Jl 14,15:3
York, John C, 1943, N 23,25:3
York, John L, 1949, Ag 16,23:3
York, John M, 1949, Mr 2,25:1
York, Joseph H, 1943, O 14,21:2; 1946, Ja 19,14:2
York, L E Gen, 1873, Jl 2,4:7
York, Lorenzo D, 1955, F 9,25:3
York, Mary Mrs, 1943, My 22,13:6
York, S P Prof, 1903, Je 8,7:6

York, Steven W, 1961, My 31,33:1
York, Thomas, 1941, Ja 14,21:4
York, Thomas H, 1907, Mr 5,9:6
York, Thomas L, 1957, D 22,40:2
York, William A, 1952, Jl 5,15:5
Yorke, Arthur, 1957, My 22,33:2
Yorke, Augustus, 1939, D 28,21:4
Yorke, Edward C, 1944, S 11,17:3
Yorke, Field Marshal, 1880, N 22,5:6
Yorke, Gabriel S, 1957, Ja 7,25:2
Yorke, Harry, 1944, Ja 6,23:4
Yorke, L S Capt, 1884, D 13,5:2
Yorke, Oswald, 1943, Ja 26,19:4
Yorke, Thomas, 1943, Ja 11,15:1
Yorke, William P, 1916, F 11,11:6
Yorkey, Charles J, 1953, Jl 13,25:5
Yorkey, Henry, 1941, Ja 23,21:4
Yorkney, John C, 1941, Ag 22,15:4
Yorkston, William R, 1965, Ja 18,35:4
Yorston, A P, 1903, My 1,9:5
Yorston, Frederic, 1947, Jl 31,21:1
Yosco, Robert J, 1942, S 21,15:2
Yoshida, Hideo (Jan 27), 1963, Ap 1,36:8
Yoshida, Shigeru (more details, O 21,31:1; funl, N 1,47:2), 1967, O 20,43:3
Yoshida, Yoshito, 1962, F 28,33:3
Yoshida, Zengo, 1966, N 16,47:3
Yoshihara, Shinryu, 1957, Jl 26,19:3
Yoshihito, Emperor of Japan, 1926, D 25,1:1
Yoshimoto, Kenko, 1938, My 12,23:3
Yoshioka, Yayoi, 1959, My 24,88:6
Yoshizawa, Kenkichi, 1965, Ja 6,39:1
Yosko, Joseph J, 1958, S 20,19:2
Yost, Albert H, 1940, Jl 24,21:2
Yost, Calvin D, 1942, Ap 11,13:5
Yost, Casper S (por), 1941, My 31,11:3
Yost, Charles E, 1941, My 31,11:2
Yost, David H, 1950, D 18,31:2
Yost, Elizena J Mrs, 1943, Jl 30,15:1
Yost, Ellis A, 1962, Ja 8,39:4
Yost, Fielding Harris, 1946, Ag 21,27:1
Yost, Frank H, 1958, N 16,89:1
Yost, Gaylord, 1958, O 12,86:5
Yost, Herbert A (por), 1945, O 25,21:4
Yost, John, 1937, S 11,17:4
Yost, John Mrs, 1965, Je 15,38:2
Yost, Joseph Warren, 1923, N 27,19:1
Yost, Mary, 1954, Mr 5,19:4
Yost, Merrill C, 1952, F 9,13:6
Yost, Paul M, 1968, S 21,33:4
Yost, Phillip Maj, 1924, Ja 13,23:1
Yost, Robert M, 1916, F 22,11:5
Yost, Rutherford, 1957, Ja 19,15:3
Yost, William, 1937, Je 6,II,8:7
Yott, Walter K, 1950, Ja 22,78:1
Yotta, Hannibal Mrs, 1956, F 5,86:2
Youatt, J R Mrs, 1943, S 10,23:5
Youatt, James R (por), 1942, S 1,19:1
Youdovin, Julius M, 1964, Ap 2,33:2
Youell, D R, 1955, Mr 12,35:2
Youell, George J, 1938, My 31,19:5
Youell, Rice M, 1962, Mr 17,25:1
Youhass, Frank G Mrs, 1957, S 3,27:1
Youker, Wilfred Earl, 1920, D 18,13:5
Youkov, Pietr, 1954, My 8,2:3
Youland, William E, 1963, O 1,40:1
Yould, Thomas, 1966, Mr 17,39:5
Youlden, Lissette K Mrs, 1947, O 9,25:5
Youle, G W, 1878, Je 30,5:4
Youmans, Charles L, 1960, Ja 21,31:2
Youmans, E L Prof, 1887, Ja 19,8:2
Youmans, Edward S, 1955, D 19,27:4
Youmans, Ephraim M, 1950, Jl 21,19:3
Youmans, Henry A, 1942, F 22,26:3
Youmans, John P, 1965, F 17,40:1
Youmans, Marcus J Mrs, 1943, N 5,19:3
Youmans, S A, 1879, Mr 10,8:4
Youmans, Scott Mrs, 1940, My 23,23:4
Youmans, Vincent, 1946, Ap 6,17:1
Youmans, Vincent M, 1951, Mr 15,29:5
Youmans, Wilson D, 1945, D 11,25:5
Youmans, Wilson D Mrs, 1953, Mr 16,19:1
Younan, Elias Rev, 1913, D 13,13:7
Younes, Joseph C, 1955, My 10,29:1
Young, A A (Mrs Brigham), 1882, Jl 5,8:6
Young, A A, 1929, Mr 8,25:3
Young, A B Filson, 1938, Ap 20,23:4
Young, A Murray Mrs, 1944, Ap 28,19:2
Young, Al, 1960, Mr 6,86:4
Young, Albert B Mrs, 1943, My 3,17:5
Young, Alden M, 1911, D 5,13:4
Young, Alex, 1884, N 26,1:6; 1950, O 28,17:2
Young, Alex C, 1956, O 26,29:2
Young, Alex M, 1939, Jl 10,19:4
Young, Allen R, 1956, Mr 15,31:4
Young, Amy M, 1938, Ja 23,II,9:3
Young, Andrew G, 1921, O 1,13:4
Young, Andrew M, 1937, Ja 22,22:3
Young, Andrew Murray, 1924, Je 1,8:1
Young, Andrew P, 1954, N 30,29:5
Young, Andrew P Mrs, 1945, Je 16,13:5
Young, Anna R, 1945, Ja 8,17:4
Young, Anne C Mrs, 1940, F 19,17:5
Young, Annesley T, 1942, Ap 22,24:3
Young, Annie H Mrs, 1948, D 15,33:2
Young, Annie M, 1937, Je 5,17:2
Young, Annie T Mrs, 1939, Mr 29,23:3
Young, Ansel V, 1954, O 2,17:2
Young, Anthony N Mrs, 1953, My 22,27:2
Young, Arch, 1939, Jl 25,19:2
Young, Archer E, 1951, N 30,23:1
Young, Archibald R, 1953, Mr 30,21:2
Young, Arden (Mrs C M Bardwell), 1953, O 19,23:6
Young, Art (por), 1943, D 31,15:3
Young, Art, 1944, Ja 5,17:5
Young, Arthur, 1938, O 21,23:6; 1948, Ap 4,60:7; 1949, My 31,24:3
Young, Arthur D, 1953, Ja 16,23:4
Young, Arthur E, 1951, Ja 16,29:1
Young, Arthur F, 1943, Mr 28,24:5
Young, Arthur H, 1943, Ag 28,11:2; 1964, Mr 7,23:5
Young, Arthur J, 1966, Jl 2,23:4
Young, Arthur L Mrs, 1949, Mr 23,27:4
Young, Arthur S, 1950, Ag 16,29:5
Young, Arthur William Sir, 1915, N 23,13:3
Young, August S Mrs, 1946, Ja 25,24:3
Young, Augusta C Mrs, 1952, Ap 9,31:1
Young, Austin A, 1944, Mr 23,19:1
Young, Benjamin, 1873, Ag 25,1:4
Young, Benjamin E, 1957, Ag 2,19:2
Young, Benjamin L, 1964, Je 5,31:1
Young, Benjamin P, 1958, O 11,23:3
Young, Benjamin S, 1965, F 4,31:1
Young, Bernard B, 1943, N 26,23:4
Young, Bert E, 1949, D 26,37:6
Young, Bertha K, 1956, D 1,21:1
Young, Bicknell, 1938, Mr 9,23:1
Young, Brigham, 1877, Ag 30,1:7
Young, Brigham Mrs, 1905, F 5,4:7
Young, Brigham Mrs (Harriet Amelia Folsom), 1910, D 12,9:5
Young, Brigham Mrs, 1915, Ag 22,13:5
Young, C Edwin, 1945, N 17,17:2
Young, C Higbie, 1960, N 2,39:5
Young, C Jac (por), 1940, Mr 5,23:3
Young, C Townsend, 1944, Mr 28,19:4
Young, C Walter, 1939, F 10,23:5
Young, Carl A, 1955, Ag 31,25:2
Young, Carl O Mrs, 1955, Jl 3,32:5
Young, Caryl B, 1946, Ag 22,27:4
Young, Charles, 1952, My 14,27:3; 1962, Ap 15,81:1
Young, Charles A, 1944, Mr 7,17:5; 1951, My 17,31:5; 1955, F 5,15:5
Young, Charles Augustus, 1908, Ja 5,11:2
Young, Charles B, 1952, Mr 19,29:3
Young, Charles Col, 1922, Ja 13,15:6; 1923, Je 2,11:6; 1925, F 9,17:5
Young, Charles D, 1946, N 20,31:1; 1955, My 14,19:3
Young, Charles D Mrs, 1951, O 28,84:5
Young, Charles Dr, 1917, Jl 15,15:3
Young, Charles F, 1939, Je 12,17:3; 1942, Je 2,24:2
Young, Charles H, 1948, My 26,25:3; 1948, S 24,25:1
Young, Charles J Rev Dr, 1911, D 21,11:5
Young, Charles K, 1938, S 15,25:3
Young, Charles M (details, N 16,31:3), 1964, N 15, 86:3
Young, Charles P, 1904, N 22,1:5
Young, Charles S, 1941, Mr 11,23:5
Young, Charles T, 1960, Ap 3,86:4
Young, Charles T Jr, 1962, Jl 26,27:4
Young, Charles V, 1960, N 14,31:1
Young, Charles W, 1949, My 11,29:2
Young, Charles W Mrs, 1951, Jl 25,23:5
Young, Charles W 3d Mrs, 1964, S 18,35:1
Young, Charles Willard, 1924, O 31,19:5
Young, Chauncey H, 1937, N 2,25:2
Young, Chester W, 1940, Je 18,23:2
Young, Christian Jr, 1905, My 2,1:2
Young, Clara K, 1960, O 16,88:2
Young, Clarence H, 1957, Ap 6,19:2; 1958, D 29,15:3
Young, Clarence H Mrs, 1967, Ap 7,37:2
Young, Clark D, 1964, S 26,23:5
Young, Clement C, 1947, D 27,13:1
Young, Clifford M, 1950, F 11,15:6
Young, Clifton, 1951, S 11,33:4
Young, Conrad H, 1951, N 17,17:3
Young, Cornelia H Mrs, 1942, Ap 15,21:2
Young, Cornelius, 1915, Ap 26,9:6
Young, Coulter D, 1941, O 24,23:2
Young, Dallas G, 1955, S 19,25:4
Young, Daniel, 1947, N 20,29:3
Young, Daniel A, 1951, N 8,29:4
Young, Daniel F, 1949, Ap 5,30:2
Young, Daniel R, 1945, Ap 12,23:1
Young, David, 1915, Ag 29,15:6; 1939, F 7,20:2; 1955, Ap 2,17:4
Young, David A Mrs, 1944, O 9,23:4
Young, David E, 1962, O 26,31:2
Young, David H Mrs, 1950, S 20,31:2
Young, David Jr, 1952, Ag 5,19:4
Young, David L, 1960, Je 15,41:2
Young, David Mrs, 1951, O 28,85:1
Young, David R, 1918, Mr 14,13:6
Young, David Rev, 1907, Ap 21,9:3
Young, Delmar, 1957, N 29,27:4
Young, Denton T (Cy),(funl, N 8,31:4), 1955, N 5, 19:2
Young, Desmond, 1966, Je 28,45:1
Young, Dinsdale, 1938, Ja 22,15:5
Young, Dominic Mrs, 1947, S 27,15:3
Young, Dominick, 1958, Ap 25,27:1
Young, Donald, 1962, Ja 3,33:2
Young, Doris, 1953, N 20,24:4
Young, Douglas, 1951, Jl 6,23:5
Young, Douglas H, 1943, S 11,13:5
Young, Douglas S, 1953, Ag 20,27:1
Young, Dwight E, 1967, Ap 11,41:3
Young, Dwight E Mrs, 1945, N 8,20:2
Young, Earl C, 1952, N 20,31:2
Young, Earl E, 1948, Jl 31,15:6
Young, Edgar L Mrs, 1951, Ap 20,29:2
Young, Edna C, 1944, Mr 5,36:2
Young, Edwar W, 1941, Je 28,15:4
Young, Edward, 1952, Jl 17,23:4
Young, Edward A, 1942, F 26,19:2
Young, Edward C, 1948, F 13,21:3
Young, Edward Faitoute Condict, 1908, D 7,9:5
Young, Edward H, 1958, Mr 1,17:4
Young, Edward H (Lord Kennet), 1960, Jl 12,35:4
Young, Edward L, 1916, Mr 19,19:7; 1940, Mr 25,15:3
Young, Edward M, 1948, Mr 23,25:2
Young, Edward M Mrs, 1956, Je 19,29:2
Young, Edward R, 1949, Je 12,76:2
Young, Edward S, 1938, Mr 11,19:5
Young, Edward W, 1957, Ap 1,25:4
Young, Edwin B, 1949, D 5,23:5
Young, Edwin S, 1937, S 21,25:5
Young, Eliot P, 1958, Je 8,88:6
Young, Eliza, 1902, Ag 11,7:5
Young, Elizabeth, 1948, F 11,27:1
Young, Elizabeth A Mrs, 1942, Je 13,15:6
Young, Elizabeth D, 1964, F 17,31:2
Young, Elizabeth J Mrs, 1948, Mr 20,13:6
Young, Ella, 1956, Jl 25,29:1
Young, Ellison, 1940, Ja 31,19:2
Young, Ellsworth, 1952, S 27,17:2
Young, Elmer B, 1944, S 30,13:3
Young, Elmer H, 1957, My 5,88:2
Young, Eloise S, 1952, Ag 4,15:3
Young, Erle F, 1953, Je 2,29:2
Young, Eugene J (por), 1939, F 23,23:1
Young, Eugene N L, 1918, Mr 9,13:5
Young, Eugenie E Mrs, 1950, D 11,25:1
Young, Evan E, 1946, Ja 14,19:2
Young, Evan E Mrs, 1943, Ja 11,15:2
Young, Evangeline W, 1944, D 21,21:4
Young, Everett G, 1947, Ja 11,19:5
Young, F Arnold, 1949, Ja 14,24:2
Young, F L, 1930, My 22,27:3
Young, F T B, 1940, Ap 21,43:2
Young, Floyd D, 1959, Je 17,35:1
Young, Floyd S, 1953, My 18,21:5
Young, Francis B, 1954, Mr 29,19:3
Young, Francis Wilbur Mrs, 1919, S 23,17:3
Young, Frank, 1968, Jl 6,19:1
Young, Frank C, 1946, S 21,15:4; 1957, Mr 4,27:3
Young, Frank S, 1953, My 6,31:2
Young, Franklin, 1955, N 28,31:5
Young, Frederick A Mrs, 1943, Ap 7,26:2
Young, Frederick H Mrs, 1960, N 18,31:5
Young, Frederick J, 1943, Mr 13,13:1
Young, Frederick R, 1951, Mr 27,29:1
Young, Freeman J, 1949, N 10,31:3
Young, G Alex, 1957, N 5,31:2
Young, G W, 1926, F 19,21:3
Young, George, 1906, Je 23,7:4; 1946, Ja 20,42:6; 1952, Ja 28,17:2
Young, George A, 1941, O 16,21:4; 1950, S 26,31:1
Young, George B, 1940, Ap 11,25:6; 1944, N 15,27:3; 1957, Jl 4,19:5
Young, George C, 1948, Ja 27,25:4; 1950, Jl 3,15:2
Young, George F, 1952, Mr 20,29:1; 1964, Jl 31,24:1
Young, George G, 1937, Je 1,23:5
Young, George H, 1943, D 20,25:7
Young, George J, 1950, Mr 14,25:4; 1954, Ap 10,15:2
Young, George Jr, 1956, Je 14,33:3
Young, George L, 1959, Ag 31,21:4
Young, George M, 1948, Ap 22,27:2
Young, George Mrs, 1954, D 5,88:2
Young, George P, 1960, Mr 18,25:3
Young, George S, 1956, Ap 5,29:3
Young, George Schaeffer, 1919, Ja 8,11:2
Young, George W, 1945, Ap 29,38:1; 1950, My 6,15:3; 1956, O 14,86:7
Young, George W Jr, 1941, O 26,43:3
Young, Gilbert A, 1943, Je 28,21:5
Young, Glenfield S, 1947, My 2,22:3
Young, Gordon C, 1947, Je 28,14:2
Young, Gordon R, 1948, F 11,27:3
Young, Gregory Mrs, 1948, Mr 20,13:3
Young, H Earl, 1940, N 26,23:4
Young, H Walter, 1942, O 23,21:3
Young, H Wilmot Mrs, 1937, My 28,21:6
Young, Hannah C Mrs, 1938, Je 10,21:4
Young, Hannah K J, 1909, Ag 7,9:5
Young, Harlow W, 1944, S 24,46:4
Young, Harold K Mrs, 1947, S 27,15:6
Young, Harold R (por), 1944, Jl 4,19:2
Young, Harry B, 1945, S 30,46:5

Young, Harry C, 1944, F 15,17:6
Young, Harry H, 1957, D 28,17:1
Young, Harry L, 1948, F 6,26:6
Young, Harvey C, 1945, Mr 9,19:5
Young, Harvey E, 1872, N 2,10:4
Young, Harvey R, 1947, N 20,29:1
Young, Helen, 1966, N 25,37:4
Young, Helen H, 1957, Je 3,27:5
Young, Helen L, 1942, Jl 14,19:4
Young, Henry, 1903, D 13,9:3; 1925, D 22,21:4; 1962, Mr 29,33:3
Young, Henry A, 1941, N 23,52:2; 1952, F 8,23:3
Young, Henry A F, 1938, Ja 21,20:5
Young, Henry B, 1943, Ap 3,15:2
Young, Henry E, 1939, O 25,23:5; 1947, Ap 9,25:2
Young, Henry F, 1938, Ap 6,23:2
Young, Henry J, 1940, N 2,15:5
Young, Henry Mrs, 1903, D 13,9:3
Young, Henry O, 1942, Je 13,15:4
Young, Henry S, 1955, Je 10,25:5
Young, Henry Sr, 1944, O 2,19:5
Young, Henry Sr Mrs, 1949, D 8,33:4
Young, Henry W, 1948, N 25,31:3
Young, Herbert, 1948, D 29,21:2
Young, Herbert M Mrs, 1954, O 21,27:3
Young, Hester M Mrs, 1940, Ja 20,15:2
Young, Heusted T, 1951, Ap 28,89:2
Young, Hobart C, 1941, Je 8,49:2
Young, Hoge D, 1958, D 2,38:1
Young, Horace G, 1946, Ja 1,27:3
Young, Horatio B, 1943, N 5,19:5
Young, Howard E, 1939, Je 21,23:2
Young, Howard G, 1937, O 6,25:2
Young, Howard H Mrs, 1948, Ag 10,22:2
Young, Howard I Mrs (por), 1943, S 23,21:3
Young, Howard O, 1960, Ap 26,37:3
Young, Howard S, 1951, D 9,91:1
Young, Howard T, 1941, N 20,27:4
Young, Hubert W, 1950, Ap 22,19:4
Young, Hugh A Jr, 1941, Je 8,49:2
Young, Hugh Col, 1912, O 22,11:5
Young, Hugh H (por), 1945, Ag 24,19:3
Young, Hugh W, 1938, O 28,23:3
Young, Ira Prof, 1858, S 20,1:6
Young, Irving W, 1939, Ag 31,19:4; 1956, O 1,27:5
Young, Isham, 1956, D 9,88:2
Young, J Addison, 1953, S 25,21:5
Young, J Albert, 1940, Ja 23,21:3
Young, J Arthur, 1943, S 16,21:4
Young, J B, 1928, S 27,29:3
Young, J Commodore, 1885, My 18,5:3
Young, J Harold, 1950, F 19,76:2
Young, J Henry Mrs, 1959, My 20,35:4
Young, J Herbert, 1953, Ap 24,23:3
Young, J R, 1899, Ja 18,7:5
Young, J R Mrs, 1881, Ja 5,5:1; 1883, O 23,5:3
Young, J S, 1877, F 21,5:5; 1880, Je 25,2:5
Young, J Walter, 1944, Mr 22,19:5
Young, J Walter Mrs, 1950, D 17,84:4
Young, J Warren, 1948, My 17,19:4
Young, Jacob W A, 1948, O 27,28:2
Young, James, 1883, My 15,2:6; 1940, Mr 31,44:2; 1965, Jl 28,35:4
Young, James B (por), 1946, N 17,68:4
Young, James C (por), 1945, O 29,19:1
Young, James D, 1949, Jl 27,23:5; 1965, Ag 4,35:5
Young, James E, 1941, Je 17,21:6; 1944, Je 29,23:1
Young, James F, 1953, My 27,31:4
Young, James H, 1940, Mr 8,22:2; 1946, O 11,23:2; 1952, My 16,23:2
Young, James H Mrs, 1941, Ja 20,17:1
Young, James N, 1959, Ap 4,20:1
Young, James O, 1949, D 24,15:4
Young, James R, 1961, N 17,35:3
Young, James Rankin, 1924, D 19,21:4
Young, James S Judge, 1914, F 26,9:4
Young, James Sir, 1912, O 22,11:5
Young, James W, 1950, F 2,28:2; 1961, Je 7,41:1
Young, James W Mrs, 1950, My 22,21:5
Young, Jean C, 1949, Ap 30,13:5
Young, Jennie Mrs, 1946, Jl 26,21:5
Young, Joe, 1939, Ap 22,17:6
Young, John, 1903, O 29,9:5; 1944, Ja 5,17:4; 1951, Mr 27,29:5
Young, John A, 1939, Ap 14,23:3; 1945, Mr 25,38:1; 1949, D 7,31:4; 1956, D 12,39:4
Young, John C, 1914, D 14,11:5; 1941, F 5,19:2; 1949, Mr 15,27:2
Young, John D Col, 1903, Jl 14,7:6
Young, John E, 1939, F 17,16:2; 1954, Jl 7,31:3
Young, John F, 1947, Ja 15,25:3
Young, John H Mrs, 1946, Ap 27,17:3; 1952, F 6,29:4
Young, John J, 1961, N 7,33:1
Young, John J Jr, 1937, Mr 24,25:1
Young, John L, 1938, F 16,21:4; 1947, Ja 26,53:3
Young, John L Mrs, 1943, My 9,40:7
Young, John M, 1937, Mr 1,19:6
Young, John M Mrs, 1960, N 4,33:4
Young, John Mrs, 1950, Mr 2,27:2
Young, John O Mrs, 1942, Jl 18,13:5
Young, John P, 1921, Ap 24,22:4; 1957, Jl 25,23:5
Young, John P Mrs, 1954, Jl 13,23:1
Young, John R, 1966, Jl 4,15:3
Young, John V Capt, 1937, O 24,II,8:2
Young, John W, 1941, O 30,23:1; 1948, Je 13,69:1; 1949, F 5,15:4
Young, John W Mrs, 1943, D 15,27:1
Young, John Williard, 1924, F 13,19:4
Young, Joseph, 1881, Jl 27,3:5; 1923, Ag 11,9:6; 1950, Jl 17,21:4
Young, Joseph C, 1948, D 23,19:3
Young, Joseph D C, 1938, O 21,23:5
Young, Joseph E, 1949, Ap 21,25:2
Young, Joseph G, 1954, F 13,13:3
Young, Joseph H, 1958, N 17,31:6
Young, Joseph I, 1962, F 17,19:2
Young, Joseph L, 1944, Mr 11,13:3
Young, Joseph L Mrs, 1961, Ja 13,27:1
Young, Joseph O Mrs, 1945, Ja 13,11:1
Young, Josephine D Mrs, 1942, Jl 29,17:3
Young, Joshua Rev, 1904, F 9,9:5
Young, Karl, 1943, N 18,23:5
Young, Karl T, 1959, N 16,31:3
Young, Katherine, 1944, Ja 29,13:5
Young, Katherine E (por), 1945, Ag 4,11:6
Young, L, 1926, N 16,27:1
Young, L F, 1881, O 3,8:1
Young, Leon G, 1949, Ja 18,23:2
Young, Leroy Mount, 1924, D 29,15:4
Young, Lester, 1959, Mr 16,31:5
Young, Lewis E, 1953, D 28,21:2
Young, Lewis G, 1944, Ja 13,21:5
Young, Lewis J, 1944, Ap 20,19:5
Young, Linn B, 1960, N 9,19:2
Young, Loretta, 1904, Ap 21,1:5
Young, Louis, 1941, Je 18,21:6
Young, Louis A, 1948, Jl 20,23:5
Young, Louis E, 1947, Ag 7,21:4
Young, Louis E A, 1952, Jl 30,25:3
Young, Louis W, 1967, Ja 15,84:6
Young, Louise U Mrs, 1940, D 31,15:1
Young, Lucien Adm (funl, O 5,13:6), 1912, O 4,13:6
Young, M J, 1882, Ap 16,2:7
Young, Mahonri M, 1957, N 3,88:6
Young, Malcolm, 1955, Je 18,17:5
Young, Mamie Mrs, 1948, My 12,28:3
Young, Marie C, 1959, Jl 29,29:3
Young, Marion S Mrs, 1959, Jl 12,73:1
Young, Martha Mrs, 1943, F 5,38:7
Young, Martin H, 1962, Je 16,19:4
Young, Marvin Thomas, 1968, S 28,33:1
Young, Mary A Mrs, 1937, N 12,22:1
Young, Mary Crosby Mrs, 1905, S 19,9:6
Young, Mary E, 1947, Jl 15,23:4; 1953, S 6,50:6
Young, Mary V, 1946, Ap 5,25:5
Young, Max L, 1914, D 22,13:4
Young, Milton A, 1949, Ap 14,25:2
Young, Minnie V Mrs, 1938, O 22,17:6
Young, Monroe, 1939, D 21,23:5
Young, Napoleon O, 1950, My 10,31:1
Young, Nathan, 1959, D 27,60:7
Young, Nedrick, 1968, S 18,44:3
Young, Nedrick Mrs (Frances), 1963, Ja 8,8:8
Young, Nicholas P, 1941, Mr 10,17:4
Young, Nora E, 1957, Mr 30,19:6
Young, Olive, 1940, O 5,15:5
Young, Oliver R, 1946, Jl 26,21:4
Young, Ollie Mrs, 1959, S 11,27:1
Young, Otto, 1906, D 1,9:6
Young, Owen D (funl, Jl 15,60:2), 1962, Jl 12,1:1
Young, Owen D Mrs, 1965, Ja 15,43:4
Young, P Bernard Sr, 1962, O 12,32:7
Young, Paul A, 1962, N 3,25:3
Young, Paul I, 1960, Mr 26,21:5
Young, Paul M, 1946, My 14,21:3
Young, Percy S, 1950, N 16,31:3
Young, Phil E, 1955, Je 18,17:2
Young, Philip, 1946, Je 21,23:4
Young, Polk, 1954, Ja 11,12:6
Young, R J, 1926, My 9,II,9:1
Young, R Luther, 1945, S 20,23:2
Young, R Trenor, 1964, N 24,39:1
Young, Ralph E, 1950, Ag 5,15:3
Young, Ralph G, 1905, Ap 13,1:5
Young, Ralph H, 1962, Ja 24,33:4
Young, Ralph R, 1942, Mr 20,19:3
Young, Ralph S, 1944, N 8,17:2
Young, Ray W, 1951, Ap 5,29:2
Young, Raymond Mrs, 1945, Ap 21,13:5
Young, Reginald S, 1940, N 13,23:5
Young, Richard D, 1965, Mr 24,43:2
Young, Richard Jr, 1916, F 25,11:6
Young, Richard M, 1945, F 13,23:2
Young, Richard R, 1962, Jl 9,31:5
Young, Richard W Brig-Gen, 1919, D 28,23:2
Young, Robert, 1949, Je 27,16:6; 1953, F 27,21:1; 1957, Jl 15,19:5
Young, Robert A, 1938, F 8,22:2; 1938, Je 10,21:3; 1945, D 10,21:2; 1959, Ag 24,21:4
Young, Robert F, 1948, Ja 25,56:4
Young, Robert G, 1964, Ap 11,25:5
Young, Robert G Mrs, 1952, D 2,31:4
Young, Robert H McCarter, 1951, F 8,23:6
Young, Robert Mrs, 1944, Ja 3,21:2
Young, Robert N, 1964, O 20,32:1
Young, Rockwell, 1903, Ap 21,9:5
Young, Roderick B, 1954, Ag 27,21:4
Young, Roger, 1961, F 7,33:1
Young, Roland, 1953, Je 7,84:1
Young, Roland L, 1961, Ap 10,31:4
Young, Roly, 1948, D 25,17:2
Young, Rose, 1941, Jl 8,19:2
Young, Roswell P, 1961, F 10,27:2
Young, Roy A, 1961, Ja 2,25:2
Young, S B, 1880, Mr 15,4:7
Young, S E, 1927, Mr 29,25:1
Young, S Edward Mrs, 1957, F 4,19:4
Young, S H, 1927, S 4,7:5
Young, S Hall Rev, 1915, Ja 14,11:4
Young, Samuel, 1940, F 8,23:6
Young, Samuel A Capt, 1915, Je 20,15:6
Young, Samuel A Mrs, 1953, Je 28,61:1
Young, Samuel Baldwin Marks Gen, 1924, S 2,19:4
Young, Samuel R, 1948, D 12,92:5
Young, Samuel T, 1945, Ap 13,17:4
Young, Sarsfield Edward Capt, 1912, Je 3,9:6
Young, Sherman P, 1947, Ja 31,23:4; 1963, Ap 2,48:1
Young, Sol, 1921, S 24,11:2
Young, Spencer C, 1962, Mr 24,25:6
Young, Spencer E, 1940, Ap 9,23:3
Young, Stanley H, 1956, N 30,24:1
Young, Stanton A, 1954, My 19,32:4
Young, Stark, 1963, Ja 7,15:1
Young, Stuart A, 1960, Jl 3,32:4
Young, T Basil, 1945, Ap 21,13:5
Young, T Basil Mrs, 1937, My 29,17:4
Young, T G Capt, 1875, N 24,2:3
Young, Theodore, 1953, N 20,23:2
Young, Theodore J, 1952, Mr 8,13:5
Young, Thomas, 1945, Mr 22,23:1
Young, Thomas E, 1964, O 31,29:5
Young, Thomas J, 1960, S 22,27:2
Young, Thomas K, 1954, Mr 24,27:3
Young, Thomas Mrs, 1949, Je 2,27:2
Young, Thomas W, 1967, S 8,40:1
Young, Thompson B Mrs, 1945, N 9,19:2
Young, Tom, 1963, Je 2,84:2
Young, Treat D, 1945, Jl 6,11:6
Young, Udell C, 1967, Ja 20,43:2
Young, V C, 1933, Mr 15,17:5
Young, Victor (funl plans, N 12,29:2), 1956, N 11, 86:4
Young, Victor, 1968, S 4,44:4
Young, Victoria O Mrs, 1955, Ap 10,88:1
Young, W B, 1938, My 12,23:5
Young, W Ewart, 1953, O 8,29:4
Young, Waldemar, 1938, Ag 31,15:3
Young, Walter, 1957, Ap 20,17:1
Young, Walter J, 1951, N 9,27:1
Young, Walter S (por), 1940, Ap 21,43:1
Young, Walter S Mrs, 1960, Mr 25,27:2
Young, Walter V, 1940, Mr 8,22:3
Young, Walter W Jr Mrs, 1945, Ap 17,23:5
Young, Walter X, 1941, Mr 24,19:4
Young, Walter X Mrs, 1941, Mr 24,19:4
Young, Ward, 1949, Ja 27,23:4
Young, Warren H, 1956, Jl 21,15:2
Young, Warren S (funl, N 22,13:4), 1917, N 19,11:4
Young, Wilbur F, 1944, Ag 17,17:3
Young, Wilbur F Mrs, 1960, N 2,39:3
Young, Wilbur H Mrs, 1948, Mr 6,13:4
Young, William, 1920, O 8,13:2; 1949, F 16,25:6; 1949, Ag 23,21:3
Young, William A, 1946, N 11,27:1
Young, William A Jr, 1955, Ja 4,21:1
Young, William B, 1959, Ag 16,82:1
Young, William B Mrs, 1952, S 9,31:2; 1953, Ag 18, 23:2
Young, William C, 1949, Ja 12,27:5
Young, William D, 1942, Ag 9,43:4
Young, William Dr, 1902, O 27,9:5
Young, William H, 1941, F 9,48:1; 1942, Ag 22,13:4; 1944, D 27,20:3; 1953, S 29,26:3; 1955, N 27,89:2; 1959, Jl 22,27:4; 1964, Ag 9,76:4
Young, William H Dr, 1903, D 27,10:1
Young, William H Mrs, 1958, Ap 7,21:2
Young, William H Rev Dr, 1937, My 17,26:1
Young, William Hamilton, 1908, Je 20,9:5
Young, William Hopkins, 1909, D 2,9:4
Young, William J, 1938, Ap 30,15:4; 1942, My 15, 19:4; 1948, Je 23,27:5; 1957, D 9,35:4
Young, William L, 1942, O 13,24:3; 1959, Jl 23,27:3
Young, William M, 1909, Je 12,7:5
Young, William M Jr, 1950, N 13,27:5
Young, William Mrs (F Robertson), 1942, Jl 1,25:4
Young, William Mrs, 1958, Je 12,31:4
Young, William P, 1912, Jl 29,9:5
Young, William P Mrs, 1945, Jl 28,11:6
Young, William Rev, 1871, Je 6,1:6
Young, William S Dr, 1937, Jl 24,15:4
Young, William Thomas, 1912, S 29,II,13:5
Young, William W (por), 1940, O 2,23:5
Young, William W, 1952, O 22,27:2
Young, William W Jr, 1961, Jl 10,21:5
Young, William W Mrs, 1947, N 23,76:2
Young, Willis H, 1917, S 22,11:6
Young, Wilson L, 1946, F 1,23:1
Young, Winfred, 1964, F 1,23:4
Young-Hunter, John, 1955, Ag 10,25:2

Youngberg, Clarence, 1945, My 27,26:1
Youngberg, Eric Sr, 1946, D 28,16:2
Youngblood, Adam, 1954, Mr 25,42:8
Youngblood, Addison P (por), 1937, Ap 28,23:3
Youngblood, Bonney, 1959, Ja 21,31:2
Youngblood, Charles D, 1959, Ag 3,25:4
Youngblood, Jay, 1921, Jl 23,7:6
Youngblood, Robert K, 1943, F 14,48:5
Youngdahl, Carl E, 1962, Mr 31,25:2
Younge, Henri M, 1963, S 2,15:4
Younger, Cole, 1916, Mr 22,13:6
Younger, Edward F (por), 1942, Ag 8,11:4
Younger, Edward F, 1944, S 29,21:5
Younger, Falk, 1917, Mr 13,11:5
Younger, G Dana, 1949, Ja 2,60:8
Younger, Gustavus A, 1938, Je 27,17:4
Younger, J Arthur, 1967, Je 21,47:2
Younger, John E, 1958, D 31,19:2
Younger, M, 1936, Je 28,II,9:1
Younger, Max, 1962, Jl 28,19:3
Younger, Scout, 1937, N 19,23:6
Younger, Viscount, 1946, D 5,31:3
Younger, William Sir, 1937, Jl 30,19:4
Youngert, Eugene Mrs, 1947, S 25,29:6
Youngert, Sven V G, 1939, F 28,19:4
Younggreen, Charles C, 1942, Ag 20,19:4
Youngheart, Samuel O, 1958, My 13,29:1
Youngholm, David S (por), 1942, D 5,15:5
Younghusband, Francis E (por), 1942, Ag 2,39:1
Younghusband, George J, 1944, O 3,23:2
Youngken, Heber W, 1963, Jl 21,64:6
Youngling, Henry W, 1948, Ap 4,60:2
Younglove, Edward H, 1942, S 1,19:1
Younglove, Herbert B, 1953, N 4,33:5
Younglove, T G, 1882, S 8,5:6
Youngman, Elmer H, 1948, O 15,23:3
Youngman, Harry V, 1943, F 3,19:6
Youngman, Jacob Mrs, 1964, F 20,29:1
Youngman, Robert Barber Rev, 1917, Mr 3,9:2
Youngman, W S, 1934, Ap 26,23:4
Youngmann, Elmer G H, 1961, S 9,19:5
Youngquist, G Aaron, 1959, O 31,23:3
Youngquist, Samuel, 1965, S 8,47:5
Youngs, Carey L, 1948, Ag 10,21:1
Youngs, Charles A, 1948, My 22,15:2
Youngs, Clarence H Mrs, 1950, Ap 25,31:1
Youngs, David G, 1946, Ja 26,13:3
Youngs, Frederick D Mrs, 1956, F 7,31:5
Youngs, George B, 1941, O 23,23:5
Youngs, Graham (will, Jl 9,19:5), 1937, Je 28,19:5
Youngs, Lester B Mrs, 1955, My 20,25:2
Youngs, Merle L, 1958, O 9,37:1
Youngs, William J Col (funl, Ap 30,19:5), 1916, Ap 28,11:6
Youngs, William J Mrs, 1947, Je 19,21:3
Youngs, William P Mrs, 1938, Ja 9,42:5
Youngson, A B Chief, 1903, Jl 31,7:5
Youngstein, Elias, 1955, Mr 27,86:7
Youngstein, Elias Mrs, 1952, F 29,23:1
Youngster, Cornelius C Mrs, 1961, Je 1,35:1
Youngster, Nelson C, 1962, Ja 31,31:1
Youngworth, Leo V, 1946, My 17,21:3
Younie, George S, 1941, Ag 2,15:2
Younker, Falk, 1917, Mr 16,11:5
Younker, Ira M, 1966, Ag 23,39:3
Yount, Barton K (por), 1949, Jl 12,27:3
Yount, Barton K, 1949, Jl 19,29:1
Yourieff, E A, 1928, My 1,29:4
Yourishin, John, 1954, D 24,13:2
Yourkevitch, Vladimir, 1964, D 14,35:1
Youry, William H, 1925, D 17,23:3
Yousry Pasha, Seifoullah, 1949, D 27,12:6
Youssef Bey, Amine, 1950, Ag 25,21:4
Youssoupoff, Felix Prince, 1967, S 28,47:1
Youssoupoff, Zenaide Princess, 1939, N 28,25:3
Youtie, Samuel, 1948, D 18,19:5
Yowell, Everett I, 1959, Mr 14,23:3
Ypres, Countess of, 1941, Je 23,18:3
Ypres, Earl of (J R L French), 1958, Ap 7,21:3
Ypsilanti, Thomas, 1966, D 23,25:5
Yselowitz, Joseph, 1942, S 3,21:3
Ysembourg, Karl von Princess, 1939, Ap 26,23:4
Yserentant, J, 1943, F 23,6:3
Yturbide, Angel, 1872, Ag 9,1:7
Yturralde y Orbegoso, Mariano de, 1962, Mr 6,32:6
Yu Tsune-Chi, Dr, 1968, F 27,39:5
Yu Ya-Ching, 1945, Ap 28,15:2
Yu Yu-Jen, 1964, N 11,43:3
Yuan, John J, 1939, Ja 21,15:2
Yuan Chung-hsien, 1957, F 17,92:6
Yuan-pei, Tsai, 1940, Mr 6,23:3
Yuasa, Keifu, 1944, N 23,31:4
Yuasa, Kurahei, 1940, D 25,27:5
Yucel, Hasan A, 1961, F 27,27:3
Yuckman, Morris, 1947, Jl 31,21:3
Yudain, Morris I, 1952, Ag 6,21:3
Yudain, Morris Mrs, 1966, My 7,31:3
Yudain, Theodore Mrs, 1962, Je 13,41:5
Yudelson, Albert B, 1939, Ag 28,19:4
Yudenitch, N, 1933, O 6,20:3
Yudin, Pavel A, 1956, Ap 11,33:3
Yudin, Pavel F Ex-Amb, 1968, Ap 12,35:2
Yudin, Sergei, 1954, Je 15,29:6
Yudkin, Arthur M, 1957, My 4,21:7
Yudkowsky, Peter (por), 1941, Ja 25,15:2
Yudnar, Stephen J, 1950, D 23,15:4
Yuells, Ida Mrs, 1939, Jl 7,17:3
Yuengling, George W, 1957, Jl 24,25:4
Yugow, Aaron A, 1954, F 11,29:3
Yuhas, Frank Mrs, 1950, N 30,33:2
Yuhas, John, 1943, Ja 21,21:1
Yuhl, Theodore, 1941, Ja 30,21:1
Yui, D Z T, 1936, Ja 23,21:1
Yui, O K, 1960, Je 2,33:3
Yuill, Andrew J, 1954, Je 22,27:5
Yuill, Ethan A Sr, 1946, Ap 30,21:5
Yuill, William A, 1951, S 11,30:2
Yuille, Thomas B Mrs, 1944, N 3,21:2
Yuki, Toyotaro, 1951, Ag 2,21:5
Yulch, Adam, 1950, Jl 3,15:2
Yule, Annie Lady, 1950, Jl 15,13:5
Yule, Dollie Mrs, 1948, Je 6,72:3
Yule, Gladys, 1957, Ag 27,29:4
Yule, Joe, 1950, Mr 31,31:4
Yule, John, 1903, O 27,9:6
Yule, John T, 1951, D 2,4:2
Yule, Ninnian, 1943, D 15,17:1
Yules, J Morris, 1948, O 1,26:2
Yules, Jay M Mrs, 1963, N 9,25:5
Yun, Ex-Queen of Korea (funl), 1966, F 14,12:7
Yun Gee, 1963, Je 7,31:4
Yunck, John A, 1941, Ap 8,25:2
Yundt, G, 1884, Je 4,2:6
Yung, Su Kwon, 1964, D 9,47:1
Yung Kwai, 1943, Mr 21,26:7
Yung Teh-Sun, 1952, Ag 2,15:4
Yung Tsung-ching, 1938, F 14,17:3
Yung Wing, Dr, 1912, Ap 22,11:4
Yunger, Francis J, 1962, Je 19,35:4
Yunich, Max, 1966, Ja 20,35:3
Yunich, Max Mrs, 1967, Ag 25,35:3
Yunker, Arthur H, 1938, F 11,23:2
Yunker, Elkan H, 1948, Mr 21,60:4
Yunker, John P, 1952, Ag 31,45:2
Yuraho, Leon G, 1945, S 30,46:2
Yurdin, Arthur, 1959, N 17,35:5
Yurdin, Barnett, 1953, Ag 14,19:1
Yurdin, Clay, 1959, Je 16,35:3
Yurdin, Harry G, 1953, D 16,35:4
Yurev, Boris, 1957, Mr 18,27:5
Yurgrau, Ruth, 1957, N 19,33:4
Yurin, Ivan, 1951, N 29,33:5
Yurkowitz, Isador, 1961, S 30,25:1
Yurkowitz, Joseph, 1958, S 14,84:4
Yuro, Frank J, 1946, O 22,25:6
Yurramendi, Bishop, 1949, Ja 27,23:1
Yuryev, Vasily Y, 1962, F 10,23:5
Yuryev, Yuri, 1948, Mr 15,23:4
Yushkevich, Mikhail, 1952, My 14,27:2
Yushkevich, Vasili, 1951, Mr 17,15:5
Yuska, Joseph J, 1952, My 15,31:5
Yussuf, Mac, 1924, F 15,15:6
Yust, Walter, 1960, Mr 2,37:1
Yust, William F, 1947, N 17,22:3
Yuster, Samuel T, 1958, Jl 5,17:6
Yusuf Ali, Abdullah (will), 1954, Ap 11,78:5
Yute, Henry J, 1942, N 3,24:2
Yutzy, Henry C, 1966, Ja 25,41:4
Yutzy, Thomas D, 1966, Ag 1,27:4
Yuzovsky, Josif I, 1964, D 18,34:5
Yuzzolino, Albert M, 1965, F 1,23:4
Yvelin, G G, 1876, Je 18,2:6
Yves-Guyot, M, 1928, F 22,21:4
Yvetot, Georges, 1942, Mr 13,19:3
Yzabal, Rafael, 1910, O 6,11:4
Yznaga, Ellen Mrs (funl, Fe 4,7:6), 1908, Ja 25,9:5
Yznaga, Emilie, 1944, N 2,19:5

Z

Zabel, Morton D, 1964, Ap 30,35:3
Zabel, Winifred C, 1948, Ja 4,52:7
Zabelka, John G, 1949, My 19,29:3
Zabelle, Flora (Mrs Raymond Hitchcock), 1968, O 8,47:2
Zaber, Louis, 1950, Mr 30,29:3
Zaberer, C F, 1964, Ag 28,35:5
Zabielski, Thomas, 1950, Ag 21,19:5
Zabin, Barton L, 1959, S 12,21:5
Zabin, James B Mrs, 1962, O 22,29:4
Zabotin, Nicolai Col (death reptd), 1946, Je 6,7:1
Zabransky, William, 1938, Ap 30,15:4
Zabriske, Cornelius, 1907, Jl 11,7:6
Zabriske, Edward H, 1951, Jl 31,22:6
Zabriskie, A O Chancellor, 1873, Je 29,8:4
Zabriskie, Aaron J, 1914, Ap 17,11:6
Zabriskie, Albert, 1937, N 9,23:4
Zabriskie, Albert L, 1949, My 5,28:2
Zabriskie, Albert M, 1961, Ja 4,33:5
Zabriskie, Alex C, 1956, Je 25,23:5
Zabriskie, Allen J, 1961, Mr 29,33:4
Zabriskie, Alonzo M, 1913, My 5,9:2
Zabriskie, Andrew C, 1916, S 16,11:5
Zabriskie, Angelo, 1954, Jl 20,19:6
Zabriskie, C, 1879, Jl 17,1:7
Zabriskie, Chancellor Mrs, 1872, F 11,8:4
Zabriskie, Cornelius, 1964, Je 20,25:3
Zabriskie, Cornelius Mrs, 1951, Ap 18,31:3
Zabriskie, David D Ex-Judge, 1919, O 8,19:3
Zabriskie, Edward C, 1962, N 30,34:7
Zabriskie, Edwin G, 1959, Ja 14,27:1
Zabriskie, Elmer T, 1949, D 3,15:1
Zabriskie, G, 1931, O 5,21:1
Zabriskie, George A, 1954, Ja 3,88:4
Zabriskie, George Gray, 1968, Ag 17,27:6
Zabriskie, Jeremiah L Rev, 1910, Ap 4,9:4
Zabriskie, John A, 1918, F 7,11:8
Zabriskie, John B, 1951, Jl 17,27:3
Zabriskie, John T Mrs, 1947, Je 22,52:8
Zabriskie, Joseph C, 1947, Je 3,25:1
Zabriskie, Joseph H, 1910, N 3,9:5
Zabriskie, Louise, 1957, D 14,21:5
Zabriskie, Louise G, 1963, Je 12,43:4
Zabriskie, Luther K, 1921, Ja 19,11:4
Zabriskie, Madeleine, 1902, N 7,9:5
Zabriskie, N L Mrs, 1906, Mr 12,2:6
Zabriskie, Nelson, 1920, O 28,15:5
Zabriskie, Paul, 1956, Je 29,21:4
Zabriskie, Robert L, 1949, Mr 21,23:6
Zabriskie, Seaman Mrs, 1952, Ja 9,29:3
Zabriskie, Stephen T, 1939, Ap 1,19:1
Zabriskie, Thomas V B, 1942, My 25,15:5
Zabriskie, Titus Mrs (funl, Ag 28,9:6), 1910, Ag 26, 7:5
Zabriskie, William H Mrs, 1949, Ja 21,22:2
Zabronsky, Jacob O, 1948, O 14,29:4
Zabrowski, Francis L, 1956, Je 8,25:4
Zaccardi, Vincent, 1955, Mr 2,27:4
Zacchini, Ildebrando, 1948, Jl 19,19:3
Zacchini, Ildebrando Mrs, 1963, My 21,23:7
Zacchio, John Mrs, 1952, O 17,27:4
Zacconi, Ermete, 1948, O 15,23:3
Zach, Carol Ann, 1945, N 17,32:6
Zach, Max Prof, 1921, F 4,11:2
Zachak, Dorothy, 1949, Ap 21,27:8
Zacharewitsch, Michael, 1953, D 22,31:5
Zacharia, Sason I, 1966, Ap 2,29:4
Zachariae, Henri Albert, 1875, My 3,4:7
Zachariah, Isaac Mrs, 1924, S 26,21:5
Zacharias, Ellis M, 1961, Je 29,33:2
Zacharias, George J, 1957, O 20,86:4
Zacharias, Hans, 1938, S 17,17:1
Zacharias, I A Mrs, 1958, Ap 6,88:8
Zacharias, Raymond B, 1955, Ja 23,85:1
Zacharie, Paul, 1949, O 2,51:6
Zacharin, Dr, 1898, Ja 6,9:1
Zacharius, Abraham H, 1961, F 18,19:5
Zachart, Manfred M, 1942, F 18,19:2
Zachary, George J, 1964, My 11,31:3
Zacher, Edmund Judge, 1925, F 24,19:5
Zacher, Elmer H, 1944, D 22,17:5
Zacher, L Edmund, 1945, Je 29,15:1
Zacher, L Edmund Mrs, 1939, N 2,23:2
Zacher, Louis H, 1940, D 3,25:4
Zachos, Ainsworth Y, 1874, N 11,5:3
Zachos, M Helena, 1951, Mr 2,25:4
Zachow, Otto, 1942, Jl 17,15:6
Zachry, Caroline B (por), 1945, F 24,11:4
Zachry, Elsie T Mrs, 1942, Ap 25,13:4
Zachry, Greer, 1967, Mr 20,20:5
Zachs, Myron A, 1965, Ap 3,29:3
Zack, Charles S, 1942, D 6,76:3
Zack, Joseph L, 1961, My 11,37:4
Zack, Samuel G, 1951, Ap 23,25:2
Zack, Samuel R, 1960, D 6,41:4
Zacker, Edward, 1955, Ag 18,23:5
Zacker, John L, 1962, Ja 15,27:5
Zacune, Don S, 1959, Ag 29,17:5
Zadeh, Ali, 1955, Ja 6,27:4
Zadek, Isadore Mrs, 1943, Ja 22,19:2
Zademach, Erich R, 1963, N 28,39:4
Zadig, Bertrand, 1956, My 9,33:5
Zadikoff, Henry W, 1962, Ap 10,43:1
Zadkine, Ossip J, 1967, N 26,85:1
Zadora, Michael, 1946, Jl 1,31:5
Zaehringer, Annie S Mrs, 1940, F 14,21:2
Zaengle, George J Sr, 1951, Ap 19,31:4
Zaffiro, Vincent, 1948, F 12,24:3
Zagaroli, Alfredo, 1946, S 24,29:2
Zagat, Arthur L, 1949, Ap 5,29:5
Zagat, Max, 1945, N 9,19:1
Zagat, Paul H, 1962, D 29,4:5
Zagat, Paul H Mrs, 1959, Mr 1,87:1
Zagayski, Michael M, 1967, F 19,89:2
Zager, David, 1958, Je 8,89:1
Zager, Saul, 1962, My 27,93:1
Zaghloul, Said Mrs, 1946, Ja 13,44:4
Zagier, Arthur, 1948, S 10,23:3
Zaglin, Bernard, 1962, My 16,41:4
Zagonel, Bartolo, 1951, Mr 31,15:4
Zagor, Abraham, 1966, Ag 9,37:3
Zahara, Marquis de, 1946, Je 11,23:4
Zaharias, Mildred D Mrs (Babe),(funl, S 29,19:6), 1956, S 28,1:2
Zaharoff, B, 1936, N 28,1:4
Zaharoff, Lady, 1926, F 26,21:3
Zahedi, Fazlollah, 1963, S 4,39:1
Zahle, Herluf, 1941, My 6,21:3
Zahler, Abe (cor, D 22,31:5), 1959, D 21,27:4
Zahler, Max B, 1960, N 20,86:6
Zahm, Albert F, 1954, Jl 24,13:5
Zahm, John A Dr, 1921, N 12,13:5
Zahn, A Frederick, 1963, Jl 20,19:3
Zahn, Anthony F Mrs, 1944, D 27,19:3
Zahn, Arthur, 1951, Ja 30,26:3; 1952, N 19,29:3
Zahn, David L, 1962, S 26,39:4
Zahn, Edward B, 1952, My 25,94:5
Zahn, Edward J Jr, 1962, O 7,38:4
Zahn, G Walter, 1956, Mr 9,23:2
Zahn, Henry, 1913, Ag 8,7:7
Zahn, John, 1938, O 16,45:2
Zahn, John Mrs, 1950, S 19,31:2
Zahn, Max, 1937, Je 19,17:1
Zahn, Robert, 1914, Ja 22,11:5
Zahn-Harnack, Agnes von Mrs, 1950, My 25,29:4
Zahnd, John, 1961, F 4,19:5
Zahner, Kenneth A, 1950, N 9,33:5
Zahner, Martin, 1943, Ja 16,13:1
Zahniser, Howard, 1964, My 6,47:4
Zahodiakin, Victor F, 1966, My 28,27:4
Zahradka, Lewis, 1938, N 22,23:6
Zahrn, Louis A, 1942, Ap 9,20:2
Zahrndt, William F, 1943, My 3,17:4
Zaidens, Nathan, 1959, S 29,36:2
Zaikin, Ivan, 1948, N 27,18:3
Zaimis, A, 1936, S 16,25:1
Zain, Sutan M, 1962, Ap 7,25:5
Zainetti, Dante, 1950, F 16,23:5
Zaiser, Carl J, 1946, Jl 31,27:4
Zaisser, wilhelm (Gen Gomez), 1958, Mr 7,23:2
Zaitsev, Vladimir A, 1955, O 26,31:3
Zaitzeff, Leon M, 1946, D 17,38:6
Zak, Emil R, 1949, Mr 24,27:2
Zakarian, Dickran M, 1965, Mr 13,25:1
Zakharov, Feodor, 1968, Ag 31,23:2
Zakharov, Georgi, 1957, Ja 30,29:3
Zakiff, Gedalia, 1959, N 24,37:5
Zakin, Solomon Mrs, 1965, Ap 10,30:1
Zaklasnik, Frank A Sr, 1944, Jl 5,17:6
Zakrzewski, Tadeusz P, 1961, N 29,41:5
Zaladonis, Anthony, 1950, F 22,29:3
Zalamea, Alberto, 1959, D 26,13:4
Zalaznick, Abraham, 1967, Ag 18,33:2
Zalcom, Joseph A, 1960, D 13,31:3
Zaldivar, Rafael Dr, 1922, My 15,17:7
Zaleck, Mr, 1942, Mr 24,21:3
Zales, Samuel, 1960, N 27,87:1
Zaleski, Count, 1913, D 26,9:4
Zaleski, Henry M, 1966, Mr 10,33:2
Zaleski, Kawery, 1946, My 26,32:4
Zaliels, Max, 1943, My 5,27:5
Zalinski, Edmund Louis Gray Maj, 1909, Mr 11,9:5
Zalinski, M Gray Mrs, 1915, My 22,11:6
Zalinski, Moses G Gen, 1937, Ag 29,II,7:2
Zalinsky, Joseph Mrs, 1952, Jl 14,17:4
Zalitach, Myron, 1946, My 21,23:4
Zalkin, Harry, 1968, S 11,47:1
Zalkind, Mitchell, 1952, Ja 17,27:1
Zalles, Jorge E, 1954, Mr 28,88:4
Zalles, Jorge E Mrs (trb lr, Mr 26,22:7), 1951, Mr 18,88:5
Zaloom, George B, 1943, Ap 29,21:2
Zaloom, Salim E, 1940, S 11,25:5
Zalowitz, Walter, 1950, Ja 21,17:2
Zaludkowski, Elias, 1943, Je 30,21:2
Zalunski, Joseph, 1949, D 24,15:5
Zam, Barnet Mrs, 1951, F 15,31:4
Zamaris, Frank, 1958, Ag 29,23:4
Zambarano, Louise A, 1947, S 20,15:2
Zambarano, Ubaldo E, 1950, My 31,29:4
Zambiasi, Richard, 1952, D 24,17:5
Zambo, Andrew, 1952, Ag 14,23:4
Zamboni, Frank Mrs, 1963, Ap 16,35:3
Zambounis, Constantine, 1954, Ap 10,15:5
Zambrowsky, S Joshua, 1939, Ag 27,35:4
Zamecnik, John S, 1953, Je 14,85:2
Zamenhof, Ludwig Dr, 1917, Ap 16,13:5
Zamenick, Paul, 1951, Ja 15,17:4
Zametkin, Joel M, 1943, N 15,19:5
Zamlyachka, Rozalia S, 1947, Ja 23,23:6
Zammiello, Frank Mrs, 1946, Ag 21,27:2
Zamora, Alcala Mrs, 1939, My 16,23:6
Zamora, Jose A, 1938, Mr 22,10:2
Zamora, Juilo, 1923, Ap 12,19:4
Zamora, Zenon, 1952, Ja 9,29:5
Zampariello, Gaetano, 1959, Ag 5,27:3
Zampatori, Angelo, 1949, Jl 5,23:4
Zamustin, Marcus, 1945, Je 10,32:4
Zamyatin, Nikolai, 1951, S 12,31:2
Zanardelli, Premier of Italy, 1903, D 27,4:3
Zanardi-Landi, Charles Count, 1953, Ag 2,73:1
Zanarini, Frank, 1955, Ag 14,80:2
Zand, Stephen J (Jan 23), 1963, Ap 1,36:8
Zander, Gustav Dr, 1920, Je 20,18:4
Zander, Harry R, 1937, Je 16,24:1
Zander, Henry G, 1937, O 14,25:5
Zander, Walter E, 1952, S 19,23:1
Zandonai, Riccardo, 1944, Je 24,13:6
Zane, Franklin A, 1949, Mr 13,76:6
Zane, Hysler J, 1953, Mr 27,23:2
Zane, Ira (mem ser plans), 1959, F 11,39:4
Zane, John M, 1937, D 8,25:4
Zanes, Pearl, 1943, Ja 15,18:1
Zanetti, Anthony A, 1952, F 16,13:2
Zanft, John, 1960, N 20,86:6
Zang, Anselm, 1942, Ja 4,48:4
Zangerle, John A, 1956, O 2,35:4
Zangwill, I, 1926, Ag 2,1:2
Zangwill, Israel Mrs, 1945, My 9,23:5
Zangwill, Louis, 1938, Je 1,23:4
Zaniboni, Tito, 1960, D 28,4:7
Zanin, Mario, 1958, Ag 5,27:1
Zanker, John H, 1947, S 3,26:3
Zanlunghi, Charles Mrs, 1966, Ja 10,44:8
Zanlunghi, Vicki, 1966, Ja 10,44:8
Zanoni, Angelo, 1942, S 16,23:4
Zanou, Thalia (A Lachmund), 1956, Ag 8,25:6
Zantzinger, Clarence C, 1954, S 27,21:2
Zantzinger, Clarence C Mrs, 1958, Ja 17,25:3
Zanzibar, Sultan of (Seyyid Sir Khalifa bin Harub bin Thwain), 1960, O 10,31:2
Zanzibar, Sultan of (Seyyid Sir Abdullah bin Khalifa), 1963, Jl 2,29:4
Zap, Edward F, 1952, D 15,25:2
Zapata, Emiliano Mrs, 1964, F 19,39:5; 1968, Ag 11, 72:6
Zapata, Jantonion, 1946, O 10,27:5
Zapf, Herman R, 1948, O 14,29:4
Zaph, Stamatis D, 1947, Mr 8,13:5
Zapke, Edward, 1940, Mr 11,15:1
Zapolin, Jack Mrs, 1950, Ja 13,23:3
Zapotocky, Antonin President (funl plans, N 14,33:4), 1957, N 13,1:2
Zappa, Antonio, 1957, N 21,33:2
Zappala, Joseph, 1942, D 29,21:2
Zappas, James L, 1946, Jl 23,25:5
Zappey, John F, 1956, Jl 5,25:3
Zappone, Ricardo D, 1951, Mr 10,31:2
Zarankiewicz, Kazimer, 1959, S 6,72:8
Zardini, Sergio, 1966, F 22,17:3
Zardo, Eric, 1956, Ja 9,25:4
Zareh I, Catolicos, 1963, F 19,8:8
Zarek, Otto, 1958, Ag 22,21:1
Zareko, John, 1942, S 10,48:3
Zaret, Leon, 1958, Je 10,33:3
Zaretski, Louis E, 1958, F 26,27:1
Zaretsky, Benjamin, 1950, Jl 11,32:2
Zaretzki, Sol, 1952, My 9,23:3
Zaretzky, Morris, 1944, Ap 9,34:4
Zaretzky, Samuel Mrs, 1953, My 19,29:3
Zari, Angelo B, 1956, Ap 16,27:3
Zaritsky, Max, 1959, My 11,27:2
Zarnekau, Anna Countess, 1959, O 24,21:6
Zarnocay, Samuel, 1950, Je 17,15:1
Zarnower, Teresa, 1949, My 3,25:2
Zaro, Henry C, 1949, Ag 7,61:2
Zarobsky, Ivan F, 1953, Ag 14,19:2
Zaroubin, Georgi, 1958, N 26,29:1
Zarrillo, Michael C, 1965, My 26,47:1
Zartman, George W, 1943, Mr 4,21:7
Zartman, Rufus C, 1946, My 17,22:3
Zartman, Samuel B, 1959, Ag 2,81:1
Zary, Henry P, 1946, F 14,26:3
Zarzecki, Walter, 1945, Jl 31,19:3
Zaslav, Louis M, 1948, Jl 23,19:2
Zaslavsky, David I, 1965, Mr 29,36:2
Zaslaw, Myer, 1943, Ja 23,13:3

Zaslawsky, Georges, 1953, Ja 30,21:1
Zasloff, Ira B, 1967, Jl 22,25:5
Zaslowsky, David R, 1947, D 4,31:2
Zasofsky, Paul, 1923, F 21,15:4
Zasowski, Anthony F, 1962, Ap 29,86:5
Zastron, Heinrich Adolf Von, 1875, Ag 14,1:1
Zastrow, Irvin E, 1958, O 14,37:2
Zasyadko, Aleksandr F, 1963, S 6,29:2
Zathureczky, Ede, 1959, Je 1,27:5
Zatkovitch, Gregory I, 1967, Mr 29,45:4
Zatkowsky, Benjamin, 1950, Jl 26,25:4
Zatrapeznoff, Peter Mrs, 1943, Ap 24,13:4
Zauderer, George, 1940, N 5,25:6
Zauderer, Irving, 1967, D 5,50:8
Zaugg, John L, 1958, Jl 4,19:2
Zaugg, John L Mrs, 1951, S 19,31:1
Zaumeyer, Robert J, 1951, O 20,15:3
Zaun, William, 1905, D 31,2:3
Zauner, Henry, 1944, Ja 16,41:7
Zauner, Joseph, 1954, Ja 26,27:1
Zauner, Leslie A, 1952, Je 24,29:4
Zauner, Waldo R, 1953, My 13,29:3
Zausner, Meyer, 1954, Ap 4,88:1
Zaustinsky, Michael V, 1959, D 6,86:4
Zavadovsky, Mikhail M, 1957, Mr 31,88:1
Zavadsky, Charles, 1949, N 12,15:2
Zavala, Luis V, 1958, Jl 25,19:2
Zavarine, Igor N, 1961, Ag 22,29:1
Zavatsky, Mary Mrs, 1955, My 3,31:2
Zavatta, Mantova R, 1940, Ap 4,23:4
Zavell, Lawrence S, 1957, D 23,23:3
Zavell, Sol, 1946, D 25,29:1
Zavell, Sol Mrs, 1940, F 8,23:3
Zavenyagin, Avraamy P, 1957, Ja 2,27:1
Zavodoff, Fred E, 1952, N 11,29:1
Zavoico, Stephen V, 1958, Ap 6,88:6
Zavoico, Vassily S, 1947, Je 9,21:3
Zawadzki, Aleksander, 1964, Ag 8,19:4
Zawadzki, Bohdan, 1966, S 24,23:2
Zawistowski, Rene Rev, 1968, Ap 25,47:3
Zayas, A, 1934, Ap 12,23:4
Zayas, A Octavio, 1942, S 15,23:5
Zayas, Alfredo Mrs, 1962, Mr 25,88:6
Zayas, Jose de Mrs, 1913, D 22,9:6
Zayas, Oscar, 1943, Mr 28,24:4
Zayas y Ayala, Juan B, 1939, Ag 19,15:4
Zayats, Nikolai, 1950, Ja 4,35:1
Zaytoun, Nasimia Mrs, 1955, N 23,23:2
Zazeela, Herman A, 1966, Je 5,86:8
Zazove, Frederick, 1963, N 11,31:6
Zazzarino, Leonard, 1949, F 14,19:2
Zazzaro, Anthony P, 1945, My 22,19:3
Zazzaro, Michael R, 1956, D 4,39:5
Zbarsky, Boris I, 1954, O 16,17:2
Zbawiony, Ignatius, 1946, O 2,29:5
Zborowski, Margaret Countess (Mrs Wm Elliott), 1911, Jl 11,7:5
Zbranak, Joseph, 1954, Ja 12,23:4
Zbyszko, Stanislaus, 1967, S 24,84:4
Zbyszko, Wladek C, 1968, Je 11,44:2
Zdaniecki, Francis E, 1956, Ag 20,21:4
Zdrubek, Frank B, 1911, S 16,7:7
Zdunek, Edward W, 1963, D 13,36:1
Zealand, Jonathan, 1953, Mr 19,29:4
Zealand, Joseph G Father, 1904, F 19,9:6
Zeamer, Jay, 1955, Ag 26,19:6
Zeamer, Jay Sr Mrs, 1954, S 9,31:3
Zeamer, Wisler G, 1939, S 11,19:5
Zearfaus, George, 1954, Je 19,15:5
Zebalios, Estanislao Dr, 1923, O 5,19:1
Zebina, Anna B, 1952, O 29,29:5
Zebrowski, Wladyslaw, 1947, My 9,21:4
Zecchino, Frank, 1948, D 17,27:2
Zech, Nicholas P, 1947, N 10,29:2
Zech-Burkersroda, Julius Count von, 1946, O 24,27:3
Zechiel, George, 1951, Mr 26,23:4
Zechnowitz, Jacob, 1965, Ag 23,31:4
Zechnowitz, Samuel, 1942, Ag 22,13:5
Zeckel, Adolph, 1955, Mr 19,15:6
Zeckendorf, Erich, 1965, S 16,47:2
Zeckendorf, William Sr Mrs (will, Mr 28,21:6), 1968, Mr 7,16:3
Zecker, Aaron Rabbi, 1925, Ap 27,17:5
Zeckwer, Camille W, 1924, Ag 9,11:6
Zeddies, Robert F Sr, 1962, My 31,27:4
Zedeikis, Povilas, 1957, My 14,10:1
Zeder, Fred M, 1951, F 25,84:3
Zederbaum, Michael C, 1944, Ja 26,19:3
Zedlitz-Truetzschler, Robert, 1942, Jl 18,13:6
Zedtwitz, Elizabeth von Baroness, 1910, D 23,13:4
Zee, John K, 1910, My 27,9:3
Zeech, Peter P, 1948, Je 9,29:2
Zeeder, Adrian, 1965, F 22,21:2
Zeeman, Abraham, 1955, Jl 31,68:5
Zeeman, Henry, 1963, Jl 18,27:4
Zeeman, Pieter, 1943, O 13,23:1
Zeffner-Spitzenberg, Baron, 1938, Ag 7,25:4
Zegada, Jose, 1955, O 21,12:4
Zegar, Frances Mrs, 1941, D 29,15:2
Zegarra, Enrique Coronel, 1919, O 17,17:5
Zegers, Theodore S Mrs, 1955, My 26,31:3
Zegreckis, Paul Sr, 1949, S 24,13:5
Zeh, Frank L, 1961, Ja 16,27:3
Zeh, Fred, 1947, N 27,31:4
Zeh, William A, 1964, My 12,37:6
Zehder, Henry J, 1960, O 13,37:3
Zehe, Paul E (will), 1943, N 6,16:1
Zehetner, Francis (Bro Aubert), 1960, Ja 22,25:1
Zehlein, Edward Mrs, 1956, Ap 17,31:1
Zehmer, George B, 1961, Ja 16,27:6
Zehnbauer, Leonard Mrs, 1959, O 22,37:2
Zehnder, A Charles, 1955, D 3,17:5
Zehner, Dorothy, 1965, Ja 18,35:2
Zehner, Harry H, 1957, N 23,19:7
Zehrer, Hans, 1966, Ag 25,37:4
Zehrer, Theodor A Mrs, 1956, D 2,86:1
Zei, Fred W, 1940, Jl 25,17:3
Zeichen, Catherine V, 1950, N 22,25:1
Zeichen, Peter, 1949, O 16,88:5
Zeichner, Nathan, 1968, Ag 24,29:5
Zeide, Asher, 1944, Mr 5,36:2
Zeidler, Frank W, 1964, S 26,23:5
Zeidler, Gilbert F, 1952, F 7,27:5
Zeidler, Michael Mrs, 1950, Ap 10,19:2
Zeidler, William A, 1943, Jl 24,13:4
Zeigen, Frederick H, 1942, My 27,23:5
Zeiger, Joseph J, 1963, S 5,31:1
Zeigler, J Henry, 1951, My 2,31:4
Zeigler, J Henry Mrs, 1968, Ja 28,76:4
Zeigler, Jacob B, 1946, D 9,25:4
Zeigler, James N, 1967, S 16,33:4
Zeigler, Loyall P, 1962, S 30,86:7
Zeigler, Raymond L, 1956, S 10,27:5
Zeigner, Joseph, 1965, Ag 27,29:2
Zeileis, Valentin, 1939, Jl 18,19:5
Zeilenbach, William, 1939, D 29,15:1
Zeiler, A Herman, 1943, Jl 17,13:5
Zeilin, Jacob (see also N 19), 1880, N 22,5:2
Zeilin, W F, 1880, Je 6,5:4
Zeiner, Edward J A, 1942, N 25,23:5
Zeinz, Henry J, 1944, Je 23,19:6
Zeis, Peter A, 1921, S 22,17:6
Zeisberg, Carl F L, 1950, Je 8,31:2
Zeisberg, Frederick C, 1938, N 13,45:2
Zeisel, Oscar, 1958, Jl 26,15:6
Zeiser, Adlow, 1953, Jl 29,23:5
Zeiser, Blasius J, 1951, My 11,27:4
Zeiser, Dagobert, 1925, Ap 9,23:4
Zeiser, Henry E, 1950, Mr 5,92:5
Zeiser, Matthew Sr, 1960, S 3,17:6
Zeishold, Frederick H, 1947, F 9,61:1
Zeisler, Joseph Dr, 1919, S 1,7:4
Zeisler, Max H Mrs, 1961, S 2,15:6
Zeismann, Hirsh, 1903, My 18,2:5
Zeiss, August W Mrs, 1959, Ap 27,27:2
Zeiter, John E, 1956, S 25,33:4
Zeitfuchs, Edward, 1950, N 4,17:4
Zeitler, Frank H, 1940, Ag 1,21:5
Zeitler, Fred A, 1946, Ja 1,27:2
Zeitlin, Alexandre, 1946, Mr 5,25:4
Zeitlin, Florence, 1905, S 8,6:6
Zeitlin, Isaac Mrs, 1951, O 9,29:2
Zeitlin, Jacob H, 1963, D 21,23:2
Zeitlin, Jacob Prof, 1937, D 9,25:4
Zeitlin, Louis, 1951, Je 21,27:1
Zeitlin, Zalman Mrs, 1967, Je 11,86:3
Zeitsoff, Dave, 1955, F 2,27:3
Zeitz, Barney, 1946, S 24,30:3
Zeitz, Herman A, 1939, Ag 1,19:5
Zeitz, Julius C, 1943, S 1,19:2
Zeitz, Louis Mrs, 1951, Ag 21,27:3
Zeitz, Marvin, 1946, Jl 19,19:4
Zeitz, Milton M, 1962, My 4,33:1
Zeitz, William, 1952, S 28,77:2
Zeitzmann, William G, 1951, My 15,31:3
Zelada, Alberto, 1939, Mr 21,23:1
Zelaya, Carlos A, 1951, D 16,90:6
Zelaya, Jose Santos Gen, 1919, My 19,17:5
Zelcer, F William, 1960, Mr 31,33:5
Zeldin, Isidor, 1948, D 22,23:1
Zeldin, Samuel, 1961, Ag 29,31:4
Zeldow, Louis, 1944, O 28,15:2
Zelenko, Michael, 1950, Ja 28,13:3
Zeleny, Charles, 1939, D 22,19:5
Zeleny, John, 1951, Je 20,27:1
Zelezinski, John F, 1957, S 28,17:1
Zelie, John S, 1942, N 11,25:4
Zeligowski, Lucjan, 1947, Jl 11,15:5
Zelinka, Max, 1957, Je 11,35:4
Zelinski, Benjamin P, 1951, F 11,88:3
Zelinsky, Charles S, 1952, S 5,27:3
Zelinsky, Nicolai, 1953, Ag 2,72:7
Zell, David Mrs, 1958, Mr 15,17:3
Zell, Joan, 1961, Jl 13,61:3
Zelle, Charles E, 1937, Ap 2,23:5
Zeller, Albert T, 1950, D 10,104:6
Zeller, Alex R, 1954, Je 16,31:2
Zeller, Ben, 1963, D 10,43:3
Zeller, Edward Mrs, 1954, Jl 30,17:2
Zeller, Frank B, 1964, My 7,37:2
Zeller, Frank L, 1952, My 5,23:6
Zeller, Frank Mrs, 1944, O 29,43:1
Zeller, George A, 1938, Je 30,23:5
Zeller, Harry L Mrs, 1955, Ja 1,13:5
Zeller, Henry C, 1942, S 9,23:3
Zeller, Herman A, 1942, S 29,23:3
Zeller, John, 1946, F 15,26:3
Zeller, John G, 1939, Ja 3,18:1
Zeller, Joseph A, 1964, Jl 11,25:1
Zeller, Joseph W, 1961, D 11,31:5
Zeller, Julius C, 1938, Mr 12,17:6
Zeller, Julius C Mrs, 1946, Ap 28,44:5
Zeller, Louis W, 1951, O 24,32:2
Zeller, Theodore Commodore, 1901, Jl 1,7:5
Zeller, Walter P, 1957, Ag 27,29:1
Zeller, William F, 1951, N 16,25:2
Zeller, William G, 1950, Je 13,27:1
Zellerbach, Eugene, 1961, Jl 23,68:3
Zellerbach, Isadore Mrs, 1965, O 30,35:2
Zellerbach, James D (funl, Ag 5,29:3), 1963, Ag 4, 81:2
Zellermayer, Abraham, 1949, D 21,29:1
Zellers, Annie W Mrs, 1948, S 1,24:3
Zellers, Emlen H Jr, 1957, O 22,33:2
Zellers, John A, 1954, Ap 30,24:3
Zelley, Henry J, 1942, Mr 18,23:3
Zelley, Samuel Z, 1955, F 4,15:4
Zellman, Charles J, 1950, Ap 19,29:5
Zellmer, John, 1944, S 2,11:5
Zellner, Arthur J, 1952, S 10,29:6
Zellweger, Frederic C, 1944, Mr 25,15:3
Zelnick, Phil, 1958, N 10,29:2
Zelony, Isaac, 1956, D 9,88:5
Zelt, Albert R, 1950, My 8,23:4
Zelter, Alfred R, 1951, Mr 18,88:5
Zeltner, Charles H (cor, S 2,21:1), 1937, S 1,19:5
Zeltner, Edward, 1964, My 5,43:4
Zeltner, Henry, 1963, S 13,29:2
Zeltner, Louis, 1953, My 13,29:5
Zeltner, Louis Mrs, 1959, N 11,35:1
Zeluff, Czar E, 1945, My 29,15:4
Zelwerowicz, Aleksander, 1955, Je 26,77:1
Zelzer, Rudolph S, 1952, S 26,21:2
Zema, Demetrius B (por), 1948, F 3,25:5
Zema, Gabriel A, 1959, Ag 14,21:4
Zema, Walter S, 1952, S 7,83:1
Zemachson, Arnold, 1956, Je 25,23:3
Zeman, Anton T, 1954, Ap 24,17:4
Zeman, Bernard R, 1944, Je 13,19:5
Zeman, Frank J, 1941, Ja 3,19:5
Zeman, Martin, 1951, F 14,29:1
Zemansky, Abraham P Mrs, 1946, F 9,13:3
Zembach, Nahum, 1939, S 9,17:5
Zemko, Ludwig, 1944, O 3,23:1
Zemlinsky, Alex von, 1942, Mr 17,21:4
Zemsky, Alex, 1945, Mr 14,19:1
Zemukhamedov, G A, 1951, Ag 22,23:1
Zemurray, Samuel, 1961, D 2,23:2
Zemurray, Samuel Jr Mrs, 1968, Je 29,29:5
Zenatello, Giovanni, 1949, F 12,18:3
Zenatello, Maria G (por), 1943, Jl 31,13:3
Zendman, Isaac Jr, 1944, Je 9,15:3
Zendt, Oliver M, 1954, Mr 22,27:2
Zener, Karl E, 1964, S 28,29:5
Zener, Virgil, 1952, Ag 14,23:5
Zengals, Gustav (por), 1939, Ja 8,42:7
Zengerle, Walter C, 1954, D 7,33:3
Zengevald, Stephen, 1950, Mr 15,29:3
Zeni, Luisa, 1940, Jl 25,17:4
Zenker, Charles, 1956, Je 11,31:3
Zenker, Rudolph, 1952, Jl 8,27:4
Zenneck, Junius F, 1944, My 31,19:5
Zenner, David R, 1950, O 18,33:5
Zenner, Phil, 1956, Je 27,31:4
Zenner, Philip M, 1960, Je 20,31:5
Zennstroem, M Gustava Mrs, 1954, Mr 7,90:8
Zenos, Andrew C, 1942, Ja 26,15:4
Zentgraf, George J, 1957, Ja 23,29:2
Zentmayer, William, 1958, Mr 20,29:4
Zentner, Julius, 1953, Ja 8,27:3
Zentner, Morris M, 1940, D 10,25:5
Zenzinov, Vladimir, 1953, O 21,29:4
Zepeda, Gustavo, 1948, My 5,25:1
Zepeda, Maximo H, 1946, Je 12,27:1
Zepf, Albert E, 1942, My 28,17:1
Zepf, Herman E, 1950, Ap 26,29:3
Zepf, William G, 1938, N 17,25:3
Zeph, Charles F, 1947, D 26,15:2
Zeph, Jules E Sr, 1947, S 25,29:5
Zepin, George, 1963, Ap 11,33:2
Zepin, George Mrs, 1955, Ja 4,21:1
Zepp, Charles A (will), 1953, F 26,27:6
Zepp, Clarence P Sr, 1964, O 3,29:3
Zepp, Maynard E, 1938, Jl 15,17:6
Zeppelin, Ferdinand von Count (funl, Mr 13,11:4), 1917, Mr 9,7:1
Zeppelin, Ferdinand von Count, 1937, O 29,22:2
Zeramby, Jacob, 1959, Je 2,35:1
Zeratsky, A W, 1940, F 13,23:2
Zerbarini, Angelo J, 1950, F 19,76:8
Zerbas, Napoleon, 1957, D 11,31:3
Zerbato, Angelo, 1942, D 16,25:5
Zerbe, Arthur J, 1951, O 6,19:4
Zerbe, Farran, 1949, D 27,23:1
Zerbe, John I, 1940, Je 17,15:6
Zerbe, William H, 1943, Ja 6,25:6
Zerbee, Leigh F J, 1952, Je 8,85:1
Zerbey, Joseph Jr, 1945, F 18,34:6
Zerbey, Joseph R 3d, 1958, Jl 4,19:5

Zerbo, Valerio, 1963, D 18,41:3
Zerbst, Frederick G, 1950, Ja 26,27:6
Zeredny, Mikita, 1950, My 12,27:4
Zerega, Alfred L B di, 1920, Ja 13,13:3
Zerega, Augustus Mrs, 1909, Mr 28,13:5
Zerega, Frank L, 1967, Ap 18,41:3
Zerega, Richard A, 1956, My 14,25:4
Zerega di Zerega, Louis A, 1949, Mr 16,27:2
Zerfas, Milton R, 1950, Ap 19,29:5
Zerfass, Julius, 1956, Mr 26,29:2
Zerfing, Wilson, 1955, Ja 16,92:5
Zerk, Oscar Ulysses, 1968, D 10,77:2
Zerkowitz, Emil, 1923, Mr 9,15:4
Zerman, Morris, 1951, N 20,31:4
Zernatto, Guido, 1943, F 10,25:2
Zernentsch, Joseph M, 1955, Ap 8,21:2
Zerner, Charles S, 1956, Ag 18,17:1
Zerner, Ernest Mrs, 1948, N 28,92:3
Zerner, Ernst, 1966, D 28,43:1
Zernike, Frits, 1966, Mr 16,45:3
Zernov, Pavel M, 1964, F 10,27:5
Zeromski, Stefan, 1925, N 24,25:3
Zerr, Andrew F, 1958, F 26,27:5
Zerr, George A, 1953, Ja 23,19:3
Zerrahn, Carl, 1909, D 30,9:5
Zerrener, Nicholas, 1915, Je 5,9:6
Zerrett, W R Rev, 1902, My 5,9:6
Zervakos, Chris E, 1945, Ap 13,17:2
Zervas, Alex, 1957, D 11,31:3
Zerweck, James W, 1960, S 2,23:1
Zess, William, 1951, Mr 4,25:1
Zetek, James, 1959, Je 4,31:2
Zetena, Dominick F, 1954, Ag 27,21:6
Zeth, John L Mrs, 1950, S 23,17:5
Zetka, Joseph B, 1950, Jl 16,69:2
Zetkin, C, 1933, Je 21,17:4
Zetland, Lord, 1929, Mr 12,29:1
Zetland, Marquess of (L J L Dundas), 1961, F 7,33:2
Zetlin, Carlton H, 1906, My 8,9:6
Zetosch, Harry, 1937, Je 14,38:4
Zett, Robert N Mrs, 1951, My 20,88:6
Zettlein, George, 1905, My 24,9:6
Zettler, Emil, 1946, Ja 12,15:4
Zettler, Joseph A, 1956, O 27,21:3
Zettler, Oscar, 1953, My 20,29:5
Zetumer, Samuel, 1964, Mr 30,29:3
Zetzmann, William G, 1962, Ap 14,25:3
Zeuch, William E, 1963, Je 4,39:4
Zeuner, Frederick E, 1963, N 7,37:5
Zevaez, Alexandre, 1953, F 22,60:8
Zevely, J W, 1927, Je 11,19:2
Zevhel, Franz, 1949, F 24,23:3
Zewin, Mordecai Rabbi, 1923, Jl 28,7:6
Zhavoronkov, Semen F, 1967, Je 11,87:2
Zhdanov, Andrei A, 1948, S 1,1:5
Zhebrak, Anton R, 1965, My 23,85:1
Zhelesnik, Joseph J, 1949, Ja 14,24:3
Zhelesnik, Sandor, 1952, Ja 4,23:2
Zhigarev, Pavel, 1963, O 5,25:1
Zhilat, A Edward, 1952, D 10,35:2
Zhitlowsky, Chaim, 1943, My 7,19:4
Zholtovsky, Ivan V, 1959, Jl 17,21:3
Zhrun, Johana Sister, 1952, Ja 3,27:3
Zhuk, Sergei Y, 1957, Mr 9,7:1
Zhukov, Gavril V, 1957, Ja 11,23:3
Zhukov, Vsevolod V, 1955, Je 2,29:2
Zhupanchich, Oton, 1949, Je 13,19:2
Zicarelli, Joseph, 1948, Je 30,25:4
Zicha, August R, 1944, S 11,17:2
Zichella, Ralph, 1959, Ap 13,31:4
Zichim, Inez, 1917, Ag 6,9:3
Zichner, Hugo, 1945, Mr 31,19:5
Zichy, Geza Count, 1924, Ja 16,19:6
Zichy, Maria P, 1962, Ag 14,31:2
Zickl, Rupert T, 1956, S 26,33:1
Zickler, James A, 1949, F 14,19:1
Zickler, James A Mrs, 1941, D 17,27:6
Zicok, William, 1905, Mr 22,9:6
Zicovich, Maximilian J, 1951, S 27,31:2
Zide, William, 1956, Mr 28,31:5
Ziebelli, Louis, 1949, My 19,30:3
Zieber, Phil S, 1940, Jl 3,17:5
Zieckler, Ernest, 1954, F 2,27:5
Ziefle, John F, 1942, Je 16,23:4
Ziegel, Ferdinand, 1910, S 3,7:6
Ziegelmeier, Arthur, 1945, F 20,19:3
Ziegenbein, Leopold, 1950, Je 23,26:2
Ziegener, August, 1955, My 3,31:3
Ziegenfus, Frank A Mrs, 1941, Mr 10,17:5
Ziegenhein, William J, 1965, Jl 10,25:5
Zieger, Ernest, 1950, Ja 8,77:1
Ziegfeld, Carl Mrs, 1949, S 23,24:3
Ziegfeld, F, 1932, Jl 23,1:3
Ziegfeld, Hugo, 1952, Ag 23,13:6
Ziegfeld, Robert L, 1966, Ja 12,21:5
Ziegfield, Carl, 1921, Ag 8,11:7
Ziegfield, Florenz Dr, 1923, My 21,15:5
Ziegler, Anna E Mrs, 1944, Ja 8,13:3
Ziegler, Augustus B, 1960, Ap 17,92:7
Ziegler, Carl A, 1952, O 22,27:6
Ziegler, Carl A Mrs, 1961, Je 5,31:4
Ziegler, Charles E, 1950, Ap 28,21:2
Ziegler, Charles F, 1957, S 23,27:6
Ziegler, Charles T, 1943, S 23,21:3
Ziegler, Christian H, 1957, S 2,13:5
Ziegler, E Willard, 1950, Ag 17,28:3
Ziegler, Edouard, 1941, Ap 5,17:2
Ziegler, Edward, 1941, My 22,21:3; 1947, O 26,68:5
Ziegler, Edward Mrs, 1943, O 15,19:2
Ziegler, Edward P, 1950, Ja 8,77:1
Ziegler, Elias, 1959, Mr 22,86:8
Ziegler, Ferd, 1961, Ja 25,33:4
Ziegler, Frances A Mrs, 1942, Je 11,23:3
Ziegler, Frank P, 1939, D 23,15:4
Ziegler, Frederick J, 1966, Ap 28,43:3
Ziegler, Fridolin, 1959, Ja 31,19:4
Ziegler, George, 1920, Ap 6,11:6
Ziegler, Gottlieb D, 1961, Je 25,76:5
Ziegler, Helen T, 1940, Jl 15,15:4
Ziegler, Herman, 1943, Ap 3,15:1
Ziegler, Israel, 1956, S 8,17:1
Ziegler, Jay L, 1961, N 16,39:1
Ziegler, Jerome I, 1950, Je 18,76:3
Ziegler, Jerome M, 1941, Ag 26,19:5
Ziegler, Jerome M Mrs, 1962, Jl 7,17:4
Ziegler, Jesse A, 1947, N 17,21:3
Ziegler, John W, 1938, Jl 25,15:6
Ziegler, Joseph, 1939, N 10,23:1
Ziegler, Joseph D, 1954, O 22,27:2
Ziegler, Lee W, 1952, Je 17,28:4
Ziegler, Lloyd H, 1945, Ja 10,23:6
Ziegler, Louis, 1950, Mr 18,13:2
Ziegler, Marcus W, 1959, Ja 11,88:2
Ziegler, Nelson T, 1951, O 31,29:1
Ziegler, Orville B, 1947, Mr 27,27:4
Ziegler, Otto, 1952, S 6,17:6
Ziegler, Phil E, 1957, Ap 22,25:1
Ziegler, Samuel H, 1947, Mr 11,27:2
Ziegler, W Sr Mrs, 1932, S 2,15:1
Ziegler, William, 1905, My 25,1:1
Ziegler, William (est appr), 1906, N 4,1:6
Ziegler, William, 1937, Ag 4,19:5; 1945, Ja 16,19:2
Ziegler, William H, 1953, Ja 24,15:6
Ziegler, William Jr, 1957, Je 22,15:2
Ziegler, William Jr (trb lr, Mr 13,28:5), 1958, Mr 4, 29:1
Zieglschmid, A J, 1950, Ap 16,104:5
Ziegner, Herman R, 1964, Je 20,25:2
Ziegner, Martin E, 1964, D 11,42:1
Ziegra, Louis A, 1952, N 23,88:1
Zielie, Mart W, 1946, F 2,13:3
Zielinski, John, 1945, Ag 31,17:3
Zielinski, John F, 1952, Ja 26,13:2
Zielinski, Michael, 1948, F 2,19:5
Zielonka, Samuel, 1947, Ag 27,23:3
Ziem, Felix, 1911, N 11,13:5
Ziemak, John W, 1960, Ap 8,31:3
Zieman, Albert Mrs, 1958, Ja 18,15:6
Zieman, Gustave A, 1948, F 17,26:2
Ziemann, P P W, 1960, O 10,31:2
Ziemba, Joseph V, 1949, Ag 2,19:4
Ziemer, Gustav, 1944, Mr 30,21:6
Ziemer, Gustav T, 1947, D 31,15:3
Ziemssen, Hugo von Dr, 1902, Ja 21,9:5
Ziengenfus, William C, 1937, Ap 11,II,9:2
Zier, Calvin V, 1954, S 1,27:2
Ziernicki, Anthony, 1949, F 27,69:1
Zierolshofen, Paul H von, 1948, Ja 21,26:3
Zieschang, Rudolph A, 1961, D 25,23:4
Ziesing, Aug, 1942, F 17,21:3
Ziesing, Richard Jr, 1968, Ja 11,37:2
Zieske, Arthur H, 1951, O 26,23:3
Ziesse, Elizabeth, 1941, Ag 24,34:1
Zietsman, Johannes, 1924, Jl 16,11:5
Zietz, Hyman Mrs, 1939, O 11,27:2
Zietz, Morris, 1953, My 7,32:3
Ziev, Harry, 1950, Ag 22,27:2
Ziff, Joseph, 1954, Ag 5,23:3
Ziff, William B, 1953, D 21,31:1
Zifferblatt, George Mrs, 1955, D 27,23:1
Zigel, Samuel, 1944, F 21,15:3
Zigmund-Cerbu, Anton, 1964, Mr 11,39:4
Zigmund-Cerbu, Anton Mrs, 1965, Ag 17,33:2
Zijl, L, 1947, Ja 18,15:5
Zilahy, Michael, 1949, N 29,20:6
Zilber, Lev A, 1966, N 12,29:4
Zilbert, Jack, 1953, Jl 3,19:2
Zilberts, Zavel (por), 1949, Ap 26,25:3
Zilboorg, Gregory, 1959, S 18,31:2
Zilcher, Hermann, 1948, Ja 18,60:8
Zilenziger, Carl B, 1938, D 18,49:2
Zilevicius, Joseph Mrs, 1951, Je 1,23:3
Zilinskas, George, 1957, Mr 18,27:6
Zilkha, Khedoury, 1956, Jl 1,56:5
Zilkha, Maurice K, 1964, My 28,37:1
Zilliacus, Konni (lr on obit, Jl 15,24:4), 1967, Jl 7, 33:1
Zillig, Friedrich K, 1950, O 3,31:1
Zillig, William J, 1945, My 24,19:4
Zillmann, Harold A, 1958, Mr 3,27:1
Zilow, Janina Mrs, 1957, F 11,29:5
Ziman, Bernard M, 1967, S 9,31:3
Zimand, Savel, 1967, D 19,47:2
Zimand, Savel Mrs, 1966, My 11,47:2
Zimbalist, Aaron Mrs, 1951, Je 24,73:1
Zimbalist, Alma G (will), 1938, D 16,28:7
Zimbalist, Efrem Jr Mrs, 1950, Ja 20,25:2
Zimbalist, Sam, 1958, N 5,39:1
Zimbalist, Samuel, 1956, D 27,25:4
Zimber, Isaac, 1956, Ja 27,23:2
Zimbler, Josef, 1959, Ap 12,86:3
Zimel, Heyman, 1966, Ja 1,17:3
Zimet, David J, 1944, Ag 26,11:2
Zimet, Henry, 1959, Je 22,25:5
Zimetbaum, Israel (por), 1946, F 5,23:4
Ziminsky, Honora O Mrs, 1942, Ag 11,19:5
Ziminsky, Victor D Mrs, 1961, S 25,33:3
Zimmer, Alvah J, 1941, Ja 7,23:4
Zimmer, Benedict F, 1941, Mr 17,17:3
Zimmer, Clement (death laid to fall, Mr 15,4:4), 1955, Mr 13,20:5
Zimmer, David, 1943, S 8,23:5
Zimmer, Delmer S, 1946, Ja 21,23:3
Zimmer, Donald Dr, 1968, Ag 13,36:3
Zimmer, Edward G, 1944, Ag 18,13:5
Zimmer, Eugene J, 1943, Ja 14,21:5
Zimmer, Frederick H, 1952, Jl 15,21:1; 1967, D 1,47:3
Zimmer, Frederick W, 1940, S 22,49:1
Zimmer, H Ward, 1955, Ja 29,15:1
Zimmer, Harrison, 1938, D 19,23:4
Zimmer, Henry J Msgr, 1920, Ag 29,20:5
Zimmer, Henry R, 1943, Mr 21,27:1
Zimmer, Jacob, 1957, Ja 6,88:8
Zimmer, John C, 1964, My 19,37:3
Zimmer, John T, 1957, Ja 7,25:1
Zimmer, John T Mrs, 1945, O 12,23:3
Zimmer, Joseph J, 1950, Ap 21,23:3
Zimmer, Louis Lee, 1906, Ja 15,2:7
Zimmer, Michael, 1952, D 7,88:4
Zimmer, Morris A Dr, 1937, Ja 17,II,8:3
Zimmer, Myron J, 1949, F 8,25:2
Zimmer, R N, 1957, Ja 6,57:4
Zimmer, Verne A, 1946, D 26,26:2
Zimmer, Virginia, 1946, D 26,2:5
Zimmer, Walter F, 1949, O 29,15:5
Zimmer, William, 1948, Je 10,25:5
Zimmer, William B, 1945, F 7,21:6
Zimmer, William B (por), 1948, S 9,27:3
Zimmer, William C, 1961, Ag 12,17:2
Zimmer, William J Mrs, 1950, Ag 29,27:5
Zimmerer, Carl P, 1953, Ap 25,15:5
Zimmerer, Edmund G, 1963, Jl 3,27:2
Zimmering, Paul, 1956, O 18,33:1
Zimmerli, Adolph, 1967, D 21,37:4
Zimmerman, A Wallace, 1964, My 12,37:5
Zimmerman, Aaron M, 1954, Jl 8,23:5
Zimmerman, Adam H, 1967, N 1,47:2
Zimmerman, Albert, 1960, Mr 1,33:4
Zimmerman, Albert C, 1945, Ja 21,40:2
Zimmerman, Albert G, 1947, F 22,13:5
Zimmerman, Alfred, 1945, Mr 25,37:2; 1950, Ap 16, 104:7
Zimmerman, Alfred Mrs, 1957, Je 29,17:4
Zimmerman, Alfred R, 1939, Jl 3,13:5
Zimmerman, Amelia V, 1941, My 28,25:2
Zimmerman, Andrew S Mrs, 1952, Ja 4,23:2
Zimmerman, Arthur C, 1945, S 8,15:1
Zimmerman, Aug E, 1954, Ja 3,90:4
Zimmerman, Benjamin A, 1959, N 17,35:4
Zimmerman, Burt E, 1941, My 13,23:6
Zimmerman, Carl, 1941, Ap 5,17:2
Zimmerman, Catherine M Mrs, 1945, Je 21,19:3
Zimmerman, Charles, 1906, Ja 24,2:7; 1943, D 8,23:4
Zimmerman, Charles A Lt, 1916, Ja 17,11:3
Zimmerman, Charles H, 1952, My 23,21:1
Zimmerman, Charles J, 1950, Ag 5,15:6
Zimmerman, Charles N, 1943, Jl 22,19:4
Zimmerman, Clarence A, 1960, S 21,32:3
Zimmerman, Conrad W, 1942, D 25,18:2
Zimmerman, Dale E, 1953, F 18,31:3
Zimmerman, David, 1952, Ap 24,31:4
Zimmerman, E Dr, 1926, Jl 10,11:5
Zimmerman, Earl W, 1952, D 16,31:4
Zimmerman, Edward M Mrs, 1953, My 11,27:4
Zimmerman, Edwin H, 1962, O 9,42:1
Zimmerman, Elvina A B Mrs, 1941, N 4,23:3
Zimmerman, Emma R W Mrs, 1942, S 9,23:5
Zimmerman, Erich K, 1966, D 31,19:3
Zimmerman, F Fithian, 1942, F 16,17:3
Zimmerman, Franklin, 1952, D 17,33:3
Zimmerman, Franklin L, 1947, Ag 15,17:4
Zimmerman, Franklyn Mrs, 1954, F 1,23:4
Zimmerman, Franz, 1944, My 15,19:4
Zimmerman, Fred, 1925, O 6,27:3
Zimmerman, Fred R, 1954, D 15,31:4
Zimmerman, Fred W, 1944, Mr 19,42:1
Zimmerman, Frederick, 1967, Ag 9,39:4
Zimmerman, Frederick D, 1946, S 24,29:3
Zimmerman, Fulton Dr, 1925, Ag 22,11:5
Zimmerman, G A Prof, 1903, Ja 6,9:5
Zimmerman, George, 1942, N 21,13:6
Zimmerman, George E, 1939, Ap 4,25:4
Zimmerman, George J, 1953, Je 2,29:5
Zimmerman, Godfrey, 1948, Jl 22,23:2
Zimmerman, Harry S, 1957, Ag 11,80:7
Zimmerman, Herbert G (por), 1949, Jl 11,17:1
Zimmerman, Herbert P, 1962, Ja 30,29:3
Zimmerman, Homer G (est appr), 1965, Ap 23,36:1
Zimmerman, Ira Mrs, 1941, O 28,23:5

Zimmerman, Irving Mrs, 1955, F 17,27:4
Zimmerman, Isaac, 1949, Mr 9,25:5
Zimmerman, Israel, 1946, Je 1,13:4
Zimmerman, Ivan, 1950, F 8,27:1
Zimmerman, J A, 1877, My 13,6:7
Zimmerman, J Fred Jr, 1948, D 14,29:3
Zimmerman, James F (por), 1944, O 22,46:4
Zimmerman, Jane, 1961, D 12,43:2
Zimmerman, Jeremiah Rev Dr, 1937, F 20,17:3
Zimmerman, John H Mrs, 1949, Ja 3,23:2
Zimmerman, John J, 1942, S 12,13:4
Zimmerman, John J Mrs, 1958, Mr 7,24:1
Zimmerman, John L, 1942, My 4,19:3; 1943, Ag 21, 11:5
Zimmerman, John R, 1939, Je 9,21:2
Zimmerman, Joseph, 1953, N 14,17:6; 1963, Jl 5,19:2
Zimmerman, Joseph J, 1951, O 13,17:5
Zimmerman, Karl A, 1941, Ap 4,21:1
Zimmerman, Leonard J, 1953, D 21,31:4
Zimmerman, Leopold, 1944, Mr 16,19:4
Zimmerman, Leroy, 1944, Mr 25,21:5
Zimmerman, Lewis, 1942, D 17,29:5
Zimmerman, Louis A, 1954, Je 17,29:3
Zimmerman, Louis D, 1952, Ja 31,27:1
Zimmerman, Mary, 1953, D 25,17:4
Zimmerman, Mason W, 1956, Ag 14,25:4
Zimmerman, Mathew M, 1966, Ja 3,27:3
Zimmerman, Matthew H, 1950, O 15,104:2
Zimmerman, Maurice, 1957, My 16,31:4
Zimmerman, Meda S Mrs (will), 1940, Mr 28,25:7
Zimmerman, Michael J, 1925, Je 10,23:5
Zimmerman, Morris Mrs, 1948, O 27,27:3
Zimmerman, Moses, 1913, Ap 2,11:3
Zimmerman, Nathan, 1944, Je 11,45:2
Zimmerman, Nathan B, 1951, Ap 24,29:2
Zimmerman, Orville, 1948, Ap 8,25:3
Zimmerman, Paul B, 1962, Je 1,28:1
Zimmerman, Paul G, 1962, Mr 30,33:4
Zimmerman, Paul I Mrs, 1937, O 31,II,11:3
Zimmerman, Percy W, 1958, Ag 16,17:6
Zimmerman, Peter, 1915, Ja 18,9:5
Zimmerman, Peter J, 1950, N 15,32:2
Zimmerman, Robert Mrs, 1955, Je 13,23:5
Zimmerman, Robert W, 1938, My 14,15:4; 1956, My 29,27:3
Zimmerman, Rosa von Baroness, 1917, Ap 26,13:6
Zimmerman, Rufus E, 1955, Je 22,29:2
Zimmerman, S R, 1944, S 19,21:5
Zimmerman, Simon, 1959, Mr 2,27:3
Zimmerman, Sylvanus, 1962, O 8,23:3
Zimmerman, Thomas W, 1937, D 11,19:1
Zimmerman, Victor L, 1959, F 4,23:1
Zimmerman, Walter, 1937, Ja 31,II,8:5
Zimmerman, Wilbur, 1941, Mr 7,21:4
Zimmerman, William, 1967, D 1,47:4
Zimmerman, William D, 1951, Je 5,31:2; 1952, O 5, 88:8
Zimmerman, William F, 1955, Jl 12,25:5; 1956, Ap 10, 31:1
Zimmerman, William G, 1944, Mr 17,17:5
Zimmerman, William H, 1941, O 30,23:4
Zimmerman, William S, 1964, Ap 16,37:2
Zimmermann, Albert, 1961, Jl 26,31:2
Zimmermann, Alfred F M (por), 1940, Je 8,15:1
Zimmermann, Alphonse W, 1920, Jl 22,11:5
Zimmermann, Charles Mrs, 1904, N 20,11:4
Zimmermann, George J, 1938, S 15,25:5
Zimmermann, George M, 1940, Jl 21,28:7
Zimmermann, Gustav, 1937, S 20,23:2; 1958, S 17,37:1
Zimmermann, John E (por), 1943, My 31,17:1
Zimmermann, L, 1931, S 16,23:3
Zimmermann, William J, 1964, My 24,93:2
Zimmern, Alfred, 1957, N 25,31:1
Zimmern, Alfred E Mrs, 1963, O 19,25:1
Zimmern, Alice, 1939, Mr 24,21:4
Zinberg, Leonard (Ed Lacy), 1968, Ja 8,35:1
Zinberg, Louis R, 1965, Ja 10,92:6
Zincke, Walter A, 1944, Je 9,15:4
Zindel, John H, 1882, My 5,5:5
Zindell, Richard E, 1920, S 24,15:4
Zinger, Albert A, 1952, F 2,13:3
Zingg, Charles J, 1906, Jl 17,7:6
Zingg, Julius Mrs, 1937, Mr 29,19:2
Zingg, Paul P, 1944, F 6,41:2
Zingher, Joseph M, 1957, Ag 21,27:1
Zink, Elmer, 1951, F 27,27:3
Zink, Harold, 1962, Je 22,25:2
Zink, Homer C, 1959, Ap 21,38:1
Zink, J Charles, 1963, Ag 23,25:6
Zink, William C, 1964, Je 18,35:4
Zinke, Robert, 1947, Ja 4,15:5
Zinman, Jacob, 1954, Jl 1,25:5
Zinman, Meyer E, 1962, D 5,47:1
Zinman, William S, 1947, My 28,26:3
Zinn, Adolph, 1913, D 14,III,15:5
Zinn, Arthur, 1944, N 21,25:5
Zinn, Herman, 1958, Ja 17,25:1
Zinn, Howard W, 1954, S 30,31:3
Zinn, Manvel K, 1961, D 31,48:5
Zinn, Martin, 1941, D 5,23:2
Zinn, Max, 1951, N 23,30:2
Zinn, Oscar, 1938, F 9,19:1
Zinnecker, Wesley D, 1952, S 12,21:4
Zinner, Otto J, 1949, Jl 2,15:3
Zinovieff, G E, 1936, Ag 25,3:5
Zinovoy, George J, 1939, N 23,27:6
Zins, Isi, 1958, N 6,37:2
Zinser, Eliakum, 1913, S 23,11:5
Zinser, Melford E, 1955, Ja 27,23:4
Zinserling, Gustave Maj, 1914, My 6,11:7
Zinsler, Leopold Rabbi, 1922, Ap 26,19:5
Zinsmaster, Warren W, 1954, F 15,23:3
Zinsmeister, Howard F, 1955, My 2,21:5
Zinsser, Aug, 1948, S 27,23:5
Zinsser, Ferdinand, 1952, Ja 6,93:1
Zinsser, Frederick G, 1956, Ja 21,21:7
Zinsser, Frederick G Mrs, 1966, Je 8,47:3
Zinsser, Hans, 1940, S 5,23:1
Zinsser, Rudolph (por), 1955, Ag 15,15:5
Zio, Louis R, 1942, F 14,15:4
Ziolkowski, Stanislaw, 1952, O 12,89:1
Zion, Harry F, 1952, S 12,21:4
Zion, Irving, 1968, Je 11,47:2
Zior, Frederick, 1955, Ag 30,27:2
Ziperlin, Adolph Dr, 1905, Mr 1,9:5
Zipf, Carl H, 1951, Jl 22,60:2
Zipf, Edward, 1940, Ag 27,21:2
Zipf, Frederick W, 1941, Ja 4,13:2
Zipf, George K, 1950, S 27,31:4
Zipf, George P, 1954, S 3,17:4
Zipf, John Sr, 1948, Mr 28,48:6
Zipfel, John C, 1946, Ag 4,45:2
Zipkin, David (cor, Ag 9,21:2), 1945, Ag 8,23:5
Zipp, Clarence, 1948, F 21,13:2
Zipp, Harvey C, 1947, My 17,15:3
Zipprodt, Roy R, 1947, Je 22,52:3
Zipse, William F, 1962, Mr 15,35:1
Zipser, Max A, 1955, O 25,33:4
Zirbes, Laura H, 1967, Je 11,87:1
Zirbes, William J, 1943, Ja 11,15:4
Zirganos, Jason, 1959, S 28,9:5
Zirinsky, Leopold, 1945, Mr 13,23:3
Zirkman, Arthur, 1942, Ja 7,20:3
Zirlin, Samuel C, 1959, S 20,86:2
Zirm, John Mrs, 1948, S 2,23:4
Zirn, Harry, 1953, Jl 13,25:6
Ziroli, Angelo, 1948, N 16,30:3
Zirpolo, Carmine, 1951, Jl 5,34:3
Zirrilli, Anthony, 1967, Jl 30,64:8
Zisch, Peter J, 1946, F 5,23:5
Ziselman, Samuel I, 1948, O 27,27:4
Ziser, Thomas, 1949, N 19,17:5
Zises, Benjamin, 1958, S 21,87:1
Zises, Louis, 1967, My 5,39:2
Zisette, Reginald R, 1958, My 29,27:4
Zisgen, Catherine M, 1949, F 19,15:4
Zisk, Harry J, 1961, D 10,88:4
Ziskin, Daniel E (por), 1948, O 23,15:5
Ziskind, Jacob, 1950, O 19,31:1
Zisling, Aharon, 1964, Ja 17,43:3
Zismer, Gustave G, 1952, Je 9,23:5
Ziswasser, Alex, 1946, D 6,23:4
Zita, Arthur R, 1950, Ag 1,23:5
Zitlinger, Peter, 1937, Jl 31,15:6
Zito, Frank J, 1955, F 4,19:8
Zito, Rocco V, 1952, My 1,29:4
Zitoli, Frank Sr, 1945, Ja 8,19:8
Zitomirsky, Ignaz, 1957, N 14,33:2
Zitowitz, Joseph, 1944, O 10,23:4
Zitrin, Joseph K, 1966, D 5,45:3
Zitt, Joseph, 1952, My 5,23:4
Zittau, Henry J, 1962, O 7,82:7
Zittel, Andrew E, 1962, Ag 25,19:2
Zittel, Carl F (por), 1943, Ja 31,44:1
Zittel, Frederick, 1920, Jl 15,7:2
Zittel, Karl Alfred von Prof, 1904, Ja 7,9:5
Zittel, Theodore H, 1950, Ap 28,21:4
Zittell, Frank M, 1955, N 3,31:4
Zitzelsberger, Max L, 1956, F 17,21:2
Zitzer, J J, 1883, O 31,4:6
Zitzmann, Philip, 1961, F 16,31:5
Ziv, Rose S Mrs, 1953, My 17,88:1
Zivan, Morton Mrs, 1964, Ag 11,33:4
Zivkovitch, Petar, 1947, F 7,23:5
Ziwer Pasha, Ahmed, 1945, Ag 23,23:2
Zizelman, Frank, 1943, F 21,32:6
Zizmor, David Mrs, 1957, Ap 6,19:6
Zlatchin, Philip J, 1959, Jl 4,15:5
Zlatin, Mois, 1952, O 11,19:4
Zlatoff-Mirsky, Alex, 1960, N 20,87:2
Zlinkoff, Joseph N, 1945, Jl 14,11:7
Zlobin, Benjamin, 1952, Jl 21,19:6
Zlobin, Stepan P, 1965, S 20,7:1
Zlosky, Joseph, 1955, Je 29,29:5
Znamenacek, Jaroslav, 1944, My 3,19:6
Znaniecki, Florian W, 1958, Mr 25,33:2
Zobel, Frederick C, 1943, N 21,56:1
Zobel, Henry L, 1943, N 7,57:3
Zobel, Robert P, 1954, Jl 21,27:5
Zober, Richard O, 1941, O 9,23:3
Zobler, Abraham, 1957, N 10,87:1
Zocchi, Arnaldo, 1940, Jl 19,19:3
Zocchi, Louis A Sr, 1962, Ag 4,19:4
Zoccola, Atilio, 1953, N 25,23:1
Zock, Anthony J, 1957, N 24,86:7
Zoebisch, Alfred T, 1957, D 18,35:2
Zoeckler, Mary A, 1954, Je 15,29:1
Zoehrer, Ernest, 1949, Jl 24,53:1
Zoehrns, Carl, 1967, My 3,45:1
Zoeliner, J C F, 1882, Ap 30,9:4
Zoeller, Charles J Mrs, 1957, N 19,30:2
Zoeller, Frank P, 1946, F 26,25:5
Zoeller, Henry A, 1968, Ag 10,27:3
Zoeller, Lee J, 1937, N 14,II,11:2
Zoellner, Albert, 1947, S 5,20:3
Zoellner, Antoinette, 1962, Mr 14,39:4
Zoellner, Joseph Sr, 1950, Ja 25,27:3
Zoellner, L, 1934, N 19,17:4
Zoellner, Wilhelm Dr (por), 1937, Jl 18,II,6:6
Zoerlein, William E, 1945, My 16,19:3
Zoern, Jule C, 1950, S 30,17:4
Zoetzl, Joseph A, 1942, S 27,49:2
Zoffman, George F, 1957, Je 6,31:1
Zog I, Ex-King of Albania (funl, Ap 12,41:3), 1961, Ap 10,31:1
Zogbaum, Baird L Mrs (B Leonard), 1941, Ja 24,17:4
Zogbaum, Ferdinand, 1948, F 27,22:3
Zogbaum, Frank H, 1949, O 26,27:3
Zogbaum, Harry S, 1954, F 22,19:5
Zogbaum, Rufus Fairchild, 1925, O 24,15:6
Zogbaum, Wilfrid M, 1965, Ja 8,29:5
Zografos, George Mrs, 1955, F 27,86:2
Zographos, Nicholas, 1953, Ap 23,6:5
Zoizumi, Shinzo, 1966, My 12,45:4
Zokovitch, Joseph B, 1953, N 24,29:2
Zola, Alberto, 1942, My 13,19:6
Zola, Emile Mrs, 1925, Ap 28,21:4
Zola, Louis J Sr, 1955, Je 5,85:2
Zoldat, Basil Rev, 1937, My 6,25:4
Zoline, Elijah N, 1924, F 29,17:6
Zolkiewicz, Thaddeus S, 1964, S 5,8:8
Zollara, E V Dr, 1916, F 12,11:5
Zoller, Abram, 1962, My 26,25:6
Zoller, Bonaventure, 1938, My 26,25:5
Zoller, Carl A Jr, 1959, Ap 27,27:4
Zoller, Charles Mrs, 1949, Ja 8,15:6
Zoller, Christian H, 1958, Mr 31,27:5
Zoller, Frederick W, 1943, O 19,19:4
Zoller, Herman, 1949, O 2,81:1
Zolli, Eugenio, 1956, Mr 4,88:7
Zollinger, John H, 1955, D 3,17:2
Zollinhofer, Clinton A, 1960, S 25,88:5
Zollner, Theodore, 1952, Ap 26,23:6
Zollschan, Ignatz, 1948, D 28,21:4
Zolnay, George J (por), 1949, My 2,25:5
Zolnay, George Julian Mrs, 1968, Ag 17,27:3
Zolotar, George, 1968, Je 5,47:2
Zolotkoff, Leon, 1938, Ag 1,13:4
Zolotnitzky, Jacques, 1945, Ja 2,19:4
Zolotorofe, Irving, 1953, O 2,21:4
Zolotow, Harry, 1963, Jl 14,61:2
Zolt, Elias, 1946, F 10,42:2
Zoltan, Wolfe Mrs, 1967, Je 7,47:2
Zolubas, John Mrs, 1947, F 11,27:5
Zolzer, Henry W, 1956, O 15,25:5
Zomerowitz, Louis, 1944, My 25,21:3
Zon, Raphael (trb lr, N 12,28:7), 1956, O 30,34:2
Zondek, Bernhard, 1966, N 9,40:1
Zone, Morris, 1962, Je 8,31:4
Zonghi, Giovanni M, 1941, Ag 9,15:2
Zonino, Fred, 1946, D 3,31:3
Zons, Frederick W, 1960, D 5,31:4
Zontlein, Leo Mrs, 1952, Mr 9,93:1
Zook, Frank, 1943, Je 15,21:2
Zook, George F, 1951, Ag 19,84:3
Zook, John G, 1942, Ja 31,17:3
Zook, John M, 1937, Mr 12,24:3
Zook, Justine S Mrs, 1941, Je 10,23:4
Zophy, Gabriel, 1947, S 10,27:1
Zoppe, Secondo, 1951, Ja 16,29:2
Zoppi, Gaetano, 1948, O 21,27:1
Zoppi, Oscar, 1955, Ja 31,19:5
Zora, Tooma A, 1956, Ag 4,15:6
Zorach, Marguerite, 1968, Je 29,29:3
Zorach, William, 1966, N 17,47:1
Zoras, Athina G Mrs, 1943, Ja 1,23:6
Zorbaugh, George L, 1943, Ag 19,19:2
Zorbaugh, Harvey W, 1965, Ja 22,43:2
Zorek, Ben C, 1953, Ap 23,29:2
Zorian, Carekin, 1939, Mr 8,21:2
Zorian, Vahan, 1937, Je 10,23:3
Zorilla, M R, 1895, Je 14,5:1
Zork, Carl T, 1947, Ja 19,53:3
Zorn, Anders Leonard, 1920, Ag 23,11:5
Zorn, Andrew, 1943, Mr 10,19:5
Zorn, Burton A, 1968, F 23,34:1
Zorn, Carl J Mrs, 1953, Mr 9,8:1
Zorn, Edwin G, 1949, Ag 22,21:4
Zorn, Errol M, 1949, Ag 7,61:2
Zorn, Frederick (por), 1948, N 2,25:3
Zorn, Harvey C, 1941, N 19,23:3
Zorn, Leroy J, 1947, Ap 28,23:4
Zorn, Sidney Mrs, 1948, Mr 26,21:5
Zorna, Joseph W, 1938, Jl 7,19:5
Zornow, Theodore A, 1954, S 5,51:1
Zoschenko, Leonard, 1956, Ap 9,27:2
Zoshchenko, Mikhail, 1958, Jl 25,19:1
Zoss, Benjamin, 1952, S 15,25:3
Zott, Robert Capt, 1949, Je 26,35:2

[illegible] 1947, My 27,25:4
Z[illegible]eorge, 1942, Jl 28,17:5
[illegible] Thomas F, 1946, Je 20,23:2
[illegible]ll, Joseph T, 1961, Ag 24,29:5
[illegible]z, Charles R Mrs, 1947, Ag 18,17:2
[illegible]ouain, Louis, 1950, F 19,77:1
Zouck, George P, 1937, F 6,17:5
Zoyara, Ella (Omar Kingsley), 1879, My 28,5:4
Zoylner, Christian F, 1951, Mr 15,29:2
Zozula, Fyodor V, 1964, Ap 23,39:5
Zraick, Ishac, 1965, Ja 4,29:5
Zrike, Salim, 1943, Je 28,21:2
Zsamboky, Paul, 1952, Jl 21,19:5
Zsasskovsky, Joseph Prince, 1917, My 31,11:4
Zscheigner, Max H, 1940, Ja 26,17:4
Zsiga, Bela J, 1951, F 1,25:4
Zsoldos, Sandor, 1955, F 2,27:1
Zsolnay, Paul von, 1961, My 14,86:6
Zu Wied, Marie Princess, 1902, Mr 25,9:6
Zuber, Frank, 1956, S 27,35:5
Zuber, Henry W, 1947, Je 27,21:4
Zuber, Nathan Mrs, 1955, Ja 18,27:4
Zuber, Robert, 1963, N 21,39:4
Zuber, Walter B, 1953, F 26,25:5
Zubizarreta, Octavio, 1941, My 10,15:5
Zubler, Leroy, 1949, Je 14,31:2
Zubov, Konstantin A, 1956, N 25,88:7
Zucca, Antonio, 1922, Ap 15,15:6
Zucca, Paul A, 1948, My 23,68:7
Zucca, Paul C, 1951, Ag 10,15:4
Zucco, George, 1960, My 29,56:3
Zucco, Ross B, 1960, S 29,71:4
Zuchovitz, Achilles, 1956, N 15,35:4
Zuck, John H, 1952, Ap 19,15:5
Zuck, Morris L, 1949, Je 12,76:7
Zucker, Abraham, 1964, O 19,33:3
Zucker, Abraham W Mrs, 1968, O 30,47:4
Zucker, Arthur A, 1945, Je 11,15:5
Zucker, Arthur A Mrs, 1966, S 13,47:1
Zucker, David G, 1956, My 17,31:4
Zucker, Edward D, 1943, Jl 6,21:5
Zucker, Elizabeth B Mrs, 1961, N 29,30:7
Zucker, Frederick A, 1957, Mr 6,31:3
Zucker, Henry L, 1958, S 6,17:6
Zucker, Jacob L, 1937, Ag 1,II,7:4
Zucker, James M, 1955, N 27,88:7
Zucker, Joseph H, 1954, F 10,29:4
Zucker, Ludwig G, 1963, My 17,33:4
Zucker, Max, 1957, My 27,31:2
Zucker, Morris Mrs, 1943, O 25,15:4
Zucker, Paul B, 1967, Ag 20,88:3
Zucker, Peter, 1925, S 5,13:6
Zucker, Ray F Mrs, 1941, N 20,27:5
Zucker, Richard D Mrs, 1952, My 19,17:4
Zucker, Simon D, 1950, Je 11,92:8
Zucker, William, 1952, My 30,15:6
Zucker, William J, 1968, N 14,47:4
Zucker-Hale, Herbert, 1960, Ja 29,25:2
Zuckerberg, Robert K Mrs, 1964, O 5,33:1
Zuckerbrod, Joseph, 1945, Jl 11,11:6
Zuckerbrot, Frank, 1966, My 1,87:4
Zuckerkandl, Victor, 1965, Ap 29,35:1
Zuckerkandl, Victor Mrs, 1965, O 15,45:2
Zuckerkane, Otto Prof, 1921, Jl 4,9:6
Zuckerman, Belle, 1955, My 29,44:5
Zuckerman, George, 1966, My 21,31:5
Zuckerman, Harry, 1951, Ja 13,15:5; 1955, D 12,31:4
Zuckerman, Isaac, 1940, Ja 19,19:3
Zuckerman, Jack, 1962, My 5,27:5
Zuckerman, Jacob, 1951, Ja 15,17:2
Zuckerman, Jacob Mrs, 1949, Ap 9,17:4
Zuckerman, Jerome, 1956, Jl 23,23:5
Zuckerman, Lavar, 1922, Je 18,28:3
Zuckerman, Louis H, 1957, My 14,35:2
Zuckerman, Paul S, 1965, D 4,31:5
Zuckerman, Samuel (Mar 9), 1963, Ap 1,36:8
Zuckerman, Sigmund, 1951, N 13,30:2
Zuckerman, Stanley, 1949, Ja 16,68:4
Zuckerman, William Mrs, 1953, Je 22,21:2
Zuckermandel, Samuel, 1953, Mr 19,29:5
Zuckert, Maurice, 1959, N 16,31:2
Zuckerwar, Jacob A Mrs, 1948, Ap 19,23:3
Zuckoschay, Bartholomew, 1948, Ja 5,19:3
Zueblin, Charles, 1924, S 16,23:4
Zuelzer, George L (por), 1949, O 20,29:4
Zuercher, Joseph P, 1957, Ag 25,31:4
Zug, Charles, 1910, O 22,11:4
Zug, George B, 1943, F 13,11:4
Zugsmith, Robert G Mrs, 1941, F 25,23:3
Zuhr, Frank, 1939, D 15,25:4
Zukerman, William, 1961, O 6,35:3
Zukor, Abram, 1943, Je 11,19:5
Zukor, Adolph Mrs, 1956, Ap 8,84:1
Zukowsky, Ethel Mrs, 1950, Ap 26,29:4
Zukowsky, John, 1950, S 26,31:1
Zulauf, G Walter, 1939, My 10,23:3
Zulauf, John, 1937, Mr 8,19:1
Zulauf, John C, 1938, F 4,21:4
Zulauf, Robert, 1947, F 26,25:4
Zulawski, Zygmunt, 1949, S 10,17:2
Zulch, Frederick W, 1956, Ap 7,19:3
Zulflacht, Jerome J Mrs, 1965, Ja 28,29:3
Zulick, Thomas C Sr, 1946, My 20,23:4
Zullinger, A Henry, 1945, O 1,19:5
Zullo, Joseph Mrs, 1963, S 15,87:1
Zuloaga, Ignazio (por), 1945, N 1,23:1
Zuluaga, Julio, 1951, O 4,33:1
Zulueta, Luis de, 1964, Ag 5,33:3
Zum Felde, Emilio, 1951, S 19,31:4
Zumbrook, Paul W Mrs, 1951, Mr 14,33:4
Zumpe, Hermann, 1903, S 5,7:6
Zumsteg, Roberto E, 1959, Ja 17,19:5
Zumstein, Frank C, 1937, Ja 16,17:1
Zumwalt, I G, 1950, D 13,35:3
Zundalek, Charles A, 1952, Ag 28,23:2
Zundel, Frederick R, 1963, O 31,33:3
Zundel, Frederick R Mrs, 1949, N 15,25:4
Zuniga, Evaristo M, 1941, N 3,19:2
Zuniga, Horacio, 1956, S 15,17:4
Zuniga Huete, Jose A, 1953, Ap 15,31:2
Zunino, Giovanni, 1954, Ap 5,32:1
Zunino, Julius, 1956, Ja 19,33:2
Zunker, Gilbert A, 1938, D 20,26:2
Zunser, Charles Mrs, 1951, O 12,27:4
Zunser, Fannie Mrs, 1939, Mr 22,23:5
Zunser, Philip, 1944, D 12,23:4
Zunser, Shomer, 1965, Je 11,31:2
Zupan, John I, 1950, Je 17,15:3
Zupan, Louis J, 1966, F 5,60:5
Zuppke, Robert C (funl, D 25,31:4; will, D 31,18:6), 1957, D 23,23:2
Zur Helle, Helen Baroness, 1950, D 7,33:3
Zuraw, Andrew, 1953, Mr 10,29:4
Zurawski, Kasimir, 1949, Ja 28,21:3
Zuray, Irwin Mrs, 1947, Mr 4,25:4
Zurbrick, John L, 1942, D 28,20:2
Zurbrugg, Theophilus, 1912, N 22,13:3
Zurcher, Emil Jr, 1949, F 16,25:1
Zurgena, Marquis of (J Gomes Acebo Modet), 1950, Ja 15,84:4
Zurhellen, Joseph O, 1965, F 28,88:5
Zurke, Bob, 1944, F 18,17:4
Zurlinden, Cyril, 1957, My 9,31:4
Zurmuhlen, Frederick H (funl, Ja 24,29:4), 1961, Ja 20,29:3
Zuro, L, 1934, Mr 29,23:1
Zusi, Chris, 1956, N 18,43:5
Zusi, Frank, 1952, Je 24,29:4
Zusi, Leonard B Mrs, 1942, D 17,29:4
Zustra, Ebro, 1951, Ag 2,11:1
Zuurmond, John P (por), 1955, Ag 1,19:4
Zuver, Blaine, 1941, Ap 9,25:3
Zuylen van Nyvelt van der Haar, Egmont van, 1960, D 22,23:3
Zuza, Vincent Mrs, 1947, Je 24,23:2
Zuzak, Josephine Mrs (will), 1954, N 24,25:4
Zvaifler, Nathan, 1959, O 19,29:4
Zvara, Michael Mrs, 1945, D 16,41:1
Zverkov, Nikolai K, 1954, F 26,20:3
Zvirka, Petras, 1947, My 7,31:1
Zwack, John, 1958, S 25,33:2
Zwanenberg, Saal van Mrs, 1961, Ap 16,86:4
Zwanzig, Carl, 1938, Mr 23,23:4
Zwarun, Michael Mrs, 1952, Mr 21,23:2
Zwarych, John, 1949, Ap 13,29:3
Zweben, Sidney Mrs, 1966, Mr 21,33:2
Zwee, Joseph H, 1952, N 11,29:1
Zwee, Samuel R, 1950, F 28,29:1
Zweifach, Aaron, 1964, D 29,27:2
Zweifach, Abraham Mrs, 1961, Ag 6,84:3
Zweifel, Henry, 1940, D 1,61:2
Zweifler, Irving, 1962, N 4,88:1
Zweig, Annie Mrs, 1940, D 28,15:1
Zweig, Arnold, 1968, N 27,47:1
Zweig, Myron, 1964, Ag 19,37:5
Zwemer, Samuel M, 1952, Ap 3,35:5
Zwemer, Samuel M Mrs, 1937, Ja 26,21:2
Zwerdling, Joseph, 1956, My 14,25:3
Zwerdling, Solomon S, 1944, Jl 8,11:5
Zwerin, Stanley, 1957, Ja 29,31:2
Zwetchkenbaum, Edward A, 1963, S 10,39:3
Zwetz, Roy G, 1957, D 28,17:4
Zweybrueck, Emmy (Mrs E A Prochaska), 1956, Je 5,35:2
Zwick, Clemence, 1937, Mr 2,21:4
Zwicker, Henry F, 1945, N 27,23:4
Zwicker, Henry F Mrs, 1942, Ja 8,21:5
Zwicker, M B (Dick), 1954, Ap 30,23:3
Zwiefka, Vincent S, 1942, S 7,19:5
Zwier, George J, 1946, Ag 21,27:6
Zwierlein, Cornelius A, 1942, F 19,19:3
Zwietusch, William Y, 1947, Ap 13,60:1
Zwigard, Ernest R, 1959, Ag 7,23:1
Zwigard, Frank J, 1964, Ap 2,33:5
Zwigard, Frank J Sr, 1955, Ap 15,24:4
Zwilling, Elihu J, 1964, Ja 24,27:2
Zwilling, Paul R, 1955, Mr 6,89:1
Zwillinger, Jack, 1960, Ag 6,19:5
Zwinak, John V, 1949, My 24,28:5
Zwinge, William P, 1943, O 26,23:5
Zwirner, William T, 1952, Ap 3,35:3
Zwirz, Frederick F E, 1962, Jl 8,65:2
Zwissler, Phil Mrs, 1950, O 7,19:2
Zwissler, Philip Jr, 1959, Mr 10,35:3
Zwissler, Robert, 1950, F 20,25:2
Zwoyer, Ellsworth B A, 1946, D 20,24:3
Zygielbojm, Szmul, 1943, My 15,15:4
Zygmunt, Laurence F, 1941, D 10,25:1
Zysman, Hans, 1951, Jl 20,21:6